Racehorse Record

FLAT 2000

Raceform's A-Z Guide to horses which ran during the 2000 Flat Season
(November 7th 1999 - November 4th 2000)

Editor	Ashley Rumney
Comments by	Richard Lowther, David Bellingham, Andrew Ayres, Ashley Rumney, Steffan Edwards
Production Assistants	Nicki Bowen, David Bellingham, Steffan Edwards
Raceform Ratings	Walter Glynn, Simon Turner, Nicki Bowen
Design	Daniel Di Pol, Ashley Rumney, Mike Shaw
Photographs	Edward Whitaker, Allsport

Typeset and Published by Raceform Ltd,
Compton, Newbury, Berkshire, RG20 6NL
Tel: 01635 578080
Fax: 01635 578101
Web http://www.raceform.co.uk
EMail: raceform@raceform.co.uk
Printed by Polestar Wheatons Ltd, Exeter

RaceformLimited is a wholly owned subsidiary of MGN Limited

ISBN 1 901100 87 1

£22.00

CONTENTS

Introduction.. iv
Raceform Ratings... vi
Official table of Weight-For-Age... vii
Top Rated Horses of 2000... viii
Main Text... 1-792
Course Maps... 793-828
Jockey Statistics.. 829-838
Trainer Statistics... 839-851
Draw Analysis... 853-873
Front Runners... 875-879
Median Times 2001... 881-884
Winners of Principal Races.. 885-888
Stamina of Sires' Progeny.. 889-892

Full details of all Raceform services and publications are available from
Raceform, Compton, Newbury, Berkshire RG20 6NL.
Tel: 01635 578080 Fax: 01635 578101.
Web http://www.raceform.co.uk
Email: raceform@raceform.co.uk

Cover Photo: Edward Whitaker
Sinndar (Johnny Murtagh) wins the Vodafone Derby from Sakhee (Richard Hills)

INTRODUCTION

Racehorse Record is a companion publication to Raceform Annual for 2001, but is also incorporated as part of the Raceform Weekly Form Book subscription and we hope this will prove a popular addition to our subscribers' reference libraries. The book is designed not only as an historical reference, but also as a guide to the future.
As Flat racing becomes more global, it is also useful to have information on the top horses racing around the world and, to this end, we have included all horses trained abroad which appeared in Raceform, The Form Book and attained a rating of 90 or above.

The horses are listed in alphabetical order, together with their suffix. This is followed by the current Raceform Master Rating (RR) for the Flat (i.e. 74f), along with an All-Weather Master Rating if applicable (i.e. 65a). The figures after this are the Official BHB Ratings (Turf, and All-Weather where applicable) as at the end of the season (4th November), as long as the horse has been entered in a handicap during the season (otherwise a BHB Rating is not issued). It should be noted that BHB Handicappers officially rate no horse above 120 after September (100 for two-year-olds) in preparation for the International Classifications. The number to the far right is the number of the last race in the Form Book in which the horse competed, with finishing position. This allows the reader to refer quickly and easily to Racehorse Record's companion title, Raceform Flat Annual For 2001.

The second line displays the age, colour, sex and pedigree of the horse. The Sire's name and suffix is followed by the average winning distance of his progeny (excluding two-year-olds). This figure is the mean average winning distance of all wins by horses he has sired, displayed to the nearest tenth of a furlong. The number in BOLD type in parentheses which follows is the average highest winning rating of his progeny in the last 12 months. The same set of figures is given for the Grandsire (sire of dam), in his role as a Grandsire.

Full form figures are shown for the 2000 campaign, rather than just the last six runs, as trends often reveal themselves through the course of a season. For horses trained outside GB and Ireland, the figures relate only to races published in Raceform, The Official Form Book and Computer Raceform.

The win and total prizemoney is followed by the horse's win record, which displays the year, month, course, going, race type (H=Handicap, C=Claimer, S=Seller, L=listed, G1=Group One, G2=Group Two and G3=Group Three), distance to the nearest tenth of a furlong, BHB and Raceform Rating. Please note, the BHB Rating is the original mark of the horse at entry and NOT adjusted for such factors as overweight and penalties that may have been incurred. An asterisk (*) at the start of the line indicates that the win was for the horse's current trainer, whilst an arrow at the end (<) indicates that it was the highest Raceform Rating gained thus far in its career.

The line directly above the narrative shows a breakdown of the runs in 2000 on Turf and All-Weather, listing the different distances and goings on which it raced, together with success rate.

The narrative itself produces an analysis of all the horse's runs and gives an assessment of physical attributes and ability. Distances at which the horse is effective, its optimum distance, going preferences, effectiveness in headgear, course preferences and best performance in the current season are all listed here. N.B. the going preferences shown are based on the Raceform going rather than the Official, as the latter is often called into question, whereas Raceform's is based on race times and takes into account other external influences. Where appropriate, the editorial also features an assessment of how the horse has run and views on its future prospects.

The final line details the trainer with wins-to-runs ratio in parentheses, followed by the owner's name. If the horse has been with more than one handler during its career, the previous trainer is shown, again with wins-to-runs ratio. N.B. National Hunt performances are included in the horse's total run figures for the trainer, for additional information.

ABBREVIATIONS AND THEIR MEANINGS

hvy	=	heavy	frm	=	firm
sft	=	soft	hrd	=	hard
g-s	=	good to soft	Equi	=	Equitrack All-Weather
gd	=	good	Fibr	=	Fibresand All-Weather
g-f	=	good to firm			

"acts on gd to frm, best on g-f" = horse is able to act effectively on any ground between good and firm, but is best when the ground is actually good to firm.
"Turf high" = this season's best performance rating
"AW high 68" = this season's performance rating if achieved on an All-Weather surface.
"(18 Aug Pont g-f RF 3637)" = the date, racecourse, going, and Raceform number in the Form Book where a horse achieved its highest rating.
"(1st run)" = indicates if a horse's rating was achieved on its first run on that surface.
"l.h. tracks" = courses with left-handed bends.
"r.h. tracks" = courses with right-handed bends.
"tight tracks" = courses with tight bends. (Raceform assess bend tightness, and these are not necessarily the tracks with the tightest circumference.

The tracks with the tightest bends are :-

Bath	Goodwood	Ripon
Catterick	Hamilton	Thirsk
Chester	Lingfield	Windsor
Epsom	Musselburgh	Wolverhampton
Folkestone	Redcar	Yarmouth

RACEFORM RATINGS

Raceform Ratings for each horse indicate the actual level of performance attained in that race. The figure shown after RR in the text represents the BEST public form that our Handicappers still believe each horse is capable of reproducing.

To use the ratings constructively in determining those horses best-in in future events, the following procedure should be followed:

(i) In races where all runners are the same age and are set to carry the same weight, no calculations are necessary. The horse with the highest rating is the horse best in.

(ii) In races where all runners are the same age but are set to carry different weights, add one point to the Raceform rating for every pound less than 10 stone to be carried, deduct one point for every pound more than 10 stone.

For example

Horse	Age & weight	Adjustment from 10 stone	RR base Rating	Adjusted Rating
Rivervale	3-10-1	-1	78	77
Marita Anne	3-9-13	+1	80	81
Foxcopse	3-9-7	+7	71	78
Seapatrick	3-8-11	+17	60	77

Therefore Marita Anne is top-rated (best-in)

(iii) In races concerning horses of different ages the procedure in example (ii) should again be followed, but reference must also be made to the Official Scale of Weight-For-Age (see page facing).

For example

12 furlongs July 20th

Horse	Age & weight	Adjust fr 10 st	RPH Rating	Adjust Rating	W-F-A deduct	Final Rating
Dance the Blues	5-10-0	0	90	90	Nil	90
Sunfly	4-9-9	+5	83	88	Nil	88
Cousin Flo	3-9-4	+10	85	95	-12	83
Gallopade	4-8-7	+21	73	94	Nil	94

Therefore Gallopade is top-rated (best-in)

(A 3-y.o is deemed 12lb less mature than a 4-y.o or older horse on 20th July over 12f. Therefore, the deduction of 12 points is necessary).

The following symbols are used in conjunction with the ratings:

++ almost certain to prove better
+ likely to prove better
d disappointing (has run well below best recently)
? form hard to evaluate - rating may prove unreliable
t tentative rating based on race time

The Official Scale of Weight, Age & Distance (Flat)

The following scale should only be used in conjunction with the Official ratings published in this book. Use of any other scale will introduce errors into calculations. The allowances are expressed as the number of pounds that is deemed the average horse in each group falls short of maturity at different dates and distances.

Dist		Jan		Feb		Mar		Apr		May		Jun		Jul		Aug		Sep		Oct		Nov		Dec	
(fur)	Age	1-15	16-31	1-14	15-28	1-15	16-31	1-15	16-30	1-15	16-31	1-15	16-30	1-15	16-31	1-15	16-31	1-15	16-30	1-15	16-31	1-15	16-30	1-15	16-31
5	2	-	-	-	-	-	47	44	41	38	36	34	32	30	28	26	24	22	20	19	18	17	17	16	16
	3	15	15	14	14	13	12	11	10	9	8	7	6	5	4	3	2	1	1	-	-	-	-	-	-
6	2	-	-	-	-	-	-	-	-	44	41	38	36	33	31	28	26	24	22	21	20	19	18	17	17
	3	16	16	15	15	14	13	12	11	10	9	8	7	6	5	4	3	2	2	1	1	-	-	-	-
7	2	-	-	-	-	-	-	-	-	-	-	-	-	38	35	32	30	27	25	23	22	21	20	19	19
	3	18	18	17	17	16	15	14	13	12	11	10	9	8	7	6	5	4	3	2	2	1	1	-	-
8	2	-	-	-	-	-	-	-	-	-	-	-	-	-	-	37	34	31	28	26	24	23	22	21	20
	3	20	20	19	19	18	17	15	14	13	12	11	10	9	8	7	6	5	4	3	3	2	2	1	1
9	3	22	22	21	21	20	19	17	15	14	13	12	11	10	9	8	7	6	5	4	4	3	3	2	2
	4	1	1	-	-	-	-	-	-	-	-	-	-	-	-	-	-	-	-	-	-	-	-	-	-
10	3	23	23	22	22	21	20	19	17	15	14	13	12	11	10	9	8	7	6	5	5	4	4	3	3
	4	2	2	1	1	-	-	-	-	-	-	-	-	-	-	-	-	-	-	-	-	-	-	-	-
11	3	24	24	23	23	22	21	20	19	17	15	14	13	12	11	10	9	8	7	6	6	5	5	4	4
	4	3	3	2	2	1	1	-	-	-	-	-	-	-	-	-	-	-	-	-	-	-	-	-	-
12	3	25	25	24	24	23	22	21	20	19	17	15	14	13	12	11	10	9	8	7	7	6	6	5	5
	4	4	4	3	3	2	2	1	1	-	-	-	-	-	-	-	-	-	-	-	-	-	-	-	-
13	3	26	26	25	25	24	23	22	21	20	19	17	15	14	13	12	11	10	9	8	8	7	7	6	6
	4	5	5	4	4	3	3	2	1	-	-	-	-	-	-	-	-	-	-	-	-	-	-	-	-
14	3	27	27	26	26	25	24	23	22	21	20	19	17	15	14	13	12	11	10	9	9	8	8	7	7
	4	6	6	5	5	4	4	3	2	1	-	-	-	-	-	-	-	-	-	-	-	-	-	-	-
15	3	28	28	27	27	26	25	24	23	22	21	20	19	17	15	14	13	12	11	10	9	8	8	7	7
	4	6	6	5	5	4	4	3	3	2	1	-	-	-	-	-	-	-	-	-	-	-	-	-	-
16	3	29	29	28	28	27	26	25	24	23	22	21	20	19	17	15	14	13	12	11	10	9	9	8	8
	4	7	7	6	6	5	5	4	4	3	2	1	-	-	-	-	-	-	-	-	-	-	-	-	-
18	3	31	31	30	30	29	28	27	26	25	24	23	22	21	20	18	16	14	13	12	11	10	10	9	9
	4	8	8	7	7	6	6	5	5	4	3	2	1	-	-	-	-	-	-	-	-	-	-	-	-
20	3	33	33	32	32	31	30	29	28	27	26	25	24	23	22	20	18	16	14	13	12	11	11	10	10
	4	9	9	8	8	7	7	6	6	5	4	3	2	1	-	-	-	-	-	-	-	-	-	-	-

RACEFORM TOP RATED THREE-YEAR-OLDS AND UPWARDS OF 2000

Horse	Rating
Dubai Millennium	136
Montjeu (IRE)	124
Sinndar (IRE)	130
Giant's Causeway(IRE)	124
Shiva (JPN)	129
Tiznow (USA)	129
Kalanisi (IRE)	129
Observatory (USA)	128
King's Best (USA)	127
Sakhee (USA)	127
Fantastic Light	126
Endless Hall	126
Fusaichi Pegasus(USA)	126
Dansili	125
Samum (GER)	125
Mutafaweq (USA)	125
Affirmed Success	125
War Chant (USA)	125
North East Bound	124
Dansili	124
Quiet Resolve (USA)	124
Fruits of Love	124
Muhtathir	124
Crimplene (IRE)	124
Indian Lodge (IRE)	124
Mutamam	124
Greek Dance (IRE)	124
Egyptband (USA)	124
John's Call	124
Kona Gold (USA)	124
Petrushka (IRE)	124
Nuclear Debate (USA)	123
Ciro (USA)	123
Holding Court	123
Captain Steve (USA)	123
Albert The Great	123

AA-YOUKNOWNOTHING BHB 64f68a **RR 58f 68a** 1187[18]
4 b g Superpower 6.6f **(58)** - Bad Payer (Tanfirion) 7f **(61)**
Form - 033416274230
Record 2000 - 1st:0 2nd:2 3rd:1 Ran:7
Pre2000 - 1st:3 2nd:3 3rd:4 Ran:25
Win Prizemoney £8,695 *Total Prizemoney* £15,799
Wins * 1999 *Dec Lingfi (STD) H 5f 62 64*
1998 May Thirsk (GD) 5f 68 <
1998 Apr Mussel (G-S) 5f 68 <
2000 Turf 0-3: (5f 3) (hvy, gd, hrd) 2000 AW 0-4: (5f 4) (Equi 3, Fibr)
Workmanlike, above-average gelding, effective 5f, - acts on AW, has worn blinkers, likes left handed tracks, likes tight tracks. Turf high 58. AW high 70 - 2nd of 8 giving 10lb to Frilly Front (26 Jan Lingfield 5f Equi RF 0164). Pacey sprint handicapper who wins in his turn.
**Miss J F Craze [1-24] T Marshall (from M W Easterby [2-8] Aug 1998).*

ABAJANY BHB 69f65a **RR 71f 65a** 5166[2]
6 b g Akarad (FR) 9.7f **(73)** -Miss Ivory Coast (USA) (Sir Ivor) 10.2f **(70)**
Form - 887702
Record 2000 - 1st:0 2nd:1 3rd:0 Ran:6
Pre2000 - 1st:4 2nd:4 3rd:8 Ran:48
Win Prizemoney £18,444 *Total Prizemoney* £44,734
Wins * 1998 Aug Ayr (G-S) H 8f 78 85 <
* 1998 Jly Bath (GD) 10.2f 78
* 1997 Spt Sandow (G-F) H 8.1f 71 77
* 1997 Aug Leices (GD) H 8f 66 72
2000 Turf 0-6: (8f 6) (sft, g-s, gd 3, g-f)
Above-average gelding, effective 8f, acts on frm, likes right handed tracks. Turf high 71 (began Aug).
**M R Channon [4-61] John White and Partners.*

ABALON (GER) RR 107f 2581a[7]
3 b c Darshaan 11.9f **(81)** - Anna Leone (Caerleon (USA)) 8.6f **(71)**
Form - 27
2000 Turf 0-2: (10f, 12f) (sft, gd)
Currently Pattern-class colt. Turf high 107. **P Lautner in GER [0-2].*

ABBAJABBA BHB 80f68a **RR 82f 68a** 4865[4]
4 b g Barrys Gamble 7f **(50)** - Bo' Babbity (Strong Gale) 5.6f **(66)**
Form - 031131204
Record 2000 - 1st:3 2nd:1 3rd:2 Ran:8
Pre2000 - 1st:0 2nd:1 3rd:0 Ran:14
Win Prizemoney £16,913 *Total Prizemoney* £21,996
Wins * **2000** Aug Ayr (GD) 6f 65
* **2000** Apr Epsom (HVY) H 6f 74 81 <
* **2000** Apr Hamilt (GD) H 6f 63 76
2000 Turf 3-8: (5f, 6f 3-7) (sft 1-2, gd 1-3, g-f 2, frm 1-1)
Workmanlike, decent gelding, effective 5 to 6f, best at 6f, acts on sft to g-f. Turf high 81 - 1st of 14 giving 1lb to Carlton (26 Apr Epsom RF 0877) - also 1st of 18 getting 10lb from Unshaken (8 Apr Hamilton RF 0641). Enjoyed a good season and should pay his way again next term.
**C W Fairhurst [3-22] North Cheshire Trading & Storage Ltd.*

ABBOT RR 51f 5223[12]
2 b g Bishop of Cashel - Gifted **(22f)** (Shareef Dancer (USA)) 9.9f **(73)**
Form - 0
Record 2000 - 1st:0 2nd:0 3rd:0 Ran:1
2000 Turf 0-1: (6f) (gd)
Currently fair gelding. **B J Meehan [0-1] Abbott Racing Ltd.*

ABBY GOA (IRE) BHB 68f **RR 73f** 5027[12]
2 b f Dr Devious (IRE) 9.9f **(74)** - Spring Reel (Mill Reef (USA)) 10.5f **(78)**
Form - 45730
Record 2000 - 1st:0 2nd:0 3rd:1 Ran:5
Win Prizemoney £0 *Total Prizemoney* £820
2000 Turf 0-5: (6f, 7f 3, 8f) (g-s 2, frm 3)
Above-average filly, has worn blinkers. Turf high 73 (began Jly).
**B Hanbury [0-5] Mrs Joan Root.*

ABCO BOY (IRE) BHB 37f **RR 44f** 3380[17]
3 b g Full Extent (USA) 5.2f **(50)** - Double Stitch (Wolver Hollow) 8f **(56)**
Form - 800600
Record 2000 - 1st:0 2nd:0 3rd:0 Ran:6
Pre2000 - 1st:0 2nd:0 3rd:0 Ran:1
2000 Turf 0-6: (5f, 6f 4, 7f) (gd, g-f 2, frm 3)
Unfurnished, moderate gelding, often wears blinkers. Turf high 44.
**Martyn Wane [0-7] E Sidebottom.*

ABDERIAN (IRE) BHB 99f **RR 99f** 2291[2]
3 b c Machiavellian (USA) 9.8f **(83)** - Aminata (Glenstal (USA)) 10.1f **(64)**
Form - 502
Record 2000 - 1st:0 2nd:1 3rd:0 Ran:3
Pre2000 - 1st:1 2nd:1 3rd:0 Ran:3
Win Prizemoney £3,707 *Total Prizemoney* £8,416
Wins * 1999 Aug Ripon (GD) 6f 77 <
2000 Turf 0-3: (6f, 7f, 8f) (gd 2, g-f)
Workmanlike, very useful colt, effective 6 to 7f, acts on g-f. Turf high 99 - 2nd of 8 giving 4lb to Dandy Night (26 Jun Yarmouth 6f g-f RF 2291). Beat a big field of maidens on his Ripon debut over six furlongs in 1999. Best effort last term was in a classified event at Yarmouth, but he appeared to be feeling the ground there and has not been seen since. **J Noseda [1-6] Hesmonds Stud.*

ABERFOLLY BHB 47f **RR 54f** 4215[14]
2 b f Minshaanshu Amad (USA) 11.3f **(53)** - Mississipi Maid (All Systems Go)
Form - 7670
Record 2000 - 1st:0 2nd:0 3rd:0 Ran:4
2000 Turf 0-4: (6f, 7f 2, 8f) (frm 4)
Fair filly. Turf high 54 (began Jly). **P D Evans [0-4] T Jarvis.*

ABERKEEN BHB 65f63a **RR 67+f 63a** 4195[22]
5 ch g Keen 11.1f **(58)** - Miss Aboyne (Lochnager) 6f **(59)**
Form - 321221200
Record 2000 - 1st:2 2nd:4 3rd:0 Ran:8
Pre2000 - 1st:2 2nd:3 3rd:4 Ran:27
Win Prizemoney £11,390 *Total Prizemoney* £21,199
Wins * **2000** Mar Southw (GD) H 7f 59 67 <
* ***2000*** *Jan Southw (STD) H 7f 53 63*
* 1999 May Doncas (G-F) H 7f 56 60
* 1997 Jun Pontef (G-F) 6f 57
2000 Turf 1-4: (7f 1-4) (gd, g-f, frm 1-2) 2000 AW 1-4: (7f 1-3, 8f) (Fibr 1-4)
Above-average gelding, effective 7f, acts on gd to frm - acts on Fibr, has worn blinkers, likes left handed tracks. Turf high 67 - 2nd of 16 getting 4lb from Nooshman (6 May Thirsk 7f gd RF 1065) - also 1st of 16 giving 5lb to Melodian (31 Mar Southwell RF 0583). AW high 72 - 2nd of 11 giving 1lb to Mystic Ridge (7 Feb Southwell 7f Fibr RF 0240) - also 1st of 12 from Mutabari (21 Jan Southwell RF 0129). **M Dods [4-35] N A Riddell.*

ABERNANT LADY BHB 20f **RR 4f** 3571[10]
3 gr f Absalom 7.1f **(56)** - Hosting (Thatching) 8f **(66)**
Form - 050
Record 2000 - 1st:0 2nd:0 3rd:0 Ran:3
2000 Turf 0-2: (8f, 10f) (g-f, frm) 2000 AW 0-1: (9f) (Fibr)
Scopey, currently very poor filly. Turf high 4.
**G A Ham [0-3] Derek Walker.*

ABIKAN (IRE) RR 98f 5355a[6]
3 ch f Erins Isle 8.3f **(76)** - Megastart (USA) (Private Account (USA)) 8.5f **(74)**
Form - 17005136
2000 Turf 2-8: (7f, 8f 2, 9f 1-1, 10f 1-3, 12f) (hvy 1-3, sft 1-1, g-s 3, gd)
Very useful filly, effective 8 to 9f, acts on sft to g-s, often wears blinkers (very effectively). Turf high 98 - 1st of 10 from Bibi Karam (14 Oct Gowran Park RF 5043a).
**J S Bolger in IRE [2-8] D H W Dobson.*

ABITARA (IRE) RR 108f 5090a[3]
4 ch f Rainbow Quest (USA) 11.2f **(81)** - Arastou (GER) (Surumu (GER)) 10f **(83)**
Form - 123
2000 Turf 1-3: (10f 2, 12f 1-1) (hvy, gd, g-f 1-1)
Currently Pattern-class filly. Turf high 108 (1st run) (began Jly) - 1st of 10 giving 12lb to Chez Cherie (22 Jly Newmarket RF 3031). This globetrotting filly landed a listed race on the July Course and was later placed in Group Two company.
**A Wohler in GER [1-2] Gestut Ittlingen (from FR [0-1] Spt 2000).*

A BIT SPECIAL RR 69f 5310[3]
2 b f Rahy (USA) 9.1f **(80)** - Speedybird (IRE) **(67+f 65a)** (Danehill (USA)) 10f **(72)**
Form - 3
Record 2000 - 1st:0 2nd:0 3rd:1 Ran:1
Win Prizemoney £0 *Total Prizemoney* £512
2000 Turf 0-1: (7f) (g-s)
Currently average filly.
**H R A Cecil [0-1] The Thoroughbred Corporation.*

ABLE AYR BHB 55f **RR 67f** 5083[11]
3 ch c Formidable (USA) 7.8f **(60)** - Ayr Classic (Local Suitor (USA)) 8.4f **(67)**
Form - 070580000000
Record 2000 - 1st:0 2nd:0 3rd:0 Ran:12
Pre2000 - 1st:1 2nd:0 3rd:1 Ran:8
Win Prizemoney £2,771 *Total Prizemoney* £3,694
Wins * 1999 Jun Carlis (GD) 5f 74 <
2000 Turf 0-12: (5f 2, 6f 8, 7f 2) (hvy, sft 2, g-f 5, frm 4)
Workmanlike, average colt, effective 5f, acts on g-f. Turf high 67.
**J S Goldie [1-20] Frank Brady.*

ABLE MASTER (NZ) RR 101f 578a[10]
5 m
Form - 0
2000 Turf 0-1: (12f) (gd)
Currently very useful. **B Wallace in NZ [0-1].*

ABLE MILLENIUM (IRE) BHB 50f52a **RR 48f 52a** 5063[9]
4 ch g Be My Guest (USA) 10.2f **(66)** - Miami Life (Miami Springs) 9.9f **(59)**
Form - 387000
Record 2000 - 1st:0 2nd:0 3rd:0 Ran:4
Pre2000 - 1st:0 2nd:0 3rd:3 Ran:4
Win Prizemoney £0 *Total Prizemoney* £1,184
2000 Turf 0-2: (10f 2) (sft, g-f) 2000 AW 0-2: (8f, 9f) (Fibr 2)
Unfurnished, moderate gelding, has worn blinkers. Turf high 48 (began Aug). AW high 49. **R W Armstrong [0-8] Dr Cornel Li.*

ABLE NATIVE (IRE) BHB 47f57a **RR 68f 57a** 5154[9]
3 b f Thatching 7.8f **(69)** - Native Joy (IRE) (Be My Native (USA)) 10.2f **(71)**
Form - 721704060
Record 2000 - 1st:1 2nd:1 3rd:0 Ran:9
Pre2000 - 1st:0 2nd:1 3rd:0 Ran:3
Win Prizemoney £2,821 *Total Prizemoney* £5,015
Wins * **2000** *Jun Lingfi (STD) H* *12f* 65 66 <
2000 Turf 0-4: (10f, 12f 2, 14f) (g-f 2, frm 2) 2000 AW 1-5: (7f, 12f 1-4) (Equi 1-3, Fibr 2)
Scopey, average filly, effective 7 to 12f, acts on g-s to frm - acts on Equi, often wears blinkers. Turf high 68 (1st run) - 2nd of 11 getting 6lb from Omniheat (2 Jun Brighton 10f frm RF 1651). AW high 66 - 1st of 10 giving 13lb to The Girls' Filly (27 Jun Lingfield RF 2305). Narrow winner on the Lingfield Equitrack in June.
**R W Armstrong [1-12] Dr Cornel Li.*

ABLE PETE BHB 23f33a **RR 24f 33a** 4221[10]
4 b g Formidable (USA) 7.8f **(60)** - An Empress (USA) (Affirmed (USA)) 9.3f **(79)**
Form - 805021468000
Record 2000 - 1st:1 2nd:1 3rd:0 Ran:11
Pre2000 - 1st:0 2nd:0 3rd:0 Ran:8
Win Prizemoney £1,456 *Total Prizemoney* £2,312
Wins * **2000** *Feb Wolver (STD) H* *12f* 33 36 <
2000 Turf 0-3: (10f, 12f 2) (gd, frm 2) 2000 AW 1-8: (8f, 10f, 11f 3, 12f 1-3) (Equi, Fibr 1-7)
Workmanlike, moderate gelding. Turf high 24. AW high 41.
**A G Newcombe [1-12] Alex Gorrie (from D J S Cosgrove [0-5] May 1999).*

ABLE SEAMAN (USA) BHB 56f **RR 68f** 4696[10]
3 b br g Northern Flagship (USA) 12.2f **(72)** - Love At Dawn (USA) (Grey Dawn II) 11.1f **(72)**
Form - 0453334364720
Record 2000 - 1st:0 2nd:1 3rd:4 Ran:13
Win Prizemoney £0 *Total Prizemoney* £4,249
2000 Turf 0-13: (7f, 10f 5, 11f, 12f 3, 14f 2, 16f) (sft, gd 2, g-f 8, frm 2)
Average gelding, effective 10 to 14f, acts on g-f to frm, best on g-f, has worn blinkers, prefers tight tracks. Turf high 68.
**C E Brittain [0-13] C E Brittain.*

A B MY BOY BHB 43f **RR 41f** 4675[17]
2 ch c Young Ern - Whitstar (Whitstead) 11.5f **(63)**
Form - 67060
Record 2000 - 1st:0 2nd:0 3rd:0 Ran:5
2000 Turf 0-5: (5f 2, 6f 2, 7f) (g-s, gd 3, frm)
Moderate colt. Turf high 41. **E A Wheeler [0-5] C Hales.*

ABOARD (FR) RR 110f 4944a[1]
5 b h Hero's Honor (USA) 9.2f **(76)** - Abordable (USA) (Formidable (USA)) 9.2f **(63)**
Form - 721
2000 Turf 1-3: (10f 1-3) (sft, g-s 1-1, gd)
Group-class colt. Turf high 110 (began Jly) - 1st of 9 giving 6lb to Rosolaw (3 Oct Hoppegarten RF 4944a). High-class German ten-furlong horse with a bright turn of foot.
**W Figge in GER [1-3] H von Finck.*

A BOB LIGHT (IRE) BHB 47f **RR 46f** 1899[5]
3 br f Bob's Return (IRE) - Light Hand (Star Appeal) 9.6f **(65)**
Form - 065
Record 2000 - 1st:0 2nd:0 3rd:0 Ran:3
Pre2000 - 1st:0 2nd:1 3rd:0 Ran:6
Win Prizemoney £0 *Total Prizemoney* £1,688
2000 Turf 0-3: (8f 3) (gd, frm 2)
Moderate filly, effective 7f, acts on frm. Turf high 45. Becoming disappointing. **M H Tompkins [0-9] Robert Levitt.*

ABOO HOM BHB 55f **RR 68?f** 45[4]
6 b h Sadler's Wells (USA) 11.3f **(87)** - Maria Waleska (Filiberto (USA)) 9.5f **(66)**
Form - 7314
Record 2000 - 1st:1 2nd:0 3rd:0 Ran:2
Pre2000 - 1st:0 2nd:0 3rd:2 Ran:9
Win Prizemoney £2,795 *Total Prizemoney* £3,871
Wins * **2000** *Jan Southw (STD) H* *16f* 49 53 <
2000 AW 1-2: (16f 1-2) (Fibr 1-2)
Average horse. AW high 55.
**S Dow [1-6] Byerley Bloodstock (from A C Stewart [0-6] Oct 1997).*

ABOU SAFIAN (IRE) RR 104f 5206a[2]
4 ch c Bluebird (USA) 7.9f **(71)** - Kind of Cute (Prince Sabo) 7.2f **(62)**
Form - 2
2000 Turf 0-1: (10f) (hvy)
Currently very useful colt. (1st run) - 2nd of 11 getting 3lb from Right Wing (20 Oct Bordeaux 10f hvy RF 5206a).
**Miss V Dissaux in FR [0-1] D Al Johar.*

ABOVE BOARD BHB 56a **RR 28f** 1438[11]
5 b g Night Shift (USA) 8.1f **(73)** - Bundled Up (USA) (Sharpen Up) 8.3f **(67)**
Form - 556587822033060
Record 2000 - 1st:0 2nd:2 3rd:2 Ran:12
Pre2000 - 1st:0 2nd:0 3rd:1 Ran:19
Win Prizemoney £0 *Total Prizemoney* £3,277
2000 Turf 0-2: (5f, 6f) (g-s, gd) 2000 AW 0-10: (5f, 6f 5, 7f 3, 8f) (Fibr 10)
Fair gelding, effective 5 to 6f, best at 6f, - acts on Fibr, has worn blinkers (effectively). AW high 54 - 3rd of 8 giving 17lb to Lydia's Look (27 Mar Southwell 5f Fibr RF 0513). Inconsistent.
**R F Marvin [0-24] R A B Saville (from J Hanson [0-5] Spt 1998).*

ABRACADABJAR BHB 55f **RR 62f** 4675[15]
2 b c Royal Abjar (USA) - Celt Song (IRE) (Unfuwain (USA))
Form - 850
Record 2000 - 1st:0 2nd:0 3rd:0 Ran:3
2000 Turf 0-3: (7f, 8f, 9f) (g-s, g-f, frm)
Currently average colt. Turf high 65 (began Aug).
**P Mitchell [0-3] Woodcote Stud Ltd.*

ABSCOND (USA) RR 97f 2445[8]
3 b f Unbridled (USA) - Lemhi Go (USA) (Lemhi Gold (USA))
Form - 5178
Record 2000 - 1st:1 2nd:0 3rd:0 Ran:4

Pre2000 - 1st:0 2nd:2 3rd:0 Ran:2
Win Prizemoney £4,007 *Total Prizemoney* £8,362
Wins *** 2000** May Beverl (GD) 9.9f 84 <
2000 Turf 1-4: (10f 1-2, 11f, 12f) (gd 1-1, g-f 2, frm)
Scopey, very useful filly, effective 7 to 11f, best at 7f, acts on g-f to frm, best on frm. Turf high 97. Basically a disappointing sort, she was last of five in the Cheshire Oaks, but was found an easy opening in a Beverley maiden. That proved to be her only win.
**Sir Michael Stoute [1-6] Cheveley Park Stud.*

ABSENT FRIENDS BHB 65a **RR 61f** 5112[22]
3 b c Rock City 8.8f **(62)** - Green Supreme (Primo Dominie) 6.2f **(80)**
Form - 04075300
Record 2000 - 1st:0 2nd:0 3rd:1 Ran:8
Pre2000 - 1st:0 2nd:0 3rd:1 Ran:4
Win Prizemoney £0 *Total Prizemoney* £1,605
2000 Turf 0-7: (5f 5, 6f 2) (g-s 2, gd 3, g-f, frm) 2000 AW 0-1: (6f) (Fibr)
Lengthy, average colt. Turf high 61. Inconsistent.
**J Cullinan [0-12] Miss L Vollaro.*

ABSINTHER BHB 55f58a **RR 55f 58a** 5016[5]
3 b g Presidium 7.5f **(56)** - Heavenly Queen (Scottish Reel) 7f **(61)**
Form - 02705312525
Record 2000 - 1st:1 2nd:3 3rd:1 Ran:11
Pre2000 - 1st:0 2nd:0 3rd:1 Ran:4
Win Prizemoney £3,445 *Total Prizemoney* £7,157
Wins *** 2000** Aug Mussel (G-F) C 9f 46 <
2000 Turf 1-9: (6f, 7f 3, 8f 2, 9f 1-2, 10f) (g-s, gd 3, g-f, frm 1-4) 2000 AW 0 2: (9f 2) (Fibr 2)
Fair gelding, effective 8 to 9f, acts on frm - acts on Fibr, has worn blinkers, prefers tight tracks. Turf high 59 - 2nd of 9 giving 20lb to Philagain (26 Jun Musselburgh 8f frm RF 2274). AW high 59 (1st run) (began Oct) - 2nd of 12 getting 9lb from Faraway Look (3 Oct Wolverhampton 9f Fibr RF 4785). Consistent.
**E J Alston [1-15] J E Abbey.*

ABSOLUTE FANTASY BHB 64f60a **RR 60f 60a** 5112[2]
4 b f Beveled (USA) 6.9f **(64)** - Sharp Venita (Sharp Edge) 10f **(56)**
Form - 46268281473428242127510 2
Record 2000 - 1st:3 2nd:7 3rd:1 Ran:23
Pre2000 - 1st:0 2nd:0 3rd:0 Ran:4
Win Prizemoney £9,286 *Total Prizemoney* £15,996
Wins *** 2000** Spt Goodwo (HVY) H 5f 56 60 <
*** 2000** Aug Newbur (G-F) H 6f 50 53
*** 2000** May Bright (FRM) H 6f 44 45
2000 Turf 3-19: (5f 1-9, 6f 2-8, 7f 2) (g-s, gd 1-6, g-f 2, frm 2-9, hrd)
2000 AW 0-4: (6f 3, 8f) (Equi 3, Fibr)
Average filly, effective 5 to 6f, best at 5f, acts on gd to hrd, best on gd, mostly wears blinkers (very effectively), and excels at Newbury. Turf high 60 - 2nd of 25 giving 12lb to Frampant (20 Oct Newbury 5f gd RF 5112) - also 1st of 21 giving 13lb to Mutasawwar (20 Spt Goodwood RF 4543). AW high 43.
**E A Wheeler [3-27] The Red Square Partnership.*

ABSOLUTE MAJORITY BHB 44f51a **RR 35f 51a** 412[5]
5 ch g Absalom 7.1f **(56)** - Shall We Run (Hotfoot) 10.5f **(59)**
Form - 04725135
Record 2000 - 1st:1 2nd:1 3rd:1 Ran:5
Pre2000 - 1st:1 2nd:0 3rd:1 Ran:11
Win Prizemoney £4,715 *Total Prizemoney* £5,929
Wins **2000** *Jan Southw (STD) S* *12f* *56*
1999 *Feb Wolver (STD)* *9.4f* *66+* <
2000 AW 1-5: (9f, 11f, 12f 1-3) (Fibr 1-5)
Fair gelding, effective 9 to 12f, - acts on Fibr, favours left handed tracks. AW high 56.
**H S Howe [0-2] George Searle (from P Howling [1-11] Jan 2000).*

ABSTRACT (IRE) BHB 36a **RR 32f** 3617[11]
4 b f Perugino (USA) - Kalapa (FR) (Mouktar)
Form - 070834000
Record 2000 - 1st:0 2nd:0 3rd:1 Ran:9
Pre2000 - 1st:0 2nd:0 3rd:0 Ran:15
Win Prizemoney £0 *Total Prizemoney* £847
2000 Turf 0-8: (5f, 6f 2, 7f 3, 8f 2) (gd, g-f 4, frm 2, hrd) 2000 AW 0-1: (8f) (Fibr)
Small, very moderate filly, effective 8f, - acts on Fibr, often wears blinkers, likes left handed tracks. Turf high 32. (1st run) - 3rd of 12 giving 9lb to Bewildered (13 Jly Wolverhampton 8f Fibr RF 2777).
**J S Wainwright [0-19] Mrs Kay Harrison (from D J S Cosgrove [0-5] Spt 1998).*

ABTAAL BHB 38f38a **RR 52f 38a** 4759[11]
10 b g Green Desert (USA) 7.8f **(78)** - Stufida (Bustino) 10.4f **(64)**
Form - 681360867670
Record 2000 - 1st:1 2nd:0 3rd:1 Ran:12
Pre2000 - 1st:8 2nd:4 3rd:6 Ran:58
Win Prizemoney £20,175 *Total Prizemoney* £28,422
Wins *** 2000** *May Southw (STD) S* *7f* *46*
* 1999 *May Wolver (STD) H* *7f* *59* *63*
* 1999 *Mar Wolver (STD) C* *7f* *58*
* 1999 *Feb Southw (STD) S* *7f* *50*
* 1998 *Aug Southw (STD) C* *7f* *59+*
* 1998 Aug Bright (FRM) 7f 64
1998 Jly Bright (G-F) C 7f 50
1997 Jun Lingfi (G-F) SH 7f 49 48
2000 Turf 0-1: (7f) (gd) 2000 AW 1-11: (6f, 7f 1-7, 8f 3) (Fibr 1-11)
Fair gelding, effective 6 to 7f, best at 7f, - acts on Fibr, often wears blinkers (effectively), favours left handed tracks, favours tight tracks, and likes Southwell. AW high 55 - 3rd of 14 giving 5lb to High Esteem (22 May Southwell 6f Fibr RF 1377).
**Mrs N Macauley [6-38] Andy Peake (from R J Hodges [2-25] Jly 1998).*

ABU CAMP BHB 45f40a **RR 41f 40a** 25[6]
5 b g Indian Ridge 7.6f **(74)** - Artistic Licence (High Top) 10.2f **(67)**
Form - 6
Record 2000 - 1st:0 2nd:0 3rd:0 Ran:1
Pre2000 - 1st:0 2nd:0 3rd:1 Ran:12
Win Prizemoney £0 *Total Prizemoney* £474
2000 AW 0-1: (8f) (Equi)
Moderate gelding, has worn blinkers. Consistent.
**C G Cox [0-3] John Manser (from M J Heaton-Ellis [0-12] Jly 1999).*

ABUZAID (USA) BHB 85f **RR 87f** 4063[4]
3 br c Nureyev (USA) 8.4f **(84)** - Elle Seule (USA) (Exclusive Native (USA)) 9.1f **(81)**
Form - 00015324
Record 2000 - 1st:1 2nd:1 3rd:1 Ran:8
Pre2000 - 1st:1 2nd:0 3rd:0 Ran:3
Win Prizemoney £7,635 *Total Prizemoney* £12,707
Wins *** 2000** Jun Salisb (G-F) H 9.9f 78 80 <
* 1999 Oct Newcas (G-S) 6f 79
2000 Turf 1-8: (7f 2, 8f, 10f 1-3, 11f, 12f) (gd, g-f 2, frm 1-5)
Well made, useful colt, effective 6 to 11f, best at 10f, acts on g-f to frm, best on frm. Turf high 87 - 4th of 10 giving 5lb to Andromedes (29 Aug Ripon 10f frm RF 4063) - also 1st of 10 getting 14lb from Clarendon (29 Jun Salisbury RF 2380). Improving. Bounced back to form when winning at Salisbury in June, and seemed to find twelve furlongs too far next time. Held since.
**J L Dunlop [2-11] Hamdan Al Maktoum.*

ABYSSINIAN WOLF **RR 42f** 5100[18]
2 ch c Dr Devious (IRE) 9.9f **(74)** - Guilty Secret (IRE) (Kris) 9.5f **(73)**
Form - 0
Record 2000 - 1st:0 2nd:0 3rd:0 Ran:1
2000 Turf 0-1: (7f) (gd)
Currently moderate colt. **J R Fanshawe [0-1] Abdulla Al Khalifa.*

ACADEMIC ACCURACY **RR 67f** 3079[6]
2 b f Environment Friend 7.5f **(67)** - Branitska (Mummy's Pet) 7.7f **(60)**
Form - 76
Record 2000 - 1st:0 2nd:0 3rd:0 Ran:2
2000 Turf 0-2: (6f, 7f) (gd, frm)
Currently average filly. Turf high 67. **R Hannon [0-2] W J Gredley.*

ACADEMIC GOLD (IRE) **RR 64f** 3842[3]
2 ch c Royal Academy (USA) 7.8f **(77)** - Penultimate (USA) (Roberto (USA)) 10f **(76)**
Form - 3
Record 2000 - 1st:0 2nd:0 3rd:1 Ran:1
Win Prizemoney £0 *Total Prizemoney* £537
2000 Turf 0-1: (8f) (gd)
Currently average colt. **K R Burke [0-1] Nigel Shields.*

ACADEMIC RECORD BHB 58f **RR 41f** 4181[5]
2 b g Royal Academy (USA) 7.8f **(77)** - Bala Monaafis (IRE) **(54f)** (In

The Wings)
Form - 785
Record 2000 - 1st:0 2nd:0 3rd:0 Ran:3
2000 Turf 0-3: (5f, 7f 2) (g-s, gd, g-f)
Currently average gelding. Turf high 41 (began Aug).
**K R Burke [0-3] Nigel Shields.*

ACAMANI (GER) RR 112f
4842a[4]
3 b c Winged Love (IRE) - Adjani (GER) (Surumu (GER)) 10f **(83)**
Form - 3464
2000 Turf 0-4: (12f 3, 14f) (hvy 2, sft, gd)
Strong, Group-class colt. Turf high 112 (1st run) (began Jly) - 3rd of 20 to Samum (2 Jly Hamburg 12f sft RF 2581a).
**A Schutz in GER [0-4].*

A C AZURE (IRE) BHB 73f74a RR 72f 74a
5015[2]
2 br g Dolphin Street (FR) - Kelvedon (General Assembly (USA)) 10f **(68)**
Form - 65372
Record 2000 - 1st:0 2nd:1 3rd:1 Ran:5
Win Prizemoney £0 *Total Prizemoney* £1,096
2000 Turf 0-4: (6f 2, 7f 2) (sft, gd, g-f, frm) 2000 AW 0-1: (6f) (Fibr)
Above-average gelding. Turf high 72 (began Aug). (1st run) - 2nd of 9 to Tumbleweed Tenor (17 Oct Wolverhampton 6f Fibr RF 5015).
**P D Evans [0-5] P M Mooney.*

ACCEPTING BHB 83f RR 86f
1132[4]
3 b c Mtoto 11.5f **(71)** - D'Azy (Persian Bold) 9.3f **(66)**
Form - 64
Record 2000 - 1st:0 2nd:0 3rd:0 Ran:2
Pre2000 - 1st:0 2nd:1 3rd:0 Ran:2
Win Prizemoney £0 *Total Prizemoney* £1,578
2000 Turf 0-2: (10f, 12f) (gd, g-f)
Workmanlike, useful colt. Turf high 86 - 4th of 10 giving 10lb to Kaiapoi (10 May Chester 12f g-f RF 1132).
**J H M Gosden [0-4] George Strawbridge.*

ACCOUNTING BHB 62f RR 31f
962[10]
4 b f Sillery (USA) - Fabulous Account (USA) (Private Account (USA)) 8.5f **(74)**
Form - 0
Record 2000 - 1st:0 2nd:0 3rd:0 Ran:1
2000 Turf 0-1: (12f) (gd)
Very moderate filly.
**Miss H C Knight [0-5] Christopher Shirley Brasher.*

ACCYSTAN BHB 44f52a RR 37f 52a
1958[8]
5 ch g Efisio 7.7f **(69)** - Amia (CAN) (Nijinsky (CAN)) 10.3f **(77)**
Form - 06271633508
Record 2000 - 1st:1 2nd:1 3rd:2 Ran:11
Pre2000 - 1st:3 2nd:0 3rd:4 Ran:15
Win Prizemoney £7,924 *Total Prizemoney* £11,161

Wins								
*** 2000**	*Mar*	*Southw*	*(STD)*	*H*	*12f*	*50*	*54*	
***** 1999	*Jly*	*Southw*	*(STD)*	*S*	*12f*		*45*	
1998	*Feb*	*Southw*	*(STD)*	*H*	*11f*	*60*	*67+*	<
1998	*Jan*	*Wolver*	*(STD)*	*C*	*9.4f*		*66*	

2000 Turf 0-2: (12f, 14f) (g-s, frm) 2000 AW 1-9: (9f, 11f 4, 12f 1-3, 16f) (Fibr 1-9)
Fair gelding, effective 11 to 16f, best at 11f, - acts on Fibr, favours left handed tracks. Turf high 37. AW high 54 - 3rd of 9 giving 19lb to Preposition (27 Mar Southwell 11f Fibr RF 0515) - also 1st of 10 giving 8lb to Malwina (6 Mar Southwell RF 0413).
**M D Hammond [3-21] G Heap (from P C Haslam [2-12] Jly 1998).*

ACEBO LYONS (IRE) BHB 56f38a RR 60f 38a
5227[4]
5 b m Waajib 8.9f **(67)** - Etage (Ile de Bourbon (USA)) 10.1f **(67)**
Form - 0166584732014
Record 2000 - 1st:2 2nd:1 3rd:1 Ran:12
Pre2000 - 1st:1 2nd:2 3rd:2 Ran:21
Win Prizemoney £7,608 *Total Prizemoney* £13,108

Wins								
*** 2000**	Oct	Yarmou	(SFT)	C	14.1f		38+	
*** 2000**	Mar	Doncas	(G-F)	H	10.3f	56	59	
* 1998	Aug	Haydoc	(GD)		10.5f		70	<

2000 Turf 2-12: (10f 1-5, 12f 5, 14f 1-1, 16f)(sft 1-1, gd 3, g-f 3, frm 1-5)
Average filly, effective 10 to 16f, best at 10f, acts on g-f to frm, best on g-f, has worn blinkers, likes left handed tracks, likes tight tracks, excels at Yarmouth. Turf high 60 - 5th of 15 giving 5lb to Sifat (31 May Yarmouth 10f g-f RF 1613) - also 1st of 20 getting 14lb from Noukari (23 Mar Doncaster RF 0478).
**A P Jarvis [3-33] Terence Lyons II.*

ACE OF PARKES BHB 68f65a RR 80f 65a
5014[9]
4 b g Teenoso (USA) 10.5f **(62)** - Summerhill Spruce (Windjammer (USA)) 7f **(59)**
Form - 50650030080
Record 2000 - 1st:0 2nd:0 3rd:1 Ran:11
Pre2000 - 1st:3 2nd:0 3rd:1 Ran:13
Win Prizemoney £16,831 *Total Prizemoney* £24,758

Wins						
1998	Aug	Cheste	(G-S)	6.1f	98	<
1998	Jly	Cheste	(G-F)	6.1f	98	<
1998	Jly	Hamilt	(FRM)	5f	91+	

2000 Turf 0-10: (5f 3, 6f 6, 7f) (g-s, gd, g-f 5, frm 3) 2000 AW 0-1: (6f) (Fibr)
Scopey, decent gelding. Turf high 83.
**A Berry [0-11] Joseph Heler (from J Berry [3-13] Spt 1999).*

ACE OF TRUMPS BHB 48f37a RR 50f 37a
5299[8]
4 ch g First Trump - Elle Reef (Shareef Dancer (USA)) 9.9f **(73)**
Form - 0100071203072564352321 8
Record 2000 - 1st:3 2nd:4 3rd:3 Ran:22
Pre2000 - 1st:3 2nd:3 3rd:3 Ran:25
Win Prizemoney £14,922 *Total Prizemoney* £23,066

Wins								
*** 2000**	Oct	Mussel	(SFT)	H	9f	43	47	
*** 2000**	May	Hamilt	(G-F)	C	9.2f		50	
*** 2000**	Mar	Mussel	(GD)	SH	9f	50	51	
1999	May	Warwic	(SFT)	C	10.5f		59	
1999	May	Nottin	(FRM)	SH	8.2f	55	59	
1998	Aug	Newmar	(FRM)	S	7f		68	<

2000 Turf 3-22: (7f, 8f 3, 9f 3-11, 10f 3, 11f 4) (hvy 3, g-s 2, gd 2-8, g-f 1-4, frm 5)
Neat, fair gelding, effective 8 to 11f, acts on sft to g-f, has worn blinkers, likes right handed tracks, favours tight tracks, and excels at Musselburgh. Turf high 51 (1st run) - 1st of 16 getting 10lb from Celestial Key (30 Mar Musselburgh RF 0568) - also 1st of 10 giving 14lb to Chez Bonito (7 May Hamilton RF 1076).
**J Hetherton [3-33] C D Barber-Lomax (from W J Haggas [3-14] May 1999).*

ACERBIC (USA) RR 96f
4567a[3]
4 b c Lear Fan (USA) 10.4f **(80)** - Averti (USA) **(97f)** (Known Fact (USA)) 7.4f **(67)**
Form - 3
2000 Turf 0-1: (7f) (gd)
Currently very useful colt. (1st run) - 3rd of 15 giving 4lb to Touch Of The Blues (16 Spt Longchamp 7f gd RF 4567a). **in FR [0-1].*

ACHILLES SKY BHB 72f RR 73f
4380[12]
4 b c Hadeer 8.9f **(58)** - Diva Madonna (Chief Singer) 8.9f **(66)**
Form - 10023870
Record 2000 - 1st:1 2nd:1 3rd:1 Ran:8
Pre2000 - 1st:1 2nd:0 3rd:0 Ran:6
Win Prizemoney £8,449 *Total Prizemoney* £11,129

Wins								
*** 2000**	Mar	Southw	(GD)	H	12f	71	73+	<
* 1999	Jly	Nottin	(GD)	H	10f	68	71	

2000 Turf 1-8: (10f 3, 12f 1-4, 14f) (g-s, gd, g-f 3, frm 1-3)
Scopey, above-average colt, effective 10 to 12f, best at 12f, acts on g-f to frm, best on g-f, has worn blinkers, prefers left handed tracks. Turf high 73 - 2nd of 4 to Captain's Log (16 Jun York 12f g-f RF 2036) - also 1st of 4 getting 6lb from Jamaican Flight (31 Mar Southwell RF 0585).
**K R Burke [2-14] Achilles International.*

ACHILLES SPIRIT (IRE) BHB 77f RR 79f
4818[8]
2 b c Deploy 11.4f **(67)** - Scenic Spirit (IRE) (Scenic)
Form - 01368
Record 2000 - 1st:1 2nd:0 3rd:1 Ran:5
Win Prizemoney £4,153 *Total Prizemoney* £5,903

Wins						
*** 2000**	Jly	Epsom	(G-S)	6f	76	<

2000 Turf 1-5: (6f 1-2, 7f, 8f 2) (g-s 2, gd 1-1, g-f, frm)
Above-average colt. Turf high 79 - 3rd of 13 giving 3lb to Forever My Lord (5 Aug Goodwood 7f g-f RF 3392) - also 1st of 9 from Seductive (13 Jly Epsom RF 2760). Improved from his debut to win an Epsom maiden auction event on his second start.
**K R Burke [1-5] Achilles International.*

ACHILLES SUN BHB 62f63a **RR 62f 63a** 4808[15]
2 b g Deploy 11.4f **(67)** - Tsungani (Cure The Blues (USA)) 9.5f **(63)**
Form - U40870
Record 2000 - 1st:0 2nd:0 3rd:0 Ran:6
Win Prizemoney £0 *Total Prizemoney* £511
2000 Turf 0-5: (6f, 7f 4) (g-s 2, gd, g-f, frm) 2000 AW 0-1: (8f) (Fibr)
Average gelding. Turf high 62 (began Jly).
**K R Burke [0-6] Achilles International.*

ACHILLES WINGS (USA) BHB 70f69a **RR 71f 69a** 1813[12]
4 b g Irish River (FR) 9f **(77)** - Shirley Valentine (Shirley Heights) 10.3f **(74)**
Form - 3442020
Record 2000 - 1st:0 2nd:2 3rd:1 Ran:7
Win Prizemoney £0 *Total Prizemoney* £3,060
2000 Turf 0-5: (8f, 10f 2, 13f 2) (g-s, gd 2, g-f 2) 2000 AW 0-2: (8f, 10f) (Equi, Fibr)
Workmanlike, above-average gelding, effective 10 to 13f, best at 10f, acts on g-s to gd - acts on Equi, prefers left handed tracks. Turf high 71 - 2nd of 13 getting 5lb from Turtle Soup (31 May Newbury 13f g-s RF 1592). AW high 71 (1st run) - 3rd of 10 giving 21lb to You da Man (4 Mar Lingfield 10f Equi RF 0400).
**K R Burke [0-7] Achilles International.*

ACID TEST BHB 54f53a **RR 54f 53a** 4538[10]
5 ch g Sharpo 7.5f **(68)** - Clunk Click (Star Appeal) 9.6f **(65)**
Form - 8663007300758670
Record 2000 - 1st:0 2nd:0 3rd:2 Ran:16
Pre2000 - 1st:8 2nd:5 3rd:1 Ran:43
Win Prizemoney £32,180 *Total Prizemoney* £39,876

Wins								
*	1999	Jun	Cheste	(SFT)	H	7f	70	78 <
*	1999	May	Catter	(FRM)	H	7f	67	72
*	*1999*	*Jan*	*Lingfi*	*(STD)*	*H*	*6f*	*62*	*67*
*	*1999*	*Jan*	*Lingfi*	*(STD)*	*H*	*6f*	*58*	*64*
*	*1998*	*Dec*	*Lingfi*	*(STD)*	*H*	*6f*	*52*	*60*
	1998	Jun	Lingfi	(GD)		7f		72
	1997	Aug	Newmar	(G-F)	H	7f	65	69
	1997	Jly	Lingfi	(G-F)	S	6f		63

2000 Turf 0-13: (6f, 7f 8, 8f 3, 10f) (g-s 2, gd, g-f 4, frm 5, hrd) 2000 AW 0-3: (6f, 7f, 8f) (Equi 3)
Fair gelding, effective 7f, acts on g-s to frm, has worn blinkers, likes left handed tracks, likes tight tracks. Turf high 67. AW high 46. Consistent.
**M A Buckley [5-37] Fair Price Racing (from W R Muir [3-22] Oct 1998).*

ACORN CATCHER BHB 60f65a **RR 61df 65a** 4993[3]
2 b f Emarati (USA) 6.6f **(63)** - Anytime Baby **(55f 40a)** (Bairn (USA)) 7.7f **(59)**
Form - 0138713
Record 2000 - 1st:2 2nd:0 3rd:2 Ran:7
Win Prizemoney £3,846 *Total Prizemoney* £4,740

Wins								
*	***2000***	*Spt*	*Wolver*	*(STD)*	*S*	*5f*		*64* <
*	**2000**	Jly	Leices	(G-F)	S	5f		61

2000 Turf 1-5: (5f 1-4, 6f) (sft, frm 1-4) 2000 AW 1-2: (5f 1-1, 6f) (Fibr 1-2)
Average filly, effective 5 to 6f, best at 5f, acts on frm - acts on Fibr. Turf high 61 - 1st of 8 from Screamin' Georgina (8 Jly Leicester RF 2638). AW high 64 (1st run) (began Spt) - 1st of 12 getting 5lb from Justalord (30 Spt Wolverhampton RF 4762).
**B Palling [2-7] N C Phillips & T Davies.*

ACQUITTAL (IRE) BHB 27f29a **RR 44f 29a** 4328[6]
8 b g Danehill (USA) 9.1f **(79)** - Perfect Alibi (Law Society (USA)) 9.9f **(70)**
Form - 004453876
Record 2000 - 1st:0 2nd:0 3rd:1 Ran:9
Pre2000 - 1st:1 2nd:5 3rd:6 Ran:39
Win Prizemoney £2,668 *Total Prizemoney* £10,526
2000 Turf 0-9: (11f, 12f 5, 14f, 16f 2) (g-s, g-f 2, frm 6)
Moderate gelding, effective 10 to 14f, best at 10f, acts on g-f to frm, best on frm, often wears blinkers (effectively), prefers left handed tracks, favours tight tracks. Turf high 44.
**P L Clinton [0-9] In The Clear Racing (from A Streeter [0-28] Spt 1999).*

ACROBATIC BHB 100f **RR 104f** 1894[2]
3 br c Warning 8.1f **(77)** - Ayodhya (IRE) (Astronef)
Form - 622
Record 2000 - 1st:0 2nd:2 3rd:0 Ran:3
Pre2000 - 1st:1 2nd:0 3rd:0 Ran:2
Win Prizemoney £4,792 *Total Prizemoney* £10,454

Wins							
*	1999	Spt	Newbur	(G-F)	6f		85 <

2000 Turf 0-3: (7f 2, 8f) (gd 2, frm)
Scopey, very useful colt. Turf high 104 - 2nd of 8 giving 4lb to Spencers Wood (7 May Newmarket 7f frm RF 1081). Made a decent reappearance at the Craven meeting and ran very well when just beaten in a classified event at the same track next time. Not seen out after June.
**J R Fanshawe [1-5] Dr Catherine Wills.*

ACTION JACKSON BHB 23f24a **RR 29f 24a** 3520[7]
8 ch g Hadeer 8.9f **(58)** - Water Woo (USA) (Tom Rolfe) 9.4f **(75)**
Form - 0587
Record 2000 - 1st:0 2nd:0 3rd:0 Ran:4
Pre2000 - 1st:2 2nd:10 3rd:2 Ran:51
Win Prizemoney £4,854 *Total Prizemoney* £13,234

Wins							
1996	Spt	Pontef	(GD)	S	10f		45
1996	Jly	Nottin	(G-F)	S	10f		55 <

2000 Turf 0-3: (12f, 13f, 14f) (g-f 2, frm) 2000 AW 0-1: (16f) (Fibr)
Little account gelding, effective 14f, - acts on Fibr, favours left handed tracks. Turf high 29 (began Jly).
**A W Carroll [0-4] D Morgan (from B J McMath [2-45] Jly 1999).*

ACTIVIST RR 51f 4386[8]
2 ch c Diesis 9f **(80)** - Shicklah (USA) (The Minstrel (CAN)) 10f **(72)**
Form - 8
Record 2000 - 1st:0 2nd:0 3rd:0 Ran:1
2000 Turf 0-1: (7f) (gd)
Currently fair colt.
**M L W Bell [0-1] Highclere Thoroughbred Racing Ltd.*

ACT OF REFORM (USA) BHB 85f85a **RR 82f 85a** 4651[1]
2 b c Lit de Justice (USA) - Bionic Soul (USA) (Bionic Light (USA))
Form - 51431
Record 2000 - 1st:2 2nd:0 3rd:1 Ran:5
Win Prizemoney £6,331 *Total Prizemoney* £8,029

Wins							
*	***2000***	*Spt*	*Southw*	*(STD)*	*8f*		*86* <
*	***2000***	*Aug*	*Wolver*	*(STD)*	*7f*		*86* <

2000 Turf 0-3: (6f, 8f 2) (gd, frm 2) 2000 AW 2-2: (7f 1-1, 8f 1-1) (Fibr 2-2)
Useful colt. Turf high 82 (began Jly) - 4th of 13 giving 6lb to Flit About (4 Spt Bath 8f frm RF 4203). AW high 86 (began Aug) - 1st of 8 giving 2lb to Alphaeus (26 Spt Southwell RF 4651) - also 1st of 9 giving 5lb to Jamila (19 Aug Wolverhampton RF 3810).
**R Charlton [2-5] Highclere Thoroughbred Racing Ltd.*

ACTUALLY (IRE) BHB 22f36a **RR ?f 36a** 4329[8]
3 b f Namaqualand (USA) - Extra Time **(75f 51a)** (Shadeed (USA)) 8.2f **(70)**
Form - 8008
Record 2000 - 1st:0 2nd:0 3rd:0 Ran:2
Pre2000 - 1st:0 2nd:0 3rd:0 Ran:6
2000 Turf 0-2: (10f, 11f) (gd, g-f)
Light-framed, little account filly, has worn blinkers. (began Aug). Becoming disappointing. **Andrew Reid [0-8] A S Reid.*

ADAMAS (IRE) BHB 67f **RR 94f** 5101[13]
3 b f Fairy King (USA) 7.7f **(75)** - Corynida (USA) (Alleged (USA)) 10f **(76)**
Form - 7410843F00
Record 2000 - 1st:1 2nd:0 3rd:1 Ran:10
Pre2000 - 1st:0 2nd:1 3rd:0 Ran:1
Win Prizemoney £3,850 *Total Prizemoney* £6,113

Wins							
*	**2000**	Jun	Beverl	(G-F)	8.5f		57+ <

2000 Turf 1-10: (8f 1-4, 10f 4, 11f, 12f) (gd 4, g-f, frm 1-5)
Useful filly, likes tight tracks. Turf high 94. Becoming disappointing. Got off the mark in cosy style at Beverley in June, but failed to build on that. She has dropped considerably in the handicap as a result. **Andrew Turnell [1-11] Mrs Claire Hollowood.*

ADAWAR (IRE) BHB 79f **RR 80f** 2664[6]
3 b c Perugino (USA) - Adalya (IRE) (Darshaan) 9.9f **(84)**
Form - 562136
Record 2000 - 1st:1 2nd:1 3rd:1 Ran:6
Win Prizemoney £3,893 *Total Prizemoney* £5,885

Wins * 2000 Jun Beverl (G-F) 7.5f 80+ <
2000 Turf 1-6: (7f 1-1, 8f, 10f 4) (g-s, gd 2, g-f 2, hrd 1-1)
Scopey, decent colt, effective 7 to 10f, acts on g-f to hrd, best on g-f. Turf high 80 - 3rd of 7 getting 1lb from Linden Grace (30 Jun Newcastle 8f g-f RF 2405) - also 1st of 7 from Golden Chance (14 Jun Beverley RF 1953). **Sir Michael Stoute [1-6] H H Aga Khan.*

A DAY ON THE DUB BHB 42f41a RR 54f 41a 5294[9]
7 b g Presidium 7.5f **(56)** - Border Mouse (Border Chief)
Form - 5644014075050
Record 2000 - 1st:1 2nd:0 3rd:0 Ran:12
Pre2000 - 1st:3 2nd:2 3rd:0 Ran:12
Win Prizemoney £10,217 *Total Prizemoney* £13,041
Wins * **2000** May Nottin (G-S) H 10f 47 54 <
* 1999 Oct Redcar (SFT) C 11f 50
* 1999 Oct Newcas (G-S) CH 8f 36 40
* 1999 *Jan Southw (STD) 12f 39*
2000 Turf 1-12: (8f 2, 9f 2, 10f 1-5, 11f, 12f 2) (sft, g-s 2, gd 1-4, g-f 2, frm 2, hrd)
Fair gelding, effective 8 to 11f, acts on g-s to gd, best on gd, prefers left handed tracks, likes tight tracks, excels at Nottingham. Turf high 54 - 1st of 17 getting 13lb from Divorce Action (19 May Nottingham RF 1309). **D Eddy [6-33] Revblayd.*

ADDICKS ADDICTS RR 251[8]
3 b c King's Signet (USA) 7f **(51)** - Alzamina (Alzao (USA)) 7.1f **(68)**
Form - 8
Record 2000 - 1st:0 2nd:0 3rd:0 Ran:1
2000 AW 0-1: (5f) (Equi)
Scopey, currently poor colt. **J R Best [0-1] Charlton Racing.*

ADDITION BHB 50f RR 52f 4275[12]
4 b f Dilum (USA) 7.1f **(56)** - Cedar Lady (Telsmoss)
Form - 00460
Record 2000 - 1st:0 2nd:0 3rd:0 Ran:5
Pre2000 - 1st:1 2nd:1 3rd:2 Ran:15
Win Prizemoney £4,199 *Total Prizemoney* £6,876
Wins * 1999 Jly Warwic (G-F) H 6.8f 52 60 <
2000 Turf 0-5: (5f, 7f 3, 8f) (gd 2, g-f, frm 2)
Neat, fair filly, effective 7f, acts on g-f to frm. Turf high 52 - 4th of 10 getting 5lb from Aploy (28 Jly Salisbury 7f frm RF 3181). **R J Hodges [1-20] J W Mursell.*

ADELPHI BOY (IRE) BHB 71f95a RR 71f 95a 5126[4]
4 ch g Ballad Rock 7.2f **(63)** - Toda (Absalom) 7.2f **(58)**
Form - 03146002104
Record 2000 - 1st:2 2nd:1 3rd:1 Ran:11
Pre2000 - 1st:3 2nd:3 3rd:3 Ran:24
Win Prizemoney £20,325 *Total Prizemoney* £32,901
Wins * **2000** Spt Yarmou (G-F) H 8f 67 71
* **2000** *Feb Wolver (STD) 9.4f 95* <
* 1998 *Dec Lingfi (STD) H 5f 85 82*
* 1998 *Dec Southw (STD) H 5f 79 84*
* 1998 *Dec Southw (STD) 5f 71*
2000 Turf 1-7: (6f, 7f 2, 8f 1-2, 9f, 12f) (sft, g-s, gd 2, g-f, frm 1-2) 2000 AW 1-4: (7f, 8f 2, 9f 1-1) (Fibr 1-4)
Workmanlike, very useful gelding, effective 7 to 9f, best at 8f, acts on gd - acts on Fibr, likes tight tracks. Turf high 71. AW high 95 - 1st of 4 from Weet-A-Minute (8 Feb Wolverhampton RF 0244). Inconsistent. He showed some decent form on sand at the end of 1998, but as a result is rated high on sand and his opportunities are limited. Much better weighted on turf, and won a handicap at Yarmouth in September. Likes to race up with the pace.
**M C Chapman [5-35] Barry Brown.*

ADILABAD (USA) BHB 114f RR 118+f 4839a[3]
3 b c Gulch (USA) 9.6f **(79)** - Adaiyka (IRE) **(103f)** (Doyoun) 9f **(69)**
Form - 5113
Record 2000 - 1st:2 2nd:0 3rd:1 Ran:4
Pre2000 - 1st:2 2nd:0 3rd:0 Ran:2
Win Prizemoney £52,646 *Total Prizemoney* £59,305
Wins * **2000** Aug Windso (G-F) G3 10f 118 <
* **2000** Aug Goodwo (GD) L 8f 112
* 1999 Oct Newmar (GD) 7f 82+
* 1999 Spt Sandow (GD) 7.1f 91+
2000 Turf 2-4: (8f 1-2, 10f 1-2) (gd 1-3, g-f 1-1)
Scopey, high-class colt, effective 8 to 10f, acts on gd to g-f. Turf high 118 - 1st of 9 getting 8lb from Albarahin (26 Aug Windsor RF 4004) - also 1st of 5 from Summoner (5 Aug Goodwood RF 3393). Well beaten on soft ground in the Craven on his comeback, he returned to land a listed race in August and stepped up on that form in Windsor's Winter Hill Stakes. Looked a progressive colt, but put in a lacklustre effort in France on his final outing.
**Sir Michael Stoute [4-6] Aga Khan.*

ADIOS RR 85f 3964[5]
2 b c Lycius (USA) 8.8f **(71)** -Itqan (IRE) (Sadler's Wells (USA)) 10f **(76)**
Form - 5
Record 2000 - 1st:0 2nd:0 3rd:0 Ran:1
2000 Turf 0-1: (7f) (g-f)
Currently useful colt. (1st run) - 5th of 10 to Fair Question (25 Aug Newmarket 7f g-f RF 3964).
**H R A Cecil [0-1] The Thoroughbred Corporation.*

ADIRPOUR (IRE) BHB 34f27a RR 42f 27a 2192[11]
6 gr g Nishapour (FR) 11.1f **(58)** - Adira (IRE) (Ballad Rock) 7.8f **(63)**
Form - 86730065841547837804360
Record 2000 - 1st:1 2nd:0 3rd:2 Ran:18
Pre2000 - 1st:2 2nd:2 3rd:4 Ran:39
Win Prizemoney £6,250 *Total Prizemoney* £9,458
Wins * **2000** *Feb Southw (STD) C 12f 43*
* 1999 May Newcas (G-F) C 7f 60 <
* 1999 Apr Leices (G-S) S 7f 53
2000 Turf 0-2: (8f, 12f) (gd 2) 2000 AW 1-16: (7f, 8f 2, 9f 2, 11f 4, 12f 1-7) (Fibr 1-16)
Moderate gelding, effective 6 to 8f, acted on gd to frm, had worn blinkers. Turf high 42. AW high 43. (DEAD)
**R Hollinshead [3-47] R Hollinshead (from Noel Chance [0-2] Dec 1998).*

ADJAWAR (IRE) RR 4f 5151[14]
2 b c Ashkalani (IRE) - Adjriyna (Top Ville) 11.7f **(68)**
Form - 0
Record 2000 - 1st:0 2nd:0 3rd:0 Ran:1
2000 Turf 0-1: (7f) (g-s)
Currently very poor colt. **Sir Michael Stoute [0-1] H H Aga Khan.*

ADJOURNMENT (USA) BHB 84f RR 86f 4203[11]
2 b br c Patton (USA) - Miss Cabell Co (USA) (Junction (USA))
Form - 716240
Record 2000 - 1st:1 2nd:1 3rd;0 Ran:6
Win Prizemoney £4,192 *Total Prizemoney* £6,882
Wins * **2000** Jun Sandow (G-F) 7.1f 76 <
2000 Turf 1-6: (6f, 7f 1-4, 8f) (gd 2, g-f 1-1, frm 2, hrd)
Useful colt, effective 7f, acts on g-f to hrd. Turf high 86 - 2nd of 7 to Barking Mad (28 Jly Thirsk 7f hrd RF 3195). Stepped up on his debut to make all at Sandown, but held in better company next time although he would have finished closer but for being hampered. **P F I Cole [1-6] The Blandford Partnership.*

ADJUTANT BHB 89f RR 98df 5126[5]
5 b g Batshoof 9.5f **(66)** - Indian Love Song (Be My Guest (USA)) 9.3f **(67)**
Form - 303120687265
Record 2000 - 1st:1 2nd:2 3rd:2 Ran:12
Pre2000 - 1st:3 2nd:3 3rd:4 Ran:19
Win Prizemoney £30,501 *Total Prizemoney* £54,881
Wins * **2000** May Lingfi (G-S) H 7f 93 97 <
1999 Oct Leices (SFT) 7f 97 <
1998 Spt Haydoc (G-F) H 7.1f 86 88
1998 May Goodwo (G-F) H 7f 83 88
2000 Turf 1-12: (7f 1-9, 8f 2, 10f) (sft 1-1, g-s 5, gd 3, g-f, frm 2)
Very useful gelding, effective 7 to 8f, best at 7f, acts on sft to frm, best on gd, excels at Kempton. Turf high 98 - also 1st of 11 giving 12lb to Mister Rambo (13 May Lingfield RF 1195). Becoming disappointing. He does most of his racing over seven furlongs and is a useful handicapper at that trip. Scored in a handicap at Lingfield in May, but struggled in higher grade during the summer. Goes well with cut in the ground.
**N P Littmoden [1-11] J R Good (from B J Meehan [3-20] Mar 2000).*

ADMIRALS FLAME (IRE) BHB 58f60a RR 58f 60a 4492[17]
9 b g Doulab (USA) 7.4f **(61)** - Fan The Flame (Grundy) 10.3f **(65)**
Form - 71330
Record 2000 - 1st:1 2nd:0 3rd:2 Ran:5

Pre2000 - 1st:6 2nd:3 3rd:4 Ran:51
Win Prizemoney £23,614 *Total Prizemoney* £32,956
Wins * **2000** Jun Nottin (SFT) H 8.2f 55 58
* 1999 Jun Leices (G-S) H 8f 55 62
* 1998 Jun Windso (SFT) H 8.3f 55 60+
* 1996 Aug Windso (G-F) H 8.3f 74 80 <
2000 Turf 1-5: (8f 1-5) (g-s 1-1, gd, g-f 2, frm)
Fair gelding, effective 8f, acts on g-s to frm, prefers tight tracks. Turf high 58 - 1st of 7 giving 15lb to Dinar (2 Jun Nottingham RF 1667). With a plethora of moderate efforts he fell down the handicap last season, but bounced back with a victory at Leicester on his second start this term. He likes cut in the ground.
**C F Wall [7-56] Mrs C A Wall.*

ADMIRALS PLACE (IRE) BHB 69f71a **RR 69f 71a** 5134[10]
4 ch c Perugino (USA) - Royal Daughter (High Top) 10.2f **(67)**
Form - 51223142853220
Record 2000 - 1st:2 2nd:5 3rd:2 Ran:13
Pre2000 - 1st:2 2nd:3 3rd:2 Ran:12
Win Prizemoney £10,842 *Total Prizemoney* £24,829
Wins * **2000** Apr Folkes (SFT) H 9.7f 64 67 <
* **2000** *Jan Lingfi (STD) 10f 57*
1999 Spt Beverl (SFT) H 9.9f 55 60
1999 *Jun Lingfi (STD) H 8f 54 58*
2000 Turf 1-9: (10f 1-9) (sft, g-s 1-3, gd 2, g-f 3) 2000 AW 1-4: (10f 1-3, 12f) (Equi 1-4)
Neat, above-average colt, effective 10f, acts on g-s to g-f - acts on Equi, best on g-s. Turf high 69 - 2nd of 14 getting 2lb from Pedro Pete (6 Oct York 10f g-s RF 4829) - also 1st of 15 giving 1lb to Hindi (18 Apr Folkestone RF 0765). AW high 67 - 2nd of 11 getting 4lb from Forty Forte (26 Jan Lingfield 10f Equi RF 0161).
**H J Collingridge [2-14] C G Donovan (from R W Armstrong [2-11] Oct 1999).*

ADMIRALS SECRET (USA) BHB 46f36a **RR 49f 36a** 2847[10]
11 ch g Secreto (USA) 9.9f **(72)** - Noble Mistress (USA) (Vaguely Noble) 10.1f **(72)**
Form - 571060
Record 2000 - 1st:1 2nd:0 3rd:0 Ran:6
Pre2000 - 1st:9 2nd:7 3rd:4 Ran:67
Win Prizemoney £28,606 *Total Prizemoney* £38,216
Wins * **2000** May Yarmou (GD) H 11.5f 47 49
* 1998 Jun Lingfi (GD) H 11.5f 64 68
* 1998 Jun Lingfi (GD) H 11.5f 62 61
* 1998 Apr Bright (GD) H 11.9f 47 57
* 1997 Jly Windso (G-F) H 11.6f 50 53
2000 Turf 1-6: (11f 1-1, 12f 5) (g-f 1-4, frm 2)
Moderate gelding, effective 11f, acts on g-f, likes left handed tracks, likes tight tracks. Turf high 49 - 1st of 16 giving 3lb to Nosey Native (31 May Yarmouth RF 1612). Consistent.
**C F Wall [10-75] Mrs C A Wall.*

ADOBE BHB 78f70a **RR 83f 70a** 5317[20]
5 b g Green Desert (USA) 7.8f **(78)** - Shamshir (Kris) 9.5f **(73)**
Form - 810242111133341211750800
Record 2000 - 1st:8 2nd:3 3rd:2 Ran:22
Pre2000 - 1st:2 2nd:2 3rd:4 Ran:25
Win Prizemoney £39,685 *Total Prizemoney* £51,441
Wins * **2000** Aug Haydoc (GD) H 8.1f 77 83+ <
* **2000** Aug Thirsk (G-F) H 8f 72 78
* **2000** Jly Doncas (G-F) H 8f 68 71
* **2000** Jun Goodwo (GD) H 8f 53 61
* **2000** Jun Bath (G-F) H 8f 53 60
* **2000** Jun Hamilt (GD) 8.3f 55
* **2000** May Hamilt (G-F) H 8.3f 49 53
* **2000** *Mar Wolver (STD) H 7f 47 54*
* 1999 Jly Nottin (G-F) H 8.2f 51 55
* 1999 Jun Bath (GD) H 8f 45 54
2000 Turf 7-18: (7f 2, 8f 7-15, 9f) (sft 2, g-s, gd 1-5, g-f 2-5, frm 3-4, hrd 1-1) 2000 AW 1-4: (7f 1-3, 8f) (Fibr 1-4)
Decent gelding, effective 8f, acts on gd to frm, best on gd, likes left handed tracks, likes tight tracks, and excels at Bath. Turf high 83 - 1st of 11 getting 10lb from Tony Tie (12 Aug Haydock RF 3587) - also 1st of 7 getting 12lb from Colway Ritz (5 Aug Thirsk RF 3409). AW high 55. Becoming disappointing. Like most of his stablemates, he was in fantastic form last term, winning no fewer than eight times. He is suited by a mile on fast ground.
**W M Brisbourne [10-43] P R Kirk (from J H M Gosden [0-4] Aug 1998).*

Adobe won eight races in 2000

ADORABLE BHB 38f30a **RR 32f 30a** 248[11]
4 b f Dalul - Helleborus (King of Spain) 7.8f **(52)**
Form - 0
Record 2000 - 1st:0 2nd:0 3rd:0 Ran:1
Pre2000 - 1st:0 2nd:0 3rd:0 Ran:3
2000 AW 0-1: (6f) (Equi)
Workmanlike, very moderate filly.
**T D McCarthy [0-1] Ken Butler (from S Dow [0-3] Dec 1998).*

ADRIANA BHB 45f37a **RR 46f 37a** 3923[13]
3 b f Tragic Role (USA) 9.4f **(63)** - Beatle Song **(49f 41a)** (Song) 7.2f **(61)**
Form - 800817140
Record 2000 - 1st:2 2nd:0 3rd:0 Ran:9
Win Prizemoney £4,746 *Total Prizemoney* £4,746
Wins * **2000** Jly Bright (FRM) H 10f 42 46 <
* **2000** Jun Lingfi (FRM) H 11.5f 39 46 <
2000 Turf 2-8: (6f, 8f, 10f 1-4, 11f 1-1, 12f) (hvy, gd, g-f 3, frm 2-3) 2000 AW 0-1: (12f) (Equi)
Light-framed, moderate filly, effective 10 to 11f, acts on frm, prefers left handed tracks, favours tight tracks. Turf high 46 - 1st of 11 getting 12lb from Crown Mint (14 Jun Lingfield RF 1970) - also 1st of 13 getting 18lb from Shaman (25 Jly Brighton RF 3089).
**C E Brittain [2-9] R A Pledger.*

ADRIFT (USA) BHB 57a **RR 63f** 5116[10]
3 ch f Irish River (FR) 9f **(77)** - Dream Play (USA) (Blushing Groom (FR)) 10.3f **(76)**
Form - 872030
Record 2000 - 1st:0 2nd:1 3rd:1 Ran:6
Win Prizemoney £0 *Total Prizemoney* £1,448
2000 Turf 0-4: (7f, 8f 2, 10f) (gd 2, g-f 2) 2000 AW 0-2: (8f, 9f) (Fibr 2)
Scopey, average filly, effective 8f, acts on g-f. Turf high 63 - 2nd of 7 to Bloody Mary (11 Aug Salisbury 8f g-f RF 3564). AW high 47 (began Oct). **B Hanbury [0-6] Mrs Sonia Rogers.*

ADULATION (USA) BHB 48f74a **RR 27f 74a** 2586[16]
6 ch g Sheikh Albadou 9.2f **(75)** - Pedestal (High Line) 10.3f **(70)**
Form - 0000

Record	2000 -	1st:0	2nd:0	3rd:0	Ran:4
	Pre2000 -	1st:0	2nd:3	3rd:2	Ran:11

Win Prizemoney £0 *Total Prizemoney* £4,725

2000 Turf 0-4: (7f 3, 9f) (gd, g-f 2, frm)

Above-average gelding, effective 8f, acts on g-f - acts on Fibr, has worn blinkers, likes tight tracks. Turf high 27. Becoming disappointing.

**J J O'Neill [0-9] Mrs Jane Chapple-Hyam & A K Collins (from P W Chapple-Hyam [0-11] Oct 1999).*

ADWEB BHB 66f **RR 68f** 5129[10]

2 b f Muhtarram (USA) - What A Present (Pharly (FR)) 9.8f **(68)**

Form - 084170

Record	2000 -	1st:1	2nd:0	3rd:0	Ran:6

Win Prizemoney £4,660 *Total Prizemoney* £4,944

Wins	* 2000	Spt	Sandow (SFT)	H	5f	56	68	<

2000 Turf 1-6: (5f 1-3, 6f 3) (sft, g-s 1-1, gd 2, frm 2)

Average filly, effective 5 to 6f, acts on g-s to gd. Turf high 68 - 7th of 22 getting 16lb from Idle Power (12 Oct Newmarket 6f gd RF 4932) - also 1st of 10 getting 25lb from Kyllachy (30 Spt Sandown RF 4751). **J Cullinan [1-6] Adweb Ltd.*

AEGEAN DREAM (IRE) BHB 88f **RR 90+f** 4740[13]

4 b f Royal Academy (USA) 7.8f **(77)** - L'Ideale (USA) (Alysheba (USA)) 9f **(84)**

Form - 23443311740

Record	2000 -	1st:2	2nd:1	3rd:3	Ran:11
	Pre2000 -	1st:1	2nd:3	3rd:0	Ran:8

Win Prizemoney £21,717 *Total Prizemoney* £33,673

Wins								
* 2000	Aug	Goodwo (G-F)	H	9f	81	86	<
* 2000	Jly	Newbur (G-F)	H	9f	78	80	
* 1999	Spt	Epsom (GD)		8.5f		81	

2000 Turf 2-11: (8f, 9f 2-4, 10f 4, 12f 2) (g-s, gd 1-2, g-f 1-5, frm 3)

Lengthy, useful filly, effective 9 to 10f, best at 9f, acts on gd to g-f, best on g-f, prefers left handed tracks. Turf high 90 - 4th of 17 giving 4lb to Komistar (16 Spt Newbury 10f g-f RF 4464) - also 1st of 10 giving 26lb to Common Consent (2 Aug Goodwood RF 3319). Consistent. Looked a progressive filly when winning twice in the summer, and ran another good race at Newbury in September. Suited by nine or ten furlongs and fast ground, and goes best with hold-up tactics. **R Hannon [3-19] Theobalds Stud.*

AEGEAN FLAME BHB 58f **RR 61f** 1272[14]

4 ch f Anshan 8.2f **(63)** - Dizzydaisy **(38f 52a)** (Sharpo) 7.7f **(59)**

Form - 600

Record	2000 -	1st:0	2nd:0	3rd:0	Ran:3
	Pre2000 -	1st:2	2nd:2	3rd:2	Ran:14

Win Prizemoney £9,309 *Total Prizemoney* £13,166

Wins							
1998	Jly	Newbur (GD)		5.2f		78	<
1998	Jly	Ripon (GD)		5f		77	

2000 Turf 0-3: (7f 3) (gd 2, frm)

Leggy, average filly, effective 5f, acts on g-s. Turf high 49.

**R M Flower [0-3] Theobalds Stud (from B J Meehan [0-6] Spt 1999).*

AEGEAN FLOWER BHB 48f **RR 48f** 4403[3]

3 b g Robellino (USA) 9.5f **(68)** - Bercheba (Bellypha) 9.8f **(73)**

Form - 0480003403

Record	2000 -	1st:0	2nd:0	3rd:2	Ran:10

Win Prizemoney £0 *Total Prizemoney* £1,311

2000 Turf 0-10: (7f 3, 8f 5, 9f, 12f) (gd 2, g-f 5, frm 2, hrd)

Scopey, moderate gelding, effective 7 to 8f, best at 8f, acts on g-f to frm, best on g-f, mostly wears blinkers (extremely effectively). Turf high 48 - 3rd of 13 getting 18lb from Evergreen (28 Jly Salisbury 8f frm RF 3183). Inconsistent. **R M Flower [0-10] K Panos.*

AEGEAN WIND BHB 62f **RR 68df** 3732[12]

3 b c Dolphin Street (FR) - Perdicula (IRE) (Persian Heights)

Form - 5070

Record	2000 -	1st:0	2nd:0	3rd:0	Ran:4
	Pre2000 -	1st:0	2nd:0	3rd:0	Ran:1

2000 Turf 0-4: (10f, 12f, 14f 2) (g-f, frm 3)

Light-framed, average colt. Turf high 57.

**J L Dunlop [0-5] Theobalds Stud.*

AESKULAP (GER) **RR 109f** 4842a[2]

3 b c Acatenango (GER) - Aerope (GER) (Celestial Storm (USA))

Form - 2

2000 Turf 0-1: (14f) (hvy)

Currently Pattern-class colt. (1st run) - 2nd of 8 giving 4lb to Moonlady (1 Oct Dortmund 14f hvy RF 4842a).

**H Blume in GER [0-1] Gestut Sommerberg.*

AFAAN (IRE) BHB 85f84a **RR 98f 84a** 5127[11]

7 ch h Cadeaux Genereux 7.9f **(76)** - Rawaabe (USA) (Nureyev (USA)) 8.7f **(78)**

Form - 433806402040075000

Record	2000 -	1st:0	2nd:1	3rd:0	Ran:14
	Pre2000 -	1st:6	2nd:8	3rd:5	Ran:42

Win Prizemoney £21,548 *Total Prizemoney* £44,062

Wins							
* 1998	Jly	Newmar (GD)	H	5f	76	91+	<
* 1998	Jly	Catter (FRM)	H	5f	73	79	
* 1997	*Dec*	*Southw (STD)*	*H*	*5f*	*65*	*72+*	
* 1997	Nov	Redcar (GD)		5f		79	
* 1997	Oct	Pontef (G-S)	H	5f	62	67	
* 1997	May	Redcar (G-F)	H	6f	56	64	

2000 Turf 0-14: (5f 11, 6f 3) (g-s 2, gd 4, g-f 5, frm 3)

Very useful horse, effective 5 to 6f, best at 5f, acts on g-s to frm, best on g-f, often wears blinkers (extremely effectively), and does well at Yarmouth. Turf high 98 - 4th of 8 to Lord Kintyre (28 Jly Newmarket 5f g-f RF 3176). Exceptionally speedy, he is best at the minimum trip but proved very difficult to place. He usually blazes a trail. **R F Marvin [6-56] Afaan Partnership.*

AFFARATI BHB 72f **RR 73f** 3855[10]

2 b g Emarati (USA) 6.6f **(63)** - Affairiste (IRE) (Simply Great (FR)) 8.2f **(65)**

Form - 216750

Record	2000 -	1st:1	2nd:1	3rd:0	Ran:6

Win Prizemoney £5,974 *Total Prizemoney* £7,380

Wins	* 2000	May	Pontef (GD)		6f		70+	<

2000 Turf 1-6: (5f 2, 6f 1-2, 7f 2) (gd 3, g-f 1-1, frm 2)

Above-average gelding, effective 6 to 7f, acts on g-f to frm. Turf high 73 - 5th of 6 giving 4lb to Dominaite (29 Jly Redcar 7f frm RF 3221) - also 1st of 6 from Wilson Blyth (26 May Pontefract RF 1472). **J L Eyre [1-6] David Scott.*

AFFIANCED (IRE) **RR 90f** 4252a[7]

2 bb f Erins Isle 8.3f **(76)** - La Meilleure (Lord Gayle (USA)) 8.8f **(62)**

Form - 2117

2000 Turf 2-4: (7f 2-4) (gd 2-3, g-f)

Useful filly, often wears blinkers. Turf high 90 - 1st of 13 from Sequoyah (20 Aug Curragh RF 3889a). Short-headed Sequoyah in a listed race but was never going behind that filly in the Group One Moyglare Stud Stakes. **J S Bolger in IRE [2-4] A G Moylan.*

AFFIRMED SUCCESS (USA) **RR 125f** 5327a[4]

6 b g Affirmed (USA) 10.3f **(75)** - Towering Success (USA) (Irish Tower (USA))

Form - 324

2000 Turf 0-3: (8f 3) (frm 3)

Top-class gelding. Turf high 125 (began Spt) - 4th of 14 giving 3lb to War Chant (4 Nov Churchill Downs 8f frm RF 5327a).

**R Schosberg in USA [0-5] A Fried Jnr.*

AFGHAN (USA) BHB 80f **RR 83f** 5310[2]

2 ch c Hennessy (USA) - Affirm The Gold (USA) (Golden Act (USA)) 8.8f **(67)**

Form - 002

Record	2000 -	1st:0	2nd:1	3rd:0	Ran:3

Win Prizemoney £0 *Total Prizemoney* £1,025

2000 Turf 0-3: (6f 2, 7f) (sft, g-s, gd)

Currently decent colt. Turf high 83 (began Oct) - 2nd of 18 to Chancellor (3 Nov Doncaster 7f g-s RF 5310).

**J H M Gosden [0-3] Sheikh Mohammed.*

AFRICA (IRE) BHB 60a **RR 47f** 4008[4]

3 b f Namaqualand (USA) - Tannerrun (IRE) **(70df)** (Runnett) 7f **(59)**

Form - 16741684

Record	2000 -	1st:2	2nd:0	3rd:0	Ran:8
	Pre2000 -	1st:1	2nd:1	3rd:2	Ran:12

Win Prizemoney £7,151 *Total Prizemoney* £9,260

Wins							
* 2000	Jly	Beverl (G-F)	C	7.5f		47+	
* 2000	*May*	*Southw (STD)*	*H*	*7f*	*56*	*62*	<
* 1999	Jly	Catter (GD)	S	7f		57	

2000 Turf 1-6: (7f 1-3, 8f 3) (g-f 4, frm 1-2) 2000 AW 1-2: (7f 1-2) (Fibr 1-2)
Scopey, average filly, effective 7f, acts on gd to hrd - acts on Fibr, best on frm, has worn blinkers, prefers left handed tracks, excels at Catterick. Turf high 47. AW high 62 (1st run) - 1st of 16 giving 15lb to Rio's Diamond (8 May Southwell RF 1091).
**T D Barron [3-20] Laurence O'Kane.*

AFRICAN CZAR (IRE) BHB 76a **RR 76a** 5013[2]

2 b c Inzar (USA) - African Grace (IRE) (Fayruz)
Form - 2

Record	**2000 -**	1st:0	2nd:1	3rd:0	Ran:1

Win Prizemoney £0 *Total Prizemoney* £502
2000 AW 0-1: (6f) (Fibr)
Currently above-average colt. (1st run) - 2nd of 9 to Moyne Pleasure (17 Oct Wolverhampton 6f Fibr RF 5013).
**M L W Bell [0-1] P A Philipps.*

AFRICAN PETE BHB 54f **RR 59f** 4403[18]

3 b g Lugana Beach 7f **(63)** - Highland Bonnie (Dreams to Reality (USA)) 6.4f **(73)**
Form - 6726570

Record	**2000 -**	1st:0	2nd:1	3rd:0	Ran:7
	Pre2000 -	1st:0	2nd:0	3rd:1	Ran:3

Win Prizemoney £0 *Total Prizemoney* £961
2000 Turf 0-7: (7f, 8f 2, 10f 4) (gd, g-f 4, frm 2)
Light-framed, fair gelding, effective 10f, acts on frm, has worn blinkers, prefers tight tracks. Turf high 63 - 2nd of 16 giving 20lb to Chaka Zulu (1 Jly Bath 10f frm RF 2426). Consistent.
**G G Margarson [0-10] Dr Neil Dorward.*

AFTER EIGHT BHB 33f46a **RR 37f 46a** 83[10]

5 b g Presidium 7.5f **(56)** - Vickenda (Giacometti) 11.2f **(56)**
Form - 0

Record	**2000 -**	1st:0	2nd:0	3rd:0	Ran:1
	Pre2000 -	1st:1	2nd:1	3rd:1	Ran:24

Win Prizemoney £1,838 *Total Prizemoney* £2,938

Wins	* 1998	*Feb*	*Lingfi*	*(STD)*	*S*	*6f*	*63* <

2000 AW 0-1: (8f) (Fibr)
Moderate gelding, effective 6f, acts on gd, often wears blinkers (extremely effectively), likes left handed tracks. Inconsistent. Successfully dropped into selling company on the Lingfield Equitrack in February, beating a very poor field easily.
**M S Saunders [1-19] M S Saunders (from R W Armstrong [0-6] Jan 1998).*

AFTERJACKO (IRE) BHB 99f **RR 99f** 4461[1]

4 ch g Seattle Dancer (USA) 10.1f **(74)** - Shilka (Soviet Star (USA))
Form - 5127056421

Record	**2000 -**	1st:2	2nd:2	3rd:0	Ran:10
	Pre2000 -	1st:1	2nd:0	3rd:1	Ran:5

Win Prizemoney £29,990 *Total Prizemoney* £51,055

Wins	*** 2000**	Spt	Newbur	(G-F)	H	13.3f	95	99	<
	*** 2000**	May	Salisb	(G-F)	H	14.1f	83	85	
	* 1999	Spt	Bath	(FRM)		11.7f		84	

2000 Turf 2-10: (12f 2, 13f 1-1, 14f 1-4, 15f, 16f 2) (gd 3, g-f 2-5, frm 2)
Scopey, very useful gelding, effective 12 to 16f, acts on gd to frm, best on g-f, prefers left handed tracks, excels at Ascot. Turf high 99 - 1st of 15 giving 7lb to Masamadas (16 Spt Newbury RF 4461). Consistent. He gained reward for some good efforts when landing Newbury's Autumn Cup on his final start. May be an interesting prospect over hurdles one day.
**D R C Elsworth [3-15] McDowell Racing.*

AFTER THE BLUE (IRE) BHB 67f **RR 74f** 5069[18]

3 b c Last Tycoon 9.4f **(73)** - Sudden Interest (FR) (Highest Honor (FR))
Form - 0064122451227040

Record	**2000 -**	1st:2	2nd:4	3rd:0	Ran:16
	Pre2000 -	1st:0	2nd:0	3rd:0	Ran:1

Win Prizemoney £5,431 *Total Prizemoney* £12,994

Wins	*** 2000**	Aug	Salisb	(G-F)	H	12f	66	74	<
	*** 2000**	Jun	Nottin	(G-F)		10f		64	

2000 Turf 2-16: (8f 2, 10f 1-4, 12f 1-10) (g-s 4, gd 5, g-f 2-4, frm 3)
Workmanlike, above-average colt, effective 10 to 12f, best at 12f, acts on g-s to frm, best on g-f, prefers right handed tracks, excels at Salisbury. Turf high 74 - 1st of 9 getting 3lb from Exile (11 Aug Salisbury RF 3565). Consistent. Running well this term, he is suited by a mile and a half and fast ground.
**M R Channon [2-17] Timberhill Racing Partnership.*

AGENT LE BLANC (IRE) BHB 70f **RR 71df** 3142[8]

5 b g Kahyasi 12.9f **(74)** - White Witch (USA) (Nureyev (USA)) 8.7f **(78)**
Form - P8

Record	**2000 -**	1st:0	2nd:0	3rd:0	Ran:2
	Pre2000 -	1st:0	2nd:2	3rd:0	Ran:7

Win Prizemoney £0 *Total Prizemoney* £1,944
2000 Turf 0-2: (14f, 18f) (g-f, frm)
Above-average gelding, effective 15 to 16f, acts on g-f to frm. (began Jly).
**Ian Williams [0-2] E Oliver (from T J Etherington [0-7] Aug 1999).*

AGENT MULDER BHB 63f55a **RR 67f 55a** 4756[2]

6 b g Kylian (USA) 8.1f **(66)** - Precious Caroline (IRE) **(26a)** (The Noble Player (USA)) 6.5f **(67)**
Form - 23382

Record	**2000 -**	1st:0	2nd:2	3rd:2	Ran:5
	Pre2000 -	1st:5	2nd:2	3rd:1	Ran:23

Win Prizemoney £19,466 *Total Prizemoney* £26,078

Wins	* 1999	Jun	Salisb	(GD)	H	6f	70	77	<
	* 1999	Apr	Nottin	(SFT)	H	6.1f	64	70	
	* 1998	Oct	Nottin	(SFT)		6.1f		58	
	* 1998	Oct	Nottin	(SFT)		6.1f		62	
	* 1997	Jun	Windso	(G-F)	H	8.3f	55	61	

2000 Turf 0-5: (5f, 6f 3, 7f) (sft 2, g-s, gd, g-f)
Average gelding, effective 6f, acts on gd to g-f, best on gd, often wears blinkers (effectively). Turf high 67. A winner twice last season, he has a fine winning record at Nottingham. Six furlongs and cut in the ground seem to suit. **P D Cundell [5-28] P D Cundell.*

AGILE DANCER (IRE) BHB 50f45a **RR 54f 45a** 4930[26]

2 ch f Eagle Eyed (USA) - Be Nimble (Wattlefield) 5.8f **(71)**
Form - 0050

Record	**2000 -**	1st:0	2nd:0	3rd:0	Ran:4

2000 Turf 0-4: (5f 2, 7f 2) (gd, g-f, frm, hrd)
Fair filly. Turf high 54. **N A Graham [0-4] Second Millennium Racing.*

AGIOTAGE BHB 54f45a **RR 55f 45a** 4361[13]

4 br g Zafonic (USA) 9f **(83)** - Rakli **(85+f)** (Warning)
Form - 00016155440

Record	**2000 -**	1st:2	2nd:0	3rd:0	Ran:11
	Pre2000 -	1st:1	2nd:0	3rd:0	Ran:8

Win Prizemoney £9,232 *Total Prizemoney* £10,180

Wins	*** 2000**	Jly	Mussel	(FRM)	H	8f	54	55	
	*** 2000**	Jun	Mussel	(FRM)	H	9f	50	55	
	1998	Nov	Redcar	(G-S)		7f		84+	<

2000 Turf 2-9: (8f 1-4, 9f 1-2, 10f, 12f, 15f) (g-s, gd, g-f, frm 2-6) 2000 AW 0-2: (10f, 16f) (Equi, Fibr)
Scopey, fair gelding, has worn blinkers, likes right handed tracks, favours tight tracks. Turf high 55. AW high 35. Easily won a Redcar maiden on his final start at two, and is worth keeping an eye on as his trainer does not have that many handicappers.
**S C Williams [2-11] The Cherry Pickers Syndicate II (from H R A Cecil [1-8] Aug 1999).*

AGNES FOR RANSOM (USA) **RR 45f** 5223[13]

2 b br f Red Ransom (USA) 8.6f **(83)** - Golden Rhyme (Dom Racine (FR)) 9.2f **(62)**
Form - 0

Record	**2000 -**	1st:0	2nd:0	3rd:0	Ran:1

2000 Turf 0-1: (6f) (gd)
Currently moderate filly. **J L Dunlop [0-1] Mrs Maria Mai Goransson.*

AGNES WORLD (USA) **RR 121+f** 5328a[8]

5 h Danzig (USA) 8.1f **(88)** - Mysteries (USA) (Seattle Slew (USA)) 9.4f **(76)**
Form - 218
2000 Turf 1-2: (5f, 6f 1-1) (gd 1-2) 2000 AW 0-1: (6f) (Dirt)
Very high-class colt. Turf high 121 - 1st of 11 giving 6lb to Lincoln Dancer (13 Jly Newmarket RF 2773). Trained in Japan, he ran a tremendous race from an unfavourable draw when runner-up in the King's Stand on his first run of last season's European campaign, and followed that with a narrow win in a desperate finish to the July Cup. He disappointed in the Breeders' Cup Sprint on dirt and has now been retired to stud. **H Mori in JPN [2-4] T Watanabe.*

Agnes World (near side), was a narrow winner of the July Cup

AGO RR 41f 3220[8]
2 ch f Rudimentary (USA) 8.2f **(66)** - Amidst **(74f)** (Midyan (USA)) 6f **(60)**
Form - 8
Record 2000 - 1st:0 2nd:0 3rd:0 Ran:1
2000 Turf 0-1: (6f) (frm)
Currently moderate filly.
**T D Easterby [0-1] Sir Evelyn De Rothschild.*

AGOL LACK (USA) RR 118f 4562a[1]
4 ch c Gulch (USA) 9.6f **(79)** - Garvin's Gal (USA) (Seattle Slew (USA)) 9.4f **(76)**
Form - 5211
2000 Turf 2-4: (10f 2-4) (g-s, gd 2-3)
High-class colt. Turf high 118 - 1st of 8 giving 3lb to Mont Rocher (13 Spt Maisons-laffitte RF 4562a) - also 1st of 8 from Tijiyr (12 Aug Deauville RF 3734a). **A Fabre in FR [2-5] Sultan Al Kabeer.*

AGRIPPINA BHB 100f **RR 105f** 1218[8]
3 b f Timeless Times (USA) 6.1f **(56)** - Boadicea's Chariot (Commanche Run) 8.5f **(58)**
Form - 08
Record 2000 - 1st:0 2nd:0 3rd:0 Ran:2
Pre2000 - 1st:2 2nd:1 3rd:0 Ran:3
Win Prizemoney £15,951 *Total Prizemoney* £17,101
Wins * 1999 Oct Newmar (SFT) L 7f 95 **<**
* 1999 Spt Ayr (G-S) 7f 77
2000 Turf 0-2: (8f, 10f) (g-f, frm)
Workmanlike, Pattern-class filly. Turf high 105. A listed winner at two, she made no impression in either the 1000 Guineas or the Musidora in the spring.
**A Bailey [2-5] Mrs Fiona Williams.*

AGUA CABALLO (IRE) BHB 59f51a **RR 50f 51a** 335[5]
3 b g Petorius 8f **(66)** - Beauty Appeal (USA) (Shadeed (USA)) 8.2f **(70)**
Form - 075
Record 2000 - 1st:0 2nd:0 3rd:0 Ran:3
Pre2000 - 1st:2 2nd:0 3rd:1 Ran:11
Win Prizemoney £5,246 *Total Prizemoney* £6,264
Wins * 1999 Jly Beverl (G-F) C 5f 82 **<**
* 1999 Jun Carlis (GD) 5f 69
2000 AW 0-3: (7f 2, 8f) (Equi, Fibr 2)
Scopey, fair gelding, effective 5f, acted on gd. AW high 50. Consistent. (DEAD) **S E Kettlewell [2-14] Middleham Park Racing XII.*

AHOUOD BHB 32f29a **RR 34f 29a** 3260[13]
4 b f Merdon Melody 6.8f **(56)** - Balidilemma (Balidar) 7.9f **(63)**
Form - 42256040860
Record 2000 - 1st:0 2nd:2 3rd:0 Ran:11
Pre2000 - 1st:0 2nd:0 3rd:1 Ran:5
Win Prizemoney £0 *Total Prizemoney* £2,092
2000 Turf 0-5: (7f, 10f, 11f 2, 12f) (sft, gd 2, g-f, frm) 2000 AW 0-6: (7f, 8f 2, 9f 2, 10f) (Equi, Fibr 5)
Workmanlike, very moderate filly, effective 6 to 9f, acts on frm - acts on Fibr. Turf high 37. AW high 44. **K Mahdi [0-16] Solaiman Alsaiary.*

AHRAAR (USA) RR 71f 4969[11]
2 b c Gulch (USA) 9.6f **(79)** - Saffaanh (USA) (Shareef Dancer (USA)) 9.9f **(73)**
Form - 0
Record 2000 - 1st:0 2nd:0 3rd:0 Ran:1
2000 Turf 0-1: (8f) (gd)
Currently above-average colt. Caught the eye on his only run.
**M P Tregoning [0-1] Hamdan Al Maktoum.*

AILINCALA (IRE) BHB 64f **RR 64f** 4675[6]
2 b f Pursuit of Love 9.5f **(69)** - Diabaig **(70f)** (Precocious) 8.6f **(62)**
Form - U856
Record 2000 - 1st:0 2nd:0 3rd:0 Ran:4
2000 Turf 0-4: (6f 2, 7f 2) (g-s, gd, g-f 2)
Average filly. Turf high 64 (began Jun). **C F Wall [0-4] M Sinclair.*

AINTNECESSARILYSO BHB 69f **RR 71f** 5197[4]
2 ch g So Factual (USA) - Ovideo **(58f)** (Domynsky) 8f **(82)**
Form - 886723704
Record 2000 - 1st:0 2nd:1 3rd:1 Ran:9
Win Prizemoney £0 *Total Prizemoney* £2,033
2000 Turf 0-9: (6f 8, 7f) (gd 3, g-f 4, frm 2)
Above-average gelding, effective 6f, acts on gd, has worn blinkers. Turf high 71 - 4th of 8 getting 9lb from Barathiki (26 Oct Windsor 6f gd RF 5197). Consistent. **D R C Elsworth [0-9] Richard Marker.*

AIRA FORCE (USA) BHB 68f75a **RR 80df 75a** 4703[27]
3 ch g Dehere (USA) - Cinnamon Splendor (USA) (Trempolino (USA)) 12f **(71)**
Form - 2000
Record 2000 - 1st:0 2nd:1 3rd:0 Ran:4
Pre2000 - 1st:1 2nd:0 3rd:2 Ran:5
Win Prizemoney £3,805 *Total Prizemoney* £5,807

Wins * 1999 Spt Haydoc (G-F) 5f 81 <
2000 Turf 0-3: (5f 3) (g-f 3) 2000 AW 0-1: (5f) (Equi)
Workmanlike, decent gelding, effective 5f, acts on g-f - acts on Equi. Turf high 59. (1st run) - 2nd of 7 getting 1lb from Bold Effort (29 Mar Lingfield 5f Equi RF 0553). Becoming disappointing. Got off the mark in a fast-ground Haydock maiden last term. and ran pretty well to finish runner-up on the Lingfield Equitrack on his reappearance. **J Noseda [1-9] Mrs H Raw.*

AIR DEFENCE BHB 93f **RR 96f** 4740[7]

3 br c Warning 8.1f **(77)** - Cruising Height (Shirley Heights) 10.3f **(74)**
Form - 210028

Record					
2000 -	1st:1	2nd:2	3rd:0	Ran:6
Pre2000 -	1st:0	2nd:1	3rd:0	Ran:1

Win Prizemoney £8,125 *Total Prizemoney* £16,991
Wins * **2000** May Cheste (GD) 10.0f 70 <
2000 Turf 1-6: (9f, 10f 1-4, 12f) (gd 3, g-f 1-2, frm)
Well made, very useful colt, effective 10f, acts on gd to frm. Turf high 96 - 2nd of 19 getting 3lb from Bound For Pleasure (9 Spt Doncaster 10f frm RF 4311). He got his head in front in a messy maiden at the Chester May meeting, but was off the track for more than two months afterwards. Ran his best race since returning when touched off at Doncaster. **B W Hills [1-7] K Abdulla.*

AIRLINE (USA) RR 108f 4847a[7]

3 br f Woodman (USA) 9.7f **(77)** - Action Francaise (USA) (Nureyev (USA)) 8.7f **(78)**
Form - 17
2000 Turf 1-2: (8f 1-1, 10f) (sft 1-1, gd)
Currently Pattern-class filly. Turf high 108 (began Spt) - also 1st of 13 getting 5lb from Blue Moon (6 Spt Chantilly RF 4408a).
**A Fabre in FR [1-2].*

AIR MAIL BHB 62f77a **RR 57f 77a** 5105[5]

3 b g Night Shift (USA) 8.1f **(73)** - Wizardry (Shirley Heights) 10.3f **(74)**
Form - 2105080818205

Record				
2000 -	1st:2	2nd:2	3rd:0	Ran:13

Win Prizemoney £5,244 *Total Prizemoney* £7,160
Wins **2000** *Spt Wolver (STD) C 7f 61+*
2000 *Mar Lingfi (STD) 7f 67* <
2000 Turf 0-8: (6f 2, 7f 4, 8f, 10f) (gd 2, g-f 3, frm 3) 2000 AW 2-5: (6f, 7f 2-2, 8f 2) (Equi 1-2, Fibr 1-3)
Scopey, above-average gelding, effective 7 to 8f, - acts on Equi, has worn blinkers, prefers left handed tracks, prefers tight tracks. Turf high 57. AW high 73 - 5th of 12 giving 18lb to Tapage (12 May Lingfield 8f Equi RF 1168) - also 1st of 7 giving 5lb to Woodwind Down (8 Mar Lingfield RF 0422).
**Mrs N Macauley [0-4] Mrs N Macauley (from J M P Eustace [2-9] Spt 2000).*

AIR MARSHALL (IRE) BHB 115f **RR 119f** 4310[2]

3 ch c In The Wings 11.2f **(77)** - Troyanna (Troy) 10.4f **(68)**
Form - 2212

Record				
2000 -	1st:1	2nd:3	3rd:0	Ran:4
Pre2000 -	1st:1	2nd:1	3rd:0	Ran:3

Win Prizemoney £93,660 *Total Prizemoney* £204,160
Wins * **2000** Aug York (GD) G2 11.9f 117+ <
* 1999 Spt Goodwo (G-F) 8f 91+
2000 Turf 1-4: (12f 1-3, 15f) (gd 1-2, g-f, frm)
Scopey, high-class colt, effective 12 to 15f, best at 12f, acts on gd to frm. Turf high 119 (began Jly) - 2nd of 11 to Millenary (9 Spt Doncaster 15f frm RF 4310) - also 1st of 5 from Marienbard (22 Aug York RF 3853). Looked in need of the run when going down by a head on his belated return and stepped up on that effort when touched off by Millenary at Glorious Goodwood. Ran out an authoritative winner of the Great Voltigeur to set himself up for a crack at the Leger, in which he was outbattled by Millenary after his stamina seemed to give way. Remains a useful prospect.
**Sir Michael Stoute [2-7] Lord Weinstock.*

AIR OF ESTEEM BHB 63f66a **RR 69df 66a** 3812[2]

4 b g Forzando 7.2f **(63)** - Shadow Bird (Martinmas) 7.6f **(59)**
Form - 357452

Record				
2000 -	1st:0	2nd:1	3rd:1	Ran:6
Pre2000 -	1st:2	2nd:3	3rd:1	Ran:12

Win Prizemoney £6,576 *Total Prizemoney* £11,884
Wins * 1999 Jun Haydoc (SFT) H 8.1f 09 80 <
* 1999 *Jan Lingfi (STD) 8f 60*
2000 Turf 0-3: (7f, 8f, 11f) (gd 2, frm) 2000 AW 0-3: (8f 3) (Fibr 3)
Scopey, average gelding, effective 8f, acts on gd, has worn blinkers, likes tight tracks. Turf high 69. AW high 67.
**P C Haslam [2-18] Middleham Park Racing XV.*

AIR SHAKUR (JPN) RR 117f 3203[5]

3 b c Sunday Silence (USA) - I Dreamed A Dream (USA) (Well Decorated (USA)) 7.6f **(64)**
Form - 125
2000 Turf 1-3: (10f 1-1, 12f 2) (gd 1-2, frm)
Currently high-class colt. Turf high 117. A Classic winner in his native country, he never really threatened when fifth in the King George at Ascot. **H Mori in JPN [1-3] Lucky Field Co Ltd.*

AISLE BHB 55f49a **RR 60f 49a** 5165[4]

3 b g Arazi (USA) 9.2f **(74)** - Chancel (USA) **(47f 50a)** (Al Nasr (FR)) 9.3f **(68)**
Form - 60522558500084

Record				
2000 -	1st:0	2nd:2	3rd:0	Ran:12
Pre2000 -	1st:2	2nd:0	3rd:1	Ran:9

Win Prizemoney £6,077 *Total Prizemoney* £8,264
Wins * 1999 Nov Nottin (SFT) H 6.1f 55 58
* 1999 *Oct Southw (STD) H 6f 53 61* <
2000 Turf 0-6: (5f, 6f, 7f 3, 8f) (hvy, g-s, gd 2, g-f 2) 2000 AW 0-6: (6f 4, 7f 2) (Fibr 6)
Light-framed, average gelding, effective 6 to 7f, best at 6f, acts on hvy to gd - acts on Fibr, has worn blinkers (extremely effectively), likes left handed tracks. Turf high 60 - 5th of 19 giving 3lb to Balfour (12 Apr Warwick 7f hvy RF 0687). AW high 59.
**S R Bowring [2-18] S R Bowring (from I A Balding [0-3] Jly 1999).*

AIWIN BHB 56f60a **RR 57f 60a** 3811[2]

3 b c Forzando 7.2f **(63)** - Great Aim (Great Nephew) 9.9f **(64)**
Form - 04530532

Record				
2000 -	1st:0	2nd:1	3rd:2	Ran:8

Win Prizemoney £0 *Total Prizemoney* £1,577
2000 Turf 0-3: (6f, 8f, 10f) (g-s 2, frm) 2000 AW 0-5: (8f, 9f 3, 11f) (Fibr 5)
Light-framed, average colt, effective 8 to 9f, - acted on Fibr, preferred left handed tracks, favoured tight tracks. Turf high 57. AW high 68. (DEAD) **G C H Chung [0-8] The Happy Valley Leisure Club.*

AIX EN PROVENCE (USA) BHB 55f50a **RR 51df 50a** 4333[5]

5 b g Geiger Counter (USA) 7.8f **(85)** - Low Hill (Rousillon (USA)) 8.2f **(74)**
Form - 075

Record				
2000 -	1st:0	2nd:0	3rd:0	Ran:1
Pre2000 -	1st:3	2nd:0	3rd:1	Ran:19

Win Prizemoney £8,595 *Total Prizemoney* £10,953

Air Marshall won the Great Voltigeur

Wins * 1999 Aug Yarmou (FRM) SH 8f 55 62
1997 Aug Ripon (G-F) 6f 84+
1997 Jun Ayr (GD) 6f 85+ <
2000 Turf 0-1: (7f) (frm)
Fair gelding, has broken blood-vessels, effective 8f, acts on g-f.
**C A Dwyer [1-7] Mrs Shelley Dwyer (from M Johnston [2-13] Jun 1999).*

AJDAR BHB 29f31a **RR 24f 31a** 412[10]
9 b g Slip Anchor 12.7f **(75)** - Loucoum (FR) (Iron Duke (FR)) 8.8f **(60)**
Form - 000
Record 2000 - 1st:0 2nd:0 3rd:0 Ran:1
Pre2000 - 1st:2 2nd:3 3rd:1 Ran:38
Win Prizemoney £3,957 *Total Prizemoney* £6,935
Wins * 1998 *Jan Southw (STD) H 12f 44 46+* <
1996 Jan Southw (STD) H 11f 42 44
2000 AW 0-1: (12f) (Fibr)
Very moderate gelding, has worn blinkers. Becoming disappointing.
**Mrs S Lamyman [1-32] P Lamyman (from Miss Gay Kelleway [1-11] Jly 1996).*

AJJAE (IRE) BHB 33f34a **RR 29f 34a** 1642[13]
4 b g High Estate 10.5f **(66)** - Lake Ormond (Kings Lake (USA)) 10.8f **(67)**
Form - 0000
Record 2000 - 1st:0 2nd:0 3rd:0 Ran:3
Pre2000 - 1st:1 2nd:2 3rd:0 Ran:13
Win Prizemoney £2,402 *Total Prizemoney* £3,928
Wins * 1999 Aug Beverl (GD) C 7.5f 46 <
2000 Turf 0-3: (8f, 9f, 11f) (g-f 2, frm)
Strong, little account gelding, effective 7 to 9f, acts on frm, mostly wears blinkers (effectively), likes right handed tracks. Turf high 29.
**I Semple [1-17] Andy Dickie.*

AJNAD (IRE) BHB 54f63a **RR 55f 63a** 4834[23]
6 b g Efisio 7.7f **(69)** - Lotte Lenta (Gorytus (USA)) 7.8f **(60)**
Form - 0887506604730
Record 2000 - 1st:0 2nd:0 3rd:1 Ran:13
Pre2000 - 1st:1 2nd:4 3rd:4 Ran:23
Win Prizemoney £3,582 *Total Prizemoney* £9,790
Wins * 1999 *Jan Lingfi (STD) 6f 67* <
2000 Turf 0-7: (5f 3, 6f 4) (g-s, gd, g-f 3, frm 2) 2000 AW 0-6: (6f 5, 7f) (Fibr 6)
Average gelding, effective 6f, - acts on AW, best on Equi, has worn blinkers, prefers left handed tracks, prefers tight tracks. Turf high 55. AW high 57. He runs a lot, but has just a solitary Equitrack victory to his name in recent seasons.
**R F Marvin [1-35] J Shine (from C J Benstead [0-1] Aug 1996).*

AJWAA (IRE) BHB 93f **RR 90f** 5228[4]
2 ch c Mujtahid (USA) 7.4f **(69)** - Nouvelle Star (AUS) (Luskin Star (AUS)) 6.3f **(71)**
Form - 214
Record 2000 - 1st:1 2nd:1 3rd:0 Ran:3
Win Prizemoney £7,397 *Total Prizemoney* £9,461
Wins * 2000 Oct Newmar (SFT) 6f 90 <
2000 Turf 1-3: (6f 1-3) (gd 1-3)
Currently useful colt. Turf high 90 (began Spt) - 1st of 29 from Ishiguru (12 Oct Newmarket RF 4935).
**M P Tregoning [1-3] Hamdan Al Maktoum.*

AJYAAL (USA) BHB 70f **RR 63f** 4703[28]
3 b g Dayjur (USA) 6.8f **(79)** - Arjuzah (IRE) **(108f)** (Ahonoora) 8.1f **(73)**
Form - 0030
Record 2000 - 1st:0 2nd:0 3rd:1 Ran:4
Win Prizemoney £0 *Total Prizemoney* £672
2000 Turf 0-4: (5f, 6f 3) (gd, g-f, frm 2)
Strong, average gelding, has worn blinkers. Turf high 63.
**J H M Gosden [0-4] Hamdan Al Maktoum.*

AKALIM BHB 60f55a **RR 51f 55a** 4619[14]
7 b g Petong 7.6f **(58)** - Tiszta Sharok (Song) 7.2f **(61)**
Form - 0500
Record 2000 - 1st:0 2nd:0 3rd:0 Ran:4
Pre2000 - 1st:4 2nd:5 3rd:3 Ran:35
Win Prizemoney £14,164 *Total Prizemoney* £19,712
Wins * 1999 Oct Newbur (SFT) H 7f 62 69
* 1998 Spt Chepst (G-S) H 7.1f 56 60
2000 Turf 0-4: (7f 4) (g-s, gd 2, g-f)
Average gelding, effective 7f, acts on g-s to gd, best on gd, has worn blinkers. Turf high 51.
**L G Cottrell [2-29] Mrs Lucy Halloran (from D Morley [2-10] Jly 1996).*

AKATIB (IRE) **RR 22f** 1528[8]
2 b f Lahib (USA) 8f **(69)** - Daltak (Night Shift (USA)) 7.2f **(69)**
Form - 08
Record 2000 - 1st:0 2nd:0 3rd:0 Ran:2
2000 Turf 0-2: (5f 2) (gd 2)
Currently little account filly. Turf high 22.
**N Tinkler [0-2] A Cute Group.*

AKBAR (IRE) BHB 99f **RR 102f** 4722a[1]
4 bb h Doyoun 10.7f **(69)** - Akishka (Nishapour (FR)) 9.1f **(61)**
Form - 1106411
Record 2000 - 1st:4 2nd:0 3rd:0 Ran:7
Pre2000 - 1st:1 2nd:3 3rd:3 Ran:10
Win Prizemoney £41,428 *Total Prizemoney* £62,376
Wins * **2000** Spt Dielsd (GD) 12.4f 100+
* **2000** Aug Dielsd (GD) 16f 100+
* **2000** Jun Frauen (GD) 12f 106 <
* **2000** Apr Dielsd (GD) 12.4f 106 <
1998 Oct Tipper (HVY) 7f 57
2000 Turf 4-7: (10f, 12f 3-5, 16f 1-1) (gd 4-6, g-f)
Very useful colt, effective 10 to 16f, best at 12f, acts on gd to g-f, best on gd, does well at Dielsdorf. Turf high 106 - 1st of 6 from Harishon (12 Jun Frauenfeld RF 2197a) - also 1st of 12 from Galtee (30 Apr Dielsdorf RF 1034a). Consistent. He scored four times in Switzerland and clearly likes Dielsdorf's sharp track. Finished in midfield at Royal Ascot and ran well on unsuitably fast ground in the Old Newton Cup.
**M Johnston [4-9] Markus Graff (from FR [0-1] Spt 1999).*

AKEBONO (IRE) BHB 52f **RR 51f** 5185[5]
4 ch g Case Law 6f **(64)** - Elanmatina (IRE) (Burslem) 8.8f **(53)**
Form - 14100005
Record 2000 - 1st:2 2nd:0 3rd:0 Ran:8
Pre2000 - 1st:0 2nd:0 3rd:0 Ran:4
Win Prizemoney £10,005 *Total Prizemoney* £10,465
Wins 2000 Jly Leopar (G-F) H 6f 58 63 <
2000 Jun Tipper (G-S) H 5f 53 53
2000 Turf 2-8: (5f 1-3, 6f 1-2, 7f 3) (g-s 1-2, gd 2, g-f 1-4)
Fair gelding, effective 5 to 6f, acts on g-s to g-f, has worn blinkers. Turf high 63 - 1st of 7 getting 19lb from Discreet Option (8 Jly Leopardstown RF 2720a).
**P Burgoyne [0-5] Philip Saunders (from D Gillespie in IRE [2-7] Jly 2000).*

AKEED (USA) **RR 100f** 4936[19]
3 ch c Affirmed (USA) 10.3f **(75)** - Victorious Lil (CAN) (Vice Regent (CAN)) 8.7f **(74)**
Form - 550
Record 2000 - 1st:0 2nd:0 3rd:0 Ran:3
Pre2000 - 1st:1 2nd:0 3rd:0 Ran:3
Win Prizemoney £6,758 *Total Prizemoney* £11,741
Wins * 1999 Spt York (G-F) 7f 85++ <
2000 Turf 0-3: (8f, 10f, 12f) (g-s, gd, g-f)
Well made, very useful colt, effective 7f, acts on g-s. Turf high 83.
**P F I Cole [1-6] H R H Prince Fahd Salman.*

AKER WOOD BHB 77f **RR 82f** 4642[21]
2 b f Bin Ajwaad (IRE) - Wannaplantatree **(73df 59a)** (Niniski (USA)) 10.6f **(65)**
Form - 727500
Record 2000 - 1st:0 2nd:1 3rd:0 Ran:6
Win Prizemoney £0 *Total Prizemoney* £1,338
2000 Turf 0-6: (6f, 7f 5) (gd 2, g-f 3, frm)
Decent filly, effective 7f, acts on g-f. Turf high 82 - 2nd of 13 to Caribbeandriftwood (12 Jly Kempton 7f g-f RF 2734).
**A P Jarvis [0-6] A M Tombs.*

AKHIRA BHB 75f **RR 87f** 5021[2]
3 b f Emperor Jones (USA) - Fakhira (IRE) **(29f)** (Jareer (USA)) 5.9f

(75)
Form - 02
Record 2000 - 1st:0 2nd:1 3rd:0 Ran:2
Pre2000 - 1st:0 2nd:0 3rd:0 Ran:2
Win Prizemoney £0 *Total Prizemoney* £15,019
2000 Turf 0-2: (7f 2) (g-s, gd)
Scopey, useful filly. Turf high 73. **S P C Woods [0-4] Dennis Yardy.*

ALABAMA WURLEY BHB 40f55a **RR 48f 55a** 3968[11]
3 b f Environment Friend 7.5f **(67)** - Logarithm (King of Spain) 7.8f **(52)**
Form - 800060018400
Record 2000 - 1st:1 2nd:0 3rd:0 Ran:12
Pre2000 - 1st:1 2nd:2 3rd:2 Ran:9
Win Prizemoney £5,724 *Total Prizemoney* £7,577
Wins * 2000 Jly Yarmou (G-F) S 7f 45
* 1999 Aug Newmar (GD) S 7f 70 <
2000 Turf 1-11: (7f 1-4, 8f 6, 10f) (gd 4, g-f 5, frm 1-2) 2000 AW 0-1: (8f) (Fibr)
Light-framed, average filly, effective 7 to 8f, best at 7f, acts on g-s to frm - acts on Fibr, best on g-f, has worn blinkers, excels at Yarmouth. Turf high 53. **D Morris [2-21] Wacky Racing.*

ALABAMY SOUND (IRE) BHB 30f **RR 42f** 5056[15]
4 ch f Superlative 8.8f **(57)** - Salt Peanuts (IRE) (Salt Dome (USA))
Form - 40480
Record 2000 - 1st:0 2nd:0 3rd:0 Ran:5
Win Prizemoney £0 *Total Prizemoney* £188
2000 Turf 0-4: (8f 3, 9f) (sft, gd 2, g-f) 2000 AW 0-1: (8f) (Fibr)
Moderate filly. Turf high 42. **K A Morgan [0-5] S Giles.*

ALAGAZAM RR 56f 3268[8]
2 ch g Alhijaz 7.7f **(57)** - Maziere **(30f)** (Mazilier (USA))
Form - 078
Record 2000 - 1st:0 2nd:0 3rd:0 Ran:3
2000 Turf 0-3: (6f, 7f 2) (gd, g-f, frm)
Currently fair gelding. Turf high 56. **B I Case [0-3] Paul Rackham.*

ALAKANANDA BHB 71f **RR 72+f** 5189[2]
2 br f Hernando (FR) - Alouette (Darshaan) 9.9f **(84)**
Form - 222
Record 2000 - 1st:0 2nd:3 3rd:0 Ran:3
Win Prizemoney £0 *Total Prizemoney* £3,189
2000 Turf 0-3: (7f 2, 8f) (hvy, gd, g-f)
Currently above-average filly. Turf high 72 (1st run) (began Spt) - 2nd of 10 to Blushing Bride (1 Spt Epsom 7f g-f RF 4142).
**Sir Mark Prescott [0-3] Miss K Rausing.*

ALAMEIN (USA) BHB 39f60a **RR 46f 60a** 4194[18]
7 ch g Roi Danzig (USA) 10.5f **(62)** - Pollination (Pentotal) 7f **(53)**
Form - 80002301040
Record 2000 - 1st:1 2nd:1 3rd:1 Ran:11
Pre2000 - 1st:5 2nd:3 3rd:7 Ran:34
Win Prizemoney £16,059 *Total Prizemoney* £26,250
Wins * 2000 Aug Hamilt (SFT) C 9.2f 42
1999 Feb Lingfi (STD) H 7f 65 66+
1999 Feb Lingfi (STD) C 7f 57
1998 Mar Southw (STD) C 7f 72+
1996 Jun Thirsk (FRM) 7f 78 <
1996 Jun Catter (GD) 7f 73
2000 Turf 1-11: (8f 3, 9f 1-6, 10f, 12f) (gd 1-2, g-f 7, frm 2)
Average gelding, effective 7f, - acts on Equi, has worn blinkers, likes left handed tracks, likes tight tracks. Turf high 46.
**W Storey [1-14] R J H Ltd (from D Nicholls [3-19] Jly 1999).*

ALASAN (IRE) BHB 75f **RR 75+f** 1704[12]
3 b c Zilzal (USA) 8.5f **(79)** - Alasana (IRE) (Darshaan) 9.9f **(84)**
Form - 00
Record 2000 - 1st:0 2nd:0 3rd:0 Ran:2
Pre2000 - 1st:0 2nd:0 3rd:1 Ran:1
Win Prizemoney £0 *Total Prizemoney* £636
2000 Turf 0-2: (6f, 7f) (g-s, gd)
Currently above-average colt. Turf high 50.
**Sir Michael Stoute [0-2] H H Aga Khan (from L M Cumani [0-1] Aug 1999).*

ALASTAIR SMELLIE BHB 69f **RR 84f** 4449[18]
4 ch g Sabrehill (USA) 8.5f **(64)** - Reel Foyle (USA) (Irish River (FR))
8.6f **(78)**
Form - 005040000
Record 2000 - 1st:0 2nd:0 3rd:0 Ran:9
Pre2000 - 1st:1 2nd:0 3rd:3 Ran:13
Win Prizemoney £5,394 *Total Prizemoney* £11,199
Wins 1998 Spt Ayr (G-S) H 6f 75 79 <
2000 Turf 0-9: (6f 8, 7f) (gd 6, g-f 2, frm)
Workmanlike, decent gelding. Turf high 84. He is a useful handicapper at six or seven furlongs on his day, but is a tricky customer who tends to find trouble in running.
**D Nicholls [0-4] G Vettraino & Fayzad Thoroughbreds II (from B W Hills [1-18] Jly 2000).*

AL AWAALAH BHB 45f **RR 46f** 5229[3]
3 b f Mukaddamah (USA) 7.6f **(74)** - Zippy Zoe (Rousillon (USA)) 8.2f **(74)**
Form - 80803
Record 2000 - 1st:0 2nd:0 3rd:1 Ran:5
Win Prizemoney £0 *Total Prizemoney* £562
2000 Turf 0-5: (8f 4, 10f) (gd 2, g-f 2, frm)
Scopey, moderate filly. Turf high 46 - 3rd of 24 getting 23lb from Eve (27 Oct Newmarket 8f gd RF 5229).
**M Salaman [0-5] J P M & J W Cook.*

ALAWAR BHB 52f **RR 52f** 5229[21]
3 ch c Wolfhound (USA) 7.3f **(71)** - Ghassanah (Pas de Seul) 9.1f **(67)**
Form - 70044450
Record 2000 - 1st:0 2nd:0 3rd:0 Ran:8
Pre2000 - 1st:0 2nd:0 3rd:1 Ran:3
Win Prizemoney £0 *Total Prizemoney* £1,365
2000 Turf 0-8: (6f 2, 7f 2, 8f 4) (sft, g-s 2, gd 2, frm 3)
Scopey, fair colt. Turf high 65. Has shown ability in maidens and ordinary handicaps. **C G Cox [0-11] Sheikh Amin Dahlawi.*

ALAZAN BHB 30f **RR 36f** 2867[7]
5 ch g Risk Me (FR) 8f **(53)** - Gunnard (Gunner B) 11.2f **(58)**
Form - 007
Record 2000 - 1st:0 2nd:0 3rd:0 Ran:3
Pre2000 - 1st:0 2nd:0 3rd:0 Ran:7
Win Prizemoney £0 *Total Prizemoney* £740
2000 Turf 0-3: (8f, 10f 2) (g-f 2, frm)
Very moderate gelding. Becoming disappointing.
**W de Best-Turner [0-6] The Spanish Connection (from D M Hyde [0-4] May 1998).*

AL AZHAR BHB 75f **RR 85df** 5026[8]
6 b g Alzao (USA) 9.8f **(73)** - Upend (Main Reef) 9.6f **(57)**
Form - 50668
Record 2000 - 1st:0 2nd:0 3rd:0 Ran:5
Pre2000 - 1st:3 2nd:3 3rd:2 Ran:16
Win Prizemoney £34,856 *Total Prizemoney* £48,418
Wins 1997 Oct Doncas (GD) H 12f 91 96
1996 Spt Doncas (G-F) H 8f 85 98+ <
1996 Aug Chepst (GD) 8.1f 86+
2000 Turf 0-5: (10f 4, 12f) (g-s 4, frm)
Useful gelding, effective 8 to 12f, best at 12f, acts on g-s to frm, best on g-s, prefers tight tracks. Turf high 90. Becoming disappointing.
**M Dods [0-5] Mrs Karen Pratt (from I A Balding [3-16] Oct 1999).*

ALBANECK BHB 71f **RR 69f** 3036[2]
2 gr g Timeless Times (USA) 6.1f **(56)** - Strawberry Pink (Absalom) 7.2f **(58)**
Form - 7642
Record 2000 - 1st:0 2nd:1 3rd:0 Ran:4
Win Prizemoney £0 *Total Prizemoney* £1,333
2000 Turf 0-4: (5f 4) (g-s, g-f 2, frm)
Average gelding. Turf high 69 - 2nd of 6 to Majestic Quest (22 Jly Ripon 5f g-f RF 3036). (DEAD) **T D Easterby [0-4] Ron George.*

ALBARAHIN (USA) BHB 116f **RR 120f** 5239[1]
5 b h Silver Hawk (USA) 11.2f **(85)** - My Dear Lady (USA) (Mr Prospector (USA)) 8.8f **(78)**
Form - 2121211
Record 2000 - 1st:4 2nd:3 3rd:0 Ran:7
Pre2000 - 1st:3 2nd:3 3rd:1 Ran:9
Win Prizemoney £78,577 *Total Prizemoney* £132,609

Wins *** 2000** Oct Newmar (SFT) L 8f 120 <
*** 2000** Oct Newmar (SFT) L 9f 120 <
*** 2000** Spt Goodwo (HVY) L 9.9f 118+
*** 2000** Aug Sandow (GD) 9f 108+
* 1999 Oct Newbur (HVY) H 9f 96 108+
* 1999 Aug Sandow (GD) H 10f 88 93++
* 1999 Aug Leices (GD) H 10f 80 90

2000 Turf 4-7: (8f 1-1, 9f 2-2, 10f 1-4) (g-s 1-1, gd 3-6)

Very high-class colt, effective 8 to 10f, acts on g-s to gd, best on gd, prefers tight tracks, and does well at Sandown. Turf high 120 (began Jly) - 1st of 11 giving 11lb to Rosse (28 Oct Newmarket RF 5239) - also 1st of 11 giving 8lb to Summer View (13 Oct Newmarket RF 4967). Improving. He developed into a most admirable racehorse in 2000, never out of the first two in seven starts. Well placed to win three times in listed company, he also acquitted himself well in a Longchamp Group Two.

**M P Tregoning [7-12] Hamdan Al Maktoum (from S bin Suroor [0-4] Oct 1998).*

Albarahin was never out of the frame

ALBARAN (GER) RR 107f $2384a^{2}$

7 b h Sure Blade (USA) 10.6f **(66)** - Araqueen (GER) (Konigsstuhl (GER)) 11.2f **(76)**
Form - 2
2000 Turf 0-1: (11f) (hvy)

Pattern-class horse. (1st run) - 2nd of 5 giving 2lb to Flamingo Road (25 Jun Hamburg 11f hvy RF 2384a). Consistent. A very useful performer over middle distances in Scandinavia.

**Catherine Erichsen in NOR [3-8] Stall Albaran.*

ALBARDEN BHB 42f RR 48f 3497^{6}

3 ch g Mujtahid (USA) 7.4f **(69)** - Aljood (Kris) 9.5f **(73)**
Form - 55076
Record 2000 - 1st:0 2nd:0 3rd:0 Ran:5
Pre2000 - 1st:0 2nd:0 3rd:0 Ran:2
Win Prizemoney £0 *Total Prizemoney* £243
2000 Turf 0-5: (10f 2, 12f, 14f, 16f) (sft, g-f 3, frm)

Leggy, moderate gelding. Turf high 48.

**T D Easterby [0-7] C H Newton Jnr Ltd.*

ALBARSHA RR 51f 4632^{5}

3 br f Mtoto 11.5f **(71)** - Walimu (IRE) (Top Ville) 11.7f **(68)**
Form - 5
Record 2000 - 1st:0 2nd:0 3rd:0 Ran:1
2000 Turf 0-1: (10f) (g-s)

Scopey, currently average filly.

**M P Tregoning [0-1] Sheikh Ahmed Al Maktoum.*

ALBASHOOSH BHB 84f RR 83f 4379^{2}

2 b c Cadeaux Genereux 7.9f **(76)** - Annona (USA) **(68f)** (Diesis) 9.3f **(69)**
Form - 032
Record 2000 - 1st:0 2nd:1 3rd:1 Ran:3
Win Prizemoney £0 *Total Prizemoney* £1,692
2000 Turf 0-3: (7f 2, 8f) (g-f, frm 2)

Currently decent colt. Turf high 83 (began Jly) - 2nd of 17 to Rebel Storm (13 Spt Yarmouth 7f frm RF 4379).

**E A L Dunlop [0-3] Khalifa Sultan.*

ALBERGO (IRE) BHB 34f49a RR 36f 49a 4489^{12}

3 b g Deploy 11.4f **(67)** - River Dove (USA) (Riverman (USA)) 9.1f **(76)**
Form - 500280400
Record 2000 - 1st:0 2nd:1 3rd:0 Ran:9
Pre2000 - 1st:0 2nd:0 3rd:0 Ran:2
Win Prizemoney £0 *Total Prizemoney* £634
2000 Turf 0-7: (8f, 10f 3, 12f 3) (g-s 2, gd, g-f 2, frm, hrd) 2000 AW 0-2: (8f, 9f) (Fibr 2)

Scopey, average gelding, effective 8f, - acts on Fibr, has worn blinkers, likes tight tracks. Turf high 38. AW high 62 - 2nd of 13 giving 4lb to Ride The Tiger (11 May Wolverhampton 8f Fibr RF 1147). Inconsistent. **M Blanshard [0-11] Goldring Hotels Ltd.*

ALBERICH (IRE) BHB 91f RR 96f 1216^{4}

5 b g Night Shift (USA) 8.1f **(73)** - Tetradonna (IRE) (Teenoso (USA)) 9.9f **(72)**
Form - 15054
Record 2000 - 1st:0 2nd:0 3rd:0 Ran:4
Pre2000 - 1st:4 2nd:1 3rd:2 Ran:13
Win Prizemoney £39,464 *Total Prizemoney* £47,085
Wins * 1999 *Nov Lingfi (STD) 12f 88+*
* 1999 Spt Newbur (G-F) H 13.3f 90 92 <
* 1998 Spt York (GD) H 11.9f 86 89
* 1997 Aug Beverl (GD) 8.5f 80+

2000 Turf 0-3: (12f 3) (gd, g-f, frm) 2000 AW 0-1: (12f) (Equi)

Very useful gelding, effective 12 to 13f, best at 12f, acts on g-f to frm - acts on Equi, best on frm, Turf high 96 - 5th of 18 getting 5lb from Rainbow Ways (7 May Newmarket 12f frm RF 1082).

**M Johnston [4-17] David Abell.*

ALBERKINNIE BHB 43f26a RR 45f 26a 1880^{25}

5 b m Ron's Victory (USA) 9.2f **(52)** - Trojan Desert (Troy) 10.4f **(68)**
Form - 87253321000
Record 2000 - 1st:1 2nd:2 3rd:2 Ran:10
Pre2000 - 1st:0 2nd:2 3rd:0 Ran:23
Win Prizemoney £4,101 *Total Prizemoney* £8,045
Wins * 2000 May Nottin (G-S) H 10f 31 45 <

2000 Turf 1-4: (10f 1-1, 11f, 12f 2) (gd 1-1, g-f, frm 2) 2000 AW 0-6: (8f, 9f, 12f 3, 13f) (Equi 2, Fibr 4)

Moderate filly, effective 9 to 10f, acts on gd, likes left handed tracks, likes tight tracks. Turf high 45 (1st run) - 1st of 10 getting 26lb from Itsanothergirl (2 May Nottingham RF 0971). AW high 26.

**J L Harris [1-33] Paddy Barrett.*

ALBERT THE BEAR BHB 52f80a RR 57df 80a 5003^{6}

7 b g Puissance 7.1f **(60)** - Florentynna Bay (Aragon) 8.1f **(60)**
Form - 060830726086
Record 2000 - 1st:0 2nd:1 3rd:1 Ran:12
Pre2000 - 1st:8 2nd:6 3rd:4 Ran:53
Win Prizemoney £41,272 *Total Prizemoney* £58,047
Wins 1999 Jly Pontef (G-S) H 6f 62 64
1999 Jun Carlis (G-F) S 5.9f 52
1997 Jun Cheste (G-F) H 7f 84 87 <
1997 May Cheste (HVY) H 7.6f 78 87 <
1996 Jun Cheste (G-F) H 7f 77 77

2000 Turf 0-12: (5f 3, 6f 8, 7f) (g-s, gd, g-f 4, frm 5, hrd)

Fair gelding, effective 6 to 7f, best at 6f, acts on g-f to frm, best on frm, often wears blinkers (extremely effectively), excels at Carlisle, does well at Pontefract. Turf high 57 - 2nd of 16 getting 7lb from Bundy (11 Jly Pontefract 6f frm RF 2696).

**A Berry [0-12] Chris & Antonia Deuters (from J Berry [8-56] Nov 1999).*

ALBERT THE GREAT (USA) RR $5332a^{4}$

3 b c Go For Gin (USA) - Bright Feather (USA) (Fappiano (USA)) 8.7f **(77)**
Form - 24
2000 AW 0-2: (10f 2) (Dirt 2)

Currently very high-class colt. AW high 123 (began Aug) - 4th of 13 to Tiznow (4 Nov Churchill Downs 10f Dirt RF 5332a).

**N Zito in USA [0-2] Tracy Farmer.*

ALBINONA (IRE) BHB 34f RR 40f 2435^{8}

3 b f Distinctly North (USA) 7.4f **(63)** - Across The Ring (IRE) (Auction

Ring (USA)) 8.6f **(65)**
Form - 6258
Record 2000 - 1st:0 2nd:1 3rd:0 Ran:4
Pre2000 - 1st:0 2nd:0 3rd:0 Ran:3
Win Prizemoney £0 *Total Prizemoney* £524
2000 Turf 0-1: (10f) (frm) 2000 AW 0-3: (12f 2, 13f) (Equi 3)
Moderate filly, effective 12f, - acts on Equi, likes left handed tracks. AW high 49 (1st run) - 2nd of 7 to Bee Gee (27 May Lingfield 12f Equi RF 1503).
**M H Tompkins [0-4] The Double-Barrelled Syndicate (from M J Byrne in IRE [0-3] Aug 1999).*

ALBUHERA (IRE) BHB 83f RR 85f 5293[1]

2 b c Desert Style (IRE) - Morning Welcome (IRE) (Be My Guest (USA)) 9.3f **(67)**
Form - 261
Record 2000 - 1st:1 2nd:1 3rd:0 Ran:3
Win Prizemoney £2,323 *Total Prizemoney* £4,043
Wins * 2000 Nov Mussel (G-S) 7.1f 85 <
2000 Turf 1-3: (6f, 7f 1-2) (g-s 1-2, g-f)
Currently useful colt. Turf high 85 (began Spt) - 1st of 8 from Ecclesiastical (1 Nov Musselburgh RF 5293).
**M Johnston [1-3] D J & F A Jackson.*

ALBURACK BHB 61f RR 49f 5156[11]

2 b c Rock City 8.8f **(62)** - Suzannah's Song (Song) 7.2f **(61)**
Form - 700
Record 2000 - 1st:0 2nd:0 3rd:0 Ran:3
2000 Turf 0-3: (5f, 6f 2) (g-s, gd, frm)
Currently moderate colt. Turf high 49.
**G G Margarson [0-3] P E Axon.*

ALCAYDE BHB 50f RR 56f 5161[2]

5 ch g Alhijaz 7.7f **(57)** - Lucky Flinders (Free State) 8.7f **(61)**
Form - 0753502
Record 2000 - 1st:0 2nd:1 3rd:1 Ran:7
Pre2000 - 1st:1 2nd:3 3rd:1 Ran:8
Win Prizemoney £3,420 *Total Prizemoney* £9,058
Wins 1998 Jly Newcas (G-F) H 10.1f 77 77 <
2000 Turf 0-7: (10f 2, 12f, 14f 2, 16f 2) (sft, g-s, gd 2, g-f 2, frm)
Fair gelding. Turf high 56. Inconsistent.
**J Akehurst [0-8] A D Spence (from J L Dunlop [1-8] Oct 1998).*

ALCONLEIGH BHB 39f81a RR 28f 81a 582[11]

5 ch g Pursuit of Love 9.5f **(69)** - Serotina (IRE) (Mtoto)
Form - 0
Record 2000 - 1st:0 2nd:0 3rd:0 Ran:1
Pre2000 - 1st:2 2nd:5 3rd:3 Ran:29
Win Prizemoney £8,600 *Total Prizemoney* £21,720
Wins 1997 Jly Thirsk (GD) 7f 90 <
1997 May Ripon (G-S) 6f 77
2000 Turf 0-1: (6f) (frm)
Average gelding, effective 8f, acts on g-f to frm, best on frm, has worn blinkers.
**B Ellison [0-9] Alconleigh Partnership (from M Johnston [2-21] Jly 1999).*

ALCOVE BHB 40f RR 42f 3435[10]

9 ch g Faustus (USA) 9.1f **(54)** - Cubby Hole (Town And Country) 8.1f **(68)**
Form - 007000
Record 2000 - 1st:0 2nd:0 3rd:0 Ran:6
Pre2000 - 1st:2 2nd:2 3rd:4 Ran:17
Win Prizemoney £7,885 *Total Prizemoney* £14,674
2000 Turf 0-6: (8f 2, 9f, 10f 2, 12f) (gd 2, g-f 2, frm 2)
Moderate gelding, has worn blinkers. Turf high 46.
**R F JohnsonHoughton [0-7] Mrs H JohnsonHoughton (from R Hannon [2-17] Oct 1994).*

ALDEBARAN (USA) RR 100+f 5100[1]

2 b c Mr Prospector (USA) 8.6f **(88)** - Chimes of Freedom (USA) (Private Account (USA)) 8.5f **(74)**
Form - 1
Record 2000 - 1st:1 2nd:0 3rd:0 Ran:1
Win Prizemoney £3,477 *Total Prizemoney* £3,477
Wins * 2000 Oct Doncas (GD) 7f 100+ <
2000 Turf 1-1: (7f 1-1) (gd 1-1)
Currently very useful colt. (1st run) - 1st of 21 from Take To Task (20 Oct Doncaster RF 5100). Out of a top-class mare, won his maiden in style and looks useful. **H R A Cecil [1-1] Niarchos Family.*

ALDWYCH RR 90+f 5110[1]

2 ch c In The Wings 11.2f **(77)** - Arderelle (FR) (Pharly (FR)) 9.8f **(68)**
Form - 81
Record 2000 - 1st:1 2nd:0 3rd:0 Ran:2
Win Prizemoney £6,612 *Total Prizemoney* £6,612
Wins * 2000 Oct Newbur (SFT) 8f 90+ <
2000 Turf 1-2: (7f, 8f 1-1) (gd 1-1, g-f)
Currently useful colt. Turf high 90 (began Spt) - 1st of 11 getting 3lb from Black Knight (20 Oct Newbury RF 5110). A half-brother to Spout amongst others, he improved on his Newmarket debut when scoring in good style at Newbury, and looks a progressive sort. **R Charlton [1-2] Lady Rothschild.*

ALDWYCH ARROW (IRE) BHB 36f46a RR 41f 46a 5020[4]

5 ch g Rainbows For Life (CAN) 9.3f **(64)** - Shygate (Shy Groom (USA)) 10f **(66)**
Form - 780067254
Record 2000 - 1st:0 2nd:1 3rd:0 Ran:9
Pre2000 - 1st:3 2nd:8 3rd:4 Ran:34
Win Prizemoney £11,474 *Total Prizemoney* £22,638
Wins * 1999 Apr Catter (SFT) H 12f 60 66
1998 Jun Mussel (SFT) H 14f 63 66
1998 Jun Ayr (GD) H 13.1f 60 67 <
2000 Turf 0-8: (10f, 12f 4, 14f 2, 16f) (g-s, gd 3, g-f 2, frm 2) 2000 AW 0-1: (12f) (Fibr)
Moderate gelding, effective 12 to 14f, best at 12f, acts on gd to g-f, best on g-f, has worn blinkers, favours tight tracks. Turf high 48 .
**M A Buckley [1-24] M A Buckley (from M L W Bell [2-19] Spt 1998).*

ALEANBH (IRE) BHB 26f RR 42?f 67[9]

5 ch g Classic Secret (USA) 8.8f **(56)** - Highdrive (Ballymore) 7.3f **(64)**
Form - 6070
Record 2000 - 1st:0 2nd:0 3rd:0 Ran:1
Pre2000 - 1st:0 2nd:0 3rd:0 Ran:5
2000 AW 0-1: (9f) (Fibr)
Moderate gelding.
**R A Fahey [0-5] Tommy Staunton (from Miss Gay Kelleway [0-1] Mar 1998).*

ALEGRIA RR 85f 4150[10]

4 b f Night Shift (USA) 8.1f **(73)** - High Habit (Slip Anchor) 9.8f **(73)**
Form - 7106000
Record 2000 - 1st:1 2nd:0 3rd:0 Ran:7
Pre2000 - 1st:1 2nd:1 3rd:2 Ran:10
Win Prizemoney £9,855 *Total Prizemoney* £16,537
Wins * 2000 Jun Windso (GD) 6f 85 <
***** 1998 Jly Windso (GD) 6f 84
2000 Turf 1-7: (5f, 6f 1-6) (g-s, gd 2, g-f 1-3, hrd)
Scopey, useful filly, effective 5 to 6f, best at 6f, acts on gd to frm, best on g-f, has worn blinkers. Turf high 85 - also 1st of 7 giving 5lb to Argent Facile (5 Jun Windsor RF 1732). She scored at Windsor before finishing an excellent ninth in the Wokingham at Ascot. **J M P Eustace [2-17] J C Smith.*

ALEXANDER STAR (IRE) BHB 67f RR 69f 4628[10]

2 b br f Inzar (USA) - Business Centre (IRE) (Digamist (USA))
Form - 430
Record 2000 - 1st:0 2nd:0 3rd:1 Ran:3
Win Prizemoney £0 *Total Prizemoney* £767
2000 Turf 0-3: (5f, 6f 2) (gd, g-f, frm)
Currently average filly. Turf high 69.
**J A R Toller [0-3] Mrs N O'Callaghan.*

ALEXANDRINE (IRE) BHB 72f70a RR 75f 70a 4779[4]

3 b f Nashwan (USA) 10.3f **(79)** - Alruccaba (Crystal Palace (FR)) 12.5f **(76)**
Form - 11411434
Record 2000 - 1st:4 2nd:0 3rd:1 Ran:8
Pre2000 - 1st:0 2nd:0 3rd:0 Ran:3
Win Prizemoney £11,339 *Total Prizemoney* £12,756
Wins * 2000 Jly Ayr (FRM) 13.1f 64+
*** 2000** Jly Carlis (FM) 12f 31++
*** 2000** Jun Mussel (FRM) H 12f 58 75 <

*** 2000** Jun Yarmou (G-F) H 10.1f 52 67
2000 Turf 4-7: (10f 1-1, 11f, 12f 2-4, 13f 1-1) (gd 2, g-f 1-1, frm 2-3, hrd 1-1) 2000 AW 0-1: (12f) (Fibr)
Tall, above-average filly, effective 10 to 12f, best at 12f, acts on gd to frm - acts on Fibr, prefers tight tracks. Turf high 75 - 1st of 8 giving 11lb to Cosmic Case (26 Jun Musselburgh RF 2271) - also 1st of 17 getting 18lb from Julius (15 Jun Yarmouth RF 1999). (1st run) - 4th of 11 giving 11lb to Failed To Hit (3 Oct Wolverhampton 12f Fibr RF 4779). Four times a winner on fast ground during the summer, she is another from her yard to take advantage of some favourable handicapping and a step up in trip.
**Sir Mark Prescott [4-11] Miss K Rausing.*

ALFAHAAL (IRE) BHB 26f56a **RR 47f 56a** 4272[17]

7 b g Green Desert (USA) 7.8f **(78)** - Fair of the Furze (Ela-Mana-Mou) 10.1f **(70)**
Form - 08000800

Record	**2000 -**	1st:0	2nd:0	3rd:0	Ran:8
	Pre2000 -	1st:3	2nd:2	3rd:2	Ran:37

Win Prizemoney £10,405 *Total Prizemoney* £14,300

Wins	1999	May	Yarmou	(FRM)	H	7f	51	52	
	1997	Oct	Leices	(SFT)		8f		63	<
	1997	Jly	Doncas	(GD)	H	8f	52	56	

2000 Turf 0-8: (6f 3, 7f 2, 8f 3) (gd 2, g-f 3, frm 3)
Fair gelding, effective 7 to 10f, acts on gd to g-f, best on g-f, has worn blinkers. Turf high 47.
**J Pearce [0-3] M M Foulger (from C A Dwyer [1-28] Jun 2000).*

ALFAHAD BHB 33f **RR 29f** 1476[12]

7 b g Doyoun 10.7f **(69)** - Moogie (Young Generation) 7.7f **(63)**
Form - 800

Record	**2000 -**	1st:0	2nd:0	3rd:0	Ran:3
	Pre2000 -	1st:0	2nd:0	3rd:0	Ran:2

2000 Turf 0-2: (11f 2) (gd, g-f) 2000 AW 0-1: (14f) (Fibr)
Little account gelding, has worn blinkers. Turf high 29.
**J L Eyre [0-3] J L Eyre (from Miss Gay Kelleway [0-2] Jun 1996).*

ALFAILAK BHB 89f **RR 96f** 4219[8]

3 b c Green Desert (USA) 7.8f **(78)** - Great Inquest **(79f)** (Shernazar) 10.2f **(73)**
Form - 75068

Record	**2000 -**	1st:0	2nd:0	3rd:0	Ran:5
	Pre2000 -	1st:1	2nd:1	3rd:1	Ran:7

Win Prizemoney £4,467 *Total Prizemoney* £15,659
Wins * 1999 Apr Newmar (GD) 5f 85 <
2000 Turf 0-5: (5f, 6f 4) (gd, g-f 2, frm, hrd)
Light-framed, very useful colt, effective 5f, acts on gd to g-f, has worn blinkers. Turf high 96 (began Jly). Becoming disappointing. A speedy juvenile in '99, when in the frame in pattern races, he ran well at Newbury in July but was generally disappointing last term.
**M R Channon [1-12] Sheikh Mohammed Obaid Al Maktoum.*

ALFALFA BHB 35f **RR 32f** 5067[15]

2 b g Rudimentary (USA) 8.2f **(66)** - Zalfa (Luthier) 9.8f **(71)**
Form - 000
Record 2000 - 1st:0 2nd:0 3rd:0 Ran:3
2000 Turf 0-3: (6f, 7f 2) (g-s 2, gd)
Currently very moderate gelding. Turf high 32 (began Oct).
**G B Balding [0-3] Mrs Mrs Gulliver Perrin Balding.*

ALFANO (IRE) BHB 67f62a **RR 70f 62a** 5076[5]

2 b c Priolo (USA) 10.9f **(71)** - Sartigila **(51f)** (Efisio)
Form - 55
Record 2000 - 1st:0 2nd:0 3rd:0 Ran:2
2000 Turf 0-2: (8f 2) (g-s, gd)
Currently above-average colt. Turf high 70 (began Spt) - 5th of 8 giving 5lb to Among Women (19 Oct Brighton 8f g-s RF 5076).
**P Mitchell [0-2] Alleynian Racing Partnership.*

ALFASEL (USA) **RR 69f** 3048[6]

2 b c Silver Hawk (USA) 11.2f **(85)** - Good Example (FR) (Crystal Glitters (USA)) 11.3f **(79)**
Form - 06
Record 2000 - 1st:0 2nd:0 3rd:0 Ran:2
2000 Turf 0-2: (7f 2) (frm 2)
Currently average colt. Turf high 69 (began Jly).
**M P Tregoning [0-2] Hamdan Al Maktoum.*

ALFIE BOY (IRE) BHB 99f **RR 106f** 1264[9]

4 b g Forest Wind (USA) - Ballinlee (IRE) (Skyliner) 7.3f **(53)**
Form - 0

Record	**2000 -**	1st:0	2nd:0	3rd:0	Ran:1
	Pre2000 -	1st:1	2nd:0	3rd:1	Ran:3

Win Prizemoney £3,835 *Total Prizemoney* £7,405
Wins * 1999 Jun Goodwo (G-S) 7f 87 <
2000 Turf 0-1: (8f) (g-f)
Scopey, Pattern-class gelding. **A P Jarvis [1-4] Mrs Ann Jarvis.*

ALFIE LEE (IRE) BHB 80f **RR 88f** 4025[5]

3 ch c Case Law 6f **(64)** - Nordic Living (IRE) (Nordico (USA)) 6.5f **(62)**
Form - 075875

Record	**2000 -**	1st:0	2nd:0	3rd:0	Ran:6
	Pre2000 -	1st:1	2nd:0	3rd:0	Ran:5

Win Prizemoney £4,123 *Total Prizemoney* £5,474
Wins * 1999 May Goodwo (GD) 5f 74 <
2000 Turf 0-6: (5f, 6f 5) (gd, g-f 2, frm 3)
Neat, useful colt. Turf high 88. Becoming disappointing. Off the track after Royal Ascot as a juvenile, he has not shown a great deal this season. **C N Allen [1-11] ShadowfaxRacing Com.*

ALFINI **RR 95+f** 1060[P]

3 ch c Selkirk (USA) 7.9f **(76)** - Vivre En Paix (Nureyev (USA)) 8.7f **(78)**
Form - P

Record	**2000 -**	1st:0	2nd:0	3rd:0	Ran:1
	Pre2000 -	1st:1	2nd:1	3rd:0	Ran:2

Win Prizemoney £5,708 *Total Prizemoney* £10,316
Wins * 1999 Oct Newmar (GD) 6f 95+ <
2000 Turf 0-1: (8f) (gd)
Scopey, very useful colt. A tank of a horse, he caught the eye on his two starts in 1999, winning very impressively at Newmarket in October. He was held in high regard, but sadly broke a leg in the the 2000 Guineas. (DEAD)
**D R C Elsworth [1-3] A Heaney & A Tuckerman.*

AL GHABRAA BHB 69f67a **RR 89f 67a** 3803[10]

3 ch f Pursuit of Love 9.5f **(69)** - Tenderetta (Tender King) 6.8f **(54)**
Form - 65870

Record	**2000 -**	1st:0	2nd:0	3rd:0	Ran:5
	Pre2000 -	1st:1	2nd:0	3rd:0	Ran:1

Win Prizemoney £3,414 *Total Prizemoney* £3,741
Wins * 1999 Oct Redcar (GD) 8f 81+ <
2000 Turf 0-5: (8f 3, 9f, 10f) (sft, g-f 2, frm 2)
Rangy, useful filly, effective 8f, acts on frm. Turf high 89. Ran green when a narrow winner of a Redcar maiden in the autumn, but has shown little at three and tends not to settle.
**J W Hills [1-6] Hassan Ahmadi.*

ALHAWA (USA) BHB 75f **RR 81f** 4987[28]

7 ch g Mt Livermore (USA) 7.7f **(90)** - Petrava (NZ) (Imposing (AUS)) 7.7f **(74)**
Form - 25B0480

Record	**2000 -**	1st:0	2nd:1	3rd:0	Ran:7
	Pre2000 -	1st:6	2nd:0	3rd:4	Ran:34

Win Prizemoney £27,674 *Total Prizemoney* £36,874

Wins	1999	Aug	Newmar	(G-F)	H	16.1f	76	81	<
	1999	Jly	Newmar	(G-F)	H	14.8f	70	72	
	1999	Jly	Newmar	(G-F)	H	14.8f	61	68	
	1999	Jly	Doncas	(G-F)	H	12f	61	67	
	1996	May	Lingfi	(G-F)		7.6f		81	<

2000 Turf 0-7: (12f, 14f, 15f, 16f 2, 18f, 20f) (gd 3, g-f 2, frm 2)
Decent gelding, effective 12 to 17f, acts on gd to g-f, best on gd, has worn blinkers, excels at Newmarket. Turf high 83 (1st run) - 2nd of 21 getting 14lb from Mowelga (19 Apr Newmarket 12f gd RF 0796). Inconsistent. Held last term, if running respectably. He was brought down at Royal Ascot, ending Kieren Fallon's season.
**K R Burke [0-7] DGH Partnership (from N P Littmoden [4-12] Oct 1999).*

ALHESN (USA) BHB 42f58a **RR 42f 58a** 570[6]

5 b br g Woodman (USA) 9.7f **(77)** - Deceit Princess (CAN) (Vice Regent (CAN)) 8.7f **(74)**
Form - 015413236

Record	**2000 -**	1st:1	2nd:1	3rd:2	Ran:6
	Pre2000 -	1st:5	2nd:2	3rd:1	Ran:21

Win Prizemoney £18,453 *Total Prizemoney* £23,324
Wins * **2000** *Jan Wolver (STD) H 16.2f 67 71* <
* 1999 *Dec Wolver (STD) H 16.2f 65 70*
* 1999 *Spt Wolver (STD) H 16.2f 57 63*
* 1999 *Aug Lingfi (STD) H 16f 45 52*
* 1999 Jly Yarmou (FRM) H 16f 33 41
* 1999 Jly Yarmou (FRM) H 14.1f 40 43
2000 Turf 0-1: (16f) (gd) 2000 AW 1-5: (16f 1-5) (Equi 2, Fibr 1-3)
Average gelding, effective 15 to 16f, best at 16f, - acts on AW, best on Fibr, favours left handed tracks, favours tight tracks, excels at Wolverhampton and does well at Lingfield. AW high 71 - 1st of 9 giving 7lb to Pipe Music (18 Jan Wolverhampton RF 0109). Consistent. He is well suited by both Equitrack and the Wolverhampton Fibresand, but is not so effective on turf and has disappointed when tried at Southwell. Ideally needs two miles and a truly-run race.
**C N Allen [6-27] J T B Racing.*

ALHUFOOF (USA) BHB 95f RR 105f 4376[6]
3 b f Dayjur (USA) 6.8f **(79)** - Cheval Volant (USA) (Kris S (USA)) 7.9f **(71)**
Form - 4046
Record 2000 - 1st:0 2nd:0 3rd:0 Ran:4
Pre2000 - 1st:1 2nd:0 3rd:1 Ran:2
Win Prizemoney £6,905 *Total Prizemoney* £10,177
Wins * 1999 Jly Goodwo (G-F) 6f 91+ <
2000 Turf 0-4: (6f 2, 7f 2) (g-s, gd 2, frm)
Scopey, Pattern-class filly. Turf high 105. Ran very well until blowing up in the Nell Gwyn Stakes on her return, but failed to progress from that in conditions races.
**M P Tregoning [1-0] Hamdan Al Maktoum.*

ALHUWBILL BHB 37f33a RR 37f 33a 4694[7]
5 b g Full Extent (USA) 5.2f **(50)** - Hale Lane (Comedy Star (USA)) 7.5f **(50)**
Form - 607437
Record 2000 - 1st:0 2nd:0 3rd:1 Ran:6
Pre2000 - 1st:0 2nd:0 3rd:0 Ran:11
Win Prizemoney £0 *Total Prizemoney* £662
2000 Turf 0-6: (6f, 7f 3, 9f, 10f) (gd 3, g-f 3)
Very moderate gelding, has worn blinkers. Turf high 36.
**J J Bridger [0-19] W R Shere.*

ALICIAN SUNHILL BHB 52f48a RR 57f 48a 5117[9]
2 br f Piccolo - Midnight Spell **(65f 77a)** (Night Shift (USA)) 7.2f **(69)**
Form - 8384430
Record 2000 - 1st:0 2nd:0 3rd:2 Ran:7
Win Prizemoney £0 *Total Prizemoney* £1,042
2000 Turf 0-6: (5f 6) (g-s 2, g-f 2, frm 2) 2000 AW 0-1: (5f) (Fibr)
Fair filly, effective 5f, acts on g-f, has worn blinkers. Turf high 57 - 4th of 10 to White Star Lady (24 Aug Musselburgh 5f g-f RF 3926).
**Mrs A Duffield [0-7] Harry Whitton.*

ALIGN BHB 44f45a RR 42f 45a 1854[13]
4 gr f Petong 7.6f **(58)** - Affirmation (Tina's Pet) 6.8f **(59)**
Form - 00
Record 2000 - 1st:0 2nd:0 3rd:0 Ran:2
Pre2000 - 1st:1 2nd:0 3rd:0 Ran:8
Win Prizemoney £2,123 *Total Prizemoney* £2,123
Wins 1999 *Apr Southw (STD) 8f 72* <
2000 Turf 0-1: (8f) (g-f) 2000 AW 0-1: (7f) (Fibr)
Neat, moderate filly, effective 8f, - acts on Fibr, likes left handed tracks, likes tight tracks.
**Mrs A Duffield [0-2] Wyck Hall Stud (from J W Hills [1-8] Oct 1999).*

AL IHSAS (IRE) RR 92f 2149[2]
2 b f Danehill (USA) 9.1f **(79)** - Simaat (USA) (Mr Prospector (USA)) 8.8f **(78)**
Form - 22
Record 2000 - 1st:0 2nd:2 3rd:0 Ran:2
Win Prizemoney £0 *Total Prizemoney* £13,746
2000 Turf 0-2: (5f, 6f) (gd 2)
Currently useful filly. Turf high 92 - 2nd of 20 to Romantic Myth (21 Jun Ascot 5f gd RF 2149). A high-class filly, she was runner-up to Romantic Myth in the Queen Mary at Ascot but was not seen out again. She will be suited by six furlongs plus.
**J H M Gosden [0-2] Hamdan Al Maktoum.*

ALINGA (IRE) BHB 97f RR 86f 4990[9]
2 b f King's Theatre (IRE) - Cheyenne Spirit **(106f)** (Indian Ridge)
Form - 51372180
Record 2000 - 1st:2 2nd:1 3rd:1 Ran:8
Win Prizemoney £6,630 *Total Prizemoney* £10,199
Wins * **2000** Aug Hamilt (SFT) 6f 81 <
* **2000** Jun Ayr (GD) 6f 72
2000 Turf 2-8: (5f, 6f 2-6, 7f) (gd 1-6, frm 1-2)
Useful filly, effective 6f, acts on gd to frm, best on gd. Turf high 86 - 3rd of 10 to In The Woods (1 Jly Newmarket 6f frm RF 2450) - also 1st of 4 getting 8lb from Blue Forest (22 Aug Hamilton RF 3846). She has shown some decent form at a modest level, winning small events at Ayr and Hamilton so far, but was out of her depth when tried in Pattern company.
**M L W Bell [2-8] Peter Ward.*

ALI OOP RR 4624[8]
3 b g Shareef Dancer (USA) 10.1f **(67)** - Happydrome (Ahonoora) 8.1f **(73)**
Form - 648
Record 2000 - 1st:0 2nd:0 3rd:0 Ran:3
Win Prizemoney £0 *Total Prizemoney* £321
2000 Turf 0-3: (10f, 12f 2) (gd, frm 2)
Lengthy, currently very poor gelding. (began Aug).
**J D Bethell [0-3] Robert Gibbons.*

ALI'S IMAGES BHB 54f46a RR 62f 46a 5109[6]
2 b f Mind Games - Question Ali **(46f)** (Petoski) 5.7f **(62)**
Form - 66733556
Record 2000 - 1st:0 2nd:0 3rd:2 Ran:8
Win Prizemoney £0 *Total Prizemoney* £804
2000 Turf 0-7: (5f, 6f 4, 7f 2) (g-s, gd, g-f, frm 4) 2000 AW 0-1: (5f) (Fibr)
Average filly, effective 6 to 7f, acts on g-f to frm. Turf high 62 - 3rd of 7 getting 2lb from Milliken Park (20 Jly Hamilton 6f g-f RF 2965).
**A Berry [0-8] T Bibby.*

ALJAARIF RR 37f 463[2]
6 ch h Rainbow Quest (USA) 11.2f **(81)** - Jasoorah (IRE) (Sadler's Wells (USA)) 10f **(76)**
Form - 2
2000 AW 0-1: (10f) (Equi)
Currently very useful horse. (1st run) - 2nd of 14 to Zanay (18 Mar Lingfield 10f Equi RF 0463). A prolific winner in Germany, he finished runner-up in the Winter Derby at Lingfield.
**M Hofor in GER [0-1] Galopp Club Deutschland (from C Collins in IRE [0-2] Oct 1997).*

ALJABR (USA) BHB 119f RR 125f 3317[5]
4 gr c Storm Cat (USA) 7f **(86)** - Sierra Madre (FR) **(111+f)** (Baillamont (USA)) 7f **(78)**
Form - 145
Record 2000 - 1st:1 2nd:0 3rd:0 Ran:3
Pre2000 - 1st:4 2nd:1 3rd:0 Ran:6
Win Prizemoney £293,828 *Total Prizemoney* £374,201
Wins * **2000** May Newbur (G-F) G1 8f 125
* 1999 Jly Goodwo (G-F) G1 8f 127 <
* 1998 Spt Longch (SFT) G1 7f 116
* 1998 Jly Goodwo (GD) G3 7f 117+
* 1998 Jly Sandow (GD) 7.1f 90+
2000 Turf 1-3: (8f 1-3) (gd 2, g-f 1-1)
Scopey, top-class colt, effective 8f, acts on gd to g-f, best on g-f. Turf high 125 (1st run) - 1st of 7 from Trans Island (20 May Newbury RF 1331). Consistent. Unbeaten at two, and decisive winner of the Sussex Stakes at three, he made all in the Lockinge Stakes on his reappearance. He was a little disappointing when fourth in Ascot's Queen Anne Stakes next time and did not run again after finishing fifth to Giant's Causeway in the Sussex Stakes.
**S bin Suroor [5-9] Godolphin.*

ALJAWF (USA) BHB 93f RR 95f 3787[2]
3 gr ro c Dehere (USA) - Careless Kitten (USA) (Caro)
Form - 761072
Record 2000 - 1st:1 2nd:1 3rd:0 Ran:6
Pre2000 - 1st:1 2nd:0 3rd:0 Ran:2
Win Prizemoney £11,370 *Total Prizemoney* £13,934
Wins * **2000** Jun Ripon (G-F) H 6f 84 91 <
* 1999 Spt Nottin (G-F) 6.1f 77+

2000 Turf 1-6: (6f 1-5, 7f) (gd, g-f 1-4, frm)
Scopey, very useful colt, effective 6 to 7f, acts on g-f, has worn blinkers. Turf high 95 - 2nd of 9 getting 9lb from Wahj (19 Aug Newbury 7f g-f RF 3787) - also 1st of 11 getting 4lb from Roo (21 Jun Ripon RF 2168). He had little trouble in landing a Ripon handicap, but a rise in the weights appeared to find him out later. He ran a decent race with the visor left off on his final start.
**E A L Dunlop [2-8] Hamdan Al Maktoum.*

ALJAZ BHB 53f46a **RR 17f 46a** 5118[2]

10 b g Al Nasr (FR) 9.9f **(72)** - Santa Linda (USA) (Sir Ivor) 10.2f **(70)**
Form - 234828646472
Record 2000 - 1st:0 2nd:2 3rd:0 Ran:10
Pre2000 - 1st:7 2nd:15 3rd:9 Ran:73
Win Prizemoney £19,919 *Total Prizemoney* £37,349
Wins * 1999 *May Southw (STD) H 6f* 57 61
1998 *Jun Wolver (STD) H 6f* 62 67 <
* 1998 *Jan Wolver (STD) C 5f* 52
* 1998 *Jan Wolver (STD) H 5f* 52 52
* 1996 *Aug Wolver (STD) H 5f* 42 43
2000 AW 0-10: (5f 3, 6f 6, 7f) (Equi 5, Fibr 5)
Moderate gelding, effective 5 to 6f, best at 6f, - acts on AW, best on Fibr, has worn blinkers, favours left handed tracks, favours tight tracks. AW high 61 - 2nd of 7 giving 5lb to Seren Teg (2 Feb Lingfield 5f Equi RF 0203). He has been a decent sprint handicapper in the past, but is rather long in the tooth now and if he is to win again, it will be in the very lowest grade.
**Miss Gay Kelleway [5-56] Miss Jo Crowley (from Mrs N Macauley [1-10] Jly 1998).*

ALJAZIR BHB 46f42a **RR 61f 42a** 5105[21]

3 b g Alhijaz 7.7f **(57)** - Duxyana (IRE) (Cyrano de Bergerac) 6f **(68)**
Form - 02050500000
Record 2000 - 1st:0 2nd:1 3rd:0 Ran:11
Pre2000 - 1st:0 2nd:0 3rd:1 Ran:7
Win Prizemoney £0 *Total Prizemoney* £1,623
2000 Turf 0-10: (6f 2, 7f 5, 8f 3) (hvy 2, g-s, gd 3, g-f 2, frm 2) 2000 AW 0-1: (6f) (Fibr)
Scopey, average gelding, effective 5 to 7f, acts on hvy to g-s, has worn blinkers, likes left handed tracks, likes tight tracks. Turf high 64 - 2nd of 19 to Balfour (12 Apr Warwick 7f hvy RF 0687). Inconsistent. **E J Alston [0-18] Liam & Tony Ferguson.*

ALJOHONCHA RR 3135[10]

2 b f Bigstone (IRE) - Ibda (Mtoto)
Form - 0
Record 2000 - 1st:0 2nd:0 3rd:0 Ran:1
2000 Turf 0-1: (7f) (frm)
Currently very poor filly. **C N Kellett [0-1] Sean Taylor.*

AL-KING SLAYER RR 75f 761[2]

3 b c Batshoof 9.5f **(66)** - Top Sovereign (High Top) 10.2f **(67)**
Form - 82
Record 2000 - 1st:0 2nd:1 3rd:0 Ran:2
Win Prizemoney £0 *Total Prizemoney* £756
2000 Turf 0-1: (7f) (g-s) 2000 AW 0-1: (8f) (Fibr)
Scopey, currently above-average colt.
**T P McGovern [0-1] Ahmed Abdel-Khaleq (from B Smart [0-1] Jan 2000).*

ALL BLEEVABLE RR 29f 649[11]

3 b g Presidium 7.5f **(56)** - Eve's Treasure (Bustino) 10.4f **(64)**
Form - 00
Record 2000 - 1st:0 2nd:0 3rd:0 Ran:2
2000 Turf 0-2: (8f, 10f) (g-s, gd)
Scopey, currently little account gelding. Turf high 29.
**Mrs S Lamyman [0-2] A E Blee.*

ALLEGRESSE (IRE) BHB 67f **RR 81f** 2630[4]

3 b f Alzao (USA) 9.8f **(73)** - Millie Musique (Miller's Mate) 7f **(63)**
Form - 3584
Record 2000 - 1st:0 2nd:0 3rd:1 Ran:4
Pre2000 - 1st:0 2nd:0 3rd:1 Ran:2
Win Prizemoney £0 *Total Prizemoney* £1,287
2000 Turf 0-4: (8f, 10f 3) (gd, frm 3)
Leggy, decent filly, effective 7f, acts on g-s, has worn blinkers. Turf high 81. **J L Dunlop [0-6] R J McAulay.*

ALLELUIA BHB 67f **RR 56f** 5196[8]

2 b f Caerleon (USA) 10.9f **(79)** - Alruccaba (Crystal Palace (FR)) 12.5f **(76)**
Form - 368
Record 2000 - 1st:0 2nd:0 3rd:1 Ran:3
Win Prizemoney £0 *Total Prizemoney* £494
2000 Turf 0-3: (7f 2, 8f) (sft, g-s, gd)
Currently fair filly. Turf high 56 (began Oct).
**Sir Mark Prescott [0-3] Mrs Sonia Rogers.*

ALLEN PARK (GER) RR 90f 2203a[2]

3 ch c Monsun (GER) - Alte Garde (FR) (Garde Royale)
Form - 2
2000 Turf 0-1: (12f) (gd)
Currently useful colt. (1st run) - 2nd of 9 to Tiger Groom (18 Jun Frauenfeld 12f gd RF 2203a). **in SWI [0-1].*

ALL GOOD THINGS (IRE) BHB 65f65a **RR 64f 65a** 4552[4]

3 b c Marju (IRE) 9.2f **(76)** - Garah (Ajdal (USA)) 9.2f **(89)**
Form - 4
Record 2000 - 1st:0 2nd:0 3rd:0 Ran:1
Pre2000 - 1st:0 2nd:0 3rd:0 Ran:2
Win Prizemoney £0 *Total Prizemoney* £339
2000 Turf 0-1: (10f) (g-s)
Workmanlike, currently average colt.
**R Ingram [0-1] A Rosenberg (from J L Dunlop [0-2] Oct 1999).*

ALL GRAIN RR 61f 4226[6]

2 b f Polish Precedent (USA) 9f **(73)** - Mill Line (Mill Reef (USA)) 10.5f **(78)**
Form - 6
Record 2000 - 1st:0 2nd:0 3rd:0 Ran:1
2000 Turf 0-1: (7f) (frm)
Currently average filly. **Sir Michael Stoute [0-1] R Barnett.*

ALL MINE (IRE) BHB 34f41a **RR 29f 41a** 4174[8]

3 ch g Desse Zenny (USA) 12f **(53)** - Laxey Leap (IRE) (Taufan (USA)) 7f **(57)**
Form - 686508
Record 2000 - 1st:0 2nd:0 3rd:0 Ran:6
2000 Turf 0-2: (5f, 8f) (gd, g-f) 2000 AW 0-4: (6f, 7f 3) (Fibr 4)
Moderate gelding. Turf high 29 (began Aug). AW high 42. (DEAD)
**B S Rothwell [0-6] Brian Rothwell.*

ALL ON MY OWN (USA) BHB 35f30a **RR 42f 30a** 3192[14]

5 ch g Unbridled (USA) - Some For All (USA) (One For All (USA))
Form - 38620
Record 2000 - 1st:0 2nd:1 3rd:1 Ran:5
Win Prizemoney £0 *Total Prizemoney* £1,166
2000 Turf 0-3: (12f, 14f, 16f) (gd, frm 2) 2000 AW 0-2: (11f, 16f) (Fibr 2)
Moderate gelding, has worn blinkers. Turf high 42 (1st run) - 3rd of 8 to Hullbank (2 Jun Catterick 14f frm RF 1656). AW high 23.
**J S Wainwright [0-9] Ian McInnes.*

ALLOTROPE (IRE) BHB 36f **RR 43f** 4119[12]

5 b g Nashwan (USA) 10.3f **(79)** - Graphite (USA) (Mr Prospector (USA)) 8.8f **(78)**
Form - 8700
Record 2000 - 1st:0 2nd:0 3rd:0 Ran:4
Pre2000 - 1st:1 2nd:1 3rd:0 Ran:8
Win Prizemoney £3,437 *Total Prizemoney* £4,344
Wins 1998 Aug Tralee (GD) 14f 78 <
2000 Turf 0-4: (14f, 16f 2, 17f) (frm 3, hrd)
Moderate gelding, has worn blinkers. Turf high 43 (began Jly).
**Mrs M Reveley [0-11] W J Smith, M D Dudley & Mrs M C Reveley (from J Oxx in IRE [1-4] Oct 1998).*

ALLRIGHTHEN BHB 27f45a **RR 33f 45a** 788[12]

4 b g Sizzling Melody 6.3f **(49)** - Luckifosome (Smackover) 6f **(52)**
Form - 0
Record 2000 - 1st:0 2nd:0 3rd:0 Ran:1
Pre2000 - 1st:0 2nd:0 3rd:0 Ran:12
2000 Turf 0-1: (8f) (g-s)
Light-framed, very moderate gelding.
**B P J Baugh [0-1] L R Perry (from T Wall [0-12] Jun 1999).*

ALLTHEDOTCOMS BHB 53f **RR 59f** 4223[11]
2 ch c Elmaamul (USA) 8.1f **(70)** - North Wind (IRE) (Lomond (USA)) 8.8f **(65)**
Form - 84670
Record 2000 - 1st:0 2nd:0 3rd:0 Ran:5
Win Prizemoney £0 *Total Prizemoney* £321
2000 Turf 0-5: (7f 5) (gd 3, g-f, frm)
Fair colt. Turf high 59 (began Jly).
**N A Callaghan [0-5] Mrs G R Smith.*

ALL THE GEARS (USA) BHB 85f **RR 89f** 2572[2]
3 b c Gone West (USA) 7.8f **(82)** - Buckeye Gal (USA) (Good Counsel (USA)) 6.9f **(69)**
Form - 5302
Record 2000 - 1st:0 2nd:1 3rd:1 Ran:4
Pre2000 - 1st:0 2nd:1 3rd:1 Ran:3
Win Prizemoney £0 *Total Prizemoney* £4,258
2000 Turf 0-4: (7f, 8f 3) (gd 2, frm 2)
Scopey, useful colt, effective 7 to 8f, best at 8f, acts on gd to frm, best on gd. Turf high 89 - 3rd of 21 giving 2lb to Malleus (18 May York 8f gd RF 1279). Cost $450,000, and is capable of winning races, finishing third in a warm York handicap in May.
**Sir Michael Stoute [0-7] The Thoroughbred Corporation.*

ALL THE LUCK (USA) **RR 66f** 1793[6]
3 ch f Mr Prospector (USA) 8.6f **(88)** - All At Sea (USA) (Riverman (USA)) 9.1f **(76)**
Form - 6
Record 2000 - 1st:0 2nd:0 3rd:0 Ran:1
2000 Turf 0-1: (8f) (gd)
Light-framed, currently average filly. **H R A Cecil [0-1] K Abdulla.*

ALL THE WAY (IRE) BHB 113f **RR 119f** 5207a[16]
4 b c Shirley Heights 12.1f **(76)** - Future Past (USA) (Super Concorde (USA)) 10.9f **(66)**
Form - 10
Record 2000 - 1st:1 2nd:0 3rd:0 Ran:2
Pre2000 - 1st:1 2nd:1 3rd:1 Ran:5
Win Prizemoney £147,480 *Total Prizemoney* £186,559

Wins						
2000	May	Kranji	(GD)	10f	110	<
1999	May	Newmar	(G-F)	12f	91	

2000 Turf 1-2: (10f 1-1, 12f) (gd 1-2)
Neat, high-class colt, effective 10 to 12f, acts on gd, has worn blinkers. Turf high 110 (1st run) - 1st of 14 from Super Goldluck (7 May Kranji RF 1157a). A useful performer at three for Terry Mills, he landed the Singapore Derby in May. He was sent down under to be prepared for the Melbourne Cup, but the plan was shelved after he was well beaten in his prep race.
**S bin Suroor [0-1] (from S bin Suroor in UAE [1-1] May 2000).*

ALLURING (IRE) **RR 106f** 3306a[5]
3 b f Lure (USA) - Shelbiana (USA) (Chieftain II) 10.4f **(75)**
Form - 15035
2000 Turf 1-5: (7f, 8f 1-2, 10f 2) (sft, g-s 2, g-f)
Pattern-class filly, effective 10f, acts on g-s, often wears blinkers. Turf high 106 - 3rd of 10 to Lady Upstage (1 Jly Curragh 10f g-s RF 2522a). Expensive for backers to follow in 1999, she got off the mark in a Listowel maiden over a mile on her seasonal debut and ran her best race of the season when stepped up to a mile and a quarter in a Curragh Group Two.
**A P O'Brien in IRE [1-12] Lewis Lakin.*

AL MABROOK (IRE) BHB 40f53a **RR 49f 53a** 4997[4]
5 b g Rainbows For Life (CAN) 9.3f **(64)** - Sky Lover (Ela-Mana-Mou) 10.1f **(70)**
Form - 570188803570504
Record 2000 - 1st:1 2nd:0 3rd:1 Ran:12
Pre2000 - 1st:1 2nd:1 3rd:1 Ran:19
Win Prizemoney £6,095 *Total Prizemoney* £8,030

Wins								
2000	*Jan*	*Wolver*	*(STD)*	*H*	*9.4f*	*58*	*61*	
1998	*Nov*	*Lingfi*	*(STD)*		*6f*		*66*	<

2000 Turf 0-6: (8f 3, 9f, 11f 2) (gd 2, g-f 3, frm) 2000 AW 1-6: (7f, 8f, 9f 1-2, 11f, 12f) (Equi, Fibr 1-5)
Average gelding, effective 8 to 9f, - acts on Fibr, has worn blinkers, likes left handed tracks, likes tight tracks. Turf high 48 (began Aug). AW high 61 (1st run) - 1st of 9 giving 10lb to River Ensign (6 Jan Wolverhampton RF 0031).
**K A Ryan [0-11] The Gloria Darley Racing Partnership (from K Mahdi [2-20] Jan 2000).*

AL MAMAALIQ (USA) **RR 90f** 4510a[1]
3 b c Gulch (USA) 9.6f **(79)** - Mamlakah (IRE) **(96f)** (Unfuwain (USA))
Form - 1
2000 Turf 1-1: (7f 1-1) (gd 1-1)
Currently useful colt. (1st run) - 1st of 15 giving 5lb to Sakina (14 Spt Gowran Park RF 4510a).
**D K Weld in IRE [1-1] Hamdan Al Maktoum.*

ALMAMZAR (USA) BHB 20f **RR 31f** 748[12]
10 b g Theatrical 11.5f **(78)** - Promising Risk (USA) (Exclusive Native (USA)) 9.1f **(81)**
Form - 057544700
Record 2000 - 1st:0 2nd:0 3rd:0 Ran:7
Pre2000 - 1st:1 2nd:1 3rd:2 Ran:20
Win Prizemoney £2,898 *Total Prizemoney* £8,186
2000 Turf 0-2: (16f, 22f) (sft, g-s) 2000 AW 0-5: (16f 5) (Fibr 5)
Very moderate gelding, effective 14 to 17f, acts on frm, likes left handed tracks, favours tight tracks. Turf high 31. AW high 24.
**Don Enrico Incisa [0-15] Don Enrico Incisa (from N Tinkler [0-14] Jun 1999).*

ALMASHROUK (IRE) BHB 57f **RR 55f** 4809[17]
3 b c Common Grounds 8.1f **(66)** - Red Note (Rusticaro (FR)) 8.2f **(65)**
Form - 6640650800
Record 2000 - 1st:0 2nd:0 3rd:0 Ran:10
Pre2000 - 1st:0 2nd:0 3rd:0 Ran:3
Win Prizemoney £0 *Total Prizemoney* £705
2000 Turf 0-10: (5f 2, 6f 6, 7f 2) (g-s 2, gd 4, g-f 2, frm 2)
Scopey, fair colt, has worn blinkers. Turf high 78. Inconsistent.
**K Mahdi [0-13] Greenfield Stud.*

ALMASI (IRE) BHB 71f **RR 77df** 5185[8]
8 b m Petorius 8f **(66)** - Best Niece (Vaigly Great) 7f **(58)**
Form - 534822508
Record 2000 - 1st:0 2nd:2 3rd:1 Ran:9
Pre2000 - 1st:8 2nd:7 3rd:8 Ran:57
Win Prizemoney £29,677 *Total Prizemoney* £52,344

Wins								
* 1999	Jun	Doncas	(GD)	H	6f	74	76	
* 1997	Spt	Haydoc	(G-S)		6f		88	<
* 1997	Aug	Newbur	(G-F)	H	6f	77	82	
* 1997	Jun	Salisb	(SFT)	H	6f	68	72	
* 1997	Jun	Doncas	(GD)	H	6f	62	67	
* 1996	Jun	Doncas	(GD)	H	6f	62	64	
* 1996	Apr	Nottin	(G-F)	H	6.1f	54	56	

2000 Turf 0-9: (6f 4, 7f 5) (g-s 3, gd 2, g-f 2, frm 2)
Above-average mare, effective 6 to 7f, best at 6f, acts on gd to frm, best on g-f, does well at Doncaster. Turf high 76 - 2nd of 10 giving 23lb to Daryabad (16 Aug Yarmouth 7f g-f RF 3711).
**C F Wall [8-66] The Equema Partnership.*

ALMATY (IRE) BHB 94f **RR 96f** 1864[9]
7 b h Dancing Dissident (USA) 6.8f **(65)** - Almaaseh (IRE) (Dancing Brave (USA)) 8.4f **(76)**
Form - 000
Record 2000 - 1st:0 2nd:0 3rd:0 Ran:3
Pre2000 - 1st:5 2nd:5 3rd:4 Ran:31
Win Prizemoney £60,802 *Total Prizemoney* £98,105

Wins								
* 1998	Oct	Newmar	(GD)	H	5f	105	107	
* 1998	Spt	Beverl	(G-F)		5f		97	
1997	May	Kempto	(G-F)	L	5f		108+	

2000 Turf 0-3: (5f 3) (gd, g-f, frm)
Very useful horse, effective 5f, acts on g-f to frm, best on frm, has worn blinkers. Turf high 86. Consistent.
**W R Muir [2-21] Fred Hayman, Daily Mail (from J H M Gosden [1-7] Spt 1997).*

ALMAYDAN **RR 54f** 5023[4]
2 b c Marju (IRE) 9.2f **(76)** - Cunning (Bustino) 10.4f **(64)**
Form - 4
Record 2000 - 1st:0 2nd:0 3rd:0 Ran:1
Win Prizemoney £0 *Total Prizemoney* £291
2000 Turf 0-1: (7f) (g-s)
Currently fair colt. **Sir Michael Stoute [0-1] Hamdan Al Maktoum.*

ALMAZHAR (IRE) BHB 54f79a **RR 57f 79a** 5166[18]
5 b g Last Tycoon 9.4f **(73)** - Mosaique Bleue (Shirley Heights) 10.3f **(74)**
Form - 312126223542180
Record 2000 - 1st:1 2nd:3 3rd:1 Ran:9
Pre2000 - 1st:5 2nd:5 3rd:1 Ran:28
Win Prizemoney £21,805 *Total Prizemoney* £33,283
Wins * **2000** Jun Ayr (G-F) H 8f 51 57
* 1999 *Dec Wolver (STD) H 7f 70 75* <
* 1999 *Nov Wolver (STD) H 7f 64 65*
* 1999 *Jly Southw (STD) H 7f 57 62*
* 1999 *Jun Southw (STD) H 8f 53 56*
* 1999 Jun Redcar (FRM) H 8f 48 49
2000 Turf 1-7: (7f 5, 8f 1-2) (gd, frm 1-5, hrd) 2000 AW 0-2: (7f, 8f) (Fibr 2)

Decent gelding, effective 6 to 8f, - acts on Fibr, has worn blinkers, likes left handed tracks, does well at Wolverhampton and Southwell. Turf high 57. AW high 80 (1st run) - 2nd of 16 giving 20lb to Noble Cyrano (3 Jan Southwell 8f Fibr RF 0012). He scored five times in a very busy 1999, four of which were on Fibresand. He is rated a good deal lower on turf, but can win races on that surface and did so in good style at Ayr in June. Needs plenty of driving and a strongly-run race.

**J L Eyre [6-33] Sunpak Potatoes 2 (from E A L Dunlop [0-4] Jly 1998).*

ALMERINA (IRE) BHB 60f60a **RR 56f 60a** 1200[16]
5 b m Erins Isle 8.3f **(76)** - Pennine Music (IRE) (Pennine Walk) 8.5f **(61)**
Form - 000
Record 2000 - 1st:0 2nd:0 3rd:0 Ran:3
Pre2000 - 1st:2 2nd:1 3rd:0 Ran:15
Win Prizemoney £8,250 *Total Prizemoney* £10,425
Wins 1998 Oct Cork (G-S) H 8f 77 80 <
1998 Oct Punche (SFT) 7.5f 66
2000 Turf 0-2: (7f, 8f) (g-f, frm) 2000 AW 0-1: (8f) (Fibr)

Fair filly, effective 8 to 9f, acted on gd to g-f, preferred left handed tracks. Turf high 48. (DEAD)

**J Mackie [0-9] Ms Caroline Breay (from J S Bolger in IRE [2-12] Jun 1999).*

ALMIDDINA (IRE) BHB 73f **RR 77f** 5064[9]
3 b f Selkirk (USA) 7.9f **(76)** - Arbela (IRE) (Persian Bold) 9.3f **(66)**
Form - 4810
Record 2000 - 1st:1 2nd:0 3rd:0 Ran:4
Win Prizemoney £4,199 *Total Prizemoney* £4,510
Wins * **2000** Spt Haydoc (HVY) 7.1f 77 <
2000 Turf 1-4: (7f 1-2, 8f 2) (sft 1-2, gd, frm)

Scopey, above-average filly. Turf high 77 - 1st of 7 from Russian Rhapsody (22 Spt Haydock RF 4577).

**R Charlton [1-4] James Wolfensohn.*

ALMINSTAR BHB 30f **RR 30f** 2358[9]
4 b f Minshaanshu Amad (USA) 11.3f **(53)** - Joytime (John de Coombe) 7.9f **(40)**
Form - 00
Record 2000 - 1st:0 2nd:0 3rd:0 Ran:2
Pre2000 - 1st:0 2nd:0 3rd:0 Ran:8
2000 Turf 0-2: (10f, 12f) (gd, g-f)

Light-framed, very moderate filly. Turf high 14. Becoming disappointing.

**Mrs L Richards [0-2] Mrs Shirley Bentley (from C A Cyzer [0-8] Aug 1999).*

ALMOST FREE RR 96f 1220[4]
3 b c Darshaan 11.9f **(81)** - Light Fresh Air (USA) **(87f)** (Rahy (USA))
Form - 14
Record 2000 - 1st:1 2nd:0 3rd:0 Ran:2
Win Prizemoney £3,802 *Total Prizemoney* £4,597
Wins * **2000** Apr Newcas (SFT) 12.4f 96 <
2000 Turf 1-2: (12f 1-1, 14f) (sft 1-1, g-f)

Lengthy, currently very useful colt. Turf high 96 (1st run) - 1st of 7 from Machrie Bay (24 Apr Newcastle RF 0844). Unraced at two, he won a modest Newcastle maiden easily on his debut, but was well beaten in a better race over 14 furlongs at York.

**M Johnston [1-2] Maktoum Al Maktoum.*

AL MUALLIM (USA) BHB 87f **RR 90f** 4991[10]
6 b g Theatrical 11.5f **(78)** - Gerri N Jo Go (USA) (Top Command (USA)) 10f **(77)**
Form - 307000401000040
Record 2000 - 1st:1 2nd:0 3rd:1 Ran:15
Pre2000 - 1st:3 2nd:4 3rd:2 Ran:15
Win Prizemoney £22,216 *Total Prizemoney* £44,507
Wins * **2000** Aug Epsom (G-F) H 7f 87 91
1997 Oct Newmar (G-F) H 7f 88 94 <
1997 Aug Lingfi (G-F) H 6f 80 87
1996 Oct Catter (GD) 6f 78
2000 Turf 1-15: (6f 7, 7f 1-7, 8f) (g-s 2, gd 6, g-f 3, frm 1-4)

Useful gelding, effective 6 to 7f, best at 7f, acts on gd to frm, best on gd. Turf high 97 (1st run) - 3rd of 18 giving 14lb to Passion For Life (25 Mar Kempton 6f gd RF 0502) - also 1st of 11 giving 8lb to Willoughby's Boy (17 Aug Epsom RF 3722). He is an able performer, but was on a long losing run before scoring at Epsom in August and may not be a straightforward ride. Held since in some well-contested handicaps.

**D Nicholls [1-12] Neil Smith (from J W Payne [3-18] Apr 2000).*

ALMUSHTARAK (IRE) BHB 109f **RR 113f** 4989[14]
7 b h Fairy King (USA) 7.7f **(75)** - Exciting (Mill Reef (USA)) 10.5f **(78)**
Form - 360600
Record 2000 - 1st:0 2nd:0 3rd:1 Ran:6
Pre2000 - 1st:5 2nd:6 3rd:9 Ran:39
Win Prizemoney £78,369 *Total Prizemoney* £383,494
Wins * 1998 Apr Sandow (SFT) G2 8.1f 116 <
* 1997 Spt Doncas (G-F) G3 8f 114
1996 Jly Lingfi (G-F) LH 7.6f 105 107
1996 Jun Kempto (G-F) H 7f 85 90
2000 Turf 0-6: (8f 4, 10f 2) (sft, gd 4, g-f)

Group-class horse, effective 8f, acts on sft to g-f. Turf high 115 (1st run) - 3rd of 6 to Indian Lodge (28 Apr Sandown 8f sft RF 0895). Consistent. Regularly in the frame in previous seasons, he helped put his trainer on the map. Did not really fire last term.

**K Mahdi [2-36] Hamad Al-Mutawa (from Miss Gay Kelleway [3-9] Jly 1996).*

ALMUTAN STAR RR 5198[15]
5 b m Almutanabbi - Salt of The Earth (Sterling Bay (SWE)) 5.5f **(69)**
Form - 0
Record 2000 - 1st:0 2nd:0 3rd:0 Ran:1
2000 Turf 0-1: (6f) (gd)

Currently very poor filly. **J Neville [0-1] A F Syndicate.*

ALNAAMI RR 38f 1693[17]
3 b c Nashwan (USA) 10.3f **(79)** - Tarhhib **(88+f)** (Danzig (USA)) 8.4f **(76)**
Form - 0
Record 2000 - 1st:0 2nd:0 3rd:0 Ran:1
2000 Turf 0-1: (10f) (frm)

Workmanlike, currently very moderate colt.

**J H M Gosden [0-1] Hamdan Al Maktoum.*

ALNAHAAM (IRE) RR 89f 3386[2]
2 ch c Hamas (IRE) 8f **(72)** - Abir **(64f)** (Soviet Star (USA))
Form - 62
Record 2000 - 1st:0 2nd:1 3rd:0 Ran:2
Win Prizemoney £0 *Total Prizemoney* £1,160
2000 Turf 0-2: (6f, 7f) (g-f, frm)

Currently useful colt. Turf high 89 (began Jly) - 2nd of 13 giving 5lb to Tarfshi (5 Aug Doncaster 7f frm RF 3386).

**B Hanbury [0-2] Hamdan Al Maktoum.*

ALNAHIGHER (FR) BHB 67f **RR 62f** 2115[13]
2 b f Mizoram (USA) - Petite Butterfly (Absalom) 7.2f **(58)**
Form - 6520
Record 2000 - 1st:0 2nd:1 3rd:0 Ran:4
Win Prizemoney £0 *Total Prizemoney* £830
2000 Turf 0-3: (5f 2, 7f) (g-s, frm 2) 2000 AW 0-1: (6f) (Fibr)

Average filly. Turf high 62. (1st run) - 2nd of 6 getting 5lb from Dim Sums (26 May Southwell 6f Fibr RF 1478).

**M Johnston [0-4] Ziad Galadari.*

ALNAJASHEE BHB 55f60a **RR 61f 60a** 5069[20]
4 b g Generous (IRE) 11.5f **(82)** - Tahdid (Mtoto)

Form - 145001700
Record 2000 - 1st:2 2nd:0 3rd:0 Ran:9
Pre2000 - 1st:0 2nd:1 3rd:0 Ran:6
Win Prizemoney £6,096 *Total Prizemoney* £7,405
Wins * 2000 Jun Salisb (G-F) H 14.1f 58 61
***2000** *Jan Southw (STD) H 12f 55 65+* <
2000 Turf 1-5: (11f, 12f, 14f 1-3) (g-s, g-f, frm 1-3) 2000 AW 1-4: (11f, 12f 1-2, 16f) (Fibr 1-4)
Scopey, average gelding, effective 12f, acts on hrd - acts on Fibr. Turf high 61. AW high 65 (1st run) - 1st of 9 giving 17lb to Broughtons Lure (17 Jan Southwell RF 0100).
**M R Bosley [2-10] Mrs Jean O'Connor (from P T Walwyn [0-6] Aug 1999).*

ALOWMDAH (USA) RR 76f 4935[10]
2 b c Gone West (USA) 7.8f **(82)** - Halholah (USA) (Secreto (USA)) 8.7f **(72)**
Form - 0
Record 2000 - 1st:0 2nd:0 3rd:0 Ran:1
2000 Turf 0-1: (6f) (gd)
Currently above-average colt.
**B Hanbury [0-1] Hamdan Al Maktoum.*

ALPATHAR (IRE) BHB 51f RR 57f 3250[12]
3 ch f Simply Great (FR) 11.9f **(61)** - Royal Language (USA) (Conquistador Cielo (USA)) 8.8f **(69)**
Form - 166480
Record 2000 - 1st:1 2nd:0 3rd:0 Ran:6
Pre2000 - 1st:0 2nd:1 3rd:0 Ran:7
Win Prizemoney £2,567 *Total Prizemoney* £3,347
Wins * 2000 Apr Thirsk (G-S) 7f 54 <
2000 Turf 1-6: (7f 1-4, 8f 2) (gd 1-3, g-f 2, frm)
Workmanlike, fair filly, effective 7f, acts on gd. Turf high 57. Consistent. **M Dods [1-13] Harry Whitton.*

ALPENGLOW BHB 96f RR 100f 4598[11]
4 b f Ezzoud (IRE) - Aquaglow (Caerleon (USA)) 8.6f **(71)**
Form - 30
Record 2000 - 1st:0 2nd:0 3rd:1 Ran:2
Pre2000 - 1st:2 2nd:0 3rd:1 Ran:4
Win Prizemoney £10,394 *Total Prizemoney* £16,200
Wins * 1999 Oct Leices (GD) 8f 99 <
* 1999 Apr Newmar (GD) 7f 82
2000 Turf 0-2: (8f 2) (gd, g-f)
Very useful filly, effective 8f, acts on gd. Turf high 92 (began Aug). She found her foot at the backend of last season, running a super race behind Bomb Alaska and Albarahin at Newmarket in October. Made a belated return to action at Ascot in August, looking as if ten furlongs might suit. Then found the soft ground too much on her only subsequent run. **J H M Gosden [2-6] Sheikh Mohammed.*

ALPEN WOLF (IRE) BHB 86f RR 89f 5109[10]
5 ch g Wolfhound (USA) 7.3f **(71)** - Oatfield (Great Nephew) 9.9f **(64)**
Form - 317210138000
Record 2000 - 1st:3 2nd:1 3rd:2 Ran:12
Pre2000 - 1st:6 2nd:1 3rd:4 Ran:30
Win Prizemoney £35,505 *Total Prizemoney* £43,744
Wins * 2000 Jly Newbur (G-F) H 6f 85 87 <
*** 2000** Jun Warwic (G-F) 6.8f 81
*** 2000** May Bath (G-F) 5.1f 77
* 1999 Aug Bath (GD) H 5.7f 76 79
* 1999 Apr Bright (G-F) H 6f 70 69
* 1998 Spt Bright (FRM) 7f 68
* 1998 Aug Folkes (G-F) 6f 68
* 1998 Aug Bright (G-F) H 6f 56 64
* 1998 Aug Bright (FRM) S 6f 41
2000 Turf 3-12: (5f 1-3, 6f 1-5, 7f 1-4) (gd 3, g-f 1-1, frm 2-7, hrd)
Useful gelding, effective 6 to 7f, best at 7f, acts on g-f to hrd, best on frm, has worn blinkers, prefers left handed tracks, excels at Bath. Turf high 89 - 3rd of 11 giving 1lb to Al Muallim (17 Aug Epsom 7f frm RF 3722) - also 1st of 9 giving 22lb to Hunting Tiger (21 Jly Newbury RF 3001). Best over six furlongs though he can win over five, he goes especially well at Brighton and at Bath. Very much suited by fast ground. **W R Muir [9-42] R Haim.*

ALPHACALL BHB 58f RR 54f 3717[8]
2 b f Forzando 7.2f **(63)** - Second Call (Kind of Hush) 10.1f **(62)**
Form - 458
Record 2000 - 1st:0 2nd:0 3rd:0 Ran:3
2000 Turf 0-3: (5f 2, 7f) (g-s, frm 2)
Currently fair filly. Turf high 54.
**T D Easterby [0-3] Mrs J B Mountifield.*

ALPHAEUS BHB 82f RR 82+f 4651[2]
2 b g Sillery (USA) - Aethra (USA) **(74f)** (Trempolino (USA)) 12f **(71)**
Form - 5512
Record 2000 - 1st:1 2nd:1 3rd:0 Ran:4
Win Prizemoney £3,737 *Total Prizemoney* £4,625
Wins * 2000 Aug Beverl (G-F) 8.5f 82+ <
2000 Turf 1-3: (6f 2, 8f 1-1) (gd, frm 1-2) 2000 AW 0-1: (8f) (Fibr)
Decent gelding. Turf high 82 (began Aug) - 1st of 13 from Bolshoi Ballet (27 Aug Beverley RF 4012). (1st run) - 2nd of 8 getting 2lb from Act of Reform (26 Spt Southwell 8f Fibr RF 4651).
**Sir Mark Prescott [1-4] Hesmonds Stud.*

ALPHA HEIGHTS (IRE) BHB 43f RR 47f 3080[13]
3 b f Namaqualand (USA) - Mnaafa (IRE) **(64f)** (Darshaan) 9.9f **(84)**
Form - 08580
Record 2000 - 1st:0 2nd:0 3rd:0 Ran:5
Pre2000 - 1st:0 2nd:0 3rd:1 Ran:5
Win Prizemoney £0 *Total Prizemoney* £490
2000 Turf 0-5: (7f, 10f, 11f, 12f 2) (hvy, gd, g-f 2, frm)
Light-framed, moderate filly, effective 6f, acts on frm. Turf high 47.
**Mrs P N Dutfield [0-10] Alpha Dorset Plumber Merchants.*

ALPHA NOBLE (GER) RR 102f 2581a[10]
3 f No Horse (GER) 10f **(87)** - 00
Form - 0
2000 Turf 0-1: (12f) (sft)
Currently very useful. **P Rau in GER [0-1].*

ALPHA ROSE BHB 80f62a RR 79f 62a 5227[1]
3 ch f Inchinor 8.9f **(64)** - Philgwyn (Milford) 9f **(61)**
Form - 554112531142171
Record 2000 - 1st:6 2nd:2 3rd:1 Ran:15
Pre2000 - 1st:0 2nd:0 3rd:0 Ran:1
Win Prizemoney £21,198 *Total Prizemoney* £23,509
Wins * 2000 Oct Newmar (SFT) H 12f 71 79 <
*** 2000** Aug Bright (FRM) H 11.9f 65 72
*** 2000** Jly Bright (FRM) H 11.9f 60 66+
*** 2000** *Jly Lingfi (STD) H 12f 53 60*
*** 2000** Jun Ayr (G-F) 13.1f 59
*** 2000** May Mussel (FRM) 14f 57
2000 Turf 5-12: (6f, 10f, 12f 3-5, 13f 1-1, 14f 1-3, 16f) (gd 1-2, g-f 2, frm 4-7, hrd) 2000 AW 1-3: (5f, 12f 1-2) (Equi 1-2, Fibr)
Scopey, above-average filly, effective 12f, acts on gd to hrd, likes left handed tracks, likes tight tracks, excels at Brighton. Turf high 79 - 1st of 13 getting 1lb from Cooling Off (27 Oct Newmarket RF 5227) - also 1st of 6 getting 8lb from Copyforce Girl (30 Aug Brighton RF 4099). AW high 60. Showed improvement when stepped right up in trip and won six times this season of which one was on Equitrack. Suited by fast ground and trips of at least 12 furlongs.
**M L W Bell [6-15] Richard Morris Jr (from R J R Williams [0-1] Spt 1999).*

ALPHILDA BHB 72f RR 73f 4127[14]
3 gr f Ezzoud (IRE) - Desert Delight (IRE) (Green Desert (USA)) 8.6f **(78)**
Form - 08340300
Record 2000 - 1st:0 2nd:0 3rd:2 Ran:8
Pre2000 - 1st:1 2nd:4 3rd:1 Ran:10
Win Prizemoney £2,916 *Total Prizemoney* £10,998
Wins * 1999 Jly Ayr (GD) H 6f 77 <
2000 Turf 0-8: (6f 2, 7f 6) (gd, g-f 2, frm 5)
Neat, above-average filly, effective 6f, acts on gd to frm, best on gd. Turf high 73. After some lacklustre efforts in 2000, she ran well when third at Leicester in July.
**B W Hills [1-18] S W Transport (Swindon) Ltd.*

ALPINE HIDEAWAY (IRE) BHB 43f38a RR 51f 38a 4928[6]
7 b g Tirol 8.1f **(64)** - Arbour (USA) (Graustark) 10.1f **(70)**
Form - 6
Record 2000 - 1st:0 2nd:0 3rd:0 Ran:1
Pre2000 - 1st:4 2nd:6 3rd:6 Ran:40

Win Prizemoney £10,273 *Total Prizemoney* £19,708

Wins	1999	Aug	Beverl	(GD)	C	8.5f	51	
	1997	Aug	Ripon	(G-F)	C	8f	61	
	1997	*Jly*	*Southw*	*(STD)*	*C*	*7f*	*66*	
	1996	Oct	Leices	(G-F)		7f	71	<

2000 AW 0-1: (12f) (Equi)

Fair gelding, has worn blinkers, likes tight tracks.

**K A Ryan [0-1] Peter Easterby (from M W Easterby [4-34] Aug 1999).*

ALPINE PANTHER (IRE) BHB 47f RR 61df 4750[8]

7 b g Tirol 8.1f **(64)** - Kentucky Wildcat (Be My Guest (USA)) 9.3f **(67)**

Form - 08

Record	**2000** -	1st:0	2nd:0	3rd:0	Ran:2
	Pre2000 -	1st:1	2nd:1	3rd:3	Ran:16

Win Prizemoney £3,074 *Total Prizemoney* £5,540

Wins * 1998 Mar Nottin (G-S) H 14.1f 55 63 <

2000 Turf 0-2: (14f 2) (g-s, gd)

Average gelding. Turf high 47.

**Mrs M Reveley [6-25] P D Savill (from W Jarvis [0-5] May 1996).*

ALQAWAASER (USA) BHB 60f RR 66f 4545[17]

3 b br g Dayjur (USA) 6.8f **(79)** - Alghuzaylah (Habitat) 9.4f **(70)**

Form - 56450

Record	**2000** -	1st:0	2nd:0	3rd:0	Ran:5
	Pre2000 -	1st:0	2nd:0	3rd:1	Ran:2

Win Prizemoney £0 *Total Prizemoney* £770

2000 Turf 0-5: (8f 2, 10f 2, 13f) (gd 2, frm 3)

Strong, average gelding, effective 8 to 13f, acts on frm. Turf high 66 (began Jly) - 6th of 13 giving 3lb to Evergreen (28 Jly Salisbury 8f frm RF 3183).

**Major D N Chappell [0-5] R C C Villers (from E A L Dunlop [0-2] Oct 1999).*

ALQUID NOVI (IRE) BHB 61f RR 76f 4926[11]

2 ch f Bluebird (USA) 7.9f **(71)** - Persian Myth (Persian Bold) 9.3f **(66)**

Form - 34800

Record **2000** - 1st:0 2nd:0 3rd:1 Ran:5

Win Prizemoney £0 *Total Prizemoney* £650

2000 Turf 0-4: (5f, 6f 2, 7f) (g-f 2, frm 2) 2000 AW 0-1: (6f) (Equi)

Above-average filly. Turf high 76 (1st run) - 3rd of 9 giving 4lb to Silk Law (17 Jun Nottingham 6f g-f RF 2048).

**J S Moore [0-5] P De Vere Hunt.*

AL RABEH (FR) RR 163[6]

8 ch g French Stress (USA) - Amrela (Aureole)

Form - 6

Record **2000** - 1st:0 2nd:0 3rd:0 Ran:1

2000 AW 0-1: (16f) (Equi)

Poor gelding. A winning hurdler in Belgium, he was a fair third at Fontwell on his British debut. Has faced some impossible tasks since. **G L Moore [0-4] Mrs J Moore.*

ALRASSAAM BHB 118f RR 120+f 4950a[9]

4 b c Zafonic (USA) 9f **(83)** - Lady Blackfoot (Prince Tenderfoot (USA)) 9f **(61)**

Form - 74180

Record	**2000** -	1st:1	2nd:0	3rd:0	Ran:5
	Pre2000 -	1st:3	2nd:1	3rd:0	Ran:7

Win Prizemoney £86,475 *Total Prizemoney* £101,252

Wins	*** 2000**	Jly	Currag	(GD)	G2	9f	120	<
	* 1999	Jly	Chanti	(GD)	G3	9f	107	
	* 1999	May	Haydoc	(GD)		8.1f	112	
	* 1999	Apr	Newbur	(G-F)		8f	97+	

2000 Turf 1-5: (8f 2, 9f 1-1, 10f 2) (sft, g-s, gd 1-2, frm)

Light-framed, very high-class colt, effective 8 to 10f, acts on gd. Turf high 120 - 1st of 4 giving 10lb to Jammaal (2 Jly Curragh RF 2532a). Inconsistent. He was not at his best in his first two starts of the season, but made all to win a weakish four-runner Group Two at the Curragh in July by a wide margin. He disappointed on his debut in America in October. **M A Jarvis [4-12].*

ALRIGHT POPS BHB 38f RR 21f 596[8]

4 b f Rock Hopper 10.6f **(54)** - Sea Aura (Roi Soleil) 8.7f **(57)**

Form - 8

Record	**2000** -	1st:0	2nd:0	3rd:0	Ran:1
	Pre2000 -	1st:0	2nd:0	3rd:0	Ran:6

2000 Turf 0-1: (7f) (sft)

Little account filly. (DEAD)

**R Dickin [0-8] Mrs C M Dickin & C J Dickin.*

ALRISHA (IRE) BHB 82f RR 86f 4600[15]

3 b f Persian Bold 10f **(69)** - Rifaya (IRE) (Lashkari) 9.8f **(67)**

Form - 7212430

Record **2000** - 1st:1 2nd:2 3rd:1 Ran:7

Win Prizemoney £4,036 *Total Prizemoney* £10,268

Wins *** 2000** Jly Newmar (GD) 14.8f 74+ <

2000 Turf 1-7: (10f, 12f, 14f, 15f 1-1, 16f 3) (gd, g-f 1-2, frm 4)

Scopey, useful filly, effective 14 to 16f, best at 16f, acts on g-f to frm, best on frm. Turf high 86 - 2nd of 7 getting 15lb from Quedex (14 Aug Kempton 16f frm RF 3622). Landed a weak fourteen-furlong maiden on the July Course.

**D R C Elsworth [1-7] Mrs R F Lowe.*

AL'S ALIBI BHB 59f58a RR 61f 58a 3547[13]

7 b g Alzao (USA) 9.8f **(73)** - Lady Kris (IRE) (Kris) 9.5f **(73)**

Form - 00021420

Record	**2000** -	1st:1	2nd:2	3rd:0	Ran:8
	Pre2000 -	1st:4	2nd:2	3rd:1	Ran:25

Win Prizemoney £19,976 *Total Prizemoney* £26,009

Wins	*** 2000**	*Jun*	*Southw*	*(STD)*	*C*	*12f*		*72*	
	* 1998	Aug	Bath	(FRM)	H	11.7f	74	75	
	* 1998	May	Newbur	(GD)	H	12f	72	75	
	* 1997	Aug	Carlis	(G-F)	H	12f	72	76	<
	* 1996	Apr	Newbur	(G-S)	H	12f	72	75	

2000 Turf 0-5: (12f 5) (gd 4, g-f) 2000 AW 1-3: (11f 2, 12f 1-1) (Fibr 1-3)

Above-average gelding, effective 12f, - acts on Fibr, likes left handed tracks, likes tight tracks. Turf high 61. AW high 72 - 1st of 10 giving 8lb to Steamroller Stanly (30 Jun Southwell RF 2416). Inconsistent. Bolted up on the Southwell Fibresand in June, but had the embarrassment of being beaten at odds of 1/5 at the same track next time. **W R Muir [5-33] J Haim.*

ALSHADIYAH (USA) BHB 99f RR 90f 5107[5]

2 gr f Danzig (USA) 8.1f **(88)** - Shadayid (USA) (Shadeed (USA)) 8.2f **(70)**

Form - 1315

Record **2000** - 1st:2 2nd:0 3rd:1 Ran:4

Win Prizemoney £15,917 *Total Prizemoney* £17,627

Wins	*** 2000**	Spt	Ayr	(SFT)	L	6f	90	<
	*** 2000**	Aug	Lingfi	(G-F)		6f	81+	

2000 Turf 2-4: (5f, 6f 2-3) (gd 1-2, frm 1-2)

Useful filly. Turf high 90 (began Aug) - 1st of 9 from Ash Moon (16 Spt Ayr RF 4448) - also 1st of 8 getting 5lb from Kirthar (19 Aug Lingfield RF 3785). Landed the odds easily on her Lingfield debut, but was a bit disappointing in a Salisbury conditions event next time. She handled the soft ground well when landing an Ayr Listed event but seemed unsuited by the drop to the minimum trip on her final start. **J L Dunlop [2-4] Hamdan Al Maktoum.*

ALSHAKR BHB 111f RR 113f 4989[13]

3 b f Bahri (USA) - Give Thanks (Relko) 9.9f **(59)**

Form - 13120

Record	**2000** -	1st:2	2nd:1	3rd:1	Ran:5
	Pre2000 -	1st:0	2nd:0	3rd:0	Ran:2

Win Prizemoney £40,078 *Total Prizemoney* £72,861

Wins	*** 2000**	Jly	Newmar	(GD)	G2	8f	111+	<
	*** 2000**	Apr	Newmar	(G-S)		7f	93	

2000 Turf 2-5: (7f 1-1, 8f 1-3, 10f) (gd 2-4, g-f)

Scopey, Group-class filly, effective 8f, acts on gd to g-f, best on gd. Turf high 113 - 3rd of 11 to Bluemamba (14 May Longchamp 8f gd RF 1291a) - also 1st of 10 from Croeso Cariad (12 Jly Newmarket RF 2748). Always looked the type who would do better as a three-year-old and duly landed a decent Newmarket maiden on her reappearance. Ran a blinder when beaten less than a length into third in the French Guineas, but made no mistake when overcoming a disadvantageous draw to win the Group Two Falmouth Stakes at the July meeting. Just beaten in the Sun Chariot, she finished a long way adrift in the Champion Stakes.

**B Hanbury [2-5] Hamdan Al Maktoum (from P T Walwyn [0-2] Oct 1999).*

AL'S ME TRAINER BHB 70f RR 70f 5052[5]

2 b g Emarati (USA) 6.6f **(63)** - Ray of Hope **(47f)** (Rainbow Quest (USA)) 10.4f **(75)**

Form - 405

Record 2000 - 1st:0 2nd:0 3rd:0 Ran:3
Win Prizemoney £0 *Total Prizemoney* £281
2000 Turf 0-3: (6f 2, 7f) (sft, gd, g-f)
Currently above-average gelding. Turf high 70 (began Aug).
**A Dickman [0-3] Mike Smallman.*

ALSYATI RR 74f
4321[7]
2 ch c Salse (USA) 10.9f **(71)** - Rubbiyati **(54f 51a)** (Cadeaux Genereux)
Form - 67
Record 2000 - 1st:0 2nd:0 3rd:0 Ran:2
Win Prizemoney £0 *Total Prizemoney* £164
2000 Turf 0-2: (7f 2) (g-f 2)
Currently above-average colt. Turf high 74 (began Spt).
**C E Brittain [0-2] R A Pledger.*

ALTARA (IRE) RR 59f
4227[11]
3 b f Warning 8.1f **(77)** - Altiyna (Troy) 10.4f **(68)**
Form - 460
Record 2000 - 1st:0 2nd:0 3rd:0 Ran:3
Win Prizemoney £0 *Total Prizemoney* £315
2000 Turf 0-3: (7f 2, 8f) (g-f, frm 2)
Scopey, currently fair filly. Turf high 59 (began Jly).
**W R Muir [0-3] D J Deer.*

ALTAY BHB 61f RR 60+f
4767[7]
3 b g Erins Isle 8.3f **(76)** - Aliuska (IRE) (Fijar Tango (FR))
Form - 03635117
Record 2000 - 1st:2 2nd:0 3rd:2 Ran:8
Pre2000 - 1st:0 2nd:0 3rd:0 Ran:3
Win Prizemoney £8,281 *Total Prizemoney* £9,324
Wins * **2000** Spt Epsom (GD) H 8.5f 51 60+ <
* **2000** Aug Ripon (GD) H 10f 51 60+ <
2000 Turf 2-8: (8f 2, 9f 1-1, 10f 1-2, 12f 2, 14f) (g-s, g-f 1-3, frm 1-4)
Scopey, average gelding, effective 9 to 14f, acts on g-f to frm, best on frm, prefers tight tracks. Turf high 60 - 1st of 15 getting 9lb from Entity (28 Aug Ripon RF 4053) - also 1st of 13 getting 1lb from Dusky Virgin (6 Spt Epsom RF 4267).
**R A Fahey [2-11] John Robson.*

ALTIBR (USA) RR 121f
5327a[6]
5 ch h Diesis 9f **(80)** - Love's Reward (Nonoalco (USA)) 8.5f **(66)**
Form - 6
2000 Turf 0-1: (8f) (frm)
Very high-class colt. (1st run) - 6th of 14 giving 3lb to War Chant (4 Nov Churchill Downs 8f frm RF 5327a).
**K P McLaughlin in USA [0-1] Shadwell Stable (from S bin Suroor [1-4] Jun 1999).*

AL TOWD (USA) BHB 86f RR 94f
4936[16]
3 b c Kingmambo (USA) 10.9f **(85)** - Toujours Elle (USA) (Lyphard (USA)) 9.9f **(72)**
Form - 05460
Record 2000 - 1st:0 2nd:0 3rd:0 Ran:5
Pre2000 - 1st:1 2nd:1 3rd:2 Ran:4
Win Prizemoney £3,761 *Total Prizemoney* £9,088
Wins * 1999 Spt Newcas (G-F) 7f 75+ <
2000 Turf 0-5: (8f, 10f 2, 12f 2) (gd 4, g-f)
Workmanlike, useful colt, effective 7 to 10f, acts on gd. Turf high 94 - 5th of 9 getting 2lb from King O' The Mana (2 May Bath 10f gd RF 0960). **J L Dunlop [1-9] Hamdan Al Maktoum.*

ALUSTAR BHB 59f RR 56df
3630[16]
3 b f Emarati (USA) 6.6f **(63)** - Chiming Melody (Cure The Blues (USA)) 9.5f **(63)**
Form - PU0
Record 2000 - 1st:0 2nd:0 3rd:0 Ran:3
Pre2000 - 1st:1 2nd:1 3rd:2 Ran:8
Win Prizemoney £2,379 *Total Prizemoney* £3,837
Wins * 1999 Jun Pontef (G-S) 5f 64 <
2000 Turf 0-2: (5f 2) (frm 2) 2000 AW 0-1: (5f) (Fibr)
Scopey, average filly, effective 5f, acts on g-f. Turf high 16 (began Jly). Becoming disappointing.
**M W Easterby [1-11] Bernard Bargh, Tom Beston & Tony Swain.*

ALVA GLEN (USA) RR 112+f
4985[8]
3 b c Gulch (USA) 9.6f **(79)** - Domludge (USA) (Lyphard (USA)) 9.9f **(72)**
Form - 601230168
Record 2000 - 1st:2 2nd:1 3rd:1 Ran:9
Pre2000 - 1st:1 2nd:1 3rd:0 Ran:3
Win Prizemoney £30,494 *Total Prizemoney* £50,585
Wins * **2000** Aug Goodwo (GD) L 14f 112 <
* **2000** Jun York (G-F) H 10.4f 94 98
* 1999 Oct Nottin (GD) 8.2f 88
2000 Turf 2-9: (9f, 10f 1-2, 12f 3, 14f 1-2, 16f) (g-s, gd 1-5, g-f 1-2, frm)
Scopey, Group-class colt, effective 12 to 14f, best at 14f, acts on gd to frm, best on gd, prefers tight tracks, excels at Goodwood and York. Turf high 112 - 1st of 5 from Kuwait Trooper (26 Aug Goodwood RF 3983). Progressed well last term, landing a Goodwood listed race just three days after a good effort in the Ebor. Disappointed on his final two starts when a busy season caught up with him, but remains a useful prospect.
**Sir Michael Stoute [3-12] Sheikh Mohammed.*

ALVARO (IRE) BHB 58a RR 69f
4775[11]
3 ch g Priolo (USA) 10.9f **(71)** - Gezalle (Shareef Dancer (USA)) 9.9f **(73)**
Form - 06206480
Record 2000 - 1st:0 2nd:1 3rd:0 Ran:8
Pre2000 - 1st:0 2nd:0 3rd:0 Ran:2
Win Prizemoney £0 *Total Prizemoney* £1,710
2000 Turf 0-7: (7f, 10f 3, 12f 2, 13f) (sft 2, g-s 2, gd, g-f 2) 2000 AW 0-1: (16f) (Fibr)
Average gelding, effective 12f, acts on g-s, likes left handed tracks. Turf high 69 - 2nd of 11 giving 8lb to Aljay (2 Jun Dundalk 12f g-s RF 1758a).
**M C Chapman [0-4] Sir Clement Freud (from D Gillespie in IRE [0-6] Jun 2000).*

ALWAYS ALIGHT BHB 88f RR 90f
4451[22]
6 ch g Never so Bold 7.1f **(62)** - Fire Sprite (Mummy's Game) 8.2f **(60)**
Form - 01570
Record 2000 - 1st:1 2nd:0 3rd:0 Ran:5
Pre2000 - 1st:6 2nd:3 3rd:9 Ran:45
Win Prizemoney £83,512 *Total Prizemoney* £99,374
Wins * **2000** Apr Windso (HVY) 6f 90
* 1998 Spt Ayr (G-S) H 6f 89 97 <
* 1998 Aug Ayr (G-S) 6f 87
* 1998 Mar Doncas (GD) H 6f 81 86
* 1997 Oct Newcas (G-F) H 6f 75 78
* 1997 Jun Goodwo (G-S) H 6f 72 74
* 1997 May Newbur (G-F) H 6f 62 69
2000 Turf 1-5: (6f 1-3, 7f, 8f) (g-s 1-2, gd 3)
Useful gelding, effective 6f, acts on g-s to gd, best on g-s, has worn blinkers. Turf high 90 - 1st of 14 from Hornbeam (17 Apr Windsor RF 0755). He needs a strong pilot nowadays and Kieren Fallon was the ideal man to have on board when he landed a heavy-ground Windsor classified event on his second start of the season. Ran well over seven next time, but was well held on his final start in the Ayr Gold Cup, an event he won in 1998. Usually reluctant to go to post, he has worn blinkers and a visor.
**K R Burke [7-50] R W and Mrs J A Allen.*

ALWAYS VIGILANT (USA) BHB 89f RR 90+f
5314[12]
3 b f Lear Fan (USA) 10.4f **(80)** - Crowning Ambition (USA) (Chief's Crown (USA)) 9.8f **(72)**
Form - 0310
Record 2000 - 1st:1 2nd:0 3rd:1 Ran:4
Win Prizemoney £2,951 *Total Prizemoney* £3,548
Wins * **2000** Aug Windso (GD) 8.3f 90 <
2000 Turf 1-4: (8f 1-2, 10f 2) (sft, gd, g-f 1-1, frm)
Useful filly. Turf high 90 - 1st of 12 from Cafe Opera (14 Aug Windsor RF 3631). Improving with racing, she got off the mark in a Windsor maiden in August but hung very badly on her only run thereafter. **R Charlton [1-4] K Abdulla.*

ALY'S ALLEY (USA) RR 118f
5331a[9]
4 b c Alwuhush (USA) - Aly Capri (USA) (Alydar (USA)) 9.1f **(76)**
Form - 0
2000 Turf 0-1: (12f) (frm)
Currently high-class colt, often wears blinkers. (1st run) - 9th of 13 to Kalanisi (4 Nov Churchill Downs 12f frm RF 5331a).
**J Tammaro III in USA [0-2] Eaglestone Farm Inc.*

ALYZIG (USA) RR 107f 1826a[7]
3 f No Horse (FR) 10f **(95)** - 00
Form - 57
2000 Turf 0-2: (9f, 11f) (gd 2)
Currently Pattern-class. Turf high 107 (1st run) - 5th of 7 to Ciro (14 May Longchamp 11f gd RF 1289a). *Mme C Head in FR [0-2].*

ALZITA (IRE) BHB 43f **RR 57df** 5137[5]
3 b f Alzao (USA) 9.8f **(73)** -Tiavanita (USA) (J O Tobin (USA)) 9.4f **(67)**
Form - 73885
Record 2000 - 1st:0 2nd:0 3rd:1 Ran:5
Pre2000 - 1st:0 2nd:0 3rd:0 Ran:1
Win Prizemoney £0 *Total Prizemoney* £547
2000 Turf 0-5: (8f 3, 10f, 14f) (g-s 2, g-f 2, frm)
Workmanlike, fair filly. Turf high 52. *J A R Toller [0-6] A Ilsley.*

AMACITA RR 58f 5152[8]
2 b f Shareef Dancer (USA) 10.1f **(67)** - Kina (USA) (Bering) 7.4f **(61)**
Form - 8
Record 2000 - 1st:0 2nd:0 3rd:0 Ran:1
2000 Turf 0-1: (7f) (g-s)
Currently fair filly. *Miss E C Lavelle [0-1] Investment AB Rustningen.*

AMALIA (IRE) BHB 104f **RR 110f** 2872[4]
4 b f Danehill (USA) 9.1f **(79)** - Cheviot Amble (IRE) **(97f)** (Pennine Walk) 8.5f **(61)**
Form - 0413414
Record 2000 - 1st:2 2nd:0 3rd:1 Ran:7
Pre2000 - 1st:3 2nd:2 3rd:2 Ran:10
Win Prizemoney £64,446 *Total Prizemoney* £80,252

Wins								
* **2000**	Jly	Newcas	(FRM)	L	10.1f		106	<
* **2000**	May	York	(FRM)	H	10.4f	98	102	
* 1999	Spt	Doncas	(G-F)	H	10.3f	93	96	
* 1999	Aug	Cheste	(G-S)	H	7.6f	89	91	
* 1999	Jun	Redcar	(FRM)		8f		82	

2000 Turf 2-7: (10f 2-6, 12f) (sft, g-s, gd 1-2, frm 1-3)
Light-framed, Group-class filly, effective 10 to 12f, best at 10f, acts on gd to frm, best on frm, prefers left handed tracks. Turf high 110 - 4th of 7 getting 10lb from Endless Hall (17 Jly Ayr 10f frm RF 2872) - also 1st of 8 from Claxon (1 Jly Newcastle RF 2445). Improving. A notably tough filly, effective on any ground, she showed her customary battling qualities when scoring at York and Newcastle. *P W Harris [5-17] Mrs P W Harris.*

AMAMACKEMMUSH (IRE) BHB 59f59a **RR 70f 59a** 4780[4]
2 b g General Monash (USA) - Paganina (FR) (Galetto (FR)) 13.1f **(60)**
Form - 022352074
Record 2000 - 1st:0 2nd:3 3rd:1 Ran:9
Win Prizemoney £0 *Total Prizemoney* £3,175
2000 Turf 0-7: (5f 7) (g-f 3, frm 3, hrd) 2000 AW 0-2: (5f, 6f) (Fibr 2)
Above-average gelding, effective 5f, acts on g-f to frm, best on g-f. Turf high 69 - 2nd of 11 getting 2lb from Candothat (3 Jly Pontefract 5f frm RF 2473). AW high 58 (began Spt).
K A Ryan [0-9] Roses Racing Club.

AMANCIO (USA) BHB 68f **RR 70f** 4692[4]
9 b g Manila (USA) 10f **(81)** - Kerry Ring (USA) (Ack Ack (USA)) 12.7f **(82)**
Form - 234
Record 2000 - 1st:0 2nd:1 3rd:1 Ran:3
Pre2000 - 1st:2 2nd:2 3rd:2 Ran:9
Win Prizemoney £10,211 *Total Prizemoney* £17,033
2000 Turf 0-3: (14f 3) (gd 2, g-f)
Above-average gelding. Turf high 70. Consistent.
Mrs A J Perrett [4-15] Lady Harrison, S Cohn, P H Locke (from G Harwood [3-14] Spt 1995).

AMARANTH (IRE) BHB 90f83a **RR 92f 83a** 5127[4]
4 b g Mujadil (USA) 7.7f **(70)** - Zoes Delight (IRE) (Hatim (USA))
Form - 707012658144
Record 2000 - 1st:2 2nd:1 3rd:0 Ran:12
Pre2000 - 1st:3 2nd:2 3rd:1 Ran:13
Win Prizemoney £17,245 *Total Prizemoney* £27,661

Wins								
* **2000**	Aug	Newmar	(G-F)	H	5f	82	85	<
* **2000**	Jun	Ayr	(G-F)	H	6f	74	80	
* 1999	Aug	Newmar	(G-F)	H	5f	77	80	
* 1999	Jun	Newcas	(G-F)	H	6f	77	83	
* 1998	Oct	Redcar	(SFT)		5f		79	

2000 Turf 2-11: (5f 1-6, 6f 1-5) (g-s 2, gd 2, g-f 2-4, frm 3) 2000 AW 0-1: (5f) (Equi)
Scopey, useful gelding, effective 5 to 6f, best at 5f, acts on g-s to frm, excels at Newmarket. Turf high 92 - 4th of 20 getting 6lb from Dancing Mystery (12 Oct Newmarket 5f gd RF 4933) - also 1st of 12 giving 2lb to Our Fred (26 Aug Newmarket RF 3994). Consistent. A winner twice on fast ground last term, he had not shown much this season until scoring at Ayr in June when well drawn. Decent efforts afterwards and regained winning form at Newmarket in August. Handles both five and six furlongs and appears best suited by a fast ground. *J L Eyre [5-25] M Gleason.*

AMARO BHB 37f37a **RR 37f 37a** 4398[8]
4 b f Emarati (USA) 6.6f **(63)** - Redcross Miss (Tower Walk) 10f **(62)**
Form - 556360708
Record 2000 - 1st:0 2nd:0 3rd:1 Ran:8
Pre2000 - 1st:0 2nd:2 3rd:0 Ran:10
Win Prizemoney £0 *Total Prizemoney* £2,060
2000 Turf 0-4: (5f 2, 6f 2) (g-f 2, frm 2) 2000 AW 0-4: (6f 2, 7f 2) (Equi 2, Fibr 2)
Scopey, very moderate filly, effective 5f, acts on g-f to frm, best on frm. Turf high 35 (began Jly). AW high 34.
J L Harris [0-4] J Rose (from J Wharton [0-14] Feb 2000).

AMARONE RR 34f 4727[18]
2 b g Young Ern - Tendresse (IRE) **(21f)** (Tender King) 6.8f **(54)**
Form - 0600
Record 2000 - 1st:0 2nd:0 3rd:0 Ran:4
2000 Turf 0-4: (5f, 6f 3) (gd, g-f, frm 2)
Very moderate gelding, has worn blinkers. Turf high 34.
M J Ryan [0-4] P E Axon.

AMAZED BHB 60f **RR 59f** 4558[12]
3 ch f Clantime 6.6f **(57)** - Indigo (Primo Dominie) 6.2f **(80)**
Form - 4200
Record 2000 - 1st:0 2nd:1 3rd:0 Ran:4
Pre2000 - 1st:0 2nd:0 3rd:0 Ran:1
Win Prizemoney £0 *Total Prizemoney* £1,068
2000 Turf 0-4: (5f 3, 6f) (gd, g-f, frm 2)
Workmanlike, fair filly. Turf high 58 (began Jly) - 2nd of 10 getting 5lb from Santiburi Lad (19 Aug Ripon 5f g-f RF 3794).
I A Balding [0-5] D R Brotherton.

AMAZING FACT (USA) BHB 17f21a **RR 26f 21a** 1649[7]
5 b g Known Fact (USA) 8.3f **(72)** - Itsamazing (USA) (The Minstrel (CAN)) 10f **(72)**
Form - 736007
Record 2000 - 1st:0 2nd:0 3rd:1 Ran:5
Pre2000 - 1st:0 2nd:0 3rd:1 Ran:11
Win Prizemoney £0 *Total Prizemoney* £663
2000 Turf 0-3: (10f, 12f 2) (gd, g-f, frm) 2000 AW 0-2: (12f, 14f) (Fibr 2)
Little account gelding, has worn blinkers. Turf high 26. AW high 22. Inconsistent.
J M Bradley [0-12] Robert Bailey (from Lady Herries [0-6] Oct 1998).

AMBASSADOR LADY (IRE) BHB 47f **RR 46f** 4226[10]
2 b f General Monash (USA) - La Fandango (IRE) **(37f)** (Taufan (USA)) 7f **(57)**
Form - 060
Record 2000 - 1st:0 2nd:0 3rd:0 Ran:3
2000 Turf 0-3: (6f 2, 7f) (frm 3)
Currently moderate filly. Turf high 46 (began Jly).
A G Newcombe [0-3] Alex Gorrie.

AMBER BROWN BHB 61f60a **RR 61f 60a** 5061[2]
4 b f Thowra (FR) 11.2f **(47)** - High Velocity (Frimley Park) 6.5f **(67)**
Form - 01001400602
Record 2000 - 1st:2 2nd:1 3rd:0 Ran:11
Pre2000 - 1st:0 2nd:0 3rd:0 Ran:7
Win Prizemoney £7,078 *Total Prizemoney* £8,762

Wins								
* **2000**	May	Lingfi	(HVY)	H	7f	58	61	<
* **2000**	Apr	Thirsk	(SFT)	H	6f	55	57	

2000 Turf 2-11: (6f 1-8, 7f 1-3) (sft, g-s 2-2, gd 2, g-f 3, frm 3)
Lengthy, average filly, effective 6 to 7f, best at 6f, acts on sft to g-f, has worn blinkers (extremely effectively). Turf high 61 - 4th of 12 getting 13lb from Fire Dome (3 Jun Lingfield 6f g-f RF 1678) - also

1st of 15 giving 14lb to Scissor Ridge (27 May Lingfield RF 1506). Consistent. **K T Ivory [2-18] K T Ivory.*

AMBER FORT BHB 68f56a **RR 73f 56a** 4866[3]

7 gr g Indian Ridge 7.6f **(74)** - Lammastide (Martinmas) 7.6f **(59)**
Form - 32547555345004403
Record 2000 - 1st:0 2nd:1 3rd:3 Ran:17
Pre2000 - 1st:5 2nd:5 3rd:9 Ran:53
Win Prizemoney £17,848 *Total Prizemoney* £41,240

Wins								
1998	Jly	Kempto	(G-S)	H	7f	75	82	<
1998	Jun	Goodwo	(G-F)	H	7f	75	81	
1997	Jun	Goodwo	(G-S)	H	7f	74	77	
1996	Oct	Newbur	(SFT)	H	7f	69	74	
1996	*Jun*	*Lingfi*	*(STD)*	*C*	*7f*		*60*	

2000 Turf 0-17: (6f, 7f 13, 8f 3) (sft 3, g-s, gd 6, g-f 3, frm 4)
Above-average gelding, effective 7 to 8f, best at 7f, acts on sft to frm, best on frm, mostly wears blinkers (effectively), likes left handed tracks, likes tight tracks, excels at Ayr. Turf high 74 - 2nd of 20 giving 16lb to Melodian (24 Apr Newcastle 7f sft RF 0846). Consistent. He is an effective seven-furlong handicapper when everything goes right, but is on a very long losing run.
**J M Bradley [0-32] I'm Out Of Here Racing (from D R C Elsworth [4-27] Oct 1998).*

AMBER GO GO BHB 33f **RR** 2927[13]

3 ch f Rudimentary (USA) 8.2f **(66)** - Plaything (High Top) 10.2f **(67)**
Form - 000
Record 2000 - 1st:0 2nd:0 3rd:0 Ran:3
Pre2000 - 1st:0 2nd:0 3rd:1 Ran:7
Win Prizemoney £0 *Total Prizemoney* £517
2000 Turf 0-3: (5f, 12f, 14f) (g-f, frm 2)
Workmanlike, very poor filly. **K W Hogg [0-10] K W Hogg.*

AMBER ROSE (IRE) RR 67f 2064[3]

2 ch f Royal Academy (USA) 7.8f **(77)** - La Fille de Cirque **(51f 34a)** (Cadeaux Genereux)
Form - 3
Record 2000 - 1st:0 2nd:0 3rd:1 Ran:1
Win Prizemoney £0 *Total Prizemoney* £856
2000 Turf 0-1: (6f) (frm)
Currently average filly. **M Johnston [0-1] Greenland Park Ltd.*

AMBERSONG RR 62f 4861[7]

2 ch c Hernando (FR) - Stygian (USA) **(71f)** (Irish River (FR)) 8.6f **(78)**
Form - 77
Record 2000 - 1st:0 2nd:0 3rd:0 Ran:2
2000 Turf 0-2: (7f, 8f) (sft, g-f)
Currently average colt. Turf high 62 (began Spt).
**J W Hills [0-2] C New.*

AMBER TIDE (IRE) BHB 74f **RR 64f** 4553[13]

2 ch f Pursuit of Love 9.5f **(69)** - Tochar Ban (USA) (Assert) 10.6f **(85)**
Form - 340
Record 2000 - 1st:0 2nd:0 3rd:1 Ran:3
Win Prizemoney £0 *Total Prizemoney* £883
2000 Turf 0-3: (5f, 6f 2) (g-s 2, gd)
Currently average filly. Turf high 64. **M L W Bell [0-3] A Buxton.*

AMBIDEXTROUS (IRE) BHB 41f26a **RR 44f 26a** 2295[4]

8 b g Shareef Dancer (USA) 10.1f **(67)** - Amber Fizz (USA) (Effervescing (USA)) 8.1f **(79)**
Form - 02045054
Record 2000 - 1st:0 2nd:0 3rd:0 Ran:6
Pre2000 - 1st:6 2nd:9 3rd:13 Ran:81
Win Prizemoney £20,370 *Total Prizemoney* £36,510

Wins								
1999	Aug	Carlis	(G-F)	C	12f		50	
1999	Aug	Cheste	(G-S)	H	12.3f	43	47	
1997	Jly	Cheste	(G-F)	H	10.3f	58	58	<
1997	Jun	Mussel	(GD)	H	12f	45	53	
1996	Jun	Mussel	(G-F)	H	11.1f	43	48	
1996	Jun	Mussel	(FRM)	H	11.1f	43	48	

2000 Turf 0-2: (12f 2) (frm 2) 2000 AW 0-4: (12f 3, 16f) (Fibr 4)
Moderate gelding, effective 10 to 14f, best at 12f, acts on gd to frm, best on frm, has worn blinkers, likes right handed tracks, does well at Chester and Musselburgh. Turf high 44. AW high 30. Inconsistent.
**M E Sowersby [1-5] Paul Clifton (from E J Alston [8-104] Mar 2000).*

AMBITIOUS BHB 89f79a **RR 90f 79a** 5199[4]

5 b m Ardkinglass 5f **(64)** - Ayodhya (IRE) (Astronef)
Form - 81040141710004
Record 2000 - 1st:4 2nd:0 3rd:0 Ran:14
Pre2000 - 1st:5 2nd:7 3rd:1 Ran:28
Win Prizemoney £45,422 *Total Prizemoney* £55,955

Wins								
*** 2000**	Aug	Newbur	(G-F)	H	5.2f	87	90	<
*** 2000**	Jly	Sandow	(GD)	H	5f	83	87	
*** 2000**	*Jun*	*Southw*	*(STD)*	*H*	*5f*	*62*	*81*	
*** 2000**	Apr	Thirsk	(SFT)		5f		81	
* 1999	Oct	York	(G-S)	H	5f	66	76	
* 1999	Oct	Redcar	(GD)		5f		69	
* 1999	Aug	Sandow	(G-S)	H	5f	63	65	
* 1999	Jun	Sandow	(GD)	C	5f		57	
1999	*Feb*	*Southw*	*(STD)*	*H*	*6f*	*57*	*65*	

2000 Turf 3-13: (5f 3-12, 6f) (g-s 1-2, gd 3, g-f 2-5, frm 3) 2000 AW 1-1: (5f 1-1) (Fibr 1-1)
Useful filly, effective 5f, acts on g-s to g-f - acts on Fibr, best on g-f, has worn blinkers, does well at Southwell and Sandown. Turf high 90 - 4th of 20 giving 3lb to Nineacres (26 Oct Windsor 5f gd RF 5199) - also 1st of 10 giving 5lb to Brecongill Lad (6 Aug Newbury RF 3419). (1st run) - 1st of 11 giving 12lb to Kosevo (16 Jun Southwell RF 2028). Consistent. She is a little bit in and out, but was successful four times last year, including one on Fibresand. Best over the minimum trip, she is an admirably tough mare.
**K T Ivory [8-28] Dean Ivory (from J R Fanshawe [1-14] May 1999).*

AMBUSHED (IRE) BHB 58f42a **RR 58f 42a** 5299[5]

4 b g Indian Ridge 7.6f **(74)** - Surprise Move (IRE) (Simply Great (FR)) 8.2f **(65)**
Form - 08001752106315
Record 2000 - 1st:3 2nd:1 3rd:1 Ran:12
Pre2000 - 1st:0 2nd:0 3rd:0 Ran:2
Win Prizemoney £10,549 *Total Prizemoney* £11,665

Wins								
*** 2000**	Oct	Mussel	(SFT)	H	9f	54	58	<
*** 2000**	Spt	Hamilt	(SFT)	H	8.3f	46	55	
2000	*Feb*	*Southw*	*(STD)*	*H*	*8f*	*25*	*36*	

2000 Turf 2-8: (6f, 7f, 8f 1-3, 9f 1-3) (hvy 2, g-s, gd 2-3, frm 2) 2000 AW 1-4: (6f, 8f 1-1, 9f, 12f) (Fibr 1-4)
Workmanlike, fair gelding, effective 8 to 9f, acts on gd, has worn blinkers, prefers tight tracks. Turf high 58 (began Aug) - 1st of 8 getting 3lb from Kid'z'play (26 Oct Musselburgh RF 5192) - also 1st of 7 getting 22lb from Sea Squirt (4 Spt Hamilton RF 4212). AW high 36.
**P Monteith [2-8] Allan Melville (from M Johnston [1-6] Feb 2000).*

AMEERAT BHB 100f **RR 97f** 4990[6]

2 b f Mark of Esteem (IRE) - Walimu (IRE) (Top Ville) 11.7f **(68)**
Form - 126
Record 2000 - 1st:1 2nd:1 3rd:0 Ran:3
Win Prizemoney £10,920 *Total Prizemoney* £20,870
Wins * 2000 Aug Goodwo (GD) 7f 88+ <
2000 Turf 1-3: (7f 1-2, 8f) (gd 1-2, frm)
Currently very useful filly. Turf high 97 (began Aug) - 2nd of 12 to Karasta (7 Spt Doncaster 8f frm RF 4280) - also 1st of 9 from Sayedah (3 Aug Goodwood RF 3344). Looked a useful recruit when winning at Glorious Goodwood, and met trouble in running when runner-up to Karasta in the May Hill at Goodwood. She ran rather freely there, and again on her final start at Newmarket.
**M A Jarvis [1-3] Sheikh Ahmed Al Maktoum.*

AMELIA (IRE) BHB 86f77a **RR 86f 77a** 5107[7]

2 b f General Monash (USA) - Rose Tint (IRE) **(45f 38a)** (Salse (USA)) 7.5f **(66)**
Form - 4233431127
Record 2000 - 1st:2 2nd:2 3rd:3 Ran:10
Win Prizemoney £23,514 *Total Prizemoney* £28,151

Wins								
*** 2000**	Spt	Lingfi	(GD)	H	5f	71	77	<
*** 2000**	*Aug*	*Wolver*	*(STD)*		*6f*		*73*	

2000 Turf 1-8: (5f 1-8) (gd 1-4, g-f 2, hrd 2) 2000 AW 1-2: (5f, 6f 1-1) (Fibr 1-2)
Useful filly, effective 5f, acts on gd to g-f. Turf high 86 - also 1st of 15 getting 10lb from Vendome (22 Spt Lingfield RF 4582). AW high 73. Improving. Consistent form on both turf and sand, winning the Weatherbys Dash on the Wolverhampton Fibresand in August and following up in a Lingfield nursery on turf.

J Cullinan [2-10] Turf 2000 Ltd.

AMELIA JESS (IRE) BHB 49f50a **RR 45f 50a** 309[5]
3 ch f Mac's Imp (USA) 5.6f **(54)** - Vieux Carre (Pas de Seul) 9.1f **(67)**
Form - 231545
Record 2000 - 1st:1 2nd:1 3rd:1 Ran:6
Pre2000 - 1st:0 2nd:0 3rd:0 Ran:4
Win Prizemoney £1,909 *Total Prizemoney* £2,720
Wins * 2000 *Jan Southw (STD) SH 8f 46 54* <
2000 AW 1-6: (7f 2, 8f 1-3, 9f) (Fibr 1-6)
Workmanlike, moderate filly, effective 7 to 8f, best at 8f, - acts on Fibr, prefers left handed tracks, prefers tight tracks. AW high 54 - 1st of 12 giving 8lb to Cinema Point (31 Jan Southwell RF 0192). Consistent. **B S Rothwell [1-10] Michael Saunders.*

AMELIA'S FIELD BHB 69f **RR 65f** 2083[4]
3 b f Distant Relative 7f **(69)** - Atlantic Record (Slip Anchor) 9.8f **(73)**
Form - 404
Record 2000 - 1st:0 2nd:0 3rd:0 Ran:3
Win Prizemoney £0 *Total Prizemoney* £705
2000 Turf 0-3: (8f 2, 9f) (g-s, gd, frm)
Scopey, currently average filly. Turf high 65.
**S P C Woods [0-3] Dwayne Woods.*

AMELLNAA (IRE) RR 85f 3217[1]
3 gr f Sadler's Wells (USA) 11.3f **(87)** - Alydaress (USA) (Alydar (USA)) 9.1f **(76)**
Form - 1
Record 2000 - 1st:1 2nd:0 3rd:0 Ran:1
Win Prizemoney £4,771 *Total Prizemoney* £4,771
Wins * 2000 Jly Nottin (G-F) 10f 85 <
2000 Turf 1-1: (10f 1-1) (frm 1-1)
Workmanlike, currently useful filly. (1st run) - 1st of 9 from Land Ahead (29 Jly Nottingham RF 3217). **S bin Suroor [1-1] Godolphin.*

AMEN CORNER (USA) BHB 78f80a **RR 77f 80a** 5183[3]
2 ch c Mt Livermore (USA) 7.7f **(90)** - For All Seasons (USA) (Crafty Prospector (USA)) 8.2f **(104)**
Form - 4135723
Record 2000 - 1st:1 2nd:1 3rd:2 Ran:7
Win Prizemoney £3,679 *Total Prizemoney* £6,044
Wins * 2000 Jly Ayr (G-F) 6f 66+ <
2000 Turf 1-6: (5f, 6f 1-4, 7f) (g-s 2, g-f 2, frm 1-2) 2000 AW 0-1: (6f) (Fibr)
Decent colt, effective 6f, acts on g-f - acts on Fibr. Turf high 77 - 3rd of 5 giving 7lb to Rasoum (28 Jly Newmarket 6f g-f RF 3175). (1st run) - 2nd of 15 getting 6lb from Clarion (16 Oct Southwell 6f Fibr RF 5008). Had little to beat when winning an Ayr maiden on his second start. Not yet proven at seven furlongs.
**M Johnston [1-7] M Doyle.*

AMERICA (IRE) RR 105f 4847a[8]
3 ch f Arazi (USA) 9.2f **(74)** - Green Rosy (USA) (Green Dancer (USA)) 10.3f **(74)**
Form - 1618
2000 Turf 2-4: (9f 1-1, 10f 2, 12f 1-1) (hvy 1-1, g-s, gd 1-2)
Pattern-class filly. Turf high 105 - also 1st of 5 from Sadler's Flag (25 Jun Longchamp RF 2386a). A very smart French-trained filly, she was successful in Group Two and Group Three company at Longchamp. Stays 12 furlongs well. **Mme C Head in FR [2-5]*

AMERICAN COUSIN BHB 60f69a **RR 58f 69a** 4487[9]
5 b g Distant Relative 7f **(69)** - Zelda (USA) (Sharpen Up) 8.3f **(67)**
Form - 0070087501110
Record 2000 - 1st:3 2nd:0 3rd:0 Ran:13
Pre2000 - 1st:2 2nd:4 3rd:3 Ran:24
Win Prizemoney £13,244 *Total Prizemoney* £19,275
Wins * 2000 Spt Yarmou (G-F) H 6f 51 58 <
*** 2000** Spt Chepst (G-S) H 5.1f 46 53
*** 2000** Aug Salisb (G-F) H 5f 47 54
* 1999 Jly Doncas (G-F) H 5f 51 58 <
* 1999 Jun Doncas (G-F) H 6f 44 48
2000 Turf 3-13: (5f 2-9, 6f 1-4) (gd, g-f 2-6, frm 1-3, hrd 3)
Fair gelding, effective 5 to 6f, best at 6f, acts on g-f to frm, best on g-f, has worn blinkers, excels at Doncaster. Turf high 58 - 1st of 17 giving 15lb to Two Step (14 Spt Yarmouth RF 4398) - also 1st of 17 getting 4lb from Waff's Folly (31 Aug Salisbury RF 4124).
**D Nicholls [5-26] Middleham Park Racing XIV (from R F JohnsonHoughton [0-6] Aug 1998).*

AMERICAONE RR 4720a[3]
2 b f Emperor Jones (USA) - High Flying Adored (IRE) **(87f)** (In The Wings)
Form - 3
Record 2000 - 1st:0 2nd:0 3rd:1 Ran:1
Win Prizemoney £0 *Total Prizemoney* £1,562
2000 Turf 0-1: (8f) (g-s)
Currently very poor filly - 3rd of 15 getting 3lb from Baranja (24 Spt San Siro 8f g-s RF 4720a). **C F Wall [0-1].*

AMERTON HEATH RR 5246[12]
7 b m Henbit (USA) 10.2f **(46)** - Rodeo Fun (Funny Man)
Form - 0
Record 2000 - 1st:0 2nd:0 3rd:0 Ran:1
2000 AW 0-1: (8f) (Fibr)
Formerly very poor mare. **B P J Baugh [0-4] Mrs C Norlander.*

AMETHYST (IRE) RR 112f 2918a[7]
3 b f Sadler's Wells (USA) 11.3f **(87)** - Zummerudd (Habitat) 9.4f **(70)**
Form - 18207
2000 Turf 1-5: (7f 1-1, 8f 3, 12f) (sft 1-1, g-s, gd, g-f, frm)
Group-class filly, effective 7 to 8f, acts on sft to g-s. Turf high 112 - 2nd of 13 to Crimplene (28 May Curragh 8f g-s RF 1584a) - also 1st of 8 from Aretha (16 Apr Leopardstown RF 0783a). A sister to King Of Kings, she took the Leopardstown Guineas Trial with authority on her seasonal return, but could only manage eighth behind Lahan in the 1000 Guineas. Ran much better when second to Crimplene in the Irish equivalent, but dropped away to finish last in the Coronation Stakes. Appeared to stay when seventh in the Irish Oaks. **A P O'Brien in IRE [2-9] Mrs John Magnier.*

AMEZOLA BHB 60f **RR 68f** 2648[11]
4 gr g Northern Park (USA) 10f **(57)** - Yamamah (Siberian Express (USA)) 8.8f **(65)**
Form - 06600
Record 2000 - 1st:0 2nd:0 3rd:0 Ran:5
Pre2000 - 1st:1 2nd:1 3rd:1 Ran:7
Win Prizemoney £2,479 *Total Prizemoney* £5,274
Wins * 1998 Oct Bath (HVY) 8f 74 <
2000 Turf 0-5: (12f, 14f, 16f 2, 18f) (g-s 2, g-f, frm 2)
Scopey, average gelding, effective 10 to 14f, acts on gd, likes right handed tracks, likes tight tracks. Turf high 68.
**Mrs A J Perrett [1-12] Bernard Keay.*

AMICA BELLA RR 4754[17]
3 b f Environment Friend 7.5f **(67)** - Pontevecchio Bella (Main Reef) 9.6f **(57)**
Form - 0
Record 2000 - 1st:0 2nd:0 3rd:0 Ran:1
2000 Turf 0-1: (10f) (g-s)
Scopey, currently very poor filly.
**L MontagueHall [0-1] John Sparke, John Kn Brawn.*

AMICABLE (IRE) RR 87f 4702[2]
2 b c Common Grounds 8.1f **(66)** - Bahia Laura (FR) (Bellypha) 9.8f **(73)**
Form - 42
Record 2000 - 1st:0 2nd:1 3rd:0 Ran:2
Win Prizemoney £0 *Total Prizemoney* £1,987
2000 Turf 0-2: (6f, 7f) (g-f, frm)
Currently useful colt. Turf high 87 (began Spt) - 2nd of 16 to Malhub (28 Spt Newmarket 7f g-f RF 4702).
**B W Hills [0-2] Lady Harrison.*

AMIGO (IRE) BHB 68f63a **RR 70f 63a** 5017[6]
2 b c Spectrum (IRE) - Eleanor Antoinette (IRE) (Double Schwartz) 7.9f **(55)**
Form - 766
Record 2000 - 1st:0 2nd:0 3rd:0 Ran:3
2000 Turf 0-2: (7f, 8f) (g-s, g-f) 2000 AW 0-1: (7f) (Fibr)
Currently above-average colt. Turf high 70 (began Spt).
**P Mitchell [0-3] Sir Peter O'Sullevan.*

AMILYNX (FR) RR 123f 5212a[1]
4 gr c Linamix (FR) 8.2f **(64)** - Amen (USA) (Alydar (USA)) 9.1f **(76)**

Form - 27111
2000 Turf 3-5: (10f, 12f, 16f 3-3) (hvy 2-2, g-s 1-2, gd)
Very high-class colt, effective 16f, acts on hvy to g-s, best on hvy, prefers right handed tracks. Turf high 123 - 1st of 11 from San Sebastian (22 Oct Longchamp RF 5212a) - also 1st of 7 giving 7lb to Katun (30 Apr Longchamp RF 1037a). A top-class stayer, he was having his first run since May when landing the Prix Royal-Oak (French St Leger) for the second successive year. Thoroughly at home in testing ground. **A Fabre in FR [5-9] J-L Lagadere.*

AMINGTON GIRL BHB 38f36a **RR 41f 36a** 20[6]
5 b m Tragic Role (USA) 9.4f **(63)** - Millfields House (Record Token) 6.3f **(53)**
Form - 6
Record 2000 - 1st:0 2nd:0 3rd:0 Ran:1
Pre2000 - 1st:1 2nd:2 3rd:6 Ran:31
Win Prizemoney £2,637 *Total Prizemoney* £6,696
Wins * 1998 Jly Nottin (G-F) C 8.2f 45 <
2000 AW 0-1: (9f) (Fibr)
Moderate filly, effective 7 to 8f, best at 7f, acts on gd - acts on Fibr, often wears blinkers (effectively). Becoming disappointing. **P D Evans [1-32] P D Evans.*

AMIR ZAMAN RR 69f 4643[21]
2 ch c Salse (USA) 10.9f **(71)** - Colorvista (Shirley Heights) 10.3f **(74)**
Form - 00
Record 2000 - 1st:0 2nd:0 3rd:0 Ran:2
2000 Turf 0-2: (7f 2) (g-f, frm)
Currently average colt. Turf high 69 (began Spt). **J W Payne [0-2] C Cotran.*

AMI'S ANGEL (IRE) BHB 89f **RR 86?f** 4990[16]
2 b f Fayruz 6.6f **(63)** - Khunasira (FR) (Nishapour (FR)) 9.1f **(61)**
Form - 21600
Record 2000 - 1st:1 2nd:1 3rd:0 Ran:5
Win Prizemoney £6,032 *Total Prizemoney* £8,277
Wins * **2000** Aug Pontef (G-F) 5f 68 <
2000 Turf 1-5: (5f 1-2, 6f, 7f, 8f) (gd 3, frm, hrd 1-1)
Useful filly. Turf high 86. A fair juvenile, she spoilt her chances by running too free when tried in a Group Two and faced another stiff task next time, appearing not to stay the mile. **D Carroll [1-5] R McDiarmid.*

AMITGE (FR) BHB 60f **RR 35tf** 3519[9]
6 ch m Vaguely Pleasant (FR) - Ribbon In Her Hair (USA) (Sauce Boat (USA)) 8.3f **(79)**
Form - 50
Record 2000 - 1st:0 2nd:0 3rd:0 Ran:2
2000 Turf 0-2: (7f, 12f) (g-f, frm)
Very moderate mare. Turf high 35. **M C Pipe [6-26] M C Pipe.*

AMIWAIN (FR) RR 101+f 5365a[1]
2 ch c Unfuwain (USA) 11.4f **(74)** - Amen (USA) (Alydar (USA)) 9.1f **(76)**
Form - 1
2000 Turf 1-1: (7f 1-1) (hvy 1-1)
Currently very useful colt. (1st run) - 1st of 5 giving 3lb to Stunning (3 Nov Maisons-Laffitte RF 5365a). Won the Criterium de Maisons-Laffitte last backend and was being talked of as a possible Guineas prospect. On breeding he should get a little further. **A Fabre in FR [1-1] J-L Lagardere.*

AMJAD BHB 68f65a **RR 78+f 65a** 4924[6]
3 ch c Cadeaux Genereux 7.9f **(76)** - Babita (Habitat) 9.4f **(70)**
Form - 50455772006
Record 2000 - 1st:0 2nd:1 3rd:0 Ran:11
Win Prizemoney £0 *Total Prizemoney* £1,227
2000 Turf 0-10: (6f 2, 7f 2, 8f 3, 10f 2, 12f) (gd 4, g-f 3, frm 2, hrd) 2000 AW 0-1: (8f) (Equi)
Unfurnished, above-average colt, effective 6f, acts on frm, often wears blinkers (very effectively). Turf high 78. **C E Brittain [0-11] Saeed Manana.*

AMNERIS (IRE) BHB 65f **RR 82+f** 4621[8]
3 b f Alzao (USA) 9.8f **(73)** - Top Lady (IRE) **(81f)** (Shirley Heights) 10.3f **(74)**
Form - 2348
Record 2000 - 1st:0 2nd:1 3rd:1 Ran:4
Win Prizemoney £0 *Total Prizemoney* £2,289
2000 Turf 0-4: (10f, 12f 3) (gd 2, g-f, frm)
Scopey, decent filly, often wears blinkers. Turf high 82 (1st run) - 2nd of 8 to True Crystal (28 Jun Kempton 10f frm RF 2342). **R Charlton [0-4] Lord Weinstock.*

AMONG ISLANDS BHB 30f **RR 37?f** 376[10]
9 b m Jupiter Island 10.4f **(57)** -Queen of The Nile(Hittite Glory)8.7f **(50)**
Form - 0
Record 2000 - 1st:0 2nd:0 3rd:0 Ran:1
Pre2000 - 1st:0 2nd:0 3rd:0 Ran:4
2000 AW 0-1: (12f) (Fibr)
Very moderate mare.
**Mrs L Williamson [0-1] R A Hughes (from G F H Charles-Jones [0-2] Feb 1999).*

AMONG WOMEN BHB 69f **RR 70f** 5076[1]
2 b f Common Grounds 8.1f **(66)** - Key West (FR) (Highest Honor (FR))
Form - 801
Record 2000 - 1st:1 2nd:0 3rd:0 Ran:3
Win Prizemoney £2,886 *Total Prizemoney* £2,886
Wins * **2000** Oct Bright (SFT) 8f 70 <
2000 Turf 1-3: (6f 2, 8f 1-1) (g-s 1-1, gd 2)
Currently above-average filly. Turf high 70 (began Spt) - 1st of 8 getting 5lb from Art Expert (19 Oct Brighton RF 5076). **N A Callaghan [1-3] Gallagher Equine Ltd.*

AMONITA RR 105+f 4844a[1]
2 b f Anabaa (USA) - Spectacular Joke (USA) (Spectacular Bid (USA)) 11.2f **(76)**
Form - 1
2000 Turf 1-1: (8f 1-1) (gd 1-1)
Currently Pattern-class filly. (1st run) - 1st of 10 from Karasta (1 Oct Longchamp RF 4844a). Showed a terrific turn of speed to take the Prix Marcel Boussac, and will be a strong contender for the Poule d'Essai des Pouliches. **P Bary in FR [1-1] Mme P de Moussac.*

AMORAS (IRE) BHB 72f **RR 71f** 4006[1]
3 b f Hamas (IRE) 8f **(72)** - Rod Lory (Bay Express) 7.1f **(60)**
Form - 4874251
Record 2000 - 1st:1 2nd:1 3rd:0 Ran:7
Pre2000 - 1st:1 2nd:1 3rd:1 Ran:8
Win Prizemoney £11,260 *Total Prizemoney* £14,714
Wins * **2000** Aug Windso (G-F) H 8.3f 70 71
* 1999 Spt Bath (FRM) H 8f 68 74 <
2000 Turf 1-7: (7f 3, 8f 1-4) (gd 1-2, g-f, frm 4)
Workmanlike, above-average filly, effective 6 to 8f, best at 8f, acts on gd to frm, best on frm, excels at Windsor. Turf high 71 - 1st of 12 giving 2lb to Den's-Joy (26 Aug Windsor RF 4006). Consistent. She got off the mark for the season at Windsor in August and seems best on fast ground. **J W Hills [2-15] Espresso Racing.*

AMOROUS SARITA RR 9f 5060[8]
2 b f Pursuit of Love 9.5f **(69)** - Hug Me (Shareef Dancer (USA)) 9.9f **(73)**
Form - 8
Record 2000 - 1st:0 2nd:0 3rd:0 Ran:1
2000 Turf 0-1: (6f) (sft)
Currently very poor filly. **P W Harris [0-1] Cage, Derry, Fox, & Wort.*

AMPULLA RR 44f 2662[7]
2 b c Primo Dominie 7.2f **(67)** - Lead Them Lady (FR) (Lead on Time (USA)) 8f **(65)**
Form - 7
Record 2000 - 1st:0 2nd:0 3rd:0 Ran:1
2000 Turf 0-1: (6f) (gd)
Currently moderate colt. **G B Balding [0-1] The Bogie Boys.*

AMRAK AJEEB (IRE) BHB 73f **RR 77f** 4464[17]
8 b h Danehill (USA) 9.1f **(79)** - Noble Dust (USA) (Dust Commander (USA)) 10.3f **(77)**
Form - 73143820
Record 2000 - 1st:1 2nd:1 3rd:2 Ran:8
Pre2000 - 1st:5 2nd:4 3rd:2 Ran:41
Win Prizemoney £62,817 *Total Prizemoney* £89,262
Wins * **2000** Jun Chepst (FRM) H 10.2f 67 70

1996 Spt Ascot (GD) H 8f 99 105 <
1996 Aug York (GD) H 10.4f 92 98
1996 May Newbur (SFT) H 8f 85 95
2000 Turf 1-8: (10f 1-8) (gd, g-f 1-4, frm 3)
Above-average horse, effective 9 to 10f, best at 10f, acts on g-f to frm, best on frm, prefers tight tracks. Turf high 77 - 3rd of 12 getting 1lb from Polar Red (19 Jly Kempton 10f frm RF 2937) - also 1st of 11 getting 10lb from Clarendon (16 Jun Chepstow RF 2013). Consistent. A former smart handicapper, he returned from a spell in Dubai but did not show much for a period of time. However, a big drop in the handicap enabled him to perform better as the season went gone on and he finally clicked at Chepstow in June. Ran well afterwards, and is suited by ten furlongs and fast ground.
**R J Baker [1-8] B P Jones (from M R Channon [0-7] Oct 1999).*

AMRITSAR BHB 67f60a RR 77f 60a 5150^{9}

3 ch c Indian Ridge 7.6f **(74)** - Trying for Gold (USA) (Northern Baby (CAN)) 11.6f **(71)**
Form - 054323360
Record 2000 - 1st:0 2nd:1 3rd:3 Ran:9
Win Prizemoney £0 *Total Prizemoney* £3,456
2000 Turf 0-8: (7f 2, 8f, 10f 4, 12f) (g-s, gd 4, g-f 2, frm) 2000 AW 0-1: (10f) (Equi)
Neat, above-average colt, effective 7 to 12f, best at 10f, acts on g-s to frm, prefers tight tracks. Turf high 77 - 2nd of 10 giving 5lb to Jocko Glasses (25 Jun Pontefract 10f frm RF 2263). Consistent.
**P Howling [0-3] Arkland International (UK) Ltd (from Sir Michael Stoute [0-6] Jly 2000).*

AMRON BHB 28f RR 41f 5195^{9}

13 b g Bold Owl 9.7f **(47)** - Sweet Minuet (Setay) 5.7f **(103)**
Form - 80600770
Record 2000 - 1st:0 2nd:0 3rd:0 Ran:8
Pre2000 - 1st:15 2nd:9 3rd:7 Ran:119
Win Prizemoney £75,919 *Total Prizemoney* £96,160
Wins 1999 Aug Ayr (G-F) H 10f 50 53
1999 May Redcar (SFT) H 8f 49 59
1998 Oct Redcar (SFT) H 8f 45 48
1997 Mar Newcas (GD) H 5f 57 63
2000 Turf 0-8: (8f 2, 9f 3, 10f, 11f, 12f) (hvy, sft 2, gd 2, g-f, frm 2)
Moderate gelding, effective 8 to 10f, acts on gd to frm. Turf high 41. Inconsistent. This popular veteran still retains ability.
**A Berry [0-8] Roy Peebles (from J Berry [15-119] Oct 1999).*

AMSARA (IRE) BHB 25f20a RR 23f 20a 5082^{12}

4 b f Taufan (USA) 8.3f **(65)** - Legend of Spain (USA) (Alleged (USA)) 10f **(76)**
Form - 060008200
Record 2000 - 1st:0 2nd:1 3rd:0 Ran:9
Pre2000 - 1st:1 2nd:1 3rd:0 Ran:14
Win Prizemoney £2,301 *Total Prizemoney* £3,748
Wins 1999 Apr Pontef (G-S) S 12f 52 <
2000 Turf 0-3: (12f, 16f, 22f) (hvy, sft, gd) 2000 AW 0-6: (11f, 12f 2, 14f 2, 16f) (Fibr 6)
Rangy, little account filly, effective 12f, acts on gd, has worn blinkers. Turf high 23.
**D W Chapman [0-19] David Chapman (from M R Channon [1-4] Apr 1999).*

AMULETTE RR 33f 4480^{13}

2 ch f Mark of Esteem (IRE) - Charmante (USA) (Alydar (USA)) 9.1f **(76)**
Form - 0
Record 2000 - 1st:0 2nd:0 3rd:0 Ran:1
2000 Turf 0-1: (7f) (g-s)
Currently very moderate filly.
**J H M Gosden [0-1] Sheikh Mohammed.*

AMWELL STAR (USA) BHB 45f RR 49f 5024^{8}

2 gr f Silver Buck (USA) - Markham Fair (CAN) (Woodman (USA)) 9f **(74)**
Form - 8
Record 2000 - 1st:0 2nd:0 3rd:0 Ran:1
2000 Turf 0-1: (6f) (g-s)
Currently moderate filly.
**J R Jenkins [0-1] Amwell Racing.*

AMY DEE BHB 48f RR 54f 5169^{9}

2 b f Be My Chief (USA) 10.2f **(62)** - Baileys by Name (Nomination) 7f **(60)**
Form - 6000
Record 2000 - 1st:0 2nd:0 3rd:0 Ran:4
2000 Turf 0-4: (6f 4) (g-s, gd 2, frm)
Fair filly. Turf high 54. **N Tinkler [0-4] R Midgley.*

AMY G (IRE) RR 44f 4365^{6}

2 b f Common Grounds 8.1f **(66)** - Queen Canute (IRE) (Ahonoora) 8.1f **(73)**
Form - 06
Record 2000 - 1st:0 2nd:0 3rd:0 Ran:2
2000 Turf 0-2: (5f, 6f) (g-f 2)
Currently moderate filly. Turf high 44 (began Spt).
**N Tinkler [0-2] Mike Gosse.*

ANALYSER (IRE) RR 78f 4935^{9}

2 ch c Royal Academy (USA) 7.8f **(77)** - Mountain Ash (Dominion) 8.5f **(63)**
Form - 40
Record 2000 - 1st:0 2nd:0 3rd:0 Ran:2
Win Prizemoney £0 *Total Prizemoney* £430
2000 Turf 0-2: (6f, 7f) (gd, g-f)
Currently above-average colt. Turf high 78 (began Spt).
**J H M Gosden [0-2] R E Sangster & A K Collins.*

ANALYTICAL BHB 63f RR 59f 3246^{8}

4 b g Pursuit of Love 9.5f **(69)** - Risha Flower (Kris) 9.5f **(73)**
Form - 00838
Record 2000 - 1st:0 2nd:0 3rd:1 Ran:5
Pre2000 - 1st:1 2nd:0 3rd:2 Ran:5
Win Prizemoney £3,260 *Total Prizemoney* £5,141
Wins * 1999 Jly Nottin (G-F) 8.2f 67+ <
2000 Turf 0-5: (7f 3, 8f 2) (gd 2, g-f 2, frm)
Scopey, fair gelding, effective 8f, acts on g-f, has worn blinkers. Turf high 59. Unraced at two, he won a modest Nottingham maiden easily on his second start last season and was third next time, but disappointed afterwards. **R Charlton [1-10] Martin Myers.*

ANALYZE (FR) BHB 72f RR 74f 3792^{2}

2 b c Anabaa (USA) - Bramosia (Forzando) 7.6f **(59)**
Form - 03572
Record 2000 - 1st:0 2nd:1 3rd:1 Ran:5
Win Prizemoney £0 *Total Prizemoney* £2,487
2000 Turf 0-5: (6f 3, 7f 2) (gd, g-f 3, frm)
Above-average colt. Turf high 74 - 2nd of 9 getting 12lb from Times Square (19 Aug Newbury 7f frm RF 3792).
**M R Channon [0-5] Mrs A M Jones.*

ANASTASIA VENTURE BHB 51f68a RR 49f 68a 4374^{9}

3 b f Lion Cavern (USA) 7.5f **(74)** - Our Shirley (Shirley Heights) 10.3f **(74)**
Form - 5324530
Record 2000 - 1st:0 2nd:1 3rd:2 Ran:7
Win Prizemoney £0 *Total Prizemoney* £2,306
2000 Turf 0-5: (8f 2, 9f, 10f 2) (gd, g-f, frm 3) 2000 AW 0-2: (9f, 12f) (Equi, Fibr)
Unfurnished, average filly, has worn blinkers. Turf high 78. AW high 66. **S P C Woods [0-7] Dr Frank Chao.*

ANCHOR VENTURE BHB 18f18a RR 24f 18a 337^{10}

7 b g Slip Anchor 12.7f **(75)** - Ski Michaela (USA) (Devil's Bag (USA)) 12.4f **(78)**
Form - 00000
Record 2000 - 1st:0 2nd:0 3rd:0 Ran:3
Pre2000 - 1st:1 2nd:1 3rd:4 Ran:31
Win Prizemoney £2,406 *Total Prizemoney* £5,197
Wins 1997 Jun Pontef (G-F) S 10f 45 <
2000 AW 0-3: (8f 2, 9f) (Fibr 3)
Little account gelding, has worn blinkers.
**D W Chapman [0-15] David Chapman (from S P C Woods [1-19] May 1998).*

ANCIENT ALMU (IRE) BHB 40f RR 53f 377^{12}

4 ch g Mac's Imp (USA) 5.6f **(54)** - Elite Exhibition (Exhibitioner) 8.7f **(61)**

Form - 00

Record	**2000**	1st:0	2nd:0	3rd:0	Ran:2
	Pre2000 -	1st:0	2nd:0	3rd:0	Ran:3

2000 AW 0-2: (11f, 12f) (Fibr 2)

Fair gelding, has worn blinkers. AW high 9.

**D Shaw [0-2] Mrs P Roberts (from T Carmody in IRE [0-3] Jun 1998).*

ANDREYEV (IRE) BHB 111f RR 109f 5324[1]

6 ch g Presidium 7.5f **(56)** - Missish (Mummy's Pet) 7.7f **(60)**

Form - 10058413621

Record	**2000 -**	1st:3	2nd:1	3rd:1	Ran:11
	Pre2000 -	1st:7	2nd:2	3rd:3	Ran:33

Win Prizemoney £113,989 *Total Prizemoney* £175,911

Wins							
* **2000**	Nov Doncas	(HVY)	L	6f		109	
* **2000**	Aug York	(GD)	H	6f	105	109+	
* **2000**	Mar Doncas	()	L	6f		108	
* 1998	Aug Deauvi	(GD)	G3	6f		119	<
* 1998	Jun Newcas	(SFT)	L	6f		117	
* 1998	Apr Kempto	(SFT)		6f		107+	
* 1997	May Newmar	(GD)	L	7f		100	
* 1996	Oct Ascot	(GD)		7f		102+	
* 1996	Aug Cheste	(G-S)		6.1f		104+	
* 1996	Jun Windso	(G-F)		5f		88	

2000 Turf 3-11: (5f 3, 6f 3-8) (sft 1-1, g-s 2, gd 2-4, g-f 3, frm)

Pattern-class gelding, effective 5 to 6f, best at 6f, acts on sft to frm, best on gd, has worn blinkers (very effectively), and likes Newmarket. Turf high 109 - 1st of 11 giving 3lb to Further Outlook (4 Nov Doncaster RF 5324) - also 1st of 13 giving 14lb to Night Flight (10 Aug York RF 4108). Consistent. Best on easy ground, he goes very well when fresh in the past and was returning from a break when scoring at York in August. He is not particularly consistent but is very able on his day.

**R Hannon [10-44] J Palmer-Brown.*

ANDROMEDA'S WAY BHB 55f RR 65f 4547[14]

2 b f Kris 10f **(75)** - Titania's Way **(89f)** (Fairy King (USA)) 7.7f **(59)**

Form - 64000

Record	**2000 -**	1st:0	2nd:0	3rd:0	Ran:5

Win Prizemoney £0 *Total Prizemoney* £214

2000 Turf 0-5: (6f 3, 7f, 8f) (g-s, g-f, frm 3)

Average filly. Turf high 65. **R Charlton [0-5] Mrs Alexandra Chandris.*

ANDROMEDES (USA) BHB 84f RR 91f 4063[1]

3 b c Sadler's Wells (USA) 11.3f **(87)** - Utr (USA) **(56tf)** (Mr Prospector (USA)) 8.8f **(78)**

Form - 431761

Record	**2000 -**	1st:2	2nd:0	3rd:1	Ran:6
	Pre2000 -	1st:0	2nd:0	3rd:1	Ran:1

Win Prizemoney £10,283 *Total Prizemoney* £11,907

Wins							
* **2000**	Aug Ripon	(GD)	H	10f	80	86+	
* **2000**	Jun Warwic	(G-F)		12.3f		90	<

2000 Turf 2-6: (10f 1-2, 11f, 12f 1-2, 15f) (g-s, gd, g-f 1-2, frm 1-2)

Scopey, useful colt, effective 10 to 12f, best at 12f, acts on g-f to frm, best on frm. Turf high 91 - also 1st of 4 from Capa (19 Jun Warwick RF 2102). Made the most of an easy task in a four-runner Warwick maiden in June but was well beaten in a fourteen-furlong listed race next time. Subsequently dropped in trip, he scrambled home in a ten-furlong handicap at Ripon.

**H R A Cecil [2-7] M Tabor & Mrs John Magnier.*

ANDY'S ELECTIVE BHB 63f60a RR 62f 60a 3910[8]

3 b c Democratic (USA) - English Mint (Jalmood (USA)) 10.1f **(52)**

Form - 36051878

Record	**2000 -**	1st:1	2nd:0	3rd:1	Ran:8
	Pre2000 -	1st:0	2nd:0	3rd:0	Ran:3

Win Prizemoney £3,178 *Total Prizemoney* £4,049

Wins							
* **2000**	Jun Bright	(FRM)	H	7f	60	62	<

2000 Turf 1-7: (7f 1-4, 8f 3) (gd 3, g-f 2, frm 1-2) 2000 AW 0-1: (7f) (Equi)

Scopey, average colt, has worn blinkers (very effectively). Turf high 74. **J R Jenkins [1-11] Mrs Stella Peirce.*

ANEEFAH RR 71f 5070[7]

3 b f Unfuwain (USA) 11.4f **(74)** - Kronengold (USA) (Golden Act (USA)) 8.8f **(67)**

Form - 57

Record	**2000 -**	1st:0	2nd:0	3rd:0	Ran:2

2000 Turf 0-2: (12f 2) (g-s, frm)

Scopey, currently above-average filly, often wears blinkers. Turf high 71 (began Spt). **M P Tregoning [0-2] Sheikh Ahmed Al Maktoum.*

ANEMOS (IRE) BHB 69f76a RR 70f 76a 2486[8]

5 ch g Be My Guest (USA) 10.2f **(66)** - Frendly Persuasion (General Assembly (USA)) 10f **(68)**

Form - 123426348

Record	**2000 -**	1st:0	2nd:2	3rd:2	Ran:8
	Pre2000 -	1st:2	2nd:2	3rd:5	Ran:18

Win Prizemoney £6,339 *Total Prizemoney* £21,132

Wins							
* 1999	*Dec Lingfi*	*(STD)*	*H*	*10f*	*71*	*78+*	<
* 1999	Aug Nottin	(G-F)		10f		75	

2000 Turf 0-4: (8f 3, 10f) (gd, g-f 2, frm) 2000 AW 0-4: (10f 4) (Equi 4)

Above-average gelding, effective 10f, acts on gd - acts on Equi, has worn blinkers, prefers left handed tracks, excels at Lingfield. Turf high 70. AW high 00 (1st run) - 2nd of 13 getting 10lb from White Plains (2 Jan Lingfield 10f Equi RF 0005). Consistent.

**M A Jarvis [2-25] Andreas Michael (from M H Tompkins [0-1] Spt 1997).*

ANGE D'HONOR (FR) BHB 52f RR 56f 2627[10]

5 b g Hero's Honor (USA) 9.2f **(76)** - Surfing Angel (FR) (Monseigneur (USA)) 7.7f **(63)**

Form - 6840

Record	**2000 -**	1st:0	2nd:0	3rd:0	Ran:4
	Pre2000 -	1st:0	2nd:1	3rd:1	Ran:5

Win Prizemoney £0 *Total Prizemoney* £1,914

2000 Turf 0-4: (12f, 14f 2, 18f) (g-f 3, frm)

Fair gelding, effective 14f, acts on frm, likes tight tracks. Turf high 56.

**E L James [0-6] Forever Blue (from S E H Sherwood [0-7] Oct 1999).*

ANGELA'S HUSBAND (IRE) BHB 51f46a RR 61f 46a 4993[12]

2 b g Up and At 'em - Lake Poopo (IRE) (Persian Heights)

Form - 68035000

Record	**2000 -**	1st:0	2nd:0	3rd:1	Ran:8

Win Prizemoney £0 *Total Prizemoney* £372

2000 Turf 0-7: (5f 5, 6f, 7f) (gd, g-f 4, frm 2) 2000 AW 0-1: (6f) (Fibr)

Average gelding, often wears blinkers. Turf high 61.

**A Dickman [0-8] Mike Smallman.*

ANGELA'S PET (IRE) BHB 43f40a RR 48f 40a 3727[11]

3 ch f Ridgewood Ben - Centenary Year (Malinowski (USA)) 10f **(56)**

Form - 66660

Record	**2000 -**	1st:0	2nd:0	3rd:0	Ran:3
	Pre2000 -	1st:0	2nd:0	3rd:0	Ran:9

2000 Turf 0-3: (6f 2, 8f) (gd, g-f, frm)

Scopey, moderate filly. Turf high 48 (began Jly). Inconsistent.

**J C Fox [0-12] Christy Kissane.*

ANGEL DUST (FR) RR 23f 5054[12]

4 b f Cadoudal (FR) - Silicity (FR) (Son of Silver)

Form - 5600

Record	**2000 -**	1st:0	2nd:0	3rd:0	Ran:4

2000 Turf 0-4: (10f 3, 12f) (sft, g-s, g-f, frm)

Little account filly. Turf high 23 (began Jly).

**C Grant [0-3] AKV Cladding Fabrications Ltd (from G M McCourt [1-6] Jly 2000).*

ANGEL HILL BHB 61f61a RR 63f 61a 4782[7]

5 ch m King's Signet (USA) 7f **(51)** - Tawny (Grey Ghost) 9.9f **(60)**

Form - 0887610040147

Record	**2000 -**	1st:2	2nd:0	3rd:0	Ran:13
	Pre2000 -	1st:2	2nd:2	3rd:5	Ran:25

Win Prizemoney £13,173 *Total Prizemoney* £23,694

Wins							
* **2000**	Spt Catter	(SFT)	H	7f	53	63	
2000	Jun Newcas	(FRM)	H	6f	52	52	
1999	Jly Newcas	(G-F)	H	6f	74	76	<
1997	May Newcas	(GD)		5f		63+	

2000 Turf 2-11: (5f 4, 6f 1-4, 7f 1-3) (sft, g-s 1-2, gd 3, frm 1-5) 2000 AW 0-2: (7f, 8f) (Fibr 2)

Average filly, effective 5 to 6f, best at 6f, acts on gd to hrd, has worn blinkers. Turf high 63. AW high 63 (began Spt). She has made the frame on several occasions in the last couple of seasons, but did not get her head in front until landing a four-runner handicap at Newcastle last July when blinkered for the first time.

**K A Ryan [1-5] Keith Taylor (from R A Fahey [2-25] Jly 2000).*

ANGEL LANE BHB 41f **RR 42f** 4824[15]
3 b f Merdon Melody 6.8f **(56)** - Young Whip (Bold Owl) 8.5f **(45)**
Form - 07480
Record 2000 - 1st:0 2nd:0 3rd:0 Ran:5
Pre2000 - 1st:0 2nd:0 3rd:0 Ran:5
Win Prizemoney £0 *Total Prizemoney* £327
2000 Turf 0-5: (8f 4, 10f) (gd, g-f 3, frm)
Workmanlike, moderate filly. Turf high 42.
**A W Carroll [0-10] Aramis Racing Syndicate.*

ANGELS VENTURE BHB 68f63a **RR 77f 63a** 4585[4]
4 ch c Unfuwain (USA) 11.4f **(74)** - City of Angels (Woodman (USA)) 9f **(74)**
Form - 07043264
Record 2000 1st:0 2nd:1 3rd:1 Ran:8
Pre2000 - 1st:2 2nd:2 3rd:6 Ran:13
Win Prizemoney £6,711 *Total Prizemoney* £16,901
Wins 1999 Oct Bright (GD) H 11.9f 80 84 <
1999 Jly Yarmou (FRM) 11.5f 79
2000 Turf 0-7: (12f 6, 14f) (gd 4, g-f, frm 2) 2000 AW 0-1: (12f) (Equi)
Well made, above-average colt, effective 8 to 14f, best at 12f, acts on g-s to hrd, best on gd, prefers left handed tracks, likes tight tracks, excels at Salisbury. Turf high 77 - 11th of 15 giving 7lb to Wait For The Will (18 May Salisbury 12f gd RF 1274).
**J R Jenkins [1-12] Tony Hayward (from S P C Woods [2-13] Oct 1999).*

ANGIE BABY BHB 68f **RR 62f** 1909[4]
4 b f Puissance 7.1f **(60)** - Hyde Princess (Touch Paper) 6.8f **(57)**
Form - 4
Record 2000 - 1st:0 2nd:0 3rd:0 Ran:1
Pre2000 - 1st:5 2nd:4 3rd:0 Ran:22
Win Prizemoney £15,930 *Total Prizemoney* £27,190
Wins 1999 Apr Ripon (G-S) C 5f 75
1998 Aug Lingfi (FRM) 5f 87 <
1998 Jly Hamilt (FRM) 5f 86+
1998 May Nottin (G-F) 5.1f 87 <
1998 Apr Redcar (SFT) 5f 60
2000 Turf 0-1: (5f) (frm)
Average filly, effective 5 to 6f, best at 5f, acts on gd to frm, best on gd. Consistent.
**R Ingram [0-9] The Barracuda Boys (from J Berry [5-14] Jly 1999).*

ANGIE MARINIE BHB 58f42a **RR 60f 42a** 2801[7]
4 b f Sabrehill (USA) 8.5f **(64)** - Lambast (Relkino) 8.9f **(65)**
Form - 067
Record 2000 - 1st:0 2nd:0 3rd:0 Ran:3
Pre2000 - 1st:1 2nd:1 3rd:2 Ran:10
Win Prizemoney £2,110 *Total Prizemoney* £5,322
Wins 1999 Apr Nottin (SFT) S 8.2f 53 <
2000 Turf 0-3: (10f, 12f 2) (gd, g-f 2)
Unfurnished, average filly, effective 8 to 12f, acts on sft to frm. Turf high 60 (1st run) - 10th of 12 getting 12lb from Veridian (11 May Chester 12f g-f RF 1139).
**M C Pipe [5-17] C R Fleet (from R A Fahey [1-5] Apr 1999).*

ANGIES QUEST BHB 74f **RR 68f** 4170[4]
3 b f Inchinor 8.9f **(64)** - Chanson D'Avril **(39f)** (Chief Singer) 8.9f **(66)**
Form - 24
Record 2000 - 1st:0 2nd:1 3rd:0 Ran:2
Pre2000 - 1st:0 2nd:0 3rd:1 Ran:3
Win Prizemoney £0 *Total Prizemoney* £2,230
2000 Turf 0-2: (8f 2) (gd, g-f)
Scopey, average filly. Turf high 68.
**H R A Cecil [0-2] High Havens Stables (from K R Burke [0-3] Spt 1999).*

ANGIOLINI (USA) RR 66f 800[20]
3 ch c Woodman (USA) 9.7f **(77)** - Danse Royale (IRE) (Caerleon (USA)) 8.6f **(71)**
Form - 0
Record 2000 - 1st:0 2nd:0 3rd:0 Ran:1
2000 Turf 0-1: (8f) (gd)
Workmanlike, currently average colt.
**H R A Cecil [0-1] Mrs John Magnier & M Tabor.*

ANGUS-G BHB 68f **RR 67f** 5168[1]
8 br g Chief Singer 8.6f **(62)** - Horton Line (High Line) 10.3f **(70)**
Form - 80081
Record 2000 - 1st:1 2nd:0 3rd:0 Ran:5
Pre2000 - 1st:4 2nd:3 3rd:4 Ran:19
Win Prizemoney £27,417 *Total Prizemoney* £51,471
Wins * 2000 Oct Redcar (SFT) 10f 66
* 1997 May York (GD) H 11.9f 88 93 <
* 1997 Apr Newmar (GD) H 12f 82 87
* 1996 Aug Newmar (G-F) H 10f 73 78
* 1996 Jly Newmar (G-F) H 10f 71 74
2000 Turf 1-5: (10f 1-2, 12f, 14f 2) (gd 1-3, g-f 2)
Average gelding, effective 10f, acts on gd, likes left handed tracks. Turf high 67 (began Aug). Consistent.
**Mrs M Reveley [5-24] W Ginzel.*

ANGUS THE BOLD BHB 22f **RR 29f** 3807[11]
4 b g Puissance 7.1f **(60)** - Floral Spark **(61f 72a)** (Forzando) 7.6f **(59)**
Form - 00060
Record 2000 - 1st:0 2nd:0 3rd:0 Ran:5
Pre2000 - 1st:0 2nd:1 3rd:0 Ran:3
Win Prizemoney £0 *Total Prizemoney* £642
2000 Turf 0-4: (6f, 7f, 8f 2) (g-f 2, frm 2) 2000 AW 0-1: (12f) (Fibr)
Light-framed, little account gelding, has worn blinkers. Turf high 29. **P D Evans [0-5] Miss D L Wisbey (from J L Eyre [0-2] Jun 1999).*

ANIMAL CRACKER BHB 85f **RR 75?f** 2659[5]
2 gr f Primo Dominie 7.2f **(67)** - Child Star (FR) **(32f 39a)** (Bellypha) 9.8f **(73)**
Form - 85155
Record 2000 - 1st:1 2nd:0 3rd:0 Ran:5
Win Prizemoney £4,446 *Total Prizemoney* £5,008
Wins * 2000 May Newbur (SFT) 5.2f 72 <
2000 Turf 1-5: (5f 1-4, 6f) (gd 1-3, g-f 2)
Above-average filly. Turf high 75 - also 1st of 9 getting 5lb from Game N Gifted (31 May Newbury RF 1587). He got off the mark with a narrow victory in a soft-ground Newbury maiden in May, but has faced some stiff tasks otherwise. **D Marks [1-5] D Marks.*

AN JOLIEN BHB 42f **RR 21f** 4677[18]
3 b f Aragon 7.7f **(58)** - Joli's Girl (Mansingh (USA)) 7.4f **(55)**
Form - 400000
Record 2000 - 1st:0 2nd:0 3rd:0 Ran:6
Pre2000 - 1st:0 2nd:0 3rd:0 Ran:4
2000 Turf 0-6: (6f, 7f 4, 10f) (hvy, g-s 2, gd, g-f, frm)
Unfurnished, little account filly, effective 7f, acts on hvy, has worn blinkers. Turf high 61 (1st run) - 4th of 19 giving 3lb to Balfour (12 Apr Warwick 7f hvy RF 0687). **M J Ryan [0-10] & Mrs W J Foley.*

ANKASAMEN BHB 50f **RR 52f** 5073[9]
2 b f Muhtarram (USA) - Arusha (IRE) (Dance of Life (USA)) 7f **(66)**
Form - 000
Record 2000 - 1st:0 2nd:0 3rd:0 Ran:3
2000 Turf 0-3: (6f, 7f 2) (g-s, g-f, frm)
Currently fair filly. Turf high 52 (began Aug).
**M L W Bell [0-3] Raymond Tooth.*

AN LU ABU (IRE) BHB 52f34a **RR 39f 34a** 3300a[13]
4 b g Distinctly North (USA) 7.4f **(63)** - Dunbally (Dunphy) 9.4f **(57)**
Form - 00708405500
Record 2000 - 1st:0 2nd:0 3rd:0 Ran:9
Pre2000 - 1st:0 2nd:1 3rd:1 Ran:16
Win Prizemoney £0 *Total Prizemoney* £1,136
2000 Turf 0-7: (8f 3, 9f 3, 10f) (sft, g-s, gd, g-f 2, frm) 2000 AW 0-2: (8f, 12f) (Fibr 2)
Very moderate gelding, effective 8f, acts on gd to frm, has worn blinkers, likes left handed tracks. Turf high 39. AW high 21.
**M Halford in IRE [0-21] Mrs Anne Campbell (from K R Burke [0-4] Jan 2000).*

ANNADAWI BHB 81f53a **RR 86f 53a** 5133[5]
5 b g Sadler's Wells (USA) 11.3f **(87)** - Prayers'n Promises (USA) (Foolish Pleasure (USA)) 8.9f **(72)**
Form - 444475463222172236331727 5
Record 2000 - 1st:2 2nd:6 3rd:4 Ran:23
Pre2000 - 1st:0 2nd:0 3rd:0 Ran:6
Win Prizemoney £9,741 *Total Prizemoney* £21,570

Wins * 2000 Spt Pontef (G-S) H 10f 49 80 <
* 2000 May Leices (G-S) H 10f 45 49
2000 Turf 2-18: (7f, 8f, 9f 2, 10f 2-10, 11f 4) (hvy, sft 4, g-s, gd 2-6, g-f 3, frm 3) 2000 AW 0-5: (7f, 8f, 9f 2, 11f) (Fibr 5)
Useful gelding, effective 9 to 10f, acts on sft to gd, has worn blinkers. Turf high 86 - 2nd of 20 giving 22lb to Greenaway Bay (7 Oct York 9f sft RF 4864) - also 1st of 10 giving 1lb to Golden Way (21 Spt Pontefract RF 4556). AW high 36. Inconsistent. Caused a 50/1 surprise when winning a rated stakes at Pontefract in September.
**C N Kellett [2-31] Sean Taylor.*

ANNA ELISE (IRE) RR 100f 5048a[2]

4 b f Nucleon (USA) - Tormented (USA) (Alleged (USA)) 10f **(76)**
Form - 1D220410102
2000 Turf 3-11: (6f 3-5, 7f 3, 8f 2, 9f) (sft 1-2, g-s 3, gd 1-5)
Very useful filly, effective 6f, acts on g-s. Turf high 100 - 2nd of 11 getting 3lb from Cobourg Lodge (15 Oct Curragh 6f g-s RF 5048a) - also 1st of 14 giving 9lb to Reptar (16 Spt Curragh RF 4519a).
**J A Flynn in IRE [4-18] L Tucker.*

ANNAKAYE BHB 32f RR 35f 3425[15]

3 b f Aragon 7.7f **(58)** - Annaceramic (Horage) 10.3f **(61)**
Form - 075050
Record 2000 - 1st:0 2nd:0 3rd:0 Ran:6
2000 Turf 0-5: (5f, 6f, 7f 3) (gd, g-f, frm 2, hrd) 2000 AW 0-1: (5f) (Fibr)
Leggy, very moderate filly, effective 5f, acts on g-f. Turf high 35.
**M W Easterby [0-6] Howard Johnson.*

ANNANDALE (IRE) BHB 36f36a RR 39f 36a 1856[2]

4 ch f Balla Cove - Gruinard Bay (Doyoun) 9f **(69)**
Form - 002
Record 2000 - 1st:0 2nd:1 3rd:0 Ran:3
Pre2000 - 1st:0 2nd:0 3rd:1 Ran:10
Win Prizemoney £0 *Total Prizemoney* £1,250
2000 AW 0-3: (7f, 8f, 9f) (Fibr 3)
Leggy, very moderate filly, effective 8f, - acts on Fibr, has worn blinkers, likes tight tracks. AW high 35 - 2nd of 7 getting 21lb from Shady Point (9 Jun Southwell 8f Fibr RF 1856). Inconsistent.
**M C Chapman [0-2] R J Hayward (from D Nicholls [0-2] Jan 2000).*

ANNAPURNA (IRE) RR 104f 5133[9]

4 b f Brief Truce (USA) 9.1f **(73)** - National Ballet (Shareef Dancer (USA)) 9.9f **(73)**
Form - 823400400
Record 2000 - 1st:0 2nd:1 3rd:1 Ran:9
Pre2000 - 1st:1 2nd:3 3rd:0 Ran:7
Win Prizemoney £4,413 *Total Prizemoney* £21,606
Wins * 1998 Spt Kempto (SFT) 7f 89 <
2000 Turf 0-9: (8f 2, 9f 4, 10f 3) (hvy, sft 2, g-s 3, gd 2, g-f)
Very useful filly, effective 8 to 9f, acts on gd to g-f, has worn blinkers. Turf high 104 - 2nd of 6 to Cape Grace (5 May Newmarket 9f g-f RF 1049). Inconsistent. She made the frame in listed races, but is the sort of filly for whom opportunities are hard to find.
**B J Meehan [1-16] Usk Valley Stud.*

ANNATTO (USA) BHB 85f RR 82f 4643[12]

2 b br f Mister Baileys - Miss Rossi (Artaius (USA)) 9f **(69)**
Form - 24230
Record 2000 - 1st:0 2nd:2 3rd:1 Ran:5
Win Prizemoney £0 *Total Prizemoney* £4,251
2000 Turf 0-5: (6f 2, 7f 3) (g-f, frm 4)
Decent filly. Turf high 82 (began Jly) - 3rd of 8 to Palatial (15 Spt Newbury 7f frm RF 4437). **I A Balding [0-5] George Strawbridge.*

ANNELIINA BHB 52f40a RR 53f 40a 1362[12]

4 b f Cadeaux Genereux 7.9f **(76)** - Blasted Heath (Thatching) 8f **(66)**
Form - 0700
Record 2000 - 1st:0 2nd:0 3rd:0 Ran:4
Pre2000 - 1st:0 2nd:1 3rd:0 Ran:9
Win Prizemoney £0 *Total Prizemoney* £1,780
2000 Turf 0-1: (13f) (frm) 2000 AW 0-3: (7f, 8f, 9f) (Fibr 3)
Neat, fair filly. AW high 18. **C N Allen [0-13] Mrs K A Hyytiainen.*

ANNE MCCOL RR 32f 4322[17]

2 b f Faustus (USA) 9.1f **(54)** - Dona Marina (IRE) (Belmez (USA))
Form - 80
Record 2000 - 1st:0 2nd:0 3rd:0 Ran:2
2000 Turf 0-2: (5f, 7f) (g-f, hrd)
Currently very moderate filly. Turf high 32 (began Aug).
**A J Chamberlain [0-2] Mike Ledbury.*

ANNE-SOPHIE BHB 49f RR 52f 4580[13]

2 ch f First Trump - Hardiprincess **(35f)** (Keen)
Form - 700
Record 2000 - 1st:0 2nd:0 3rd:0 Ran:3
2000 Turf 0-3: (5f, 6f 2) (gd, g-f, frm)
Currently fair filly. Turf high 49 (began Aug).
**M L W Bell [0-3] Mrs Anne Yearley.*

ANNESPRIDE BHB 30f RR 24f 2654[14]

3 b f Komaite (USA) 6.9f **(61)** - Lindrake's Pride (Mandrake Major) 7.6f **(53)**
Form - 550
Record 2000 - 1st:0 2nd:0 3rd:0 Ran:3
Pre2000 - 1st:0 2nd:0 3rd:0 Ran:1
2000 Turf 0-3: (7f, 8f 2) (g-s, gd, frm)
Lengthy, little account filly. Turf high 24.
**Mrs M Reveley [0-4] Mrs Muriel Ward.*

ANNETTE VALLON (IRE) BHB 88f RR 86f 3033[2]

3 b f Efisio 7.7f **(69)** - Christine Daae (Sadler's Wells (USA)) 10f **(76)**
Form - 2132
Record 2000 - 1st:1 2nd:2 3rd:1 Ran:4
Win Prizemoney £2,884 *Total Prizemoney* £7,107
Wins * 2000 Jun Folkes (FRM) 5f 75 <
2000 Turf 1-4: (5f 1-4) (gd 2, g-f 1-2)
Well made, useful filly. Turf high 86 - 2nd of 6 getting 15lb from Guinea Hunter (22 Jly Newmarket 5f g-f RF 3033). Unraced at two, she got off the mark in a Folkestone maiden on very fast ground in July and ran very well to finish third in a competitive sprint handicap at the Newmarket July meeting next time.
**P W Harris [1-4] Mrs P W Harris.*

ANNIE APPLE (IRE) BHB 44f53a RR 48f 53a 5155[7]

4 ch f Petardia 8.2f **(58)** - Art Duo (Artaius (USA)) 9f **(69)**
Form - 770058457014237
Record 2000 - 1st.1 2nd:1 3rd:1 Ran:14
Pre2000 - 1st:2 2nd:3 3rd:2 Ran:22
Win Prizemoney £5,886 *Total Prizemoney* £11,171
Wins * 2000 Aug Bright (FRM) S 7f 44
1999 *Jan Lingfi (STD) S 8f 60* <
1998 Aug Folkes (G-F) S 7f 60 <
2000 Turf 1-10: (7f 1-5, 8f 3, 9f 2) (sft, gd 2, g-f 2, frm 4, hrd 1-1) 2000 AW 0-4: (6f, 7f 2, 8f) (Equi 4)
Leggy, fair filly, effective 7 to 8f, acts on frm - acts on Equi, has worn blinkers. Turf high 48. AW high 48.
**N Hamilton [1-19] City Industrial Supplies Ltd (from G Lewis [0-4] Jly 1999).*

ANNIEIRWIN (IRE) RR 98f 4796a[8]

4 ch f Perugino (USA) - Elsaca (Ela-Mana-Mou) 10.1f **(70)**
Form - 6184008
2000 Turf 1-7: (8f 2, 9f 1-1, 10f 3, 12f) (sft, gd 4, g-f 1-1)
Very useful filly, effective 9f, acts on g-f, has worn blinkers. Turf high 98 - also 1st of 5 getting 6lb from Free To Speak (14 Jun Leopardstown RF 2132a). **F Ennis in IRE [1-7] M E McElroy.*

ANNIE RUAN BHB 71f RR 76f 4582[14]

2 b f So Factual (USA) - Sans Diablo (IRE) (Mac's Imp (USA))
Form - 03440
Record 2000 - 1st:0 2nd:0 3rd:1 Ran:5
Win Prizemoney £0 *Total Prizemoney* £749
2000 Turf 0-5: (5f 2, 6f 3) (gd 3, hrd 2)
Above-average filly. Turf high 76.
**D HaydnJones [0-5] The Lamorran Partnership.*

ANNIJAZ BHB 59f53a RR 60f 53a 4729[4]

3 b f Alhijaz 7.7f **(57)** - Figment (Posse (USA)) 8.9f **(61)**
Form - 5000463301735234
Record 2000 - 1st:1 2nd:1 3rd:4 Ran:16
Pre2000 - 1st:0 2nd:2 3rd:1 Ran:4
Win Prizemoney £5,255 *Total Prizemoney* £11,494
Wins * 2000 Jly Epsom (GD) H 7f 48 60 <
2000 Turf 1-14: (6f, 7f 1-9, 8f 3, 10f) (g-s 2, gd 3, g-f 1-3, frm 5, hrd)

2000 AW 0-2: (6f, 7f) (Equi 2)
Workmanlike, average filly, likes left handed tracks. Turf high 60. AW high 57.
**J G Portman [1-10] Christopher Shankland (from G M McCourt [0-6] Jun 2000).*

ANNIVERSARY DAY BHB 39f RR 54f 5164[13]

4 ch g Lion Cavern (USA) 7.5f **(74)** - Doyce **(72f)** (Formidable (USA)) 9.2f **(63)**
Form - 00
Record 2000 - 1st:0 2nd:0 3rd:0 Ran:2
Pre2000 - 1st:0 2nd:1 3rd:0 Ran:7
Win Prizemoney £0 *Total Prizemoney* £1,050
2000 Turf 0-2: (10f, 11f) (sft, gd)
Lengthy, fair gelding, has worn blinkers. Becoming disappointing.
**W S Cunningham [0-10] Mrs Ann Bell.*

ANNO DOMINI BHB 73f RR 53f 2568[10]

4 b c Primo Dominie 7.2f **(67)** - Jalopy (Jalmood (USA)) 10.1f **(52)**
Form - 00
Record 2000 - 1st:0 2nd:0 3rd:0 Ran:2
Pre2000 - 1st:1 2nd:1 3rd:0 Ran:4
Win Prizemoney £3,907 *Total Prizemoney* £9,352
Wins * 1998 Jun Pontef (GD) 5f 81 <
2000 Turf 0-2: (5f, 7f) (g-f 2)
Workmanlike, fair colt. Turf high 53. Returned to the fray in 2000 after missing a season. **P F I Cole [1-6] P F I Cole Ltd.*

ANN'S MILL BHB 39f34a RR 54f 34a 2554[8]

3 b f Pelder (IRE) - Honey Mill (Milford) 9f **(61)**
Form - 047078
Record 2000 - 1st:0 2nd:0 3rd:0 Ran:6
Pre2000 - 1st:1 2nd:0 3rd:0 Ran:5
Win Prizemoney £2,810 *Total Prizemoney* £2,810
Wins 1999 Aug Thirsk (G-F) S 7f 64 <
2000 Turf 0-6: (7f 4, 8f, 10f) (gd 2, g-f, frm 3)
Leggy, fair filly, effective 7f, acts on hrd. Turf high 54.
**J S Moore [0-6] Mrs A Anidjah (from Derrick Morris [0-1] Oct 1999).*

ANN SUMMERS (USA) BHB 48f RR 34f 5196[14]

2 b f Dehere (USA) - Upper Class Lady (USA) (Upper Nile (USA)) 8.5f **(75)**
Form - 040
Record 2000 - 1st:0 2nd:0 3rd:0 Ran:3
2000 Turf 0-2: (6f, 8f) (gd, frm) 2000 AW 0-1: (9f) (Fibr)
Currently very moderate filly. Turf high 34 (began Aug).
**B J Meehan [0-3] Gold Group International Ltd.*

ANONYMITY RR 39f 5186[16]

2 ch c Exit To Nowhere (USA) 8.7f **(77)** - Wind Of Roses (USA) (Lomond (USA)) 8.8f **(65)**
Form - 00
Record 2000 - 1st:0 2nd:0 3rd:0 Ran:2
2000 Turf 0-2: (7f 2) (g-s 2)
Currently very moderate colt. Turf high 39 (began Oct).
**Sir Michael Stoute [0-2] Cheveley Park Stud.*

ANOTHER ARTHUR BHB 19f24a RR 34f 24a 1040[6]

4 b g Puissance 7.1f **(60)** - Traumatic Laura (Pragmatic)
Form - 6
Record 2000 - 1st:0 2nd:0 3rd:0 Ran:1
Pre2000 - 1st:0 2nd:0 3rd:0 Ran:3
2000 Turf 0-1: (16f) (frm)
Leggy, very moderate gelding. **W McKeown [0-6] Miss Susan Blain.*

ANOTHER BEVELED BHB 43f RR 42f 3168[U]

5 ch g Beveled (USA) 6.9f **(64)** - Cotehele (Paddy's Stream)
Form - 04U
Record 2000 - 1st:0 2nd:0 3rd:0 Ran:3
Pre2000 - 1st:0 2nd:0 3rd:0 Ran:3
2000 Turf 0-2: (12f 2) (g-f, frm) 2000 AW 0-1: (10f) (Equi)
Moderate gelding. Turf high 42 (began Jly).
**G L Moore [0-3] Mrs P A Wilkins (from A P Jones [0-3] Jly 1998).*

ANOTHER DIAMOND (IRE) RR 54f 5312[9]

2 b f First Trump - Rockin' Rosie (Song) 7.2f **(61)**
Form - 0
Record 2000 - 1st:0 2nd:0 3rd:0 Ran:1
2000 Turf 0-1: (8f) (g-s)
Currently fair filly. **P Howling [0-1] Mrs P Reditt.*

ANOTHER MONK (IRE) BHB 49f49a RR 47f 49a 1734[10]

9 br g Supreme Leader 10.9f **(66)** - Royal Demon (Tarboosh (USA)) 10f **(55)**
Form - 284141120
Record 2000 - 1st:3 2nd:1 3rd:0 Ran:7
Pre2000 - 1st:2 2nd:3 3rd:2 Ran:11
Win Prizemoney £11,898 *Total Prizemoney* £16,609
Wins * **2000** May Windso (G-S) H 10f 44 47
* **2000** *Apr Lingfi (STD) H 13f 41 43*
* **2000** *Jan Lingfi (STD) S 16f 39*
* 1997 *Nov Lingfi (STD) H 12f 27 48* <
* 1997 *Nov Lingfi (STD) H 16f 27 37*
2000 Turf 1-2: (10f 1-1, 12f) (gd 1-1, g-f) 2000 AW 2-5: (12f, 13f 1-3, 16f 1-1) (Equi 2-5)
Fair gelding, effective 10 to 16f, best at 12f, acts on gd - acts on AW, best on Equi, has worn blinkers, likes left handed tracks, does well at Lingfield. Turf high 47 (1st run) - 1st of 21 giving 3lb to Second Paige (2 May Windsor RF 0978). AW high 50 - 2nd of 10 getting 22lb from Pluralist (3 Jun Lingfield 12f Equi RF 1679). Consistent.
**R Ingram [5-11] D G Wheatley (from B R Johnson [0-7] Dec 1999).*

ANOTHER NIGHTMARE (IRE) BHB 49f49a RR 46f 49a 23[1]

8 b m Treasure Kay 6.5f **(53)** - Carange (Known Fact (USA)) 7.4f **(67)**
Form - 74031
Record 2000 - 1st:1 2nd:0 3rd:0 Ran:1
Pre2000 - 1st:10 2nd:6 3rd:7 Ran:99
Win Prizemoney £26,770 *Total Prizemoney* £36,259
Wins * **2000** *Jan Lingfi (STD) H 6f 44 47*
* 1999 Aug Hamilt (G-F) H 5f 40 45
* 1999 May Hamilt (G-F) H 5f 37 48
* 1999 *Jan Lingfi (STD) H 6f 44 49*
* 1999 *Jan Wolver (STD) H 6f 37 46*
1997 Aug Thirsk (GD) SH 6f 44 50
1997 Jly Hamilt (SFT) H 5f 41 46
1997 *Mar Wolver (STD) H 6f 41 42*
1996 Aug Ripon (SFT) H 6f 47 53 <
1996 Aug Hamilt (G-F) H 6f 39 48
2000 AW 1-1: (6f 1-1) (Equi 1-1)
Moderate mare, effective 5 to 6f, best at 6f, acts on g-f to frm - acts on AW, best on Equi, has worn blinkers, excels at Hamilton, likes Lingfield. (1st run) - 1st of 9 getting 21lb from Brutal Fantasy (5 Jan Lingfield RF 0023).
**D W Barker [5-25] GM Engineering (from R M McKellar [5-64] Aug 1998).*

ANOTHER RAINBOW (IRE) BHB 63f36a RR 62?f 36a 108[5]

4 br f Rainbows For Life (CAN) 9.3f **(64)** - Phylella (Persian Bold) 9.3f **(66)**
Form - 50835
Record 2000 - 1st:0 2nd:0 3rd:1 Ran:3
Pre2000 - 1st:0 2nd:3 3rd:1 Ran:13
Win Prizemoney £0 *Total Prizemoney* £4,053
2000 AW 0-3: (11f, 12f 2) (Fibr 3)
Workmanlike, average filly, effective 10f, acts on gd, likes left handed tracks. AW high 35.
**Miss Gay Kelleway [0-16] Pot Of Gold Racing.*

ANOTHER SECRET BHB 70f RR 68f 4821[9]

2 b f Efisio 7.7f **(69)** - Secrets of Honour (Belmez (USA))
Form - 4740
Record 2000 - 1st:0 2nd:0 3rd:0 Ran:4
Win Prizemoney £0 *Total Prizemoney* £658
2000 Turf 0-4: (6f 3, 7f) (gd, g-f 2, frm)
Average filly. Turf high 68 (began Aug).
**R Hannon [0-4] Jubert Family.*

ANOTHER TIME BHB 82f84a RR 84f 84a 4380[10]

8 ch g Clantime 6.6f **(57)** - Another Move (Farm Walk) 11.6f **(55)**
Form - 75043520
Record 2000 - 1st:0 2nd:1 3rd:1 Ran:8
Pre2000 - 1st:10 2nd:4 3rd:3 Ran:59
Win Prizemoney £56,086 *Total Prizemoney* £91,452
Wins * 1999 Aug Leices (G-F) H 10f 81 82

* 1998 Aug Lingfi (G-F) 10f 93 <
* 1998 Jun Ascot (G-S) H 10f 87 90
* 1997 Jly Newbur (G-F) H 9f 84 89
* 1997 Apr Pontef (G-F) H 8f 80 84
* 1996 Aug Lingfi (G-F) H 10f 70 77
* 1996 Jun Ripon (G-F) 10f 73

2000 Turf 0-8: (10f 8) (gd 4, g-f 2, frm 2)

Decent gelding, effective 10f, acts on gd to frm, prefers right handed tracks, excels at Sandown, does well at Newmarket. Turf high 84 - 2nd of 9 getting 1lb from Blue Sugar (26 Aug Newmarket 10f g-f RF 3991). Consistent. He is suited by coming off a fast pace and rather needs things his own way.

**S P C Woods [10-63] W J P Jackson (from Miss S E Hall [0-5] May 1995).*

ANOTHER VICTIM BHB 40f RR 43f 2928[10]

6 ch g Beveled (USA) 6.9f **(64)** - Ragtime Rose (Ragstone) 9.6f **(59)**

Form - 00387820

Record 2000 - 1st:0 2nd:1 3rd:1 Ran:8
Pre2000 - 1st:0 2nd:0 3rd:0 Ran:2

Win Prizemoney £0 *Total Prizemoney* £904

2000 Turf 0-8: (5f 2, 6f 5, 7f) (gd 2, g-f 3, frm 3)

Moderate gelding, effective 5 to 6f, best at 6f, acts on gd to frm, best on gd. Turf high 43 - 3rd of 10 giving 9lb to Doctor Dennis (26 May Brighton 6f gd RF 1458).

**M R Bosley [0-9] John Hughes (from M Blanshard [0-1] May 1997).*

ANSAR (IRE) RR 94+f 4987[8]

4 b g Kahyasi 12.9f **(74)** - Anaza (Darshaan) 9.9f **(84)**

Form - 720118

2000 Turf 2-6: (14f 1-1, 16f 2, 17f 1-1, 18f, 19f) (sft 1-2, gd 1-2, g-f, frm)

Useful gelding, effective 12 to 19f, acts on sft to frm, has worn blinkers, likes Curragh. Turf high 94 - 1st of 9 giving 5lb to Morning Breeze (4 Aug Galway RF 3474a) - also 1st of 8 giving 7lb to Moscow Express (24 Aug Tralee RF 4079a). Consistent. An Irish-trained stayer, he failed by the minimum margin to get up and win the Chester Cup and compiled a hat-trick in August, the first win coming over hurdles. Never made an impression when eighth in the Cesarewitch.

**D K Weld in IRE [3-9] Michael Watt (from J Oxx in IRE [1-7] Oct 1999).*

ANSARI (IRE) BHB 85f RR 91f 1125a[2]

3 b c Selkirk (USA) 7.9f **(76)** - Anaza (Darshaan) 9.9f **(84)**

Form - 322

2000 Turf 0-3: (8f, 9f 2) (hvy, sft, gd)

Well made, useful colt, effective 8 to 9f, best at 9f, acts on hvy to gd. Turf high 91 - 2nd of 14 giving 12lb to Tushna (7 May Gowran Park 8f gd RF 1125a).

**J Oxx in IRE [0-3] H H Aga Khan (from L M Cumani [1-4] Oct 1999).*

ANSELLAD (IRE) BHB 77f69a RR 83f 69a 4537[10]

3 b g Dancing Dissident (USA) 6.8f **(65)** - Dutch Queen (Ahonoora) 8.1f **(73)**

Form - 072500

Record 2000 - 1st:0 2nd:1 3rd:0 Ran:6
Pre2000 - 1st:1 2nd:1 3rd:3 Ran:7

Win Prizemoney £3,533 *Total Prizemoney* £8,846

Wins 1999 Jun Bath (GD) 5.1f 84 <

2000 Turf 0-6: (5f 5, 6f) (g-s 2, gd 2, g-f, hrd)

Unfurnished, decent gelding, effective 5 to 6f, best at 5f, acts on g-f to hrd, best on g-f. Turf high 83 - 2nd of 10 giving 3lb to Bandanna (20 Jly Bath 5f hrd RF 2956).

**A Berry [0-6] Ansells of Watford (from J Berry [1-7] Spt 1999).*

ANSELLMAN BHB 58f78a RR 63f 78a 5068[10]

10 gr g Absalom 7.1f **(56)** - Grace Poole (Sallust) 8.4f **(63)**

Form - 025470145332050

Record 2000 - 1st:1 2nd:2 3rd:2 Ran:15
Pre2000 - 1st:10 2nd:15 3rd:10 Ran:105

Win Prizemoney £40,970 *Total Prizemoney* £99,679

Wins * 2000 Jly Bath (FRM) C 5.1f 56
1999 Aug Bath (HRD) H 5.1f 69 72
1998 May Redcar (GD) C 6f 84
1997 Spt Leices (G-F) H 5f 78 80
1997 Apr Ripon (G-F) C 5f 77
1996 Jly Chepst (G-F) H 5.1f 75 77
1996 Apr Bath (GD) H 5.1f 70 78

2000 Turf 1-15: (5f 1-10, 6f 5) (g-s 2, gd 2, g-f 2, frm 8, hrd 1-1)

Average gelding, effective 5 to 6f, best at 5f, acts on g-f to frm, best on frm, often wears blinkers, likes left handed tracks. Turf high 63.

**A Berry [1-15] Ansells of Watford (from J Berry [8-88] Nov 1999).*

ANSHAAM (IRE) RR 89f 1057[6]

3 b c Alzao (USA) 9.8f **(73)** -Anna of Saxony (Ela-Mana-Mou) 10.1f **(70)**

Form - 6

Record 2000 - 1st:0 2nd:0 3rd:0 Ran:1
Pre2000 - 1st:1 2nd:1 3rd:0 Ran:2

Win Prizemoney £0 *Total Prizemoney* £17,388

Wins 1999 Aug Deauvi (SFT) 8f 89 <

2000 Turf 0-1: (12f) (gd)

Currently useful colt.

**S bin Suroor [0-1] Godolphin (from D R Loder in FR [1-2] Aug 1999).*

ANSHAN SQUAW RR 39f 5100[17]

2 b f Anshan 8.2f **(63)** - Natchez Trace (Commanche Run) 8.5f **(58)**

Form - 0

Record 2000 - 1st:0 2nd:0 3rd:0 Ran:1

2000 Turf 0-1: (7f) (gd)

Currently very moderate filly. **I A Balding [0-1] Dr J A E Hobby.*

AN SMEARDUBH (IRE) BHB 24f RR 25f 4022[11]

4 b f Dolphin Street (FR) - Forest Berries (IRE) (Thatching) 8f **(66)**

Form - 706860

Record 2000 - 1st:0 2nd:0 3rd:0 Ran:6
Pre2000 - 1st:0 2nd:0 3rd:0 Ran:5

2000 Turf 0-5: (10f, 12f 3, 14f) (gd 2, g-f, frm 2) 2000 AW 0-1: (12f) (Fibr)

Little account filly, had worn blinkers. Turf high 36. (DEAD)

**M J Ryan [0-11] & Mrs W J Foley.*

ANSTAND BHB 39f RR 48f 4396[13]

5 b g Anshan 8.2f **(63)** - Pussy Foot (Red Sunset) 8.2f **(63)**

Form - 006000700

Record 2000 - 1st:0 2nd:0 3rd:0 Ran:9
Pre2000 - 1st:2 2nd:0 3rd:1 Ran:19

Win Prizemoney £10,209 *Total Prizemoney* £11,429

Wins 1998 Oct York (GD) 6f 76
1998 May Ripon (GD) H 6f 66 86 <

2000 Turf 0-9: (5f, 6f 3, 7f 4, 8f) (g-s, gd 2, g-f 2, frm 4)

Moderate gelding, has worn blinkers. Turf high 48. Inconsistent.

**M S Saunders [0-14] Earl Toups (from Mrs J R Ramsden [2-14] Oct 1998).*

ANTHEMION (IRE) BHB 70f70a RR 73f 70a 2233[4]

3 ch g Night Shift (USA) 8.1f **(73)** - New Sensitive (Wattlefield) 5.8f **(71)**

Form - 03114

Record 2000 - 1st:2 2nd:0 3rd:1 Ran:5
Pre2000 - 1st:0 2nd:0 3rd:1 Ran:4

Win Prizemoney £6,013 *Total Prizemoney* £7,312

Wins * 2000 Jun Haydoc (G-S) H 7.1f 65 73 <
*** 2000** *May Wolver (STD) H 7f 65 69*

2000 Turf 1-3: (7f 1-3) (gd 1-2, frm) 2000 AW 1-2: (6f, 7f 1-1) (Fibr 1-2)

Above-average gelding, effective 7f, acts on gd - acts on Fibr. Turf high 73 - 1st of 16 giving 21lb to Swynford Elegance (8 Jun Haydock RF 1810). AW high 69 - 1st of 11 from Manxwood (20 May Wolverhampton RF 1353). **P C Haslam [2-9] Lord Scarsdale.*

ANTHONY MON AMOUR (USA) BHB 67f67a RR 70f 67a 4832[19]

5 b g Nicholas (USA) 6.1f **(63)** - Reine de La Ciel (USA) (Conquistador Cielo (USA)) 8.8f **(69)**

Form - 0041713567000

Record 2000 - 1st:2 2nd:0 3rd:1 Ran:13
Pre2000 - 1st:2 2nd:2 3rd:3 Ran:15

Win Prizemoney £16,025 *Total Prizemoney* £21,035

Wins * 2000 Jly Pontef (G-F) H 5f 66 70
*** 2000** Jly Catter (G-F) H 5f 56 71
1998 Jly Southw (STD) 6f 69
1998 Jly Chepst (GD) H 6.1f 56 74 <

2000 Turf 2-12: (5f 2-9, 6f 3) (g-s, gd 5, g-f 3, frm 2-3) 2000 AW 0-1: (6f) (Fibr)

Above-average gelding, effective 5 to 6f, best at 5f, acts on g-s to frm - acts on Fibr, best on frm, likes left handed tracks. Turf high 74 - 3rd of 11 to Ring Dancer (27 Jly Bath 6f frm RF 3150) - also 1st

of 15 getting 2lb from Swynford Dream (5 Jly Catterick RF 2541).
**D Nicholls [2-13] David Faulkner (from W J Haggas [2-15] Oct 1999).*

ANTHONY ROYLE BHB 62f52a **RR 69f 52a** 5117[10]
2 ch c King's Signet (USA) 7f **(51)** - La Thuile **(34f 24a)** (Statoblest)
Form - 6655800
Record 2000 - 1st:0 2nd:0 3rd:0 Ran:7
Win Prizemoney £0 *Total Prizemoney* £885
2000 Turf 0-6: (5f 3, 6f 2, 7f) (gd, g-f 3, frm, hrd) 2000 AW 0-1: (5f) (Fibr)
Average colt, has worn blinkers. Turf high 69 (began Jly).
**A Berry [0-7] Alan Berry.*

ANTICLES (FR) BHB 96f **RR 92f** 4734[10]
3 f Barathea (IRE) - Alexandra Fair (USA) (Green Dancer (USA)) 10.3f **(74)**
Form - 560
Record 2000 - 1st:0 2nd:0 3rd:0 Ran:3
Win Prizemoney £0 *Total Prizemoney* £1,153
2000 Turf 0-3: (10f, 12f, 13f) (gd 3)
Currently useful. Turf high 92 (began Aug).
**Ian Williams [0-3] A Stennett & Mrs J M Stennett.*

ANTIGONEL (IRE) BHB 56f **RR 59f** 1803[12]
3 b f Fairy King (USA) 7.7f **(75)** - Euromill (Shirley Heights) 10.3f **(74)**
Form - 7370
Record 2000 - 1st:0 2nd:0 3rd:1 Ran:4
Pre2000 - 1st:0 2nd:0 3rd:0 Ran:2
Win Prizemoney £0 *Total Prizemoney* £370
2000 Turf 0-4: (7f 2, 8f 2) (sft, gd 3)
Workmanlike, fair filly, effective 8f, acts on sft. Turf high 59 - 3rd of 17 getting 3lb from Bold Raider (24 Apr Nottingham 8f sft RF 0852). **R Hannon [0-6] Stonethorn Stud Farms Ltd.*

ANTINNAZ (IRE) RR 113f 5285a[7]
4 ch f Thatching 7.8f **(69)** - Tootling (IRE) (Pennine Walk) 8.5f **(61)**
Form - 067
2000 Turf 0-3: (5f 2, 6f) (hvy, gd 2)
Group-class filly, effective 5f, acts on sft to gd. Turf high 92 (began Jly). **T Stack in IRE [2-12] Mrs T Stack.*

ANTIPODES (USA) RR 58f 3766[9]
2 gr f Pleasant Colony (USA) 12.4f **(88)** - La Grande Epoque (USA) (Lyphard (USA)) 9.9f **(72)**
Form - 0
Record 2000 - 1st:0 2nd:0 3rd:0 Ran:1
2000 Turf 0-1: (7f) (g-f)
Currently fair filly. **J L Dunlop [0-1] Robin Scully.*

ANTONIA'S DILEMMA BHB 77f **RR 75f** 3345[3]
2 ch f Primo Dominie 7.2f **(67)** - Antonia's Folly **(53f 53a)** (Music Boy) 6.8f **(57)**
Form - 813
Record 2000 - 1st:1 2nd:0 3rd:1 Ran:3
Win Prizemoney £3,477 *Total Prizemoney* £4,657
Wins * 2000 Jly Lingfi (G-F) 5f 67 <
2000 Turf 1-3: (5f 1-3) (hvy, gd, frm 1-1)
Currently above-average filly. Turf high 75 - 3rd of 8 giving 4lb to Soldier On (3 Aug Goodwood 5f gd RF 3345) - also 1st of 6 getting 5lb from Warlingham (1 Jly Lingfield RF 2436).
**A Berry [1-3] Slatch Farm Stud.*

ANTONIA'S DOUBLE BHB 73f67a **RR 75df 67a** 4299[17]
5 ch m Primo Dominie 7.2f **(67)** - Mainly Sunset (Red Sunset) 8.2f **(63)**
Form - 50003002030
Record 2000 - 1st:0 2nd:1 3rd:2 Ran:11
Pre2000 - 1st:4 2nd:5 3rd:1 Ran:19
Win Prizemoney £21,197 *Total Prizemoney* £35,999

Wins	1999	Jly	Newcas	(G-F)	H	5f	74	74 <
	1999	Jun	Salisb	(FRM)	H	5f	66	69
	1999	Jun	Redcar	(FRM)	H	5f	59	61
	1998	Jly	Newcas	(G-F)		5f		61

2000 Turf 0-10: (5f 10) (gd 3, g-f 7) 2000 AW 0-1: (5f) (Fibr)
Above-average filly, effective 5f, acts on g-f to frm - acts on Fibr, best on g-f, excels at Newcastle, does well at Wolverhampton. Turf high 75 - 3rd of 18 getting 17lb from Henry Hall (30 Jun Newcastle 5f g-f RF 2404). He is speedy, but often hampers himself by missing the break.
**A Berry [0-11] Chris & Antonia Deuters (from J Berry [4-19] Aug 1999).*

ANTONIO CANOVA BHB 78f **RR 78f** 3856[2]
4 ch g Komaite (USA) 6.9f **(61)** - Joan's Venture (Beldale Flutter (USA)) 9.7f **(71)**
Form - 30012
Record 2000 - 1st:1 2nd:1 3rd:1 Ran:5
Pre2000 - 1st:0 2nd:2 3rd:1 Ran:4
Win Prizemoney £7,670 *Total Prizemoney* £18,078
Wins * 2000 Jly Newmar (GD) H 6f 70 76 <
2000 Turf 1-5: (6f 1-4, 7f) (gd 3, g-f 1-1, frm)
Workmanlike, above-average gelding, effective 6f, acts on gd to g-f, best on g-f. Turf high 78 - 2nd of 23 getting 11lb from Night Flight (22 Aug York 6f gd RF 3856) - also 1st of 17 getting 6lb from Bahamian Pirate (28 Jly Newmarket RF 3177). Relatively lightly raced, he showed improved form to win a handicap over six furlongs at Newmarket in July.
**Bob Jones [1-9] The Antonio Canova Partnership.*

ANUGRAHA (IRE) RR 148[9]
7 gr g Supreme Leader 10.9f **(66)** - Nanny Kehoe (IRE) (Sexton Blake) 12f **(51)**
Form - 0
Record 2000 - 1st:0 2nd:0 3rd:0 Ran:1
2000 AW 0-1: (12f) (Fibr)
Poor gelding. **V Soane [0-3] I C M (Europe) Ltd.*

ANYHOW (IRE) BHB 67f62a **RR 74f 62a** 4729[12]
3 b f Distant Relative 7f **(69)** - Fast Chick (Henbit (USA)) 9f **(61)**
Form - 741070
Record 2000 - 1st:1 2nd:0 3rd:0 Ran:6
Pre2000 - 1st:0 2nd:0 3rd:1 Ran:1
Win Prizemoney £1,893 *Total Prizemoney* £2,738
Wins * 2000 Jly Lingfi (GD) H 7f 62 74+ <
2000 Turf 1-5: (7f 1-4, 8f) (g-s, gd 2, g-f 1-1, frm) 2000 AW 0-1: (8f) (Fibr)
Unfurnished, above-average filly, effective 7f, acts on g-f. Turf high 74 - 1st of 14 getting 3lb from Toyon (12 Jly Lingfield RF 2742).
**Andrew Reid [1-7] A S Reid.*

ANZARI (IRE) RR 102f 1251a[1]
3 b c Nicolotte - Anazara (USA) **00**
Form - 31
2000 Turf 1-2: (7f, 8f 1-1) (sft, g-f 1-1)
Very useful colt, effective 8f, acts on g-f. Turf high 102 - 1st of 9 from Jammaal (14 May Leopardstown RF 1251a). Not seen again after a game win in a Curragh listed race.
**J Oxx in IRE [3-6] H H Aga Khan.*

ANZILLERO (GER) RR 106f 5211a[3]
3 b c Law Society (USA) 11.6f **(71)** - Anzille (GER) (Plugged Nickle (USA)) 7.8f **(68)**
Form - 383
2000 Turf 0-3: (11f, 12f 2) (sft 2, gd)
Currently Pattern-class colt. Turf high 106.
**D Richardson in GER [0-3].*

APACHE POINT (IRE) RR 68f 805[14]
3 ch c Indian Ridge 7.6f **(74)** - Ausherra (USA) (Diesis) 9.3f **(69)**
Form - 0
Record 2000 - 1st:0 2nd:0 3rd:0 Ran:1
2000 Turf 0-1: (7f) (gd)
Workmanlike, currently average colt.
**H R A Cecil [0-1] H R H Prince Fahd Salman.*

APADI (USA) BHB 64f70a **RR 23f 70a** 1588[13]
4 ch g Diesis 9f **(80)** - Ixtapa (USA) (Chief's Crown (USA)) 9.8f **(72)**
Form - 68000
Record 2000 - 1st:0 2nd:0 3rd:0 Ran:2
Pre2000 - 1st:0 2nd:0 3rd:0 Ran:3
2000 Turf 0-2: (7f 2) (gd 2)
Above-average gelding. Turf high 23.
**W R Muir [0-5] John Mills.*

APLESTEDE BHB 60f **RR 65f** 2951[4]
3 b f Thowra (FR) 11.2f **(47)** - Mummy's Chick (Mummy's Pet) 7.7f **(60)**

Form - 004
Record 2000 - 1st:0 2nd:0 3rd:0 Ran:3
Win Prizemoney £0 *Total Prizemoney* £287
2000 Turf 0-3: (7f, 8f 2) (gd, g-f 2)
Workmanlike, currently average filly. Turf high 65.
**I A Wood [0-3] Brian Cantle.*

APLOY BHB 75f **RR 76f** 4743[8]

3 b f Deploy 11.4f **(67)** - Amidst **(74f)** (Midyan (USA)) 6f **(60)**
Form - 644512268
Record 2000 - 1st:1 2nd:2 3rd:0 Ran:9
Pre2000 - 1st:0 2nd:1 3rd:1 Ran:4
Win Prizemoney £4,582 *Total Prizemoney* £11,275
Wins * 2000 Jly Salisb (FRM) H 7f 65 68 <
2000 Turf 1-9: (7f 1-6, 8f 3) (g-s, g-f 2, frm 1-6)
Neat, above-average filly, effective 6 to 7f, best at 7f, acts on g-f to frm, best on frm, has worn blinkers. Turf high 76 - 2nd of 14 getting 2lb from Cream Tease (31 Aug Salisbury 7f frm RF 4127) - also 1st of 10 getting 3lb from Amoras (28 Jly Salisbury RF 3181).
**R F JohnsonHoughton [1-13] Mrs P Robeson.*

APOLLO BAY (USA) BHB 70f72a **RR 71f 72a** 449[5]

4 b c Farma Way (USA) 12f **(65)** - Ottomwa (USA) (Strawberry Road (AUS))
Form - 15
Record 2000 - 1st:1 2nd:0 3rd:0 Ran:2
Pre2000 - 1st:0 2nd:0 3rd:3 Ran:7
Win Prizemoney £3,867 *Total Prizemoney* £5,002
Wins * 2000 *Jan Wolver (STD) H 12f 67 70+* <
2000 AW 1-2: (12f 1-2) (Fibr 1-2)
Above-average colt, effective 8 to 12f, best at 8f, acts on g-s to gd - acts on Fibr, often wears blinkers (extremely effectively), prefers left handed tracks. AW high 70 (1st run) - 1st of 11 getting 5lb from Failed To Hit (27 Jan Wolverhampton RF 0168). Inconsistent.
**P Mitchell [1-2] The Chint Racing Club (from D K Weld in IRE [0-7] Spt 1999).*

APOLLO RED BHB 50f72a **RR 54f 72a** 2940[4]

11 ch g Dominion 8.9f **(65)** - Woolpack (Golden Fleece (USA)) 7.9f **(74)**
Form - 76131261104
Record 2000 - 1st:3 2nd:1 3rd:0 Ran:7
Pre2000 - 1st:13 2nd:9 3rd:20 Ran:100
Win Prizemoney £44,143 *Total Prizemoney* £63,429

Wins									
*	**2000**	*Feb*	*Lingfi*	*(STD)*	*C*	*7f*		*61*	
*	**2000**	*Feb*	*Lingfi*	*(STD)*	*H*	*7f*	*68*	*77*	
*	**2000**	*Jan*	*Lingfi*	*(STD)*	*S*	*8f*		*56*	
*	1999	*Dec*	*Lingfi*	*(STD)*	*S*	*7f*		*49*	
*	1998	Jly	Bright	(GD)	H	7f	68	72	
*	1997	*Dec*	*Lingfi*	*(STD)*	*H*	*6f*	*85*	*87*	<
*	1997	*Nov*	*Lingfi*	*(STD)*	*H*	*6f*	*80*	*83*	
*	1997	May	Bright	(G-F)	H	7f	68	76	
*	1997	*Apr*	*Lingfi*	*(STD)*	*H*	*6f*	*72*	*79*	
	1997	*Feb*	*Lingfi*	*(STD)*	*H*	*6f*	*60*	*65*	
	1996	*Dec*	*Lingfi*	*(STD)*	*H*	*7f*	*58*	*62*	
	1996	*Nov*	*Lingfi*	*(STD)*	*C*	*7f*		*59*	
	1996	May	Lingfi	(G-F)	H	7f	54	57	
	1996	Apr	Bright	(FRM)	H	5.3f	51	53	

2000 Turf 0-1: (7f) (frm) 2000 AW 3-6: (7f 2-5, 8f 1-1) (Equi 3-6)
Above-average gelding, effective 7f, - acts on Equi, has worn blinkers, prefers left handed tracks, prefers tight tracks. AW high 77 - 1st of 10 giving 24lb to Reachforyourpocket (12 Feb Lingfield RF 0269). **G L Moore [10-54] A Moore (from A Moore [6-42] Jan 1997).*

APOLLO VICTORIA (FR) **RR 104f** 5212a[11]

3 b c Sadler's Wells (USA) 11.3f **(87)** - Dame Solitaire (CAN) (Halo (USA)) 10.6f **(75)**
Form - 2485650
2000 Turf 0-7: (9f, 10f 3, 11f 2, 16f) (hvy, g-s 3, gd 2)
Very useful colt, effective 7 to 11f, acts on sft to g-s, best on g-s, has worn blinkers. Turf high 104 - 4th of 8 to Saddler's Quest (13 May Lingfield 11f g-s RF 1193). Inconsistent. He was beaten a short-head by Grand Finale when 1/5 at Gowran Park on his return, and was a little disappointing in the Lingfield Derby Trial. Lost his way subsequently. **A P O'Brien in IRE [1-8].*

APOLLO WELLS **RR 109f** 2205a[9]

5 b h Sagal Wells - Sharrara (CAN) (Blushing Groom (FR)) 10.3f **(76)**
Form - 30
2000 Turf 0-2: (12f 2) (g-f 2)
Pattern-class colt. Turf high 107 (1st run) - 3rd of 9 to Hamond (28 May Capannelle 12f g-f RF 1634a). **R Brogi in ITY [0-6].*

APORTO BHB 54f **RR 59f** 5008[12]

2 ch c Clantime 6.6f **(57)** - Portvally (Import) 6.6f **(68)**
Form - 803041740
Record 2000 - 1st:1 2nd:0 3rd:1 Ran:9
Win Prizemoney £3,094 *Total Prizemoney* £3,612
Wins * 2000 Spt Catter (SFT) H 7f 51 59 <
2000 Turf 1-8: (5f 2, 6f 2, 7f 1-3, 8f) (g-s 1-2, gd, g-f 3, frm, hrd) 2000 AW 0-1: (6f) (Fibr)
Fair colt, effective 6 to 7f, acts on g-s to g-f. Turf high 59 (began Jly) - 1st of 17 getting 9lb from Blushing Spur (16 Spt Catterick RF 4460). Inconsistent. **D W Barker [1-9] D W Barker.*

APPELLATION BHB 93f **RR 92f** 4550[1]

2 b c Clantime 6.6f **(57)** - Chablisse (Radetzky) 9.8f **(56)**
Form - 6411
Record 2000 - 1st:2 2nd:0 3rd:0 Ran:4
Win Prizemoney £9,116 *Total Prizemoney* £9,403
Wins * 2000 Spt Goodwo (SFT) 6f 92 <
*** 2000** Spt Goodwo (GD) 6f 92 <
2000 Turf 2-4: (5f 2, 6f 2-2) (g-s 1-1, gd 1-1, frm 2)
Useful colt. Turf high 92 (began Jly) - 1st of 6 giving 3lb to Zhitomir (21 Spt Goodwood RF 4550) - also 1st of 12 from Ajwaa (8 Spt Goodwood RF 4300). He missed the break on his first two runs but looked a promising sort when recording a brace of wins in September. **R Hannon [2-4] Noodles Racing.*

APPLES AND PEARS (IRE) BHB 39f37a **RR 39f 37a** 4174[5]

4 b f High Estate 10.5f **(66)** - Tiempo (King of Spain) 7.8f **(52)**
Form - 050077045
Record 2000 - 1st:0 2nd:0 3rd:0 Ran:9
Pre2000 - 1st:0 2nd:1 3rd:1 Ran:12
Win Prizemoney £0 *Total Prizemoney* £1,048
2000 Turf 0-6: (5f 4, 6f 2) (gd 2, g-f 2, frm 2) 2000 AW 0-3: (5f 2, 6f) (Equi, Fibr 2)
Unfurnished, moderate filly, effective 5f, acts on gd to frm - acts on Fibr. Turf high 39. AW high 34.
**M H Tompkins [0-21] www raceworld co uk.*

APPLE TOWN BHB 83f **RR 93+f** 4815[4]

3 br f Warning 8.1f **(77)** - Applecross (Glint of Gold) 9.3f **(66)**
Form - 32114
Record 2000 - 1st:2 2nd:1 3rd:1 Ran:5
Win Prizemoney £11,456 *Total Prizemoney* £13,535
Wins * 2000 Spt Haydoc (HVY) H 11.9f 76 93 <
*** 2000** Aug Bright (GD) 11.9f 76+
2000 Turf 2-5: (12f 2-5) (sft 1-1, g-s, gd, g-f 1-1, frm)
Neat, useful filly. Turf high 93 - 1st of 8 getting 3lb from Mini Lodge (22 Spt Haydock RF 4576). She had little to beat when winning a Brighton maiden, but was quite impressive when following up in a Haydock handicap on heavy ground and may be able to handle a step up in class. **H R A Cecil [2-5] Dr Catherine Wills.*

APPROACHABLE (USA) BHB 35f46a **RR 47df 46a** 3812[6]

5 b br h Known Fact (USA) 8.3f **(72)** - Western Approach (USA) (Gone West (USA)) 6.5f **(75)**
Form - 2472544232422543202336
Record 2000 - 1st:0 2nd:7 3rd:4 Ran:19
Pre2000 - 1st:3 2nd:1 3rd:2 Ran:16
Win Prizemoney £6,419 *Total Prizemoney* £12,939
Wins * 1999 *Jly Wolver (STD) C 8.5f 65* <
* 1999 *Jly Wolver (STD) C 9.4f 61+*
1999 *Mar Wolver (STD) H 7f 49 57*
2000 Turf 0-1: (10f) (hrd) 2000 AW 0-18: (8f 6, 9f, 10f, 11f 4, 12f 6) (Equi, Fibr 17)
Fair colt, effective 7 to 9f, - acts on Fibr, has worn blinkers, favours left handed tracks. AW high 51. A winner three times on the Wolverhampton Fibresand in 1999, he has changed stables since then and, though making the frame on numerous occasions, keeps on finding one or two to beat him.
**K A Morgan [2-8] R G Marriott (from Miss S J Wilton [0-21] May 2000).*

APPROBATION (USA) BHB 52f47a **RR 71df 47a** 5101[20]

3 ch c With Approval (CAN) 8.7f **(80)** - Exotic Beauty (USA) (Java Gold

(USA))
Form - 0
Record 2000 - 1st:0 2nd:0 3rd:0 Ran:1
Pre2000 - 1st:0 2nd:0 3rd:0 Ran:3
Win Prizemoney £0 *Total Prizemoney* £229
2000 Turf 0-1: (10f) (gd)
Leggy, above-average colt.
**P W Harris [0-4] Atkinson, Rodway and Mrs P W Harris.*

APPROVED QUALITY (IRE) BHB 35f **RR 52f** 360[9]
7 b m Persian Heights 10.5f **(61)** - Greatest Pleasure (Be My Guest (USA)) 9.3f **(67)**
Form - 0
Record 2000 - 1st:0 2nd:0 3rd:0 Ran:1
Pre2000 - 1st:0 2nd:1 3rd:2 Ran:14
Win Prizemoney £0 *Total Prizemoney* £1,174
2000 AW 0-1: (12f) (Fibr)
Fair mare, has worn blinkers. Inconsistent.
**M J Polglase [0-1] Dr Frederick Cody (from Ferdy Murphy [0-2] Mar 1999).*

APPYABO BHB 25f23a **RR 26f 23a** 2256[7]
5 ch g Never so Bold 7.1f **(62)** - Cardinal Palace (Royal Palace) 9f **(56)**
Form - 78772136577
Record 2000 - 1st:1 2nd:1 3rd:1 Ran:8
Pre2000 - 1st:0 2nd:4 3rd:3 Ran:27
Win Prizemoney £1,526 *Total Prizemoney* £6,923
Wins * **2000** *Feb Lingfi (STD) SH 13f 28 33 <*
2000 AW 1-8: (11f, 12f 4, 13f 1-3) (Equi 1-5, Fibr 3)
Very moderate gelding, has worn blinkers. AW high 33.
**M Quinn [1-33] M Quinn (from M R Channon [0-5] Aug 1997).*

APRIL ACE BHB 44f50a **RR 40f 50a** 2043[15]
4 ch g First Trump - Champ d'Avril (Northfields (USA)) 9f **(72)**
Form - 000800
Record 2000 - 1st:0 2nd:0 3rd:0 Ran:6
Pre2000 - 1st:3 2nd:3 3rd:4 Ran:26
Win Prizemoney £12,593 *Total Prizemoney* £18,064
Wins * 1999 Aug Bright (G-F) H 8f 54 56
* 1999 Jly Nottin (FRM) H 8.2f 52 49
* 1998 Jun Bath (G-S) 5.7f 70 <
2000 Turf 0-5: (7f, 8f 4) (gd, g-f, frm 2, hrd) 2000 AW 0-1: (10f) (Equi)
Unfurnished, average gelding, effective 7 to 9f, best at 9f, acts on gd to frm, best on frm, has worn blinkers. Turf high 40. Inconsistent. **M Quinn [3-32] John Breslin.*

APRIL LEE **RR 58f** 5320[10]
2 b f Superpower 6.6f **(58)** - Petitesse (Petong) 6.6f **(58)**
Form - 675525283080
Record 2000 - 1st:0 2nd:2 3rd:1 Ran:12
Win Prizemoney £0 *Total Prizemoney* £2,218
2000 Turf 0-10: (5f, 6f, 7f 7, 8f) (sft, g-s 2, gd 4, g-f 3) 2000 AW 0-2: (5f 2) (Fibr 2)
Above-average filly, effective 7f, acts on gd, always wears blinkers. Turf high 71. AW high 49. **K McAuliffe [0-12] E P Jameson.*

APRIL'S COMAIT BHB 42f40a **RR 46f 40a** 3193[12]
3 br f Komaite (USA) 6.9f **(61)** - Sweet Caroline **(29f 35a)** (Squill (USA))
Form - 36853300856800
Record 2000 - 1st:0 2nd:0 3rd:2 Ran:13
Pre2000 - 1st:0 2nd:0 3rd:1 Ran:8
Win Prizemoney £0 *Total Prizemoney* £833
2000 Turf 0-9: (5f 6, 6f 2, 8f) (gd 3, g-f, frm 3, hrd 2) 2000 AW 0-4: (5f 3, 6f) (Equi, Fibr 3)
Leggy, moderate filly, effective 5f, acts on gd to frm - acts on Fibr, has worn blinkers. Turf high 55 (1st run) - 3rd of 10 getting 3lb from Bennochy (29 Mar Catterick 5f gd RF 0544). AW high 47 - 3rd of 7 getting 11lb from Tropical King (20 Mar Southwell 5f Fibr RF 0469). **Miss J F Craze [0-21] K Briggs And Holgate Four.*

APRIL STAR **RR 48f** 4877[13]
3 ch f Deploy 11.4f **(67)** - Cabaret Artiste (Shareef Dancer (USA)) 9.9f **(73)**
Form - 05700
Record 2000 - 1st:0 2nd:0 3rd:0 Ran:5
2000 Turf 0-5: (6f, 7f 2, 10f 2) (g-s, gd, g-f 2, frm)
Scopey, moderate filly. Turf high 48. **G G Margarson [0-5] P E Axon.*

APRIL STOCK BHB 78f **RR 86+f** 2114[14]
5 ch m Beveled (USA) 6.9f **(64)** - Stockline (Capricorn Line) 14.6f **(62)**
Form - 510
Record 2000 - 1st:1 2nd:0 3rd:0 Ran:3
Pre2000 - 1st:2 2nd:3 3rd:2 Ran:12
Win Prizemoney £14,996 *Total Prizemoney* £20,031
Wins * **2000** May Chepst (HVY) H 12.1f 73 86 <
* 1999 Oct Windso (G-S) 11.6f 74
1999 Apr Folkes (HVY) 12f 68
2000 Turf 1-3: (10f, 12f 1-2) (sft, g-s 1-1, gd)
Useful filly, effective 12f, acts on g-s, prefers tight tracks. Turf high 86 - 1st of 4 giving 14lb to Sure Quest (29 May Chepstow RF 1518).
**G A Butler [2-5] Stock Hill Racing (from Miss Gay Kelleway [1-10] Jun 1999).*

APTITUDE (USA) RR 2001a[2]
3 br c A P Indy (USA) - Dokki (USA) (Northern Dancer) 9.6f **(80)**
Form - 22
2000 AW 0-2: (10f, 12f) (Dirt 2)
Currently very high-class colt. AW high 124 (1st run) - 2nd of 19 to Fusaichi Pegasus (6 May Churchill Downs 10f Dirt RF 1154a). He finished second to Fusaichi Pegasus in the Kentucky Derby, and followed that by filling the same place behind Commendable in the Belmont Stakes. **R Frankel in USA [0-2] Juddmonte Farms.*

AQUADAM BHB 30f **RR 30f** 4489[11]
3 b g Namaqualand (USA) - Bahiadin (FR) (Sarhoob (USA))
Form - 080
Record 2000 - 1st:0 2nd:0 3rd:0 Ran:3
2000 Turf 0-2: (8f, 10f) (g-f 2) 2000 AW 0-1: (9f) (Fibr)
Light-framed, currently very moderate gelding. Turf high 30 (began Aug). **B Palling [0-3] Mrs R M Williams.*

AQUARIUS (IRE) **RR 78+f** 2866[5]
2 b c Royal Academy (USA) 7.8f **(77)** - Rafha (Kris) 9.5f **(73)**
Form - 5
Record 2000 - 1st:0 2nd:0 3rd:0 Ran:1
2000 Turf 0-1: (7f) (g-f)
Currently above-average colt. **J L Dunlop [0-1] Prince A A Faisal.*

AQUAVITA BHB 32f29a **RR 23f 29a** 3575[6]
6 b gr m Kalaglow 11.2f **(67)** - Aigua Blava (USA) (Solford (USA)) 13f **(71)**
Form - 0354416
Record 2000 - 1st:1 2nd:0 3rd:1 Ran:7
Pre2000 - 1st:1 2nd:3 3rd:2 Ran:23
Win Prizemoney £3,932 *Total Prizemoney* £7,523
Wins * **2000** *Jly Southw (STD) H 16f 27 30*
1998 *May Lingfi (STD) C 16f 54 <*
2000 Turf 0-1: (16f) (frm) 2000 AW 1-6: (13f, 14f 2, 15f, 16f 1-2) (Equi, Fibr 1-5)
Very moderate mare, effective 16f, - acts on Fibr. AW high 31 - 4th of 13 getting 18lb from Vincent (13 Jly Wolverhampton 16f Fibr RF 2782) - also 1st of 16 getting 29lb from Pipe Music (28 Jly Southwell RF 3192).
**Miss K M George [1-14] Miss K George (from J S Moore [2-24] Spt 1998).*

AQUIRE NOT DESIRE (USA) BHB 50f **RR 48f** 4696[8]
4 ch g Woodman (USA) 9.7f **(77)** - Forladiesonly (USA) (Sovereign Dancer (USA)) 11.2f **(68)**
Form - 58
Record 2000 - 1st:0 2nd:0 3rd:0 Ran:2
Win Prizemoney £0 *Total Prizemoney* £378
2000 Turf 0-2: (8f, 12f) (g-s, g-f)
Moderate gelding. Turf high 48 (began Spt).
**G L Moore [0-2] Brighthelm Racing.*

ARABELLA GIRL BHB 50f45a **RR 48f 45a** 2480[16]
3 ch f Aragon 7.7f **(58)** - Bella Helena (Balidar) 7.9f **(63)**
Form - 0
Record 2000 - 1st:0 2nd:0 3rd:0 Ran:1
Pre2000 - 1st:0 2nd:0 3rd:0 Ran:3
2000 AW 0-1: (8f) (Fibr)
Light-framed, moderate filly.
**J G Smyth-Osbourne [0-1] Mrs F A Veasey (from P D Evans [0-3] Jly 1999).*

ARABESQUE BHB 102f **RR 99f** 4966[13]
3 b f Zafonic (USA) 9f **(83)** - Prophecy (IRE) **(99f)** (Warning)
Form - 3140410
Record 2000 - 1st:2 2nd:0 3rd:1 Ran:7
Pre2000 - 1st:0 2nd:1 3rd:1 Ran:2
Win Prizemoney £21,011 *Total Prizemoney* £26,496
Wins * 2000 Aug Pontef (G-F) L 6f 99 <
*** 2000** May Salisb (G-F) 6f 91+
2000 Turf 2-7: (6f 2-5, 7f, 8f) (gd 3, g-f 1-2, frm, hrd 1-1)
Scopey, very useful filly, effective 6 to 8f, best at 6f, acts on gd to hrd. Turf high 99 - 1st of 13 from Jezebel (20 Aug Pontefract RF 3828) - also 1st of 20 from Effervescent (7 May Salisbury RF 1084). She showed plenty of ability in maiden company, winning at Salisbury, and went on to land a Listed event at Pontefract in August. Six furlongs and fast ground suit her best.
**H R A Cecil [2-9] K Abdulla.*

ARAB GOLD BHB 42f40a **RR 36f 40a** 3908[6]
5 b g Presidium 7.5f **(56)** - Parklands Belle (Stanford) 7.9f **(56)**
Form - 00003031448683400302б
Record 2000 - 1st:1 2nd:1 3rd:4 Ran:19
Pre2000 - 1st:0 2nd:0 3rd:1 Ran:15
Win Prizemoney £1,897 *Total Prizemoney* £4,764
Wins * 2000 *Mar Lingfi (STD) H 6f 36 38* <
2000 Turf 0-8: (5f 4, 6f 4) (gd 2, frm 5, hrd) 2000 AW 1-11: (5f 6, 6f 1-3, 7f 2) (Equi 1-5, Fibr 6)
Very moderate gelding, has worn blinkers. Turf high 36. AW high 51. Consistent.
**M Quinn [1-29] W Trezise (from Miss S E Hall [0-5] Jly 1000).*

ARABIAN LIGHT (USA) RR 5330a[5]
2 ch f Fly So Free (USA) - Heartlight (USA) (Majestic Light (USA)) 10.6f **(75)**
Form - 5
2000 AW 0-1: (9f) (Dirt)
Currently very useful. (1st run) - 5th of 14 to Macho Uno (4 Nov Churchill Downs 9f Dirt RF 5330a).
**B Baffert in USA [0-1] The Thoroughbred Corporation.*

ARABIAN MOON (IRE) BHB 90f **RR 91f** 3155[4]
4 ch c Barathea (IRE) - Excellent Alibi (USA) (Exceller (USA)) 12.5f **(74)**
Form - 035134
Record 2000 - 1st:1 2nd:0 3rd:2 Ran:6
Pre2000 - 1st:2 2nd:1 3rd:1 Ran:12
Win Prizemoney £16,693 *Total Prizemoney* £20,537
Wins * 2000 Jun Pontef (G-F) 10f 91 <
* 1999 Jly Windso (G-F) H 11.6f 78 84
* 1999 Jun Ripon (G-F) H 12.3f 68 80
2000 Turf 1-6: (10f 1-2, 12f 3, 14f) (g-s, gd, g-f 3, frm 1-1)
Scopey, useful colt, effective 10 to 16f, best at 12f, acts on gd to frm, likes tight tracks. Turf high 91 - 3rd of 14 getting 2lb from Rada's Daughter (8 Jly Haydock 12f gd RF 2633) - also 1st of 7 giving 11lb to Mynah (25 Jun Pontefract RF 2266). He scored over ten furlongs at Pontefract, but is better over further and finished third in the twelve-furlong Old Newton Cup next time.
**C E Brittain [3-18] Salem Suhail.*

ARABIAN WATERS RR 50f 3920[7]
2 b f Muhtarram (USA) - Secret Waters (Pharly (FR)) 9.8f **(68)**
Form - 07
Record 2000 - 1st:0 2nd:0 3rd:0 Ran:2
2000 Turf 0-2: (6f, 7f) (gd, g-f)
Currently fair filly. Turf high 50 (began Aug).
**R F JohnsonHoughton [0-2] R Crutchley.*

ARAGANT (FR) BHB 30f **RR 30f** 3085[6]
4 b br g Aragon 7.7f **(58)** - Soolaimon (IRE) **(68f)** (Shareef Dancer (USA)) 9.9f **(73)**
Form - 000006
Record 2000 - 1st:0 2nd:0 3rd:0 Ran:6
Pre2000 - 1st:0 2nd:0 3rd:2 Ran:6
Win Prizemoney £0 *Total Prizemoney* £2,126
2000 Turf 0-6: (8f 2, 10f 2, 12f 2) (gd 2, g-f, frm 3)
Unfurnished, very moderate gelding, effective 8 to 10f, acts on g-f, has worn blinkers, likes left handed tracks. Turf high 30.
**R J Hodges [0-8] R J Hodges (from P W Chapple-Hyam [0-5] Aug 1999).*

ARANA BHB 15f25a **RR 18f 25a** 4328[15]
5 b m Noble Patriarch 12.2f **(43)** - Pod's Daughter (IRE) (Tender King) 6.8f **(54)**
Form - 080006070
Record 2000 - 1st:0 2nd:0 3rd:0 Ran:7
Pre2000 - 1st:0 2nd:0 3rd:0 Ran:10
Win Prizemoney £0 *Total Prizemoney* £143
2000 Turf 0-7: (6f, 8f, 11f, 12f 2, 16f 2) (gd 2, g-f 2, frm 2, hrd)
Poor filly, has worn blinkers. Turf high 18.
**W de Best-Turner [0-15] The Spanish Connection (from D M Hyde [0-2] Dec 1997).*

ARANUI (IRE) BHB 55f48a **RR 54f 48a** 4474[9]
3 b c Pursuit of Love 9.5f **(69)** - Petite Rosanna (Ile de Bourbon (USA)) 10.1f **(67)**
Form - 08350
Record 2000 - 1st:0 2nd:0 3rd:1 Ran:4
Pre2000 - 1st:0 2nd:0 3rd:0 Ran:1
Win Prizemoney £0 *Total Prizemoney* £500
2000 Turf 0-3: (8f, 9f, 10f) (g-f, frm 2) 2000 AW 0-1: (8f) (Fibr)
Workmanlike, fair colt. Turf high 54 (began Jly).
**R Hollinshead [0-5] J D Graham.*

ARANYI (USA) BHB 89f **RR 89f** 4736[5]
3 gr c El Gran Senor (USA) 8.9f **(85)** - Heather's It (USA) (Believe It (USA)) 9.4f **(70)**
Form - 541332165
Record 2000 - 1st:2 2nd:1 3rd:2 Ran:9
Pre2000 - 1st:0 2nd:0 3rd:0 Ran:3
Win Prizemoney £10,874 *Total Prizemoney* £15,078
Wins * 2000 Aug Ripon (GD) H 9f 83 88 <
*** 2000** Jun Ripon (G-S) 9f 81
2000 Turf 2-9: (8f 4, 9f 2-3, 10f, 12f) (gd 4, g-f 1-1, frm 1-4)
Strong, useful colt, effective 8 to 9f, best at 8f, acts on gd to frm, best on frm. Turf high 89 - 5th of 11 giving 2lb to Lagoon (29 Spt Newmarket 8f gd RF 4736) - also 1st of 6 giving 23lb to Wilfram (7 Aug Ripon RF 3431). He won twice over Ripon's nine furlongs last year and seemed suited by bowling along in front on the second occasion. **J L Dunlop [2-12] Benny Andersson.*

ARAVONIAN BHB 76f **RR 72f** 5196[3]
2 ch f Night Shift (USA) 8.1f **(73)** - Age of Reality (USA) **(55f)** (Alleged (USA)) 10f **(76)**
Form - 563
Record 2000 - 1st:0 2nd:0 3rd:1 Ran:3
Win Prizemoney £0 *Total Prizemoney* £641
2000 Turf 0-3: (7f, 8f 2) (g-s, gd 2)
Currently above-average filly. Turf high 72 (began Spt) - 3rd of 16 to Jumaireyah (26 Oct Windsor 8f gd RF 5196).
**R Hannon [0-3] Mrs Perle O'Rourke.*

ARAWAK PRINCE (IRE) BHB 80f **RR 84f** 403[12]
4 ch g College Chapel - Alpine Symphony (Northern Dancer) 9.6f **(80)**
Form - 0
Record 2000 - 1st:0 2nd:0 3rd:0 Ran:1
Pre2000 - 1st:1 2nd:0 3rd:0 Ran:3
Win Prizemoney £2,866 *Total Prizemoney* £3,037
Wins 1999 Aug Windso (GD) 10f 70 <
2000 AW 0-1: (10f) (Equi)
Strong, decent gelding, has worn blinkers.
**D G Bridgwater [0-2] Andy Mavrou (from J Noseda [1-3] Spt 1999).*

ARBENIG (IRE) BHB 50f42a **RR 49f 42a** 5020[6]
5 b m Anita's Prince 6f **(62)** - Out On Her Own (Superlative) 7.2f **(56)**
Form - 03105274826
Record 2000 - 1st:1 2nd:2 3rd:1 Ran:11
Pre2000 - 1st:2 2nd:3 3rd:6 Ran:33
Win Prizemoney £6,633 *Total Prizemoney* £13,174
Wins * 2000 Jun Leices (G-S) C 8f 47
* 1998 May Salisb (FRM) C 7f 60+
* 1997 *Oct Wolver (STD) 6f 77* <
2000 Turf 1-9: (7f, 8f 1-6, 9f, 11f) (gd 1-3, g-f, frm 4, hrd) 2000 AW 0-2: (7f, 12f) (Fibr 2)
Moderate filly, effective 7 to 11f, best at 7f, acts on gd to frm, best on gd, has worn blinkers, and excels at Leicester. Turf high 49 -

2nd of 19 giving 10lb to Priory Gardens (14 Jly Chepstow 8f frm RF 2792). AW high 35. Consistent. **B Palling [3-44] Andrew Smallwood.*

ARC (IRE) BHB 70a **RR 68f** 2327[11]

6 b g Archway (IRE) 8.5f **(60)** - Columbian Sand (IRE) (Salmon Leap (USA)) 11f **(61)**

Form - 24242412010

Record 2000 - 1st:2 2nd:3 3rd:0 Ran:9
Pre2000 - 1st:2 2nd:8 3rd:3 Ran:35

Win Prizemoney £11,079 *Total Prizemoney* £21,877

Wins	*** 2000**	Jun	Carlis	(SFT)	H	8f	64	68+	<
	*** 2000**	Apr	Mussel	(G-S)	H	8f	60	65	
	1999	Jly	Carlis	(GD)		8f		61	
	1999	*Feb*	*Wolver*	*(STD)*	*H*	*7f*	*62*	*65*	

2000 Turf 2-5: (8f 2-5) (sft, gd 1-1, g-f 1-1, frm, hrd) 2000 AW 0-4: (8f 2, 9f 2) (Fibr 4)

Average gelding, effective 7 to 9f, best at 8f, acts on gd to hrd - acts on Fibr, has worn blinkers, favours tight tracks, excels at Carlisle and Wolverhampton. Turf high 68 - 1st of 4 giving 28lb to Nobby Barnes (5 Jun Carlisle RF 1711) - also 1st of 8 giving 7lb to Mr Perry (13 Apr Musselburgh RF 0699). AW high 68 - 2nd of 9 giving 4lb to Danakil (16 Mar Wolverhampton 9f Fibr RF 0451). Consistent. A fair handicapper at around a mile on turf and sand, he has not appeared to stay when tried over further.

**G M Moore [2-9] Mrs A Roddis (from F Jordan [2-24] Nov 1999).*

ARCADIAN CHIEF BHB 25f20a **RR 42f 20a** 4116[18]

3 b g Be My Chief (USA) 10.2f **(62)** - May Hinton (Main Reef) 9.6f **(57)**

Form - 0557000

Record 2000 - 1st:0 2nd:0 3rd:0 Ran:7
Pre2000 - 1st:0 2nd:0 3rd:0 Ran:5

2000 Turf 0-7: (5f 4, 6f 2, 7f) (gd 2, g-f 2, frm 3)

Leggy, moderate gelding. Turf high 42. Becoming disappointing.

**B A Pearce [0-2] J Salter (from K T Ivory [0-10] Jly 2000).*

ARC EN CIEL BHB 69f **RR 68f** 4822[17]

2 b c Rainbow Quest (USA) 11.2f **(81)** - Nadia Nerina (CAN) (Northern Dancer) 9.6f **(80)**

Form - 0640

Record 2000 - 1st:0 2nd:0 3rd:0 Ran:4

Win Prizemoney £0 *Total Prizemoney* £313

2000 Turf 0-4: (7f 2, 9f, 10f) (g-f 4)

Average colt. Turf high 68 (began Jly).

**J L Dunlop [0-4] Philip Wroughton.*

ARCHDUKE FERDINAND (FR) BHB 100f **RR 91f** 4301[5]

2 ch c Dernier Empereur (USA) - Lady Norcliffe (USA) (Norcliffe (CAN)) 14f **(72)**

Form - 0155

Record 2000 - 1st:1 2nd:0 3rd:0 Ran:4

Win Prizemoney £7,020 *Total Prizemoney* £10,862

Wins	*** 2000**	Aug	Goodwo	(GD)	7f	84	<

2000 Turf 1-4: (7f 1-2, 8f 2) (gd 2, g-f 1-2)

Useful colt. Turf high 92 - 5th of 10 to Equerry (19 Aug Deauville 8f g-f RF 3944a) - also 1st of 11 from Tamburlaine (5 Aug Goodwood RF 3397). Got off the mark at Goodwood on his second start, but did not enjoy a clear passage in a Deauville listed event next time. Beaten under two lengths in a Goodwood listed race on his final run. **P F I Cole [1-4] C Wright & The Hon Mrs J M Corbett.*

ARCHELLO (IRE) BHB 45f37a **RR 53f 37a** 2698[10]

6 b m Archway (IRE) 8.5f **(60)** - Golden Room (African Sky) 7.7f **(50)**

Form - 01080730

Record 2000 - 1st:1 2nd:0 3rd:1 Ran:7
Pre2000 - 1st:1 2nd:4 3rd:4 Ran:33

Win Prizemoney £6,481 *Total Prizemoney* £13,572

Wins	*** 2000**	May	Carlis	(FRM)	H	5.9f	43	53	<
	1997	Aug	Ripon	(G-F)		5f		46+	

2000 Turf 1-7: (6f 1-4, 7f, 8f 2) (gd, g-f 2, frm 1-4)

Fair mare, effective 6f, acts on frm, has worn blinkers. Turf high 53 (1st run) - 1st of 15 getting 10lb from Nineacres (12 May Carlisle RF 1167).

**M Brittain [1-19] Robert Cook (from G R Oldroyd [1-21] Spt 1998).*

ARCHIE BABE (IRE) BHB 79f **RR 81f** 5085[1]

4 ch g Archway (IRE) 8.5f **(60)** - Frensham Manor (Le Johnstan) 7.4f **(55)**

Form - 6501710182500381

Record 2000 - 1st:4 2nd:1 3rd:1 Ran:16
Pre2000 - 1st:4 2nd:2 3rd:3 Ran:20

Win Prizemoney £30,538 *Total Prizemoney* £37,672

Wins	*** 2000**	Oct	Newcas	(HVY)	H	10.1f	73	79	
	*** 2000**	Jly	Pontef	(GD)		10f		80	<
	*** 2000**	Jun	Newcas	(SFT)	H	10.1f	67	73	
	*** 2000**	May	Pontef	(GD)	H	12f	63	67	
	* 1999	Nov	Redcar	(G-S)	H	11f	65	66	
	* 1999	May	Pontef	(GD)	H	10f	56	61	
	* 1999	May	Redcar	(SFT)	H	10f	56	63	
	* 1998	Spt	Thirsk	(GD)		7f		75	

2000 Turf 4-16: (10f 3-8, 12f 1-8) (hvy 1-1, sft 1-2, g-s 2, gd 4, g-f 1-3, frm 1-3, hrd)

Light-framed, decent gelding, effective 10 to 12f, best at 10f, acts on hvy to frm, best on frm, prefers left handed tracks, excels at Newcastle and Redcar and Pontefract. Turf high 81 - 2nd of 7 giving 10lb to Sense of Freedom (9 Aug Pontefract 12f frm RF 3503) - also 1st of 6 giving 13lb to Astronaut (11 Jly Pontefract RF 2699). Inconsistent. A fair handicapper, he managed to win four times last season. Effective from ten to 12 furlongs and suited by forcing tactics. **J J Quinn [8-36] Mrs K Mapp.*

ARCHIRONDEL BHB 40f **RR 31f** 5293[7]

2 b c Bin Ajwaad (IRE) - Penang Rose (NZ) (Kingdom Bay (NZ))

Form - 887

Record 2000 - 1st:0 2nd:0 3rd:0 Ran:3

2000 Turf 0-3: (5f, 6f, 7f) (g-s 2, gd)

Currently very moderate colt. Turf high 31 (began Oct).

**John Berry [0-3] D J Huelin.*

ARC ROYAL (GER) **RR 105f** 3158a[2]

3 ch c Big Shuffle (USA) - Alepha (GER) (Celestial Storm (USA))

Form - 2

2000 Turf 0-1: (7f) (gd)

Currently Pattern-class colt. (1st run) - 2nd of 8 to Sunderland (22 Jly Hoppegarten 7f gd RF 3158a).

**C Sprengel in GER [0-2] Frau B Stenzel.*

ARCTIC CHAR BHB 98f **RR 100f** 3362[6]

4 br f Polar Falcon (USA) 9f **(74)** - Breadcrumb (Final Straw) 7.9f **(64)**

Form - 0176

Record 2000 - 1st:1 2nd:0 3rd:0 Ran:4
Pre2000 - 1st:2 2nd:2 3rd:1 Ran:7

Win Prizemoney £25,609 *Total Prizemoney* £39,659

Wins	*** 2000**	May Haydoc	(GD)	L	7.1f	100	<
	* 1999	May Kempto	(GD)		6f	96	
	* 1999	Apr Leices	(G-S)		7f	80	

2000 Turf 1-4: (7f 1-4) (g-s, gd 1-2, g-f)

Light-framed, very useful filly, effective 6 to 7f, best at 7f, acts on gd to frm, best on gd, likes Newmarket. Turf high 100 - 1st of 5 giving 7lb to Selking (6 May Haydock RF 1052). Consistent. She came back to her best when just winning a Haydock Listed event on her second start of the season, but ran below that form on her two subsequent outings. **B J Meehan [3-11] Miss Gloria Abbey.*

ARCTIC HIGH BHB 39f55a **RR 48f 55a** 4551[8]

3 b f Polar Falcon (USA) 9f **(74)** - Oublier L'Ennui (FR) (Bellman (FR)) 8.4f **(77)**

Form - 3230388008

Record 2000 - 1st:0 2nd:1 3rd:3 Ran:10

Win Prizemoney £0 *Total Prizemoney* £1,973

2000 Turf 0-5: (7f, 8f 2, 10f, 12f) (g-s, gd, g-f, frm 2) 2000 AW 0-5: (7f 2, 8f, 9f 2) (Equi, Fibr 4)

Scopey, average filly, effective 8 to 9f, - acts on Fibr, likes left handed tracks, favours tight tracks. Turf high 48. AW high 63. Becoming disappointing. **M S Saunders [0-10] D T Horn.*

ARCTIC OWL BHB 116f **RR 120f** 4520a[1]

6 b g Most Welcome 8.6f **(66)** - Short Rations (Lorenzaccio) 10f **(64)**

Form - 3711

Record 2000 - 1st:2 2nd:0 3rd:1 Ran:4
Pre2000 - 1st:7 2nd:4 3rd:3 Ran:17

Win Prizemoney £272,677 *Total Prizemoney* £342,954

Wins	*** 2000**	Spt	Currag	(G-S)	G1	14f	120	
	*** 2000**	Aug	Ascot	(G-F)		12f	117	
	* 1999	May	Sandow	(GD)	G3	16.4f	123	<
	* 1998	Oct	Newmar	()	G3	16f	120	

* 1998	Aug	Deauvi	(SFT)	G2	15f		115
* 1998	Jun	York	(G-S)	H	13.9f	100	114
* 1998	May	Newmar	(GD)	H	12f	95	99
* 1997	Spt	York	(SFT)	H	11.9f	88	95
* 1997	Jun	Windso	(G-F)		10f		78

2000 Turf 2-4: (12f 1-1, 14f 1-1, 16f, 20f) (g-s 1-2, gd 1-1, g-f)

Very high-class gelding, effective 12 to 20f, best at 16f, acts on g-s to frm, likes Sandown and York and Newmarket and Ascot. Turf high 120 - 1st of 8 from Yavana's Pace (16 Spt Curragh RF 4520a) - also 1st of 6 from Murghem (12 Aug Ascot RF 3581). Consistent. A classy stayer, he bounced back to form to land the valuable Shergar Cup Classic, although the twelve furlongs of that race is a bare minimum for him. He went on to gain Group One honours in the Irish St Leger, getting the better of Yavana's Pace after a protracted duel, before ending his season with a most creditable fifth in the Melbourne Cup. A credit to connections.

**J R Fanshawe [9-21] The Owl Society.*

Arctic Owl, a credit to connections

ARDANZA (IRE) BHB 66f **RR 73f** 4680[2]

3 b f Hernando (FR) - Arrastra (Bustino) 10.4f **(64)**

Form - 24652

Record 2000 -	1st:0	2nd:2	3rd:0	Ran:5	

Win Prizemoney £0 — *Total Prizemoney* £2,330

2000 Turf 0-5: (8f 2, 10f 2, 12f) (hvy, gd 2, g-f, frm)

Leggy, above-average filly. Turf high 73 (1st run) - 2nd of 13 to Revival (18 May Salisbury 10f gd RF 1267).

**B Hanbury [0-4] Mrs Mette Campbell-Andenaes (from Lady Herries [0-1] May 2000).*

ARDARROCH PRINCE BHB 40f **RR 32f** 3314[10]

9 b g Chief Singer 8.6f **(62)** - Queen's Eyot (Grundy) 10.3f **(65)**

Form - 80

Record	**2000 -**	1st:0	2nd:0	3rd:0	Ran:2
	Pre2000 -	1st:0	2nd:1	3rd:0	Ran:4

Win Prizemoney £0 — *Total Prizemoney* £1,159

2000 Turf 0-2: (14f, 16f) (g-f 2)

Very moderate gelding. Turf high 32 (began Jly).

**Mrs M Reveley [1-14] W G McHarg.*

ARDENT BHB 40f43a **RR 46f 43a** 4723[4]

6 b g Aragon 7.7f **(58)** - Forest of Arden (Tap On Wood) 10.3f **(65)**

Form - 2206648005134

Record	**2000 -**	1st:1	2nd:0	3rd:1	Ran:9
	Pre2000 -	1st:3	2nd:7	3rd:2 *	Ran:36

Win Prizemoney £12,418 — *Total Prizemoney* £19,166

Wins	*** 2000**	Aug	Bright	(FRM)	H	10f	42	45	
	* 1999	Jun	Windso	(G-F)	H	8.3f	46	49	
	* 1999	May	Kempto	(G-F)	H	9f	46	50	
	1998	Apr	Bright	(GD)	H	8f	47	54	<

2000 Turf 1-7: (8f 4, 10f 1-3) (g-f 3, frm 3, hrd 1-1) 2000 AW 0-2: (12f 2) (Equi 2)

Moderate gelding, effective 8 to 10f, best at 10f, acts on gd to hrd - acts on Equi, has worn blinkers, favours tight tracks. Turf high 46. AW high 41. Consistent.

**Miss B Sanders [3-24] R Lamb (from C J Bonstead [1-21] Nov 1998).*

ARDUINE BHB 72f **RR 80f** 5135[4]

3 ch f Diesis 9f **(80)** - Ardisia (USA) (Affirmed (USA)) 9.3f **(79)**

Form - 3303384

Record	**2000 -**	1st:0	2nd:0	3rd:4	Ran:7
	Pre2000 -	1st:0	2nd:0	3rd:0	Ran:1

Win Prizemoney £0 — *Total Prizemoney* £3,468

2000 Turf 0-7: (8f, 9f, 10f 4, 11f) (sft, gd 2, g-f 3, frm)

Lengthy, decent filly, effective 9 to 10f, best at 10f, acts on g-f to frm, best on g-f. Turf high 80 - 3rd of 20 getting 5lb from Subtle Power (20 May Newbury 10f g-f RF 1333).

**J H M Gosden [0-8] Sheikh Mohammed.*

AREION (GER) **RR 108f** 2580a[1]

5 b h Big Shuffle (USA) - Aerleona (GER) (Caerleon (USA)) 8.6f **(71)**

Form - 1

2000 Turf 1-1: (6f 1-1) (sft 1-1)

Pattern-class colt. (1st run) - 1st of 11 getting 4lb from Gorse (1 Jly Hamburg RF 2580a). **A Wohler in GER [3-5] Frau M Haller.*

AREISH (IRE) BHB 45f53a **RR 34f 53a** 4763[7]

7 b m Keen 11.1f **(58)** - Cool Combination (Indian King (USA)) 7.4f **(64)**

Form - 20511121356807

Record	**2000 -**	1st:4	2nd:1	3rd:1	Ran:12
	Pre2000 -	1st:4	2nd:5	3rd:4	Ran:32

Win Prizemoney £23,098 — *Total Prizemoney* £29,671

Wins	*** 2000**	*Feb*	*Wolver*	*(STD)*	*H*	*9.4f*	*55*	*57*	<
	*** 2000**	*Feb*	*Wolver*	*(STD)*	*H*	*9.4f*	*54*	*55*	
	*** 2000**	*Jan*	*Wolver*	*(STD)*	*H*	*9.4f*	*48*	*53*	
	*** 2000**	*Jan*	*Wolver*	*(STD)*	*H*	*9.4f*	*50*	*53*	
	* 1999	*Feb*	*Southw*	*(STD)*	*H*	*8f*	*48*	*52*	
	* 1999	*Jan*	*Wolver*	*(STD)*	*S*	*9.4f*		*51*	
	1998	*Spt*	*Wolver*	*(STD)*	*SH*	*12f*	*39*	*41*	
	1998	*Jan*	*Southw*	*(STD)*	*H*	*11f*	*38*	*43*	

2000 Turf 0-1: (11f) (g-f) 2000 AW 4-11: (8f 2, 9f 4-9) (Fibr 4-11)

Fair mare, effective 8 to 9f, best at 9f, - acts on Fibr, has worn blinkers, excels at Wolverhampton. AW high 57 - 1st of 12 getting 28lb from Pantar (29 Feb Wolverhampton RF 0380) - also 1st of 7 giving 8lb to Roi de Danse (3 Feb Wolverhampton RF 0210).

**J Balding [6-26] Mrs J Coghlan-Everitt (from M C Pipe [1-1] Spt 1998).*

ARETHA (IRE) **RR 107f** 5048a[4]

3 ch f Indian Ridge 7.6f **(74)** - Smaoineamh (Tap On Wood) 10.3f **(65)**

Form - 24244354

2000 Turf 0-8: (5f, 6f 4, 7f 3) (sft 2, g-s, gd 2, g-f, frm)

Pattern-class filly, effective 5 to 6f, best at 6f, acts on gd to frm, best on gd, has worn blinkers. Turf high 107 - 4th of 8 getting 7lb from Eastern Purple (13 Aug Leopardstown 6f gd RF 3675a). Consistent. Regularly in the frame in listed and Group Three company.

**J S Bolger in IRE [1-14] D H W Dobson.*

ARETINO (IRE) BHB 76f **RR 78f** 4049[4]

3 ch c Common Grounds 8.1f **(66)** - Inonder (Belfort (FR)) 6.8f **(63)**

Form - 058500264

Record	**2000 -**	1st:0	2nd:1	3rd:0	Ran:9
	Pre2000 -	1st:1	2nd:2	3rd:1	Ran:5

Win Prizemoney £3,321 — *Total Prizemoney* £10,338

Wins	* 1999	Jly	Pontef	(G-F)		6f		83+	<

2000 Turf 0-9: (6f 2, 7f 6, 8f) (gd 2, g-f 2, frm 5)
Scopey, above-average colt, effective 6 to 7f, best at 6f, acts on g-s to frm, best on frm, excels at Kempton. Turf high 78 - 5th of 14 giving 8lb to Shadow Prince (28 Jun Kempton 7f frm RF 2345). He pulled too hard over seven and a half furlongs at Lingfield, and showed speed back over six at Kempton. Has since been ridden more positively, which has seemed to suit him. On a reasonable mark now. **P W Harris [1-14] Mrs A M Palmer.*

AREYDHA BHB 94f **RR 95f** 5228[3]

3 b f Cadeaux Genereux 7.9f **(76)** - Elaine's Honor (USA) (Chief's Crown (USA)) 9.8f **(72)**
Form - 07263
Record 2000 - 1st:0 2nd:1 3rd:1 Ran:5
Pre2000 - 1st:1 2nd:0 3rd:0 Ran:3
Win Prizemoney £7,115 *Total Prizemoney* £12,025
Wins * 1999 May York (G-S) 5f 87+ <
2000 Turf 0-5: (6f 3, 7f, 8f) (g-s, gd 4)
Workmanlike, very useful filly, effective 5 to 6f, acts on g-s to gd. Turf high 95. After trying longer trips, she reverted to sprinting in the early autumn and ran better as a result.
**M R Channon [1-8] Sheikh Ahmed Al Maktoum.*

ARGENTAN (USA) BHB 86f **RR 88f** 3601[4]

3 b c Gulch (USA) 9.6f **(79)** - Honfleur (IRE) **(97f)** (Sadler's Wells (USA)) 10f **(76)**
Form - 220144
Record 2000 - 1st:1 2nd:2 3rd:0 Ran:6
Pre2000 - 1st:0 2nd:0 3rd:2 Ran:2
Win Prizemoney £3,883 *Total Prizemoney* £9,734
Wins * 2000 Jly Doncas (GD) 8f 80 <
2000 Turf 1-6: (7f, 8f 1-5) (gd 3, g-f 2, frm 1-1)
Scopey, useful colt, effective 7 to 8f, best at 8f, acts on gd to frm, best on g-f, has worn blinkers. Turf high 88 - 4th of 13 getting 3lb from Jathaabeh (22 Jly Newmarket 8f g-f RF 3032) - also 1st of 14 getting 9lb from Invader (13 Jly Doncaster RF 2756). Consistent. He has looked reluctant at times and needs plenty of driving, but is progressing well and, having won his maiden at Doncaster in July, looks capable of scoring in handicap company, possibly over ten furlongs.
**J H M Gosden [1-6] R E Sangster & A K Collins (from A G Foster [0-1] Oct 1999).*

ARGENT FACILE (IRE) BHB 87f **RR 94f** 4026[5]

3 b c Midhish - Rosinish (IRE) (Lomond (USA)) 8.8f **(65)**
Form - 220223055
Record 2000 - 1st:0 2nd:4 3rd:1 Ran:9
Pre2000 - 1st:1 2nd:1 3rd:0 Ran:8
Win Prizemoney £2,882 *Total Prizemoney* £14,941
Wins * 1999 Jly Leices (G-F) H 5f 87 <
2000 Turf 0-9: (5f 6, 6f 3) (g-s 2, gd 4, g-f 2, frm)
Workmanlike, useful colt, effective 5 to 6f, best at 5f, acts on g-s to frm. Turf high 94 - 3rd of 18 giving 12lb to Compton Banker (24 Jun Ascot 5f gd RF 2237). He ran a series of good races without reward, and could be best at a stiff five furlongs.
**D J S Cosgrove [1-17] Winning Circle Racing Club Ltd.*

ARHAAFF (IRE) **RR 87f** 1687[2]

2 b f Danehill (USA) 9.1f **(79)** - Mosaique Bleue (Shirley Heights) 10.3f **(74)**
Form - 2
Record 2000 - 1st:0 2nd:1 3rd:0 Ran:1
Win Prizemoney £0 *Total Prizemoney* £1,616
2000 Turf 0-1: (6f) (frm)
Currently useful filly. (1st run) - 2nd of 17 getting 5lb from Volata (3 Jun Newmarket 6f frm RF 1687). Made a debut full of promise in the summer, but was not seen subsequently.
**M R Channon [0-1] Sheikh Ahmed Al Maktoum.*

ARIALA BHB 50f **RR 56f** 5200[2]

3 b f Arazi (USA) 9.2f **(74)** - Kashtala (Lord Gayle (USA)) 8.8f **(62)**
Form - 677372
Record 2000 - 1st:0 2nd:1 3rd:1 Ran:6
Win Prizemoney £0 *Total Prizemoney* £995
2000 Turf 0-6: (8f, 10f 4, 12f) (g-s 3, gd 3)
Scopey, fair filly, effective 10f, acts on g-s. Turf high 60.
**K R Burke [0-6] Leydens Farm Stud.*

ARIES FIRECRACKER (IRE) **RR 24f** 3739[14]

2 b g Petardia 8.2f **(58)** - Red Riding Hood (FR) (Mummy's Pet) 7.7f **(60)**
Form - 00000
Record 2000 - 1st:0 2nd:0 3rd:0 Ran:5
2000 Turf 0-5: (5f, 6f 2, 7f 2) (gd, g-f 3, frm)
Little account gelding, has worn blinkers. Turf high 24.
**J Norton [0-5] J B Thomson.*

ARISTAEUS **RR** 3998[9]

2 b c Mistertopogigo (IRE) - Zealous (Hard Fought) 8.8f **(62)**
Form - 0
Record 2000 - 1st:0 2nd:0 3rd:0 Ran:1
2000 Turf 0-1: (7f) (g-f)
Currently very poor colt. **D Carroll [0-1] Roger Langley.*

ARISTOCRAT BHB 81f **RR 83f** 1219[13]

3 b c Bin Ajwaad (IRE) - Bereeka (Main Reef) 9.6f **(57)**
Form - 40
Record 2000 - 1st:0 2nd:0 3rd:0 Ran:2
Pre2000 - 1st:0 2nd:0 3rd:1 Ran:2
Win Prizemoney £0 *Total Prizemoney* £760
2000 Turf 0-2: (10f 2) (g-f, frm)
Decent colt. Turf high 83 (1st run) - 4th of 16 to Cover Up (10 Apr Windsor 10f frm RF 0653). (DEAD) **R Hannon [0-4] Noodles Racing.*

ARISTOTLE (IRE) **RR 115f** 1863[10]

3 b c Sadler's Wells (USA) 11.3f **(87)** - Flamenco Wave (USA) (Desert Wine (USA)) 9.7f **(80)**
Form - 30
2000 Turf 0-2: (11f, 12f) (hvy, gd)
High-class colt. Turf high 106 (1st run) - 3rd of 7 to Rhenium (23 Apr Longchamp 11f hvy RF 0891a). He looked a high-class staying prospect when beating stablemate Lermontov in the Racing Post Trophy in 1999, and passed the post first on his three-year-old bow in the Prix Greffulhe at Longchamp. Disqualified that day after hanging left, he was well beaten in the Derby. He was subsequently sold to race in Singapore
**A P O'Brien in IRE [2-4] Mrs John Magnier.*

ARIUS BHB 43f **RR 40f** 2792[16]

4 ch g Royal Academy (USA) 7.8f **(77)** - Ville Eternelle (USA) (Slew O' Gold (USA)) 8f **(75)**
Form - 00060
Record 2000 - 1st:0 2nd:0 3rd:0 Ran:5
Pre2000 - 1st:0 2nd:0 3rd:0 Ran:1
2000 Turf 0-5: (6f 2, 7f, 8f 2) (gd, g-f 2, frm 2)
Moderate gelding, has worn blinkers. Turf high 40.
**G G Margarson [0-5] E M Thornton (from P J Hobbs [0-1] Oct 1999).*

ARIZONA LADY BHB 67f66a **RR 71f 66a** 5016[11]

3 ch f Lion Cavern (USA) 7.5f **(74)** - Unfuwaanah **(67f)** (Unfuwain (USA))
Form - 107321570240
Record 2000 - 1st:2 2nd:2 3rd:1 Ran:12
Pre2000 - 1st:0 2nd:0 3rd:1 Ran:5
Win Prizemoney £6,365 *Total Prizemoney* £10,406
Wins * 2000 Jly Hamilt (G-F) H 9.2f 63 66 <
*** 2000** Apr Mussel (G-S) 9f 66 <
2000 Turf 2-9: (8f 3, 9f 2-5, 10f) (gd 1-3, g-f 1-4, frm 2) 2000 AW 0-3: (9f 2, 12f) (Fibr 3)
Leggy, above-average filly, effective 7 to 9f, best at 9f, acts on gd to frm - acts on Fibr, prefers right handed tracks. Turf high 71 - 2nd of 5 getting 5lb from Granted (28 Jun Hamilton 8f g-f RF 2338) - also 1st of 8 getting 5lb from High Topper (13 Apr Musselburgh RF 0702). AW high 68 (1st run) (began Spt) - 2nd of 12 getting 6lb from Just Wiz (30 Spt Wolverhampton 9f Fibr RF 4763). She looked to have improved when scoring over nine furlongs at Musselburgh on her reappearance, but her effort over an extra furlong at Pontefract next time was too bad to be true. Perhaps she cannot cope with genuinely soft ground. **I Semple [2-17] Ian Crawford.*

ARJAN (IRE) BHB 68f65a **RR 71f 65a** 734[16]

5 gr m Paris House 5.9f **(64)** - Forest Berries (IRE) (Thatching) 8f **(66)**
Form - 70
Record 2000 - 1st:0 2nd:0 3rd:0 Ran:2
Pre2000 - 1st:2 2nd:1 3rd:0 Ran:15

Win Prizemoney £7,323 *Total Prizemoney* £10,117
Wins 1998 May Catter (SFT) H 5f 73 81? <
1997 Oct Catter (SFT) 5f 75
2000 Turf 0-1: (5f) (gd) 2000 AW 0-1: (5f) (Fibr)
Above-average filly. Becoming disappointing.
**J L Eyre [0-2] Whitestonecliffe Racing Partnership (from J Berry [2-15] Nov 1998).*

ARJAY BHB 86f **RR 82f** 5052[1]
2 b g Shaamit (IRE) - Jenny's Call (Petong) 6.6f **(58)**
Form - 5621
Record 2000 - 1st:1 2nd:1 3rd:0 Ran:4
Win Prizemoney £3,334 *Total Prizemoney* £4,324
Wins * 2000 Oct Newcas (HVY) 6f 82 <
2000 Turf 1-4: (6f 1-3, 7f) (sft 1-1, gd, g-f, frm)
Decent gelding. Turf high 82 - 1st of 14 giving 5lb to Rosalia (18 Oct Newcastle RF 5052). **Andrew Turnell [1-4] Dr John Hollowood.*

ARKADIAN HERO (USA) BHB 120f **RR 119f** 5327a[14]
5 ch h Trempolino (USA) 11.9f **(77)** - Careless Kitten (USA) (Caro)
Form - 48416120
Record 2000 - 1st:2 2nd:1 3rd:0 Ran:8
Pre2000 - 1st:5 2nd:1 3rd:1 Ran:17
Win Prizemoney £123,940 *Total Prizemoney* £253,521
Wins * 2000 Aug Newbur (G-F) G3 7.3f 119 <
*** 2000** Jly Newmar (G-F) G3 7f 114
* 1999 Aug Newmar (G-F) L 6f 114+
* 1999 Jly Newbur (G-F) L 6f 116+
* 1997 Spt Newbur (G-S) G2 6f 99
* 1997 Aug Ripon (G-F) L 6f 104+
* 1997 Jly Goodwo (G-F) 6f 102
2000 Turf 2-8: (5f, 6f 2, 7f 2-2, 8f 3) (gd 4, g-f 1-1, frm 1-3)
High-class colt, effective 6 to 8f, acts on g-f to frm, best on g-f, and excels at Newbury. Turf high 119 - 2nd of 13 giving 2lb to Riviera (10 Spt Woodbine 8f frm RF 4424a) - also 1st of 8 giving 8lb to Cape Town (18 Aug Newbury RF 3759). Began the campaign as a sprinter, but showed improved form when stepped up in trip. Landed Group Three prizes over seven furlongs in the Criterion and Hungerford Stakes, and ran very well over a mile, just touched off at Woodbine and not beaten far in the Sussex Stakes and Breeders' Cup Mile. Usually held up, he has been slow to leave the stalls more than once. **L M Cumani [7-25] Miss L Regis.*

ARMAGNAC BHB 85f **RR 87f** 4932[14]
2 b c Young Ern - Arianna Aldini (Habitat) 9.4f **(70)**
Form - 64042551280
Record 2000 - 1st:1 2nd:2 3rd:0 Ran:11
Win Prizemoney £3,893 *Total Prizemoney* £10,192
Wins * 2000 Spt Ayr (SFT) 6f 83 <
2000 Turf 1-11: (5f, 6f 1-9, 8f) (gd 1-8, g-f 2, frm)
Useful colt, effective 6 to 8f, best at 6f, acts on gd to g-f, best on gd. Turf high 87 - 2nd of 11 giving 4lb to Soldier On (15 Spt Ayr 6f gd RF 4425) - also 1st of 17 giving 6lb to Second Venture (14 Spt Ayr RF 4382). Not winning out of turn at Ayr, and just beaten there next time. Goes well with some cut.
**M H Tompkins [1-6] High Havens Stables (from D Sasse [0-5] Jly 2000).*

ARM AND A LEG (IRE) BHB 41f41a **RR 41f 41a** 531[11]
5 ch g Petardia 8.2f **(58)** - Ikala (Lashkari) 9.8f **(67)**
Form - 0
Record 2000 - 1st:0 2nd:0 3rd:0 Ran:1
Pre2000 - 1st:1 2nd:2 3rd:2 Ran:26
Win Prizemoney £2,239 *Total Prizemoney* £5,102
Wins 1997 May Yarmou (G-F) S 5.2f 61 <
2000 AW 0-1: (9f) (Fibr)
Fair gelding, has worn blinkers. Inconsistent.
**C F C Jackson [0-2] C F C Jackson (from C A Dwyer [1-26] Spt 1998).*

ARMEN (FR) BHB 72f **RR 82f** 4156[14]
3 b c Kaldoun (FR) 9.9f **(84)** - Anna Edes (FR) (Fabulous Dancer (USA)) 9.4f **(70)**
Form - 220
Record 2000 - 1st:0 2nd:2 3rd:0 Ran:3
Pre2000 - 1st:0 2nd:0 3rd:0 Ran:1
Win Prizemoney £0 *Total Prizemoney* £2,434
2000 Turf 0-3: (12f, 14f 2) (sft, g-f 2)
Strong, decent colt. Turf high 82 (1st run) - 2nd of 7 to Total Care (14 Jun Kempton 12f g-f RF 1966). Runner-up in two maidens during the summer, stamina looks his strong suit.
**M C Pipe [0-4] T M Hely-Hutchinson.*

ARMENIA (IRE) BHB 54a **RR 57f** 5071[2]
3 ch f Arazi (USA) 9.2f **(74)** - Atlantic Flyer (USA) (Storm Bird (CAN)) 10.3f **(74)**
Form - 2143208700702
Record 2000 - 1st:1 2nd:3 3rd:1 Ran:13
Pre2000 - 1st:0 2nd:0 3rd:1 Ran:4
Win Prizemoney £2,847 *Total Prizemoney* £6,412
Wins 2000 *Jan Southw (STD) 8f 65* <
2000 Turf 0-6: (8f 2, 10f 3, 11f) (g-s 2, gd 2, g-f, frm) 2000 AW 1-7: (8f 1-3, 9f, 10f 3) (Equi 4, Fibr 1-3)
Fair filly, effective 8f, - acts on Fibr. Turf high 57 (began Aug). AW high 65 - 1st of 9 getting 5lb from Air Mail (28 Jan Southwell RF 0178). **A G Newcombe [0-8] A Newby (from R Hannon [1-8] Apr 2000).*

ARMIDA BHB 45f **RR 51f** 4965[27]
2 b f Lycius (USA) 8.8f **(71)** - Ma Petite Cherie (USA) (Caro)
Form - 000700
Record 2000 - 1st:0 2nd:0 3rd:0 Ran:6
2000 Turf 0-6: (5f, 6f 3, 7f, 8f) (gd 2, g-f 2, frm 2)
Fair filly. Turf high 51.
**G G Margarson [0-5] Stableside Racing Partnership 3 (from W R Muir [0-1] May 2000).*

AROB PETE BHB 52f40a **RR 63f 40a** 2964[0]
3 b c Robellino (USA) 9.5f **(68)** - An Empress (USA) (Affirmed (USA)) 9.3f **(79)**
Form - 80688
Record 2000 - 1st:0 2nd:0 3rd:0 Ran:5
Pre2000 - 1st:0 2nd:0 3rd:0 Ran:1
2000 Turf 0-3: (9f, 10f 2) (g-f 2, frm) 2000 AW 0-2: (9f, 10f) (Equi, Fibr)
Leggy, average colt. Turf high 63. AW high 30.
**A J McNae [0-6] Paul Locke.*

AROGANT PRINCE BHB 51f **RR 64f** 4320[11]
3 ch c Aragon 7.7f **(58)** - Versaillesprincess (Legend of France (USA)) 9.5f **(61)**
Form - 04316700403800
Record 2000 - 1st:1 2nd:0 3rd:2 Ran:14
Pre2000 - 1st:0 2nd:0 3rd:1 Ran:5
Win Prizemoney £7,592 *Total Prizemoney* £9,312
Wins * 2000 May Windso (G-S) H 5f 53 64 <
2000 Turf 1-14: (5f 1-11, 6f 3) (gd 2, g-f 1-8, frm 4)
Workmanlike, average colt, effective 5f, acts on g-f. Turf high 64 - 1st of 15 getting 7lb from Corblets (22 May Windsor RF 1383).
**J J Bridger [1-19] Miss Julie Self.*

ARONA (IRE) BHB 56f **RR 52f** 5169[12]
2 b f Spectrum (IRE) - Divine Valse (FR) (Groom Dancer (USA))
Form - 7050
Record 2000 - 1st:0 2nd:0 3rd:0 Ran:4
2000 Turf 0-4: (6f 2, 7f 2) (g-s, gd 3)
Fair filly. Turf high 52 (began Spt).
**J G Given [0-4] & Mrs G Middlebrook.*

AROUND ALONE RR 97f 4409a[2]
3 b c Rudimentary (USA) 8.2f **(66)** - Mistress Thames **(64f)** (Sharpo) 7.7f **(59)**
Form - 25122
2000 Turf 1-5: (8f 2, 10f 1-3) (hvy 1-2, sft, gd, g-f)
Very useful colt, effective 10f, acts on hvy to g-f. Turf high 97 - 2nd of 9 to Shibuni's Falcon (2 Jly San Siro 10f g-f RF 2585a) - also 1st of 5 giving 4lb to Fairy Sensazione (14 May San Siro RF 1293a).
**R Feligioni in ITY [1-7].*

ARPEGGIO BHB 74f69a **RR 78f 69a** 4991[9]
5 b g Polar Falcon (USA) 9f **(74)** - Hilly (Town Crier) 10.2f **(55)**
Form - 000410313700
Record 2000 - 1st:2 2nd:0 3rd:2 Ran:12
Pre2000 - 1st:1 2nd:2 3rd:1 Ran:12
Win Prizemoney £13,909 *Total Prizemoney* £20,110
Wins * 2000 Spt Lingfi (G-F) H 7.6f 69 74 <
*** 2000** Jly Catter (G-F) 7f 64
* 1999 May Thirsk (Sft) 6f 72

2000 Turf 2-11: (5f, 6f, 7f 1-8, 8f 1-1) (gd 3, g-f 1-2, frm 1-6) 2000 AW 0-1: (6f) (Fibr)
Above-average gelding, effective 6 to 8f, acts on gd to frm, best on frm, has worn blinkers. Turf high 78 - 3rd of 21 to Norfolk Reed (7 Spt Doncaster 7f frm RF 4284) - also 1st of 17 getting 3lb from Copplestone (5 Spt Lingfield RF 4224).
**D Nicholls [3-18] Lhendup Dorji (from R Hannon [0-6] May 1998).*

ARRAN MIST BHB 60f RR 65?f 5102[9]

2 b f Alhijaz 7.7f **(57)** - Saraswati (Mansingh (USA)) 7.4f **(55)**
Form - 03760
Record 2000 - 1st:0 2nd:0 3rd:1 Ran:5
Win Prizemoney £0 *Total Prizemoney* £328
2000 Turf 0-5: (5f 2, 6f 3) (gd 2, g-f 2, frm)
Average filly. Turf high 65. **D W Barker [0-5] D W Barker.*

ARROGANT BHB 39f RR 41f 3486[10]

3 b g Aragon 7.7f **(58)** - Miss Ark Royal (Broadsword (USA))
Form - 030
Record 2000 - 1st:0 2nd:0 3rd:1 Ran:2
Pre2000 - 1st:0 2nd:0 3rd:0 Ran:7
Win Prizemoney £0 *Total Prizemoney* £533
2000 Turf 0-2: (10f 2) (g-f, frm)
Leggy, moderate gelding, effective 10f, acts on frm, likes tight tracks. Turf high 41 (1st run) (began Jly) - 3rd of 13 getting 5lb from Adriana (25 Jly Brighton 10f frm RF 3089).
**R M Flower [0-9] The Secret Circle II.*

ARTERXERXES BHB 71f75a RR 77f 75a 4196[4]

7 b g Anshan 8.2f **(63)** - Hanglands (Bustino) 10.4f **(64)**
Form - 030044
Record 2000 - 1st:0 2nd:0 3rd:1 Ran:5
Pre2000 - 1st:4 2nd:6 3rd:1 Ran:33
Win Prizemoney £13,585 *Total Prizemoney* £27,136
Wins 1999 Jly Kempto (G-F) H 8f 72 76
1998 Aug Folkes (G-F) H 6.9f 73 76
1997 Aug Yarmou (G-F) H 7f 75 81 <
1996 Apr Folkes (FRM) 6.9f 71
2000 Turf 0-5: (8f 5) (g-f 5)
Above-average gelding, effective 7 to 8f, best at 8f, acts on g-f to frm, best on frm, has worn blinkers, excels at Kempton. Turf high 77 (1st run) - 3rd of 17 getting 6lb from Silca Blanka (11 May Chester 8f g-f RF 1138). Inconsistent. A front-runner, he is suited by fast ground and a mile.
**C G Cox [0-8] S P Tindall & Partners (from M J Heaton-Ellis [4-30] Aug 1999).*

ART EXPERT (FR) BHB 72f RR 74f 5219[5]

2 b c Pursuit of Love 9.5f **(69)** - Celtic Wing (Midyan (USA)) 6f **(60)**
Form - 0225
Record 2000 - 1st:0 2nd:2 3rd:0 Ran:4
Win Prizemoney £0 *Total Prizemoney* £2,940
2000 Turf 0-4: (8f 3, 10f) (sft 2, g-s, g-f)
Above-average colt, has worn blinkers. Turf high 74 (began Spt) - 2nd of 8 giving 5lb to Among Women (19 Oct Brighton 8f g-s RF 5076). **P F I Cole [0-4] Richard Green (Fine Paintings).*

ARTFUL DANE (IRE) BHB 56f50a RR 52f 50a 5072[20]

8 b g Danehill (USA) 9.1f **(79)** - Art Age (Artaius (USA)) 9f **(69)**
Form - 857307110
Record 2000 - 1st:2 2nd:0 3rd:1 Ran:9
Pre2000 - 1st:4 2nd:4 3rd:3 Ran:50
Win Prizemoney £47,184 *Total Prizemoney* £61,571
Wins * 2000 Spt Chepst (G-S) S 8.1f 52
*** 2000** Aug Ripon (GD) C 8f 43
1997 Mar Doncas (G-F) H 8f 72 79 <
1996 Spt Newbur (G-F) H 8f 64 72
1996 Aug Bath (G-F) H 8f 62 66
2000 Turf 2-9: (8f 2-7, 10f 2) (g-s 2, gd 2, g-f 1-2, frm 1-2, hrd)
Fair gelding, effective 8f, acts on g-f to frm, best on g-f, often wears blinkers (effectively). Turf high 52 - 1st of 18 from Ertlon (7 Spt Chepstow RF 4272). Inconsistent. Once a decent handicapper, but had to be dropped in grade in order to regain winning form, landing a Ripon claimer and a Chepstow seller in the autumn.
**C G Cox [2-10] S P Lansdown Racing (from M J Heaton-Ellis [4-49] Aug 1999).*

ARTHUR-K BHB 47f RR 65f 3905[3]

3 ch g Greensmith - Classy Miss (Homeboy) 6.6f **(55)**
Form - 6483
Record 2000 - 1st:0 2nd:0 3rd:1 Ran:4
Win Prizemoney £0 *Total Prizemoney* £607
2000 Turf 0-4: (12f 2, 14f, 17f) (gd, g-f 2, frm)
Workmanlike, average gelding. Turf high 65.
**H Morrison [0-4] Kavanagh Roofing Southern Ltd.*

ARTHURS KINGDOM (IRE) BHB 56f63a RR 65f 63a 3044[3]

4 b g Roi Danzig (USA) 10.5f **(62)** - Merrie Moment (IRE) (Taufan (USA)) 7f **(57)**
Form - 0304463
Record 2000 - 1st:0 2nd:0 3rd:2 Ran:7
Pre2000 - 1st:0 2nd:1 3rd:2 Ran:10
Win Prizemoney £0 *Total Prizemoney* £3,277
2000 Turf 0-7: (10f, 11f, 12f 2, 13f 3) (gd, g-f 5, frm)
Workmanlike, average gelding, effective 10 to 13f, acts on gd to frm - acts on Fibr, best on g-f, has worn blinkers, prefers right handed tracks. Turf high 65 - 3rd of 9 giving 1lb to Swagger (19 May Hamilton 13f g-f RF 1301). **A P Jarvis [0-17] Mrs Ann Jarvis.*

ARTHUR'S QUAY (IRE) RR 514[6]

3 gr g College Chapel - Originality (Godswalk (USA)) 7.3f **(58)**
Form - 6
Record 2000 - 1st:0 2nd:0 3rd:0 Ran:1
2000 AW 0-1: (7f) (Fibr)
Currently very poor gelding. **B J Meehan [0-1] Mrs Eithne Meehan.*

ARTIC COURIER BHB 47f57a RR 42f 57a 3923[11]

9 gr g Siberian Express (USA) 9f **(58)** - La Reine de France (Queen's Hussar) 11.6f **(58)**
Form - 1144140
Record 2000 - 1st:3 2nd:0 3rd:0 Ran:7
Pre2000 - 1st:3 2nd:15 3rd:12 Ran:64
Win Prizemoney £19,807 *Total Prizemoney* £54,684
Wins * 2000 Jly Windso (G-F) SH 11.6f 45 42
*** 2000** *Mar Wolver (STD) S 12f 52*
*** 2000** *Feb Wolver (STD) S 12f 36*
* 1996 Jly Epsom (G-F) H 12f 80 85 <
* 1996 May Kempto (G-F) H 12f 76 80
2000 Turf 1-3: (12f 1-3) (g-f 2, frm 1-1) 2000 AW 2-4: (12f 2-4) (Fibr 2-4)
Fair gelding, effective 12f, acts on frm - acts on Fibr, has worn blinkers. Turf high 42 (1st run) (began Jly). AW high 52 - 1st of 11 giving 5lb to Approachable (2 Mar Wolverhampton RF 0395).
**D J S Cosgrove [6-71] D J S Cosgrove.*

ARTIFACT RR 58f 5129[17]

2 b f So Factual (USA) - Ancient Secret (Warrshan (USA))
Form - 3070
Record 2000 - 1st:0 2nd:0 3rd:1 Ran:4
Win Prizemoney £0 *Total Prizemoney* £450
2000 Turf 0-4: (6f 3, 7f) (sft, g-s, g-f 2)
Fair filly. Turf high 58 (began Aug). **R Hannon [0-4] J C Smith.*

ARTYFACTUAL BHB 48f RR 39f 4680[5]

3 ch c Factual (USA) - Ring of Pearl (Auction Ring (USA)) 8.6f **(65)**
Form - 005
Record 2000 - 1st:0 2nd:0 3rd:0 Ran:3
2000 Turf 0-3: (6f 2, 8f) (hvy, frm 2)
Currently very moderate colt. Turf high 24 (began Aug).
**G L Moore [0-3] Dr Melvyn Walters.*

ARZILLO BHB 48f50a RR 56f 50a 5116[8]

4 b g Forzando 7.2f **(63)** - Titania's Dance (IRE) **(49a)** (Fairy King (USA)) 7.7f **(59)**
Form - 034040305802678
Record 2000 - 1st:0 2nd:1 3rd:2 Ran:15
Pre2000 - 1st:0 2nd:0 3rd:1 Ran:9
Win Prizemoney £0 *Total Prizemoney* £2,136
2000 Turf 0-13: (6f 4, 7f 5, 8f 3, 10f) (g-s, gd, g-f 4, frm 6, hrd) 2000 AW 0-2: (7f, 8f) (Equi, Fibr)
Neat, fair gelding, effective 7 to 8f, acts on frm, has worn blinkers. Turf high 56 - 2nd of 15 getting 11lb from Blakeset (13 Spt Yarmouth 7f frm RF 4378). AW high 33 (began Oct).
**J M Bradley [0-15] M G Ridley & Partners (from S Dow [0-9] Aug*

1999).

ASAAL BHB 89f **RR 85f** 4433[9]
3 b c Machiavellian (USA) 9.8f **(83)** - Rawaabe (USA) (Nureyev (USA)) 8.7f **(78)**
Form - 5600
Record 2000 - 1st:0 2nd:0 3rd:0 Ran:4
Pre2000 - 1st:2 2nd:0 3rd:1 Ran:4
Win Prizemoney £9,883 *Total Prizemoney* £11,310
Wins * 1999 Spt Salisb (HVY) 6f 93+ <
* 1999 Aug Pontef (G-F) 6f 76+
2000 Turf 0-4: (6f 2, 7f, 8f) (g-s 2, gd, frm)
Scopey, useful colt, effective 6f, acts on g-s. Turf high 85.
**B W Hills [2-8] Hamdan Al Maktoum.*

ASAKIR BHB 102f **RR 96f** 3200[9]
5 ch h Nashwan (USA) 10.3f **(79)** - Yaqut (USA) (Northern Dancer) 9.6f **(80)**
Form - 80
Record 2000 - 1st:0 2nd:0 3rd:0 Ran:2
Pre2000 - 1st:2 2nd:1 3rd:0 Ran:3
Win Prizemoney £9,297 *Total Prizemoney* £27,254
Wins 1997 Oct Leices (SFT) 10f 88+ <
1997 Spt Nottin (G-F) 8.2f 84+
2000 Turf 0-2: (8f, 10f) (gd 2)
Very useful colt. Turf high 96 (began Jly).
**M P Tregoning [0-2] Hamdan Al Maktoum (from S bin Suroor [2-3] Nov 1997).*

ASAREER (USA) RR 73f 5098[7]
2 b f Gone West (USA) 7.8f **(82)** - Leo's Lucky Lady (USA) (Seattle Slew (USA)) 9.4f **(76)**
Form - 7
Record 2000 - 1st:0 2nd:0 3rd:0 Ran:1
2000 Turf 0-1: (8f) (gd)
Currently above-average filly.
**M P Tregoning [0-1] Hamdan Al Maktoum.*

ASCARI BHB 55f56a **RR 61f 56a** 4493[12]
4 br g Presidium 7.5f **(56)** - Ping Pong (Petong) 6.6f **(58)**
Form - 8273880
Record 2000 - 1st:0 2nd:1 3rd:1 Ran:7
Pre2000 - 1st:1 2nd:2 3rd:1 Ran.16
Win Prizemoney £3,330 *Total Prizemoney* £8,243
Wins 1999 Oct Nottin (GD) H 10f 55 62 <
2000 Turf 0-7: (8f 3, 10f 4) (g-f 5, frm 2)
Light-framed, average gelding, effective 8 to 10f, best at 10f, acts on gd to frm, has worn blinkers, likes left handed tracks, likes tight tracks. Turf high 65.
**W Jarvis [0-7] M C Banks (from P W Harris [1-16] Oct 1999).*

ASCENSION (IRE) RR 104+f 5203a[2]
2 ch f Night Shift (USA) 8.1f **(73)** - Outeniqua (Bold Lad (IRE)) 8.4f **(68)**
Form - 11162
Record 2000 - 1st:3 2nd:1 3rd:0 Ran:5
Win Prizemoney £39,290 *Total Prizemoney* £46,975
Wins * **2000** Aug Deauvi (G-S) G3 7f 104+ <
* **2000** Jly Newbur (G-F) L 6f 85+
2000 May Leopar (G-F) 6f 81
2000 Turf 3-5: (6f 2-2, 7f 1-1, 8f 2) (hvy, g-s 1-1, gd, g-f 1-1, hrd 1-1)
Very useful filly. Turf high 104 - 1st of 7 from Wooden Doll (27 Aug Deauville RF 4137a). Sold after her winning debut in Ireland, she was an impressive winner at Newbury before taking a listed race at Deauville. Just found wanting in the Prix Marcel Boussac, but ran well at Deauville on he final start. She has a bright turn of foot and should be kept on the right side.
**M R Channon [2-4] N Cheng (from D Wachman in IRE [1-1] May 2000).*

AS GOOD AS IT GETS RR 29f 4828[17]
2 b f Alhijaz 7.7f **(57)** - Iota **(53f 46a)** (Niniski (USA)) 10.6f **(65)**
Form - 0
Record 2000 - 1st:0 2nd:0 3rd:0 Ran:1
2000 Turf 0-1: (8f) (g-s)
Currently little account filly.
**C Smith [0-1] Mrs S V Hansell.*

ASH RR 20f 5318[18]
2 b f Salse (USA) 10.9f **(71)** - Thundercloud (Electric) 10.1f **(61)**
Form - 0
Record 2000 - 1st:0 2nd:0 3rd:0 Ran:1
2000 Turf 0-1: (6f) (sft)
Currently little account filly. **L M Cumani [0-1] L Marinopoulos.*

ASHA FALLS BHB 50a **RR 58f 50a** 5065[9]
2 ch c River Falls 8.2f **(56)** - Saint Navarro (Raga Navarro (ITY)) 8f **(64)**
Form - 0
Record 2000 - 1st:0 2nd:0 3rd:0 Ran:1
2000 Turf 0-1: (8f) (g-s)
Currently fair colt. **B Palling [0-1] S R Carter.*

ASH BOLD (IRE) BHB 39f49a **RR 45f 49a** 5005[8]
3 ch g Persian Bold 10f **(69)** - Pasadena Lady (Captain James) 5f **(59)**
Form - 708
Record 2000 - 1st:0 2nd:0 3rd:0 Ran:2
Pre2000 - 1st:0 2nd:0 3rd:0 Ran:3
2000 Turf 0-1: (8f) (g-s) 2000 AW 0-1: (6f) (Fibr)
Workmanlike, moderate gelding.
**R M Whitaker [0-5] Harvey Ashworth.*

ASHGAR (USA) BHB 80f **RR 103f** 4469[6]
4 ch c Bien Bien (USA) - Ardisia (USA) (Affirmed (USA)) 9.3f **(79)**
Form - 756404866
Record 2000 - 1st:0 2nd:0 3rd:0 Ran:9
Pre2000 - 1st:1 2nd:1 3rd:1 Ran:6
Win Prizemoney £3,057 *Total Prizemoney* £10,359
Wins * 1999 Jun Redcar (FRM) 14.1f 86 <
2000 Turf 0-9: (12f, 13f 2, 14f, 16f 4, 20f) (hvy, g-s 2, gd, g-f 4, frm)
Leggy, very useful colt, effective 16f, acts on g-s to g-f, has worn blinkers, likes left handed tracks. Turf high 103 - 4th of 6 getting 6lb from Amilynx (21 May Longchamp 16f g-s RF 1451a). Becoming disappointing. He put in a couple of useful efforts in '99, notably when a very creditable fourth in York's Lonsdale Stakes over two miles, but showed little in the face of some stiff tasks last season. **C E Brittain [1-15] Prince Abdul Aziz Bin Saud.*

ASH HAB (USA) BHB 66f **RR 66f** 4191[12]
2 b c A P Indy (USA) - Histoire (FR) (Riverman (USA)) 9.1f **(76)**
Form - 700
Record 2000 - 1st:0 2nd:0 3rd:0 Ran:3
2000 Turf 0-3: (7f 2, 8f) (g-f, frm 2)
Currently average colt. Turf high 66 (began Jly).
**J L Dunlop [0-3] Hamdan Al Maktoum.*

ASHKAAL (IRE) RR 48f 4828[9]
2 b c Sheikh Albadou 9.2f **(75)** - Three Piece (Jaazeiro (USA)) 9.2f **(54)**
Form - 00
Record 2000 - 1st:0 2nd:0 3rd:0 Ran:2
2000 Turf 0-2: (8f 2) (g-s, gd)
Currently moderate colt. Turf high 48 (began Spt).
**M R Channon [0-2] Sheikh Ahmed Al Maktoum.*

ASHLEEN BHB 60f **RR 58f** 4227[16]
3 ch f Chilibang 7f **(55)** - Bergliot (Governor General)
Form - 4700
Record 2000 - 1st:0 2nd:0 3rd:0 Ran:4
Win Prizemoney £0 *Total Prizemoney* £275
2000 Turf 0-4: (6f 2, 7f 2) (gd, frm 3)
Scopey, fair filly. Turf high 58 (began Jly).
**V Soane [0-4] Mrs C L Rivenaes.*

ASHLEIGH BAKER (IRE) BHB 45f43a **RR 52f 43a** 4750[6]
5 b br m Don't Forget Me 9.5f **(66)** - Gayla Orchestra (Lord Gayle (USA)) 8.8f **(62)**
Form - 64737161244056
Record 2000 - 1st:2 2nd:1 3rd:1 Ran:14
Pre2000 - 1st:1 2nd:0 3rd:2 Ran:18
Win Prizemoney £8,367 *Total Prizemoney* £11,607
Wins * **2000** Jly Hamilt (G-F) H 12.1f 42 49
* **2000** Jly Mussel (G-S) H 12f 43 44+
1998 Jly Ayr (SFT) H 10.9f 60 66 <
2000 Turf 2-14: (9f, 10f 3, 12f 2-7, 14f 2, 16f) (gd 1-6, g-f 1-3, frm 5)
Fair filly, effective 8 to 12f, acts on gd to frm, best on frm, has worn blinkers, prefers right handed tracks, excels at Musselburgh.

Turf high 53 - 4th of 12 getting 7lb from Dark Shadows (7 Aug Ripon 12f frm RF 3430) - also 1st of 6 getting 11lb from Little John (20 Jly Hamilton RF 2970). Consistent.
**M Johnston [2-20] The David James Partnership (from A Bailey [1-12] Nov 1998).*

ASHLINN (IRE) BHB 89f RR 80f 4990[14]
2 ch f Ashkalani (IRE) - Always Far (USA) (Alydar (USA)) 9.1f **(76)**
Form - 2170
Record 2000 - 1st:1 2nd:1 3rd:0 Ran:4
Win Prizemoney £4,065 *Total Prizemoney* £5,577
Wins * 2000 Aug Newmar (G-F) 7f 79 <
2000 Turf 1-4: (6f, 7f 1-3) (gd, g-f 1-3)
Decent filly. Turf high 80 (1st run) (began Jun) - 2nd of 8 to Enthused (30 Jun Newmarket 6f g-f RF 2410) - also 1st of 9 from Nafisah (18 Aug Newmarket RF 3766). Went down by the minimum margin to Enthused on her debut, and made all at Newmarket next time. Fair effort in a Listed race.
**S Dow [1-4] R E Anderson, J M Connolly & W Thornton.*

ASH MOON (IRE) BHB 97f RR 88f 4965[10]
2 ch f General Monash (USA) - Jarmar Moon **(55f)** (Unfuwain (USA))
Form - 1103720
Record 2000 - 1st:2 2nd:1 3rd:1 Ran:7
Win Prizemoney £7,754 *Total Prizemoney* £13,248
Wins * 2000 Jun Carlis (FRM) 5.9f 77+
*** 2000** May Haydoc (SFT) 5f 79 <
2000 Turf 2-7: (5f 1-1, 6f 1-6) (g-s 1-1, gd 4, g-f 1-1, frm)
Useful filly, effective 5 to 6f, acts on g-s to gd. Turf high 88 - also 1st of 9 from Fair Princess (27 May Haydock RF 1494). Winner of ordinary events at Haydock and Carlisle on her first two starts, but has struggled since taking on rather better company.
**K R Burke [2-7] David Morgan.*

ASHNAYA (FR) RR 55f 5236[12]
2 b f Ashkalani (IRE) - Upend (Main Reef) 9.6f **(57)**
Form - 0
Record 2000 - 1st:0 2nd:0 3rd:0 Ran:1
2000 Turf 0-1: (7f) (g-s)
Currently fair filly. **J L Dunlop [0-1] George Galazka & Robert Scott.*

ASHOVER AMBER BHB 73f67a RR 67f 67a 511[4]
4 b f Green Desert (USA) 7.8f **(78)** - Zafaaf **(98df)** (Kris) 9.5f **(73)**
Form - 45234
Record 2000 - 1st:0 2nd:1 3rd:1 Ran:5
Pre2000 - 1st:3 2nd:1 3rd:4 Ran:13
Win Prizemoney £9,109 *Total Prizemoney* £13,318
Wins * 1999 Jly Carlis (FRM) 5f 67
* 1999 Jun Carlis (G-F) H 5f 61 64
* 1999 *Feb Southw (STD) 6f 69* <
2000 AW 0-5: (5f 3, 6f 2) (Equi, Fibr 4)
Strong, average filly, effective 5 to 6f, best at 6f, acts on frm to hrd - acts on Fibr, likes left handed tracks, likes tight tracks, and excels at Carlisle. AW high 67 (1st run) - 4th of 9 giving 7lb to Days of Grace (7 Jan Southwell 6f Fibr RF 0041). Consistent.
**T D Barron [3-18] Timothy Cox.*

ASHVILLE LAD BHB 30f RR 3831[19]
3 b c Bigstone (IRE) - Hooray Lady (Ahonoora) 8.1f **(73)**
Form - 0
Record 2000 - 1st:0 2nd:0 3rd:0 Ran:1
2000 Turf 0-1: (8f) (hrd)
Workmanlike, currently poor colt.
**B A McMahon [0-1] Mrs Rita Gibson.*

ASIAN HEIGHTS RR 83+f 5151[1]
2 b c Hernando (FR) - Miss Rinjani **(88f)** (Shirley Heights) 10.3f **(74)**
Form - 1
Record 2000 - 1st:1 2nd:0 3rd:0 Ran:1
Win Prizemoney £3,549 *Total Prizemoney* £3,549
Wins * 2000 Oct Lingfi (HVY) 7f 83+ <
2000 Turf 1-1: (7f 1-1) (g-s 1-1)
Currently decent colt. (1st run) - 1st of 18 from Wannabe Around (23 Oct Lingfield RF 5151). **G Wragg [1-1] J L C Pearce.*

ASKHAM (USA) RR 75f 4607[3]
2 b c El Gran Senor (USA) 8.9f **(85)** - Konvincha (USA) (Cormorant (USA)) 8.2f **(104)**
Form - 3
Record 2000 - 1st:0 2nd:0 3rd:1 Ran:1
Win Prizemoney £0 *Total Prizemoney* £2,282
2000 Turf 0-1: (7f) (g-s)
Currently above-average colt. (1st run) - 3rd of 8 to Lunar Crystal (24 Spt Ascot 7f g-s RF 4607). Very promising debut at Ascot.
**L M Cumani [0-1] M J Dawson.*

ASLY (USA) BHB 100f RR 108+f 4633[7]
3 b br c Riverman (USA) 9.7f **(78)** - La Pepite (USA) (Mr Prospector (USA)) 8.8f **(78)**
Form - 21187
Record 2000 - 1st:2 2nd:1 3rd:0 Ran:5
Win Prizemoney £16,750 *Total Prizemoney* £18,350
Wins * 2000 Jly Ascot (G-F) 10f 108+ <
*** 2000** Jun York (G-F) 7.9f 88+
2000 Turf 2-5: (8f 1-3, 9f, 10f 1-1) (g-s, gd, g-f 2-2, frm)
Well made, Pattern-class colt. Turf high 108 - 1st of 5 giving 3lb to Hiddnah (30 Jly Ascot RF 3228). Landed an ordinary York maiden before winning a five-runner Ascot classified stakes. Not disgraced in a listed race before disappointing in soft ground on his final start. **Sir Michael Stoute [2-5] Hamdan Al Maktoum.*

ASPIRANT DANCER BHB 64f69a RR 71f 69a 5322[4]
5 b g Marju (IRE) 9.2f **(76)** - Fairy Ballerina (Fairy King (USA)) 7.7f **(59)**
Form - 074
Record 2000 - 1st:0 2nd:0 3rd:0 Ran:3
Pre2000 - 1st:6 2nd:4 3rd:3 Ran:24
Win Prizemoney £30,189 *Total Prizemoney* £37,695
Wins * 1999 Spt Pontef (GD) 10f 71+ <
* 1999 Jly Pontef (G-S) 10f 71+ <
* 1999 Apr Pontef (G-S) H 10f 63 69+
* 1998 May Haydoc (GD) H 10.5f 65 69
* 1998 Apr Folkes (SFT) H 9.7f 57 63
* 1998 *Apr Southw (STD) H 11f 49 63*
2000 Turf 0-3: (10f 2, 17f) (sft, g-s, g-f)
Above-average gelding, effective 10 to 12f, best at 10f, acts on gd to frm - acts on Fibr, likes tight tracks, likes Pontefract. Turf high 62 (began Spt). **M L W Bell [6-27] Peter Coe.*

ASSURANCE (IRE) RR 48f 5021[8]
3 b c Green Desert (USA) 7.8f **(78)** - Self Assured (IRE) (Ahonoora) 8.1f **(73)**
Form - 508
Record 2000 - 1st:0 2nd:0 3rd:0 Ran:3
2000 Turf 0-3: (7f 2, 8f) (g-s 2, g-f)
Scopey, currently moderate colt. Turf high 48 (began Jly).
**C E Brittain [0-3] Ali Saeed.*

ASSURED PHYSIQUE BHB 53f56a RR 68f 56a 4499[10]
3 b c Salse (USA) 10.9f **(71)** - Metaphysique (FR) (Law Society (USA)) 9.9f **(70)**
Form - 753665567460
Record 2000 - 1st:0 2nd:0 3rd:1 Ran:12
Pre2000 - 1st:0 2nd:0 3rd:0 Ran:4
Win Prizemoney £0 *Total Prizemoney* £595
2000 Turf 0-11: (7f, 8f 4, 9f, 10f 3, 11f 2) (g-s 2, gd 3, g-f 3, frm 3) 2000 AW 0-1: (8f) (Equi)
Scopey, average colt, effective 11f, acts on gd, has worn blinkers, likes left handed tracks. Turf high 68 - 3rd of 11 getting 4lb from Fantastic Fantasy (7 Jun Yarmouth 11f gd RF 1792).
**C E Brittain [0-16] Peter Head Racing Ltd.*

ASTAIREDOTCOM (IRE) BHB 58f65a RR 59f 65a 4993[1]
2 b f Lake Coniston (IRE) - Romantic Overture (USA) (Stop The Music (USA)) 9.2f **(71)**
Form - 4504721
Record 2000 - 1st:1 2nd:1 3rd:0 Ran:7
Win Prizemoney £2,275 *Total Prizemoney* £3,288
Wins * 2000 *Oct Wolver (STD) C 6f 66* <
2000 Turf 0-6: (5f 2, 6f 3, 7f) (gd 2, g-f 2, frm 2) 2000 AW 1-1: (6f 1-1) (Fibr 1-1)
Average filly, effective 6f, acts on gd - acts on Fibr, has worn blinkers. Turf high 59 - 2nd of 18 getting 17lb from Clanbroad (29 Spt Lingfield 6f gd RF 4727). (1st run) - 1st of 12 getting 2lb from Blue Lady (14 Oct Wolverhampton RF 4993).
**K R Burke [1-7] Astaire & Partners (Holdings) Ltd.*

ASTER FIELDS (IRE) BHB 52f **RR 46f** 4182[5]
2 b f Common Grounds 8.1f **(66)** - North Telstar (Sallust) 8.4f **(63)**
Form - 0685
Record 2000 - 1st:0 2nd:0 3rd:0 Ran:4
Win Prizemoney £0 *Total Prizemoney* £226
2000 Turf 0-4: (5f 4) (hvy, g-s, gd, frm)
Moderate filly. Turf high 46. **D Shaw [0-4] J C Fretwell.*

ASTONISHED BHB 95f **RR 113f** 4700[2]
4 ch g Weldnaas (USA) 8.4f **(55)** - Indigo (Primo Dominie) 6.2f **(80)**
Form - 1472
2000 Turf 1-4: (5f 1-4) (gd 1-1, g-f, frm 2)
Scopey, Group-class gelding, effective 5 to 6f, best at 5f, acts on gd to g-f, best on gd. Turf high 113 (1st run) - 1st of 12 getting 1lb from Proud Native (10 Jun Epsom RF 1864). Very speedy off a fast pace, he won in France before a spectacular effort in Epsom's Vodafone Dash. Best effort in listed races subsequently when beaten a whisker at Newmarket in September.
**J E Hammond in FR [2-6] D R Brotherton (from Mrs J R Ramsden [2-5] Oct 1998).*

ASTON MARA BHB 45f40a **RR 67f 40a** 3497[8]
3 b g Bering 9.6f **(80)** - Coigach **(97f)** (Niniski (USA)) 10.6f **(65)**
Form - 787078
Record 2000 - 1st:0 2nd:0 3rd:0 Ran:6
Pre2000 - 1st:1 2nd:0 3rd:0 Ran:3
Win Prizemoney £3,468 *Total Prizemoney* £3,878
Wins 1999 Jun Newcas (GD) 7f 75+ <
2000 Turf 0-5: (11f 2, 12f, 14f, 16f) (hvy, gd, g-f 2, frm) 2000 AW 0-1: (12f) (Fibr)
Strong, average gelding, effective 7f, acts on frm, often wears blinkers. Turf high 67.
**Mrs M Reveley [0-1] Mrs D J Buckley (from M Johnston [1-8] Jly 2000).*

ASTRAC (IRE) BHB 52f75a **RR 55f 75a** 4825[13]
9 b g Nordico (USA) 8.2f **(59)** -Shirleen (Daring Display (USA)) 6.9f **(69)**
Form - 33513007000700
Record 2000 - 1st:1 2nd:0 3rd:1 Ran:11
Pre2000 - 1st:11 2nd:2 3rd:10 Ran:73
Win Prizemoney £106,195 *Total Prizemoney* £121,019

Wins							
* 2000	*Jan*	*Wolver*	*(STD)*	*C*	*6f*		*77+*
* 1999	Oct	Catter	(SFT)		6f		83
1998	Spt	Hamilt	(SFT)		6f		95
1998	May	Ayr	(GD)	H	6f	85	93
1996	Nov	Evry	(SFT)	L	6f		113 <
1996	Nov	Doncas	(SFT)	L	6f		111
1996	Oct	Nottin	(SFT)		6.1f		92+

2000 Turf 0-8: (5f, 6f 5, 7f 2) (sft, gd 3, g-f 4) 2000 AW 1-3: (6f 1-2, 7f) (Fibr 1-3)
Decent gelding, effective 6f, acts on gd to frm - acts on Fibr, has worn blinkers, likes left handed tracks, likes tight tracks, excels at Wolverhampton. Turf high 65. AW high 84 - 3rd of 13 giving 7lb to Daawe (17 Feb Wolverhampton 6f Fibr RF 0298) - also 1st of 10 from Takhlid (27 Jan Wolverhampton RF 0167). An admirable veteran sprint handicapper, he appreciates cut in the ground on turf and goes on Fibresand, scoring in a claimer at Wolverhampton in January.
**A J McNae [2-25] Clive Titcomb (from D Nicholls [2-14] May 1999).*

ASTRAL PRINCE BHB 72f **RR 73f** 5132[5]
2 ch c Efisio 7.7f **(69)** - Val d'Erica (Ashmore (FR)) 8.5f **(65)**
Form - 005
Record 2000 - 1st:0 2nd:0 3rd:0 Ran:3
2000 Turf 0-3: (6f, 7f 2) (sft, g-f 2)
Currently above-average colt. Turf high 73 (began Jly).
**B J Meehan [0-3] Matham Investments.*

ASTROLOVE (IRE) BHB 39f **RR 36f** 5138[12]
2 ch f Bigstone (IRE) - Pizzazz **(48f)** (Unfuwain (USA))
Form - 0
Record 2000 - 1st:0 2nd:0 3rd:0 Ran:1
2000 Turf 0-1: (8f) (g-s)
Currently very moderate filly.
**M H Tompkins [0-1] Mystic Meg Ltd.*

ASTRONAUT BHB 70f **RR 77f** 5101[15]
3 b g Sri Pekan (USA) - Wild Abandon (USA) (Graustark) 10.1f **(70)**
Form - 84122640
Record 2000 - 1st:1 2nd:2 3rd:0 Ran:8
Win Prizemoney £2,834 *Total Prizemoney* £5,725
Wins * 2000 *May Wolver (STD) 9.4f 74* <
2000 Turf 0-7: (6f, 7f, 10f 3, 12f 2) (sft, gd 4, g-f, frm) 2000 AW 1-1: (9f 1-1) (Fibr 1-1)
Scopey, above-average gelding, effective 9 to 12f, best at 10f, acts on gd to frm - acts on Fibr, has worn blinkers, prefers tight tracks. Turf high 77 - 2nd of 10 getting 3lb from Zibeline (6 Jly Chepstow 10f g-f RF 2567). (1st run) - 1st of 11 giving 5lb to Anastasia Venture (20 May Wolverhampton RF 1351). Appreciated the step up to an extended nine furlongs when getting off the mark on the Wolverhampton Fibresand in May, and has run well on turf since.
**W J Haggas [1-8] Highclere Thoroughbred Racing Ltd.*

ASTURIAN LADY (IRE) BHB 92f **RR 88f** 1881[11]
3 b f Zieten (USA) - Thubut (USA) (Tank's Prospect (USA))
Form - 0
Record 2000 - 1st:0 2nd:0 3rd:0 Ran:1
Pre2000 - 1st:1 2nd:0 3rd:0 Ran:4
Win Prizemoney £3,063 *Total Prizemoney* £4,875
Wins 1999 Aug Nottin (G-F) 6.1f 88 <
2000 Turf 0-1: (8f) (frm)
Scopey, useful filly.
**J W Hills [0-1] Mrs Julio Mitchell (from A P Jarvis [1-4] Spt 1999).*

ASWHATILLDOIS (IRE) BHB 67f74a **RR 60f 74a** 5017[1]
2 b f Blues Traveller (IRE) - Reasonably French (Reasonable (FR))
Form - 0581
Record 2000 - 1st:1 2nd:0 3rd:0 Ran:4
Win Prizemoney £2,219 *Total Prizemoney* £2,219
Wins * 2000 *Oct Wolver (STD) 7f 70* <
2000 Turf 0-3: (5f, 6f 2) (gd, g-f, frm) 2000 AW 1-1: (7f 1-1) (Fibr 1-1)
Above-average filly. Turf high 60 (began Spt). (1st run) - 1st of 9 getting 11lb from Foreign Affairs (17 Oct Wolverhampton RF 5017). Got off the mark in a Wolverhampton maiden in October, a race that may be rather hotter than it seemed at the time.
**D J S Cosgrove [1-4] The Cosgrove Group.*

AS YOU LIKE (USA) **RR 95f** 1636a[18]
3 b c Trempolino (USA) 11.9f **(77)** - Duchess Kiss (USA) (Cox's Ridge (USA)) 8f **(68)**
Form - 040
2000 Turf 0-2: (8f, 12f) (sft, g-f)
Very useful colt. Turf high 95. **B Grizzetti in ITY [1-5].*

ATALYA BHB 60f58a **RR 65f 58a** 4474[11]
3 ch g Afzal - Sandy Looks (Music Boy) 6.8f **(57)**
Form - 672452800
Record 2000 - 1st:0 2nd:2 3rd:0 Ran:7
Pre2000 - 1st:0 2nd:0 3rd:0 Ran:3
Win Prizemoney £0 *Total Prizemoney* £2,395
2000 Turf 0-3: (7f, 8f, 10f) (gd, g-f, frm) 2000 AW 0-4: (8f 2, 9f 2) (Fibr 4)
Unfurnished, average gelding, effective 9f, - acts on Fibr, favours left handed tracks. Turf high 65 (began Jly). AW high 67 (1st run) - 2nd of 9 to You're Special (13 Jan Wolverhampton 9f Fibr RF 0080). **G A Ham [0-4] W E Catstrey (from F Jordan [0-6] Mar 2000).*

ATAMANA (IRE) **RR 69f** 4363[2]
2 b f Lahib (USA) 8f **(69)** - Dance Ahead (Shareef Dancer (USA)) 9.9f **(73)**
Form - 22
Record 2000 - 1st:0 2nd:2 3rd:0 Ran:2
Win Prizemoney £0 *Total Prizemoney* £2,430
2000 Turf 0-2: (6f, 7f) (g-f 2)
Currently average filly. Turf high 69 (began Aug) - 2nd of 12 to Love Everlasting (13 Spt Beverley 7f g-f RF 4363).
**M P Tregoning [0-2] Sheikh Ahmed Al Maktoum.*

ATAVUS BHB 78f **RR 84f** 5240[7]
3 b c Distant Relative 7f **(69)** - Elysian (Northfields (USA)) 9f **(72)**
Form - 4183580077
Record 2000 - 1st:1 2nd:0 3rd:1 Ran:10

Pre2000 - 1st:1 2nd:0 3rd:1 Ran:3
Win Prizemoney £19,174 *Total Prizemoney* £31,898
Wins 2000 May Newmar (GD) H 8f 79 84 <
1999 Oct Lingfi (G-F) 7f 75+
2000 Turf 1-10: (8f 1-7, 9f 3) (g-s 2, gd 2, g-f 4, frm 1-2)
Neat, decent colt, effective 6 to 9f, best at 8f, acts on gd to frm. Turf high 87 - 3rd of 13 getting 4lb from Jathaabeh (22 Jly Newmarket 8f g-f RF 3032) - also 1st of 28 getting 6lb from Red N' Socks (7 May Newmarket RF 1078). Consistent. Gained a battling victory over a big field in a Newmarket handicap in May. Suited by a mile and fast ground.
**G G Margarson [0-7] Stableside Racing Partnership II (from W R Muir [2-6] May 2000).*

A TEEN BHB 59a RR 59a 2174[7]

2 ch c Presidium 7.5f **(56)** - Very Good (Noalto) 5.7f **(49)**
Form - 7
Record 2000 - 1st:0 2nd:0 3rd:0 Ran:1
2000 AW 0-1: (6f) (Fibr)
Currently fair colt. **C N Allen [0-1] Mrs A K Petersen.*

ATEMME BHB 51f RR 49f 4822[21]

2 b f Up and At 'em - Petersford Girl (IRE) **(70f)** (Taufan (USA)) 7f **(57)**
Form - 037R00
Record 2000 - 1st:0 2nd:0 3rd:1 Ran:6
Win Prizemoney £0 *Total Prizemoney* £590
2000 Turf 0-6: (5f 3, 6f 2, 10f) (gd, g-f 3, frm 2)
Moderate filly, has worn blinkers. Turf high 49 (began Jly). She has given problems at the start several times.
**Miss Jacqueline Doyle [0-6] The Hopeful Seven Partnership.*

ATHLETIC SAM (IRE) RR 48f 4969[27]

2 b c Definite Article - No Hard Feelings (IRE) (Alzao (USA)) 7.1f **(68)**
Form - 0
Record 2000 - 1st:0 2nd:0 3rd:0 Ran:1
2000 Turf 0-1: (8f) (gd)
Currently moderate colt. **T G Mills [0-1] J E Harley.*

ATLANTIC ACE BHB 73f RR 80?f 5316[18]

3 b g First Trump - Risalah **(37f)** (Marju (IRE))
Form - 180
Record 2000 - 1st:1 2nd:0 3rd:0 Ran:3
Pre2000 - 1st:0 2nd:0 3rd:0 Ran:1
Win Prizemoney £2,912 *Total Prizemoney* £2,912
Wins * 2000 Oct Pontef (HVY) 8f 80? <
2000 Turf 1-3: (8f 1-3) (g-s 1-3)
Unfurnished, decent gelding. Turf high 80 (1st run) (began Oct) - 1st of 8 giving 5lb to Dena (2 Oct Pontefract RF 4769).
**B Smart [1-4] Richard Page.*

ATLANTIC CHARTER (USA) BHB 55f65a RR 62f 65a 4538[9]

4 b g Gone West (USA) 7.8f **(82)** - Silk Slippers (USA) (Nureyev (USA)) 8.7f **(78)**
Form - 065500
Record 2000 - 1st:0 2nd:0 3rd:0 Ran:6
Pre2000 - 1st:1 2nd:0 3rd:1 Ran:8
Win Prizemoney £6,157 *Total Prizemoney* £6,740
Wins 1999 Oct Redcar (GD) H 10f 66 72 <
2000 Turf 0-6: (8f 2, 10f 3, 11f) (sft, g-s 3, gd, g-f)
Scopey, average gelding, effective 7 to 10f, best at 10f, acts on g-f to frm, best on frm, prefers left handed tracks, prefers tight tracks. Turf high 62. Becoming disappointing.
**J J O'Neill [0-6] Strathayr Publishing Ltd (from A G Foster [0-1] Oct 1999).*

ATLANTIC EAGLE (USA) RR 71f 5099[8]

2 b c Mt Livermore (USA) 7.7f **(90)** - Lyphdum (USA) (Lyphard (USA)) 9.9f **(72)**
Form - 08
Record 2000 - 1st:0 2nd:0 3rd:0 Ran:2
2000 Turf 0-2: (6f, 7f) (gd 2)
Currently above-average colt. Turf high 71 (began Oct).
**M Johnston [0-2] Atlantic Racing Ltd.*

ATLANTIC MYSTERY (IRE) BHB 70f66a RR 63f 66a 5052[3]

2 ch f Cadeaux Genereux 7.9f **(76)** - Nottash (IRE) **(72f)** (Royal Academy (USA))
Form - 353
Record 2000 - 1st:0 2nd:0 3rd:2 Ran:3
Win Prizemoney £0 *Total Prizemoney* £985
2000 Turf 0-3: (6f 3) (sft, g-s, gd)
Currently average filly. Turf high 63 (began Spt).
**M Johnston [0-3] Atlantic Racing Ltd.*

ATLANTIC RHAPSODY (FR) BHB 99f90a RR 103f 90a 5240[2]

3 b g Machiavellian (USA) 9.8f **(83)** - First Waltz (FR) (Green Dancer (USA)) 10.3f **(74)**
Form - 1744125605462042
Record 2000 - 1st:2 2nd:3 3rd:0 Ran:16
Pre2000 - 1st:0 2nd:3 3rd:1 Ran:4
Win Prizemoney £46,696 *Total Prizemoney* £79,583
Wins * 2000 May Haydoc (SFT) H 8.1f 86 95 <
*** 2000** *Mar Southw (STD) 8f 90*
2000 Turf 1-15: (7f 2, 8f 1-7, 9f 4, 10f 2) (sft 2, g-s 1-4, gd 5, g-f 3, frm)
2000 AW 1-1: (8f 1-1) (Fibr 1-1)
Scopey, very useful gelding, effective 7 to 9f, best at 8f, acts on sft to frm, has worn blinkers, likes left handed tracks, likes tight tracks, excels at Goodwood. Turf high 103 - 2nd of 30 giving 25lb to Greenaway Bay (28 Oct Newmarket 8f g-s RF 5240) - also 1st of 16 getting 8lb from Vintage Premium (27 May Haydock RF 1491). (1st run). He landed a very valuable handicap in soft ground at Haydock in May, and ran well in a series of warm events later. Capable of winning another good prize on easy ground, although a note of caution is advised in that he has hung on more than one occasion. **M Johnston [2-20] Atlantic Racing Ltd.*

ATLANTIC VIKING (IRE) BHB 82f RR 83f 3796[18]

5 b g Danehill (USA) 9.1f **(79)** - Hi Bettina (Henbit (USA)) 9f **(61)**
Form - 0074040
Record 2000 - 1st:0 2nd:0 3rd:0 Ran:7
Pre2000 - 1st:3 2nd:3 3rd:2 Ran:23
Win Prizemoney £16,747 *Total Prizemoney* £26,156
Wins * 1999 Aug Ripon (G-F) H 6f 85 86
*** 1999** Jly Pontef (G-F) H 5f 80 82
1997 Jun Newcas (FRM) 5f 97+ <
2000 Turf 0-7: (5f 5, 6f 2) (g-f 5, frm 2)
Decent gelding, effective 5 to 6f, best at 5f, acts on g-f to frm, best on frm, has worn blinkers (very effectively). Turf high 81. Consistent.
**D Nicholls [2-16] David Faulkner (from M Johnston [1-14] Oct 1998).*

ATLANTIS PRINCE BHB 100f RR 102f 4610[1]

2 ch c Tagula (IRE) - Zoom Lens (IRE) (Caerleon (USA)) 8.6f **(71)**
Form - 1111
Record 2000 - 1st:4 2nd:0 3rd:0 Ran:4
Win Prizemoney £95,397 *Total Prizemoney* £95,397
Wins * 2000 Spt Ascot (SFT) G2 8f 102 <
*** 2000** Spt Goodwo (GD) L 8f 94
*** 2000** Aug Newmar (GD) 7f 92
*** 2000** Jly Epsom (GD) 7f 74+
2000 Turf 4-4: (7f 2-2, 8f 2-2) (g-s 1-1, gd 1-1, g-f 1-1, frm 1-1)
Very useful colt. Turf high 102 (began Jly) - 1st of 8 from Turnberry Isle (24 Spt Ascot RF 4610) - also 1st of 8 giving 5lb to Chaguaramas (8 Spt Goodwood RF 4301). Notably tough and game, he completed a four-timer with a pillar-to-post win in the Royal Lodge Stakes at Ascot. His second win, at Newmarket, was a comeback winner after his plane crash for Frankie Dettori, who later described the colt as a true professional. Subsequently sold to Godolphin, this scopey individual is a bright prospect at up to a mile and a quarter. **S P C Woods [4-4] Lucayan Stud.*

AT LARGE (IRE) BHB 70f RR 72f 4430[9]

6 b g Night Shift (USA) 8.1f **(73)** - Lady Donna (Dominion) 8.5f **(63)**
Form - 86171070000
Record 2000 - 1st:2 2nd:0 3rd:0 Ran:11
Pre2000 - 1st:1 2nd:4 3rd:3 Ran:18
Win Prizemoney £14,013 *Total Prizemoney* £22,142
Wins * 2000 May Leices (SFT) H 6f 69 72
*** 2000** May Windso (GD) H 6f 66 70
1997 Oct Nottin (G-F) H 6.1f 74 77 <
2000 Turf 2-11: (5f 3, 6f 2-6, 7f 2) (sft, gd 1-4, g-f 1-5, hrd)
Above-average gelding, effective 5 to 6f, best at 6f, acted on gd to frm, best on gd, had worn blinkers. Turf high 72 - 1st of 14 giving 19lb to Blushing Grenadier (29 May Leicester RF 1521) - also 1st of

25 giving 7lb to Blue Kite (8 May Windsor RF 1097). (DEAD)
**W J Musson [2-11] The Square Table (from J A R Toller [0-10] Spt 1999).*

ATMOSPHERIC (USA) BHB 100f **RR 101f** 4862[1]

2 ch c Irish River (FR) 9f **(77)** - Magic Feeling (IRE) (Magical Wonder (USA))
Form - 12101
Record 2000 - 1st:3 2nd:1 3rd:0 Ran:5
Win Prizemoney £50,109 *Total Prizemoney* £51,149
Wins * 2000 Oct York (HVY) L 6f 101 <
*** 2000** Jun Epsom (GD) L 6f 89
*** 2000** May Pontef (SFT) 5f 77+
2000 Turf 3-5: (5f 1-1, 6f 2-3, 7f) (sft 1-1, gd 2-4)
Very useful colt, has worn blinkers. Turf high 101 - 1st of 4 giving 5lb to Nearly A Fool (7 Oct York RF 4862). Made a winning debut, but was unable to concede 5lb to the useful Bram Stoker next time. Landed a listed race at Epsom on Derby day, but finished last in a Group three race. His win at York came in a bog.
**P F I Cole [3-5] Highclere Thoroughbred Racing Ltd.*

A TOUCH OF FROST BHB 80f **RR 84f** 5242[11]

5 gr m Distant Relative 7f **(69)** - Pharland (FR) (Bellypha) 9.8f **(73)**
Form - 1480
Record 2000 - 1st:1 2nd:0 3rd:0 Ran:4
Pre2000 - 1st:4 2nd:1 3rd:0 Ran:13
Win Prizemoney £31,820 *Total Prizemoney* £34,108
Wins * 2000 Jun Thirsk (SFT) 7f 84+ <
* 1999 Spt Salisb (G-F) H 7f 73 79
* 1999 Jly York (G-F) H 7f 71 74
* 1999 Jun Salisb (GD) CH 7f 58 64
* 1998 Aug Salisb (G-F) 8f 68
2000 Turf 1-4: (7f 1-4) (sft, g-s, gd 1-1, g-f)
Decent filly, effective 7f, acts on gd to frm, best on gd, often wears blinkers (extremely effectively), excels at Salisbury. Turf high 84 (1st run) - 1st of 4 from Boomerang Blade (5 Jun Thirsk RF 1726).
**G G Margarson [5-17] Mrs Patricia Williams.*

ATTACHE BHB 107f **RR 95f** 5214a[5]

2 ch c Wolfhound (USA) 7.3f **(71)** - Royal Passion (Ahonoora) 8.1f **(73)**
Form - 2115
Record 2000 - 1st:2 2nd:1 3rd:0 Ran:4
Win Prizemoney £8,570 *Total Prizemoney* £9,648
Wins * 2000 Spt Sandow (G-F) 7.1f 87 <
*** 2000** Aug Redcar (FRM) 7f 85+
2000 Turf 2-4: (7f 2-3, 8f) (hvy, gd, g-f 1-1, frm 1-1)
Very useful colt. Turf high 95 (began Aug) - 5th of 6 to Count Dubois (22 Oct San Siro 8f hvy RF 5214a) - also 1st of 5 giving 8lb to Dilshaan (13 Spt Sandown RF 4371). Gradually improving and has looked pretty good in fast-ground victories over seven furlongs at Redcar and Sandown. **M Johnston [2-4].*

ATTACKER (USA) BHB 38f **RR 24f** 4766[12]

3 b g Defensive Play (USA) - Bold Ballerina (Sadler's Wells (USA)) 10f **(76)**
Form - 06000
Record 2000 - 1st:0 2nd:0 3rd:0 Ran:5
2000 Turf 0-5: (8f, 10f, 12f 2, 17f) (g-s 3, gd, g-f)
Little account gelding. Turf high 24 (began Aug).
**Miss L C Siddall [0-5] Mrs Ann Morgan.*

ATTO (IRE) BHB 45f **RR 42f** 4204[9]

6 b g Mandalus - Deep Cristina (Deep Run) 18f **(46)**
Form - 060
Record 2000 - 1st:0 2nd:0 3rd:0 Ran:3
2000 Turf 0-3: (8f, 10f, 12f) (gd, frm 2)
Moderate gelding. Turf high 42 (began Jly).
**J S King [0-10] S Clough.*

ATTORNEY BHB 82f **RR 82f** 3525[2]

2 ch g Wolfhound (USA) 7.3f **(71)** - Princess Sadie **(75df)** (Shavian)
Form - 0222
Record 2000 - 1st:0 2nd:3 3rd:0 Ran:4
Win Prizemoney £0 *Total Prizemoney* £2,945
2000 Turf 0-4: (5f 3, 6f) (g-s, gd, frm 2)
Decent gelding. Turf high 82 - 2nd of 11 to Kyllachy (10 Aug Chepstow 5f frm RF 3525). **M A Jarvis [0-4] J R Good.*

ATYLAN BOY (IRE) BHB 59f66a **RR 69f 66a** 4676[5]

3 b g Efisio 7.7f **(69)** - Gold Flair (Tap On Wood) 10.3f **(65)**
Form - 00315246805
Record 2000 - 1st:1 2nd:1 3rd:1 Ran:11
Pre2000 - 1st:0 2nd:0 3rd:0 Ran:4
Win Prizemoney £2,816 *Total Prizemoney* £5,263
Wins * 2000 *Jun Lingfi (STD) 7f 79* <
2000 Turf 0-9: (7f 5, 8f 4) (g-s 4, gd, g-f 2, frm 2) 2000 AW 1-2: (7f 1-2) (Equi 1-1, Fibr)
Scopey, above-average gelding, effective 7f, - acts on Equi, has worn blinkers, likes tight tracks. Turf high 69. AW high 79 (1st run) - 1st of 8 giving 3lb to Diva (6 Jun Lingfield RF 1741). A winner on Equitrack in June, he has not run too badly on turf since. He is probably worth another try at a mile.
**B J Meehan [1-15] Mrs Sheila Tucker.*

AUBERGADE (FR) **RR 108f** 3949a[7]

4 gr f Kaldoun (FR) 9.9f **(84)** - Anna Edes (FR) (Fabulous Dancer (USA)) 9.4f **(70)**
Form - 537
2000 Turf 0-3: (12f, 14f, 15f) (sft, g-s 2)
Pattern-class filly. Turf high 108 - 3rd of 8 giving 13lb to Interlude (30 Jly Deauville 14f g-s RF 3352a).
**Mme M Bollack-Badel in FR [0-5].*

AUBRIETA (USA) BHB 48f57a **RR 44f 57a** 5245[5]

4 b f Dayjur (USA) 6.8f **(79)** - Fennel (Slew O' Gold (USA)) 8f **(75)**
Form - 17528457114085
Record 2000 - 1st:2 2nd:1 3rd:0 Ran:13
Pre2000 - 1st:1 2nd:0 3rd:4 Ran:18
Win Prizemoney £7,891 *Total Prizemoney* £12,408
Wins * 2000 *Jun Lingfi (STD) C 6f 60* <
*** 2000** *Jun Lingfi (STD) C 7f 50*
* 1999 *Nov Lingfi (STD) 6f 58*
2000 Turf 0-4: (6f 3, 7f) (gd, g-f, frm 2) 2000 AW 2-9: (6f 1-5, 7f 1-3, 8f) (Equi 2-4, Fibr 5)
Leggy, fair filly, effective 6 to 7f, best at 6f, acts on g-f to frm - acts on Equi, often wears blinkers, likes left handed tracks, likes tight tracks, excels at Lingfield. Turf high 44. AW high 60 - 1st of 8 giving 10lb to Palo Blanco (14 Jun Lingfield RF 1969).
**D HaydnJones [3-20] P F Crowley (from C E Brittain [0-11] Jly 1999).*

AUCHONVILLERS BHB 81f **RR 82f** 2183[20]

3 b g Deploy 11.4f **(67)** - Forbearance (Bairn (USA)) 7.7f **(59)**
Form - 170
Record 2000 - 1st:1 2nd:0 3rd:0 Ran:3
Pre2000 - 1st:0 2nd:0 3rd:0 Ran:1
Win Prizemoney £3,835 *Total Prizemoney* £3,835
Wins * 2000 Mar Nottin (GD) 8.2f 77 <
2000 Turf 1-3: (8f 1-3) (gd 1-3)
Leggy, decent gelding. Turf high 82 - also 1st of 15 getting 17lb from Sloane (29 Mar Nottingham RF 0557).
**B A McMahon [1-4] Major W R Paton-Smith and Partners.*

AUCTIONEERS CO UK (IRE) **RR 66f** 3809[P]

2 br c Anita's Prince 6f **(62)** - Carmelina (Habitat) 9.4f **(70)**
Form - 3P
Record 2000 - 1st:0 2nd:0 3rd:1 Ran:2
Win Prizemoney £0 *Total Prizemoney* £352
2000 Turf 0-1: (6f) (hrd) 2000 AW 0-1: (6f) (Fibr)
Currently average colt. (1st run) - 3rd of 6 giving 5lb to Magical Flute (20 Jly Bath 6f hrd RF 2953). (DEAD)
**B Palling [0-2] Merthyr Motor Auctions.*

AUDACIEUSE **RR 113f** 5306a[1]

3 b f Rainbow Quest (USA) 11.2f **(81)** - Sarah Georgina (Persian Bold) 9.3f **(66)**
Form - 61
2000 Turf 1-2: (10f, 11f 1-1) (g-s 1-1, gd)
Currently Group-class filly. Turf high 113 (began Oct) - 1st of 8 from Beyond The Waves (24 Oct Saint-cloud RF 5306a).
**E Lellouche in FR [1-3] Ecurie Woodcote Stud.*

AUDACITY BHB 23f28a **RR 52f 28a** 4228[8]

4 b g Minshaanshu Amad (USA) 11.3f **(53)** - Glory Isle (Hittite Glory) 8.7f **(50)**

Form - 5008
Record 2000 - 1st:0 2nd:0 3rd:0 Ran:4
Pre2000 - 1st:0 2nd:0 3rd:0 Ran:8
2000 Turf 0-3: (10f, 12f, 16f) (g-s, g-f, frm) 2000 AW 0-1: (12f) (Equi)
Strong, fair gelding. Turf high 52. Becoming disappointing.
**N Hamilton [0-9] City Industrial Supplies Ltd (from G Lewis [0-3] Aug 1998).*

AUENKLANG (GER) RR 118+f 4157[11]

3 b c Big Shuffle (USA) - Auenglocke (GER) (Surumu (GER)) 10f **(83)**
Form - 120
Record 2000 - 1st:1 2nd:1 3rd:0 Ran:3
Pre2000 - 1st:1 2nd:1 3rd:0 Ran:2
Win Prizemoney £51,896 *Total Prizemoney* £84,966
Wins * **2000** Jly Newbur (G-F) L 6f 118+ <
1999 Spt Baden- (GD) G2 6f 114+
2000 Turf 1-3: (6f 1-3) (g-s, gd, hrd 1-1)
High-class colt, mostly wears blinkers. Turf high 118 (1st run) (began Jly) - 1st of 11 getting 5lb from Harmonic Way (22 Jly Newbury RF 3021). Purchased by Godolphin after showing high-class form in Germany at two, he bolted up at Newbury on his British debut, breaking the track record, but was just pipped by Bernstein in the Shergar Cup Sprint and was left floundering in the heavy ground at Haydock.
**S bin Suroor [1-3] Godolphin (from H Hiller in GER [1-2] Spt 1999).*

Auenklang blitzed the opposition

AUENZAR (GER) RR 111f 2581a[5]

3 b c Shirley Heights 12.1f **(76)** - Auenmaid (Luciano) 11.2f **(65)**
Form - 25
2000 Turf 0-2: (11f, 12f) (sft, gd)
Currently Group-class colt. Turf high 111 - 5th of 20 to Samum (2 Jly Hamburg 12f sft RF 2581a). **U Ostmann in GER [0-2].*

AUNT DORIS BHB 56f RR 55+f 3485[5]

3 b f Distant Relative 7f **(69)** - Nevis (Connaught) 7.7f **(63)**
Form - 600425
Record 2000 - 1st:0 2nd:1 3rd:0 Ran:6
Pre2000 - 1st:1 2nd:0 3rd:1 Ran:4
Win Prizemoney £2,094 *Total Prizemoney* £3,924
Wins 1999 Aug Leices (GD) S 5f 66 <
2000 Turf 0-6: (5f, 6f 4, 7f) (gd, g-f 2, frm 3)
Unfurnished, fair filly, effective 5 to 6f, acts on g-f. Turf high 55. Consistent.
**R F JohnsonHoughton [0-6] Dr J A E Hobby (from J Berry [1-4] Spt 1999).*

AUNT RUBY (USA) BHB 67f RR 77f 5121[6]

2 ch f Rubiano (USA) 7.1f **(87)** -Redress (USA) **(82f)** (Storm Cat (USA))
Form - 02606
Record 2000 - 1st:0 2nd:1 3rd:0 Ran:5
Win Prizemoney £0 *Total Prizemoney* £1,320
2000 Turf 0-5: (6f 3, 7f 2) (g-s, gd, g-f 2, frm)
Above-average filly. Turf high 77 (began Jly) - 2nd of 9 getting 2lb from Midnight Venture (26 Aug Goodwood 6f gd RF 3987). Hung right when odds-on on her third start.
**M L W Bell [0-5] Stamford Bridge Partnership.*

AUNT SUSAN RR 3809[12]

2 b f Distant Relative 7f **(69)** - Lawn Order **(44f)** (Efisio)
Form - 0
Record 2000 - 1st:0 2nd:0 3rd:0 Ran:1
2000 AW 0-1: (6f) (Fibr)
Currently very poor filly. **K McAuliffe [0-1] Miss J Hall.*

AUNTY ROSE (IRE) BHB 101f RR 106f 4698[11]

3 b f Caerleon (USA) 10.9f **(79)** - Come on Rosi (Valiyar) 8.5f **(73)**
Form - 300
Record 2000 - 1st:0 2nd:0 3rd:1 Ran:3
Pre2000 - 1st:1 2nd:0 3rd:1 Ran:3
Win Prizemoney £5,061 *Total Prizemoney* £12,636
Wins * 1999 Jly Newmar (G-F) 7f 78+ <
2000 Turf 0-3: (7f, 8f 2) (gd, g-f, frm)
Scopey, Pattern-class filly. Turf high 106. A half-sister to Bin Rosie, she made a promising return when third in the Nell Gwyn but was well held in the Guineas. Off for nearly five months afterwards, and made no show in a listed race.
**J L Dunlop [1-6] Wafic Said.*

AURA OF GRACE (USA) BHB 70f RR 73f 5191[1]

3 b br f Southern Halo (USA) - Avarice (USA) (Manila (USA)) 9.3f **(71)**
Form - 6501
Record 2000 - 1st:1 2nd:0 3rd:0 Ran:4
Pre2000 - 1st:0 2nd:0 3rd:0 Ran:1
Win Prizemoney £2,726 *Total Prizemoney* £2,986
Wins * **2000** Oct Mussel (SFT) 8f 73 <
2000 Turf 1-4: (7f, 8f 1-2, 9f) (gd 1-3, g-f)
Leggy, above-average filly. Turf high 73 - 1st of 6 getting 5lb from For Heavens Sake (26 Oct Musselburgh RF 5191).
**M Johnston [1-1] R N Bracher (from R W Armstrong [0-4] Jly 2000).*

AURATUM (USA) RR 88f 1875[4]

3 ch f Carson City (USA) - Gilded Lilly (USA) (What A Pleasure (USA)) 8.4f **(61)**
Form - P4
Record 2000 - 1st:0 2nd:0 3rd:0 Ran:2
Win Prizemoney £0 *Total Prizemoney* £1,205
2000 Turf 0-2: (6f, 7f) (g-s 2)
Tall, currently useful filly. Turf high 88.
**S bin Suroor [0-2] Godolphin.*

AURIGNY BHB 67f68a RR 73f 68a 2692[9]

5 b m Timeless Times (USA) 6.1f **(56)** - Dear Glenda (Gold Song) 5.5f **(61)**
Form - 55080640480
Record 2000 - 1st:0 2nd:0 3rd:0 Ran:9
Pre2000 - 1st:3 2nd:1 3rd:5 Ran:28
Win Prizemoney £21,620 *Total Prizemoney* £47,487
Wins * 1999 Jly Goodwo (G-F) 5f 62+
* 1997 Aug Newbur (G-F) L 5.2f 91 <
* 1997 May Bright (G-F) 5.3f 80+
2000 Turf 0-7: (5f 7) (gd 4, g-f, frm 2) 2000 AW 0-2: (5f, 6f) (Equi, Fibr)
Above-average filly, effective 5f, acts on gd to frm, has worn blinkers. Turf high 73. AW high 58. A very useful sprinting juvenile in 1997, she has been difficult to place since.
**S Dow [3-37] J & S Kelly.*

AUTONOMY (IRE) BHB 106f RR 108f 4698[12]

3 b c Doyoun 10.7f **(69)** - Debbie's Next (USA) (Arctic Tern (USA)) 8.9f **(69)**
Form - 320
Record 2000 - 1st:0 2nd:1 3rd:1 Ran:3
Pre2000 - 1st:2 2nd:0 3rd:0 Ran:3
Win Prizemoney £9,392 *Total Prizemoney* £17,237
Wins * 1999 Oct Newmar (G-S) 8f 95 <
* 1999 Aug Sandow (G-S) 7.1f 74+
2000 Turf 0-3: (8f, 9f, 10f) (gd, g-f, frm)
Scopey, Pattern-class colt, effective 9 to 10f, acts on gd to frm. Turf high 108 (began Aug) - 2nd of 9 getting 12lb from Right Wing (30 Aug York 9f gd RF 4105). Lightly raced, he was a good second in a listed race in August but disappointed on his final start. Likely to prove capable of better.
**M L W Bell [2-6] Deln Ltd.*

AUTUMNAL (IRE) RR 96f 4990[8]
2 b f Indian Ridge 7.6f **(74)** - Please Believe Me (Try My Best (USA)) 7.6f **(67)**
Form - 3112348
Record 2000 - 1st:2 2nd:1 3rd:2 Ran:7
Win Prizemoney £23,826 *Total Prizemoney* £49,019
Wins * **2000** Jun Ascot (G-F) 5f 96 <
* **2000** Jun Haydoc (G-S) 5f 79
2000 Turf 2-7: (5f 2-3, 6f 3, 7f) (g-s 1-1, gd 1-4, g-f 2)
Very useful filly, effective 5 to 6f, best at 6f, acts on gd to g-f, best on gd. Turf high 96 - 2nd of 9 to Enthused (29 Jly Ascot 6f gd RF 3201) - also 1st of 11 getting 3lb from Give Back Calais (23 Jun Ascot RF 2210). She got up close home to win the Windsor Castle at Ascot and later ran well behind Enthused in both the Princess Margaret and Lowther. She was a good fourth in the Cheveley Park Stakes but did not run up to her best over seven furlongs on her final outing. **B J Meehan [2-7] Paul & Jenny Green.*

AUTUMN COVER BHB 60f51a **RR 72f 51a** 4763[11]
8 gr g Nomination 7.3f **(57)** - Respray (Rusticaro (FR)) 8.2f **(65)**
Form - 00
Record 2000 - 1st:0 2nd:0 3rd:0 Ran:2
Pre2000 - 1st:7 2nd:1 3rd:3 Ran:39
Win Prizemoney £56,269 *Total Prizemoney* £63,350
Wins * 1998 Apr Bright (GD) 8f 78
* 1997 May Kempto (GD) H 8f 75 79 <
* 1996 Spt Goodwo (G-F) H 9f 70 74
* 1996 Jly Goodwo (G-F) H 8f 64 70
* 1996 Jun Sandow (FRM) H 8.1f 55 58
1996 Apr Bright (FRM) H 8f 50 54
1996 Apr Bright (FRM) H 8f 43 51
2000 Turf 0-1: (8f) (frm) 2000 AW 0-1: (9f) (Fibr)
Above-average gelding, has worn blinkers.
**P R Hedger [5-29] G A Alexander (from R M Flower [2-15] May 1996).*

AUTUMN LEAVES BHB 25a **RR 38f** 148[10]
4 b f Warning 8.1f **(77)** - Misty Goddess (IRE) **(51df 37a)** (Godswalk (USA)) 7.3f **(58)**
Form - 0670
Record 2000 - 1st:0 2nd:0 3rd:0 Ran:2
Pre2000 - 1st:0 2nd:0 3rd:0 Ran:4
2000 AW 0-2: (8f, 12f) (Fibr 2)
Neat, very moderate filly. AW high 17.
**N P Littmoden [0-6] J R Good.*

AUTUMN RAIN (USA) BHB 77f **RR 78f** 4046[10]
3 br c Dynaformer (USA) 12f **(82)** - Edda (USA) (Ogygian (USA))
Form - 20130
Record 2000 - 1st:1 2nd:1 3rd:1 Ran:5
Pre2000 - 1st:0 2nd:0 3rd:0 Ran:2
Win Prizemoney £3,282 *Total Prizemoney* £5,046
Wins * **2000** May Lingfi (G-S) 7f 78 <
2000 Turf 1-5: (7f 1-2, 8f 2, 10f) (g-s 2, gd 1-3)
Workmanlike, above-average colt, effective 7 to 8f, acts on gd. Turf high 81 (1st run) - 2nd of 16 to Moon Emperor (5 Apr Ripon 8f gd RF 0621) - also 1st of 17 from Innkeeper (12 May Lingfield RF 1172). Ran a race full of promise when runner-up in a Ripon maiden on his reappearance over a mile, but was well beaten over an extra two furlongs in a much better race at Newmarket next time. Scraped home at Lingfield before finding a Nottingham handicap too competitive in June. Appears to need easy ground.
**E A L Dunlop [1-7] Khalifa Sultan.*

AUTUMN RHYTHM RR 104+f 5138[1]
2 b f Hernando (FR) - Fextal (USA) (Alleged (USA)) 10f **(76)**
Form - 1
Record 2000 - 1st:1 2nd:0 3rd:0 Ran:1
Win Prizemoney £3,233 *Total Prizemoney* £3,233
Wins * **2000** Oct Yarmou (HVY) 8f 104+ <
2000 Turf 1-1: (8f 1-1) (g-s 1-1)
Currently very useful filly. (1st run) - 1st of 12 from Perfect Pirouette (22 Oct Yarmouth RF 5138). A runaway winner of her maiden on heavy ground, she was made favourite for the Oaks on the strength of that performance. She shows a knee action and there must be some doubt about her handling fast ground.
**H R A Cecil [1-1] Niarchos Family.*

AVANTI BHB 66f63a **RR 73f 63a** 4934[27]
4 gr c Reprimand 8.2f **(63)** - Dolly Bevan (Another Realm) 6.6f **(55)**
Form - 0
Record 2000 - 1st:0 2nd:0 3rd:0 Ran:1
Pre2000 - 1st:1 2nd:1 3rd:0 Ran:6
Win Prizemoney £4,474 *Total Prizemoney* £5,664
Wins 1999 May Sandow (GD) H 7.1f 70 72 <
2000 Turf 0-1: (8f) (gd)
Scopey, above-average colt, effective 7 to 8f, acts on frm.
**Dr J R J Naylor [0-1] A R M Galbraith (from P J Makin [1-6] Aug 1999).*

AVERHAM STAR BHB 27f32a **RR 28f 32a** 4054[11]
5 ch g Absalom 7.1f **(56)** - Upper Sister (Upper Case (USA)) 8.2f **(55)**
Form - 00068700
Record 2000 - 1st:0 2nd:0 3rd:0 Ran:8
Pre2000 - 1st:0 2nd:0 3rd:1 Ran:25
Win Prizemoney £0 *Total Prizemoney* £619
2000 Turf 0-7: (8f, 10f 3, 11f 3) (g-s, gd 2, g-f 2, frm 2) 2000 AW 0-1: (9f) (Fibr)
Little account gelding, has worn blinkers. Turf high 28.
**G Barnett [0-9] Lee Heath (from W Clay [0-8] Spt 1999).*

AVERY RING BHB 77f **RR 71f** 3907[7]
2 b c Magic Ring (IRE) 6.5f **(64)** - Thatcherella **(65f)** (Thatching) 8f **(66)**
Form - 62347
Record 2000 - 1st:0 2nd:1 3rd:1 Ran:5
Win Prizemoney £0 *Total Prizemoney* £1,070
2000 Turf 0-5: (5f 2, 6f 2, 8f) (frm 5)
Above-average colt.Turf high 71- 2nd of 13 to Western Hero (17 Jly Windsor 5f frm RF 2875). **A P Jarvis [0-5] Avebury Ring Partnership.*

AVONDALE GIRL (IRE) BHB 61f47a **RR 61f 47a** 1902[2]
4 ch f Case Law 6f **(64)** - Battle Queen (Kind of Hush) 10.1f **(62)**
Form - 07885787632
Record 2000 - 1st:0 2nd:1 3rd:1 Ran:10
Pre2000 - 1st:3 2nd:1 3rd:4 Ran:15
Win Prizemoney £6,583 *Total Prizemoney* £11,351
Wins * 1999 Jun Thirsk (G-F) H 6f 66 68
1999 Mar Wolver (STD) S 5f 60
1998 Jun Yarmou (GD) S 5.2f 79+ <
2000 Turf 0-6: (5f 4, 6f 2) (sft, g-s, gd 2, frm 2) 2000 AW 0-4: (5f 3, 6f) (Fibr 4)
Light-framed, average filly, has broken blood-vessels, effective 5 to 6f, best at 6f, acts on gd to frm - acts on Fibr, has worn blinkers, likes left handed tracks, likes tight tracks. Turf high 61. AW high 36. **M Dods [1-14] C A Lynch (from C A Dwyer [2-11] May 1999).*

AWAKE BHB 98f **RR 99f** 4933[11]
3 ch c First Trump - Pluvial (Habat) 7.6f **(61)**
Form - 4042731400
Record 2000 - 1st:1 2nd:1 3rd:1 Ran:9
Pre2000 - 1st:2 2nd:1 3rd:0 Ran:4
Win Prizemoney £18,622 *Total Prizemoney* £39,172
Wins * **2000** Jly Newbur (G-F) H 6f 97 99 <
* 1999 Oct Newbur (HVY) H 6f 81 91+
* 1999 Aug Epsom (GD) 6f 73
2000 Turf 1-9: (5f 4, 6f 1-5) (hvy, g-s 2, gd 4, g-f 1-2)
Very useful colt, effective 5 to 6f, best at 6f, acts on sft to g-f, best on g-f. Turf high 99 - 1st of 9 getting 7lb from Kayo (16 Jly Newbury RF 2864).
**M Johnston [3-12] Lord Hartington (from M A Johnson [0-1] Nov 1999).*

AWAY WIN RR 52f 4028[9]
2 b f Common Grounds 8.1f **(66)** - Cafe Glace **(38f 41a)** (Beldale Flutter (USA)) 9.7f **(71)**
Form - 50
Record 2000 - 1st:0 2nd:0 3rd:0 Ran:2
2000 Turf 0-2: (7f, 8f) (frm 2)
Currently fair filly. Turf high 52. **B Palling [0-2] Albert Yemm.*

AWESOME VENTURE BHB 30f31a **RR 23f 31a** 369[8]
10 b g Formidable (USA) 7.8f **(60)** - Pine Ridge (High Top) 10.2f **(67)**
Form - 088
Record 2000 - 1st:0 2nd:0 3rd:0 Ran:3
Pre2000 - 1st:4 2nd:16 3rd:11 Ran:123
Win Prizemoney £10,287 *Total Prizemoney* £28,590
Wins * 1996 *May Southw (STD) C 7f 73* <

* 1996	*Apr*	*Southw*	*(STD)*	*C*	*8f*		*69*
* 1996	*Apr*	*Southw*	*(STD)*	*H*	*8f*	*62*	*63*

2000 AW 0-3: (7f, 8f, 11f) (Fibr 3)

Little account gelding, effective 6 to 8f, best at 7f, - acts on Fibr, has worn blinkers, likes left handed tracks, likes tight tracks. AW high 15.

**M C Chapman [3-130] Market Rasen Racing Club (from J A R Toller [1-9] Oct 1994).*

AWTAAN (USA) BHB 75f RR 82df 3782[1]

3 b f Arazi (USA) 9.2f **(74)** - Bashayer (USA) (Mr Prospector (USA)) 8.8f **(78)**

Form - 41

Record 2000 - 1st:1 2nd:0 3rd:0 Ran:2
Pre2000 - 1st:0 2nd:0 3rd:1 Ran:2

Win Prizemoney £2,834 *Total Prizemoney* £3,602

Wins * **2000** Aug Lingfi (G-F) 14f 71 <

2000 Turf 1-2: (12f, 14f 1-1) (g-s, frm 1-1)

Scopey, decent filly. Turf high 71.

**M P Tregoning [1-4] Hamdan Al Maktoum.*

AYMARA BHB 80f RR 76+f 4963[13]

3 b f Darshaan 11.9f **(81)** - Chipaya (Northern Prospect (USA)) 9.5f **(71)**

Form - 42210

Record 2000 - 1st:1 2nd:2 3rd:0 Ran:5

Win Prizemoney £3,068 *Total Prizemoney* £6,034

Wins * **2000** Spt Mussel (G-S) 12f 76+ <

2000 Turf 1-5: (8f, 11f, 12f 1-3) (gd 1-4, g-f)

Scopey, above-average filly. Turf high 76 (began Jly) - 1st of 15 getting 5lb from Tolstoy (24 Spt Musselburgh RF 4624). Gradually improving, she made short work of a field of maidens at Musselburgh on her fourth start.

**J H M Gosden [1-5] Lord Hartington.*

AZAAN (IRE) RR 80+f 3989[2]

3 ch c Lure (USA) - Crystal Cross (USA) **(73f)** (Roberto (USA)) 10f **(76)**

Form - 22

Record 2000 - 1st:0 2nd:2 3rd:0 Ran:2

Win Prizemoney £0 *Total Prizemoney* £2,874

2000 Turf 0-2: (8f, 10f) (gd, g-f)

Scopey, currently decent colt. Turf high 80 (began Aug) - 2nd of 17 giving 5lb to You Are The One (26 Aug Newmarket 8f g-f RF 3989). **M P Tregoning [0-2] Hamdan Al Maktoum.*

AZIRA BHB 45f RR 53f 3899[10]

3 ch f Arazi (USA) 9.2f **(74)** - Free City (USA) (Danzig (USA)) 8.4f **(76)**

Form - 60860

Record 2000 - 1st:0 2nd:0 3rd:0 Ran:4
Pre2000 - 1st:0 2nd:0 3rd:0 Ran:2

2000 Turf 0-4: (5f 3, 6f) (g-f, frm 2, hrd)

Neat, fair filly. Turf high 53. **P R Chamings [0-6] Mrs Ann Jenkins.*

AZIZ PRESENTING (IRE) BHB 90f RR 87f 2798[3]

2 br f Charnwood Forest (IRE) - Khalatara (IRE) (Kalaglow) 9.8f **(67)**

Form - 271023

Record 2000 - 1st:1 2nd:2 3rd:1 Ran:6

Win Prizemoney £3,120 *Total Prizemoney* £8,439

Wins * **2000** Jun Salisb (G-F) 5f 76+ <

2000 Turf 1-6: (5f 1-5, 6f) (g-s, gd 3, g-f, frm 1-1)

Useful filly, effective 5 to 6f, acts on gd to g-f. Turf high 87 - 3rd of 6 getting 2lb from Red Millennium (14 Jly Chester 5f g-f RF 2798).

**M R Channon [1-6] Coriolan Partnership.*

AZIZZI BHB 86f RR 93df 4468[9]

8 ch g Indian Ridge 7.6f **(74)** - Princess Silca Key (Grundy) 10.3f **(65)**

Form - 000

Record 2000 - 1st:0 2nd:0 3rd:0 Ran:3
Pre2000 - 1st:4 2nd:3 3rd:2 Ran:17

Win Prizemoney £22,232 *Total Prizemoney* £43,103

Wins								
	* 1999	Oct	Windso	(SFT)	H	5f	79	89+
	* 1999	Oct	Pontef	(GD)	H	5f	79	82
	* 1999	Aug	Newmar	(GD)	C	7f		69+
	* 1996	Apr	Kempto	(G-F)		7f		91 <

2000 Turf 0-3: (5f 2, 6f) (g-s, gd, g-f)

Useful gelding, effective 5f, acts on g-s to g-f. Turf high 80 (began Spt). **C R Egerton [4-20] Chris Brasher.*

AZKABAN (IRE) BHB 90f RR 83f 4643[10]

2 ch c Ashkalani (IRE) - Lanasara (Generous (IRE))

Form - 3250

Record 2000 - 1st:0 2nd:1 3rd:1 Ran:4

Win Prizemoney £0 *Total Prizemoney* £3,001

2000 Turf 0-4: (7f 3, 8f) (g-f 3, frm)

Decent colt. Turf high 83 (began Aug). In the frame in seven-furlong maidens. **B J Meehan [0-4] Mrs Susan Roy.*

AZOUZ PASHA (USA) BHB 107f RR 110f 4297[4]

4 b c Lyphard (USA) 10.6f **(75)** -Empress Club (ARG) (Farnesio (ARG))

Form - 5534

Record 2000 - 1st:0 2nd:0 3rd:1 Ran:4
Pre2000 - 1st:3 2nd:1 3rd:0 Ran:6

Win Prizemoney £56,216 *Total Prizemoney* £61,674

Wins								
	* 1999	Spt	Doncas	(G-F)	L	12f		109 <
	* 1999	Jly	Goodwo	(FRM)	H	9.9f	96	100
	* 1999	Jun	Lingfi	(GD)		10f		87+

2000 Turf 0-4: (10f 2, 12f 2) (sft, gd 2, g-f)

Scopey, Group-class colt, effective 10 to 12f, best at 12f, acts on gd to frm, best on g-f, has worn blinkers, and excels at Windsor. Turf high 110. Consistent. A useful if enigmatic sort, he ran well on each of his four starts in 2000 without getting his head in front. Best on fast ground. **H R A Cecil [3-10] Wafic Said.*

AZTEC FLYER (USA) BHB 43f36a RR 50f 36a 651[14]

7 b g Alwasmi (USA) 12.9f **(77)** - Jetta J (USA) (Super Concorde (USA)) 10.9f **(66)**

Form - 0

Record 2000 - 1st:0 2nd:0 3rd:0 Ran:1
Pre2000 - 1st:4 2nd:0 3rd:2 Ran:29

Win Prizemoney £13,037 *Total Prizemoney* £15,338

Wins								
	1998	Aug	Yarmou	(FRM)	H	14.1f	49	52
	1997	Aug	Warwic	(SFT)	H	16.1f	56	56 <
	1997	Aug	Nottin	(G-F)	H	16f	50	53
	1997	Jly	Yarmou	(G-F)	H	14.1f	45	56 <

2000 Turf 0-1: (16f) (g-s)

Fair gelding, often wears blinkers.

**Mrs M Reveley [2-22] R Meredith (from C E Brittain [4-18] Spt 1998).*

AZUR (IRE) BHB 62f RR 64f 4539[9]

3 b f Brief Truce (USA) 9.1f **(73)** - Bayadere (USA) (Green Dancer (USA)) 10.3f **(74)**

Form - 00780

Record 2000 - 1st:0 2nd:0 3rd:0 Ran:5
Pre2000 - 1st:1 2nd:0 3rd:0 Ran:2

Win Prizemoney £3,509 *Total Prizemoney* £3,509

Wins * 1999 Oct Lingfi (G-F) 7f 75+ <

2000 Turf 0-5: (8f 2, 10f, 12f 2) (gd 2, g-f, frm 2)

Scopey, average filly, effective 7f, acts on gd, has worn blinkers. Turf high 64. She got off the mark in a Lingfield maiden on her second start at two but has not shown much in 2000.

**J R Fanshawe [1-7] B M Guerin.*

AZZAN (USA) BHB 48f RR 52f 690[17]

4 b br g Gulch (USA) 9.6f **(79)** - Dixieland Dream (USA) (Dixieland Band (USA)) 7f **(74)**

Form - 680

Record 2000 - 1st:0 2nd:0 3rd:0 Ran:2
Pre2000 - 1st:0 2nd:0 3rd:0 Ran:9

Win Prizemoney £0 *Total Prizemoney* £845

2000 Turf 0-1: (11f) (hvy) 2000 AW 0-1: (8f) (Fibr)

Workmanlike, fair gelding, effective 8f, acts on gd to frm, has worn blinkers.

**T Keddy [0-5] Brensway Partnership (from J L Dunlop [0-8] Spt 1999).*

BAAJIL BHB 39f41a RR 44f 41a 1971[12]

5 b g Marju (IRE) 9.2f **(76)** - Arctic River (FR) (Arctic Tern (USA)) 8.9f **(69)**

Form - 14680000

Record 2000 - 1st:0 2nd:0 3rd:0 Ran:5
Pre2000 - 1st:1 2nd:3 3rd:1 Ran:12

Win Prizemoney £1,798 *Total Prizemoney* £6,183

Wins * 1999 *Nov Lingfi (STD) 10f 61* <

2000 AW 0-5: (8f, 9f, 10f 2, 12f) (Equi 4, Fibr)

Moderate gelding, effective 10f, - acts on Equi. AW high 47. Becoming disappointing.

D J S Cosgrove [1-17] Crown Pkg & Mailing Svs Ltd (from L M Cumani [0-1] Oct 1997).

BAARIDD BHB 100f **RR 105f** 4699[6]
2 b c Halling (USA) - Millstream (USA) **(107f)** (Dayjur (USA))
Form - 12516
Record 2000 - 1st:2 2nd:1 3rd:0 Ran:5
Win Prizemoney £18,002 *Total Prizemoney* £27,812
Wins * 2000 Aug Ripon (GD) L 6f 96 <
*** 2000** May Goodwo (G-S) 5f 79
2000 Turf 2-5: (5f 1-1, 6f 1-2, 7f 2) (g-s 1-1, gd 2, g-f, frm 1-1)
Pattern-class colt. Turf high 105 - also 1st of 4 getting 3lb from Piccolo Player (28 Aug Ripon RF 4051). Out of a mare who was a very quick juvenile and won Group races at two and three, he got home in the last stride at Goodwood on his debut. Stepped up to seven furlongs at Ascot, there was no disgrace in his defeat by Celtic Silence, but he was a little disappointing at Goodwood. Regained winning form at Ripon when dropped back to six furlongs before finishing sixth in the Group One Middle Park Stakes on his final run. *M A Jarvis [2-5] Sheikh Ahmed Al Maktoum.*

BABA AU RHUM (IRE) BHB 60f **RR 54f** 3982[11]
8 b g Baba Karam 8.1f **(71)** - Spring About (Hard Fought) 8.8f **(62)**
Form - 80
Record 2000 - 1st:0 2nd:0 3rd:0 Ran:2
Pre2000 - 1st:2 2nd:1 3rd:1 Ran:15
Win Prizemoney £6,726 *Total Prizemoney* £8,528
Wins * 1997 Aug Haydoc (G-F) H 8.1f 66 71 <
*** 1997** Jun Sandow (G-F) H 8.1f 60 67
2000 Turf 0-2: (8f, 9f) (gd, frm)
Fair gelding. Turf high 54 (began Aug). Consistent.
Ian Williams [5-26] Horses For Courses Partnership.

BABY BARRY BHB 70f **RR 81f** 5317[9]
3 b c Komaite (USA) 6.9f **(61)** - Malcesine (IRE) **(38f 31a)** (Auction Ring (USA)) 8.6f **(65)**
Form - 703430335080700
Record 2000 - 1st:0 2nd:0 3rd:4 Ran:15
Pre2000 - 1st:1 2nd:4 3rd:3 Ran:12
Win Prizemoney £2,547 *Total Prizemoney* £22,520
Wins * 1999 Oct Redcar (GD) 5f **77** <
2000 Turf 0-15: (5f 2, 6f 8, 7f 5) (sft 2, g-s 2, gd 4, g-f 4, frm 3)
Workmanlike, decent colt, effective 5 to 7f, best at 6f, acts on gd to frm - acts on Fibr, best on frm, has worn blinkers (effectively). Turf high 84 - 3rd of 8 to Mersey Mirage (13 Aug Leicester 6f frm RF 3610). Inconsistent. *Mrs G S Rees [1-27] John Barry.*

BABY BUNTING RR 63f 4001[4]
2 b f Wolfhound (USA) 7.3f **(71)** - Flitteriss Park (Beldale Flutter (USA)) 9.7f **(71)**
Form - 444
Record 2000 - 1st:0 2nd:0 3rd:0 Ran:3
Win Prizemoney £0 *Total Prizemoney* £952
2000 Turf 0-3: (5f 2, 6f) (gd 2, g-f)
Currently average filly. Turf high 63 - 4th of 9 getting 5lb from Whale Beach (26 Aug Windsor 6f g-f RF 4001).
M L W Bell [0-3] Miss Farr, Farr, Gray.

BABY MAYBE (USA) BHB 49f **RR 61f** 4495[5]
2 b f Known Fact (USA) 8.3f **(72)** - Bai Shun (USA) (Fappiano (USA)) 8.7f **(77)**
Form - 705
Record 2000 - 1st:0 2nd:0 3rd:0 Ran:3
2000 Turf 0-3: (5f 2, 6f) (g-s, gd, g-f)
Currently average filly. Turf high 61 (began Jly).
T H Caldwell [0-3] R S G Jones.

BACCHUS RR 72f 4864[14]
6 b g Prince Sabo 6.6f **(64)** - Bonica (Rousillon (USA)) 8.2f **(74)**
Form - 2322156020
Record 2000 - 1st:1 2nd:4 3rd:1 Ran:10
Pre2000 - 1st:3 2nd:0 3rd:0 Ran:15
Win Prizemoney £17,395 *Total Prizemoney* £25,226
Wins * 2000 Jly Cheste (G-S) H 10.3f 69 74
* 1999 Aug Beverl (GD) H 7.5f 58 63
* 1999 Jly Beverl (G-F) SH 7.5f 54 58
1997 Jly Newmar (G-S) 6f 80 <
2000 Turf 1-10: (8f 2, 9f 3, 10f 1-5) (sft, gd, g-f 1-5, frm 2, hrd)
Above-average gelding, effective 8 to 10f, best at 10f, acts on gd to hrd, has worn blinkers, likes right handed tracks, prefers tight tracks, does well at Beverley, likes Redcar. Turf high 74 - 1st of 11 giving 21lb to Paarl Rock (15 Jly Chester RF 2835). Ran decent races to make the frame early on last season and deservedly got his head in front at Chester in July when visored for the first time.
Miss J A Camacho [3-19] L A Bolingbroke (from A C Stewart [1-6] Oct 1997).

BACCURA (IRE) BHB 89f **RR 82f** 3279[2]
2 b c Dolphin Street (FR) - Luzzara (IRE) (Tate Gallery (USA)) 7.4f **(67)**
Form - 0212
Record 2000 - 1st:1 2nd:2 3rd:0 Ran:4
Win Prizemoney £3,302 *Total Prizemoney* £7,686
Wins * 2000 Jly Pontef (G-F) 6f 62 <
2000 Turf 1-4: (5f 2, 6f 1-2) (g-f, frm 1-3)
Decent colt. Turf high 82 - 2nd of 8 giving 2lb to Piccolo Player (1 Aug Goodwood 6f g-f RF 3279). Runner-up in a decent nursery at Glorious Goodwood. Yet to tackle soft ground.
A P Jarvis [1-4] Jalal Harake.

BACH (IRE) RR 108f 1826a[2]
3 b c Caerleon (USA) 10.9f **(79)** - Producer (USA) (Nashua) 10.3f **(67)**
Form - 122
2000 Turf 1-3: (8f 1-1, 9f, 10f) (sft 1-1, gd, g-f)
Pattern-class colt. Turf high 108 - also 1st of 4 giving 3lb to Legal Jousting (16 Apr Leopardstown RF 0782a). Bred to be something special, he easily won on his juvenile debut, but had to work to follow up in the Chesham Stakes at Royal Ascot. Off the track for the rest of the year, he narrowly made a winning return in the a Leopardstown Listed event, but just found Sinndar too good when stepped up to ten furlongs at the same track. No match for Suances in the Prix Jean Prat.
A P O'Brien in IRE [3-5] Satish K Sanan & Mrs John Magnier.

BACHELORS PAD BHB 52f57a **RR 60df 57a** 5164[4]
6 b g Pursuit of Love 9.5f **(69)** - Note Book (Mummy's Pet) 7.7f **(60)**
Form - 821121414234618774
Record 2000 - 1st:5 2nd:3 3rd:1 Ran:18
Pre2000 - 1st:1 2nd:5 3rd:3 Ran:32
Win Prizemoney £15,382 *Total Prizemoney* £31,267
Wins * 2000 Aug Cheste (GD) H 12.3f 56 60
*** 2000** Apr Southw (G-S) H 11f 54 60+
*** 2000** *Feb Wolver (STD) S 9.4f 47*
*** 2000** *Feb Wolver (STD) C 9.4f 61*
2000 *Jan Wolver (STD) C 9.4f 61*
1996 Spt Goodwo (G-F) 6f 96+ <
2000 Turf 2-10: (10f 4, 11f 1-3, 12f 1-3) (sft, g-s 1-3, gd 3, g-f 1-3) 2000 AW 3-8: (8f 2, 9f 3-4, 11f, 12f) (Fibr 3-8)
Average gelding, effective 7 to 12f, acts on g-s to hrd - acts on Fibr, has worn blinkers, excels at Ayr and Wolverhampton and Southwell, does well at Chester. Turf high 60 (1st run) - 1st of 16 getting 14lb from Pluralist (10 Apr Southwell RF 0646) - also 1st of 8 getting 3lb from Jamaican Flight (18 Aug Chester RF 3749). AW high 61 - 4th of 15 giving 11lb to Generate (15 May Southwell 11f Fibr RF 1209) - also 1st of 12 giving 4lb to Tyler's Toast (1 Feb Wolverhampton RF 0196).
Miss S J Wilton [4-15] John Pointon and Sons (from D Nicholls [1-17] Jan 2000).

BACHIR (IRE) BHB 118f **RR 120f** 3985[5]
3 b c Desert Style (IRE) - Morning Welcome (IRE) (Be My Guest (USA)) 9.3f **(67)**
Form - 121165
Record 2000 - 1st:3 2nd:1 3rd:0 Ran:6
Pre2000 - 1st:2 2nd:0 3rd:2 Ran:4
Win Prizemoney £331,483 *Total Prizemoney* £424,343
Wins * 2000 May Currag (G-S) G1 8f 120 <
*** 2000** May Longch (HVY) G1 8f 119
2000 *Feb Nad Al (FST) 8f 111*
1999 Jly Goodwo (G-F) G2 6f 103+
1999 Jly Chepst (G-F) 6.1f 84++
2000 Turf 2-4: (8f 2-4) (g-s 1-1, gd 1-3) 2000 AW 1-2: (8f 1-1, 9f) (Dirt 1-2)
Very high-class colt, effective 8 to 9f, best at 8f, acts on g-s to gd - acts on Dirt, excels at Nad Al Sheba. Turf high 120 - 1st of 8 from Giant's Causeway (27 May Curragh RF 1576a) - also 1st of 7 from Berine's Son (14 May Longchamp RF 1290a). AW high 117 - 2nd of

16 to China Visit (25 Mar Nad Al Sheba 9f Dirt RF 0576a) - also 1st of 11 giving 6lb to Interrogate (20 Feb Nad Al Sheba RF 0353a). He was in action in Dubai in the spring, winning once and finishing second to China Visit in the UAE Derby. He battled on well to win the French Guineas, and completed the Guineas double under a canny ride from Dettori at the Curragh. A little disappointing at Royal Ascot, although he was reported lame the following day, he was again below par at Goodwood in August. He was subsequently retired to the Kildangan Stud at a fee of IR£10,000.
**S bin Suroor [2-4] Godolphin (from S bin Suroor in UAE [1-2] Mar 2000).*

BACKEND CHARLIE BHB 20f **RR 27df** 2251[10]

6 b g Sylvan Express 9.6f **(45)** - Red Eska (Smackover) 6f **(52)**
Form - 00
Record 2000 - 1st:0 2nd:0 3rd:0 Ran:2
Pre2000 - 1st:0 2nd:0 3rd:0 Ran:2
2000 Turf 0-2: (12f, 14f) (gd, frm)
Little account gelding, has broken blood-vessels. Turf high 23.
**B W Murray [0-8] G Bulmer.*

BACK PASS (USA) **RR 68f** 3231[9]

2 b br f Quest for Fame 12.8f **(75)** - Skiable (IRE) (Niniski (USA)) 10.6f **(65)**
Form - 0
Record 2000 - 1st:0 2nd:0 3rd:0 Ran:1
2000 Turf 0-1: (7f) (g-f)
Currently average filly. **B W Hills [0-1] K Abdulla.*

BACKWOODS BHB 43f62a **RR 62a** 5161[16]

7 ch g In The Wings 11.2f **(77)** - Kates Cabin (Habitat) 9.4f **(70)**
Form - 0
Record 2000 - 1st:0 2nd:0 3rd:0 Ran:1
Pre2000 - 1st:3 2nd:0 3rd:0 Ran:15
Win Prizemoney £10,160 *Total Prizemoney* £10,160
Wins * 1996 Oct Nottin (GD) H 16f 55 65 <
* 1996 Oct Catter (GD) H 15.8f 55 64
* 1996 *Aug Wolver (STD) H 14.8f 56 52*
2000 Turf 0-1: (16f) (sft)
Very poor gelding.
**W M Brisbourne [3-15] P R Kirk (from G Wragg [0-1] Nov 1995).*

BADAAWAH **RR 62f** 4146[5]

3 ch f Lion Cavern (USA) 7.5f **(74)** - Wanisa (USA) (Topsider (USA)) 8.3f **(71)**
Form - 25
Record 2000 - 1st:0 2nd:1 3rd:0 Ran:2
Win Prizemoney £0 *Total Prizemoney* £1,076
2000 Turf 0-2: (7f, 9f) (g-f, frm)
Scopey, currently average filly. Turf high 62 (1st run) (began Aug) - 2nd of 13 getting 5lb from Burgundy (17 Aug Salisbury 7f frm RF 3731). **B Hanbury [0-2] Hamdan Al Maktoum.*

BAD AS I WANNA BE (IRE) BHB 119f **RR 108f** 4699[4]

2 ch c Common Grounds 8.1f **(66)** - Song of The Glens (Horage) 10.3f **(61)**
Form - 01144
Record 2000 - 1st:2 2nd:0 3rd:0 Ran:5
Win Prizemoney £80,586 *Total Prizemoney* £92,128
Wins * 2000 Aug Deauvi (G-S) G1 6f 115 <
*** 2000** Jly Windso (G-F) 5f 90
2000 Turf 2-5: (5f 1-1, 6f 1-3, 7f) (g-s 1-1, gd, g-f 2, frm 1-1)
Pattern-class colt. Turf high 115 - 1st of 6 from Endless Summer (20 Aug Deauville RF 3947a). He looked good when bolting up in a Windsor maiden before proving a revelation in the Prix Morny, crushing his field by six lengths and more. He was helped by racing on the best ground there, and his two subsequent runs were disappointing in the light of that performance, as he failed to settle in the Prix de la Salamandre, his only attempt at seven furlongs, and could not produce a turn of foot in the Middle Park Stakes. He may be best when allowed an uncontested lead.
**B J Meehan [2-5] Joe Allbritton.*

BADERNA **RR 49f** 5157[14]

2 b c Rainbow Quest (USA) 11.2f **(81)** - Baaderah (IRE) **(102df)** (Cadeaux Genereux)
Form - 0
Record 2000 - 1st:0 2nd:0 3rd:0 Ran:1
2000 Turf 0-1: (8f) (sft)
Currently moderate colt.
**M R Channon [0-1] Sheikh Ahmed Al Maktoum.*

BADRINATH (IRE) BHB 49f36a **RR 49f 36a** 2455[19]

6 b g Imperial Frontier (USA) 7f **(65)** - Badedra (Kings Lake (USA)) 10.8f **(67)**
Form - 063200250
Record 2000 - 1st:0 2nd:2 3rd:1 Ran:8
Pre2000 - 1st:3 2nd:4 3rd:3 Ran:28
Win Prizemoney £9,566 *Total Prizemoney* £15,322
Wins * 1998 Spt Redcar (G-F) SH 10f 47 53
* 1998 Jun Newmar (GD) H 8f 40 48
* 1998 *Jan Lingfi (STD) 10f 55* <
2000 Turf 0-5: (8f 3, 10f 2) (g-s, gd, g-f 2, frm) 2000 AW 0-3: (9f, 10f 2) (Equi 2, Fibr)
Moderate gelding, effective 10f, acts on g-f to frm, best on g-f. Turf high 49. AW high 46. Inconsistent.
**H J Collingridge [3-33] D Burke (from J Pearce [0-3] Jan 1999).*

BADR RAINBOW BHB 82f **RR 80f** 3777[1]

3 b c Rainbow Quest (USA) 11.2f **(81)** - Baaderah (IRE) **(102df)** (Cadeaux Genereux)
Form - 31
Record 2000 - 1st:1 2nd:0 3rd:1 Ran:2
Pre2000 - 1st:0 2nd:1 3rd:0 Ran:4
Win Prizemoney £3,867 *Total Prizemoney* £6,511
Wins * 2000 Aug Haydoc (G-S) 8.1f 70 <
2000 Turf 1-2: (8f 1-1, 10f) (gd 1-1, g-f)
Workmanlike, decent colt, effective 7 to 8f, best at 8f, acts on g-s to gd, best on gd. Turf high 79 (began Jly).
**M A Jarvis [1-6] Sheikh Ahmed Al Maktoum.*

BAHAMAS (IRE) BHB 71f72a **RR 71f 72a** 5137[4]

3 b g Barathea (IRE) - Rum Cay (USA) (Our Native (USA)) 11.2f **(63)**
Form - 1233117624
Record 2000 - 1st:3 2nd:2 3rd:2 Ran:10
Pre2000 - 1st:0 2nd:0 3rd:0 Ran:4
Win Prizemoney £7,581 *Total Prizemoney* £10,196
Wins * 2000 *Jly Southw (STD) H 11f 60 75* <
*** 2000** *Jly Southw (STD) H 12f 60 66*
*** 2000** Jun Redcar (G-F) H 10f 58 65
2000 Turf 1-7: (10f 1-3, 12f 3, 14f) (g-s 3, gd, g-f 2, frm 1-1) 2000 AW 2-3: (11f 1-1, 12f 1-2) (Fibr 2-3)
Scopey, above-average gelding, effective 10 to 12f, best at 12f, acts on g-s to frm - acts on Fibr, often wears blinkers (effectively), prefers left handed tracks, prefers tight tracks. Turf high 71 - 2nd of 16 giving 10lb to Bollin Nellie (3 Oct Catterick 12f g-s RF 4775). AW high 75 (began Jly) - 1st of 11 giving 2lb to Kara Sea (28 Jly Southwell RF 3186) - also 1st of 10 giving 6lb to Furness (21 Jly Southwell RF 3015).
**Sir Mark Prescott [3-14] Eclipse Thoro'breds House III.*

BAHAMIAN PIRATE (USA) BHB 110f87a **RR 109+f 87a** 4966[1]

5 ch g Housebuster (USA) 7f **(81)** - Shining Through (USA) (Deputy Minister (CAN)) 7.4f **(80)**
Form - 011222130151
Record 2000 - 1st:5 2nd:3 3rd:1 Ran:12
Pre2000 - 1st:1 2nd:2 3rd:1 Ran:9
Win Prizemoney £94,158 *Total Prizemoney* £106,688
Wins * 2000 Oct Newmar (SFT) L 6f 109+ <
*** 2000** Spt Ayr (SFT) H 6f 86 91
*** 2000** Aug Newmar (G-F) H 6f 78 85
*** 2000** *Jly Southw (STD) H 6f 58 78*
*** 2000** May Carlis (FRM) H 5.9f 62 69
* 1999 Aug Ripon (GD) 5f 68
2000 Turf 4-11: (5f 2, 6f 4-8, 7f) (gd 2-5, g-f 3, frm 2-3) 2000 AW 1-1: (6f 1-1) (Fibr 1-1)
Pattern-class gelding, effective 6f, acts on gd. Turf high 109 - 1st of 15 from Andreyev (13 Oct Newmarket RF 4966). (1st run). Improving. He enjoyed a fine season and gained his big payday when running out the authoritative winner of the Ayr Gold Cup. Graduated successfully to Listed company on his final start.
**D Nicholls [6-19] Lhendup Dorji (from C Collins in IRE [0-2] May 1998).*

BAHAMIAN PRINCE (IRE) BHB 38f **RR 17f** 192[7]

3 b g Night Shift (USA) 8.1f **(73)** - Fairy Water **(82f)** (Warning)
Form - 7067
Record 2000 - 1st:0 2nd:0 3rd:0 Ran:3
Pre2000 - 1st:0 2nd:0 3rd:0 Ran:2
2000 AW 0-3: (8f 2, 9f) (Equi, Fibr 2)
Scopey, very moderate gelding, has worn blinkers. AW high 35.
**J Noseda [0-4] Lucayan Stud (from H R A Cecil [0-1] Aug 1999).*

BAHRAIN (IRE) BHB 61a RR 61df 4782[10]

4 ch c Lahib (USA) 8f **(69)** - Twin Island (IRE) (Standaan (FR)) 7f **(55)**
Form - 480862310
Record 2000 - 1st:1 2nd:1 3rd:1 Ran:9
Pre2000 - 1st:0 2nd:0 3rd:0 Ran:3
Win Prizemoney £3,080 *Total Prizemoney* £4,099
Wins * **2000** *Spt Wolver (STD) H 8.5f 57 60* <
2000 Turf 0-6: (7f 2, 8f 2, 10f 2) (g-s, gd, g-f 2, frm 2) 2000 AW 1-3: (8f 1-3) (Fibr 1-3)
Scopey, average colt, effective 8f, acts on g-f - acts on Fibr, likes tight tracks. Turf high 61 - 8th of 18 giving 1lb to Danakil (8 May Windsor 8f g-f RF 1102). AW high 60 (began Spt) - 1st of 13 giving 10lb to Sharp Belline (16 Spt Wolverhampton RF 4474).
**N P Littmoden [1-4] Mrs Julie Mitchell (from J W Hills [0-5] Jun 2000).*

BAILAMOS (IRE) RR 27f 4318[8]

2 ch c Bluebird (USA) 7.9f **(71)** - Majieda (Kashmir II) 11.7f **(48)**
Form - 8
Record 2000 - 1st:0 2nd:0 3rd:0 Ran:1
2000 Turf 0-1: (8f) (gd)
Currently little account colt. **Miss Gay Kelleway [0-1] A P Griffin.*

BAILEYS CREAM BHB 85f RR 74+f 4595[8]

2 ch f Mister Baileys - Exclusive Life (USA) (Exclusive Native (USA)) 9.1f **(81)**
Form - 0218
Record 2000 - 1st:1 2nd:1 3rd:0 Ran:4
Win Prizemoney £3,087 *Total Prizemoney* £4,177
Wins * **2000** Aug Ayr (GD) 7f 74+ <
2000 Turf 1-4: (6f, 7f 1-2, 8f) (gd, frm 1-3)
Above-average filly. Turf high 74 - 1st of 12 getting 5lb from Magnusson (15 Aug Ayr RF 3638). She is improving with experience and showed the right attitude to score at Ayr.
**M Johnston [1-4] G R Bailey Ltd (Baileys Horse Foods).*

Ayr Gold Cup winner Bahamian Pirate (far side)

BAILEYS ON LINE BHB 53f46a RR 61+f 46a 5150[8]

3 b f Shareef Dancer (USA) 10.1f **(67)** - Three Stars (Star Appeal) 9.6f **(65)**
Form - 0802308
Record 2000 - 1st:0 2nd:1 3rd:1 Ran:7
Win Prizemoney £0 *Total Prizemoney* £1,532
2000 Turf 0-5: (6f, 7f 2, 12f, 14f) (gd 3, g-f, frm) 2000 AW 0-2: (10f, 12f) (Equi, Fibr)
Neat, average filly, effective 12 to 14f, acts on gd to frm. Turf high 61 - 2nd of 9 getting 14lb from Spectrometer (5 Jly Brighton 12f gd RF 2536). AW high 35 (began Oct).
**M Johnston [0-7] G R Bailey Ltd (Baileys Horse Feeds).*

BAILEYS PRIZE (USA) BHB 80f RR 86f 3991[7]

3 ch c Mister Baileys - Mar Mar (USA) (Forever Casting (USA))
Form - 271462223147
Record 2000 - 1st:2 2nd:4 3rd:1 Ran:12
Pre2000 - 1st:0 2nd:0 3rd:0 Ran:2
Win Prizemoney £10,167 *Total Prizemoney* £19,408
Wins * **2000** Jly Newmar (G-F) H 10f 79 86 <
* **2000** May Redcar (G-F) H 10f 70 72
2000 Turf 2-11: (8f, 10f 2-8, 11f, 12f) (g-s, gd 1-5, g-f 2, frm 1-3) 2000 AW 0-1: (8f) (Fibr)
Scopey, useful colt, effective 10 to 12f, best at 10f, acts on gd to frm, prefers right handed tracks, prefers tight tracks, excels at Redcar and Goodwood. Turf high 86 - 1st of 9 getting 10lb from Mynah (21 Jly Newmarket RF 3006). Consistent. He got off the mark in a handicap over ten furlongs on fast ground at Redcar in May before running up a sequence of second placings during the summer. Back in the winning groove when awarded a race at Newmarket in July, he was disappointing there in August.
**M Johnston [2-14] Mrs Val Armstrong.*

BAILEY'S WHIRLWIND (USA) BHB 88f RR 91f 4732[12]

3 b f Mister Baileys - Tornado Cat (USA) (Storm Cat (USA))
Form - 503444460
Record 2000 - 1st:0 2nd:0 3rd:1 Ran:9
Pre2000 - 1st:2 2nd:0 3rd:0 Ran:4
Win Prizemoney £9,324 *Total Prizemoney* £14,768
Wins * 1999 Spt Yarmou (SFT) 6f 80+
* 1999 Aug Windso (GD) 6f 90+ <
2000 Turf 0-9: (6f 5, 7f 4) (gd 4, g-f 2, frm 3)
Light-framed, useful filly, effective 6 to 7f, best at 6f, acts on gd to frm, excels at Yarmouth. Turf high 92 - 3rd of 8 getting 1lb from Dandy Night (26 Jun Yarmouth 6f g-f RF 2291). Consistent.
**M L W Bell [2-13] W J P Jackson.*

BAILLIESTON (USA) BHB 85f RR 85f 5001[9]

2 ch g Indian Ridge 7.6f **(74)** - Bathilde (IRE) **(101f)** (Generous (IRE))
Form - 33510
Record 2000 - 1st:1 2nd:0 3rd:2 Ran:5
Win Prizemoney £3,770 *Total Prizemoney* £5,012
Wins * **2000** Oct Ayr (HVY) 7f 67+ <
2000 Turf 1-5: (6f, 7f 1-2, 8f 2) (hvy 1-1, sft, g-s, gd 2)
Useful gelding. Turf high 85 (began Aug). (DEAD)
**J S Goldie [1-5] Martin Delaney & Frank Brady.*

BAISSE D'ARGENT (IRE) BHB 48f RR 51f 3261[3]

4 b g Common Grounds 8.1f **(66)** - Fabulous Pet (Somethingfabulous (USA)) 9.5f **(75)**
Form - 3232483
Record 2000 - 1st:0 2nd:2 3rd:3 Ran:7
Pre2000 - 1st:1 2nd:0 3rd:0 Ran:8
Win Prizemoney £3,184 *Total Prizemoney* £7,520
Wins * 1998 Spt Mussel (GD) 8f 74 <
2000 Turf 0-4: (16f 2, 17f, 18f) (gd 2, frm 2) 2000 AW 0-3: (13f, 16f 2) (Equi 3)
Workmanlike, fair gelding, effective 18f, acts on frm, has worn blinkers, likes left handed tracks, likes tight tracks. Turf high 51 - 4th of 13 getting 2lb from Bustling Rio (25 Jun Pontefract 18f frm RF 2264). AW high 50. Consistent.
**D J S Cosgrove [3-19] Winning Circle Racing Club Ltd.*

BAJAN BELLE (IRE) BHB 54f68a RR 70f 68a 4809[15]

3 b f Efisio 7.7f **(69)** - With Love (Be My Guest (USA)) 9.3f **(67)**
Form - 084038022500
Record 2000 - 1st:0 2nd:2 3rd:1 Ran:12
Pre2000 - 1st:1 2nd:0 3rd:1 Ran:2
Win Prizemoney £2,697 *Total Prizemoney* £5,877
Wins * 1999 Jly Carlis (FRM) 5f 71+ <
2000 Turf 0-11: (6f 5, 7f 6) (g-s 3, gd, g-f, frm 6) 2000 AW 0-1: (6f) (Fibr)
Scopey, above-average filly, effective 5f, acts on frm, likes right handed tracks. Turf high 70. **M Johnston [1-14] R H A Smith.*

BAJAN BLUE BHB 54f RR 59f 5004[13]

2 b f Lycius (USA) 8.8f **(71)** - Serotina (IRE) (Mtoto)
Form - 63330
Record 2000 - 1st:0 2nd:0 3rd:3 Ran:5

Win Prizemoney £0 *Total Prizemoney* £1,584
2000 Turf 0-5: (6f 2, 7f 2, 8f) (g-s, g-f 3, frm)
Fair filly. Turf high 59 (began Jly) - 3rd of 7 getting 8lb from Scotish Law (16 Aug Epsom 6f g-f RF 3690).
**M Johnston [0-5] Mrs Louise Boggs.*

BAJAN BROKER (IRE) BHB 56f **RR 61f** 5071[4]

3 br f Turtle Island (IRE) - Foxrock (Ribero) 9.3f **(56)**
Form - 0405604
Record 2000 - 1st:0 2nd:0 3rd:0 Ran:7
Pre2000 - 1st:0 2nd:0 3rd:1 Ran:2
Win Prizemoney £0 *Total Prizemoney* £717
2000 Turf 0-7: (8f 3, 9f, 10f 3) (g-s 2, gd, g-f, frm 3)
Leggy, average filly, effective 7 to 10f, acts on gd. Turf high 61 - 5th of 13 giving 1lb to Paarl Rock (21 Aug Nottingham 10f gd RF 3843).
**E Stanners [0-4] P D Burnett (from N A Callaghan [0-3] Jly 2000).*

BAJAN SUNSET (IRE) BHB 47f **RR 51f** 4493[16]

3 ch c Mujtahid (USA) 7.4f **(69)** - Dubai Lady (Kris) 9.5f **(73)**
Form - 0622000
Record 2000 - 1st:0 2nd:2 3rd:0 Ran:7
Pre2000 - 1st:0 2nd:0 3rd:0 Ran:1
Win Prizemoney £0 *Total Prizemoney* £1,980
2000 Turf 0-7: (8f 5, 10f 2) (gd, g-f 3, frm 3)
Scopey, fair colt, effective 8f, acts on frm. Turf high 51 - 2nd of 13 getting 16lb from Evergreen (28 Jly Salisbury 8f frm RF 3183). Becoming disappointing. **J D Bethell [0-8] Mrs John Lee.*

BALACLAVA (IRE) BHB 30f41a **RR 28f 41a** 1260[13]

5 b g Balla Cove - Little Cynthia (Wolver Hollow) 8f **(56)**
Form - 0
Record 2000 - 1st:0 2nd:0 3rd:0 Ran:1
Pre2000 - 1st:0 2nd:1 3rd:1 Ran:14
Win Prizemoney £0 *Total Prizemoney* £1,641
2000 Turf 0-1: (7f) (g-f)
Moderate gelding, has worn blinkers. Inconsistent.
**A J McNae [0-6] J Willoughby (from I Semple [0-3] Feb 1998).*

BALANITA (IRE) BHB 48f56a **RR 42f 56a** 4875[11]

5 b g Anita's Prince 6f **(62)** - Ballybannon (Ballymore) 7.3f **(64)**
Form - 00025430
Record 2000 - 1st:0 2nd:1 3rd:1 Ran:7
Pre2000 - 1st:2 2nd:1 3rd:0 Ran:17
Win Prizemoney £6,353 *Total Prizemoney* £8,857
Wins * 1998 Jly Windso (GD) H 6f 67 76 <
* 1997 Oct Bright (G-F) H 7f 60 67
2000 Turf 0-7: (6f 5, 8f 2) (g-s, gd, g-f 3, frm 2)
Fair gelding, effective 7f, acts on frm, has worn blinkers. Turf high 57. Inconsistent. **B Palling [2-24] Mrs Anita Quinn.*

BALANOU BHB 50f **RR 48f** 5237[14]

2 b br f Valanour (IRE) - Batalya (BEL) (Boulou) 8.2f **(48)**
Form - 00
Record 2000 - 1st:0 2nd:0 3rd:0 Ran:2
2000 Turf 0-2: (7f, 8f) (g-s 2)
Currently moderate filly. Turf high 48 (began Oct).
**S C Williams [0-2] Mrs V Vilain.*

BALDAQUIN BHB 85f **RR 93f** 2755[11]

3 b c Barathea (IRE) - Nibbs Point (IRE) (Sure Blade (USA)) 11.3f **(67)**
Form - 04150
Record 2000 - 1st:1 2nd:0 3rd:0 Ran:5
Win Prizemoney £4,231 *Total Prizemoney* £4,231
Wins * 2000 Jun Goodwo (GD) 9.9f 85 <
2000 Turf 1-5: (8f, 10f 1-3, 12f) (gd 1-2, g-f, frm 2)
Strong, useful colt. Turf high 93 - 5th of 16 getting 10lb from Give The Slip (22 Jun Ascot 12f g-f RF 2182) - also 1st of 6 from Speed Venture (1 Jun Goodwood RF 1626). Ran very well in a handicap at Royal Ascot, if rather one-paced, after landing a maiden. Something was obviously amiss on his final start.
**J H M Gosden [1-5] Sheikh Mohammed.*

BALFOUR (IRE) BHB 68f **RR 67f** 4115[9]

3 b c Green Desert (USA) 7.8f **(78)** - Badawi (USA) (Diesis) 9.3f **(69)**
Form - 156034310
Record 2000 - 1st:2 2nd:0 3rd:2 Ran:9
Pre2000 - 1st:0 2nd:0 3rd:0 Ran:3
Win Prizemoney £6,724 *Total Prizemoney* £8,670
Wins * 2000 Aug Lingfi (G-F) H 7.6f 61 67 <
* 2000 Apr Warwic (HVY) H 6.8f 57 64
2000 Turf 2-9: (5f, 6f 3, 7f 1-3, 8f 1-2) (hvy 1-1, gd 2, g-f, frm 1-5)
Unfurnished, average colt, effective 6 to 8f, acts on hvy to frm, best on frm, has worn blinkers. Turf high 67 - 1st of 17 getting 17lb from Cedar Master (23 Aug Lingfield RF 3910) - also 1st of 19 from Aljazir (12 Apr Warwick RF 0687).
**C E Brittain [2-12] Sheikh Marwan Al Maktoum.*

BALI BATIK (IRE) BHB 79f **RR 86f** 5026[16]

3 b g Barathea (IRE) - Miss Garuda (Persian Bold) 9.3f **(66)**
Form - 4310440
Record 2000 - 1st:1 2nd:0 3rd:1 Ran:7
Pre2000 - 1st:0 2nd:0 3rd:0 Ran:1
Win Prizemoney £3,282 *Total Prizemoney* £5,499
Wins * 2000 May Lingfi (G-S) 7f 86 <
2000 Turf 1-7: (7f 1-3, 9f, 10f 3) (g-s 2, gd 1-2, g-f 2, frm)
Scopey, useful gelding, effective 7 to 10f, best at 7f, acts on gd to frm. Turf high 86 - 1st of 17 from Break The Glass (12 May Lingfield RF 1170). **G Wragg [1-8] J L C Pearce.*

BALIDARE BHB 36f **RR 35f** 4320[16]

3 b f King's Signet (USA) 7f **(51)** - Baligay (Balidar) 7.9f **(63)**
Form - 0800800
Record 2000 - 1st:0 2nd:0 3rd:0 Ran:7
Pre2000 - 1st:0 2nd:0 3rd:0 Ran:2
2000 Turf 0-7: (5f 4, 6f, 7f 2) (g-s, gd, g-f 3, frm, hrd)
Scopey, very moderate filly. Turf high 35. Inconsistent.
**M J Weeden [0-9] E W Carnell.*

BALI ROYAL BHB 55f **RR 58f** 5067[4]

2 b f King's Signet (USA) 7f **(51)** - Baligay (Balidar) 7.9f **(63)**
Form - 2878024
Record 2000 - 1st:0 2nd:2 3rd:0 Ran:7
Win Prizemoney £0 *Total Prizemoney* £1,240
2000 Turf 0-7: (5f 3, 6f 4) (g-s 2, gd 2, g-f, frm 2)
Fair filly, effective 5f, acts on g-s. Turf high 58.
**J M Bradley [0-7] Mrs R J Manning.*

BALI-STAR BHB 47f **RR 46f** 2848[2]

5 b g Alnasr Alwasheek 9.4f **(62)** - Baligay (Balidar) 7.9f **(63)**
Form - 207002
Record 2000 - 1st:0 2nd:2 3rd:0 Ran:6
Pre2000 - 1st:0 2nd:0 3rd:0 Ran:3
Win Prizemoney £0 *Total Prizemoney* £1,680
2000 Turf 0-6: (6f 5, 7f) (g-s, gd, g-f 2, frm 2)
Moderate gelding, effective 6f, acts on g-f. Turf high 47.
**M J Weeden [0-9] E W Carnell.*

BALLA D'AIRE (IRE) BHB 30f **RR 32f** 247[5]

5 b br g Balla Cove - Silius (Junius (USA)) 7.7f **(65)**
Form - 5
Record 2000 - 1st:0 2nd:0 3rd:0 Ran:1
Pre2000 - 1st:0 2nd:0 3rd:0 Ran:13
Win Prizemoney £0 *Total Prizemoney* £242
2000 AW 0-1: (13f) (Equi)
Very moderate gelding, has worn blinkers.
**B R Johnson [0-13] Miss Julie Reeves (from M L W Bell [0-6] Spt 1998).*

BALLADEER (IRE) BHB 80f74a **RR 72f 74a** 3728[4]

2 b c King's Theatre (IRE) - Carousel Music **(36f)** (On Your Mark) 7.7f **(58)**
Form - 04
Record 2000 - 1st:0 2nd:0 3rd:0 Ran:2
Win Prizemoney £0 *Total Prizemoney* £225
2000 Turf 0-2: (7f 2) (g-f, frm)
Currently above-average colt. Turf high 72 (began Jly) - 4th of 9 getting 2lb from Bourgainville (17 Aug Salisbury 7f frm RF 3728).
**J W Hills [0-2] Scott Hardy Partnership.*

BALLADONIA BHB 91f **RR 94f** 4647[8]

4 b f Primo Dominie 7.2f **(67)** - Susquehanna Days (USA) (Chief's Crown (USA)) 9.8f **(72)**

Form - 65458
Record 2000 - 1st:0 2nd:0 3rd:0 Ran:5
Pre2000 - 1st:1 2nd:4 3rd:1 Ran:10
Win Prizemoney £4,381 *Total Prizemoney* £18,973
Wins * 1999 May Goodwo (GD) 9f 82 <
2000 Turf 0-5: (10f 3, 12f 2) (g-s, gd, g-f 2, frm)
Scopey, useful filly, effective 10 to 12f, best at 10f, acts on g-s to frm, best on gd. Turf high 94 (began Aug) - 5th of 15 giving 3lb to Courting (12 Spt Yarmouth 10f gd RF 4330). Consistent.
**Lady Herries [1-15] D K R & Mrs J B C Oliver.*

BALLET HIGH (IRE) BHB 65f **RR 32f** 5111[12]
7 b g Sadler's Wells (USA) 11.3f **(87)** - Marie D'Argonne (FR) (Jefferson) 7.9f **(89)**
Form - 0
Record 2000 - 1st:0 2nd:0 3rd:0 Ran:1
Pre2000 - 1st:0 2nd:1 3rd:3 Ran:5
Win Prizemoney £0 *Total Prizemoney* £3,813
2000 Turf 0-1: (16f) (gd)
Very moderate gelding.
**R Dickin [1-6] Wholebuild Ltd (from I A Balding [0-4] Spt 1996).*

BALLET MASTER (USA) BHB 75f **RR ?f** 857[9]
4 ch c Kingmambo (USA) 10.9f **(85)** - Danse Royale (IRE) (Caerleon (USA)) 8.6f **(71)**
Form - 0
Record 2000 - 1st:0 2nd:0 3rd:0 Ran:1
Pre2000 - 1st:1 2nd:0 3rd:0 Ran:2
Win Prizemoney £3,157 *Total Prizemoney* £3,582
Wins 1998 Oct Yarmou (SFT) 7f 78++ <
2000 Turf 0-1: (7f) (hvy)
Tall, very poor colt. He looked a decent sort early on in his career when with Henry Cecil, but he has had his problems and is now with Mick Easterby. Yet to really show that he retains much ability.
**M W Easterby [0-2] Guy Reed & Winton Bloodstock (from H R A Cecil [1-2] Apr 1999).*

BALLETS RUSSES (IRE) BHB 40f30a **RR 52f 30a** 5122[12]
3 b f Marju (IRE) 9.2f **(76)** -Elminya (IRE) (Sure Blade (USA)) 11.3f **(67)**
Form - 43008060
Record 2000 - 1st:0 2nd:0 3rd:1 Ran:8
Pre2000 - 1st:0 2nd:0 3rd:0 Ran:3
Win Prizemoney £0 *Total Prizemoney* £638
2000 Turf 0-8: (5f, 6f 2, 7f 3, 8f 2) (g-s, gd 2, g-f 3, frm, hrd)
Lengthy, fair filly, effective 7f, acts on g-f. Turf high 52 - 3rd of 11 giving 11lb to Rio's Diamond (19 Jun Warwick 7f g-f RF 2100). Inconsistent. **H J Collingridge [0-11] G B Amy.*

BALL GAMES BHB 64f **RR 70?f** 5296[4]
2 b c Mind Games - Deb's Ball **(43f)** (Glenstal (USA)) 10.1f **(64)**
Form - 6468404
Record 2000 - 1st:0 2nd:0 3rd:0 Ran:7
Win Prizemoney £0 *Total Prizemoney* £725
2000 Turf 0-7: (5f 3, 6f, 7f, 8f 2) (hvy, g-s, gd 4, frm)
Above-average colt, effective 8f, acts on hvy. Turf high 70.
**D Moffatt [0-7] Cartmel Bloodstock.*

BALLINA LAD (IRE) BHB 42f52a **RR 40f 52a** 4396[8]
4 b g Mac's Imp (USA) 5.6f **(54)** - Nationalartgallery (IRE) (Tate Gallery (USA)) 7.4f **(67)**
Form - 005068
Record 2000 - 1st:0 2nd:0 3rd:0 Ran:6
Pre2000 - 1st:2 2nd:0 3rd:1 Ran:13
Win Prizemoney £5,344 *Total Prizemoney* £6,151
Wins * 1999 May Ripon (G-F) H 6f 58 60
* 1998 May Newcas (G-S) 5f 81+
2000 Turf 0-5: (6f 5) (g-f, frm 2, hrd 2) 2000 AW 0-1: (6f) (Fibr)
Neat, moderate gelding, effective 6f, acts on frm, has worn blinkers. Turf high 40 (began Jly). **J G FitzGerald [2-19] Mike Browne.*

BALLISTIC BOY BHB 58f **RR 62f** 1851[10]
3 ch g First Trump - Be Discreet (Junius (USA)) 7.7f **(65)**
Form - 0830
Record 2000 - 1st:0 2nd:0 3rd:1 Ran:4
Pre2000 - 1st:0 2nd:0 3rd:0 Ran:3
Win Prizemoney £0 *Total Prizemoney* £400
2000 Turf 0-4: (8f 3, 9f) (g-s, gd, g-f, frm)
Leggy, average gelding, effective 9f, acts on frm. Turf high 62 - 3rd of 8 giving 3lb to Sham Sharif (1 Jun Ayr 9f frm RF 1618).
**J J O'Neill [0-4] A J Oliver (from A T Murphy [0-3] Oct 1999).*

BALLYCROY RIVER BHB 28f35a **RR 42f 35a** 355[11]
4 b g Sizzling Melody 6.3f **(49)** - Little Tich (Great Nephew) 9.9f **(64)**
Form - 080
Record 2000 - 1st:0 2nd:0 3rd:0 Ran:3
Pre2000 - 1st:0 2nd:0 3rd:1 Ran:9
Win Prizemoney £0 *Total Prizemoney* £198
2000 AW 0-3: (8f 2, 16f) (Fibr 3)
Light-framed, moderate gelding, has worn blinkers. AW high 21. Becoming disappointing. **B A McMahon [0-14] C G Conway.*

BALLY CYRANO BHB 36f44a **RR 4f 44a** 3976[11]
3 b g Cyrano de Bergerac 7.3f **(58)** - Iolite (Forzando) 7.6f **(59)**
Form - 0000
Record 2000 - 1st:0 2nd:0 3rd:0 Ran:4
Pre2000 - 1st:0 2nd:0 3rd:1 Ran:4
Win Prizemoney £0 *Total Prizemoney* £376
2000 Turf 0-2: (5f, 8f) (gd, frm) 2000 AW 0-2: (5f, 6f) (Fibr 2)
Scopey, very poor gelding, has worn blinkers. Turf high 4 (began Aug). Becoming disappointing. **B A McMahon [0-8] C G Conway.*

BALLYKISSANN BHB 30f **RR 29f** 2792[11]
5 ch g Ballacashtal (CAN) 7.9f **(51)** - Mybella Ann (Anfield) 8.5f **(59)**
Form - 7000
Record 2000 - 1st:0 2nd:0 3rd:0 Ran:4
Pre2000 - 1st:0 2nd:0 3rd:1 Ran:10
Win Prizemoney £0 *Total Prizemoney* £336
2000 Turf 0-4: (8f 3, 10f) (gd 2, frm, hrd)
Little account gelding, has worn blinkers. Turf high 29. Becoming disappointing.
**J C Tuck [0-12] Paul De Weck (from D J S ffrenchDavis [0-10] Aug 1998).*

BALLYMORRIS BOY (IRE) BHB 45f37a **RR 47f 37a** 373[5]
4 b c Dolphin Street (FR) - Solas Abu (IRE) (Red Sunset) 8.2f **(63)**
Form - 75343468305
Record 2000 - 1st:0 2nd:0 3rd:2 Ran:7
Pre2000 - 1st:0 2nd:1 3rd:3 Ran:20
Win Prizemoney £0 *Total Prizemoney* £2,730
2000 AW 0-7: (7f 3, 8f 2, 10f, 12f) (Equi 3, Fibr 4)
Leggy, moderate colt, effective 6 to 7f, best at 7f, acts on frm to hrd, best on frm, has worn blinkers, likes left handed tracks, likes tight tracks. AW high 48.
**J Pearce [0-26] Saracen Racing (from W R Muir [0-1] Oct 1998).*

BALLY PRIDE (IRE) BHB 100f **RR 101f** 3578[5]
3 ch g Pips Pride 6.7f **(70)** - Ballysnip (Ballymore) 7.3f **(64)**
Form - 4035
Record 2000 - 1st:0 2nd:0 3rd:1 Ran:4
Pre2000 - 1st:1 2nd:2 3rd:2 Ran:9
Win Prizemoney £59,000 *Total Prizemoney* £89,647
Wins * 1999 Jun Currag (G-F) 6.3f 93 <
2000 Turf 0-4: (6f 3, 7f) (g-s, gd, g-f, frm)
Scopey, very useful gelding, effective 6 to 7f, best at 6f, acts on gd to frm, has worn blinkers. Turf high 101. Consistent. Effective at up to seven furlongs, he showed useful form as a juvenile but did not prove easy to place in a light campaign last season.
**T D Easterby [1-13] G Siu.*

BALMAINE (USA) RR 47f 4129[10]
2 b f Gulch (USA) 9.6f **(79)** - Silk Slippers (USA) (Nureyev (USA)) 8.7f **(78)**
Form - 0
Record 2000 - 1st:0 2nd:0 3rd:0 Ran:1
2000 Turf 0-1: (7f) (frm)
Currently moderate filly. **J H M Gosden [0-1] R E Sangster.*

BALSOX BHB 75f **RR 79f** 879[10]
4 b g Alzao (USA) 9.8f **(73)** - Bobbysoxer (Valiyar) 8.5f **(73)**
Form - 0
Record 2000 - 1st:0 2nd:0 3rd:0 Ran:1
Pre2000 - 1st:1 2nd:1 3rd:0 Ran:9
Win Prizemoney £3,419 *Total Prizemoney* £7,256
Wins 1999 Mar Nottin (G-S) 8.2f 76+ <

2000 Turf 0-1: (12f) (sft)
Workmanlike, above-average gelding, effective 8f, acts on g-s, has worn blinkers, favours tight tracks.
**S Dow [0-3] Nil Desperandum (from J L Dunlop [1-9] Spt 1999).*

BAMBOO GARDEN (USA) BHB 38f58a **RR 52f 58a** 5244[8]
4 b g Desert Secret (IRE) - Miss Mischievous (USA) (Brazen Brother (USA))
Form - 08
Record 2000 - 1st:0 2nd:0 3rd:0 Ran:2
Pre2000 - 1st:1 2nd:0 3rd:1 Ran:8
Win Prizemoney £1,872 *Total Prizemoney* £2,341
Wins * 1999 *Feb Southw (STD) SH 8f 55 59* <
2000 AW 0-2: (12f, 14f) (Fibr 2)
Well made, fair gelding, effective 8f, - acts on Fibr, often wears blinkers. AW high 7 (began Oct). Becoming disappointing.
**G C H Chung [1-10] J Tse.*

BAMBOOZLE BHB 35f **RR 42f** 5182[11]
4 b f Alhijaz 7.7f **(57)** - Frustration **(105f)** (Salse (USA)) 7.5f **(66)**
Form - 0500060
Record 2000 - 1st:0 2nd:0 3rd:0 Ran:7
2000 Turf 0-6: (8f, 10f, 12f 2, 14f 2) (sft, g-s, g-f 3, frm) 2000 AW 0-1: (15f) (Fibr)
Scopey, moderate filly. Turf high 58.
**Lady Herries [0-7] The High Flying Partnership.*

BAMFORD CASTLE (IRE) RR 90f 5180a[9]
5 b g Scenic 10.6f **(66)** - Allorette (Ballymore) 7.3f **(64)**
Form - 81120
2000 Turf 2-4: (11f, 12f, 14f 2-2) (g-s 1-2, gd 1-2)
Useful gelding, effective 12 to 14f, best at 14f, acts on g-s to gd, best on gd, likes right handed tracks. Turf high 90 - 2nd of 15 giving 12lb to Tragic Lover (2 Jly Curragh 12f gd RF 2533a) - also 1st of 7 giving 18lb to Keeping The Faith (25 Jun Gowran Park RF 2323a). **P Mullins in IRE [8-33] John Brophy.*

BANAFSAJYH (IRE) BHB 79f **RR 83f** 3555[1]
3 b f Lion Cavern (USA) 7.5f **(74)** - Arylh (USA) (Lyphard (USA)) 9.9f **(72)**
Form - 10481
Record 2000 - 1st:2 2nd:0 3rd:0 Ran:5
Pre2000 - 1st:0 2nd:1 3rd:1 Ran:3
Win Prizemoney £10,308 *Total Prizemoney* £12,332
Wins *** 2000** Aug Lingfi (G-F) H 6f 75 79
*** 2000** May Nottin (G-F) 6.1f 83 <
2000 Turf 2-5: (6f 2-4, 7f) (g-f 2, frm 2-3)
Scopey, decent filly, effective 6f, acts on g-f to frm, best on frm. Turf high 83 (1st run) - 1st of 20 getting 5lb from Parker (12 May Nottingham RF 1175) - also 1st of 12 giving 1lb to Chiquita (11 Aug Lingfield RF 3555). **A C Stewart [2-8] Hamdan Al Maktoum.*

BANBURY (USA) BHB 94f92a **RR 96f 92a** 796[8]
6 b g Silver Hawk (USA) 11.2f **(85)** - Sugar Hollow (USA) (Val de L'Orne (FR)) 12f **(75)**
Form - 8
Record 2000 - 1st:0 2nd:0 3rd:0 Ran:1
Pre2000 - 1st:4 2nd:5 3rd:3 Ran:18
Win Prizemoney £11,992 *Total Prizemoney* £36,674
Wins * 1999 *Mar Lingfi (STD) 12f 79*
* 1999 *Feb Lingfi (STD) H 12f 72 74*
* 1999 *Jan Lingfi (STD) C 12f 65+*
1997 May Redcar (GD) 10f 94 <
2000 Turf 0-1: (12f) (gd)
Very useful gelding, effective 12 to 14f, best at 12f, acts on gd to g-f, best on g-f, has worn blinkers. (1st run) - 8th of 21 giving 1lb to Mowelga (19 Apr Newmarket 12f gd RF 0796). A tough and useful middle-distance handicapper, he has been hard to train.
**C A Dwyer [3-12] Cedar Lodge Syndicate (from M Johnston [0-2] Jly 1998).*

BANCO SUIVI (IRE) BHB 83f82a **RR 86f 82a** 4936[8]
3 b f Nashwan (USA) 10.3f **(79)** - Pay the Bank (High Top) 10.2f **(67)**
Form - 2723138
Record 2000 - 1st:1 2nd:2 3rd:2 Ran:7
Pre2000 - 1st:0 2nd:0 3rd:0 Ran:1
Win Prizemoney £4,192 *Total Prizemoney* £10,416
Wins *** 2000** Aug Doncas (G-F) 12f 86 <
2000 Turf 1-7: (10f, 11f 3, 12f 1-2, 14f) (sft, gd 2, g-f 1-2, frm 2)
Light-framed, useful filly, effective 7 to 14f, acts on sft to frm, best on g-f. Turf high 86 - 3rd of 6 getting 16lb from Jardines Lookout (16 Spt Newmarket 14f g-f RF 4469) - also 1st of 6 from Second Affair (5 Aug Doncaster RF 3387). Consistent. Not winning out of turn when successful at Doncaster, she is suited by forcing tactics over a mile and a half. **B W Hills [1-8] Wafic Said.*

BANDANNA BHB 84f **RR 83f** 4483[4]
3 gr f Bandmaster (USA) - Gratclo (Belfort (FR)) 6.8f **(63)**
Form - 006516354
Record 2000 - 1st:1 2nd:0 3rd:1 Ran:9
Pre2000 - 1st:1 2nd:1 3rd:1 Ran:6
Win Prizemoney £9,198 *Total Prizemoney* £18,985
Wins *** 2000** Jly Bath (FRM) H 5.1f 79 83 <
* 1999 May Chepst (GD) S 6.1f 68+
2000 Turf 1-9: (5f 1-4, 6f 4, 7f) (g-s 2, gd 2, g-f 2, frm 2, hrd 1-1)
Lengthy, decent filly, effective 5 to 6f, best at 5f, acts on g-s to hrd, excels at Bath. Turf high 83 - also 1st of 10 getting 3lb from Ansellad (20 Jly Bath RF 2956). Consistent. Won a Chepstow seller on her two-year-old debut, but was not disgraced in much better company afterwards. Some decent efforts last term, landing a showcase handicap at Bath in July.
**R J Hodges [2-15] Miss R Dobson.*

BANDARELLO RR 55f 3525[6]
2 b f Distant Relative 7f **(69)** - Bangles **(62f 61a)** (Chilibang)
Form - 6
Record 2000 - 1st:0 2nd:0 3rd:0 Ran:1
2000 Turf 0-1: (5f) (frm)
Currently fair filly. **D J Coakley [0-1] J Rose.*

BANDBOX (IRE) BHB 67f63a **RR 68f 63a** 4618[5]
5 ch g Imperial Frontier (USA) 7f **(65)** - Dublah (USA) (Private Account (USA)) 8.5f **(74)**
Form - 1278730673062361255
Record 2000 - 1st:2 2nd:3 3rd:3 Ran:19
Pre2000 - 1st:2 2nd:8 3rd:6 Ran:37
Win Prizemoney £10,897 *Total Prizemoney* £24,283
Wins *** 2000** Aug Folkes (G-F) 6f 61
*** 2000** *Feb Southw (STD) C 7f 60*
* 1999 Aug Leices (GD) 6f 66
1997 Oct Leices (GD) 6f 78 <
2000 Turf 1-16: (5f 3, 6f 1-10, 7f 2, 8f) (gd 1-7, g-f 4, frm 5) 2000 AW 1-3: (7f 1-3) (Fibr 1-3)
Average gelding, effective 5 to 7f, best at 6f, acts on gd to frm - acts on Fibr, best on g-f, has worn blinkers, excels at Chepstow, does well at Leicester and Southwell. Turf high 68 - 2nd of 20 giving 17lb to American Cousin (7 Spt Chepstow 5f g-f RF 4276) - also 1st of 12 from Double Bounce (24 Aug Folkestone RF 3924). AW high 63 - 2nd of 11 giving 2lb to Distinctive Dream (28 Feb Southwell 7f Fibr RF 0368) - also 1st of 8 giving 15lb to Guest Envoy (14 Feb Southwell RF 0277). Consistent.
**M Salaman [3-45] Brookes, Else, Salaman (from S Mellor [1-11] Oct 1997).*

BANDIDA (GER) BHB 27f **RR 24f** 4122[10]
6 ch m Neshad (USA) 5.5f **(59)** - Bula (GER) (Wildschutz (GER))
Form - 760700
Record 2000 - 1st:0 2nd:0 3rd:0 Ran:6
2000 Turf 0-6: (5f 4, 7f, 8f) (sft, frm 4, hrd)
Little account mare. Turf high 24.
**Mrs D Thomson [0-10] Mrs Jean McGregor.*

BANDIDO RR 4272[14]
3 b g Piccolo - Ideal Candidate **(69df 57a)** (Celestial Storm (USA))
Form - 0
Record 2000 - 1st:0 2nd:0 3rd:0 Ran:1
2000 Turf 0-1: (8f) (g-f)
Currently very poor gelding. **Miss K M George [0-1] R J Matthews.*

BAND IS PASSING (USA) RR 579a[11]
4 m No Horse (FR) 10f **(95)** - 00
Form - 0
2000 AW 0-1: (12f) (Dirt)
Currently very useful. **S Ersoff in USA [0-1].*

BANDLER CHING (IRE) BHB 72f **RR 78+f** 4734[13]
3 b g Sri Pekan (USA) - Stanerra's Wish (IRE) (Caerleon (USA)) 8.6f **(71)**
Form - 521340
Record 2000 - 1st:1 2nd:1 3rd:1 Ran:6
Pre2000 - 1st:0 2nd:1 3rd:3 Ran:5
Win Prizemoney £5,044 *Total Prizemoney* £11,332
Wins * 2000 Aug Leices (G-F) H 10f 68 78+ <
2000 Turf 1-6: (10f 1-5, 11f) (gd, g-f, frm 1-4)
Above-average gelding, effective 7 to 10f, best at 10f, acts on g-f to frm, best on frm. Turf high 78 (began Jly) - 1st of 14 giving 6lb to Eastwood Drifter (9 Aug Leicester RF 3490).
**C N Allen [1-8] Newmarket Connections Ltd (from Pat Mitchell [0-3] Oct 1999).*

BANDORE (IRE) BHB 48f **RR** 5069[19]
6 ch g Salse (USA) 10.9f **(71)** - Key Tothe Minstrel (USA) (The Minstrel (CAN)) 10f **(72)**
Form - 00
Record 2000 - 1st:0 2nd:0 3rd:0 Ran:2
Pre2000 - 1st:1 2nd:0 3rd:0 Ran:8
Win Prizemoney £4,201 *Total Prizemoney* £4,431
Wins 1996 Spt Lingfi (FRM) 7.6f 72 <
2000 Turf 0-2: (12f, 14f) (g-s, gd)
Very poor gelding. (began Spt).
**M Blanshard [0-5] C McKenna (from D R Loder [1-8] Spt 1997).*

BANGALORE BHB 92f **RR 93f** 4438[1]
4 ch c Sanglamore (USA) 12.9f **(67)** - Ajuga (USA) (The Minstrel (CAN)) 10f **(72)**
Form - 3171
Record 2000 - 1st:2 2nd:0 3rd:1 Ran:4
Pre2000 - 1st:1 2nd:1 3rd:2 Ran:9
Win Prizemoney £74,774 *Total Prizemoney* £81,449
Wins * 2000 Spt Newbur (G-F) H 16f 90 93 <
*** 2000** May Cheste (GD) H 18.7f 81 88
1999 Apr Pontef (SFT) 10f 85
2000 Turf 2-4: (16f 1-2, 19f 1-1, 20f) (sft, gd, g-f 1-1, frm 1-1)
Scopey, useful colt, effective 10 to 19f, acts on sft to frm, best on g-f, prefers left handed tracks, prefers tight tracks. Turf high 93 - 1st of 9 giving 17lb to First Officer (15 Spt Newbury RF 4438) - also 1st of 18 getting 1lb from Ansar (10 May Chester RF 1129). Consistent. Useful under both codes, he won two of his three starts on the level including the Chester Cup. He stays well.
**Mrs A J Perrett [4-8] Mike Dawson (from B W Hills [1-9] Oct 1999).*

BANGLED BHB 43f50a **RR 42f 50a** 5120[8]
3 ch g Beveled (USA) 6.9f **(64)** - Bangles **(62f 61a)** (Chilibang)
Form - 080030428
Record 2000 - 1st:0 2nd:1 3rd:1 Ran:9
Pre2000 - 1st:0 2nd:0 3rd:1 Ran:5
Win Prizemoney £0 *Total Prizemoney* £1,782
2000 Turf 0-5: (5f, 6f 4) (gd, g-f 2, frm 2) 2000 AW 0-4: (6f 4) (Equi, Fibr 3)
Unfurnished, fair gelding. Turf high 42. AW high 50.
**D J Coakley [0-14] J J Henderson.*

BANITA RR 40f 4324[9]
2 b f Balnibarbi - Something Speedy (IRE) **(31f 40a)** (Sayf El Arab (USA)) 7.1f **(54)**
Form - 80
Record 2000 - 1st:0 2nd:0 3rd:0 Ran:2
2000 Turf 0-2: (6f, 7f) (gd, g-f)
Currently moderate filly. Turf high 40 (began Jly).
**B Palling [0-2] A Quinn, M Palling, P McCormack & P Kerr.*

BANIYAR (IRE) BHB 102f **RR 104f** 2206[5]
3 ch c Alzao (USA) 9.8f **(73)** - Banaja (IRE) (Sadler's Wells (USA)) 10f **(76)**
Form - 415
Record 2000 - 1st:1 2nd:0 3rd:0 Ran:3
Pre2000 - 1st:0 2nd:0 3rd:0 Ran:1
Win Prizemoney £4,914 *Total Prizemoney* £5,251
Wins * 2000 May Hamilt (G-F) 11.1f 72+ <
2000 Turf 1-3: (11f 1-2, 12f) (sft, gd, g-f 1-1)
Well made, very useful colt. Turf high 104 - 5th of 7 to Subtle Power (23 Jun Ascot 12f gd RF 2206). Easily landed a Hamilton maiden, and made the steep climb to Group Two level at Ascot next time. By no means disgraced in finishing fifth, he was not seen again. **Sir Michael Stoute [1-4] H H Aga Khan.*

BANJO BAY (IRE) BHB 66f **RR 63f** 4313[10]
2 b c Common Grounds 8.1f **(66)** - Thirlmere (Cadeaux Genereux)
Form - 53050
Record 2000 - 1st:0 2nd:0 3rd:1 Ran:5
Win Prizemoney £0 *Total Prizemoney* £1,090
2000 Turf 0-5: (5f 4, 7f) (gd 3, g-f, frm)
Average colt. Turf high 63. Showed up well on his debut, and is from a yard whose juveniles have made a good start.
**B A McMahon [0-5] Mrs C P Lees-Jones.*

BANK BUSTER BHB 20f **RR** 2339[11]
3 b g Mutamarrid - Miss Brook (Meadowbrook)
Form - 000
Record 2000 - 1st:0 2nd:0 3rd:0 Ran:3
2000 Turf 0-3: (8f, 9f, 12f) (gd, g-f 2)
Currently very poor gelding, has worn blinkers.
**W T Kemp [0-3] G Lofthouse.*

BANK ON HIM BHB 48f73a **RR 43f 73a** 205[6]
5 b g Elmaamul (USA) 8.1f **(70)** - Feather Flower (Relkino) 8.9f **(65)**
Form - 6
Record 2000 - 1st:0 2nd:0 3rd:0 Ran:1
Pre2000 - 1st:3 2nd:4 3rd:3 Ran:20
Win Prizemoney £12,535 *Total Prizemoney* £17,061
Wins * 1999 *Feb Lingfi (STD) H 10f 74 75* <
* 1999 *Jan Lingfi (STD) H 10f 67 75* <
* 1998 *Spt Wolver (STD) H 8.5f 56 63*
2000 AW 0-1: (10f) (Equi)
Above-average gelding, effective 10f, - acts on Equi, prefers left handed tracks. Becoming disappointing.
**G L Moore [3-22] Allen House Partnership.*

BANNERET (USA) BHB 32f38a **RR 19f 38a** 1372[6]
7 b g Imperial Falcon (CAN) 9.2f **(72)** - Dashing Partner (Formidable (USA)) 9.2f **(63)**
Form - 4217532646
Record 2000 - 1st:1 2nd:2 3rd:1 Ran:9
Pre2000 - 1st:5 2nd:2 3rd:2 Ran:22
Win Prizemoney £12,721 *Total Prizemoney* £15,735
Wins * 2000 *Jan Wolver (STD) C 12f 48*
* 1999 *Oct Wolver (STD) H 12f 56 63*
* 1999 *Spt Southw (STD) C 11f 60+*
* 1998 *Jly Southw (STD) S 12f 64*
1998 *Jly Wolver (STD) S 12f 64*
1998 *Mar Wolver (STD) 9.4f 72+* <
2000 AW 1-9: (12f 1-7, 14f, 16f) (Fibr 1-9)
Moderate gelding, effective 11 to 12f, best at 12f, - acts on Fibr, has worn blinkers. AW high 51.
**Miss S J Wilton [4-22] John Pointon and Sons (from G Woodward [2-5] Jly 1998).*

BANNINGHAM BLIZ BHB 52f **RR 58df** 3489[3]
2 ch f Inchinor 8.9f **(64)** - Mary From Dunlow (Nicholas Bill) 10.1f **(56)**
Form - 0065438223
Record 2000 - 1st:0 2nd:2 3rd:2 Ran:10
Win Prizemoney £0 *Total Prizemoney* £1,615
2000 Turf 0-10: (5f 4, 6f 4, 7f 2) (gd 5, g-f, frm 4)
Fair filly, effective 6 to 7f, acts on frm, has worn blinkers (extremely effectively). Turf high 54. **D Shaw [0-10] Crown Select.*

BANNISTER RR 95f 4699[10]
2 ch c Inchinor 8.9f **(64)** - Shall We Run (Hotfoot) 10.5f **(59)**
Form - 2210
Record 2000 - 1st:1 2nd:2 3rd:0 Ran:4
Win Prizemoney £72,500 *Total Prizemoney* £75,146
Wins * 2000 Aug York (GD) G2 6f 95 <
2000 Turf 1-4: (6f 1-4) (g-f 2, frm 1-2)
Very useful colt. Turf high 95 - 1st of 10 from Zilch (23 Aug York RF 3915). Runner-up in two decent six-furlong maidens, he got off the mark in the Gimcrack at York, collaring stablemate Zilch close home. He finished last in the Middle Park on his final run and may not be easy to place at three.

**R Hannon [1-4] The Royal Ascot Racing Club.*

BANSTEAD (USA) RR 53f 5023[5]
2 b c Known Fact (USA) 8.3f **(72)** - Rapid Raja (USA) (Darby Creek Road (USA)) 9.5f **(77)**
Form - 5
Record 2000 - 1st:0 2nd:0 3rd:0 Ran:1
2000 Turf 0-1: (7f) (g-s)
Currently fair colt. **T G Mills [0-1] M J Joyce.*

BANYUMANIK (IRE) RR 117f 4951a[2]
4 b c Perugino (USA) - Bennetta (FR) (Top Ville) 11.7f **(68)**
Form - 2122
2000 Turf 1-4: (8f 2, 9f 1-2) (sft 3, gd 1-1)
High-class colt, effective 8 to 11f, best at 8f, acts on sft to gd, best on sft. Turf high 117 - 1st of 10 getting 4lb from Elle Danzig (18 Jun Dortmund RF 2202a). **M Hofer in GER [1-7] Stall Sorpresa.*

BAPTISMAL ROCK (IRE) BHB 51f42a **RR 51f 42a** 391[11]
6 ch g Ballad Rock 7.2f **(63)** - Flower From Heaven (Baptism) 10f **(59)**
Form - 7850
Record 2000 - 1st:0 2nd:0 3rd:0 Ran:3
Pre2000 - 1st:3 2nd:6 3rd:5 Ran:37
Win Prizemoney £10,212 *Total Prizemoney* £20,807
Wins * 1999 *Jan Southw (STD) H 6f 44 57* <
* 1999 *Jan Lingfi (STD) H 6f 44 54*
* 1999 *Jan Wolver (STD) H 6f 37 37*
2000 AW 0-3: (5f, 6f 2) (Fibr 3)
Fair gelding, effective 5 to 6f, best at 6f, acts on gd to frm - acts on AW, best on Fibr, likes tight tracks, excels at Southwell, likes Lingfield. AW high 42.
**A G Newcombe [3-24] M Patel (from B J Curley [0-9] Aug 1998).*

BAQUERIZO (IRE) RR 710a[8]
3 f
Form - 8
Record 2000 - 1st:0 2nd:0 3rd:0 Ran:1
2000 Turf 0-1: (8f) (hvy)
Currently very poor filly - 8th of 10 getting 8lb from Karpaasi (9 Apr San Siro 8f hvy RF 0710a). **L M Cumani [0-1].*

BARABASCHI BHB 74f **RR 78f** 4597[16]
4 b g Elmaamul (USA) 8.1f **(70)** - Hills' Presidium (Presidium)
Form - 2261200
Record 2000 - 1st:1 2nd:3 3rd:0 Ran:7
Pre2000 - 1st:0 2nd:4 3rd:2 Ran:10
Win Prizemoney £3,412 *Total Prizemoney* £11,046
Wins * 2000 Aug Ayr (G-F) 8f 64+ <
2000 Turf 1-7: (7f 2, 8f 1-5) (g-s, gd 2, g-f 2, frm 1-2)
Leggy, above-average gelding, effective 7 to 8f, best at 8f, acts on gd to g-f, best on g-f, has worn blinkers. Turf high 76 - 2nd of 9 giving 32lb to Warring (20 Aug Bath 8f g-f RF 3814). Consistent. He had had plenty of chances before winning a maiden in August. Respectable efforts since.
**J H M Gosden [1-7] Dr Ornella Carlini Cozzi (from A G Foster [0-2] Oct 1999).*

BARAGUEY (FR) BHB 75f **RR 67f** 1112[13]
6 ch g Marignan (USA) - Liberty Nell (Weavers' Hall) 9.8f **(53)**
Form - 00
Record 2000 - 1st:0 2nd:0 3rd:0 Ran:2
2000 Turf 0-2: (8f, 10f) (sft, g-f)
Average gelding. Turf high 67. **C R Egerton [0-4] Andy Smith.*

BARAKANA (IRE) BHB 74f **RR 76f** 4675[7]
2 b c Barathea (IRE) - Safkana (IRE) (Doyoun) 9f **(69)**
Form - 33263507
Record 2000 - 1st:0 2nd:1 3rd:3 Ran:8
Win Prizemoney £0 *Total Prizemoney* £4,475
2000 Turf 0-8: (5f, 6f 2, 7f 4, 8f) (g-s 3, g-f, frm 4)
Above-average colt, effective 7f, acts on frm, often wears blinkers (very effectively). Turf high 76 - 3rd of 8 giving 8lb to Meriden Mist (24 Jly Brighton 7f frm RF 3075). **B J Meehan [0-8] Merlyn II.*

BARAKULA BHB 90f **RR 88f** 4470[8]
3 b f Barathea (IRE) - Bright Generation (IRE) (Rainbow Quest (USA)) 10.4f **(75)**
Form - 8
Record 2000 - 1st:0 2nd:0 3rd:0 Ran:1
Pre2000 - 1st:1 2nd:0 3rd:0 Ran:2
Win Prizemoney £4,981 *Total Prizemoney* £8,456
Wins * 1999 Jun Windso (G-F) 6f 75+ <
2000 Turf 0-1: (10f) (g-f)
Scopey, currently useful filly.
**P F I Cole [1-3] H R H Prince Fahd Salman.*

BARANN BHB 14f18a **RR 35f 18a** 3213[12]
4 ch g Henbit (USA) 10.2f **(46)** - Opalkino (Relkino) 8.9f **(65)**
Form - 00000
Record 2000 - 1st:0 2nd:0 3rd:0 Ran:3
Pre2000 - 1st:0 2nd:0 3rd:0 Ran:4
2000 Turf 0-1: (14f) (frm) 2000 AW 0-2: (12f, 13f) (Equi, Fibr)
Unfurnished, very moderate gelding.
**J M Bradley [0-7] Mrs Ann Tomlinson.*

BARANOVA (IRE) RR 76f 4214[1]
2 b f Caerleon (USA) 10.9f **(79)** - Lacandona (USA) **(62f 60a)** (Septieme Ciel (USA))
Form - 51
Record 2000 - 1st:1 2nd:0 3rd:0 Ran:2
Win Prizemoney £3,887 *Total Prizemoney* £3,887
Wins * 2000 Spt Leices (G-F) 8f 76 <
2000 Turf 1-2: (7f, 8f 1-1) (g-f, frm 1-1)
Currently above-average filly. Turf high 76 (began Aug) - 1st of 6 from Guardia (5 Spt Leicester RF 4214).
**J H M Gosden [1-2] R E Sangster.*

BARATHEA GUEST BHB 114f **RR 117f** 4989[15]
3 b c Barathea (IRE) - Western Heights (Shirley Heights) 10.3f **(74)**
Form - 1348555430
Record 2000 - 1st:1 2nd:0 3rd:2 Ran:10
Pre2000 - 1st:3 2nd:1 3rd:0 Ran:5
Win Prizemoney £69,150 *Total Prizemoney* £182,661
Wins 2000 Apr Newmar (G-S) G3 7f 112 <
1999 Aug Deauvi (HVY) L 8f 90
1999 Aug Salisb (G-S) 7f 100
1999 Jun Yarmou (G-F) 6f 82
2000 Turf 1-10: (7f 1-1, 8f 5, 10f 3, 12f) (sft 2, g-s, gd 1-6, frm)
Workmanlike, high-class colt, effective 7 to 10f, best at 8f, acts on sft to gd. Turf high 117 - also 1st of 7 from Distant Music (18 Apr Newmarket RF 0766). Consistent. A very smart two-year-old, he edged out Distant Music in the Greenham at Newmarket on his reappearance and reached the frame in the Guineas at Newmarket and the Curragh. Tackled the best without success subsequently, leaving George Margarson's yard after his fifth start. Probably best at a mile.
**M R Channon [0-5] John Guest (from G G Margarson [4-10] Jly 2000).*

BARATHEASTAR RR 82f 4738[6]
2 ch f Barathea (IRE) - Sueboog (IRE) (Darshaan) 9.9f **(84)**
Form - 56
Record 2000 - 1st:0 2nd:0 3rd:0 Ran:2
Win Prizemoney £0 *Total Prizemoney* £591
2000 Turf 0-2: (7f 2) (g-f 2)
Currently decent filly. Turf high 82 (began Spt).
**C E Brittain [0-2] Mohamed Obaida.*

BARATHIKI BHB 81f **RR 83f** 5197[1]
2 gr f Barathea (IRE) - Tagiki (IRE) (Doyoun) 9f **(69)**
Form - 146281
Record 2000 - 1st:2 2nd:1 3rd:0 Ran:6
Win Prizemoney £11,115 *Total Prizemoney* £14,992
Wins * 2000 Oct Windso (HVY) H 6f 79 83 <
*** 2000** May York (G-F) 6f 76+
2000 Turf 2-6: (6f 2-4, 7f, 8f) (hvy, gd 1-3, g-f, frm 1-1)
Decent filly, effective 6 to 7f, best at 6f, acts on gd to frm, best on gd, has worn blinkers. Turf high 83 - 1st of 8 giving 1lb to Captain Gibson (26 Oct Windsor RF 5197) - also 1st of 8 getting 4lb from Celtic Island (16 May York RF 1221). Disappointing since winning on her York debut. **P F I Cole [2-6] Axom Barathiki Partnership.*

BARBA PAPA (IRE) BHB 94f **RR 96f** 4987[3]
6 b g Mujadil (USA) 7.7f **(70)** - Baby's Smile (Shirley Heights) 10.3f **(74)**
Form - 13
2000 Turf 1-2: (18f, 20f 1-1) (gd 1-2)

Very useful gelding, effective 18 to 20f, acts on gd. Turf high 96 - 3rd of 33 giving 8lb to Heros Fatal (14 Oct Newmarket 18f gd RF 4987) - also 1st of 24 giving 16lb to Seliana (21 Jun Ascot RF 2153). Trained at one time by Luca Cumani, he was lightly raced in 2000. A cosy winner of the Ascot Stakes in June, he stayed on strongly into third in the Cesarewitch having won over hurdles in the interim.
**A J Martin in IRE [2-4] G Devlin (from D T Hughes in IRE [1-12] Aug 1999).*

BARBASON BHB 70f54a RR 70f 54a 3556[4]

8 ch g Polish Precedent (USA) 9f **(73)** - Barada (USA) (Damascus (USA)) 8.9f **(71)**
Form - 313725515534
Record 2000 - 1st:1 2nd:1 3rd:1 Ran:8
Pre2000 - 1st:14 2nd:6 3rd:13 Ran:64
Win Prizemoney £45,430 *Total Prizemoney* £59,929

Wins * **2000** Jun Goodwo (GD) H 9f 65 70
* 1999 *Dec Lingfi (STD) 10f 66*
* 1999 Spt Bright (G-F) C 8f 64
* 1999 Jly Sandow (G-F) C 8.1f 67
* 1999 Jun Newbur (GD) H 10f 68 71
* 1999 *Feb Lingfi (STD) C 8f 71*
* 1998 Jun Bright (FRM) H 8f 66 71
* 1998 *Jan Lingfi (STD) H 8f 69 72* <
* 1997 Jly Bright (FRM) H 7f 64 68
* 1997 Apr Bright (FRM) H 7f 59 67
* 1997 Apr Lingfi (FRM) H 7f 50 62
* 1997 *Mar Lingfi (STD) H 8f 57 68*
* 1997 *Mar Lingfi (STD) 7f 60*
* 1997 *Feb Lingfi (STD) H 7f 53 56*
1996 *Feb Lingfi (STD) 7f 52+*

2000 Turf 1-4: (8f, 9f 1-1, 10f 2) (gd 1-2, frm 2) 2000 AW 0-4: (8f, 10f 3) (Equi 3, Fibr)
Above-average gelding, effective 8 to 10f, best at 8f, acts on gd to frm - acts on Equi, has worn blinkers (effectively). Turf high 70 - 4th of 10 giving 15lb to Fashion (11 Aug Lingfield 10f frm RF 3556) - also 1st of 19 giving 25lb to Sammy's Shuffle (9 Jun Goodwood RF 1842). AW high 57.
**G L Moore [14-59] A Moore (from A Moore [1-11] Jan 1997).*

BARBERELLO (IRE) RR 30f 5153[5]

2 b f Bigstone (IRE) - Missish (Mummy's Pet) 7.7f **(60)**
Form - 05
Record 2000 - 1st:0 2nd:0 3rd:0 Ran:2
2000 Turf 0-2: (5f, 7f) (g-s, frm)
Currently very moderate filly. Turf high 30 (began Aug).
**Miss E C Lavelle [0-2] Investment AB Rustningen.*

BARBOLA (USA) RR 119f 630a[3]

5 ch h Diesis 9f **(80)** - Barboukh (Night Shift (USA)) 7.2f **(69)**
Form - 3
2000 Turf 0-1: (10f) (g-s)
High-class colt, effective 10f, acts on hvy to gd, best on g-s. (1st run) - 3rd of 5 to Indian Danehill (2 Apr Longchamp 10f g-s RF 0630a). A high-class performer in France before being sent to America. **J deRoualle in FR [1-7] 6C Racing Ltd.*

BARCELONA BHB 85f80a RR 81f 80a 4047[1]

3 b c Barathea (IRE) - Pipitina (Bustino) 10.4f **(64)**
Form - 311631
Record 2000 - 1st:3 2nd:0 3rd:2 Ran:6
Pre2000 - 1st:0 2nd:0 3rd:1 Ran:3
Win Prizemoney £10,592 *Total Prizemoney* £12,357

Wins * **2000** Aug Newcas (SFT) H 14.4f 78 81 <
* **2000** Jun Kempto (G-F) 14.4f 78
* **2000** May Nottin (G-F) H 14.1f 68 73

2000 Turf 3-5: (14f 3-4, 16f) (g-s 1-1, gd 2, g-f 2-2) 2000 AW 0-1: (12f) (Fibr)
Scopey, decent colt, effective 14f, acts on g-s to g-f. Turf high 81 - 1st of 5 giving 12lb to Lady Coldunell (28 Aug Newcastle RF 4047) - also 1st of 7 getting 19lb from Wait For The Will (14 Jun Kempton RF 1965). Put a disappointing run on sand behind him when getting off the mark over 14 furlongs at Nottingham and followed up over the same trip in a Kempton classified event. Suited by fast ground, he looks a progressive stayer. **J Noseda [3-9] K Y Lim.*

BARDEN LADY BHB 56f RR 66f 3078[11]

3 b f Presidium 7.5f **(56)** - Pugilistic (Hard Fought) 8.8f **(62)**
Form - 800
Record 2000 - 1st:0 2nd:0 3rd:0 Ran:3
Pre2000 - 1st:0 2nd:0 3rd:0 Ran:2
2000 Turf 0-3: (6f, 7f, 8f) (gd, g-f, frm)
Scopey, average filly. Turf high 66. **B C Morgan [0-5] D G Blagden.*

BAREFOOTED FLYER (USA) BHB 62f58a RR 54f 58a 4334[9]

2 ch f Fly So Free (USA) - Carmelita (USA) (Mogambo (USA))
Form - 02430
Record 2000 - 1st:0 2nd:1 3rd:1 Ran:5
Win Prizemoney £0 *Total Prizemoney* £1,464
2000 Turf 0-4: (5f, 6f 2, 7f) (gd 2, g-f, frm) 2000 AW 0-1: (6f) (Fibr)
Fair filly. Turf high 54. **T D Barron [0-5] Peter Jones.*

BARITONE BHB 32f RR 27f 3641[8]

6 b g Midyan (USA) 9.9f **(64)** - Zinzi (Song) 7.2f **(61)**
Form - 074341536008
Record 2000 - 1st:1 2nd:0 3rd:2 Ran:11
Pre2000 - 1st:1 2nd:3 3rd:7 Ran:40
Win Prizemoney £5,349 *Total Prizemoney* £11,920

Wins * **2000** *Feb Wolver (STD) H 5f 38 43*
* 1999 *Feb Southw (STD) H 6f 47 57* <

2000 Turf 0-3: (5f, 6f 2) (frm 2, hrd) 2000 AW 1-8: (5f 1-3, 6f 5) (Equi 4, Fibr 1-4)
Moderate gelding, effective 6f, - acts on AW, best on Equi, often wears blinkers (effectively), likes left handed tracks, likes tight tracks. Turf high 27 (began Jly). AW high 43.
**S E Kettlewell [2-40] Hollinbridge Racing (from J W Watts [0-11] Jly 1997).*

BARKING MAD (USA) BHB 100f RR 95f 4747[7]

2 b br c Dayjur (USA) 6.8f **(79)** - Avian Assembly (USA) (General Assembly (USA)) 10f **(68)**
Form - 31621367
Record 2000 - 1st:2 2nd:1 3rd:2 Ran:8
Win Prizemoney £13,304 *Total Prizemoney* £27,530

Wins * **2000** Jly Thirsk (FRM) 7f 89 <
* **2000** May York (FRM) 6f 80

2000 Turf 2-8: (5f, 6f 1-3, 7f 1-3, 8f) (gd 3, g-f 3, frm 1-1, hrd 1-1)
Very useful colt, effective 6 to 8f, best at 7f, acts on gd to hrd, best on g-f. Turf high 95 - 6th of 8 getting 4lb from Noverre (8 Spt Doncaster 7f g-f RF 4296) - also 1st of 7 from Adjournment (28 Jly Thirsk RF 3195). He was a decent juvenile, a winner twice and placed in pattern company. Suited by fast ground.
**M L W Bell [2-8] Christopher Wright.*

BARNABY BHB 26f RR 8f 5070[15]

3 b g Theatrical Charmer 10.9f **(63)** - Fruitful Affair (IRE) **(35df 30a)** (Taufan (USA)) 7f **(57)**
Form - 00
Record 2000 - 1st:0 2nd:0 3rd:0 Ran:2
Pre2000 - 1st:0 2nd:0 3rd:0 Ran:1
2000 Turf 0-2: (10f, 12f) (g-s 2)
Unfurnished, currently very poor gelding. (began Spt) - 15th of 20 to Maniatis (19 Oct Bath 12f g-s RF 5070).
**P Hayward [0-2] The Ann & Daisy George Partnership (from J R Arnold [0-1] Jly 1999).*

BARNEY KNOWS (IRE) RR 63f 4624[5]

5 b g In The Wings 11.2f **(77)** - Afeefa (Lyphard (USA)) 9.9f **(72)**
Form - 5
Record 2000 - 1st:0 2nd:0 3rd:0 Ran:1
Pre2000 - 1st:0 2nd:0 3rd:0 Ran:1
2000 Turf 0-1: (12f) (gd)
Average gelding.
**R A Fahey [0-1] C N Barnes (from M A Peill [2-5] May 1999).*

BARNIE RUBBLE BHB 65f RR 70f 2216[2]

4 ch g Pharly (FR) 11.5f **(64)** - Sharp Fairy (Sharpo) 7.7f **(59)**
Form - 642
Record 2000 - 1st:0 2nd:1 3rd:0 Ran:3
Pre2000 - 1st:0 2nd:0 3rd:0 Ran:1
Win Prizemoney £0 *Total Prizemoney* £1,500
2000 Turf 0-3: (7f 3) (g-s 2, frm)

Lengthy, above-average gelding. Turf high 70 - 2nd of 8 giving 9lb to Capricho (23 Jun Ayr 7f frm RF 2216). He has been gradually getting it together in maiden company and should find a small handicap in time. **A Bailey [0-4] A H Bennett.*

BARNINGHAM BHB 61f **RR 58f** 3687[5]
2 b g Emperor Jones (USA) - Lady Anchor (Slip Anchor) 9.8f **(73)**
Form - 645
Record 2000 - 1st:0 2nd:0 3rd:0 Ran:3
Win Prizemoney £0 *Total Prizemoney* £231
2000 Turf 0-3: (7f 3) (gd, g-f 2)
Currently fair gelding. Turf high 58 (began Jly).
**J D Bethell [0-3] WWW Clarendon Racing Com.*

BARON CROCODILE BHB 78f **RR 79f** 5153[3]
2 b g Puissance 7.1f **(60)** - Glow Again (The Brianstan) 5.9f **(55)**
Form - 224582472183
Record 2000 - 1st:1 2nd:4 3rd:1 Ran:12
Win Prizemoney £1,974 *Total Prizemoney* £6,975
Wins * 2000 Spt Lingfi (GD) 5f 73 <
2000 Turf 1-12: (5f 1-11, 6f) (hvy, sft, g-s, gd 1-2, g-f 3, frm 2, hrd 2)
Above-average gelding, effective 5f, acts on hvy to frm, has worn blinkers, does well at Lingfield. Turf high 79 - 3rd of 5 getting 5lb from Clarion (23 Oct Lingfield 5f g-s RF 5153) - also 1st of 16 from Nosy Be (22 Spt Lingfield RF 4580).
**A Berry [1-12] Chris & Antonia Deuters.*

BARON DE PICHON (IRE) BHB 57f72a **RR 64f 72a** 5006[4]
4 b g Perugino (USA) - Ariadne (Bustino) 10.4f **(64)**
Form - 10014
Record 2000 - 1st:2 2nd:0 3rd:0 Ran:5
Pre2000 - 1st:5 2nd:4 3rd:0 Ran:19
Win Prizemoney £24,286 *Total Prizemoney* £28,348
Wins 2000 *Spt Wolver (STD) C 7f 63*
2000 *Jly Southw (STD) C 8f 70+*
1999 *Feb Lingfi (STD) H 8f* 75 84 <
1999 *Jan Southw (STD) H 7f* 62 70
1999 *Jan Wolver (STD) H 8.5f* 62 74
1999 *Jan Wolver (STD) H 7f* 60 66
1999 *Jan Wolver (STD) H 8.5f* 54 67
2000 Turf 0-1: (7f) (g-f) 2000 AW 2-4: (7f 1-1, 8f 1-2, 9f) (Fibr 2-4)
Scopey, decent gelding, effective 8f, - acts on AW, best on Fibr, has worn blinkers, prefers left handed tracks, prefers tight tracks, and excels at Wolverhampton. AW high 70 (1st run) (began Jly).
**Andrew Reid [0-1] A S Reid (from K R Burke [2-4] Spt 2000).*

BAROSSA VALLEY (IRE) BHB 30f40a **RR 40a** 1842[19]
9 b g Alzao (USA) 9.8f **(73)** - Night of Wind (Tumble Wind (USA)) 7.5f **(57)**
Form - 000
Record 2000 - 1st:0 2nd:0 3rd:0 Ran:1
Pre2000 - 1st:3 2nd:3 3rd:1 Ran:29
Win Prizemoney £10,200 *Total Prizemoney* £15,100
Wins * 1996 *Dec Lingfi (STD) H 10f* 70 80
* 1996 *Dec Lingfi (STD) C 10f* 79
2000 Turf 0-1: (9f) (gd)
Very moderate gelding, has worn blinkers. Becoming disappointing.
**P Butler [2-16] P Butler (from P W Chapple-Hyam [1-14] Aug 1995).*

BARR BEACON BHB 58f53a **RR 54f 53a** 74[7]
4 br g Puissance 7.1f **(60)** - Lominda (IRE) (Lomond (USA)) 8.8f **(65)**
Form - 7
Record 2000 - 1st:0 2nd:0 3rd:0 Ran:1
Pre2000 - 1st:0 2nd:1 3rd:0 Ran:5
Win Prizemoney £0 *Total Prizemoney* £585
2000 AW 0-1: (6f) (Equi)
Light-framed, fair gelding, has worn blinkers.
**T G Mills [0-6] Thorpe Vernon.*

BARRETTSTOWN BHB 64f48a **RR 70f 48a** 3256[2]
5 ch g Cadeaux Genereux 7.9f **(76)** - Sagar (Habitat) 9.4f **(70)**
Form - 2
Record 2000 - 1st:0 2nd:1 3rd:0 Ran:1
Pre2000 - 1st:0 2nd:1 3rd:1 Ran:4
Win Prizemoney £0 *Total Prizemoney* £2,020
2000 Turf 0-1: (10f) (frm)
Above-average gelding. (1st run) - 2nd of 21 giving 1lb to Queen's Pageant (31 Jly Windsor 10f frm RF 3256).
**P R Chamings [0-1] Ralph Peters (from M C Pipe [0-6] Jly 1999).*

BARRIER REEF (IRE) **RR 107f** 4422a[2]
3 b c Perugino (USA) - Singing Millie (Millfontaine)
Form - 2
2000 Turf 0-1: (12f) (gd)
Pattern-class colt, effective 8 to 12f, best at 8f, acts on hvy to gd. (1st run) - 2nd of 10 getting 9lb from Valley Chapel (10 Spt Taby 12f gd RF 4422a).
**A Hyldmo in NOR [0-1] Mrs E M Stockwell (from A P O'Brien in IRE [2-6] Oct 1999).*

BARRINGER (IRE) BHB 70f **RR 83df** 5068[9]
3 b g Nicolotte - Prosaic Star (IRE) (Common Grounds)
Form - 45300000
Record 2000 - 1st:0 2nd:0 3rd:1 Ran:8
Pre2000 - 1st:3 2nd:2 3rd:0 Ran:9
Win Prizemoney £13,191 *Total Prizemoney* £18,505
Wins * 1999 May Windso (GD) 5f 89 <
* 1999 Apr Nottin (HVY) 5.1f 86++
* 1999 Apr Hamilt (HVY) 5f 89+
2000 Turf 0-8: (5f 5, 6f 3) (g-s 5, gd 3)
Scopey, decent gelding, effective 5 to 6f, best at 5f, acts on hvy to g-f. Turf high 83 - 5th of 14 getting 11lb from Always Alight (17 Apr Windsor 6f g-s RF 0755). Becoming disappointing.
**M R Channon [3-17] Imperial Racing.*

BARROW (SWI) BHB 70f **RR 78+f** 3618[6]
3 br c Caerleon (USA) 10.9f **(79)** - Bestow (Shirley Heights) 10.3f **(74)**
Form - 70126
Record 2000 - 1st:1 2nd:1 3rd:0 Ran:5
Pre2000 - 1st:0 2nd:0 3rd:1 Ran:3
Win Prizemoney £3,640 *Total Prizemoney* £5,526
Wins * 2000 Jun Newcas (FRM) H 16.1f 65 70+ <
2000 Turf 1-5: (12f 2, 16f 1-3) (g-s, frm 1-4)
Scopey, above-average colt, effective 16f, acts on frm. Turf high 78 - 2nd of 9 giving 18lb to Jack Dawson (14 Jly Chepstow 16f frm RF 2793) - also 1st of 6 getting 4lb from Little Docker (29 Jun Newcastle RF 2370). **J L Dunlop [1-8] Mrs S Egloff.*

BARROW CREEK BHB 58f56a **RR 112f 56a** 5307a[2]
6 ch h Cadeaux Genereux 7.9f **(76)** -Breadcrumb (Final Straw) 7.9f **(64)**
Form - 1102
2000 Turf 2-4: (6f 2-3, 7f) (sft 2, gd 2-2)
Group-class horse. Turf high 112 - 1st of 9 from Kaka (30 Aug Baden-Baden RF 4286a). Inconsistent.
**P Schiergen in GER [2-4] (from G Wragg [0-5] May 1998).*

BARRYS DOUBLE BHB 40f47a **RR 42f 47a** 4634[11]
3 br g Barrys Gamble 7f **(50)** - Pennine Star (IRE) (Pennine Walk) 8.5f **(61)**
Form - 8404000
Record 2000 - 1st:0 2nd:0 3rd:0 Ran:4
Pre2000 - 1st:0 2nd:0 3rd:1 Ran:8
Win Prizemoney £0 *Total Prizemoney* £658
2000 Turf 0-3: (8f 3) (g-s, gd, frm) 2000 AW 0-1: (7f) (Fibr)
Neat, moderate gelding, has worn blinkers. Turf high 33 (began Aug). Inconsistent.
**P Burgoyne [0-3] R J Apperley (from C W Fairhurst [0-9] Jan 2000).*

BARTEX (FR) **RR 108f** 705a[3]
6 b h Groom Dancer (USA) 9.5f **(75)** - Belisonde (FR) (Gay Mecene (USA)) 8.6f **(69)**
Form - 3
2000 Turf 0-1: (8f) (g-s)
Pattern-class horse, has worn blinkers. (1st run) - 3rd of 6 getting 5lb from Dansili (5 Apr Saint-cloud 8f g-s RF 0705a).
**T Clout in FR [0-2] (from P Barbe in FR [0-2] Jun 1999).*

BARTON MISS BHB 32f **RR 26f** 1175[17]
3 ch f Whittingham (IRE) - Miss Derby (USA) (Master Derby (USA)) 9.5f **(69)**
Form - 0
Record 2000 - 1st:0 2nd:0 3rd:0 Ran:1
Pre2000 - 1st:0 2nd:0 3rd:0 Ran:2

2000 Turf 0-1: (6f) (frm)
Neat, currently little account filly.
**T E Powell [0-1] Robin Rayfield (from G L Moore [0-2] Oct 1999).*

BARTON SANDS (IRE) BHB 86f **RR 89f** 5133[11]
3 b c Tenby 10.4f **(76)** - Hetty Green (Bay Express) 7.1f **(60)**
Form - 21260
Record 2000 - 1st:1 2nd:2 3rd:0 Ran:5
Win Prizemoney £2,808 *Total Prizemoney* £6,915
Wins * 2000 May Hamilt (FRM) 9.2f 82 <
2000 Turf 1-5: (8f, 9f 1-2, 10f, 12f) (sft, g-s, gd 2, frm 1-1)
Workmanlike, useful colt. Turf high 89 - 2nd of 22 giving 10lb to Shrivar (29 Spt Newmarket 10f gd RF 4734) - also 1st of 7 from Night Sight (11 May Hamilton RF 1143). Unraced at two, he showed promise on his debut and had little difficulty landing a Hamilton maiden. Sure to improve and worth watching out for in handicap company. **L M Cumani [1-5] Stanley Clarke.*

BASE LINE RR 1f 2941[9]
2 b c Rudimentary (USA) 8.2f **(66)** - Hemline (Sharpo) 7.7f **(59)**
Form - 0
Record 2000 - 1st:0 2nd:0 3rd:0 Ran:1
2000 Turf 0-1: (6f) (frm)
Currently very poor colt. **R M Flower [0-1] Atlas Public Relations Ltd.*

BASHER JACK BHB 36f45a **RR 22f 45a** 564[7]
4 b g Suave Dancer (USA) 10.7f **(68)** - Possessive Lady (Dara Monarch) 8.8f **(59)**
Form - 77
Record 2000 - 1st:0 2nd:0 3rd:0 Ran:2
Pre2000 - 1st:1 2nd:0 3rd:0 Ran:9
Win Prizemoney £1,815 *Total Prizemoney* £2,018
Wins * 1999 *Aug Wolver (STD) H 12f 44 46* <
2000 Turf 0-1: (12f) (g-f) 2000 AW 0-1: (12f) (Fibr)
Neat, little account gelding, effective 12f, - acts on Fibr, likes left handed tracks. Becoming disappointing.
**C N Allen [1-11] J T B Racing.*

BASHKIR (USA) RR 100f 2921a[6]
3 b c Nureyev (USA) 8.4f **(84)** - Palestrina (USA) 6f **(63)**
Form - 2526
2000 Turf 0-4: (7f, 8f 2, 9f) (g-s, g-f 3)
Very useful colt, effective 7 to 9f, best at 7f, acts on sft to g-f, often wears blinkers (extremely effectively). Turf high 100 (1st run) - 2nd of 4 giving 3lb to Jammaal (24 Apr Cork 9f g-s RF 0980a). Ran perhaps his best race of the campaign when runner-up in a Leopardstown Group Three in June.
**A P O'Brien in IRE [1-7] Mrs John Magnier.*

BASIC INSTINCT BHB 32f **RR 32?f** 556[10]
3 ch f Prince Sabo 6.6f **(64)** - Constant Delight (Never so Bold) 6.3f **(66)**
Form - 078840
Record 2000 - 1st:0 2nd:0 3rd:0 Ran:4
Pre2000 - 1st:0 2nd:0 3rd:1 Ran:5
Win Prizemoney £0 *Total Prizemoney* £278
2000 Turf 0-1: (8f) (gd) 2000 AW 0-3: (6f, 7f 2) (Fibr 3)
Neat, very moderate filly. AW high 32.
**R Brotherton [0-6] William Day (from M H Tompkins [0-3] Spt 1999).*

BASINET BHB 74f70a **RR 68f 70a** 5019[4]
2 b c Alzao (USA) 9.8f **(73)** - Valiancy (Grundy) 10.3f **(65)**
Form - 034
Record 2000 - 1st:0 2nd:0 3rd:1 Ran:3
Win Prizemoney £0 *Total Prizemoney* £515
2000 Turf 0-2: (6f 2) (gd 2) 2000 AW 0-1: (7f) (Fibr)
Currently average colt. Turf high 68 (began Aug) - 3rd of 14 giving 5lb to Rich Gift (21 Spt Pontefract 6f gd RF 4554).
**D W Barker [0-3] P R C Morrison.*

BASMAN (IRE) BHB 72f **RR 84f** 3271[7]
6 b h Persian Heights 10.5f **(61)** - Gepares (IRE) (Mashhor Dancer (USA)) 10f **(65)**
Form - 6057
Record 2000 - 1st:0 2nd:0 3rd:0 Ran:4
Pre2000 - 1st:1 2nd:2 3rd:1 Ran:12
Win Prizemoney £3,993 *Total Prizemoney* £12,641
Wins * 1997 Oct Nottin (SFT) 10f 101 <
2000 Turf 0-4: (8f, 10f, 12f 2) (gd 3, g-f)
Decent horse. Turf high 84. Becoming disappointing. Showed useful form in '97, but has had his training problems and has been tried over hurdles and fences since. Little promise on the Flat in the last couple of seasons.
**B Smart [2-23] Nelson, Edmondson And Partners.*

BATALEUR BHB 38f39a **RR 36f 39a** 2281[16]
7 b g Midyan (USA) 9.9f **(64)** - Tinkerbird (Music Boy) 6.8f **(57)**
Form - 6548070
Record 2000 - 1st:0 2nd:0 3rd:0 Ran:7
Pre2000 - 1st:3 2nd:1 3rd:2 Ran:28
Win Prizemoney £8,157 *Total Prizemoney* £10,029
Wins * 1999 Nov Catter (SFT) C 5f 49
* 1998 Oct Newcas (SFT) H 6f 45 49
1996 Spt Hamilt (G-S) H 6f 55 56 <
2000 Turf 0-6: (5f 2, 6f 4) (hvy, g-f 2, frm 3) 2000 AW 0-1: (6f) (Fibr)
Very moderate gelding, effective 5f, acts on g-s, has worn blinkers. Turf high 48. He does not win that often, but when he does it is when the ground is soft and he is worth watching out for under those conditions.
**G Woodward [2-27] Michael Worth (from Miss J Bower [1-8] May 1997).*

BATCHWORTH BELLE BHB 93f84a **RR 89?f 84a** 835[R]
5 b m Interrex (CAN) 7.7f **(51)** - Treasurebound (Beldale Flutter (USA)) 9.7f **(71)**
Form - 23R
Record 2000 - 1st:0 2nd:1 3rd:1 Ran:3
Pre2000 - 1st:5 2nd:5 3rd:11 Ran:35
Win Prizemoney £25,477 *Total Prizemoney* £56,213
Wins * 1999 Jly Newmar (G-F) H 5f 88 92 <
* 1999 *Apr Lingfi (STD) H 5f 75 76*
* 1998 Spt Epsom (SFT) H 5f 77 80
* 1998 Aug Bright (G-F) H 5.3f 73 76
* 1997 *Dec Lingfi (G-S) 6f 66*
2000 Turf 0-2: (5f 2) (g-s, frm) 2000 AW 0-1: (5f) (Equi)
Useful filly, effective 5f, acts on gd to frm, best on frm, has worn blinkers. Turf high 89. **E A Wheeler [5-38] Mrs Diana Price.*

BATCHWORTH BREEZE RR 24f 3079[12]
2 ch f Beveled (USA) 6.9f **(64)** - Batchworth Dancer (Ballacashtal (CAN)) 5.3f **(50)**
Form - 00
Record 2000 - 1st:0 2nd:0 3rd:0 Ran:2
2000 Turf 0-2: (5f, 6f) (gd, frm)
Currently little account filly. Turf high 24 (began Jly).
**E A Wheeler [0-2] Mrs Diana Price.*

BATCHWORTH LOCK RR 47f 3255[10]
2 b g Beveled (USA) 6.9f **(64)** - Treasurebound (Beldale Flutter (USA)) 9.7f **(71)**
Form - 080
Record 2000 - 1st:0 2nd:0 3rd:0 Ran:3
2000 Turf 0-3: (5f 3) (frm 3)
Currently moderate gelding. Turf high 47.
**E A Wheeler [0-3] Austin Stroud & Co Ltd.*

BATHWICK BABE (IRE) BHB 65f58a **RR 76f 58a** 5323[12]
3 b f Sri Pekan (USA) - Olean (Sadler's Wells (USA)) 10f **(76)**
Form - 20
Record 2000 - 1st:0 2nd:1 3rd:0 Ran:2
Pre2000 - 1st:0 2nd:0 3rd:0 Ran:2
Win Prizemoney £0 *Total Prizemoney* £1,248
2000 Turf 0-2: (12f 2) (sft, g-f)
Above-average filly. Turf high 76 (1st run) (began Jly) - 2nd of 6 to Solo Performance (2 Jly Goodwood 12f g-f RF 2460). Showed nothing in two runs a juvenile, but stayed on well into second in a Goodwood maiden in July.
**E J O'Neill [0-2] W Clifford (from B Smart [0-2] Oct 1999).*

BATHWICK DREAM BHB 30f **RR 2f** 3731[13]
3 b f Tragic Role (USA) 9.4f **(63)** - Trina **(39f)** (Malaspina)
Form - 0
Record 2000 - 1st:0 2nd:0 3rd:0 Ran:1
2000 Turf 0-1: (7f) (frm)
Unfurnished, currently poor filly. **Dr J R J Naylor [0-1] W Clifford.*

BATOUTOFTHEBLUE BHB 45f60a **RR 45f 60a** 2782[10]
7 br g Batshoof 9.5f **(66)** - Action Belle (Auction Ring (USA)) 8.6f **(65)**
Form - 1340

Record					
	2000 -	1st:1	2nd:0	3rd:1	Ran:4
	Pre2000 -	1st:4	2nd:3	3rd:3	Ran:34

Win Prizemoney £15,142 *Total Prizemoney* £21,834

Wins								
* **2000**	Mar	Mussel	(GD)	H	16f	42	45	
* 1999	Apr	Mussel	(GD)	H	16f	43	47	
1998	Aug	Pontef	(G-F)	H	17.1f	39	43	
* 1996	*Spt*	*Wolver*	*(STD)*		*14.8f*		*67*	<
* 1996	*Spt*	*Southw*	*(STD)*	*H*	*14f*	*58*	*62*	

2000 Turf 1-3: (14f, 16f 1-2) (gd 1-1, g-f, frm) 2000 AW 0-1: (16f) (Fibr)
Average gelding, effective 16 to 18f, best at 16f, acts on gd to frm, best on g-f, has worn blinkers, likes right handed tracks, favours tight tracks, excels at Musselburgh and Pontefract. Turf high 45 (1st run) - 1st of 11 getting 23lb from Indiana Princess (30 Mar Musselburgh RF 0570).
**W W Haigh [4-36] Mrs I Gibson (from J M Jefferson [0-1] Oct 1998).*

BATSWING BHB 85f **RR 85f** 5323[1]
5 b g Batshoof 9.5f **(66)** - Magic Milly (Simply Great (FR)) 8.2f **(65)**
Form - 7728120021

Record					
	2000 -	1st:2	2nd:3	3rd:0	Ran:10
	Pre2000 -	1st:1	2nd:2	3rd:1	Ran:19

Win Prizemoney £31,291 *Total Prizemoney* £43,410

Wins								
* **2000**	Nov	Doncas	(HVY)	H	12f	80	85	<
* **2000**	Jun	Cheste	(G-S)	H	10.3f	66	74	
1997	Jun	Lingfi	(SFT)		5f		66+	

2000 Turf 2-10: (10f 1-2, 12f 1-7, 14f) (sft 1-1, g-s, gd 1-3, g-f 4, frm)
Useful gelding, effective 12f, acts on sft to g-f, best on g-f, has worn blinkers, prefers left handed tracks. Turf high 85 - 1st of 20 getting 6lb from Carlys Quest (4 Nov Doncaster RF 5323). Suited by soft ground, he is an able handicapper who gained his biggest payday in the November Handicap at Doncaster. Suited by patient tactics.
**B Ellison [2-11] Ashley Carr (from B R Millman [1-11] Spt 1999).*

BATTLE GREEN LAD BHB 25f **RR** 5158[9]
3 b g Presidium 7.5f **(56)** - Antouna (Clantime)
Form - 00

Record					
	2000 -	1st:0	2nd:0	3rd:0	Ran:2

2000 Turf 0-1: (8f) (sft) 2000 AW 0-1: (7f) (Fibr)
Workmanlike, currently very poor gelding.
**J Balding [0-2] G D and Mrs M Brumby.*

BATTLE WARNING BHB 55f **RR 56f** 1880[31]
5 b g Warning 8.1f **(77)** - Royal Ballet (IRE) (Sadler's Wells (USA)) 10f **(76)**
Form - 200

Record					
	2000 -	1st:0	2nd:1	3rd:0	Ran:3
	Pre2000 -	1st:0	2nd:0	3rd:0	Ran:6

Win Prizemoney £0 *Total Prizemoney* £1,244
2000 Turf 0-3: (8f, 10f, 12f) (g-f 2, frm)
Fair gelding, effective 10f, acts on g-f to hrd, prefers tight tracks. Turf high 56 (1st run) - 2nd of 12 getting 19lb from Total Delight (30 Mar Leicester 10f g-f RF 0566).
**M D Hammond [0-3] Mrs Alex Hammond (from H Candy [0-5] Oct 1999).*

BATWINK BHB 32f **RR 23f** 3793[5]
3 b f Batshoof 9.5f **(66)** - Quick As A Wink (Glint of Gold) 9.3f **(66)**
Form - 08805

Record					
	2000 -	1st:0	2nd:0	3rd:0	Ran:5

Win Prizemoney £0 *Total Prizemoney* £268
2000 Turf 0-5: (8f, 10f 2, 12f 2) (g-f 2, frm 3)
Scopey, little account filly. Turf high 23 (began Jly).
**P D Cundell [0-5] I J Heseltine.*

BAWSIAN BHB 73f75a **RR 84f 75a** 5323[17]
5 b g Persian Bold 10f **(69)** - Bawaeth (USA) (Blushing Groom (FR)) 10.3f **(76)**
Form - 400

Record					
	2000 -	1st:0	2nd:0	3rd:0	Ran:3
	Pre2000 -	1st:5	2nd:3	3rd:2	Ran:28

Win Prizemoney £30,734 *Total Prizemoney* £47,104

Wins								
* 1998	May	York	(GD)	H	10.4f	90	96	<
* 1998	Mar	Doncas	(GD)	H	10.3f	81	90	
* 1998	*Jan*	*Wolver*	*(STD)*	*H*	*8.5f*	*80*	*82*	
* 1998	*Jan*	*Wolver*	*(STD)*	*H*	*8.5f*	*75*	*77*	
* 1997	Nov	Redcar	(GD)	H	8f	65	72	

2000 Turf 0-3: (10f, 12f 2) (sft, g-s 2)
Useful gelding, effective 10 to 12f, best at 12f, acts on sft to frm - acts on Fibr, prefers left handed tracks. Turf high 84. Inconsistent. Brought down on his final start of '99, he made an encouraging return to action in April but was then off the course for more than six months. He stays a mile and a half and appreciates easy ground.
**J L Eyre [5-31] David Scott.*

BAYARD LADY BHB 25f35a **RR 28f 35a** 3333[6]
4 b f Robellino (USA) 9.5f **(68)** - Lurking (Formidable (USA)) 9.2f **(63)**
Form - 0700005006

Record					
	2000 -	1st:0	2nd:0	3rd:0	Ran:9
	Pre2000 -	1st:1	2nd:0	3rd:2	Ran:19

Win Prizemoney £3,074 *Total Prizemoney* £4,079

Wins								
1998	May	Hamilt	(GD)		5f		67	<

2000 Turf 0-9: (5f, 6f 2, 7f 3, 8f, 9f, 10f) (g-s 2, gd 3, g-f 3, frm)
Unfurnished, little account filly, effective 12f, acts on g-f, has worn blinkers, likes right handed tracks. Turf high 28. Improving.
**L R Lloyd-James [0-13] L R Lloyd-James (from D Moffatt [1-16] Aug 1999).*

BAY OF BENGAL (IRE) BHB 44f **RR 43f** 4626[14]
4 ch f Persian Bold 10f **(69)** - Adjamiya (USA) (Shahrastani (USA)) 8.8f **(72)**
Form - 03286038400

Record					
	2000 -	1st:0	2nd:1	3rd:2	Ran:11
	Pre2000 -	1st:2	2nd:0	3rd:1	Ran:10

Win Prizemoney £4,778 *Total Prizemoney* £7,644

Wins								
* 1999	Jun	Pontef	(GD)	SH	12f	47	50	<
* 1999	May	Nottin	(FRM)	SH	10f	43	44	

2000 Turf 0-11: (8f, 9f 4, 10f 4, 12f 2) (gd 5, g-f 3, frm 3)
Scopey, moderate filly, effective 10 to 12f, acts on g-f to frm, likes left handed tracks, favours tight tracks. Turf high 40. Inconsistent.
**J S Wainwright [2-16] Barry Ross (from H Alexander [0-5] Spt 1998).*

Northumberland Plate winner
Bay of Islands

BAY OF ISLANDS BHB 97f **RR 98f** 4295[3]
8 b g Jupiter Island 10.4f **(57)** - Lawyer's Wave (USA) (Advocator) 10.9f **(80)**
Form - 0831303

Record					
	2000 -	1st:1	2nd:0	3rd:3	Ran:7
	Pre2000 -	1st:4	2nd:2	3rd:4	Ran:22

Win Prizemoney £95,261 *Total Prizemoney* £133,185

Wins								
* **2000**	Jly	Newcas	(FRM)	H	16.1f	90	97	<
* 1999	May	Nottin	(FRM)	H	14.1f	80	82	
* 1998	Jun	Doncas	(GD)	H	12f	78	84	
* 1997	Jun	Cheste	(G-F)	H	10.3f	75	81	

2000 Turf 1-7: (12f, 13f, 14f 3, 15f, 16f 1-1) (gd 2, g-f 3, frm 1-2)
Very useful gelding, effective 14 to 16f, acts on gd to frm, has worn blinkers (extremely effectively), prefers left handed tracks, excels at Newcastle, likes York. Turf high 98 - 3rd of 13 giving 11lb

to Romantic Affair (8 Spt Doncaster 15f g-f RF 4295) - also 1st of 18 giving 8lb to Temple Way (1 Jly Newcastle RF 2442). Consistent. He put in an eyecatching run at York on his third start of the campaign before running out the clear-cut winner of the Northumberland Plate. Touched off next time, he was badly drawn in the Ebor but ran well at Doncaster in September. He stays two miles and appreciates fast ground, but has some speed so could win a decent event over middle distances.
**D Morris [4-26] Bloomsbury Stud (from C E Brittain [1-3] Aug 1995).*

BAYONET BHB 55f50a **RR 51f 50a** 2976^{15}
4 b f Then Again 7.4f **(52)** - Lambay (Lorenzaccio) 10f **(64)**
Form - 02170
Record 2000 - 1st:1 2nd:1 3rd:0 Ran:5
Pre2000 - 1st:0 2nd:2 3rd:0 Ran:11
Win Prizemoney £2,940 *Total Prizemoney* £5,565
Wins * 2000 Jun Chepst (FRM) H 6.1f 51 51 <
2000 Turf 1-5: (6f 1-5) (gd, g-f 1-1, frm 3)
Light-framed, fair filly, effective 6f, acts on frm, has worn blinkers. Turf high 51. Inconsistent. She looked a sharp sort in her early starts at two, but has become a bit disappointing.
**Jane Southcombe [1-8] Mark Savill (from R F JohnsonHoughton [0-8] Jly 1999).*

BAYRAMI BHB 48f **RR 50f** 3441^{11}
2 ch f Emarati (USA) 6.6f **(63)** - Music Mistress (IRE) **(40f 46a)** (Classic Music (USA))
Form - 75800440
Record 2000 - 1st:0 2nd:0 3rd:0 Ran:8
2000 Turf 0-6: (5f 4, 6f 2) (g-s, gd 2, frm 3) 2000 AW 0-2: (5f 2) (Fibr 2)
Fair filly. Turf high 50. AW high 2. Inconsistent.
**S E Kettlewell [0-8] John Chilton & Middleham Park Racing XI.*

BAYSWATER BHB 70f **RR 76f** 4065^{5}
3 b f Caerleon (USA) 10.9f **(79)** - Shining Water (Kalaglow) 9.8f **(67)**
Form - 02215
Record 2000 - 1st:1 2nd:2 3rd:0 Ran:5
Win Prizemoney £4,212 *Total Prizemoney* £6,224
Wins * 2000 Aug Cheste (GD) 12.3f 76 <
2000 Turf 1-5: (10f, 12f 1-2, 14f, 16f) (g-f 1-2, frm 3)
Scopey, above-average filly, has worn blinkers. Turf high 76 - 1st of 5 from Aymara (18 Aug Chester RF 3748).
**B W Hills [1-5] K Abdulla.*

BAYTOWN RHAPSODY BHB 55f58a **RR 60f 58a** 1146^{12}
3 b f Emperor Jones (USA) - Sing a Rainbow (IRE) (Rainbow Quest (USA)) 10.4f **(75)**
Form - 32131310
Record 2000 - 1st:3 2nd:1 3rd:3 Ran:8
Pre2000 - 1st:0 2nd:1 3rd:0 Ran:6
Win Prizemoney £6,302 *Total Prizemoney* £8,939
Wins 2000 *Mar Southw (STD) S 7f 60 <*
2000 *Feb Southw (STD) H 6f 55 60 <*
2000 *Jan Wolver (STD) H 6f 47 52*
2000 AW 3-8: (6f 2-4, 7f 1-3, 8f) (Equi, Fibr 3-7)
Leggy, average filly, effective 6 to 7f, best at 7f, - acts on Fibr, prefers left handed tracks, prefers tight tracks. AW high 60 - 1st of 8 giving 19lb to Paddywack (14 Feb Southwell RF 0281) - also 1st of 9 getting 5lb from Priceless Second (17 Mar Southwell RF 0461).
**J Balding [0-1] P S J Croft (from P S McEntee [3-13] Mar 2000).*

BAY VIEW BHB 55f **RR 53f** 4813^{5}
5 b m Slip Anchor 12.7f **(75)** - Carmita (Caerleon (USA)) 8.6f **(71)**
Form - 300005
Record 2000 - 1st:0 2nd:0 3rd:1 Ran:6
Pre2000 - 1st:0 2nd:1 3rd:0 Ran:2
Win Prizemoney £0 *Total Prizemoney* £1,645
2000 Turf 0-6: (8f 3, 9f, 10f, 12f) (g-s, gd 3, g-f, frm)
Fair filly, effective 8 to 10f, acts on g-s to gd. Turf high 74 (1st run) - 3rd of 15 giving 14lb to Gargalhada Final (6 Apr Leicester 10f gd RF 0628). **K Mahdi [0-8] Greenfield Stud.*

BEACH BABY BHB 34f38a **RR 49f 38a** 1918^{10}
3 ch f Mizoram (USA) - Kina (USA) (Bering) 7.4f **(61)**
Form - 0707800070
Record 2000 - 1st:0 2nd:0 3rd:0 Ran:8
Pre2000 - 1st:0 2nd:0 3rd:0 Ran:2
2000 Turf 0-7: (5f, 6f, 7f 3, 8f 2) (sft, g-s 2, gd, g-f 2, frm) 2000 AW 0-1: (10f) (Equi)
Workmanlike, moderate filly. Turf high 49. Becoming disappointing. **J J Bridger [0-10] K J Walls.*

BEACON OF LIGHT (IRE) BHB 37f **RR 45f** 4215^{16}
2 b f Lake Coniston (IRE) - Deydarika (IRE) (Kahyasi)
Form - 0780
Record 2000 - 1st:0 2nd:0 3rd:0 Ran:4
2000 Turf 0-4: (5f, 6f, 7f, 8f) (gd, g-f 2, frm)
Moderate filly. Turf high 45.
**P C Haslam [0-4] The Jack Of All Trades Partnership.*

BEACONS A LIGHT RR 38f 3919^{14}
2 b g Whittingham (IRE) - Poly Static (IRE) **(37f)** (Statoblest)
Form - 00
Record 2000 - 1st:0 2nd:0 3rd:0 Ran:2
2000 Turf 0-2: (5f, 7f) (gd, frm)
Currently very moderate gelding. Turf high 38 (began Aug).
**P J Hobbs [0-2] P J Hobbs.*

BEADING BHB 70f **RR 70f** 5240^{27}
3 b f Polish Precedent (USA) 9f **(73)** - Silver Braid (USA) (Miswaki (USA)) 9f **(81)**
Form - 07251430
Record 2000 - 1st:1 2nd:1 3rd:1 Ran:8
Pre2000 - 1st:0 2nd:0 3rd:0 Ran:1
Win Prizemoney £4,836 *Total Prizemoney* £8,468
Wins * 2000 Aug Newmar (G-F) H 8f 65 67 <
2000 Turf 1-8: (7f 5, 8f 1-3) (g-s 2, gd, g-f 2, frm 1-3)
Leggy, above-average filly, effective 7 to 8f, best at 8f, acts on g-s to frm, best on frm. Turf high 70 - 4th of 14 getting 2lb from Cream Tease (31 Aug Salisbury 7f frm RF 4127) - also 1st of 14 giving 13lb to Jessinca (12 Aug Newmarket RF 3592). Showed little in maidens, but has run better in handicap company and on faster ground and scored in decisive style at Newmarket.
**J W Hills [1-9] Wyck Hall Stud.*

BEANBOY BHB 30f **RR 19f** 5024^{11}
2 ch c Clantime 6.6f **(57)** - Lady Blues Singer (Chief Singer) 8.9f **(66)**
Form - 60
Record 2000 - 1st:0 2nd:0 3rd:0 Ran:2
2000 Turf 0-2: (5f, 6f) (g-s 2)
Currently poor colt. Turf high 19 (began Spt).
**R F Marvin [0-2] A Snipe.*

BEAT ALL (USA) BHB 116f **RR 120df** 4594^{5}
4 b br h Dynaformer (USA) 12f **(82)** - Spirited Missus (USA) (Distinctive (USA)) 10.7f **(70)**
Form - 43245
Record 2000 - 1st:0 2nd:1 3rd:1 Ran:5
Pre2000 - 1st:2 2nd:1 3rd:1 Ran:5
Win Prizemoney £15,855 *Total Prizemoney* £231,242
Wins * 1999 Apr Newmar (GD) L 10f 107 <
* 1998 Spt Chepst (G-S) 7.1f 93
2000 Turf 0-5: (10f 3, 12f 2) (g-s, gd 3, frm)
Unfurnished, very high-class colt, effective 10 to 12f, acts on gd to frm. Turf high 120. Consistent. Third in the 1999 Derby, he was a big disappointment last term, his best performances being a well beaten third to Dubai Millennium at Royal Ascot, and a fourth to Montjeu in the King George VI & Queen Elizabeth Diamond Stakes. He is best on fast ground. **Sir Michael Stoute [2-10] Saeed Suhail.*

BEAT HOLLOW BHB 117f **RR 120f** 2387a^{1}
3 b c Sadler's Wells (USA) 11.3f **(87)** - Wemyss Bight (Dancing Brave (USA)) 8.4f **(76)**
Form - 131
Record 2000 - 1st:2 2nd:0 3rd:1 Ran:3
Pre2000 - 1st:1 2nd:0 3rd:0 Ran:1
Win Prizemoney £135,758 *Total Prizemoney* £251,258
Wins * 2000 Jun Longch (GD) G1 10f 118+ <
*** 2000** May Newmar (GD) L 10f 115+
* 1999 Spt Yarmou (SFT) 8f 93++
2000 Turf 2-3: (10f 2-2, 12f) (gd 1-2, g-f 1-1)
Light-framed, very high-class colt. Turf high 120 - 3rd of 15 to Sinndar (10 Jun Epsom 12f gd RF 1863) - also 1st of 7 from Premier Pas (25 Jun Longchamp RF 2387a). Winner of a Yarmouth maiden on his only start at two, he beat stablemate Sandmason in

good style on his return at Newmarket. Finished third in the Derby before landing the Grand Prix de Paris back at ten furlongs, but did not reappear. He remains in training and could prove a major contender for the big middle-distance races next summer.
**H R A Cecil [3-4] K Abdulla.*

BEAT IT (USA) RR 18f
4365[15]

2 b f Diesis 9f **(80)** - Drums of Freedom (USA) (Green Forest (USA)) 9.9f **(68)**
Form - 0
Record 2000 - 1st:0 2nd:0 3rd:0 Ran:1
2000 Turf 0-1: (5f) (g-f)
Currently poor filly. **Sir Mark Prescott [0-1] Sir Edmund Loder.*

BEAT THE RING (IRE) BHB 45a RR 45a
5243[11]

2 br c Tagula (IRE) - Pursue (Auction Ring (USA)) 8.6f **(65)**
Form - 0
Record 2000 - 1st:0 2nd:0 3rd:0 Ran:1
2000 AW 0-1: (6f) (Fibr)
Currently moderate colt. **G Brown [0-1] Mrs K W Sneath.*

BEAU CANADIEN (FR) RR 99f
260a[2]

4 m
Form - 2
2000 Turf 0-1: (13f) (gd)
Currently very useful. (1st run) - 2nd of 12 getting 5lb from Ben Ewar (2 Feb Cagnes-sur-mer 13f gd RF 0260a). **in FR [0-2].*

BEAUCHAMP MAGIC BHB 40f50a RR 33f 50a
4112[6]

5 b g Northern Park (USA) 10f **(57)** - Beauchamp Buzz (High Top) 10.2f **(67)**
Form - 81604854371116

Record					
2000 -	1st:3	2nd:0	3rd:1	Ran:11	
Pre2000 -	1st:1	2nd:1	3rd:1	Ran:18	

Win Prizemoney £9,543 *Total Prizemoney* £11,094

Wins								
*** 2000**	Aug	Thirsk	(GD)	H	16f	30	33	
**** 2000***	*Aug*	*Wolver*	*(STD)*	*H*	*14.8f*	*30*	*37*	<
*** 2000**	Jly	Bright	(FRM)	SH	11.9f	25	29	
** 1999*	*Dec*	*Wolver*	*(STD)*	*H*	*16.2f*	*33*	*34*	

2000 Turf 2-4: (12f 1-1, 16f 1-3) (gd, frm 2-3) 2000 AW 1-7: (15f 1-1, 16f 6) (Equi 2, Fibr 1-5)
Fair gelding, has worn blinkers, favours left handed tracks, favours tight tracks. Turf high 33 (began Jly). AW high 37.
**M D I Usher [4-19] The Magic And Dance Partnership (from G A Butler [0-9] Jun 1999).*

BEAUCHAMP NYX BHB 28f RR 25f
5244[9]

4 b f Northern Park (USA) 10f **(57)** - Beauchamp Image (Midyan (USA)) 6f **(60)**
Form - 6080

Record				
2000 -	1st:0	2nd:0	3rd:0	Ran:3
Pre2000 -	1st:0	2nd:0	3rd:0	Ran:4

2000 Turf 0-1: (10f) (g-s) 2000 AW 0-2: (12f, 14f) (Fibr 2)
Scopey, little account filly. AW high 8 (began Oct).
**P A Pritchard [0-3] P A Pritchard (from G A Butler [0-4] Nov 1999).*

BEAUCHAMP PILOT RR
5114[8]

2 ch g Inchinor 8.9f **(64)** - Beauchamp Image (Midyan (USA)) 6f **(60)**
Form - 8
Record 2000 - 1st:0 2nd:0 3rd:0 Ran:1
2000 AW 0-1: (9f) (Fibr)
Currently very moderate gelding. **G A Butler [0-1] E Penser.*

BEAU CHEVALIER BHB 45f RR 39df
3385[13]

4 b g Up and At 'em - Exceptional Beauty (Sallust) 8.4f **(63)**
Form - 0

Record				
2000 -	1st:0	2nd:0	3rd:0	Ran:1
Pre2000 -	1st:0	2nd:0	3rd:0	Ran:5

2000 Turf 0-1: (7f) (frm)
Scopey, very moderate gelding, effective 5f, acts on gd.
**J L Eyre [0-6] Mark Ford & Nick Tritton.*

BEAU DUCHESS (FR) BHB 67f RR 63f
2661[7]

3 ch f Bering 9.6f **(80)** - Turkish Coffee (FR) (Gay Mecene (USA)) 8.6f **(69)**
Form - 867
Record 2000 - 1st:0 2nd:0 3rd:0 Ran:3
2000 Turf 0-3: (10f 2, 12f) (g-f, frm 2)
Scopey, currently average filly. Turf high 63.
**P W Harris [0-3] Derbyshire,Elliott,Merritt & Seagroat.*

BEAUMONT (IRE) BHB 60f50a RR 65df 50a
46[9]

10 br g Be My Native (USA) 11.2f **(62)** - Say Yes (Junius (USA)) 7.7f **(65)**
Form - 0

Record				
2000 -	1st:0	2nd:0	3rd:0	Ran:1
Pre2000 -	1st:9	2nd:3	3rd:3	Ran:50

Win Prizemoney £38,396 *Total Prizemoney* £46,050

Wins							
1997	Jly	Newmar	(GD)	H	14.8f	67	72
1996	Oct	York	(GD)	H	13.9f	61	69+
1996	Spt	Cheste	(GD)	H	15.9f	59	66
1996	*Jan*	*Wolver*	*(STD)*	*H*	*12f*	*56*	*66*

2000 AW 0-1: (16f) (Equi)
Average gelding, has worn blinkers. Becoming disappointing.
**N A Callaghan [0-3] P Cunningham (from J E Banks [6-38] Oct 1999).*

BEAU SAUVAGE BHB 56f53a RR 62f 53a
5081[16]

2 b g Wolfhound (USA) 7.3f **(71)** - Maestrale (Top Ville) 11.7f **(68)**
Form - 08500
Record 2000 - 1st:0 2nd:0 3rd:0 Ran:5
2000 Turf 0-5: (5f, 6f 3, 7f) (hvy, g-s, gd 2, g-f)
Average gelding. Turf high 62 (began Aug).
**M W Easterby [0-5] Guy Reed.*

BEAUTIFUL BUSINESS BHB 47f RR 45f
3091[5]

2 b f Deploy 11.4f **(67)** - Jade Mistress (Damister (USA)) 9f **(73)**
Form - 0335
Record 2000 - 1st:0 2nd:0 3rd:2 Ran:4
Win Prizemoney £0 *Total Prizemoney* £587
2000 Turf 0-4: (6f, 7f 3) (g-f 2, frm 2)
Moderate filly, has worn blinkers. Turf high 45.
**M Quinn [0-4] Ms H Rees & J Marks.*

BEAUTIFUL PLEASURE (USA) RR
5325a[6]

5 b m General Meeting - Beautiful Bid (USA) (Baldski (USA))
Form - 6
2000 AW 0-1: (9f) (Dirt)
Currently high-class filly. Winner of the Breeders' Cup distaff in 1999, failed to repeat the performance last season.
**J Ward Jnr in USA [1-3] J Oxley.*

BEAUTY ROSE (USA) RR 45f
3613[3]

3 ch f Bien Bien (USA) - Small World (USA) (Transworld (USA))
Form - 3
Record 2000 - 1st:0 2nd:0 3rd:1 Ran:1
Win Prizemoney £0 *Total Prizemoney* £456
2000 Turf 0-1: (9f) (frm)
Rangy, currently moderate filly. (1st run) - 3rd of 10 to Berzoud (13 Aug Redcar 9f frm RF 3613).
**J H M Gosden [0-1] J Toffan & T McCaffery.*

BEBE DE CHAM BHB 40f65a RR 45f 65a
4053[13]

3 b f Tragic Role (USA) 9.4f **(63)** - Champenoise (Forzando) 7.6f **(59)**
Form - 80607066600

Record				
2000 -	1st:0	2nd:0	3rd:0	Ran:11
Pre2000 -	1st:2	2nd:1	3rd:0	Ran:11

Win Prizemoney £8,344 *Total Prizemoney* £10,280

Wins								
* 1999	Aug	Thirsk	(G-F)	H	6f	68	78	<
* 1999	Apr	Thirsk	(GD)		5f		67	

2000 Turf 0-10: (6f, 7f 2, 8f 4, 9f, 10f, 12f) (g-s 2, gd 3, g-f, frm 3, hrd)
2000 AW 0-1: (7f) (Equi)
Leggy, moderate filly, effective 6 to 7f, acts on frm to hrd, has worn blinkers. Turf high 45. A winner twice at Thirsk as a juvenile, but she has been well held on most of her other starts.
**J L Eyre [2-22] Lovely Bubbly Racing.*

BECKETT (IRE) RR 107f
4527a[1]

2 b c Fairy King (USA) 7.7f **(75)** - Groom Order 00
Form - 131
2000 Turf 2-3: (6f 1-1, 7f 1-2) (g-s, g-f 1-1)
Currently Pattern-class colt. Turf high 107 - 1st of 9 from King's County (17 Spt Curragh RF 4527a). Made a winning debut at Leopardstown before finishing third in a good race at the Curragh. One of four O'Brien runners in the Group One National Stakes, he

caused something of a surprise by winning with authority by three lengths from stablemate King's County. Reportedly to be aimed at the 2000 Guineas, he looks unlikely to stay beyond a mile.
**A P O'Brien in IRE [2-3] Mrs John Magnier.*

BECKON BHB 39f51a **RR 44df 51a** 5077[4]
4 ch f Beveled (USA) 6.9f **(64)** - Carolynchristensen (Sweet Revenge) 7.2f **(54)**
Form - 1354571586184
Record 2000 - 1st:2 2nd:0 3rd:0 Ran:11
Pre2000 - 1st:1 2nd:0 3rd:2 Ran:12
Win Prizemoney £6,240 *Total Prizemoney* £7,048
Wins * 2000 Aug Bright (FRM) H 10f 36 39
*** 2000** *Jun Lingfi (STD) H 10f 47 52* <
* 1999 *Nov Lingfi (STD) S 10f 44+*
2000 Turf 1-6: (8f, 10f 1-3, 11f, 12f) (g-s, g-f 2, frm 1-3) 2000 AW 1-5: (10f 1-2, 12f 3) (Equi 1-5)
Leggy, fair filly, effective 10 to 12f, best at 10f, - acts on Equi, favours left handed tracks, favours tight tracks. Turf high 39. AW high 52 - also 1st of 14 giving 4lb to Approachable (27 Jun Lingfield RF 2300).
**B R Johnson [3-17] B A Whittaker (from T D Barron [0-6] Jun 1999).*

BECKY SIMMONS BHB 81f **RR 86f** 4642[10]
2 b f Mujadil (USA) 7.7f **(70)** - Jolies Eaux (Shirley Heights) 10.3f **(74)**
Form - 111500
Record 2000 - 1st:3 2nd:0 3rd:0 Ran:6
Win Prizemoney £13,509 *Total Prizemoney* £13,902
Wins * 2000 Aug Redcar (FRM) H 6f 80 86 <
*** 2000** Jly Salisb (GD) 6f 79
*** 2000** Jun Hamilt (GD) 5f 66
2000 Turf 3-6: (5f 1-1, 6f 2-3, 7f 2) (gd, g-f 1-3, frm 2-2)
Useful filly, effective 6f, acts on g-f to frm. Turf high 86 - 1st of 15 giving 13lb to Milliken Park (13 Aug Redcar RF 3614) - also 1st of 10 from Sibla (15 Jly Salisbury RF 2845). She won her first three starts before being found out in better company at Chester and Doncaster. **A P Jarvis [3-6] Mrs D B Brazier.*

BEDARA BHB 87f **RR 95f** 4931[12]
3 b f Barathea (IRE) - Cutting Reef (IRE) (Kris) 9.5f **(73)**
Form - 14560
Record 2000 - 1st:1 2nd:0 3rd:0 Ran:5
Pre2000 - 1st:0 2nd:1 3rd:0 Ran:2
Win Prizemoney £3,545 *Total Prizemoney* £9,064
Wins * 2000 Apr Warwic (SFT) 10.5f 73 <
2000 Turf 1-5: (10f, 11f 1-2, 12f 2) (sft 1 1, g-s 2, gd 2)
Light-framed, very useful filly, effective 8 to 12f, acts on g-s to gd. Turf high 95 - 5th of 9 getting 15lb from Katiykha (7 Jun Gowran Park 12f g-s RF 1934a). Had to work hard to win a weak Warwick maiden on her return, and has been held in listed company since.
**B W Hills [1-6] John Poynton (from Trained [0-1] Jun 2000).*

BEDAZZLING (IRE) BHB 102f **RR 108f** 5239[6]
3 gr f Darshaan 11.9f **(81)** - Dazzlingly Radiant (Try My Best (USA)) 7.6f **(67)**
Form - 014846
Record 2000 - 1st:1 2nd:0 3rd:0 Ran:6
Pre2000 - 1st:1 2nd:1 3rd:1 Ran:5
Win Prizemoney £9,094 *Total Prizemoney* £97,017
Wins * 2000 Jun Leices (G-S) 7f 100+ <
* 1999 Spt Kempto (HVY) 7f 90+
2000 Turf 1-6: (7f 1-3, 8f 3) (g-s 2, gd 1-3, g-f)
Scopey, Pattern-class filly, effective 7 to 8f, best at 7f, acts on g-s to gd, best on gd. Turf high 108 - 4th of 8 getting 3lb from Mount Abu (21 Spt Goodwood 7f g-s RF 4549) - also 1st of 7 giving 4lb to Total Love (5 Jun Leicester RF 1717). She made no show in the Nell Gwyn on her return, but won a Leicester conditions event by the minimum margin next time. Ran really well in a Group Two at Newmarket, beaten under two lengths into fourth, and seven furlongs in soft ground look her conditions.
**J R Fanshawe [2-11] B McAllister.*

BEDEVILLED BHB 64f61a **RR 63f 61a** 5112[19]
5 ch g Beveled (USA) 6.9f **(64)** - Putout (Dowsing (USA))
Form - 272510027716030
Record 2000 - 1st:2 2nd:3 3rd:1 Ran:15
Pre2000 - 1st:1 2nd:2 3rd:1 Ran:14
Win Prizemoney £9,867 *Total Prizemoney* £16,025
Wins 2000 Aug Catter (G-S) C 5f 57
2000 Mar Newcas (GD) H 5f 67 74 <
1999 Aug Beverl (GD) 5f 68
2000 Turf 2-11: (5f 2-9, 6f 2) (gd 1-5, g-f 1-4, frm 2) 2000 AW 0-4: (5f 3, 6f) (Fibr 4)
Above-average gelding, has broken blood-vessels, effective 5 to 6f, best at 5f, acts on gd to frm - acts on Fibr, has worn blinkers. Turf high 74 (1st run) - 1st of 15 getting 4lb from Mungo Park (28 Mar Newcastle RF 0525). AW high 70 - 2nd of 8 giving 13lb to Off Hire (29 Feb Wolverhampton 5f Fibr RF 0383).
**J Pearce [0-4] Treble Chance Partnership (from T D Barron [3-16] Aug 2000).*

BEDEY (USA) BHB 82f **RR 80f** 3831[1]
3 b c Red Ransom (USA) 8.6f **(83)** - Mount Helena (Danzig (USA)) 8.4f **(76)**
Form - 4221
Record 2000 - 1st:1 2nd:2 3rd:0 Ran:4
Win Prizemoney £4,543 *Total Prizemoney* £7,685
Wins * 2000 Aug Pontef (G-F) 8f 74+ <
2000 Turf 1-4: (8f 1-3, 10f) (gd 2, g-f, hrd 1-1)
Scopey, decent colt. Turf high 80 (began Jly) - 2nd of 7 giving 5lb to May Ball (15 Jly Ascot 8f gd RF 2831) - also 1st of 19 from Mush (20 Aug Pontefract RF 3831).
**A C Stewart [1-4] Sheikh Ahmed Al Maktoum.*

BEDFORD FALLS RR 1731[9]
2 b f Mind Games - Dancing Diana (Raga Navarro (ITY)) 8f **(64)**
Form - 0
Record 2000 - 1st:0 2nd:0 3rd:0 Ran:1
2000 Turf 0-1: (5f) (g-f)
Currently very poor filly.
**A J McNae [0-1] Astaire & Partners (Holdings) Ltd.*

BEDOUIN QUEEN BHB 43f53a **RR 60f 53a** 4877[3]
3 ch f Aragon 7.7f **(58)** - Petra's Star **(55f)** (Rock City)
Form - 705706002083
Record 2000 - 1st:0 2nd:1 3rd:1 Ran:9
Pre2000 - 1st:0 2nd:0 3rd:1 Ran:6
Win Prizemoney £0 *Total Prizemoney* £1,306
2000 Turf 0-8: (8f 5, 10f 3) (g-s 2, gd 2, g-f 3, frm) 2000 AW 0-1: (8f) (Equi)
Neat, average filly, has worn blinkers. Turf high 60. Becoming disappointing.
**R F JohnsonHoughton [0-15] Zara Campbell-Harris & Partners.*

BEE GEE BHB 33f **RR 44f** 5059[3]
3 b f Beveled (USA) 6.9f **(64)** - Bunny Gee **(54f)** (Last Tycoon) 8.5f **(62)**
Form - 71438588433
Record 2000 - 1st:1 2nd:0 3rd:3 Ran:11
Pre2000 - 1st:0 2nd:0 3rd:0 Ran:4
Win Prizemoney £1,834 *Total Prizemoney* £2,790
Wins * 2000 *May Lingfi (STD) S 12f 51* <
2000 Turf 0-8: (8f, 10f 2, 11f, 12f 2, 14f, 16f) (sft, gd 2, g-f 2, frm 3)
2000 AW 1-3: (11f, 12f 1-2) (Equi 1-2, Fibr)
Unfurnished, fair filly, effective 11 to 12f, acts on frm - acts on Equi, likes left handed tracks, likes tight tracks. Turf high 44 - 4th of 11 giving 1lb to Adriana (14 Jun Lingfield 11f frm RF 1970). AW high 51 (1st run) - 1st of 7 from Albinona (27 May Lingfield RF 1503). **M Blanshard [1-15] Mara Racing.*

BEE J GEE BHB 61f63a **RR 71f 63a** 5074[12]
2 b c Dilum (USA) 7.1f **(56)** - Sound Check **(55f)** (Formidable (USA)) 9.2f **(63)**
Form - 60040
Record 2000 - 1st:0 2nd:0 3rd:0 Ran:5
2000 Turf 0-5: (5f 2, 7f 2, 8f) (g-s, gd 2, g-f, frm)
Above-average colt. Turf high 71 - 4th of 10 giving 6lb to Paula's Pride (24 Spt Brighton 8f gd RF 4615). **J Pearce [0-5] B J Goldsmith.*

BEEKEEPER RR 91f 4643[5]
2 b c Rainbow Quest (USA) 11.2f **(81)** - Chief Bee **(89f)** (Chief's Crown (USA)) 9.8f **(72)**
Form - 55
Record 2000 - 1st:0 2nd:0 3rd:0 Ran:2
Win Prizemoney £0 *Total Prizemoney* £9,168
2000 Turf 0-2: (7f 2) (g-f, frm)

Currently useful colt. Turf high 91 (began Spt). Showed plenty of promise in two outings at the back-end and should not be long in getting off the mark. He should stay ten furlongs.
**Sir Michael Stoute [0-2] Highclere Thoroughbred Racing Ltd.*

BEE KING BHB 60f **RR 62f** 5067^{6}

2 ch c First Trump - Fine Honey (USA) (Drone) 10.3f **(74)**
Form - 008033286
Record 2000 - 1st:0 2nd:1 3rd:2 Ran:9
Win Prizemoney £0 *Total Prizemoney* £2,214
2000 Turf 0-9: (5f, 6f 7, 7f) (sft, g-s 3, gd 3, frm 2)
Average colt, effective 6f, acts on sft to g-s, has worn blinkers. Turf high 62 - 2nd of 9 giving 2lb to Inzacure (27 Spt Brighton 6f g-s RF 4673).
**M R Channon [0-6] John Breslin (from M Quinn [0-3] Jun 2000).*

BEENABOUTABIT BHB 70f **RR 75f** 5156^{7}

2 b f Komaite (USA) 6.9f **(61)** - Tassagh Bridge (IRE) **(16df 19a)** (Double Schwartz) 7.9f **(55)**
Form - 027
Record 2000 - 1st:0 2nd:1 3rd:0 Ran:3
Win Prizemoney £0 *Total Prizemoney* £895
2000 Turf 0-3: (5f 2, 6f) (g-s, gd, g-f)
Currently above-average filly. Turf high 75 (began Spt) - 2nd of 19 to Princess Chloe (6 Oct Windsor 6f g-f RF 4821).
**R Ingram [0-3] The Banter Boyz.*

BEE ONE (IRE) BHB 84f **RR 79f** 4201^{2}

2 b f Catrail (USA) - Ruwy **(69f)** (Soviet Star (USA))
Form - 548452
Record 2000 - 1st:0 2nd:1 3rd:0 Ran:6
Win Prizemoney £0 *Total Prizemoney* £1,866
2000 Turf 0-6: (5f 4, 6f 2) (g-s 2, gd 2, frm 2)
Above-average filly, effective 6f, acts on gd. Turf high 79.
**D R C Elsworth [0-6] J Wotherspoon.*

BE GONE BHB 80f77a **RR 83f 77a** 2153^{11}

5 ch g Be My Chief (USA) 10.2f **(62)** - Hence (USA) (Mr Prospector (USA)) 8.8f **(78)**
Form - 381370
Record 2000 - 1st:1 2nd:0 3rd:1 Ran:4
Pre2000 - 1st:1 2nd:0 3rd:3 Ran:10
Win Prizemoney £6,182 *Total Prizemoney* £10,715
Wins * **2000** *Jan Wolver (STD) H 16.2f 82 86*
1998 Aug Newcas (GD) 9f 89 <
2000 Turf 0-1: (20f) (gd) 2000 AW 1-3: (12f, 16f 1-2) (Equi, Fibr 1-2)
Useful gelding, effective 12f, acts on gd, has worn blinkers, likes tight tracks. AW high 86. Inconsistent.
**C A Dwyer [2-10] Costas Kyriacou (from H R A Cecil [1-8] Aug 1999).*

BEGORRAT (IRE) BHB 58f **RR 61f** 478^{12}

6 ch g Ballad Rock 7.2f **(63)** - Hada Rani (Jaazeiro (USA)) 9.2f **(54)**
Form - 0
Record 2000 - 1st:0 2nd:0 3rd:0 Ran:1
Pre2000 - 1st:3 2nd:2 3rd:1 Ran:30
Win Prizemoney £8,948 *Total Prizemoney* £15,680
Wins * 1998 Oct Ayr (G-S) H 10f 58 65
1997 Oct Ayr (SFT) C 10.9f 69 <
1997 Aug Haydoc (G-F) S 8.1f 68
2000 Turf 0-1: (10f) (frm)
Average gelding, effective 10f, acts on frm, has worn blinkers (very effectively), likes left handed tracks.
**J S Goldie [2-23] S Bruce (from D Moffatt [1-12] Aug 1998).*

BEGUILE BHB 46f50a **RR 48f 50a** 3003^{16}

6 b g Most Welcome 8.6f **(66)** - Captivate (Mansingh (USA)) 7.4f **(55)**
Form - 24106300
Record 2000 - 1st:1 2nd:1 3rd:1 Ran:8
Pre2000 - 1st:0 2nd:0 3rd:2 Ran:9
Win Prizemoney £2,341 *Total Prizemoney* £4,189
Wins * **2000** *Mar Wolver (STD) H 7f 48 50* <
2000 Turf 0-4: (6f, 8f 3) (gd 2, g-f, frm) 2000 AW 1-4: (7f 1-3, 10f) (Equi 3, Fibr 1-1)
Fair gelding, effective 7 to 8f, best at 7f, acts on frm - acts on AW, prefers left handed tracks, prefers tight tracks. Turf high 48 - 3rd of 14 getting 16lb from Moon At Night (4 May Brighton 8f frm RF 1016). AW high 57 (1st run) - 2nd of 12 giving 5lb to Superchief (2 Feb Lingfield 7f Equi RF 0202) - also 1st of 12 giving 1lb to Puppet Play (4 Mar Wolverhampton RF 0406). Inconsistent.
**R Ingram [1-14] D G Wheatley (from B R Johnson [0-3] Feb 1999).*

BEHARI (IRE) **RR 33f** 148^{8}

6 b g Kahyasi 12.9f **(74)** - Berhala (IRE) (Doyoun) 9f **(69)**
Form - 8
Record 2000 - 1st:0 2nd:0 3rd:0 Ran:1
Pre2000 - 1st:0 2nd:0 3rd:0 Ran:1
2000 AW 0-1: (12f) (Fibr)
Very moderate gelding. **R Hollinshead [0-8] John Marriott.*

BEHRENS (USA) **RR** $3545a^{3}$

6 b h Pleasant Colony (USA) 12.4f **(88)** - Hot Novel (USA) (Mari's Book (USA))
Form - 123
2000 AW 1-3: (9f, 10f 1-2) (Dirt 1-3)
Top-class horse, effective 9 to 10f, - acts on Dirt, has worn blinkers. AW high 126. Inconsistent. He ran his best race of the season when chasing home Dubai Millennium in the Dubai World Cup.
**H J Bond in USA [2-8].*

BEIDERBECKE **RR 63f** 5223^{14}

2 ch c Inchinor 8.9f **(64)** - Dancing Tide (Pharly (FR)) 9.8f **(68)**
Form - 060
Record 2000 - 1st:0 2nd:0 3rd:0 Ran:3
2000 Turf 0-3: (6f 3) (gd 2, frm)
Currently average colt. Turf high 63 (began Spt).
**R Charlton [0-3] Michael Pescod.*

BELANDO BHB 43f38a **RR 39f 38a** 5010^{16}

2 b g Forzando 7.2f **(63)** - Bella Helena (Balidar) 7.9f **(63)**
Form - 000
Record 2000 - 1st:0 2nd:0 3rd:0 Ran:3
2000 Turf 0-2: (5f 2) (gd, frm) 2000 AW 0-1: (7f) (Fibr)
Currently very moderate gelding. Turf high 39.
**P D Evans [0-3] Mrs F A Veasey.*

BELIEVING BHB 47f69a **RR 61f 69a** 5120^{11}

3 b f Belmez (USA) 11.4f **(65)** - Australia Fair (AUS)(Without Fear (FR)) 5.9f **(55)**
Form - 46000000
Record 2000 - 1st:0 2nd:0 3rd:0 Ran:8
Pre2000 - 1st:1 2nd:0 3rd:0 Ran:4
Win Prizemoney £2,529 *Total Prizemoney* £2,774
Wins * 1999 Jly Bright (FRM) 5.3f 71+ <
2000 Turf 0-6: (6f 3, 7f 3) (gd, g-f 2, frm 3) 2000 AW 0-2: (5f, 6f) (Fibr 2)
Unfurnished, average filly, effective 5f, acts on hrd, likes left handed tracks, likes tight tracks. Turf high 61. AW high 46. Winner of a Brighton maiden as a juvenile, failed to make an impression last season. **R Hannon [1-12] R Hannon.*

BELINDA BHB 63a **RR 50f** 4652^{11}

3 ch f Mizoram (USA) - Mountain Dew (Pharly (FR)) 9.8f **(68)**
Form - 748100300
Record 2000 - 1st:1 2nd:0 3rd:1 Ran:9
Win Prizemoney £2,737 *Total Prizemoney* £3,177
Wins * **2000** *Jun Southw (STD) 8f 64* <
2000 Turf 0-3: (7f, 8f, 10f) (gd, g-f, frm) 2000 AW 1-6: (7f, 8f 1-4, 11f) (Fibr 1-6)
Light-framed, average filly, effective 8f, - acts on Fibr, favours left handed tracks, likes tight tracks. Turf high 50. AW high 64 - 1st of 7 getting 5lb from Guarded Secret (16 Jun Southwell RF 2029).
**K Bell [1-9] North Farm Stud.*

BELLA BELLISIMO (IRE) BHB 67f **RR 75f** 5072^{9}

3 b f Alzao (USA) 9.8f **(73)** - Bella Vitessa (IRE) **(60df)** (Thatching) 8f **(66)**
Form - 7067400
Record 2000 - 1st:0 2nd:0 3rd:0 Ran:7
Pre2000 - 1st:1 2nd:1 3rd:1 Ran:6
Win Prizemoney £5,498 *Total Prizemoney* £9,712
Wins 1999 Jun York (G-S) 6f 78 <
2000 Turf 0-7: (7f, 8f 2, 10f 4) (g-s 2, g-f 4, frm)
Scopey, above-average filly, effective 6 to 8f, acts on gd to g-f, best on gd, has worn blinkers, likes left handed tracks. Turf high 75. **J W Hills [0-3] Wyck Hall Stud (from T D Easterby [1-10] Jly 2000).*

BELLA LAMBADA BHB 82f **RR 88f** 2037[1]
3 ch f Lammtarra (USA) - Bella Colora (Bellypha) 9.8f **(73)**
Form - 61
Record 2000 - 1st:1 2nd:0 3rd:0 Ran:2
Win Prizemoney £5,642 *Total Prizemoney* £5,642
Wins * **2000** Jun York (GD) 10.4f 88 <
2000 Turf 1-2: (7f, 10f 1-1) (g-f 1-2)
Well made, currently useful filly. Turf high 88 - 1st of 6 getting 12lb from Helen's Day (16 Jun York RF 2037).
**Sir Michael Stoute [1-2] Helena Springfield Ltd.*

BELLA PAVLINA BHB 57f **RR 58f** 5197[5]
2 ch f Sure Blade (USA) 10.6f **(66)** - Pab's Choice **(51f 55a)** (Telsmoss)
Form - 0765
Record 2000 - 1st:0 2nd:0 3rd:0 Ran:4
2000 Turf 0-4: (5f 2, 6f 2) (gd 3, g-f)
Fair filly. Turf high 58 (began Spt). **P Mitchell [0-4] C Papaioannou.*

BELLAS GATE BOY BHB 49f46a **RR 43f 46a** 2499[5]
8 b g Doulab (USA) 7.4f **(61)** - Celestial Air (Rheingold) 10.4f **(62)**
Form - 000305
Record 2000 - 1st:0 2nd:0 3rd:1 Ran:6
Pre2000 - 1st:4 2nd:6 3rd:1 Ran:42
Win Prizemoney £10,307 *Total Prizemoney* £18,503
Wins * 1999 *Jun Wolver (STD) H 8.5f 40 42*
* 1999 May Warwic (SFT) H 7.7f 49 63? <
* 1998 May Lingfi (GD) H 7f 46 52
* 1997 May Lingfi (G-F) H 7f 46 51
2000 Turf 0-5: (7f 3, 8f, 10f) (hvy, g-f 2, frm, hrd) 2000 AW 0-1: (8f) (Fibr)
Moderate gelding, effective 8f, acts on sft, has worn blinkers, likes left handed tracks, likes tight tracks. Turf high 43.
**J Pearce [4-36] Miss Ann Pauline Meadows (from G Lewis [0-3] Jly 1995).*

BELLE AMOUR BHB 48f **RR 20f** 5158[6]
3 b f Inchinor 8.9f **(64)** - Mossy Rose (King of Spain) 7.8f **(52)**
Form - 6
Record 2000 - 1st:0 2nd:0 3rd:0 Ran:1
2000 Turf 0-1: (8f) (sft)
Lengthy, currently moderate filly.
**M P Tregoning [0-1] Stanley Sharp.*

BELLE DANCER BHB 20f25a **RR 25a** 3524[15]
6 b m Rambo Dancer (CAN) 8.4f **(59)** - Warning Bell (Bustino) 10.4f **(64)**
Form - 0
Record 2000 - 1st:0 2nd:0 3rd:0 Ran:1
Pre2000 - 1st:0 2nd:0 3rd:0 Ran:3
2000 Turf 0-1: (8f) (frm)
Formerly very poor mare. **T Wall [0-13] R Pitchford.*

BELLE OF HEARTS BHB 29f30a **RR 18f 30a** 2280[18]
4 gr f Belfort (FR) 6.7f **(53)** - Three of Hearts **(56f 50a)** (Governor General)
Form - 00000
Record 2000 - 1st:0 2nd:0 3rd:0 Ran:5
Pre2000 - 1st:0 2nd:1 3rd:3 Ran:14
Win Prizemoney £0 *Total Prizemoney* £2,041
2000 Turf 0-4: (6f 2, 7f, 8f) (gd 2, g-f, frm) 2000 AW 0-1: (8f) (Fibr)
Light-framed, poor filly. Turf high 18. Becoming disappointing.
**Ronald Thompson [0-5] Mrs Valerie Dixon (from C B B Booth [0-3] Oct 1999).*

BELLE ROUGE **RR 42f** 5236[19]
2 b f Celtic Swing - Gunner's Belle (Gunner B) 11.2f **(58)**
Form - 0
Record 2000 - 1st:0 2nd:0 3rd:0 Ran:1
2000 Turf 0-1: (7f) (g-s)
Currently moderate filly. **Major D N Chappell [0-1] Mrs B Woodford.*

BELLINO EMPRESARIO (IRE) BHB 44f **RR 30f** 4482[7]
2 b g Robellino (USA) 9.5f **(68)** - The Last Empress (IRE) (Last Tycoon) 8.5f **(62)**
Form - 07
Record 2000 - 1st:0 2nd:0 3rd:0 Ran:2
2000 Turf 0-2: (7f, 8f) (g-s, gd)
Currently very moderate gelding. Turf high 30 (began Aug).
**I A Wood [0-2] Happy Days Partnership.*

BELLS ARE RINGING (USA) **RR 92f** 5181a[11]
3 b f Sadler's Wells (USA) 11.3f **(87)** - Trolley Song (USA) (Caro)
Form - 64040
2000 Turf 0-4: (7f, 8f 2, 10f) (sft, g-s 2, gd)
Useful filly, effective 7f, acts on hvy, has worn blinkers. Turf high 92. **A P O'Brien in IRE [1-7] Miss Katherine Magnier.*

BELLS BEACH (IRE) BHB 42f **RR** 3189[10]
2 ch f General Monash (USA) - Clifton Beach (Auction Ring (USA)) 8.6f **(65)**
Form - 8330
Record 2000 - 1st:0 2nd:0 3rd:2 Ran:4
Win Prizemoney £0 *Total Prizemoney* £520
2000 Turf 0-1: (6f) (gd) 2000 AW 0-3: (5f, 6f 2) (Fibr 3)
Fair filly. AW high 52. **A Berry [0-4] Alex Gorrie.*

BELSTANE BADGER (IRE) **RR 38f** 5189[7]
2 b f Blues Traveller (IRE) - Brigadina (Brigadier Gerard) 9.3f **(58)**
Form - 7
Record 2000 - 1st:0 2nd:0 3rd:0 Ran:1
2000 Turf 0-1: (7f) (gd)
Currently very moderate filly.
**I Semple [0-1] Belstane Racing Partnership (Two).*

BELSTANE FOX (IRE) **RR 25f** 5189[8]
2 ch f General Monash (USA) - Countess Kildare (Dominion) 8.5f **(63)**
Form - 8
Record 2000 - 1st:0 2nd:0 3rd:0 Ran:1
2000 Turf 0-1: (7f) (gd)
Currently little account filly.
**I Semple [0-1] Belstane Racing Partnership (One).*

BELTANE **RR 36f** 4321[15]
2 b c Magic Ring (IRE) 6.5f **(64)** - Sally's Trust (IRE) (Classic Secret (USA))
Form - 00
Record 2000 - 1st:0 2nd:0 3rd:0 Ran:2
2000 Turf 0-2: (6f, 7f) (g-f 2)
Currently very moderate colt. Turf high 36 (began Aug).
**W de Best-Turner [0-2] Mrs Gillian Swanton.*

BEL TEMPO **RR 30f** 4222[12]
2 b f Petong 7.6f **(58)** - Mystic Tempo (USA) **(73?f 60a)** (El Gran Senor (USA)) 9.6f **(76)**
Form - 70
Record 2000 - 1st:0 2nd:0 3rd:0 Ran:2
2000 Turf 0-2: (6f, 7f) (g-f, frm)
Currently very moderate filly. Turf high 30 (began Aug).
**S Dow [0-2] Mrs A M Upsdell.*

BE MY TINKER BHB 65f **RR 66f** 3376[2]
2 ch f Be My Chief (USA) 10.2f **(62)** - Tinkerbird (Music Boy) 6.8f **(57)**
Form - 622
Record 2000 - 1st:0 2nd:2 3rd:0 Ran:3
Win Prizemoney £0 *Total Prizemoney* £2,249
2000 Turf 0-3: (5f 2, 6f) (g-f, frm 2)
Currently average filly. Turf high 66 (began Jly).
**G Brown [0-3] J Cleeve.*

BE MY WISH BHB 64f68a **RR 62f 68a** 4471[8]
5 b m Be My Chief (USA) 10.2f **(62)** - Spinner (Blue Cashmere) 6.4f **(54)**
Form - 453225188
Record 2000 - 1st:1 2nd:2 3rd:1 Ran:7
Pre2000 - 1st:1 2nd:1 3rd:3 Ran:22
Win Prizemoney £9,008 *Total Prizemoney* £14,884
Wins * **2000** Aug Newmar (G-F) H 6f 59 62
1998 Aug Ascot (G-F) 7f 77 <
2000 Turf 1-7: (6f 1-3, 7f 4) (gd, g-f 1-4, frm 2)
Above-average filly, effective 6 to 8f, best at 6f, acts on g-f to frm - acts on Equi, has worn blinkers. Turf high 62 - 1st of 15 getting 9lb from Double Splendour (25 Aug Newmarket RF 3969).
**W A O'Gorman [1-9] W A O'Gorman (from S P C Woods [0-6] Jun*

1999).

BENATOM (USA) BHB 95f RR 93f 1129[13]

7 gr g Hawkster (USA) 12.4f **(71)** - Dance Til Two (USA) (Sovereign Dancer (USA)) 11.2f **(68)**

Form - 0

Record	**2000 -**	1st:0	2nd:0	3rd:0	Ran:1
	Pre2000 -	1st:5	2nd:3	3rd:2	Ran:29

Win Prizemoney £39,065 *Total Prizemoney* £59,474

Wins	* 1999	Jly	Newmar	(GD)	H	16.1f	90	95	
	1997	Jly	York	(GD)	LH	13.9f	90	97	<
	1996	Aug	Goodwo	(G-F)	H	14f	90	95	
	1996	Jly	Newmar	(GD)	H	16.1f	85	90	
	1996	Apr	Thirsk	(G-F)		12f		76	

2000 Turf 0-1: (19f) (g-f)

Useful gelding, effective 14 to 20f, best at 16f, acts on gd to frm, best on frm, has worn blinkers, likes right handed tracks, excels at Kempton.

**D R C Elsworth [2-23] Lordship Stud (from H R A Cecil [4-15] Jly 1997).*

BENBYAS BHB 50f40a RR 58f 40a 5316[5]

3 b g Rambo Dancer (CAN) 8.4f **(59)** - Light the Way (Nicholas Bill) 10.1f **(56)**

Form - 061804305

Record	**2000 -**	1st:1	2nd:0	3rd:1	Ran:9
	Pre2000 -	1st:0	2nd:0	3rd:0	Ran:5

Win Prizemoney £2,352 *Total Prizemoney* £4,063

Wins	* **2000**	Jun	Carlis	(SFT)		5.9f		58	<

2000 Turf 1-8: (6f 1-3, 8f 5) (g-s 3, gd, g-f 1-3, frm) 2000 AW 0-1: (8f) (Fibr)

Scopey, fair gelding, often wears blinkers (effectively). Turf high 58. **J L Eyre [1-14] C H Stephenson & Partners.*

BENEDICTINE RR 85f 4149[2]

2 b c Primo Dominie 7.2f **(67)** - Benedicite (Lomond (USA)) 8.8f **(65)**

Form - 2

Record	**2000 -**	1st:0	2nd:1	3rd:0	Ran:1

Win Prizemoney £0 *Total Prizemoney* £1,426

2000 Turf 0-1: (5f) (gd)

Currently useful colt. (1st run) - 2nd of 14 to King's Ballet (1 Spt Haydock 5f gd RF 4149). **R Hannon [0-1] N Ahamad.*

BENEVOLENCE (IRE) BHB 69f RR 61f 3561[6]

2 b f Lahib (USA) 8f **(69)** - Fyors Gift (IRE) **(64f 58a)** (Cadeaux Genereux)

Form - 046

Record	**2000 -**	1st:0	2nd:0	3rd:0	Ran:3

Win Prizemoney £0 *Total Prizemoney* £336

2000 Turf 0-3: (6f 2, 7f) (gd, frm 2)

Currently average filly. Turf high 61 (began Jly).

**S P C Woods [0-3] R A Dawson.*

BEN EWAR RR 113f 2982a[P]

6 b h Old Vic 12.8f **(72)** - Sunset Reef (Mill Reef (USA)) 10.5f **(78)**

Form - 13P

2000 Turf 1-3: (12f, 13f 1-2) (sft, gd 1-2)

Group-class horse, has broken blood-vessels. Turf high 113 - 3rd of 6 giving 3lb to Daring Miss (11 Jun Chantilly 12f gd RF 2006a) - also 1st of 12 giving 5lb to Beau Canadien (2 Feb Cagnes-sur-mer RF 0260a). **F Doumen in FR [2-6].*

BENJAMIN (IRE) RR 61f 2845[10]

2 b c Night Shift (USA) 8.1f **(73)** - Best Academy (USA) (Roberto (USA)) 10f **(76)**

Form - 000

Record	**2000 -**	1st:0	2nd:0	3rd:0	Ran:3

2000 Turf 0-3: (5f, 6f, 7f) (g-f, frm 2)

Currently average colt. Turf high 61. **P Mitchell [0-3] Richard Cohen.*

BENNOCHY BHB 41f RR 53f 5057[9]

3 ch g Factual (USA) - Agreloui (Tower Walk) 10f **(62)**

Form - 105745460000

Record	**2000 -**	1st:1	2nd:0	3rd:0	Ran:12
	Pre2000 -	1st:0	2nd:0	3rd:0	Ran:6

Win Prizemoney £2,254 *Total Prizemoney* £2,797

Wins	* **2000**	Mar	Catter	(GD)		5f		61	<

2000 Turf 1-12: (5f 1-9, 6f 3) (sft 2, gd 1-3, g-f 5, frm 2)

Neat, fair gelding, effective 5 to 6f, best at 5f, acts on gd to frm. Turf high 61 (1st run) - 1st of 10 giving 3lb to College Maid (29 Mar Catterick RF 0544). Becoming disappointing.

**A Berry [1-12] Mrs Norma Peebles (from J Berry [0-6] Nov 1999).*

BENOUI SPRINGS (IRE) RR 70f 3960[4]

3 br c Caerleon (USA) 10.9f **(79)** - Afrique Bleu Azur (USA) (Sagace (FR)) 8f **(124)**

Form - 4

Record	**2000 -**	1st:0	2nd:0	3rd:0	Ran:1
	Pre2000 -	1st:0	2nd:0	3rd:0	Ran:1

Win Prizemoney £0 *Total Prizemoney* £281

2000 Turf 0-1: (7f) (hrd)

Neat, currently above-average colt.

**J H M Gosden [0-1] R E Sangster & A K Collins (from P W Chapple-Hyam [0-1] Spt 1999).*

BENOVIA (IRE) RR 93f 5283a[5]

3 b g Ridgewood Ben - Zinovia (USA) (Ziggy's Boy (USA))

Form - 656012025

2000 Turf 1-9: (8f 1-5, 10f 3, 11f) (hvy 2, g-s, gd 3, g-f 2, frm 1-1)

Useful gelding, effective 10 to 11f, acts on hvy to gd, has worn blinkers, likes left handed tracks. Turf high 93.

**Miss Frances Crowley in IRE [2-14] Eight Hills Syndicate.*

BENTICO BHB 35f46a RR 41f 46a 1092[13]

11 b g Nordico (USA) 8.2f **(59)** - Bentinck Hotel (Red God) 8.5f **(65)**

Form - 74240

Record	**2000 -**	1st:0	2nd:1	3rd:0	Ran:5
	Pre2000 -	1st:16	2nd:14	3rd:12	Ran:114

Win Prizemoney £50,262 *Total Prizemoney* £72,104

Wins	* 1997	*Dec*	*Southw*	*(STD)*	*C*	*8f*		*63*	
	* 1997	*Jun*	*Lingfi*	*(STD)*		*8f*		*73*	<
	* 1997	*Jun*	*Wolver*	*(STD)*	*C*	*7f*		*68*	
	* 1996	*Jun*	*Wolver*	*(STD)*	*H*	*8.5f*	*68*	*69*	

2000 AW 0-5: (8f 3, 9f, 12f) (Fibr 5)

Fair gelding, often wears blinkers. AW high 52. Inconsistent.

**Mrs N Macauley [11-91] Mrs N Macauley (from M A Jarvis [5-28] Spt 1994).*

BENTYHEATH LANE BHB 50f RR 51f 4535[11]

3 b g Puissance 7.1f **(60)** - Eye Sight (Roscoe Blake) 11f **(66)**

Form - 00

Record	**2000 -**	1st:0	2nd:0	3rd:0	Ran:2
	Pre2000 -	1st:0	2nd:0	3rd:0	Ran:2

2000 Turf 0-2: (8f, 16f) (g-s, gd)

Lengthy, fair gelding.

**M Mullineaux [0-4] Exors of the late Lord Leverhulme.*

BENVOLIO RR 2267[7]

3 br g Cidrax (FR) - Miss Capulet (Commanche Run) 8.5f **(58)**

Form - 7

Record	**2000 -**	1st:0	2nd:0	3rd:0	Ran:1

2000 Turf 0-1: (12f) (frm)

Formerly very poor gelding - 7th of 9 to Bid For Fame (25 Jun Pontefract 12f frm RF 2267). **C N Kellett [0-1] 7 A D Racing.*

BENZOE (IRE) BHB 55f RR 55f 4276[6]

10 b g Taufan (USA) 8.3f **(65)** - Saintly Guest (What A Guest) 7f **(62)**

Form - 506153046

Record	**2000 -**	1st:1	2nd:0	3rd:1	Ran:9
	Pre2000 -	1st:10	2nd:9	3rd:10	Ran:103

Win Prizemoney £58,688 *Total Prizemoney* £90,259

Wins	* **2000**	Jly	Haydoc	(G-F)	H	5f	52	54
	1999	Jly	Leices	(G-F)	H	6f	62	61
	1998	Spt	Redcar	(G-F)	H	6f	70	74
	1998	May	Thirsk	(G-F)	H	6f	68	73
	1997	Jly	Thirsk	(GD)	H	6f	73	77
	1997	Jun	Thirsk	(G-F)	H	5f	64	65
	1996	Aug	Thirsk	(G-F)	H	6f	77	81
	1996	May	Thirsk	(G-F)	H	6f	69	72

2000 Turf 1-9: (5f 1-5, 6f 4) (gd 2, g-f, frm 1-6)

Fair gelding, has broken blood-vessels, effective 5 to 6f, best at 5f, acts on g-f to frm, best on frm, has worn blinkers. Turf high 55 - 4th of 17 getting 4lb from Northern Svengali (25 Aug Thirsk 5f frm RF 3975) - also 1st of 19 getting 21lb from Mungo Park (16 Jly

Haydock RF 2859).
**D Nicholls [1-9] Tony Fawcett (from Andrew Turnell [1-14] Oct 1999).*

BERBERIS BHB 28f RR 29f 3171[16]

4 b g Green Desert (USA) 7.8f **(78)** - Babita (Habitat) 9.4f **(70)**
Form - 80000
Record 2000 - 1st:0 2nd:0 3rd:0 Ran:5
Pre2000 - 1st:0 2nd:0 3rd:0 Ran:3
2000 Turf 0-5: (7f 2, 8f 2, 12f) (gd 2, g-f, frm, hrd)
Workmanlike, little account gelding, has worn blinkers. Turf high 29. Becoming disappointing.
**J M Bradley [0-5] Mrs Marion Morgan (from C E Brittain [0-3] Oct 1999).*

BERENICA (IRE) RR 95f 4795a[5]

3 b f College Chapel - Berenice (ITY) 00
Form - 7731685
2000 Turf 1-7: (5f 2, 6f 1-3, 7f 2) (sft 4, g-s 1-1, gd)
Very useful filly, effective 6f, acts on g-s to gd, has worn blinkers. Turf high 95 - 1st of 9 giving 13lb to Antrim Coast (4 Jun Naas RF 1768a). **J S Bolger in IRE [2-15] Sporting Quest Racing Club.*

BEREZINA BHB 61f RR 66f 4460[15]

2 b f Brief Truce (USA) 9.1f **(73)** - Lithe Spirit (IRE) **(31f 38a)** (Dancing Dissident (USA))
Form - 56481080
Record 2000 - 1st:1 2nd:0 3rd:0 Ran:8
Win Prizemoney £2,779 *Total Prizemoney* £2,779
Wins * 2000 Jly Redcar (G-F) 6f 66 **<**
2000 Turf 1-8: (5f 3, 6f 1-4, 7f) (sft, g-s, gd, g-f 2, frm 1-3)
Average filly, effective 6f, acts on g-f to frm. Turf high 66 - 4th of 14 getting 7lb from Our Destiny (7 Jly Haydock 6f g-f RF 2593) - also 1st of 9 from Micklow Magic (29 Jly Redcar RF 3220). Inconsistent.
**T D Easterby [1-8] Chris & Antonia Deuters.*

BERGAMO BHB 54f RR 63df 1673[7]

4 b g Robellino (USA) 9.5f **(68)** - Pretty Thing (Star Appeal) 9.6f **(65)**
Form - 08057
Record 2000 - 1st:0 2nd:0 3rd:0 Ran:5
Pre2000 - 1st:3 2nd:0 3rd:3 Ran:20
Win Prizemoney £9,653 *Total Prizemoney* £14,036

Wins								
	1999	Jun Yarmou	(GD)	H	14.1f	74	79	**<**
	1999	May Beverl	(GD)	H	12f	70	73	
	1998	Spt Bath	(G-S)		10.2f		78	

2000 Turf 0-5: (12f 2, 13f, 14f 2) (g-s 2, gd, g-f, frm)
Workmanlike, average gelding, effective 12 to 16f, best at 14f, acts on gd to hrd, often wears blinkers (extremely effectively), favours tight tracks, does well at Kempton. Turf high 63. Becoming disappointing.
**B Ellison [0-5] Ashley Young (from J Noseda [3-20] Spt 1999).*

BERGEN (IRE) BHB 63f RR 65f 4452[11]

5 b g Ballad Rock 7.2f **(63)** - Local Custom (IRE) (Be My Native (USA)) 10.2f **(71)**
Form - 8500
Record 2000 - 1st:0 2nd:0 3rd:0 Ran:4
Pre2000 - 1st:1 2nd:2 3rd:1 Ran:13
Win Prizemoney £3,485 *Total Prizemoney* £8,028
Wins 1997 Jly Pontef (G-F) 6f 86+ **<**
2000 Turf 0-4: (5f, 7f 2, 8f) (gd 3, frm)
Average gelding, effective 8 to 9f, acts on g-f to frm, likes left handed tracks, likes tight tracks. Turf high 65. Fair performer at around a mile for Barry Hills, he has not won since 1997 and has shown little since joining Dandy Nicholls.
**D Nicholls [0-4] J Hanson (from B W Hills [0-6] Oct 1999).*

BERINE'S SON (USA) RR 116f 1826a[6]

3 b c Irish River (FR) 9f **(77)** - Berine (FR) (Bering) 7.4f **(61)**
Form - 126
2000 Turf 1-3: (8f 1-2, 9f) (hvy 1-1, gd 2)
Currently high-class colt. Turf high 116 - 2nd of 7 to Bachir (14 May Longchamp 8f gd RF 1290a) - also 1st of 8 from Premier Pas (23 Apr Longchamp RF 0890a). Won a trial before chasing home Bachir in the French Guineas. Well beaten in heavy ground in the Prix Jean Prat.
**A Fabre in FR [1-3].*

BERISKAIO (IRE) RR 100f 1447a[3]

3 b c Bering 9.6f **(80)** - Boubskaia (FR) (Niniski (USA)) 10.6f **(65)**
Form - 3
2000 Turf 0-1: (9f) (g-s)
Currently very useful colt. (1st run) - 3rd of 6 to Suances (18 May Longchamp 9f g-s RF 1447a). **A Fabre in FR [0-1] Paul Lau.*

BERKELEY DIDO (IRE) BHB 52f45a RR 52f 45a 182[8]

3 b f Foxhound (USA) - Dignified Air (FR) (Wolver Hollow) 8f **(56)**
Form - 88
Record 2000 - 1st:0 2nd:0 3rd:0 Ran:2
Pre2000 - 1st:0 2nd:0 3rd:1 Ran:5
Win Prizemoney £0 *Total Prizemoney* £497
2000 AW 0-2: (7f, 8f) (Equi, Fibr)
Light-framed, fair filly, has worn blinkers. AW high 15.
**M L W Bell [0-7] Capt B W Bell.*

BERKELEY HALL BHB 63f48a RR 60f 48a 4275[13]

3 b f Saddlers' Hall (IRE) 10.5f **(65)** - Serious Affair (Valiyar) 8.5f **(73)**
Form - 001260
Record 2000 - 1st:1 2nd:1 3rd:0 Ran:6
Pre2000 - 1st:0 2nd:0 3rd:1 Ran:3
Win Prizemoney £2,198 *Total Prizemoney* £3,364
Wins * 2000 May Nottin (G-F) H 6.1f 56 60 **<**
2000 Turf 1-5: (6f 1-3, 7f 2) (hvy, g-f, frm 1-3) 2000 AW 0-1: (9f) (Fibr)
Workmanlike, average filly, effective 6f, acts on frm, has worn blinkers. Turf high 60 - 1st of 18 getting 3lb from Myttons Mistake (12 May Nottingham RF 1182). Inconsistent.
**B Palling [1-9] Glyn and Albert Yemm.*

BERLIN (IRE) RR 96f 4527a[5]

2 b c Common Grounds 8.1f **(66)** - Carranza
Form - 135
2000 Turf 1-3: (6f 1-2, 7f) (gd 1-2)
Currently very useful colt. Turf high 96 (1st run) (began Jun) - 1st of 11 from Mowassel (30 Jun Curragh RF 2515a). Impressed in a valuable sales race on his debut, and looked in need of further when third in a Group Three over six furlongs. Stepped up to Group One company over seven on his third run, he was never a threat. **E Lynam in IRE [1-3] R P Behan.*

BERNARDO BELLOTTO (IRE) BHB 44f52a RR 54f 52a 4949a[2]

5 b g High Estate 10.5f **(66)** - Naivity (IRE) (Auction Ring (USA)) 8.6f **(65)**
Form - 77008822
Record 2000 - 1st:0 2nd:2 3rd:0 Ran:8
Pre2000 - 1st:3 2nd:5 3rd:2 Ran:22
Win Prizemoney £8,274 *Total Prizemoney* £19,740

Wins							
	1999	Jun Mussel	(GD)	C	7.1f	59	
	1999	May Redcar	(FRM)	S	7f	56	
	1997	Aug Epsom	(GD)		6f	78	**<**

2000 Turf 0-5: (7f 5) (g-s, gd 2, frm 2) 2000 AW 0-3: (6f, 7f, 12f) (Fibr 2, Dirt)
Fair gelding, effective 7f, acts on g-f to frm, has worn blinkers (extremely effectively). Turf high 42. AW high 43. Inconsistent.
**P R Haley in SPA [0-1] (from D Nicholls [2-15] Jly 2000).*

BERNARDON (GER) RR 116f 4713a[1]

4 b c Suave Dancer (USA) 10.7f **(68)** - Bejaria () (Konigsstuhl (GER)) 11.2f **(76)**
Form - 23211
2000 Turf 2-5: (8f 2-5) (hvy, sft 2-2, gd 2)
High-class colt, effective 8f, acts on hvy to gd, best on sft. Turf high 116 - 1st of 9 giving 9lb to Proudwings (29 Aug Baden-Baden RF 4285a) - also 1st of 10 from Banyumanik (23 Spt Cologne RF 4713a). **P Schiergen in GER [2-6] Gestut Schlenderhan.*

BERNSTEIN (USA) RR 110f 4805a[1]

3 b c Storm Cat (USA) 7f **(86)** - La Affirmed (USA) (Affirmed (USA)) 9.3f **(79)**
Form - 0101
2000 Turf 2-4: (5f, 6f 1-1, 7f 1-1, 8f) (sft 1-1, gd 1-3)
Group-class colt, effective 6 to 7f, best at 6f, acts on sft to gd, best on gd, has worn blinkers. Turf high 110 - 1st of 11 getting 2lb from Cobourg Lodge (1 Oct Cork RF 4805a) - also 1st of 9 getting 6lb from Auenklang (12 Aug Ascot RF 3578). High-class at two, his

form last season was patchy. Well beaten in the 2000 Guineas, he landed the Shergar Cup Sprint over six furlongs at Ascot, was well beaten over five in the Nunthorpe, but won a Group Three at Cork when stepped back up to seven.

**A P O'Brien in IRE [4-7] Michael Tabor.*

BERTOLINI (USA) BHB 120f **RR 119f** 4845a[7]
4 b c Danzig (USA) 8.1f **(88)** - Aquilegia (USA) (Alydar (USA)) 9.1f **(76)**
Form - 23627
Record **2000** - 1st:0 2nd:2 3rd:1 Ran:5
Pre2000 - 1st:2 2nd:4 3rd:3 Ran:14
Win Prizemoney £35,410 *Total Prizemoney* £323,225
Wins 1999 Apr Newmar (GD) LH 7f 113 113 <
1998 Jly Newmar (G-F) G3 6f 106+
2000 Turf 0-4: (5f 3, 6f) (gd 4) 2000 AW 0-1: (6f) (Dirt)
Scopey, high-class colt, effective 5 to 7f, acts on hvy to frm, often wears blinkers. Turf high 119 - 2nd of 13 to Nuclear Debate (24 Aug York 5f gd RF 3935). A very able sprinter, he often runs well in the highest class, such as when chasing home Nuclear Debate in the Nunthorpe, but has not won a race since landing the Free Handicap on his reappearance at three. Probably best over six furlongs.
**S bin Suroor [0-4] Godolphin (from S bin Suroor in UAE [0-1] Mar 2000).*

BERTY BOY BHB 30f **RR ?f** 3547[20]
4 ch g Alhijaz 7.7f **(57)** - Bridge Player (The Noble Player (USA)) 6.5f **(67)**
Form - 00
Record **2000** - 1st:0 2nd:0 3rd:0 Ran:2
Pre2000 - 1st:0 2nd:0 3rd:0 Ran:4
2000 Turf 0-2: (12f, 17f) (g-f, frm)
Scopey, very poor gelding, has worn blinkers.
**W M Brisbourne [0-1] Miss Marjorie Thompson (from Mrs G S Rees [0-5] Jun 2000).*

BERZOUD BHB 75f **RR 66f** 3613[1]
3 b f Ezzoud (IRE) - Bertie's Girl (Another Realm) 6.6f **(55)**
Form - 021
Record **2000** - 1st:1 2nd:1 3rd:0 Ran:3
Win Prizemoney £2,964 *Total Prizemoney* £4,274
Wins *** 2000** Aug Redcar (FRM) 9f 49 <
2000 Turf 1-3: (8f 2, 9f 1-1) (gd, g-f, frm 1-1)
Light-framed, currently average filly. Turf high 66 - 2nd of 14 to Tango Two Thousand (10 Jly Windsor 8f gd RF 2684).
**J Noseda [1-3] Mike Sullivan.*

BESCABY BLUE (IRE) BHB 60f52a **RR 64f 52a** 180[2]
3 b f Blues Traveller (IRE) - Nurse Tyra (USA) (Dr Blum (USA)) 9.8f **(70)**
Form - 02662
Record **2000** - 1st:0 2nd:1 3rd:0 Ran:3
Pre2000 - 1st:2 2nd:2 3rd:0 Ran:10
Win Prizemoney £5,070 *Total Prizemoney* £7,062
Wins * 1999 Oct Redcar (GD) C 7f 64
* 1999 *May Southw (STD) 5f 76* <
2000 AW 0-3: (6f, 7f 2) (Equi, Fibr 2)
Scopey, average filly, effective 5f, acts on gd - acts on Fibr, has worn blinkers. AW high 57. **J Wharton [2-13] John Wharton.*

BE SEEING YOU (IRE) **RR 103f** 5283a[3]
3 b c Turtle Island - Winning Feature (Red Alert) 7.6f **(66)**
Form - 103
2000 Turf 1-3: (7f 1-1, 8f 2) (hvy, sft, gd 1-1)
Very useful colt. Turf high 103. **C Collins in IRE [1-4] Mrs C Collins.*

BEST BOND BHB 55f51a **RR 65f 51a** 4655[10]
3 ch c Cadeaux Genereux 7.9f **(76)** - My Darlingdaughter **(18f)** (Night Shift (USA)) 7.2f **(69)**
Form - 0380056063060
Record **2000** - 1st:0 2nd:0 3rd:2 Ran:13
Pre2000 - 1st:0 2nd:0 3rd:0 Ran:3
Win Prizemoney £0 *Total Prizemoney* £1,040
2000 Turf 0-12: (5f 5, 6f 5, 7f 2) (sft, gd 2, g-f 4, frm 5) 2000 AW 0-1: (6f) (Fibr)
Well made, average colt, effective 5f, acts on gd, has worn blinkers. Turf high 65 - 3rd of 17 getting 9lb from Queen of The May (2 May Windsor 5f gd RF 0976).
**N P Littmoden [0-13] Miss Vanessa Church (from J L Dunlop [0-3] Spt 1999).*

BEST EVER **RR 54f** 2886[13]
3 ch g Rock City 8.8f **(62)** - Better Still (IRE) (Glenstal (USA)) 10.1f **(64)**
Form - 000250
Record **2000** - 1st:0 2nd:1 3rd:0 Ran:6
Pre2000 - 1st:0 2nd:2 3rd:1 Ran:10
Win Prizemoney £0 *Total Prizemoney* £5,292
2000 Turf 0-6: (8f 4, 10f 2) (gd 4, frm, hrd)
Fair gelding, effective 7 to 8f, best at 7f, acts on g-f to hrd, best on frm. Turf high 54. Inconsistent.
**M W Easterby [0-16] Mrs Jean Turpin.*

BEST GREY **RR 107f** 1634a[5]
4 gr c Ezzoud (IRE) - Best Girl Friend (Sharrood (USA)) 10.5f **(72)**
Form - 5
2000 Turf 0-1: (12f) (g-f)
Currently Pattern-class colt. **V Caruso in ITY [0-3].*

BEST GUEST (IRE) BHB 53f **RR 51f** 4725[9]
2 b c Barathea (IRE) - Common Rumpus (IRE) **(81f)** (Common Grounds)
Form - 800
Record **2000** - 1st:0 2nd:0 3rd:0 Ran:3
2000 Turf 0-3: (6f, 7f, 8f) (gd 3)
Currently fair colt. Turf high 51 (began Aug).
**G G Margarson [0-3] John Guest.*

BEST KEPT SECRET BHB 16f32a **RR 19f 32a** 571[8]
9 b g Petong 7.6f **(58)** - Glenfield Portion (Mummy's Pet) 7.7f **(60)**
Form - 8
Record **2000** - 1st:0 2nd:0 3rd:0 Ran:1
Pre2000 - 1st:6 2nd:9 3rd:13 Ran:80
Win Prizemoney £17,921 *Total Prizemoney* £33,410
2000 Turf 0-1: (5f) (gd)
Very moderate gelding, had worn blinkers. (DEAD)
**D A Nolan [0-18] Mrs J McFadyen-Murray (from L J Barratt [0-7] Aug 1997).*

BEST MUSIC METROFM BHB 50f40a **RR 40a** 80[9]
3 b g Governor General 6.8f **(45)** - Dancing May (Tina's Pet) 6.8f **(59)**
Form - 00
Record **2000** - 1st:0 2nd:0 3rd:0 Ran:2
Pre2000 - 1st:0 2nd:0 3rd:1 Ran:1
Win Prizemoney £0 *Total Prizemoney* £452
2000 AW 0-2: (6f, 9f) (Fibr 2)
Workmanlike, currently very poor gelding.
**E J Alston [0-2] J Laughton (from D Eddy [0-1] Apr 1999).*

BEST OF THE BESTS (IRE) BHB 120f **RR 121f** 4596[3]
3 ch c Machiavellian (USA) 9.8f **(83)** - Sueboog (IRE) (Darshaan) 9.9f **(84)**
Form - 344133
Record **2000** - 1st:1 2nd:0 3rd:3 Ran:6
Pre2000 - 1st:1 2nd:1 3rd:1 Ran:3
Win Prizemoney £44,893 *Total Prizemoney* £243,651
Wins *** 2000** Aug Deauvi (G-F) G2 10f 115+ <
1999 Aug Sandow (GD) G3 7.1f 112+
2000 Turf 1-6: (8f, 10f 1-4, 12f) (gd 4, g-f 1-2)
Workmanlike, very high-class colt, effective 7 to 10f, best at 10f, acts on sft to g-f, best on gd, excels at Ascot. Turf high 121 - 3rd of 7 to Giant's Causeway (9 Spt Leopardstown 10f gd RF 4355a) - also 1st of 5 getting 5lb from Kutub (15 Aug Deauville RF 3939a). Consistent. A high-class juvenile for Clive Brittain, he was third in the Dante Stakes on his reappearance, his first run for Godolphin, but saw the front too soon in the Derby and faded into fourth. He filled the same position behind Beat Hollow in the Grand Prix de Paris but confirmed himself a very smart colt when landing a Deauville Group Two in August. He finished a good third in the Irish Champion Stakes and was supplemented for £25,000 for the QE2 at Ascot, in which he finished third.
**S bin Suroor [1-6] Godolphin (from C E Brittain [1-3] Spt 1999).*

BEST PORT (IRE) BHB 33f **RR 40f** 5012[5]
4 b g Be My Guest (USA) 10.2f **(66)** - Portree (Slip Anchor) 9.8f **(73)**

Form - 7834377212705

Record	**2000 -**	1st:1	2nd:2	3rd:2	Ran:13
	Pre2000 -	1st:0	2nd:0	3rd:0	Ran:9

Win Prizemoney £2,296 *Total Prizemoney* £5,106

Wins * **2000** Aug Beverl (G-F) SH 16.2f 31 35 <

2000 Turf 1-10: (12f 2, 13f, 14f 4, 16f 1-3) (g-s, gd 3, g-f 3, frm 1-3)

2000 AW 0-3: (12f 2, 14f) (Fibr 3)

Neat, moderate gelding, effective 12 to 16f, best at 16f, acts on gd to frm - acts on Fibr, best on frm. Turf high 42 - also 1st of 11 giving 16lb to Swandale Flyer (17 Aug Beverley RF 3714). AW high 34 - 5th of 16 getting 5lb from Half Tide (16 Oct Southwell 14f Fibr RF 5012). Consistent.

**J Parkes [1-20] W A Sellers (from M A Jarvis [0-2] Nov 1998).*

BEST QUEST BHB 59f67a RR 60f 67a 466[7]

5 b h Salse (USA) 10.9f **(71)** - Quest for the Best (Rainbow Quest (USA)) 10.4f **(75)**

Form - 20031233358227

Record	**2000 -**	1st:1	2nd:3	3rd:4	Ran:11
	Pre2000 -	1st:2	2nd:3	3rd:3	Ran:25

Win Prizemoney £9,355 *Total Prizemoney* £18,577

Wins	* **2000**	*Jan*	*Lingfi*	*(STD)*	*C*	*6f*		*59*	
	* 1998	*Dec*	*Lingfi*	*(STD)*	*H*	*7f*	*68*	*70*	<
	1998	Oct	Doncas	(SFT)	C	7f		55	

2000 AW 1-11: (5f, 6f 1-6, 7f 4) (Equi 1-5, Fibr 6)

Best of the Bests tried hard to live up to his name

Average colt, effective 5 to 7f, - acts on AW, best on Equi, has worn blinkers. AW high 69 - 3rd of 8 giving 9lb to Frilly Front (26 Jan Lingfield 5f Equi RF 0164). Consistent.

**K R Burke [2-26] Nigel Shields (from J H M Gosden [1-10] Oct 1998).*

BETACHANCE DOT COM BHB 46f RR 47f 3066[14]

3 b f Safawan 6.6f **(60)** - Alipampa (IRE) (Glenstal (USA)) 10.1f **(64)**

Form - 0800

Record **2000 -** 1st:0 2nd:0 3rd:0 Ran:4

2000 Turf 0-4: (10f 2, 14f, 16f) (g-f 3, frm)

Scopey, moderate filly. Turf high 47.

**J Pearce [0-4] Betachance com plc.*

BETCHWORTH SAND BHB 39f34a RR 26f 34a 4221[11]

4 ch g Aragon 7.7f **(58)** - Gay Patricia (Gay Fandango (USA)) 8.5f **(59)**

Form - 000000

Record	**2000 -**	1st:0	2nd:0	3rd:0	Ran:5
	Pre2000 -	1st:0	2nd:0	3rd:0	Ran:1

2000 Turf 0-4: (6f, 7f, 8f, 10f) (g-s, gd, frm 2) 2000 AW 0-1: (10f) (Equi)

Little account gelding, has worn blinkers. Turf high 26.

**B R Johnson [0-5] Peter Crate (from T E Powell [0-1] Nov 1999).*

BETHANIA RR 55f 4935[24]

2 gr f Mark of Esteem (IRE) - Anneli Rose (Superlative) 7.2f **(56)**

Form - 0

Record **2000 -** 1st:0 2nd:0 3rd:0 Ran:1

2000 Turf 0-1: (6f) (gd)

Currently fair filly. **Mrs A J Perrett [0-1] Usk Valley Stud.*

BE THANKFULL (IRE) BHB 91f RR 98?f 5226[7]

4 gr f Linamix (FR) 8.2f **(64)** - Thank One's Stars (Alzao (USA)) 7.1f **(68)**

Form - 536037

Record	**2000 -**	1st:0	2nd:0	3rd:2	Ran:6
	Pre2000 -	1st:2	2nd:1	3rd:0	Ran:5

Win Prizemoney £13,354 *Total Prizemoney* £21,114

Wins	* 1999	Oct	Newmar	(G-S)	H	10f	81	85	<
	* 1999	Jly	Ascot	(G-F)		8f		76	

2000 Turf 0-6: (10f 2, 12f 3, 16f) (gd 3, g-f 2, frm)

Unfurnished, very useful filly, effective 12f, acts on g-f. Turf high 98 - 6th of 8 giving 11lb to Miss Lorilaw (6 Aug Newbury 12f g-f RF 3420). **Major D N Chappell [2-11] Mrs G C Maxwell.*

BE THE CHIEF BHB 50f RR 64f 4782[11]

4 ch c Be My Chief (USA) 10.2f **(62)** - Blink Naskra (USA) (Naskra (USA)) 8.8f **(69)**

Form - 00

Record	**2000 -**	1st:0	2nd:0	3rd:0	Ran:2
	Pre2000 -	1st:1	2nd:1	3rd:0	Ran:5

Win Prizemoney £3,494 *Total Prizemoney* £14,769

Wins 1998 May Doncas (GD) 6f 97+ <

2000 Turf 0-1: (8f) (gd) 2000 AW 0-1: (8f) (Fibr)

Workmanlike, average colt, has worn blinkers. He looked a colt of some potential when runner-up behind Red Sea in the 1998 Coventry Stakes, but missed the rest of the season after injuring a pastern, and showed very little on his return.

**W Clay [0-7] William Cooper (from T G Mills [1-5] Aug 1999).*

BETHESDA BHB 75f RR 63f 5198[5]

3 gr f Distant Relative 7f **(69)** - Anneli Rose (Superlative) 7.2f **(56)**

Form - 645

Record	**2000 -**	1st:0	2nd:0	3rd:0	Ran:3
	Pre2000 -	1st:0	2nd:1	3rd:0	Ran:3

Win Prizemoney £0 *Total Prizemoney* £2,149

2000 Turf 0-3: (6f 3) (g-s, gd 2)

Leggy, average filly. Turf high 63.

**Mrs A J Perrett [0-1] Usk Valley Stud (from J M P Eustace [0-5] Jun 2000).*

BET ME BEST (USA) RR 577a[3]

4 ch c Barberstown (USA) - Tough Wendy (USA) (Tough Assignment (USA))

Form - 3

2000 AW 0-1: (6f) (Dirt)

Currently Group-class colt, always wears blinkers.

**W E Walden in USA [0-1].*

BET ON SUNSHINE (USA) RR 5328a[3]
8 Bet Big (USA) - My Own Sunshine (USA) (In Reality) 7.4f **(74)**
Form - 3
2000 AW 0-1: (6f) (Dirt)
Currently very high-class. (1st run) - 3rd of 14 to Kona Gold (4 Nov Churchill Downs 6f Dirt RF 5328a). Ran a fine third in the Breeders' Cup Sprint. **P McGee in USA [0-2] David Holloway.*

BETTER MOMENT (IRE) BHB 61f **RR 47tf** 4009[4]
3 b g Turtle Island (IRE) - Snoozeandyoulose (IRE) **(65f)** (Scenic)
Form - 474
Record 2000 - 1st:0 2nd:0 3rd:0 Ran:3
Win Prizemoney £0 *Total Prizemoney* £585
2000 Turf 0-3: (10f, 12f 2) (gd, frm 2)
Currently moderate gelding. Turf high 47 (began Jly).
**J G FitzGerald [0-3] Marquesa de Moratalla.*

BETTER OFF BHB 66a **RR 66a** 5015[5]
2 ch g Bettergeton - Miami Pride (Miami Springs) 9.9f **(59)**
Form - 55
Record 2000 - 1st:0 2nd:0 3rd:0 Ran:2
2000 AW 0-2: (5f, 6f) (Fibr 2)
Currently average gelding. AW high 63 (began Oct).
**Mrs N Macauley [0-2] J Teasdale.*

BETTINA BLUE (IRE) BHB 47f60a **RR 54f 60a** 4825[19]
3 b f Paris House 5.9f **(64)** - Born to Fly (IRE) (Last Tycoon) 8.5f **(62)**
Form - 566000760
Record 2000 - 1st:0 2nd:0 3rd:0 Ran:8
Pre2000 - 1st:0 2nd:0 3rd:0 Ran:4
2000 Turf 0-8: (5f, 6f 4, 7f 2, 8f) (gd, g-f 3, frm 4)
Scopey, fair filly. Turf high 55.
**R Ingram [0-12] Epsom Sporting Proposals Ltd.*

BETTY BATHWICK (IRE) BHB 61f53a **RR 52f 53a** 5185[11]
3 b f Common Grounds 8.1f **(66)** - Tynaghmile (IRE) (Lyphard's Special (USA)) 10.3f **(72)**
Form - 00100
Record 2000 - 1st:1 2nd:0 3rd:0 Ran:5
Pre2000 - 1st:0 2nd:1 3rd:0 Ran:4
Win Prizemoney £2,310 *Total Prizemoney* £2,925
Wins * 2000 Oct Catter (SFT) 6f 50 <
2000 Turf 1-4: (6f 1-1, 7f 2, 8f) (g-s 1-2, g-f, hrd) 2000 AW 0-1: (7f) (Equi)
Unfurnished, fair filly, effective 6f, acts on g-s. Turf high 52 (began Aug) - also 1st of 11 getting 5lb from Champfis (3 Oct Catterick RF 4774). Inconsistent.
**E J O'Neill [1-5] The Parrot Club (from B Smart [0-4] Aug 1999).*

BETTYJOE BHB 45f **RR 36f** 1598[13]
3 ch f Inchinor 8.9f **(64)** - Jay Gee Ell (Vaigly Great) 7f **(58)**
Form - 800
Record 2000 - 1st:0 2nd:0 3rd:0 Ran:3
Pre2000 - 1st:0 2nd:1 3rd:2 Ran:8
Win Prizemoney £0 *Total Prizemoney* £1,868
2000 Turf 0-3: (6f 2, 7f) (gd, g-f, frm)
Scopey, very moderate filly, effective 6f, acts on gd. Turf high 35. Inconsistent. **J S Goldie [0-11] Martin Delaney.*

BE VALIANT BHB 26f28a **RR 16f 28a** 322[10]
6 gr g Petong 7.6f **(58)** - Fetlar (Pharly (FR)) 9.8f **(68)**
Form - 60
Record 2000 - 1st:0 2nd:0 3rd:0 Ran:2
Pre2000 - 1st:1 2nd:1 3rd:0 Ran:13
Win Prizemoney £2,295 *Total Prizemoney* £2,963
Wins 1998 Jly Ripon (GD) S 10f 50 <
2000 AW 0-2: (9f, 15f) (Fibr 2)
Poor gelding, has worn blinkers. AW high 8. Becoming disappointing.
**C L Popham [0-2] Mrs S Wiltshire (from Mrs N Macauley [0-7] May 1999).*

BEVEL BLUE BHB 55f **RR 56f** 4724[13]
2 b g Beveled (USA) 6.9f **(64)** - Blue Angel (Lord Gayle (USA)) 8.8f **(62)**
Form - 000
Record 2000 - 1st:0 2nd:0 3rd:0 Ran:3
2000 Turf 0-3: (5f 2, 6f) (gd 2, frm)
Currently fair gelding. Turf high 56 (began Jly).
**G B Balding [0-3] Rocaro Partnership.*

BEVELED HAWTHORN BHB 32f31a **RR 28f 31a** 443[12]
5 b m Beveled (USA) 6.9f **(64)** - Sideloader Special (Song) 7.2f **(61)**
Form - 40
Record 2000 - 1st:0 2nd:0 3rd:0 Ran:2
Pre2000 - 1st:1 2nd:0 3rd:0 Ran:4
Win Prizemoney £3,013 *Total Prizemoney* £3,013
Wins * 1999 Spt Thirsk (FRM) H 5f 25 28 <
2000 AW 0-2: (5f 2) (Fibr 2)
Little account filly. AW high 20.
**D Nicholls [1-4] Mrs Margaret Dunning (from M P Bielby [0-2] Jun 1998).*

BEVELENA BHB 64f **RR 56f** 1893[15]
4 ch f Beveled (USA) 6.9f **(64)** - Bella Helena (Balidar) 7.9f **(63)**
Form - 0000
Record 2000 - 1st:0 2nd:0 3rd:0 Ran:4
Pre2000 - 1st:2 2nd:3 3rd:1 Ran:10
Win Prizemoney £6,134 *Total Prizemoney* £9,809
Wins * 1999 Apr Catter (SFT) H 5f 74 79 <
* 1998 Aug Haydoc (G-S) H 5f 62 76
2000 Turf 0-4: (5f 3, 6f) (gd 4)
Unfurnished, average filly, effective 5 to 6f, acts on gd to frm, has worn blinkers. Turf high 56. **P D Evans [2-14] Mrs F A Veasey.*

BEVERLEY MACCA BHB 78f **RR 75f** 2487[7]
2 ch f Piccolo - Kangra Valley **(41f 54a)** (Indian Ridge)
Form - 221147
Record 2000 - 1st:2 2nd:2 3rd:0 Ran:6
Win Prizemoney £4,539 *Total Prizemoney* £6,249
Wins * 2000 May Redcar (G-F) 5f 75 <
*** 2000** *May Wolver (STD) 5f 65+*
2000 Turf 1-4: (5f 1-4) (hvy, gd, frm 1-2) 2000 AW 1-2: (5f 1-2)(Fibr 1-2)
Above-average filly, effective 5f, acts on frm - acts on Fibr. Turf high 75 - 1st of 10 getting 1lb from Fantasy Believer (15 May Redcar RF 1197). AW high 65. **A Berry [2-6] Mrs Margaret Forsyth.*

BEVERLEY MONKEY (IRE) BHB 29f30a **RR 40df 30a** 2392[6]
4 b f Fayruz 6.6f **(63)** - Godly Light (FR) (Vayrann) 9.7f **(74)**
Form - 00006
Record 2000 - 1st:0 2nd:0 3rd:0 Ran:5
Pre2000 - 1st:3 2nd:2 3rd:2 Ran:20
Win Prizemoney £6,898 *Total Prizemoney* £9,560
Wins 1998 Aug Lingfi (FRM) C 6f 66
1998 Jun Hamilt (GD) C 5f 47+
1998 May Newcas (G-F) C 6f 83+ <
2000 Turf 0-3: (6f 3) (gd, g-f, frm) 2000 AW 0-2: (6f, 7f) (Equi, Fibr)
Scopey, moderate filly, effective 6f, acts on g-f, has worn blinkers. Turf high 24. AW high 9. Inconsistent.
**J M Bradley [0-5] W E Jones (from J Berry [3-20] Spt 1999).*

BEWARE BHB 49a **RR 59f** 2044[11]
5 br g Warning 8.1f **(77)** - Dancing Spirit (IRE) (Ahonoora) 8.1f **(73)**
Form - 38366154560
Record 2000 - 1st:1 2nd:0 3rd:1 Ran:9
Pre2000 - 1st:1 2nd:3 3rd:5 Ran:23
Win Prizemoney £7,237 *Total Prizemoney* £15,064
Wins * 2000 *Feb Southw (STD) S 6f 50*
1997 Oct Newbur (G-S) H 6f 81 84 <
2000 Turf 0-4: (5f 2, 6f 2) (g-s, g-f 2, hrd) 2000 AW 1-5: (6f 1-3, 7f 2) (Fibr 1-5)
Fair gelding, effective 5 to 6f, acts on gd, has worn blinkers. Turf high 57. AW high 50.
**D Nicholls [1-20] A A Bloodstock Ltd (from R W Armstrong [1-12] Aug 1998).*

BE WARNED BHB 48f42a **RR 58f 42a** 5007[7]
9 b g Warning 8.1f **(77)** - Sagar (Habitat) 9.4f **(70)**
Form - 04750127017
Record 2000 - 1st:2 2nd:1 3rd:0 Ran:11
Pre2000 - 1st:11 2nd:13 3rd:11 Ran:93
Win Prizemoney £46,282 *Total Prizemoney* £76,293
Wins * 2000 *Spt Southw (STD) C 11f 47+*
*** 2000** *Mar Southw (STD) C 8f 60*
1999 *Oct Wolver (STD) C 12f 68+*

1998 Oct Newbur (HVY) H 7f 56 66
1998 Mar Southw (STD) H 8f 73 79 <
1998 Mar Wolver (STD) H 9.4f 69 73
1998 Feb Wolver (STD) H 9.4f 62 69
1998 Jan Southw (STD) H 7f 55 55+
1997 Spt Yarmou (FRM) H 6f 44 49
2000 AW 2-11: (8f 1-6, 11f 1-2, 12f 3) (Fibr 2-11)
Average gelding, has broken blood-vessels, effective 9 to 12f, best at 12f, - acts on AW, best on Fibr, mostly wears blinkers, prefers left handed tracks, prefers tight tracks, and likes Wolverhampton. AW high 61.
**R Brotherton [2-11] Paul Stringer (from J Pearce [7-42] Oct 1999).*

BEWILDERED (IRE) BHB 36a RR 35f 2777[1]

3 br f Prince Sabo 6.6f **(64)** - Collage (Ela-Mana-Mou) 10.1f **(70)**
Form - 007500067301
Record 2000 - 1st:1 2nd:0 3rd:1 Ran:12
Pre2000 - 1st:0 2nd:0 3rd:0 Ran:3
Win Prizemoney £2,275 *Total Prizemoney* £2,769
Wins * 2000 *Jly Wolver (STD) H 8.5f 36 37 <*
2000 Turf 0-7: (6f, 7f 2, 8f 3, 10f) (gd, g-f 2, frm 4) 2000 AW 1-5: (6f 2, 8f 1-2, 9f) (Fibr 1-5)
Scopey, very moderate filly, has broken blood-vessels, has worn blinkers (very effectively), likes left handed tracks, likes tight tracks. Turf high 35. AW high 37.
**D W Chapman [1-12] T S Redman (from G Lewis [0-3] Jun 1999).*

BEYOND CALCULATION (USA) BHB 67f61a RR 68f 61a 4027[10]

6 ch g Geiger Counter (USA) 7.8f **(85)** -Placer Queen (Habitat) 9.4f **(70)**
Form - 515016442000
Record 2000 - 1st:2 2nd:1 3rd:0 Ran:12
Pre2000 - 1st:5 2nd:3 3rd:3 Ran:36
Win Prizemoney £29,561 *Total Prizemoney* £38,718
Wins * 2000 Jun Windso (G-F) H 6f 64 68
*** 2000** May Nottin (G-S) 6.1f 66
* 1999 Aug Bright (FRM) H 6f 62 73
* 1999 Jly Thirsk (FRM) H 6f 57 64
* 1999 Jly Bath (FRM) H 5.7f 54 60
* 1999 Jun Windso (G-F) H 6f 47 52
1997 Oct Redcar (G-F) 6f 74 <
2000 Turf 2-12: (5f 4, 6f 2-8) (gd 1-2, g-f 1-5, frm 4, hrd)
Average gelding, effective 5 to 6f, best at 6f, acts on gd to frm, best on frm, likes left handed tracks, and likes Bath. Turf high 68 - 2nd of 18 giving 3lb to Beyond The Clouds (26 Aug Beverley 5f frm RF 3978) - also 1st of 16 giving 6lb to Thatcham (26 Jun Windsor RF 2283). Consistent. Six furlongs on fast ground are ideal, and he likes to go from the front.
**J M Bradley [6-40] E A Hayward (from P W Harris [1-8] Oct 1997).*

BEYOND THE CLOUDS (IRE) BHB 70f RR 67f 4332[9]

4 b g Midhish - Tongabezi (IRE) (Shernazar) 10.2f **(73)**
Form - 80261414210
Record 2000 - 1st:3 2nd:2 3rd:0 Ran:11
Pre2000 - 1st:0 2nd:0 3rd:1 Ran:8
Win Prizemoney £13,032 *Total Prizemoney* £16,065
Wins * 2000 Aug Beverl (FRM) H 5f 65 67 <
*** 2000** Jly Windso (GD) H 5f 55 60
*** 2000** Jun Hamilt (GD) H 5f 50 51
2000 Turf 3-11: (5f 3-9, 6f, 8f) (sft, g-s, gd 2, g-f 3, frm 3-4)
Average gelding, effective 5f, acts on g-f to frm, best on g-f, has worn blinkers. Turf high 67 - 1st of 18 getting 3lb from Beyond Calculation (26 Aug Beverley RF 3978) - also 1st of 13 getting 11lb from Mousehole (17 Jly Windsor RF 2880).
**J S Wainwright [3-19] P Charalambous.*

BEYOND THE WAVES (USA) RR 110f 5306a[2]

3 b f Ocean Crest (USA) - Excedent (FR) (Exceller (USA)) 12.5f **(74)**
Form - 3422
2000 Turf 0-4: (9f, 10f, 11f, 13f) (hvy, g-s, gd, g-f)
Group-class filly. Turf high 110 - 2nd of 11 to Mouramara (30 Spt Longchamp 13f gd RF 4837a).
**J E Pease in FR [0-4] George Strawbridge.*

BEZZA (IRE) RR 52f 5136[11]

2 ch f Bob Back (USA) 11.5f **(71)** - Lady Lord (IRE) (Coquelin (USA)) 8.4f **(58)**
Form - 00
Record 2000 - 1st:0 2nd:0 3rd:0 Ran:2
2000 Turf 0-2: (8f 2) (g-s, gd)
Currently fair filly. Turf high 52 (began Oct).
**M H Tompkins [0-2] Mrs Beryl Lockey.*

BEZZAAF BHB 86f RR 94f 4606[5]

3 b f Machiavellian (USA) 9.8f **(83)** - Maid of Kashmir (IRE) **(86f)** (Dancing Brave (USA)) 8.4f **(76)**
Form - 15P705
Record 2000 - 1st:1 2nd:0 3rd:0 Ran:6
Win Prizemoney £4,316 *Total Prizemoney* £4,316
Wins * 2000 May Windso (GD) 10f 80 <
2000 Turf 1-6: (10f 1-5, 11f) (gd 3, g-f 1-3)
Scopey, useful filly. Turf high 94. Unraced at two, she won a Windsor maiden in clear-cut fashion on her debut, but has been comfortably held in Listed company since then, though she was pulled up after the rider lost his irons on her third run.
**M A Jarvis [1-6] Sheikh Ahmed Al Maktoum.*

BHUTAN (IRE) RR 72f 5297[3]

5 b g Polish Patriot (USA) 7.8f **(70)** - Bustinetta (Bustino) 10.4f **(64)**
Form - 160712423
Record 2000 - 1st:2 2nd:2 3rd:1 Ran:9
Pre2000 - 1st:5 2nd:0 3rd:6 Ran:24
Win Prizemoney £28,715 *Total Prizemoney* £38,762
Wins * 2000 Aug Catter (G-F) H 13.8f 66 68
*** 2000** May Hamilt (G-F) H 13f 65 68
* 1999 Oct Catter (GD) 13.8f 50
* 1999 Jly Newcas (FRM) H 12.4f 64 67
1998 Oct Currag (SFT) H 8f 66 71 <
1998 Jly Killar (GD) H 11f 56 71+
1998 Jun Cork (G-S) H 9f 53 71 <
2000 Turf 2-9: (9f, 12f 2, 13f 1-1, 14f 1-3, 16f, 17f) (sft, g-s, gd, g-f 1-3, frm 1-3)
Above-average gelding, effective 10 to 16f, best at 14f, acts on sft to frm, best on frm, likes right handed tracks, prefers tight tracks, and excels at Beverley and Catterick. Turf high 72 - 2nd of 6 giving 27lb to Manzoni (24 Aug Musselburgh 14f frm RF 3927) - also 1st of 12 giving 15lb to Sing And Dance (8 Aug Catterick RF 3450). Consistent. He is an effective sort in modest middle-distance handicaps, winning two in 1999 and scoring at Hamilton and Catterick last year. Appreciates fast ground and a decent pace.
**Mrs M Reveley [8-31] P D Savill (from C Collins in IRE [3-13] Oct 1998).*

BIANCHI (USA) RR 67f 3162[4]

2 b f Gulch (USA) 9.6f **(79)** - Northern Trick (USA) (Northern Dancer) 9.6f **(80)**
Form - 4
Record 2000 - 1st:0 2nd:0 3rd:0 Ran:1
Win Prizemoney £0 *Total Prizemoney* £624
2000 Turf 0-1: (6f) (g-f)
Currently average filly. **P F I Cole [0-1] Mrs Belinda Strudwick.*

BIBI KARAM (IRE) RR 96f 5043a[2]

3 b f Persian Bold 10f **(69)** - Lady Pavlova (Ballymore) 7.3f **(64)**
Form - 881262
2000 Turf 1-6: (8f 1-5, 9f) (sft, g-s, gd 3, g-f 1-1)
Very useful filly, effective 8 to 9f, acts on sft to g-s. Turf high 96 - 2nd of 10 to Abikan (14 Oct Gowran Park 9f sft RF 5043a).
**J G Burns in IRE [1-6] Cordell Family Syndicate.*

BIBLE BOX (IRE) RR 48f 2075[7]

2 b f Bin Ajwaad (IRE) - Addie Pray (IRE) **(63f 60a)** (Great Commotion (USA))
Form - 7
Record 2000 - 1st:0 2nd:0 3rd:0 Ran:1
2000 Turf 0-1: (6f) (hrd)
Currently moderate filly. **J Pearce [0-1] M Sinclair.*

BICTON PARK BHB 24f25a RR ?f 25a 2880[12]

6 b g Distant Relative 7f **(69)** - Merton Mill (Dominion) 8.5f **(63)**
Form - 00000
Record 2000 - 1st:0 2nd:0 3rd:0 Ran:2
Pre2000 - 1st:0 2nd:1 3rd:0 Ran:27
Win Prizemoney £0 *Total Prizemoney* £858
2000 Turf 0-1: (5f) (frm) 2000 AW 0-1: (8f) (Fibr)

Little account gelding, effective 7f, - acts on Fibr, has worn blinkers, likes left handed tracks.
**K C Comerford [0-25] The Old Style Partnership (from D Morley [0-4] Nov 1996).*

BID FOR FAME (USA) BHB 85f **RR 88f** 3396[7]
3 b br c Quest for Fame 12.8f **(75)** - Shroud (USA) (Vaguely Noble) 10.1f **(72)**
Form - 538137
Record 2000 - 1st:1 2nd:0 3rd:2 Ran:6
Win Prizemoney £2,860 *Total Prizemoney* £4,689
Wins * 2000 Jun Pontef (G-F) 12f 82 <
2000 Turf 1-6: (10f, 11f, 12f 1-2, 13f, 14f) (g-s, gd 2, g-f 2, frm 1-1)
Scopey, useful colt, effective 12 to 14f, acts on g-f to frm, best on g-f. Turf high 88 - 3rd of 10 giving 2lb to Duchamp (22 Jly Newbury 13f g-f RF 3026) - also 1st of 9 giving 5lb to Sense of Freedom (25 Jun Pontefract RF 2267). **T G Mills [1-6] T G Mills.*

BID ME WELCOME BHB 79f **RR 82f** 4987[20]
4 b g Alzao (USA) 9.8f **(73)** - Blushing Barada (USA) (Blushing Groom (FR)) 10.3f **(76)**
Form - 005231520630
Record 2000 - 1st:1 2nd:2 3rd:2 Ran:12
Pre2000 - 1st:3 2nd:1 3rd:2 Ran:14
Win Prizemoney £23,902 *Total Prizemoney* £32,411
Wins * 2000 Jly Newbur (G-F) H 16f 75 82 <
1999 Oct Newmar (GD) H 14.8f 77 81
1999 Aug Nottin (G-F) H 14.1f 69 75
1999 May Warwic (GD) H 12.5f 67 73
2000 Turf 1-12: (12f, 13f, 14f 2, 15f 2, 16f 1-5, 18f) (gd 3, g-f 5, frm 1-4)
Workmanlike, decent gelding, effective 13 to 16f, best at 16f, acts on gd to frm, best on frm, likes left handed tracks, and excels at Newbury and Warwick. Turf high 83 - 2nd of 5 giving 10lb to Fait Le Jojo (25 Aug Newmarket 15f g-f RF 3967) - also 1st of 8 giving 19lb to Renaissance Lady (21 Jly Newbury RF 3000). Consistent. Suited by front-running tactics, he scored at Newbury in July and ran a couple of good races in September. Sometimes gets worked up in the preliminaries.
**Miss D A McHale [1-12] P Burban (from H J Collingridge [3-13] Oct 1999).*

BIEN ENTENDU RR 101f 2867[3]
3 b c Hernando (FR) - Entente Cordiale (USA) (Affirmed (USA)) 9.3f **(79)**
Form - 13
Record 2000 - 1st:1 2nd:0 3rd:1 Ran:2
Win Prizemoney £5,252 *Total Prizemoney* £6,434
Wins * 2000 Apr Newmar (G-S) 10f 100+ <
2000 Turf 1-2: (10f 1-2) (gd 1-1, g-f)
Well made, currently very useful colt. Turf high 101 - also 1st of 16 from Air Defence (18 Apr Newmarket RF 0773). Unraced at two, he made a very impressive start to his career when winning a ten-furlong Newmarket maiden in April, but was a big disappointment in a Newbury conditions event next time after a three-month break. He will probably be out of action in 2001 after undergoing an operation. **H R A Cecil [1-2] Niarchos Family.*

BIENNALE (IRE) BHB 105f **RR 109f** 4575[2]
4 b c Caerleon (USA) 10.9f **(79)** - Malvern Beauty (Shirley Heights) 10.3f **(74)**
Form - 445352
Record 2000 - 1st:0 2nd:1 3rd:1 Ran:6
Pre2000 - 1st:1 2nd:3 3rd:1 Ran:5
Win Prizemoney £3,566 *Total Prizemoney* £29,315
Wins * 1999 May Hamilt (GD) 11.1f 73 <
2000 Turf 0-6: (12f, 14f 2, 16f 3) (hvy, sft, g-s, gd, frm 2)
Scopey, Pattern-class colt, effective 14 to 16f, best at 16f, acts on g-s to frm. Turf high 109 - 3rd of 9 giving 12lb to Dominant Duchess (12 Aug Ascot 16f gd RF 3577). Consistent. He ran some fine races without winning, but is basically too high in the handicap and not good enough for Pattern races.
**Sir Michael Stoute [1-11] M Tabor & Mrs John Magnier.*

BIFF-EM (IRE) BHB 34f **RR 40f** 5194[6]
6 ch g Durgam (USA) 12.3f **(53)** - Flash The Gold (Ahonoora) 8.1f **(73)**
Form - 50304260000506
Record 2000 - 1st:0 2nd:1 3rd:1 Ran:14
Pre2000 - 1st:2 2nd:2 3rd:7 Ran:37
Win Prizemoney £6,707 *Total Prizemoney* £14,193
Wins * 1998 Jly Hamilt (FRM) H 6f 37 45
* 1996 Jun Hamilt (GD) 5f 61 <
2000 Turf 0-14: (5f 8, 6f 4, 7f 2) (hvy, sft, gd 3, g-f 4, frm 4, hrd)
Moderate gelding, effective 5 to 6f, best at 6f, acts on gd to frm, best on g-f, excels at Hamilton. Turf high 40 - 3rd of 13 getting 5lb from Jacmar (19 May Hamilton 5f g-f RF 1296).
**Miss L A Perratt [2-51] Cree Lodge Racing Club.*

BIG AL (IRE) BHB 50f **RR 47f** 1848[2]
4 b g Shalford (IRE) 7.8f **(63)** - Our Pet (Mummy's Pet) 7.7f **(60)**
Form - 2
Record 2000 - 1st:0 2nd:1 3rd:0 Ran:1
Pre2000 - 1st:1 2nd:0 3rd:0 Ran:10
Win Prizemoney £2,304 *Total Prizemoney* £2,882
Wins 1998 Jly Haydoc (G-S) S 6f 72 <
2000 Turf 0-1: (11f) (g-s)
Moderate gelding. (DEAD)
**M D Hammond [0-5] Stef Stefanou (from R A Fahey [0-8] Nov 1999).*

BIG CHIEF RR 33f 658[18]
4 ch g Be My Chief (USA) 10.2f **(62)** - Grove Daffodil (IRE) (Salt Dome (USA))
Form - 0
Record 2000 - 1st:0 2nd:0 3rd:0 Ran:1
Pre2000 - 1st:0 2nd:0 3rd:0 Ran:12
2000 Turf 0-1: (10f) (g-s)
Workmanlike, very moderate gelding, has worn blinkers.
**M E Sowersby [0-7] M E Sowersby (from M H Tompkins [0-11] Aug 1999).*

BIG E (IRE) RR 2030[5]
3 ch g Port Lucaya - Lucayan Sunshine (USA) **(81f)** (Sunshine Forever (USA))
Form - 45
Record 2000 - 1st:0 2nd:0 3rd:0 Ran:2
2000 AW 0-2: (11f, 12f) (Equi, Fibr)
Leggy, currently very moderate gelding, always wears blinkers. AW high 36. **S P C Woods [0-2] Lucayan Stud.*

BIG FUTURE BHB 94f **RR 95f** 5240[24]
3 b c Bigstone (IRE) - Star of the Future (USA) (El Gran Senor (USA)) 9.6f **(76)**
Form - 141533010
Record 2000 - 1st:3 2nd:0 3rd:2 Ran:9
Win Prizemoney £18,541 *Total Prizemoney* £22,939
Wins * 2000 Oct York (SFT) H 7f 90 95 <
*** 2000** Jly Lingfi (G-F) H 7f 79 88+
*** 2000** Apr Kempto (SFT) 7f 80
2000 Turf 3-9: (7f 3-7, 8f 2) (sft 1-1, g-s 1-2, gd 2, g-f, frm 1-3)
Scopey, very useful colt, effective 7f, acts on g-s to frm. Turf high 95 - 1st of 9 getting 12lb from Granny's Pet (5 Oct York RF 4817) - also 1st of 11 giving 13lb to Royal Ivy (1 Jly Lingfield RF 2437). Unraced at two, he made a winning debut on soft ground at Kempton and bolted up on his handicap debut at Lingfield. Continued to run well in warm company and scored in soft ground on his penultimate run. **Mrs A J Perrett [3-9] K Abdulla.*

BIGGLES (IRE) RR 64f 2775[9]
3 b g Desert Style (IRE) - Excruciating (CAN) (Bold Forbes (USA)) 8.9f **(59)**
Form - 40
Record 2000 - 1st:0 2nd:0 3rd:0 Ran:2
Win Prizemoney £0 *Total Prizemoney* £266
2000 Turf 0-2: (8f, 10f) (gd, g-f)
Workmanlike, currently average gelding. Turf high 64.
**Andrew Turnell [0-2] Mrs Claire Hollowood.*

BIG ISSUE BHB 60f55a **RR 50f 55a** 425[9]
3 b c First Trump - Hollow Heart (Wolver Hollow) 8f **(56)**
Form - 0
Record 2000 - 1st:0 2nd:0 3rd:0 Ran:1
Pre2000 - 1st:1 2nd:0 3rd:0 Ran:4
Win Prizemoney £2,164 *Total Prizemoney* £2,164
Wins * 1999 Oct Bath (SFT) S 5.7f
2000 AW 0-1: (7f) (Equi)

Fair colt. **B Smart [1-4] Willie McKay (from K McAuliffe [0-1] Jly 1999).*

BIG JAG (USA) RR 108f 577a[1]

7 m Kleven (USA) - In Hopes (USA) (Affirmed (USA)) 9.3f **(79)**
Form - 31
2000 AW 1-1: (6f 1-1) (Dirt 1-1)
Currently very high-class. (1st run) - 1st of 14 from Bertolini (25 Mar Nad Al Sheba RF 0577a). A high-class American sprinter, she was a decisive winner of the big sprint at Nad Al Sheba on Dubai World Cup day from Bertolini. **T Pinfield in USA [1-3] J H Zolezzi.*

BIG JOHN (IRE) RR 71f 2064[7]

2 ch c Cadeaux Genereux 7.9f **(76)** - India Atlanta (Ahonoora) 8.1f **(73)**
Form - 47
Record 2000 - 1st:0 2nd:0 3rd:0 Ran:2
Win Prizemoney £0 *Total Prizemoney* £267
2000 Turf 0-2: (6f 2) (g-f, frm)
Currently above-average colt. Turf high 71.
**J S Goldie [0-2] John Pitt.*

BIG MOMENT RR 89+f 4701[2]

2 ch c Be My Guest (USA) 10.2f **(66)** - Petralona (USA) **(96f)** (Alleged (USA)) 10f **(76)**
Form - 2
Record 2000 - 1st:0 2nd:1 3rd:0 Ran:1
Win Prizemoney £0 *Total Prizemoney* £1,570
2000 Turf 0-1: (7f) (g-f)
Currently useful colt. (1st run) - 2nd of 17 to Demophilos (28 Spt Newmarket 7f g-f RF 4701). **B W Hills [0-1] K Abdulla.*

BIGWIG (IRE) BHB 37f40a RR 22f 40a 420[5]

7 ch g Thatching 7.8f **(69)** - Sabaah (USA) (Nureyev (USA)) 8.7f **(78)**
Form - 55
Record 2000 - 1st:0 2nd:0 3rd:0 Ran:1
Pre2000 - 1st:2 2nd:0 3rd:0 Ran:10
Win Prizemoney £5,418 *Total Prizemoney* £5,418
Wins * 1999 *Mar Lingfi (STD) H 13f 40 45* <
* 1999 *Feb Lingfi (STD) H 13f 25 43*
2000 AW 0-1: (16f) (Equi)
Moderate gelding, has broken blood-vessels, effective 13 to 14f, best at 13f, - acts on AW, best on Equi, often wears blinkers.
**G L Moore [4-32] Mrs Elizabeth Kiernan (from A Moore [0-4] Dec 1996).*

BIJA BHB 16f RR 8f 222[10]

5 b g Librate 10.4f **(37)** - Guilty Sparkle (Roc Imp)
Form - 0800
Record 2000 - 1st:0 2nd:0 3rd:0 Ran:4
Pre2000 - 1st:0 2nd:0 3rd:0 Ran:8
2000 AW 0-4: (8f, 9f, 12f, 13f) (Equi, Fibr 3)
Very poor gelding, effective 9f, acts on g-f.
**J M Bradley [0-13] Martyn James.*

BIJAN (IRE) BHB 75f72a RR 71f 72a 4307[4]

2 b f Mukaddamah (USA) 7.6f **(74)** - Alkariyh (USA) (Alydar (USA)) 9.1f **(76)**
Form - 53104
Record 2000 - 1st:1 2nd:0 3rd:1 Ran:5
Win Prizemoney £2,977 *Total Prizemoney* £4,014
Wins * 2000 Jun Carlis (G-F) 5f 70 <
2000 Turf 1-5: (5f 1-2, 6f 3) (g-s, gd, g-f 1-1, frm 2)
Above-average filly. Turf high 71 - also 1st of 15 from Extra Guest (29 Jun Carlisle RF 2361). **R Hollinshead [1-5] Geoff Lloyd.*

BILLADDIE BHB 65f58a RR 66f 58a 4810[10]

7 b g Touch of Grey 8.1f **(47)** - Young Lady (Young Generation) 7.7f **(63)**
Form - 0
Record 2000 - 1st:0 2nd:0 3rd:0 Ran:1
Pre2000 - 1st:5 2nd:4 3rd:8 Ran:33
Win Prizemoney £20,975 *Total Prizemoney* £31,978
Wins * 1998 Oct Newbur (HVY) H 10f 66 70 <
* 1998 Spt Kempto (G-S) H 12f 58 61
* 1998 Jun Newmar (GD) H 12f 52 58
* 1998 *Jan Lingfi (STD) H 10f 51 61*
1996 *Jan Lingfi (STD) 8f 53*
2000 AW 0-1: (12f) (Equi)
Average gelding.
**R M Flower [4-26] Richard Gurr (from R Boss [1-8] Mar 1997).*

BILLICHANG BHB 28f38a RR 51f 38a 4928[15]

4 b c Chilibang 7f **(55)** - Swing O'The Kilt (Hotfoot) 10.5f **(59)**
Form - 01233334426180445420
Record 2000 - 1st:1 2nd:3 3rd:4 Ran:18
Pre2000 - 1st:1 2nd:2 3rd:2 Ran:18
Win Prizemoney £4,627 *Total Prizemoney* £10,102
Wins * 2000 *Mar Lingfi (STD) S 10f 55* <
* 1999 *Dec Lingfi (STD) 10f 44*
2000 Turf 0-1: (12f) (frm) 2000 AW 1-17: (8f 3, 9f 3, 10f 1-5, 12f 6) (Equi 1-8, Fibr 9)
Workmanlike, fair colt, effective 8 to 10f, - acts on AW, best on Fibr, has worn blinkers, favours left handed tracks, favours tight tracks. AW high 59 - also 1st of 10 giving 4lb to Badrinath (29 Mar Lingfield RF 0554).
**P Howling [2-36] Paul Howling Racing Syndicate.*

BILLIE H BHB 61f RR 64f 1223[10]

2 ch f Cool Jazz - Rachels Eden (Ring Bidder)
Form - 707610
Record 2000 - 1st:1 2nd:0 3rd:0 Ran:6
Win Prizemoney £2,775 *Total Prizemoney* £2,775
Wins * 2000 Aug Bright (FRM) 7f 64 <
2000 Turf 1-5: (5f, 7f 1-4) (gd, g-f 2, frm, hrd 1-1) 2000 AW 0-1: (5f) (Fibr)
Average filly, effective 7f, acts on g-f to hrd. Turf high 61 - 1st of 6 getting 6lb from Nun Left (23 Aug Brighton RF 3895).
**C E Brittain [1-6] C E Brittain.*

BILLY BATHWICK (IRE) BHB 60f58a RR 66f 58a 5125[15]

3 ch c Fayruz 6.6f **(63)** - Cut it Fine (USA) (Big Spruce (USA)) 11f **(71)**
Form - 555281700324450
Record 2000 - 1st:1 2nd:2 3rd:1 Ran:15
Pre2000 - 1st:0 2nd:0 3rd:0 Ran:6
Win Prizemoney £2,743 *Total Prizemoney* £6,465
Wins * 2000 Jun Carlis (G-F) 5.9f 66 <
2000 Turf 1-14: (6f 1-5, 7f 3, 8f, 9f, 10f 2, 12f 2) (hvy, g-s 3, gd 2, g-f 1-3, frm 5) 2000 AW 0-1: (9f) (Fibr)
Neat, average colt, effective 6 to 10f, best at 6f, acts on gd to frm, best on g-f, has worn blinkers, likes tight tracks. Turf high 66 - 2nd of 15 giving 6lb to Flyover (1 Spt Epsom 10f g-f RF 4144) - also 1st of 8 giving 5lb to Davey's Panacea (29 Jun Carlisle RF 2362). Effective between six and ten furlongs, he made a winning debut for his current yard at Carlisle in June and has run some fair races since stepping up in trip.
**E J O'Neill [1-10] W Clifford (from B Smart [0-11] May 2000).*

BILLYJO (IRE) BHB 50f48a RR 55f 48a 4478[5]

2 b g Idris (IRE) - Village Countess (IRE) (Reasonable (FR))
Form - 66445
Record 2000 - 1st:0 2nd:0 3rd:0 Ran:5
2000 Turf 0-3: (5f, 6f, 7f) (gd, frm 2) 2000 AW 0-2: (5f, 7f) (Equi, Fibr)
Fair gelding, has worn blinkers. Turf high 55. AW high 52.
**B J Meehan [0-5] Bill Bigmore.*

BILLY'S BLUNDER (IRE) BHB 38f39a RR 6f 39a 1857[13]

3 b f Hamas (IRE) 8f **(72)** - Open Date (IRE) (Thatching) 8f **(66)**
Form - 07327445400
Record 2000 - 1st:0 2nd:1 3rd:1 Ran:9
Pre2000 - 1st:0 2nd:0 3rd:0 Ran:2
Win Prizemoney £0 *Total Prizemoney* £1,347
2000 Turf 0-1: (6f) (g-f) 2000 AW 0-8: (5f 2, 6f 2, 7f 3, 8f) (Fibr 8)
Moderate filly, has worn blinkers. AW high 48.
**P D Evans [0-11] Colin Booth.*

BIN ALMOOJID BHB 14f RR 232[9]

4 b g Almoojid 7f **(36)** - Stella Royale (Astronef)
Form - 0
Record 2000 - 1st:0 2nd:0 3rd:0 Ran:1
Pre2000 - 1st:0 2nd:0 3rd:0 Ran:2
2000 AW 0-1: (15f) (Fibr)
Scopey, formerly very poor gelding, has worn blinkers.
**A D Smith [0-3] Duckhaven Stud (from Miss Kate Whitehouse [0-1] Apr 1998).*

BINA RIDGE RR 99+f 1870^{5}
3 b f Indian Ridge 7.6f **(74)** - Balabina (USA) (Nijinsky (CAN)) 10.3f **(77)**
Form - 15
Record 2000 - 1st:1 2nd:0 3rd:0 Ran:2
Win Prizemoney £5,330 *Total Prizemoney* £5,330
Wins * 2000 May Goodwo (SFT) 9f 99+ <
2000 Turf 1-2: (9f 1-1, 10f) (g-s 1-1, gd)
Scopey, currently very useful filly. Turf high 99 (1st run) - 1st of 8 from May Ball (25 May Goodwood RF 1432).
**H R A Cecil [1-2] K Abdulla.*

BINT ALJOOD BHB 56f46a **RR 62f 46a** 1481^{11}
3 b f Bin Ajwaad (IRE) - Shareehan (Dancing Brave (USA)) 8.4f **(76)**
Form - 0
Record 2000 - 1st:0 2nd:0 3rd:0 Ran:1
Pre2000 - 1st:0 2nd:0 3rd:0 Ran:6
Win Prizemoney £0 *Total Prizemoney* £276
2000 AW 0-1: (7f) (Fibr)
Light-framed, average filly, effective 6f, acts on gd to frm.
**B A McMahon [0-7] Khalifa Dasmal.*

BINTALREEF (USA) RR 88++f 1080^{18}
3 ch f Diesis 9f **(80)** - Solar Star (USA) (Lear Fan (USA)) 8.5f **(73)**
Form - 0
Record 2000 - 1st:0 2nd:0 3rd:0 Ran:1
Pre2000 - 1st:1 2nd:0 3rd:0 Ran:1
Wins 1999 Oct Deauvi (GD) 7f 88++ <
2000 Turf 0-1: (8f) (frm)
Currently useful filly. A winner of her only juvenile run in France, she burst into the Classic picture when running away with one of the Godolphin private trials, but finished last in the 1000 Guineas when she reportedly pulled a muscle leaving the stalls. She could still be anything.
**S bin Suroor [0-1] Godolphin (from D R Loder in FR [1-1] Oct 1999).*

BINTANG TIMOR (USA) BHB 69f68a **RR 72f 68a** 5242^{2}
6 ch g Mt Livermore (USA) 7.7f **(90)** - Frisky Kitten (USA) (Isopach (USA)) 6f **(84)**
Form - 7346250000012
Record 2000 - 1st:1 2nd:2 3rd:1 Ran:13
Pre2000 - 1st:3 2nd:6 3rd:4 Ran:35
Win Prizemoney £18,127 *Total Prizemoney* £37,405
Wins * 2000 Oct Yarmou (HVY) H 6f 62 66
* 1999 Oct Yarmou (G-S) H 7f 62 65
* 1999 May Newmar (G-F) H 7f 64 68
* 1998 Jly Leices (GD) H 6f 67 70 <
2000 Turf 1-13: (6f 1-6, 7f 7) (g-s 1-4, gd 3, g-f 3, frm 3)
Above-average gelding, effective 6 to 7f, best at 7f, acts on g-s to frm, best on frm, excels at Yarmouth, likes Newmarket. Turf high 72 - 2nd of 15 getting 2lb from Celtic Exit (9 Jun Goodwood 7f gd RF 1845) - also 1st of 13 giving 10lb to Brevity (22 Oct Yarmouth RF 5141). Inconsistent.
**W J Musson [4-43] Goodey & Broughton (from P F I Cole [0-5] May 1997).*

BINT HABIBI BHB 51f56a **RR 54f 56a** 5071^{12}
3 b f Bin Ajwaad (IRE) - High Stepping (IRE) (Taufan (USA)) 7f **(57)**
Form - 816631530300
Record 2000 - 1st:2 2nd:0 3rd:3 Ran:12
Pre2000 - 1st:0 2nd:1 3rd:0 Ran:4
Win Prizemoney £4,469 *Total Prizemoney* £6,953
Wins 2000 Jly Leices (G-F) S 8f 50
2000 Jun Chepst (FRM) C 7.1f 54 <
2000 Turf 2-12: (7f 1-4, 8f 1-8) (g-s 4, g-f 1-5, frm 1-2, hrd)
Workmanlike, average filly, effective 7f, acts on frm. Turf high 54. Inconsistent. Successful in a claimer and a seller so far this season, she proved she stays a mile on the second occasion. Suited by fast ground.
**J Pearce [0-6] Mrs Linda Leech (from M R Channon [2-10] Jly 2000).*

BINT ROYAL (IRE) BHB 62f **RR 68f** 5060^{11}
2 ch f Royal Abjar (USA) - Living Legend (USA) (Septieme Ciel (USA))
Form - 810
Record 2000 - 1st:1 2nd:0 3rd:0 Ran:3
Win Prizemoney £2,730 *Total Prizemoney* £2,730
Wins * 2000 Oct Catter (SFT) 5f 68 <
2000 Turf 1-3: (5f 1-2, 6f) (sft, gd 1-1, g-f)
Currently average filly. Turf high 68 (began Spt) - 1st of 12 getting 5lb from Siamo Disperati (3 Oct Catterick RF 4771).
**J A Glover [1-3] Miss V Haigh.*

BIRCHWOOD SUN BHB 45f54a **RR 52f 54a** 3406^{13}
10 b g Bluebird (USA) 7.9f **(71)** - Shapely Test (USA) (Elocutionist (USA)) 8f **(77)**
Form - 334030
Record 2000 - 1st:0 2nd:0 3rd:3 Ran:6
Pre2000 - 1st:13 2nd:11 3rd:10 Ran:102
Win Prizemoney £38,888 *Total Prizemoney* £54,353
Wins * 1999 Apr Pontef (SFT) S 6f 61
* 1998 Jun Carlis (G-S) S 5.9f 58
* 1998 May Newcas (G-S) C 7f 61
* 1998 Apr Redcar (SFT) S 7f 62
* 1998 Apr Carlis (G-S) H 5.9f 48 52
* 1997 May Carlis (G-S) H 5.9f 49 59
2000 Turf 0-6: (6f 4, 7f 2) (g-s, gd 3, g-f, hrd)
Fair gelding, effective 6 to 7f, best at 6f, acts on sft to frm, mostly wears blinkers. Turf high 56 (1st run) - 3rd of 12 giving 9lb to Patsy Culsyth (28 Mar Newcastle 6f gd RF 0523). A stiff six furlongs suits him best, though he has won over seven. He needs holding up until the last possible moment, and is not an ideal investment for anyone with a weak heart.
**M Dods [10-92] Mrs C E Dods (from R Hollinshead [3-16] May 1993).*

BIRDSAND BHB 54f **RR 62f** 2367^{6}
3 ch f Bluebird (USA) 7.9f **(71)** - Nottash (IRE) **(72f)** (Royal Academy (USA))
Form - 6766
Record 2000 - 1st:0 2nd:0 3rd:0 Ran:4
Pre2000 - 1st:0 2nd:0 3rd:0 Ran:1
2000 Turf 0-4: (7f 2, 8f 2) (g-s, gd, g-f 2)
Lengthy, average filly. Turf high 62.
**J R Fanshawe [0-5] Lord Vestey.*

BIRDSONG (IRE) BHB 68f **RR 66f** 4442^{7}
3 b f Dolphin Street (FR) - Gay France (FR) (Sir Gaylord) 10.6f **(64)**
Form - 001317
Record 2000 - 1st:2 2nd:0 3rd:1 Ran:6
Win Prizemoney £8,378 *Total Prizemoney* £8,933
Wins * 2000 Aug Lingfi (G-F) H 6f 65 66 <
2000 Jun Newcas (FRM) 6f 60
2000 Turf 2-6: (6f 2-4, 7f, 10f) (gd, g-f 1-3, frm 1-2)
Scopey, average filly, effective 6f, acts on g-f to frm, best on g-f. Turf high 66 - 1st of 20 giving 5lb to Toldya (31 Aug Lingfield RF 4116) - also 1st of 6 from Daylily (30 Jun Newcastle RF 2407).
**C F Wall [1-3] Mrs A G Kavanagh (from R Guest [1-3] Jun 2000).*

BIRTH OF THE BLUES BHB 44f **RR 61f** 5054^{18}
4 ch c Efisio 7.7f **(69)** - Great Steps **(70f)** (Vaigly Great) 7f **(58)**
Form - 80075070
Record 2000 - 1st:0 2nd:0 3rd:0 Ran:8
Pre2000 - 1st:1 2nd:0 3rd:0 Ran:8
Win Prizemoney £3,574 *Total Prizemoney* £3,574
Wins 1999 Apr Leices (HVY) H 8f 65 73 <
2000 Turf 0-8: (8f 4, 10f 3, 12f) (sft 2, gd 2, g-f, frm 2, hrd)
Average colt, effective 8f, acts on sft, has worn blinkers. Turf high 61. Becoming disappointing.
**Mark Campion [0-1] Supreme Racing Ltd (from D R C Elsworth [0-7] Jly 2000).*

BISHOP'S BLADE BHB 43f **RR 51f** 5070^{17}
3 b g Sure Blade (USA) 10.6f **(66)** - Myrtilla (Beldale Flutter (USA)) 9.7f **(71)**
Form - 800
Record 2000 - 1st:0 2nd:0 3rd:0 Ran:3
2000 Turf 0-3: (9f, 12f 2) (g-s, g-f 2)
Scopey, currently fair gelding. Turf high 51 (began Aug).
**J S King [0-3] Robert Long.*

BISHOPS COURT BHB 109f **RR 107f** 2053^{1}
6 ch g Clantime 6.6f **(57)** - Indigo (Primo Dominie) 6.2f **(80)**
Form - 051
Record 2000 - 1st:1 2nd:0 3rd:0 Ran:3
Pre2000 - 1st:5 2nd:6 3rd:7 Ran:25
Win Prizemoney £81,672 *Total Prizemoney* £138,193

Wins * 2000 Jun Sandow (G-F) 5f 106
1998 Oct Longch (HVY) G3 5f 115
1998 Oct Newmar () L 5f 116 <
1998 Jun Epsom (GD) LH 5f 102 103
1997 May Cheste (SFT) H 6.1f 83 88++
1996 Spt Hamilt (GD) 5f 78+
2000 Turf 1-3: (5f 1-3) (gd 2, g-f 1-1)
Pattern-class gelding. Turf high 106. Consistent. A very useful sprinter in '98 when trained by Lynda Ramsden, he missed all the following season. Landed a conditions race at Sandown in June, but was not seen again. Retains plenty of ability but clearly has his problems.
**I A Balding [1-3] D R Brotherton (from Mrs J R Ramsden [5-25] Oct 1998).*

BISHOP'S SECRET BHB 52f **RR 56f** 4930[5]
2 b c Bishop of Cashel - Secret Rapture (USA) (Woodman (USA)) 9f **(74)**
Form - 0005
Record 2000 - 1st:0 2nd:0 3rd:0 Ran:4
2000 Turf 0-4: (6f, 7f 2, 8f) (gd 3, hrd)
Fair colt, has worn blinkers. Turf high 56.
**M H Tompkins [0-4] John Bull.*

BISHOPSTONE MAN BHB 66f **RR 69f** 5105[14]
3 b g Piccolo - Auntie Gladys (Great Nephew) 9.9f **(64)**
Form - 470351028035760
Record 2000 - 1st:1 2nd:1 3rd:2 Ran:15
Pre2000 - 1st:0 2nd:0 3rd:1 Ran:5
Win Prizemoney £3,168 *Total Prizemoney* £5,973
Wins * 2000 Jly Leices (G-F) H 8f 64 67 <
2000 Turf 1-15: (6f, 7f 7, 8f 1-7) (sft, gd 4, g-f 4, frm 1-6)
Neat, average gelding, effective 6 to 8f, acts on g-f to frm, best on g-f. Turf high 69 - 3rd of 19 giving 5lb to Mister Clinton (13 Jun Salisbury 7f g-f RF 1923) - also 1st of 14 giving 15lb to Bajan Sunset (8 Jly Leicester RF 2643). Won at Leicester in July, and ran well on the same track the following month. Acts well on a fast surface. **S Mellor [1-20] The Bishopstone Ducks.*

BISHOPSTONE POND (IRE) BHB 34f28a **RR 33f 28a** 510[10]
4 b f Persian Bold 10f **(69)** - Swift And Early (IRE) (Alzao (USA)) 7.1f **(68)**
Form - 0
Record 2000 - 1st:0 2nd:0 3rd:0 Ran:1
Pre2000 - 1st:0 2nd:0 3rd:1 Ran:10
Win Prizemoney £0 *Total Prizemoney* £331
2000 AW 0-1: (16f) (Fibr)
Unfurnished, very moderate filly. Inconsistent.
**S Mellor [0-18] The Bishopstone Ducks.*

BISQUE **RR 51f** 5312[12]
2 ch f Inchinor 8.9f **(64)** - Biscay **(62f)** (Unfuwain (USA))
Form - 0
Record 2000 - 1st:0 2nd:0 3rd:0 Ran:1
2000 Turf 0-1: (8f) (g-s)
Currently fair filly. **R Charlton [0-1] Lady Rothschild.*

BISQUET-DE-BOUCHE BHB 27f **RR 28f** 1185[14]
6 ch m Most Welcome 8.6f **(66)** - Larive (Blakeney) 10.5f **(64)**
Form - 0
Record 2000 - 1st:0 2nd:0 3rd:0 Ran:1
Pre2000 - 1st:0 2nd:0 3rd:1 Ran:9
Win Prizemoney £0 *Total Prizemoney* £732
2000 Turf 0-1: (16f) (hrd)
Little account mare.
**A W Carroll [1-11] Martin Brook (from R Dickin [0-7] Jly 1997).*

BITTER SWEET BHB 56a **RR 49f** 4695[7]
4 gr f Deploy 11.4f **(67)** - Julia Flyte (Drone) 10.3f **(74)**
Form - 8483540057667
Record 2000 - 1st:0 2nd:0 3rd:1 Ran:13
Pre2000 - 1st:0 2nd:1 3rd:1 Ran:12
Win Prizemoney £0 *Total Prizemoney* £2,471
2000 Turf 0-11: (8f, 10f 8, 11f, 12f) (gd 5, g-f 4, frm 2) 2000 AW 0-2: (9f 2) (Fibr 2)
Unfurnished, moderate filly, effective 9 to 10f, acts on g-s to g-f, has worn blinkers, likes left handed tracks. Turf high 49. AW high 23.
**J L Spearing [0-16] Masonaires (from D R C Elsworth [0-12] Oct 1999).*

BITTY MARY BHB 19f **RR 26f** 4455[7]
3 ch f Be My Chief (USA) 10.2f **(62)** - Souadah (USA) (General Holme (USA)) 5.7f **(63)**
Form - 780056087
Record 2000 - 1st:0 2nd:0 3rd:0 Ran:9
Pre2000 - 1st:0 2nd:0 3rd:0 Ran:4
2000 Turf 0-9: (9f, 10f 2, 12f 4, 14f 2) (g-s, gd 2, g-f, frm 4, hrd)
Neat, little account filly, has worn blinkers. Turf high 46.
**J D Bethell [0-13] M W Territt.*

BLACK ARMY BHB 60f66a **RR 57f 66a** 5165[14]
5 b g Aragon 7.7f **(58)** - Morgannwg (IRE) (Simply Great (FR)) 8.2f **(65)**
Form - 38051560
Record 2000 - 1st:1 2nd:0 3rd:0 Ran:6
Pre2000 - 1st:1 2nd:0 3rd:2 Ran:13
Win Prizemoney £6,655 *Total Prizemoney* £7,749
Wins 2000 Jly Catter (G-F) S 6f 39
1999 May Beverl (GD) H 5f 69 72 <
2000 Turf 1-5: (5f, 6f 1-3, 7f) (gd, g-f, frm 1-3) 2000 AW 0-1: (6f) (Fibr)
Above-average gelding, effective 5 to 6f, best at 5f, acts on sft to gd - acts on Fibr, has worn blinkers. Turf high 57. A lightly-raced maiden, he has shown ability.
**K A Ryan [0-3] Crewe And Nantwich Racing Club (from J M P Eustace [2-16] Jly 2000).*

BLACKFOOT (IRE) BHB 59f52a **RR 16f 52a** 33[9]
4 br g River Falls 8.2f **(56)** - Northern Amber (Shack (USA)) 5.8f **(53)**
Form - 00
Record 2000 - 1st:0 2nd:0 3rd:0 Ran:1
Pre2000 - 1st:0 2nd:2 3rd:0 Ran:5
Win Prizemoney £0 *Total Prizemoney* £1,746
2000 AW 0-1: (5f) (Fibr)
Scopey, poor gelding, effective 5f, - acts on Fibr, mostly wears blinkers (very effectively). **J Balding [0-6] John Balding.*

BLACK HAWK **RR 118f** 1286a[2]
6 b h Nureyev (USA) 8.4f **(84)** - Silver Lane (USA) (Silver Hawk (USA)) 8.6f **(70)**
Form - 2
2000 Turf 0-1: (7f) (frm)
Currently high-class horse. (1st run) - 2nd of 18 giving 9lb to Stinger (14 May Fuchu 7f frm RF 1286a). **S Kunioda in JPN [0-2].*

BLACKHEATH (IRE) **RR 79f** 3369[8]
4 ch c Common Grounds 8.1f **(66)** - Queen Caroline (USA) (Chief's Crown (USA)) 9.8f **(72)**
Form - 80888
Record 2000 - 1st:0 2nd:0 3rd:0 Ran:5
Pre2000 - 1st:1 2nd:1 3rd:3 Ran:8
Win Prizemoney £3,786 *Total Prizemoney* £11,105
Wins * 1999 Jun Lingfi (GD) 6f 79 <
2000 Turf 0-5: (6f 5) (g-s, g-f 3, frm)
Scopey, above-average colt, effective 6f, acts on gd to frm, best on frm, has worn blinkers. Turf high 79. Consistent.
**J A R Toller [1-13] G H Toller.*

BLACK ICE BOY (IRE) BHB 33f28a **RR 47f 28a** 5311[7]
9 b g Law Society (USA) 11.6f **(71)** - Hogan's Sister (USA) (Speak John) 10.7f **(72)**
Form - P500807406072307
Record 2000 - 1st:0 2nd:1 3rd:1 Ran:15
Pre2000 - 1st:4 2nd:0 3rd:3 Ran:27
Win Prizemoney £12,971 *Total Prizemoney* £16,275
Wins * 1999 Oct Pontef (SFT) H 17.1f 39 48 <
* 1998 Apr Pontef (G-S) H 21.6f 36 42
* 1997 Jly Beverl (HVY) H 16.2f 32 37
* 1997 Jun Carlis (G-F) H 17.2f 28 31
2000 Turf 0-12: (14f, 15f, 16f 3, 17f 5, 18f, 22f) (sft 4, g-s 4, gd, frm, hrd 2) 2000 AW 0-3: (16f 3) (Fibr 3)
Moderate gelding, effective 17f, acts on g-s to gd, best on gd, mostly wears blinkers, favours left handed tracks, likes tight tracks. Turf high 47 - 2nd of 14 getting 2lb from Martha Reilly (2 Oct Pontefract 17f g-s RF 4766). AW high 30. Requires a real test of stamina. **R Bastiman [4-52] Mrs Judith Marshall.*

BLACK JACK GIRL (IRE) RR 3241[12]

3 br f Ridgewood Ben - Shiyra (Darshaan) 9.9f **(84)**
Form - 0
Record 2000 - 1st:0 2nd:0 3rd:0 Ran:1
Pre2000 - 1st:0 2nd:0 3rd:0 Ran:1
2000 Turf 0-1: (10f) (frm)
Scopey, currently very poor filly.
**J S Wainwright [0-2] Adrian Goodings.*

BLACK KNIGHT BHB 96f RR 88f 5110[2]

2 b br c Contract Law (USA) 8.9f **(54)** - Another Move (Farm Walk) 11.6f **(55)**
Form - 3116632
Record 2000 - 1st:2 2nd:1 3rd:2 Ran:7
Win Prizemoney £6,830 *Total Prizemoney* £11,188
Wins * **2000** Jly Beverl (GD) 7.5f 75+
* **2000** Jun Folkes (FRM) 7f 88+ <
2000 Turf 2-7: (7f 2-4, 8f 3) (g-s, gd, g-f 2-4, frm)
Useful colt, effective 7 to 8f, best at 8f, acts on g-s to frm. Turf high 88 - 2nd of 11 giving 3lb to Aldwych (20 Oct Newbury 8f gd RF 5110) - also 1st of 12 giving 5lb to Fadhah (30 Jun Folkestone RF 2390). **S P C Woods [2-7] Rex Norton.*

BLACK MARK RR 27f 2192[10]

6 b g Daring March 9f **(54)** - Munequita (Marching On) 6f **(60)**
Form - 60
Record 2000 - 1st:0 2nd:0 3rd:0 Ran:2
2000 Turf 0-1: (10f) (gd) 2000 AW 0-1: (11f) (Fibr)
Little account gelding. **C N Kellett [0-4] Sean Taylor.*

BLACK MINNALOUSHE (USA) RR 93f 4530a[1]

2 b c Storm Cat (USA) 7f **(86)** - Coral Dance (FR) (Green Dancer (USA)) 10.3f **(74)**
Form - 11
2000 Turf 2-2: (6f 2-2) (g-f 1-1)
Currently useful colt. Turf high 93 (began Aug) - 1st of 8 getting 3lb from Imperial Dancer (17 Spt Curragh RF 4530a) - also 1st of 6 giving 5lb to La Stellina (7 Aug Cork RF 3644a). A half-brother to Pennekamp, he won his first two starts, including a listed race, and could still be anything.
**A P O'Brien in IRE [2-2] Mrs John Magnier.*

BLACKPOOL MAMMA'S BHB 43f38a RR 62f 38a 5056[13]

3 b f Merdon Melody 6.8f **(56)** - Woodland Steps (Bold Owl) 8.5f **(45)**
Form - 01020060660600
Record 2000 - 1st:1 2nd:1 3rd:0 Ran:14
Pre2000 - 1st:3 2nd:3 3rd:2 Ran:11
Win Prizemoney £10,144 *Total Prizemoney* £14,981
Wins * **2000** Apr Warwic (SFT) 6.8f 68
1999 Jun Chepst (G-F) C 6.1f 71 <
1999 May Newcas (G-F) C 6f 67
1999 Apr Mussel (GD) 5f 68
2000 Turf 1-13: (6f 3, 7f 1-6, 8f 4) (sft 1-3, g-s, gd, g-f 5, frm 3) 2000 AW 0-1: (5f) (Fibr)
Unfurnished, average filly, effective 5 to 6f, best at 5f, acts on gd to g-f - acts on Fibr. Turf high 70. Becoming disappointing.
**J M Bradley [1-14] D J & L & Mrs C R M Gardiner (from J Berry [3-11] Jly 1999).*

BLACK ROCKET (IRE) BHB 45f52a RR 52f 52a 2623[12]

4 br f Perugino (USA) - Betelgeuse (Kalaglow) 9.8f **(67)**
Form - 8671700
Record 2000 - 1st:0 2nd:0 3rd:0 Ran:2
Pre2000 - 1st:1 2nd:0 3rd:0 Ran:13
Win Prizemoney £2,696 *Total Prizemoney* £2,696
Wins * 1999 *Dec Wolver (STD) 8.5f 45* <
2000 Turf 0-2: (10f 2) (g-f 2)
Fair filly, effective 8f, - acts on Fibr, likes left handed tracks, favours tight tracks. Turf high 36 (began Jun). **K Mahdi [1-15] Hamad Al-Mutawa.*

BLACK SAINT RR 4995[6]

3 br g Perpendicular - Fool's Errand (Milford) 9f **(61)**
Form - 6
Record 2000 - 1st:0 2nd:0 3rd:0 Ran:1
2000 AW 0-1: (7f) (Fibr)
Workmanlike, currently very moderate gelding.
**B A McMahon [0-1] Trio Racing.*

BLACK SILK BHB 93f RR 98f 4597[15]

4 b g Zafonic (USA) 9f **(83)** - Mademoiselle Chloe (Night Shift (USA)) 7.2f **(69)**
Form - 16340
Record 2000 - 1st:1 2nd:0 3rd:1 Ran:5
Pre2000 - 1st:1 2nd:4 3rd:3 Ran:14
Win Prizemoney £11,205 *Total Prizemoney* £26,201
Wins * **2000** Jun Goodwo (GD) 8f 90 <
* 1999 Jly Warwic (G-F) 7.7f 75+
2000 Turf 1-5: (7f 2, 8f 1-3) (gd 1-4, frm)
Very useful gelding, effective 7 to 8f, best at 8f, acts on gd to frm, best on gd. Turf high 98 - 6th of 32 getting 6lb from Caribbean Monarch (21 Jun Ascot 8f gd RF 2151) - also 1st of 7 giving 11lb to French Lieutenant (1 Jun Goodwood RF 1621). Consistent. Not an easy ride, he did nothing wrong when winning a Goodwood classified event on his belated return and was an excellent sixth in the Hunt Cup next time. He continued to run well but looked in the Handicapper's grip. **C F Wall [2-19] S Fustok.*

BLACK WEASEL (IRE) BHB 37f35a RR 40f 35a 4535[5]

5 b g Lahib (USA) 8f **(69)** - Glowlamp (IRE) (Glow (USA)) 6.7f **(71)**
Form - 5247562555
Record 2000 - 1st:0 2nd:1 3rd:0 Ran:7
Pre2000 - 1st:1 2nd:1 3rd:1 Ran:17
Win Prizemoney £2,736 *Total Prizemoney* £6,390
Wins 1998 Jly Pontef (G-F) 10f 61 <
2000 Turf 0-5: (16f 4, 17f) (g-s, gd 2, g-f 2) 2000 AW 0-2: (15f, 16f) (Fibr 2)
Fair gelding, effective 14f, - acts on Fibr, has worn blinkers. Turf high 40 (began Jly). AW high 42 (began Jly).
**A Bailey [1-12] S A Pritchard (from Miss J F Craze [0-9] Jun 1999).*

BLAIR (IRE) BHB 32f30a RR 42tf 30a 3312[14]

3 b g Persian Bold 10f **(69)** - Zara's Birthday (IRE) (Waajib)
Form - 074075750
Record 2000 - 1st:0 2nd:0 3rd:0 Ran:9
Pre2000 - 1st:0 2nd:0 3rd:0 Ran:1
2000 Turf 0-7: (8f, 10f 2, 11f 2, 12f 2) (g-s, g-f 2, frm 4) 2000 AW 0-2: (8f 2) (Fibr 2)
Unfurnished, moderate gelding. Turf high 42. AW high 25.
**W W Haigh [0-10] Alan Swinbank.*

BLAKESET BHB 64f94a RR 61f 94a 4378[1]

5 ch g Midyan (USA) 9.9f **(64)** - Penset (Red Sunset) 8.2f **(63)**
Form - 12055100006001
Record 2000 - 1st:2 2nd:0 3rd:0 Ran:11
Pre2000 - 1st:2 2nd:6 3rd:2 Ran:24
Win Prizemoney £11,147 *Total Prizemoney* £26,094
Wins * **2000** Spt Yarmou (G-F) H 7f 58 60
2000 *Mar Wolver (STD) C 7f 79* <
1999 *Nov Lingfi (STD) H 7f 74 75*
1997 Apr Newmar (G-F) 5f 76
2000 Turf 1-8: (6f 3, 7f 1-4, 8f) (sft, gd 3, frm 1-3, hrd) 2000 AW 1-3: (7f 1-2, 8f) (Equi, Fibr 1-2)
Useful gelding, effective 6 to 8f, acts on g-f to frm - acts on AW, has worn blinkers (extremely effectively), prefers left handed tracks, excels at Lingfield. Turf high 61. AW high 80 (1st run) - 5th of 15 giving 5lb to Nautical Warning (15 Jan Lingfield 7f Equi RF 0098) - also 1st of 10 giving 4lb to Royal Cascade (16 Mar Wolverhampton RF 0447).
**T D Barron [1-8] Nigel Shields (from T G Mills [2-6] Mar 2000).*

BLAKESHALL BOY BHB 74f RR 83f 5129[8]

2 b g Piccolo - Giggleswick Girl **(55f 50a)** (Full Extent (USA))
Form - 34140321353008
Record 2000 - 1st:2 2nd:1 3rd:4 Ran:14
Win Prizemoney £7,114 *Total Prizemoney* £12,457
Wins * **2000** Aug Sandow (GD) H 5f 76 83 <
* **2000** May Bright (G-F) 5.3f 67
2000 Turf 2-14: (5f 2-8, 6f 6) (sft, gd 1-5, g-f 4, frm 1-4)
Decent gelding, effective 5 to 6f, best at 5f, acts on gd to frm. Turf high 83 - 1st of 10 getting 5lb from Clarion (9 Aug Sandown RF 3507). Consistent form in a busy season.
**M R Channon [2-14] M Bishop.*

BLAKESHALL JOE RR 508[4]
2 ch c Fraam - Lorcanjo **(35df 36a)** (Hallgate)
Form - 4
Record 2000 - 1st:0 2nd:0 3rd:0 Ran:1
2000 AW 0-1: (5f) (Fibr)
Currently little account colt. **M R Channon [0-1] M Bishop.*

BLAKEY (IRE) BHB 60a **RR 23f** 3385[14]
4 b g Maledetto (IRE) - Villars (Home Guard (USA)) 9.3f **(66)**
Form - 0008050
Record 2000 - 1st:0 2nd:0 3rd:0 Ran:7
Pre2000 - 1st:0 2nd:2 3rd:1 Ran:13
Win Prizemoney £0 *Total Prizemoney* £2,177
2000 Turf 0-7: (5f 2, 6f 3, 7f, 8f) (gd 2, g-f 2, frm 3)
Little account gelding, effective 5f, acts on g-f, has worn blinkers. Turf high 23.
**J M Bradley [0-7] E R Griffiths (from J Berry [0-13] Spt 1999).*

BLAYNEY DANCER BHB 35f39a **RR 37f 39a** 4583[7]
3 b c Contract Law (USA) 8.9f **(54)** - Lady Poly **(127f 18a)** (Dunbeath (USA)) 7.8f **(70)**
Form - 7736500387
Record 2000 - 1st:0 2nd:0 3rd:2 Ran:9
Pre2000 - 1st:0 2nd:0 3rd:0 Ran:3
Win Prizemoney £0 *Total Prizemoney* £746
2000 Turf 0-4: (12f 2, 14f, 16f) (g-s, g-f 2, frm) 2000 AW 0-5: (8f, 10f 3, 16f) (Equi 5)
Scopey, fair colt. Turf high 37. AW high 56.
**J R Poulton [0-14] Mrs M Liston.*

BLAZING BILLY BHB 33f27a **RR 27f 27a** 202[12]
5 ch g Anshan 8.2f **(63)** - Worthy Venture (Northfields (USA)) 9f **(72)**
Form - 0
Record 2000 - 1st:0 2nd:0 3rd:0 Ran:1
Pre2000 - 1st:0 2nd:0 3rd:0 Ran:11
2000 AW 0-1: (7f) (Equi)
Little account gelding, has worn blinkers.
**C A Dwyer [0-13] R West.*

BLAZING IMP (USA) BHB 28f **RR 23f** 2156[8]
7 ch g Imp Society (USA) 7.1f **(63)** - Marital (USA) (Marine Patrol (USA)) 5f **(52)**
Form - 08
Record 2000 - 1st:0 2nd:0 3rd:0 Ran:2
Pre2000 - 1st:2 2nd:0 3rd:1 Ran:29
Win Prizemoney £6,034 *Total Prizemoney* £6,618
Wins 1998 Jly Hamilt (FRM) S 5f 49
1997 Jun Mussel (G-S) 5f 52 <
2000 Turf 0-2: (5f 2) (sft, frm)
Little account gelding. Turf high 4.
**M Dods [0-2] Mrs J Szuszkewicz (from Mrs J Jordan [2-25] Spt 1999).*

BLAZING PEBBLES BHB 25f **RR 28f** 1885[9]
3 ch f Pebble Powder - Wrightway Blues (Majority Blue)
Form - 0708008800
Record 2000 - 1st:0 2nd:0 3rd:0 Ran:7
Pre2000 - 1st:0 2nd:0 3rd:0 Ran:6
2000 Turf 0-3: (6f, 8f, 10f) (gd 2, frm) 2000 AW 0-4: (5f, 6f, 7f 2) (Equi 2, Fibr 2)
Neat, little account filly, has worn blinkers. Turf high 28. AW high 10. **P S McEntee [0-13] Mrs S van der Meulen.*

BLAZING ROCK BHB 25a **RR 25a** 143[5]
3 b g Rock Hopper 10.6f **(54)** - Blazing Pearl (Blazing Saddles (AUS)) 6.7f **(46)**
Form - 005
Record 2000 - 1st:0 2nd:0 3rd:0 Ran:1
Pre2000 - 1st:0 2nd:0 3rd:0 Ran:2
2000 AW 0-1: (9f) (Fibr)
Unfurnished, currently very poor gelding, has worn blinkers.
**P S McEntee [0-3] C E Thompson.*

BLENHEIM TERRACE BHB 40f **RR 56f** 5294[12]
7 b g Rambo Dancer (CAN) 8.4f **(59)** - Boulevard Girl (Nicholas Bill) 10.1f **(56)**
Form - 10
Record 2000 - 1st:1 2nd:0 3rd:0 Ran:2
Pre2000 - 1st:2 2nd:5 3rd:1 Ran:19
Win Prizemoney £8,082 *Total Prizemoney* £14,228
Wins * 2000 Oct Redcar (SFT) C 11f 43
1997 Spt Mussel (G-F) H 12f 52 56 <
1996 Jly Mussel (GD) 11.1f 50
2000 Turf 1-2: (11f 1-1, 12f) (g-s, gd 1-1)
Fair gelding. Turf high 43 (1st run) (began Oct). Consistent. He needs holding up.
**W H Tinning [1-4] W H Tinning (from C B B Booth [2-19] Spt 1997).*

BLESS BHB 38f39a **RR 51f 39a** 3565[9]
3 ch f Beveled (USA) 6.9f **(64)** -Ballystate (Ballacashtal (CAN)) 5.3f **(50)**
Form - 076003300
Record 2000 - 1st:0 2nd:0 3rd:2 Ran:9
Pre2000 - 1st:0 2nd:0 3rd:0 Ran:5
Win Prizemoney £0 *Total Prizemoney* £848
2000 Turf 0-8: (10f 4, 11f, 12f 3) (gd 2, g-f 4, frm 2) 2000 AW 0-1: (10f) (Equi)
Unfurnished, fair filly, has worn blinkers. Turf high 52.
**M Madgwick [0-14] Gail Gaisford And Friends.*

BLESSINGINDISGUISE BHB 72f **RR 77df** 4832[15]
7 b g Kala Shikari 6f **(48)** - Blowing Bubbles (Native Admiral (USA)) 5f **(80)**
Form - 5028628000
Record 2000 - 1st:0 2nd:2 3rd:0 Ran:10
Pre2000 - 1st:9 2nd:5 3rd:3 Ran:49
Win Prizemoney £64,958 *Total Prizemoney* £88,593
Wins * 1999 Spt Newcas (G-F) H 5f 73 76
* 1998 Jly Ascot (G-F) H 5f 97 100 <
* 1998 Jly York (G-F) H 5f 92 97
* 1997 Jly Ascot (GD) H 5f 76 94
* 1997 Jly Ayr (G-F) H 5f 76 80+
* 1997 Jly Haydoc (GD) H 5f 70 71+
* 1997 Jun Ripon (GD) H 5f 64 67
* 1997 May Redcar (G-F) H 5f 58 61
2000 Turf 0-10: (5f 10) (g-s, gd 4, g-f 4, frm)
Above-average gelding, effective 5f, acts on gd to frm, mostly wears blinkers (effectively). Turf high 78 - 2nd of 14 giving 3lb to Eastern Trumpeter (14 Jly York 5f gd RF 2820). Inconsistent.
**M W Easterby [9-59] A G Black.*

BLESS THE BRIDE (IRE) BHB 70f **RR 78f** 5227[8]
3 b f Darshaan 11.9f **(81)** - Feather Bride (IRE) (Groom Dancer (USA))
Form - 18858
Record 2000 - 1st:1 2nd:0 3rd:0 Ran:5
Pre2000 - 1st:0 2nd:0 3rd:0 Ran:3
Win Prizemoney £2,821 *Total Prizemoney* £3,039
Wins * 2000 May Bath (G-S) H 10.2f 72 78 <
2000 Turf 1-5: (10f 1-1, 12f 4) (gd 1-3, g-f 2)
Scopey, above-average filly, effective 10f, acts on gd, likes tight tracks. Turf high 78 (1st run) - 1st of 15 giving 4lb to Distant Prospect (2 May Bath RF 0965).
**J L Dunlop [1-8] Mrs Dan Abbott (Susan Ab Racing) II.*

BLEU D'ALTAIR (FR) RR 117f 4565a[2]
3 c Green Tune (USA) - Parannda (Bold Lad (IRE)) 8.4f **(68)**
Form - 452
2000 Turf 0-3: (10f 2, 11f) (hvy 2, gd)
Currently high-class colt. Turf high 112 - 2nd of 7 to Hightori (16 Spt Longchamp 10f gd RF 4565a).
**D Smaga in FR [0-3] Ecurie du Club Galop.*

BLINDING MISSION (IRE) BHB 54f **RR 73f** 4583[5]
3 b f Marju (IRE) 9.2f **(76)** - Blinding (IRE) (High Top) 10.2f **(67)**
Form - 030605
Record 2000 - 1st:0 2nd:0 3rd:1 Ran:6
Pre2000 - 1st:0 2nd:0 3rd:0 Ran:2
Win Prizemoney £0 *Total Prizemoney* £651
2000 Turf 0-5: (8f 2, 9f 2, 10f) (gd, g-f 2, frm 2) 2000 AW 0-1: (16f) (Equi)
Scopey, above-average filly, effective 9f, acts on g-f. Turf high 73 - 3rd of 8 to Tarabaya (21 Jun Kempton 9f g-f RF 2165). Inconsistent. **J Noseda [0-8] B McAllister.*

BLIND SPOT BHB 57f **RR 60f** 5319[9]
2 ch c Inchinor 8.9f **(64)** - High Tern (High Line) 10.3f **(70)**

Form - 000
Record 2000 - 1st:0 2nd:0 3rd:0 Ran:3
2000 Turf 0-3: (6f, 7f 2) (sft, g-s, gd)
Currently average colt. Turf high 60 (began Aug).
**E A L Dunlop [0-3] Abdullah Ali.*

BLOOD ORANGE BHB 50a **RR 30df** 3385[10]

6 ch g Ron's Victory (USA) 9.2f **(52)** - Little Bittern (USA) (Riva Ridge (USA)) 8.2f **(68)**
Form - 0
Record 2000 - 1st:0 2nd:0 3rd:0 Ran:1
Pre2000 - 1st:0 2nd:0 3rd:0 Ran:11
2000 Turf 0-1: (7f) (frm)
Fair gelding. **G G Margarson [0-12] G G Margarson.*

BLOODY MARY (IRE) BHB 59f **RR 65f** 4823[18]

3 ch f Prince of Birds (USA) - Royaltess (Royal And Regal (USA)) 9.5f **(60)**
Form - 01000
Record 2000 - 1st:1 2nd:0 3rd:0 Ran:5
Pre2000 - 1st:0 2nd:2 3rd:2 Ran:7
Win Prizemoney £3,640 *Total Prizemoney* £6,307
Wins * 2000 Aug Salisb (G-F) 8f 65 <
2000 Turf 1-5: (8f 1-4, 10f) (gd 2, g-f 1-2, frm)
Workmanlike, average filly, effective 6f, acts on g-f. Turf high 65. Scored at Salisbury in August on her first run for four months.
**R Hannon [1-12] Gamahada Partners.*

BLOOM BHB 39f **RR 39f** 4215[17]

2 b f Clantime 6.6f **(57)** - Miami Dolphin (Derrylin) 8.8f **(54)**
Form - 50000
Record 2000 - 1st:0 2nd:0 3rd:0 Ran:5
2000 Turf 0-5: (5f 3, 7f, 8f) (gd 2, g-f, frm 2)
Very moderate filly. Turf high 39.
**J Hetherton [0-3] Ms A Hartley (from D Moffatt [0-2] Jun 2000).*

BLOOMING AMAZING BHB 51f46a **RR 51f 46a** 1951[5]

6 b g Mazilier (USA) 8.5f **(56)** - Cornflower Blue (Tyrnavos) 10.1f **(55)**
Form - 30076850505
Record 2000 - 1st:0 2nd:0 3rd:0 Ran:9
Pre2000 - 1st:4 2nd:6 3rd:5 Ran:41
Win Prizemoney £16,396 *Total Prizemoney* £24,398
Wins 1998 Aug Pontef (G-F) H 8f 78 85 <
1998 Aug Beverl (G-F) H 7.5f 70 77
1998 May Beverl (GD) H 7.5f 70 77
1997 Apr Beverl (G-F) H 8.5f 72 76
2000 Turf 0-5: (7f 2, 8f 3) (g-s, gd 2, g-f, hrd) 2000 AW 0-4: (7f, 8f 2, 9f) (Fibr 4)
Fair gelding, effective 8f, acts on gd to g-f, best on g-f, has worn blinkers (very effectively), likes right handed tracks. Turf high 51. AW high 44.
**G Woodward [0-11] P C Smith (from J L Eyre [4-39] Spt 1999).*

BLOSSOM WHISPERS BHB 54f **RR 71df** 3925[8]

3 b f Ezzoud (IRE) - Springs Welcome (Blakeney) 10.5f **(64)**
Form - 0643238
Record 2000 - 1st:0 2nd:1 3rd:2 Ran:7
Win Prizemoney £0 *Total Prizemoney* £2,653
2000 Turf 0-7: (10f 2, 12f 2, 15f, 16f 2) (sft, g-f 5, frm)
Scopey, above-average filly, effective 12 to 15f, acts on g-f. Turf high 71. **C A Cyzer [0-7] R M Cyzer.*

BLOWING AWAY (IRE) BHB 28f22a **RR 29f 22a** 5182[4]

6 b br m Last Tycoon 9.4f **(73)** - Taken By Force (Persian Bold) 9.3f **(66)**
Form - 700503104
Record 2000 - 1st:1 2nd:0 3rd:1 Ran:9
Pre2000 - 1st:1 2nd:2 3rd:6 Ran:24
Win Prizemoney £5,167 *Total Prizemoney* £9,350
Wins * 2000 Aug Bright (G-F) SH 11.9f 23 28
1997 Oct Leices (GD) C 8f 54 <
2000 Turf 1-6: (11f, 12f 1-3, 14f, 16f) (sft, g-s, gd, g-f 1-1, frm 2) 2000 AW 0-3: (11f, 12f, 16f) (Fibr 3)
Little account mare, effective 12 to 14f, acts on sft to g-f, has worn blinkers, likes left handed tracks. Turf high 29 - 4th of 13 getting 2lb from Acebo Lyons (25 Oct Yarmouth 14f sft RF 5182) - also 1st of 12 from Remember Star (10 Aug Brighton RF 3520). AW high 19.

Improving.
**J Pearce [1-11] & Mrs S Fernandes (from M H Tompkins [2-25] Oct 1998).*

BLU AIR FORCE (IRE) RR 112f 2148[10]

3 b c Sri Pekan (USA) - Carillon Miss (USA) (The Minstrel (CAN)) 10f **(72)**
Form - 10
2000 Turf 1-2: (7f 1-2) (gd 1-2)
Currently Group-class colt. Turf high 112 (1st run) - 1st of 11 getting 11lb from Warningford (25 May Longchamp RF 1629a). Useful Italian-trained colt, down the field in the Jersey Stakes at the Royal meeting. **B Grizzetti in ITY [1-3] Daniel Wildenstein.*

BLUE (IRE) BHB 94f **RR 99+f** 4464[15]

4 b c Bluebird (USA) 7.9f **(71)** - Watership (USA) (Foolish Pleasure (USA)) 8.9f **(72)**
Form - 15100
Record 2000 - 1st:2 2nd:0 3rd:0 Ran:5
Pre2000 - 1st:0 2nd:2 3rd:0 Ran:4
Win Prizemoney £30,855 *Total Prizemoney* £33,080
Wins * 2000 Jun Ascot (G-F) H 10f 90 99 <
*** 2000** Apr Doncas (G-S) 10.3f 84
2000 Turf 2-5: (10f 2-4, 12f) (gd 2-3, g-f, frm)
Strong, very useful colt. Turf high 99 - 1st of 14 getting 2lb from Sharp Play (24 Jun Ascot RF 2239). Absent for the whole of 1999, he looked fit for his Doncaster reappearance and won well, but was a shade disappointing when upped in class. Bounced back to land a valuable Ascot handicap but was held subsequently.
**Mrs A J Perrett [2-9] K J Buchanan.*

BLUE ACE (NZ) BHB 45f **RR 45f** 3569[10]

7 gr g Spectacular Love (USA) - Nursery Rhyme (NZ) (Namnan (USA))
Form - 5080666460
Record 2000 - 1st:0 2nd:0 3rd:0 Ran:10
Win Prizemoney £0 *Total Prizemoney* £281
2000 Turf 0-10: (6f 2, 7f 4, 8f 2, 9f, 10f) (hvy, gd 4, g-f 4, frm)
Moderate gelding. Turf high 61. Consistent.
**A W Carroll [0-12] D Timmins.*

BLUE AWAY (IRE) RR 51f 5186[10]

2 b br g Blues Traveller (IRE) - Lomond Heights (IRE) (Lomond (USA)) 8.8f **(65)**
Form - 0
Record 2000 - 1st:0 2nd:0 3rd:0 Ran:1
2000 Turf 0-1: (7f) (g-s)
Currently fair gelding. **C F Wall [0-1] N Ahamad.*

BLUEBEL (IRE) BHB 43f **RR 38f** 2500[4]

2 b f Lake Coniston (IRE) - Sainte Adresse (USA) (Steinlen)
Form - 504
Record 2000 - 1st:0 2nd:0 3rd:0 Ran:3
2000 Turf 0-3: (5f, 6f 2) (gd 2, g-f)
Currently very moderate filly. Turf high 38.
**J S Moore [0-3] Richard Hannon Jnr.*

BLUEBELL WOOD (IRE) BHB 81f **RR 80f** 2182[12]

3 ch f Bluebird (USA) 7.9f **(71)** - Jungle Jezebel (Thatching) 8f **(66)**
Form - 1114400
Record 2000 - 1st:3 2nd:0 3rd:0 Ran:7
Pre2000 - 1st:0 2nd:0 3rd:0 Ran:1
Win Prizemoney £9,848 *Total Prizemoney* £10,143
Wins * 2000 *Feb Lingfi (STD) H 10f 73 78+* <
*** 2000** *Feb Lingfi (STD) H 10f 67 71+*
*** 2000** *Jan Lingfi (STD) 10f 54*
2000 Turf 0-3: (11f, 12f 2) (g-s 2, g-f) 2000 AW 3-4: (9f, 10f 3-3) (Equi 3-3, Fibr)
Scopey, decent filly, effective 10 to 11f, best at 10f, acts on g-s - acts on Equi, prefers left handed tracks. Turf high 80. AW high 78 - 1st of 5 getting 2lb from Service Star (12 Feb Lingfield RF 0275) - also 1st of 3 giving 9lb to Colombe d'Or (5 Feb Lingfield RF 0225). She completed a hat-trick over ten furlongs on Equitrack at the start of the year, but did not take to Fibresand. Fair fourth in a French listed event in March, but was completely out of her depth in the Oaks. May appreciate quicker ground on turf.
**G C Bravery [3-7] Dr Omar Zawawi (from A J McNae [0-1] Oct 1999).*

BLUEBERRY FOREST (IRE) BHB 97f **RR 96f** 4850a[3]
2 br c Charnwood Forest (IRE) - Abstraction (Rainbow Quest (USA)) 10.4f **(75)**
Form - 1222613
Record 2000 - 1st:2 2nd:3 3rd:1 Ran:7
Win Prizemoney £10,378 *Total Prizemoney* £26,966
Wins * **2000** Spt Ayr (SFT) 7f 96 <
* **2000** May Doncas (G-S) 6f 82+
2000 Turf 2-7: (6f 1-2, 7f 1-3, 8f 2) (hvy, gd 2-4, g-f, hrd)
Very useful colt, effective 7f, acts on gd. Turf high 96 - 1st of 4 giving 12lb to Denise Best (15 Spt Ayr RF 4429). Made a winning debut before finishing second to Marine in a decent event at Newbury. Ran up against promising juveniles on his next two runs before scoring in soft ground at Ayr. He stays very well.
**J L Dunlop [2-7].*

BLUE CAVALIER (IRE) BHB 39f41a **RR 41f 41a** 2569[7]
3 b c Blues Traveller (IRE) - Age of Elegance (Troy) 10.4f **(68)**
Form - 600747
Record 2000 - 1st:0 2nd:0 3rd:0 Ran:4
Pre2000 - 1st:0 2nd:0 3rd:0 Ran:2
2000 Turf 0-2: (12f, 18f) (gd, g-f) 2000 AW 0-2: (7f, 12f) (Fibr 2)
Strong, moderate colt, effective 12f, - acts on Fibr. Turf high 41. AW high 37 - 4th of 8 getting 7lb from Xellance (22 Jun Southwell 12f Fibr RF 2196). **S Dow [0-6] G Steinberg.*

BLUE DOVE (IRE) BHB 45f **RR 53f** 4116[11]
3 b f Bluebird (USA) 7.9f **(71)** - Paradise Forum (Prince Sabo) 7.2f **(62)**
Form - 0000
Record 2000 - 1st:0 2nd:0 3rd:0 Ran:4
Pre2000 - 1st:0 2nd:0 3rd:0 Ran:1
2000 Turf 0-4: (6f 3, 7f) (g-f 2, frm 2)
Fair filly. Turf high 53. (DEAD) **C A Horgan [0-5] Mrs B Sumner.*

BLUE FALCON (IRE) BHB 52f **RR 49f** 4048[15]
2 b c Eagle Eyed (USA) - Indian Sand (Indian King (USA)) 7.4f **(64)**
Form - 860
Record 2000 - 1st:0 2nd:0 3rd:0 Ran:3
2000 Turf 0-3: (5f, 6f, 7f) (frm 2, hrd)
Currently moderate colt. Turf high 49 (began Jly).
**M A Buckley [0-3] Stamford Bridge Partnership.*

BLUE FOREST (IRE) BHB 80f74a **RR 81f 74a** 3846[2]
2 b c Charnwood Forest (IRE) - Vian (USA) (Far Out East (USA)) 8.4f **(65)**
Form - 12
Record 2000 - 1st:1 2nd:1 3rd:0 Ran:2
Win Prizemoney £3,419 *Total Prizemoney* £4,533
Wins * **2000** Mar Newcas (GD) 5f 62+ <
2000 Turf 1-2: (5f 1-1, 6f) (gd 1-2)
Currently decent colt. Turf high 81 - 2nd of 4 giving 8lb to Alinga (22 Aug Hamilton 6f gd RF 3846). **J Noseda [1-2] Hesmonds Stud.*

BLUE GODDESS (IRE) **RR 84+f** 4091a[1]
2 b br f Blues Traveller (IRE) - Classic Goddess (IRE) (Classic Secret (USA))
Form - 111
Record 2000 - 1st:3 2nd:0 3rd:0 Ran:3
Win Prizemoney £106,146 *Total Prizemoney* £106,146
Wins * **2000** Aug Currag (G-S) 6f 84+ <
* **2000** Jly Windso (GD) 6f 77+
* **2000** Jun Chepst (GD) 6.1f 77
2000 Turf 3-3: (6f 3-3) (g-s 1-1, gd 1-1, frm 1-1)
Currently decent filly. Turf high 84 - 1st of 24 from Sweet Dilemma (26 Aug Curragh RF 4091a) - also 1st of 7 giving 2lb to Myhat (17 Jly Windsor RF 2878). Won her first two starts at Chepstow and Windsor, before giving her trainer a fifth consecutive winner of a valuable sales race at the Curragh. Has given the impression that she does not want the ground too fast. **R Hannon [3-3] David Mort.*

BLUE GOLD BHB 103f **RR 107f** 4297[3]
3 b c Rainbow Quest (USA) 11.2f **(81)** - Relatively Special **(105f)** (Alzao (USA)) 7.1f **(68)**
Form - 420120123
Record 2000 - 1st:2 2nd:3 3rd:1 Ran:9
Pre2000 - 1st:1 2nd:0 3rd:2 Ran:4
Win Prizemoney £59,986 *Total Prizemoney* £72,150
Wins * **2000** Aug Goodwo (G-F) H 12f 97 104 <
* **2000** Jun Sandow (G-F) H 10f 95 97
* 1999 Jly Sandow (G-F) 7.1f 83+
2000 Turf 2-9: (9f, 10f 1-5, 12f 1-3) (sft, g-s, gd 1-3, g-f 3, frm 1-1)
Workmanlike, Pattern-class colt, effective 10 to 12f, best at 12f, acts on gd to frm, best on gd, likes right handed tracks, likes tight tracks, excels at Doncaster and Sandown. Turf high 107 - 3rd of 5 getting 9lb from Lear Spear (8 Spt Doncaster 12f g-f RF 4297) - also 1st of 10 giving 1lb to Zafonic's Song (2 Aug Goodwood RF 3318). Consistent. He did not seem to handle the soft ground when fourth of five in the Blue Riband Trial on his return. Ran rather better when runner-up on faster ground at Salisbury next time, and regained winning form at Sandown in June. Enjoyed a nice payday when landing the Tote Gold Trophy at Glorious Goodwood, where he impressed with his attitude, and ran well in a listed race on his final start. **R Hannon [3-13] Mohamed Suhail.*

BLUEGRASS MOUNTAIN BHB 53f60a **RR 46f 60a** 2299[17]
3 b g Primo Dominie 7.2f **(67)** - Florentynna Bay (Aragon) 8.1f **(60)**
Form - 000030
Record 2000 - 1st:0 2nd:0 3rd:1 Ran:6
Pre2000 - 1st:0 2nd:0 3rd:1 Ran:3
Win Prizemoney £0 *Total Prizemoney* £980
2000 Turf 0-5: (5f, 6f 3, 7f) (g-s, gd 2, g-f, frm) 2000 AW 0-1: (6f) (Fibr)
Scopey, moderate gelding, has worn blinkers. Turf high 46. Inconsistent. **T D Easterby [0-9] T G Holdcroft.*

BLUE HAWAII (IRE) BHB 40f30a **RR 54f 30a** 1151[7]
3 ch g Up and At 'em - Astral Way (Hotfoot) 10.5f **(59)**
Form - 207
Record 2000 - 1st:0 2nd:1 3rd:0 Ran:3
Pre2000 - 1st:0 2nd:0 3rd:1 Ran:5
Win Prizemoney £0 *Total Prizemoney* £1,462
2000 Turf 0-2: (10f, 15f) (gd 2) 2000 AW 0-1: (12f) (Fibr)
Leggy, fair gelding, effective 6 to 10f, acts on gd. Turf high 54 (1st run) - 2nd of 25 getting 5lb from Boss Tweed (5 Apr Ripon 10f gd RF 0622). Inconsistent.
**S R Bowring [0-3] David Garner (from B S Rothwell [0-5] Nov 1999).*

BLUE HAWK (IRE) BHB 47f **RR 57?f** 4007[8]
3 ch g Prince of Birds (USA) - Classic Queen (IRE) (Classic Secret (USA))
Form - 8868
Record 2000 - 1st:0 2nd:0 3rd:0 Ran:4
Pre2000 - 1st:0 2nd:0 3rd:1 Ran:6
Win Prizemoney £0 *Total Prizemoney* £557
2000 Turf 0-4: (7f, 8f, 10f, 12f) (gd 2, frm 2)
Scopey, fair gelding. Turf high 62.
**R Hollinshead [0-10] Mrs Dianne Edwards.*

BLUE HOLLY (IRE) BHB 75f70a **RR 80df 70a** 5003[17]
3 b f Blues Traveller (IRE) - Holly Bird (Runnett) 7f **(59)**
Form - 520100000
Record 2000 - 1st:1 2nd:1 3rd:0 Ran:9
Pre2000 - 1st:1 2nd:3 3rd:2 Ran:9
Win Prizemoney £6,494 *Total Prizemoney* £13,243
Wins * **2000** Jun Chepst (GD) H 5.1f 76 80
* 1999 Oct Lingfi (G-F) 5f 87 <
2000 Turf 1-9: (5f 1-8, 6f) (g-s 2, gd 1-3, g-f 2, frm 2)
Workmanlike, decent filly, effective 5f, acts on gd. Turf high 80 - 1st of 14 giving 5lb to Sea Haze (8 Jun Chepstow RF 1799).
**J S Moore [2-18] Alan Chatfield.*

BLUE KITE BHB 55f77a **RR 63f 77a** 4825[20]
5 ch g Silver Kite (USA) 10.2f **(51)** - Gold And Blue (IRE) (Bluebird (USA)) 7.5f **(69)**
Form - 3261166034510024600
Record 2000 - 1st:2 2nd:1 3rd:1 Ran:15
Pre2000 - 1st:3 2nd:10 3rd:2 Ran:43
Win Prizemoney £17,223 *Total Prizemoney* £36,059
Wins * **2000** *Mar Southw (STD) H 6f 78 84* <
* **2000** *Jan Wolver (STD) H 6f 72 79+*
* 1999 *Dec Southw (SLW) H 6f 69 71*
* 1999 *Spt Wolver (STD) H 6f 59 66*
* 1997 *Spt Wolver (STD) 5f 72*
2000 Turf 0-6: (5f, 6f 5) (gd, g-f 4, frm) 2000 AW 2-9: (5f 3, 6f 2-5, 7f) (Equi, Fibr 2-8)

Above-average gelding, effective 5 to 6f, best at 6f, - acts on Fibr, has worn blinkers, likes left handed tracks, likes tight tracks. Turf high 63. AW high 84 - 1st of 16 from James Dee (6 Mar Southwell RF 0416) - also 1st of 13 getting 3lb from Pips Song (4 Jan Wolverhampton RF 0019). Inconsistent.
**N P Littmoden [5-52] T Clarke (from P D Evans [0-6] Jun 1999).*

BLUE LADY (IRE) BHB 59f59a **RR 62f 59a** 4993[2]

2 b f College Chapel - Dancing Bluebell (IRE) **(81f)** (Bluebird (USA)) 7.5f **(69)**
Form - 7650633612
Record 2000 - 1st:1 2nd:1 3rd:2 Ran:10
Win Prizemoney £1,736 *Total Prizemoney* £6,401
Wins * 2000 *Oct Wolver (STD) C 6f 58* **<**
2000 Turf 0-5: (5f 2, 6f 2, 7f) (hvy, gd, g-f 2, frm) 2000 AW 1-5: (5f, 6f 1-3, 8f) (Fibr 1-5)
Average filly, effective 6f, - acts on Fibr, likes left handed tracks, prefers tight tracks. Turf high 62. AW high 65 - 2nd of 12 giving 2lb to Astairedotcom (14 Oct Wolverhampton 6f Fibr RF 4993) - also 1st of 12 getting 4lb from Flowing Rio (3 Oct Wolverhampton RF 4778). **N P Littmoden [1-10] T Clarke.*

BLUE LEGEND (IRE) BHB 39f56a **RR 41f 56a** 4186[6]

3 b f Blues Traveller (IRE) - Swoon Along (Dunphy) 9.4f **(57)**
Form - 8456
Record 2000 - 1st:0 2nd:0 3rd:0 Ran:4
Pre2000 - 1st:1 2nd:1 3rd:0 Ran:8
Win Prizemoney £2,571 *Total Prizemoney* £3,231
Wins 1999 Jly Bright (FRM) C 7f 65 **<**
2000 Turf 0-4: (8f, 9f 3) (g-s, gd, frm 2)
Leggy, moderate filly, effective 7f, acts on gd to frm, likes tight tracks. Turf high 41.
**B Mactaggart [0-4] Mrs Hilary MacTaggart (from J S Moore [1-8] Oct 1999).*

BLUE LINE LADY (IRE) BHB 37f **RR 42f** 4768[11]

3 b f Common Grounds 8.1f **(66)** - Best Academy (USA) (Roberto (USA)) 10f **(76)**
Form - 705700050
Record 2000 - 1st:0 2nd:0 3rd:0 Ran:9
Pre2000 - 1st:0 2nd:2 3rd:0 Ran:8
Win Prizemoney £0 *Total Prizemoney* £2,872
2000 Turf 0-9: (5f 2, 6f 3, 7f 2, 8f 2) (g-s, gd 2, g-f 4, frm, hrd)
Unfurnished, moderate filly, effective 5 to 6f, acts on g-f to frm, has worn blinkers. Turf high 47. Inconsistent.
**K A Ryan [0-3] Peter Tingey (from R A Fahey [0-14] Jun 2000).*

BLUEMAMBA (USA) **RR 114f** 3542a[8]

3 b f Kingmambo (USA) 10.9f **(85)** - Black Penny (West Partisan)
Form - 138
2000 Turf 1-3: (7f, 8f 1-2) (gd 1-3)
Currently Group-class filly. Turf high 114 (1st run) - 1st of 11 from Peony (14 May Longchamp RF 1291a). A tough filly, she landed the French Guineas, but it was a messy race and they all finished in a heap. **P Bary in FR [1-3].*

BLUE MOON (FR) **RR 108f** 4408a[2]

3 ch f Lomitas - To The Rainbow (FR) (Rainbow Quest (USA)) 10.4f **(75)**
Form - 02
2000 Turf 0-2: (8f 2) (sft, gd)
Currently Pattern-class filly. Turf high 108 (1st run) - 9th of 11 to Bluemamba (14 May Longchamp 8f gd RF 1291a).
**X Nakkachdji in FR [0-3].*

BLUE MOUNTAIN **RR 109f** 4986[5]

3 ch c Elmaamul (USA) 8.1f **(70)** -Glenfinlass (Lomond (USA)) 8.8f **(65)**
Form - 52211028135
Record 2000 - 1st:3 2nd:3 3rd:1 Ran:11
Pre2000 - 1st:0 2nd:1 3rd:1 Ran:3
Win Prizemoney £25,133 *Total Prizemoney* £44,101
Wins * 2000 Spt Goodwo (GD) 7f 100 **<**
*** 2000** Jly Goodwo (GD) H 6f 88 93+
*** 2000** Jun Kempto (G-F) H 6f 84 88
2000 Turf 3-11: (6f 2-5, 7f 1-5, 8f) (gd 1-6, g-f 2-5)
Workmanlike, Pattern-class colt, effective 7f, acts on gd to g-f. Turf high 109 - 3rd of 9 getting 3lb from Warningford (16 Spt Newbury 7f g-f RF 4462) - also 1st of 8 getting 3lb from Welcome Friend (8 Spt Goodwood RF 4303). He was running with credit over as far as a mile earlier this season, but did well after being returned to six furlongs, winning handicaps at Kempton and Goodwood. Never in the hunt when favourite in the Stewards' Cup, he was a good second in the Great St Wilfrid at Ripon and benefited from tackling an extra furlong when winning at Goodwood. Acquitted himself well in pattern company on his last two runs.
**R F JohnsonHoughton [3-14] Mrs Hue Williams.*

BLUE ORLEANS BHB 54f65a **RR 54f 65a** 4400[6]

2 b g Dancing Spree (USA) 8f **(59)** - Blues Player (Jaazeiro (USA)) 9.2f **(54)**
Form - 3087606
Record 2000 - 1st:0 2nd:0 3rd:1 Ran:7
Win Prizemoney £0 *Total Prizemoney* £320
2000 Turf 0-4: (5f, 7f 2, 8f) (gd, g-f, frm, hrd) 2000 AW 0-3: (5f 2, 7f) (Fibr 3)
Fair gelding. Turf high 54. AW high 56.
**A G Newcombe [0-7] Advanced Marketing Services Ltd.*

BLUE PLANET (IRE) BHB 87f **RR 84f** 5167[5]

2 b c Bluebird (USA) 7.9f **(71)** - Millie Musique (Miller's Mate) 7f **(63)**
Form - 135
Record 2000 - 1st:1 2nd:0 3rd:1 Ran:3
Win Prizemoney £3,789 *Total Prizemoney* £4,859
Wins * 2000 Jun Hamilt (G-F) 6f 64+ **<**
2000 Turf 1-3: (6f 1-1, 7f 2) (gd 2, g-f 1-1)
Currently decent colt. Turf high 84 - 5th of 7 giving 7lb to Lanesborough (24 Oct Redcar 7f gd RF 5167).
**Sir Mark Prescott [1-3] Meg Dennis,Michael B Brown.*

BLUE POOL **RR 30f** 5140[12]

2 b f Saddlers' Hall (IRE) 10.5f **(65)** - Blue Brocade (Reform) 8.9f **(62)**
Form - 80 -
Record 2000 - 1st:0 2nd:0 3rd:0 Ran:2
2000 Turf 0-2: (6f, 7f) (g-s 2)
Currently very moderate filly. Turf high 30 (began Oct).
**J A R Toller [0-2] Alan Gibson.*

BLUEPRINT (IRE) BHB 115f89a **RR 121f 89a** 2207[3]

5 b h Generous (IRE) 11.5f **(82)** - Highbrow (Shirley Heights) 10.3f **(74)**
Form - 13
Record 2000 - 1st:1 2nd:0 3rd:1 Ran:2
Pre2000 - 1st:6 2nd:2 3rd:2 Ran:16
Win Prizemoney £116,066 *Total Prizemoney* £152,600
Wins * 2000 May Newmar (GD) G2 12f 118 **<**
* 1999 Jun Newmar (G-F) L 12f 116+
* 1999 Jun Ascot (G-F) H 12f 99 104
* 1999 May Newmar (G-F) H 12f 92 94
1998 Aug York (G-F) H 13.9f 89 93
1998 *May Lingfi (STD) H 12f 65 78+*
1998 *May Southw (STD) H 12f 65 69+*
2000 Turf 1-2: (12f 1-2) (gd, g-f 1-1)
Very high-class colt, effective 12 to 13f, best at 12f, acts on gd to frm, best on g-f, has worn blinkers. Turf high 121 - 3rd of 9 to Fruits of Love (23 Jun Ascot 12f gd RF 2207) - also 1st of 11 from Casamasa (5 May Newmarket RF 1047). He made a winning return in the Jockey Club Stakes and, after finishing third in the Hardwicke Stakes at Royal Ascot, was sent to race in America.
**Sir Michael Stoute [4-7] The Queen (from Lord Huntingdon [3-11] Oct 1998).*

BLUE REIGNS BHB 89f **RR 90f** 4932[2]

2 b c Whittingham (IRE) - Gold And Blue (IRE) (Bluebird (USA)) 7.5f **(69)**
Form - 5112
Record 2000 - 1st:2 2nd:1 3rd:0 Ran:4
Win Prizemoney £30,558 *Total Prizemoney* £32,822
Wins * 2000 Spt Doncas (G-F) 6f 83 **<**
*** 2000** Jly Sandow (G-F) 5f 73
2000 Turf 2-4: (5f 1-2, 6f 1-2) (hvy, gd, g-f 2-2)
Useful colt. Turf high 90 - 2nd of 22 giving 4lb to Idle Power (12 Oct Newmarket 6f gd RF 4932) - also 1st of 21 giving 5lb to Fair Princess (8 Spt Doncaster RF 4293). A brother to Blue Star, he is progressing well and won a valuable prize at Doncaster. Has the size and scope to make a nice three-year-old.
**N P Littmoden [2-4] J R Salter.*

BLUE SAPPHIRE (IRE) BHB 34f RR 41f 3639[10]

3 b f Blues Traveller (IRE) - Era (Dalsaan) 9.8f **(64)**
Form - 0600036300
Record 2000 - 1st:0 2nd:0 3rd:2 Ran:9
Pre2000 - 1st:0 2nd:0 3rd:1 Ran:9
Win Prizemoney £0 *Total Prizemoney* £999
2000 Turf 0-9: (5f, 6f 3, 7f 3, 8f 2) (gd, g-f 2, frm 5, hrd)
Tall, moderate filly. Turf high 41. **D W Barker [0-18] D W Barker.*

BLUE SNAKE (USA) BHB 95f RR 89f 575a[9]

4 br c Gone West (USA) 7.8f **(82)** - Dabaweyaa (Shareef Dancer (USA)) 9.9f **(73)**
Form - 10
2000 AW 1-2: (8f 1-2) (Dirt 1-2)
Scopey, Pattern-class colt. AW high 106 (1st run) - 1st of 5 getting 2lb from Running Stag (12 Mar Nad Al Sheba RF 0454a).
**S bin Suroor in UAE [1-2] (from S bin Suroor [1-4] Jly 1999).*

BLUE STAR BHB 65f92a RR 74f 92a 4743[18]

4 b g Whittingham (IRE) - Gold And Blue (IRE) (Bluebird (USA)) 7.5f **(69)**
Form - 5241512200000
Record 2000 - 1st:2 2nd:3 3rd:0 Ran:13
Pre2000 - 1st:1 2nd:2 3rd:3 Ran:18
Win Prizemoney £37,112 *Total Prizemoney* £47,291

Wins							
* 2000	*Mar*	*Wolver*	*(STD)*	*H*	*6f*	*85*	*88* <
* 2000	*Feb*	*Wolver*	*(STD)*	*H*	*6f*	*81*	*84*
* 1998	*Aug*	*Wolver*	*(STD)*		*6f*		*87*

2000 Turf 0-6: (6f 3, 7f 2, 8f) (sft, gd 2, g-f 3) 2000 AW 2-7: (6f 2-4, 7f 3) (Equi, Fibr 2-6)
Rangy, useful gelding, effective 6 to 7f, best at 6f, - acts on Fibr, often wears blinkers, prefers left handed tracks, prefers tight tracks. Turf high 76. AW high 92 - 2nd of 15 giving 26lb to Santandre (17 Mar Southwell 7f Fibr RF 0460) - also 1st of 13 getting 2lb from First Maite (11 Mar Wolverhampton RF 0432). Becoming disappointing. Kept very busy, he is a fair sort on turf, but is much better on Fibresand and scored twice on that surface at the start of 2000. Stays seven furlongs but is better over six.
**N P Littmoden [3-31] T Clarke.*

BLUE STREAK (IRE) BHB 68a RR 75f 4474[0]

3 ch c Bluebird (USA) 7.9f **(71)** - Fleet Amour (USA) (Afleet (CAN))
Form - 784468
Record 2000 - 1st:0 2nd:0 3rd:0 Ran:6
Win Prizemoney £0 *Total Prizemoney* £631
2000 Turf 0-5: (7f 2, 8f 2, 9f) (gd 3, g-f 2) 2000 AW 0-1: (8f) (Fibr)
Well made, above-average colt, has worn blinkers. Turf high 84.
**Sir Michael Stoute [0-6] Mrs Denis Haynes.*

BLUE STREET BHB 42f39a RR 59f 39a 4645[10]

4 b g Deploy 11.4f **(67)** - Kumzar (Hotfoot) 10.5f **(59)**
Form - 8860231680
Record 2000 - 1st:1 2nd:1 3rd:1 Ran:10
Win Prizemoney £2,310 *Total Prizemoney* £4,482

Wins							
* 2000	Aug	Beverl	(G-F)	H	12f		53 <

2000 Turf 1-10: (7f 2, 10f 3, 11f, 12f 1-4) (hvy, g-s 2, gd 2, g-f 1-5)
Scopey, fair gelding, effective 10 to 12f, best at 12f, acts on g-f. Turf high 60 - 2nd of 8 getting 2lb from Mini Lodge (22 Jly Ripon 10f g-f RF 3037) - also 1st of 8 giving 13lb to Lady Donatella (16 Aug Beverley RF 3689). Steadily improving, although his win came in a weak race. **S C Williams [1-10] Tyrnest Ltd.*

BLUE STYLE (IRE) BHB 59f53a RR 66f 53a 5111[15]

4 ch g Bluebird (USA) 7.9f **(71)** - Style For Life (IRE) (Law Society (USA)) 9.9f **(70)**
Form - 61210080
Record 2000 - 1st:2 2nd:1 3rd:0 Ran:8
Pre2000 - 1st:0 2nd:0 3rd:0 Ran:1
Win Prizemoney £9,411 *Total Prizemoney* £12,726

Wins							
* 2000	May	Kempto	(G-S)	H	12f	60	65+
2000	Apr	Bright	(G-S)	C	11.9f		66 <

2000 Turf 2-7: (11f, 12f 2-5, 16f) (sft, g-s 1-1, gd 1-5) 2000 AW 0-1: (8f) (Fibr)
Average gelding, effective 12f, acts on sft to gd, has worn blinkers, prefers tight tracks. Turf high 66 - 2nd of 11 getting 24lb from Zilarator (26 Apr Epsom 12f sft RF 0879) - also 1st of 14 giving 7lb to Ei Ei (13 Apr Brighton RF 0693). Inconsistent. Formerly trained in France and Ireland, he bolted up in a modest Brighton claimer in April after which he was claimed by Philip Mitchell. Unlucky in running in a handicap at Epsom, he made no mistake at Kempton next time. Later became disappointing.
**P Mitchell [1-6] M C Mason & D S Nevison (from J R Poulton [1-2] Apr 2000).*

BLUE SUGAR (USA) BHB 94f RR 94+f 3991[1]

3 ch c Shuailaan (USA) - Chelsea My Love (USA) **(23f)** (Opening Verse (USA))
Form - 42221
Record 2000 - 1st:1 2nd:3 3rd:0 Ran:5
Pre2000 - 1st:1 2nd:0 3rd:0 Ran:1
Win Prizemoney £12,936 *Total Prizemoney* £25,364

Wins							
* 2000	Aug	Newmar	(G-F)	H	10f	89	94+ <
* 1999	Aug	Lingfi	(G-F)		7.6f		88+

2000 Turf 1-5: (7f, 8f 2, 10f 1-2) (sft, g-s, g-f 1-2, frm)
Scopey, useful colt, effective 7 to 10f, best at 8f, acts on g-s to frm, best on g-f. Turf high 94 - 1st of 9 giving 1lb to Another Time (26 Aug Newmarket RF 3991). Ended a frustrating run of seconds when winning a rated stakes at Newmarket in August on his first attempt at ten furlongs. There should be more to come if he returns to training. **J R Fanshawe [2-6] G Algranti.*

BLUES WHISPERER (IRE) BHB 45f RR 55df 2084[10]

3 b g Blues Traveller (IRE) - Princess Roxanne (Prince Tenderfoot (USA)) 9f **(61)**
Form - 0000
Record 2000 - 1st:0 2nd:0 3rd:0 Ran:4
Pre2000 - 1st:0 2nd:0 3rd:0 Ran:1
2000 Turf 0-4: (8f 2, 10f 2) (gd 2, frm 2)
Leggy, fair gelding. Turf high 55.
**B R Millman [0-5] The Blues Whisperer Partnership.*

BLUE VELVET BHB 92f RR 94f 5109[3]

3 gr f Formidable (USA) 7.8f **(60)** - Sweet Whisper **(14f 46a)** (Petong) 6.6f **(58)**
Form - 6000011657623063
Record 2000 - 1st:2 2nd:1 3rd:2 Ran:16
Pre2000 - 1st:2 2nd:4 3rd:1 Ran:15
Win Prizemoney £25,443 *Total Prizemoney* £54,872

Wins							
* 2000	Jly	Newmar	(G-S)	H	6f	79	89 <
* 2000	Jly	Sandow	(GD)	H	5f	79	86
* 1999	Spt	Newmar	(G-S)	H	5f	78	81
* 1999	*Jun*	*Southw*	*(STD)*		*5f*		*65*

2000 Turf 2-16: (5f 1-3, 6f 1-12, 7f) (g-s 4, gd 1-5, g-f 1-3, frm 4)
Useful filly, effective 5 to 7f, best at 6f, acts on g-s to frm. Turf high 94 - 2nd of 9 to Femme Fatale (13 Spt Yarmouth 6f frm RF 4376) - also 1st of 14 getting 2lb from Glenrock (11 Jly Newmarket RF 2691). Consistent. A speedy sort, she was in fine form in July, successful in two decent handicaps, but paid the penalty handicap-wise. Goes well for apprentice Craig Carver, and is suited by some give in the ground. **K T Ivory [4-31] K T Ivory.*

BLUNDELL LANE (IRE) BHB 60f59a RR 74f 59a 4098[4]

5 ch g Shalford (IRE) 7.8f **(63)** - Rathbawn Realm (Doulab (USA)) 9.8f **(65)**
Form - 00180604784
Record 2000 - 1st:1 2nd:0 3rd:0 Ran:9
Pre2000 - 1st:3 2nd:1 3rd:2 Ran:27
Win Prizemoney £21,249 *Total Prizemoney* £26,214

Wins							
* 2000	May	Bright	(G-F)	H	6f	67	74
* 1999	May	Warwic	(Gd)		6f		74
* 1998	May	Cheste	(GD)	H	6.1f	75	86+ <
* 1997	Oct	Redcar	(G-F)	H	6f	69	76

2000 Turf 1-9: (5f 3, 6f 1-5, 7f) (gd, g-f 3, frm 1-5)
Above-average gelding, effective 5 to 6f, best at 6f, acts on gd to frm - acts on Fibr, best on frm, has worn blinkers, likes left handed tracks, likes tight tracks. Turf high 74 (1st run) - 1st of 12 giving 1lb to Ivory Dawn (4 May Brighton RF 1013). A pacey front runner who is suited by six furlongs on a turning left-hand track, his strike-rate has been very moderate in recent seasons.
**A P Jarvis [4-36] Nick Coverdale.*

BLUSHING BRIDE RR 92+f 5241[3]

2 b f Distant Relative 7f **(69)** - Dime Bag (High Line) 10.3f **(70)**
Form - 1123

Record 2000 - 1st:2 2nd:1 3rd:1 Ran:4
Win Prizemoney £10,525 *Total Prizemoney* £17,028
Wins * **2000** Spt Goodwo (HVY) 7f 83+ <
* **2000** Spt Epsom (GD) 7f 76+
2000 Turf 2-4: (7f 2-3, 8f) (sft, g-s, gd 1-1, g-f 1-1)
Useful filly. Turf high 92 (began Spt) - 3rd of 9 to La Vita E Bella (28 Oct Newmarket 8f g-s RF 5241) - also 1st of 9 getting 5lb from Loyal Tycoon (20 Spt Goodwood RF 4541). Scored twice in September, quickening right away from her field on her second start at Goodwood. Looked unlucky in a listed event at Newbury next time. **J Noseda [2-4] Mrs D M Solomon.*

BLUSHING GRENADIER (IRE) BHB 48f53a **RR 46f 53a**
4759[7]
8 ch g Salt Dome (USA) 6.5f **(59)** - La Duse (Junius (USA)) 7.7f **(65)**
Form - 34033433716667217827
Record 2000 - 1st:2 2nd:2 3rd:4 Ran:17
Pre2000 - 1st:8 2nd:6 3rd:8 Ran:71
Win Prizemoney £28,636 *Total Prizemoney* £39,341

Wins								
* **2000**	Jun	Catter	(GD)	C	6f		39	
* **2000**	*Feb*	*Southw*	*(STD)*	*SH*	*6f*	*50*	*51*	
* 1999	Jun	Carlis	(GD)	C	5.9f		57	
* 1999	May	Redcar	(SFT)	C	6f		65	<
* 1998	Oct	Newcas	(SFT)	H	6f	56	62	
* 1998	Spt	Haydoc	(GD)	SH	6f	50	55	
1998	Jun	Warwic	(GD)	C	6f		47	
1998	*Mar*	*Wolver*	*(STD)*	*S*	*6f*		*56*	
1996	Jly	Windso	(GD)	H	6f	46	57?	

2000 Turf 1-6: (5f, 6f 1-5) (g-s, gd 2, g-f 2, frm 1-1) 2000 AW 1-11: (5f 3, 6f 1-4, 7f 3, 8f) (Fibr 1-11)
Fair gelding, effective 6f, acts on gd to g-f, best on gd, mostly wears blinkers. Turf high 46. AW high 58.
**S R Bowring [6-47] S R Bowring (from M J Fetherston-Godley [4-40] Jun 1998).*

BLUSHING PRINCE (IRE) **RR 68f** 5184[6]
2 b c Priolo (USA) 10.9f **(71)** - Eliade (IRE) (Flash of Steel) 7.2f **(53)**
Form - 6
Record 2000 - 1st:0 2nd:0 3rd:0 Ran:1
2000 Turf 0-1: (8f) (g-s)
Currently average colt. **J Noseda [0-1] Mrs D M Solomon.*

BLUSHING SPUR BHB 62f69a **RR 66f 69a** 5008[6]
2 b g Flying Spur (AUS) - Bogus John (CAN) (Blushing John (USA))
Form - 5025236
Record 2000 - 1st:0 2nd:2 3rd:1 Ran:7
Win Prizemoney £0 *Total Prizemoney* £2,240
2000 Turf 0-5: (6f 4, 7f) (g-s 2, gd 3) 2000 AW 0-2: (6f, 7f) (Fibr 2)
Above-average gelding, effective 7f, acts on g-s - acts on Fibr. Turf high 66 - 2nd of 17 giving 9lb to Aporto (16 Spt Catterick 7f g-s RF 4460). AW high 71 (1st run) (began Jly) - 2nd of 10 to Mujalina (3 Jly Southwell 7f Fibr RF 2483). **D Shaw [0-7] J C Fretwell.*

BLUSIENKA (IRE) BHB 92f **RR 100df** 4872[3]
3 b f Blues Traveller (IRE) - Pudgy Poppet (Danehill (USA)) 10f **(72)**
Form - 435403
Record 2000 - 1st:0 2nd:0 3rd:2 Ran:6
Pre2000 - 1st:1 2nd:0 3rd:0 Ran:1
Win Prizemoney £3,225 *Total Prizemoney* £8,474
Wins * 1999 Nov Doncas (SFT) 8f 80 <
2000 Turf 0-6: (8f 4, 10f 2) (hvy, sft, g-s, gd, frm 2)
Lengthy, very useful filly, effective 8f, acts on sft. Turf high 100 - 3rd of 7 to Lady Upstage (22 Apr Kempton 8f sft RF 0829). By no means disgraced in the Group One Prix Saint-Alary earlier in the season, but was rather disappointing latterly. She does not want the ground too fast. **G A Butler [1-7] Mrs Renata Tanaka.*

BOADICEA THE RED (IRE) BHB 50f55a **RR 62f 55a** 5122[11]
3 gr f Inchinor 8.9f **(64)** - Kanika (Be My Chief (USA))
Form - 35000
Record 2000 - 1st:0 2nd:0 3rd:0 Ran:4
Pre2000 - 1st:0 2nd:2 3rd:1 Ran:6
Win Prizemoney £0 *Total Prizemoney* £2,105
2000 Turf 0-3: (6f 2, 7f) (sft, g-s, g-f) 2000 AW 0-1: (7f) (Fibr)
Leggy, above-average filly, effective 5 to 6f, best at 6f, acts on g-f - acts on Equi. Turf high 37 (began Spt). Becoming disappointing.
**B S Rothwell [0-10] Mrs D E Sharp.*

BOANERGES (IRE) BHB 75f **RR 79f** 5313[19]
3 br c Caerleon (USA) 10.9f **(79)** - Sea Siren (Slip Anchor) 9.8f **(73)**
Form - 0071130604070
Record 2000 - 1st:2 2nd:0 3rd:1 Ran:13
Pre2000 - 1st:0 2nd:1 3rd:1 Ran:3
Win Prizemoney £8,866 *Total Prizemoney* £12,167
Wins * **2000** Jun Newmar (G-F) H 5f 77 79 <
* **2000** Jun Goodwo (G-F) H 6f 72 73
2000 Turf 2-13: (5f 1-4, 6f 1-7, 7f, 8f) (sft, g-s 3, gd 2, g-f 2-6, frm)
Workmanlike, above-average colt, effective 5 to 6f, best at 5f, acts on gd to g-f, best on g-f, has worn blinkers. Turf high 79 - 1st of 8 giving 2lb to La Caprice (30 Jun Newmarket RF 2413) - also 1st of 8 getting 3lb from Magelta (16 Jun Goodwood RF 2019).
**R Guest [2-13] P A & D G Sakal (from J Noseda [0-3] Oct 1999).*

BOAST BHB 99f **RR 99f** 3828[4]
3 ch f Most Welcome 8.6f **(66)** - Bay Bay (Bay Express) 7.1f **(60)**
Form - 6351034
Record 2000 - 1st:1 2nd:0 3rd:2 Ran:7
Pre2000 - 1st:2 2nd:1 3rd:0 Ran:6
Win Prizemoney £13,835 *Total Prizemoney* £24,050
Wins * **2000** Jun Newmar (G-F) - 6f 99 <
* 1999 Jly Newmar (GD) 6f 87
* 1999 May Nottin (GD) 5.1f 69+
2000 Turf 1-7: (6f 1-4, 7f 3) (g-s, gd 3, g-f 1-1, frm, hrd)
Scopey, very useful filly, effective 6 to 7f, best at 6f, acts on g-s to hrd. Turf high 99 - 1st of 8 giving 3lb to Flowington (30 Jun Newmarket RF 2414). Consistent. Ran well all season, showing a bright turn of foot to win at Newmarket.
**R F JohnsonHoughton [3-13] Lady Rothschild.*

BOASTED **RR** 4696[15]
3 b f Subotica (FR) - Besotted (Shirley Heights) 10.3f **(74)**
Form - 00
Record 2000 - 1st:0 2nd:0 3rd:0 Ran:2
2000 Turf 0-2: (10f, 12f) (g-f 2)
Currently very poor filly. (began Spt). **B I Case [0-2] S C Rucklidge.*

BOATER BHB 57f73a **RR 55f 73a** 2013[6]
6 b g Batshoof 9.5f **(66)** - Velvet Beret (IRE) (Dominion) 8.5f **(63)**
Form - 36
Record 2000 - 1st:0 2nd:0 3rd:1 Ran:2
Pre2000 - 1st:1 2nd:3 3rd:4 Ran:20
Win Prizemoney £3,044 *Total Prizemoney* £10,685
Wins 1997 Apr Bright (FRM) H 8f 69 71 <
2000 Turf 0-2: (10f 2) (gd, g-f)
Above-average gelding, has worn blinkers. Turf high 55.
**A T Murphy [3-20] Childcraft (from R G Frost [0-3] Aug 1998).*

BOBANVI BHB 51f53a **RR 53?f 53a** 4890[6]
2 b f Timeless Times (USA) 6.1f **(56)** - Bobanlyn (IRE) **(65f)** (Dance of Life (USA)) 7f **(66)**
Form - 548036556
Record 2000 - 1st:0 2nd:0 3rd:1 Ran:9
Win Prizemoney £0 *Total Prizemoney* £266
2000 Turf 0-7: (5f, 6f 2, 7f, 8f 3) (hvy, sft, gd 2, g-f 2, frm) 2000 AW 0-2: (5f, 7f) (Fibr 2)
Fair filly, effective 7 to 8f, acts on hvy - acts on Fibr. Turf high 53 - 6th of 10 getting 12lb from Oriental Mist (10 Oct Ayr 8f hvy RF 4890). AW high 49 - 3rd of 11 to Visitation (28 Jly Southwell 7f Fibr RF 3190). **J S Wainwright [0-9] S Pedersen.*

BOBBYDAZZLE BHB 51f56a **RR 52f 56a** 5116[2]
5 ch m Rock Hopper 10.6f **(54)** - Billie Blue (Ballad Rock) 7.8f **(63)**
Form - 32440340402
Record 2000 - 1st:0 2nd:2 3rd:1 Ran:10
Pre2000 - 1st:2 2nd:1 3rd:2 Ran:21
Win Prizemoney £33,943 *Total Prizemoney* £40,056
Wins 1998 Jun Newcas (SFT) H 8f 76 79+ <
1997 Aug Newcas (GD) H 8f 74 78
2000 Turf 0-6: (8f 5, 10f) (g-s, gd 3, g-f, frm) 2000 AW 0-4: (8f 4)(Fibr 4)
Fair filly, has worn blinkers. Turf high 54. AW high 58.
**C A Dwyer [0-6] Ms Bobby Cohen (from Dr J D Scargill [2-25] May 2000).*

BOBONA BHB 21f23a **RR 29f 23a** 1371[6]
4 b c Interrex (CAN) 7.7f **(51)** - Puella Bona **(48df)** (Handsome Sailor)

Form - 1026506
Record 2000 - 1st:0 2nd:1 3rd:0 Ran:6
Pre2000 - 1st:1 2nd:0 3rd:1 Ran:10
Win Prizemoney £1,829 *Total Prizemoney* £2,690
Wins * 1999 *Dec Southw (STD) C 11f 35* <
2000 AW 0-6: (11f, 12f 3, 14f, 16f) (Fibr 6)
Scopey, very moderate colt, effective 11f, - acts on Fibr, has worn blinkers. AW high 30. Inconsistent. **M D I Usher [1-16] Mrs J Black.*

BOB'S BUSTER BHB 50f38a **RR 53f 38a** 127[5]

4 b g Bob's Return (IRE) - Saltina (Bustino) 10.4f **(64)**
Form - 055
Record 2000 - 1st:0 2nd:0 3rd:0 Ran:3
Pre2000 - 1st:0 2nd:1 3rd:1 Ran:11
Win Prizemoney £0 *Total Prizemoney* £1,253
2000 AW 0-3: (8f 2, 9f) (Fibr 3)
Leggy, fair gelding. AW high 41.
**J Wharton [0-9] Eric Atkinson (from J L Harris [0-5] Spt 1998).*

BOCA CHICA BHB 20f **RR 3f** 4179[12]

3 gr f Environment Friend 7.5f **(67)** - Scoffera **(49f 30a)** (Scottish Reel) 7f **(61)**
Form - 70
Record 2000 - 1st:0 2nd:0 3rd:0 Ran:2
Pre2000 - 1st:0 2nd:0 3rd:0 Ran:4
2000 Turf 0-1: (12f) (frm) 2000 AW 0-1: (12f) (Fibr)
Neat, very poor filly.
**M Mullineaux [0-2] Michael Mullineaux (from N Tinkler [0-4] Spt 1999).*

BODFARI ANNA BHB 54f40a **RR 55f 40a** 5194[4]

4 br f Casteddu 7.4f **(54)** - Lowrianna (IRE) (Cyrano de Bergerac) 6f **(68)**
Form - 3054501083143072004
Record 2000 - 1st:2 2nd:1 3rd:3 Ran:19
Pre2000 - 1st:2 2nd:5 3rd:1 Ran:30
Win Prizemoney £10,634 *Total Prizemoney* £18,584

Wins	* **2000**	Jly	Cheste	(G-S)	H	7.6f	52	56
	* **2000**	May	Southw	(HVY)	H	7f	46	52
	* 1999	Spt	Haydoc	(G-F)	SH	6f	45	46
	1998	Aug	Nottin	(G-F)	S	6.1f		64 <

2000 Turf 2-14: (7f 1-11, 8f 1-3) (hvy, g-s 2, gd 1-5, g-f 1-4, frm, hrd)
2000 AW 0-5: (6f 3, 7f 2) (Fibr 5)
Light-framed, fair filly, effective 6 to 8f, best at 7f, acts on gd to hrd, mostly wears blinkers (effectively), prefers right handed tracks, excels at Musselburgh, likes Haydock. Turf high 56 - 1st of 18 from Caution (15 Jly Chester RF 2837) - also 1st of 15 giving 5lb to Tayovullin (31 May Southwell RF 1604). AW high 40. Inconsistent.
**J L Eyre [3-35] The Haydock Badgeholders (from M W Easterby [1-14] Oct 1998).*

BODFARI JET (IRE) BHB 47f49a **RR 41f 49a** 1598[21]

3 b f Grand Lodge (USA) - River Jet (USA) (Lear Fan (USA)) 8.5f **(73)**
Form - 00
Record 2000 - 1st:0 2nd:0 3rd:0 Ran:2
Pre2000 - 1st:0 2nd:0 3rd:0 Ran:3
Win Prizemoney £0 *Total Prizemoney* £279
2000 Turf 0-1: (6f) (g-f) 2000 AW 0-1: (6f) (Fibr)
Light-framed, moderate filly. **M W Easterby [0-5] Bodfari Stud Ltd.*

BODFARI KOMAITE BHB 70f **RR 72f** 5313[15]

4 b g Komaite (USA) 6.9f **(61)** - Gypsy's Barn Rat (Balliol) 5f **(43)**
Form - 211347700
Record 2000 - 1st:2 2nd:1 3rd:1 Ran:9
Pre2000 - 1st:3 2nd:0 3rd:1 Ran:18
Win Prizemoney £17,923 *Total Prizemoney* £22,784

Wins	* **2000**	Jun	Catter	(GD)	H	5f	67	69 <
	* **2000**	May	Thirsk	(GD)	H	5f	61	62
	* 1999	Jly	Doncas	(G-F)	H	5f	59	61
	* 1999	Jun	Mussel	(GD)	H	5f	56	58
	* 1998	Spt	Redcar	(G-F)	H	5f	62	68

2000 Turf 2-9: (5f 2-9) (g-s 3, gd 1-3, g-f, frm 1-1, hrd)
Scopey, above-average gelding, effective 5f, acts on gd to frm, best on gd. Turf high 72 - 4th of 19 getting 29lb from Repertory (28 Aug Epsom 5f gd RF 4037) - also 1st of 12 getting 5lb from Brecongill Lad (2 Jun Catterick RF 1658). In fine form early in the summer, he is suited by five furlongs and fast ground.
**M W Easterby [5-27] Bodfari Stud Ltd.*

BODFARI MILLENNIUM **RR 54f** 3384[9]

2 b g Tragic Role (USA) 9.4f **(63)** - Petomania (Petong) 6.6f **(58)**
Form - 0
Record 2000 - 1st:0 2nd:0 3rd:0 Ran:1
2000 Turf 0-1: (7f) (frm)
Currently fair gelding. **M W Easterby [0-1] Bodfari Stud Ltd.*

BODFARI PRIDE (IRE) BHB 78f69a **RR 81f 69a** 4776[2]

5 b g Pips Pride 6.7f **(70)** - Renata's Ring (IRE) (Auction Ring (USA)) 8.6f **(65)**
Form - 00011620022
Record 2000 - 1st:2 2nd:3 3rd:0 Ran:11
Pre2000 - 1st:2 2nd:1 3rd:2 Ran:12
Win Prizemoney £30,000 *Total Prizemoney* £43,299

Wins	* **2000**	Jun	Cheste	(G-S)	H	5.1f	64	81 <
	* **2000**	Jun	Goodwo	(G-S)	H	6f	64	68
	1998	May	Cheste	(GD)	H	7.6f	68	76
	1998	Apr	Redcar	(SFT)		7f		76

2000 Turf 2-10: (5f 1-4, 6f 1-5, 8f) (sft, g-s 2, gd 2-6, g-f) 2000 AW 0-1: (6f) (Fibr)
Decent gelding, effective 5 to 6f, best at 5f, acts on g-s to gd, best on gd, likes left handed tracks, likes tight tracks. Turf high 81 - 1st of 10 giving 7lb to Retaliator (7 Jun Chester RF 1785).
**D Nicholls [2-11] Bodfari Stud Ltd (from A Bailey [2-12] Nov 1998).*

BODFARI SIGNET BHB 25f44a **RR 44f 44a** 3607[8]

4 ch g King's Signet (USA) 7f **(51)** - Darakah **(37f 46a)** (Doulab (USA)) 9.8f **(65)**
Form - 00070000608
Record 2000 - 1st:0 2nd:0 3rd:0 Ran:10
Pre2000 - 1st:1 2nd:2 3rd:0 Ran:21
Win Prizemoney £3,712 *Total Prizemoney* £5,446
Wins 1999 Jun Hamilt (GD) H 8.3f 52 54 <
2000 Turf 0-10: (7f, 8f 5, 9f, 10f 2, 11f) (sft, g-s 2, g-f 3, frm 4)
Scopey, moderate gelding, effective 8f, acts on frm, often wears blinkers, likes right handed tracks. Turf high 44.
**B P J Baugh [0-14] Mrs Sylvia Knobbs (from M W Easterby [1-20] Jly 1999).*

BODFARI TIMES BHB 27f61a **RR 26f 61a** 3339[10]

4 ch f Clantime 6.6f **(57)** - Tendency (Ballad Rock) 7.8f **(63)**
Form - 0000000
Record 2000 - 1st:0 2nd:0 3rd:0 Ran:7
Pre2000 - 1st:0 2nd:1 3rd:0 Ran:9
Win Prizemoney £0 *Total Prizemoney* £2,041
2000 Turf 0-6: (5f 3, 6f 2, 7f) (gd 2, g-f 3, frm) 2000 AW 0-1: (5f) (Fibr)
Light-framed, very moderate filly. Turf high 26. Sure to win a sprint maiden. **L J Barratt [0-9] L J Barratt (from A Bailey [0-7] Nov 1998).*

BOGUS DREAMS (IRE) BHB 100f **RR 99f** 1393[3]

3 ch c Lahib (USA) 8f **(69)** - Dreams Are Free (IRE) (Caerleon (USA)) 8.6f **(71)**
Form - 53
Record 2000 - 1st:0 2nd:0 3rd:1 Ran:2
Pre2000 - 1st:2 2nd:0 3rd:1 Ran:3
Win Prizemoney £15,728 *Total Prizemoney* £21,558

Wins	* 1999	Spt	Ascot	(HVY)	7f		98 <
	* 1999	Spt	Thirsk	(FRM)	7f		84+

2000 Turf 0-2: (8f, 10f) (sft, g-s)
Lengthy, very useful colt. Turf high 99. Successful on firm and heavy ground at two, he looked a bit one-paced in Listed company on his final start. Well beaten in a Kempton Listed event on his return, but ran better in a similar race at Goodwood.
**S P C Woods [2-5] Dwayne Woods.*

BOGUS MIX (IRE) BHB 60f **RR 59f** 2537[5]

3 gr f Linamix (FR) 8.2f **(64)** - La Kermesse (USA) (Storm Bird (CAN)) 10.3f **(74)**
Form - 055
Record 2000 - 1st:0 2nd:0 3rd:0 Ran:3
2000 Turf 0-3: (8f, 10f, 12f) (gd 2, g-f)
Light-framed, currently fair filly. Turf high 59.
**S P C Woods [0-3] Northmore Stud.*

BOGUS PENNY (IRE) BHB 78f **RR 77f** 4642[8]

2 b f Pennekamp (USA) - Dreams Are Free (IRE) (Caerleon (USA))

8.6f **(71)**
Form - 4228
Record 2000 - 1st:0 2nd:2 3rd:0 Ran:4
Win Prizemoney £0 *Total Prizemoney* £2,973
2000 Turf 0-4: (6f, 7f 3) (gd, g-f 2, frm)
Above-average filly. Turf high 77 - 2nd of 17 to Lilium (11 Spt Warwick 7f g-f RF 4322). **S P C Woods [0-4] Northmore Stud.*

BOHEMIAN SPIRIT (IRE) BHB 62f **RR 60f** 959[10]

2 b g Eagle Eyed (USA) - Tuesday Morning (Sadler's Wells (USA)) 10f **(76)**
Form - 540
Record 2000 - 1st:0 2nd:0 3rd:0 Ran:3
2000 Turf 0-3: (5f 3) (gd 3)
Currently average gelding. Turf high 60.
**P G Murphy [0-3] Mrs Dianne Abel.*

BOILING POINT RR 4812[17]

4 b f Beveled (USA) 6.9f **(64)** - A Little Hot (Petong) 6.6f **(58)**
Form - 0
Record 2000 - 1st:0 2nd:0 3rd:0 Ran:1
2000 Turf 0-1: (8f) (g-s)
Scopey, currently very poor filly.
**E A Wheeler [0-1] You're Having A Laugh Racing Club.*

BOIRA (USA) RR 74f 3231[6]

2 b f Diesis 9f **(80)** - Noblissima (IRE) **(77f)** (Sadler's Wells (USA)) 10f **(76)**
Form - 6
Record 2000 - 1st:0 2nd:0 3rd:0 Ran:1
2000 Turf 0-1: (7f) (g-f)
Currently above-average filly. **D Morris [0-1] Cuadra Africa.*

BOISDALE (IRE) RR 82f 4728[1]

2 b c Common Grounds 8.1f **(66)** - Alstomeria (Petoski) 5.7f **(62)**
Form - 0064011
Record 2000 - 1st:2 2nd:0 3rd:0 Ran:7
Win Prizemoney £10,037 *Total Prizemoney* £10,037
Wins * 2000 Spt Lingfi (SFT) H 7f 65 82 <
*** 2000** Spt Cheste (SFT) H 7f 65 73+
2000 Turf 2-7: (6f 3, 7f 2-4) (g-s 1-1, gd 1-1, frm 5)
Decent colt, effective 7f, acts on g-s to gd. Turf high 82 (began Jly) - 1st of 18 from Looking For Love (29 Spt Lingfield RF 4728) - also 1st of 9 getting 9lb from Pasithea (20 Spt Chester RF 4534).
**G C Bravery [2-7] OTT Partnership.*

BOIS DE CITRON (USA) BHB 91f **RR 86f** 4448[6]

2 b f Woodman (USA) 9.7f **(77)** - Lemon Souffle **(103f)** (Salse (USA)) 7.5f **(66)**
Form - 34176
Record 2000 - 1st:1 2nd:0 3rd:1 Ran:5
Win Prizemoney £3,601 *Total Prizemoney* £5,109
Wins * 2000 Aug Leices (G-F) 5f 74+ <
2000 Turf 1-5: (5f 1-2, 6f 3) (gd, g-f 1-3, frm)
Useful filly. Turf high 86. Ran over six furlongs in her first two starts, but seemed to be suited by the drop back to five when dismissing a poor field with ease by ten lengths in a Leicester maiden. Well beaten when tried at Listed level.
**R Hannon [1-5] Fieldspring Racing.*

BOISMORAND (FR) RR 97f 1262[3]

4 ch f Sheikh Albadou 9.2f **(75)** - Coupole (USA) (Vaguely Noble) 10.1f **(72)**
Form - 3
2000 Turf 0-1: (10f) (g-f)
Currently very useful filly. (1st run) - 3rd of 8 to Lafite (17 May York 10f g-f RF 1262). Third in a York listed race in May.
**M F Mathet in FR [0-1] M Clifford.*

BOKAY BHB 43f **RR 31f** 1328[14]

3 b f Prince Sabo 6.6f **(64)** - Bassmaat (USA) **(69f 74a)** (Cadeaux Genereux)
Form - 000
Record 2000 - 1st:0 2nd:0 3rd:0 Ran:3
2000 Turf 0-3: (6f 2, 7f) (gd 3)
Neat, currently very moderate filly. Turf high 31.
**B J Meehan [0-3] Total (Bloodstock) Ltd.*

BOLD AMUSEMENT BHB 61f74a **RR 63f 74a** 5168[6]

10 ch g Never so Bold 7.1f **(62)** - Hysterical (High Top) 10.2f **(67)**
Form - 208166
Record 2000 - 1st:1 2nd:1 3rd:0 Ran:6
Pre2000 - 1st:6 2nd:7 3rd:1 Ran:41
Win Prizemoney £24,947 *Total Prizemoney* £36,011
Wins * 2000 Jly Beverl (GD) H 9.9f 60 63
* 1999 Jun Newcas (GD) H 10.1f 58 60
* 1999 Jun Newcas (G-F) H 10.1f 55 58
* 1998 Nov Redcar (G-S) H 10f 55 60
2000 Turf 1-6: (8f, 9f, 10f 1-3, 12f) (gd 2, g-f 1-3, frm)
Average gelding, effective 8 to 12f, best at 10f, acts on gd to frm, has worn blinkers, excels at Newcastle. Turf high 70 (1st run) - 2nd of 11 to Wilton (8 Apr Hamilton 8f gd RF 0644) - also 1st of 14 giving 12lb to Khuchn (8 Jly Beverley RF 2623). Consistent.
**W S Cunningham [5-40] Mrs Ann Bell (from Mrs M Reveley [2-12] Spt 1994).*

BOLD ARISTOCRAT (IRE) BHB 35f35a **RR 24f 35a** 4655[13]

9 b g Bold Arrangement 8.7f **(57)** - Wyn Mipet (Welsh Saint) 7.6f **(64)**
Form - 00400
Record 2000 - 1st:0 2nd:0 3rd:0 Ran:5
Pre2000 - 1st:11 2nd:10 3rd:17 Ran:103
Win Prizemoney £23,619 *Total Prizemoney* £36,529
Wins * 1999 *Feb Southw (STD) S 6f 65*
* 1999 *Feb Southw (STD) C 6f 64*
* 1998 *Mar Southw (STD) S 6f 61*
* 1998 *Feb Southw (STD) S 6f 60*
* 1998 *Feb Southw (STD) S 6f 56*
* 1997 *Jun Southw (STD) 6f 68*
* 1997 *Feb Southw (STD) SH 6f 60 60*
* 1996 *Feb Southw (STD) SH 6f 50 46*
* 1996 *Jan Southw (STD) C 6f 48*
2000 Turf 0-2: (5f, 6f) (frm 2) 2000 AW 0-3: (6f 2, 7f) (Fibr 3)
Little account gelding, effective 6f, - acts on Fibr, prefers left handed tracks, prefers tight tracks. Turf high 24 (began Jly). AW high 49. Becoming disappointing. **R Hollinshead [11-108] Mrs J Hughes.*

BOLD BAHAMIAN (IRE) BHB 60f56a **RR 58f 56a** 4923[4]

3 b g Persian Bold 10f **(69)** - Nordic Pride (Horage) 10.3f **(61)**
Form - 644
Record 2000 - 1st:0 2nd:0 3rd:0 Ran:3
Pre2000 - 1st:0 2nd:0 3rd:0 Ran:3
Win Prizemoney £0 *Total Prizemoney* £481
2000 Turf 0-1: (10f) (g-s) 2000 AW 0-2: (13f, 16f) (Equi 2)
Light-framed, fair gelding. AW high 56 (began Spt).
**J Noseda [0-6] Lucayan Stud.*

BOLD BYZANTIUM BHB 27f **RR 27f** 5198[13]

4 b f Bold Arrangement 8.7f **(57)** - Raunchy Rita (Brigadier Gerard) 9.3f **(58)**
Form - 700
Record 2000 - 1st:0 2nd:0 3rd:0 Ran:3
Pre2000 - 1st:0 2nd:0 3rd:0 Ran:1
2000 Turf 0-3: (6f, 8f 2) (hvy, g-s, gd)
Little account filly. Turf high 27 (began Spt).
**K Bell [0-3] T A Couchman (from E J Alston [0-1] Oct 1998).*

BOLD CARDOWAN (IRE) BHB 35f **RR 38f** 5082[2]

4 br g Persian Bold 10f **(69)** - Moving Trend (IRE) (Be My Guest (USA)) 9.3f **(67)**
Form - 7000402
Record 2000 - 1st:0 2nd:1 3rd:0 Ran:7
Pre2000 - 1st:1 2nd:0 3rd:2 Ran:11
Win Prizemoney £3,038 *Total Prizemoney* £5,424
Wins * 1999 Spt Lingfi (HVY) H 16f 40 53 <
2000 Turf 0-7: (13f, 14f 2, 16f 2, 17f 2) (hvy, sft, g-s 2, g-f 3)
Workmanlike, very moderate gelding, effective 11 to 16f, acts on g-s, has worn blinkers, likes left handed tracks, favours tight tracks. Turf high 42. Consistent. **John Berry [1-18] J McCarthy.*

BOLD CONQUEROR BHB 17f **RR 26f** 1512[11]

4 br f Anshan 8.2f **(63)** - Freudenau (Wassl) 9.7f **(62)**
Form - 0
Record 2000 - 1st:0 2nd:0 3rd:0 Ran:1
Pre2000 - 1st:0 2nd:0 3rd:0 Ran:6

2000 Turf 0-1: (11f) (hvy)
Leggy, little account filly.
**P D Evans [0-1] A Shields (from J M Bradley [0-6] Jun 1999).*

BOLD EDGE BHB 117f **RR 119f** 5095a[8]
5 ch h Beveled (USA) 6.9f **(64)** - Daring Ditty (Daring March) 7.1f **(61)**
Form - 034108

Record	**2000 -**	1st:1	2nd:0	3rd:1	Ran:6
	Pre2000 -	1st:7	2nd:4	3rd:2	Ran:22

Win Prizemoney £216,398 *Total Prizemoney* £296,003

Wins							
	* **2000**	Aug Deauvi	(GD)	G1	6.5f	119	<
	* 1999	Spt Ascot	(HVY)	G2	6f	118	
	* 1999	Jun Ascot	(G-F)	G2	6f	119	<
	* 1999	Apr Newmar	(GD)	L	6f	108+	
	* 1998	Oct Newmar	(GD)	L	6f	108	
	* 1998	May Newbur	(GD)		6f	107	
	* 1998	Apr Leices	(SFT)		6f	100	
	* 1997	May Newbur	(SFT)		6f	94+	

2000 Turf 1-5: (6f 3, 7f 1-2) (sft, g-s, gd 1-3) 2000 AW 0-1: (6f) (Dirt)
High-class colt, effective 6 to 7f, best at 6f, acts on sft to frm, excels at Ascot. Turf high 119 - 1st of 11 from Lend A Hand (6 Aug Deauville RF 3542a). He ran very well in both the Duke Of York and Cork And Orrery earlier last season, but gained his biggest success when the clear-cut winner of the Group One Prix Maurice de Gheest at Deauville. Ran poorly in heavy ground at Haydock, and although he has won on soft, he is reported by his trainer to be better suited by a sound surface. Seven furlongs on soft was too much for him on his final run.
**R Hannon [0-20].*

BOLD EFFORT (FR) BHB 81f74a **RR 80f 74a** 5109[12]
8 b g Bold Arrangement 8.7f **(57)** - Malham Tarn (Riverman (USA)) 9.1f **(76)**
Form - 004001005218501000

Record	**2000 -**	1st:3	2nd:1	3rd:0	Ran:18
	Pre2000 -	1st:11	2nd:9	3rd:5	Ran:80

Win Prizemoney £135,009 *Total Prizemoney* £167,752

Wins								
	* **2000**	Aug Bath	(GD)	H	5.7f	78	80	
	* **2000**	Jun Salisb	(G-F)	H	6f	76	80	
	* **2000**	*Mar Lingfi*	*(STD)*	*H*	*5f*	*70*	*77*	
	* 1999	*Feb Lingfi*	*(STD)*	*H*	*6f*	*86*	*97*	<
	* 1998	Jly Sandow	(G-S)	H	5f	92	95	
	* 1998	May Kempto	(G-F)	H	6f	89	91	
	* 1997	*May Wolvor*	*(STD)*	*H*	*6f*	*90*	*94*	
	* 1996	*Dec Lingfi*	*(STD)*	*H*	*6f*	*82*	*89*	
	* 1996	Spt Maison	(SFT)	H	6f		80	
	* 1996	Aug Claire	(SFT)		8f		78	

2000 Turf 2-12: (5f 2, 6f 2-9, 7f) (sft, g-s, gd 6, g-f 2-4) 2000 AW 1-6: (5f 1-1, 6f 5) (Equi 1-3, Fibr 3)
Decent gelding, effective 6f, - acts on Equi, often wears blinkers, likes left handed tracks. Turf high 80. AW high 77. Becoming disappointing. He is an inconsistent sprint handicapper, but capable of useful form on both turf and sand on his day. Requires luck in running as he comes from behind.
**K O Cunningham-Brown [14-98] A J Richards.*

BOLD EMMA BHB 48f **RR 48f** 4491[8]
3 b f Emarati (USA) 6.6f **(63)** - Nevita (Never so Bold) 6.3f **(66)**
Form - 006008

Record	**2000 -**	1st:0	2nd:0	3rd:0	Ran:5
	Pre2000 -	1st:0	2nd:0	3rd:0	Ran:1

2000 Turf 0-5: (6f 4, 7f) (gd, g-f, frm 3)
Leggy, moderate filly. Turf high 56.
**D J S ffrenchDavis [0-6] Bill Allan.*

BOLDER ALEXANDER (IRE) BHB 30f **RR 24f** 3486[11]
3 b g Persian Bold 10f **(69)** - Be Yourself (USA) (Noalcoholic (FR)) 7.3f **(62)**
Form - 0000S0

Record	**2000 -**	1st:0	2nd:0	3rd:0	Ran:6
	Pre2000 -	1st:1	2nd:1	3rd:2	Ran:12

Win Prizemoney £1,850 *Total Prizemoney* £3,074

Wins							
	1999	Jun Bright	(GD)	S	7f	62	<

2000 Turf 0-6: (10f 3, 12f 3) (sft, g-f, frm 4)
Neat, very moderate gelding, effective 5 to 7f, acts on gd to g-f, has worn blinkers. Turf high 24. Becoming disappointing.
**F Jordan [0-6] M W Doyle (from G L Moore [0-8] Nov 1999).*

BOLD EWAR (IRE) BHB 75f75a **RR 78f 75a** 4934[26]
3 ch c Persian Bold 10f **(69)** - Hot Curry (USA) (Sharpen Up) 8.3f **(67)**
Form - 4153250527150060

Record	**2000 -**	1st:1	2nd:2	3rd:1	Ran:14
	Pre2000 -	1st:1	2nd:1	3rd:1	Ran:9

Win Prizemoney £5,960 *Total Prizemoney* £15,241

Wins								
	* **2000**	Aug Bright	(G-F)	H	8f	75	81	<
	* 1999	*Nov Southw*	*(STD)*	*H*	*8f*	*70*	*74*	

2000 Turf 1-12: (8f 1-7, 9f, 10f 3, 12f) (g-s 2, gd 2, g-f 1-8) 2000 AW 0-2: (8f 2) (Equi, Fibr)
Workmanlike, above-average colt, effective 7 to 10f, acts on gd to frm - acts on Fibr, best on g-f, mostly wears blinkers (very effectively), excels at Newmarket. Turf high 82 (1st run) - 2nd of 14 getting 11lb from King's Mill (20 Apr Newmarket 10f gd RF 0801) - also 1st of 8 giving 24lb to Dusky Virgin (10 Aug Brighton RF 3521). AW high 69. Ten furlongs looks as far as he wants, and he gained his only victory of the season so far over a mile at Brighton in August.
**C E Brittain [2-23] A J Richards.*

BOLD FELICITER BHB 27f **RR 17f** 2046[12]
4 ch f Bold Arrangement 8.7f **(57)** - Jersey Maid (On Your Mark) 7.7f **(58)**
Form - 0

Record	**2000 -**	1st:0	2nd:0	3rd:0	Ran:1
	Pre2000 -	1st:0	2nd:0	3rd:0	Ran:13

2000 Turf 0-1: (14f) (g-f)
Leggy, poor filly, effective 12f, acts on gd to frm, has worn blinkers. Becoming disappointing.
**D Moffatt [0 17] C Lowio.*

BOLD GUEST (IRE) BHB 69f62a **RR 78f 62a** 5119[9]
3 ch c Be My Guest (USA) 10.2f **(66)** - Cross Question (USA) (Alleged (USA)) 10f **(76)**
Form - 033400

Record	**2000 -**	1st:0	2nd:0	3rd:2	Ran:6

Win Prizemoney £0 *Total Prizemoney* £1,282
2000 Turf 0-5: (7f, 8f, 10f 3) (g-s, gd 3, frm) 2000 AW 0-1: (12f) (Fibr)
Scopey, above-average colt. Turf high 78.
**J W Hills [0-6] George Tong.*

BOLD HUNTER BHB 37f **RR 31f** 288[5]
6 b g Polish Precedent (USA) 9f **(73)** - Pumpona (USA) (Sharpen Up) 8.3f **(67)**
Form - 05

Record	**2000 -**	1st:0	2nd:0	3rd:0	Ran:2
	Pre2000 -	1st:1	2nd:3	3rd:2	Ran:23

Win Prizemoney £2,740 *Total Prizemoney* £7,515

Wins							
	1997	Jun Sligo	(FRM)		6.5f	77	<

2000 AW 0-2: (8f, 12f) (Equi, Fibr)
Very moderate gelding, often wears blinkers. AW high 28. Consistent.
**E L James [0-2] V R Bedley (from Mrs P N Dutfield [0-16] Jly 1999).*

BOLD KING BHB 89f83a **RR 97f 83a** 5240[4]
5 br g Anshan 8.2f **(63)** - Spanish Heart (King of Spain) 7.8f **(52)**
Form - 103000164

Record	**2000 -**	1st:2	2nd:0	3rd:1	Ran:9
	Pre2000 -	1st:2	2nd:6	3rd:2	Ran:19

Win Prizemoney £47,331 *Total Prizemoney* £66,159

Wins								
	* **2000**	Spt Goodwo	(SFT)		8f		90	
	* **2000**	May Ascot	(G-S)	H	7f	86	97	<
	* 1999	Aug Newbur	(GD)	H	7f	81	87	
	* 1998	*Apr Southw*	*(STD)*		*8f*		*72+*	

2000 Turf 2-9: (7f 1-4, 8f 1-5) (g-s 1-2, gd 1-5, g-f 2)
Very useful gelding, effective 7 to 8f, best at 8f, acts on g-s to gd, best on g-s. Turf high 97 (1st run) - 1st of 22 getting 4lb from Hornbeam (3 May Ascot RF 1001) - also 1st of 6 giving 1lb to Penang Pearl (21 Spt Goodwood RF 4548).
**J W Hills [4-28] The Farleigh Court Racing Partnership.*

BOLDLY GOES BHB 85f **RR 89f** 5324[5]
4 b c Bold Arrangement 8.7f **(57)** - Reine de Thebes (FR) (Darshaan) 9.9f **(84)**
Form - 00604317067140065

Record	**2000 -**	1st:2	2nd:0	3rd:1	Ran:17
	Pre2000 -	1st:4	2nd:0	3rd:1	Ran:7

Win Prizemoney £36,819 *Total Prizemoney* £40,929

Wins							
	* **2000**	Aug Newcas	(SFT)	H	7f	80	87

* **2000** Jun York (G-F) H 6f 78 83
* 1998 Aug Ripon (G-F) L 6f 98+ <
* 1998 Jly Thirsk (FRM) 7f 88
* 1998 *Jun Wolver (STD) 6f 87*
* 1998 Apr Pontef (G-S) 5f 62
2000 Turf 2-16: (6f 1-10, 7f 1-6) (sft 2, g-s 1-2, gd 6, g-f 2, frm 1-4)
2000 AW 0-1: (10f) (Equi)
Workmanlike, useful colt, effective 7f, acts on sft to g-s, often wears blinkers (very effectively). Turf high 87 - 4th of 13 giving 7lb to Prince Babar (2 Spt Haydock 7f sft RF 4158) - also 1st of 12 giving 14lb to Jeffrey Anotherred (28 Aug Newcastle RF 4046). Consistent. Formerly a useful juvenile, he failed to recapture his best in just two starts at three but forced a dead-heat in a competitive York handicap in June when blinkered for the first time. Best over six furlongs on fast ground.
**C W Fairhurst [6-24] G H & S Leggott.*

BOLD MCLAUGHLAN BHB 64f RR 62f 4120[8]
2 b c Mind Games - Stoneydale (Tickled Pink) 6.5f **(59)**
Form - 8086548
Record 2000 - 1st:0 2nd:0 3rd:0 Ran:7
Win Prizemoney £0 *Total Prizemoney* £233
2000 Turf 0-7: (5f 7) (gd, g-f 2, frm 3, hrd)
Average colt. Turf high 62.
**J S Goldie [0-7] Martin Delaney & Frank Brady.*

BOLD PRECEDENT BHB 70f RR 71f 5079[8]
3 b g Polish Precedent (USA) 9f **(73)** - Shining Water (USA) (Riverman (USA)) 9.1f **(76)**
Form - 43478
Record 2000 - 1st:0 2nd:0 3rd:1 Ran:5
Pre2000 - 1st:0 2nd:0 3rd:0 Ran:1
Win Prizemoney £0 *Total Prizemoney* £1,080
2000 Turf 0-5: (10f 3, 12f 2) (g-s, g-f, frm 3)
Workmanlike, above-average gelding, effective 10f, acts on frm. Turf high 71 (1st run) - 4th of 13 giving 5lb to Janet (19 Jun Windsor 10f frm RF 2108). **P W Harris [0-6] The Shining Examples.*

BOLD RAIDER RR 73f 4824[1]
3 b g Rudimentary (USA) 8.2f **(66)** - Spanish Heart (King of Spain) 7.8f **(52)**
Form - 1234351
Record 2000 - 1st:2 2nd:1 3rd:2 Ran:7
Pre2000 - 1st:0 2nd:0 3rd:0 Ran:3
Win Prizemoney £5,379 *Total Prizemoney* £7,769
Wins * 2000 Oct Windso (G-S) 8.3f 57
*** 2000** Apr Nottin (HVY) H 8.2f 60 63 <
2000 Turf 2-7: (8f 2-7) (sft 1-2, g-s 2, gd 2, g-f 1-1)
Scopey, above-average gelding, effective 8f, acts on sft to gd, best on gd, likes tight tracks. Turf high 73 - 3rd of 19 getting 1lb from Sweet Reward (18 Spt Kempton 8f g-s RF 4484).
**I A Balding [2-10] The Farleigh Court Racing Partnership.*

BOLD SABOTEUR BHB 41f RR 43f 3786[17]
3 b g Prince Sabo 6.6f **(64)** - Latest Flame (IRE) (Last Tycoon) 8.5f **(62)**
Form - 0700
Record 2000 - 1st:0 2nd:0 3rd:0 Ran:4
Pre2000 - 1st:0 2nd:0 3rd:0 Ran:3
2000 Turf 0-4: (6f 3, 7f) (gd, g-f, frm 2)
Scopey, moderate gelding. Turf high 43.
**Mark Campion [0-1] Woodhaven Racing Syndicate (from D R C Elsworth [0-6] Aug 2000).*

BOLD STATE BHB 70f RR 68f 3521[5]
3 b g Never so Bold 7.1f **(62)** - Multi-Sofft **(42f)** (Northern State (USA))
Form - 08811225
Record 2000 - 1st:2 2nd:2 3rd:0 Ran:8
Pre2000 - 1st:1 2nd:3 3rd:1 Ran:10
Win Prizemoney £13,153 *Total Prizemoney* £18,061
Wins * 2000 Jun Hamilt (G-F) 8.3f 66
*** 2000** Jun Nottin (G-F) H 8.2f 63 66
* 1999 Spt York (G-F) 7.9f 80 <
2000 Turf 2-8: (8f 2-4, 9f, 10f 2, 12f) (gd 4, g-f 1-2, frm 1-2)
Workmanlike, average gelding, effective 5 to 8f, best at 7f, acts on gd to frm, best on g-f, has worn blinkers. Turf high 68. Consistent.
**M H Tompkins [3-18] The Toy Boy Partnership.*

BOLD WILLY BHB 35f RR 50f 1542[14]
3 b g Never so Bold 7.1f **(62)** - Indian Star (Indian King (USA)) 7.4f **(64)**
Form - 00
Record 2000 - 1st:0 2nd:0 3rd:0 Ran:2
Pre2000 - 1st:0 2nd:0 3rd:0 Ran:3
2000 Turf 0-2: (8f, 12f) (gd 2)
Scopey, fair gelding. **C W Fairhurst [0-5] William Hill.*

BOLEYN CASTLE (USA) BHB 89f RR 92f 4933[19]
3 ch g River Special (USA) - Dance Skirt (CAN) (Caucasus (USA)) 8.2f **(74)**
Form - 05080
Record 2000 - 1st:0 2nd:0 3rd:0 Ran:5
Pre2000 - 1st:1 2nd:0 3rd:0 Ran:3
Win Prizemoney £3,485 *Total Prizemoney* £3,800
Wins * 1999 Apr Windso (G-S) 5f 78 <
2000 Turf 0-5: (5f 4, 6f) (hvy, gd 2, g-f, frm)
Scopey, useful gelding, effective 6f, acts on frm. Turf high 92. Inconsistent. **T G Mills [1-8] Shipman Racing Ltd.*

BOLHAM LADY BHB 44f RR 3f 5010[5]
2 b f Timeless Times (USA) 6.1f **(56)** - Stratford Lady (Touching Wood (USA)) 8.2f **(55)**
Form - 705
Record 2000 - 1st:0 2nd:0 3rd:0 Ran:3
2000 Turf 0-1: (5f) (g-s) 2000 AW 0-2: (6f, 7f) (Fibr 2)
Currently very moderate filly. AW high 36 (began Spt).
**J Balding [0-3] J M Lacey.*

BOLINGBROKE CASTLE (IRE) RR 65f 5319[20]
2 ch g Goldmark (USA) - Ruby River (Red God) 8.5f **(65)**
Form - 50
Record 2000 - 1st:0 2nd:0 3rd:0 Ran:2
2000 Turf 0-2: (5f, 6f) (sft, gd)
Currently average gelding. Turf high 65.
**Miss J A Camacho [0-1] L A Bolingbroke (from B R Millman [0-1] May 2000).*

BOLLIN ANN BHB 60f RR 66f 4299[11]
5 b m Anshan 8.2f **(63)** - Bollin Zola (Alzao (USA)) 7.1f **(68)**
Form - 0172306850
Record 2000 - 1st:1 2nd:1 3rd:1 Ran:10
Pre2000 - 1st:2 2nd:3 3rd:2 Ran:27
Win Prizemoney £9,555 *Total Prizemoney* £15,944
Wins * 2000 May Newcas (GD) H 5f 58 66 <
* 1999 Jly Beverl (G-F) H 5f 51 55
* 1998 Aug Ripon (G-F) 5f 64
2000 Turf 1-10: (5f 1-9, 6f) (gd 1-3, g-f 2, frm 4, hrd)
Average filly, effective 5 to 6f, best at 5f, acts on gd to frm, best on frm. Turf high 67 - 3rd of 15 getting 4lb from Double Oscar (1 Jly Newcastle 5f frm RF 2446) - also 1st of 20 giving 18lb to Tancred Times (25 May Newcastle RF 1443). Goes on all types of ground, and best suited by the minimum. She had the draw to suit when scoring at Newcastle in May. **T D Easterby [3-37] Lady Westbrook.*

BOLLIN NELLIE BHB 63f RR 62f 5101[10]
3 ch f Rock Hopper 10.6f **(54)** - Bollin Magdalene (Teenoso (USA)) 9.9f **(72)**
Form - 45758216210
Record 2000 - 1st:2 2nd:2 3rd:0 Ran:11
Pre2000 - 1st:0 2nd:0 3rd:1 Ran:4
Win Prizemoney £6,250 *Total Prizemoney* £8,910
Wins * 2000 Oct Catter (SFT) H 12f 57 62+ <
*** 2000** Aug Haydoc (GD) H 11.9f 50 54
2000 Turf 2-11: (9f, 10f 4, 12f 2-5, 14f) (g-s 1-1, gd 4, g-f 1-1, frm 4, hrd)
Neat, average filly, effective 10 to 12f, best at 12f, acts on g-s to frm, prefers tight tracks. Turf high 62 - 1st of 16 getting 10lb from Bahamas (3 Oct Catterick RF 4775) - also 1st of 20 getting 4lb from Skyers A Kite (11 Aug Haydock RF 3547).
**T D Easterby [2-15] Lady Westbrook.*

BOLLIN RITA BHB 56f RR 59df 4457[10]
4 b f Rambo Dancer (CAN) 8.4f **(59)** -Bollin Harriet (Lochnager) 6f **(59)**
Form - 0000204030
Record 2000 - 1st:0 2nd:1 3rd:1 Ran:10
Pre2000 - 1st:1 2nd:4 3rd:2 Ran:15

Win Prizemoney £3,548 *Total Prizemoney* £13,509
Wins * 1000 Apr Thirsk (OD) 0f 72 <
2000 Turf 0-10: (5f 4, 6f 5, 7f) (g-s 2, gd 2, frm 5, hrd)
Leggy, fair filly, effective 6f, acts on gd to g-f, best on g-f, has worn blinkers. Turf high 60. **T D Easterby [1-25] Lady Westbrook.*

BOLLIN ROBERTA BHB 67f **RR 70f** 4427[5]

4 b f Bob's Return (IRE) - Bollin Emily (Lochnager) 6f **(59)**
Form - 528531225
Record 2000 - 1st:1 2nd:3 3rd:1 Ran:9
Pre2000 - 1st:1 2nd:4 3rd:2 Ran:18
Win Prizemoney £6,616 *Total Prizemoney* £16,853
Wins * **2000** Aug Beverl (GD) H 8.5f 60 62 <
* 1999 Spt Mussel (G-F) 7.1f 46
2000 Turf 1-9: (7f 4, 8f 1-2, 10f 3) (g-s, gd 1-2, frm 6)
Scopey, above-average filly, effective 6 to 10f, best at 10f, acts on gd to frm, best on frm, prefers right handed tracks, excels at Musselburgh, likes Beverley. Turf high 70 - 2nd of 9 getting 7lb from Summer Song (27 Aug Beverley 10f frm RF 4013) - also 1st of 8 getting 7lb from Kass Alhawa (1 Aug Beverley RF 3271). Took an age in getting off the mark, but managed it at the sixteenth attempt when landing a seven-furlong Musselburgh maiden in September '99. Running well last term prior to her win at Beverley.
**T D Easterby [2-27] Lady Westbrook.*

BOLLIN ROCK **RR 36f** 3976[6]

3 b g Rock City 8.8f **(62)** - Bollin Zola (Alzao (USA)) 7.1f **(68)**
Form - 56
Record 2000 - 1st:0 2nd:0 3rd:0 Ran:2
2000 Turf 0-2: (5f, 7f) (frm, hrd)
Scopey, currently very moderate gelding. Turf high 36 (began Jly).
**T D Easterby [0-2] Sir Neil Westbrook.*

BOLLIN THOMAS BHB 56f **RR 68f** 5004[7]

2 b g Alhijaz 7.7f **(57)** - Bollin Magdalene (Teenoso (USA)) 9.9f **(72)**
Form - 7787
Record 2000 - 1st:0 2nd:0 3rd:0 Ran:4
2000 Turf 0-4: (6f, 7f, 8f 2) (g-s, g-f, frm 2)
Average gelding. Turf high 68 (began Jly).
**T D Easterby [0-4] Sir Neil Westbrook.*

BOLLIN TOBY BHB 50f **RR 58f** 5081[10]

2 ch c Timeless Times (USA) 6.1f **(56)** - Bollin Emily (Lochnager) 6f **(59)**
Form - 070650
Record 2000 - 1st:0 2nd:0 3rd:0 Ran:6
2000 Turf 0-6: (5f 3, 6f 2, 7f) (hvy, g-s, gd, frm 3)
Fair colt, often wears blinkers. Turf high 57 (began Jly).
**T D Easterby [0-6] Sir Neil Westbrook.*

BOLSHOI (IRE) BHB 100f **RR 102f** 2597[4]

8 br g Royal Academy (USA) 7.8f **(77)** - Mainly Dry (The Brianstan) 5.9f **(55)**
Form - 08004
Record 2000 - 1st:0 2nd:0 3rd:0 Ran:5
Pre2000 - 1st:9 2nd:4 3rd:2 Ran:46
Win Prizemoney £166,604 *Total Prizemoney* £224,000
Wins 1998 Jun Ascot (G-S) G2 5f 120 <
1998 May Sandow (G-F) G2 5f 118
1998 May Beverl (GD) 5f 101
1997 Apr Beverl (G-F) 5f 102
1996 Spt Ascot (GD) H 5f 88 94
1996 Jly Ascot (G-F) H 5f 83 89
1996 Jly Beverl (G-F) H 5f 73 80
1996 May Doncas (G-F) C 5f 68
2000 Turf 0-5: (5f 3, 6f 2) (g-s, gd 3, g-f)
Very useful gelding, often wears blinkers. Turf high 102. Consistent. A high-class sprinter in 1998, he returned to the track following a serious injury and could not recapture his best form, although he was never discredited. He has reportedly been retired.
**A Berry [0-5] Mrs David Brown (from J Berry [9-46] Nov 1998).*

BOLSHOI BALLET BHB 73f **RR 75f** 5004[4]

2 b c Dancing Spree (USA) 8f **(59)** - Broom Isle **(54df 53a)** (Damister (USA)) 9f **(73)**
Form - 033224
Record 2000 - 1st:0 2nd:2 3rd:2 Ran:6
Win Prizemoney £0 *Total Prizemoney* £3,326
2000 Turf 0-6: (6f, 7f 2, 8f 3) (g-s, gd, g-f 2, frm 2)
Above-average colt, effective 8f, acts on g-s to frm. Turf high 75.
**J L Dunlop [0-6] C A Washbourn.*

BOLT FROM THE BLUE BHB 51a **RR 32f** 4870[9]

4 b g Grand Lodge (USA) - Lightning Legacy (USA) (Super Concorde (USA)) 10.9f **(66)**
Form - 00856060
Record 2000 - 1st:0 2nd:0 3rd:0 Ran:7
Pre2000 - 1st:0 2nd:2 3rd:1 Ran:15
Win Prizemoney £0 *Total Prizemoney* £2,141
2000 Turf 0-7: (10f, 11f, 12f 3, 13f, 14f) (hvy, g-s, g-f 3, frm 2)
Light-framed, very moderate gelding, effective 11f, acts on sft to g-f, has worn blinkers, likes left handed tracks, likes tight tracks. Turf high 42.
**Don Enrico Incisa [0-14] Don Enrico Incisa (from N Tinkler [0-8] May 1999).*

BOMB ALASKA BHB 100f **RR 104df** 4967[9]

5 br g Polar Falcon (USA) 9f **(74)** - So True (So Blessed) 8.7f **(67)**
Form - 4434800600
Record 2000 - 1st:0 2nd:0 3rd:1 Ran:10
Pre2000 - 1st:5 2nd:5 3rd:1 Ran:18
Win Prizemoney £57,325 *Total Prizemoney* £104,449
Wins * 1999 Oct Newmar (SFT) L 8f 109 <
* 1999 May Goodwo (GD) H 8f 85 95
* 1999 Apr Newbur (G-F) H 8f 77 85+
* 1999 Mar Doncas (G-S) H 8f 73 79
* 1998 Spt Newbur (gd) 8f 81
2000 Turf 0-10: (7f, 8f 3, 9f 4, 10f 2) (sft, g-s 2, gd 4, g-f 2, frm)
Very useful gelding, effective 8 to 10f, best at 10f, acts on sft to gd, best on gd, likes Newmarket. Turf high 110 - 3rd of 8 to Little Rock (29 Apr Sandown 10f sft RF 0929). He enjoyed a fantastic season in 1999 but was not able to replicate it last term, losing his way after a couple of promising efforts in the spring. He is proven on everything bar firm ground. **G B Balding [5-28] Miss B Swire.*

BOMBAY BINNY BHB 42f **RR 45f** 4360[15]

2 b f First Trump - Bombay Sapphire **(50f)** (Be My Chief (USA))
Form - 7275550
Record 2000 - 1st:0 2nd:1 3rd:0 Ran:7
Win Prizemoney £0 *Total Prizemoney* £1,075
2000 Turf 0-7: (5f 2, 6f 2, 7f 3) (sft, gd, g-f 3, frm 2)
Moderate filly, has worn blinkers. Turf high 45.
**T D Easterby [0-7] Henderson (Co Durham).*

BONAGUIL (USA) BHB 95f **RR 95f** 5134[1]

3 b g Septieme Ciel (USA) - Chateaubrook (USA) (Alleged (USA)) 10f **(76)**
Form - 1113428231
Record 2000 - 1st:4 2nd:2 3rd:2 Ran:10
Pre2000 - 1st:0 2nd:0 3rd:0 Ran:2
Win Prizemoney £23,957 *Total Prizemoney* £50,186
Wins * **2000** Oct Newbur (HVY) H 10f 91 95 <
* **2000** May Kempto (G-S) H 9f 82 89+
* **2000** Mar Sandow (GD) H 8.1f 78 80+
* ***2000*** *Feb Lingfi (STD)* *8f* *75*
2000 Turf 3-9: (8f 1-1, 9f 1-1, 10f 1-4, 11f, 12f 2) (sft 1-2, g-s 1-1, gd, g-f 1-4, frm) 2000 AW 1-1: (8f 1-1) (Equi 1-1)
Scopey, very useful gelding, effective 9 to 12f, best at 10f, acts on sft to frm, likes left handed tracks, excels at Newbury. Turf high 96 - 4th of 16 getting 8lb from Give The Slip (22 Jun Ascot 12f g-f RF 2182) - also 1st of 14 giving 8lb to Gentleman Venture (21 Oct Newbury RF 5134). (1st run). Consistent. A progressive middle-distance handicapper, he hung left on more than one occasion but is genuine. Yet to convince that he truly stays twelve furlongs.
**C F Wall [4-12] Mrs R M S Neave.*

BON AMI (IRE) BHB 84f **RR 82f** 5055[4]

4 b c Paris House 5.9f **(64)** - Felin Special (Lyphard's Special (USA)) 10.3f **(72)**
Form - 004080034602400704
Record 2000 - 1st:0 2nd:1 3rd:1 Ran:18
Pre2000 - 1st:3 2nd:8 3rd:3 Ran:23
Win Prizemoney £10,612 *Total Prizemoney* £59,958
Wins 1998 Aug Ripon (G-F) 6f 88
1998 Aug Newcas (GD) H 6f 100? <

1998 Apr Leices (SFT) 5f 77
2000 Turf 0-18: (5f 3, 6f 14, 7f) (hvy, sft 2, g-s, gd 7, g-f 5, frm 2)
Leggy, decent colt, effective 5 to 7f, best at 6f, acts on gd to frm, best on gd, has worn blinkers. Turf high 92. A useful sprint handicapper but on a long losing run, he was short-headed in the '99 Great St Wilfrid and finished second in last term's Stewards' Cup. A horse who has to be dropped in front on the line, he handles any ground and stays an easy seven furlongs.
**A Berry [0-18] K T Ivory (from J Berry [3-23] Spt 1999).*

BONANZA PEAK (USA) BHB 56f54a **RR 68f 54a** 15[9]

7 b g Houston (USA) 7.7f **(65)** - Bunnicula (USA) (Shadeed (USA)) 8.2f **(70)**
Form - 0
Record 2000 - 1st:0 2nd:0 3rd:0 Ran:1
Pre2000 - 1st:1 2nd:2 3rd:2 Ran:12
Win Prizemoney £2,708 *Total Prizemoney* £6,068
Wins 1997 Aug Bath (GD) H 10.2f 61 66 <
2000 AW 0-1: (8f) (Fibr)
Average gelding, has worn blinkers. Becoming disappointing.
**D Burchell [0-5] Primeshade Contracts Ltd (from Mrs J Cecil [1-12] Nov 1998).*

BOND BOY BHB 69f **RR 71f** 5313[3]

3 b c Piccolo - Arabellajill (Aragon) 8.1f **(60)**
Form - 4510073
Record 2000 - 1st:1 2nd:0 3rd:1 Ran:7
Pre2000 - 1st:0 2nd:1 3rd:1 Ran:4
Win Prizemoney £3,809 *Total Prizemoney* £12,358
Wins * 2000 Jly Beverl (GD) 5f 42 <
2000 Turf 1-7: (5f 1-6, 6f) (g-s 4, gd 2, frm 1-1)
Scopey, above-average colt, effective 5f, acts on g-s. Turf high 71. Inconsistent. **B Smart [1-11] R C Bond.*

BOND DIAMOND BHB 52f67a **RR 53f 67a** 3837[12]

3 gr g Prince Sabo 6.6f **(64)** - Alsiba (Northfields (USA)) 9f **(72)**
Form - 1750000300
Record 2000 - 1st:1 2nd:0 3rd:1 Ran:10
Pre2000 - 1st:0 2nd:0 3rd:0 Ran:4
Win Prizemoney £2,278 *Total Prizemoney* £3,135
Wins * 2000 *Jan Southw (STD) 7f 69* <
2000 Turf 0-7: (6f, 7f 3, 10f 3) (g-s, gd, g-f 2, frm 3) 2000 AW 1-3: (7f 1-2, 8f) (Equi, Fibr 1-2)
Workmanlike, average gelding, effective 7f, - acts on Fibr, likes left handed tracks, likes tight tracks. Turf high 53. AW high 69 (1st run) - 1st of 8 getting 13lb from Fanny Parnell (31 Jan Southwell RF 0190). Inconsistent. **B Smart [1-14] R C Bond.*

BONDI BAY (IRE) BHB 51f **RR 50f** 2271[5]

3 b f Catrail (USA) - Sodium's Niece (Northfields (USA)) 9f **(72)**
Form - 35201705
Record 2000 - 1st:1 2nd:1 3rd:0 Ran:6
Pre2000 - 1st:0 2nd:0 3rd:1 Ran:8
Win Prizemoney £2,450 *Total Prizemoney* £3,410
Wins * 2000 May Beverl (G-F) S 9.9f 50 <
2000 Turf 1-5: (8f 3, 10f 1-1, 12f) (gd, frm 3, hrd 1-1) 2000 AW 0-1: (8f) (Fibr)
Leggy, fair filly, effective 8f, acts on gd, has worn blinkers, likes tight tracks. Turf high 61 (1st run) - 2nd of 10 getting 5lb from Lago di Levico (29 Mar Nottingham 8f gd RF 0556).
**J J O'Neill [1-6] A J Oliver (from A T Murphy [0-8] Nov 1999).*

BOND MILLENNIUM RR 54f 4828[7]

2 ch c Piccolo - Farmer's Pet (Sharrood (USA)) 10.5f **(72)**
Form - 07
Record 2000 - 1st:0 2nd:0 3rd:0 Ran:2
2000 Turf 0-2: (6f, 8f) (g-s, g-f)
Currently fair colt. Turf high 54 (began Spt).
**B Smart [0-2] R C Bond.*

BONDS GULLY (IRE) BHB 49f59a **RR 52f 59a** 2358[4]

4 b c Pips Pride 6.7f **(70)** - Classic Ring (IRE) (Auction Ring (USA)) 8.6f **(65)**
Form - 3284404
Record 2000 - 1st:0 2nd:1 3rd:1 Ran:7
Pre2000 - 1st:0 2nd:0 3rd:0 Ran:5
Win Prizemoney £0 *Total Prizemoney* £1,202
2000 Turf 0-5: (10f, 12f 3, 13f) (gd, g-f 2, frm 2) 2000 AW 0-2: (7f, 10f) (Equi 2)
Scopey, fair colt, effective 7f, acts on gd. Turf high 53. AW high 54. Consistent. **R W Armstrong [0-12] Mrs L Alexander.*

BONELLA (IRE) BHB 46f **RR 52f** 5236[21]

2 gr f Eagle Eyed (USA) - Mettlesome (Lomond (USA)) 8.8f **(65)**
Form - 700
Record 2000 - 1st:0 2nd:0 3rd:0 Ran:3
2000 Turf 0-3: (6f 2, 7f) (g-s, g-f 2)
Currently fair filly. Turf high 52 (began Jun).
**J Pearce [0-3] Mrs Anne Holman-Chappell.*

BONELLI BHB 40f36a **RR 43f 36a** 2030[10]

4 ch c Casteddu 7.4f **(54)** - Tawnais (Artaius (USA)) 9f **(69)**
Form - 60
Record 2000 - 1st:0 2nd:0 3rd:0 Ran:2
Pre2000 - 1st:0 2nd:0 3rd:0 Ran:6
Win Prizemoney £0 *Total Prizemoney* £238
2000 Turf 0-1: (10f) (gd) 2000 AW 0-1: (11f) (Fibr)
Workmanlike, moderate colt. Inconsistent.
**J R Arnold [0-8] Lofal Partnership.*

BON GUEST (IRE) BHB 36f50a **RR 24f 50a** 4479[4]

6 ch g Kefaah (USA) 11.2f **(64)** - Uninvited Guest (Be My Guest (USA)) 9.3f **(67)**
Form - 0004
Record 2000 - 1st:0 2nd:0 3rd:0 Ran:4
Pre2000 - 1st:4 2nd:4 3rd:5 Ran:33
Win Prizemoney £8,716 *Total Prizemoney* £13,048
Wins 1998 *Nov Lingfi (STD) C 12f 54*
1998 *Feb Lingfi (SLW) C 12f 63* <
1998 *Jan Lingfi (STD) H 10f 58 62*
1997 May Nottin (GD) H 8.2f 52 56
2000 Turf 0-2: (10f, 11f) (g-f, frm) 2000 AW 0-2: (10f, 12f) (Equi, Fibr)
Very moderate gelding, has worn blinkers. Turf high 24 (began Aug). AW high 30.
**M P Muggeridge [0-3] A Liddiard (from C R Egerton [0-1] Jun 2000).*

BONIFACIO RR 550[4]

4 br c Zafonic (USA) 9f **(83)** - Bonne Ile (Ile de Bourbon (USA)) 10.1f **(67)**
Form - 4
Record 2000 - 1st:0 2nd:0 3rd:0 Ran:1
Win Prizemoney £0 *Total Prizemoney* £209
2000 AW 0-1: (10f) (Equi)
Very moderate colt. (DEAD) **P F I Cole [0-1] Faisal Salman.*

BONNARD (IRE) RR 100f 5124[3]

2 b c Nureyev (USA) 8.4f **(84)** - Utr (USA) **(56tf)** (Mr Prospector (USA)) 8.8f **(78)**
Form - 132283
2000 Turf 1-6: (6f 1-1, 7f 4, 8f) (g-s 2, gd 1-3)
Very useful colt, effective 7 to 8f, best at 7f, acts on g-s to gd, best on g-s, has worn blinkers. Turf high 100 - 3rd of 10 to Dilshaan (21 Oct Doncaster 8f g-s RF 5124). This well-bred colt was long odds-on when scraping home on his Fairyhouse debut. Third in a Newmarket listed race in July, he appeared a little one-paced. He has run some solid races since, but does not look amongst the best from his stable.
**A P O'Brien in IRE [1-6] M Tabor & Mrs John Magnier.*

BONNET ROUGE (FR) RR 104f 4840a[5]

3 b c Pistolet Bleu (IRE) - French Free Star (FR) (Carmarthen (FR))
Form - 25
2000 Turf 0-2: (12f, 15f) (g-s, gd)
Currently very useful colt. Turf high 104 - 5th of 7 to Epitre (30 Spt Longchamp 15f gd RF 4840a). **E Lellouche in FR [0-2].*

BONNIE DUNDEE BHB 42a **RR 32f** 4102[6]

4 b f Rock City 8.8f **(62)** - Shy Dolly (Cajun) 5.2f **(54)**
Form - 0057074566
Record 2000 - 1st:0 2nd:0 3rd:0 Ran:10
Pre2000 - 1st:1 2nd:1 3rd:0 Ran:14
Win Prizemoney £2,458 *Total Prizemoney* £3,310
Wins 1999 May Salisb (G-F) C 7f 60 <
2000 Turf 0-8: (6f, 7f 5, 8f 2) (gd, g-f 2, frm 5) 2000 AW 0-2: (7f, 8f)

(Equi 2)
Neat, very moderate filly, effective 7f, acts on frm, often wears blinkers. Turf high 32. AW high 9.
**E A Wheeler [0-10] Graham Racing (from M Kettle [1-14] Oct 1999).*

BONNIE FLORA BHB 45f **RR 65f** 4479[11]
4 b f Then Again 7.4f **(52)** - My Minnie **(46f 62a)** (Kind of Hush) 10.1f **(62)**
Form - 703U000
Record 2000 - 1st:0 2nd:0 3rd:1 Ran:7
Pre2000 - 1st:0 2nd:0 3rd:0 Ran:2
Win Prizemoney £0 *Total Prizemoney* £616
2000 Turf 0-6: (10f 4, 12f 2) (gd, g-f, frm 4) 2000 AW 0-1: (12f) (Fibr)
Well made, average filly, effective 10f, acts on frm, likes tight tracks. Turf high 65. Becoming disappointing.
**K Bishop [0-7] Mrs W J B Protheroe-Beynon (from D R C Elsworth [0-2] Jun 1999).*

BONNYELLA BHB 42f **RR 49f** 4478[9]
2 b f Phountzi (USA) 9.6f **(60)** - Diavalezza (Connaught) 7.7f **(63)**
Form - 500
Record 2000 - 1st:0 2nd:0 3rd:0 Ran:3
2000 Turf 0-2: (5f, 6f) (frm 2) 2000 AW 0-1: (7f) (Fibr)
Currently moderate filly. Turf high 49 (began Jly).
**B Palling [0-3] The Saturday Seven.*

BONVIVANT (GER) RR 109f 4842a[5]
3 ch c Sternkonig (IRE) - Bonne Chance (GER) (Surumu (GER)) 10f **(83)**
Form - 35
2000 Turf 0-2: (12f, 14f) (hvy, gd)
Currently Pattern-class colt. Turf high 109 (1st run) (began Aug) - 3rd of 4 giving 4lb to Wild Side (13 Aug Hoppegarten 12f gd RF 3737a).
**H Horwart in GER [0-2].*

BOOGY WOOGY BHB 60f **RR 63f** 4749[7]
4 ch g Rock Hopper 10.6f **(54)** - Primulette (Mummy's Pet) 7.7f **(60)**
Form - 7
Record 2000 - 1st:0 2nd:0 3rd:0 Ran:1
Pre2000 - 1st:3 2nd:1 3rd:6 Ran:22
Win Prizemoney £12,772 *Total Prizemoney* £19,736
Wins * 1999 Jly Thirsk (FRM) H 12f 66 70 <
* 1998 Oct Doncas (HVY) H 7f 64 68
* 1998 Oct Redcar (g-s) C 7f 66
2000 Turf 0-1: (10f) (gd)
Scopey, average gelding, effective 11 to 14f, best at 11f, acts on g-f to frm, best on frm, mostly wears blinkers (extremely effectively), likes left handed tracks, prefers tight tracks, excels at Redcar. Consistent.
**T D Easterby [4-26] Mrs P D Croft.*

BOOMERANG BLADE BHB 83f **RR 79f** 5324[8]
4 b f Sure Blade (USA) 10.6f **(66)** - Opuntia (Rousillon (USA)) 8.2f **(74)**
Form - 06622667518
Record 2000 - 1st:1 2nd:2 3rd:0 Ran:11
Pre2000 - 1st:2 2nd:2 3rd:2 Ran:15
Win Prizemoney £184,450 *Total Prizemoney* £197,621
Wins * 2000 Oct Catter (SFT) 6f 60
* 1998 Spt Doncas (GD) 6f 97 <
* 1998 Jly Folkes (GD) 6f 73
2000 Turf 1-11: (6f 1-5, 7f 6) (hvy, sft 2, g-s 1-4, gd 2, g-f 2)
Scopey, above-average filly, effective 7f, acts on frm. Turf high 80. Earned a huge payday when winning Doncaster's St Leger Yearling Stakes as a two-year-old, and ran respectably against the top fillies in the Fred Darling and 1000 Guineas on her first two starts of 1999. Below-par afterwards, she ran respectably last term but is not an easy filly to place.
**B Smart [3-26] John Ford.*

BOOMSHADOW BHB 35f55a **RR 30f 55a** 5119[6]
3 ch g Imperial Frontier (USA) 7f **(65)** - Marie de Sologne (Lashkari) 9.8f **(67)**
Form - 680056
Record 2000 - 1st:0 2nd:0 3rd:0 Ran:6
Pre2000 - 1st:0 2nd:0 3rd:0 Ran:2
2000 Turf 0-4: (6f, 8f 2, 10f) (g-s, gd, frm 2) 2000 AW 0-2: (7f, 12f) (Equi, Fibr)
Leggy, very moderate gelding. Turf high 30. AW high 29.
**J L Eyre [0-8] Miss C King.*

BOP BHB 40f **RR 51f** 5062[7]
3 b br f Darkwood Bay (USA) - Call of the Night (IRE) **(68f)** (Night Shift (USA)) 7.2f **(69)**
Form - 77
Record 2000 - 1st:0 2nd:0 3rd:0 Ran:2
2000 Turf 0-2: (7f, 10f) (sft, g-f)
Rangy, currently fair filly. Turf high 51 (began Jly).
**D R C Elsworth [0-2] Raymond Tooth.*

BORDER ARROW BHB 116f **RR 119f** 4989[6]
5 ch h Selkirk (USA) 7.9f **(76)** - Nibbs Point (IRE) (Sure Blade (USA)) 11.3f **(67)**
Form - 62376
Record 2000 - 1st:0 2nd:1 3rd:1 Ran:5
Pre2000 - 1st:2 2nd:0 3rd:4 Ran:6
Win Prizemoney £19,503 *Total Prizemoney* £227,433
Wins * 1998 Apr Newmar (SFT) L 9f 104+ <
* 1997 Oct Newmar (G-S) 8f 95++
2000 Turf 0-5: (10f 3, 12f 2) (g-s 2, gd, g-f, frm)
High-class colt, effective 10 to 12f, best at 10f, acts on g-s to g-f, best on g-s. Turf high 119 - 3rd of 4 to Daliapour (9 Jun Epsom 12f g-s RF 1831). Consistent. He has performed with great credit in the highest class in recent seasons, but has had his problems and his opportunities of landing a top-class prize look to have passed him by.
**I A Balding [2-11] R P B Michaelson & Wafic Said.*

BORDER COMET RR 88f 1101[2]
2 b c Selkirk (USA) 7.9f **(76)** - Starlet (Teenoso (USA)) 9.9f **(72)**
Form - 42
Record 2000 - 1st:0 2nd:1 3rd:0 Ran:2
Win Prizemoney £0 *Total Prizemoney* £1,863
2000 Turf 0-2: (7f, 8f) (g-f 2)
Currently useful colt. Turf high 88 (began Jly) - 2nd of 15 to Hill Country (3 Spt Kempton 8f g-f RF 4191).
**Sir Michael Stoute [0-2] The Queen.*

BORDER EDGE BHB 49f55a **RR 58f 55a** 5218[7]
2 b c Beveled (USA) 6.9f **(64)** - Seymour Ann (Krayyan) 8.5f **(49)**
Form - 04757067
Record 2000 - 1st:0 2nd:0 3rd:0 Ran:8
2000 Turf 0-5: (5f, 6f, 8f 2, 10f) (sft, g-s, gd, g-f 2) 2000 AW 0-3. (5f, 7f 2) (Fibr 3)
Fair colt, has worn blinkers. Turf high 58. AW high 56.
**K McAuliffe [0-8] Allsorts.*

BORDER GLEN BHB 53f51a **RR 59f 51a** 5248[11]
4 b g Selkirk (USA) 7.9f **(76)** - Sulitelma (USA) (The Minstrel (CAN)) 10f **(72)**
Form - 334362670577537643360
Record 2000 - 1st:0 2nd:1 3rd:4 Ran:18
Pre2000 - 1st:2 2nd:0 3rd:2 Ran:17
Win Prizemoney £5,350 *Total Prizemoney* £8,814
Wins 1999 Jun Mussel (G-F) H 8f 51 55
1999 Jun Southw (STD) H 8f 51 56 <
2000 Turf 0-10: (5f 6, 6f 4) (g-s, gd 3, g-f, frm 4, hrd) 2000 AW 0-8: (6f, 7f 3, 8f 2, 9f, 10f) (Equi 5, Fibr 3)
Scopey, fair gelding, effective 5 to 9f, best at 8f, acts on g-s to hrd - acts on AW, best on Equi, often wears blinkers (effectively), prefers left handed tracks, likes tight tracks, and excels at Bath and Southwell. Turf high 59 (began Jly) - 3rd of 7 to Cauda Equina (25 Aug Bath 5f hrd RF 3953). AW high 60 - 2nd of 9 giving 6lb to Superchief (26 Feb Lingfield 8f Equi RF 0366).
**J J Bridger [0-17] J J Bridger (from D HaydnJones [0-8] Jan 2000).*

BORDERLINE BHB 49f **RR 66tf** 5105[17]
3 ch c Polish Precedent (USA) 9f **(73)** - Brecon Beacons (IRE) (Shirley Heights) 10.3f **(74)**
Form - 70700
Record 2000 - 1st:0 2nd:0 3rd:0 Ran:5
2000 Turf 0-5: (7f, 8f 2, 10f 2) (g-s, gd 2, g-f, frm)
Scopey, average colt. Turf high 66.
**M C Chapman [0-4] Jalons Partnership (from H R A Cecil [0-1] Apr 2000).*

BORDER RUN BHB 58f53a **RR 63df 53a** 4479[7]
3 b g Missed Flight - Edraianthus (Windjammer (USA)) 7f **(59)**

Form - 50036037
Record 2000 - 1st:0 2nd:0 3rd:2 Ran:8
Pre2000 - 1st:0 2nd:0 3rd:0 Ran:3
Win Prizemoney £0 *Total Prizemoney* £1,013
2000 Turf 0-6: (8f, 10f 2, 11f, 12f 2) (g-s, gd, g-f, frm 3) 2000 AW 0-2: (10f, 12f) (Equi, Fibr)
Scopey, average gelding, effective 12f, acts on frm, has worn blinkers, likes tight tracks. Turf high 63 - 3rd of 20 getting 4lb from Fanfare (15 May Windsor 12f frm RF 1214). AW high 31.
**B J Meehan [0-11] N B Attenborough.*

BORDERS BELLE (IRE) BHB 77f RR 74f 5103[1]

2 b f Pursuit of Love 9.5f **(69)** - Sheryl Lynn (Miller's Mate) 7f **(63)**
Form - 4320671
Record 2000 - 1st:1 2nd:1 3rd:1 Ran:7
Win Prizemoney £5,050 *Total Prizemoney* £6,939
Wins * 2000 Oct Doncas (GD) H 8f 72 74 <
2000 Turf 1-7: (6f 2, 7f 3, 8f 1-2) (g-s 2, gd 1-1, g-f, frm 3)
Above-average filly, effective 7 to 8f, best at 7f, acts on g-s to g-f. Turf high 74 (began Jly) - 1st of 12 giving 10lb to King's Crest (20 Oct Doncaster RF 5103). **J D Bethell [1-7] M J Dawson.*

BORDER SUBJECT BHB 92f RR 91+f 4597[21]

3 b c Selkirk (USA) 7.9f **(76)** - Topicality (USA) (Topsider (USA)) 8.3f **(71)**
Form - 60110
Record 2000 - 1st:2 2nd:0 3rd:0 Ran:5
Win Prizemoney £10,071 *Total Prizemoney* £10,071
Wins * 2000 Aug Windso (G-F) H 8.3f 87 91 <
*** 2000** Aug Chepst (G-F) 7.1f 71+
2000 Turf 2-5: (7f 1-2, 8f 1-3) (gd 1-4, frm 1-1)
Well made, useful colt. Turf high 91 - 1st of 9 getting 7lb from Welsh Wind (26 Aug Windsor RF 4005). Came good in August with two victories on fast ground, looking very progressive, but was down the field in a hot handicap on his last run.
**R Charlton [2-5] K Abdulla.*

BORDER TERRIER (IRE) BHB 60f RR 66f 4381[7]

2 b c Balnibarbi - Ring Side (IRE) (Alzao (USA)) 7.1f **(68)**
Form - 7427
Record 2000 - 1st:0 2nd:1 3rd:0 Ran:4
Win Prizemoney £0 *Total Prizemoney* £967
2000 Turf 0-4: (7f 2, 8f 2) (g-s, gd, frm 2)
Average colt. Turf high 66 (began Jly) - 2nd of 11 giving 5lb to Fazzani (28 Aug Newcastle 8f g-s RF 4044).
**R A Fahey [0-4] Stephen Laidlaw.*

BOREAS BHB 111f RR 115+f 5321[1]

5 b g In The Wings 11.2f **(77)** - Reamur (Top Ville) 11.7f **(68)**
Form - 1231
Record 2000 - 1st:2 2nd:1 3rd:1 Ran:4
Pre2000 - 1st:1 2nd:0 3rd:1 Ran:5
Win Prizemoney £28,622 *Total Prizemoney* £70,143
Wins * 2000 Nov Doncas (HVY) L 12f 115+ <
*** 2000** Jly York (GD) H 11.9f 82 89
* 1998 Aug Ripon (G-F) 10f 84
2000 Turf 2-4: (12f 2-3, 14f) (sft 1-2, gd 1-1, frm)
High-class gelding. Turf high 115 (began Jly) - 1st of 4 from Zilarator (4 Nov Doncaster RF 5321). Improving. Had some decent form in 1998, but was not seen again until winning easily at York in July of 2000. Sent of a warm favourite for the Ebor the following month, he found only Give The Slip too good. Ran a cracker when stepped up in class to a Newbury Group Three, handling the heavy ground well, and bolted up on his final start. May still have improvement in him. **L M Cumani [3-9] Aston House Stud.*

BORN SOMETHING (IRE) RR 97f 4844a[5]

2 f
Form - 5
2000 Turf 0-1: (8f) (gd)
Currently very useful. (1st run) - 5th of 10 to Amonita (1 Oct Longchamp 8f gd RF 4844a). **Mme C Head in FR [0-1].*

BORN TO RULE BHB 52f RR 52f 3484[8]

3 ch g Mujtahid (USA) 7.4f **(69)** - Born To Glamour (Ajdal (USA)) 9.2f **(89)**
Form - 000500808
Record 2000 - 1st:0 2nd:0 3rd:0 Ran:9
Pre2000 - 1st:0 2nd:0 3rd:0 Ran:3
Win Prizemoney £0 *Total Prizemoney* £535
2000 Turf 0-9: (5f 6, 6f 2, 7f) (hvy, gd 2, g-f 4, frm 2)
Small, fair gelding, has worn blinkers. Turf high 58.
**M S Saunders [0-12] Naylor,B McFadzean,M Mulchrone.*

BORN WILD (FR) RR 17f 4363[12]

2 b f Exit To Nowhere (USA) 8.7f **(77)** - Passerella (FR) (Brustolon)
Form - 0
Record 2000 - 1st:0 2nd:0 3rd:0 Ran:1
2000 Turf 0-1: (7f) (g-f)
Currently poor filly. **J G FitzGerald [0-1] Tony Fawcett.*

BOSPORUS (IRE) RR 100f 4411a[2]

5 ch h Night Shift (USA) 8.1f **(73)** - Rain Again (Relko) 9.9f **(59)**
Form - 2
2000 Turf 0-1: (8f) (gd)
Currently very useful colt. **M Yuksel in TUR [0-1].*

BOSRA BADGER BHB 60f57a RR 65f 57a 4724[8]

2 ch c Emarati (USA) 6.6f **(63)** - Mrs McBadger **(50f 45a)** (Weldnaas (USA))
Form - 000058
Record 2000 - 1st:0 2nd:0 3rd:0 Ran:6
2000 Turf 0-6: (5f 3, 6f 3) (gd 3, g-f, frm 2)
Average colt. Turf high 65. **Mrs L C Jewell [0-6] Godelpus.*

BOSSCAT BHB 48f RR 61f 5162[12]

3 b g Presidium 7.5f **(56)** - Belltina (Belfort (FR)) 6.8f **(63)**
Form - 05000
Record 2000 - 1st:0 2nd:0 3rd:0 Ran:5
Pre2000 - 1st:0 2nd:0 3rd:0 Ran:4
2000 Turf 0-5: (7f, 10f 3, 11f) (sft, gd 2, g-f, frm)
Scopey, average gelding, has worn blinkers. Turf high 61 (began Jly). Inconsistent.
**K McAuliffe [0-9] Boss Racing.*

BOSS TWEED (IRE) BHB 56f54a RR 65f 54a 4814[7]

3 b g Persian Bold 10f **(69)** - Betty Kenwood **(43f 35a)** (Dominion) 8.5f **(63)**
Form - 011431050307
Record 2000 - 1st:3 2nd:0 3rd:2 Ran:11
Pre2000 - 1st:0 2nd:0 3rd:0 Ran:4
Win Prizemoney £7,126 *Total Prizemoney* £7,858
Wins * 2000 Apr Ripon (SFT) H 10f 59 65 <
**** 2000** Jan Lingfi (STD) H 8f 52 62+*
***2000** Jan Southw (STD) S 8f 60+*
2000 Turf 1-6: (8f, 10f 1-5) (g-s 2, gd 1-4) 2000 AW 2-5: (8f 2-3, 11f 2) (Equi 1-1, Fibr 1-4)
Scopey, average gelding, effective 8 to 10f, best at 8f, acts on gd - acts on AW, likes tight tracks. Turf high 65 (1st run) - 1st of 25 giving 5lb to Blue Hawaii (5 Apr Ripon RF 0622). AW high 62 - 1st of 8 giving 3lb to Legendaire (19 Jan Lingfield RF 0116) - also 1st of 11 giving 5lb to Imari (10 Jan Southwell RF 0064). Inconsistent.
**Ronald Thompson [2-10] B Bruce (from G C Bravery [1-5] Jan 2000).*

BOSSY SPICE BHB 33f RR 48f 2426[13]

3 br f Emperor Jones (USA) - Million Heiress (Auction Ring (USA)) 8.6f **(65)**
Form - 0000
Record 2000 - 1st:0 2nd:0 3rd:0 Ran:4
Pre2000 - 1st:0 2nd:0 3rd:0 Ran:4
2000 Turf 0-4: (10f, 12f, 13f, 14f) (gd, g-f, frm 2)
Light-framed, moderate filly, has worn blinkers. Turf high 48.
**N M Babbage [0-6] B Babbage (from M R Channon [0-2] Apr 1999).*

BOTTELINO JOE (IRE) BHB 40f RR 44f 4277[12]

3 b br g Bluebird (USA) 7.9f **(71)** - My-O-My (IRE) **(84f)** (Waajib)
Form - 00070
Record 2000 - 1st:0 2nd:0 3rd:0 Ran:5
Pre2000 - 1st:0 2nd:0 3rd:0 Ran:4
Win Prizemoney £0 *Total Prizemoney* £267
2000 Turf 0-4: (7f 4) (hvy, gd, g-f 2) 2000 AW 0-1: (7f) (Fibr)
Moderate gelding, has worn blinkers. Turf high 44.
**M S Saunders [0-9] Il Bottelino.*

BOUCHRA (IRE) BHB 70f64a **RR 74f 64a** 5320[21]
2 ch f Inchinor 8.9f **(64)** - My Darlingdaughter **(18f)** (Night Shift (USA)) 7.2f **(69)**
Form - 220360
Record 2000 - 1st:0 2nd:2 3rd:1 Ran:6
Win Prizemoney £0 *Total Prizemoney* £5,645
2000 Turf 0-6: (5f, 6f, 7f 3, 8f) (sft, gd, g-f 4)
Above-average filly, effective 6 to 7f, best at 7f, acts on g-f. Turf high 74 (began Aug) - 3rd of 22 getting 18lb from Palatial (26 Spt Newmarket 7f g-f RF 4642). **M L W Bell [0-6] Wafic Said.*

BOULDER (IRE) BHB 73f **RR 74f** 5104[9]
3 b c Bigstone (IRE) - Tendermark (Prince Tenderfoot (USA)) 9f **(61)**
Form - 6454440
Record 2000 - 1st:0 2nd:0 3rd:0 Ran:7
Win Prizemoney £0 *Total Prizemoney* £1,909
2000 Turf 0-7: (10f 3, 12f 2, 14f, 15f) (gd 3, g-f, frm 3)
Scopey, above-average colt, effective 10 to 14f, acted on gd to g-f, had worn blinkers. Turf high 74. (DEAD)
**L M Cumani [0-7] Anglia Bloodstock Syndicate 1998.*

BOUNCING BOWDLER BHB 100f **RR 102f** 4463[1]
2 b c Mujadil (USA) 7.7f **(70)** - Prima Volta **(65f)** (Primo Dominie) 6.2f **(80)**
Form - 322122211
Record 2000 - 1st:3 2nd:5 3rd:1 Ran:9
Win Prizemoney £51,524 *Total Prizemoney* £79,310

Wins	*** 2000**	Spt	Newbur	(G-F)	G2	6f	102	<
	*** 2000**	Aug	York	(GD)	L	5f	97	
	*** 2000**	May	Ripon	(GD)		5f	76+	

2000 Turf 3-9: (5f 2-8, 6f 1-1) (gd 4, g-f 2-4, frm 1-1)
Very useful colt, effective 5 to 6f, best at 5f, acts on g-f to frm, best on g-f. Turf high 102 - 1st of 7 from Pomfret Lad (16 Spt Newbury RF 4463) - also 1st of 7 from Senior Minister (23 Aug York RF 3916). Improving. Tough and speedy, he was extremely consistent in his first season and ended the campaign with victory in the Group Two Mill Reef Stakes, albeit a substandard version. That win proved he stays six furlongs, but he might find opportunities hard to come by at three. **M Johnston [3-9] Paul Dean.*

BOUND BHB 73f85a **RR 73f 85a** 5218[9]
2 b c Kris 10f **(75)** - Tender Moment (IRE) (Caerleon (USA)) 8.6f **(71)**
Form - 0003610
Record 2000 - 1st:1 2nd:0 3rd:1 Ran:7
Win Prizemoney £2,737 *Total Prizemoney* £3,804

Wins	*** 2000**	*Oct*	*Wolver*	*(STD)*	*9.4f*	*73+*	<

2000 Turf 0-6: (7f 3, 8f 3) (sft, g-s, g-f 2, frm 2) 2000 AW 1-1: (9f 1-1) (Fibr 1-1)
Above-average colt, effective 8 to 9f, best at 8f, acts on g-s to frm - acts on Fibr, prefers tight tracks. Turf high 73 (began Jly) - 3rd of 13 getting 3lb from Flit About (4 Spt Bath 8f frm RF 4203). (1st run) - 1st of 8 giving 5lb to Kestle Imp (20 Oct Wolverhampton RF 5114). **B W Hills [1-7] Ray Richards.*

BOUND FOR PLEASURE (IRE) BHB 91f **RR 92+f** 4740[24]
4 gr c Barathea (IRE) - Dazzlingly Radiant (Try My Best (USA)) 7.6f **(67)**
Form - 23110
Record 2000 - 1st:2 2nd:1 3rd:1 Ran:5
Pre2000 - 1st:1 2nd:1 3rd:0 Ran:7
Win Prizemoney £27,087 *Total Prizemoney* £33,019

Wins	*** 2000**	Spt	Doncas	(G-F)	H	10.3f	86	92	<
	*** 2000**	Aug	Goodwo	(GD)	H	9f	75	88	
	1998	Oct	Lingfi	(HVY)		7f		82	

2000 Turf 2-5: (8f, 9f 1-3, 10f 1-1) (gd 1-2, g-f 2, frm 1-1)
Scopey, useful colt, effective 9 to 10f, acts on gd to frm, has worn blinkers. Turf high 92 (began Jly) - 1st of 19 giving 3lb to Air Defence (9 Spt Doncaster RF 4311) - also 1st of 14 giving 12lb to Thatchmaster (26 Aug Goodwood RF 3982). In good heart in the summer, he ran very well at Glorious Goodwood and bolted up in an amateur riders' event at the same track next time. Continued his improvement to win a valuable Doncaster handicap.
**J H M Gosden [2-5] Action Bloodstock (from G L Moore [1-7] Jun 1999).*

BOUND TO PLEASE BHB 51f62a **RR 56f 62a** 5245[10]
5 b g Warrshan (USA) 9.7f **(59)** - Hong Kong Girl (Petong) 6.6f **(58)**
Form - 13110
Record 2000 - 1st:2 2nd:0 3rd:0 Ran:3
Pre2000 - 1st:1 2nd:1 3rd:1 Ran:14
Win Prizemoney £6,357 *Total Prizemoney* £7,792

Wins	*** 2000**	Oct	Windso	(G-S)	H	6f	48	52	
	*** 2000**	*Jan*	*Southw*	*(STD)*	*H*	*7f*	*55*	*63*	<
	* 1999	*Nov*	*Southw*	*(STD)*	*H*	*7f*	*48*	*61*	

2000 Turf 1-1: (6f 1-1) (g-f 1-1) 2000 AW 1-2: (7f 1-2) (Fibr 1-2)
Average gelding, effective 7f, - acts on Fibr. (1st run). AW high 63 (1st run) - 1st of 9 giving 2lb to Aberkeen (10 Jan Southwell RF 0060). Inconsistent. **P J Makin [3-17] Mrs P J Makin.*

BOURGAINVILLE BHB 97f **RR 83+f** 4733[10]
2 b c Pivotal - Petonica (IRE) (Petoski) 5.7f **(62)**
Form - 110
Record 2000 - 1st:2 2nd:0 3rd:0 Ran:3
Win Prizemoney £9,276 *Total Prizemoney* £9,276

Wins	*** 2000**	Spt	Kempto	(GD)	7f	83+	<
	*** 2000**	Aug	Salisb	(G-F)	7f	81+	

2000 Turf 2-3: (7f 2-3) (gd, g-f 1-1, frm 1-1)
Currently decent colt. Turf high 83 (began Aug) - also 1st of 8 from Azkaban (2 Spt Kempton RF 4163). Won an ordinary race at Salisbury on his debut, but was very impressive when following up in a Kempton conditions event. Faded disappointingly in a Group Three on his final run, but may have had excuses and should be given the chance to atone.
**I A Balding [2-3] Robert Hitchins.*

BOURGEOIS RR 103f 3940a[2]
3 ch c Sanglamore (USA) 12.9f **(67)** - Bourbon Girl (Ile de Bourbon (USA)) 10.1f **(67)**
Form - 32
2000 Turf 0-2: (13f, 15f) (gd, g-f)
Currently very useful colt. Turf high 103 (1st run) - 3rd of 5 to Lycitus (28 Jun Chantilly 13f gd RF 2577a).
**Mme C Head in FR [0-2].*

BOURKAN BHB 68f **RR 68f** 3434[4]
3 gr c Linamix (FR) 8.2f **(64)** - North Wind (IRE) (Lomond (USA)) 8.8f **(65)**
Form - 874
Record 2000 - 1st:0 2nd:0 3rd:0 Ran:3
Win Prizemoney £0 *Total Prizemoney* £270
2000 Turf 0-3: (10f, 11f, 14f) (g-s 2, frm)
Strong, currently average colt. Turf high 68.
**A C Stewart [0-3] Sheikh Ahmed Al Maktoum.*

BOUTRON (FR) RR 108f 3347a[1]
3 b c Exit To Nowhere (USA) 8.7f **(77)** - Vindelonde (FR) (No Lute (FR))
Form - 2241
2000 Turf 1-4: (9f 1-2, 10f, 11f) (hvy, sft 1-1, g-s, gd)
Pattern-class colt, effective 9 to 11f, best at 9f, acts on hvy to g-s. Turf high 108 - also 1st of 8 from Crystal D'Ass (25 Jly Chantilly RF 3347a). **P Costes in FR [2-6] Gary Tanaka.*

BOWCLIFFE BHB 60f60a **RR 60f 60a** 4194[21]
9 b g Petoski 10.4f **(56)** - Gwiffina (Welsh Saint) 7.6f **(64)**
Form - 843682210010
Record 2000 - 1st:2 2nd:2 3rd:1 Ran:12
Pre2000 - 1st:7 2nd:7 3rd:5 Ran:62
Win Prizemoney £43,140 *Total Prizemoney* £68,611

Wins	*** 2000**	Aug	Redcar	(FRM)		8f		44	
	*** 2000**	Jun	Carlis	(G-F)		8f		60	
	* 1999	Apr	Mussel	(G-F)		8f		66	
	* 1998	Spt	Doncas	(GD)	H	8f	62	68	<
	* 1998	*Jan*	*Wolver*	*(STD)*	*H*	*9.4f*	*63*	*62+*	
	* 1997	Jly	Carlis	(GD)	H	8f	51	62	
	* 1997	Jun	Pontef	(G-F)	H	8f	46	54	
	1996	May	Mussel	(G-S)	H	8.1f	44	50	

2000 Turf 2-8: (8f 2-4, 9f 3, 10f) (g-s, g-f 1-3, frm 1-4) 2000 AW 0-4: (8f, 9f 3) (Fibr 4)
Average gelding, effective 8 to 10f, best at 8f, acts on g-f to frm - acts on Fibr, has worn blinkers, likes right handed tracks, excels at Musselburgh. Turf high 60 - 2nd of 9 giving 6lb to Agiotage (19 Jun Musselburgh 9f frm RF 2095) - also 1st of 7 from Sparky (29 Jun Carlisle RF 2367). AW high 68 - 4th of 7 giving 14lb to Areish (3 Feb Wolverhampton 9f Fibr RF 0210). A winner twice over a mile last season, he is suited by a strongly-run race and fast ground.

**E J Alston [7-58] Philip Davies (from Mrs A M Naughton [1-9] Nov 1996).*

BOWCLIFFE GRANGE (IRE) BHB 28f32a **RR 27f 32a**3931[5]

8 b g Dominion Royale 7.8f **(63)** - Cala-Vadella (Mummy's Pet) 7.7f **(60)**
Form - 2808003006085
Record 2000 - 1st:0 2nd:0 3rd:1 Ran:9
Pre2000 - 1st:6 2nd:4 3rd:7 Ran:59
Win Prizemoney £16,494 *Total Prizemoney* £23,930
Wins * 1999 Spt Hamilt (G-F) H 5f 35 36
* 1999 *Mar Lingfi (STD) H 5f 37 40*
* 1996 Jly Doncas (G-F) H 5f 44 50 <
* 1996 Jly Windso (G-F) H 5f 44 50 <
* 1996 Jun Lingfi (FRM) H 5f 34 39
* 1996 Jun Beverl (G-F) H 5f 23 25
2000 Turf 0-6: (5f 6) (gd 2, g-f, frm 3) 2000 AW 0-3: (5f 3) (Equi, Fibr 2)
Little account gelding, effective 5f, acts on frm - acts on Equi, has worn blinkers. Turf high 27. AW high 26.
**D W Chapman [6-67] David Chapman (from J Hanson [0-1] Oct 1994).*

BOWFELL BHB 63f60a **RR 62f 60a** 5295[1]

2 b f Alflora (IRE) - April City **(30a)** (Lidhame) 9.2f **(50)**
Form - 0601
Record 2000 - 1st:1 2nd:0 3rd:0 Ran:4
Win Prizemoney £2,268 *Total Prizemoney* £2,268
Wins * 2000 Nov Mussel (G-S) H 5f 58 62 <
2000 Turf 1-4: (5f 1-1, 6f 2, 7f) (g-s 1-1, gd, frm 2)
Average filly. Turf high 62 - 1st of 10 giving 3lb to Grand Houdini (1 Nov Musselburgh RF 5295). **C Smith [1-4] & Mrs T I Gourley.*

BOWLERS BOY BHB 62f66a **RR 62f 66a** 5083[1]

7 ch g Risk Me (FR) 8f **(53)** - Snow Wonder (Music Boy) 6.8f **(57)**
Form - 7241215403521
Record 2000 - 1st:3 2nd:3 3rd:1 Ran:13
Pre2000 - 1st:7 2nd:8 3rd:5 Ran:61
Win Prizemoney £35,872 *Total Prizemoney* £53,779
Wins * 2000 Oct Newcas (HVY) H 6f 56 62
*** 2000** Jun Hamilt (GD) H 6f 52 56
*** 2000** Jun Carlis (SFT) H 5f 52 56
* 1998 Nov Redcar (G-S) 5f 65
* 1998 Oct Pontef (SFT) H 5f 68 74 <
* 1998 Jun Pontef (SFT) H 6f 68 70
* 1997 Aug Ripon (GD) H 6f 67 71
* 1997 Jly Beverl (HVY) H 5f 66 68
* 1996 Spt Pontef (G-F) H 5f 68 69
* 1996 Jly Pontef (G-F) 6f 64
2000 Turf 3-13: (5f 1-4, 6f 2-8, 7f) (hvy 1-1, g-s, gd 5, g-f 2-4, frm 2)
Average gelding, effective 5 to 6f, best at 5f, acts on hvy to frm, has worn blinkers, likes Pontefract. Turf high 62 - 1st of 19 giving 22lb to Superfrills (19 Oct Newcastle RF 5083) - also 1st of 12 giving 9lb to Dazzling Quintet (5 Jun Carlisle RF 1714).
**J J Quinn [10-74] Bowlers Racing.*

BOW PEEP (IRE) BHB 51f62a **RR 54f 62a** 4558[15]

5 b br m Shalford (IRE) 7.8f **(63)** - Gale Force Seven (Strong Gale) 5.6f **(66)**
Form - 124080
Record 2000 - 1st:1 2nd:1 3rd:0 Ran:6
Pre2000 - 1st:2 2nd:0 3rd:0 Ran:17
Win Prizemoney £9,701 *Total Prizemoney* £11,387
Wins * 2000 Mar Mussel (GD) H 5f 46 48
* 1998 Jly Nottin (G-F) 5.1f 63 <
* 1998 Jly Ripon (GD) H 6f 60 63 <
2000 Turf 1-6: (5f 1-4, 6f 2) (g-s, gd 1-2, frm 3)
Fair filly, effective 5 to 6f, acts on g-s to gd, has worn blinkers (very effectively). Turf high 54 - 2nd of 23 to Amber Brown (14 Apr Thirsk 6f g-s RF 0724) - also 1st of 12 getting 16lb from Aa-Youknownothing (30 Mar Musselburgh RF 0571). In good form in 2000, she is effective at five and six furlongs.
**M W Easterby [3-23] Mrs Anne Jarvis.*

BOW STRADA BHB 80f **RR 81f** 5104[14]

3 ch c Rainbow Quest (USA) 11.2f **(81)** - La Strada (Niniski (USA)) 10.6f **(65)**
Form - 570
Record 2000 - 1st:0 2nd:0 3rd:0 Ran:3
Pre2000 - 1st:2 2nd:0 3rd:0 Ran:2
Win Prizemoney £8,774 *Total Prizemoney* £8,774
Wins * 1999 Oct Leices (G-S) 10f 86 <
* 1999 Aug Yarmou (GD) 8f 79+
2000 Turf 0-3: (10f, 12f, 15f) (g-s, gd, g-f)
Scopey, decent colt. Turf high 81.
**P W Harris [2-5] Doolan, Haygarth, Rice & Strachan.*

BOXBERRY BHB 34f **RR 38f** 2743[11]

3 b f Owington - Chatterberry (Aragon) 8.1f **(60)**
Form - 400
Record 2000 - 1st:0 2nd:0 3rd:0 Ran:3
Pre2000 - 1st:0 2nd:0 3rd:0 Ran:5
Win Prizemoney £0 *Total Prizemoney* £263
2000 Turf 0-3: (5f 2, 7f) (g-f, frm 2)
Light-framed, very moderate filly, has worn blinkers. Turf high 38. Inconsistent. **N A Callaghan [0-8] Peter Bickmore.*

BOX BUILDER BHB 80f **RR 90f** 5111[9]

3 ch c Fraam - Ena Olley (Le Moss)
Form - 33514480
Record 2000 - 1st:1 2nd:0 3rd:2 Ran:8
Win Prizemoney £4,173 *Total Prizemoney* £7,290
Wins * 2000 Jly Sandow (GD) 14f 85 <
2000 Turf 1-8: (11f, 12f, 14f 1-4, 15f, 16f) (g-s, gd 1-3, g-f 4)
Workmanlike, useful colt, effective 11 to 14f, best at 14f, acts on g-s to g-f. Turf high 90 - 4th of 8 giving 4lb to Fanfare (5 Aug Goodwood 14f g-f RF 3396) - also 1st of 7 from Takwin (7 Jly Sandown RF 2608). Beat Takwin in a Sandown maiden before a decent effort at Goodwood. A mile and three-quarters seems his trip. **M R Channon [1-8] M Hutchinson.*

BOX CAR (IRE) BHB 54f **RR 67f** 4621[7]

3 b g Blues Traveller (IRE) - Racey Naskra (USA) (Star de Naskra (USA)) 9.7f **(65)**
Form - 625322006087
Record 2000 - 1st:0 2nd:2 3rd:1 Ran:10
Pre2000 - 1st:0 2nd:1 3rd:0 Ran:6
Win Prizemoney £0 *Total Prizemoney* £4,246
2000 Turf 0-8: (9f, 10f 2, 12f 5) (g-s, gd 3, g-f 2, frm 2) 2000 AW 0-2: (10f 2) (Equi 2)
Workmanlike, average gelding, effective 12f, acts on g-s to g-f, likes tight tracks. Turf high 67 - 2nd of 12 getting 20lb from River Bann (8 May Windsor 12f g-f RF 1100). AW high 58.
**G L Moore [0-16] R Kiernan.*

BOY BAND (IRE) **RR 50f** 5237[6]

2 b c Desert Style (IRE) - Arab Scimetar (IRE) (Sure Blade (USA)) 11.3f **(67)**
Form - 06
Record 2000 - 1st:0 2nd:0 3rd:0 Ran:2
2000 Turf 0-2: (8f 2) (g-s, g-f)
Currently fair colt. Turf high 50 (began Spt).
**M R Channon [0-2] John Livock.*

BRADY BOYS (USA) **RR 80f** 5062[2]

3 b g Cozzene (USA) 10.1f **(87)** - Elvia (USA) (Roberto (USA)) 10f **(76)**
Form - 02
Record 2000 - 1st:0 2nd:1 3rd:0 Ran:2
Win Prizemoney £0 *Total Prizemoney* £1,060
2000 Turf 0-2: (10f 2) (sft, g-s)
Scopey, currently decent gelding, often wears blinkers. Turf high 80 (began Spt) - 2nd of 8 giving 5lb to Eaton Place (18 Oct Nottingham 10f sft RF 5062). **J H M Gosden [0-2] Harry Taylor.*

BRAINWAVE **RR 55f** 4724[4]

2 b f Mind Games - Thorner Lane (Tina's Pet) 6.8f **(59)**
Form - 4
Record 2000 - 1st:0 2nd:0 3rd:0 Ran:1
Win Prizemoney £0 *Total Prizemoney* £300
2000 Turf 0-1: (5f) (gd)
Currently fair filly. **H Candy [0-1] Henry Candy & Partners.*

BRAITHWELL BHB 54f49a **RR 58f 49a** 4770[16]

2 b c Mujadil (USA) 7.7f **(70)** - Promise Fulfilled (USA) **(72df 61a)** (Bet Twice (USA))
Form - 0770
Record 2000 - 1st:0 2nd:0 3rd:0 Ran:4
2000 Turf 0-4: (5f 3, 6f) (g-s, g-f 2, frm)

Fair colt. Turf high 58. **T D Easterby [0-4] A K Smeaton.*

BRAMBLE BEAR BHB 57f51a **RR 60f 51a** 4825[18]

6 b m Beveled (USA) 6.9f **(64)** - Supreme Rose (Frimley Park) 6.5f **(67)**
Form - 466267710483323610
Record 2000 - 1st:2 2nd:2 3rd:3 Ran:18
Pre2000 - 1st:4 2nd:3 3rd:8 Ran:43
Win Prizemoney £19,501 *Total Prizemoney* £32,420
Wins * 2000 Spt Bright (SFT) H 6f 50 60
*** 2000** May Bright (G-S) H 6f 47 49
* 1998 May Lingfi (GD) H 5f 65 72 <
* 1997 May Catter (G-F) H 5f 62 67
* 1997 May Windso (SFT) H 5f 62 64
* 1996 Jly Bath (FRM) 5.1f 67
2000 Turf 2-14: (5f 3, 6f 2-11) (gd 2-5, g-f 4, frm 4, hrd) 2000 AW 0-4: (5f 2, 6f 2) (Equi 4)
Average mare, effective 5 to 6f, best at 5f, acts on gd to frm, best on gd, does well at Brighton. Turf high 60 - 1st of 16 getting 17lb from Doctor Dennis (24 Spt Brighton RF 4618). AW high 48.
**M Blanshard [6-61] Vino Veritas.*

BRAMBLES WAY BHB 28f44a **RR 42f 44a** 3062[8]

11 ch g Clantime 6.6f **(57)** - Streets Ahead (Ovid) 10f **(32)**
Form - 8
Record 2000 - 1st:0 2nd:0 3rd:0 Ran:1
Pre2000 - 1st:3 2nd:4 3rd:4 Ran:47
Win Prizemoney £8,439 *Total Prizemoney* £12,888
Wins 1997 Oct Newcas (G-F) H 10.1f 45 53
1997 Apr Beverl (G-F) H 9.9f 50 54 <
1996 Spt Redcar (FRM) SH 10f 41 49
2000 Turf 0-1: (11f) (frm)
Moderate gelding, has worn blinkers. Becoming disappointing.
**Miss Lucinda Russell [0-8] The Pharkula Partnership (from F Jordan [1-8] Jun 1999).*

BRAM STOKER (IRE) BHB 100f **RR 101f** 4699[7]

2 ch c General Monash (USA) - Taniokey (Grundy) 10.3f **(65)**
Form - 211233337
Record 2000 - 1st:2 2nd:2 3rd:4 Ran:9
Win Prizemoney £6,292 *Total Prizemoney* £38,509
Wins * 2000 May Nottin (G-S) 6.1f 80+
*** 2000** Apr Doncas (G-S) 5f 91 <
2000 Turf 2-9: (5f 1-2, 6f 1-7) (hvy, gd 2-5, g-f 2, frm)
Very useful colt, effective 5 to 6f, best at 6f, acts on hvy to g-f. Turf high 101. Consistent. In the frame in Pattern races, he was a smart juvenile and more races will surely come his way, though possibly at a slightly lower level. His wins have been when the ground has been on the easy side.
**R Hannon [2-9] Alessandro Gaucci.*

BRANCASTER (USA) BHB 107f **RR 108df** 2762[2]

4 br c Riverman (USA) 9.7f **(78)** - Aseltine's Angels (USA) (Fappiano (USA)) 8.7f **(77)**
Form - 52
Record 2000 - 1st:0 2nd:1 3rd:0 Ran:2
Pre2000 - 1st:2 2nd:1 3rd:0 Ran:6
Win Prizemoney £23,793 *Total Prizemoney* £47,200
Wins 1998 Oct Newbur (HVY) G3 7.3f 104 <
1998 Spt Haydoc (G-F) 7.1f 94++
2000 Turf 0-2: (9f, 10f) (gd 2)
Leggy, Pattern-class colt, effective 8 to 9f, best at 8f, acts on gd to frm, has worn blinkers. Turf high 108 (1st run) - 5th of 11 to Indian Lodge (19 Apr Newmarket 9f gd RF 0795). High-class at two and three, he ran just twice for his new yard in 2000, running a good race at Sandown but beaten at odds-on in a minor race next time.
**Sir Michael Stoute [0-2] The Royal Ascot Racing Club (from P W Chapple-Hyam [2-6] Jun 1999).*

BRAND NEW DAY (IRE) **RR 9f** 5310[18]

2 b c Robellino (USA) 9.5f **(68)** - Nawaji (USA) **(40f 40a)** (Trempolino (USA)) 12f **(71)**
Form - 00
Record 2000 - 1st:0 2nd:0 3rd:0 Ran:2
2000 Turf 0-2: (6f, 7f) (sft, g-s)
Currently very poor colt. Turf high 9 (began Oct).
**D W P Arbuthnot [0-2] Banfield Cronin Thompson.*

BRANDON MAGIC BHB 40f41a **RR 48f 41a** 3423[5]

7 ch g Primo Dominie 7.2f **(67)** - Silk Stocking (Pardao) 8.6f **(60)**
Form - 00385575
Record 2000 - 1st:0 2nd:0 3rd:1 Ran:8
Pre2000 - 1st:4 2nd:4 3rd:3 Ran:25
Win Prizemoney £17,803 *Total Prizemoney* £36,460
Wins * 1999 *Feb Southw (STD) C 8f 37*
2000 Turf 0-5: (8f 3, 9f, 10f) (gd, g-f, frm 3) 2000 AW 0-3: (8f 2, 12f) (Fibr 3)
Moderate gelding, effective 8 to 9f, acts on frm, has worn blinkers. Turf high 48 (1st run) - 3rd of 17 getting 4lb from Almazhar (2 Jun Ayr 8f frm RF 1642). AW high 17.
**D Nicholls [1-10] The David Nicholls Racing Club (from I A Balding [3-26] Aug 1997).*

BRANDON ROCK BHB 62f **RR 73df** 5068[16]

3 b g Robellino (USA) 9.5f **(68)** - The Kings Daughter (Indian King (USA)) 7.4f **(64)**
Form - 000
Record 2000 - 1st:0 2nd:0 3rd:0 Ran:3
Pre2000 - 1st:1 2nd:0 3rd:0 Ran:4
Win Prizemoney £3,777 *Total Prizemoney* £3,777
Wins * 1999 Spt Sandow (G-F) 5f 82 <
2000 Turf 0-3: (5f 2, 6f) (g-s, gd, g-f)
Strong, above-average gelding, effective 5f, acts on gd. Turf high 61.
**I A Balding [1-7] R P B Michaelson.*

BRANDONVILLE BHB 37f30a **RR 35f 30a** 1007[5]

7 b g Never so Bold 7.1f **(62)** - Enduring (Sadler's Wells (USA)) 10f **(76)**
Form - 0007005
Record 2000 - 1st:0 2nd:0 3rd:0 Ran:5
Pre2000 - 1st:2 2nd:0 3rd:0 Ran:18
Win Prizemoney £6,113 *Total Prizemoney* £6,848
Wins 1997 Jly Haydoc (G-S) H 7.1f 56 60 <
* 1997 May Ayr (SFT) H 7f 52 56
2000 Turf 0-3: (8f 3) (hvy, g-s, g-f) 2000 AW 0-2: (7f, 8f) (Fibr 2)
Very moderate gelding. Turf high 35. AW high 22. Inconsistent.
**N Tinkler [2-20] Philip Grundy (from I A Balding [0-3] Oct 1995).*

BRANDON WIZZARD (IRE) **RR 73f** 4365[2]

2 b c Tagula (IRE) - Topmost (IRE) (Top Ville) 11.7f **(68)**
Form - 002
Record 2000 - 1st:0 2nd:1 3rd:0 Ran:3
Win Prizemoney £0 *Total Prizemoney* £1,259
2000 Turf 0-3: (5f, 6f 2) (g-s, g-f, frm)
Currently above-average colt. Turf high 73 (began Aug) - 2nd of 19 to Prince Pyramus (13 Spt Beverley 5f g-f RF 4365).
**I A Balding [0-3] R P B Michaelson.*

BRANDY COVE BHB 69f **RR 50f** 5158[2]

3 b c Lugana Beach 7f **(63)** - Tender Moment (IRE) (Caerleon (USA)) 8.6f **(71)**
Form - 02
Record 2000 - 1st:0 2nd:1 3rd:0 Ran:2
Win Prizemoney £0 *Total Prizemoney* £1,420
2000 Turf 0-2: (8f, 10f) (sft, g-f)
Lengthy, currently fair colt. Turf high 50 (began Spt).
**B Smart [0-2] Miss N Jefford.*

BRANICKI (IRE) **RR 80+f** 4472[1]

2 b f Spectrum (IRE) - Karinski (USA) (Palace Music (USA))
Form - 31
Record 2000 - 1st:1 2nd:0 3rd:1 Ran:2
Win Prizemoney £5,525 *Total Prizemoney* £6,061
Wins * 2000 Spt Newmar (SFT) 8f 80+ <
2000 Turf 1-2: (8f 1-2) (g-f 1-1, frm)
Currently decent filly. Turf high 80 (began Aug) - 1st of 5 from Guaranda (16 Spt Newmarket RF 4472).
**J H M Gosden [1-2] R E Sangster.*

BRANSTON FIZZ BHB 73f72a **RR 74+f 72a** 4449[14]

3 b f Efisio 7.7f **(69)** - Tuxford Hideaway (Cawston's Clown) 8f **(60)**
Form - 347017100
Record 2000 - 1st:2 2nd:0 3rd:0 Ran:8
Pre2000 - 1st:0 2nd:2 3rd:1 Ran:3
Win Prizemoney £6,316 *Total Prizemoney* £8,666
Wins * 2000 Aug Yarmou (G-F) H 7f 65 74+ <

* 2000 *Jly Southw (STD) 6f 71*
2000 Turf 1-7: (5f 2, 6f 2, 7f 1-2, 8f) (sft, g-s, gd 1-2, frm 2, hrd) 2000 AW 1-1: (6f 1-1) (Fibr 1-1)
Neat, above-average filly, effective 6 to 7f, best at 6f, acts on gd - acts on Fibr. Turf high 74 - 1st of 9 getting 5lb from Sea Drift (27 Aug Yarmouth RF 4024). (1st run) - 1st of 11 from Layan (28 Jly Southwell RF 3188). **M Johnston [2-11] David Abell.*

BRANSTON GEM BHB 61f55a **RR 63f 55a** 5295[4]
2 br f So Factual (USA) - Branston Jewel (IRE) **(87f)** (Prince Sabo) 7.2f **(62)**
Form - 085024
Record 2000 - 1st:0 2nd:1 3rd:0 Ran:6
Win Prizemoney £0 *Total Prizemoney* £530
2000 Turf 0-4: (5f 3, 6f)(g-s, gd, g-f, frm) 2000 AW 0-2: (5f 2)(Equi, Fibr)
Average filly, effective 5f, acts on g-s - acts on Equi. Turf high 63 (began Aug). AW high 56 (began Spt) - 2nd of 10 getting 5lb from Pat The Builder (11 Oct Lingfield 5f Equi RF 4927).
**M Johnston [0-6] David Abell.*

BRANSTON LUCY BHB 53f46a **RR 58f 46a** 4992[9]
3 b f Prince Sabo 6.6f **(64)** - Softly Spoken (Mummy's Pet) 7.7f **(60)**
Form - 008212243000
Record 2000 - 1st:1 2nd:3 3rd:1 Ran:12
Pre2000 - 1st:1 2nd:0 3rd:1 Ran:5
Win Prizemoney £5,759 *Total Prizemoney* £8,964
Wins 2000 Jly Mussel (G-S) H 5f 55 56
1999 Spt Redcar (G-F) H 5f 56 62 <
2000 Turf 1-9: (5f 1-8, 6f) (gd 1-1, g-f 5, frm 3) 2000 AW 0-3: (5f, 6f 2) (Fibr 3)
Leggy, fair filly, effective 5f, acts on gd to frm - acts on Fibr, has worn blinkers. Turf high 58 - 2nd of 9 getting 3lb from Pleasure Time (4 Aug Nottingham 5f g-f RF 3375) - also 1st of 14 getting 2lb from Garnock Valley (10 Jly Musselburgh RF 2671). AW high 59 - 4th of 11 giving 3lb to Sotonian (11 Aug Wolverhampton 5f Fibr RF 3570).
**J Pearce [0-3] Mrs Jennifer Marsh (from M Johnston [0-1] Aug 2000).*

BRANSTON PICKLE BHB 59f74a **RR 62f 74a** 5188[6]
3 ch g Piccolo - Indefinite Article (IRE) (Indian Ridge)
Form - 120007008120006
Record 2000 - 1st:1 2nd:2 3rd:0 Ran:14
Pre2000 - 1st:3 2nd:0 3rd:1 Ran:10
Win Prizemoney £10,932 *Total Prizemoney* £14,835
Wins * 2000 Spt Hamilt (SFT) H 5f 59 61+
1999 *Nov Wolver (STD) C 6f 78*
1999 Nov Catter (SFT) H 6f 69 80 <
1999 *Oct Wolver (STD) S 5f 69*
2000 Turf 1-11: (5f 1-10, 6f) (sft, g-s, gd 1-6, g-f 2, frm) 2000 AW 0-3: (6f 3) (Fibr 3)
Workmanlike, above-average gelding, effective 6f, acts on g-s - acts on Fibr, has worn blinkers, prefers left handed tracks, prefers tight tracks. Turf high 61. AW high 80 (1st run) - 2nd of 11 giving 8lb to Feast of Romance (6 Jan Wolverhampton 6f Fibr RF 0036).
**M Johnston [1-7] David Abell (from T J Etherington [3-17] Aug 2000).*

BRATBY (IRE) BHB 33f35a **RR 35a** 2031[12]
4 b g Distinctly North (USA) 7.4f **(63)** - Aridje (Mummy's Pet) 7.7f **(60)**
Form - 800
Record 2000 - 1st:0 2nd:0 3rd:0 Ran:3
Pre2000 - 1st:1 2nd:0 3rd:0 Ran:12
Win Prizemoney £1,891 *Total Prizemoney* £1,891
Wins 1999 *Jan Lingfi (STD) H 8f 42 44* <
2000 Turf 0-1: (6f) (g-s) 2000 AW 0-2: (7f, 12f) (Fibr 2)
Light-framed, very poor gelding, effective 8f, - acts on Equi, likes left handed tracks, likes tight tracks.
**M C Chapman [0-4] W P Gaff (from D R C Elsworth [0-4] Oct 1999).*

BRAVADO BHB 102f **RR 95f** 3024[3]
2 b c Zafonic (USA) 9f **(83)** - Brave Revival **(93f)** (Dancing Brave (USA)) 8.4f **(76)**
Form - 1143
Record 2000 - 1st:2 2nd:0 3rd:1 Ran:4
Win Prizemoney £6,557 *Total Prizemoney* £10,251
Wins * 2000 Jly Doncas (GD) 6f 95+ <
*** 2000** *Jun Wolver (STD) 6f 77+*
2000 Turf 1-3: (6f 1-3) (gd, g-f 1-1, hrd) 2000 AW 1-1: (6f 1-1) (Fibr 1-1)
Very useful colt. Turf high 95 (1st run) (began Jly) - 1st of 3 giving 1lb to Kachina Doll (2 Jly Doncaster RF 2458). (1st run). He was placed to win two small events with plenty to spare and ran very well when upped in class in Newmarket's July Stakes. A little disappointing on fast ground on his final run in July.
**Sir Mark Prescott [2-4] Cheveley Park Stud.*

BRAVE BURT (IRE) BHB 90f **RR 87f** 2062[8]
3 ch c Pips Pride 6.7f **(70)** - Friendly Song (Song) 7.2f **(61)**
Form - 0388
Record 2000 - 1st:0 2nd:0 3rd:1 Ran:4
Pre2000 - 1st:2 2nd:0 3rd:1 Ran:4
Win Prizemoney £6,600 *Total Prizemoney* £11,417
Wins 1999 May Bath (GD) 5.1f 92 <
1999 May Carlis (FRM) 5f 81+
2000 Turf 0-4: (5f 2, 6f 2) (hvy, gd 2, frm)
Workmanlike, useful colt, effective 5f, acts on g-f. Turf high 87.
**D Nicholls [0-2] Lucayan Stud (from J Noseda [0-2] May 2000).*

BRAVE EDGE BHB 83f **RR 87f** 3395[28]
9 b g Beveled (USA) 6.9f **(64)** - Daring Ditty (Daring March) 7.1f **(61)**
Form - 03382304230
Record 2000 - 1st:0 2nd:2 3rd:4 Ran:11
Pre2000 - 1st:7 2nd:11 3rd:9 Ran:80
Win Prizemoney £58,267 *Total Prizemoney* £154,209
Wins * 1998 Jly Newbur (GD) H 6f 98 100
* 1997 Spt Hamilt (GD) 6f 90
* 1996 Jun Kempto (G-F) L 5f 107 <
2000 Turf 0-11: (5f, 6f 6, 7f 4) (hvy, g-s, gd 3, g-f 3, frm 3)
Useful gelding, effective 6 to 7f, best at 6f, acts on g-s to frm, excels at York and Newbury. Turf high 87 - 2nd of 14 giving 21lb to Dolphinelle (31 May Newbury 7f gd RF 1588). Consistent. He is a useful sprint handicapper, but is on a long losing run and difficult to win with. Effective on any ground, he has often gone well for Pat Eddery. **R Hannon [7-91] Horris Vale Racing Partnership.*

BRAVE KNIGHT BHB 46f **RR 45f** 4872[6]
3 b c Presidium 7.5f **(56)** - Agnes Jane (Sweet Monday) 8.3f **(25)**
Form - 36
Record 2000 - 1st:0 2nd:0 3rd:1 Ran:2
Pre2000 - 1st:0 2nd:0 3rd:0 Ran:1
Win Prizemoney £0 *Total Prizemoney* £780
2000 Turf 0-2: (8f, 10f) (hvy, frm)
Workmanlike, currently moderate colt. Turf high 42 (1st run) (began Aug) - 3rd of 10 to First Back (27 Aug Beverley 10f frm RF 4014). **N Bycroft [0-3] Piers Casimir-Mrowczynski.*

BRAVE TORNADO BHB 75f **RR 80f** 5111[8]
9 ch g Dominion 8.9f **(65)** - Accuracy (Gunner B) 11.2f **(58)**
Form - 12245378
Record 2000 - 1st:1 2nd:2 3rd:1 Ran:8
Pre2000 - 1st:2 2nd:0 3rd:0 Ran:9
Win Prizemoney £13,927 *Total Prizemoney* £22,519
Wins * 2000 Apr Newbur (SFT) H 16f 65 72
2000 Turf 1-8: (16f 1-6, 17f, 18f) (sft, g-s 1-2, gd 4, frm)
Decent gelding, effective 16 to 18f, best at 16f, acts on sft to frm, excels at Kempton. Turf high 80 - 2nd of 10 giving 3lb to Wave of Optimism (29 Apr Doncaster 17f gd RF 0910) - also 1st of 9 from Bridie's Pride (14 Apr Newbury RF 0717). Consistent. A fair sort over hurdles, he won on the Flat at Newbury in April and has run well since. Needs very soft ground.
**G B Balding [10-34] Miss B Swire.*

BRAVO RR 5f 5189[12]
2 b br c Efisio 7.7f **(69)** - Apache Squaw (Be My Guest (USA)) 9.3f **(67)**
Form - 0
Record 2000 - 1st:0 2nd:0 3rd:0 Ran:1
2000 Turf 0-1: (7f) (gd)
Currently very poor colt. **C W Thornton [0-1] Guy Reed.*

BRAVURA RR 51f 4808[14]
2 ch g Never so Bold 7.1f **(62)** - Sylvan Song (Song) 7.2f **(61)**
Form - 0080
Record 2000 - 1st:0 2nd:0 3rd:0 Ran:4
2000 Turf 0-4: (5f 3, 6f) (g-s, gd, frm 2)
Fair gelding. Turf high 51 (began Jly). **G L Moore [0-4] R Kiernan.*

BRAZILIAN MOOD (IRE) BHB 66f70a **RR 70f 70a** 2403[9]

4 b g Doyoun 10.7f **(69)** - Sea Mistress (Habitat) 9.4f **(70)**
Form - 1050
Record 2000 - 1st:0 2nd:0 3rd:0 Ran:2
Pre2000 - 1st:1 2nd:1 3rd:0 Ran:4
Win Prizemoney £2,879 *Total Prizemoney* £3,647
Wins * 1999 *Nov Lingfi (STD) 10f 58* <
2000 Turf 0-2: (10f 2) (g-f, frm)
Lengthy, above-average gelding, effective 10f, acts on frm. Turf high 66 (1st run) - 5th of 9 getting 13lb from Blue Gold (16 Jun Sandown 10f frm RF 2023). **C E Brittain [1-6] C E Brittain.*

BREAD WINNER BHB 54f58a **RR 57f 58a** 657[4]

4 b g Reprimand 8.2f **(63)** - Khubza (Green Desert (USA)) 8.6f **(78)**
Form - 422234
Record 2000 - 1st:0 2nd:3 3rd:1 Ran:6
Pre2000 - 1st:0 2nd:3 3rd:2 Ran:14
Win Prizemoney £0 *Total Prizemoney* £5,696
2000 Turf 0-1: (8f) (frm) 2000 AW 0-5: (7f, 8f 2, 9f 2) (Equi, Fibr 4)
Average gelding, effective 6 to 10f, acted on gd to frm - acted on Fibr, best on frm, often wore blinkers (effectively), excelled at Wolverhampton, liked Lingfield. AW high 60. (DEAD) **I A Balding [0-20] Anthony & Valerie Hogarth.*

BREAKFAST BAY (IRE) BHB 80f **RR 76f** 4643[14]

2 b br f Charnwood Forest (IRE) - Diavolina (USA) (Lear Fan (USA)) 8.5f **(73)**
Form - 310
Record 2000 - 1st:1 2nd:0 3rd:1 Ran:3
Win Prizemoney £4,407 *Total Prizemoney* £5,009
Wins * **2000** Aug Folkes (G-F) 7f 76 <
2000 Turf 1-3: (7f 1-3) (gd 1-1, g-f 2)
Currently above-average filly. Turf high 76 (began Jly) - 1st of 9 from Bogus Penny (24 Aug Folkestone RF 3920). Battled on well to win a Folkestone maiden by the minimum margin on her second start. **R Charlton [1-3] F M Alger.*

BREAKIN GLASS BHB 37f44a **RR 37f 44a** 3847[16]

3 b f Ardkinglass 5f **(64)** - Bee Dee Dancer (Ballacashtal (CAN)) 5.3f **(50)**
Form - 5540
Record 2000 - 1st:0 2nd:0 3rd:0 Ran:4
Win Prizemoney £0 *Total Prizemoney* £299
2000 Turf 0-4: (7f 2, 8f, 10f) (gd, g-f, frm, hrd)
Workmanlike, very moderate filly, has worn blinkers. Turf high 37. **A Bailey [0-4] Mrs Frank Campbell.*

BREAKING NEWS BHB 78f **RR 71f** 4726[2]

2 b c Emperor Jones (USA) - Music Khan (Music Boy) 6.8f **(57)**
Form - 382
Record 2000 - 1st:0 2nd:1 3rd:1 Ran:3
Win Prizemoney £0 *Total Prizemoney* £1,435
2000 Turf 0-3: (5f, 6f 2) (gd, frm 2)
Currently above-average colt. Turf high 71 (began Spt) - 2nd of 15 to Sunny Glenn (29 Spt Lingfield 6f gd RF 4726). **M A Jarvis [0-3] Jaber Abdullah.*

BREAK THE GLASS (USA) BHB 78f **RR 82f** 4680[3]

3 b br g Dynaformer (USA) 12f **(82)** - Greek Wedding (USA) (Blushing Groom (FR)) 10.3f **(76)**
Form - 3233
Record 2000 - 1st:0 2nd:1 3rd:3 Ran:4
Pre2000 - 1st:0 2nd:0 3rd:0 Ran:2
Win Prizemoney £0 *Total Prizemoney* £3,578
2000 Turf 0-4: (7f 2, 8f, 11f) (hvy, g-s, gd 2)
Scopey, decent gelding, effective 7 to 11f, best at 7f, acts on g-s to gd, best on gd. Turf high 82 - 3rd of 6 giving 5lb to Polar Red (26 May Haydock 11f g-s RF 1466). **E A L Dunlop [0-6] Maktoum Al Maktoum.*

BREAK THE RULES BHB 53f46a **RR 39f 46a** 3749[7]

8 b g Dominion 8.9f **(65)** - Surf Bird (Shareef Dancer (USA)) 9.9f **(73)**
Form - 77
Record 2000 - 1st:0 2nd:0 3rd:0 Ran:2
Pre2000 - 1st:8 2nd:5 3rd:6 Ran:46
Win Prizemoney £46,538 *Total Prizemoney* £57,166

Wins								
	1998	May	Cheste	(GD)	H	10.3f	66	71+
	1997	Jun	Cheste	(SFT)	C	10.3f		70
	1997	May	Cheste	(SFT)	H	10.3f	79	83 <
	1997	Mar	Doncas	(G-F)	H	10.3f	73	82
	1996	Oct	Doncas	(GD)	C	10.3f		79
	1996	Jly	Cheste	(G-F)	H	12.3f		68+

2000 Turf 0-1: (12f) (g-f) 2000 AW 0-1: (14f) (Fibr)
Very moderate gelding, has worn blinkers. Becoming disappointing.
**A G Juckes [0-10] Whistlejacket Partnership (from D Nicholls [1-22] Jun 1998).*

BREAKWATER (USA) BHB 73f **RR 79df** 2628[3]

3 b f Boundary (USA) - Flippers (USA) (Coastal (USA)) 11.5f **(72)**
Form - 453
Record 2000 - 1st:0 2nd:0 3rd:1 Ran:3
Pre2000 - 1st:0 2nd:0 3rd:0 Ran:2
Win Prizemoney £0 *Total Prizemoney* £1,120
2000 Turf 0-3: (7f 2, 8f) (gd, g-f, frm)
Scopey, above-average filly. Turf high 60.
**L M Cumani [0-5] Flippers Partnership.*

BREATHLESS DREAMS (IRE) BHB 74f **RR 75f** 1596[12]

3 ch c College Chapel - Foston Bridge (Relkino) 8.9f **(65)**
Form - 580
Record 2000 - 1st:0 2nd:0 3rd:0 Ran:3
Pre2000 - 1st:1 2nd:1 3rd:0 Ran:2
Win Prizemoney £2,495 *Total Prizemoney* £3,363
Wins 1999 Jun Salisb (FRM) 7f 75 <
2000 Turf 0-3: (8f, 10f 2) (sft, g-f 2)
Scopey, above-average colt. Turf high 71.
**S E Kettlewell [0-3] Cable Media Consultancy Ltd (from M L W Bell [1-2] Jun 1999).*

BREATHTAKING VIEW (USA) **RR 107f** 578a[8]

4 m
Form - 28
2000 Turf 0-2: (12f 2) (gd)
Currently Pattern-class. Turf high 107 (1st run) - 2nd of 7 getting 5lb from High-Rise (24 Feb Nad Al Sheba 12f RF 0426a). **S bin Suroor in UAE [0-2].*

BRECONGILL LAD BHB 85f **RR 85f** 4865[18]

8 b g Clantime 6.6f **(57)** - Chikala (Pitskelly) 8.5f **(53)**
Form - 303220031202300
Record 2000 - 1st:1 2nd:4 3rd:4 Ran:15
Pre2000 - 1st:7 2nd:7 3rd:11 Ran:61
Win Prizemoney £48,929 *Total Prizemoney* £82,431

Wins								
	* **2000**	Jly	Newcas	(G-F)	H	5f	77	80 <
	* 1999	Spt	Goodwo	(G-F)	H	6f	68	74
	* 1999	Aug	Yarmou	(GD)	H	5.2f	62	65+
	* 1999	Aug	Pontef	(GD)	H	5f	56	59+
	* 1999	Aug	Catter	(FRM)	H	5f	50	53+
	1996	Aug	Beverl	(GD)	H	5f	65	67

2000 Turf 1-15: (5f 1-10, 6f 5) (sft, gd 5, g-f 1-6, frm 3)
Useful gelding, effective 5 to 6f, best at 5f, acts on gd to g-f, best on g-f, has worn blinkers, excels at Newbury. Turf high 85 - 2nd of 10 getting 5lb from Ambitious (6 Aug Newbury 5f g-f RF 3419) - also 1st of 8 giving 6lb to Antonia's Double (29 Jly Newcastle RF 3211). Consistent. Yet another performer to be sprinkled with the Dandy Nicholls magic dust, he was consistent last season, but only managed a solitary victory at Newcastle in July. Best over five furlongs but does stay six.
**D Nicholls [5-22] P Davidson-Brown (from M D Hammond [0-16] Jun 1999).*

BREEZE HOME BHB 60f **RR 71f** 4328[13]

4 b g Homo Sapien - Poppy's Pride (Uncle Pokey) 10.1f **(49)**
Form - 54D0
Record 2000 - 1st:0 2nd:0 3rd:0 Ran:4
Win Prizemoney £0 *Total Prizemoney* £312
2000 Turf 0-4: (10f 2, 11f, 16f) (g-f 2, frm 2)
Above-average gelding. Turf high 71 (1st run) (began Jly) - 5th of 15 giving 15lb to Eurolink Artemis (20 Jly Leicester 10f frm RF 2973). **C M Kinane [0-4] Mrs M Mann.*

BREEZY LOUISE BHB 54f58a **RR 55f 58a** 4768[15]

3 b f Dilum (USA) 7.1f **(56)** - Louise Moillon (Mansingh (USA)) 7.4f **(55)**
Form - 1866800

Record 2000 - 1st:1 2nd:0 3rd:0 Ran:7
Pre2000 - 1st:1 2nd:1 3rd:0 Ran:9
Win Prizemoney £4,236 *Total Prizemoney* £6,514
Wins * 2000 Apr Folkes (SFT) C 5f **71 <**
* 1999 Jun Windso (G-F) S 5f 69+
2000 Turf 1-7: (5f 1-5, 6f 2) (g-s 1-2, gd 2, g-f 2, frm)
Light-framed, fair filly, effective 5f, acts on g-s to frm, has worn blinkers. Turf high 71 (1st run) - 1st of 7 getting 17lb from Argent Facile (18 Apr Folkestone RF 0759). **R J Hodges [2-16] R J Hodges.*

BREMRIDGE (IRE) BHB 65f **RR 79f** 4220[16]
3 ch g Ridgewood Ben - Eimkar (Junius (USA)) 7.7f **(65)**
Form - 580
Record 2000 - 1st:0 2nd:0 3rd:0 Ran:3
Pre2000 - 1st:0 2nd:1 3rd:0 Ran:5
Win Prizemoney £0 *Total Prizemoney* £856
2000 Turf 0-3: (10f 3) (gd, g-f, frm)
Light-framed, above-average gelding, effective 8f, acts on g-f. Turf high 36. Becoming disappointing.
**J A Osborne [0-3] Anglia Bloodstock Syndicate 1998 (from A G Foster [0-1] Oct 1999).*

BRENDA'S DELIGHT (IRE) BHB 40f **RR 39f** 5110[11]
2 b f Blues Traveller (IRE) - Tara's Delight (Dunbeath (USA)) 7.8f **(70)**
Form - 0000
Record 2000 - 1st:0 2nd:0 3rd:0 Ran:4
2000 Turf 0-4: (6f, 7f, 8f 2) (gd, g-f 3)
Very moderate filly. Turf high 39 (began Jly).
**P Butler [0-4] E H Whatmough.*

BREVITY BHB 61f **RR 56f** 5141[2]
5 b g Tenby 10.4f **(76)** - Rive (USA) (Riverman (USA)) 9.1f **(76)**
Form - 70002
Record 2000 - 1st:0 2nd:1 3rd:0 Ran:5
Pre2000 - 1st:1 2nd:3 3rd:0 Ran:16
Win Prizemoney £3,727 *Total Prizemoney* £8,362
Wins 1999 Aug Newbur (GD) H 6f 49 57 <
2000 Turf 0-5: (6f 4, 7f) (g-s, g-f 2, frm 2)
Fair gelding, effective 6f, acts on g-s to frm. Turf high 56 - 2nd of 13 getting 10lb from Bintang Timor (22 Oct Yarmouth 6f g-s RF 5141).
**E J O'Neill [0-1] Christopher Ranson (from D Sasse [1-18] Jly 2000).*

BREW BHB 48f **RR 46f** 3976[7]
4 b c Primo Dominie 7.2f **(67)** - Boozy (Absalom) 7.2f **(58)**
Form - 060777
Record 2000 - 1st:0 2nd:0 3rd:0 Ran:6
Pre2000 - 1st:0 2nd:2 3rd:0 Ran:9
Win Prizemoney £0 *Total Prizemoney* £1,902
2000 Turf 0-6: (5f 5, 6f) (gd 2, g-f, frm 3)
Workmanlike, moderate colt, effective 5f, acts on g-f. Turf high 46.
**A Berry [0-1] Heathavon Stables Ltd (from R Hannon [0-14] Aug 2000).*

BREYDON BHB 26f44a **RR 30f 44a** 1040[8]
7 ch g Be My Guest (USA) 10.2f **(66)** - Palmella (USA) (Grundy) 10.3f **(65)**
Form - 088
Record 2000 - 1st:0 2nd:0 3rd:0 Ran:3
Pre2000 - 1st:1 2nd:4 3rd:6 Ran:32
Win Prizemoney £2,346 *Total Prizemoney* £7,459
Wins * 1998 May Hamilt (SFT) SH 12.1f 26 32 <
2000 Turf 0-3: (14f, 16f 2) (gd 2, frm)
Moderate gelding. Turf high 30.
**P Monteith [4-41] The Dregs Of Humanity (from M H Tompkins [0-8] Aug 1996).*

BRIAN'S BLUE (IRE) BHB 30f **RR 5f** 535[9]
5 ch g Statoblest 6.4f **(63)** - Lamya (Hittite Glory) 8.7f **(50)**
Form - 0
Record 2000 - 1st:0 2nd:0 3rd:0 Ran:1
Pre2000 - 1st:0 2nd:0 3rd:0 Ran:5
2000 AW 0-1: (5f) (Fibr)
Poor gelding.
**B P J Baugh [0-4] M J Lyons (from P Eccles [0-2] Feb 1998).*

BRIDAL WHITE BHB 31f31a **RR 31df 31a** 3265[12]
4 b f Robellino (USA) 9.5f **(68)** - Alwatar (USA) (Caerleon (USA)) 8.6f **(71)**
Form - 0000
Record 2000 - 1st:0 2nd:0 3rd:0 Ran:4
Pre2000 - 1st:0 2nd:0 3rd:2 Ran:13
Win Prizemoney £0 *Total Prizemoney* £1,265
2000 Turf 0-3: (7f, 10f, 11f) (hvy, g-s, gd) 2000 AW 0-1: (8f) (Fibr)
Workmanlike, very moderate filly. Turf high 15.
**M J Ryan [0-14] Peter Scott (from K G Wingrove [0-5] Spt 1998).*

BRIDIE'S PRIDE BHB 70f49a **RR 73f 49a** 5322[8]
9 b g Alleging (USA) 8.8f **(57)** - Miss Monte Carlo (Reform) 8.9f **(62)**
Form - 2408
Record 2000 - 1st:0 2nd:1 3rd:0 Ran:4
Pre2000 - 1st:2 2nd:5 3rd:3 Ran:26
Win Prizemoney £8,575 *Total Prizemoney* £22,313
Wins * 1998 Jun Ascot (G-S) H 16.2f 50 57 <
* 1997 Jly Chepst (G-S) H 18f 46 50
2000 Turf 0-4: (16f 2, 17f, 18f) (sft 2, g-s, gd)
Above-average gelding, effective 16f, acts on sft to g-f, best on g-s. Turf high 73 - 4th of 10 giving 9lb to Captain Miller (22 Apr Kempton 16f sft RF 0831). Inconsistent. A tough stayer who runs from the front, he was in fine form in 1998, but rather lost his way the following year. Made a good return to action when second at Newbury in April, and stayed on after leading for a long way in the Queen's Prize. Absent for nearly six months, he made little impression in two efforts in the autumn. **G A Ham [2-38] K C White.*

BRIEF CALL (IRE) BHB 47f40a **RR 53f 40a** 1647[8]
3 ch f Case Law 6f **(64)** - Collected (IRE) (Taufan (USA)) 7f **(57)**
Form - 0608
Record 2000 - 1st:0 2nd:0 3rd:0 Ran:4
Pre2000 - 1st:0 2nd:0 3rd:2 Ran:9
Win Prizemoney £0 *Total Prizemoney* £598
2000 Turf 0-1: (5f) (gd) 2000 AW 0-3: (5f 3) (Equi, Fibr 2)
Fair filly, has worn blinkers. AW high 21. Inconsistent.
**B Palling [0-13] The Lanebrook Partners.*

BRIEF CONTACT (IRE) BHB 47f **RR 47f** 5151[8]
2 b g Brief Truce (USA) 9.1f **(73)** - Incommunicado (IRE) (Sadler's Wells (USA)) 10f **(76)**
Form - 008
Record 2000 - 1st:0 2nd:0 3rd:0 Ran:3
2000 Turf 0-3: (6f, 7f 2) (g-s 2, gd)
Currently moderate gelding. Turf high 47 (began Spt).
**J R Poulton [0-3] George H Gibson & Seamus M McAnulty.*

BRIEF KEY (IRE) RR 31f 4744[12]
2 b f Brief Truce (USA) 9.1f **(73)** - Latch Key Lady (USA) **(12f 48a)** (Tejano (USA))
Form - 0
Record 2000 - 1st:0 2nd:0 3rd:0 Ran:1
2000 Turf 0-1: (7f) (gd)
Currently very moderate filly. **N Tinkler [0-1] David Scott.*

BRIEF STAR (IRE) BHB 52f **RR 41f** 4965[26]
2 b f Brief Truce (USA) 9.1f **(73)** - Millionetta (IRE) (Danehill (USA)) 10f **(72)**
Form - 83580
Record 2000 - 1st:0 2nd:0 3rd:1 Ran:5
Win Prizemoney £0 *Total Prizemoney* £378
2000 Turf 0-4: (5f 3, 6f) (gd 4) 2000 AW 0-1: (5f) (Fibr)
Fair filly. Turf high 41. **M Brittain [0-5] Northgate Lodge Racing Club.*

BRIERY MEC BHB 51f **RR 46f** 3174[1]
5 b g Ron's Victory (USA) 9.2f **(52)** - Briery Fille (Sayyaf)
Form - 015031
Record 2000 - 1st:2 2nd:0 3rd:1 Ran:6
Pre2000 - 1st:0 2nd:1 3rd:2 Ran:11
Win Prizemoney £6,403 *Total Prizemoney* £9,003
Wins * 2000 Jly Newmar (GD) H 10f 45 46 <
*** 2000** May Bright (SFT) H 10f 41 45
2000 Turf 2-6: (10f 2-4, 11f, 12f) (hvy, gd 1-1, g-f 1-2, frm 2)
Moderate gelding, effective 10f, acts on gd to g-f, best on gd. Turf high 46 - 1st of 17 getting 1lb from Roffey Spinney (28 Jly Newmarket RF 3174) - also 1st of 13 giving 3lb to Sammy's Shuffle (26 May Brighton RF 1459). Consistent.

*H J Collingridge [2-17] N H Gardner.

BRIGHELLA (GER) RR 92f 2199a[7]
3 f
Form - 7
2000 Turf 0-1: (11f) (gd)
Currently useful filly. *in GER [0-1].

BRIGHT BLADE BHB 31f **RR 38f** 3185[12]
4 b c Sure Blade (USA) 10.6f **(66)** - Gay Gem (Sparkler)
Form - 700
Record 2000 - 1st:0 2nd:0 3rd:0 Ran:2
Pre2000 - 1st:0 2nd:0 3rd:0 Ran:3
2000 Turf 0-2: (12f, 14f) (frm 2)
Unfurnished, very moderate colt. (began Jly).
*P Mitchell [0-5] Mrs Sara Sorby.

BRIGHT BLUE RR 4054[15]
4 b g Precocious 7.2f **(54)** - Wrightway Blues (Majority Blue)
Form - 00
Record 2000 - 1st:0 2nd:0 3rd:0 Ran:2
2000 Turf 0-2: (7f, 11f) (gd, frm)
Currently very poor gelding. (began Aug) - 15th of 18 to Divorce Action (28 Aug Warwick 11f gd RF 4054).
*P S McEntee [0-2] Mrs S van der Meulen.

BRIGHT HOPE (IRE) BHB 82f **RR 82+f** 2412[9]
4 b f Danehill (USA) 9.1f **(79)** - Crystal Cross (USA) **(73f)** (Roberto (USA)) 10f **(76)**
Form - 0
Record 2000 - 1st:0 2nd:0 3rd:0 Ran:1
Pre2000 - 1st:1 2nd:0 3rd:1 Ran:3
Win Prizemoney £3,875 *Total Prizemoney* £4,553
Wins * 1999 Spt Pontef (G-F) 10f 82+ <
2000 Turf 0-1: (10f) (g-f)
Tall, decent filly. *P W Harris [1-4] Mrs P W Harris.

BRIGHT QUESTION BHB 75f **RR 77f** 2615[9]
3 ch c Nashwan (USA) 10.3f **(79)** - Ozone Friendly (USA) (Green Forest (USA)) 9.9f **(68)**
Form - 0
Record 2000 - 1st:0 2nd:0 3rd:0 Ran:1
Pre2000 - 1st:0 2nd:0 3rd:0 Ran:2
2000 Turf 0-1: (8f) (gd)
Well made, currently above-average colt.
*B W Hills [0-3] Maktoum Al Maktoum.

BRIGMOUR BHB 20f **RR 19f** 3311[11]
4 gr f Aydimour - Briglen (Swing Easy (USA)) 6.5f **(55)**
Form - 00008000
Record 2000 - 1st:0 2nd:0 3rd:0 Ran:8
2000 Turf 0-8: (7f, 8f 4, 9f, 10f 2) (g-s 2, gd 2, g-f 3, frm)
Poor filly. Turf high 22. *N Wilson [0-8] Steven Downes.

BRIG O'TURK BHB 60f **RR 72f** 4228[4]
3 ch g Inchinor 8.9f **(64)** - Sharmood (USA) (Sharpen Up) 8.3f **(67)**
Form - 434
Record 2000 - 1st:0 2nd:0 3rd:1 Ran:3
Pre2000 - 1st:0 2nd:0 3rd:0 Ran:1
Win Prizemoney £0 *Total Prizemoney* £657
2000 Turf 0-2: (10f 2) (gd, g-f) 2000 AW 0-1: (12f) (Equi)
Workmanlike, above-average gelding. Turf high 72 (1st run) - 4th of 11 to Pentagonal (13 May Lingfield 10f gd RF 1190).
*Mrs A J Perrett [0-4] Mrs G Harwood.

BRILLIANCY (USA) BHB 30f **RR 25f** 2046[13]
5 b g Alleged (USA) 11.8f **(81)** - Crystal Gazing (USA) (El Gran Senor (USA)) 9.6f **(76)**
Form - 3550
Record 2000 - 1st:0 2nd:0 3rd:1 Ran:4
Win Prizemoney £0 *Total Prizemoney* £430
2000 Turf 0-3: (8f, 12f, 14f) (g-s, gd, g-f) 2000 AW 0-1: (12f) (Equi)
Moderate gelding. Turf high 25. (1st run) - 3rd of 14 giving 4lb to Fusul (5 Jan Lingfield 12f Equi RF 0028).
*Mrs A E Johnson [0-6] Mrs Joy Johnson.

BRILLIANT RED BHB 98f97a **RR 102f 97a** 4968[17]
7 b g Royal Academy (USA) 7.8f **(77)** - Red Comes Up (USA) (Blushing Groom (FR)) 10.3f **(76)**
Form - 1000362000
Record 2000 - 1st:0 2nd:1 3rd:1 Ran:9
Pre2000 - 1st:8 2nd:5 3rd:7 Ran:37
Win Prizemoney £106,635 *Total Prizemoney* £154,939

Wins							
* 1999	*Nov*	*Lingfi*	*(STD)*		*10f*		92
* 1999	Jly	Sandow	(G-F)	H	8.1f	97	99 <
* 1999	Jun	Ascot	(G-F)	H	10f	95	98
1998	Spt	Newbur	(GD)	H	10f	92	95
1998	*Feb*	*Lingfi*	*(SLW)*	*H*	*10f*	*85*	92
1998	*Feb*	*Lingfi*	*(SLW)*	*H*	*10f*	*78*	*81*
1997	Jly	Lingfi	(G-F)		7.6f		83

2000 Turf 0-9: (8f 4, 9f, 10f 4) (g-s, gd 4, g-f 4)
Very useful gelding, effective 8 to 10f, best at 10f, acts on gd to frm, best on gd, likes tight tracks, excels at Newbury and does well at Sandown. Turf high 102 - 6th of 9 giving 18lb to Happy Diamond (29 Jly Ascot 10f gd RF 3200).
*Mrs L Richards [3-19] Mrs M J George (from P R Hedger [4-21] Oct 1998).

BRILLIANTRIO BHB 77f **RR 83df** 4555[6]
2 ch f Selkirk (USA) 7.9f **(76)** - Loucoum (FR) (Iron Duke (FR)) 8.8f **(60)**
Form - 106
Record 2000 - 1st:1 2nd:0 3rd:0 Ran:3
Win Prizemoney £6,955 *Total Prizemoney* £6,955
Wins * 2000 Jly Newcas (G-F) 7f 83+ <
2000 Turf 1-3: (7f 1-2, 8f) (gd, g-f 1-1, frm)
Currently decent filly. Turf high 83 (1st run) (began Jly) - 1st of 13 giving 6lb to That's Jazz (29 Jly Newcastle RF 3209).
*Miss J A Camacho [1-3] Brian Nordan.

BRILLYANT DANCER RR 64f 4744[9]
2 b f Environment Friend 7.5f **(67)** - Brillyant Glen (IRE) (Glenstal (USA)) 10.1f **(64)**
Form - 00
Record 2000 - 1st:0 2nd:0 3rd:0 Ran:2
2000 Turf 0-2: (6f, 7f) (gd, frm)
Currently average filly. Turf high 64 (began Aug).
*Mrs A Duffield [0-2] Clarks New Town.

BRIMSTONE (IRE) BHB 45f50a **RR 50f 50a** 4396[10]
5 ch g Ballad Rock 7.2f **(63)** -Blazing Glory (IRE) (Glow (USA)) 6.7f **(71)**
Form - 0860000
Record 2000 - 1st:0 2nd:0 3rd:0 Ran:4
Pre2000 - 1st:1 2nd:2 3rd:0 Ran:12
Win Prizemoney £3,485 *Total Prizemoney* £6,276
Wins 1997 Jly Sandow (G-F) 5f 78 <
2000 Turf 0-3: (5f, 6f 2) (g-f 3) 2000 AW 0-1: (10f) (Equi)
Fair gelding, has worn blinkers. Turf high 50 (began Jly).
*P L Gilligan [0-3] Miss Linsey Knocker (from H J Collingridge [0-6] Jan 2000).

BRING PLENTY (USA) BHB 100f **RR 95f** 4844a[10]
2 b f Southern Halo (USA) - Alcando (Alzao (USA)) 7.1f **(68)**
Form - 013240
Record 2000 - 1st:1 2nd:1 3rd:1 Ran:6
Win Prizemoney £3,900 *Total Prizemoney* £13,000
Wins * 2000 Jun Goodwo (G-F) 6f 76 <
2000 Turf 1-6: (6f 1-2, 7f 2, 8f 2) (gd 2, g-f 1-2, frm 2)
Very useful filly, effective 7 to 8f, best at 7f, acts on g-f to frm, best on frm, has worn blinkers. Turf high 95 - 3rd of 12 to Silver Jorden (27 Jly Sandown 7f g-f RF 3153). Won readily at Goodwood on her second start and has run well in useful company since. She will stay ten furlongs. *J H M Gosden [1-6].

BRING SWEETS BHB 85f **RR 91df** 5317[22]
4 b g Sabrehill (USA) 8.5f **(64)** - Che Gambe (USA) (Lyphard (USA)) 9.9f **(72)**
Form - 0
Record 2000 - 1st:0 2nd:0 3rd:0 Ran:1
Pre2000 - 1st:2 2nd:1 3rd:2 Ran:8
Win Prizemoney £8,217 *Total Prizemoney* £14,950
Wins 1998 Nov Doncas (SFT) 8f 87 <
1998 Oct Redcar (HVY) 8f 79
2000 Turf 0-1: (7f) (sft)
Scopey, useful gelding, has worn blinkers.
*B Ellison [0-1] Spring Cottage Syndicate (from B W Hills [2-8] May

1999).

BRIONEY (IRE) BHB 72f **RR 73f** 3217[4]
3 ch f Barathea (IRE) - La Vigie (King of Clubs) 7.1f **(57)**
Form - 884
Record 2000 - 1st:0 2nd:0 3rd:0 Ran:3
Win Prizemoney £0 *Total Prizemoney* £367
2000 Turf 0-3: (8f 2, 10f) (gd, g-f, frm)
Currently above-average filly. Turf high 73.
**J H M Gosden [0-3] Lady Vestey.*

BRISBANE ROAD (IRE) RR 71f 4373[10]
3 b g Blues Traveller (IRE) - Eva Fay (IRE) (Fayruz)
Form - 451200
Record 2000 - 1st:1 2nd:1 3rd:0 Ran:6
Pre2000 - 1st:0 2nd:0 3rd:0 Ran:2
Win Prizemoney £2,886 *Total Prizemoney* £4,646
Wins * 2000 Jly Bath (G-S) H 11.7f 60 62 <
2000 Turf 1-6: (8f, 10f, 12f 1-1, 14f 3) (sft, gd 1-2, frm 3)
Scopey, above-average gelding, effective 12 to 14f, acts on gd, favours left handed tracks, favours tight tracks. Turf high 71 - 2nd of 7 getting 8lb from Fantastic Fantasy (21 Aug Nottingham 14f gd RF 3841) - also 1st of 18 getting 1lb from Lanzlo (10 Jly Bath RF 2666). She looked to possess plenty of stamina when winning a Bath maiden handicap in July. **I A Balding [1-8] Lord Lloyd-Webber.*

BRITANNIA (USA) RR 100?f 1426[6]
3 b f Sea Hero (USA) - Brave And True (USA) (Fappiano (USA)) 8.7f **(77)**
Form - 6
Record 2000 - 1st:0 2nd:0 3rd:0 Ran:1
Pre2000 - 1st:0 2nd:2 3rd:2 Ran:4
Win Prizemoney £0 *Total Prizemoney* £44,794
2000 Turf 0-1: (10f) (gd)
Workmanlike, very useful filly. In the frame in all four of her starts at two, she looked unlucky when touched-off in a maiden at Sandown and was only beaten narrowly in the Group One Fillies' Mile at Ascot on her final start. Poor effort in the Lupe Stakes on her sole start at three. **I A Balding [0-5] Mrs Paul Mellon.*

BRITTAS BAY (IRE) RR 24f 2085[7]
2 b f Idris (IRE) - Nyali Beach (IRE) **(54f 42a)** (Treasure Kay)
Form - 7
Record 2000 - 1st:0 2nd:0 3rd:0 Ran:1
2000 Turf 0-1: (5f) (frm)
Currently little account filly. **M H Tompkins [0-1] Michael Keogh.*

BRITTAS BLUES (IRE) BHB 45f **RR 49f** 4870[5]
3 b f Blues Traveller (IRE) - Missish (Mummy's Pet) 7.7f **(60)**
Form - 7345035
Record 2000 - 1st:0 2nd:0 3rd:2 Ran:7
Win Prizemoney £0 *Total Prizemoney* £1,497
2000 Turf 0-7: (6f 5, 9f, 10f) (hvy, g-s, gd, g-f, frm 3)
Rangy, moderate filly, effective 9f, acts on g-s. Turf high 49.
**M Johnston [0-7] J M Cullinan.*

BROADWAY LEGEND (IRE) BHB 85f **RR 92f** 4041[10]
3 b f Caerleon (USA) 10.9f **(79)** - Tetradonna (IRE) (Teenoso (USA)) 9.9f **(72)**
Form - 18020
Record 2000 - 1st:1 2nd:1 3rd:0 Ran:5
Pre2000 - 1st:0 2nd:0 3rd:1 Ran:2
Win Prizemoney £4,004 *Total Prizemoney* £6,674
Wins * 2000 May Haydoc (GD) 10.5f 85 <
2000 Turf 1-5: (8f, 10f 3, 11f 1-1) (g-s, gd 1-3, frm)
Scopey, useful filly, effective 10 to 11f, acts on gd to frm. Turf high 93 - 2nd of 11 getting 4lb from Happy Diamond (13 Jly Doncaster 10f frm RF 2755) - also 1st of 6 from Lucky Lady (6 May Haydock RF 1054). Made all in a Haydock maiden on her seasonal debut. Well held in listed races since, not looking a straightforward ride.
**J W Hills [1-7] Freddy Bienstock and Martin Boase.*

BROCHE (USA) RR 112f 1863[12]
3 b c Summer Squall (USA) 7f **(80)** - Ribbonwood (USA) (Diesis) 9.3f **(69)**
Form - 70150
Record 2000 - 1st:1 2nd:0 3rd:0 Ran:5
Pre2000 - 1st:1 2nd:0 3rd:0 Ran:1
Win Prizemoney £15,953 *Total Prizemoney* £27,961
Wins * **2000** May Doncas (G-S) 10.3f 100+ <
1999 Jun Currag (GD) 7f 96+
2000 Turf 1-4: (8f, 10f 1-1, 12f 2) (gd 1-4) 2000 AW 0-1: (9f) (Dirt)
Group-class colt. Turf high 112. Winner of a Curragh maiden for John Oxx on his sole start at two, he then joined Godolphin. Well beaten in the UAE Derby at Nad Al Sheba on his return, he finished down the field in the Guineas but looked good when landing a conditions event at Doncaster. Ran a respectable fifth in the Prix du Jockey-Club at Chantilly, but was understandably well beaten in the Epsom Derby six days later.
**S bin Suroor [1-4] Godolphin (from S bin Suroor in UAE [0-1] Mar 2000).*

BROCKHALL LAD RR 2753[12]
2 b g Primo Dominie 7.2f **(67)** - Cremets (Mummy's Pet) 7.7f **(60)**
Form - 00
Record 2000 - 1st:0 2nd:0 3rd:0 Ran:2
2000 Turf 0-2: (5f, 6f) (frm 2)
Currently very poor gelding. (began Jly) - 12th of 12 to Caustic Wit (13 Jly Doncaster 6f frm RF 2753).
**J J Quinn [0-2] Brockhall Village Ltd.*

BROCTUNE GOLD BHB 35f56a **RR 41f 56a** 4122[9]
9 b g Superpower 6.6f **(58)** - Golden Sunlight (Ile de Bourbon (USA)) 10.1f **(67)**
Form - 504050
Record 2000 - 1st:0 2nd:0 3rd:0 Ran:6
Pre2000 - 1st:12 2nd:10 3rd:6 Ran:68
Win Prizemoney £32,883 *Total Prizemoney* £47,964

Wins							
* 1998	Aug	Catter	(GD)	H	7f	58	59
* 1998	Jun	Mussel	(SFT)	H	8f	54	57
* 1997	Jly	Mussel	(GD)	C	7.1f		62
* 1997	Jun	Mussel	(GD)	C	7.1f		56+
* 1996	Aug	Beverl	(GD)	C	8.5f		64
* 1996	Jly	Mussel	(G-F)	H	8.1f	60	68
* 1996	Jun	Mussel	(FRM)	C	7.1f		61
* 1996	May	Thirsk	(G-F)	S	7f		55

2000 Turf 0-6: (7f 2, 8f 4) (g-f, frm 5)
Moderate gelding, effective 7 to 8f, best at 8f, acts on frm, prefers left handed tracks. Turf high 41 (1st run) - 5th of 17 getting 9lb from Almazhar (2 Jun Ayr 8f frm RF 1642).
**Mrs M Reveley [12-73] Mrs M B Thwaites (from B W Hills [0-1] Aug 1997).*

BROCTUNE LINE BHB 30f47a **RR 6f 47a** 1513[11]
6 ch g Safawan 6.6f **(60)** - Ra Ra (Lord Gayle (USA)) 8.8f **(62)**
Form - 0
Record 2000 - 1st:0 2nd:0 3rd:0 Ran:1
Pre2000 - 1st:2 2nd:2 3rd:3 Ran:26
Win Prizemoney £5,208 *Total Prizemoney* £7,861
Wins 1997 *Apr Southw (STD) H 11f 55 58* <
1997 *Jan Southw (STD) H 8f 45 46*
2000 Turf 0-1: (15f) (hvy)
Moderate gelding, effective 8 to 11f, - acts on Fibr, has worn blinkers, prefers left handed tracks. Inconsistent.
**T Keddy [0-6] M Sweeney (from Mrs M Reveley [2-33] May 1999).*

BROKENBOROUGH BHB 51f **RR 47f** 1179[12]
3 ch g Beveled (USA) 6.9f **(64)** - Swilly Express (Ballacashtal (CAN)) 5.3f **(50)**
Form - 050
Record 2000 - 1st:0 2nd:0 3rd:0 Ran:3
Pre2000 - 1st:0 2nd:0 3rd:0 Ran:4
2000 Turf 0-3: (10f, 12f, 14f) (sft, gd, g-f)
Scopey, moderate gelding. Turf high 47.
**M Blanshard [0-7] Brig Parker Bowles.*

BROKEN SPECTRE RR 57f 5142[5]
3 b f Rainbow Quest (USA) 11.2f **(81)** - Armeria (USA) (Northern Dancer) 9.6f **(80)**
Form - 75
Record 2000 - 1st:0 2nd:0 3rd:0 Ran:2
2000 Turf 0-2: (10f, 11f) (g-s 2)
Scopey, currently fair filly. Turf high 57 (began Spt).
**J H M Gosden [0-2] K Abdulla.*

BROKE ROAD (IRE) BHB 46f48a **RR 42f 48a** 1613[10]
4 b g Deploy 11.4f **(67)** - Shamaka **(57df 41a)** (Kris) 9.5f **(73)**
Form - 0
Record 2000 - 1st:0 2nd:0 3rd:0 Ran:1
Pre2000 - 1st:1 2nd:1 3rd:4 Ran:13
Win Prizemoney £2,944 *Total Prizemoney* £5,923
Wins 1999 Spt Hamilt (SFT) H 8.3f 40 42+ <
2000 Turf 0-1: (10f) (g-f)
Unfurnished, moderate gelding, effective 7 to 12f, best at 8f, acts on gd to frm - acts on Fibr, has worn blinkers (extremely effectively), likes right handed tracks, likes Beverley. Consistent.
**Mrs V C Ward [1-6] Broke Road Partnership (from T D Barron [1-13] Oct 1999).*

BROMEIGAN BHB 42f **RR 36f** 3486[8]
3 b f Mtoto 11.5f **(71)** - Penlanfeigan (Abutammam)
Form - 0768
Record 2000 - 1st:0 2nd:0 3rd:0 Ran:4
2000 Turf 0-4: (8f, 10f 3) (gd, g-f 3)
Unfurnished, very moderate filly. Turf high 36.
**R Guest [0-4] The Flying Whippet Society.*

BROMPTON BARRAGE BHB 42f **RR 51f** 5229[11]
3 b g Rudimentary (USA) 8.2f **(66)** - Song of Hope (Chief Singer) 8.9f **(66)**
Form - 00800040
Record 2000 - 1st:0 2nd:0 3rd:0 Ran:0
Pre2000 - 1st:0 2nd:0 3rd:0 Ran:4
Win Prizemoney £0 *Total Prizemoney* £528
2000 Turf 0-8: (6f, 7f 5, 8f 2) (gd 4, g-f 2, frm 2)
Workmanlike, fair gelding, has worn blinkers. Turf high 66. Has shown some ability in maidens and handicaps, and is one to keep an eye on when dropped in grade.
**R Hannon [0-12] Thurloe Thoroughbreds.*

BRONZINO BHB 51f **RR ?f** 5000[16]
5 ch g Midyan (USA) 9.9f **(64)** - Indubitable (Sharpo) 7.7f **(59)**
Form - 0
Record 2000 - 1st:0 2nd:0 3rd:0 Ran:1
Pre2000 - 1st:1 2nd:0 3rd:3 Ran:20
Win Prizemoney £3,127 *Total Prizemoney* £4,638
Wins * 1999 Aug Salisb (G-S) H 9.9f 52 56 <
2000 Turf 0-1: (10f) (g-s)
Very poor gelding, effective 10f, acted on gd, had worn blinkers, favoured tight tracks.(DEAD) **G B Balding [1-30] Miss B Swire.*

BROOKFURLONG BHB 36f **RR 11f** 4678[7]
4 br f Rock City 8.8f **(62)** - Call of the Night (IRE) **(68f)** (Night Shift (USA)) 7.2f **(69)**
Form - 7
Record 2000 - 1st:0 2nd:0 3rd:0 Ran:1
Pre2000 - 1st:0 2nd:0 3rd:0 Ran:2
2000 Turf 0-1: (8f) (g-s)
Workmanlike, currently poor filly.
**D R C Elsworth [0-1] Raymond Tooth (from J R Fanshawe [0-2] Spt 1999).*

BROTHER TOM BHB 27f **RR 40df** 4491[20]
3 b c Prince Sabo 6.6f **(64)** - Danseuse Davis (FR) **(46f 42a)** (Glow (USA)) 6.7f **(71)**
Form - 0
Record 2000 - 1st:0 2nd:0 3rd:0 Ran:1
Pre2000 - 1st:0 2nd:0 3rd:0 Ran:5
2000 Turf 0-1: (6f) (g-f)
Unfurnished, moderate colt.
**J M Bradley [0-1] Mrs H Raw (from P D Evans [0-5] Aug 1999).*

BROUGHTON BELLE BHB 12f **RR** 3515[16]
4 b f Chaddleworth (IRE) - Broughtons Pet (IRE) (Cyrano de Bergerac) 6f **(68)**
Form - 08000
Record 2000 - 1st:0 2nd:0 3rd:0 Ran:5
Pre2000 - 1st:0 2nd:0 3rd:0 Ran:3
2000 Turf 0-2: (8f 2) (g-f, frm) 2000 AW 0-3: (7f, 8f 2) (Equi, Fibr 2)
Very poor filly, effective 12f, acts on gd.
**W J Musson [0-8] Broughton Thermal Insulation.*

BROUGHTON MAGIC (IRE) BHB 36f39a **RR 39f 39a** 2479[14]
5 ch g Archway (IRE) 8.5f **(60)** - Magic Green (Magic Mirror)
Form - 51000
Record 2000 - 1st:1 2nd:0 3rd:0 Ran:5
Pre2000 - 1st:0 2nd:0 3rd:0 Ran:6
Win Prizemoney £2,326 *Total Prizemoney* £2,326
Wins * 2000 *Feb Southw (STD) H 8f 33 43* <
2000 AW 1-5: (7f 2, 8f 1-3) (Fibr 1-5)
Moderate gelding. AW high 43 - 1st of 12 getting 19lb from Ellway Prince (11 Feb Southwell RF 0263).
**W J Musson [1-11] Broughton Thermal Insulation.*

BROUGHTONS FLUSH RR 54f 5312[14]
2 b g First Trump - Glowing Reference (Reference Point) 6.8f **(70)**
Form - 00
Record 2000 - 1st:0 2nd:0 3rd:0 Ran:2
2000 Turf 0-2: (6f, 8f) (g-s, g-f)
Currently fair gelding. Turf high 54 (began Spt).
**W J Musson [0-2] Broughton Thermal Insulation.*

BROUGHTONS LURE (IRE) BHB 36f30a **RR 34f 30a** 360[8]
6 ch m Archway (IRE) 8.5f **(60)** - Vaal Salmon (IRE) (Salmon Leap (USA)) 11f **(61)**
Form - 52288
Record 2000 - 1st:0 2nd:1 3rd:0 Ran:3
Pre2000 - 1st:0 2nd:3 3rd:0 Ran:15
Win Prizemoney £0 *Total Prizemoney* £3,959
2000 AW 0-3: (12f 2, 16f) (Fibr 3)
Very moderate mare. AW high 33.
**W J Musson [0-18] Broughton Bloodstock.*

BROUGHTONS MILL BHB 38f27a **RR 44f 27a** 3807[6]
5 ch g Ron's Victory (USA) 9.2f **(52)** - Sandra's Desire (Grey Desire) 8.7f **(50)**
Form - 08423606
Record 2000 - 1st:0 2nd:1 3rd:1 Ran:8
Pre2000 - 1st:0 2nd:0 3rd:1 Ran:5
Win Prizemoney £0 *Total Prizemoney* £1,376
2000 Turf 0-5: (10f, 11f 2, 12f, 13f) (g-s, gd 2, g-f, frm) 2000 AW 0-3: (8f, 9f, 12f) (Fibr 3)
Moderate gelding, effective 10 to 13f, acts on g-s to frm. Turf high 44 - 2nd of 20 giving 8lb to Vanborough Lad (4 Jun Warwick 11f g-s RF 1703). AW high 14. Inconsistent.
**W J Musson [0-13] Windmill Racing.*

BROUGHTONS MOTTO BHB 63f68a **RR 57f 68a** 2740[6]
2 b f Mtoto 11.5f **(71)** - Ice Chocolate (USA) (Icecapade (USA)) 11f **(62)**
Form - 0146
Record 2000 - 1st:1 2nd:0 3rd:0 Ran:4
Win Prizemoney £2,233 *Total Prizemoney* £2,233
Wins * 2000 *May Southw (STD) 5f 62* <
2000 Turf 0-3: (5f, 6f 2) (g-f 3) 2000 AW 1-1: (5f 1-1) (Fibr 1-1)
Average filly. Turf high 57 - 6th of 10 getting 20lb from Norcroft Lady (12 Jly Lingfield 6f g-f RF 2740). (1st run) - 1st of 14 giving 1lb to Miss Verity (15 May Southwell RF 1207).
**W J Musson [1-4] Broughton Thermal Insulation.*

BROUGHTON STORM BHB 43f **RR 41f** 4002[14]
2 ch g Chaddleworth (IRE) - Rainy Day Song **(58f 40a)** (Persian Bold) 9.3f **(66)**
Form - 0060
Record 2000 - 1st:0 2nd:0 3rd:0 Ran:4
2000 Turf 0-4: (5f 2, 7f 2) (gd, g-f, frm 2)
Moderate gelding. Turf high 41 (began Jly).
**W J Musson [0-4] Broughton Thermal Insulation.*

BROWN HOLLY BHB 40f **RR 15f** 4724[14]
2 br c So Factual (USA) - Scarlett Holly (Red Sunset) 8.2f **(63)**
Form - 00
Record 2000 - 1st:0 2nd:0 3rd:0 Ran:2
2000 Turf 0-2: (5f 2) (gd, frm)
Currently fair colt. Turf high 15 (began Spt).
**H E Haynes [0-2] F J Sainsbury.*

BROWNING BHB 58f56a **RR 61f 56a** 5154[6]

5 b g Warrshan (USA) 9.7f **(59)** - Mossy Rose (King of Spain) 7.8f **(52)**
Form - 206
Record 2000 - 1st:0 2nd:1 3rd:0 Ran:3
Pre2000 - 1st:1 2nd:5 3rd:0 Ran:18
Win Prizemoney £3,013 *Total Prizemoney* £9,335
Wins 1998 Aug Windso (G-F) H 11.6f 54 60 <
2000 Turf 0-2: (8f, 10f) (frm 2) 2000 AW 0-1: (12f) (Equi)
Average gelding, effective 10 to 12f, best at 12f, acts on frm, favours tight tracks. Turf high 60 (1st run) (began Aug) - 2nd of 16 getting 4lb from Guarded Secret (16 Aug Salisbury 10f frm RF 3705).
**M P Tregoning [0-3] Stanley Sharp (from D J Coakley [0-6] Jly 1999).*

BROWNS DELIGHT BHB 46f50a RR 48f 50a 3955[1]
3 b f Runnett 6.7f **(56)** - Fearless Princess (Tyrnavos) 10.1f **(55)**
Form - 77448065800241
Record 2000 - 1st:1 2nd:1 3rd:0 Ran:13
Pre2000 - 1st:0 2nd:1 3rd:0 Ran:5
Win Prizemoney £2,289 *Total Prizemoney* £4,465
Wins * 2000 Aug Bath (FRM) S 11.7f 40 <
2000 Turf 1-9: (7f, 8f 4, 9f, 10f 2, 12f 1-1) (gd 3, g-f 3, frm 2, hrd 1-1)
2000 AW 0-4: (7f 2, 10f 2) (Equi 4)
Workmanlike, moderate filly, effective 6f, - acts on Equi, has worn blinkers, likes left handed tracks, likes tight tracks. Turf high 48. AW high 47. **S Dow [1-18] Cecil Brown.*

BROWN'S FLIGHT BHB 41f52a RR 46f 52a 2698[12]
4 b f Jupiter Island 10.4f **(57)** - Fearless Princess (Tyrnavos) 10.1f **(55)**
Form - 0070
Record 2000 - 1st:0 2nd:0 3rd:0 Ran:4
Pre2000 - 1st:0 2nd:1 3rd:1 Ran:16
Win Prizemoney £0 *Total Prizemoney* £1,792
2000 Turf 0-4: (8f 2, 11f, 16f) (sft, gd, frm 2)
Light-framed, moderate filly, effective 10f, acts on frm, has worn blinkers, likes tight tracks. Turf high 46.
**M G Quinlan [0-5] D J Nice (from S Dow [0-16] Aug 1999).*

BROWSER (IRE) BHB 76f RR 70f 5001[8]
2 b g Rubiano (USA) 7.1f **(87)** - Just Looking (IRE) (Marju (IRE))
Form - 0318
Record 2000 - 1st:1 2nd:0 3rd:1 Ran:4
Win Prizemoney £1,694 *Total Prizemoney* £2,056
Wins * 2000 *Oct Wolver (STD) 8.5f 70* <
2000 Turf 0-3: (6f, 7f, 8f) (g-s, g-f 2) 2000 AW 1-1: (8f 1-1) (Fibr 1-1)
Above-average gelding. Turf high 70. (1st run) - 1st of 9 giving 1lb to My Very Own (3 Oct Wolverhampton RF 4783).
**K R Burke [1-4] Mrs Julie Mitchell.*

BRUNNHILDE BHB 63f RR 53f 4602[5]
2 ch f Wolfhound (USA) 7.3f **(71)** - Vilanika (FR) (Top Ville) 11.7f **(68)**
Form - 005
Record 2000 - 1st:0 2nd:0 3rd:0 Ran:3
2000 Turf 0-3: (5f, 6f, 8f) (gd, g-f, hrd)
Currently fair filly. Turf high 53. **John Berry [0-3] H R Moszkowicz.*

BRUTAL FANTASY (IRE) BHB 58f57a RR 52f 57a 2175[13]
6 b g Distinctly North (USA) 7.4f **(63)** - Flash Donna (USA) (Well Decorated (USA)) 7.6f **(64)**
Form - 7025214830600070
Record 2000 - 1st:1 2nd:1 3rd:1 Ran:12
Pre2000 - 1st:7 2nd:6 3rd:2 Ran:49
Win Prizemoney £29,912 *Total Prizemoney* £41,931
Wins * 2000 *Jan Lingfi (STD) 6f 69*
* 1999 Aug Ascot (SFT) H 5f 65 67
1999 May Lingfi (G-F) H 5f 68 70
1997 Apr Catter (GD) H 5f 78 83 <
1997 Mar Doncas (G-F) H 5f 72 78
1997 *Feb Wolver (STD) H 5f 72 72*
1997 *Jan Southw (STD) H 6f 65 74*
1996 May Mussel (G-S) S 5f 65+
2000 Turf 0-3: (5f 3) (gd, g-f, frm) 2000 AW 1-9: (5f 3, 6f 1-4, 7f 2) (Equi 1-8, Fibr)
Fair gelding, effective 5 to 6f, best at 5f, acts on gd to g-f - acts on Equi, best on gd, has worn blinkers, does well at Lingfield. Turf high 52. AW high 71 - 3rd of 5 giving 2lb to Prince Prospect (22 Jan Lingfield 6f Equi RF 0137) - also 1st of 6 getting 4lb from Mister Tricky (8 Jan Lingfield RF 0049).
**P Howling [2-25] C Hammond (from P G Murphy [1-7] Jun 1999).*

BRYNA (IRE) RR 134[8]
3 b f Ezzoud (IRE) - Suekar (IRE) (Don't Forget Me) 8.3f **(74)**
Form - 08
Record 2000 - 1st:0 2nd:0 3rd:0 Ran:2
2000 AW 0-2: (8f, 10f) (Equi 2)
Neat, currently very poor filly, wears blinkers.
**E J O'Neill [0-2] J P & T Syndicate.*

BRYNKIR BHB 27f41a RR 45f 41a 2041[13]
6 b g Batshoof 9.5f **(66)** - Felinwen (White Mill) 16.2f **(66)**
Form - 000
Record 2000 - 1st:0 2nd:0 3rd:0 Ran:3
Pre2000 - 1st:1 2nd:0 3rd:1 Ran:16
Win Prizemoney £2,085 *Total Prizemoney* £2,642
Wins 1998 *Feb Wolver (STD) H 16.2f 44 53* <
2000 Turf 0-2: (16f, 17f) (g-s, hrd) 2000 AW 0-1: (12f) (Fibr)
Moderate gelding, has worn blinkers. Turf high 13. Becoming disappointing.
**B J Llewellyn [0-7] Miss Emily Jane Jones (from D J G MurraySmith [1-14] Oct 1998).*

BUCKMINSTER (USA) RR 88+f 2860[6]
3 br c Silver Hawk (USA) 11.2f **(85)** - Buckarina (USA) (Buckaroo (USA))
Form - 3106
Record 2000 - 1st:1 2nd:0 3rd:1 Ran:4
Pre2000 - 1st:0 2nd:0 3rd:0 Ran:1
Win Prizemoney £2,936 *Total Prizemoney* £3,640
Wins * 2000 May Redcar (G-F) 10f 88 <
2000 Turf 1-4: (10f 1-2, 12f 2) (g-f, frm 1-3)
Useful colt. Turf high 88 - 1st of 6 from Luxor (15 May Redcar RF 1198). Held in the King George V Handicap after winning his maiden.
**J H M Gosden [1-5] Sheikh Mohammed.*

BUDDELIEA RR 5017[5]
2 b f Pivotal - Fernlea (USA) (Sir Ivor) 10.2f **(70)**
Form - 5
Record 2000 - 1st:0 2nd:0 3rd:0 Ran:1
2000 AW 0-1: (7f) (Fibr)
Currently fair filly. **J S Moore [0-1] J S Moore.*

BUDELLI (IRE) BHB 79f RR 81f 5141[4]
3 b c Elbio 9f **(62)** - Eves Temptation (IRE) (Glenstal (USA)) 10.1f **(64)**
Form - 362312502084
Record 2000 - 1st:1 2nd:3 3rd:2 Ran:12
Pre2000 - 1st:0 2nd:0 3rd:0 Ran:1
Win Prizemoney £3,298 *Total Prizemoney* £8,412
Wins * 2000 May Lingfi (G-S) 6f 77 <
2000 Turf 1-12: (5f 2, 6f 1-9, 7f) (sft, g-s 2, gd 1-3, g-f 4, frm 2)
Strong, decent colt, effective 5 to 6f, best at 6f, acts on sft to frm. Turf high 81 - 2nd of 14 getting 6lb from Blue Mountain (14 Jun Kempton 6f g-f RF 1962) - also 1st of 17 giving 5lb to Villa Via (20 May Lingfield RF 1328). Landed a Lingfield maiden in May and has shown up well in six-furlong handicaps since.
**M R Channon [1-13] Mrs C Roper.*

BUGGY RIDE (IRE) BHB 80f87a RR 67f 87a 1110[17]
3 b c Blues Traveller (IRE) - Tambora (Darshaan) 9.9f **(84)**
Form - 242211060
Record 2000 - 1st:2 2nd:1 3rd:0 Ran:6
Pre2000 - 1st:0 2nd:2 3rd:1 Ran:8
Win Prizemoney £6,214 *Total Prizemoney* £10,134
Wins * 2000 *Jan Lingfi (STD) H 8f 75 91* <
*** 2000** *Jan Lingfi (STD) 8f 75*
2000 Turf 0-1: (8f) (g-f) 2000 AW 2-5: (8f 2-3, 10f 2) (Equi 2-4, Dirt)
Workmanlike, useful colt, effective 8f, - acts on Equi, has worn blinkers (extremely effectively), likes left handed tracks, likes tight tracks. AW high 91 - 1st of 5 giving 17lb to Will Iveson (26 Jan Lingfield RF 0162). Took time to find his form, but showed himself to be a decent sort at around a mile on Equitrack, albeit at a modest level. Found it all too much when sent for a race at Nad Al Sheba in February and made the running for a mile in the Winter Derby. Well beaten in one run on turf.
**Miss Gay Kelleway [2-9] & Mrs Gary Pinchen (from R Charlton [0-5] Oct 1999).*

BUGIA (ITY) RR 91?f 2002a[1]
2 b f Kendor (FR) 12.2f **(66)** - Bugiarda (Fabulous Dancer (USA)) 9.4f **(70)**
Form - 1
2000 Turf 1-1: (6f 1-1) (g-f 1-1)
Currently useful filly. (1st run) - 1st of 10 from Pursuit Of Life (10 Jun San Siro RF 2002a). **L Brogi in ITY [1-1] Scuderia Nordovest.*

BULA ROSE (IRE) BHB 56f **RR 70f** 4460[17]
2 ch f Alphabatim (USA) 10.9f **(74)** - Titled Dancer (IRE) (Where To Dance (USA))
Form - 5231400
Record 2000 - 1st:1 2nd:1 3rd:1 Ran:7
Win Prizemoney £1,841 *Total Prizemoney* £2,971
Wins 2000 Jun Redcar (FRM) S 7f 55 <
2000 Turf 1-7: (6f 2, 7f 1-5) (g-s 2, g-f, frm 1-4)
Above-average filly, effective 6 to 7f, best at 7f, acts on frm. Turf high 55 - 1st of 9 from Eastern Red (24 Jun Redcar RF 2250).
**E W Tuer [0-3] E Tuer (from W G M Turner [1-4] Jun 2000).*

BULAWAYO BHB 60f67a **RR 68f 67a** 4049[19]
3 b c Prince Sabo 6.6f **(64)** - Ra Ra Girl (Shack (USA)) 5.8f **(53)**
Form - 61404650
Record 2000 - 1st:1 2nd:0 3rd:0 Ran:7
Pre2000 - 1st:0 2nd:0 3rd:0 Ran:2
Win Prizemoney £2,795 *Total Prizemoney* £3,302
Wins * 2000 *Jan Wolver (STD)* *7f* *69* <
2000 Turf 0-4: (6f 3, 7f) (gd, g-f, frm 2) 2000 AW 1-3: (6f, 7f 1-2) (Fibr 1-3)
Above-average colt, effective 7f, - acts on Fibr. Turf high 68. AW high 74 - also 1st of 12 giving 5lb to Night And Day (20 Jan Wolverhampton RF 0123). Inconsistent.
**B A McMahon [1-9] D J Allen.*

BULLSEFIA (USA) RR 90f 4321[2]
2 gr c Holy Bull (USA) - Yousefia (USA) (Danzig (USA)) 8.4f **(76)**
Form - 32
Record 2000 - 1st:0 2nd:1 3rd:1 Ran:2
Win Prizemoney £0 *Total Prizemoney* £1,840
2000 Turf 0-2: (6f, 7f) (g-f 2)
Currently useful colt. Turf high 90 (began Jly).
**B W Hills [0-2] Maktoum Al Maktoum.*

BUNDY BHB 65f67a **RR 68f 67a** 5057[6]
4 b g Ezzoud (IRE) - Sanctuary Cove (Habitat) 9.4f **(70)**
Form - 15311703086
Record 2000 - 1st:3 2nd:0 3rd:2 Ran:11
Pre2000 - 1st:2 2nd:0 3rd:4 Ran:20
Win Prizemoney £19,535 *Total Prizemoney* £23,776

Wins	*** 2000**	Jly	Pontef	(GD)	H	6f	64	64
	*** 2000**	Jun	Pontef	(G-F)	H	6f	60	62
	*** 2000**	Mar	Nottin	(GD)	H	6.1f	56	60
	* 1998	Aug	Warwic	(G-F)	H	6f	69	71 <
	1998	Jly	Newcas	(G-F)	S	6f		68

2000 Turf 3-11: (5f 2, 6f 3-6, 7f 3) (sft, gd 3, g-f 1-4, frm 2-3)
Light-framed, average gelding, effective 6 to 7f, best at 6f, acts on sft to frm, has worn blinkers. Turf high 68 - 3rd of 24 getting 3lb from Style Dancer (3 Spt York 7f g-f RF 4195) - also 1st of 16 giving 7lb to Albert The Bear (11 Jly Pontefract RF 2696).
**M Dods [4-25] A J Henderson (from M R Channon [1-6] Jly 1998).*

BUNKUM BHB 53f **RR 54f** 5217[8]
2 b c Robellino (USA) 9.5f **(68)** - Spinning Mouse **(62f 55a)** (Bustino) 10.4f **(64)**
Form - 008
Record 2000 - 1st:0 2nd:0 3rd:0 Ran:3
2000 Turf 0-3: (6f, 7f 2) (sft, g-s, frm)
Currently fair colt. Turf high 54 (began Spt).
**M L W Bell [0-3] Lord Hartington.*

BUNTY BHB 32f32a **RR 23f 32a** 4268[7]
4 b f Presidium 7.5f **(56)** - Shirlstar Investor (Some Hand) 9f **(50)**
Form - 6406040007
Record 2000 - 1st:0 2nd:0 3rd:0 Ran:9
Pre2000 - 1st:2 2nd:1 3rd:1 Ran:25
Win Prizemoney £6,795 *Total Prizemoney* £8,578

Wins	1999	Nov	Nottin	(SFT)	H	8.2f	46	50 <
	1999	Jly	Epsom	(G-F)	H	8.5f	42	47

2000 Turf 0-6: (8f 4, 10f, 12f) (g-s, gd, g-f 2, frm 2) 2000 AW 0-3: (8f 3) (Fibr 3)
Small, very moderate filly, effective 8 to 9f, best at 8f, acts on gd to frm, best on gd, has worn blinkers, likes tight tracks. Turf high 31. AW high 29.
**R C Spicer [0-2] John Purcell (from Mrs S Lamyman [0-7] May 2000).*

BURCOT GIRL (IRE) BHB 26f **RR 28f** 3896[15]
3 b f Petardia 8.2f **(58)** - Phoenix Forli (USA) (Forli (ARG)) 9.6f **(67)**
Form - 000300
Record 2000 - 1st:0 2nd:0 3rd:1 Ran:6
Pre2000 - 1st:0 2nd:0 3rd:0 Ran:3
Win Prizemoney £0 *Total Prizemoney* £389
2000 Turf 0-6: (6f, 7f 2, 8f 2, 10f) (g-f 2, frm 3, hrd)
Leggy, little account filly, effective 8f, acts on frm, has worn blinkers. Turf high 28 - 3rd of 7 getting 15lb from Speedfit Free (29 Jly Nottingham 8f frm RF 3215).
**J L Spearing [0-9] Exors of the late Colin Ross.*

BURGUNDIAN RED (USA) BHB 68f **RR 62f** 1493[7]
3 b c Red Ransom (USA) 8.6f **(83)** - Chesa Plana (Niniski (USA)) 10.6f **(65)**
Form - 077
Record 2000 - 1st:0 2nd:0 3rd:0 Ran:3
Pre2000 - 1st:0 2nd:0 3rd:0 Ran:3
Win Prizemoney £0 *Total Prizemoney* £210
2000 Turf 0-3: (7f 3) (g-s, g-f, frm)
Workmanlike, average colt. Turf high 62.
**A Berry [0-3] Dr G W W Tsoi (from R W Armstrong [0-3] Oct 1999).*

BURGUNDY RR 73++f 3731[1]
3 b g Lycius (USA) 8.8f **(71)** - Decant **(61f)** (Rousillon (USA)) 8.2f **(74)**
Form - 1
Record 2000 - 1st:1 2nd:0 3rd:0 Ran:1
Win Prizemoney £3,497 *Total Prizemoney* £3,497
Wins * 2000 Aug Salisb (G-F) 7f 73++ <
2000 Turf 1-1: (7f 1-1) (frm 1-1)
Scopey, currently above-average gelding. (1st run) - 1st of 13 giving 5lb to Badaawah (17 Aug Salisbury RF 3731).
**R Charlton [1-1] Highclere Thoroughbred Racing Ltd.*

BURMA TIGER (IRE) RR 93f 4523a[3]
3 b c Indian Ridge 7.6f **(74)** - Eva Luna (IRE) **(96f)** (Double Schwartz) 7.9f **(55)**
Form - 13
2000 Turf 1-2: (5f 1-2) (g-s 1-1)
Currently useful colt. Turf high 93 (1st run) (began Aug) - 1st of 13 giving 5lb to Vasanta (26 Aug Curragh RF 4088a).
**J Oxx in IRE [1-2] Mrs Chryss O'Reilly.*

BURNING (USA) BHB 34f34a **RR 17f 34a** 3999[12]
8 b g Bering 9.6f **(80)** - Larnica (USA) (Alydar (USA)) 9.1f **(76)**
Form - 00000030
Record 2000 - 1st:0 2nd:0 3rd:1 Ran:8
Pre2000 - 1st:5 2nd:4 3rd:3 Ran:44
Win Prizemoney £14,530 *Total Prizemoney* £22,623

Wins	1999	Jun	Doncas	(G-F)	H	10.3f	53	55
	1999	*Jan*	*Wolver*	*(STD)*	*S*	*8.5f*		*51+*
	1998	*Dec*	*Wolver*	*(STD)*	*S*	*8.5f*		*55*
	1998	Aug	Bright	(G-F)	C	10f		63

2000 Turf 0-7: (8f, 10f 3, 11f 2, 12f) (hvy, gd 3, g-f, frm, hrd) 2000 AW 0-1: (8f) (Fibr)
Poor gelding, effective 8 to 10f, best at 10f, acts on gd to frm - acts on Fibr, has worn blinkers, likes left handed tracks. Turf high 26.
**B D Leavy [0-10] Joe Singh (from C N Kellett [0-5] Aug 1999).*

BURNING DAYLIGHT (IRE) BHB 50f **RR 54f** 3090[7]
3 b g Bigstone (IRE) - Ma N'Ieme Biche (USA) (Key to the Kingdom (USA)) 8.3f **(65)**
Form - 057
Record 2000 - 1st:0 2nd:0 3rd:0 Ran:3
2000 Turf 0-3: (10f, 11f, 12f) (frm 3)
Scopey, currently fair gelding. Turf high 54.
**M H Tompkins [0-3] Mrs Jane Bailey.*

BURNING ROMA (USA) RR 5330a[4]

2 b f Rubiano (USA) 7.1f **(87)** - While Rome Burns (USA) (Overskate (USA))

Form - 4

2000 AW 0-1: (9f) (Dirt)

Currently very useful. (1st run) - 4th of 14 to Macho Uno (4 Nov Churchill Downs 9f Dirt RF 5330a). **A Dutrow in USA [0-1] H Queen.*

BURNING SUNSET BHB 89f **RR 94f** 4227[1]

3 ch f Caerleon (USA) 10.9f **(79)** - Lingerie (Shirley Heights) 10.3f **(74)**

Form - 302231

Record 2000 - 1st:1 2nd:2 3rd:2 Ran:6
Pre2000 - 1st:0 2nd:0 3rd:1 Ran:2

Win Prizemoney £4,179 *Total Prizemoney* £9,524

Wins * 2000 Spt Lingfi (G-F) 7f 72+ <

2000 Turf 1-6: (7f 1-1, 9f, 10f 4) (sft, gd, g-f, frm 1-3)

Leggy, useful filly, effective 9 to 10f, best at 10f, acts on sft to frm. Turf high 91 - 2nd of 6 getting 4lb from Common Place (17 Jun Sandown 9f g-f RF 2056). A half-sister to Shiva, she did not get off the mark until winning a Lingfield maiden in September. Later joined French trainer D. Sepulchre.

**H R A Cecil [1-8] Niarchos Family.*

BURNING TRUTH (USA) BHB 65f75a **RR 62f 75a** 5113[4]

6 ch g Known Fact (USA) 8.3f **(72)** - Galega (Sure Blade (USA)) 11.3f **(67)**

Form - 6020014

Record 2000 - 1st:1 2nd:1 3rd:0 Ran:7
Pre2000 - 1st:0 2nd:5 3rd:5 Ran:20

Win Prizemoney £2,534 *Total Prizemoney* £16,287

Wins * 2000 *Oct Wolver (STD) H 8.5f 60 66* <

2000 Turf 0-5: (8f 3, 9f, 10f) (gd 3, frm 2) 2000 AW 1-2: (8f 1-2) (Fibr 1-2)

Above-average gelding, effective 8 to 10f, best at 8f, acts on gd to frm - acts on Fibr, does well at Redcar. Turf high 62 - 2nd of 16 getting 15lb from Gralmano (30 Jly Ripon 9f frm RF 3240). AW high 66 (1st run) (began Oct) - 1st of 12 giving 7lb to Robbies Dream (14 Oct Wolverhampton RF 4997).

**Mrs A Duffield [1-22] Middleham Park Racing IV (from R Charlton [0-7] Spt 1997).*

BURN PARK BHB 45f **RR 53df** 2426[16]

3 ch f Fraam - Dewberry (Bay Express) 7.1f **(60)**

Form - 00

Record 2000 - 1st:0 2nd:0 3rd:0 Ran:2
Pre2000 - 1st:1 2nd:0 3rd:0 Ran:4

Win Prizemoney £1,884 *Total Prizemoney* £1,973

Wins 1999 Apr Nottin (G-S) S 5.1f 56 <

2000 Turf 0-2: (8f, 10f) (gd, frm)

Light-framed, fair filly, effective 5f, acts on sft.

**P Bowen [0-2] Seasons Holidays (from B R Millman [1-4] Oct 1999).*

BUSTLE (USA) RR 55f 4821[12]

2 ch f Chief Honcho (USA) - Parliament House (USA) (General Assembly (USA)) 10f **(68)**

Form - 00

Record 2000 - 1st:0 2nd:0 3rd:0 Ran:2

2000 Turf 0-2: (6f, 7f) (g-f, frm)

Currently fair filly. Turf high 55 (began Spt).

**J A R Toller [0-2] P C J Dalby.*

BUSTLING RIO (IRE) BHB 74f66a **RR 74f 66a** 3826[3]

4 b g Up and At 'em - Une Venitienne (FR) (Green Dancer (USA)) 10.3f **(74)**

Form - 211580111513

Record 2000 - 1st:5 2nd:0 3rd:1 Ran:10
Pre2000 - 1st:3 2nd:1 3rd:2 Ran:13

Win Prizemoney £31,587 *Total Prizemoney* £34,271

Wins * 2000 Aug Beverl (G-F) H 16.2f 65 72 <
*** 2000** Jly Doncas (GD) H 16.5f 60 64+
*** 2000** Jly Beverl (GD) H 16.2f 60 65
*** 2000** Jun Pontef (G-F) H 18f 55 57
*** 2000** *Jan Southw (STD) H 16f 61 66*
* 1999 *Nov Southw (STD) H 16f 55 60*
* 1999 May Pontef (GD) H 12f 55 56
* 1999 *Feb Southw (STD) H 11f 47 55*

2000 Turf 4-8: (16f 2-2, 17f 1-3, 18f 1-2, 20f) (gd 3, g-f 2-2, frm 2-2, hrd) 2000 AW 1-2: (16f 1-2) (Fibr 1-2)

Above-average gelding, effective 16 to 20f, acts on gd to hrd - acts on Fibr, likes tight tracks, and excels at Pontefract and Beverley. Turf high 74 - 3rd of 14 giving 15lb to Keep Ikis (20 Aug Pontefract 17f hrd RF 3826) - also 1st of 7 getting 14lb from Star Rage (16 Aug Beverley RF 3685). AW high 66 (1st run) - 1st of 11 giving 9lb to Kent (31 Jan Southwell RF 0191). A winner on the All-Weather and turf, he stepped up successfully to two miles at Southwell during the winter. He was in fine form in the summer, completing a hat-trick in staying handicap.

**P C Haslam [8-23] Rio Stainless Engineering Ltd.*

BUSTOPHER JONES BHB 47f49a **RR 47f 49a** 972[8]

6 b g Robellino (USA) 9.5f **(68)** - Catkin (USA) (Sir Ivor) 10.2f **(70)**

Form - 8

Record 2000 - 1st:0 2nd:0 3rd:0 Ran:1
Pre2000 - 1st:1 2nd:0 3rd:1 Ran:5

Win Prizemoney £2,463 *Total Prizemoney* £2,900

Wins * 1998 *Mar Southw (STD) H 11f 45 46* <

2000 Turf 0-1: (14f) (gd)

Moderate gelding.

**C R Egerton [1-6] Chris Brasher.*

BUSY BUSY BEE BHB 45f55a **RR 33f 55a** 5119[4]

3 gr f Batshoof 9.5f **(66)** - Rectitude (Runnymede) 9.3f **(50)**

Form - 50464

Record 2000 - 1st:0 2nd:0 3rd:0 Ran:5
Pre2000 - 1st:0 2nd:1 3rd:0 Ran:3

Win Prizemoney £0 *Total Prizemoney* £1,108

2000 AW 0-5: (9f 2, 12f 3) (Equi, Fibr 4)

Light-framed, fair filly, effective 7f, - acts on Fibr. AW high 50 (began Aug).

**N P Littmoden [0-8] The Busy Bee Partnership.*

BUSY LIZZIE (IRE) BHB 94f **RR 97f** 5226[8]

3 b f Sadler's Wells (USA) 11.3f **(87)** - Impatiente (USA) (Vaguely Noble) 10.1f **(72)**

Form - 206251168

Record 2000 - 1st:2 2nd:2 3rd:0 Ran:9
Pre2000 - 1st:0 2nd:0 3rd:0 Ran:2

Win Prizemoney £11,576 *Total Prizemoney* £14,494

Wins * 2000 Spt Ayr (SFT) H 15f 90 97 <
*** 2000** Aug Cheste (GD) H 15.9f 79 91

2000 Turf 2-9: (12f 3, 14f 2, 15f 1-1, 16f 1-3) (g-s, gd 2-6, g-f 2)

Light-framed, very useful filly, effective 15 to 16f, acts on gd, likes tight tracks. Turf high 97 - 1st of 8 giving 10lb to Royal Minstrel (14 Spt Ayr RF 4385) - also 1st of 10 getting 5lb from Jaseur (20 Aug Chester RF 3823). Tough and genuine staying filly.

**J L Dunlop [2-11] Nigel Clark (Susan A Racing).*

BUTRINTO BHB 61f58a **RR 65f 58a** 5155[4]

6 ch g Anshan 8.2f **(63)** - Bay Bay (Bay Express) 7.1f **(60)**

Form - 850611402322054

Record 2000 - 1st:2 2nd:3 3rd:1 Ran:14
Pre2000 - 1st:3 2nd:2 3rd:1 Ran:33

Win Prizemoney £14,918 *Total Prizemoney* £21,115

Wins * 2000 May Bright (FRM) H 7f 46 58
*** 2000** May Bright (FRM) H 7f 46 50
1998 *Dec Lingfi (STD) H 7f 70 70*
1998 May Newbur (GD) H 6f 71 74 <
1997 Aug Salisb (G-F) 6f 69

2000 Turf 2-10: (7f 2-5, 8f 5) (gd 3, g-f 1-3, frm 1-4) 2000 AW 0-4: (7f 2, 8f, 16f) (Equi, Fibr 3)

Average gelding, effective 7 to 8f, acts on g-f - acts on Fibr, has worn blinkers, likes left handed tracks, likes tight tracks. Turf high 65 - 2nd of 9 giving 3lb to Hail The Chief (10 Aug Brighton 7f g-f RF 3519). AW high 60. Consistent.

**B R Johnson [2-11] Miss Julie Reeves (from J Pearce [2-31] Jan 2000).*

BUTTERSCOTCH BHB 44f37a **RR 49f 37a** 3598[10]

4 b g Aragon 7.7f **(58)** - Gwiffina (Welsh Saint) 7.6f **(64)**

Form - 0033570

Record 2000 - 1st:0 2nd:0 3rd:2 Ran:7
Pre2000 - 1st:0 2nd:1 3rd:3 Ran:17

Win Prizemoney £0 *Total Prizemoney* £4,191

2000 Turf 0-5: (10f 4, 12f) (gd, g-f 2, frm, hrd) 2000 AW 0-2: (8f, 11f) (Fibr 2)
Moderate gelding, effective 7 to 10f, acts on gd to frm, likes right handed tracks, favours tight tracks. Turf high 49. AW high 8.
**J L Eyre [0-28] Sunpak Potatoes.*

BUTTERWICK CHIEF BHB 43f **RR 52f** 4213[16]
3 b g Be My Chief (USA) 10.2f **(62)** - Swift Return (Double Form) 7.3f **(58)**
Form - 0400
Record 2000 - 1st:0 2nd:0 3rd:0 Ran:4
Win Prizemoney £0 *Total Prizemoney* £259
2000 Turf 0-4: (8f 2, 11f, 12f) (g-s 2, gd, hrd)
Workmanlike, fair gelding, has worn blinkers. Turf high 52.
**R A Fahey [0-4] P S Cresswell.*

BUXTED'S FIRST BHB 45f47a **RR 52f 47a** 5220[4]
3 gr f Mystiko (USA) 7.7f **(59)** - Sea Fairy (Wollow) 8.2f **(61)**
Form - 033804
Record 2000 - 1st:0 2nd:0 3rd:2 Ran:6
Pre2000 - 1st:0 2nd:0 3rd:0 Ran:2
Win Prizemoney £0 *Total Prizemoney* £1,321
2000 Turf 0-5: (8f 2, 9f, 10f 2) (sft, g-s, gd 2, frm) 2000 AW 0-1: (12f) (Equi)
Leggy, fair filly, effective 9f, acts on frm, likes tight tracks. Turf high 52 - 3rd of 4 getting 17lb from Den's-Joy (14 Jun Lingfield 9f frm RF 1973). Becoming disappointing.
**G L Moore [0-8] Buxted Partnership.*

BUY A VOWEL (USA) BHB 67f **RR 62f** 4970[10]
2 b br c Capote (USA) 9.1f **(84)** - Monaassabaat (USA) **(103f)** (Zilzal (USA))
Form - 7600
Record 2000 - 1st:0 2nd:0 3rd:0 Ran:4
2000 Turf 0-4: (7f 3, 8f) (g-s, gd 2, g-f)
Average colt. Turf high 78 (began Jly).
**Sir Michael Stoute [0-4] Maktoum Al Maktoum.*

BUYING A DREAM (IRE) BHB 75f **RR 75f** 1390[17]
3 ch g Prince of Birds (USA) - Cartagena Lady (IRE) (Prince Rupert (FR))
Form - 30
Record 2000 - 1st:0 2nd:0 3rd:1 Ran:2
Pre2000 - 1st:1 2nd:1 3rd:0 Ran:4
Win Prizemoney £2,526 *Total Prizemoney* £5,966
Wins * 1999 Jun Thirsk (G-F) 7f 56+ <
2000 Turf 0-2: (8f, 10f) (gd 2)
Scopey, above-average gelding, effective 8f, acts on gd. Turf high 75 (1st run) - 3rd of 13 getting 12lb from Safarando (1 Apr Haydock 8f gd RF 0590).
**Andrew Turnell [1-6] Mrs Claire Hollowood.*

BUZ KIRI (USA) BHB 53f **RR 31f** 5075[7]
2 b c Gulch (USA) 9.6f **(79)** - White Corners (USA) (Caro)
Form - 7
Record 2000 - 1st:0 2nd:0 3rd:0 Ran:1
2000 Turf 0-1: (8f) (g-s)
Currently average colt. **A W Carroll [0-1] Serafino Agodino.*

BUZZ THE AGENT BHB 35f **RR 35df** 3738[6]
5 b g Prince Sabo 6.6f **(64)** - Chess Mistress (USA) (Run The Gantlet (USA)) 12.1f **(59)**
Form - 2706
Record 2000 - 1st:0 2nd:1 3rd:0 Ran:4
Pre2000 - 1st:1 2nd:2 3rd:2 Ran:24
Win Prizemoney £3,036 *Total Prizemoney* £6,716
Wins * 1998 Spt Beverl (G-F) H 12f 51 56 <
2000 Turf 0-4: (8f, 10f, 12f 2) (gd, g-f, frm 2)
Very moderate gelding, effective 10 to 12f, acts on g-s to frm, best on frm, often wears blinkers (extremely effectively). Turf high 31 (began Aug). Consistent. **M W Easterby [1-29] Alan Black & Co.*

B W LEADER BHB 47f **RR 30f** 4366[8]
3 b g Owington - Showery **(73+f)** (Rainbow Quest (USA)) 10.4f **(75)**
Form - 8
Record 2000 - 1st:0 2nd:0 3rd:0 Ran:1
Pre2000 - 1st:0 2nd:0 3rd:0 Ran:1

2000 Turf 0-1: (5f) (g-f)
Leggy, currently very moderate gelding.
**Miss D A McHale [0-1] Watmore-Davis/Mackintosh-Amon Racing (from P F I Cole [0-1] Apr 1999).*

BY DEFINITION (IRE) **RR 52f** 2257[12]
2 gr b f Definite Article - Miss Goodbody (Castle Keep) 8.3f **(57)**
Form - 00
Record 2000 - 1st:0 2nd:0 3rd:0 Ran:2
2000 Turf 0-2: (6f, 7f) (frm 2)
Currently fair filly. Turf high 52. **P W Harris [0-2] The Definite Dozen.*

BYLAW (USA) BHB 78f **RR 76f** 5136[3]
2 b f Lear Fan (USA) 10.4f **(80)** - Byre Bird (USA) (Diesis) 9.3f **(69)**
Form - 273
Record 2000 - 1st:0 2nd:1 3rd:1 Ran:3
Win Prizemoney £0 *Total Prizemoney* £1,841
2000 Turf 0-3: (7f 2, 8f) (g-s, gd, frm)
Currently above-average filly. Turf high 76 (began Aug) - 3rd of 11 to Heavenly Whisper (22 Oct Yarmouth 8f g-s RF 5136).
**J H M Gosden [0-3] Sheikh Mohammed.*

BYO (IRE) BHB 92f **RR 100f** 5123[8]
2 gr c Paris House 5.9f **(64)** - Navan Royal (IRE) (Dominion Royale)
Form - 01512435648
Record 2000 - 1st:2 2nd:1 3rd:1 Ran:11
Win Prizemoney £6,178 *Total Prizemoney* £11,213
Wins * **2000** Jly Bovorl (GD) 5f 85 <
* **2000** Jun Ripon (G-F) 5f 71
2000 Turf 2-11: (5f 2-8, 6f 3) (g-s 2, gd 2, g-f 1-2, frm 1-5)
Very useful colt, effective 5f, acts on gd to g-f. Turf high 100 - 3rd of 9 giving 32lb to Effervesce (10 Aug Haydock 5f gd RF 3531).
**M C Chapman [2-11] Jalons Partnership.*

BY THE GLASS BHB 25f **RR 35f** 5166[12]
4 b g Ardkinglass 5f **(64)** - Mia Fillia (Formidable (USA)) 9.2f **(63)**
Form - 67076840
Record 2000 - 1st:0 2nd:0 3rd:0 Ran:8
Pre2000 - 1st:1 2nd:0 3rd:1 Ran:20
Win Prizemoney £2,721 *Total Prizemoney* £3,222
Wins 1998 May Leices (GD) 5f 73 <
2000 Turf 0-8: (7f 4, 8f 4) (hvy, gd 3, g-f, frm 2, hrd)
Average gelding, has worn blinkers. Turf high 35.
**N Tinkler [0-9] Don Enrico Incisa (from Don Enrico Incisa [0-11] Aug 2000).*

BYZANTIUM BHB 71a **RR 70f** 4484[17]
6 b g Shirley Heights 12.1f **(76)** - Dulceata (IRE) (Rousillon (USA)) 8.2f **(74)**
Form - 5430
Record 2000 - 1st:0 2nd:0 3rd:1 Ran:4
Pre2000 - 1st:4 2nd:3 3rd:4 Ran:25
Win Prizemoney £11,560 *Total Prizemoney* £20,011
Wins 1999 Aug Windso (G-F) H 8.3f 59 63
1998 *Dec Lingfi (STD) H 10f 64 67*
1998 *Nov Lingfi (STD) H 10f 57 61*
1997 May Kempto (GD) 8f 78 <
2000 Turf 0-4: (8f 3, 9f) (g-s, g-f, frm 2)
Above-average gelding, effective 8 to 9f, best at 8f, acts on g-f to frm, best on frm, has worn blinkers, excels at Newmarket and Lingfield. Turf high 69 (began Aug) - 3rd of 17 getting 2lb from Arpeggio (5 Spt Lingfield 8f frm RF 4224). Consistent.
**W Jarvis [0-4] R Van Gelder (from M J Fetherston-Godley [1-12] Oct 1999).*

CABALLE (USA) BHB 76f **RR 77f** 4734[17]
3 ch f Opening Verse (USA) 11.8f **(70)** - Attirance (FR) (Crowned Prince (USA)) 10.1f **(67)**
Form - 23322130
Record 2000 - 1st:1 2nd:3 3rd:3 Ran:8
Pre2000 - 1st:0 2nd:1 3rd:0 Ran:1
Win Prizemoney £2,717 *Total Prizemoney* £8,649
Wins * **2000** Aug Bright (G-F) 10f 41++ <
2000 Turf 1-8: (8f 3, 10f 1-4, 12f) (g-s, gd 3, g-f 1-1, frm 3)
Workmanlike, above-average filly, effective 8 to 12f, acts on g-s to frm, best on frm. Turf high 78 (1st run) - 2nd of 8 to Inforapenny (11 Apr Pontefract 10f g-s RF 0660). Regularly in the frame,

but her only win to date came in a very poor maiden at Brighton in August. **S P C Woods [1-9] B Allen/R Hine/R Dawson/A Duke.*

CABARET QUEST BHB 43f **RR 42f** 3954[2]
4 ch g Pursuit of Love 9.5f **(69)** - Cabaret Artiste (Shareef Dancer (USA)) 9.9f **(73)**
Form - 0000683362
Record 2000 - 1st:0 2nd:1 3rd:2 Ran:10
Pre2000 - 1st:1 2nd:0 3rd:1 Ran:8
Win Prizemoney £2,742 *Total Prizemoney* £5,014
Wins 1999 May Leices (G-F) C 8f 57 <
2000 Turf 0-10: (8f 7, 10f 2, 11f) (hvy, gd 3, g-f 3, frm, hrd 2)
Scopey, moderate gelding, effective 8f, acts on frm. Turf high 42.
**J M Bradley [0-10] Miss S Howell (from R Hannon [1-8] Jun 1999).*

CABCHARGE BLUE BHB 37f30a **RR ?f 30a** 5063[15]
8 b m Midyan (USA) 9.9f **(64)** - Mashobra (Vision (USA)) 9f **(64)**
Form - 0
Record 2000 - 1st:0 2nd:0 3rd:0 Ran:1
Pre2000 - 1st:8 2nd:6 3rd:5 Ran:61
Win Prizemoney £20,136 *Total Prizemoney* £29,052
Wins 1999 May Bright (FRM) H 11.9f 43 45
1997 Oct Bright (G-F) SH 10f 36 48
1996 Jan Southw (STD) H 8f 48 52
2000 Turf 0-1: (10f) (sft)
Little account mare, effective 10 to 12f, best at 12f, acts on g-f to frm, best on g-f. Inconsistent.
**M Kettle [0-1] Johnny Wise (from T J Naughton [4-52] Spt 1999).*

CABOTO (IRE) RR 4413a[2]
2 b g Sri Pekan (USA) - Fiction (Dominion) 8.5f **(63)**
Form - 2
Record 2000 - 1st:0 2nd:1 3rd:0 Ran:1
Win Prizemoney £0 *Total Prizemoney* £1,789
2000 Turf 0-1: (7f) (gd)
Currently very poor gelding - 2nd of 8 to Dolphin Tattoo (10 Spt Cascine 7f gd RF 4413a). **M Quinlan [0-1].*

CABRIAC BHB 85f **RR 85f** 526[2]
3 b br c Machiavellian (USA) 9.8f **(83)** - Chief Bee **(89f)** (Chief's Crown (USA)) 9.8f **(72)**
Form - 2
Record 2000 - 1st:0 2nd:1 3rd:0 Ran:1
Pre2000 - 1st:0 2nd:1 3rd:0 Ran:2
Win Prizemoney £0 *Total Prizemoney* £2,354
2000 Turf 0-1: (7f) (gd)
Well made, currently useful colt. (1st run) - 2nd of 16 to Dancing Bay (28 Mar Newcastle 7f gd RF 0526).
**J L Dunlop [0-3] Benny Andersson.*

CACOPHONY BHB 41f46a **RR 51df 46a** 4649[15]
3 b g Son Pardo - Ansellady **(62f 60a)** (Absalom) 7.2f **(58)**
Form - 38335462200
Record 2000 - 1st:0 2nd:2 3rd:0 Ran:7
Pre2000 - 1st:0 2nd:0 3rd:3 Ran:10
Win Prizemoney £0 *Total Prizemoney* £1,907
2000 Turf 0-1: (10f) (sft) 2000 AW 0-6: (6f 2, 7f 2, 8f, 11f) (Equi 2, Fibr 4)
Unfurnished, fair gelding, has worn blinkers. AW high 46.
**S R Bowring [0-2] Roland Wheatley (from S Dow [0-15] Mar 2000).*

CADEAUX CHER BHB 81f **RR 83f** 4258[5]
6 ch g Cadeaux Genereux 7.9f **(76)** - Home Truth (Known Fact (USA)) 7.4f **(67)**
Form - 220081075055
Record 2000 - 1st:1 2nd:2 3rd:0 Ran:12
Pre2000 - 1st:5 2nd:2 3rd:0 Ran:37
Win Prizemoney £68,246 *Total Prizemoney* £83,156
Wins * **2000** Jly Warwic (G-F) H 6.1f 78 82
* 1998 Spt Doncas (GD) H 5.6f 89 93 <
* 1998 Aug Ripon (G-F) H 6f 79 86
* 1998 Aug Leices (GD) 6f 76
* 1998 Jly Doncas (G-F) 6f 78?
* 1997 Mar Doncas (G-F) 6f 76
2000 Turf 1-12: (6f 1-12) (gd 6, g-f 1-6)
Decent gelding, effective 6f, acts on gd to g-f, best on g-f, has worn blinkers. Turf high 83 - 5th of 22 giving 8lb to William's Well (19 Aug Ripon 6f g-f RF 3796) - also 1st of 9 giving 11lb to Eventuality (22 Jly Warwick RF 3046). A winner four times in 1998, including the Great St Wilfrid and the Portland, he has not sparkled since. Needs to be produced late.
**B W Hills [6-49] N N Browne.*

CADILLAC JUKEBOX (USA) BHB 53f **RR 51f** 1162[4]
5 b br g Alleged (USA) 11.8f **(81)** - Symphonic Music (USA) (Al Nasr (FR)) 9.3f **(68)**
Form - 04
Record 2000 - 1st:0 2nd:0 3rd:0 Ran:2
Pre2000 - 1st:1 2nd:0 3rd:1 Ran:9
Win Prizemoney £2,140 *Total Prizemoney* £2,890
Wins 1998 Aug Pontef (G-F) 12f 69 <
2000 Turf 0-2: (12f, 14f) (g-f, frm)
Fair gelding, has worn blinkers. Turf high 51. Consistent.
**G M Moore [0-8] North Briton Racing (from J W Hills [1-9] Oct 1998).*

CA'D'ORO BHB 65f **RR 66f** 5316[15]
7 ch g Cadeaux Genereux 7.9f **(76)** - Palace Street (USA) (Secreto (USA)) 8.7f **(72)**
Form - 0302840
Record 2000 - 1st:0 2nd:1 3rd:1 Ran:7
Pre2000 - 1st:6 2nd:6 3rd:5 Ran:49
Win Prizemoney £26,483 *Total Prizemoney* £39,519
Wins * 1999 Aug Kempto (SFT) H 7f 64 69 <
* 1998 Oct Nottin () H 8.2f 59 63
* 1997 Oct Nottin (G-S) H 8.2f 58 64
* 1997 Jun Goodwo (G-S) H 8f 53 59
* 1997 Jun Newbur (GD) H 8f 53 57
* 1996 Aug Bath (GD) H 8f 56 60
2000 Turf 0-7: (7f 3, 8f 4) (sft 3, g-s 2, gd, g-f)
Average gelding, effective 7 to 8f, best at 7f, acts on sft to g-f. Turf high 66. A grand handicapper who really earns his keep, he is best at distances of seven furlongs plus, and goes particularly well with some give in the ground. **G B Balding [6-56] Miss B Swire.*

CAERDYDD FACH BHB 26f31a **RR 23f 31a** 4922[15]
4 b f Bluebird (USA) 7.9f **(71)** - Waitingformargaret (Kris) 9.5f **(73)**
Form - 047770
Record 2000 - 1st:0 2nd:0 3rd:0 Ran:6
Pre2000 - 1st:0 2nd:0 3rd:1 Ran:19
Win Prizemoney £0 *Total Prizemoney* £245
2000 Turf 0-4: (8f 2, 10f, 11f) (gd, g-f 2, frm) 2000 AW 0-2: (7f, 10f) (Equi 2)
Light-framed, little account filly, effective 10f, acts on gd. Turf high 23. AW high 14 (began Jly).
**M Quinn [0-1] M B Clemence (from Mrs A E Johnson [0-5] Aug 2000).*

CAERNARFON BAY (IRE) BHB 42f49a **RR 45f 49a** 521[13]
5 ch g Royal Academy (USA) 7.8f **(77)** - Bay Shade (USA) (Sharpen Up) 8.3f **(67)**
Form - 2000
Record 2000 - 1st:0 2nd:0 3rd:0 Ran:2
Pre2000 - 1st:2 2nd:4 3rd:3 Ran:21
Win Prizemoney £4,936 *Total Prizemoney* £9,893
Wins 1999 Apr Bright (G-F) H 11.9f 46 49
1999 Jan Lingfi (STD) H 10f 48 53 <
2000 Turf 0-1: (12f) (frm) 2000 AW 0-1: (12f) (Equi)
Fair gelding, effective 10 to 12f, best at 10f, acts on g-f to frm - acts on Equi, has worn blinkers, prefers left handed tracks, favours tight tracks, excels at Brighton, likes Lingfield. A fair handicapper in modest company, he has been successful on Equitrack and on turf at Brighton so far this year. Goes well for an amateur rider.
**A Barrow [0-2] Alan Harrington (from G L Moore [2-13] Jan 2000).*

CAFE GRANDE (IRE) **RR 71f** 4964[2]
2 b c Grand Lodge (USA) - Olean (Sadler's Wells (USA)) 10f **(76)**
Form - 2
Record 2000 - 1st:0 2nd:1 3rd:0 Ran:1
Win Prizemoney £0 *Total Prizemoney* £2,871
2000 Turf 0-1: (7f) (gd)
Currently above-average colt. **M A Jarvis [0-1] Ivan Allan.*

CAFE OPERA (USA) BHB 84f **RR 86f** 5368a[5]
3 b f Sadler's Wells (USA) 11.3f **(87)** - Takreem (USA) **(51f)** (Mr Prospector (USA)) 8.8f **(78)**

Form - 021055
Record 2000 - 1st:1 2nd:1 3rd:0 Ran:6
Pre2000 - 1st:0 2nd:1 3rd:0 Ran:2
Win Prizemoney £3,760 *Total Prizemoney* £6,496
Wins * 2000 Aug Newcas (SFT) 8f 81 <
2000 Turf 1-6: (8f 1-5, 10f) (hvy, sft, g-s 1-2, gd, g-f)
Leggy, useful filly, effective 8f, acts on g-s to g-f. Turf high 86 - also 1st of 8 from Land Ahead (28 Aug Newcastle RF 4045). Landed a soft-ground maiden at Newcastle in August, when front-running tactics worked well. **J W Hills [1-8].*

CAFETERIA BAY (USA) BHB 100f RR 94f 5108[5]

2 ch c Sky Classic (CAN) 10f **(83)** - Go On Zen (USA) (Zen (USA))
Form - 1315
Record 2000 - 1st:2 2nd:0 3rd:1 Ran:4
Win Prizemoney £7,660 *Total Prizemoney* £8,740
Wins * 2000 Spt Leices (G-S) 7f 89 <
* 2000 Aug Yarmou (G-F) 6f 77+
2000 Turf 2-4: (6f 1-1, 7f 1-3) (gd 2, g-f 2-2)
Useful colt. Turf high 94 (began Aug) - also 1st of 5 from Steel Band (18 Spt Leicester RF 4488). He is progressing well, and his defeats have come at the hands of some useful opponents. **K R Burke [2-4] Kenneth Lau.*

CAFFE LATTE (USA) RR 119f 5329a[9]

4 m Seattle Dancer (USA) 10.1f **(74)** - Debbie's Next (USA) (Arctic Tern (USA)) 8.9f **(69)**
Form - 0
2000 Turf 0-1: (11f) (frm)
Neat, currently high-class.
**B Baffert in USA [0-1] Stonerside Stable (from J Canani in USA [0-1] Nov 1999).*

CAIRN DHU BHB 22f31a RR 22f 31a 4494[13]

6 ch g Presidium 7.5f **(56)** - My Precious Daisy (Sharpo) 7.7f **(59)**
Form - 2000007500
Record 2000 - 1st:0 2nd:0 3rd:0 Ran:8
Pre2000 - 1st:1 2nd:1 3rd:0 Ran:20
Win Prizemoney £1,634 *Total Prizemoney* £2,518
Wins 1997 Apr Nottin (G-F) S 6.1f 62+ <
2000 Turf 0-8: (6f 3, 7f, 8f 3, 12f) (g-s 2, gd, g-f 2, frm 3)
Very moderate gelding, has worn blinkers. Turf high 22.
**D W Barker [0-21] Mrs S J Barker (from Mrs J R Ramsden [1-8] May 1997).*

CAIR PARAVEL (IRE) BHB 84f RR 86f 4732[11]

3 b br c Dolphin Street (FR) - Queen's Ransom (IRE) **(66f)** (Last Tycoon) 8.5f **(62)**
Form - 530071000
Record 2000 - 1st:1 2nd:0 3rd:1 Ran:9
Pre2000 - 1st:2 2nd:0 3rd:0 Ran:2
Win Prizemoney £12,614 *Total Prizemoney* £13,794
Wins * **2000** Jly Salisb (GD) H 8f 82 86 <
* 1999 Jun Doncas (G-S) 6f 71+
* 1999 Jun Leices (GD) 5f 78+
2000 Turf 1-9: (6f, 7f 5, 8f 1-3) (sft, gd 2, g-f 1-5, frm)
Workmanlike, useful colt, effective 5 to 8f, best at 7f, acts on g-f, has worn blinkers. Turf high 86 - 1st of 10 giving 8lb to Pretrail (15 Jly Salisbury RF 2846). Consistent. **R Hannon [3-11] Mrs Caroline Parker.*

CAITANO RR 121f 4412a[1]

6 b h Niniski (USA) 13.2f **(67)** - Eversince (USA) (Foolish Pleasure (USA)) 8.9f **(72)**
Form - 234541
2000 Turf 1-6: (10f, 12f 1-5) (gd 1-5, g-f)
Very high-class horse, effective 10 to 12f, best at 12f, acts on sft to gd, best on gd, has worn blinkers. Turf high 121 (1st run) - 2nd of 16 giving 2lb to Fantastic Light (25 Mar Nad Al Sheba 12f gd RF 0578a). A high-class German-trained colt, he has competed in most of the top races around the world for the past four years. He finished fifth in the 1998 Arc and recorded successive Group Two victories in his native Germany in 1999, on one occasion beating the top-class Tiger Hill. He once again contested the major international races last year, ending the season with a good third in the Hong Kong Vase.
**A Schutz in GER [3-16] G Tanaka (from B Schutz in GER [3-7] Nov 1997).*

CAJOLE (IRE) BHB 56f RR 71df 591[14]

4 ch f Barathea (IRE) - Frendly Persuasion (General Assembly (USA)) 10f **(68)**
Form - 0
Record 2000 - 1st:0 2nd:0 3rd:0 Ran:1
Pre2000 - 1st:0 2nd:1 3rd:0 Ran:6
Win Prizemoney £0 *Total Prizemoney* £1,103
2000 Turf 0-1: (7f) (gd)
Workmanlike, above-average filly, effective 7f, acts on frm.
**R F JohnsonHoughton [0-7] Mrs Hue Williams.*

CAKESTOWN LADY (IRE) RR 95f 5283a[4]

3 br f Petorius 8f **(66)** - Sally Gone (IRE) (Last Tycoon) 8.5f **(62)**
Form - 1282824
2000 Turf 1-7: (7f 1-4, 8f 3) (hvy, sft 1-1, g-s 4, g-f)
Very useful filly, effective 8f, acts on g-s. Turf high 94 - 2nd of 13 getting 3lb from Molly-O (22 Oct Naas 8f g-s RF 5181a).
**G Keane in IRE [1-10] Mrs D Thornton.*

CALANDA RR 62f 3952[6]

2 b f Aragon 7.7f **(58)** - Henceforth (Full of Hope) 8.5f **(64)**
Form - 6
Record 2000 - 1st:0 2nd:0 3rd:0 Ran:1
2000 Turf 0-1: (5f) (hrd)
Currently average filly. **H Candy [0-1] Henry Candy.*

CALANDRELLA BHB 35f27a RR 34f 27a 4543[21]

7 b m Sizzling Melody 6.3f **(49)** - Maravilla (Mandrake Major) 7.6f **(53)**
Form - 770063308000
Record 2000 - 1st:0 2nd:0 3rd:2 Ran:12
Pre2000 - 1st:1 2nd:2 3rd:2 Ran:33
Win Prizemoney £2,736 *Total Prizemoney* £5,929
Wins 1999 Aug Mussel (G-S) H 5f 38 38 <
2000 Turf 0-10: (5f 6, 6f 4) (gd 4, g-f, frm 5) 2000 AW 0-2: (5f 2) (Equi, Fibr)
Very moderate mare, effective 5 to 6f, best at 5f, acts on gd to frm. Turf high 37 - 3rd of 11 getting 23lb from Perigeux (5 Jly Brighton 5f gd RF 2539). AW high 10.
**I A Wood [0-5] M B Clemence (from A G Newcombe [1-18] Jly 2000).*

CALCAVELLA BHB 62f59a RR 62f 59a 4195[5]

4 b f Pursuit of Love 9.5f **(69)** - Brightside (IRE) **(84f)** (Last Tycoon) 8.5f **(62)**
Form - 4750425
Record 2000 - 1st:0 2nd:1 3rd:0 Ran:7
Pre2000 - 1st:0 2nd:2 3rd:1 Ran:7
Win Prizemoney £0 *Total Prizemoney* £5,755
2000 Turf 0-7: (7f 7) (gd, g-f, frm 5)
Workmanlike, average filly, effective 7f, acts on g-f to frm, best on frm. Turf high 62 (began Jly) - 5th of 24 getting 7lb from Style Dancer (3 Spt York 7f g-f RF 4195). Consistent.
**M Kettle [0-14] Pillar To Post Racing Partnership (III).*

CALCINATE (IRE) RR 102f 5090a[5]

3 b f Tirol 8.1f **(64)** - Sea of Sand (Henbit (USA)) 9f **(61)**
Form - 25005
2000 Turf 0-5: (8f 2, 10f 2, 11f) (hvy 2, sft, gd 2)
Very useful filly. Turf high 102 - 5th of 18 to Xua (30 Apr Capannelle 8f sft RF 1031a).
**L Camici in ITY [0-3] (from F Camici in ITY [0-2] May 2000).*

CALCUTTA BHB 92f RR 95f 3934[8]

4 b c Indian Ridge 7.6f **(74)** - Echoing (Formidable (USA)) 9.2f **(63)**
Form - 0806308
Record 2000 - 1st:0 2nd:0 3rd:1 Ran:7
Pre2000 - 1st:3 2nd:2 3rd:3 Ran:13
Win Prizemoney £26,160 *Total Prizemoney* £50,706
Wins * 1999 Spt Doncas (G-F) H 8f 93 98+ <
* 1999 Jly Newmar (G-F) H 8f 83 86
* 1998 Jly Ayr (GD) 6f 80
2000 Turf 0-7: (8f 6, 9f) (sft, g-s, gd 2, g-f 2, frm)
Well made, very useful colt, effective 8f, acts on gd to frm, best on frm, has worn blinkers. Turf high 95 - 3rd of 11 to Free Option (23 Jly Kempton 8f frm RF 3051). Inconsistent. A useful handicapper in '99, he showed his best form last year in July. He is now back on a winning mark and, given a mile on fast ground could well

bounce back to winning ways.
**B W Hills [3-20] The Hon Mrs J M Corbett & C Wright.*

CALDEY ISLAND (IRE) BHB 36f60a **RR 43?f 60a** 4922[14]
3 b c Turtle Island (IRE) - Lady Taufan (IRE) (Taufan (USA)) 7f **(57)**
Form - 0000005750
Record 2000 - 1st:0 2nd:0 3rd:0 Ran:10
Pre2000 - 1st:0 2nd:0 3rd:2 Ran:10
Win Prizemoney £0 *Total Prizemoney* £1,868
2000 Turf 0-9: (6f, 7f 3, 8f 5) (sft, gd, g-f 2, frm 4, hrd) 2000 AW 0-1: (7f) (Equi)
Unfurnished, moderate colt, effective 6 to 7f, acts on g-f, has worn blinkers. Turf high 43.
**A G Newcombe [0-10] Alex Gorrie (from D W P Arbuthnot [0-10] Oct 1999).*

CALDIZ BHB 36f **RR 36tf** 4877[11]
3 b c Warning 8.1f **(77)** - Segovia **(93f)** (Groom Dancer (USA))
Form - 666480
Record 2000 - 1st:0 2nd:0 3rd:0 Ran:6
2000 Turf 0-6: (8f, 9f, 10f 3, 12f) (g-s, g-f 2, frm 3)
Workmanlike, very moderate colt. Turf high 62.
**Mrs M Bridgwater [0-4] Michael Appleby (from Mrs A J Perrett [0-3] Aug 2000).*

CALEB'S BOY BHB 34f **RR 50f** 2356[10]
3 b g Son Pardo - Lon Isa **(39f 47a)** (Grey Desire) 8.7f **(50)**
Form - 00
Record 2000 - 1st:0 2nd:0 3rd:0 Ran:2
Pre2000 - 1st:0 2nd:0 3rd:0 Ran:2
2000 Turf 0-2: (7f, 11f) (g-f 2)
Light-framed, fair gelding. Turf high 27.
**A G Juckes [0-2] H Weeks (from B Palling [0-2] Oct 1999).*

CALEDONIAN EXPRESS BHB 44f48a **RR 56df 48a** 555[9]
5 b m Northern Park (USA) 10f **(57)** - New Edition (Great Nephew) 9.9f **(64)**
Form - 0
Record 2000 - 1st:0 2nd:0 3rd:0 Ran:1
Pre2000 - 1st:0 2nd:0 3rd:1 Ran:8
Win Prizemoney £0 *Total Prizemoney* £434
2000 AW 0-1: (8f) (Equi)
Fair filly. Becoming disappointing.
**J R Best [1-12] Mercato Ltd (from J L Dunlop [0-6] Jly 1998).*

CALIBAN (IRE) BHB 60a **RR 68f** 5004[9]
2 ch g Rainbows For Life (CAN) 9.3f **(64)** - Amour Toujours (IRE) (Law Society (USA)) 9.9f **(70)**
Form - 75820
Record 2000 - 1st:0 2nd:1 3rd:0 Ran:5
Win Prizemoney £0 *Total Prizemoney* £552
2000 Turf 0-4: (6f, 8f 3) (g-s, gd, g-f 2) 2000 AW 0-1: (7f) (Fibr)
Average gelding. Turf high 63 (began Aug).
**N P Littmoden [0-5] Joy and Valentine Feerick.*

CALICO BHB 46f **RR 60f** 3374[14]
3 b f Barathea (IRE) - Craigmill **(78f)** (Slip Anchor) 9.8f **(73)**
Form - 080
Record 2000 - 1st:0 2nd:0 3rd:0 Ran:3
Pre2000 - 1st:0 2nd:0 3rd:0 Ran:4
2000 Turf 0-3: (11f, 12f, 16f) (hvy, g-f, frm)
Leggy, average filly. Turf high 35.
**J G Smyth-Osbourne [0-7] J H Henderson.*

CALIFORNIA SON (IRE) BHB 25f **RR 35f** 3044[8]
4 ch g Lycius (USA) 8.8f **(71)** - Madame Nureyev (USA) (Nureyev (USA)) 8.7f **(78)**
Form - U88
Record 2000 - 1st:0 2nd:0 3rd:0 Ran:3
Pre2000 - 1st:0 2nd:1 3rd:0 Ran:4
Win Prizemoney £0 *Total Prizemoney* £808
2000 Turf 0-3: (11f, 13f, 16f) (g-s, g-f 2)
Workmanlike, very moderate gelding. Turf high 35.
**C L Popham [0-3] C L Popham (from M Quinn [0-3] Oct 1999).*

CALIWAG (IRE) BHB 62f **RR 67f** 5159[16]
4 b g Lahib (USA) 8f **(69)** - Mitsubishi Style (Try My Best (USA)) 7.6f **(67)**
Form - 700
Record 2000 - 1st:0 2nd:0 3rd:0 Ran:3
Pre2000 - 1st:0 2nd:0 3rd:0 Ran:4
Win Prizemoney £0 *Total Prizemoney* £223
2000 Turf 0-3: (6f, 7f, 8f) (sft, gd, g-f)
Rangy, average gelding. Turf high 67.
**J R Poulton [0-1] Lottie Collins Partnership (from D R C Elsworth [0-6] May 2000).*

CALKO BHB 56f66a **RR 56f 66a** 1370[13]
3 ch g Timeless Times (USA) 6.1f **(56)** - Jeethgaya (USA) (Critique (USA))
Form - 153111700
Record 2000 - 1st:3 2nd:0 3rd:1 Ran:7
Pre2000 - 1st:1 2nd:0 3rd:2 Ran:8
Win Prizemoney £9,978 *Total Prizemoney* £11,094

Wins							
* **2000**	*Feb*	*Southw*	*(STD)*	*H*	*8f*	*62*	*67*
* **2000**	*Jan*	*Southw*	*(STD)*	*C*	*8f*		*69* <
* **2000**	*Jan*	*Southw*	*(STD)*	*S*	*7f*		*66*
* 1999	*Nov*	*Southw*	*(STD)*	*S*	*6f*		*60*

2000 Turf 0-2: (8f 2) (gd, frm) 2000 AW 3-5: (6f, 7f 1-1, 8f 2-3) (Fibr 3-5)
Unfurnished, average gelding, effective 6 to 8f, best at 8f, - acts on Fibr, often wears blinkers (extremely effectively), prefers left handed tracks, prefers tight tracks. Turf high 27. AW high 69 - 1st of 8 getting 3lb from Maid To Love (24 Jan Southwell RF 0146) - also 1st of 7 getting 5lb from National Dance (18 Feb Southwell RF 0309). Becoming disappointing. **T D Barron [4-15] T Calver.*

CALLAS BHB 60f **RR 65f** 5069[6]
3 b f Mtoto 11.5f **(71)** - Ower (IRE) (Lomond (USA)) 8.8f **(65)**
Form - 00566
Record 2000 - 1st:0 2nd:0 3rd:0 Ran:5
Pre2000 - 1st:0 2nd:0 3rd:0 Ran:2
Win Prizemoney £0 *Total Prizemoney* £276
2000 Turf 0-5: (6f, 7f, 8f, 10f, 12f) (g-s, gd 2, frm 2)
Scopey, average filly, effective 10f, acts on gd. Turf high 65 - 6th of 14 giving 11lb to Middlethorpe (7 Spt Chepstow 10f gd RF 4274).
**R F JohnsonHoughton [0-7] Dr J A E Hobby.*

CALLDAT SEVENTEEN BHB 70f65a **RR 80f 65a** 4864[9]
4 b g Komaite (USA) 6.9f **(61)** - Westminster Waltz (Dance In Time (CAN)) 8.9f **(59)**
Form - 7024676081R0
Record 2000 - 1st:1 2nd:1 3rd:0 Ran:11
Pre2000 - 1st:3 2nd:0 3rd:2 Ran:15
Win Prizemoney £13,185 *Total Prizemoney* £17,205

Wins							
* **2000**	Spt	Nottin	(SFT)		10f		73+
* 1999	Aug	Epsom	(GD)	H	8.5f	75	80 <
* 1999	Apr	Epsom	(SFT)		8.5f		79
* 1999	*Feb*	*Lingfi*	*(STD)*		*8f*		*70*

2000 Turf 1-11: (8f 3, 9f 2, 10f 1-6) (sft 2, gd 1-3, g-f 5, hrd)
Scopey, decent gelding, effective 7 to 10f, best at 9f, acts on g-s to frm - acts on Equi, best on g-f, likes tight tracks, excels at Epsom, likes Nottingham and Newmarket. Turf high 80 - 2nd of 7 giving 3lb to Lady Angharad (12 May Nottingham 10f g-f RF 1180) - also 1st of 15 giving 10lb to Ma Vie (15 Spt Nottingham RF 4446). Inconsistent. Dropped in the handicap before winning very easily on soft ground at Nottingham in September.
**P W D'Arcy [4-26] Keith Harrison & Terry Miller.*

CALLER ONE (USA) RR 5328a[4]
3 b c Phone Trick (USA) 7f **(62)** - Baltic Sea (USA) (Danzig (USA)) 8.4f **(76)**
Form - 4
2000 AW 0-1: (6f) (Dirt)
Currently Group-class colt. (1st run) - 4th of 14 getting 2lb from Kona Gold (4 Nov Churchill Downs 6f Dirt RF 5328a).
**James Chapman in USA [0-1] Carolyn Chapman & Theresa Mc Arthur.*

CALLING DOT COM (IRE) RR 39+f 4440[7]
2 ch c Halling (USA) - Rawya (USA) **(71df 76a)** (Woodman (USA)) 9f **(74)**
Form - 7
Record 2000 - 1st:0 2nd:0 3rd:0 Ran:1
2000 Turf 0-1: (6f) (gd)
Currently very moderate colt. **Sir Michael Stoute [0-1] Larry Yung.*

CALLING THE SHOTS BHB 51f49a **RR 53f 49a** 5084[11]
3 b c Democratic (USA) - Two Shots (Dom Racine (FR)) 9.2f **(62)**
Form - 07784240
Record 2000 - 1st:0 2nd:1 3rd:0 Ran:8
Pre2000 - 1st:0 2nd:0 3rd:0 Ran:3
Win Prizemoney £0 *Total Prizemoney* £1,564
2000 Turf 0-8: (5f, 7f 3, 8f 3, 9f) (hvy, gd 2, g-f 2, frm 3)
Scopey, fair colt, effective 7 to 8f, best at 7f, acts on gd to frm, best on frm, has worn blinkers. Turf high 53 - 2nd of 10 getting 21lb from Cowboys And Angels (17 Jly Ayr 7f frm RF 2871).
**W Storey [0-11] Gremlin Racing.*

CALLMEMRWOO RR 29f 4554[13]
2 ch g Rock City 8.8f **(62)** - Samana Cay **(40f 32a)** (Pharly (FR)) 9.8f **(68)**
Form - 00
Record 2000 - 1st:0 2nd:0 3rd:0 Ran:2
2000 Turf 0-2: (6f 2) (gd, g-f)
Currently little account gelding. Turf high 29 (began Spt).
**J G Given [0-2] Michael Ng.*

CALUKI RR 98f 1636a[17]
3 b c Kris 10f **(75)** - Chevisaunce (Fabulous Dancer (USA)) 9.4f **(70)**
Form - 30
2000 Turf 0-2: (8f, 12f) (sft, g-f)
Currently very useful colt. Turf high 98. **L Camici in ITY [0-2].*

CAMAIR CRUSADER (IRE) BHB 26f **RR 33f** 3495[13]
6 br g Jolly Jake (NZ) - Sigrid's Dream (USA) (Triple Bend (USA))
Form - 4353500
Record 2000 - 1st:0 2nd:0 3rd:2 Ran:7
Pre2000 - 1st:0 2nd:0 3rd:1 Ran:6
Win Prizemoney £0 *Total Prizemoney* £1,275
2000 Turf 0-7: (9f, 11f, 12f 4, 17f) (gd 2, g-f 2, frm 3)
Very moderate gelding. Turf high 39.
**W McKeown [0-24] Colin German.*

CAMARADERIE BHB 46f **RR 48f** 3547[7]
4 b g Most Welcome 8.6f **(66)** - Secret Valentine (Wollow) 8.2f **(61)**
Form - 337
Record 2000 - 1st:0 2nd:0 3rd:2 Ran:3
Pre2000 - 1st:0 2nd:0 3rd:1 Ran:8
Win Prizemoney £0 *Total Prizemoney* £1,744
2000 Turf 0-3: (10f, 11f, 12f) (sft, g-f, frm)
Light-framed, moderate gelding. Turf high 48.
**Mrs M Reveley [0-11] T S Child.*

CAMBERLEY (IRE) BHB 93f **RR 97+f** 4597[6]
3 b c Sri Pekan (USA) - Nsx **(56df)** (Roi Danzig (USA))
Form - 322106
Record 2000 - 1st:1 2nd:2 3rd:1 Ran:6
Pre2000 - 1st:0 2nd:1 3rd:0 Ran:2
Win Prizemoney £32,500 *Total Prizemoney* £45,384
Wins * 2000 May Goodwo (SFT) H 7f 88 97+ <
2000 Turf 1-6: (6f, 7f 1-4, 8f) (gd 1-4, g-f 2)
Neat, very useful colt, has broken blood-vessels, effective 7 to 8f, best at 7f, acts on gd to g-f, best on gd. Turf high 97 - 1st of 18 getting 7lb from Strahan (24 May Goodwood RF 1427). A good mover, he was a bit unlucky to be narrowly beaten in two competitive handicaps before winning one at Goodwood in May. Disappointed at Glorious Goodwood on his return from a break, before a decent effort at Ascot. Acts on easy ground and could become a formidable contender in high-class handicaps this season.
**P F I Cole [1-6] H R H Sultan Ahmad Shah (from Miss Gay Kelleway [0-2] Oct 1999).*

CAMBIADO (IRE) RR 77f 4323[3]
2 ch g Ashkalani (IRE) - Changed Around (IRE) (Doulab (USA)) 9.8f **(65)**
Form - 03
Record 2000 - 1st:0 2nd:0 3rd:1 Ran:2
Win Prizemoney £0 *Total Prizemoney* £345
2000 Turf 0-2: (6f 2) (g-f 2)
Currently above-average gelding. Turf high 77 (began Jly) - 3rd of 16 getting 4lb from Flint River (11 Spt Warwick 6f g-f RF 4323).
**J R Fanshawe [0-2] Mrs David Russell.*

CAMZO (USA) RR 49f 5157[13]
2 ch c Diesis 9f **(80)** - Cary Grove (USA) (Theatrical)
Form - 0
Record 2000 - 1st:0 2nd:0 3rd:0 Ran:1
2000 Turf 0-1: (8f) (sft)
Currently moderate colt. **P W Harris [0-1] Mrs P W Harris.*

CANADA RR 85f 5184[2]
2 b c Ezzoud (IRE) - Chancel (USA) **(47f 50a)** (Al Nasr (FR)) 9.3f **(68)**
Form - 422
Record 2000 - 1st:0 2nd:2 3rd:0 Ran:3
Win Prizemoney £0 *Total Prizemoney* £2,995
2000 Turf 0-3: (7f 2, 8f) (g-s, gd, g-f)
Currently useful colt. Turf high 85 (began Jly) - 2nd of 17 to Caughnawaga (25 Oct Yarmouth 8f g-s RF 5184).
**B W Hills [0-3] W J Gredley.*

CANADIAN APPROVAL (USA) BHB 50f63a **RR 55df 63a** 4113[6]
4 ch f With Approval (CAN) 8.7f **(80)** - A Taste For Lace (USA) (Laomedonte (USA))
Form - 1044002114816
Record 2000 - 1st:4 2nd:1 3rd:0 Ran:13
Pre2000 - 1st:1 2nd:0 3rd:3 Ran:10
Win Prizemoney £11,988 *Total Prizemoney* £15,893

Wins								
	2000	*Aug*	*Wolver*	*(STD)*	*S*	*9.4f*		*55*
	2000	*Jun*	*Southw*	*(STD)*	*C*	*11f*		*55*
	2000	*Jun*	*Southw*	*(STD)*	*S*	*11f*		*45*
	2000	*Jan*	*Lingfi*	*(STD)*	*H*	*8f*	*72*	*74*
	1998	Aug	Lingfi	(FRM)		7.6f		82 <

2000 Turf 0-2: (8f, 9f) (sft, frm) 2000 AW 4-11: (8f 1-5, 9f 1-1, 10f, 11f 2-3, 12f) (Equi 1-3, Fibr 3-8)
Light-framed, fair filly, effective 8f, acts on gd - acts on Equi, has worn blinkers, likes left handed tracks, prefers tight tracks. Turf high 10. AW high 74 (1st run) - 1st of 12 giving 12lb to Ursa Major (15 Jan Lingfield RF 0097).
**K McAuliffe [0-1] Mrs Mary O'Connor (from I A Wood [3-11] Aug 2000).*

CANCUN CARIBE (IRE) BHB 68f **RR 76f** 4823[16]
3 ch g Port Lucaya - Miss Tuko (Good Times (ITY)) 6.6f **(54)**
Form - 0430
Record 2000 - 1st:0 2nd:0 3rd:1 Ran:4
Win Prizemoney £0 *Total Prizemoney* £602
2000 Turf 0-2: (7f, 10f) (sft, g-f) 2000 AW 0-2: (8f, 10f) (Equi, Fibr)
Leggy, above-average gelding. Turf high 76 (1st run) - 3rd of 10 to Big Future (24 Apr Kempton 7f sft RF 0840). AW high 56.
**K McAuliffe [0-4] Michael Keogh.*

CANDICE (IRE) BHB 100f **RR 96f** 4280[3]
2 br f Caerleon (USA) 10.9f **(79)** - Criquette (Shirley Heights) 10.3f **(74)**
Form - 3313
Record 2000 - 1st:1 2nd:0 3rd:3 Ran:4
Win Prizemoney £3,484 *Total Prizemoney* £9,455
Wins * 2000 Aug Chepst (G-F) 8.1f 81 <
2000 Turf 1-4: (7f 2, 8f 1-2) (g-f 2, frm 1-2)
Very useful filly. Turf high 96 (began Jly) - 3rd of 12 to Karasta (7 Spt Doncaster 8f frm RF 4280). A late foal who improved towards the backend, her best effort was a third in the May Hill Stakes at Doncaster. She is bred to get middle distances at least and may well be up to Pattern class.
**E A L Dunlop [1-4] Maktoum Al Maktoum.*

CANDLERIGGS (IRE) BHB 92f **RR 96f** 5109[14]
4 ch g Indian Ridge 7.6f **(74)** - Ridge Pool (IRE) (Bluebird (USA)) 7.5f **(69)**
Form - 120
Record 2000 - 1st:1 2nd:1 3rd:0 Ran:3
Pre2000 - 1st:1 2nd:2 3rd:0 Ran:8
Win Prizemoney £20,048 *Total Prizemoney* £27,025

Wins								
	*** 2000**	Spt	Kempto	(GD)	H	6f	84	87 <
	* 1999	Apr	Kempto	(GD)	H	6f	79	81

2000 Turf 1-3: (5f, 6f 1-2) (gd 2, g-f 1-1)
Workmanlike, very useful gelding, effective 5 to 6f, acts on gd to g-f. Turf high 96 (began Spt) - 2nd of 20 getting 6lb from Dancing Mystery (12 Oct Newmarket 5f gd RF 4933) - also 1st of 24 giving 8lb to Ivory Dawn (2 Spt Kempton RF 4164). He made a winning reappearance over six furlongs at Kempton in '99 and overcame a

14-month break before winning over the same course and distance in September. Obviously goes well fresh.
**E A L Dunlop [2-11] The Right Angle Club.*

CANDLE SMILE (USA) BHB 55f52a **RR 64f 52a** 5161[12]
8 b g Pleasant Colony (USA) 12.4f **(88)** - Silent Turn (USA) (Silent Cal (USA)) 14.5f **(91)**
Form - 65360
Record 2000 - 1st:0 2nd:0 3rd:1 Ran:5
Pre2000 - 1st:2 2nd:4 3rd:2 Ran:16
Win Prizemoney £11,746 *Total Prizemoney* £26,295
Wins 1996 Spt Goodwo (G-F) H 16f 90 97 <
1996 May Ayr (GD) 13.1f 76
2000 Turf 0-5: (16f 4, 17f) (sft, g-s, gd 2, frm)
Average gelding, has worn blinkers. Turf high 64 (began Aug). Consistent.
**G Barnett [0-9] J C Bradbury (from Sir Michael Stoute [2-12] Oct 1996).*

CANDOTHAT BHB 77f **RR 81f** 4697[11]
2 b c Thatching 7.8f **(69)** - Yo-Cando (IRE) **(50df)** (Cyrano de Bergerac) 6f **(68)**
Form - 761515000
Record 2000 - 1st:2 2nd:0 3rd:0 Ran:9
Win Prizemoney £7,215 *Total Prizemoney* £7,215
Wins * **2000** Aug Mussel (GD) H 5f 80 81 <
* **2000** Jly Pontef (GD) 5f 75+
2000 Turf 2-9: (5f 2-4, 6f 5) (gd 2, g-f 4, frm 2-3)
Decent colt, effective 5 to 6f, best at 5f, acts on g-f to frm, best on frm. Turf high 81 - 1st of 10 giving 4lb to Blakeshall Boy (2 Aug Musselburgh RF 3337) - also 1st of 11 giving 2lb to Amamackemmush (3 Jly Pontefract RF 2473).
**P W Harris [2-9] The Thatchers.*

CANFORD (IRE) BHB 87f **RR 92f** 5125[19]
3 b c Caerleon (USA) 10.9f **(79)** - Veronica (Persian Bold) 9.3f **(66)**
Form - 1355520
Record 2000 - 1st:1 2nd:1 3rd:1 Ran:7
Pre2000 - 1st:0 2nd:0 3rd:0 Ran:1
Win Prizemoney £4,368 *Total Prizemoney* £9,218
Wins * **2000** May Sandow (HVY) 10f 86+ <
2000 Turf 1-7: (10f 1-2, 12f 4, 15f) (sft, g-s 1-3, gd 2, g-f)
Leggy, useful colt, effective 10 to 15f, best at 12f, acts on g-s to gd, best on gd. Turf high 93 - 5th of 9 giving 5lb to Cephalonia (12 Jly Newmarket 15f gd RF 2745) - also 1st of 11 getting 14lb from Victory Roll (30 May Sandown RF 1559).
**W Jarvis [1-8] Woodcote Stud Ltd.*

CANNY CHIFTANE BHB 56f60a **RR 66f 60a** 276[3]
4 b g Be My Chief (USA) 10.2f **(62)** - Prudence (Grundy) 10.3f **(65)**
Form - 3
Record 2000 - 1st:0 2nd:0 3rd:1 Ran:1
Pre2000 - 1st:1 2nd:0 3rd:1 Ran:7
Win Prizemoney £2,297 *Total Prizemoney* £3,223
Wins 1999 *Spt Wolver (STD) H 12f 50 50+* <
2000 AW 0-1: (12f) (Fibr)
Unfurnished, average gelding.
**J I A Charlton [0-3] & Mrs Raymond Anderson Green (from M A Jarvis [1-7] Spt 1999).*

CANNY HILL BHB 42f54a **RR 43f 54a** 4868[7]
3 ch g Bold Arrangement 8.7f **(57)** - Jersey Maid (On Your Mark) 7.7f **(58)**
Form - 4300507
Record 2000 - 1st:0 2nd:0 3rd:1 Ran:6
Pre2000 - 1st:0 2nd:0 3rd:0 Ran:3
Win Prizemoney £0 *Total Prizemoney* £378
2000 Turf 0-5: (7f, 9f 2, 10f, 11f) (hvy, gd 4) 2000 AW 0-1: (8f) (Fibr)
Workmanlike, average gelding. Turf high 43.
**D Moffatt [0-9] The Sheroot Partnership.*

CANOPY RR 72f 4701[9]
2 b f Ezzoud (IRE) - Zenith (Shirley Heights) 10.3f **(74)**
Form - 50
Record 2000 - 1st:0 2nd:0 3rd:0 Ran:2
2000 Turf 0-2: (6f, 7f) (g-f 2)
Currently above-average filly. Turf high 72 (began Jly).
**R Hannon [0-2] The Queen.*

CANOVAS HEART BHB 77f65a **RR 84f 65a** 4866[P]
11 b g Balidar 6.5f **(58)** - Worthy Venture (Northfields (USA)) 9f **(72)**
Form - P
Record 2000 - 1st:0 2nd:0 3rd:0 Ran:1
Pre2000 - 1st:11 2nd:2 3rd:3 Ran:44
Win Prizemoney £67,336 *Total Prizemoney* £71,912
Wins * 1999 Oct York (SFT) H 7f 79 81
* 1998 Spt Nottin (G-F) H 6.1f 82 86 <
* 1997 Oct York (GD) H 5f 79 86 <
* 1997 May Ripon (G-S) H 5f 78 84
* 1996 Spt Yarmou (GD) H 5.2f 72 73
* 1996 Jun York (GD) H 5f 70 71
* 1996 May Folkes (GD) H 5f 65 68
* 1996 Apr Warwic (GD) H 5f 60 66
2000 Turf 0-1: (7f) (sft)
Decent gelding, effective 6 to 7f, best at 6f, acts on gd to frm.
**Bob Jones [11-48] D S Blake And M J Osborne.*

CANOVAS KINGDOM BHB 53f **RR 55f** 5310[17]
2 ch c Aragon 7.7f **(58)** - Joan's Venture (Beldale Flutter (USA)) 9.7f **(71)**
Form - 050
Record 2000 - 1st:0 2nd:0 3rd:0 Ran:3
2000 Turf 0-3: (6f, 7f, 8f) (sft, g-s, gd)
Currently fair colt. Turf high 55 (began Spt).
**Bob Jones [0-3] The Canova's Kingdom Partnership.*

CANTERLOUPE (IRE) BHB 75f **RR 70f** 5060[4]
2 b f Wolfhound (USA) 7.3f **(71)** - Missed Again (High Top) 10.2f **(67)**
Form - 14
Record 2000 - 1st:1 2nd:0 3rd:0 Ran:2
Win Prizemoney £2,918 *Total Prizemoney* £2,918
Wins * **2000** Spt Bath (SFT) 5.7f 70 <
2000 Turf 1-2: (6f 1-2) (sft, gd 1-1)
Currently above-average filly. Turf high 70 (1st run) (began Spt) - 1st of 15 from Lochsprite (25 Spt Bath RF 4628). Won her maiden on easy ground, but was a little disappointing next time. Likely to be placed to best advantage as a three-year-old.
**P J Makin [1-2] R A Ballin & The Billinomas.*

CANTGETYOURBREATH (IRE) BHB 41f27a **RR 28f 27a** 536[12]
4 ch g College Chapel - Cathy Garcia (IRE) (Be My Guest (USA)) 9.3f **(67)**
Form - 0517000
Record 2000 - 1st:0 2nd:0 3rd:0 Ran:4
Pre2000 - 1st:2 2nd:2 3rd:3 Ran:24
Win Prizemoney £3,540 *Total Prizemoney* £6,541
Wins * 1999 *Dec Southw (STD) S 6f 48*
1998 *Nov Southw (STD) S 6f 69* <
2000 AW 0-4: (6f 2, 7f 2) (Fibr 4)
Unfurnished, little account gelding, effective 6f, - acts on Fibr, mostly wears blinkers, likes left handed tracks, likes tight tracks. AW high 40.
**B P J Baugh [1-7] M J Lyons (from Mrs N Macauley [0-11] Oct 1999).*

CANTINA BHB 93f72a **RR 95f 72a** 4282[11]
6 b m Tina's Pet 7.4f **(56)** - Real Claire (Dreams to Reality (USA)) 6.4f **(73)**
Form - 20014311170
Record 2000 - 1st:4 2nd:0 3rd:1 Ran:9
Pre2000 - 1st:4 2nd:1 3rd:4 Ran:27
Win Prizemoney £40,205 *Total Prizemoney* £46,727
Wins * **2000** Aug Cheste (GD) H 7f 88 95 <
* **2000** Aug Cheste (GD) H 7.6f 72 90
* **2000** Aug Carlis (GD) H 6.9f 72 83
* **2000** May Beverl (G-F) H 7.5f 66 70
* 1999 Jly Redcar (FRM) 7f 68
* 1998 Aug Lingfi (G-F) H 7.6f 73 77
* 1998 Jly Cheste (G-F) H 7.6f 69 72
* 1997 Spt Catter (G-F) 7f 62
2000 Turf 4-8: (7f 3-6, 8f 1-2) (g-s, gd, g-f 3-4, frm, hrd 1-1) 2000 AW 0-1: (7f) (Equi)
Very useful mare, effective 7 to 8f, acts on g-f. Turf high 95 - 1st of 7 giving 3lb to Rayyaan (18 Aug Chester RF 3746) - also 1st of 17 giving 27lb to Shaanxi Romance (6 Aug Chester RF 3413). Made all

to win at Beverley on her second start of last season and completed a hat-trick in August, winning at Carlisle and Chester twice. Seven furlongs and fast ground suit her admirably, and she is hard to peg back when on song.
**A Bailey [8-36] R Kinsey,Mrs M Kinsey & Miss B Roberts.*

CAPA RR 81f 2102[2]
3 b c Salse (USA) 10.9f **(71)** - Pippas Song (Reference Point) 6.8f **(70)**
Form - 452
Record 2000 - 1st:0 2nd:1 3rd:0 Ran:3
Pre2000 - 1st:0 2nd:2 3rd:0 Ran:2
Win Prizemoney £0 *Total Prizemoney* £4,226
2000 Turf 0-3: (12f 3) (g-s, gd, g-f)
Lengthy, decent colt. Turf high 81.
**B W Hills [0-5] R J McCreery & S P Tindall.*

CAPACOOSTIC BHB 42f30a RR 42f 30a 4874[9]
3 ch f Savahra Sound 7.8f **(55)** - Cocked Hat Girl (Ballacashtal (CAN)) 5.3f **(50)**
Form - 0002700
Record 2000 - 1st:0 2nd:1 3rd:0 Ran:6
Pre2000 - 1st:0 2nd:0 3rd:0 Ran:3
Win Prizemoney £0 *Total Prizemoney* £975
2000 Turf 0-5: (6f, 8f 4) (g-s, g-f, frm 3) 2000 AW 0-1: (11f) (Fibr)
Workmanlike, moderate filly, effective 8f, acts on frm. Turf high 42 - 2nd of 15 getting 14lb from Datura (8 Jly Leicester 8f frm RF 2637). **S R Bowring [0-9] J E Reed & P M Sedgwick.*

CAPAL GARMON (IRE) BHB 96f RR 94f 5238[2]
2 b c Caerleon (USA) 10.9f **(79)** - Elevate (Ela-Mana-Mou) 10.1f **(70)**
Form - 4312
Record 2000 - 1st:1 2nd:1 3rd:1 Ran:4
Win Prizemoney £3,415 *Total Prizemoney* £9,272
Wins * 2000 Spt Bath (SFT) 10.2f 87+ <
2000 Turf 1-4: (7f, 8f, 10f 1-2) (g-s 1-2, g-f 2)
Useful colt. Turf high 94 (began Spt) - 2nd of 9 getting 5lb from Worthily (28 Oct Newmarket 10f g-s RF 5238) - also 1st of 9 from Tamiami Trail (25 Spt Bath RF 4631). Out of a half-sister to Sun Princess and Saddlers' Hall, he progressed steadily before scoring in style on easy ground at Bath. Should appreciate even further next season. **J H M Gosden [1-4] R E Sangster & A K Collins.*

CAP COZ (IRE) RR 111f 3542a[6]
3 f Indian Ridge 7.6f **(74)** - Pont-Aven (Try My Best (USA)) 7.6f **(67)**
Form - 26
2000 Turf 0-2: (7f 2) (gd 2)
Group-class, often wears blinkers. Turf high 111 (1st run) - 2nd of 9 getting 12lb from Josr Algarhoud (25 Jun Longchamp 7f gd RF 2388a). Chased home Josr Algarhoud in a Group Three at Longchamp in June. **R Collet in FR [0-4].*

CAPE COAST (IRE) BHB 69f60a RR 69f 60a 5185[15]
3 b g Common Grounds 8.1f **(66)** - Strike It Rich (FR) (Rheingold) 10.4f **(62)**
Form - 00163042112630
Record 2000 - 1st:3 2nd:2 3rd:2 Ran:14
Pre2000 - 1st:0 2nd:1 3rd:0 Ran:2
Win Prizemoney £13,052 *Total Prizemoney* £17,355
Wins * 2000 Spt Epsom (GD) H 7f 60 68 <
2000 Aug Epsom (GD) C 6f 62
2000 May Nottin (G-S) S 6.1f 63
2000 Turf 3-13: (6f 2-8, 7f 1-5) (g-s 3, gd 2-3, g-f 1-5, frm 2) 2000 AW 0-1: (6f) (Fibr)
Average gelding, effective 6 to 7f, best at 6f, acts on g-s to frm, has worn blinkers. Turf high 69 - 3rd of 19 giving 8lb to Toldya (4 Oct Lingfield 6f g-s RF 4809) - also 1st of 12 getting 5lb from Hail The Chief (6 Spt Epsom RF 4265). Inconsistent.
**N P Littmoden [1-5] Miss Vanessa Church (from R M Beckett [1-3] Aug 2000).*

CAPE COD (IRE) BHB 66f RR 74f 4441[3]
2 b f Unfuwain (USA) 11.4f **(74)** - Haboobti (Habitat) 9.4f **(70)**
Form - 403
Record 2000 - 1st:0 2nd:0 3rd:1 Ran:3
Win Prizemoney £0 *Total Prizemoney* £788
2000 Turf 0-3: (6f, 7f, 8f) (gd, g-f, frm)
Currently above-average filly. Turf high 74 (began Aug).
**J W Hills [0-3] Wright, Whitehouse, Murrell.*

CAPE GRACE (IRE) BHB 100f RR 107f 5225[8]
4 b f Priolo (USA) 10.9f **(71)** - Saffron (FR) (Fabulous Dancer (USA)) 9.4f **(70)**
Form - 6158524028
Record 2000 - 1st:1 2nd:2 3rd:0 Ran:10
Pre2000 - 1st:1 2nd:1 3rd:0 Ran:5
Win Prizemoney £20,586 *Total Prizemoney* £35,274
Wins * 2000 May Newmar (GD) L 9f 107 <
* 1998 Jly Ascot (G-F) 6f 86t
2000 Turf 1-10: (9f 1-1, 10f 7, 11f, 12f) (sft, g-s, gd 3, g-f 1-4, frm)
Scopey, Pattern-class filly, effective 9 to 10f, best at 10f, acts on gd to frm, has worn blinkers. Turf high 107 - 1st of 6 from Annapurna (5 May Newmarket RF 1049). Inconsistent. Winner of a Newmarket Listed event on her second start of the season, she has been found out in Group company. Failed to settle and finished tailed off when tried at a mile and a half.
**R Hannon [2-15] George Strawbridge.*

CAPE LODGE (USA) RR 68f 1800[5]
3 b f Lear Fan (USA) 10.4f **(80)** - Charmie Carmie (USA) (Lyphard (USA)) 9.9f **(72)**
Form - 65
Record 2000 - 1st:0 2nd:0 3rd:0 Ran:2
2000 Turf 0-2: (8f, 10f) (gd, g-f)
Neat, currently average filly. Turf high 68.
**D W P Arbuthnot [0-2] Christopher Wright.*

CAPERCAILLIE BHB 30a RR 35f 3192[13]
5 ch g Deploy 11.4f **(67)** - Tee Gee Jay **(36f 36a)** (Northern Tempest (USA))
Form - 0640
Record 2000 - 1st:0 2nd:0 3rd:0 Ran:4
Pre2000 - 1st:0 2nd:2 3rd:3 Ran:18
Win Prizemoney £0 *Total Prizemoney* £2,384
2000 Turf 0-1: (10f) (g-f) 2000 AW 0-3: (11f, 12f, 16f) (Fibr 3)
Very moderate gelding, effective 10f, acted on gd to frm, had worn blinkers. (DEAD)
**D E Cantillon [0-5] Future Electrical Services Ltd (from J E Banks [0-3] Jun 1999).*

CAPE ROSE (USA) RR 71f 4222[7]
2 b f Mt Livermore (USA) 7.7f **(90)** - Devil's Needle (USA) (Nureyev (USA)) 8.7f **(78)**
Form - 57
Record 2000 - 1st:0 2nd:0 3rd:0 Ran:2
2000 Turf 0-2: (7f 2) (g-f, frm)
Currently above-average filly. Turf high 71 (began Aug).
**J L Dunlop [0-2] Blue Blood And Wentworth Racing.*

CAPE SOCIETY RR 52f 4820[17]
2 ch f Imp Society (USA) 7.1f **(63)** - La Noisette (Rock Hopper)
Form - 0
Record 2000 - 1st:0 2nd:0 3rd:0 Ran:1
2000 Turf 0-1: (6f) (g-f)
Currently fair filly.
**J G Smyth-Osbourne [0-1] Mrs F A Veasey.*

CAPE TOWN (IRE) BHB 115f RR 119f 4986[3]
3 gr c Desert Style (IRE) - Rossaldene (Mummy's Pet) 7.7f **(60)**
Form - 10302333
Record 2000 - 1st:1 2nd:1 3rd:4 Ran:8
Pre2000 - 1st:1 2nd:1 3rd:0 Ran:2
Win Prizemoney £21,152 *Total Prizemoney* £79,569
Wins * 2000 Apr Newmar (G-S) LH 7f 105 112 <
* 1999 Oct Lingfi (G-S) 7f 85+
2000 Turf 1-8: (7f 1-3, 8f 5) (g-s, gd 1-5, g-f, frm)
Scopey, high-class colt, effective 7 to 8f, best at 8f, acts on g-s to frm. Turf high 119 - 3rd of 6 to Medicean (26 Aug Goodwood 8f gd RF 3985) - also 1st of 8 from Catchy Word (19 Apr Newmarket RF 0797). Consistent. Impressive winner of the Free Handicap on his return, he failed to win afterwards despite making the frame on several occasions in Group company. Probably his best effort was when third behind Bachir in the Irish Guineas.
**R Hannon [2-10] S A Six.*

CAPITALIST BHB 48f38a **RR 29f 38a** 88[6]
4 br g Bigstone (IRE) - Pinkie Rose (FR) (Kenmare (FR)) 6.5f **(72)**
Form - 6
Record 2000 - 1st:0 2nd:0 3rd:0 Ran:1
Pre2000 - 1st:0 2nd:0 3rd:1 Ran:17
Win Prizemoney £0 *Total Prizemoney* £1,099
2000 AW 0-1: (16f) (Fibr)
Scopey, very moderate gelding, effective 11f, acts on frm, has worn blinkers, likes left handed tracks, likes tight tracks. Becoming disappointing.
**R M Whitaker [0-13] GRP Group (from Mrs J R Ramsden [0-8] Oct 1998).*

CAPITAL LAD (IRE) RR 70f 4783[6]
2 b c Charnwood Forest (IRE) - Casla (Lomond (USA)) 8.8f **(65)**
Form - 846
Record 2000 - 1st:0 2nd:0 3rd:0 Ran:3
Win Prizemoney £0 *Total Prizemoney* £330
2000 Turf 0-2: (6f, 7f) (g-f 2) 2000 AW 0-1: (8f) (Fibr)
Currently above-average colt. Turf high 70 (began Aug).
**G Brown [0-3] Capital Accomodation Ltd.*

CAPOSO (IRE) RR 64f 5132[15]
2 gr f Common Grounds 8.1f **(66)** -High Mare (FR)(Highest Honor (FR))
Form - 70
Record 2000 - 1st:0 2nd:0 3rd:0 Ran:2
2000 Turf 0-2: (6f 2) (sft, g-f)
Currently average filly. Turf high 64 (began Oct).
**P W Harris [0-2] The Mare High Club.*

CAPPELLINA (IRE) BHB 53f42a **RR 56f 42a** 5248[13]
3 b f College Chapel - Santa Ana Wind (Busted) 10.2f **(61)**
Form - 70427780
Record 2000 - 1st:0 2nd:1 3rd:0 Ran:8
Pre2000 - 1st:0 2nd:0 3rd:0 Ran:2
Win Prizemoney £0 *Total Prizemoney* £975
2000 Turf 0-5: (6f, 7f, 8f, 10f 2) (gd, g-f 2, frm 2) 2000 AW 0-3: (6f 3) (Fibr 3)
Light-framed, fair filly, effective 7 to 8f, acts on g-f to frm. Turf high 56 - 4th of 9 getting 17lb from Lake Sunbeam (26 Jly Sandown 8f g-f RF 3139). AW high 45 (began Spt).
**P G Murphy [0-10] Mrs John Spielman.*

CAPPUCINO LADY BHB 35f26a **RR 16f 26a** 4543[18]
3 b f Prince Sabo 6.6f **(64)** - Cubist (IRE) (Tate Gallery (USA)) 7.4f **(67)**
Form - 805000500
Record 2000 - 1st:0 2nd:0 3rd:0 Ran:8
Pre2000 - 1st:0 2nd:0 3rd:1 Ran:6
Win Prizemoney £0 *Total Prizemoney* £602
2000 Turf 0-5: (5f 2, 6f, 7f, 8f) (gd, g-f 2, frm 2) 2000 AW 0-3: (5f, 6f, 7f) (Equi 3)
Unfurnished, poor filly. Turf high 16. AW high 11.
**J J Bridger [0-14] J J Bridger.*

CAPRI BHB 113f **RR 117f** 3779[2]
5 ch h Generous (IRE) 11.5f **(82)** - Island Jamboree (USA) (Explodent (USA)) 9.4f **(87)**
Form - 202
Record 2000 - 1st:0 2nd:2 3rd:0 Ran:3
Pre2000 - 1st:4 2nd:3 3rd:1 Ran:10
Win Prizemoney £79,374 *Total Prizemoney* £105,630
Wins * 1999 Jun Chanti (G-S) G2 12f 117 <
* 1998 Spt Ascot (G-F) G3 12f 113
* 1998 May Newmar (G-S) 12f 99+
* 1998 Apr Newmar (G-S) 12f 93+
2000 Turf 0-3: (12f 2, 13f) (hvy, gd, g-f)
High-class colt, effective 12f, acts on hvy to g-f. Turf high 117 (1st run) - 2nd of 11 giving 2lb to Yavana's Pace (22 Apr Haydock 12f hvy RF 0821). Lightly raced in the last couple of campaigns, he just lost out to a race-fit rival in the John Porter on his return last season, but was tailed off next time. Having his first run for 100 days when runner-up at Haydock in August, but did not reappear.
**H R A Cecil [4-13] H R H Prince Fahd Salman.*

CAPRICCIO (IRE) BHB 73f **RR 76f** 5323[7]
3 gr g Robellino (USA) 9.5f **(68)** - Yamamah (Siberian Express (USA)) 8.8f **(65)**
Form - 43525287
Record 2000 - 1st:0 2nd:2 3rd:1 Ran:8
Win Prizemoney £0 *Total Prizemoney* £4,305
2000 Turf 0-8: (7f, 8f, 10f 3, 11f 2, 12f) (sft, gd 5, g-f 2)
Scopey, above-average gelding, effective 8 to 11f, best at 11f, acts on gd to g-f, best on gd. Turf high 76 - 2nd of 7 getting 16lb from Polar Red (10 Aug Haydock 11f gd RF 3534). Consistent. A maiden, he has looked short of pace so far and is worth a try at a mile and a half.
**C G Cox [0-8] Axom.*

CAPRICE BHB 35a **RR 15f 35a** 318[11]
3 gr f Mystiko (USA) 7.7f **(59)** - Tebre (USA) (Sir Ivor) 10.2f **(70)**
Form - 00
Record 2000 - 1st:0 2nd:0 3rd:0 Ran:2
Pre2000 - 1st:0 2nd:0 3rd:0 Ran:1
2000 AW 0-2: (6f, 7f) (Fibr 2)
Workmanlike, currently very moderate filly. AW high 30.
**S C Williams [0-3] Bruce Wyatt.*

CAPRICHO (IRE) BHB 90f **RR 92+f** 4732[1]
3 gr g Lake Coniston (IRE) - Star Spectacle (Spectacular Bid (USA)) 11.2f **(76)**
Form - 2112001
Record 2000 - 1st:3 2nd:2 3rd:0 Ran:7
Win Prizemoney £19,137 *Total Prizemoney* £29,369
Wins * **2000** Spt Newmar (GD) H 7f 86 92 <
* **2000** Jly Newmar (G-F) H 7f 74 92 <
* **2000** Jun Ayr (GD) 7f 78
2000 Turf 3-7: (6f 2, 7f 3-5) (g-s, gd 1-2, g-f 1-3, frm 1-1)
Light-framed, useful gelding, effective 6 to 7f, best at 7f, acts on gd to g-f, best on g-f. Turf high 92 - 1st of 17 getting 14lb from Strahan (29 Spt Newmarket RF 4732) - also 1st of 13 getting 1lb from Pageant (22 Jly Newmarket RF 3029). A progressive sort, he won well at Newmarket in July on his handicap debut. Fine effort to finish runner-up in a valuable handicap at Glorious Goodwood and met trouble in running at York. Drawn on the wrong side at Kempton next time, he returned to winning form at Newmarket in September. He was unraced as a juvenile, and should have improvement in him. There are good races to be won next season, and he may even make listed class. **W J Haggas [3-7] M Tabor.*

CAPRIOLO (IRE) BHB 80f75a **RR 80f 75a** 5125[2]
4 ch g Priolo (USA) 10.9f **(71)** - Carroll's Canyon (IRE) (Hatim (USA))
Form - 670163132
Record 2000 - 1st:2 2nd:1 3rd:2 Ran:9
Pre2000 - 1st:2 2nd:3 3rd:3 Ran:16
Win Prizemoney £22,733 *Total Prizemoney* £34,327
Wins * **2000** Aug York (GD) H 11.9f 70 74+ <
* **2000** Jly Cheste (SFT) 12.3f 57
* 1999 Oct Leices (GD) H 10f 69 72
* 1999 Jun Salisb (FRM) H 9.9f 62 67
2000 Turf 2-9: (10f 3, 12f 2-6) (g-s, gd 1-3, g-f 1-4, frm)
Decent gelding, effective 10 to 12f, best at 12f, acts on g-s to frm, best on gd, often wears blinkers (extremely effectively), likes left handed tracks, does well at Salisbury. Turf high 80 - 2nd of 19 giving 5lb to Norcroft Joy (21 Oct Doncaster 12f g-s RF 5125) - also 1st of 11 giving 20lb to Simple Ideals (30 Aug York RF 4104). Got off the mark last term under an inspired Richard Hughes ride at Chester and front-running tactics again proved successful at York.
**R Hannon [4-25] Taylor Homer Racing.*

CAPTAIN BOYCOTT (IRE) RR 38f 636[12]
3 b g Petardia 8.2f **(58)** - Duck Hands (IRE) (Prince Tenderfoot (USA)) 9f **(61)**
Form - 0
Record 2000 - 1st:0 2nd:0 3rd:0 Ran:1
2000 Turf 0-1: (7f) (gd)
Strong, currently very moderate gelding.
**D J S Cosgrove [0-1] Global Racing Club.*

CAPTAIN BRADY (IRE) BHB 48f **RR 56df** 5054[8]
5 ch g Soviet Lad (USA) 9.4f **(63)** - Eight Mile Rock (Dominion) 8.5f **(63)**
Form - 136808
Record 2000 - 1st:1 2nd:0 3rd:1 Ran:6
Pre2000 - 1st:2 2nd:2 3rd:4 Ran:19
Win Prizemoney £15,573 *Total Prizemoney* £20,965
Wins * **2000** Aug Hamilt (SFT) H 11.1f 51 55 <
* 1999 Aug Ripon (GD) H 9f 50 55 <

* 1999 May Hamilt (Sft) H 8.3f 44 52
2000 Turf 1-6: (8f, 10f 3, 11f 1-2) (sft, g-s, gd 1-3, frm)
Fair gelding, effective 8 to 11f, acts on g-s to frm, has worn blinkers, prefers right handed tracks, favours tight tracks, and excels at Ripon. Turf high 56 (began Aug) - 3rd of 10 getting 19lb from Andromedes (29 Aug Ripon 10f frm RF 4063) - also 1st of 9 giving 5lb to Ocean Drive (16 Aug Hamilton RF 3700). Inconsistent.
**J S Goldie [4-24] Frank Brady (from W G M Turner [0-6] Oct 1997).*

CAPTAIN CRUSOE RR 54f 4969[22]
2 b g Selkirk (USA) 7.9f **(76)** - Desert Girl (Green Desert (USA)) 8.6f **(78)**
Form - 0
Record 2000 - 1st:0 2nd:0 3rd:0 Ran:1
2000 Turf 0-1: (8f) (gd)
Currently fair gelding. **C A Horgan [0-1] Mrs B Sumner.*

CAPTAIN GIBSON BHB 79f RR 81f 5197[2]
2 b g Beveled (USA) 6.9f **(64)** - Little Egret (Carwhite) 7.2f **(61)**
Form - 5086212
Record 2000 - 1st:1 2nd:2 3rd:0 Ran:7
Win Prizemoney £1,820 *Total Prizemoney* £4,114
Wins * 2000 Oct Pontef (HVY) 6f 72 <
2000 Turf 1-7: (6f 1-6, 7f) (g-s 1-2, gd, g-f 3, frm)
Decent gelding, effective 6f, acts on g-s to gd, best on g-s, has worn blinkers. Turf high 81 - 2nd of 8 getting 1lb from Barathiki (26 Oct Windsor 6f gd RF 5197) - also 1st of 10 getting 6lb from Travel Tardia (16 Oct Pontefract RF 4998).
**D J S ffrenchDavis [1-7] M Duthie.*

CAPTAIN KOZANDO BHB 63f RR 59f 4999[1]
2 b g Komaite (USA) 6.9f **(61)** - Times Zando **(13f 47a)** (Forzando) 7.6f **(59)**
Form - 521
Record 2000 - 1st:1 2nd:1 3rd:0 Ran:3
Win Prizemoney £1,820 *Total Prizemoney* £2,510
Wins * 2000 Oct Pontef (HVY) 6f 59 <
2000 Turf 1-3: (6f 1-2, 8f) (g-s 1-1, gd, g-f)
Currently fair gelding. Turf high 59 (began Aug) - 1st of 9 getting 2lb from Darwin Tower (16 Oct Pontefract RF 4999). Steadily improving and got off the mark in a Pontefract maiden on his third start. **Mrs G S Rees [1-3] Capt James Wilson.*

CAPTAIN LOGAN (IRE) BHB 49f40a RR 56f 40a 181[14]
5 b h Fairy King (USA) 7.7f **(75)** - Heaven High (High Line) 10.3f **(70)**
Form - 00
Record 2000 - 1st:0 2nd:0 3rd:0 Ran:1
Pre2000 - 1st:1 2nd:2 3rd:0 Ran:10
Win Prizemoney £3,548 *Total Prizemoney* £6,594
Wins 1998 Jun Ayr (GD) 7f 91 <
2000 AW 0-1: (8f) (Fibr)
Fair colt, has worn blinkers. Becoming disappointing.
**A Kelleway [0-2] Don Brennan (from J Noseda [0-3] Oct 1999).*

CAPTAIN MCCLOY (USA) BHB 45f40a RR 45f 40a 4220[12]
5 ch g Lively One (USA) - Fly Me First (USA) (Herbager) 13f **(65)**
Form - 576333010
Record 2000 - 1st:1 2nd:0 3rd:3 Ran:7
Pre2000 - 1st:1 2nd:1 3rd:4 Ran:29
Win Prizemoney £5,081 *Total Prizemoney* £8,978
Wins * 2000 Aug Windso (GD) H 10f 41 45 <
1999 Jly Warwic (G-F) SH 10.5f 33 38
2000 Turf 1-7: (8f, 10f 1-5, 11f) (gd 2, g-f 1-4, frm)
Moderate gelding, effective 10 to 11f, best at 10f, acts on gd to g-f, best on g-f, often wears blinkers, favours tight tracks. Turf high 45 - 3rd of 20 getting 1lb from Westgate Run (19 Jun Warwick 11f g-f RF 2097) - also 1st of 7 getting 13lb from Night City (14 Aug Windsor RF 3637). Consistent.
**P Mitchell [1-4] D W Smith (from N E Berry [1-25] Jly 2000).*

CAPTAIN MILLER BHB 78f RR 83f 5323[6]
4 b g Batshoof 9.5f **(66)** - Miller's Gait (Mill Reef (USA)) 10.5f **(78)**
Form - 1206
Record 2000 - 1st:1 2nd:1 3rd:0 Ran:4
Pre2000 - 1st:4 2nd:2 3rd:0 Ran:18
Win Prizemoney £25,205 *Total Prizemoney* £29,392
Wins * 2000 Apr Kempto (SFT) H 16f 67 75
1999 May Ripon (G-F) C 8f 70
1999 Apr Hamilt (HVY) 8.3f 69++
1999 Apr Leices (G-S) H 7f 62 70
1998 Jun Lingfi (G-S) 7f 82+ <
2000 Turf 1-4: (12f 2, 16f 1-1, 20f) (sft 1-2, gd, frm)
Light-framed, decent gelding, effective 12 to 16f, acts on sft to frm. Turf high 83 - 2nd of 18 getting 24lb from Rainbow Ways (7 May Newmarket 12f frm RF 1082) - also 1st of 10 getting 13lb from Brave Tornado (22 Apr Kempton RF 0831). Returned from a successful campaign over hurdles to land the Queen's Prize at Kempton in April, and went down narrowly next time. Never in the hunt at Royal Ascot.
**N J Henderson [4-11] W H Ponsonby (from M R Channon [4-18] Jun 1999).*

CAPTAIN SCOTT (IRE) BHB 90f92a RR 92f 92a 5240[P]
6 b g Polar Falcon (USA) 9f **(74)** - Camera Girl (Kalaglow) 9.8f **(67)**
Form - 0P
Record 2000 - 1st:0 2nd:0 3rd:0 Ran:2
Pre2000 - 1st:3 2nd:2 3rd:3 Ran:15
Win Prizemoney £39,245 *Total Prizemoney* £59,437
Wins 1999 *Mar Wolver (STD) H 8.5f 85 94* <
1997 Jly Ayr (G-F) 10f 84
1997 *Mar Southw (STD) 8f 70+*
2000 Turf 0-2: (7f, 8f) (g-s, gd)
Useful gelding, effective 8 to 10f, best at 8f, acts on gd to frm - acts on Fibr. Turf high 85 (began Oct). Inconsistent.
**G A Butler [0-2] The Write State Partnership (from J A Glover [3 16] Jly 1999).*

CAPTAIN'S FOLLY BHB 40f RR 46f 3971[13]
2 b f Mind Games - Miss Petella (Dunphy) 9.4f **(57)**
Form - 08570
Record 2000 - 1st:0 2nd:0 3rd:0 Ran:5
2000 Turf 0-5: (5f 4, 7f) (gd, frm 3, hrd)
Moderate filly. Turf high 46.
**J S Wainwright [0-2] Steve Dalton (from Miss J F Craze [0-3] Jly 2000).*

CAPTAIN'S LOG BHB 80f RR 86f 4268[2]
5 b g Slip Anchor 12.7f **(75)** - Cradle of Love (USA) (Roberto (USA)) 10f **(76)**
Form - 42511415042
Record 2000 - 1st:3 2nd:2 3rd:0 Ran:11
Pre2000 - 1st:2 2nd:2 3rd:0 Ran:20
Win Prizemoney £25,250 *Total Prizemoney* £42,247
Wins * 2000 Jly Newcas (G-F) 12.4f 82 <
*** 2000** Jun York (GD) 11.9f 80+
*** 2000** Jun Windso (GD) H 10f 75 78
* 1998 Jun Newcas (GD) H 9f 73 76
* 1998 May Warwic (GD) 8f 74
2000 Turf 3-11: (10f 1-8, 12f 2-3) (sft, g-s, gd 1-2, g-f 2-7)
Useful gelding, effective 10 to 12f, best at 10f, acts on gd to frm, best on g-f, likes left handed tracks, likes tight tracks, and excels at York. Turf high 86 - 2nd of 7 giving 3lb to Riberac (6 Spt Epsom 10f g-f RF 4268) - also 1st of 7 giving 4lb to Hunters Tweed (9 Jly Newcastle RF 2653). Consistent. Effective at ten or twelve furlongs, he hit form in the early summer, winning three times in just over a month. His come-from-behind style means he sometimes finds trouble in running. **M L W Bell [5-31] Christopher Wright.*

CAPTAIN STEVE (USA) RR 5332a[3]
3 f Fly So Free (USA) - Sparkling Delite (USA) (Vice Regent (CAN)) 8.7f **(74)**
Form - 3
2000 AW 0-1: (10f) (Dirt)
Currently very high-class, often wears blinkers. (1st run) - 3rd of 13 to Tiznow (4 Nov Churchill Downs 10f Dirt RF 5332a).
**B Baffert in USA [0-2] Mike Pegram.*

CAPTIVATING (IRE) BHB 25f60a RR 31f 60a 4269[22]
5 b m Wolfhound (USA) 7.3f **(71)** - Winning Appeal (FR) (Law Society (USA)) 9.9f **(70)**
Form - 70070
Record 2000 - 1st:0 2nd:0 3rd:0 Ran:5
Pre2000 - 1st:0 2nd:0 3rd:1 Ran:15
Win Prizemoney £0 *Total Prizemoney* £311
2000 Turf 0-3: (12f, 16f, 17f) (g-f 2, hrd) 2000 AW 0-2: (8f, 11f) (Fibr 2)

Very moderate filly, has worn blinkers. Turf high 31 - 7th of 14 getting 23lb from Keep Ikis (20 Aug Pontefract 17f hrd RF 3826). AW high 8. Inconsistent.
**R C Spicer [0-4] John Purcell (from C A Dwyer [0-1] Feb 2000).*

CAQUI D'OR (IRE) BHB 67f RR 71f 5151[10]

2 b c Danehill (USA) 9.1f **(79)** - Ghaiya (USA) (Alleged (USA)) 10f **(76)**
Form - 000
Record 2000 - 1st:0 2nd:0 3rd:0 Ran:3
2000 Turf 0-3: (7f 3) (g-s, g-f 2)
Currently above-average colt. Turf high 71 (began Spt).
**J L Dunlop [0-3] Windflower Overseas Holdings Inc.*

CARAMBO BHB 60f50a RR 51f 50a 312[11]

5 b m Rambo Dancer (CAN) 8.4f **(59)** - Light the Way (Nicholas Bill) 10.1f **(56)**
Form - 0706430
Record 2000 - 1st:0 2nd:0 3rd:1 Ran:4
Pre2000 - 1st:3 2nd:5 3rd:4 Ran:38
Win Prizemoney £9,861 *Total Prizemoney* £18,849
Wins 1999 Spt Nottin (G-F) H 6.1f 56 61
1997 *Oct Wolver (STD) H 7f 82 86* <
1997 *Jly Wolver (STD) H 6f 77*
2000 AW 0-4: (6f 3, 8f) (Equi 2, Fibr 2)
Fair filly, effective 6 to 7f, best at 7f, acts on gd to frm, best on frm, has worn blinkers (effectively), likes left handed tracks. AW high 47. **T D Barron [0-8] Nigel Shields (from J L Eyre [3-34] Oct 1999).*

CARAMELLE (IRE) BHB 34f29a RR 20f 29a 5182[6]

4 ch f Be My Guest (USA) 10.2f **(66)** - Lobbino (Bustino) 10.4f **(64)**
Form - 7006
Record 2000 - 1st:0 2nd:0 3rd:0 Ran:4
2000 Turf 0-3: (10f, 12f, 14f) (sft, g-f, frm) 2000 AW 0-1: (10f) (Equi)
Leggy, little account filly. Turf high 20 (began Aug).
**G L Moore [0-4] Frederick Ellis.*

CARBON COPY RR 60f 4382[5]

2 ch f Pivotal - Astolat (Rusticaro (FR)) 8.2f **(65)**
Form - 35
Record 2000 - 1st:0 2nd:0 3rd:1 Ran:2
Win Prizemoney £0 *Total Prizemoney* £434
2000 Turf 0-2: (6f 2) (gd 2)
Currently average filly. Turf high 60 (1st run) (began Aug) - 3rd of 18 giving 4lb to St Antim (10 Aug Haydock 6f gd RF 3535).
**W J Haggas [0-2] HTTP Partnership Ltd.*

CARD GAMES BHB 83f RR 85f 5317[21]

3 b f First Trump - Pericardia **(60df)** (Petong) 6.6f **(58)**
Form - 000120050200
Record 2000 - 1st:1 2nd:2 3rd:0 Ran:12
Pre2000 - 1st:2 2nd:1 3rd:2 Ran:9
Win Prizemoney £11,049 *Total Prizemoney* £30,959
Wins * 2000 May Redcar (G-S) H 5f 75 80
1999 Aug Pontef (GD) H 6f 78 85 <
1999 Jly Salisb (G-F) 6f 76
2000 Turf 1-12: (5f 1-2, 6f 7, 7f 3) (sft 3, gd 1-8, g-f)
Unfurnished, useful filly, effective 5 to 7f, best at 6f, acts on sft to frm, has worn blinkers, excels at Salisbury, likes York. Turf high 85 - 5th of 29 giving 6lb to Lady Boxer (16 Spt Ayr 6f gd RF 4449) - also 1st of 23 giving 4lb to Whizz Kid (4 May Redcar RF 1020). Inconsistent. Took advantage of a lenient mark to score at Redcar in May and ran into a useful sort next time, but has been disappointing since.
**M W Easterby [1-12] M W Easterby (from I A Balding [2-9] Oct 1999).*

CARDIFF ARMS (NZ) RR 97f 3200[4]

6 b g Lowell (USA) - Shuzohra (NZ) (Tom's Shu (USA))
Form - 2885054
Record 2000 - 1st:0 2nd:1 3rd:0 Ran:7
Pre2000 - 1st:0 2nd:0 3rd:0 Ran:1
Win Prizemoney £0 *Total Prizemoney* £4,056
2000 Turf 0-7: (8f 4, 9f, 10f 2) (g-s 3, gd 3, frm)
Very useful gelding, effective 8 to 10f, acts on g-s to gd. Turf high 97 (1st run) - 2nd of 7 to Sharmy (3 May Ascot 8f g-s RF 1003). A useful middle-distance performer in his native New Zealand, he has been found out in decent company in this country, but was a staying-on fifth in the John Smith's Cup at York. He ran well at Ascot after that and looks quite capable of winning in good company now he has had time to acclimatise.
**M Johnston [0-8] The Winning Line.*

CARDINAL FAIR (IRE) BHB 45f45a RR 45a 481[5]

3 b f Namaqualand (USA) - Irish Affaire (IRE) (Fairy King (USA)) 7.7f **(59)**
Form - 0548735
Record 2000 - 1st:0 2nd:0 3rd:1 Ran:5
Pre2000 - 1st:0 2nd:0 3rd:0 Ran:2
Win Prizemoney £0 *Total Prizemoney* £319
2000 AW 0-5: (7f, 8f 4) (Fibr 5)
Leggy, moderate filly, has worn blinkers. AW high 47.
**B P J Baugh [0-7] Mrs Joan Chrimes.*

CARDINAL VENTURE (IRE) RR 68f 4382[4]

2 b c Bishop of Cashel - Phoenix Venture (IRE) **(59f 63a)** (Thatching) 8f **(66)**
Form - 04
Record 2000 - 1st:0 2nd:0 3rd:0 Ran:2
Win Prizemoney £0 *Total Prizemoney* £299
2000 Turf 0-2: (6f, 7f) (gd, frm)
Currently average colt. Turf high 68 (began Aug).
**K A Ryan [0-2] Tony Fawcett.*

CAREFULLY RR 60f 3726[6]

2 ch c Caerleon (USA) 10.9f **(79)** - Sabaah Elfull **(46f)** (Kris) 9.5f **(73)**
Form - 006
Record 2000 - 1st:0 2nd:0 3rd:0 Ran:3
2000 Turf 0-3: (6f 2, 7f) (g-f 2, frm)
Currently average colt. Turf high 60. **N A Graham [0-3] Paul Jacobs.*

CAREL RR 56f 5184[8]

2 b c Polish Precedent (USA) 9f **(73)** - Castle Peak (Darshaan) 9.9f **(84)**
Form - 8
Record 2000 - 1st:0 2nd:0 3rd:0 Ran:1
2000 Turf 0-1: (8f) (g-s)
Currently fair colt. **M L W Bell [0-1] Baron F C Oppenheim.*

CARELESS BHB 58f RR 62f 5174a[8]

3 b f Robellino (USA) 9.5f **(68)** - Life's Too Short (IRE) **(51f)** (Astronef)
Form - 4042717258
Record 2000 - 1st:1 2nd:2 3rd:0 Ran:10
Pre2000 - 1st:0 2nd:0 3rd:0 Ran:3
Win Prizemoney £7,312 *Total Prizemoney* £9,568
Wins 2000 Jly Newmar (GD) C 10f 53 <
2000 Turf 1-10: (7f, 8f 2, 9f, 10f 1-4, 12f 2) (hvy, g-s, gd, g-f 1-5, frm 2)
Workmanlike, average filly, effective 7 to 12f, acts on g-s to frm, best on frm, has worn blinkers, prefers right handed tracks. Turf high 62. Consistent.
**A J Martin in IRE [0-5] Red Ned's Racing Club (from T D Easterby [1-6] Jly 2000).*

CARELLA BOY RR 3251[6]

3 br g Symbolic - Fidget (Workboy) 7.3f **(46)**
Form - 6
Record 2000 - 1st:0 2nd:0 3rd:0 Ran:1
2000 Turf 0-1: (12f) (g-f)
Lengthy, currently very poor gelding. **N Wilson [0-1] J B Slatcher.*

CARENS HERO (IRE) BHB 76f RR 88f 5078[11]

3 ch g Petardia 8.2f **(58)** - Clear Glade (Vitiges (FR)) 8.2f **(59)**
Form - 317460
Record 2000 - 1st:1 2nd:0 3rd:1 Ran:6
Pre2000 - 1st:0 2nd:0 3rd:0 Ran:1
Win Prizemoney £1,869 *Total Prizemoney* £3,107
Wins * 2000 May Bath (G-F) 8f 73 <
2000 Turf 1-6: (8f 1-3, 9f, 10f 2) (g-s 2, gd, g-f, frm 1-2)
Well made, useful gelding, has worn blinkers. Turf high 88.
**Mrs A J Perrett [1-7] Mrs R Doel.*

CAREQUICK BHB 41f35a RR 34f 35a 352[6]

4 ch f Risk Me (FR) 8f **(53)** - Miss Serlby (Runnett) 7f **(59)**
Form - 053356
Record 2000 - 1st:0 2nd:0 3rd:1 Ran:3
Pre2000 - 1st:0 2nd:0 3rd:1 Ran:12
Win Prizemoney £0 *Total Prizemoney* £545

2000 AW 0-3: (6f, 7f 2) (Equi, Fibr 2)
Light-framed, very moderate filly, effective 8f, - acts on Fibr, has worn blinkers, favours left handed tracks, favours tight tracks. AW high 30. Consistent. **A Bailey [0-15] Carequick Ltd-Conser Units.*

CARESSING (USA) RR 5326a[1]

2 br f Honour And Glory (USA) - Loving Touch (USA) (Majestic Prince (USA)) 10f **(74)**
Form - 1
2000 AW 1-1: (9f 1-1) (Dirt 1-1)
Currently very useful filly. (1st run) - 1st of 12 from Platinum Tiara (4 Nov Churchill Downs RF 5326a).
**D Vance in USA [1-1] Carl Pollard.*

CAREW CASTLE (IRE) BHB 53f RR 50f 5009[2]

3 b g Fayruz 8.0f **(63)** - Mirmande (Kris) 9.5f **(70)**
Form - 550002
Record 2000 - 1st:0 2nd:1 3rd:0 Ran:6
Win Prizemoney £0 *Total Prizemoney* £484
2000 Turf 0-5: (5f, 6f 2, 7f 2) (sft, gd 3, frm) 2000 AW 0-1: (6f) (Fibr)
Scopey, fair gelding, has worn blinkers. Turf high 66.
**D W P Arbuthnot [0-6] Derrick Broomfield.*

CARHUE LASS (IRE) RR 97f 1926a[8]

6 b m Common Grounds 8.1f **(66)** - Return Journey (IRE) (Pennine Walk) 8.5f **(61)**
Form - 308
2000 Turf 0-3: (5f 3) (g-s, gd 2)
Very useful mare, effective 5f, acts on g-s to gd. Turf high 97. She has plenty of early pace and is a useful sprinter on easy ground. She was lightly raced in 2000, and did not make much impression in Pattern company. **P O'Leary in IRE [2-23] P O'Leary.*

CARIBBEANDRIFTWOOD (USA) BHB 86f RR 84f 4042[5]

2 ch f Woodman (USA) 9.7f **(77)** - Drifting (USA) (Lyphard (USA)) 9.9f **(72)**
Form - 2105
Record 2000 - 1st:1 2nd:1 3rd:0 Ran:4
Win Prizemoney £4,348 *Total Prizemoney* £5,662
Wins * 2000 Jly Kempto (G-S) 7f 84 <
2000 Turf 1-4: (7f 1-3, 8f) (gd, g-f 1-2, frm)
Decent filly. Turf high 84 - 1st of 13 from Aker Wood (12 Jly Kempton RF 2734). Got off the mark at Kempton on her second start, but has since been found out in better company.
**P F I Cole [1-4] Christopher Wright.*

CARIBBEAN MONARCH (IRE) BHB 109f RR 110f 3343[8]

5 b g Fairy King (USA) 7.7f **(75)** - Whos The Blonde (Cure The Blues (USA)) 9.5f **(63)**
Form - 4321108
Record 2000 - 1st:2 2nd:1 3rd:1 Ran:7
Pre2000 - 1st:2 2nd:0 3rd:0 Ran:7
Win Prizemoney £108,581 *Total Prizemoney* £123,081
Wins * 2000 Jly Sandow (GD) H 8.1f 102 110 <
*** 2000** Jun Ascot (G-F) H 8f 96 107
* 1998 Jun Windso (G-F) 6f 93
* 1998 Apr Newmar (G-S) 6f 83
2000 Turf 2-7: (7f 3, 8f 2-4) (gd 1-5, g-f 1-2)
Group-class gelding, effective 8f, acts on gd to g-f, best on gd. Turf high 110 - 1st of 18 getting 1lb from Speedfit Too (9 Jly Sandown RF 2658) - also 1st of 32 giving 1lb to John Ferneley (21 Jun Ascot RF 2151). He ran very well in his early starts last season, but is a horse who needs to be produced just at the right time and he finally managed to get it right in the Royal Hunt Cup. Followed up at Sandown, but disappointed again afterwards.
**Sir Michael Stoute [4-14] Pierpont Scott & C H Scott.*

CARIBBEAN SUMMER RR 21f 3900[9]

3 b g Bold Arrangement 8.7f **(57)** - Poppadom (Rapid River) 5.7f **(51)**
Form - 00
Record 2000 - 1st:0 2nd:0 3rd:0 Ran:2
2000 Turf 0-2: (12f 2) (g-f, frm)
Rangy, currently little account gelding. Turf high 21 (began Aug).
**J R Turner [0-2] Mrs Sylvia Blakeley.*

CARINTHIA (IRE) BHB 63f57a RR 64f 57a 4586[3]

5 br m Tirol 8.1f **(64)** - Hot Lavender (CAN) (Shadeed (USA)) 8.2f **(70)**
Form - 002023
Record 2000 - 1st:0 2nd:2 3rd:1 Ran:6
Pre2000 - 1st:1 2nd:1 3rd:2 Ran:11
Win Prizemoney £2,981 *Total Prizemoney* £11,084
Wins * 1998 Aug Salisb (G-F) H 6f 68 70 <
2000 Turf 0-6: (6f, 7f 2, 8f 3) (gd 4, g-f, frm)
Average filly. Turf high 64. Inconsistent.
**C F Wall [1-17] Hintlesham Thoroughbreds.*

CARIOCA DREAM (USA) RR 74+f 5196[2]

2 b f Diesis 9f **(80)** - Highland Ceilidh (IRE) (Scottish Reel) 7f **(61)**
Form - 2
Record 2000 - 1st:0 2nd:1 3rd:0 Ran:1
Win Prizemoney £0 *Total Prizemoney* £1,282
2000 Turf 0-1: (8f) (gd)
Currently above-average filly. (1st run) - 2nd of 16 to Jumaireyah (26 Oct Windsor 8f gd RF 5196). **W J Haggas [0-1] Cyril Humphris.*

CARK BHB 65f RR 67f 3775[11]

2 b g Farfelu - Precious Girl **(64f)** (Precious Metal)
Form - 1450
Record 2000 - 1st:1 2nd:0 3rd:0 Ran:4
Win Prizemoney £2,834 *Total Prizemoney* £3,046
Wins * 2000 Jun Carlis (SFT) 5f 60+ <
2000 Turf 1-4: (5f 1-3, 6f) (gd, g-f 1-2, frm)
Average gelding. Turf high 67 - also 1st of 4 from First Sight (5 Jun Carlisle RF 1709). **A Berry [1-4] Andrew Gorton.*

CARLISLE BAY (IRE) BHB 45f RR 1f 523[12]

6 b g Darshaan 11.9f **(81)** - My Potters (USA) (Irish River (FR)) 8.6f **(78)**
Form - 0
Record 2000 - 1st:0 2nd:0 3rd:0 Ran:1
Pre2000 - 1st:1 2nd:0 3rd:1 Ran:8
Win Prizemoney £6,850 *Total Prizemoney* £9,100
Wins 1996 Spt Currag (GD) 6f 85 <
2000 Turf 0-1: (6f) (gd)
Very poor gelding, has worn blinkers. Becoming disappointing.
**J S Goldie [0-3] Martin Delaney (from J Oxx in IRE [1-6] Jun 1998).*

CARLTON (IRE) BHB 54a RR 82f 5199[2]

6 ch g Thatching 7.8f **(69)** - Hooray Lady (Ahonoora) 8.1f **(73)**
Form - 1214207247056182
Record 2000 - 1st:1 2nd:3 3rd:0 Ran:13
Pre2000 - 1st:8 2nd:6 3rd:8 Ran:42
Win Prizemoney £29,606 *Total Prizemoney* £50,337
Wins * 2000 Spt Sandow (SFT) C 5f 82 <
* 1999 *Nov Wolver (STD)* *6f* *69*
* 1999 *Nov Southw (STD) H* *6f* *54 73*
* 1999 Nov Windso (G-S) H 6f 70 72
* 1999 Oct Windso (G-S) H 6f 60 65
1999 Jly Epsom (G-F) H 6f 57 59
1998 Jly Newbur (G-F) H 7f 60 62
1998 Jun Windso (GD) H 6f 55 58
1997 May Beverl (GD) H 7.5f 53 60
2000 Turf 1-13: (5f 1-2, 6f 4, 7f 6, 8f) (sft 2, g-s 1-2, gd 4, g-f, frm 4)
Decent gelding, effective 5 to 6f, best at 5f, acts on g-s to frm, best on g-s, often wears blinkers, likes left handed tracksprefers right handed tracks, likes tight tracks, excels at Windsor. Turf high 87 (1st run) - 4th of 14 giving 3lb to Always Alight (17 Apr Windsor 6f g-s RF 0755) - also 1st of 17 giving 15lb to Agent Mulder (30 Spt Sandown RF 4756).
**D R C Elsworth [5-20] City Slickers (from G Lewis [4-35] Aug 1999).*

CARLYS QUEST BHB 89f80a RR 92f 80a 5323[2]

6 ch g Primo Dominie 7.2f **(67)** - Tuppy (USA) (Sharpen Up) 8.3f **(67)**
Form - 3130047552
Record 2000 - 1st:1 2nd:1 3rd:2 Ran:10
Pre2000 - 1st:2 2nd:5 3rd:7 Ran:29
Win Prizemoney £18,421 *Total Prizemoney* £59,599
Wins * 2000 May Newbur (G-F) H 12f 82 87 <
* 1998 May Warwic (G-F) H 10.8f 70 79
* 1998 May Newmar (G-S) H 10f 64 70
2000 Turf 1-10: (12f 1-8, 13f, 18f) (hvy, sft, gd 1-5, g-f, frm 2)
Useful gelding, effective 12 to 18f, best at 12f, acts on sft to frm, often wears blinkers, excels at Newbury and Newmarket and Doncaster. Turf high 92 - 3rd of 7 giving 5lb to Three Green Leaves (3 Jun Newmarket 12f frm RF 1691) - also 1st of 14 giving 23lb to

Morgans Orchard (19 May Newbury RF 1304). Consistent. His style of racing makes it difficult for him as he lacks early pace and often finds himself caught for a turn of foot before staying on towards the finish, but the race was run to suit him when he scored at Newbury in May. Ran a good race in the Cesarewitch, but was just found out by the extended trip. He ended the season by finishing runner-up in the November Handicap for the third successive year.
**J Neville [3-45] Yorkeys Knob Racing Club.*

Carlys Quest (right) is second best, again!

CARMARTHEN (IRE) BHB 43a **RR 27f** 3487[11]

4 ch g Hamas (IRE) 8f **(72)** - Solar Attraction (IRE) (Salt Dome (USA))
Form - 444808080000
Record 2000 - 1st:0 2nd:0 3rd:0 Ran:9
Pre2000 - 1st:0 2nd:2 3rd:3 Ran:18
Win Prizemoney £0 *Total Prizemoney* £2,964
2000 Turf 0-7: (5f 5, 6f, 8f) (gd, frm 5, hrd) 2000 AW 0-2: (5f 2) (Fibr 2)
Neat, very moderate gelding, effective 5f, acts on gd to hrd - acts on Equi. Turf high 29. AW high 19. Inconsistent.
**L R Lloyd-James [0-6] Nelson Unit Ltd (from K R Burke [0-10] Apr 2000).*

CARNAGE (IRE) BHB 51f **RR 46f** 3910[12]

3 b g Catrail (USA) - Caranina (USA) (Caro)
Form - 08260
Record 2000 - 1st:0 2nd:1 3rd:0 Ran:5
Pre2000 - 1st:0 2nd:0 3rd:0 Ran:3
Win Prizemoney £0 *Total Prizemoney* £925
2000 Turf 0-5: (6f 2, 8f 2, 9f) (sft, gd 2, frm 2)
Workmanlike, moderate gelding, effective 6f, acts on frm. Turf high 46 - 6th of 13 getting 15lb from Ravine (24 Jly Windsor 6f frm RF 3078).
**Mrs P N Dutfield [0-8] Mrs C A Clarke.*

CARNBREA DANCER BHB 70f **RR 79f** 3234[4]

3 b f Suave Dancer (USA) 10.7f **(68)** - Carnbrea Belle (IRE) **(72f)** (Kefaah (USA))
Form - 524
Record 2000 - 1st:0 2nd:1 3rd:0 Ran:3
Win Prizemoney £0 *Total Prizemoney* £1,254
2000 Turf 0-3: (10f, 14f, 15f) (gd, g-f 2)
Workmanlike, currently above-average filly. Turf high 79.
**W J Haggas [0-3] Mrs S M Crompton.*

CARNIVAL DANCER **RR 82+f** 5224[4]

2 b c Sadler's Wells (USA) 11.3f **(87)** - Red Carnival (USA) **(103df)** (Mr Prospector (USA)) 8.8f **(78)**
Form - 4
Record 2000 - 1st:0 2nd:0 3rd:0 Ran:1
Win Prizemoney £0 *Total Prizemoney* £492
2000 Turf 0-1: (8f) (gd)
Currently decent colt. (1st run) - 4th of 10 getting 2lb from Welsh Border (27 Oct Newmarket 8f gd RF 5224).
**Sir Michael Stoute [0-1] Cheveley Park Stud.*

CARNIVAL LAD (USA) BHB 76f78a **RR 74+f 78a** 4475[2]

2 ch c Caerleon (USA) 10.9f **(79)** - Fun Crowd (USA) (Easy Goer (USA))
Form - 2532
Record 2000 - 1st:0 2nd:2 3rd:1 Ran:4
Win Prizemoney £0 *Total Prizemoney* £2,636
2000 Turf 0-2: (6f 2) (gd 2) 2000 AW 0-2: (7f, 8f) (Fibr 2)
Above-average colt. Turf high 74 (1st run) - 2nd of 6 giving 5lb to Grove Dancer (31 May Yarmouth 6f gd RF 1610). AW high 77 (began Aug) - 2nd of 10 to Seductive (16 Spt Wolverhampton 8f Fibr RF 4475). **Sir Michael Stoute [0-4] Saeed Suhail.*

CARNOT (IRE) BHB 73f **RR 79f** 4890[10]

2 b g General Monash (USA) - Pamiers (Huntercombe) 7.3f **(56)**
Form - 85100
Record 2000 - 1st:1 2nd:0 3rd:0 Ran:5
Win Prizemoney £2,763 *Total Prizemoney* £2,763
Wins * **2000** Aug Bright (GD) 7f 79 <
2000 Turf 1-5: (6f 3, 7f 1-1, 8f) (hvy, g-f 1-4)
Above-average gelding. Turf high 79 (began Jly) - 1st of 10 giving 3lb to Soona (9 Aug Brighton RF 3481).
**G C Bravery [1-5] OTT Partnership.*

CAROLE'S DOVE BHB 40f **RR 35f** 1513[9]

4 b f Manhal - Nimble Dove (Starch Reduced) 11.5f **(52)**
Form - 0000
Record 2000 - 1st:0 2nd:0 3rd:0 Ran:4
Pre2000 - 1st:0 2nd:0 3rd:0 Ran:1
2000 Turf 0-4: (5f, 6f, 8f, 15f) (hvy, sft, gd 2)
Neat, very moderate filly. Turf high 35.
**C J Price [0-5] Mrs C A Crawford.*

CAROLS CHOICE BHB 57f65a **RR 59f 65a** 5068[18]

3 ch f Emarati (USA) 6.6f **(63)** - Lucky Song (Lucky Wednesday) 8f **(50)**
Form - 42033235620
Record 2000 - 1st:0 2nd:3 3rd:3 Ran:11
Pre2000 - 1st:0 2nd:0 3rd:1 Ran:5
Win Prizemoney £0 *Total Prizemoney* £4,847
2000 Turf 0-4: (5f 3, 6f) (g-s, gd, g-f 2) 2000 AW 0-7: (5f 2, 6f 4, 7f) (Fibr 7)
Neat, average filly, effective 5 to 6f, best at 6f, acts on gd to g-f - acts on Fibr, has worn blinkers, likes left handed tracks, prefers tight tracks, excels at Wolverhampton. Turf high 59 - 3rd of 14 getting 14lb from Blue Holly (8 Jun Chepstow 5f gd RF 1799). AW high 68 - 2nd of 11 to Diamond Rachael (19 Feb Wolverhampton 6f Fibr RF 0318). **D HaydnJones [0-16] Monolithic Refractories Ltd.*

CAROUSING BHB 80f **RR 92+f** 4936[14]

3 b c Selkirk (USA) 7.9f **(76)** - Moon Carnival **(96f)** (Be My Guest (USA)) 9.3f **(67)**
Form - 15001040
Record 2000 - 1st:2 2nd:0 3rd:0 Ran:8
Pre2000 - 1st:2 2nd:0 3rd:0 Ran:3
Win Prizemoney £23,976 *Total Prizemoney* £24,658

Wins							
	2000	Spt	Ayr	(SFT)	C	9.1f	70
	2000	Jun	Pontef	(SFT)		10f	92+ <
	1999	Jly	Goodwo	(FRM)	H	7f	86+
	1999	Jun	Lingfi	(GD)		7f	79+

2000 Turf 2-8: (9f 1-1, 10f 1-3, 11f 2, 12f 2) (hvy, sft, gd 2-4, g-f 2)
Workmanlike, useful colt, effective 7 to 10f, best at 10f, acts on gd to g-f, best on g-f, has worn blinkers, likes tight tracks. Turf high 92 - 5th of 6 getting 1lb from Alva Glen (17 Jun York 10f g-f RF 2063) - also 1st of 4 getting 4lb from Foreign Secretary (4 Jun Pontefract RF 1699).
**R M Beckett [0-3] Willie McKay (from M Johnston [4-8] Spt 2000).*

CARPET LADY (IRE) BHB 69f **RR 75f** 4751[5]

2 b f Night Shift (USA) 8.1f **(73)** - Lucky Fountain (IRE) (Lafontaine (USA)) 8.7f **(49)**
Form - 3305
Record 2000 - 1st:0 2nd:0 3rd:2 Ran:4
Win Prizemoney £0 *Total Prizemoney* £2,023
2000 Turf 0-4: (5f, 6f 3) (g-s, g-f 2, frm)
Above-average filly. Turf high 75 (began Jly) - 3rd of 7 to Early Morning Mist (13 Aug Ascot 6f g-f RF 3605).
**Mrs P N Dutfield [0-4] Axminster Carpets Ltd.*

CARPET PRINCESS (IRE) **RR 62f** 3079[9]

2 gr ro f Prince of Birds (USA) - Krayyalei (IRE) **(73f)** (Krayyan) 8.5f

(49)
Form - 40
Record 2000 - 1st:0 2nd:0 3rd:0 Ran:2
Win Prizemoney £0 *Total Prizemoney* £448
2000 Turf 0-2: (6f 2) (frm 2)
Currently average filly. Turf high 62 (began Jly).
**Mrs P N Dutfield [0-2] Axminster Carpets Ltd.*

CARRABAN (IRE) BHB 67f **RR 65f** 4822[12]

2 b f Mujadil (USA) 7.7f **(70)** - Bayazida (Bustino) 10.4f **(64)**
Form - 5336230
Record 2000 - 1st:0 2nd:1 3rd:3 Ran:7
Win Prizemoney £0 *Total Prizemoney* £2,295
2000 Turf 0-5: (5f, 6f 2, 7f, 10f) (gd 3, g-f, frm) 2000 AW 0-2: (7f, 8f) (Fibr 2)
Average filly, effective 7 to 8f, acts on Fibr. Turf high 65. AW high 67 (began Aug) - 3rd of 10 getting 5lb from Seductive (16 Spt Wolverhampton 8f Fibr RF 4475). **B J Meehan [0-7] C J Foy.*

CARRACA (IRE) BHB 59f **RR 57f** 5080[4]

2 b g Alzao (USA) 9.8f **(73)** - Honey Bun (Unfuwain (USA))
Form - 004
Record 2000 - 1st:0 2nd:0 3rd:0 Ran:3
Win Prizemoney £0 *Total Prizemoney* £264
2000 Turf 0-3: (6f, 7f, 8f) (hvy, g-f, frm)
Currently fair gelding, has worn blinkers. Turf high 57.
**J D Bethell [0-2] M J Dawson (from L M Cumani [0-1] Jun 2000).*

CARRADIUM BHB 53f **RR** 4624[7]

4 b g Presidium 7.5f **(56)** - Carrapateira (Gunner B) 11.2f **(58)**
Form - 67
Record 2000 - 1st:0 2nd:0 3rd:0 Ran:2
Pre2000 - 1st:0 2nd:0 3rd:0 Ran:5
2000 Turf 0-2: (8f, 12f) (gd, hrd)
Workmanlike, very poor gelding. (began Aug).
**C W Fairhurst [0-7] R Shiels.*

CARRICK LADY (IRE) BHB 41f **RR 44f** 5237[5]

2 ch f Fayruz 6.6f **(63)** - Mantlepicce (IRE) (Common Grounds)
Form - 80805
Record 2000 - 1st:0 2nd:0 3rd:0 Ran:5
2000 Turf 0-4: (5f 2, 6f, 8f) (g-s 2, g-f, frm) 2000 AW 0-1: (5f) (Equi)
Moderate filly, has worn blinkers. Turf high 44 (began Aug).
**G P Enright [0-5] The Carrick Partnership.*

CARRICK VIEW (IRE) BHB 56f **RR 49f** 1287a[3]

5 b h Posen (USA) 8.6f **(59)** - Linda's Fantasy (Raga Navarro (ITY)) 8f **(64)**
Form - 3
2000 AW 0-1: (5f) (Dirt)
Very useful colt. (1st run) - 3rd of 10 to Rolo Tomasi (14 May Jagersro 5f Dirt RF 1287a).
**in SWE [0-1] (from P Calver [0-4] Spt 1997).*

CARRIE CAN CAN BHB 61f67a **RR 59f 67a** 5142[4]

3 b f Green Tune (USA) - Maidenhair (IRE) (Darshaan) 9.9f **(84)**
Form - 653854
Record 2000 - 1st:0 2nd:0 3rd:1 Ran:6
Win Prizemoney £0 *Total Prizemoney* £1,268
2000 Turf 0-6: (8f 2, 10f 3, 11f) (g-s 2, gd, g-f 2, hrd)
Leggy, average filly. Turf high 59 (began Aug).
**J G Given [0-6] A W Robinson & Ian Robinson.*

CARRIE POOTER BHB 76f75a **RR 76+f 75a** 4183[1]

4 b f Tragic Role (USA) 9.4f **(63)** - Ginny Binny (Ahonoora) 8.1f **(73)**
Form - 1680000111
Record 2000 - 1st:4 2nd:0 3rd:0 Ran:10
Pre2000 - 1st:3 2nd:6 3rd:3 Ran:23
Win Prizemoney £31,854 *Total Prizemoney* £40,943

Wins								
	*** 2000**	Spt	Hamilt	(SFT)	H	6f	70	76 <
	*** 2000**	Jly	Thirsk	(FRM)	H	6f	65	67
	*** 2000**	Jly	Pontef	(GD)	H	6f	57	65
	*** 2000**	*Mar*	*Southw*	*(STD)*	*H*	*6f*	*69*	*70*
	* 1999	Jly	Hamilt	(G-F)	H	6f	63	65
	* 1999	*Mar*	*Southw*	*(SLW)*	*H*	*7f*	*59*	*62+*
	* 1998	May	Redcar	(G-F)		6f		73

2000 Turf 3-9: (6f 3-7, 7f 2) (g-s 1-2, gd 2, g-f, frm 1-3, hrd 1-1) 2000 AW 1-1: (6f 1-1) (Fibr 1-1)
Tall, above-average filly, effective 6 to 7f, best at 6f, acts on sft to hrd - acts on Fibr, often wears blinkers (extremely effectively), excels at Hamilton and likes Thirsk. Turf high 76 - 1st of 12 giving 21lb to Rouge Etoile (3 Spt Hamilton RF 4183) - also 1st of 10 giving 19lb to Dominelle (28 Jly Thirsk RF 3198). (1st run) - 1st of 9 giving 17lb to Marengo (20 Mar Southwell RF 0471). Inconsistent. Scored on the Southwell Fibresand in March and, after some disappointing efforts, landed a hat-trick in the summer at Pontefract, Thirsk and Hamilton. Suited by six furlongs.
**T D Barron [7-33] Stephen Woodall.*

CARRY THE FLAG BHB 104f **RR 118f** 429a[3]

5 b h Tenby 10.4f **(76)** - Tamassos (Dance In Time (CAN)) 8.9f **(59)**
Form - 3
2000 Turf 0-1: (10f) (gd)
High-class colt, effective 10f, acts on gd. (1st run) - 3rd of 14 to Ouzo (5 Mar Kranji 10f gd RF 0429a).
**M Kent in SIN [0-1] (from P F I Cole [4-13] Spt 1999).*

CARTMEL PARK BHB 60f73a **RR 71f 73a** 4756[14]

4 ch g Skyliner 6.8f **(51)** - Oh My Oh My (Ballacashtal (CAN)) 5.3f **(50)**
Form - 050018300480
Record 2000 - 1st:1 2nd:0 3rd:1 Ran:12
Pre2000 - 1st:4 2nd:5 3rd:2 Ran:21
Win Prizemoney £19,451 *Total Prizemoney* £26,797

Wins								
	*** 2000**	*Jun*	*Wolver*	*(STD)*	*H*	*5f*	*74*	*81* <
	1999	Oct	Catter	(GD,)	H	5f	73	79?
	1999	Jly	Sandow	(GD)	H	5f	74	77
	1998	Spt	Newcas	(GD)		5f		60+
	1998	Jly	Mussel	(GD)		5f		69

2000 Turf 0-11: (5f 11) (g-s 3, gd 2, frm 5, hrd) 2000 AW 1-1: (5f 1-1) (Fibr 1-1)
Leggy, decent gelding, effective 5f, acts on gd to hrd - acts on Fibr, has worn blinkers (effectively). Turf high 73 - 3rd of 13 giving 10lb to Flak Jacket (26 Jly Catterick 5f frm RF 3129). (1st run) - 1st of 13 getting 2lb from Teyaar (21 Jun Wolverhampton RF 2175). Inconsistent. A winner twice over five furlongs on good ground in 1999, he seems best when able to dominate and was able to use those tactics when winning on the Wolverhampton Fibresand in July.
**A Berry [1-12] P G Airey & R R Whitton (from J Berry [4-21] Oct 1999).*

CARTMEL PRINCE BHB 54f **RR 62f** 2870[7]

2 b c Prince Daniel (USA) 11.4f **(46)** - Oh My Oh My (Ballacashtal (CAN)) 5.3f **(50)**
Form - 607277
Record 2000 - 1st:0 2nd:1 3rd:0 Ran:6
Win Prizemoney £0 *Total Prizemoney* £840
2000 Turf 0-6: (5f 5, 7f) (gd 2, g-f 3, frm)
Average colt, effective 5f, acts on g-f. Turf high 62 - 2nd of 6 giving 5lb to Last Impression (15 Jun Hamilton 5f g-f RF 1981).
**D Moffatt [0-6] P G Airey & R R Whitton.*

CARUSO'S BHB 50f **RR 58f** 3272[15]

2 b f Be My Guest (USA) 10.2f **(66)** - Courtisane (Persepolis (FR)) 6.4f **(67)**
Form - 08360
Record 2000 - 1st:0 2nd:0 3rd:1 Ran:5
Win Prizemoney £0 *Total Prizemoney* £325
2000 Turf 0-5: (5f 3, 6f 2) (gd, g-f, frm 3)
Fair filly. Turf high 58 - 3rd of 7 giving 2lb to Deceitful (19 Jun Brighton 5f frm RF 2085). **E J O'Neill [0-5] The Ballybrit Partnership.*

CASAMASA (IRE) **RR 116f** 1047[2]

4 b c Sadler's Wells (USA) 11.3f **(87)** - Millieme (Mill Reef (USA)) 10.5f **(78)**
Form - 2
2000 Turf 0-1: (12f) (g-f)
High-class colt, has worn blinkers. (1st run) - 2nd of 11 to Blueprint (5 May Newmarket 12f g-f RF 1047). He stays well and, being from a late maturing family, is open to further improvement.
**E Lellouche in FR [0-4] Wafic Said.*

CASE THE JOINT (IRE) **RR 42f** 4579[15]

2 b c Case Law 6f **(64)** - Chesham Lady (IRE) (Fayruz)
Form - 0

Record 2000 - 1st:0 2nd:0 3rd:0 Ran:1
2000 Turf 0-1: (5f) (gd)
Currently moderate colt.
**R M Beckett [0-1] The Millennium Madness Partnership.*

CASH RR 4382[17]

2 b g Bishop of Cashel - Ballad Island (Ballad Rock) 7.8f **(63)**
Form - 0
Record 2000 - 1st:0 2nd:0 3rd:0 Ran:1
2000 Turf 0-1: (6f) (gd)
Currently very poor gelding. **M Brittain [0-1] Northgate Autumn.*

CASHAPLENTY BHB 41f43a RR 14f 43a 131[9]

7 ch g Ballacashtal (CAN) 7.9f **(51)** - Storm of Plenty (Billion (USA)) 12f **(43)**
Form - 40

Record	**2000 -**	1st:0	2nd:0	3rd:0	Ran:2
	Pre2000 -	1st:1	2nd:1	3rd:0	Ran:9

Win Prizemoney £2,713 *Total Prizemoney* £3,234

Wins	* 1997	*Feb*	*Wolver*	*(STD)*	*12f*	*44+*	<

2000 AW 0-2: (12f 2) (Fibr 2)
Moderate gelding. AW high 43 (1st run) - 4th of 11 giving 17lb to Manful (4 Jan Wolverhampton 12f Fibr RF 0021).
**N P Littmoden [4-25] J R Salter.*

CASHDOWN (IRE) RR 4806[15]

2 b g Bishop of Cashel - Ashdown (Pharly (FR)) 9.8f **(68)**
Form - 0
Record 2000 - 1st:0 2nd:0 3rd:0 Ran:1
2000 Turf 0-1: (7f) (g-s)
Currently very poor gelding. **I A Wood [0-1] Neardown Stables.*

CASHIKI (IRE) BHB 34f22a RR 42f 22a 3714[4]

4 ch f Case Law 6f **(64)** - Nishiki (USA) (Brogan (USA))
Form - 80682826174

Record	**2000 -**	1st:1	2nd:2	3rd:0	Ran:9
	Pre2000 -	1st:3	2nd:4	3rd:1	Ran:25

Win Prizemoney £10,138 *Total Prizemoney* £15,215

Wins	*** 2000**	Jly	Mussel	(G-S)	C	16f		37	
	* 1998	Aug	Pontef	(G-F)	H	6f	70	73	<
	* 1998	Jun	Chepst	(G-S)	C	6.1f		61	
	* 1998	Jun	Lingfi	(GD)	S	6f		58	

2000 Turf 1-9: (10f, 11f 2, 12f 2, 14f, 16f 1-3) (sft, g-s 2, gd 1-2, g-f 2, frm 2)
Light-framed, moderate filly, likes right handed tracks. Turf high 42. **B Palling [4-34] The Valley Commandos.*

CASHMERE LADY BHB 56f62a RR 59f 62a 4456[12]

8 b m Hubbly Bubbly (USA) 9.5f **(43)** - Choir (High Top) 10.2f **(67)**
Form - 5011027480

Record	**2000 -**	1st:2	2nd:1	3rd:0	Ran:9
	Pre2000 -	1st:9	2nd:7	3rd:3	Ran:62

Win Prizemoney £40,204 *Total Prizemoney* £59,703

Wins	*** 2000**	Jly	Haydoc	(G-F)	H	11.9f	61	53	
	*** 2000**	Apr	Ripon	(SFT)	H	12.3f	54	60	
	* 1999	Spt	Haydoc	(G-F)	H	10.5f	60	63	
	* 1998	Apr	Thirsk	(G-S)	H	8f	73	78	
	* 1998	*Mar*	*Southw*	*(STD)*	*H*	*12f*	*87*	*89*	<
	* 1997	Aug	Redcar	(FRM)	H	8f	72	78	
	* 1997	*Jun*	*Wolver*	*(STD)*	*H*	*8.5f*	*76*	*89*	<
	* 1997	Jun	Thirsk	(GD)	H	8f	65	70	
	* 1996	*Mar*	*Wolver*	*(STD)*	*H*	*8.5f*	*72*	*77+*	

2000 Turf 2-9: (12f 2-9) (g-s, gd 1-3, frm 1-5)
Average mare, effective 11 to 12f, acts on g-f to frm, likes tight tracks. Turf high 62. Won an amateurs' event at Haydock in 1999, but it took a drop in the weights for her to return to the winner's enclosure at Ripon in April. Was off for three months before coming back to score under a well-timed ride at Haydock, but has been held since. **J L Eyre [11-76] Mrs Sybil Howe.*

CASHNEEM (IRE) BHB 84f RR 81f 4547[7]

2 b c Case Law 6f **(64)** - Haanem (Mtoto)
Form - 4127
Record 2000 - 1st:1 2nd:1 3rd:0 Ran:4
Win Prizemoney £2,604 *Total Prizemoney* £3,500

Wins	*** 2000**	Aug	Mussel	(GD)	7.1f	72+	<

2000 Turf 1-4: (7f 1-3, 8f) (g-s, g-f, frm 1-2)
Decent colt. Turf high 81 (began Jly) - 2nd of 9 giving 1lb to Harrier (17 Aug Beverley 7f frm RF 3717) - also 1st of 6 giving 5lb to Ocean Love (2 Aug Musselburgh RF 3336).
**P W Harris [1-4] Law Abiding Citizens.*

CASING (IRE) RR 4651[7]

2 gr f Case Law 6f **(64)** - Singhana (IRE) (Mouktar)
Form -
Record 2000 - 1st:0 2nd:0 3rd:0 Ran:3
2000 Turf 0-2: (g-s, frm) 2000 AW 0-1: (Fibr)
Currently moderate gelding. Turf high 48 (began Jly).
**R M Whitaker [0-3] J F Coupland.*

CASPIAN BHB 72f RR 67f 3855[13]

2 b f Spectrum (IRE) - Sinking Sun **(67f)** (Danehill (USA)) 10f **(72)**
Form - 210
Record 2000 - 1st:1 2nd:1 3rd:0 Ran:3
Win Prizemoney £3,575 *Total Prizemoney* £4,865

Wins	*** 2000**	Jly	Doncas	(G-F)	7f	67	<

2000 Turf 1-3: (7f 1-3) (gd, g-f, frm 1-1)
Currently average filly. Turf high 67 - 1st of 4 from St Florent (1 Jly Doncaster RF 2428). Made hard work of winning a four-runner Doncaster maiden on her second start. **B W Hills [1-3] K Abdulla.*

CASSANDRA RR 58f 5000[9]

4 b f Catrail (USA) - Circo (High Top) 10.2f **(67)**
Form - 258200400

Record	**2000 -**	1st:0	2nd:2	3rd:0	Ran:9
	Pre2000 -	1st:0	2nd:0	3rd:0	Ran:6

Win Prizemoney £0 *Total Prizemoney* £2,222
2000 Turf 0-9: (8f, 10f 7, 12f) (g-s 2, gd, g-f 2, frm 4)
Tall, fair filly. Turf high 58. **M Brittain [0-15] Mel Brittain.*

CASSANDRA GO (IRE) BHB 110f RR 110f 3276[1]

4 gr f Indian Ridge 7.6f **(74)** -Rahaam (USA) (Secreto (USA)) 8.7f **(72)**
Form - 12621

Record	**2000 -**	1st:2	2nd:2	3rd:0	Ran:5
	Pre2000 -	1st:2	2nd:0	3rd:1	Ran:8

Win Prizemoney £53,061 *Total Prizemoney* £68,192

Wins	*** 2000**	Aug	Goodwo	(G-F)	G3	5f	109	<
	*** 2000**	May	Bath	(G-S)	L	5.1f	102	
	* 1999	Jun	Newmar	(G-F)		6f	94	
	* 1999	Apr	Newmar	(GD)		7f	89	

2000 Turf 2-5: (5f 2-4, 6f) (g-s, gd 1-3, g-f 1-1)
Light-framed, Group-class filly, effective 5 to 6f, best at 5f, acts on g-s to g-f, does well at Newmarket. Turf high 110 - 2nd of 9 getting 6lb from Rudi's Pet (5 Jun Leopardstown 5f g-s RF 1926a) - also 1st of 13 getting 8lb from Eastern Purple (1 Aug Goodwood RF 3276). Consistent. She proved herself a smart sprinter last season, successful in the King George Stakes at Glorious Goodwood but was not seen after. A free-runner, she ran well both with and without a tongue-strap. **G Wragg [4-13] Trevor Stewart.*

Cassandra Go certainly went

CASSIUS RR 74+f 5099[16]

2 b g Machiavellian (USA) 9.8f **(83)** - Chain Dance (Shareef Dancer (USA)) 9.9f **(73)**
Form - 50
Record 2000 - 1st:0 2nd:0 3rd:0 Ran:2
2000 Turf 0-2: (7f 2) (gd, g-f)
Currently above-average gelding. Turf high 74 (began Spt).
**J R Fanshawe [0-2] J M Greetham.*

CASTANEA SATIVA (IRE) BHB 48f RR 43f 1551[11]

3 b f In The Wings 11.2f **(77)** - Chesnut Tree (USA) (Shadeed (USA)) 8.2f **(70)**
Form - 0450
Record 2000 - 1st:0 2nd:0 3rd:0 Ran:4
Pre2000 - 1st:0 2nd:1 3rd:0 Ran:4
Win Prizemoney £0 *Total Prizemoney* £1,313
2000 Turf 0-4: (10f, 12f, 14f 2) (g-s, gd, g-f, frm)
Lengthy, moderate filly, effective 7f, acts on g-s, has worn blinkers, favours tight tracks. Turf high 43. Consistent.
**T D Easterby [0-8] Chris & Antonia Deuters.*

CASTIYA (IRE) RR 110f 5202a[2]

3 gr f Bluebird (USA) 7.9f **(71)** - Comme D'Habitude (USA) (Caro)
Form - 722
2000 Turf 0-3: (7f 2, 8f) (hvy 2, gd)
Group-class filly. Turf high 110 (1st run) - 7th of 11 to Bluemamba (14 May Longchamp 8f gd RF 1291a). She made the frame in a couple of French Listed races last season. **C Laffon-Parias in FR [1-4].*

CASTLEBAR BHB 61f RR 53f 953[20]

3 b g Formidable (USA) 7.8f **(60)** - Nineteenth of May (Homing) 7.8f **(59)**
Form - 1700
Record 2000 - 1st:1 2nd:0 3rd:0 Ran:4
Win Prizemoney £2,769 *Total Prizemoney* £2,769
Wins ** **2000** Feb Southw (STD) 6f 57 <*
2000 Turf 0-3: (6f, 7f 2) (hvy 2, sft) 2000 AW 1-1: (6f 1-1) (Fibr 1-1)
Fair gelding. Turf high 53. (1st run) - 1st of 9 getting 15lb from Above Board (7 Feb Southwell RF 0236).
**Miss Gay Kelleway [1-4] & Mrs Gary Pinchen.*

CASTLE BEAU BHB 27f RR 35f 2954[11]

5 ch g Safawan 6.6f **(60)** - Castle Maid **(28f)** (Castle Keep) 8.3f **(57)**
Form - 0008000
Record 2000 - 1st:0 2nd:0 3rd:0 Ran:7
Pre2000 - 1st:0 2nd:0 3rd:0 Ran:1
2000 Turf 0-7: (6f 4, 7f, 8f, 12f) (gd 3, g-f, frm 2, hrd)
Very moderate gelding. Turf high 37.
**R J Hodges [0-8] R T Sercombe.*

CASTLEBRIDGE BHB 50f44a RR 79f 44a 5154[16]

3 b g Batshoof 9.5f **(66)** - Super Sisters (AUS) (Call Report (USA))
Form - 08001161530450000
Record 2000 - 1st:3 2nd:0 3rd:1 Ran:14
Pre2000 - 1st:0 2nd:0 3rd:0 Ran:3
Win Prizemoney £6,666 *Total Prizemoney* £7,286

Wins	**2000**	Apr Warwic	(HVY) H	10.5f	69	74 <
	2000	*Feb Wolver*	*(STD) S*	*9.4f*		*69++*
	2000	*Jan Wolver*	*(STD) S*	*8.5f*		*64+*

2000 Turf 1-8: (8f, 10f 4, 11f 1-2, 12f) (hvy 1-2, gd 3, g-f 2, frm) 2000 AW 2-6: (8f 1-4, 9f 1-1, 12f) (Equi, Fibr 2-5)
Unfurnished, above-average gelding, effective 9 to 11f, best at 11f, acts on hvy to gd - acts on Fibr, best on hvy, often wears blinkers (extremely effectively), favours left handed tracks. Turf high 79 - 3rd of 11 giving 9lb to Desert Island Disc (27 May Warwick 11f hvy RF 1510) - also 1st of 11 giving 17lb to Stafford King (24 Apr Warwick RF 0855). AW high 69. Becoming disappointing.
**M D I Usher [0-4] P Sweeting (from M C Pipe [2-9] Aug 2000).*

CASTLE FRIEND BHB 51f RR 55f 439[10]

5 b g Durgam (USA) 12.3f **(53)** - Furry Friend (USA) (Bold Bidder) 8.8f **(67)**
Form - 0
Record 2000 - 1st:0 2nd:0 3rd:0 Ran:1
Pre2000 - 1st:0 2nd:1 3rd:2 Ran:8
Win Prizemoney £0 *Total Prizemoney* £1,657
2000 AW 0-1: (8f) (Fibr)
Fair gelding. He is still a maiden, but has enough ability to be able to land a small race. Whatever he does on the Flat, he should find races when tried over hurdles.
**M D Hammond [0-8] G Heap (from P C Haslam [0-4] Spt 1997).*

CASTLES BURNING (USA) BHB 51f63a RR 59f 63a 4811[1]

6 b br g Minshaanshu Amad (USA) 11.3f **(53)** - Major Overhaul (Known Fact (USA)) 7.4f **(67)**
Form - 1
Record 2000 - 1st:1 2nd:0 3rd:0 Ran:1
Pre2000 - 1st:8 2nd:6 3rd:7 Ran:49
Win Prizemoney £23,300 *Total Prizemoney* £32,614

Wins	* **2000**	*Oct Lingfi*	*(STD) S*	*8f*		*45*
	* 1999	*Jun Lingfi*	*(STD)*	*8f*		*71*
	* 1999	*Mar Lingfi*	*(STD)*	*8f*		*67*
	* 1998	*Dec Lingfi*	*(STD)*	*10f*		*65*
	* 1998	*Dec Lingfi*	*(STD) H*	*10f*	*59*	*65*
	* 1998	Aug Bright	(FRM) H	10f	50	56
	* 1997	*Oct Lingfi*	*(STD) H*	*10f*	*65*	*67*
	* 1997	Aug Bright	(FRM) H	11.9f	50	54
	* 1997	*Mar Lingfi*	*(STD) H*	*8f*	*69*	*78 <*

2000 AW 1-1: (8f 1-1) (Equi 1-1)
Average gelding, effective 8 to 10f, best at 8f, - acts on AW, best on Equi, has worn blinkers (effectively). (1st run). He is probably a better horse on Equitrack, but has also shown a liking for the turf at Brighton. Obviously suited by a sharp left-handed track.
**C A Cyzer [9-50] R M Cyzer.*

CASTLE SECRET BHB 35f48a RR 42?f 48a 234[11]

14 b g Castle Keep 10.5f **(58)** - Baffle (Petingo) 11f **(72)**
Form - 00
Record 2000 - 1st:0 2nd:0 3rd:0 Ran:1
Pre2000 - 1st:2 2nd:6 3rd:1 Ran:32
Win Prizemoney £12,226 *Total Prizemoney* £17,915
Wins ** 1997 May Wolver (STD) H 16.2f 47 52 <*
2000 AW 0-1: (16f) (Fibr)
Moderate gelding, has worn blinkers. Becoming disappointing. A useful stayer on Fibresand in the past, but is at the veteran stage now and does not have the speed for the Flat.
**D Burchell [9-67] Mrs Ruth Burchell (from J L Dunlop [1-5] Aug 1990).*

CASTLE SEMPILL BHB 68f68a RR 66f 68a 5014[10]

3 b g Presidium 7.5f **(56)** - La Suquet **(60f 60a)** (Puissance)
Form - 431121351060040360
Record 2000 - 1st:3 2nd:1 3rd:2 Ran:15
Pre2000 - 1st:2 2nd:1 3rd:4 Ran:12
Win Prizemoney £24,307 *Total Prizemoney* £30,160

Wins	**2000**	Apr Windso	(GD) H	6f	73	82 <
	2000	*Feb Wolver*	*(STD) H*	*6f*	*70*	*77*
	* **2000**	*Jan Lingfi*	*(STD) H*	*5f*	*67*	*70*
	* 1999	*Dec Lingfi*	*(STD) H*	*6f*	*64*	*68*
	1999	Oct Newmar	(GD) S	7f		67

2000 Turf 1-7: (5f 2, 6f 1-4, 7f) (sft, gd, g-f, frm 1-4) 2000 AW 2-8: (5f 1-1, 6f 1-5, 7f 2) (Equi 1-4, Fibr 1-4)
Above-average gelding, effective 5 to 6f, best at 6f, acts on g-f to frm - acts on AW, often wears blinkers, likes Lingfield. Turf high 82 (1st run) - 1st of 21 giving 18lb to Watergrasshill (10 Apr Windsor RF 0655). AW high 77 - 2nd of 5 getting 1lb from Illusive (2 Feb Lingfield 6f Equi RF 0207) - also 1st of 8 giving 9lb to Stop The Traffic (8 Feb Wolverhampton RF 0243). A tough and useful sprint handicapper on turf and sand, he has won over five furlongs, but looks better suited by six and was victorious over that trip when returned to turf at Windsor in April. Did not recapture his best after a three-month break.
**R M H Cowell [4-19] Mrs J M Penney (from J R Fanshawe [1-8] Oct 1999).*

CASTLESHANE (IRE) RR 87f 5283a[11]

3 b c Kris 10f **(75)** - Ahbab (IRE) (Ajdal (USA)) 9.2f **(89)**
Form - 636855430
2000 Turf 0-9: (7f, 8f, 10f 4, 12f 3) (hvy 3, sft, g-s, gd 2, g-f, frm)
Useful colt, effective 10f, acts on hvy to g-s, likes right handed tracks. Turf high 95 - 6th of 11 giving 21lb to Turn Turtle (1 Jly Curragh 10f g-s RF 2520a). Consistent.
**K Prendergast in IRE [2-17] A D Brennan.*

CASTLETOWN COUNT BHB 35f **RR 36f** 527[6]
8 b g Then Again 7.4f **(52)** - Pepeke (Mummy's Pet) 7.7f **(60)**
Form - 6
Record 2000 - 1st:0 2nd:0 3rd:0 Ran:1
Pre2000 - 1st:1 2nd:1 3rd:0 Ran:14
Win Prizemoney £2,679 *Total Prizemoney* £3,426
2000 Turf 0-1: (16f) (g-s)
Very moderate gelding. A modest handicapper, he seems to reserve his best for Catterick. Suited by trips of around two and a half miles.
**M W Easterby [2-12] Abbots Salford Carav Park (from K W Hogg [1-13] Jun 1996).*

CASTRATO BHB 25f **RR 22f** 5122[22]
4 b g Rock City 8.8f **(62)** - Vocalist (Crooner) 9.9f **(49)**
Form - 880000
Record 2000 - 1st:0 2nd:0 3rd:0 Ran:6
2000 Turf 0-4: (6f, 7f 3) (g-s, gd, frm 2) 2000 AW 0-2: (9f 2) (Fibr 2)
Leggy, little account gelding. Turf high 22.
**B N Doran [0-3] P N Exton (from G M McCourt [0-3] Mar 2000).*

CATALAN BAY BHB 30f **RR 39f** 4622[12]
2 b br f Risk Me (FR) 8f **(53)** - Astrid Gilberto (Runnett) 7f **(59)**
Form - 008000
Record 2000 - 1st:0 2nd:0 3rd:0 Ran:6
2000 Turf 0-6: (5f 4, 6f 2) (g-s, gd 2, frm 3)
Very moderate filly. Turf high 39.
**R Bastiman [0-6] New Kids on the Rock Ltd.*

CATALONIA (IRE) RR 66df 5139[2]
3 ch f Catrail (USA) - Shakanda (IRE) (Shernazar) 10.2f **(73)**
Form - 502
Record 2000 - 1st:0 2nd:1 3rd:0 Ran:3
Pre2000 - 1st:0 2nd:0 3rd:0 Ran:2
Win Prizemoney £0 *Total Prizemoney* £1,230
2000 Turf 0-3: (7f, 8f 2) (g-s, g-f 2)
Neat, average filly. Turf high 60 (began Aug).
**M L W Bell [0-3] B H Farr (from J A Glover [0-2] Oct 1999).*

CATAMARAN BHB 57f **RR 70f** 4679[8]
5 ch g Rainbow Quest (USA) 11.2f **(81)** - Cattermole (USA) (Roberto (USA)) 10f **(76)**
Form - 457008
Record 2000 - 1st:0 2nd:0 3rd:0 Ran:6
Pre2000 - 1st:0 2nd:0 3rd:1 Ran:2
Win Prizemoney £0 *Total Prizemoney* £876
2000 Turf 0-6: (7f 3, 8f 2, 12f) (sft, g-s, gd 2, g-f 2)
Above-average gelding, effective 7f, acts on sft, has worn blinkers. Turf high 72 (1st run) - 4th of 10 giving 13lb to Big Future (24 Apr Kempton 7f sft RF 0840). Becoming disappointing.
**Lady Herries [0-6] D Heath (from J H M Gosden [0-2] Spt 1999).*

CATCHTHEBATCH BHB 52f52a **RR 50f 52a** 963[17]
4 b g Beveled (USA) 6.9f **(64)** - Batchworth Dancer (Ballacashtal (CAN)) 5.3f **(50)**
Form - 08050
Record 2000 - 1st:0 2nd:0 3rd:0 Ran:4
Pre2000 - 1st:1 2nd:0 3rd:1 Ran:13
Win Prizemoney £2,583 *Total Prizemoney* £3,151
Wins * 1999 *Jan Lingfi (STD) 6f* 77 <
2000 Turf 0-1: (5f) (gd) 2000 AW 0-3: (5f 2, 6f) (Equi 3)
Workmanlike, fair gelding, effective 6f, - acts on Equi, has worn blinkers, likes left handed tracks, likes tight tracks. AW high 47.
**E A Wheeler [1-17] The Over The Bridge Partnership.*

CATCH THE CHRON BHB 68f **RR 61f** 4770[11]
2 b f Clantime 6.6f **(57)** - Emerald Gulf (IRE) (Wassl) 9.7f **(62)**
Form - 27401620
Record 2000 - 1st:1 2nd:2 3rd:0 Ran:8
Win Prizemoney £2,646 *Total Prizemoney* £4,498
Wins * 2000 Aug Hamilt (SFT) S 5f 60 <
2000 Turf 1-8: (5f 1-4, 6f 4) (sft, g-s 2, gd 1-2, g-f, frm 2)
Average filly, effective 5 to 6f, acts on sft to gd. Turf high 61 - 2nd of 10 getting 5lb from Church Mice (22 Spt Haydock 6f sft RF 4574) - also 1st of 11 from Sean's Honor (16 Aug Hamilton RF 3697). Inconsistent. **N Tinkler [1-8] The Oldham Chronicle Racing Club.*

CATCH THE DRAGON (IRE) RR 95f 5355a[10]
5 b h Sharp Victor (USA) 10f **(56)** - Roblanna (Roberto (USA)) 10f **(76)**
Form - 006250
2000 Turf 0-6: (7f, 8f, 9f, 10f 2, 12f) (hvy, sft, g-s 4)
Very useful colt, effective 9 to 12f, acts on g-s. Turf high 95 - 2nd of 13 getting 1lb from Winged Hussar (28 May Curragh 12f g-s RF 1586a). He returned from ten months off early in 2000, and his best effort was when runner-up in a valuable handicap at the Curragh. His best form is on easy ground, so he is likely to be in action before the ground dires up. **L Browne in IRE [2-14] Mrs P K Cooper.*

CATCHY WORD BHB 101f **RR 99f** 4470[1]
3 ch c Cadeaux Genereux 7.9f **(76)** - Lora's Guest (Be My Guest (USA)) 9.3f **(67)**
Form - 20540831
Record 2000 - 1st:1 2nd:1 3rd:1 Ran:8
Pre2000 - 1st:2 2nd:0 3rd:1 Ran:4
Win Prizemoney £15,909 *Total Prizemoney* £27,715
Wins * 2000 Spt Newmar (SFT) 10f 99
* 1999 Oct Yarmou (G-F) 7f 105 <
* 1999 Jun Haydoc (SFT) 6f 78+
2000 Turf 1-8: (7f 5, 8f, 10f 1-2) (sft, g-s, gd 3, g-f 1-1, frm 2)
Scopey, very useful colt, effective 7 to 10f, best at 7f, acts on gd to g-f, best on g-f, has worn blinkers. Turf high 104 (1st run) - 2nd of 8 to Cape Town (19 Apr Newmarket 7f gd RF 0797) - also 1st of 10 getting 8lb from Cape Grace (16 Spt Newmarket RF 4470). Consistent. A decent second in the Free Handicap on his return, he was a disappointing favourite in the Italian Guineas. Held in Listed company since, he won a decent conditions race on his final start. He does not want the ground too firm.
**E A L Dunlop [3-12] Abdullah Ali.*

CATEEL BAY RR 59f 4828[10]
2 ch f Most Welcome 8.6f **(66)** - Calachuchi (Martinmas) 7.6f **(59)**
Form - 60
Record 2000 - 1st:0 2nd:0 3rd:0 Ran:2
2000 Turf 0-2: (7f, 8f) (g-s 2)
Currently fair filly. Turf high 59 (began Aug).
**Miss J A Camacho [0-2] Stuart Postill.*

CATELLA (GER) RR 120f 5329a[3]
4 ch f Generous (IRE) 11.5f **(82)** - Crystal Ring (IRE) (Kris) 9.5f **(73)**
Form - 12231233
2000 Turf 2-8: (11f 2, 12f 2-6) (hvy, sft 2, gd 2-3, g-f, frm)
Very high-class filly, effective 10 to 12f, best at 12f, acts on hvy to frm, excels at Frankfurt. Turf high 120 - 2nd of 11 giving 7lb to Samum (3 Spt Baden-Baden 12f hvy RF 4289a) - also 1st of 9 giving 9lb to Paolini (13 Aug Gelsenkirchen-Horst RF 3736a). Consistent. Probably the best middle-distance filly of her generation in Germany, this strong galloper won three Group races in 1999 and returned to action with a Group Two win in Cologne. Suited by a sound surface, she won her first Group One in August and was also placed in five other races at the top level, including the Breeders' Cup Filly & Mare Turf.
**P Schiergen in GER [5-11] Gestut Schlenderhan.*

CATHERINA (IRE) RR 92f 5355a[5]
4 b f Sadler's Wells (USA) 11.3f **(87)** - Katie McLain (USA) **00**
Form - 26101565
2000 Turf 2-8: (9f, 10f 3, 12f 2, 14f 2-2) (hvy 1-2, sft, g-s 2, gd, g-f 1-2)
Useful filly, effective 9 to 14f, acts on sft to g-f, often wears blinkers, and excels at Gowran Park. Turf high 92 - also 1st of 11 getting 10lb from Gaudi (14 Jun Leopardstown RF 2134a). Consistent. She was tried a number of times in Pattern company in 2000, but found that level a little beyond her. She won two qualified riders' events over 14 furlongs, and seemed unaffected by the state of the ground. **D K Weld in IRE [3-14] Mrs C L Weld.*

CATOKI (USA) RR 108f 4713a[5]
7 b h Storm Cat (USA) 7f **(86)** - Matoki (USA) (Hail To Reason) 10.1f **(82)**
Form - 5
2000 Turf 0-1: (8f) (sft)
Pattern-class horse. (1st run) - 5th of 10 getting 2lb from Bernardon (23 Spt Cologne 8f sft RF 4713a).
**P Lautner in GER [0-3] (from H Steguweit in GER [0-1] Aug 1997).*

CATSTREET (IRE) BHB 47f **RR 39f** 4935[28]
2 b c Catrail (USA) - Catherinofaragon (USA) (Chief's Crown (USA)) 9.8f **(72)**
Form - 0
Record 2000 - 1st:0 2nd:0 3rd:0 Ran:1
2000 Turf 0-1: (6f) (gd)
Currently fair colt. **R W Armstrong [0-1] Horst Geicke.*

CAT THIEF (USA) RR 117f 5332a[7]
4 ch c Storm Cat (USA) 7f **(86)** - Train Robbery (USA) (Alydar (USA)) 9.1f **(76)**
Form - 27
2000 AW 0-2: (9f, 10f) (Dirt 2)
Top-class colt, has worn blinkers. AW high 117 (began Aug). The winner of the 1999 Breeders' Cup Classic, he did not enjoy the clearest of runs in last year's renewal when seventh behind Tiznow. **D W Lukas in USA [1-5] Overbrook Farm.*

CATZ (IRE) RR 95f 2143a[3]
3 b f Catrail (USA) - Alriyaah (Shareef Dancer (USA)) 9.9f **(73)**
Form - 143
2000 Turf 1-4: (7f 1-1, 8f 2, 9f) (sft, gd 1-2, g-f)
Very useful filly, effective 8f, acts on g-f, has worn blinkers. Turf high 95 - 4th of 9 getting 3lb from Anzari (14 May Leopardstown 8f g-f RF 1251a). Winner of a Gowran maiden on her return to action in 2000, she ran fair races afterwards but was absent after June. **J S Bolger in IRE [1-6] Mrs J M Ryan.*

CAUDA EQUINA BHB 77f **RR 83f** 4991[21]
6 gr g Statoblest 6.4f **(63)** - Sea Fret (Habat) 7.6f **(61)**
Form - 020056043827480465211305700
Record 2000 - 1st:2 2nd:3 3rd:2 Ran:27
Pre2000 - 1st:9 2nd:7 3rd:8 Ran:62
Win Prizemoney £37,935 *Total Prizemoney* £67,561
Wins * 2000 Aug Goodwo (GD) 7f 55+
*** 2000** Aug Bath (FRM) 5.1f 66+
* 1999 Aug Lingfi (GD) 5f 79
* 1999 Jun Bath (GD) 5.1f 81 <
* 1999 May Bath (GD) 5.1f 79
* 1998 Spt Bath (GD) H 5.7f 64 76
* 1998 Spt Salisb (GD) H 5f 62 67
* 1998 Aug Bath (GD) C 5.7f 64
* 1997 Jly Ripon (GD) H 6f 75 76
* 1997 May Bath (G-S) 5.1f 71
* 1997 Apr Bath (G-F) S 5.1f 63
2000 Turf 2-27: (5f 1-7, 6f 17, 7f 1-3) (sft 2, g-s 2, gd 8, g-f 1-5, frm 8, hrd 1-2)
Decent gelding, effective 5 to 6f, best at 6f, acts on gd to frm, best on frm, has worn blinkers, likes left handed tracks, excels at Bath. Turf high 83 - 3rd of 18 giving 13lb to Petarga (4 Spt Bath 6f frm RF 4207). A genuine sprinter who is kept very busy, he goes particularly well at Bath. Scored twice in three days at the end of August. **M R Channon [11-89] Michael Foy.*

CAUGHNAWAGA (FR) RR 86+f 5184[1]
2 b c Indian Ridge 7.6f **(74)** - Wakria (IRE) (Sadler's Wells (USA)) 10f **(76)**
Form - 61
Record 2000 - 1st:1 2nd:0 3rd:0 Ran:2
Win Prizemoney £3,932 *Total Prizemoney* £3,932
Wins * 2000 Oct Yarmou (SFT) 8f 86+ <
2000 Turf 1-2: (8f 1-2) (g-s 1-1, gd)
Currently useful colt. Turf high 86 (began Oct) - 1st of 17 from Canada (25 Oct Yarmouth RF 5184). **H R A Cecil [1-2] Lady Harrison.*

CAUNTON BHB 48f **RR 68?f** 5142[11]
3 b f Suave Dancer (USA) 10.7f **(68)** - Arminda (Blakeney) 10.5f **(64)**
Form - 80000
Record 2000 - 1st:0 2nd:0 3rd:0 Ran:5
Pre2000 - 1st:0 2nd:0 3rd:0 Ran:3
Win Prizemoney £0 *Total Prizemoney* £270
2000 Turf 0-5: (10f 3, 11f, 12f) (g-s 2, gd, g-f, frm)
Scopey, average filly. Turf high 68. Becoming disappointing. Ran her best race as a juvenile in High Walden's Leicester maiden. **P Howling [0-5] Miss J E Leggett (from M L W Bell [0-3] Oct 1999).*

CAUSTIC WIT (IRE) BHB 98f **RR 96f** 5123[6]
2 b c Cadeaux Genereux 7.9f **(76)** - Baldemosa (FR) (Lead on Time (USA)) 8f **(65)**
Form - 501216
Record 2000 - 1st:2 2nd:1 3rd:0 Ran:6
Win Prizemoney £12,619 *Total Prizemoney* £18,619
Wins * 2000 Spt Newmar (GD) H 6f 92 96 <
*** 2000** Jly Doncas (GD) 6f 87
2000 Turf 2-6: (5f, 6f 2-5) (g-s, gd, g-f 1-1, frm 1-3)
Very useful colt, effective 6f, acts on g-f to frm, best on frm. Turf high 96 - 1st of 19 giving 2lb to Threezedzz (30 Spt Newmarket RF 4742) - also 1st of 12 from Ridge Runner (13 Jly Doncaster RF 2753). Comfortable winner of a Doncaster maiden, having finished last at Royal Ascot on his previous run. Useful form in nurseries since including a fine win at Newmarket. Suited by six furlongs and good ground. **E A L Dunlop [2-6] Maktoum Al Maktoum.*

CAUTION BHB 54f52a **RR 56f 52a** 5166[7]
6 b m Warning 8.1f **(77)** - Fairy Flax (IRE) (Dancing Brave (USA)) 8.4f **(76)**
Form - 6068004225233347
Record 2000 - 1st:0 2nd:3 3rd:3 Ran:16
Pre2000 - 1st:4 2nd:6 3rd:4 Ran:34
Win Prizemoney £13,910 *Total Prizemoney* £30,182
Wins * 1998 Oct Redcar (HVY) 5f 65
1997 Jly Beverl (G-F) C 7.5f 61+
1997 Jun Cheste (G-F) C 6.1f 70
1996 Spt Ayr (G-F) 6f 70 <
2000 Turf 0-15: (6f 5, 7f, 8f 9) (g-s, gd 7, g-f 3, frm 4) 2000 AW 0-1: (6f) (Fibr)
Fair mare, effective 5 to 6f, best at 5f, acts on g-s to frm, best on frm, has worn blinkers, likes left handed tracks, likes tight tracks. Turf high 56. Consistent. She tries hard, but has a poor winning record in recent seasons. Goes on fast ground, but handles heavy extremely well.
**S Gollings [1-44] Ian & Mrs Irene Thomas (from Mrs J R Ramsden [3-6] Jly 1997).*

CAUTIONARY (IRE) BHB 71f **RR 63f** 4183[8]
3 b f Warning 8.1f **(77)** - Iltimas (USA) **(90f)** (Dayjur (USA))
Form - 068
Record 2000 - 1st:0 2nd:0 3rd:0 Ran:3
Pre2000 - 1st:1 2nd:3 3rd:0 Ran:5
Win Prizemoney £3,403 *Total Prizemoney* £6,377
Wins 1999 May Hamilt (GD) 5f 70+ <
2000 Turf 0-3: (6f 3) (g-s, frm 2)
Neat, average filly, effective 5 to 6f, acts on gd to g-f. Turf high 63 (began Jly). Consistent. **A Berry [0-3] Mrs J M Berry (from J Berry [1-5] Jly 1999).*

CAUTIOUS JOE BHB 65f60a **RR 69f 60a** 5063[2]
3 b f First Trump - Jomel Amou (IRE) (Ela-Mana-Mou) 10.1f **(70)**
Form - 7008355830112
Record 2000 - 1st:2 2nd:1 3rd:2 Ran:12
Pre2000 - 1st:1 2nd:0 3rd:0 Ran:3
Win Prizemoney £8,040 *Total Prizemoney* £9,764
Wins * 2000 Oct Leices (HVY) 8f 69 <
*** 2000** Spt Leices (G-S) 8f 54
* 1999 May Newcas (G-F) 5f 64+
2000 Turf 2-11: (5f 4, 6f, 7f 2, 8f 2-3, 10f) (sft, g-s 1-1, gd 3, g-f 1-3, frm 3) 2000 AW 0-1: (6f) (Fibr)
Leggy, above-average filly, effective 5 to 10f, acts on sft to frm, excels at Leicester. Turf high 69 - 1st of 18 getting 4lb from Martello (9 Oct Leicester RF 4875). **R A Fahey [3-15] Tommy Staunton.*

CAUVERY BHB 100f **RR 95f** 5124[9]
2 ch c Exit To Nowhere (USA) 8.7f **(77)** -Triple Zee (USA) (Zilzal (USA))
Form - 217370
Record 2000 - 1st:1 2nd:1 3rd:1 Ran:6
Win Prizemoney £3,575 *Total Prizemoney* £5,255
Wins * 2000 Jun Newcas (FRM) 7f 86+ <
2000 Turf 1-6: (6f, 7f 1-4, 8f) (g-s, gd 2, frm 1-3)
Very useful colt, effective 7f, acts on gd to frm, best on frm. Turf high 95 - 7th of 13 to King Charlemagne (29 Spt Newmarket 7f gd RF 4733) - also 1st of 5 from Double Honour (29 Jun Newcastle RF 2368). An easy winner of a firm-ground Newcastle maiden on his second start, he was not right when down the field in Group com-

pany next time, but there were no excuses when he was comfortably beaten in a Sandown novice stakes. Fair effort in a Group Three, looking as if a mile would suit.
**S P C Woods [1-6] W J P Jackson.*

CAVANIA (IRE) BHB 65f **RR 59f** 4486[15]

3 ch f Lion Cavern (USA) 7.5f **(74)** - Ma Pavlova (USA) (Irish River (FR)) 8.6f **(78)**
Form - 340
Record 2000 - 1st:0 2nd:0 3rd:1 Ran:3
Win Prizemoney £0 *Total Prizemoney* £935
2000 Turf 0-3: (10f 2, 12f) (g-s, g-f 2)
Unfurnished, currently fair filly. Turf high 59 (began Jly).
**W R Muir [0-3] D J Deer.*

CAVERNARA (IRE) BHB 68f **RR 54+f** 3810[4]

2 b f Lion Cavern (USA) 7.5f **(74)** - Rainbow Ring (Rainbow Quest (USA)) 10.4f **(75)**
Form - 454
Record 2000 - 1st:0 2nd:0 3rd:0 Ran:3
Win Prizemoney £0 *Total Prizemoney* £552
2000 Turf 0-2: (6f, 7f) (frm 2) 2000 AW 0-1: (7f) (Fibr)
Currently average filly. Turf high 54. **T D Barron [0-3] Nigel Shields.*

CAVERSFIELD BHB 36f49a **RR 42f 49a** 4922[9]

5 ch h Tina's Pet 7.4f **(56)** - Canoodle (Warpath) 12.3f **(52)**
Form - 707760300
Record 2000 - 1st:0 2nd:0 3rd:1 Ran:9
Pre2000 - 1st:2 2nd:3 3rd:7 Ran:32
Win Prizemoney £6,643 *Total Prizemoney* £13,508
Wins 1997 Oct Leices (GD) H 7f 75 76 <
1997 Aug Windso (G-F) H 6f 72 76 <
2000 Turf 0-7: (6f, 7f 3, 8f 3) (sft, g-s, gd, g-f 3, frm) 2000 AW 0-2: (7f, 8f) (Equi 2)
Moderate colt, effective 7f, acts on g-f to frm, best on frm, has worn blinkers. Turf high 42. AW high 44.
**J M Bradley [0-8] S E Hall (from Miss E C Lavelle [0-4] Jan 2000).*

CAXTON LAD BHB 83f **RR 87f** 5199[15]

3 b c Cyrano de Bergerac 7.3f **(58)** - Urania **(54f)** (Most Welcome)
Form - 1000
Record 2000 - 1st:0 2nd:0 3rd:0 Ran:3
Pre2000 - 1st:2 2nd:0 3rd:1 Ran:6
Win Prizemoney £6,331 *Total Prizemoney* £6,856
Wins * 1999 *Dec Southw (STD) H 5f 78 94+* <
* 1999 *Oct Haydoc (HVY) H 5f 65 78+*
2000 Turf 0-3: (5f 3) (g-s 2, gd)
Neat, useful colt, effective 5f, - acts on Fibr. Turf high 79 (began Spt). Inconsistent. Winner of two nurseries in 1999, he was having his first start for nine months when not running at all badly in a valuable sprint handicap at Ascot in September. Failed to build on that in two subsequent runs, but has dropped a little in the weights and could well find a race or two next season.
**P J Makin [2-9] Four Seasons Racing Ltd.*

CAYMAN EXPRESSO (IRE) BHB 82f **RR 76f** 3023[12]

2 b f Fayruz 6.6f **(63)** - Cappuchino (IRE) **(59a)** (Roi Danzig (USA))
Form - 6350
Record 2000 - 1st:0 2nd:0 3rd:1 Ran:4
Win Prizemoney £0 *Total Prizemoney* £516
2000 Turf 0-4: (5f 4) (g-f 2, frm, hrd)
Above-average filly. Turf high 76. She has shown plenty of dash in five-furlong maidens. **R Hannon [0-4] The Cayman 'A' Team.*

CAYMAN SUNSET (IRE) BHB 99f **RR 102f** 5126[2]

3 ch f Night Shift (USA) 8.1f **(73)** - Robinia (USA) (Roberto (USA)) 10f **(76)**
Form - 1642
Record 2000 - 1st:1 2nd:1 3rd:0 Ran:4
Win Prizemoney £4,134 *Total Prizemoney* £8,734
Wins * **2000** Jly Kempto (G-S) 7f 81+ <
2000 Turf 1-4: (7f 1-3, 8f) (g-s, g-f 1-2, frm)
Scopey, very useful filly. Turf high 95 (began Jly) - 4th of 11 to Kalindi (7 Spt Doncaster 7f frm RF 4282). Unraced at two, she bolted up in a Kempton maiden on her debut, but was found out in Listed company afterwards. Still relatively inexperienced, she ran the useful Umistim close at Doncaster, and she may well improve over the winter. **E A L Dunlop [1-4] M P Burke.*

CAYOKE (FR) RR 110f 2004a[1]

3 b c Always Fair (USA) 14f **(61)** - Sarah Annita (FR) (Pharly (FR)) 9.8f **(68)**
Form - 1
2000 Turf 1-1: (8f 1-1) (gd 1-1)
Currently Group-class colt. (1st run) - 1st of 8 from Indian Prospector (11 Jun Chantilly RF 2004a). Scored in a Chantilly Group Three during the summer.
**H-A Pantall in FR [1-1] Mme P-D Beck.*

CAZOULIAS (FR) RR 111f 5209a[2]

3 b g Rasi Brasak - Cazouls (FR) (Gairloch) 7f **(63)**
Form - 32
2000 Turf 0-2: (7f, 10f) (hvy)
Currently Group-class gelding. Turf high 111 - 2nd of 9 getting 5lb from Inglenook (21 Oct Saint-cloud 10f hvy RF 5209a).
**Mrs N Rossio in FR [0-2].*

CD EUROPE (IRE) BHB 100f **RR 107f** 5124[8]

2 ch c Royal Academy (USA) 7.8f **(77)** - Woodland Orchid (IRE) (Woodman (USA)) 9f **(74)**
Form - 11248
Record 2000 - 1st:2 2nd:1 3rd:0 Ran:5
Win Prizemoney £40,426 *Total Prizemoney* £73,032
Wins * **2000** Jun Ascot (G-F) G3 6f 97 <
* **2000** May Goodwo (SFT) 6f 80+
2000 Turf 2-5: (6f 2-2, 7f, 8f 2) (sft, g-s, gd 2-2, g-f)
Pattern-class colt. Turf high 107. Sent off at 25/1 for his Goodwood debut, but won well despite meeting trouble in running and stepped up on that to land the Coventry at Royal Ascot. Absent through the summer, he put in decent efforts to finish runner-up in the Champagne Stakes and fourth in the Grand Criterium, but weakened in testing ground in the Racing Post Trophy on his final start. **M R Channon [2-5] Circular Distributors Ltd.*

CD FLYER (IRE) BHB 75f **RR 74f** 5061[3]

3 ch g Grand Lodge (USA) - Pretext (Polish Precedent (USA)) 10.2f **(60)**
Form - 0644633803
Record 2000 - 1st:0 2nd:0 3rd:3 Ran:10
Pre2000 - 1st:2 2nd:0 3rd:2 Ran:10
Win Prizemoney £10,592 *Total Prizemoney* £15,939
Wins * 1999 Oct Newmar (SFT) H 6f 75 80 <
* 1999 May Thirsk (G-S) 5f 77
2000 Turf 0-10: (5f 4, 6f 5, 7f) (sft 2, gd 2, g-f 2, frm 4)
Workmanlike, above-average gelding, effective 5 to 7f, best at 5f, acts on sft to frm, best on gd, prefers right handed tracks, does well at Windsor. Turf high 74 - 3rd of 12 getting 7lb from Molly Brown (12 Jly Doncaster 6f frm RF 2728). Consistent.
**M R Channon [2-20] Circular Distributors Ltd.*

CEARNACH BHB 67f **RR 66f** 4970[21]

2 b c Night Shift (USA) 8.1f **(73)** - High Matinee (Shirley Heights) 10.3f **(74)**
Form - 005430
Record 2000 - 1st:0 2nd:0 3rd:1 Ran:6
Win Prizemoney £0 *Total Prizemoney* £1,294
2000 Turf 0-6: (6f 3, 7f, 8f 2) (g-s, gd 2, g-f, frm 2)
Average colt, effective 7 to 8f, acts on g-s to frm. Turf high 66 (began Jly) - 3rd of 16 giving 9lb to Monica Geller (21 Spt Goodwood 8f g-s RF 4547).
**B J Meehan [0-6] The Part-Time Partnership.*

CEDAR BILL BHB 45f **RR 38f** 1620[4]

2 ch c So Factual (USA) - Toffee **(74?f)** (Midyan (USA)) 6f **(60)**
Form - 504
Record 2000 - 1st:0 2nd:0 3rd:0 Ran:3
Win Prizemoney £0 *Total Prizemoney* £262
2000 Turf 0-3: (5f 2, 6f) (gd 3)
Currently very moderate colt. Turf high 38.
**R J O'Sullivan [0-3] R O S Racing Club Epsom.*

CEDAR CHIEF BHB 38f **RR 47f** 757[13]

3 b c Saddlers' Hall (IRE) 10.5f **(65)** - Dame Ashfield (Grundy) 10.3f **(65)**

Form - 0
Record 2000 - 1st:0 2nd:0 3rd:0 Ran:1
Pre2000 - 1st:0 2nd:0 3rd:0 Ran:4
2000 Turf 0-1: (12f) (g-s)
Unfurnished, moderate colt. **R J O'Sullivan [0-5] R O S Racing.*

CEDAR FLAG (IRE) BHB 39f41a **RR 44f 41a** 2758[7]

6 br g Jareer (USA) 10.2f **(54)** - Sasha Lea (Cawston's Clown) 8f **(60)**
Form - 7603243108407
Record 2000 - 1st:1 2nd:1 3rd:2 Ran:10
Pre2000 - 1st:0 2nd:0 3rd:0 Ran:3
Win Prizemoney £1,799 *Total Prizemoney* £3,450
Wins ** **2000** Mar Southw (STD) H 12f 40 44* **<**
2000 Turf 0-4: (11f 2, 12f 2) (g-s, gd, g-f, frm) 2000 AW 1-6: (12f 1-2, 13f, 16f 3) (Equi 3, Fibr 1-3)
Moderate gelding, effective 11 to 12f, best at 12f, acts on g-s - acts on Fibr. Turf high 44 - 4th of 20 giving 9lb to Vanborough Lad (4 Jun Warwick 11f g-s RF 1703). AW high 44 - 1st of 9 getting 7lb from Winsome George (17 Mar Southwell RF 0455).
**R J O'Sullivan [1-15] R O S Racing.*

CEDAR GROVE BHB 53f **RR 58f** 3374[9]

3 b c Shirley Heights 12.1f **(76)** - Trojan Desert (Troy) 10.4f **(68)**
Form - 004040
Record 2000 - 1st:0 2nd:0 3rd:0 Ran:6
Win Prizemoney £0 *Total Prizemoney* £587
2000 Turf 0-6: (10f 2, 12f 2, 14f, 16f) (g-s, gd, g-f 2, frm 2)
Rangy, fair colt, effective 14f, acts on frm. Turf high 58.
**A C Stewart [0-6] M J C Hawkes & P E Barrett.*

CEDAR JENEVA BHB 41f **RR 27f** 4226[P]

2 b f Muhtarram (USA) - Soba Up **(70f)** (Persian Heights)
Form - 0U8P
Record 2000 - 1st:0 2nd:0 3rd:0 Ran:4
2000 Turf 0-4: (5f 3, 7f) (g-s 2, frm 2)
Very moderate filly. Turf high 27. **R J O'Sullivan [0-4] Robert Allen.*

CEDAR LIGHT (IRE) BHB 39f47a **RR 48f 47a** 4221[9]

3 b g Dolphin Street (FR) - Maxencia (FR) (Tennyson (FR)) 12.1f **(50)**
Form - 0000350
Record 2000 - 1st:0 2nd:0 3rd:1 Ran:7
Pre2000 - 1st:0 2nd:0 3rd:0 Ran:1
Win Prizemoney £0 *Total Prizemoney* £340
2000 Turf 0-5: (6f 3, 7f, 8f) (g-s, gd, g-f 2, frm) 2000 AW 0-2: (6f, 10f) (Equi 2)
Leggy, moderate gelding. Turf high 48. AW high 34.
**R J O'Sullivan [0-8] R O S Racing.*

CEDAR LORD BHB 45f **RR 48f** 3484[18]

3 b g Emperor Jones (USA) - Bint Damascus (USA) (Damascus (USA)) 8.9f **(71)**
Form - 67700
Record 2000 - 1st:0 2nd:0 3rd:0 Ran:5
Pre2000 - 1st:0 2nd:0 3rd:0 Ran:1
2000 Turf 0-5: (7f, 8f, 10f 3) (g-s, g-f, frm 3)
Workmanlike, moderate gelding, has worn blinkers. Turf high 48.
**R J O'Sullivan [0-6] Never Ever Bet Partnership.*

CEDAR MASTER (IRE) BHB 76f **RR 81f** 5078[4]

3 b c Soviet Lad (USA) 9.4f **(63)** - Samriah (IRE) (Wassl) 9.7f **(62)**
Form - 7556032704
Record 2000 - 1st:0 2nd:1 3rd:1 Ran:10
Pre2000 - 1st:1 2nd:1 3rd:4 Ran:10
Win Prizemoney £2,864 *Total Prizemoney* £23,815
Wins * 1999 May Chepst (GD) 6.1f 83 **<**
2000 Turf 0-10: (7f 3, 8f 6, 10f) (sft, g-s, gd 4, g-f 2, frm 2)
Unfurnished, decent colt, effective 5 to 7f, acts on g-f, often wears blinkers. Turf high 90. Consistent. He stood up well to an arduous campaign at two in 1999, running his best race to finish third in the Weatherbys Super Sprint. He appears to stay a mile, but failed to score in 2000. However, he is on a reasonable mark as a result. Appears to go well on sharp tracks.
**R J O'Sullivan [1-20] Robert Allen.*

CEDAR PRINCE (IRE) BHB 52f **RR 54f** 4729[14]

3 b c Namaqualand (USA) - Supreme Crown (USA) (Chief's Crown (USA)) 9.8f **(72)**

Form - 0006000800
Record 2000 - 1st:0 2nd:0 3rd:0 Ran:10
Pre2000 - 1st:1 2nd:2 3rd:1 Ran:8
Win Prizemoney £5,875 *Total Prizemoney* £8,881
Wins * 1999 Aug Ascot (GD) H 7f 69 77 **<**
2000 Turf 0-10: (7f 4, 8f 2, 9f 2, 10f 2) (g-s 2, gd 2, g-f 3, frm 3)
Scopey, fair colt, effective 7f, acts on gd to g-f, often wears blinkers (effectively). Turf high 66. **R J O'Sullivan [1-18] B S Chatwal.*

CEDAR RANGERS (USA) BHB 78f **RR 75f** 4305[9]

2 b c Anabaa (USA) - Chelsea (USA) (Miswaki (USA)) 9f **(81)**
Form - 510
Record 2000 - 1st:1 2nd:0 3rd:0 Ran:3
Win Prizemoney £4,023 *Total Prizemoney* £4,023
Wins * **2000** Jly Lingfi (GD) 6f 75 **<**
2000 Turf 1-3: (5f, 6f 1-2) (gd, g-f 1-2)
Currently above-average colt. Turf high 75 - 1st of 7 from Midnight Venture (14 Jly Lingfield RF 2810). Caught the eye on his Lingfield debut and got off the mark there next time.
**R J O'Sullivan [1-3] "We Are QPR" Racing Partnership.*

CEDAR TREBLE RR 38f 5217[3]

2 b c Emperor Jones (USA) - Tjakka (USA) (Little Missouri (USA))
Form - 3
Record 2000 - 1st:0 2nd:0 3rd:1 Ran:1
Win Prizemoney £0 *Total Prizemoney* £568
2000 Turf 0-1: (6f) (sft)
Currently very moderate colt.
**R J O'Sullivan [0-1] R O S Racing Club Epsom.*

CEDAR TSAR (IRE) BHB 56f59a **RR 62f 59a** 5010[12]

2 b c Inzar (USA) - The Aspecto Girl (IRE) **(30f 40a)** (Alzao (USA)) 7.1f **(68)**
Form - 6202133310700
Record 2000 - 1st:2 2nd:2 3rd:3 Ran:13
Win Prizemoney £4,610 *Total Prizemoney* £7,225
Wins ** **2000** Jly Southw (STD) H 6f 79* **<**
__2000__ Jun Southw (STD) S 7f 67+
2000 Turf 0-9: (5f, 6f 6, 7f 2) (gd, g-f 2, frm 6) 2000 AW 2-4: (6f 1-2, 7f 1-2) (Fibr 2-4)
Above-average colt, effective 6f, - acts on Fibr, likes left handed tracks, likes tight tracks. Turf high 62. AW high 79 (began Jun) - 1st of 10 from Orchard Raider (28 Jly Southwell RF 3189). Becoming disappointing.
**D W Chapman [1-8] Michael Hill (from Andrew Reid [1-3] Jun 2000).*

CEDAR WELLS (USA) BHB 41f51a **RR 47f 51a** 3088[4]

4 b g Desert Secret (IRE) - Sans Sorrow (USA) (Barachois (CAN)) 8.3f **(63)**
Form - 0060064
Record 2000 - 1st:0 2nd:0 3rd:0 Ran:7
Pre2000 - 1st:1 2nd:2 3rd:1 Ran:14
Win Prizemoney £2,778 *Total Prizemoney* £5,824
Wins 1998 *Dec Lingfi (STD) H 7f 55 64* **<**
2000 Turf 0-6: (7f 6) (gd, g-f, frm 4) 2000 AW 0-1: (9f) (Fibr)
Scopey, moderate gelding, has broken blood-vessels, effective 8 to 9f, best at 8f, acts on g-f to hrd, has worn blinkers, prefers left handed tracks, likes tight tracks. Turf high 47. Showed improved form when switched to Equitrack at the end of last year, and got off the mark in a small nursery on that surface.
**J M Bradley [0-7] Martyn James, Pete S Jenkins (from G Lewis [1-14] Spt 1999).*

CEEPIO (IRE) BHB 100f **RR 95f** 5123[5]

2 b c Pennekamp (USA) - Boranwood (IRE) (Exhibitioner) 8.7f **(61)**
Form - 3135
Record 2000 - 1st:1 2nd:0 3rd:2 Ran:4
Win Prizemoney £3,575 *Total Prizemoney* £9,783
Wins * **2000** Jun Nottin (G-F) 6.1f 93+ **<**
2000 Turf 1-4: (6f 1-4) (g-s, gd, g-f, frm 1-1)
Very useful colt. Turf high 95 - 3rd of 8 to Endless Summer (3 Aug Goodwood 6f gd RF 3341) - also 1st of 6 giving 5lb to Palatial (26 Jun Nottingham RF 2277). An attractive colt, he followed an encouraging debut by taking his maiden. A good third in the Richmond Stakes at Goodwood, his only disappointment was on easy ground at Doncaster. He should benefit from a light campaign as a juvenile and should win races. He may be able to win at listed level, although he may have to go abroad to do it.

**T G Mills [1-4] Mrs C Stephens.*

CEINWEN BHB 25f **RR 11f** 1257[9]
5 ch m Keen 11.1f **(58)** - Drudwen (Sayf El Arab (USA)) 7.1f **(54)**
Form - 000
Record 2000 - 1st:0 2nd:0 3rd:0 Ran:3
2000 Turf 0-2: (7f 2) (g-s, g-f) 2000 AW 0-1: (8f) (Fibr)
Currently poor filly. Turf high 11. **J M Bradley [0-3] C F Basterfield.*

CELANDINE BHB 41f65a **RR 40df 65a** 3041[6]
7 b m Warning 8.1f **(77)** - Silly Bold (Rousillon (USA)) 8.2f **(74)**
Form - 0006
Record 2000 - 1st:0 2nd:0 3rd:0 Ran:4
Pre2000 - 1st:3 2nd:2 3rd:4 Ran:36
Win Prizemoney £9,709 *Total Prizemoney* £14,226
Wins * 1998 Spt Catter (G-F) H 7f 56 61
* 1998 Jly Warwic (G-F) H 7f 51 57
2000 Turf 0-4: (7f 4) (g-f, frm 3)
Average mare, effective 7f, acts on gd, has worn blinkers, likes tight tracks. Turf high 40.
**Andrew Turnell [2-32] Mrs Claire Hollowood (from J L Eyre [0-4] Jun 1996).*

CELEBES BHB 54f60a **RR 51f 60a** 2012[8]
3 b g Weldnaas (USA) 8.4f **(55)** - Shift Over (USA) (Night Shift (USA)) 7.2f **(69)**
Form - 34640008
Record 2000 - 1st:0 2nd:0 3rd:1 Ran:8
Pre2000 - 1st:0 2nd:0 3rd:0 Ran:3
Win Prizemoney £0 *Total Prizemoney* £1,130
2000 Turf 0-6: (7f 2, 8f 3, 10f) (gd 2, g-f 3, frm) 2000 AW 0-2: (8f, 9f) (Equi, Fibr)
Scopey, average gelding, effective 9f, - acts on Fibr, has worn blinkers. Turf high 70. AW high 66 - 4th of 9 getting 4lb from Favorisio (23 Mar Wolverhampton 9f Fibr RF 0482).
**I A Balding [0-11] Robert Hitchins.*

CELEBRATION TOWN (IRE) BHB 91f **RR 90f** 4831[1]
3 b br g Case Law 6f **(64)** - Battle Queen (Kind of Hush) 10.1f **(62)**
Form - 1016121
Record 2000 - 1st:4 2nd:1 3rd:0 Ran:7
Pre2000 - 1st:0 2nd:0 3rd:0 Ran:3
Win Prizemoney £24,972 *Total Prizemoney* £29,972
Wins * **2000** Oct York (SFT) H 7.9f 86 90 <
* **2000** Aug Newmar (GD) H 7f 76 85
* **2000** May Sandow (HVY) H 7.1f 72 78
* **2000** Apr Southw (G-S) H 7f 67 69
2000 Turf 4-7: (7f 3-5, 8f 1-2) (g-s 2-2, gd 2, g-f 1-1, frm 1-2)
Scopey, useful gelding, effective 7 to 8f, best at 7f, acts on g-s to frm. Turf high 90 - 1st of 6 from Great News (6 Oct York RF 4831) - also 1st of 14 giving 10lb to Shather (5 Aug Newmarket RF 3400). Improving. A winner three times over seven furlongs this season, he continues to rise in the weights as a result and will find life tougher. Suited by soft ground.
**D Morris [4-7] Meadowcrest Ltd (from J J O'Neill [0-3] Aug 1999).*

CELEBRE BLU BHB 55f56a **RR 67f 56a** 4767[9]
3 b g Suave Dancer (USA) 10.7f **(68)** - Taufan Blu (IRE) **(83df 69a)** (Taufan (USA)) 7f **(57)**
Form - 6333087360
Record 2000 - 1st:0 2nd:0 3rd:4 Ran:10
Win Prizemoney £0 *Total Prizemoney* £1,819
2000 Turf 0-9: (6f, 7f 5, 8f 2, 9f) (g-s, gd 3, g-f, frm 4) 2000 AW 0-1: (8f) (Fibr)
Workmanlike, average gelding, effective 6f, acts on gd. Turf high 67. **K A Ryan [0-10] Mrs J Lewis & K Lewis.*

CELERIC BHB 115f **RR 113f** 2180[9]
8 b g Mtoto 11.5f **(71)** - Hot Spice (Hotfoot) 10.5f **(59)**
Form - 370
Record 2000 - 1st:0 2nd:0 3rd:1 Ran:3
Pre2000 - 1st:13 2nd:7 3rd:4 Ran:39
Win Prizemoney £365,847 *Total Prizemoney* £465,152
Wins * 1999 Aug York (GD) G3 15.9f 115
* 1999 Apr Ascot (GD) G3 16.2f 111
1997 Jun Ascot (GD) G1 20f 121 <
1997 May York (GD) G2 13.9f 115
1996 Oct Newmar (G-F) G3 16f 112
1996 Aug York (GD) L 15.9f 113+
1996 Jly York (GD) LH 13.9f 102 104
1996 Jun Newcas (FRM) H 16.1f 96 100
1996 May York (G-F) H 13.9f 90 94+
2000 Turf 0-3: (14f, 16f, 20f) (g-s, gd, g-f)
Group-class gelding, effective 16 to 20f, best at 16f, acts on g-s to g-f, best on g-f. Turf high 113 (1st run) - 3rd of 9 giving 3lb to Orchestra Stall (3 May Ascot 16f g-s RF 1000). This most likeable of racehorses, winner of the 1997 Gold Cup, a Jockey Club Cup, and a Yorkshire Cup among a total of five wins at the Knavesmire, he raced just three times last season and a ninth in the Ascot Gold Cup proved to be his swansong.
**J L Dunlop [2-16] Christopher Spence (from D Morley [11-26] Oct 1997).*

CELERITY (IRE) BHB 40f **RR 39f** 5008[7]
2 b f Fairy King (USA) 7.7f **(75)** - Three Terns (USA) (Arctic Tern (USA)) 8.9f **(69)**
Form - 0607
Record 2000 - 1st:0 2nd:0 3rd:0 Ran:4
2000 Turf 0-2: (6f 2) (frm 2) 2000 AW 0-2: (6f, 8f) (Fibr 2)
Average filly. Turf high 39 (began Aug). AW high 36 (began Spt).
**M J Polglase [0-4] Gen Sir G Howlett, M Doury & T Swift.*

CELESTIAL KEY (USA) BHB 61f46a **RR 78f 46a** 2198a[1]
10 br g Star de Naskra (USA) 8.8f **(63)** - Casa Key (USA) (Cormorant (USA)) 8.2f **(104)**
Form - 20721
Record 2000 - 1st:1 2nd:2 3rd:0 Ran:5
Pre2000 - 1st:11 2nd:7 3rd:8 Ran:79
Win Prizemoney £74,326 *Total Prizemoney* £112,470
Wins * **2000** Jun Frauen (GD) 9.3f 78
* 1998 Aug Dielsd (GD) 9f 89
* 1997 Spt Dielsd (GD) 8f 96
* 1997 Aug Dielsd (GD) 8f 89
2000 Turf 1-2: (9f 1-2) (gd 1-2) 2000 AW 0-3: (8f 3) (Equi, Fibr 2)
Above-average gelding, effective 9f, acts on gd, has worn blinkers. Turf high 78 - 1st of 9 from For Pleasure (12 Jun Frauenfeld RF 2198a). AW high 46. A versatile performer, his wins in recent seasons have been in Switzerland.
**M Johnston [8-59] Markus Graff (from S G Norton [4-28] Spt 1994).*

CELESTIAL POWER RR 23f 1877[9]
2 b f Superpower 6.6f **(58)** - Heavenly Queen (Scottish Reel) 7f **(61)**
Form - 00
Record 2000 - 1st:0 2nd:0 3rd:0 Ran:2
2000 Turf 0-2: (5f 2) (g-s, frm)
Currently little account filly. Turf high 23.
**A Bailey [0-2] Mrs V Farrington.*

CELESTIAL WELCOME BHB 70f **RR 73f** 4156[13]
5 b m Most Welcome 8.6f **(66)** - Choral Sundown (Night Shift (USA)) 7.2f **(69)**
Form - 6100800
Record 2000 - 1st:1 2nd:0 3rd:0 Ran:7
Pre2000 - 1st:7 2nd:2 3rd:0 Ran:22
Win Prizemoney £69,617 *Total Prizemoney* £72,241
Wins * **2000** Apr Haydoc (HVY) 10.5f 84
* 1999 Jly Haydoc (G-S) H 11.9f 85 92 <
* 1999 Jun Haydoc (G-S) H 10.5f 80 86
* 1999 Apr Newcas (GD) H 8f 71 76
* 1998 May Redcar (GD) H 7f 62 74
* 1998 May Newcas (G-S) H 8f 62 65
* 1998 Apr Carlis (G-S) H 9.3f 54 56
* 1998 Apr Hamilt (HVY) 8.3f 52
2000 Turf 1-7: (10f 2, 11f 1-1, 12f 3, 14f) (hvy 1-1, sft, g-s, gd 2, g-f 2)
Above-average filly, effective 10 to 12f, best at 12f, acts on hvy to frm, best on gd, favours left handed tracks, prefers tight tracks, excels at Haydock. Turf high 84 - 1st of 7 getting 5lb from Mantusis (22 Apr Haydock RF 0820). Consistent. A useful handicapper on her day, she returned to winning form at her beloved Haydock in April, but has made little show since.
**Mrs M Reveley [8-29] The Welcome Alliance.*

CELLO SOLO RR 65f 4813[3]
3 b c Piccolo - Whirling Words (Sparkler)
Form - 3

Record 2000 - 1st:0 2nd:0 3rd:1 Ran:1
Win Prizemoney £0 *Total Prizemoney* £394
2000 Turf 0-1: (8f) (g-s)
Scopey, currently average colt. (1st run) - 3rd of 18 to Hindaam (4 Oct Lingfield 8f g-s RF 4813). **P J Makin [0-1] Mrs P J Makin.*

CELOTTI (IRE) BHB 73f RR 74f 4697[14]
2 b f Celtic Swing - Zalotti (IRE) **(69f)** (Polish Patriot (USA))
Form - 3517200
Record 2000 - 1st:1 2nd:1 3rd:1 Ran:7
Win Prizemoney £2,205 *Total Prizemoney* £3,860
Wins * 2000 *Jly Southw (STD) 5f 61 <*
2000 Turf 0-6: (5f 3, 6f 3) (gd 2, g-f 2, frm 2) 2000 AW 1-1: (5f 1-1) (Fibr 1-1)
Above-average filly, effective 5f, acts on g-f. Turf high 74 - 2nd of 11 giving 19lb to Cozzie (16 Aug Beverley 5f g-f RF 3684). (1st run). **R Hollinshead [1-7] P D Savill.*

CELTIC BAY (USA) BHB 60f RR 67f 4033[5]
3 b f Green Dancer (USA) 11.9f **(77)** - Taylor Park (USA) (Sir Gaylord) 10.6f **(64)**
Form - 66665
Record 2000 - 1st:0 2nd:0 3rd:0 Ran:5
2000 Turf 0-5: (8f, 10f 3, 12f) (gd, g-f, frm 3)
Lengthy, average filly. Turf high 67. **J W Hills [0-5] D J Deer.*

CELTIC EXIT (FR) BHB 78f RR 81f 2055[5]
6 b g Exit To Nowhere (USA) 8.7f **(77)** - Amour Celtique (Northfields (USA)) 9f **(72)**
Form - 515
Record 2000 - 1st:1 2nd:0 3rd:0 Ran:3
Win Prizemoney £11,163 *Total Prizemoney* £11,163
Wins * 2000 Jun Goodwo (GD) H 7f 73 81 <
2000 Turf 1-3: (7f 1-2, 8f) (gd 1-2, g-f)
Currently decent gelding, has broken blood-vessels. Turf high 81 - 1st of 15 giving 2lb to Bintang Timor (9 Jun Goodwood RF 1845). Formerly trained in France, he broke a blood vessel on his British debut, but came fast and late to win a Goodwood handicap on his second start. **I A Balding [1-3] Action Bloodstock.*

CELTIC FLING BHB 75f RR 76f 730[9]
4 b f Lion Cavern (USA) 7.5f **(74)** - Celtic Ring (Welsh Pageant) 10f **(65)**
Form - 0
Record 2000 - 1st:0 2nd:0 3rd:0 Ran:1
Pre2000 - 1st:1 2nd:1 3rd:0 Ran:2
Win Prizemoney £2,541 *Total Prizemoney* £3,809
Wins * 1999 Nov Windso (G-S) 8.3f 76 <
2000 Turf 0-1: (8f) (gd)
Light-framed, currently above-average filly. **Lady Herries [1-3] Chris Hardy.*

CELTIC ISLAND BHB 94f RR 85f 4642[16]
2 b f Celtic Swing - Chief Island **(58f)** (Be My Chief (USA))
Form - 212281480
Record 2000 - 1st:2 2nd:3 3rd:0 Ran:9
Win Prizemoney £13,547 *Total Prizemoney* £20,150
Wins * 2000 Jun Salisb (G-F) 7f 79 <
*** 2000** Apr Pontef (HVY) 5f 71
2000 Turf 2-9: (5f 1-3, 6f, 7f 1-4, 8f) (sft 1-1, gd 2, g-f 4, frm 1-2)
Useful filly, effective 7f, acts on g-f. Turf high 96 - 4th of 12 giving 2lb to Silver Jorden (27 Jly Sandown 7f g-f RF 3153). Consistent. A winner at Pontefract and Salisbury as a juvenile, she appeared to lose her way towards the end of the season. She may not be easy to place from her current mark. **W G M Turner [2-9] Bill Brown.*

CELTIC LEGEND RR 24f 2439[10]
2 b f Celtic Swing - No Reprieve (NZ) (Deputy Governor (USA))
Form - 000
Record 2000 - 1st:0 2nd:0 3rd:0 Ran:3
2000 Turf 0-3: (5f, 6f 2) (gd, g-f, frm)
Currently little account filly. Turf high 24. **W Storey [0-3] Dr P and Mrs D M Johnson.*

CELTIC MISS BHB 68f RR 70f 5312[6]
2 b f Celtic Swing - Regent Miss (CAN) (Vice Regent (CAN)) 8.7f **(74)**
Form - 036
Record 2000 - 1st:0 2nd:0 3rd:1 Ran:3
Win Prizemoney £0 *Total Prizemoney* £540
2000 Turf 0-3: (6f, 7f, 8f) (g-s 2, frm)
Currently above-average filly. Turf high 70 (began Spt). **J L Dunlop [0-3] R Barnett.*

CELTIC MISSION (USA) BHB 79f77a RR 84+f 77a 5298[1]
2 ch g Cozzene (USA) 10.1f **(87)** - Norfolk Lavender (CAN) **(56f)** (Ascot Knight (CAN))
Form - 7531
Record 2000 - 1st:1 2nd:0 3rd:1 Ran:4
Win Prizemoney £3,526 *Total Prizemoney* £3,843
Wins * 2000 Nov Mussel (G-S) 8f 84+ <
2000 Turf 1-3: (7f 2, 8f 1-1) (g-s 1-1, frm 2) 2000 AW 0-1: (7f) (Fibr)
Decent gelding. Turf high 84 (began Spt) - 1st of 7 from Sungio (1 Nov Musselburgh RF 5298). **M Johnston [1-4] C H Racing Partnership.*

CELTIC SEAL BHB 56f42a RR 59f 42a 410[8]
4 br f Lugana Beach 7f **(63)** - Celtic Bird (Celtic Cone) 9.8f **(43)**
Form - 578
Record 2000 - 1st:0 2nd:0 3rd:0 Ran:3
Pre2000 - 1st:1 2nd:0 3rd:0 Ran:8
Win Prizemoney £2,295 *Total Prizemoney* £2,554
Wins * 1998 *Nov Southw (STD) 5f 54 <*
2000 AW 0-3: (5f 3) (Fibr 3)
Scopey, fair filly, has worn blinkers. AW high 27. Becoming disappointing. **I Balding [1-11] Mrs Paula Haigh.*

CELTIC SILENCE RR 90+f 2152[1]
2 b c Celtic Swing - Smart 'n Noble (USA) (Smarten (USA))
Form - 11
Record 2000 - 1st:2 2nd:0 3rd:0 Ran:2
Win Prizemoney £27,300 *Total Prizemoney* £27,300
Wins * 2000 Jun Ascot (G-F) L 7f 93+ <
*** 2000** Jun Ayr (G-F) 6f 85+
2000 Turf 2-2: (6f 1-1, 7f 1-1) (gd 1-1, g-f 1-1)
Currently useful colt. Turf high 93 - 1st of 16 getting 2lb from Baaridd (21 Jun Ascot RF 2152) - also 1st of 9 from Snowstorm (2 Jun Ayr RF 1637). Won a better than average event at Ayr, and followed up in the Chesham Stakes at Royal Ascot. Was bought by Godolphin after that race but was not seen again. He has the looks and build of a high-class colt, and is an interesting prospect. **M Johnston [2-2] P D Savill.*

CELTIC SPRING RR 16f 4043[12]
2 b c Celtic Swing - Brookhead Lady **(40f 48a)** (Petong) 6.6f **(58)**
Form - 0
Record 2000 - 1st:0 2nd:0 3rd:0 Ran:1
2000 Turf 0-1: (7f) (g-s)
Poor colt. (DEAD) **W S Cunningham [0-1] Mrs Ann Bell.*

CELTIC VENTURE BHB 42f42a RR 39f 42a 4100[6]
5 ch g Risk Me (FR) 8f **(53)** - Celtic River (IRE) (Caerleon (USA)) 8.6f **(71)**
Form - 80661086
Record 2000 - 1st:1 2nd:0 3rd:0 Ran:6
Pre2000 - 1st:1 2nd:1 3rd:0 Ran:8
Win Prizemoney £4,594 *Total Prizemoney* £5,335
Wins * 2000 Jly Bright (FRM) C 7f 39
***** 1999 Apr Bright (GD) C 5.3f 47 <
2000 Turf 1-4: (6f, 7f 1-2, 8f) (g-f, frm 1-2, hrd) 2000 AW 0-2: (5f, 6f) (Equi, Fibr)
Very moderate gelding, effective 5 to 7f, acts on frm, likes left handed tracks, likes tight tracks. Turf high 39 (1st run) (began Jly) - 1st of 11 giving 4lb to Hi Mujtahid (25 Jly Brighton RF 3088). AW high 33. Consistent. **J C Poulton [2-11] Gerald West (from M R Channon [0-3] Aug 1997).*

CELTS DAWN RR 55f 2841[7]
2 b f Celtic Swing - Susie's Baby (Balidar) 7.9f **(63)**
Form - 7
Record 2000 - 1st:0 2nd:0 3rd:0 Ran:1
2000 Turf 0-1: (6f) (frm)
Currently fair filly. **J G Smyth-Osbourne [0-1] W H Joyce.*

CENTAUR SPIRIT BHB 55f **RR 40f** 5162[11]
3 b g Distant Relative 7f **(69)** - Winnie Reckless (Local Suitor (USA)) 8.4f **(67)**
Form - 740710
Record 2000 - 1st:1 2nd:0 3rd:0 Ran:6
Pre2000 - 1st:0 2nd:0 3rd:0 Ran:1
Win Prizemoney £1,974 *Total Prizemoney* £1,974
Wins * 2000 Oct Leices (HVY) S 10f 40+ <
2000 Turf 1-6: (8f 2, 10f 1-4) (sft, g-s 1-1, gd, g-f, frm 2)
Light-framed, moderate gelding, effective 8 to 10f, acts on g-s to frm, prefers tight tracks. Turf high 40 - 1st of 17 from Royal Exposure (9 Oct Leicester RF 4877).
**A Streeter [1-7] Centaur Racing Ltd.*

CENTER STAGE (IRE) BHB 74f **RR 71f** 3631[6]
3 ch c In The Wings 11.2f **(77)** - Secret Feeling (USA) (Riverman (USA)) 9.1f **(76)**
Form - 6
Record 2000 - 1st:0 2nd:0 3rd:0 Ran:1
Pre2000 - 1st:0 2nd:0 3rd:0 Ran:2
Win Prizemoney £0 *Total Prizemoney* £320
2000 Turf 0-1: (8f) (g-f)
Above-average colt. (DEAD) **R Hannon [0-3] Mrs Derek Strauss.*

CENTRAL COAST (IRE) BHB 75f **RR 69f** 3164[18]
4 b c Hamas (IRE) 8f **(72)** - Clairification (IRE) **(56f 58a)** (Shernazar) 10.2f **(73)**
Form - 0000
Record 2000 - 1st:0 2nd:0 3rd:0 Ran:4
Pre2000 - 1st:2 2nd:2 3rd:0 Ran:11
Win Prizemoney £10,866 *Total Prizemoney* £16,004
Wins * 1999 Jly Newbur (G-F) H 6f 77 79
* 1998 Aug Nottin (G-F) 6.1f 82 <
2000 Turf 0-4: (5f, 6f 3) (gd, g-f 3)
Strong, average colt, effective 6f, acted on g-f to frm. Turf high 69. (DEAD) **J M P Eustace [2-15] R Carstairs.*

CENTURY STAR (IRE) BHB 50f **RR 43f** 4727[17]
2 b g Bigstone (IRE) - Miss Willow Bend (USA) (Willow Hour (USA)) 5.6f **(71)**
Form - 0860
Record 2000 - 1st:0 2nd:0 3rd:0 Ran:4
2000 Turf 0-4: (5f 2, 6f, 7f) (gd 3, g-f)
Moderate gelding, has worn blinkers. Turf high 43.
**J M P Eustace [0-4] J C Smith.*

CEPHALONIA BHB 98f **RR 101f** 5226[3]
3 b f Slip Anchor 12.7f **(75)** - Cephira (FR) (Abdos) 10f **(77)**
Form - 1161703
Record 2000 - 1st:3 2nd:0 3rd:1 Ran:7
Pre2000 - 1st:0 2nd:0 3rd:0 Ran:3
Win Prizemoney £27,394 *Total Prizemoney* £30,331
Wins * 2000 Jly Newmar (GD) L 14.8f 95 <
*** 2000** May Newbur (G-F) H 12f 85 95+
*** 2000** May Pontef (SFT) H 12f 75 80+
2000 Turf 3-7: (12f 2-4, 15f 1-2, 16f) (g-s 2, gd 2-4, g-f 1-1)
Scopey, very useful filly, effective 12 to 16f, best at 15f, acts on gd to g-f, best on gd. Turf high 101 - 3rd of 12 getting 6lb from Romantic Affair (27 Oct Newmarket 16f gd RF 5226) - also 1st of 9 getting 5lb from Samsaam (12 Jly Newmarket RF 2745). Looked a most progressive filly when scoring at Pontefract on her reappearance, appreciating the soft ground and twelve-furlong trip, but showed that she could handle much faster ground when following up in a Newbury rated stakes. The steep rise in the handicap looked to have found her out at Haydock on her third start, but she bounced back when upped in trip to land a Newmarket Listed race. Decent effort when upped in trip on her final run.
**J L Dunlop [3-10] Exors of the late Lord Howard de Walden.*

CERALBI (IRE) BHB 64f **RR 71f** 5320[9]
2 b c Goldmark (USA) - Siwana (IRE) (Dom Racine (FR)) 9.2f **(62)**
Form - 622000
Record 2000 - 1st:0 2nd:2 3rd:0 Ran:6
Win Prizemoney £0 *Total Prizemoney* £2,015
2000 Turf 0-6: (6f 3, 7f 2, 8f) (sft, g-s, g-f 2, frm 2)
Above-average colt, effective 6f, acts on g-f to frm. Turf high 71 (began Jly). **R Hollinshead [0-6] L & R Roadlines.*

CERTAIN JUSTICE (USA) RR 100+f 1212[1]
2 gr c Lit de Justice (USA) - Pure Misk (Rainbow Quest (USA)) 10.4f **(75)**
Form - 11
Record 2000 - 1st:2 2nd:0 3rd:0 Ran:2
Win Prizemoney £12,222 *Total Prizemoney* £12,222
Wins * 2000 May Windso (G-F) 5f 100+ <
*** 2000** Apr Newmar (SFT) 5f 81
2000 Turf 2-2: (5f 2-2) (gd 1-1, frm 1-1)
Currently very useful colt. Turf high 100 - 1st of 7 giving 2lb to Threezedzz (15 May Windsor RF 1212).
**P F I Cole [2-2] The Blenheim Partnership.*

CERTAINLY SO RR 57f 4480[7]
2 ch f So Factual (USA) - Indubitable (Sharpo) 7.7f **(59)**
Form - 07
Record 2000 - 1st:0 2nd:0 3rd:0 Ran:2
2000 Turf 0-2: (6f, 7f) (g-s, g-f)
Currently fair filly. Turf high 57. **G B Balding [0-2] Miss B Swire.*

CEZZARO (IRE) BHB 79f **RR 77f** 4643[15]
2 ch c Ashkalani (IRE) - Sept Roses (USA) (Septieme Ciel (USA))
Form - 57300
Record 2000 - 1st:0 2nd:0 3rd:1 Ran:5
Win Prizemoney £0 *Total Prizemoney* £550
2000 Turf 0-5: (6f, 7f 3, 8f) (g-s, gd, g-f 2, frm)
Above-average colt, has worn blinkers. Turf high 77.
**A C Stewart [0-5] Fayzad Thoroughbred Ltd.*

CHAFAYA (IRE) RR 76f 5236[18]
2 ch f Mark of Esteem (IRE) - Matila (IRE) (Persian Bold) 9.3f **(66)**
Form - 30
Record 2000 - 1st:0 2nd:0 3rd:1 Ran:2
Win Prizemoney £0 *Total Prizemoney* £467
2000 Turf 0-2: (7f 2) (g-s 2)
Currently above-average filly. Turf high 76 (1st run) (began Spt) - 3rd of 15 to Lipica (18 Spt Kempton 7f g-s RF 4480). Made an encouraging first appearance at Kempton, and can improve in time. **R W Armstrong [0-2] Hamdan Al Maktoum.*

CHAGALL RR 109+f 4698[7]
3 ch c Fraam - Pooka (Dominion) 8.5f **(63)**
Form - 27
2000 Turf 0-2: (7f, 8f) (g-f, frm)
Strong, currently Pattern-class colt, has worn blinkers. Turf high 109 (1st run) (began Jly) - 2nd of 9 getting 8lb from Arkadian Hero (1 Jly Newmarket 7f frm RF 2449). A winner at Listed level in his native Germany, he ran very well to chase home Arkadian Hero in a Newmarket Group Three in July.
**B Hellier in GER [1-3] Stall Florian.*

CHAGUARAMAS (IRE) BHB 100f **RR 88f** 4738[8]
2 b f Mujadil (USA) 7.7f **(70)** - Sabaniya (FR) (Lashkari) 9.8f **(67)**
Form - 115428
Record 2000 - 1st:2 2nd:1 3rd:0 Ran:6
Win Prizemoney £7,208 *Total Prizemoney* £13,916
Wins * 2000 Jly Bath (FRM) 5.1f 74 <
*** 2000** Jun Windso (G-F) 6f 74+
2000 Turf 2-6: (5f 1-1, 6f 1-1, 7f 3, 8f) (gd, g-f 1-3, frm 1-2)
Useful filly, effective 8f, acts on gd. Turf high 88. Scored on her Windsor debut, but may have found the step back to the minimum trip against her when only narrowly justifying long odds-on at Bath next time. Showed steering problems when beaten in a Newmarket Listed race, but has since run very well in a Group Three and a Listed event at Goodwood. Needs a mile.
**R Hannon [2-6] Dr A Haloute.*

CHAHAYA TIMOR (IRE) BHB 44f54a **RR 54a** 124[3]
8 b g Slip Anchor 12.7f **(75)** - Roxy Hart (High Top) 10.2f **(67)**
Form - 433
Record 2000 - 1st:0 2nd:0 3rd:2 Ran:2
Pre2000 - 1st:3 2nd:1 3rd:1 Ran:13
Win Prizemoney £6,978 *Total Prizemoney* £9,474
Wins * 1998 *Feb Wolver (STD) S 16.2f 59++*
1998 *Jan Wolver (STD) S 14.8f 62*
2000 AW 0-2: (15f, 16f) (Fibr 2)

Moderate gelding. AW high 46. Consistent.
**Miss S J Wilton [1-6] John Pointon and Sons (from R Simpson [1-3] Jan 1998).*

CHAIN **RR 36tf** 3532[8]
3 b c Last Tycoon 9.4f **(73)** - Trampship (High Line) 10.3f **(70)**
Form - 8
Record 2000 - 1st:0 2nd:0 3rd:0 Ran:1
2000 Turf 0-1: (11f) (gd)
Currently very moderate colt. **R Charlton [0-1] K Abdulla.*

CHAIRMAN BOBBY BHB 65f **RR 67f** 4760[5]
2 ch g Clantime 6.6f **(57)** - Formidable Liz **(31f 45a)** (Formidable (USA)) 9.2f **(63)**
Form - 385
Record 2000 - 1st:0 2nd:0 3rd:1 Ran:3
Win Prizemoney £0 *Total Prizemoney* £411
2000 Turf 0-2: (5f, 6f) (g-f, frm) 2000 AW 0-1: (6f) (Fibr)
Currently average gelding. Turf high 67 (1st run) (began Aug) - 3rd of 12 giving 5lb to Yellow Trumpet (23 Aug Carlisle 5f frm RF 3901). **T D Barron [0-3] J Johnson.*

CHAI-YO BHB 58f **RR 39f** 4757[18]
10 b g Rakaposhi King 9.3f **(55)** - Ballysax Lass (Main Reef) 9.6f **(57)**
Form - 0
Record 2000 - 1st:0 2nd:0 3rd:0 Ran:1
Pre2000 - 1st:0 2nd:1 3rd:0 Ran:5
Win Prizemoney £0 *Total Prizemoney* £1,938
2000 Turf 0-1: (10f) (g-s)
Very moderate gelding. **J A B Old [7-30] Nick Viney.*

CHAKA ZULU BHB 69f65a **RR 76f 65a** 4779[9]
3 b g Muhtarram (USA) - African Dance (USA) (El Gran Senor (USA)) 9.6f **(76)**
Form - 13113120
Record 2000 - 1st:4 2nd:1 3rd:2 Ran:8
Pre2000 - 1st:0 2nd:0 3rd:0 Ran:3
Win Prizemoney £11,734 *Total Prizemoney* £13,839

Wins									
	* 2000	Aug	Newcas	(FRM)	H	12.4f	65	67+	
	* 2000	Jly	Newcas	(GD)	H	12.4f	52	70	<
	* 2000	Jly	Catter	(G-F)	H	12f	44	60	
	* 2000	Jly	Bath	(FRM)	H	10.2f	40	44	

2000 Turf 4-7: (10f 1-2, 12f 3-5) (g-f 1-1, frm 3-6) 2000 AW 0-1: (12f) (Fibr)
Workmanlike, above-average gelding, effective 12f, acts on g-f to frm, best on frm, prefers left handed tracks, likes tight tracks. Turf high 76 (began Jly) - 2nd of 3 giving 8lb to Slaneyside (31 Aug Musselburgh 12f frm RF 4118) - also 1st of 7 getting 13lb from Haystacks (31 Jly Newcastle RF 3253). Inconsistent. A decent piece of placement saw him gain four victories in modest handicaps during the summer. Best over 12 furlongs and suited by fast ground. **W J Haggas [4-11] J D Ashenheim.*

CHAKRA BHB 49f36a **RR 49f 36a** 4543[16]
6 gr g Mystiko (USA) 7.7f **(59)** - Maracuja (USA) (Riverman (USA)) 9.1f **(76)**
Form - 76506106800021382166550
Record 2000 - 1st:3 2nd:2 3rd:1 Ran:23
Pre2000 - 1st:3 2nd:1 3rd:4 Ran:38
Win Prizemoney £14,648 *Total Prizemoney* £19,600

Wins									
	* 2000	Aug	Bright	(GD)	H	6f	45	48	
	2000	Jun	Folkes	(FRM)	C	6f		38	
	2000	*Mar*	*Lingfi*	*(STD)*	*H*	*6f*	*32*	*37*	
	1998	Aug	Warwic	(G-F)	H	5f	47	52	<
	1998	Jly	Warwic	(G-F)	H	5f	42	46	
	1997	Jly	Bright	(FRM)	H	5.3f	45	48	

2000 Turf 2-16: (5f 5, 6f 2-9, 7f 2) (gd 4, g-f 2-6, frm 6) 2000 AW 1-7: (5f 3, 6f 1-4) (Equi 1-5, Fibr 2)
Moderate gelding, effective 5 to 7f, best at 6f, acts on gd to frm, best on g-f, excels at Ayr and does well at Brighton. Turf high 49 - also 1st of 15 getting 5lb from Absolute Fantasy (9 Aug Brighton RF 3485). AW high 37.
**M S Saunders [1-9] Brian McFadzean (from J M Bradley [4-43] Jun 2000).*

CHALCEDONY BHB 49f57a **RR 56f 57a** 5007[13]
4 ch g Highest Honor (FR) 10.9f **(72)** - Sweet Holland (USA) (Alydar (USA)) 9.1f **(76)**
Form - 12474036210
Record 2000 - 1st:2 2nd:2 3rd:1 Ran:11
Pre2000 - 1st:2 2nd:0 3rd:2 Ran:10
Win Prizemoney £11,010 *Total Prizemoney* £16,728

Wins									
	* **2000**	*Spt*	*Lingfi*	*(STD)*		*12f*		*51*	
	2000	*Jan*	*Southw*	*(STD)*	*H*	*11f*	*66*	*69*	<
	1999	*Apr*	*Southw*	*(STD)*	*H*	*11f*	*60*	*63*	
	1999	*Jan*	*Lingfi*	*(STD)*	*H*	*10f*	*55*	*59*	

2000 Turf 0-4: (10f, 12f 2, 14f) (g-s, gd 2, g-f) 2000 AW 2-7: (11f 1-2, 12f 1-5) (Equi 1-3, Fibr 1-4)
Leggy, above-average gelding, effective 11 to 12f, best at 11f, - acts on AW, best on Fibr, has worn blinkers, prefers left handed tracks, favours tight tracks, excels at Lingfield and Southwell. Turf high 56. AW high 79 - 2nd of 9 giving 1lb to Ursa Major (12 Feb Lingfield 12f Equi RF 0274).
**G L Moore [1-4] Lancing Racing Syndicate (from T D Barron [3-17] May 2000).*

CHALLENOR BHB 50f **RR 41f** 4828[18]
2 ch c Casteddu 7.4f **(54)** - Expletive (Shiny Tenth) 9.2f **(56)**
Form - 600
Record 2000 - 1st:0 2nd:0 3rd:0 Ran:3
2000 Turf 0-3: (5f, 8f 2) (g-s, g-f, frm)
Currently moderate colt. Turf high 41 (began Jly).
**J Pearce [0-3] Paul Sandy.*

CHALOM (IRE) BHB 77f **RR 68f** 5131[10]
2 b c Mujadil (USA) 7.7f **(70)** - The Poachers Lady (IRE) (Salmon Leap (USA)) 11f **(61)**
Form - 060
Record 2000 - 1st:0 2nd:0 3rd:0 Ran:3
Win Prizemoney £0 *Total Prizemoney* £311
2000 Turf 0-3: (6f, 7f 2) (sft, g-s, g-f)
Currently average colt. Turf high 68 (began Spt).
**B J Meehan [0-3] Maagar UK Ltd.*

CHALUZ BHB 37f42a **RR 31f 42a** 459[5]
6 b g Night Shift (USA) 8.1f **(73)** - Laluche (USA) (Alleged (USA)) 10f **(76)**
Form - 2554255545
Record 2000 - 1st:0 2nd:1 3rd:0 Ran:7
Pre2000 - 1st:4 2nd:5 3rd:3 Ran:41
Win Prizemoney £7,791 *Total Prizemoney* £12,741

Wins									
	1999	*Feb*	*Wolver*	*(STD)*	*C*	*6f*		*50*	
	1998	*Jan*	*Southw*	*(STD)*	*H*	*7f*	*53*	*59*	<
	1998	*Jan*	*Southw*	*(STD)*	*H*	*8f*	*53*	*55*	
	1997	*Nov*	*Southw*	*(STD)*	*H*	*7f*	*48*	*53*	

2000 AW 0-7: (6f 2, 7f 3, 8f 2) (Equi, Fibr 6)
Very moderate gelding, effective 5 to 7f, - acts on Fibr, has worn blinkers. AW high 50. Consistent. A modest performer overall, he does win from time to time on Fibresand. He had shown form over seven furlongs and a mile, but has been dropped successfully in trip recently, his early pace being a big help to him.
**N P Littmoden [0-19] Miss Vanessa Church (from K R Burke [4-25] Feb 1999).*

CHAMBOLLE MUSIGNY (USA) BHB 37f **RR 54df** 217[8]
4 b f Majestic Light (USA) 9.5f **(78)** - Bridal Up (USA) (Sharpen Up) 8.3f **(67)**
Form - 3778
Record 2000 - 1st:0 2nd:0 3rd:1 Ran:4
Pre2000 - 1st:0 2nd:0 3rd:0 Ran:7
Win Prizemoney £0 *Total Prizemoney* £328
2000 AW 0-4: (8f 2, 9f, 12f) (Fibr 4)
Unfurnished, fair filly, effective 11f, acts on frm, has worn blinkers, likes left handed tracks, favours tight tracks. AW high 39. Becoming disappointing.
**M J Polglase [0-4] M J Polglase (from P F I Cole [0-7] Spt 1999).*

CHAMELEON BHB 68f **RR 70f** 4824[10]
4 b f Green Desert (USA) 7.8f **(78)** - Old Domesday Book (High Top) 10.2f **(67)**
Form - 105260
Record 2000 - 1st:1 2nd:1 3rd:0 Ran:6
Pre2000 - 1st:0 2nd:0 3rd:0 Ran:1
Win Prizemoney £2,588 *Total Prizemoney* £4,798

Wins									
	* **2000**	*Feb*	*Wolver*	*(STD)*		*7f*		*67+*	<

2000 Turf 0-5: (6f, 7f, 8f, 10f, 11f) (sft, gd 2, g-f 2) 2000 AW 1-1: (7f 1-1) (Fibr 1-1)
Scopey, above-average filly, effective 7f, - acts on Fibr. Turf high 70 (began Jly). (1st run) - 1st of 8 getting 5lb from Palawan (8 Feb Wolverhampton RF 0242). **M L W Bell [1-7] Lordship Stud.*

CHAMLANG RR 54f 5319[19]
2 b f Petong 7.6f **(58)** - Makalu (Godswalk (USA)) 7.3f **(58)**
Form - 00
Record 2000 - 1st:0 2nd:0 3rd:0 Ran:2
2000 Turf 0-2: (6f 2) (sft, gd)
Currently fair filly. Turf high 54 (began Oct).
**N A Graham [0-2] Flying Colours Racing.*

CHAMPAGNE BHB 63a **RR 40f** 2682[4]
4 b g Efisio 7.7f **(69)** - Success Story **(47f 55a)** (Sharrood (USA)) 10.5f **(72)**
Form - 850301004
Record 2000 - 1st:1 2nd:0 3rd:1 Ran:9
Pre2000 - 1st:1 2nd:0 3rd:0 Ran:4
Win Prizemoney £4,926 *Total Prizemoney* £5,533
Wins * 2000 *May Wolver (STD) H 8.5f 55 61+*
1999 Aug Leices (GD) C 10f 65 <
2000 Turf 0-4: (8f 2, 11f 2) (sft, g-s, gd, frm) 2000 AW 1-5: (7f, 8f 1-3, 9f) (Fibr 1-5)
Workmanlike, average gelding, effective 8 to 10f, acts on gd - acts on Fibr, often wears blinkers, likes tight tracks. Turf high 40. AW high 61 - 1st of 13 getting 1lb from Malchik (20 May Wolverhampton RF 1356). Landed a handicap in good style on the Wolverhampton Fibresand in May.
**Andrew Reid [1-10] A S Reid (from R Charlton [1-3] Aug 1999).*

CHAMPAGNE N DREAMS BHB 38f34a **RR 45df 34a** 4811[8]
8 b m Rambo Dancer (CAN) 8.4f **(59)** - Pink Sensation (Sagaro) 9.7f **(55)**
Form - U6780058
Record 2000 - 1st:0 2nd:0 3rd:0 Ran:8
Pre2000 - 1st:3 2nd:2 3rd:6 Ran:40
Win Prizemoney £8,497 *Total Prizemoney* £13,837
Wins 1999 Spt Catter (G-F) H 7f 51 55
1998 Aug Chepst (G-F) H 8.1f 48 54
2000 Turf 0-7: (7f 4, 8f 3) (g-s, gd, frm 3, hrd 2) 2000 AW 0-1: (8f) (Equi)
Moderate mare, effective 7 to 10f, acts on g-f to frm, best on frm, has worn blinkers, prefers left handed tracks, prefers tight tracks. Turf high 45.
**N Tinkler [0-8] P D R Construction Ltd (from W W Haigh [1-7] Oct 1999).*

CHAMPAGNE RIDER BHB 70f66a **RR 80f 66a** 5317[6]
4 b c Presidium 7.5f **(56)** - Petitesse (Petong) 6.6f **(58)**
Form - 0000068004026
Record 2000 - 1st:0 2nd:1 3rd:0 Ran:13
Pre2000 - 1st:3 2nd:0 3rd:3 Ran:21
Win Prizemoney £17,465 *Total Prizemoney* £30,989
Wins * 1999 Aug Leices (G-F) H 6f 86 89 <
* 1998 May Kempto (GD) 6f 83
* 1998 Apr Kempto (HVY) 5f 74
2000 Turf 0-13: (6f 4, 7f 8, 8f) (sft 2, g-s 2, gd 3, g-f 4, frm 2)
Leggy, decent colt, effective 6 to 7f, best at 6f, acts on g-s to frm, best on frm, has worn blinkers. Turf high 80 - 2nd of 22 giving 8lb to Mantles Pride (21 Oct Doncaster 7f g-s RF 5122).
**K McAuliffe [3-34] Highgrove Developments Ltd.*

CHAMPFIS BHB 67f58a **RR 77+f 58a** 4774[2]
3 b g Efisio 7.7f **(69)** - Champ d'Avril (Northfields (USA)) 9f **(72)**
Form - 4252
Record 2000 - 1st:0 2nd:2 3rd:0 Ran:4
Pre2000 - 1st:0 2nd:0 3rd:1 Ran:2
Win Prizemoney £0 *Total Prizemoney* £2,561
2000 Turf 0-4: (6f, 7f, 8f 2) (g-s 2, gd, frm)
Strong, above-average gelding, effective 7f, acts on g-s. Turf high 77 (began Jly) - 2nd of 8 to Material Witness (16 Spt Catterick 7f g-s RF 4458). He caught the eye at Newcastle in July and just failed to get up next time. Should find a race.
**M Johnston [0-6] Henderson (Co Durham).*

CHAMPION LODGE (IRE) BHB 92f **RR 97f** 4465[15]
3 b c Sri Pekan (USA) - Legit (IRE) (Runnett) 7f **(59)**
Form - 211700
Record 2000 - 1st:2 2nd:1 3rd:0 Ran:6
Win Prizemoney £15,723 *Total Prizemoney* £17,623
Wins * 2000 May Thirsk (GD) 8f 97 <
*** 2000** May Newmar (GD) 8f 96
2000 Turf 2-6: (8f 2-5, 10f) (gd 1-2, g-f, frm 1-3)
Workmanlike, very useful colt, effective 8f, acts on gd to frm, best on gd. Turf high 97 - 1st of 4 from Elghani (20 May Thirsk RF 1345) - also 1st of 19 from Hymn (7 May Newmarket RF 1083). Unraced at two, he progressed well early last season with wins at Newmarket and Thirsk, but was been found out in better company afterwards.
**J A R Toller [2-6] P C J Dalby.*

CHANCELLOR (IRE) BHB 85f **RR 89+f** 5310[1]
2 ch c Halling (USA) - Isticanna (USA) (Far North (CAN)) 9.7f **(75)**
Form - 01
Record 2000 - 1st:1 2nd:0 3rd:0 Ran:2
Win Prizemoney £3,331 *Total Prizemoney* £3,331
Wins * 2000 Nov Doncas (HVY) 7f 89+ <
2000 Turf 1-2: (7f 1-2) (g-s 1-1, g-f)
Currently useful colt. Turf high 89 (began Spt) - 1st of 18 from Afghan (3 Nov Doncaster RF 5310). **B W Hills [1-2] W J Gredley.*

CHANCE REMARK (IRE) RR 28f 5160[8]
2 ch f Goldmark (USA) - Fair Chance (Young Emperor) 10.1f **(63)**
Form - 08
Record 2000 - 1st:0 2nd:0 3rd:0 Ran:2
2000 Turf 0-1: (8f) (sft) 2000 AW 0-1: (7f) (Fibr)
Currently little account filly. **Martyn Wane [0-2] B Batey.*

CHANCERY (USA) BHB 48f **RR 79f** 3588[3]
4 ch g St Jovite (USA) 11.8f **(75)** - Big E Dream (USA) (Persian Bold) 9.3f **(66)**
Form - 23
Record 2000 - 1st:0 2nd:1 3rd:1 Ran:2
Pre2000 - 1st:0 2nd:1 3rd:1 Ran:5
Win Prizemoney £0 *Total Prizemoney* £2,990
2000 Turf 0-2: (12f 2) (g-f, frm)
Above-average gelding, effective 9 to 12f, best at 9f, acts on g-s to g-f, has worn blinkers, prefers right handed tracks. Turf high 79 (1st run) - 2nd of 14 to Pollardsfield (22 May Roscommon 12f g-f RF 1561a).
**A King [0-1] The Golden Anorak Partnership (from J S Bolger in IRE [0-6] May 2000).*

CHANCY DEAL (IRE) RR 11f 628[15]
3 b f Namaqualand (USA) - Broadway Gal (USA) (Foolish Pleasure (USA)) 8.9f **(72)**
Form - 80
Record 2000 - 1st:0 2nd:0 3rd:0 Ran:2
2000 Turf 0-1: (10f) (gd) 2000 AW 0-1: (8f) (Fibr)
Light-framed, currently poor filly.
**Miss M E Rowland [0-2] Goldliner Racing Club.*

CHANGE OF IMAGE BHB 62f57a **RR 47f 57a** 2193[11]
2 b f Spectrum (IRE) - Reveuse du Soir (Vision (USA)) 9f **(64)**
Form - 640
Record 2000 - 1st:0 2nd:0 3rd:0 Ran:3
Win Prizemoney £0 *Total Prizemoney* £200
2000 Turf 0-2: (6f 2) (g-f 2) 2000 AW 0-1: (5f) (Fibr)
Currently moderate filly. Turf high 47. **J M P Eustace [0-3] J Shack.*

CHANGING SCENE (USA) BHB 85f **RR 85+f** 4818[P]
2 b c Theatrical 11.5f **(78)** - Routilante (Rousillon (USA)) 8.2f **(74)**
Form - 051P
Record 2000 - 1st:1 2nd:0 3rd:0 Ran:4
Win Prizemoney £4,075 *Total Prizemoney* £4,075
Wins * 2000 Spt Epsom (GD) 8.5f 85+ <
2000 Turf 1-4: (7f 2, 8f, 9f 1-1) (g-s, g-f 1-3)
Useful colt. Turf high 85 (began Jly) - 1st of 7 giving 5lb to Zanzibar (6 Spt Epsom RF 4264). (DEAD)
**I A Balding [1-4] George Strawbridge.*

CHANTAIGNE (IRE) BHB 66f **RR 58f** 5121[8]
2 ch f General Monash (USA) - Blue Vista (IRE) (Pennine Walk) 8.5f

(61)
Form - 8538
Record 2000 - 1st:0 2nd:0 3rd:1 Ran:4
Win Prizemoney £0 *Total Prizemoney* £685
2000 Turf 0-4: (5f, 7f 2, 8f) (g-s, gd 2, frm)
Fair filly. Turf high 58. **A Bailey [0-4] Ray Bailey.*

CHANTRESS LORELEI RR 66f 5131[5]
2 b f So Factual (USA) - Sound of the Sea (Windjammer (USA)) 7f **(59)**
Form - 05
Record 2000 - 1st:0 2nd:0 3rd:0 Ran:2
2000 Turf 0-2: (6f 2) (sft, gd)
Currently average filly. Turf high 66 (began Oct).
**Mrs A J Perrett [0-2] Mrs O'Brien, Broad, Ambler.*

CHAPEL ROYALE (IRE) BHB 78f RR 87df 5240[19]
3 gr c College Chapel - Merci Royale (Fairy King (USA)) 7.7f **(59)**
Form - 5772031070330000
Record 2000 - 1st:1 2nd:1 3rd:3 Ran:16
Pre2000 - 1st:1 2nd:0 3rd:0 Ran:3
Win Prizemoney £9,528 *Total Prizemoney* £15,177
Wins * 2000 Jly Newmar (G-S) H 8f 78 85
1999 Spt Newcas (SFT) 7f 87+ <
2000 Turf 1-16: (7f, 8f 1-11, 9f 3, 10f) (sft, g-s 3, gd 1-7, g-f 4, frm)
Workmanlike, useful colt, effective 7 to 9f, best at 8f, acts on g-s to frm, best on gd, prefers right handed tracks, prefers tight tracks, excels at Goodwood and Windsor. Turf high 87 - 3rd of 6 getting 1lb from Bold King (21 Spt Goodwood 8f g-s RF 4548) - also 1st of 13 getting 1lb from Resounding (13 Jly Newmarket RF 2772). He faced some stiff tasks in handicap company earlier on this season, but bounced back to form with victory over a mile at the Newmarket July meeting. Good effort at Goodwood in September. Needs cut in the ground.
**K Mahdi [1-14] Prospect Estates Ltd (from D Nicholls [0-2] May 2000).*

CHARENTE (USA) BHB 68f68a RR 71f 68a 4822[3]
2 ch c Hennessy (USA) - Zalamalec (USA) **(82f)** (Septieme Ciel (USA))
Form - 5803
Record 2000 - 1st:0 2nd:0 3rd:1 Ran:4
Win Prizemoney £0 *Total Prizemoney* £398
2000 Turf 0-4: (6f 3, 10f) (g-f, frm 3)
Above-average colt. Turf high 71 - 3rd of 21 getting 1lb from Trumpington (6 Oct Windsor 10f g-f RF 4822).
**M C Pipe [0-4] Lord Donoughmore.*

CHARGE BHB 57f60a RR 61f 60a 2942[11]
4 gr g Petong 7.6f **(58)** - Madam Petoski (Petoski) 5.7f **(62)**
Form - 167722150850
Record 2000 - 1st:1 2nd:2 3rd:0 Ran:10
Pre2000 - 1st:1 2nd:0 3rd:3 Ran:9
Win Prizemoney £6,114 *Total Prizemoney* £9,735
Wins * 2000 *Mar Lingfi (STD) H 6f 62 78+* <
1999 *Nov Lingfi (STD) 6f 55*
2000 Turf 0-4: (5f 2, 6f 2) (g-f, frm 3) 2000 AW 1-6: (5f 2, 6f 1-4) (Equi 1-5, Fibr)
Light-framed, above-average gelding, effective 6f, - acts on Equi, likes left handed tracks, likes tight tracks. Turf high 61. AW high 78 - 1st of 12 giving 15lb to Bramble Bear (18 Mar Lingfield RF 0464). **K R Burke [1-8] Nigel Shields (from B Smart [1-11] Jan 2000).*

CHARITY CRUSADER BHB 30f RR 30f 3599[5]
9 b g Rousillon (USA) 10.4f **(69)** - Height of Folly (Shirley Heights) 10.3f **(74)**
Form - 005
Record 2000 - 1st:0 2nd:0 3rd:0 Ran:3
Pre2000 - 1st:4 2nd:7 3rd:2 Ran:35
Win Prizemoney £16,535 *Total Prizemoney* £27,202
Wins * 1998 Aug Mussel (G-F) H 16f 48 51
* 1997 Aug Redcar (G-F) C 14.1f 41
2000 Turf 0-3: (12f 2, 14f) (gd, frm, hrd)
Very moderate gelding, effective 12 to 14f, acts on frm, often wears blinkers, prefers left handed tracks. Turf high 30. Consistent.
**Mrs M Reveley [5-45] The Mary Reveley Racing Club (from P W Chapple-Hyam [2-10] Jun 1995).*

CHARLATAN (IRE) RR 24f 2686[11]
2 b c Charnwood Forest (IRE) - Taajreh (IRE) (Mtoto)
Form - 0
Record 2000 - 1st:0 2nd:0 3rd:0 Ran:1
2000 Turf 0-1: (7f) (gd)
Currently little account colt. **C A Dwyer [0-1] John Purcell.*

CHARLEM BHB 37f41a RR 20f 41a 3266[11]
3 br f Petardia 8.2f **(58)** - La Neva (FR) (Arctic Tern (USA)) 8.9f **(69)**
Form - 66602000
Record 2000 - 1st:0 2nd:1 3rd:0 Ran:8
Pre2000 - 1st:0 2nd:0 3rd:0 Ran:2
Win Prizemoney £0 *Total Prizemoney* £650
2000 Turf 0-4: (8f, 9f, 10f 2) (gd, g-f 2, frm) 2000 AW 0-4: (8f 2, 9f, 12f) (Fibr 4)
Leggy, moderate filly, effective 8f, - acts on Fibr, often wears blinkers (effectively), likes left handed tracks, likes tight tracks. Turf high 20 (began Jly). AW high 40. Becoming disappointing.
**D Shaw [0-10] R A B Saville.*

CHARLIE BIGTIME BHB 25f33a RR 40f 33a 376[8]
10 b g Norwick (USA) 9.4f **(51)** - Sea Aura (Roi Soleil) 8.7f **(57)**
Form - 8
Record 2000 - 1st:0 2nd:0 3rd:0 Ran:1
Pre2000 - 1st:5 2nd:3 3rd:11 Ran:64
Win Prizemoney £15,396 *Total Prizemoney* £22,716
2000 AW 0-1: (12f) (Fibr)
Moderate gelding, has worn blinkers. Inconsistent.
**B J Llewellyn [0-2] Miss Emily Jane Jones (from I Campbell [0-8] Oct 1997).*

CHARLIE PARKES BHB 99f RR 94f 1439[2]
2 ch c Pursuit of Love 9.5f **(69)** - Lucky Parkes **(97f)** (Full Extent (USA))
Form - 222
Record 2000 - 1st:0 2nd:3 3rd:0 Ran:3
Win Prizemoney £0 *Total Prizemoney* £5,379
2000 Turf 0-3: (5f 3) (gd 2, g-f)
Currently useful colt. Turf high 94 - 2nd of 7 giving 2lb to Romantic Myth (9 May Chester 5f g-f RF 1109). Runner-up on his three starts as a juvenile, beaten under a length each time, he looked as if fast ground would suit. However, he was absent from the end of May, having been withdrawn on his intended return in August.
**A Berry [0-3] Joseph Heler.*

CHARLIE SILLETT BHB 44f70a RR 16f 70a 2280[20]
8 ch g Handsome Sailor 6.6f **(53)** -Bystrouska (Gorytus (USA)) 7.8f **(60)**
Form - 080
Record 2000 - 1st:0 2nd:0 3rd:0 Ran:3
Pre2000 - 1st:5 2nd:0 3rd:1 Ran:29
Win Prizemoney £28,436 *Total Prizemoney* £29,095
Wins 1997 Jun Cheste (SFT) H 6.1f 80 88 <
1996 Oct Chepst (SFT) H 6.1f 80 82
2000 Turf 0-3: (6f 2, 8f) (gd 2, frm)
Moderate gelding, has worn blinkers. Turf high 16. Becoming disappointing.
**J Mackie [0-3] John Sillett (from B W Hills [5-29] Aug 1999).*

CHARLIE'S QUEST BHB 38f RR 56f 5119[10]
4 b g Kylian (USA) 8.1f **(66)** - Pleasure Quest (Efisio)
Form - 00
Record 2000 - 1st:0 2nd:0 3rd:0 Ran:2
Pre2000 - 1st:0 2nd:0 3rd:0 Ran:3
2000 Turf 0-1: (10f) (g-s) 2000 AW 0-1: (12f) (Fibr)
Leggy, fair gelding.
**D W P Arbuthnot [0-5] Miss P E Decker.*

CHARLOTTE RUSSE BHB 35f RR 23f 3780[14]
3 b f Rudimentary (USA) 8.2f **(66)** - Do Run Run (Commanche Run) 8.5f **(58)**
Form - 00
Record 2000 - 1st:0 2nd:0 3rd:0 Ran:1
Pre2000 - 1st:0 2nd:0 3rd:0 Ran:3
2000 Turf 0-1: (11f) (gd)
Scopey, little account filly, has worn blinkers.
**R A Fahey [0-1] Appleby Racing (from Mrs N Macauley [0-3] Nov 1999).*

CHARLOTTEVALENTINA (IRE) BHB 75f **RR 78f** 4533[5]
3 ch f Perugino (USA) - The Top Diesis (USA) (Diesis) 9.3f **(69)**
Form - 020005
Record 2000 - 1st:0 2nd:1 3rd:0 Ran:6
Pre2000 - 1st:1 2nd:0 3rd:0 Ran:6
Win Prizemoney £2,770 *Total Prizemoney* £7,160
Wins * 1999 Jun Catter (G-F) 6f 65 <
2000 Turf 0-6: (5f, 6f 5) (sft, g-s, g-f 2, frm 2)
Strong, above-average filly, effective 6f, acts on g-f, has worn blinkers, prefers left handed tracks. Turf high 78 - 2nd of 16 giving 6lb to Railroader (10 May Chester 6f g-f RF 1127). Showed a return to form when runner-up in a competitive handicap at Chester in May. Finished well that day, but held since.
**P D Evans [1-12] Global Racing Club.*

CHARLTON IMP (USA) BHB 25f **RR 18f** 3526[10]
7 b m Imp Society (USA) 7.1f **(63)** - Percentage (USA) (Vaguely Noble) 10.1f **(72)**
Form - 00
Record 2000 - 1st:0 2nd:0 3rd:0 Ran:2
Pre2000 - 1st:2 2nd:1 3rd:2 Ran:24
Win Prizemoney £4,818 *Total Prizemoney* £6,736
Wins * 1996 Aug Bath (GD) S 8f 40
* 1996 Jly Chepst (G-F) S 8.1f 56 <
2000 Turf 0-2: (7f, 8f) (frm 2)
Poor mare, has worn blinkers. Turf high 18 (began Jly). Inconsistent. **R J Hodges [2-26] Miss R Dobson.*

CHARMED BHB 43f **RR 46f** 4323[11]
2 ch c Savahra Sound 7.8f **(55)** - Sweet And Lucky (Lucky Wednesday) 8f **(50)**
Form - 000
Record 2000 - 1st:0 2nd:0 3rd:0 Ran:3
2000 Turf 0-3: (5f, 6f 2) (g-f 2, hrd)
Currently moderate colt. Turf high 46 (began Jly).
**N P Littmoden [0-3] Paul Dixon.*

CHARMER VENTURE RR 75+f 5098[4]
2 ch f Zilzal (USA) 8.5f **(79)** - City of Angels (Woodman (USA)) 9f **(74)**
Form - 4
Record 2000 - 1st:0 2nd:0 3rd:0 Ran:1
Win Prizemoney £0 *Total Prizemoney* £336
2000 Turf 0-1: (8f) (gd)
Currently above-average filly. **S P C Woods [0-1] Dr Frank Chao.*

CHARMING ADMIRAL (IRE) BHB 52f36a **RR 55f 36a** 5002[9]
7 b g Shareef Dancer (USA) 10.1f **(67)** - Lilac Charm (Bustino) 10.4f **(64)**
Form - 812003030
Record 2000 - 1st:1 2nd:1 3rd:2 Ran:9
Pre2000 - 1st:0 2nd:4 3rd:4 Ran:20
Win Prizemoney £3,029 *Total Prizemoney* £12,459
Wins * **2000** Apr Pontef (G-S) H 17.1f 48 59 <
2000 Turf 1-7: (14f, 16f, 17f 1-3, 18f, 22f) (sft, g-s 1-2, gd 3, g-f) 2000 AW 0-2: (16f 2) (Fibr 2)
Fair gelding, effective 17 to 22f, best at 17f, acts on sft to gd, has worn blinkers (very effectively), likes left handed tracks. Turf high 61 - 2nd of 17 giving 7lb to Imad (17 Apr Pontefract 22f sft RF 0748) - also 1st of 15 from Protocol (11 Apr Pontefract RF 0663). AW high 23.
**Mrs A Duffield [6-35] The Old Spice Girls (from C F Wall [0-9] Jly 1997).*

CHARMING LOTTE BHB 62f57a **RR 67f 57a** 5061[5]
3 b f Nicolotte - Courtisane (Persepolis (FR)) 6.4f **(67)**
Form - 000513035
Record 2000 - 1st:1 2nd:0 3rd:2 Ran:9
Pre2000 - 1st:1 2nd:1 3rd:2 Ran:8
Win Prizemoney £7,448 *Total Prizemoney* £10,322
Wins * **2000** Jun Cheste (G-S) C 6.1f 60
1999 Oct Ayr (SFT) H 6f 66 76 <
2000 Turf 1-9: (6f 1-6, 7f 3) (sft, g-s, gd 1-3, g-f 3, frm)
Light-framed, average filly, effective 5 to 6f, best at 6f, acts on sft to gd, best on gd, often wears blinkers. Turf high 67 - 3rd of 18 getting 7lb from Tom Tun (16 Aug Hamilton 6f gd RF 3698). Suited by the drop back to six furlongs when winning a Chester claimer in June.

**N Tinkler [1-9] Mike Gosse (from P Shakespeare [1-8] Oct 1999).*

C-HARRY (IRE) BHB 56f43a **RR 57f 43a** 2479[6]
6 ch h Imperial Frontier (USA) 7f **(65)** - Desert Gale (Taufan (USA)) 7f **(57)**
Form - 04138352542657 5006
Record 2000 - 1st:0 2nd:2 3rd:0 Ran:12
Pre2000 - 1st:13 2nd:12 3rd:12 Ran:74
Win Prizemoney £30,265 *Total Prizemoney* £47,843
Wins * 1999 *Nov Southw (STD) S 7f 66*
* 1999 *Spt Wolver (STD) C 7f 58*
* 1999 *Jun Wolver (STD) H 6f 58 64*
* 1999 May Leices (G-F) SH 6f 52 56
* 1999 *Jan Wolver (STD) C 7f 67* <
* 1999 *Jan Southw (STD) C 7f 62*
* 1998 *Dec Wolver (SLW) H 7f 56 59*
* 1998 *Nov Wolver (STD) S 7f 57*
* 1997 Jly Ayr (G-F) H 7f 60 64
* 1997 *Mar Wolver (STD) H 6f 68 67* <
* 1997 *Feb Wolver (STD) H 7f 64 64*
* 1996 May Haydoc (G-S) S 5f 51
* 1996 *May Wolver (STD) S 6f 51*
2000 AW 0-12: (6f, 7f 9, 8f 2) (Fibr 12)
Fair horse, effective 6 to 7f, best at 7f, - acts on Fibr, has worn blinkers. AW high 64 - 2nd of 7 giving 10lb to Elite Hope (6 Jan Wolverhampton 7f Fibr RF 0035). Becoming disappointing. A useful performer over seven furlongs on the Wolverhampton Fibresand, especially in claimers, he has won under different conditions but is not particularly consistent these days.
**R Hollinshead [13-86] D Coppenhall.*

CHARTER FLIGHT BHB 63a **RR 45f** 1181[17]
4 b g Cosmonaut - Irene's Charter (Persian Bold) 9.3f **(66)**
Form - 747070
Record 2000 - 1st:0 2nd:0 3rd:0 Ran:6
Pre2000 - 1st:1 2nd:1 3rd:1 Ran:5
Win Prizemoney £2,409 *Total Prizemoney* £3,595
Wins * 1999 *Spt Wolver (STD) H 8.5f 61 63* <
2000 Turf 0-3: (8f, 10f 2) (sft, gd, g-f) 2000 AW 0-3: (8f, 9f 2) (Fibr 3)
Fair gelding, effective 8f, - acts on Fibr, likes left handed tracks, favours tight tracks. Turf high 45. AW high 58.
**A G Newcombe [1-11] D Bass.*

CHARTERHOUSE RR 61f 1692[5]
3 b c Shirley Heights 12.1f **(76)** - Time Charter (Saritamer (USA)) 9.5f **(63)**
Form - 05
Record 2000 - 1st:0 2nd:0 3rd:0 Ran:2
2000 Turf 0-2: (10f, 12f) (g-f, frm)
Scopey, currently average colt. Turf high 61.
**J W Hills [0-2] K Y Lim & R Barnett.*

CHARTLEYS PRINCESS BHB 63f **RR 61f** 4965[22]
2 b f Prince Sabo 6.6f **(64)** - Ethel Knight (Thatch (USA)) 9.8f **(62)**
Form - 533570
Record 2000 - 1st:0 2nd:0 3rd:2 Ran:6
Win Prizemoney £0 *Total Prizemoney* £864
2000 Turf 0-6: (5f 5, 6f) (g-s, gd, g-f, frm 3)
Average filly, effective 5f, acts on g-f to frm. Turf high 61 - 3rd of 6 to Eastern Promise (19 Jun Musselburgh 5f frm RF 2091).
**K R Burke [0-6] M Nelmes-Crocker.*

CHARTWELL BHB 35f **RR** 3909[14]
3 ch g Chilibang 7f **(55)** - Star Connection (Faustus (USA)) 10f **(58)**
Form - 760
Record 2000 - 1st:0 2nd:0 3rd:0 Ran:3
2000 Turf 0-1: (6f) (frm) 2000 AW 0-2: (6f, 8f) (Equi 2)
Strong, currently little account gelding. AW high 22.
**T M Jones [0-3] Robert Le Blanc.*

CHASE THE BLUES (IRE) BHB 54f **RR 69f** 3786[18]
3 b c Blues Traveller (IRE) - Highdrive (Ballymore) 7.3f **(64)**
Form - 65700
Record 2000 - 1st:0 2nd:0 3rd:0 Ran:5
2000 Turf 0-5: (5f, 6f 2, 7f, 8f) (g-f 3, frm 2)
Leggy, average colt. Turf high 69 (began Jly).
**H Akbary [0-5] Egerton Stud Farm Ltd.*

CHASETOWN CAILIN BHB 36f27a **RR 34f 27a** 1375[8]
5 b m Suave Dancer (USA) 10.7f **(68)** - Kilvarnet (Furry Glen) 8.9f **(63)**
Form - 68
Record 2000 - 1st:0 2nd:0 3rd:0 Ran:2
Pre2000 - 1st:0 2nd:1 3rd:1 Ran:19
Win Prizemoney £0 *Total Prizemoney* £1,497
2000 AW 0-2: (7f, 8f) (Fibr 2)
Very moderate filly, effective 8 to 10f, acts on g-f to frm, likes left handed tracks, likes tight tracks. AW high 17.
**N Tinkler [0-2] Don Enrico Incisa (from Don Enrico Incisa [0-13] Oct 1999).*

CHATER FLAIR BHB 59f **RR 63f** 4192[8]
3 b g Efisio 7.7f **(69)** - Native Flair (Be My Native (USA)) 10.2f **(71)**
Form - 74178
Record 2000 - 1st:1 2nd:0 3rd:0 Ran:5
Pre2000 - 1st:0 2nd:0 3rd:0 Ran:2
Win Prizemoney £4,426 *Total Prizemoney* £4,426
Wins 2000 Jly Epsom (G-S) H 12f 55 63 <
2000 Turf 1-5: (10f, 12f 1-3, 14f) (gd 1-2, g-f, frm 2)
Workmanlike, average gelding, effective 12f, acts on gd to frm. Turf high 69 - also 1st of 12 giving 3lb to Half Tide (5 Jly Epsom RF 2546). Improved in midsummer to win an ordinary handicap at Epsom.
**W R Muir [0-1] Hong Kong Cricket Club (from A P Jarvis [1-6] Jly 2000).*

CHAUNTRY GOLD (IRE) BHB 89f **RR 69f** 3559[1]
2 b g Desert Style (IRE) - Ervedya (IRE) (Doyoun) 9f **(69)**
Form - 00321
Record 2000 - 1st:1 2nd:1 3rd:1 Ran:5
Win Prizemoney £3,445 *Total Prizemoney* £5,001
Wins * **2000** Aug Newmar (G-F) S 7f 68+ <
2000 Turf 1-5: (6f 2, 7f 1-3) (gd, g-f, frm 1-3)
Average gelding, has worn blinkers. Turf high 69 - 2nd of 4 to Mamore Gap (25 Jly Brighton 7f frm RF 3084) - also 1st of 7 from Tip The Scales (11 Aug Newmarket RF 3559).
**B J Meehan [1-5] J S Dunningham.*

CHAWENG BEACH BHB 66f59a **RR 72+f 59a** 5074[3]
2 ro f Chaddleworth (IRE) - Swallow Bay (Penmarric (USA))
Form - 016451103
Record 2000 - 1st:3 2nd:0 3rd:1 Ran:9
Win Prizemoney £12,023 *Total Prizemoney* £12,722
Wins * **2000** Spt Lingfi (G-F) H 7f 56 65
* **2000** Aug Epsom (GD) H 7f 56 72+ <
* **2000** May Lingfi (G-S) S 6f 43
2000 Turf 3-9: (5f, 6f 1-4, 7f 2-4) (g-s, gd 2-3, g-f 4, frm 1-1)
Above-average filly, effective 7f, acts on gd to frm. Turf high 72 - 1st of 9 getting 16lb from Shining Oasis (28 Aug Epsom RF 4040) - also 1st of 16 getting 13lb from Paso Doble (5 Spt Lingfield RF 4223). **R Hannon [3-9] F Coen.*

CHEEK TO CHEEK BHB 48f38a **RR 59f 38a** 3236[7]
6 b m Shavian 7.7f **(67)** - Intoxication (Great Nephew) 9.9f **(64)**
Form - 5524437
Record 2000 - 1st:0 2nd:1 3rd:1 Ran:7
Pre2000 - 1st:3 2nd:4 3rd:2 Ran:23
Win Prizemoney £14,150 *Total Prizemoney* £20,944
Wins * 1998 Jly Yarmou (GD) H 14.1f 60 63 <
* 1998 May Bath (FRM) H 13.1f 59 63 <
* *1998 Apr Wolver (STD) 12f 49*
2000 Turf 0-7: (12f, 13f, 14f 2, 15f, 16f 2) (gd 2, g-f 2, frm 3)
Fair mare, effective 14 to 16f, acted on gd to frm, best on frm. Turf high 59 - 2nd of 6 getting 21lb from Total Delight (17 Jun Sandown 14f g-f RF 2057). (DEAD) **C A Cyzer [3-30] R M Cyzer.*

CHEERFUL GROOM (IRE) BHB 29f29a **RR 35f 29a** 532[7]
9 ch g Shy Groom (USA) 8.2f **(59)** - Carange (Known Fact (USA)) 7.4f **(67)**
Form - 07
Record 2000 - 1st:0 2nd:0 3rd:0 Ran:2
Pre2000 - 1st:5 2nd:7 3rd:10 Ran:87
Win Prizemoney £14,961 *Total Prizemoney* £23,787
Wins *1998 Jly Wolver (STD) H 8.5f 56 59* <
1998 Jun Wolver (STD) H 8.5f 51 52
1998 May Wolver (STD) H 8.5f 41 50
1996 May Doncas (G-F) H 7f 36 42
2000 AW 0-2: (8f 2) (Fibr 2)
Very moderate gelding, has worn blinkers. AW high 32. Inconsistent. He has enjoyed a fair amount of success at around a mile on Fibresand, especially over Wolverhampton's extended mile, but the signs are that time has caught up with him.
**J Mackie [1-39] Bill Cahill (from D Shaw [3-43] Spt 1999).*

CHELONIA (IRE) BHB 63f **RR 63f** 4217[18]
3 gr f Turtle Island (IRE) - Whirl (Bellypha) 9.8f **(73)**
Form - 856370
Record 2000 - 1st:0 2nd:0 3rd:1 Ran:6
Pre2000 - 1st:0 2nd:0 3rd:1 Ran:1
Win Prizemoney £0 *Total Prizemoney* £1,388
2000 Turf 0-6: (7f, 8f, 9f, 10f 3) (gd, g-f 2, frm 3)
Scopey, average filly, effective 7 to 10f, acts on g-f to frm. Turf high 63 - 3rd of 10 giving 2lb to Santiburi Girl (6 Aug Newbury 10f g-f RF 3421). She should stay beyond ten furlongs, and could require some cut in the ground. **B W Hills [0-7] A N Foster.*

CHELSEA MANOR RR 116f 4562a[4]
4 b c Grand Lodge (USA) - Docklands (Theatrical)
Form - 233274
2000 Turf 0-6: (8f 2, 9f, 10f 2, 11f) (hvy 2, g-s 2, gd, g-f)
High-class colt, effective 8 to 10f, acts on hvy to gd, best on g-s. Turf high 116 - 3rd of 5 to Sendawar (21 May Longchamp 9f g-s RF 1453a). He kept on making the frame in small-field Group events last season without managing to win one. **P Bary in FR [1-7].*

CHEMCAST BHB 42f45a **RR 37f 45a** 132[5]
7 ch g Chilibang 7f **(55)** - Golden October (Young Generation) 7.7f **(63)**
Form - 1075
Record 2000 - 1st:0 2nd:0 3rd:0 Ran:1
Pre2000 - 1st:8 2nd:5 3rd:6 Ran:69
Win Prizemoney £24,277 *Total Prizemoney* £32,440
Wins * *1999 Nov Lingfi (STD) H 5f 45 46*
* 1997 Mar Mussel (SFT) H 5f 68 68? <
* *1996 Nov Lingfi (STD) H 5f 63 64*
1996 Jun Mussel (FRM) H 5f 65 66
1996 Jan Lingfi (STD) C 5f 65
1996 Jan Lingfi (STD) H 5f 55 62
2000 AW 0-1: (5f) (Equi)
Very moderate gelding, effective 5f, acted on gd - acted on Equi, often wore blinkers. (DEAD)
**J L Eyre [3-45] Neil Midgley (from D Nicholls [3-14] Aug 1996).*

CHEMICALATTRACTION (IRE) BHB 56f **RR 63f** 4460[10]
2 b g Definite Article - Domino's Nurse (Dom Racine (FR)) 9.2f **(62)**
Form - 884700
Record 2000 - 1st:0 2nd:0 3rd:0 Ran:6
Win Prizemoney £0 *Total Prizemoney* £238
2000 Turf 0-6: (5f, 7f 5) (g-s, gd, g-f, frm 3)
Average gelding. Turf high 63. **D W Barker [0-6] George Murray.*

CHEM'S TRUCE (IRE) BHB 78f **RR 84df** 5026[6]
3 b c Brief Truce (USA) 9.1f **(73)** - In the Rigging (USA) (Topsider (USA)) 8.3f **(71)**
Form - 38003454436
Record 2000 - 1st:0 2nd:0 3rd:3 Ran:11
Pre2000 - 1st:1 2nd:1 3rd:0 Ran:3
Win Prizemoney £2,882 *Total Prizemoney* £9,786
Wins * 1999 Nov Catter (SFT) 7f 82+ <
2000 Turf 0-11: (8f 4, 9f, 10f 5, 11f) (sft, g-s 4, gd 2, g-f 3, frm)
Scopey, decent colt, effective 6 to 10f, acts on g-s to frm, has worn blinkers. Turf high 84. Consistent. He was found wanting in some warm handicaps last year, but ran better when third at Salisbury in July. Stays 12 furlongs. **W R Muir [1-14] The Parkside Partnership.*

CHERISH ME BHB 73f80a **RR 66f 80a** 81[2]
4 b f Polar Falcon (USA) 9f **(74)** - Princess Zepoli (Persepolis (FR)) 6.4f **(67)**
Form - 112
Record 2000 - 1st:0 2nd:1 3rd:0 Ran:1
Pre2000 - 1st:2 2nd:1 3rd:1 Ran:6
Win Prizemoney £5,104 *Total Prizemoney* £8,988
Wins * *1999 Dec Wolver (STD) H 6f 70 78+* <

* 1999 *Nov Wolver (STD) 6f 70+*
2000 AW 0-1: (6f) (Fibr)
Scopey, above-average filly, effective 6f, - acts on Fibr.
**J G Given [2-7] J R Good.*

CHEROKEE FLIGHT BHB 53f50a RR 53f 50a 1181[11]
6 b g Green Desert (USA) 7.8f **(78)** - Totham (Shernazar) 10.2f **(73)**
Form - 0
Record 2000 - 1st:0 2nd:0 3rd:0 Ran:1
Pre2000 - 1st:4 2nd:2 3rd:3 Ran:35
Win Prizemoney £12,703 *Total Prizemoney* £17,298

Wins								
1998	Aug	Chepst	(G-F)	H	10.2f	59	63	
1997	*Aug*	*Wolver*	*(STD)*	*H*	*9.4f*	*61*	*64*	<
1997	*Jly*	*Wolver*	*(STD)*	*H*	*9.4f*	*55*	*60*	
1996	Jly	Nottin	(G-F)		5.1f		63	

2000 Turf 0-1: (10f) (g-f)
Fair gelding, has worn blinkers. Inconsistent.
**N P Littmoden [0-1] Silver Knight Exhibitions Ltd (from S Mellor [3-31] Spt 1999).*

CHEROKEEINTHEHILLS (USA) RR 4406a[3]
3 b c Cherokee Colony (USA) - Key To The Hill (USA) (Mokhieba (USA))
Form - 3
2000 AW 0-1: (9f) (Dirt)
Currently very useful colt. (1st run) - 3rd of 10 getting 8lb from Pine Dance (4 Spt Philadelphia Park 9f Dirt RF 4406a).
**R Sweeney in IRE [0-1].*

CHERRY FLYER RR 49f 1702[6]
2 b f Formidable (USA) 7.8f **(60)** - Portvasco (Sharpo) 7.7f **(59)**
Form - 6
Record 2000 - 1st:0 2nd:0 3rd:0 Ran:1
2000 Turf 0-1: (5f) (g-s)
Currently moderate filly.
**S C Williams [0-1] The Cherry Pickers Syndicate II.*

CHESHIRE RR 105f 3733a[1]
3 b g Warning 8.1f **(77)** - Dance to the Top **(93f)** (Sadler's Wells (USA)) 10f **(76)**
Form - 1
2000 Turf 1-1: (10f 1-1) (gd 1-1)
Currently Pattern-class gelding. (1st run) - 1st of 9 from Skipping (12 Aug Deauville RF 3733a). **J E Hammond in FR [1-1] P Willmott.*

CHESTER HOUSE (USA) BHB 119f RR 126f 3942a[1]
5 b h Mr Prospector (USA) 8.6f **(88)** - Toussaud (USA) (El Gran Senor (USA)) 9.6f **(76)**
Form - 1
2000 Turf 1-1: (10f 1-1) (g-s 1-1)
Top-class colt, effective 10f, acts on g-s to frm - acts on Dirt. (1st run) - 1st of 7 from Manndar (19 Aug Arlington Park RF 3942a). Consistent. After finishing third to Royal Anthem in the Juddmonte International of 1999, he was sent to the US, where he made his debut in the Breeders' Cup Classic and ran an astonishing race. Down on his nose at the start and virtually tailed off after two furlongs, he made up an enormous amount of ground to finish fourth. He built on that promise last year with his finest moment coming with a comfortable win in the Arlington Million.
**R Frankel in USA [1-2] Juddmonte Farms (from H R A Cecil [5-14] Aug 1999).*

CHESTERS BOY BHB 44f RR 49f 5160[15]
2 ch g Casteddu 7.4f **(54)** - Pear Drop (Bustino) 10.4f **(64)**
Form - 06000
Record 2000 - 1st:0 2nd:0 3rd:0 Ran:5
2000 Turf 0-4: (7f 3, 8f) (sft, g-f, frm 2) 2000 AW 0-1: (6f) (Fibr)
Moderate gelding, has worn blinkers. Turf high 49 (began Aug).
**B D Leavy [0-5] I Norman.*

CHEVENING LODGE BHB 60f70a RR 46f 70a 5027[5]
2 ch g Eagle Eyed (USA) - Meadmore Magic (Mansingh (USA)) 7.4f **(55)**
Form - 467835
Record 2000 - 1st:0 2nd:0 3rd:1 Ran:6
Win Prizemoney £0 *Total Prizemoney* £733
2000 Turf 0-6: (5f 3, 6f, 8f 2) (g-s, gd 2, g-f 3)
Average gelding, effective 8f, acts on g-f. Turf high 46 - 3rd of 10 getting 22lb from Snowey Mountain (14 Spt Yarmouth 8f g-f RF 4400). **K R Burke [0-6] Nigel Shields.*

CHEWIT BHB 76f95a RR 69f 95a 2397[R]
8 gr g Beveled (USA) 6.9f **(64)** - Sylvan Song (Song) 7.2f **(61)**
Form - 356040R
Record 2000 - 1st:0 2nd:0 3rd:0 Ran:5
Pre2000 - 1st:9 2nd:8 3rd:5 Ran:50
Win Prizemoney £48,433 *Total Prizemoney* £72,593

Wins								
* 1998	May	Goodwo	(G-F)	H	7f	84	90	
** 1998*	*Mar*	*Wolver*	*(STD)*		*7f*		*89*	
** 1997*	*Dec*	*Wolver*	*(STD)*	*H*	*7f*	*99*	*102*	<
* 1997	Aug	Ascot	(GD)	H	7f	82	83	
1996	Spt	Lingfi	(FRM)		7.6f		79+	
1996	Spt	Lingfi	(G-F)	H	7f	77	75	
1996	*Feb*	*Lingfi*	*(STD)*	*H*	*6f*	*90*	*88*	
1996	*Jan*	*Lingfi*	*(STD)*	*H*	*6f*	*80*	*88+*	

2000 Turf 0-5: (7f 4, 8f) (g-s, gd 4)
Very useful gelding, has worn blinkers. Turf high 85. Inconsistent. Not the force he was a few years ago and has not won since May 1998. He ran pretty well on his Newmarket reappearance in 2000, but seemed to have fallen out of love with the game afterwards, being recalcitrant on more than one occasion.
**G L Moore [4-31] Ballard (1834) Ltd (from A Moore [5-24] Dec 1996).*

CHEZ BONITO (IRE) BHB 43f33a RR 44f 33a 4695[18]
3 br f Persian Bold 10f **(69)** - Tycoon Aly (IRE) (Last Tycoon) 8.5f **(62)**
Form - 52054885410
Record 2000 - 1st:1 2nd:1 3rd:0 Ran:11
Win Prizemoney £2,324 *Total Prizemoney* £3,076

Wins								
* 2000	Spt	Yarmou	(G-F)	C	11.5f		44	<

2000 Turf 1-11: (7f, 9f, 10f 7, 11f 1-1, 12f) (gd 1-4, g-f 4, frm 3)
Moderate filly, effective 10 to 12f, best at 10f, acts on gd to frm, best on g-f, prefers tight tracks. Turf high 44 - 1st of 10 getting 11lb from Emali (12 Spt Yarmouth RF 4329). Consistent.
**J M Bradley [1-9] David Lewis (from J A Osborne [0-2] May 2000).*

CHEZ CHERIE BHB 102f RR 107f 3031[2]
3 ch f Wolfhound (USA) 7.3f **(71)** - Gerante (USA) (Private Account (USA)) 8.5f **(74)**
Form - 04432
Record 2000 - 1st:0 2nd:1 3rd:1 Ran:5
Pre2000 - 1st:1 2nd:0 3rd:0 Ran:3
Win Prizemoney £10,650 *Total Prizemoney* £25,339

Wins								
1999	Jly	Goodwo	(G-F)		7f		95+	<

2000 Turf 0-5: (8f, 10f 2, 12f 2) (gd, g-f 2, frm 2)
Workmanlike, Pattern-class filly, effective 10 to 12f, best at 12f, acts on gd to frm. Turf high 107 - 2nd of 10 getting 12lb from Abitara (22 Jly Newmarket 12f g-f RF 3031). Consistent. Ninth in the 1000 Guineas, she seemed suited by the step up to 12 furlongs when third in the Lancashire Oaks and ran well in a listed race over that trip on her final run.
**L M Cumani [0-5] Ivan Allan (from P W Chapple-Hyam [1-3] Oct 1999).*

CHIANG MAI (IRE) RR 113f 5212a[4]
3 b f Sadler's Wells (USA) 11.3f **(87)** - Eljazzi (Artaius (USA)) 9f **(69)**
Form - 118164
2000 Turf 2-5: (8f 1-2, 11f 1-1, 13f, 16f) (hvy, g-s 1-2, gd)
Group-class filly, effective 11 to 16f, acts on gd, and does well at Longchamp. Turf high 113 - 4th of 11 getting 12lb from Amilynx (22 Oct Longchamp 16f hvy RF 5212a) - also 1st of 6 getting 3lb from Chimes At Midnight (17 Spt Curragh RF 4525a). Winner of a Listed event on her return to action, she never got into contention in the Irish 1000 Guineas but showed better form when stepped up in trip on her next start, winning the Group Three Blandford Stakes. Emphasised that stamina is her stength when fourth in the Prix Royal-Oak on her final run. **A P O'Brien in IRE [4-7].*

CHIANTI (IRE) BHB 100f RR 103f 4988[7]
2 b c Danehill (USA) 9.1f **(79)** - Sabaah (USA) (Nureyev (USA)) 8.7f **(78)**
Form - 11637
Record 2000 - 1st:2 2nd:0 3rd:1 Ran:5
Win Prizemoney £16,166 *Total Prizemoney* £24,666

Wins								
* 2000	Jly	York	(GD)		7f		98+	<
* 2000	Jun	York	(G-F)		6f		85+	

2000 Turf 2-5: (6f 1-1, 7f 1-4) (gd 1-3, g-f, frm 1-1)

Very useful colt. Turf high 103 - also 1st of 3 giving 5lb to Rizerie (15 Jly York RF 2851). A full-brother to Desert King, he won well at York on his debut and had a simple task over a furlong more there next time. Faded disappointingly after making the running at Goodwood and pulled too hard in Doncaster's Champagne Stakes. Never got into the race when held up in the Dewhurst. He will have to learn to settle if he is to be anywhere near as good as his brother, but maturity may well enable him to do that.
**J L Dunlop [2-5] Wafic Said.*

CHIARO RR 25f 2353[13]

3 b f Safawan 6.6f **(60)** - Bold Dove (Never so Bold) 6.3f **(66)**
Form - 00
Record 2000 - 1st:0 2nd:0 3rd:0 Ran:2
2000 Turf 0-2: (7f 2) (g-f, frm)
Workmanlike, currently little account filly. Turf high 25.
**C R Egerton [0-2] Shefford Valley Stud.*

CHICAGO BEAR (IRE) BHB 46f RR 30f 130[5]

4 ch g Night Shift (USA) 8.1f **(73)** - Last Drama (IRE) (Last Tycoon) 8.5f **(62)**
Form - 5
Record 2000 - 1st:0 2nd:0 3rd:0 Ran:1
Pre2000 - 1st:1 2nd:0 3rd:0 Ran:8
Win Prizemoney £2,788 *Total Prizemoney* £2,788
Wins 1999 Jun Sandow (GD) C 10f 63 <
2000 AW 0-1: (11f) (Fibr)
Scopey, very moderate gelding, effective 10f, acts on g f, often wears blinkers (very effectively). Becoming disappointing.
**J Mackie [0-6] The Festival Dream Partnership (from P F I Cole [1-6] Jun 1999).*

CHICAGO BULLS (IRE) RR 83f 5238[5]

2 b c Darshaan 11.9f **(81)** - Celestial Melody (USA) (The Minstrel (CAN)) 10f **(72)**
Form - 45
Record 2000 - 1st:0 2nd:0 3rd:0 Ran:2
Win Prizemoney £0 *Total Prizemoney* £1,321
2000 Turf 0-2: (8f, 10f) (g-s 2)
Currently decent colt. Turf high 83 (began Spt).
**C F Wall [0-2] Ettore Landi.*

CHICAGO SOX (IRE) RR 4719a[3]

2 b c Grand Lodge (USA) - Elle Meme **(19f)** (Ela-Mana-Mou) 10.1f **(70)**
Form - 3
Record 2000 - 1st:0 2nd:0 3rd:1 Ran:1
Win Prizemoney £0 *Total Prizemoney* £1,562
2000 Turf 0-1: (8f) (g-s)
Currently very poor colt - 3rd of 10 getting 4lb from Shy Dream (24 Spt San Siro 8f g-s RF 4719a). **C F Wall [0-1].*

CHICAMBA (IRE) RR 101f 1031a[6]

3 f
Form - 6
2000 Turf 0-1: (8f) (sft)
Currently very useful filly. (1st run) - 6th of 18 to Xua (30 Apr Capannelle 8f sft RF 1031a). **M Guarnieri in ITY [0-1].*

CHICANE (IRE) RR 59f 5318[4]

2 ch c Mark of Esteem (IRE) - Rapid Repeat (IRE) (Exactly Sharp (USA))
Form - 4
Record 2000 - 1st:0 2nd:0 3rd:0 Ran:1
Win Prizemoney £0 *Total Prizemoney* £258
2000 Turf 0-1: (6f) (sft)
Currently fair colt. *L M Cumani [0-1] Lord Hartington.*

CHICANERY (IRE) BHB 45f RR 59f 5198[11]

3 b g Irish River (FR) 9f **(77)** - Deceive **(87f)** (Machiavellian (USA))
Form - 600
Record 2000 - 1st:0 2nd:0 3rd:0 Ran:3
2000 Turf 0-3: (6f, 7f 2) (g-s, gd, g-f)
Scopey, currently fair gelding. Turf high 59 (began Aug).
**Mrs L Stubbs [0-3] F W Swain.*

CHICARA BHB 60f54a RR 46f 54a 2098[8]

2 ch f Beveled (USA) 6.9f **(64)** - Chili Lass **(8f)** (Chilibang)
Form - 38
Record 2000 - 1st:0 2nd:0 3rd:1 Ran:2
Win Prizemoney £0 *Total Prizemoney* £595
2000 Turf 0-2: (5f 2) (gd, g-f)
Currently fair filly. Turf high 46. **T R Watson [0-2] J Rose.*

CHICKASAW TRAIL BHB 53f43a RR 47f 43a 4363[7]

2 ch f Be My Chief (USA) 10.2f **(62)** - Maraschino **(49f 36a)** (Lycius (USA))
Form - 887
Record 2000 - 1st:0 2nd:0 3rd:0 Ran:3
2000 Turf 0-3: (7f 3) (gd 2, g-f)
Currently moderate filly. Turf high 47 (began Aug).
**R Hollinshead [0-3] Anthony White.*

CHIEF CASHIER BHB 76f RR 86f 5134[6]

5 b g Persian Bold 10f **(69)** - Kentfield (Busted) 10.2f **(61)**
Form - 5007146006
Record 2000 - 1st:1 2nd:0 3rd:0 Ran:10
Pre2000 - 1st:3 2nd:2 3rd:1 Ran:17
Win Prizemoney £23,860 *Total Prizemoney* £28,953
Wins * 2000 Jly Bath (G-S) H 10.2f 74 79+
* 1999 Apr Epsom (SFT) H 10.1f 75 83+ <
* 1998 Spt Epsom (SFT) H 10.1f 71 75
* 1998 Jly Epsom (G-F) H 10.1f 69 72
2000 Turf 1-10: (10f 1-9, 12f) (sft 2, gd 1-3, g-f 3, frm 2)
Useful gelding, effective 10 to 13f, best at 10f, acts on g-s to frm, prefers tight tracks. Turf high 82 - 4th of 12 giving 4lb to Polar Red (19 Jly Kempton 10f frm RF 2937) - also 1st of 11 giving 4lb to Real Estate (10 Jly Bath RF 2664). Becoming disappointing. A useful handicapper on his day, he landed the City And Suburban Handicap on his second start of '99 and has a fine record at Epsom. Suited by soft ground, conditions just came right for him before winning at Bath in July. **G B Balding [4-30] Surgical Spirits.*

CHIEF JUSTICE RR 35f 143[4]

3 b g Be My Chief (USA) 10.2f **(62)** - Supreme Kingdom (Take A Reef) 7.5f **(59)**
Form - 884
Record 2000 - 1st:0 2nd:0 3rd:0 Ran:3
Pre2000 - 1st:0 2nd:0 3rd:0 Ran:1
2000 AW 0-3: (7f, 8f, 9f) (Fibr 3)
Leggy, very moderate gelding. AW high 12.
**N P Littmoden [0-4] J R Good.*

CHIEF MONARCH BHB 76f RR 77f 2061[12]

6 b g Be My Chief (USA) 10.2f **(62)** - American Beauty (Mill Reef (USA)) 10.5f **(78)**
Form - 250230
Record 2000 - 1st:0 2nd:2 3rd:1 Ran:6
Pre2000 - 1st:1 2nd:1 3rd:1 Ran:14
Win Prizemoney £3,517 *Total Prizemoney* £15,979
Wins 1997 Jly Sandow (G-F) 8.1f 75 <
2000 Turf 0-6: (8f 2, 10f 3, 12f) (sft, g-s 2, gd, g-f, frm)
Above-average gelding. Turf high 77.
**R A Fahey [3-20] Tommy Staunton (from B Smart [1-8] Spt 1997).*

CHIEF OF JUSTICE BHB 64f69a RR 73f 69a 5016[7]

3 b c Be My Chief (USA) 10.2f **(62)** - Clare Court (Glint of Gold) 9.3f **(66)**
Form - 113807
Record 2000 - 1st:2 2nd:0 3rd:1 Ran:6
Pre2000 - 1st:0 2nd:0 3rd:0 Ran:3
Win Prizemoney £4,865 *Total Prizemoney* £5,267
Wins * 2000 *Mar Wolver (STD) H 12f 63 74* <
*** 2000** *Feb Southw (STD) H 11f 58 61*
2000 Turf 0-3: (12f 2, 15f) (g-s, gd, frm) 2000 AW 2-3: (9f, 11f 1-1, 12f 1-1) (Fibr 2-3)
Leggy, above-average colt, effective 12f, acts on frm - acts on Fibr, prefers left handed tracks, prefers tight tracks. Turf high 73 (1st run) - 3rd of 10 giving 2lb to Merryvale Man (29 Mar Catterick 12f frm RF 0549). AW high 74 - 1st of 5 getting 6lb from Merryvale Man (4 Mar Wolverhampton RF 0411). **D Shaw [2-9] J C Fretwell.*

CHIEF WALLAH BHB 54f RR 61df 5111[11]

4 b g Be My Chief (USA) 10.2f **(62)** - Arusha (IRE) (Dance of Life (USA)) 7f **(66)**

Form - 042600
Record 2000 - 1st:0 2nd:1 3rd:0 Ran:6
Pre2000 - 1st:0 2nd:0 3rd:0 Ran:1
Win Prizemoney £0 *Total Prizemoney* £1,456
2000 Turf 0-5: (12f, 14f, 16f 2, 17f) (g-s, gd, g-f 2, hrd) 2000 AW 0-1: (12f) (Equi)
Average gelding, effective 17f, acts on hrd, likes tight tracks. Turf high 61 (began Jly). **D R C Elsworth [0-7] Raymond Tooth.*

CHIEF WARDANCE BHB 59f **RR 57f** 4216[10]
6 ch g Profilic - Dolly Wardance (Warpath) 12.3f **(52)**
Form - 530
Record 2000 - 1st:0 2nd:0 3rd:1 Ran:3
Win Prizemoney £0 *Total Prizemoney* £633
2000 Turf 0-3: (10f 2, 11f) (gd, frm 2)
Fair gelding. Turf high 57 (began Aug).
**Mrs S Lamyman [3-21] Mrs Jennifer Woodward.*

CHIKO BHB 55f59a **RR 62f 59a** 3505[14]
3 b g Afif - Walsham Witch (Music Maestro) 7.7f **(66)**
Form - 000
Record 2000 - 1st:0 2nd:0 3rd:0 Ran:2
Pre2000 - 1st:1 2nd:0 3rd:0 Ran:9
Win Prizemoney £2,221 *Total Prizemoney* £3,044
Wins 1999 Mar Doncas (G-S) S 5f 62 <
2000 Turf 0-2: (8f 2) (g-f, frm)
Unfurnished, average gelding, effective 5 to 6f, acts on g-s, often wears blinkers. Turf high 28 (began Aug). Becoming disappointing. **J G Given [0-2] J Starbuck (from J L Harris [1-9] Nov 1999).*

CHILDREN'S CHOICE (IRE) BHB 30f42a **RR 34f 42a** 3213[11]
9 b m Taufan (USA) 8.3f **(65)** - Alice Brackloon (USA) (Melyno) 10.4f **(55)**
Form - 2631340800
Record 2000 - 1st:1 2nd:0 3rd:2 Ran:8
Pre2000 - 1st:9 2nd:9 3rd:6 Ran:69
Win Prizemoney £34,841 *Total Prizemoney* £47,359
Wins * **2000** *Jan Wolver (STD) S 14.8f . 47*
* 1999 Aug Redcar (G-S) S 14.1f 39
* 1999 Aug Bright (G-F) SH 11.9f 41 42
1998 Oct Newmar (G-S) H 12f 50 54
1997 Oct Nottin (G-F) H 14.1f 50 57
1997 Jly Yarmou (G-F) H 16f 49 51
1996 Aug Yarmou (G-F) H 14.1f 52 56
2000 Turf 0-4: (12f 2, 14f 2) (g-f, frm 3) 2000 AW 1-4: (15f 1-2, 16f 2) (Fibr 1-4)
Moderate mare, effective 12 to 17f, best at 16f, acts on gd to hrd - acts on Fibr, has worn blinkers, likes left handed tracks, and likes Nottingham. Turf high 34. AW high 47 - 1st of 9 getting 5lb from Swan Hunter (20 Jan Wolverhampton RF 0124).
**J Pearce [3-25] & Mrs S Fernandes (from D Morris [1-11] Jan 1999).*

CHILI PEPPER BHB 48f56a **RR 50df 56a** 4654[9]
3 b f Chilibang 7f **(55)** - Game Germaine (Mummy's Game) 8.2f **(60)**
Form - 610300
Record 2000 - 1st:1 2nd:0 3rd:1 Ran:6
Pre2000 - 1st:0 2nd:1 3rd:0 Ran:7
Win Prizemoney £2,194 *Total Prizemoney* £3,255
Wins * **2000** *Mar Wolver (STD) H 6f 53 55* <
2000 Turf 0-2: (6f, 7f) (hvy, g-f) 2000 AW 1-4: (6f 1-2, 7f, 8f) (Fibr 1-4)
Unfurnished, fair filly, effective 5f, acts on gd, has worn blinkers. Turf high 17. AW high 55. **A Smith [1-13] Mrs R Auchterlounie.*

CHILLI BHB 41f43a **RR 52df 43a** 5025[12]
3 br g Most Welcome 8.6f **(66)** - So Saucy **(35f 41a)** (Teenoso (USA)) 9.9f **(72)**
Form - 33233035750
Record 2000 - 1st:0 2nd:1 3rd:5 Ran:11
Pre2000 - 1st:0 2nd:0 3rd:0 Ran:4
Win Prizemoney £0 *Total Prizemoney* £2,996
2000 Turf 0-6: (10f 3, 11f 2, 14f) (sft, g-s, gd 2, g-f 2) 2000 AW 0-5: (8f 3, 10f 2) (Equi 3, Fibr 2)
Workmanlike, fair gelding, effective 8f, - acts on Equi, has worn blinkers. Turf high 54. AW high 52 (1st run) - 3rd of 9 getting 4lb from Will Iveson (29 Jan Lingfield 8f Equi RF 0182). Inconsistent.
**C E Brittain [0-15] C E Brittain.*

CHILLIAN BHB 25f **RR 22f** 3429[16]
4 b g Chilibang 7f **(55)** - Five Islands (Bairn (USA)) 7.7f **(59)**
Form - 85000000
Record 2000 - 1st:0 2nd:0 3rd:0 Ran:8
Pre2000 - 1st:0 2nd:0 3rd:0 Ran:8
2000 Turf 0-6: (5f 3, 6f, 7f 2) (gd 2, frm 3, hrd) 2000 AW 0-2: (5f, 6f) (Fibr 2)
Scopey, little account gelding. Turf high 22. AW high 18.
**M Brittain [0-16] Mel Brittain.*

CHILLI BOY RR 49f 3739[7]
2 gr g Belfort (FR) 6.7f **(53)** - Con Carni (Blakeney) 10.5f **(64)**
Form - 787
Record 2000 - 1st:0 2nd:0 3rd:0 Ran:3
2000 Turf 0-2: (6f, 7f) (g-f, frm) 2000 AW 0-1: (5f) (Fibr)
Currently moderate gelding. Turf high 49 (began Jly).
**J R Turner [0-3] J R Turner.*

CHILWORTH (IRE) BHB 43f48a **RR 61f 48a** 5162[10]
3 ch g Shalford (IRE) 7.8f **(63)** - Close the Till (Formidable (USA)) 9.2f **(63)**
Form - 08560427003700
Record 2000 - 1st:0 2nd:1 3rd:1 Ran:14
Pre2000 - 1st:0 2nd:0 3rd:0 Ran:3
Win Prizemoney £0 *Total Prizemoney* £1,107
2000 Turf 0-12: (7f 8, 8f 2, 9f, 10f) (sft 3, g-f 6, frm 2, hrd) 2000 AW 0-2: (7f 2) (Equi 2)
Scopey, average gelding, effective 7f, acts on g-f, often wears blinkers. Turf high 61. AW high 27. **T M Jones [0-17] John Crouch.*

CHIMES AT MIDNIGHT (USA) RR 110f 5355a[12]
3 b c Danzig (USA) 8.1f **(88)** - Surely Georgie's (USA) (Alleged (USA)) 10f **(76)**
Form - 541310023620
2000 Turf 2-12: (8f 2, 10f 1-3, 11f, 12f 1-3, 14f 2, 15f) (hvy, g-s, gd 2-7, g-f, frm)
Group-class colt, effective 11 to 15f, acts on frm, often wears blinkers (effectively). Turf high 118 - 3rd of 11 to Millenary (9 Spt Doncaster 15f frm RF 4310). Inconsistent. Irish-trained, he had a busy season and won twice in July, but his best effort was when third in the St Leger. Ended the season disappointingly when asked to race on very soft ground.
**L Comer in IRE [1-9] L Comer (from A P O'Brien in IRE [1-3] Jly 2000).*

CHIMNEY DUST BHB 80f **RR 82f** 1670[8]
3 b c Pelder (IRE) - Evening Falls **(45f 60a)** (Beveled (USA)) 9f **(59)**
Form - 08
Record 2000 - 1st:0 2nd:0 3rd:0 Ran:2
Pre2000 - 1st:1 2nd:1 3rd:0 Ran:5
Win Prizemoney £2,048 *Total Prizemoney* £3,725
Wins * 1999 Aug Warwic (GD) 6.8f 82 <
2000 Turf 0-2: (7f 2) (g-s, g-f)
Leggy, decent colt, effective 7f, acts on g-s to frm. Turf high 74.
**G C H Chung [1-7] Osvaldo Pedroni.*

CHINABERRY BHB 44f38a **RR 44f 38a** 4123[5]
6 b m Soviet Star (USA) 8.6f **(74)** - Crimson Conquest (USA) (Diesis) 9.3f **(69)**
Form - 040025
Record 2000 - 1st:0 2nd:1 3rd:0 Ran:6
Pre2000 - 1st:1 2nd:3 3rd:3 Ran:30
Win Prizemoney £2,788 *Total Prizemoney* £8,930
Wins * 1999 *Jan Southw (STD) H 8f 48 56* <
2000 Turf 0-3: (7f, 8f 2) (g-s, frm 2) 2000 AW 0-3: (7f, 8f 2) (Fibr 3)
Moderate mare, effective 8f, - acts on Fibr. Turf high 44. AW high 26. Inconsistent. Won his first start of last year on Fibresand, but did not add to it.
**M Brittain [1-32] Northgate Lodge Racing Club (from C E Brittain [0-4] Jly 1997).*

CHINA CASTLE BHB 51f90a **RR 51f 90a** 404[1]
7 b g Sayf El Arab (USA) 8.2f **(57)** - Honey Plum (Kind of Hush) 10.1f **(62)**
Form - 25476621
Record 2000 - 1st:1 2nd:1 3rd:0 Ran:5
Pre2000 - 1st:18 2nd:4 3rd:7 Ran:63
Win Prizemoney £90,553 *Total Prizemoney* £101,699

Wins * 2000 *Mar Lingfi (STD) H* 12f 86 89
* 1999 Jly Hamilt (FRM) H 11.1f 48 51
* 1999 *Mar Southw (STD) H* 12f 101 103 <
* 1999 *Feb Wolver (STD) H* 12f 94 96
* 1999 *Feb Wolver (STD) H* 12f 90 94
* 1999 *Jan Wolver (STD) H* 12f 73 86
* 1999 *Jan Southw (STD) H* 11f 73 93
* 1999 *Jan Southw (STD)* 12f 76
* 1999 *Jan Southw (STD) H* 11f 73 73
* 1998 *Jan Wolver (STD) H* 12f 71 75
* 1998 *Jan Southw (STD)* 12f 75
* 1997 *Jan Southw (STD) H* 12f 67 82+
* 1997 *Jan Southw (STD) H* 11f 67 87
* 1997 *Jan Southw (STD) H* 11f 67 77
* 1996 *Feb Southw (STD) C* 11f 67+
* 1996 *Jan Wolver (STD) H* 8.5f 68 72
* 1996 *Jan Lingfi (STD) H* 10f 54 64
* 1996 *Jan Southw (STD) H* 7f 54 72
2000 AW 1-5: (8f, 11f, 12f 1-3) (Equi 1-3, Fibr 2)
Useful gelding, effective 9 to 12f, best at 12f, - acts on Fibr, likes left handed tracks, excels at Southwell, likes Wolverhampton. AW high 89. Consistent. Modest on the Turf, he is a smart handicapper on the All-Weather, being particularly effective on Fibresand. Best over a mile and a half these days, especially early in the year, he needs plenty of driving but is genuine in a finish.
**P C Haslam [19-71] J M Davis & Middleham Park Racing I.*

CHINA FAIN (IRE) RR 2564[6]
2 b f Emarati (USA) 6.6f **(63)** - Oriental Air (IRE) **(49f 48a)** (Taufan (USA)) 7f **(57)**
Form - 6
Record 2000 - 1st:0 2nd:0 3rd:0 Ran:1
2000 Turf 0-1: (6f) (g-f)
Currently very poor filly. **K McAuliffe [0-1] Mrs H Raw.*

CHINA RED (USA) BHB 70f87a RR 72f 87a 5159[6]
6 br g Red Ransom (USA) 8.6f **(83)** - Akamare (FR) (Akarad (FR)) 9f **(76)**
Form - 770010076
Record 2000 - 1st:1 2nd:0 3rd:0 Ran:9
Pre2000 - 1st:5 2nd:3 3rd:1 Ran:21
Win Prizemoney £38,283 *Total Prizemoney* £46,706
Wins 2000 Aug Epsom (GD) C 8.5f 72
1999 *May Lingfi (STD) H* 8f 90 95 <
1999 *May Lingfi (STD) H* 8f 78 89
1998 Jly Goodwo (GD) H 8f 82 85
1998 May Goodwo (G-F) H 8f 78 82
1997 Apr Nottin (G-F) 8.2f 85
2000 Turf 1-8: (7f 2, 8f 2, 9f 1-4) (sft 2, g-s, gd 2, g-f 1-2, frm) 2000 AW 0-1: (9f) (Dirt)
Useful gelding, effective 8f, - acts on Equi, prefers left handed tracks, prefers tight tracks. Turf high 72. He is a game front-runner and goes particularly well on turning tracks (Goodwood suits him admirably). Best on fast ground, he should win another race or two. **J J Quinn [0-4] Mrs Marie Taylor (from J W Hills [6-26] Aug 2000).*

CHINATOWN (IRE) RR 105f 2238[3]
3 br c Marju (IRE) 9.2f **(76)** - Sunley Saint (Artaius (USA)) 9f **(69)**
Form - 53
Record 2000 - 1st:0 2nd:0 3rd:1 Ran:2
Pre2000 - 1st:1 2nd:0 3rd:1 Ran:3
Win Prizemoney £3,452 *Total Prizemoney* £13,748
Wins 1999 Aug Newcas (GD) 7f 90 <
2000 Turf 0-2: (9f, 10f) (gd 2)
Scopey, Pattern-class colt. Turf high 104 - 3rd of 8 to Port Vila (24 Jun Ascot 10f gd RF 2238). Fair eforts in listed company, but the sort of horse for whom opportunities are limited.
**Sir Michael Stoute [0-2] Ivan Allan & Sir Alex Ferguson (from P W Chapple-Hyam [1-3] Spt 1999).*

CHINA VISIT (USA) RR 108f 2111[10]
3 b c Red Ransom (USA) 8.6f **(83)** -Furajet (USA) (The Minstrel (CAN)) 10f **(72)**
Form - 160
Record 2000 - 1st:1 2nd:0 3rd:0 Ran:3
Win Prizemoney £182,297 *Total Prizemoney* £182,297
Wins 2000 *Mar Nad Al (FST)* 9f 125 <
2000 Turf 0-1: (8f) (gd) 2000 AW 1-2: (9f 1-1, 10f) (Dirt 1-2)
Currently top-class colt. AW high 125 (1st run) - 1st of 16 from Bachir (25 Mar Nad Al Sheba RF 0576a). He was hugely impressive when slamming a big field in the UAE Derby, but could finish only sixth in the Kentucky Derby. He was then very disappointing at Ascot, where something looked amiss, and subsequently failed to reappear.
**S bin Suroor [0-1] Godolphin (from S bin Suroor in UAE [1-2] May 2000).*

CHIN UP (IRE) BHB 55f RR 62f 1481[7]
3 b f Port Lucaya - Tiempo (King of Spain) 7.8f **(52)**
Form - 07
Record 2000 - 1st:0 2nd:0 3rd:0 Ran:2
Pre2000 - 1st:0 2nd:0 3rd:0 Ran:3
2000 Turf 0-1: (5f) (hrd) 2000 AW 0-1: (7f) (Fibr)
Scopey, average filly. **M H Tompkins [0-5] www raceworld co uk.*

CHIPPEWA (FR) RR 13f 4679[9]
6 b m Cricket Ball (USA) 7.9f **(75)** - Vaika (FR) (Cosmopolitan (FR))
Form - 0
Record 2000 - 1st:0 2nd:0 3rd:0 Ran:1
2000 Turf 0-1: (12f) (g-s)
Poor mare. **M C Pipe [4-15] The Dionysius Partnership.*

CHIQUITA (IRE) BHB 79f79a RR 79f 79a 5141[6]
3 ch f College Chapel - Council Rock (General Assembly (USA)) 10f **(68)**
Form - 50082106
Record 2000 - 1st:1 2nd:1 3rd:0 Ran:8
Pre2000 - 1st:2 2nd:1 3rd:1 Ran:5
Win Prizemoney £12,302 *Total Prizemoney* £15,713
Wins * **2000** Aug Ripon (GD) H 6f 76 79 <
1999 Oct Sandow (HVY) H 5f **75 75**
1999 *Spt Wolver (STD) H* 5f 73 74
2000 Turf 1-8: (6f 1-6, 7f 2) (g-s 3, gd, g-f 2, frm 1-2)
Unfurnished, above-average filly, effective 5 to 6f, best at 6f, acts on sft to frm - acts on Fibr, best on frm. Turf high 79 - 1st of 19 getting 2lb from Budelli (28 Aug Ripon RF 4049). Consistent.
**J A R Toller [1-8] Buckingham Thoroughbreds I (from W J Haggas [2-5] Oct 1999).*

CHISPA BHB 72f78a RR 71f 78a 5117[5]
2 b f Imperial Frontier (USA) 7f **(65)** - Digamist Girl (IRE) (Digamist (USA))
Form - 8075
Record 2000 - 1st:0 2nd:0 3rd:0 Ran:4
2000 Turf 0-3: (5f 2, 6f) (g-s, g-f 2) 2000 AW 0-1: (5f) (Fibr)
Useful filly. Turf high 71. **R Hannon [0-4] Mrs Betty Valentine.*

CHIST (USA) BHB 103f RR 107?f 4450[4]
5 b br h Lear Fan (USA) 10.4f **(80)** - Morna (Blakeney) 10.5f **(64)**
Form - 4
Record 2000 - 1st:0 2nd:0 3rd:0 Ran:1
Pre2000 - 1st:1 2nd:1 3rd:1 Ran:6
Win Prizemoney £3,655 *Total Prizemoney* £10,168
Wins * 1998 Apr Leices (SFT) 10f 86+ <
2000 Turf 0-1: (11f) (gd)
Pattern-class colt. (DEAD) **M H Tompkins [1-7] Mrs Jane Bailey.*

CHOC ICE (IRE) RR 100f 4844a[3]
2 b f Kahyasi 12.9f **(74)** - Sherkiya (IRE) (Goldneyev (USA))
Form - 333
2000 Turf 0-3: (8f 3) (gd 2, g-f)
Currently very useful filly. Turf high 100 (began Aug) - 3rd of 10 to Amonita (1 Oct Longchamp 8f gd RF 4844a). A high-class juvenile in 1999, her best effort was when in the frame in the Marcel Boussac. She should get a little further next season, and should be up to winning in Pattern company.
**R Collet in FR [0-3] Mlle M Vidal.*

CHOCOLATE FOG (USA) RR 48f 3810[7]
2 b f Mt Livermore (USA) 7.7f **(90)** - Native Fancy (USA) (Our Native (USA)) 11.2f **(63)**
Form - 05857
Record 2000 - 1st:0 2nd:0 3rd:0 Ran:5
2000 Turf 0-4: (5f, 6f 2, 7f) (gd, g-f 2, frm) 2000 AW 0-1: (7f) (Fibr)
Moderate filly. Turf high 48.

**R M H Cowell [0-5] Dr St John Collier & Mrs Sherry Collier.*

CHOCOLATE ICE BHB 46f52a RR 52a 3044[P]

7 b g Shareef Dancer (USA) 10.1f **(67)** - Creake (Derring-Do) 11.1f **(64)**
Form - P
Record 2000 - 1st:0 2nd:0 3rd:0 Ran:1
Pre2000 - 1st:0 2nd:0 3rd:3 Ran:16
Win Prizemoney £0 *Total Prizemoney* £2,649
2000 Turf 0-1: (13f) (g-f)
Very poor gelding, had worn blinkers. (DEAD)
**F Jordan [0-1] Graham Brown (from R J O'Sullivan [0-4] Jly 1997).*

CHOCSTAW (IRE) BHB 62f66a RR 66a 5007[1]

3 b c Mtoto 11.5f **(71)** - Cwm Deri (IRE) (Alzao (USA)) 7.1f **(68)**
Form - 70541
Record 2000 - 1st:1 2nd:0 3rd:0 Ran:5
Win Prizemoney £2,296 *Total Prizemoney* £2,566
Wins * 2000 *Oct Southw (STD) 12f 68+* <
2000 Turf 0-4: (8f 2, 12f 2) (g-s, g-f, frm 2) 2000 AW 1-1: (12f 1-1) (Fibr 1-1)
Workmanlike, average colt. Turf high 72. (1st run) - 1st of 16 getting 7lb from Love Diamonds (16 Oct Southwell RF 5007).
**Sir Michael Stoute [1-5] Sir Evelyn De Rothschild.*

CHOK-DI BHB 29f41a RR 31f 41a 1960[15]

4 b g Beveled (USA) 6.9f **(64)** - Pendona (Blue Cashmere) 6.4f **(54)**
Form - 4780000000
Record 2000 - 1st:0 2nd:0 3rd:0 Ran:10
Pre2000 - 1st:0 2nd:0 3rd:0 Ran:11
Win Prizemoney £0 *Total Prizemoney* £219
2000 Turf 0-7: (5f 3, 6f 2, 7f, 9f) (sft, gd 2, g-f, frm 3) 2000 AW 0-3: (5f, 6f 2) (Fibr 3)
Leggy, moderate gelding, effective 6f, acts on frm, has worn blinkers. Turf high 31. AW high 40.
**Mrs M Reveley [0-21] The Desert Rats Racing Club.*

CHOOKIE HEITON (IRE) RR 63f 2803[2]

2 br g Fumo Di Londra (IRE) - Royal Wolff (Prince Tenderfoot (USA)) 9f **(61)**
Form - 2
Record 2000 - 1st:0 2nd:1 3rd:0 Ran:1
Win Prizemoney £0 *Total Prizemoney* £1,075
2000 Turf 0-1: (5f) (g-f)
Currently average gelding. (1st run) - 2nd of 6 to River Raven (14 Jly Hamilton 5f g-f RF 2803).
**I Semple [0-1] Hamilton Park Members Syndicate.*

CHORALLI RR 54f 5132[17]

2 ch f Inchinor 8.9f **(64)** - Salanka (IRE) **(65df 56a)** (Persian Heights)
Form - 00
Record 2000 - 1st:0 2nd:0 3rd:0 Ran:2
2000 Turf 0-2: (6f 2) (sft, g-f)
Currently fair filly. Turf high 54 (began Oct).
**D R C Elsworth [0-2] Sir Stanley and Lady Grinstead.*

CHORUS BHB 70f65a RR 71f 65a 5199[12]

3 b f Bandmaster (USA) - Name That Tune **(43f 36a)** (Fayruz)
Form - 200632321670100
Record 2000 - 1st:2 2nd:3 3rd:2 Ran:15
Pre2000 - 1st:0 2nd:2 3rd:0 Ran:11
Win Prizemoney £7,074 *Total Prizemoney* £14,347
Wins * 2000 Oct Windso (G-S) H 5f 67 70 <
*** 2000** Aug Sandow (GD) 5f 70 <
2000 Turf 2-14: (5f 2-10, 6f 4) (hvy, g-s 2, gd 1-5, g-f 1-3, frm 3) 2000 AW 0-1: (6f) (Fibr)
Strong, above-average filly, effective 5 to 6f, best at 5f, acts on hvy to frm, has worn blinkers, likes right handed tracks, likes Windsor. Turf high 79 (1st run) - 2nd of 15 to Footprints (12 Apr Warwick 6f hvy RF 0688) - also 1st of 7 from Star Princess (9 Aug Sandown RF 3508).
**B R Millman [2-26] In The Know.*

CHORUS GIRL BHB 43f RR 50f 3739[8]

2 ch f Dancing Spree (USA) 8f **(59)** - Better Still (IRE) (Glenstal (USA)) 10.1f **(64)**
Form - 543846508
Record 2000 - 1st:0 2nd:0 3rd:1 Ran:9
Win Prizemoney £0 *Total Prizemoney* £888
2000 Turf 0-9: (5f 2, 6f 3, 7f 4) (g-s, gd 2, g-f 4, frm 2)
Fair filly. Turf high 50. Consistent.
**K A Ryan [0-6] W B Imison (from M W Easterby [0-3] Jun 2000).*

CHOTO MATE (IRE) BHB 85f RR 89f 4968[12]

4 ch c Brief Truce (USA) 9.1f **(73)** - Greatest Pleasure (Be My Guest (USA)) 9.3f **(67)**
Form - 04107080
Record 2000 - 1st:1 2nd:0 3rd:0 Ran:8
Pre2000 - 1st:1 2nd:0 3rd:1 Ran:6
Win Prizemoney £19,108 *Total Prizemoney* £20,763
Wins * 2000 Jun Sandow (G-F) H 7.1f 86 89 <
* 1998 May Goodwo (G-F) 5f 85+
2000 Turf 1-8: (6f 2, 7f 1-3, 8f 3) (g-s 2, gd 2, g-f 1-2, frm 2)
Scopey, useful colt, effective 7 to 8f, acts on g-f to frm. Turf high 89 - 1st of 11 giving 4lb to Temeraire (17 Jun Sandown RF 2055). A winner on fast ground at Goodwood as a juvenile, but then lost his form completely and missed the whole of the following season. Caused something of a surprise when winning at Sandown on his third start of last term. Best on fast ground.
**R Hannon [2-14] Vernon Carl Matalon.*

CHRIS'S LITTLE LAD (IRE) BHB 61f56a RR 70f 56a 3016[12]

3 ch g Hamas (IRE) 8f **(72)** - Jeema (Thatch (USA)) 9.8f **(62)**
Form - 2770
Record 2000 - 1st:0 2nd:1 3rd:0 Ran:4
Pre2000 - 1st:0 2nd:0 3rd:0 Ran:3
Win Prizemoney £0 *Total Prizemoney* £536
2000 Turf 0-3: (8f 3) (gd, frm 2) 2000 AW 0-1: (8f) (Fibr)
Workmanlike, above-average gelding, effective 8f, acts on frm. Turf high 70 (1st run) - 2nd of 9 to Mamzug (22 May Bath 8f frm RF 1357).
**W R Muir [0-7] Hugh Smith.*

CHRISTENSEN (IRE) BHB 44f44a RR 37f 44a 4663a[8]

4 ch f Simply Great (FR) 11.9f **(61)** - Waterstown Girl (Ahonoora) 8.1f **(73)**
Form - 0077408
Record 2000 - 1st:0 2nd:0 3rd:0 Ran:7
Pre2000 - 1st:0 2nd:1 3rd:1 Ran:10
Win Prizemoney £0 *Total Prizemoney* £1,978
2000 Turf 0-6: (5f, 6f, 7f 3, 8f) (hvy, sft, g-s, gd, g-f, frm) 2000 AW 0-1: (6f) (Fibr)
Very moderate filly, effective 6 to 8f, acts on g-s to frm, has worn blinkers. Turf high 37.
**E Lynam in IRE [0-15] Eugene O'Connell (from D Nicholls [0-2] Apr 2000).*

CHRISTIANSTED (IRE) BHB 78f RR 83f 4987[11]

5 ch g Soviet Lad (USA) 9.4f **(63)** - How True (Known Fact (USA)) 7.4f **(67)**
Form - 617570
Record 2000 - 1st:1 2nd:0 3rd:0 Ran:6
Pre2000 - 1st:3 2nd:1 3rd:2 Ran:10
Win Prizemoney £15,450 *Total Prizemoney* £23,349
Wins * 2000 Jun Mussel (FRM) H 16f 78 83
* 1999 Jun Nottin (GD) H 14.1f 68 75
* 1999 Apr Ripon (G-F) H 12.3f 63 69
1998 May Killar (SFT) C 12f 90 <
2000 Turf 1-6: (12f, 16f 1-3, 18f, 20f) (gd 3, frm 1-3)
Decent gelding, effective 14 to 16f, best at 16f, acts on gd to frm, best on frm, excels at Newcastle. Turf high 83 - 1st of 6 getting 2lb from Star Rage (3 Jun Musselburgh RF 1682). Consistent. He scored in good style on very fast ground at Musselburgh on his second start of the campaign and was not disgraced in the Northumberland Plate. Stayed on after meeting trouble in running at Sandown.
**Ferdy Murphy [6-15] John Duddy (from Ms J Morgan in IRE [0-1] Spt 1998).*

CHRISTMAS MORNING (IRE) BHB 49f RR 56f 5004[15]

2 b g Brief Truce (USA) 9.1f **(73)** - Maid O'Cannie **(56f 68a)** (Efisio)
Form - 70000
Record 2000 - 1st:0 2nd:0 3rd:0 Ran:5
2000 Turf 0-5: (5f 2, 6f, 7f, 8f) (g-s 2, g-f, frm, hrd)
Fair gelding, has worn blinkers. Turf high 56.
**M W Easterby [0-5] Lord & Lady Manton.*

CHRISTOPHERSSISTER BHB 44f50a **RR 40f 50a** 4871[7]

3 br f Timeless Times (USA) 6.1f **(56)** - Petite Elite (Anfield) 8.5f **(59)**
Form - 2717004000067
Record 2000 - 1st:1 2nd:0 3rd:0 Ran:11
Pre2000 - 1st:0 2nd:1 3rd:0 Ran:6
Win Prizemoney £2,091 *Total Prizemoney* £3,019
Wins 2000 *Jan Southw (STD) C 6f 59 <*
2000 Turf 0-7: (5f 3, 6f 3, 7f) (sft, gd, g-f 2, frm 2, hrd) 2000 AW 1-4: (5f, 6f 1-3) (Fibr 1-4)
Scopey, fair filly, effective 6f, - acts on Fibr, has worn blinkers. Turf high 58. AW high 59 (1st run) - 1st of 12 getting 9lb from Risky Gem (31 Jan Southwell RF 0189).
**N Bycroft [0-14] Paul Dixon (from D Nicholls [0-2] Mar 2000).*

CHRYSOLITE (IRE) BHB 30f60a **RR 42f 60a** 4757[10]

5 ch g Kris 10f **(75)** - Alamiya (IRE) (Doyoun) 9f **(69)**
Form - 00
Record 2000 - 1st:0 2nd:0 3rd:0 Ran:2
Pre2000 - 1st:1 2nd:0 3rd:1 Ran:13
Win Prizemoney £5,711 *Total Prizemoney* £6,865
Wins * 1998 May Lingfi (GD) H 9f 74 78 <
2000 Turf 0-2: (10f 2) (g-s, gd)
Moderate gelding. Turf high 42. Becoming disappointing.
**B W Hills [1-14] Mrs B W Hills (from M E Sowersby [0-8] Jun 2000).*

CHURCH BELLE (IRE) **RR 60f** 4642[17]

2 gr f College Chapel - Siva (FR) (Bellypha) 9.8f **(73)**
Form - 8278660
Record 2000 - 1st:0 2nd:1 3rd:0 Ran:7
Win Prizemoney £0 *Total Prizemoney* £809
2000 Turf 0-7: (5f 2, 6f 2, 7f 3) (gd 2, g-f 3, frm 2)
Average filly, effective 7f, acts on gd. Turf high 60.
**R Hannon [0-7] E K Cleveland.*

CHURCH FARM FLYER (IRE) BHB 56f61a **RR 58f 61a** 587[4]

3 b f College Chapel - Young Isabel (IRE) (Last Tycoon) 8.5f **(62)**
Form - 6311236324
Record 2000 - 1st:0 2nd:2 3rd:2 Ran:6
Pre2000 - 1st:2 2nd:0 3rd:1 Ran:7
Win Prizemoney £5,457 *Total Prizemoney* £9,061
Wins * 1999 *Dec Wolver (STD) H 7f 46 58 <*
* 1999 *Dec Lingfi (STD) S 8f 58 <*
2000 Turf 0-1: (10f) (gd) 2000 AW 0-5: (7f 2, 8f 2, 9f) (Equi, Fibr 4)
Light-framed, above-average filly, effective 8f, - acts on Fibr, prefers left handed tracks, prefers tight tracks. AW high 77 - 3rd of 8 giving 6lb to Lord Harley (29 Feb Wolverhampton 8f Fibr RF 0382). Modest form on turf, but got off the mark in a seller on the Lingfield Equitrack in December. Followed up in a better race at Wolverhampton and is a bit better than a plater, but is pretty much exposed. **C N Allen [2-13] Felix Snell.*

CHURCHILL'S SHADOW (IRE) BHB 48f45a **RR 31f 45a** 3609[14]

6 b g Polish Precedent (USA) 9f **(73)** - Shy Princess (USA) (Irish River (FR)) 8.6f **(78)**
Form - 35000
Record 2000 - 1st:0 2nd:0 3rd:0 Ran:4
Pre2000 - 1st:4 2nd:3 3rd:1 Ran:25
Win Prizemoney £10,104 *Total Prizemoney* £13,727
Wins * 1999 Jly Chepst (G-F) SH 8.1f 45 47
* 1998 May Doncas (GD) H 7f 45 49
* 1997 *Nov Lingfi (STD) H 7f 44 53 <*
* 1997 *Nov Lingfi (STD) H 7f 44 46*
2000 Turf 0-1: (8f) (frm) 2000 AW 0-3: (8f 3) (Equi 3)
Very moderate gelding, effective 7 to 8f, best at 7f, acts on g-f to frm, best on frm. AW high 37. Consistent.
**B A Pearce [4-35] A Leg Each Partnership.*

CHURCH MICE (IRE) BHB 79f **RR 75f** 5320[2]

2 br f Petardia 8.2f **(58)** - Negria (IRE) (Al Hareb (USA))
Form - 24215364132
Record 2000 - 1st:2 2nd:3 3rd:2 Ran:11
Win Prizemoney £6,323 *Total Prizemoney* £10,540
Wins 2000 Spt Haydoc (HVY) H 6f 70 68 <
2000 May Leices (SFT) 5f 67
2000 Turf 2-8: (5f 1-3, 6f 1-3, 7f 2) (sft 1-3, g-s, gd 1-1, g-f 2, frm) 2000 AW 0-3: (5f, 6f, 7f) (Fibr 3)
Above-average filly, effective 6 to 7f, acts on sft to g-s, mostly wears blinkers (extremely effectively). Turf high 81 - 2nd of 22 giving 8lb to Leatherback (4 Nov Doncaster 7f sft RF 5320). AW high 67. Consistent. Fairly consistent at a modest level, she might not stay seven furlongs.
**W H Tinning [0-1] W H Tinning (from M L W Bell [2-10] Oct 2000).*

CHURLISH CHARM BHB 114f **RR 119f** 4985[6]

5 b h Niniski (USA) 13.2f **(67)** - Blushing Storm (USA) (Blushing Groom (FR)) 10.3f **(76)**
Form - 732361246
Record 2000 - 1st:1 2nd:2 3rd:2 Ran:9
Pre2000 - 1st:4 2nd:1 3rd:1 Ran:10
Win Prizemoney £104,285 *Total Prizemoney* £154,133
Wins * 2000 Aug Salisb (G-F) 14.1f 109+
* 1999 May York (SFT) G2 13.9f 115 <
* 1998 Spt Newbur (GD) H 10f 00 101
* 1998 Jun Goodwo (GD) 12f 95
* 1998 May Newmar (G-F) 12f 81
2000 Turf 1-9: (12f, 14f 1-3, 16f 3, 18f, 20f) (g-s 2, gd 4, g-f, frm 1-2)
High-class colt, effective 14 to 20f, acts on g-s to frm, best on gd, excels at York. Turf high 119 - 2nd of 7 giving 5lb to Persian Punch (29 May Sandown 16f g-s RF 1535). Consistent. Surprise winner of last season's Yorkshire Cup, he has been campaigned in the top staying events since. He has often run well, such as when just beaten by Enzeli in the Doncaster Cup, but his only victory came in a Salisbury conditions event. **R Hannon [5-19] Mohamed Suhail.*

Churlish Charm was consistent but only managed the one success last season.

CIBENZE BHB 63f53a **RR 69f 53a** 3767[8]

3 b f Owington - Maria Cappuccini (Siberian Express (USA)) 8.8f **(65)**
Form - 0642672688
Record 2000 - 1st:0 2nd:2 3rd:0 Ran:10
Pre2000 - 1st:0 2nd:1 3rd:1 Ran:5
Win Prizemoney £0 *Total Prizemoney* £4,199
2000 Turf 0-10: (6f 2, 7f 6, 8f, 9f) (gd, g-f 4, frm 5)
Scopey, average filly, effective 7 to 8f, best at 7f, acts on g-f to frm, best on frm. Turf high 69 - 2nd of 21 giving 10lb to Magic Babe (8 Jun Newbury 7f frm RF 1816).
**M R Channon [0-15] Miletrian Plc.*

CICATRIX RR 127^{6}
6 ch g Anvari - Like Amber (Aragon) 8.1f **(60)**
Form - 6
Record 2000 - 1st:0 2nd:0 3rd:0 Ran:1
2000 AW 0-1: (8f) (Fibr)
Formerly very poor gelding. **J L Eyre [0-4] John Ashcroft.*

CIEL DE REVE (USA) BHB 25f35a **RR ?f 35a** 3451^{11}
6 b g Septieme Ciel (USA) - Reve de Reine (USA) (Lyphard (USA)) 9.9f **(72)**
Form - 0000
Record 2000 - 1st:0 2nd:0 3rd:0 Ran:3
Pre2000 - 1st:0 2nd:0 3rd:0 Ran:9
2000 Turf 0-2: (10f, 12f) (gd, frm) 2000 AW 0-1: (9f) (Fibr)
Very moderate gelding, has worn blinkers. Becoming disappointing. **K C Comerford [0-14] Alan Brackley.*

CIELITO LINDO RR 86f 5128^{7}
2 b f Pursuit of Love 9.5f **(69)** - Seal Indigo (IRE) (Glenstal (USA)) 10.1f **(64)**
Form - 27
Record 2000 - 1st:0 2nd:1 3rd:0 Ran:2
Win Prizemoney £0 *Total Prizemoney* £1,735
2000 Turf 0-2: (6f, 7f) (sft, g-f)
Currently useful filly. Turf high 86 (began Spt).
**R Hannon [0-2] Geoff Howard-Spink & Lindy Regis.*

CINCINNATI (IRE) RR 3839^{14}
2 ch c Tagula (IRE) - Pretty Sally (IRE) **(18f 50a)** (Polish Patriot (USA))
Form - 0
Record 2000 - 1st:0 2nd:0 3rd:0 Ran:1
2000 Turf 0-1: (6f) (g-f)
Currently very poor colt. **B S Rothwell [0-1] Norman Jackson.*

CINDER HILLS BHB 62f60a **RR 62f 60a** 527^{2}
5 ch m Deploy 11.4f **(67)** - Dame du Moulin (Shiny Tenth) 9.2f **(56)**
Form - 2
Record 2000 - 1st:0 2nd:1 3rd:0 Ran:1
Pre2000 - 1st:2 2nd:2 3rd:1 Ran:14
Win Prizemoney £6,610 *Total Prizemoney* £10,743
Wins * 1998 Apr Ripon (SFT) H 12.3f 53 64 <
* 1998 Apr Ripon (SFT) H 10f 53 60
2000 Turf 0-1: (16f) (g-s)
Average filly. (1st run) - 2nd of 15 giving 16lb to Swiftway (28 Mar Newcastle 16f g-s RF 0527).
**M W Easterby [3-22] Winton Bloodstock Ltd.*

CINDESTI (IRE) BHB 37f60a **RR 40f 60a** 4779^{10}
4 b c Barathea (IRE) - Niamh Cinn Oir (IRE) (King of Clubs) 7.1f **(57)**
Form - 700000
Record 2000 - 1st:0 2nd:0 3rd:0 Ran:6
Pre2000 - 1st:2 2nd:0 3rd:0 Ran:7
Win Prizemoney £4,496 *Total Prizemoney* £4,793
Wins * 1999 *Spt Wolver (STD) 14.8f 64* <
* 1999 *Spt Wolver (STD) H 12f 56 58*
2000 Turf 0-5: (14f 2, 16f 2, 17f) (g-s 2, gd 3) 2000 AW 0-1: (12f) (Fibr)
Scopey, average colt, effective 12 to 15f, - acts on Fibr, has worn blinkers, likes left handed tracks, likes tight tracks. Turf high 45. Becoming disappointing. Showed much-improved form when tried on Fibresand, winning twice at Wolverhampton in September. He seemed to get the extended 14 furlongs well on the second occasion. Has since won over hurdles, but his efforts on turf since returning to the Flat have not been encouraging.
**B A McMahon [3-15] Mrs J McMahon (from L M Cumani [0-2] Oct 1998).*

CINDY'S HERO (USA) RR $5326a^{4}$
2 br f Sea Hero (USA) - Cindazanno (USA) (Alleged (USA)) 10f **(76)**
Form - 4
2000 AW 0-1: (9f) (Dirt)
Currently very useful filly. (1st run) - 4th of 12 to Caressing (4 Nov Churchill Downs 9f Dirt RF 5326a).
**D Hofmans in USA [0-1] E & T Baxter.*

CINEMA POINT (IRE) BHB 35f42a **RR 33f 42a** 2086^{14}
3 b g Doyoun 10.7f **(69)** - Airport (Warpath) 12.3f **(52)**
Form - 82040
Record 2000 - 1st:0 2nd:1 3rd:0 Ran:5
Pre2000 - 1st:0 2nd:0 3rd:0 Ran:3
Win Prizemoney £0 *Total Prizemoney* £545
2000 Turf 0-2: (8f, 10f) (frm, hrd) 2000 AW 0-3: (8f, 10f, 11f) (Equi, Fibr 2)
Lengthy, moderate gelding, effective 8f, - acts on Fibr, has worn blinkers, likes tight tracks. Turf high 5. AW high 41 - 2nd of 12 getting 8lb from Amelia Jess (31 Jan Southwell 8f Fibr RF 0192). Inconsistent. **M H Tompkins [0-8] www raceworld co uk.*

CINNAMON COURT (IRE) BHB 62f **RR 54f** 2639^{11}
3 b f College Chapel - Henrietta Street (IRE) **(53f)** (Royal Academy (USA))
Form - 100000
Record 2000 - 1st:1 2nd:0 3rd:0 Ran:6
Pre2000 - 1st:0 2nd:0 3rd:0 Ran:2
Win Prizemoney £3,965 *Total Prizemoney* £3,965
Wins * **2000** Mar Leices (GD) 7f 67 <
2000 Turf 1-6: (7f 1-4, 8f 2) (gd 1-2, g-f 2, frm 2)
Light-framed, fair filly, effective 7f, acts on gd. Turf high 68 - also 1st of 14 from Night Empress (30 Mar Leicester RF 0567). Consistent. Showed little in two starts at two, but caused a real surprise when winning a Leicester maiden on her reappearance at 33/1. There seemed no fluke about it but she was then found out in handicap company. **J R Arnold [1-8] Prof Green.*

CIRCLE OF LIGHT BHB 93f **RR 104f** 4145^{7}
3 b f Anshan 8.2f **(63)** - Cockatoo Island (High Top) 10.2f **(67)**
Form - 3233847
Record 2000 - 1st:0 2nd:1 3rd:3 Ran:7
Pre2000 - 1st:1 2nd:0 3rd:0 Ran:2
Win Prizemoney £2,165 *Total Prizemoney* £13,389
Wins * 1999 Aug Lingfi (G-F) 7.6f 85+ <
2000 Turf 0-7: (7f, 8f 3, 10f 2, 12f) (g-s, gd 2, g-f 4)
Scopey, very useful filly, effective 8 to 10f, best at 10f, acts on gd to g-f, best on gd. Turf high 104 - 2nd of 14 to Whitefoot (19 May Newbury 10f gd RF 1305). A half sister to Champion Hurdle winner Collier Bay, she ran some good races in listed company but is rather one-paced. **P W D'Arcy [1-9] Lord Derby.*

CIRCLE OF WOLVES RR 72f 2257^{10}
2 ch c Wolfhound (USA) 7.3f **(71)** - Misty Halo (High Top) 10.2f **(67)**
Form - 00
Record 2000 - 1st:0 2nd:0 3rd:0 Ran:2
2000 Turf 0-2: (6f, 7f) (g-f, frm)
Currently above-average colt. Turf high 72.
**Bob Jones [0-2] The Circle of Wolves Partnership.*

CIRCLET RR 41f 3436^{9}
2 ch f Lion Cavern (USA) 7.5f **(74)** - Chiltern Court (USA) (Topsider (USA)) 8.3f **(71)**
Form - 0
Record 2000 - 1st:0 2nd:0 3rd:0 Ran:1
2000 Turf 0-1: (6f) (g-f)
Currently moderate filly. **J W Hills [0-1] Wyck Hall Stud.*

CIRCUIT LIFE (IRE) BHB 53f **RR 59f** 4890^{3}
2 ch g Rainbows For Life (CAN) 9.3f **(64)** - Alicedale (USA) (Trempolino (USA)) 12f **(71)**
Form - 853066623433
Record 2000 - 1st:0 2nd:1 3rd:4 Ran:12
Win Prizemoney £0 *Total Prizemoney* £2,922
2000 Turf 0-11: (5f, 6f 5, 7f 3, 8f 2) (hvy, gd, g-f 4, frm 5) 2000 AW 0-1: (6f) (Fibr)
Fair gelding, effective 6 to 8f, acts on hvy to frm, has worn blinkers. Turf high 59. **A Berry [0-12] David Fish.*

CIRCUS DANCE RR 112f $3939a^{4}$
3 b c Sadler's Wells (USA) 11.3f **(87)** - Dance by Night (Northfields (USA)) 9f **(72)**
Form - 34
2000 Turf 0-2: (10f, 12f) (gd, g-f)
Currently Group-class colt. Turf high 112. **A Fabre in FR [0-2].*

CIRCUS PARADE (IRE) BHB 75f65a **RR 74f 65a** 4584^{5}
3 b c Night Shift (USA) 8.1f **(73)** - Circus Maid (IRE) (High Top) 10.2f

(67)
Form - 50365
Record 2000 - 1st:0 2nd:0 3rd:1 Ran:5
Win Prizemoney £0 *Total Prizemoney* £610
2000 Turf 0-4: (9f, 10f 2, 11f) (gd, g-f, frm 2) 2000 AW 0-1: (10f) (Equi)
Unfurnished, above-average colt. Turf high 74.
**J H M Gosden [0-5] R E Sangster & A K Collins.*

CIRO (USA) RR 123f 5331a[6]
3 ch c Woodman (USA) 9.7f **(77)** - Gioconda (ARG) (Good Manners (USA))
Form - 3163116
2000 Turf 3-7: (10f 1-1, 11f 1-2, 12f 1-4) (hvy, g-s 1-1, gd 1-3, frm 1-2)
Very high-class colt, effective 10 to 12f, best at 12f, acts on g-s to frm, best on frm, has worn blinkers. Turf high 123 - 6th of 13 getting 4lb from Kalanisi (4 Nov Churchill Downs 12f frm RF 5331a) - also 1st of 10 giving 8lb to Whata Brainstorm (24 Spt Belmont Park RF 4835a). Improving. Awarded a weak renewal of the Group One Grand Criterium on the controversial disqualification of Barathea Guest in 1999, he was sent to France for his first runs last term, winning the Prix Lupin in heavy ground before finishing a well-beaten sixth in the French Derby. He then finished a distant third in the Irish Derby before being transferred to America, where he took his first two starts, including the Grade One Secretariat Stakes, before finishing sixth in the Breeders' Cup Turf. Looks likely to develop into a top Turf horse next year.
**C Clement in USA [1-2] Jayeff B Stables (from A P O'Brien in IRE [4-8] Aug 2000).*

Currently little account filly. Turf high 27.
**P C Haslam [0-3] Mrs B M Hawkins.*

CITRUS MAGIC BHB 57f **RR 60f** 4923[3]
3 b c Cosmonaut - Up All Night **(6f)** (Green Desert (USA)) 8.6f **(78)**
Form - 487723
Record 2000 - 1st:0 2nd:1 3rd:1 Ran:6
Win Prizemoney £0 *Total Prizemoney* £1,537
2000 Turf 0-4: (9f, 10f 2, 12f) (g-f 2, frm 2) 2000 AW 0-2: (13f, 16f) (Equi 2)
Scopey, average colt. Turf high 60. AW high 61 (began Spt).
**K Bell [0-6] Brian Footer.*

CITY BANK DUDLEY BHB 36f32a **RR 41f 32a** 5168[8]
3 b g Noble Patriarch 12.2f **(43)** - Derry's Delight (Mufrij)
Form - 03646477508
Record 2000 - 1st:0 2nd:0 3rd:1 Ran:11
Win Prizemoney £0 *Total Prizemoney* £623
2000 Turf 0-10: (6f 2, 7f 2, 8f 4, 10f 2) (sft, gd 2, g-f 4, frm 2, hrd) 2000 AW 0-1: (8f) (Fibr)
Light-framed, moderate gelding. Turf high 53.
**N Wilson [0-11] J B Slatcher.*

CITY FLYER BHB 50f60a **RR 55f 60a** 4492[9]
3 br c Night Shift (USA) 8.1f **(73)** - Al Guswa (Shernazar) 10.2f **(73)**
Form - 5000601000
Record 2000 - 1st:1 2nd:0 3rd:0 Ran:10

Ciro (centre), spent most of his time in France and is now hitting the right note in America

CIRO'S PEARL (IRE) BHB 31f **RR 37f** 2569[8]
6 b m Petorius 8f **(66)** - Cut it Fine (USA) (Big Spruce (USA)) 11f **(71)**
Form - 8
Record 2000 - 1st:0 2nd:0 3rd:0 Ran:1
Pre2000 - 1st:2 2nd:1 3rd:3 Ran:25
Win Prizemoney £8,067 *Total Prizemoney* £15,469
Wins 1997 Jun Goodwo (GD) H 12f 77 79 <
1997 May Lingfi (G-F) H 10f 74 78
2000 Turf 0-1: (18f) (g-f)
Very moderate mare, has worn blinkers.
**A W Carroll [0-10] Mrs J Lewis (from M H Tompkins [2-20] Nov 1998).*

CITRUS (IRE) RR 27f 2250[7]
2 b br f Idris (IRE) - Law Student (Precocious) 8.6f **(62)**
Form - 047
Record 2000 - 1st:0 2nd:0 3rd:0 Ran:3
2000 Turf 0-2: (5f, 7f) (gd, frm) 2000 AW 0-1: (6f) (Fibr)

Pre2000 - 1st:0 2nd:0 3rd:0 Ran:5
Win Prizemoney £3,029 *Total Prizemoney* £3,548
Wins * 2000 Aug Carlis (GD) H 8f 45 55 <
2000 Turf 1-9: (7f 3, 8f 1-4, 10f 2) (gd 2, g-f 1-4, frm 3) 2000 AW 0-1: (9f) (Fibr)
Light-framed, fair colt, effective 6f, acts on frm, has worn blinkers, likes right handed tracks. Turf high 55.
**J D Bethell [1-15] N D Fisher.*

CITY GAMBLER BHB 53f62a **RR 50f 62a** 3612[9]
6 b m Rock City 8.8f **(62)** - Sun Street (Ile de Bourbon (USA)) 10.1f **(67)**
Form - 507100
Record 2000 - 1st:1 2nd:0 3rd:0 Ran:6
Pre2000 - 1st:3 2nd:3 3rd:6 Ran:39
Win Prizemoney £12,388 *Total Prizemoney* £21,842
Wins * 2000 Jly Yarmou (GD) H 10.1f 46 50
* 1998 Aug Leices (GD) H 10f 57 62
* 1997 Aug Leices (GD) H 8f 67 73 <

* 1997 Aug Lingfi (G-F) 7.6f 57
2000 Turf 1-6: (8f, 10f 1-4, 12f) (gd 1-3, g-f, frm 2)
Fair mare, effective 10 to 12f, acts on gd to frm, likes left handed tracks, favours tight tracks. Turf high 50.
**G C Bravery [4-45] J J May.*

CITY GUILD BHB 39f **RR 26f** 2614[16]
4 b g Saddlers' Hall (IRE) 10.5f **(65)** - Indubitable (Sharpo) 7.7f **(59)**
Form - 000
Record 2000 - 1st:0 2nd:0 3rd:0 Ran:3
Pre2000 - 1st:0 2nd:0 3rd:0 Ran:4
Win Prizemoney £0 *Total Prizemoney* £353
2000 Turf 0-3: (10f, 11f 2) (gd 2, g-f)
Scopey, little account gelding. Turf high 26.
**G B Balding [0-10] Miss B Swire.*

CITY OF LONDON (IRE) RR 46f 4441[6]
2 ch c Grand Lodge (USA) - Penny Fan **(34f)** (Nomination) 7f **(60)**
Form - 6
Record 2000 - 1st:0 2nd:0 3rd:0 Ran:1
2000 Turf 0-1: (6f) (gd)
Currently moderate colt. **J W Payne [0-1] C Cotran.*

CITY PLAYER BHB 81f **RR 46f** 5243[8]
2 ch c Komaite (USA) 6.9f **(61)** - Blink Naskra (USA) (Naskra (USA)) 8.8f **(69)**
Form - 08
Record 2000 - 1st:0 2nd:0 3rd:0 Ran:2
2000 Turf 0-1: (6f) (sft) 2000 AW 0-1: (6f) (Fibr)
Currently fair colt. **Sir Mark Prescott [0-2] Ne'er Do Wells II.*

CITY PURSUIT BHB 49f **RR 52f** 1352[P]
4 b g Pursuit of Love 9.5f **(69)** - Diabaig **(70f)** (Precocious) 8.6f **(62)**
Form - P0P
Record 2000 - 1st:0 2nd:0 3rd:0 Ran:3
Pre2000 - 1st:0 2nd:0 3rd:0 Ran:3
Win Prizemoney £0 *Total Prizemoney* £256
2000 Turf 0-2: (10f, 11f) (hvy, g-f) 2000 AW 0-1: (12f) (Fibr)
Lengthy, fair gelding. Turf high 15.
**J Pearce [0-6] Harvey White Partnership II.*

CITY REACH BHB 59f69a **RR 50f 69a** 4992[1]
4 b g Petong 7.6f **(58)** - Azola (IRE) (Alzao (USA)) 7.1f **(68)**
Form - 3241305103311
Record 2000 - 1st:4 2nd:0 3rd:3 Ran:11
Pre2000 - 1st:0 2nd:2 3rd:1 Ran:7
Win Prizemoney £9,565 *Total Prizemoney* £12,883
Wins *** 2000** *Oct Wolver (STD) H* *6f 64 70* <
*** 2000** *Spt Wolver (STD) H* *6f 56 63*
*** 2000** Jly Bright (FRM) 5.3f 50
*** 2000** *Jan Southw (STD)* *7f 60*
2000 Turf 1-4: (5f 1-2, 6f, 7f) (g-s, g-f, frm 1-1, hrd) 2000 AW 3-7: (6f 2-4, 7f 1-3) (Fibr 3-7)
Scopey, above-average gelding, effective 6 to 7f, best at 6f, - acts on Fibr, often wears blinkers (extremely effectively), likes left handed tracks, likes tight tracks. Turf high 50. AW high 70 - 1st of 13 giving 2lb to Teofilio (14 Oct Wolverhampton RF 4992) - also 1st of 12 getting 7lb from Gay Breeze (30 Spt Wolverhampton RF 4758). **P J Makin [4-18] T W Wellard Partnership.*

CITY STANDARD (IRE) BHB 60f **RR 58f** 668[8]
4 b g Rainbow Quest (USA) 11.2f **(81)** - City Fortress (Troy) 10.4f **(68)**
Form - 008
Record 2000 - 1st:0 2nd:0 3rd:0 Ran:3
Pre2000 - 1st:0 2nd:0 3rd:2 Ran:5
Win Prizemoney £0 *Total Prizemoney* £1,319
2000 Turf 0-2: (13f, 14f) (gd 2) 2000 AW 0-1: (14f) (Fibr)
Workmanlike, fair gelding, effective 12f, acts on frm, has worn blinkers, favours tight tracks. Turf high 37. Becoming disappointing.
**S Dow [0-3] Byerley Bloodstock (from Sir Michael Stoute [0-5] Spt 1999).*

CITY ZIP (USA) RR 5330a[7]
2 ch f Carson City (USA) - Baby Zip (USA) (Relaunch (USA)) 6f **(92)**
Form - 7
2000 AW 0-1: (9f) (Dirt)
Currently very useful. (1st run) - 7th of 14 to Macho Uno (4 Nov Churchill Downs 9f Dirt RF 5330a).
**Linda Rice in USA [0-1] Bowling, Lakeland Farm & C Thompson.*

CIVIL LIBERTY BHB 56f64a **RR 55f 64a** 238[P]
7 b g Warning 8.1f **(77)** - Libertine (Hello Gorgeous (USA)) 9.7f **(63)**
Form - 45P
Record 2000 - 1st:0 2nd:0 3rd:0 Ran:3
Pre2000 - 1st:3 2nd:6 3rd:0 Ran:29
Win Prizemoney £9,166 *Total Prizemoney* £17,544
Wins * 1999 *Spt Wolver (STD) H* *9.4f 56 71*
1997 Spt Nottin (G-F) H 10f 60 64
1996 Aug Windso (G-F) 8.3f 79 <
2000 AW 0-3: (8f, 9f, 11f) (Fibr 3)
Average gelding, effective 9f, - acted on Fibr, had worn blinkers, liked left handed tracks, liked tight tracks. AW high 66. (DEAD)
**D Sasse [1-12] Christopher Ranson (from G Lewis [2-20] Oct 1997).*

CLADANTOM (IRE) BHB 34f41a **RR 34f 41a** 1529[19]
4 b f High Estate 10.5f **(66)** - Riflebird (IRE) (Runnett) 7f **(59)**
Form - 0600000
Record 2000 - 1st:0 2nd:0 3rd:0 Ran:5
Pre2000 - 1st:1 2nd:1 3rd:0 Ran:9
Win Prizemoney £4,238 *Total Prizemoney* £5,045
Wins * 1999 Jly Thirsk (FRM) 7f 68 <
2000 Turf 0-4: (7f 4) (gd 2, frm 2) 2000 AW 0-1: (7f) (Fibr)
Leggy, very moderate filly, effective 7f, acts on frm, has worn blinkers, likes left handed tracks, likes tight tracks. Turf high 34. Becoming disappointing.
**D W Barker [1-11] L H Gilmurray & T J Docherty (from W Jarvis [0-1] May 1999).*

CLAIM GEBAL CLAIM BHB 40f51a **RR 42f 51a** 4209[4]
4 b g Ardkinglass 5f **(64)** - Infra Blue (IRE) **(35f)** (Bluebird (USA)) 7.5f **(69)**
Form - 081673234
Record 2000 - 1st:1 2nd:1 3rd:2 Ran:9
Pre2000 - 1st:0 2nd:1 3rd:3 Ran:16
Win Prizemoney £2,772 *Total Prizemoney* £6,115
Wins *** 2000** Jly Hamilt (G-F) C 9.2f 39 <
2000 Turf 1-9: (8f 3, 9f 1-5, 11f) (gd 4, g-f 1-2, frm 3)
Neat, moderate gelding, effective 7f, acts on gd, has worn blinkers, likes tight tracks. Turf high 42 (began Jly). Consistent.
**P Monteith [1-9] Stan Moffat (from Mrs A Duffield [0-16] Aug 1999).*

CLANBROAD BHB 76f73a **RR 79f 73a** 4727[1]
2 ch c Clantime 6.6f **(57)** - Under the Wing (Aragon) 8.1f **(60)**
Form - 41401
Record 2000 - 1st:2 2nd:0 3rd:0 Ran:5
Win Prizemoney £6,631 *Total Prizemoney* £6,845
Wins *** 2000** Spt Lingfi (SFT) C 6f 79 <
*** 2000** Aug Leices (G-F) 6f 73
2000 Turf 2-5: (6f 2-4, 7f) (gd 1-1, frm 1-3, hrd)
Above-average colt. Turf high 79 (began Jly) - 1st of 18 giving 17lb to Astairedotcom (29 Spt Lingfield RF 4727) - also 1st of 13 getting 9lb from Kai One (9 Aug Leicester RF 3488).
**Mrs A J Perrett [2-5] Derek Broad.*

CLAN CHIEF BHB 57f **RR 59f** 5112[21]
7 b g Clantime 6.6f **(57)** - Mrs Meyrick (Owen Dudley) 8.3f **(61)**
Form - 028050
Record 2000 - 1st:0 2nd:1 3rd:0 Ran:6
Pre2000 - 1st:4 2nd:6 3rd:4 Ran:27
Win Prizemoney £29,113 *Total Prizemoney* £44,233
Wins 1996 Spt Goodwo (GD) H 6f 79 81 <
1996 Aug Goodwo (G-F) H 5f 63 75
1996 Jly Sandow (G-F) H 5f 63 70
1996 Jly Sandow (G-F) H 5f 58 60
2000 Turf 0-6: (5f 4, 6f 2) (gd 2, g-f, frm 3)
Fair gelding, has worn blinkers. Turf high 59. Enjoyed a great season in 1996, with four victories culminating in the valuable William Hill Sprint Cup at Goodwood. He has found life harder since, but is weighted to win again.
**M Blanshard [0-3] Gathering Of The Clan (from J R Arnold [4-30] Jly 2000).*

CLANSINGE BHB 57f52a **RR 60f 52a** 5008[14]
2 ch f Clantime 6.6f **(57)** - North Pine (Import) 6.6f **(68)**
Form - 5313400672360
Record 2000 - 1st:1 2nd:1 3rd:3 Ran:13
Win Prizemoney £2,352 *Total Prizemoney* £4,922
Wins * 2000 Jun Beverl (G-F) C 5f 51 <
2000 Turf 1-11: (5f 1-8, 6f 3) (g-s, gd 4, g-f 2, frm 3, hrd 1-1) 2000 AW 0-2: (6f 2) (Fibr 2)
Average filly, effective 5 to 6f, best at 6f, acts on gd to hrd, best on gd, has worn blinkers. Turf high 60 - 2nd of 20 getting 4lb from Piccolo Rose (22 Spt Lingfield 6f gd RF 4581) - also 1st of 9 giving 10lb to Fayz Slipper (14 Jun Beverley RF 1949). AW high 30 (began Oct). **A Berry [1-13] The Monkey Partnership.*

CLANSMAN BHB 30f **RR 46f** 4877[9]
3 ch g Clantime 6.6f **(57)** - Chili Lass **(8f)** (Chillibang)
Form - 0007000
Record 2000 - 1st:0 2nd:0 3rd:0 Ran:7
Pre2000 - 1st:0 2nd:0 3rd:0 Ran:4
Win Prizemoney £0 *Total Prizemoney* £275
2000 Turf 0-7: (5f 4, 6f 2, 10f) (g-s 2, gd 2, g-f, frm, hrd)
Scopey, moderate gelding, has worn blinkers. Turf high 46. Becoming disappointing.
**J L Harris [0-2] J L Harris (from T R Watson [0-9] Aug 2000).*

CLARA BLUE BHB 28f **RR 15f** 4372[13]
4 gr f Alhijaz 7.7f **(57)** - Hazy Kay (IRE) (Treasure Kay)
Form - 00600
Record 2000 - 1st:0 2nd:0 3rd:0 Ran:4
Pre2000 - 1st:1 2nd:0 3rd:0 Ran:15
Win Prizemoney £2,070 *Total Prizemoney* £2,070
Wins 1998 Oct Folkes (G-S) 5f 76 <
2000 Turf 0-3: (5f 2, 6f) (g-f, frm 2) 2000 AW 0-1: (7f) (Equi)
Neat, little account filly. Turf high 15 (began Jun).
**R Ingram [0-10] Epsom Sporting Proposals Ltd (from T D McCarthy [1-9] May 1999).*

CLARANET BHB 98f78a **RR 107f 78a** 4549[6]
3 ch f Arazi (USA) 9.2f **(74)** - Carmita (Caerleon (USA)) 8.6f **(71)**
Form - 3310002546
Record 2000 - 1st:1 2nd:1 3rd:2 Ran:10
Pre2000 - 1st:0 2nd:0 3rd:1 Ran:2
Win Prizemoney £4,459 *Total Prizemoney* £17,702
Wins * 2000 Apr Windso (HVY) 8.3f **74** <
2000 Turf 1-9: (6f, 7f 3, 8f 1-4, 10f) (g-s 1-3, gd 3, g-f, frm 2) 2000 AW 0-1: (9f) (Fibr)
Workmanlike, Pattern-class filly, effective 7f, acts on gd, likes tight tracks. Turf high 107. Inconsistent. Stepped up on her previous form when a fine second at Glorious Goodwood, and by no means disgraced in her subsequent runs.
**K Mahdi [1-12] Greenfield Stud.*

CLARENDON (IRE) BHB 75f **RR 78f** 4461[14]
4 ch c Forest Wind (USA) - Sparkish (IRE) (Persian Bold) 9.3f **(66)**
Form - 706223030
Record 2000 - 1st:0 2nd:2 3rd:2 Ran:9
Pre2000 - 1st:2 2nd:0 3rd:1 Ran:14
Win Prizemoney £12,234 *Total Prizemoney* £19,021
Wins * 1999 Jly Ascot (G-F) H 10f 69 73 <
* 1999 Jun Chepst (G-F) H 10.2f 62 65+
2000 Turf 0-9: (10f 4, 12f 3, 13f 2) (g-s, gd 2, g-f 5, frm)
Well made, above-average colt, effective 10 to 12f, best at 10f, acts on gd to frm, has worn blinkers, likes right handed tracks, excels at Chepstow. Turf high 78 - 3rd of 11 giving 7lb to Capriolo (30 Aug York 12f gd RF 4104). Consistent. He has run some good races this term and has been suited by the drop back to ten furlongs. Needs a little help from the Handicapper.
**V Soane [2-15] Mrs Jane Gillett (from J D Bethell [0-8] Nov 1998).*

CLARINCH CLAYMORE BHB 58f62a **RR 56f 62a** 5294[1]
4 b g Sabrehill (USA) 8.5f **(64)** - Salu **(58f)** (Ardross) 10.6f **(68)**
Form - 72380421
Record 2000 - 1st:1 2nd:2 3rd:1 Ran:7
Pre2000 - 1st:1 2nd:1 3rd:1 Ran:13
Win Prizemoney £7,217 *Total Prizemoney* £10,060
Wins * 2000 Nov Mussel (G-S) H 12f 51 56 <
* 1999 Aug Beverl (GD) H 8.5f 47 55
2000 Turf 1-4: (10f, 11f, 12f 1-2) (g-s 1-2, gd, frm) 2000 AW 0-3: (11f, 12f, 16f) (Fibr 3)
Scopey, average gelding, effective 8 to 12f, best at 12f, acts on g-s to g-f - acts on Fibr, best on g-s, likes left handed tracks. Turf high 56 (began Spt) - 1st of 16 giving 7lb to Ocean Drive (1 Nov Musselburgh RF 5294). AW high 54 - 3rd of 11 getting 9lb from Swagger (28 Jan Southwell 12f Fibr RF 0176).
**J M Jefferson [2-20] John Donald.*

CLARION BHB 89f92a **RR 90f 92a** 5153[1]
2 ch c First Trump - Area Girl (Jareer (USA)) 5.9f **(75)**
Form - 21213111
Record 2000 - 1st:5 2nd:2 3rd:1 Ran:8
Win Prizemoney £15,652 *Total Prizemoney* £18,747
Wins * 2000 Oct Lingfi (HVY) 5f 90 <
*** 2000** *Oct Southw (STD) H 6f 85 88*
*** 2000** *Oct Wolver (STD) C 6f 83*
*** 2000** Aug Sandow (G-F) H 5f 81 81
*** 2000** Jly Yarmou (G-F) 5.2f 76
2000 Turf 3-5: (5f 3-5) (g-s 1-1, gd, g-f 1-1, frm 1-2) 2000 AW 2-3: (5f, 6f 2-2) (Fibr 2-3)
Useful colt, effective 5 to 6f, best at 5f, acts on g-s to frm - acts on Fibr, likes Sandown. Turf high 90 (began Jly) - 1st of 5 giving 10lb to Milly's Lass (23 Oct Lingfield RF 5153) - also 1st of 7 getting 1lb from Fair Princess (18 Aug Sandown RF 3769). AW high 88 (began Jly) - 1st of 15 giving 6lb to Amen Corner (16 Oct Southwell RF 5008) - also 1st of 11 giving 8lb to Erracht (3 Oct Wolverhampton RF 4700). Consistent. Was well placed by his astute trainer to win five races on varying ground as a juvenile.
**Sir Mark Prescott [5-8] Neil Greig.*

CLASSIC COLOURS (USA) BHB 26f34a **RR 30f 34a** 3213[13]
7 ch g Blushing John (USA) 8.9f **(75)** - All Agleam (USA) (Gleaming (USA)) 11.5f **(75)**
Form - 0780
Record 2000 - 1st:0 2nd:0 3rd:0 Ran:4
Pre2000 - 1st:0 2nd:3 3rd:3 Ran:27
Win Prizemoney £0 *Total Prizemoney* £5,371
2000 Turf 0-4: (10f, 11f, 12f, 14f) (hvy, g-f, frm 2)
Very moderate gelding, effective 11f, acts on gd, has worn blinkers. Turf high 30.
**G H Yardley [0-25] Philip Jones (from R Harris [0-5] Spt 1996).*

CLASSIC CONKERS (IRE) BHB 36f **RR 43f** 4306[9]
6 b g Conquering Hero (USA) 10.6f **(50)** - Erck (Sun Prince) 12.4f **(52)**
Form - 7160240
Record 2000 - 1st:1 2nd:1 3rd:0 Ran:7
Pre2000 - 1st:1 2nd:1 3rd:0 Ran:21
Win Prizemoney £4,852 *Total Prizemoney* £6,661
Wins * 2000 Jly Warwic (GD) H 12.3f 30 36
* 1998 Oct Yarmou (G-S) SH 11.5f 45 49 <
2000 Turf 1-7: (12f 1-6, 17f) (gd 1-2, g-f 4, frm)
Moderate gelding, effective 12f, acts on gd to g-f, best on g-f, favours tight tracks. Turf high 43 - 2nd of 12 getting 9lb from Rayik (7 Aug Windsor 12f g-f RF 3435). Inconsistent. He tends to find his stride all too late, but unfortunately that stride is pretty slow.
**Pat Mitchell [2-29] Steven Rees.*

CLASSIC DEFENCE (IRE) BHB 38f32a **RR 40f 32a** 4327[5]
7 b g Cyrano de Bergerac 7.3f **(58)** - My Alanna (Dalsaan) 9.8f **(64)**
Form - 3735
Record 2000 - 1st:0 2nd:0 3rd:2 Ran:4
Pre2000 - 1st:2 2nd:1 3rd:1 Ran:11
Win Prizemoney £6,561 *Total Prizemoney* £8,907
Wins 1996 Jun Goodwo (G-F) H 10f 69 74 <
1996 Apr Mussel (GD) 8.1f 62+
2000 Turf 0-4: (11f, 12f 3) (g-f, frm 3)
Moderate gelding. Turf high 40 (began Jly). Inconsistent.
**B J Llewellyn [0-4] The Welsh Valleys Syndicate (from J W Hills [3-12] Spt 1997).*

CLASSIC EAGLE BHB 32f **RR 41f** 5011[11]
7 b g Unfuwain (USA) 11.4f **(74)** - La Lutine (My Swallow) 9.2f **(71)**
Form - 8000540050
Record 2000 - 1st:0 2nd:0 3rd:0 Ran:10
Pre2000 - 1st:1 2nd:0 3rd:0 Ran:13
Win Prizemoney £3,855 *Total Prizemoney* £4,722
2000 Turf 0-8: (8f 2, 9f, 10f 3, 11f, 16f) (gd 3, g-f 2, frm 3) 2000 AW 0-2:

(14f, 16f) (Fibr 2)

Moderate gelding, effective 8 to 16f, acts on frm - acts on Fibr, has worn blinkers, likes tight tracks. Turf high 41. AW high 37 (1st run) (began Spt) - 5th of 16 getting 16lb from Vincent (26 Spt Southwell 16f Fibr RF 4648).

**Pat Mitchell [0-13] Classic Bloodstock Plc (from I Campbell [0-2] Oct 1997).*

CLASSIC LORD BHB 51f **RR 52f** 5037a[5]

3 b g Wolfhound (USA) 7.3f **(71)** - Janaat (Kris) 9.5f **(73)**

Form - 8003U20365

Record 2000 - 1st:0 2nd:1 3rd:2 Ran:10
Pre2000 - 1st:0 2nd:1 3rd:0 Ran:5

Win Prizemoney £0 *Total Prizemoney* £2,844

2000 Turf 0-10: (8f 3, 9f 4, 10f 2, 12f) (sft, gd 4, g-f 2, frm 3)

Scopey, fair gelding, has worn blinkers. Turf high 53. Inconsistent.

**T G McCourt in IRE [0-3] Conor Clarkson (from M Johnston [0-12] Jun 2000).*

CLASSIC MILLENNIUM BHB 52f **RR 53f** 5004[11]

2 b f Midyan (USA) 9.9f **(64)** - Classic Colleen (IRE) **(78f)** (Sadler's Wells (USA)) 10f **(76)**

Form - 00000

Record 2000 - 1st:0 2nd:0 3rd:0 Ran:5

2000 Turf 0-5: (5f, 6f, 7f, 8f 2) (g-s, g-f, frm 3)

Fair filly. Turf high 53 (began Jly).

**Pat Mitchell [0-5] Classic Bloodstock Plc.*

CLASSIC REFERENDUM (IRE) BHB 42f38a **RR 23f 38a** 1015[14]

6 ch g Classic Music (USA) 7.2f **(57)** - My Alanna (Dalsaan) 9.8f **(64)**

Form - 00000

Record 2000 - 1st:0 2nd:0 3rd:0 Ran:3
Pre2000 - 1st:2 2nd:5 3rd:3 Ran:21

Win Prizemoney £6,359 *Total Prizemoney* £12,241

Wins 1999 Jun Wexfor (G-F) H 13f 63 74+
1999 Jun Leopar (G-S) 14f 78 <

2000 Turf 0-3: (12f, 14f, 15f) (g-s, gd, frm)

Little account gelding, effective 12 to 14f, best at 14f, acts on gd to g-f, best on gd, has worn blinkers. Turf high 23. Inconsistent.

**B J Curley [0-10] Mrs B J Curley (from L Browne in IRE [2-4] Jly 1999).*

CLASSY ACT BHB 77f **RR 75f** 5320[20]

2 ch f Lycius (USA) 8.8f **(71)** - Stripanoora (Ahonoora) 8.1f **(73)**

Form - 2301610

Record 2000 - 1st:2 2nd:1 3rd:1 Ran:7

Win Prizemoney £8,298 *Total Prizemoney* £9,761

Wins * **2000** Oct Catter (SFT) H 7f 73 75 <
* **2000** Spt Hamilt (SFT) H 6f 69 73

2000 Turf 2-7: (6f 1-4, 7f 1-3) (sft, g-s 1-2, gd 1-2, g-f 2)

Above-average filly, effective 6 to 7f, best at 6f, acts on g-s to g-f. Turf high 75 - 1st of 14 getting 2lb from Pasithea (3 Oct Catterick RF 4773) - also 1st of 7 getting 2lb from Joint Instruction (4 Spt Hamilton RF 4210). **A Berry [2-7] Shine, Cunningham, Lambert.*

CLASSY CLEO (IRE) BHB 70f82a **RR 76f 82a** 5313[5]

5 b m Mujadil (USA) 7.7f **(70)** - Sybaris (Crowned Prince (USA)) 10.1f **(67)**

Form - 324230700704640018030405

Record 2000 - 1st:1 2nd:1 3rd:2 Ran:22
Pre2000 - 1st:10 2nd:15 3rd:11 Ran:75

Win Prizemoney £54,084 *Total Prizemoney* £96,853

Wins * **2000** Aug Cheste (GD) H 5.1f 69 72
* 1999 Nov Redcar (G-S) H 6f 82 83
* 1998 Nov Redcar (G-S) H 6f 90 93
* 1998 Jly Cheste (G-F) H 5.1f 85 88
* 1998 May Cheste (GD) H 5.1f 85 87
* 1997 *Nov Lingfi (STD) H 5f 87 105* <
* 1997 *Nov Southw (STD) H 6f 87 86*
* 1997 Oct Yarmou (FRM) H 5.2f 79 86
1997 Spt Haydoc (G-S) C 6f 68
1997 Apr Pontef (GD) 5f 79
1997 Apr Beverl (G-F) 5f 79

2000 Turf 1-16: (5f 1-8, 6f 7, 7f) (sft, g-s 4, gd 1-4, g-f 2, frm 4, hrd)

2000 AW 0-6: (5f, 6f 4, 7f) (Equi 2, Fibr 4)

Useful filly, effective 5 to 7f, best at 7f, acts on frm - acts on AW, best on Equi, likes left handed tracks, likes tight tracks, excels at Lingfield and Wolverhampton. Turf high 76. AW high 93 - 3rd of 11 giving 5lb to Dil (25 Jan Wolverhampton 5f Fibr RF 0155). Vigorously campaigned like many of her stablemates, she is a tough sprint handicapper who acts on just about any surface, but does not win very often these days. A suitable mount for inexperienced riders, she often gets going too late.

**P D Evans [8-87] J E Abbey (from R Hannon [3-10] Spt 1997).*

CLASSY IRISH (USA) BHB 75f **RR 82f** 4444[6]

3 ch c Irish River (FR) 9f **(77)** - Steal The Thunder (CAN) (Lyphard (USA)) 9.9f **(72)**

Form - 6246

Record 2000 - 1st:0 2nd:1 3rd:0 Ran:4

Win Prizemoney £0 *Total Prizemoney* £1,417

2000 Turf 0-4: (8f 2, 10f 2) (gd, frm 3)

Well made, decent colt. Turf high 82.

**L M Cumani [0-4] Robert Smith.*

CLAUDIUS TERTIUS BHB 44f43a **RR 50f 43a** 4194[26]

3 b g Rudimentary (USA) 8.2f **(66)** - Sanctuary Cove (Habitat) 9.4f **(70)**

Form - 00034200

Record 2000 - 1st:0 2nd:1 3rd:1 Ran:8
Pre2000 - 1st:0 2nd:0 3rd:0 Ran:5

Win Prizemoney £0 *Total Prizemoney* £1,103

2000 Turf 0-6: (8f 3, 9f, 10f, 12f) (gd, g-f 3, frm 2) 2000 AW 0-2: (6f, 9f) (Fibr 2)

Scopey, fair gelding. Turf high 50. AW high 40. Inconsistent.

**M E Sowersby [0-2] Newland Paint Partnership (from M A Jarvis [0-11] Jly 2000).*

CLAXON BHB 108f **RR 106f** 5090a[1]

4 b f Caerleon (USA) 10.9f **(79)** - Bulaxie **(103f)** (Bustino) 10.4f **(64)**

Form - 211

Record 2000 - 1st:2 2nd:1 3rd:0 Ran:3
Pre2000 - 1st:3 2nd:1 3rd:1 Ran:6

Win Prizemoney £95,556 *Total Prizemoney* £107,242

Wins * **2000** Oct Capann (HVY) G2 10f 110 <
* **2000** Jly Newbur (G-F) L 10f 106
* 1999 May Goodwo (GD) L 9.9f 106
* 1999 Apr Kempto (GD) L 8f 101
* 1998 Oct Ayr (SFT) 8f 82

2000 Turf 2-3: (10f 2-3) (hvy 1-1, g-f 1-1, frm)

Scopey, Pattern-class filly, effective 8 to 10f, best at 10f, acts on hvy to frm. Turf high 110 (began Jly) - 1st of 13 giving 4lb to Ustimona (15 Oct Capannelle RF 5090a) - also 1st of 6 giving 5lb to Trumpet Sound (22 Jly Newbury RF 3025). Back to her best when making all to win a Newbury Listed event on her second start, she was a game winner in Italy on her final run before being retired to the paddocks. **J L Dunlop [5-9] Hesmonds Stud.*

Claxon never gave connections cause for alarm

CLEAR AMBITION BHB 70f **RR 74f** 4828[15]
2 ch g Definite Article - Canlubang **(20f)** (Mujtahid (USA))
Form - 7800
Record 2000 - 1st:0 2nd:0 3rd:0 Ran:4
2000 Turf 0-4: (7f 2, 8f 2) (g-s, g-f 3)
Above-average gelding. Turf high 74 (began Aug).
**B J Meehan [0-4] N B Attenborough.*

CLEAR CRYSTAL BHB 41f32a **RR 48f 32a** 4378[10]
3 b f Zilzal (USA) 8.5f **(79)** - Shoot Clear (Bay Express) 7.1f **(60)**
Form - 607667660
Record 2000 - 1st:0 2nd:0 3rd:0 Ran:9
Pre2000 - 1st:0 2nd:0 3rd:0 Ran:3
2000 Turf 0-8: (6f 2, 7f 4, 10f 2) (g-s, gd 2, g-f, frm 4) 2000 AW 0-1: (8f) (Fibr)
Unfurnished, moderate filly, has worn blinkers. Turf high 48.
**R M H Cowell [0-12] Bottisham Heath Stud.*

CLEARING BHB 100f **RR 104f** 5108[1]
2 b c Zafonic (USA) 9f **(83)** - Bright Spells (USA) (Alleged (USA)) 10f **(76)**
Form - 2211
Record 2000 - 1st:2 2nd:2 3rd:0 Ran:4
Win Prizemoney £24,672 *Total Prizemoney* £26,985
Wins * 2000 Oct Newbur (SFT) G3 7f 104 <
*** 2000** Spt Cheste (SFT) 7f 89+
2000 Turf 2-4: (7f 2-4) (gd 2-2, g-f, frm)
Very useful colt. Turf high 104 - 1st of 9 from Prizeman (20 Oct Newbury RF 5108). Came up against a highly-rated opponent in Golan on his second start, and had no trouble landing the odds at Chester next time. A decisive winner of a possibly sub-standard Horris Hill next time, he looks to have more improvement in him and should get further as a three-year-old.
**J H M Gosden [2-4] K Abdulla.*

CLEAR MOON (IRE) BHB 35f **RR 39f** 4871[20]
3 b g Lake Coniston (IRE) - Tenea (Reform) 8.9f **(62)**
Form - 585880RR0
Record 2000 - 1st:0 2nd:0 3rd:0 Ran:9
Pre2000 - 1st:0 2nd:0 3rd:1 Ran:5
Win Prizemoney £0 *Total Prizemoney* £550
2000 Turf 0-9: (5f, 6f 2, 7f 5, 9f) (sft, gd 2, g-f 2, frm 4)
Scopey, very moderate gelding, effective 6f, acts on gd, has worn blinkers. Turf high 48. Becoming disappointing.
**Miss L A Perratt [0-14] C D Barber-Lomax.*

CLEAR NIGHT BHB 55f55a **RR 50f 55a** 419[2]
4 b c Night Shift (USA) 8.1f **(73)** - Clarista (USA) (Riva Ridge (USA)) 8.2f **(68)**
Form - 02422
Record 2000 - 1st:0 2nd:2 3rd:0 Ran:3
Pre2000 - 1st:1 2nd:1 3rd:1 Ran:15
Win Prizemoney £2,346 *Total Prizemoney* £4,956
Wins 1999 Jun Chepst (G-F) S 8.1f 63 <
2000 AW 0-3: (7f, 8f 2) (Fibr 3)
Workmanlike, fair colt, effective 8f, acts on g-f - acts on Fibr, has worn blinkers. AW high 55 - 2nd of 13 giving 8lb to Godmersham Park (6 Mar Southwell 8f Fibr RF 0419). Failed to add to his score in an All-Weather campaign last winter, despite running well in general.
**J J Sheehan [0-8] Mrs Eileen Sheehan (from R Hannon [1-10] Jun 1999).*

CLEAR PROSPECT (USA) BHB 60f **RR 70f** 5101[16]
3 b g Virginia Rapids (USA) - Cameo Performance (USA) (Be My Guest (USA)) 9.3f **(67)**
Form - 074040
Record 2000 - 1st:0 2nd:0 3rd:0 Ran:6
Pre2000 - 1st:0 2nd:0 3rd:1 Ran:3
Win Prizemoney £0 *Total Prizemoney* £1,592
2000 Turf 0-6: (10f 4, 12f 2) (gd 3, g-f, frm 2)
Scopey, above-average gelding, effective 10f, acts on gd. Turf high 70. Inconsistent.
**M A Buckley [0-6] C C Buckley (from A G Foster [0-1] Oct 1999).*

CLEF OF SILVER BHB 76f **RR 72f** 3050[9]
5 b h Indian Ridge 7.6f **(74)** - Susquehanna Days (USA) (Chief's Crown (USA)) 9.8f **(72)**
Form - 80
Record 2000 - 1st:0 2nd:0 3rd:0 Ran:2
Pre2000 - 1st:2 2nd:4 3rd:0 Ran:10
Win Prizemoney £5,266 *Total Prizemoney* £13,476
Wins * 1998 Oct Catter (gd,) 6f 74
* 1997 Aug Catter (G-F) H 6f 80 85 <
2000 Turf 0-2: (6f 2) (frm 2)
Above-average colt. Turf high 72 (began Jly). Consistent. Lightly raced in recent seasons and has obviously had his problems.
**W Jarvis [2-12] Silver Clef Racing Venture.*

CLEPSYDRA BHB 75f **RR 79f** 4545[11]
3 b f Sadler's Wells (USA) 11.3f **(87)** - Quandary (USA) **(92+f)** (Blushing Groom (FR)) 10.3f **(76)**
Form - 223510
Record 2000 - 1st:1 2nd:2 3rd:1 Ran:6
Win Prizemoney £4,153 *Total Prizemoney* £6,957
Wins * 2000 Aug Epsom (G-F) 12f 76 <
2000 Turf 1-6: (10f 3, 12f 1-3) (g-s, gd 2, frm 1-3)
Light-framed, above-average filly, effective 12f, acts on g-s to frm, best on frm, has worn blinkers. Turf high 79 - 2nd of 4 to Riyafa (26 May Haydock 12f g-s RF 1468) - also 1st of 4 from South Sea Pearl (17 Aug Epsom RF 3724). **H R A Cecil [1-6] K Abdulla.*

CLEVER GIRL (IRE) BHB 67f **RR 88f** 4864[8]
3 b f College Chapel - Damezao (Alzao (USA)) 7.1f **(68)**
Form - 4028084305008
Record 2000 - 1st:0 2nd:1 3rd:1 Ran:13
Pre2000 - 1st:3 2nd:1 3rd:1 Ran:9
Win Prizemoney £11,260 *Total Prizemoney* £17,284
Wins * 1999 Oct Ayr (SFT) H 8f 82 90 <
* 1999 Jly Ayr (GD) H 7f 77
* 1999 Jun Pontef (G-S) 6f 65
2000 Turf 0-13: (7f 2, 8f 7, 9f 4) (sft 3, g-s 2, gd 6, g-f, frm)
Workmanlike, useful filly, effective 8f, acts on sft to g-s, has worn blinkers, prefers left handed tracks, prefers tight tracks. Turf high 88 - 2nd of 8 giving 23lb to It Can Be Done (2 Jun Nottingham 8f g-s RF 1666). Becoming disappointing. Disqualified after finishing first in a Nottingham handicap in June, she has run respectably since. Likes cut in the ground. **T D Easterby [3-22] Peter Bourke.*

CLICK-ON (IRE) RR 80f 4935[6]
2 b c Danehill (USA) 9.1f **(79)** - Bold Flawless (USA) (Bold Bidder) 8.8f **(67)**
Form - 6
Record 2000 - 1st:0 2nd:0 3rd:0 Ran:1
2000 Turf 0-1: (6f) (gd)
Currently decent colt. **J Noseda [0-1] Ivan Allan.*

CLIFTON WOOD (IRE) BHB 34f **RR 37f** 2792[19]
5 b g Paris House 5.9f **(64)** - Millie's Lady (IRE) (Common Grounds)
Form - 6000
Record 2000 - 1st:0 2nd:0 3rd:0 Ran:4
Pre2000 - 1st:0 2nd:0 3rd:0 Ran:5
2000 Turf 0-4: (8f 3, 9f) (gd 2, frm, hrd)
Very moderate gelding. Turf high 37. Becoming disappointing.
**R J Baker [0-6] Horses Away Racing Club (from J A Glover [0-5] Spt 1998).*

CLIMBING ROSE (USA) RR 72f 4873[3]
2 b f Quest for Fame 12.8f **(75)** - Abeer (USA) (Dewan (USA)) 7.4f **(65)**
Form - 53
Record 2000 - 1st:0 2nd:0 3rd:1 Ran:2
Win Prizemoney £0 *Total Prizemoney* £496
2000 Turf 0-2: (7f 2) (g-s, frm)
Currently above-average filly. Turf high 72 (began Aug) - 3rd of 11 to Goncharova (9 Oct Leicester 7f g-s RF 4873).
**R Charlton [0-2] K Abdulla.*

CLIPPER BHB 95f **RR 98f** 4613[8]
3 b f Salse (USA) 10.9f **(71)** - Yawl **(93f)** (Rainbow Quest (USA)) 10.4f **(75)**
Form - 308888
Record 2000 - 1st:0 2nd:0 3rd:1 Ran:6

Pre2000 - 1st:1 2nd:0 3rd:0 Ran:2
Win Prizemoney £3,574 *Total Prizemoney* £6,654
Wins * 1999 Oct Ayr (SFT) 8f 76 <
2000 Turf 0-6: (10f, 12f 4, 15f) (g-s 2, gd, g-f 2, frm)
Scopey, very useful filly, effective 10f, acts on frm, has worn blinkers. Turf high 98 (1st run) - 3rd of 8 to Melikah (7 May Newmarket 10f frm RF 1079). Out of a Group-winning daughter of an Oaks winner, she ran well to finish third in the Pretty Polly on her return but was well beaten at Epsom and subsequently in Pattern company.
**B W Hills [1-8] R D Hollingsworth.*

CLOCHE CALL RR 56f

5310[6]
2 b f Anabaa (USA) - Fur Hat (Habitat) 9.4f **(70)**
Form - 6
Record 2000 - 1st:0 2nd:0 3rd:0 Ran:1
2000 Turf 0-1: (7f) (g-s)
Currently fair filly. **W Jarvis [0-1] Mrs J Cecil.*

CLOG DANCE BHB 102f RR 102f

2551[2]
3 b f Pursuit of Love 9.5f **(69)** - Discomatic (USA) (Roberto (USA)) 10f **(76)**
Form - 2202
Record 2000 - 1st:0 2nd:3 3rd:0 Ran:4
Pre2000 - 1st:0 2nd:1 3rd:1 Ran:2
Win Prizemoney £0 *Total Prizemoney* £17,690
2000 Turf 0-4: (8f, 10f 2, 12f) (g-s, gd, frm 2)
Scopey, very useful filly, effective 7 to 10f, acts on gd to frm. Turf high 102 - 2nd of 8 to Melikah (7 May Newmarket 10f frm RF 1079). A big, scopey filly, she is still a maiden but is useful, having gone down by just a neck to the subsequent 1000 Guineas winner Lahan in the Rockfel in 1999, and just being pipped in the Pretty Polly on her second start of last season. **B W Hills [0-6] K Abdulla.*

CLOHAMON BHB 28f43a RR 22f 43a

3847[7]
5 b g Aragon 7.7f **(58)** - Almadaniyah (Dunbeath (USA)) 7.8f **(70)**
Form - 6857
Record 2000 - 1st:0 2nd:0 3rd:0 Ran:4
Pre2000 - 1st:0 2nd:0 3rd:0 Ran:11
Win Prizemoney £0 *Total Prizemoney* £204
2000 Turf 0-4: (5f, 7f, 8f 2) (gd 2, frm 2)
Little account gelding, has worn blinkers. Turf high 22.
**R A Fahey [0-3] C N Barnes (from M A Peill [0-4] Jun 2000).*

CLONOE BHB 39f49a RR 39f 49a

4147[8]
6 b g Syrtos 8.1f **(57)** - Anytime Anywhere (Daring March) 7.1f **(61)**
Form - 240410005358
Record 2000 - 1st:1 2nd:1 3rd:1 Ran:12
Pre2000 - 1st:4 2nd:5 3rd:6 Ran:45
Win Prizemoney £11,884 *Total Prizemoney* £19,518
Wins * 2000 *Feb Lingfi (STD) S 8f 63?* <
* 1999 Jly Folkes (G-F) H 7f 39 48
* 1999 *Jan Lingfi (STD) H 10f 37 43*
* 1998 Aug Kempto (G-F) H 8f 43 46
* 1998 Apr Folkes (SFT) H 6f 36 47?
2000 Turf 0-5: (7f 3, 8f 2) (gd 2, g-f, frm 2) 2000 AW 1-7: (7f, 8f 1-3, 9f, 10f 2) (Equi 1-4, Fibr 3)
Average gelding, effective 8f, - acts on Equi, has worn blinkers. Turf high 39 (began Jly). AW high 63 - 1st of 11 from Malchik (23 Feb Lingfield RF 0343). **R Ingram [5-58] P McKernan.*

CLOONDESH BHB 50f RR 45f

5169[8]
2 b g Forzando 7.2f **(63)** - Shalati (FR) (High Line) 10.3f **(70)**
Form - 5078
Record 2000 - 1st:0 2nd:0 3rd:0 Ran:4
2000 Turf 0-4: (5f 3, 6f) (gd 2, g-f 2)
Moderate gelding. Turf high 45. **R A Fahey [0-4] Tommy Staunton.*

CLOPTON GREEN BHB 51f44a RR 50f 44a

4871[8]
3 b g Presidium 7.5f **(56)** - Silkstone Lady (Puissance)
Form - 30603335278
Record 2000 - 1st:0 2nd:1 3rd:3 Ran:8
Pre2000 - 1st:0 2nd:0 3rd:1 Ran:3
Win Prizemoney £0 *Total Prizemoney* £1,768
2000 Turf 0-2: (5f 2) (sft, g-f) 2000 AW 0-6: (5f 5, 6f) (Equi 4, Fibr 2)
Scopey, fair gelding, effective 5f, - acts on AW, best on Equi, often wears blinkers (extremely effectively). Turf high 50 (began Spt). AW high 52 - 2nd of 7 getting 6lb from Tropical King (20 Mar Southwell 5f Fibr RF 0469). **J W Payne [0-11] T W Morley.*

CLOTH OF GOLD RR 69f

839[8]
3 b c Barathea (IRE) - Bustinetta (Bustino) 10.4f **(64)**
Form - 8
Record 2000 - 1st:0 2nd:0 3rd:0 Ran:1
Pre2000 - 1st:0 2nd:0 3rd:0 Ran:1
2000 Turf 0-1: (11f) (sft)
Workmanlike, currently average colt.
**Lady Herries [0-2] Mrs H A Cameron-Rose.*

CLOTTED CREAM (USA) BHB 76f RR 80f

5185[7]
3 gr f Eagle Eyed (USA) - Seattle Victory (USA) (Seattle Song (USA)) 9f **(77)**
Form - 31237
Record 2000 - 1st:1 2nd:1 3rd:2 Ran:5
Pre2000 - 1st:0 2nd:0 3rd:1 Ran:2
Win Prizemoney £3,705 *Total Prizemoney* £7,509
Wins * 2000 May Pontef (GD) 6f 64+ <
2000 Turf 1-5: (6f 1-2, 7f 3) (g-s 2, gd, g-f 1-1, frm)
Decent filly, effective 5 to 7f, acts on g-s to frm. Turf high 78 - 2nd of 10 giving 12lb to Carrie Pooter (3 Jly Pontefract 6f frm RF 2476).
**P J Makin [1-7] Admin of the late C Stelling.*

CLOUD HOPPING (USA) BHB 81f RR 76f

4734[16]
3 ch c Mr Prospector (USA) 8.6f **(88)** - Skimble (USA) (Lyphard (USA)) 9.9f **(72)**
Form - 610
Record 2000 - 1st:1 2nd:0 3rd:0 Ran:3
Win Prizemoney £4,329 *Total Prizemoney* £4,329
Wins * 2000 Jly Sandow (G-F) 10f 74+ <
2000 Turf 1-3: (10f 1-3) (gd 2, g-f 1-1)
Well made, currently above-average colt. Turf high 76 (began Jly) - also 1st of 4 from Shadowblaster (26 Jly Sandown RF 3143). Hard to assess after winning a four-horse maiden at Sandown on his second start. **H R A Cecil [1-3] K Abdulla.*

CLOUD INSPECTOR (IRE) BHB 28f40a RR 49df 40a

311[6]
9 b g Persian Bold 10f **(69)** - Timbale d'Argent (Petingo) 11f **(72)**
Form - 246
Record 2000 - 1st:0 2nd:1 3rd:0 Ran:3
Pre2000 - 1st:2 2nd:5 3rd:1 Ran:21
Win Prizemoney £20,936 *Total Prizemoney* £36,821
Wins * 1997 Aug Dielsd (GD) 15f 89+ <
* 1997 Jly Goodwo (G-F) H 20f 75 82
2000 AW 0-3: (13f, 16f 2) (Equi, Fibr 2)
Moderate gelding, has worn blinkers. AW high 32. An Ex-German and Irish performer who won the Goodwood Handicap last year, he has been beaten in Switzerland and in a couple of warm handicaps this term. **M Johnston [2-24] Markus Graff.*

CLOUDY RR 69f

3963[7]
2 b f Ashkalani (IRE) - Shady Leaf (IRE) (Glint of Gold) 9.3f **(66)**
Form - 567
Record 2000 - 1st:0 2nd:0 3rd:0 Ran:3
2000 Turf 0-3: (6f 2, 7f) (gd, g-f 2)
Currently average filly. Turf high 69 (1st run) (began Jly) - 5th of 10 getting 9lb from Dominus (12 Jly Newmarket 6f gd RF 2749).
**R F JohnsonHoughton [0-3] Lady Rothschild.*

COASTAL BLUFF BHB 90f RR 95f

4933[10]
8 gr g Standaan (FR) 5.4f **(46)** - Combattente (Reform) 8.9f **(62)**
Form - 5721020404470
Record 2000 - 1st:1 2nd:2 3rd:0 Ran:13
Pre2000 - 1st:7 2nd:2 3rd:1 Ran:28
Win Prizemoney £189,786 *Total Prizemoney* £213,090
Wins * 2000 Jun Nottin (G-F) H 5.1f 78 80
1997 Aug York (GD) G1 5f 115 <
1997 Jly Newmar (G-F) 5f 108+
1996 Spt Ayr (G-F) H 6f 104 115+
1996 Aug Goodwo (G-F) H 6f 88 101+
1996 Jly York (GD) H 5f 88 91+
2000 Turf 1-13: (5f 1-10, 6f 3) (gd 1-5, g-f 7, frm)
Very useful gelding, effective 5f, acts on g-f, has worn blinkers. Turf high 102 - 2nd of 8 to Lord Kintyre (28 Jly Newmarket 5f g-f RF 3176). This fine stamp of a gelding dead-heated with Ya Malak in a sensational Nunthorpe in 1997, with rider Kevin Darley per-

forming miracles after the bit broke early on. He regressed badly after that, was tubed and changed stables, but he rediscovered some of his talent in the summer.

**N P Littmoden [1-22] Paul Dixon (from T D Barron [7-19] Jun 1998).*

COASTGUARDS HERO BHB 15f38a **RR 17f 38a** 222[9]

7 ch g Chilibang 7f **(55)** - Aldwick Colonnade **(43f 41a)** (Kind of Hush) 10.1f **(62)**

Form - 20

Record 2000 - 1st:0 2nd:1 3rd:0 Ran:2
Pre2000 - 1st:4 2nd:3 3rd:4 Ran:50

Win Prizemoney £8,279 *Total Prizemoney* £12,973

Wins 1998 *Jun Lingfi (STD) SH 13f 30 36*
1998 *Feb Lingfi (SLW) SH 16f 35 36*
1998 *Jan Lingfi (STD) H 13f 30 35*
1996 *Feb Southw (STD) 6f 45* <

2000 AW 0-2: (13f, 16f) (Equi 2)

Very moderate gelding, effective 16f, - acts on Equi. AW high 36 (1st run) - 2nd of 10 to Another Monk (26 Jan Lingfield 16f Equi RF 0163). **L A Dace [0-3] D Newman (from B A Pearce [1-27] Jly 1999).*

COBOURG LODGE (IRE) RR 110f 5048a[1]

4 b c Unblest - Rachel Pringle (IRE) 00

Form - 0121077344621

2000 Turf 3-12: (6f 1-3, 7f 2-6, 8f 2, 9f) (sft 2-4, g-s 1-4, gd 3)

Group-class colt, effective 6 to 7f, acts on sft to g-s, has worn blinkers, likes right handed tracks. Turf high 110 - 2nd of 11 giving 2lb to Bernstein (1 Oct Cork 7f sft RF 4805a) - also 1st of 11 giving 3lb to Anna Elise (15 Oct Curragh RF 5048a). A useful handicapper at the beginning of last season, he progressed enough in the autumn to give Bernstein a good race in a Group Three at Cork before winning a listed event at the Curragh. He acts on easy ground and could well be a major contender early in early season Pattern events. **J T Gorman in IRE [5-32] Andrews Syndicate.*

COCCOLONA (IRE) BHB 65f **RR 61f** 4808[11]

2 b f Idris (IRE) - Fair Siobahn (Petingo) 11f **(72)**

Form - 4060

Record 2000 - 1st:0 2nd:0 3rd:0 Ran:4

Win Prizemoney £0 *Total Prizemoney* £231

2000 Turf 0-4: (6f 2, 7f 2) (g-s 2, g-f, frm)

Average filly. Turf high 61. **D HaydnJones [0-4] Mrs William Byrne.*

COCHITI BHB 12f18a **RR 13f 18a** 350[8]

6 b m Kris 10f **(75)** - Sweet Jaffa (Never so Bold) 6.3f **(66)**

Form - 0558

Record 2000 - 1st:0 2nd:0 3rd:0 Ran:4
Pre2000 - 1st:0 2nd:0 3rd:1 Ran:15

Win Prizemoney £0 *Total Prizemoney* £342

2000 AW 0-4: (12f 2, 15f, 16f) (Equi, Fibr 3)

Poor mare, effective 12f, acts on g-f, has worn blinkers. AW high 3.

**P W Hiatt [0-38] P W Hiatt (from C W Thornton [0-9] Spt 1997).*

COCO (USA) RR 98f 3340[7]

3 ch f Storm Bird (CAN) 8.5f **(82)** - Fond Romance (USA) (Fappiano (USA)) 8.7f **(77)**

Form - 1437

Record 2000 - 1st:1 2nd:0 3rd:1 Ran:4
Pre2000 - 1st:0 2nd:0 3rd:0 Ran:1

Win Prizemoney £3,488 *Total Prizemoney* £7,026

Wins * **2000** May Nottin (G-F) 8.2f 87 <

2000 Turf 1-4: (7f 2, 8f 1-2) (gd 3, g-f 1-1)

Unfurnished, very useful filly. Turf high 98 - 7th of 11 to Danceabout (3 Aug Goodwood 7f gd RF 3340). Won her maiden at the start of last season, and in a light campaign, ran fair races in listed events without setting the world alight.

**Sir Michael Stoute [1-5] Philip Newton.*

COCO DE MER RR 57f 3975[14]

3 ch g Prince Sabo 6.6f **(64)** - Musica **(78df)** (Primo Dominie) 6.2f **(80)**

Form - 0800000

Record 2000 - 1st:0 2nd:0 3rd:0 Ran:7
Pre2000 - 1st:1 2nd:4 3rd:0 Ran:9

Win Prizemoney £4,120 *Total Prizemoney* £11,186

Wins 1999 Jly Cheste (G-F) 5.1f 70 <

2000 Turf 0-7: (5f 7) (g-s, gd 3, g-f, frm, hrd)

Strong, fair gelding, effective 5f, acts on g-f. Turf high 57.

**R A Fahey [0-7] Mrs Julie Mitchell (from A P Jarvis [1-9] Spt 1999).*

COCO GIRL BHB 36f **RR 50f** 2435[7]

4 ch f Mystiko (USA) 7.7f **(59)** - Cantico (Green Dancer (USA)) 10.3f **(74)**

Form - 4287

Record 2000 - 1st:0 2nd:1 3rd:0 Ran:3
Pre2000 - 1st:0 2nd:0 3rd:0 Ran:9

Win Prizemoney £0 *Total Prizemoney* £897

2000 AW 0-3: (13f 2, 16f) (Equi 3)

Unfurnished, fair filly. AW high 38. Inconsistent.

**Mrs A E Johnson [0-8] Chasers IV (from I A Balding [0-5] May 1999).*

COCO LOCO BHB 85f **RR 87+f** 5322[1]

3 b f Bin Ajwaad (IRE) - Mainly Me **(17f)** (Huntingdale)

Form - 6706502111

Record 2000 - 1st:3 2nd:1 3rd:0 Ran:10
Pre2000 - 1st:0 2nd:0 3rd:0 Ran:1

Win Prizemoney £14,213 *Total Prizemoney* £15,037

Wins * **2000** Nov Doncas (HVY) H 16.5f 70 87+ <
* **2000** Oct Yarmou (HVY) H 14.1f 61 68+
* **2000** Spt Catter (SFT) H 15.8f 52 60

2000 Turf 3-10: (8f, 10f 3, 12f 2, 14f 1-1, 16f 1-2, 17f 1-1) (hvy, sft 1-2, g-s 2-2, g-f 3, frm 2)

Leggy, useful filly, effective 17f, acts on sft, prefers left handed tracks. Turf high 87 - 1st of 12 from Mr Fortywinks (4 Nov Doncaster RF 5322). Showed improved form in testing ground in the autumn. **J Pearce [3 11] & Mrs J Matthews.*

CODICIL BHB 39f **RR 37f** 4333[12]

4 ch f Then Again 7.4f **(52)** - Own Free Will (Nicholas Bill) 10.1f **(56)**

Form - 0034100

Record 2000 - 1st:1 2nd:0 3rd:1 Ran:7
Pre2000 - 1st:1 2nd:0 3rd:2 Ran:13

Win Prizemoney £4,922 *Total Prizemoney* £7,383

Wins * **2000** Aug Ayr (G-F) SH 7f 36 36
1998 Jly Redcar (G-S) 5f 72+ <

2000 Turf 1-7: (7f 1-2, 8f 3, 10f 2) (gd 2, g-f 2, frm 1-3)

Scopey, very moderate filly, effective 10f, acts on g-f, likes left handed tracks, favours tight tracks. Turf high 37.

**M Dods [1-11] Harry Whitton (from Mrs J R Ramsden [1-9] Oct 1998).*

CO DOT UK BHB 65f60a **RR 71f 60a** 5247[6]

2 b g Distant Relative 7f **(69)** - Cubist (IRE) (Tate Gallery (USA)) 7.4f **(67)**

Form - 5301345020236

Record 2000 - 1st:1 2nd:2 3rd:3 Ran:13

Win Prizemoney £3,523 *Total Prizemoney* £7,035

Wins * **2000** May Southw (HVY) 6f 66 <

2000 Turf 1-10: (5f 2, 6f 1-4, 7f 2, 8f 2) (g-s, gd 1-5, g-f, frm 3) 2000 AW 0-3: (7f 2, 8f) (Fibr 3)

Above-average gelding, effective 6 to 8f, acts on gd - acts on Fibr, has worn blinkers, prefers left handed tracks, likes tight tracks. Turf high 71 - 2nd of 14 giving 5lb to Rathkenny (14 Spt Ayr 8f gd RF 4381) - also 1st of 12 from Young Jack (31 May Southwell RF 1600). AW high 62 (began Spt) - 2nd of 16 giving 6lb to Little Task (16 Oct Southwell 7f Fibr RF 5010). **K A Ryan [1-13] Tony Fawcett.*

COEUR DE LA MER (IRE) BHB 87f **RR 84+f** 1699[3]

3 b f Caerleon (USA) 10.9f **(79)** - Cochineal (USA) (Vaguely Noble) 10.1f **(72)**

Form - 3

Record 2000 - 1st:0 2nd:0 3rd:1 Ran:1
Pre2000 - 1st:1 2nd:0 3rd:1 Ran:2

Win Prizemoney £3,078 *Total Prizemoney* £4,639

Wins 1999 Oct Windso (SFT) 8.3f 84+ <

2000 Turf 0-1: (10f) (gd)

Scopey, currently decent filly.

**J H M Gosden [0-1] R E Sangster (from A G Foster [1-2] Oct 1999).*

COHIBA BHB 38f31a **RR 48?f 31a** 972[15]

7 b g Old Vic 12.8f **(72)** - Circus Ring (High Top) 10.2f **(67)**

Form - 670

Record 2000 - 1st:0 2nd:0 3rd:0 Ran:3
Pre2000 - 1st:3 2nd:2 3rd:0 Ran:25

Win Prizemoney £7,144 *Total Prizemoney* £9,199

Wins 1999 Jly Nottin (FRM) SH 14.1f 37 41

1998 May Bright (G-F) H 11.9f 38 44 <
1997 Jly Nottin (G-F) SH 14.1f 34 42
2000 Turf 0-1: (14f) (gd) 2000 AW 0-2: (12f 2) (Fibr 2)
Moderate gelding, effective 12 to 14f, acts on frm - acts on Fibr, has worn blinkers. AW high 39 (1st run) - 6th of 11 giving 14lb to Manful (4 Jan Wolverhampton 12f Fibr RF 0021). Inconsistent.
**A G Juckes [0-8] D W Thorne (from B J Curley [3-18] Jly 1999).*

COIS CUAIN (IRE) RR 102f 5283a[2]
3 b f Night Shift (USA) 8.1f **(73)** - Pitmarie (Pitskelly) 8.5f **(53)**
Form - 3543071642
2000 Turf 1-10: (6f, 7f 1-5, 8f 4) (hvy, sft 3, g-s 1-4, g-f)
Very useful filly, effective 6 to 8f, best at 7f, acts on sft to g-f, best on g-s, has worn blinkers. Turf high 100 - also 1st of 4 from Topsy Morning (6 Spt Galway RF 4343a). **J Oxx in IRE [2-12] E Keena.*

COLD CLIMATE BHB 53f **RR 55f** 3560[5]
5 b g Pursuit of Love 9.5f **(69)** - Sharpthorne (USA) (Sharpen Up) 8.3f **(67)**
Form - 5000485
Record 2000 - 1st:0 2nd:0 3rd:0 Ran:7
Pre2000 - 1st:1 2nd:2 3rd:3 Ran:20
Win Prizemoney £4,503 *Total Prizemoney* £9,894
Wins * 1999 Aug Newmar (GD) H 6f 55 56 <
2000 Turf 0-7: (6f 4, 7f 3) (sft, g-s, gd 2, g-f, frm 2)
Fair gelding, effective 5 to 7f, best at 6f, acts on gd to frm, best on g-f, has worn blinkers, and excels at Windsor. Turf high 60.
**Bob Jones [1-24] Sandbaggers Club (from R Charlton [0-3] May 1998).*

COLD ENCOUNTER (IRE) BHB 45f **RR 13f** 4306[15]
5 ch g Polar Falcon (USA) 9f **(74)** - Scene Galante (FR) (Sicyos (USA))
Form - 00
Record 2000 - 1st:0 2nd:0 3rd:0 Ran:2
2000 Turf 0-2: (10f, 12f) (gd, frm)
Poor gelding, often wears blinkers. Turf high 13 (began Aug).
**S Mellor [0-2] Anthony Hibbard and Joe Baker.*

COLERIDGE BHB 28f31a **RR 35f 31a** 415[10]
12 gr g Bellypha 11.9f **(66)** - Quay Line (High Line) 10.3f **(70)**
Form - 080
Record 2000 - 1st:0 2nd:0 3rd:0 Ran:3
Pre2000 - 1st:11 2nd:14 3rd:9 Ran:96
Win Prizemoney £31,377 *Total Prizemoney* £52,313
Wins * 1999 *Feb Southw (STD) H 16f 47 53*
* 1998 *Dec Lingfi (STD) H 16f 45 50*
* 1997 *Feb Lingfi (STD) H 16f 51 55*
* 1996 May Bath (G-F) H 17.2f 47 56
2000 AW 0-3: (16f 3) (Fibr 3)
Very moderate gelding, effective 16f, - acts on Fibr, mostly wears blinkers, favours left handed tracks, favours tight tracks. AW high 34. **J J Sheehan [6-79] P J Sheehan (from D Shaw [4-17] Feb 1993).*

COLETTE (IRE) BHB 63f **RR 70f** 5070[6]
3 b f Nicolotte - Ascensiontide (Ela-Mana-Mou) 10.1f **(70)**
Form - 86
Record 2000 - 1st:0 2nd:0 3rd:0 Ran:2
Pre2000 - 1st:0 2nd:0 3rd:0 Ran:1
2000 Turf 0-2: (10f, 12f) (g-s 2)
Scopey, currently above-average filly. Turf high 63 (began Spt).
**Major D N Chappell [0-3] Super Sprinters.*

COLEY BHB 48a **RR 44f** 4811[7]
3 ch f Pursuit of Love 9.5f **(69)** - Cole Slaw (Absalom) 7.2f **(58)**
Form - 35607
Record 2000 - 1st:0 2nd:0 3rd:1 Ran:5
Pre2000 - 1st:1 2nd:0 3rd:0 Ran:4
Win Prizemoney £1,708 *Total Prizemoney* £1,967
Wins 1999 Spt Lingfi (HVY) C 6f 63 <
2000 Turf 0-1: (7f) (gd) 2000 AW 0-4: (6f 2, 7f, 8f) (Equi 3, Fibr)
Scopey, moderate filly, effective 6f, acts on g-s, has worn blinkers. AW high 49,
**B A Pearce [0-1] Mike Culling (from L MontagueHall [0-6] Apr 2000).*

COLIN COOK RR 4454[12]
2 b c Presidium 7.5f **(56)** - Horton Lady **(43+f)** (Midyan (USA)) 6f **(60)**
Form - 0
Record 2000 - 1st:0 2nd:0 3rd:0 Ran:1
2000 Turf 0-1: (6f) (g-s)
Currently very poor colt. **M Brittain [0-1] Robert Cook.*

COLLARD RR 72+f 5100[6]
2 ch f Wolfhound (USA) 7.3f **(71)** - Collide (High Line) 10.3f **(70)**
Form - 6
Record 2000 - 1st:0 2nd:0 3rd:0 Ran:1
2000 Turf 0-1: (7f) (gd)
Currently above-average filly. **H Candy [0-1] Major M G Wyatt.*

COLLECTIVITY BHB 65f **RR 68f** 5318[10]
2 b f Dr Devious (IRE) 9.9f **(74)** - Loch Quest (Lochnager) 6f **(59)**
Form - 00
Record 2000 - 1st:0 2nd:0 3rd:0 Ran:2
2000 Turf 0-2: (6f, 7f) (sft, g-f)
Currently average filly. Turf high 68 (began Spt).
**B W Hills [0-2] W J Gredley.*

COLLECT THE CASH (USA) RR 102f 5329a[11]
3 b f Dynaformer (USA) 12f **(82)** - Worldly Possession (USA) (Valis Appeal (USA))
Form - 0
2000 Turf 0-1: (11f) (frm)
Currently very useful. **J Orseno in USA [0-1] Stronach Stables.*

COLLEGE BLUE (IRE) BHB 70f53a **RR 71f 53a** 424[5]
4 b f College Chapel - Mitsubishi Centre (IRE) (Thatching) 8f **(66)**
Form - 2871075
Record 2000 - 1st:1 2nd:1 3rd:0 Ran:7
Pre2000 - 1st:0 2nd:3 3rd:1 Ran:7
Win Prizemoney £2,081 *Total Prizemoney* £7,060
Wins * 2000 *Feb Lingfi (STD) C 6f 60* <
2000 AW 1-7: (6f 1-5, 7f, 8f) (Equi 1-5, Fibr 2)
Workmanlike, above-average filly, effective 5 to 6f, - acts on Equi, has worn blinkers. AW high 60 - 1st of 11 getting 5lb from Palacegate Touch (9 Feb Lingfield RF 0248).
**G L Moore [1-4] Danny Bloor (from T G Mills [0-10] Jan 2000).*

COLLEGE DEAN (IRE) BHB 30f **RR 55f** 4891[9]
4 ch g College Chapel - Phyllode **(53f)** (Pharly (FR)) 9.8f **(68)**
Form - 67870
Record 2000 - 1st:0 2nd:0 3rd:0 Ran:5
Pre2000 - 1st:1 2nd:0 3rd:1 Ran:17
Win Prizemoney £3,192 *Total Prizemoney* £3,918
Wins 1998 Aug Hamilt (SFT) H 6f 70 <
2000 Turf 0-5: (6f, 8f, 9f 2, 11f) (hvy, g-s, gd 2, g-f)
Scopey, fair gelding, has worn blinkers. Turf high 55. Inconsistent.
**P Monteith [0-5] P Monteith (from J J O'Neill [1-17] Aug 1999).*

COLLEGE FACT RR 44f 1796[8]
2 b c So Factual (USA) - Starfida **(39f)** (Soviet Star (USA))
Form - 8
Record 2000 - 1st:0 2nd:0 3rd:0 Ran:1
2000 Turf 0-1: (6f) (gd)
Currently moderate colt. **E J O'Neill [0-1] Mrs Christine Dunnett.*

COLLEGE GALLERY BHB 33f38a **RR 14f 38a** 2417[9]
3 b g College Chapel - Gallarus (IRE) (Standaan (FR)) 7f **(55)**
Form - 00000
Record 2000 - 1st:0 2nd:0 3rd:0 Ran:3
Pre2000 - 1st:0 2nd:0 3rd:0 Ran:4
2000 Turf 0-2: (6f, 8f) (gd, g-f) 2000 AW 0-1: (6f) (Fibr)
Unfurnished, very moderate gelding, has worn blinkers. Turf high 14. **B I Case [0-5] E R Arkwright (from C G Cox [0-1] Aug 1999).*

COLLEGE KING (IRE) BHB 47f **RR 57f** 1553[13]
4 b c College Chapel - Genetta (Green Desert (USA)) 8.6f **(78)**
Form - 00
Record 2000 - 1st:0 2nd:0 3rd:0 Ran:2
Pre2000 - 1st:0 2nd:0 3rd:0 Ran:3
Win Prizemoney £0 *Total Prizemoney* £261
2000 Turf 0-2: (8f, 9f) (g-f, frm)
Workmanlike, fair colt. Turf high 21. **M Brittain [0-5] Mel Brittain.*

COLLEGE MAID (IRE) RR 69f 5313[10]
3 b f College Chapel - Maid of Mourne (Fairy King (USA)) 7.7f **(59)**

Form - 2082112501805804002010
Record 2000 - 1st:4 2nd:4 3rd:0 Ran:22
Pre2000 - 1st:1 2nd:3 3rd:2 Ran:14
Win Prizemoney £23,347 *Total Prizemoney* £31,750
Wins * **2000** Oct Newcas (HVY) H 6f 64 69
* **2000** Jun Ayr (GD) H 5f 65 71 <
* **2000** Jun Catter (GD) H 5f 53 60
* **2000** May Ripon (GD) H 6f 53 59
* 1999 May Mussel (G-F) 5f 61
2000 Turf 4-22: (5f 1-13, 6f 3-9) (sft 1-2, g-s 3, gd 1-7, g-f 1-2, frm 1-8)
Leggy, average filly, effective 5 to 6f, best at 5f, acts on sft to frm, excels at Catterick. Turf high 71 - 1st of 11 getting 3lb from Elvington Boy (24 Jun Ayr RF 2247) - also 1st of 20 getting 16lb from Downland (18 Oct Newcastle RF 5055).
**J S Goldie [5-36] S Bruce.*

COLLEGE PRINCESS BHB 28f52a RR 32f 52a 971[7]
6 b m Anshan 8.2f **(63)** - Tinkers Fairy (Myjinski (USA)) 9.5f **(54)**
Form - 47
Record 2000 - 1st:0 2nd:0 3rd:0 Ran:2
Pre2000 - 1st:1 2nd:1 3rd:4 Ran:24
Win Prizemoney £2,337 *Total Prizemoney* £4,878
Wins 1997 Jly Redcar (G-F) SH 5f 47 46 <
2000 Turf 0-2: (8f, 10f) (g-s, gd)
Very moderate mare. Turf high 28. Consistent.
**E J O'Neill [0-2] Mrs Christine Dunnett (from S C Williams [1-18] Jly 1999).*

COLLEGE QUEEN BHB 58f RR 34f 5319[13]
2 b f Lugana Beach 7f **(63)** - Eccentric Dancer **(41f 20a)** (Rambo Dancer (CAN))
Form - 0
Record 2000 - 1st:0 2nd:0 3rd:0 Ran:1
2000 Turf 0-1: (6f) (sft)
Currently average filly. **J G Given [0-1] J F Coupland.*

COLLEGE ROCK BHB 63f46a RR 65f 46a 5064[3]
3 ch g Rock Hopper 10.6f **(54)** - Sea Aura (Roi Soleil) 8.7f **(57)**
Form - 042637641461374243
Record 2000 - 1st:2 2nd:2 3rd:3 Ran:18
Pre2000 - 1st:0 2nd:2 3rd:2 Ran:8
Win Prizemoney £4,823 *Total Prizemoney* £8,917
Wins * **2000** Aug Leices (G-F) C 8f 60 <
* **2000** Jly Chepst (G-F) S 8.1f 60 <
2000 Turf 2-15: (8f 2-8, 9f, 10f 6) (sft, g-s, gd 3, g-f 2-7, frm 3) 2000 AW 0-3: (7f, 9f, 10f) (Equi 2, Fibr)
Small, average gelding, effective 7 to 10f, acts on gd to frm, best on gd, often wears blinkers, and excels at Leicester. Turf high 65 - also 1st of 15 giving 11lb to Sweet Haven (2 Aug Leicester RF 3330). AW high 49. Consistent.
**R Brotherton [2-13] Ms Gerardine O'Reilly (from Mrs A E Johnson [0-6] May 2000).*

COLLEGE STAR BHB 54f49a RR 48f 49a 4651[7]
2 b g Lugana Beach 7f **(63)** - Alis Princess (Sayf El Arab (USA)) 7.1f **(54)**
Form - 057
Record 2000 - 1st:0 2nd:0 3rd:0 Ran:3
2000 Turf 0-2: (6f 2) (g-s, frm) 2000 AW 0-1: (8f) (Fibr)
Currently moderate gelding. Turf high 48 (began Jly).
**R M Whitaker [0-3] J F Coupland.*

COLLIERS TREASURE RR 4632[13]
3 b f Manhal - Indian Treasure (IRE) **(8f 25a)** (Treasure Kay)
Form - 0
Record 2000 - 1st:0 2nd:0 3rd:0 Ran:1
2000 Turf 0-1: (10f) (g-s)
Unfurnished, currently very poor filly.
**K Bell [0-1] Chasing Rainbows Partnership.*

COLLINE DE FEU BHB 57f50a RR 58f 50a 5137[7]
3 ch f Sabrehill (USA) 8.5f **(64)** - Band of Fire (USA) (Chief's Crown (USA)) 9.8f **(72)**
Form - 0407
Record 2000 - 1st:0 2nd:0 3rd:0 Ran:4
Win Prizemoney £0 *Total Prizemoney* £306
2000 Turf 0-4: (8f, 10f, 12f, 14f) (g-s, gd, g-f 2)
Scopey, fair filly. Turf high 58. **Mrs P Sly [0-4] David Bayliss.*

COLLISION RR 49f 2684[10]
3 ch f Wolfhound (USA) 7.3f **(71)** - Collide (High Line) 10.3f **(70)**
Form - 60
Record 2000 - 1st:0 2nd:0 3rd:0 Ran:2
2000 Turf 0-2: (7f, 8f) (gd, frm)
Leggy, currently moderate filly. Turf high 49.
**H Candy [0-2] Major M G Wyatt.*

COLLISION TIME BHB 45f RR 42f 3425[16]
3 b f Timeless Times (USA) 6.1f **(56)** - Kaleidophone (Kalaglow) 9.8f **(67)**
Form - 00080
Record 2000 - 1st:0 2nd:0 3rd:0 Ran:5
Pre2000 - 1st:0 2nd:0 3rd:3 Ran:6
Win Prizemoney £0 *Total Prizemoney* £1,260
2000 Turf 0-5: (5f 3, 6f 2) (gd, frm 4)
Neat, moderate filly, effective 5f, acts on g-f, has worn blinkers. Turf high 42. **P D Evans [0-11] D Maloney.*

COLNE VALLEY AMY BHB 70f RR 69f 5240[28]
3 b f Mizoram (USA) - Panchellita (USA) **(34f 44a)** (Pancho Villa (USA))
Form - 2114325100
Record 2000 - 1st:3 2nd:2 3rd:1 Ran:10
Pre2000 - 1st:0 2nd:0 3rd:0 Ran:3
Win Prizemoney £12,919 *Total Prizemoney* £15,190
Wins * **2000** Spt Sandow (G-F) H 8.1f 67 69 <
* **2000** Jly Salisb (G-S) H 8f 52 61
* **2000** Jun Salisb (G-F) H 8f 50 54
2000 Turf 3-10: (7f 2, 8f 3-7, 10f) (g-s 2, gd 1-1, g-f 2, frm 2-5)
Workmanlike, average filly, effective 8 to 10f, best at 8f, acts on gd to frm, best on frm. Turf high 69 - 1st of 12 getting 12lb from Ogilia (13 Spt Sandown RF 4369) - also 1st of 18 getting 10lb from Hand Chime (7 Jly Salisbury RF 2598). Scored twice at Salisbury in the summer and added another victory at Sandown in September. A mile and fast ground suit her best.
**G L Moore [3-13] Colne Valley Golf (Deluxeward Ltd).*

COLOMBE D'OR BHB 39f41a RR 55df 41a 4650[4]
3 gr g Petong 7.6f **(58)** - Deep Divide **(74f)** (Nashwan (USA))
Form - 622607734
Record 2000 - 1st:0 2nd:2 3rd:1 Ran:8
Pre2000 - 1st:0 2nd:0 3rd:0 Ran:4
Win Prizemoney £0 *Total Prizemoney* £1,927
2000 Turf 0-4: (8f, 10f, 12f, 17f) (gd, g-f, frm 2) 2000 AW 0-4: (8f, 10f, 11f 2) (Equi, Fibr 3)
Workmanlike, fair gelding, effective 8 to 10f, - acts on AW, has worn blinkers, likes left handed tracks, likes tight tracks. Turf high 45. AW high 58 - 2nd of 3 getting 9lb from Bluebell Wood (5 Feb Lingfield 10f Equi RF 0225).
**P C Haslam [0-13] Middleham Park Racing.*

COLONEL CUSTER BHB 32f42a RR 26f 42a 4650[7]
5 ch g Komaite (USA) 6.9f **(61)** - Mohican (Great Nephew) 9.9f **(64)**
Form - 5001310057650406077
Record 2000 - 1st:1 2nd:0 3rd:1 Ran:15
Pre2000 - 1st:3 2nd:1 3rd:1 Ran:18
Win Prizemoney £8,199 *Total Prizemoney* £10,074
Wins 2000 *Jan Wolver (STD) SH 12f 48 54*
1999 *Dec Wolver (STD) S 12f 48+*
1999 *Feb Southw (STD) H 11f 57 60*
1997 *Jly Southw (STD) 6f 61* <
2000 Turf 0-4: (8f, 11f 2, 12f) (g-s 2, g-f, hrd) 2000 AW 1-11: (6f, 7f 2, 11f, 12f 1-7) (Fibr 1-11)
Fair gelding, effective 11 to 12f, - acts on Fibr, has worn blinkers, favours left handed tracks, favours tight tracks. Turf high 30. AW high 54 - 1st of 12 giving 19lb to Hill Farm Dancer (27 Jan Wolverhampton RF 0169).
**R Brotherton [0-13] Paul Stringer (from J Pearce [3-12] Jan 2000).*

COLONEL KURTZ (USA) BHB 39f RR 17f 5318[19]
2 b c Slip Anchor 12.7f **(75)** - Rustaka (USA) (Riverman (USA)) 9.1f **(76)**
Form - 00
Record 2000 - 1st:0 2nd:0 3rd:0 Ran:2

2000 Turf 0-2: (6f 2) (sft 2)
Currently poor colt. Turf high 17 (began Oct).
John Berry [0-2] The 1997 Partnership.

COLONEL NORTH (IRE) BHB 54f53a **RR 66f 53a** 4997[6]

4 b g Distinctly North (USA) 7.4f **(63)** - Tricky (Song) 7.2f **(61)**
Form - 64787066554576
Record 2000 - 1st:0 2nd:0 3rd:0 Ran:11
Pre2000 - 1st:2 2nd:0 3rd:0 Ran:10
Win Prizemoney £7,692 *Total Prizemoney* £7,692
Wins * 1999 Jun Carlis (G-F) H 8f 64 73 <
1999 Jun Newmar (G-F) C 8f 67
2000 Turf 0-8: (8f 6, 10f 2) (gd, g-f 3, frm 4) 2000 AW 0-3: (8f, 10f, 13f) (Equi 2, Fibr)
Leggy, average gelding, effective 8f, acts on frm to hrd. Turf high 66. AW high 45.
Andrew Reid [1-17] A S Reid (from W R Muir [1-5] Jun 1999).

COLONEL SAM BHB 39f37a **RR 39f 37a** 3551[16]

4 b g Puissance 7.1f **(60)** -Indian Summer (Young Generation) 7.7f **(63)**
Form - 0800850040R30
Record 2000 - 1st:0 2nd:0 3rd:1 Ran:13
Pre2000 - 1st:0 2nd:1 3rd:1 Ran:16
Win Prizemoney £0 *Total Prizemoney* £2,162
2000 Turf 0-10: (5f 3, 6f 4, 7f, 8f 2) (g-s, gd, g-f 5, frm 3) 2000 AW 0-3: (5f, 6f, 7f) (Fibr 3)
Very moderate gelding, effective 5 to 7f, acts on frm to hrd, has worn blinkers. Turf high 43. AW high 22. Inconsistent.
S R Bowring [0-13] W I Derry (from J A Glover [0-16] Spt 1999).

COLONIAL RULE (USA) BHB 75f **RR 86f** 4741[16]

3 b g Pleasant Colony (USA) 12.4f **(88)** - Musicale (USA) (The Minstrel (CAN)) 10f **(72)**
Form - 77860
Record 2000 - 1st:0 2nd:0 3rd:0 Ran:5
Pre2000 - 1st:1 2nd:1 3rd:1 Ran:4
Win Prizemoney £3,954 *Total Prizemoney* £5,711
Wins 1999 Oct Bright (GD) 8f 87+ <
2000 Turf 0-5: (10f, 12f 3, 14f) (g-s 2, gd, g-f 2)
Scopey, useful gelding, effective 7 to 8f, best at 8f, acts on gd, has worn blinkers. Turf high 86.
J H M Gosden [0-5] R E Sangster & A K Collins (from A G Foster [1-1] Oct 1999).

COLORFUL AMBITION BHB 34f63a **RR 36f 63a** 88[5]

10 b g Slip Anchor 12.7f **(75)** - Reprocolor (Jimmy Reppin) 8.8f **(64)**
Form - 5
Record 2000 - 1st:0 2nd:0 3rd:0 Ran:1
Pre2000 - 1st:3 2nd:4 3rd:3 Ran:24
Win Prizemoney £9,315 *Total Prizemoney* £15,440
2000 AW 0-1: (16f) (Fibr)
Very moderate gelding.
W W Haigh [0-4] Alan Swinbank (from Mrs A Duffield [5-27] Spt 1996).

COLOUR KEY (USA) BHB 32f **RR 29f** 3260[16]

6 b g Red Ransom (USA) 8.6f **(83)** - Trend (USA) (Ray's Word (USA))
Form - 00
Record 2000 - 1st:0 2nd:0 3rd:0 Ran:2
Pre2000 - 1st:0 2nd:0 3rd:0 Ran:4
2000 Turf 0-2: (12f 2) (frm 2)
Little account gelding. Turf high 29 (began Jly).
P Hayward [0-5] P Hayward (from D R C Elsworth [0-3] Jun 1997).

COLOUR SERGEANT (USA) **RR 68f** 498[3]

2 ch c Candy Stripes (USA) - Princess Afleet (USA) (Afleet (CAN))
Form - 3
Record 2000 - 1st:0 2nd:0 3rd:1 Ran:1
Win Prizemoney £0 *Total Prizemoney* £642
2000 Turf 0-1: (5f) (gd)
Currently average colt. *M L W Bell [0-1] Mrs Evelyn Hankinson.*

COLSTAR (USA) **RR 112f** 5329a[7]

4 b f Opening Verse (USA) 11.8f **(70)** - Ascend (USA) (Risen Star (USA))
Form - 7
2000 Turf 0-1: (11f) (frm)
Currently Group-class. (1st run) - 7th of 14 to Perfect Sting (4 Nov Churchill Downs 11f frm RF 5329a).
P Fout in USA [0-1] Beverley Steinman.

COLUMBINE (IRE) BHB 84f79a **RR 73f 79a** 4781[3]

2 b f Pivotal - Heart of India (IRE) (Try My Best (USA)) 7.6f **(67)**
Form - 133
Record 2000 - 1st:1 2nd:0 3rd:2 Ran:3
Win Prizemoney £3,510 *Total Prizemoney* £5,766
Wins * **2000** Jly Doncas (G-F) 5f 66+ <
2000 Turf 1-2: (5f 1-1, 6f) (g-f, frm 1-1) 2000 AW 0-1: (5f) (Fibr)
Currently above-average filly. Turf high 73 (began Jly) - also 1st of 7 getting 4lb from Extra Guest (19 Jly Doncaster RF 2931). Battled on well to make a winning debut at Doncaster, but was comfortably held in a Chester conditions event next time.
A Berry [1-3] Miss Lilo Blum.

COLUMBUS (IRE) **RR 78f** 3685[6]

3 b c Sadler's Wells (USA) 11.3f **(87)** - Northern Script (USA) (Arts And Letters (USA)) 12.7f **(68)**
Form - 64176
Record 2000 - 1st:1 2nd:0 3rd:0 Ran:5
Pre2000 - 1st:0 2nd:0 3rd:0 Ran:1
Win Prizemoney £3,450 *Total Prizemoney* £3,710
Wins 2000 Jly Roscom (GD) 16f 78 <
2000 Turf 1-5: (12f 2, 14f, 16f 1-2) (g-s, gd 1-2, g-f 2)
Above-average colt, effective 12 to 16f, acts on g-s to gd, often wears blinkers. Turf high 78 (1st run) - 6th of 7 to Independence Hall (5 Jun Leopardstown 12f g-s RF 1927a) - also 1st of 13 from Circus Maximus (10 Jly Roscommon RF 2897a).
C Grant [0-2] C E Whiteley (from A P O'Brien in IRE [1-4] Jly 2000).

COLWAY RITZ BHB 80f **RR 85f** 4745[15]

6 b g Rudimentary (USA) 8.2f **(66)** - Million Heiress (Auction Ring (USA)) 8.6f **(65)**
Form - 036112024580
Record 2000 - 1st:2 2nd:2 3rd:1 Ran:12
Pre2000 - 1st:5 2nd:3 3rd:8 Ran:42
Win Prizemoney £42,875 *Total Prizemoney* £63,135
Wins * **2000** Jun Ripon (G-F) H 10f 78 78+
* **2000** Jun Ripon (G-S) H 10f 75 78
* 1999 Jun Redcar (FRM) H 10f 78 82 <
* 1999 May Redcar (FRM) H 10f 74 78
* 1999 May Ripon (G-S) H 10f 69 75
* 1998 Jly Beverl (GD) H 8.5f 68 70
1997 Oct Doncas (GD) H 7f 65 69
2000 Turf 2-12: (8f 3, 10f 2-9) (g-s, gd 3, g-f 2-2, frm 5, hrd)
Useful gelding, effective 8 to 12f, best at 10f, acts on frm, has worn blinkers, prefers right handed tracks, prefers tight tracks, excels at Ripon and does well at Beverley. Turf high 90 - 2nd of 6 giving 12lb to Gralmano (24 Jun Redcar 10f frm RF 2252). A winner three times in '99 at ten furlongs, including the Zetland Gold Cup, he paid for that by climbing the handicap, but eventually dropped to a favourable mark and regained winning form with two wins over his ideal trip at Ripon in June. He acts on easy ground, but looks ideally suited by a fast surface.
W Storey [6-45] Mrs M Tindale & Tom Park (from J W Watts [1-12] Oct 1997).

COL-WOODY BHB 51f45a **RR 49f 45a** 1512[3]

4 ch g Safawan 6.6f **(60)** - Sky Fighter (Hard Fought) 8.8f **(62)**
Form - 873
Record 2000 - 1st:0 2nd:0 3rd:1 Ran:3
Pre2000 - 1st:0 2nd:3 3rd:1 Ran:14
Win Prizemoney £0 *Total Prizemoney* £4,250
2000 Turf 0-2: (10f, 11f) (hvy, g-s) 2000 AW 0-1: (12f) (Fibr)
Workmanlike, moderate gelding, effective 8 to 12f, acts on g-f, has worn blinkers, favours tight tracks. Turf high 41. Becoming disappointing.
J G Portman [0-6] Christopher Shankland (from A P Jarvis [0-14] Aug 1999).

COMANCHE QUEEN BHB 34f **RR 18f** 3686[9]

3 ch f Totem (USA) 5f **(38)** - Chess Mistress (USA) (Run The Gantlet (USA)) 12.1f **(59)**
Form - 00000
Record 2000 - 1st:0 2nd:0 3rd:0 Ran:5
Pre2000 - 1st:0 2nd:0 3rd:0 Ran:4
2000 Turf 0-5: (8f, 9f, 10f, 12f, 14f) (gd 2, g-f 2, frm)

Light-framed, poor filly, has worn blinkers. Turf high 18.
**K W Hogg [0-9] Hurn Racing Club.*

COMBINED VENTURE (IRE) BHB 29f RR 39f 3807[10]

4 b c Dolphin Street (FR) - Centinela **(47f)** (Caerleon (USA)) 8.6f **(71)**
Form - 0
Record 2000 - 1st:0 2nd:0 3rd:0 Ran:1
Pre2000 - 1st:0 2nd:1 3rd:3 Ran:16
Win Prizemoney £0 *Total Prizemoney* £2,470
2000 AW 0-1: (12f) (Fibr)
Very moderate colt, effective 10 to 11f, acts on gd to frm, prefers left handed tracks.
**K A Morgan [0-4] Mrs Joanne Woods (from E Weymes [0-13] Aug 1999).*

COMEONMOM (USA) RR 427a[3]

4 b c
Form - 3
2000 AW 0-1: (10f) (Dirt)
Group-class colt. **S bin Suroor in UAE [0-1].*

COME ON MURGY BHB 48f43a RR 42f 43a 514[3]

3 b f Weldnaas (USA) 8.4f **(55)** - Forest Song (Forzando) 7.6f **(59)**
Form - 1314447543
Record 2000 - 1st:1 2nd:0 3rd:1 Ran:8
Pre2000 - 1st:1 2nd:0 3rd:1 Ran:10
Win Prizemoney £3,445 *Total Prizemoney* £3,971
Wins * 2000 *Jan Southw (STD) S 7f 51+* **<**
*1999 *Dec Wolver (STD) S 7f 48*
2000 AW 1-8: (6f 2, 7f 1-6) (Fibr 1-8)
Light-framed, moderate filly, effective 7 to 8f, best at 7f, - acts on AW, best on Fibr, has worn blinkers, likes left handed tracks, likes tight tracks. AW high 51 - also 1st of 9 giving 5lb to Sounds Crazy (7 Jan Southwell RF 0044). Consistent. **A Bailey [2-18] K W Weale.*

COME ON PEKAN (IRE) RR 80f 4607[4]

2 b c Sri Pekan (USA) - Landrail (USA) (Storm Bird (CAN)) 10.3f **(74)**
Form - 24
Record 2000 - 1st:0 2nd:1 3rd:0 Ran:2
Win Prizemoney £0 *Total Prizemoney* £2,265
2000 Turf 0-2: (7f 2) (sft, g-s)
Currently decent colt. Turf high 80 (began Spt) - 4th of 8 to Lunar Crystal (24 Spt Ascot 7f g-s RF 4607). **M A Jarvis [0-2] Ivan Allan.*

COMEOUTOFTHEFOG (IRE) BHB 44f34a RR 45f 34a 5113[6]

5 b g Mujadil (USA) 7.7f **(70)** - Local Belle (Ballymore) 7.3f **(64)**
Form - 25715086
Record 2000 - 1st:1 2nd:0 3rd:0 Ran:7
Pre2000 - 1st:3 2nd:5 3rd:5 Ran:38
Win Prizemoney £9,055 *Total Prizemoney* £15,236
Wins 2000 *Feb Wolver (STD) S 7f 52*
1999 *Jun Lingfi (STD) SH 7f 52 59*
1998 *Feb Lingfi (SLW) C 8f 68* **<**
1998 *Feb Lingfi (SLW) C 7f 61+*
2000 AW 1-7: (7f 1-4, 8f 3) (Equi 2, Fibr 1-5)
Moderate gelding, effective 7 to 8f, best at 7f, - acts on AW, best on Equi, has worn blinkers, prefers left handed tracks, prefers tight tracks. AW high 55 (1st run) - 5th of 12 getting 12lb from Canadian Approval (15 Jan Lingfield 8f Equi RF 0097) - also 1st of 11 giving 5lb to Diletto (22 Feb Wolverhampton RF 0336).
**Miss S J Wilton [0-4] John Pointon and Sons (from S Dow [1-4] Feb 2000).*

COMEUPPANCE (IRE) BHB 53f RR 57f 3973[6]

2 b g General Monash (USA) - Press Reception (Beldale Flutter (USA)) 9.7f **(71)**
Form - 686
Record 2000 - 1st:0 2nd:0 3rd:0 Ran:3
2000 Turf 0-3: (6f, 7f 2) (g-f, frm 2)
Currently fair gelding. Turf high 57 (began Jly).
**T D Barron [0-3] Alex Gorrie.*

COMEX FLYER (IRE) BHB 51f RR 48f 3425[9]

3 ch g Prince of Birds (USA) - Smashing Pet (Mummy's Pet) 7.7f **(60)**
Form - 406701080
Record 2000 - 1st:1 2nd:0 3rd:0 Ran:9
Pre2000 - 1st:0 2nd:0 3rd:0 Ran:4
Win Prizemoney £1,855 *Total Prizemoney* £2,311
Wins * **2000** Jun Catter (G-S) 7f 48 **<**
2000 Turf 1-9: (6f 3, 7f 1-3, 8f 2, 11f) (gd 1-3, g-f 2, frm 4)
Scopey, moderate gelding, has worn blinkers, likes tight tracks. Turf high 60. **D Nicholls [1-9] Neil Smith (from J Berry [0-4] Spt 1999).*

COMING UP ROSES BHB 35f RR 45f 1480[16]

3 b f Sabrehill (USA) 8.5f **(64)** - Peaches Polly **(87?f 58a)** (Slip Anchor) 9.8f **(73)**
Form - 00
Record 2000 - 1st:0 2nd:0 3rd:0 Ran:2
Pre2000 - 1st:0 2nd:0 3rd:0 Ran:1
2000 Turf 0-1: (6f) (gd) 2000 AW 0-1: (8f) (Fibr)
Unfurnished, currently moderate filly.
**D Shaw [0-2] Mrs Dyanne Benjamin (from B W Hills [0-1] Jun 1999).*

COMMANDER BHB 57f RR 63f 2345[14]

4 b g Puissance 7.1f **(60)** - Tarkhana (IRE) (Dancing Brave (USA)) 8.4f **(76)**
Form - 5030
Record 2000 - 1st:0 2nd:0 3rd:1 Ran:4
Pre2000 - 1st:0 2nd:0 3rd:0 Ran:2
Win Prizemoney £0 *Total Prizemoney* £398
2000 Turf 0-4: (7f 2, 8f 2) (gd 2, g-f, frm)
Scopey, average gelding. Turf high 63.
**M Kettle [0-4] A Parker & A Buckley (from H R A Cecil [0-2] Oct 1999).*

COMMANDER COLLINS (IRE) BHB 109f RR 112f 4940a[11]

4 b c Sadler's Wells (USA) 11.3f **(87)** - Kanmary (FR) (Kenmare (FR)) 6.5f **(72)**
Form - 43340
Record 2000 - 1st:0 2nd:0 3rd:2 Ran:5
Pre2000 - 1st:2 2nd:1 3rd:0 Ran:5
Win Prizemoney £107,407 *Total Prizemoney* £151,099
Wins 1998 Oct Doncas (HVY) G1 8f 112 **<**
1998 Jly Newmar (FRM) L 7f 102+
2000 Turf 0-5: (10f, 12f 4) (sft, gd 3, frm)
Well made, Group-class colt, effective 10 to 12f, best at 12f, acts on sft to gd, best on gd. Turf high 112 - 3rd of 4 to Montjeu (10 Spt Longchamp 12f gd RF 4416a). Consistent. He won a weak renewal of the Racing Post Trophy as a juvenile and was probably overrated at the end of that season. He has run respectably this year, but is not proving easy to place.
**J H M Gosden [0-5] (from P W Chapple-Hyam [2-5] Aug 1999).*

COMMENDABLE (USA) RR 4135a[3]

3 ch c Gone West (USA) 7.8f **(82)** - Bought Twice (USA) (In Reality) 7.4f **(74)**
Form - 13
2000 AW 1-2: (10f, 12f 1-1) (Dirt 1-2)
Currently high-class colt, often wears blinkers. AW high 117 (1st run) - 1st of 11 from Aptitude (10 Jun Belmont Park RF 2001a).
**D W Lukas in USA [1-2].*

COMMONBIRD BHB 36f RR 46f 2539[8]

3 b f Common Grounds 8.1f **(66)** - Queenbird **(63f 52a)** (Warning)
Form - 8588
Record 2000 - 1st:0 2nd:0 3rd:0 Ran:4
Pre2000 - 1st:0 2nd:0 3rd:1 Ran:11
Win Prizemoney £0 *Total Prizemoney* £504
2000 Turf 0-4: (5f, 6f, 7f 2) (gd 2, g-f, frm)
Scopey, moderate filly, effective 6f, acts on g-f, has worn blinkers, likes left handed tracks, likes tight tracks. Turf high 46.
**Andrew Reid [0-15] A S Reid.*

COMMON CAUSE BHB 72f RR 76f 3030[8]

4 b f Polish Patriot (USA) 7.8f **(70)** - Alongside (Slip Anchor) 9.8f **(73)**
Form - 44558
Record 2000 - 1st:0 2nd:0 3rd:0 Ran:5
Pre2000 - 1st:2 2nd:1 3rd:2 Ran:8
Win Prizemoney £11,002 *Total Prizemoney* £13,522
Wins * 1999 Aug Leices (GD) H 11.8f 72 74+ **<**
* 1999 Jun Lingfi (GD) H 11.5f 65 67
2000 Turf 0-5: (10f 2, 12f 2, 15f) (g-f 3, frm 2)
Light-framed, above-average filly, effective 10 to 12f, best at 12f, acts on gd to frm, likes tight tracks, excels at Windsor and Leicester. Turf high 76 - 4th of 14 giving 11lb to Lidakiya (8 Jun

Newbury 10f g-f RF 1814). **C F Wall [2-13] T Taniguchi.*

COMMON CONSENT (IRE) BHB 52f **RR 53f** 4616[13]
4 b f Common Grounds 8.1f **(66)** - Santella Bell (Ballad Rock) 7.8f **(63)**
Form - 7610420600
Record 2000 - 1st:1 2nd:1 3rd:0 Ran:10
Pre2000 - 1st:0 2nd:1 3rd:2 Ran:10
Win Prizemoney £2,954 *Total Prizemoney* £9,030
Wins * 2000 Jun Folkes (FRM) H 9.7f 52 54 <
2000 Turf 1-10: (8f 4, 9f 2, 10f 1-3, 12f) (gd 4, g-f 1-2, frm 4)
Scopey, fair filly, effective 8 to 11f, best at 11f, acts on gd to frm, best on frm, likes right handed tracks, favours tight tracks. Turf high 56 - 2nd of 10 getting 26lb from Aegean Dream (2 Aug Goodwood 9f gd RF 3319) - also 1st of 13 giving 1lb to Silver Queen (30 Jun Folkestone RF 2396). She took a long time in getting off the mark, but managed to win a handicap at Folkestone in June. Suited by very fast ground.
**S Woodman [1-20] Mrs Fiona Gordon & Mrs Jenny Carter.*

COMMON KRIS (IRE) RR 90f 5180a[3]
5 ch g Common Grounds 8.1f **(66)** - Lotte Lenta (Gorytus (USA)) 7.8f **(60)**
Form - 7662033
2000 Turf 0-7: (8f, 9f, 10f 2, 11f, 12f 2) (g-s 3, gd 2, g-f, frm)
Useful gelding, effective 9 to 12f, acts on g-s to frm, excels at Naas. Turf high 90 - 2nd of 13 to Media Puzzle (13 Jly Down Royal 12f frm RF 2905a). Was punished by the Handicapper for two wins in August 1999, and has continued to run well from a higher mark without winning since.
**P Casey in IRE [3-18] Mrs Margaret McManus.*

COMMON PLACE BHB 94f89a **RR 96f 89a** 3228[4]
3 b g Common Grounds 8.1f **(66)** - One Wild Oat **(53f 43a)** (Shareef Dancer (USA)) 9.9f **(73)**
Form - 56113214
Record 2000 - 1st:3 2nd:1 3rd:1 Ran:8
Pre2000 - 1st:1 2nd:0 3rd:0 Ran:7
Win Prizemoney £21,498 *Total Prizemoney* £26,008
Wins * 2000 Jun Sandow (G-F) H 9f 90 96 <
*** 2000** Apr Kempto (SFT) H 9f 85 91
*** 2000** Mar Kempto (GD) H 9f 87
***** 1999 Aug Goodwo (GD) H 7f 77 79
2000 Turf 3-6: (9f 3-3, 10f 2, 11f) (sft 1-1, g-s, gd 1-1, g-f 1-3) 2000 AW 0-2: (8f, 9f) (Fibr 2)
Small, very useful gelding, effective 9 to 11f, acts on sft to g-f, best on g-f, prefers right handed tracks, prefers tight tracks, excels at Kempton. Turf high 96 - also 1st of 6 giving 4lb to Burning Sunset (17 Jun Sandown RF 2056). AW high 74. Improving. Ran into Primo Valentino and Bachir in his first two starts at two in 1999, and finally got off the mark in a Goodwood nursery. He was in fine form during the spring of 2000, winning twice over nine furlongs at Kempton and ran well afterwards, adding another victory over that specialist trip at Sandown. Not seen after July, if all is well he could be one to consider for the Cambridgeshire next autumn.
**C F Wall [4-15] Tim Yau.*

COMMONWOOD BHB 44f **RR 65f** 4677[11]
3 b g Rudimentary (USA) 8.2f **(66)** - Mira Lady (Henbit (USA)) 9f **(61)**
Form - 4807060
Record 2000 - 1st:0 2nd:0 3rd:0 Ran:7
Pre2000 - 1st:0 2nd:1 3rd:1 Ran:8
Win Prizemoney £0 *Total Prizemoney* £1,557
2000 Turf 0-5: (8f 3, 10f 2)(g-s, g-f, frm 3) 2000 AW 0-2: (8f, 12f)(Fibr 2)
Light-framed, average gelding, effective 5f, acts on g-f. Turf high 65. AW high 28 (began Spt). Becoming disappointing.
**J G Smyth-Osbourne [0-15] Highfields Partnership I.*

COMO (USA) RR 77f 5236[D]
2 b br f Cozzene (USA) 10.1f **(87)** - Merida (Warning)
Form - 4D
Record 2000 - 1st:0 2nd:0 3rd:0 Ran:2
Win Prizemoney £0 *Total Prizemoney* £272
2000 Turf 0-2: (7f 2) (g-s 2)
Currently above-average filly. Turf high 77 (began Oct).
**R Charlton [0-2] K Abdulla.*

COMPANION BHB 71f69a **RR 76f 69a** 4475[4]
2 b f Most Welcome 8.6f **(66)** - Benazir (High Top) 10.2f **(67)**
Form - 464
Record 2000 - 1st:0 2nd:0 3rd:0 Ran:3
Win Prizemoney £0 *Total Prizemoney* £274
2000 Turf 0-2: (8f 2) (g-s, frm) 2000 AW 0-1: (8f) (Fibr)
Currently above-average filly. Turf high 76 (began Aug). (1st run) - 4th of 10 getting 5lb from Seductive (16 Spt Wolverhampton 8f Fibr RF 4475). **W J Haggas [0-3] J M Greetham.*

COMPATRIOT (IRE) BHB 61a **RR 67f** 5154[4]
4 b g Bigstone (IRE) - Campestral (USA) (Alleged (USA)) 10f **(76)**
Form - 246025361064
Record 2000 - 1st:1 2nd:2 3rd:1 Ran:12
Pre2000 - 1st:0 2nd:2 3rd:3 Ran:13
Win Prizemoney £2,534 *Total Prizemoney* £10,942
Wins * 2000 *Spt Wolver (STD) H 8.5f 57 62 <*
2000 Turf 0-8: (7f, 8f 5, 10f, 12f) (gd 3, g-f 2, frm 2, hrd) 2000 AW 1-4: (8f 1-3, 12f) (Equi, Fibr 1-3)
Well made, average gelding, effective 5 to 7f, acts on gd to frm, has worn blinkers, likes left handed tracks. Turf high 67. AW high 62 (began Jly). Possesses plenty of ability, but has proved a little disappointing.
**P S Felgate [1-12] Foreneish Racing (from N A Callaghan [0-13] Oct 1999).*

COMPRADORE BHB 66f **RR 72+f** 5061[7]
5 b m Mujtahid (USA) 7.4f **(69)** - Keswa (Kings Lake (USA)) 10.8f **(67)**
Form - 8321103003837
Record 2000 - 1st:2 2nd:1 3rd:4 Ran:13
Pre2000 - 1st:2 2nd:2 3rd:2 Ran:29
Win Prizemoney £14,369 *Total Prizemoney* £22,827
Wins * 2000 May Bright (SFT) 7f 72+
*** 2000** May Salisb (GD) H 7f 61 68
***** 1998 Oct Folkes (G-S) 6f 69
***** 1997 May Newbur (G-F) 5.2f 82 <
2000 Turf 2-13: (6f 2, 7f 2-8, 8f 3) (sft 2, gd 2-6, g-f 4, frm)
Above-average filly, effective 7 to 8f, best at 7f, acts on gd to frm, excels at Salisbury and Brighton, likes Newbury. Turf high 72 - 1st of 8 giving 10lb to Kinsman (24 May Brighton RF 1424) - also 1st of 20 getting 1lb from Feather 'n Lace (18 May Salisbury RF 1272). A fair handicapper on her day, she gained consecutive victories at Salisbury and Brighton in May. Best over seven furlongs.
**M Blanshard [4-42] C McKenna.*

COMPTON ACE BHB 116f90a **RR 118f 90a** 2180[3]
4 ch c Pharly (FR) 11.5f **(64)** - Mountain Lodge (Blakeney) 10.5f **(64)**
Form - 23
Record 2000 - 1st:0 2nd:1 3rd:1 Ran:2
Pre2000 - 1st:2 2nd:2 3rd:1 Ran:8
Win Prizemoney £32,546 *Total Prizemoney* £69,115
Wins * 1999 Jly Goodwo (G-F) G3 12f 118 <
***** 1999 May Newbur (G-F) H 13.3f 80 83+
2000 Turf 0-2: (10f, 20f) (g-s, g-f)
Workmanlike, high-class colt, effective 10 to 20f, acts on g-s to frm. Turf high 118 - 3rd of 11 getting 2lb from Kayf Tara (22 Jun Ascot 20f g-f RF 2180). Improving. He was much improved in '99, winning the Gordon Stakes at Glorious Goodwood. Unfortunately, he sustained a fractured knee in the process and that was him finished for the season. Ran pretty well in a Newbury conditions event on his return before finishing a fine third in the Ascot Gold Cup. Stays very well. **G A Butler [2-10] E Penser.*

COMPTON ARROW (IRE) BHB 72f68a **RR 74f 68a** 5242[3]
4 b g Petardia 8.2f **(58)** - Impressive Lady (Mr Fluorocarbon) 6f **(55)**
Form - 00000053
Record 2000 - 1st:0 2nd:0 3rd:1 Ran:8
Pre2000 - 1st:2 2nd:0 3rd:4 Ran:13
Win Prizemoney £10,452 *Total Prizemoney* £17,095
Wins * 1998 Oct Ascot (SFT) 6f 95 <
***** 1998 Aug Haydoc (G-S) 6f 86+
2000 Turf 0-7: (7f 3, 8f 4) (g-s 3, gd 2, g-f, frm) 2000 AW 0-1: (8f) (Equi)
Scopey, above-average gelding, effective 7 to 8f, acts on g-f to frm. Turf high 74. **G A Butler [2-21] E Penser.*

COMPTON AVIATOR BHB 75f75a **RR 80df 75a** 4922[1]
4 ch g First Trump - Rifada (Ela-Mana-Mou) 10.1f **(70)**

Form - 0701
Record 2000 - 1st:1 2nd:0 3rd:0 Ran:4
Pre2000 - 1st:0 2nd:0 3rd:2 Ran:3
Win Prizemoney £1,785 *Total Prizemoney* £3,415
Wins * **2000** *Oct Lingfi (STD) C 7f 50+* <
2000 Turf 0-3: (10f, 16f 2) (gd, frm 2) 2000 AW 1-1: (7f 1-1) (Equi 1-1)
Scopey, decent gelding, effective 10 to 16f, acts on frm. Turf high 80 (began Spt) - 7th of 9 getting 10lb from Bangalore (15 Spt Newbury 16f frm RF 4438). (1st run). **G A Butler [1-7] E Penser.*

COMPTON BANKER (IRE) BHB 96f RR 98+f 4700[12]

3 br c Distinctly North (USA) 7.4f **(63)** - Mary Hinge **(96f)** (Dowsing (USA))
Form - 051024410
Record 2000 - 1st:2 2nd:1 3rd:0 Ran:9
Pre2000 - 1st:0 2nd:0 3rd:0 Ran:3
Win Prizemoney £40,007 *Total Prizemoney* £60,155
Wins * **2000** Spt Doncas (GD) H 5.6f 89 98 <
* **2000** Jun Ascot (G-F) H 5f 77 86
2000 Turf 2-9: (5f 1-4, 6f 1-5) (gd 2-4, g-f 4, frm)
Scopey, very useful colt, effective 5 to 6f, acts on gd to frm. Turf high 98 - 1st of 22 getting 1lb from Delegate (6 Spt Doncaster RF 4258). Landed a well contested handicap over the minimum trip at Ascot in June and was possibly unlucky not to win a very valuable handicap at the same track later the same month, but made no mistake in the Portland at Doncaster. Suited by six furlongs or a stiff five, his come-from-behind style means he meets more than his fair share of trouble in running. **G A Butler [2-12] E Penser.*

COMPTON BOLTER (IRE) BHB 109f RR 113f 5239[4]

3 b c Red Sunset 9f **(57)** - Milk And Honey (So Blessed) 8.7f **(67)**
Form - 485045174
Record 2000 - 1st:1 2nd:0 3rd:0 Ran:9
Pre2000 - 1st:1 2nd:2 3rd:2 Ran:5
Win Prizemoney £12,279 *Total Prizemoney* £53,814
Wins * **2000** Spt Newbur (G-F) 9f 103 <
* 1999 Spt Chepst (GD) 8.1f 85
2000 Turf 1-7: (8f 3, 9f 1-1, 10f 3) (hvy, g-s 2, gd 3, g-f 1-1) 2000 AW 0-2: (8f, 9f) (Dirt 2)
Scopey, Group-class colt, effective 9f, acts on g-f, has worn blinkers. Turf high 113. AW high 109. Consistent. He has run fine races in the face of some stiff tasks this season, but did not win until landing a Newbury conditions event in September with a tongue tie fitted for the first time. **G A Butler [2-14] E Penser.*

Compton Bolter had some stiff tasks

COMPTON CHICK (IRE) RR 53f 5293[5]

2 b f Dolphin Street (FR) - Cecina (Welsh Saint) 7.6f **(64)**
Form - 75
Record 2000 - 1st:0 2nd:0 3rd:0 Ran:2
2000 Turf 0-2: (6f, 7f) (sft, g-s)
Currently fair filly. Turf high 53 (began Oct). **G A Butler [0-2] E Penser.*

COMPTON COMMANDER BHB 81f RR 80f 5219[1]

2 ch c Barathea (IRE) - Triode (USA) (Sharpen Up) 8.3f **(67)**
Form - 831
Record 2000 - 1st:1 2nd:0 3rd:1 Ran:3
Win Prizemoney £2,873 *Total Prizemoney* £3,398
Wins * **2000** Oct Bright (SFT) 10f 80 <
2000 Turf 1-3: (7f, 10f 1-2) (sft 1-1, g-s, g-f)
Currently decent colt. Turf high 80 (began Jly) - 1st of 7 giving 5lb to English Harbour (27 Oct Brighton RF 5219). **G A Butler [1-3] E Penser.*

CONCIERGE (IRE) BHB 39f RR 50f 4649[14]

3 b g Catrail (USA) - Monterana (Sallust) 8.4f **(63)**
Form - 7700
Record 2000 - 1st:0 2nd:0 3rd:0 Ran:4
2000 Turf 0-2: (8f 2) (g-f, frm) 2000 AW 0-2: (8f, 11f) (Fibr 2)
Workmanlike, fair gelding. Turf high 50. AW high 23 (began Jly). **D W Chapman [0-3] Michael Hill (from P F I Cole [0-1] Jun 2000).*

CONCINO (FR) BHB 35f RR 29f 5012[6]

3 b g Zafonic (USA) 9f **(83)** -Petronella (USA) (Nureyev (USA)) 8.7f **(78)**
Form - 0300706
Record 2000 - 1st:0 2nd:0 3rd:1 Ran:7
Pre2000 - 1st:0 2nd:0 3rd:0 Ran:3
Win Prizemoney £0 *Total Prizemoney* £426
2000 Turf 0-6: (8f 2, 10f 2, 14f 2) (gd, g-f, frm 3, hrd) 2000 AW 0-1: (14f) (Fibr)
Tall, moderate gelding, effective 14f, - acts on Fibr, likes left handed tracks, likes tight tracks. Turf high 27. (1st run) - 6th of 16 getting 5lb from Half Tide (16 Oct Southwell 14f Fibr RF 5012). **Miss A Stokell [0-7] T J Ford (from P W Harris [0-4] Mar 2000).*

CONDOR HERO (IRE) RR 64f 2613[6]

3 b g Catrail (USA) - Rince Deas (IRE) (Alzao (USA)) 7.1f **(68)**
Form - 36
Record 2000 - 1st:0 2nd:0 3rd:1 Ran:2
Win Prizemoney £0 *Total Prizemoney* £647
2000 Turf 0-2: (6f, 7f) (gd, frm)
Workmanlike, average gelding. Turf high 64. (DEAD) **W Jarvis [0-2] N S Yong.*

CONFLICT (FR) BHB 98f RR 97f 575a[1]

4 b c Warning 8.1f **(77)** - La Dama Bonita (USA) (El Gran Senor (USA)) 9.6f **(76)**
Form - 1
2000 AW 1-1: (8f 1-1) (Dirt 1-1)
Leggy, Pattern-class colt, effective 8f, - acts on Dirt. (1st run) - 1st of 13 from Iftitah (25 Mar Nad Al Sheba RF 0575a). **N Robb in UAE [1-1] Sheikh Marwan Al Maktoum (from C E Brittain [2-9] Aug 1999).*

CONFRONTER BHB 35f45a RR 28f 45a 1459[9]

11 ch g Bluebird (USA) 7.9f **(71)** - Grace Darling (USA) (Vaguely Noble) 10.1f **(72)**
Form - 6450700
Record 2000 - 1st:0 2nd:0 3rd:0 Ran:4
Pre2000 - 1st:12 2nd:20 3rd:11 Ran:123
Win Prizemoney £40,036 *Total Prizemoney* £76,111
Wins * 1999 *Apr Lingfi (STD) H 10f 58 61*
* 1999 *Jan Lingfi (STD) H 10f 55 60*
* 1997 *Nov Lingfi (STD) H 10f 52 54*
* 1997 *Jun Bath (G-F) H 8f 53 57*
2000 Turf 0-1: (10f) (gd) 2000 AW 0-3: (10f, 12f 2) (Equi 3)
Moderate gelding, effective 10f, - acts on Equi, has worn blinkers (extremely effectively), favours left handed tracks, favours tight tracks. AW high 41. Becoming disappointing. He scored at Bath in June, though he showed little else on turf in '97. He scored on the Lingfield Equitrack in November, when the ten-furlong trip looked

plenty far enough, but did not perform so well at Wolverhampton when he seemed not to get home over the extended nine-furlongs. Decent efforts back on turf.
**S Dow [9-110] Hatfield Ltd (from P F I Cole [3-17] Spt 1992).*

CONGENIALITY (USA) BHB 52f RR 55f 4773[13]
2 b f Katowice (USA) - Popularity (General Assembly (USA)) 10f **(68)**
Form - 0040
Record 2000 - 1st:0 2nd:0 3rd:0 Ran:4
Win Prizemoney £0 *Total Prizemoney* £285
2000 Turf 0-4: (6f, 7f 3) (g-s, gd, g-f, frm)
Fair filly. Turf high 53 (began Jly).
**T D Easterby [0-4] Manchester United Racing Club.*

CONISTON RR 1374[14]
2 b g Lake Coniston (IRE) - Allyana (IRE) **(62df)** (Thatching) 8f **(66)**
Form - 0
Record 2000 - 1st:0 2nd:0 3rd:0 Ran:1
2000 AW 0-1: (5f) (Fibr)
Currently very poor gelding.
**Ronald Thompson [0-1] Haggswood Partnerships.*

CONISTON MILL (IRE) BHB 65f56a RR 71f 56a 5022[4]
3 b f Lake Coniston (IRE) - Haiti Mill (Free State) 8.7f **(61)**
Form - 34
Record 2000 - 1st:0 2nd:0 3rd:1 Ran:2
Win Prizemoney £0 *Total Prizemoney* £903
2000 Turf 0-2: (7f 2) (sft, g-s)
Lengthy, currently above-average filly. Turf high 71 (began Spt).
**W R Muir [0-2] Timothy Chick.*

CONNECT RR 79f 4703[13]
3 b g Petong 7.6f **(58)** - Natchez Trace (Commanche Run) 8.5f **(58)**
Form - 7000430560
Record 2000 - 1st:0 2nd:0 3rd:1 Ran:10
Pre2000 - 1st:1 2nd:1 3rd:1 Ran:4
Win Prizemoney £2,944 *Total Prizemoney* £7,157
Wins * 1999 Spt Pontef (G-F) 5f 79 <
2000 Turf 0-10: (5f 6, 6f 3, 7f) (g-s, gd, g-f 4, frm 3, hrd)
Workmanlike, above-average gelding, effective 5f, acts on gd to frm, best on gd, has worn blinkers. Turf high 79 - 3rd of 8 giving 1lb to Boanerges (30 Jun Newmarket 5f g-f RF 2413).
**M H Tompkins [1-14] www raceworld co uk.*

CONORMARA (USA) RR 112f 5048a[8]
3 bb c Carr de Naskra (USA) 10.4f **(76)** - Teeming Shore (USA) (L'Emigrant (USA)) 10.5f **(62)**
Form - 0115238
2000 Turf 2-7: (5f, 6f 2-4, 7f 2) (sft, g-s 1-3, gd 1-3)
Group-class colt, effective 6 to 7f, best at 6f, acts on sft to gd, best on gd. Turf high 112 - 2nd of 8 getting 4lb from Eastern Purple (13 Aug Leopardstown 6f gd RF 3675a) - also 1st of 12 getting 18lb from One Won One (2 Jly Curragh RF 2529a). Progressed into a useful sprinter last season.
**D Hanley in IRE [2-9] Timothy Rooney.*

CONQUERING LOVE (IRE) BHB 59f RR 66f 4675[13]
2 b c Pursuit of Love 9.5f **(69)** - Susquehanna Days (USA) (Chief's Crown (USA)) 9.8f **(72)**
Form - 000
Record 2000 - 1st:0 2nd:0 3rd:0 Ran:3
2000 Turf 0-3: (7f 2, 8f) (g-s, gd, g-f)
Currently average colt. Turf high 66 (began Aug).
**M L W Bell [0-3] Nicholas Hodges.*

CONSIDERATION (IRE) BHB 44f40a RR 51f 40a 5018[6]
3 ch f Perugino (USA) - Reflection Time (IRE) (Fayruz)
Form - 024420006
Record 2000 - 1st:0 2nd:2 3rd:0 Ran:9
Pre2000 - 1st:0 2nd:1 3rd:0 Ran:4
Win Prizemoney £0 *Total Prizemoney* £2,617
2000 Turf 0-8: (5f 2, 6f 5, 8f) (g-s, g-f 5, frm 2) 2000 AW 0-1: (7f) (Fibr)
Neat, fair filly, effective 5 to 6f, acts on g-f to frm. Turf high 54 - 2nd of 4 getting 5lb from Scafell (21 Jun Hamilton 5f frm RF 2157). Becoming disappointing.
**D Burchell [0-3] Mrs S Geen (from A Berry [0-6] Jly 2000).*

CONSORT BHB 51f60a RR 57f 60a 1686[21]
7 b h Groom Dancer (USA) 9.5f **(75)** - Darnelle (Shirley Heights) 10.3f **(74)**
Form - 7300000000
Record 2000 - 1st:0 2nd:0 3rd:0 Ran:7
Pre2000 - 1st:2 2nd:5 3rd:3 Ran:35
Win Prizemoney £27,496 *Total Prizemoney* £70,782
Wins 1997 Nov Newmar (G-F) H 8f 84 89 <
1996 Aug Salisb (G-F) 7f 74
2000 Turf 0-5: (8f 5) (gd, g-f, frm 3) 2000 AW 0-2: (8f, 10f) (Equi 2)
Fair horse, effective 7 to 8f, acts on g-f to frm. Turf high 57. AW high 43.
**A J McNae [0-10] Mrs C Stewart-Moore (from Mrs A J Perrett [1-26] Nov 1999).*

CONSPICUOUS (IRE) BHB 77f86a RR 80f 86a 2221[6]
10 b g Alzao (USA) 9.8f **(73)** - Mystery Lady (USA) (Vaguely Noble) 10.1f **(72)**
Form - 8666
Record 2000 - 1st:0 2nd:0 3rd:0 Ran:4
Pre2000 - 1st:9 2nd:12 3rd:7 Ran:67
Win Prizemoney £55,143 *Total Prizemoney* £102,035
Wins * 1999 Oct Ascot (G-S) H 12f 78 81
* 1999 Spt Kempto (HVY) H 9f 73 75+
* 1998 Nov Bright (SFT) H 10f 83 89
* 1997 Oct Newbur (GD) H 10f 86 91 <
* 1997 Aug Salisb (G-F) H 8f 82 89
* 1996 Aug Goodwo (GD) 9f 84
2000 Turf 0-4: (9f, 12f 3) (g-s, gd 2, g-f)
Decent gelding, effective 9 to 12f, best at 12f, acts on g-s to gd, best on gd, has worn blinkers. Turf high 80 - 6th of 14 to Carlys Quest (19 May Newbury 12f gd RF 1304).
**L G Cottrell [8-58] Mrs Jenny Hopkins (from P F I Cole [1-13] Jly 1993).*

CONSPIRACY THEORY BHB 33f RR 42f 4200[12]
2 b f Fraam - Dewberry (Bay Express) 7.1f **(60)**
Form - 634648000
Record 2000 - 1st:0 2nd:0 3rd:1 Ran:9
Win Prizemoney £0 *Total Prizemoney* £580
2000 Turf 0-8: (5f 2, 6f 4, 7f, 8f) (gd, g-f 4, frm 3) 2000 AW 0-1: (7f) (Fibr)
Moderate filly. Turf high 42.
**A J Lockwood [0-3] A J Lockwood (from A Berry [0-6] Jly 2000).*

CONSPIRE (IRE) RR 85f 4148[4]
2 b f Turtle Island (IRE) - Mild Intrigue (USA) (Sir Ivor) 10.2f **(70)**
Form - 34
Record 2000 - 1st:0 2nd:0 3rd:1 Ran:2
Win Prizemoney £0 *Total Prizemoney* £1,044
2000 Turf 0-2: (8f 2) (g-s, frm)
Currently useful filly. Turf high 85 (1st run) (began Aug) - 3rd of 4 getting 6lb from Crystal Music (18 Aug Sandown 8f frm RF 3771).
**G A Butler [0-2] Anthony Rogers.*

CONSTANT BHB 50f RR 72f 5072[13]
3 b g Deploy 11.4f **(67)** - Avowal (Kris) 9.5f **(73)**
Form - 85000500
Record 2000 - 1st:0 2nd:0 3rd:0 Ran:8
Pre2000 - 1st:0 2nd:0 3rd:0 Ran:3
2000 Turf 0-7: (10f 2, 12f 4, 13f) (g-s, gd 2, g-f 3, frm) 2000 AW 0-1: (12f) (Fibr)
Strong, above-average gelding, effective 8f, acts on gd. Turf high 72. Inconsistent. **B W Hills [0-11] Kennet Valley Thoroughbreds III.*

CONSULTANT BHB 33f48a RR 20f 48a 5006[15]
4 b g Man of May - Avenita Lady (Free State) 8.7f **(61)**
Form - 000832872006000
Record 2000 - 1st:0 2nd:2 3rd:1 Ran:12
Pre2000 - 1st:2 2nd:2 3rd:1 Ran:20
Win Prizemoney £5,188 *Total Prizemoney* £11,741
Wins 1998 *Spt Wolver (STD)* *6f* *82* <
1998 *Apr Wolver (STD) S* *5f* *60+*
2000 Turf 0-4: (7f, 8f 3) (sft, frm 2, hrd) 2000 AW 0-8: (8f 6, 9f, 10f) (Equi, Fibr 7)
Leggy, moderate gelding, effective 5f, - acts on Fibr. Turf high 20. AW high 58. Becoming disappointing. Showed ability on the

Wolverhampton Fibresand at two, winning twice as well as running some fine races in defeat, and his best form of this season has again been on that track.
**D Carroll [0-1] J W C Coxon (from C N Kellett [0-12] Jun 2000).*

CONTACT (IRE) RR 80f 4743[6]

3 br g Grand Lodge (USA) - Pink Cashmere (IRE) (Polar Falcon (USA))
Form - 0806
Record 2000 - 1st:0 2nd:0 3rd:0 Ran:4
Pre2000 - 1st:1 2nd:0 3rd:1 Ran:4
Win Prizemoney £6,900 *Total Prizemoney* £7,320
Wins 1999 Spt Leopar (SFT) 6f 87+ <
2000 Turf 0-4: (6f, 7f, 8f, 10f) (gd 2, g-f, frm)
Decent gelding, effective 6 to 7f, acts on gd to g-f, has worn blinkers. Turf high 80 (began Aug). Consistent.
**M Wigham [0-4] Michael Wigham (from J S Bolger in IRE [1-4] Oct 1999).*

CONTEXTE (USA) RR 93f 452a[2]

3 ch c Septieme Ciel (USA) - Company (USA) (Nureyev (USA)) 8.7f **(78)**
Form - 2
2000 Turf 0-1: (7f) (hvy)
Currently useful colt. (1st run) - 2nd of 7 to Igman (7 Mar Maisons-laffitte 7f hvy RF 0452a). **J-C Rouget in FR [0-2] Oct 1999).*

CONTINUATION (IRE) RR 84+f 5186[2]

2 b c Sadler's Wells (USA) 11.3f **(87)** - Sequel (IRE) (Law Society (USA)) 9.9f **(70)**
Form - 2
Record 2000 - 1st:0 2nd:1 3rd:0 Ran:1
Win Prizemoney £0 *Total Prizemoney* £1,280
2000 Turf 0-1: (7f) (g-s)
Currently decent colt. (1st run) - 2nd of 16 to Halland (25 Oct Yarmouth 7f g-s RF 5186). **J H M Gosden [0-1] Sheikh Mohammed.*

CONTRABAND RR 75f 4701[10]

2 b c Red Ransom (USA) 8.6f **(83)** - Shortfall **(98f)** (Last Tycoon) 8.5f **(62)**
Form - 0
Record 2000 - 1st:0 2nd:0 3rd:0 Ran:1
2000 Turf 0-1: (7f) (g-f)
Currently above-average colt.
**W J Haggas [0-1] Highclere Thoroughbred Racing Ltd.*

CONTRARY MARY BHB 66f61a RR 65f 61a 4586[4]

5 b m Mujadil (USA) 7.7f **(70)** - Love Street (Mummy's Pet) 7.7f **(60)**
Form - 005122714
Record 2000 - 1st:2 2nd:2 3rd:0 Ran:9
Pre2000 - 1st:3 2nd:2 3rd:3 Ran:28
Win Prizemoney £17,292 *Total Prizemoney* £25,405
Wins * **2000** Spt Epsom (GD) H 7f 62 65
* **2000** Jun Salisb (G-F) H 6f 53 62
* 1999 Apr Folkes (SFT) 7f 66
* 1998 Aug Lingfi (G-F) H 7f 65 71
1997 May Lingfi (G-F) 5f 82+ <
2000 Turf 2-9: (6f 1-5, 7f 1-4) (g-s 2, gd 2, g-f 1-3, frm 1-2)
Average filly, effective 6 to 7f, best at 7f, acts on sft to frm, excels at Epsom and Salisbury. Turf high 65 - 1st of 16 giving 10lb to Annijaz (1 Spt Epsom RF 4147) - also 1st of 17 giving 3lb to Magique Etoile (28 Jun Salisbury RF 2351).
**J Akehurst [4-28] Flisher Foods (from S P C Woods [0-3] May 1998).*

CONWY CASTLE BHB 87f RR 85+f 4617[1]

3 b c Sri Pekan (USA) - Dumayla (Shernazar) 10.2f **(73)**
Form - 551
Record 2000 - 1st:1 2nd:0 3rd:0 Ran:3
Win Prizemoney £2,857 *Total Prizemoney* £2,857
Wins * **2000** Spt Bright (SFT) 11.9f 85 <
2000 Turf 1-3: (8f, 10f, 12f 1-1) (gd 1-1, g-f, frm)
Scopey, currently useful colt. Turf high 85 (began Jly) - 1st of 7 from Machrie Bay (24 Spt Brighton RF 4617).
**J H M Gosden [1-3] John Gosden.*

COOL AFFAIR (IRE) BHB 40f RR 33f 3625[15]

5 ch g Statoblest 6.4f **(63)** - Ukraine's Affair (USA) (The Minstrel (CAN)) 10f **(72)**
Form - 00
Record 2000 - 1st:0 2nd:0 3rd:0 Ran:2
Pre2000 - 1st:0 2nd:0 3rd:0 Ran:4
2000 Turf 0-2: (7f, 8f) (frm 2)
Very moderate gelding. Turf high 33 (began Aug).
**J G Given [0-2] S J Crawford (from K W Hogg [0-2] Jun 1999).*

COOLING OFF (IRE) BHB 72f RR 76f 5227[2]

3 b f Brief Truce (USA) 9.1f **(73)** - Lovers' Parlour (Beldale Flutter (USA)) 9.7f **(71)**
Form - 735742
Record 2000 - 1st:0 2nd:1 3rd:1 Ran:6
Win Prizemoney £0 *Total Prizemoney* £3,043
2000 Turf 0-6: (8f 4, 10f, 12f) (g-s, gd 2, g-f 2, frm)
Scopey, above-average filly, effective 10 to 12f, acts on gd. Turf high 76 (began Jly). **G Wragg [0-6] Mrs H H Morriss.*

COOL INVESTMENT (IRE) BHB 92f RR 95f 5321[4]

3 b c Prince of Birds (USA) - Superb Investment (IRE) (Hatim (USA))
Form - 28644135184
Record 2000 - 1st:2 2nd:1 3rd:1 Ran:11
Pre2000 - 1st:1 2nd:0 3rd:0 Ran:1
Win Prizemoney £18,410 *Total Prizemoney* £28,754
Wins * **2000** Spt Lucern (HVY) 15f 95+ <
* **2000** Jly Windso (SFT) 11.6f 91+
* 1999 Spt Mussel (G-F) 8f 48+
2000 Turf 2-11: (8f, 9f, 10f 2, 12f 1-5, 15f 1-2) (hvy 1-1, sft, g-s, gd 1-7, g-f)
Strong, very useful colt, effective 9 to 15f, best at 12f, acts on hvy to gd, best on gd, has worn blinkers. Turf high 95 - 3rd of 8 getting 1lb from Wait For The Will (29 Jly Ascot 12f gd RF 3206) - also 1st of 8 from Etbash (3 Spt Lucerne RF 4292a). He flew too high earlier in the season, including being tried on the continent, but found things a bit easier when winning a Windsor classified event in July. He subsequently won the Swiss St Leger, but that run seemed to take its toll as he performed poorly on his next two outings. **M Johnston [3-12] Markus Graff.*

COOL LOCATION BHB 17f RR 9f 3374[15]

3 b f Pelder (IRE) - Hello Lady (Wolverlife) 9.3f **(54)**
Form - 00760
Record 2000 - 1st:0 2nd:0 3rd:0 Ran:4
Pre2000 - 1st:0 2nd:0 3rd:0 Ran:4
2000 Turf 0-4: (10f, 11f, 12f, 16f) (gd, g-f, frm 2)
Light-framed, very poor filly, has worn blinkers. Turf high 9.
**M Quinn [0-8] V K Cox.*

COOL PROSPECT BHB 56f48a RR 53f 48a 3975[6]

5 b g Mon Tresor 7.9f **(60)** - I Ran Lovely (Persian Bold) 9.3f **(66)**
Form - 05754104232270306
Record 2000 - 1st:1 2nd:3 3rd:2 Ran:17
Pre2000 - 1st:1 2nd:4 3rd:3 Ran:29
Win Prizemoney £4,908 *Total Prizemoney* £18,352
Wins * **2000** May Mussel (FRM) H 5f 47 51 <
* 1999 Jun Redcar (FRM) H 6f 44 49
2000 Turf 1-11: (5f 1-5, 6f 5, 7f) (gd 3, frm 1-7, hrd) 2000 AW 0-6: (5f, 7f 2, 8f 2, 10f) (Equi, Fibr 5)
Fair gelding, effective 6f, acts on frm - acts on Fibr, has worn blinkers. Turf high 57 - 2nd of 19 getting 7lb from Full Spate (6 Jly Haydock 6f frm RF 2573). AW high 47. Consistent.
**K A Ryan [2-40] Mrs Candice Reilly (from A B Mulholland [0-6] Apr 1998).*

COOL SPICE BHB 51f RR 56f 5072[11]

3 b f Karinga Bay - Cool Run (Deep Run) 18f **(46)**
Form - 046570
Record 2000 - 1st:0 2nd:0 3rd:0 Ran:6
Win Prizemoney £0 *Total Prizemoney* £290
2000 Turf 0-6: (7f 2, 8f 2, 10f 2) (g-s 2, gd, g-f, frm 2)
Workmanlike, fair filly, effective 8f, acts on g-f. Turf high 56 (began Jly). **B Palling [0-6] Celtic Racing.*

COOL TEMPER BHB 67f71a RR 77f 71a 4934[23]

4 b g Magic Ring (IRE) 6.5f **(64)** - Ovideo **(58f)** (Domynsky) 8f **(82)**
Form - 555754400
Record 2000 - 1st:0 2nd:0 3rd:0 Ran:9

Pre2000 - 1st:0 2nd:6 3rd:0 Ran:6
Win Prizemoney £0 *Total Prizemoney* £7,623
2000 Turf 0-8: (7f 4, 8f 3, 10f) (sft 2, gd 2, g-f 2, frm 2) 2000 AW 0-1: (8f) (Fibr)
Workmanlike, above-average gelding, effective 6 to 8f, best at 6f, acts on sft to frm, best on frm, excels at Warwick. Turf high 77 - 5th of 14 giving 14lb to Dolphinelle (31 May Newbury 7f gd RF 1588).
**J M P Eustace [0-9] The Academy (from J E Banks [0-6] Jly 1999).*

COOL VIBES BHB 29f63a **RR 37f 63a** 5182[12]
5 br g Rock City 8.8f **(62)** - Meet Again (Lomond (USA)) 8.8f **(65)**
Form - 8070030
Record 2000 - 1st:0 2nd:0 3rd:1 Ran:7
Pre2000 - 1st:1 2nd:0 3rd:1 Ran:6
Win Prizemoney £4,737 *Total Prizemoney* £5,874
Wins 1998 Aug Newmar (G-F) 8f 83 <
2000 Turf 0-5: (8f 2, 10f, 12f, 14f) (sft, g-s, gd, g-f, frm) 2000 AW 0-2: (8f, 12f) (Fibr 2)
Moderate gelding, effective 10f, acts on frm, has worn blinkers. Turf high 37. AW high 42.
**Mrs N Macauley [0-9] G Wiltshire (from J Pearce [1-6] Jun 1999).*

COPCOURT ROYALE BHB 59a **RR 59a** 5114[5]
2 b f Rock City 8.8f **(62)** - Royal Meeting (Dara Monarch) 8.8f **(59)**
Form - 65
Record 2000 - 1st:0 2nd:0 3rd:0 Ran:2
2000 AW 0-2: (8f, 9f) (Fibr 2)
Currently average filly. AW high 35 (began Spt).
**D J G MurraySmith [0-2] Mrs Susan Nash.*

COPPELIUS (USA) RR 49f 4028[11]
2 b f Pleasant Colony (USA) 12.4f **(88)** - Lilian Bayliss (IRE) (Sadler's Wells (USA)) 10f **(76)**
Form - 0
Record 2000 - 1st:0 2nd:0 3rd:0 Ran:1
2000 Turf 0-1: (8f) (frm)
Currently moderate filly. **J H M Gosden [0-1] R E Sangster.*

COPPER CARNIVAL (FR) RR 112f 630a[4]
4 b c Petit Loup (USA) - Lailati (USA) (Mr Prospector (USA)) 8.8f **(78)**
Form - 4
2000 Turf 0-1: (10f) (g-s)
Currently Group-class colt. (1st run) - 4th of 5 to Indian Danehill (2 Apr Longchamp 10f g-s RF 0630a). **C Laffon-Parias in FR [0-1].*

COPPER COOKIE BHB 30f23a **RR 37f 23a** 38[8]
5 ch m Selkirk (USA) 7.9f **(76)** - Festival Fanfare (Ile de Bourbon (USA)) 10.1f **(67)**
Form - 8
Record 2000 - 1st:0 2nd:0 3rd:0 Ran:1
Pre2000 - 1st:0 2nd:0 3rd:1 Ran:20
Win Prizemoney £0 *Total Prizemoney* £717
2000 AW 0-1: (15f) (Fibr)
Very moderate filly. Inconsistent. **M J Polglase [0-22] M J Polglase.*

COPPER SHELL BHB 52f60a **RR 44?f 60a** 200[9]
6 ch g Beveled (USA) 6.9f **(64)** - Luly My Love (Hello Gorgeous (USA)) 9.7f **(63)**
Form - 70
Record 2000 - 1st:0 2nd:0 3rd:0 Ran:1
Pre2000 - 1st:4 2nd:2 3rd:0 Ran:16
Win Prizemoney £8,074 *Total Prizemoney* £9,899
Wins * 1999 *Feb Wolver (STD) H 12f 65 66* <
* 1999 *Jan Southw (STD) H 12f 59 66* <
* 1999 *Jan Southw (STD) H 11f 55 60*
* 1999 *Jan Southw (STD) H 12f 50 58*
2000 AW 0-1: (12f) (Fibr)
Average gelding, effective 11 to 12f, best at 12f, - acts on Fibr, favours left handed tracks, and excels at Southwell. Becoming disappointing.
**Mrs L C Jewell [4-20] Gallagher Equine Ltd (from A P Jones [0-6] Oct 1997).*

COPPLESTONE (IRE) BHB 72f **RR 75f** 4378[12]
4 b g Second Set (IRE) 9.2f **(67)** - Queen of the Brush (Averof) 8.2f **(62)**
Form - 72440432220
Record 2000 - 1st:0 2nd:4 3rd:1 Ran:11
Pre2000 - 1st:0 2nd:0 3rd:3 Ran:7
Win Prizemoney £0 *Total Prizemoney* £14,188
2000 Turf 0-11: (7f, 8f 5, 9f 3, 10f 2) (g-s, gd 3, g-f 3, frm 4)
Leggy, above-average gelding, effective 8 to 10f, best at 8f, acts on gd to frm, has worn blinkers, prefers left handed tracks, prefers tight tracks, excels at Lingfield. Turf high 75 - 2nd of 12 getting 7lb from Riberac (28 Aug Epsom 9f gd RF 4035).
**P W Harris [0-18] Mrs P W Harris.*

COPY-CAT BHB 60f **RR 54f** 3750[12]
2 b f Lion Cavern (USA) 7.5f **(74)** - Imperial Jade (Lochnager) 6f **(59)**
Form - 400
Record 2000 - 1st:0 2nd:0 3rd:0 Ran:3
2000 Turf 0-3: (5f, 6f 2) (gd 2, g-f)
Currently fair filly. Turf high 54. **W R Muir [0-3] Timothy Chick.*

COPYFORCE BOY BHB 44f35a **RR 47f 35a** 384[4]
4 ch g Mystiko (USA) 7.7f **(59)** - Surpassing (Superlative) 7.2f **(56)**
Form - 04
Record 2000 - 1st:0 2nd:0 3rd:0 Ran:2
Pre2000 - 1st:0 2nd:0 3rd:0 Ran:4
Win Prizemoney £0 *Total Prizemoney* £209
2000 AW 0-2: (8f, 10f) (Equi 2)
Workmanlike, moderate gelding. AW high 23.
**Miss B Sanders [0-6] Copy Xpress Ltd.*

COPYFORCE GIRL BHB 65f60a **RR 65f 60a** 4099[2]
4 b f Elmaamul (USA) 8.1f **(70)** - Sabaya (USA) (Seattle Dancer (USA))
Form - 1322262
Record 2000 - 1st:1 2nd:4 3rd:1 Ran:7
Pre2000 - 1st:0 2nd:1 3rd:1 Ran:11
Win Prizemoney £2,776 *Total Prizemoney* £10,237
Wins * 2000 Jun Bright (FRM) 11.9f 55 <
2000 Turf 1-7: (12f 1-4, 14f 2, 16f) (gd 3, g-f, frm 1-3)
Unfurnished, average filly, has broken blood-vessels, effective 11 to 16f, best at 12f, acts on gd to frm, best on frm, favours tight tracks, excels at Epsom and Brighton and Sandown. Turf high 66 - 3rd of 12 giving 16lb to Chater Flair (5 Jly Epsom 12f gd RF 2546). Consistent. Running well in ordinary company, winning at Brighton in June and placed regularly since. Just lacks a turn of foot. **Miss B Sanders [1-19] Copy Xpress Ltd.*

CORAL SHELLS BHB 30f **RR 41f** 4402[13]
3 b f Formidable (USA) 7.8f **(60)** - Elle Reef (Shareef Dancer (USA)) 9.9f **(73)**
Form - 887006800
Record 2000 - 1st:0 2nd:0 3rd:0 Ran:9
Pre2000 - 1st:0 2nd:1 3rd:0 Ran:5
Win Prizemoney £0 *Total Prizemoney* £1,416
2000 Turf 0-9: (7f 2, 8f 4, 10f 2, 12f) (g-s, gd, g-f 2, frm 5)
Leggy, moderate filly, has worn blinkers. Turf high 41.
**R M Flower [0-9] R M Flower (from P T Walwyn [0-5] Oct 1999).*

CORAL WATERS (IRE) BHB 42f37a **RR 37f 37a** 8[10]
4 b f College Chapel - Premier Leap (IRE) (Salmon Leap (USA)) 11f **(61)**
Form - 0
Record 2000 - 1st:0 2nd:0 3rd:0 Ran:1
Pre2000 - 1st:0 2nd:0 3rd:1 Ran:11
Win Prizemoney £0 *Total Prizemoney* £280
2000 AW 0-1: (7f) (Fibr)
Scopey, moderate filly, has worn blinkers. Becoming disappointing. **R Curtis [0-4] Mrs R A Smith (from C A Cyzer [0-9] Jun 1999).*

CORBETTA (IRE) RR 92f 1031a[15]
3 ch f Polar Falcon (USA) 9f **(74)** - Kiska (USA) (Bering) 7.4f **(61)**
Form - 10
2000 Turf 1-2: (8f 1-2) (hvy 1-1, sft)
Currently useful filly. Turf high 92 (1st run) - 1st of 9 from Calcinate (2 Apr San Siro RF 0631a). **M Guarnieri in ITY [1-2].*

CORBLETS BHB 56f60a **RR 69f 60a** 4543[6]
3 b f Timeless Times (USA) 6.1f **(56)** - Dear Glenda (Gold Song) 5.5f **(61)**
Form - 322570836306
Record 2000 - 1st:0 2nd:2 3rd:3 Ran:12

Pre2000 - 1st:0 2nd:1 3rd:0 Ran:4
Win Prizemoney £0 *Total Prizemoney* £6,279
2000 Turf 0-11: (5f 9, 6f 2) (gd 3, g-f 6, frm 2) 2000 AW 0-1: (5f) (Equi)
Workmanlike, average filly, effective 5f, acts on gd to g-f, best on g-f. Turf high 69 - 2nd of 15 giving 7lb to Arogant Prince (22 May Windsor 5f g-f RF 1383). **S Dow [0-16] J & S Kelly.*

CORINIUM (IRE) BHB 108f **RR 111f** 1832[6]
3 br f Turtle Island (IRE) - Searching Star (Rainbow Quest (USA)) 10.4f **(75)**
Form - 16
Record 2000 - 1st:1 2nd:0 3rd:0 Ran:2
Pre2000 - 1st:2 2nd:0 3rd:1 Ran:3
Win Prizemoney £34,738 *Total Prizemoney* £40,220
Wins * 2000 May Goodwo (SFT) L 8f 111 <
* 1999 Oct Newbur (HVY) L 7.3f 100+
* 1999 Spt Warwic (SFT) 7.7f 88+
2000 Turf 1-2: (8f 1-1, 12f) (g-s 1-2)
Workmanlike, Group-class filly. Turf high 111 (1st run) - 1st of 6 giving 3lb to Eurolink Raindance (25 May Goodwood RF 1436). Bolted up in a soft-ground Warwick maiden on her second start at two, though the opposition did not look up to much, and followed up by short-heading Iftiraas in a Listed race on heavy ground at Newbury. Won a similar race over a mile on her return to action, before finishing a respectable sixth in the Oaks.
**H R A Cecil [3-5] Derek D & Mrs Jean P Clee.*

CORK HARBOUR (FR) BHB 73f **RR 71f** 5134[11]
4 ch g Grand Lodge (USA) - Irish Sea (Irish River (FR)) 8.6f **(78)**
Form - 10
Record 2000 - 1st:1 2nd:0 3rd:0 Ran:2
Pre2000 - 1st:0 2nd:0 3rd:1 Ran:2
Win Prizemoney £3,282 *Total Prizemoney* £3,828
Wins * 2000 Spt Bright (SFT) 8f 71 <
2000 Turf 1-2: (8f 1-1, 10f) (sft, g-s 1-1)
Scopey, above-average gelding. Turf high 71 (1st run) (began Spt) - 1st of 9 giving 4lb to Digital (27 Spt Brighton RF 4678).
**Mrs N Smith [1-2] Martin Ingram (from B W Hills [0-2] Oct 1999).*

CORNDAVON (USA) BHB 85f **RR 86f** 2440[1]
4 b f Sheikh Albadou 9.2f **(75)** - Ferber's Follies (USA) (Saratoga Six (USA)) 7f **(73)**
Form - 2047121
Record 2000 - 1st:2 2nd:2 3rd:0 Ran:7
Pre2000 - 1st:1 2nd:2 3rd:2 Ran:14
Win Prizemoney £28,028 *Total Prizemoney* £34,511
Wins * 2000 Jly Newcas (FRM) H 6f 80 86 <
*** 2000** Jun Doncas (G-F) H 6f 66 74
1999 Jly Warwic (G-F) 6f 76
2000 Turf 2-7: (5f, 6f 2-3, 7f 3) (g-s, gd, g-f 2, frm 2-3)
Leggy, useful filly, effective 6f, acts on g-f to frm. Turf high 86 - 1st of 19 giving 8lb to Smart Predator (1 Jly Newcastle RF 2440). Improving. Returned to her best with a convincing victory at Doncaster in June, but went up a stone in the handicap and was unable to justify favouritism in a Warwick classified event next time. Suited by fast ground.
**M L W Bell [2-7] Anne Lady Scott (from M J Fetherston-Godley [1-14] Oct 1999).*

CORN DOLLY (IRE) BHB 39f48a **RR 40f 48a** 2892[5]
4 ch f Thatching 7.8f **(69)** - Keepers Lock (USA) (Sunny's Halo (CAN)) 6.7f **(70)**
Form - 412500005
Record 2000 - 1st:0 2nd:1 3rd:0 Ran:7
Pre2000 - 1st:1 2nd:0 3rd:0 Ran:5
Win Prizemoney £2,691 *Total Prizemoney* £3,486
Wins * 1999 *Dec Lingfi (STD) 7f* 50 <
2000 Turf 0-5: (6f, 7f 3, 8f) (gd, frm 4) 2000 AW 0-2: (6f, 7f) (Equi 2)
Fair filly, effective 6 to 7f, - acts on Equi, has worn blinkers, prefers left handed tracks, likes tight tracks. Turf high 40. AW high 49 (1st run) - 2nd of 9 getting 6lb from Dolphinelle (5 Jan Lingfield 6f Equi RF 0024). Inconsistent.
**R F JohnsonHoughton [1-12] Bob Lanigan.*

CORNELIAN PRINCE RR 4296[8]
3 b c Sri Pekan (USA) - Silent Girl (Krayyan) 8.5f **(49)**
Form - 6
Record 2000 - 1st:0 2nd:0 3rd:0 Ran:1
Win Prizemoney £0 *Total Prizemoney* £0
2000 Turf 0-1: (7f) (hvy)
Currently poor colt **A Senior [0-1] .*

CORNELIUS BHB 102f **RR 108f** 5133[1]
3 b c Barathea (IRE) - Rainbow Mountain **(75f)** (Rainbow Quest (USA)) 10.4f **(75)**
Form - 250274011
Record 2000 - 1st:2 2nd:2 3rd:0 Ran:9
Pre2000 - 1st:1 2nd:0 3rd:1 Ran:3
Win Prizemoney £23,012 *Total Prizemoney* £37,689
Wins * 2000 Oct Newbur (HVY) H 9f 97 101 <
*** 2000** Oct Ayr (HVY) 8f 100
* 1999 May York (SFT) 6f 81+
2000 Turf 2-9: (8f 1-4, 9f 1-1, 10f 4) (hvy 1-1, sft 1-1, gd 5, g-f, frm)
Light-framed, Pattern-class colt, effective 8 to 10f, best at 8f, acts on hvy to gd. Turf high 109 - 2nd of 7 to Fanaar (7 Jly Sandown 8f gd RF 2607) - also 1st of 11 giving 7lb to Highland Reel (21 Oct Newbury RF 5133). Consistent. He took time to find his form, but won twice when the mud was flying in October. He enjoys bowling along in front. **P F I Cole [3-12] Sir George Meyrick.*

CORNER HOUSE (IRE) RR 78f 772[3]
3 gr f Lion Cavern (USA) 7.5f **(74)** - Snowing (USA) (Icecapade (USA)) 11f **(62)**
Form - 3
Record 2000 - 1st:0 2nd:0 3rd:1 Ran:1
Win Prizemoney £0 *Total Prizemoney* £780
2000 Turf 0-1: (6f) (gd)
Scopey, currently above-average filly. (1st run) - 3rd of 11 to May Contessa (18 Apr Newmarket 6f gd RF 0772). Unraced at two, she showed a deal of promise in a Newmarket maiden on her debut.
**A C Stewart [0-1] Cliveden Stud.*

CORNISH ECLIPSE BHB 25f **RR 4f** 4272[18]
3 b g Formidable (USA) 7.8f **(60)** - Julie's Star (IRE) (Thatching) 8f **(66)**
Form - 600
Record 2000 - 1st:0 2nd:0 3rd:0 Ran:3
Pre2000 - 1st:0 2nd:0 3rd:0 Ran:3
2000 Turf 0-2: (6f, 8f) (g-f, frm) 2000 AW 0-1: (6f) (Fibr)
Strong, poor gelding. (began Jly).
**M D I Usher [0-6] Kinsmen Racing.*

CORRIDOR CREEPER (FR) BHB 82f **RR 89f** 4332[17]
3 ch g Polish Precedent (USA) 9f **(73)** - Sonia Rose (USA) (Superbity (USA))
Form - 73786380
Record 2000 - 1st:0 2nd:0 3rd:2 Ran:8
Pre2000 - 1st:1 2nd:2 3rd:0 Ran:4
Win Prizemoney £3,598 *Total Prizemoney* £13,958
Wins * 1999 Oct Bright (G-S) 6f 74+ <
2000 Turf 0-8: (5f 5, 6f 3) (g-s, gd 3, g-f, frm 3)
Lengthy, useful gelding, effective 5 to 6f, best at 6f, acts on gd to frm, best on frm, has worn blinkers. Turf high 89 - 3rd of 30 getting 18lb from Hunting Lion (3 Jun Newmarket 6f frm RF 1690).
**P W Harris [1-12] T Rattee & Mrs P W Harris.*

CORSECAN BHB 28f38a **RR 16df 38a** 1737[8]
5 ch g Phountzi (USA) 9.6f **(60)** - Sagareina (Sagaro) 9.7f **(55)**
Form - 008
Record 2000 - 1st:0 2nd:0 3rd:0 Ran:3
Pre2000 - 1st:1 2nd:0 3rd:2 Ran:17
Win Prizemoney £1,850 *Total Prizemoney* £2,583
Wins * 1998 *Feb Lingfi (SLW) H 8f 50 67+* <
2000 Turf 0-2: (7f, 10f) (gd, frm) 2000 AW 0-1: (7f) (Equi)
Average gelding. Turf high 5. Becoming disappointing.
**Miss Z C Davison [0-3] Four In Hand Club (from S Dow [1-17] Aug 1998).*

CORUNNA BHB 75f **RR 74f** 4049[13]
3 b g Puissance 7.1f **(60)** - Kind of Shy (Kind of Hush) 10.1f **(62)**
Form - 331316600
Record 2000 - 1st:2 2nd:0 3rd:3 Ran:9
Pre2000 - 1st:0 2nd:4 3rd:1 Ran:10
Win Prizemoney £10,335 *Total Prizemoney* £18,140
Wins * 2000 Jun Lingfi (G-F) H 6f 76 80 <
*** 2000** Jun Mussel (FRM) 5f 69

2000 Turf 2-9: (5f 1-3, 6f 1-6) (gd 2, g-f 1-4, frm 1-2, hrd)
Scopey, above-average gelding, effective 5 to 6f, best at 6f, acts on gd to hrd, best on g-f. Turf high 80 - 1st of 11 getting 9lb from Melanzana (27 Jun Lingfield RF 2304). Consistent. It took him a long time to get off the mark, but he managed to do so at Musselburgh in June and he added rather a better race over six furlongs at Lingfield later the same month. Well beaten since. Best on fast ground.
**A Berry [2-9] Chris & Antonia Deuters (from J Berry [0-10] Spt 1999).*

CORUSCATING BHB 60f60a **RR 72f 60a** 5150[4]
3 gr g Highest Honor (FR) 10.9f **(72)** - Mytilene (IRE) **(94f)** (Soviet Star (USA))
Form - 841004
Record 2000 - 1st:1 2nd:0 3rd:0 Ran:6
Pre2000 - 1st:0 2nd:0 3rd:0 Ran:3
Win Prizemoney £2,860 *Total Prizemoney* £3,316
Wins ** 2000 Spt Lingfi (STD) 10f 67* <
2000 Turf 0-3: (8f 2, 10f) (g-s, g-f 2) 2000 AW 1-3: (8f, 10f 1-2) (Equi 1-2, Fibr)
Scopey, above-average gelding, effective 10f, acts on g-f - acts on Equi, likes left handed tracks, likes tight tracks. Turf high 67 (began Aug) - 4th of 15 giving 9lb to Flyover (1 Spt Epsom 10f g-f RF 4144). AW high 67 (1st run) (began Spt) - 1st of 12 from Noble Calling (22 Spt Lingfield RF 4584). Inconsistent.
**Sir Mark Prescott [1-9] Mrs F R Watts.*

COSI FAN TUTTE RR 84+f 2686[3]
2 b c Inchinor 8.9f **(64)** - Bumpkin (Free State) 8.7f **(61)**
Form - 3
Record 2000 - 1st:0 2nd:0 3rd:1 Ran:1
Win Prizemoney £0 *Total Prizemoney* £955
2000 Turf 0-1: (7f) (gd)
Currently decent colt. (1st run) - 3rd of 11 to Londoner (11 Jly Newmarket 7f gd RF 2686). Ran an eyecatching debut in a decent Newmarket maiden. **B Hanbury [0-1] Lord Clinton.*

COSMIC BUZZ BHB 40f70a **RR 43f 70a** 3170[4]
3 ch g Cosmonaut - G'Ime a Buzz (Electric) 10.1f **(61)**
Form - 070074
Record 2000 - 1st:0 2nd:0 3rd:0 Ran:6
Pre2000 - 1st:1 2nd:0 3rd:0 Ran:8
Win Prizemoney £2,318 *Total Prizemoney* £2,704
Wins * 1999 Aug Salisb (G-S) C 7f 78? <
2000 Turf 0-6: (10f, 11f, 12f 2, 16f 2) (sft, g-s, gd, frm 3)
Scopey, moderate gelding, effective 7f, acts on gd, has worn blinkers. Turf high 44. Inconsistent.
**A T Murphy [1-14] Exmoor Racing Partnership.*

COSMIC CASE BHB 43f **RR 41f** 5294[5]
5 b m Casteddu 7.4f **(54)** - La Fontainova (IRE) (Lafontaine (USA)) 8.7f **(49)**
Form - 504074211345
Record 2000 - 1st:2 2nd:1 3rd:1 Ran:12
Pre2000 - 1st:1 2nd:0 3rd:5 Ran:27
Win Prizemoney £7,834 *Total Prizemoney* £13,125
Wins * **2000** Jly Hamilt (G-F) H 12.1f 37 39
* **2000** Jly Mussel (FRM) H 16f 37 39
* 1998 May Mussel (G-F) H 8f 57 64 <
2000 Turf 2-12: (9f, 10f, 12f 1-6, 13f 2, 14f, 16f 1-1) (g-s 2, gd, g-f 1-2, frm 1-7)
Moderate filly, effective 11 to 16f, acts on g-f to frm, best on g-f, has worn blinkers, favours right handed tracks, favours tight tracks, and excels at Hamilton. Turf high 41 - 3rd of 11 getting 20lb from Spectrometer (14 Jly Hamilton 13f g-f RF 2807) - also 1st of 4 giving 13lb to Urgent Reply (3 Jly Musselburgh RF 2466). Consistent. **J S Goldie [4-53] The Cosmic Cases.*

COSMIC DANCER RR 5070[14]
3 b g Cosmonaut - Djanila (Fabulous Dancer (USA)) 9.4f **(70)**
Form - 060
Record 2000 - 1st:0 2nd:0 3rd:0 Ran:3
2000 Turf 0-3: (8f 2, 12f) (g-s 2, g-f)
Scopey, currently very poor gelding. (began Spt) - 14th of 20 to Maniatis (19 Oct Bath 12f g-s RF 5070).
**D J S ffrenchDavis [0-3] L F Hoare.*

COSMIC MILLENNIUM (IRE) BHB 85f **RR 74f** 3412[1]
2 b c In The Wings 11.2f **(77)** - Windmill Princess (Gorytus (USA)) 7.8f **(60)**
Form - 61
Record 2000 - 1st:1 2nd:0 3rd:0 Ran:2
Win Prizemoney £3,575 *Total Prizemoney* £3,575
Wins * **2000** Aug Cheste (GD) 7f 74 <
2000 Turf 1-2: (7f 1-2) (g-f 1-2)
Currently above-average colt. Turf high 74 (began Jly) - 1st of 9 giving 5lb to Borders Belle (6 Aug Chester RF 3412). Improved from his debut to score in good style over seven furlongs at Chester in August. Ought to stay a mile.
**R Guest [1-2] Cosmic Greyhound Racing Partnership III.*

COSMIC PEARL BHB 38f **RR 34f** 4615[10]
2 b f Cosmonaut - Bebe Altesse (GER) (Alpenkonig (GER)) 10.8f **(76)**
Form - 050
Record 2000 - 1st:0 2nd:0 3rd:0 Ran:3
2000 Turf 0-3: (7f, 8f 2) (gd 2, frm)
Currently very moderate filly. Turf high 34 (began Aug).
**A G Newcombe [0-3] D Bass.*

COSMIC RANGER BHB 67f **RR 66f** 4615[6]
2 b c Magic Ring (IRE) 6.5f **(64)** - Lismore (Relkino) 8.9f **(65)**
Form - 0506
Record 2000 - 1st:0 2nd:0 3rd:0 Ran:4
2000 Turf 0-4: (6f 3, 8f) (gd, g-f, frm 2)
Average colt. Turf high 66 (began Aug).
**N P Littmoden [0-4] Wetherby Racing Bureau 44.*

COSMIC SONG BHB 37f45a **RR 52f 45a** 5162[8]
3 b f Cosmonaut - Hotaria **(52df)** (Sizzling Melody)
Form - 5563514468508
Record 2000 - 1st:1 2nd:0 3rd:1 Ran:12
Pre2000 - 1st:0 2nd:0 3rd:0 Ran:3
Win Prizemoney £2,977 *Total Prizemoney* £3,723
Wins * **2000** Jun Carlis (SFT) H 9.3f 44 46 <
2000 Turf 1-10: (8f 4, 9f 1-2, 10f 4) (sft 2, gd, g-f 1-3, frm 4) 2000 AW 0-2: (7f, 9f) (Fibr 2)
Lengthy, fair filly, effective 8 to 10f, acts on gd to frm, likes tight tracks. Turf high 52 - 4th of 15 getting 8lb from Bahamas (13 Jun Redcar 10f frm RF 1915) - also 1st of 9 getting 12lb from Marvel (5 Jun Carlisle RF 1712). AW high 34. Becoming disappointing. She seemed to appreciate the soft ground when getting off the mark in a nine-furlong Carlisle handicap in June.
**R M Whitaker [1-15] R M Whitaker.*

COSMOCRAT RR 84f 5066[2]
2 b g Cosmonaut - Bella Coola **(23f 20a)** (Northern State (USA))
Form - 02
Record 2000 - 1st:0 2nd:1 3rd:0 Ran:2
Win Prizemoney £0 *Total Prizemoney* £714
2000 Turf 0-2: (7f, 8f) (g-s, g-f)
Currently decent gelding. Turf high 84 (began Spt) - 2nd of 16 to Flying Lyric (19 Oct Bath 8f g-s RF 5066).
**B J Meehan [0-2] A E Smith & Co.*

COSMOGRAPHE (FR) RR 107f 1825a[9]
3 b c Lomitas - Volcania (FR) (Neustrien (FR))
Form - 0
2000 Turf 0-1: (12f) (gd)
Currently Pattern-class colt. **J M Beguigne in FR [0-2].*

COSMO JACK (IRE) BHB 42f **RR 66f** 4179[7]
4 b g Balla Cove - Foolish Law (IRE) (Law Society (USA)) 9.9f **(70)**
Form - 0250007
Record 2000 - 1st:0 2nd:1 3rd:0 Ran:7
Pre2000 - 1st:4 2nd:1 3rd:2 Ran:18
Win Prizemoney £9,644 *Total Prizemoney* £11,792
Wins * 1999 Spt Chepst (GD) S 8.1f 46
* 1999 Aug Haydoc (GD) S 8.1f 55
* 1998 Aug Sandow (G-F) SH 7.1f 68 68 <
1998 Jly Bath (GD) S 5.1f 68 <
2000 Turf 0-6: (8f, 10f 2, 12f 3) (gd 2, g-f 3, frm) 2000 AW 0-1: (12f) (Fibr)
Lengthy, average gelding, effective 12f, acts on gd, often wears blinkers (very effectively). Turf high 66.

**M C Pipe [7-27] Kammac Plc (from B J Meehan [1-6] Jly 1998).*

COST AUDITING BHB 39f50a **RR 50df 50a** 5248[12]
3 ch f Bluebird (USA) 7.9f **(71)** - Elabella (Ela-Mana-Mou) 10.1f **(70)**
Form - 50070
Record 2000 - 1st:0 2nd:0 3rd:0 Ran:5
Pre2000 - 1st:0 2nd:1 3rd:0 Ran:7
Win Prizemoney £0 *Total Prizemoney* £1,237
2000 Turf 0-3: (6f, 7f, 8f) (gd, g-f 2) 2000 AW 0-2: (6f, 9f) (Fibr 2)
Scopey, fair filly, effective 5f, - acts on Fibr. Turf high 31. AW high 28 (began Aug).
**Andrew Reid [0-5] A S Reid (from Sir Mark Prescott [0-7] Oct 1999).*

COTE SOLEIL BHB 76f **RR 82f** 4743[23]
3 ch c Inchinor 8.9f **(64)** - Sunshine Coast (Posse (USA)) 8.9f **(61)**
Form - 330005000
Record 2000 - 1st:0 2nd:0 3rd:2 Ran:9
Pre2000 - 1st:1 2nd:1 3rd:0 Ran:8
Win Prizemoney £2,723 *Total Prizemoney* £9,052
Wins 1999 Apr Nottin (G-S) 5.1f 66 <
2000 Turf 0-9: (7f 4, 8f 4, 9f) (g-s 2, gd 3, g-f 4)
Leggy, decent colt, effective 6 to 9f, acts on g-s to frm, has worn blinkers, likes left handed tracks, prefers tight tracks, likes Haydock. Turf high 86 (1st run) - 3rd of 5 to Going Global (5 Apr Ripon 9f gd RF 0618). Inconsistent.
**M L W Bell [0-9] Mrs Evelyn Hankinson (from M R Channon [1-8] Spt 1999).*

COTTAM LILLY BHB 35f **RR 26f** 4775[10]
3 b f Sabrehill (USA) 8.5f **(64)** - Karminski (Pitskelly) 8.5f **(53)**
Form - 800
Record 2000 - 1st:0 2nd:0 3rd:0 Ran:3
Pre2000 - 1st:0 2nd:0 3rd:0 Ran:1
2000 Turf 0-3: (5f, 6f, 12f) (g-s, g-f, frm)
Leggy, little account filly. Turf high 26 (began Aug).
**M W Easterby [0-4] Peter Easterby.*

COTTON HOUSE (IRE) BHB 100f **RR 99f** 2822[6]
3 b f Mujadil (USA) 7.7f **(70)** - Romanovna (Mummy's Pet) 7.7f **(60)**
Form - 15150
Record 2000 - 1st:2 2nd:0 3rd:0 Ran:5
Pre2000 - 1st:1 2nd:1 3rd:0 Ran:3
Win Prizemoney £47,912 *Total Prizemoney* £50,591
Wins * **2000** Jun York (G-F) H 6f 95 99 <
* **2000** May Leices (G-S) 6f 97
* 1999 Apr Warwic (GD) 5f 88+
2000 Turf 2-5: (5f, 6f 2-4) (g-s, gd 1-2, frm 1-2)
Scopey, very useful filly, effective 6f, acts on gd to frm. Turf high 99 - 1st of 23 giving 15lb to Railroader (17 Jun York RF 2062) - also 1st of 4 getting 3lb from Argent Facile (30 May Leicester RF 1546). She ran three times early on in 1999, winning on her Warwick debut, but was not seen out after June owing to suffering a fractured pelvis. She easily won a four-runner Leicester classified event on her return last season, and gained her biggest victory in York's William Hill Trophy on her handicap debut. Found the drop to five furlongs against her at Sandown and was a little disappointing back over six at York. Might continue to struggle in listed races. **M R Channon [3-8] Michael Foy.*

COTTONTAIL BHB 50f **RR 42f** 4861[6]
2 b c Alzao (USA) 9.8f **(73)** - Height of Passion (Shirley Heights) 10.3f **(74)**
Form - 806
Record 2000 - 1st:0 2nd:0 3rd:0 Ran:3
2000 Turf 0-3: (6f, 7f, 8f) (sft, gd, frm)
Currently moderate colt. Turf high 42.
**N Tinkler [0-3] Mrs D Wright.*

COUGHLAN'S GIFT BHB 63f57a **RR 63f 57a** 5063[1]
4 ch f Alnasr Alwasheek 9.4f **(62)** - Superfrost (Tickled Pink) 6.5f **(59)**
Form - 5700U05011
Record 2000 - 1st:2 2nd:0 3rd:0 Ran:9
Pre2000 - 1st:1 2nd:3 3rd:1 Ran:16
Win Prizemoney £7,647 *Total Prizemoney* £10,663
Wins * **2000** Oct Nottin (SFT) 10f 63 <
* **2000** Spt Salisb (SFT) H 9.9f 49 57
* 1999 Oct Bath (SFT) H 8f 55 58
2000 Turf 2-8: (8f 3, 10f 2-5) (sft 1-1, g-s, gd 1-3, g-f, frm 2) 2000 AW 0-1: (10f) (Equi)
Light-framed, average filly, effective 7 to 10f, best at 8f, acts on sft to g-f, best on gd, likes left handed tracks, does well at Nottingham, likes Salisbury. Turf high 63 - 1st of 15 giving 1lb to Cautious Joe (18 Oct Nottingham RF 5063) - also 1st of 18 getting 12lb from Two Socks (27 Spt Salisbury RF 4695).
**J C Fox [3-25] Mrs J A Cleary.*

COULD BE EXPENSIVE BHB 38f38a **RR 38df 38a** 2641[10]
3 b g Pursuit of Love 9.5f **(69)** - High Typha **(53f)** (Dowsing (USA))
Form - 66400
Record 2000 - 1st:0 2nd:0 3rd:0 Ran:5
Pre2000 - 1st:0 2nd:0 3rd:0 Ran:3
2000 Turf 0-2: (8f, 10f) (gd, frm) 2000 AW 0-3: (6f 2, 8f) (Fibr 3)
Very moderate gelding, effective 8f, - acts on Fibr, has worn blinkers. Turf high 30. AW high 37 - 4th of 14 getting 12lb from Just The Job Too (21 Feb Southwell 8f Fibr RF 0324).
**M H Tompkins [0-8] M H Tompkins.*

COULTHARD (IRE) BHB 84f **RR 80f** 825[7]
7 ch g Glenstal (USA) 10f **(59)** - Royal Aunt (Martinmas) 7.6f **(59)**
Form - 7
Record 2000 - 1st:0 2nd:0 3rd:0 Ran:1
Pre2000 - 1st:2 2nd:1 3rd:0 Ran:11
Win Prizemoney £11,022 *Total Prizemoney* £12,504
Wins * 1999 Apr Haydoc (SFT) H 11.9f 85 89 <
* 1998 Jun Windso (SFT) 10f 84
2000 Turf 0-1: (12f) (hvy)
Decent gelding, has worn blinkers. Inconsistent.
**Mrs P Sly [5-21] R Brazier (from A Leahy in IRE [0-8] Aug 1997).*

COUNT CALYPSO BHB 60f66a **RR 53f 66a** 3769[7]
2 ch g King's Signet (USA) 7f **(51)** - Atlantic Air (Air Trooper) 9.1f **(63)**
Form - 00037
Record 2000 - 1st:0 2nd:0 3rd:1 Ran:5
Win Prizemoney £0 *Total Prizemoney* £315
2000 Turf 0-4: (5f 4) (g-f 2, frm, hrd) 2000 AW 0-1: (5f) (Fibr)
Above-average gelding. Turf high 53.
**D J Coakley [0 5] Count Calypso Racing.*

COUNT DE MONEY (IRE) BHB 35f76a **RR 37f 76a** 668[1]
5 b g Last Tycoon 9.4f **(73)** - Menominee (Soviet Star (USA))
Form - 5221231211
Record 2000 - 1st:3 2nd:2 3rd:1 Ran:6
Pre2000 - 1st:7 2nd:5 3rd:4 Ran:31
Win Prizemoney £23,030 *Total Prizemoney* £30,009
Wins * **2000** *Apr Southw (STD) H 14f 72 73* <
* **2000** *Mar Wolver (STD) 12f 71*
2000 *Feb Southw (STD) C 12f 54*
1999 *Dec Southw (SLW) H 12f 57 63*
1999 *Oct Southw (STD) 12f 56+*
1999 *Jun Southw (STD) C 11f 59*
1999 *Jun Southw (STD) C 11f 50*
1999 *May Wolver (STD) C 12f 65*
1999 *Feb Southw (STD) H 12f 53 57*
1998 *Nov Southw (STD) H 12f 44 53*
2000 AW 3-6: (12f 2-4, 14f 1-1, 15f) (Fibr 3-6)
Above-average gelding, effective 12 to 15f, - acts on Fibr, favours left handed tracks, favours tight tracks, excels at Southwell, likes Wolverhampton. AW high 73 - 1st of 8 giving 12lb to Cresset (11 Apr Southwell RF 0668) - also 1st of 6 giving 2lb to Sea Danzig (16 Mar Wolverhampton RF 0449). He is a very effective middle-distance handicapper on Fibresand, especially over a mile and a half at Southwell, and added to his six wins in 1999 with three more early last year. He is a tough sort, and hopefully there will be more to come.
**Miss S J Wilton [2-3] John Pointon and Sons (from S R Bowring [8-26] Feb 2000).*

COUNT DUBOIS BHB 113f **RR 102f** 5214a[1]
2 b c Zafonic (USA) 9f **(83)** - Madame Dubois (Legend of France (USA)) 9.5f **(61)**
Form - 12331
Record 2000 - 1st:2 2nd:1 3rd:2 Ran:5
Win Prizemoney £66,748 *Total Prizemoney* £116,140
Wins * **2000** Oct San Si (HVY) G1 8f 102 <
* **2000** Aug Haydoc (G-S) 6f 80+

2000 Turf 2-5: (6f 1-1, 7f 2, 8f 1-2) (hvy 1-1, sft, gd 1-2, g-f)
Very useful colt, has worn blinkers. Turf high 102 (began Aug) - 1st of 6 from King's County (22 Oct San Siro RF 5214a). Placed in warm company before landing the Gran Criterium in Milan on bad ground. **W J Haggas [2-5] Wentworth Racing (Pty) Ltd.*

COUNTESS BANKES BHB 49f49a **RR 45f 49a** 847[6]

2 b f Son Pardo - Lowrianna (IRE) (Cyrano de Bergerac) 6f **(68)**
Form - 416
Record 2000 - 1st:1 2nd:0 3rd:0 Ran:3
Win Prizemoney £1,831 *Total Prizemoney* £1,831
Wins * 2000 *Apr Southw (STD) S 5f 52 <*
2000 Turf 0-1: (5f) (sft) 2000 AW 1-2: (5f 1-2) (Fibr 1-2)
Currently fair filly, has worn blinkers. AW high 52 - 1st of 9 getting 5lb from Sand Bankes (10 Apr Southwell RF 0647).
**W G M Turner [1-3] T Lightbowne.*

COUNTESS COLDUNELL BHB 50f **RR 53f** 5135[10]

3 b f Bin Ajwaad (IRE) - Beau's Delight (USA) (Lypheor) 12f **(71)**
Form - 60
Record 2000 - 1st:0 2nd:0 3rd:0 Ran:2
2000 Turf 0-2: (8f, 10f) (sft, g-s)
Scopey, currently fair filly. Turf high 53 (began Oct).
**J W Payne [0-2] John Dunsdon.*

COUNTESS PARKER BHB 38f **RR 40f** 3834[15]

4 ch f First Trump - Hoist (IRE) **(72df 63a)** (Bluebird (USA)) 7.5f **(69)**
Form - 700000
Record 2000 - 1st:0 2nd:0 3rd:0 Ran:6
Pre2000 - 1st:0 2nd:1 3rd:0 Ran:3
Win Prizemoney £0 *Total Prizemoney* £1,407
2000 Turf 0-6: (6f 2, 7f, 8f 3) (gd, g-f, frm 3, hrd)
Leggy, moderate filly, effective 8f, acts on gd. Turf high 40. Inconsistent.
**J M Bradley [0-6] I'm Out Of Here Racing (from H R A Cecil [0-3] Spt 1999).*

COUNT FREDERICK BHB 42a **RR 46df** 2300[6]

4 b g Anshan 8.2f **(63)** - Minteen (Teenoso (USA)) 9.9f **(72)**
Form - 006
Record 2000 - 1st:0 2nd:0 3rd:0 Ran:3
Pre2000 - 1st:0 2nd:2 3rd:2 Ran:11
Win Prizemoney £0 *Total Prizemoney* £2,859
2000 Turf 0-2: (11f, 12f) (hvy, frm) 2000 AW 0-1: (10f) (Equi)
Moderate gelding, effective 10f, acts on frm, likes tight tracks. Turf high 26. Some decent efforts in handicap company last season without managing to win, but has shown little this term.
**J R Jenkins [0-14] Mrs Stella Peirce.*

COUNT ON THUNDER (USA) BHB 38f31a **RR 54f 31a** 5150[12]

3 ch c Thunder Gulch (USA) - Count On A Change (USA) (Time For A Change (USA))
Form - 5650600
Record 2000 - 1st:0 2nd:0 3rd:0 Ran:7
Pre2000 - 1st:0 2nd:0 3rd:0 Ran:3
2000 Turf 0-6: (10f 2, 11f, 12f 3) (hvy, gd 4, g-f) 2000 AW 0-1: (10f) (Equi)
Leggy, fair colt. Turf high 54. Becoming disappointing.
**J Hetherton [0-4] C D Barber-Lomax (from E A L Dunlop [0-6] Jly 2000).*

COUNTRY BUMPKIN BHB 20f **RR 21f** 2276[12]

4 ch g Village Star (FR) 5.7f **(61)** - Malham Tarn (Riverman (USA)) 9.1f **(76)**
Form - 0
Record 2000 - 1st:0 2nd:0 3rd:0 Ran:1
Pre2000 - 1st:0 2nd:0 3rd:0 Ran:2
2000 Turf 0-1: (8f) (g-f)
Unfurnished, currently little account gelding.
**H E Haynes [0-1] Lainey Hilder & Vyv Attwood (from K O Cunningham-Brown [0-2] Aug 1999).*

COUNTRY GARDEN BHB 81f **RR 103f** 3941a[3]

5 b m Selkirk (USA) 7.9f **(76)** - Totham (Shernazar) 10.2f **(73)**
Form - 33
2000 Turf 0-1: (10f) (g-s)
Very useful filly. (1st run) - 3rd of 10 to Snow Polina (19 Aug Arlington Park 10f g-s RF 3941a). Improving.
**Michael Harte in USA [0-1] Edward McGrath (from W Greenman in USA [0-1] Dec 1999).*

COUNTRYSIDE FRIEND RR 28tf 1051[2]

3 ch c Sabrehill (USA) 8.5f **(64)** - Well Proud (IRE) (Sadler's Wells (USA)) 10f **(76)**
Form - 2
Record 2000 - 1st:0 2nd:1 3rd:0 Ran:1
2000 Turf 0-1: (8f) (g-f)
Scopey, currently little account colt. (1st run) - 2nd of 2 giving 5lb to May Ball (5 May Newmarket 8f g-f RF 1051).
**M C Pipe [0-1] W J Gredley.*

COUNTRYWIDE PRIDE (IRE) BHB 69a **RR 65f** 5115[5]

2 ch c Eagle Eyed (USA) - Lady's Dream (Mazilier (USA))
Form - 675
Record 2000 - 1st:0 2nd:0 3rd:0 Ran:3
2000 Turf 0-2: (7f, 8f) (gd 2) 2000 AW 0-1: (8f) (Fibr)
Currently average colt. Turf high 65 (began Aug). (1st run) - 5th of 13 giving 6lb to Forum Finale (20 Oct Wolverhampton 8f Fibr RF 5115). **K R Burke [0-3] Countrywide Steel & Tubes Ltd.*

COUNT TIROL (IRE) BHB 47f **RR 25f** 3837[11]

3 b g Tirol 8.1f **(64)** - Bid High (IRE) (High Estate)
Form - 000
Record 2000 - 1st:0 2nd:0 3rd:0 Ran:3
Pre2000 - 1st:0 2nd:0 3rd:1 Ran:3
Win Prizemoney £0 *Total Prizemoney* £336
2000 Turf 0-3: (8f 2, 10f) (g-f 2, frm)
Scopey, little account gelding. Turf high 25.
**C G Cox [0-3] Elite Racing Club (from M J Heaton-Ellis [0-3] Jly 1999).*

COUNT TONY BHB 52f69a **RR 65?f 69a** 651[16]

6 ch g Keen 11.1f **(58)** - Turtle Dove (Gyr (USA)) 9.5f **(65)**
Form - 0
Record 2000 - 1st:0 2nd:0 3rd:0 Ran:1
Pre2000 - 1st:2 2nd:1 3rd:0 Ran:10
Win Prizemoney £5,591 *Total Prizemoney* £6,947
Wins 1997 Aug Yarmou (G-F) 10.1f 65
1997 Mar Warwic (G-F) H 10.8f 66 69 <
2000 Turf 0-1: (16f) (g-s)
Average gelding, has worn blinkers. Inconsistent.
**P Bowen [1-8] Brian Collett (from S P C Woods [2-10] Aug 1997).*

COURAGE UNDER FIRE BHB 40f44a **RR 46f 44a** 1592[10]

5 b g Risk Me (FR) 8f **(53)** - Dreamtime Quest (Blakeney) 10.5f **(64)**
Form - 000
Record 2000 - 1st:0 2nd:0 3rd:0 Ran:3
Pre2000 - 1st:1 2nd:2 3rd:2 Ran:13
Win Prizemoney £2,206 *Total Prizemoney* £4,747
Wins * 1998 *Jun Southw (STD) H 12f 44 45 <*
2000 Turf 0-3: (10f, 12f, 13f) (sft, g-s, frm)
Moderate gelding, has worn blinkers. Turf high 24. Becoming disappointing. **D W P Arbuthnot [1-22] Mrs Adrian Ireland.*

COURT CHAMPAGNE BHB 23f **RR 27f** 2569[10]

4 b f Batshoof 9.5f **(66)** - Fairfield's Breeze (Buckskin (FR))
Form - 006000
Record 2000 - 1st:0 2nd:0 3rd:0 Ran:6
Pre2000 - 1st:0 2nd:0 3rd:0 Ran:2
2000 Turf 0-6: (8f, 10f, 11f, 12f 2, 18f) (hvy, gd 2, g-f 3)
Little account filly. Turf high 32.
**R J Price [1-8] Derek & Cheryl Holder (from R Dickin [0-2] Oct 1998).*

COURT EXPRESS BHB 52a **RR 80f** 4740[21]

6 b g Then Again 7.4f **(52)** - Moon Risk (Risk Me (FR)) 5.9f **(53)**
Form - 1620530440
Record 2000 - 1st:1 2nd:1 3rd:1 Ran:10
Pre2000 - 1st:7 2nd:2 3rd:2 Ran:33
Win Prizemoney £37,609 *Total Prizemoney* £45,580
Wins * 2000 May Beverl (G-F) H 8.5f 75 79 <
* 1999 Aug Redcar (FRM) H 8f 72 74
* 1999 Jly Beverl (G-F) H 9.9f 68 69
* 1999 Jly Hamilt (FRM) H 9.2f 62 66
* 1999 Jun Carlis (GD) H 8f 57 59

* 1999 May Hamilt (GD) H 8.3f 50 51
1997 Jun Carlis (G-F) H 5.9f 63 68
1997 Jun Carlis (FRM) 5.9f 61

2000 Turf 1-10: (8f 1-6, 9f, 10f 3) (gd 2, g-f 3, frm 3, hrd 1-2)

Decent gelding, effective 8 to 10f, best at 8f, acts on g-f to hrd, has worn blinkers, prefers right handed tracks, prefers tight tracks, excels at Ripon and Hamilton, likes Beverley and Redcar. Turf high 80 - 3rd of 8 giving 18lb to Mini Lodge (22 Jly Ripon 10f g-f RF 3037) - also 1st of 16 giving 12lb to It's Our Secret (13 May Beverley RF 1188). Consistent.

**W W Haigh [6-22] Tim Hawkins (from J M Jefferson [0-3] Oct 1998).*

COURT FLIRT RR 29f 556[9]

3 b f Charmer 9f **(59)** - Willow Court (USA) (Little Current (USA)) 9.6f **(75)**

Form - 0

Record 2000 - 1st:0 2nd:0 3rd:0 Ran:1
Pre2000 - 1st:0 2nd:0 3rd:0 Ran:1

2000 Turf 0-1: (8f) (gd)

Leggy, currently little account filly.

**C W Fairhurst [0-2] David Hawes.*

COURT HOUSE BHB 30f26a RR 30f 26a 3224[20]

6 b g Reprimand 8.2f **(63)** - Chalet Girl (Double Form) 7.3f **(58)**

Form - 00

Record 2000 - 1st:0 2nd:0 3rd:0 Ran:2
Pre2000 - 1st:1 2nd:0 3rd:0 Ran:21

Win Prizemoney £2,448 *Total Prizemoney* £2,448

Wins 1997 Jun Pontef (GD) S 8f 60 <

2000 Turf 0-1: (7f) (frm) 2000 AW 0-1: (8f) (Fibr)

Very moderate gelding, has broken blood-vessels. Inconsistent.

**R J Price [0-5] R J Price (from B R Johnson [0-2] Aug 1999).*

COURTING RR 104f 4330[1]

3 gr f Pursuit of Love 9.5f **(69)** - Doctor's Glory (USA) **(90f)** (Elmaamul (USA))

Form - 3121

Record 2000 - 1st:2 2nd:1 3rd:1 Ran:4
Pre2000 - 1st:4 2nd:0 3rd:0 Ran:6

Win Prizemoney £46,293 *Total Prizemoney* £54,258

Wins * 2000 Spt Yarmou (G-F) L 10.1f 104 <
*** 2000** Jly Bordea (GD) L 8f 93
1999 Jly Newmar (G-F) 7f 87+
1999 Jly Thirsk (FRM) 7f 90+
1999 Jly Catter (FRM) 7f 77+
1999 Jun Catter (G-F) 7f 77+

2000 Turf 2-4: (8f 1-3, 10f 1-1) (gd 2-3, g-f)

Scopey, very useful filly, effective 8 to 10f, best at 8f, acts on gd to g-f, best on gd, does well at Catterick and Ascot. Turf high 104 - 1st of 15 giving 4lb to Sacred Song (12 Spt Yarmouth RF 4330). Reportedly in foal to Danzero, she increased her paddock value when scoring at listed level at Bordeaux on her second start of last season and added another success at that level at Yarmouth.

**W J Haggas [2-4] Cheveley Park Stud (from Sir Mark Prescott [4-6] Spt 1999).*

COURTLEDGE BHB 36f RR 51f 1204[15]

5 b g Unfuwain (USA) 11.4f **(74)** - Tremellick (Mummy's Pet) 7.7f **(60)**

Form - 0

Record 2000 - 1st:0 2nd:0 3rd:0 Ran:1
Pre2000 - 1st:0 2nd:0 3rd:0 Ran:8

2000 AW 0-1: (14f) (Fibr)

Fair gelding. Becoming disappointing.

**Miss J A Camacho [0-9] B P Skirton.*

COURTNEY GYM (IRE) BHB 24f24a RR 13f 24a 3077[8]

5 ch g Shalford (IRE) 7.8f **(63)** - Fair Or Foul (Patch) 11.5f **(51)**

Form - 0008

Record 2000 - 1st:0 2nd:0 3rd:0 Ran:4
Pre2000 - 1st:0 2nd:3 3rd:0 Ran:26

Win Prizemoney £0 *Total Prizemoney* £2,026

2000 Turf 0-2: (6f, 7f) (gd, frm) 2000 AW 0-2: (6f, 7f) (Equi, Fibr)

Poor gelding, effective 6f, acts on gd to hrd, often wears blinkers (effectively), likes left handed tracks, likes tight tracks. Turf high 13 (began Jly). AW high 6.

**P Burgoyne [0-25] R J Apperley (from M R Channon [0-5] Oct 1997).*

COURT OF APPEAL RR 89f 4829[4]

3 ch c Bering 9.6f **(80)** - Hiawatha's Song (USA) (Chief's Crown (USA)) 9.8f **(72)**

Form - 01884

Record 2000 - 1st:1 2nd:0 3rd:0 Ran:5
Pre2000 - 1st:0 2nd:0 3rd:0 Ran:1

Win Prizemoney £4,524 *Total Prizemoney* £5,089

Wins * 2000 May Kempto (SFT) 8f 89 <

2000 Turf 1-5: (8f 1-3, 10f 2) (sft, g-s 1-2, g-f, frm)

Lengthy, useful colt, effective 8 to 10f, acts on g-s. Turf high 89 - 1st of 12 from Mahfooth (27 May Kempton RF 1502).

**J R Fanshawe [1-6] Mrs Susan Davis.*

COURT OF JUSTICE (USA) BHB 64f RR 67f 5137[6]

4 b g Alleged (USA) 11.8f **(81)** - Captive Island (Northfields (USA)) 9f **(72)**

Form - 576

Record 2000 - 1st:0 2nd:0 3rd:0 Ran:3
Pre2000 - 1st:0 2nd:0 3rd:0 Ran:1

2000 Turf 0-3: (10f 2, 14f) (g-s, gd, g-f)

Scopey, average gelding. Turf high 67.

**K A Morgan [0-3] Pryke, Simpson, Butl Simcox (from P W Chapple-Hyam [0-1] Apr 1999).*

COURT ONE BHB 40f RR 34f 3633[7]

2 b c Shareef Dancer (USA) 10.1f **(67)** - Fairfields Cone (Celtic Cone) 9.8f **(43)**

Form - 007

Record 2000 - 1st:0 2nd:0 3rd:0 Ran:3

2000 Turf 0-3: (6f 2, 7f) (g-f 2, frm)

Currently very moderate colt. Turf high 34.

**R J Price [0-2] Derek & Cheryl Holder (from M Quinn [0-1] May 2000).*

COURT SHAREEF BHB 78f RR 81f 3275[15]

5 b g Shareef Dancer (USA) 10.1f **(67)** - Fairfields Cone (Celtic Cone) 9.8f **(43)**

Form - 1311020

Record 2000 - 1st:3 2nd:1 3rd:1 Ran:7
Pre2000 - 1st:2 2nd:0 3rd:2 Ran:16

Win Prizemoney £31,266 *Total Prizemoney* £39,311

Wins * 2000 Jun Carlis (G-F) H 12f 62 79 <
*** 2000** Jun Goodwo (GD) H 12f 63 72
*** 2000** Jun Windso (GD) H 11.6f 54 64
1998 May Leices (GD) H 11.8f 66 75
1998 May Windso (G-F) H 11.6f 58 62

2000 Turf 3-7: (10f, 12f 3-5, 14f) (gd, g-f 3-4, frm 2)

Decent gelding, effective 12f, acts on g-f to frm, best on g-f, likes right handed tracks, prefers tight tracks. Turf high 81 - 2nd of 5 getting 11lb from Mantusis (26 Jly Leicester 12f frm RF 3136) - also 1st of 15 giving 13lb to Octane (29 Jun Carlisle RF 2363). A drop in the handicap helped him return to his best and was in brilliant form this summer, winning three times including a clear-cut victory in the Cumberland Plate. Suited by 12 furlongs, he may not have stopped winning yet.

**R J Price [3-7] Derek & Cheryl Holder (from R Dickin [2-16] Oct 1999).*

COUTURE BHB 60f RR 69f 4827[23]

3 ch f Night Shift (USA) 8.1f **(73)** - Classic Design (Busted) 10.2f **(61)**

Form - 2550

Record 2000 - 1st:0 2nd:1 3rd:0 Ran:4

Win Prizemoney £0 *Total Prizemoney* £1,050

2000 Turf 0-4: (5f, 8f, 9f, 10f) (g-s, g-f, frm 2)

Workmanlike, average filly. Turf high 69 (1st run) (began Aug) - 2nd of 4 to Seeking Success (9 Aug Pontefract 8f frm RF 3500).

**N A Callaghan [0-4] M Tabor & Mrs John Magnier.*

COVENT GARDEN RR 67f 4807[7]

2 b c Sadler's Wells (USA) 11.3f **(87)** - Temple Row (Ardross) 10.6f **(68)**

Form - 7

Record 2000 - 1st:0 2nd:0 3rd:0 Ran:1

2000 Turf 0-1: (7f) (g-s)

Currently average colt. **Sir Michael Stoute [0-1] Lord Hartington.*

COVER UP (IRE) BHB 93f RR 97f 5226[9]

3 b g Machiavellian (USA) 9.8f **(83)** - Sought Out (IRE) (Rainbow Quest (USA)) 10.4f **(75)**

Form - 1030710
Record **2000** - 1st:2 2nd:0 3rd:1 Ran:7
Pre2000 - 1st:0 2nd:1 3rd:1 Ran:2
Win Prizemoney £11,557 *Total Prizemoney* £16,056
Wins * **2000** Spt Mussel (G-S) H 16f 89 94+ <
* **2000** Apr Windso (GD) 10f 90+
2000 Turf 2-7: (10f 1-1, 12f, 14f 2, 15f, 16f 1-2) (gd 1-2, g-f 4, frm 1-1)
Well made, very useful gelding, effective 10 to 16f, acts on gd to frm, has worn blinkers. Turf high 97 - 3rd of 8 giving 11lb to Fanfare (5 Aug Goodwood 14f g-f RF 3396) - also 1st of 9 giving 7lb to Heracles (24 Spt Musselburgh RF 4625). Out of a mare who won the Prix du Cadran, he narrowly got off the mark in a Windsor maiden on his return, but was highly tried several times after. Better effort upped to 14 furlongs at Goodwood, and scored again in a valuable Musselburgh handicap over two miles. Staying is obviously his game, but needs to improve to be a contender for the top long-distance handicaps.
**Sir Michael Stoute [2-9] Lord Weinstock.*

COWBOYS AND ANGELS BHB 75f69a **RR 77f 69a** 4533[6]

3 b g Bin Ajwaad (IRE) - Halimah (Be My Guest (USA)) 9.3f **(67)**
Form - 336010241206
Record **2000** - 1st:2 2nd:2 3rd:2 Ran:12
Pre2000 - 1st:0 2nd:1 3rd:1 Ran:3
Win Prizemoney £5,521 *Total Prizemoney* £10,397
Wins * **2000** Jly Ayr (G-F) H 7f 70 74 <
* **2000** May Salisb (GD) C 7f 74 <
2000 Turf 2-10: (6f, 7f 2-4, 8f 3, 10f 2) (g-s, gd 1-4, g-f 2, frm 1-3) 2000 AW 0-2: (8f, 9f) (Fibr 2)
Unfurnished, above-average gelding, effective 5 to 8f, best at 5f, acts on sft to frm, excels at Salisbury. Turf high 77 - 2nd of 12 giving 4lb to Hand Chime (2 Aug Kempton 7f g-f RF 3325) - also 1st of 20 giving 13lb to Sonbelle (18 May Salisbury RF 1273). AW high 63.
**W G M Turner [2-15] Mascalls Stud.*

COY DEBUTANTE (IRE) BHB 35f **RR 37f** 5077[11]

6 ch m Archway (IRE) 8.5f **(60)** - Presentable (Sharpen Up) 8.3f **(67)**
Form - 0000
Record **2000** - 1st:0 2nd:0 3rd:0 Ran:4
Pre2000 - 1st:0 2nd:0 3rd:1 Ran:7
Win Prizemoney £0 *Total Prizemoney* £390
2000 Turf 0-4: (10f 2, 12f 2) (g-s 2, gd, g-f)
Very moderate mare, effective 10 to 11f, acts on g-f to frm, favours tight tracks. Turf high 37. Inconsistent.
**W J Musson [0-11] The Flying Temple Partnership.*

COYOTE **RR 52f** 4876[4]

2 b f Indian Ridge 7.6f **(74)** - Caramba **(111+f)** (Belmez (USA))
Form - 4
Record **2000** - 1st:0 2nd:0 3rd:0 Ran:1
Win Prizemoney £0 *Total Prizemoney* £247
2000 Turf 0-1: (7f) (g-s)
Currently fair filly. **Sir Michael Stoute [0-1] Lord Carnarvon.*

COZZIE BHB 59f66a **RR 57f 66a** 4305[6]

2 ch f Cosmonaut - Royal Deed (USA) (Shadeed (USA)) 8.2f **(70)**
Form - 3751166146
Record **2000** - 1st:3 2nd:0 3rd:1 Ran:10
Win Prizemoney £8,025 *Total Prizemoney* £8,848
Wins * **2000** Aug Beverl (G-F) H 5f 56 56
* **2000** *Jun Lingfi (STD) S 5f 57* <
* **2000** Jun Mussel (FRM) S 5f 56
2000 Turf 2-8: (5f 2-7, 6f) (gd 2, g-f 1-2, frm 1-4) 2000 AW 1-2: (5f 1-2) (Equi 1-1, Fibr)
Fair filly, effective 5f, acts on g-f to frm - acts on AW, best on frm. Turf high 57 - also 1st of 11 getting 19lb from Celotti (16 Aug Beverley RF 3684). AW high 57 - 1st of 8 from Some Dust (14 Jun Lingfield RF 1972). Consistent. **J G Given [3-10] D Bass.*

CRACK ON CHERYL RR 1267[13]

6 b m Rakaposhi King 9.3f **(55)** - Furstin (Furry Glen) 8.9f **(63)**
Form - 00
Record **2000** - 1st:0 2nd:0 3rd:0 Ran:2
2000 Turf 0-1: (10f) (gd) 2000 AW 0-1: (9f) (Fibr)
Formerly very poor mare.
**F Jordan [0-10] F K Jennings.*

CRACOW (IRE) BHB 89f **RR 92f** 4936[15]

3 b c Polish Precedent (USA) 9f **(73)** - Height of Secrecy (Shirley Heights) 10.3f **(74)**
Form - 431052100
Record **2000** - 1st:2 2nd:1 3rd:1 Ran:9
Pre2000 - 1st:0 2nd:1 3rd:0 Ran:3
Win Prizemoney £17,475 *Total Prizemoney* £23,895
Wins * **2000** Aug York (GD) H 11.9f 88 92 <
* **2000** May Bright (SFT) 11.9f 75+
2000 Turf 2-9: (10f 2, 11f, 12f 2-5, 13f) (gd 2-6, g-f 3)
Scopey, useful colt, effective 10 to 12f, best at 12f, acts on gd to g-f, best on gd, likes left handed tracks. Turf high 92 - 2nd of 6 getting 16lb from Westender (18 Aug Newbury 11f g-f RF 3758) - also 1st of 4 getting 5lb from Kiftsgate (30 Aug York RF 4107). Got off the mark when faced with a simple task in a soft-ground Brighton maiden but was inevitably outclassed in the Derby. Decent efforts in handicaps afterwards, making all to win at York in September. He can be placed to win a good race at around 12 furlongs next season. **J W Hills [2-12] N N Browne.*

CRAFTY PICK (IRE) BHB 51f **RR 50f** 1918[4]

3 b f Thatching 7.8f **(69)** - Lucky Pick (Auction Ring (USA)) 8.6f **(65)**
Form - 70034
Record **2000** - 1st:0 2nd:0 3rd:1 Ran:5
Win Prizemoney £0 *Total Prizemoney* £310
2000 Turf 0-5: (6f 3, 7f 2) (gd 3, g-f 2)
Leggy, fair filly. Turf high 50. **R Hannon [0-5] Mrs D M Wight.*

CRAIGARY BHB 26f **RR 26f** 5193[1]

9 b g Dunbeath (USA) 9.9f **(53)** - Velvet Pearl (Record Token) 6.3f **(53)**
Form - 0501
Record **2000** - 1st:1 2nd:0 3rd:0 Ran:4
Pre2000 - 1st:1 2nd:1 3rd:3 Ran:18
Win Prizemoney £4,754 *Total Prizemoney* £6,681
Wins * **2000** Oct Mussel (SFT) H 13f 17 26
1997 Spt Hamilt (GD) SH 12.1f 37 41 <
2000 Turf 1-4: (12f, 13f 1-2, 16f) (gd 1-1, g-f, frm 2)
Little account gelding, has worn blinkers (extremely effectively). Turf high 26.
**D A Nolan [1-3] James Cringan (from Mrs A Duffield [3-35] Jun 2000).*

CRAIGSTEEL BHB 117f **RR 119f** 4948a[2]

5 b h Suave Dancer (USA) 10.7f **(68)** - Applecross (Glint of Gold) 9.3f **(66)**
Form - 2
2000 Turf 0-1: (12f) (frm)
High-class colt. (1st run) - 2nd of 12 to John's Call (7 Oct Belmont Park 12f frm RF 4948a). Improving.
**C Clement in USA [0-1] (from H R A Cecil [4-10] Oct 1999).*

CRASH CALL LADY BHB 31f30a **RR 23f 30a** 79[11]

4 b f Batshoof 9.5f **(66)** - Petite Louie (Chilibang)
Form - 43200
Record **2000** - 1st:0 2nd:0 3rd:0 Ran:2
Pre2000 - 1st:1 2nd:3 3rd:3 Ran:25
Win Prizemoney £2,211 *Total Prizemoney* £4,846
Wins * 1999 *Feb Wolver (STD) 12f 64* <
2000 AW 0-2: (16f 2) (Fibr 2)
Scopey, very moderate filly, effective 12f, - acts on Fibr, has worn blinkers. AW high 11. Inconsistent. **C N Allen [1-28] Crash Call Ltd.*

CRAZY LARRYS (USA) BHB 96f **RR 94f** 3623[1]

2 ch c Mutakddim (USA) - No Fear Of Flying (USA) (Super Concorde (USA)) 10.9f **(66)**
Form - 121
Record **2000** - 1st:2 2nd:1 3rd:0 Ran:3
Win Prizemoney £10,942 *Total Prizemoney* £13,340
Wins * **2000** Aug Kempto (G-F) 7f 94 <
* **2000** Jly Newcas (G-F) 7f 77
2000 Turf 2-3: (7f 2-3) (gd 1-1, frm 1-2)
Currently useful colt. Turf high 94 (began Jly) - 1st of 4 giving 8lb to Khitaam (14 Aug Kempton RF 3623). Won an ordinary race on his debut and, by no means disgraced in chasing home the subsequent Royal Lodge winner next time. He then took a conditions event at Kempton. There looks to be more to come.
**J Noseda [2-3] Crazy Radio Ltd.*

CREAM TEASE BHB 78f **RR 80f** 4127[1]
3 b f Pursuit of Love 9.5f **(69)** - Contralto (Busted) 10.2f **(61)**
Form - 00771
Record 2000 - 1st:1 2nd:0 3rd:0 Ran:5
Pre2000 - 1st:1 2nd:0 3rd:0 Ran:5
Win Prizemoney £15,804 *Total Prizemoney* £16,208
Wins * 2000 Aug Salisb (G-F) H 7f 73 78
* 1999 Aug Salisb (GD) 7f 80 <
2000 Turf 1-5: (7f 1-2, 8f 2, 10f) (gd 2, g-f, frm 1-2)
Scopey, decent filly, effective 7f, acts on frm, has worn blinkers. Turf high 80. Inconsistent. **D J S ffrenchDavis [2-10] Badgers Holt.*

CREDENZA MOMENT BHB 46f **RR 54f** 5131[12]
2 b c Pyramus (USA) - Mystoski **(41f 36a)** (Petoski) 5.7f **(62)**
Form - 000
Record 2000 - 1st:0 2nd:0 3rd:0 Ran:3
2000 Turf 0-3: (6f, 7f, 8f) (sft, gd, frm)
Currently fair colt. Turf high 54 (began Spt).
**R Hannon [0-3] Mrs J Wood.*

CREDIBILITY RR 64f 3334[3]
2 ch f Komaite (USA) 6.9f **(61)** - Integrity (Reform) 8.9f **(62)**
Form - 3
Record 2000 - 1st:0 2nd:0 3rd:1 Ran:1
Win Prizemoney £0 *Total Prizemoney* £430
2000 Turf 0 1: (6f) (frm)
Currently average filly.
**Sir Mark Prescott [0-1] Sharp But Fair Partnership.*

CREME DE CASSIS BHB 39f33a **RR 40f 33a** 224[7]
4 ch f Alhijaz 7.7f **(57)** - Lucky Flinders (Free State) 8.7f **(61)**
Form - 57
Record 2000 - 1st:0 2nd:0 3rd:0 Ran:1
Pre2000 - 1st:0 2nd:0 3rd:1 Ran:11
Win Prizemoney £0 *Total Prizemoney* £275
2000 AW 0-1: (13f) (Equi)
Neat, moderate filly, effective 10f, acts on g-f, likes left handed tracks, favours tight tracks. Inconsistent.
**P J Makin [0-12] Mrs Pauline Smith & Four Seasons Racing.*

CRESSET BHB 63a **RR 23f** 2989[7]
4 ch g Arazi (USA) 9.2f **(74)** - Mixed Applause (USA) (Nijinsky (CAN)) 10.3f **(77)**
Form - 68212122007
Record 2000 - 1st:2 2nd:4 3rd:0 Ran:10
Pre2000 - 1st:0 2nd:0 3rd:0 Ran:4
Win Prizemoney £4,340 *Total Prizemoney* £7,873
Wins * 2000 *Feb Southw (STD) H 12f 46 61* <
2000 *Jan Wolver (STD) SH 12f 54 61* <
2000 Turf 0-3: (13f, 14f, 22f) (sft, g-f, hrd) 2000 AW 2-7: (12f 2-5, 14f, 16f) (Fibr 2-7)
Tall, average gelding, effective 12 to 16f, - acts on Fibr, often wears blinkers (extremely effectively), prefers left handed tracks, favours tight tracks, excels at Wolverhampton and Southwell. Turf high 23. AW high 65 - 2nd of 11 giving 13lb to Kent (11 Feb Southwell 16f Fibr RF 0268) - also 1st of 6 getting 21lb from Jibereen (4 Feb Southwell RF 0220). Becoming disappointing.
**D W Chapman [1-7] Michael Hill (from W Jarvis [1-7] Jan 2000).*

Crimplene was made of the right material

CRESSIDA RR 66f 5236[20]
2 ch f Polish Precedent (USA) 9f **(73)** - Regent's Folly (IRE) (Touching Wood (USA)) 8.2f **(55)**
Form - 00
Record 2000 - 1st:0 2nd:0 3rd:0 Ran:2
2000 Turf 0-2: (7f, 8f) (g-s 2)
Currently average filly. Turf high 66 (began Oct).
**Sir Mark Prescott [0-2] Lord Roborough.*

CRETAN GIFT BHB 106f103a **RR 111f 103a** 4966[4]
9 ch g Cadeaux Genereux 7.9f **(76)** - Caro's Niece (USA) (Caro)
Form - 7351465772344558084
Record 2000 - 1st:1 2nd:1 3rd:2 Ran:19
Pre2000 - 1st:14 2nd:20 3rd:6 Ran:102
Win Prizemoney £110,527 *Total Prizemoney* £199,646
Wins * 2000 Apr Newmar (G-S) L 6f 111 <
* 1999 Aug Yarmou (GD) 6f 100
* 1999 Jly Ascot (FRM) H 6f 95 102
* 1998 *Mar Wolver (STD) H 5f 98 103*
* 1997 Aug Leopar (G-S) G3 6f 102
* 1997 Jun Newcas (HVY) H 6f 93 96
* 1997 *Feb Southw (STD) H 6f 90 97*
* 1996 Nov Redcar (G-F) H 6f 73 81
* 1996 Spt Ayr (G-F) H 6f 68 70
* 1996 Spt Nottin (FRM) H 5.1f 66 69
* 1996 *Jun Wolver (STD) H 6f 85 86*
* 1996 *Apr Wolver (STD) C 5f 82*
2000 Turf 1-18: (5f 2, 6f 1-15, 7f) (g-s 3, gd 1-7, g-f 5, frm 2, hrd) 2000 AW 0-1: (6f) (Fibr)
Group-class gelding, effective 6 to 7f, best at 6f, acts on gd to frm, best on gd, mostly wears blinkers (effectively), excels at Yarmouth, likes Newmarket. Turf high 111 - 1st of 12 getting 6lb from Warningford (18 Apr Newmarket RF 0768). A grand old campaigner who is kept very busy, he ran well to finish third in the Cammidge Trophy at Doncaster in March and everything went right for him when returning to winning form in the Abernant at the Craven meeting. Finds genuine Group company a bit too tough, but owes no-one a thing. Best when finishing late from off a fast pace and six furlongs is his trip.
**N P Littmoden [15-114] T Clarke (from John Harris [0-4] Jun 1994).*

CREUX NOIR (IRE) RR 92f 5286a[2]
4 b c Be My Guest (USA) 10.2f **(66)** -Sanndila (IRE) (Lashkari) 9.8f **(67)**
Form - 125530162
2000 Turf 2-9: (8f 1-4, 9f 1-3, 10f 2) (hvy 3, sft 1-2, g-s 2, gd)
Useful colt, effective 8 to 10f, acts on g-s, often wears blinkers (extremely effectively), excels at Curragh. Turf high 92 - 1st of 18 getting 1lb from Kerataka (16 Spt Curragh RF 4522a) - also 1st of 18 giving 15lb to Hill Port (2 Apr Fairyhouse RF 0615a). Consistent.
**D K Weld in IRE [4-21] Michael Smurfit.*

CRICKETERS CLUB BHB 56f **RR 49f** 3907[15]
2 b c Dancing Spree (USA) 8f **(59)** - Alacrity **(58df)** (Alzao (USA)) 7.1f **(68)**
Form - 000
Record 2000 - 1st:0 2nd:0 3rd:0 Ran:3
2000 Turf 0-3: (5f, 6f, 8f) (gd, frm 2)
Currently moderate colt. Turf high 52.
**B C Morgan [0-3] Cricketers Club Owners Group (2000).*

CRILLON (FR) RR 112f 4416a[2]
4 br c Saumarez 15.1f **(87)** - Shangrila (FR) (Nijinsky (CAN)) 10.3f **(77)**
Form - 2252
2000 Turf 0-4: (12f 3, 13f) (hvy, sft, g-s, gd)
Group-class colt. Turf high 112 - 2nd of 4 to Montjeu (10 Spt Longchamp 12f gd RF 4416a). **E Lellouche in FR [0-4] Mlle Y Shen.*

CRIMPLENE (IRE) BHB 121f **RR 124+f** 5325a[4]
3 ch f Lion Cavern (USA) 7.5f **(74)** - Crimson Conquest (USA) (Diesis) 9.3f **(69)**
Form - 6331111484
Record 2000 - 1st:4 2nd:0 3rd:2 Ran:10
Pre2000 - 1st:2 2nd:1 3rd:2 Ran:6
Win Prizemoney £398,283 *Total Prizemoney* £533,827
Wins * 2000 Aug Goodwo (GD) G1 9.9f 119+
*** 2000** Jun Ascot (G-F) G1 8f 124+ <

*** 2000**	May	Currag	(G-S)	G1	8f	115
*** 2000**	May	Dussel	(GD)	G2	8f	105
* 1999	Spt	Salisb	(G-F)		6f	88
* 1999	Jun	Redcar	(FRM)		6f	72+

2000 Turf 4-8: (7f, 8f 3-6, 10f 1-1) (sft, g-s 1-2, gd 2-3, g-f 1-2) 2000 AW 0-2: (9f 2) (Dirt 2)

Scopey, very high-class filly, effective 8 to 10f, best at 8f, acts on g-s to g-f, likes right handed tracks. Turf high 124 - 1st of 9 from Princess Ellen (23 Jun Ascot RF 2208) - also 1st of 7 getting 9lb from Ela Athena (5 Aug Goodwood RF 3394). AW high 111. Sixth behind China Visit at Nad Al Sheba on her reappearance, she finished third in the Fred Darling next time and then went on to prove herself a high-class filly. An unlucky third in the Italian Guineas before winning both the German and Irish versions, she added the Coronation Stakes at Ascot and the Nassau at Goodwood. Her stamina seemed to be giving out at the end of the ten furlongs there, and she returned to a mile when below-par at Deauville and Ascot. A really tough filly, she put up another game effort in the Breeders' Cup Distaff in which she finished fourth.

**C E Brittain [6-16] Darley Stud Management Inc.*

CRIMSON GLORY BHB 70a **RR 68f** 279[9]

4 ch f Lycius (USA) 8.8f **(71)** - Crimson Conquest (USA) (Diesis) 9.3f **(69)**

Form - 120

Record	**2000 -**	1st:1	2nd:1	3rd:0	Ran:3
	Pre2000 -	1st:0	2nd:1	3rd:1	Ran:8

Win Prizemoney £2,808 *Total Prizemoney* £6,430

Wins *** 2000** *Jan Wolver (STD) 8.5f 68* <

2000 AW 1-3: (8f 1-3) (Equi, Fibr 1-2)

Neat, average filly, effective 7 to 8f, best at 8f, acts on g-f to frm - acts on Fibr, best on frm. AW high 69 - also 1st of 10 giving 20lb to Mantilla (27 Jan Wolverhampton RF 0170). Inconsistent.

**G C Bravery [1-3] G C Bravery (from C E Brittain [0-8] Spt 1999).*

CRIMSON QUEST (IRE) RR 115f 5094a[1]

3 ch c Rainbow Quest (USA) 11.2f **(81)** - Bex (USA) (Explodent (USA)) 9.4f **(87)**

Form - 27221

2000 Turf 1-5: (10f, 11f, 12f 1-3) (hvy, sft 1-1, gd 3)

High-class colt. Turf high 114 - 1st of 5 from Slew The Red (15 Oct Longchamp RF 5094a). **A Fabre in FR [1-5] Sultan Al Kabeer.*

CRIMSON RIDGE BHB 67f **RR 65f** 3627[2]

2 b f King's Signet (USA) 7f **(51)** - Cloudy Reef (Cragador) 6f **(67)**

Form - 3642

Record **2000 -** 1st:0 2nd:1 3rd:1 Ran:4

Win Prizemoney £0 *Total Prizemoney* £1,567

2000 Turf 0-4: (5f 4) (g-f 2, frm 2)

Average filly. Turf high 65 - 2nd of 14 to Forever Times (14 Aug Thirsk 5f frm RF 3627). **R Hollinshead [0-4] M Johnson.*

CRIMSON TIDE (IRE) BHB 100f98a **RR 103f 98a** 5225[7]

6 b h Sadler's Wells (USA) 11.3f **(87)** - Sharata (IRE) (Darshaan) 9.9f **(84)**

Form - 35777

Record	**2000 -**	1st:0	2nd:0	3rd:1	Ran:5
	Pre2000 -	1st:5	2nd:2	3rd:5	Ran:17

Win Prizemoney £110,575 *Total Prizemoney* £125,929

Wins	* 1998	Spt	Epsom	(SFT)	G3	12f	102	
	* 1997	Nov	Capann	(HVY)	G2	8f	114	<
	* 1997	Oct	Dussel	(SFT)	G2	8.5f	109	
	* 1997	Spt	Bath	(G-F)		8f	100	
	* 1996	Oct	Newmar	(GD)		7f	92	

2000 Turf 0-5: (8f 3, 10f 2) (gd 4, g-f)

Very useful horse. Turf high 103 (began Aug). He won a weak Group Three at Epsom in September 1998 when the soft ground was in his favour, but missed the whole of the following season. Faced some stiff tasks in 2000, but showed that he retains ability.

**J W Hills [5-22] C Wright & Partners.*

CRIPSEY BROOK BHB 69f **RR 67f** 2811[12]

2 ch c Lycius (USA) 8.8f **(71)** - Duwon (IRE) **(53df)** (Polish Precedent (USA)) 10.2f **(60)**

Form - 450

Record **2000 -** 1st:0 2nd:0 3rd:0 Ran:3

Win Prizemoney £0 *Total Prizemoney* £340

2000 Turf 0-3: (6f 2, 7f) (gd, g-f, frm)

Currently average colt. Turf high 67.

**R J O'Sullivan [0-3] Normandy Developments (London).*

CRISOS IL MONACO (IRE) RR 117f 1456a[8]

5 b h Common Grounds 8.1f **(66)** - Gayshuka (Lord Gayle (USA)) 8.8f **(62)**

Form - 528

2000 Turf 0-2: (8f, 10f) (g-s, gd)

High-class colt. Turf high 117 (1st run) - 2nd of 9 to Timboroa (14 May Capannelle 10f gd RF 1284a).

**L Camici in ITY [1-7] (from F Camici in ITY [0-1] Nov 1999).*

CRISS CROSS (IRE) RR 79f 3593[5]

3 b c Lahib (USA) 8f **(69)** - La Belle Katherine (USA) (Lyphard (USA)) 9.9f **(72)**

Form - 22245415

Record	**2000 -**	1st:1	2nd:3	3rd:0	Ran:8
	Pre2000 -	1st:0	2nd:0	3rd:0	Ran:1

Win Prizemoney £4,368 *Total Prizemoney* £8,461

Wins *** 2000** Jly Kempto (G-S) 6f 76 <

2000 Turf 1-8: (6f 1-3, 7f 4, 8f) (hvy 2, sft, gd, g-f 1-1, frm 3)

Scopey, above-average colt, effective 6 to 8f, best at 7f, acts on hvy to g-f, best on hvy. Turf high 79 - 2nd of 6 getting 15lb from Redoubtable (1 May Warwick 7f sft RF 0952) - also 1st of 3 from Whistler (12 Jly Kempton RF 2733). **R Hannon [1-9] Michael Pescod.*

CRISTOFORO (IRE) BHB 51f **RR** 5246[5]

3 b g Perugino (USA) - Red Barons Lady (IRE) (Electric) 10.1f **(61)**

Form - 05

Record **2000 -** 1st:0 2nd:0 3rd:0 Ran:2

2000 AW 0-2: (7f, 8f) (Fibr 2)

Scopey, currently moderate gelding. AW high 49 (began Oct).

**B J Curley [0-2] P Byrne.*

CROESO ADREF BHB 36f40a **RR 28f 40a** 5018[11]

3 ch f Most Welcome 8.6f **(66)** - Grugiar (Red Sunset) 8.2f **(63)**

Form - 3123643480700

Record	**2000 -**	1st:1	2nd:1	3rd:2	Ran:12
	Pre2000 -	1st:0	2nd:0	3rd:1	Ran:4

Win Prizemoney £2,299 *Total Prizemoney* £4,171

Wins **2000** *Jan Wolver (STD) H 7f 42 44* <

2000 Turf 0-4: (6f, 7f, 8f, 10f) (gd 2, frm 2) 2000 AW 1-8: (7f 1-5, 8f 2, 10f) (Equi 4, Fibr 1-4)

Light-framed, moderate filly, effective 7 to 10f, best at 7f, acts on gd - acts on AW, has worn blinkers. Turf high 46 (1st run) - 3rd of 8 getting 21lb from Fantastic Fantasy (31 Mar Southwell 10f gd RF 0587). AW high 51 - 2nd of 9 getting 9lb from Lucky Star (8 Jan Lingfield 7f Equi RF 0048) - also 1st of 12 getting 5lb from Lion's Domane (4 Jan Wolverhampton RF 0018).

**A B Mulholland [0-3] Miss K Watson (from S C Williams [1-13] May 2000).*

CROESO CARIAD BHB 105f **RR 109f** 2748[2]

3 b f Most Welcome 8.6f **(66)** - Colorsnap (Shirley Heights) 10.3f **(74)**

Form - 5042

Record	**2000 -**	1st:0	2nd:1	3rd:0	Ran:4
	Pre2000 -	1st:2	2nd:1	3rd:0	Ran:6

Win Prizemoney £19,230 *Total Prizemoney* £49,466

Wins	* 1999	Spt	San Si	(GD)	L	7f	97+	<
	* 1999	Aug	Chepst	(G-F)		5.1f	86+	

2000 Turf 0-4: (7f, 8f, 11f, 12f) (gd 3, g-f)

Scopey, Pattern-class filly, effective 8 to 12f, acts on gd to g-f. Turf high 109 - 2nd of 10 to Alshakr (12 Jly Newmarket 8f gd RF 2748). A useful fillly, she ran well in a light campaign, reaching the frame in the Ribblesdale and Falmouth Stakes.

**M L W Bell [2-10] Usk Valley Stud.*

CROESO CROESO RR 33f 5156[12]

2 b f Most Welcome 8.6f **(66)** - Croeso-I-Cymru **(93f)** (Welsh Captain) 5f **(60)**

Form - 0

Record **2000 -** 1st:0 2nd:0 3rd:0 Ran:1

2000 Turf 0-1: (5f) (g-s)

Currently very moderate filly. **J L Spearing [0-1] Mrs Richard Evans.*

CROMABOO COUNTESS BHB 25f **RR 11f** 4489[17]

3 b f Makbul - La Belle Epoque (Tachypous) 8.6f **(55)**

Form - 70
Record 2000 - 1st:0 2nd:0 3rd:0 Ran:1
Pre2000 - 1st:0 2nd:0 3rd:0 Ran:4
2000 Turf 0-1: (10f) (g-f)
Light-framed, poor filly. **B D Leavy [0-5] John Wardle.*

CROMER PIER BHB 26f38a RR 28f 38a 564[10]

5 b g Reprimand 8.2f **(63)** - Fleur du Val (Valiyar) 8.5f **(73)**
Form - 0
Record 2000 - 1st:0 2nd:0 3rd:0 Ran:1
Pre2000 - 1st:0 2nd:1 3rd:2 Ran:16
Win Prizemoney £0 *Total Prizemoney* £1,496
2000 Turf 0-1: (12f) (g-f)
Little account gelding, often wears blinkers.
**G Fierro [0-10] M D Benniston (from M H Tompkins [0-11] Oct 1998).*

CROOKFORD WATER BHB 44f RR 55df 2818[3]

3 b g Rock City 8.8f **(62)** - Blue Nile (IRE) **(69f)** (Bluebird (USA)) 7.5f **(69)**
Form - 043
Record 2000 - 1st:0 2nd:0 3rd:1 Ran:3
Pre2000 - 1st:0 2nd:0 3rd:0 Ran:3
Win Prizemoney £0 *Total Prizemoney* £258
2000 Turf 0-2: (10f, 11f) (g-f 2) 2000 AW 0-1: (12f) (Fibr)
Light-framed, fair gelding. Turf high 44.
**J A Glover [0-6] Vic Atherton.*

CROSBY DONJOHN BHB 60f57a RR 68f 57a 126[7]

3 ch c Magic Ring (IRE) 6.5f **(64)** - Ovideo **(58f)** (Domynsky) 8f **(82)**
Form - 0267
Record 2000 - 1st:0 2nd:0 3rd:0 Ran:2
Pre2000 - 1st:0 2nd:1 3rd:0 Ran:8
Win Prizemoney £0 *Total Prizemoney* £1,280
2000 AW 0-2: (6f, 7f) (Fibr 2)
Scopey, average colt, effective 7f, - acts on Fibr, has worn blinkers (very effectively), likes left handed tracks, likes tight tracks. AW high 45. Inconsistent. **E Weymes [0-10] Don Raper.*

CROSS DALL (IRE) BHB 53f RR 63f 3185[4]

3 b f Blues Traveller (IRE) - Faapette (Runnett) 7f **(59)**
Form - 33180584
Record 2000 - 1st:1 2nd:0 3rd:1 Ran:7
Pre2000 - 1st:0 2nd:0 3rd:1 Ran:4
Win Prizemoney £2,352 *Total Prizemoney* £3,197
Wins * 2000 May Windso (G-S) 11.6f 63 <
2000 Turf 1-6: (11f, 12f 1-4, 14f) (sft, gd 1-1, g-f, frm 3) 2000 AW 0-1: (12f) (Fibr)
Workmanlike, average filly, effective 12f, acts on gd, often wears blinkers, favours tight tracks. Turf high 63 - 1st of 11 getting 3lb from Fliquet Bay (2 May Windsor RF 0974).
**Lady Herries [1-7] Global Racing Club (from R Ingram [0-4] Nov 1999).*

CROSS FINGERS (IRE) RR 2250[9]

2 ch f Idris (IRE) - Light Hand (Star Appeal) 9.6f **(65)**
Form - 60
Record 2000 - 1st:0 2nd:0 3rd:0 Ran:2
2000 Turf 0-1: (7f) (frm) 2000 AW 0-1: (5f) (Equi)
Currently very poor filly.
**M H Tompkins [0-2] Robert Levitt.*

CROSS LUGANA BHB 45f RR 49f 2357[11]

4 b f Lugana Beach 7f **(63)** - Cross Mags **(45f)** (Hasty Word)
Form - 800
Record 2000 - 1st:0 2nd:0 3rd:0 Ran:3
Pre2000 - 1st:0 2nd:0 3rd:0 Ran:1
2000 Turf 0-3: (7f, 10f, 12f) (g-s, gd, g-f)
Neat, moderate filly. Turf high 49.
**P D Evans [0-3] H K Strickland (from D Burchell [0-1] May 1998).*

CROSSWAYS RR 45f 5184[13]

2 b c Mister Baileys - Miami Dancer (Miami Springs) 9.9f **(59)**
Form - 00
Record 2000 - 1st:0 2nd:0 3rd:0 Ran:2
2000 Turf 0-2: (7f, 8f) (g-s, frm)
Currently moderate colt. Turf high 45 (began Spt). **C F Wall [0-2] N Ahamad.*

CROWDED AVENUE BHB 73f00a RR 77f 80a 4756[12]

8 b g Sizzling Melody 6.3f **(49)** - Lady Bequick (Sharpen Up) 8.3f **(67)**
Form - 0032800
Record 2000 - 1st:0 2nd:1 3rd:1 Ran:6
Pre2000 - 1st:6 2nd:5 3rd:5 Ran:40
Win Prizemoney £39,805 *Total Prizemoney* £69,251
Wins * 1996 Aug Sandow (GD) H 5f 95 93 <
2000 Turf 0-6: (5f 6) (g-s, frm 5)
Above-average gelding, effective 5f, acts on frm, has worn blinkers (very effectively). Turf high 77. Inconsistent. Has not won for donkey's years, and spurned a clear chance in a claimer at Sandown. **P J Makin [6-46] T W Wellard.*

CROWN LODGE (IRE) BHB 86f RR 89f 5134[7]

3 ch f Grand Lodge (USA) - Itqan (IRE) (Sadler's Wells (USA)) 10f **(76)**
Form - 215757
Record 2000 - 1st:1 2nd:1 3rd:0 Ran:6
Win Prizemoney £3,984 *Total Prizemoney* £6,019
Wins * 2000 Jun Haydoc (G-S) 8.1f 82 <
2000 Turf 1-6: (8f 1-4, 10f 2) (sft, g-s 1-3, gd, g-f)
Useful filly, effective 8f, acts on g-s to gd. Turf high 89 - 5th of 14 getting 6lb from Riberac (23 Spt Ascot 8f gd RF 4598) - also 1st of 6 getting 5lb from Grey Eminence (10 Jun Haydock RF 1879). Unraced at two, she won an ordinary Haydock maiden on her second start. The fast ground was not in her favour next time, and she was found wanting in listed races. **L M Cumani [1-6] Robert Smith.*

CROWN MINT (USA) BHB 50f45a RR 56f 45a 2790[10]

3 gr c Chief's Crown (USA) 10.2f **(75)** - Add Mint (USA) (Vigors (USA)) 10f **(72)**
Form - 8200
Record 2000 - 1st:0 2nd:1 3rd:0 Ran:3
Pre2000 - 1st:0 2nd:0 3rd:0 Ran:3
Win Prizemoney £0 *Total Prizemoney* £675
2000 Turf 0-3: (11f, 12f 2) (g-f, frm 2)
Workmanlike, fair colt, effective 11f, acts on frm. Turf high 56 (1st run) - 2nd of 11 giving 12lb to Adriana (14 Jun Lingfield 11f frm RF 1970). **R T Phillips [0-6] Wilwyn Racing.*

CRUAGH EXPRESS (IRE) BHB 53f51a RR 54f 51a 4924[3]

4 b g Unblest - Cry In The Dark (Godswalk (USA)) 7.3f **(58)**
Form - 56081163
Record 2000 - 1st:2 2nd:0 3rd:1 Ran:8
Pre2000 - 1st:0 2nd:0 3rd:2 Ran:10
Win Prizemoney £5,262 *Total Prizemoney* £6,378
Wins * 2000 Spt Goodwo (HVY) CH 8f 50 54 <
2000 *Spt Lingfi (STD) SH 10f 43 46*
2000 Turf 1-5: (8f 1-2, 10f 3) (gd 1-3, g-f 2) 2000 AW 1-3: (8f 2, 10f 1-1) (Equi 1-2, Fibr)
Fair gelding, effective 6 to 10f, best at 8f, acts on g-s to g-f - acts on Equi, has worn blinkers (extremely effectively), prefers left handed tracks, prefers tight tracks, excels at Lingfield. Turf high 54 - 1st of 17 giving 4lb to Magical Bailiwick (20 Spt Goodwood RF 4544). AW high 55 (began Aug) - 3rd of 12 getting 6lb from Tapage (11 Oct Lingfield 8f Equi RF 4924).
**G L Moore [1-3] C F Sparrowhawk (from P L Gilligan [1-5] Spt 2000).*

CRUISE RR 60f 4676[14]

3 ch c Prince Sabo 6.6f **(64)** - Mistral's Dancer (Shareef Dancer (USA)) 9.9f **(73)**
Form - 510500170
Record 2000 - 1st:1 2nd:0 3rd:0 Ran:7
Pre2000 - 1st:1 2nd:0 3rd:0 Ran:2
Win Prizemoney £4,572 *Total Prizemoney* £4,572
Wins * 2000 Aug Bright (FRM) 7f 62 <
*1999 *Dec Lingfi (STD) 6f 61+*
2000 Turf 1-7: (6f, 7f 1-5, 8f) (g-s, gd, g-f 2, frm 1-3)
Workmanlike, average colt, effective 6 to 7f, acts on frm - acts on Equi, prefers left handed tracks, prefers tight tracks. Turf high 62 - 1st of 10 giving 3lb to Sangra (30 Aug Brighton RF 4103).
**R Hannon [2-9] Heathavon Stables Ltd.*

CRUSTY LILY BHB 43f RR 43f 4396[6]

4 gr f Whittingham (IRE) - Miss Crusty **(35df)** (Belfort (FR)) 6.8f **(63)**
Form - 04200663056
Record 2000 - 1st:0 2nd:1 3rd:1 Ran:11

Pre2000 - 1st:1 2nd:1 3rd:0 Ran:9
Win Prizemoney £3,132 *Total Prizemoney* £5,530
Wins 1999 Aug Yarmou (GD) H 6f 39 42 <
2000 Turf 0-11: (5f, 6f 7, 7f 3) (g-f 2, frm 8, hrd)
Light-framed, moderate filly, effective 6 to 7f, best at 6f, acts on gd to frm, best on frm, excels at Yarmouth. Turf high 45 - 2nd of 10 getting 6lb from Muja's Magic (5 Jly Yarmouth 6f frm RF 2556). Inconsistent.
**J M Bradley [0-11] Three Of A Kind Racing (from N P Littmoden [1-8] Oct 1999).*

CRUZ SANTA BHB 34f27a **RR 31f 27a** 2559[2]

7 b m Lord Bud 8.2f **(52)** - Linpac Mapleleaf (Dominion) 8.5f **(63)**
Form - 2
Record 2000 - 1st:0 2nd:1 3rd:0 Ran:1
Pre2000 - 1st:1 2nd:1 3rd:1 Ran:26
Win Prizemoney £2,085 *Total Prizemoney* £4,656
Wins 1998 *Jan Southw (STD) 11f 40* <
2000 Turf 0-1: (16f) (g-f)
Moderate mare.
**Mrs M Reveley [1-8] The Mary Reveley Racing Club (from M C Chapman [1-16] Aug 1998).*

CRYFIELD BHB 67f55a **RR 66f 55a** 5229[8]

3 b g Efisio 7.7f **(69)** - Ciboure (Norwick (USA)) 7.2f **(56)**
Form - 050271310062428
Record 2000 - 1st:2 2nd:3 3rd:1 Ran:15
Win Prizemoney £5,700 *Total Prizemoney* £9,217
Wins * 2000 Jun Carlis (G-F) H 5.9f 58 62 <
*** 2000** May Redcar (G-S) H 6f 51 55
2000 Turf 2-13: (5f, 6f 2-7, 7f 4, 8f) (sft, g-s 2, gd 6, g-f 1-1, frm 1-2, hrd) 2000 AW 0-2: (6f 2) (Fibr 2)
Average gelding, effective 6 to 7f, best at 6f, acts on g-s to frm, has worn blinkers (very effectively). Turf high 66 - 2nd of 21 giving 12lb to Printsmith (20 Oct Doncaster 7f gd RF 5105) - also 1st of 11 giving 2lb to Pacific Place (28 Jun Carlisle RF 2328). AW high 51.
**N Tinkler [2-15] & Mrs G Middlebrook.*

CRYHAVOC BHB 88f **RR 87f** 4451[15]

6 b g Polar Falcon (USA) 9f **(74)** - Sarabah (IRE) (Ela-Mana-Mou) 10.1f **(70)**
Form - 6003732021028000600
Record 2000 - 1st:1 2nd:3 3rd:2 Ran:19
Pre2000 - 1st:7 2nd:3 3rd:2 Ran:31
Win Prizemoney £38,229 *Total Prizemoney* £62,789
Wins * 2000 Jly Epsom (G-S) H 6f 85 97 <
* 1999 Jly Beverl (SFT) H 5f 73 88+
* 1999 Jun Catter (G-F) H 7f 71 83
* 1999 Jun Windso (G-F) H 6f 63 75+
* 1999 Jun Goodwo (G-F) H 6f 58 68
* 1999 Jun Yarmou (GD) H 6f 58 61
1996 Oct Newmar (G-F) H 6f 86 96
1996 Spt Epsom (G-F) 6f 83
2000 Turf 1-19: (5f 7, 6f 1-12) (sft, gd 1-9, g-f 7, frm 2)
Useful gelding, effective 5 to 7f, best at 6f, acts on gd to g-f, best on g-f, has worn blinkers, prefers left handed tracks, likes tight tracks. Turf high 97 - 1st of 8 giving 10lb to Cauda Equina (5 Jly Epsom RF 2549). Consistent. He suddenly hit an extraordinary vein of form in the summer of '99, winning five times. Not surprisingly the Handicapper took a dim view, but he ran well enough early in 2000 and was successful at Epsom in July. However, another hike in the ratings was enough to prevent further success. He is returning to a reasonable mark though.
**D Nicholls [6-34] John Gilbertson (from J R Arnold [2-16] Oct 1998).*

CRYSTAL CANYON BHB 57f **RR 61f** 1708[7]

3 ch f Efisio 7.7f **(69)** - Manor Adventure **(26f 47a)** (Smackover) 6f **(52)**
Form - 7
Record 2000 - 1st:0 2nd:0 3rd:0 Ran:1
Pre2000 - 1st:0 2nd:0 3rd:0 Ran:2
2000 Turf 0-1: (5f) (g-s)
Workmanlike, currently average filly. **B Smart [0-3] Mrs Julie Martin.*

CRYSTAL CHANDELIER BHB 30f **RR 23f** 4454[8]

2 ch f Pivotal - Whittle Woods Girl **(74f 60a)** (Emarati (USA))
Form - 08
Record 2000 - 1st:0 2nd:0 3rd:0 Ran:2
2000 Turf 0-2: (5f, 6f) (g-s, hrd)
Currently little account filly. Turf high 23 (began Aug).
**B W Murray [0-2] John Jackson.*

CRYSTAL CREEK (IRE) BHB 72f **RR 77f** 4934[13]

4 b g River Falls 8.2f **(56)** - Dazzling Maid (IRE) (Tate Gallery (USA)) 7.4f **(67)**
Form - 06800
Record 2000 - 1st:0 2nd:0 3rd:0 Ran:5
Pre2000 - 1st:2 2nd:1 3rd:2 Ran:11
Win Prizemoney £10,126 *Total Prizemoney* £14,545
Wins * 1999 Jun Bath (FRM) H 8f 84 85 <
* 1999 May Kempto (G-F) 8f 80
2000 Turf 0-5: (8f 3, 10f 2) (sft, gd 2, g-f, frm)
Scopey, above-average gelding, effective 8 to 10f, best at 8f, acts on gd to hrd. Turf high 77.
**Mrs A J Perrett [2-16] Fred Cotton & Mrs Gaynor Scruton.*

CRYSTAL D'ASS (FR) **RR 108f** 4411a[3]

3 f Northern Crystal - Asslana (FR) (Al Nasr (FR)) 9.3f **(68)**
Form - 2323
2000 Turf 0-3: (8f 2, 9f) (sft, gd 2)
Pattern-class, effective 8 to 9f, best at 9f, acts on hvy to gd, has worn blinkers. Turf high 108 (1st run) - 3rd of 8 to Cayoke (11 Jun Chantilly 8f gd RF 2004a).
**T Clout in FR [0-6] (from F Chappet in FR [1-3] Aug 1999).*

CRYSTAL FLITE (IRE) BHB 54f47a **RR 63df 47a** 4692[5]

3 b f Darshaan 11.9f **(81)** - Crystal City (Kris) 9.5f **(73)**
Form - 7026055
Record 2000 - 1st:0 2nd:1 3rd:0 Ran:7
Pre2000 - 1st:0 2nd:0 3rd:1 Ran:5
Win Prizemoney £0 *Total Prizemoney* £1,738
2000 Turf 0-7: (10f 2, 12f 4, 14f) (gd 2, g-f 2, frm 3)
Workmanlike, average filly, effective 7f, acts on g-f. Turf high 68.
**W R Muir [0-12] The Wheet Partnership.*

CRYSTAL LASS BHB 40f57a **RR 40f 57a** 4652[7]

4 b f Ardkinglass 5f **(64)** - That's Rich (Hot Spark) 7.6f **(62)**
Form - 405705050407
Record 2000 - 1st:0 2nd:0 3rd:0 Ran:11
Pre2000 - 1st:1 2nd:2 3rd:2 Ran:17
Win Prizemoney £2,814 *Total Prizemoney* £5,894
Wins * 1999 *Jun Southw (STD) H 8f 63 73+* <
2000 Turf 0-8: (6f 4, 7f 3, 8f) (gd, frm 4, hrd 3) 2000 AW 0-3: (7f, 8f 2) (Fibr 3)
Rangy, average filly, effective 8f, - acts on Fibr, has worn blinkers, likes left handed tracks, likes tight tracks. Turf high 40. AW high 49. **J Balding [1-28] White House Racing Club.*

CRYSTAL MUSIC (USA) BHB 100f **RR 98f** 4595[1]

2 b f Nureyev (USA) 8.4f **(84)** - Crystal Spray (Beldale Flutter (USA)) 9.7f **(71)**
Form - 111
Record 2000 - 1st:3 2nd:0 3rd:0 Ran:3
Win Prizemoney £126,150 *Total Prizemoney* £126,150
Wins * 2000 Spt Ascot (G-S) G1 8f 98 <
*** 2000** Aug Sandow (G-F) 8.1f 96+
*** 2000** Jly Newmar (G-F) 7f 80++
2000 Turf 3-3: (7f 1-1, 8f 2-2) (gd 2-2, frm 1-1)
Currently very useful filly. Turf high 98 (began Jly) - 1st of 9 from Summer Symphony (23 Spt Ascot RF 4595) - also 1st of 4 giving 3lb to Zaheemah (18 Aug Sandown RF 3771). From a good family, she won her first two races in useful style, before stepping up in class to take the Fillies' Mile at Ascot. She has plenty of scope and looks classic material although, as ten furlongs may be the limit of her stamina, she is reportedly to be aimed at the Prix de Diane rather than the Oaks. **J H M Gosden [3-3] Lord Lloyd-Webber.*

CUBISM (USA) BHB 102f **RR 104f** 4933[18]

4 b c Miswaki (USA) 8.1f **(81)** - Seattle Kat (USA) (Seattle Song (USA)) 9f **(77)**
Form - 735380
Record 2000 - 1st:0 2nd:0 3rd:2 Ran:6
Pre2000 - 1st:4 2nd:1 3rd:0 Ran:14
Win Prizemoney £32,173 *Total Prizemoney* £54,879
Wins * 1999 May Haydoc (GD) LH 6f 96 98 <
* 1999 May Salisb (G-F) H 6f 87 91

* 1998 Aug Windso (G-F) H 6f 85 89
* 1998 Jly Yarmou (GD) 6f 77+
2000 Turf 0-6: (5f, 6f 5) (gd 2, g-f 4)
Small, very useful colt, effective 5 to 6f, best at 6f, acts on g-f to frm, best on g-f. Turf high 104 - 3rd of 30 giving 10lb to Tayseer (5 Aug Goodwood 6f g-f RF 3395). An able sprinter, he ran his best race of the campaign when third in the Stewards' Cup.
**J W Hills [4-20] K Y Lim.*

CUIGIU (IRE) BHB 50f46a **RR 57f 46a** 4403[12]
3 b g Persian Bold 10f **(69)** - Homosassa (Burslem) 8.8f **(53)**
Form - 407542054782300
Record 2000 - 1st:0 2nd:2 3rd:1 Ran:13
Pre2000 - 1st:0 2nd:1 3rd:0 Ran:8
Win Prizemoney £0 *Total Prizemoney* £3,041
2000 Turf 0-9: (6f, 7f, 8f 5, 9f, 10f) (gd 3, g-f 2, frm 4) 2000 AW 0-4: (7f 2, 8f 2) (Fibr 4)
Fair gelding, effective 8f, acts on g-s, has worn blinkers. Turf high 57. AW high 46.
**D Carroll [0-12] Miss Diane Allman (from Noel Chance [0-3] Jan 2000).*

CULMINATE BHB 38f **RR 44tf** 5150[13]
3 ch g Afzal - Straw Blade (Final Straw) 7.9f **(64)**
Form - 00000
Record 2000 - 1st:0 2nd:0 3rd:0 Ran:5
2000 Turf 0-4: (8f 2, 9f, 10f) (g-s, g-f 2, frm) 2000 AW 0-1: (10f) (Equi)
Workmanlike, moderate gelding. Turf high 55 (began Jly).
**J E Long [0-5] J King.*

CULTURED PEARL (IRE) BHB 58f53a **RR 58f 53a** 4474[12]
3 ch f Lammtarra (USA) - Culture Vulture (USA) (Timeless Moment (USA)) 6f **(72)**
Form - 360700
Record 2000 - 1st:0 2nd:0 3rd:1 Ran:6
Pre2000 - 1st:0 2nd:0 3rd:0 Ran:1
Win Prizemoney £0 *Total Prizemoney* £536
2000 Turf 0-4: (7f 2, 8f, 10f) (g-f 2, frm 2) 2000 AW 0-2: (8f, 9f) (Fibr 2)
Scopey, fair filly, has worn blinkers. Turf high 58. AW high 58.
**P F I Cole [0-7] Christopher Wright.*

CULZEAN (IRE) BHB 85f **RR 90f** 5187[5]
4 b g Machiavellian (USA) 9.8f **(83)** - Eileen Jenny (IRE) (Kris) 9.5f **(73)**
Form - 536704120362005
Record 2000 - 1st:1 2nd:2 3rd:2 Ran:15
Pre2000 - 1st:1 2nd:1 3rd:2 Ran:12
Win Prizemoney £9,784 *Total Prizemoney* £22,882
Wins * 2000 Jun Newmar (G-F) H 10f 78 84 <
* 1998 Spt Leices (G-S) 7f 80+
2000 Turf 1-15: (8f 4, 9f, 10f 1-9, 11f) (hvy, sft, g-s 2, gd 3, g-f 1-7, frm)
Leggy, useful gelding, effective 8 to 11f, best at 10f, acts on sft to frm, has worn blinkers, excels at Doncaster and Newbury, does well at Newmarket. Turf high 90 - 2nd of 13 giving 4lb to Green Card (6 Spt Doncaster 10f gd RF 4262) - also 1st of 10 getting 1lb from Second Wind (30 Jun Newmarket RF 2412). Consistent. He ran some good races last term and landed a Newmarket rated stakes in July. Suited by ten furlongs, but probably needs to come down a few pounds in the handicap on turf.
**R Hannon [2-27] Stonethorn Stud Farms Ltd.*

CUMBRIAN CASPER (IRE) RR 848[4]
2 b g Tagula (IRE) - More Mirth (Main Reef) 9.6f **(57)**
Form - 4
Record 2000 - 1st:0 2nd:0 3rd:0 Ran:1
2000 Turf 0-1: (5f) (sft)
Currently very poor gelding.
**T D Easterby [0-1] Cumbrian Industrials Ltd.*

CUMBRIAN HARMONY (IRE) BHB 66f **RR 72f** 4257[13]
2 b f Distinctly North (USA) 7.4f **(63)** - Sawaki (Song) 7.2f **(61)**
Form - 0237552100
Record 2000 - 1st:1 2nd:2 3rd:1 Ran:10
Win Prizemoney £3,445 *Total Prizemoney* £5,573
Wins * 2000 Jly Newcas (GD) 6f 72+ <
2000 Turf 1-10: (5f 5, 6f 1-3, 7f 2) (sft, gd 2, g-f 1-4, frm 2, hrd)
Above-average filly, effective 5 to 6f, best at 6f, acts on g-f to hrd, best on g-f. Turf high 72 - 1st of 8 getting 7lb from Ceralbi (31 Jly Newcastle RF 3249). **T D Easterby [1-10] Cumbrian Industrials Ltd.*

CUMBRIAN PRINCESS BHB 38f **RR 35f** 4275[18]
3 gr f Mtoto 11.5f **(71)** - Cumbrian Melody (Petong) 6.6f **(58)**
Form - 0006850
Record 2000 - 1st:0 2nd:0 3rd:0 Ran:7
Pre2000 - 1st:1 2nd:0 3rd:0 Ran:5
Win Prizemoney £3,366 *Total Prizemoney* £3,366
Wins * 1999 Oct Pontef (SFT) H 6f 57 60 <
2000 Turf 0-7: (7f 4, 10f 3) (g-s, gd, g-f 4, frm)
Light-framed, very moderate filly, effective 6f, acts on gd. Turf high 52. **M Blanshard [1-12] David Sykes.*

CUPBOARD LOVER BHB 58f61a **RR 58f 61a** 4928[2]
4 ch g Risk Me (FR) 8f **(53)** - Galejade **(50df 37a)** (Sharrood (USA)) 10.5f **(72)**
Form - 6566314142
Record 2000 - 1st:2 2nd:1 3rd:1 Ran:10
Pre2000 - 1st:2 2nd:0 3rd:1 Ran:12
Win Prizemoney £11,639 *Total Prizemoney* £14,489
Wins * 2000 *Spt Wolver (STD) H 12f 48 59*
*** 2000** Aug Chepst (G-F) H 12.1f 50 54
* 1999 Spt Nottin (GD) H 14.1f 58 60 <
* 1999 Jun Hamilt (GD) H 12.1f 59 60 <
2000 Turf 1-6: (12f 1-2, 13f, 14f 3) (gd 2, g-f 2, frm 1-2) 2000 AW 1-4: (12f 1-3, 14f) (Equi, Fibr 1-3)
Average gelding, effective 12 to 14f, best at 12f, acts on gd to frm - acts on AW, has worn blinkers, likes left handed tracks, excels at Wolverhampton. Turf high 50. AW high 65 - 2nd of 18 to Rogue Spirit (11 Oct Lingfield 12f Equi RF 4928) - also 1st of 12 getting 12lb from Desert Spa (16 Spt Wolverhampton RF 4479). Improving.
**D HaydnJones [4-22] Mrs Judy Mihalop.*

CUPERCOY (FR) **RR 96f** 3349a[4]
2 f
Form - 4
2000 Turf 0-1: (6f) (hvy)
Currently very useful. **H Carlus in FR [0-1].*

CUPIDS CHARM BHB 80f **RR 79f** 5307a[3]
3 b f Cadeaux Genereux 7.9f **(76)** - Chapka (IRE) (Green Desert (USA)) 8.6f **(78)**
Form - 0817168843
Record 2000 - 1st:2 2nd:0 3rd:1 Ran:10
Pre2000 - 1st:0 2nd:0 3rd:0 Ran:1
Win Prizemoney £6,550 *Total Prizemoney* £8,646
Wins * 2000 Jun Carlis (G-F) H 5f 71 75 <
*** 2000** May Bright (FRM) H 5.3f 65 70
2000 Turf 2-10: (5f 2-3, 6f 6, 7f) (sft, g-s, gd 2, g-f 2-4, frm 2)
Unfurnished, above-average filly, effective 5 to 7f, acts on sft to g-f, best on g-f. Turf high 79 - 3rd of 6 getting 3lb from Irish Fire (29 Oct Cologne 6f sft RF 5307a) - also 1st of 12 giving 16lb to Maron (29 Jun Carlisle RF 2364). Lightly-raced, she has been given time to gain experience on the smaller tracks, winning twice at the minimum trip. May well improve considerably.
**R Guest [2-10] (from P W Chapple-Hyam [0-1] Spt 1999).*

CUPID'S DART BHB 54a **RR 52f** 4584[8]
3 ch g Pursuit of Love 9.5f **(69)** - Tisza (Kris) 9.5f **(73)**
Form - 365235237005048
Record 2000 - 1st:0 2nd:2 3rd:2 Ran:13
Pre2000 - 1st:0 2nd:1 3rd:3 Ran:11
Win Prizemoney £0 *Total Prizemoney* £5,273
2000 Turf 0-4: (7f 2, 8f 2) (frm 3, hrd) 2000 AW 0-9: (5f, 6f, 7f 2, 8f 3, 10f 2) (Equi 8, Fibr)
Workmanlike, fair gelding, effective 6 to 7f, acts on gd to frm, has worn blinkers. Turf high 52. AW high 61.
**P Howling [0-14] Paul Howling Racing Syndicate 2 (from B J Meehan [0-10] Nov 1999).*

CURRENCY **RR 3f** 5198[10]
3 b c Sri Pekan (USA) - On Tiptoes (Shareef Dancer (USA)) 9.9f **(73)**
Form - 60
Record 2000 - 1st:0 2nd:0 3rd:0 Ran:2
2000 Turf 0-2: (6f 2) (gd, frm)
Workmanlike, currently very poor colt. Turf high 38 (began Spt).
**J M Bradley [0-2] Robert Bailey.*

CURTSEY RR 4629[15]
2 b f Mark of Esteem (IRE) - Tabyan (USA) (Topsider (USA)) 8.3f **(71)**
Form - 0
Record 2000 - 1st:0 2nd:0 3rd:0 Ran:1
2000 Turf 0-1: (6f) (gd)
Currently very poor filly. **R Charlton [0-1] Mountgrange Stud.*

CURULE (USA) RR 4135a[9]
3 b c Go For Gin (USA) - Reservation (USA) (Cryptoclearance (USA))
Form - 37P0
Record 2000 - 1st:0 2nd:0 3rd:1 Ran:4
Win Prizemoney £0 *Total Prizemoney* £30,488
2000 AW 0-4: (9f, 10f 2, 12f) (Dirt 4)
High-class colt. AW high 117.
**S bin Suroor [0-2] (from S bin Suroor in UAE [0-1] May 2000).*

CUSIN BHB 64f **RR 72f** 5122[5]
4 ch g Arazi (USA) 9.2f **(74)** - Fairy Tern (Mill Reef (USA)) 10.5f **(78)**
Form - 703050005285
Record 2000 - 1st:0 2nd:1 3rd:1 Ran:12
Pre2000 - 1st:1 2nd:2 3rd:0 Ran:10
Win Prizemoney £3,956 *Total Prizemoney* £9,883
Wins 1999 Spt Salisb (G-F) H 8f 70 74 <
2000 Turf 0-12: (5f, 7f 9, 8f, 9f) (g-s 2, gd 3, g-f 3, frm 4)
Neat, above-average gelding, effective 7 to 8f, best at 7f, acts on g-f to frm, best on frm. Turf high 72 - 3rd of 22 getting 4lb from I Cried For You (10 Jun Doncaster 7f frm RF 1869). Formerly trained by James Fanshawe, he is now with Dandy Nicholls and has hinted at a return to form though it has yet to come to fruition.
**D Nicholls [0-12] London Ebor Developments Plc (from J R Fanshawe [1-7] Oct 1999).*

CUTE CAROLINE BHB 41f36a **RR 52f 36a** 4121[4]
4 ch f First Trump - Hissma (Midyan (USA)) 6f **(60)**
Form - 3506238074
Record 2000 - 1st:0 2nd:1 3rd:2 Ran:10
Pre2000 - 1st:0 2nd:0 3rd:1 Ran:5
Win Prizemoney £0 *Total Prizemoney* £2,053
2000 Turf 0-8: (7f, 8f 6, 9f) (gd, g-f 2, frm 5) 2000 AW 0-2: (8f 2) (Fibr 2)
Neat, fair filly, has worn blinkers. Turf high 52. AW high 24.
**A Berry [0-10] Murray Grubb (from C W Thornton [0-4] Spt 1999).*

CUT QUARTZ (FR) RR 104f 5206a[3]
3 b c Johann Quatz (FR) - Cutlass (IRE) (Sure Blade (USA)) 11.3f **(67)**
Form - 63
2000 Turf 0-2: (10f, 11f) (hvy 2)
Currently very useful colt, often wears blinkers. Turf high 104 - 3rd of 11 getting 6lb from Right Wing (20 Oct Bordeaux 10f hvy RF 5206a). **R Gibson in FR [0-2] Mme A Kavanagh.*

CUT RATE (USA) RR 57f 5100[10]
2 ch c Diesis 9f **(80)** - Itsamazing (USA) (The Minstrel (CAN)) 10f **(72)**
Form - 0
Record 2000 - 1st:0 2nd:0 3rd:0 Ran:1
2000 Turf 0-1: (7f) (gd)
Currently fair colt. **Mrs A J Perrett [0-1] K Abdulla.*

CYBER BABE (IRE) BHB 60f54a **RR 59f 54a** 5007[10]
3 b f Persian Bold 10f **(69)** - Ervedya (IRE) (Doyoun) 9f **(69)**
Form - 7072100213170
Record 2000 - 1st:3 2nd:2 3rd:1 Ran:11
Pre2000 - 1st:0 2nd:2 3rd:0 Ran:12
Win Prizemoney £9,535 *Total Prizemoney* £12,350
Wins * 2000 Aug Salisb (GD) H 12f 56 59 <
*** 2000** Jly Bright (FRM) H 10f 52 53
2000 *May Wolver (STD) S 9.4f 53*
2000 Turf 2-7: (7f, 8f, 10f 1-2, 12f 1-3) (gd 3, g-f, frm 2-3) 2000 AW 1-4: (8f, 9f 1-2, 12f) (Fibr 1-4)
Light-framed, fair filly, effective 7 to 12f, acts on g-f to frm, has worn blinkers. Turf high 59 - 1st of 10 getting 9lb from Sweet Angeline (16 Aug Salisbury RF 3707). AW high 53. She has progressed from winning a seller in May to taking a Class D handicap at Salisbury in August. She is a trier, and can continue to progress.
**A G Newcombe [2-8] Advanced Marketing Services Ltd (from Andrew Reid [1-10] May 2000).*

CYBER SANTA BHB 50f **RR 62f** 5189[10]
2 b c Celtic Swing - Qualitair Ridge **(49f 37a)** (Indian Ridge)
Form - 500
Record 2000 - 1st:0 2nd:0 3rd:0 Ran:3
2000 Turf 0-3: (7f 2, 8f) (g-s, gd, g-f)
Currently average colt. Turf high 62 (began Spt).
**J Hetherton [0-3] Qualitair Holdings Ltd.*

CYBERTECHNOLOGY BHB 59f **RR 62f** 4361[10]
6 b g Environment Friend 7.5f **(67)** - Verchinina (Star Appeal) 9.6f **(65)**
Form - 00803161860
Record 2000 - 1st:2 2nd:0 3rd:1 Ran:11
Pre2000 - 1st:4 2nd:5 3rd:1 Ran:35
Win Prizemoney £29,161 *Total Prizemoney* £39,302
Wins * 2000 Aug Ayr (G-F) H 9.1f 58 62
*** 2000** Jun Beverl (G-F) H 9.9f 53 57
* 1999 Jly Doncas (G-F) H 8f 65 68
1998 Jly Redcar (G-S) H 7f 80 82
1997 Aug Newmar (G-F) H 7f 77 80
1996 Oct York (GD) 7.9f 84 <
2000 Turf 2-11: (8f 5, 9f 1-2, 10f 1-4) (sft, g-s, g-f 3, frm 2-5, hrd)
Average gelding, effective 7 to 9f, best at 8f, acts on g-f to frm, best on frm, has worn blinkers, excels at Ayr. Turf high 62 - 1st of 12 giving 21lb to Kestral (4 Aug Ayr RF 3358).
**M Dods [3-23] Exors of the late Mrs H M Carr (from Mrs J Cecil [1-13] Oct 1998).*

CYCLONE CONNIE RR 73f 2241[3]
2 ch f Dr Devious (IRE) 9.9f **(74)** - Cutpurse Moll **(71f)** (Green Desert (USA)) 8.6f **(78)**
Form - 23
Record 2000 - 1st:0 2nd:1 3rd:1 Ran:2
Win Prizemoney £0 *Total Prizemoney* £2,252
2000 Turf 0-2: (6f 2) (gd, g-f)
Currently above-average filly. Turf high 73.
**C A Cyzer [0-2] Mrs E A Cyzer.*

CYMBAL MELODY BHB 10f **RR 31f** 256[6]
4 b f Merdon Melody 6.8f **(56)** - Cymbal (Ribero) 9.3f **(56)**
Form - 0576
Record 2000 - 1st:0 2nd:0 3rd:0 Ran:4
Pre2000 - 1st:0 2nd:0 3rd:0 Ran:11
2000 AW 0-4: (15f 3, 16f) (Fibr 4)
Workmanlike, very moderate filly. Becoming disappointing.
**R Hollinshead [0-9] Mrs Norman Hill (from J R Jenkins [0-8] Jun 1999).*

CYMMERIAD O GYMRU BHB 27f **RR 23f** 5198[12]
5 b g Sparky Lad - Fleur Power (IRE) (The Noble Player (USA)) 6.5f **(67)**
Form - 000
Record 2000 - 1st:0 2nd:0 3rd:0 Ran:3
Pre2000 - 1st:0 2nd:0 3rd:0 Ran:3
2000 Turf 0-3: (5f, 6f, 8f) (gd, g-f, hrd)
Little account gelding. Turf high 23 (began Aug).
**R Brotherton [0-3] Davies and Bridgeman (from B Palling [0-3] Oct 1998).*

CYNARA BHB 66f **RR 65f** 5103[7]
2 b f Imp Society (USA) 7.1f **(63)** - Reina (Homeboy) 6.6f **(55)**
Form - 85215517
Record 2000 - 1st:2 2nd:1 3rd:0 Ran:8
Win Prizemoney £5,850 *Total Prizemoney* £6,390
Wins * 2000 Spt Pontef (G-S) H 8f 62 65 <
*** 2000** Aug Newcas (GD) H 7f 54 59
2000 Turf 2-8: (6f 2, 7f 1-4, 8f 1-2) (gd 1-2, g-f 1-1, frm 5)
Average filly, effective 7 to 8f, best at 7f, acts on gd to frm. Turf high 65 - 1st of 13 getting 3lb from Espana (21 Spt Pontefract RF 4555) - also 1st of 16 getting 20lb from Perfect Plum (9 Aug Newcastle RF 3494). **G M Moore [2-8] R I Graham.*

CYPRESS CREEK (IRE) BHB 37f **RR 44f** 2228[16]
3 b f College Chapel - Akayid **(73f)** (Old Vic)
Form - 00700
Record 2000 - 1st:0 2nd:0 3rd:0 Ran:5
Pre2000 - 1st:0 2nd:0 3rd:0 Ran:4
2000 Turf 0-5: (8f, 10f 2, 12f 2) (g-s, g-f 2, frm 2)

Light-framed, moderate filly, has worn blinkers. Turf high 44.
**J S Moore [0-9] Geoffrey Morgan.*

CYRAN PARK BHB 28f52a **RR 44f 52a** 4061[14]

4 b g Cyrano de Bergerac 7.3f **(58)** - Kimberley Park (Try My Best (USA)) 7.6f **(67)**

Form - 04807400000

Record 2000 - 1st:0 2nd:0 3rd:0 Ran:11
Pre2000 - 1st:0 2nd:0 3rd:0 Ran:7

Win Prizemoney £0 *Total Prizemoney* £263

2000 Turf 0-11: (6f, 7f 4, 8f 5, 9f) (gd 3, g-f, frm 6, hrd)

Workmanlike, moderate gelding, has worn blinkers. Turf high 44.
**W Storey [0-13] Richardson Kelly O'Gara Partnership (from W Jarvis [0-7] Jly 1999).*

CYRAZY BHB 65f **RR 59f** 3376[4]

2 b f Cyrano de Bergerac 7.3f **(58)** - Hazy Kay (IRE) (Treasure Kay)

Form - 304

Record 2000 - 1st:0 2nd:0 3rd:1 Ran:3

Win Prizemoney £0 *Total Prizemoney* £650

2000 Turf 0-3: (5f 3) (gd, g-f, hrd)

Currently fair filly. Turf high 59. **J G Given [0-3] Mrs R E Digby.*

CZAR WARS BHB 50f65a **RR 41df 65a** 5122[13]

5 b g Warrshan (USA) 9.7f **(59)** - Dutch Czarina (Prince Sabo) 7.2f **(62)**

Form - 58440003461370

Record 2000 - 1st:1 2nd:0 3rd:2 Ran:10
Pre2000 - 1st:1 2nd:2 3rd:1 Ran:35

Win Prizemoney £4,745 *Total Prizemoney* £8,988

Wins 2000 Aug Haydoc (GD) C 6f 41
1997 Aug Warwic (G-S) 7f 70 <

2000 Turf 1-7: (6f 1-4, 7f 3) (g-s, gd 2, g-f 1-2, frm, hrd) 2000 AW 0-3: (6f 2, 7f) (Fibr 3)

Average gelding, has broken blood-vessels, effective 5 to 11f, acts on g-s to frm - acts on Fibr, often wears blinkers. Turf high 41 - 1st of 12 getting 3lb from Cape Coast (11 Aug Haydock RF 3546). AW high 40.
**J Balding [0-3] Men Behaving Badly (from P T Dalton [2-42] Aug 2000).*

DAAWE (USA) BHB 65f92a **RR 73f 92a** 5003[18]

9 b h Danzig (USA) 8.1f **(88)** - Capo Di Monte (Final Straw) 7.9f **(64)**

Form - 1116306100575000580

Record 2000 - 1st:4 2nd:0 3rd:1 Ran:19
Pre2000 - 1st:13 2nd:5 3rd:6 Ran:81

Win Prizemoney £73,527 *Total Prizemoney* £88,215

Wins * **2000** May Doncas (G-S) H 6f 68 72
* **2000** *Feb Wolver (STD) H 5f 80 93+* <
* **2000** *Feb Wolver (STD) H 6f 70 79*
* **2000** *Feb Southw (STD) H 6f 70 76*
* 1999 Spt Newcas (SFT) H 5f 54 59
* 1999 Spt Pontef (GD) H 5f 54 57
1998 May Doncas (GD) 6f 84
1998 Apr Thirsk (G-S) 5f 77
1997 Jun Redcar (GD) H 6f 75 78
1997 *Apr Southw (STD) H 5f 70 75*
1996 Jun York (GD) H 6f 63 66
1996 *May Southw (STD) H 5f 65 72*
1996 May Doncas (G-F) H 6f 56 63
1996 *Mar Southw (STD) H 6f 58 57*
1996 *Jan Southw (STD) H 6f 52 57*

2000 Turf 1-14: (5f 10, 6f 1-4) (g-s 3, gd 8, g-f 1-3) 2000 AW 3-5: (5f 1-1, 6f 2-4) (Fibr 3-5)

Useful horse, effective 5 to 6f, - acts on Fibr, often wears blinkers (effectively), prefers left handed tracks, prefers tight tracks, excels at Wolverhampton. Turf high 72. AW high 94 - 3rd of 13 giving 11lb to Blue Star (11 Mar Wolverhampton 6f Fibr RF 0432) - also 1st of 11 giving 11lb to Tom Tun (24 Feb Wolverhampton RF 0348). Completed a Fibresand hat-trick in February and scored on turf at Doncaster in June. Wins his races from the front and is equally effective over five and six furlongs. Getting on now, and a little high in the handicap, but not one to discard lightly.
**D Nicholls [6-25] Mrs Andrea Mallinson (from J A Glover [2-27] Aug 1999).*

DA BOSS BHB 42f **RR 66?f** 1092[14]

5 ch g Be My Chief (USA) 10.2f **(62)** - Lady Kris (IRE) (Kris) 9.5f **(73)**

Form - 000

Record 2000 - 1st:0 2nd:0 3rd:0 Ran:3
Pre2000 - 1st:0 2nd:0 3rd:4 Ran:11

Win Prizemoney £0 *Total Prizemoney* £2,053

2000 Turf 0-2: (10f, 11f) (g-s, gd) 2000 AW 0-1: (12f) (Fibr)

Average gelding. Turf high 37. (DEAD) **W R Muir [0-14] R Haim.*

DABUS BHB 75f **RR 59f** 4262[13]

5 b g Kris 10f **(75)** - Licorne (Sadler's Wells (USA)) 10f **(76)**

Form - 00

Record 2000 - 1st:0 2nd:0 3rd:0 Ran:2
Pre2000 - 1st:1 2nd:0 3rd:3 Ran:5

Win Prizemoney £3,598 *Total Prizemoney* £6,436

Wins 1998 Jly Sandow (G-F) 10f 84+ <

2000 Turf 0-2: (10f 2) (gd, frm)

Fair gelding. Turf high 59 (began Aug).
**M C Chapman [3-18] Alan Mann (from H R A Cecil [1-4] Jun 1999).*

D'ACCORD BHB 85a **RR 79f** 4832[4]

3 ch g Beveled (USA) 6.9f **(64)** - National Time (USA) (Lord Avie (USA)) 5.3f **(61)**

Form - 1153506424

Record 2000 - 1st:0 2nd:1 3rd:1 Ran:8
Pre2000 - 1st:2 2nd:0 3rd:1 Ran:6

Win Prizemoney £5,293 *Total Prizemoney* £8,961

Wins 1999 *Dec Lingfi (STD) H 5f 71 80* <
1999 *Dec Lingfi (STD) 6f 80* <

2000 Turf 0-6: (5f 4, 6f 2) (g-s, g-f 5) 2000 AW 0-2: (6f 2) (Equi, Fibr)

Unfurnished, useful gelding, effective 5 to 6f, best at 6f, acts on g-f - acts on Equi. Turf high 79 - 2nd of 30 getting 3lb from Whistler (28 Spt Newmarket 5f g-f RF 4703). AW high 87 - 3rd of 5 giving 14lb to Illusive (2 Feb Lingfield 6f Equi RF 0207). He has won a couple of races on Equitrack, but does not look to be progressing.
**M Kettle [0-6] Dagfell Properties Ltd (from E A Wheeler [2-8] Feb 2000).*

Daawe has been a fine servant to Dandy Nicholls

DAHLIDYA BHB 35f59a **RR 30f 59a** 4992[7]

5 b m Midyan (USA) 9.9f **(64)** - Dahlawise (IRE) (Caerleon (USA)) 8.6f **(71)**

Form - 5317346110150313307007O7

Record 2000 - 1st:4 2nd:0 3rd:4 Ran:20
Pre2000 - 1st:3 2nd:1 3rd:4 Ran:34

Win Prizemoney £19,840 *Total Prizemoney* £25,345

Wins * **2000** *Mar Southw (STD) H 6f 60 63* <
* **2000** *Feb Southw (STD) C 6f 60*
* **2000** *Feb Southw (STD) S 6f 61*
* **2000** *Feb Wolver (STD) S 6f 49*
* 1999 *Dec Southw (STD) H 6f 45 59*
* 1998 *Dec Southw (STD) H 6f 43 56*
* 1998 *Feb Wolver (STD) H 5f 39 52*

2000 Turf 0-2: (6f, 7f) (gd, frm) 2000 AW 4-18: (6f 4-12, 7f 6) (Fibr 4-18)
Average filly, effective 6 to 7f, best at 6f, - acts on Fibr, has worn blinkers, favours left handed tracks, favours tight tracks, and likes Southwell. Turf high 30. AW high 65 - 3rd of 13 getting 2lb from Teyaar (15 Apr Wolverhampton 6f Fibr RF 0745) - also 1st of 10 getting 4lb from Russian Romeo (20 Mar Southwell RF 0470). Inconsistent. She is a prolific winner of modest Fibresand events in recent seasons. Six furlongs at Southwell are her ideal conditions, though she tends to get behind in her races.
**M J Polglase [7-54] The Lovatt Partnership.*

DAILY TONIC RR 61f — 5062[3]

3 ch c Sanglamore (USA) 12.9f **(67)** - Woodwardia (USA) (El Gran Senor (USA)) 9.6f **(76)**
Form - 3
Record 2000 - 1st:0 2nd:0 3rd:1 Ran:1
Win Prizemoney £0 *Total Prizemoney* £530
2000 Turf 0-1: (10f) (sft)
Well made, currently average colt. **Mrs A J Perrett [0-1] K Abdulla.*

DAJAM VU BHB 39f RR 32f — 3443[7]

3 ch f Lyphento (USA) - Dancing Diamond (IRE) **(41f 54a)** (Alzao (USA)) 7.1f **(68)**
Form - 0087
Record 2000 - 1st:0 2nd:0 3rd:0 Ran:4
2000 Turf 0-4: (10f 3, 12f) (gd 3, frm)
Unfurnished, very moderate filly. Turf high 32.
**J S King [0-4] Dajam Ltd.*

DAKHIRA RR 58f — 4270[6]

2 b f Emperor Jones (USA) - Fakhira (IRE) **(29f)** (Jareer (USA)) 5.9f **(75)**
Form - 6
Record 2000 - 1st:0 2nd:0 3rd:0 Ran:1
2000 Turf 0-1: (7f) (g-f)
Currently fair filly.
**D R C Elsworth [0-1] Teviot Stud,Ann Cole Watson.*

DAKISI ROYALE BHB 40f39a RR 42f 39a — 3193[14]

3 ch f King's Signet (USA) 7f **(51)** - Marcroft (Crofthall) 6.3f **(59)**
Form - 57600
Record 2000 - 1st:0 2nd:0 3rd:0 Ran:3
Pre2000 - 1st:0 2nd:1 3rd:1 Ran:12
Win Prizemoney £0 *Total Prizemoney* £948
2000 Turf 0-3: (8f 3) (gd, g-f, hrd)
Neat, moderate filly, effective 7f, acts on g-f to hrd, has worn blinkers (effectively), likes left handed tracks, likes tight tracks. Turf high 42.
**L J Barratt [0-3] L J Barratt (from R M Whitaker [0-12] Nov 1999).*

DAKOTA SIOUX (IRE) BHB 73f RR 73f — 4866[10]

3 ch f College Chapel - Batilde (IRE) (Victory Piper (USA))
Form - 36011810
Record 2000 - 1st:3 2nd:0 3rd:1 Ran:8
Pre2000 - 1st:0 2nd:0 3rd:1 Ran:1
Win Prizemoney £20,131 *Total Prizemoney* £20,955

Wins								
* **2000**	Spt	Haydoc	(HVY)	H	7.1f	61	73	<
* **2000**	Aug	Haydoc	(G-S)	H	7.1f	51	58	
* **2000**	Jly	Newcas	(GD)	H	7f	51	60	

2000 Turf 3-8: (6f, 7f 3-4, 8f 3) (sft, g-s, gd 2-2, g-f 1-1, frm 3)
Scopey, above-average filly, effective 5 to 7f, acts on gd to frm, often wears blinkers (extremely effectively). Turf high 73 - 1st of 11 getting 16lb from Celebration Town (23 Spt Haydock RF 4604). Inconsistent. Adopting forcing tactics did the trick when she won at Newcastle and Haydock during the summer and handled the heavy ground well when winning a valuable handicap at Haydock in September. **R A Fahey [3-9] Mrs Una Towell.*

DALAMPOUR (IRE) BHB 111f RR 114f — 4310[5]

3 b c Shernazar 11.8f **(71)** - Dalara (IRE) **(113f)** (Doyoun) 9f **(69)**
Form - 71135
Record 2000 - 1st:2 2nd:0 3rd:1 Ran:5
Win Prizemoney £40,758 *Total Prizemoney* £57,258

Wins							
* **2000**	Jun	Ascot	(G-F)	G3	16.2f	103	<
* **2000**	Jun	Newmar	(G-F)		12f	90+	

2000 Turf 2-5: (10f, 12f 1-2, 15f, 16f 1-1) (gd 1-2, g-f, frm 1-2)
Scopey, Group-class colt. Turf high 114 - 5th of 11 to Millenary (9 Spt Doncaster 15f frm RF 4310). A half-brother to Daliapour, he progressed nicely and looked a stayer with a future when landing the Queen's Vase at Ascot. A decent third in the Great Voltigeur, he may have found the 12 furlongs inadequate.
**Sir Michael Stoute [2-5] H H Aga Khan.*

DALBY OF YORK BHB 56f50a RR 58f 50a — 974[6]

4 ch g Polar Falcon (USA) 9f **(74)** - Miller's Creek (USA) (Star de Naskra (USA)) 9.7f **(65)**
Form - 6
Record 2000 - 1st:0 2nd:0 3rd:0 Ran:1
Pre2000 - 1st:2 2nd:1 3rd:2 Ran:14
Win Prizemoney £5,350 *Total Prizemoney* £7,357

Wins								
* 1999	May	Mussel	(FRM)		14f		70?	<
* 1999	Apr	Windso	(G-F)	H	11.6f	55	60+	

2000 Turf 0-1: (12f) (gd)
Scopey, fair gelding, effective 12 to 15f, acts on g-f to frm, best on frm, has worn blinkers. Consistent.
**P F I Cole [2-15] Richard Green (Fine Paintings).*

DALIAPOUR (IRE) BHB 120f RR 123f — 5097a[3]

4 b c Sadler's Wells (USA) 11.3f **(87)** - Dalara (IRE) **(113f)** (Doyoun) 9f **(69)**
Form - 11343
Record 2000 - 1st:2 2nd:0 3rd:2 Ran:5
Pre2000 - 1st:3 2nd:3 3rd:1 Ran:9
Win Prizemoney £210,810 *Total Prizemoney* £786,917

Wins							
* **2000**	Jun	Epsom	(G-S)	G1	12f	121+	<
* **2000**	May	Cheste	(GD)	G3	13.4f	117+	
1999	Apr	Epsom	(SFT)		10.1f	111+	
1998	Oct	Ascot	(SFT)	L	8f	98+	
1998	Aug	Chepst	(G-F)		8.1f	78	

2000 Turf 2-5: (12f 1-4, 13f 1-1) (hvy, g-s 1-1, gd, g-f 1-1, frm)
Neat, very high-class colt, effective 11 to 13f, best at 12f, acts on g-s to frm, best on gd, likes left handed tracks, does well at Epsom. Turf high 121 - 3rd of 12 to Mutafaweq (15 Oct Woodbine 12f frm RF 5097a) - also 1st of 4 from Fantastic Light (9 Jun Epsom RF 1831). Consistent. Runner-up in both Epsom and Irish Derbys for Luca Cumani in 1999 before suffering a bad cut to his near-fore when last in the King George, an injury which forced him to miss the remainder of the season, he was switched to Sir Michael Stoute for last season's campaign. He bounced back to run out a worthy winner of Chester's Ormonde Stakes before making all in a tactical race for the Coronation Cup. He later finished third to Montjeu in the King George.
**Sir Michael Stoute [2-5] (from L M Cumani [3-9] Jly 1999).*

Daliapour was back to winning ways at Chester

DALLACHIO (IRE) BHB 27f RR 7f — 1476[5]

9 ch g Shernazar 11.8f **(71)** - Mafiosa (Miami Springs) 9.9f **(59)**
Form - 85
Record 2000 - 1st:0 2nd:0 3rd:0 Ran:1
Pre2000 - 1st:0 2nd:0 3rd:0 Ran:3
2000 AW 0-1: (14f) (Fibr)
Little account gelding.

**A G Newcombe [0-8] C T Brinson (from P J Hobbs [0-1] Apr 1995).*

DALWHINNIE BHB 39f27a **RR 40f 27a** 304[6]
7 b m Persian Bold 10f **(69)** - Land Line (High Line) 10.3f **(70)**
Form - 846
Record 2000 - 1st:0 2nd:0 3rd:0 Ran:1
Pre2000 - 1st:2 2nd:3 3rd:2 Ran:32
Win Prizemoney £4,155 *Total Prizemoney* £9,587
Wins 1998 Oct Yarmou (SFT) C 14.1f 47
1998 Jan Southw (STD) 12f 51+ <
2000 AW 0-1: (16f) (Fibr)
Moderate mare, effective 14f, acts on g-f, has worn blinkers (extremely effectively), favours left handed tracks. Inconsistent.
**J G Given [0-8] A Clarke (from J Wharton [2-19] Jun 1999).*

DALYAN (IRE) BHB 45f **RR 52f** 4499[9]
3 b g Turtle Island (IRE) - Salette (Sallust) 8.4f **(63)**
Form - 8047500
Record 2000 - 1st:0 2nd:0 3rd:0 Ran:7
Pre2000 - 1st:0 2nd:0 3rd:0 Ran:4
Win Prizemoney £0 *Total Prizemoney* £675
2000 Turf 0-7: (8f, 10f 2, 11f, 12f 3) (g-s 2, gd 2, frm 3)
Workmanlike, fair gelding, effective 8f, acts on frm. Turf high 55.
**T D Easterby [0-12] Mrs J B Mountifield.*

DAMAGES BHB 30a **RR 15f 30a** 4820[19]
2 b f Contract Law (USA) 8.9f **(54)** - Treasure Time (IRE) (Treasure Kay)
Form - 0
Record 2000 - 1st:0 2nd:0 3rd:0 Ran:1
2000 Turf 0-1: (6f) (g-f)
Currently little account filly. **P D Evans [0-1] Red & Black Racing.*

DAMALIS (IRE) BHB 97f **RR 95f** 4612[18]
4 b f Mukaddamah (USA) 7.6f **(74)** - Art Age (Artaius (USA)) 9f **(69)**
Form - 461081803550
Record 2000 - 1st:2 2nd:0 3rd:1 Ran:12
Pre2000 - 1st:3 2nd:1 3rd:3 Ran:18
Win Prizemoney £39,520 *Total Prizemoney* £57,527
Wins * 2000 Jun Cheste (G-F) H 5.1f 93 95 <
*** 2000** May Cheste (GD) H 5.1f 88 93
* 1999 Apr Sandow (SFT) H 5f 93 93
* 1998 Spt Ripon (SFT) 5f 86
* 1998 May Cheste (G-F) 5.1f 86
2000 Turf 2-12: (5f 2-9, 6f 3) (g-s, gd 4, g-f 1-3, frm 1-3, hrd)
Strong, very useful filly, effective 5 to 6f, best at 5f, acts on g-s to hrd, prefers left handed tracks, excels at Chester. Turf high 95 - 1st of 16 giving 25lb to The Gay Fox (28 Jun Chester RF 2332) - also 1st of 12 giving 5lb to Sunley Sense (11 May Chester RF 1133). A pacey sprinter, she goes well at Chester and scored twice there last year. Seems to handle any ground.
**E J Alston [5-30] Liam & Tony Ferguson.*

DAMASQUINER BHB 52f53a **RR 57f 53a** 552[6]
3 b f Casteddu 7.4f **(54)** - Hymn Book (IRE) (Darshaan) 9.9f **(84)**
Form - 6416356
Record 2000 - 1st:1 2nd:0 3rd:1 Ran:6
Pre2000 - 1st:0 2nd:0 3rd:0 Ran:6
Win Prizemoney £2,289 *Total Prizemoney* £2,579
Wins * 2000 *Feb Lingfi (STD) C 7f* 62 <
2000 AW 1-6: (7f 1-4, 8f 2) (Equi 1-6)
Unfurnished, fair filly, effective 7f, - acts on Equi, likes left handed tracks, likes tight tracks. AW high 62 - 1st of 9 getting 3lb from John Company (5 Feb Lingfield RF 0223). Inconsistent.
**T E Powell [1-12] Miss P I Westbrook.*

DAME FONTEYN BHB 59f **RR 61f** 5137[8]
3 b f Suave Dancer (USA) 10.7f **(68)** - Her Honour (Teenoso (USA)) 9.9f **(72)**
Form - P2261308
Record 2000 - 1st:1 2nd:2 3rd:1 Ran:8
Pre2000 - 1st:0 2nd:0 3rd:0 Ran:3
Win Prizemoney £2,404 *Total Prizemoney* £4,630
Wins * 2000 May Redcar (G-S) H 14.1f 58 61 <
2000 Turf 1-8: (12f 4, 14f 1-4) (sft 2, g-s, gd 3, g-f 1-2)
Light-framed, average filly, effective 12 to 14f, acts on gd to g-f, likes left handed tracks, likes tight tracks. Turf high 61 - 1st of 15 giving 8lb to Ptah (30 May Redcar RF 1551).
**M L W Bell [1-11] Frank Farrant.*

DAME HATTIE BHB 60f **RR 55f** 3387[6]
5 b m Hatim (USA) 7.8f **(56)** - Camden Grove (Uncle Pokey) 10.1f **(49)**
Form - 556
Record 2000 - 1st:0 2nd:0 3rd:0 Ran:3
2000 Turf 0-3: (10f, 12f, 14f) (g-s, g-f 2)
Fair filly. Turf high 55. **A Scott [0-6] G M Abercrombie.*

DAME JUDE BHB 50f **RR 44f** 1421[8]
4 ch f Dilum (USA) 7.1f **(56)** - Three Lucky (IRE) (Final Straw) 7.9f **(64)**
Form - 008
Record 2000 - 1st:0 2nd:0 3rd:0 Ran:3
Pre2000 - 1st:2 2nd:0 3rd:1 Ran:19
Win Prizemoney £5,724 *Total Prizemoney* £7,853
Wins 1998 Aug Sandow (G-F) 5f 78 <
1998 Apr Bright (GD) 5.3f 67
2000 Turf 0-3: (5f, 6f, 7f) (gd 2, frm)
Light-framed, moderate filly, effective 6f, acts on g-f, likes left handed tracks. Turf high 44.
**G G Margarson [0-3] D Lancaster-Smith (from W R Muir [2-19] Spt 1999).*

DAM ELHANAH BHB 60f50a **RR 62f 50a** 1344[5]
2 b f Mind Games - Kimberley Park (Try My Best (USA)) 7.6f **(67)**
Form - 245
Record 2000 - 1st:0 2nd:1 3rd:0 Ran:3
Win Prizemoney £0 *Total Prizemoney* £756
2000 Turf 0-3: (5f 3) (gd 3)
Currently average filly. Turf high 62 (1st run) - 2nd of 6 getting 2lb from Nifty Alice (30 Mar Musselburgh 5f gd RF 0569).
**R A Fahey [0-3] Basheer Kielany.*

DANAKIL BHB 65f67a **RR 66f 67a** 1728[7]
5 b g Warning 8.1f **(77)** - Danilova (USA) (Lyphard (USA)) 9.9f **(72)**
Form - 5663516127
Record 2000 - 1st:2 2nd:1 3rd:1 Ran:10
Pre2000 - 1st:1 2nd:0 3rd:2 Ran:8
Win Prizemoney £9,798 *Total Prizemoney* £12,435
Wins * 2000 May Windso (GD) H 8.3f 63 66
*** 2000** *Mar Wolver (STD) H 9.4f 64 66*
1999 *Mar Wolver (STD) 9.4f 68* <
2000 Turf 1-3: (8f 1-3) (g-s, gd, g-f 1-1) 2000 AW 1-7: (8f 5, 9f 1-2) (Fibr 1-7)
Average gelding, effective 8 to 9f, best at 8f, acts on g-s to frm - acts on Fibr, has worn blinkers, favours tight tracks, and excels at Windsor. Turf high 66 - 2nd of 13 giving 4lb to Kanz Wood (24 May Goodwood 8f g-s RF 1430) - also 1st of 18 giving 8lb to Fuegian (8 May Windsor RF 1102). AW high 66 - 3rd of 8 giving 2lb to Internal Affair (15 Feb Wolverhampton 8f Fibr RF 0287) - also 1st of 9 getting 4lb from Arc (16 Mar Wolverhampton RF 0451).
**K R Burke [2-10] The Danakilists (from J E Banks [1-7] Jly 1999).*

DANAKIM BHB 51f52a **RR 39f 52a** 4776[12]
3 b g Emarati (USA) 6.6f **(63)** - Kangra Valley **(41f 54a)** (Indian Ridge)
Form - 00824050000
Record 2000 - 1st:0 2nd:1 3rd:0 Ran:11
Pre2000 - 1st:0 2nd:1 3rd:0 Ran:6
Win Prizemoney £0 *Total Prizemoney* £2,502
2000 Turf 0-7: (5f 4, 6f 3) (sft, g-s, gd, frm 3, hrd) 2000 AW 0-4: (6f 2, 8f 2) (Fibr 4)
Workmanlike, very moderate gelding, effective 5 to 6f, best at 5f, acts on g-f to frm, best on g-f, has worn blinkers. Turf high 61. AW high 37. Inconsistent.
**J R Weymes [0-11] John Weymes Racing (from E Weymes [0-3] Spt 1999).*

DANAMALA BHB 70f **RR 69f** 1534[4]
4 b f Danehill (USA) 9.1f **(79)** - Carmelized (CAN) (Key To The Mint (USA)) 9.4f **(75)**
Form - 24
Record 2000 - 1st:0 2nd:1 3rd:0 Ran:2
Pre2000 - 1st:0 2nd:0 3rd:2 Ran:4
Win Prizemoney £0 *Total Prizemoney* £2,554
2000 Turf 0-2: (7f, 8f) (sft, g-s)
Scopey, average filly, effective 8f, acts on sft. Turf high 69 (1st

run) - 2nd of 9 giving 13lb to Kanaka Creek (1 May Warwick 8f sft RF 0955). **R Hannon [0-6] Ananda Krishnan.*

DANANEYEV (FR) RR 105f 704a[1]

4 br c Goldeneyev (USA) - Danagroom (USA) (Groom Dancer (USA))
Form - 1
2000 Turf 1-1: (6f 1-1) (hvy 1-1)
Currently Pattern-class colt. (1st run) - 1st of 11 getting 4lb from Halmahera (4 Apr Maisons-laffitte RF 0704a).
**C Laffon-Parias in FR [1-3] Wertheimer Brothers.*

DANCEABOUT BHB 109f RR 109f 4739[1]

3 b f Shareef Dancer (USA) 10.1f **(67)** - Putupon (Mummy's Pet) 7.7f **(60)**
Form - 153121
Record 2000 - 1st:3 2nd:1 3rd:1 Ran:6
Win Prizemoney £63,172 *Total Prizemoney* £77,942
Wins * **2000** Spt Newmar (GD) G2 8f 109 <
* **2000** Aug Goodwo (GD) L 7f 104
* **2000** May Goodwo (SFT) 7f 78+
2000 Turf 3-6: (7f 2-3, 8f 1-3) (gd 2-5, g-f 1-1)
Scopey, Pattern-class filly, effective 7 to 8f, best at 8f, acts on gd to g-f, best on gd. Turf high 109 - 1st of 9 getting 3lb from Alshakr (30 Spt Newmarket RF 4739) - also 1st of 11 from Claranet (3 Aug Goodwood RF 3340). Unraced at two, she progressed well and ended the camapign on a high note by landing the Sun Chariot Stakes at Newmarket on her final start. That was a weak Group Two, however, and she was all out to hold off Alshakr.
**G Wragg [3-6] Bloomsbury Stud.*

DANCE DIRECTOR (IRE) BHB 88f RR 84+f 4486[1]

3 b c Sadler's Wells (USA) 11.3f **(87)** - Memories (USA) (Hail the Pirates (USA)) 11f **(78)**
Form - 421
Record 2000 - 1st:1 2nd:1 3rd:0 Ran:3
Win Prizemoney £4,062 *Total Prizemoney* £6,437
Wins * **2000** Spt Kempto (SFT) 12f 84+ <
2000 Turf 1-3: (10f, 11f, 12f 1-1) (g-s 1-1, gd, g-f)
Workmanlike, currently decent colt. Turf high 84 (began Aug) - 1st of 19 giving 5lb to Saluem (18 Spt Kempton RF 4486).
**J H M Gosden [1-3] R E Sangster & A K Collins.*

DANCE IN THE DAY (IRE) RR 55f 5184[11]

2 b c Caerleon (USA) 10.9f **(79)** - One to One **(62f)** (Shirley Heights) 10.3f **(74)**
Form - 00
Record 2000 - 1st:0 2nd:0 3rd:0 Ran:2
2000 Turf 0-2: (7f, 8f) (g-s, frm)
Currently fair colt. Turf high 55 (began Spt).
**E A L Dunlop [0-2] Khalid Ali.*

DANCE IN TUNE BHB 83f79a RR 82df 79a 3808[12]

3 ch g Mujtahid (USA) 7.4f **(69)** - Dancing Prize (IRE) (Sadler's Wells (USA)) 10f **(76)**
Form - 50
Record 2000 - 1st:0 2nd:0 3rd:0 Ran:2
Pre2000 - 1st:2 2nd:1 3rd:2 Ran:7
Win Prizemoney £7,137 *Total Prizemoney* £10,380
Wins * 1999 Aug Mussel (G-F) H 7.1f 83 90 <
* 1999 *Aug Wolver (STD) 7f 79+*
2000 Turf 0-1: (10f) (frm) 2000 AW 0-1: (9f) (Fibr)
Scopey, decent gelding, effective 7 to 8f, acts on g-f to frm.
**Sir Mark Prescott [2-9] Cheveley Park Stud.*

DANCE LITTLE LADY (IRE) BHB 54f50a RR 57f 50a 4654[14]

3 b f Common Grounds 8.1f **(66)** - Kentucky Tears (USA) (Cougar (CHI)) 12.6f **(64)**
Form - 6401600
Record 2000 - 1st:1 2nd:0 3rd:0 Ran:5
Pre2000 - 1st:0 2nd:0 3rd:0 Ran:7
Win Prizemoney £3,315 *Total Prizemoney* £3,315
Wins * **2000** Jun Redcar (G-F) H 6f 52 53 <
2000 Turf 1-4: (5f, 6f 1-3) (g-f, frm 1-2, hrd) 2000 AW 0-1: (6f) (Fibr)
Fair filly, effective 5 to 6f, acts on gd to frm. Turf high 53 - 1st of 18 getting 11lb from Distinctly Blu (13 Jun Redcar RF 1911).
**M W Easterby [1-5] G B Stuart (from J Berry [0-7] Dec 1999).*

DANCE MELODY BHB 20f29a RR ?f 29a 3904[12]

6 b m Rambo Dancer (CAN) 8.4f **(59)** - Cateryne (Ballymoss) 8.5f **(55)**
Form - 0
Record 2000 - 1st:0 2nd:0 3rd:0 Ran:1
Pre2000 - 1st:0 2nd:0 3rd:0 Ran:12
2000 Turf 0-1: (8f) (frm)
Very poor mare, has worn blinkers. Becoming disappointing.
**N Tinkler [0-1] C J Nunn (from G R Oldroyd [0-15] May 1998).*

DANCEMMA BHB 51f60a RR 62f 60a 4826[8]

3 ch f Emarati (USA) 6.6f **(63)** - Hanglands (Bustino) 10.4f **(64)**
Form - 700250084088
Record 2000 - 1st:0 2nd:1 3rd:0 Ran:12
Pre2000 - 1st:0 2nd:2 3rd:1 Ran:8
Win Prizemoney £0 *Total Prizemoney* £4,329
2000 Turf 0-11: (5f 4, 6f 6, 8f) (g-s 2, gd 5, g-f 2, frm 2) 2000 AW 0-1: (6f) (Fibr)
Unfurnished, average filly, effective 5 to 6f, best at 6f, acts on gd. Turf high 62. **M Blanshard [0-20] M Blanshard.*

DANCE OF LOVE (IRE) RR 100f 5181a[5]

3 b f Pursuit of Love 9.5f **(69)** - Ducking **(68f 60a)** (Reprimand)
Form - 554405
2000 Turf 0-6: (8f 3, 9f 2, 10f) (sft, g-s 2, gd, g-f)
Very useful filly, effective 8f, acts on gd to g-f. Turf high 100 (1st run) - 5th of 9 getting 7lb from Preseli (14 May Leopardstown 8f g-f RF 1250a). **C O'Brien in IRE [1-10] Gerard Callanan.*

DANCE ON BHB 99f RR 90f 5128[4]

2 ch f Caerleon (USA) 10.9f **(79)** - Dance Sequence (USA) **(104df)** (Mr Prospector (USA)) 8.8f **(78)**
Form - 1761834
Record 2000 - 1st:2 2nd:0 3rd:1 Ran:7
Win Prizemoney £9,306 *Total Prizemoney* £13,142
Wins * **2000** Jly Yarmou (GD) 5.2f 89 <
* **2000** Jun Leices (G-S) 5f 80++
2000 Turf 2-7: (5f 2-4, 6f 2, 7f) (sft, gd 2-4, g-f, frm)
Useful filly, effective 5 to 6f, best at 5f, acts on gd. Turf high 90 - 3rd of 9 giving 3lb to Alshadiyah (16 Spt Ayr 6f gd RF 4448) - also 1st of 6 giving 6lb to Tissaly (31 Jly Yarmouth RF 3262). Out of a mare who won the Lowther Stakes and was in the frame in the Queen Mary and Cheveley Park, she won a Leicester maiden first time up, and landed a Yarmouth conditions event in July, but has just seemed to find Pattern company too much for her otherwise. Suited by the minimum trip.
**Sir Michael Stoute [2-7] Cheveley Park Stud.*

DANCE ON THE TOP BHB 84f RR 87f 4643[20]

2 ch c Caerleon (USA) 10.9f **(79)** - Fern (Shirley Heights) 10.3f **(74)**
Form - 61200
Record 2000 - 1st:1 2nd:1 3rd:0 Ran:5
Win Prizemoney £4,533 *Total Prizemoney* £8,033
Wins * **2000** Jly Kempto (G-F) 7f 80 <
2000 Turf 1-5: (6f, 7f 1-3, 8f) (g-s, gd, g-f 2, frm 1-1)
Useful colt. Turf high 87 - 2nd of 13 giving 9lb to Forever My Lord (5 Aug Goodwood 7f g-f RF 3392) - also 1st of 15 from Gleaming Blade (23 Jly Kempton RF 3048). He seemed to appreciate the seven furlongs when making all to win at Kempton on his second start. **E A L Dunlop [1-5] Khalifa Sultan.*

DANCE QUEEN BHB 41f RR 54f 5053[7]

2 b f Puissance 7.1f **(60)** - Lorlanne (Bustino) 10.4f **(64)**
Form - 60060867
Record 2000 - 1st:0 2nd:0 3rd:0 Ran:8
2000 Turf 0-8: (5f 2, 6f, 7f 4, 8f) (hvy, sft 2, g-f, frm 4)
Fair filly. Turf high 54. **D Moffatt [0-8] David Doughty.*

DANCE TO THE BEAT BHB 37f45a RR 39f 45a 86[12]

5 b m Batshoof 9.5f **(66)** - Woodleys (Tyrnavos) 10.1f **(55)**
Form - 0
Record 2000 - 1st:0 2nd:0 3rd:0 Ran:1
Pre2000 - 1st:1 2nd:2 3rd:0 Ran:21
Win Prizemoney £1,998 *Total Prizemoney* £3,382
Wins 1997 *Dec Wolver (STD) S 6f 60* <
2000 AW 0-1: (11f) (Fibr)
Moderate filly, effective 12f, acts on AW, often wears blinkers (effectively), prefers tight tracks.

P Shakespeare [0-8] The Country Life Partnership (from M Meade [1-14] Jly 1998).

DANCE WEST (USA) BHB 83f **RR 87+f** 3992[8]

3 b c Gone West (USA) 7.8f **(82)** - Danzante (USA) (Danzig (USA)) 8.4f **(76)**

Form - 774218

Record 2000 - 1st:1 2nd:1 3rd:0 Ran:6

Win Prizemoney £3,737 *Total Prizemoney* £5,403

Wins * 2000 Jly Yarmou (GD) 7f 87 <

2000 Turf 1-6: (7f 1-4, 8f 2) (sft, g-f 1-2, frm 3)

Scopey, useful colt, effective 7f, acts on g-f to frm. Turf high 87 - also 1st of 8 from Shadowblaster (19 Jly Yarmouth RF 2951). He has improved with racing, and got off the mark over seven at Yarmouth. **H R A Cecil [1-6] K Abdulla.*

DANCE WITH ME BHB 47f **RR 29f** 1994[4]

2 b g Dancing Spree (USA) 8f **(59)** - So Saucy **(35f 41a)** (Teenoso (USA)) 9.9f **(72)**

Form - 004

Record 2000 - 1st:0 2nd:0 3rd:0 Ran:3

2000 Turf 0-3: (5f, 6f, 7f) (g-s, g-f 2)

Currently little account gelding, has worn blinkers. Turf high 29. **B J Meehan [0-3] Bill Bigmore.*

DANCING BAY BHB 89f **RR 93f** 4892[1]

3 b g Suave Dancer (USA) 10.7f **(80)** - Kabayil **(74f)** (Dancing Brave (USA)) 8.4f **(76)**

Form - 11041

Record 2000 - 1st:3 2nd:0 3rd:0 Ran:5
Pre2000 - 1st:0 2nd:0 3rd:0 Ran:2

Win Prizemoney £18,375 *Total Prizemoney* £18,934

Wins * 2000 Oct Ayr (HVY) H 13.1f 87 93 <
*** 2000** May Pontef (SFT) H 10f 80 89
*** 2000** Mar Newcas (GD) 7f 86+

2000 Turf 3-5: (7f 1-1, 10f 1-3, 13f 1-1) (hvy 1-1, gd 2-3, g-f)

Useful gelding, effective 7 to 13f, acts on hvy to gd, best on gd. Turf high 93 - 1st of 7 giving 9lb to Subtle Influence (10 Oct Ayr RF 4892) - also 1st of 12 giving 19lb to Rhodamine (3 May Pontefract RF 1008). Lightly raced, he showed improved form when stepped up to 13 furlongs at Ayr in October. The bottomless ground held no terrors for him there. **Miss J A Camacho [3-7] Elite Racing Club.*

DANCING DERVISH BHB 40f **RR 44f** 3044[12]

5 b g Shareef Dancer (USA) 10.1f **(67)** - Taj Victory (Final Straw) 7.9f **(64)**

Form - 70

Record 2000 - 1st:0 2nd:0 3rd:0 Ran:2
Pre2000 - 1st:1 2nd:2 3rd:1 Ran:14

Win Prizemoney £2,913 *Total Prizemoney* £5,122

Wins 1998 Aug Bright (G-F) H 8f 55 59 <

2000 Turf 0-2: (11f, 13f) (hvy, g-f)

Moderate gelding, often wears blinkers. Turf high 44. Inconsistent. **D Burchell [0-1] Vivian Guy (from S Mellor [0-19] Apr 2000).*

DANCING DREAMS (IRE) RR 1083[19]

3 b g Dancing Dissident (USA) 6.8f **(65)** - Siwana (IRE) (Dom Racine (FR)) 9.2f **(62)**

Form - 0

Record 2000 - 1st:0 2nd:0 3rd:0 Ran:1

2000 Turf 0-1: (8f) (frm)

Workmanlike, currently very poor gelding . **B A Pearce [0-1] J Salter.*

DANCING EMPRESS BHB 70f78a **RR 80f 78a** 4703[25]

3 b f Emperor Jones (USA) - Music Khan (Music Boy) 6.8f **(57)**

Form - 21712406000

Record 2000 - 1st:1 2nd:1 3rd:0 Ran:9
Pre2000 - 1st:1 2nd:3 3rd:2 Ran:9

Win Prizemoney £5,954 *Total Prizemoney* £11,748

Wins * 2000 *May Wolver (STD) H 6f 75 80* <
***** *1999 Dec Southw (STD) 5f 75*

2000 Turf 0-7: (5f, 6f 6) (hvy, sft, g-s 2, gd, g-f, frm) 2000 AW 1-2: (5f, 6f 1-1) (Fibr 1-2)

Decent filly, effective 5 to 6f, best at 6f, acts on g-s to frm - acts on Fibr, has worn blinkers, does well at Wolverhampton. Turf high 80 - 2nd of 8 giving 17lb to Trump Street (29 May Chepstow 6f g-s RF 1520). AW high 80 (1st run) - 1st of 12 giving 11lb to Stop The Traffic (4 May Wolverhampton RF 1025). **M A Jarvis [2-18] The C H F Partnership.*

DANCING JACK BHB 38f44a **RR 39f 44a** 4372[12]

7 ch g Clantime 6.6f **(57)** - Sun Follower (Relkino) 8.9f **(65)**

Form - 07765070

Record 2000 - 1st:0 2nd:0 3rd:0 Ran:4
Pre2000 - 1st:1 2nd:5 3rd:4 Ran:64

Win Prizemoney £2,211 *Total Prizemoney* £8,947

2000 Turf 0-2: (5f 2) (frm, hrd) 2000 AW 0-2: (6f 2) (Equi 2)

Very moderate gelding, has worn blinkers. Turf high 36 (began Aug). AW high 11. **J J Bridger [1-68] Mrs J M Stamp.*

DANCING KING (IRE) BHB 25f **RR 52f** 4624[11]

4 b g Fairy King (USA) 7.7f **(75)** - Zariysha (IRE) (Darshaan) 9.9f **(84)**

Form - 0

Record 2000 - 1st:0 2nd:0 3rd:0 Ran:1
Pre2000 - 1st:0 2nd:0 3rd:0 Ran:2

2000 Turf 0-1: (12f) (gd)

Light-framed, currently fair gelding. **J D Bethell [0-1] M J Dawson (from L M Cumani [0-2] May 1999).*

DANCING KRIS BHB 90f **RR 97df** 4740[35]

7 b g Kris 10f **(75)** - Liska's Dance (USA) (Riverman (USA)) 9.1f **(76)**

Form - 70

Record 2000 - 1st:0 2nd:0 3rd:0 Ran:2
Pre2000 1st:1 2nd:1 3rd:1 Ran:5

Win Prizemoney £18,299 *Total Prizemoney* £30,223

Wins * 1999 Aug Deauvi (HVY) H 8f 97+ <

2000 Turf 0-2: (8f, 9f) (g-f, frm)

Very useful gelding, effective 8 to 10f, best at 8f, acts on hvy to g-f, best on hvy, has worn blinkers. Turf high 51. **Ian Williams [1-9] & Mrs John Poynton (from Mme C Head in FR [0-1] May 1998).*

DANCING LAWYER BHB 30f37a **RR 30f 37a** 646[11]

9 b g Thowra (FR) 11.2f **(47)** - Miss Lawsuit (Neltino) 7.6f **(54)**

Form - 080

Record 2000 - 1st:0 2nd:0 3rd:0 Ran:3
Pre2000 - 1st:7 2nd:7 3rd:10 Ran:78

Win Prizemoney £19,446 *Total Prizemoney* £36,409

Wins 1998 May Warwic (GD) H 8f 44 56
1998 Apr Bright (GD) H 8f 44 52
1996 *Jan Lingfi (STD) C 8f 81* <

2000 Turf 0-2: (9f, 11f) (g-s, gd) 2000 AW 0-1: (7f) (Fibr)

Moderate gelding, effective 9 to 11f, acts on gd to g-f, has worn blinkers, likes tight tracks. Turf high 24. **B Ellison [0-17] Brian Ellison Racing Club (from K R Burke [2-14] Spt 1998).*

DANCING LILY BHB 40f38a **RR 42f 38a** 3910[15]

3 ch f Clantime 6.6f **(57)** - Sun Follower (Relkino) 8.9f **(65)**

Form - 087028570

Record 2000 - 1st:0 2nd:1 3rd:0 Ran:9
Pre2000 - 1st:0 2nd:0 3rd:0 Ran:7

Win Prizemoney £0 *Total Prizemoney* £538

2000 Turf 0-9: (5f, 6f 3, 7f 3, 8f 2) (g-s 2, g-f 2, frm 5)

Neat, moderate filly. Turf high 42. **J J Bridger [0-16] Mrs J M Stamp.*

DANCING MAESTRO (USA) BHB 100f **RR 104f** 4966[15]

4 gr c Nureyev (USA) 8.4f **(84)** - Ancient Regime (USA) (Olden Times) 11.4f **(67)**

Form - 063280

Record 2000 - 1st:0 2nd:1 3rd:1 Ran:6

Win Prizemoney £0 *Total Prizemoney* £3,521

2000 Turf 0-6: (5f 3, 6f 3) (gd 2, g-f 2, frm 2)

Very useful colt, effective 5 to 6f, best at 6f, acts on gd to g-f, best on g-f. Turf high 104 (began Jly) - 2nd of 6 to Deep Space (27 Aug Yarmouth 6f gd RF 4025). A decent sort in France, he has run a couple of fair races in conditions events over here without setting the world alight. **N A Callaghan [0-6] Wafic Said.*

DANCING MARY BHB 44f35a **RR 51f 35a** 5012[9]

3 gr f Sri Pekan (USA) - Fontenoy (USA) (Lyphard's Wish (FR)) 9f **(74)**

Form - 373574360

Record 2000 - 1st:0 2nd:0 3rd:3 Ran:9

Pre2000 - 1st:0 2nd:0 3rd:0 Ran:4
Win Prizemoney £0 *Total Prizemoney* £1,211
2000 Turf 0-5: (12f 5) (g-s, g-f, frm 2, hrd) 2000 AW 0-4: (8f, 10f, 12f, 14f) (Equi, Fibr 3)
Leggy, fair filly. Turf high 58. AW high 55. Consistent.
**B Smart [0-13] R Bond.*

DANCING MASTER (IRE) RR 66+f 4163^{3}

2 b c Nashwan (USA) 10.3f **(79)** - Dance Time (IRE) (Sadler's Wells (USA)) 10f **(76)**
Form - 3
Record 2000 - 1st:0 2nd:0 3rd:1 Ran:1
Win Prizemoney £0 *Total Prizemoney* £1,204
2000 Turf 0-1: (7f) (g-f)
Currently average colt. **Sir Michael Stoute [0-1] Lord Weinstock.*

DANCING MILLY RR 24f 3441^{17}

2 ch f Dancing Spree (USA) 8f **(59)** - Maid Welcome **(53f 55a)** (Mummy's Pet) 7.7f **(60)**
Form - U60
Record 2000 - 1st:0 2nd:0 3rd:0 Ran:3
2000 Turf 0-3: (5f, 6f 2) (gd, frm 2)
Currently little account filly. Turf high 24 (began Jly).
**B J Meehan [0-3] Mrs Anna Sanders.*

DANCING MIRAGE (IRE) BHB 76f RR 82f 4734^{19}

3 ch f Machiavellian (USA) 9.8f **(83)** - Kraemer (USA) (Lyphard (USA)) 9.9f **(72)**
Form - 630
Record 2000 - 1st:0 2nd:0 3rd:1 Ran:3
Pre2000 - 1st:1 2nd:2 3rd:1 Ran:6
Win Prizemoney £5,199 *Total Prizemoney* £10,305
Wins * 1999 Spt Salisb (G-F) 7f 82+ <
2000 Turf 0-3: (8f, 10f 2) (gd, g-f, frm)
Decent filly, effective 6 to 8f, best at 7f, acts on frm. Turf high 78.
**R Hannon [1-9] Mohamed Suhail.*

DANCING MYSTERY BHB 104f98a RR 106f 98a 5127^{1}

6 b g Beveled (USA) 6.9f **(64)** - Batchworth Dancer (Ballacashtal (CAN)) 5.3f **(50)**
Form - 707335173014011211
Record 2000 - 1st:6 2nd:1 3rd:3 Ran:17
Pre2000 - 1st:8 2nd:7 3rd:6 Ran:49
Win Prizemoney £80,529 *Total Prizemoney* £104,767

Wins									
	* **2000**	Oct	Doncas	(SFT)	H	5f	100	106	<
	* **2000**	Oct	Newmar	(SFT)	H	5f	96	104	
	* **2000**	Spt	Newmar	(SFT)	H	5f	82	91	
	* **2000**	Spt	Yarmou	(G-F)	H	5.2f	82	90	
	* **2000**	Aug	Ascot	(G-F)	H	5f	80	82	
	* **2000**	Jun	Salisb	(G-F)	H	5f	73	78	
	* 1999	Nov	Redcar	(G-S)		5f		68+	
	* 1999	Jly	Warwic	(G-F)	H	5f	63	67	
	* 1999	*Jun*	*Southw*	*(STD)*	*H*	*5f*	*73*	*78*	
	* 1999	May	Lingfi	(G-F)	H	5f	57	59	
	* 1998	Spt	Goodwo	(G-F)	H	5f	51	56	
	* 1998	Jly	Windso	(GD)	H	5f	48	50	
	* 1997	*Nov*	*Lingfi*	*(STD)*	*H*	*5f*	*65*	*67*	
	* 1997	*Oct*	*Southw*	*(STD)*		*6f*		*63*	

2000 Turf 6-17: (5f 6-14, 6f 3) (g-s 1-2, gd 1-3, g-f 2-7, frm 2-5)
Pattern-class gelding, effective 5f, acts on g-s to gd, has worn blinkers, excels at Newmarket. Turf high 106 - 1st of 18 giving 8lb to Now Look Here (21 Oct Doncaster RF 5127) - also 1st of 20 giving 6lb to Candleriggs (12 Oct Newmarket RF 4933). A consistent come-from-behind sprinter, he was in blinding form in 2000, winning six times at the minimum trip, and rising 31lb in the ratings as a result. A credit to connections, his handicap mark means he will probably be mainly confined to listed and conditions events in the new season. **E A Wheeler [14-66] Austin Stroud & Co Ltd.*

DANCING PENNEY (IRE) BHB 57f58a RR 58f 58a 4993^{4}

2 b f General Monash (USA) - Penultimate Cress (IRE) (My Generation)
Form - 508122166034
Record 2000 - 1st:2 2nd:2 3rd:1 Ran:12
Win Prizemoney £4,200 *Total Prizemoney* £5,501

Wins								
	* **2000**	Aug	Redcar	(FRM)	S	6f	58	<
	* **2000**	Jly	Catter	(G-F)	S	5f	58	<

2000 Turf 2-9: (5f 1-5, 6f 1-3, 7f) (g-s, gd 3, g-f 1-3, frm, hrd 1-1) 2000 AW 0-3: (5f, 6f 2) (Fibr 3)
Average filly, effective 5 to 6f, best at 6f, acts on g-f to hrd - acts on Fibr, best on g-f, has worn blinkers. Turf high 58 - 1st of 9 giving 1lb to Late At Night (12 Aug Redcar RF 3595) - also 1st of 8 from Fair Step (6 Jly Catterick RF 2558). AW high 58 (began Jly) - 4th of 12 getting 2lb from Astairedotcom (14 Oct Wolverhampton 6f Fibr RF 4993). Consistent. **K A Ryan [2-12] Robert Chambers.*

DANCING RIDGE (IRE) BHB 44f RR 27f 2364^{10}

3 b c Ridgewood Ben - May We Dance (IRE) **(14f)** (Dance of Life (USA)) 7f **(66)**
Form - 070
Record 2000 - 1st:0 2nd:0 3rd:0 Ran:3
Pre2000 - 1st:0 2nd:1 3rd:0 Ran:6
Win Prizemoney £0 *Total Prizemoney* £651
2000 Turf 0-3: (5f, 6f 2) (gd, g-f, frm)
Little account colt. Turf high 27.
**P D Evans [0-6] Michael Duffy (from G Lewis [0-2] Spt 1999).*

DANCING TSAR RR 47f 4629^{6}

2 b c Salse (USA) 10.9f **(71)** - Lunda (IRE) **(60?f)** (Soviet Star (USA))
Form - 6
Record 2000 - 1st:0 2nd:0 3rd:0 Ran:1
2000 Turf 0-1: (6f) (gd)
Currently moderate colt. **G A Butler [0-1] R J Styles.*

DANCING VENTURE BHB 70f RR 66f 4890^{7}

2 b f Shareef Dancer (USA) 10.1f **(67)** - Adeptation (USA) (Exceller (USA)) 12.5f **(74)**
Form - 54327
Record 2000 - 1st:0 2nd:1 3rd:1 Ran:5
Win Prizemoney £0 *Total Prizemoney* £1,705
2000 Turf 0-5: (6f, 7f 2, 8f 2) (hvy, g-f 2, frm, hrd)
Average filly. Turf high 66 - 2nd of 10 getting 9lb from Snowey Mountain (14 Spt Yarmouth 8f g-f RF 4400).
**S P C Woods [0-5] Dr Frank Chao.*

DANDE'S RAMBO BHB 46f40a RR 54f 40a 5154^{11}

3 gr g Rambo Dancer (CAN) 8.4f **(59)** - Kajetana (FR) (Caro)
Form - 5636042650
Record 2000 - 1st:0 2nd:1 3rd:1 Ran:10
Pre2000 - 1st:0 2nd:0 3rd:0 Ran:2
Win Prizemoney £0 *Total Prizemoney* £2,668
2000 Turf 0-8: (8f, 10f 2, 11f, 12f 3, 14f) (sft, gd 2, g-f, frm 4) 2000 AW 0-2: (12f, 16f) (Equi 2)
Rangy, fair gelding, effective 10 to 12f, acts on frm, has worn blinkers. Turf high 54 - 3rd of 11 getting 20lb from Romantic Affair (16 Jun Sandown 11f frm RF 2025). AW high 42 (began Oct).
**D W P Arbuthnot [0-12] Noel Cronin.*

Dancing Mystery lorded it over his rivals

DANDILUM BHB 75f RR 78f 5242^{13}

3 b c Dilum (USA) 7.1f **(56)** - Renira (Relkino) 8.9f **(65)**
Form - 40200
Record 2000 - 1st:0 2nd:1 3rd:0 Ran:5
Pre2000 - 1st:0 2nd:3 3rd:1 Ran:5
Win Prizemoney £0 *Total Prizemoney* £4,574

2000 Turf 0-5: (7f 3, 8f 2) (g-s 2, gd 2, frm)
Workmanlike, above-average colt, effective 6f, acts on g-f to frm. Turf high 84. Inconsistent. *V Soane [0-10] The Dandy Cavaliers.*

DANDY NIGHT BHB 96f RR 100f 4735[6]

3 b f Lion Cavern (USA) 7.5f **(74)** - Desert Venus (Green Desert (USA)) 8.6f **(78)**
Form - 7138686
Record 2000 - 1st:1 2nd:0 3rd:1 Ran:7
Pre2000 - 1st:1 2nd:1 3rd:0 Ran:4
Win Prizemoney £13,629 *Total Prizemoney* £16,359
Wins * **2000** Jun Yarmou (FRM) 6f 98 <
* 1999 May Newmar (G-F) 5f 89
2000 Turf 1-7: (6f 1-6, 7f) (gd 3, g-f 1-2, frm, hrd)
Neat, very useful filly, effective 6f, acts on g-f to hrd, best on g-f. Turf high 101 - 3rd of 8 giving 10lb to Boast (30 Jun Newmarket 6f g-f RF 2414) - also 1st of 8 getting 4lb from Abderian (26 Jun Yarmouth RF 2291). Consistent. A decent filly at around six furlongs, she generally performed well last term but might strugle from the sort of mark she ended the season on.
B Hanbury [2-11] Abdullah Ali.

DANDY REGENT BHB 56f26a RR 63f 26a 5165[5]

6 b g Green Desert (USA) 7.8f **(78)** - Tahilla (Moorestyle) 6.9f **(64)**
Form - 1710040035
Record 2000 - 1st:2 2nd:0 3rd:1 Ran:10
Pre2000 - 1st:1 2nd:3 3rd:1 Ran:27
Win Prizemoney £8,661 *Total Prizemoney* £13,199
Wins * **2000** May Thirsk (GD) S 7f 63
* **2000** Mar Leices (GD) S 7f 49
1998 Apr Bright (GD) H 7f 65 73 <
2000 Turf 2-10: (6f 2, 7f 2-8) (g-s, gd 2-4, g-f, frm 4)
Average gelding, effective 7f, acts on gd to g-f. Turf high 63 - 1st of 16 giving 5lb to Erupt (19 May Thirsk RF 1316).
J L Harris [2-23] J L Harris (from C A Cyzer [1-14] Aug 1998).

DANE DANCING (IRE) BHB 63f55a RR 68f 55a 5320[12]

2 b f Danehill (USA) 9.1f **(79)** - My Ballerina (USA) (Sir Ivor) 10.2f **(70)**
Form - 578730
Record 2000 - 1st:0 2nd:0 3rd:1 Ran:6
Win Prizemoney £0 *Total Prizemoney* £708
2000 Turf 0-6: (6f 3, 7f 3) (sft, gd 2, g-f 2, frm)
Average filly, effective 7f, acts on gd. Turf high 68 (began Aug).
J H M Gosden [0-6] Lady Bamford.

DANE FLYER (IRE) BHB 70f RR 67tf 4629[8]

2 b c Danehill (USA) 9.1f **(79)** - Old Domesday Book (High Top) 10.2f **(67)**
Form - 708
Record 2000 - 1st:0 2nd:0 3rd:0 Ran:3
2000 Turf 0-3: (6f 3) (gd 2, frm)
Currently average colt. Turf high 67 (began Jly).
M R Channon [0-3] John Carey.

DANE FRIENDLY RR 114f 4956a[4]

4 b c Danehill (USA) 9.1f **(79)** - Always Friendly (High Line) 10.3f **(70)**
Form - 34
2000 Turf 0-2: (8f 2) (sft, g-s)
Scopey, Group-class colt. Turf high 114 - 4th of 9 to Faberger (8 Oct San Siro 8f sft RF 4956a).
O Pessi in ITY [0-2] (from P W Chapple-Hyam [0-2] May 1999).

DANEGOLD (IRE) BHB 49f68a RR 58f 68a 4630[9]

8 b g Danehill (USA) 9.1f **(79)** - Cistus (Sun Prince) 12.4f **(52)**
Form - 045407846380
Record 2000 - 1st:0 2nd:0 3rd:1 Ran:12
Pre2000 - 1st:10 2nd:5 3rd:9 Ran:67
Win Prizemoney £52,072 *Total Prizemoney* £71,401
Wins * 1999 Jly Ascot (G-F) H 16.2f 64 66
* 1999 Mar Doncas (G-S) H 18f 65 68
* 1998 Oct Ascot (SFT) H 16.2f 58 65+
* 1998 Oct Catter (gd,) H 15.8f 58 58
* 1998 Spt Goodwo (G-F) H 16f 52 58
* 1998 Jly Yarmou (G-F) H 16f 50 52
2000 Turf 0-12: (14f 3, 16f 6, 17f 2, 18f) (g-s, gd 5, g-f 2, frm 3, hrd)
Average gelding, effective 14 to 22f, acts on g-s to frm, often wears blinkers (extremely effectively), excels at Doncaster. Turf high 58. A prolific scorer over the years, he likes to come late, but his style of racing means that he occasionally finds trouble when trying to get a run. Decent hurdler.
M R Channon [16-102] Circular Distributors Ltd (from J W Hills [0-5] Oct 1994).

DANEHURST BHB 100f RR 105+f 5107[1]

2 b f Danehill (USA) 9.1f **(79)** - Miswaki Belle (USA) **(64+f)** (Miswaki (USA)) 9f **(81)**
Form - 111
Record 2000 - 1st:3 2nd:0 3rd:0 Ran:3
Win Prizemoney £23,567 *Total Prizemoney* £23,567
Wins * **2000** Oct Newbur (SFT) G3 5f 105+ <
* **2000** *Oct Wolver (STD) 5f 104+*
* **2000** Jun Warwic (G-F) 5f 72
2000 Turf 2-2: (5f 2-2) (gd 1-1, g-f 1-1) 2000 AW 1-1: (5f 1-1) (Fibr 1-1)
Currently Pattern-class filly. Turf high 105 - 1st of 17 getting 5lb from Fromsong (20 Oct Newbury RF 5107). (1st run) - 1st of 7 from Prince of Blues (3 Oct Wolverhampton RF 4781). Made a winning debut at Warwick and broke the course record when following up at Wolverhampton four months later. She completed the hat-trick when landing the Cornwallis Stakes, which was run in 2000 at Newbury rather than Ascot.
Sir Mark Prescott [3-3] Cheveley Park Stud.

DANE'S LADY (IRE) BHB 66f RR 66f 4991[18]

4 b f Danehill (USA) 9.1f **(79)** - Lady Ellen (Horage) 10.3f **(61)**
Form - 400
Record 2000 - 1st:0 2nd:0 3rd:0 Ran:3
Pre2000 - 1st:1 2nd:3 3rd:0 Ran:9
Win Prizemoney £2,484 *Total Prizemoney* £5,949
Wins 1999 Aug Roscom (G-F) 7f 68 <
2000 Turf 0-3: (6f 2, 7f) (g-s, gd, frm)
Average filly, effective 7f, acts on gd to g-f, best on g-f. Turf high 66 (began Aug). Consistent. A winner over seven furlongs at Roscommon in '99.
E J Alston [0-3] Mrs Chris Harrington (from K Prendergast in IRE [1-9] Aug 1999).

DANESTAR BHB 40f30a RR 37f 30a 4906a[15]

5 b m Danehill (USA) 9.1f **(79)** - Ministra (USA) (Deputy Minister (CAN)) 7.4f **(80)**
Form - 06000
Record 2000 - 1st:0 2nd:0 3rd:0 Ran:4
Pre2000 - 1st:0 2nd:0 3rd:0 Ran:7
2000 Turf 0-3: (9f, 14f, 16f) (hvy, sft, gd) 2000 AW 0-1: (8f) (Fibr)
Very moderate filly, has worn blinkers. (began Spt). Becoming disappointing.
Ms V Charlton in IRE [0-3] Paul Phelan (from K R Burke [0-5] Jan 2000).

DANGER BABY BHB 48f45a RR 51f 45a 3245[6]

10 ch g Bairn (USA) 9.4f **(55)** - Swordlestown Miss (USA) (Apalachee (USA)) 9.4f **(71)**
Form - 0625216
Record 2000 - 1st:1 2nd:2 3rd:0 Ran:6
Pre2000 - 1st:2 2nd:1 3rd:2 Ran:12
Win Prizemoney £9,331 *Total Prizemoney* £12,612
Wins * **2000** Jly Folkes (GD) H 16.4f 46 48
* 1999 Spt Bath (G-S) H 17.2f 37 51 <
2000 Turf 1-6: (15f, 16f 1-3, 18f 2) (gd 1-2, g-f 2, frm 2)
Fair gelding, effective 16 to 18f, acts on gd to g-f, best on gd, has worn blinkers, prefers left handed tracks, excels at Chepstow. Turf high 51 (1st run) - 6th of 14 getting 27lb from Eastwell Hall (8 Jun Chepstow 18f gd RF 1804) - also 1st of 13 giving 13lb to Ziggy Stardust (13 Jly Folkestone RF 2767). Consistent. He fell out of love with fences, but nonetheless has ability on the level. Stays well. *P Bowen [9-38] Shark Racing (from Bob Jones [1-8] Aug 1993).*

DANGERMAN (IRE) BHB 38f36a RR 51f 36a 151[9]

5 ch g Pips Pride 6.7f **(70)** - Two Magpies (Doulab (USA)) 9.8f **(65)**
Form - 30
Record 2000 - 1st:0 2nd:0 3rd:1 Ran:2
Pre2000 - 1st:1 2nd:1 3rd:0 Ran:14
Win Prizemoney £3,183 *Total Prizemoney* £4,662
Wins * 1998 Oct Nottin () H 10f 37 43 <
2000 AW 0-2: (8f, 11f) (Fibr 2)
Fair gelding. AW high 22. *M W Easterby [2-25] Stephen Curtis.*

DANGEROUS DEPLOY BHB 59f54a **RR 62f 54a** 5059[1]
3 b g Deploy 11.4f **(67)** - Emily-Mou (IRE) **(72f 75a)** (Cadeaux Genereux)
Form - 550851
Record 2000 - 1st:1 2nd:0 3rd:0 Ran:6
Win Prizemoney £1,817 *Total Prizemoney* £1,817
Wins * **2000** Oct Nottin (SFT) SH 14.1f 57 57 <
2000 Turf 1-6: (7f, 8f, 10f 2, 12f, 14f 1-1) (sft 1-1, gd, g-f 3, frm)
Neat, average gelding, effective 10 to 14f, acts on sft to g-f, best on g-f. Turf high 62 (began Jly) - 5th of 16 giving 6lb to Final Lap (28 Spt Newmarket 12f g-f RF 4696) - also 1st of 6 giving 18lb to Gypsy Song (18 Oct Nottingham RF 5059).
**D R C Elsworth [1-6] Del & Jake Partnership.*

DANGEROUS FORTUNE (USA) BHB 70f78a **RR 74f 78a** 4934[22]
4 b g Barathea (IRE) - Miss Demure (Shy Groom (USA)) 10f **(66)**
Form - 67800
Record 2000 - 1st:0 2nd:0 3rd:0 Ran:5
Pre2000 - 1st:1 2nd:2 3rd:1 Ran:6
Win Prizemoney £3,179 *Total Prizemoney* £6,308
Wins * 1999 Spt Redcar (G-F) 7f 81 <
2000 Turf 0-5: (7f, 8f 4) (sft, g-s, gd, g-f 2)
Workmanlike, above-average gelding, effective 7 to 8f, best at 8f, acts on gd to frm, best on frm. Turf high 74. Consistent.
**J W Hills [1-11] Sara Warren, Amanda Hills.*

DANGEROUS LADY RR 440[6]
3 ch f Rock Hopper 10.6f **(54)** - Society Arch (CAN) (Legal Bid (USA))
Form - 86
Record 2000 - 1st:0 2nd:0 3rd:0 Ran:2
2000 AW 0-2: (8f, 11f) (Equi, Fibr)
Workmanlike, currently very poor filly. AW high 4.
**J R Best [0-2] Angley Stud.*

DANGEROUS MIND (IRE) RR 99f 2204a[2]
4 b f Platini (GER) - Desert Squaw (Commanche Run) 8.5f **(58)**
Form - 12
2000 Turf 0-1: (12f) (g-f)
Currently very useful filly. (1st run) - 2nd of 11 giving 13lb to Sailing (18 Jun San Siro 12f g-f RF 2204a).
**H Blume in GER [1-2] Gestut Sommerberg.*

DANGER OVER RR 112f 4564a[1]
3 b c Warning 8.1f **(77)** - Danilova (USA) (Lyphard (USA)) 9.9f **(72)**
Form - 1221
2000 Turf 2-4: (6f 1-3, 7f 1-1) (hvy, g-s, gd 1-1)
Group-class colt. Turf high 112 - 1st of 7 giving 3lb to Khasayl (15 Spt Chantilly RF 4564a). **P Bary in FR [2-4] K Abdulla.*

DANIAVI (IRE) RR 38f 5100[20]
2 ch c Kris 10f **(75)** - Danishara (IRE) (Slew O' Gold (USA)) 8f **(75)**
Form - 0
Record 2000 - 1st:0 2nd:0 3rd:0 Ran:1
2000 Turf 0-1: (7f) (gd)
Currently very moderate colt.
**Sir Michael Stoute [0-1] H H Aga Khan.*

DANIEL DERONDA BHB 56f55a **RR 57f 55a** 1734[17]
6 b g Danehill (USA) 9.1f **(79)** - Kilvarnet (Furry Glen) 8.9f **(63)**
Form - 00
Record 2000 - 1st:0 2nd:0 3rd:0 Ran:2
Pre2000 - 1st:1 2nd:3 3rd:0 Ran:13
Win Prizemoney £4,354 *Total Prizemoney* £6,902
Wins 1999 Jly Nottin (FRM) H 10f 54 57 <
2000 Turf 0-2: (10f, 12f) (gd, g-f)
Fair gelding, effective 10 to 12f, acts on gd to frm, best on frm, has worn blinkers, favours tight tracks. Turf high 42. Inconsistent.
**P Burgoyne [0-2] R J Apperley (from J Cullinan [1-7] Jly 1999).*

DANIELLA RIDGE (IRE) BHB 53f47a **RR 53f 47a** 5116[11]
4 b f Indian Ridge 7.6f **(74)** - Daniella Drive (USA) (Shelter Half (USA)) 7.9f **(79)**
Form - 0082540
Record 2000 - 1st:0 2nd:1 3rd:0 Ran:7
Pre2000 - 1st:0 2nd:0 3rd:4 Ran:7
Win Prizemoney £0 *Total Prizemoney* £3,924
2000 Turf 0-6: (8f 3, 9f, 10f 2) (g-f 3, frm 2, hrd) 2000 AW 0-1: (8f) (Fibr)
Scopey, fair filly, effective 8 to 10f, best at 8f, acts on g-f to frm, best on frm, has worn blinkers. Turf high 53. Inconsistent.
**R Hannon [0-14] A F Harrington.*

DANIELLE'S LAD BHB 93f81a **RR 97f 81a** 4691[17]
4 b g Emarati (USA) 6.6f **(63)** - Cactus Road (FR) (Iron Duke (FR)) 8.8f **(60)**
Form - 8747110406860
Record 2000 - 1st:2 2nd:0 3rd:0 Ran:12
Pre2000 - 1st:2 2nd:2 3rd:3 Ran:18
Win Prizemoney £22,767 *Total Prizemoney* £31,011
Wins * **2000** May Kempto (SFT) H 6f 86 97 <
* **2000** May Goodwo (SFT) H 6f 86 91
* 1998 Nov Doncas (SFT) H 5f 81 84
* 1998 Aug Goodwo (G-F) 5f 77
2000 Turf 2-12: (5f 2, 6f 2-10) (g-s 1-3, gd 1-7, g-f 2)
Strong, very useful gelding, effective 5 to 6f, best at 6f, acts on g-s to g-f, best on gd, excels at Chepstow and Kempton. Turf high 97 - 1st of 13 giving 27lb to Sarena Pride (27 May Kempton RF 1501) - also 1st of 16 giving 6lb to Return of Amin (24 May Goodwood RF 1428). He struck form in May, winning sprint handicaps at Goodwood and Kempton in the space of four days. Held afterwards, he goes well in soft ground. **B Palling [4-30] Mrs P K Chick.*

DANISH RHAPSODY (IRE) BHB 113f **RR 114f** 1135[3]
7 b g Danehill (USA) 9.1f **(79)** - Ardmelody (Law Society (USA)) 9.9f **(70)**
Form - 3
Record 2000 - 1st:0 2nd:0 3rd:1 Ran:1
Pre2000 - 1st:9 2nd:3 3rd:3 Ran:26
Win Prizemoney £145,755 *Total Prizemoney* £178,411
Wins * 1999 Jly Goodwo (FRM) LH 12f 110 114 <
* 1999 Jly Newbur (G-F) 10f 109
* 1998 Spt Goodwo (G-F) L 9.9f 101
* 1998 May Haydoc (GD) L 10.5f 110
* 1997 Spt Goodwo (G-F) L 10f 105
* 1997 Spt Goodwo (GD) H 9f 95 100
* 1997 Jly Goodwo (G-F) H 10f 90 95
* 1997 Jly Lingfi (G-F) 10f 96
* 1997 May Folkes (G-F) H 9.7f 80 85
2000 Turf 0-1: (13f) (g-f)
Group-class gelding, effective 10 to 13f, acted on g-f to frm, best on g-f. (1st run) - 3rd of 9 to Daliapour (11 May Chester 13f g-f RF 1135). Consistent. (DEAD)
**Lady Herries [9-27] Chris Hardy & Friends.*

DANITY FAIR BHB 35f **RR 8f** 3238[11]
2 b f Cool Jazz - Flute Royale (Horage) 10.3f **(61)**
Form - 400
Record 2000 - 1st:0 2nd:0 3rd:0 Ran:3
2000 Turf 0-1: (6f) (frm) 2000 AW 0-2: (5f, 6f) (Fibr 2)
Currently moderate filly. AW high 43.
**R Bastiman [0-3] J M Barraclough.*

DANIYSHA (IRE) BHB 73f **RR 72f** 4024[3]
3 b f Doyoun 10.7f **(69)** - Danishara (IRE) (Slew O' Gold (USA)) 8f **(75)**
Form - 431063
Record 2000 - 1st:1 2nd:0 3rd:2 Ran:6
Pre2000 - 1st:0 2nd:0 3rd:0 Ran:1
Win Prizemoney £4,104 *Total Prizemoney* £6,122
Wins * **2000** Jly Chepst (G-F) 7.1f 71 <
2000 Turf 1-6: (7f 1-5, 8f) (gd 3, g-f, frm 1-2)
Scopey, above-average filly, effective 6 to 7f, best at 7f, acts on gd to frm, best on gd. Turf high 72 - also 1st of 5 from Prinisha (8 Jly Chepstow RF 2628). **Sir Michael Stoute [1-7] H H Aga Khan.*

DANKA BHB 32f34a **RR 33f 34a** 4757[19]
6 gr g Petong 7.6f **(58)** - Angel Drummer (Dance In Time (CAN)) 8.9f **(59)**
Form - 70580
Record 2000 - 1st:0 2nd:0 3rd:0 Ran:2
Pre2000 - 1st:1 2nd:0 3rd:2 Ran:24
Win Prizemoney £1,813 *Total Prizemoney* £3,036
Wins * 1999 *Mar Southw (STD) S 11f 47* <
2000 Turf 0-1: (10f) (g-s) 2000 AW 0-1: (16f) (Fibr)
Very moderate gelding, effective 11f, - acts on Fibr, often wears

blinkers. Inconsistent.
**K C Comerford [1-18] S J V Construction (from P T Walwyn [0-8] Dec 1997).*

DANNI BHB 24f **RR** 1480[10]
7 ch m Clantime 6.6f **(57)** - Kasu (Try My Best (USA)) 7.6f **(67)**
Form - 00
Record 2000 - 1st:0 2nd:0 3rd:0 Ran:2
Pre2000 - 1st:0 2nd:0 3rd:0 Ran:1
2000 AW 0-2: (6f, 8f) (Fibr 2)
Poor mare. AW high 13. **J L Harris [0-4] J L Harris.*

DANNY DEEVER BHB 18f **RR 4f** 5086[12]
4 b g Deploy 11.4f **(67)** - Yes (Blakeney) 10.5f **(64)**
Form - 000
Record 2000 - 1st:0 2nd:0 3rd:0 Ran:2
Pre2000 - 1st:0 2nd:1 3rd:0 Ran:17
Win Prizemoney £0 *Total Prizemoney* £1,366
2000 Turf 0-2: (7f, 12f) (hvy, g-s)
Strong, very poor gelding, effective 12f, acts on frm, has worn blinkers. (began Spt). Becoming disappointing.
**Miss J F Craze [0-2] D T Thom (from D T Thom [0-19] Nov 1999).*

DANO-MAST RR 111f 4717a[4]
4 b c Unfuwain (USA) 11.4f **(74)** - Camera Girl (Kalaglow) 9.8f **(67)**
Form - 134
2000 Turf 1-3: (9f 1-1, 12f 2) (stt, gd)
Currently Group-class colt. Turf high 111. **F Poulsen in DEN [1-3].*

DANSILI RR 126f 5327a[3]
4 h Danehill (USA) 9.1f **(79)** - Hasili (IRE) **(103?f)** (Kahyasi)
Form - 1122623
2000 Turf 2-7: (7f, 8f 2-6) (sft 2, g-s 2-2, gd 2, frm)
Top-class colt, effective 7 to 8f, best at 8f, acts on hvy to frm, best on gd, and likes Saint-cloud and Deauville. Turf high 125 - 3rd of 14 giving 3lb to War Chant (4 Nov Churchill Downs 8f frm RF 5327a) - also 1st of 5 from Kingsalsa (1 May Saint-cloud RF 1152a). Consistent. A high-class miler in France, he gained two wins at Saint-Cloud early in the season and was an excellent second to Kalanisi in the Queen Anne at Ascot. He ran into the mighty Giant's Causeway in the Sussex Stakes and was unsuited by the soft ground on both visits to Longchamp, but he bounced back to form on fast ground when an unlucky third in the Breeders' Cup Mile. **A Fabre in FR [5-14] Juddmonte Farms.*

DANZA MONTANA (USA) RR 68f 1884[8]
2 ch f Diesis 9f **(80)** - Valsora (IRE) (Tate Gallery (USA)) 7.4f **(67)**
Form - 78
Record 2000 - 1st:0 2nd:0 3rd:0 Ran:2
2000 Turf 0-2: (5f, 6f) (gd, frm)
Currently average filly. Turf high 68.
**J A Osborne [0-2] Mrs Belinda Strudwick.*

DANZAS BHB 40f30a **RR 47f 30a** 4759[6]
6 b g Polish Precedent (USA) 9f **(73)** - Dancing Rocks (Green Dancer (USA)) 10.3f **(74)**
Form - 676467618326257466576
Record 2000 - 1st:1 2nd:2 3rd:1 Ran:21
Pre2000 - 1st:1 2nd:3 3rd:3 Ran:30
Win Prizemoney £4,227 *Total Prizemoney* £10,209

Wins								
* 2000	Apr	Bright	(G-S)	H	7f	40	47	<
* 1999	May	Nottin	(FRM)	H	8.2f	40	44	

2000 Turf 1-13: (7f 1-4, 8f 9) (hvy, sft, gd 1-4, g-f 3, frm 2, hrd 2) 2000 AW 0-8: (7f 4, 8f 2, 9f 2) (Equi, Fibr 7)
Moderate gelding, effective 7 to 8f, best at 8f, acts on gd to hrd, best on gd, often wears blinkers, does well at Brighton. Turf high 47 (1st run) - 1st of 18 getting 1lb from Stitch In Time (13 Apr Brighton RF 0696). AW high 41. Consistent.
**J M Bradley [2-51] Martyn James, Pete S Jenkins (from R Charlton [0-6] Oct 1997).*

DANZIGAWAY (USA) RR 114f 5095a[4]
4 b f Danehill (USA) 9.1f **(79)** - Blushing Away (FR) (Blushing Groom (FR)) 10.3f **(76)**
Form - 2064
2000 Turf 0-4: (7f, 8f 3) (sft, g-s, gd, g-f)
Group-class filly, effective 7 to 8f, best at 8f, acts on g-s, has worn blinkers. Turf high 110 (1st run) (began Jly) - 2nd of 13 giving 8lb to Lady Of Chad (30 Jly Deauville 8f g-s RF 3351a).
**Mme C Head in FR [2-9].*

DANZIGEUSE (IRE) BHB 39f **RR 50f** 4491[14]
3 b f Zieten (USA) - Baliana **(47df)** (Midyan (USA)) 6f **(60)**
Form - 08400
Record 2000 - 1st:0 2nd:0 3rd:0 Ran:5
Pre2000 - 1st:0 2nd:0 3rd:0 Ran:3
Win Prizemoney £0 *Total Prizemoney* £277
2000 Turf 0-5: (6f 3, 7f 2) (g-f 3, frm 2)
Neat, fair filly. Turf high 50. Inconsistent.
**C B B Booth [0-4] A Kay (from R Charlton [0-4] Apr 2000).*

DANZIG FLYER (IRE) BHB 18f55a **RR 6f 55a** 2027[8]
5 h h Roi Danzig (USA) 10.5f **(62)** - Fenland Express (IRE) (Reasonable (FR))
Form - 08
Record 2000 - 1st:0 2nd:0 3rd:0 Ran:2
Pre2000 - 1st:0 2nd:1 3rd:1 Ran:19
Win Prizemoney £0 *Total Prizemoney* £1,365
2000 Turf 0-1: (11f) (g-s) 2000 AW 0-1: (14f) (Fibr)
Very poor colt, has worn blinkers.
**B P J Baugh [0-14] Mrs Renee Farrington-Kirkham (from P W Harris [0-13] Oct 1998).*

DANZIG WITHWOLVES (USA) BHB 70f **RR 72f** 5239[9]
3 b f Danzig (USA) 8.1f **(88)** - Strategic Maneuver (USA) (Cryptoclearance (USA))
Form - 440
Record 2000 - 1st:0 2nd:0 3rd:0 Ran:3
Win Prizemoney £0 *Total Prizemoney* £522
2000 Turf 0-3: (8f 3) (g-s 2, g-f)
Scopey, currently above-average filly. Turf high 72 (1st run) (began Jly) - 4th of 8 getting 13lb from Invader (27 Jly Sandown 8f g-f RF 3156). **H R A Cecil [0-3] Shane Ryan.*

DANZINO (IRE) BHB 45f85a **RR 85a** 4761[P]
5 b g Roi Danzig (USA) 10.5f **(62)** - Luvi Ullmann (Thatching) 8f **(66)**
Form - 0PP
Record 2000 - 1st:0 2nd:0 3rd:0 Ran:3
Pre2000 - 1st:5 2nd:3 3rd:3 Ran:24
Win Prizemoney £19,960 *Total Prizemoney* £31,486

Wins								
* 1998	*Dec*	*Lingfi*	*(STD)*		*10f*		*82*	
* 1998	*Nov*	*Wolver*	*(STD)*	*H*	*8.5f*	*89*	*92*	<
* 1998	*Jun*	*Wolver*	*(STD)*	*H*	*9.4f*	*83*	*85*	
* 1998	*Feb*	*Lingfi*	*(SLW)*	*H*	*10f*	*64*	*72*	
* 1998	*Jan*	*Southw*	*(STD)*		*8f*		*72*	

2000 AW 0-3: (9f, 12f 2) (Fibr 3)
Very poor gelding, mostly wears blinkers. (began Jun).
**Mrs N Macauley [5-22] Godfrey Horsford (from A P Jarvis [0-5] Oct 1997).*

DAPHNE'S DOLL (IRE) BHB 46f49a **RR 47f 49a** 3054[17]
5 b m Polish Patriot (USA) 7.8f **(70)** - Helietta (Tyrnavos) 10.1f **(55)**
Form - 417087030
Record 2000 - 1st:0 2nd:0 3rd:1 Ran:7
Pre2000 - 1st:2 2nd:1 3rd:2 Ran:16
Win Prizemoney £4,579 *Total Prizemoney* £7,603

Wins								
* 1999	*Dec*	*Lingfi*	*(STD)*	*H*	*10f*	*48*	*50*	
1998	*Dec*	*Lingfi*	*(STD)*		*7f*		*65*	<

2000 Turf 0-4: (7f, 8f 3) (gd 2, g-f 2) 2000 AW 0-3: (8f, 9f, 10f) (Equi 2, Fibr)
Moderate filly, effective 7 to 10f, acts on gd to frm - acts on Equi. Turf high 47 - 3rd of 18 getting 1lb from Colne Valley Amy (7 Jly Salisbury 8f gd RF 2598). AW high 28.
**Dr J R J Naylor [1-9] Mrs S P Elphick (from Miss Gay Kelleway [1-14] Nov 1999).*

DARAKIYLA (IRE) RR 93f 1282a[3]
3 b f Last Tycoon 9.4f **(73)** - Daralinsha (USA) (Empery (USA)) 11.2f **(69)**
Form - 3
2000 Turf 0-1: (7f) (g-s)
Currently useful filly.
**A deRoyerDupre in FR [1-3] Aga Khan.*

DARARIYNA (IRE) BHB 80f **RR 81f** 4815[5]
3 b f Shirley Heights 12.1f **(76)** - Dararita (IRE) (Halo (USA)) 10.6f **(75)**
Form - 2215105
Record 2000 - 1st:2 2nd:2 3rd:0 Ran:7
Win Prizemoney £8,105 *Total Prizemoney* £10,927
Wins * **2000** Aug Beverl (FRM) 12f 79 <
* **2000** Jun Cheste (G-F) 13.4f 51+
2000 Turf 2-7: (11f, 12f 1-4, 13f 1-1, 14f) (g-s 2, gd, g-f, frm 2-3)
Scopey, decent filly, effective 11 to 12f, acts on g-s to frm. Turf high 81 - also 1st of 10 getting 3lb from Octavius Caesar (26 Aug Beverley RF 3979). She got off the mark in a four-runner Chester maiden in June, but ran poorly on her handicap debut and regained winning form in a Beverley limited event. Her wins have been on fast ground, but she may be better with some cut.
**Sir Michael Stoute [2-7] H H Aga Khan.*

DARAYDAN (IRE) BHB 80f **RR 41f** 2153[19]
8 b g Kahyasi 12.9f **(74)** - Delsy (FR) (Abdos) 10f **(77)**
Form - 0
Record 2000 - 1st:0 2nd:0 3rd:0 Ran:1
Pre2000 - 1st:1 2nd:2 3rd:1 Ran:13
Win Prizemoney £11,053 *Total Prizemoney* £34,396
2000 Turf 0-1: (20f) (gd)
Moderate gelding. Becoming disappointing. Much better known as a jumper, he makes infrequent appearances on the Flat.
**M C Pipe [10-38] Martin Pipe Racing Club (from Lady Herries [1-9] Aug 1996).*

DARCY DANCER BHB 42f **RR 46f** 3374[17]
3 b g Be My Chief (USA) 10.2f **(62)** - Little White Star (Mill Reef (USA)) 10.5f **(78)**
Form - 0800
Record 2000 - 1st:0 2nd:0 3rd:0 Ran:4
Pre2000 - 1st:0 2nd:0 3rd:1 Ran:3
Win Prizemoney £0 *Total Prizemoney* £542
2000 Turf 0-4: (11f, 12f 2, 16f) (hvy, g-f 2, frm)
Leggy, moderate gelding, has worn blinkers. Turf high 42.
**A J McNae [0-4] J P Racing (from Martyn Wane [0-3] Spt 1999).*

DARCY ROAD DANCER RR 46f 2938[8]
3 b g Shareef Dancer (USA) 10.1f **(67)** - Handy Dancer (Green God) 9.6f **(68)**
Form - 78
Record 2000 - 1st:0 2nd:0 3rd:0 Ran:2
2000 Turf 0-2: (9f, 12f) (frm 2)
Workmanlike, currently moderate gelding. Turf high 46 (began Jly). **G L Moore [0-2] Bryan Pennick.*

DARDANUS RR 77f 5027[3]
2 ch c Komaite (USA) 6.9f **(61)** - Dance On A Cloud (USA) **(76f)** (Capote (USA))
Form - 4043
Record 2000 - 1st:0 2nd:0 3rd:1 Ran:4
Win Prizemoney £0 *Total Prizemoney* £988
2000 Turf 0-4: (7f, 8f 3) (g-s, gd 2, g-f)
Above-average colt. Turf high 77 (began Aug) - 3rd of 12 giving 2lb to Port Moresby (17 Oct Yarmouth 8f g-s RF 5027).
**E A L Dunlop [0-4] Hesmonds Stud.*

DARE BHB 54f54a **RR 58f 54a** 2194[11]
5 b g Beveled (USA) 6.9f **(64)** - Run Amber Run (Run The Gantlet (USA)) 12.1f **(59)**
Form - 301008322070358738460
Record 2000 - 1st:0 2nd:2 3rd:3 Ran:15
Pre2000 - 1st:5 2nd:0 3rd:1 Ran:22
Win Prizemoney £17,684 *Total Prizemoney* £24,226
Wins * 1999 *Nov Southw (STD) H 8f 57 61* <
* 1999 Oct Leices (SFT) H 8f 47 55
* 1999 *Oct Southw (STD) H 8f 47 51*
* 1999 Spt Salisb (HVY) H 9.9f 35 46+
* 1999 Spt Hamilt (SFT) H 8.3f 35 44+
2000 Turf 0-6: (8f, 10f 3, 11f, 12f) (g-s 2, gd 2, g-f 2) 2000 AW 0-9: (8f 2, 9f 6, 12f) (Fibr 9)
Average gelding, effective 8 to 12f, best at 9f, acts on g-s to g-f - acts on Fibr, often wears blinkers, likes right handed tracks, and likes Wolverhampton. Turf high 58 - 7th of 12 getting 15lb from Veridian (11 May Chester 12f g-f RF 1139). AW high 65 - 3rd of 11 getting 5lb from Tyler's Toast (4 Mar Wolverhampton 9f Fibr RF 0408). **P D Evans [6-28] J E Potter (from E L James [0-12] Jun 1999).*

DARE HUNTER (USA) BHB 76f **RR 81f** 5078[6]
3 ch g Gulch (USA) 9.6f **(79)** - Dabaweyaa (Shareef Dancer (USA)) 9.9f **(73)**
Form - 024086
Record 2000 - 1st:0 2nd:1 3rd:0 Ran:6
Pre2000 - 1st:1 2nd:0 3rd:0 Ran:3
Win Prizemoney £4,143 *Total Prizemoney* £7,213
Wins * 1999 Jly Sandow (G-F) 7.1f 85+ <
2000 Turf 0-6: (8f 4, 9f, 10f) (sft, g-s, gd, g-f 2, frm)
Scopey, decent gelding, effective 7f, acts on frm, likes tight tracks. Turf high 81. **B W Hills [1-9] Mohamed Obaida.*

DARGO BHB 60f61a **RR 47f 61a** 141[6]
6 b g Formidable (USA) 7.8f **(60)** - Mountain Memory (High Top) 10.2f **(67)**
Form - 6
Record 2000 - 1st:0 2nd:0 3rd:0 Ran:1
Pre2000 - 1st:1 2nd:4 3rd:2 Ran:17
Win Prizemoney £2,284 *Total Prizemoney* £6,223
Wins * 1999 *Feb Wolver (STD) H 16.2f 43 77+* <
2000 AW 0-1: (16f) (Fibr)
Above-average gelding.
**D G Bridgwater [2-7] The Rule Racing Syndicate (from C W Thornton [0-13] Nov 1998).*

DARIALANN (IRE) RR 91f 4356a[11]
5 b g Kahyasi 12.9f **(74)** - Delsy (FR) (Abdos) 10f **(77)**
Form - 30450
2000 Turf 0-5: (14f 3, 16f 2) (sft, gd 4)
Useful gelding, effective 12 to 17f, acts on hvy to g-f, mostly wears blinkers, excels at Galway. Turf high 91 - 4th of 26 giving 17lb to Gamekeeper (31 Jly Galway 16f gd RF 3454a).
**D K Weld in IRE [4-17] S Mulryan.*

DARING MISS RR 115f 5212a[9]
4 b f Sadler's Wells (USA) 11.3f **(87)** - Bourbon Girl (Ile de Bourbon (USA)) 10.1f **(67)**
Form - 12270
2000 Turf 1-5: (12f 1-3, 13f, 16f) (hvy, g-s, gd 1-3)
High-class filly, effective 12 to 13f, best at 12f, acts on hvy to gd, best on gd, excels at Deauville. Turf high 115 - also 1st of 6 getting 8lb from First Magnitude (11 Jun Chantilly RF 2006a). Tough and consistent, she landed a Group Two at Chantilly before splitting Arc winners Montjeu and Sagamix in the Grand Prix de Saint-Cloud. Just beaten in the Group-Two Grand Prix de Deauville.
**A Fabre in FR [3-8].*

DARK DOLORES BHB 44f **RR 46f** 5160[9]
2 b f Inchinor 8.9f **(64)** - Pingin (Corvaro (USA)) 9f **(53)**
Form - 000
Record 2000 - 1st:0 2nd:0 3rd:0 Ran:4
2000 Turf 0-3: (6f, 7f, 8f) (sft, g-s, frm) 2000 AW 0-1: (6f) (Equi)
Moderate filly. Turf high 48 (began Spt).
**M R Channon [0-4] J D Knight & Mrs V A Knight.*

DARK FINISH (IRE) RR 60f 4149[4]
2 b f Night Shift (USA) 8.1f **(73)** - Varnish (Final Straw) 7.9f **(64)**
Form - 4
Record 2000 - 1st:0 2nd:0 3rd:0 Ran:1
Win Prizemoney £0 *Total Prizemoney* £356
2000 Turf 0-1: (5f) (gd)
Currently average filly. **B A McMahon [0-1] Mrs C P Lees-Jones.*

DARK MENACE BHB 48f41a **RR 53f 41a** 3073[2]
8 br g Beveled (USA) 6.9f **(64)** - Sweet and Sure (Known Fact (USA)) 7.4f **(67)**
Form - 710886018002
Record 2000 - 1st:1 2nd:1 3rd:0 Ran:10
Pre2000 - 1st:5 2nd:8 3rd:8 Ran:66
Win Prizemoney £14,360 *Total Prizemoney* £23,091
Wins * **2000** May Bright (G-S) H 8f 49 53 <
* 1999 *Dec Lingfi (STD) S 7f 48*
* 1999 May Bright (FRM) H 7f 42 47
* 1998 *Jun Southw (STD) SH 7f 32 37*

* 1997 Jun Bright (FRM) H 7f 47 52
* 1996 Jly Bright (FRM) H 6f 45 47
2000 Turf 1-5: (7f 2, 8f 1-3) (gd 1-3, g-f, frm) 2000 AW 0-5: (7f 5) (Equi 3, Fibr 2)
Fair gelding, effective 7 to 8f, best at 8f, acted on gd to hrd - acted on Equi to Fibr, mostly wore blinkers (very effectively), liked left handed tracks, favoured tight tracks, and excelled at Brighton. Turf high 53 - 1st of 14 giving 5lb to Danzas (24 May Brighton RF 1419). AW high 36. (DEAD)
**E A Wheeler [6-64] M V Kirby (from S Mellor [0-12] Spt 1995).*

DARK SHADOWS BHB 60f **RR 62f** 4750[11]
5 b g Machiavellian (USA) 9.8f **(83)** - Instant Desire (USA) (Northern Dancer) 9.6f **(80)**
Form - 536310
Record 2000 - 1st:1 2nd:0 3rd:2 Ran:6
Win Prizemoney £2,941 *Total Prizemoney* £4,760
Wins * 2000 Aug Ripon (GD) H 12.3f 58 62 <
2000 Turf 1-6: (10f 2, 11f, 12f 1-2, 14f) (sft, gd 2, g-f 2, frm 1-1)
Average gelding, effective 10 to 12f, acts on gd to frm. Turf high 62 - 1st of 12 giving 20lb to Jonloz (7 Aug Ripon RF 3430).
**W Storey [1-10] D O Cremin.*

DARK SOCIETY BHB 69f **RR 71f** 5151[13]
2 b c Imp Society (USA) 7.1f **(63)** - No Candles Tonight (Star Appeal) 9.0f **(65)**
Form - 400
Record 2000 - 1st:0 2nd:0 3rd:0 Ran:3
Win Prizemoney £0 *Total Prizemoney* £257
2000 Turf 0-3: (6f 2, 7f) (g-s, gd 2)
Currently above-average colt. Turf high 71 (began Spt).
**P W Harris [0-3] Skelltools Ltd.*

DARK TROJAN (IRE) BHB 85f **RR 96f** 3454a[3]
4 b c Darshaan 11.9f **(81)** - Trojan Miss (Troy) 10.4f **(68)**
Form - 3
2000 Turf 0-1: (16f) (gd)
Scopey, very useful colt, effective 16f, acts on gd. (1st run) - 3rd of 26 giving 20lb to Gamekeeper (31 Jly Galway 16f gd RF 3454a).
**P Hughes in IRE [1-6] Mrs G T McKey (from Sir Michael Stoute [0-6] Oct 1999).*

DARK VICTOR (IRE) BHB 55f70a **RR 53df 70a** 5166[3]
4 b g Cadeaux Genereux 7.9f **(76)** - Dimmer (Kalaglow) 9.8f **(67)**
Form - 4857106623
Record 2000 - 1st:1 2nd:1 3rd:1 Ran:10
Win Prizemoney £3,926 *Total Prizemoney* £5,639
Wins * 2000 Apr Doncas (G-S) H 10.3f 47 53 <
2000 Turf 1-7: (8f 2, 10f 1-3, 11f, 12f) (sft, g-s 2, gd 1-3, frm) 2000 AW 0-3: (6f, 9f, 12f) (Fibr 3)
Above-average gelding, effective 8 to 10f, best at 10f, acts on sft to gd, best on gd, has worn blinkers. Turf high 53 - 1st of 20 getting 18lb from Achilles Wings (29 Apr Doncaster RF 0908). AW high 40.
**D Shaw [1-12] J C Fretwell.*

DARLING COREY BHB 68f **RR 66f** 566[12]
4 b f Caerleon (USA) 10.9f **(79)** - Tass (Soviet Star (USA))
Form - 0
Record 2000 - 1st:0 2nd:0 3rd:0 Ran:1
Pre2000 - 1st:0 2nd:1 3rd:0 Ran:3
Win Prizemoney £0 *Total Prizemoney* £1,628
2000 Turf 0-1: (10f) (g-f)
Scopey, average filly.
**E A L Dunlop [0-1] Lindy Regis & Geoff Howard-Spink (from R Charlton [0-3] Spt 1999).*

DARVAN BHB 50f **RR 57f** 549[9]
3 b g Efisio 7.7f **(69)** - Do You Miss Me (CAN) (El Gran Senor (USA)) 9.6f **(76)**
Form - 0
Record 2000 - 1st:0 2nd:0 3rd:0 Ran:1
Pre2000 - 1st:0 2nd:0 3rd:0 Ran:5
Win Prizemoney £0 *Total Prizemoney* £197
2000 Turf 0-1: (12f) (frm)
Scopey, fair gelding.
**M W Easterby [0-6] Guy Reed.*

DARWELL'S FOLLY (USA) BHB 40f42a **RR 37f 42a** 5077[18]
5 ch g Blushing John (USA) 8.9f **(75)** - Hispanolia (FR) (Kris) 9.5f **(73)**
Form - 30000
Record 2000 - 1st:0 2nd:0 3rd:1 Ran:5
Pre2000 - 1st:5 2nd:1 3rd:0 Ran:16
Win Prizemoney £15,985 *Total Prizemoney* £17,401
Wins * 1999 *Oct Wolver (STD) C* 7f 56
* 1999 Spt Leices (FRM) H 7f 62 66
* 1998 *Mar Wolver (STD) H* 7f 83 87 <
* 1998 *Feb Wolver (STD) H* 6f 77 82
* 1997 Jly Newcas (GD) 6f 79
2000 Turf 0-4: (7f 2, 8f, 10f) (g-s, gd, g-f, frm) 2000 AW 0-1: (7f) (Fibr)
Fair gelding, effective 7f, acts on frm - acts on Fibr, has worn blinkers. Turf high 37 (began Spt).
**M Johnston [5-21] S & P Darwell Ltd.*

DARWIN (IRE) RR 100+f 5124[4]
2 b c Danehill (USA) 9.1f **(79)** - Armorique (IRE) (Top Ville) 11.7f **(68)**
Form - 164
2000 Turf 1-3: (6f 1-1, 7f, 8f) (g-s 1-2)
Currently very useful colt. Turf high 100 (1st run) - 1st of 10 giving 5lb to Ventura (28 May Curragh RF 1580a). Most impressive on his Curragh debut at the end of May before being put away for an autumn campaign, he was a disappointing sixth to stablemate Beckett in the National Stakes, but was reported to have finished lame. Did too much in the testing ground in the Racing Post Trophy on his final start.
**A P O'Brien in IRE [1-3] M Tabor & Mrs John Magnier*

DARWIN TOWER BHB 55f52a **RR 61f 52a** 5169[2]
2 gr c Bin Ajwaad (IRE) - Floria Tosca **(14f)** (Petong) 6.6f **(58)**
Form - 00000022
Record 2000 - 1st:0 2nd:2 3rd:0 Ran:8
Win Prizemoney £0 *Total Prizemoney* £1,420
2000 Turf 0-8: (5f, 6f 5, 7f 2) (g-s 2, gd 3, g-f 2, frm)
Average colt, effective 6f, acts on g-s, has worn blinkers. Turf high 61.
**B W Murray [0-8] John Jackson.*

DARYABAD (IRE) BHB 54f67a **RR 56f 67a** 4929[6]
8 b g Thatching 7.8f **(69)** - Dayanata (Shirley Heights) 10.3f **(74)**
Form - 160738131336
Record 2000 - 1st:2 2nd:0 3rd:4 Ran:10
Pre2000 - 1st:4 2nd:2 3rd:1 Ran:29
Win Prizemoney £20,704 *Total Prizemoney* £26,801
Wins * 2000 Aug Yarmou (G-F) H 7f 50 55
*** 2000** Jly Yarmou (GD) H 7f 44 46
1999 *Nov Lingfi (STD) H* 7f 64 69
1999 *Oct Lingfi (STD)* 7f 59
1998 Jly Catter (GD) 7f 64
1996 Aug Redcar (G-F) H 7f 72 73 <
2000 Turf 2-9: (7f 2-6, 8f 3) (gd 1-2, g-f 1-3, frm 3, hrd) 2000 AW 0-1: (8f) (Equi)
Average gelding, effective 7 to 8f, best at 7f, - acts on Equi, often wears blinkers (very effectively). Turf high 56. (1st run) - 6th of 12 getting 4lb from Padhams Green (11 Oct Lingfield 8f Equi RF 4929).
**N A Graham [2-10] The Three Amigos (from R McGhin [3-17] Dec 1999).*

DASHIBA BHB 91f **RR 97f** 4598[14]
4 gr f Dashing Blade 7.9f **(80)** - Alsiba (Northfields (USA)) 9f **(72)**
Form - 30662570
Record 2000 - 1st:0 2nd:1 3rd:1 Ran:8
Pre2000 - 1st:2 2nd:3 3rd:6 Ran:15
Win Prizemoney £18,725 *Total Prizemoney* £37,751
Wins * 1999 Aug Goodwo (GD) H 9f 83 96 <
* 1999 Aug Sandow (GD) 10f 80
2000 Turf 0-8: (8f, 10f 6, 12f) (gd 3, g-f, frm 4)
Scopey, very useful filly, effective 9 to 10f, best at 10f, acts on g-f to frm, best on frm, likes tight tracks, excels at Sandown. Turf high 98 - 6th of 8 to Amalia (1 Jly Newcastle 10f frm RF 2445). Consistent. A useful filly, if somewhat difficult to win with, she is best around ten furlongs and was just touched off over that trip in a Salisbury listed race. **D R C Elsworth [2-23] J C Smith.*

DASHING BLUE BHB 89f **RR 91f** 4037[18]
7 ch g Dashing Blade 7.9f **(80)** - Blubella (Balidar) 7.9f **(63)**

Form - 060000
Record 2000 - 1st:0 2nd:0 3rd:0 Ran:6
Pre2000 - 1st:7 2nd:7 3rd:11 Ran:47
Win Prizemoney £61,056 *Total Prizemoney* £151,603
Wins * 1999 Jun Sandow (GD) 5f 103
* 1997 Oct Newmar (GD) L 5f 108
* 1997 Spt Doncas (G-F) H 5.6f 105 111 <
* 1997 Jly York (GD) H 5f 99 103
* 1996 Apr Sandow (GD) H 5f 93 94
2000 Turf 0-6: (5f 5, 6f) (gd 2, g-f 2, frm 2)
Useful gelding, effective 5f, acts on gd to frm, has worn blinkers. Turf high 92. Inconsistent. He does not win that often these days despite giving his all on every occasion, and finds winning in pattern company a bit too much for him. However, as he is a long way below his last winning mark, the Handicapper has given him a chance if he can regain his old form.
**I A Balding [7-53] Mrs Duncan Allen.*

DASHING CHIEF (IRE) BHB 70f RR 67f 2256[3]
5 b g Darshaan 11.9f **(81)** - Calaloo Sioux (USA) (Our Native (USA)) 11.2f **(63)**
Form - 3
Record 2000 - 1st:0 2nd:0 3rd:1 Ran:1
Pre2000 - 1st:1 2nd:0 3rd:3 Ran:14
Win Prizemoney £3,915 *Total Prizemoney* £12,215
Wins 1997 Oct Pontef (G-F) 10f 87 <
2000 AW 0-1: (12f) (Equi)
Average gelding. Becoming disappointing.
**W J Musson [0-5] Magnificent Seven (from M A Jarvis [1-10] Aug 1998).*

DASH OF MAGIC RR 18f 5060[6]
2 b f Magic Ring (IRE) 6.5f **(64)** - Praglia (IRE) **(59f)** (Darshaan) 9.9f **(84)**
Form - 6
Record 2000 - 1st:0 2nd:0 3rd:0 Ran:1
2000 Turf 0-1: (6f) (sft)
Currently poor filly. **E J Alston [0-1] 21st Century Racing.*

DATIN STAR BHB 51f RR 58f 4770[15]
2 ch f Inchinor 8.9f **(64)** - Halimah (Be My Guest (USA)) 9.3f **(67)**
Form - 606480
Record 2000 - 1st:0 2nd:0 3rd:0 Ran:6
Win Prizemoney £0 *Total Prizemoney* £213
2000 Turf 0-6: (6f, 7f 5) (g-s, g-f 3, frm, hrd)
Fair filly. Turf high 58. **D J Coakley [0-6] David Wilson.*

DATO STAR (IRE) BHB 89f RR 99?f 1129[12]
9 br g Accordion 11.3f **(75)** - Newgate Fairy (Flair Path) 7.8f **(79)**
Form - 0
Record 2000 - 1st:0 2nd:0 3rd:0 Ran:1
Pre2000 - 1st:1 2nd:2 3rd:3 Ran:12
Win Prizemoney £5,468 *Total Prizemoney* £24,553
Wins * 1998 Oct Ayr (HVY) H 13.1f 85 99 <
2000 Turf 0-1: (19f) (g-f)
Very useful gelding. Inconsistent.
**J M Jefferson [10-29] Kath Riley, Mrs M Guthrie & Joe Donald.*

DATURA BHB 74a RR 57f 2968[3]
3 b f Darshaan 11.9f **(81)** - Realize **(77f)** (Al Nasr (FR)) 9.3f **(68)**
Form - 806413
Record 2000 - 1st:1 2nd:0 3rd:1 Ran:5
Pre2000 - 1st:0 2nd:1 3rd:1 Ran:6
Win Prizemoney £3,168 *Total Prizemoney* £5,152
Wins * **2000** Jly Leices (G-F) H 8f 56 56 <
2000 Turf 1-5: (7f, 8f 1-2, 9f, 10f) (gd, g-f 2, frm 1-2)
Scopey, fair filly, effective 6 to 7f, acts on g-f to frm, has worn blinkers. Turf high 57.
**M L W Bell [1-5] Lord Hartington (from J H M Gosden [0-6] Nov 1999).*

DAUNTED (IRE) BHB 47f62a RR 60f 62a 5079[5]
4 b g Priolo (USA) 10.9f **(71)** - Dauntess (Formidable (USA)) 9.2f **(63)**
Form - 870275
Record 2000 - 1st:0 2nd:1 3rd:0 Ran:5
Pre2000 - 1st:3 2nd:4 3rd:4 Ran:25
Win Prizemoney £8,580 *Total Prizemoney* £16,901
Wins * 1999 *Jan Lingfi (STD) C 8f 83+*
* 1998 *Dec Lingfi (STD) 8f 84* <
* 1998 *Nov Lingfi (STD) 8f 80*
2000 Turf 0-1: (12f) (g-s) 2000 AW 0-4: (10f, 12f 3) (Equi 4)
Scopey, average gelding, effective 7 to 12f, - acts on AW, best on Fibr, mostly wears blinkers (effectively), prefers left handed tracks, favours tight tracks. AW high 65.
**G L Moore [3-31] David Allen.*

DAUNTING ASSEMBLY BHB 25f RR 18f 4009[10]
5 ch m Presidium 7.5f **(56)** - Dauntless Flight (Golden Mallard) 5.7f **(38)**
Form - 0
Record 2000 - 1st:0 2nd:0 3rd:0 Ran:1
Pre2000 - 1st:0 2nd:0 3rd:0 Ran:2
2000 Turf 0-1: (10f) (frm)
Poor filly. (DEAD) **B W Murray [0-3] B Murray.*

DAVEYSFIRE BHB 35f RR 26f 4381[12]
2 b f Gildoran 11.6f **(58)** - Doubtfire (Jalmood (USA)) 10.1f **(52)**
Form - 630
Record 2000 - 1st:0 2nd:0 3rd:1 Ran:3
Win Prizemoney £0 *Total Prizemoney* £309
2000 Turf 0-3: (5f, 6f, 8f) (gd, g-f 2)
Currently little account filly. Turf high 26.
**Miss L A Perratt [0-3] J A Davidson.*

DAVEY'S PANACEA (IRE) BHB 55f45a RR 52f 45a 4366[7]
3 ch f Paris House 5.9f **(64)** - Pampoushka (Pampabird) 7.5f **(73)**
Form - 2533377
Record 2000 - 1st:0 2nd:1 3rd:3 Ran:7
Win Prizemoney £0 *Total Prizemoney* £2,315
2000 Turf 0-7: (5f 4, 6f 3) (g-f 5, frm 2)
Fair filly, effective 5f, acts on g-f. Turf high 52 - 3rd of 10 getting 5lb from Santiburi Lad (19 Aug Ripon 5f g-f RF 3794).
**R D Wylie [0-7] Daveys Chemists (Lpool) Ltd.*

DAVID (USA) RR 1823a[3]
4 ch c Mt Livermore (USA) 7.7f **(90)** - Fateful Beauty (USA) (Turkoman (USA))
Form - 3
2000 AW 0-1: (9f) (Dirt)
Currently Group-class colt. (1st run) - 3rd of 8 getting 3lb from Running Stag (3 Jun Suffolk Downs 9f Dirt RF 1823a).
**B K Schwartz in USA [0-1].*

DAVID COPPERFIELD (USA) RR 108f 5210a[2]
3 br c Halo (USA) 10.9f **(67)** - Bannockburn (USA) (Count Brook (USA))
Form - 2
2000 Turf 0-1: (9f) (frm)
Currently Pattern-class colt. (1st run) - 2nd of 5 to Sign of Hope (21 Oct Santa Anita 9f frm RF 5210a). **J Shirreffs in USA [0-1].*

DAVIDE UMBRO (ITY) RR 107f 1636a[4]
3 b c In The Wings 11.2f **(77)** - Afreeta (ITY) (Afleet (CAN))
Form - 14
2000 Turf 1-2: (8f 1-1, 12f) (sft 1-1, g-f)
Currently Pattern-class colt. Turf high 107 (1st run) - 1st of 13 from Golden Indigo (30 Apr Capannelle RF 1032a). Surprise winner of the Italian 2000 Guineas, he kept the race on a technicality despite failing the dope test. **E Russo in ITY [1-2].*

DAVID WYNNE BHB 56f RR 51f 5099[13]
2 b c Dolphin Street (FR) - Statuette **(55f)** (Statoblest)
Form - 0
Record 2000 - 1st:0 2nd:0 3rd:0 Ran:1
2000 Turf 0-1: (7f) (gd)
Currently fair colt. **L M Cumani [0-1] Mrs Luca Cumani.*

DA VINCI (IRE) BHB 78f RR 81f 4751[6]
2 b c Inzar (USA) - Tuft Hill (Grundy) 10.3f **(65)**
Form - 17016
Record 2000 - 1st:2 2nd:0 3rd:0 Ran:5
Win Prizemoney £6,893 *Total Prizemoney* £6,893
Wins * **2000** Spt Hamilt (SFT) H 5f 70 81 <
* **2000** Jun Pontef (SFT) 5f 70+
2000 Turf 2-5: (5f 2-5) (g-s 1-2, gd 1-1, hrd 2)
Decent colt. Turf high 81 - 1st of 12 giving 25lb to Mr Pertemps (3 Spt Hamilton RF 4182). **J A Osborne [2-5] Andy Miller.*

DAVIS ROCK BHB 48f58a **RR 51f 58a** 4874[4]

6 ch m Rock City 8.8f **(62)** - Sunny Davis (USA)(Alydar (USA)) 9.1f **(76)**
Form - 55110166264
Record 2000 - 1st:3 2nd:1 3rd:0 Ran:9
Pre2000 - 1st:5 2nd:12 3rd:6 Ran:44
Win Prizemoney £20,990 *Total Prizemoney* £34,835

Wins * **2000** *Feb Southw (STD) H 8f 60 66*
* **2000** *Jan Southw (STD) C 7f 65*
* **2000** *Jan Southw (STD) C 7f 59*
* 1999 Nov Nottin (SFT) H 8.2f 45 51
* 1998 *Nov Wolver (STD) S 7f 64*
* 1998 *Jan Lingfi (STD) H 7f 64 67*
* 1997 Oct Folkes (GD) S 6.9f 52
1996 *Oct Wolver (STD)* 6f 69 <

2000 Turf 0-3: (7f 2, 8f) (g-s 2, g-f) 2000 AW 3-6: (7f 2-3, 8f 1-0) (Fibr 3 6)

Average mare, effective 7 to 8f, best at 7f, - acts on Fibr, likes left handed tracks, likes tight tracks. Turf high 47 (began Spt). AW high 66 - 1st of 9 getting 10lb from Rutland Chantry (28 Feb Southwell RF 0371) - also 1st of 11 giving 11lb to French Connection (17 Jan Southwell RF 0102). She is a consistent sort over seven furlongs on turf or sand.
**W R Muir [7-44] Gordon Cunningham (from R M McKellar [0-5] Aug 1998).*

DAWARI (IRE) BHB 07f **RR 82f** 4969[4]

2 b c In The Wings 11.2f **(77)** - Dawala (IRE) (Lashkari) 9.8f **(67)**
Form - 734
Record 2000 - 1st:0 2nd:0 3rd:1 Ran:3
Win Prizemoney £0 *Total Prizemoney* £1,478
2000 Turf 0-3: (8f 3) (gd 2, g-f)

Currently decent colt. Turf high 82 (began Spt) - 4th of 29 to Terrestrial (13 Oct Newmarket 8f gd RF 4969).
**Sir Michael Stoute [0-3] H H Aga Khan.*

DAWN BHB 60f **RR 68f** 4834[20]

3 b f Owington - Realisatrice (USA) (Raja Baba (USA)) 10f **(64)**
Form - 360360
Record 2000 - 1st:0 2nd:0 3rd:2 Ran:6
Pre2000 - 1st:0 2nd:0 3rd:1 Ran:3
Win Prizemoney £0 *Total Prizemoney* £2,055
2000 Turf 0-6: (5f 5, 6f) (g-s 2, gd 2, g-f, hrd)

Neat, average filly, effective 5f, acts on gd. Turf high 68 (1st run) - 3rd of 23 getting 5lb from Card Games (4 May Redcar 5f gd RF 1020). Slowly away in her performances to date, has yet to show any notable ability.
**J S Wainwright [0-6] Matthew Sharkey (from N A Graham [0-3] Jun 1999).*

DAWN ROMANCE (IRE) BHB 56f **RR 66f** 4108[6]

2 b br f Fraam - Whispering Dawn **(59f 64a)** (Then Again)
Form - 5757666
Record 2000 - 1st:0 2nd:0 3rd:0 Ran:7
2000 Turf 0-7: (6f 3, 7f 3, 8f) (gd 2, g-f, frm 4)

Average filly. Turf high 66. **M R Channon [0-7] W H Ponsonby.*

DAWN'S DANCER (IRE) BHB 60f **RR 58f** 2437[7]

3 b f Petardia 8.2f **(58)** - Cree's Figurine (Creetown) 6.9f **(50)**
Form - 0637
Record 2000 - 1st:0 2nd:0 3rd:1 Ran:4
Pre2000 - 1st:0 2nd:1 3rd:1 Ran:3
Win Prizemoney £0 *Total Prizemoney* £1,840
2000 Turf 0-4: (6f, 7f 3) (gd, frm 3)

Workmanlike, fair filly, effective 5 to 7f, acts on frm to hrd. Turf high 58 - 3rd of 11 giving 2lb to Andy's Elective (19 Jun Brighton 7f frm RF 2090).
**G C H Chung [0-7] Mrs D J Murphy.*

DAWN TRAVELLER (IRE) BHB 38f **RR 37f** 4403[10]

3 b f Blues Traveller (IRE) - All Alright (Alzao (USA)) 7.1f **(68)**
Form - 00500
Record 2000 - 1st:0 2nd:0 3rd:0 Ran:5
2000 Turf 0-5: (7f 2, 8f 2, 10f) (g-s, g-f 3, hrd)

Unfurnished, very moderate filly. Turf high 37.
**H J Collingridge [0-5] D Burke.*

DA WOLF (IRE) RR 49f 5065[12]

2 ch c Wolfhound (USA) 7.3f **(71)** - Lady Joyce (FR) (Galetto (FR)) 13.1f **(60)**
Form - 60
Record 2000 - 1st:0 2nd:0 3rd:0 Ran:2
2000 Turf 0-2: (6f, 8f) (g-s 2)

Currently moderate colt. Turf high 49 (began Spt).
**W R Muir [0-2] J Haim.*

DAY-BOY BHB 64f58a **RR 70f 58a** 5299[9]

4 b g Prince Sabo 6.6f **(64)** - Lady Day (FR) (Lightning (FR)) 7.9f **(74)**
Form - 3744400
Record 2000 - 1st:0 2nd:0 3rd:1 Ran:7
Pre2000 - 1st:1 2nd:0 3rd:1 Ran:9
Win Prizemoney £2,804 *Total Prizemoney* £6,251

Wins * 1998 May Ayr (GD) 6f 70 <

2000 Turf 0-7: (6f 2, 7f 4, 8f) (sft, g-s 3, gd, frm 2)

Scopey, above-average gelding, effective 7f, acts on g-s to frm, best on g-f, prefers tight tracks. Turf high 70 - 4th of 16 giving 9lb to Persian Fayre (1 Jun Ayr 7f frm RF 1617).
**Denys Smith [1-17] P & I Darling.*

DAYGLOW DANCER BHB 104f **RR 89f** 5315[2]

2 b c Fraam - Fading (Pharly (FR)) 9.8f **(68)**
Form - 1324252262
Record 2000 - 1st:1 2nd:5 3rd:1 Ran:10
Win Prizemoney £2,812 *Total Prizemoney* £23,712

Wins * **2000** Apr Nottin (HVY) 5.1f 63 <

2000 Turf 1-10: (5f 1-1, 6f 2, 7f 2, 8f 4, 9f) (sft 1-1, g-s 3, gd 2, g-f 2, frm 2)

Useful colt, effective 6 to 9f, best at 8f, acts on g-s to frm, best on g-s. Turf high 89 - 2nd of 7 to Panis (30 Spt Longchamp 9f gd RF 4838a). Consistent. Won a weak race on heavy ground and has shown much better form in small fields since, in the frame in Group races. **M R Channon [1-10] Surrey Laminators Ltd.*

DAY JOURNEY (USA) BHB 102f **RR 102f** 1217[6]

3 b c Dayjur (USA) 6.8f **(79)** - Dayflower (USA) (Majestic Light (USA)) 10.6f **(75)**
Form - 346
Record 2000 - 1st:0 2nd:0 3rd:1 Ran:3
Pre2000 - 1st:2 2nd:1 3rd:0 Ran:5
Win Prizemoney £9,972 *Total Prizemoney* £18,157

Wins * 1999 Aug Haydoc (G-S) 6f 87 <
* 1999 Jly Newmar (G-F) 6f 81+

2000 Turf 0-3: (6f 2, 7f) (g-s, gd, g-f)

Well made, very useful colt. Turf high 102. He ran well in a couple of six-furlong conditions events, and was not disgraced on his one run over seven. Not seen after May.
**E A L Dunlop [2-8] Maktoum Al Maktoum.*

DAYLILY (IRE) BHB 54f **RR 66f** 4871[6]

3 ch f Pips Pride 6.7f **(70)** - Leaping Water (Sure Blade (USA)) 11.3f **(67)**
Form - 006033235036
Record 2000 - 1st:0 2nd:1 3rd:4 Ran:12
Win Prizemoney £0 *Total Prizemoney* £3,537
2000 Turf 0-12: (5f 4, 6f 6, 7f, 8f) (sft 2, g-s 3, g-f 4, frm 3)

Strong, average filly, effective 5 to 6f, acts on g-f to frm. Turf high 66. Becoming disappointing. **T D Easterby [0-12] Mrs Jean Connew.*

DAYNABEE BHB 33f34a **RR 29f 34a** 5120[9]

5 b m Common Grounds 8.1f **(66)** - Don't Wary (FR) (Lomond (USA)) 8.8f **(65)**
Form - 54252515463540
Record 2000 - 1st:1 2nd:0 3rd:1 Ran:9
Pre2000 - 1st:4 2nd:7 3rd:4 Ran:43
Win Prizemoney £12,168 *Total Prizemoney* £19,819

Wins **2000** *Jan Wolver (STD) S 7f 44*
1998 Jly Windso (G-F) H 6f 52 56
1997 Aug Nottin (G-F) C 5.1f 64 <
1997 Jly Newcas (GD) S 6f 61
1997 Jly Leices (GD) S 5f 59

2000 AW 1-9: (6f 3, 7f 1-5, 8f) (Fibr 1-9)

Very moderate filly, effective 6 to 7f, best at 7f, acts on g-s to frm - acts on AW, best on Fibr, and does well at Lingfield. AW high 49 - 3rd of 11 to Comeoutofthefog (22 Feb Wolverhampton 7f Fibr RF

0336) - also 1st of 10 getting 10lb from C-Harry (25 Jan Wolverhampton RF 0152). Consistent.
**Miss S J Wilton [0-6] John Pointon and Sons (from A J McNae [2-29] Feb 2000).*

DAYS OF GRACE BHB 69f68a **RR 72f 68a** 5014[5]
5 gr m Wolfhound (USA) 7.3f **(71)** - Inshirah (USA) (Caro)
Form - 242123132200531142065
Record 2000 - 1st:4 2nd:5 3rd:3 Ran:19
Pre2000 - 1st:3 2nd:1 3rd:6 Ran:26
Win Prizemoney £19,530 *Total Prizemoney* £33,072
Wins *** 2000** Aug Lingfi (G-F) H 6f 59 62
*** 2000** Aug Salisb (G-F) H 6f 52 56
** **2000** Feb Wolver (STD) H 6f 64 61*
** **2000** Jan Southw (STD) H 6f 61 64*
* 1999 *Oct Wolver (STD) H 6f 57 60*
* 1999 *Spt Southw (STD) H 6f 50 52*
1997 May Redcar (FRM) 5f 69 <
2000 Turf 2-10: (6f 2-8, 7f 2) (gd 5, g-f 1-3, frm 1-2) 2000 AW 2-9: (6f 2-8, 7f) (Equi 2, Fibr 2-7)
Above-average filly, effective 6f, acts on gd to frm - acts on Fibr, prefers left handed tracks, prefers tight tracks, excels at Wolverhampton and Southwell, does well at Salisbury. Turf high 72 - 6th of 17 getting 10lb from Fire Dome (27 Spt Salisbury 6f gd RF 4691). AW high 67 - also 1st of 9 getting 2lb from Muja's Magic (7 Jan Southwell RF 0041).
**L MontagueHall [6-32] Stephen & Michelle Bayless (from M Meade [1-13] Jly 1998).*

DAYS OF THUNDER BHB 20f40a **RR 31f 40a** 395[10]
12 ch g Vaigly Great - Silent Prayer (Queen's Hussar) 11.6f **(58)**
Form - 0
Record 2000 - 1st:0 2nd:0 3rd:0 Ran:1
Pre2000 - 1st:0 2nd:0 3rd:0 Ran:11
Win Prizemoney £0 *Total Prizemoney* £235
2000 AW 0-1: (12f) (Fibr)
Very moderate gelding. (DEAD)
**Mrs P Ford [0-7] Advantage Chemicals Holdings Ltd (from J White [4-23] Mar 1995).*

DAY STAR BHB 67f64a **RR 65f 64a** 119[10]
4 b f Dayjur (USA) 6.8f **(79)** - Krisalya (Kris) 9.5f **(73)**
Form - 0
Record 2000 - 1st:0 2nd:0 3rd:0 Ran:1
Pre2000 - 1st:1 2nd:0 3rd:0 Ran:6
Win Prizemoney £4,670 *Total Prizemoney* £4,948
Wins * 1999 Oct Redcar (GD) H 6f 62 65 <
2000 AW 0-1: (6f) (Equi)
Unfurnished, average filly, effective 6f, acts on frm.
**C F Wall [1-7] A E Oppenheimer.*

DAZZLING DAISY BHB 39f **RR 39f** 4679[12]
3 b f Shareef Dancer (USA) 10.1f **(67)** - Mariette (Blushing Scribe (USA)) 6f **(45)**
Form - 44060
Record 2000 - 1st:0 2nd:0 3rd:0 Ran:5
Win Prizemoney £0 *Total Prizemoney* £444
2000 Turf 0-5: (8f 3, 10f, 12f) (g-s, g-f 4)
Neat, very moderate filly. Turf high 40 (began Aug).
**Pat Mitchell [0-5] Miss H M A Omersa.*

DAZZLING QUINTET BHB 43f38a **RR 47f 38a** 5112[12]
4 ch f Superlative 8.8f **(57)** - Miss Display (Touch Paper) 6.8f **(57)**
Form - 67210000
Record 2000 - 1st:1 2nd:1 3rd:0 Ran:8
Pre2000 - 1st:1 2nd:1 3rd:2 Ran:16
Win Prizemoney £5,584 *Total Prizemoney* £8,158
Wins *** 2000** Jun Beverl (G-F) H 5f 43 47
* 1998 Jly Beverl (GD) 5f 78 <
2000 Turf 1-8: (5f 1-8) (gd 3, g-f 2, frm, hrd 1-2)
Moderate filly, effective 5 to 6f, best at 5f, acts on gd to hrd. Turf high 47 - 1st of 15 getting 3lb from Marino Street (14 Jun Beverley RF 1954). **C Smith [2-24] Roman Bath V.*

DEAD AIM (IRE) BHB 45f **RR 33f** 3270[6]
6 b g Sadler's Wells (USA) 11.3f **(87)** -Dead Certain (Absalom) 7.2f **(58)**
Form - 06
Record 2000 - 1st:0 2nd:0 3rd:0 Ran:2
Pre2000 - 1st:1 2nd:2 3rd:4 Ran:17
Win Prizemoney £3,467 *Total Prizemoney* £7,889
Wins 1997 Aug Windso (G-F) H 11.6f 75 78 <
2000 Turf 0-2: (11f, 12f) (gd, g-f)
Very moderate gelding, has worn blinkers. Turf high 33 (began Jly). Becoming disappointing.
**J J Quinn [0-2] Mrs Karan Ridley (from Mrs J Brown [0-8] Jly 1999).*

DEADLY NIGHTSHADE (IRE) RR 96?f 1261[23]
4 b f Night Shift (USA) 8.1f **(73)** - Dead Certain (Absalom) 7.2f **(58)**
Form - 00
Record 2000 - 1st:0 2nd:0 3rd:0 Ran:2
Pre2000 - 1st:2 2nd:1 3rd:0 Ran:5
Win Prizemoney £7,146 *Total Prizemoney* £16,171
Wins * 1998 Spt Goodwo (G-F) 6f 88+ <
* 1998 Aug Bath (FRM) 5.1f 74+
2000 Turf 0-2: (5f 2) (gd, frm)
Scopey, very useful filly. Turf high 78. **D R C Elsworth [2-7] M Tabor & Mrs John Magnier.*

DEADLY SERIOUS BHB 56a **RR 42f** 1909[7]
4 ch c Emarati (USA) 6.6f **(63)** - Bentinck Hotel (Red God) 8.5f **(65)**
Form - 433807
Record 2000 - 1st:0 2nd:0 3rd:2 Ran:6
Win Prizemoney £0 *Total Prizemoney* £1,009
2000 Turf 0-2: (5f, 6f) (g-f, frm) 2000 AW 0-4: (6f 3, 7f) (Equi 2, Fibr 2)
Scopey, fair colt. Turf high 42. AW high 51.
**D R C Elsworth [0-6] G V Wright.*

DEAR DAUGHTER RR 82f 5136[4]
2 ch f Polish Precedent (USA) 9f **(73)** - Darayna (IRE) (Shernazar) 10.2f **(73)**
Form - 34
Record 2000 - 1st:0 2nd:0 3rd:1 Ran:2
Win Prizemoney £0 *Total Prizemoney* £1,021
2000 Turf 0-2: (7f, 8f) (g-s, frm)
Currently decent filly. Turf high 82 (1st run) (began Aug) - 3rd of 11 to Up On Points (31 Aug Salisbury 7f frm RF 4129).
**Sir Michael Stoute [0-2] Philip Newton.*

DEAR GIRL (IRE) RR 81+f 4216[3]
3 b f Fairy King (USA) 7.7f **(75)** - Alidiva (Chief Singer) 8.9f **(66)**
Form - 3
Record 2000 - 1st:0 2nd:0 3rd:1 Ran:1
Win Prizemoney £0 *Total Prizemoney* £642
2000 Turf 0-1: (10f) (frm)
Workmanlike, currently decent filly. (1st run) - 3rd of 17 to Jalisco (5 Spt Leicester 10f frm RF 4216).
**H R A Cecil [0-1] Greenbay Stables Ltd.*

DEAR PICKLES BHB 72f82a **RR 67f 82a** 4760[4]
2 b f Piccolo - Freddie's Recall **(27f)** (Warrshan (USA))
Form - 6284
Record 2000 - 1st:0 2nd:1 3rd:0 Ran:4
Win Prizemoney £0 *Total Prizemoney* £1,140
2000 Turf 0-3: (6f 2, 7f) (g-s, gd, g-f) 2000 AW 0-1: (6f) (Fibr)
Useful filly. Turf high 67 (began Aug) - 2nd of 9 getting 5lb from Whale Beach (26 Aug Windsor 6f g-f RF 4001). (1st run) - 4th of 13 to Ella's Pal (30 Spt Wolverhampton 6f Fibr RF 4760).
**J G Portman [0-4] Christopher Shankland.*

DEAR PRUDENCE BHB 38f **RR 57f** 763[16]
4 b f Puissance 7.1f **(60)** - Coir 'a' Ghaill (Jalmood (USA)) 10.1f **(52)**
Form - 00
Record 2000 - 1st:0 2nd:0 3rd:0 Ran:2
Pre2000 - 1st:0 2nd:0 3rd:0 Ran:3
2000 Turf 0-2: (12f, 15f) (g-s, frm)
Leggy, fair filly. Turf high 8. **J G Portman [0-5] Mrs Heather Murat.*

DEBBIE'S WARNING BHB 80f **RR 94?f** 4991[15]
4 b c Warning 8.1f **(77)** - Lomond Blossom (Lomond (USA)) 8.8f **(65)**
Form - 064076005000
Record 2000 - 1st:0 2nd:0 3rd:0 Ran:12
Pre2000 - 1st:1 2nd:1 3rd:2 Ran:9
Win Prizemoney £3,907 *Total Prizemoney* £12,468
Wins * 1999 May Kempto (G-F) 8f 80 <

2000 Turf 0-11: (6f 3, 7f 4, 8f 3, 10f) (sft, gd 6, g-f 2, frm 2) 2000 AW 0-1: (8f) (Fibr)

Tall, useful colt, effective 8f, acts on g-f to frm. Turf high 97. Becoming disappointing. Unraced at two, he looked a Group-class horse in the spring of 1999, but lost his way after being set a series of impossible tasks. Tried at a variety of trips, he ran several good races in handicap company last season. Looks best at around seven furlongs, and has slipped to a competitive mark.

**K Mahdi [1-21] Greenfield Stud.*

DEBRIEF (IRE) RR 3703[12]

2 b g Brief Truce (USA) 9.1f **(73)** - Dahsala (Top Ville) 11.7f **(68)**

Form - 0

Record 2000 - 1st:0 2nd:0 3rd:0 Ran:1

2000 Turf 0-1: (7f) (frm)

Currently very poor gelding.

**Mrs P N Dutfield [0-1] Theruened Partnership.*

DEB'S SON BHB 48f RR 56f 3776[10]

3 b g Minster Son 10.9f **(56)** - Deb's Ball **(43f)** (Glenstal (USA)) 10.1f **(64)**

Form - 6660

Record 2000 - 1st:0 2nd:0 3rd:0 Ran:4
Pre2000 - 1st:0 2nd:0 3rd:0 Ran:3

Win Prizemoney £0 *Total Prizemoney* £269

2000 Turf 0-4: (10f, 12f, 14f, 16f) (gd 2, g-f 2)

Leggy, fair gelding. Turf high 56. **D Moffatt [0-7] & Mrs A G Milligan.*

DECARCHY (USA) BHB 94f RR 90f 1484[3]

3 b c Distant View (USA) - Toussaud (USA) (El Gran Senor (USA)) 9.6f **(76)**

Form - 53

Record 2000 - 1st:0 2nd:0 3rd:1 Ran:2
Pre2000 - 1st:1 2nd:0 3rd:0 Ran:1

Win Prizemoney £3,752 *Total Prizemoney* £5,492

Wins * 1999 Spt Yarmou (G-S) 7f 76++ <

2000 Turf 0-2: (8f, 10f) (gd 2)

Scopey, currently useful colt. Turf high 90. Closely related to Chester House, he won impressively at Yarmouth on his only airing at two in 1999, but was disappointing twice at Doncaster in the spring and was not seen afterwards. **H R A Cecil [1-3] K Abdulla.*

DECEITFUL BHB 63f RR 65f 2564[4]

2 ch g Most Welcome 8.6f **(66)** - Sure Care **(66f 49a)** (Caerleon (USA)) 8.6f **(71)**

Form - 134

Record 2000 - 1st:1 2nd:0 3rd:1 Ran:3

Win Prizemoney £2,278 *Total Prizemoney* £3,398

Wins * 2000 Jun Bright (FRM) 5.3f 60 <

2000 Turf 1-3: (5f 1-1, 6f 2) (g-f 2, frm 1-1)

Currently average gelding. Turf high 65 - also 1st of 7 giving 5lb to London Eye (19 Jun Brighton RF 2085).

**Sir Mark Prescott [1-3] A S Reid.*

DECEIVES THE EYE BHB 56f RR 34f 2419[6]

2 b g Dancing Spree (USA) 8f **(59)** - Lycius Touch **(41f 40a)** (Lycius (USA))

Form - 245716

Record 2000 - 1st:1 2nd:1 3rd:0 Ran:6

Win Prizemoney £1,813 *Total Prizemoney* £2,340

Wins * 2000 *Jun Wolver (STD) S 6f 65* <

2000 Turf 0-2: (5f, 6f) (g-s, gd) 2000 AW 1-4: (5f, 6f 1-2, 7f) (Fibr 1-4)

Average gelding, effective 6f, - acts on Fibr, has worn blinkers. Turf high 34. AW high 65 - 1st of 8 from Running For Me (21 Jun Wolverhampton RF 2176). **J G Given [1-6] Mrs Trude Cutler.*

DECISION MAID (USA) BHB 97f RR 101f 2208[7]

3 b f Diesis 9f **(80)** - Robellino Miss (USA) (Robellino (USA)) 7.6f **(80)**

Form - 747

Record 2000 - 1st:0 2nd:0 3rd:0 Ran:3
Pre2000 - 1st:1 2nd:0 3rd:0 Ran:2

Win Prizemoney £4,987 *Total Prizemoney* £6,386

Wins * 1999 Oct Lingfi (HVY) 7f 81+ <

2000 Turf 0-3: (7f, 8f 2) (g-s, gd 2)

Scopey, very useful filly. Turf high 101 - 4th of 6 getting 3lb from Corinium (25 May Goodwood 8f g-s RF 1436). She was not easy to place and faced some stiff tasks.

**G Wragg [1-5] The Eclipse Partnership - 2.*

DEE DIAMOND (USA) BHB 31f RR 46f 5162[14]

3 b f Eagle Eyed (USA) - Noumea (USA) (Plugged Nickle (USA)) 7.8f **(68)**

Form - 8075800

Record 2000 - 1st:0 2nd:0 3rd:0 Ran:7
Pre2000 - 1st:0 2nd:0 3rd:0 Ran:2

Win Prizemoney £0 *Total Prizemoney* £248

2000 Turf 0-7: (8f, 10f 2, 11f, 12f 2, 16f) (sft, g-s, gd 2, g-f, frm 2)

Scopey, moderate filly. Turf high 46.

**Andrew Turnell [0-10] Mrs Claire Hollowood.*

DEEP BLUE RR 60?f 5198[1]

3 b c Lake Coniston (IRE) - Billie Blue (Ballad Rock) 7.8f **(63)**

Form - 1

Record 2000 - 1st:1 2nd:0 3rd:0 Ran:1
Pre2000 - 1st:0 2nd:2 3rd:1 Ran:5

Win Prizemoney £3,006 *Total Prizemoney* £5,996

Wins * 2000 Oct Windso (HVY) 6f 47 <

2000 Turf 1-1: (6f 1-1) (gd 1-1)

Light-framed, average colt, effective 5f, acts on g-s to g-f. (1st run). **Dr J D Scargill [1-6] R A Dalton.*

DEE PEE TEE CEE (IRE) BHB 72f RR 67f 5323[10]

6 b g Tidaro (USA) 8.2f **(75)** - Silver Glimpse (Petingo) 11f **(72)**

Form - 00000

Record 2000 - 1st:0 2nd:0 3rd:0 Ran:5
Pre2000 - 1st:11 2nd:0 3rd:1 Ran:31

Win Prizemoney £66,263 *Total Prizemoney* £67,602

Wins								
* 1999	Aug	York	(GD)	H	11.9f	82	86	<
* 1999	Jun	Hamilt	(GD)	H	9.2f	70	82	
* 1999	Jun	York	(G-S)	H	8.9f	70	78	
* 1999	Jun	Pontef	(SFT)	H	10f	63	74+	
* 1999	Jun	Cheste	(SFT)	H	10.3f	63	66	
* 1997	Jly	Mussel	(GD)	H	8f	62	74+	
* 1997	Jly	Beverl	(HVY)	H	8.5f	62	74	
* 1997	Jun	Carlis	(GD)		8f		65	
* 1997	Jun	Redcar	(GD)	H	9f	54	58	
* 1997	Jun	Beverl	(SFT)	H	7.5f	46	54	
* 1996	Jun	Redcar	(G-F)	S	7f		59+	

2000 Turf 0-5: (8f 2, 9f, 12f 2) (hvy, sft 3, frm)

Average gelding, effective 9 to 12f, best at 9f, acts on gd to g-f, best on g-f, likes left handed tracks, likes tight tracks. Turf high 67. Inconsistent. Enjoyed a fine season in '99 and carried on the good work over hurdles, but was well below-par on the level in 2000.

**M W Easterby [13-44] Mrs M E Curtis.*

DEEP SPACE (IRE) BHB 104f RR 106f 4376[3]

5 br g Green Desert (USA) 7.8f **(78)** - Dream Season (USA) (Mr Prospector (USA)) 8.8f **(78)**

Form - 63543013

Record 2000 - 1st:1 2nd:0 3rd:3 Ran:8
Pre2000 - 1st:5 2nd:3 3rd:0 Ran:21

Win Prizemoney £88,578 *Total Prizemoney* £107,377

Wins								
*** 2000**	Aug	Yarmou	(G-F)		6f		105+	
* 1999	Aug	Nottin	(G-F)		6.1f		106	<
* 1999	Jun	Ascot	(G-F)	H	6f	88	97	
* 1999	May	Lingfi	(G-F)	H	7f	82	88	
* 1998	Aug	Newmar	(FRM)	H	6f	79	85	
* 1998	Jly	Sandow	(GD)	H	5f	73	79	

2000 Turf 1-8: (6f 1-8) (g-s, gd 1-3, g-f 2, frm 2)

Pattern-class gelding, effective 6f, acts on g-s to frm, best on gd, excels at Yarmouth. Turf high 106 - also 1st of 6 from Dancing Maestro (27 Aug Yarmouth RF 4025). Consistent. A narrow winner of the Wokingham in '99, he ran well in listed company and some hot handicaps before landing a minor race at Yarmouth.

**E A L Dunlop [6-29] Maktoum Al Maktoum.*

DEEP WATER (USA) BHB 65f RR 69f 1492[7]

6 b g Diesis 9f **(80)** - Water Course (USA) (Irish River (FR)) 8.6f **(78)**

Form - 27

Record 2000 - 1st:0 2nd:1 3rd:0 Ran:2
Pre2000 - 1st:0 2nd:1 3rd:4 Ran:8

Win Prizemoney £0 *Total Prizemoney* £4,216

2000 Turf 0-2: (11f, 14f) (g-s, gd)

Average gelding. Turf high 49.

**M D Hammond [4-11] The County Set (from P F I Cole [0-8] Oct 1997).*

DEFIANCE BHB 25f20a **RR 42f 20a** 5122[17]
5 b g Warning 8.1f **(77)** - Princess Athena (Ahonoora) 8.1f **(73)**
Form - 00008700
Record 2000 - 1st:0 2nd:0 3rd:0 Ran:8
Pre2000 - 1st:0 2nd:0 3rd:2 Ran:11
Win Prizemoney £0 *Total Prizemoney* £1,032
2000 Turf 0-7: (5f, 6f 2, 7f 2, 8f 2) (g-s, g-f 2, frm 4) 2000 AW 0-1: (6f) (Fibr)
Moderate gelding, has worn blinkers. Turf high 42. Inconsistent.
**A P James [0-15] Anne & Mahendra Ramkaran (from B W Hills [0-4] May 1998).*

DEFIANT BHB 69f **RR 72f** 5022[5]
3 b c Indian Ridge 7.6f **(74)** - Centaine **(100f)** (Royal Academy (USA))
Form - 075
Record 2000 - 1st:0 2nd:0 3rd:0 Ran:3
2000 Turf 0-3: (7f 2, 8f) (g-s 2, g-f)
Workmanlike, currently above-average colt. Turf high 72 (began Spt). **P W D'Arcy [0-3] & Mrs G M Vergette.*

DEFINITE GUEST (IRE) BHB 66f **RR 67f** 4808[16]
2 gr c Definite Article - Nicea (IRE) (Dominion) 8.5f **(63)**
Form - 6040
Record 2000 - 1st:0 2nd:0 3rd:0 Ran:4
Win Prizemoney £0 *Total Prizemoney* £282
2000 Turf 0-4: (6f 2, 7f 2) (g-s, gd, frm 2)
Average colt. Turf high 67 (began Jly).
**G G Margarson [0-4] John Guest.*

DEFINITE RETURN (IRE) BHB 55f **RR 64f** 5066[12]
2 ch f Definite Article - Keen Note (Sharpo) 7.7f **(59)**
Form - 740
Record 2000 - 1st:0 2nd:0 3rd:0 Ran:3
2000 Turf 0-2: (6f, 8f) (g-s, gd) 2000 AW 0-1: (8f) (Fibr)
Currently average filly. Turf high 64 (began Spt).
**B Palling [0-3] B A Evans.*

DEGREE OF POWER BHB 52f46a **RR 46f 46a** 5115[11]
2 b f Sure Blade (USA) 10.6f **(66)** - One Degree (Crooner) 9.9f **(49)**
Form - 4000
Record 2000 - 1st:0 2nd:0 3rd:0 Ran:4
Win Prizemoney £0 *Total Prizemoney* £273
2000 Turf 0-3: (5f, 7f 2) (sft, g-f 2) 2000 AW 0-1: (8f) (Fibr)
Moderate filly. Turf high 46.
**Miss D A McHale [0-3] Manor Boys (from A W Carroll [0-1] May 2000).*

DEHOUSH (USA) BHB 104f **RR 110+f** 3583[7]
4 ch c Diesis 9f **(80)** - Dream Play (USA) (Blushing Groom (FR)) 10.3f **(76)**
Form - 1037
Record 2000 - 1st:1 2nd:0 3rd:1 Ran:4
Pre2000 - 1st:2 2nd:1 3rd:1 Ran:7
Win Prizemoney £24,519 *Total Prizemoney* £44,927
Wins * 2000 May Newbur (SFT) 10f 110+ <
* 1999 Apr Kempto (GD) L 8f 104
* 1998 Jun Newmar (GD) 6f 76+
2000 Turf 1-4: (10f 1-3, 11f) (g-s 1-1, gd 2, g-f)
Scopey, Group-class colt, effective 8 to 10f, best at 10f, acts on g-s to g-f, best on g-s. Turf high 110 (1st run) - 1st of 5 getting 12lb from Compton Ace (31 May Newbury RF 1590). He goes well fresh, and began this year with a victory in a Newbury conditions race. Decent efforts subsequently.
**A C Stewart [3-11] Sheikh Ahmed Al Maktoum.*

DEIDAMIA (USA) BHB 60f **RR 60f** 4751[8]
2 b f Dayjur (USA) 6.8f **(79)** - Home Again (USA) (Forty Niner (USA))
Form - 4748
Record 2000 - 1st:0 2nd:0 3rd:0 Ran:4
Win Prizemoney £0 *Total Prizemoney* £600
2000 Turf 0-4: (5f 4) (g-s, g-f 2, hrd)
Average filly. Turf high 60 (began Aug).
**P W Harris [0-4] Mrs A Palmer & Mrs S Harris.*

DEKELSMARY BHB 45f37a **RR 43f 37a** 113[11]
5 b m Komaite (USA) 6.9f **(61)** - Final Call (Town Crier) 10.2f **(55)**
Form - 860
Record 2000 - 1st:0 2nd:0 3rd:0 Ran:2
Pre2000 - 1st:2 2nd:2 3rd:5 Ran:34
Win Prizemoney £5,934 *Total Prizemoney* £10,214
Wins * 1999 Aug Thirsk (G-F) H 5f 41 43
* 1998 *Nov Southw (STD) H 7f 45 48* <
2000 AW 0-2: (6f, 7f) (Fibr 2)
Moderate filly, effective 5 to 7f, best at 5f, acts on hrd - acts on Fibr, has worn blinkers, likes left handed tracks, likes tight tracks. AW high 19. **J Balding [2-36] Derrick Moss.*

DELAMERE (USA) RR 84f 4190[4]
3 b f Brocco (USA) - Shelia Dacre (USA) (Nureyev (USA)) 8.7f **(78)**
Form - 643124
Record 2000 - 1st:1 2nd:1 3rd:1 Ran:6
Pre2000 - 1st:0 2nd:0 3rd:0 Ran:1
Win Prizemoney £3,848 *Total Prizemoney* £7,226
Wins * 2000 Jly Ayr (G-F) 10f 81 <
2000 Turf 1-6: (7f, 8f, 10f 1-3, 12f) (gd 2, g-f 2, frm 1-2)
Decent filly, effective 8 to 12f, best at 10f, acts on gd to frm, best on g-f. Turf high 84 - 4th of 7 getting 18lb from Ulundi (3 Spt Kempton 12f g-f RF 4190) - also 1st of 5 getting 5lb from Tigre (17 Jly Ayr RF 2874).
**J H M Gosden [1-6] R E Sangster, H Lester & R Clifton (from A G Foster [0-1] Oct 1999).*

DELAWARE TOWNSHIP (USA) RR 5328a[10]
4 ch c Notebook (USA) - Sunny Mimosa (USA) (Sunny North (USA))
Form - 0
2000 AW 0-1: (6f) (Dirt)
Currently Pattern-class colt. **B Perkins in USA [0-1] Kinsman Stable.*

DELEGATE BHB 88f85a **RR 92f 85a** 5127[5]
7 ch g Polish Precedent (USA) 9f **(73)** - Dangora (USA) (Sovereign Dancer (USA)) 11.2f **(68)**
Form - 864202005
Record 2000 - 1st:0 2nd:2 3rd:0 Ran:9
Pre2000 - 1st:0 2nd:1 3rd:2 Ran:7
Win Prizemoney £0 *Total Prizemoney* £25,937
2000 Turf 0-9: (5f 2, 6f 6, 7f) (g-s, gd 6, g-f, frm)
Useful gelding, effective 6f, acts on gd. Turf high 92. Without a win for a long time, there are not many miles on the clock and his performances last term suggest there are still races to be won with him. **N A Callaghan [0-9] Mrs P Reditt (from J E Banks [0-6] Oct 1999).*

DEL MAR SHOW (USA) RR 105f 3159a[3]
3 b c Theatrical 11.5f **(78)** - Prankstress (Foolish Pleasure (USA)) 8.9f **(72)**
Form - 3
2000 Turf 0-1: (10f) (frm)
Currently Pattern-class colt. (1st run) - 3rd of 4 to Pine Dance (23 Jly Arlington Park 10f frm RF 3159a). **W Mott in USA [0-1].*

DELPHYLLIA BHB 45f **RR 59f** 5067[12]
2 b f Mind Games - Euphyllia **(52f 44a)** (Superpower)
Form - 007000
Record 2000 - 1st:0 2nd:0 3rd:0 Ran:6
2000 Turf 0-6: (5f 4, 6f 2) (g-s, gd 3, g-f, frm)
Fair filly. Turf high 59. **G G Margarson [0-6] The Del Boys.*

DELTA GEORGIA BHB 40f **RR 49f** 1548[12]
4 ch f Tina's Pet 7.4f **(56)** - Bacolet (Dominion) 8.5f **(63)**
Form - 000
Record 2000 - 1st:0 2nd:0 3rd:0 Ran:3
Pre2000 - 1st:0 2nd:1 3rd:0 Ran:4
Win Prizemoney £0 *Total Prizemoney* £656
2000 Turf 0-3: (6f, 8f, 11f) (hvy, gd, g-f)
Moderate filly. Turf high 24. **A Bailey [0-7] David English.*

DELTA SOLEIL (USA) BHB 50f70a **RR 43f 70a** 2838[9]
8 b h Riverman (USA) 9.7f **(78)** - Sunny Roberta (USA) (Robellino (USA)) 7.6f **(80)**
Form - 000000
Record 2000 - 1st:0 2nd:0 3rd:0 Ran:6
Pre2000 - 1st:4 2nd:3 3rd:2 Ran:46
Win Prizemoney £27,054 *Total Prizemoney* £39,424
Wins * 1999 May Kempto (GD) H 6f 71 76
* 1998 Jly Newbur (G-F) H 6f 71 75

* 1998 Jun Salisb (G-S) H 6f 65 71
2000 Turf 0-6: (6f 5, 7f) (gd, g-f, frm 4)
Average horse, effective 6f, acts on frm, has worn blinkers. Turf high 43.
**V Soane [3-30] American Quartet (from P W Harris [1-22] Nov 1997).*

DELTA SONG BHB 88f **RR 87f** 4690[2]
2 b f Delta Dancer - Song of Gold (Song) 7.2f **(61)**
Form - 12112
Record 2000 - 1st:3 2nd:2 3rd:0 Ran:5
Win Prizemoney £11,449 *Total Prizemoney* £14,697
Wins * 2000 Spt Goodwo (GD) H 6f 74 87 <
*** 2000** Spt Epsom (GD) H 6f 74 81
2000 Aug Lingfi (G-F) S 6f 59+
2000 Turf 3-5: (5f, 6f 3-4) (gd 1-3, g-f 1-1, frm 1-1)
Useful filly. Turf high 87 (began Aug) - 2nd of 6 getting 1lb from Inspector General (27 Spt Salisbury 6f gd RF 4690) - also 1st of 14 giving 2lb to Soldier On (8 Spt Goodwood RF 4305). Enjoyed a good season, winning three times at six furlongs and running well in defeat.
**G L Moore [2-4] Richard Green (Fine Paintings) (from W R Muir [1-1] Aug 2000).*

DEMOCRACY (IRE) BHB 42f53a **RR 51f 53a** 3834[11]
4 ch g Common Grounds 8.1f **(66)** - Inonder (Belfort (FR)) 6.8f **(63)**
Form - 000537700005340400
Record 2000 - 1st:0 2nd:0 3rd:2 Ran:17
Pre2000 - 1st:1 2nd:3 3rd:5 Ran:13
Win Prizemoney £3,779 *Total Prizemoney* £10,339
Wins 1999 Spt Bath (FRM) 5.7f 78 <
2000 Turf 0-11: (5f, 7f 5, 8f 5) (sft, gd 3, g-f 2, frm 5) 2000 AW 0-6: (6f, 7f 2, 8f 3) (Equi, Fibr 5)
Lengthy, fair gelding, effective 6 to 9f, acts on gd to frm, best on frm, often wears blinkers (extremely effectively), likes Brighton. Turf high 51. AW high 52.
**P G Murphy [0-18] The Golden Anorak Partnership (from R Hannon [1-12] Spt 1999).*

DEMOLITION JO BHB 70f63a **RR 78?f 63a** 4183[7]
5 gr m Petong 7.6f **(58)** - Fire Sprite (Mummy's Game) 8.2f **(60)**
Form - 8060006027
Record 2000 - 1st:0 2nd:1 3rd:0 Ran:9
Pre2000 - 1st:3 2nd:13 3rd:4 Ran:58
Win Prizemoney £13,160 *Total Prizemoney* £48,994
Wins 1998 Jun Cheste (G-S) H 7f 69 71
1997 Oct Newmar (G-S) H 6f 77 81 <
1997 Aug Mussel (G-F) 7.1f 73
2000 Turf 0-9: (5f, 6f 6, 8f 2) (g-s, gd 3, g-f 4, frm)
Above-average filly, effective 5 to 6f, best at 6f, acts on gd to g-f, best on gd, mostly wears blinkers. Turf high 84 - 6th of 7 getting 5lb from Yorkies Boy (6 Aug Chester 6f g-f RF 3415). Inconsistent.
**W M Brisbourne [0-5] John Pugh (from P D Evans [3-62] May 2000).*

DEMOPHILOS **RR 90+f** 4701[1]
2 b c Dr Devious (IRE) 9.9f **(74)** - Graecia Magna (USA) (Private Account (USA)) 8.5f **(74)**
Form - 1
Record 2000 - 1st:1 2nd:0 3rd:0 Ran:1
Win Prizemoney £5,102 *Total Prizemoney* £5,102
Wins * 2000 Spt Newmar (GD) 7f 90+ <
2000 Turf 1-1: (7f 1-1) (g-f 1-1)
Currently useful colt. (1st run) - 1st of 17 from Big Moment (28 Spt Newmarket RF 4701). **Mrs A J Perrett [1-1] Athos Christodoulou.*

DENA BHB 61f **RR 69+f** 5168[5]
3 b f Deploy 11.4f **(67)** - Isabena (Star Appeal) 9.6f **(65)**
Form - 025
Record 2000 - 1st:0 2nd:1 3rd:0 Ran:3
Pre2000 - 1st:0 2nd:0 3rd:0 Ran:1
Win Prizemoney £0 *Total Prizemoney* £896
2000 Turf 0-3: (8f, 10f, 12f) (g-s 2, gd)
Average filly. Turf high 65 (began Spt). **W Jarvis [0-4] Cuadra Africa.*

DENARIUS SECUNDUS BHB 51f **RR 54f** 4544[10]
3 ch c Barathea (IRE) - Penny Drops **(109f)** (Sharpo) 7.7f **(59)**
Form - 7000
Record 2000 - 1st:0 2nd:0 3rd:0 Ran:4
2000 Turf 0-4: (7f, 8f 2, 10f) (gd 2, frm 2)
Scopey, fair colt, has worn blinkers. Turf high 54 (began Jly).
**M P Tregoning [0-4] Stanley Sharp.*

DENBRAE (IRE) BHB 49f49a **RR 50f 49a** 696[17]
8 b g Sure Blade (USA) 10.6f **(66)** - Fencing (Viking (USA)) 6.7f **(65)**
Form - 0
Record 2000 - 1st:0 2nd:0 3rd:0 Ran:1
Pre2000 - 1st:6 2nd:5 3rd:9 Ran:59
Win Prizemoney £17,201 *Total Prizemoney* £29,339
Wins * 1999 May Hamilt (SFT) H 6f 47 51
** 1999 Mar Southw (STD) H 7f 46 49*
1997 Aug Leices (GD) 7f 68
1996 Jun Chepst (G-F) H 6.1f 68 69 <
2000 Turf 0-1: (7f) (gd)
Fair gelding, effective 6 to 8f, acts on gd - acts on AW, likes left handed tracks, likes tight tracks.
**J Pearce [2-11] Jeff Pearce (from D J G MurraySmith [4-49] Oct 1998).*

DENISE BEST (IRE) BHB 75f70a **RR 78f 70a** 5315[5]
2 ch f Goldmark (USA) - Titchwell Lass **(58f)** (Lead on Time (USA)) 8f **(65)**
Form - 72485
Record 2000 - 1st:0 2nd:1 3rd:0 Ran:5
Win Prizemoney £0 *Total Prizemoney* £2,897
2000 Turf 0-4: (7f, 8f 3) (g-s 2, gd, frm) 2000 AW 0-1: (8f) (Fibr)
Above-average filly. Turf high 78 (began Aug) - 4th of 6 getting 8lb from Elnahaar (20 Spt Chester 8f g-s RF 4536).
**A Berry [0-5] Alan Berry.*

DENNIS BERGKAMP (IRE) BHB 43f33a **RR 58df 33a** 4575[8]
3 b g Night Shift (USA) 8.1f **(73)** - Indian Express **(59f)** (Indian Ridge)
Form - 0808
Record 2000 - 1st:0 2nd:0 3rd:0 Ran:4
Pre2000 - 1st:0 2nd:0 3rd:1 Ran:6
Win Prizemoney £0 *Total Prizemoney* £290
2000 Turf 0-2: (10f, 14f) (sft, gd) 2000 AW 0-2: (8f, 9f) (Fibr 2)
Workmanlike, fair gelding, has worn blinkers. Turf high 12 (began Spt). Becoming disappointing.
**W Clay [0-6] Dave Dutton (from M R Channon [0-5] Aug 1999).*

DENNIS EL MENACE BHB 79f **RR 78f** 3965[3]
2 b c College Chapel - Spanish Craft (IRE) **(38f)** (Jareer (USA)) 5.9f **(75)**
Form - 04643203
Record 2000 - 1st:0 2nd:1 3rd:2 Ran:8
Win Prizemoney £0 *Total Prizemoney* £3,215
2000 Turf 0-6: (5f 2, 7f 3, 8f) (gd 3, g-f 3) 2000 AW 0-2: (5f, 7f) (Fibr 2)
Above-average colt, effective 7 to 8f, best at 7f, acts on gd to g-f, best on g-f, has worn blinkers. Turf high 78 - 3rd of 10 giving 4lb to Siena Star (25 Aug Newmarket 8f g-f RF 3965). AW high 58.
**W R Muir [0-8] Brian & Helen Moss.*

DENNIS OUR MENACE BHB 81f **RR 82f** 4970[20]
2 b c Piccolo - Free on Board (Free State) 8.7f **(61)**
Form - 0330
Record 2000 - 1st:0 2nd:0 3rd:2 Ran:4
Win Prizemoney £0 *Total Prizemoney* £1,449
2000 Turf 0-4: (7f 2, 8f 2) (gd, g-f 2, frm)
Decent colt. Turf high 82 - 3rd of 6 to Rosi's Boy (18 Aug Newmarket 8f g-f RF 3765). **S Dow [0-4] G Steinberg.*

DENSIM BLUE (IRE) BHB 73f **RR 76f** 4582[7]
2 b c Lake Coniston (IRE) - Surprise Visitor (IRE) (Be My Guest (USA)) 9.3f **(67)**
Form - 024145247
Record 2000 - 1st:1 2nd:2 3rd:0 Ran:9
Win Prizemoney £2,832 *Total Prizemoney* £5,287
Wins * 2000 May Bright (G-S) 5.3f 76 <
2000 Turf 1-9: (5f 1-7, 6f 2) (gd 1-3, g-f 2, frm 3, hrd)
Above-average colt, effective 5 to 6f, best at 6f, acts on gd to hrd, best on gd. Turf high 76 - 1st of 10 giving 5lb to Church Belle (24 May Brighton RF 1420). **J Pearce [1-9] Double M Partnership.*

DEN'S-JOY BHB 63f60a **RR 64f 60a** 4824[13]
4 b f Archway (IRE) 8.5f **(60)** - Bonvin (Taufan (USA)) 7f **(57)**
Form - 53881001200547200

Record 2000 - 1st:2 2nd:2 3rd:1 Ran:16
Pre2000 - 1st:0 2nd:0 3rd:1 Ran:2
Win Prizemoney £7,813 *Total Prizemoney* £11,835
Wins * 2000 Jun Lingfi (FRM) H 9f 57 60 <
*** 2000** May Windso (G-S) H 8.3f 56 60 <
2000 Turf 2-14: (7f 3, 8f 1-7, 9f 1-3, 10f) (g-s, gd 1-5, g-f 2, frm 1-6)
2000 AW 0-2: (11f, 12f) (Fibr 2)
Workmanlike, average filly, effective 7 to 9f, best at 8f, acts on gd to frm, best on gd, prefers right handed tracks, prefers tight tracks, excels at Windsor. Turf high 64 - 2nd of 12 getting 2lb from Amoras (26 Aug Windsor 8f gd RF 4006) - also 1st of 4 giving 1lb to Sifat (14 Jun Lingfield RF 1973). AW high 62.
**Miss D A McHale [2-14] N T Davis & M Watmore (from H J Collingridge [0-4] Jan 2000).*

DENTON LADY BHB 36f39a RR 41f 39a 2092[10]

3 br f Inchinor 8.9f **(64)** - Lammastide (Martinmas) 7.6f **(59)**
Form - 67003000
Record 2000 - 1st:0 2nd:0 3rd:1 Ran:8
Pre2000 - 1st:0 2nd:0 3rd:0 Ran:9
Win Prizemoney £0 *Total Prizemoney* £1,094
2000 Turf 0-7: (6f, 7f 2, 8f 2, 9f, 11f) (gd 3, g-f 2, frm 2) 2000 AW 0-1: (7f) (Fibr)
Light-framed, moderate filly, often wears blinkers. Turf high 41. Inconsistent. **W T Kemp [0-17] Mrs M Irwin.*

DEREK'S PRIDE (IRE) RR 5010[15]

2 b f General Monash (USA) - Likeness (Young Generation) 7.7f **(63)**
Form - 0
Record 2000 - 1st:0 2nd:0 3rd:0 Ran:1
2000 AW 0-1: (7f) (Fibr)
Currently very poor filly. **J Parkes [0-1] P J Sweeney.*

DERIVATIVE (IRE) RR 91f 5279a[1]

2 bb c Erins Isle 8.3f **(76)** - Our Hope 00
Form - 1441
2000 Turf 2-4: (7f 1-2, 8f, 9f 1-1) (sft 1-1, g-s 2, gd 1-1)
Useful colt, has worn blinkers. Turf high 91 (began Jly) - 1st of 18 giving 7lb to Turtle Dancer (27 Oct Fairyhouse RF 5279a) - also 1st of 14 giving 5lb to Echo Canyon (16 Jly Curragh RF 2917a).
**J S Bolger in IRE [2-4] D H W Dobson.*

DERRYQUIN BHB 73f RR 70f 4609[18]

5 b g Lion Cavern (USA) 7.5f **(74)** - Top Berry (High Top) 10.2f **(67)**
Form - 0102048110
Record 2000 - 1st:3 2nd:1 3rd:0 Ran:10
Pre2000 - 1st:2 2nd:0 3rd:0 Ran:15
Win Prizemoney £23,593 *Total Prizemoney* £24,980
Wins * 2000 Aug Redcar (FRM) H 8f 64 70
*** 2000** Aug Leices (G-F) H 8f 56 66
*** 2000** May Redcar (G-F) H 8f 52 55
1997 Nov Doncas (GD) 8f 95 <
1997 Oct Lingfi (GD) 7f 81
2000 Turf 3-10: (6f, 8f 3-9) (g-s, gd, g-f 1-4, frm 2-3, hrd)
Above-average gelding, effective 8f, acts on g-f to frm, often wears blinkers (very effectively). Turf high 70 - 1st of 12 giving 3lb to Ryefield (26 Aug Redcar RF 3997) - also 1st of 14 getting 19lb from Flitwick (13 Aug Leicester RF 3609).
**P L Gilligan [3-16] Lady Bland (from R Charlton [2-9] Oct 1998).*

DESAMO (USA) BHB 79f RR 73f 2249[1]

3 br c Chief's Crown (USA) 10.2f **(75)** - Green Heights (USA) (Miswaki (USA)) 9f **(81)**
Form - 331
Record 2000 - 1st:1 2nd:0 3rd:2 Ran:3
Win Prizemoney £2,814 *Total Prizemoney* £3,923
Wins * 2000 Jun Redcar (FRM) 6f 69+ <
2000 Turf 1-3: (6f 1-2, 7f) (gd, frm 1-2)
Scopey, currently above-average colt. Turf high 73 - 3rd of 12 to Lakeland Paddy (8 Jun Newbury 6f frm RF 1812) - also 1st of 4 from Pacific Place (24 Jun Redcar RF 2249).
**J Noseda [1-3] K Y Lim.*

DESARU (USA) BHB 95f RR 92f 3021[11]

4 br c Chief's Crown (USA) 10.2f **(75)** - Team Colors (USA) (Mr Prospector (USA)) 8.8f **(78)**
Form - 000
Record 2000 - 1st:0 2nd:0 3rd:0 Ran:3
Pre2000 - 1st:1 2nd:1 3rd:1 Ran:5
Win Prizemoney £5,552 *Total Prizemoney* £19,882
Wins * 1998 Spt Doncas (GD) 7f 99+ <
2000 Turf 0-3: (6f, 7f, 9f) (gd, frm, hrd)
Scopey, useful colt. Turf high 92. Consistent.
**J Noseda [1-8] K Y Lim.*

DESERT CHARM BHB 31f RR 40f 793[12]

3 b f Desert Style (IRE) - Autumn Fall (USA) (Sanglamore (USA))
Form - 0
Record 2000 - 1st:0 2nd:0 3rd:0 Ran:1
Pre2000 - 1st:0 2nd:0 3rd:0 Ran:3
2000 Turf 0-1: (12f) (g-s)
Scopey, moderate filly. **N Tinkler [0-4] & Mrs G Middlebrook.*

DESERT FIGHTER BHB 62f RR 63f 3410[2]

9 b g Green Desert (USA) 7.8f **(78)** - Jungle Rose (Shirley Heights) 10.3f **(74)**
Form - 0010212
Record 2000 - 1st:2 2nd:2 3rd:0 Ran:7
Pre2000 - 1st:9 2nd:3 3rd:6 Ran:34
Win Prizemoney £34,780 *Total Prizemoney* £43,733
Wins * 2000 Jly Catter (G-F) 12f 58
*** 2000** May Thirsk (GD) C 12f 51
* 1999 Jly Catter (FRM) C 12f 65
* 1999 Jly Hamilt (FRM) C 11.1f 55
* 1999 Jly Haydoc (G-S) C 11.9f 68
* 1999 May Thirsk (G-S) C 12f 50
* 1997 May Newcas (G-F) H 12.4f 68 75
* 1997 Apr Thirsk (G-F) 12f 76
2000 Turf 2-7: (10f 2, 12f 2-5) (g-s, gd 1-2, g-f, frm 1-3)
Above-average gelding, effective 12f, acts on gd to hrd, favours tight tracks, and excels at Thirsk. Turf high 63 - 2nd of 3 getting 4lb from Waseem (5 Aug Thirsk 12f frm RF 3410).
**Mrs M Reveley [12-55] A Frame (from D Nicholson [0-5] May 1995).*

DESERT FURY BHB 73f RR 89f 5242[10]

3 b c Warning 8.1f **(77)** - Number One Spot (Reference Point) 6.8f **(70)**
Form - 30006846540
Record 2000 - 1st:0 2nd:0 3rd:1 Ran:11
Pre2000 - 1st:1 2nd:0 3rd:1 Ran:2
Win Prizemoney £7,067 *Total Prizemoney* £10,417
Wins * 1999 May Cheste (G-F) 5.1f 82+ <
2000 Turf 0-11: (6f 4, 7f 2, 8f 4, 10f) (g-s 4, gd, g-f 3, frm 3)
Small, useful colt, effective 6f, acts on frm. Turf high 94.
**B Hanbury [1-13] B Hanbury.*

DESERT INVADER (IRE) BHB 29f24a RR 24f 24a 2485[12]

9 br g Lead on Time (USA) 7.5f **(69)** - Aljood (Kris) 9.5f **(73)**
Form - 008050
Record 2000 - 1st:0 2nd:0 3rd:0 Ran:6
Pre2000 - 1st:9 2nd:13 3rd:13 Ran:104
Win Prizemoney £23,046 *Total Prizemoney* £38,610
Wins * 1998 *Jun Wolver (STD) H 6f 60 63*
* 1998 *Jun Southw (STD) H 7f 55 60*
* 1997 *Jun Wolver (STD) H 6f 63 70* <
* 1997 *May Southw (STD) C 7f 63*
* 1997 *May Wolver (STD) C 6f 56+*
* 1996 *Feb Southw (STD) H 7f 57 61*
2000 AW 0-6: (6f 2, 7f 4) (Fibr 6)
Little account gelding, effective 6 to 7f, - acts on Fibr, has worn blinkers. AW high 17.
**D W Chapman [8-106] David Chapman (from A A Scott [1-4] Jly 1994).*

DESERT ISLAND DISC BHB 68f58a RR 71f 58a 1510[1]

3 b f Turtle Island (IRE) - Distant Music (Darshaan) 9.9f **(84)**
Form - 651
Record 2000 - 1st:1 2nd:0 3rd:0 Ran:3
Pre2000 - 1st:0 2nd:0 3rd:0 Ran:3
Win Prizemoney £4,030 *Total Prizemoney* £4,030
Wins * 2000 May Warwic (HVY) H 10.5f 66 71 <
2000 Turf 1-3: (8f 2, 11f 1-1) (hvy 1-1, gd 2)
Unfurnished, above-average filly, effective 8 to 11f, acts on hvy to gd. Turf high 71 - 1st of 11 getting 4lb from Distinctly Well (27 May Warwick RF 1510). **N A Graham [1-6] Flying Colours Racing.*

DESERT KNIGHT BHB 100f **RR 97f** 1052[5]
4 b c Green Desert (USA) 7.8f **(78)** - Green Leaf (USA) (Alydar (USA)) 9.1f **(76)**
Form - 315
Record 2000 - 1st:1 2nd:0 3rd:1 Ran:3
Pre2000 - 1st:1 2nd:1 3rd:0 Ran:2
Win Prizemoney £10,441 *Total Prizemoney* £14,493
Wins * 2000 Apr Warwic (HVY) 6.8f 91+
* 1999 Aug Pontef (GD) 8f 92+ <
2000 Turf 1-3: (7f 1-2, 8f) (hvy 1-1, gd, frm)
Rangy, very useful colt. Turf high 97 (1st run) - 3rd of 8 giving 5lb to Hasty Words (23 Mar Doncaster 8f frm RF 0476) - also 1st of 9 giving 4lb to Muchea (24 Apr Warwick RF 0857). A winner at Warwick on his second start of last year, he finished last on his only subsequent run. Wore bandages on all his starts and may not be the easiest to train. **J Noseda [2-5] Sheikh Khaled Duaij Al Sabah.*

DESERT MAGIC (IRE) RR 101f 3576[9]
4 bb m Green Desert (USA) 7.8f **(78)** - Gracieuse Majeste (FR) (Saint Cyrien (FR)) 8.4f **(80)**
Form - 120
2000 Turf 1-3: (6f 2, 7f 1-1) (sft 1-1, gd 2)
Very useful filly, effective 6 to 7f, acts on sft to gd. Turf high 101 - 2nd of 9 giving 1lb to Namid (8 May Cork 6f gd RF 1223a) - also 1st of 7 giving 15lb to Yara (1 May Curragh RF 1121a).
**N Clement in FR [0-1] Marquesa de Moratalla (from C Collins in IRE [3-12] May 2000).*

DESERT MUSIC BHB 32f **RR 31f** 3999[7]
4 b f Ardkinglass 5f **(64)** - Musical Princess (Cavo Doro) 10.6f **(57)**
Form - 755507
Record 2000 - 1st:0 2nd:0 3rd:0 Ran:6
2000 Turf 0-6: (11f, 12f 4, 14f) (g-f 4, frm 2)
Scopey, very moderate filly. Turf high 31.
**J R Weymes [0-6] Mrs N Napier.*

DESERT NORTH (IRE) RR 61f 1090[11]
3 b g Desert Style (IRE) - Ever so (Mummy's Pet) 7.7f **(60)**
Form - 00
Record 2000 - 1st:0 2nd:0 3rd:0 Ran:2
2000 Turf 0-2: (6f 2) (gd, g-f)
Workmanlike, average gelding. Turf high 61. (DEAD)
**R J O'Sullivan [0-2] Normandy Developments (London).*

DESERT RAGE RR 88f 1391[3]
3 b c Polish Precedent (USA) 9f **(73)** - Shore Line (High Line) 10.3f **(70)**
Form - 53
Record 2000 - 1st:0 2nd:0 3rd:1 Ran:2
Win Prizemoney £0 *Total Prizemoney* £880
2000 Turf 0-2: (8f 2) (g-s, frm)
Scopey, currently useful colt. Turf high 88.
**E A L Dunlop [0-2] Abdullah Ali.*

DESERT RECRUIT BHB 46f **RR 45f** 2096[5]
4 b g Marju (IRE) 9.2f **(76)** - Storm Gayle (IRE) (Sadler's Wells (USA)) 10f **(76)**
Form - 553665
Record 2000 - 1st:0 2nd:0 3rd:1 Ran:6
Pre2000 - 1st:1 2nd:0 3rd:0 Ran:9
Win Prizemoney £2,780 *Total Prizemoney* £3,962
Wins 1999 Jly Hamilt (G-F) H 11.1f 42 42 <
2000 Turf 0-6: (10f, 12f, 13f, 14f 3) (g-s 2, gd, frm 3)
Workmanlike, moderate gelding, likes right handed tracks. Turf high 45. Consistent.
**D Nicholls [0-6] David McKenzie (from I Semple [1-9] Aug 1999).*

DESERT SAFARI (IRE) BHB 71f70a **RR 74f 70a** 4604[10]
3 b f Desert Style (IRE) - Dublah (USA) (Private Account (USA)) 8.5f **(74)**
Form - 05480113670
Record 2000 - 1st:2 2nd:0 3rd:1 Ran:11
Pre2000 - 1st:1 2nd:1 3rd:2 Ran:11
Win Prizemoney £9,707 *Total Prizemoney* £12,443
Wins * 2000 Jly Catter (G-F) H 7f 71 74 <
*** 2000** Jun Carlis (FRM) H 6.9f 67 74 <
* 1999 Spt Mussel (G-F) 5f 72
2000 Turf 2-10: (6f, 7f 2-6, 8f 3) (hvy, g-s, gd 3, g-f 2-2, frm 3) 2000 AW 0-1: (6f) (Fibr)
Scopey, above-average filly, effective 5 to 8f, best at 7f, acts on hvy to frm - acts on Fibr, best on g-f, has worn blinkers, likes left handed tracks, likes tight tracks. Turf high 74 - 1st of 11 getting 2lb from Lady of Windsor (18 Jun Carlisle RF 2069) - also 1st of 10 giving 8lb to Dihatjum (6 Jly Catterick RF 2561). (1st run) - 4th of 12 getting 4lb from Dancing Empress (4 May Wolverhampton 6f Fibr RF 1025). Inconsistent.
**E J Alston [3-22] The Burlington Partnership.*

DESERT SPA (USA) BHB 40f60a **RR 39df 60a** 4779[7]
5 b g Sheikh Albadou 9.2f **(75)** - Healing Waters (USA) (Temperence Hill (USA)) 11f **(58)**
Form - 821181027
Record 2000 - 1st:3 2nd:1 3rd:0 Ran:7
Pre2000 - 1st:1 2nd:1 3rd:2 Ran:14
Win Prizemoney £8,975 *Total Prizemoney* £11,462
Wins * 2000 *May Wolver (STD) C 12f 58* <
*** 2000** *Feb Wolver (STD) H 12f 55 58* <
*** 2000** *Jan Wolver (STD) H 12f 51 54*
1998 *Spt Wolver (STD) H 12f 51 55*
2000 Turf 0-2: (10f, 12f) (gd, frm) 2000 AW 3-5: (12f 3-5) (Fibr 3-5)
Average gelding, effective 12f, - acts on Fibr, has worn blinkers, favours left handed tracks. Turf high 29. AW high 61 - 2nd of 12 giving 12lb to Cupboard Lover (16 Spt Wolverhampton 12f Fibr RF 4479) - also 1st of 8 giving 13lb to Irish Cream (20 May Wolverhampton RF 1352).
**P J Makin [0-0] D M Ahier (from P W Harris [1-12] Nov 1998).*

DESERT VALENTINE BHB 54f **RR 49f** 4692[P]
5 b g Midyan (USA) 9.9f **(64)** - Mo Ceri (Kampala) 8.4f **(56)**
Form - 0251P
Record 2000 - 1st:1 2nd:1 3rd:0 Ran:5
Pre2000 - 1st:1 2nd:0 3rd:0 Ran:12
Win Prizemoney £7,170 *Total Prizemoney* £8,025
Wins * 2000 Spt Goodwo (GD) H 12f 43 49
* 1998 Spt Goodwo (G-S) H 8f 55 60 <
2000 Turf 1-5: (7f, 12f 1-2, 14f 2) (gd 1-2, frm 3)
Moderate gelding, effective 12 to 14f, best at 12f, acts on gd to frm, best on frm, prefers tight tracks. Turf high 49 (began Jly) - 1st of 16 getting 3lb from Chalcedony (8 Spt Goodwood RF 4306).
**L G Cottrell [2-17] Mrs Lucy Halloran.*

DESIRE ME BHB 46f **RR 47f** 4114[5]
2 b f Silca Blanka (IRE) - Dazzle Me **(20df)** (Kalaglow) 9.8f **(67)**
Form - 575
Record 2000 - 1st:0 2nd:0 3rd:0 Ran:3
2000 Turf 0-3: (5f 2, 6f) (frm 3)
Currently moderate filly. Turf high 47 (began Jly).
**A D Smith [0-3] Duckhaven Stud.*

DESIRE'S GOLD BHB 28f **RR 42f** 58[10]
5 br g Grey Desire 9.3f **(49)** - Glory Gold (Hittite Glory) 8.7f **(50)**
Form - 00
Record 2000 - 1st:0 2nd:0 3rd:0 Ran:1
Pre2000 - 1st:0 2nd:0 3rd:0 Ran:12
2000 AW 0-1: (8f) (Fibr)
Moderate gelding. **M Brittain [0-13] Mel Brittain.*

DESRAYA (IRE) BHB 76f **RR 75+f** 4449[26]
3 b g Desert Style (IRE) - Madaraya (USA) (Shahrastani (USA)) 8.8f **(72)**
Form - 7602311180
Record 2000 - 1st:3 2nd:1 3rd:1 Ran:10
Pre2000 - 1st:0 2nd:0 3rd:0 Ran:5
Win Prizemoney £13,536 *Total Prizemoney* £15,289
Wins * 2000 Jly Ripon (G-F) H 6f 71 75+ <
*** 2000** Jly Hamilt (G-F) H 6f 56 61
*** 2000** Jly Ripon (G-S) H 6f 56 57
2000 Turf 3-10: (5f, 6f 3-7, 8f, 12f) (g-s 1-1, gd 3, g-f 1-2, frm 1-4)
Scopey, above-average gelding, effective 6f, acts on frm, often wears blinkers (extremely effectively). Turf high 75 - 1st of 14 giving 1lb to Elvington Boy (30 Jly Ripon RF 3239). Dropped in the handicap during the summer and completed a hat trick in July at Hamilton and Ripon twice. He has shot up the weights again as a result and will find life much tougher.
**K A Ryan [3-15] Pendle Inn Partnership.*

DESTINATION BHB 79f64a **RR 81f 64a** 5311[2]
3 ch g Deploy 11.4f **(67)** - Veuve (Tirol)
Form - 52445322
Record 2000 - 1st:0 2nd:3 3rd:1 Ran:8
Pre2000 - 1st:0 2nd:0 3rd:0 Ran:1
Win Prizemoney £0 *Total Prizemoney* £5,106
2000 Turf 0-5: (10f 2, 12f 2, 15f) (sft, g-s, gd 2, g-f) 2000 AW 0-3: (10f, 13f, 16f) (Equi 3)
Unfurnished, decent gelding, effective 10 to 15f, acts on sft to g-f. Turf high 81 - 2nd of 10 getting 3lb from Jardines Lookout (3 Nov Doncaster 15f sft RF 5311). AW high 68. **C A Cyzer [0-9] R M Cyzer.*

DETACHING (IRE) **RR 53f** 5073[8]
2 b f Thatching 7.8f **(69)** - David's Star (Welsh Saint) 7.6f **(64)**
Form - 08
Record 2000 - 1st:0 2nd:0 3rd:0 Ran:2
2000 Turf 0-2: (7f 2) (g-s 2)
Currently fair filly. Turf high 53 (began Oct).
**I A Balding [0-2] D H Caslon.*

DETECTIVE BHB 48f **RR 54f** 4827[14]
4 ch g Wolfhound (USA) 7.3f **(71)** - Ivoronica (Targowice (USA)) 11.4f **(70)**
Form - 5700
Record 2000 - 1st:0 2nd:0 3rd:0 Ran:4
Pre2000 - 1st:0 2nd:1 3rd:0 Ran:7
Win Prizemoney £0 *Total Prizemoney* £806
2000 Turf 0-4: (5f, 6f 3) (g-f 3, frm)
Workmanlike, fair gelding, has worn blinkers. Turf high 54 (began Jly).
**Dr J D Scargill [0-7] A C Edwards (from J H M Gosden [0-4] Jly 1999).*

DE TRAMUNTANA BHB 69f **RR 76f** 5058[5]
3 b f Alzao (USA) 9.8f **(73)** - Glamour Game (Nashwan (USA))
Form - 242505
Record 2000 - 1st:0 2nd:2 3rd:0 Ran:6
Pre2000 - 1st:0 2nd:0 3rd:0 Ran:2
Win Prizemoney £0 *Total Prizemoney* £4,150
2000 Turf 0-6: (10f 6) (sft, gd, g-f 2, frm 2)
Light-framed, above-average filly, effective 10f, acts on g-f, favours tight tracks. Turf high 76 - 2nd of 15 getting 5lb from Kiftsgate (9 Jly Sandown 10f g-f RF 2661). Nearly beat Air Defence at Chester, but that is the nearest she has come to a victory.
**W Jarvis [0-8] P A Howell.*

DETROIT CITY (IRE) BHB 32f40a **RR 43f 40a** 4123[7]
5 b g Distinctly North (USA) 7.4f **(63)** - Moyhora (IRE) (Nashamaa) 7.1f **(66)**
Form - 4202040007
Record 2000 - 1st:0 2nd:2 3rd:0 Ran:10
Pre2000 - 1st:3 2nd:2 3rd:1 Ran:31
Win Prizemoney £8,006 *Total Prizemoney* £11,178
Wins * 1999 Apr Mussel (G-F) H 7.1f 54 56
* 1998 Jly Beverl (G-F) C 7.5f 62 <
* 1998 Jun Mussel (SFT) 7.1f 57
2000 Turf 0-10: (6f, 7f 6, 8f 3) (g-f 3, frm 6, hrd)
Moderate gelding, effective 7f, acts on g-f, has worn blinkers, likes right handed tracks. Turf high 43.
**B S Rothwell [3-36] Mrs Liz Hunt (from J Berry [0-6] Apr 1998).*

DEUCE OF TRUMPS (IRE) BHB 84f **RR 87f** 4765[1]
2 b c Desert Style (IRE) - Mauras Pride (IRE) (Cadeaux Genereux)
Form - 351
Record 2000 - 1st:1 2nd:0 3rd:1 Ran:3
Win Prizemoney £3,828 *Total Prizemoney* £4,266
Wins * 2000 Oct Pontef (HVY) 10f 80 <
2000 Turf 1-3: (8f 2, 10f 1-1) (g-s 1-2, gd)
Currently useful colt. Turf high 87 (1st run) (began Spt) - 3rd of 15 to Morshdi (1 Spt Haydock 8f g-s RF 4148) - also 1st of 9 giving 5lb to English Harbour (2 Oct Pontefract RF 4765).
**J Noseda [1-3] & Mrs John Poynton.*

DEVELOPMENT (IRE) **RR 104f** 5089a[1]
5 b h Dancing Dissident (USA) 6.8f **(65)** - Gay's Flutter (Beldale Flutter (USA)) 9.7f **(71)**
Form - 21
2000 Turf 1-2: (5f 1-2) (hvy 1-1, g-f)
Currently very useful colt. Turf high 100 (began Jly) - 1st of 7 from Onice Nero (14 Oct San Siro RF 5089a).
**L Mele in ITY [1-2] Scuderia Becco & Becco.*

DEVIL LEADER (USA) BHB 72f **RR 70f** 3390[4]
3 ch f Diesis 9f **(80)** - Shihama (USA) (Shadeed (USA)) 8.2f **(70)**
Form - 753214
Record 2000 - 1st:1 2nd:1 3rd:1 Ran:6
Win Prizemoney £4,290 *Total Prizemoney* £6,359
Wins * 2000 Jly Warwic (G-F) 8.1f 70 <
2000 Turf 1-6: (8f 1-4, 10f 2) (gd 3, g-f 1-3)
Lengthy, above-average filly, effective 8 to 10f, best at 8f, acts on gd to g-f, best on g-f. Turf high 70 - 1st of 6 getting 5lb from Atalya (22 Jly Warwick RF 3047). Gradually improving and got off the mark with a convincing win in a weak maiden at Warwick in July.
**B W Hills [1-6] Mohamed Obaida.*

DEVILS NIGHT BHB 8f **RR 9f** 88[9]
5 b g Faustus (USA) 9.1f **(54)** - Up All Night **(6f)** (Green Desert (USA)) 8.6f **(78)**
Form - 80
Record 2000 - 1st:0 2nd:0 3rd:0 Ran:1
Pre2000 - 1st:0 2nd:0 3rd:0 Ran:4
2000 AW 0-1: (16f) (Fibr)
Poor gelding. **K Bell [0-5] Brian Footer.*

DEVON HEIGHTS (USA) **RR 112f** 3351a[10]
3 ch f Mt Livermore (USA) 7.7f **(90)** - Devon Diva (USA) (The Minstrel (CAN)) 10f **(72)**
Form - 30
2000 Turf 0-2: (8f 2) (g-s, gd)
Currently Group-class filly. Turf high 112 (1st run) - 3rd of 13 to Zarkiya (4 Jun Chantilly 8f gd RF 1827a). **A Fabre in FR [0-2].*

DEXTROUS **RR 87f** 5135[3]
3 gr c Machiavellian (USA) 9.8f **(83)** - Heavenly Cause (USA) (Grey Dawn II) 11.1f **(72)**
Form - 33
Record 2000 - 1st:0 2nd:0 3rd:2 Ran:2
Win Prizemoney £0 *Total Prizemoney* £1,596
2000 Turf 0-2: (8f, 10f) (sft, frm)
Workmanlike, currently useful colt. Turf high 87.
**H R A Cecil [0-2] H R H Prince Fahd Salman.*

DHAUDELOUP (FR) BHB 65f **RR 60+f** 5323[13]
5 ch g Mister Sicy (FR) - Debolouve (FR) (Yours)
Form - 40
Record 2000 - 1st:0 2nd:0 3rd:0 Ran:2
Win Prizemoney £0 *Total Prizemoney* £1,140
2000 Turf 0-2: (12f 2) (sft, g-s)
Average gelding. Turf high 60 (began Oct). Better known as a hurdler, he has won on the Flat in France and ran well on the level at Doncaster in October. **R A Fahey [1-8] G H Leatham.*

DIABLO DANCER (IRE) BHB 64f **RR 69f** 1315[7]
4 b g Deploy 11.4f **(67)** - Scharade (Lombard (GER)) 10.5f **(66)**
Form - 0517
Record 2000 - 1st:1 2nd:0 3rd:0 Ran:4
Pre2000 - 1st:2 2nd:2 3rd:3 Ran:18
Win Prizemoney £9,059 *Total Prizemoney* £18,858
Wins * 2000 May Warwic (SFT) H 10.5f 62 69
* 1998 Jly Lingfi (G-F) 7f 82 <
* 1998 Apr Nottin (G-S) 5.1f 75
2000 Turf 1-4: (10f, 11f 1-1, 14f, 15f) (hvy, sft 1-1, gd 2)
Strong, average gelding, effective 10f, acts on frm, has worn blinkers, likes tight tracks. Turf high 69.
**B R Millman [3-23] Kentisbeare Quartet.*

DIABOLO (IRE) BHB 49f **RR 52f** 5052[11]
2 b c Magic Ring (IRE) 6.5f **(64)** - First Play **(45df)** (Primo Dominie) 6.2f **(80)**
Form - 700
Record 2000 - 1st:0 2nd:0 3rd:0 Ran:3
2000 Turf 0-3: (5f, 6f 2) (sft, gd 2)
Currently fair colt. Turf high 52 (began Spt).
**M W Easterby [0-3] Guy Reed.*

DIAMANTE (GER) RR 101f 2581a[14]
3 f
Form - 40
2000 Turf 0-2: (11f, 12f) (sft, gd)
Currently very useful. Turf high 101. **A Wohler in GER [0-2].*

DIAMOND RR 69f 3387[4]
4 b f Rainbow Quest (USA) 11.2f **(81)** - Key Flyer (USA) (Nijinsky (CAN)) 10.3f **(77)**
Form - 04
Record 2000 - 1st:0 2nd:0 3rd:0 Ran:2
Win Prizemoney £0 *Total Prizemoney* £322
2000 Turf 0-2: (10f, 12f) (g-f, frm)
Currently average filly. Turf high 52.
**H R A Cecil [0-2] H R H Prince Fahd Salman.*

DIAMOND CROWN (IRE) BHB 24f44a **RR 39f 44a** 3335[4]
9 ch g Kris 10f **(75)** - State Treasure (USA) (Secretariat (USA)) 9f **(79)**
Form - 02004
Record 2000 - 1st:0 2nd:1 3rd:0 Ran:5
Pre2000 - 1st:7 2nd:8 3rd:13 Ran:79
Win Prizemoney £16,782 *Total Prizemoney* £29,973

Wins								
* 1999	Jly	Hamilt	(FRM)	H	13f	39	42	
* 1998	Aug	Newcas	(GD)	S	12.4f		47	
* 1998	Jly	Ayr	(GD)	S	10.9f		47	
* 1997	Jun	Nottin	(GD)	SH	10f	42	45	
* 1996	Oct	Newcas	(G-F)	CH	0f	11	11	

2000 Turf 0-5: (12f, 13f 2, 14f, 16f) (gd, g-f, frm 3)
Very moderate gelding, effective 13 to 14f, best at 13f, acts on gd to frm, best on frm, has worn blinkers, favours tight tracks, excels at Catterick and does well at Hamilton. Turf high 39 - 2nd of 6 getting 10lb from Night City (9 Jun Catterick 14f gd RF 1837).
**Martyn Wane [7-89] B R Bradbury (from P F I Cole [0-2] Jly 1993).*

DIAMOND DECORUM (IRE) BHB 64f68a **RR 68f 68a** 5061[13]
4 ch g Fayruz 6.6f **(63)** - Astra Adastra (Mount Hagen (FR)) 8.4f **(70)**
Form - 61860000
Record 2000 - 1st:1 2nd:0 3rd:0 Ran:8
Pre2000 - 1st:2 2nd:1 3rd:0 Ran:23
Win Prizemoney £19,213 *Total Prizemoney* £26,223

Wins								
* 2000	May	Thirsk	(GD)	H	6f	66	68	
* 1999	Jun	Lingfi	(GD)	H	6f	73	77	<
* 1998	Aug	Thirsk	(G-F)		5f		77	<

2000 Turf 1-8: (5f 3, 6f 1-5) (hvy, sft, gd 1-1, g-f 2, frm 3)
Leggy, average gelding, effective 6 to 7f, acts on g-f to frm. Turf high 68. **P D Evans [3-31] Diamond Racing Ltd.*

DIAMOND FLAME BHB 40f53a **RR 45f 53a** 5056[10]
6 b g Suave Dancer (USA) 10.7f **(68)** - Eternal Flame (Primo Dominie) 6.2f **(80)**
Form - 800487000
Record 2000 - 1st:0 2nd:0 3rd:0 Ran:9
Pre2000 - 1st:2 2nd:1 3rd:1 Ran:24
Win Prizemoney £6,775 *Total Prizemoney* £9,157

Wins							
1998	*Mar*	*Wolver*	*(STD)*	*9.4f*		*87*	<
1998	*Feb*	*Lingfi*	*(SLW)*	*10f*		*83+*	

2000 Turf 0-7: (8f, 10f 3, 11f 2, 12f) (sft, g-s 2, gd, g-f 2, frm) 2000 AW 0-2: (9f 2) (Fibr 2)
Fair gelding, has worn blinkers. Turf high 50. AW high 55. Becoming disappointing.
**A B Mulholland [0-6] Mark Fearn (from P W Harris [2-27] Apr 2000).*

DIAMOND GEEZER (IRE) BHB 67f77a **RR 71f 77a** 5068[4]
4 br c Tenby 10.4f **(76)** - Unaria (Prince Tenderfoot (USA)) 9f **(61)**
Form - 212350244386142240784
Record 2000 - 1st:1 2nd:3 3rd:1 Ran:17
Pre2000 - 1st:5 2nd:5 3rd:2 Ran:31
Win Prizemoney £18,896 *Total Prizemoney* £30,263

Wins								
* 2000	Jly	Windso	(GD)	H	6f	63	64	
* 1999	*Nov*	*Lingfi*	*(STD)*	*H*	*6f*	*57*	*62*	
* 1999	Jly	Windso	(G-F)	H	6f	64	65	<
* 1999	Jly	Windso	(GD)	H	6f	61	62	
* 1999	*Jan*	*Lingfi*	*(STD)*	*H*	*6f*	*48*	*57*	
* 1998	Spt	Sandow	(G-S)	C	5f		62	

2000 Turf 1-15: (5f 9, 6f 1-6) (g-s, gd 2, g-f 7, frm 1-5) 2000 AW 0-2: (6f 2) (Equi 2)
Workmanlike, above-average colt, effective 5 to 6f, best at 5f, acts on g-f to frm acts on Equi, best on g-f, has worn blinkers, likes right handed tracks, and likes Windsor. Turf high 71 - 2nd of 12 giving 1lb to Mousehole (26 Jly Sandown 5f g-f RF 3144) - also 1st of 15 giving 4lb to Contrary Mary (3 Jly Windsor RF 2490). AW high 67 - 2nd of 9 getting 3lb from Mister Tricky (12 Apr Lingfield 6f Equi RF 0681). Kept very busy, he is equally effective on turf and Equitrack. Scored four times in 1999 and returned to winning form at Windsor in July. Six furlongs is his trip.
**R Hannon [6-48] J B R Leisure Ltd.*

DIAMOND GEORGIA (IRE) BHB 35f32a **RR 53f 32a** 1611[6]
3 ch f Soviet Lad (USA) 9.4f **(63)** - Secret Assignment (Vitiges (FR)) 8.2f **(59)**
Form - 0050806
Record 2000 - 1st:0 2nd:0 3rd:0 Ran:6
Pre2000 - 1st:0 2nd:0 3rd:0 Ran:3
2000 Turf 0-3: (10f, 12f, 16f) (gd, g-f, frm) 2000 AW 0-3: (7f, 8f 2) (Equi 2, Fibr)
Unfurnished, fair filly, often wears blinkers. Turf high 35. AW high 23. **John Berry [0-9] Diamond Racing Ltd.*

DIAMOND JAYNE (IRE) BHB 40f **RR 26f** 5060[7]
2 ch f Royal Abjar (USA) - Valiant Friend (USA) (Shahrastani (USA)) 8.8f **(72)**
Form - 007
Record 2000 - 1st:0 2nd:0 3rd:0 Ran:3
2000 Turf 0-3: (5f 2, 6f) (sft, gd, g-f)
Currently little account filly. Turf high 26 (bogan Spt)
**J Hetherton [0-3] Diamond Racing Ltd.*

DIAMOND KISS (IRE) BHB 48f **RR 46f** 2792[6]
3 b f Perugino (USA) - Kunuz (Ela-Mana-Mou) 10.1f **(70)**
Form - 8006
Record 2000 - 1st:0 2nd:0 3rd:0 Ran:4
Pre2000 - 1st:0 2nd:0 3rd:0 Ran:1
2000 Turf 0-4: (7f, 8f, 10f 2) (sft, g-f, frm 2)
Scopey, moderate filly. Turf high 46.
**Mrs P N Dutfield [0-5] Mrs Nerys Dutfield.*

DIAMOND LOOK (USA) BHB 84f **RR 87f** 1427[12]
3 b c Dayjur (USA) 6.8f **(79)** - Pedestal (High Line) 10.3f **(70)**
Form - 130
Record 2000 - 1st:1 2nd:0 3rd:1 Ran:3
Pre2000 - 1st:0 2nd:1 3rd:0 Ran:1
Win Prizemoney £2,713 *Total Prizemoney* £5,315

Wins								
* 2000	Apr	Lingfi	(G-S)		7f		75	<

2000 Turf 1-3: (7f 1-3) (gd 1-3)
Scopey, useful colt. Turf high 87 - 3rd of 21 giving 2lb to Rayyaan (18 Apr Newmarket 7f gd RF 0770). Comes from an excellent family, and showed ability on his sole start at two when runner-up in a Newbury maiden. He was not particularly impressive when landing the odds on his Lingfield reappearance, and probably achieved more in finishing third in a decent Newmarket handicap next time.
**E A L Dunlop [1-4] Jaber Abdullah.*

DIAMOND MAX (IRE) BHB 75f **RR 77f** 5320[3]
2 b c Nicolotte - Kawther (Tap On Wood) 10.3f **(65)**
Form - 74145513
Record 2000 - 1st:2 2nd:0 3rd:1 Ran:8
Win Prizemoney £4,851 *Total Prizemoney* £6,267

Wins								
* 2000	Oct	Redcar	(SFT)	H	6f	61	77	<
* 2000	Apr	Nottin	(HVY)	S	5.1f		68	

2000 Turf 2-8: (5f 1-5, 6f 1-1, 7f 2) (sft 1-2, gd 1-2, g-f 2, frm 2)
Above-average colt, effective 5 to 7f, acts on sft to gd, best on sft. Turf high 77 - 3rd of 22 giving 5lb to Leatherback (4 Nov Doncaster 7f sft RF 5320) - also 1st of 12 giving 12lb to Darwin Tower (24 Oct Redcar RF 5169). **P D Evans [2-8] Diamond Racing Ltd.*

DIAMOND MILLENNIUM BHB 43f **RR 50f** 2638[6]
2 ch f Clantime 6.6f **(57)** - Innocent Abroad (DEN) (Viking (USA)) 6.7f **(65)**
Form - 5753336
Record 2000 - 1st:0 2nd:0 3rd:3 Ran:7
Win Prizemoney £0 *Total Prizemoney* £849
2000 Turf 0-6: (5f 3, 6f 3) (g-s, g-f, frm 4) 2000 AW 0-1: (5f) (Fibr)
Fair filly, has worn blinkers. Turf high 50.
**P D Evans [0-7] Diamond Racing Ltd.*

DIAMOND MURPHY RR 22f 4478[8]
2 gr f Petong 7.6f **(58)** - Amathus Glory (Mummy's Pet) 7.7f **(60)**
Form - 08
Record 2000 - 1st:0 2nd:0 3rd:0 Ran:2
2000 Turf 0-1: (5f) (gd) 2000 AW 0-1: (7f) (Fibr)
Moderate filly. (DEAD)
**P G Murphy [0-2] Diamond Racing Ltd.*

DIAMOND OLIVIA BHB 61f46a **RR 60f 46a** 5229[5]
3 b f Beveled (USA) 6.9f **(64)** - Queen of the Quorn **(51df 45a)** (Governor General)
Form - 3476250135
Record 2000 - 1st:1 2nd:1 3rd:2 Ran:10
Pre2000 - 1st:0 2nd:0 3rd:1 Ran:4
Win Prizemoney £3,640 *Total Prizemoney* £5,575
Wins * 2000 Spt Lingfi (SFT) H 7f 53 59 <
2000 Turf 1-9: (7f 1-5, 8f 4) (hvy, sft, gd 1-3, g-f 2, frm, hrd) 2000 AW 0-1: (7f) (Fibr)
Light-framed, average filly, effective 5 to 8f, best at 7f, acts on hvy to g-f - acts on Fibr, best on gd. Turf high 60 - 5th of 24 getting 6lb from Eve (27 Oct Newmarket 8f gd RF 5229) - also 1st of 17 getting 7lb from Air Mail (29 Spt Lingfield RF 4729).
**John Berry [1-10] Diamond Racing Ltd (from W G M Turner [0-4] Oct 1999).*

DIAMOND PROMISE (IRE) BHB 52f46a **RR 61f 46a** 4827[22]
3 b f Fayruz 6.6f **(63)** - Cupid Miss (Anita's Prince)
Form - 52741000
Record 2000 - 1st:1 2nd:1 3rd:0 Ran:7
Pre2000 - 1st:3 2nd:5 3rd:1 Ran:14
Win Prizemoney £9,081 *Total Prizemoney* £14,111

Wins							
2000	Jun	Bath	(G-S)	C	5.1f		61
1999	Spt	Lingfi	(HVY)	C	6f		69 <
1999	May	Leices	(GD)	C	5f		69 <
1999	Apr	Thirsk	(GD)	C	5f		69+

2000 Turf 1-5: (5f 1-3, 6f 2) (gd 1-3, g-f, frm) 2000 AW 0-2: (5f, 6f) (Equi, Fibr)
Light-framed, average filly, effective 5 to 6f, best at 5f, acts on g-s to g-f, best on gd, excels at Thirsk, likes Lingfield. Turf high 61. AW high 49. Nippy sort, effective in claimers.
**Mrs P N Dutfield [0-3] Simon Dutfield (from P D Evans [4-18] Jun 2000).*

DIAMOND RACHAEL (IRE) BHB 63f67a **RR 64f 67a** 5245[1]
3 b f Shalford (IRE) 7.8f **(63)** - Brown Foam (Horage) 10.3f **(61)**
Form - 34712366712001
Record 2000 - 1st:3 2nd:2 3rd:1 Ran:12
Pre2000 - 1st:0 2nd:0 3rd:1 Ran:3
Win Prizemoney £9,912 *Total Prizemoney* £13,334

Wins							
*** 2000**	*Oct*	*Wolver*	*(STD)*	*H*	*7f*	*63*	*68 <*
*** 2000**	Jly	Leices	(G-F)	H	7f	58	58
*** 2000**	*Feb*	*Wolver*	*(STD)*		*6f*		*68 <*

2000 Turf 1-5: (6f, 7f 1-3, 8f) (gd 2, g-f, frm 1-2) 2000 AW 2-7: (5f, 6f 1-4, 7f 1-2) (Fibr 2-7)
Lengthy, average filly, effective 6 to 8f, best at 6f, acts on g-f to frm - acts on Fibr, mostly wears blinkers (extremely effectively), prefers left handed tracks, likes tight tracks. Turf high 64 (began Jly) - 2nd of 9 getting 17lb from Jawla (5 Aug Doncaster 8f g-f RF 3390). AW high 68 - 1st of 12 getting 5lb from Teofilio (28 Oct Wolverhampton RF 5245) - also 1st of 11 from Carols Choice (19 Feb Wolverhampton RF 0318).
**Mrs N Macauley [3-15] Diamond Racing Ltd.*

DIAMOND ROAD (IRE) BHB 68f **RR 73f** 4319[7]
3 b c Dolphin Street (FR) - Tiffany's Case (IRE) **(58f)** (Thatching) 8f **(66)**
Form - 332607
Record 2000 - 1st:0 2nd:1 3rd:2 Ran:6
Pre2000 - 1st:0 2nd:0 3rd:0 Ran:1
Win Prizemoney £0 *Total Prizemoney* £2,514
2000 Turf 0-6: (8f, 9f, 10f 2, 12f 2) (gd 2, g-f 3, frm)
Scopey, above-average colt, effective 9 to 10f, acts on gd to g-f, prefers right handed tracks. Turf high 73 - 2nd of 4 to Forest Heath (30 Jun Goodwood 10f gd RF 2402).
**C A Horgan [0-7] John Kelsey-Fry.*

DIAMOND SNAKE (IRE) RR 97f 1635a[2]
5 b h Thatching 7.8f **(69)** - Dorothy Harding (ITY) (Chief Singer) 8.9f **(66)**
Form - 2
2000 Turf 0-1: (7f) (g-f)
Very useful colt. (1st run) - 2nd of 11 giving 3lb to Fay Breeze (28 May Capannelle 7f g-f RF 1635a). **G Colleo in ITY [0-5] Spt 1998).*

DIAMOND VANESSA (IRE) BHB 40f46a **RR 49f 46a** 852[16]
3 b f Distinctly North (USA) 7.4f **(63)** - Elegant Act (USA) (Shecky Greene (USA)) 8f **(50)**
Form - 80500
Record 2000 - 1st:0 2nd:0 3rd:0 Ran:3
Pre2000 - 1st:0 2nd:0 3rd:0 Ran:3
2000 Turf 0-2: (8f, 10f) (sft, gd) 2000 AW 0-1: (7f) (Fibr)
Neat, moderate filly. Turf high 26.
**J Hetherton [0-6] Diamond Racing Ltd.*

DIAMOND WHITE BHB 104f100a **RR 110f 100a** 5225[5]
5 b m Robellino (USA) 9.5f **(68)** - Diamond Wedding (USA) (Diamond Shoal) 9.1f **(66)**
Form - 823456454533055
Record 2000 - 1st:0 2nd:1 3rd:3 Ran:15
Pre2000 - 1st:6 2nd:6 3rd:10 Ran:49
Win Prizemoney £89,082 *Total Prizemoney* £210,471

Wins							
***** 1999	Oct	Longch	(HVY)	G2	9.3f		113 <
***** 1999	Spt	Goodwo	(HVY)	L	9.9f		108+
1998	Nov	Doncas	(SFT)		10.3f		91
1998	Spt	Nottin	(G-F)		10f		90
1998	Jun	Folkes	(G-F)	H	7f	85	95+
1997	Aug	Newmar	(G-F)	L	7f		85

2000 Turf 0-14: (9f 3, 10f 10, 11f) (sft, g-s 3, gd 6, g-f 2, frm 2) 2000 AW 0-1: (9f) (Dirt)
Group-class filly, effective 9 to 11f, best at 9f, acts on sft to frm, best on sft, has worn blinkers, prefers right handed tracks, likes tight tracks, excels at Goodwood, does well at Sandown. Turf high 113 - 2nd of 8 giving 2lb to Little Rock (29 Apr Sandown 10f sft RF 0929). A model of consistency in an extremely busy '99 campaign, she failed to score last season, but always tried her best and is a credit to her connections' attacking policy.
**M J Ryan [2-37] Peter Scott (from P W D'Arcy [0-1] Mar 1999).*

DIAMOND ZOE BHB 45f **RR 43f** 5312[18]
2 b f Whittingham (IRE) - Sharp Gazelle **(42f 44a)** (Beveled (USA)) 9f **(59)**
Form - 440
Record 2000 - 1st:0 2nd:0 3rd:0 Ran:3
Win Prizemoney £0 *Total Prizemoney* £210
2000 Turf 0-3: (5f 2, 8f) (g-s, gd 2)
Currently moderate filly. Turf high 43 (began Oct).
**J L Eyre [0-3] Diamond Racing Ltd.*

DIANEME BHB 52f **RR 61f** 4767[15]
3 b f Primo Dominie 7.2f **(67)** - Aunt Jemima (Busted) 10.2f **(61)**
Form - 384500203040
Record 2000 - 1st:0 2nd:1 3rd:2 Ran:12
Win Prizemoney £0 *Total Prizemoney* £2,907
2000 Turf 0-12: (6f 2, 7f 3, 8f 5, 10f 2) (g-s 2, gd 3, g-f 3, frm 3, hrd)
Rangy, average filly, effective 7f, acts on frm, likes tight tracks. Turf high 62. Inconsistent.
**T D Easterby [0-12] The Snailwell Stud Company Ltd.*

DIATRIBE (AUS) RR 120f 5207a[1]
4 b c Brief Truce (USA) 9.1f **(73)** - Gabbing Gloria (USA) (Desert Wine (USA)) 9.7f **(80)**
Form - 1
2000 Turf 1-1: (12f 1-1) (gd 1-1)
Currently very high-class colt. (1st run) - 1st of 18 giving 1lb to Kaapstad Way (21 Oct Caulfield RF 5207a).
**G Hanlon in AUS [1-1] J Thompson.*

DI CANIO RR 23f 3126[9]
2 ch c Piccolo - Conquista (Aragon) 8.1f **(60)**
Form - 0
Record 2000 - 1st:0 2nd:0 3rd:0 Ran:1
2000 Turf 0-1: (6f) (frm)
Currently little account colt. **B Smart [0-1] W Mckay & P Di Canio.*

DICKIE DEADEYE BHB 70f **RR 74f** 5201[2]

3 b g Distant Relative 7f **(69)** - Accuracy (Gunner B) 11.2f **(58)**
Form - 756560152
Record 2000 - 1st:1 2nd:1 3rd:0 Ran:9
Win Prizemoney £2,103 *Total Prizemoney* £3,287
Wins * 2000 Spt Salisb (SFT) H 9.9f 65 73 <
2000 Turf 1-9: (8f 4, 10f 1-4, 12f) (hvy, g-s, gd 1-3, g-f 3, frm)
Light-framed, above-average gelding, effective 10 to 12f, acts on gd, likes tight tracks. Turf high 74 - also 1st of 17 giving 3lb to Fort Sumter (27 Spt Salisbury RF 4694). **G B Balding [1-9] Miss B Swire.*

DID YOU MISS ME (IRE) **RR 62f** 1795[5]

3 ch f Indian Ridge 7.6f **(74)** - Upward Trend (Salmon Leap (USA)) 11f **(61)**
Form - 75
Record 2000 - 1st:0 2nd:0 3rd:0 Ran:2
2000 Turf 0-2: (6f 2) (gd, g-f)
Workmanlike, currently average filly. Turf high 62.
**J Noseda [0-2] Paul & Jenny Green.*

DIETRICH (USA) **RR 90f** 4913a[10]

2 br f Storm Cat (USA) 7f **(86)** - Piquetnol (USA) **(95f)** (Private Account (USA)) 8.5f **(74)**
Form - 24180
2000 Turf 1-5: (5f 1-3, 6f 2) (sft, g-s, gd, g-f 1-2)
Useful filly. Turf high 90 - also 1st of 8 from Patinnam (23 Jly Tipperary RF 3123a). Landed long odds-on when winning at Tipperary on her third start before finishing a respectable eighth in the Cheveley Park. **A P O'Brien in IRE [1-5] Michael Tabor.*

DIFFERENTIAL (USA) BHB 93f **RR 87f** 3388[4]

3 b br c Known Fact (USA) 8.3f **(72)** - Talk About Home (USA) (Elocutionist (USA)) 8f **(77)**
Form - 554
Record 2000 - 1st:0 2nd:0 3rd:0 Ran:3
Pre2000 - 1st:1 2nd:0 3rd:1 Ran:4
Win Prizemoney £3,647 *Total Prizemoney* £6,804
Wins * 1999 Jly Windso (G-F) 5f 82+ <
2000 Turf 0-3: (5f, 6f 2) (g-f 2, frm)
Workmanlike, useful colt, effective 5f, acts on gd to g-f. Turf high 86 (began Jly). Won on his debut at Windsor as a juvenile, but looked in need of the race on his belated first two runs of last term. **B Smart [1-7] Peter Nelson And Partners.*

DIGITAL BHB 80f **RR 84f** 5064[1]

3 ch g Safawan 6.6f **(60)** - Heavenly Goddess (Soviet Star (USA))
Form - 423021
Record 2000 - 1st:1 2nd:2 3rd:1 Ran:6
Win Prizemoney £3,172 *Total Prizemoney* £6,434
Wins * 2000 Oct Nottin (SFT) H 8.2f 74 84 <
2000 Turf 1-6: (7f, 8f 1-5) (sft 1-1, g-s, g-f 2, frm 2)
Scopey, decent gelding, effective 8f, acts on sft. Turf high 84 (began Jly) - 1st of 14 giving 7lb to My Retreat (18 Oct Nottingham RF 5064). **M R Channon [1-6] W G R Wightman.*

DIGITAL IMAGE BHB 60f **RR 69f** 1782[8]

3 b c Presidium 7.5f **(56)** - Sally Tadpole (Jester)
Form - 6008
Record 2000 - 1st:0 2nd:0 3rd:0 Ran:4
Pre2000 - 1st:1 2nd:0 3rd:0 Ran:4
Win Prizemoney £7,422 *Total Prizemoney* £7,602
Wins * 1999 May Cheste (G-F) 5.1f 92+ <
2000 Turf 0-4: (7f 3, 8f) (gd 3, g-f)
Workmanlike, average colt, effective 5f, acts on g-f. Turf high 69.
**R Hannon [1-8] Kellco Ltd.*

DIGNIFY (IRE) **RR 101f** 3580[5]

3 b f Rainbow Quest (USA) 11.2f **(81)** - Her Ladyship **(115df)** (Polish Precedent (USA)) 10.2f **(60)**
Form - 45
Record 2000 - 1st:0 2nd:0 3rd:0 Ran:2
Pre2000 - 1st:2 2nd:0 3rd:1 Ran:4
Win Prizemoney £23,681 *Total Prizemoney* £28,280
Wins 1999 Spt Chanti (GD) G3 8f 88 <
1999 Jly Chanti (GD) 7f
2000 Turf 0-2: (11f, 12f) (gd 2)
Very useful filly, effective 11f, acts on gd. Turf high 101 (1st run) - 4th of 18 to Timi (21 May San Siro 11f gd RF 1455a). She was a close fourth in the Italian Oaks on her comeback but disappointed at Ascot three months later.
**S bin Suroor [0-2] Godolphin (from D R Loder in FR [2-4] Oct 1999).*

DIGON DA BHB 62f **RR 61f** 1210[12]

4 ch g Sparky Lad - Fleur Power (IRE) (The Noble Player (USA)) 6.5f **(67)**
Form - 00
Record 2000 - 1st:0 2nd:0 3rd:0 Ran:2
Pre2000 - 1st:0 2nd:0 3rd:1 Ran:6
Win Prizemoney £0 *Total Prizemoney* £933
2000 Turf 0-2: (8f, 10f) (g-f, frm)
Workmanlike, average gelding, effective 8f, acts on gd to frm, favours tight tracks. Turf high 42. Becoming disappointing.
**B Palling [0-8] Davies and Bridgeman.*

DIHATJUM BHB 55f **RR 64f** 5122[8]

3 b g Mujtahid (USA) 7.4f **(69)** - Rosie Potts (Shareef Dancer (USA)) 9.9f **(73)**
Form - 3247123378
Record 2000 - 1st:1 2nd:2 3rd:3 Ran:10
Pre2000 - 1st:0 2nd:1 3rd:2 Ran:9
Win Prizemoney £2,299 *Total Prizemoney* £7,757
Wins * 2000 Aug Carlis (FRM) C 6.9f 62 <
2000 Turf 1-10: (7f 1-6, 8f 4) (g-s, g-f 5, frm 1-4)
Leggy, average gelding, effective 6 to 7f, best at 7f, acts on g-f to hrd, best on frm, has worn blinkers, excels at Newcastle. Turf high 65 - 2nd of 10 getting 8lb from Desert Safari (6 Jly Catterick 7f g-f RF 2561) - also 1st of 6 giving 5lb to Bajan Belle (7 Aug Carlisle RF 3427).
**T D Easterby [1-19] The Gordon Partnership.*

DIKTAT BHB 117f **RR 123f** 4596[6]

5 br h Warning 8.1f **(77)** - Arvola (Sadler's Wells (USA)) 10f **(76)**
Form - 6236
Record 2000 - 1st:0 2nd:1 3rd:1 Ran:4
Pre2000 - 1st:7 2nd:1 3rd:0 Ran:10
Win Prizemoney £249,654 *Total Prizemoney* £509,167
Wins * 1999 Spt Haydoc (G-F) G1 6f 120
* 1999 Aug Deauvi (HVY) G1 6.5f 123 <
* 1999 Jun Newmar (G-F) G3 7f 118
* 1999 May Goodwo (GD) 7f 121+
1998 Jun Ascot (GD) G3 7f 114
1998 May Leices (GD) 7f 115+
1998 Apr Newmar (SFT) 7f 90+
2000 Turf 0-4: (7f, 8f 3) (sft, gd, frm 2)
Very high-class colt, effective 6 to 8f, best at 7f, acts on frm, does well at Longchamp. Turf high 117 - 3rd of 8 to Indian Lodge (3 Spt Longchamp 8f sft RF 4290a). Consistent. Showed high-class form at six and seven furlongs in 1999, winning the Haydock Sprint Cup, and ran with credit abroad last year if not managing a win. He has now been retired to Dalham Hall Stud at a fee of £10,000.
**S bin Suroor [4-9] Godolphin (from D R Loder [3-5] Jly 1998).*

DIL BHB 55f79a **RR 58f 79a** 1187[20]

5 b g Primo Dominie 7.2f **(67)** - Swellegant (Midyan (USA)) 6f **(60)**
Form - 5730180800
Record 2000 - 1st:1 2nd:0 3rd:0 Ran:7
Pre2000 - 1st:5 2nd:1 3rd:2 Ran:29
Win Prizemoney £28,750 *Total Prizemoney* £32,481
Wins * 2000 *Jan Wolver (STD) H 5f 89 91*
* 1999 *Apr Wolver (STD) H 5f 90 95* <
* 1999 *Mar Southw (SLW) H 5f 83 85*
* 1998 Spt Leices (G-F) H 5f 78 82
* 1998 Jly Doncas (G-F) H 6f 73 76
1998 May Doncas (GD) 5f 74
2000 Turf 0-2: (5f, 6f) (g-f, hrd) 2000 AW 1-5: (5f 1-2, 6f 3) (Fibr 1-5)
Useful gelding, effective 5f, - acts on Fibr, has worn blinkers, likes left handed tracks, likes tight tracks. Turf high 39. AW high 91 - 1st of 11 giving 25lb to Yabint El Sham (25 Jan Wolverhampton RF 0155). Effective over five and six furlongs, he reserves his best for Fibresand sprints these days, especially the minimum trip at Wolverhampton.
**Mrs N Macauley [5-27] Mrs N Macauley (from B Hanbury [1-9] Jun 1998).*

DILETIA BHB 56f **RR 60f** 5054[13]
3 b f Dilum (USA) 7.1f **(56)** - Miss Laetitia (IRE) **(36f)** (Entitled)
Form - 045674140
Record 2000 - 1st:1 2nd:0 3rd:0 Ran:9
Pre2000 - 1st:0 2nd:0 3rd:0 Ran:2
Win Prizemoney £2,051 *Total Prizemoney* £2,051
Wins * 2000 Spt Leices (G-S) S 10f 51+ <
2000 Turf 1-9: (7f, 8f 4, 10f 1-4) (sft, g-s, gd 3, g-f 1-1, frm 3)
Scopey, average filly, often wears blinkers (very effectively), likes tight tracks. Turf high 60. Consistent.
**N A Graham [1-11] T H Chadney.*

DILETTO (IRE) BHB 35f60a **RR 40f 60a** 2560[9]
4 b f Mujadil (USA) 7.7f **(70)** - Avidal Park (Horage) 10.3f **(61)**
Form - 08602617680
Record 2000 - 1st:1 2nd:1 3rd:0 Ran:11
Pre2000 - 1st:0 2nd:2 3rd:6 Ran:28
Win Prizemoney £1,960 *Total Prizemoney* £8,415
Wins * 2000 Mar Catter (GD) S 7f 35 <
2000 Turf 1-5: (7f 1-4, 8f) (gd 2, g-f, frm 1-2) 2000 AW 0-6: (7f, 8f 3, 11f, 12f) (Fibr 6)
Lengthy, moderate filly, effective 8f, acts on g-f, has worn blinkers. Turf high 40. AW high 46. **E J Alston [1-39] Liam & Tony Ferguson.*

DILKUSHA (IRE) BHB 74f76a **RR 77f 76a** 4284[8]
5 b g Indian Ridge 7.6f **(74)** - Crimson Glen (Glenstal (USA)) 10.1f **(64)**
Form - 60843548
Record 2000 - 1st:0 2nd:0 3rd:1 Ran:7
Pre2000 - 1st:3 2nd:1 3rd:2 Ran:23
Win Prizemoney £11,337 *Total Prizemoney* £16,725
Wins * 1999 Jly Newbur (G-F) H 7f 75 76 <
* 1999 Jun Kempto (G-F) H 7f 73 75
* 1998 Aug Bright (FRM) H 7f 67 72
2000 Turf 0-7: (7f 6, 8f) (g-f 2, frm 5)
Above-average gelding, effective 7f, acts on g-f to frm, best on frm, has worn blinkers, excels at Kempton. Turf high 77 - 3rd of 8 giving 15lb to Hail The Chief (31 Jly Folkestone 7f frm RF 3246). Consistent. **B J Meehan [3-30] Trevor Painting.*

DILLY RR 75f 4334[1]
2 br f Dilum (USA) 7.1f **(56)** - Princess Rosananti (IRE) (Shareef Dancer (USA)) 9.9f **(73)**
Form - 2431
Record 2000 - 1st:1 2nd:1 3rd:1 Ran:4
Win Prizemoney £4,543 *Total Prizemoney* £5,943
Wins * 2000 Spt Yarmou (G-F) H 7f 66 75 <
2000 Turf 1-4: (7f 1-4) (gd, g-f, frm 1-2)
Above-average filly. Turf high 75 (began Jly) - 1st of 15 giving 7lb to Monica Geller (12 Spt Yarmouth RF 4334).
**P R Chamings [1-4] Mrs J E L Wright.*

DILSAA BHB 59f60a **RR 67f 60a** 4929[9]
3 ch g Night Shift (USA) 8.1f **(73)** - Llia **(86f)** (Shirley Heights) 10.3f **(74)**
Form - 58786460
Record 2000 - 1st:0 2nd:0 3rd:0 Ran:8
Pre2000 - 1st:0 2nd:1 3rd:0 Ran:4
Win Prizemoney £0 *Total Prizemoney* £1,515
2000 Turf 0-7: (7f 3, 8f 3, 9f) (gd 2, g-f, frm 4) 2000 AW 0-1: (8f) (Equi)
Lengthy, average gelding, effective 7f, acts on g-s, has worn blinkers, likes tight tracks. Turf high 72. Consistent.
**P W Harris [0-12] G Knight & D Patel.*

DILSHAAN RR 106+f 5124[1]
2 b c Darshaan 11.9f **(81)** - Avila (Ajdal (USA)) 9.2f **(89)**
Form - 21
Record 2000 - 1st:1 2nd:1 3rd:0 Ran:2
Win Prizemoney £105,000 *Total Prizemoney* £106,512
Wins * 2000 Oct Doncas (SFT) G1 8f 106+ <
2000 Turf 1-2: (7f, 8f 1-1) (g-s 1-1, frm)
Currently Pattern-class colt. Turf high 106 (began Spt) - 1st of 10 from Tamburlaine (21 Oct Doncaster RF 5124). Ran green when runner-up at Sandown on his debut and looked a high-class prospect when landing the Racing Post Trophy next time. Gives the impression he should get further, but whether he will stay the Derby distance must be open to doubt considering his dam's side.
**Sir Michael Stoute [1-2] Saeed Suhail.*

DIM DOT BHB 42a **RR 43f 42a** 4927[8]
2 b c Inzar (USA) - Plucky Pet **(40f 28a)** (Petong) 6.6f **(58)**
Form - 08
Record 2000 - 1st:0 2nd:0 3rd:0 Ran:2
2000 Turf 0-1: (5f) (gd) 2000 AW 0-1: (5f) (Equi)
Currently moderate colt. **B Palling [0-2] Mrs D J Hughes.*

DIMMING OF THE DAY BHB 50f59a **RR 51f 59a** 523[11]
3 ch f Muhtarram (USA) - Darkness At Noon (USA) (Night Shift (USA)) 7.2f **(69)**
Form - 1330
Record 2000 - 1st:0 2nd:0 3rd:0 Ran:1
Pre2000 - 1st:1 2nd:3 3rd:3 Ran:11
Win Prizemoney £1,850 *Total Prizemoney* £4,311
Wins 1999 *Nov Wolver (STD) S 5f 65* <
2000 Turf 0-1: (6f) (gd)
Strong, average filly, effective 5f, - acts on Fibr, often wears blinkers, prefers left handed tracks.
**J J O'Neill [0-1] A J Oliver (from A T Murphy [0-2] Dec 1999).*

DIM OFAN BHB 49f60a **RR 55f 60a** 4695[11]
4 b f Petong 7.6f **(58)** - Wilsonic (Damister (USA)) 9f **(73)**
Form - 64106007480
Record 2000 - 1st:1 2nd:0 3rd:0 Ran:10
Pre2000 - 1st:2 2nd:2 3rd:1 Ran:17
Win Prizemoney £10,025 *Total Prizemoney* £13,215
Wins * 2000 *Jan Southw (STD) H 8f 60 62*
1998 Oct Nottin (SFT) 6.1f 84? <
* 1998 Jly Chepst (GD) 6.1f 69
2000 Turf 0-5: (7f, 8f, 10f 2, 12f) (g-s, gd, frm 3) 2000 AW 1-5: (8f 1-3, 9f 2) (Fibr 1-5)
Fair filly, effective 6 to 8f, best at 6f, acts on gd - acts on Fibr, has worn blinkers. Turf high 55. AW high 62 - 1st of 11 giving 6lb to Kass Alhawa (14 Jan Southwell RF 0087). Inconsistent.
**B Palling [3-27] Mrs J E Morton.*

DI MOI OUI RR 111+f 4847a[5]
3 b f Warning 8.1f **(77)** - Biosphere (Pharly (FR)) 9.8f **(68)**
Form - 0115
2000 Turf 2-4: (9f 1-1, 10f 1-2, 11f) (gd 1-3, g-f 1-1)
Group-class filly. Turf high 111 - 1st of 6 from Tres Ravi (19 Aug Deauville RF 3945a) - also 1st of 11 from Premiere Creation (30 Jun Chantilly RF 2578a). **P Bary in FR [2-4].*

DIM SUMS (USA) BHB 100f **RR 99f** 4747[1]
2 b g Repriced (USA) - Regal Baby (USA) (Northern Baby (CAN)) 11.6f **(71)**
Form - 21111
Record 2000 - 1st:4 2nd:1 3rd:0 Ran:5
Win Prizemoney £119,128 *Total Prizemoney* £119,758
Wins * 2000 Spt Redcar (SFT) 6f 97+
* 2000 Aug Newmar (GD) H 6f 91 99 <
* 2000 Jly Pontef (GD) H 6f 81+
* 2000 *May Southw (STD) 6f 72*
2000 Turf 3-3: (6f 3-3) (gd 1-1, frm 2-2) 2000 AW 1-2: (5f, 6f 1-1) (Fibr 1-2)
Very useful gelding. Turf high 99 (began Jly) - 1st of 12 giving 2lb to Caustic Wit (5 Aug Newmarket RF 3402) - also 1st of 23 getting 3lb from Zietunzeen (30 Spt Redcar RF 4747). AW high 72. Took a maiden on Fibresand, and was a convincing winner of Pontefract and Newmarket nurseries after switching to Turf. He ended the season with a comfortable victory in the valuable juvenile sales race at Redcar. He was subsequently sold to race in the United States. **T D Barron [4-5] Executive Network (P Group).*

DINAR (USA) BHB 64f **RR 62+f** 2682[1]
5 b h Dixieland Band (USA) 10.1f **(80)** - Bold Jessie (Never so Bold) 6.3f **(66)**
Form - 30282711
Record 2000 - 1st:2 2nd:2 3rd:1 Ran:8
Pre2000 - 1st:1 2nd:1 3rd:1 Ran:10
Win Prizemoney £9,491 *Total Prizemoney* £12,324
Wins * 2000 Jly Windso (SFT) H 8.3f 48 62 <
* 2000 Jly Windso (GD) H 8.3f 46 50
1999 Spt Kempto (G-F) H 12f 36 42
2000 Turf 2-8: (7f, 8f 2-4, 10f, 11f 2) (hvy, sft, g-s, gd 1-1, g-f, frm 1-2, hrd)

Average colt, effective 8f, acts on gd, likes tight tracks. Turf high 62 - 1st of 16 getting 8lb from Compatriot (10 Jly Windsor RF 2682). **R Brotherton [2-8] J Rees (from P Bowen [1-10] Nov 1999).*

DINKY BHB 27f RR 28f 4329[7]

3 ch f Floose 16f **(5)** - Marinsky (USA) (Diesis) 9.3f **(69)**
Form - 7008008807
Record 2000 - 1st:0 2nd:0 3rd:0 Ran:8
Pre2000 - 1st:0 2nd:0 3rd:0 Ran:5
2000 Turf 0-7: (8f, 10f 2, 11f, 12f 3) (gd 2, g-f, frm 4) 2000 AW 0-1: (8f) (Fibr)
Little account filly, effective 12f, acts on frm. Turf high 28 - 8th of 18 getting 21lb from Artic Courier (24 Jly Windsor 12f frm RF 3080). **M J Ryan [0-13] M J Ryan.*

DINOFELIS BHB 61f RR 59f 4689[7]

2 b c Rainbow Quest (USA) 11.2f **(81)** - Revonda (IRE) (Sadler's Wells (USA)) 10f **(76)**
Form - 057
Record 2000 - 1st:0 2nd:0 3rd:0 Ran:3
2000 Turf 0-3: (8f 3) (g-s, gd 2)
Currently fair colt. Turf high 59 (began Spt).
**P W Harris [0-3] Mrs P W Harris.*

DINO'S GIRL BHB 40f RR 30f 1038[15]

3 ch f Sabrehill (USA) 8.5f **(64)** - Nashya (Rousillon (USA)) 8.2f **(74)**
Form - 0
Record 2000 - 1st:0 2nd:0 3rd:0 Ran:1
Pre2000 - 1st:0 2nd:0 3rd:0 Ran:3
2000 Turf 0-1: (5f) (frm)
Scopey, very moderate filly. **W T Kemp [0-4] W T Kemp.*

DION DEE BHB 43f39a RR 50f 39a 4269[15]

4 ch f Anshan 8.2f **(63)** - Jade Mistress (Damister (USA)) 9f **(73)**
Form - 87300361825640
Record 2000 - 1st:1 2nd:1 3rd:2 Ran:14
Pre2000 - 1st:0 2nd:0 3rd:1 Ran:4
Win Prizemoney £2,968 *Total Prizemoney* £5,410
Wins * **2000** Jun Nottin (G-F) H 10f 39 42 <
2000 Turf 1-10: (10f 1-6, 11f, 12f 3) (gd 3, g-f 1-4, frm 3) 2000 AW 0-4: (10f, 12f 3) (Equi 2, Fibr 2)
Leggy, fair filly, effective 10 to 12f, best at 10f, acts on gd to frm. Turf high 50 - 2nd of 9 getting 13lb from Summer Song (13 Jly Folkestone 10f gd RF 2770) - also 1st of 10 getting 8lb from Pursuivant (17 Jun Nottingham RF 2049). AW high 47.
**Dr J R J Naylor [1-14] B C Mills (from A P Jarvis [0-4] May 1999).*

DIRECT DEAL BHB 49f RR 50f 3260[10]

4 b g Rainbow Quest (USA) 11.2f **(81)** - Al Najah (USA) (Topsider (USA)) 8.3f **(71)**
Form - 70000810
Record 2000 - 1st:1 2nd:0 3rd:0 Ran:8
Pre2000 - 1st:1 2nd:0 3rd:2 Ran:7
Win Prizemoney £5,998 *Total Prizemoney* £7,691
Wins * **2000** Jly Windso (GD) S 11.6f 50
1999 Jly Bath (G-F) 10.2f 72+ <
2000 Turf 1-8: (8f, 10f 4, 12f 1-3) (g-s, gd, g-f, frm 1-5)
Scopey, fair gelding, effective 10f, acts on hrd, has worn blinkers, favours tight tracks. Turf high 69.
**G M McCourt [1-8] Mrs B Taylor (from E A L Dunlop [1-7] Aug 1999).*

DIRECT REACTION (IRE) BHB 64f78a RR 60f 78a 4177[10]

3 b g College Chapel - Mary's Way (GR) **(78df)** (Night Shift (USA)) 7.2f **(69)**
Form - 533514114280
Record 2000 - 1st:3 2nd:1 3rd:1 Ran:10
Pre2000 - 1st:0 2nd:1 3rd:1 Ran:7
Win Prizemoney £8,989 *Total Prizemoney* £12,423
Wins * **2000** *Mar Lingfi (STD) H 7f 73 79* <
* **2000** *Feb Lingfi (STD) H 7f 69 74*
* **2000** *Jan Lingfi (STD) 6f 64+*
2000 Turf 0-3: (6f, 7f 2) (frm 3) 2000 AW 3-7: (6f 1-2, 7f 2-4, 8f) (Equi 3-5, Fibr 2)
Scopey, above-average gelding, effective 5 to 8f, best at 7f, acts on g-f - acts on Equi, often wears blinkers, likes left handed tracks, likes tight tracks, excels at Lingfield. Turf high 60 (began Aug). AW high 79 - 1st of 8 getting 1lb from First Venture (1 Mar Lingfield RF 0386) - also 1st of 11 giving 11lb to Legendaire (9 Feb Lingfield RF 0252). **Miss Gay Kelleway [3-17] A P Griffin.*

DISGLAIR RR 41f 1440[10]

2 b f River Falls 8.2f **(56)** - Bold Dove (Never so Bold) 6.3f **(66)**
Form - 070
Record 2000 - 1st:0 2nd:0 3rd:0 Ran:3
2000 Turf 0-2: (5f, 6f) (gd, frm) 2000 AW 0-1: (5f) (Fibr)
Currently moderate filly. Turf high 41.
**C W Thornton [0-3] Mrs Jill Murphy.*

DISPOL CHIEFTAN BHB 70f RR 71f 5081[4]

2 b c Clantime 6.6f **(57)** - Ski Baby (Petoski) 5.7f **(62)**
Form - 8550374
Record 2000 - 1st:0 2nd:0 3rd:1 Ran:7
Win Prizemoney £0 *Total Prizemoney* £474
2000 Turf 0-7: (5f 7) (hvy, gd 3, frm 3)
Above-average colt, effective 5f, acts on frm. Turf high 71.
**S E Kettlewell [0-7] W B Imison.*

DISPOL FOXTROT BHB 49f RR 48f 4996[3]

2 ch f Alhijaz 7.7f **(57)** - Foxtrot Pie (Shernazar) 10.2f **(73)**
Form - 0463
Record 2000 - 1st:0 2nd:0 3rd:1 Ran:4
Win Prizemoney £0 *Total Prizemoney* £537
2000 Turf 0-3: (6f, 8f 2) (gd 2, frm) 2000 AW 0-1: (8f) (Fibr)
Fair filly. Turf high 48 (began Aug). **S E Kettlewell [0-4] W B Imison.*

DISPOL JAZZ BHB 56f RR 62df 3035[8]

3 ch f Alhijaz 7.7f **(57)** - Foxtrot Pie (Shernazar) 10.2f **(73)**
Form - 37008
Record 2000 - 1st:0 2nd:0 3rd:1 Ran:5
Pre2000 - 1st:3 2nd:2 3rd:2 Ran:12
Win Prizemoney £10,075 *Total Prizemoney* £14,502
Wins * 1999 Oct Catter (SFT) H 7f 64 74 <
* 1999 Jly Carlis (GD) 5.9f 70
* 1999 May Thirsk (G-F) S 6f 64
2000 Turf 0-5: (7f, 8f 3, 10f) (gd, g-f 2, frm 2)
Light-framed, average filly, effective 6 to 7f, best at 6f, acts on gd to frm, best on frm. Turf high 63. Becoming disappointing.
**S E Kettlewell [3-17] W B Imison.*

DISPOL LAIRD RR 43f 3055[8]

2 ch c Clantime 6.6f **(57)** - She's a Breeze (Crofthall) 6.3f **(59)**
Form - 588
Record 2000 - 1st:0 2nd:0 3rd:0 Ran:3
2000 Turf 0-3: (5f 2, 7f) (gd 2, g-f)
Currently moderate colt. Turf high 43.
**S E Kettlewell [0-3] W B Imison.*

DISPOL MISS CHIEF BHB 43f RR 38f 1551[14]

3 ch f Be My Chief (USA) 10.2f **(62)** - Tino-Ella (Bustino) 10.4f **(64)**
Form - 0
Record 2000 - 1st:0 2nd:0 3rd:0 Ran:1
Pre2000 - 1st:0 2nd:0 3rd:0 Ran:3
2000 Turf 0-1: (14f) (g-f)
Scopey, very moderate filly.
**S E Kettlewell [0-1] W B Imison (from P Calver [0-3] Oct 1999).*

DISPOL ROCK (IRE) BHB 57f RR 63f 5168[9]

4 b g Ballad Rock 7.2f **(63)** - Havana Moon (Ela-Mana-Mou) 10.1f **(70)**
Form - 0000
Record 2000 - 1st:0 2nd:0 3rd:0 Ran:4
Pre2000 - 1st:2 2nd:2 3rd:2 Ran:11
Win Prizemoney £5,373 *Total Prizemoney* £9,781
Wins 1999 Aug Ripon (GD) H 10f 69 71+ <
1998 Spt Newcas (GD) 7f 66
2000 Turf 0-4: (9f, 10f 3) (sft, g-s, gd 2)
Workmanlike, average gelding, effective 9 to 10f, best at 10f, acts on g-f to frm, best on frm. Turf high 63. Becoming disappointing.
**S E Kettlewell [0-4] W B Imison (from P Calver [2-11] Oct 1999).*

DISTANT COUSIN BHB 78f RR 80f 5111[13]

3 b c Distant Relative 7f **(69)** - Tinaca (USA) (Manila (USA)) 9.3f **(71)**
Form - 2310
Record 2000 - 1st:1 2nd:1 3rd:1 Ran:4
Win Prizemoney £2,973 *Total Prizemoney* £4,488

Wins * **2000** *Spt Lingfi (STD) 13f 80* **<**
2000 Turf 0-3: (11f, 12f, 16f) (g-s, gd, frm) 2000 AW 1-1: (13f 1-1) (Equi 1-1)
Scopey, decent colt. Turf high 80 (began Aug) - 3rd of 19 to Dance Director (18 Spt Kempton 12f g-s RF 4486). (1st run) - 1st of 13 from Citrus Magic (29 Spt Lingfield RF 4730). Showed promise on turf before bolting up in a maiden on the Lingfield Equitrack in September. Could develop into a fair staying handicapper.
**H R A Cecil [1-4] Wafic Said.*

DISTANT DAWN BHB 51f RR 55f 4114[4]
2 b f Petong 7.6f **(58)** - Turbo Rose (Taufan (USA)) 7f **(57)**
Form - 4026004
Record 2000 - 1st:0 2nd:1 3rd:0 Ran:7
Win Prizemoney £0 *Total Prizemoney* £627
2000 Turf 0-7: (5f 2, 6f 3, 7f 2) (hvy, g-s, g-f, frm 4)
Fair filly, often wears blinkers. Turf high 55.
**B R Millman [0-7] Dean Ivory.*

DISTANT DECREE (USA) RR 53f 5098[22]
2 ch f Distant View (USA) - Nobile Decretum (USA) (Noble Decree (USA)) 10.2f **(76)**
Form - 0
Record 2000 - 1st:0 2nd:0 3rd:0 Ran:1
2000 Turf 0-1: (8f) (gd)
Currently fair filly. **J A Osborne [0-1] Wood Hall Stud Ltd.*

DISTANT FLAME BHB 31f RR 33f 5077[12]
3 b f Distant Relative 7f **(69)** - Brockton Flame **(65f)** (Emarati (USA))
Form - 07005600
Record 2000 - 1st:0 2nd:0 3rd:0 Ran:8
Pre2000 - 1st:0 2nd:0 3rd:0 Ran:1
2000 Turf 0-8: (6f 2, 7f 2, 8f 2, 10f, 11f) (g-s 2, gd 2, g-f 2, frm 2)
Workmanlike, very moderate filly, has worn blinkers. Turf high 50. Inconsistent. **N A Graham [0-9] First Millennium Racing.*

DISTANT GUEST BHB 59f RR 74f 5071[1]
3 b c Distant Relative 7f **(69)** - Teacher's Game (Mummy's Game) 8.2f **(60)**
Form - 2024050701
Record 2000 - 1st:1 2nd:2 3rd:0 Ran:10
Pre2000 - 1st:0 2nd:0 3rd:0 Ran:3
Win Prizemoney £2,289 *Total Prizemoney* £4,010
Wins * **2000** Oct Bath (GD) H 8f 54 60 <
2000 Turf 1-10: (7f 5, 8f 1-5) (hvy, sft, g-s 1-2, gd 3, g-f, frm, hrd)
Neat, above-average colt, effective 7f, acts on gd, often wears blinkers (very effectively). Turf high 74 - 2nd of 9 giving 3lb to Santiburi Girl (20 May Lingfield 7f gd RF 1326).
**G G Margarson [1-13] John Guest.*

DISTANT KING BHB 49f43a RR 42tf 43a 4776[11]
7 b g Distant Relative 7f **(69)** - Lindfield Belle (IRE) (Fairy King (USA)) 7.7f **(59)**
Form - 0000008800068080500
Record 2000 - 1st:0 2nd:0 3rd:0 Ran:18
Pre2000 - 1st:3 2nd:0 3rd:1 Ran:39
Win Prizemoney £7,950 *Total Prizemoney* £8,664
Wins * 1998 Jly Beverl (G-F) H 5f 49 54 <
* 1998 Jly Carlis (G-F) H 5f 43 45
* 1998 Jun Beverl (GD) H 5f 31 43
2000 Turf 0-18: (5f 8, 6f 3, 7f 5, 8f, 9f)(hvy, g-s 2, gd 3, g-f 4, frm 7, hrd)
Moderate gelding, has worn blinkers. Turf high 46. **G P Kelly [3-57] A Barrett (from S Coathup [0-1] Aug 1995).*

DISTANT MUSIC (USA) RR 123f 5327a[10]
3 b c Distant View (USA) - Musicanti (USA) (Nijinsky (CAN)) 10.3f **(77)**
Form - 28130
Record 2000 - 1st:1 2nd:1 3rd:1 Ran:5
Pre2000 - 1st:3 2nd:0 3rd:0 Ran:3
Win Prizemoney £203,120 *Total Prizemoney* £254,020
Wins * **2000** Spt Doncas (G-F) G3 8f 119 <
* 1999 Oct Newmar (GD) G1 7f 114+
* 1999 Spt Doncas (G-F) G2 7f 119+
* 1999 Jly Doncas (G-F) 7f 95++
2000 Turf 1-5: (7f, 8f 1-3, 10f) (gd 3, frm 1-2)
Scopey, very high-class colt, effective 7 to 10f, acts on gd to frm, best on frm. Turf high 123 - 3rd of 15 getting 5lb from Kalanisi (14 Oct Newmarket 10f gd RF 4989) - also 1st of 5 from Valentino (7 Spt Doncaster RF 4279). Consistent. Impressive when winning a maiden and the Champagne Stakes at Doncaster in his first two starts, he completed his juvenile programme with victory in Newmarket's Dewhurst Stakes though he did not impress everyone. Slightly disappointing when just touched off in the Greenham on his return, and again when only eighth in the Guineas. Returned after a lengthy absence to win a Group Three at the St Leger meeting, and was a good third in the Dubai Champion Stakes. Never dangerous in the Breeders' Cup Mile.
**B W Hills [4-8] Juddmonte Farms.*

DISTANT PROSPECT (IRE) BHB 84f RR 84f 5111[1]
3 b c Namaqualand (USA) - Ukraine's Affair (USA) (The Minstrel (CAN)) 10f **(72)**
Form - 2354111
Record 2000 - 1st:3 2nd:1 3rd:1 Ran:7
Pre2000 - 1st:0 2nd:0 3rd:1 Ran:4
Win Prizemoney £18,443 *Total Prizemoney* £20,606
Wins * **2000** Oct Newbur (SFT) H 16f 79 84 <
* **2000** Oct York (HVY) H 13.9f 74 81
* **2000** Spt Bath (GD) H 13.1f 69 74
2000 Turf 3-7: (10f, 12f 3, 13f 1-1, 14f 1-1, 16f 1-1) (sft 1-1, g-s, gd 1-3, g-f, frm 1-1)
Leggy, decent colt, effective 13 to 16f, acts on sft to frm, prefers left handed tracks. Turf high 84 - 1st of 15 giving 3lb to Mane Frame (20 Oct Newbury RF 5111) - also 1st of 14 getting 2lb from Kadoun (7 Oct York RF 4863).
**I A Balding [3-3] The Rae Smiths and Pauline Gale (from J R Arnold [0-8] Jly 2000).*

DISTANT STORM BHB 49f42a RR 53f 42a 3823[7]
7 ch g Pharly (FR) 11.5f **(64)** - Candle in the Wind (Thatching) 8f **(66)**
Form - 407
Record 2000 - 1st:0 2nd:0 3rd:0 Ran:3
Pre2000 - 1st:1 2nd:6 3rd:3 Ran:18
Win Prizemoney £2,243 *Total Prizemoney* £11,111
2000 Turf 0-3: (14f, 16f, 18f) (gd 2, g-f)
Fair gelding, effective 16 to 18f, best at 18f, acts on g-s to g-f, mostly wears blinkers (very effectively), prefers left handed tracks. Turf high 53 (1st run) - 4th of 12 getting 16lb from Royal Expression (24 Mar Doncaster 18f gd RF 0487). Consistent.
**B J Llewellyn [6-63] D H Driscoll (from M L W Bell [1-7] Aug 1996).*

DISTILLERY (USA) RR 58f 5075[4]
2 ch c Mister Baileys - Respectable (USA) (Northrop (USA))
Form - 4
Record 2000 - 1st:0 2nd:0 3rd:0 Ran:1
Win Prizemoney £0 *Total Prizemoney* £222
2000 Turf 0-1: (8f) (g-s)
Currently fair colt.
**P F I Cole [0-1] Highclere Thoroughbred Racing Ltd.*

DISTINCTIVE DREAM (IRE) BHB 58f55a RR 70f 55a 5316[9]
6 b g Distinctly North (USA) 7.4f **(63)** - Green Side (USA) (Green Dancer (USA)) 10.3f **(74)**
Form - 62153417367260804050 08270
Record 2000 - 1st:2 2nd:3 3rd:2 Ran:25
Pre2000 - 1st:7 2nd:7 3rd:0 Ran:38
Win Prizemoney £26,801 *Total Prizemoney* £44,850
Wins * **2000** *Feb Southw (STD) H 7f 63 65*
* **2000** *Feb Wolver (STD) S 7f 57*
1999 Jly Haydoc (FRM) 7.1f 73
1997 Spt Kempto (G-F) H 6f 73 79 <
1997 Aug Windso (GD) H 5f 63 70
1997 *Jly Southw (STD) H 5f 56 66*
1997 Jly Windso (G-F) H 6f 49 61
1997 Jly Salisb (FRM) CH 6f 43 53
1997 Jly Windso (GD) H 6f 45 50
2000 Turf 0-15: (6f 8, 7f 3, 8f 4) (sft, g-s, gd, g-f 7, frm 5) 2000 AW 2-10: (6f 4, 7f 2-5, 8f) (Equi, Fibr 2-9)
Above-average gelding, effective 6 to 8f, best at 7f, acts on g-f to frm, best on frm, often wears blinkers (extremely effectively), excels at Kempton. Turf high 70 - 2nd of 18 giving 16lb to Xanadu (7 May Hamilton 6f g-f RF 1073). AW high 65.
**A Bailey [2-25] A Thomson (from Lady Herries [1-13] Jly 1999).*

DISTINCTIVE MANNA (IRE) BHB 30f **RR 2f** 3971[14]
2 b g Ezzoud (IRE) - Butterwick Belle (IRE) **(48f 48a)** (Distinctly North (USA))
Form - 00
Record 2000 - 1st:0 2nd:0 3rd:0 Ran:2
2000 Turf 0-2: (5f, 7f) (frm, hrd)
Currently very poor gelding. Turf high 2 (began Aug).
**P C Haslam [0-2] Mrs B M Hawkins.*

DISTINCTLY BLU (IRE) BHB 70f63a **RR 71f 63a** 3630[13]
3 b f Distinctly North (USA) 7.4f **(63)** - Stifen (Burslem) 8.8f **(53)**
Form - 616252180
Record 2000 - 1st:2 2nd:2 3rd:0 Ran:9
Pre2000 - 1st:0 2nd:0 3rd:0 Ran:2
Win Prizemoney £11,336 *Total Prizemoney* £13,386
Wins * 2000 Jly Cheste (SFT) H 5.1f 64 71 <
*** 2000** Apr Mussel (G-S) H 5f 57 60
2000 Turf 2-7: (5f 2-4, 6f 3) (gd 1-1, g-f 1-2, frm 4) 2000 AW 0-2: (5f, 6f) (Fibr 2)
Scopey, above-average filly, effective 5 to 6f, best at 6f, acts on g-f to frm, best on g-f. Turf high 71 - 1st of 11 getting 16lb from Imperialist (14 Jly Chester RF 2797). AW high 60. She won a very poor event at Musselburgh in April, but landed a much better race at Chester in July. Very pacey from the stalls, she is suited by the minimum trip and cut in the ground.
**K A Ryan [2-11] The Gloria Darley Racing Partnership.*

DISTINCTLY CHIC (IRE) RR 77f 1614[2]
2 b f Distinctly North (USA) 7.4f **(63)** - Dane's Lane (IRE) (Danehill (USA)) 10f **(72)**
Form - 612
Record 2000 - 1st:1 2nd:1 3rd:0 Ran:3
Win Prizemoney £3,146 *Total Prizemoney* £4,215
Wins * 2000 May Hamilt (G-F) 5f 77 <
2000 Turf 1-3: (5f 1-2, 6f) (g-f 1-3)
Above-average filly. Turf high 77 - 2nd of 11 giving 2lb to Waterpark (1 Jun Ayr 6f g-f RF 1614) - also 1st of 10 giving 4lb to Shatin Dollybird (19 May Hamilton RF 1297). (DEAD)
**A P Jarvis [1-3] Christopher Shankland.*

DISTINCTLY DANCER (IRE) RR 106f 4715a[2]
2 b c Distinctly North (USA) 7.4f **(63)** - Shadow Casting **(68f)** (Warning)
Form - 372
2000 Turf 0-3: (5f, 6f 2) (hvy, g-s 2)
Currently Pattern-class colt. Turf high 106 (began Jly) - 2nd of 7 giving 3lb to Sign Of Nike (23 Spt San Siro 6f g-s RF 4715a).
**A Peraino in ITY [0-3] Jly 2000).*

DISTINCTLY EAST (IRE) BHB 56f **RR 57f** 2552[6]
3 b g Distinctly North (USA) 7.4f **(63)** - Raggy (Smoggy) 8f **(50)**
Form - 84056
Record 2000 - 1st:0 2nd:0 3rd:0 Ran:5
Pre2000 - 1st:1 2nd:1 3rd:0 Ran:7
Win Prizemoney £3,146 *Total Prizemoney* £6,314
Wins * 1999 Apr Ripon (G-F) 5f 74 <
2000 Turf 0-5: (7f, 8f 2, 10f 2) (gd 3, frm 2)
Workmanlike, fair gelding, effective 5 to 6f, acts on g-s to g-f, has worn blinkers. Turf high 57. Consistent.
**M H Tompkins [1-12] P F Riseborough.*

DISTINCTLY WELL (IRE) BHB 71f79a **RR 74f 79a** 1783[6]
3 b g Distinctly North (USA) 7.4f **(63)** - Brandywell (Skyliner) 7.3f **(53)**
Form - 23026
Record 2000 - 1st:0 2nd:2 3rd:1 Ran:5
Pre2000 - 1st:1 2nd:3 3rd:0 Ran:16
Win Prizemoney £6,092 *Total Prizemoney* £12,540
Wins * 1999 Aug Cheste (G-S) H 7f 70 77 <
2000 Turf 0-5: (9f, 10f, 11f, 12f 2) (hvy, g-s, gd 2, g-f)
Neat, above-average gelding, effective 5 to 12f, acts on hvy to g-f - acts on Fibr, has worn blinkers, likes tight tracks. Turf high 74 - 2nd of 11 giving 4lb to Desert Island Disc (27 May Warwick 11f hvy RF 1510). **P D Evans [1-21] The Bears Syndicate.*

DIVA BHB 68f65a **RR 66+f 65a** 2809[4]
3 b f Exit To Nowhere (USA) 8.7f **(77)** - Opera Lover (IRE) **(97f)** (Sadler's Wells (USA)) 10f **(76)**
Form - 6052214
Record 2000 - 1st:1 2nd:2 3rd:0 Ran:7
Win Prizemoney £3,126 *Total Prizemoney* £4,707
Wins * 2000 Jly Beverl (GD) H 9.9f 64 66 <
2000 Turf 1-3: (6f, 7f, 10f 1-1) (gd, frm 1-2) 2000 AW 0-4: (7f, 9f 2, 12f) (Equi 2, Fibr 2)
Rangy, average filly, effective 9 to 10f, acts on frm - acts on Fibr. Turf high 66 - 1st of 11 giving 9lb to Careless (7 Jly Beverley RF 2591). AW high 61 - 2nd of 13 giving 6lb to Perfect Moment (21 Jun Wolverhampton 9f Fibr RF 2177).
**Sir Mark Prescott [1-7] Cheveley Park Stud.*

DIVA'S ROBE (IRE) RR 71f 2998[6]
2 b f Robellino (USA) 9.5f **(68)** - High Note **(76f)** (Shirley Heights) 10.3f **(74)**
Form - 66
Record 2000 - 1st:0 2nd:0 3rd:0 Ran:2
2000 Turf 0-2: (7f 2) (frm 2)
Currently above-average filly. Turf high 71.
**N A Graham [0-2] Paul Jacobs.*

DIVE BHB 54f **RR 54f** 1029[8]
3 b g Slip Anchor 12.7f **(75)** - Delightful Chime (IRE) (Alzao (USA)) 7.1f **(68)**
Form - 8
Record 2000 - 1st:0 2nd:0 3rd:0 Ran:1
Pre2000 - 1st:0 2nd:0 3rd:0 Ran:3
2000 AW 0-1: (12f) (Fibr)
Well made, fair gelding. (DEAD) **Sir Mark Prescott [0-4] B Haggas.*

DIVEBOMB BHB 40f **RR 54f** 5237[9]
2 b f Rudimentary (USA) 8.2f **(66)** - Buzzbomb (Bustino) 10.4f **(64)**
Form - 00080
Record 2000 - 1st:0 2nd:0 3rd:0 Ran:5
2000 Turf 0-4: (5f, 6f, 8f 2) (g-s 2, gd, g-f) 2000 AW 0-1: (7f) (Fibr)
Fair filly, has worn blinkers. Turf high 54.
**R F JohnsonHoughton [0-5] R F JohnsonHoughton.*

DIVER'S PEARL (FR) BHB 81f **RR 83+f** 4755[13]
3 b f Prince Sabo 6.6f **(64)** - Seek the Pearl **(90df)** (Rainbow Quest (USA)) 10.4f **(75)**
Form - 213810
Record 2000 - 1st:2 2nd:1 3rd:1 Ran:6
Pre2000 - 1st:0 2nd:0 3rd:1 Ran:2
Win Prizemoney £9,014 *Total Prizemoney* £11,285
Wins * 2000 Spt Thirsk (GD) H 8f 75 83 <
*** 2000** *Apr Wolver (STD) 7f 80+*
2000 Turf 1-5: (6f, 7f, 8f 1-3) (g-s, gd 1-2, g-f, frm) 2000 AW 1-1: (7f 1-1) (Fibr 1-1)
Unfurnished, decent filly, effective 6 to 8f, acts on gd to frm - acts on Fibr. Turf high 83 - 1st of 7 giving 23lb to Falls O'Moness (2 Spt Thirsk RF 4170). (1st run) - 1st of 11 from Hoxton Square (28 Apr Wolverhampton RF 0900). She was successful at Thirsk in September to supplement her victory on the Wolverhampton Fibresand in April. A mile and a bit of cut in the ground may be her ideal conditions on turf. **J R Fanshawe [2-8] Cheveley Park Stud.*

DIVIDE AND RULE BHB 35f28a **RR 26f 28a** 83[12]
6 b h Puissance 7.1f **(60)** - Indivisible (Remainder Man) 11.2f **(45)**
Form - 0000
Record 2000 - 1st:0 2nd:0 3rd:0 Ran:2
Pre2000 - 1st:1 2nd:0 3rd:4 Ran:34
Win Prizemoney £3,028 *Total Prizemoney* £5,616
Wins * 1996 Jun Ripon (G-F) 5f 71 <
2000 AW 0-2: (5f, 8f) (Fibr 2)
Little account horse. **R Hollinshead [1-36] M Johnson.*

DIVINE APPEAL BHB 49f **RR 57f** 4459[14]
5 b m El Gran Senor (USA) 8.9f **(85)** - Maribiya (FR) (Natroun (FR))
Form - 06700
Record 2000 - 1st:0 2nd:0 3rd:0 Ran:5
2000 Turf 0-5: (10f 2, 12f 2, 16f) (sft, g-s, frm 3)
Fair filly. Turf high 57. **Martyn Wane [0-5] W N Smith.*

DIVINE HOSTESS BHB 34f **RR 29f** 5164[10]
3 br f Batshoof 9.5f **(66)** - Divina Mia **(65f)** (Dowsing (USA))
Form - 0
Record 2000 - 1st:0 2nd:0 3rd:0 Ran:1

Pre2000 - 1st:0 2nd:0 3rd:0 Ran:3
Win Prizemoney £0 *Total Prizemoney* £266
2000 Turf 0-1: (11f) (gd)
Leggy, little account filly. **M W Easterby [0-4] W H Jackson.*

DIVINE PROSPECT (IRE) BHB 65f **RR 71f** 4824[11]
3 b br f Namaqualand (USA) - Kayu (Tap On Wood) 10.3f **(65)**
Form - 6564023500
Record 2000 - 1st:0 2nd:1 3rd:1 Ran:10
Pre2000 - 1st:1 2nd:0 3rd:1 Ran:8
Win Prizemoney £4,581 *Total Prizemoney* £7,407
Wins * 1999 Aug Newmar (GD) H 7f 70 76 <
2000 Turf 0-10: (8f 2, 9f 2, 10f 3, 11f, 12f 2) (g-s, gd 3, g-f 3, frm 3)
Above-average filly, effective 7 to 11f, acts on g-f to frm, best on g-f, likes tight tracks. Turf high 72. Becoming disappointing.
**A P Jarvis [1-18] Christopher Shankland.*

DIVINE WIND BHB 61f **RR 74f** 5121[5]
2 ch f Clantime 6.6f **(57)** - Breezy Day (Day Is Done) 6.3f **(67)**
Form - 14733407702005
Record 2000 - 1st:1 2nd:1 3rd:2 Ran:14
Win Prizemoney £3,705 *Total Prizemoney* £6,602
Wins * 2000 Mar Doncas (GD) 5f 67 <
2000 Turf 1-14: (5f 1-7, 6f 3, 7f 3, 8f) (g-s 2, gd 1-6, g-f 4, frm, hrd)
Above-average filly, effective 5 to 6f, best at 5f, acts on gd to g-f, best on g-f. Turf high 74 - also 1st of 17 getting 5lb from Squirrel Nutkin (25 Mar Doncaster RF 0491). A sharp sort, she rather lost her way after a winning debut but came back after a break to run a couple of better races. Likely to be best over the minimum trip.
**B A McMahon [1-14] Mrs J McMahon.*

DIVORCE ACTION (IRE) BHB 60f60a **RR 67f 60a** 4054[1]
4 b g Common Grounds 8.1f **(66)** - Overdue Reaction (Be My Guest (USA)) 9.3f **(67)**
Form - 0250051
Record 2000 - 1st:1 2nd:1 3rd:0 Ran:7
Pre2000 - 1st:1 2nd:0 3rd:1 Ran:10
Win Prizemoney £4,848 *Total Prizemoney* £6,212
Wins * 2000 Aug Warwic (GD) S 10.9f 54
1999 Aug Kempto (G-F) C 9f 67 <
2000 Turf 1-6: (8f, 9f, 10f 3, 11f 1-1) (gd 1-3, frm 3) 2000 AW 0-1: (12f) (Equi)
Strong, average gelding, effective 9 to 11f, best at 10f, acts on gd to frm, favours tight tracks. Turf high 67 (1st run) - 2nd of 17 giving 13lb to A Day On The Dub (19 May Nottingham 10f gd RF 1309).
**R M Stronge [1-1] Kevin Elliott (from P R Hedger [1-13] Jly 2000).*

DIVULGE (USA) RR 89f 4755[18]
3 b c Diesis 9f **(80)** - Avira **(8f)** (Dancing Brave (USA)) 8.4f **(76)**
Form - 51400
Record 2000 - 1st:1 2nd:0 3rd:0 Ran:5
Win Prizemoney £3,900 *Total Prizemoney* £4,455
Wins * 2000 Jun Goodwo (G-F) 8f 86 <
2000 Turf 1-5: (8f 1-4, 9f) (g-s, g-f 1-2, frm 2)
Well made, useful colt. Turf high 89 - also 1st of 5 from Krantor (16 Jun Goodwood RF 2018). After a promising debut, he accomplished a simple task at Goodwood but his limitations have been exposed since. **J H M Gosden [1-5] K Abdulla.*

DIWAN (IRE) RR 67f 5157[9]
2 b c Be My Guest (USA) 10.2f **(66)** - Nectarine (IRE) (Darshaan) 9.9f **(84)**
Form - 00
Record 2000 - 1st:0 2nd:0 3rd:0 Ran:2
2000 Turf 0-2: (6f, 8f) (sft, gd)
Currently average colt. Turf high 67 (began Spt).
**R W Armstrong [0-2] Hamdan Al Maktoum.*

DIXIE FLYER (IRE) BHB 42f **RR 41f** 143[3]
3 b f Blues Traveller (IRE) - African Cousin (Kampala) 8.4f **(56)**
Form - 03
Record 2000 - 1st:0 2nd:0 3rd:1 Ran:2
Pre2000 - 1st:0 2nd:0 3rd:0 Ran:5
Win Prizemoney £0 *Total Prizemoney* £215
2000 AW 0-2: (7f, 9f) (Fibr 2)
Neat, moderate filly, has worn blinkers. AW high 1.
**E J Alston [0-7] The Burlington Partnership.*

DIXIELAKE (IRE) BHB 80f **RR 80f** 4755[15]
3 b f Lake Coniston (IRE) - Rathvindon (Realm) 8.1f **(65)**
Form - 1330
Record 2000 - 1st:1 2nd:0 3rd:2 Ran:4
Pre2000 - 1st:0 2nd:0 3rd:0 Ran:1
Win Prizemoney £4,013 *Total Prizemoney* £5,771
Wins * **2000** May Chepst (HVY) 8.1f 68 <
2000 Turf 1-4: (7f, 8f 1-2, 9f) (g-s 1-2, g-f, frm)
Decent filly. Turf high 80 - 3rd of 14 giving 3lb to Pips Way (12 Jly Kempton 9f g-f RF 2732). Scored in heavy ground at Chepstow on her reappearance and ran well on her handicap debut at Kempton in July.
**H Candy [1-5] C G P Wyatt.*

DIXIE'S DARTS RR 52f 4965[24]
2 b g Mistertopogigo (IRE) - Maestrette (Manado) 9.6f **(63)**
Form - 00
Record 2000 - 1st:0 2nd:0 3rd:0 Ran:2
2000 Turf 0-2: (6f 2) (gd, frm)
Currently fair gelding. Turf high 52 (began Spt).
**M H Tompkins [0-2] Yours For A Day Ltd.*

DIZZIE LIZZIE BHB 45f **RR 17tf** 3909[11]
3 b f Elmaamul (USA) 8.1f **(70)** - Linpac North Moor (Moorestyle) 6.9f **(64)**
Form - 880
Record 2000 - 1st:0 2nd:0 3rd:0 Ran:3
2000 Turf 0-3: (6f, 7f, 9f) (g-f 2, frm)
Unfurnished, currently poor filly. Turf high 17.
**T J Naughton [0-3] Mrs S Leech.*

DIZZY KNIGHT BHB 59f **RR 61f** 4774[9]
3 b f Distant Relative 7f **(69)** - Top Treat (USA) (Topsider (USA)) 8.3f **(71)**
Form - 400
Record 2000 - 1st:0 2nd:0 3rd:0 Ran:3
Pre2000 - 1st:0 2nd:0 3rd:0 Ran:1
Win Prizemoney £0 *Total Prizemoney* £312
2000 Turf 0-3: (6f 2, 8f) (g-s, gd, frm)
Scopey, average filly. Turf high 61 (began Aug).
**B Palling [0-3] Derek D & Mrs Jean P Clee (from M J Fetherston-Godley [0-1] Spt 1999).*

DIZZY TILLY BHB 32f26a **RR 54f 26a** 5244[10]
6 b m Anshan 8.2f **(63)** - Nadema (Artaius (USA)) 9f **(69)**
Form - 00043381860000
Record 2000 - 1st:1 2nd:0 3rd:2 Ran:14
Pre2000 - 1st:3 2nd:3 3rd:5 Ran:38
Win Prizemoney £11,042 *Total Prizemoney* £18,182
Wins * **2000** Jly Windso (GD) H 11.6f 44 50
* **1999** Jun Windso (G-F) H 11.6f 43 46
1997 Jun Windso (G-S) 10f 66 <
1997 Jun Windso (G-F) H 11.6f 57 64+
2000 Turf 1-11: (9f, 10f 2, 12f 1-7, 14f) (sft, gd, g-f, frm 1-7, hrd) 2000 AW 0-3: (12f 3) (Fibr 3)
Fair mare, effective 10 to 12f, best at 12f, acts on g-s to frm, best on frm, has worn blinkers, likes right handed tracks, favours tight tracks, and does well at Kempton. Turf high 54 - also 1st of 8 getting 4lb from Misconduct (3 Jly Windsor RF 2489). AW high 34. Becoming disappointing.
**A J McNae [2-30] L R Gotch (from T J Naughton [2-25] Oct 1998).*

DJAIS (FR) BHB 54f60a **RR 30f 60a** 5182[7]
11 ch g Vacarme (USA) - Dame de Carreau (FR) (Targowice (USA)) 11.4f **(70)**
Form - 127
Record 2000 - 1st:1 2nd:1 3rd:0 Ran:3
Pre2000 - 1st:1 2nd:1 3rd:3 Ran:15
Win Prizemoney £22,831 *Total Prizemoney* £25,158
Wins * **2000** *Jun Southw (STD) C 16f 60*
2000 Turf 0-1: (14f) (sft) 2000 AW 1-2: (16f 1-2) (Fibr 1-2)
Average gelding, has worn blinkers. AW high 60 (1st run). Inconsistent.
**J R Jenkins [5-41] Christopher Shankland (from R T Phillips [0-3] Jly 1995).*

DJIBOUTI (GER) RR 93f 1285a[2]
3 b c Dashing Blade 7.9f **(80)** - Diana Dancer (FR) (Fabulous Dancer (USA)) 9.4f **(70)**
Form - 2
2000 Turf 0-1: (8f) (gd)
Useful colt. (1st run) - 2nd of 11 to Pacino (14 May Cologne 8f gd RF 1285a). Runner-up in the German 2000 Guineas.
**M Trybuhl in GER [0-1] Stall Elite.*

DOBAANDI SECRET BHB 28f **RR 34f** 124[8]
4 b g Reprimand 8.2f **(63)** - Secret Dance (Sadler's Wells (USA)) 10f **(76)**
Form - 8
Record 2000 - 1st:0 2nd:0 3rd:0 Ran:1
Pre2000 - 1st:0 2nd:0 3rd:0 Ran:5
2000 AW 0-1: (15f) (Fibr)
Leggy, very moderate gelding. (DEAD)
**A Bailey [0-4] Smiley Partnership (from P D Evans [0-2] Nov 1998).*

DOBERMAN (IRE) BHB 46f45a **RR 44f 45a** 4101[7]
5 br g Dilum (USA) 7.1f **(56)** - Switch Blade (IRE) (Robellino (USA)) 7.6f **(80)**
Form - 8440350317822207
Record 2000 - 1st:1 2nd:3 3rd:2 Ran:14
Pre2000 - 1st:0 2nd:5 3rd:1 Ran:26
Win Prizemoney £2,166 *Total Prizemoney* £9,286
Wins * **2000** *Feb Wolver (STD) C* 8.5f 47 <
2000 Turf 0-4: (7f, 8f 2, 10f) (g-f, frm 3) 2000 AW 1-10: (7f 2, 8f 1-7, 9f) (Fibr 1-10)
Moderate gelding, effective 8f, acts on frm - acts on Fibr, often wears blinkers. Turf high 44 (began Jly). AW high 47 - 1st of 13 getting 6lb from Sharp Shuffle (19 Feb Wolverhampton RF 0319).
**P D Evans [1-27] Mrs I M Folkes (from S A Brookshaw [0-5] Jun 1999).*

DOC DAVIS (IRE) RR 32f 5099[18]
2 ch c Dr Devious (IRE) 9.9f **(74)** - Miracle of Love (USA) (Nureyev (USA)) 8.7f **(78)**
Form - 00
Record 2000 - 1st:0 2nd:0 3rd:0 Ran:2
2000 Turf 0-2. (7f 2) (gd, g-f)
Currently very moderate colt. Turf high 32 (began Spt).
**B W Hills [0-2] A N Foster.*

DOCKLANDS ROLLER (IRE) RR 49f 2250[8]
2 b g Inzar (USA) - Zestino (Shack (USA)) 5.8f **(53)**
Form - 058
Record 2000 - 1st:0 2nd:0 3rd:0 Ran:3
2000 Turf 0-3: (6f, 7f 2) (gd, frm 2)
Currently moderate gelding. Turf high 49.
**N Tinkler [0-3] Mrs Lisa Olley.*

DOC RYAN'S BHB 63f72a **RR 67f 72a** 14[5]
6 b h Damister (USA) 9.1f **(66)** - Jolimo (Fortissimo) 11.8f **(61)**
Form - 5
Record 2000 - 1st:0 2nd:0 3rd:0 Ran:1
Pre2000 - 1st:7 2nd:4 3rd:6 Ran:36
Win Prizemoney £21,841 *Total Prizemoney* £28,202
Wins * 1999 *Jun Wolver (STD) C* 12f 73 <
* 1999 *Jun Wolver (STD) C* 16.2f 73 <
* 1999 *Jun Southw (STD) C* 14f 73 <
* 1999 *May Southw (STD) H* 16f 62 73+
* 1999 *May Southw (STD) H* 14f 62 66+
* 1998 Jun Mussel (SFT) H 12f 61 68
* 1997 Nov Mussel (G-S) H 12f 61 67
2000 AW 0-1: (16f) (Fibr)
Above-average horse, effective 12 to 16f, acts on frm - acts on Fibr, often wears blinkers (very effectively), prefers left handed tracks, prefers tight tracks, excels at Wolverhampton, likes Southwell. **M J Ryan [8-45] Paul Blows.*

DOCTOR DENNIS (IRE) BHB 69f72a **RR 70f 72a** 4809[11]
3 b g Last Tycoon 9.4f **(73)** - Noble Lustre (USA) (Lyphard's Wish (FR)) 9f **(74)**
Form - 00021271224420
Record 2000 - 1st:2 2nd:5 3rd:0 Ran:14
Pre2000 - 1st:0 2nd:1 3rd:0 Ran:7
Win Prizemoney £5,138 *Total Prizemoney* £10,853
Wins * **2000** Jly Windso (SFT) H 6f 60 57 <
* **2000** May Bright (SFT) S 6f 48
2000 Turf 2-13: (6f 2-11, 7f, 8f) (sft, g-s, gd 2-4, g-f 3, frm 4) 2000 AW 0-1: (6f) (Fibr)
Unfurnished, above-average gelding, effective 6 to 7f, best at 6f, acts on gd to frm - acts on Fibr, best on frm, has worn blinkers, likes left handed tracks, excels at Lingfield and does well at Brighton. Turf high 70 - 4th of 12 getting 6lb from Banafsajyh (11 Aug Lingfield 6f frm RF 3555). (1st run) - 2nd of 8 giving 4lb to Nite-Owl Mate (13 Jly Wolverhampton 6f Fibr RF 2779).
**B J Meehan [2-21] Mrs Judith Mendonca.*

DOCTOR JOHN BHB 55f **RR 60f** 3015[4]
3 ch g Handsome Sailor 6.6f **(53)** - Bollin Sophie **(33f)** (Efisio)
Form - 0744
Record 2000 - 1st:0 2nd:0 3rd:0 Ran:4
Win Prizemoney £0 *Total Prizemoney* £220
2000 Turf 0-3: (10f, 12f 2) (gd 2, frm) 2000 AW 0-1: (12f) (Fibr)
Leggy, average gelding. Turf high 60.
**Andrew Turnell [0-4] Dr John Hollowood.*

DOCTOR SPIN (IRE) BHB 105f **RR 106f** 3514[2]
4 b c Namaqualand (USA) - Madam Loving (Vaigly Great) 7f **(58)**
Form - 1502
Record 2000 - 1st:1 2nd:1 3rd:0 Ran:4
Pre2000 - 1st:2 2nd:0 3rd:1 Ran:9
Win Prizemoney £16,800 *Total Prizemoney* £27,622
Wins * **2000** May Newmar (GD) H 6f 98 103 <
* 1998 May Lingfi (GD) 5f 93+
* 1998 May Windso (G-F) 5f 82
2000 Turf 1-4: (6f 1-4) (gd 2, g-f, frm 1-1)
Leggy, Pattern-class colt, effective 6f, acts on gd to frm. Turf high 106 - 5th of 10 getting 4lb from Lend A Hand (18 May York 6f gd RF 1276) - also 1st of 13 giving 3lb to Sheer Viking (7 May Newmarket RF 1077). He put up a fine performance to win a competitive rated stakes at Newmarket on his return and stepped up on that with an excellent fifth in the Group Two Duke of York Stakes, but was down the field in the Wokingham. Better run on his final start. He tends to sweat profusely before his races, but it does not affect his running. **R F JohnsonHoughton [3-13] Anthony Pye-Jeary.*

DODONA BHB 61f **RR 62f** 5320[7]
2 b f Lahib (USA) 8f **(69)** - Dukrame (Top Ville) 11.7f **(68)**
Form - 400407
Record 2000 - 1st:0 2nd:0 3rd:0 Ran:6
Win Prizemoney £0 *Total Prizemoney* £587
2000 Turf 0-6: (6f, 7f 4, 8f) (sft, gd 2, g-f 2, frm)
Average filly. Turf high 73 (began Jly).
**T D McCarthy [0-6] A D Spence.*

DOLFINESSE (IRE) BHB 37f **RR 51f** 4403[7]
3 ch f Dolphin Street (FR) - Gortadoo (USA) (Sharpen Up) 8.3f **(67)**
Form - 05234062067
Record 2000 - 1st:0 2nd:2 3rd:1 Ran:11
Pre2000 - 1st:0 2nd:0 3rd:0 Ran:6
Win Prizemoney £0 *Total Prizemoney* £2,320
2000 Turf 0-11: (7f, 8f 10) (gd 2, g-f 5, frm 4)
Neat, fair filly, effective 7f, acts on g-f, often wears blinkers (effectively), likes right handed tracks. Turf high 51 - 3rd of 11 getting 17lb from Desert Safari (18 Jun Carlisle 7f g-f RF 2069).
**M Brittain [0-17] Steven Box.*

DOLLAR BIRD (IRE) BHB 93f **RR 102f** 5311[3]
3 b f Kris 10f **(75)** - High Spirited (Shirley Heights) 10.3f **(74)**
Form - 3280203
Record 2000 - 1st:0 2nd:2 3rd:2 Ran:7
Pre2000 - 1st:1 2nd:0 3rd:0 Ran:3
Win Prizemoney £4,695 *Total Prizemoney* £17,142
Wins * 1999 Spt Nottin (GD) 8.2f 84 <
2000 Turf 0-7: (10f, 11f, 12f 3, 14f, 15f) (sft, g-s, gd 3, g-f 2)
Well made, very useful filly, effective 11 to 14f, acts on gd to g-f. Turf high 102 - 2nd of 7 to Film Script (13 May Lingfield 11f gd RF 1191). She gained black type when a gallant second in a sub-standard Lingfield Oaks Trial, but was well beaten in better company. Decent effort in a 14-furlong handicap at Goodwood.
**J L Dunlop [1-10] Sir Thomas Pilkington.*

DOLPHIN BEECH (IRE) BHB 35f **RR 39f** 5243^{10}
2 b f Dolphin Street (FR) - Prenom Carmen (IRE) (Persian Bold) 9.3f **(66)**
Form - 00
Record 2000 - 1st:0 2nd:0 3rd:0 Ran:2
2000 Turf 0-1: (6f) (g-f) 2000 AW 0-1: (6f) (Fibr)
Currently moderate filly. **R Dickin [0-2] Clifford Beech.*

DOLPHINELLE (IRE) BHB 58f46a **RR 66+f 46a** 5185^{9}
4 b g Dolphin Street (FR) - Mamie's Joy (Prince Tenderfoot (USA)) 9f **(61)**
Form - 654104544373473160000

Record	**2000 -**	1st:2	2nd:0	3rd:3	Ran:18
	Pre2000 -	1st:1	2nd:2	3rd:2	Ran:24

Win Prizemoney £11,261 *Total Prizemoney* £15,293

Wins							
*** 2000**	May Newbur	(SFT)	H	7f	62	66+	
2000	*Jan Lingfi*	*(STD)*	*H*	*6f*	*55*	*55*	
1999	Jun Bright	(G-F)	H	6f	66	71	<

2000 Turf 1-8: (7f 1-3, 8f 5) (g-s 3, gd 1-2, g-f 2, frm) 2000 AW 1-10: (5f, 6f 1-5, 7f 4) (Equi 1-8, Fibr 2)
Unfurnished, average gelding, effective 6 to 7f, best at 7f, acts on gd to frm, best on frm, has worn blinkers. Turf high 66 - 1st of 14 getting 21lb from Brave Edge (31 May Newbury RF 1588). AW high 55 (1st run). Had a very busy first half of the year, scoring on the Lingfield Equitrack in January and on soft ground at Newbury in May.
**J R Poulton [1-8] Mrs G M Temmerman (from R Hannon [2-34] Apr 2000).*

2000 Turf 1-11: (5f 4, 7f 1-4, 8f 3) (sft, g-s, gd 6, g-f, frm 1-2)
Decent gelding, effective 7 to 8f, best at 8f, acts on g-s to frm, best on gd, excels at Newcastle. Turf high 82 - 2nd of 21 giving 3lb to Regatta Point (13 Oct Newmarket 8f gd RF 4970).
**M W Easterby [1-11] B Bargh, T Beston, J Walsh & S Godber.*

DOMINANT DUCHESS BHB 95f **RR 97f** 4987^{23}
6 b m Old Vic 12.8f **(72)** - Andy's Find (USA) (Buckfinder (USA)) 8.1f **(71)**
Form - 11100

Record	**2000 -**	1st:3	2nd:0	3rd:0	Ran:5
	Pre2000 -	1st:3	2nd:4	3rd:0	Ran:18

Win Prizemoney £62,738 *Total Prizemoney* £91,237

Wins							
*** 2000**	Aug Ascot	(G-F)	H	16.2f	92	97	<
*** 2000**	Jun Ascot	(G-F)		22.2f		92	
*** 2000**	May York	(FRM)	H	13.9f	82	84	
* 1999	May Kempto	(G-F)	H	14.4f	75	78	
* 1997	Apr Nottin	(G-F)		10f		73+	
* 1997	Mar Warwic	(G-F)	C	12.5f		61+	

2000 Turf 3-5: (14f 1-1, 16f 1-1, 18f 2, 22f 1-1) (gd 2-3, g-f 1-1, frm)
Very useful mare, has broken blood-vessels, effective 16 to 22f, acts on gd. Turf high 97 - 1st of 9 getting 13lb from Spirit of Love (12 Aug Ascot RF 3577) - also 1st of 8 getting 10lb from Three Cheers (23 Jun Ascot RF 2211). Inconsistent. She made a winning reappearance last season on her favoured fast ground at York, and followed up in fine style in the Queen Alexandra. Returned to Ascot to land the Shergar Cup Stayers, but was well beaten in the Doncaster Cup and the Cesarewitch. She stays extreme distances.
**J W Hills [6-23] Mrs Diana Patterson.*

Dominant Duchess (near side) had the upper hand at Ascot

DOLYDILLE (IRE) RR 106f $4796a^{1}$
4 b f Dolphin Street (FR) - Gradille (Home Guard (USA)) 9.3f **(66)**
Form - 2033410121
2000 Turf 3-9: (8f, 9f, 10f 2-5, 12f 1-2) (sft, g-s 3, gd 3-4, frm)
Pattern-class filly, effective 10 to 12f, acts on gd, prefers right handed tracks, and excels at Gowran Park. Turf high 106 - 1st of 9 giving 10lb to Fantasia Girl (30 Spt Curragh RF 4796a) - also 1st of 9 getting 1lb from Jammaal (5 Spt Galway RF 4339a). Improving. Showed steady improvement to end the season as a listed performer.
**J S Bolger in IRE [7-21] Mrs K Twomey.*

DOMINAITE BHB 80f **RR 82f** 5320^{8}
2 b g Komaite (USA) 6.9f **(61)** - Fairy Kingdom (Prince Sabo) 7.2f **(62)**
Form - 00321323238
Record 2000 - 1st:1 2nd:3 3rd:4 Ran:11
Win Prizemoney £4,595 *Total Prizemoney* £16,416

Wins							
*** 2000**	Jly Redcar	(G-F)	H	7f		72	<

DOMINELLE BHB 48f45a **RR 48f 45a** 5248^{10}
8 b m Domynsky 7.8f **(58)** - Gymcrak Lovebird (Taufan (USA)) 7f **(57)**
Form - 0004048610050

Record	**2000 -**	1st:1	2nd:0	3rd:0	Ran:13
	Pre2000 -	1st:8	2nd:12	3rd:9	Ran:88

Win Prizemoney £30,246 *Total Prizemoney* £54,224

Wins							
*** 2000**	Jly Thirsk	(FRM)	H	6f	46		
* 1998	Aug Ripon	(G-F)	H	6f	65	67	<
* 1998	Aug Redcar	(G-F)	H	6f	53	63	
* 1998	Aug Pontef	(G-F)	H	5f	54	58	
* 1998	Jun Doncas	(GD)	H	6f	48	49	
* 1996	Jun Beverl	(G-F)	H	5f	45	46	

2000 Turf 1-12: (5f 7, 6f 1-5) (sft, gd 2, g-f, frm 4, hrd 1-4) 2000 AW 0-1: (6f) (Fibr)
Moderate mare, effective 5 to 6f, best at 5f, acts on gd to frm, best on frm, prefers left handed tracks, prefers tight tracks, excels at Pontefract. Turf high 46. Inconsistent.
**T D Easterby [6-79] Mrs Sue Tindall (from M H Easterby [3-22] Oct*

1995).

DOMINION PRINCE BHB 64f **RR 54f** 5121[9]
2 b c First Trump - Lammastide (Martinmas) 7.6f **(59)**
Form - 00770
Record 2000 - 1st:0 2nd:0 3rd:0 Ran:5
2000 Turf 0-5: (6f 2, 7f 2, 8f) (g-s, gd, g-f, frm 2)
Fair colt. Turf high 54 (began Aug).
**R Hannon [0-5] Major A M Everett.*

DOMINIQUE **RR 75f** 2038[3]
2 ch f Primo Dominie 7.2f **(67)** - Tender Loving Care (Final Straw) 7.9f **(64)**
Form - 03
Record 2000 - 1st:0 2nd:0 3rd:1 Ran:2
Win Prizemoney £0 *Total Prizemoney* £404
2000 Turf 0-2: (5f, 6f) (gd, hrd)
Currently above-average filly. Turf high 75 - 3rd of 10 to Nashira (17 Jun Bath 5f hrd RF 2038). **R Hannon [0-2] Park Walk Racing.*

DOMINO FLYER BHB 44f45a **RR 49f 45a** 1356[9]
7 b g Warrshan (USA) 9.7f **(59)** - Great Dilemma (Vaigly Great) 7f **(58)**
Form - 0040
Record 2000 - 1st:0 2nd:0 3rd:0 Ran:3
Pre2000 - 1st:6 2nd:4 3rd:3 Ran:40
Win Prizemoney £14,785 *Total Prizemoney* £19,082

Wins							
* 1998	*Jun Southw*	*(STD)*	*H*	*8f*	*56*	*61*	
* 1997	Mar Newcas	(GD)	H	10.1f	66	72	<
* 1997	*Jan Southw*	*(STD)*	*H*	*8f*	*58*	*56*	
* 1996	*Nov Southw*	*(STD)*		*8f*		*62*	
* 1996	May Hamilt	(SFT)		9.2f		63	
* 1996	*Apr Southw*	*(STD)*	*H*	*7f*	*52*	*59*	

2000 AW 0-3: (8f 3) (Fibr 3)
Moderate gelding, effective 8f, - acts on Fibr, has worn blinkers, favours left handed tracks. AW high 35. Becoming disappointing.
**Mrs A Duffield [6-44] S Smith.*

DOMINUS BHB 100f **RR 98f** 4296[8]
2 b c Primo Dominie 7.2f **(67)** - Howlin' (USA) (Alleged (USA)) 10f **(76)**
Form - 221658
Record 2000 - 1st:1 2nd:2 3rd:0 Ran:6
Win Prizemoney £6,012 *Total Prizemoney* £11,688
Wins * **2000** Jly Newmar (GD) 6f 85 <
2000 Turf 1-6: (5f 2, 6f 1-3, 7f) (gd 1-4, g-f 2)
Very useful colt, effective 5 to 6f, acts on gd. Turf high 91 - also 1st of 10 giving 4lb to Red Magic (12 Jly Newmarket RF 2749). Ran really well against decent sorts in the spring and finally got off the mark in a maiden at the July meeting. Rather outclassed in Pattern events afterwards. **R Hannon [1-6] Noodles Racing.*

DOM MIGUEL (FR) BHB 29f **RR 36f** 4723[11]
3 b g Fairy King (USA) 7.7f **(75)** - Damasquine (USA) (Damascus (USA)) 8.9f **(71)**
Form - 70070060
Record 2000 - 1st:0 2nd:0 3rd:0 Ran:8
Pre2000 - 1st:0 2nd:0 3rd:0 Ran:2
2000 Turf 0-7: (7f 3, 9f 2, 10f, 12f) (g-s, gd, g-f 3, frm 2) 2000 AW 0-1: (12f) (Equi)
Workmanlike, very moderate gelding. Turf high 48. Inconsistent.
**P W Harris [0-10] The Fairy Kings.*

DOM SHADEED BHB 53f64a **RR 52f 64a** 2939[1]
5 b g Shadeed (USA) 7.7f **(72)** - Fair Dominion (Dominion) 8.5f **(63)**
Form - 1
Record 2000 - 1st:1 2nd:0 3rd:0 Ran:1
Pre2000 - 1st:1 2nd:0 3rd:0 Ran:9
Win Prizemoney £6,779 *Total Prizemoney* £6,779

Wins							
* **2000**	Jly Kempto	(G-F)	H	8f	50	52	
1998	*Dec Wolver*	*(STD)*		*8.5f*		*62*	<

2000 Turf 1-1: (8f 1-1) (frm 1-1)
Average gelding, has worn blinkers. (1st run).
**R J Baker [1-3] Graham Brown (from R Charlton [0-5] Jun 1999).*

DON ALFRED (IRE) BHB 70f **RR 76f** 5027[10]
2 b c Mark of Esteem (IRE) - Jezyah (USA) **(75f)** (Chief's Crown (USA)) 9.8f **(72)**
Form - 57330
Record 2000 - 1st:0 2nd:0 3rd:2 Ran:5
Win Prizemoney £0 *Total Prizemoney* £1,195
2000 Turf 0-5: (7f 2, 8f 2, 10f) (g-s 2, gd 2, frm)
Above-average colt. Turf high 76 (began Jly).
**P F I Cole [0-5] Alessandro Gaucci.*

DONATUS (IRE) BHB 68f **RR 74f** 4461[7]
4 b g Royal Academy (USA) 7.8f **(77)** - La Dame du Lac (USA) (Round Table) 9.5f **(81)**
Form - 27
Record 2000 - 1st:0 2nd:1 3rd:0 Ran:2
Pre2000 - 1st:0 2nd:2 3rd:1 Ran:10
Win Prizemoney £0 *Total Prizemoney* £8,056
2000 Turf 0-1: (13f) (g-f) 2000 AW 0-1: (10f) (Equi)
Above-average gelding, effective 8 to 10f, acts on g-s to frm - acts on Equi, prefers tight tracks. (1st run) - 2nd of 10 giving 21lb to You da Man (4 Mar Lingfield 10f Equi RF 0400). Consistent.
**S Dow [0-14] Michael A J Hall & Miss M Shields (from C O'Brien in IRE [0-3] Oct 1998).*

DON BOSCO (IRE) BHB 58f53a **RR 65f 53a** 4929[2]
4 ch g Grand Lodge (USA) - Suyayeb (USA) (The Minstrel (CAN)) 10f **(72)**
Form - 0080308102
Record 2000 - 1st:1 2nd:1 3rd:1 Ran:10
Pre2000 - 1st:1 2nd:0 3rd:0 Ran:5
Win Prizemoney £9,134 *Total Prizemoney* £10,219

Wins							
2000	Aug Lingfl	(G-F)	C	10f		45+	
1999	Jun Ripon	(G-F)	H	6f	68	72	<

2000 Turf 1-8: (5f, 6f, 7f 4, 8f, 10f 1-1) (sft, gd, g-f, frm 1-5) 2000 AW 0-2: (8f, 12f) (Equi 2)
Average gelding, effective 6 to 7f, acts on g-f to frm, has worn blinkers. Turf high 65. AW high 57 (began Spt).
**E Stanners [0-2] Mrs Patricia Cunningham (from N A Callaghan [1-8] Aug 2000).*

DONE AND DUSTED (IRE) BHB 67f66a **RR 54f 66a** 1254[10]
4 ch f Up and At 'em - Florentink (USA) (The Minstrel (CAN)) 10f **(72)**
Form - 76810631560
Record 2000 - 1st:1 2nd:0 3rd:1 Ran:7
Pre2000 - 1st:5 2nd:1 3rd:4 Ran:26
Win Prizemoney £18,120 *Total Prizemoney* £20,658

Wins							
* **2000**	*Feb Wolver*	*(STD)*	*H*	*7f*	*62*	*65*	
* 1999	*Dec Wolver*	*(STD)*	*H*	*6f*	*59*	*63*	
* 1999	Apr Windso	(GD)	H	6f	60	68+	
* 1999	*Feb Lingfl*	*(STD)*	*H*	*7f*	*62*	*70*	<
* 1998	*Dec Lingfl*	*(STD)*	*C*	*7f*		*67*	
1998	*Nov Southw*	*(STD)*	*S*	*7f*		*54*	

2000 Turf 0-1: (8f) (g-f) 2000 AW 1-6: (6f 2, 7f 1-3, 8f) (Equi, Fibr 1-5)
Light-framed, average filly. AW high 65.
**R Brotherton [5-23] Paul Stringer (from J Berry [1-10] Nov 1998).*

DONE WELL (USA) BHB 22f **RR 22f** 1984[7]
8 b g Storm Bird (CAN) 8.5f **(82)** - Suspicious Toosome (USA) (Secretariat (USA)) 9f **(79)**
Form - 0077007
Record 2000 - 1st:0 2nd:0 3rd:0 Ran:7
Pre2000 - 1st:1 2nd:3 3rd:1 Ran:15
Win Prizemoney £4,557 *Total Prizemoney* £8,762
2000 Turf 0-7: (8f, 9f 2, 11f, 12f 2, 14f) (gd 2, g-f, frm 4)
Little account gelding, effective 12f, acts on frm. Turf high 22.
**P Monteith [2-28] Allan Melville (from E A L Dunlop [0-3] Jly 1995).*

DONNA DOUGHNUT **RR 37f** 2781[5]
2 ch f Imp Society (USA) 7.1f **(63)** - Louisville Belle (IRE) **(41f)** (Ahonoora) 8.1f **(73)**
Form - 05
Record 2000 - 1st:0 2nd:0 3rd:0 Ran:2
2000 Turf 0-1: (6f) (g-f) 2000 AW 0-1: (5f) (Fibr)
Currently very moderate filly. **M D I Usher [0-2] M D I Usher.*

DONNA'S DOUBLE BHB 68f61a **RR 72f 61a** 5165[13]
5 ch g Weldnaas (USA) 8.4f **(55)** - Shadha (Shirley Heights) 10.3f **(74)**
Form - 056352103402400
Record 2000 - 1st:1 2nd:2 3rd:2 Ran:15
Pre2000 - 1st:4 2nd:5 3rd:4 Ran:33
Win Prizemoney £26,400 *Total Prizemoney* £46,318

Wins * **2000** Jly York (GD) H 7f 63 66 <
* 1999 Oct Redcar (SFT) H 8f 62 65
* 1999 Oct Catter (GD,) H 7f 58 62
* 1998 Spt Hamilt (SFT) H 8.3f 49 54
* 1998 Spt Mussel (GD) H 7.1f 44 54

2000 Turf 1-15: (7f 1-6, 8f 6, 9f, 10f 2) (sft, g-s 2, gd 1-4, g-f 6, frm 2)
Above-average gelding, effective 7 to 10f, acts on gd to frm, best on g-f, likes left handed tracks, and excels at York. Turf high 72 - 4th of 19 getting 17lb from Bound For Pleasure (9 Spt Doncaster 10f frm RF 4311) - also 1st of 21 getting 15lb from Karameg (15 Jly York RF 2852).
**D Eddy [5-39] James Adams (from Don Enrico Incisa [0-5] Jun 1998).*

DONNINI (IRE) RR 30f 1664[8]

3 ch g Kris 10f **(75)** - La Luna (USA) (Lyphard (USA)) 9.9f **(72)**
Form - 8
Record 2000 - 1st:0 2nd:0 3rd:0 Ran:1
2000 Turf 0-1: (8f) (g-s)
Currently very moderate gelding. **P W Harris [0-1] Mrs P W Harris.*

DON PUCCINI BHB 94f RR 101f 5324[9]

3 ch c Piccolo - Baileys by Name (Nomination) 7f **(60)**
Form - 5000
Record 2000 - 1st:0 2nd:0 3rd:0 Ran:4
Pre2000 - 1st:2 2nd:0 3rd:1 Ran:4
Win Prizemoney £76,876 *Total Prizemoney* £77,750
Wins * 1999 Jly Newbur (G-F) 5.2f 101 <
* 1999 May Kempto (G-F) 6f 90

2000 Turf 0-4: (5f 2, 6f 2) (sft, g-s, g-f, hrd)
Unfurnished, very useful colt, effective 5f, acts on g-f. Turf high 101. Inconsistent. Missed the second half of his juvenile campaign with a stress fracture, and failed to recapture his form on returning. **B Smart [2-8] The Tenors.*

DON QUIXOTE (IRE) BHB 32f38a RR 35f 38a 3385[9]

4 b g Waajib 8.9f **(67)** - Maimiti (Goldhill) 8.5f **(55)**
Form - 860770
Record 2000 - 1st:0 2nd:0 3rd:0 Ran:6
Pre2000 - 1st:0 2nd:0 3rd:1 Ran:5
Win Prizemoney £0 *Total Prizemoney* £428
2000 Turf 0-6: (5f, 6f 4, 7f) (gd, g-f, frm 3, hrd)
Well made, moderate gelding, has worn blinkers. Turf high 35.
**D Nicholls [0-6] Insideracing (from L M Cumani [0-5] Jly 1999).*

DON RUBINI BHB 35f RR 27f 5076[8]

2 b c Emarati (USA) 6.6f **(63)** - Emerald Ring (Auction Ring (USA)) 8.6f **(65)**
Form - 8
Record 2000 - 1st:0 2nd:0 3rd:0 Ran:1
2000 Turf 0-1: (8f) (g-s)
Currently very moderate colt. **B Smart [0-1] The Tenors 2000.*

DONTBESOBOLD (IRE) BHB 56f56a RR 57f 56a 3536[15]

3 b g River Falls 8.2f **(56)** - Jarmar Moon **(55f)** (Unfuwain (USA))
Form - 743662440502860
Record 2000 - 1st:0 2nd:2 3rd:1 Ran:15
Pre2000 - 1st:0 2nd:0 3rd:0 Ran:7
Win Prizemoney £0 *Total Prizemoney* £2,585
2000 Turf 0-8: (7f 3, 8f 2, 9f, 10f, 11f) (hvy, g-s, gd 5, g-f) 2000 AW 0-7: (7f 2, 8f 2, 9f, 11f, 12f) (Fibr 7)
Scopey, above-average gelding, effective 7 to 8f, best at 8f, acts on sft to gd - acts on Fibr, has worn blinkers, likes tight tracks. Turf high 67 (1st run) - 4th of 11 getting 15lb from Wilton (8 Apr Hamilton 8f gd RF 0644). AW high 72 - 2nd of 8 getting 18lb from Ulundi (11 Mar Wolverhampton 8f Fibr RF 0433). Becoming disappointing. **B S Rothwell [0-22] Premier Protection Services Ltd.*

DON'T SURRENDER (IRE) BHB 90f RR 93f 5285a[6]

3 b c Zieten (USA) - St Clair Star (Sallust) 8.4f **(63)**
Form - 0230076
Record 2000 - 1st:0 2nd:1 3rd:1 Ran:7
Pre2000 - 1st:2 2nd:2 3rd:0 Ran:4
Win Prizemoney £8,521 *Total Prizemoney* £16,988
Wins 1999 Oct Newmar (G-S) 6f 85 <
1999 Oct Lingfi (G-F) 6f 80

2000 Turf 0-7: (6f 6, 7f) (hvy, g-s, gd 4, g-f)
Workmanlike, useful colt, effective 6f, acts on gd to g-f, has worn blinkers. Turf high 93 - 2nd of 12 giving 5lb to Duke of Modena (7 May Salisbury 6f g-f RF 1087). Gained battling victories at Lingfield and Newmarket as a juvenile in 1999, both over six furlongs. Some encouraging efforts early on last season, but failed to regain his form after a mid-term break. He is a real battler and is well named.
**W M Roper in IRE [0-1] B Demuyser (from J L Dunlop [2-10] Spt 2000).*

DONT WORRY BOUT ME (IRE) BHB 50f47a RR 57f 47a 4928[16]

3 b g Brief Truce (USA) 9.1f **(73)** - Coggle **(65f)** (Kind of Hush) 10.1f **(62)**
Form - 7016262800
Record 2000 - 1st:1 2nd:2 3rd:0 Ran:9
Pre2000 - 1st:0 2nd:1 3rd:2 Ran:7
Win Prizemoney £2,808 *Total Prizemoney* £6,609
Wins * **2000** *Feb Lingfi (STD) 12f 67* <

2000 Turf 0-4: (10f 2, 11f, 12f) (g-f, frm 3) 2000 AW 1-5: (9f, 10f, 12f 1-3) (Equi 1-4, Fibr)
Neat, average gelding, effective 5 to 6f, acts on g-f to frm, often wears blinkers. Turf high 57 (began Jly). AW high 67. Becoming disappointing. **T G Mills [1-16] Thorpe Vernon.*

DOODLE BUG BHB 65f60a RR 72f 60a 5104[6]

3 b f Missed Flight - Kaiserlinde (GER) (Frontal) 6.4f **(64)**
Form - 3536
Record 2000 - 1st:0 2nd:0 3rd:2 Ran:4
Pre2000 - 1st:0 2nd:0 3rd:1 Ran:2
Win Prizemoney £0 *Total Prizemoney* £1,561
2000 Turf 0-4: (11f, 12f, 13f, 15f) (sft, gd, g-f 2)
Light-framed, above-average filly, effective 7 to 15f, acts on sft to g-f, best on g-f. Turf high 72 - 3rd of 13 getting 9lb from Kennet (20 Aug Bath 13f g-f RF 3818). **T R Watson [0-6] Miss S Hoare.*

DOOWALEY (IRE) RR 108f 819a[3]

4 m Sadler's Wells (USA) 11.3f **(87)** - Dwell (USA) (Habitat) 9.4f **(70)**
Form - 3
2000 Turf 0-1: (10f) (hvy)
Currently Pattern-class.
**M Osthaus in ITY [0-1] (from M R Channon [1-2] Spt 1999).*

DORA CARRINGTON (IRE) RR 102f 3674a[3]

2 b f Sri Pekan (USA) - Dorothea Brooke (IRE) **(88df)** (Dancing Brave (USA)) 8.4f **(76)**
Form - 113
Record 2000 - 1st:2 2nd:0 3rd:1 Ran:3
Win Prizemoney £34,141 *Total Prizemoney* £50,241
Wins **2000** Jly Newmar (G-S) G2 6f 102 <
2000 Jun Pontef (G-F) 6f 76+

2000 Turf 2-3: (6f 2-3) (gd 1-2, frm 1-1)
Currently very useful filly. Turf high 102 - 1st of 9 from Enthused (11 Jly Newmarket RF 2688). Put up a good performance to beat Enthused in the Princess Margaret Stakes at the July meeting, and kept on to finish third in the Group One Phoenix Stakes on her final run. A half-sister to the stable's Primo Valentino, she might be hard to place successfully in her second season.
**P R Harriss [0-1] Mrs P W Harris (from P W Harris [2-2] Jly 2000).*

DORANFIELD LADY BHB 22a RR 22a 442[6]

5 b m Gildoran 11.6f **(58)** - Outfield (Monksfield)
Form - 7856
Record 2000 - 1st:0 2nd:0 3rd:0 Ran:4
2000 AW 0-4: (6f, 7f, 9f, 11f) (Fibr 4)
Poor filly. AW high 15.
**J L Spearing [0-5] Roger Nicholls & Thomas Smith.*

DORCHESTER RR 86f 4258[14]

3 b g Primo Dominie 7.2f **(67)** - Penthouse Lady (Last Tycoon) 8.5f **(62)**
Form - 0000530
Record 2000 - 1st:0 2nd:0 3rd:1 Ran:7
Pre2000 - 1st:3 2nd:1 3rd:1 Ran:9
Win Prizemoney £8,761 *Total Prizemoney* £18,424
Wins * 1999 Jly Doncas (G-F) 5f 86 <
* *1999 Jly Southw (STD) H 5f 79*
* 1999 Jly Nottin (GD) 5.1f 80

2000 Turf 0-7: (5f 4, 6f 3) (gd 3, g-f 2, frm 2)
Useful gelding, effective 5 to 6f, best at 5f, acts on gd to frm, has

worn blinkers. Turf high 86 - 3rd of 11 getting 7lb from See You Later (19 Aug Sandown 5f gd RF 3805).
**Sir Mark Prescott [3-16] Cheveley Park Stud.*

DORISSIO (IRE) BHB 62f **RR 67f** 4864[18]
4 b f Efisio 7.7f **(69)** - Floralia (Auction Ring (USA)) 8.6f **(65)**
Form - 33360300
Record 2000 - 1st:0 2nd:0 3rd:4 Ran:8
Pre2000 - 1st:2 2nd:0 3rd:0 Ran:9
Win Prizemoney £10,599 *Total Prizemoney* £12,761
Wins * 1999 Oct Pontef (SFT) H 8f 54 66+ <
* 1999 Spt Bath (FRM) SH 8f 50 54
2000 Turf 0-8: (7f 2, 8f 5, 9f) (sft, g-s, gd 4, g-f, frm)
Strong, average filly, effective 8f, acts on gd to frm, best on gd, likes right handed tracks, prefers tight tracks, excels at Bath. Turf high 67 - 3rd of 7 giving 8lb to Den's-Joy (2 May Windsor 8f gd RF 0975). **I A Balding [2-17] Miss A V Hill.*

DOROTHEA SHARP (IRE) BHB 36f **RR 25f** 2305[9]
3 b br f Foxhound (USA) - Captain's Niece (Vitiges (FR)) 8.2f **(59)**
Form - 057000
Record 2000 - 1st:0 2nd:0 3rd:0 Ran:6
Pre2000 - 1st:0 2nd:0 3rd:0 Ran:3
2000 Turf 0-3: (7f, 8f, 10f) (gd, g-f, frm) 2000 AW 0-3: (7f, 10f, 12f) (Equi 2, Fibr)
Neat, moderate filly, has worn blinkers. Turf high 25. AW high 41. Inconsistent. **N P Littmoden [0-9] Turf 2000 Ltd.*

DOROTHY ALLEN BHB 38f26a **RR 36f 26a** 101[11]
4 b f Mon Tresor 7.9f **(60)** - Anytime Anywhere (Daring March) 7.1f **(61)**
Form - 080
Record 2000 - 1st:0 2nd:0 3rd:0 Ran:1
Pre2000 - 1st:0 2nd:0 3rd:1 Ran:6
Win Prizemoney £0 *Total Prizemoney* £270
2000 AW 0-1: (8f) (Fibr)
Neat, very moderate filly.
**P D Evans [0-1] Ron Monte-Colombo (from R Ingram [0-2] Dec 1999).*

DOUBLE ACTION BHB 60f65a **RR 64f 65a** 4894[7]
6 br g Reprimand 8.2f **(63)** - Final Shot (Dalsaan) 9.8f **(64)**
Form - 4047532660600667
Record 2000 - 1st:0 2nd:1 3rd:1 Ran:16
Pre2000 - 1st:3 2nd:4 3rd:5 Ran:41
Win Prizemoney £27,190 *Total Prizemoney* £67,769
Wins * 1997 Spt York (SFT) H 6f 90 104 <
* 1997 Jun Ripon (GD) H 6f 86 88
* 1996 May Thirsk (G-F) 5f 71
2000 Turf 0-15: (6f 9, 7f 3, 8f 3) (sft 2, g-s 4, gd 2, g-f 2, frm 4, hrd)
2000 AW 0-1: (7f) (Fibr)
Average gelding, effective 7f, acts on g-f, has worn blinkers, likes left handed tracks, likes tight tracks. Turf high 64. He is on a long losing run, but is tumbling down the handicap and makes the frame from time to time. Seven furlongs is probably his best trip these days. **T D Easterby [3-57] C H Stevens.*

DOUBLE BANGER (IRE) BHB 75f73a **RR 80f 73a** 935[3]
3 b c Ela-Mana-Mou 12.7f **(72)** - Penny Banger (IRE) (Pennine Walk) 8.5f **(61)**
Form - 133
Record 2000 - 1st:0 2nd:0 3rd:2 Ran:2
Pre2000 - 1st:1 2nd:0 3rd:1 Ran:3
Win Prizemoney £2,840 *Total Prizemoney* £5,625
Wins * 1999 *Dec Lingfi (STD) 10f 74+* <
2000 Turf 0-1: (15f) (gd) 2000 AW 0-1: (10f) (Equi)
Scopey, decent colt. (1st run) - 3rd of 5 giving 2lb to Kathakali (29 Jan Lingfield 10f Equi RF 0183). (DEAD)
**M Johnston [1-5] R W Huggins & P H Wilkerson.*

DOUBLE BID BHB 55f **RR 60?f** 3241[9]
3 b g Rudimentary (USA) 8.2f **(66)** - Bidweaya (USA) (Lear Fan (USA)) 8.5f **(73)**
Form - 270
Record 2000 - 1st:0 2nd:1 3rd:0 Ran:3
Win Prizemoney £0 *Total Prizemoney* £1,286
2000 Turf 0-3: (8f, 10f 2) (gd, frm 2)
Rangy, currently average gelding. Turf high 60 (1st run) - 2nd of 5 giving 5lb to Poetic (5 Jun Thirsk 8f gd RF 1727).

**T P Tate [0-3] Mrs Sylvia Clegg.*

DOUBLE BLADE BHB 68f **RR 66f** 3999[1]
5 b g Kris 10f **(75)** - Sesame (Derrylin) 8.8f **(54)**
Form - 2011
Record 2000 - 1st:2 2nd:1 3rd:0 Ran:4
Pre2000 - 1st:0 2nd:2 3rd:3 Ran:13
Win Prizemoney £8,300 *Total Prizemoney* £13,575
Wins * 2000 Aug Redcar (FRM) H 11f 64 66 <
*** 2000** Jly Doncas (G-F) H 12f 60 61
2000 Turf 2-4: (11f 1-1, 12f 1-2, 14f) (gd, g-f 1-1, frm 1-2)
Average gelding, effective 11 to 16f, acts on g-f to frm, best on frm, has worn blinkers. Turf high 66 - 1st of 12 giving 5lb to Freedom Quest (26 Aug Redcar RF 3999) - also 1st of 7 getting 3lb from Forest Heath (19 Jly Doncaster RF 2930). Out of a prolific middle-distance winner, he looks to have his own ideas about the game.
**Mrs M Reveley [6-12] The Mary Reveley Racing Club (from M Johnston [0-10] Oct 1998).*

DOUBLE BOUNCE BHB 60f **RR 59f** 4217[19]
10 b g Interrex (CAN) 7.7f **(51)** - Double Gift (Cragador) 6f **(67)**
Form - 020
Record 2000 - 1st:0 2nd:1 3rd:0 Ran:3
Pre2000 - 1st:6 2nd:2 3rd:4 Ran:41
Win Prizemoney £45,874 *Total Prizemoney* £73,514
Wins 1996 Jun Newcas (FRM) H 6f 84 85 <
2000 Turf 0-3: (6f 2, 7f) (gd, frm 2)
Fair gelding, has worn blinkers. Turf high 59 (began Aug). Consistent.
**H Morrison [0-6] Mrs P Scott-Dunn (from H Candy [0-3] Nov 1998).*

DOUBLE BREW BHB 80f **RR 77f** 4697[6]
2 ch c Primo Dominie 7.2f **(67)** - Boozy (Absalom) 7.2f **(58)**
Form - 3422546
Record 2000 - 1st:0 2nd:2 3rd:1 Ran:7
Win Prizemoney £0 *Total Prizemoney* £6,643
2000 Turf 0-7: (5f 2, 6f 5) (g-s, g-f 5, frm)
Above-average colt, effective 5 to 6f, best at 6f, acts on g-f to frm, best on g-f. Turf high 77 - 6th of 14 getting 1lb from Muja Farewell (28 Spt Newmarket 5f g-f RF 4697).
**R Hannon [0-7] Heathavon Stables Ltd.*

DOUBLE CROSSED **RR 68+f** 5196[4]
2 b f Caerleon (USA) 10.9f **(79)** - Quandary (USA) **(92+f)** (Blushing Groom (FR)) 10.3f **(76)**
Form - 4
Record 2000 - 1st:0 2nd:0 3rd:0 Ran:1
Win Prizemoney £0 *Total Prizemoney* £320
2000 Turf 0-1: (8f) (gd)
Currently average filly. (1st run) - 4th of 16 to Jumaireyah (26 Oct Windsor 8f gd RF 5196). **H R A Cecil [0-1] K Abdulla.*

DOUBLE DESTINY BHB 46f44a **RR 50f 44a** 3327[8]
4 b g Anshan 8.2f **(63)** - Double Gift (Cragador) 6f **(67)**
Form - 0788308
Record 2000 - 1st:0 2nd:0 3rd:1 Ran:7
Pre2000 - 1st:0 2nd:0 3rd:0 Ran:3
Win Prizemoney £0 *Total Prizemoney* £744
2000 Turf 0-6: (7f 3, 8f 2, 10f) (gd 2, g-f, frm 2, hrd) 2000 AW 0-1: (6f) (Fibr)
Fair gelding, often wears blinkers. Turf high 50.
**K T Ivory [0-7] Mrs P Scott-Dunn (from H Candy [0-3] Spt 1999).*

DOUBLE DIGIT BHB 30f **RR 35f** 4365[19]
2 b f Timeless Times (USA) 6.1f **(56)** - Kagram Queen **(54df)** (Prince Ragusa)
Form - 8000
Record 2000 - 1st:0 2nd:0 3rd:0 Ran:4
2000 Turf 0-4: (5f 2, 6f, 7f) (gd, g-f 2, frm)
Very moderate filly. Turf high 35. **M Brittain [0-4] Too Many Cooks.*

DOUBLE ECLIPSE (IRE) BHB 110f **RR 110f** 2447[2]
8 b h Ela-Mana-Mou 12.7f **(72)** - Solac (FR) (Gay Lussac (ITY)) 16.7f **(109)**
Form - 2
Record 2000 - 1st:0 2nd:1 3rd:0 Ran:1
Pre2000 - 1st:7 2nd:5 3rd:2 Ran:18

Win Prizemoney £126,349 *Total Prizemoney* £184,099
Wins * 1997 Aug York (GD) G3 15.9f 117 <
* 1996 May Longch (SFT) G2 15.5f 117 <
* 1996 Apr Longch (GD) G3 15f 108
* 1996 Apr Haydoc (GD) 16.2f 100
2000 Turf 0-1: (12f) (frm)
Group-class horse. (1st run) - 2nd of 4 getting 3lb from Murghem (1 Jly Newmarket 12f frm RF 2447). Consistent. A full-brother to Double Trigger, he was a high-class stayer but his career was blighted by injury problems. He returned last year after spending two seasons in retirement, but was only seen the once, and failed to take part in the Cup races.
**M Johnston [7-19] The Middleham Partnership.*

DOUBLE ENTRY BHB 28f **RR 21f** 2325[14]
3 b g Rambo Dancer (CAN) 8.4f **(59)** - Andbracket (Import) 6.6f **(68)**
Form - 000
Record 2000 - 1st:0 2nd:0 3rd:0 Ran:3
Pre2000 - 1st:0 2nd:0 3rd:0 Ran:3
2000 Turf 0-3: (6f, 8f, 9f) (g-f, frm 2)
Little account gelding. Turf high 10.
**J J O'Neill [0-3] Deeteecee Eff Partnership (from D Nicholls [0-3] Oct 1999).*

DOUBLE FANTASY BHB 80f **RR 85f** 5153[4]
2 b f Mind Games - Song's Best (Never so Bold) 6.3f **(66)**
Form - 06104
Record 2000 - 1st:1 2nd:0 3rd:0 Ran:5
Win Prizemoney £3,503 *Total Prizemoney* £3,770
Wins * **2000** Aug Bath (FRM) 5.1f 85 <
2000 Turf 1-5: (5f 1-4, 6f) (g-s, gd 2, frm, hrd 1-1)
Useful filly. Turf high 85 - 1st of 8 from Fair Princess (25 Aug Bath RF 3952). Last of 20 at Royal Ascot on her debut, she got off the mark at Bath. **B Smart [1-5] Willie McKay.*

DOUBLE FAULT (IRE) BHB 39f30a **RR 52f 30a** 5200[5]
3 br f Zieten (USA) - Kashapour (Nishapour (FR)) 9.1f **(61)**
Form - 500330007455
Record 2000 - 1st:0 2nd:0 3rd:2 Ran:12
Pre2000 - 1st:0 2nd:1 3rd:0 Ran:6
Win Prizemoney £0 *Total Prizemoney* £2,120
2000 Turf 0-11: (7f 4, 8f 5, 10f 2) (hvy, sft, g-s, gd 3, g-f 3, frm 2) 2000 AW 0-1: (7f) (Fibr)
Fair filly, effective 5 to 8f, best at 8f, acts on sft to frm, often wears blinkers, likes tight tracks. Turf high 54 (1st run) - 5th of 17 getting 5lb from Bold Raider (24 Apr Nottingham 8f sft RF 0852). Inconsistent.
**J A Gilbert [0-7] Terry Connors (from T D Easterby [0-12] Jun 2000).*

DOUBLE GUN BHB 65f **RR 65f** 1920[7]
3 b c Puissance 7.1f **(60)** - Star of Jupiter (Jupiter Island) 14f **(62)**
Form - 0657
Record 2000 - 1st:0 2nd:0 3rd:0 Ran:4
Pre2000 - 1st:0 2nd:0 3rd:1 Ran:3
Win Prizemoney £0 *Total Prizemoney* £702
2000 Turf 0-4: (6f 2, 7f 2) (hvy 2, g-f, frm)
Scopey, average colt. Turf high 64.
**R Hannon [0-7] Heathavon Stables Ltd.*

DOUBLE HEART (FR) **RR 116f** 1453a[4]
4 b c Akarad (FR) 9.7f **(73)** - No Horse (FR) (No Horse (USA))
Form - 334
2000 Turf 0-3: (8f, 9f, 10f) (g-s 3)
High-class colt. Turf high 116 - 4th of 5 to Sendawar (21 May Longchamp 9f g-s RF 1453a). **Miss V Dissaux in FR [0-4].*

DOUBLE HONOUR (FR) BHB 82f **RR 82f** 4208[1]
2 gr c Highest Honor (FR) 10.9f **(72)** - Silver Cobra (USA) (Silver Hawk (USA)) 8.6f **(70)**
Form - 241
Record 2000 - 1st:1 2nd:1 3rd:0 Ran:3
Win Prizemoney £3,461 *Total Prizemoney* £4,879
Wins * **2000** Spt Hamilt (SFT) 8.3f 82 <
2000 Turf 1-3: (7f 2, 8f 1-1) (gd 1-1, g-f, frm)
Currently decent colt. Turf high 82 - 1st of 5 giving 5lb to Exotic Fan (4 Spt Hamilton RF 4208). Did not look happy on fast ground on his second run, but revelled on an easy surface when scoring at Hamilton. **M Johnston [1-3] The 4th Middleham Partnership.*

DOUBLE KAY (IRE) **RR 48f** 1680[5]
2 gr g Treasure Kay 6.5f **(53)** - Heart to Heart (IRE) **(36f)** (Double Schwartz) 7.9f **(55)**
Form - 05
Record 2000 - 1st:0 2nd:0 3rd:0 Ran:2
2000 Turf 0-2: (5f 2) (gd, frm)
Currently moderate gelding. Turf high 48.
**J A Glover [0-2] J A Glover.*

DOUBLE M BHB 60f57a **RR 73f 57a** 4476[11]
3 ch c First Trump - Girton Degree (Balliol) 5f **(43)**
Form - 060
Record 2000 - 1st:0 2nd:0 3rd:0 Ran:3
Pre2000 - 1st:1 2nd:1 3rd:0 Ran:7
Win Prizemoney £3,655 *Total Prizemoney* £5,055
Wins * 1999 Jly Nottin (G-F) 5.1f 83+ <
2000 Turf 0-2: (5f 2) (frm, hrd) 2000 AW 0-1: (6f) (Fibr)
Scopey, above-average colt, effective 5f, acts on frm, often wears blinkers (effectively). Turf high 52. Becoming disappointing.
**J L Spearing [1-10] Bryan Mathieson.*

DOUBLE MARCH BHB 54f60a **RR 58f 60a** 3144[11]
7 b g Weldnaas (USA) 8.4f **(55)** - Double Gift (Cragador) 6f **(67)**
Form - 0500
Record 2000 - 1st:0 2nd:0 3rd:0 Ran:4
Pre2000 - 1st:3 2nd:2 3rd:3 Ran:32
Win Prizemoney £12,423 *Total Prizemoney* £19,062
Wins * 1998 Oct Nottin (SFT) H 6.1f 67 68 <
* 1998 Jun Windso (SFT) H 6f 56 58
* 1998 May Nottin (G-F) H 6.1f 50 53
2000 Turf 0-4: (5f, 6f 3) (gd 2, g-f 2)
Fair gelding, effective 6f, acts on g-f, has worn blinkers. Turf high 57. **K T Ivory [3-21] Mrs P Scott-Dunn (from H Candy [0-5] Oct 1999).*

DOUBLE-O BHB 66f68a **RR 68?f 68a** 1479[5]
6 b g Sharpo 7.5f **(68)** - Ktolo (Tolomeo) 5.6f **(60)**
Form - 3748735
Record 2000 - 1st:0 2nd:0 3rd:1 Ran:5
Pre2000 - 1st:6 2nd:1 3rd:3 Ran:32
Win Prizemoney £23,277 *Total Prizemoney* £26,635
Wins * 1999 Oct Bright (G-S) H 5.3f 64 68?
* 1998 *Feb Wolver (STD) H 5f 79 85* <
* 1998 *Feb Wolver (STD) H 6f 74 75*
* 1997 *Dec Wolver (STD) H 6f 69 75*
* 1997 *Mar Southw (STD) H 6f 70 73*
* 1996 *Dec Wolver (STD) 6f 78*
2000 Turf 0-2: (5f 2) (g-s, gd) 2000 AW 0-3: (5f 2, 6f) (Fibr 3)
Average gelding, effective 5 to 6f, best at 5f, acts on gd to g-f - acts on Equi, often wears blinkers (extremely effectively). Turf high 51. AW high 63. **W Jarvis [6-37] Canisbay Bloodstock Ltd.*

DOUBLE OSCAR (IRE) BHB 71f87a **RR 77f 87a** 3796[15]
7 ch g Royal Academy (USA) 7.8f **(77)** - Broadway Rosie (Absalom) 7.2f **(58)**
Form - 00056321700
Record 2000 - 1st:1 2nd:1 3rd:1 Ran:11
Pre2000 - 1st:11 2nd:10 3rd:10 Ran:82
Win Prizemoney £52,267 *Total Prizemoney* £80,496
Wins * **2000** Jly Newcas (FRM) H 5f 70 73
* 1999 Jun Ayr (GD) H 5f 74 78
* 1998 Aug Ascot (G-F) H 5f 73 84+
* 1998 Jly Goodwo (G-S) H 5f 73 80
* 1998 *Apr Wolver (STD) H 5f 84 88* <
* 1998 *Jan Lingfi (STD) C 6f 75+*
* 1997 Aug Carlis (FRM) H 5f 75 80
* 1997 Aug Pontef (G-F) H 5f 62 76
* 1997 Aug Catter (G-F) H 5f 62 69
* 1997 Jly Folkes (G-F) H 6f 48 61+
* 1997 Apr Nottin (G-F) C 5.1f 53
2000 Turf 1-10: (5f 1-7, 6f 3) (gd 2, g-f 4, frm 1-4) 2000 AW 0-1: (6f) (Fibr)
Above-average gelding, effective 5 to 6f, best at 5f, acts on gd to frm, best on gd, often wears blinkers (effectively), excels at Newcastle, does well at Goodwood. Turf high 73 - 1st of 15 giving 1lb to Referendum (1 Jly Newcastle RF 2446). A multiple winner of sprint handicaps on turf and sand, he needs covering up before

being delivered late off a strong pace, but needs the gaps to appear at the right time. He had the right jockey on board when giving Alex Greaves a winner on her first day back in action at Newcastle.

**D Nicholls [11-79] Trilby Racing (from M Johnston [1-14] Aug 1996).*

DOUBLE PING BHB 49f RR 48f 4553[11]

2 ch f Petong 7.6f **(58)** - Paircullis (Tower Walk) 10f **(62)**
Form - 050
Record 2000 - 1st:0 2nd:0 3rd:0 Ran:3
2000 Turf 0-3: (5f, 6f 2) (gd, frm 2)
Currently moderate filly. Turf high 48 (began Aug).
**M W Easterby [0-3] Andrew Scott.*

DOUBLE PLATINUM BHB 75f RR 74f 3909[3]

3 ch f Seeking the Gold (USA) 7.4f **(80)** - Band (USA) (Northern Dancer) 9.6f **(80)**
Form - 36223
Record 2000 - 1st:0 2nd:2 3rd:2 Ran:5
Pre2000 - 1st:0 2nd:1 3rd:0 Ran:2
Win Prizemoney £0 *Total Prizemoney* £5,185
2000 Turf 0-5: (5f, 6f 3, 7f) (gd 2, g-f, frm 2)
Light-framed, above-average filly, effective 6f, acts on gd. Turf high 74.
**J H M Gosden [0-5] Lord Lloyd-Webber (from A G Foster [0-1] Oct 1999).*

DOUBLE RED (IRE) RR 66f 5085[4]

3 b f Thatching 7.8f **(69)** - Local Custom (IRE) (Be My Native (USA)) 10.2f **(71)**
Form - 2300164
Record 2000 - 1st:1 2nd:1 3rd:1 Ran:7
Pre2000 - 1st:0 2nd:2 3rd:0 Ran:5
Win Prizemoney £3,575 *Total Prizemoney* £6,857
Wins * 2000 Spt Goodwo (HVY) H 9.9f 56 61 <
2000 Turf 1-7: (10f 1-5, 12f 2) (hvy, g-s, gd 1-4, g-f)
Scopey, average filly, effective 8 to 10f, best at 10f, acts on g-s to g-f, best on gd, likes tight tracks. Turf high 66 (1st run) - 2nd of 8 getting 5lb from Fantastic Fantasy (31 Mar Southwell 10f gd RF 0587) - also 1st of 19 getting 18lb from Capriccio (20 Spt Goodwood RF 4545).
**M L W Bell [1-12] Terry Neill.*

DOUBLE ROCK BHB 37f RR 34f 3632[2]

4 b f Rock Hopper 10.6f **(54)** - Rockin' Rosie (Song) 7.2f **(61)**
Form - 542
Record 2000 - 1st:0 2nd:1 3rd:0 Ran:3
Win Prizemoney £0 *Total Prizemoney* £901
2000 Turf 0-3: (11f, 12f 2) (g-f, frm 2)
Very moderate filly. Turf high 34 (began Jly) - 2nd of 9 giving 2lb to Titus Bramble (14 Aug Windsor 12f g-f RF 3632).
**P Howling [0-5] Mrs P Reditt.*

DOUBLE RUSH (IRE) BHB 42f45a RR 42f 45a 2359[7]

8 b g Doulab (USA) 7.4f **(61)** - Stanza Dancer (Stanford) 7.9f **(56)**
Form - 0612347
Record 2000 - 1st:1 2nd:1 3rd:1 Ran:6
Pre2000 - 1st:7 2nd:4 3rd:5 Ran:57
Win Prizemoney £19,650 *Total Prizemoney* £28,093

Wins								
2000	Mar	Nottin	(GD)	H	14.1f	36	42	
1998	Jly	Bath	(GD)	S	11.7f		48	
1996	*Nov*	*Lingfi*	*(STD)*	*H*	*10f*	*53*	*61*	<
1996	*Nov*	*Lingfi*	*(STD)*		*10f*		*59+*	
1996	Aug	Bright	(FRM)	H	10f	48	56	
1996	Aug	Bright	(FRM)	H	10f	40	48+	

2000 Turf 1-5: (14f 1-2, 16f 3) (sft, g-s 2, gd 1-1, g-f) 2000 AW 0-1: (16f) (Equi)
Moderate gelding, effective 12 to 16f, best at 14f, acted on sft to frm, had worn blinkers, and excelled at Nottingham. Turf high 42 - 3rd of 17 getting 13lb from My Legal Eagle (24 Apr Nottingham 14f sft RF 0851) - also 1st of 15 getting 17lb from My Legal Eagle (29 Mar Nottingham RF 0561). (DEAD)
**G A Ham [0-2] The Barneby Partnership (from T Keddy [1-24] Apr 2000).*

DOUBLE SPLENDOUR (IRE) BHB 68f68a RR 72f 68a 4195[16]

10 b g Double Schwartz 7f **(60)** - Princess Pamela (Dragonara Palace (USA)) 6.1f **(55)**
Form - 0007620
Record 2000 - 1st:0 2nd:1 3rd:0 Ran:7
Pre2000 - 1st:9 2nd:8 3rd:4 Ran:54
Win Prizemoney £42,068 *Total Prizemoney* £77,049

Wins								
* 1999	Jly	Newmar	(G-F)	H	6f	82	86	
* 1998	May	Newmar	(GD)	H	6f	95	100	<
* 1996	Jly	York	(GD)	H	6f	82	87	
* 1996	Apr	Nottin	(G-F)	H	6.1f	70	83+	

2000 Turf 0-7: (6f 4, 7f 3) (gd, g-f 2, frm 4)
Above-average gelding, effective 6f, acts on g-f to frm, best on frm. Turf high 72.
**P S Felgate [9-61] M Heywood, E Rollinson & J Spooner.*

DOUBLE STYLE BHB 40f RR 46?f 1899[13]

3 ch c Presidium 7.5f **(56)** - Sorrowful (Moorestyle) 6.9f **(64)**
Form - 0
Record 2000 - 1st:0 2nd:0 3rd:0 Ran:1
Pre2000 - 1st:0 2nd:0 3rd:0 Ran:2
2000 Turf 0-1: (8f) (frm)
Unfurnished, currently moderate colt. **J L Eyre [0-3] K Birkinshaw.*

DOUBTLESS RISK BHB 26f RR 17f 5194[8]

3 b g Risk Me (FR) 8f **(53)** - Doubtfire (Jalmood (USA)) 10.1f **(52)**
Form - 008
Record 2000 - 1st:0 2nd:0 3rd:0 Ran:3
Pre2000 - 1st:0 2nd:0 3rd:0 Ran:7
Win Prizemoney £0 *Total Prizemoney* £226
2000 Turf 0-3: (6f, 7f 2) (sft, gd, frm)
Workmanlike, poor gelding, has worn blinkers. Turf high 15 (began Aug). **Miss L A Perratt [0-10] J A Davidson.*

DOVEBRACE BHB 53f47a RR 56f 47a 3977[11]

7 b g Dowsing (USA) 7f **(61)** - Naufrage (Main Reef) 9.6f **(57)**
Form - 321216662380
Record 2000 - 1st:2 2nd:3 3rd:2 Ran:12
Pre2000 - 1st:3 2nd:1 3rd:3 Ran:41
Win Prizemoney £23,940 *Total Prizemoney* £32,529

Wins							
*** 2000**	Jly	Catter	(G-F)	H	7f	48	55
*** 2000**	Jun	Ayr	(GD)	SH	8f	38	47

2000 Turf 2-12: (7f 1-5, 8f 1-6, 9f) (gd, g-f 3, frm 2-8)
Average gelding, effective 7 to 9f, acts on g-f to frm, best on frm, has worn blinkers, likes left handed tracks, favours tight tracks, excels at Ayr. Turf high 56 - 2nd of 10 getting 16lb from Eastern Spice (27 Jly Bath 8f frm RF 3148) - also 1st of 10 getting 10lb from Rymer's Rascal (5 Jly Catterick RF 2543).
**A Bailey [5-39] Dovebrace Ltd Air-Conditioning-Projects (from T D Barron [0-16] Aug 1998).*

DOVEDON SUPREME RR 35f 5223[16]

2 b f Emperor Jones (USA) - Secreto Bold (Never so Bold) 6.3f **(66)**
Form - 0
Record 2000 - 1st:0 2nd:0 3rd:0 Ran:1
2000 Turf 0-1: (6f) (gd)
Currently very moderate filly. **H Akbary [0-1] Michael Whatley.*

DOVE'S DOMINION BHB 48f48a RR 46f 48a 3524[8]

3 b g Primo Dominie 7.2f **(67)** - Dame Helene (USA) (Sir Ivor) 10.2f **(70)**
Form - 50005588
Record 2000 - 1st:0 2nd:0 3rd:0 Ran:8
Pre2000 - 1st:0 2nd:0 3rd:0 Ran:3
Win Prizemoney £0 *Total Prizemoney* £268
2000 Turf 0-7: (7f, 8f 4, 10f, 12f) (gd 3, g-f 2, frm 2) 2000 AW 0-1: (8f) (Fibr)
Moderate gelding, effective 7f, acts on gd, has worn blinkers. Turf high 59 (1st run) - 5th of 13 to Northern Times (7 Apr Lingfield 7f gd RF 0638).
**D Burchell [0-5] D N Carey (from M R Channon [0-6] May 2000).*

DOWNLAND (IRE) BHB 82f RR 82f 5317[18]

4 b c Common Grounds 8.1f **(66)** - Boldabsa (Persian Bold) 9.3f **(66)**
Form - 860220
Record 2000 - 1st:0 2nd:2 3rd:0 Ran:6
Pre2000 - 1st:1 2nd:2 3rd:0 Ran:7
Win Prizemoney £3,622 *Total Prizemoney* £10,189

Wins 1999 Jly Lingfi (G-F) 6f 78++ <
2000 Turf 0-6: (6f 5, 7f) (sft 2, g-s, gd 3)
Well made, decent colt, effective 6 to 8f, best at 6f, acts on sft to frm, has worn blinkers. Turf high 82 - 2nd of 20 giving 16lb to College Maid (18 Oct Newcastle 6f sft RF 5055). Bolted up in a six-furlong Lingfield maiden last term, but has failed to make an impact in handicap company and connections seem to be having trouble identifying his best trip.
**S C Williams [0-1] Stuart Williams (from G Wragg [1-12] Oct 2000).*

DOWNPOUR (USA) BHB 60f RR 38f 5151[5]

2 b g Torrential (USA) - Juliac (USA) (Accipiter (USA))
Form - 705
Record 2000 - 1st:0 2nd:0 3rd:0 Ran:3
2000 Turf 0-3: (6f, 7f 2) (g-s, gd 2)
Currently very moderate gelding. Turf high 38 (began Spt).
**Sir Mark Prescott [0-3] Sturt Osborne House III.*

DOWN THE AISLE (USA) RR 119f 5331a[12]

7 gr h Runaway Groom (CAN) 8.1f **(69)** - That's My Hon (CAN) (L'Enjoleur (CAN)) 8f **(65)**
Form - 30
2000 Turf 0-1: (12f) (frm) 2000 AW 0-1: (9f) (Dirt)
Currently high-class horse. **W Mott in USA [0-3] C H Deters.*

DOWN TO THE WOODS (USA) BHB 100f RR 99f 5123[2]

2 ch c Woodman (USA) 9.7f **(77)** - Riviera Wonder (USA) (Batonnier (USA))
Form - 15142
Record 2000 - 1st:2 2nd:1 3rd:0 Ran:5
Win Prizemoney £10,367 *Total Prizemoney* £20,875
Wins * **2000** Spt Doncas (G-F) 6f 94+ <
* **2000** Jun Doncas (G-F) 6f 91+
2000 Turf 2-5: (6f 2-3, 7f 2) (g-s 2, frm 2-2)
Very useful colt. Turf high 99 - 2nd of 10 to Shaard (21 Oct Doncaster 6f g-s RF 5123) - also 1st of 6 giving 2lb to Freefourinternet (9 Spt Doncaster RF 4307). Made a winning debut but was held when stepped up in class at the Curragh. Won nicely at Doncaster and ran a rather better race when returned to the Curragh in the National Stakes, before being touched off in a listed event back at Doncaster. Goes well at the South Yorkshire track, but also looks more effective on fast ground.
**M Johnston [2-5] Miller/Richards Partnership.*

DRAFT OF VINTAGE (IRE) RR 98f 5286a[14]

7 b g Imperial Frontier (USA) 7f **(65)** - Kelly's Vintage (Persian Bold) 9.3f **(66)**
Form - 0461071370
2000 Turf 2-10: (7f 2, 8f 2, 9f 1-4, 10f, 11f 1-1) (hvy, sft, g-s 1-3, gd 1-4)
Very useful gelding, effective 7 to 11f, best at 7f, acts on g-s to g-f, best on g-f, prefers left handed tracks, and excels at Leopardstown. Turf high 98 - 3rd of 16 giving 18lb to Tarakan (9 Spt Leopardstown 7f gd RF 4353a) - also 1st of 11 giving 9lb to Goldstreet (13 Aug Leopardstown RF 3677a). Invariably held-up, he landed a couple of decent handicaps last summer. Has since been tried over hurdles. **J E Mulhern in IRE [7-45] J E Mulhern.*

DRAGNET (IRE) RR 78f 5138[5]

2 ch f Rainbow Quest (USA) 11.2f **(81)** - River Dancer (Irish River (FR)) 8.6f **(78)**
Form - 65
Record 2000 - 1st:0 2nd:0 3rd:0 Ran:2
2000 Turf 0-2: (7f, 8f) (g-s, g-f)
Currently above-average filly. Turf high 78 (1st run) (began Spt) - 6th of 17 getting 5lb from Demophilos (28 Spt Newmarket 7f g-f RF 4701). **Sir Michael Stoute [0-2] Lord Weinstock.*

DRAGON STAR BHB 56f52a RR 51f 52a 386[6]

3 b f Rudimentary (USA) 8.2f **(66)** - Nazakat (Known Fact (USA)) 7.4f **(67)**
Form - 656
Record 2000 - 1st:0 2nd:0 3rd:0 Ran:1
Pre2000 - 1st:0 2nd:0 3rd:1 Ran:4
Win Prizemoney £0 *Total Prizemoney* £535
2000 AW 0-1: (7f) (Equi)
Scopey, fair filly. **J W Payne [0-5] T H Barma.*

DRAMA CLASS (IRE) BHB 100f RR 103f 4963[6]

3 ch f Caerleon (USA) 10.9f **(79)** - Stage Struck (IRE) **(81f)** (Sadler's Wells (USA)) 10f **(76)**
Form - 21356
Record 2000 - 1st:1 2nd:1 3rd:1 Ran:5
Win Prizemoney £3,760 *Total Prizemoney* £7,275
Wins * **2000** Jly Bath (G-S) 10.2f 86 <
2000 Turf 1-5: (10f 1-3, 12f 2) (g-s, gd 1-2, frm 2)
Rangy, very useful filly. Turf high 103 (began Jly). Unraced as a juvenile, she got off the mark in a Bath maiden on her second start, but subsequent events showed she was not up to Pattern class. **Sir Michael Stoute [1-5] Lord Weinstock.*

DRAMA CRITIC (USA) RR 118f 4410a[3]

4 b c Theatrical 11.5f **(78)** - Guiza (USA) (Golden Act (USA)) 8.8f **(67)**
Form - 3
2000 Turf 0-1: (11f)
Currently high-class colt. (1st run) - 3rd of 8 to Fantastic Light (9 Spt Belmont Park 11f RF 4410a). **M Hennig in USA [0-1].*

DRAMA PREMIERE BHB 65f60a RR 62f 60a 4935[16]

2 br f Emarati (USA) 6.6f **(63)** - Dramatic Mood (Jalmood (USA)) 10.1f **(52)**
Form - 00
Record 2000 - 1st:0 2nd:0 3rd:0 Ran:2
2000 Turf 0-2: (6f 2) (gd, g-f)
Currently average filly. Turf high 62 (began Spt).
**I A Balding [0-2] Ann Plummer & Friends.*

DRAMATIC QUEST BHB 100f RR 105f 4298[5]

3 b c Zafonic (USA) 9f **(83)** - Ultra Finesse (USA) (Rahy (USA))
Form - 5
Record 2000 - 1st:0 2nd:0 3rd:0 Ran:1
Pre2000 - 1st:2 2nd:0 3rd:0 Ran:4
Win Prizemoney £11,625 *Total Prizemoney* £11,625
Wins * 1999 Jly Ascot (G-F) 7f 105+ <
* 1999 May Pontef (G-F) 6f 84+
2000 Turf 0-1: (8f) (g-f)
Scopey, Pattern-class colt. (1st run) - 5th of 7 getting 3lb from El Gran Papa (8 Spt Doncaster 8f g-f RF 4298). A tough and able juvenile in 1999, he was only seen once last season following a year off the track. **M Johnston [2-5] Maktoum Al Maktoum.*

DRAPLOY (GER) RR 97f 1033a[6]

4 m
Form - 6
2000 Turf 0-1: (12f) (gd)
Currently very useful. **A Schutz in GER [0-2].*

DR COOL BHB 48f60a RR 59f 60a 4431[9]

3 b c Ezzoud (IRE) - Vayavaig (Damister (USA)) 9f **(73)**
Form - 3054000
Record 2000 - 1st:0 2nd:0 3rd:0 Ran:6
Pre2000 - 1st:0 2nd:0 3rd:1 Ran:2
Win Prizemoney £0 *Total Prizemoney* £428
2000 Turf 0-6: (8f, 11f 2, 12f 2, 17f) (hvy, g-s, gd 2, g-f, frm)
Light-framed, average colt, effective 11 to 12f, acts on hvy to g-f, has worn blinkers. Turf high 59 - 5th of 11 getting 10lb from Desert Island Disc (27 May Warwick 11f hvy RF 1510). Becoming disappointing. **W Jarvis [0-8] Canisbay Bloodstock Ltd.*

DR DIGNITY RR 94f 4524a[2]

2 bb c Dr Devious (IRE) 9.9f **(74)** - Ard Na Sighe 00
Form - 422
2000 Turf 0-3: (6f 2, 7f) (gd 2)
Currently useful colt. Turf high 94 (began Jly) - 2nd of 17 to Juniper (17 Spt Curragh 6f RF 4524a). Came up against O'Brien juveniles in all three of his outings, being touched off in the last. Will stay middle distances at three and should have no trouble finding a race or two. **C Collins in IRE [0-3] Stal Statenprojekt B V.*

DR DUKE (IRE) BHB 44f39a RR 51f 39a 1310[6]

3 b g Dolphin Street (FR) - Diamond Lake (Kings Lake (USA)) 10.8f **(67)**
Form - 554064006
Record 2000 - 1st:0 2nd:0 3rd:0 Ran:7
Pre2000 - 1st:0 2nd:1 3rd:3 Ran:13

Win Prizemoney £0 *Total Prizemoney* £1,727
2000 Turf 0-2: (8f, 10f) (gd, hrd) 2000 AW 0-5: (8f 2, 9f, 10f, 11f) (Equi 2, Fibr 3)
Neat, fair gelding, effective 5 to 7f, best at 7f, acts on frm, has worn blinkers. Turf high 44. AW high 53.
**M Wigham [0-2] Stephen Roots (from Mrs N Macauley [0-11] Feb 2000).*

DREAM CARRIER (IRE) BHB 25f25a **RR 40f 25a** 2420[9]
12 b g Doulab (USA) 7.4f **(61)** - Dream Trader (Auction Ring (USA)) 8.6f **(65)**
Form - 007000
Record 2000 - 1st:0 2nd:0 3rd:0 Ran:6
Pre2000 - 1st:11 2nd:13 3rd:13 Ran:126
Win Prizemoney £37,821 *Total Prizemoney* £59,439
Wins * 1997 *Jun Southw (STD) H 7f 39 45*
2000 AW 0-6: (7f, 8f 3, 11f, 12f) (Fibr 6)
Moderate gelding, has worn blinkers. AW high 25.
**R E Peacock [1-47] R E Peacock (from J G M O'Shea [0-9] Jly 1995).*

DREAMIE BATTLE BHB 62f **RR 62f** 4534[5]
2 br f Makbul - Highland Rossie (Pablond) 5.9f **(42)**
Form - 33575
Record 2000 - 1st:0 2nd:0 3rd:2 Ran:5
Win Prizemoney £0 *Total Prizemoney* £1,303
2000 Turf 0-5: (6f, 7f 3, 8f) (g c, g-f, frm 3)
Average filly. Turf high 75 (began Jly) - 3rd of 8 getting 5lb from Zeloso (11 Aug Haydock 7f g-f RF 3550).
**R Hollinshead [0-5] Tim Leadbeater.*

DREAM MAGIC BHB 74f **RR 78f** 5027[11]
2 b g Magic Ring (IRE) 6.5f **(64)** - Pip's Dream **(56df 30a)** (Glint of Gold) 9.3f **(66)**
Form - 0640
Record 2000 - 1st:0 2nd:0 3rd:0 Ran:4
Win Prizemoney £0 *Total Prizemoney* £268
2000 Turf 0-4: (6f, 7f 2, 8f) (sft, g-s, gd, frm)
Above-average gelding. Turf high 78 (began Spt) - 6th of 17 to Rebel Storm (13 Spt Yarmouth 7f frm RF 4379).
**M J Ryan [0-4] P E Axon.*

DREAM ON ME BHB 38f49a **RR 50f 49a** 2082[6]
4 b f Prince Sabo 6.6f **(64)** - Holens Dreamgirl (Caerleon (USA)) 8.6f **(71)**
Form - 435816
Record 2000 - 1st:1 2nd:0 3rd:0 Ran:2
Pre2000 - 1st:3 2nd:4 3rd:3 Ran:21
Win Prizemoney £8,790 *Total Prizemoney* £11,941
Wins * 2000 *Jan Wolver (STD) S 12f 37+*
1999 Jly Leices (G-F) S 8f 50
1999 *Jan Lingfi (STD) H 7f 56 62* <
1998 *Dec Lingfi (STD) S 8f 58*
2000 Turf 0-1: (12f) (frm) 2000 AW 1-1: (12f 1-1) (Fibr 1-1)
Unfurnished, fair filly, effective 7 to 8f, best at 8f, - acts on Equi. (1st run).
**H J Manners [1-12] H J Manners (from G L Moore [3-11] Jly 1999).*

DREAM QUEST BHB 94f **RR 101f** 4953a[2]
3 ch f Rainbow Quest (USA) 11.2f **(81)** - Dreamawhile (Known Fact (USA)) 7.4f **(67)**
Form - 1332
Record 2000 - 1st:1 2nd:1 3rd:2 Ran:4
Win Prizemoney £4,524 *Total Prizemoney* £15,308
Wins * 2000 Apr Sandow (SFT) 10f 86 <
2000 Turf 1-4: (10f 1-2, 11f, 12f) (sft 1-2, gd, frm)
Scopey, very useful filly. Turf high 101 - 2nd of 9 to Space Quest (8 Oct Longchamp 12f sft RF 4953a). Unraced at two, she battled on really well to make a winning debut on soft ground at Sandown. She looked sure to improve, but did not reach the anticipated level when only third in a sub-standard Lingfield Oaks Trial. In the frame in listed races since. **J L Dunlop [1-4].*

DREAMS DESIRE BHB 90f **RR 80+f** 2149[16]
2 b f Mind Games - Champenoise (Forzando) 7.6f **(59)**
Form - 110
Record 2000 - 1st:2 2nd:0 3rd:0 Ran:3
Win Prizemoney £7,549 *Total Prizemoney* £7,549
Wins * 2000 May Thirsk (GD) 5f 80+ <
*** 2000** May Doncas (G-S) 5f 71
2000 Turf 2-3: (5f 2-3) (gd 1-2, g-f 1-1)
Currently decent filly. Turf high 80 - 1st of 8 from Muja Farewell (20 May Thirsk RF 1348) - also 1st of 13 from Franica (1 May Doncaster RF 0931). **J A Glover [2-3] Sports Mania.*

DREAM SUPREME (USA) RR 5328a[6]
3 br f Seeking the Gold (USA) 7.4f **(80)** - Spinning Round (USA) (Dixieland Band (USA)) 7f **(74)**
Form - 6
2000 AW 0-1: (6f) (Dirt)
Currently Pattern-class. **W Mott in USA [0-1] Kinsman Stable.*

DREAM TIME RR 52f 5098[23]
2 b f Rainbow Quest (USA) 11.2f **(81)** - Grey Angel (Kenmare (FR)) 6.5f **(72)**
Form - 0
Record 2000 - 1st:0 2nd:0 3rd:0 Ran:1
2000 Turf 0-1: (8f) (gd)
Currently fair filly. **Sir Michael Stoute [0-1] The Queen.*

DR EDGAR BHB 40f41a **RR 53?f 41a** 253[10]
8 b g Most Welcome 8.6f **(66)** - African Dancer (Nijinsky (CAN)) 10.3f **(77)**
Form - 040
Record 2000 - 1st:0 2nd:0 3rd:0 Ran:2
Pre2000 - 1st:3 2nd:6 3rd:6 Ran:35
Win Prizemoney £13,287 *Total Prizemoney* £21,935
2000 AW 0-2: (12f 2) (Fibr 2)
Fair gelding, has worn blinkers. AW high 46.
**J L Eyre [0-8] A G Watson (from M Dods [0-22] Apr 1997).*

DRESS CODE (IRE) BHB 88f **RR 80f** 4643[7]
2 b f Barathea (IRE) - Petite Epaulette (Night Shift (USA)) 7.2f **(69)**
Form - 317047
Record 2000 - 1st:1 2nd:0 3rd:1 Ran:6
Win Prizemoney £6,955 *Total Prizemoney* £7,992
Wins * 2000 May Cheste (GD) 5.1f 78 <
2000 Turf 1-6: (5f 1-2, 6f 3, 7f) (g-s, gd, g-f 2, frm 1-2)
Decent filly, effective 5 to 6f, acts on g-f to frm. Turf high 80 - also 1st of 11 from Miss Brief (11 May Chester RF 1137). Won at Chester on her second outing, but had a hard race in the process, and has not achieved much since. **W Jarvis [1-6] Anthony Foster.*

DRESS REHEARSAL RR 71f 3964[9]
2 b c Machiavellian (USA) 9.8f **(83)** - Dance to the Top **(93f)** (Sadler's Wells (USA)) 10f **(76)**
Form - 0
Record 2000 - 1st:0 2nd:0 3rd:0 Ran:1
2000 Turf 0-1: (7f) (g-f)
Currently above-average colt.
**Sir Michael Stoute [0-1] Cheveley Park Stud.*

DR GORDON (IRE) RR 52f 4191[13]
2 b c Definite Article - Bristle (Thatch (USA)) 9.8f **(62)**
Form - 0
Record 2000 - 1st:0 2nd:0 3rd:0 Ran:1
2000 Turf 0-1: (8f) (g-f)
Currently fair colt. **C E Brittain [0-1] Alessandro Gaucci.*

DR GREENFIELD (IRE) RR 74f 4969[8]
2 ch c Dr Devious (IRE) 9.9f **(74)** - Memory Green (USA) (Green Forest (USA)) 9.9f **(68)**
Form - 8
Record 2000 - 1st:0 2nd:0 3rd:0 Ran:1
2000 Turf 0-1: (8f) (gd)
Currently useful colt. **G A Butler [0-1] Alan Lillingston.*

DRIPPING IN GOLD (IRE) BHB 25f **RR 46f** 1325[12]
2 ch f Alhijaz 7.7f **(57)** - Fanny's Choice (IRE) **(78f)** (Fairy King (USA)) 7.7f **(59)**
Form - 3700
Record 2000 - 1st:0 2nd:0 3rd:1 Ran:4
Win Prizemoney £0 *Total Prizemoney* £318
2000 Turf 0-4: (5f 3, 6f) (sft, gd 3)
Moderate filly. Turf high 46. **J J Bridger [0-4] K J Walls.*

DRIVE ASSURED BHB 50f **RR 45f** 4788a[15]
6 gr g Mystiko (USA) 7.7f **(59)** - Black Ivor (USA) (Sir Ivor) 10.2f **(70)**
Form - 740000
Record 2000 - 1st:0 2nd:0 3rd:0 Ran:6
Pre2000 - 1st:1 2nd:2 3rd:4 Ran:20
Win Prizemoney £2,577 *Total Prizemoney* £7,627
Wins 1998 Oct Bright (GD) H 8f 65 71+ <
2000 Turf 0-5: (7f, 8f, 9f 2, 12f) (sft, g-s 3, g-f) 2000 AW 0-1: (12f) (Fibr)
Moderate gelding. Turf high 45 (began Jly). Inconsistent. Has joined Kevin Morgan.
**Patrick Kelly in IRE [0-5] Mrs J O'Kane (from K A Morgan [1-13] May 2000).*

DR MARTENS (IRE) BHB 38f **RR 35f** 3834[9]
6 b g Mtoto 11.5f **(71)** - Suyayeb (USA) (The Minstrel (CAN)) 10f **(72)**
Form - 0000
Record 2000 - 1st:0 2nd:0 3rd:0 Ran:4
Pre2000 - 1st:1 2nd:1 3rd:0 Ran:10
Win Prizemoney £3,642 *Total Prizemoney* £4,832
Wins 1997 Aug Windso (G-F) 8.3f 84 <
2000 Turf 0-4: (8f 2, 10f 2) (g-s, gd 2, g-f)
Moderate gelding, has worn blinkers. Turf high 35. Becoming disappointing.
**W J Musson [0-8] R Griggs Group Ltd (from J A Glover [0-2] Aug 1998).*

DR STRANGELOVE (IRE) RR 78f 4109[6]
2 ch c Dr Devious (IRE) 9.9f **(74)** - Renzola (Dragonara Palace (USA)) 6.1f **(55)**
Form - 56
Record 2000 - 1st:0 2nd:0 3rd:0 Ran:2
2000 Turf 0-2: (7f 2) (gd, frm)
Currently above-average colt. Turf high 78 (began Aug).
**B W Hills [0-2] Wafic Said.*

(67)
Form - 007000
Record 2000 - 1st:0 2nd:0 3rd:0 Ran:6
Pre2000 - 1st:0 2nd:3 3rd:0 Ran:21
Win Prizemoney £0 *Total Prizemoney* £2,048
2000 Turf 0-5: (8f 2, 10f 2, 11f) (hvy, gd 3, hrd) 2000 AW 0-1: (7f) (Fibr)
Workmanlike, little account gelding, has worn blinkers. Turf high 22.
**Mrs M Bridgwater [0-6] Mrs Mary Bridgwater (from K S Bridgwater [0-1] Aug 1999).*

DRYING GRASS MOON BHB 58f49a **RR 65f 49a** 285[4]
4 b f Be My Chief (USA) 10.2f **(62)** - Sickle Moon (Shirley Heights) 10.3f **(74)**
Form - 4
Record 2000 - 1st:0 2nd:0 3rd:0 Ran:1
Pre2000 - 1st:0 2nd:0 3rd:0 Ran:2
Win Prizemoney £0 *Total Prizemoney* £254
2000 AW 0-1: (12f) (Fibr)
Workmanlike, currently average filly.
**J R Fanshawe [0-3] The Snailwell Stud Company Ltd.*

DUBAI MILLENNIUM BHB 136f136a **RR 133+f 136a** 2150[1]
4 b c Seeking the Gold (USA) 7.4f **(80)** - Colorado Dancer (Shareef Dancer (USA)) 9.9f **(73)**
Form - 111
Record 2000 - 1st:3 2nd:0 3rd:0 Ran:3
Pre2000 - 1st:6 2nd:0 3rd:0 Ran:7
Win Prizemoney £2,752,610 *Total Prizemoney* £2,752,610

Wins								
	*** 2000**	Jun	Ascot	(G-F)	G1	10f	133+	
	2000	*Mar*	*Nad Al*	*(FST)*	*G1*	*10f*	*136+*	<
	2000	*Mar*	*Nad Al*	*(FST)*	*L*	*10f*	*125+*	
	* 1999	Spt	Ascot	(HVY)	G1	8f	124+	
	* 1999	Aug	Deauvi	(HVY)	G1	8f	124	
	* 1999	Jly	Maison	(GD)	G2	10f	120	
	* 1999	May	Goodwo	(GD)	L	9.9f	113+	
	* 1999	May	Doncas	(G-F)		8f	114++	
	1998	Oct	Yarmou	(SFT)		8f	103++	

2000 Turf 1-1: (10f 1-1) (gd 1-1) 2000 AW 2-2: (10f 2-2) (Dirt 2-2)

Dubai Millennium, Godolphin's flagship

DRURIDGE BAY (IRE) BHB 25f43a **RR 22f 43a** 2819[11]
4 b g Turtle Island (IRE) - Lady of Shalott (Kings Lake (USA)) 10.8f

Exceptional colt, effective 10f, acts on gd - acts on Dirt, likes Nad Al Sheba and Ascot. (1st run) - 1st of 6 from Sumitas (21 Jun Ascot RF 2150). AW high 136 - 1st of 13 from Behrens (25 Mar Nad Al Sheba RF 0580a). Following his disappointing run in the 1999 Derby, he went on to prove himself a top-class miler with victories in the Prix Jacques Le Marois and Queen Elizabeth II Stakes at Ascot. He started off last season with an easy victory on sand in a prep race for the Dubai World Cup, and then put up an awesome performance to land the big event itself. He returned to Europe for the Prince of Wales's Stakes and galloped his rivals into the ground, after which he was acclaimed by Sheikh Mohammed as the best horse he had ever had. Sadly, an eagerly awaited clash with Montjeu was denied to racing fans when it was revealed the Godolphin colt had suffered a fracture in his off-hind. He was deservedly recognised as the best racehorse of last year in the International Classifications.
**S bin Suroor [6-7] Godolphin (from S bin Suroor in UAE [2-2] Mar 2000).*

DUBAI NURSE BHB 32f **RR 40f** 3131[7]
6 ch m Handsome Sailor 6.6f **(53)** - Lady Eccentric (IRE) (Magical Wonder (USA))
Form - 746007
Record 2000 - 1st:0 2nd:0 3rd:0 Ran:6
Pre2000 - 1st:0 2nd:4 3rd:0 Ran:16
Win Prizemoney £0 *Total Prizemoney* £3,341
2000 Turf 0-5: (5f 5) (gd, frm 4) 2000 AW 0-1: (5f) (Fibr)
Moderate mare, has worn blinkers. Turf high 40.
**A R Dicken [0-24] M G Mackenzie.*

DUBAI SEVEN STARS BHB 84f **RR 85f** 4642[5]
2 ch f Suave Dancer (USA) 10.7f **(68)** - Her Honour (Teenoso (USA)) 9.9f **(72)**
Form - 45225
Record 2000 - 1st:0 2nd:2 3rd:0 Ran:5
Win Prizemoney £0 *Total Prizemoney* £1,577
2000 Turf 0-5: (5f, 7f 2, 8f 2) (hvy, gd, g-f 2, frm)
Useful filly. Turf high 85 - 5th of 22 getting 5lb from Palatial (26 Spt Newmarket 7f g-f RF 4642). **M C Pipe [0-5] Mrs Alison Farrant.*

DUBAI TWO THOUSAND **RR 94f** 2113[7]
3 b c Nashwan (USA) 10.3f **(79)** - Queen's View (FR) (Lomond (USA)) 8.8f **(65)**
Form - 67
Record 2000 - 1st:0 2nd:0 3rd:0 Ran:2
Win Prizemoney £0 *Total Prizemoney* £900
2000 Turf 0-2: (11f, 16f) (g-s, gd)
Scopey, currently useful colt. Turf high 94. An attractive colt with a big reputation over the winter, he failed to deliver in the Lingfield Derby Trial and was not seen after being well beaten at Royal Ascot. **S bin Suroor [0-2] Godolphin.*

DUCHAMP (USA) BHB 83f **RR 87f** 4461[10]
3 b c Pine Bluff (USA) - Higher Learning (USA) (Fappiano (USA)) 8.7f **(77)**
Form - 54721500
Record 2000 - 1st:1 2nd:1 3rd:0 Ran:8
Pre2000 - 1st:1 2nd:2 3rd:0 Ran:5
Win Prizemoney £14,642 *Total Prizemoney* £21,266
Wins * 2000 Jly Newbur (G-F) H 13.3f 83 87 <
* 1999 Oct York (G-S) H 7.9f 76 85
2000 Turf 1-8: (10f 2, 12f 2, 13f 1-2, 14f 2) (gd, g-f 1-6, frm)
Scopey, useful colt, effective 8 to 13f, acts on gd to frm, best on g-f, has worn blinkers, prefers left handed tracks. Turf high 88 - 2nd of 4 getting 7lb from Firecrest (28 Jun Salisbury 12f frm RF 2352) - also 1st of 10 getting 12lb from Masamadas (22 Jly Newbury RF 3026). He is an improving handicapper and won readily at Newbury in July when tackling thirteen furlongs for the first time. Fair run at York, but failed to settle there next time in a first-time visor. **I A Balding [2-13] Mrs Paul Mellon.*

DUCHCOV **RR 68f** 3007[3]
2 ch f Caerleon (USA) 10.9f **(79)** - Amandine (IRE) (Darshaan) 9.9f **(84)**
Form - 3
Record 2000 - 1st:0 2nd:0 3rd:1 Ran:1
Win Prizemoney £0 *Total Prizemoney* £656
2000 Turf 0-1: (7f) (gd)
Currently average filly. **L M Cumani [0-1] Raimon Bloodstock.*

DUCIE BHB 61f **RR 63f** 1006[8]
3 b f Distant Relative 7f **(69)** - Ellebanna (Tina's Pet) 6.8f **(59)**
Form - 088
Record 2000 - 1st:0 2nd:0 3rd:0 Ran:3
Pre2000 - 1st:0 2nd:3 3rd:0 Ran:5
Win Prizemoney £0 *Total Prizemoney* £3,869
2000 Turf 0-3: (5f, 6f 2) (gd 2, frm)
Scopey, average filly, effective 5f, acts on g-s to frm. Turf high 55.
**I A Balding [0-8] Robert Hitchins.*

DUCK ROW (USA) BHB 105f **RR 114f** 5225[4]
5 ch g Diesis 9f **(80)** - Sunny Moment (USA) (Roberto (USA)) 10f **(76)**
Form - 12232734
Record 2000 - 1st:1 2nd:3 3rd:2 Ran:8
Pre2000 - 1st:2 2nd:0 3rd:3 Ran:11
Win Prizemoney £21,742 *Total Prizemoney* £86,749
Wins * 2000 May Haydoc (G-S) 8.1f 106
* 1999 Apr Ascot (GD) 8f 109 <
* 1997 Spt Newbur (SFT) 8f 100
2000 Turf 1-8: (8f 1-4, 9f 3, 10f) (g-s 1-1, gd 5, g-f 2)
Group-class gelding, effective 8 to 9f, best at 8f, acts on g-s to g-f, best on g-f, excels at Ascot. Turf high 114 - 2nd of 5 getting 5lb from Trans Island (10 Jun Epsom 9f gd RF 1862) - also 1st of 4 from Exeat (26 May Haydock RF 1464). Consistent. Just falls short of Group class despite trying his best, and his victories in recent seasons have been in small-field conditions events. Suited by a mile on easy ground. **J A R Toller [3-19] Duke of Devonshire.*

DUC'S DREAM BHB 72f **RR 69?f** 5184[5]
2 b c Bay Tern (USA) - Kala's Image (Kala Shikari) 8.4f **(54)**
Form - 45
Record 2000 - 1st:0 2nd:0 3rd:0 Ran:2
Win Prizemoney £0 *Total Prizemoney* £392
2000 Turf 0-2: (7f, 8f) (g-s, gd)
Currently average colt. Turf high 69 (began Jly).
**D Morris [0-2] Mrs S I Parry.*

DUELLO BHB 56f70a **RR 60f 70a** 3754[1]
9 b g Sure Blade (USA) 10.6f **(66)** - Royal Loft (Homing) 7.8f **(59)**
Form - 33311
Record 2000 - 1st:2 2nd:0 3rd:3 Ran:5
Pre2000 - 1st:5 2nd:13 3rd:8 Ran:86
Win Prizemoney £27,202 *Total Prizemoney* £51,178
Wins * 2000 Aug Folkes (G-F) S 12f 44+
* 2000 Jly Bath (FRM) S 11.7f 38
1999 Oct Leices (GD) C 11.8f 53
1998 Spt Nottin (G-F) H 14.1f 56 59
1996 Spt Newbur (G-F) H 7.3f 64 66 <
1996 May Newbur (SFT) H 7.3f 60 62
2000 Turf 2-5: (12f 2-5) (gd, g-f 1-3, hrd 1-1)
Average gelding, effective 12f, acts on gd to g-f, best on gd, has worn blinkers, excels at Brighton. Turf high 60 (1st run) - 3rd of 14 giving 19lb to Fuero Real (24 May Brighton 12f gd RF 1422).
**M C Pipe [2-10] T M Hely-Hutchinson (from M Blanshard [6-94] Oct 1999).*

DUEMILA (IRE) BHB 40f **RR 50f** 4146[7]
3 b g Forest Wind (USA) - Kotaya (IRE) (Kahyasi)
Form - 007
Record 2000 - 1st:0 2nd:0 3rd:0 Ran:3
2000 Turf 0-3: (8f, 9f, 10f) (g-f, frm 2)
Workmanlike, currently fair gelding. Turf high 50 (began Jly).
**M J Haynes [0-3] SFB Racing.*

DUKE D'ALBA (GER) **RR 100f** 4842a[6]
3 c
Form - 66
2000 Turf 0-2: (11f, 14f) (hvy, gd)
Currently very useful. Turf high 100. **W Figge in GER [0-2].*

DUKE OF MODENA BHB 100f **RR 101f** 5109[4]
3 ch g Salse (USA) 10.9f **(71)** - Palace Street (USA) (Secreto (USA)) 8.7f **(72)**
Form - 115144614
Record 2000 - 1st:4 2nd:0 3rd:0 Ran:9
Pre2000 - 1st:0 2nd:0 3rd:1 Ran:3

Win Prizemoney £71,065 *Total Prizemoney* £82,277

Wins	*** 2000**	Spt Ascot	(G-S)	H	7f	95	101	<
	*** 2000**	Jun Newbur	(G-F)	H	7f	92	96	
	*** 2000**	May Salisb	(G-F)	H	6f	85	91	
	*** 2000**	Apr Kempto	(SFT)	H	6f	79	85	

2000 Turf 4-9: (6f 2-3, 7f 2-6) (sft 1-1, gd 1-4, g-f 2-3, frm)

Neat, very useful gelding, effective 6 to 7f, best at 7f, acts on gd to frm. Turf high 101 - 1st of 26 giving 2lb to Nice One Clare (23 Spt Ascot RF 4597) - also 1st of 4 getting 10lb from Delegate (15 Jun Newbury RF 1990). Consistent. He always looked as if he could step up on his two-year-old form and that proved to be the case last season. A winner four times including a very valuable handicap at Ascot in September, he may find further opportunities in handicap company limited. **G B Balding [4-12] Miss B Swire.*

DULCIFICATION RR 55f

1141[4]

2 b c So Factual (USA) - Dunloe (IRE) **(54f)** (Shaadi (USA))

Form - 74

Record	**2000 -**	1st:0	2nd:0	3rd:0	Ran:2

Win Prizemoney £0 *Total Prizemoney* £217

2000 Turf 0-2: (5f 2) (gd, frm)

Currently fair colt. Turf high 57. **J R Weymes [0-2] Mrs R L Heaton.*

DULZIE BHB 42f50a RR 58f 50a

4489[10]

3 b f Safawan 6.6f **(60)** - Dulzura (Daring March) 7.1f **(61)**

Form - 2465500

Record	**2000 -**	1st:0	2nd:1	3rd:0	Ran:7
	Pre2000 -	1st:0	2nd:0	3rd:0	Ran:2

Win Prizemoney £0 *Total Prizemoney* £737

2000 Turf 0-4: (9f, 10f 2, 11f) (g-f, frm 3) 2000 AW 0-3: (7f 2, 8f) (Equi, Fibr 2)

Light-framed, fair filly, effective 9f, acts on frm, likes tight tracks. Turf high 58 (1st run) - 5th of 8 to Sham Sharif (1 Jun Ayr 9f frm RF 1618). AW high 52. Becoming disappointing. **A P Jarvis [0-9] Mrs D B Brazier.*

DUMARAN (IRE) RR

1987[17]

2 b c Be My Chief (USA) 10.2f **(62)** - Pine Needle **(84f)** (Kris) 9.5f **(73)**

Form - 0

Record	**2000 -**	1st:0	2nd:0	3rd:0	Ran:1

2000 Turf 0-1: (6f) (g-f)

Currently very poor colt. **I A Balding [0-1] Robert Hitchins.*

DUN DISTINCTLY (IRE) BHB 39f45a RR 49f 45a

1151[6]

3 b g Distinctly North (USA) 7.4f **(63)** - Dunbally (Dunphy) 9.4f **(57)**

Form - 742656

Record	**2000 -**	1st:0	2nd:1	3rd:0	Ran:5
	Pre2000 -	1st:0	2nd:0	3rd:0	Ran:5

Win Prizemoney £0 *Total Prizemoney* £1,265

2000 Turf 0-2: (12f 2) (sft, frm) 2000 AW 0-3: (8f, 11f, 12f) (Fibr 3)

Moderate gelding, effective 11f, - acts on Fibr, has worn blinkers, likes left handed tracks, likes tight tracks. Turf high 37. AW high 46. **P C Haslam [0-10] Sir Timothy Kitson & G F Armitage.*

DUNKELD CHAMP BHB 35f RR 12f

1300[8]

3 br g Be My Chief (USA) 10.2f **(62)** - Callipoli (USA) (Green Dancer (USA)) 10.3f **(74)**

Form - 088

Record	**2000 -**	1st:0	2nd:0	3rd:0	Ran:3
	Pre2000 -	1st:0	2nd:0	3rd:0	Ran:2

2000 Turf 0-3: (7f, 8f, 12f) (gd, g-f, frm)

Workmanlike, poor gelding. Turf high 2. **A R Dicken [0-5] J W D Campbell.*

DUNKELLIN HOUSE (IRE) BHB 49f55a RR 54f 55a

2883[11]

3 gr g Petorius 8f **(66)** - More Magnanimous (King Persian)

Form - 800

Record	**2000 -**	1st:0	2nd:0	3rd:0	Ran:3
	Pre2000 -	1st:0	2nd:0	3rd:0	Ran:3

2000 Turf 0-2: (5f 2) (frm, hrd) 2000 AW 0-1: (5f) (Fibr)

Lengthy, fair gelding. Turf high 38. **R A Fahey [0-6] Tommy Staunton.*

DUNKIRK SPIRIT BHB 58f RR 60f

5223[18]

2 b c Whittingham (IRE) - Ruda (FR) (Free Round (USA)) 11.7f **(70)**

Form - 7070

Record	**2000 -**	1st:0	2nd:0	3rd:0	Ran:4

2000 Turf 0-4: (6f 3, 8f) (g-s 2, gd, g-f)

Average colt. Turf high 60 (began Aug). **J Pearce [0-4] B & G Racing.*

DURAID (IRE) BHB 87f84a RR 89f 84a

5317[4]

8 ch g Irish River (FR) 9f **(77)** - Fateful Princess (USA) (Vaguely Noble) 10.1f **(72)**

Form - 4214165644

Record	**2000 -**	1st:2	2nd:1	3rd:0	Ran:10
	Pre2000 -	1st:5	2nd:2	3rd:0	Ran:34

Win Prizemoney £46,957 *Total Prizemoney* £63,041

Wins	*** 2000**	Jly York	(GD)	H	7.9f	82	83	<
	*** 2000**	Jun Catter	(SFT)	H	7f	78	79	
	* 1999	Nov Catter	(SFT)	H	7f	70	75	
	* 1999	Aug Ripon	(GD)	H	8f	66	68	
	* 1999	Jly Beverl	(G-F)	H	8.5f	65	65	
	* 1997	Spt Haydoc	(GD)	H	8.1f	76	82	
	* 1997	Jun Newcas	(GD)	H	8f	64	73	

2000 Turf 2-10: (7f 1-2, 8f 1-8) (sft, g-s 1-1, gd 1-4, g-f 2, frm 2)

Useful gelding, effective 7 to 8f, best at 8f, acts on g-s to frm, best on frm, has worn blinkers, likes left handed trackslikes right handed tracks, excels at Ripon, does well at Catterick and York. Turf high 89 - 5th of 16 to Peartree House (24 Aug York 8f g-f RF 3934) - also 1st of 8 getting 8lb from Swan Knight (14 Jly York RF 2824). Consistent. He is suited by seven furlongs or a mile and a strongly-run race, but does have a bit of a mind of his own. **Denys Smith [11-53] A Suddes.*

DURHAM BHB 55f58a RR 60f 58a

4192[3]

9 ch g Caerleon (USA) 10.9f **(79)** - Sanctuary (Welsh Pageant) 10f **(65)**

Form - 01573

Record	**2000 -**	1st:1	2nd:0	3rd:1	Ran:5
	Pre2000 -	1st:7	2nd:12	3rd:9	Ran:57

Win Prizemoney £28,705 *Total Prizemoney* £45,791

Wins	*** 2000**	Jun Nottin	(G-F)	SH	14.1f	56	60	
	* 1999	Jun Goodwo	(G-F)	H	14f	60	62	
	* 1998	Jly Sandow	(G-F)	H	14f	60	64	
	* 1997	Aug Yarmou	(G-F)	H	14.1f	59	64	
	1996	Spt Ayr	(G-F)	H	13.1f	60	68	<
	1996	Spt Kempto	(GD)	H	14.4f	54	61	
	1996	Aug Lingfi	(G-F)	S	14f		55	
	1996	Jun Nottin	(G-F)	H	14.1f	48	56	

2000 Turf 1-5: (14f 1-4, 16f) (gd 2, g-f 1-3)

Average gelding, effective 14 to 17f, best at 14f, acts on gd to frm, best on frm, mostly wears blinkers (effectively), likes right handed tracks, excels at Kempton. Turf high 60 - 1st of 18 giving 21lb to Cashiki (17 Jun Nottingham RF 2046). Something of a character, he is a fair sort in modest staying handicaps, but he needs fast ground and is not one to totally rely on. **G L Moore [4-39] Wessex House Racing (from H S Howe [2-4] Oct 1996).*

DURLSTON BAY BHB 50f RR 58f

3185[7]

3 b c Welsh Captain 7.2f **(54)** - Nelliellamay (Super Splash (USA)) 7.3f **(54)**

Form - 30877

Record	**2000 -**	1st:0	2nd:0	3rd:1	Ran:5
	Pre2000 -	1st:0	2nd:0	3rd:0	Ran:1

Win Prizemoney £0 *Total Prizemoney* £604

2000 Turf 0-5: (10f, 12f 2, 14f 2) (g-s, gd 2, g-f, frm)

Workmanlike, fair colt, effective 12f, acts on gd. Turf high 74 (1st run) - 3rd of 9 to Pompeii (6 Apr Leicester 12f gd RF 0627). **R Ingram [0-6] M G Mackenzie.*

DUSKY SWALLOW BHB 30f RR 18f

5243[12]

2 b f Factual (USA) - Sarah Carter (Reesh)

Form - 00

Record	**2000 -**	1st:0	2nd:0	3rd:0	Ran:2

2000 Turf 0-1: (6f) (gd) 2000 AW 0-1: (6f) (Fibr)

Currently poor filly, often wears blinkers. **J L Spearing [0-2] Mrs K J Buckley.*

DUSKY VIRGIN BHB 59f RR 60f

4369[8]

3 b f Missed Flight - Rosy Sunset (IRE) (Red Sunset) 8.2f **(63)**

Form - 0740212328

Record	**2000 -**	1st:1	2nd:3	3rd:1	Ran:10
	Pre2000 -	1st:1	2nd:0	3rd:0	Ran:5

Win Prizemoney £6,481 *Total Prizemoney* £10,414

Wins * **2000** Aug Epsom (GD) H 8.5f 51 58
1999 Aug Bright (FRM) S 7f 59 <
2000 Turf 1-10: (6f, 7f 2, 8f 4, 9f 1-2, 10f) (g-f 1-4, frm 5, hrd)
Light-framed, average filly, effective 7 to 9f, best at 9f, acts on g-f to hrd, best on g-f, prefers left handed tracks, prefers tight tracks. Turf high 60 - 2nd of 13 giving 1lb to Altay (6 Spt Epsom 9f g-f RF 4267) - also 1st of 6 getting 16lb from Rasmalai (16 Aug Epsom RF 3691). Consistent. Landed an Epsom handicap in August and is a different horse on an undulating track.
**S Woodman [1-10] Mrs W Edgar (from M Quinn [1-5] Aug 1999).*

DUST ON THE BOTTLE (USA) RR 5332a[11]
5 b h Temperance Hill (USA) - Princely Proof (USA) (Princely Pleasure (USA))
Form - 0
2000 AW 0-1: (10f) (Dirt)
Currently Pattern-class colt, always wears blinkers.
**G Hild in USA [0-1] Sharon Hild.*

DUSTY CARPET BHB 80f RR 78f 5103[8]
2 ch g Pivotal - Euridice (IRE) (Woodman (USA)) 9f **(74)**
Form - 64643038
Record 2000 - 1st:0 2nd:0 3rd:2 Ran:8
Win Prizemoney £0 *Total Prizemoney* £2,836
2000 Turf 0-8: (6f 3, 7f 3, 8f 2) (g-s, gd 3, g-f 3, frm)
Above average gelding, effective 7 to 8f, acts on g-s to g-f. Turf high 82 - 3rd of 6 giving 2lb to Lil's Jessy (10 Aug Chester 7f g-f RF 3747). **C A Dwyer [0-8] Mrs C M Goode.*

DUSTY DEMOCRAT BHB 40f42a RR 15f 42a 4689[18]
2 b g Democratic (USA) - Two Shots (Dom Racine (FR)) 9.2f **(62)**
Form - D800
Record 2000 - 1st:0 2nd:0 3rd:0 Ran:4
2000 Turf 0-2: (8f 2) (gd, frm) 2000 AW 0-2: (5f, 7f) (Fibr 2)
Moderate gelding, has worn blinkers. Turf high 15 (began Aug). AW high 47. **W G M Turner [0-4] T O C S Ltd.*

DUSTY PRINCESS BHB 35f RR 7f 4048[16]
2 gr f Aragon 7.7f **(58)** -Lady Seren (IRE) **(27f)** (Doulab (USA)) 9.8f **(65)**
Form - 060
Record 2000 - 1st:0 2nd:0 3rd:0 Ran:3
2000 Turf 0-2: (6f 2) (gd, frm) 2000 AW 0-1: (5f) (Fibr)
Currently very moderate filly, has worn blinkers. Turf high 7.
**J G Given [0-3] David Wright.*

DUSTY SHOES RR 70f 4319[4]
3 b f Shareef Dancer (USA) 10.1f **(67)** - Run Faster (IRE) (Commanche Run) 8.5f **(58)**
Form - 34
Record 2000 - 1st:0 2nd:0 3rd:1 Ran:2
Win Prizemoney £0 *Total Prizemoney* £877
2000 Turf 0-2: (8f, 10f) (gd, g-f)
Scopey, currently above-average filly. Turf high 70 (began Aug).
**D R C Elsworth [0-2] C J Harper.*

DUTCH DYANE BHB 41f26a RR 45f 26a 5161[14]
7 b m Midyan (USA) 9.9f **(64)** - Double Dutch (Nicholas Bill) 10.1f **(56)**
Form - 5380
Record 2000 - 1st:0 2nd:0 3rd:1 Ran:4
Pre2000 - 1st:0 2nd:2 3rd:2 Ran:12
Win Prizemoney £0 *Total Prizemoney* £2,790
2000 Turf 0-4: (15f, 16f 3) (hvy, sft, gd 2)
Moderate mare, effective 15 to 16f, best at 16f, acts on hvy to gd. Turf high 45 - 3rd of 12 giving 3lb to Elsie Bamford (27 May Warwick 15f hvy RF 1513).
**G P Enright [3-31] Miss Fuller, Ross, Neil Kenworthy.*

DUTCH HARRIER (IRE) RR 102f 4092a[5]
3 ch c Barathea (IRE) - Fanny Blankers 00
Form - 831224305
2000 Turf 1-9: (10f, 12f 1-4, 14f 3, 16f) (g-s 3, gd 4, g-f 1-2)
Very useful colt, effective 12 to 16f, best at 14f, acts on gd to g-f, best on gd. Turf high 102 - 5th of 8 getting 14lb from Katiykha (26 Aug Curragh 14f gd RF 4092a). He stays well, and ran one of his best races of the season when runner-up to Dalampour in the Queen's Vase over two miles.
**K Prendergast in IRE [1-9] Magnus Berger.*

DUTCH LAD BHB 65f62a RR 76f 62a 0003[12]
5 b g Alnasr Alwasheek 9.4f **(62)** - Double Dutch (Nicholas Bill) 10.1f **(56)**
Form - 00
Record 2000 - 1st:0 2nd:0 3rd:0 Ran:2
Pre2000 - 1st:1 2nd:4 3rd:2 Ran:15
Win Prizemoney £2,600 *Total Prizemoney* £10,156
Wins * 1998 Apr Mussel (G-S) 12f 68+ <
2000 Turf 0-1: (12f) (gd) 2000 AW 0-1: (11f) (Fibr)
Above-average gelding, has worn blinkers. Becoming disappointing. **M H Tompkins [1-19] D J Anderson.*

D W MCCEE BHB 34f37a RR 24f 37a 2425[15]
4 b g Keen 11.1f **(58)** - Miss Coco (Swing Easy (USA)) 6.5f **(55)**
Form - 0000
Record 2000 - 1st:0 2nd:0 3rd:0 Ran:4
Pre2000 - 1st:0 2nd:0 3rd:0 Ran:4
2000 Turf 0-3: (6f, 8f 2) (sft, g-f, frm) 2000 AW 0-1: (7f) (Fibr)
Workmanlike, little account gelding, has worn blinkers. Turf high 22.
**C G Cox [0-4] Ms Dawn Stagg (from Miss Gay Kelleway [0-4] Oct 1999).*

DYNAMIC DREAM (USA) BHB 85f RR 83f 4016[4]
3 b f Dynaformer (USA) 12f **(82)** - Hip Hip Hur Rahy (USA) (Rahy (USA))
Form - 354
Record 2000 - 1st:0 2nd:0 3rd:1 Ran:3
Pre2000 - 1st:1 2nd:0 3rd:0 Ran:1
Win Prizemoney £4,597 *Total Prizemoney* £7,131
Wins * 1999 Aug Folkes (GD) 7f 80 <
2000 Turf 0-3: (8f, 9f, 10f) (g-f, frm 2)
Scopey, decent filly. Turf high 83 (began Jly).
**P W Harris [1-4] Dynamic Dozen.*

DYNAMISM (FR) BHB 80f70a RR 88f 70a 63[11]
5 b g Caerleon (USA) 10.9f **(79)** - Fextal (USA) (Alleged (USA)) 10f **(76)**
Form - 060
Record 2000 - 1st:0 2nd:0 3rd:0 Ran:1
Pre2000 - 1st:1 2nd:0 3rd:1 Ran:11
Win Prizemoney £3,582 *Total Prizemoney* £6,390
Wins 1998 May Ripon (GD) 10f 77 <
2000 AW 0-1: (11f) (Fibr)
Useful gelding, effective 10f, acts on g-f, has worn blinkers. Inconsistent.
**Mrs L Stubbs [0-10] M S & C S Griffiths (from H R A Cecil [1-2] May 1998).*

EAGALITY (IRE) BHB 52f RR 51f 4215[15]
2 b f Eagle Eyed (USA) - Originality (Godswalk (USA)) 7.3f **(58)**
Form - 700670
Record 2000 - 1st:0 2nd:0 3rd:0 Ran:6
2000 Turf 0-6: (5f, 6f 3, 7f, 8f) (g-f 3, frm 2, hrd)
Fair filly, has worn blinkers. Turf high 51.
**B J Meehan [0-6] Mrs Eithne Meehan.*

EAGER ANGEL (IRE) BHB 54f RR 53f 4200[15]
2 b f Up and At 'em - Seanee Squaw (Indian Ridge)
Form - 580
Record 2000 - 1st:0 2nd:0 3rd:0 Ran:3
2000 Turf 0-3: (5f 2, 6f) (g-f 2, hrd)
Currently fair filly. Turf high 53 (began Aug).
**D Carroll [0-3] C I S Racing.*

EAGLERIDER (IRE) RR 55f 5318[6]
2 b c Eagle Eyed (USA) - What A Summer (USA) (What Luck (USA)) 8.1f **(79)**
Form - 36
Record 2000 - 1st:0 2nd:0 3rd:1 Ran:2
Win Prizemoney £0 *Total Prizemoney* £343
2000 Turf 0-2: (5f, 6f) (sft, gd)
Currently fair colt. Turf high 55 (began Oct).
**J G Given [0-2] & Mrs G Calder.*

EAGLES CACHE BHB 75f70a RR 78f 70a 4784[5]
2 b c Eagle Eyed (USA) - Cache (Bustino) 10.4f **(64)**

Form - 4362623025
Record 2000 - 1st:0 2nd:3 3rd:2 Ran:10
Win Prizemoney £0 *Total Prizemoney* £4,084
2000 Turf 0-9: (5f, 6f 6, 7f 2) (gd 3, g-f 4, frm 2) 2000 AW 0-1: (8f) (Fibr)
Above-average colt, effective 6f, acts on gd. Turf high 78 - 3rd of 8 giving 10lb to Joint Instruction (28 Aug Warwick 6f gd RF 4056).
**A Berry [0-10] W R Milner.*

EAGLE'S CROSS (USA) BHB 84f **RR 90f** 3950a[2]

5 b h Trempolino (USA) 11.9f **(77)** - Shining Bright (Rainbow Quest (USA)) 10.4f **(75)**
Form - 2
2000 Turf 0-1: (16f) (gd)
Useful colt. (1st run) - 2nd of 6 getting 5lb from Akbar (20 Aug Dielsdorf 16f gd RF 3950a).
**in SWI [0-1] (from R Charlton [1-8] Oct 1998).*

EAGLET (IRE) BHB 59f **RR 68?f** 4062[8]

2 b c Eagle Eyed (USA) - Justice System (USA) (Criminal Type (USA))
Form - 000545508
Record 2000 - 1st:0 2nd:0 3rd:0 Ran:9
Win Prizemoney £0 *Total Prizemoney* £251
2000 Turf 0-9: (5f, 6f 3, 7f 5) (g-s, gd 2, g-f, frm 4, hrd)
Average colt. Turf high 68. Inconsistent. **A Scott [0-9] Andy Scott.*

EARLENE (IRE) **RR 98f** 3172[6]

3 b f In The Wings 11.2f **(77)** - Ela Romara (Ela-Mana-Mou) 10.1f **(70)**
Form - 6
Record 2000 - 1st:0 2nd:0 3rd:0 Ran:1
Pre2000 - 1st:1 2nd:2 3rd:0 Ran:3
Win Prizemoney £9,750 *Total Prizemoney* £19,660
Wins 1999 Spt Currag (SFT) 8f 90+ <
2000 Turf 0-1: (10f) (frm)
Very useful filly. She had one run on unsuitable ground for Godolphin.
**S bin Suroor [0-1] Godolphin (from J Oxx in IRE [1-3] Oct 1999).*

EARLEY SESSION (IRE) BHB 35f30a **RR 41df 30a** 4811[11]

3 b g Puissance 7.1f **(60)** - Shabby Doll (Northfields (USA)) 9f **(72)**
Form - 88700
Record 2000 - 1st:0 2nd:0 3rd:0 Ran:4
Pre2000 - 1st:0 2nd:0 3rd:0 Ran:3
2000 Turf 0-3: (6f 2, 8f) (g-f, frm 2) 2000 AW 0-1: (8f) (Equi)
Light-framed, moderate gelding, has worn blinkers. Turf high 41.
**J C Tuck [0-7] The Cat & Custard Partnership.*

EARL GREY BHB 101f **RR 92f** 4643[6]

2 b c Twining (USA) - Regal Peace (Known Fact (USA)) 7.4f **(67)**
Form - 1466
Record 2000 - 1st:1 2nd:0 3rd:0 Ran:4
Win Prizemoney £3,688 *Total Prizemoney* £14,654
Wins * 2000 May Leices (G-S) 6f 79+ <
2000 Turf 1-4: (6f 1-2, 7f 2) (gd 1-3, g-f)
Useful colt. Turf high 92 - 4th of 12 to Cd Europe (20 Jun Ascot 6f gd RF 2112). Looked the most backward in the field when scoring on his debut, and improved for the experience when running a close fourth in the Coventry Stakes at Royal Ascot. Disappointed next time, but ran reasonably after a break in a valuable sales race at Newmarket. Looks capable of winning a decent race or two, and may be best caught first time up. **W Jarvis [1-4] The Tea Clippers.*

EARLY MORNING MIST (IRE) BHB 85f **RR 82f** 3605[1]

2 b f Alzao (USA) 9.8f **(73)** - Welsh Mist **(93f)** (Damister (USA)) 9f **(73)**
Form - 31
Record 2000 - 1st:1 2nd:0 3rd:1 Ran:2
Win Prizemoney £6,760 *Total Prizemoney* £7,312
Wins * 2000 Aug Ascot (G-F) 6f 82 <
2000 Turf 1-2: (6f 1-2) (g-f 1-1, frm)
Currently decent filly. Turf high 82 (began Jly) - 1st of 7 from Farha (13 Aug Ascot RF 3605). She got off the mark in an Ascot maiden on her second start despite not enjoying the clearest of runs and should improve further. **M Johnston [1-2] Alan Lillingston.*

EARLY WARNING (USA) RR 1628a[2]

5 b h Summer Squall (USA) 7f **(80)** - Vid Kid (USA) (Pleasant Colony (USA)) 7f **(70)**
Form - 2
2000 AW 0-1: (9f) (Dirt)
Currently Pattern-class colt. (1st run) - 2nd of 6 getting 6lb from Running Stag (24 May Belmont Park 9f Dirt RF 1628a).
**in USA [0-1].*

EARLY WISH (USA) BHB 72f68a **RR 79f 68a** 5115[6]

2 ch f Rahy (USA) 9.1f **(80)** - Heaven's Nook (USA) (Great Above (USA))
Form - 63306
Record 2000 - 1st:0 2nd:0 3rd:2 Ran:5
Win Prizemoney £0 *Total Prizemoney* £1,460
2000 Turf 0-4: (5f, 6f, 7f 2) (g-s, g-f 2, frm) 2000 AW 0-1: (8f) (Fibr)
Above-average filly. Turf high 74 - 3rd of 12 to Dora Carrington (25 Jun Pontefract 6f frm RF 2262). **B Hanbury [0-5] Abdullah Ali.*

EASAAR BHB 114f **RR 105df** 2151[19]

4 b c Machiavellian (USA) 9.8f **(83)** - Matila (IRE) (Persian Bold) 9.3f **(66)**
Form - 280
Record 2000 - 1st:0 2nd:1 3rd:0 Ran:3
Pre2000 - 1st:1 2nd:1 3rd:0 Ran:3
Win Prizemoney £8,217 *Total Prizemoney* £253,287
Wins * 1998 Oct Newmar () 7f 91+ <
2000 Turf 0-2: (8f, 10f) (g-s, gd) 2000 AW 0-1: (12f) (Dirt)
Scopey, very high-class colt. Turf high 83. (1st run) - 2nd of 11 to Rhythm Band (25 Mar Nad Al Sheba 12f Dirt RF 0579a). He finished tenth to stablemate Island Sands in the 2000 Guineas in 1999, but did not reappear until racing successfully in Dubai in the winter. The heavy ground seemed against him when last at Sandown on his European return, but he was well beaten in the Hunt Cup next time.
**S bin Suroor [1-5] Godolphin (from S bin Suroor in UAE [0-1] Mar 2000).*

EAST CAPE BHB 77f **RR 76f** 2772[9]

3 b c Bering 9.6f **(80)** - Reine de Danse (USA) (Nureyev (USA)) 8.7f **(78)**
Form - 54210
Record 2000 - 1st:1 2nd:1 3rd:0 Ran:5
Win Prizemoney £4,179 *Total Prizemoney* £5,813
Wins * 2000 Jun Windso (G-F) 8.3f 76 <
2000 Turf 1-5: (8f 1-2, 9f 2, 10f) (hvy, gd, g-f 1-3)
Above-average colt. Turf high 76 - 1st of 13 giving 5lb to Eve (26 Jun Windsor RF 2287). Has gradually improved from his debut in Italy, and got off the mark in a Windsor maiden. From a yard who often do well with progressive three-year-olds in handicaps.
**L M Cumani [1-5] Mrs M Schulthess.*

EASTER BONNET RR 1467[9]

2 ch f My Generation 6.5f **(68)** - Flower Othe Forest (Indian Forest (USA))
Form - 0
Record 2000 - 1st:0 2nd:0 3rd:0 Ran:1
2000 Turf 0-1: (5f) (gd)
Currently very poor filly. **N M Babbage [0-1] B Babbage.*

EASTER ISLAND (IRE) BHB 59a **RR 62f** 4927[7]

2 b br f Turtle Island (IRE) - Port Queen (IRE) **(54f)** (Nashamaa) 7.1f **(66)**
Form - 0070017
Record 2000 - 1st:1 2nd:0 3rd:0 Ran:7
Win Prizemoney £1,884 *Total Prizemoney* £1,884
Wins * 2000 Spt Bright (SFT) S 5.3f 62 <
2000 Turf 1-6: (5f 1-3, 6f 3) (g-s 1-2, gd, g-f 2, frm) 2000 AW 0-1: (5f) (Equi)
Average filly, effective 5f, acts on g-s. Turf high 62 - 1st of 9 from Bali Royal (27 Spt Brighton RF 4674).
**B R Millman [1-3] Normandy Developments (London) (from R J O'Sullivan [0-4] Jun 2000).*

EASTERN BREEZE (IRE) RR 76f 5309[3]

2 b c Sri Pekan (USA) - Elegant Bloom (IRE) (Be My Guest (USA)) 9.3f **(67)**
Form - 373
Record 2000 - 1st:0 2nd:0 3rd:2 Ran:3
Win Prizemoney £0 *Total Prizemoney* £1,048

2000 Turf 0-3: (6f, 7f 2) (g-s, gd 2)
Currently above-average colt. Turf high 76 (began Spt).
**P W Harris [0-3] Brosnan, Cage, Coppen & Lupson.*

EASTERN CHAMP (USA) BHB 59f70a **RR 59f 70a** 5006[5]

4 ch c Star de Naskra (USA) 8.8f **(63)** - Dance Troupe (USA) (Native Charger) 10.7f **(63)**
Form - 0020634665
Record 2000 - 1st:0 2nd:1 3rd:1 Ran:9
Pre2000 - 1st:1 2nd:4 3rd:0 Ran:11
Win Prizemoney £3,387 *Total Prizemoney* £11,045
Wins * 1999 Aug Redcar (GD) 9f 78+ <
2000 Turf 0-6: (8f 4, 9f, 10f) (g-s 2, g-f, frm 3) 2000 AW 0-3: (8f 3) (Equi, Fibr 2)
Workmanlike, above-average colt, effective 8 to 9f, best at 9f, acts on frm - acts on AW, prefers left handed tracks, prefers tight tracks. Turf high 59. AW high 72 (1st run) - 2nd of 12 giving 25lb to Tapage (12 May Lingfield 8f Equi RF 1168).
**S P C Woods [1-20] P K L Chu.*

EASTERN JEWEL **RR 55f** 5312[16]

2 b f Anshan 8.2f **(63)** - China's Pearl **(33df)** (Shirley Heights) 10.3f **(74)**
Form - 00
Record 2000 - 1st:0 2nd:0 3rd:0 Ran:2
2000 Turf 0-2: (8f 2) (g-s, gd)
Currently fair filly. Turf high 55 (began Oct).
**Mrs A J Perrett [0-2] C Duncan.*

EASTERN LILAC **RR 38f** 4744[11]

2 b f Mistertopogigo (IRE) - Rosy Diamond (Jalmood (USA)) 10.1f **(52)**
Form - 0
Record 2000 - 1st:0 2nd:0 3rd:0 Ran:1
2000 Turf 0-1: (7f) (gd)
Currently very moderate filly. **K A Ryan [0-1] T C Chiang.*

EASTERN PROMISE **RR 63f** 3407[10]

2 gr f Factual (USA) - Indian Crystal **(45f 42a)** (Petong) 6.6f **(58)**
Form - 24140
Record 2000 - 1st:1 2nd:1 3rd:0 Ran:5
Win Prizemoney £2,795 *Total Prizemoney* £3,992
Wins * 2000 Jun Mussel (FRM) 5f 63 <
2000 Turf 1-5: (5f 1-5) (gd 2, frm 1-2, hrd)
Average filly. Turf high 63 (1st run) - 2nd of 6 getting 4lb from Milly's Lass (2 May Nottingham 5f gd RF 0968) - also 1st of 6 from Peyto Princess (19 Jun Musselburgh RF 2091).
**A Berry [1-5] Mrs B A Matthews.*

EASTERN PROPHETS BHB 53f45a **RR 56f 45a** 4378[8]

7 b g Emarati (USA) 6.6f **(63)** - Four Love (Pas de Seul) 9.1f **(67)**
Form - 3007744018
Record 2000 - 1st:1 2nd:0 3rd:1 Ran:10
Pre2000 - 1st:6 2nd:11 3rd:8 Ran:72
Win Prizemoney £27,353 *Total Prizemoney* £52,606
Wins * 2000 Aug Newcas (G-F) H 6f 49 52
* 1999 May Nottin (GD) H 6.1f 61 58
1998 May Doncas (G-F) C 6f 70
1997 Mar Kempto (G-F) H 6f 79 82
2000 Turf 1-10: (5f 2, 6f 1-6, 7f 2) (g-f 3, frm 4, hrd 1-3)
Fair gelding, effective 5 to 7f, best at 5f, acts on g-f to frm, best on frm, often wears blinkers (very effectively), does well at Carlisle. Turf high 56.
**M Dods [2-27] Graham and Barbara Spencer (from G Lewis [5-45] Oct 1998).*

EASTERN PURPLE (IRE) BHB 117f **RR 117f** 4434[2]

5 b g Petorius 8f **(66)** - Broadway Rosie (Absalom) 7.2f **(58)**
Form - 83705621862
Record 2000 - 1st:1 2nd:2 3rd:1 Ran:11
Pre2000 - 1st:3 2nd:1 3rd:2 Ran:24
Win Prizemoney £65,481 *Total Prizemoney* £108,612
Wins * 2000 Aug Leopar (GD) G3 6f 112 <
* 1999 May Currag (GD) G3 6f 111
1998 May Haydoc (G-S) LH 6f 93 106
1997 Aug Newcas (G-F) 6f 71+
2000 Turf 1-11: (5f 7, 6f 1-4) (g-s 2, gd 1-6, g-f 2, frm)
High-class gelding, effective 5 to 6f, best at 6f, acts on gd to frm, best on g-f, has worn blinkers, excels at Ascot. Turf high 117 - 2nd of 13 giving 8lb to Cassandra Go (1 Aug Goodwood 5f g-f RF 3276) - also 1st of 8 giving 4lb to Conormara (13 Aug Leopardstown RF 3675a). He is a few pounds below the leading sprinters, but he was in good heart in the summer and deserved his Group Three success at Leopardstown. He is effective over both five and six furlongs. **K A Ryan [2-20] T C Chiang (from R A Fahey [2-15] Nov 1998).*

EASTERN RAINBOW (IRE) BHB 38f **RR 38f** 2928[5]

4 b g Bluebird (USA) 7.9f **(71)** - Insaf (USA) (Raise A Native) 11.2f **(69)**
Form - 002365
Record 2000 - 1st:0 2nd:1 3rd:1 Ran:6
Pre2000 - 1st:0 2nd:0 3rd:0 Ran:4
Win Prizemoney £0 *Total Prizemoney* £1,171
2000 Turf 0-6: (5f 2, 6f 2, 10f, 12f) (gd, g-f, frm 4)
Leggy, very moderate gelding, effective 5f, acted on frm, often wore blinkers (very effectively). Turf high 38 - 5th of 14 getting 1lb from Noble Patriot (19 Jly Doncaster 5f frm RF 2928). (DEAD)
**K A Ryan [0-10] T C Chiang.*

EASTERN RED BHB 50f **RR 48f** 4783[3]

2 b f Contract Law (USA) 8.9f **(54)** - Gagajulu **(31f 58a)** (Al Hareb (USA))
Form - 05620546233
Record 2000 - 1st:0 2nd:2 3rd:2 Ran:11
Win Prizemoney £0 *Total Prizemoney* £1,678
2000 Turf 0-9: (5f 3, 6f 3, 7f 2, 8f) (g-s, gd 2, g-f 2, frm 4) 2000 AW 0-2: (6f, 8f) (Fibr 2)
Moderate filly, effective 7 to 8f, acts on g-f to frm, has worn blinkers. Turf high 48 - 3rd of 16 getting 11lb from The Fancy Man (13 Spt Beverley 7f g-f RF 4360). AW high 40 (began Jly). Consistent.
**K A Ryan [0-11] T C Chiang.*

EASTERN SPICE BHB 79f **RR 81f** 4035[10]

3 b c Polish Precedent (USA) 9f **(73)** - Mithl Al Hawa (Salse (USA)) 7.5f **(66)**
Form - 02138100
Record 2000 - 1st:2 2nd:1 3rd:1 Ran:8
Pre2000 - 1st:0 2nd:1 3rd:1 Ran:6
Win Prizemoney £11,004 *Total Prizemoney* £14,749
Wins * 2000 Jly Bath (FRM) H 8f 77 81 <
*** 2000** Jun Goodwo (GD) 9f 75
2000 Turf 2-8: (8f 1-5, 9f 1-3) (g-s, gd 3, g-f 1-2, frm 1-2)
Workmanlike, decent colt, effective 7 to 9f, best at 8f, acts on gd to frm, best on frm, excels at Bath. Turf high 81 - 1st of 10 giving 16lb to Dovebrace (27 Jly Bath RF 3148) - also 1st of 7 from Flying Treaty (23 Jun Goodwood RF 2223). Suited by a mile and fast ground. **R Hannon [2-14] Mohamed Suhail.*

EASTERN TRUMPETER BHB 79f77a **RR 81f 77a** 5199[16]

4 b c First Trump - Oriental Air (IRE) **(49f 48a)** (Taufan (USA)) 7f **(57)**
Form - 141000211113821837040
Record 2000 - 1st:7 2nd:2 3rd:2 Ran:21
Pre2000 - 1st:2 2nd:1 3rd:4 Ran:19
Win Prizemoney £47,244 *Total Prizemoney* £57,748
Wins * 2000 Jly York (GD) H 5f 73 79 <
*** 2000** Jun Ripon (G-S) H 5f 70 73
*** 2000** May Redcar (G-S) H 5f 66 69
*** 2000** May Lingfi (G-S) H 5f 62 66
*** 2000** May Carlis (FRM) 5f 68
*** 2000** *Mar Wolver (STD) H 5f 66 69*
*** 2000** *Feb Wolver (STD) H 5f 61 66*
* 1999 Jun Ayr (SFT) H 5f 62 62
* 1999 Apr Folkes (SFT) C 5f 70
2000 Turf 5-17: (5f 5-17) (sft, g-s, gd 2-7, g-f 2-5, frm 1-3) 2000 AW 2-4: (5f 2-4) (Fibr 2-4)
Decent colt, effective 5f, acts on gd to frm, best on gd. Turf high 81 - 3rd of 10 getting 8lb from Ambitious (6 Aug Newbury 5f g-f RF 3419) - also 1st of 14 getting 3lb from Blessingindisguise (14 Jly York RF 2820). AW high 69. A winner twice at Wolverhampton at the start of the year, he is a most effective sprint handicapper. Best at the minimum trip, as four wins in a row in the space of a month in the spring testify, he has continued to run well since and won a decent handicap at York in July. Another example of Milton Bradley's skill, especially with sprinters.
**J M Bradley [9-38] R G G Racing (from G Lewis [0-2] Aug 1998).*

EASTER OGIL (IRE) BHB 71f **RR 80f** 5068[14]

5 ch g Pips Pride 6.7f **(70)** - Piney Pass (Persian Bold) 9.3f **(66)**

Form - 500641257704000

Record 2000 - 1st:1 2nd:1 3rd:0 Ran:15
Pre2000 - 1st:3 2nd:4 3rd:3 Ran:28

Win Prizemoney £17,292 *Total Prizemoney* £31,700

Wins * **2000** May Doncas (G-S) 6f 80
* 1999 Spt Bath (FRM) H 5.7f 78 85 <
* 1998 Spt Sandow (GD) 7.1f 83
* 1998 Apr Beverl (SFT) 5f 83

2000 Turf 1-15: (5f 2, 6f 1-8, 7f 5) (sft 2, g-s 2, gd 1-5, g-f 2, frm 3, hrd)

Decent gelding, effective 6 to 7f, best at 6f, acts on gd to frm, often wears blinkers, excels at Kempton. Turf high 85 (1st run) - 5th of 17 giving 2lb to Premier Baron (25 Mar Kempton 7f gd RF 0499) - also 1st of 8 giving 12lb to La Caprice (27 May Doncaster RF 1486). Becoming disappointing. He wins in his turn, but is not the most consistent of sorts. Performed well in the spring including a victory at Doncaster, but has not done so well since. Looks best suited by six furlongs. **I A Balding [4-43] I A Balding.*

EAST OF JAVA BHB 70f **RR 84f** 5156[9]

2 b c Greensmith - Krakatoa (Shirley Heights) 10.3f **(74)**

Form - 8300

Record 2000 - 1st:0 2nd:0 3rd:1 Ran:4

Win Prizemoney £0 *Total Prizemoney* £495

2000 Turf 0-4: (5f, 6f 3) (g-s, gd 3)

Decent colt. Turf high 84 (began Aug) - 3rd of 12 giving 5lb to Farha (15 Spt Nottingham 6f gd RF 4440). **K R Burke [0-4] Snowdrop 2000 Partnership.*

EAST ROSE RR 1559[11]

4 b f Keen 11.1f **(58)** - Rashah (Blakeney) 10.5f **(64)**

Form - 0

Record 2000 - 1st:0 2nd:0 3rd:0 Ran:1

2000 Turf 0-1: (10f) (g-s)

Scopey, currently very poor filly. **M D I Usher [0-1] R Torre.*

EASTWAYS BHB 82f **RR 88f** 4311[7]

3 ch c Efisio 7.7f **(69)** - Helens Dreamgirl (Caerleon (USA)) 8.6f **(71)**

Form - 7030000742247

Record 2000 - 1st:0 2nd:2 3rd:1 Ran:13
Pre2000 - 1st:1 2nd:2 3rd:2 Ran:5

Win Prizemoney £8,732 *Total Prizemoney* £25,830

Wins * 1999 Jun Beverl (GD) 5f 80+ <

2000 Turf 0-13: (6f 5, 7f 4, 8f, 10f 3) (g-s, gd 3, g-f 4, frm 5)

Useful colt, effective 6 to 10f, acts on g-s to frm, does well at Newmarket. Turf high 89. Consistent. Generally running well during the summer without managing to win, a mile looks to be his best trip. **M Johnston [1-18] B E P Partnership.*

EASTWELL HALL BHB 84f **RR 87f** 5226[5]

5 b g Saddlers' Hall (IRE) 10.5f **(65)** - Kinchenjunga (Darshaan) 9.9f **(84)**

Form - 515205

Record 2000 - 1st:1 2nd:1 3rd:0 Ran:6
Pre2000 - 1st:3 2nd:2 3rd:1 Ran:16

Win Prizemoney £14,393 *Total Prizemoney* £25,375

Wins * **2000** Jun Chepst (GD) H 18f 78 84 <
1998 May Warwic (GD) H 12.5f 53 68
1998 Apr Bath (SFT) H 10.2f 53 70+
1998 Apr Folkes (GD) H 9.7f 47 52

2000 Turf 1-6: (16f 2, 18f 1-3, 20f) (g-s, gd 1-4, g-f)

Useful gelding, effective 17 to 18f, best at 18f, acts on gd to g-f, best on gd. Turf high 87 - 2nd of 4 giving 14lb to King Flyer (14 Spt Yarmouth 18f g-f RF 4399) - also 1st of 14 giving 4lb to Stormy Skye (8 Jun Chepstow RF 1804).

**T P McGovern [3-18] Eastwell Manor Racing (from R Curtis [3-13] Spt 1998).*

EASTWELL MANOR RR 69f 4191[10]

2 b c Dancing Spree (USA) 8f **(59)** - Kinchenjunga (Darshaan) 9.9f **(84)**

Form - 70

Record 2000 - 1st:0 2nd:0 3rd:0 Ran:2

2000 Turf 0-2: (7f, 8f) (g-f 2)

Currently average colt. Turf high 69 (began Aug). **Derrick Morris [0-2] Eastwell Manor Racing.*

EASTWELL MINSTREL BHB 30f34a **RR 34a** 3826[14]

5 ch g Risk Me (FR) 8f **(53)** - Ramz (IRE) (The Minstrel (CAN)) 10f **(72)**

Form - 00

Record 2000 - 1st:0 2nd:0 3rd:0 Ran:2
Pre2000 - 1st:1 2nd:0 3rd:0 Ran:6

Win Prizemoney £1,984 *Total Prizemoney* £1,984

Wins 1997 Jly Folkes (SFT) S 5f 65 <

2000 Turf 0-1: (17f) (hrd) 2000 AW 0-1: (6f) (Fibr)

Very poor gelding, had worn blinkers. (DEAD)

**A J Lockwood [0-9] Mrs Lynne Lumley (from K Mahdi [0-3] Nov 1998).*

EASTWOOD DRIFTER (USA) BHB 55f53a **RR 66f 53a** 4730[9]

3 ch g Woodman (USA) 9.7f **(77)** - Mandarina (USA) **(93f)** (El Gran Senor (USA)) 9.6f **(76)**

Form - 30362625730

Record 2000 - 1st:0 2nd:2 3rd:3 Ran:11
Pre2000 - 1st:0 2nd:0 3rd:0 Ran:3

Win Prizemoney £0 *Total Prizemoney* £4,261

2000 Turf 0-9: (8f 2, 9f, 10f 5, 12f) (gd 4, g-f, frm 4) 2000 AW 0-2: (13f, 16f) (Equi 2)

Scopey, average gelding, effective 8 to 12f, best at 10f, acts on gd to frm, best on frm, has worn blinkers, favours tight tracks. Turf high 66 (1st run) - 3rd of 10 getting 4lb from Sporty Mo (13 Apr Brighton 8f gd RF 0694). AW high 62 (began Spt).

**W R Muir [0-14] M J Caddy.*

EASY DOLLAR BHB 81f **RR 96f** 4933[12]

8 ch g Gabitat 8.5f **(44)** - Burglars Girl (Burglar) 7.2f **(49)**

Form - 6070550050

Record 2000 - 1st:0 2nd:0 3rd:0 Ran:10
Pre2000 - 1st:3 2nd:7 3rd:5 Ran:46

Win Prizemoney £39,459 *Total Prizemoney* £77,987

Wins * 1999 Spt Nottin (GD) H 6.1f 85 88

2000 Turf 0-10: (5f, 6f 6, 7f 3) (gd 4, g-f 4, frm 2)

Very useful gelding, effective 6 to 7f, acts on gd to g-f, mostly wears blinkers. Turf high 96. He remains a useful six and seven-furlong handicapper, despite failing to trouble the judge last season. Unsuited by soft ground, he is game, and has dropped to a mark off which he is capable of winning.

**B Gubby [3-56] Brian Gubby Ltd.*

EASY ENIGMA (IRE) RR 74f 3412[5]

2 ch c Selkirk (USA) 7.9f **(76)** - Moonlight Saunter (USA) **(82f)** (Woodman (USA)) 9f **(74)**

Form - 85

Record 2000 - 1st:0 2nd:0 3rd:0 Ran:2

2000 Turf 0-2: (7f 2) (g-f 2)

Currently above-average colt. Turf high 74 (began Jly).

**B W Hills [0-2] Maktoum Al Maktoum.*

EASY FREE BHB 45f **RR 40f** 4169[10]

2 b f Bin Ajwaad (IRE) - Essex Girl **(60df)** (Dominion) 8.5f **(63)**

Form - 800

Record 2000 - 1st:0 2nd:0 3rd:0 Ran:3

2000 Turf 0-3: (5f, 7f 2) (g-s, gd, frm)

Currently moderate filly. Turf high 40.

**T D Easterby [0-3] B E W Higgins.*

EASY TO LOVE (USA) RR 75f 5314[7]

4 b f Diesis 9f **(80)** - La Sky (IRE) (Law Society (USA)) 9.9f **(70)**

Form - 38417

Record 2000 - 1st:1 2nd:0 3rd:1 Ran:5
Pre2000 - 1st:0 2nd:0 3rd:0 Ran:1

Win Prizemoney £3,094 *Total Prizemoney* £4,473

Wins * **2000** Oct Yarmou (HVY) 11.5f 70+ <

2000 Turf 1-5: (10f 4, 11f 1-1) (sft, g-s 1-2, gd 2)

Light-framed, above-average filly, effective 10 to 11f, best at 10f, acts on g-s to g-f. Turf high 75 - also 1st of 13 giving 6lb to Youhadyourwarning (22 Oct Yarmouth RF 5142).

**H R A Cecil [1-6] Lordship Stud.*

EATON PLACE (IRE) BHB 79f **RR 78+f** 5314[11]

3 b f Zafonic (USA) 9f **(83)** - One Way Street (Habitat) 9.4f **(70)**

Form - 10

Record 2000 - 1st:1 2nd:0 3rd:0 Ran:2

Win Prizemoney £3,445 *Total Prizemoney* £3,445

Wins * **2000** Oct Nottin (SFT) 10f 78 <

2000 Turf 1-2: (10f 1-2) (sft 1-2)

Light-framed, currently above-average filly. Turf high 78 (1st run) (began Oct) - 1st of 8 getting 5lb from Brady Boys (18 Oct Nottingham RF 5062). **H R A Cecil [1-2] H R H Prince Fahd Salman.*

EAU ROUGE BHB 70f **RR 59f** 2324[2]

2 ch f Grand Lodge (USA) - Tarsa (Ballad Rock) 7.8f **(63)**
Form - 722
Record 2000 - 1st:0 2nd:2 3rd:0 Ran:3
Win Prizemoney £0 *Total Prizemoney* £2,040
2000 Turf 0-3: (5f, 6f 2) (gd, g-f, frm)
Currently fair filly. Turf high 59 - 2nd of 10 getting 5lb from Mon Secret (28 Jun Carlisle 6f frm RF 2324).
**M A Jarvis [0-3] Miss D F Fleming.*

EBBA BHB 84f **RR 88f** 3045[5]

3 ch f Elmaamul (USA) 8.1f **(70)** - Strawberry Song (Final Straw) 7.9f **(64)**
Form - 74035
Record 2000 - 1st:0 2nd:0 3rd:1 Ran:5
Pre2000 - 1st:3 2nd:0 3rd:0 Ran:7
Win Prizemoney £12,255 *Total Prizemoney* £15,014
Wins * 1999 Jly Yarmou (FRM) 5.2f 83 <
* 1999 Jun Yarmou (GD) 6f 82+
* 1999 May Catter (G-F) 5f 69
2000 Turf 0-5: (5f, 7f, 8f 3) (gd 3, g-f, frm)
Useful filly, effective 5 to 7f, acts on gd to frm. Turf high 88.
**M L W Bell [3-12] Mrs Anne Yearley.*

E B PEARL BHB 35f38a **RR 34f 38a** 3931[6]

4 ch f Timeless Times (USA) 6.1f **(56)** - Petite Elite (Anfield) 8.5f **(59)**
Form - 76510605500426
Record 2000 - 1st:1 2nd:1 3rd:0 Ran:14
Pre2000 - 1st:2 2nd:1 3rd:2 Ran:29
Win Prizemoney £7,052 *Total Prizemoney* £9,476
Wins 2000 *Mar Wolver (STD) H 5f 38 37*
1999 Jly Redcar (FRM) SH 5f 41 44
1999 *Apr Southw (STD) C 5f 51* <
2000 Turf 0-7: (5f 5, 6f 2) (gd 2, g-f 3, frm, hrd) 2000 AW 1-7: (5f 1-4, 6f 2, 7f) (Fibr 1-7)
Unfurnished, very moderate filly, effective 5 to 7f, best at 5f, acts on hrd - acts on Fibr, has worn blinkers. Turf high 34. AW high 37. Regained winning ways when dropped to the minimum trip at Wolverhampton.
**A Dickman [0-3] Mike Smallman (from N Bycroft [3-40] Jun 2000).*

EBULLIENCE BHB 76f **RR 73f** 3951[3]

2 b f Makbul - Steadfast Elite (IRE) **(46f)** (Glenstal (USA)) 10.1f **(64)**
Form - 01203
Record 2000 - 1st:1 2nd:1 3rd:1 Ran:5
Win Prizemoney £2,600 *Total Prizemoney* £4,159
Wins * **2000** Jun Salisb (G-F) 6f 61 <
2000 Turf 1-5: (5f, 6f 1-4) (g-f 1-4, hrd)
Above-average filly. Turf high 73 - 2nd of 10 getting 9lb from Norcroft Lady (12 Jly Lingfield 6f g-f RF 2740).
**R Charlton [1-5] Beckhampton Partnership.*

ECCENTRICITY **RR 38f** 3919[11]

2 b f Emarati (USA) 6.6f **(63)** - Lady Electric (Electric) 10.1f **(61)**
Form - 00
Record 2000 - 1st:0 2nd:0 3rd:0 Ran:2
2000 Turf 0-2: (5f, 7f) (gd, frm)
Currently very moderate filly. Turf high 38 (began Aug).
**R J Hodges [0-2] A J Coombes.*

ECCLESIASTICAL **RR 84f** 5293[2]

2 b c Bishop of Cashel - Rachael Tennessee (USA) (Matsadoon (USA))
Form - 02
Record 2000 - 1st:0 2nd:1 3rd:0 Ran:2
Win Prizemoney £0 *Total Prizemoney* £715
2000 Turf 0-2: (7f 2) (g-s, gd)
Currently decent colt. Turf high 84 (began Jly) - 2nd of 8 to Albuhera (1 Nov Musselburgh 7f g-s RF 5293).
**J R Fanshawe [0-2] Cheveley Park Stud.*

ECKSCLUSIVE STORY (IRE) BHB 52f **RR 55f** 4048[11]

2 ch f Definite Article - Mint Addition (Tate Gallery (USA)) 7.4f **(67)**
Form - 0447640
Record 2000 - 1st:0 2nd:0 3rd:0 Ran:7
Win Prizemoney £0 *Total Prizemoney* £241
2000 Turf 0-7: (5f 2, 6f 3, 7f 2) (gd, g-f 2, frm 4)
Fair filly, effective 7f, acts on g-f to frm, has worn blinkers. Turf high 55 - 4th of 14 to Petit Tor (18 Aug Catterick 7f g-f RF 3739).
**J J Quinn [0-7] Mark Rabone.*

ECLECTIC BHB 37f **RR 56f** 650[13]

4 b f Emarati (USA) 6.6f **(63)** - Great Aim (Great Nephew) 9.9f **(64)**
Form - 0
Record 2000 - 1st:0 2nd:0 3rd:0 Ran:1
Pre2000 - 1st:0 2nd:0 3rd:0 Ran:4
2000 Turf 0-1: (10f) (g-s)
Workmanlike, fair filly. **S Dow [0-5] Harold Nass.*

ECOLOGY (IRE) BHB 98f **RR 91f** 4301[7]

2 b c Sri Pekan (USA) - Ecco Mi (IRE) (Priolo (USA))
Form - 211187
Record 2000 - 1st:3 2nd:1 3rd:0 Ran:6
Win Prizemoney £14,569 *Total Prizemoney* £15,977
Wins * **2000** Jly Doncas (GD) 7f 91 <
* **2000** Jun Kempto (G-F) 6f 81
* **2000** Jun Ripon (G-S) 6f 80
2000 Turf 3-6: (6f 2-3, 7f 1-2, 8f) (gd 2, g-f 1-2, frm 2-2)
Useful colt, effective 6 to 7f, acts on frm. Turf high 91 - 1st of 5 giving 3lb to Imperial Dancer (12 Jly Doncaster RF 2727). Found out by a useful juvenile on his debut, he progressed well afterwards by completing a hat trick at Ripon, Kempton and Doncaster, but was unable to handle a step up in class in Pattern events at Goodwood. Will probably need to go abroad if he is to score at that level. **J L Dunlop [3-6] Hesmonds Stud.*

ECSTASY BHB 75f **RR 80f** 5101[7]

3 b f Pursuit of Love 9.5f **(69)** - Gong (Bustino) 10.4f **(64)**
Form - 01387
Record 2000 - 1st:1 2nd:0 3rd:1 Ran:5
Pre2000 - 1st:1 2nd:1 3rd:1 Ran:7
Win Prizemoney £6,916 *Total Prizemoney* £12,017
Wins * **2000** May Bath (G-F) 10.2f 79 <
1999 Jly Warwic (G-F) 6.8f 78+
2000 Turf 1-5: (9f, 10f 1-4) (gd 3, g-f, frm 1-1)
Light-framed, decent filly, effective 6 to 10f, acts on gd to frm, best on g-f. Turf high 80 - 3rd of 6 getting 12lb from Common Place (17 Jun Sandown 9f g-f RF 2056) - also 1st of 6 getting 3lb from Mingling (22 May Bath RF 1361).
**R M Beckett [1-5] A D G Oldrey (from P T Walwyn [1-7] Oct 1999).*

ECSTATIC BHB 88f **RR 82f** 5217[1]

2 ch f Nashwan (USA) 10.3f **(79)** - Divine Quest **(84f)** (Kris) 9.5f **(73)**
Form - 24331
Record 2000 - 1st:1 2nd:1 3rd:2 Ran:5
Win Prizemoney £3,693 *Total Prizemoney* £6,916
Wins * **2000** Oct Bright (SFT) 6f 64+ <
2000 Turf 1-5: (5f, 6f 1-3, 7f) (sft 1-1, g-s, gd, g-f 2)
Decent filly. Turf high 82.
**R Hannon [1-5] Exors of the late Lord Howard de Walden.*

ECTON PARK (USA) RR 580a[5]

4 ch c Forty Niner (USA) 8.8f **(73)** - Daring Danzig (USA) (Danzig (USA)) 8.4f **(76)**
Form - 35
2000 AW 0-2: (9f, 10f) (Dirt 2)
Currently Group-class colt, has worn blinkers. AW high 113.
**W E Walden in USA [0-3].*

ECUDAMAH (IRE) BHB 50f62a **RR 52f 62a** 4825[7]

4 ch g Mukaddamah (USA) 7.6f **(74)** - Great Land (USA) (Friend's Choice (USA)) 8.6f **(57)**
Form - 124600064033700047
Record 2000 - 1st:0 2nd:0 3rd:2 Ran:14
Pre2000 - 1st:1 2nd:4 3rd:2 Ran:21
Win Prizemoney £2,762 *Total Prizemoney* £9,288
Wins * 1999 *Nov Wolver (STD) H 5f 60 64* <
2000 Turf 0-12: (5f 7, 6f 4, 7f) (g-s 2, gd, g-f 5, frm 4) 2000 AW 0-2: (5f, 6f) (Equi, Fibr)
Strong, fair gelding, effective 5f, acts on gd - acts on AW, has worn blinkers, likes left handed tracks, likes tight tracks. Turf high

57. AW high 37.
**Miss Jacqueline Doyle [1-20] Sanford Racing (from K Bell [0-5] Aug 1999).*

EDDIE ROYALE (IRE) BHB 57f62a **RR 45f 62a** 2439[7]
2 b g Elbio 9f **(62)** - Persian Royale (Persian Bold) 9.3f **(66)**
Form - 057
Record 2000 - 1st:0 2nd:0 3rd:0 Ran:3
2000 Turf 0-2: (5f, 6f) (gd, frm) 2000 AW 0-1: (5f) (Fibr)
Currently fair gelding. Turf high 45. **D Nicholls [0-3] Mike Browne.*

EDDYS LAD RR 73f 3447[3]
2 b c Lahib (USA) 8f **(69)** - Glamour Model (Last Tycoon) 8.5f **(62)**
Form - 23
Record 2000 - 1st:0 2nd:1 3rd:1 Ran:2
Win Prizemoney £0 *Total Prizemoney* £1,378
2000 Turf 0-2: (7f 2) (g-f, frm)
Currently above-average colt. Turf high 73 (began Jly).
**R M H Cowell [0-2] C Akers.*

EDE'IFF BHB 46f51a **RR 46df 51a** 3709[2]
3 b f Tragic Role (USA) 9.4f **(63)** - Flying Amy (Norwick (USA)) 7.2f **(56)**
Form - 6850552
Record 2000 - 1st:0 2nd:1 3rd:0 Ran:7
Pre2000 - 1st:1 2nd:0 3rd:0 Ran:3
Win Prizemoney £2,326 *Total Prizemoney* £2,950
Wins * 1999 Nov Windso (G-S) S 8.3f 64 <
2000 Turf 0-6: (7f, 8f 3, 10f 2) (g-f 5, frm) 2000 AW 0-1: (7f) (Equi)
Neat, moderate filly, effective 8f, acts on gd, likes tight tracks. Turf high 46. **W G M Turner [1-11] Ede's (UK) Ltd.*

EDHKERINI RR 72f 1468[3]
3 ch f Lammtarra (USA) - Walesiana (GER) (Star Appeal) 9.6f **(65)**
Form - 3
Record 2000 - 1st:0 2nd:0 3rd:1 Ran:1
Win Prizemoney £0 *Total Prizemoney* £586
2000 Turf 0-1: (12f) (g-s)
Tall, currently above-average filly. (1st run) - 3rd of 4 to Riyafa (26 May Haydock 12f g-s RF 1468).
**M A Jarvis [0-1] Sheikh Ahmed Al Maktoum.*

EDIFICE (JPN) BHB 51f46a **RR 57f 46a** 5025[11]
4 ch c Carroll House - Moon Tosho (JPN) (Steel Heart) 8.3f **(58)**
Form - 560000
Record 2000 - 1st:0 2nd:0 3rd:0 Ran:6
Pre2000 - 1st:0 2nd:0 3rd:0 Ran:7
Win Prizemoney £0 *Total Prizemoney* £310
2000 Turf 0-5: (10f 4, 11f) (g-s, gd, g-f 2, frm) 2000 AW 0-1: (8f) (Fibr)
Workmanlike, fair colt, effective 8 to 10f, best at 10f, acts on g-f to frm, best on g-f, has worn blinkers, likes right handed tracks, prefers tight tracks. Turf high 68 (1st run) - 5th of 10 giving 16lb to Swinging The Blues (26 Jun Yarmouth 10f g-f RF 2293). Becoming disappointing. **A C Stewart [0-13] Teiji Takasaki.*

EDIPO RE BHB 37f **RR 32f** 1513[10]
8 b g Slip Anchor 12.7f **(75)** - Lady Barrister (Law Society (USA)) 9.9f **(70)**
Form - 00
Record 2000 - 1st:0 2nd:0 3rd:0 Ran:2
Pre2000 - 1st:2 2nd:1 3rd:0 Ran:7
Win Prizemoney £22,701 *Total Prizemoney* £25,178
2000 Turf 0-2: (14f, 15f) (hvy, gd)
Very moderate gelding. Turf high 32. Becoming disappointing.
**Ian Williams [1-7] Tony Eaves (from P J Hobbs [0-6] Oct 1998).*

EDMO HEIGHTS BHB 38f **RR 42f** 3070[10]
4 ch g Keen 11.1f **(58)** - Bodham (Bustino) 10.4f **(64)**
Form - 00800
Record 2000 - 1st:0 2nd:0 3rd:0 Ran:5
Pre2000 - 1st:3 2nd:2 3rd:0 Ran:18
Win Prizemoney £7,964 *Total Prizemoney* £9,455
Wins * 1999 Jly Beverl (G-F) 9.9f 69
* 1999 Jun Redcar (FRM) H 9f 62 63
* 1998 Spt Beverl (G-F) 7.5f 73 <
2000 Turf 0-5: (8f, 10f 3, 12f) (g-f 2, frm, hrd 2)
Scopey, moderate gelding, effective 9 to 10f, acts on g-f to frm, has worn blinkers, favours tight tracks. Turf high 42.
**T D Easterby [3-23] Edmolift UK Ltd.*

EFFERVESCE (IRE) BHB 75f **RR 75f** 4697[10]
2 b f Sri Pekan (USA) - Arctic Winter (CAN) (Briartic (CAN)) 9.5f **(84)**
Form - 4681200
Record 2000 - 1st:1 2nd:1 3rd:0 Ran:7
Win Prizemoney £3,108 *Total Prizemoney* £4,670
Wins * 2000 Aug Haydoc (G-S) H 5f 67 73 <
2000 Turf 1-7: (5f 1-5, 6f 2) (g-s, gd 1-4, g-f, frm)
Above-average filly, effective 5f, acts on gd. Turf high 75 - 2nd of 12 giving 8lb to Time Maite (19 Aug Haydock 5f gd RF 3775) - also 1st of 9 from Love Tune (10 Aug Haydock RF 3531).
**M A Buckley [1-7] C C Buckley.*

EFFERVESCENT RR 78f 4483[22]
3 b f Efisio 7.7f **(69)** - Sharp Chief (Chief Singer) 8.9f **(66)**
Form - 82341300
Record 2000 - 1st:1 2nd:1 3rd:2 Ran:8
Win Prizemoney £2,730 *Total Prizemoney* £5,322
Wins * 2000 Jly Catter (G-F) 6f 49 <
2000 Turf 1-8: (6f 1-5, 7f 3) (g-s 2, g-f 2, frm 1-4)
Scopey, above-average filly. Turf high 78.
**I A Balding [1-8] J C Smith.*

EFIDIUM BHB 63f63a **RR 64f 63a** 5008[10]
2 b c Presidium 7.5f **(56)** - Efipetite **(11f 20a)** (Efisio)
Form - 5770
Record 2000 - 1st:0 2nd:0 3rd:0 Ran:4
2000 Turf 0-3: (5f 2, 6f) (g-s, frm 2) 2000 AW 0-1: (6f) (Fibr)
Average colt. Turf high 64 (began Aug).
**N Bycroft [0-4] Hambleton Racing Partnership.*

EGYPT BHB 52f **RR 42f** 5217[9]
2 b c Green Desert (USA) 7.8f **(78)** - Just You Wait (Nonoalco (USA)) 8.5f **(66)**
Form - 070
Record 2000 - 1st:0 2nd:0 3rd:0 Ran:3
2000 Turf 0-3: (6f 3) (sft 2, gd)
Currently moderate colt. Turf high 42 (began Spt).
**Sir Mark Prescott [0-3] H R H Prince Fahd Salman.*

EGYPTBAND (USA) RR 124f 4846a[2]
3 b f Dixieland Band (USA) 10.1f **(80)** - Egyptown (FR) (Top Ville) 11.7f **(68)**
Form - 132
2000 Turf 1-3: (11f 1-1, 12f 2) (gd 1-3)
Strong, currently very high-class filly. Turf high 124 - 2nd of 10 getting 3lb from Sinndar (1 Oct Longchamp 12f gd RF 4846a) - also 1st of 14 from Volvoreta (11 Jun Chantilly RF 2005a). A top-class French filly, she beat Volvoreta comfortably in the French Oaks, but was only third behind that filly over the extra quarter-mile of the Prix Vermeille. Left that form behind when finding only Sinndar too good in the Arc, and there should be a big race in her if she trains on satisfactorily at four.
**Mme C Head in FR [1-3] Wertheimer Brothers.*

EI EI BHB 37f29a **RR 46f 29a** 2946[10]
5 b g North Briton 8.2f **(53)** - Branitska (Mummy's Pet) 7.7f **(60)**
Form - 072466240580
Record 2000 - 1st:0 2nd:2 3rd:0 Ran:11
Pre2000 - 1st:1 2nd:0 3rd:2 Ran:17
Win Prizemoney £1,720 *Total Prizemoney* £3,927
Wins 1998 Apr Folkes (SFT) 7f 86 <
2000 Turf 0-5: (10f 4, 12f) (gd, g-f 2, frm 2) 2000 AW 0-6: (8f 2, 9f, 10f, 11f, 12f) (Equi 2, Fibr 4)
Moderate gelding, has worn blinkers. Turf high 46. AW high 30.
**G L Moore [0-17] John Hetherington (from B W Hills [1-10] Oct 1998).*

EIGHT (IRE) BHB 54f49a **RR 64f 49a** 4997[11]
4 ch g Thatching 7.8f **(69)** - Up To You (Sallust) 8.4f **(63)**
Form - 035403000
Record 2000 - 1st:0 2nd:0 3rd:2 Ran:9
Pre2000 - 1st:0 2nd:0 3rd:2 Ran:6
Win Prizemoney £0 *Total Prizemoney* £2,567
2000 Turf 0-8: (8f 2, 9f, 10f 5) (g-s, gd, g-f 4, frm 2) 2000 AW 0-1: (8f) (Fibr)
Average gelding, effective 8 to 9f, best at 8f, acts on gd to frm, has

worn blinkers, likes left handed tracks, prefers tight tracks. Turf high 64 - 3rd of 19 getting 1lb from Barbason (9 Jun Goodwood 9f gd RF 1842).
**C G Cox [0-11] Mrs Anthony Andrews (from M J Heaton-Ellis [0-4] Jly 1999).*

EIGHTY TWO (USA) BHB 81f **RR 58f** 5111[14]
4 br c Theatrical 11.5f **(78)** - Heaven Knows Why (USA) (Star de Naskra (USA)) 9.7f **(65)**
Form - 00
Record 2000 - 1st:0 2nd:0 3rd:0 Ran:2
2000 Turf 0-2: (12f, 16f) (gd, g-f)
Currently decent colt. Turf high 58 (began Spt).
**S P C Woods [0-2] P K L Chu.*

EILEAN SHONA BHB 96f **RR 103f** 5226[11]
4 b f Suave Dancer (USA) 10.7f **(68)** - Moidart **(88f)** (Electric) 10.1f **(61)**
Form - 054570
Record 2000 - 1st:0 2nd:0 3rd:0 Ran:6
Pre2000 - 1st:3 2nd:1 3rd:1 Ran:8
Win Prizemoney £23,574 *Total Prizemoney* £31,224
Wins * 1999 Oct Newmar (G-S) LH 16.1f 87 91 <
* 1999 Spt Redcar (G-F) H 14.1f 84 85
* 1998 Spt Redcar (G-F) 9f 75
2000 Turf 0-6: (16f 3, 18f, 19f, 22f) (g-s, gd 3, g-f, frm)
Scopey, very useful filly, effective 16f, acts on gd. Turf high 103. A useful stayer, she ran her best races of the season in the Henry II Stakes at Ascot and a Shergar Cup race at Ascot.
**J R Fanshawe [3-14] Dr Catherine Wills.*

EJDER (IRE) BHB 40f **RR 39f** 4654[13]
4 b f Indian Ridge 7.6f **(74)** - Eskaroon (Artaius (USA)) 9f **(69)**
Form - 00000
Record 2000 - 1st:0 2nd:0 3rd:0 Ran:4
Pre2000 - 1st:0 2nd:0 3rd:0 Ran:1
2000 Turf 0-3: (6f 2, 8f) (g-f 2, frm) 2000 AW 0-1: (6f) (Fibr)
Very moderate filly. Turf high 39.
**E A Wheeler [0-4] S Shefket (from E Sheehy in IRE [0-1] Nov 1999).*

EJTITHAAB (IRE) BHB 75f **RR 89f** 4063[9]
3 ch c Arazi (USA) 9.2f **(74)** - Cunning (Bustino) 10.4f **(64)**
Form - 440030
Record 2000 - 1st:0 2nd:0 3rd:1 Ran:6
Pre2000 - 1st:0 2nd:0 3rd:0 Ran:1
Win Prizemoney £0 *Total Prizemoney* £1,417
2000 Turf 0-6: (8f 2, 10f 3, 12f) (gd 4, g-f, frm)
Tall, useful colt, effective 8 to 12f, acts on gd, has worn blinkers. Turf high 89 - 4th of 6 getting 3lb from Wellbeing (6 May Newmarket 12f gd RF 1057).
**R W Armstrong [0-6] Hamdan Al Maktoum (from P T Walwyn [0-1] Oct 1999).*

EKRAAR (USA) BHB 118f **RR 122+f** 4315[1]
3 b c Red Ransom (USA) 8.6f **(83)** - Sacahuista (USA) (Raja Baba (USA)) 10f **(64)**
Form - 34111
Record 2000 - 1st:3 2nd:0 3rd:1 Ran:5
Pre2000 - 1st:1 2nd:1 3rd:1 Ran:4
Win Prizemoney £80,035 *Total Prizemoney* £109,976
Wins * **2000** Spt Goodwo (GD) G3 9.9f 122 <
* **2000** Aug Haydoc (GD) G3 10.5f 114
* **2000** Jly Newbur (G-F) 10f 113
* 1999 Jly Goodwo (G-F) G3 7f 113+
2000 Turf 3-5: (8f 2, 10f 2-2, 11f 1-1) (gd 2-4, g-f 1-1)
Well made, very high-class colt, effective 7 to 11f, best at 10f, acts on gd to frm, best on gd, has worn blinkers. Turf high 122 - 1st of 5 getting 4lb from National Anthem (9 Spt Goodwood RF 4315) - also 1st of 9 from Forbearing (12 Aug Haydock RF 3583). Consistent. A decent two-year-old, he was not disgraced in the Craven and French Guineas on his first two starts of last season, considering his stable was in the doldrums. He looked back to something like his best when making all to land a Newbury conditions event in July on his first attempt at ten furlongs and followed up in Group Three events at Haydock and Goodwood.
**M P Tregoning [4-9] Hamdan Al Maktoum.*

ELAANDO BHB 58f **RR 52f** 3804[7]
5 b g Darshaan 11.9f **(81)** - Evocatrice (Persepolis (FR)) 6.4f **(67)**
Form - 87
Record 2000 - 1st:0 2nd:0 3rd:0 Ran:2
Pre2000 - 1st:0 2nd:0 3rd:0 Ran:1
2000 Turf 0-2: (12f, 14f) (g-f 2)
Fair gelding. Turf high 52 (began Aug).
**Mrs Merrita Jones [4-17] F J Sainsbury.*

ELA-ARISTOKRATI (IRE) BHB 91f **RR 73f** 3004[4]
8 b h Danehill (USA) 9.1f **(79)** - Dubai Lady (Kris) 9.5f **(73)**
Form - 64
Record 2000 - 1st:0 2nd:0 3rd:0 Ran:2
Pre2000 - 1st:3 2nd:5 3rd:3 Ran:20
Win Prizemoney £47,929 *Total Prizemoney* £110,657
Wins 1996 Jun Epsom (GD) H 10.1f 109 112 <
2000 Turf 0-2: (10f, 12f) (gd, g-f)
Above-average horse. Turf high 73 (began Jly). Consistent. A one-time useful performer on the level, he has appeared infrequently in recent years.
**M A Jarvis [0-2] Andreas Michael (from M H Tompkins [0-5] Aug 1997).*

ELA ATHENA BHB 113f **RR 119f** 4948a[3]
4 gr f Ezzoud (IRE) - Crodelle (IRE) (Formidable (USA)) 9.2f **(63)**
Form - 0412523
Record 2000 - 1st:1 2nd:2 3rd:1 Ran:7
Pre2000 - 1st:2 2nd:2 3rd:0 Ran:4
Win Prizemoney £41,445 *Total Prizemoney* £238,972
Wins * **2000** Jly Haydoc (G-F) G3 11.9f 109+ <
* 1999 Jly Chepst (G-F) L 10.2f 107
* 1999 Apr Newbur (G-F) 10f 79
2000 Turf 1-7: (10f 2, 11f, 12f 1-4) (g-s, gd 1-1, g-f 2, frm 2)
Leggy, high-class filly, effective 10 to 12f, acts on frm, prefers left handed tracks, excels at Belmont Park. Turf high 116 - 2nd of 7 giving 9lb to Crimplene (5 Aug Goodwood 10f g-f RF 3394) - also 1st of 11 giving 13lb to Solaia (8 Jly Haydock RF 2632). Consistent. Well beaten in the Jockey Club Stakes at Newmarket on her reappearance, she ran better over an inadequate trip in the Pretty Polly at the Curragh before putting the three-year-olds firmly in their place in the Lancashire Oaks. Best over 12 furlongs these days, she stayed on well into second in the Nassau Stakes over ten. Embarked on a world tour in the autumn, showing high-class form in top international events. **M A Jarvis [3-11] Andreas Michael .*

ELABORATE (USA) RR 5328a[11]
5 ch h Gilded Time (USA) 7f **(76)** - Jeanie's Gift (USA) (Gulch (USA)) 8f **(81)**
Form - 0
2000 AW 0-1: (6f) (Dirt)
Currently very useful colt.
**J Gonzalez in USA [0-1] Trudy McCaffrey & John Toffan.*

EL ACTOR RR 76f 4965[17]
2 ch g Forzando 7.2f **(63)** - Irish Impulse (USA) (Irish River (FR)) 8.6f **(78)**
Form - 10
Record 2000 - 1st:1 2nd:0 3rd:0 Ran:2
Win Prizemoney £4,880 *Total Prizemoney* £4,880
Wins 2000 Spt Turin (GD) 6f
2000 Turf 1-2: (6f 1-2) (gd 1-2)
Currently above-average gelding. Turf high 76 (began Spt).
**M G Quinlan [0-1] Mario Lanfranchi (from M Quinlan [1-1] Spt 2000).*

ELA-DARLIN-MOU BHB 63f **RR 57f** 4432[12]
2 gr f Mtoto 11.5f **(71)** - Ancestry (Persepolis (FR)) 6.4f **(67)**
Form - 080
Record 2000 - 1st:0 2nd:0 3rd:0 Ran:3
2000 Turf 0-3: (6f, 7f 2) (frm 3)
Currently fair filly. Turf high 57.
**K T Ivory [0-3] Mrs Andry Muinos.*

ELAFLAAK (USA) BHB 101f **RR 98f** 3576[10]
3 b f Gulch (USA) 9.6f **(79)** - Catnip (USA) (Flying Paster (USA))
Form - 0
Record 2000 - 1st:0 2nd:0 3rd:0 Ran:1
Pre2000 - 1st:3 2nd:0 3rd:0 Ran:4

Win Prizemoney £20,690 *Total Prizemoney* £20,690
Wins * 1999 Aug Newbur (GD) L 5.2f 98+ <
* 1999 Jly Newbur (G-F) 6f 91+
* 1999 Jly Beverl (G-F) 5f 80+
2000 Turf 0-1: (6f) (gd)
Workmanlike, very useful filly. She impressed when winning her first three starts at two but did not train on.
**M P Tregoning [3-5] Hamdan Al Maktoum.*

ELAINE'S REBECCA BHB 50f RR 43f 1297[6]
2 ch f Missed Flight - Pretty Scarce **(23a)** (Handsome Sailor)
Form - 6206
Record 2000 - 1st:0 2nd:1 3rd:0 Ran:4
Win Prizemoney £0 *Total Prizemoney* £550
2000 Turf 0-4: (5f 4) (sft, gd, g-f, frm)
Moderate filly. Turf high 54. **W T Kemp [0-4] Realm (UK).*

ELBA MAGIC (IRE) BHB 41f54a RR 12f 54a 3266[13]
5 b m Faustus (USA) 9.1f **(54)** - Dependable (Formidable (USA)) 9.2f **(63)**
Form - 800000
Record 2000 - 1st:0 2nd:0 3rd:0 Ran:6
Pre2000 - 1st:4 2nd:4 3rd:7 Ran:33
Win Prizemoney £10,091 *Total Prizemoney* £17,530
Wins * 1999 Spt Beverl (GD) H 8.5f 58 60
* 1998 Aug Ripon (G-F) H 10f 63 66 <
* 1998 Jly Yarmou (GD) H 10.1f 60 63
* 1998 *Apr Southw (STD) H 7f 55 63*
2000 Turf 0-5: (8f 2, 9f, 10f 2) (g-s, gd 2, g-f, hrd) 2000 AW 0-1: (8f) (Fibr)
Very moderate filly, effective 8 to 10f, best at 10f, acts on g-s to frm, has worn blinkers, prefers tight tracks. Turf high 12. Inconsistent. A fair handicapper on her day, she has shown absolutely nothing so far this season.
**C A Dwyer [4-34] Graham Mitchell (from Mrs N Macauley [0-4] Jun 2000).*

EL CURIOSO (USA) BHB 85f RR 95f 4968[15]
3 b g El Gran Senor (USA) 8.9f **(85)** - Curious (USA) (Rare Performer (USA))
Form - 01683870
Record 2000 - 1st:1 2nd:0 3rd:1 Ran:8
Pre2000 - 1st:1 2nd:1 3rd:0 Ran:6
Win Prizemoney £14,422 *Total Prizemoney* £17,081
Wins * 2000 May Lingfi (G-S) 7.6f 95 <
* 1999 Spt Warwic (SFT) H 7.7f 85 87
2000 Turf 1-8: (8f 1-7, 10f) (g-s, gd 1-5, frm 2)
Workmanlike, very useful gelding, effective 8f, acts on sft to frm, has worn blinkers. Turf high 95 - 1st of 6 getting 10lb from Welsh Wind (12 May Lingfield RF 1171). Becoming disappointing. He returned to winning ways in a Lingfield classified event on his second start last season, and continued to run well without adding to his score. Goes quite well with cut, but handles faster ground.
**P W Harris [2-14] The Curious Twelve.*

EL DIVINO (GER) RR 110f 5225[9]
5 b h Platini (GER) - Eivissa (GER) (Frontal) 6.4f **(64)**
Form - 50
2000 Turf 0-2: (8f, 10f) (gd 2)
Group-class colt, effective 8 to 9f, best at 8f, acts on sft to gd, best on gd. Turf high 99 (began Jly).
**Chr Recke in GER [0-1] Stall Gaisberg (from M Hofer in GER [1-5] Jly 2000).*

ELEANOR J BHB 42f RR 7f 1723[7]
2 ch f Imp Society (USA) 7.1f **(63)** - Moniques Venture **(31f)** (Midyan (USA)) 6f **(60)**
Form - 3607
Record 2000 - 1st:0 2nd:0 3rd:1 Ran:4
Win Prizemoney £0 *Total Prizemoney* £263
2000 Turf 0-2: (6f 2) (gd 2) 2000 AW 0-2: (5f 2) (Fibr 2)
Very moderate filly, has worn blinkers. Turf high 7. AW high 37.
**K R Burke [0-4] James Ryan.*

ELEGANT DANCE BHB 52f38a RR 44f 38a 1354[13]
6 ch m Statoblest 6.4f **(63)** - Furry Dance (USA) (Nureyev (USA)) 8.7f **(78)**
Form - 80640
Record 2000 - 1st:0 2nd:0 3rd:0 Ran:3
Pre2000 - 1st:1 2nd:1 3rd:1 Ran:18
Win Prizemoney £3,096 *Total Prizemoney* £4,812
Wins * 1998 Jun Salisb (G-F) H 6f 61 62 <
2000 Turf 0-1: (6f) (frm) 2000 AW 0-2: (6f, 7f) (Equi, Fibr)
Moderate mare, effective 6f, acts on frm. AW high 4. Inconsistent.
**J J Sheehan [1-21] Mrs Christina Dowling.*

ELEGANT ESCORT (USA) BHB 60f65a RR 60f 65a 4050[12]
3 b c Take Me Out (USA) - Get With It (USA) (King Pellinore (USA)) 8.2f **(68)**
Form - 160
Record 2000 - 1st:0 2nd:0 3rd:0 Ran:2
Pre2000 - 1st:1 2nd:0 3rd:1 Ran:2
Win Prizemoney £2,794 *Total Prizemoney* £3,103
Wins * 1999 *Dec Southw (STD) 8f 74+* <
2000 Turf 0-2: (8f, 11f) (gd, frm)
Leggy, above-average colt. Turf high 60 (began Aug).
**Mrs G S Rees [1-4] Times of Wigan.*

ELEGANT LADY RR 83df 5199[20]
4 ch f Selkirk (USA) 7.9f **(76)** - Prompting (Primo Dominie) 6.2f **(80)**
Form - 0
Record 2000 - 1st:0 2nd:0 3rd:0 Ran:1
Pre2000 - 1st:1 2nd:1 3rd:1 Ran:9
Win Prizemoney £10,866 *Total Prizemoney* £13,678
Wins * 1999 May Cheste (G-F) H 6.1f 80 82 <
2000 Turf 0-1: (5f) (gd)
Lengthy, decent filly, effective 5 to 6f, acts on gd to g-f.
**J H M Gosden [1-10] Platt Promotions Ltd.*

ELEGIA PRIMA BHB 56f RR 61f 3147[6]
3 ch f Mon Tresor 7.9f **(60)** - Miss Milton (Young Christopher) 6f **(61)**
Form - 74206
Record 2000 - 1st:0 2nd:1 3rd:0 Ran:5
Pre2000 - 1st:1 2nd:0 3rd:0 Ran:4
Win Prizemoney £2,477 *Total Prizemoney* £3,956
Wins * 1999 Jun Salisb (FRM) 7f 69+ <
2000 Turf 0-5: (10f, 13f, 14f, 15f, 17f) (g-s, gd 2, frm 2)
Strong, average filly, effective 7 to 14f, acts on g-s to frm, has worn blinkers. Turf high 61 - 2nd of 6 getting 21lb from Samsaam (9 Jun Haydock 14f g-s RF 1850). Inconsistent.
**Major D N Chappell [1-9] C V Cruden.*

EL EMEL (USA) BHB 87f RR 31f 5323[18]
3 b g Green Dancer (USA) 11.9f **(77)** - Moivouloirtoi (USA) **(89f)** (Bering) 7.4f **(61)**
Form - 0
Record 2000 - 1st:0 2nd:0 3rd:0 Ran:1
2000 Turf 0-1: (12f) (sft)
Currently very moderate gelding.
**I A Balding [0-1] Rodger Sargent.*

EL EMPERADOR BHB 72f RR 72f 4812[3]
3 b g Emperor Jones (USA) - Car Stop (USA) (Stop The Music (USA)) 9.2f **(71)**
Form - 5453
Record 2000 - 1st:0 2nd:0 3rd:1 Ran:4
Pre2000 - 1st:0 2nd:0 3rd:0 Ran:1
Win Prizemoney £0 *Total Prizemoney* £715
2000 Turf 0-4: (7f, 8f 2, 10f) (g-s, g-f, frm, hrd)
Light-framed, above-average gelding. Turf high 72 - 3rd of 18 to Glory Quest (4 Oct Lingfield 8f g-s RF 4812).
**J R Fanshawe [0-5] H R H Prince Fahd Salman.*

ELENII BHB 25f RR 24f 247[8]
4 b f Risk Me (FR) 8f **(53)** - Sunday Sport's Pet (Mummy's Pet) 7.7f **(60)**
Form - 08
Record 2000 - 1st:0 2nd:0 3rd:0 Ran:1
Pre2000 - 1st:0 2nd:0 3rd:0 Ran:4
2000 AW 0-1: (13f) (Equi)
Light-framed, little account filly, has worn blinkers.
**T T Clement [0-3] Mrs M Liston (from Miss Gay Kelleway [0-3] Apr 1999).*

EL FLAMENCO RR 1295a[6]

3 f
Form - 6
Record 2000 - 1st:0 2nd:0 3rd:0 Ran:1
2000 Turf 0-1: (8f) (hvy)
Currently very poor filly - 6th of 8 getting 4lb from Fonic Joy (14 May San Siro 8f hvy RF 1295a). **M Quinlan [0-1].*

ELGHANI BHB 94f RR 96f 5240[10]

3 br c Lahib (USA) 8f **(69)** - Fawaakeh (USA) **(75f)** (Lyphard (USA)) 9.9f **(72)**
Form - 01210
Record 2000 - 1st:2 2nd:1 3rd:0 Ran:5
Win Prizemoney £12,070 *Total Prizemoney* £15,060
Wins * 2000 Oct Newmar (SFT) H 8f 90 96 <
*** 2000** May Windso (O C) 8.3f 80
2000 Turf 2-5: (7f, 8f 2-4) (g-s, gd 2-4)
Very useful colt. Turf high 96 - 1st of 21 giving 17lb to Melodian (13 Oct Newmarket RF 4968) - also 1st of 16 from Blue Mountain (2 May Windsor RF 0977). Unraced at two, he improved from his debut to win a Windsor maiden over a mile in good style next time. Came back from nearly five months off with an injured splint bone to cause an upset in a Newmarket handicap, but was unable to follow up in a hot handicap over the same course and distance next time. Open to improvement.
**R W Armstrong [2-5] Hamdan Al Maktoum.*

EL GIZA (USA) RR 49f 4935[25]

2 ch c Cozzene (USA) 10.1f **(87)** - Gazayil (USA) (Irish River (FR)) 8.6f **(78)**
Form - 0
Record 2000 - 1st:0 2nd:0 3rd:0 Ran:1
2000 Turf 0-1: (6f) (gd)
Currently moderate colt. **D R C Elsworth [0-1] Raymond Tooth.*

EL GRAN LODE (ARG) RR 94f 5213a[3]

5 ch h Lode (USA) - La Pastoral (ARG) (Cinco Grande (USA))
Form - 118323
2000 Turf 2-6: (5f, 6f 2-3, 7f 2) (hvy, sft, gd 2)
Useful colt, effective 6 to 7f, acts on sft to gd. Turf high 94. A useful Scandinavian trained Group class sprinter, who will continue to be a threat to foreign invaders next season.
**Diego Lowther in SWE [2-6] Lowther Racing.*

EL GRAN PAPA (USA) BHB 103f RR 106f 5210a[3]

3 b c El Gran Senor (USA) 8.9f **(85)** - Banner Hit (USA) (Oh Say (USA))
Form - 211020133
Record 2000 - 1st:3 2nd:2 3rd:2 Ran:9
Pre2000 - 1st:0 2nd:0 3rd:1 Ran:2
Win Prizemoney £46,566 *Total Prizemoney* £102,448
Wins * 2000 Spt Doncas (G-F) 8f 103+ <
*** 2000** Jun Ascot (G-F) H 8f 85 99
*** 2000** Jun Newbur (G-F) 8f 86
2000 Turf 3-9: (6f, 7f 2, 8f 3-5, 9f) (gd 1-3, g-f 1-3, frm 1-3)
Well made, Pattern-class colt, effective 7 to 9f, acts on gd to frm, excels at Ascot. Turf high 106 - 2nd of 24 getting 14lb from Tillerman (29 Jly Ascot 7f gd RF 3202) - also 1st of 7 giving 3lb to Soviet Flash (8 Spt Doncaster RF 4298). He justified favouritism in the hugely competitive Britannia Handicap at Ascot and ran well in most subsequent starts. Tough, with a touch of class, he is now trained in America by Bobby Frankel. **J H M Gosden [3-11].*

ELGRIA (IRE) RR 69f 1429[3]

2 b br c Distinctly North (USA) 7.4f **(63)** - Perfect Swinger (Shernazar) 10.2f **(73)**
Form - 3
Record 2000 - 1st:0 2nd:0 3rd:1 Ran:1
Win Prizemoney £0 *Total Prizemoney* £681
2000 Turf 0-1: (6f) (gd)
Currently average colt. **R Hannon [0-1] Mrs Betty Valentine.*

EL HAMRA (IRE) BHB 70f78a RR 69f 78a 4784[1]

2 gr c Royal Abjar (USA) - Cherlinoa (FR) (Crystal Palace (FR)) 12.5f **(76)**
Form - 503335231
Record 2000 - 1st:1 2nd:1 3rd:4 Ran:9
Win Prizemoney £1,694 *Total Prizemoney* £4,238
Wins * 2000 *Oct Wolver (STD) 8.5f 71+* <
2000 Turf 0-4: (6f, 7f 3) (gd, g-f 2, frm) 2000 AW 1-5: (5f, 6f, 7f, 8f 1-2) (Fibr 1-5)
Above-average colt, effective 7 to 8f, best at 8f, acts on g-f - acts on Fibr, likes left handed tracks, prefers tight tracks. Turf high 68 - 3rd of 10 giving 3lb to Sister Celestine (13 Spt Beverley 7f g-f RF 4362). AW high 71 - 1st of 9 getting 3lb from Hawkes Run (3 Oct Wolverhampton RF 4784). **B A McMahon [1-9] R Thornhill.*

ELITE HOPE (USA) BHB 57f60a RR 47f 60a 157[8]

8 ch m Moment of Hope (USA) 6.9f **(80)** - Chervil (USA) (Greenough (USA)) 6.9f **(85)**
Form - 2418
Record 2000 - 1st:1 2nd:0 3rd:0 Ran:2
Pre2000 - 1st:10 2nd:10 3rd:6 Ran:58
Win Prizemoney £27,002 *Total Prizemoney* £38,310
Wins * 2000 *Jan Wolver (STD) S 7f 56*
* 1999 *Feb Southw (STD) C 7f 66*
* 1999 *Feb Southw (STD) H 7f 62 67*
* 1998 *Apr Wolver (STD) C 7f 66*
* 1998 *Mar Wolver (STD) C 7f 67*
* 1998 *Jan Wolver (STD) C 7f 77*
* 1997 *Nov Wolver (STD) C 6f 60*
* 1997 *Jan Wolver (SLW) H 7f 67 71*
* 1996 *Dec Wolver (STD) H 7f 64 66*
* 1996 *Nov Wolver (STD) H 7f 52 60*
2000 AW 1-2: (7f 1-2) (Fibr 1-2)
Fair mare, effective 6 to 7f, best at 7f, - acts on Fibr, has worn blinkers, and excels at Wolverhampton. AW high 56 (1st run). Consistent. She is an effective sort on sand when able to dominate. Seven furlongs is her best trip, especially at Wolverhampton, though she has won over that trip at Southwell as well.
**N Tinkler [10-44] Elite Racing Club (from C R Egerton [1-16] Spt 1996).*

ELJOHAR (IRE) RR 80f 2831[3]

3 ch c Nashwan (USA) 10.3f **(79)** - Mehthaaf (USA) **(122f)** (Nureyev (USA)) 8.7f **(78)**
Form - 3
Record 2000 - 1st:0 2nd:0 3rd:1 Ran:1
Win Prizemoney £0 *Total Prizemoney* £828
2000 Turf 0-1: (8f) (gd)
Scopey, currently decent colt. (1st run) - 3rd of 7 giving 5lb to May Ball (15 Jly Ascot 8f gd RF 2831). **S bin Suroor [0-1] Godolphin.*

EL KARIM (USA) BHB 48f RR ?f 3611[5]

4 ch c Storm Cat (USA) 7f **(86)** - Gmaasha (IRE) (Kris) 9.5f **(73)**
Form - 05
Record 2000 - 1st:0 2nd:0 3rd:0 Ran:2
Pre2000 - 1st:0 2nd:0 3rd:1 Ran:4
Win Prizemoney £0 *Total Prizemoney* £807
2000 Turf 0-2: (8f, 12f) (gd, g-f)
Workmanlike, very poor colt. (began Aug).
**R Ford [0-2] R Burgess (from J L Dunlop [0-4] Jun 1999).*

ELLA'S PAL RR 4760[1]

2 ch f Alhijaz 7.7f **(57)** - Rattle Along (Tap On Wood) 10.3f **(65)**
Form - 1
Record 2000 - 1st:1 2nd:0 3rd:0 Ran:1
Win Prizemoney £2,404 *Total Prizemoney* £2,404
Wins * 2000 *Spt Wolver (STD) 6f 76* <
2000 AW 1-1: (6f 1-1) (Fibr 1-1)
Currently above-average filly. (1st run) - 1st of 13 getting 5lb from Lilleman (30 Spt Wolverhampton RF 4760).
**W Jarvis [1-1] Miss E G Macgregor.*

ELLA-TINO BHB 71f RR 69f 5053[4]

2 b f Reprimand 8.2f **(63)** - Tino-Ella (Bustino) 10.4f **(64)**
Form - 654
Record 2000 - 1st:0 2nd:0 3rd:0 Ran:3
Win Prizemoney £0 *Total Prizemoney* £255
2000 Turf 0-3: (7f 2, 8f) (sft, gd 2)
Currently average filly. Turf high 69 (began Spt).
**J A Glover [0-3] B H Farr.*

ELLE DANZIG (GER) RR 118+f 4572a[1]

5 b m Roi Danzig (USA) 10.5f **(62)** - Elegie (GER) (Teotepec (GER))

Form - 172411
2000 Turf 2-5: (9f, 10f 2-4) (sft, g-s, gd 2-3)
High-class filly, effective 9 to 10f, best at 10f, acts on hvy to gd, best on gd, and does well at Capannelle. Turf high 116 - 1st of 10 giving 4lb to Hangover Square (25 Aug Baden-Baden RF 4131a) - also 1st of 8 getting 3lb from Aboard (17 Spt Frankfurt RF 4572a). Consistent. Top-class filly in Germany.
**A Schutz in GER [9-16] Gestut Wittekindshof.*

ELLENDUNE GIRL BHB 61f **RR 68f** 4965^{15}
2 b f Mistertopogigo (IRE) - Perfidy (FR) (Persian Bold) 9.3f **(66)**
Form - 050400
Record 2000 - 1st:0 2nd:0 3rd:0 Ran:6
Win Prizemoney £0 *Total Prizemoney* £315
2000 Turf 0-6: (5f 4, 6f 2) (gd 2, g-f 2, frm 2)
Average filly. Turf high 68.
**D J S ffrenchDavis [0-6] Wroughton Racing Partnership.*

ELLENS ACADEMY (IRE) BHB 77f **RR 90f** 4933^{17}
5 b g Royal Academy (USA) 7.8f **(77)** - Lady Ellen (Horage) 10.3f **(61)**
Form - 043830400
Record 2000 - 1st:0 2nd:0 3rd:2 Ran:9
Pre2000 - 1st:2 2nd:2 3rd:1 Ran:14
Win Prizemoney £14,189 *Total Prizemoney* £20,402
Wins * 1999 Jly Newmar (G-F) H 6f 73 78 <
* 1999 May Newbur (G-F) H 6f 63 71+
2000 Turf 0-9: (5f 4, 6f 3, 7f 2) (g-s, gd 2, g-f 3, frm 2, hrd)
Useful gelding, effective 5f, acts on hrd, has worn blinkers. Turf high 90 - 3rd of 6 getting 7lb from Flanders (13 May Beverley 5f hrd RF 1186). A useful handicapper in '99, he was knocking at the door in the summer. Suited by coming from behind.
**E J Alston [2-20] Mrs Chris Harrington (from D K Weld in IRE [0-3] Jly 1998).*

ELLENS LAD (IRE) BHB 108f **RR 107f** 4612^{1}
6 b g Polish Patriot (USA) 7.8f **(70)** - Lady Ellen (Horage) 10.3f **(61)**
Form - 057150117501
Record 2000 - 1st:4 2nd:0 3rd:0 Ran:12
Pre2000 - 1st:6 2nd:3 3rd:4 Ran:38
Win Prizemoney £107,017 *Total Prizemoney* £121,273
Wins * 2000 Spt Ascot (SFT) H 5f 103 107 <
*** 2000** Jly Ascot (GD) H 5f 100 103
*** 2000** Jly Doncas (GD) H 5f 96 98
*** 2000** May York (FRM) H 5f 92 96
* 1999 Oct Newmar (GD) H 5f 87 94
* 1999 Spt Haydoc (G-F) H 5f 84 86
* 1999 Aug Newbur (GD) H 5.2f 80 81
1998 Jly Newmar (G-F) H 5f 81 86
1996 Nov Newmar (GD) H 5f 77 86
1996 Spt Folkes (G-F) H 5f 72 76
2000 Turf 4-12: (5f 4-10, 6f 2) (g-s 1-3, gd 1-2, g-f 1-4, frm 1-3)
Pattern-class gelding, effective 5f, acts on g-s to g-f, has worn blinkers, excels at Ascot. Turf high 107 - 1st of 19 giving 9lb to Dancing Mystery (24 Spt Ascot RF 4612) - also 1st of 15 giving 17lb to Sunley Sense (15 Jly Ascot RF 2828). A five-furlong specialist, he enjoyed a fine season in handicaps and looks capable of making his mark in listed races.
**W J Musson [7-27] Mrs Rita Brown (from E J Alston [1-10] Oct 1998).*

ELLIEBERRY (IRE) RR 4772^{12}
2 ch f Lucky Guest - Persian Flower **(50f 42a)** (Persian Heights)
Form - 0
Record 2000 - 1st:0 2nd:0 3rd:0 Ran:1
2000 Turf 0-1: (5f) (gd)
Currently very poor filly.
**B Ellison [0-1] E J Berry.*

ELLPEEDEE BHB 43f **RR 49f** 2467^{11}
3 b g Wolfhound (USA) 7.3f **(71)** - Kilvarnet (Furry Glen) 8.9f **(63)**
Form - 0656700
Record 2000 - 1st:0 2nd:0 3rd:0 Ran:7
Pre2000 - 1st:0 2nd:0 3rd:1 Ran:6
Win Prizemoney £0 *Total Prizemoney* £560
2000 Turf 0-7: (5f 4, 6f 2, 8f) (g-s, gd 4, frm 2)
Leggy, moderate gelding, effective 5f, acts on gd. Turf high 56.
**N Tinkler [0-13] Leeds Plywood and Doors Ltd.*

ELLWAY HEIGHTS BHB 58f **RR 61f** 4364^{5}
3 b g Shirley Heights 12.1f **(76)** - Amina (Brigadier Gerard) 9.3f **(58)**
Form - 7645
Record 2000 - 1st:0 2nd:0 3rd:0 Ran:4
Win Prizemoney £0 *Total Prizemoney* £322
2000 Turf 0-4: (9f 3, 12f) (g-f 3, frm)
Scopey, average gelding. Turf high 61 (began Aug).
**I A Balding [0-4] Ellway Racing.*

ELLWAY PRINCE BHB 49f63a **RR 53f 63a** 3517^{13}
5 b g Prince Sabo 6.6f **(64)** - Star Arrangement (Star Appeal) 9.6f **(65)**
Form - 8847022625011432400
Record 2000 - 1st:2 2nd:4 3rd:1 Ran:15
Pre2000 - 1st:1 2nd:6 3rd:1 Ran:33
Win Prizemoney £7,973 *Total Prizemoney* £19,656
Wins * 2000 *Apr Lingfi (STD) H 10f 48 62* <
*** 2000** *Mar Lingfi (STD) H 8f 48 62* <
1998 *Nov Lingfi (STD) 6f 61*
2000 Turf 0-5: (7f 2, 8f 3) (gd, g-f 2, frm 2) 2000 AW 2-10: (6f, 8f 1-7, 9f, 10f 1-1) (Equi 2-5, Fibr 5)
Average gelding, effective 6 to 10f, - acts on Equi, often wears blinkers, likes left handed tracks, likes tight tracks. Turf high 53. AW high 65 - 4th of 12 giving 19lb to Tapage (12 May Lingfield 8f Equi RF 1168) - also 1st of 13 giving 2lb to Consultant (7 Apr Lingfield RF 0639).
**M Wigham [2-8] Stephen Roots (from Mrs N Macauley [1-32] Mar 2000).*

ELLWAY QUEEN (USA) BHB 74f **RR 75f** 3711^{9}
3 b f Bahri (USA) - Queen Linear (USA) (Polish Navy (USA)) 8f **(67)**
Form - 8610
Record 2000 - 1st:1 2nd:0 3rd:0 Ran:4
Win Prizemoney £3,055 *Total Prizemoney* £3,055
Wins * 2000 Aug Nottin (G-F) 8.2f 75 <
2000 Turf 1-4: (7f 2, 8f 1-1, 10f) (gd, g-f 1-3)
Workmanlike, above-average filly. Turf high 75 (began Jly) - 1st of 7 getting 5lb from Musical Heath (4 Aug Nottingham RF 3378).
**B Hanbury [1-4] Ellway Racing.*

EL MAXIMO (IRE) BHB 71f **RR 74f** 5129^{19}
2 b g First Trump - Kentucky Starlet (USA) (Cox's Ridge (USA)) 8f **(68)**
Form - 6326152400
Record 2000 - 1st:1 2nd:2 3rd:1 Ran:10
Win Prizemoney £1,778 *Total Prizemoney* £4,619
Wins * 2000 Jly Folkes (GD) 7f 81 <
2000 Turf 1-10: (5f 2, 6f 5, 7f 1-3) (sft, gd 1-4, g-f 3, frm, hrd)
Above-average gelding, effective 6 to 7f, best at 7f, acts on gd to g-f, best on gd. Turf high 81 - 1st of 9 giving 5lb to Pertemps Thatcher (13 Jly Folkestone RF 2765). Consistent. Won at Folkestone in July, and was short-headed there the following month. Good run at Newmarket in September.
**M G Quinlan [1-10] Mario Lanfranchi.*

ELMHURST BOY BHB 84f81a **RR 86f 81a** 4609^{23}
4 b c Merdon Melody 6.8f **(56)** - Young Whip (Bold Owl) 8.5f **(45)**
Form - 215456601037452771550
Record 2000 - 1st:2 2nd:1 3rd:1 Ran:19
Pre2000 - 1st:2 2nd:4 3rd:4 Ran:15
Win Prizemoney £17,053 *Total Prizemoney* £33,175
Wins * 2000 Spt Kempto (GD) H 10f 79 86 <
*** 2000** Jun Bright (G-F) H 7f 75 77
* 1999 *Dec Lingfi (STD) H 7f 78 82*
* 1999 Aug Epsom (GD) 7f 77
2000 Turf 2-16: (6f 2, 7f 1-7, 8f 4, 10f 1-3) (sft, g-s 2, gd 4, g-f 1-5, frm 1-4) 2000 AW 0-3: (7f, 8f 2) (Equi 3)
Workmanlike, useful colt, effective 7 to 10f, best at 7f, acts on gd to frm - acts on Equi, best on g-f, often wears blinkers (very effectively), likes left handed tracksprefers right handed tracks, prefers tight tracks, excels at Kempton, does well at Goodwood and Lingfield. Turf high 86 - 1st of 19 getting 6lb from Milligan (2 Spt Kempton RF 4167) - also 1st of 7 giving 22lb to Milady Lillie (2 Jun Brighton RF 1654). AW high 81 - 4th of 7 giving 1lb to Salty Jack (9 Feb Lingfield 8f Equi RF 0249). He does not look at all keen on occasions, but definitely has ability. It looked as though seven furlongs was his ideal trip until he scored over ten furlongs at Kempton in September. **S Dow [4-34] R E Anderson.*

ELMONJED (USA) BHB 84f RR 82f 5103[5]
2 b c Gulch (USA) 9.6f **(79)** - Aqaarid (USA) **(109f)** (Nashwan (USA))
Form - 87215
Record 2000 - 1st:1 2nd:1 3rd:0 Ran:5
Win Prizemoney £4,280 *Total Prizemoney* £5,588
Wins * **2000** Spt Goodwo (GD) 8f 82 <
2000 Turf 1-5: (7f 3, 8f 1-2) (gd 1-3, g-f, frm)
Decent colt. Turf high 82 - 1st of 8 from Spanish Spur (9 Spt Goodwood RF 4318). **J L Dunlop [1-5] Hamdan Al Maktoum.*

ELMS SCHOOLGIRL BHB 60f68a RR 63f 68a 4330[15]
4 ch f Emarati (USA) 6.6f **(63)** - Ascend (IRE) (Glint of Gold) 9.3f **(66)**
Form - 206764520
Record 2000 - 1st:0 2nd:2 3rd:0 Ran:9
Pre2000 - 1st:3 2nd:0 3rd:2 Ran:12
Win Prizemoney £12,001 *Total Prizemoney* £16,221
Wins * 1999 Aug Bright (G-F) H 11.9f 61 64 <
* 1999 Jly Bright (FRM) H 10f 59 60
* 1999 Jun Bright (G-F) 10f 55
2000 Turf 0-9: (10f 4, 12f 4, 14f) (gd 3, g-f 4, frm 2)
Light-framed, average filly, effective 10 to 14f, best at 12f, acts on gd to hrd, best on g-f, prefers left handed tracks, prefers tight tracks, excels at Brighton, does well at Yarmouth. Turf high 64 - 6th of 10 giving 13lb to Swinging The Blues (26 Jun Yarmouth 10f g-f RF 2293). Something of a Brighton specialist, she is not as good away from the Sussex track. **J M P Eustace [3-21] J D Moore.*

ELMS SCHOOLPREFECT BHB 38f RR 50f 2891[19]
3 b f Emarati (USA) 6.6f **(63)** - Ascend (IRE) (Glint of Gold) 9.3f **(66)**
Form - 00
Record 2000 - 1st:0 2nd:0 3rd:0 Ran:2
Pre2000 - 1st:0 2nd:0 3rd:0 Ran:4
2000 Turf 0-2: (10f, 12f) (gd, frm)
Fair filly. (DEAD) **J M P Eustace [0-6] Park Lodge Racing.*

ELMUTABAKI BHB 102f RR 107f 5225[11]
4 b c Unfuwain (USA) 11.4f **(74)** - Bawaeth (USA) (Blushing Groom (FR)) 10.3f **(76)**
Form - 5760
Record 2000 - 1st:0 2nd:0 3rd:0 Ran:4
Pre2000 - 1st:2 2nd:2 3rd:0 Ran:8
Win Prizemoney £49,315 *Total Prizemoney* £54,820
Wins * 1999 Jly Haydoc (G-S) L 11.9f 102+ <
* 1999 Jun Ascot (G-F) H 12f 90 100+
2000 Turf 0-4: (10f 2, 12f, 13f) (gd 2, g-f 2)
Scopey, Pattern-class colt, effective 12f, acts on gd to g-f, best on gd. Turf high 106 - 7th of 14 giving 17lb to Rada's Daughter (8 Jly Haydock 12f gd RF 2633). He evidently had his problems and failed to fire in a light campaign.
**B W Hills [2-12] Hamdan Al Maktoum.*

ELNAHAAR (USA) RR 92+f 4536[1]
2 b c Silver Hawk (USA) 11.2f **(85)** - Futuh (USA) (Diesis) 9.3f **(69)**
Form - 11
Record 2000 - 1st:2 2nd:0 3rd:0 Ran:2
Win Prizemoney £9,452 *Total Prizemoney* £9,452
Wins * **2000** Spt Cheste (SFT) 7.6f 92+ <
* **2000** Jly Salisb (GD) 7f 77+
2000 Turf 2-2: (7f 1-1, 8f 1-1) (g-s 1-1, g-f 1-1)
Currently useful colt. Turf high 92 (began Jly) - 1st of 6 from Dayglow Dancer (20 Spt Chester RF 4536).
**E A L Dunlop [2-2] Hamdan Al Maktoum.*

ELREHAAN BHB 98f RR 90f 5241[6]
2 b f Sadler's Wells (USA) 11.3f **(87)** - Moss (USA) (Woodman (USA)) 9f **(74)**
Form - 2176
Record 2000 - 1st:1 2nd:1 3rd:0 Ran:4
Win Prizemoney £2,834 *Total Prizemoney* £4,465
Wins * **2000** Aug Redcar (FRM) 7f 90+ <
2000 Turf 1-4: (7f 1-2, 8f 2) (g-s, gd, frm, hrd 1-1)
Useful filly. Turf high 90 (began Jly) - 1st of 6 from Princess Titania (12 Aug Redcar RF 3596). Toyed with the opposition when winning a Redcar maiden on her second start, but was well beaten in better company afterwards.
**J L Dunlop [1-4] Hamdan Al Maktoum.*

ELSAAMRI (USA) RR 79f 4807[3]
2 b br c Silver Hawk (USA) 11.2f **(85)** - Muhbubh (USA) (Blushing Groom (FR)) 10.3f **(76)**
Form - 43
Record 2000 - 1st:0 2nd:0 3rd:1 Ran:2
Win Prizemoney £0 *Total Prizemoney* £843
2000 Turf 0-2: (7f 2) (g-s, g-f)
Currently above-average colt. Turf high 79 (began Spt) - 3rd of 18 giving 5lb to Paiyda (4 Oct Lingfield 7f g-s RF 4807).
**M P Tregoning [0-2] Hamdan Al Maktoum.*

EL SALIDA (IRE) BHB 63f68a RR 68f 68a 3959[12]
4 b g Second Set (IRE) 9.2f **(67)** - Tradescantia (GER) (Windwurf (GER)) 12.7f **(72)**
Form - 47700
Record 2000 - 1st:0 2nd:0 3rd:0 Ran:4
Pre2000 - 1st:0 2nd:0 3rd:1 Ran:4
Win Prizemoney £0 *Total Prizemoney* £1,290
2000 Turf 0-4: (8f, 9f, 10f 2) (g-s 2, frm 2)
Workmanlike, average gelding, effective 8f, acts on gd. Turf high 68. **J G FitzGerald [2-13] David Fulton.*

ELSA'S PRIDE RR 38f 3356[3]
5 b g Mon Tresor 7.9f **(60)** - Elsa (Green Ruby (USA))
Form - 3
Record 2000 - 1st:0 2nd:0 3rd:1 Ran:1
Win Prizemoney £0 *Total Prizemoney* £525
2000 Turf 0-1: (8f) (frm)
Very moderate gelding. **J M Jefferson [1-12] Mrs M E Dixon.*

ELSIE BAMFORD BHB 52f42a RR 53f 42a 3245[5]
4 b f Tragic Role (USA) 9.4f **(63)** - Sara Sprint (Formidable (USA)) 9.2f **(63)**
Form - 063843112333334325
Record 2000 - 1st:2 2nd:2 3rd:8 Ran:16
Pre2000 - 1st:0 2nd:0 3rd:2 Ran:18
Win Prizemoney £6,970 *Total Prizemoney* £13,947
Wins * **2000** Jun Catter (SFT) H 13.8f 41 47+ <
* **2000** May Warwic (HVY) H 14.6f 38 45
2000 Turf 2-15: (12f 3, 13f 5, 14f 1-1, 15f 1-2, 16f 2, 17f 2) (hvy 1-1, g-s 1-1, gd, g-f 5, frm 6, hrd) 2000 AW 0-1: (14f) (Fibr)
Leggy, fair filly, effective 7 to 17f, acts on hvy to hrd - acts on Fibr, best on g-f, likes right handed tracks, , excels at Bath, does well at Hamilton and likes Newcastle. Turf high 53 - 4th of 11 getting 7lb from Spectrometer (14 Jly Hamilton 13f g-f RF 2807) - also 1st of 14 getting 6lb from Hasta la Vista (3 Jun Catterick RF 1673). Consistent.
**M Johnston [2-21] Mrs Sheila Ramsden (from J Berry [0-13] Aug 1999).*

ELSIE PLUNKETT BHB 97f RR 91f 4747[10]
2 b f Mind Games - Snow Eagle (IRE) **(45f)** (Polar Falcon (USA))
Form - 5111324430
Record 2000 - 1st:3 2nd:1 3rd:2 Ran:10
Win Prizemoney £11,439 *Total Prizemoney* £60,747
Wins * **2000** May Newbur (G-F) 5.2f 86+ <
* **2000** May Nottin (G-F) 5.1f 81+
* **2000** Apr Sandow (SFT) 5f 77
2000 Turf 3-10: (5f 3-8, 6f 2) (hvy, g-s 1-2, gd 1-4, g-f, frm 1-1, hrd)
Useful filly, effective 5 to 6f, best at 5f, acts on gd to frm, best on gd. Turf high 91 - 3rd of 12 getting 2lb from Vicious Dancer (14 Spt Ayr 5f gd RF 4383) - also 1st of 7 giving 3lb to Fair Princess (19 May Newbury RF 1303). Consistent. She improved from her debut to land a hat-trick, but disappointed in heavy ground at Sandown. Ran much better on fast ground at Newbury, finding only Superstar Leo too good, and has run sound races since if just looking held. After a relatively busy season as a juvenile, she may be the type who does not improve as a three-year-old.
**R Hannon [3-10] C J M Partnership.*

ELTARS BHB 37f30a RR 28f 30a 4403[19]
3 ch g Elmaamul (USA) 8.1f **(70)** - Iradah (USA) **(55df)** (Topsider (USA)) 8.3f **(71)**
Form - 70800
Record 2000 - 1st:0 2nd:0 3rd:0 Ran:5
Pre2000 - 1st:0 2nd:0 3rd:0 Ran:1
2000 Turf 0-3: (5f, 6f, 8f) (g-s, g-f, frm) 2000 AW 0-2: (6f 2) (Fibr 2)

Leggy, little account gelding, has worn blinkers. Turf high 28. AW high 7.
**K A Morgan [0-1] The Eltars Partnership (from R F Marvin [0-4] Jun 2000).*

ELTON LEDGER (IRE) BHB 41f51a **RR 40f 51a** 2838[11]

11 b g Cyrano de Bergerac 7.3f **(58)** - Princess of Nashua (Crowned Prince (USA)) 10.1f **(67)**
Form - 621222735776470
Record 2000 - 1st:1 2nd:4 3rd:1 Ran:14
Pre2000 - 1st:17 2nd:24 3rd:8 Ran:106
Win Prizemoney £41,375 *Total Prizemoney* £68,110
Wins * 2000 *Jan Southw (STD) S 6f 51*
* 1999 *Jan Southw (STD) S 6f 64*
* 1998 *Dec Southw (STD) C 5f 63+*
* 1998 *Dec Southw (STD) S 6f 70*
* 1998 *Dec Southw (STD) H 6f 67 69*
* 1998 *Nov Southw (STD) C 5f 67*
* 1998 *Jun Southw (STD) 6f 71* <
* 1998 *Mar Southw (STD) SH 6f 58 64*
* 1997 *Feb Southw (STD) S 6f 71* <
* 1997 *Jan Southw (STD) H 6f 70 69*
* 1996 *Spt Southw (STD) C 5f 71* <
* 1996 *Jun Southw (STD) H 5f 63 66*
* 1996 *Apr Southw (STD) 7f 45*
* 1996 *Mar Southw (STD) H 6f 55 56*
2000 Turf 0-2: (6f 2) (frm 2) 2000 AW 1-12: (5f, 6f 1-9, 7f, 8f) (Fibr 1-12)
Moderate gelding, effective 6f, - acts on Fibr, often wears blinkers, favours left handed tracks, likes tight tracks. Turf high 40. AW high 61 - 2nd of 5 giving 5lb to Dahlidya (7 Feb Southwell 6f Fibr RF 0239). Consistent. He owes his connections nothing, having won a multitude of races over the years, especially on the Southwell Fibresand, and is still capable in modest company on that surface.
**Mrs N Macauley [15-93] Mrs N Macauley (from A A Scott [2-17] May 1994).*

EL UNO (IRE) BHB 56f50a **RR 68f 50a** 5169[7]

2 ch c Elmaamul (USA) 8.1f **(70)** - Fawaakeh (USA) **(75f)** (Lyphard (USA)) 9.9f **(72)**
Form - 806577
Record 2000 - 1st:0 2nd:0 3rd:0 Ran:6
2000 Turf 0-5: (5f, 6f 2, 7f 2) (gd 3, g-f, frm) 2000 AW 0-1: (8f) (Fibr)
Average colt, has worn blinkers. Turf high 68.
**J L Eyre [0-5] E Richmond (from Miss J F Craze [0-1] Jun 2000).*

ELVINGTON BOY BHB 75f **RR 74f** 5313[13]

3 ch g Emarati (USA) 6.6f **(63)**-Catherines Well (Junius (USA)) 7.7f **(65)**
Form - 083262200
Record 2000 - 1st:0 2nd:3 3rd:1 Ran:9
Pre2000 - 1st:1 2nd:2 3rd:0 Ran:6
Win Prizemoney £2,970 *Total Prizemoney* £10,571
Wins * 1999 Aug Ripon (GD) 5f 73 <
2000 Turf 0-9: (5f 6, 6f 3) (g-s 2, gd 2, g-f, frm 3, hrd)
Workmanlike, above-average gelding, effective 5 to 6f, best at 5f, acts on gd to frm, best on frm, excels at Carlisle, does well at Ripon. Turf high 74 - 2nd of 14 giving 28lb to Pips Star (5 Aug Doncaster 5f frm RF 3391). Inconsistent.
**M W Easterby [1-15] K Hodgson & Mrs J Hodgson.*

ELVIS REIGNS BHB 48f **RR 57f** 3242[9]

4 b g Rock City 8.8f **(62)** - Free Rein (Sagaro) 9.7f **(55)**
Form - 000700
Record 2000 - 1st:0 2nd:0 3rd:0 Ran:6
Pre2000 - 1st:1 2nd:0 3rd:1 Ran:2
Win Prizemoney £3,860 *Total Prizemoney* £4,497
Wins 1998 Spt Ayr (G-S) 7f 85+ <
2000 Turf 0-6: (8f 2, 10f, 12f 3) (g-s, gd, g-f 3, frm)
Scopey, fair gelding. Turf high 61. Inconsistent.
**M D Hammond [0-6] A G Chappell (from Mrs J R Ramsden [1-2] Spt 1998).*

ELYSIAN FIELDS (IRE) **RR 51f** 5017[8]

2 br f Marju (IRE) 9.2f **(76)** - Suspiria (IRE) (Glenstal (USA)) 10.1f **(64)**
Form - 08
Record 2000 - 1st:0 2nd:0 3rd:0 Ran:2
2000 Turf 0-1: (6f) (g-f) 2000 AW 0-1: (7f) (Fibr)
Currently fair filly. **G C Bravery [0-2] The TT Partnership.*

EL ZITO (IRE) BHB 83f **RR 89f** 4380[15]

3 b g Mukaddamah (USA) 7.6f **(74)** - Samite (FR) (Tennyson (FR)) 12.1f **(50)**
Form - 3021103300
Record 2000 - 1st:2 2nd:1 3rd:2 Ran:9
Pre2000 - 1st:0 2nd:1 3rd:1 Ran:2
Win Prizemoney £10,114 *Total Prizemoney* £16,737
Wins * 2000 Jun Beverl (G-F) H 12f 75 85 <
*** 2000** Jun Cheste (G-S) 10.3f 84
2000 Turf 2-9: (10f 1-6, 12f 1-3) (gd 1-3, g-f 3, frm 2, hrd 1-1)
Useful gelding, effective 10 to 12f, best at 10f, acts on gd to hrd, likes left handed tracks, prefers tight tracks. Turf high 89 - 3rd of 5 getting 1lb from Golconda (31 Jly Folkestone 10f frm RF 3247) - also 1st of 9 giving 6lb to High Topper (14 Jun Beverley RF 1950). Inconsistent. A winner at Chester and Beverley in June, he has run some decent races since despite a rise in the handicap, but ran very badly at Haydock in August.
**M G Quinlan [2-9] Mario Lanfranchi (from B J Meehan [0-2] Nov 1999).*

EMALI BHB 47f **RR 56f** 4877[12]

3 b g Emarati (USA) 6.6f **(63)** - Princess Poquito (Hard Fought) 8.8f **(62)**
Form - 2204303250
Record 2000 - 1st:0 2nd:3 3rd:2 Ran:10
Pre2000 - 1st:0 2nd:0 3rd:0 Ran:2
Win Prizemoney £0 *Total Prizemoney* £3,496
2000 Turf 0-10: (8f 2, 10f 7, 11f) (g-s, gd, g-f 4, frm 3, hrd)
Strong, fair gelding, effective 8 to 10f, best at 8f, acts on frm, has worn blinkers, likes left handed tracks. Turf high 63 (began Jly) - 2nd of 10 giving 14lb to Fisher Island (15 Jly Nottingham 10f frm RF 2843). Inconsistent. **C E Brittain [0-12] C E Brittain.*

EMAN'S JOY BHB 63f **RR 68f** 4824[17]

3 b f Lion Cavern (USA) 7.5f **(74)** - Carolside (Music Maestro) 7.7f **(66)**
Form - 3514530
Record 2000 - 1st:1 2nd:0 3rd:2 Ran:7
Win Prizemoney £3,672 *Total Prizemoney* £5,704
Wins * 2000 Jly Warwic (GD) 6f 68 <
2000 Turf 1-7: (6f 1-2, 7f 3, 8f 2) (gd 1-3, g-f 2, frm 2)
Light-framed, average filly, effective 6 to 8f, best at 6f, acts on gd to frm, best on gd. Turf high 68 (1st run) - 3rd of 8 to Pageant (7 Jun Yarmouth 6f gd RF 1795) - also 1st of 7 getting 11lb from Kuwait Rose (7 Jly Warwick RF 2613).
**J R Fanshawe [1-7] Arashan Ali.*

EMBODY **RR 106f** 1456a[2]

5 b h Indian Ridge 7.6f **(74)** - Kamakha (ITY) (Natroun (FR))
Form - 12
2000 Turf 1-2: (8f 1-2) (hvy 1-1, g-s)
Pattern-class colt. Turf high 106 - also 1st of 9 from Hurricane Louis (7 May San Siro RF 1160a). Improving.
**B Grizzetti in ITY [1-8] Scuderia Cocktail.*

EMBRACED BHB 106f **RR 101f** 2748[10]

3 b f Pursuit of Love 9.5f **(69)** - Tromond **(92f)** (Lomond (USA)) 8.8f **(65)**
Form - 160
Record 2000 - 1st:1 2nd:0 3rd:0 Ran:3
Pre2000 - 1st:1 2nd:0 3rd:0 Ran:1
Win Prizemoney £19,365 *Total Prizemoney* £20,040
Wins * 2000 May Ascot (G-S) L 8f 101+ <
* 1999 Oct Nottin (SFT) 8.2f 79+
2000 Turf 1-3: (8f 1-2, 10f) (g-s 1-1, gd, g-f)
Lengthy, very useful filly. Turf high 101 - also 1st of 12 from Verbose (3 May Ascot RF 0999). She looked a very nice prospect when winning an Ascot Listed race on her return, but was held in a couple of hot races later. **J R Fanshawe [2-4] Cheveley Park Stud.*

EMBRACE ME **RR 50f** 5138[10]

2 ch f Nashwan (USA) 10.3f **(79)** - Zilayah (USA) **(67f)** (Zilzal (USA))
Form - 0
Record 2000 - 1st:0 2nd:0 3rd:0 Ran:1
2000 Turf 0-1: (8f) (g-s)
Currently fair filly. **E A L Dunlop [0-1] Saeed Suhail.*

EMBRYONIC (IRE) BHB 55f **RR 70f** 4459[15]

8 b g Prince Rupert (FR) 10.4f **(60)** - Belle Viking (FR) (Riverman

(USA)) 9.1f **(76)**
Form - 70686200
Record 2000 - 1st:0 2nd:1 3rd:0 Ran:8
Pre2000 - 1st:4 2nd:6 3rd:4 Ran:29
Win Prizemoney £15,658 *Total Prizemoney* £36,569
Wins 1997 Jun Newcas (FRM) H 16.1f 78 83 <
1997 May Doncas (GD) H 16.5f 76 81
2000 Turf 0-8: (13f, 14f, 15f, 16f 3, 17f, 19f) (g-s, gd 3, g-f, frm 3)
Above-average gelding, effective 16f, acted on frm, favoured tight tracks. Turf high 70. (DEAD)
**R F Fisher [2-21] Mrs D Miller (from M Todhunter [2-16] May 2000).*

EMERALD IMP (IRE) BHB 48f48a **RR 50f 48a** 2351[16]

3 ch f Mac's Imp (USA) 5.6f **(54)** - Lady Montekin (Montekin) 11.1f **(55)**
Form - 600
Record 2000 - 1st:0 2nd:0 3rd:0 Ran:3
Pre2000 - 1st:0 2nd:0 3rd:0 Ran:2
Win Prizemoney £0 *Total Prizemoney* £244
2000 Turf 0-2: (6f, 7f) (frm 2) 2000 AW 0-1: (9f) (Fibr)
Unfurnished, fair filly. Turf high 28. **M S Saunders [0-5] Chris Scott.*

EMERALD PALM RR 74f 5140[6]

2 b f Green Desert (USA) 7.8f **(78)** - Opus One **(61f 51a)** (Slip Anchor) 9.8f **(73)**
Form - 66
Record 2000 - 1st:0 2nd:0 3rd:0 Ran:2
2000 Turf 0-2: (6f 2) (g-s, g-f)
Currently above-average filly. Turf high 74 (began Spt).
**J Noseda [0-2] Robert Ogden.*

EMERALD PEACE (IRE) BHB 103f **RR 95f** 4700[4]

3 b f Green Desert (USA) 7.8f **(78)** - Puck's Castle **(85f)** (Shirley Heights) 10.3f **(74)**
Form - 00164
Record 2000 - 1st:1 2nd:0 3rd:0 Ran:5
Pre2000 - 1st:2 2nd:2 3rd:0 Ran:5
Win Prizemoney £15,230 *Total Prizemoney* £28,325
Wins * 2000 Spt Leices (G-F) 5f 95 <
* 1999 Aug Lingfi (G-F) 5f 87+
* 1999 Aug Lingfi (GD) 5f 87+
2000 Turf 1-5: (5f 1-5) (gd, g-f 2, frm 1-2)
Very useful filly, effective 5f, acts on g-f to frm, best on frm. Turf high 95 (began Aug) - also 1st of 9 from Presentation (5 Spt Leicester RF 4219). Consistent. Progressive at two, just touched off in the Fling Childers, she showed early pace on her belated return at Goodwood. Well held in the Nunthorpe but won well when dropped in class at Leicester. Did not fare badly in listed class afterwards, and looks capable of scoring at that level.
**M A Jarvis [3-10] M P Burke.*

EMERGING MARKET BHB 82f **RR 83f** 4284[13]

8 b g Emarati (USA) 6.6f **(63)** - Flitteriss Park (Beldale Flutter (USA)) 9.7f **(71)**
Form - 7005280
Record 2000 - 1st:0 2nd:1 3rd:0 Ran:7
Pre2000 - 1st:3 2nd:6 3rd:3 Ran:41
Win Prizemoney £57,059 *Total Prizemoney* £91,009
Wins * 1996 Jun Ascot (G-F) H 6f 95 98 <
2000 Turf 0-7: (6f 4, 7f 3) (gd 3, g-f, frm 3)
Decent gelding, effective 6f, acts on g-f to frm, best on frm. Turf high 84. Consistent. He has run some good races in well-contested sprint handicaps in the last couple of seasons, but has not won for four years. **J L Dunlop [3-48] Philip Wroughton.*

EMINENCE (IRE) RR 102df 4643[R]

2 b c Machiavellian (USA) 9.8f **(83)** - Divine Danse (FR) (Kris) 9.5f **(73)**
Form - 32R
Record 2000 - 1st:0 2nd:1 3rd:1 Ran:3
Win Prizemoney £0 *Total Prizemoney* £8,073
2000 Turf 0-3: (6f, 7f 2) (gd, g-f, frm)
Currently very useful colt. Turf high 102 (began Aug) - 2nd of 5 getting 5lb from Hemingway (22 Aug York 7f gd RF 3850). Showed distinct promise on his debut and ran into a decent sort at York next time, but refused to race at Newmarket. He is one of the best maidens around, but is one to have reservations about.
**Sir Michael Stoute [0-3] Sheikh Mohammed.*

EMINENCE GRISE (IRE) BHB 05f **RR 99f** 4295[4]

5 b g Sadler's Wells (USA) 11.3f **(87)** - Impatiente (USA) (Vaguely Noble) 10.1f **(72)**
Form - 821074
Record 2000 - 1st:1 2nd:1 3rd:0 Ran:6
Pre2000 - 1st:1 2nd:2 3rd:2 Ran:13
Win Prizemoney £25,916 *Total Prizemoney* £47,955
Wins * 2000 Jly York (GD) LH 13.9f 95 96 <
* 1999 May Kempto (G-F) H 16f 73 77
2000 Turf 1-6: (12f, 14f 1-4, 15f) (gd 1-1, g-f 3, frm 2)
Very useful gelding, effective 14 to 22f, best at 14f, acts on gd to frm, best on g-f, has worn blinkers, prefers left handed tracks, excels at York. Turf high 99 - 2nd of 10 giving 11lb to Inch Perfect (16 Jun York 14f g-f RF 2034) - also 1st of 9 giving 1lb to Musician (15 Jly York RF 2853). Consistent. Progressive in '99, he ran well at York on his second start of last season and came out best in a four-way photo in a listed event at the same track next time. An honest sort, he is best at 14 furlongs. **H R A Cecil [2-19] Wafic Said.*

EMISSARY BHB 58f53a **RR 66f 53a** 5320[19]

2 gr c Primo Dominie 7.2f **(67)** - Misty Goddess (IRE) **(51df 37a)** (Godswalk (USA)) 7.3f **(58)**
Form - 66402450
Record 2000 - 1st:0 2nd:1 3rd:0 Ran:8
Win Prizemoney £0 *Total Prizemoney* £1,337
2000 Turf 0-8: (5f 3, 6f 4, 7f) (sft, g-s, gd 3, g-f, frm 2)
Average colt, effective 5 to 6f, acts on gd to frm. Turf high 66. Inconsistent. **M Johnston [0-0] J R Good.*

EMLEY BHB 40f **RR 42f** 3385[5]

4 b f Safawan 6.6f **(60)** - Bit of a State (Free State) 8.7f **(61)**
Form - 60705
Record 2000 - 1st:0 2nd:0 3rd:0 Ran:5
Pre2000 - 1st:0 2nd:0 3rd:1 Ran:3
Win Prizemoney £0 *Total Prizemoney* £515
2000 Turf 0-5: (5f, 6f, 7f 2, 8f) (gd, frm 4)
Unfurnished, moderate filly. Turf high 45. Consistent.
**A Berry [0-5] J Wilkins (from D Nicholls [0-3] Aug 1999).*

EMMA AMOUR BHB 35f **RR 33f** 4360[17]

3 b br f Emarati (USA) 6.6f **(63)** - Ella Mon Amour (Ela-Mana-Mou) 10.1f **(70)**
Form - 50000780
Record 2000 - 1st:0 2nd:0 3rd:0 Ran:7
Pre2000 - 1st:0 2nd:1 3rd:0 Ran:3
Win Prizemoney £0 *Total Prizemoney* £584
2000 Turf 0-7: (5f 5, 6f 2) (gd 3, g-f, frm 3)
Workmanlike, fair filly, effective 6f, acts on frm, has worn blinkers. Turf high 33. She finished runner-up in a Lingfield maiden on her racecourse debut at two but has not shown too much since.
**M W Easterby [0-9] K Wreglesworth (from J R Fanshawe [0-1] Aug 1999).*

EMMA CLARE (IRE) BHB 56f51a **RR 68f 51a** 5247[3]

2 b f Namaqualand (USA) - Medicosma (USA) (The Minstrel (CAN)) 10f **(72)**
Form - 8872410063
Record 2000 - 1st:1 2nd:1 3rd:1 Ran:10
Win Prizemoney £3,428 *Total Prizemoney* £4,427
Wins * 2000 Aug Mussel (G-F) 8f 49 <
2000 Turf 1-8: (6f 2, 7f 3, 8f 1-2, 10f) (gd 2, g-f 3, frm 1-3) 2000 AW 0-2: (8f 2) (Fibr 2)
Average filly, effective 7f, acts on frm, has worn blinkers, prefers tight tracks. Turf high 68 - 2nd of 11 giving 2lb to Fazzani (4 Aug Thirsk 7f frm RF 3384). AW high 52 (began Oct).
**J A Osborne [1-10] Mrs K Sherry.*

EMMAJOUN BHB 50f38a **RR 40f 38a** 152[4]

5 b m Emarati (USA) 6.6f **(63)** - Parijoun (Manado) 9.6f **(63)**
Form - 3625734
Record 2000 - 1st:0 2nd:0 3rd:1 Ran:3
Pre2000 - 1st:1 2nd:3 3rd:2 Ran:21
Win Prizemoney £3,006 *Total Prizemoney* £5,837
Wins * 1999 *Mar Lingfi (STD) 5f 57 <*
2000 AW 0-3: (6f, 7f 2) (Equi, Fibr 2)
Moderate filly, effective 5 to 6f, acts on frm - acts on Equi, has worn blinkers, likes left handed tracks, likes tight tracks. AW high

37. *W G M Turner [1-21] P Nabavi (from A P Jarvis [0-3] Spt 1997).*

EMMA-LYNE BHB 35f40a **RR 34f 40a** 1255[15]

4 b f Emarati (USA) 6.6f **(63)** - Moreton's Martha (Derrylin) 8.8f **(54)**
Form - 000
Record 2000 - 1st:0 2nd:0 3rd:0 Ran:3
Pre2000 - 1st:0 2nd:2 3rd:1 Ran:10
Win Prizemoney £0 *Total Prizemoney* £2,104
2000 Turf 0-2: (7f, 10f) (gd, g-f) 2000 AW 0-1: (6f) (Equi)
Light-framed, very moderate filly, has worn blinkers. Turf high 5. Becoming disappointing.
Derrick Morris [0-3] K Powell (from A P Jarvis [0-10] Oct 1999).

EMMAS HOPE BHB 25f27a **RR 22f 27a** 2801[8]

3 b f Emarati (USA) 6.6f **(63)** - Ray of Hope **(47f)** (Rainbow Quest (USA)) 10.4f **(75)**
Form - 50808
Record 2000 - 1st:0 2nd:0 3rd:0 Ran:4
Pre2000 - 1st:0 2nd:0 3rd:0 Ran:8
2000 Turf 0-3: (10f, 11f, 12f) (g-f 2, frm) 2000 AW 0-1: (6f) (Equi)
Light-framed, little account filly, has worn blinkers. Turf high 15.
B P J Baugh [0-10] D E Simpson (from P D Evans [0-2] Jan 2000).

EMMA'S SUNSET (IRE) **RR 1f** 4014[10]

4 ch f Red Sunset 9f **(57)** - Rose A Village (River Beauty) 8.6f **(77)**
Form - 0
Record 2000 - 1st:0 2nd:0 3rd:0 Ran:1
Pre2000 - 1st:0 2nd:0 3rd:0 Ran:2
2000 Turf 0-1: (10f) (frm)
Neat, currently very poor filly.
J S Wainwright [0-1] Ms Julie French (from N Tinkler [0-2] Jun 1998).

EMMA THOMAS BHB 38f47a **RR 50f 47a** 5295[10]

2 b f Puissance 7.1f **(60)** - Clan Scotia **(46f)** (Clantime)
Form - 7080300
Record 2000 - 1st:0 2nd:0 3rd:1 Ran:7
Win Prizemoney £0 *Total Prizemoney* £281
2000 Turf 0-5: (5f 3, 6f, 7f) (g-s 2, gd, g-f, frm) 2000 AW 0-2: (6f, 7f) (Fibr 2)
Fair filly. Turf high 50 (began Jly). AW high 50 (began Spt).
A Berry [0-7] Alan Berry.

EMMS (USA) BHB 95f **RR 88+f** 4610[8]

2 gr c Fastness (IRE) - Carnation (FR) (Carwhite) 7.2f **(61)**
Form - 23128
Record 2000 - 1st:1 2nd:2 3rd:1 Ran:5
Win Prizemoney £4,163 *Total Prizemoney* £15,365
Wins * **2000** Aug Newmar (G-F) 7f 82 <
2000 Turf 1-5: (5f, 7f 1-2, 8f 2) (g-s 2, gd 2, frm 1-1)
Useful colt. Turf high 88 - 2nd of 18 giving 14lb to Perfect Plum (28 Aug Newcastle 8f g-s RF 4042) - also 1st of 10 from Muqtadi (11 Aug Newmarket RF 3561). Runner-up in his first two starts, he got off the mark at Newmarket in August when seeming to appreciate the step up to seven furlongs. A fine runner-up in a valuable Newcastle nursery when beating the group on his side of the track, he was found wanting in a Group Two on his last run.
P F I Cole [1-5] Sir George Meyrick.

EMPERORS FOLLY **RR 22f** 4614[8]

2 b c Emperor Jones (USA) - Highest Bid (FR) (Highest Honor (FR))
Form - 8
Record 2000 - 1st:0 2nd:0 3rd:0 Ran:1
2000 Turf 0-1: (8f) (gd)
Currently little account colt. *C A Dwyer [0-1] Roalco Ltd.*

EMPEROR'S GOLD BHB 28f28a **RR 34f 28a** 421[13]

5 gr g Petong 7.6f **(58)** - Tarnside Rosal **(56f)** (Mummy's Game) 8.2f **(60)**
Form - 8364550
Record 2000 - 1st:0 2nd:0 3rd:1 Ran:6
Pre2000 - 1st:2 2nd:2 3rd:4 Ran:19
Win Prizemoney £3,463 *Total Prizemoney* £6,295
Wins 1998 *Jan Southw (STD) S 8f 68+* <
1997 *Nov Wolver (STD) SH 8.5f 58 64*
2000 AW 0-6: (9f 3, 10f, 11f, 12f) (Equi 2, Fibr 4)
Very moderate gelding, has worn blinkers. AW high 34.
M G Quinlan [0-8] Emperor's Gold Partnership (from M J Polglase [0-5] Oct 1998).

EMPIRE DREAM BHB 64f **RR 71f** 4775[16]

3 b c Alzao (USA) 9.8f **(73)** - Triste Oeil (USA) (Raise A Cup (USA)) 7.6f **(74)**
Form - 422000
Record 2000 - 1st:0 2nd:2 3rd:0 Ran:6
Win Prizemoney £0 *Total Prizemoney* £2,403
2000 Turf 0-6: (8f, 10f 2, 12f 3) (g-s, g-f 2, frm 2, hrd)
Scopey, above-average colt, effective 12f, acts on frm. Turf high 71 - 2nd of 5 giving 5lb to Zibilene (11 Jly Pontefract 12f frm RF 2697). Improving steadily in maidens. *M Johnston [0-6] Abdullah Ali.*

EMPIRE STATE (IRE) BHB 44f39a **RR 44f 39a** 228[9]

5 b g High Estate 10.5f **(66)** - Palm Dove (USA) (Storm Bird (CAN)) 10.3f **(74)**
Form - 60
Record 2000 - 1st:0 2nd:0 3rd:0 Ran:2
Pre2000 - 1st:2 2nd:2 3rd:1 Ran:27
Win Prizemoney £6,074 *Total Prizemoney* £8,224
Wins 1998 Jly Catter (GD) H 6f 63 72 <
1998 Jun Carlis (G-S) H 5.9f 63 68
2000 AW 0-2: (9f, 12f) (Fibr 2)
Moderate gelding, effective 11f, acts on g-f, has worn blinkers, likes left handed tracks, likes tight tracks. AW high 39.
R A Fahey [1-12] E O'Malley (from P S Felgate [0-6] Jly 1999).

EMPORIO BHB 70f **RR 73f** 5312[15]

2 b c Emperor Jones (USA) - Lykoa (Shirley Heights) 10.3f **(74)**
Form - 040
Record 2000 - 1st:0 2nd:0 3rd:0 Ran:3
2000 Turf 0-3: (7f 2, 8f) (g-s 2, g-f)
Currently above-average colt. Turf high 73 (began Spt).
L M Cumani [0-3] Mrs V Shelton.

EMPRESS OF AUSTRIA (USA) BHB 59f **RR 60f** 5074[16]

2 ch f Foxhound (USA) - Falabella (Steel Heart) 8.3f **(58)**
Form - 30670
Record 2000 - 1st:0 2nd:0 3rd:1 Ran:5
Win Prizemoney £0 *Total Prizemoney* £554
2000 Turf 0-5: (5f 2, 6f 2, 7f) (g-s 2, gd, g-f, frm)
Average filly. Turf high 60 (began Aug).
Miss Gay Kelleway [0-5] Mrs Jackie Ward Ramos.

ENCHANTING (IRE) **RR 33f** 4599[10]

2 b f Bigstone (IRE) - Spire (Shirley Heights) 10.3f **(74)**
Form - 0
Record 2000 - 1st:0 2nd:0 3rd:0 Ran:1
2000 Turf 0-1: (7f) (gd)
Currently very moderate filly. *B J Meehan [0-1] Fieldspring Racing.*

ENCORE DU CRISTAL (USA) **RR 69f** 800[17]

3 b f Quiet American (USA) 7.9f **(60)** - Elegant Champagne (USA) (Alleged (USA)) 10f **(76)**
Form - 0
Record 2000 - 1st:0 2nd:0 3rd:0 Ran:1
2000 Turf 0-1: (8f) (gd)
Workmanlike, currently average filly.
J H M Gosden [0-1] Thomas Tatham.

ENCOUNTER BHB 52f43a **RR 52f 43a** 5190[2]

4 br g Primo Dominie 7.2f **(67)** - Dancing Spirit (IRE) (Ahonoora) 8.1f **(73)**
Form - 040740085211716054502
Record 2000 - 1st:3 2nd:2 3rd:0 Ran:20
Pre2000 - 1st:2 2nd:2 3rd:2 Ran:27
Win Prizemoney £14,940 *Total Prizemoney* £19,850
Wins * **2000** Aug Thirsk (G-F) SH 6f 51 52
* **2000** Jly Catter (G-F) H 7f 44 47
* **2000** Jly Hamilt (G-F) H 6f 41 47
* 1999 Aug Hamilt (G-F) H 6f 44 53 <
* 1999 Aug Ayr (G-F) S 7f 45
2000 Turf 3-20: (6f 2-11, 7f 1-8, 8f) (hvy, gd 3, g-f 1-7, frm 1-8, hrd 1-1)
Scopey, fair gelding, effective 6 to 7f, best at 7f, acts on gd to hrd, best on g-f, and likes Musselburgh. Turf high 52 - 2nd of 8 getting 4lb from Lady of Windsor (26 Oct Musselburgh 7f gd RF 5190) - also 1st of 24 giving 17lb to E B Pearl (5 Aug Thirsk RF 3406).

**J Hetherton [5-42] Qualitair Holdings Ltd (from C E Brittain [0-5] Oct 1998).*

ENCYCLOPEDIA BHB 59f **RR 51f** 4365[5]
2 b f So Factual (USA) - Wakayi (Persian Bold) 9.3f **(66)**
Form - 505
Record 2000 - 1st:0 2nd:0 3rd:0 Ran:3
2000 Turf 0-3: (5f 3) (gd, g-f, frm)
Currently fair filly. Turf high 51 (began Aug).
**T D Easterby [0-3] Lady Halifax.*

ENDEAVOUR TO DO (USA) RR 3f 2766[8]
3 ch c Fly So Free (USA) - Shady Street (USA) (Shadeed (USA)) 8.2f **(70)**
Form - 8
Record 2000 - 1st:0 2nd:0 3rd:0 Ran:1
2000 Turf 0-1: (7f) (gd)
Very poor colt. (DEAD) **Miss Gay Kelleway [0-1] A P Griffin.*

ENDLESS HALL RR 126+f 2872[1]
4 b c Saddlers' Hall (IRE) 10.5f **(65)** - Endless Joy (Law Society (USA)) 9.9f **(70)**
Form - 5811
Record 2000 - 1st:2 2nd:0 3rd:0 Ran:4
Pre2000 - 1st:2 2nd:1 3rd:2 Ran:5
Win Prizemoney £153,790 *Total Prizemoney* £174,228

Wins							
*** 2000**	Jly	Ayr	(G-F)	G3	10f	126	<
*** 2000**	Jun	San Si	(G-F)	G1	12f	122+	
* 1999	Oct	San Si	(YLD)		12f	98	
* 1999	Jly	San Si	(G-F)	L	10f	97	

2000 Turf 2-4: (8f, 10f 1-2, 12f 1-1) (hvy 2, g-f 1-1, frm 1-1)
Top-class colt, effective 10 to 12f, acts on g-f to frm. Turf high 126 - 1st of 7 giving 7lb to Beat All (17 Jly Ayr RF 2872) - also 1st of 9 giving 3lb to Catella (18 Jun San Siro RF 2205a). Inconsistent. He improved when moved to Luca Cumani and developed into a high-class middle-distance performer on fast ground. He was impressive in the Gran Premio di Milano, although that was not a strong Group One, and followed up by taking a Group Three at Ayr in a desperate finish with Beat All.
**L M Cumani [4-7] Il Paralupo (from G Verricelli in ITY [0-2] Spt 1998).*

ENDLESS SUMMER BHB 100f **RR 114f** 4699[2]
2 b c Zafonic (USA) 9f **(83)** - Well Away (IRE) (Sadler's Wells (USA)) 10f **(76)**
Form - 1122
Record 2000 - 1st:2 2nd:2 3rd:0 Ran:4
Win Prizemoney £33,992 *Total Prizemoney* £98,612

Wins							
*** 2000**	Aug	Goodwo	(GD)	G2	6f	102+	<
*** 2000**	Jly	Newbur	(G-F)		6f	84++	

2000 Turf 2-4: (6f 2-4) (g-s, gd 1-1, g-f, frm 1-1)
Group-class colt. Turf high 114 (began Jly) - 2nd of 10 to Minardi (28 Spt Newmarket 6f g-f RF 4699). Successful in Goodwood's Richmond Stakes, he was beaten a long way by Bad As I Wanna Be in the Prix Morny when the soft ground may not have suited him. Ran a much better race in the Middle Park, only going down to Minardi. **J H M Gosden [2-4] K Abdulla.*

END OF STORY (IRE) BHB 36f50a **RR 32f 50a** 4192[11]
4 b g Doubletour (USA) 12f **(46)** - Baliana (CAN) (Riverman (USA)) 9.1f **(76)**
Form - 0000
Record 2000 - 1st:0 2nd:0 3rd:0 Ran:3
Pre2000 - 1st:0 2nd:0 3rd:0 Ran:8
Win Prizemoney £0 *Total Prizemoney* £223
2000 Turf 0-3: (7f 2, 14f) (gd, g-f 2)
Light-framed, very moderate gelding. Turf high 22. Becoming disappointing. **P Butler [0-6] P Butler (from R Hannon [0-7] Oct 1999).*

END OF THE DAY (IRE) BHB 58f70a **RR 71f 70a** 4559[19]
4 br g Night Shift (USA) 8.1f **(73)** - Huldine (Cure The Blues (USA)) 9.5f **(63)**
Form - 00
Record 2000 - 1st:0 2nd:0 3rd:0 Ran:1
Pre2000 - 1st:0 2nd:0 3rd:1 Ran:5
Win Prizemoney £0 *Total Prizemoney* £367
2000 Turf 0-1: (10f) (gd)
Above-average gelding, effective 8f, acts on sft.
**D Carroll [0-1] J J Devaney (from L Browne in IRE [0-5] Nov 1999).*

ENDORSEMENT BHB 91f **RR 103f** 3031[6]
4 b f Warning 8.1f **(77)** - Overdrive (Shirley Heights) 10.3f **(74)**
Form - 086
Record 2000 - 1st:0 2nd:0 3rd:0 Ran:3
Pre2000 - 1st:2 2nd:0 3rd:1 Ran:4
Win Prizemoney £39,801 *Total Prizemoney* £40,811

Wins							
* 1999	Jun	Ascot	(G-F)	G3	16.2f	98	<
* 1999	May	Thirsk	(G-S)		12f	63+	

2000 Turf 0-3: (12f 2, 20f) (gd, g-f 2)
Scopey, very useful filly, effective 16f, acts on g-f. Turf high 96. She put up a smashing performance for an inexperienced filly when winning the Queen's Vase at Royal Ascot in 1999, but showed little in a light campaign last season. Would probably benefit from a return to two miles. **H R A Cecil [2-7] Cliveden Stud.*

ENDYMION (IRE) BHB 55f **RR 57f** 5068[20]
3 ch f Paris House 5.9f **(64)** - Vaguely Jade (Corvaro (USA)) 9f **(53)**
Form - 000304600
Record 2000 - 1st:0 2nd:0 3rd:1 Ran:9
Pre2000 - 1st:0 2nd:0 3rd:2 Ran:8
Win Prizemoney £0 *Total Prizemoney* £2,096
2000 Turf 0-9: (5f 3, 6f 6) (g-s, g-f 3, frm 5)
Leggy, fair filly. Turf high 57. Unlucky at Kempton in August when unshipping his rider, he should get his head in front at three.
**Mrs P N Dutfield [0-17] Matt Tompkins.*

ENFILADE BHB 71f **RR 78f** 5137[3]
4 b g Deploy 11.4f **(67)** - Bargouzine (Hotfoot) 10.5f **(59)**
Form - 5816503
Record 2000 - 1st:1 2nd:0 3rd:1 Ran:7
Pre2000 - 1st:2 2nd:0 3rd:3 Ran:13
Win Prizemoney £16,423 *Total Prizemoney* £20,236

Wins							
*** 2000**	May	Haydoc	(SFT)	H	14f	71	76 <
* 1999	Jly	Haydoc	(G-S)	H	14f	72	75
* 1999	May	Cheste	(G-F)	H	12.3f	66	69

2000 Turf 1-7: (12f 2, 13f, 14f 1-4) (g-s 1-2, gd, g-f 3, frm)
Strong, above-average gelding, effective 11 to 14f, best at 14f, acts on g-s to frm, has worn blinkers, prefers tight tracks. Turf high 76 - 1st of 11 giving 21lb to Fletcher (27 May Haydock RF 1492). He improved as he has was stepped up in trip in 1999, and appreciated the return to 14 furlongs when winning at Haydock last season.
**B Hanbury [3-20] H Channon.*

Endless Summer basked in glory

ENGLAND'S LEGEND (FR) RR 109f 3351a[7]
3 b f Lure (USA) - Mystery Tune (IRE) (Commanche Run) 8.5f **(58)**
Form - 17
2000 Turf 1-2: (8f 1-2) (g-s, gd 1-1)
Currently Pattern-class filly. Turf high 109 (1st run) - 1st of 7 from Starine (17 May Saint-cloud RF 1445a). **A Fabre in FR [1-2].*

ENGLISH HARBOUR RR 75f 5219[2]
2 ch f Sabrehill (USA) 8.5f **(64)** - Water Woo (USA) (Tom Rolfe) 9.4f **(75)**
Form - 884222
Record 2000 - 1st:0 2nd:3 3rd:0 Ran:6
Win Prizemoney £0 *Total Prizemoney* £3,255
2000 Turf 0-6: (7f 2, 8f 2, 10f 2) (sft, g-s 2, gd 2, g-f)
Above-average filly, effective 8 to 10f, best at 10f, acts on sft to gd. Turf high 75 (began Aug) - 4th of 12 getting 5lb from Tiyoun (21 Spt Pontefract 8f gd RF 4557). **B W Hills [0-6] W J Gredley.*

EN GRISAILLE BHB 38f43a **RR 42f 43a** 4694[12]
4 gr f Mystiko (USA) 7.7f **(59)** - Hickleton Lady (IRE) **(60f 60a)** (Kala Shikari) 8.4f **(54)**
Form - 0700
Record 2000 - 1st:0 2nd:0 3rd:0 Ran:4
Pre2000 - 1st:2 2nd:0 3rd:0 Ran:11
Win Prizemoney £4,194 *Total Prizemoney* £4,194
Wins * 1999 Aug Yarmou (GD) C 10.1f 44
1998 Aug Folkes (G-F) S 6f 56 <
2000 Turf 0-3: (10f 3) (gd, g-f 2) 2000 AW 0-1: (10f) (Equi)
Scopey, moderate filly, effective 10f, acts on gd to g-f, favours tight tracks. Turf high 42 (1st run) - 7th of 15 getting 8lb from Sifat (31 May Yarmouth 10f g-f RF 1613).
**John Berry [1-9] H R Moszkowicz (from Sir Mark Prescott [1-6] Spt 1998).*

ENRICH (USA) RR 90f 4793a[3]
2 b f Dynaformer (USA) 12f **(82)** - Eternal Reve (USA) **(108f)** (Diesis) 9.3f **(69)**
Form - 13
2000 Turf 1-2: (6f 1-1, 7f) (sft, gd 1-1)
Currently useful filly. Turf high 90 (began Spt) - 3rd of 12 to Imagine (30 Spt Curragh 7f sft RF 4793a) - also 1st of 16 getting 5lb from Tiger Trap (2 Spt Cork RF 4245a).
**J Oxx in IRE [1-2] Sheikh Mohammed.*

ENTAIL (USA) BHB 75f **RR 71f** 4678[3]
3 b br f Riverman (USA) 9.7f **(78)** - Estala **(87f)** (Be My Guest (USA)) 9.3f **(67)**
Form - 5343
Record 2000 - 1st:0 2nd:0 3rd:2 Ran:4
Pre2000 - 1st:0 2nd:0 3rd:1 Ran:1
Win Prizemoney £0 *Total Prizemoney* £2,241
2000 Turf 0-4: (7f 2, 8f 2) (g-s, g-f 2, frm)
Neat, above-average filly. Turf high 69.
**J H M Gosden [0-5] K Abdulla.*

ENTHUSED (USA) BHB 100f **RR 103+f** 4644[6]
2 b f Seeking the Gold (USA) 7.4f **(80)** - Magic of Life (USA) (Seattle Slew (USA)) 9.4f **(76)**
Form - 12116
Record 2000 - 1st:3 2nd:1 3rd:0 Ran:5
Win Prizemoney £75,314 *Total Prizemoney* £88,264
Wins * **2000** Aug York (GD) G2 6f 103+ <
* **2000** Jly Ascot (G-F) G3 6f 103+ <
* **2000** Jun Newmar (G-F) 6f 80+
2000 Turf 3-5: (6f 3-5) (gd 2-3, g-f 1-2)
Very useful filly. Turf high 103 (began Jun) - 1st of 7 giving 3lb to Khulan (24 Aug York RF 3933) - also 1st of 9 from Autumnal (29 Jly Ascot RF 3201). Showed a nice attitude on her Newmarket debut and ran Dora Carrington to half a length in the Cherry Hinton there next time. Looked a very smart filly when winning the Princess Margaret at Ascot and was especially impressive in the Lowther. Finished sixth to stablemate Regal Rose in the Cheveley Park, when the yielding ground was against her.
**Sir Michael Stoute [3-5] Niarchos Family.*

ENTISAR RR 99f 1397[1]
3 b br c Nashwan (USA) 10.3f **(79)** - Fawaayid (USA) (Vaguely Noble) 10.1f **(72)**
Form - 31
Record 2000 - 1st:1 2nd:0 3rd:1 Ran:2
Win Prizemoney £4,192 *Total Prizemoney* £7,223
Wins * **2000** May Goodwo (GD) 12f 84 <
2000 Turf 1-2: (10f, 12f 1-1) (g-s 1-1, g-f)
Well made, currently very useful colt. Turf high 99. Showed plenty of ability in a light campaign last season, and looks capable of better. **S bin Suroor [1-2] Godolphin.*

ENTITY BHB 72f **RR 74+f** 4767[13]
3 ch g Rudimentary (USA) 8.2f **(66)** - Desert Ditty (Green Desert (USA)) 8.6f **(78)**
Form - 7003R775771 2110
Record 2000 - 1st:3 2nd:1 3rd:1 Ran:15
Pre2000 - 1st:0 2nd:0 3rd:0 Ran:5
Win Prizemoney £11,043 *Total Prizemoney* £14,099
Wins * **2000** Spt Beverl (HVY) H 8.5f 63 74+ <
* **2000** Spt Hamilt (SFT) H 9.2f 60 61+
* **2000** Aug Hamilt (SFT) H 8.3f 54 56
2000 Turf 3-15: (7f 5, 8f 2-6, 9f 1-1, 10f 3) (g-s 2-4, gd 1-4, frm 7)
Lengthy, above-average gelding, effective 8 to 10f, acts on g-s to frm, has worn blinkers, prefers right handed tracks, prefers tight tracks. Turf high 74 - 1st of 16 giving 8lb to Rudetski (19 Spt Beverley RF 4498). Showed ability on a couple of occasions at two without being given a hard time. Achieved little on fast ground earlier in the season, but has been a revelation since encountering very soft ground, winning twice at Hamilton and once at Beverley. Obviously very useful when conditions are right.
**T D Barron [3-20] Mrs J Hazell.*

ENTROPY BHB 37a **RR 52f** 3954[13]
4 b f Brief Truce (USA) 9.1f **(73)** - Distant Isle (IRE) (Bluebird (USA)) 7.5f **(69)**
Form - 05000230510360
Record 2000 - 1st:1 2nd:1 3rd:2 Ran:11
Pre2000 - 1st:1 2nd:1 3rd:3 Ran:19
Win Prizemoney £5,642 *Total Prizemoney* £10,381
Wins * **2000** Jly Bath (FRM) CH 8f 43 47+
1998 Aug Bath (FRM) H 5.7f 73 73+ <
2000 Turf 1-9: (6f, 7f 3, 8f 1-5) (gd, g-f 2, frm 1-3, hrd 3) 2000 AW 0-2: (7f, 8f) (Equi 2)
Light-framed, fair filly. Turf high 52. AW high 36.
**B A Pearce [1-14] T M J Keep (from R Hannon [1-16] Spt 1999).*

ENVY (IRE) RR 150[13]
4 gr f Paris House 5.9f **(64)** - Rhett's Choice (Beveled (USA)) 9f **(59)**
Form - 000
Record 2000 - 1st:0 2nd:0 3rd:0 Ran:2
Pre2000 - 1st:0 2nd:0 3rd:0 Ran:1
2000 AW 0-2: (6f 2) (Fibr 2)
Very poor filly. AW high 3. **J G Given [0-4] Thegreenwith Partnership.*

ENZELI (IRE) RR 120f 4848a[5]
5 b h Kahyasi 12.9f **(74)** - Ebaziya (IRE) (Darshaan) 9.9f **(84)**
Form - 2815
2000 Turf 1-4: (14f, 18f 1-1, 20f 2) (gd 2, g-f, frm 1-1)
Very high-class colt, effective 18 to 20f, best at 20f, acts on gd to frm, has worn blinkers. Turf high 120 - 1st of 9 giving 7lb to Churlish Charm (7 Spt Doncaster RF 4281). Consistent. A half-brother to Ebadiyla, he won a highly competitive renewal of the Ascot Gold Cup in 1999. He was only just beaten in a Leopardstown Listed event on his return, but was well beaten in the Gold Cup. He bounced back to form to take the Doncaster Cup but ran poorly in the Prix du Cadran and was well below his best in the Melourne Cup. **J Oxx in IRE [6-13].*

EPERNAY BHB 64f69a **RR 67f 69a** 1609[14]
4 b f Lion Cavern (USA) 7.5f **(74)** - Decant **(61f)** (Rousillon (USA)) 8.2f **(74)**
Form - 1570
Record 2000 - 1st:1 2nd:0 3rd:0 Ran:4
Pre2000 - 1st:0 2nd:1 3rd:0 Ran:2
Win Prizemoney £2,651 *Total Prizemoney* £3,377
Wins * **2000** *Feb Southw (STD)* *8f* 74+ <
2000 Turf 0-2: (7f, 8f) (gd 2) 2000 AW 1-2: (8f 1-2) (Fibr 1-2)
Light-framed, above-average filly, effective 8f, acted on sft - acted on Fibr. Turf high 36. AW high 74 (1st run) - 1st of 10 getting 5lb from Kustom Kit Kevin (4 Feb Southwell RF 0217). (DEAD)
**J R Fanshawe [1-6] Mrs E Fanshawe.*

EPITRE (FR) RR 112f 4840a[1]
3 b c Common Grounds 8.1f **(66)** - Epistolienne (Law Society (USA))

9.9f **(70)**
Form - 42111
2000 Turf 3-5: (11f, 13f 1-2, 15f 2-2) (sft 1-1, gd 2-4)
Group-class colt. Turf high 112 - 1st of 7 from Riddlesdown (30 Spt Longchamp RF 4840a) - also 1st of 5 from Mister Kick (3 Spt Longchamp RF 4291a). Developed into a promising young stayer, winning two good races at Longchamp. Likely to be brought back to middle distances next year, he probably has more improvement in him. **A Fabre in FR [3-5] Baron E de Rothschild.*

EPONA RR 32f 1899[14]

3 ch f Inchinor 8.9f **(64)** - Zelda (USA) (Sharpen Up) 8.3f **(67)**
Form - 0600
Record 2000 - 1st:0 2nd:0 3rd:0 Ran:2
Pre2000 - 1st:0 2nd:0 3rd:0 Ran:3
2000 Turf 0-2: (6f, 8f) (g-f, frm)
Lengthy, very moderate filly.
**T D Easterby [0-5] Keith Wills & Middleham Park Racing.*

EPWORTH BHB 34f36a RR 35f 36a 228[11]

6 b m Unfuwain (USA) 11.4f **(74)** - Positive Attitude (Red Sunset) 8.2f **(63)**
Form - 0
Record 2000 - 1st:0 2nd:0 3rd:0 Ran:1
Pre2000 - 1st:0 2nd:4 3rd:2 Ran:23
Win Prizemoney £0 *Total Prizemoney* £6,725
2000 AW 0-1. (12f) (Fibr)
Very moderate mare, has worn blinkers.
**L J Barratt [0-14] Ray Bailey (from J A Glover [0-9] Oct 1997).*

EQUAL BALANCE BHB 46f RR 31f 5010[3]

2 ch c Pivotal - Thatcher's Era (IRE) **(63f 53a)** (Never so Bold) 6.3f **(66)**
Form - 003
Record 2000 - 1st:0 2nd:0 3rd:1 Ran:3
Win Prizemoney £0 *Total Prizemoney* £281
2000 Turf 0-2: (7f, 8f) (gd, g-f) 2000 AW 0-1: (7f) (Fibr)
Currently moderate colt, has worn blinkers. Turf high 31 (began Spt). **V Soane [0-3] Michael Hancock.*

EQUERRY (USA) RR 98f 4415a[1]

2 br c St Jovite (USA) 11.8f **(75)** - Colour Chart (USA) (Mr Prospector (USA)) 8.8f **(78)**
Form - 11
2000 Turf 2-2: (8f 2-2) (gd 1-1, g-f 1-1)
Currently very useful colt. Turf high 98 (1st run) (began Aug) - 1st of 10 from Pares (19 Aug Deauville RF 3944a). Twice a Pattern winner over a mile in France last season, he looks likely to make up into a nice three-year-old, although his pedigree suggests there is doubt about him staying much further.
**A Fabre in FR [2-2] Sheikh Mohammed.*

EREBUS (IRE) BHB 66f RR 67f 2766[9]

3 b c Desert Style (IRE) - Almost A Lady (IRE) (Entitled)
Form - 06340
Record 2000 - 1st:0 2nd:0 3rd:1 Ran:5
Win Prizemoney £0 *Total Prizemoney* £267
2000 Turf 0-5: (7f, 8f 2, 9f, 10f) (hvy, gd 2, frm 2)
Average colt. Turf high 67 - 3rd of 9 to Carens Hero (22 May Bath 8f frm RF 1358). Unraced at two, he has shown some ability but did not seem to stay when tried over ten furlongs in soft ground. Looks to have improvement in him.
**M H Tompkins [0-5] Mrs Janis MacPherson.*

ERIN ANAM CARA (IRE) BHB 36f30a RR 40f 30a 4877[15]

3 ch f Exit To Nowhere (USA) 8.7f **(77)** - Honey Heather (IRE) (Kris) 9.5f **(73)**
Form - 7870530
Record 2000 - 1st:0 2nd:0 3rd:1 Ran:7
Pre2000 - 1st:0 2nd:0 3rd:1 Ran:7
Win Prizemoney £0 *Total Prizemoney* £835
2000 Turf 0-6: (8f 2, 10f 2, 12f 2) (g-s, gd, g-f, frm 3) 2000 AW 0-1: (8f) (Fibr)
Moderate filly, effective 7 to 8f, acts on gd to frm, has worn blinkers. Turf high 40.
**D J S Cosgrove [0-15] Prayer And A Song Syndicate.*

ERITH'S CHILL WIND DI IB 40f12a RR 49f 42a 5288a[12]

4 b f Be My Chief (USA) 10.2f **(62)** - William's Bird (USA) (Master Willie) 7f **(70)**
Form - 44430
Record 2000 - 1st:0 2nd:0 3rd:1 Ran:3
Pre2000 - 1st:1 2nd:2 3rd:2 Ran:14
Win Prizemoney £3,308 *Total Prizemoney* £5,779
Wins 1999 Aug Bright (G-F) H 10f 43 49 <
2000 Turf 0-1: (9f) (hvy) 2000 AW 0-2: (9f, 12f) (Equi, Fibr)
Workmanlike, moderate filly, effective 9 to 10f, best at 10f, acts on g-s to hrd - acts on AW, best on frm, has worn blinkers, likes left handed tracks, prefers tight tracks, excels at Brighton. AW high 43 (1st run) - 4th of 13 getting 5lb from Areish (11 Jan Wolverhampton 9f Fibr RF 0066).
**T Carmody in IRE [0-1] Mark Barrett (from G L Moore [1-12] Jan 2000).*

ERRACHT BHB 78f73a RR 75+f 73a 4780[2]

2 gr f Emarati (USA) 6.6f **(63)** - Port Na Blath (On Your Mark) 7.7f **(58)**
Form - 2162
Record 2000 - 1st:1 2nd:2 3rd:0 Ran:4
Win Prizemoney £2,408 *Total Prizemoney* £3,870
Wins * **2000** Aug Beverl (GD) 5f 75+ <
2000 Turf 1-3: (5f 1-2, 6f) (sft, gd 1-1, g-f) 2000 AW 0-1: (6f) (Fibr)
Above-average filly. Turf high 75 - 1st of 16 giving 3lb to Peyto Princess (1 Aug Beverley RF 3272). (1st run) - 2nd of 11 getting 8lb from Clarion (3 Oct Wolverhampton 6f Fibr RF 4780).
**P C Haslam [1-4] Lord Bolton.*

ERRO CODIGO BHB 53f51a RR 52f 51a 11[6]

5 b g Formidable (USA) 7.8f **(60)** - Home Wrecker (DEN) (Affiliation Order (USA)) 6f **(70)**
Form - 00346
Record 2000 - 1st:0 2nd:0 3rd:0 Ran:1
Pre2000 - 1st:2 2nd:4 3rd:5 Ran:31
Win Prizemoney £7,193 *Total Prizemoney* £15,056
Wins * 1999 Oct Lingfi (G-F) H 6f 49 52
* 1998 *Feb Southw (STD) 6f 62* <
2000 AW 0-1: (6f) (Fibr)
Fair gelding, effective 6f, acts on gd, has worn blinkers. Inconsistent.
**S E Kettlewell [2-25] D Neale (from Mrs J R Ramsden [0-7] Aug 1997).*

ERTLON BHB 50f46a RR 45f 46a 4811[9]

10 b g Shareef Dancer (USA) 10.1f **(67)** - Sharpina (Sharpen Up) 8.3f **(67)**
Form - 0007603551200
Record 2000 - 1st:1 2nd:1 3rd:1 Ran:13
Pre2000 - 1st:5 2nd:10 3rd:11 Ran:82
Win Prizemoney £24,216 *Total Prizemoney* £50,269
Wins * **2000** Aug Bright (FRM) C 8f 43
* 1997 *Mar Lingfi (STD) C 7f 76*
2000 Turf 1-11: (7f 3, 8f 1-4, 10f 3, 11f) (g-s, gd 4, g-f 3, frm 1-2, hrd)
2000 AW 0-2: (8f, 10f) (Equi 2)
Moderate gelding, effective 10f, - acts on Equi, has worn blinkers, likes left handed tracks, likes tight tracks. Turf high 45. AW high 17. **C E Brittain [6-95] C E Brittain.*

ERUPT BHB 51f38a RR 56f 38a 4492[7]

7 b g Beveled (USA) 6.9f **(64)** - Sparklingsovereign (Sparkler)
Form - 7628421130000407
Record 2000 - 1st:2 2nd:2 3rd:1 Ran:14
Pre2000 - 1st:3 2nd:5 3rd:1 Ran:49
Win Prizemoney £14,545 *Total Prizemoney* £22,531
Wins **2000** May Southw (HVY) C 7f 55
2000 May Mussel (FRM) H 7.1f 50 52
1999 Spt Newcas (SFT) H 8f 47 50
1998 May Mussel (GD) H 7.1f 56 62
2000 Turf 2-12: (6f, 7f 2-8, 8f, 10f, 11f) (gd 1-4, g-f 2, frm 1-5, hrd) 2000 AW 0-2: (8f 2) (Fibr 2)
Fair gelding, effective 7 to 8f, best at 7f, acts on gd to frm - acts on Fibr, best on gd, has worn blinkers, likes right handed tracks, and excels at Musselburgh. Turf high 56 - also 1st of 12 giving 17lb to Maydoro (31 May Southwell RF 1599). AW high 38.
**Miss S J Wilton [0-8] John Pointon and Sons (from M Brittain [4-33] May 2000).*

ESCALADE BHB 60f **RR 63f** 2072[12]
3 b g Green Desert (USA) 7.8f **(78)** - Sans Escale (USA) (Diesis) 9.3f **(69)**
Form - 0
Record 2000 - 1st:0 2nd:0 3rd:0 Ran:1
Pre2000 - 1st:0 2nd:0 3rd:1 Ran:5
Win Prizemoney £0 *Total Prizemoney* £435
2000 Turf 0-1: (7f) (hrd)
Scopey, average gelding, effective 7f, acts on gd.
**M A Jarvis [0-6] Mohammed Bin Hendi.*

ESHER COMMON (IRE) RR 80+f 4159[1]
2 b c Common Grounds 8.1f **(66)** - Alsahah (IRE) **(61f)** (Unfuwain (USA))
Form - 51
Record 2000 - 1st:1 2nd:0 3rd:0 Ran:2
Win Prizemoney £3,991 *Total Prizemoney* £3,991
Wins * 2000 Spt Haydoc (HVY) 7.1f 80+ <
2000 Turf 1-2: (7f 1-2) (sft 1-1, frm)
Currently decent colt. Turf high 80 (began Aug) - 1st of 13 from Come On Pekan (2 Spt Haydock RF 4159).
**T G Mills [1-2] David Archer.*

ESHTIAAL (USA) BHB 55f **RR 62f** 168[9]
6 b br h Riverman (USA) 9.7f **(78)** - Lady Cutlass (USA) (Cutlass (USA)) 8.5f **(76)**
Form - 3240
Record 2000 - 1st:0 2nd:0 3rd:0 Ran:1
Pre2000 - 1st:4 2nd:2 3rd:4 Ran:15
Win Prizemoney £19,190 *Total Prizemoney* £22,434
Wins 1997 Spt Pontef (G-F) H 10f 94 99 <
1997 Aug Beverl (G-S) H 9.9f 84 94
1997 Aug Haydoc (G-F) H 10.5f 84 94
1997 Jly Ayr (G-F) 10f 72+
2000 AW 0-1: (12f) (Fibr)
Average horse, mostly wore blinkers. (DEAD)
**G L Moore [1-11] Graham Parker (from J L Dunlop [4-9] May 1998).*

ESPADA (IRE) RR 93f 4732[15]
4 b c Mukaddamah (USA) 7.6f **(74)** - Folk Song (CAN) (The Minstrel (CAN)) 10f **(72)**
Form - 62100800
Record 2000 - 1st:1 2nd:1 3rd:0 Ran:8
Pre2000 - 1st:3 2nd:3 3rd:0 Ran:13
Win Prizemoney £45,042 *Total Prizemoney* £56,412
Wins * 2000 May Kempto (G-S) H 8f 85 93 <
1999 Spt Ayr (G-S) H 7f 83 84
1999 May Thirsk (G-F) 7f 80
1998 Aug Ripon (G-F) 6f 79
2000 Turf 1-8: (7f, 8f 1-7) (sft, g-s 1-1, gd 5, g-f)
Useful colt, effective 7 to 8f, best at 8f, acts on sft to gd, has worn blinkers, likes left handed tracks. Turf high 93 - 1st of 17 getting 17lb from Pulau Tioman (1 May Kempton RF 0941). Scored twice over seven furlongs in 1999 and finished on the heels of the principals in the Lincoln on his return. Finished well to be a close second to Pulau Tioman in the Rosebery over a mile at Kempton, but reversed the form with the winner in a valuable event over the same course and distance next time. He failed to run up to that form afterwards though.
**M H Tompkins [1-8] Mrs Janis MacPherson (from P Calver [3-13] Oct 1999).*

ESPANA RR 67f 5004[14]
2 gr f Hernando (FR) - Pamela Peach (Habitat) 9.4f **(70)**
Form - 737520
Record 2000 - 1st:0 2nd:1 3rd:1 Ran:6
Win Prizemoney £0 *Total Prizemoney* £1,496
2000 Turf 0-6: (6f 3, 8f 3) (g-s, gd 2, g-f 2, frm)
Average filly, effective 8f, acts on gd. Turf high 67 (began Jly) - 2nd of 13 giving 3lb to Cynara (21 Spt Pontefract 8f gd RF 4555).
**B W Hills [0-6] The Hon Mrs J M Corbett & C Wright.*

ESPERE D'OR BHB 25f34a **RR 22f 34a** 3250[18]
3 b c Golden Heights 7.1f **(50)** - Drummer's Dream (IRE) **(9f 36a)** (Drumalis) 12f **(54)**
Form - 00005000600000
Record 2000 - 1st:0 2nd:0 3rd:0 Ran:13
Pre2000 - 1st:0 2nd:0 3rd:0 Ran:1
2000 Turf 0-8: (7f 4, 8f, 10f, 11f, 14f) (hvy, gd, g-f, frm 5) 2000 AW 0-5: (6f 2, 8f, 9f 2) (Fibr 5)
Neat, very moderate colt. Turf high 22. AW high 35.
**T Wall [0-14] Snax Catering Services Ltd.*

ESPERTO BHB 35f40a **RR 42f 40a** 5077[9]
7 b g Risk Me (FR) 8f **(53)** - Astrid Gilberto (Runnett) 7f **(59)**
Form - 80061044070
Record 2000 - 1st:1 2nd:0 3rd:0 Ran:11
Pre2000 - 1st:2 2nd:4 3rd:3 Ran:15
Win Prizemoney £6,095 *Total Prizemoney* £9,528
Wins * 2000 May Leices (SFT) SH 10f 37 42
* 1997 May Nottin (GD) S 10f 53 <
* 1996 Apr Nottin (GD) SH 10f 40 44
2000 Turf 1-10: (8f, 9f, 10f 1-6, 11f 2) (g-s 2, gd 1-3, g-f 3, frm 2) 2000 AW 0-1: (9f) (Fibr)
Moderate gelding, effective 10 to 11f, best at 10f, acts on gd to frm. Turf high 42 - 4th of 11 giving 16lb to Titus Bramble (19 Jly Yarmouth 10f g-f RF 2946) - also 1st of 17 giving 5lb to Lunar Lord (29 May Leicester RF 1522). Inconsistent.
**J Pearce [3-26] Mrs Anne Holman-Chappell.*

ESSENCE BHB 38f45a **RR 12f 45a** 4215[18]
2 b f Be My Chief (USA) 10.2f **(62)** - Shamaka **(57df 41a)** (Kris) 9.5f **(73)**
Form - 0860
Record 2000 - 1st:0 2nd:0 3rd:0 Ran:4
2000 Turf 0-2: (6f, 8f) (frm, hrd) 2000 AW 0-2: (7f 2) (Fibr 2)
Very moderate filly. Turf high 12. AW high 39 (began Jly).
**M J Polglase [0-4] Nilesh Unadkat.*

ESSIE BHB 52f48a **RR 48f 48a** 1703[17]
3 b f Ezzoud (IRE) - Safari Park (Absalom) 7.2f **(58)**
Form - 0
Record 2000 - 1st:0 2nd:0 3rd:0 Ran:1
Pre2000 - 1st:0 2nd:1 3rd:0 Ran:5
Win Prizemoney £0 *Total Prizemoney* £575
2000 Turf 0-1: (11f) (g-s)
Light-framed, moderate filly, effective 6f, acts on g-f, often wears blinkers.
**H J Collingridge [0-1] Ms D A Stevens (from C E Brittain [0-5] Spt 1999).*

ESTABELLA (IRE) BHB 55f58a **RR 50f 58a** 4583[1]
3 ch f Mujtahid (USA) 7.4f **(69)** - Lady In Green (Shareef Dancer (USA)) 9.9f **(73)**
Form - 2130555401
Record 2000 - 1st:2 2nd:1 3rd:1 Ran:10
Pre2000 - 1st:0 2nd:0 3rd:0 Ran:4
Win Prizemoney £5,705 *Total Prizemoney* £6,760
Wins * 2000 *Spt Lingfi (STD) H 16f 51 62+*
* 2000 Apr Beverl (HVY) H 12f 55 64 <
2000 Turf 1-6: (10f 2, 11f, 12f 1-3) (g-s 1-1, gd 3, g-f, frm) 2000 AW 1-4: (12f 3, 16f 1-1) (Equi 1-3, Fibr)
Scopey, average filly, effective 12 to 16f, best at 12f, acts on g-s to gd - acts on AW, has worn blinkers, prefers tight tracks. Turf high 64 - 1st of 12 getting 5lb from Windmill Lane (19 Apr Beverley RF 0793). AW high 62 - 1st of 14 giving 11lb to Ptah (22 Spt Lingfield RF 4583).
**S P C Woods [2-14] Ben Allen & Mrs Catherine Hine.*

ESTABLISHED BHB 34a **RR 52f** 4328[3]
3 b g Not in Doubt (USA) - Copper Trader (Faustus (USA)) 10f **(58)**
Form - 85035501313
Record 2000 - 1st:2 2nd:0 3rd:3 Ran:11
Pre2000 - 1st:0 2nd:0 3rd:0 Ran:7
Win Prizemoney £5,867 *Total Prizemoney* £6,881
Wins * 2000 Aug Lingfi (G-F) H 16f 43 49 <
* 2000 Aug Nottin (G-F) H 16f 34 44
2000 Turf 2-9: (11f, 12f 3, 14f, 16f 2-4) (g-s, g-f 1-5, frm 1-3) 2000 AW 0-2: (12f, 13f) (Equi, Fibr)
Fair gelding, has worn blinkers, likes left handed tracks, likes tight tracks. Turf high 52. AW high 30.
**J R Best [2-15] Teapot Lane Partnership (from H Candy [0-3] Jly 1999).*

ESTABLISHMENT BHB 60f62a **RR 68f 62a** 3897[6]
3 b g Muhtarram (USA) - Uncharted Waters **(57f 43a)** (Celestial Storm (USA))
Form - 640215666
Record 2000 - 1st:1 2nd:1 3rd:0 Ran:9
Pre2000 - 1st:0 2nd:0 3rd:0 Ran:3
Win Prizemoney £2,927 *Total Prizemoney* £3,816
Wins * **2000** Jun Bright (FRM) H 11.9f 65 68 <
2000 Turf 1-7: (8f, 10f 2, 11f, 12f 1-3) (gd 2, frm 1-4, hrd) 2000 AW 0-2: (10f, 12f) (Equi 2)
Workmanlike, above-average gelding, effective 10 to 12f, acts on frm - acts on Equi, has worn blinkers, prefers left handed tracks, favours tight tracks. Turf high 68 - also 1st of 7 giving 11lb to Jack Dawson (15 Jun Brighton RF 1979). AW high 72 (1st run) - 2nd of 8 getting 2lb from Rich Vein (27 May Lingfield 10f Equi RF 1508). Becoming disappointing **C A Cyzer [1-12] R M Cyzer.*

ESTACADO (IRE) BHB 42f **RR 42f** 5002[11]
4 b f Dolphin Street (FR) - Raubritter (Levmoss) 11.4f **(66)**
Form - 50
Record 2000 - 1st:0 2nd:0 3rd:0 Ran:2
Pre2000 - 1st:0 2nd:0 3rd:0 Ran:6
Win Prizemoney £0 *Total Prizemoney* £75
2000 Turf 0-2: (16f, 18f) (g-s 2)
Neat, moderate filly, has worn blinkers. Turf high 38 (began Spt). Becoming disappointing.
**J W Mullins [3-14] Woodford Valley Racing (from B Gubby [0-6] Jly 1999).*

ESTIHAN (USA) RR 65f 4222[6]
2 b f Silver Hawk (USA) 11.2f **(85)** - Dance Image (IRE) (Sadler's Wells (USA)) 10f **(76)**
Form - 6
Record 2000 - 1st:0 2nd:0 3rd:0 Ran:1
2000 Turf 0-1: (7f) (frm)
Currently average filly. **C E Brittain [0-1] Saeed Manana.*

ESTOPPED (IRE) BHB 26f20a **RR 40f 20a** 9[14]
5 b g Case Law 6f **(64)** - Action Belle (Auction Ring (USA)) 8.6f **(65)**
Form - 000
Record 2000 - 1st:0 2nd:0 3rd:0 Ran:1
Pre2000 - 1st:0 2nd:0 3rd:2 Ran:20
Win Prizemoney £0 *Total Prizemoney* £1,190
2000 AW 0-1: (11f) (Fibr)
Moderate gelding, has worn blinkers. Becoming disappointing.
**M Quinn [0-17] Mrs S G Davies (from M R Channon [0-5] Jly 1997).*

ESTUARY (USA) RR 38f 2224[15]
5 ch g Riverman (USA) 9.7f **(78)** - Ocean Ballad (Grundy) 10.3f **(65)**
Form - 2300
Record 2000 - 1st:0 2nd:1 3rd:1 Ran:4
Win Prizemoney £0 *Total Prizemoney* £1,282
2000 Turf 0-2: (8f, 10f) (gd, frm) 2000 AW 0-2: (10f, 12f) (Equi 2)
Average gelding. Turf high 38. AW high 65 (1st run) - 2nd of 11 giving 24lb to Dont Worry Bout Me (5 Feb Lingfield 12f Equi RF 0221). **Mrs A E Johnson [0-5] D W Haggie.*

ESYOUEFFCEE (IRE) BHB 99f **RR 92f** 5241[2]
2 b f Alzao (USA) 9.8f **(73)** - Familiar (USA) (Diesis) 9.3f **(69)**
Form - 2182
Record 2000 - 1st:1 2nd:2 3rd:0 Ran:4
Win Prizemoney £3,705 *Total Prizemoney* £9,659
Wins * **2000** Aug Beverl (FRM) 7.5f 82++ <
2000 Turf 1-4: (7f 1-2, 8f 2) (g-s, g-f, frm 1-2)
Useful filly. Turf high 92 (began Aug) - 2nd of 9 to La Vita E Bella (28 Oct Newmarket 8f g-s RF 5241). Well beaten in a Group Three after winning her maiden in good style. She is a rather keen sort. **M W Easterby [1-4] M P Burke.*

ETBASH (RUS) RR 95f 4292a[2]
3 b c
Form - 12
2000 Turf 1-2: (8f 1-1, 15f) (hvy, gd 1-1)
Currently very useful colt. Turf high 95 (1st run) - 1st of 10 from Pamir (7 May Dielsdorf RF 1155a). Winner of the Swiss equivalent of the 2000 Guineas, and runner up in the Swiss St Leger. **in SWI [0-2] .*

ETERNAL SPRING (IRE) BHB 103f **RR 103f** 1193[5]
3 b c Persian Bold 10f **(69)** - Emerald Waters (Kings Lake (USA)) 10.8f **(67)**
Form - 15
Record 2000 - 1st:1 2nd:0 3rd:0 Ran:2
Pre2000 - 1st:1 2nd:2 3rd:1 Ran:4
Win Prizemoney £16,587 *Total Prizemoney* £21,135
Wins * **2000** Apr Epsom (HVY) 10.1f 103 <
* 1999 Aug Beverl (GD) 7.5f 80+
2000 Turf 1-2: (10f 1-1, 11f) (sft 1-1, g-s)
Very useful colt, effective 10f, acts on sft. Turf high 103 (1st run) - 1st of 5 from Modish (26 Apr Epsom RF 0878). He ploughed through the mud in good style to win Epsom's Blue Riband Trial on his return but was found wanting in the Lingfield Derby trial next time and did not resurface. **E A L Dunlop [2-0] Paul & Jenny Green.*

ETHMAAR (USA) BHB 94f **RR 97f** 4936[6]
3 b c Silver Hawk (USA) 11.2f **(85)** - Minifah (USA) (Nureyev (USA)) 8.7f **(78)**
Form - 4506
Record 2000 - 1st:0 2nd:0 3rd:0 Ran:4
Pre2000 - 1st:1 2nd:0 3rd:1 Ran:2
Win Prizemoney £9,269 *Total Prizemoney* £12,031
Wins * 1999 Spt Newbur (G-F) 8f 99+ <
2000 Turf 0-4: (10f 2, 12f 2) (gd 2, g-f, frm)
Scopey, very useful colt, effective 0 to 12f, acts on frm. Turf high 97 - 5th of 15 giving 5lb to Takwin (9 Spt Doncaster 12f frm RF 4308). After a fair effort behind Beat Hollow in a Newmarket Listed event on his return, he competed in handicaps for the remainder of a light campaign, giving the impression that he was best suited by fast ground. **M P Tregoning [1-6] Hamdan Al Maktoum.*

ETIENNE LADY (IRE) BHB 78f **RR 75f** 3594[1]
3 gr f Imperial Frontier (USA) 7f **(65)** - Petula **(94f)** (Petong) 6.6f **(58)**
Form - 61
Record 2000 - 1st:1 2nd:0 3rd:0 Ran:2
Win Prizemoney £4,065 *Total Prizemoney* £4,065
Wins * **2000** Aug Newmar (G-F) 6f 75 <
2000 Turf 1-2: (6f 1-2) (gd, frm 1-1)
Light-framed, currently above-average filly. Turf high 75 - 1st of 6 from Double Platinum (12 Aug Newmarket RF 3594).
**J H M Gosden [1-2] Owen Promotions Ltd.*

ETISALAT (IRE) BHB 53f51a **RR 63f 51a** 2687[12]
5 b g Lahib (USA) 8f **(69)** - Sweet Repose (High Top) 10.2f **(67)**
Form - 103126311130000
Record 2000 - 1st:4 2nd:1 3rd:3 Ran:13
Pre2000 - 1st:2 2nd:1 3rd:0 Ran:14
Win Prizemoney £15,687 *Total Prizemoney* £17,866
Wins * **2000** May Carlis (FRM) H 9.3f 46 58
* **2000** May Hamilt (G-F) H 8.3f 46 62 <
* **2000** May Mussel (FRM) H 7.1f 46 48
* **2000** *Jan Wolver (STD) H 9.4f 49 56*
* 1999 *Nov Lingfi (STD) H 10f 42 49*
* 1999 Jun Yarmou (G-F) SH 8f 40 50+
2000 Turf 3-8: (7f 1-1, 8f 1-6, 9f 1-1) (gd, g-f 2-3, frm 1-3, hrd) 2000 AW 1-5: (8f 2, 9f 1-3) (Fibr 1-5)
Average gelding, effective 8 to 9f, best at 8f, acts on g-f - acts on Fibr, prefers tight tracks, excels at Hamilton, does well at Wolverhampton. Turf high 63 - 3rd of 10 giving 14lb to Adobe (19 May Hamilton 8f g-f RF 1298) - also 1st of 15 getting 1lb from Gablesea (7 May Hamilton RF 1071). AW high 56 - 3rd of 11 giving 22lb to Wellcome Inn (28 Mar Wolverhampton 9f Fibr RF 0531) - also 1st of 13 giving 2lb to Perchancer (27 Jan Wolverhampton RF 0166). Completed a quickfire hat-trick in May, but has been held by the handicapper since.
**J Pearce [6-24] Mrs E M Clarke (from R W Armstrong [0-3] Oct 1998).*

EUCALYPTUS (IRE) RR 54f 1170[11]
3 ch c Mujtahid (USA) 7.4f **(69)** - Imprecise **(49f)** (Polish Precedent (USA)) 10.2f **(60)**
Form - 0
Record 2000 - 1st:0 2nd:0 3rd:0 Ran:1
2000 Turf 0-1: (7f) (gd)
Currently fair colt. **S Dow [0-1] G Steinberg.*

EURO DANDY BHB 40f **RR 52f** 146[8]
3 b g Rambo Dancer (CAN) 8.4f **(59)** - Kagram Queen **(54df)** (Prince Ragusa)
Form - 8
Record 2000 - 1st:0 2nd:0 3rd:0 Ran:1
Pre2000 - 1st:0 2nd:0 3rd:0 Ran:4
2000 AW 0-1: (8f) (Fibr)
Strong, fair gelding. **D Nicholls [0-5] W G Swiers.*

EURO IMPORT BHB 39f **RR 32f** 1887[8]
2 ch g Imp Society (USA) 7.1f **(63)** - Upper Club (IRE) **(14f 35a)** (Taufan (USA)) 7f **(57)**
Form - 008
Record 2000 - 1st:0 2nd:0 3rd:0 Ran:3
2000 Turf 0-3: (5f 2, 6f) (g-s, gd, g-f)
Currently very moderate gelding. Turf high 32.
**D Nicholls [0-3] W G Swiers.*

EUROLINK APACHE (IRE) BHB 55f63a **RR 60f 63a** 2279[6]
5 b g Be My Chief (USA) 10.2f **(62)** - Eurolink Dancer (Petoski) 5.7f **(62)**
Form - 24056
Record 2000 - 1st:0 2nd:1 3rd:0 Ran:5
Pre2000 - 1st:0 2nd:1 3rd:0 Ran:1
Win Prizemoney £0 *Total Prizemoney* £2,055
2000 Turf 0-3: (12f, 16f 2) (gd, g-f 2) 2000 AW 0-2: (12f 2) (Fibr 2)
Average gelding, has broken blood-vessels, has worn blinkers. Turf high 60. AW high 50.
**D R C Elsworth [0-7] Eurolink Group Plc (from M Johnston [0-1] Aug 1998).*

EUROLINK ARTEMIS BHB 70f **RR 79f** 4545[16]
3 b f Common Grounds 8.1f **(66)** - Taiga (Northfields (USA)) 9f **(72)**
Form - 435140
Record 2000 - 1st:1 2nd:0 3rd:1 Ran:6
Win Prizemoney £2,520 *Total Prizemoney* £4,278
Wins * 2000 Jly Leices (G-F) 10f 74+ <
2000 Turf 1-6: (7f, 8f, 9f, 10f 1-3) (g-s 2, gd 2, frm 1-2)
Scopey, above-average filly, effective 10f, acts on frm. Turf high 81 - also 1st of 15 from Marenka (20 Jly Leicester RF 2973). Appreciated the faster ground and step up in trip when winning at Leicester. **J L Dunlop [1-6] Eurolink Group Plc.*

EUROLINK MAYFLY BHB 58f **RR 61f** 636[11]
3 b f Night Shift (USA) 8.1f **(73)** - North Kildare (USA) (Northjet) 10.3f **(74)**
Form - 0
Record 2000 - 1st:0 2nd:0 3rd:0 Ran:1
Pre2000 - 1st:0 2nd:0 3rd:0 Ran:2
2000 Turf 0-1: (7f) (gd)
Neat, currently average filly.
**E A L Dunlop [0-1] Eurolink Group Plc (from J L Dunlop [0-2] Spt 1999).*

EUROLINK MOUSSAKA BHB 50f74a **RR 32f 74a** 2678[15]
5 b g Superlative 8.8f **(57)** - Albiflora (USA) (Manila (USA)) 9.3f **(71)**
Form - 50
Record 2000 - 1st:0 2nd:0 3rd:0 Ran:2
Pre2000 - 1st:2 2nd:0 3rd:0 Ran:7
Win Prizemoney £5,000 *Total Prizemoney* £5,000
Wins * 1999 *Feb Southw (STD) H 8f 65 75* <
* 1998 *Dec Wolver (STD) 7f 69*
2000 Turf 0-2: (8f 2) (g-s, g-f)
Above-average gelding, effective 8f, - acted on Fibr. Turf high 32. (DEAD) **J L Eyre [2-7] Peter Watson (from C F Wall [0-2] Spt 1998).*

EUROLINK RAINDANCE (IRE) BHB 105f **RR 110f** 1989[2]
3 b f Alzao (USA) 9.8f **(73)** - Eurolink Mischief **(81f)** (Be My Chief (USA))
Form - 3022
Record 2000 - 1st:0 2nd:2 3rd:1 Ran:4
Pre2000 - 1st:2 2nd:2 3rd:0 Ran:5
Win Prizemoney £12,631 *Total Prizemoney* £31,435
Wins * 1999 Jun Salisb (FRM) 7f 91+ <
* 1999 Jun Chepst (GD) 6.1f 74+
2000 Turf 0-4: (7f, 8f 2, 10f) (sft, g-s, gd, g-f)
Workmanlike, Group-class filly, effective 8 to 10f, acts on g-s to g-f. Turf high 110 - 2nd of 9 to Littlepacepaddocks (15 Jun Newbury 10f g-f RF 1989). A fair third in the Free Handicap on her return, she was beaten a long way in the Italian Guineas but bounced back with good efforts in listed comapny. She was not seen after June. **J L Dunlop [2-9] Eurolink Group Plc.*

EUROLINK SUNDANCE BHB 79f **RR 76f** 4143[3]
2 ch f Night Shift (USA) 8.1f **(73)** - Eurolink Mischief **(81f)** (Be My Chief (USA))
Form - 01343
Record 2000 - 1st:1 2nd:0 3rd:2 Ran:5
Win Prizemoney £4,407 *Total Prizemoney* £6,347
Wins * 2000 Jly Goodwo (GD) 6f 69 <
2000 Turf 1-5: (5f, 6f 1-4) (gd, g-f 1-4)
Above-average filly. Turf high 76 - also 1st of 14 getting 5lb from Double Brew (2 Jly Goodwood RF 2463).
**J L Dunlop [1-5] Eurolink Group Plc.*

EUROLINK ZANTE (IRE) RR 59f 4812[8]
4 b g Turtle Island (IRE) - Lady Eurolink (Kala Shikari) 8.4f **(54)**
Form - 58
Record 2000 - 1st:0 2nd:0 3rd:0 Ran:2
2000 Turf 0-2: (8f 2) (g-s, g-f)
Scopey, currently fair gelding. Turf high 59 (began Aug).
**G C Bravery [0-2] Eurolink Group Plc.*

EUROPRIME GAMES RR 45f 4830[8]
2 b c Mind Games - Flower Princess (Slip Anchor) 9.8f **(73)**
Form - 8
Record 2000 - 1st:0 2nd:0 3rd:0 Ran:1
2000 Turf 0-1: (6f) (g-s)
Currently moderate colt. **Miss L A Perratt [0-1] Europrime Racing.*

EURO VENTURE BHB 74f70a **RR 79f 70a** 4487[14]
5 b g Prince Sabo 6.6f **(64)** - Brave Advance (USA) (Bold Laddie (USA)) 5.6f **(69)**
Form - 00006701614480
Record 2000 - 1st:2 2nd:0 3rd:0 Ran:14
Pre2000 - 1st:4 2nd:4 3rd:2 Ran:20
Win Prizemoney £31,458 *Total Prizemoney* £45,790
Wins * 2000 Jly Beverl (GD) H 5f 70 72
*** 2000** Jun Redcar (FRM) H 6f 66 70
* 1999 Jun Carlis (G-F) H 6.9f 68 70
* 1999 May Thirsk (Sft) H 6f 63 67
* 1999 *Feb Southw (STD) H 6f 67 72*
* 1998 *Jan Wolver (STD) 6f 75* <
2000 Turf 2-13: (5f 1-5, 6f 1-6, 7f 2) (gd 4, g-f 3, frm 2-6) 2000 AW 0-1: (6f) (Fibr)
Above-average gelding, effective 5 to 7f, best at 6f, acts on gd to frm - acts on Fibr, likes Southwell. Turf high 76 - 4th of 14 giving 4lb to Eastern Trumpeter (14 Jly York 5f gd RF 2820) - also 1st of 10 getting 3lb from Mungo Park (8 Jly Beverley RF 2622). Stays seven furlongs, but is probably better over six, so it was surprising to see him score over Beverley's stiff five in July.
**D Nicholls [6-34] W G Swiers.*

EVANDER (IRE) BHB 82f **RR 86f** 3236[5]
5 ch g Indian Ridge 7.6f **(74)** - Heavenly Hope (Glenstal (USA)) 10.1f **(64)**
Form - 865
Record 2000 - 1st:0 2nd:0 3rd:0 Ran:3
Pre2000 - 1st:1 2nd:2 3rd:2 Ran:11
Win Prizemoney £5,071 *Total Prizemoney* £12,986
Wins * 1998 May Goodwo (G-F) 8f 79 <
2000 Turf 0-3: (12f 2, 15f) (gd 2, g-f)
Useful gelding, effective 10 to 12f, best at 12f, acts on sft to frm. Turf high 86 - 6th of 14 giving 8lb to Hannibal Lad (15 Jly Ascot 12f gd RF 2826). Consistent. Suited by forcing the pace, he looks short of a finishing punch over a mile and a half.
**P F I Cole [1-14] Anthony Speelman.*

EVE RR 74f 5316[4]
3 b f Rainbow Quest (USA) 11.2f **(81)** - Fade (Persepolis (FR)) 6.4f **(67)**
Form - 42343071114
Record 2000 - 1st:3 2nd:1 3rd:2 Ran:11
Win Prizemoney £8,523 *Total Prizemoney* £11,822
Wins * 2000 Oct Newmar (SFT) H 8f 68 74 <
*** 2000** Oct Leices (HVY) H 8f 64 70

* 2000	Spt	Bright	(SFT)		8f	65

2000 Turf 3-11: (8f 3-8, 10f 2, 12f) (g-s 2-4, gd 1-2, g-f 2, frm 2, hrd)
Scopey, above-average filly, effective 8 to 10f, best at 8f, acts on g-s to frm. Turf high 74 - 1st of 24 from Harmonic (27 Oct Newmarket RF 5229) - also 1st of 20 getting 6lb from Natalie Jay (9 Oct Leicester RF 4874). **M L W Bell [3-11] Lady Carolyn Warren.*

EVENING CHORUS (USA) RR 30f
2329[11]

5 b g Shadeed (USA) 7.7f **(72)** - Evening Air (USA) (J O Tobin (USA)) 9.4f **(67)**
Form - 0
Record 2000 - 1st:0 2nd:0 3rd:0 Ran:1
Pre2000 - 1st:0 2nd:0 3rd:0 Ran:8
Win Prizemoney £0 *Total Prizemoney* £631
2000 Turf 0-1: (17f) (frm)
Very moderate gelding. Becoming disappointing. He has been hopelessly outclassed so far.
**R Ford [3-13] Ken Liscombe (from R Simpson [0-8] Spt 1998).*

EVENING SCENT BHB 59f45a RR 65f 45a
5294[10]

4 b f Ardkinglass 5f **(64)** - Fresh Line (High Line) 10.3f **(70)**
Form - 6032716411560
Record 2000 - 1st:3 2nd:1 3rd:1 Ran:13
Pre2000 - 1st:1 2nd:0 3rd:1 Ran:7
Win Prizemoney £19,873 *Total Prizemoney* £22,100

Wins									
	* 2000	Oct	York	(SFT)	H	11.9f	55	65+	<
	* 2000	Spt	Haydoc	(HVY)	H	14f	48	50	
	* 2000	Jun	Hamilt	(GD)	H	13f	45	48	
	* 1999	Spt	Catter	(G-F)	S	13.8f	46		

2000 Turf 3-11: (12f 1-6, 13f 1-1, 14f 1-3, 16f) (sft 2, g-s 1-3, gd 1-3, frm 1-3) 2000 AW 0-2: (11f, 14f) (Fibr 2)
Small, average filly, effective 12 to 14f, acts on g-s to gd. Turf high 65 - 1st of 19 giving 2lb to Five of Wands (5 Oct York RF 4819) - also 1st of 12 from Simple Ideals (23 Spt Haydock RF 4603). AW high 31. **J Hetherton [4-23] N Hetherton.*

EVENTUALITY BHB 67f69a RR 71f 69a
4442[9]

4 b f Petoski 10.4f **(56)** - Queen's Tickle (Tickled Pink) 6.5f **(59)**
Form - 50012070
Record 2000 - 1st:1 2nd:1 3rd:0 Ran:8
Pre2000 - 1st:2 2nd:0 3rd:1 Ran:10
Win Prizemoney £11,076 *Total Prizemoney* £16,006

Wins									
	* 2000	Jly	Lingfi	(GD)	H	6f	61	63	
	* 1999	Spt	Epsom	(GD)	H	7f	61	68	<
	* 1999	Jly	Salisb	(FRM)	H	7f	56	63	

2000 Turf 1-8: (6f 1-6, 7f 2) (gd 3, g-f 1-3, frm 2)
Workmanlike, above-average filly, effective 6 to 7f, best at 6f, acts on g-f to frm, best on g-f. Turf high 71 - 2nd of 9 getting 11lb from Cadeaux Cher (22 Jly Warwick 6f g-f RF 3046) - also 1st of 13 giving 11lb to Palo Blanco (14 Jly Lingfield RF 2812).
**R F JohnsonHoughton [3-18] Anthony Harrison.*

EVERBOLD BHB 28f RR 21f
4491[11]

3 b f Never so Bold 7.1f **(62)** - Out of Hours (Lochnager) 6f **(59)**
Form - 700
Record 2000 - 1st:0 2nd:0 3rd:0 Ran:3
2000 Turf 0-3: (6f, 7f 2) (g-f 2, frm)
Unfurnished, currently little account filly. Turf high 21 (began Aug). **D McCain [0-3] Mrs D McCain.*

EVEREST (IRE) BHB 87f RR 89f
4755[17]

3 ch c Indian Ridge 7.6f **(74)** - Reine D'Beaute (Caerleon (USA)) 8.6f **(71)**
Form - 23211150
Record 2000 - 1st:3 2nd:2 3rd:1 Ran:8
Pre2000 - 1st:0 2nd:1 3rd:0 Ran:1
Win Prizemoney £26,604 *Total Prizemoney* £34,418

Wins									
	* 2000	Aug	Goodwo	(GD)	H	9f	85	89	<
	* 2000	Aug	Pontef	(G-F)	H	8f	84	87	
	* 2000	May	Thirsk	(GD)		8f		84	

2000 Turf 3-8: (8f 2-5, 9f 1-2, 11f) (sft 2, g-s, gd 1-3, g-f 1-1, hrd 1-1)
Useful colt, effective 8 to 9f, best at 8f, acts on sft to hrd. Turf high 89 - 1st of 11 from Kathir (27 Aug Goodwood RF 4016) - also 1st of 4 getting 1lb from Sir Ferbet (20 Aug Pontefract RF 3830). A winner at Thirsk in May, he was having his first run for three months when following up at Pontefract and went on to complete the hat-trick with a game success at Goodwood. Found the extended ten furlongs on heavy ground at Haydock too much of a mountain to climb. **P F I Cole [3-9] H R H Prince Fahd Salman.*

EVERGREEN (IRE) RR 73f
4369[9]

3 ch f Lammtarra (USA) - Nettle (Kris) 9.5f **(73)**
Form - 3504702160
Record 2000 - 1st:1 2nd:1 3rd:1 Ran:10
Pre2000 - 1st:0 2nd:0 3rd:2 Ran:6
Win Prizemoney £3,266 *Total Prizemoney* £6,494

Wins									
	* 2000	Jly	Salisb	(FRM)	H	8f	67	70	<

2000 Turf 1-10: (7f, 8f 1-6, 9f, 10f, 11f) (hvy, gd 4, g-f, frm 1-4)
Above-average filly, effective 6 to 10f, best at 6f, acts on gd to frm, best on gd, likes left handed tracks. Turf high 73 - 4th of 11 to Omniheat (2 Jun Brighton 10f frm RF 1651) - also 1st of 13 giving 16lb to Bajan Sunset (28 Jly Salisbury RF 3183). She took a long time in getting off the mark, but finally managed it in a Salisbury handicap on very fast ground in July. **R Hannon [1-16] The Queen.*

EVER IN LOVE (FR) RR 104f
3948a[3]

3 b f Neverneyev (USA) - French Love (FR) (Zino) 12.9f **(54)**
Form - 33
2000 Turf 0-2: (7f, 8f) (hvy, g-s)
Currently very useful filly. Turf high 104 (began Jly) - 3rd of 9 giving 4lb to May Ball (20 Aug Deauville 8f g-s RF 3948a).
**Francois Rohaut in FR [0-2].*

EVERLASTING LOVE BHB 100f RR 102f
2148[16]

3 b f Pursuit of Love 9.5f **(69)** - Now And Forever (IRE) (Kris) 9.5f **(73)**
Form - 5560
Record 2000 - 1st:0 2nd:0 3rd:0 Ran:4
Pre2000 - 1st:1 2nd:1 3rd:0 Ran:5
Win Prizemoney £4,232 *Total Prizemoney* £14,031

Wins								
	* 1999	Aug	Redcar	(G-F)	7f		82+	<

2000 Turf 0-4: (7f, 9f, 10f 2) (g-s, gd, g-f, frm)
Very useful filly, effective 8 to 10f, best at 10f, acts on g-f to frm, best on g-f. Turf high 102 - 5th of 9 to Kalypso Katie (16 May York 10f g-f RF 1218). Inconsistent. Not beaten far in a couple of Oaks trials, she was held subsequently after being dropped in trip.
**M L W Bell [1-9] DGH Partnership.*

EVERMOORE BHB 51f RR 55f
4930[15]

2 b f Thatching 7.8f **(69)** - Ganador **(42f 41a)** (Weldnaas (USA))
Form - 046470
Record 2000 - 1st:0 2nd:0 3rd:0 Ran:6
Win Prizemoney £0 *Total Prizemoney* £454
2000 Turf 0-6: (5f 2, 6f 2, 7f 2) (sft, gd 3, frm 2)
Fair filly. Turf high 55. **J S Moore [0-6] W J Wyatt.*

EVER REVIE (IRE) BHB 48f41a RR 54f 41a
4497[11]

3 b f Hamas (IRE) 8f **(72)** - Lucy Limelight (Hot Spark) 7.6f **(62)**
Form - 8014000
Record 2000 - 1st:1 2nd:0 3rd:0 Ran:7
Pre2000 - 1st:1 2nd:0 3rd:0 Ran:5
Win Prizemoney £4,290 *Total Prizemoney* £4,400

Wins								
	2000	May	Southw	(HVY)	C	7f	54+	
	1999	Jly	Beverl	(SFT)	S	7.5f	59	<

2000 Turf 1-5: (7f 1-2, 8f 2, 10f) (sft, g-s 2, gd 1-2) 2000 AW 0-2: (6f, 8f) (Fibr 2)
Scopey, fair filly, effective 7f, acts on gd, often wears blinkers (extremely effectively). Turf high 54 - 1st of 11 getting 10lb from King Tut (31 May Southwell RF 1601). AW high 20. Becoming disappointing.
**Miss S J Wilton [0-4] John Pointon and Sons (from T D Easterby [2-8] May 2000).*

EVERY RIGHT (IRE) RR 32f
3009[10]

2 b c Common Grounds 8.1f **(66)** - Incendio (Siberian Express (USA)) 8.8f **(65)**
Form - 0
Record 2000 - 1st:0 2nd:0 3rd:0 Ran:1
2000 Turf 0-1: (6f) (frm)
Currently very moderate colt. **T D Easterby [0-1] J Hanson.*

EVEZIO RUFO BHB 45f52a RR 44f 52a
1301[8]

8 b g Blakeney 11.9f **(53)** - Empress Corina (Free State) 8.7f **(61)**
Form - 54651314511518
Record 2000 - 1st:5 2nd:0 3rd:1 Ran:13
Pre2000 - 1st:7 2nd:7 3rd:10 Ran:69

Win Prizemoney £28,788 *Total Prizemoney* £37,001

Wins *** 2000** May Bright (G-F) H 11.9f 41 44
*** 2000** *Mar Wolver (STD) H 12f 54 59*
*** 2000** *Mar Southw (STD) H 12f 50 52*
*** 2000** *Feb Wolver (STD) H 12f 46 52*
*** 2000** *Feb Wolver (STD) H 12f 38 50+*
* 1999 *Mar Wolver (STD) H 12f 39 44*
* 1999 *Jan Wolver (STD) S 14.8f 45*
* 1998 *Apr Wolver (STD) H 12f 54 57*
* 1998 *Feb Southw (STD) H 12f 44 61*
* 1998 *Jan Lingfi (STD) SH 13f 44 47*
* 1997 *May Southw (STD) H 11f 45 50*

2000 Turf 1-2: (12f 1-1, 13f) (g-f, frm 1-1) 2000 AW 4-11: (11f, 12f 4-9, 13f) (Equi, Fibr 4-10)

Fair gelding, effective 12f, - acts on Fibr, mostly wears blinkers (effectively), favours left handed tracks, does well at Wolverhampton. Turf high 44 (1st run). AW high 59 - 1st of 10 giving 7lb to Summer Bounty (25 Mar Wolverhampton RF 0509) - also 1st of 6 getting 11lb from Morgans Orchard (22 Feb Wolverhampton RF 0331). A real Fibresand regular, he remains capable of winning modest middle-distance events on that surface, but does not seem to like being crowded by other horses. He is therefore probably not suited by large fields.

**N P Littmoden [12-95] O A Gunter (from J L Dunlop [1-4] Apr 1995).*

EVIL EMPIRE (GER) RR 107f

5088a[12]

4 ch f Acatenango (GER) - Elea (GER) (Dschingis Khan) 11.3f **(75)**

Form - 430

Record	**2000** -	1st:0	2nd:0	3rd:1	Ran:3
	Pre2000 -	1st:1	2nd:0	3rd:2	Ran:4

Win Prizemoney £26,173 *Total Prizemoney* £54,933

Wins 1999 Spt Hanove (GD) G3 12f 100 <

2000 Turf 0-3: (12f 3) (g-s, g-f 2)

Pattern-class filly, effective 11 to 13f, best at 12f, acts on hvy to g-f, best on g-f. Turf high 107 - 3rd of 10 to Abitara (22 Jly Newmarket 12f g-f RF 3031). Ex-German, she finished fourth in an Italian Group Two on her first run for Godolphin. Ran a good race at Newmarket before being sent for an autumn campaign in Australia, but plans for a crack at the Melbourne Cup were shelved.

**S bin Suroor [0-3] (from A Schutz in GER [1-4] Oct 1999).*

EVIYRN (IRE) BHB 38f RR 54?f

4204[10]

4 b g In The Wings 11.2f **(77)** - Evrana (USA) (Nureyev (USA)) 8.7f **(78)**

Form - 860

Record	**2000** -	1st:0	2nd:0	3rd:0	Ran:3
	Pre2000 -	1st:0	2nd:0	3rd:0	Ran:2

Win Prizemoney £0 *Total Prizemoney* £200

2000 Turf 0-2: (12f 2) (gd, frm) 2000 AW 0-1: (8f) (Fibr)

Fair gelding. Turf high 20.

**J R Jenkins [0-8] Home Counties Finance Ltd (from J Oxx in IRE [0-2] Oct 1999).*

EXALT BHB 48f53a RR 53f 53a

1209[15]

4 b g Puissance 7.1f **(60)** - Gild the Lily (Ile de Bourbon (USA)) 10.1f **(67)**

Form - 0

Record	**2000** -	1st:0	2nd:0	3rd:0	Ran:1
	Pre2000 -	1st:0	2nd:0	3rd:0	Ran:4

2000 AW 0-1: (11f) (Fibr)

Scopey, fair gelding, has worn blinkers.

**J Balding [0-2] Mrs J Coghlan-Everitt (from A W Carroll [0-3] Apr 1999).*

EXALTED (IRE) BHB 59f77a RR 64f 77a

5297[7]

7 b g High Estate 10.5f **(66)** - Heavenward (USA) (Conquistador Cielo (USA)) 8.8f **(69)**

Form - 15657

Record	**2000** -	1st:1	2nd:0	3rd:0	Ran:5
	Pre2000 -	1st:1	2nd:1	3rd:3	Ran:17

Win Prizemoney £14,616 *Total Prizemoney* £20,057

Wins *** 2000** Apr Hamilt (GD) H 13f 60 64

2000 Turf 1-5: (13f 1-2, 14f, 16f 2) (hvy 2, g-s, gd 1-2)

Average gelding, effective 13f, acts on gd. Turf high 64 (1st run) - 1st of 14 from Mr Fortywinks (8 Apr Hamilton RF 0642).

**T A K Cuthbert [3-23] Railway-Lochmaben (from W Jenks [1-14] Jun 1998).*

EXBOURNE'S WISH (USA) BHB 81f RR 92+f

4420a[1]

5 b h Exbourne (USA) - Social Wish (USA) (Lyphard's Wish (FR)) 9f **(74)**

Form - 1

2000 Turf 1-1: (8f 1-1) (gd 1-1)

Useful colt. (1st run) - 1st of 10 from Royal Dancer (10 Spt Taby RF 4420a).

**A Lund in NOR [2-2] Stall Bonne Nuit (from B W Hills [1-7] Oct 1997).*

EXCEPTIONAL PADDY (IRE) BHB 69f64a RR 72f 64a

5052[6]

2 b c Common Grounds 8.1f **(66)** - Itkan (IRE) **(48f)** (Marju (IRE))

Form - 36

Record	**2000** -	1st:0	2nd:0	3rd:1	Ran:2

Win Prizemoney £0 *Total Prizemoney* £517

2000 Turf 0-2: (6f 2) (sft, gd)

Currently above-average colt. Turf high 72 (1st run) (began Spt) - 3rd of 15 giving 5lb to Sabo Rose (21 Spt Pontefract 6f gd RF 4553).

**J A Osborne [0-2] Durkan Ltd.*

EXCLUSION ZONE RR

4228[1]

3 ch g Exit To Nowhere (USA) 8.7f **(77)** - Exclusive Virtue (USA) (Shadeed (USA)) 8.2f **(70)**

Form - 1

Record	**2000** -	1st:1	2nd:0	3rd:0	Ran:1

Win Prizemoney £2,257 *Total Prizemoney* £2,257

Wins *** 2000** *Spt Lingfi (STD) 12f 73* <

2000 AW 1-1: (12f 1-1) (Equi 1-1)

Scopey, currently useful gelding. (1st run) - 1st of 12 from Quiet Reading (5 Spt Lingfield RF 4228). **M Johnston [1-1] Sir John Robb.*

EXEAT (USA) RR 105df

4746[2]

4 b br h Dayjur (USA) 6.8f **(79)** - By Your Leave (USA) (Private Account (USA)) 8.5f **(74)**

Form - 20062

Record	**2000** -	1st:0	2nd:2	3rd:0	Ran:5
	Pre2000 -	1st:1	2nd:4	3rd:2	Ran:11

Win Prizemoney £3,631 *Total Prizemoney* £60,596

Wins 1998 Jly Haydoc (G-F) 6f 84+ <

2000 Turf 0-5: (7f 3, 8f 2) (g-s, gd 4)

Workmanlike, Pattern-class colt, effective 7 to 8f, best at 8f, acts on g-s to frm, best on g-f, has worn blinkers. Turf high 105 (1st run) - 2nd of 4 to Duck Row (26 May Haydock 8f g-s RF 1464). Becoming disappointing. He left John Gosden after a couple of moderate efforts, and is in the right yard to recapture some of his old sparkle.

**D Nicholls [0-2] Lady Harrison (from J H M Gosden [1-14] Jly 2000).*

EXECUTIVE GHOST BHB 60f RR 61f

4809[13]

3 gr g Executive Man 8.9f **(52)** - Armalou (Ardoon) 7.3f **(53)**

Form - 07400

Record	**2000** -	1st:0	2nd:0	3rd:0	Ran:5

Win Prizemoney £0 *Total Prizemoney* £336

2000 Turf 0-5: (5f, 6f 3, 8f) (g-s, gd 2, g-f, frm)

Workmanlike, average gelding. Turf high 61.

**Mrs D Haine [0-4] Terry Rowley (from D Sasse [0-1] Jun 2000).*

EXECUTIVE ORDER BHB 84f RR 89df

2661[4]

3 b c Rainbow Quest (USA) 11.2f **(81)** - Exclusive Order (USA) (Exclusive Native (USA)) 9.1f **(81)**

Form - 424

Record	**2000** -	1st:0	2nd:1	3rd:0	Ran:3

Win Prizemoney £0 *Total Prizemoney* £2,356

2000 Turf 0-3: (8f, 10f 2) (g-f, frm 2)

Scopey, currently useful colt. Turf high 89 (1st run) - 4th of 19 to Champion Lodge (7 May Newmarket 8f frm RF 1083).

**Sir Michael Stoute [0-3] Cheveley Park Stud.*

EXECUTIVE PROFILES (IRE) RR

5244[11]

5 ch m Executive Perk 9.5f **(58)** - Vague Logic (Corvaro (USA)) 9f **(53)**

Form - 00

Record	**2000** -	1st:0	2nd:0	3rd:0	Ran:2

2000 AW 0-2: (12f 2) (Equi, Fibr)

Formerly very poor filly.

**C N Kellett [0-1] R P Kernohan (from Miss K M George [0-6] Jun 2000).*

EXECUTIVE WISH BHB 38f **RR 12f** 4333[16]
3 b f Executive Man 8.9f **(52)** -Tria Romantica (Another Realm)6.6f **(55)**
Form - 7700
Record 2000 - 1st:0 2nd:0 3rd:0 Ran:4
2000 Turf 0-2: (6f, 7f) (frm 2) 2000 AW 0-2: (6f 2) (Fibr 2)
Lengthy, poor filly. Turf high 12 (began Aug). AW high 13 (began Jun). **Mrs D Haine [0-2] Terry Rowley (from D Sasse [0-2] Jly 2000).*

EXELLENT ADVENTURE RR 31f 1858[5]
2 ch c Gold Dust - Freedom Weekend (USA) (Shahrastani (USA)) 8.8f **(72)**
Form - 665
Record 2000 - 1st:0 2nd:0 3rd:0 Ran:3
2000 Turf 0-1: (5f) (gd) 2000 AW 0 2: (6f 2) (Fibr 2)
Currently very moderate colt. AW high 29.
**P D Evans [0-3] Mrs D L Smith-Hooper.*

EX GRATIA (USA) BHB 85f **RR 88f** 2456[5]
4 b g Exbourne (USA) - Populi (USA) (Star Envoy (USA)) 9.6f **(78)**
Form - 05
Record 2000 - 1st:0 2nd:0 3rd:0 Ran:2
Pre2000 - 1st:2 2nd:1 3rd:0 Ran:7
Win Prizemoney £10,216 *Total Prizemoney* £13,381
Wins * 1999 Spt Doncas (G-F) 10.3f 88 <
* 1999 Jun Haydoc (GD-) 8.1f 79
2000 Turf 0-2: (10f 2) (gd, g-f)
Well made, useful gelding, effective 8 to 12f, acts on gd to g-f, best on gd. Turf high 81. **B W Hills [2-9] K Abdulla.*

EXHIBITION GIRL (IRE) BHB 60f **RR 76f** 2684[14]
3 ch f Perugino (USA) - Shy Jinks (Shy Groom (USA)) 10f **(66)**
Form - 570
Record 2000 - 1st:0 2nd:0 3rd:0 Ran:3
2000 Turf 0-3: (8f, 9f, 10f) (gd 2, g-f)
Workmanlike, currently above-average filly. Turf high 76.
**Andrew Turnell [0-3] Mrs Kate Dalton.*

EXILE BHB 73f **RR 72f** 3565[2]
3 b g Emperor Jones (USA) - Silver Venture (USA) (Silver Hawk (USA)) 8.6f **(70)**
Form - 25212
Record 2000 1st:1 2nd:3 3rd:0 Ran:5
Pre2000 - 1st:0 2nd:0 3rd:0 Ran:7
Win Prizemoney £3,415 *Total Prizemoney* £7,919
Wins * **2000** Aug Kempto (G-F) H 12f 69 71 <
2000 Turf 1-5: (10f, 11f, 12f 1-3) (g-f 1-2, frm 3)
Strong, above-average gelding, effective 11 to 12f, best at 12f, acts on g-f to frm, best on g-f, has worn blinkers, prefers tight tracks. Turf high 72 (began Jly) - 2nd of 9 giving 3lb to After The Blue (11 Aug Salisbury 12f g-f RF 3565) - also 1st of 9 giving 4lb to Acebo Lyons (2 Aug Kempton RF 3322). Consistent.
**R T Phillips [1-5] Ellangowan Racing Partners (from W J Haggas [0-2] Oct 1999).*

EXORCET (FR) BHB 85f **RR 78f** 5199[18]
3 b f Selkirk (USA) 7.9f **(76)** -Stack Rock **(105df)** (Ballad Rock) 7.8f **(63)**
Form - 100
Record 2000 - 1st:1 2nd:0 3rd:0 Ran:3
Pre2000 - 1st:0 2nd:0 3rd:0 Ran:2
Win Prizemoney £3,822 *Total Prizemoney* £3,822
Wins * **2000** Apr Thirsk (SFT) 6f 78 <
2000 Turf 1-3: (5f, 6f 1-2) (g-s 1-1, gd, g-f)
Scopey, above-average filly. Turf high 78 (1st run) - 1st of 21 getting 5lb from Mi Amigo (14 Apr Thirsk RF 0723).
**I A Balding [1-5] J C Smith.*

EXOTIC FAN (USA) BHB 71f **RR 69f** 4822[13]
2 b br f Lear Fan (USA) 10.4f **(80)** - Green Moon (FR) (Shirley Heights) 10.3f **(74)**
Form - 4720
Record 2000 - 1st:0 2nd:1 3rd:0 Ran:4
Win Prizemoney £0 *Total Prizemoney* £1,353
2000 Turf 0-4: (7f 2, 8f, 10f) (gd, g-f 3)
Average filly. Turf high 69 (began Jly) - 2nd of 5 getting 5lb from Double Honour (4 Spt Hamilton 8f gd RF 4208).
**R Guest [0-4] S Lury.*

EXPEDIENT BHB 47f **RR 52f** 850[10]
3 ch g Polish Precedent (USA) 9f **(73)** - Widows Walk (Habitat) 9.4f **(70)**
Form - 00
Record 2000 - 1st:0 2nd:0 3rd:0 Ran:2
Pre2000 - 1st:0 2nd:0 3rd:0 Ran:2
2000 Turf 0-2: (8f, 10f) (sft, gd)
Scopey, fair gelding. Turf high 52. **J L Dunlop [0-4] Ian Cameron.*

EXPLODE BHB 104f **RR 104f** 5225[3]
3 b c Zafonic (USA) 9f **(83)** - Didicoy (USA) (Danzig (USA)) 8.4f **(76)**
Form - 3113
Record 2000 - 1st:2 2nd:0 3rd:2 Ran:4
Win Prizemoney £10,260 *Total Prizemoney* £13,358
Wins * **2000** Jly Epsom (G-S) 10.1f 95 <
* **2000** Jun Salisb (G-F) 9.9f 84
2000 Turf 2-4: (8f, 10f 2-3) (gd 1-3, frm 1-1)
Neat, very useful colt. Turf high 104 - also 1st of 4 getting 6lb from Brancaster (13 Jly Epsom RF 2762). Unraced at two, he was impressive when winning a Salisbury maiden on his second start and benefited from a fine tactical ride to beat Brancaster in an Epsom conditions event. After being withdrawn at the start of the Gordon Stakes, he was absent for over three months, and looked to have benefited from the break. He showed enough to suggest he will be able to pick up races in Pattern company next season.
**R Charlton [2-4] K Abdulla.*

EXPLOSIVE RR 57f 3561[8]
2 b g Saddlers' Hall (IRE) 10.5f **(65)** - Pursuit of Glory **(83f)** (Shirley Heights) 10.3f **(74)**
Form - 08
Record 2000 - 1st:0 2nd:0 3rd:0 Ran:2
2000 Turf 0-2: (7f 2) (gd, frm)
Currently fair gelding. Turf high 57 (began Jly).
**C A Cyzer [0-2] Mrs E A Cyzer.*

EXTRA GUEST BHB 72f **RR 91?f** 5320[5]
2 b f Fraam - Gibaltarik (IRE) **(63f)** (Jareer (USA)) 5.9f **(75)**
Form - 4326222422233445
Record 2000 - 1st:0 2nd:7 3rd:3 Ran:16
Win Prizemoney £0 *Total Prizemoney* £15,298
2000 Turf 0-16: (5f 8, 6f 6, 7f 2) (hvy, sft 2, g-s, gd 4, g-f 4, frm 3, hrd)
Useful filly, effective 6f, acts on gd. Turf high 91 - 4th of 30 giving 7lb to Goodie Twosues (13 Oct Newmarket 6f gd RF 4965).
**N Tinkler [0-1] James Marshall & Mrs Susan Marshall (from M R Channon [0-15] Oct 2000).*

EYECATCHER RR 68f 4227[4]
3 b c Green Desert (USA) 7.8f **(78)** - Reuval (Sharpen Up) 8.3f **(67)**
Form - 4
Record 2000 - 1st:0 2nd:0 3rd:0 Ran:1
Win Prizemoney £0 *Total Prizemoney* £321
2000 Turf 0-1: (7f) (frm)
Scopey, currently average colt.
**J R Fanshawe [0-1] Dr Catherine Wills.*

EYELETS ECHO BHB 62f **RR 68f** 5101[12]
3 b g Inchinor 8.9f **(64)** - Kinkajoo (Precocious) 8.6f **(62)**
Form - 007150600
Record 2000 - 1st:1 2nd:0 3rd:0 Ran:9
Pre2000 - 1st:0 2nd:0 3rd:0 Ran:1
Win Prizemoney £3,607 *Total Prizemoney* £3,607
Wins * **2000** Jun Newcas (FRM) H 9f 66 68 <
2000 Turf 1-9: (7f, 8f 2, 9f 1-2, 10f 2, 11f, 12f) (sft, gd 4, g-f 2, frm 1-2)
Workmanlike, average gelding, effective 9f, acts on frm, has worn blinkers. Turf high 77 - also 1st of 5 giving 13lb to French Master (29 Jun Newcastle RF 2373). **D Morris [1-10] Mrs G M Peel.*

EYE OF GOLD RR 74f 4187[5]
2 b f Wolfhound (USA) 7.3f **(71)** - Blade of Grass (Kris) 9.5f **(73)**
Form - 5
Record 2000 - 1st:0 2nd:0 3rd:0 Ran:1
2000 Turf 0-1: (6f) (g-f)
Currently above-average filly.
**J R Fanshawe [0-1] The Snailwell Stud Company Ltd.*

EYES DONT LIE (IRE) BHB 50f **RR 57f** 4890[9]
2 b g Namaqualand (USA) - Avidal Park (Horage) 10.3f **(61)**

Form - 0480860
Record 2000 - 1st:0 2nd:0 3rd:0 Ran:7
Win Prizemoney £0 *Total Prizemoney* £242
2000 Turf 0-7: (5f 2, 6f, 7f 2, 8f 2) (hvy, g-f 3, frm 3)
Fair gelding, has worn blinkers. Turf high 57.
**I Semple [0-7] James Cringan.*

FABERGER (GER) RR 120f 4956a[1]

4 b c Dashing Blade 7.9f **(80)** - Friedrichslust (GER) (Caerleon (USA)) 8.6f **(71)**
Form - 3181
2000 Turf 2-4: (8f 2-4) (hvy 1-1, sft 1-1, gd, g-f)
Very high-class colt. Turf high 120 - 1st of 9 from Sumitas (8 Oct San Siro RF 4956a) - also 1st of 9 from Chelsea Manor (8 Jly Deauville RF 2787a). This German-trained horse beat compatriot Sumitas to land the Group One Premio Vittorio Du Capua at San Siro. **Frau E Mader in GER [2-4] Gestut Etzean.*

FABI RR 4061[15]

5 br g Rock City 8.8f **(62)** - Shadiyama (Nishapour (FR)) 9.1f **(61)**
Form - 0
Record 2000 - 1st:0 2nd:0 3rd:0 Ran:1
2000 Turf 0-1: (8f) (frm)
Currently very poor gelding. **F Watson [0-1] F Watson.*

FACE D FACTS BHB 73f RR 77f 4932[3]

2 b f So Factual (USA) - Water Well (Sadler's Wells (USA)) 10f **(76)**
Form - 5130243
Record 2000 - 1st:1 2nd:1 3rd:2 Ran:7
Win Prizemoney £3,640 *Total Prizemoney* £6,661
Wins * 2000 Jun Lingfi (G-F) 5f 68 <
2000 Turf 1-7: (5f 1-3, 6f 4) (gd 3, g-f 1-2, frm 2)
Above-average filly, effective 5 to 6f, best at 6f, acts on gd to frm. Turf high 77 - 2nd of 9 getting 4lb from Samadilla (29 Aug Ripon 6f frm RF 4062) - also 1st of 20 getting 3lb from Lai See (27 Jun Lingfield RF 2302). **C F Wall [1-7] The Boardroom Syndicate.*

FACILE TIGRE BHB 48f38a RR 49f 38a 4827[9]

5 gr g Efisio 7.7f **(69)** - Dancing Diana (Raga Navarro (ITY)) 8f **(64)**
Form - 44668600705067557380023600
Record 2000 - 1st:0 2nd:1 3rd:2 Ran:22
Pre2000 - 1st:2 2nd:3 3rd:0 Ran:39
Win Prizemoney £4,650 *Total Prizemoney* £10,901
Wins 1998 Nov Bright (SFT) H 6f 63 68
1998 Jun Bright (FRM) H 5.3f 67 74 <
2000 Turf 0-17: (5f 12, 6f 5) (gd 4, g-f 6, frm 7) 2000 AW 0-5: (6f 4, 7f) (Equi 2, Fibr 3)
Moderate gelding, effective 5 to 6f, best at 5f, acts on gd to hrd. Turf high 51 - 3rd of 9 getting 13lb from Sharp Hat (17 Jly Ayr 5f frm RF 2873). AW high 41.
**R Hollinshead [0-1] Miss Sarah Hollinshead (from P Monteith [0-16] Spt 2000).*

FACT OR FICTION RR 2679[5]

3 b f Polar Falcon (USA) 9f **(74)** - Round Midnight (Star Appeal) 9.6f **(65)**
Form - 5
Record 2000 - 1st:0 2nd:0 3rd:0 Ran:1
2000 Turf 0-1: (8f) (g-s)
Rangy, currently very poor filly. **Miss I Foustok [0-1] S Fustok.*

FACTUAL LAD BHB 87f RR 85f 5129[14]

2 b c So Factual (USA) - Surprise Surprise (Robellino (USA)) 7.6f **(80)**
Form - 2332310600
Record 2000 - 1st:1 2nd:2 3rd:3 Ran:10
Win Prizemoney £2,788 *Total Prizemoney* £14,140
Wins * 2000 Jly Chepst (G-F) 6.1f 74 <
2000 Turf 1-10: (5f 4, 6f 1-6) (hvy, sft, gd 3, g-f, frm 1-4)
Useful colt, effective 6f, acts on gd. Turf high 85 - 6th of 22 to Goggles (6 Spt Doncaster 6f gd RF 4259). He was not winning out of turn when successful at Chepstow and has run creditably since. Should stay seven. **B R Millman [1-10] Tarka Racing.*

FADHAH BHB 66f RR 69f 5074[10]

2 b f Mukaddamah (USA) 7.6f **(74)** - Ishtiyak **(72f)** (Green Desert (USA)) 8.6f **(78)**
Form - 5200
Record 2000 - 1st:0 2nd:1 3rd:0 Ran:4
Win Prizemoney £0 *Total Prizemoney* £711
2000 Turf 0-4: (6f 2, 7f 2) (g-s, g-f 2, frm)
Average filly. Turf high 69.
**L M Cumani [0-4] Sheikh Mohammed Obaid Al Maktoum.*

FAERIE REALM (IRE) RR 71+f 4873[5]

2 b f Fairy King (USA) 7.7f **(75)** - Marie Noelle (FR) (Brigadier Gerard) 9.3f **(58)**
Form - 5
Record 2000 - 1st:0 2nd:0 3rd:0 Ran:1
2000 Turf 0-1: (7f) (g-s)
Currently above-average filly.
**Sir Michael Stoute [0-1] Mrs Belinda Strudwick.*

FAGIN BHB 72f RR 81df 1381[13]

3 b g Formidable (USA) 7.8f **(60)** - Rich Pickings (Dominion) 8.5f **(63)**
Form - 0
Record 2000 - 1st:0 2nd:0 3rd:0 Ran:1
Pre2000 - 1st:0 2nd:0 3rd:1 Ran:3
Win Prizemoney £0 *Total Prizemoney* £555
2000 Turf 0-1: (12f) (g-f)
Decent gelding.
**M H Tompkins [0-1] P Heath (from B J Meehan [0-3] Oct 1999).*

FAHAN (IRE) BHB 44f42a RR 55f 42a 4583[10]

3 b f Sri Pekan (USA) - Damemill (IRE) (Danehill (USA)) 10f **(72)**
Form - 055500
Record 2000 - 1st:0 2nd:0 3rd:0 Ran:6
Pre2000 - 1st:0 2nd:0 3rd:1 Ran:4
Win Prizemoney £0 *Total Prizemoney* £830
2000 Turf 0-4: (8f, 10f 2, 12f) (gd, frm 3) 2000 AW 0-2: (8f, 16f) (Equi, Fibr)
Unfurnished, fair filly, has worn blinkers. Turf high 55. AW high 16 (began Spt). Becoming disappointing. **B W Hills [0-10] John Grant.*

FAHS (USA) BHB 75f80a RR 85f 80a 4810[3]

8 b br g Riverman (USA) 9.7f **(78)** - Tanwi (Vision (USA)) 9f **(64)**
Form - 3125712115003
Record 2000 - 1st:3 2nd:2 3rd:1 Ran:11
Pre2000 - 1st:5 2nd:5 3rd:13 Ran:49
Win Prizemoney £24,986 *Total Prizemoney* £62,259

Wins	*** 2000**	Aug	Leices	(G-F)		11.8f		85	<
	*** 2000**	Aug	Newmar	(GD)	H	12f	75	79	
	*** 2000**	Jly	Yarmou	(GD)	H	11.5f	69	73	
	* 1999	*Dec*	*Lingfi*	*(STD)*	*H*	*13f*	*78*	*72+*	
	* 1999	Jun	Yarmou	(G-F)	H	10.1f	68	71	
	1998	*Nov*	*Lingfi*	*(STD)*	*H*	*12f*	*73*	*75*	
	1997	Oct	Yarmou	(GD)	H	10.1f	75	79	
	1997	May	Sandow	(G-F)	H	10f	70	80	

2000 Turf 3-8: (9f, 10f 3, 11f 1-1, 12f 2-3) (gd 1-2, g-f 2-5, frm) 2000 AW 0-3: (12f 3) (Equi 3)
Useful gelding, effective 10 to 12f, best at 12f, acts on gd to frm - acts on Equi, and excels at Lingfield. Turf high 85 (began Jly) - 1st of 8 giving 4lb to Angels Venture (13 Aug Leicester RF 3611) - also 1st of 10 giving 30lb to Ordained (4 Aug Newmarket RF 3372). AW high 83 (1st run) - 2nd of 11 giving 29lb to Hawksbill Henry (15 Jan Lingfield 12f Equi RF 0093). Consistent. He is a consistent sort in modest middle-distance handicaps on sand and turf. In very good form during the summer, winning at Yarmouth, Newmarket and Leicester. Best when held up for a late run.
**N Hamilton [5-23] City Industrial Supplies Ltd (from G Lewis [1-15] Nov 1998).*

FAILED TO HIT BHB 45f66a RR 40f 66a 5244[1]

7 b g Warrshan (USA) 9.7f **(59)** - Missed Again (High Top) 10.2f **(67)**
Form - 51522423281634365263151
Record 2000 - 1st:3 2nd:3 3rd:4 Ran:18
Pre2000 - 1st:9 2nd:6 3rd:7 Ran:54
Win Prizemoney £31,741 *Total Prizemoney* £45,858

Wins	*** 2000**	*Oct*	*Wolver*	*(STD)*	*C*	*12f*		*71*	<
	*** 2000**	*Oct*	*Wolver*	*(STD)*	*H*	*12f*	*54*	*61*	
	*** 2000**	*Feb*	*Wolver*	*(STD)*	*C*	*12f*		*59*	
	* 1999	*Nov*	*Lingfi*	*(STD)*	*C*	*12f*		*60*	
	* 1999	*Jan*	*Wolver*	*(STD)*	*H*	*12f*	*66*	*71*	<
	* 1998	*Dec*	*Wolver*	*(STD)*	*H*	*9.4f*	*62*	*65*	
	* 1998	*Oct*	*Lingfi*	*(STD)*		*12f*		*60*	
	* 1998	*Mar*	*Wolver*	*(STD)*	*H*	*9.4f*	*60*	*66*	

* 1998	*Feb Lingfi*	*(SLW)*	*10f*		*62*	
* 1998	*Feb Wolver*	*(STD) C*	*8.5f*		*65+*	
* 1998	*Feb Lingfi*	*(STD) H*	*8f*	*43*	*51*	
1996	Aug Folkes	(G-F)	6f		67	

2000 AW 3-18: (9f, 11f 2, 12f 3-13, 14f, 15f) (Equi 7, Fibr 3-11)
Above-average gelding, effective 10 to 12f, best at 12f, - acts on AW, best on Fibr, mostly wears blinkers (effectively), favours left handed tracks, and likes Southwell and Wolverhampton. AW high 71 - 1st of 11 giving 4lb to Toujours Riviera (28 Oct Wolverhampton RF 5244). An effective and game front runner on both types of artificial surface on his day, he ran one or two moody races last year and cannot be totally relied upon.
**N P Littmoden [11-68] M C S D Racing Ltd (from Sir Mark Prescott [1-5] Oct 1996).*

FAIRFIELD BAY BHB 21f10a RR 30?f 18a 1969[8]

4 b g Emarati (USA) 6.6f **(63)** - Navarino Bay (Averof) 8.2f **(62)**
Form - 00008

Record	**2000 -**	1st:0	2nd:0	3rd:0	Ran:5
	Pre2000 -	1st:0	2nd:0	3rd:0	Ran:5

2000 Turf 0-4: (7f, 8f 2, 12f) (g-s, gd, g-f, frm) 2000 AW 0-1: (6f) (Equi)
Scopey, very moderate gelding, has worn blinkers.
**Miss A M Newton-Smith [0-6] The Fairfield Partnership (from Mrs P N Dutfield [0-5] Aug 1998).*

FAIR FINNISH (IRE) RR 43f 2279[9]

6 b g Commanche Run 10.3f **(63)** - Karelia (USA) (Sir Ivor) 10.2f **(70)**
Form - 0

Record	**2000 -**	1st:0	2nd:0	3rd:0	Ran:1
	Pre2000 -	1st:0	2nd:0	3rd:0	Ran:1

2000 Turf 0-1: (16f) (g-f)
Moderate gelding.
**G Barnett [2-7] Lee Heath (from Lord Huntingdon [0-1] Feb 1998).*

FAIRGAME MAN BHB 89f RR 61f 4383[11]

2 ch c Clantime 6.6f **(57)** - Thalya (Crofthall) 6.3f **(59)**
Form - 31130

Record	**2000 -**	1st:2	2nd:0	3rd:2	Ran:5

Win Prizemoney £6,435 *Total Prizemoney* £7,954

Wins	*** 2000**	Aug Cheste	(GD)	H	6.1f	75	89+	<
	*** 2000**	Jly Carlis	(FM)		5f		77	

2000 Turf 2-5: (5f 1-3, 6f 1-2) (gd, g-f 1-2, frm, hrd 1-1)
Average colt. Turf high 89 (began Jly) - 3rd of 5 getting 2lb from Healey (19 Aug Ripon 6f g-f RF 3795) - also 1st of 9 giving 11lb to Love Tune (6 Aug Chester RF 3411). Twice a comfortable winner, he would not want any further than six furlongs at this stage.
**A Berry [2-5] Robert Ogden.*

FAIR IMPRESSION (IRE) BHB 79f RR 80f 5317[16]

3 ch f Arazi (USA) 9.2f **(74)** - Al Najah (USA) (Topsider (USA)) 8.3f **(71)**
Form - 0011050

Record	**2000 -**	1st:2	2nd:0	3rd:0	Ran:7
	Pre2000 -	1st:0	2nd:1	3rd:0	Ran:2

Win Prizemoney £7,926 *Total Prizemoney* £8,906

Wins	*** 2000**	Jly Haydoc	(G-F)	7.1f	63	
	*** 2000**	Jly Bright	(G-S)	8f	78	<

2000 Turf 2-7: (7f 1-5, 8f 1-1, 9f) (sft 2, g-s, gd 1-2, g-f, frm 1-1)
Light-framed, decent filly, effective 7 to 8f, best at 7f, acts on g-s to gd, best on gd. Turf high 80 - 5th of 22 giving 17lb to Weetman's Weigh (28 Oct Newmarket 7f g-s RF 5242) - also 1st of 6 from Devil Leader (5 Jly Brighton RF 2537). Inconsistent.
**E A L Dunlop [2-9] Maktoum Al Maktoum.*

FAIR LADY BHB 69a RR 79df 5150[1]

3 b f Machiavellian (USA) 9.8f **(83)** - Just Cause (Law Society (USA)) 9.9f **(70)**
Form - 16304281

Record	**2000 -**	1st:2	2nd:1	3rd:1	Ran:8
	Pre2000 -	1st:0	2nd:1	3rd:0	Ran:3

Win Prizemoney £5,553 *Total Prizemoney* £9,879

Wins	*** 2000**	*Oct Lingfi*	*(STD)*	*H*	*10f*	*69*	*76+*	<
	*** 2000**	*Feb Wolver*	*(STD)*		*9.4f*		*71*	

2000 Turf 0-6: (8f, 10f 4, 11f) (gd, g-f 5) 2000 AW 2-2: (9f 1-1, 10f 1-1) (Equi 1-1, Fibr 1-1)
Scopey, above-average filly, effective 7 to 11f, acts on gd to frm - acts on AW, best on g-f, prefers tight tracks. Turf high 79 (began Jly) - 3rd of 6 giving 22lb to Winged Angel (23 Jly Redcar 11f g-f RF 3056). AW high 76 - 1st of 13 giving 24lb to Snatch (23 Oct Lingfield RF 5150) - also 1st of 5 getting 5lb from You da Man (5 Feb Wolverhampton RF 0231).
**B W Hills [2-11] Maktoum Al Maktoum.*

FAIRLY SURE (IRE) BHB 30f24a RR 26f 24a 2160[7]

7 b m Red Sunset 9f **(57)** - Mirabiliary (USA) (Crow (FR)) 7.4f **(75)**
Form - 07

Record	**2000 -**	1st:0	2nd:0	3rd:0	Ran:2
	Pre2000 -	1st:2	2nd:0	3rd:0	Ran:28

Win Prizemoney £5,013 *Total Prizemoney* £5,211

Wins	* 1999	Jly Bath	(FRM)	H	10.2f	26	35	
	* 1996	Aug Lingfi	(G-F)	H	7.6f	46	39	<

2000 Turf 0-2: (8f, 12f) (gd, g-f)
Very moderate mare, effective 10f, acts on frm, likes left handed tracks. Turf high 17.
**N E Berry [2-30] The Purple People Racing Partnership.*

FAIR PRINCESS RR 80f 5129[20]

2 b f Efisio 7.7f **(69)** - Fair Attempt (IRE) (Try My Best (USA)) 7.6f **(67)**
Form - 22062220

Record	**2000 -**	1st:0	2nd:5	3rd:0	Ran:8

Win Prizemoney £0 *Total Prizemoney* £16,593
2000 Turf 0-8: (5f 6, 6f 2) (sft, g-s, gd 3, g-f 2, hrd)
Decent filly, effective 5 to 6f, best at 5f, acts on g-s to hrd, best on g-f. Turf high 80 - 2nd of 7 giving 1lb to Clarion (18 Aug Sandown 5f g-f RF 3769). She has been running well, but is still a maiden and has finished runner-up on far too many occasions.
**B W Hills [0-8] Stephen Crown.*

FAIR QUESTION (IRE) RR 89f 4435[4]

2 b c Rainbow Quest (USA) 11.2f **(81)** - Fair of the Furze (Ela-Mana-Mou) 10.1f **(70)**
Form - 14

Record	**2000 -**	1st:1	2nd:0	3rd:0	Ran:2

Win Prizemoney £4,862 *Total Prizemoney* £5,675

Wins	*** 2000**	Aug Newmar (G-F)	7f	89+	<

2000 Turf 1-2: (7f 1-1, 8f) (g-f 1-1, frm)
Currently useful colt. Turf high 89 (began Aug) - also 1st of 10 from Nation (25 Aug Newmarket RF 3964). This half-brother to White Muzzle showed a nice turn of foot to score on his debut before going on to finish fourth behind Nayef at Newbury.
**J L Dunlop [1-2] Tessona Racing Ltd.*

FAIR STEP BHB 48f RR 55f 4060[5]

2 ch f King's Signet (USA) 7f **(51)** - Miss Hocroft (Dominion) 8.5f **(63)**
Form - 2385

Record	**2000 -**	1st:0	2nd:1	3rd:1	Ran:4

Win Prizemoney £0 *Total Prizemoney* £812
2000 Turf 0-4: (5f 3, 6f) (g-f 2, frm 2)
Fair filly. Turf high 55 (1st run) (began Jly) - 2nd of 8 to Dancing Penney (6 Jly Catterick 5f g-f RF 2558).
**W W Haigh [0-4] David Young.*

FAIRTOTO BHB 42f RR 48f 5161[7]

4 b g Mtoto 11.5f **(71)** - Fairy Feet (Sadler's Wells (USA)) 10f **(76)**
Form - 37

Record	**2000 -**	1st:0	2nd:0	3rd:1	Ran:2
	Pre2000 -	1st:0	2nd:0	3rd:1	Ran:6

Win Prizemoney £0 *Total Prizemoney* £744
2000 Turf 0-2: (16f 2) (sft, g-s)
Moderate gelding. Turf high 47 (began Oct).
**D J Wintle [1-13] Mrs Joan Egan (from Mrs J R Ramsden [0-3] Spt 1998).*

FAIR WARNING (GER) BHB 88f RR 90f 4936[5]

4 b g Warning 8.1f **(77)** - Fairy Bluebird (Be My Guest (USA)) 9.3f **(67)**
Form - 507105

Record	**2000 -**	1st:1	2nd:0	3rd:0	Ran:6
	Pre2000 -	1st:2	2nd:1	3rd:4	Ran:11

Win Prizemoney £17,183 *Total Prizemoney* £25,269

Wins	*** 2000**	Aug Newbur	(G-F)	12f	90	
	* 1999	Oct York	(G-S)	11.9f	91	
	* 1999	Jun Yarmou	(G-F)	8f	95	<

2000 Turf 1-6: (12f 1-6) (sft, gd, g-f 2, frm 1-2)
Workmanlike, useful gelding, effective 8 to 12f, best at 12f, acts on gd to frm, best on gd, likes left handed tracks. Turf high 90 - 1st of 5 giving 6lb to Kiftsgate (19 Aug Newbury RF 3793). Inconsistent.

He showed nothing in his early starts last season, but returned to winning form in a Newbury classified event in August. Suited by 12 furlongs. **J W Hills [3-17] Wauchope,Sir Simon D Cottam.*

FAIRWAY (AUS) RR 122f 5207a[3]

4 br g Danzero (AUS) - Our Caddy (NZ) (Cocky Golfer (USA))
Form - 3
2000 Turf 0-1: (12f) (gd)
Currently very high-class gelding. (1st run) - 3rd of 18 giving 5lb to Diatribe (21 Oct Caulfield 12f gd RF 5207a). **J Denham in AUS [0-1].*

FAIRY CHARM RR 95f 4851a[3]

3 b c Fairy King (USA) 7.7f **(75)** - Fatal Charm (USA) (Sham (USA)) 9.5f **(68)**
Form - 13
2000 Turf 1-2: (9f 1-2) (hvy 1-2)
Currently very useful colt. Turf high 95 - 3rd of 9 getting 3lb from Tamora (1 Oct San Siro 9f hvy RF 4851a).
**G Vericalli in ITY [0-1] (from G Verricelli in ITY [1-1] Apr 2000).*

FAIRY GEM (IRE) BHB 92f RR 97f 3986[R]

3 b f Fairy King (USA) 7.7f **(75)** - Cajo (IRE) (Tirol)
Form - 74677R
Record 2000 - 1st:0 2nd:0 3rd:0 Ran:6
Pre2000 - 1st:1 2nd:1 3rd:0 Ran:7
Win Prizemoney £5,157 *Total Prizemoney* £11,562
Wins * 1999 May Salisb (G-F) 5f 83 <
2000 Turf 0-6: (6f, 7f 3, 8f 2) (sft, g-s, gd 3, g-f)
Light-framed, very useful filly, effective 7f, acts on g-s, has worn blinkers. Turf high 97 - 4th of 13 getting 12lb from Hot Tin Roof (13 May Lingfield 7f g-s RF 1192). Inconsistent.
**R Hannon [1-13] Jubert Family.*

FAIRY GODMOTHER BHB 108f RR 109f 1049[5]

4 b f Fairy King (USA) 7.7f **(75)** - Highbrow (Shirley Heights) 10.3f **(74)**
Form - 25
Record 2000 - 1st:0 2nd:1 3rd:0 Ran:2
Pre2000 - 1st:2 2nd:0 3rd:0 Ran:2
Win Prizemoney £18,749 *Total Prizemoney* £27,041
Wins * 1999 Jun Newbur (GD) L 10f 104+ <
* 1999 May Newbur (SFT) 10f 97
2000 Turf 0-2: (9f 2) (gd, g-f)
Scopey, Pattern-class filly. Turf high 109 (1st run) - 2nd of 11 getting 3lb from Indian Lodge (19 Apr Newmarket 9f gd RF 0795). Off the track for ten months before finishing runner-up in the Earl Of Sefton on her return, she was well beaten in a listed race and was not seen again. **R Charlton [2-4] The Queen.*

FAIRY KING PRAWN (AUS) RR 117f 1828a[1]

5 b g Danehill (USA) 9.1f **(79)** - Twiglet (AUS) (Twig Moss (FR))
Form - 11
2000 Turf 1-1: (8f 1-1) (frm 1-1)
Currently high-class gelding. (1st run) - 1st of 18 from Diktat (4 Jun Fuchu RF 1828a). A brilliant performer in Japan, effective at up to a mile, he will be interesting should plans to send him to Europe come to fruition. **P F Yiu in HK [2-2] & Mrs Lau Sak Hong.*

FAIRY PRINCE (IRE) BHB 60f57a RR 59df 57a 4827[20]

7 b g Fairy King (USA) 7.7f **(75)** - Danger Ahead (Mill Reef (USA)) 10.5f **(78)**
Form - 04510044300
Record 2000 - 1st:1 2nd:0 3rd:1 Ran:11
Pre2000 - 1st:5 2nd:11 3rd:2 Ran:49
Win Prizemoney £16,930 *Total Prizemoney* £34,858
Wins * **2000** Jun Nottin (G-F) H 6.1f 56 62
* 1998 Jly Beverl (GD) 5f 67
* 1997 Jly Doncas (GD) 6f 72 <
* 1997 Jly Nottin (G-F) 5.1f 65
* 1997 Jly Pontef (G-F) 6f 67
* 1996 Jun Carlis (FRM) H 5.9f 54 54
2000 Turf 1-11: (5f 4, 6f 1-7) (gd, g-f 5, frm 1-5)
Fair gelding, effective 5 to 8f, best at 6f, acts on gd to frm, best on frm, has worn blinkers, excels at Kempton, does well at Goodwood. Turf high 62 - 1st of 20 from Be My Wish (26 Jun Nottingham RF 2280). Inconsistent.
**Mrs A L M King [6-60] All The Kings Horses.*

FAIRYTIME BHB 29f38a RR 39f 38a 4922[5]

4 b f Efisio 7.7f **(69)** - Fairy Flax (IRE) (Dancing Brave (USA)) 8.4f **(76)**
Form - 00805
Record 2000 - 1st:0 2nd:0 3rd:0 Ran:5
Pre2000 - 1st:0 2nd:0 3rd:1 Ran:6
Win Prizemoney £0 *Total Prizemoney* £568
2000 Turf 0-4: (6f 4) (gd, g-f, frm 2) 2000 AW 0-1: (7f) (Equi)
Very moderate filly, has worn blinkers. Turf high 40. Inconsistent.
**J G Portman [0-3] A H Robinson (from J R Arnold [0-8] Jun 2000).*

FAITH AGAIN (IRE) BHB 34f RR 47f 3147[8]

4 b f Namaqualand (USA) - Intricacy (Formidable (USA)) 9.2f **(63)**
Form - 88
Record 2000 - 1st:0 2nd:0 3rd:0 Ran:2
Pre2000 - 1st:0 2nd:1 3rd:1 Ran:10
Win Prizemoney £0 *Total Prizemoney* £1,612
2000 Turf 0-2: (14f, 17f) (gd, frm)
Moderate filly, effective 8f, acts on g-f, has worn blinkers (very effectively). Turf high 37. Consistent.
**A Streeter [3-11] Racing For You (from C F Wall [0-10] Aug 1999).*

FAITHFUL WARRIOR (USA) BHB 75f RR 71f 5132[4]

2 ch c Diesis 9f **(80)** - Dabaweyaa (Shareef Dancer (USA)) 9.9f **(73)**
Form - 454
Record 2000 - 1st:0 2nd:0 3rd:0 Ran:3
Win Prizemoney £0 *Total Prizemoney* £776
2000 Turf 0-3: (5f, 6f 2) (sft, frm 2)
Currently above-average colt. Turf high 71 (began Jly).
**B W Hills [0-3] Mohamed Obaida.*

FAIT LE JOJO (FR) BHB 86f80a RR 87f 80a 3967[1]

3 b g Pistolet Bleu (IRE) - Pretty Davis (USA) (Trempolino (USA)) 12f **(71)**
Form - 45411351
Record 2000 - 1st:3 2nd:0 3rd:1 Ran:8
Pre2000 - 1st:1 2nd:0 3rd:2 Ran:3
Win Prizemoney £24,223 *Total Prizemoney* £27,083
Wins * **2000** Aug Newmar (G-F) H 14.8f 82 87 <
* **2000** Jun Goodwo (G-F) H 14f 80 85
* **2000** Jun Salisb (G-F) H 14.1f 77 81+
* 1999 *Spt Wolver (STD) 8.5f* 79+
2000 Turf 3-8: (10f, 11f, 12f, 14f 2-3, 15f 1-1, 16f) (gd 1-3, g-f 1-3, frm 1-2)
Leggy, useful gelding, effective 8 to 16f, acts on gd to frm - acts on Fibr, best on g-f, excels at Newmarket and Goodwood and Windsor. Turf high 87 - 1st of 5 getting 10lb from Bid Me Welcome (25 Aug Newmarket RF 3967) - also 1st of 4 getting 19lb from Total Delight (30 Jun Goodwood RF 2399). Improving. Now hurdling with Philip Hobbs. **S P C Woods [4-11] G A Roberts.*

FALCON FLIGHT (FR) RR 119f 1153a[2]

4 b c Persian Bold 10f **(69)** - Flying Circus (FR) (Gay Mecene (USA)) 8.6f **(69)**
Form - 2
2000 Turf 0-1: (9f)
High-class colt. (1st run) - 2nd of 8 giving 4lb to Manndar (6 May Churchill Downs 9f RF 1153a). He finished runner-up to Manndar in the Turf Classic at Churchill Downs in May.
**in USA [0-1] (from P Bary in FR [2-3] Jun 1999).*

FALCON GOA (IRE) BHB 75f RR 71f 3809[2]

2 b f Sri Pekan (USA) - Minden (IRE) (Bluebird (USA)) 7.5f **(69)**
Form - 04162
Record 2000 - 1st:1 2nd:1 3rd:0 Ran:5
Win Prizemoney £3,152 *Total Prizemoney* £11,211
Wins * **2000** Jun Pontef (SFT) 5f 71 <
2000 Turf 1-4: (5f 1-3, 6f) (gd 1-3, g-f) 2000 AW 0-1: (6f) (Fibr)
Above-average filly. Turf high 71 - also 1st of 8 from Hard To Lay (4 Jun Pontefract RF 1694). (1st run) - 2nd of 13 to Amelia (19 Aug Wolverhampton 6f Fibr RF 3809). **N Tinkler [1-5] Racingclub co uk.*

FALCONIDAE BHB 80f RR 85+f 4755[8]

3 ch c Polar Falcon (USA) 9f **(74)** - Barbary Court (Grundy) 10.3f **(65)**
Form - 05127U8
Record 2000 - 1st:1 2nd:1 3rd:0 Ran:7
Pre2000 - 1st:0 2nd:0 3rd:0 Ran:2
Win Prizemoney £6,987 *Total Prizemoney* £9,467

Wins * **2000** Jly Bath (FRM) H 8f 77 85 <
2000 Turf 1-7: (7f, 8f 1-6) (g-s, gd, g-f 2, frm 1-3)
Scopey, useful colt, effective 7 to 8f, acts on g-f to frm. Turf high 85 - 2nd of 12 giving 2lb to Rushmore (26 Jly Sandown 7f g-f RF 3141) - also 1st of 11 getting 15lb from Strasbourg (1 Jly Bath RF 2424). Got off the mark in a Bath handicap on fast ground having shown promise in maiden company. **P J Makin [1-9] A W Schiff.*

FALCON SPIRIT BHB 45f **RR 52f** 5119[5]
4 b g Polar Falcon (USA) 9f **(74)** - Amina (Brigadier Gerard) 9.3f **(58)**
Form - 8047505
Record 2000 - 1st:0 2nd:0 3rd:0 Ran:7
Pre2000 - 1st:0 2nd:2 3rd:2 Ran:8
Win Prizemoney £0 *Total Prizemoney* £2,989
2000 Turf 0-4: (10f 2, 11f, 12f) (g-s, g-f 2, frm) 2000 AW 0-3: (12f 3) (Fibr 3)
Scopey, fair gelding, effective 8 to 12f, acts on g-f - acts on AW, often wears blinkers (extremely effectively), likes left handed tracks, likes tight tracks. Turf high 52 (began Jly). AW high 52 (began Spt).
**G M Moore [0-9] R Wardlaw (from W J Haggas [0-8] Oct 1999).*

FALLACHAN (USA) BHB 62f58a **RR 82f 58a** 5185[14]
4 ch g Diesis 9f **(80)** - Afaff (USA) (Nijinsky (CAN)) 10.3f **(77)**
Form - 044030070
Record 2000 - 1st:0 2nd:0 3rd:1 Ran:9
Pre2000 - 1st:2 2nd:3 3rd:0 Ran:11
Win Prizemoney £6,067 *Total Prizemoney* £18,542
Wins * 1999 Apr Nottin (G-S) H 8.2f 63 78+ <
* 1999 Apr Mussel (GD) H 8f 63 68+
2000 Turf 0-9: (7f 4, 8f 4, 9f) (sft, g-s 4, gd, g-f 2, frm)
Lengthy, decent gelding, effective 7 to 8f, best at 8f, acts on g-s to frm, best on frm. Turf high 82 - 4th of 15 getting 3lb from Silk St John (26 May Haydock 8f g-s RF 1465). Becoming disappointing. Running quite well in 2000, he just lacks a turn of foot and does not want the ground too soft.
**M A Jarvis [2-20] & Mrs Raymond Anderson Green.*

FALL HABIT (IRE) **RR 103f** 5090a[8]
3 b f Hamas (IRE) 8f **(72)** - Hard Bob (FR) (Hard Fought) 8.8f **(62)**
Form - 288
2000 Turf 0-3: (10f 2, 12f) (hvy, gd 2)
Currently very useful filly. Turf high 103 (1st run) (began Aug) - 2nd of 12 to Hidalguia (5 Aug Deauville 10f gd RF 3540a).
**L Camici in ITY [0-3].*

FALLS O'MONESS (IRE) BHB 45f41a **RR 48f 41a** 5084[6]
6 b m River Falls 8.2f **(56)** - Sevens Are Wild (Petorius) 7.3f **(61)**
Form - 208200802706
Record 2000 - 1st:0 2nd:3 3rd:0 Ran:12
Pre2000 - 1st:4 2nd:3 3rd:8 Ran:57
Win Prizemoney £12,100 *Total Prizemoney* £28,526
Wins * 1999 Aug Thirsk (SFT) SH 8f 46 50
* 1998 Spt Hamilt (SFT) H 8.3f 48 50
* 1998 Aug Thirsk (G-F) SH 8f 40 48
1997 Spt Ayr (G-S) C 9f 65 <
2000 Turf 0-12: (7f, 8f 9, 9f, 10f) (hvy, g-s, gd 3, g-f 4, frm 3)
Moderate mare, effective 8f, acts on gd to frm, best on gd, has worn blinkers, likes left handed tracks, likes tight tracks. Turf high 54 - 2nd of 8 getting 14lb from Poppadam (20 Jun Thirsk 8f frm RF 2120). She is a bit of a character who is on a long losing run, despite making the frame from time to time. She seems to run her best races over a mile at Thirsk.
**E J Alston [3-37] Piquet Opera House Partnership (from K R Burke [1-32] Jun 1998).*

FALSE PROMISE BHB 56f **RR 62f** 5157[12]
2 b c Bluebird (USA) 7.9f **(71)** - Funoon (IRE) (Kris) 9.5f **(73)**
Form - 000
Record 2000 - 1st:0 2nd:0 3rd:0 Ran:3
2000 Turf 0-3: (7f, 8f 2) (sft, gd, frm)
Currently average colt. Turf high 62 (began Spt).
**E A L Dunlop [0-3] Khalifa Sultan.*

FAME AT LAST (USA) BHB 95f **RR 97f** 4931[7]
3 b f Quest for Fame 12.8f **(75)** - Ranales (USA) (Majestic Light (USA)) 10.6f **(75)**
Form - 4777
Record 2000 - 1st:0 2nd:0 3rd:0 Ran:4
Pre2000 - 1st:1 2nd:0 3rd:0 Ran:1
Win Prizemoney £3,988 *Total Prizemoney* £6,188
Wins * 1999 Oct Doncas (G-S) 7f 82+ <
2000 Turf 0-4: (10f 2, 11f, 12f) (gd 3, g-f)
Lengthy, very useful filly. Turf high 97 (1st run) - 4th of 5 to Solaia (10 May Chester 11f g-f RF 1130). Finished fourth of five in the Cheshire Oaks in the spring, but was held in better company afterwards. **B W Hills [1-5] K Abdulla.*

FAMOUS (FR) BHB 27f28a **RR 36f 28a** 4694[6]
7 b g Tropular - Famous Horse (FR) (Labus (FR)) 12.8f **(52)**
Form - 45720075008000876
Record 2000 - 1st:0 2nd:0 3rd:0 Ran:13
Pre2000 - 1st:2 2nd:5 3rd:2 Ran:40
Win Prizemoney £5,592 *Total Prizemoney* £10,061
Wins * 1999 Oct Sandow (SFT) H 10f 43 48 <
* 1999 Aug Bright (G-S) H 10f 35 39
2000 Turf 0-11: (8f, 10f 4, 12f 6) (sft, g-s, gd 4, g-f 2, frm 3) 2000 AW 0-2: (12f 2) (Equi, Fibr)
Moderate gelding, effective 8 to 10f, acts on g-s - acts on Equi, has worn blinkers. Turf high 42. AW high 29. Inconsistent.
**J J Bridger [2-53] J J Bridger (from G L Moore [0-1] May 1998).*

FANAAR BHB 107f **RR 110f** 4105[3]
3 ch c Unfuwain (USA) 11.4f **(74)** - Catalonda (African Sky) 7.7f **(50)**
Form - 1813
Record 2000 - 1st:2 2nd:0 3rd:1 Ran:4
Win Prizemoney £12,555 *Total Prizemoney* £15,885
Wins * **2000** Jly Sandow (GD) 8.1f 110 <
* **2000** Apr Newmar (G-S) 8f 98
2000 Turf 2-4: (8f 2-3, 9f) (gd 2-4)
Well made, Group-class colt. Turf high 110 - 1st of 7 from Cornelius (7 Jly Sandown RF 2607). Unraced at two, he ran out the clear-cut winner of the Wood Ditton on his debut, form which has been franked numerous times. Finished eighth when taking on the big guns in the St James's Palace Stakes, but was back at his right level when winning a Sandown conditions event next time. He was slightly disappointing when only third in a York Listed event over ten furlongs on his final start.
**J Noseda [2-4] Saleh Al Homeizi.*

FANCY A FORTUNE (IRE) BHB 48f44a **RR 42f 44a** 195[7]
6 b g Fools Holme (USA) 10.3f **(64)** - Fancy's Girl (FR) (Nadjar (FR)) 7.2f **(49)**
Form - 577
Record 2000 - 1st:0 2nd:0 3rd:0 Ran:3
Pre2000 - 1st:3 2nd:7 3rd:6 Ran:43
Win Prizemoney £7,907 *Total Prizemoney* £17,976
Wins * 1998 Jly Beverl (GD) SH 7.5f 52 60
* 1998 May Thirsk (GD) S 7f 56
* 1997 Aug Thirsk (GD) H 7f 60 64 <
2000 AW 0-3: (7f, 8f 2) (Fibr 3)
Moderate gelding, effective 7 to 8f, best at 8f, acts on gd to hrd, often wears blinkers (very effectively), excels at Thirsk. AW high 35. **D Nicholls [3-37] V Greaves (from J Pearce [0-9] Oct 1996).*

FANDANGO DREAM (IRE) BHB 35f **RR 37f** 4112[8]
4 ch g Magical Wonder (USA) 7.2f **(60)** - Fandikos (IRE) (Taufan (USA)) 7f **(57)**
Form - 04574413558
Record 2000 - 1st:1 2nd:0 3rd:1 Ran:11
Pre2000 - 1st:0 2nd:0 3rd:0 Ran:13
Win Prizemoney £2,268 *Total Prizemoney* £3,763
Wins * **2000** Jly Chepst (G-F) H 12.1f 27 31 <
2000 Turf 1-11: (11f, 12f 1-6, 14f, 16f 2, 18f) (g-s, gd, g-f 3, frm 1-6)
Neat, very moderate gelding, effective 8f, acts on gd, has worn blinkers. Turf high 37. Consistent.
**M D I Usher [1-24] Midweek Racing.*

FANFARE **RR 89f** 4741[10]
3 b f Deploy 11.4f **(67)** - Tashinsky (USA) (Nijinsky (CAN)) 10.3f **(77)**
Form - 711824160
Record 2000 - 1st:3 2nd:1 3rd:0 Ran:9
Pre2000 - 1st:0 2nd:0 3rd:0 Ran:2
Win Prizemoney £17,332 *Total Prizemoney* £19,941
Wins * **2000** Aug Goodwo (GD) H 14f 81 87 <

* 2000 May Sandow (HVY) H 10f 72 75
* 2000 May Windso (G-F) H 11.6f 63 70
2000 Turf 3-9: (8f, 10f 1-1, 11f, 12f 1-2, 14f 1-3, 15f) (g-s 1-2, gd, g-f 1-4, frm 1-2)
Light-framed, useful filly, effective 12 to 15f, acts on gd to g-f, best on g-f, likes right handed tracks, prefers tight tracks. Turf high 89 - 4th of 9 to Cephalonia (12 Jly Newmarket 15f gd RF 2745) - also 1st of 8 getting 14lb from Dollar Bird (5 Aug Goodwood RF 3396). She is a useful handicapper at up to 14 furlongs and scored three times last season. Suited by come-from-behind tactics.
**G A Butler [3-11] T D Holland-Martin.*

FANNY PARNELL BHB 50a **RR 50a** 470[8]

4 b f Local Suitor (USA) 9.7f **(58)** - Heart Broken **(58f 74a)** (Bustino) 10.4f **(64)**
Form - 0828
Record 2000 - 1st:0 2nd:1 3rd:0 Ran:3
Pre2000 - 1st:0 2nd:0 3rd:0 Ran:1
Win Prizemoney £0 *Total Prizemoney* £651
2000 AW 0-3: (6f, 7f 2) (Fibr 3)
Strong, fair filly. AW high 50. **J G FitzGerald [0-4] J G FitzGerald.*

FANTAIL BHB 66f **RR 72f** 3803[6]

6 b g Taufan (USA) 8.3f **(65)** - Eleganza (IRE) (Kings Lake (USA)) 10.8f **(67)**
Form - 08866
Record 2000 - 1st:0 2nd:0 3rd:0 Ran:5
Pre2000 - 1st:5 2nd:0 3rd:2 Ran:23
Win Prizemoney £21,759 *Total Prizemoney* £31,189
Wins * 1998 Jun Beverl (GD) H 12f 83 87 <
* 1997 Nov Redcar (GD) H 11f 78 84+
* 1997 Jly Redcar (G-S) H 10f 76 79
* 1997 Jun Hamilt (SFT) H 11.1f 73 77
* 1997 May Redcar (G-F) H 11f 67 77
2000 Turf 0-5: (10f 2, 11f, 12f 2) (g-f 4, frm)
Above-average gelding, has worn blinkers. Turf high 72. Consistent. **M H Tompkins [5-28] The Hon Mrs Tritton.*

FANTASIA GIRL (IRE) **RR 95f** 5355a[7]

3 b f Caerleon (USA) 10.9f **(79)** - Dreamboat (USA) **(76f)** (Mr Prospector (USA)) 8.8f **(78)**
Form - 21123237
2000 Turf 2-8: (7f, 9f 1-2, 10f 1-4, 12f) (hvy, sft, gd 3, g-f 2-3)
Very useful filly, effective 9 to 12f, acts on sft to g-f, best on g-f, often wears blinkers. Turf high 100 (began Jly) - 2nd of 13 to Firecrest (24 Aug York 12f g-f RF 3932) - also 1st of 12 from Cutting The Edge (23 Jly Tipperary RF 3124a).
**J Oxx in IRE [2-8] Sheikha Hassa.*

FANTASTIC FANTASY (IRE) BHB 79f **RR 80f** 4373[11]

3 b f Lahib (USA) 8f **(69)** - Gay Fantasy (Troy) 10.4f **(68)**
Form - 116210
Record 2000 - 1st:3 2nd:1 3rd:0 Ran:6
Pre2000 - 1st:0 2nd:0 3rd:1 Ran:3
Win Prizemoney £12,429 *Total Prizemoney* £15,239
Wins * 2000 Aug Nottin (GD) H 14.1f 76 80 <
*** 2000** Jun Yarmou (GD) H 11.5f 71 75
*** 2000** Mar Southw (GD) H 10f 67 73+
2000 Turf 3-6: (10f 1-1, 11f 1-2, 12f, 14f 1-2) (gd 3-3, g-f, frm 2)
Scopey, decent filly, effective 10 to 14f, best at 11f, acts on gd to g-f, best on gd, likes tight tracks. Turf high 80 - 1st of 7 giving 8lb to Brisbane Road (21 Aug Nottingham RF 3841) - also 1st of 11 getting 6lb from Full Ahead (7 Jun Yarmouth RF 1792).
**J L Dunlop [3-9] Windflower Overseas Holdings Inc.*

FANTASTIC LIGHT (USA) **RR 126f** 5331a[5]

4 b c Rahy (USA) 9.1f **(80)** - Jood (USA) (Nijinsky (CAN)) 10.3f **(77)**
Form - 1252145
Record 2000 - 1st:2 2nd:2 3rd:0 Ran:7
Pre2000 - 1st:5 2nd:1 3rd:2 Ran:10
Win Prizemoney £1,048,636 *Total Prizemoney* £1,398,089
Wins * **2000** Spt Belmon (FST) G1 11f 120+
2000 Mar Nad Al (GD) G3 12f 125 <
1999 Spt Newbur (G-S) L 11f 125 <
1999 Aug York (GD) G2 11.9f 121
1999 Apr Sandow (SFT) G3 10f 108
1998 Aug Sandow (G-F) 8.1f 93
1998 Aug Sandow (GD) 7.1f 82+
2000 Turf 2-7: (10f, 11f 1-1, 12f 1-5) (g-s, gd 1-2, frm 3)
Scopey, top-class colt, effective 10 to 12f, best at 12f, acts on frm, best on gd, and excels at Ascot. Turf high 126 - 2nd of 7 to Montjeu (29 Jly Ascot 12f gd RF 3203) - also 1st of 16 getting 2lb from Caitano (25 Mar Nad Al Sheba RF 0578a). Consistent. Effective on Turf and sand, he took on the best all season, and is a thoroughly admirable colt.
**S bin Suroor [1-6] Godolphin (from Sir Michael Stoute [6-11] Mar 2000).*

FANTASY ADVENTURER BHB 37f62a **RR 50f 62a** 5083[14]

3 b g Magic Ring (IRE) 6.5f **(64)** - Delicious **(53f)** (Dominion) 8.5f **(63)**
Form - 00048400000
Record 2000 - 1st:0 2nd:0 3rd:0 Ran:11
Pre2000 - 1st:0 2nd:0 3rd:0 Ran:3
Win Prizemoney £0 *Total Prizemoney* £905
2000 Turf 0-11: (5f, 6f 6, 7f 2, 8f 2) (hvy, g-s, g-f 6, frm 3)
Leggy, fair gelding. Turf high 50. Becoming disappointing.
**J J Quinn [0-14] The Fantasy Fellowship.*

FANTASY BELIEVER BHB 76f **RR 76f** 4742[16]

2 b g Sure Blade (USA) 10.6f **(66)** - Delicious **(53f)** (Dominion) 8.5f **(63)**
Form - 3242216020
Record 2000 - 1st:1 2nd:4 3rd:1 Ran:10
Win Prizemoney £2,808 *Total Prizemoney* £7,864
Wins * **2000** Jly Mussel (G-S) 5f 72 <
2000 Turf 1-10: (5f 1-9, 6f) (hvy, g-s, gd 1-2, g-f, frm 5)
Above-average gelding, effective 5f, acts on hvy to frm, excels at Haydock and Hamilton. Turf high 76 - 2nd of 5 giving 3lb to Muja Farewell (19 Jun Windsor 5f frm RF 2107) - also 1st of 8 from Baron Crocodile (10 Jly Musselburgh RF 2668). Consistent. An honest five-furlong juvenile, he seems to act on any ground.
**J J Quinn [1-10] The Fantasy Fellowship.*

FANTASY HILL (IRE) BHB 97f **RR 99f** 3577[4]

4 b g Danehill (USA) 9.1f **(79)** - Gay Fantasy (Troy) 10.4f **(68)**
Form - 534814
Record 2000 - 1st:1 2nd:0 3rd:1 Ran:6
Pre2000 - 1st:1 2nd:1 3rd:2 Ran:8
Win Prizemoney £21,338 *Total Prizemoney* £45,802
Wins * **2000** Aug Cheste (GD) H 18.7f 95 98+ <
* 1999 May Nottin (FRM) H 14.1f 81 87
2000 Turf 1-6: (14f, 16f 3, 19f 1-2) (g-s, gd 2, g-f 1-2, frm)
Unfurnished, very useful gelding, effective 14 to 19f, best at 16f, acts on gd to frm, has worn blinkers, prefers left handed tracks, excels at Chester. Turf high 99 - 4th of 9 giving 3lb to Dominant Duchess (12 Aug Ascot 16f gd RF 3577) - also 1st of 6 giving 7lb to Virgin Soldier (6 Aug Chester RF 3414). In the frame in the Chester Cup and the Northumberland Plate, he gained his reward when given a fine ride by Eddery to win at Chester in August. He looks capable of winning a big staying handicap.
**J L Dunlop [2-14] Windflower Overseas Holdings Inc.*

FANTASY PARK **RR 85f** 964[1]

3 b c Sanglamore (USA) 12.9f **(67)** - Fantasy Flyer (USA) (Lear Fan (USA)) 8.5f **(73)**
Form - 1
Record 2000 - 1st:1 2nd:0 3rd:0 Ran:1
Win Prizemoney £3,945 *Total Prizemoney* £3,945
Wins * **2000** May Bath (G-S) 10.2f 85 <
2000 Turf 1-1: (10f 1-1) (gd 1-1)
Strong, currently useful colt. (1st run) - 1st of 15 from Trahern (2 May Bath RF 0964). **Mrs A J Perrett [1-1] K Abdulla.*

FANTASY RIDGE BHB 99f **RR 98?f** 4990[10]

2 ch f Indian Ridge 7.6f **(74)** - Footlight Fantasy (USA) **(66f)** (Nureyev (USA)) 8.7f **(78)**
Form - 150
Record 2000 - 1st:1 2nd:0 3rd:0 Ran:3
Win Prizemoney £3,815 *Total Prizemoney* £3,815
Wins * **2000** Aug Salisb (G-F) 7f 98+ <
2000 Turf 1-3: (7f 1-3) (gd, g-f 1-2)
Currently very useful filly. Turf high 98 (1st run) (began Aug) - 1st of 15 from S W Three (11 Aug Salisbury RF 3567). She won by eight lengths on her debut, but her bubble was burst in a Group Three at Goodwood and the Rockfel at Newmarket. Needs to take a drop in class. **M R Channon [1-3] Helena Springfield Ltd.*

FANTAZIA BHB 95f **RR 102f** 4740[23]
4 b f Zafonic (USA) 9f **(83)** - Trescalini (IRE) (Sadler's Wells (USA)) 10f **(76)**
Form - 250
Record 2000 - 1st:0 2nd:1 3rd:0 Ran:3
Pre2000 - 1st:3 2nd:0 3rd:2 Ran:9
Win Prizemoney £22,295 *Total Prizemoney* £30,662
Wins * 1999 Aug Newmar (G-F) H 10f 81 84 <
* 1999 Aug Redcar (GD) H 11f 76 79
* 1999 Jly Redcar (FRM) H 10f 73 79
2000 Turf 0-3: (9f, 10f, 12f) (g-f 3)
Very useful filly, effective 10 to 12f, acts on g-f. Turf high 102 (1st run) - 2nd of 8 to Lafite (17 May York 10f g-f RF 1262). Completed a summer hat-trick in '99, and had been off the track for nine months before being caught on the line on her York reappearance. Ridden to get the trip when tried over twelve furlongs next time and was never a threat in the Cambridgeshire. She is suited by fast ground.
**J R Fanshawe [3-9] Byerley Turf (from M Johnston [0-3] Oct 1998).*

FAN-TC GEM BHB 35f34a **RR 41f 34a** 128[7]
4 b f Lugana Beach 7f **(63)** - Florac (IRE) **(27df 32a)** (Sayf El Arab (USA)) 7.1f **(54)**
Form - 06077
Record 2000 - 1st:0 2nd:0 3rd:0 Ran:4
Pre2000 - 1st:0 2nd:0 3rd:0 Ran:4
2000 AW 0-4: (7f 3, 8f) (Fibr 4)
Strong, moderate filly. AW high 30.
**J Balding [0-8] Spring Hill Syndicate.*

FAR AHEAD BHB 68f65a **RR 68f 65a** 2061[13]
8 b g Soviet Star (USA) 8.6f **(74)** - Cut Ahead (Kalaglow) 9.8f **(67)**
Form - 070
Record 2000 - 1st:0 2nd:0 3rd:0 Ran:3
Pre2000 - 1st:6 2nd:4 3rd:6 Ran:28
Win Prizemoney £123,429 *Total Prizemoney* £133,679
Wins * 1997 Aug York (GD) H 13.9f 82 92 <
* 1997 Jun Beverl (G-F) H 12f 82 86
* 1996 Spt Thirsk (G-F) H 12f 79 83
* 1996 Aug Thirsk (G-F) H 12f 74 77
2000 Turf 0-3: (12f 3) (gd 2, g-f)
Average gelding. Turf high 68. Becoming disappointing.
**J L Eyre [8-34] Sunpak Potatoes (from Mrs V A Aconley [0-2] Jly 1995).*

FARAUDE BHB 47f42a **RR 53f 42a** 5160[13]
2 b f Farfelu - Pennine Star (IRE) (Pennine Walk) 8.5f **(61)**
Form - 740
Record 2000 - 1st:0 2nd:0 3rd:0 Ran:3
Win Prizemoney £0 *Total Prizemoney* £469
2000 Turf 0-3: (6f, 7f, 8f) (sft, gd 2)
Currently fair filly. Turf high 53 (began Spt).
**W R Muir [0-3] John O'Mulloy.*

FARAWAY JOHN (IRE) RR 4581[P]
2 b c Farhaan - Indiana Dancer (Hallgate)
Form - P
Record 2000 - 1st:0 2nd:0 3rd:0 Ran:1
2000 Turf 0-1: (6f) (gd)
Currently very moderate colt. **G P Enright [0-1] Neil Kenworthy.*

FARAWAY LOOK (USA) BHB 78f85a **RR 62f 85a** 5016[1]
3 br c Distant View (USA) - Summer Trip (USA) (L'Emigrant (USA)) 10.5f **(62)**
Form - 42711
Record 2000 - 1st:2 2nd:1 3rd:0 Ran:5
Win Prizemoney £5,139 *Total Prizemoney* £6,666
Wins * **2000** *Oct Wolver (STD) H 9.4f 71 88+* <
* **2000** *Oct Wolver (STD) H 9.4f 64 69*
2000 Turf 0-3: (7f, 8f 2) (gd 2, g-f) 2000 AW 2-2: (9f 2-2) (Fibr 2-2)
Scopey, useful colt. Turf high 62 (began Aug). AW high 88 (began Oct) - 1st of 11 giving 13lb to Shalbeblue (17 Oct Wolverhampton RF 5016). **J R Fanshawe [2-5] Cheveley Park Stud.*

FARCE RR 51f 5157[11]
2 b f King's Theatre (IRE) - Satiric (IRE) (Doyoun) 9f **(69)**
Form - 0
Record 2000 - 1st:0 2nd:0 3rd:0 Ran:1
2000 Turf 0-1: (8f) (sft)
Currently fair filly. **B Smart [0-1] B H Simpson.*

FAR CRY (IRE) BHB 118f90a **RR 119f 90a** 3342[2]
5 b g Pharly (FR) 11.5f **(64)** - Darabaka (IRE) (Doyoun) 9f **(69)**
Form - 22
Record 2000 - 1st:0 2nd:2 3rd:0 Ran:2
Pre2000 - 1st:8 2nd:2 3rd:1 Ran:16
Win Prizemoney £117,938 *Total Prizemoney* £191,263
Wins * 1999 Spt Doncas (G-F) G3 18f 105 <
* 1999 Jun Newcas (G-F) H 16.1f 89 95
* 1999 Apr Kempto (GD) H 16f 85 87
1999 Mar Wolver (STD) H 16.2f 82 102
1999 Feb Southw (STD) H 16f 73 89+
1998 Dec Southw (STD) H 12f 67 74
1998 Dec Southw (STD) 14f 71+
1998 Nov Southw (STD) 12f 67+
2000 Turf 0-2: (16f, 20f) (gd, g-f)
High-class gelding, effective 16 to 20f, acts on gd to g-f. Turf high 119 - 2nd of 8 to Royal Rebel (3 Aug Goodwood 16f gd RF 3342). After a rather disappointing hurdling campaign, he only found Kayf Tara too strong on his return to the Flat in the Ascot Gold Cup and was only just beaten in the Goodwood Cup. Unfortunately, he ran badly in the Melbourne Cup but reportedly finished lame.
**M C Pipe [4-11] Mrs Nicky Chambers (from Sir Mark Prescott [5-10] Mar 1999).*

FAREHAM RR 32f 4580[16]
2 b f Komaite (USA) 6.9f **(61)** - Lizzy Cantle (Homing) 7.8f **(59)**
Form - 780
Record 2000 - 1st:0 2nd:0 3rd:0 Ran:3
2000 Turf 0-3: (5f, 6f, 7f) (gd, g-f, frm)
Currently very moderate filly, has worn blinkers. Turf high 32 (began Aug). **G G Margarson [0-3] Brian Cantle.*

FARFALA (FR) BHB 99f **RR 101f** 4330[14]
4 gr f Linamix (FR) 8.2f **(64)** - Fragrant Hill (Shirley Heights) 10.3f **(74)**
Form - 52370
Record 2000 - 1st:0 2nd:1 3rd:1 Ran:5
Pre2000 - 1st:1 2nd:0 3rd:1 Ran:4
Win Prizemoney £15,070 *Total Prizemoney* £36,567
Wins 1999 Spt Chanti (GD) L 12f 98 <
2000 Turf 0-5: (10f 3, 12f 2) (gd, g-f 4)
Very useful filly, effective 10 to 12f, best at 12f, acts on sft to g-f, best on g-f. Turf high 101 - 2nd of 8 giving 11lb to Miss Lorilaw (6 Aug Newbury 12f g-f RF 3420). In the frame in listed races at ten and twelve furlongs.
**P F I Cole [0-5] M Arbib (from A Fabre in FR [1-4] Oct 1999).*

FARHA (USA) BHB 80f **RR 86+f** 4440[1]
2 b f Nureyev (USA) 8.4f **(84)** - Arutua (USA) (Riverman (USA)) 9.1f **(76)**
Form - 321
Record 2000 - 1st:1 2nd:1 3rd:1 Ran:3
Win Prizemoney £3,217 *Total Prizemoney* £5,820
Wins * **2000** Spt Nottin (G-S) 6.1f 86+ <
2000 Turf 1-3: (5f, 6f 1-2) (gd 1-1, g-f, frm)
Currently useful filly. Turf high 86 (began Jly) - 1st of 12 from Hiraeth (15 Spt Nottingham RF 4440).
**B Hanbury [1-3] Hamdan Al Maktoum.*

FARMOST BHB 83f88a **RR 85+f 88a** 3681a[1]
7 ch g Pharly (FR) 11.5f **(64)** - Dancing Meg (USA) (Marshua's Dancer (USA)) 8.6f **(75)**
Form - 11
Record 2000 - 1st:1 2nd:0 3rd:0 Ran:1
Pre2000 - 1st:15 2nd:6 3rd:1 Ran:35
Win Prizemoney £91,153 *Total Prizemoney* £99,976
Wins * **2000** Aug Tramor (G-F) H 9f 80+
* 1999 *Nov Lingfi (STD) H 10f 85 87*
* 1999 Jly Redcar (FRM) 9f 74
* 1999 Jly Cheste (G-F) H 10.3f 70 71
* 1999 Jun Chepst (GD) H 10.2f 67 70
* 1997 *Dec Wolver (STD) L 9.4f 100* <
* 1997 *Nov Wolver (STD) H 8.5f 82 87*
* 1997 *Spt Wolver (STD) H 9.4f 70 84*

* 1997 Spt Bright (FRM) H 10f 80 85
* 1997 Jly Bath (FRM) 10.2f 78
* 1996 *Aug Wolver (STD) H 9.4f 66 71*
* 1996 Jly Bright (FRM) H 8f 75 79
* 1996 Jun Folkes (G-F) 6.9f 78
* 1996 May Bright (GD) 7f 76
* 1996 May Sandow (GD) H 7.1f 61 69
* 1996 *Jan Wolver (STD) 6f 56*

2000 Turf 1-1: (9f 1-1) (g-f 1-1)
Very useful gelding, effective 9 to 10f, acts on g-f - acts on Equi, prefers left handed tracks. (1st run) - 1st of 7 getting 5lb from Molly-O (13 Aug Tramore RF 3681a). He was banned from racing out of stalls in Britain, so his shrewd connections sent him for a race at Tramore which was started by flag. He has since been retired. **Sir Mark Prescott [16-36] Neil Greig/Osborne House III.*

FARRFESHEENA (USA) BHB 95f RR 99f 5314[4]

3 ch f Rahy (USA) 9.1f **(80)** - Bevel (USA) (Mr Prospector (USA)) 8.8f **(78)**
Form - 24
Record 2000 - 1st:0 2nd:1 3rd:0 Ran:2
Pre2000 - 1st:0 2nd:0 3rd:0 Ran:1
Win Prizemoney £0 *Total Prizemoney* £2,605
2000 Turf 0-2: (8f, 10f) (sft, g-f)
Scopey, currently very useful filly. Turf high 99 (1st run) (began Jly) - 2nd of 4 to Velvet Lady (30 Jly Ascot 8f g-f RF 3230). Was having her first run for 13 months when narrowly beaten in an Ascot maiden in July. Did not run for another three months after and has clearly had her problems.
**S bin Suroor [0-2] Godolphin (from D R Loder in FR [0-1] Jun 1999).*

FARRIER'S GAMBLE BHB 44f RR 40f 4396[16]

4 ch f Belmez (USA) 11.4f **(65)** - Chrisanthy (So Blessed) 8.7f **(67)**
Form - 58050
Record 2000 - 1st:0 2nd:0 3rd:0 Ran:5
Pre2000 - 1st:0 2nd:0 3rd:0 Ran:1
2000 Turf 0-5: (5f, 6f 3, 7f) (g-s, g-f, frm 3)
Small, moderate filly, has worn blinkers. Turf high 40.
**R M Flower [0-6] D Leadbetter & J M Gamble.*

FAR SOUTH TRADER RR 70f 5076[4]

2 gr c Blushing Flame (USA) - Podrida (Persepolis (FR)) 6.4f **(67)**
Form - 04
Record 2000 - 1st:0 2nd:0 3rd:0 Ran:2
Win Prizemoney £0 *Total Prizemoney* £222
2000 Turf 0-2: (6f, 8f) (g-s, gd)
Currently above-average colt. Turf high 70 (began Spt) - 4th of 8 giving 5lb to Among Women (19 Oct Brighton 8f g-s RF 5076).
**R J O'Sullivan [0-2] Isle of Wight Bloodstock And Racing.*

FAS BHB 19f23a RR 25f 23a 3972[4]

4 ch g Weldnaas (USA) 8.4f **(55)** - Polly's Teahouse (Shack (USA)) 5.8f **(53)**
Form - 675040770874
Record 2000 - 1st:0 2nd:0 3rd:0 Ran:12
Pre2000 - 1st:0 2nd:0 3rd:0 Ran:8
Win Prizemoney £0 *Total Prizemoney* £509
2000 Turf 0-9: (7f 2, 8f 4, 9f 2, 12f) (gd, g-f 4, frm 4) 2000 AW 0-3: (7f, 8f 2) (Fibr 3)
Workmanlike, little account gelding, often wears blinkers. Turf high 30. AW high 26. **J D Bethell [0-20] F & T Walton.*

FASHION BHB 75f RR 75+f 3686[1]

3 b f Bin Ajwaad (IRE) - New Generation (Young Generation) 7.7f **(63)**
Form - 11
Record 2000 - 1st:2 2nd:0 3rd:0 Ran:2
Pre2000 - 1st:1 2nd:0 3rd:2 Ran:4
Win Prizemoney £10,684 *Total Prizemoney* £11,701
Wins * **2000** Aug Beverl (G-F) H 9.9f 66 75+ <
* **2000** Aug Lingfi (G-F) 10f 70+
* 1999 Oct Pontef (GD) H 8f 62 70

2000 Turf 2-2: (10f 2-2) (g-f 1-1, frm 1-1)
Lengthy, above-average filly, effective 8 to 10f, best at 10f, acts on g-f to frm, best on g-f. Turf high 75 (began Aug) - 1st of 10 giving 11lb to Noble Calling (16 Aug Beverley RF 3686) - also 1st of 10 getting 6lb from Keltic Bard (11 Aug Lingfield RF 3556).
**Sir Mark Prescott [3-6] H R H Prince Fahd Salman.*

FASTBEAT RACING BHB 20f RR 3607[13]

3 b f Safawan 6.6f **(60)** - Little Vixen (Aragon) 8.1f **(60)**
Form - 00
Record 2000 - 1st:0 2nd:0 3rd:0 Ran:2
Pre2000 - 1st:0 2nd:0 3rd:0 Ran:1
2000 Turf 0-2: (7f, 10f) (frm 2)
Light-framed, currently very poor filly. (began Jly) - 13th of 13 to Term of Endearment (13 Aug Leicester 7f frm RF 3607).
**T Keddy [0-2] J S Camilleri (from A Senior [0-1] Aug 1999).*

FAST BUCK (IRE) RR 52f 3127[9]

2 b br g Petardia 8.2f **(58)** - Lady Montekin (Montekin) 11.1f **(55)**
Form - 000500
Record 2000 - 1st:0 2nd:0 3rd:0 Ran:6
2000 Turf 0-6: (5f, 6f 3, 7f 2) (gd 2, g-f, frm 3)
Fair gelding, had worn blinkers. Turf high 52. (DEAD)
**J J Quinn [0-6] Carlton Partnership.*

FASTESTBARBERALIVE RR 25[9]

5 b g Full Extent (USA) 5.2f **(50)** - Please Please Me (IRE) (Tender King) 6.8f **(54)**
Form - 0
Record 2000 - 1st:0 2nd:0 3rd:0 Ran:1
Pre2000 - 1st:0 2nd:0 3rd:0 Ran:1
2000 AW 0-1: (8f) (Equi)
Currently very poor gelding.
**M Madgwick [0-2] Trevor Mitchell (from J J Bridger [0-1] Oct 1999).*

FAST FOIL (IRE) BHB 76f RR 70f 3418[9]

2 b f Lahib (USA) 8f **(69)** - Fast Chick (Henbit (USA)) 9f **(61)**
Form - 32630
Record 2000 - 1st:0 2nd:1 3rd:2 Ran:5
Win Prizemoney £0 *Total Prizemoney* £2,670
2000 Turf 0-5: (5f, 6f 3, 7f) (g-s, gd, g-f, frm 2)
Above-average filly. Turf high 70.
**M R Channon [0-5] The Savoyards.*

FAST FORTUNE BHB 47f40a RR 36f 40a 5015[8]

2 ch f Forzando 7.2f **(63)** - High Cut **(66df)** (Dashing Blade)
Form - 78
Record 2000 - 1st:0 2nd:0 3rd:0 Ran:2
2000 Turf 0-1: (5f) (gd) 2000 AW 0-1: (6f) (Fibr)
Currently very moderate filly. **J M P Eustace [0-2] J C Smith.*

FAST FORWARD FRED BHB 52f42a RR 54f 42a 4112[4]

9 gr g Sharrood (USA) 11.1f **(67)** - Sun Street (Ile de Bourbon (USA)) 10.1f **(67)**
Form - 803524
Record 2000 - 1st:0 2nd:1 3rd:1 Ran:6
Pre2000 - 1st:3 2nd:3 3rd:0 Ran:18
Win Prizemoney £9,697 *Total Prizemoney* £13,654
Wins * 1998 Aug Sandow (G-F) H 16.4f 48 57 <
* 1998 Aug Bath (FRM) H 17.2f 48 52
* 1998 Jly Chepst (GD) H 18f 43 49

2000 Turf 0-6: (15f, 16f 3, 17f, 18f) (gd, g-f, frm 3, hrd)
Fair gelding, effective 15 to 17f, acts on frm to hrd, best on frm, prefers tight tracks. Turf high 54 - 2nd of 7 giving 3lb to Our Monogram (25 Aug Bath 17f hrd RF 3956).
**L MontagueHall [3-23] Freddie And The Dreamers (from G Lewis [0-2] Oct 1994).*

FASTINA (DEN) RR 87f 4555[5]

2 b f Dunphy - Farandole (DEN) (Gay Baron)
Form - 437345
Record 2000 - 1st:0 2nd:0 3rd:2 Ran:6
Win Prizemoney £0 *Total Prizemoney* £1,667
2000 Turf 0-6: (6f, 7f 3, 8f 2) (gd 2, g-f 2, frm, hrd)
Useful filly. Turf high 87.
**R Guest [0-6] Bo Ejler Rasmussen & Jan Hansen.*

FASTRACK TIME BHB 38f RR 41f 4396[14]

3 ch g Clantime 6.6f **(57)** - Bitch **(37f 32a)** (Risk Me (FR)) 5.9f **(53)**
Form - 000000
Record 2000 - 1st:0 2nd:0 3rd:0 Ran:6
Pre2000 - 1st:0 2nd:0 3rd:0 Ran:5
2000 Turf 0-5: (5f 2, 6f 3) (g-f 3, frm 2) 2000 AW 0-1: (5f) (Fibr)
Light-framed, moderate gelding, has worn blinkers. Turf high 41.

**S Mellor [0-11] R N Fearnall.*

FAST TRACK (IRE) BHB 101f **RR 105f** 1882[6]

3 b c Doyoun 10.7f **(69)** - Manntika (Kalamoun) 10.4f **(67)**
Form - 36
Record 2000 - 1st:0 2nd:0 3rd:1 Ran:2
Pre2000 - 1st:1 2nd:0 3rd:0 Ran:1
Win Prizemoney £3,330 *Total Prizemoney* £6,695
Wins * 1999 Oct Yarmou (G-S) 7f 87+ <
2000 Turf 0-2: (10f 2) (gd, frm)
Scopey, currently Pattern-class colt. Turf high 105 (1st run) - 3rd of 6 getting 6lb from Hataab (18 May York 10f gd RF 1278). Ran just twice in listed company, running a decent race in the first of them at York. **Sir Michael Stoute [1-3] Maktoum Al Maktoum.*

FASTWAN BHB 20f **RR 15f** 5195[8]

4 ch g Nashwan (USA) 10.3f **(79)** - Jammaayil (IRE) (Lomond (USA)) 8.8f **(65)**
Form - 70005000008
Record 2000 - 1st:0 2nd:0 3rd:0 Ran:11
Pre2000 - 1st:0 2nd:1 3rd:0 Ran:13
Win Prizemoney £0 *Total Prizemoney* £1,429
2000 Turf 0-11: (7f 3, 8f 2, 9f 4, 12f 2) (gd 6, g-f, frm 4)
Scopey, poor gelding, effective 9 to 11f, acts on g-f, has worn blinkers, likes tight tracks. Turf high 19 (began Jly).
**J S Goldie [0-24] Frank Brady.*

FATEHALKHAIR (IRE) BHB 64f59a **RR 66f 59a** 4171[4]

8 ch g Kris 10f **(75)** - Midway Lady (USA) (Alleged (USA)) 10f **(76)**
Form - 48231504
Record 2000 - 1st:1 2nd:1 3rd:1 Ran:8
Pre2000 - 1st:4 2nd:4 3rd:3 Ran:25
Win Prizemoney £22,835 *Total Prizemoney* £33,817
Wins * **2000** Jun Thirsk (FRM) H 12f 62 68 <
* 1999 Spt Thirsk (FRM) H 12f 58 61
* 1999 Jun Catter (G-F) H 12f 49 52
* 1999 Jun Catter (GD) H 12f 45 47
* 1999 Apr Redcar (G-S) H 11f 34 42
2000 Turf 1-7: (12f 1-6, 14f) (gd 3, g-f 2, frm 1-2) 2000 AW 0-1: (12f) (Fibr)
Average gelding, effective 12f, acts on gd to hrd, has worn blinkers, prefers left handed tracks, , excels at Thirsk, does well at Catterick, likes York. Turf high 68 - 1st of 5 giving 2lb to Ile Distinct (20 Jun Thirsk RF 2119). Consistent. A useful hurdler/chaser, he has ability on the Flat too, winning several times over the years, and scored at Thirsk in June. He has sometimes not appeared to relish being put under pressure, but must have a left-handed track and fast ground to show his best. **B Ellison [14-61] R Wagner.*

FATH (USA) BHB 110f **RR 107f** 3966[4]

3 b c Danzig (USA) 8.1f **(88)** - Desirable (Lord Gayle (USA)) 8.8f **(62)**
Form - 0614
Record 2000 - 1st:1 2nd:0 3rd:0 Ran:4
Pre2000 - 1st:1 2nd:1 3rd:0 Ran:2
Win Prizemoney £22,030 *Total Prizemoney* £48,585
Wins * **2000** Aug Doncas (G-F) 6f 105+ <
1999 Aug York (GD) 6f 96++
2000 Turf 1-4: (6f 1-2, 7f, 8f) (gd 2, g-f, frm 1-1)
Strong, Pattern-class colt, effective 6f, acts on gd to frm. Turf high 107 - 4th of 8 getting 3lb from Vision of Night (25 Aug Newmarket 6f g-f RF 3966) - also 1st of 7 getting 12lb from Proud Native (5 Aug Doncaster RF 3388). Snaffled by Godolphin, he won their private Guineas trial in April but finished down the field in the big race itself. Better effort in the Jersey Stakes at Ascot, although he failed to settle,and he won a minor race at Doncaster comfortably. Something seemed amiss on his final start.
**S bin Suroor [1-4] Godolphin (from M P Tregoning [1-2] Spt 1999).*

FATHER JUNINHO (IRE) BHB 87f **RR 98f** 4461[5]

3 b c Distinctly North (USA) 7.4f **(63)** - Shane's Girl (IRE) (Marktingo)
Form - 76523354045
Record 2000 - 1st:0 2nd:1 3rd:2 Ran:11
Pre2000 - 1st:2 2nd:2 3rd:0 Ran:7
Win Prizemoney £9,637 *Total Prizemoney* £27,775
Wins * 1999 Spt Doncas (G-F) H 7f 78 84 <
* 1999 Jly Redcar (FRM) H 7f 84 <
2000 Turf 0-11: (8f, 9f, 10f 5, 11f, 12f 2, 13f) (sft, g-s 2, gd 2, g-f 5, frm)
Workmanlike, very useful colt, effective 8 to 11f, best at 10f, acts on g-s to g-f, best on gd, has worn blinkers, likes left handed tracks. Turf high 99 - 3rd of 13 getting 1lb from Moon Solitaire (12 Jly Newmarket 10f gd RF 2747). Consistent. Progressed throughout his juvenile season and has continued to run well last season, but is found it hard to put his head in front where it matters. Promises to stay a mile and a half plus.
**A P Jarvis [2-18] Haleray Ltd.*

FATHER SEAMUS BHB 55f50a **RR 55f 50a** 5110[10]

2 b g Bin Ajwaad (IRE) - Merry Rous (Rousillon (USA)) 8.2f **(74)**
Form - 00073870
Record 2000 - 1st:0 2nd:0 3rd:1 Ran:8
Win Prizemoney £0 *Total Prizemoney* £313
2000 Turf 0-8: (6f 2, 7f 4, 8f 2) (g-s, gd 2, g-f 4, frm)
Fair gelding. Turf high 55. **P Butler [0-8] P Butler.*

FATHERS FOOTSTEPS BHB 40f **RR 32f** 5100[8]

2 ch c Clantime 6.6f **(57)** - Cousin Jenny (Midyan (USA)) 6f **(60)**
Form - 00008
Record 2000 - 1st:0 2nd:0 3rd:0 Ran:5
2000 Turf 0-4: (5f 3, 6f) (gd 2, frm, hrd) 2000 AW 0-1: (5f) (Fibr)
Very moderate colt. Turf high 32. **C Smith [0-5] A E Needham.*

FATHER TED (IRE) BHB 33f **RR 36tf** 3484[17]

3 b g Catrail (USA) - Firey Encounter (IRE) (Kris) 9.5f **(73)**
Form - 00000
Record 2000 - 1st:0 2nd:0 3rd:0 Ran:5
2000 Turf 0-5: (6f, 7f 3, 8f) (gd, g-f 3, frm)
Very moderate gelding. Turf high 36.
**P Mitchell [0-5] Craggy Island Partnership.*

FATHER THAMES RR 94+f 5073[1]

2 b c Bishop of Cashel - Mistress Thames **(64f)** (Sharpo) 7.7f **(59)**
Form - 31
Record 2000 - 1st:1 2nd:0 3rd:1 Ran:2
Win Prizemoney £3,157 *Total Prizemoney* £3,689
Wins * **2000** Oct Bright (SFT) 7f 94+ <
2000 Turf 1-2: (6f, 7f 1-1) (g-s 1-1, gd)
Currently useful colt. Turf high 94 (began Spt) - 1st of 13 from Lucefer (19 Oct Brighton RF 5073). **J R Fanshawe [1-2] Mrs Denis Haynes.*

FAUTE DE MIEUX BHB 77f62a **RR 78f 62a** 2828[14]

5 ch g Beveled (USA) 6.9f **(64)** - Supreme Rose (Frimley Park) 6.5f **(67)**
Form - 860103320
Record 2000 - 1st:1 2nd:1 3rd:2 Ran:8
Pre2000 - 1st:1 2nd:4 3rd:0 Ran:17
Win Prizemoney £5,443 *Total Prizemoney* £15,027
Wins 2000 Apr Folkes (SFT) 5f 71+ <
1999 Jun Windso (SFT) 5f 71+ <
2000 Turf 1-7: (5f 1-6, 7f) (hvy, g-s 1-1, gd 2, g-f, frm 2) 2000 AW 0-1: (5f) (Fibr)
Above-average gelding, effective 5f, acts on g-s to frm, best on frm, has worn blinkers, excels at Sandown. Turf high 78 - 2nd of 14 getting 9lb from Ambitious (7 Jly Sandown 5f g-f RF 2604) - also 1st of 7 giving 3lb to Corndavon (18 Apr Folkestone RF 0760). Inconsistent.
**M Kettle [0-4] Dagfell Properties Ltd (from E A Wheeler [1-5] Apr 2000).*

FAVORISIO BHB 60f75a **RR 57f 75a** 4864[20]

3 br g Efisio 7.7f **(69)** - Dixie Favor (USA) (Dixieland Band (USA)) 7f **(74)**
Form - 116000
Record 2000 - 1st:2 2nd:0 3rd:0 Ran:6
Pre2000 - 1st:0 2nd:0 3rd:0 Ran:2
Win Prizemoney £5,577 *Total Prizemoney* £5,577
Wins * **2000** *Mar Wolver (STD) H 9.4f 73 77++* <
* **2000** *Feb Wolver (STD) 9.4f 74*
2000 Turf 0-4: (8f 2, 9f, 11f) (hvy, sft, gd, g-f) 2000 AW 2-2: (9f 2-2) (Fibr 2-2)
Above-average gelding, effective 9f, - acts on Fibr. Turf high 44. AW high 77 - 1st of 9 giving 7lb to Shamsan (23 Mar Wolverhampton RF 0482) - also 1st of 11 giving 5lb to Arctic High (29 Feb Wolverhampton RF 0379). Inconsistent.
**Miss J A Camacho [2-8] Elite Racing Club.*

FAY (IRE) BHB 72f **RR 68f** 1267[6]
3 ch f Polish Precedent (USA) 9f **(73)** - My Ballerina (USA) (Sir Ivor) 10.2f **(70)**
Form - 656
Record 2000 - 1st:0 2nd:0 3rd:0 Ran:3
2000 Turf 0-3: (10f, 11f, 12f) (sft, g-s, gd)
Scopey, currently average filly. Turf high 68 - 6th of 13 to Revival (18 May Salisbury 10f gd RF 1267).
**P F I Cole [0-3] H R H Prince Fahd Salman.*

FAY BREEZE (IRE) RR 94f 1635a[1]
4 b c Fayruz 6.6f **(63)** - Loma Breeze (Cure The Blues (USA)) 9.5f **(63)**
Form - 51
2000 Turf 1-2: (7f 1-1, 8f) (g-s, g-f 1-1)
Currently useful colt. Turf high 94 - 1st of 11 getting 3lb from Diamond Snake (28 May Capannelle RF 1635a).
**L d'Auria in ITY [1-3] Signora Dettori.*

FAY KING RR 5018[12]
3 ch g King's Signet (USA) 7f **(51)** - Fay Eden (IRE) (Fayruz)
Form - 00
Record 2000 - 1st:0 2nd:0 3rd:0 Ran:2
2000 Turf 0-1: (10f) (g-s) 2000 AW 0-1: (7f) (Fibr)
Scopey, currently very poor gelding.
**J W Mullins [0-2] The Learners.*

FAYRWAY RHYTHM (IRE) BHB 79f80a **RR 79f 80a** 3573[3]
3 b c Fayruz 6.6f **(63)** - The Way She Moves (North Stoke) 10.4f **(55)**
Form - 445183
Record 2000 - 1st:1 2nd:0 3rd:1 Ran:6
Pre2000 - 1st:0 2nd:2 3rd:0 Ran:5
Win Prizemoney £4,231 *Total Prizemoney* £8,441
Wins * 2000 Jun Carlis (FRM) 9.3f 79 <
2000 Turf 1-5: (9f 1-1, 10f 2, 12f 2) (sft, gd, g-f 1-2, frm) 2000 AW 0-1: (8f) (Fibr)
Above-average colt, effective 7 to 12f, best at 8f, acts on sft to g-f - acts on Fibr, best on g-f. Turf high 79 - 1st of 4 from East Cape (18 Jun Carlisle RF 2071). (1st run) - 3rd of 7 giving 6lb to Inver Gold (11 Aug Wolverhampton 8f Fibr RF 3573). Consistent. Had been running with credit before getting off the mark at Carlisle when dropping in trip and encountering fast ground for the first time.
**M A Jarvis [1-11] Yusof Sepiuddin.*

FAYZ SLIPPER (IRE) BHB 47f **RR 52f** 3697[5]
2 b f Fayruz 6.6f **(63)** - Farriers Slipper (Prince Tenderfoot (USA)) 9f **(61)**
Form - 780424555
Record 2000 - 1st:0 2nd:1 3rd:0 Ran:9
Win Prizemoney £0 *Total Prizemoney* £672
2000 Turf 0-9: (5f 8, 6f) (sft, gd 4, g-f 3, hrd)
Fair filly, effective 5f, acts on g-f. Turf high 52 - 4th of 8 to Dancing Penney (6 Jly Catterick 5f g-f RF 2558).
**T D Easterby [0-9] Ryedale Partners No 2.*

FAZENDA RR 3809[7]
2 b f Piccolo - Petra's Star **(55f)** (Rock City)
Form - 7
Record 2000 - 1st:0 2nd:0 3rd:0 Ran:1
2000 AW 0-1: (6f) (Fibr)
Currently moderate filly. **K McAuliffe [0-1] Miss J Hall.*

FAZZANI (IRE) BHB 74f **RR 74f** 5121[14]
2 b f Shareef Dancer (USA) 10.1f **(67)** - Taj Victory (Final Straw) 7.9f **(64)**
Form - 044437121220
Record 2000 - 1st:2 2nd:3 3rd:1 Ran:12
Win Prizemoney £5,132 *Total Prizemoney* £12,743
Wins 2000 Aug Newcas (SFT) C 8f 67
2000 Aug Thirsk (GD) C 7f 68 <
2000 Turf 2-12: (5f 2, 6f, 7f 1-6, 8f 1-3) (g-s 1-4, gd, g-f 2, frm 1-5)
Above-average filly, effective 7 to 8f, best at 7f, acts on g-s to frm, best on frm. Turf high 74 - 2nd of 11 getting 3lb from Lady Bear (5 Oct York 8f g-s RF 4818) - also 1st of 11 getting 2lb from Emma Clare (4 Aug Thirsk RF 3384).
**M W Easterby [0-3] Chris Brasher (from P C Haslam [1-2] Aug 2000).*

FEARBY CROSS (IRE) BHB 76f **RR 79f** 4865[21]
4 b g Unblest - Two Magpies (Doulab (USA)) 9.8f **(65)**
Form - 134100780
Record 2000 - 1st:2 2nd:0 3rd:1 Ran:9
Pre2000 - 1st:1 2nd:0 3rd:1 Ran:12
Win Prizemoney £15,966 *Total Prizemoney* £20,063
Wins * 2000 May Newbur (SFT) H 6f 75 79
*** 2000** Mar Sandow (G-F) H 5f 70 76
1998 Spt Ayr (G-S) 6f 91+ <
2000 Turf 2-9: (5f 1-3, 6f 1-6) (sft, gd 1-6, g-f 1-2)
Lengthy, above-average gelding, effective 5 to 6f, best at 6f, acts on gd to g-f, best on gd, has worn blinkers. Turf high 79 - 1st of 16 giving 2lb to Bold Effort (31 May Newbury RF 1589) - also 1st of 16 getting 7lb from Prince Prospect (28 Mar Sandown RF 0530). A change of yard saw him in good form in the spring, winning twice. Has won at five furlongs, but appears to need a stiff six at least. Handles fast ground, but looks most effective on an easier surface.
**W J Musson [2-9] Mrs Rita Brown (from J D Bethell [1-12] Oct 1999).*

FEARSOME FACTOR (USA) BHB 56f52a **RR 69f 52a** 4335a[1]
5 b g Alleged (USA) 11.8f **(81)** - Spark of Success (USA) (Topsider (USA)) 8.3f **(71)**
Form - 87402105231
Record 2000 - 1st:2 2nd:2 3rd:1 Ran:10
Pre2000 - 1st:1 2nd:0 3rd:1 Ran:9
Win Prizemoney £12,266 *Total Prizemoney* £15,933
Wins * 2000 Spt Galway (GD) H 12f 70 69
2000 *Feb Wolver (STD) H 16.2f 52 58*
1998 Oct Leopar (HVY) 10f 86+ <
2000 Turf 1-5: (12f 1-4, 16f) (g-s, gd 1-3, g-f) 2000 AW 1-5: (8f, 9f, 12f, 16f 1-2) (Fibr 1-5)
Average gelding, effective 9 to 12f, best at 12f, acts on sft to gd, has worn blinkers, prefers right handed tracks. Turf high 69 (began Jly) - 2nd of 11 giving 3lb to She's Wonderful (2 Aug Galway 12f g-s RF 3462a) - also 1st of 12 giving 3lb to Siamsa (4 Spt Galway RF 4335a). AW high 60.
**M Halford in IRE [1-5] M Woods (from B J Curley [1-6] Feb 2000).*

FEAST OF ROMANCE BHB 57f72a **RR 62f 72a** 4533[9]
3 b g Pursuit of Love 9.5f **(69)** - June Fayre (Sagaro) 9.7f **(55)**
Form - 131656060300400
Record 2000 - 1st:1 2nd:0 3rd:1 Ran:13
Pre2000 - 1st:1 2nd:0 3rd:1 Ran:5
Win Prizemoney £8,915 *Total Prizemoney* £9,569
Wins * 2000 *Jan Wolver (STD) H 6f 72 75* <
*** 1999** *Nov Southw (STD) 6f 74*
2000 Turf 0-10: (5f, 6f 8, 7f) (g-s, g-f 5, frm 4) 2000 AW 1-3: (6f 1-1, 7f 2) (Fibr 1-3)
Workmanlike, above-average gelding, effective 6f, - acts on Fibr, has worn blinkers, likes left handed tracks, likes tight tracks. Turf high 62. AW high 79 - also 1st of 11 getting 8lb from Branston Pickle (6 Jan Wolverhampton RF 0036).
**Miss Gay Kelleway [2-18] K & W Racing Partnership.*

FEATHER 'N LACE (IRE) BHB 63f65a **RR 64f 65a** 2948[10]
4 b f Green Desert (USA) 7.8f **(78)** - Report 'em (USA) (Staff Writer (USA)) 10f **(54)**
Form - 2240
Record 2000 - 1st:0 2nd:2 3rd:0 Ran:4
Pre2000 - 1st:1 2nd:0 3rd:5 Ran:12
Win Prizemoney £4,305 *Total Prizemoney* £10,221
Wins * 1999 Aug Newmar (G-F) C 7f 60 <
2000 Turf 0-3: (7f, 8f 2) (gd, g-f, frm) 2000 AW 0-1: (8f) (Equi)
Light-framed, average filly, effective 6 to 8f, acts on gd to frm - acts on Equi, has worn blinkers, excels at Lingfield. Turf high 64 (1st run) - 2nd of 20 giving 1lb to Compradore (18 May Salisbury 7f gd RF 1272). (1st run) - 2nd of 12 giving 16lb to Tapage (14 Jun Lingfield 8f Equi RF 1971). Consistent. **C A Cyzer [1-16] R M Cyzer.*

FEATHERSTONE LANE BHB 38f51a **RR 35f 51a** 5248[9]
9 b g Siberian Express (USA) 9f **(58)** - Try Gloria (Try My Best (USA)) 7.6f **(67)**
Form - 4584425222316336343502O
Record 2000 - 1st:1 2nd:5 3rd:5 Ran:20
Pre2000 - 1st:7 2nd:17 3rd:21 Ran:133
Win Prizemoney £19,501 *Total Prizemoney* £48,777
Wins * 2000 *May Wolver (STD) H 7f 50 52*

* 1998	*Apr Wolver*	*(STD) C*	*5f*		*67*	
* 1998	*Apr Wolver*	*(STD) C*	*5f*		*65*	
* 1998	*Mar Wolver*	*(STD) S*	*5f*		*60*	
* 1998	*Jan Wolver*	*(STD) H*	*5f*	*49*	*51*	
* 1997	*Aug Wolver*	*(STD) S*	*5f*		*44*	
* 1996	*Feb Wolver*	*(STD) H*	*5f*	*64*	*65*	

2000 AW 1-20: (5f, 6f 13, 7f 1-5, 8f) (Equi 2, Fibr 1-18)

Fair gelding, effective 6 to 7f, best at 6f, - acts on Fibr, often wears blinkers (very effectively), favours left handed tracks, favours tight tracks, and likes Southwell. AW high 59 - 3rd of 8 to Garnock Valley (21 Jly Southwell 6f Fibr RF 3019) - also 1st of 11 getting 14lb from Rock Island Line (11 May Wolverhampton RF 1148).

**Miss L C Siddall [8-153] Miss L C Siddall.*

FEATHERTIME BHB 54f RR 55f 908[3]

4 b f Puissance 7.1f **(60)** - Midnight Owl (FR) (Ardross) 10.6f **(68)**

Form - 533

Record 2000 - 1st:0 2nd:0 3rd:2 Ran:3
Pre2000 - 1st:1 2nd:0 3rd:1 Ran:9

Win Prizemoney £2,410 *Total Prizemoney* £4,043

Wins * 1999 Oct Newcas (G-S) CH 8f 45 52 <

2000 Turf 0-3: (7f, 8f, 10f) (gd 3)

Neat, fair filly, effective 8 to 10f, best at 8f, acts on gd, prefers left handed tracks. Turf high 53 - 3rd of 16 getting 11lb from Itsanothergirl (15 Apr Thirsk 8f gd RF 0739). Consistent.

**Mrs G S Rees [1-11] Brooke Rankin (from P Shakespeare [0-1] Jan 1999).*

FEEL NO FEAR BHB 44f52a RR 47f 52a 2089[6]

7 b m Fearless Action (USA) 8f **(44)** - Charm Bird (Daring March) 7.1f **(61)**

Form - 266

Record 2000 - 1st:0 2nd:0 3rd:0 Ran:1
Pre2000 - 1st:3 2nd:4 3rd:2 Ran:29

Win Prizemoney £7,890 *Total Prizemoney* £12,835

Wins 1999 *Oct Lingfi (STD) S 8f 50*
1999 *Aug Lingfi (STD) SH 8f 44 48*
1998 Jly Newmar (G-F) H 8f 50 55 <

2000 Turf 0-1: (8f) (frm)

Fair mare, effective 7 to 10f, best at 8f, acts on g-f - acts on Equi, has worn blinkers.

**Miss Gay Kelleway [0-3] Crocs Racing (from B J Meehan [2-7] Nov 1999).*

FEEL THE STEEL BHB 24f RR 4374[10]

3 b f Sure Blade (USA) 10.6f **(66)** - Flair Park (Frimley Park) 6.5f **(67)**

Form - 00

Record 2000 - 1st:0 2nd:0 3rd:0 Ran:2

2000 Turf 0-2: (8f, 10f) (g-f, frm)

Workmanlike, currently very poor filly. (began Aug).

**Mrs A E Johnson [0-2] Colin Waldock.*

FEE MAIL BHB 72f RR 70f 1592[13]

4 b f Danehill (USA) 9.1f **(79)** - Wizardry (Shirley Heights) 10.3f **(74)**

Form - 33120

Record 2000 - 1st:1 2nd:1 3rd:2 Ran:5
Pre2000 - 1st:1 2nd:1 3rd:1 Ran:8

Win Prizemoney £6,775 *Total Prizemoney* £10,749

Wins * **2000** May Carlis (FRM) 12f 67 <
* 1999 Oct Windso (SFT) H 11.6f 61 63

2000 Turf 1-5: (12f 1-3, 13f 2) (g-s, gd, g-f 1-1, frm 2)

Neat, above-average filly, effective 8 to 13f, acts on gd to frm, best on frm, prefers tight tracks, excels at Windsor. Turf high 70 - 2nd of 12 getting 4lb from Pulau Pinang (22 May Bath 13f frm RF 1362) - also 1st of 6 from Santa Lucia (12 May Carlisle RF 1162).

**I A Balding [2-13] Gary Coull.*

FEMME FATALE RR 101f 4700[16]

3 b f Fairy King (USA) 7.7f **(75)** - Red Rita (IRE) **(75f)** (Kefaah (USA))

Form - 410

Record 2000 - 1st:1 2nd:0 3rd:0 Ran:3
Pre2000 - 1st:1 2nd:1 3rd:1 Ran:4

Win Prizemoney £18,747 *Total Prizemoney* £23,556

Wins * **2000** Spt Yarmou (G-F) 6f 93+
* 1999 Spt Ayr (G-S) L 6f 100+ <

2000 Turf 1-3: (5f, 6f 1-2) (g-f 2, frm 1-1)

Scopey, very useful filly, effective 6f, acts on gd to frm. Turf high 101 (began Aug) - also 1st of 9 from Blue Velvet (13 Spt Yarmouth RF 4376). Useful at two, when she won the Listed Firth Of Clyde Stakes at Ayr, she ran an encouraging race on her belated return to action in 2000. Showed the right attitude to win a conditions event, but was held in a listed race on her final start.

**W Jarvis [2-7] Anthony Foster.*

FENWICKS PRIDE (IRE) BHB 87f RR 78f 4833[1]

2 b g Imperial Frontier (USA) 7f **(65)** - Stunt Girl (IRE) (Thatching) 8f **(66)**

Form - 5332661851

Record 2000 - 1st:2 2nd:1 3rd:2 Ran:10

Win Prizemoney £9,662 *Total Prizemoney* £11,516

Wins * **2000** Oct York (SFT) H 6f 74 78 <
* **2000** Aug Ripon (GD) 5f 72

2000 Turf 2-10: (5f 1-7, 6f 1-3) (sft, g-s 1-1, gd 4, g-f, frm 1-2, hrd)

Above-average gelding, effective 5 to 6f, best at 5f, acts on g-s to frm, best on frm, has worn blinkers. Turf high 78 - 1st of 7 from Prince Pyramus (6 Oct York RF 4833) - also 1st of 11 from Baron Crocodile (29 Aug Ripon RF 4060). Consistent.

**B S Rothwell [2-10] J H Tattersall.*

FERNDOWN (IRE) BHB 46f RR 41f 3901[10]

2 b f Inzar (USA) - Musical Gem (USA) (The Minstrel (CAN)) 10f **(72)**

Form - 4600

Record 2000 - 1st:0 2nd:0 3rd:0 Ran:4

Win Prizemoney £0 *Total Prizemoney* £276

2000 Turf 0-4: (5f, 6f 2, 7f) (g-f, frm, hrd 2)

Moderate filly. Turf high 41 (began Jly).

**Denys Smith [0-4] Vic Roper.*

FERNS MEMORY BHB 15f RR 22f 339[7]

5 ch m Beveled (USA) 6.9f **(64)** - Sharp Venita (Sharp Edge) 10f **(56)**

Form - 07

Record 2000 - 1st:0 2nd:0 3rd:0 Ran:2
Pre2000 - 1st:0 2nd:0 3rd:0 Ran:3

2000 AW 0-2: (7f, 13f) (Equi 2)

Little account filly, has worn blinkers. AW high 7.

**J J Bridger [0-2] J J Bridger (from W J Musson [0-3] Jun 1998).*

FERNY FACTORS BHB 30f41a RR 26f 41a 2674[19]

4 ch g King Among Kings 7.4f **(49)** -Market Blues (Porto Bello) 8.9f **(43)**

Form - 800000

Record 2000 - 1st:0 2nd:0 3rd:0 Ran:6
Pre2000 - 1st:3 2nd:0 3rd:0 Ran:13

Win Prizemoney £8,139 *Total Prizemoney* £8,139

Wins * 1999 Jun Beverl (GD) H 12f 54 56
* 1999 May Beverl (GD) S 9.9f 46
* 1998 Jly Beverl (GD) S 7.5f 57 <

2000 Turf 0-5: (10f 3, 11f, 12f) (hvy, g-s, gd, g-f, frm) 2000 AW 0-1: (12f) (Fibr)

Lengthy, little account gelding, effective 10 to 12f, acts on gd, has worn blinkers, prefers right handed tracks, favours tight tracks. Turf high 26. Inconsistent. **Ronald Thompson [3-19] B Bruce.*

FERZAO (IRE) BHB 88f92a RR 94f 92a 4968[14]

3 b c Alzao (USA) 9.8f **(73)** - Fer de Lance (IRE) (Diesis) 9.3f **(69)**

Form - 3150040

Record 2000 - 1st:1 2nd:0 3rd:1 Ran:7
Pre2000 - 1st:1 2nd:0 3rd:0 Ran:2

Win Prizemoney £10,382 *Total Prizemoney* £11,975

Wins * **2000** May Windso (GD) 10f 94 <
* 1999 Oct Leices (GD) 7f 84+

2000 Turf 1-7: (8f 4, 10f 1-3) (g-s, gd 3, g-f 1-2, frm)

Scopey, useful colt, effective 7 to 10f, best at 8f, acts on gd to frm. Turf high 94 - 1st of 5 getting 12lb from Kuster (8 May Windsor RF 1099). Won his maiden in good style at Leicester in 1999 and made a promising seasonal debut at Windsor. Returned to winning form with a battling victory on the same track next time when fitted with a cross-noseband, but has been well held in the face of stiff tasks subsequently. **Mrs A J Perrett [2-9] Clive Batt & Mrs Elaine Batt.*

FESTINO (IRE) RR 26f 968[4]

2 b f Lake Coniston (IRE) - Cresalin (Coquelin (USA)) 8.4f **(58)**

Form - 04

Record 2000 - 1st:0 2nd:0 3rd:0 Ran:2

2000 Turf 0-1: (5f) (gd) 2000 AW 0-1: (5f) (Fibr)

Currently little account filly.

**N P Littmoden [0-2] Joy and Valentine Feerick.*

FESTIVE AFFAIR RR 46f 4747[20]

2 b c Mujadil (USA) 7.7f **(70)** - Christmas Kiss **(91df)** (Taufan (USA)) 7f **(57)**
Form - 80
Record 2000 - 1st:0 2nd:0 3rd:0 Ran:2
2000 Turf 0-2: (5f, 6f) (gd, g-f)
Currently moderate colt. Turf high 50 (began Aug).
**B Smart [0-2] The Hackers.*

FFIFFIFFER (IRE) RR 63f 4169[9]

2 b c Definite Article - Merry Twinkle (Martinmas) 7.6f **(59)**
Form - 40
Record 2000 - 1st:0 2nd:0 3rd:0 Ran:2
2000 Turf 0-2: (7f, 8f) (gd, hrd)
Currently average colt. Turf high 63 (began Aug).
**A Dickman [0-2] Mike Smallman.*

FFYNNON GOLD BHB 44f50a RR 62f 50a 5198[4]

3 b f Beveled (USA) 6.9f **(64)** - Sparklingsovereign (Sparkler)
Form - 000006044
Record 2000 - 1st:0 2nd:0 3rd:0 Ran:9
Win Prizemoney £0 *Total Prizemoney* £231
2000 Turf 0-8: (6f 2, 8f 5, 10f) (g-s, gd 3, g-f 3, frm) 2000 AW 0-1: (6f) (Fibr)
Light-framed, average filly. Turf high 62. Inconsistent.
**J G Portman [0-9] The Faraway Partnership.*

FIAMMA ROYALE (IRE) BHB 76f RR 75f 4367[1]

2 b f Fumo Di Londra (IRE) - Ariadne (Bustino) 10.4f **(64)**
Form - 322524201
Record 2000 - 1st:1 2nd:4 3rd:1 Ran:9
Win Prizemoney £3,688 *Total Prizemoney* £7,814
Wins * **2000** Spt Sandow (G-F) 5f 75 <
2000 Turf 1-9: (5f 1-6, 6f 3) (hvy, sft, g-s, gd, g-f 2, frm 1-3)
Above-average filly, effective 5f, acts on hvy to frm, best on frm, excels at Warwick. Turf high 75 - 1st of 16 giving 3lb to Little Callian (13 Spt Sandown RF 4367). Improving.
**Mrs P N Dutfield [1-9] Royal Oak Racing Partnership.*

FIDDLER'S MOLL (IRE) RR 65f 4969[13]

2 b f Dr Devious (IRE) 9.9f **(74)** - Belle Bleue (Blazing Saddles (AUS)) 6.7f **(46)**
Form - 40
Record 2000 - 1st:0 2nd:0 3rd:0 Ran:2
Win Prizemoney £0 *Total Prizemoney* £233
2000 Turf 0-2: (7f, 8f) (g-s, gd)
Currently average filly. Turf high 65 (began Spt).
**B J Meehan [0-2] Miss Gloria Abbey.*

FIDDLER'S ROCK (IRE) BHB 65f RR 54f 5003[13]

5 b g Ballad Rock 7.2f **(63)** - Rockbourne (Midyan (USA)) 6f **(60)**
Form - 66000
Record 2000 - 1st:0 2nd:0 3rd:0 Ran:5
Pre2000 - 1st:2 2nd:3 3rd:1 Ran:17
Win Prizemoney £10,275 *Total Prizemoney* £15,376
Wins 1998 Apr Cork (HVY) 6f 108 <
1997 Apr Leopar (GD) 5f 86
2000 Turf 0-5: (5f, 7f 2, 9f, 10f) (sft, g-s, gd 3)
Fair gelding, effective 5 to 7f, best at 7f, acts on hvy to sft, best on hvy, has worn blinkers. Turf high 54. Becoming disappointing.
**D Nicholls [0-1] Mrs C Gilsenan & P Platt (from G M Lyons in IRE [2-27] Jun 2000).*

FIELD MASTER (IRE) BHB 50f70a RR 54f 70a 3506[7]

3 ch c Foxhound (USA) - Bold Avril (IRE) (Persian Bold) 9.3f **(66)**
Form - 8322187050007
Record 2000 - 1st:1 2nd:2 3rd:1 Ran:13
Pre2000 - 1st:0 2nd:0 3rd:0 Ran:5
Win Prizemoney £2,717 *Total Prizemoney* £8,428
Wins * **2000** *Mar Lingfi (STD) 10f 62* <
2000 Turf 0-11: (8f 3, 9f, 10f 4, 11f, 12f 2) (sft, g-s, gd 5, g-f 2, frm 2)
2000 AW 1-2: (10f 1-2) (Equi 1-1, Dirt)
Leggy, average colt, effective 7 to 10f, best at 10f, acts on g-s to gd - acts on Dirt, likes left handed tracks. Turf high 72 - 3rd of 17 getting 1lb from Shericaine (6 Feb Cagnes-sur-mer 10f g-s RF 0261a). AW high 67 (1st run) - 2nd of 12 to Sheer Tenby (23 Feb Cagnes-sur-mer 10f Dirt RF 0397a). Inconsistent.
**S Dow [1-13] Zero 3 Racing (from A C Stewart [0-5] Oct 1999).*

FIELD OF VISION (IRE) BHB 38f55a RR 53f 55a 5164[5]

10 b g Vision (USA) 10.4f **(57)** - Bold Meadows (Persian Bold) 9.3f **(66)**
Form - 02432145222415
Record 2000 - 1st:2 2nd:5 3rd:1 Ran:14
Pre2000 - 1st:9 2nd:10 3rd:8 Ran:65
Win Prizemoney £39,135 *Total Prizemoney* £62,899
Wins * **2000** Spt Beverl (HVY) S 12f 40
* **2000** Jun Carlis (SFT) C 12f 45+
* 1998 May Beverl (G-F) H 12f 68 74 <
* 1998 May Hamilt (G-S) H 13f 65 66
1996 Apr Hamilt (G-S) C 9.2f 64
1996 Jan Wolver (STD) H 9.4f 63 72
1996 Jan Wolver (STD) H 9.4f 63 65
2000 Turf 2-14: (11f 2, 12f 2-9, 13f, 14f 2) (g-s 1-2, gd 2, g-f 1-2, frm 8)
Fair gelding, effective 11 to 14f, acts on gd to frm, best on frm, has worn blinkers, likes right handed tracks, favours tight tracks, excels at Hamilton, does well at Catterick. Turf high 53 - 2nd of 11 giving 8lb to Hasta la Vista (13 Apr Musselburgh 14f gd RF 0703) - also 1st of 7 giving 6lb to Wafir (5 Jun Carlisle RF 1710).
**Mrs A Duffield [7-51] Mrs L J Tounsend (from M Johnston [7-40] Apr 1996).*

FIENNES (USA) BHB 63f RR 67f 3965[10]

2 b br g Dayjur (USA) 6.8f **(79)** - Artic Strech (USA) (Arctic Tern (USA)) 8.9f **(69)**
Form - 576360
Record 2000 - 1st:0 2nd:0 3rd:1 Ran:6
Win Prizemoney £0 *Total Prizemoney* £594
2000 Turf 0-5: (5f 4, 8f) (g-s, gd, g-f 2, frm) 2000 AW 0-1: (6f) (Fibr)
Average gelding, effective 5f, acts on frm. Turf high 67 - 3rd of 14 to Wally McArthur (7 Jly Beverley 5f frm RF 2587).
**M L W Bell [0-6] The Royal Ascot Racing Club.*

FIERY WATERS BHB 48f61a RR 50f 61a 4695[8]

4 b g Rudimentary (USA) 8.2f **(66)** - Idle Waters (Mill Reef (USA)) 10.5f **(78)**
Form - 076008
Record 2000 - 1st:0 2nd:0 3rd:0 Ran:6
Pre2000 - 1st:0 2nd:0 3rd:1 Ran:5
Win Prizemoney £0 *Total Prizemoney* £353
2000 Turf 0-6: (10f 2, 12f 3, 15f) (g-s, gd 2, g-f 3)
Workmanlike, fair gelding, effective 10f, acts on g-f, has worn blinkers, likes right handed tracks, favours tight tracks. Turf high 50. Becoming disappointing.
**D W P Arbuthnot [0-11] R Crutchley.*

FIFE AND DRUM (USA) BHB 66f61a RR 53f 61a 5154[1]

3 b br g Rahy (USA) 9.1f **(80)** - Fife (IRE) (Lomond (USA)) 8.8f **(65)**
Form - 0001701
Record 2000 - 1st:2 2nd:0 3rd:0 Ran:7
Pre2000 - 1st:0 2nd:0 3rd:0 Ran:3
Win Prizemoney £5,852 *Total Prizemoney* £5,852
Wins * **2000** *Oct Lingfi (STD) H 12f 57 64* <
2000 Jun Nottin (G-F) H 10f 50 53
2000 Turf 1-6: (10f 1-3, 12f 3) (g-s, gd 3, g-f 1-2) 2000 AW 1-1: (12f 1-1) (Equi 1-1)
Workmanlike, average gelding, effective 12f, - acts on Equi, has worn blinkers, likes tight tracks. Turf high 53. (1st run) - 1st of 17 getting 13lb from Fusul (23 Oct Lingfield RF 5154).
**J Akehurst [1-2] Last Order's Partnership (from E A L Dunlop [1-8] Jun 2000).*

FIFTEEN REDS BHB 38f44a RR 32f 44a 3905[10]

5 b g Jumbo Hirt (USA) 15.8f **(44)** - Dominance (Dominion) 8.5f **(63)**
Form - 260
Record 2000 - 1st:0 2nd:1 3rd:0 Ran:3
Pre2000 - 1st:0 2nd:0 3rd:0 Ran:6
Win Prizemoney £0 *Total Prizemoney* £860
2000 Turf 0-1: (17f) (frm) 2000 AW 0-2: (16f 2) (Fibr 2)
Moderate gelding, often wears blinkers. AW high 45.
**P C Haslam [0-1] J Roundtree (from D Shaw [0-12] Jan 2000).*

FIFTH EDITION BHB 40f RR 42f 5154[12]

4 b f Rock Hopper 10.6f **(54)** - Glossary (Reference Point) 6.8f **(70)**
Form - 0000
Record 2000 - 1st:0 2nd:0 3rd:0 Ran:4
Pre2000 - 1st:0 2nd:0 3rd:0 Ran:5
Win Prizemoney £0 *Total Prizemoney* £279
2000 Turf 0-3: (8f, 10f 2) (gd, g-f, frm) 2000 AW 0-1: (12f) (Equi)
Scopey, moderate filly, effective 7f, acts on frm. Turf high 42 (began Jly). **C F Wall [0-9] M Ng.*

FIGURA BHB 85f **RR 90f** 4738[10]

2 b f Rudimentary (USA) 8.2f **(66)** - Dream Baby (Master Willie) 7f **(70)**
Form - 61640
Record 2000 - 1st:1 2nd:0 3rd:0 Ran:5
Win Prizemoney £1,778 *Total Prizemoney* £2,893
Wins * 2000 Jly Folkes (GD) 7f 74+ <
2000 Turf 1-5: (7f 1-5) (gd 1-1, g-f 4)
Useful filly. Turf high 90 (began Jun) - 6th of 12 getting 3lb from Silver Jorden (27 Jly Sandown 7f g-f RF 3153). Decisive winner of a moderate race on her second run, she finished a close sixth in listed company next time. Not really up to that level, she is likely to be better off in handicaps. **K McAuliffe [1-5] Alex Fraser.*

FILIAL (IRE) BHB 53f52a **RR 56f 52a** 515[9]

7 b g Danehill (USA) 9.1f **(79)** - Sephira (Luthier) 9.8f **(71)**
Form - 0
Record 2000 - 1st:0 2nd:0 3rd:0 Ran:1
Pre2000 - 1st:7 2nd:7 3rd:4 Ran:37
Win Prizemoney £17,844 *Total Prizemoney* £25,396

Wins								
	1998	Oct	Redcar	(SFT)	C	11f		70
	1998	May	Hamilt	(GD)	H	13f	68	73
	1998	Apr	Ripon	(SFT)	H	12.3f	60	66
	1998	*Mar*	*Southw*	*(STD)*	C	*12f*		*61*
	1997	*Nov*	*Wolver*	*(STD)*	C	*12f*		*72*
	1996	*Dec*	*Lingfi*	*(STD)*	H	*12f*	*80*	*86* <
	1996	Aug	Sandow	(G-F)		10f		75

2000 AW 0-1: (11f) (Fibr)
Fair gelding, has worn blinkers.
**Mrs A Duffield [1-11] Mrs Ann Duffield (from J Pearce [5-18] Oct 1998).*

FILLE DE BUCHERON (USA) **RR 82+f** 4226[2]

2 b f Woodman (USA) 9.7f **(77)** - Special Secreto (USA) (Secreto (USA)) 8.7f **(72)**
Form - 2
Record 2000 - 1st:0 2nd:1 3rd:0 Ran:1
Win Prizemoney £0 *Total Prizemoney* £935
2000 Turf 0-1: (7f) (frm)
Currently decent filly. (1st run) - 2nd of 11 to Velvet Glade (5 Spt Lingfield 7f frm RF 4226).
**H R A Cecil [0-1] Clark Industrial Services Partnership.*

FILLE DE DAUPHIN (IRE) BHB 35f **RR 30f** 5010[14]

2 b f Dolphin Street (FR) - Asturiana (Julio Mariner) 7.2f **(57)**
Form - 0800
Record 2000 - 1st:0 2nd:0 3rd:0 Ran:4
2000 Turf 0-3: (5f, 6f, 7f) (g-s, g-f 2) 2000 AW 0-1: (7f) (Fibr)
Very moderate filly. Turf high 30 (began Aug).
**N Bycroft [0-4] 21st Century Racing I.*

FILM SCRIPT BHB 103f **RR 107f** 4613[4]

3 b f Unfuwain (USA) 11.4f **(74)** - Success Story **(47f 55a)** (Sharrood (USA)) 10.5f **(72)**
Form - 611361354
Record 2000 - 1st:3 2nd:0 3rd:2 Ran:9
Win Prizemoney £33,744 *Total Prizemoney* £43,541

Wins								
	*** 2000**	Jly	Chepst	(FRM)	L	10.2f	103	<
	*** 2000**	May	Lingfi	(G-S)	L	11.5f	103	<
	*** 2000**	May	Salisb	(G-F)		12f	81	

2000 Turf 3-9: (10f 1-1, 11f 1-2, 12f 1-5, 15f) (sft, g-s, gd 1-3, g-f 1-3, frm 1-1)
Unfurnished, Pattern-class filly, effective 10 to 15f, best at 12f, acts on g-s to frm, best on g-f, has worn blinkers, likes Ascot. Turf high 107 - 3rd of 16 giving 1lb to Give The Slip (22 Jun Ascot 12f g-f RF 2182) - also 1st of 7 getting 10lb from Cape Grace (28 Jly Chepstow RF 3172). Consistent. A tough and genuine filly, winner of two listed races including the Lingfield Oaks Trial, she lacks a turn of foot and is better over 12 furlongs than ten.
**R Charlton [3-9] The Queen.*

FINAL DIVIDEND (IRE) BHB 61f64a **RR 74df 64a** 5026[12]

4 b g Second Set (IRE) 9.2f **(67)** - Prime Interest (IRE) (Kings Lake (USA)) 10.8f **(67)**
Form - 045000
Record 2000 - 1st:0 2nd:0 3rd:0 Ran:5
Pre2000 - 1st:2 2nd:0 3rd:2 Ran:16
Win Prizemoney £6,385 *Total Prizemoney* £7,580

Wins									
	1999	Spt	Beverl	(SFT)	H	8.5f	69	70	<
	1999	May	Salisb	(G-F)	H	8f	67	70+	

2000 Turf 0-5: (7f, 8f 2, 10f 2) (g-s 2, g-f, frm 2)
Workmanlike, above-average gelding, effective 7 to 10f, best at 8f, acts on g-s to frm, best on frm. Turf high 74 (1st run) - 4th of 20 giving 18lb to Acebo Lyons (23 Mar Doncaster 10f frm RF 0478).
**J M P Eustace [0-8] Charles Curtis (from M J Fetherston-Godley [2-15] Oct 1999).*

FINAL EXAM (IRE) **RR 100f** 5048a[5]

3 ch c College Chapel - It Takes Two 00
Form - 3125
2000 Turf 1-4: (6f 1-2, 7f 2) (sft 2, g-s 1-2)
Very useful colt, effective 6 to 7f, acts on sft to g-s, mostly wears blinkers (extremely effectively). Turf high 100 - 5th of 11 getting 1lb from Cobourg Lodge (15 Oct Curragh 6f g-s RF 5048a).
**D K Weld in IRE [2-7] Bertram Firestone.*

FINAL KISS (IRE) BHB 52f **RR 42f** 1923[F]

3 b c Dolphin Street (FR) - Mystery Train (Bay Express) 7.1f **(60)**
Form - PF
Record 2000 - 1st:0 2nd:0 3rd:0 Ran:2
Pre2000 - 1st:0 2nd:0 3rd:0 Ran:4
2000 Turf 0-2: (7f 2) (g-s, g-f)
Workmanlike, moderate colt, has broken blood-vessels.
**J R Jenkins [0-6] Mrs Stella Garrad.*

FINAL LAP BHB 50f42a **RR 53f 42a** 5137[10]

4 b g Batshoof 9.5f **(66)** - Lap of Honour (Final Straw) 7.9f **(64)**
Form - 50000010
Record 2000 - 1st:1 2nd:0 3rd:0 Ran:7
Pre2000 - 1st:0 2nd:1 3rd:0 Ran:5
Win Prizemoney £5,021 *Total Prizemoney* £6,737
Wins * 2000 Spt Newmar (GD) C 12f 53 <
2000 Turf 1-7: (8f, 10f 3, 12f 1-2, 14f) (g-s 2, gd, g-f 1-3, hrd)
Workmanlike, fair gelding, effective 8f, acts on sft to gd, likes left handed tracks. Turf high 58. Consistent.
**W Jarvis [1-12] T C Blackwell And Partners.*

FINAL PURSUIT BHB 94f **RR 85f** 4644[12]

2 b f Pursuit of Love 9.5f **(69)** - Final Shot (Dalsaan) 9.8f **(64)**
Form - 71000
Record 2000 - 1st:1 2nd:0 3rd:0 Ran:5
Win Prizemoney £3,562 *Total Prizemoney* £3,562
Wins * 2000 Jun Bath (G-S) 5.7f 85+ <
2000 Turf 1-5: (5f 2, 6f 1-3) (gd 1-3, g-f 2)
Useful filly. Turf high 85 - 1st of 17 from Al Ihsas (2 Jun Bath RF 1644). Won a Bath maiden on her second start, but was well beaten at Royal Ascot and in the St Leger Yearling Stakes at Doncaster. **D HaydnJones [1-5] Jack Brown (Bookmaker) Ltd.*

FINAL SETTLEMENT (IRE) BHB 66f **RR 70f** 4535[8]

5 b g Soviet Lad (USA) 9.4f **(63)** - Tender Time (Tender King) 6.8f **(54)**
Form - 16534148
Record 2000 - 1st:2 2nd:0 3rd:1 Ran:8
Pre2000 - 1st:2 2nd:0 3rd:3 Ran:10
Win Prizemoney £20,412 *Total Prizemoney* £23,773

Wins									
	*** 2000**	Jly	Newmar	(G-F)	H	14.8f	65	68	<
	*** 2000**	Mar	Kempto	(GD)	H	14.4f	61	64	
	*** 1998**	Jly	Lingfi	(G-F)	H	11.5f	60	64	
	*** 1998**	Jun	Windso	(GD)	H	8.3f	58	60	

2000 Turf 2-8: (12f 3, 14f 1-1, 15f 1-2, 16f 2) (sft, g-s, gd 1-2, g-f 1-3, frm)
Above-average gelding, effective 10 to 15f, best at 12f, acts on g-s to frm, best on g-f, likes right handed tracks, and excels at Newmarket. Turf high 70 - also 1st of 8 getting 17lb from Fiori (22 Jly Newmarket RF 3030). Consistent. Landed a 14-furlong handicap at Kempton in March, having been successful over hurdles at that track during the winter, and benefited from the return to that

trip when scoring at Newmarket.
**J R Jenkins [5-20] The Meek Partnership.*

FINCH BHB 44f38a **RR 39f 38a** 305[8]
3 b f Inchinor 8.9f **(64)** - Wryneck (Niniski (USA)) 10.6f **(65)**
Form - 08
Record 2000 - 1st:0 2nd:0 3rd:0 Ran:2
Pre2000 - 1st:0 2nd:0 3rd:0 Ran:3
2000 AW 0-2: (8f, 11f) (Equi, Fibr)
Neat, very moderate filly. AW high 12.
**R Charlton [0-5] Lady Sophia Topley.*

FIND THE KING (IRE) RR 61f 5309[11]
2 b c King's Theatre (IRE) - Undiscovered (Tap On Wood) 10.3f **(65)**
Form - 40
Record 2000 - 1st:0 2nd:0 3rd:0 Ran:2
Win Prizemoney £0 *Total Prizemoney* £513
2000 Turf 0-2: (7f, 8f) (sft, g-s)
Currently average colt. Turf high 61 (began Oct).
**D W P Arbuthnot [0-2] J S Gutkin.*

FINE HONOR (FR) RR 100f 2386a[4]
3 f
Form - 4
2000 Turf 0-1: (12f) (gd)
Currently very useful filly. (1st run) - 4th of 5 to America (25 Jun Longchamp 12f gd RF 2386a). **C Laffon-Parias in FR [0-1].*

FINE MELODY BHB 71f79a **RR 74f 79a** 4834[19]
3 b f Green Desert (USA) 7.8f **(78)** - Sit Alkul (USA) (Mr Prospector (USA)) 8.8f **(78)**
Form - 3114000
Record 2000 - 1st:2 2nd:0 3rd:1 Ran:7
Win Prizemoney £5,406 *Total Prizemoney* £6,126
Wins * 2000 *Mar Lingfi (STD) H 7f 65 75+* <
*** 2000** *Feb Lingfi (STD) 7f 54*
2000 Turf 0-4: (5f, 6f 3) (g-s, gd 2, g-f) 2000 AW 2-3: (6f, 7f 2-2) (Equi 2-2, Fibr)
Light-framed, above-average filly, effective 7f, - acts on Equi. Turf high 74. AW high 75 - 1st of 6 giving 21lb to French Fancy (29 Mar Lingfield RF 0552). Won twice on the Equitrack early in the year but has not been so effective since returning to turf.
**B W Hills [2-7] Maktoum Al Maktoum.*

FINERY (IRE) BHB 49f60a **RR 53f 60a** 4471[21]
3 ch g Barathea (IRE) - Micky's Pleasure (USA) (Foolish Pleasure (USA)) 8.9f **(72)**
Form - 6424010023003400
Record 2000 - 1st:1 2nd:2 3rd:2 Ran:16
Win Prizemoney £2,191 *Total Prizemoney* £5,822
Wins 2000 *May Southw (STD) C 11f 56* <
2000 Turf 0-10: (7f 3, 8f 2, 9f, 10f 2, 11f, 14f) (gd 2, g-f 6, frm 2) 2000 AW 1-6: (7f, 8f, 10f 2, 11f 1-2) (Equi 2, Fibr 1-4)
Leggy, average gelding, effective 10 to 11f, best at 10f, - acts on AW, best on Equi, has worn blinkers, prefers left handed tracks, prefers tight tracks. Turf high 55. AW high 66 - 4th of 10 to You da Man (4 Mar Lingfield 10f Equi RF 0400). Inconsistent.
**C A Dwyer [0-10] Costas Kyriacou (from W Jarvis [1-6] May 2000).*

FINISHED ARTICLE (IRE) BHB 75f **RR 82f** 4934[19]
3 b c Indian Ridge 7.6f **(74)** - Summer Fashion (Moorestyle) 6.9f **(64)**
Form - 46352100
Record 2000 - 1st:1 2nd:1 3rd:1 Ran:8
Pre2000 - 1st:0 2nd:0 3rd:0 Ran:2
Win Prizemoney £4,095 *Total Prizemoney* £6,487
Wins * 2000 Aug Epsom (G-F) 8.5f 81 <
2000 Turf 1-8: (7f, 8f 3, 9f 1-1, 10f 3) (sft, gd, g-f 5, frm 1-1)
Workmanlike, decent colt, effective 8 to 10f, acts on g-f to frm, best on g-f. Turf high 82 - 6th of 20 to Subtle Power (20 May Newbury 10f g-f RF 1333) - also 1st of 6 from Musical Heath (17 Aug Epsom RF 3721). Got off the mark in an ordinary Epsom maiden. **D R C Elsworth [1-10] Dr D B Davis.*

FINLAYS FOLLY RR 12f 4216[15]
3 b g Fremont Boy - Twiglette (Aragon) 8.1f **(60)**
Form - 00
Record 2000 - 1st:0 2nd:0 3rd:0 Ran:2
2000 Turf 0-2: (7f, 10f) (frm 2)
Workmanlike, poor gelding. Turf high 12 (began Aug).
**P R Hedger [0-2] B Williams.*

FINMAR BHB 71f **RR 70f** 4429[4]
2 b c Efisio 7.7f **(69)** - Patiala (IRE) **(22f)** (Nashwan (USA))
Form - 5004
Record 2000 - 1st:0 2nd:0 3rd:0 Ran:4
Win Prizemoney £0 *Total Prizemoney* £550
2000 Turf 0-4: (6f 3, 7f) (gd, g-f, frm 2)
Above-average colt. Turf high 70 (began Aug).
**Miss L A Perratt [0-4] T P Finch.*

FINN MCCOOL (IRE) BHB 54f57a **RR 52f 57a** 5247[2]
2 b g Blues Traveller (IRE) - Schonbein (IRE) (Persian Heights)
Form - 6102
Record 2000 - 1st:1 2nd:1 3rd:0 Ran:4
Win Prizemoney £1,970 *Total Prizemoney* £2,498
Wins * 2000 *Spt Wolver (STD) S 7f 64* <
2000 Turf 0-2: (7f 2) (gd, frm) 2000 AW 1-2: (7f 1-1, 8f) (Fibr 1-2)
Average gelding. Turf high 52 (began Aug). AW high 64 (1st run) (began Spt) - 1st of 12 giving 5lb to Red Fanfare (16 Spt Wolverhampton RF 4478). **R A Fahey [1-4] R A Fahey.*

FIONN DE COOL (IRE) BHB 43f **RR 44f** 4130[14]
9 b g Mazaad 8.5f **(53)** - Pink Fondant (Northfields (USA)) 9f **(72)**
Form - 00530
Record 2000 - 1st:0 2nd:0 3rd:1 Ran:5
Pre2000 - 1st:3 2nd:4 3rd:5 Ran:43
Win Prizemoney £17,108 *Total Prizemoney* £28,519
Wins * 1998 Jly Chepst (GD) H 8.1f 58 63
1997 Aug Epsom (GD) H 8.5f 59 64
2000 Turf 0-5: (7f, 8f 4) (gd 3, frm 2)
Moderate gelding, effective 8f, acts on frm, likes tight tracks. Turf high 44.
**J Akehurst [1-19] Canisbay Bloodstock Ltd (from R Akehurst [2-29] Spt 1997).*

FIORA (IRE) RR 31f 5022[11]
3 b f Sri Pekan (USA) - Fleuretta (USA) (The Minstrel (CAN)) 10f **(72)**
Form - 00
Record 2000 - 1st:0 2nd:0 3rd:0 Ran:2
2000 Turf 0-2: (7f 2) (g-s, g-f)
Neat, currently very moderate filly. Turf high 31.
**R W Armstrong [0-2] Mrs Robert Armstrong.*

FIORI BHB 82f80a **RR 85f 80a** 5104[15]
4 b g Anshan 8.2f **(63)** - Fen Princess (IRE) (Trojan Fen) 8.1f **(62)**
Form - 628064413220
Record 2000 - 1st:1 2nd:3 3rd:1 Ran:12
Pre2000 - 1st:3 2nd:4 3rd:4 Ran:17
Win Prizemoney £23,145 *Total Prizemoney* £44,225
Wins * 2000 Jun Ayr (GD) H 15f 77 80
* 1999 Jun York (G-S) H 10.4f 80 88 <
* 1999 Jun Beverl (SFT) H 12f 80 85+
* 1999 May Hamilt (G-F) 9.2f 64
2000 Turf 1-10: (10f 2, 12f 3, 15f 1-4, 16f) (g-s 2, gd 3, g-f 1-4, frm)
2000 AW 0-2: (11f, 16f) (Fibr 2)
Scopey, useful gelding, effective 10 to 16f, acts on g-s to frm - acts on Fibr, best on gd, likes right handed tracks, excels at Newmarket, does well at York. Turf high 85 - 2nd of 7 giving 8lb to Turnpole (12 Jly Newmarket 16f gd RF 2751) - also 1st of 5 giving 9lb to Urgent Swift (24 Jun Ayr RF 2246). AW high 81 - 2nd of 6 getting 9lb from Wilcuma (22 Jan Wolverhampton 16f Fibr RF 0141). Consistent. Scored over 15 furlongs at Ayr in June when allowed his own way out in front. Running well since, but he does not have much in the way of pace these days.
**P C Haslam [4-30] I Wilson.*

FIRE BELLE (IRE) BHB 30f **RR 18f** 5067[17]
2 ch f Lake Coniston (IRE) - Blackpool Belle (The Brianstan) 5.9f **(55)**
Form - 8050
Record 2000 - 1st:0 2nd:0 3rd:0 Ran:4
2000 Turf 0-4: (5f, 6f 3) (g-s, g-f, frm 2)
Poor filly. Turf high 18.
**H S Howe [0-4] Jonathan Leigh.*

FIRECREST (IRE) BHB 105f **RR 105f** 4963[4]
3 b f Darshaan 11.9f **(81)** - Trefoil (FR) (Blakeney) 10.5f **(64)**
Form - 711114144
Record 2000 - 1st:5 2nd:0 3rd:0 Ran:9
Pre2000 - 1st:0 2nd:0 3rd:0 Ran:2
Win Prizemoney £45,500 *Total Prizemoney* £51,155

Wins									
	*** 2000**	Aug	York	(GD)	L	11.9f		105	<
	*** 2000**	Jun	Salisb	(G-F)	H	12f	90	98	
	*** 2000**	Jun	Newbur	(G-F)	H	12f	76	92	
	*** 2000**	Jun	Leices	(G-S)	H	11.8f	63	81+	
	*** 2000**	May	Leices	(G-S)	H	11.8f	63	74	

2000 Turf 5-9: (10f, 12f 5-8) (gd 2-4, g-f 2-3, frm 1-2)
Pattern-class filly, effective 12f, acts on gd to frm, best on g-f, and excels at Newmarket. Turf high 105 - 4th of 15 to Sacred Song (13 Oct Newmarket 12f gd RF 4963) - also 1st of 13 from Fantasia Girl (24 Aug York RF 3932). Improving. She had her three runs in maidens to qualify for a handicap mark and really found her feet once stepped up in trip, completing a fine four-timer despite a huge rise in the handicap. Handled the step up to Listed company when winning at York but was held in Group Threes.
**J L Dunlop [5-11] Sir Thomas Pilkington.*

FIRE DOME (IRE) BHB 90f86a **RR 98f 86a** 4933[16]
8 ch g Salt Dome (USA) 6.5f **(59)** - Penny Habit (Habitat) 9.4f **(70)**
Form - 833111107130
Record 2000 - 1st:5 2nd:0 3rd:3 Ran:12
Pre2000 - 1st:7 2nd:5 3rd:4 Ran:41
Win Prizemoney £103,748 *Total Prizemoney* £125,117

Wins									
	*** 2000**	Spt	Salisb	(SFT)	H	6f	87	89	
	*** 2000**	Jun	Epsom	(GD)	H	6f	80	87+	
	*** 2000**	Jun	Lingfi	(G-S)	H	6f	75	79	
	2000	May	Windso	(G-S)	C	6f		66	
	2000	May	Redcar	(G-F)	C	6f		65	
	1999	Oct	Redcar	(GD)	C	6f		68+	
	1999	Oct	Sandow	(HVY)	C	5f		82	
	1998	Jly	Sandow	(G-S)	L	5f		109	<
	1998	Apr	Thirsk	(G-S)		6f		106	
	1996	Mar	Doncas	(SFT)	L	6f		107	

2000 Turf 5-11: (5f 2, 6f 5-9) (sft, gd 2-4, g-f 2-5, frm 1-1) 2000 AW 0-1: (7f) (Fibr)
Very useful gelding, has worn blinkers, excels at Redcar. Turf high 89. He was claimed by Andrew Reid for £10,000 after winning a Windsor claimer in May. Won a decent Lingfield handicap for his new yard the following month and gained a big payday when winning a very valuable handicap at Epsom on Derby day. He was struck into when running poorly at York next time, but returned to winning form at Salisbury in September. Best over six furlongs these days, he is suited by coming off a fast pace.
**Andrew Reid [3-7] A S Reid (from D Nicholls [6-29] May 2000).*

FIRE PRINCESS BHB 40f **RR** 5067[18]
2 b f Emarati (USA) 6.6f **(63)** - Redcross Miss (Tower Walk) 10f **(62)**
Form - 500
Record 2000 - 1st:0 2nd:0 3rd:0 Ran:3
2000 Turf 0-1: (6f) (g-s) 2000 AW 0-2: (5f, 6f) (Fibr 2)
Currently very moderate filly. AW high 38.
**P S Felgate [0-2] P Willett (from J Wharton [0-1] Mar 2000).*

FIRE THUNDER (USA) RR 575a[5]
5 m
Form - 5
2000 AW 0-1: (8f) (Dirt)
Currently Pattern-class. (1st run) - 5th of 13 to Conflict (25 Mar Nad Al Sheba 8f Dirt RF 0575a). **P L Rudkin in UAE [0-1].*

FIREWIRE RR 57f 5151[18]
2 b c Blushing Flame (USA) - Bay Risk **(37f)** (Risk Me (FR)) 5.9f **(53)**
Form - 00
Record 2000 - 1st:0 2nd:0 3rd:0 Ran:2
2000 Turf 0-2: (7f, 8f) (g-s, gd)
Currently fair colt. Turf high 57 (began Oct).
**N Hamilton [0-2] Miss Jennie Wisher.*

FIREWORK BHB 82f77a **RR 77f 77a** 4926[9]
2 b c Primo Dominie 7.2f **(67)** - Prancing **(96f)** (Prince Sabo) 7.2f **(62)**
Form - 2230
Record 2000 - 1st:0 2nd:2 3rd:1 Ran:4
Win Prizemoney £0 *Total Prizemoney* £5,012
2000 Turf 0-3: (5f, 6f 2) (g-s, gd, frm) 2000 AW 0-1: (6f) (Equi)
Above-average colt. Turf high 77 - 2nd of 13 to Barking Mad (17 May York 6f frm RF 1265).
**W J Haggas [0-4] Exors of the late M H Wilson.*

FIRST BACK (IRE) BHB 53f **RR 65f** 4014[1]
3 b g Fourstars Allstar (USA) - Par Un Nez (IRE) (Cyrano de Bergerac) 6f **(68)**
Form - 407301
Record 2000 - 1st:1 2nd:0 3rd:1 Ran:6
Pre2000 - 1st:0 2nd:0 3rd:0 Ran:3
Win Prizemoney £4,095 *Total Prizemoney* £4,766

Wins									
	*** 2000**	Aug	Beverl	(G-F)		9.9f		48	<

2000 Turf 1-6: (10f 1-2, 11f, 12f 2, 16f) (gd 3, frm 1-3)
Leggy, average gelding, favours tight tracks. Turf high 65.
**C W Fairhurst [1-9] Twinacre Nurseries Ltd.*

FIRST BALLOT (IRE) BHB 84f **RR 88f** 5111[3]
4 b g Perugino (USA) - Election Special **(62f)** (Chief Singer) 8.9f **(66)**
Form - 000363
Record 2000 - 1st:0 2nd:0 3rd:2 Ran:6
Pre2000 - 1st:2 2nd:0 3rd:0 Ran:6
Win Prizemoney £16,796 *Total Prizemoney* £19,843

Wins									
	*** 1999**	Aug	Ascot	(GD)	H	16.2f	87	89	<
	*** 1999**	Jly	Newbur	(G-F)		12f		83	

2000 Turf 0-6: (12f 2, 16f 3, 19f) (gd 3, g-f 2, frm)
Workmanlike, useful gelding, effective 10 to 16f, acts on gd to frm, best on gd, excels at Newbury, likes Ascot. Turf high 89. Enjoyed a good season at three, but suffered in the handicap as a result and was out of sorts in the first part of 2000. Better efforts in the autumn. **D R C Elsworth [2-12] J C Smith.*

FIRST DEGREE BHB 52f **RR 55f** 4890[5]
2 br f Sabrehill (USA) 8.5f **(64)** - Degree **(53f 54a)** (Warning)
Form - 0005
Record 2000 - 1st:0 2nd:0 3rd:0 Ran:4
2000 Turf 0-4: (5f 2, 6f, 8f) (hvy, gd, g-f, frm)
Fair filly. Turf high 55 - 5th of 10 getting 12lb from Oriental Mist (10 Oct Ayr 8f hvy RF 4890). **S C Williams [0-4] D A Shekells.*

FIRST DRAW (IRE) BHB 68f **RR 67f** 5350a[3]
3 b f Night Shift (USA) 8.1f **(73)** - Brook's Quest 00
Form - 020023
Record 2000 - 1st:0 2nd:2 3rd:1 Ran:6
Pre2000 - 1st:0 2nd:0 3rd:1 Ran:4
Win Prizemoney £0 *Total Prizemoney* £3,270
2000 Turf 0-6: (5f 4, 6f, 7f) (hvy 2, gd, g-f 3)
Average filly, effective 5 to 6f, best at 5f, acts on hvy to g-f, best on hvy. Turf high 67 - 3rd of 11 getting 17lb from Miracle Ridge (30 Oct Leopardstown 5f hvy RF 5350a). Inconsistent.
**T J Taaffe in IRE [0-6] Gerard Callanan (from J R Fanshawe [0-4] Spt 2000).*

FIRST FANTASY BHB 95f **RR 99f** 4931[6]
4 b f Be My Chief (USA) 10.2f **(62)** - Dreams **(80df)** (Rainbow Quest (USA)) 10.4f **(75)**
Form - 0518501766
Record 2000 - 1st:2 2nd:0 3rd:0 Ran:10
Pre2000 - 1st:4 2nd:1 3rd:1 Ran:10
Win Prizemoney £45,123 *Total Prizemoney* £50,077

Wins									
	*** 2000**	Aug	Salisb	(GD)	L	9.9f		95	<
	*** 2000**	Jun	Warwic	(G-S)		10.5f		80+	
	* 1999	Spt	Yarmou	(G-S)	H	10.1f	77	79	
	* 1999	Aug	Folkes	(G-S)	H	9.7f	71	76+	
	* 1999	Jly	Yarmou	(FRM)	H	10.1f	67	72	
	* 1999	Jly	Warwic	(G-F)	H	10.5f	62	64	

2000 Turf 2-10: (9f, 10f 1-8, 11f 1-1) (sft, g-s 1-1, gd 4, g-f, frm 1-3)
Scopey, very useful filly, effective 10f, acts on frm, likes left handed tracks, likes tight tracks, excels at Warwick, likes Yarmouth. Turf high 99 - 5th of 8 to Amalia (1 Jly Newcastle 10f frm RF 2445) - also 1st of 10 from Dashiba (16 Aug Salisbury RF 3704). She ended '99 in brilliant form, winning four of her last five starts, all over ten furlongs. She was held in handicap company last season, but managed to win a Warwick conditions event and came from last to first to win a listed event at Salisbury. She flashes her tail, but has shown she can battle when required and goes in most ground except for very soft.

**J R Fanshawe [6-20] Nigel & Carolyn Elwes.*

FIRST GOLD BHB 22f36a **RR 26df 36a** 2366[10]
11 gr g Absalom 7.1f **(56)** - Cindys Gold (Sonnen Gold) 6.6f **(47)**
Form - 00
Record 2000 - 1st:0 2nd:0 3rd:0 Ran:2
Pre2000 - 1st:9 2nd:8 3rd:6 Ran:93
Win Prizemoney £26,175 *Total Prizemoney* £37,046

Wins							
1997	Mar	Leices	(G-F)	S	7f	37	
1996	May	Carlis	(G-F)	C	6.9f	61	
1996	*Jan*	*Southw*	*(STD)*	*S*	*7f*	*51*	

2000 Turf 0-1: (7f) (g-f) 2000 AW 0-1: (6f) (Fibr)
Little account gelding, has worn blinkers. Inconsistent.
**A Smith [0-14] Alfred Smith (from J Wharton [9-93] Dec 1997).*

FIRST IMPRESSION BHB 72f **RR 76f** 5142[6]
5 b g Saddlers' Hall (IRE) 10.5f **(65)** - First Sapphire (Simply Great (FR)) 8.2f **(65)**
Form - 20206
Record 2000 - 1st:0 2nd:2 3rd:0 Ran:5
Pre2000 - 1st:0 2nd:1 3rd:0 Ran:6
Win Prizemoney £0 *Total Prizemoney* £3,481
2000 Turf 0-5: (11f, 12f 3, 13f) (g-s, g-f 3, frm)
Above-average gelding, effective 12f, acts on g-f to frm, prefers tight tracks. Turf high 76 - 2nd of 11 giving 8lb to Kennet (14 Aug Windsor 12f g-f RF 3634).
**Mrs A J Perrett [0-5] Ms Elaine Reffo (from Lady Herries [0-6] Jly 1999).*

FIRST LEGACY BHB 26f **RR 31f** 3683[10]
4 ch f First Trump - Loving Legacy **(62f)** (Caerleon (USA)) 8.6f **(71)**
Form - 007060
Record 2000 - 1st:0 2nd:0 3rd:0 Ran:6
Pre2000 - 1st:0 2nd:0 3rd:0 Ran:4
2000 Turf 0-6: (6f, 8f 2, 10f 2, 12f) (g-s 2, g-f 3, hrd)
Unfurnished, very moderate filly, has worn blinkers. Turf high 31.
**M Brittain [0-10] Mel Brittain.*

FIRST MAGNITUDE (IRE) RR 120f 2006a[2]
4 ch c Arazi (USA) 9.2f **(74)** - Crystal Cup (USA) (Nijinsky (CAN)) 10.3f **(77)**
Form - 112
2000 Turf 2-3: (12f 2-3) (hvy 1-1, sft 1-1, gd)
Very high-class colt, effective 12f, acts on gd, likes right handed tracks. Turf high 120 - 2nd of 6 giving 8lb to Daring Miss (11 Jun Chantilly 12f gd RF 2006a) - also 1st of 7 giving 9lb to Crillon (27 Apr Longchamp RF 1030a). He was successful in a Group Three and Group Two in France over 12 furlongs last season before finishing runner-up in the Grand Prix de Chantilly.
**A Fabre in FR [3-8] D Wildenstein.*

FIRST MAITE BHB 79f85a **RR 95f 85a** 5055[10]
7 b g Komaite (USA) 6.9f **(61)** - Marina Plata (Julio Mariner) 7.2f **(57)**
Form - 15404083244650034007800
Record 2000 - 1st:0 2nd:1 3rd:2 Ran:20
Pre2000 - 1st:12 2nd:9 3rd:5 Ran:69
Win Prizemoney £93,199 *Total Prizemoney* £129,325

Wins								
* *1999*	*Nov*	*Southw*	*(STD)*	*H*	*7f*	*84*	*88*	
* 1999	Spt	Ascot	(HVY)	H	5f	99	103+	<
* 1999	Aug	Haydoc	(SFT)	H	5f	95	101	
* 1999	May	York	(SFT)	H	6f	92	97	
* 1998	Oct	Ascot	(SFT)	H	5f	85	93	
* *1998*	*Jly*	*Southw*	*(STD)*	*H*	*7f*	*77*	*83*	
* 1998	May	Ripon	(G-F)	H	5f	83	84	
* 1997	May	Beverl	(GD)	H	5f	72	75	
* *1997*	*Apr*	*Wolver*	*(STD)*	*C*	*5f*		*67*	
* *1996*	*Feb*	*Southw*	*(STD)*	*H*	*6f*	*70*	*77*	
* *1996*	*Feb*	*Southw*	*(STD)*	*H*	*6f*	*70*	*78*	

2000 Turf 0-14: (5f 5, 6f 7, 7f 2) (sft 2, g-s 3, gd 3, g-f 3, frm 3) 2000 AW 0-6: (5f, 6f 3, 7f 2) (Fibr 6)
Very useful gelding, effective 5 to 7f, best at 5f, acts on sft to g-f, best on gd, mostly wears blinkers, excels at Haydock. Turf high 101 (1st run) - 4th of 14 to Andreyev (25 Mar Doncaster 6f gd RF 0495). AW high 88. Inconsistent. Best on easy ground, he was impressive when winning three valuable sprint handicaps in '99. Never fired last term, but is on a lenient mark if he can recapture his form. He acts on Fibresand, but needs six or seven furlongs on that surface.
**S R Bowring [12-89] S R Bowring.*

FIRST MANASSAS (USA) BHB 79f **RR 82f** 1835[6]
3 b c Sea Hero (USA) - Ispahan (USA) (Majestic Light (USA)) 10.6f **(75)**
Form - 086
Record 2000 - 1st:0 2nd:0 3rd:0 Ran:3
Pre2000 - 1st:1 2nd:1 3rd:1 Ran:4
Win Prizemoney £2,920 *Total Prizemoney* £4,488

Wins							
* 1999	Spt	Haydoc	(G-F)	8.1f	82	<

2000 Turf 0-3: (10f, 12f 2) (g-s, g-f 2)
Workmanlike, decent colt, effective 8f, acts on gd to g-f, best on g-f. Turf high 78. **I A Balding [1-7] Mrs Paul Mellon.*

FIRST MEETING BHB 58f **RR 53f** 4454[4]
2 b f Contract Law (USA) 8.9f **(54)** - Sunday News'n'echo (USA) **(60f 47a)** (Trempolino (USA)) 12f **(71)**
Form - 2504
Record 2000 - 1st:0 2nd:1 3rd:0 Ran:4
Win Prizemoney £0 *Total Prizemoney* £1,046
2000 Turf 0-4: (6f, 7f 2, 8f) (g-s 2, frm 2)
Fair filly. Turf high 53. **M Dods [0-4] D C Batey.*

FIRST MUSICAL BHB 71f **RR 82f** 5055[18]
4 ch f First Trump - Musical Sally (USA) (The Minstrel (CAN)) 10f **(72)**
Form - 850050
Record 2000 - 1st:0 2nd:0 3rd:0 Ran:6
Pre2000 - 1st:4 2nd:5 3rd:0 Ran:18
Win Prizemoney £14,771 *Total Prizemoney* £36,131

Wins						
* 1998	Jly	Windso	(GD)	6f	89+	<
* 1998	Jun	Pontef	(GD)	6f	89	
* 1998	Jun	Ayr	(G-F)	5f	83	
* 1998	Jun	Pontef	(G-S)	5f	74+	

2000 Turf 0-6: (5f, 6f 5) (sft, g-s, gd 3, hrd)
Light-framed, decent filly, effective 6f, acts on gd. Turf high 82. Becoming disappointing.
**M Brittain [4-24] Bob Abson BJK Partnership.*

FIRST OFFICER (USA) RR 88f 4600[10]
3 b c Lear Fan (USA) 10.4f **(80)** - Trampoli (USA) (Trempolino (USA)) 12f **(71)**
Form - 02176320
Record 2000 - 1st:1 2nd:2 3rd:1 Ran:8
Win Prizemoney £4,043 *Total Prizemoney* £9,088

Wins						
* 2000	May	Haydoc	(SFT)	10.5f	82	<

2000 Turf 1-8: (10f 2, 11f 1-1, 12f 2, 14f, 16f 2) (g-s 1-2, gd 4, frm 2)
Scopey, useful colt, effective 10 to 16f, acts on g-s to frm. Turf high 88 - 2nd of 9 getting 17lb from Bangalore (15 Spt Newbury 16f frm RF 4438) - also 1st of 9 giving 5lb to Darariyna (27 May Haydock RF 1495). Unraced at two, he got off the mark in a soft-ground Haydock maiden on his third start. Held since, but looks the sort who could eventually turn into a decent middle-distance handicapper. **J R Fanshawe [1-8] H R H Prince Fahd Salman.*

FIRST SIGHT (IRE) BHB 41f **RR 49tf** 3207[9]
2 ch g Eagle Eyed (USA) - Madaraka (USA) **(53f)** (Arctic Tern (USA)) 8.9f **(69)**
Form - 200
Record 2000 - 1st:0 2nd:1 3rd:0 Ran:3
Win Prizemoney £0 *Total Prizemoney* £872
2000 Turf 0-3: (5f, 6f 2) (g-f 3)
Currently moderate gelding, has worn blinkers. Turf high 49.
**J J O'Neill [0-3] A J Oliver.*

FIRST STEPS (IRE) BHB 60f **RR 63f** 5319[7]
2 b f Brief Truce (USA) 9.1f **(73)** - Wilsonic (Damister (USA)) 9f **(73)**
Form - 67
Record 2000 - 1st:0 2nd:0 3rd:0 Ran:2
2000 Turf 0-2: (6f 2) (sft 2)
Currently average filly. Turf high 63 (began Oct).
**B Smart [0-2] Martin Padfield.*

FIRST TRUTH BHB 86f **RR 91f** 4452[5]
3 b c Rudimentary (USA) 8.2f **(66)** - Pursuit of Truth (USA) (Irish River (FR)) 8.6f **(78)**
Form - 6427465
Record 2000 - 1st:0 2nd:1 3rd:1 Ran:7
Pre2000 - 1st:1 2nd:1 3rd:0 Ran:6
Win Prizemoney £4,005 *Total Prizemoney* £11,446

Wins * 1999 Spt Pontef (GD) 8f 81 <

2000 Turf 0-7: (8f 3, 11f 2, 12f, 13f) (hvy, sft, gd 4, g-f)

Scopey, useful colt, effective 8 to 11f, best at 8f, acts on hvy to g-f, prefers left handed tracks, prefers tight tracks. Turf high 91 - 2nd of 7 getting 8lb from Holding Court (22 Apr Haydock 11f hvy RF 0824). Consistent. Won a Pontefract maiden over a mile at two but, despite chasing home subsequent French Derby winner Holding Court at Haydock in April, failed to make much impression last season. He barely seems to get ten furlongs, let alone further.

**A Bailey [1-13] Ray Bailey.*

FIRST VENTURE BHB 55f67a **RR 57f 67a** 5005[2]

3 b g Formidable (USA) 7.8f **(60)** - Diamond Wedding (USA) (Diamond Shoal) 9.1f **(66)**

Form - 22300442082

Record 2000 - 1st:0 2nd:4 3rd:1 Ran:11
Pre2000 - 1st:0 2nd:2 3rd:1 Ran:6

Win Prizemoney £0 *Total Prizemoney* £7,368

2000 Turf 0-9: (5f 3, 6f 3, 7f 2, 8f) (g-s, gd 2, g-f 3, frm 3) 2000 AW 0-2: (6f, 7f) (Equi, Fibr)

Scopey, above-average gelding, effective 7f, - acts on AW, often wears blinkers, likes left handed tracks, likes tight tracks. Turf high 73. AW high 79 (1st run) - 2nd of 8 giving 1lb to Direct Reaction (1 Mar Lingfield 7f Equi RF 0386). Has yet to win a race, but he has shown ability on both turf and sand.

**C N Allen [0-17] Pelicas Partnership.*

FISHER ISLAND (IRE) BHB 47f48a **RR 52f 48a** 5016[3]

3 b br f Sri Pekan (USA) - Liberty Song (IRE) (Last Tycoon) 8.5f **(62)**

Form - 63440471853

Record 2000 - 1st:1 2nd:0 3rd:2 Ran:11
Pre2000 - 1st:0 2nd:0 3rd:1 Ran:8

Win Prizemoney £3,005 *Total Prizemoney* £4,907

Wins * **2000** Jly Nottin (G-F) H 10f 49 52 <

2000 Turf 1-6: (8f, 9f, 10f 1-4) (g-s, gd, g-f, frm 1-3) 2000 AW 0-5: (8f, 9f 3, 12f) (Fibr 5)

Scopey, fair filly, effective 6 to 10f, best at 6f, acts on gd to frm - acts on Fibr. Turf high 52 - 1st of 10 getting 14lb from Emali (15 Jly Nottingham RF 2843). AW high 52 - 3rd of 11 getting 20lb from Faraway Look (17 Oct Wolverhampton 9f Fibr RF 5016). Consistent. **R Hollinshead [1-19] The C H F Partnership.*

FISHERMAN'S COVE (USA) **RR 67f** 703[11]

5 b g Caerleon (USA) 10.9f **(79)** - Free At Last (Shirley Heights) 10.3f **(74)**

Form - 0

Record 2000 - 1st:0 2nd:0 3rd:0 Ran:1
Pre2000 - 1st:0 2nd:1 3rd:1 Ran:7

Win Prizemoney £0 *Total Prizemoney* £1,731

2000 Turf 0-1: (14f) (gd)

Average gelding, effective 12 to 17f, acts on gd to frm, prefers tight tracks. Inconsistent.

**J J O'Neill [0-1] Four Clubs (from L Lungo [0-8] Oct 1999).*

FIVE OF WANDS BHB 63f **RR 71f** 5294[14]

3 b f Caerleon (USA) 10.9f **(79)** - Overact (IRE) **(88f)** (Law Society (USA)) 9.9f **(70)**

Form - 23020

Record 2000 - 1st:0 2nd:2 3rd:1 Ran:5
Pre2000 - 1st:0 2nd:0 3rd:0 Ran:1

Win Prizemoney £0 *Total Prizemoney* £4,085

2000 Turf 0-5: (12f 4, 14f) (g-s 2, g-f 3)

Light-framed, above-average filly, effective 12f, acts on g-s to g-f. Turf high 71 (began Jly).

**W Jarvis [0-5] Woodcote Stud Ltd (from J L Dunlop [0-1] Oct 1999).*

FIVE STAR DAY (USA) **RR** 5328a[14]

4 ch c Carson City (USA) - Reggie V (USA) (Vanlandingham (USA))

Form - 0

2000 AW 0-1: (6f) (Dirt)

Currently very useful colt.

**C B Greely in USA [0-1] Columbine Stable & Kitchwa Stable.*

FIZZLE BHB 70f **RR 61f** 2650[2]

3 ch c Efisio 7.7f **(69)** - Altaia (FR) (Sicyos (USA))

Form - 572

Record 2000 - 1st:0 2nd:1 3rd:0 Ran:3

Win Prizemoney £0 *Total Prizemoney* £1,596

2000 Turf 0-3: (7f, 8f 2) (gd, frm 2)

Neat, currently average colt. Turf high 61 - 2nd of 6 to Riparian (9 Jly Newcastle 8f gd RF 2650).

**M Johnston [0-3] H H Racing Partnership.*

FLAG FEN (USA) BHB 49f54a **RR 65f 54a** 4269[18]

9 b br g Riverman (USA) 9.7f **(78)** - Damascus Flag (USA) (Damascus (USA)) 8.9f **(71)**

Form - 0627680

Record 2000 - 1st:0 2nd:1 3rd:0 Ran:7
Pre2000 - 1st:4 2nd:3 3rd:3 Ran:40

Win Prizemoney £14,870 *Total Prizemoney* £22,920

Wins * 1999 Jly Yarmou (GD) H 10.1f 65 68 <
* 1998 Spt Newmar (GD) H 10f 57 60+
* 1998 Jly Newmar (G-F) H 10f 54 60
1997 May Ripon (G-S) S 8f 65

2000 Turf 0-7: (8f, 10f 5, 12f) (gd 3, g-f 2, frm 2)

Average gelding, effective 10f, acts on gd to g-f, best on gd, has worn blinkers, likes tight tracks. Turf high 65 - 2nd of 7 giving 16lb to Julius (12 Jun Nottingham 10f gd RF 1897).

**H J Collingridge [3-21] Mrs Carol Dolan (from J Parkes [1-9] Feb 1998).*

FLAK JACKET BHB 69f **RR 73df** 4832[14]

5 b g Magic Ring (IRE) 6.5f **(64)** - Vaula (Henbit (USA)) 9f **(61)**

Form 00002111300000

Record 2000 - 1st:3 2nd:1 3rd:1 Ran:14
Pre2000 - 1st:2 2nd:1 3rd:1 Ran:13

Win Prizemoney £33,608 *Total Prizemoney* £41,780

Wins * **2000** Aug Goodwo (GD) H 6f 62 71+
* **2000** Jly Catter (G-F) H 5f 62 72+
* **2000** Jly Pontef (G-F) 6f 69
1998 Jly Haydoc (G-F) H 6f 80 83 <
1998 Jun Kempto (HVY) H 6f 70 79

2000 Turf 3-14: (5f 1-9, 6f 2-4, 7f) (g-s 3, gd 5, g-f 1-3, frm 2-3)

Above-average gelding, effective 5 to 6f, best at 6f, acts on gd to frm, best on gd, has worn blinkers, excels at Goodwood. Turf high 75 - 3rd of 13 getting 7lb from Dancing Mystery (13 Aug Ascot 5f g-f RF 3604). Inconsistent. Effective over six furlongs on fast ground, he is still well handicapped on his best form.

**D Nicholls [3-14] The Knavesmire Alliance (from B J Meehan [2-13] Oct 1999).*

FLAMBE BHB 68f76a **RR 52f 76a** 3405[7]

2 b c Whittingham (IRE) - Uae Flame (IRE) (Polish Precedent (USA)) 10.2f **(60)**

Form - 037

Record 2000 - 1st:0 2nd:0 3rd:1 Ran:3

Win Prizemoney £0 *Total Prizemoney* £340

2000 Turf 0-2: (5f 2) (g-f, hrd) 2000 AW 0-1: (5f) (Fibr)

Currently above-average colt. Turf high 52 (began Jly).

**P C Haslam [0-3] Mrs B M Hawkins.*

FLAMEBIRD (IRE) BHB 50f **RR 34f** 4277[13]

3 b f Mukaddamah (USA) 7.6f **(74)** - Flamenco (USA) (Dance Spell (USA)) 9.6f **(75)**

Form - 7050

Record 2000 - 1st:0 2nd:0 3rd:0 Ran:4

2000 Turf 0-4: (7f 2, 8f 2) (gd, g-f 3)

Leggy, very moderate filly. Turf high 34.

**Mrs A L M King [0-4] Mrs L R Lovell.*

FLAMENCO RED BHB 87f **RR 88f** 4736[3]

3 b f Warning 8.1f **(77)** - Spanish Wells (IRE) (Sadler's Wells (USA)) 10f **(76)**

Form - 42183

Record 2000 - 1st:1 2nd:1 3rd:1 Ran:5
Pre2000 - 1st:1 2nd:1 3rd:2 Ran:5

Win Prizemoney £10,394 *Total Prizemoney* £16,789

Wins * **2000** Aug Thirsk (G-F) 8f 43
* 1999 Jun Nottin (GD) 6.1f 74 <

2000 Turf 1-5: (8f 1-4, 10f) (g-s, gd, frm 1-3)

Useful filly, effective 8f, acts on gd to frm, has worn blinkers. Turf high 88 (began Jly) - 3rd of 11 getting 1lb from Lagoon (29 Spt Newmarket 8f gd RF 4736). Scored at 1/25 at Thirsk but was held in a listed race next time when tackling ten furlongs.

**R Charlton [2-10] K Abdulla.*

FLAME OF TRUTH BHB 72f **RR 76f** 5070[2]
3 b f Rainbow Quest (USA) 11.2f **(81)** - River Lullaby (USA) (Riverman (USA)) 9.1f **(76)**
Form - 3222
Record 2000 - 1st:0 2nd:3 3rd:1 Ran:4
Win Prizemoney £0 *Total Prizemoney* £4,509
2000 Turf 0-4: (10f, 12f 3) (g-s 2, g-f, frm)
Scopey, above-average filly. Turf high 76 (began Aug).
**J H M Gosden [0-4] K Abdulla.*

FLAME THROWER (USA) RR 5330a[8]
2 ch f Saint Ballado (USA) - Metromane (USA) (Metrogrand (USA))
Form - 8
2000 AW 0-1: (9f) (Dirt)
Currently useful. **B Baffert in USA [0-1] G Garber.*

FLAMINGO ROAD (GER) RR 108f 4138a[6]
4 m Acatenango (GER) - Fabula Dancer (Northern Dancer) 9.6f **(80)**
Form - 43146
2000 Turf 1-5: (11f 1-2, 12f 2, 13f) (hvy 1-1, sft, g-s, gd 2)
Pattern-class filly, effective 11 to 12f, best at 12f, acts on hvy to gd, best on gd. Turf high 108. Consistent. A smart German-trained filly, she made all in a Group Two in heavy ground.
**A Schutz in GER [2-10].*

FLAMME DE LA VIE BHB 65f65a **RR 77f 65a** 5312[17]
2 b g Blushing Flame (USA) - La Belle Vie (Indian King (USA)) 7.4f **(64)**
Form - 40
Record 2000 - 1st:0 2nd:0 3rd:0 Ran:2
Win Prizemoney £0 *Total Prizemoney* £178
2000 Turf 0-2: (8f 2) (g-s 2)
Currently above-average gelding. Turf high 77 (began Oct).
**G A Butler [0-2] David Mills.*

FLANDERS (IRE) RR 98f 3576[7]
4 b f Common Grounds 8.1f **(66)** - Family At War (USA) (Explodent (USA)) 9.4f **(87)**
Form - 1077
Record 2000 - 1st:1 2nd:0 3rd:0 Ran:4
Pre2000 - 1st:5 2nd:4 3rd:1 Ran:15
Win Prizemoney £121,671 *Total Prizemoney* £236,786
Wins * **2000** May Beverl (G-F) 5f 98
* 1999 Spt Doncas (G-F) L 5f 102 <
* 1998 Jly Newbur (G-F) 5.2f 94
* 1998 Jun Ascot (G-S) 5f 98+
* 1998 Jun Beverl (G-S) 5f 99++
* 1998 May Beverl (G-F) 5f 74+
2000 Turf 1-4: (5f 1-3, 6f) (gd 2, g-f, hrd 1-1)
Workmanlike, very useful filly, effective 5f, acts on g-f. Turf high 98. A speedy filly, she returned to land the odds in a Beverley conditions event, but failed to make an impression in the King's Stand or a listed race at Chester, although she did not run at all badly when tried over six on her final run.
**T D Easterby [6-19] Mrs Jean Connew.*

FLAPDOODLE BHB 56f **RR 30f** 4628[14]
2 b f Superpower 6.6f **(58)** - My Concordia (Belfort (FR)) 6.8f **(63)**
Form - 00
Record 2000 - 1st:0 2nd:0 3rd:0 Ran:2
2000 Turf 0-2: (5f, 6f) (gd, frm)
Currently fair filly. Turf high 30 (began Jly).
**A W Carroll [0-2] John Halsey.*

FLASH BACK (IRE) RR 59f 3028[9]
2 b c Anabaa (USA) - Embracing **(93f)** (Reference Point) 6.8f **(70)**
Form - 0
Record 2000 - 1st:0 2nd:0 3rd:0 Ran:1
2000 Turf 0-1: (6f) (g-f)
Currently fair colt. **Sir Michael Stoute [0-1] Saeed Suhail.*

FLASHFEET BHB 30f25a **RR 36f 25a** 3569[8]
10 b g Rousillon (USA) 10.4f **(69)** - Miellita (King Emperor (USA)) 9.4f **(58)**
Form - 00000046074060008
Record 2000 - 1st:0 2nd:0 3rd:0 Ran:16
Pre2000 - 1st:1 2nd:4 3rd:7 Ran:42
Win Prizemoney £2,519 *Total Prizemoney* £10,127
2000 Turf 0-7: (7f 4, 8f 3) (gd 2, g-f 4, frm) 2000 AW 0-9: (7f 2, 8f 3, 9f 3, 11f) (Equi, Fibr 8)
Very moderate gelding, effective 7f, acts on g-f, has worn blinkers. Turf high 36. AW high 22.
**P D Purdy [0-24] P D Purdy (from K Bishop [1-14] May 1997).*

FLASH OF LIGHT (IRE) BHB 58f53a **RR 66f 53a** 4125[8]
2 b f Brief Truce (USA) 9.1f **(73)** - Dancing Light (Dancers Image (USA)) 9.3f **(71)**
Form - 08
Record 2000 - 1st:0 2nd:0 3rd:0 Ran:2
2000 Turf 0-2: (7f 2) (g-f, frm)
Currently average filly. Turf high 66 (began Aug).
**R Hannon [0-2] D Boocock.*

FLASHTALKIN' FLOOD BHB 37f32a **RR 39f 32a** 4764[12]
6 ch g Then Again 7.4f **(52)** - Linguistic (Porto Bello) 8.9f **(43)**
Form - 004020
Record 2000 - 1st:0 2nd:1 3rd:0 Ran:6
Pre2000 - 1st:2 2nd:0 3rd:2 Ran:15
Win Prizemoney £6,047 *Total Prizemoney* £7,758
Wins 1998 May Hamilt (G-S) H 8.3f 59 63
1997 Jun Nottin (SFT) SH 8.2f 57 70+ <
2000 Turf 0-6: (8f 3, 9f, 11f, 12f) (g-s 2, g-f 3, frm)
Very moderate gelding, effective 8f, acts on g-f to frm. Turf high 39 - 4th of 20 giving 8lb to Kierchem (21 Jun Ripon 8f g-f RF 2166).
**J L Eyre [0-6] Wessex House Racing (from Mrs M Reveley [1-7] Oct 1998).*

FLAVIA (IRE) BHB 36f40a **RR 43f 40a** 5227[13]
3 b f Lahib (USA) 8f **(69)** - Gustavia (IRE) **(79df 83a)** (Red Sunset) 8.2f **(63)**
Form - 667530
Record 2000 - 1st:0 2nd:0 3rd:1 Ran:6
Win Prizemoney £0 *Total Prizemoney* £388
2000 Turf 0-3: (7f, 8f, 12f) (gd, g-f 2) 2000 AW 0-3: (9f, 12f 2) (Equi, Fibr 2)
Lengthy, moderate filly, effective 12f, - acted on Fibr, often wore blinkers. Turf high 43 (began Jly). AW high 47 (began Aug). (DEAD)
**R W Armstrong [0-6] Mrs Robert Armstrong.*

FLAVIAN BHB 96f **RR 97f** 4282[8]
4 b f Catrail (USA) - Fatah Flare (USA) (Alydar (USA)) 9.1f **(76)**
Form - 87188
Record 2000 - 1st:1 2nd:0 3rd:0 Ran:5
Pre2000 - 1st:1 2nd:1 3rd:0 Ran:3
Win Prizemoney £10,067 *Total Prizemoney* £11,649
Wins * **2000** Jly Yarmou (FRM) 7f 94+ <
* 1998 Oct Newmar (G-S) 6f 87
2000 Turf 1-5: (5f, 6f, 7f 1-3) (gd 2, g-f 1-2, frm)
Scopey, very useful filly, effective 7f, acts on gd to g-f. Turf high 97 - 8th of 11 giving 6lb to Danceabout (3 Aug Goodwood 7f gd RF 3340) - also 1st of 7 getting 7lb from Jarn (4 Jly Yarmouth RF 2501). Consistent. She has had her problems, but suddenly bounced back to form with an impressive win on very fast ground at Yarmouth in July. By no means disgraced in the face of a stiff task at Goodwood, she sweated up when well beaten in a similar event at Doncaster. **H Candy [2-8] Major M G Wyatt.*

FLAWLY RR 99f 2788a[3]
3 b f Old Vic 12.8f **(72)** - Flawlessly (USA) (Rainbow Quest (USA)) 10.4f **(75)**
Form - 23
2000 Turf 0-2: (12f, 13f) (g-s, gd)
Currently very useful filly. Turf high 99 (1st run) - 2nd of 6 to Sadler's Flag (3 Jun Chantilly 12f gd RF 1821a). A reasonable record in Group events in France.
**E Lellouche in FR [0-2] Gary Tanaka.*

FLAXEN PRIDE (IRE) BHB 35f **RR 36f** 1912[18]
5 ch m Pips Pride 6.7f **(70)** - Fair Chance (Young Emperor) 10.1f **(63)**
Form - 800
Record 2000 - 1st:0 2nd:0 3rd:0 Ran:3
Pre2000 - 1st:1 2nd:1 3rd:0 Ran:15
Win Prizemoney £3,096 *Total Prizemoney* £3,931

Wins * 1999 Aug Leices (G-F) H 8f 37 41 <
2000 Turf 0-3: (8f 2, 9f) (frm 3)
Very moderate filly, effective 8 to 9f, best at 8f, acts on g-f to frm, best on g-f. Turf high 28. Inconsistent.
**Mrs M Reveley [1-21] Evans, Bailey, Playf Snaith.*

FLEDGLING BHB 82f **RR 80+f** 5366a[13]
3 b f Efisio 7.7f **(69)** - Nest (Sharpo) 7.7f **(59)**
Form - 510
Record 2000 - 1st:1 2nd:0 3rd:0 Ran:3
Win Prizemoney £4,173 *Total Prizemoney* £4,173
Wins * 2000 Jun Haydoc (G-S) 7.1f 80+ <
2000 Turf 1-3: (6f, 7f 1-1, 8f) (hvy, gd 1-1, g-f)
Scopey, currently decent filly. Turf high 80 - 1st of 4 getting 5lb from Argentan (8 Jun Haydock RF 1806). **A C Stewart [1-3].*

FLEETING FANCY BHB 49f **RR 52f** 4116[11]
3 b f Thatching 7.8f **(69)** - Fleetwood Fancy (Taufan (USA)) 7f **(57)**
Form - 030757400
Record 2000 - 1st:0 2nd:0 3rd:1 Ran:9
Pre2000 - 1st:0 2nd:0 3rd:0 Ran:2
Win Prizemoney £0 *Total Prizemoney* £693
2000 Turf 0-9: (6f 7, 7f, 8f) (gd 3, g-f, frm 4, hrd)
Unfurnished, fair filly, effective 6f, acts on frm. Turf high 52.
**S Dow [0-11] N Boyle.*

FLEETING FOOTSTEPS BHB 30f32a **RR 15f 32a** 100[9]
8 b h Komaite (USA) 6.9f **(61)** - Hyperion Palace (Dragonara Palace (USA)) 6.1f **(55)**
Form - 0
Record 2000 - 1st:0 2nd:0 3rd:0 Ran:1
Pre2000 - 1st:0 2nd:0 3rd:0 Ran:5
2000 AW 0-1: (12f) (Fibr)
Poor horse.
**C N Kellett [0-1] B G Peacock (from D Shaw [0-2] May 1997).*

FLETCHER BHB 64f60a **RR 68f 60a** 5297[10]
6 b g Salse (USA) 10.9f **(71)** - Ballet Classique (USA) (Sadler's Wells (USA)) 10f **(76)**
Form - 707802232115102700
Record 2000 - 1st:3 2nd:4 3rd:1 Ran:17
Pre2000 - 1st:2 2nd:5 3rd:4 Ran:36
Win Prizemoney £18,618 *Total Prizemoney* £36,153
Wins * 2000 Aug Salisb (G-F) H 14.1f 63 67
*** 2000** Jly Sandow (G-F) H 14f 58 61
*** 2000** Jly Salisb (GD) H 12f 55 58
* 1998 Oct Ascot (SFT) H 12f 74 78
1996 Apr Newmar (G-F) 5f 83+ <
2000 Turf 3-17: (12f 1-4, 14f 2-9, 15f, 16f 2, 18f) (hvy, sft, g-s 2, gd 6, g-f 2-2, frm 1-5)
Average gelding, effective 12 to 14f, best at 12f, acts on g-s to frm, has worn blinkers, prefers right handed tracks, excels at Salisbury and Sandown. Turf high 68 - 2nd of 13 getting 3lb from Hambleden (13 Spt Sandown 14f frm RF 4373) - also 1st of 16 giving 11lb to Misconduct (17 Aug Salisbury RF 3732). Consistent. He has enjoyed a good season, winning three times, but has looked held since. He has on occasions not always looked to put it all in, but has been well handled by Richard Hughes.
**H Morrison [4-53] Lady Margadale (from P F I Cole [1-7] Oct 1996).*

FLICKER BHB 30f25a **RR 17?f 25a** 196[12]
5 b m Unfuwain (USA) 11.4f **(74)** - Lovers Light (Grundy) 10.3f **(65)**
Form - 0
Record 2000 - 1st:0 2nd:0 3rd:0 Ran:1
Pre2000 - 1st:0 2nd:0 3rd:1 Ran:11
Win Prizemoney £0 *Total Prizemoney* £1,661
2000 AW 0-1: (9f) (Fibr)
Poor filly, has broken blood-vessels, has worn blinkers. Becoming disappointing.
**W Clay [0-10] B Baggott & H Clewlow (from Lord Huntingdon [0-9] Nov 1998).*

FLIGHT FOR FREEDOM BHB 42f50a **RR 55f 50a** 325[7]
5 b m Saddlers' Hall (IRE) 10.5f **(65)** - Anatroccolo (Ile de Bourbon (USA)) 10.1f **(67)**
Form - 7
Record 2000 - 1st:0 2nd:0 3rd:0 Ran:1
Pre2000 - 1st:0 2nd:1 3rd:0 Ran:8
Win Prizemoney £0 *Total Prizemoney* £1,196
2000 AW 0-1: (12f) (Fibr)
Fair filly.
**D W P Arbuthnot [0-2] Miss Samantha Dare (from Ferdy Murphy [1-11] Jun 1999).*

FLIGHT OF DREAMS (IRE) BHB 41f **RR 43f** 4378[4]
3 b f College Chapel - Lady Portobello (Porto Bello) 8.9f **(43)**
Form - 806134
Record 2000 - 1st:1 2nd:0 3rd:1 Ran:6
Pre2000 - 1st:0 2nd:0 3rd:0 Ran:3
Win Prizemoney £2,467 *Total Prizemoney* £2,787
Wins * 2000 Aug Bright (GD) H 7f 32 41 <
2000 Turf 1-6: (6f 2, 7f 1-3, 12f) (sft, g-f 1-3, frm 2)
Scopey, moderate filly, effective 7f, acts on g-f, has worn blinkers. Turf high 43 - also 1st of 18 getting 13lb from Master Luke (9 Aug Brighton RF 3484).
**M Wigham [1-5] Cable Media Consultancy Ltd (from B S Rothwell [0-4] Apr 2000).*

FLIGHT OF FANCY **RR 87+f** 4125[1]
2 b f Sadler's Wells (USA) 11.3f **(87)** - Phantom Gold **(115f)** (Machiavellian (USA))
Form - 21
Record 2000 - 1st:1 2nd:1 3rd:0 Ran:2
Win Prizemoney £5,044 *Total Prizemoney* £6,633
Wins * 2000 Aug Salisb (G-F) 7f 82++ <
2000 Turf 1-2: (7f 1-2) (g-f, frm 1-1)
Currently useful filly. Turf high 87 (1st run) (began Jly) - 2nd of 11 to Summer Symphony (30 Jly Newmarket 7f g-f RF 3231) - also 1st of 10 from Roofer (31 Aug Salisbury RF 4125). She just failed to catch Summer Splendour on her debut and made no mistake next time. A very promising filly. **Sir Michael Stoute [1-2] The Queen.*

FLIGHT REFUND BHB 40f **RR 38f** 5062[6]
3 ch g Missed Flight - Settlement (USA) (Irish River (FR)) 8.6f **(78)**
Form - 0006
Record 2000 - 1st:0 2nd:0 3rd:0 Ran:3
Pre2000 - 1st:0 2nd:0 3rd:0 Ran:3
2000 Turf 0-3: (8f 2, 10f) (sft, gd, g-f)
Leggy, very moderate gelding. Turf high 38.
**R Hollinshead [0-6] Mrs A L Wood.*

FLIGHT SEQUENCE BHB 74f **RR 75f** 4269[6]
4 b f Polar Falcon (USA) 9f **(74)** - Doubles (Damister (USA)) 9f **(73)**
Form - 682016
Record 2000 - 1st:1 2nd:1 3rd:0 Ran:6
Pre2000 - 1st:0 2nd:2 3rd:0 Ran:4
Win Prizemoney £4,173 *Total Prizemoney* £8,257
Wins * 2000 Aug Epsom (GD) 10.1f 75 <
2000 Turf 1-6: (7f, 8f, 9f 2, 10f 1-1, 12f) (sft, g-f 1-4, frm)
Leggy, above-average filly, effective 8 to 10f, acts on g-f to frm, best on g-f, has worn blinkers. Turf high 75 - 2nd of 9 getting 5lb from Fredora (28 Jun Kempton 9f frm RF 2346) - also 1st of 9 giving 6lb to Pheisty (16 Aug Epsom RF 3693). Consistent.
**Lady Herries [1-10] Tony Perkins.*

FLINT (IRE) BHB 70f **RR 70f** 3614[11]
2 b g Fayruz 6.6f **(63)** - Full of Sparkle (IRE) (Persian Heights)
Form - 754150
Record 2000 - 1st:1 2nd:0 3rd:0 Ran:6
Win Prizemoney £2,380 *Total Prizemoney* £2,619
Wins * 2000 Jly Beverl (G-F) C 5f 70 <
2000 Turf 1-6: (5f 1-5, 6f) (gd, g-f 1-1, frm 3, hrd)
Above-average gelding, effective 5f, acts on g-f to frm. Turf high 70 - 5th of 10 getting 6lb from Candothat (2 Aug Musselburgh 5f frm RF 3337) - also 1st of 12 giving 7lb to Patrician Fox (24 Jly Beverley RF 3067). **M W Easterby [1-6] Guy Reed.*

FLINT RIVER BHB 84f **RR 83+f** 4742[9]
2 b c Red Ransom (USA) 8.6f **(83)** - She's All Class (USA) (Rahy (USA))
Form - 220210
Record 2000 - 1st:1 2nd:3 3rd:0 Ran:6
Win Prizemoney £2,415 *Total Prizemoney* £6,901
Wins * 2000 Spt Warwic (G-F) 6.1f 83+ <

2000 Turf 1-6: (5f 4, 6f 1-2) (gd 2, g-f 1-3, hrd)
Decent colt, effective 6f, acts on g-f. Turf high 83 - 1st of 16 giving 9lb to Halcyon Magic (11 Spt Warwick RF 4323). Scored a deserved win at Warwick after meeting trouble in running.
**R F JohnsonHoughton [1-6] Mrs Hue Williams.*

FLINTSTONE BHB 44f RR 33f 4011[14]
3 b g First Trump - South Rock **(97f)** (Rock City)
Form - 000
Record 2000 - 1st:0 2nd:0 3rd:0 Ran:3
Pre2000 - 1st:0 2nd:0 3rd:1 Ran:2
Win Prizemoney £0 *Total Prizemoney* £367
2000 Turf 0-3: (8f, 12f, 14f) (gd, g-f, frm)
Workmanlike, very moderate gelding, has worn blinkers. Turf high 33. **J A Glover [0-5] Mrs Andrea Mallinson.*

FLIPSIDE (IRE) RR 25f 5065[15]
2 b c Dolphin Street (FR) - Trinity Hall **(62f)** (Hallgate)
Form - 80
Record 2000 - 1st:0 2nd:0 3rd:0 Ran:2
2000 Turf 0-2: (7f, 8f) (g-s, frm)
Currently little account colt. Turf high 25 (began Aug).
**J W Hills [0-2] The Dan Abbott Racing Partnership.*

FLIQUET BAY (IRE) BHB 50f RR 64f 4696[3]
3 b g Namaqualand (USA) - Thatcherite (Final Straw) 7.9f **(64)**
Form - 420303
Record 2000 - 1st:0 2nd:1 3rd:2 Ran:6
Pre2000 - 1st:0 2nd:0 3rd:0 Ran:3
Win Prizemoney £0 *Total Prizemoney* £1,864
2000 Turf 0-6: (12f 4, 14f, 16f) (g-s, gd, g-f 3, frm)
Unfurnished, average gelding, effective 12f, acts on gd to g-f, often wears blinkers (extremely effectively). Turf high 64 - 2nd of 11 giving 3lb to Cross Dall (2 May Windsor 12f gd RF 0974). Inconsistent.
**Mrs A J Perrett [0-9] Mrs S L Whitehead.*

FLIT ABOUT (USA) BHB 79f75a RR 78f 75a 4555[7]
2 ch f Fly So Free (USA) - Oxava (FR) (Antheus (USA))
Form - 23517
Record 2000 - 1st:1 2nd:1 3rd:1 Ran:5
Win Prizemoney £6,938 *Total Prizemoney* £8,492
Wins * 2000 Spt Bath (GD) H 8f 77 78 <
2000 Turf 1-4: (6f, 7f, 8f 1-2) (gd, g-f, frm 1-2) 2000 AW 0-1: (7f) (Fibr)
Above-average filly. Turf high 78 (began Jly) - 1st of 13 getting 3lb from Murrendi (4 Spt Bath RF 4203). **I A Balding [1-5] Robin Scully.*

FLITE OF ARABY BHB 60f RR 59f 3492[6]
3 b c Green Desert (USA) 7.8f **(78)** - Allegedly Blue (USA) (Alleged (USA)) 10f **(76)**
Form - 346
Record 2000 - 1st:0 2nd:0 3rd:1 Ran:3
Pre2000 - 1st:0 2nd:0 3rd:0 Ran:3
Win Prizemoney £0 *Total Prizemoney* £718
2000 Turf 0-3: (12f 3) (frm 2, hrd)
Scopey, fair colt, effective 12f, acts on frm. Turf high 59 - 4th of 7 getting 8lb from Double Blade (19 Jly Doncaster 12f frm RF 2930).
**W R Muir [0-6] The Wheet Partnership.*

FLITE OF LIFE BHB 60f63a RR 62df 63a 563[18]
4 gr g Forzando 7.2f **(63)** - Frighten The Life (Kings Lake (USA)) 10.8f **(67)**
Form - 051600
Record 2000 - 1st:0 2nd:0 3rd:0 Ran:3
Pre2000 - 1st:1 2nd:1 3rd:0 Ran:12
Win Prizemoney £1,871 *Total Prizemoney* £4,341
Wins * *1999 Dec Southw (STD) H 8f 57 72* <
2000 Turf 0-1: (7f) (gd) 2000 AW 0-2: (8f 2) (Fibr 2)
Unfurnished, above-average gelding, effective 8f, - acts on Fibr, likes left handed tracks. AW high 61.
**W R Muir [1-15] Mrs Irene White.*

FLITWICK BHB 83f RR 85f 3609[2]
3 b c Warning 8.1f **(77)** - Flit (USA) (Lyphard (USA)) 9.9f **(72)**
Form - 8162
Record 2000 - 1st:1 2nd:1 3rd:0 Ran:4
Win Prizemoney £3,497 *Total Prizemoney* £5,787
Wins * 2000 May Ripon (GD) 10f 80 <
2000 Turf 1-4: (8f, 9f, 10f 1-2) (sft, g-f 1-1, frm 2)
Scopey, useful colt. Turf high 85 - 2nd of 14 giving 19lb to Derryquin (13 Aug Leicester 8f frm RF 3609) - also 1st of 8 giving 5lb to Sense of Freedom (31 May Ripon RF 1597). Ordinary handicap form after winning his maiden, and is likely to prove better at ten furlongs than a mile. **H R A Cecil [1-4] K Abdulla.*

FLOATING CHARGE BHB 84a RR 82+f 4831[4]
6 b g Sharpo 7.5f **(68)** - Poyle Fizz (Damister (USA)) 9f **(73)**
Form - 2U88114
Record 2000 - 1st:2 2nd:1 3rd:0 Ran:7
Pre2000 - 1st:3 2nd:2 3rd:1 Ran:17
Win Prizemoney £28,982 *Total Prizemoney* £37,328
Wins * 2000 Spt Newbur (G-F) H 7.3f 77 82+ <
*** 2000** Spt Kempto (GD) H 7f 74 78
* 1999 Spt Kempto (HVY) H 8f 71 76
* 1999 Apr Windso (GD) H 8.3f 65 69+
* 1998 Jly Redcar (G-F) 9f 62
2000 Turf 2-5: (7f 2-2, 8f 3) (g-s 2, g-f 1-2, frm 1-1) 2000 AW 0-2: (7f, 8f) (Fibr 2)
Useful gelding, effective 7 to 8f, best at 7f, acts on g-s to frm - acts on Fibr, has worn blinkers, likes right handed tracks. Turf high 82 - 1st of 16 from Goodenough Mover (15 Spt Newbury RF 4433) - also 1st of 16 giving 1lb to Hill Magic (3 Spt Kempton RF 4188). AW high 85 (1st run) - 2nd of 11 giving 10lb to One Dinar (24 Feb Wolverhampton 8f Fibr RF 0349). He won very nicely at Kempton in September and followed up in good style at Newbury.
**J R Fanshawe [5-24] The Leonard Curtis Partnership.*

FLOATING EMBER BHB 38f RR 44f 2474[3]
3 b f Rambo Dancer (CAN) 8.4f **(59)** - Spark (IRE) **(62df 47a)** (Flash of Steel) 7.2f **(53)**
Form - 08103
Record 2000 - 1st:1 2nd:0 3rd:1 Ran:5
Pre2000 - 1st:0 2nd:0 3rd:0 Ran:5
Win Prizemoney £3,591 *Total Prizemoney* £3,918
Wins * 2000 Jun Pontef (SFT) S 10f 44 <
2000 Turf 1-5: (8f 2, 10f 1-2, 12f) (gd 1-2, g-f, frm 2)
Neat, moderate filly, effective 10f, acts on gd, likes tight tracks. Turf high 44 - 1st of 13 getting 18lb from Hot Potato (4 Jun Pontefract RF 1695). **J L Eyre [1-10] Martin West.*

FLOORSO'THEFOREST (IRE) BHB 37f RR 58f 5056[12]
4 ch g Forest Wind (USA) - Ravensdale Rose (IRE) (Henbit (USA)) 9f **(61)**
Form - 655265277750000
Record 2000 - 1st:0 2nd:2 3rd:0 Ran:15
Pre2000 - 1st:1 2nd:1 3rd:2 Ran:11
Win Prizemoney £4,380 *Total Prizemoney* £8,733
Wins * 1999 Jly Hamilt (G-F) H 9.2f 65 59 <
2000 Turf 0-15: (8f 7, 9f 6, 10f, 11f) (sft 2, gd 3, g-f 6, frm 4)
Workmanlike, fair gelding, effective 9 to 10f, acts on g-f to frm, likes left handed tracks, likes tight tracks. Turf high 60. Inconsistent. **Miss L A Perratt [1-26] Miss L A Perratt.*

FLOOT BHB 66f RR 67f 4728[3]
2 b c Piccolo - Midnight Owl (FR) (Ardross) 10.6f **(68)**
Form - 8803
Record 2000 - 1st:0 2nd:0 3rd:1 Ran:4
Win Prizemoney £0 *Total Prizemoney* £477
2000 Turf 0-4: (6f 2, 7f, 8f) (gd 2, frm 2)
Average colt. Turf high 67.
**J L Dunlop [0-4] Mrs Patrick Darling(Susa Racing).*

FLORA DREAMBIRD BHB 20f15a RR 38f 15a 748[9]
6 b m Mandalus - Dame Flora (Celtic Cone) 9.8f **(43)**
Form - 6085660
Record 2000 - 1st:0 2nd:0 3rd:0 Ran:6
Pre2000 - 1st:0 2nd:1 3rd:0 Ran:5
Win Prizemoney £0 *Total Prizemoney* £512
2000 Turf 0-1: (22f) (sft) 2000 AW 0-5: (13f, 16f 4) (Equi 3, Fibr 2)
Very moderate mare, effective 16f, acts on frm, has worn blinkers, favours left handed tracks, favours tight tracks. AW high 17.
**P W Hiatt [1-33] P W Hiatt.*

FLORIDA (IRE) BHB 42f40a RR 41f 40a 4480[14]
2 b f Sri Pekan (USA) - Florinda (CAN) (Vice Regent (CAN)) 8.7f **(74)**

Form - 000
Record 2000 - 1st:0 2nd:0 3rd:0 Ran:3
2000 Turf 0-3: (6f, 7f 2) (g-s, frm 2)
Currently moderate filly. Turf high 41 (began Aug).
**I A Wood [0-3] Neardown Stables.*

FLOSSY BHB 100f94a **RR 101f 94a** 5323[15]
4 b f Efisio 7.7f **(69)** - Sirene Bleu Marine (USA) (Secreto (USA)) 8.7f **(72)**
Form - 04410233120
Record 2000 - 1st:2 2nd:2 3rd:2 Ran:11
Pre2000 - 1st:6 2nd:3 3rd:0 Ran:14
Win Prizemoney £60,949 *Total Prizemoney* £85,964
Wins * **2000** Spt Newmar (G-S) H 12f 89 95 <
* **2000** Aug Cheste (GD) H 12.3f 84 87+
* 1999 Nov Doncas (SFT) H 12f 82 86
* 1999 Spt Haydoc (G-F) H 11.9f 75 81
* 1999 Aug Newcas (GD) H 12.4f 66 70
* 1999 Jly Newbur (G-F) H 10f 51 59+
* 1999 Jly Mussel (G-S) H 12f 43 57+
* 1999 Jly Beverl (G-F) H 9.9f 43 47
2000 Turf 2-11: (10f 2, 12f 2-7, 13f, 14f) (sft, g-s 2, gd 4, g-f 2-2, frm 2)
Leggy, very useful filly, effective 10 to 13f, best at 12f, acts on g-s to g-f, and excels at Newcastle. Turf high 101 - 2nd of 20 giving 11lb to Seren Hill (12 Oct Newmarket 12f gd RF 4936) - also 1st of 18 getting 2lb from Ormelie (26 Spt Newmarket RF 4647). Consistent. Suddenly hit form in July of '99 and went on to pass the post first seven times, culminating in landing the November Handicap. Back to winning ways at Chester in August, she continued to run well through the autumn, scoring again at Newmarket and being touched off over the same track next time. Appeared to be over the top when trying to repeat her 1999 win at Doncaster, but 12 furlongs and cut in the ground are ideal.
**C W Thornton [8-25] Guy Reed.*

FLOTSAM RR 24f 4128[8]
4 ch g Beveled (USA) 6.9f **(64)** - Parrot Fashion (Pieces of Eight) 7.8f

Flossy gained a smooth success at Newmarket

(51)
Form - 8
Record 2000 - 1st:0 2nd:0 3rd:0 Ran:1
Pre2000 - 1st:0 2nd:0 3rd:0 Ran:1
2000 Turf 0-1: (14f) (frm)
Leggy, currently little account gelding.
**J G Portman [0-1] Mrs Gina Newman (from M D I Usher [0-1] Spt 1999).*

FLOW BEAU BHB 32f **RR 41f** 5012[7]
3 b f Mtoto 11.5f **(71)** - Radiance (FR) (Blakeney) 10.5f **(64)**
Form - 406007
Record 2000 - 1st:0 2nd:0 3rd:0 Ran:6
Win Prizemoney £0 *Total Prizemoney* £192
2000 Turf 0-5: (7f 2, 8f, 9f, 10f) (gd 2, g-f 2, frm) 2000 AW 0-1: (14f) (Fibr)
Unfurnished, moderate filly, effective 14f, - acts on Fibr, has worn blinkers. Turf high 41. (1st run) - 7th of 16 getting 5lb from Half Tide (16 Oct Southwell 14f Fibr RF 5012).

**D Shaw [0-3] J Saul (from G Woodward [0-3] Jun 2000).*

FLOWER O'CANNIE (IRE) BHB 70f **RR 60f** 546[12]
5 b m Mujadil (USA) 7.7f **(70)** -Baby's Smile (Shirley Heights) 10.3f **(74)**
Form - 0
Record 2000 - 1st:0 2nd:0 3rd:0 Ran:1
Pre2000 - 1st:5 2nd:4 3rd:6 Ran:34
Win Prizemoney £25,090 *Total Prizemoney* £36,895
Wins * 1999 Jun York (G-S) H 11.9f 75 76
* 1998 Nov Mussel (SFT) H 12f 68 81
* 1998 Oct Newcas (SFT) H 12.4f 68 75
* 1997 Jly Beverl (HVY) 7.5f 89? <
* 1997 Jun Hamilt (SFT) 6f 69
2000 Turf 0-1: (14f) (frm)
Average filly, effective 11 to 12f, best at 12f, acts on hvy to g-f. Consistent. **M W Easterby [5-36] Mrs E Rhind.*

FLOWING RIO BHB 68f **RR 72f** 4778[2]
2 b f First Trump - Deanta in Eirinn (Red Sunset) 8.2f **(63)**
Form - 0153302
Record 2000 - 1st:1 2nd:1 3rd:2 Ran:7
Win Prizemoney £3,526 *Total Prizemoney* £5,096
Wins * **2000** Jun Hamilt (GD) 6f 72 <
2000 Turf 1-6: (5f, 6f 1-2, 7f 3) (gd 2, g-f 1-1, frm 3) 2000 AW 0-1: (6f) (Fibr)
Above-average filly, effective 6 to 7f, acts on g-f to frm. Turf high 72 - 3rd of 6 giving 3lb to Dominaite (29 Jly Redcar 7f frm RF 3221) - also 1st of 8 giving 4lb to Katies Dolphin (15 Jun Hamilton RF 1982). **P C Haslam [1-7] Rio Stainless Engineering Ltd.*

FLOWINGTON (IRE) BHB 93f **RR 97f** 4376[4]
3 b f Owington - Persian Flower **(50f 42a)** (Persian Heights)
Form - 50426304
Record 2000 - 1st:0 2nd:1 3rd:1 Ran:8
Pre2000 - 1st:2 2nd:0 3rd:1 Ran:6
Win Prizemoney £4,808 *Total Prizemoney* £14,068
Wins * 1999 Jun Warwic (G-F) 6.8f 71 <
* 1999 *Jun Wolver (STA) S 5f 62*
2000 Turf 0-8: (6f 8) (gd 2, g-f 3, frm 2, hrd)
Light-framed, very useful filly, effective 6f, acts on gd to frm, best on g-f. Turf high 97 - 3rd of 10 getting 5lb from Littlefeather (4 Aug Newmarket 6f g-f RF 3370). A decent filly, she is not quite up to listed class. Just caught by Boast in a conditions event at Newmarket in June, she faced one or two stiff tasks subsequently.
**N P Littmoden [2-14] Linane.*

FLOWLINE RIVER RR 17f 3441[18]
2 b f Awesome - Gymcrak Dancer (Pennine Walk) 8.5f **(61)**
Form - 800
Record 2000 - 1st:0 2nd:0 3rd:0 Ran:3
2000 Turf 0-2: (5f 2) (frm 2) 2000 AW 0-1: (7f) (Fibr)
Currently poor filly. Turf high 17 (began Jly).
**D Burchell [0-3] Mrs J A Davies.*

FLUME BHB 78f **RR 74f** 1779[3]
3 br f Zafonic (USA) 9f **(83)** - Rainy Sky (Rainbow Quest (USA)) 10.4f **(75)**
Form - 3
Record 2000 - 1st:0 2nd:0 3rd:1 Ran:1
Pre2000 - 1st:0 2nd:0 3rd:0 Ran:2
Win Prizemoney £0 *Total Prizemoney* £1,642
2000 Turf 0-1: (7f) (gd)
Above-average filly. (DEAD) **B W Hills [0-3] K Abdulla.*

FLUMMOX BHB 83f **RR 74+f** 2694[4]
2 b c Rudimentary (USA) 8.2f **(66)** - Pluvial (Habat) 7.6f **(61)**
Form - 1344
Record 2000 - 1st:1 2nd:0 3rd:1 Ran:4
Win Prizemoney £2,804 *Total Prizemoney* £4,104
Wins * **2000** May Warwic (HVY) 5f 74+ <
2000 Turf 1-4: (5f 1-3, 6f) (hvy 1-1, gd, frm 2)
Above-average colt. Turf high 74 (1st run) - 1st of 7 giving 5lb to Fiamma Royale (27 May Warwick RF 1511).
**M Johnston [1-4] Lord Hartington.*

FLUSH (FR) BHB 45f36a **RR 31f 36a** 1375[10]
5 b br m Warning 8.1f **(77)** - Garden Pink (FR) (Bellypha) 9.8f **(73)**

Form - 00500
Record 2000 - 1st:0 2nd:0 3rd:0 Ran:3
Pre2000 - 1st:1 2nd:0 3rd:2 Ran:15
Win Prizemoney £2,700 *Total Prizemoney* £4,267
Wins 1998 Oct Leices (SFT) C 8f 73 <
2000 Turf 0-1: (10f) (g-f) 2000 AW 0-2: (8f, 12f) (Fibr 2)
Very moderate filly. AW high 30.
**Miss S J Wilton [1-8] John Pointon and Sons (from R E Peacock [0-3] Dec 1999).*

FLUTED BHB 60f RR 73f 5027[6]

2 ch c Piccolo - Champagne Grandy **(77f 75a)** (Vaigly Great) 7f **(58)**
Form - 40373406
Record 2000 - 1st:0 2nd:0 3rd:2 Ran:8
Win Prizemoney £0 *Total Prizemoney* £1,334
2000 Turf 0-8: (6f, 7f 6, 8f) (g-s, gd, g-f 3, frm 3)
Above-average colt, effective 7f, acts on gd. Turf high 73 (began Jun). **M R Channon [0-8] Michael Hills.*

FLUXUS RR 96f 4409a[1]

3 b c Night Shift (USA) 8.1f **(73)** - Fracassina (Rusticaro (FR)) 8.2f **(65)**
Form - 3331
2000 Turf 1-4: (9f, 10f 1-3) (hvy 2, gd 1-1, g-f)
Very useful colt. Turf high 96 - 3rd of 9 to Shibuni's Falcon (2 Jly San Siro 10f g-f RF 2585a). **B Grizzetti in ITY [1-4] Scuderia Jemncha.*

FLY BOY FLY (USA) BHB 73f70a RR 70f 70a 5015[4]

2 b c Chief's Crown (USA) 10.2f **(75)** - Gillingham (USA) (Hatchet Man (USA)) 6.3f **(51)**
Form - 4644
Record 2000 - 1st:0 2nd:0 3rd:0 Ran:4
Win Prizemoney £0 *Total Prizemoney* £529
2000 Turf 0-3: (5f, 6f, 7f) (gd 2, g-f) 2000 AW 0-1: (6f) (Fibr)
Above-average colt. Turf high 71 (1st run) (began Jly) - 4th of 9 to Achilles Spirit (13 Jly Epsom 6f gd RF 2760).
**M Johnston [0-4] M J Pilkington.*

FLY FOR AVIE (USA) RR 120f 5329a[6]

5 br m Lord Avie (USA) - Fly For Baby (USA) (Arctic Tern (USA)) 8.9f **(69)**
Form - 16
2000 Turf 1-2: (10f 1-1, 11f) (frm 1-2)
Currently very high-class filly. Turf high 120 (1st run) (began Oct) - 1st of 6 giving 6lb to Lady Upstage (15 Oct Woodbine RF 5096a).
**D Bell in CAN [1-2] I Dalos.*

FLYING BACK (FR) BHB 60f RR 68f 3533[11]

3 b g Efisio 7.7f **(69)** - Flying Sauce (Sauce Boat (USA)) 8.3f **(79)**
Form - 440
Record 2000 - 1st:0 2nd:0 3rd:0 Ran:3
Win Prizemoney £0 *Total Prizemoney* £652
2000 Turf 0-3: (7f 2, 8f) (gd, g-f 2)
Scopey, currently average gelding. Turf high 68.
**R Hannon [0-3] Lady Whent and Friends.*

FLYING CARPET RR 69f 4170[7]

3 b f Barathea (IRE) - Flying Squaw **(90f)** (Be My Chief (USA))
Form - 6703137
Record 2000 - 1st:1 2nd:0 3rd:2 Ran:7
Pre2000 - 1st:0 2nd:0 3rd:0 Ran:1
Win Prizemoney £6,077 *Total Prizemoney* £8,297
Wins * 2000 Jly Beverl (GD) H 8.5f 58 67 <
2000 Turf 1-7: (6f, 7f 2, 8f 1-4) (g-s, gd 3, g-f 1-2, frm)
Leggy, average filly, effective 8f, acts on g-f. Turf high 69 - 3rd of 11 getting 11lb from Kirovski (30 Jly Newmarket 8f g-f RF 3233) - also 1st of 11 getting 15lb from Bold Ewar (8 Jly Beverley RF 2620). **T D Easterby [1-8] Burton Agnes Bloodstock.*

FLYING EAGLE BHB 72f74a RR 77f 74a 3749[8]

9 b g Shaadi (USA) 8.1f **(75)** - Fly Me (FR) (Luthier) 9.8f **(71)**
Form - 8
Record 2000 - 1st:0 2nd:0 3rd:0 Ran:1
Pre2000 - 1st:7 2nd:2 3rd:3 Ran:25
Win Prizemoney £26,507 *Total Prizemoney* £30,286
Wins 1999 Aug Epsom (GD) H 12f 67 76
1998 Jly Epsom (G-F) H 12f 74 82 <
1998 Jly Nottin (G-F) H 10f 74 75
1998 Jly Bright (GD) C 10f 69+
1998 Jun Warwic (G-S) S 10.8f 65+
1998 Jun Bath (G-S) C 10.2f 65
1998 May Nottin (G-F) S 10f 57+
2000 Turf 0-1: (12f) (g-f)
Above-average gelding, effective 10 to 12f, best at 12f, acts on gd to g-f, best on g-f. Inconsistent.
**D McCain [1-5] D Charlesworth (from G L Moore [1-10] Oct 1999).*

FLYING FAISAL (USA) BHB 64f RR 55f 5019[6]

2 b c Alydeed (CAN) 8f **(81)** - Peaceful Silence (USA) (Proper Reality (USA))
Form - 06
Record 2000 - 1st:0 2nd:0 3rd:0 Ran:2
2000 Turf 0-1: (8f) (g-f) 2000 AW 0-1: (7f) (Fibr)
Currently average colt. **J A Osborne [0-2] S Hussain.*

FLYING GREEN (FR) BHB 40f RR 84f 744[11]

7 ch g Persian Bold 10f **(69)** - Flying Sauce (Sauce Boat (USA)) 8.3f **(79)**
Form - 0
Record 2000 - 1st:0 2nd:0 3rd:0 Ran:1
Pre2000 - 1st:1 2nd:1 3rd:0 Ran:6
Win Prizemoney £3,803 *Total Prizemoney* £5,198
Wins 1996 Jly Bath (G-F) 10.2f 84 <
2000 AW 0-1: (9f) (Fibr)
Decent gelding, has worn blinkers.
**B P J Baugh [0-2] Stan Baugh (from N J H Walker [0-2] Aug 1996).*

FLYING HIGH (IRE) BHB 27f29a RR 2f 29a 1480[5]

5 b g Fayruz 6.6f **(63)** - Shayista **(47f)** (Tap On Wood) 10.3f **(65)**
Form - 76403805
Record 2000 - 1st:0 2nd:0 3rd:1 Ran:7
Pre2000 - 1st:0 2nd:0 3rd:0 Ran:8
Win Prizemoney £0 *Total Prizemoney* £258
2000 Turf 0-1: (8f) (frm) 2000 AW 0-6: (6f, 7f 2, 8f 3) (Fibr 6)
Little account gelding, has worn blinkers. AW high 40.
**B Ellison [0-15] B Batey (from Ferdy Murphy [0-3] Jun 1997).*

FLYING LYRIC (IRE) RR 89f 5066[1]

2 b c Definite Article - Lyric Junction (IRE) (Classic Secret (USA))
Form - 41
Record 2000 - 1st:1 2nd:0 3rd:0 Ran:2
Win Prizemoney £2,320 *Total Prizemoney* £2,599
Wins * 2000 Oct Bath (GD) 8f 89 <
2000 Turf 1-2: (8f 1-2) (g-s 1-1, g-f)
Currently useful colt. Turf high 89 (began Spt) - 1st of 16 from Cosmocrat (19 Oct Bath RF 5066).
**S P C Woods [1-2] Mrs Marian Borsberry.*

FLYING MEMORY BHB 31f RR 32f 3380[13]

4 b f Greensmith - Flying (Head for Heights) 9.6f **(55)**
Form - 00
Record 2000 - 1st:0 2nd:0 3rd:0 Ran:2
Pre2000 - 1st:0 2nd:0 3rd:0 Ran:6
2000 Turf 0-2: (6f, 7f) (frm 2)
Leggy, very moderate filly. Turf high 13 (began Jly). Inconsistent.
**J M Bradley [0-2] Avon & West Racing Club Ltd (from N P Littmoden [0-3] Spt 1999).*

FLYING MILLIE (IRE) BHB 93f RR 82f 3201[7]

2 b f Flying Spur (AUS) - Sweet Pleasure (Sweet Revenge) 7.2f **(54)**
Form - 167
Record 2000 - 1st:1 2nd:0 3rd:0 Ran:3
Win Prizemoney £4,504 *Total Prizemoney* £4,504
Wins * 2000 May Windso (G-S) 5f 82 <
2000 Turf 1-3: (5f 1-2, 6f) (gd 2, g-f 1-1)
Currently decent filly. Turf high 82 - also 1st of 18 from Superstar Leo (22 May Windsor RF 1380). Made a winning debut at Windsor, and finished sixth in the Queen Mary at Ascot after a slow start. Had her limitations exposed behind Enthused next time.
**R Hannon [1-3] John Guest.*

FLYING OFFICER BHB 94a RR 96f 94a 1996[4]

4 ch g Efisio 7.7f **(69)** - Area Girl (Jareer (USA)) 5.9f **(75)**
Form - 4
Record 2000 - 1st:0 2nd:0 3rd:0 Ran:1

Pre2000 - 1st:4 2nd:3 3rd:0 Ran:10
Win Prizemoney £16,755 *Total Prizemoney* £21,192
Wins * 1999 *Mar Wolver (STD)* *7f* *108+* <
* 1999 *Jan Wolver (STD)* *6f* *106++*
* 1999 *Jan Wolver (STD) H* *7f* *80* *102+*
* 1998 *Dec Lingfi (STD)* *6f* *88+*
2000 Turf 0-1: (6f) (g-f)
Workmanlike, Pattern-class gelding, effective 6 to 7f, best at 7f, - acted on Fibr. (DEAD) **Sir Mark Prescott [4-11] Neil Greig.*

FLYING PENNANT (IRE) BHB 43f39a **RR 46f 39a** 4277[5]

7 ch g Waajib 8.9f **(67)** - Flying Beckee (IRE) (Godswalk (USA)) 7.3f **(58)**
Form - 553861036305
Record 2000 - 1st:1 2nd:0 3rd:3 Ran:12
Pre2000 - 1st:2 2nd:3 3rd:5 Ran:41
Win Prizemoney £11,621 *Total Prizemoney* £19,010
Wins * **2000** Jly Bright (SFT) H 7f 36 38
* 1998 Jun Chepst (G-S) H 7.1f 50 54
1996 May Salisb (G-F) C 7f 63 <
2000 Turf 1-12: (7f 1-12) (gd 1-4, g-f 3, frm 5)
Moderate gelding, effective 7f, acts on gd to frm, best on gd, often wears blinkers (effectively), excels at Beverley. Turf high 46 - 3rd of 14 getting 25lb from Tribal Prince (18 Aug Folkestone 7f gd RF 3752) - also 1st of 10 getting 24lb from Rainbow Rain (5 Jly Brighton RF 2538). Consistent.
**J M Bradley [?-49] F A Hayward (from R Hannon [1-10] Oct 1996).*

FLYING PETREL (USA) RR 65f 5156[4]

2 b f Storm Bird (CAN) 8.5f **(82)** - Olatha (USA) (Miswaki (USA)) 9f **(81)**
Form - 84
Record 2000 - 1st:0 2nd:0 3rd:0 Ran:2
Win Prizemoney £0 *Total Prizemoney* £351
2000 Turf 0-2: (5f, 6f) (g-s, frm)
Currently average filly. Turf high 65 (began Aug).
**M Johnston [0-2] M J Pilkington.*

FLYING ROMANCE (IRE) BHB 58f **RR 61f** 4773[10]

2 b f Flying Spur (AUS) - State Romance (Free State) 8.7f **(61)**
Form - 8553740
Record 2000 - 1st:0 2nd:0 3rd:1 Ran:7
Win Prizemoney £0 *Total Prizemoney* £404
2000 Turf 0-7: (5f 3, 6f 2, 7f 2) (g-s 2, g-f 3, frm 2)
Average filly, effective 5 to 7f, acts on g-s to frm. Turf high 61 - 4th of 17 giving 9lb to Aporto (16 Spt Catterick 7f g-s RF 4460).
**D W Barker [0-7] Swift Racing.*

FLYING RUN (IRE) BHB 31f54a **RR 37f 54a** 4730[10]

3 b f Lake Coniston (IRE) - Kaskazi (Dancing Brave (USA)) 8.4f **(76)**
Form - 800007370
Record 2000 - 1st:0 2nd:0 3rd:1 Ran:9
Pre2000 - 1st:0 2nd:0 3rd:0 Ran:4
Win Prizemoney £0 *Total Prizemoney* £605
2000 Turf 0-7: (7f 2, 8f 3, 10f 2) (g-s 2, g-f 3, frm 2) 2000 AW 0-2: (7f, 13f) (Equi, Fibr)
Very moderate filly, has worn blinkers. Turf high 37. AW high 30.
**J G Portman [0-4] A H Robinson (from J R Arnold [0-9] Jly 2000).*

FLYING TACKLE BHB 48f **RR 50f** 4365[11]

2 ch c First Trump - Frighten The Life (Kings Lake (USA)) 10.8f **(67)**
Form - 000
Record 2000 - 1st:0 2nd:0 3rd:0 Ran:3
2000 Turf 0-3: (5f 2, 6f) (g-f 2, frm)
Currently fair colt. Turf high 50 (began Jly).
**J S Wainwright [0-3] Neil Harrison.*

FLYING TRAPEZE (USA) RR 47f 4935[27]

2 ch c Trempolino (USA) 11.9f **(77)** - Loen (USA) (Accipiter (USA))
Form - 0
Record 2000 - 1st:0 2nd:0 3rd:0 Ran:1
2000 Turf 0-1: (6f) (gd)
Currently moderate colt. **J Noseda [0-1] W L Armitage.*

FLYING TREATY (USA) BHB 68f61a **RR 75f 61a** 3723[7]

3 br c You and I (USA) 8.5f **(78)** - Cherie's Hope (USA) (Flying Paster (USA))
Form - 5237

Record 2000 - 1st:0 2nd:1 3rd:1 Ran:4
Win Prizemoney £0 *Total Prizemoney* £2,333
2000 Turf 0-4: (8f 2, 9f, 10f) (gd, g-f, frm 2)
Light-framed, above-average colt. Turf high 75.
**J H M Gosden [0-4] R E Sangster and B V Sangster.*

FLYING TURK (IRE) BHB 72f **RR 72f** 4808[12]

2 ch c Flying Spur (AUS) - Empress Wu (High Line) 10.3f **(70)**
Form - 3044660
Record 2000 - 1st:0 2nd:0 3rd:1 Ran:7
Win Prizemoney £0 *Total Prizemoney* £2,372
2000 Turf 0-7: (6f 6, 7f) (sft, g-s, gd 2, g-f, frm, hrd)
Above-average colt. Turf high 72. **J A Osborne [0-7] S Hussain.*

FLY LIKE A BIRD BHB 27f34a **RR 29f 34a** 5025[10]

4 ch f Keen 11.1f **(58)** - Turtle Dove (Gyr (USA)) 9.5f **(65)**
Form - 0407550
Record 2000 - 1st:0 2nd:0 3rd:0 Ran:7
Pre2000 - 1st:0 2nd:0 3rd:1 Ran:6
Win Prizemoney £0 *Total Prizemoney* £452
2000 Turf 0-4: (11f, 12f, 13f, 14f) (g-s, gd, g-f, frm) 2000 AW 0-3: (12f 2, 16f) (Fibr 3)
Small, very moderate filly, effective 12f, acts on frm. Turf high 29. AW high 37. Consistent.
**S P C Woods [0-13] One Dream Partnership.*

FLY LIKE THE WIND BHB 73f **RR 74f** 4703[21]

3 br f Cyrano de Bergerac 7.3f **(58)** - Thulium (Mansingh (USA)) 7.4f **(55)**
Form - 223100
Record 2000 - 1st:1 2nd:2 3rd:1 Ran:6
Pre2000 - 1st:0 2nd:0 3rd:0 Ran:1
Win Prizemoney £2,247 *Total Prizemoney* £4,840
Wins * **2000** Jly Lingfi (GD) 5f 72+ <
2000 Turf 1-6: (5f 1-6) (gd, g-f 1-4, hrd)
Scopey, above-average filly, effective 5f, acts on gd to g-f, best on g-f. Turf high 74 - 2nd of 9 to Jodeeka (27 May Doncaster 5f gd RF 1485) - also 1st of 8 getting 5lb from Our Fred (12 Jly Lingfield RF 2741). **M A Jarvis [1-7] Cosmic Greyhound Racing Partnership III.*

FLY MORE BHB 69f **RR 70+f** 4320[5]

3 ch g Lycius (USA) 8.8f **(71)** - Double River (USA) (Irish River (FR)) 8.6f **(78)**
Form - 455155
Record 2000 - 1st:1 2nd:0 3rd:0 Ran:6
Win Prizemoney £3,250 *Total Prizemoney* £3,546
Wins * **2000** Jly Ripon (G-F) H 6f 64 70 <
2000 Turf 1-6: (5f, 6f 1-4, 7f) (gd 3, g-f 1-2, frm)
Scopey, above-average gelding, effective 6f, acts on g-f. Turf high 70 - 1st of 19 giving 17lb to Tawn Again (22 Jly Ripon RF 3040).
**J M Bradley [1-6] E A Hayward.*

FLYOVER RR 63f 4616[4]

3 b f Presidium 7.5f **(56)** - Flash-By (Ilium)
Form - 0751614
Record 2000 - 1st:2 2nd:0 3rd:0 Ran:7
Pre2000 - 1st:1 2nd:1 3rd:1 Ran:7
Win Prizemoney £11,285 *Total Prizemoney* £12,498
Wins * **2000** Spt Epsom (GD) H 10.1f 57 63
* **2000** Aug Bath (G-F) H 11.7f 54 54
* 1999 Jun Salisb (GD) 6f 74 <
2000 Turf 2-7: (8f 3, 10f 1-2, 12f 1-2) (gd 2, g-f 1-2, frm 1-3)
Neat, average filly, effective 6f, acts on g-f to frm, has worn blinkers. Turf high 63. **B R Millman [3-14] R J Tory.*

FLY TO THE STARS BHB 114f **RR 125df** 4290a[4]

6 b h Bluebird (USA) 7.9f **(71)** - Rise and Fall (Mill Reef (USA)) 10.5f **(78)**
Form - 754
Record 2000 - 1st:0 2nd:0 3rd:0 Ran:3
Pre2000 - 1st:6 2nd:5 3rd:3 Ran:20
Win Prizemoney £221,956 *Total Prizemoney* £337,898
Wins * 1999 May Newbur (SFT) G1 8f 122
* 1998 Oct Longch (SFT) G2 8f 125 <
* 1998 Jly Deauvi (G-S) G3 8f 120
1997 Jly Goodwo (G-F) H 8f 106 112
1997 Jun Ascot (GD) H 8f 100 105

1997 Mar Doncas (G-F) 8f 92+
2000 Turf 0-2: (8f, 9f) (sft, gd) 2000 AW 0-1: (12f) (Dirt)
Top-class horse, effective 8f, acts on sft to gd. Turf high 117 - 4th of 8 to Indian Lodge (3 Spt Longchamp 8f sft RF 4290a). Finished seventh in the Dubai Duty Free on his 2000 bow, but flopped badly in the Diomed at Epsom. He ran better when third behind Indian Lodge in the Prix du Moulin.
**S bin Suroor [3-9] (from S bin Suroor in UAE [0-3] Mar 2000).*

FLY WITH ME RR 64f
4807[10]
2 b c Pharly (FR) 11.5f **(64)** - Nelly Do Da (Derring-Do) 11.1f **(64)**
Form - 60
Record 2000 - 1st:0 2nd:0 3rd:0 Ran:2
2000 Turf 0-2: (7f, 8f) (g-s, g-f)
Currently average colt. Turf high 64 (began Spt).
**T G Mills [0-2] John Humphreys (Turf Accountants) Ltd.*

FOCUSED ATTRACTION (IRE) BHB 72f68a RR 69f 68a
4305[13]
2 b g Eagle Eyed (USA) - Seattle Siren (USA) (Seattle Slew (USA)) 9.4f **(76)**
Form - 6540
Record 2000 - 1st:0 2nd:0 3rd:0 Ran:4
Win Prizemoney £0 *Total Prizemoney* £456
2000 Turf 0-4: (5f 3, 6f) (gd, frm 3)
Average gelding. Turf high 69.
**R Hannon [0-4] Mrs Teresa Moriarty.*

FOIST BHB 40f42a RR 40f 42a
5084[3]
8 b g Efisio 7.7f **(69)** - When The Saints (Bay Express) 7.1f **(60)**
Form - 0065026703
Record 2000 - 1st:0 2nd:1 3rd:1 Ran:10
Pre2000 - 1st:8 2nd:1 3rd:3 Ran:43
Win Prizemoney £31,161 *Total Prizemoney* £36,086
Wins * 1998 May Warwic (GD) 6f 65
* 1998 May Hamilt (G-S) H 6f 56 61
* 1997 May Hamilt (SFT) H 6f 59 68+ <
* 1997 Apr Hamilt (G-S) H 6f 50 64
* 1997 Mar Catter (GD) H 7f 46 50
* 1996 *Apr Southw (STD) H 6f 40 58*
* 1996 *Apr Wolver (STD) H 6f 40 51+*
* 1996 *Mar Southw (STD) H 6f 30 36*
2000 Turf 0-5: (6f, 7f 3, 8f) (hvy, sft, gd, g-f, hrd) 2000 AW 0-5: (6f 4, 7f) (Fibr 5)
Moderate gelding, effective 6f, acts on g-f, has worn blinkers. Turf high 39. AW high 48.
**M W Easterby [8-53] D F Spence.*

FOLAANN (IRE) RR 32f
4806[11]
2 ch c Pennekamp (USA) - Chaturanga (Night Shift (USA)) 7.2f **(69)**
Form - 0
Record 2000 - 1st:0 2nd:0 3rd:0 Ran:1
2000 Turf 0-1: (7f) (g-s)
Currently very moderate colt.
**M A Jarvis [0-1] Sheikh Ahmed Al Maktoum.*

FOLEY MILLENNIUM (IRE) BHB 80f RR 80f
4143[8]
2 ch c Tagula (IRE) - Inshirah (USA) (Caro)
Form - 551341358
Record 2000 - 1st:2 2nd:0 3rd:2 Ran:9
Win Prizemoney £6,182 *Total Prizemoney* £7,976
Wins *** 2000** Aug Newbur (G-F) 5.2f 78 <
*** 2000** Jly Haydoc (G-F) C 6f 76+
2000 Turf 2-9: (5f 1-2, 6f 1-7) (gd, g-f 1-5, frm 1-2, hrd)
Decent colt, effective 5 to 6f, best at 6f, acts on g-f to frm, best on g-f. Turf high 80 - 3rd of 10 giving 3lb to Becky Simmons (15 Jly Salisbury 6f g-f RF 2845) - also 1st of 4 giving 3lb to Miss Domuch (6 Aug Newbury RF 3417).
**M Quinn [2-9] Mrs S G Davies.*

FOLIE DANSE (FR) RR 109f
5094a[3]
3 b f Petit Loup (USA) - Folle Envie (USA) (Un Desperado (FR))
Form - 12513
2000 Turf 2-5: (10f, 11f 1-2, 12f, 13f 1-1) (sft, g-s 2-3, gd)
Pattern-class filly. Turf high 109 - also 1st of 7 from Playact (9 Jly Deauville RF 2788a).
**Y de Nicolay in FR [2-5].*

FOLK DANCE (USA) RR
422[7]
3 b f Bertrando (USA) - Lady Ferial (FR) (Carwhite) 7.2f **(61)**
Form - 607
Record 2000 - 1st:0 2nd:0 3rd:0 Ran:3
2000 AW 0-3: (7f 2, 9f) (Equi, Fibr 2)
Light-framed, currently very poor filly. AW high 9.
**P W Hiatt [0-3] P W Hiatt.*

FOLLOW A DREAM (USA) BHB 76f RR 67f
5053[2]
2 b f Gone West (USA) 7.8f **(82)** - Dance a Dream **(107f)** (Sadler's Wells (USA)) 10f **(76)**
Form - 632
Record 2000 - 1st:0 2nd:1 3rd:1 Ran:3
Win Prizemoney £0 *Total Prizemoney* £1,487
2000 Turf 0-3: (7f 3) (sft, g-s, frm)
Currently average filly. Turf high 67 (began Aug) - 2nd of 14 to Shaanara (18 Oct Newcastle 7f sft RF 5053).
**Sir Michael Stoute [0-3] Cheveley Park Stud.*

FOLLOWEROFFASHION (IRE) RR 20f
4754[13]
3 b c Unfuwain (USA) 11.4f **(74)** - Al Theraab (USA) (Roberto (USA)) 10f **(76)**
Form - 00
Record 2000 - 1st:0 2nd:0 3rd:0 Ran:2
2000 Turf 0-2: (10f, 12f) (g-s 2)
Scopey, currently little account colt. Turf high 20 (began Spt).
**V Soane [0-2] The Highrollers.*

FOLLOW FREDDY BHB 62f RR 60f
5052[12]
2 ch g Factual (USA) - Forgiving (Jellaby) 6.4f **(58)**
Form - 070
Record 2000 - 1st:0 2nd:0 3rd:0 Ran:3
2000 Turf 0-3: (6f 3) (sft, gd, g-f)
Currently average gelding. Turf high 60 (began Aug).
**M Johnston [0-3] Mrs S J Brookhouse.*

FOLLOW LAMMTARRA (IRE) BHB 86f RR 85f
5226[6]
3 ch g Lammtarra (USA) - Felawnah (USA) (Mr Prospector (USA)) 8.8f **(78)**
Form - 3616
Record 2000 - 1st:1 2nd:0 3rd:1 Ran:4
Win Prizemoney £4,192 *Total Prizemoney* £5,186
Wins *** 2000** Jun Haydoc (G-S) 14f 74 <
2000 Turf 1-4: (12f, 14f 1-2, 16f) (g-s 1-1, gd 3)
Tall, useful gelding. Turf high 85. Unraced at two, he looked a potentially useful stayer when winning a Haydock maiden in fine style in June. **M R Channon [1-4] Sheikh Ahmed Al Maktoum.*

FOLLOW SUIT BHB 77f RR 74f
3992[7]
3 ch c First Trump - Indian Lament **(34df)** (Indian Ridge)
Form - 07
Record 2000 - 1st:0 2nd:0 3rd:0 Ran:2
Pre2000 - 1st:1 2nd:0 3rd:0 Ran:2
Win Prizemoney £6,524 *Total Prizemoney* £6,524
Wins * 1999 Jly York (G-F) 6f 79 <
2000 Turf 0-2: (6f, 7f) (g-f 2)
Unfurnished, above-average colt. Turf high 74.
**J L Dunlop [1-4] The Earl Cadogan.*

FOLLOW YOUR STAR BHB 74f RR 78f
4673[7]
2 ch c Pursuit of Love 9.5f **(69)** - Possessive Artiste **(69f)** (Shareef Dancer (USA)) 9.9f **(73)**
Form - 66777
Record 2000 - 1st:0 2nd:0 3rd:0 Ran:5
2000 Turf 0-5: (6f 2, 7f 3) (g-s, gd 2, g-f 2)
Above-average colt, has worn blinkers. Turf high 78 (began Jly).
**P W Harris [0-5] Mrs P W Harris.*

FOODBROKER FANCY (IRE) BHB 80f RR 79f
4018[2]
2 ch f Halling (USA) - Red Rita (IRE) **(75f)** (Kefaah (USA))
Form - 24172
Record 2000 - 1st:1 2nd:2 3rd:0 Ran:5
Win Prizemoney £4,290 *Total Prizemoney* £8,066
Wins *** 2000** Jly Newmar (G-F) 6f 79 <
2000 Turf 1-5: (5f, 6f 1-3, 7f) (gd, g-f 1-3, frm)
Above-average filly. Turf high 79 - 2nd of 6 giving 7lb to Loner (27

Aug Goodwood 7f g-f RF 4018) - also 1st of 11 from Lady Miletrian (22 Jly Newmarket RF 3028). Put her previous experience to good use when winning a six-furlong maiden at Newmarket on her third start, and did not get any sort of run behind Dim Sums next time.
**D R C Elsworth [1-5] Food Brokers Ltd.*

FOOL ON THE HILL BHB 74f **RR 77f** 4813[8]
3 b g Reprimand 8.2f **(63)** - Stock Hill Lass (Air Trooper) 9.1f **(63)**
Form - 428
Record 2000 - 1st:0 2nd:1 3rd:0 Ran:3
Pre2000 - 1st:0 2nd:0 3rd:0 Ran:2
Win Prizemoney £0 *Total Prizemoney* £1,702
2000 Turf 0-3: (7f, 8f 2) (g-s 2, g-f)
Above-average gelding. Turf high 77 - 2nd of 8 to Hilltop Warning (15 Jun Newbury 7f g-f RF 1991). **L G Cottrell [0-5] E Gadsden.*

FOOLS PARADISE (IRE) BHB 30f40a **RR 40a** 2256[8]
3 ch g Barathea (IRE) - Sadly Sober (IRE) **(59f 60a)** (Roi Danzig (USA))
Form - 06608
Record 2000 - 1st:0 2nd:0 3rd:0 Ran:4
Pre2000 - 1st:0 2nd:0 3rd:0 Ran:1
2000 Turf 0-1: (10f) (frm) 2000 AW 0-3: (10f, 11f, 12f) (Equi 2, Fibr)
Workmanlike, very moderate gelding. AW high 36.
**C A Cyzer [0-5] R M Cyzer.*

FOOTPRINTS (IRE) DI ID 70f **RR 74f** 4991[25]
3 b f College Chapel - Near Miracle (Be My Guest (USA)) 9.3f **(67)**
Form - 100271600
Record 2000 - 1st:2 2nd:1 3rd:0 Ran:9
Pre2000 - 1st:1 2nd:1 3rd:0 Ran:3
Win Prizemoney £8,970 *Total Prizemoney* £10,664

Wins								
	2000	Aug	Leices	(G-F)	C	7f		67
	2000	Apr	Warwic	(HVY)		6f		79 <
	1999	Oct	Redcar	(SFT)		5f		75

2000 Turf 2-9: (6f 1-2, 7f 1-5, 8f 2) (hvy 1-1, sft 2, g-s, gd, g-f, frm 1-3)
Workmanlike, above-average filly, effective 5 to 8f, acts on hvy to frm, excels at Redcar, does well at Warwick. Turf high 79 (1st run) - 1st of 15 from Chorus (12 Apr Warwick RF 0688). Inconsistent.
**W R Muir [0-3] Mrs P A Garner (from M Johnston [3-9] Aug 2000).*

FORBEARING (IRE) BHB 111f98a **RR 115f 98a** 4450[2]
3 b c Bering 9.6f **(80)** - For Example (USA) (Northern Baby (CAN)) 11.6f **(71)**
Form - 11871112232
Record 2000 - 1st:3 2nd:3 3rd:1 Ran:9
Pre2000 - 1st:2 2nd:0 3rd:0 Ran:4
Win Prizemoney £47,259 *Total Prizemoney* £73,719

Wins								
	* **2000**	Jly	Salisb	(G-S)		9.9f		108
	* **2000**	Jun	Goodwo	(G-F)	H	9.9f	88	104+
	* **2000**	Jun	Epsom	(G-S)	H	10.1f	88	104++
	* 1999	*Dec*	*Wolver*	*(STD)*		*8.5f*		*92+*
	* 1999	*Nov*	*Lingfi*	*(STD)*		*8f*		*81*

2000 Turf 3-9: (9f, 10f 3-6, 11f 2) (g-s 2-3, gd 5, g-f 1-1)
Scopey, high-class colt, effective 10 to 11f, best at 10f, acts on g-s to gd, best on gd, likes left handed tracks, prefers tight tracks. Turf high 115 - 3rd of 9 to Adilabad (26 Aug Windsor 10f gd RF 4004) - also 1st of 4 getting 1lb from Turaath (7 Jly Salisbury RF 2602). Consistent. After winning a couple of times on sand, it took a couple of runs before he found his form on turf last season, but when he did find his feet he did so with a bang, completing a fine hat-trick. Ran really well in defeat afterwards including making the frame in Group company. Suited by ten furlongs.
**Sir Mark Prescott [5-13] Eclipse Thoroughbreds - Osborne House IV.*

FORBIDDEN APPLE (USA) **RR 121f** 5327a[7]
5 br h Pleasant Colony (USA) 12.4f **(88)** - North of Eden (USA) (Northfields (USA)) 9f **(72)**
Form - 17
2000 Turf 1-2: (8f 1-2) (frm 1-2)
Currently very high-class colt. Turf high 121 (began Oct) - 7th of 14 giving 3lb to War Chant (4 Nov Churchill Downs 8f frm RF 5327a) - also 1st of 9 getting 4lb from Affirmed Success (8 Oct Belmont Park RF 4950a). **C Clement in USA [1-2] A I Appleton.*

FOREIGN AFFAIRS BHB 85f **RR** 5017[2]
2 ch c Hernando (FR) - Entente Cordiale (USA) (Affirmed (USA)) 9.3f **(79)**
Form - 2
Record 2000 - 1st:0 2nd:1 3rd:0 Ran:1
Win Prizemoney £0 *Total Prizemoney* £634
2000 AW 0-1: (7f) (Fibr)
Currently decent colt. (1st run) - 2nd of 9 giving 11lb to Aswhatilldois (17 Oct Wolverhampton 7f Fibr RF 5017).
**Sir Mark Prescott [0-1] The Speculators.*

FOREIGN EDITOR BHB 62f80a **RR 67f 80a** 4558[16]
4 ch g Magic Ring (IRE) 6.5f **(64)** - True Precision **(61f 59a)** (Presidium)
Form - 411D11332000
Record 2000 - 1st:2 2nd:1 3rd:2 Ran:9
Pre2000 - 1st:2 2nd:0 3rd:1 Ran:12
Win Prizemoney £14,695 *Total Prizemoney* £18,195

Wins								
	2000	*Jan*	*Lingfl*	*(STD)*	H	*7f*	*73*	*75*
	2000	*Jan*	*Wolver*	*(STD)*	H	*7f*	*65*	*77+* <
	1999	*Dec*	*Wolver*	*(STD)*	H	*6f*	*52*	*72*
	1999	*Dec*	*Wolver*	*(STD)*	H	*7f*	*46*	*53*

2000 Turf 0-4: (5f, 6f, 7f 2) (gd, frm 3) 2000 AW 2-5: (6f 2, 7f 2-3) (Equi 1-2, Fibr 1-3)
Workmanlike, above-average gelding, effective 6 to 7f, best at 7f, - acts on AW, best on Fibr, has worn blinkers, prefers left handed tracks, prefers tight tracks, excels at Wolverhampton and Lingfield. Turf high 67. AW high 78 - 3rd of 16 getting 2lb from Blue Kite (6 Mar Southwell 6f Fibr RF 0416) - also 1st of 10 getting 15lb from Blue Star (20 Jan Wolverhampton RF 0125). Becoming disappointing. He has been in fine form on Fibresand during the winter, winning three times at Wolverhampton and once at Lingfield so far. Equally effective over six or seven furlongs, he is most effective when able to dominate. If he can transfer that ability on to turf he is extremely well handicapped.
**K A Ryan [0-1] Pride Of Yorkshire Racing Club (from R A Fahey [4-20] May 2000).*

FOREIGN SECRETARY (USA) BHB 89f **RR 101f** 4470[9]
3 b c Kingmambo (USA) 10.9f **(85)** - Misinskie (USA) (Nijinsky (CAN)) 10.3f **(77)**
Form - 12600
Record 2000 - 1st:1 2nd:1 3rd:0 Ran:5
Pre2000 - 1st:0 2nd:0 3rd:0 Ran:1
Win Prizemoney £4,017 *Total Prizemoney* £6,532

Wins								
	* **2000**	May	Newbur	(G-F)		8f		87 <

2000 Turf 1-5: (8f 1-1, 10f 3, 12f) (gd 1-2, g-f 3)
Scopey, very useful colt, effective 10 to 12f, acts on gd to g-f. Turf high 101 - 6th of 16 to Give The Slip (22 Jun Ascot 12f g-f RF 2182). Was a fine sixth in the King George V Handicap at Ascot when stepped up to twelve furlongs but was beaten over shorter on his two subsequent runs. **Sir Michael Stoute [1-6] W J Gredley.*

FOREST BUCK (USA) BHB 107f **RR 108f** 2205a[7]
7 ch h Green Forest (USA) 7.4f **(73)** - Perlee (FR) (Margouillat (FR)) 10.2f **(76)**
Form - 277
2000 Turf 0-3: (10f 2, 12f) (hvy, gd, g-f)
Pattern-class horse. Turf high 105. Consistent.
**P Billeri in ITY [0-3] (from B Grizzetti in ITY [0-2] Aug 1998).*

FOREST DANCER (IRE) BHB 81f90a **RR 79f 90a** 5197[7]
2 b c Charnwood Forest (IRE) - Forest Berries (IRE) (Thatching) 8f **(66)**
Form - 3577
Record 2000 - 1st:0 2nd:0 3rd:1 Ran:4
Win Prizemoney £0 *Total Prizemoney* £619
2000 Turf 0-4: (6f 4) (gd 3, g-f)
Useful colt. Turf high 79 (began Jly).
**R Hannon [0-4] Nicholas Hodges.*

FOREST DREAM BHB 36f28a **RR 50f 28a** 5154[15]
5 b m Warrshan (USA) 9.7f **(59)** - Sirenivo (USA) (Sir Ivor) 10.2f **(70)**
Form - 24080007823072740
Record 2000 - 1st:0 2nd:2 3rd:1 Ran:14
Pre2000 - 1st:1 2nd:4 3rd:1 Ran:19
Win Prizemoney £3,088 *Total Prizemoney* £8,861

Wins								
	1999	Aug	Lingfi	(G-F)	H	10f	53	56 <

2000 Turf 0-10: (10f 4, 11f 2, 12f 4) (gd 2, g-f 3, frm 5) 2000 AW 0-4: (10f, 12f 3) (Equi 3, Fibr)
Fair filly, effective 10 to 12f, best at 10f, acts on gd to frm - acts on Fibr, favours tight tracks. Turf high 50. AW high 41.

**L A Dace [0-15] Eddie Davess (from Lady Herries [1-18] Nov 1999).*

FOREST ECHO (IRE) RR 88[13]

6 gr g Wood Chanter - Arboe Lass (IRE) (Mandalus)
Form - 0
Record 2000 - 1st:0 2nd:0 3rd:0 Ran:1
2000 AW 0-1: (16f) (Fibr)
Formerly very poor gelding. **Miss A Stokell [0-3] T J Ford.*

FOREST FIRE (SWE) BHB 81f RR 85f 2640[6]

5 b m Never so Bold 7.1f **(62)** - Mango Sampaquita (SWE) (Colombian Friend (USA)) 8.5f **(64)**
Form - 27736

Record	**2000** -	1st:0	2nd:1	3rd:1	Ran:5	
	Pre2000 -	1st:4	2nd:1	3rd:2	Ran:19	

Win Prizemoney £17,615 *Total Prizemoney* £22,675

Wins	* 1999	Jly	Newmar (G-F)	H	12f	78	83	<
	* 1999	Jly	Newmar (G-F)	H	10f	74	79	
	* 1998	Spt	Sandow (GD)	H	8.1f	65	69	
	* 1998	Aug	Sandow (G-F)	C	9f		58	

2000 Turf 0-5: (10f, 12f 3, 14f) (g-s, g-f 2, frm 2)
Useful filly, effective 10 to 14f, best at 12f, acts on g-s to frm, prefers right handed tracks. Turf high 85.
**B Hanbury [4-23] Mrs Mette Campbell-Andenaes (from P Mooney [0-1] Oct 1997).*

FOREST FRIENDLY BHB 63f RR 74df 4220[14]

3 b f Unfuwain (USA) 11.4f **(74)** - Butsova (Formidable (USA)) 9.2f **(63)**
Form - 00570

Record	**2000** -	1st:0	2nd:0	3rd:0	Ran:5
	Pre2000 -	1st:0	2nd:0	3rd:0	Ran:1

Win Prizemoney £0 *Total Prizemoney* £289
2000 Turf 0-5: (8f 2, 9f, 10f 2) (gd 3, frm 2)
Above-average filly, effective 7f, acted on gd. Turf high 74. (DEAD)
**R A Fahey [0-2] R A Fahey (from B W Hills [0-4] Jun 2000).*

FOREST HEATH (IRE) BHB 82f RR 81f 5125[12]

3 gr g Common Grounds 8.1f **(66)** - Caroline Lady (JPN) (Caro)
Form - 21220

Record	**2000** -	1st:1	2nd:3	3rd:0	Ran:5
	Pre2000 -	1st:0	2nd:0	3rd:0	Ran:2

Win Prizemoney £4,114 *Total Prizemoney* £8,218
Wins * 2000 Jun Goodwo (G-F) 9.9f 73 <
2000 Turf 1-5: (8f, 10f 1-2, 12f 2) (g-s 2, gd 1-1, g-f, frm)
Decent gelding, effective 10 to 12f, best at 10f, acts on gd to frm. Turf high 81 - 2nd of 19 getting 7lb from Julius (26 Spt Newmarket 10f g-f RF 4645) - also 1st of 4 from Diamond Road (30 Jun Goodwood RF 2402).
**H J Collingridge [1-5] Forest Heath Partnership (from J E Banks [0-2] Oct 1999).*

FOREST KITTEN (IRE) RR 5f 1892[9]

2 b br f Marju (IRE) 9.2f **(76)** - Forest Cat (IRE) **(98f)** (Petorius) 7.3f **(61)**
Form - 0
Record 2000 - 1st:0 2nd:0 3rd:0 Ran:1
2000 Turf 0-1: (5f) (gd)
Currently very poor filly. **E Stanners [0-1] George Ward.*

FOREST LIGHT (IRE) RR 51f 4643[22]

2 gr f Rainbow Quest (USA) 11.2f **(81)** - Woodland Garden (Godswalk (USA)) 7.3f **(58)**
Form - 00
Record 2000 - 1st:0 2nd:0 3rd:0 Ran:2
2000 Turf 0-2: (6f, 7f) (g-f, frm)
Currently fair filly. Turf high 51 (began Spt).
**R F JohnsonHoughton [0-2] Bob Lanigan.*

FOREST MOON BHB 54f51a RR 58f 51a 4926[10]

2 b f Charnwood Forest (IRE) - Moon Watch (Night Shift (USA)) 7.2f **(69)**
Form - 660100
Record 2000 - 1st:1 2nd:0 3rd:0 Ran:6
Win Prizemoney £1,865 *Total Prizemoney* £1,865
Wins 2000 Jun Windso (G-F) S 6f 58 <
2000 Turf 1-5: (5f 2, 6f 1-3) (sft, g-s, gd, g-f, frm 1-1) 2000 AW 0-1: (6f) (Equi)
Fair filly, effective 6f, acts on frm. Turf high 58 - 1st of 8 from Immaculate Charlie (19 Jun Windsor RF 2104).
**Andrew Reid [0-2] A S Reid (from P D Evans [1-4] Jun 2000).*

FOREST QUEEN BHB 30f RR 33f 5190[8]

3 b f Risk Me (FR) 8f **(53)** - Grey Cree (Creetown) 6.9f **(50)**
Form - 00000868

Record	**2000** -	1st:0	2nd:0	3rd:0	Ran:8
	Pre2000 -	1st:0	2nd:1	3rd:1	Ran:9

Win Prizemoney £0 *Total Prizemoney* £2,197
2000 Turf 0-8: (5f, 6f, 7f 3, 10f, 11f, 12f) (hvy, gd 2, g-f 4, frm)
Light-framed, very moderate filly, effective 5f, acts on frm. Turf high 33. **K W Hogg [0-17] P W Cooper.*

FOREVER FABULOUS BHB 45f RR 44f 4778[10]

2 b c Timeless Times (USA) 6.1f **(56)** - Judys Girl (IRE) (Simply Great (FR)) 8.2f **(65)**
Form - 600
Record 2000 - 1st:0 2nd:0 3rd:0 Ran:3
2000 Turf 0-2: (6f 2) (frm, hrd) 2000 AW 0-1: (6f) (Fibr)
Currently moderate colt. Turf high 44 (began Aug).
**W Jarvis [0-3] Sales Race 2000 Syndicate.*

FOREVER MY LORD BHB 75f RR 79f 5106[13]

2 b c Be My Chief (USA) 10.2f **(62)** - In Love Again (IRE) **(67f)** (Prince Rupert (FR))
Form - 67111700
Record 2000 - 1st:3 2nd:0 3rd:0 Ran:8
Win Prizemoney £21,671 *Total Prizemoney* £21,671

Wins	*** 2000**	Aug	Goodwo (GD)	H	7f	75	79	<
	*** 2000**	Jly	Newmar (GD)	H	7f		69	
	*** 2000**	Jly	Newmar (GD)	S	7f		67+	

2000 Turf 3-8: (5f, 6f 2, 7f 3-4, 8f) (hvy, g-s, gd 1-3, g-f 2-3)
Above-average colt, effective 7f, acts on g-f. Turf high 79 - 1st of 13 getting 9lb from Dance On The Top (5 Aug Goodwood RF 3392).
**R F JohnsonHoughton [3-8] W H Ponsonby.*

FOREVER TIMES BHB 73f RR 73f 5129[4]

2 b f So Factual (USA) - Simply Times (USA) (Dodge (USA))
Form - 36221833704
Record 2000 - 1st:1 2nd:2 3rd:3 Ran:11
Win Prizemoney £3,038 *Total Prizemoney* £12,420
Wins * 2000 Aug Thirsk (GD) 5f 71+ <
2000 Turf 1-11: (5f 1-3, 6f 5, 7f 3) (sft, gd 5, g-f, frm 1-2, hrd 2)
Above-average filly, effective 5 to 7f, best at 6f, acts on gd to hrd, best on gd, excels at Thirsk. Turf high 73 (1st run) (began Jly) - 3rd of 8 to Green Tambourine (8 Jly Haydock 6f gd RF 2631) - also 1st of 14 from Crimson Ridge (14 Aug Thirsk RF 3627). Consistent. Pretty consistent at a modest level, but her only victory to date came in a Thirsk maiden in August.
**T D Easterby [1-11] Times of Wigan.*

FORGOTTEN TIMES (USA) BHB 74f71a RR 74f 71a 4605[10]

6 ch m Nabeel Dancer (USA) 6.1f **(65)** - Etoile D'Amore (USA) (The Minstrel (CAN)) 10f **(72)**
Form - 206221206003100

Record	**2000** -	1st:2	2nd:4	3rd:1	Ran:15
	Pre2000 -	1st:9	2nd:3	3rd:2	Ran:50

Win Prizemoney £36,158 *Total Prizemoney* £46,946

Wins	*** 2000**	Spt	Epsom (GD)	H	5f	72	74	<
	*** 2000**	Jun	Lingfi (G-F)	H	5f	69	73	
	* 1999	Spt	Goodwo (HVY)	H	5f	60	61+	
	* 1999	Aug	Bright (G-F)	H	5.3f	51	59	
	* 1999	Aug	Windso (SFT)	H	5f	51	64	
	* 1999	Jly	Salisb (G-S)	H	5f	50	50	
	* 1999	May	Folkes (G-F)	H	5f	43	45	
	* 1999	May	Goodwo (Gd)	H	5f	43	51	
	* 1998	*Feb*	*Lingfi (SLW)*	*H*	*6f*	*67*	*71*	
	1997	*Feb*	*Lingfi (STD)*	*H*	*6f*	*69*	*71*	
	1997	*Jan*	*Lingfi (STD)*		*6f*		*59*	

2000 Turf 2-15: (5f 2-13, 6f 2) (g-s 2, gd 7, g-f 1-2, frm 1-4)
Above-average mare, effective 5f, acts on g-s to frm, best on frm, often wears blinkers (extremely effectively), excels at Brighton, likes Goodwood. Turf high 74 - 1st of 13 getting 6lb from Rita's Rock Ape (6 Spt Epsom RF 4266) - also 1st of 20 giving 16lb to Sihafi (25 Jun Lingfield RF 2259). Obviously suited by a sharp downhill track and acts on Equitrack.
**K T Ivory [9-48] John Crook (from T M Jones [2-15] Spt 1997).*

FOR HEAVENS SAKE BHB 60a RR 60f 5191[2]

3 b g Rambo Dancer (CAN) 8.4f **(59)** - Angel Fire (Nashwan (USA))
Form - 466432602323562
Record 2000 - 1st:0 2nd:4 3rd:3 Ran:12
Pre2000 - 1st:0 2nd:0 3rd:0 Ran:4
Win Prizemoney £0 *Total Prizemoney* £4,341
2000 Turf 0-6: (7f 3, 8f 2, 12f) (gd 3, g-f, frm 2) 2000 AW 0-6: (7f, 8f 3, 12f 2) (Equi, Fibr 5)
Average gelding, effective 7 to 12f, best at 8f, acts on gd to frm - acts on Fibr, has worn blinkers, favours tight tracks, and excels at Wolverhampton. Turf high 60 - 3rd of 14 getting 2lb from Perpetuo (13 Spt Beverley 12f g-f RF 4364). AW high 62 - 2nd of 13 getting 2lb from Compatriot (2 Spt Wolverhampton 8f Fibr RF 4175).
**C W Thornton [0-16] Guy Reed.*

FORMAL BID (USA) BHB 65f RR 72df 3329[6]

3 b br c Dynaformer (USA) 12f **(82)** - Fantastic Bid (USA) (Auction Ring (USA)) 8.6f **(65)**
Form - 806
Record 2000 - 1st:0 2nd:0 3rd:0 Ran:3
Pre2000 - 1st:0 2nd:0 3rd:1 Ran:2
Win Prizemoney £0 *Total Prizemoney* £712
2000 Turf 0-3: (7f, 8f, 10f) (gd, g-f 2)
Well made, above-average colt. Turf high 68 (began Jly).
**P J Makin [0-3] Dr Carlos Stelling (from P W Chapple-Hyam [0-2] Spt 1999).*

FORMAL PARTY BHB 55f RR 62f 5152[11]

2 ch f Formidable (USA) 7.8f **(60)** - Tea Colony (USA) (Pleasant Colony (USA)) 7f **(70)**
Form - 66300
Record 2000 - 1st:0 2nd:0 3rd:1 Ran:5
Win Prizemoney £0 *Total Prizemoney* £397
2000 Turf 0-5: (6f 3, 7f 2) (g-s, gd, frm 2, hrd)
Average filly. Turf high 62 - 3rd of 9 to Berezina (29 Jly Redcar 6f frm RF 3220).
**T D McCarthy [0-1] A D Spence (from J L Dunlop [0-4] Aug 2000).*

FORMIDABLE FLAME BHB 30f29a RR 31f 29a 2627[11]

7 ch g Formidable (USA) 7.8f **(60)** - Madiyla (Darshaan) 9.9f **(84)**
Form - 0
Record 2000 - 1st:0 2nd:0 3rd:0 Ran:1
Pre2000 - 1st:0 2nd:0 3rd:3 Ran:21
Win Prizemoney £0 *Total Prizemoney* £961
2000 Turf 0-1: (18f) (frm)
Moderate gelding, has worn blinkers.
**G A Ham [0-17] G B J Humphries (from W J Musson [0-17] Jly 1998).*

FORMULA VENETTA (IRE) RR 56f 3687[6]

2 ch c Fumo Di Londra (IRE) - So Stylish (Great Nephew) 9.9f **(64)**
Form - 8576
Record 2000 - 1st:0 2nd:0 3rd:0 Ran:4
2000 Turf 0-4: (6f, 7f 3) (g-f, frm 2, hrd)
Fair colt. Turf high 56 (began Jly). **T D Easterby [0-4] J J Swan.*

FORTHECHOP BHB 35f40a RR 23f 40a 3981[9]

3 b g Minshaanshu Amad (USA) 11.3f **(53)** - Cousin Jenny (Midyan (USA)) 6f **(60)**
Form - 06454370
Record 2000 - 1st:0 2nd:0 3rd:1 Ran:6
Pre2000 - 1st:0 2nd:0 3rd:0 Ran:4
Win Prizemoney £0 *Total Prizemoney* £337
2000 Turf 0-1: (10f) (frm) 2000 AW 0-5: (7f 2, 8f 3) (Fibr 5)
Scopey, moderate gelding, effective 8f, - acts on Fibr, favours left handed tracks. AW high 42. Inconsistent.
**Mrs H L Walton [0-10] J P McCarthy.*

FORT KNOX (IRE) BHB 28f38a RR 17f 38a 3367[11]

9 b g Treasure Kay 6.5f **(53)** - Single Viking (Viking (USA)) 6.7f **(65)**
Form - 660
Record 2000 - 1st:0 2nd:0 3rd:0 Ran:3
Pre2000 - 1st:6 2nd:8 3rd:6 Ran:69
Win Prizemoney £17,084 *Total Prizemoney* £29,431

Wins	1996	*Mar Lingfi*	*(STD)*		*7f*		*66*	<
	1996	*Mar Lingfi*	*(STD)*	*H*	*8f*	*56*	*57*	

2000 Turf 0-2: (8f 2) (g-f, frm) 2000 AW 0-1: (8f) (Equi)
Little account gelding, often wears blinkers. Turf high 17 (began Jly).
**J R Poulton [0-14] Mrs D M Hickling (from R M Flower [7-75] May 1999).*

FORT SUMTER (USA) BHB 58a RR 65df 5072[15]

4 b g Sea Hero (USA) - Gray And Red (USA) (Wolf Power (SAF))
Form - 620
Record 2000 - 1st:0 2nd:1 3rd:0 Ran:3
Pre2000 - 1st:0 2nd:2 3rd:1 Ran:9
Win Prizemoney £0 *Total Prizemoney* £3,117
2000 Turf 0-2: (10f 2) (g-s, gd) 2000 AW 0-1: (8f) (Fibr)
Scopey, average gelding. Turf high 60 (began Spt). Inconsistent.
**P R Hedger [0-10] E Whelan (from I A Balding [0-3] Spt 1998).*

FORTUNA RR 17f 2570[9]

2 b c Fairy King (USA) 7.7f **(75)** - Local Lass (Local Suitor (USA)) 8.4f **(67)**
Form - 850
Record 2000 - 1st:0 2nd:0 3rd:0 Ran:3
2000 Turf 0-1: (6f) (frm) 2000 AW 0-2: (6f 2) (Fibr 2)
Currently fair colt. AW high 52.
**Sir Mark Prescott [0-3] G S Shropshire.*

FORTUNE FOUND (IRE) RR 5312[21]

2 b f Fumo Di Londra (IRE) - Trillick (IRE) (Treasure Kay)
Form - 0
Record 2000 - 1st:0 2nd:0 3rd:0 Ran:1
2000 Turf 0-1: (8f) (g-s)
Currently very poor filly.
**C G Cox [0-1] Mrs T L Cox.*

FORTUNE HOPPER BHB 29f RR 27f 3451[8]

6 br g Rock Hopper 10.6f **(54)** - Lots of Luck (Neltino) 7.6f **(54)**
Form - 8
Record 2000 - 1st:0 2nd:0 3rd:0 Ran:1
Pre2000 - 1st:0 2nd:0 3rd:3 Ran:8
Win Prizemoney £0 *Total Prizemoney* £903
2000 Turf 0-1: (12f) (frm)
Little account gelding, has worn blinkers.
**M Todhunter [0-17] UGM Racing Club (from J Pearce [0-7] Jly 1997).*

FORTUNE POINT (IRE) RR 73f 4601[2]

2 ch c Cadeaux Genereux 7.9f **(76)** - Mountains of Mist (IRE) **(91f)** (Shirley Heights) 10.3f **(74)**
Form - 42
Record 2000 - 1st:0 2nd:1 3rd:0 Ran:2
Win Prizemoney £0 *Total Prizemoney* £1,542
2000 Turf 0-2: (7f 2) (sft, gd)
Currently above-average colt. Turf high 73 (began Spt) - 2nd of 5 to Turku (23 Spt Haydock 7f gd RF 4601).
**J Noseda [0-2] Lucayan Stud.*

FORTY FORTE BHB 73f64a RR 74f 64a 1112[8]

4 b g Pursuit of Love 9.5f **(69)** - Cominna (Dominion) 8.5f **(63)**
Form - 132056162441538
Record 2000 - 1st:2 2nd:1 3rd:1 Ran:11
Pre2000 - 1st:3 2nd:4 3rd:2 Ran:14
Win Prizemoney £22,234 *Total Prizemoney* £32,226

Wins	*** 2000**	Mar Nottin	(GD)	H	10f	71	78	<
	*** 2000**	*Jan Lingfi*	*(STD)*	*H*	*10f*	*69*	*73*	
	* 1999	*Nov Lingfi*	*(STD)*	*H*	*10f*	*68*	*69*	
	* 1999	*Apr Beverl*	*(GD)*	*H*	*7.5f*	*72*	*76*	
	1999	*Mar Nottin*	*(G-S)*	*S*	*8.2f*		*76+*	

2000 Turf 1-4: (9f, 10f 1-3) (sft, gd 1-2, g-f) 2000 AW 1-7: (7f, 8f, 10f 1-4, 12f) (Equi 1-7)
Leggy, above-average gelding, effective 7 to 10f, best at 8f, acts on sft to frm - acts on Equi, best on gd, favours tight tracks, and excels at Nottingham. Turf high 78 (1st run) - 1st of 13 getting 7lb from Spring Pursuit (29 Mar Nottingham RF 0559). AW high 73 - 1st of 11 giving 4lb to Admirals Place (26 Jan Lingfield RF 0161). Consistent.
**K R Burke [4-21] Nigel Shields (from M R Channon [1-4] Mar 1999).*

FORUM CHRIS (IRE) BHB 80f RR 80f 2468[1]

3 ch g Trempolino (USA) 11.9f **(77)** - Memory Green (USA) (Green Forest (USA)) 9.9f **(68)**

Form - 743311
Record 2000 - 1st:2 2nd:0 3rd:2 Ran:6
Win Prizemoney £7,588 *Total Prizemoney* £8,861
Wins * 2000 Jly Mussel (FRM) H 14f 66 80+ <
* **2000** Jun Hamilt (G-F) H 13f 66 73+
2000 Turf 2-6: (10f, 12f 2, 13f 1-1, 14f 1-2) (g-s, gd 2, g-f 1-2, frm 1-1)
Rangy, decent gelding, effective 13 to 14f, acts on g-f to frm. Turf high 80 - 1st of 6 giving 1lb to Fletcher (3 Jly Musselburgh RF 2468) - also 1st of 7 getting 12lb from Once More for Luck (28 Jun Hamilton RF 2341). **M Johnston [2-6] Mrs Jacqueline Conroy.*

FORUM FINALE (USA) BHB 67f **RR 65f** 5115[1]

2 b f Silver Hawk (USA) 11.2f **(85)** - Silk Masque (USA) **(90f)** (Woodman (USA)) 9f **(74)**
Form - 25881
Record 2000 - 1st:1 2nd:1 3rd:0 Ran:5
Win Prizemoney £2,772 *Total Prizemoney* £3,892
Wins * 2000 *Oct Wolver (STD) H 8.5f 63 66* <
2000 Turf 0-4: (6f 2, 7f, 8f) (g-s, gd 2, frm) 2000 AW 1-1: (8f 1-1) (Fibr 1-1)
Average filly. Turf high 65. (1st run) - 1st of 13 getting 7lb from Thomas Smythe (20 Oct Wolverhampton RF 5115).
**M Johnston [1-5] Mrs Jacqueline Conroy.*

FORWOOD (IRE) BHB 100f **RR 95f** 4733[4]

2 b c Charnwood Forest (IRE) - Silver Hut (USA) **(73f)** (Silver Hawk (USA)) 8.6f **(70)**
Form - 1144
Record 2000 - 1st:2 2nd:0 3rd:0 Ran:4
Win Prizemoney £11,248 *Total Prizemoney* £16,498
Wins * 2000 Jly Ascot (GD) 7f 88+ <
* **2000** Jun Newbur (G-F) 6f 87+
2000 Turf 2-4: (6f 1-1, 7f 1-2, 8f) (gd 1-3, g-f 1-1)
Very useful colt. Turf high 95 - 4th of 13 to King Charlemagne (29 Spt Newmarket 7f gd RF 4733) - also 1st of 4 giving 3lb to Smith And Western (15 Jly Ascot RF 2829). Won what turned out to be a hot maiden on his debut and faced a simple task when following up, but just found the company a bit hot in the Shergar Cup Juvenile. Decent effort in a Group Three on his final run.
**M A Jarvis [2-4] & Mrs Raymond Anderson Green.*

FOR YOUR EYES ONLY BHB 90f **RR 101?f** 4740[29]

6 b g Pursuit of Love 9.5f **(69)** - Rivers Rhapsody (Dominion) 8.5f **(63)**
Form - 00
Record 2000 - 1st:0 2nd:0 3rd:0 Ran:2
Pre2000 - 1st:5 2nd:4 3rd:4 Ran:32
Win Prizemoney £103,641 *Total Prizemoney* £134,575
Wins 1998 Jly Goodwo (G-S) H 8f 102 108 <
1998 Jly Sandow (GD) H 8.1f 97 103
1998 May Sandow (GD) H 8.1f 90 102
1996 Jun Beverl (G-F) 5f 91+
1996 May Ripon (GD) 6f 78
2000 Turf 0-2: (8f, 9f) (g-s, g-f)
Very useful gelding, often wears blinkers. Turf high 69. Becoming disappointing.
**C E Brittain [0-5] H E Sheikh Rashid Bin Mohammed (from T D Easterby [5-29] Oct 1998).*

FORZA FIGLIO BHB 60f **RR 76f** 4934[18]

7 b g Warning 8.1f **(77)** - Wish You Well (Sadler's Wells (USA)) 10f **(76)**
Form - 0334400
Record 2000 - 1st:0 2nd:0 3rd:2 Ran:7
Pre2000 - 1st:1 2nd:3 3rd:2 Ran:14
Win Prizemoney £4,793 *Total Prizemoney* £17,458
Wins 1996 May Goodwo (GD) 8f 76 <
2000 Turf 0-7: (8f, 9f 2, 10f 4) (gd 2, g-f 5)
Above-average gelding, has worn blinkers. Turf high 76.
**M Kettle [0-7] Taylor Parker Associates Ltd (from R Akehurst [0-2] Oct 1997).*

FOSTON FOX BHB 41f39a **RR 43f 39a** 4768[8]

3 b f Foxhound (USA) - Enaam (Shirley Heights) 10.3f **(74)**
Form - 6405876705748
Record 2000 - 1st:0 2nd:0 3rd:0 Ran:11
Pre2000 - 1st:0 2nd:0 3rd:0 Ran:5
Win Prizemoney £0 *Total Prizemoney* £200
2000 Turf 0-10: (6f 2, 7f, 8f 6, 12f) (g-s, gd 3, g-f 4; frm 2) 2000 AW 0-1: (8f) (Fibr)
Neat, moderate filly, often wears blinkers. Turf high 43.
**C B B Booth [0-16] The Foston Partnership.*

FOSTON SECOND (IRE) BHB 28f **RR 36f** 4455[9]

3 ch f Lycius (USA) 8.8f **(71)** - Gentle Guest (IRE) (Be My Guest (USA)) 9.3f **(67)**
Form - 42430
Record 2000 - 1st:0 2nd:1 3rd:1 Ran:5
Pre2000 - 1st:0 2nd:0 3rd:0 Ran:2
Win Prizemoney £0 *Total Prizemoney* £1,252
2000 Turf 0-5: (11f, 12f 2, 14f 2) (g-s 2, g-f 2, frm)
Strong, very moderate filly, effective 11 to 12f, best at 12f, acts on g-s to frm. Turf high 36 (began Jly).
**C B B Booth [0-7] The Foston Partnership.*

FOUETTE RR 46f 4969[24]

2 b f Saddlers' Hall (IRE) 10.5f **(65)** - Tight Spin (High Top) 10.2f **(67)**
Form - 0
Record 2000 - 1st:0 2nd:0 3rd:0 Ran:1
2000 Turf 0-1: (8f) (gd)
Currently moderate filly.
**N A Graham [0-1] Matthews Breeding and Racing.*

FOUND AT LAST BHB 56f44a **RR 54f 44a** 4834[11]

4 b g Aragon 7.7f **(58)** - Girton (Balidar) 7.9f **(63)**
Form - 3073502224352200
Record 2000 - 1st:0 2nd:5 3rd:3 Ran:16
Pre2000 - 1st:0 2nd:0 3rd:0 Ran:6
Win Prizemoney £0 *Total Prizemoney* £5,628
2000 Turf 0-12: (5f, 6f 8, 7f 3) (g-s, gd 2, g-f, frm 8) 2000 AW 0-4: (5f, 6f 2, 7f) (Fibr 4)
Scopey, fair gelding, effective 6f, acts on frm, has worn blinkers. Turf high 58 (1st run) - 3rd of 8 to Pisces Lad (29 Mar Catterick 6f frm RF 0548). AW high 42. Consistent.
**J Balding [0-14] Mrs Jo Hardy (from G Woodward [0-3] Jan 2000).*

FOUNDRY LANE BHB 74f **RR 76f** 4603[3]

9 b g Mtoto 11.5f **(71)** - Eider (Niniski (USA)) 10.6f **(65)**
Form - 42133
Record 2000 - 1st:1 2nd:1 3rd:2 Ran:5
Pre2000 - 1st:4 2nd:3 3rd:5 Ran:29
Win Prizemoney £25,437 *Total Prizemoney* £57,396
Wins * 2000 Jly Haydoc (G-F) H 14f 74 74
* 1998 Oct York (GD) H 13.9f 70 75
2000 Turf 1-5: (14f 1-3, 16f 2) (g-s, gd 2, g-f 1-2)
Above-average gelding, effective 14 to 16f, best at 16f, acts on g-s to frm, best on g-f, likes left handed tracks, and excels at York. Turf high 76 - 3rd of 7 giving 11lb to Bustling Rio (16 Aug Beverley 16f g-f RF 3685) - also 1st of 4 giving 5lb to Sandbaggedagain (7 Jly Haydock RF 2594). Consistent. Has been running on the Flat, over hurdles and over fences in the last couple of years, but remains a decent staying handicapper on the level and scored in brave style at Haydock in July. **Mrs M Reveley [12-50] A Sharratt.*

FOURDANED (IRE) BHB 24f26a **RR 34df 26a** 3783[12]

7 b g Danehill (USA) 9.1f **(79)** - Pro Patria (Petingo) 11f **(72)**
Form - 5000
Record 2000 - 1st:0 2nd:0 3rd:0 Ran:3
Pre2000 - 1st:0 2nd:3 3rd:1 Ran:40
Win Prizemoney £0 *Total Prizemoney* £3,431
2000 Turf 0-3: (7f, 10f, 12f) (gd, frm 2)
Very moderate gelding, effective 11f, acts on hrd, has worn blinkers. Becoming disappointing.
**D C O'Brien [0-3] Mrs B C Knowles (from B R Johnson [0-14] Nov 1999).*

FOUR EAGLES (USA) RR 78+f 4969[5]

2 b c Lear Fan (USA) 10.4f **(80)** - Bloomingly (ARG) (Candy Stripes (USA))
Form - 5
Record 2000 - 1st:0 2nd:0 3rd:0 Ran:1
2000 Turf 0-1: (8f) (gd)
Currently above-average colt. (1st run) - 5th of 29 to Terrestrial (13 Oct Newmarket 8f gd RF 4969).
**D R C Elsworth [0-1] McDowell Racing.*

FOUR LEGS GOOD (IRE) BHB 61f **RR 59f** 4623[9]

2 b f Be My Guest (USA) 10.2f **(66)** Korino (Habitat) 9.4f **(70)**
Form - 8070
Record 2000 - 1st:0 2nd:0 3rd:0 Ran:4
2000 Turf 0-4: (6f, 7f, 8f 2) (g-s, gd, g-f 2)
Fair filly. Turf high 59 (began Jly).
**G C Bravery [0-4] Sir Clement Freud & Partners.*

FOUR MEN (IRE) BHB 37f RR 43?f 4872[9]

3 b g Nicolotte - Sound Pet (Runnett) 7f **(59)**
Form - 00706606565372060
Record 2000 - 1st:0 2nd:1 3rd:1 Ran:17
Pre2000 - 1st:0 2nd:0 3rd:0 Ran:4
Win Prizemoney £0 *Total Prizemoney* £3,166
2000 Turf 0-17: (7f 4, 8f 8, 9f 2, 10f 2, 11f) (hvy, gd 2, g-f 5, frm 9)
Leggy, moderate gelding, effective 8f, acts on frm, likes left handed tracks. Turf high 43.
**A Berry [0-17] Alan Berry (from J Berry [0-4] Aug 1999).*

FOURTH TIME LUCKY BHB 26f29a RR 27f 29a 3617[10]

4 b g Timeless Times (USA) 6.1f **(56)** - Wych Willow (Hard Fought) 8.8f **(62)**
Form - 00060
Record 2000 - 1st:0 2nd:0 3rd:0 Ran:4
Pre2000 - 1st:0 2nd:1 3rd:0 Ran:16
Win Prizemoney £0 *Total Prizemoney* £748
2000 Turf 0-3: (7f, 8f 2) (g-f, frm 2) 2000 AW 0-1: (7f) (Fibr)
Little account gelding, effective 8f, - acts on Fibr, has worn blinkers, likes left handed tracks. Turf high 27.
**B W Murray [0-21] Mrs M Lingwood.*

FOX COTTAGE (IRE) BHB 49f RR 41f 4821[17]

2 ch f So Factual (USA) - Ever So Artful (Never so Bold) 6.3f **(66)**
Form - 000
Record 2000 - 1st:0 2nd:0 3rd:0 Ran:3
2000 Turf 0-3: (5f, 6f 2) (gd, g-f, frm)
Currently moderate filly. Turf high 41 (began Spt).
**D W P Arbuthnot [0-3] Miss Samantha Dare.*

FOXDALE (FR) BHB 39f RR 47f 3077[11]

3 ch f Emarati (USA) 6.6f **(63)** - Fox Croft (FR) (Bustino) 10.4f **(64)**
Form - 5000
Record 2000 - 1st:0 2nd:0 3rd:0 Ran:4
Pre2000 - 1st:0 2nd:0 3rd:0 Ran:1
2000 Turf 0-4: (5f, 6f 2, 7f) (sft, gd, frm 2)
Unfurnished, moderate filly. Turf high 47.
**H Morrison [0-5] Mrs R Pease & Lady Margadale.*

FOXES LAIR (IRE) RR 66f 5189[4]

2 b g Muhtarram (USA) - Forest Lair (Habitat) 9.4f **(70)**
Form - 54
Record 2000 - 1st:0 2nd:0 3rd:0 Ran:2
2000 Turf 0-2: (7f, 8f) (g-s, gd)
Currently average gelding. Turf high 66 (began Oct).
**M Dods [0-2] D C Batey.*

FOXKEY BHB 55f53a RR 59f 53a 42[6]

3 ch f Foxhound (USA) - Latch Key Lady (USA) **(12f 48a)** (Tejano (USA))
Form - 66
Record 2000 - 1st:0 2nd:0 3rd:0 Ran:1
Pre2000 - 1st:2 2nd:1 3rd:0 Ran:6
Win Prizemoney £3,762 *Total Prizemoney* £4,386
Wins 1999 *Apr Southw (STD) S* 5f 59 <
1999 *Apr Catter (SFT) S* 5f 59 <
2000 AW 0-1: (7f) (Fibr)
Light-framed, fair filly, effective 5f, acts on g-s to gd - acts on Fibr, has worn blinkers.
**Miss Gay Kelleway [0-4] A P Griffin (from E J Alston [2-2] Apr 1999).*

FOX'S IDEA BHB 60f77a RR 68f 77a 4493[R]

3 b f Magic Ring (IRE) 6.5f **(64)** - Lindy Belle **(35f)** (Alleging (USA))
Form - 1330505430R
Record 2000 - 1st:1 2nd:0 3rd:3 Ran:11
Pre2000 - 1st:0 2nd:0 3rd:2 Ran:5
Win Prizemoney £3,250 *Total Prizemoney* £6,349
Wins 2000 *Jan Wolver (STD) H* 7f 70 75 <
2000 Turf 0-8: (6f, 7f 2, 8f 4, 10f) (g-s, gd 2, g-f 5) 2000 AW 1-3: (7f 1-2, 8f) (Fibr 1-3)
Above-average filly, effective 5 to 8f, acts on frm - acts on Fibr, likes left handed tracks, prefers tight tracks. Turf high 68. AW high 79 - 3rd of 9 giving 3lb to Special Promise (10 Feb Wolverhampton 8f Fibr RF 0259) - also 1st of 7 giving 10lb to Church Farm Flyer (8 Jan Wolverhampton RF 0055). Inconsistent.
**T D Barron [0-3] Nigel Shields (from D HaydnJones [1-13] Jun 2000).*

FOX STAR (IRE) BHB 33f40a RR 48f 40a 4267[13]

3 b f Foxhound (USA) - Our Pet (Mummy's Pet) 7.7f **(60)**
Form - 706070530000
Record 2000 - 1st:0 2nd:0 3rd:1 Ran:10
Pre2000 - 1st:0 2nd:0 3rd:1 Ran:9
Win Prizemoney £0 *Total Prizemoney* £1,249
2000 Turf 0-8: (7f 5, 8f, 9f, 10f) (sft, gd, g-f 3, frm 3) 2000 AW 0-2: (6f, 12f) (Equi 2)
Leggy, moderate filly, often wears blinkers. Turf high 48. AW high 31.
**J C Poulton [0-12] Mrs Elizabeth Reed (from R Hannon [0-7] Spt 1999).*

FOXY ALPHA (IRE) BHB 33f RR 16f 2886[11]

3 ch f Foxhound (USA) - Ice Baby (Grundy) 10.3f **(65)**
Form - 0580
Record 2000 - 1st:0 2nd:0 3rd:0 Ran:4
Pre2000 - 1st:0 2nd:0 3rd:0 Ran:1
2000 Turf 0-4: (6f 2, 8f 2) (g-s, g-f 2, frm)
Lengthy, poor filly. Turf high 16.
**J L Eyre [0-4] Burtree Racing Partnership (from A B Mulholland [0-1] Oct 1999).*

FOXY BROWN BHB 61a RR 16f 61a 92[4]

3 b f Factual (USA) - Miltak **(43f 40a)** (Risk Me (FR)) 5.9f **(53)**
Form - 234
Record 2000 - 1st:0 2nd:0 3rd:0 Ran:1
Pre2000 - 1st:0 2nd:2 3rd:1 Ran:4
Win Prizemoney £0 *Total Prizemoney* £1,470
2000 AW 0-1: (6f) (Fibr)
Tall, average filly. **Miss I Foustok [0-5] Miss I Foustok.*

FRAMPANT BHB 53f51a RR 52f 51a 5112[1]

3 ch f Fraam - Potent (IRE) (Pusen (USA))
Form - 4300044306001
Record 2000 - 1st:1 2nd:0 3rd:2 Ran:13
Pre2000 - 1st:1 2nd:1 3rd:0 Ran:10
Win Prizemoney £6,959 *Total Prizemoney* £10,522
Wins * 2000 Oct Newbur (SFT) H 5.2f 50 50
* 1999 Aug Windso (SFT) 5f 69 <
2000 Turf 1-11: (5f 1-5, 6f 5, 7f) (sft, g-s, gd 1-2, g-f 5, frm 2) 2000 AW 0-2: (6f, 7f) (Equi, Fibr)
Workmanlike, fair filly, effective 5 to 6f, acts on g-s to gd. Turf high 56. AW high 57. **M Quinn [2-23] The Frampant Fellows.*

FRANCESCO GUARDI (IRE) BHB 109f RR 113f 4436[2]

3 b c Robellino (USA) 9.5f **(68)** - Lamees (USA) (Lomond (USA)) 8.8f **(65)**
Form - 12
Record 2000 - 1st:1 2nd:1 3rd:0 Ran:2
Pre2000 - 1st:1 2nd:1 3rd:0 Ran:2
Win Prizemoney £13,093 *Total Prizemoney* £26,216
Wins * 2000 Spt Doncas (G-F) 10.3f 104+ <
* 1999 Oct Catter (GD,) 7f 86+
2000 Turf 1-2: (10f 1-1, 11f) (g-f 1-1, frm)
Rangy, Group-class colt. Turf high 113 (began Spt) - 2nd of 7 to Pawn Broker (15 Spt Newbury 11f frm RF 4436) - also 1st of 4 getting 2lb from Kookaburra (8 Spt Doncaster RF 4294). Lightly raced, he was successful at Doncaster in September on his belated reappearance and was only just beaten in a Newbury Listed event next time. **P F I Cole [2-4] Richard Green (Fine Paintings).*

FRANCHETTI BHB 70f RR 78?f 1056[16]

4 b g Unfuwain (USA) 11.4f **(74)** - Lady Shipley (Shirley Heights) 10.3f **(74)**
Form - 0
Record 2000 - 1st:0 2nd:0 3rd:0 Ran:1
Pre2000 - 1st:1 2nd:1 3rd:1 Ran:5
Win Prizemoney £5,500 *Total Prizemoney* £7,300

Wins 1998 Oct Leopar (SFT) 8f 84 <
2000 Turf 0-1: (14f) (gd)
Above-average gelding.
**M D Hammond [0-3] Rykneld Thoroughbred Co Ltd (from C O'Brien in IRE [1-5] Oct 1999).*

FRANCPORT BHB 69f RR 78df 5061[10]

4 b c Efisio 7.7f **(69)** - Elkie Brooks (Relkino) 8.9f **(65)**
Form - 51070306000
Record 2000 - 1st:1 2nd:0 3rd:1 Ran:11
Pre2000 - 1st:1 2nd:1 3rd:0 Ran:6
Win Prizemoney £10,810 *Total Prizemoney* £13,945
Wins * 2000 Apr Ripon (SFT) H 6f 70 78 <
1999 May Beverl (GD) 5f 70
2000 Turf 1-11: (6f 1-11) (sft, g-s, gd 1-4, g-f, frm 4)
Scopey, above-average colt, effective 5 to 6f, best at 6f, acts on gd to frm. Turf high 78 - 1st of 19 getting 7lb from Manorbier (5 Apr Ripon RF 0619).
**A Berry [1-11] R A Popely (from J Berry [1-6] Spt 1999).*

FRANGY BHB 77f RR 76f 3936[14]

3 b f Sadler's Wells (USA) 11.3f **(87)** - Fern (Shirley Heights) 10.3f **(74)**
Form - 31150
Record 2000 - 1st:2 2nd:0 3rd:1 Ran:5
Win Prizemoney £7,585 *Total Prizemoney* £8,173
Wins * 2000 Jly Bath (FRM) 11.7f 76 <
*** 2000** Jly Doncas (GD) 12f 71
2000 Turf 2-5: (12f 2-4, 14f) (g-s, gd, g-f, frm 2-2)
Lengthy, above-average filly. Turf high 76 - 1st of 6 getting 15lb from Wasp Ranger (27 Jly Bath RF 3149) - also 1st of 6 getting 5lb from Troilus (13 Jly Doncaster RF 2754). Won two small races in July but was held on her handicap bow.
**L M Cumani [2-5] Fittocks Stud.*

FRANICA (IRE) BHB 74f RR 81f 4642[18]

2 b f Inzar (USA) - Comfrey Glen (Glenstal (USA)) 10.1f **(64)**
Form - 222271522470
Record 2000 - 1st:1 2nd:6 3rd:0 Ran:12
Win Prizemoney £2,828 *Total Prizemoney* £9,147
Wins * 2000 May Mussel (FRM) 5f 68 <
2000 Turf 1-12: (5f 1-8, 6f 3, 7f) (hvy 2, sft, gd 2, g-f 3, frm 1-4)
Decent filly. Turf high 81. **A Bailey [1-12] Ms M A Rowlands.*

FRANKLIN-D BHB 44f44a RR 34f 44a 2892[11]

4 ch g Democratic (USA) - English Mint (Jalmood (USA)) 10.1f **(52)**
Form - 32340570
Record 2000 - 1st:0 2nd:1 3rd:1 Ran:7
Pre2000 - 1st:0 2nd:0 3rd:1 Ran:7
Win Prizemoney £0 *Total Prizemoney* £1,327
2000 Turf 0-1: (7f) (frm) 2000 AW 0-6: (6f, 7f 4, 8f) (Equi 3, Fibr 3)
Scopey, moderate gelding, effective 7f, - acts on AW, best on Equi, has worn blinkers, prefers left handed tracks, prefers tight tracks. AW high 43. Inconsistent. **J R Jenkins [0-14] Mrs Stella Peirce.*

FRANKLIN LAKES BHB 39f30a RR 34f 30a 3908[8]

5 ch g Sanglamore (USA) 12.9f **(67)** - Eclipsing (IRE) (Baillamont (USA)) 7f **(78)**
Form - 5783754600208
Record 2000 - 1st:0 2nd:1 3rd:1 Ran:10
Pre2000 - 1st:0 2nd:0 3rd:0 Ran:21
Win Prizemoney £0 *Total Prizemoney* £1,298
2000 Turf 0-5: (5f, 6f 3, 7f) (g-f, frm 4) 2000 AW 0-5: (7f, 8f 4) (Fibr 5)
Very moderate gelding, often wears blinkers. Turf high 34 (began Jly). AW high 32. Consistent.
**M R Bosley [0-24] M R Bosley (from C A Horgan [0-8] Aug 1998).*

FRATERNITY BHB 69f62a RR 72f 62a 1381[7]

3 b g Grand Lodge (USA) - Catawba (Mill Reef (USA)) 10.5f **(78)**
Form - 47
Record 2000 - 1st:0 2nd:0 3rd:0 Ran:2
Pre2000 - 1st:0 2nd:1 3rd:0 Ran:2
Win Prizemoney £0 *Total Prizemoney* £1,272
2000 Turf 0-2: (12f 2) (sft, g-f)
Scopey, above-average gelding. Turf high 71.
**W Jarvis [0-4] Exors of the late Lord Howard de Walden.*

FRAZER'S LAD BHB 53f RR 31f 5246[3]

3 b g Whittingham (IRE) - Loch Tain (Lochnager) 6f **(59)**
Form - 53
Record 2000 - 1st:0 2nd:0 3rd:1 Ran:2
Win Prizemoney £0 *Total Prizemoney* £446
2000 Turf 0-1: (8f) (sft) 2000 AW 0-1: (8f) (Fibr)
Currently fair gelding. **A Bailey [0-2] Gerald Williams.*

FREDDY FLINTSTONE BHB 82f RR 83f 5022[2]

3 b c Bigstone (IRE) - Daring Ditty (Daring March) 7.1f **(61)**
Form - 0478234302
Record 2000 - 1st:0 2nd:2 3rd:2 Ran:10
Pre2000 - 1st:0 2nd:0 3rd:0 Ran:2
Win Prizemoney £0 *Total Prizemoney* £6,202
2000 Turf 0-10: (7f 3, 8f 4, 9f, 10f 2) (g-s 2, gd 3, g-f 4, frm)
Scopey, decent colt, effective 7 to 10f, best at 8f, acts on gd to frm, best on g-f, and does well at Newmarket. Turf high 83 - 3rd of 16 giving 4lb to Kareeb (16 Spt Newbury 8f g-f RF 4465). Consistent. A half-brother to Bold Edge and Brave Edge, he has shown ability in maidens and handicaps, but is finding it difficult to put his head in front where it matters. **R Hannon [0-12] Lady Whent and Friends.*

FREDERICK JAMES BHB 50f47a RR 61df 47a 2461[17]

6 b g Efisio 7.7f **(69)** - Rare Roberta (USA) (Roberto (USA)) 10f **(76)**
Form - 4677000
Record 2000 - 1st:0 2nd:0 3rd:0 Ran:7
Pre2000 - 1st:1 2nd:3 3rd:6 Ran:26
Win Prizemoney £3,272 *Total Prizemoney* £12,748
Wins * 1999 Mar Nottin (G-S) H 6.1f 57 65 <
2000 Turf 0-4: (6f 2, 7f, 8f) (hvy 2, g-f, frm) 2000 AW 0-3: (6f 2, 7f) (Equi, Fibr 2)
Average gelding. Turf high 62. AW high 48.
**H E Haynes [1-26] Miss Sally Haynes (from M J Heaton-Ellis [0-7] Oct 1997).*

FREDORA BHB 80f RR 84f 5159[13]

5 ch m Inchinor 8.9f **(64)** - Ophrys (Nonoalco (USA)) 8.5f **(66)**
Form - 50024181474526800
Record 2000 - 1st:2 2nd:2 3rd:0 Ran:17
Pre2000 - 1st:3 2nd:3 3rd:2 Ran:18
Win Prizemoney £25,525 *Total Prizemoney* £39,603
Wins * 2000 Jly Epsom (G-S) H 8.5f 83 83
*** 2000** Jun Kempto (G-F) H 9f 80 81
* 1999 Jun Salisb (GD) 9.9f 86
* 1998 Aug Kempto (G-F) H 7f 87 89 <
* 1998 May Kempto (GD) 7f 82
2000 Turf 2-17: (8f 8, 9f 2-5, 10f 3, 11f) (hvy, sft 2, gd 1-5, g-f 5, frm 1-4)
Decent filly, effective 8 to 10f, best at 10f, acts on gd to frm, best on g-f, prefers right handed tracks, and does well at Kempton. Turf high 84 - 2nd of 8 giving 5lb to Willoughby's Boy (13 Spt Sandown 8f frm RF 4370) - also 1st of 9 giving 11lb to Kind Regards (13 Jly Epsom RF 2761). **M Blanshard [5-35] Peter Goldring.*

FREE BHB 58f RR 57df 3772[10]

5 ch g Gone West (USA) 7.8f **(82)** - Bemissed (USA) (Nijinsky (CAN)) 10.3f **(77)**
Form - 0010
Record 2000 - 1st:1 2nd:0 3rd:0 Ran:4
Pre2000 - 1st:1 2nd:3 3rd:3 Ran:17
Win Prizemoney £5,545 *Total Prizemoney* £10,575
Wins * 2000 Aug Newcas (GD) H 14.4f 50 54 <
* 1999 Aug Newcas (FRM) H 16.1f 51 54 <
2000 Turf 1-4: (14f 1-1, 16f 3) (g-f 1-2, frm, hrd)
Fair gelding, effective 14 to 17f, best at 16f, acts on g-f to hrd, excels at Musselburgh and Newcastle. Turf high 54 - 1st of 12 giving 6lb to Lucky Judge (9 Aug Newcastle RF 3497).
**Mrs M Reveley [6-30] P D Savill (from P F I Cole [0-2] Spt 1997).*

FREECOM NET (IRE) RR 55f 4109[7]

2 b c Zieten (USA) - Radiance (IRE) **(52f)** (Thatching) 8f **(66)**
Form - U7
Record 2000 - 1st:0 2nd:0 3rd:0 Ran:2
2000 Turf 0-2: (7f 2) (gd, g-f)
Currently fair colt. Turf high 55 (began Jly).
**A P Jarvis [0-2] A L R Morton.*

FREEDOM NOW (IRE) RR 79f 4701[7]

2 b c Sadler's Wells (USA) 11.3f **(87)** Free At Last (Shirley Heights) 10.3f **(74)**
Form - 7
Record 2000 - 1st:0 2nd:0 3rd:0 Ran:1
2000 Turf 0-1: (7f) (g-f)
Currently above-average colt. **L M Cumani [0-1] Gerald Leigh.*

FREEDOM QUEST (IRE) BHB 58f58a **RR 62f 58a** 4870[3]

5 b g Polish Patriot (USA) 7.8f **(70)** - Recherchee (Rainbow Quest (USA)) 10.4f **(75)**
Form - 44346425214874205З
Record 2000 - 1st:1 2nd:3 3rd:2 Ran:18
Pre2000 - 1st:2 2nd:7 3rd:3 Ran:23
Win Prizemoney £17,421 *Total Prizemoney* £34,291
Wins * **2000** Jly Newcas (G-F) H 10.1f 58 60
* 1999 Spt Mussel (G-F) H 12f 60 62 <
* 1999 Jly Beverl (SFT) H 9.9f 57 59
2000 Turf 1-17: (8f, 10f 1-9, 11f 2, 12f 2, 14f 2, 16f) (hvy, g-s 2, gd 1-4, g-f 6, frm 4) 2000 AW 0-1: (8f) (Fibr)
Average gelding, effective 8 to 14f, best at 12f, acts on gd to frm - acts on Fibr, best on frm, has worn blinkers, likes right handed tracks, likes tight tracks, excels at Musselburgh and likes Newcastle. Turf high 62 - 3rd of 8 getting 7lb from Plutocrat (5 May Musselburgh 12f frm RF 1042) - also 1st of 7 getting 6lb from Donna's Double (9 Jly Newcastle RF 2652). (1st run) - 2nd of 16 giving 14lb to The Third Curate (3 Jly Southwell 8f Fibr RF 2479). Consistent. He is a little hard to win with, but got his head in front at Newcastle in July. Best off a strong pace.
**B S Rothwell [3-34] B Valentine (from J M Jefferson [0-2] Spt 1998).*

FREEFOURINTERNET (USA) BHB 97f **RR 85f** 4307[2]

2 b c Tabasco Cat (USA) - Dixie Chimes (USA) (Dixieland Band (USA)) 7f **(74)**
Form - 352
Record 2000 - 1st:0 2nd:1 3rd:1 Ran:3
Win Prizemoney £0 *Total Prizemoney* £3,429
2000 Turf 0-3: (6f, 7f 2) (frm 3)
Currently useful colt. Turf high 85 (began Aug) - 2nd of 6 getting 2lb from Down To The Woods (9 Spt Doncaster 6f frm RF 4307). Still a maiden, but has been taking on some decent sorts and there are races to be won with him. **B J Meehan [0-3] Roldvale Ltd.*

FREEFOURRACING (USA) BHB 100f **RR 97f** 4017[1]

2 b f French Deputy (USA) - Gerri N Jo Go (USA) (Top Command (USA)) 10f **(77)**
Form - 1181
Record 2000 - 1st:3 2nd:0 3rd:0 Ran:4
Win Prizemoney £38,095 *Total Prizemoney* £38,095
Wins * **2000** Aug Goodwo (GD) G3 7f 97 <
* **2000** Jly Windso (GD) 6f 90
* **2000** Jun Beverl (G-S) 5f 79+
2000 Turf 3-4: (5f 1-1, 6f 1-2, 7f 1-1) (gd 1-2, g-f 1-1, frm 1-1)
Very useful filly. Turf high 97 - 1st of 6 from Summer Symphony (27 Aug Goodwood RF 4017) - also 1st of 5 giving 6lb to Makboola (3 Jly Windsor RF 2488). Caused a surprise when scoring in the Hilary Needler at Beverley on her debut, and followed up at Windsor, but ran a tame race when hoisted in class. Got back to winning ways in a Group Three at Goodwood, and was subsequently exported to America. **B J Meehan [3-4] Roldvale Ltd.*

FREE KEVIN BHB 36f **RR 17tf** 4870[15]

4 b g Midyan (USA) 9.9f **(64)** - Island Desert (IRE) (Green Desert (USA)) 8.6f **(78)**
Form - 3000
Record 2000 - 1st:0 2nd:0 3rd:1 Ran:4
Win Prizemoney £0 *Total Prizemoney* £580
2000 Turf 0-4: (9f 2, 10f, 12f) (hvy, gd, g-f 2)
Leggy, poor gelding. Turf high 17 (began Aug).
**Miss L C Siddall [0-4] Miss J A Challen.*

FREE OPTION (IRE) BHB 95f **RR 95f** 4732[7]

5 ch g Indian Ridge 7.6f **(74)** - Saneena (Kris) 9.5f **(73)**
Form - 303103677
Record 2000 - 1st:1 2nd:0 3rd:3 Ran:9
Pre2000 - 1st:5 2nd:4 3rd:3 Ran:26
Win Prizemoney £58,296 *Total Prizemoney* £76,712
Wins * **2000** Jly Kempto (G-F) H 8f 94 95+ <
* 1999 Oct Newmar (GD) H 8f 88 93
* 1999 Jly Cheste (G-F) 7f 85
* 1999 May Kempto (G-F) H 8f 91 92
* 1998 Spt Newbur (gd) H 7.3f 85 94
* 1998 Jly Lingfi (G-F) 7.6f 72+
2000 Turf 1-9: (7f 4, 8f 1-4, 9f) (gd 4, g-f 3, frm 1-2)
Very useful gelding, effective 7 to 9f, best at 8f, acts on gd to frm, best on g-f, likes right handed tracks, prefers tight tracks, and excels at Kempton. Turf high 95 - 1st of 11 giving 2lb to Pantar (23 Jly Kempton RF 3051). Consistent. Ran a blinder to finish third in a York rated stakes on his return and, though down the field in the Royal Hunt Cup, got back to winning ways with a game success at Kempton in July. Looks best over a mile and has gained the majority of his wins on turning tracks. **B Hanbury [6-35] Ahmed Ali.*

FREE RIDER BHB 106f **RR 107f** 2148[9]

3 b c Inchinor 8.9f **(64)** - Forever Roses **(62f)** (Forzando) 7.6f **(59)**
Form - 20030
Record 2000 - 1st:0 2nd:1 3rd:1 Ran:5
Pre2000 - 1st:1 2nd:2 3rd:0 Ran:3
Win Prizemoney £3,160 *Total Prizemoney* £11,725
Wins * 1999 Nov Windso (G-S) 6f 85 <
2000 Turf 0-5: (7f 4, 8f) (gd 4, frm)
Scopey, Pattern-class colt, effective 7f, acts on gd to frm. Turf high 107 - 3rd of 9 to Shibboleth (3 Jun Newmarket 7f frm RF 1689). He ran some good races in useful company, and met trouble in running more than once. Not easy to place.
**I A Balding [1-8] J C Smith.*

FREE TO SPEAK (IRE) BHB 104f **RR 106f** 4353a[13]

8 ch g Be My Guest (USA) 10.2f **(66)** - Love For Poetry (Lord Gayle (USA)) 8.8f **(62)**
Form - 8220460
2000 Turf 0-7: (6f, 7f, 8f 3, 9f 2) (sft, g-s, gd 2, g-f 3)
Pattern-class gelding, effective 8 to 9f, best at 8f, acts on g-s to gd, best on g-s, often wears blinkers (effectively), likes left handed tracks. Turf high 106 - 2nd of 9 giving 16lb to Provosky (5 Jun Leopardstown 9f g-s RF 1928a).
**D K Weld in IRE [5-35] Moyglare Stud Farm.*

FREETOWN (IRE) BHB 71f **RR 72f** 1442[2]

4 b g Shirley Heights 12.1f **(76)** - Pageantry (Welsh Pageant) 10f **(65)**
Form - 62
Record 2000 - 1st:0 2nd:1 3rd:0 Ran:2
Pre2000 - 1st:1 2nd:0 3rd:0 Ran:2
Win Prizemoney £2,745 *Total Prizemoney* £4,203
Wins 1999 Oct Ayr (SFT) C 10.9f 68 <
2000 Turf 0-2: (13f, 16f) (gd, g-f)
Workmanlike, above-average gelding. Turf high 72 - 2nd of 14 getting 11lb from Virgin Soldier (25 May Newcastle 16f gd RF 1442).
**L Lungo [0-4] Miss S Blumberg (from P F I Cole [1-2] Oct 1999).*

FREE WILL RR 72f 3500[4]

3 ch c Indian Ridge 7.6f **(74)** - Free Guest (Be My Guest (USA)) 9.3f **(67)**
Form - 5634
Record 2000 - 1st:0 2nd:0 3rd:1 Ran:4
Win Prizemoney £0 *Total Prizemoney* £835
2000 Turf 0-4: (8f, 9f, 10f 2) (gd, g-f, frm 2)
Above-average colt. Turf high 72. **L M Cumani [0-4] Fittocks Stud.*

FRENCH BRAMBLE (IRE) BHB 60f53a **RR 62f 53a** 4760[8]

2 ch f General Monash (USA) - La Mazya (IRE) (Mazaad) 7.1f **(45)**
Form - 67806448
Record 2000 - 1st:0 2nd:0 3rd:0 Ran:8
2000 Turf 0-5: (5f 2, 6f 3) (g-f 2, frm 3) 2000 AW 0-3: (5f 2, 6f) (Fibr 3)
Average filly, has worn blinkers. Turf high 62 (began Jly). AW high 49. **J Balding [0-8] Tykes And Terriers Racing Club.*

FRENCH CONNECTION BHB 48a **RR 46f** 3373[11]

5 b g Tirol 8.1f **(64)** - Heaven-Liegh-Grey (Grey Desire) 8.7f **(50)**
Form - 62000
Record 2000 - 1st:0 2nd:1 3rd:0 Ran:5
Pre2000 - 1st:2 2nd:3 3rd:0 Ran:22
Win Prizemoney £24,491 *Total Prizemoney* £31,760
Wins 1998 May Haydoc (G-S) H 8.1f 77 81 <
1998 May Hamilt (SFT) 9.2f 79
2000 Turf 0-1: (10f) (g-f) 2000 AW 0-4: (7f 2, 8f, 9f) (Fibr 4)

Fair gelding, effective 8f, acts on gd, has worn blinkers. AW high 51. Becoming disappointing.
**B D Leavy [0-6] Joe Singh (from D Nicholls [0-8] Jan 2000).*

FRENCH FANCY (IRE) BHB 37f43a **RR 38f 43a** 2976[14]

3 gr f Paris House 5.9f **(64)** - Clipping (Kris) 9.5f **(73)**
Form - 74537424074108050
Record 2000 - 1st:1 2nd:1 3rd:1 Ran:17
Pre2000 - 1st:0 2nd:0 3rd:2 Ran:13
Win Prizemoney £2,320 *Total Prizemoney* £4,390
Wins * 2000 *Jun Lingfi (STD) H 6f 45 47* <
2000 Turf 0-8: (5f, 6f 3, 7f 3, 8f) (g-s, gd 3, g-f 3, frm) 2000 AW 1-9: (6f 1-3, 7f 4, 8f 2) (Equi 1-8, Fibr)
Light-framed, moderate filly, effective 5 to 7f, acts on sft to g-f - acts on Equi, often wears blinkers. Turf high 48 (1st run) - 4th of 13 getting 12lb from Northern Times (7 Apr Lingfield 7f gd RF 0638). AW high 47 - 1st of 14 getting 15lb from Paddywack (6 Jun Lingfield RF 1738).
**B A Pearce [1-17] Richard Gray (from C A Dwyer [0-13] Oct 1999).*

FRENCH FELLOW (IRE) BHB 110f **RR 111f** 3853[4]

3 b c Suave Dancer (USA) 10.7f **(68)** - Mademoiselle Chloe (Night Shift (USA)) 7.2f **(69)**
Form - 20134
Record 2000 - 1st:1 2nd:1 3rd:1 Ran:5
Pre2000 - 1st:5 2nd:1 3rd:0 Ran:7
Win Prizemoney £58,141 *Total Prizemoney* £84,123
Wins * 2000 Jly Doncas (GD) 8f 94+
* 1999 Oct Ascot (G-S) L 8f 104 <
* 1999 Spt Doncas (G-F) H 8f 95 104 <
* 1999 Aug York (GD) H 7f 88 93+
* 1999 Aug Redcar (GD) H 6f 80 87+
* 1999 Jun Ayr (GD) 6f 73
2000 Turf 1-5: (8f 1-3, 11f, 12f) (gd 4, frm 1-1)
Scopey, Group-class colt, effective 8 to 12f, acts on gd to g-f, best on gd, excels at York and Doncaster. Turf high 111 - 4th of 5 to Air Marshall (22 Aug York 12f gd RF 3853). He justified all his connections' faith at two and would have completed a six-timer but for being badly hampered at Newcastle in August. He went down fighting behind Race Leader in the Thirsk Classic Trial on his reappearance, but was well beaten in the 2000 Guineas. Returned to winning form in a Doncaster conditions event in July and ran a sound race in a Haydock Group Three. He is a real battler, but appeared to find the trip too far in the Great Voltigeur at York. He was later sold to race abroad. **T D Easterby [6-12] T H Bennett.*

FRENCH GINGER BHB 28f21a **RR 21f 21a** 53[7]

9 ch m Most Welcome 8.6f **(66)** - French Plait (Thatching) 8f **(66)**
Form - 07
Record 2000 - 1st:0 2nd:0 3rd:0 Ran:1
Pre2000 - 1st:1 2nd:1 3rd:1 Ran:34
Win Prizemoney £2,752 *Total Prizemoney* £4,896
Wins * 1997 Spt Mussel (G-F) H 7.1f 45 54 <
2000 AW 0-1: (9f) (Fibr)
Little account mare, effective 7f, acts on g-f, has worn blinkers.
**L R Lloyd-James [1-14] L R Lloyd-James (from Don Enrico Incisa [0-9] Spt 1998).*

FRENCH GRIT (IRE) BHB 39f36a **RR 41f 36a** 1985[15]

8 b g Common Grounds 8.1f **(66)** - Charbatte (FR) (In Fijar (USA)) 7.5f **(70)**
Form - 250607060800
Record 2000 - 1st:0 2nd:0 3rd:0 Ran:10
Pre2000 - 1st:4 2nd:8 3rd:5 Ran:62
Win Prizemoney £21,683 *Total Prizemoney* £40,694
Wins 1997 Jun Pontef (G-F) H 6f 71 75
1997 Apr Ripon (G-F) H 6f 72 78
2000 Turf 0-4: (6f 4) (g-f 2, frm 2) 2000 AW 0-6: (6f 4, 7f 2) (Equi 2, Fibr 4)
Moderate gelding, effective 6f, acts on frm - acts on Fibr, has worn blinkers. Turf high 41. AW high 34.
**K A Ryan [0-12] The Gloria Darley Racing Partnership (from D W Barker [0-13] Spt 1999).*

FRENCH HORN BHB 80f **RR 95f** 4465[7]

3 b g Fraam - Runcina (Runnett) 7f **(59)**
Form - 8311077
Record 2000 - 1st:2 2nd:0 3rd:1 Ran:7
Pre2000 - 1st:1 2nd:0 3rd:0 Ran:6
Win Prizemoney £12,183 *Total Prizemoney* £12,894
Wins * 2000 May Chepst (HVY) 8.1f 95+ <
*** 2000** Apr Doncas (G-S) H 8f 66 81+
* 1999 Oct Leices (SFT) H 7f 64 71
2000 Turf 2-7: (8f 2-6, 9f) (sft, g-s 1-1, gd 1-2, g-f 2, frm)
Workmanlike, very useful gelding, effective 8f, acts on g-s. Turf high 95 - 1st of 5 getting 10lb from Barabaschi (29 May Chepstow RF 1515). Looked progressive on easy ground in the spring, winning twice, and did not do badly on a faster surface later in the season. One to keep in mind for a good handicap this term
**M J Ryan [3-13] The French Horn Hotel Ltd Sonning.*

FRENCH LIEUTENANT **RR 89f** 2183[21]

3 b c Cadeaux Genereux 7.9f **(76)** - Madame Crecy (USA) (Al Nasr (FR)) 9.3f **(68)**
Form - 620
Record 2000 - 1st:0 2nd:1 3rd:0 Ran:3
Pre2000 - 1st:0 2nd:1 3rd:1 Ran:3
Win Prizemoney £0 *Total Prizemoney* £5,679
2000 Turf 0-3: (7f, 8f 2) (gd 2, g-f)
Scopey, useful colt, effective 7 to 8f, best at 8f, acts on g-s to g-f. Turf high 89 - 2nd of 7 getting 11lb from Black Silk (1 Jun Goodwood 8f gd RF 1621). **G A Butler [0-6] Mark Armitage.*

FRENCHMANS BAY (FR) **RR 96+f** 5108[3]

2 br c Polar Falcon (USA) 9f **(74)** - River Fantasy (USA) **(48df 42a)** (Irish River (FR)) 8.6f **(78)**
Form - 3
Record 2000 - 1st:0 2nd:0 3rd:1 Ran:1
Win Prizemoney £0 *Total Prizemoney* £4,025
2000 Turf 0-1: (7f) (gd)
Currently very useful colt. **R Charlton [0-1] Michael Pescod.*

FRENCH MASTER (IRE) BHB 36f57a **RR 52f 57a** 5056[9]

3 b g Petardia 8.2f **(58)** - Reasonably French (Reasonable (FR))
Form - 433310332070600
Record 2000 - 1st:1 2nd:1 3rd:5 Ran:14
Pre2000 - 1st:0 2nd:0 3rd:2 Ran:7
Win Prizemoney £1,968 *Total Prizemoney* £5,842
Wins 2000 Mar Southw (GD) S 10f 64 <
2000 Turf 1-11: (8f, 9f 2, 10f 1-5, 11f, 12f 2) (sft, g-s 2, gd 1-2, g-f, frm 4, hrd) 2000 AW 0-3: (8f 2, 11f) (Fibr 3)
Fair gelding, effective 7 to 10f, acts on gd to frm, mostly wears blinkers (effectively). Turf high 64 (1st run) - 1st of 13 from College Rock (31 Mar Southwell RF 0586). AW high 56.
**J L Eyre [0-8] Wetherby Racing Bureau 48 (from P C Haslam [1-14] Jun 2000).*

FRENCH SPICE BHB 74f **RR** 331[4]

4 b f Cadeaux Genereux 7.9f **(76)** - Hot Spice (Hotfoot) 10.5f **(59)**
Form - 611111114
Record 2000 - 1st:6 2nd:0 3rd:0 Ran:7
Pre2000 - 1st:1 2nd:0 3rd:0 Ran:4
Win Prizemoney £15,458 *Total Prizemoney* £15,458
Wins * 2000 *Feb Southw (STD) 12f 73++*
*** 2000** *Feb Wolver (STD) H 12f 57 79* <
*** 2000** *Feb Wolver (STD) 8.5f 74+*
*** 2000** *Feb Wolver (STD) H 9.4f 57 69++*
*** 2000** *Jan Wolver (STD) H 9.4f 46 52++*
*** 2000** *Jan Wolver (STD) H 9.4f 46 48*
* 1999 *Dec Wolver (STD) H 8.5f 40 47*
2000 AW 6-7: (8f 1-1, 9f 3-3, 12f 2-3) (Fibr 6-7)
Light-framed, above-average filly, effective 8 to 12f, best at 12f, - acts on Fibr, excels at Wolverhampton. AW high 79 - 1st of 12 giving 17lb to St Lawrence (10 Feb Wolverhampton RF 0253) - also 1st of 13 giving 3lb to One Dinar (8 Feb Wolverhampton RF 0241). Inconsistent. Expertly placed to land a seven-timer on Fibresand, she has now retired to stud. **Sir Mark Prescott [7-11] J Morley.*

FREUD (USA) **RR 110f** 5124[5]

2 b c Storm Cat (USA) 7f **(86)** - Mariah's Storm (USA) (Rahy (USA))
Form - 255
2000 Turf 0-3: (6f, 7f, 8f) (g-s 2, gd)
Currently Group-class colt. Turf high 110 (began Jly) - 5th of 10 to Tobougg (14 Oct Newmarket 7f gd RF 4988). Beaten at 1/5 on his debut in a Curragh maiden, but did not fare badly when fifth in the Dewhurst. He probably found the race coming too quickly when

unplaced in the Racing Post Trophy a week later.
**A P O'Brien in IRE [0-3] M Tabor & Mrs John Magnier.*

FRIAR TUCK BHB 78f **RR 80f** 4865[14]

5 ch g Inchinor 8.9f **(64)** - Jay Gee Ell (Vaigly Great) 7f **(58)**
Form - 021830113000
Record 2000 - 1st:3 2nd:1 3rd:2 Ran:12
Pre2000 - 1st:2 2nd:2 3rd:3 Ran:25
Win Prizemoney £56,197 *Total Prizemoney* £71,076
Wins * 2000 Jly Ayr (FRM) H 6f 69 76
*** 2000** Jly Carlis (FM) 5f 57
*** 2000** Jun York (G-F) H 6f 65 70
* 1998 Jun York (G-S) H 6f 95 100 <
* 1997 Jly Ayr (G-F) 6f 81
2000 Turf 3-12: (5f 1-1, 6f 2-9, 7f 2) (sft, gd 2, g-f 2, frm 2-6, hrd 1-1)
Decent gelding, effective 5 to 6f, best at 6f, acts on gd to frm, best on frm. Turf high 80 - 3rd of 13 getting 1lb from Lago Di Varano (7 Aug Ripon 6f frm RF 3432) - also 1st of 11 from Mungo Park (24 Jly Ayr RF 3064). He had dropped a long way in the weights before forcing a dead heat in a competitive handicap at York in June and won twice within the space of three days in July at Carlisle and Ayr. Still running well, but looks held by the handicapper.
**Miss L A Perratt [5-37] Cree Lodge Racing Club.*

FRIENDLY HOSTESS RR 5024[9]

2 gr f Environment Friend 7.5f **(67)** - Gay Hostess (FR) (Direct Flight) 13.1f **(51)**
Form - 0
Record 2000 - 1st:0 2nd:0 3rd:0 Ran:1
2000 Turf 0-1: (6f) (g-s)
Currently very poor filly, always wears blinkers.
**J A Gilbert [0-1] The Black & White Partnership.*

FRILLY FRONT BHB 51f75a **RR 54f 75a** 3827[8]

4 ch f Aragon 7.7f **(58)** - So so **(56f)** (Then Again)
Form - 418P11016000500428
Record 2000 - 1st:3 2nd:1 3rd:0 Ran:15
Pre2000 - 1st:2 2nd:1 3rd:7 Ran:28
Win Prizemoney £18,545 *Total Prizemoney* £26,524
Wins * 2000 *Mar Lingfi (STD) H 5f 68 77*
*** 2000** *Feb Lingfi (STD) H 5f 60 66*
*** 2000** *Jan Lingfi (STD) H 5f 57 60*
* 1999 *Nov Wolver (STD) H 5f 54 55*
* 1998 Jun Mussel (SFT) 5f 84+ <
2000 Turf 0-8: (5f 6, 6f 2) (gd 4, g-f, frm 2, hrd) 2000 AW 3-7: (5f 3-7) (Equi 3-5, Fibr 2)
Scopey, average filly, effective 5f, acts on frm - acts on Equi, has worn blinkers, likes left handed tracks, likes tight tracks. Turf high 54. AW high 77 - 1st of 7 giving 20lb to Ready To Rock (4 Mar Lingfield RF 0402). Had a fair juvenile season, winning on her debut, but has shown improved form since being tried on sand, winning once at Wolverhampton and three times at Lingfield during the winter. Best over five furlongs but does stay six.
**T D Barron [5-43] M Dalby.*

FRISCO BAY RR 37f 1006[5]

2 b c Efisio 7.7f **(69)** - Kabayil **(74f)** (Dancing Brave (USA)) 8.4f **(76)**
Form - 5
Record 2000 - 1st:0 2nd:0 3rd:0 Ran:1
2000 Turf 0-1: (5f) (gd)
Currently very moderate colt. **T D Easterby [0-1] Elite Racing Club.*

FROMSONG (IRE) BHB 100f **RR 102f** 5107[2]

2 b c Fayruz 6.6f **(63)** - Lindas Delight **(48f)** (Batshoof)
Form - 512
Record 2000 - 1st:1 2nd:1 3rd:0 Ran:3
Win Prizemoney £2,908 *Total Prizemoney* £9,406
Wins * 2000 Spt Bath (SFT) 5.7f 97 <
2000 Turf 1-3: (5f 2, 6f 1-1) (gd 1-3)
Currently very useful colt. Turf high 102 - 2nd of 17 giving 5lb to Danehurst (20 Oct Newbury 5f gd RF 5107) - also 1st of 15 from Mootafayill (25 Spt Bath RF 4629). Looked very good when winning at Bath on his second start and was o good second in the rearranged Cornwallis Stakes at Newbury. Looks to have a future.
**B R Millman [1-3] The Fromsong Partnership.*

FRONTIER BHB 91f **RR 90f** 4755[1]

3 b c Indian Ridge 7.6f **(74)** - Adatiya (IRE) (Shardari) 11f **(46)**
Form - 533641
Record 2000 - 1st:1 2nd:0 3rd:2 Ran:6
Pre2000 - 1st:1 2nd:1 3rd:0 Ran:3
Win Prizemoney £15,793 *Total Prizemoney* £23,300
Wins * 2000 Spt Sandow (SFT) H 8.1f 86 90 <
* 1999 Oct Lingfi (G-S) 7f 84
2000 Turf 1-6: (8f 1-3, 10f 2, 11f) (g-s 1-1, gd, g-f 3, frm)
Useful colt, effective 7 to 11f, best at 8f, acts on g-s to frm, excels at Windsor. Turf high 90 - 1st of 18 giving 7lb to Scottish Spice (30 Spt Sandown RF 4755). Consistent. Fair form in ordinary handicaps last season without setting the world alight, until showing his liking for soft ground when scoring at Sandown in the autumn. Both of his wins have been gained at that time of year.
**R Hannon [2-9] Highclere Thoroughbred Racing Ltd.*

FRONTIER FLIGHT (USA) BHB 24f20a **RR 14f 20a** 5078[15]

10 b g Flying Paster (USA) - Sly Charmer (USA) (Valdez (USA)) 10.7f **(70)**
Form - 60700
Record 2000 - 1st:0 2nd:0 3rd:0 Ran:3
Pre2000 - 1st:1 2nd:0 3rd:0 Ran:15
Win Prizemoney £2,553 *Total Prizemoney* £2,771
2000 Turf 0-2: (8f, 12f) (g-s 2) 2000 AW 0-1: (14f) (Fibr)
Poor gelding. Turf high 5 (began Oct).
**P W Hiatt [1-23] S F Holder (from Miss L C Siddall [1-14] Aug 1996).*

FROSTED AIRE BHB 47f **RR 50f** 659[15]

4 ch g Chilibang 7f **(55)** - Suzannah's Song (Song) 7.2f **(61)**
Form - 00
Record 2000 - 1st:0 2nd:0 3rd:0 Ran:2
Pre2000 - 1st:0 2nd:0 3rd:0 Ran:4
2000 Turf 0-2: (6f 2) (g-s, gd)
Workmanlike, fair gelding, has broken blood-vessels.
**G G Margarson [0-6] The Shambles Partnership.*

FROZEN SEA (USA) BHB 28f35a **RR 30f 35a** 3085[7]

9 ch g Diesis 9f **(80)** - Ocean Ballad (Grundy) 10.3f **(65)**
Form - 0067
Record 2000 - 1st:0 2nd:0 3rd:0 Ran:4
Pre2000 - 1st:1 2nd:2 3rd:3 Ran:17
Win Prizemoney £2,660 *Total Prizemoney* £6,438
Wins 1996 Jun Yarmou (FRM) 14.1f 66 <
2000 Turf 0-2: (12f 2) (gd, frm) 2000 AW 0-2: (10f, 12f) (Equi 2)
Fair gelding, effective 12f, - acts on Equi, favours left handed tracks. Turf high 27. AW high 20.
**G L Moore [0-10] The Oaks Partners (from G P Enright [2-19] Spt 1997).*

FRUIT PUNCH (IRE) BHB 66f **RR 75+f** 4283[12]

2 b f Barathea (IRE) - Friendly Finance (Auction Ring (USA)) 8.6f **(65)**
Form - 5580
Record 2000 - 1st:0 2nd:0 3rd:0 Ran:4
2000 Turf 0-4: (6f, 7f 2, 8f) (g-f 2, frm 2)
Above-average filly. Turf high 75 (began Jly).
**T D Easterby [0-4] M P Burke.*

FRUITS OF LOVE (USA) RR 124+f 5331a[11]

5 b h Hansel (USA) 12.6f **(78)** - Vallee Secrete (USA) (Secretariat (USA)) 9f **(79)**
Form - 0130
Record 2000 - 1st:1 2nd:0 3rd:1 Ran:3
Pre2000 - 1st:4 2nd:3 3rd:4 Ran:19
Win Prizemoney £346,683 *Total Prizemoney* £607,525
Wins * 2000 Jun Ascot (G-F) G2 12f 124 <
* 1999 Jun Ascot (G-F) G2 12f 123
* 1999 Mar Nad Al (G-F) 12f 118
* 1998 Jly Newmar (G-F) G2 12f 114
* 1997 Aug Newcas (G-F) 7f 85+
2000 Turf 1-3: (12f 1-3) (hvy, gd 1-1, frm)
Very high-class colt, effective 12f, acts on hvy to g-f, best on gd, has worn blinkers, excels at Ascot. Turf high 124 - 3rd of 11 giving 11lb to Samum (3 Spt Baden-Baden 12f hvy RF 4289a) - also 1st of 9 giving 3lb to Yavana's Pace (23 Jun Ascot RF 2207). Consistent. A high-class international performer, he made a winning return to action in Ascot's Hardwicke Stakes in June, a race he also won in 1999. Suited by fast ground, he ran well in contrasting conditions in a Group One in Germany, but subsequently disappointed in the

Breeders' Cup and Japan Cup. **M Johnston [5-22] M Doyle.*

FUEGIAN BHB 54f37a **RR 57f 37a** 4544[13]
5 ch g Arazi (USA) 9.2f **(74)** - Well Beyond (IRE) (Don't Forget Me) 8.3f **(74)**
Form - 2010P000
Record 2000 - 1st:1 2nd:1 3rd:0 Ran:8
Pre2000 - 1st:1 2nd:2 3rd:0 Ran:16
Win Prizemoney £5,944 *Total Prizemoney* £8,420
Wins * 2000 Jun Windso (G-F) H 8.3f 56 57 <
* 1999 Jly Windso (GD) H 8.3f 48 56
2000 Turf 1-8: (8f 1-8) (gd, g-f 3, frm 1-4)
Fair gelding, effective 8f, acts on g-f to frm, best on frm, often wears blinkers, prefers right handed tracks, prefers tight tracks, excels at Windsor. Turf high 57 (1st run) - 2nd of 18 getting 8lb from Danakil (8 May Windsor 8f g-f RF 1102) - also 1st of 13 getting 7lb from Den's-Joy (19 Jun Windsor RF 2103). Becoming disappointing. He got off the mark at the twelfth attempt when making all at Windsor in July. Forcing tactics suit him.
**M Madgwick [2-23] D Knight (from R Charlton [0-2] Aug 1998).*

FUERO REAL (FR) BHB 39f **RR 42f** 1643[15]
5 b g Highest Honor (FR) 10.9f **(72)** - Highest Pleasure (USA) (Foolish Pleasure (USA)) 8.9f **(72)**
Form - 05310
Record 2000 - 1st:1 2nd:0 3rd:1 Ran:4
Pre2000 - 1st:0 2nd:2 3rd:0 Ran:7
Win Prizemoney £1,968 *Total Prizemoney* £3,601
Wins * 2000 May Bright (SFT) SH 11.9f 35 42 <
2000 Turf 1-3: (10f 2, 12f 1-1) (gd 1-2, g-f) 2000 AW 0-1: (13f) (Equi)
Moderate gelding, effective 10 to 13f, acts on gd to frm - acts on Equi, prefers left handed tracks, excels at Brighton and Lingfield. Turf high 42 - 1st of 14 giving 9lb to Grooms Gold (24 May Brighton RF 1422). (1st run) - 5th of 12 giving 8lb to Negative Equity (5 Feb Lingfield 13f Equi RF 0224).
**R J Hodges [1-15] Grandstand Jockeys.*

FUJIYAMA CREST (IRE) BHB 57f **RR 64f** 2839[5]
8 b g Roi Danzig (USA) 10.5f **(62)** -Snoozy Time (Cavo Doro) 10.6f **(57)**
Form - 07715
Record 2000 - 1st:1 2nd:0 3rd:0 Ran:5
Pre2000 - 1st:6 2nd:0 3rd:3 Ran:20
Win Prizemoney £46,681 *Total Prizemoney* £50,421
Wins * 2000 Jun Nottin (G-F) C 16f 62
1996 Spt Ascot (G-F) H 16.2f 86 92 <
2000 Turf 1-5: (14f, 16f 1-2, 17f, 18f) (gd 2, g-f 1-1, frm, hrd)
Average gelding, often wears blinkers (extremely effectively), likes left handed tracks, likes tight tracks. Turf high 64. Consistent.
**R Curtis [1-13] Glazer, Harris & Swaden (from Sir Michael Stoute [6-17] Spt 1996).*

FULHAM BHB 34f38a **RR 21f 38a** 3694[11]
4 ch c Safawan 6.6f **(60)** - Sister Sal (Bairn (USA)) 7.7f **(59)**
Form - 4280400
Record 2000 - 1st:0 2nd:1 3rd:0 Ran:7
Pre2000 - 1st:0 2nd:0 3rd:0 Ran:4
Win Prizemoney £0 *Total Prizemoney* £1,050
2000 Turf 0-3: (9f 2, 12f) (gd, g-f, frm) 2000 AW 0-4: (7f, 10f 2, 12f) (Equi 4)
Neat, moderate colt, often wears blinkers. Turf high 21 (began Jly). AW high 48. **M J Haynes [0-14] J P Saunders.*

FULL AHEAD (IRE) BHB 82f **RR 92f** 4987[25]
3 b c Slip Anchor 12.7f **(75)** - Foulard (IRE) (Sadler's Wells (USA)) 10f **(76)**
Form - 33221600
Record 2000 - 1st:1 2nd:2 3rd:2 Ran:8
Pre2000 - 1st:0 2nd:0 3rd:0 Ran:2
Win Prizemoney £2,730 *Total Prizemoney* £6,807
Wins * 2000 Jun Redcar (FRM) 14.1f 75 <
2000 Turf 1-8: (10f 2, 11f, 12f, 14f 1-2, 15f, 18f) (gd 4, g-f 3, frm 1-1)
Scopey, useful colt, effective 15f, acts on gd. Turf high 92 - 6th of 9 giving 5lb to Cephalonia (12 Jly Newmarket 15f gd RF 2745). Rather frustrating in his early starts as he always seemed to find one or two to beat him. Made the most of an easy opportunity in a four-runner Redcar maiden on very fast ground in June, and ran well in a listed race the following month. Lost his form afterwards and was sold to race over hurdles.
**M H Tompkins [1-10] thehorsesmouth co uk.*

FULL CIRCUIT (IRE) BHB 60f **RR 67?f** 1473[16]
4 ch g Keen 11.1f **(58)** - Ringawoody (Auction Ring (USA)) 8.6f **(65)**
Form - 0
Record 2000 - 1st:0 2nd:0 3rd:0 Ran:1
Pre2000 - 1st:0 2nd:0 3rd:0 Ran:5
Win Prizemoney £0 *Total Prizemoney* £262
2000 Turf 0-1: (8f) (g-f)
Average gelding. (DEAD)
**Ferdy Murphy [0-2] J Taqvi (from J Muldoon in IRE [0-5] May 1999).*

FULL EGALITE BHB 49f51a **RR 54f 51a** 4928[3]
4 gr g Ezzoud (IRE) - Milva (Jellaby) 6.4f **(58)**
Form - 0701200235D3
Record 2000 - 1st:1 2nd:2 3rd:2 Ran:12
Pre2000 - 1st:1 2nd:0 3rd:0 Ran:9
Win Prizemoney £4,946 *Total Prizemoney* £6,978
Wins * 2000 *Jun Lingfi (STD) S 12f 42*
1998 Nov Bright (SFT) 6f 72 <
2000 Turf 0-7: (10f 2, 11f, 12f 4) (gd 2, g-f 3, frm 2) 2000 AW 1-5: (12f 1-4, 13f) (Equi 1-5)
Workmanlike, fair gelding, effective 11 to 12f, acts on gd - acts on Equi, often wears blinkers (extremely effectively), likes left handed tracks, likes tight tracks. Turf high 54 - 3rd of 18 giving 5lb to Divorce Action (28 Aug Warwick 11f gd RF 4054). AW high 57.
**B R Johnson [1-12] Mrs P J Sheen (from W J Haggas [1-9] Aug 1999).*

FULL FLOW (USA) RR 112f 4698[8]
3 b c Eagle Eyed (USA) - Fast Flow (USA) (Riverman (USA)) 9.1f **(76)**
Form - 440128
Record 2000 - 1st:1 2nd:1 3rd:0 Ran:6
Pre2000 - 1st:1 2nd:1 3rd:0 Ran:3
Win Prizemoney £12,704 *Total Prizemoney* £23,566
Wins * 2000 Aug Bath (GD) 8f 99 <
* 1999 Jun Newcas (G-F) 6f 85+
2000 Turf 1-6: (7f 2, 8f 1-3, 9f) (gd 2, g-f 1-4)
Scopey, Group-class colt, effective 7 to 9f, acts on g-f. Turf high 112 - 2nd of 6 giving 9lb to Compton Bolter (16 Spt Newbury 9f g-f RF 4467). A half-brother to Auction House, he was caught in the void between handicapper and pattern-race performer last season, his only victory coming in a Bath conditions event.
**B W Hills [2-9] K Abdulla.*

FULLOPEP BHB 61f **RR 62df** 5104[12]
6 b g Dunbeath (USA) 9.9f **(53)** - Suggia (Alzao (USA)) 7.1f **(68)**
Form - 0
Record 2000 - 1st:0 2nd:0 3rd:0 Ran:1
Pre2000 - 1st:2 2nd:2 3rd:1 Ran:15
Win Prizemoney £2,617 *Total Prizemoney* £5,034
Wins * 1997 May Catter (G-F) 12f 57+ <
2000 Turf 0-1: (15f) (gd)
Average gelding. **Mrs M Reveley [5-23] & Mrs W J Williams.*

FULL SPATE RR 67f 3984[10]
5 ch h Unfuwain (USA) 11.4f **(74)** - Double River (USA) (Irish River (FR)) 8.6f **(78)**
Form - 360354103040
Record 2000 - 1st:1 2nd:0 3rd:3 Ran:12
Pre2000 - 1st:1 2nd:1 3rd:2 Ran:15
Win Prizemoney £14,737 *Total Prizemoney* £20,693
Wins * 2000 Jly Haydoc (G-F) H 6f 63 67
* 1999 May Thirsk (G-F) H 7f 73 76 <
2000 Turf 1-12: (6f 1-11, 7f) (sft, gd 3, g-f 4, frm 1-4)
Average colt, effective 6 to 7f, best at 7f, acts on sft to frm, best on frm, likes left handed tracks, likes tight tracks. Turf high 67 - 3rd of 11 getting 5lb from Friar Tuck (24 Jly Ayr 6f frm RF 3064) - also 1st of 19 giving 7lb to Cool Prospect (6 Jly Haydock RF 2573). Consistent.
**J M Bradley [2-24] E A Hayward (from R Charlton [0-3] Jun 1998).*

FULLY INVESTED (USA) RR 84+f 4806[1]
2 b f Irish River (FR) 9f **(77)** - Shirley Valentine (Shirley Heights) 10.3f **(74)**
Form - 1
Record 2000 - 1st:1 2nd:0 3rd:0 Ran:1
Win Prizemoney £3,542 *Total Prizemoney* £3,542

Wins * **2000** Oct Lingfi (SFT) 7f 84+ <
2000 Turf 1-1: (7f 1-1) (g-s 1-1)
Currently decent filly. (1st run) - 1st of 15 getting 5lb from Modrik (4 Oct Lingfield RF 4806). From an excellent family, she looks to have a future. **H R A Cecil [1-1] K Abdulla.*

FUNNY GIRL (IRE) RR 92f 4170[6]

3 b f Darshaan 11.9f **(81)** - Just For Fun (FR) (Lead on Time (USA)) 8f **(65)**
Form - 56256
Record 2000 - 1st:0 2nd:1 3rd:0 Ran:5
Pre2000 - 1st:0 2nd:0 3rd:0 Ran:2
Win Prizemoney £0 *Total Prizemoney* £1,597
2000 Turf 0-5: (8f 2, 9f, 10f 2) (g-s, gd 2, g-f, frm)
Unfurnished, useful filly Turf high 92. Showed promise in both her juvenile starts, but was inclined to run freely and failed to get home. Did not fare badly in her early starts last term in listed events, but failed to hit the target despite being dropped in class. Has slipped down the handicap and may be able to find a small race.
**W R Muir [0-7] Vicki & David Fleet.*

FUNNY VALENTINE (IRE) RR 85f 5319[5]

2 ch c Cadeaux Genereux 7.9f **(76)** - Aunt Hester (IRE) (Caerleon (USA)) 8.6f **(71)**
Form - 25
Record 2000 - 1st:0 2nd:1 3rd:0 Ran:2
Win Prizemoney £0 *Total Prizemoney* £1,570
2000 Turf 0-2: (6f 2) (sft 2)
Currently useful colt. Turf high 85 (began Oct).
**T G Mills [0-2] John Humphreys (Turf Accountants) Ltd.*

FURNESS BHB 58f58a RR 58f 58a 5011[1]

3 b g Emarati (USA) 6.6f **(63)** - Thelma (Blakeney) 10.5f **(64)**
Form - 25251
Record 2000 - 1st:1 2nd:2 3rd:0 Ran:5
Pre2000 - 1st:0 2nd:0 3rd:0 Ran:3
Win Prizemoney £2,373 *Total Prizemoney* £3,819
Wins * **2000** *Oct Southw (STD) H 14f 53 62+* <
2000 Turf 0-2: (12f, 16f) (gd, frm) 2000 AW 1-3: (12f, 14f 1-1, 15f) (Fibr 1-3)
Workmanlike, average gelding, effective 12 to 14f, - acts on Fibr. Turf high 58 (began Aug). AW high 62 (began Jly) - 1st of 16 getting 14lb from Vincent (16 Oct Southwell RF 5011).
**J G Smyth-Osbourne [1-8] T D Rootes.*

FURTHER OUTLOOK (USA) BHB 103f RR 102f 5324[2]

6 gr g Zilzal (USA) 8.5f **(79)** - Future Bright (USA) (Lyphard's Wish (FR)) 9f **(74)**
Form - 0080532536403003132
Record 2000 - 1st:1 2nd:2 3rd:5 Ran:19
Pre2000 - 1st:5 2nd:3 3rd:2 Ran:25
Win Prizemoney £75,988 *Total Prizemoney* £128,087
Wins * **2000** Oct York (HVY) H 6f 97 102 <
* 1999 Jun Doncas (G-F) H 5f 95 98
* 1999 Jun Epsom (GD,) H 6f 88 94
* 1999 Apr Pontef (G-S) H 6f 78 82
1996 Spt Hamilt (GD) 8.3f 96
1996 Aug Beverl (GD) 7.5f 85+
2000 Turf 1-19: (5f 8, 6f 1-10, 7f) (sft 1-2, g-s 3, gd 6, g-f 5, frm 3)
Very useful gelding, effective 5 to 6f, best at 6f, acts on sft to g-f, best on sft, excels at Epsom and does well at Ascot and Haydock. Turf high 102 - 1st of 22 giving 16lb to Card Games (7 Oct York RF 4865). He turned the corner once dropped to sprint distances in '99, winning three valuable handicaps. He ran well in similar company last term and made all at York in October. Already high in the weights, he had to race in conditions and listed races afterwards, running a good second at Doncaster. A game sort, he races from the front.
**D Nicholls [4-29] Mark Leatham (from Mrs A J Perrett [0-10] Oct 1998).*

FUSAICHI PEGASUS (USA) RR 5332a[6]

3 b c Mr Prospector (USA) 8.6f **(88)** - Angel Fever (USA) (Danzig (USA)) 8.4f **(76)**
Form - 126
2000 AW 1-3: (10f 1-3) (Dirt 1-3)
Currently top-class colt. AW high 126 (1st run) - 1st of 19 from Aptitude (6 May Churchill Downs RF 1154a). A high-class horse on dirt in the US, he sealed a memorable win in the Kentucky Derby with a tremendous turn of foot. He was subsequently sent off at very short odds for the Preakness Stakes but had to settle for second, and was a hot favourite for the Breeders' Cup Classic in which he failed to shine. **N Drysdale in USA [1-3] Fusao Sekiguchi.*

FUSUL (USA) BHB 52f62a RR 53df 62a 5154[2]

4 ch g Miswaki (USA) 8.1f **(81)** - Silent Turn (USA) (Silent Cal (USA)) 14.5f **(91)**
Form - 7411302502
Record 2000 - 1st:2 2nd:2 3rd:1 Ran:8

Fusaichi Pegasus sprouted wings in the Kentucky Derby

Pre2000 - 1st:0 2nd:0 3rd:0 Ran:9
Win Prizemoney £6,563 *Total Prizemoney* £9,016
Wins * **2000** *Feb Lingfi (STD) H 12f 51 61* <
* **2000** *Jan Lingfi (STD) 12f 50*
2000 Turf 0-2: (9f, 12f) (g-f, frm) 2000 AW 2-6: (10f, 12f 2-4, 13f) (Equi 2-6)
Leggy, average gelding, effective 12 to 13f, best at 12f, - acts on Equi, favours left handed tracks, favours tight tracks. Turf high 44 (began Aug). AW high 68 - 2nd of 17 giving 13lb to Fife And Drum (23 Oct Lingfield 12f Equi RF 5154) - also 1st of 8 getting 1lb from Lost Spirit (2 Feb Lingfield RF 0204).
**G L Moore [2-12] Allen,Barry Prichard Russell (from B Hanbury [0-5] Jun 1999).*

FUTURE COUP (USA) BHB 46f46a RR 50f 46a 4327[9]

4 b g Lord At War (ARG) 6.6f **(67)** - Holy Moly (USA) (Halo (USA)) 10.6f **(75)**
Form - 0004053040
Record 2000 - 1st:0 2nd:0 3rd:1 Ran:10
Pre2000 - 1st:2 2nd:2 3rd:1 Ran:8
Win Prizemoney £5,275 *Total Prizemoney* £9,020
Wins 1999 Spt Nottin (GD) SH 8.2f 51 55+
1999 Jly Beverl (G-F) C 7.5f 63 <
2000 Turf 0-7: (8f 4, 9f, 10f, 11f) (gd 3, g-f 3, hrd) 2000 AW 0-3: (8f 3) (Fibr 3)
Fair gelding, effective 7 to 10f, acts on gd to frm, best on frm, has worn blinkers. Turf high 50. AW high 44 (began Jly).
**J Norton [0-10] The Countess of Tyrone (from W J Haggas [2-8] Spt 1999).*

FUTURE FLIGHT RR 84f 5223[2]

2 b f Polar Falcon (USA) 9f **(74)** - My Branch **(103f)** (Distant Relative)
Form - 2
Record 2000 - 1st:0 2nd:1 3rd:0 Ran:1
Win Prizemoney £0 *Total Prizemoney* £1,412
2000 Turf 0-1: (6f) (gd)
Currently decent filly. (1st run) - 2nd of 21 getting 5lb from Heretic (27 Oct Newmarket 6f gd RF 5223).
**B W Hills [0-1] Wafic Said.*

FUTURE PROSPECT (IRE) BHB 51f48a RR 66f 48a 4361[11]

6 b g Marju (IRE) 9.2f **(76)** - Phazania (Tap On Wood) 10.3f **(65)**
Form - 255080
Record 2000 - 1st:0 2nd:1 3rd:0 Ran:6
Pre2000 - 1st:5 2nd:4 3rd:1 Ran:35
Win Prizemoney £14,561 *Total Prizemoney* £22,735
Wins * 1999 Jun Redcar (FRM) H 9f 62 64
* 1999 May Hamilt (G-F) H 8.3f 58 60
1998 *Jly Wolver (STD) C 8.5f 70*
1998 May Pontef (G-F) C 8f 73
1996 Jun Haydoc (G-S) 5f 81+ <
2000 Turf 0-6: (7f, 8f, 9f 4) (g-f 3, frm 2, hrd)
Average gelding, effective 7 to 10f, acts on g-f to hrd, best on frm, has worn blinkers, likes right handed tracks, excels at Redcar, likes Hamilton. Turf high 66 (1st run) - 2nd of 15 giving 2lb to Mehmaas (14 Jun Beverley 7f hrd RF 1951).
**M A Buckley [2-27] C C Buckley (from M Johnston [3-15] Spt 1998).*

F-ZERO BHB 74f RR 76f 474[13]

3 b g Bin Ajwaad (IRE) - Saluti Tutti (Trojan Fen) 8.1f **(62)**
Form - 10
Record 2000 - 1st:1 2nd:0 3rd:0 Ran:2
Pre2000 - 1st:0 2nd:1 3rd:0 Ran:3
Win Prizemoney £2,717 *Total Prizemoney* £3,577
Wins * 2000 *Mar Lingfi (STD) 8f 62* <
2000 Turf 0-1: (10f) (frm) 2000 AW 1-1: (8f 1-1) (Equi 1-1)
Scopey, above-average gelding. (1st run). Got off the mark in a weak four-runner maiden on the Lingfield Equitrack in March, but was far from impressive and looks modest.
**C F Wall [1-5] S Fustok.*

GABI (IRE) RR 42f 5152[9]

2 ch f Gabitat 8.5f **(44)** - Gabibti (IRE) (Dara Monarch) 8.8f **(59)**
Form - 0
Record 2000 - 1st:0 2nd:0 3rd:0 Ran:1
2000 Turf 0-1: (7f) (g-s)
Currently moderate filly.
**B Gubby [0-1] Brian Gubby Ltd.*

GABIDIA BHB 53f RR 63f 4505a[2]

3 br f Bin Ajwaad (IRE) - Diabaig **(70f)** (Precocious) 8.6f **(62)**
Form - 6486382
Record 2000 - 1st:0 2nd:1 3rd:1 Ran:7
Pre2000 - 1st:0 2nd:0 3rd:1 Ran:1
Win Prizemoney £0 *Total Prizemoney* £3,024
2000 Turf 0-6: (7f 2, 8f, 10f, 12f, 13f) (sft, gd 2, g-f 3) 2000 AW 0-1: (7f) (Fibr)
Leggy, average filly, effective 7f, acts on frm. Turf high 63.
**A J Martin in IRE [0-2] Mrs Ruth Fergus (from M A Jarvis [0-6] Jly 2000).*

GABLESEA BHB 40f41a RR 60f 41a 5113[12]

6 b g Beveled (USA) 6.9f **(64)** - Me Spede (Valiyar) 8.5f **(73)**
Form - 0246102858084600
Record 2000 - 1st:1 2nd:2 3rd:0 Ran:16
Pre2000 - 1st:4 2nd:5 3rd:7 Ran:47
Win Prizemoney £13,800 *Total Prizemoney* £23,019
Wins * 2000 Apr Warwic (HVY) H 10.5f 46 53
* 1998 Aug Haydoc (GD) H 8.1f 50 52
* 1998 Jly Chepst (GD) H 7.1f 44 48
* 1997 *Nov Southw (STD) H 7f 49 56* <
* 1997 *Spt Wolver (STD) H 8.5f 44 47*
2000 Turf 1-10: (8f 4, 9f, 10f 2, 11f 1-3) (hvy 1-1, sft, g-s, gd 2, g-f 4, frm) 2000 AW 0-6: (8f 4, 9f 2) (Fibr 6)
Average gelding, effective 7 to 11f, best at 8f, acts on hvy to frm - acts on Fibr, best on g-f, has worn blinkers, likes tight tracks, excels at Hamilton. Turf high 60 - 2nd of 15 giving 1lb to Etisalat (7 May Hamilton 8f g-f RF 1071) - also 1st of 19 giving 2lb to Pip's Brave (12 Apr Warwick RF 0690). AW high 51 - 6th of 12 getting 2lb from Jessinca (16 Mar Wolverhampton 8f Fibr RF 0445).
**B P J Baugh [5-64] Messrs Chrimes, Winn & Wilson.*

GADGE BHB 40f32a RR 44f 32a 545[11]

9 br g Nomination 7.3f **(57)** - Queenstyle (Moorestyle) 6.9f **(64)**
Form - 3400883870
Record 2000 - 1st:0 2nd:0 3rd:1 Ran:6
Pre2000 - 1st:9 2nd:7 3rd:11 Ran:94
Win Prizemoney £70,169 *Total Prizemoney* £88,867
Wins * 1998 Oct Bright (GD) 7f 68
* 1997 May Ayr (G-F) H 6f 66 80+ <
* 1997 May Goodwo (G-S) H 7f 66 72
* 1997 May Bath (G-S) H 8f 61 66
* 1997 May Thirsk (G-F) H 8f 58 63
* 1997 Mar Newcas (G-F) SH 8f 50 59
* 1997 *Feb Lingfi (STD) SH 8f 40 44*
2000 Turf 0-1: (7f) (frm) 2000 AW 0-5: (6f, 7f 2, 8f 2) (Equi, Fibr 4)
Moderate gelding, effective 7 to 8f, best at 7f, - acts on AW, best on Fibr, has worn blinkers, likes left handed tracks, likes tight tracks. AW high 30.
**A Bailey [7-68] J B Wilcox (from D Morris [1-22] Jun 1996).*

GAD YAKOUN BHB 31f28a RR 32f 28a 4748[16]

7 ch g Cadeaux Genereux 7.9f **(76)** - Summer Impressions (USA) (Lyphard (USA)) 9.9f **(72)**
Form - 000870000
Record 2000 - 1st:0 2nd:0 3rd:0 Ran:9
Pre2000 - 1st:1 2nd:0 3rd:1 Ran:11
Win Prizemoney £3,566 *Total Prizemoney* £4,136
Wins 1996 *Nov Lingfi (STD) 7f 69* <
2000 Turf 0-8: (5f 4, 6f 3, 7f) (g-s, gd 4, frm 3) 2000 AW 0-1: (7f) (Fibr)
Very moderate gelding. Turf high 32. Inconsistent.
**Mrs G S Rees [0-9] Capt James Wilson (from M G Meagher [1-11] Jan 1999).*

GAELIC FORAY (IRE) BHB 40f50a RR 33f 50a 5116[9]

4 b f Unblest - Rich Heiress (IRE) (Last Tycoon) 8.5f **(62)**
Form - 7035300
Record 2000 - 1st:0 2nd:0 3rd:2 Ran:7
Pre2000 - 1st:0 2nd:0 3rd:0 Ran:1
Win Prizemoney £0 *Total Prizemoney* £670
2000 Turf 0-2: (7f, 10f) (frm 2) 2000 AW 0-5: (6f, 7f 2, 8f, 10f) (Equi 4, Fibr)
Workmanlike, fair filly. Turf high 33. AW high 47.
**M R Ewer-Hoad [0-1] The Phoenix Partnership (Lewes) (from R P C Hoad [0-7] Aug 2000).*

GAELIC STORM BHB 115f95a RR 116f 95a 5324[3]

6 b g Shavian 7.7f **(67)** - Shannon Princess (Connaught) 7.7f **(63)**
Form - 0650464154712113
Record 2000 - 1st:4 2nd:1 3rd:1 Ran:16
Pre2000 - 1st:12 2nd:4 3rd:6 Ran:46
Win Prizemoney £172,668 *Total Prizemoney* £253,076
Wins * 2000 Oct Leopar (HVY) H 6f 116 <

* **2000** Oct Newbur (SFT) H 6f 107 111
* **2000** Spt Redcar (SFT) 7f 60
* **2000** Aug Klampe (GD) 6f 93+
* 1999 Oct Newmar (GD) L 6f 108
* 1999 Jly Ovrevo (GD) L 6.8f 104
* 1999 Jly Ovrevo (SFT) 6.8f 97
* 1999 May Goodwo (GD) 6f 111
* 1998 Oct Newbur (HVY) H 6f 105 109
* 1998 Oct York (GD) H 7f 102 105
* 1998 Jun Newcas (SFT) H 6f 95 98
* 1998 Jun York (G-S) H 6f 86 94
* 1997 Spt Catter (GD) 6f 76+
* 1997 Aug Epsom (GD) H 5f 81 83
* 1997 Aug Thirsk (G-F) H 5f 75 78
* 1996 Spt Sandow (G-F) 5f 84

2000 Turf 4-16: (6f 3-10, 7f 1-6) (hvy 1-1, sft 3, gd 3-6, g-f 4, frm, hrd)
High-class gelding, effective 6 to 7f, best at 6f, acts on hvy to g-f, best on gd, excels at Curragh and Newbury and Ovrevoll. Turf high 116 - 1st of 10 giving 10lb to Tiger Royal (28 Oct Leopardstown RF 5285a) - also 1st of 14 giving 15lb to Grey Eminence (20 Oct Newbury RF 5109). This globe-trotting sprinter enjoyed another good season in 2000. A tough sort, he is best coming late off a fast pace.
**M Johnston [16-62] H C Racing Club.*

Gaelic Storm, the globe-trotting sprinter

GALAPAGOS GIRL (IRE) BHB 80f **RR 76f** 4259[10]

2 b f Turtle Island (IRE) - Shabby Doll (Northfields (USA)) 9f **(72)**
Form - 120
Record 2000 - 1st:1 2nd:1 3rd:0 Ran:3
Win Prizemoney £3,688 *Total Prizemoney* £5,932
Wins * **2000** Jly Windso (G-F) 6f 77+ <
2000 Turf 1-3: (6f 1-3) (gd, g-f, frm 1-1)
Currently above-average filly. Turf high 77 (1st run) (began Jly) - 1st of 12 from Maine Lobster (24 Jly Windsor RF 3079). She made a winning debut at Windsor, but hung when beaten next time.
**B W Hills [1-3] Mrs Simon Polito.*

GALAPINO BHB 37f34a **RR 48f 34a** 5079[4]

7 b g Charmer 9f **(59)** - Carousella (Rousillon (USA)) 8.2f **(74)**
Form - 54860520804
Record 2000 - 1st:0 2nd:1 3rd:0 Ran:11
Pre2000 - 1st:7 2nd:10 3rd:6 Ran:63
Win Prizemoney £25,664 *Total Prizemoney* £49,056
Wins * 1999 Aug Sandow (G-S) H 16.4f 56 59
1998 Aug Goodwo (G-F) CH 9.9f 60 64
1997 Jun Warwic (G-F) H 12.5f 59 58
1997 Mar Doncas (G-F) H 12f 48 53
1997 *Jan Wolver (STD) C 12f 66*
1996 *Feb Wolver (STD) H 9.4f 65 76+* <
1996 *Feb Lingfi (STD) H 10f 65 69*

2000 Turf 0-11: (12f, 13f, 14f 2, 16f 6, 20f) (sft, g-s 2, gd 3, g-f 2, frm 3)
Average gelding, effective 14 to 18f, best at 16f, acts on g-s to frm, best on g-f, has worn blinkers, likes tight tracks. Turf high 48. Stays well, but lacks a turn of foot.
**J R Poulton [2-27] Glendale Partnership Ltd (from M R Channon [2-12] Jan 1999).*

GALAXY RETURNS BHB 63f **RR 69f** 5102[20]

2 ch c Alhijaz 7.7f **(57)** - Naulakha **(55f)** (Bustino) 10.4f **(64)**
Form - 7261700
Record 2000 - 1st:1 2nd:1 3rd:0 Ran:7
Win Prizemoney £3,233 *Total Prizemoney* £4,323
Wins * **2000** Aug Carlis (FRM) 5.9f 66 <
2000 Turf 1-7: (5f, 6f 1-3, 7f 2, 8f) (g-s, gd 3, g-f 1-2, frm)
Average colt, effective 6f, acts on g-f. Turf high 66 - 1st of 8 from Tefi (2 Aug Carlisle RF 3309).
**A Berry [1-7] Galaxy Moss Side Racing.*

GALI BHB 37f **RR 39f** 3437[11]

4 gr g Petong 7.6f **(58)** - Wasimah (Caerleon (USA)) 8.6f **(71)**
Form - 7000
Record 2000 - 1st:0 2nd:0 3rd:0 Ran:4
Pre2000 - 1st:0 2nd:0 3rd:1 Ran:6
Win Prizemoney £0 *Total Prizemoney* £501
2000 Turf 0-4: (8f 2, 10f 2) (g-f, frm 3)
Workmanlike, very moderate gelding, has worn blinkers. Turf high 39 (began Jly). Consistent. **C A Horgan [0 10] B R Tantoco.*

GALILEO (IRE) **RR 92f** 5282a[1]

2 b c Sadler's Wells (USA) 11.3f **(87)** - Urban Sea (USA) **(119f)** (Miswaki (USA)) 9f **(81)**
Form - 1
2000 Turf 1-1: (8f 1-1) (hvy 1-1)
Currently useful colt. (1st run) - 1st of 16 giving 5lb to Taraza (28 Oct Leopardstown RF 5282a). Bred in the purple, he could be anything. **A P O'Brien in IRE [1-1] Mrs John Magnier.*

GALLANT BHB 77f **RR 81?f** 5022[7]

3 b c Rainbow Quest (USA) 11.2f **(81)** - Gay Gallanta (USA) **(106f)** (Woodman (USA)) 9f **(74)**
Form - 347
Record 2000 - 1st:0 2nd:0 3rd:1 Ran:3
Pre2000 - 1st:0 2nd:0 3rd:0 Ran:1
Win Prizemoney £0 *Total Prizemoney* £877
2000 Turf 0-3: (7f, 8f 2) (g-s 2, gd)
Scopey, decent colt. Turf high 81 (1st run) (began Aug) - 3rd of 8 giving 5lb to Cafe Opera (28 Aug Newcastle 8f g-s RF 4045).
**Sir Michael Stoute [0-4] Cheveley Park Stud.*

GALLA PLACIDIA (IRE) **RR 74f** 4475[5]

2 b f Royal Abjar (USA) - Merrie Moment (IRE) (Taufan (USA)) 7f **(57)**
Form - 65
Record 2000 - 1st:0 2nd:0 3rd:0 Ran:2
2000 Turf 0-1: (8f) (g-f) 2000 AW 0-1: (8f) (Fibr)
Currently above-average filly. **R Ingram [0-2] Alex Fraser.*

GALLEON BEACH **RR 99df** 2823[P]

3 b c Shirley Heights 12.1f **(76)** - Music in My Life (IRE) (Law Society (USA)) 9.9f **(70)**
Form - 38P
Record 2000 - 1st:0 2nd:0 3rd:1 Ran:3
Pre2000 - 1st:1 2nd:1 3rd:2 Ran:4
Win Prizemoney £3,468 *Total Prizemoney* £11,542
Wins * 1999 Spt Hamilt (G-F) 8.3f 78 <
2000 Turf 0-3: (10f, 12f 2) (sft, gd, g-f)
Strong, very useful colt, effective 10f, acts on gd. Turf high 86.
**J W Hills [1-7] Christopher Wright.*

GALLERY GOD (FR) BHB 93f **RR 96f** 3206[2]

4 ch c In The Wings 11.2f **(77)** - El Fabulous (FR) (Fabulous Dancer (USA)) 9.4f **(70)**
Form - 063122
Record 2000 - 1st:1 2nd:2 3rd:1 Ran:6
Pre2000 - 1st:1 2nd:0 3rd:3 Ran:9
Win Prizemoney £12,233 *Total Prizemoney* £30,363
Wins * **2000** Jun Thirsk (SFT) H 12f 80 88 <

* 1999 Spt Newcas (G-F) 12.4f 82
2000 Turf 1-6: (12f 1-5, 14f) (g-s, gd 1-4, frm)
Scopey, very useful colt, effective 12f, acts on gd. Turf high 96 - 2nd of 8 giving 11lb to Wait For The Will (29 Jly Ascot 12f gd RF 3206) - also 1st of 8 getting 7lb from Rum Pointer (5 Jun Thirsk RF 1725). Improving. Despite being tried over further, he seemed best over 12 furlongs, winning at Thirsk before being touched off at Royal Ascot. Came from behind when second there at the King George meeting, but has run several good races when ridden aggressively. **G Wragg [2-15] Takashi Watanabe.*

GALLOWAY BOY (IRE) BHB 99f RR 98f 4519a[14]

3 ch c Mujtahid (USA) 7.4f **(69)** - Supportive (IRE) (Nashamaa) 7.1f **(66)**
Form - 0380
2000 Turf 0-4: (5f 2, 6f 2) (hvy, gd, g-f)
Very useful colt, effective 5f, acts on g-s. Turf high 98. Irish trained, he won twice over the minimum trip on soft ground as a juvenile in 1999, but failed to add to that in 2000. He needs to come down the handicap.
**D K Weld in IRE [0-3] C P Byrne (from S J Mahon in IRE [2-8] Apr 2000).*

GALTEE (IRE) RR 112f 1034a[2]

8 b h Be My Guest (USA) 10.2f **(66)** - Gandria (Charlottown) 10.9f **(57)**
Form - 2
2000 Turf 0-1: (12f) (gd)
Group-class horse. **in SWI [0-2].*

GALY BAY BHB 74f RR 72f 5320[11]

2 b f Bin Ajwaad (IRE) - Sylhall (Sharpo) 7.7f **(59)**
Form - 333260
Record 2000 - 1st:0 2nd:1 3rd:3 Ran:6
Win Prizemoney £0 *Total Prizemoney* £3,227
2000 Turf 0-6: (5f, 6f 2, 7f 3) (sft 2, g-s, gd 2, g-f)
Above-average filly, effective 6f, acts on sft. Turf high 72 - 2nd of 12 giving 20lb to Pharaoh Hatshepsut (9 Oct Ayr 6f sft RF 4869).
**A Bailey [0-4] D Martin (from D Morris [0-2] May 2000).*

GAME MAGIC BHB 64f RR 65f 3559[3]

2 b c Mind Games - Mia Fillia (Formidable (USA)) 9.2f **(63)**
Form - 443
Record 2000 - 1st:0 2nd:0 3rd:1 Ran:3
Win Prizemoney £0 *Total Prizemoney* £810
2000 Turf 0-3: (5f 2, 7f) (g-f, frm 2)
Currently average colt. Turf high 70.
**R Hannon [0-3] N A Woodcock.*

GAME N GIFTED BHB 99f RR 92f 4189[8]

2 b c Mind Games - Margaret's Gift **(92f)** (Beveled (USA)) 9f **(59)**
Form - 2158
Record 2000 - 1st:1 2nd:1 3rd:0 Ran:4
Win Prizemoney £2,488 *Total Prizemoney* £6,981
Wins * 2000 Jun Nottin (G-F) 5.1f 76 <
2000 Turf 1-4: (5f 1-2, 6f 2) (gd, g-f 1-2, frm)
Useful colt. Turf high 87. **B J Meehan [1-4] Margaret's Partnership.*

GAME TUFTY BHB 46f35a RR 48f 35a 5244[5]

4 b g Sirgame - Melancolia (Legend of France (USA)) 9.5f **(61)**
Form - P886225
Record 2000 - 1st:0 2nd:2 3rd:0 Ran:7
Pre2000 - 1st:1 2nd:1 3rd:3 Ran:16
Win Prizemoney £1,913 *Total Prizemoney* £5,936
Wins 1999 Oct Windso (SFT) S 10f 51 <
2000 Turf 0-6: (8f, 10f 2, 11f 3) (sft, g-s, gd, g-f, frm 2) 2000 AW 0-1: (12f) (Fibr)
Workmanlike, moderate gelding, effective 8 to 10f, acts on g-s to g-f, favours tight tracks. Turf high 48. Inconsistent.
**P Howling [0-7] Paul Howling (from J Pearce [1-16] Nov 1999).*

GAMITAS BHB 63a RR 53f 63a 5019[3]

2 b f Dolphin Street (FR) - Driftholme **(20f 26a)** (Safawan)
Form - 73
Record 2000 - 1st:0 2nd:0 3rd:1 Ran:2
Win Prizemoney £0 *Total Prizemoney* £317
2000 Turf 0-1: (8f) (frm) 2000 AW 0-1: (7f) (Fibr)
Currently average filly. (1st run) - 3rd of 9 to Monte Mayor Golf (17 Oct Wolverhampton 7f Fibr RF 5019).
**A P Jarvis [0-2] St Davids Racing Syndicate 1.*

GANDER (USA) RR 5332a[9]

4 gr c Cormorant (USA) - Lovely Nurse (USA) (Sawbones (USA))
Form - 0
2000 AW 0-1: (10f) (Dirt)
Currently Pattern-class colt, always wears blinkers.
**J P Terranova in USA [0-1] Gatsas Thoroughbred LLC.*

GARDEN IN THE RAIN (FR) RR 100f 4836a[3]

3 b f Dolphin Street (FR) - Marcotte (Nebos (GER)) 9f **(78)**
Form - 33
2000 Turf 0-2: (8f 2) (gd 2)
Very useful filly. Turf high 100 (began Jly) - 3rd of 10 to Terre A Terre (27 Spt Saint-Cloud 8f gd RF 4836a).
**A deRoyerDupre in FR [0-2].*

GARDEN OF EDEN RR 27f 4876[6]

2 b f Green Desert (USA) 7.8f **(78)** - All The Time **(57f)** (Dancing Brave (USA)) 8.4f **(76)**
Form - 6
Record 2000 - 1st:0 2nd:0 3rd:0 Ran:1
2000 Turf 0-1: (7f) (g-s)
Currently little account filly.
**Sir Michael Stoute [0-1] Capt J Macdonald-Buchanan.*

GARDEN SOCIETY (IRE) BHB 98f RR 99f 3563[6]

3 ch c Caerleon (USA) 10.9f **(79)** - Eurobird (Ela-Mana-Mou) 10.1f **(70)**
Form - 1336
Record 2000 - 1st:1 2nd:0 3rd:2 Ran:4
Win Prizemoney £4,257 *Total Prizemoney* £7,228
Wins * 2000 May Thirsk (GD) 12f 74+ <
2000 Turf 1-4: (10f 2, 12f 1-1, 14f) (gd 1-2, g-f, frm)
Unfurnished, very useful colt. Turf high 99 - 3rd of 6 getting 17lb from King Adam (10 Jun Doncaster 10f gd RF 1870). Held in conditions races since winning a maiden first time out. 12 furlongs looks his trip, but he has a bit of knee action and may be worth a try on easy ground. **J A R Toller [1-4] Duke of Devonshire.*

GARDOR (FR) BHB 68f RR 73f 5189[6]

2 b c Kendor (FR) 12.2f **(66)** - Garboesque (Priolo (USA))
Form - 44426
Record 2000 - 1st:0 2nd:1 3rd:0 Ran:5
Win Prizemoney £0 *Total Prizemoney* £1,979
2000 Turf 0-5: (6f 2, 7f 3) (gd 2, g-f 2, frm)
Above-average colt. Turf high 73 (began Jly).
**J G FitzGerald [0-5] Halewood International Ltd.*

GARDRUM (IRE) RR 4830[R]

2 ch c Lycius (USA) 8.8f **(71)** - Kafayef (USA) **(44tf)** (Secreto (USA)) 8.7f **(72)**
Form - R
Record 2000 - 1st:0 2nd:0 3rd:0 Ran:1
2000 Turf 0-1: (6f) (g-s)
Currently very poor colt. **Miss L A Perratt [0-1] David Sutherland.*

GARGALHADA FINAL BHB 100f RR 103f 4872[2]

3 b c Sabrehill (USA) 8.5f **(64)** - Secret Waters (Pharly (FR)) 9.8f **(68)**
Form - 12562
Record 2000 - 1st:1 2nd:2 3rd:0 Ran:5
Win Prizemoney £4,062 *Total Prizemoney* £8,700
Wins * 2000 Apr Leices (G-S) 10f 87+ <
2000 Turf 1-5: (8f, 10f 1-2, 12f 2) (hvy, g-s, gd 1-3)
Lengthy, very useful colt. Turf high 103 - 2nd of 9 giving 5lb to Cornelius (9 Oct Ayr 8f hvy RF 4872). Unraced at two, he was quite impressive when landing a ten-furlong Leicester maiden on his debut but was well held by Wellbeing next time. Ineffective on faster ground, he returned to some sort of form over an apparently inadequate mile on heavy in the autumn. Can build on that given easy ground next season. **J Noseda [1-5] Goncalo Borges Torrealba.*

GARGOYLE GIRL BHB 46f RR 49f 3701[3]

3 b f Be My Chief (USA) 10.2f **(62)** - May Hills Legacy (IRE) (Be My Guest (USA)) 9.3f **(67)**
Form - 0644555443
Record 2000 - 1st:0 2nd:0 3rd:1 Ran:10

Pre2000 - 1st:0 2nd:0 3rd:1 Ran:7

Win Prizemoney £0 *Total Prizemoney* £1,542

2000 Turf 0-10: (8f 2, 10f, 11f 3, 12f 3, 13f) (sft, gd, g-f, frm 5, hrd 2)

Scopey, moderate filly, effective 6f, acts on gd. Turf high 49. Consistent. **J S Goldie [0-17] J S Morrison.*

GARNOCK VALLEY BHB 65f71a RR 62f 71a 5188[1]

10 b g Dowsing (USA) 7f **(61)** - Sunley Sinner (Try My Best (USA)) 7.6f **(67)**

Form - 15216400362520138431

Record 2000 - 1st:3 2nd:2 3rd:3 Ran:17

Pre2000 - 1st:12 2nd:10 3rd:10 Ran:89

Win Prizemoney £49,167 *Total Prizemoney* £70,426

	Year	Month	Course	Going		Dist			
Wins	*** 2000**	Oct	Mussel	(SFT)	H	5f	55	62	
	*** 2000**	*Jly*	*Southw*	*(STD)*	*S*	*6f*		*67+*	
	*** 2000**	*Jan*	*Southw*	*(STD)*	*H*	*6f*	67	74	
	1999	*Nov*	*Southw*	*(STD)*	*H*	*6f*	62	66	
	1999	Oct	Newbur	(SFT)	H	5.2f	46	49	
	1999	*Apr*	*Southw*	*(STD)*		*7f*		62	
	1999	*Feb*	*Lingfi*	*(STD)*	*C*	*7f*		60	
	1999	*Feb*	*Wolver*	*(STD)*	*C*	*6f*		60	
	1998	Apr	Mussel	(G-S)	H	5f	60	64	
	1996	Oct	Haydoc	(SFT)	H	6f	74	88	<
	1996	Jun	Ayr	(G-F)	H	5f	71	74	
	1996	May	Mussel	(G-S)	H	5f	65	70	
	1996	Apr	Mussel	(CD)		5f		62	

2000 Turf 1-12: (5f 1-9, 6f 2, 7f) (hvy, sft, gd 1-5, g-f 2, frm 2, hrd) 2000 AW 2-5: (6f 2-5) (Fibr 2-5)

Above-average gelding, effective 6f, - acts on Fibr, has worn blinkers, likes left handed tracks, likes tight tracks, excels at Southwell. Turf high 62. AW high 74 (1st run) - 1st of 13 giving 29lb to Itch (3 Jan Southwell RF 0011) - also 1st of 8 giving 5lb to Purple Fling (21 Jly Southwell RF 3019). Effective on turf and sand at a modest level, he has won over an easy seven furlongs, but looks suited by shorter. **A Berry [3-17] Robert Aird (from J Berry [12-89] Dec 1999).*

GARRISON (IRE) BHB 53f44a RR 52f 44a 5295[3]

2 b f College Chapel - Milain (IRE) (Unfuwain (USA))

Form - 74763

Record 2000 - 1st:0 2nd:0 3rd:1 Ran:5

Win Prizemoney £0 *Total Prizemoney* £562

2000 Turf 0-5: (5f 3, 6f 2) (hvy, g-s 2, gd, g-f)

Fair filly. Turf high 52 (began Aug) - 3rd of 10 getting 5lb from Bowfell (1 Nov Musselburgh 5f g-s RF 5295). **Miss L A Perratt [0-5] Mrs K T McCluskey.*

GARTH POOL (IRE) BHB 69f88a RR 73f 88a 3504[2]

3 b g Sri Pekan (USA) - Millionetta (IRE) (Danehill (USA)) 10f **(72)**

Form - 511082

Record 2000 - 1st:2 2nd:1 3rd:0 Ran:6

Pre2000 - 1st:0 2nd:1 3rd:2 Ran:9

Win Prizemoney £5,023 *Total Prizemoney* £8,513

	Year	Month	Course	Going		Dist			
Wins	*** 2000**	*May*	*Southw*	*(STD)*	*H*	*6f*	72	*83++*	<
	*** 2000**	*Apr*	*Wolver*	*(STD)*	*C*	*5f*		*76+*	

2000 Turf 0-3: (5f, 6f 2) (sft, g-f, frm) 2000 AW 2-3: (5f 1-2, 6f 1-1) (Fibr 2-3)

Leggy, useful gelding, effective 5 to 6f, - acts on Fibr, has worn blinkers. Turf high 73. AW high 83 - 1st of 16 giving 21lb to Cryfield (8 May Southwell RF 1094) - also 1st of 13 giving 2lb to Noble Patriot (28 Apr Wolverhampton RF 0901). Inconsistent. Got off the mark when making all to win a claimer on the Wolverhampton Fibresand in April and those tactics look to suit him.

**A Berry [2-6] Exors of the late Lord Mostyn (from J Berry [0-9] Oct 1999).*

GASCON BHB 60f54a RR 66f 54a 4207[8]

4 b g Beveled (USA) 6.9f **(64)** - Lady Roxanne **(51+f 47a)** (Cyrano de Bergerac) 6f **(68)**

Form - 82408

Record 2000 - 1st:0 2nd:1 3rd:0 Ran:5

Win Prizemoney £0 *Total Prizemoney* £1,502

2000 Turf 0-5: (5f, 6f 4) (gd 2, g-f 2, frm)

Average gelding. Turf high 66 - 2nd of 9 giving 14lb to Najeyba (31 May Southwell 6f gd RF 1603). **D J Coakley [0-5] I E and Mrs K E D'Arcy.*

GAUDI (IRE) RR 94f 5050a[5]

4 b g In The Wings 11.2f **(77)** - Shuss (USA) (Princely Native (USA)) 8.6f **(81)**

Form - 127585

2000 Turf 1-6: (14f 2, 16f 1-3, 17f) (sft, g-s, gd 2, g-f 1-2)

Useful gelding, effective 12 to 16f, acts on g-s to g-f, best on g-f, often wears blinkers, prefers left handed tracks. Turf high 94 - 2nd of 11 giving 10lb to Catherina (14 Jun Leopardstown 14f g-f RF 2134a) - also 1st of 8 giving 5lb to Cape Clear (9 May Navan RF 1231a). Becoming disappointing. **J Oxx in IRE [1-10] Dundalk Racing Club.*

GAVEL (IRE) BHB 47f RR 46f 2228[17]

3 b g Rhoman Rule (USA) 15.1f **(64)** - Fall of The Hammer (IRE) (Auction Ring (USA)) 8.6f **(65)**

Form - 0000

Record 2000 - 1st:0 2nd:0 3rd:0 Ran:4

Pre2000 - 1st:0 2nd:0 3rd:1 Ran:4

Win Prizemoney £0 *Total Prizemoney* £285

2000 Turf 0-4: (7f, 8f 2, 10f) (gd 2, g-f, frm)

Lengthy, moderate gelding, has worn blinkers. Turf high 46. Inconsistent. **M H Tompkins [0-8] Flint Fairyhouse Partnership.*

GAY BREEZE BHB 76f RR 75f 5194[1]

7 b g Dominion 8.9f **(65)** - Judy's Dowry (Dragonara Palace (USA)) 6.1f **(55)**

Form - 3035006007221

Record 2000 - 1st:1 2nd:2 3rd:2 Ran:13

Pre2000 - 1st:5 2nd:7 3rd:3 Ran:30

Win Prizemoney £21,166 *Total Prizemoney* £40,934

	Year	Month	Course	Going		Dist			
Wins	*** 2000**	Oct	Mussel	(SFT)	H	7.1f	65	64	
	* 1998	Jun	Haydoc	(GD)	H	5f	61	70+	<
	* 1998	May	Doncas	(G-F)	H	6f	56	60	
	* 1998	Apr	Nottin	(SFT)	H	6.1f	49	56	
	* 1997	Spt	Yarmou	(FRM)	H	6f	43	48	
	* 1997	Aug	Leices	(GD)	H	5f	40	42	

2000 Turf 1-12: (5f 9, 6f 2, 7f 1-1) (sft, g-s, gd 1-5, g-f 4, frm) 2000 AW 0-1: (6f) (Fibr)

Above-average gelding, effective 5f, acts on g-s to frm, excels at Thirsk. Turf high 75 - 3rd of 18 giving 16lb to Bodfari Komaite (19 May Thirsk 5f gd RF 1322). **P S Felgate [6-37] E Rollinson (from D Nicholls [0-6] Oct 1999).*

GAY CHALLENGER BHB 51f46a RR 73f 46a 4822[9]

2 b g Young Ern - Ship of Gold (Glint of Gold) 9.3f **(66)**

Form - 504000

Record 2000 - 1st:0 2nd:0 3rd:0 Ran:6

Win Prizemoney £0 *Total Prizemoney* £318

2000 Turf 0-6: (6f, 7f 3, 8f, 10f) (g-s, g-f 4, frm)

Above-average gelding, effective 7f, acts on g-f. Turf high 73 (began Jly) - 4th of 4 getting 7lb from Londoner (9 Aug Yarmouth 7f g-f RF 3516). **N A Callaghan [0-6] N A Callaghan.*

GAYE CHARM (IRE) BHB 46f RR 48f 4402[12]

3 ch g Imp Society (USA) 7.1f **(63)** - Anoint (Connaught) 7.7f **(63)**

Form - 0600

Record 2000 - 1st:0 2nd:0 3rd:0 Ran:4

2000 Turf 0-4: (8f 3, 10f) (g-f 2, frm 2)

Moderate gelding. Turf high 48 (began Jly). **P S McEntee [0-4] M D Queripel.*

GAY HEROINE RR 73+f 4368[2]

2 b f Caerleon (USA) 10.9f **(79)** - Gay Gallanta (USA) **(106f)** (Woodman (USA)) 9f **(74)**

Form - 2

Record 2000 - 1st:0 2nd:1 3rd:0 Ran:1

Win Prizemoney £0 *Total Prizemoney* £1,302

2000 Turf 0-1: (8f) (frm)

Currently above-average filly. (1st run) - 2nd of 5 to Time Away (13 Spt Sandown 8f frm RF 4368). **Sir Michael Stoute [0-1] Cheveley Park Stud.*

GAY LOVER RR 21f 5070[13]

3 gr f Environment Friend 7.5f **(67)** - Gay Ming (Gay Meadow)

Form - 80

Record 2000 - 1st:0 2nd:0 3rd:0 Ran:2

2000 Turf 0-2: (10f, 12f) (g-s 2)

Workmanlike, currently little account filly. Turf high 21 (began Spt). **Dr J R J Naylor [0-2] W Clifford.*

GAZETTE IT TONIGHT BHB 58f48a **RR 62f 48a** 5115[10]
2 b f Merdon Melody 6.8f **(56)** - Balidilemma (Balidar) 7.9f **(63)**
Form - 556331331400
Record 2000 - 1st:2 2nd:0 3rd:4 Ran:12
Win Prizemoney £4,865 *Total Prizemoney* £6,551
Wins * 2000 Aug Thirsk (G-F) S 7f 62 <
*** 2000** Jly Catter (G-F) S 7f 52
2000 Turf 2-10: (5f 3, 6f, 7f 2-5, 8f) (g-s, gd 2, g-f 4, frm 2-3) 2000 AW 0-2: (5f, 8f) (Fibr 2)
Average filly, effective 7f, acts on g-f to frm, best on frm, prefers left handed tracks, prefers tight tracks. Turf high 62 - 1st of 14 from Petit Tor (25 Aug Thirsk RF 3971). AW high 41 (began Jly). **A Berry [2-12] The Gazetters.*

GDANSK (IRE) BHB 66f **RR 66f** 4871[15]
3 b g Pips Pride 6.7f **(70)** - Merry Twinkle (Martinmas) 7.6f **(59)**
Form - 402187400210
Record 2000 - 1st:2 2nd:2 3rd:0 Ran:12
Pre2000 - 1st:0 2nd:0 3rd:0 Ran:3
Win Prizemoney £6,994 *Total Prizemoney* £9,806
Wins * 2000 Spt Redcar (SFT) 5f 57
*** 2000** Jun Warwic (G-S) 5f 66 <
2000 Turf 2-12: (5f 2-8, 6f 2, 7f 2) (sft 2, g-s 1-1, gd 1-4, g-f 4, frm)
Workmanlike, average gelding, effective 5 to 6f, best at 5f, acts on g-s to g-f, prefers left handed tracks. Turf high 66 - 1st of 10 giving 5lb to Dancemma (4 Jun Warwick RF 1708) - also 1st of 22 getting 1lb from Whizz Kid (30 Spt Redcar RF 4748). Inconsistent.
**A Berry [2-12] Chris & Antonia Deuters (from J Berry [0-3] Nov 1999).*

GEE BEE BOY BHB 40f47a **RR 46df 47a** 3894[3]
6 ch g Beveled (USA) 6.9f **(64)** - Blue and White (Busted) 10.2f **(61)**
Form - 063
Record 2000 - 1st:0 2nd:0 3rd:1 Ran:3
Pre2000 - 1st:1 2nd:3 3rd:1 Ran:20
Win Prizemoney £2,448 *Total Prizemoney* £5,973
Wins 1997 Jun Redcar (GD) 11f 68 <
2000 Turf 0-2: (10f, 16f) (gd, hrd) 2000 AW 0-1: (10f) (Equi)
Moderate gelding. Turf high 42 (began Jly).
**G M McCourt [2-25] Daltagh Construction Ltd (from A P Jarvis [1-15] Aug 1998).*

GEEGEE EMMARR BHB 35f29a **RR 24f 29a** 124[9]
7 b m Rakaposhi King 9.3f **(55)** - Fair Sara (McIndoe) 13.8f **(32)**
Form - 0080
Record 2000 - 1st:0 2nd:0 3rd:0 Ran:3
Pre2000 - 1st:0 2nd:0 3rd:1 Ran:14
Win Prizemoney £0 *Total Prizemoney* £1,240
2000 AW 0-3: (8f, 15f, 16f) (Fibr 3)
Little account mare. Becoming disappointing.
**M J Polglase [0-4] Dr Frederick Cody (from S Gollings [0-13] Aug 1999).*

GEETEE RR 1966[7]
3 b g Good Times (ITY) 8.7f **(53)** - Sonairo (Tudor Rhythm)
Form - 7
Record 2000 - 1st:0 2nd:0 3rd:0 Ran:1
2000 Turf 0-1: (12f) (g-f)
Currently very poor gelding.
**N A Callaghan [0-1] Over The Hill Racing.*

GEETEE EIGHTYFIVE RR 44f 1811[12]
2 b c Magic Ring (IRE) 6.5f **(64)** - Versaillesprincess (Legend of France (USA)) 9.5f **(61)**
Form - 00
Record 2000 - 1st:0 2nd:0 3rd:0 Ran:2
2000 Turf 0-2: (5f 2) (gd, frm)
Currently moderate colt. Turf high 44.
**J J Bridger [0-2] Miss Julie Self.*

GEM BIEN (USA) BHB 75f **RR 60f** 5189[1]
2 b c Bien Bien (USA) - Eastern Gem (USA) (Jade Hunter (USA))
Form - 501
Record 2000 - 1st:1 2nd:0 3rd:0 Ran:3
Win Prizemoney £2,842 *Total Prizemoney* £2,842
Wins * 2000 Oct Mussel (SFT) 7.1f 60 <
2000 Turf 1-3: (6f 2, 7f 1-1) (sft, gd 1-2)
Currently average colt. Turf high 60 (began Spt) - 1st of 12 giving 5lb to Alakananda (26 Oct Musselburgh RF 5189). **Andrew Turnell [1-3] Mrs Claire Hollowood.*

GEMINI GUEST (IRE) BHB 62f **RR 66df** 5069[2]
4 ch g Waajib 8.9f **(67)** - Aldhabyih (General Assembly (USA)) 10f **(68)**
Form - 0573802
Record 2000 - 1st:0 2nd:1 3rd:1 Ran:7
Pre2000 - 1st:1 2nd:0 3rd:2 Ran:5
Win Prizemoney £3,496 *Total Prizemoney* £6,918
Wins * 1999 May Thirsk (G-F) 7f 74 <
2000 Turf 0-7: (8f, 10f, 12f 3, 13f, 14f) (g-s 2, gd 2, g-f 2, frm)
Strong, average gelding, effective 7f, acts on g-f. Turf high 66.
**G G Margarson [1-12] John Guest.*

GEM OF WISDOM BHB 48f48a **RR 49f 48a** 61[11]
3 gr c Factual (USA) - Indian Crystal **(45f 42a)** (Petong) 6.6f **(58)**
Form - 880
Record 2000 - 1st:0 2nd:0 3rd:0 Ran:1
Pre2000 - 1st:2 2nd:1 3rd:2 Ran:13
Win Prizemoney £3,690 *Total Prizemoney* £4,930
Wins 1999 *Jly Southw (STD) S 5f 55* <
1999 *Jun Southw (STD) S 5f 55* <
2000 AW 0-1: (6f) (Fibr)
Lengthy, moderate colt, effective 5f, - acts on Fibr, mostly wears blinkers (effectively).
**A Berry [0-1] Mrs B A Matthews (from J Berry [2-13] Dec 1999).*

GEMTASTIC BHB 60f68a **RR 55f 68a** 5117[2]
2 b f Tagula (IRE) - It's So Easy **(51f 31a)** (Shaadi (USA))
Form - 6833202
Record 2000 - 1st:0 2nd:2 3rd:2 Ran:7
Win Prizemoney £0 *Total Prizemoney* £2,015
2000 Turf 0-6: (5f 5, 6f) (gd 2, g-f 2, frm 2) 2000 AW 0-1: (5f) (Fibr)
Above-average filly, effective 5f, - acts on Fibr. Turf high 55. (1st run) - 2nd of 10 to Roxanne Mill (20 Oct Wolverhampton 5f Fibr RF 5117). **P D Evans [0-7] WWW GEM CARPETS CO UK.*

GENERAL ALARM RR 66f 5062[4]
3 b g Warning 8.1f **(77)** - Reprocolor (Jimmy Reppin) 8.8f **(64)**
Form - 74
Record 2000 - 1st:0 2nd:0 3rd:0 Ran:2
Win Prizemoney £0 *Total Prizemoney* £265
2000 Turf 0-2: (10f 2) (sft, g-s)
Leggy, currently average gelding. Turf high 66 (began Spt).
**J R Fanshawe [0-2] Lancen Farm Partnership.*

GENERAL DOMINION BHB 54f **RR 55tf** 4748[19]
3 b g Governor General 6.8f **(45)** - Innocent Princess (NZ) (Full On Aces (AUS))
Form - 886470
Record 2000 - 1st:0 2nd:0 3rd:0 Ran:6
2000 Turf 0-6: (5f, 6f 2, 7f, 9f, 10f) (gd 3, g-f, frm 2)
Leggy, fair gelding. Turf high 55. **Denys Smith [0-6] J Greenbank.*

GENERAL HAWK (IRE) RR 66f 1913[3]
2 b c Distinctly North (USA) 7.4f **(63)** - Sabev (USA) (Saber Thrust (CAN))
Form - 3
Record 2000 - 1st:0 2nd:0 3rd:1 Ran:1
Win Prizemoney £0 *Total Prizemoney* £412
2000 Turf 0-1: (6f) (frm)
Currently average colt. (1st run) - 3rd of 11 giving 5lb to Makboola (13 Jun Redcar 6f frm RF 1913). **R A Fahey [0-1] J E M Hawkins Ltd.*

GENERAL JACKSON BHB 67f **RR 72f** 4552[7]
3 ch c Cadeaux Genereux 7.9f **(76)** - Moidart **(88f)** (Electric) 10.1f **(61)**
Form - 04307
Record 2000 - 1st:0 2nd:0 3rd:1 Ran:5
Win Prizemoney £0 *Total Prizemoney* £1,001
2000 Turf 0-5: (7f, 8f 2, 10f 2) (g-s 2, gd, g-f 2)
Scopey, above-average colt. Turf high 72 - 3rd of 8 to Hilltop Warning (15 Jun Newbury 7f g-f RF 1991).
**D R C Elsworth [0-5] S R Leoni.*

GENERAL JANE RR 25f 1620[7]

2 ch f Be My Chief (USA) 10.2f **(62)** - Brave Advance (USA) (Bold Laddie (USA)) 5.6f **(69)**

Form - 37

Record	**2000** -	1st:0	2nd:0	3rd:1	Ran:2

Win Prizemoney £0 — *Total Prizemoney* £547

2000 Turf 0-2: (5f, 6f) (sft, gd)

Currently little account filly. Turf high 25.

**R Hannon [0-2] Miss Jane Collier.*

GENERAL KLAIRE BHB 45f68a RR 48f 68a 4652[6]

5 b br m Presidium 7.5f **(56)** - Klairover (Smackover) 6f **(52)**

Form - 56537136400146

Record	**2000** -	1st:2	2nd:0	3rd:1	Ran:10
	Pre2000 -	1st:2	2nd:5	3rd:3	Ran:33

Win Prizemoney £9,478 — *Total Prizemoney* £10,126

Wins							
* **2000**	*Jly*	*Southw*	*(STD)*	*H*	*7f*	*62*	*74*
2000	*Feb*	*Southw*	*(STD)*	*S*	*7f*		*47*
1999	*Spt*	*Southw*	*(STD)*	*H*	*7f*	*70*	*76* <
1998	*Jly*	*Wolver*	*(STD)*		*6f*		*70*

2000 Turf 0-2: (7f, 8f) (gd 2) 2000 AW 2-8: (6f, 7f 2-6, 8f) (Fibr 2-8)

Above-average filly, effective 6 to 7f, best at 7f, - acts on Fibr, favours left handed tracks, favours tight tracks, excels at Southwell. Turf high 23. AW high 74 - 1st of 12 giving 1lb to My Alibi (14 Jly Southwell RF 2819). She is a decent sort in handicaps on Fibresand, though she does not win that often. Probably better over seven furlongs than six.

**D Morris [1-3] Tommy Staunton (from R A Fahey [1-7] May 2000).*

GENERAL SONG (IRE) BHB 25f25a RR 54?f 25a 1208[13]

6 b g Fayruz 6.6f **(63)** - Daybreaker (Thatching) 8f **(66)**

Form - 0

Record	**2000** -	1st:0	2nd:0	3rd:0	Ran:1
	Pre2000 -	1st:1	2nd:0	3rd:0	Ran:11

Win Prizemoney £12,180 — *Total Prizemoney* £12,448

Wins				
* 1996	Spt	Capann	(GD)	7.5f

2000 AW 0-1: (7f) (Fibr)

Fair gelding, has worn blinkers. **K McAuliffe [1-12] K W J McAuliffe.*

GENERATE BHB 61f57a RR 59f 57a 2172[5]

4 b f Generous (IRE) 11.5f **(82)** - Ivorine (USA) (Blushing Groom (FR)) 10.3f **(76)**

Form - 16310215

Record	**2000** -	1st:3	2nd:1	3rd:1	Ran:8

Win Prizemoney £8,379 — *Total Prizemoney* £10,641

Wins							
* **2000**	Jun	Pontef	(SFT)	H	10f	57	59 <
* **2000**	*May*	*Southw*	*(STD)*	*H*	*11f*	*51*	*53*
* **2000**	*Feb*	*Wolver*	*(STD)*		*9.4f*		*41*

2000 Turf 1-4: (10f 1-3, 12f) (g-s 2, gd 1-1, g-f) 2000 AW 2-4: (7f, 9f 1-1, 11f 1-1, 12f) (Fibr 2-4)

Fair filly, effective 10 to 11f, best at 10f, acts on g-s to gd - acts on Fibr, best on g-s, favours tight tracks. Turf high 59 (1st run) - 3rd of 12 getting 8lb from Ringside Jack (19 Apr Beverley 10f g-s RF 0790) - also 1st of 12 giving 2lb to Smarter Charter (4 Jun Pontefract RF 1701). AW high 53 - 1st of 15 giving 15lb to Whistling Dixie (15 May Southwell RF 1209).

**M J Polglase [3-8] Dominic Racing.*

GENEROUS DIANA BHB 82f RR 78+f 5314[1]

4 ch f Generous (IRE) 11.5f **(82)** - Lypharitissima (FR) (Lightning (FR)) 7.9f **(74)**

Form - 211

Record	**2000** -	1st:2	2nd:1	3rd:0	Ran:3
	Pre2000 -	1st:1	2nd:2	3rd:0	Ran:4

Win Prizemoney £17,326 — *Total Prizemoney* £22,183

Wins					
* **2000**	Nov	Doncas	(HVY)	10.3f	70+
* **2000**	Oct	Yarmou	(SFT)	10.1f	78+ <
1999	Oct	Lingfi	(SFT)	9f	63

2000 Turf 2-3: (10f 2-3) (sft 2-2, g-s)

Neat, above-average filly, effective 10f, acts on sft to g-s, best on sft, prefers left handed tracks. Turf high 78 (began Oct) - 1st of 8 getting 1lb from Thundering Surf (25 Oct Yarmouth RF 5187) - also 1st of 12 giving 10lb to Ya Tarra (3 Nov Doncaster RF 5314). Unraced at two, she won a soft-ground Lingfield maiden in 1999. Switched to Henry Cecil, she did not reappear until October, but quickly made up for lost time by running second in a handicap and then taking a couple of conditions events. Should have little difficulty adding to her total if kept in training.

**H R A Cecil [2-3] Greenfield Stud (from K Mahdi [1-4] Oct 1999).*

GENEROUS TERMS BHB 92f RR 87f 1725[6]

5 ch h Generous (IRE) 11.5f **(82)** - Time Charter (Saritamer (USA)) 9.5f **(63)**

Form - 86

Record	**2000** -	1st:0	2nd:0	3rd:0	Ran:2
	Pre2000 -	1st:2	2nd:1	3rd:1	Ran:7

Win Prizemoney £9,296 — *Total Prizemoney* £15,698

Wins						
* 1998	Jun	Salisb	(G-F)	14.1f	104	<
* 1998	Jun	Leices	(GD)	11.8f	90	

2000 Turf 0-2: (12f, 13f) (gd, g-f)

Useful colt. Turf high 87. Becoming disappointing. Lightly raced, he looked a promising sort in 1998 but failed to fire last term. He ought to stay two miles, but is one to treat with caution at present.

**H Candy [2-9] H R H Prince Fahd Salman.*

GENEROUS WAYS BHB 59f53a RR 68f 53a 3927[6]

5 ch g Generous (IRE) 11.5f **(82)** - Clara Bow (USA) (Coastal (USA)) 11.5f **(72)**

Form - 4054010226

Record	**2000** -	1st:1	2nd:2	3rd:0	Ran:10
	Pre2000 -	1st:2	2nd:0	3rd:4	Ran:18

Win Prizemoney £16,093 — *Total Prizemoney* £22,716

Wins							
* **2000**	Jun	Ascot	(G-F)	H	16.2f	52	59
* 1999	Jun	Ascot	(G-F)	H	16.2f	57	62
1998	Aug	Redcar	(G-F)	H	14.1f	65	70 <

2000 Turf 1-9: (12f, 14f 2, 16f 1-6) (gd 1 3, g-f, frm 4, hrd) 2000 AW 0-1: (16f) (Fibr)

Average gelding, effective 12 to 16f, best at 16f, acts on gd to frm, has worn blinkers, excels at Ascot. Turf high 68 - 2nd of 9 getting 29lb from Virgin Soldier (11 Aug Newmarket 16f frm RF 3558) - also 1st of 16 getting 27lb from Temple Way (24 Jun Ascot RF 2242). Rather inconsistent, but won well at Ascot in June for the second year in a row. Ran two good races in the space of three days in August but was well beaten at Musselburgh at the end of that month. Best on fast ground.

**E J Alston [2-21] Honest Traders (from E A L Dunlop [1-7] Oct 1998).*

GENIUS (IRE) BHB 33f39a RR 30f 39a 904[11]

5 b g Lycius (USA) 8.8f **(71)** - Once in My Life (IRE) (Lomond (USA)) 8.8f **(65)**

Form - 0004022704050

Record	**2000** -	1st:0	2nd:2	3rd:0	Ran:8
	Pre2000 -	1st:3	2nd:1	3rd:2	Ran:38

Win Prizemoney £7,956 — *Total Prizemoney* £11,138

Wins							
1999	*Feb*	*Lingfi*	*(STD)*	*H*	*8f*	*64*	*68*
1998	*Feb*	*Lingfi*	*(SLW)*	*H*	*8f*	*69*	*73* <
1998	*Feb*	*Lingfi*	*(SLW)*	*H*	*8f*	*64*	*66*

2000 AW 0-8: (7f, 8f 4, 9f 2, 12f) (Fibr 8)

Very moderate gelding, effective 8f, - acts on Equi, has worn blinkers. AW high 45. Inconsistent.

**A G Juckes [0-3] A C W Price (from D W Chapman [0-16] Feb 2000).*

GENSCHER BHB 49f RR 57f 1958[9]

4 b g Cadeaux Genereux 7.9f **(76)** - Marienbad (FR) (Darshaan) 9.9f **(84)**

Form - 0

Record	**2000** -	1st:0	2nd:0	3rd:0	Ran:1
	Pre2000 -	1st:1	2nd:0	3rd:1	Ran:8

Win Prizemoney £4,005 — *Total Prizemoney* £5,249

Wins							
* 1999	Spt	Hamilt	(G-F)	H	12.1f	50	53 <

2000 Turf 0-1: (12f) (frm)

Scopey, fair gelding, effective 12f, acts on frm, prefers tight tracks.

**R Allan [2-14] Robert Miller-Bakewell (from M A Jarvis [0-2] Nov 1998).*

GENTLE ANNE BHB 47f43a RR 60df 43a 356[5]

3 b f Faustus (USA) 9.1f **(54)** - Gentle Stream (Sandy Creek) 8.9f **(59)**

Form - 345445

Record	**2000** -	1st:0	2nd:0	3rd:0	Ran:3
	Pre2000 -	1st:0	2nd:0	3rd:1	Ran:10

Win Prizemoney £0 — *Total Prizemoney* £537

2000 AW 0-3: (8f, 11f 2) (Fibr 3)

Unfurnished, average filly, effective 7f, acts on frm. AW high 43.

**Ronald Thompson [0-13] B Bruce.*

GENTLE MAGIC RR 50f 5223[11]
2 b f Magic Ring (IRE) 6.5f **(64)** -Gentle Stream (Sandy Creek) 8.9f **(59)**
Form - 0
Record 2000 - 1st:0 2nd:0 3rd:0 Ran:1
2000 Turf 0-1: (6f) (gd)
Currently fair filly. **H Akbary [0-1] & Mrs Kit Dudley.*

GENTLEMAN VENTURE BHB 81f **RR 85f** 5134[2]
4 b g Polar Falcon (USA) 9f **(74)** - Our Shirley (Shirley Heights) 10.3f **(74)**
Form - 36425513062
Record 2000 - 1st:1 2nd:2 3rd:2 Ran:11
Pre2000 - 1st:1 2nd:0 3rd:2 Ran:9
Win Prizemoney £10,067 *Total Prizemoney* £32,199
Wins * 2000 Aug Epsom (GD) H 12f 75 85 <
1999 May Redcar (SFT) 10f 73
2000 Turf 1-11: (10f 5, 12f 1-6) (sft, g-s 2, gd 5, g-f 1-3)
Workmanlike, useful gelding, effective 10 to 12f, best at 12f, acts on sft to frm, best on g-f, excels at Newbury and Goodwood and Newmarket. Turf high 85 - 1st of 9 giving 4lb to Mana d'Argent (16 Aug Epsom RF 3692). Consistent. Probably best over 12 furlongs, he was a very game winner at Epsom in August.
**J Akehurst [1-11] Canisbay Bloodstock Ltd (from S P C Woods [1-9] Oct 1999).*

GENTLE NIGHT RR 47f 5319[8]
2 b f Zafonic (USA) 9f **(83)** - Sahara Star (Green Desert (USA)) 8.6f **(78)**
Form - 8
Record 2000 - 1st:0 2nd:0 3rd:0 Ran:1
2000 Turf 0-1: (6f) (sft)
Currently moderate filly. **B W Hills [0-1] Maktoum Al Maktoum.*

GENUINE JOHN (IRE) BHB 23f33a **RR 32tf 33a** 4815[11]
7 b g High Estate 10.5f **(66)** - Fiscal Folly (USA) (Foolish Pleasure (USA)) 8.9f **(72)**
Form - 063324505300700
Record 2000 - 1st:0 2nd:1 3rd:2 Ran:12
Pre2000 - 1st:5 2nd:6 3rd:13 Ran:71
Win Prizemoney £14,733 *Total Prizemoney* £24,608
Wins * 1999 Apr Beverl (G-F) S 8.5f 52
* 1998 Jly Ripon (G-F) S 8f 59
* 1998 May Hamilt (GD) H 8.3f 40 50
* 1998 May Mussel (GD) H 8f 40 48
* 1997 *Mar Southw (STD) H 7f 65 64* <
2000 Turf 0-10: (10f 3, 11f 2, 12f 5) (g-s 3, gd, g-f 2, frm 3, hrd) 2000 AW 0-2: (11f, 12f) (Fibr 2)
Very moderate gelding, effective 8f, acts on frm, has worn blinkers. Turf high 40. AW high 40.
**J Parkes [5-76] Mrs G M Z Spink (from K Prendergast in IRE [0-13] Spt 1996).*

GEORGE STUBBS (USA) RR 49+f 5315[4]
2 b br c Affirmed (USA) 10.3f **(75)** - Mia Duchessa (USA) (Nijinsky (CAN)) 10.3f **(77)**
Form - 4
Record 2000 - 1st:0 2nd:0 3rd:0 Ran:1
Win Prizemoney £0 *Total Prizemoney* £468
2000 Turf 0-1: (8f) (g-s)
Currently moderate colt.
**P F I Cole [0-1] Richard Green (Fine Paintings).*

GEORGES WAY RR 58f 4532[8]
2 b c Petong 7.6f **(58)** - Glorious Aragon **(84f)** (Aragon) 8.1f **(60)**
Form - 78
Record 2000 - 1st:0 2nd:0 3rd:0 Ran:2
2000 Turf 0-2: (6f, 7f) (gd, frm)
Currently fair colt. Turf high 58 (began Aug).
**R F JohnsonHoughton [0-2] Exors of the late Lord Leverhulme.*

GERONIMO BHB 53f55a **RR 23f 55a** 4176[6]
3 b g Efisio 7.7f **(69)** - Apache Squaw (Be My Guest (USA)) 9.3f **(67)**
Form - 721666
Record 2000 - 1st:1 2nd:1 3rd:0 Ran:5
Pre2000 - 1st:0 2nd:0 3rd:0 Ran:1
Win Prizemoney £2,765 *Total Prizemoney* £3,571
Wins * 2000 *Jly Wolver (STD) 6f 71* <
2000 Turf 0-1: (9f) (frm) 2000 AW 1-4: (6f 1-2, 7f, 8f) (Fibr 1-4)
Small, above-average gelding, effective 6f, - acts on Fibr. AW high 71 (began Jun) - 1st of 8 from Resilient (13 Jly Wolverhampton RF 2780). **C W Thornton [1-6] Guy Reed.*

GET A LIFE BHB 30f **RR 25f** 3035[4]
7 gr m Old Vic 12.8f **(72)** - Sandstream (Sandford Lad) 7.8f **(54)**
Form - 050504
Record 2000 - 1st:0 2nd:0 3rd:0 Ran:6
Pre2000 - 1st:0 2nd:2 3rd:1 Ran:26
Win Prizemoney £0 *Total Prizemoney* £2,565
2000 Turf 0-6: (6f 4, 7f, 8f) (g-s, gd, g-f, frm 3)
Little account mare, has worn blinkers. Turf high 39. Inconsistent.
**G Woodward [0-12] A Jane (from M Brittain [0-12] Feb 1999).*

GET IT SORTED RR 3376[U]
2 ch f Superpower 6.6f **(58)** - Sophisticated Baby (Bairn (USA)) 7.7f **(59)**
Form - 5U
Record 2000 - 1st:0 2nd:0 3rd:0 Ran:2
2000 Turf 0-2: (5f 2) (g-f, frm)
Very poor filly. (DEAD) **M J Polglase [0-2] R D Letby.*

GET STUCK IN (IRE) BHB 82f **RR 83f** 5313[1]
4 b g Up and At 'em - Shoka (FR) (Kaldoun (FR)) 10.3f **(68)**
Form - 760544007230031
Record 2000 - 1st:1 2nd:1 3rd:2 Ran:15
Pre2000 - 1st:3 2nd:9 3rd:2 Ran:27
Win Prizemoney £35,305 *Total Prizemoney* £55,125
Wins * 2000 Nov Doncas (HVY) H 5f 73 83
* 1999 Oct York (SFT) H 6f 80 85 <
* 1999 Aug Ripon (GD) H 6f 70 75
* 1999 Jun Hamilt (GD) 6f 68
2000 Turf 1-15: (5f 1-5, 6f 10) (sft, g-s 1-2, gd 7, g-f 2, frm 3)
Scopey, decent gelding, effective 5 to 6f, best at 6f, acts on g-s to frm, has worn blinkers, excels at Ripon. Turf high 83 - 1st of 21 giving 6lb to Regal Song (3 Nov Doncaster RF 5313). Inconsistent.
**Miss L A Perratt [4-42] David Sutherland.*

GET THE POINT BHB 48f **RR 52f** 685[6]
6 b g Sadler's Wells (USA) 11.3f **(87)** - Tolmi (Great Nephew) 9.9f **(64)**
Form - 6
Record 2000 - 1st:0 2nd:0 3rd:0 Ran:1
Pre2000 - 1st:0 2nd:2 3rd:1 Ran:20
Win Prizemoney £0 *Total Prizemoney* £3,649
2000 Turf 0-1: (15f) (hvy)
Fair gelding.
**S Gollings [4-21] R L Houlton (from R Hollinshead [0-18] Spt 1997).*

GHAAZI BHB 44f51a **RR 49f 51a** 1419[13]
4 ch g Lahib (USA) 8f **(69)** - Shurooq (USA) (Affirmed (USA)) 9.3f **(79)**
Form - 431478880
Record 2000 - 1st:0 2nd:0 3rd:0 Ran:5
Pre2000 - 1st:1 2nd:0 3rd:2 Ran:11
Win Prizemoney £2,411 *Total Prizemoney* £3,603
Wins * 1999 *Nov Lingfi (STD) 8f 47* <
2000 Turf 0-2: (7f, 8f) (gd, g-f) 2000 AW 0-3: (7f, 8f 2) (Equi 2, Fibr)
Scopey, fair gelding, effective 8f, - acts on Equi, has worn blinkers. Turf high 29. AW high 42.
**Miss Gay Kelleway [1-10] A P Griffin (from E A L Dunlop [0-6] Jun 1999).*

GHADIR RR 56f 4270[8]
2 b f Bering 9.6f **(80)** - Malaika (GER) (Saumarez)
Form - 78
Record 2000 - 1st:0 2nd:0 3rd:0 Ran:2
2000 Turf 0-2: (7f 2) (g-f 2)
Currently fair filly. Turf high 56 (began Jly).
**E J O'Neill [0-2] M S Fakhry.*

GHAY (USA) RR 65f 4873[7]
2 b f Bahri (USA) - Jathibiyah (USA) (Nureyev (USA)) 8.7f **(78)**
Form - 7
Record 2000 - 1st:0 2nd:0 3rd:0 Ran:1
2000 Turf 0-1: (7f) (g-s)
Currently average filly. **M P Tregoning [0-1] Hamdan Al Maktoum.*

GHAYTH BHB 100f **RR 98f** 4600[9]
2 b c Sadler's Wells (USA) 11.3f **(87)** - Myself **(101f)** (Nashwan (USA))
Form - 6130
Record 2000 - 1st:1 2nd:0 3rd:1 Ran:4
Win Prizemoney £14,755 *Total Prizemoney* £23,255
Wins * 2000 Aug York (GD) 6f 98 **<**
2000 Turf 1-4: (6f 1-3, 7f) (gd, g-f 2, frm 1-1)
Very useful colt. Turf high 98 (began Jly) - 3rd of 8 getting 4lb from Noverre (8 Spt Doncaster 7f g-f RF 4296) - also 1st of 11 from King Charlemagne (23 Aug York RF 3917). He looked a colt with a future when landing the Convivial Maiden Stakes at York, but had his limitations exposed in Doncaster's Champagne Stakes and the Middle Park. He has stamina on his dam's side, but his dam never won beyond seven furlongs.
**Sir Michael Stoute [1-4] Hamdan Al Maktoum.*

GHAZAL (USA) RR 95+f 4737[1]
2 b f Gone West (USA) 7.8f **(82)** - Touch of Greatness (USA) (Hero's Honor (USA)) 8.2f **(86)**
Form - 21
Record 2000 - 1st:1 2nd:1 3rd:0 Ran:2
Win Prizemoney £5,638 *Total Prizemoney* £7,054
Wins * 2000 Spt Newmar (GD) 6f 95+ <
2000 Turf 1-2: (6f 1-2) (g-f 1-2)
Currently very useful filly. Turf high 95 (began Spt) - 1st of 17 from Cielito Lindo (30 Spt Newmarket RF 4737).
**Sir Michael Stoute [1-2] Hamdan Al Maktoum.*

GHUTAH BHB 24f **RR 34f** 788[8]
6 ch g Lycius (USA) 8.8f **(71)** - Barada (USA) (Damascus (USA)) 8.9f **(71)**
Form - 008
Record 2000 - 1st:0 2nd:0 3rd:0 Ran:3
Pre2000 - 1st:0 2nd:0 3rd:0 Ran:6
2000 Turf 0-1: (8f) (g-s) 2000 AW 0-2: (8f, 14f) (Fibr 2)
Very moderate gelding, has worn blinkers. AW high 1.
**Martyn Wane [0-14] J P Slattery.*

GHYRAAN (IRE) RR 99f 4841a[2]
3 b f Cadeaux Genereux 7.9f **(76)** - Karayb (IRE) **(89f)** (Last Tycoon) 8.5f **(62)**
Form - 2
2000 Turf 0-1: (10f) (gd)
Very useful filly. (1st run) - 2nd of 12 giving 4lb to Tawasila (30 Spt Longchamp 10f gd RF 4841a). **in FR [0-1].*

GIANT'S CAUSEWAY (USA) RR 129f 5332a[2]
3 ch c Storm Cat (USA) 7f **(86)** - Mariah's Storm (USA) (Rahy (USA))
Form - 1221111122
2000 Turf 6-9: (7f 1-1, 8f 2-5, 10f 3-3) (g-s 1-2, gd 4-6, frm 1-1) 2000 AW 0-1: (10f) (Dirt)
Top-class colt, effective 8 to 10f, best at 10f, acts on gd to frm - acts on Dirt, best on gd. Turf high 129 - 1st of 6 getting 8lb from Kalanisi (22 Aug York RF 3852) - also 1st of 8 getting 11lb from Kalanisi (8 Jly Sandown RF 2647). (1st run) - 2nd of 13 to Tiznow (4 Nov Churchill Downs 10f Dirt RF 5332a). Consistent. A very smart juvenile, he beat older horses on his return to action at the Curragh and looked likely to win the 2000 Guineas until he was cut down by King's Best. Filled the runner-up spot behind Bachir in the Irish Guineas and was a game winner of the St James's Palace Stakes at Royal Ascot. He appreciated the step up to ten furlongs by running out the gamest of winners of the Eclipse after a thrilling battle with Kalanisi, and maintained the sequence with another courageous win in the Sussex Stakes back at a mile. Acted out an almost identical finish to the Eclipse with Kalanisi in the Juddmonte International and the result was the same, before landing Group One number five in the Irish Champion Stakes. The sequence was broken when he was just beaten by Observatory in the Queen Elizabeth II Stakes at Ascot, but he lost no caste in defeat. He has rightly been labelled the 'Iron Horse'. He retires to stud at Coolmore in Ireland.
**A P O'Brien in IRE [9-13] Tabor/Mrs John Magnier.*

Giant's Causeway - The Iron Horse

GHOST OF A CHANCE (IRE) BHB 33f **RR 33f** 4930[25]
2 b c Indian Ridge 7.6f **(74)** - Ma N'Ieme Biche (USA) (Key to the Kingdom (USA)) 8.3f **(65)**
Form - 000
Record 2000 - 1st:0 2nd:0 3rd:0 Ran:3
2000 Turf 0-3: (6f 2, 7f) (gd 3)
Currently very moderate colt. Turf high 33 (began Spt).
**M H Tompkins [0-3] Mrs Jane Bailey.*

GHOST PATH BHB 15f **RR 24f** 256[7]
5 gr m Absalom 7.1f **(56)** - Glide Path (Sovereign Path) 9.3f **(55)**
Form - 07
Record 2000 - 1st:0 2nd:0 3rd:0 Ran:2
Pre2000 - 1st:0 2nd:1 3rd:0 Ran:4
Win Prizemoney £0 *Total Prizemoney* £1,040
2000 AW 0-2: (16f 2) (Equi, Fibr)
Little account filly.
**R J O'Sullivan [0-7] Jack Joseph (from C E Brittain [0-3] Aug 1998).*

GIBNEY'S FLYER (IRE) BHB 68f **RR 69f** 4181P
2 br f Magical Wonder (USA) 7.2f **(60)** - Wisdom to Know (Bay Express) 7.1f **(60)**
Form - 617P
Record 2000 - 1st:1 2nd:0 3rd:0 Ran:4
Win Prizemoney £2,828 *Total Prizemoney* £2,828
Wins * **2000** Aug Carlis (FRM) 5f 69+ <
2000 Turf 1-4: (5f 1-3, 6f) (g-s, g-f, frm 1-2)
Average filly. Turf high 69 (began Jly) - 1st of 6 getting 11lb from Midnight Venture (7 Aug Carlisle RF 3424). (DEAD)
**A Berry [1-4] Mrs U O'Reilly.*

GIFT OF GOLD BHB 78f64a **RR 84df 64a** 5317[7]
5 ch g Statoblest 6.4f **(63)** - Ellebanna (Tina's Pet) 6.8f **(59)**
Form - 0450013705706047
Record 2000 - 1st:1 2nd:0 3rd:1 Ran:15
Pre2000 - 1st:3 2nd:3 3rd:3 Ran:32
Win Prizemoney £28,400 *Total Prizemoney* £52,542
Wins * **2000** May Goodwo (SFT) H 7f 77 84 <
* 1999 Jun Goodwo (G-S) H 7f 80 83
1998 Jly Lingfi (G-F) H 7f 77 80
1997 Nov Mussel (G-S) 7.1f 73
2000 Turf 1-13: (6f, 7f 1-10, 8f 2) (sft 3, g-s 1-2, gd 6, g-f 2) 2000 AW 0-2: (7f, 9f) (Fibr 2)
Decent gelding, effective 7 to 8f, best at 7f, acts on g-s to g-f, best on gd, has worn blinkers, likes tight tracks, excels at Goodwood, likes Newmarket. Turf high 84 - 1st of 17 getting 3lb from Boomerang Blade (25 May Goodwood RF 1434). AW high 51. His only win of last season came at Goodwood and he returned to winning form there in May. He obviously likes that track and is suited by seven furlongs on easy ground.
**A Bailey [2-31] Classic Gold (from A Kelleway [1-8] Aug 1998).*

GIKO BHB 45f57a **RR 58f 57a** 4875[12]
6 b g Arazi (USA) 9.2f **(74)** - Gayane (Nureyev (USA)) 8.7f **(78)**
Form - 800656000030
Record 2000 - 1st:0 2nd:0 3rd:1 Ran:12
Pre2000 - 1st:3 2nd:2 3rd:5 Ran:25
Win Prizemoney £12,940 *Total Prizemoney* £29,099
Wins 1998 Jly Sandow (GD) H 8.1f 63 69
1998 Jun Goodwo (G-F) H 9f 55 60
1997 Aug Chepst (G-F) 7.1f 71 <
2000 Turf 0-12: (8f 4, 9f 3, 10f 5) (sft, g-s, gd 5, g-f 2, frm 3)
Fair gelding, effective 10f, acts on g-f, has worn blinkers (very effectively), likes tight tracks. Turf high 58 - 5th of 18 getting 18lb from Captain's Log (5 Jun Windsor 10f g-f RF 1733). Inconsistent.
**Jane Southcombe [0-2] V R V Partnership (from J R Poulton [3-34] Aug 2000).*

GILDA (IRE) BHB 75a **RR 60f 75a** 5296[5]
2 b f Goldmark (USA) - Pretty Precedent (Polish Precedent (USA)) 10.2f **(60)**
Form - 05
Record 2000 - 1st:0 2nd:0 3rd:0 Ran:2
2000 Turf 0-2: (6f, 7f) (sft, g-s)
Currently above-average filly. Turf high 60 (began Oct).
**B W Hills [0-2] E D Kessly.*

GILDED DANCER BHB 78f **RR 76f** 5066[8]
2 b c Bishop of Cashel - La Piaf (FR) (Fabulous Dancer (USA)) 9.4f **(70)**
Form - 3638
Record 2000 - 1st:0 2nd:0 3rd:2 Ran:4
Win Prizemoney £0 *Total Prizemoney* £1,012
2000 Turf 0-4: (5f, 7f 2, 8f) (g-s, gd, g-f, frm)
Above-average colt. Turf high 76.
**W R Muir [0-4] Percipacious Punters Racing Club.*

GILDERSLEVE BHB 42f28a **RR 44f 28a** 20[11]
5 ch m Gildoran 11.6f **(58)** - Fragrant Hackette (Simply Great (FR)) 8.2f **(65)**
Form - 0
Record 2000 - 1st:0 2nd:0 3rd:0 Ran:1
Pre2000 - 1st:0 2nd:1 3rd:1 Ran:15
Win Prizemoney £0 *Total Prizemoney* £1,191
2000 AW 0-1: (9f) (Fibr)
Moderate filly.
**G L Moore [0-1] Lancing Racing Syndicate (from N E Berry [0-11] Jan 1999).*

GILFOOT BREEZE (IRE) BHB 40f40a **RR 47f 40a** 442[7]
3 b g Forest Wind (USA) - Ma Bella Luna (Jalmood (USA)) 10.1f **(52)**
Form - 0747
Record 2000 - 1st:0 2nd:0 3rd:0 Ran:3
Pre2000 - 1st:0 2nd:0 3rd:0 Ran:6
2000 AW 0-3: (11f 3) (Fibr 3)
Moderate gelding, has worn blinkers. AW high 37. Inconsistent.
**J Norton [0-9] All Yorkshire Racing Club.*

GILL'S DIAMOND (IRE) BHB 56f55a **RR 56f 55a** 5008[11]
2 ch f College Chapel - Yafford (Warrshan (USA))
Form - 350030
Record 2000 - 1st:0 2nd:0 3rd:2 Ran:6
Win Prizemoney £0 *Total Prizemoney* £968
2000 Turf 0-4: (5f 2, 6f 2) (g-s, gd, g-f 2) 2000 AW 0-2: (5f, 6f) (Fibr 2)
Fair filly, has broken blood-vessels, effective 5f, - acts on Fibr. Turf high 56. AW high 53 (1st run) (began Spt) - 3rd of 12 getting 5lb from Acorn Catcher (30 Spt Wolverhampton 5f Fibr RF 4762).
**N Tinkler [0-4] W F Burton (from J J O'Neill [0-2] Aug 2000).*

GILT TRIP (IRE) BHB 50f **RR 36f** 4760[12]
2 b c Goldmark (USA) - Opening Day (Day Is Done) 6.3f **(67)**
Form - 000
Record 2000 - 1st:0 2nd:0 3rd:0 Ran:3
2000 Turf 0-2: (6f 2) (gd, frm) 2000 AW 0-1: (6f) (Fibr)
Currently very moderate colt. Turf high 36 (began Spt).
**J A Osborne [0-3] Sheer Madness Partnership.*

GILWILL RR 447[10]
5 b g Gildoran 11.6f **(58)** - Ming Blue (Primo Dominie) 6.2f **(80)**
Form - B0
Record 2000 - 1st:0 2nd:0 3rd:0 Ran:2
2000 AW 0-2: (7f, 9f) (Fibr 2)
Currently very poor gelding. **J M Bradley [0-2] R D Willis.*

GIMCO BHB 73f75a **RR 78f 75a** 3248[6]
3 b c Pelder (IRE) - Valetta **(35f)** (Faustus (USA)) 10f **(58)**
Form - 432216
Record 2000 - 1st:1 2nd:2 3rd:1 Ran:6
Pre2000 - 1st:0 2nd:0 3rd:0 Ran:1
Win Prizemoney £2,775 *Total Prizemoney* £5,489
Wins * **2000** *Jly Southw (STD) H* 12f 73 77 <
2000 Turf 0-5: (8f, 10f 3, 12f) (hvy, gd 2, g-f, frm) 2000 AW 1-1: (12f 1-1) (Fibr 1-1)
Scopey, above-average colt, effective 7 to 12f, best at 12f, acts on gd to frm - acts on Fibr. Turf high 78 - 2nd of 4 giving 5lb to Red Empress (21 Jun Ripon 12f g-f RF 2170). (1st run) - 1st of 8 giving 25lb to Niciara (3 Jly Southwell RF 2482). He has shown a little bit of ability on turf, but got off the mark on Fibresand at the first attempt at Southwell in July.
**G C H Chung [1-6] Osvaldo Pedroni (from A Kelleway [0-1] Jun 1999).*

GINA (IRE) RR 30f 5318[16]
2 b f Lahib (USA) 8f **(69)** - Relankina (IRE) (Broken Hearted)
Form - 0
Record 2000 - 1st:0 2nd:0 3rd:0 Ran:1
2000 Turf 0-1: (6f) (sft)
Currently moderate filly. **J A Glover [0-1] Countrywide Classics Ltd.*

GINGKO BHB 66f65a **RR 74f 65a** 4224[12]
3 b g Pursuit of Love 9.5f **(69)** - Arboretum (IRE) (Green Desert (USA)) 8.6f **(78)**
Form - 44460
Record 2000 - 1st:0 2nd:0 3rd:0 Ran:5
Win Prizemoney £0 *Total Prizemoney* £564
2000 Turf 0-4: (7f 2, 8f 2) (gd, g-f 2, frm) 2000 AW 0-1: (6f) (Fibr)
Lengthy, above-average gelding. Turf high 74.
**J G Smyth-Osbourne [0-5] Lady Rothschild.*

GINISKI PARK BHB 20f **RR 30f** 37[8]
4 b f Risk Me (FR) 8f **(53)** - Georgina Park (Silly Season) 9.7f **(56)**
Form - 08
Record 2000 - 1st:0 2nd:0 3rd:0 Ran:1
Pre2000 - 1st:0 2nd:0 3rd:0 Ran:5

2000 AW 0-1: (7f) (Fibr)
Very moderate filly, has worn blinkers.
**Mrs N Macauley [0-2] Appleby Lodge Stud (from J Wharton [0-4] Dec 1998).*

GINNER MORRIS BHB 48f42a **RR 48f 42a** 5166[14]
5 b g Emarati (USA) 6.6f **(63)** - Just Run (IRE) (Runnett) 7f **(59)**
Form - 70410
Record 2000 - 1st:1 2nd:0 3rd:0 Ran:5
Pre2000 - 1st:0 2nd:2 3rd:0 Ran:17
Win Prizemoney £2,922 *Total Prizemoney* £4,073
Wins * 2000 Oct Newcas (HVY) CH 8f 41 48 <
2000 Turf 1-5: (8f 1-3, 9f, 11f) (hvy 2, sft 1-1, gd, g-f)
Moderate gelding, effective 8 to 9f, acts on sft to gd, has worn blinkers, favours left handed tracks. Turf high 48 - 1st of 20 getting 7lb from King Tut (18 Oct Newcastle RF 5056). Inconsistent.
**J Hetherton [1-10] Formulated Polymer Products Ltd (from C B B Booth [0-17] May 1999).*

GINNY WOSSERNAME BHB 28f33a **RR 20f 33a** 3181[8]
6 br m Prince Sabo 6.6f **(64)** - Leprechaun Lady (Royal Blend) 11.9f **(58)**
Form - 08
Record 2000 - 1st:0 2nd:0 3rd:0 Ran:2
Pre2000 - 1st:1 2nd:1 3rd:3 Ran:17
Win Prizemoney £2,690 *Total Prizemoney* £4,220
Wins 1996 Jly Warwic (G-F) C 7f 47 <
2000 Turf 0-2: (7f, 10f) (gd, frm)
Little account mare, often wears blinkers. Turf high 20 (began Jly).
**Dr J R J Naylor [0-2] Mrs Clare Lawrence (from W G M Turner [1-12] Nov 1997).*

GINOLA'S MAGIC (IRE) BHB 103f **RR 98+f** 1285a[7]
3 b c Perugino (USA) - Simple Annie (Simply Great (FR)) 8.2f **(65)**
Form - 7
Record 2000 - 1st:0 2nd:0 3rd:0 Ran:1
Pre2000 - 1st:2 2nd:0 3rd:1 Ran:6
Win Prizemoney £7,132 *Total Prizemoney* £11,507
Wins * 1999 Jun Epsom (GD) 7f 95+
* 1999 Jun Kempto (GD) 6f 98+ <
2000 Turf 0-1: (8f) (gd)
Unfurnished, very useful colt, effective 6 to 7f, best at 6f, acts on g-f to frm, best on g-f. **R Hannon [2-7].*

GIN PALACE (IRE) RR 74f 4541[6]
2 b gr c King's Theatre (IRE) - Ikala (Lashkari) 9.8f **(67)**
Form - 6
Record 2000 - 1st:0 2nd:0 3rd:0 Ran:1
Win Prizemoney £0 *Total Prizemoney* £161
2000 Turf 0-1: (7f) (gd)
Currently above-average colt. **G L Moore [0-1] Mrs Patricia Gilmore.*

GIRARE (IRE) RR 400[6]
4 b g Arctic Tern (USA) 12.2f **(71)** - Kirova (USA) (Nijinsky (CAN)) 10.3f **(77)**
Form - 6
Record 2000 - 1st:0 2nd:0 3rd:0 Ran:1
2000 AW 0-1: (10f) (Equi)
Very moderate gelding.
**G L Moore [0-1] The Tuesday Syndicate.*

GIRL BAND (IRE) BHB 57f **RR 57f** 4129[9]
2 b f Bluebird (USA) 7.9f **(71)** - Bandit Girl **(70f)** (Robellino (USA)) 7.6f **(80)**
Form - 0680
Record 2000 - 1st:0 2nd:0 3rd:0 Ran:4
2000 Turf 0-4: (6f 2, 7f 2) (g-f, frm 3)
Fair filly, has worn blinkers. Turf high 57 (began Jly).
**M R Channon [0-4] John Livock.*

GIRL FRIDAY RR 11f 4454[11]
2 ch f Ajraas (USA) 7f **(53)** - Miss Nonnie (High Kicker (USA))
Form - 0
Record 2000 - 1st:0 2nd:0 3rd:0 Ran:1
2000 Turf 0-1: (6f) (g-s)
Currently poor filly. **Ronald Thompson [0-1] G M Pugh.*

GIRLIE SET (IRE) BHB 73f57a **RR 74f 57a** 90[10]
5 b m Second Set (IRE) 9.2f **(67)** - Heavenward (USA) (Conquistador Cielo (USA)) 8.8f **(69)**
Form - 0
Record 2000 - 1st:0 2nd:0 3rd:0 Ran:1
Pre2000 - 1st:4 2nd:1 3rd:1 Ran:13
Win Prizemoney £12,665 *Total Prizemoney* £13,998
Wins 1999 Jly Yarmou (G-F) H 8f 53 74 <
1999 Jly Lingfi (G-F) H 9f 53 64
1999 Jly Mussel (G-S) H 9f 53 58+
1999 Jun Lingfi (G-F) H 9f 47 48
2000 AW 0-1: (8f) (Fibr)
Above-average filly, effective 8 to 9f, acts on gd to frm.
**A Streeter [0-2] J T Stimpson (from Sir Mark Prescott [4-13] Jly 1999).*

GIRL'S BEST FRIEND BHB 70f75a **RR 77f 75a** 4968[21]
3 b f Nicolotte - Diamond Princess (Horage) 10.3f **(61)**
Form - 00560000
Record 2000 - 1st:0 2nd:0 3rd:0 Ran:7
Pre2000 - 1st:1 2nd:1 3rd:0 Ran:6
Win Prizemoney £3,460 *Total Prizemoney* £4,871
Wins * 1999 Oct Lingfi (HVY) 6f 87+ <
2000 Turf 0-6: (7f 3, 8f, 10f 2) (sft 2, gd 4) 2000 AW 0-1: (7f) (Fibr)
Scopey, above-average filly, effective 6 to 8f, acts on g-s to gd. Turf high 77. Inconsistent. **D W P Arbuthnot [1-13] Stephen Crown.*

GIULIA MURIEL BHB 28f **RR** 2031[14]
4 ch f Dolphin Street (FR) - Formosanta (USA) (Believe It (USA)) 9.4f **(70)**
Form - 000
Record 2000 - 1st:0 2nd:0 3rd:0 Ran:3
2000 Turf 0-1: (10f) (g-f) 2000 AW 0-2: (7f, 11f) (Fibr 2)
Currently very poor filly, has worn blinkers.
**K A Morgan [0-3] Mrs S J Storer.*

GIVE AND TAKE BHB 42f **RR 32f** 1323[12]
7 ch g Generous (IRE) 11.5f **(82)** - Starlet (Teenoso (USA)) 9.9f **(72)**
Form - 0
Record 2000 - 1st:0 2nd:0 3rd:0 Ran:1
Pre2000 - 1st:0 2nd:0 3rd:1 Ran:4
Win Prizemoney £0 *Total Prizemoney* £525
2000 Turf 0-1: (16f) (gd)
Very moderate gelding.
**J E Long [0-3] Ms Breege Gilbride (from Lord Huntingdon [0-4] Oct 1996).*

GIVE AN INCH (IRE) BHB 66f **RR 70f** 5322[11]
5 b m Inchinor 8.9f **(64)** - Top Heights (High Top) 10.2f **(67)**
Form - 800071100
Record 2000 - 1st:2 2nd:0 3rd:0 Ran:9
Pre2000 - 1st:5 2nd:3 3rd:2 Ran:23
Win Prizemoney £27,841 *Total Prizemoney* £33,446
Wins * 2000 Spt Ayr (SFT) H 17.5f 60 70 <
*** 2000** Jun Pontef (SFT) H 17.1f 58 57
* 1999 Spt Ayr (G-S) H 17.5f 65 70 <
* 1999 Jun Pontef (GD) H 18f 62 65
* 1998 Spt Ayr (G-S) H 17.5f 51 61
* 1998 Aug Ayr (G-S) H 15f 44 53+
* 1998 Jly Redcar (G-F) S 11f 45
2000 Turf 2-9: (14f, 16f 3, 17f 2-5) (sft, g-s 3, gd 2-4, g-f)
Above-average filly, effective 16 to 18f, best at 17f, acts on gd to frm, best on gd, prefers tight tracks. Turf high 70 - 1st of 11 getting 11lb from Bhutan (15 Spt Ayr RF 4431). Winner of the same event at the Ayr Western meeting three years running, ideally she needs further than two miles, and she appears to act on any ground except the extremes. **W Storey [7-32] Black Type Racing.*

GIVE BACK CALAIS (IRE) BHB 97f **RR 98f** 4432[5]
2 b c Brief Truce (USA) 9.1f **(73)** - Nichodoula (Doulab (USA)) 9.8f **(65)**
Form - 3235
Record 2000 - 1st:0 2nd:1 3rd:2 Ran:4
Win Prizemoney £0 *Total Prizemoney* £10,482
2000 Turf 0-4: (5f 2, 6f 2) (gd, g-f 2, frm)
Very useful colt. Turf high 98 - 2nd of 11 giving 3lb to Autumnal (23 Jun Ascot 5f gd RF 2210). Showed ability on his Goodwood debut and, brought back a furlong, ran a blinder to finish runner-up in the Windsor Castle next time. Suffered a low blood count

after another good effort at Sandown, and that may have accounted for a disappointing run in a maiden on his return. Connections should be able to find a suitable race for him in 2001.
**P J Makin [0-4] Peter Melotti.*

GIVE NOTICE BHB 84f RR 95+f 3936[13]

3 b c Warning 8.1f **(77)** - Princess Genista (Ile de Bourbon (USA)) 10.1f **(67)**
Form - 0611100
Record 2000 - 1st:3 2nd:0 3rd:0 Ran:7
Pre2000 - 1st:0 2nd:0 3rd:0 Ran:2
Win Prizemoney £14,020 *Total Prizemoney* £14,020
Wins * 2000 Jly Kempto (G-S) H 14.4f 72 88+
*** 2000** Jly Haydoc (G-F) H 14f 72 95 <
*** 2000** Jun Yarmou (G-F) H 14.1f 62 77
2000 Turf 3-7: (8f, 10f, 14f 3-5) (gd, g-f 2-4, frm 1-2)
Scopey, very useful colt, effective 14f, acts on g-f to frm. Turf high 95 - 1st of 7 getting 7lb from Prince Among Men (6 Jly Haydock RF 2574) - also 1st of 5 giving 4lb to Busy Lizzie (12 Jly Kempton RF 2735). Inconsistent. Little show in maidens, but he completed a fine hat-trick in progressively better handicap company once stepped up in trip. Somewhat disappointing at Goodwood, however, and was tailed off at York. On to keep in mind for handicaps in midsummer, particularly if coming down the weights in the meantime. **J L Dunlop [3-9] I H Stewart-Brown.*

GIVE THE SLIP BHB 110f RR 111+f 3914[1]

3 b c Slip Anchor 12.7f **(75)** - Falafil (FR) (Fabulous Dancer (USA)) 9.4f **(70)**
Form - 312141
Record 2000 - 1st:3 2nd:1 3rd:1 Ran:6
Pre2000 - 1st:0 2nd:0 3rd:1 Ran:2
Win Prizemoney £152,755 *Total Prizemoney* £167,224
Wins * 2000 Aug York (GD) H 13.9f 101 109+ <
*** 2000** Jun Ascot (G-F) H 12f 95 109
*** 2000** May Windso (G-F) 10f 87+
2000 Turf 3-6: (8f, 9f, 10f 1-1, 12f 1-2, 14f 1-1) (g-s, gd, g-f 1-2, frm 2-2)
Scopey, Group-class colt, effective 12 to 14f, best at 12f, acts on g-f to frm, best on g-f. Turf high 111 - 4th of 11 getting 3lb from Millenary (1 Aug Goodwood 12f g-f RF 3278) - also 1st of 22 getting 6lb from Boreas (23 Aug York RF 3914). Inconsistent. He showed progressive form, gaining a fine victory in the King George V Handicap at Royal Ascot before putting up a remarkable front-running performance to win the Ebor. An ultra-game sort who has improved as he has stepped up in trip, he is now with Godolphin and it will be interesting to see what direction they take with him. **Mrs A J Perrett [3-8] John Bodie.*

GLADIATORIAL (IRE) RR 64f 296[7]

8 b g Mazaad 8.5f **(53)** - Arena (Sallust) 8.4f **(63)**
Form - 7
Record 2000 - 1st:0 2nd:0 3rd:0 Ran:1
Pre2000 - 1st:1 2nd:0 3rd:0 Ran:1
Win Prizemoney £1,712 *Total Prizemoney* £1,712
Wins 1997 May Downpa (G-S) 13f 64 <
2000 AW 0-1: (12f) (Fibr)
Average gelding.
**Miss S E Baxter [0-3] E G Ashford (from M J Grassick in IRE [3-10] May 1997).*

GLAD MASTER (GER) RR 108f 2997[2]

3 b c Big Shuffle (USA) - Glady Star (GER) (Star Appeal) 9.6f **(65)**
Form - 072
Record 2000 - 1st:0 2nd:1 3rd:0 Ran:3
Pre2000 - 1st:1 2nd:0 3rd:0 Ran:1
Win Prizemoney £59,567 *Total Prizemoney* £63,236
Wins 1999 Oct Cologn (SFT) G3 8f
2000 Turf 0-2: (7f, 8f) (g-s, frm) 2000 AW 0-1: (9f) (Dirt)
Pattern-class colt. Turf high 108. Useful at two in Germany, he finished tenth in the UAE Derby in Dubai and was well beaten in the Irish Guineas too. Ran better when dropped back a furlong at Newbury, but looks below Pattern class.
**S bin Suroor [0-2] Godolphin (from S bin Suroor in UAE [0-1] Mar 2000).*

GLASTONBURY (IRE) BHB 36a RR 13f 2808[6]

4 b g Common Grounds 8.1f **(66)** - Harmonious (Sharrood (USA)) 10.5f **(72)**
Form - 084800503086
Record 2000 - 1st:0 2nd:0 3rd:1 Ran:12
Pre2000 - 1st:2 2nd:1 3rd:4 Ran:27
Win Prizemoney £3,592 *Total Prizemoney* £7,458
Wins * 1999 *Jan Lingfi (STD) S 7f 63*
1998 *Nov Lingfi (STD) S 7f 73 <*
2000 Turf 0-4: (5f, 6f, 7f, 8f) (gd 2, frm 2) 2000 AW 0-8: (5f 4, 6f 2, 7f 2) (Equi 4, Fibr 4)
Very moderate gelding, effective 6 to 7f, - acts on Equi, has worn blinkers, likes left handed tracks, likes tight tracks. Turf high 13. AW high 31. Becoming disappointing.
**P Howling [1-24] Jeff Lewis (from D Shaw [0-5] May 2000).*

GLEAMING BLADE (USA) BHB 100f RR 82f 4371[4]

2 ch c Diesis 9f **(80)** - Gleam of Light (IRE) **(88df)** (Danehill (USA)) 10f **(72)**
Form - 214
Record 2000 - 1st:1 2nd:1 3rd:0 Ran:3
Win Prizemoney £3,851 - *Total Prizemoney* £5,624
Wins * 2000 Aug Leices (G-F) 7f 78 <
2000 Turf 1-3: (7f 1-3) (frm 1-3)
Currently decent colt. Turf high 82 (began Jly) - also 1st of 15 giving 5lb to Single Honour (13 Aug Leicester RF 3608).
**Mrs A J Perrett [1-3] K Abdulla.*

GLEDSWOOD BHB 65f RR 81+f 4678[4]

3 ch f Selkirk (USA) 7.9f **(76)** - Horseshoe Reef (Mill Reef (USA)) 10.5f **(78)**
Form - 322634
Record 2000 - 1st:0 2nd:2 3rd:2 Ran:6
Win Prizemoney £0 *Total Prizemoney* £4,603
2000 Turf 0-6: (8f 4, 10f 2) (g-s, gd, g-f 2, frm 2)
Leggy, decent filly, effective 8 to 10f, best at 8f, acts on gd to frm, has worn blinkers. Turf high 81 - 2nd of 4 getting 5lb from Asly (17 Jun York 8f g-f RF 2065). **Lady Herries [0-6] D Davidson.*

GLENDALE RIDGE (IRE) BHB 51f46a RR 68f 46a 4825[12]

5 b g Indian Ridge 7.6f **(74)** - English Lily (Runnett) 7f **(59)**
Form - 444070040
Record 2000 - 1st:0 2nd:0 3rd:0 Ran:9
Win Prizemoney £0 *Total Prizemoney* £1,162
2000 Turf 0-9: (6f, 7f 2, 8f 3, 9f 2, 10f) (g-s, gd 4, g-f 2, frm 2)
Average gelding. Turf high 68.
**J R Poulton [0-10] Glendale Partnership Ltd.*

GLENDAMAH (IRE) BHB 52f RR 46f 5165[8]

3 b g Mukaddamah (USA) 7.6f **(74)** - Sea Glen (IRE) (Glenstal (USA)) 10.1f **(64)**
Form - 00008
Record 2000 - 1st:0 2nd:0 3rd:0 Ran:5
Pre2000 - 1st:1 2nd:1 3rd:4 Ran:11
Win Prizemoney £2,452 *Total Prizemoney* £6,524
Wins 1999 Aug Newcas (FRM) 6f 74 <
2000 Turf 0-5: (7f 3, 8f 2) (g-s 2, gd, frm 2)
Scopey, moderate gelding, effective 6f, acts on gd to hrd, has worn blinkers. Turf high 66 (began Jly). Becoming disappointing.
**J R Weymes [0-5] Mrs A Birkett (from E Weymes [1-11] Oct 1999).*

GLENHURICH (IRE) RR 30f 3960[5]

3 b f Sri Pekan (USA) - Forli's Treat (USA) (Forli (ARG)) 9.6f **(67)**
Form - 45
Record 2000 - 1st:0 2nd:0 3rd:0 Ran:2
Win Prizemoney £0 *Total Prizemoney* £349
2000 Turf 0-2: (7f, 8f) (hrd 2)
Scopey, currently very moderate filly. Turf high 30 (began Aug).
**M Johnston [0-2] J S Morrison & R A Dalglish.*

GLENQUOICH (IRE) RR 29f 3777[5]

3 ch c Indian Ridge 7.6f **(74)** - Glen Kella Manx (Tickled Pink) 6.5f **(59)**
Form - 5
Record 2000 - 1st:0 2nd:0 3rd:0 Ran:1
2000 Turf 0-1: (8f) (gd)
Leggy, currently little account colt.
**J H M Gosden [0-1] Sheikh Mohammed.*

GLENROCK BHB 81f RR 90f 4776[8]

3 ch g Muhtarram (USA) - Elkie Brooks (Relkino) 8.9f **(65)**

Form - 865028068
Record 2000 - 1st:0 2nd:1 3rd:0 Ran:9
Pre2000 - 1st:2 2nd:2 3rd:2 Ran:9
Win Prizemoney £7,587 *Total Prizemoney* £15,444
Wins 1999 Aug Cheste (G-S) 6.1f 89 <
1999 Aug Lingfi (GD) 6f 75
2000 Turf 0-9: (6f 7, 7f, 8f) (g-s 2, gd, g-f 3, frm 3)
Useful gelding, effective 6f, acts on gd to frm, best on gd. Turf high 90 - 5th of 30 getting 16lb from Hunting Lion (3 Jun Newmarket 6f frm RF 1690). He ran some good races last term, finishing second at Newmarket in July, when the draw was in his favour. Yet to prove he stays seven furlongs.
**A Berry [0-9] Glenrock Racing Ltd (from J Berry [2-9] Spt 1999).*

GLEN ROSIE (IRE) BHB 95f RR 103f 5239[8]

3 ch f Mujtahid (USA) 7.4f **(69)** - Silver Echo (Caerleon (USA)) 8.6f **(71)**
Form - 248768
Record 2000 - 1st:0 2nd:1 3rd:0 Ran:6
Pre2000 - 1st:1 2nd:0 3rd:2 Ran:5
Win Prizemoney £4,198 *Total Prizemoney* £15,243
Wins * 1999 Jly Newbur (G-F) 5.2f 70+ <
2000 Turf 0-6: (7f, 8f 4, 10f) (g-s 3, gd 2, frm)
Light-framed, very useful filly. Turf high 103. Becoming disappointing. Runner-up at a respectful distance in the Fred Darling on her return, she has been held in decent company since and seemed not to stay when tried at ten furlongs.
**B W Hills [1-11] John Grant.*

GLEN VALE WALK (IRE) BHB 43f RR 46f 5056[18]

3 ch g Balla Cove - Winter Harvest (Grundy) 10.3f **(65)**
Form - 80004822000
Record 2000 - 1st:0 2nd:2 3rd:0 Ran:11
Pre2000 - 1st:0 2nd:0 3rd:1 Ran:3
Win Prizemoney £0 *Total Prizemoney* £2,701
2000 Turf 0-11: (7f, 8f 6, 10f 3, 11f) (hvy, sft, gd 3, g-f 3, frm 2, hrd)
Leggy, moderate gelding, effective 8f, acts on gd, likes left handed tracks. Turf high 46. Inconsistent. **Mrs G S Rees [0-14] D C Brady.*

GLENWHARGEN (IRE) BHB 58f55a RR 60f 55a 111[3]

3 b f Polar Falcon (USA) 9f **(74)** - La Veine (USA) (Diesis) 9.3f **(69)**
Form - 4513
Record 2000 - 1st:1 2nd:0 3rd:1 Ran:2
Pre2000 - 1st:0 2nd:1 3rd:1 Ran:10
Win Prizemoney £2,194 *Total Prizemoney* £6,407
Wins 2000 *Jan Lingfi (STD) C 10f 57* <
2000 AW 1-2: (8f, 10f 1-1) (Equi 1-1, Fibr)
Average filly, effective 6 to 10f, acts on gd - acts on Equi, has worn blinkers. AW high 57 (1st run) - 1st of 5 getting 11lb from Shaman (8 Jan Lingfield RF 0047).
**J C Poulton [0-1] Russell Reed (from M Johnston [1-11] Jan 2000).*

GLOBAL DRAW (IRE) BHB 25f RR 31f 2101[12]

4 ch g Be My Guest (USA) 10.2f **(66)** - Almost A Lady (IRE) (Entitled)
Form - 00
Record 2000 - 1st:0 2nd:0 3rd:0 Ran:2
Pre2000 - 1st:0 2nd:0 3rd:1 Ran:8
Win Prizemoney £0 *Total Prizemoney* £412
2000 Turf 0-2: (14f, 16f) (gd, g-f)
Workmanlike, very moderate gelding, has worn blinkers. Turf high 31. **P Bowen [0-5] Mrs A M Thorpe (from J Parkes [0-2] Spt 1999).*

GLOBAL EXPLORER (IRE) BHB 57f RR 57f 4443[8]

2 b g Barathea (IRE) - Dance of Joy **(33f 33a)** (Shareef Dancer (USA)) 9.9f **(73)**
Form - 00678
Record 2000 - 1st:0 2nd:0 3rd:0 Ran:5
2000 Turf 0-5: (5f 3, 6f 2) (gd 2, g-f 2, hrd)
Fair gelding. Turf high 57.
**D J Murphy [0-4] Global Racing Club (from P Mitchell [0-1] Jun 2000).*

GLORIOUS QUEST (IRE) RR 87f 5131[7]

2 ch c Lake Coniston (IRE) - Lassalia (Sallust) 8.4f **(63)**
Form - 37
Record 2000 - 1st:0 2nd:0 3rd:1 Ran:2
Win Prizemoney £0 *Total Prizemoney* £844
2000 Turf 0-2: (6f 2) (sft, frm)
Currently useful colt. Turf high 87 (began Spt).
**M A Jarvis [0-2] & Mrs Nicholas Baker.*

GLORY DAYS (IRE) RR 74f 943[1]

2 ch c Lahib (USA) 8f **(69)** - Gloire (Thatching) 8f **(66)**
Form - 1
Record 2000 - 1st:1 2nd:0 3rd:0 Ran:1
Win Prizemoney £3,542 *Total Prizemoney* £3,542
Wins * 2000 May Kempto (G-S) 5f 74 <
2000 Turf 1-1: (5f 1-1) (g-s 1-1)
Currently above-average colt. (1st run) - 1st of 8 from Silca Legend (1 May Kempton RF 0943). A cosy winner on his Kempton debut.
**R Hannon [1-1] A F Merritt.*

GLORY OF LOVE BHB 32f RR 32f 56[10]

5 b g Belmez (USA) 11.4f **(65)** - Princess Lieven (Royal Palace) 9f **(56)**
Form - 0
Record 2000 - 1st:0 2nd:0 3rd:0 Ran:1
Pre2000 - 1st:0 2nd:0 3rd:0 Ran:7
2000 AW 0-1: (12f) (Fibr)
Very moderate gelding, has worn blinkers. Becoming disappointing. **K A Ryan [0-2] Mrs C M Barlow (from J Hetherton [0-7] Aug 1999).*

GLORY QUEST (USA) BHB 81f RR 82f 4812[1]

3 b c Quest for Fame 12.8f **(75)** - Sonseri (Prince Tenderfoot (USA)) 9f **(61)**
Form - 2234221
Record 2000 - 1st:1 2nd:4 3rd:1 Ran:7
Pre2000 - 1st:0 2nd:0 3rd:2 Ran:2
Win Prizemoney £2,561 *Total Prizemoney* £10,673
Wins * 2000 Oct Lingfi (SFT) 7.6f 77 <
2000 Turf 1-7: (7f 2, 8f 1-3, 9f, 10f) (sft, g-s 1-2, gd 3, g-f)
Rangy, decent colt, effective 6 to 10f, acts on g-s to frm, best on gd, likes Goodwood. Turf high 82 - 3rd of 15 to Takrir (19 May Newbury 8f gd RF 1307) - also 1st of 18 giving 5lb to Russian Rhapsody (4 Oct Lingfield RF 4812). Consistent.
**Miss Gay Kelleway [1-9] Quest To Win Partnership.*

GLOW BHB 39a RR 51f 2627[9]

4 br f Alzao (USA) 9.8f **(73)** - Shimmer (Bustino) 10.4f **(64)**
Form - 035240
Record 2000 - 1st:0 2nd:1 3rd:1 Ran:6
Pre2000 - 1st:0 2nd:0 3rd:0 Ran:5
Win Prizemoney £0 *Total Prizemoney* £1,247
2000 Turf 0-3: (12f, 14f, 18f) (gd, frm 2) 2000 AW 0-3: (11f, 12f, 14f) (Fibr 3)
Unfurnished, fair filly, effective 12f, acts on gd to g-f. Turf high 51 (1st run) - 5th of 8 getting 10lb from Hannibal Lad (31 May Southwell 12f gd RF 1602). AW high 42.
**M J Polglase [0-6] M J Polglase (from I A Balding [0-3] Jly 1999).*

GLOWING BHB 81f RR 80f 4735[7]

5 b m Chilibang 7f **(55)** - Juliet Bravo (Glow (USA)) 6.7f **(71)**
Form - 2024157
Record 2000 - 1st:1 2nd:2 3rd:0 Ran:7
Pre2000 - 1st:3 2nd:2 3rd:2 Ran:13
Win Prizemoney £14,886 *Total Prizemoney* £24,012
Wins * 2000 Jly Newmar (G-F) H 6f 76 79+ <
* 1999 Spt Doncas (G-F) H 5f 70 73
* 1999 Aug Nottin (G-F) H 6.1f 65 68
* 1998 Aug Folkes (G-F) 6f 67
2000 Turf 1-7: (5f, 6f 1-6) (gd 1-3, g-f, frm 3)
Decent filly, effective 5 to 6f, best at 6f, acts on gd to frm, best on gd, excels at Goodwood and Nottingham. Turf high 80 - 5th of 16 giving 2lb to Zuhair (9 Spt Goodwood 6f gd RF 4316) - also 1st of 8 giving 16lb to Carinthia (21 Jly Newmarket RF 3005). A winner twice in 1999, she returned to winning form at Newmarket in July. Suited by six furlongs and fast ground.
**J R Fanshawe [4-20] Peters Friends.*

GLYNDEBOURNE (IRE) RR 118f 2530a[2]

3 b c Sadler's Wells (USA) 11.3f **(87)** - Heaven Only Knows (High Top) 10.2f **(67)**
Form - 2112
2000 Turf 2-4: (10f 2-2, 12f 2) (g-s 2-3, gd)
High-class colt. Turf high 118 - also 1st of 5 getting 13lb from Right Wing (10 Jun Curragh RF 1942a). An improving colt, he landed a Curragh maiden before beating some established performers

in the Group Three Gallinule Stakes at the same course. Ran a cracker to finish runner-up in the Irish Derby, albeit no match for Sinndar, before being exported to race in Hong Kong.
**A P O'Brien in IRE [2-4] Michael Tabor.*

GODMERSHAM PARK BHB 41f38a RR 41f 38a 2479[4]

8 b g Warrshan (USA) 9.7f **(59)** - Brown Velvet (Mansingh (USA)) 7.4f **(55)**
Form - 03752344147014
Record 2000 - 1st:2 2nd:1 3rd:1 Ran:10
Pre2000 - 1st:6 2nd:5 3rd:7 Ran:59
Win Prizemoney £19,796 *Total Prizemoney* £28,717
Wins * **2000** Jun Ripon (G-S) S 8f 41
* **2000** *Mar Southw (STD) H 8f 45 48*
* 1998 *Feb Wolver (STD) H 8.5f 68 73* <
* 1998 *Jan Southw (STD) H 8f 54 65*
* 1998 *Jan Southw (STD) H 8f 54 63*
* 1998 *Jan Southw (STD) H 7f 54 59*
* 1997 *Dec Southw (STD) H 7f 50 54*
* 1997 *Nov Southw (STD) H 8f 46 51*
2000 Turf 1-1: (8f 1-1) (g-f 1-1) 2000 AW 1-9: (7f, 8f 1-7, 9f) (Fibr 1-9)
Moderate gelding, effective 7 to 9f, - acts on Fibr, has worn blinkers. (1st run). AW high 48. Consistent.
**P S Felgate [8-59] P S Felgate (from M J Heaton-Ellis [0-10] Oct 1996).*

GOES A TREAT (IRE) BHB 70f58a RR 77df 58a 351[12]

4 b f Common Grounds 8.1f **(66)** - Just a Treat (IRE) (Glenstal (USA)) 10.1f **(64)**
Form - 00
Record 2000 - 1st:0 2nd:0 3rd:0 Ran:2
Pre2000 - 1st:1 2nd:1 3rd:1 Ran:6
Win Prizemoney £4,270 *Total Prizemoney* £6,072
Wins 1999 Jly Warwic (G-F) 6.8f 82 <
2000 AW 0-2: (6f, 7f) (Fibr 2)
Unfurnished, above-average filly, effective 7f, acts on g-f to frm. AW high 13. Becoming disappointing.
**A Berry [0-2] David Brown (from A G Foster [0-1] Nov 1999).*

GO FOR IT SWEETIE (IRE) RR 21f 3996[7]

7 b m Brush Aside (USA) - Arctic Mistress (Quayside) 12f **(43)**
Form - 7
Record 2000 - 1st:0 2nd:0 3rd:0 Ran:1
2000 Turf 0-1: (14f) (g-f)
Little account mare. **B D Leavy [0-8] Barry Leavy.*

GOGGLES (IRE) BHB 99f RR 92f 4259[1]

2 b br c Eagle Eyed (USA) - Rock On (IRE) (Ballad Rock) 7.8f **(63)**
Form - 411
Record 2000 - 1st:2 2nd:0 3rd:0 Ran:3
Win Prizemoney £163,132 *Total Prizemoney* £163,486
Wins * **2000** Spt Doncas (GD) 6f 92 <
* **2000** Aug Goodwo (G-F) 6f 86
2000 Turf 2-3: (6f 2-3) (gd 1-1, g-f 1-2)
Currently useful colt. Turf high 92 - 1st of 22 getting 3lb from Reel Buddy (6 Spt Doncaster RF 4259) - also 1st of 7 from Mootafayill (1 Aug Goodwood RF 3281). Fourth in a hot maiden on his debut, he showed a useful turn of foot to score next time, before taking a valuable sales event at Doncaster. There looks to be more to come. **H Candy [2-3] Mrs J K Powell.*

GOG'S GIFT BHB 50f RR 47f 5318[20]

2 b g So Factual (USA) - Premium Gift **(53f)** (Most Welcome)
Form - 850
Record 2000 - 1st:0 2nd:0 3rd:0 Ran:3
2000 Turf 0-3: (5f 2, 6f) (sft, gd, hrd)
Currently moderate gelding. Turf high 47 (began Aug).
**C B B Booth [0-3] Ashley Carr.*

GOING GLOBAL (IRE) BHB 100f RR 110f 4731[5]

3 ch c Bob Back (USA) 11.5f **(71)** - Ukraine Girl (Targowice (USA)) 11.4f **(70)**
Form - 132060405
Record 2000 - 1st:1 2nd:1 3rd:1 Ran:9
Pre2000 - 1st:1 2nd:0 3rd:1 Ran:2
Win Prizemoney £10,001 *Total Prizemoney* £32,778
Wins * **2000** Apr Ripon (SFT) 9f 90 <
* 1999 Spt Goodwo (SFT) 8f 77+
2000 Turf 1-9: (9f 1-1, 10f, 11f, 12f 4, 14f, 15f) (sft, g-s, gd 1-5, g-f, frm)
Lengthy, Group-class colt, effective 11f, acts on g-s, has worn blinkers, prefers tight tracks. Turf high 110 - 2nd of 8 to Saddler's Quest (13 May Lingfield 11f g-s RF 1193). Third to Sakhee in Sandown's Classic Trial, he went down by only a neck in the Lingfield Derby Trial, but has failed to make the grade since and was well beaten in both the Derby and St Leger. He was faced with unsuitably fast ground on most of his starts, however. Now hurdling with Gary Moore. **S P C Woods [2-11] Dwayne Woods.*

GOING HOME (IRE) BHB 40f RR 18f 3312[15]

3 b g Thatching 7.8f **(69)** - Princess of Dance (IRE) (Dancing Dissident (USA))
Form - 00
Record 2000 - 1st:0 2nd:0 3rd:0 Ran:2
Pre2000 - 1st:0 2nd:0 3rd:0 Ran:5
Win Prizemoney £0 *Total Prizemoney* £193
2000 Turf 0-2: (5f, 8f) (g-f, hrd)
Strong, poor gelding, effective 5f, acts on g-f, often wears blinkers. Turf high 2 (began Jly).
**M W Easterby [0-2] Steve Macdonald (from J L Eyre [0-5] Spt 1999).*

GOING SUZUKA (JPN) RR 111f 578a[5]

7 m
Form - 5
2000 Turf 0-1: (12f) (gd)
Group-class mare.
**M Hashida in JPN [0-1].*

GOLAN (IRE) RR 4270[1]

2 b c Spectrum (IRE) - Highland Gift (IRE) **(87f)** (Generous (IRE))
Form - 1
Record 2000 - 1st:1 2nd:0 3rd:0 Ran:1
Win Prizemoney £3,877 *Total Prizemoney* £3,877
Wins * **2000** Spt Chepst (G-S) 7.1f 95++ <
2000 Turf 1-1: (7f 1-1) (g-f 1-1)
Currently very poor colt. (1st run) - 1st of 13 from Clearing (7 Spt Chepstow RF 4270). Made an impressive winning debut at Chepstow and will be suited by middle distances next term.
**Sir Michael Stoute [1-1] Lord Weinstock.*

GOLCONDA (IRE) BHB 65a RR 91f 4740[11]

4 br f Lahib (USA) 8f **(69)** - David's Star (Welsh Saint) 7.6f **(64)**
Form - 38870160
Record 2000 - 1st:1 2nd:0 3rd:1 Ran:8
Pre2000 - 1st:3 2nd:3 3rd:2 Ran:11
Win Prizemoney £23,228 *Total Prizemoney* £39,812
Wins * **2000** Jly Folkes (GD-) 9.7f 85+ <
* 1999 May Lingfi (G-F) H 10f 73 75
* 1999 May Kempto (G-F) H 9f 68 72
* 1999 *Feb Wolver (STD) 7f 63*
2000 Turf 1-8: (9f, 10f 1-7) (g-s, gd 4, g-f, frm 1-2)
Workmanlike, useful filly, effective 10f, acts on gd to g-f, has worn blinkers, likes tight tracks. Turf high 91 (1st run) - 3rd of 16 getting 10lb from National Anthem (6 May Newmarket 10f gd RF 1059). Thoroughly genuine, she developed into a smart handicapper in 1999, but the Handicapper had her measure last term, and her only win came in a conditions event at Folkestone.
**M L W Bell [4-19] Innlaw Racing.*

GOLD ACADEMY (IRE) BHB 105f RR 113f 4989[11]

4 b c Royal Academy (USA) 7.8f **(77)** - Soha (USA) (Dancing Brave (USA)) 8.4f **(76)**
Form - 666240
Record 2000 - 1st:0 2nd:1 3rd:0 Ran:6
Pre2000 - 1st:2 2nd:2 3rd:3 Ran:12
Win Prizemoney £23,809 *Total Prizemoney* £121,379
Wins * 1999 Spt York (G-F) L 8.9f 113+ <
* 1999 May Chepst (GD) 8.1f 98+
2000 Turf 0-6: (10f 5, 12f) (sft, gd 4, frm)
Scopey, Group-class colt, effective 8 to 12f, acts on gd to frm, best on gd. Turf high 113. Consistent. Yet to score beyond nine furlongs, he faced some stiff tasks last term and ran as well as could be expected when sixth in the Eclipse.
**R Hannon [2-18] George Teo.*

GOLD AIR BHB 67f63a **RR 70f 63a** 5008[8]

2 b f Sri Pekan (USA) - Pebbledash **(48f)** (Great Commotion (USA))
Form - 01028008
Record 2000 - 1st:1 2nd:1 3rd:0 Ran:8
Win Prizemoney £4,290 *Total Prizemoney* £5,359
Wins * 2000 May Sandow (HVY) 5f 61 <
2000 Turf 1-7: (5f 1-4, 6f 3) (sft, g-s 1-1, gd 2, g-f, frm 2) 2000 AW 0-1: (6f) (Fibr)
Above-average filly, effective 5f, acts on g-s, has worn blinkers. Turf high 70 - also 1st of 6 from Ecstatic (29 May Sandown RF 1538). Becoming disappointing.
**B J Meehan [1-8] Gold Group International Ltd.*

GOLDAMIX (IRE) RR 112f 5329a[10]

3 gr f Linamix (FR) 8.2f **(64)** - Gold's Dance (FR) (Goldneyev (USA))
Form - 430
2000 Turf 0-3: (10f, 11f 2) (g-s, gd, frm)
Group-class filly. Turf high 112. In the frame in the Prix Saint-Alary and Prix de Diane, both Group Ones.
**C Laffon-Parias in FR [1-4] Wertheimer et Frere.*

GOLD BLADE BHB 47f44a **RR 41f 44a** 4101[15]

11 ch g Rousillon (USA) 10.4f **(69)** - Sharp Girl (FR) (Sharpman) 11.3f **(66)**
Form - 40854610
Record 2000 - 1st:1 2nd:0 3rd:0 Ran:8
Pre2000 - 1st:14 2nd:13 3rd:9 Ran:80
Win Prizemoney £43,010 *Total Prizemoney* £58,972

Wins								
*** 2000**	Aug	Beverl	(GD)	H	9.9f	40	41	
* 1999	Jly	Pontef	(G-S)	H	10f	41	44	
* 1999	Jun	Lingfi	(G-F)	H	11.5f	40	38	
* 1996	Aug	Catter	(G-F)	H	12f	67	58+	
* 1996	Jly	Beverl	(G-F)	H	9.9f	64	68	
* 1996	Jly	Ayr	(G-F)	H	13.1f	60	61	
* 1996	Jly	Hamilt	(G-F)	H	9.2f	49	60	
* 1996	Jly	Pontef	(G-F)	H	10f	49	61+	
* 1996	Apr	Nottin	(GD)	H	10f	44	48	
* 1996	*Jan*	*Southw*	*(STD)*	*H*	*12f*	*60*	*67*	

2000 Turf 1-7: (10f 1-6, 11f) (gd 1-1, g-f 3, frm 3) 2000 AW 0-1: (12f) (Fibr)
Moderate gelding, effective 10 to 11f, best at 11f, acts on gd to hrd, best on frm, has worn blinkers, prefers tight tracks. Turf high 41 - 1st of 9 giving 4lb to Buzz The Agent (1 Aug Beverley RF 3269).
**J Pearce [12-56] Arthur Old (from N A Graham [3-32] Jly 1994).*

GOLDBRIDGE (IRE) BHB 37f **RR 41f** 4328[4]

5 b g Distinctly North (USA) 7.4f **(63)** - Bold Kate (Bold Lad (IRE)) 8.4f **(68)**
Form - 44
Record 2000 - 1st:0 2nd:0 3rd:0 Ran:2
Pre2000 - 1st:0 2nd:0 3rd:0 Ran:13
Win Prizemoney £0 *Total Prizemoney* £607
2000 Turf 0-2: (15f, 16f) (g-f, frm)
Moderate gelding, has worn blinkers. Turf high 41 (began Jly). Inconsistent.
**T P McGovern [3-16] Alan Clarke (from Miss Frances Crowley in IRE [1-5] Aug 1998).*

GOLD EDGE BHB 28f25a **RR 22f 25a** 2667[4]

6 ch m Beveled (USA) 6.9f **(64)** - Golden October (Young Generation) 7.7f **(63)**
Form - 70850607004
Record 2000 - 1st:0 2nd:0 3rd:0 Ran:9
Pre2000 - 1st:1 2nd:5 3rd:5 Ran:48
Win Prizemoney £3,631 *Total Prizemoney* £11,335
Wins 1997 Aug Chepst (G-F) H 6.1f 50 59 <
2000 Turf 0-5: (5f 2, 6f 2, 7f) (gd 2, g-f 2, frm) 2000 AW 0-4: (5f, 6f 2, 7f) (Fibr 4)
Little account mare, has worn blinkers. Turf high 22. AW high 24.
**A G Newcombe [0-11] M B Clemence (from N Tinkler [0-4] Aug 1999).*

GOLDEN ACE (IRE) BHB 28f27a **RR 28f 27a** 4494[12]

7 ch g Archway (IRE) 8.5f **(60)** - Gobolino (Don) 7.7f **(64)**
Form - 45800
Record 2000 - 1st:0 2nd:0 3rd:0 Ran:5
Pre2000 - 1st:3 2nd:3 3rd:7 Ran:41
Win Prizemoney £10,256 *Total Prizemoney* £18,714

Wins								
* 1999	Apr	Folkes	(SFT)	H	12f	39	42	
1997	Aug	Newmar	(GD)	S	8f		42	
1996	Apr	Newbur	(G-S)		8f		85	<

2000 Turf 0-5: (9f, 12f 3, 15f) (g-s 2, gd, g-f 2)
Little account gelding, effective 10 to 14f, best at 12f, acts on hvy to g-f, has worn blinkers, favours tight tracks. Turf high 37 (1st run) - 4th of 13 getting 32lb from Puzzlement (30 Mar Leicester 12f g-f RF 0564). Becoming disappointing.
**R C Spicer [1-37] G D J Linder (from R Hannon [2-9] Aug 1997).*

GOLDEN BEACH BHB 47f **RR 61f** 5067[5]

2 b f Turtle Island (IRE) - Good as Gold (IRE) (Glint of Gold) 9.3f **(66)**
Form - 0005205
Record 2000 - 1st:0 2nd:1 3rd:0 Ran:7
Win Prizemoney £0 *Total Prizemoney* £630
2000 Turf 0-7: (6f 3, 7f 4) (g-s, gd 2, g-f 2, frm 2)
Average filly, effective 7f, acts on frm. Turf high 61.
**Mrs P N Dutfield [0-7] The Carpetbaggers.*

GOLDEN BIFF (IRE) BHB 40f55a **RR 39f 55a** 5057[20]

4 ch g Shalford (IRE) 7.8f **(63)** - Capable Kate (IRE) (Alzao (USA)) 7.1f **(68)**
Form - 6067000
Record 2000 - 1st:0 2nd:0 3rd:0 Ran:6
Pre2000 - 1st:1 2nd:3 3rd:3 Ran:18
Win Prizemoney £2,250 *Total Prizemoney* £5,990
Wins * 1999 Oct Catter (SFT) 6f 52 <
2000 Turf 0-6: (5f, 6f 3, 7f 2) (sft 2, g-s 2, g-f, frm)
Scopey, moderate gelding, effective 5 to 6f, acts on gd to g-f, has worn blinkers. Turf high 39. Inconsistent.
**I Semple [1-24] Patersons of Greenoakhill.*

GOLDEN BRIEF (IRE) BHB 60f64a **RR 48f 64a** 5186[13]

2 ch g Brief Truce (USA) 9.1f **(73)** - Tiffany's Case (IRE) **(58f)** (Thatching) 8f **(66)**
Form - 00
Record 2000 - 1st:0 2nd:0 3rd:0 Ran:2
2000 Turf 0-2: (7f 2) (g-s 2)
Currently above-average gelding. Turf high 48 (began Oct).
**K R Burke [0-2] John Kelsey-Fry.*

GOLDEN CHANCE (IRE) BHB 76f **RR 86f** 3597[6]

3 b c Unfuwain (USA) 11.4f **(74)** - Golden Digger (USA) **(54f)** (Mr Prospector (USA)) 8.8f **(78)**
Form - 322138426
Record 2000 - 1st:1 2nd:3 3rd:2 Ran:9
Win Prizemoney £2,769 *Total Prizemoney* £7,969
Wins * 2000 Jun Redcar (FRM) 8f 86 <
2000 Turf 1-9: (7f 2, 8f 1-3, 10f 4) (gd 2, g-f 3, frm 1-2, hrd 2)
Workmanlike, useful colt, effective 7 to 10f, acts on gd to hrd, best on frm, excels at Beverley. Turf high 86 - 1st of 5 giving 5lb to Caballe (24 Jun Redcar RF 2254). He went close to winning on his second and third starts but made no mistake in a small Redcar maiden next time. Mixed form since. Suited by fast ground.
**M Johnston [1-9] Maktoum Al Maktoum.*

GOLDEN CHIMES (USA) BHB 60f57a **RR 65f 57a** 2989[6]

5 ch g Woodman (USA) 9.7f **(77)** - Russian Ballet (USA) (Nijinsky (CAN)) 10.3f **(77)**
Form - 1686
Record 2000 - 1st:1 2nd:0 3rd:0 Ran:4
Pre2000 - 1st:1 2nd:0 3rd:1 Ran:11
Win Prizemoney £8,622 *Total Prizemoney* £9,662

Wins								
*** 2000**	Jun	Carlis	(FRM)	H	14.1f	60	65	
1998	Spt	Listow	(G-S)		10f		87	<

2000 Turf 1-4: (12f, 14f 1-2, 18f) (g-f 1-2, frm, hrd)
Average gelding, has worn blinkers, likes right handed tracks, likes tight tracks. Turf high 65 (1st run). Began his career in Ireland, but has been disappointing over here so far this season, though he has run in some pretty competitive handicaps and put up an improved performance when tried in blinkers.
**D Nicholls [1-4] G Tuer (from Major D N Chappell [0-7] Oct 1999).*

GOLDEN DRAGONFLY (IRE) BHB 58f **RR 63f** 5004[17]

2 ch g Eagle Eyed (USA) - Shanna (BEL) **(66f)** (River Smile (USA))
Form - 0060
Record 2000 - 1st:0 2nd:0 3rd:0 Ran:4

2000 Turf 0-4: (5f 2, 6f, 8f) (g-s, gd, frm 2)
Average gelding. Turf high 63. **D Nicholls [0-4] Mrs J Phillips-Hill.*

GOLDEN FACT (USA) BHB 77f RR 92f 5283a[6]
6 b g Known Fact (USA) 8.3f **(72)** - Cosmic Sea Queen (USA) (Determined Cosmic (USA))
Form - 000073620804726
2000 Turf 0-14: (8f 9, 9f 2, 10f 2, 11f) (hvy 3, sft 2, g-s 4, gd 4)
Useful gelding, effective 8 to 11f, best at 8f, acts on g-s to g-f, best on g-f, likes right handed tracks, and excels at Galway. Turf high 96 - 2nd of 17 giving 19lb to Markskeepingfaith (4 Aug Galway 8f gd RF 3472a). Consistent. Tough and genuine, he ran his share of good races but seems to be in the Handicapper's grip.
**M McElhone in IRE [4-35] Thomas Cassidy (from R Hannon [0-10] Aug 1997).*

GOLDEN FORTUNA RR 66f 3766[7]
2 b f Turtle Island (IRE) - Shady Bank (USA) **(42f)** (Alleged (USA)) 10f **(76)**
Form - 7
Record 2000 - 1st:0 2nd:0 3rd:0 Ran:1
2000 Turf 0-1: (7f) (g-f)
Currently average filly. **J W Hills [0-1] George Tong.*

GOLDENGIRLMICHELLE (IRE) BHB 20f RR 42f 346[7]
5 b m Project Manager 7.2f **(47)** - Arbour Day (Artaius (USA)) 9f **(69)**
Form - 7
Record 2000 - 1st:0 2nd:0 3rd:0 Ran:1
Pre2000 - 1st:0 2nd:0 3rd:0 Ran:9
2000 AW 0-1: (16f) (Fibr)
Moderate filly, has worn blinkers. Inconsistent.
**J J O'Neill [0-11] The Cartmel Syndicate (from Ferdy Murphy [1-6] Apr 1999).*

GOLDEN GROOVE (USA) RR 3451[10]
4 ch f Go and Go - Smooth Edge (USA) (Meadowlake (USA))
Form - 0
Record 2000 - 1st:0 2nd:0 3rd:0 Ran:1
2000 Turf 0-1: (12f) (frm)
Formerly very poor filly, always wears blinkers.
**J Norton [0-5] Jaffa Racing Syndicate.*

GOLDEN HAWK (USA) BHB 43f RR 57f 4479[5]
5 ch g Silver Hawk (USA) 11.2f **(85)** - Crockadore (USA) (Nijinsky (CAN)) 10.3f **(77)**
Form - 5
Record 2000 - 1st:0 2nd:0 3rd:0 Ran:1
Pre2000 - 1st:0 2nd:1 3rd:1 Ran:9
Win Prizemoney £0 *Total Prizemoney* £2,610
2000 AW 0-1: (12f) (Fibr)
Fair gelding.
**C A Dwyer [0-3] David Bowkett (from S Dow [0-6] Aug 1999).*

GOLDEN HIND (USA) RR 52f 5318[5]
2 ch f Seeking the Gold (USA) 7.4f **(80)** - Min Elreeh (USA) **(76+f)** (Danzig (USA)) 8.4f **(76)**
Form - 5
Record 2000 - 1st:0 2nd:0 3rd:0 Ran:1
2000 Turf 0-1: (6f) (sft)
Currently above-average filly.
**Sir Mark Prescott [0-1] Sir Edmund Loder.*

GOLDEN INDIGO (USA) RR 100f 4956a[7]
3 ch c
Form - 3207
2000 Turf 0-3: (8f 2, 12f) (sft 2, g-f)
Very useful colt. Turf high 100 (1st run) - 2nd of 13 to Davide Umbro (30 Apr Capannelle 8f sft RF 1032a). **G Fratini in ITY [0-4].*

GOLDEN LEGEND (IRE) BHB 65f RR 71f 804[18]
3 b g Last Tycoon 9.4f **(73)** - Adjalisa (IRE) (Darshaan) 9.9f **(84)**
Form - 470
Record 2000 - 1st:0 2nd:0 3rd:0 Ran:3
Pre2000 - 1st:0 2nd:0 3rd:0 Ran:2
Win Prizemoney £0 *Total Prizemoney* £328
2000 Turf 0-3: (6f, 7f, 8f) (gd 2, frm)
Scopey, above-average gelding. Turf high 71.
**G Wragg [0-5] Mollers Racing.*

GOLDEN LOCKET RR 67f 1608[11]
3 ch f Beveled (USA) 6.9f **(64)** - Rekindled Flame (IRE) (Kings Lake (USA)) 10.8f **(67)**
Form - 480
Record 2000 - 1st:0 2nd:0 3rd:0 Ran:3
Pre2000 - 1st:0 2nd:0 3rd:0 Ran:3
Win Prizemoney £0 *Total Prizemoney* £305
2000 Turf 0-3: (7f 2, 8f) (gd 2, g-f)
Unfurnished, average filly. Turf high 67.
**M Kettle [0-3] Good Connections (from A G Foster [0-2] Oct 1999).*

GOLDEN LYRIC (IRE) BHB 27f44a RR 27f 44a 2382a[2]
5 ch g Lycius (USA) 8.8f **(71)** - Adjala (Northfields (USA)) 9f **(72)**
Form - 380742212
Record 2000 - 1st:1 2nd:3 3rd:0 Ran:6
Pre2000 - 1st:1 2nd:2 3rd:4 Ran:27
Win Prizemoney £4,193 *Total Prizemoney* £7,781

Wins							
2000	*Mar Southw*	*(STD)*	*S*	*8f*		*43*	*<*
1999	*Mar Southw*	*(SLW)*	*H*	*11f*	*39*	*42*	

2000 Turf 0-1: (9f) (g-f) 2000 AW 1-5: (8f 1-2, 9f, 11f, 12f) (Fibr 1-5)
Moderate gelding, effective 8 to 11f, best at 8f, - acts on AW, best on Fibr, has worn blinkers, favours tight tracks, excels at Wolverhampton, likes Southwell. AW high 43 - 1st of 16 from Waiting Knight (6 Mar Southwell RF 0417). Inconsistent.
**Mrs K Harvey in JER [0-1] (from J Pearce [2-22] Mar 2000).*

GOLDEN MIRACLE (FR) BHB 78f RR 78f 2677[2]
3 b g Cadeaux Genereux 7.9f **(76)** - Cheeky Charm (USA) **(47f)** (Nureyev (USA)) 8.7f **(78)**
Form - 000102
Record 2000 - 1st:1 2nd:1 3rd:0 Ran:6
Pre2000 - 1st:2 2nd:0 3rd:1 Ran:8
Win Prizemoney £20,228 *Total Prizemoney* £23,036

Wins							
* 2000	Jun Redcar	(FRM)	H	7f	75	78	<
* 1999	Spt Hamilt	(SFT)	H	6f	77	77	
* 1999	Spt Hamilt	(G-F)	H	6f	73	77	

2000 Turf 1-6: (6f 4, 7f 1-2) (sft, g-s, gd, g-f 2, frm 1-1)
Well made, above-average gelding, effective 6 to 7f, best at 7f, acts on g-s to frm, best on frm, has worn blinkers, excels at Hamilton. Turf high 78 - 1st of 9 giving 24lb to Soba Jones (23 Jun Redcar RF 2233). Inconsistent. **M Johnston [3-14] Gainsborough Stud.*

GOLDEN NEEDLE (IRE) RR 4651[4]
2 b f Prince of Birds (USA) - Royal Thimble (IRE) **(57f 60a)** (Prince Rupert (FR))
Form - 4
Record 2000 - 1st:0 2nd:0 3rd:0 Ran:1
Win Prizemoney £0 *Total Prizemoney* £222
2000 AW 0-1: (8f) (Fibr)
Currently average filly. **Noel Chance [0-1] Family Tree Syndicate.*

GOLDEN OSCAR BHB 55f RR 60?f 2171[7]
3 ch g Primo Dominie 7.2f **(67)** - Noble Destiny (Dancing Brave (USA)) 8.4f **(76)**
Form - 0737
Record 2000 - 1st:0 2nd:0 3rd:1 Ran:4
Win Prizemoney £0 *Total Prizemoney* £643
2000 Turf 0-4: (8f 4) (gd 3, g-f)
Lengthy, average gelding. Turf high 60 - 3rd of 5 giving 5lb to Poetic (5 Jun Thirsk 8f gd RF 1727).
**Andrew Turnell [0-4] Dr John Hollowood.*

GOLDEN POUND (USA) BHB 44f60a RR 45f 60a 3727[4]
8 b g Seeking the Gold (USA) 7.4f **(80)** - Coesse Express (USA) (Dewan (USA)) 7.4f **(65)**
Form - 45474
Record 2000 - 1st:0 2nd:0 3rd:0 Ran:5
Pre2000 - 1st:4 2nd:5 3rd:5 Ran:59
Win Prizemoney £14,201 *Total Prizemoney* £28,280

Wins							
* 1998	May Leices	(GD)	H	6f	72	77	
* 1997	Aug Bright	(GD)	H	6f	75	78	
* 1996	Jly Epsom	(G-F)	H	6f	77	83	<
* 1996	Apr Thirsk	(G-F)		6f		75	

2000 Turf 0-5: (5f 2, 6f 3) (gd, frm 4)
Average gelding, effective 6f, acts on g-f to frm, best on g-f, has

worn blinkers (effectively), prefers left handed tracks, likes tight tracks. Turf high 45.

**Miss Gay Kelleway [4-53] A P Griffin (from Mrs L Stubbs [0-7] May 1999).*

GOLDEN RETRIEVER (USA) BHB 57f RR 51f 3183[11]

3 b br c Red Ransom (USA) 8.6f **(83)** - Golden Rhyme (Dom Racine (FR)) 9.2f **(62)**

Form - 00000

Record 2000 - 1st:0 2nd:0 3rd:0 Ran:5
Pre2000 - 1st:0 2nd:0 3rd:0 Ran:1

2000 Turf 0-5: (7f, 8f 4) (g-s, gd 2, frm 2)

Well made, fair colt. Turf high 72. **D R C Elsworth [0-6] P D Savill.*

GOLDEN ROD BHB 44f4/a RR 66f 47a 5102[3]

3 ch g Rainbows For Life (CAN) 9.3f **(64)** - Noble Form (Double Form) 7.3f **(58)**

Form - 003460003

Record 2000 - 1st:0 2nd:0 3rd:2 Ran:9
Pre2000 - 1st:0 2nd:0 3rd:0 Ran:3

Win Prizemoney £0 *Total Prizemoney* £845

2000 Turf 0-8: (10f 3, 11f, 12f, 14f 2, 16f) (sft, gd 2, g-f, frm 4) 2000 AW 0-1: (12f) (Equi)

Scopey, average gelding, effective 10f, acts on gd. Turf high 66 - 3rd of 12 getting 1lb from River Ensign (31 May Southwell 10f gd RF 1606). Becoming disappointing. **P W Harris [0-12] Neil Rodway.*

GOLDEN SILCA BHB 114f RR 117+f 5095a[9]

4 ch f Inchinor 8.9f **(64)** - Silca-Cisa (Hallgate)

Form - 0418541750

Record 2000 - 1st:2 2nd:0 3rd:0 Ran:10
Pre2000 - 1st:5 2nd:4 3rd:1 Ran:13

Win Prizemoney £135,115 *Total Prizemoney* £281,725

Wins							
*** 2000**	Aug	Currag	(GD)	G3	8f	112+	<
*** 2000**	Jun	Epsom	(G-S)	L	8.5f	111+	
* 1998	Spt	Newbur	(GD)	G2	6f	106	
* 1998	Spt	Baden-	(SFT)	G2	6f	97	
* 1998	Jly	Newbur	(G-F)	L	6f	97	
* 1998	May	Newbur	(GD)		5.2f	81	
* 1998	Apr	Newbur	(HVY)		5.2f	84+	

2000 Turf 2-9: (7f, 8f 1-7, 9f 1-1) (sft 2, g-s 1-1, gd 1-5, g-f) 2000 AW 0-1: (12f) (Dirt)

Leggy, high-class filly, effective 8 to 9f, best at 8f, acts on g-s to g-f, best on gd, excels at Curragh. Turf high 117 (1st run) - 4th of 7 getting 3lb from Aljabr (20 May Newbury 8f g-f RF 1331) - also 1st of 3 getting 3lb from Duck Row (20 Aug Curragh RF 3888a). A game and genuine filly, she paid her way again last year, landing an Epsom Listed event and a Group Three at the Curragh. She just misses out in top company though. **M R Channon [7-23].*

Golden Silca (nearside), again paid her way

GOLDEN SNAKE (USA) BHB 115f RR 120f 5215a[1]

4 b c Danzig (USA) 8.1f **(88)** - Dubian (High Line) 10.3f **(70)**

Form - 4511

Record 2000 - 1st:2 2nd:0 3rd:0 Ran:4
Pre2000 - 1st:3 2nd:1 3rd:0 Ran:7

Win Prizemoney £262,392 *Total Prizemoney* £295,017

Wins							
*** 2000**	Oct	San Si	(HVY)	G1	12f	120	<
*** 2000**	Spt	Cologn	(SFT)	G1	12f	120	<
1999	Jun	Chanti	(SFT)	G1	9f	116	
1999	Apr	Newmar	(GD)	L	8.5f	108	
1998	Spt	Doncas	(GD)		8f	85+	

2000 Turf 2-4: (10f, 11f, 12f 2-2) (hvy 1-1, sft 1-1, g-s, gd)

Scopey, very high-class colt, effective 9 to 12f, best at 12f, acts on hvy to gd, likes Newmarket. Turf high 120 - 1st of 10 giving 9lb to Reve D'Oscar (22 Oct San Siro RF 5215a) - also 1st of 11 from Yavana's Pace (24 Spt Cologne RF 4717a). Consistent. Showed high-class form at three, winning the Group One Prix Jean Prat, but was rather disappointing in his last two starts. Switched to John Dunlop, he came into his own in the autumn with victories at the top level in Germany and Italy. A genuine sort, he should enjoy another good season at five.

**J L Dunlop [2-4] The National Stud (from B W Hills [3-7] Oct 1999).*

Golden Snake tasted victory in Germany and Italy

GOLDEN SPARROW RR 87f 5312[1]

2 ch f Elmaamul (USA) 8.1f **(70)** - Moon Spin (Night Shift (USA)) 7.2f **(69)**

Form - 21

Record 2000 - 1st:1 2nd:1 3rd:0 Ran:2

Win Prizemoney £3,997 *Total Prizemoney* £5,077

Wins * 2000 Nov Doncas (HVY) 8f 87 <

2000 Turf 1-2: (7f, 8f 1-1) (g-s 1-2)

Currently useful filly. Turf high 87 (began Oct) - 1st of 22 getting 5lb from Pole Star (3 Nov Doncaster RF 5312).

**J L Dunlop [1-2] J L Dunlop.*

GOLDEN STORM (IRE) RR 90f 4794a[10]

3 ch g Magical Wonder (USA) 7.2f **(60)** - Independent Woman 00

Form - 671610

2000 Turf 2-6: (8f, 12f 2-4, 16f) (hvy 1-1, sft 1-1, gd 2, g-f 2)

Useful gelding, effective 12f, acts on hvy to sft, prefers left handed tracks. Turf high 90 - 1st of 15 giving 15lb to Berkeley Bay (21 Spt Listowel RF 4666a).

**Miss Frances Crowley in IRE [4-11] Crock of Gold Syndicate.*

GOLDEN TOUCH (USA) BHB 50f51a RR 51f 51a 5113[2]

8 ch h Elmaamul (USA) 8.1f **(70)** - Tour D'Argent (USA) (Halo (USA))

10.6f **(75)**

Form - 62

Record	**2000 -**	1st:0	2nd:1	3rd:0	Ran:2
	Pre2000 -	1st:3	2nd:3	3rd:5	Ran:35

Win Prizemoney £9,752 *Total Prizemoney* £15,731

Wins							
1996	May Newmar	(G-F)	H	10f	60	68	<
1996	Apr Kempto	(G-F)	H	9f	60	62	
1996	*Apr Wolver*	*(STD)*	*H*	*8.5f*	*56*	*61*	

2000 Turf 0-1: (8f) (g-f) 2000 AW 0-1: (8f) (Fibr)

Fair horse. (1st run) - 2nd of 12 getting 5lb from Groesfaen Lad (20 Oct Wolverhampton 8f Fibr RF 5113). Consistent.

**H J Collingridge [0-2] Mrs Rita Godfrey (from D J S Cosgrove [0-20] Aug 1997).*

GOLDEN WAY (IRE) RR 88f 4963[12]

3 ch f Cadeaux Genereux 7.9f **(76)** - Diavolina (USA) (Lear Fan (USA)) 8.5f **(73)**

Form - 61120

Record	**2000 -**	1st:2	2nd:1	3rd:0	Ran:5
	Pre2000 -	1st:0	2nd:0	3rd:0	Ran:1

Win Prizemoney £11,264 *Total Prizemoney* £13,721

Wins							
*** 2000**	Spt Ayr	(SFT)	H	10f	80	88	<
*** 2000**	Aug Haydoc	(G-S)		10.5f		79+	

2000 Turf 2-5: (8f, 10f 1-2, 11f 1-1, 12f) (gd 2-5)

Scopey, useful filly, effective 10 to 11f, best at 10f, acts on gd. Turf high 88 (began Jly) - 1st of 7 giving 1lb to Chameleon (15 Spt Ayr RF 4427) - also 1st of 10 from Aymara (10 Aug Haydock RF 3532). Landed a Haydock maiden in August and followed up in an Ayr handicap. Very much suited by soft ground.

**E A L Dunlop [2-6] Ahmed Ali.*

GOLDEN WHISPER (IRE) BHB 54f47a RR 59f 47a 3324[6]

2 b f Priolo (USA) 10.9f **(71)** - Gold Wind (IRE) **(69f)** (Marju (IRE))

Form - 40306

Record	**2000 -**	1st:0	2nd:0	3rd:1	Ran:5

Win Prizemoney £0 *Total Prizemoney* £743

2000 Turf 0-5: (5f 3, 6f, 7f) (gd 2, g-f 2, frm)

Fair filly. Turf high 59 - 3rd of 9 getting 7lb from Da Vinci (4 Jun Pontefract 5f gd RF 1700). **I A Balding [0-5] Park House Partnership.*

GOLDEN WINGS RR 55f 4363[9]

2 b f Goldmark (USA) - Rose Chime (IRE) **(12f 25a)** (Tirol)

Form - 000

Record	**2000 -**	1st:0	2nd:0	3rd:0	Ran:3

2000 Turf 0-3: (7f 3) (sft, g-f, frm)

Currently fair filly, has worn blinkers. Turf high 55 (began Jly).

**B Smart [0-3] Michael Broke & Paul Darling.*

GOLDFAW BHB 21f RR 38f 5246[11]

3 ch g Wing Park - Sailors Moon **(33f 46a)** (Indian Ridge)

Form - 00080

Record	**2000 -**	1st:0	2nd:0	3rd:0	Ran:5
	Pre2000 -	1st:0	2nd:0	3rd:0	Ran:2

2000 Turf 0-4: (6f, 7f, 10f, 12f) (gd, g-f, frm 2) 2000 AW 0-1: (8f) (Fibr)

Workmanlike, very moderate gelding, has worn blinkers. Turf high 38. **A T Murphy [0-7] Orby Racing.*

GOLDFINCH BHB 57f53a RR 59f 53a 2948[5]

3 b f Zilzal (USA) 8.5f **(79)** - Garconniere (Gay Mecene (USA)) 8.6f **(69)**

Form - 0805

Record	**2000 -**	1st:0	2nd:0	3rd:0	Ran:4
	Pre2000 -	1st:0	2nd:0	3rd:0	Ran:1

2000 Turf 0-3: (8f 3) (gd, g-f 2) 2000 AW 0-1: (8f) (Fibr)

Fair filly. Turf high 59 - 5th of 14 getting 8lb from Sadaka (19 Jly Yarmouth 8f g-f RF 2948). **J R Fanshawe [0-5] Dr Catherine Wills.*

GOLDIE BHB 81f RR 86+f 4965[3]

2 b f Celtic Swing - Hotel California (IRE) (Last Tycoon) 8.5f **(62)**

Form - 123

Record	**2000 -**	1st:1	2nd:1	3rd:1	Ran:3

Win Prizemoney £2,762 *Total Prizemoney* £13,781

Wins							
*** 2000**	Aug Bath	(G-F)		5.7f		86+	<

2000 Turf 1-3: (6f 1-3) (gd, frm 1-1, hrd)

Currently useful filly. Turf high 86 (1st run) (began Aug) - 1st of 11 getting 5lb from Fiamma Royale (8 Aug Bath RF 3442). An easy winner on fast ground on her Bath debut, she was beaten fair and square in a novice event on the same track next time. Much better run when third of 30 in a valuable sales race.

**D J Coakley [1-3] Chris van Hoorn.*

GOLD KRIEK BHB 39f RR 41f 3267[7]

3 b g High Kicker (USA) 8.4f **(52)** - Ship of Gold (Glint of Gold) 9.3f **(66)**

Form - 88877

Record	**2000 -**	1st:0	2nd:0	3rd:0	Ran:3
	Pre2000 -	1st:0	2nd:0	3rd:0	Ran:3

2000 Turf 0-3: (10f, 12f 2) (gd 2, frm)

Leggy, moderate gelding, effective 10f, acts on frm. Turf high 41 (began Jly) - 7th of 13 getting 1lb from Adriana (25 Jly Brighton 10f frm RF 3089). **N A Callaghan [0-6] Norcroft Park Stud.*

GOLD LANCE (USA) BHB 30f27a RR 46f 27a 3168[7]

7 ch g Seeking the Gold (USA) 7.4f **(80)** - Lucky State (USA) (State Dinner (USA)) 9.4f **(74)**

Form - 56007

Record	**2000 -**	1st:0	2nd:0	3rd:0	Ran:5
	Pre2000 -	1st:4	2nd:2	3rd:4	Ran:28

Win Prizemoney £13,264 *Total Prizemoney* £16,568

Wins							
* 1997	Spt Goodwo	(GD)	H	8f	56	60	<
* 1997	Aug Windso	(G-F)	H	8.3f	53	57	
* 1997	Jly Chepst	(G-F)	SH	8.1f	48	53	
* 1997	Apr Pontef	(G-F)	SH	8f	45	53	

2000 Turf 0-5: (10f, 11f, 12f 3) (g-s, gd 2, frm 2)

Moderate gelding, effective 9f, acts on hrd, has worn blinkers, likes left handed tracks. Turf high 46. Becoming disappointing.

**R J O'Sullivan [4-44] Mrs Barbara Marchant (from Sir Michael Stoute [0-2] Jun 1996).*

GOLD MILLENIUM (IRE) BHB 45f RR 52f 4328[5]

6 gr g Kenmare (FR) 9.6f **(76)** - Gold Necklace (Golden Fleece (USA)) 7.9f **(74)**

Form - 041363125

Record	**2000 -**	1st:2	2nd:1	3rd:2	Ran:9
	Pre2000 -	1st:0	2nd:0	3rd:0	Ran:8

Win Prizemoney £4,777 *Total Prizemoney* £6,780

Wins							
*** 2000**	Aug Folkes	(G-F)	H	16.4f	44	45	<
*** 2000**	Jun Warwic	(G-F)	H	12.3f	40	41	

2000 Turf 2-9: (9f, 10f, 12f 1-2, 14f, 15f, 16f 1-3) (gd 2, g-f 2-5, frm 2)

Fair gelding, effective 16f, acts on frm, likes left handed tracks, likes tight tracks. Turf high 52 - 2nd of 18 giving 17lb to Established (31 Aug Lingfield 16f frm RF 4112). Consistent.

**C A Horgan [2-17] Mrs L M Horgan.*

GOLD QUEST (IRE) RR 86f 4647[18]

3 ch c Rainbow Quest (USA) 11.2f **(81)** - My Potters (USA) (Irish River (FR)) 8.6f **(78)**

Form - 5233130

Record	**2000 -**	1st:1	2nd:1	3rd:3	Ran:7
	Pre2000 -	1st:0	2nd:0	3rd:0	Ran:1

Win Prizemoney £3,750 *Total Prizemoney* £7,618

Wins							
*** 2000**	Jly Yarmou	(G-F)		11.5f		79	<

2000 Turf 1-7: (10f, 11f 1-1, 12f 3, 14f 2) (gd 2, g-f 2, frm 1-3)

Rangy, useful colt, effective 11 to 12f, acts on frm, prefers tight tracks. Turf high 86 - 3rd of 5 giving 10lb to Mickley (19 Aug Ripon 12f frm RF 3799) - also 1st of 7 from Troilus (25 Jly Yarmouth RF 3090). Winner of a weak Yarmouth maiden in July, he is consistent but does not look anything special.

**Sir Michael Stoute [1-8] Lady Clague.*

GOLD RIDER (IRE) BHB 35f RR 53f 2892[12]

3 b g Common Grounds 8.1f **(66)** - Baydon Belle (USA) (Al Nasr (FR)) 9.3f **(68)**

Form - 870000

Record	**2000 -**	1st:0	2nd:0	3rd:0	Ran:6

2000 Turf 0-6: (5f, 6f 2, 7f 2, 8f) (gd 2, g-f, frm 3)

Leggy, fair gelding, has worn blinkers. Turf high 53.

**G M McCourt [0-6] D J Rushen, T Stapleton & M Taylor.*

GOLD ROUND (IRE) RR 103f 4840a[7]

3 f

Form - 3107

2000 Turf 1-4: (7f 1-1, 8f, 12f, 15f) (hvy, g-s 1-2, gd)

Very useful filly. Turf high 103 - also 1st of 9 from Seattle Bay (12 May Saint-Cloud RF 1282a). A decent effort when third to Lady of Chad on her seasonal bow was followed by a decisive win over

further in the Prix Cleopatre. Never got competitive in the Oaks next time, and was well beaten on her return from a break in the autumn. Looks capable of better. **Mme C Head in FR [1-5] .*

GOLD STANDARD (IRE) RR 75f 5066[9]

2 ch c Goldmark (USA) - Miss Audimar (USA) (Mr Leader (USA)) 9.8f **(66)**
Form - 0
Record 2000 - 1st:0 2nd:0 3rd:0 Ran:1
2000 Turf 0-1: (8f) (g-s)
Currently above-average colt.
**D R C Elsworth [0-1] Black, Stott, Ferrar Watson.*

GOLD STATUETTE (IRE) BHB 75f RR 72f 4042[11]

2 ch c Caerleon (USA) 10.9f **(79)** - Nawara (Welsh Pageant) 10f **(65)**
Form - 7640
Record 2000 - 1st:0 2nd:0 3rd:0 Ran:4
Win Prizemoney £0 *Total Prizemoney* £252
2000 Turf 0-4: (7f 3, 8f) (g-s, gd 2, frm)
Above-average colt. Turf high 72. Looks the type for nurseries.
**J W Hills [0-4] Bienstock, Boase, Kerr-Dineen.*

GOLDSTREET (IRE) RR 93f 5286a[8]

3 b g Dolphin Street (FR) - Up To You (Sallust) 8.4f **(63)**
Form - 06212858
2000 Turf 1-8: (7f, 9f 3, 10f 1-3, 12f) (hvy 2, sft, g-s, gd 3, g-f 1-1)
Useful gelding, effective 9 to 10f, best at 9f, acts on gd to g-f, best on gd, likes right handed tracks. Turf high 93 - 2nd of 11 getting 9lb from Draft Of Vintage (13 Aug Leopardstown 9f gd RF 3677a) - also 1st of 11 giving 3lb to Lammas (29 Jly Curragh RF 3305a).
**Miss Frances Crowley in IRE [3-13] Crock of Gold Syndicate.*

GOLFAGENT BHB 44f RR 52f 5295[8]

2 b g Kris 10f **(75)** - Alusha **(90+f)** (Soviet Star (USA))
Form - 0008
Record 2000 - 1st:0 2nd:0 3rd:0 Ran:4
2000 Turf 0-4: (5f, 6f 2, 7f) (sft, g-s 2, frm)
Fair gelding. Turf high 52 (began Spt). **B W Hills [0-4] A L R Morton.*

GOLGOTHA BHB 49f RR 55f 3926[5]

2 gr f Presidium 7.6f **(56)** - Bright Venus (Petong) 6.6f **(58)**
Form - 05785
Record 2000 - 1st:0 2nd:0 3rd:0 Ran:5
2000 Turf 0-4: (5f 4) (gd, g-f, frm 2) 2000 AW 0-1: (5f) (Fibr)
Fair filly. Turf high 55 - 5th of 10 to White Star Lady (24 Aug Musselburgh 5f g-f RF 3926). **A Berry [0-5] William Burns.*

GOLOVIN (GER) RR 100f 5355a[2]

3 b c Bering 9.6f **(80)** - Guilinn (IRE) (Last Tycoon) 8.5f **(62)**
Form - 432
2000 Turf 0-3: (8f, 10f, 12f) (hvy, sft, g-s)
Light-framed, very useful colt. Turf high 100 - 2nd of 12 getting 7lb from Jammaal (30 Oct Leopardstown 10f hvy RF 5355a).
**M J Grassick in IRE [1-4] Mrs H Focke.*

GO MAN (IRE) BHB 22a RR 22a 62[14]

6 b g Mandalus - Cherry Park (Netherkelly) 5.6f **(46)**
Form - 00
Record 2000 - 1st:0 2nd:0 3rd:0 Ran:2
Pre2000 - 1st:0 2nd:0 3rd:0 Ran:1
2000 AW 0-2: (12f 2) (Equi, Fibr)
Very moderate gelding. **P D Evans [0-5] J E Potter.*

GOMPAS PAL BHB 47f RR 31f 5140[13]

2 b g Petong 7.6f **(58)** - Impala Lass (Kampala) 8.4f **(56)**
Form - 0
Record 2000 - 1st:0 2nd:0 3rd:0 Ran:1
2000 Turf 0-1: (6f) (g-s)
Currently moderate gelding. **K R Burke [0-1] I Russell.*

GONCHAROVA (USA) RR 64f 5241[7]

2 b f Gone West (USA) 7.8f **(82)** - Pure Grain **(114f)** (Polish Precedent (USA)) 10.2f **(60)**
Form - 17
Record 2000 - 1st:1 2nd:0 3rd:0 Ran:2
Win Prizemoney £3,224 *Total Prizemoney* £3,224
Wins * 2000 Oct Leices (HVY) 7f 79+ <
2000 Turf 1-2: (7f 1-1, 8f) (g-s 1-2)
Currently average filly. Turf high 79 (1st run) (began Oct) - 1st of 11 from Hernandita (9 Oct Leicester RF 4873). Out of a high-class racemare, she was a nice winner of her Leicester maiden, but failed to handle the step up to listed class on her only other run. Likely to appreciate middle distances.
**Sir Michael Stoute [1-2] Mrs John Magnier & M Tabor.*

GONE TOO FAR BHB 67f RR 75f 5102[13]

2 b g Reprimand 8.2f **(63)** - Blue Nile (IRE) **(69f)** (Bluebird (USA)) 7.5f **(69)**
Form - 72160
Record 2000 - 1st:1 2nd:1 3rd:0 Ran:5
Win Prizemoney £2,925 *Total Prizemoney* £4,110
Wins * 2000 Spt Thirsk (GD) 7f 75 <
2000 Turf 1-5: (6f 3, 7f 1-2) (g-s, gd 1-2, g-f, frm)
Above-average gelding. Turf high 75 (began Aug) - 1st of 13 from Gardor (2 Spt Thirsk RF 4169).
**M Dods [1-5] Exors of the late Mrs H M Carr.*

GONE WITH THE WIND (IRE) RR 45f 3756[9]

2 br f Common Grounds 8.1f **(66)** - Family At War (USA) (Explodent (USA)) 9.4f **(87)**
Form - 000
Record 2000 - 1st:0 2nd:0 3rd:0 Ran:3
2000 Turf 0-3: (5f, 6f 2) (g-f, frm 2)
Currently moderate filly. Turf high 45. **B W Hills [0-3] R J C Upton.*

GOODBYE GOLDSTONE BHB 59f47a RR 70f 47a 3692[9]

4 b g Mtoto 11.5f **(71)** - Shareehan (Dancing Brave (USA)) 8.4f **(76)**
Form - 05860
Record 2000 - 1st:0 2nd:0 3rd:0 Ran:5
Pre2000 - 1st:1 2nd:1 3rd:2 Ran:8
Win Prizemoney £2,483 *Total Prizemoney* £10,711
Wins * 1999 Apr Folkes (SFT) H 9.7f 62 69 <
2000 Turf 0-5: (10f 2, 12f 3) (gd 2, g-f 2, frm)
Light-framed, above-average gelding, effective 10 to 12f, best at 10f, acts on hvy to g-f, favours tight tracks. Turf high 70.
**T J Naughton [1-13] Ashley Carr Racing 2.*

GOODENOUGH MOVER BHB 78f RR 81f 5242[20]

4 ch g Beveled (USA) 6.9f **(64)** - Rekindled Flame (IRE) (Kings Lake (USA)) 10.8f **(67)**
Form - 011114200
Record 2000 - 1st:4 2nd:1 3rd:0 Ran:9
Pre2000 - 1st:0 2nd:0 3rd:0 Ran:5
Win Prizemoney £14,137 *Total Prizemoney* £17,125
Wins * 2000 Jly Salisb (GD) H 6f 70 80 <
*** 2000** Jly Chepst (G-F) H 8.1f 64 71+
*** 2000** Jun Chepst (FRM) H 7.1f 45 68
*** 2000** Jun Chepst (GD) H 7.1f 45 57
2000 Turf 4-9: (6f 1-1, 7f 2-6, 8f 1-2) (g-s, gd 1-1, g-f 2-3, frm 1-4)
Unfurnished, decent gelding, effective 6 to 8f, best at 7f, acts on g-f to frm, best on g-f, excels at Chepstow. Turf high 81 - 2nd of 16 to Floating Charge (15 Spt Newbury 7f frm RF 4433) - also 1st of 13 giving 24lb to Bali-Star (15 Jly Salisbury RF 2848). He progressed very well during the summer before the handicapper appeared to catch up with him. Effective from six furlongs to a mile.
**J S King [4-8] D Goodenough Removals & Transport (from G F H Charles-Jones [0-6] Apr 2000).*

GOOD EVANS ABOVE BHB 43f46a RR 46f 46a 1147[13]

3 br f Tragic Role (USA) 9.4f **(63)** - Dark Amber (Formidable (USA)) 9.2f **(63)**
Form - 600
Record 2000 - 1st:0 2nd:0 3rd:0 Ran:3
Pre2000 - 1st:0 2nd:0 3rd:0 Ran:5
2000 Turf 0-2: (7f 2) (gd 2) 2000 AW 0-1: (8f) (Fibr)
Light-framed, fair filly, effective 5f, - acts on Fibr, has worn blinkers. Turf high 39. Inconsistent. **P D Evans [0-8] David Evans.*

GOOD FRIDAY (IRE) BHB 59f RR 65f 3183[7]

3 b f Tenby 10.4f **(76)** - Sign of Peace (IRE) (Posen (USA))
Form - 656U67
Record 2000 - 1st:0 2nd:0 3rd:0 Ran:6
Pre2000 - 1st:0 2nd:0 3rd:1 Ran:5

Win Prizemoney £0 *Total Prizemoney* £490
2000 Turf 0-6: (8f 3, 11f, 12f, 13f) (g-s 2, frm 4)
Unfurnished, average filly, effective 7 to 8f, acts on g-f to frm. Turf high 65. Consistent. **Mrs P N Dutfield [0-11] Aidan Walsh.*

GOODGOLLYMISSMOLLY RR 43f 4553[8]

2 b f Factual (USA) - Chardonnay Girl **(31f 35a)** (Hubbly Bubbly (USA))
Form - 08
Record 2000 - 1st:0 2nd:0 3rd:0 Ran:2
2000 Turf 0-2: (6f, 7f) (gd, frm)
Currently moderate filly. Turf high 43 (began Aug).
**M A Allen [0-2] John Robson.*

GOODIE TWOSUES BHB 98f RR 89f 4965[1]

2 b f Fraam - Aliuska (IRE) (Fijar Tango (FR))
Form - 134561
Record 2000 - 1st:2 2nd:0 3rd:1 Ran:6
Win Prizemoney £55,222 *Total Prizemoney* £59,315
Wins * **2000** Oct Newmar (SFT) 6f 89 <
* **2000** May Goodwo (SFT) 6f 74
2000 Turf 2-6: (6f 2-5, 7f) (g-s 1-1, gd 1-2, g-f, frm 2)
Useful filly, effective 6f, acts on gd to frm. Turf high 89 - 1st of 30 giving 5lb to Miss Verity (13 Oct Newmarket RF 4965). Made a winning debut at Goodwood, but was found out in decent company before taking a valuable sales race at Headquarters.
**R Hannon [2-6] Mrs Sue Crane & Lady Davis.*

GOOD STANDING (USA) RR 82+f 5236[1]

2 b f Distant View (USA) - Storm Dove (USA) (Storm Bird (CAN)) 10.3f **(74)**
Form - 1
Record 2000 - 1st:1 2nd:0 3rd:0 Ran:1
Win Prizemoney £4,862 *Total Prizemoney* £4,862
Wins * **2000** Oct Newmar (SFT) 7f 82+ <
2000 Turf 1-1: (7f 1-1) (g-s 1-1)
Currently decent filly. (1st run) - 1st of 22 from Toffee Nosed (28 Oct Newmarket RF 5236). **B W Hills [1-1] K Abdulla.*

GOOD TIMING RR 62f 4999[3]

2 bl g Timeless Times (USA) 6.1f **(56)** - Fort Vally **(47f)** (Belfort (FR)) 6.8f **(63)**
Form - 63
Record 2000 - 1st:0 2nd:0 3rd:1 Ran:2
Win Prizemoney £0 *Total Prizemoney* £260
2000 Turf 0-2: (5f, 6f) (g-s, hrd)
Currently average gelding. Turf high 62 (began Aug).
**J J Quinn [0-2] Mrs M Lingwood.*

GOOD WHIT SON BHB 30a RR 30a 202[10]

4 b c Whittingham (IRE) - Davemma (Tachypous) 8.6f **(55)**
Form - 0780
Record 2000 - 1st:0 2nd:0 3rd:0 Ran:2
Pre2000 - 1st:0 2nd:0 3rd:0 Ran:2
2000 AW 0-2: (6f, 7f) (Equi, Fibr)
Workmanlike, little account colt.
**G F H Charles-Jones [0-4] George Smith.*

GOODWOOD BLIZZARD BHB 95f RR 98f 5239[7]

3 ch f Inchinor 8.9f **(64)** - Icecapped (Caerleon (USA)) 8.6f **(71)**
Form - 7
Record 2000 - 1st:0 2nd:0 3rd:0 Ran:1
Pre2000 - 1st:2 2nd:2 3rd:1 Ran:6
Win Prizemoney £16,921 *Total Prizemoney* £33,498
Wins * 1999 Jly Ascot (FRM) 7f 93 <
* 1999 Jun Salisb (GD) 6f 84
2000 Turf 0-1: (8f) (g-s)
Neat, very useful filly, effective 7 to 8f, best at 7f, acts on gd to g-f, best on g-f.
**J L Dunlop [2-7] Goodwood Racehorse Owners Group (Five).*

GORDONS FRIEND BHB 45f42a RR 50f 42a 4653[9]

2 ch g Clantime 6.6f **(57)** - Auntie Fay (IRE) **(25f)** (Fayruz)
Form - 6000
Record 2000 - 1st:0 2nd:0 3rd:0 Ran:4
2000 Turf 0-3: (6f 2, 7f) (g-f 2, frm) 2000 AW 0-1: (7f) (Fibr)
Fair gelding. Turf high 50 (began Aug).
**B S Rothwell [0-4] S P Hudson.*

GORECKI (USA) BHB 93f RR 91f 1155a[3]

3 b c Hermitage (USA) 8.6f **(84)** - Leading Candidate (USA) (Allen's Prospect (USA))
Form - 3
2000 Turf 0-1: (8f) (gd)
Scopey, useful colt, effective 6 to 8f, best at 6f, acts on gd to g-f, best on gd. (1st run) - 3rd of 10 to Etbash (7 May Dielsdorf 8f gd RF 1155a). **U Suter in GER [0-1] (from N A Callaghan [2-6] Aug 1999).*

GORETSKI (IRE) BHB 63f63a RR 60f 63a 5003[7]

7 b g Polish Patriot (USA) 7.8f **(70)** - Celestial Path (Godswalk (USA)) 7.3f **(58)**
Form - 80000067
Record 2000 - 1st:0 2nd:0 3rd:0 Ran:8
Pre2000 - 1st:15 2nd:8 3rd:2 Ran:71
Win Prizemoney £56,999 *Total Prizemoney* £68,377
Wins * 1999 Aug Beverl (GD) H 5f 65 73
* 1999 Aug Pontef (G-F) H 5f 65 71
* 1999 Jun Hamilt (GD) H 5f 59 66
* 1998 Aug Beverl (G-F) H 5f 70 74
* 1998 *Jly Southw (STD) H 5f 74 80* <
* 1998 *Jly Southw (STD) H 5f 67 74*
* 1998 Jun Pontef (SFT) 5f 66
* 1997 Aug Beverl (G-S) H 5f 71 78
* 1997 Jly Catter (G-F) H 5f 60 63
* 1997 Jly Bath (GD) H 5.1f 60 65+
* 1997 *Jun Southw (STD) H 5f 59 67*
* 1997 *Jun Southw (STD) H 5f 59 63*
* 1997 May Hamilt (SFT) H 5f 54 59
* 1996 Apr Catter (GD) H 5f 58 57+
2000 Turf 0-8: (5f 7, 6f) (sft, g-s 2, gd 4, g-f)
Above-average gelding, effective 5f, acts on gd to frm, best on gd, has worn blinkers. Turf high 61. Inconsistent.
**N Tinkler [15-79] P D Savill.*

GORSE BHB 112f RR 115f 3542a[3]

5 b h Sharpo 7.5f **(68)** - Pervenche (Latest Model) 6f **(62)**
Form - 36213
Record 2000 - 1st:1 2nd:1 3rd:2 Ran:5
Pre2000 - 1st:5 2nd:2 3rd:2 Ran:12
Win Prizemoney £107,722 *Total Prizemoney* £162,627
Wins * **2000** Jly Deauvi (HVY) G3 6f 114 <
* 1999 Aug Leopar (SFT) G3 6f 103
* 1999 Jly Hambur (GD) G3 12f 106+
* 1998 Nov Doncas (SFT) L 6f 111
* 1998 Oct Newmar (SFT) 6f 98
* 1998 May Salisb (G-S) 6f 100+
2000 Turf 1-5: (6f 1-4, 7f) (hvy 1-1, sft, g-s, gd 2)
High-class colt, effective 6 to 12f, best at 6f, acts on hvy to gd, best on gd, does well at Deauville and Hamburg. Turf high 115 - 3rd of 11 to Bold Edge (6 Aug Deauville 7f gd RF 3542a) - also 1st of 7 giving 10lb to Danger Over (11 Jly Deauville RF 2977a). Consistent. A very useful sprinter, he won on heavy ground at Deauville in July but just seems to find domestic Group company a bit too much for him. He will no doubt be campaigned on the continent again in 2001. **H Candy [6-17] Girsonfield Ltd.*

GO SALLY GO (IRE) BHB 28f RR 17f 3380[11]

4 b f Elbio 9f **(62)** - Pollette (Stanford) 7.9f **(56)**
Form - 0000
Record 2000 - 1st:0 2nd:0 3rd:0 Ran:2
Pre2000 - 1st:0 2nd:0 3rd:1 Ran:12
Win Prizemoney £0 *Total Prizemoney* £252
2000 Turf 0-2: (5f, 6f) (gd, frm)
Light-framed, very moderate filly. Turf high 17 (began Jly).
**Mrs G S Rees [0-2] The Bitter Fun Partnership (from Ferdy Murphy [0-6] Nov 1999).*

GOT ALOT ON (USA) BHB 59f RR 56f 4443[6]

2 b br g Charnwood Forest (IRE) - Fleety Belle (GER) (Assert) 10.6f **(85)**
Form - 0086
Record 2000 - 1st:0 2nd:0 3rd:0 Ran:4
2000 Turf 0-4: (5f, 6f 3) (gd 2, g-f, hrd)
Fair gelding. Turf high 56 (began Jly).
**J J Quinn [0-4] Mrs Jane Dwyer.*

GOTHIC REVIVAL (IRE) BHB 80f **RR 80f** 3212[5]
3 b c Indian Ridge 7.6f **(74)** - Gothic Dream (IRE) **(107df)** (Nashwan (USA))
Form - 45
Record 2000 - 1st:0 2nd:0 3rd:0 Ran:2
Pre2000 - 1st:0 2nd:0 3rd:0 Ran:2
Win Prizemoney £0 *Total Prizemoney* £1,268
2000 Turf 0-2: (8f, 9f) (g-f, frm)
Scopey, decent colt. Turf high 74 (1st run) (began Jly) - 4th of 14 to Argentan (13 Jly Doncaster 8f frm RF 2756).
**J L Dunlop [0-4] Lady Clague.*

GO THUNDER (IRE) BHB 41f **RR 48f** 5192[3]
6 b g Nordico (USA) 8.2f **(59)** - Moving Off (Henbit (USA)) 9f **(61)**
Form - 000531483
Record 2000 - 1st:1 2nd:0 3rd:2 Ran:9
Pre2000 - 1st:1 2nd:2 3rd:2 Ran:24
Win Prizemoney £15,480 *Total Prizemoney* £19,134
Wins * **2000** Spt Hamilt (SFT) S 9.2f 35
1996 Aug Tralee (Y-S) H 8f 71 90 <
2000 Turf 1-9: (6f, 7f, 8f, 9f 1-6) (hvy, gd 1-5, frm 3)
Moderate gelding, likes right handed tracks. Turf high 48.
**D A Nolan [1-14] Miss G Joughin (from W P Mullins in IRE [1-25] Spt 1998).*

GOT ONE TOO (FR) BHB 56f **RR 56f** 5079[1]
3 ch g Green Tune (USA) - Gloria Mundi (FR) (Saint Cyrien (FR)) 8.4f **(80)**
Form - 070101
Record 2000 - 1st:2 2nd:0 3rd:0 Ran:6
Pre2000 - 1st:0 2nd:0 3rd:0 Ran:6
Win Prizemoney £5,684 *Total Prizemoney* £5,876
Wins * **2000** Oct Bright (SFT) H 11.9f 50 56 <
2000 Jly Folkes (GD) H 12f 46 48
2000 Turf 2-6: (8f 2, 10f, 12f 2-3) (g-s 1-2, gd 1-1, g-f, frm 2)
Leggy, fair gelding, effective 12f, acts on g-s to gd, has worn blinkers, likes tight tracks. Turf high 56 - 1st of 9 getting 28lb from Kadoun (19 Oct Brighton RF 5079). Inconsistent.
**E J O'Neill [1-1] Christopher Ranson (from D Sasse [1-11] Jly 2000).*

GOT TO GO BHB 100f **RR 90+f** 5241[8]
2 b f Shareef Dancer (USA) 10.1f **(67)** - Ghost Tree (IRE) (Caerleon (USA)) 8.6f **(71)**
Form - 178
Record 2000 - 1st:1 2nd:0 3rd:0 Ran:3
Win Prizemoney £2,918 *Total Prizemoney* £2,918
Wins * **2000** Oct Windso (G-S) 6f 90+ <
2000 Turf 1-3: (6f 1-1, 7f, 8f) (g-s, gd, g-f 1-1)
Currently useful filly. Turf high 90 (1st run) (began Oct) - 1st of 20 from How Do I Know (6 Oct Windsor RF 4820). Cosy winner on her Windsor debut, and did not run too badly when upped in class in the Rockfel. **B W Hills [1-3] Mrs H Theodorou.*

GO WITH THE WIND BHB 35f **RR 41f** 5244[6]
7 b g Unfuwain (USA) 11.4f **(74)** - Cominna (Dominion) 8.5f **(63)**
Form - 73276
Record 2000 - 1st:0 2nd:1 3rd:1 Ran:5
Pre2000 - 1st:2 2nd:5 3rd:4 Ran:27
Win Prizemoney £7,247 *Total Prizemoney* £18,101
Wins 1999 Jly Beverl (G-F) H 12f 44 48
1996 Spt Nottin (G-F) H 16f 60 67 <
2000 Turf 0-4: (12f 2, 14f 2) (g-s, g-f, frm, hrd) 2000 AW 0-1: (12f) (Fibr)
Moderate gelding, effective 11 to 14f, acts on g-f to frm, best on frm, has worn blinkers. Turf high 41 (began Jly).
**R A Fahey [0-5] Alf Chadwick (from J S Goldie [3-15] Spt 1999).*

GRACE BHB 59a **RR 41f** 2976[17]
6 b m Buzzards Bay 8.9f **(44)** - Bingo Bongo (Petong) 6.6f **(58)**
Form - 44664866460
Record 2000 - 1st:0 2nd:0 3rd:0 Ran:11
Pre2000 - 1st:1 2nd:4 3rd:1 Ran:36
Win Prizemoney £3,048 *Total Prizemoney* £8,545
Wins * 1998 Jun Chepst (G-S) H 6.1f 50 60 <
2000 Turf 0-11: (5f, 6f 8, 7f 2) (g-s 3, gd 2, g-f, frm 3, hrd 2)
Moderate mare, effective 5 to 7f, best at 6f, acts on g-s to frm, has worn blinkers (effectively). Turf high 47 - 4th of 23 getting 5lb from Amber Brown (14 Apr Thirsk 6f g-s RF 0724).
**J M Bradley [1-47] Treevale Syndicate.*

GRACE AND POWER (IRE) BHB 77f **RR 78f** 939[10]
3 b f Brief Truce (USA) 9.1f **(73)** - Tantum Ergo (Tanfirion) 7f **(61)**
Form - 00
Record 2000 - 1st:0 2nd:0 3rd:0 Ran:2
Pre2000 - 1st:0 2nd:2 3rd:0 Ran:3
Win Prizemoney £0 *Total Prizemoney* £2,259
2000 Turf 0-2: (8f, 9f) (g-s 2)
Lengthy, above-average filly. Turf high 43.
**J L Dunlop [0-5] P J Vela.*

GRACEFUL EMPEROR RR 14f 3209[13]
2 b g Emperor Jones (USA) - Juvenka (Shirley Heights) 10.3f **(74)**
Form - 80
Record 2000 - 1st:0 2nd:0 3rd:0 Ran:2
2000 Turf 0-2: (5f, 7f) (gd, g-f)
Currently poor gelding. Turf high 14. **D Eddy [0-2] Kevin Elliott.*

GRACILIS (IRE) BHB 46f **RR 54?f** 5161[3]
3 b g Caerleon (USA) 10.9f **(79)** - Grace Note (FR) (Top Ville) 11.7f **(68)**
Form - 48053
Record 2000 - 1st:0 2nd:0 3rd:1 Ran:5
Win Prizemoney £0 *Total Prizemoney* £810
2000 Turf 0-5: (8f, 10f, 11f, 12f, 16f) (sft, g-s, gd, frm 2)
Unfurnished, fair gelding. Turf high 54 (1st run) (began Jly) - 4th of 6 to Riparian (9 Jly Newcastle 8f gd RF 2650).
**W W Haigh [0-5] K Elliott.*

GRACIOUS AIR (USA) RR 37f 4602[7]
2 b f Bahri (USA) - Simply Bell (USA) (Simply Majestic (USA))
Form - 7
Record 2000 - 1st:0 2nd:0 3rd:0 Ran:1
2000 Turf 0-1: (8f) (gd)
Currently very moderate filly. **J R Weymes [0-1] T A Scothern.*

GRACIOUS GIFT BHB 82f **RR 90f** 2209[24]
4 ch f Cadeaux Genereux 7.9f **(76)** - Gentle Persuasion (Bustino) 10.4f **(64)**
Form - 000
Record 2000 - 1st:0 2nd:0 3rd:0 Ran:3
Pre2000 - 1st:2 2nd:2 3rd:1 Ran:9
Win Prizemoney £7,621 *Total Prizemoney* £14,701
Wins * 1999 Jly Windso (G-F) H 6f 77 80 <
* 1999 Jun Salisb (G-F) 7f 75
2000 Turf 0-3: (6f 3) (gd 3)
Scopey, useful filly, effective 6f, acts on gd to g-f. Turf high 81.
**R Hannon [2-10] The Queen (from Lord Huntingdon [0-2] Oct 1998).*

GRAF PHILIPP (FR) RR 107f 428a[2]
5 b h Acatenango (GER) - Grey Pearl (GER) (Magic Mirror)
Form - 2
2000 Turf 0-1: (10f) (gd)
Pattern-class colt. (1st run) - 2nd of 14 to Timahs (5 Mar Kranji 10f gd RF 0428a).
**M Thwaites in SIN [0-1] (from A Schutz in GER [1-4] Spt 1999).*

GRAIG PARK RR 23f 4055[12]
2 b c Mind Games - Flicker Toa Flame (USA) (Empery (USA)) 11.2f **(69)**
Form - 00
Record 2000 - 1st:0 2nd:0 3rd:0 Ran:2
2000 Turf 0-2: (6f, 7f) (gd 2)
Currently little account colt. Turf high 23 (began Aug).
**A Berry [0-2] D J Goddard.*

GRAIN STORM (IRE) BHB 65f60a **RR 65f 60a** 4226[5]
2 b f Marju (IRE) 9.2f **(76)** - Zuhal (Busted) 10.2f **(61)**
Form - 085
Record 2000 - 1st:0 2nd:0 3rd:0 Ran:3
2000 Turf 0-3: (6f, 7f 2) (gd, frm 2)
Currently average filly. Turf high 65 (began Aug).
**E A L Dunlop [0-3] Jimmy Strauss.*

GRALMANO (IRE) BHB 84f90a **RR 85f 90a** 4063[6]
5 b g Scenic 10.6f **(66)** - Llangollen (IRE) (Caerleon (USA)) 8.6f **(71)**
Form - 145251641106
Record 2000 - 1st:4 2nd:1 3rd:0 Ran:12
Pre2000 - 1st:5 2nd:5 3rd:4 Ran:33
Win Prizemoney £54,299 *Total Prizemoney* £68,481
Wins * **2000** Aug Doncas (G-F) H 10.3f 80 85
* **2000** Jly Ripon (G-F) H 9f 75 78
* **2000** Jun Redcar (FRM) H 10f 72 80+
* ***2000*** *Feb Wolver (STD) H 8.5f 85 87*
* 1999 Aug Pontef (GD) H 8f 65 68
* 1999 Aug Redcar (GD) 8f 67
1998 *Feb Lingfi (SLW) 8f 91*
1997 *Dec Wolver (STD) 7f 94* <
1997 *Nov Wolver (STD) 8.5f 69*
2000 Turf 3-10: (8f 2, 9f 1-3, 10f 2-4, 12f) (gd 3, g-f 1-3, frm 2-4) 2000 AW 1-2: (8f 1-2) (Fibr 1-2)
Useful gelding, effective 8 to 10f, best at 8f, acts on g-f to frm - acts on Fibr, has worn blinkers, likes left handed tracks, excels at Wolverhampton and Redcar. Turf high 85 - 1st of 12 giving 22lb to Warning Reef (5 Aug Doncaster RF 3389). AW high 90 - 4th of 13 to The Prince (11 Mar Wolverhampton 8f Fibr RF 0435) - also 1st of 6 giving 21lb to Arc (19 Feb Wolverhampton RF 0320). Ran well last season, scoring four times, and looked to be improving even at the age of five. Suited by ten furlongs and fast ground, he is at his most dangerous when allowed to dominate.
**K A Ryan [6-16] Coleorton Moor Racing (from N P Littmoden [3-29] Jun 1999).*

GRAMPAS (USA) BHB 95f **RR 92f** 4470[4]
3 b br c El Gran Senor (USA) 8.9f **(85)** - Let There Be Light (USA) (Sunny's Halo (CAN)) 6.7f **(70)**
Form - 2164
Record 2000 - 1st:1 2nd:1 3rd:0 Ran:4
Win Prizemoney £4,387 *Total Prizemoney* £6,748
Wins * **2000** Aug Newbur (G-F) 9f 88+ <
2000 Turf 1-4: (7f, 8f, 9f 1-1, 10f) (g-f 1-4)
Strong, useful colt. Turf high 92 (began Jly) - also 1st of 9 giving 5lb to Funny Girl (6 Aug Newbury RF 3422). Landed a Newbury maiden, and ran respectably in conditions events since. Still something of an unknown quantity.
**J H M Gosden [1-4] Thomas Tatham.*

GRAND AMBITION (USA) BHB 60f **RR 56f** 4104[11]
4 b g Lear Fan (USA) 10.4f **(80)** - Longing To Dance (USA) (Nureyev (USA)) 8.7f **(78)**
Form - 5057070
Record 2000 - 1st:0 2nd:0 3rd:0 Ran:7
Pre2000 - 1st:1 2nd:1 3rd:0 Ran:5
Win Prizemoney £4,468 *Total Prizemoney* £5,944
Wins 1999 Jly Galway (G-F) 8.5f 80 <
2000 Turf 0-7: (8f 3, 10f 2, 11f, 12f) (g-s, gd 2, g-f 2, frm 2)
Fair gelding, effective 8f, acts on frm, has worn blinkers. Turf high 69. Inconsistent. A winner at Galway on firm ground in 1999, he has not really found his form since coming to Britain.
**T H Caldwell [0-7] R J & Mrs J Mills (from D K Weld in IRE [1-5] Spt 1999).*

GRAND BAHAMIAN (USA) BHB 75f70a **RR 83df 70a** 5018[4]
3 gr c Distant View (USA) - Flora Scent (USA) (Fluorescent Light (USA))
Form - 010P04
Record 2000 - 1st:1 2nd:0 3rd:0 Ran:6
Win Prizemoney £2,697 *Total Prizemoney* £2,697
Wins * **2000** Apr Lingfi (G-S) 7f 83 <
2000 Turf 1-5: (6f, 7f 1-3, 8f) (g-s, gd 1-3, frm) 2000 AW 0-1: (7f) (Fibr)
Rangy, decent colt, effective 7f, acts on gd, has worn blinkers. Turf high 83 - 1st of 16 from Leeroy (7 Apr Lingfield RF 0637). Unraced at two, he caused a surprise when making all to win a Lingfield maiden in April but was then found out in better company. **J Noseda [1-6] Lucayan Stud.*

GRAND CRU BHB 42f40a **RR 38f 40a** 5012[8]
9 ch g Kabour 6.1f **(36)** - Hydrangea (Warpath) 12.3f **(52)**
Form - 41423778146008
Record 2000 - 1st:1 2nd:1 3rd:1 Ran:12
Pre2000 - 1st:4 2nd:0 3rd:3 Ran:24
Win Prizemoney £16,444 *Total Prizemoney* £18,868
Wins * **2000** Apr Warwic (HVY) H 14.6f 37 43
* 1999 *Nov Southw (STD) 14f 54*
* 1997 May Newbur (SFT) H 16f 62 67 <
1997 *Apr Southw (STD) S 12f 67* <
1997 *Feb Southw (STD) C 14f 39*
2000 Turf 1-6: (11f, 14f, 15f 1-2, 16f 2) (hvy 1-1, sft, g-s 2, gd 2) 2000 AW 0-6: (12f, 14f, 16f 4) (Fibr 6)
Moderate gelding, effective 12 to 16f, - acts on Fibr, often wears blinkers (very effectively), likes left handed tracks, favours tight tracks. Turf high 43. AW high 54 - 2nd of 11 giving 9lb to St Lawrence (28 Jan Southwell 12f Fibr RF 0175).
**J Cullinan [3-39] Turf 2000 Ltd (from R Craggs [1-2] Apr 1997).*

GRANDERA (IRE) BHB 100f **RR 99+f** 5124[7]
2 ch c Grand Lodge (USA) - Bordighera (USA) (Alysheba (USA)) 9f **(84)**
Form - 5127
Record 2000 - 1st:1 2nd:1 3rd:0 Ran:4
Win Prizemoney £3,835 *Total Prizemoney* £11,535
Wins * **2000** Spt Warwic (G-F) 7.1f 99+ <
2000 Turf 1-4: (6f, 7f 1-2, 8f) (g-s, gd, g-f 1-1, frm)
Very useful colt. Turf high 99 (began Jly) - 1st of 16 from Bullsefia (11 Spt Warwick RF 4321). Improved from his debut when bolting up in a Warwick maiden, and just missed out in a Group Three next time. Out of his depth in the Racing Post Trophy, he will stay middle distances and can go on to better things.
**J R Fanshawe [1-4] Mrs V Shelton.*

GRAND ESTATE BHB 56f43a **RR 55f 43a** 4654[7]
5 b g Prince Sabo 6.6f **(64)** - Ultimate Dream (Kafu) 6f **(47)**
Form - 40788300545235034807
Record 2000 - 1st:0 2nd:1 3rd:3 Ran:20
Pre2000 - 1st:3 2nd:2 3rd:2 Ran:24
Win Prizemoney £9,187 *Total Prizemoney* £16,720
Wins * 1999 Jly Hamilt (FRM) H 6f 57 63
* 1999 Jun Hamilt (GD) 6f 55
1997 Aug Thirsk (G-F) H 6f 69 75 <
2000 Turf 0-14: (5f 2, 6f 12) (gd 2, g-f 3, frm 7, hrd 2) 2000 AW 0-6: (5f 2, 6f 3, 7f) (Fibr 6)
Fair gelding, effective 6f, acts on g-f to hrd - acts on Fibr, has worn blinkers, excels at Newcastle and Hamilton. Turf high 55 - 4th of 24 giving 5lb to Encounter (5 Aug Thirsk 6f hrd RF 3406). AW high 43. Consistent.
**D W Chapman [2-30] J M Chapman (from T D Easterby [1-14] Apr 1999).*

GRAND FINALE (IRE) RR 106f 3673a[1]
3 b c Sadler's Wells (USA) 11.3f **(87)** - Final Figure (USA) (Super Concorde (USA)) 10.9f **(66)**
Form - 111
2000 Turf 3-3: (9f 1-1, 10f 1-1, 12f 1-1) (sft 1-1, g-s 1-1, gd 1-1)
Pattern-class colt. Turf high 106 - 1st of 12 getting 3lb from Palace Royale (13 Aug Leopardstown RF 3673a). Enjoys the distinction of being the only horse to beat Sinndar, but was out of action for much of the season, returning to gain a hard-fought victory in a Leopardstown listed event. He has reportedly gone to be trained in America. **D K Weld in IRE [3-4] Moyglare Stud Farm.*

GRAND FIVE BHB 71f **RR 78f** 5004[8]
2 b c Spectrum (IRE) - Iberian Dancer (CAN) **(80f)** (El Gran Senor (USA)) 9.6f **(76)**
Form - 2083208
Record 2000 - 1st:0 2nd:2 3rd:1 Ran:7
Win Prizemoney £0 *Total Prizemoney* £3,064
2000 Turf 0-7: (6f 3, 7f, 8f 2, 10f) (g-s 2, gd 3, g-f, frm)
Above-average colt, effective 6 to 8f, best at 6f, acts on g-s to gd, best on gd. Turf high 78 (1st run) - 2nd of 5 to Earl Grey (30 May Leicester 6f gd RF 1543). **J S Moore [0-7] Geoffrey Morgan.*

GRAND HOUDINI BHB 58f56a **RR 57f 56a** 5295[2]
2 b g Primo Dominie 7.2f **(67)** - Cole Slaw (Absalom) 7.2f **(58)**
Form - 0502
Record 2000 - 1st:0 2nd:1 3rd:0 Ran:4
Win Prizemoney £0 *Total Prizemoney* £648
2000 Turf 0-4: (5f 2, 6f, 7f) (g-s, gd 3)
Fair gelding. Turf high 57 (began Spt) - 2nd of 10 getting 3lb from Bowfell (1 Nov Musselburgh 5f g-s RF 5295).
**M W Easterby [0-4] I Bray.*

GRAND JURY (IRE) RR 1[11]
3 ch c Grand Lodge (USA) - Scales of Justice (Final Straw) 7.9f **(64)**
Form - 0
Record 2000 - 1st:0 2nd:0 3rd:0 Ran:1
2000 AW 0-1: (10f) (Equi)
Workmanlike, currently very poor colt.
**E J O'Neill [0-1] The Ballybrit Partnership.*

GRANDMA GRIFFITHS BHB 49f RR 42f 5319[14]
2 b f Eagle Eyed (USA) - Buck Comtess (USA) (Spend A Buck (USA)) 8.5f **(38)**
Form - 800
Record 2000 - 1st:0 2nd:0 3rd:0 Ran:3
2000 Turf 0-3: (6f, 8f 2) (sft, g-s, gd)
Currently moderate filly. Turf high 38 (began Aug).
**Mrs L Stubbs [0-3] Doug Kirk,Darren Kirk,Winton Bloodstock.*

GRANDMA ULLA (IRE) BHB 48f RR 48f 3554[9]
3 b f Muhtarram (USA) - Trojan Lady (USA) (Irish River (FR)) 8.6f **(78)**
Form - 0000700
Record 2000 - 1st:0 2nd:0 3rd:0 Ran:7
Pre2000 - 1st:1 2nd:0 3rd:0 Ran:5
Win Prizemoney £3,550 *Total Prizemoney* £3,550
Wins * 1999 Jly Kempto (G-F) 6f 73 <
2000 Turf 0-7: (6f 2, 7f 3, 9f, 10f) (hvy, sft, g-s, frm 4)
Leggy, moderate filly, effective 6f, acts on frm. Turf high 55.
**R J O'Sullivan [1-12] Jack Joseph.*

GRAND MUSICA BHB 35f RR 5154[17]
7 b g Puissance 7.1f **(60)** - Vera Musica (USA) (Stop The Music (USA)) 9.2f **(71)**
Form - 000
Record 2000 - 1st:0 2nd:0 3rd:0 Ran:3
Pre2000 - 1st:2 2nd:3 3rd:0 Ran:21
Win Prizemoney £6,490 *Total Prizemoney* £13,735
Wins 1998 Jly Haydoc (G-F) H 10.5f 63 66
1996 Aug Epsom (GD) 7f 78 <
2000 Turf 0-1: (7f) (gd) 2000 AW 0-2: (7f, 12f) (Equi 2)
Very poor gelding, has broken blood-vessels, has worn blinkers. (began Oct).
**B A Pearce [0-3] A Log Each Partnership (from I A Balding [2-21] Spt 1998).*

GRAND ORO RR 84f 1083[12]
3 ch c Suave Dancer (USA) 10.7f **(68)** - Hence (USA) (Mr Prospector (USA)) 8.8f **(78)**
Form - 0
Record 2000 - 1st:0 2nd:0 3rd:0 Ran:1
Pre2000 - 1st:0 2nd:1 3rd:0 Ran:1
Win Prizemoney £0 *Total Prizemoney* £975
2000 Turf 0-1: (8f) (frm)
Lengthy, currently decent colt. **G C H Chung [0-2] Osvaldo Pedroni.*

GRAND SLAM (IRE) BHB 48f RR 42f 5294[15]
5 b g Second Set (IRE) 9.2f **(67)** - Lady In The Park (IRE) (Last Tycoon) 8.5f **(62)**
Form - 4000
Record 2000 - 1st:0 2nd:0 3rd:0 Ran:4
Pre2000 - 1st:1 2nd:5 3rd:1 Ran:18
Win Prizemoney £2,658 *Total Prizemoney* £10,367
Wins 1998 Spt Warwic (G-F) 8f 76 <
2000 Turf 0-4: (10f, 12f 2, 14f) (sft, g-s, gd, hrd)
Moderate gelding, effective 8f, acts on g-f to frm, best on frm, has worn blinkers, likes right handed tracks, prefers tight tracks. Turf high 42 (began Jly). Becoming disappointing.
**L Lungo [0-7] R J Gilbert (from R Hannon [1-18] Spt 1999).*

GRAND VIEW BHB 62f59a RR 66df 59a 4333[4]
4 ch g Grand Lodge (USA) - Hemline (Sharpo) 7.7f **(59)**
Form - 61304
Record 2000 - 1st:1 2nd:0 3rd:1 Ran:5
Pre2000 - 1st:1 2nd:1 3rd:1 Ran:12
Win Prizemoney £4,864 *Total Prizemoney* £6,727
Wins * **2000** *Mar Lingfi (STD) S 6f 59*
1999 Jly Salisb (G-F) H 6f 65 67 <
2000 Turf 0-2: (5f, 7f) (g-f, frm) 2000 AW 1-3: (6f 1-2, 7f) (Equi 1-2, Fibr)
Scopey, average gelding, effective 6f, acts on frm. Turf high 58 (began Spt). AW high 59.
**D Nicholls [1-5] The David Nicholls Racing Club (from R Hannon [1-12] Oct 1999).*

GRANITE CITY BHB 52f RR 50f 4123[6]
3 ro g Clantime 6.6f **(57)** - Alhargah (Be My Guest (USA)) 9.3f **(67)**
Form - 08077302166
Record 2000 - 1st:1 2nd:1 3rd:1 Ran:11
Pre2000 - 1st:0 2nd:0 3rd:1 Ran:9
Win Prizemoney £2,562 *Total Prizemoney* £4,609
Wins * **2000** Aug Mussel (GD) H 7.1f 48 48 <
2000 Turf 1-11: (5f 2, 7f 1-6, 8f 3) (g-f 3, frm 1-7, hrd)
Leggy, fair gelding, effective 5 to 8f, acts on g-f to hrd, likes tight tracks. Turf high 50 - 2nd of 16 to Send It To Penny (28 Jly Thirsk 8f hrd RF 3193) - also 1st of 14 giving 3lb to Red Wolf (2 Aug Musselburgh RF 3339). **J S Goldie [1-20] Aberdeenshire Racing Club.*

GRANNY RICH BHB 37f RR 45?f 4987[24]
6 ch m Ardross 12.4f **(67)** - Weareagrandmother (Prince Tenderfoot (USA)) 9f **(61)**
Form - 00
Record 2000 - 1st:0 2nd:0 3rd:0 Ran:2
Pre2000 - 1st:0 2nd:0 3rd:0 Ran:6
2000 Turf 0-2: (16f, 18f) (g-s, gd)
Moderate mare. Turf high 50 (began Spt). **P M Rich [4-20] P M Rich.*

GRANNY'S PET BHB 103f RR 105f 4817[2]
6 ch g Selkirk (USA) 7.9f **(76)** - Patsy Western (Precocious) 8.6f **(62)**
Form - 3168532
Record 2000 - 1st:1 2nd:1 3rd:2 Ran:7
Pre2000 - 1st:6 2nd:7 3rd:3 Ran:31
Win Prizemoney £60,486 *Total Prizemoney* £102,547
Wins * **2000** May Leices (G-S) 7f 105 <
* 1999 Oct Doncas (SFT) 7f 101
* 1999 Spt Goodwo (G-F) H 7f 100 103
* 1999 Aug Goodwo (GD) H 7f 98 99
* 1999 Aug Cheste (G-S) H 7f 95 98
* 1998 Spt Haydoc (GD) H 7.1f 89 99
* 1996 Jun Epsom (GD) 5f 84
2000 Turf 1-7: (7f 1-7) (g-s, gd 1-4, g-f, frm)
Pattern-class gelding, effective 7f, acts on g-s to g-f, best on gd, has worn blinkers, likes tight tracks, and excels at York and Doncaster. Turf high 105 - 2nd of 9 giving 12lb to Big Future (5 Oct York 7f g-s RF 4817) - also 1st of 3 giving 7lb to Tissifer (30 May Leicester RF 1544). Consistent. He goes well for Jimmy Fortune and returned to winning form in a three-runner conditions event at Leicester on his second start of the season. Back in good heart in the autumn, he appreciates some cut in the ground.
**P F I Cole [7-38] Mrs Denise Margot Arbib.*

GRANTED (FR) BHB 96f RR 94f 5368a[2]
3 b f Cadeaux Genereux 7.9f **(76)** - Germane **(83df)** (Distant Relative)
Form - 332114321032
Record 2000 - 1st:3 2nd:3 3rd:4 Ran:12
Pre2000 - 1st:0 2nd:0 3rd:0 Ran:2
Win Prizemoney £17,036 *Total Prizemoney* £35,106
Wins * **2000** Spt Kempto (GD) H 8f 81 84 <
* **2000** Jly Doncas (GD) H 8f 76 82
* **2000** Jun Hamilt (G-F) H 8.3f 73 76
2000 Turf 3-12: (8f 3-7, 9f 3, 10f, 11f) (hvy 2, gd 3, g-f 2-4, frm 1-3)
Light-framed, useful filly, effective 8 to 9f, best at 8f, acts on hvy to g-f, best on hvy, has worn blinkers, prefers right handed tracks. Turf high 94 - 2nd of 15 getting 3lb from Mosquera (4 Nov Cologne 8f hvy RF 5368a). Consistent. She enjoyed a good season, winning three handicaps at around a mile. **M L W Bell [3-14].*

GRANTLEY BHB 39f53a RR 48f 53a 4489[6]
3 b g Deploy 11.4f **(67)** - Matisse **(43f 39a)** (Shareef Dancer (USA)) 9.9f **(73)**
Form - 07006
Record 2000 - 1st:0 2nd:0 3rd:0 Ran:5
Pre2000 - 1st:0 2nd:0 3rd:0 Ran:2
2000 Turf 0-5: (7f, 10f 2, 12f, 14f) (gd 2, g-f 3)
Moderate gelding, has worn blinkers. Turf high 48.
**J D Bethell [0-7] WWW Clarendon Racing Co UK.*

GRASSLANDIK BHB 50f42a **RR 55f 42a** 4275[8]
4 b c Ardkinglass 5f **(64)** - Sophisticated Baby (Bairn (USA)) 7.7f **(59)**
Form - 023535074568
Record 2000 - 1st:0 2nd:0 3rd:2 Ran:10
Pre2000 - 1st:1 2nd:3 3rd:1 Ran:14
Win Prizemoney £1,934 *Total Prizemoney* £5,220
Wins * 1998 *Dec Southw (STD) S 5f 53 <*
2000 Turf 0-3: (6f 2, 7f) (gd, g-f 2) 2000 AW 0-7: (6f 7) (Fibr 7)
Fair colt, effective 5f, - acts on Equi, has worn blinkers. Turf high 55. AW high 48. **A G Newcombe [1-24] Chris Bradbury.*

GRAY PASTEL (IRE) BHB 44f **RR 32f** 2596[10]
6 gr g Al Nasr (FR) 9.9f **(72)** - Gay Pastel (FR) (No Pass No Sale) 11.9f **(85)**
Form - 0
Record 2000 - 1st:0 2nd:0 3rd:0 Ran:1
Pre2000 - 1st:1 2nd:0 3rd:0 Ran:3
Win Prizemoney £2,259 *Total Prizemoney* £2,259
Wins * 1998 Jly Leices (GD) C 11.8f 56 <
2000 Turf 0-1: (12f) (g-f)
Very moderate gelding, has worn blinkers.
**M C Pipe [3-24] Harry Saunders.*

GREAT CRAIC (IRE) RR 44[7]
3 b f Treasure Kay 6.5f **(53)** - Heart to Heart (IRE) **(36f)** (Double Schwartz) 7.9f **(55)**
Form - 7
Record 2000 - 1st:0 2nd:0 3rd:0 Ran:1
2000 AW 0-1: (7f) (Fibr)
Unfurnished, currently very poor filly.
**M H Tompkins [0-1] Michael Keogh.*

GREAT HOPPER BHB 15f **RR 26f** 1710[7]
5 b m Rock Hopper 10.6f **(54)** - Spun Gold (Thatch (USA)) 9.8f **(62)**
Form - 77
Record 2000 - 1st:0 2nd:0 3rd:0 Ran:2
Pre2000 - 1st:0 2nd:0 3rd:0 Ran:3
2000 Turf 0-2: (12f, 14f) (gd, g-f)
Little account filly. Turf high 26. **F Watson [0-5] F Watson.*

GREAT MANOEUVRE RR 53f 3244[5]
2 b f Deploy 11.4f **(67)** - Great Exception (Grundy) 10.3f **(65)**
Form - 5
Record 2000 - 1st:0 2nd:0 3rd:0 Ran:1
2000 Turf 0-1: (7f) (frm)
Currently fair filly. **H Candy [0-1] T A F Frost.*

GREAT NEWS BHB 85f80a **RR 85f 80a** 5240[8]
5 b g Elmaamul (USA) 8.1f **(70)** - Amina (Brigadier Gerard) 9.3f **(58)**
Form - 00008711128
Record 2000 - 1st:3 2nd:1 3rd:0 Ran:11
Pre2000 - 1st:3 2nd:4 3rd:4 Ran:13
Win Prizemoney £62,612 *Total Prizemoney* £76,277
Wins * **2000** Spt Lingfi (GD) H 7f 67 85 <
* **2000** Spt Ayr (SFT) H 8f 67 82+
* **2000** Spt Ayr (SFT) H 7f 67 77+
1999 Aug Windso (GD) H 8.3f 80 83
1999 Apr Ascot (GD) H 7f 77 81
1998 Oct Lingfi (SFT) H 7f 69 73
2000 Turf 3-11: (7f 2-2, 8f 1-6, 10f 3) (g-s 4, gd 3-7)
Useful gelding, effective 7 to 8f, best at 8f, acts on g-s to frm, excels at Ayr. Turf high 85 - 2nd of 6 to Celebration Town (6 Oct York 8f g-s RF 4831) - also 1st of 17 giving 18lb to Kilmeena Lad (22 Spt Lingfield RF 4586). Winner of the Victoria Cup in '99, he changed stables before last season and it took him a while to find his form, but was in irresistible form during the autumn. Landed a brilliant hat-trick with the space of a week in September, including at Ayr on consecutive days. Very much suited by soft ground.
**W J Haggas [3-11] Executive Network (P Group) (from I A Balding [3-13] Oct 1999).*

GREAT RICHES BHB 30f **RR 30f** 3312[16]
3 b g Mon Tresor 7.9f **(60)** - Glitter of Gold **(56f 52a)** (Glint of Gold) 9.3f **(66)**
Form - 00
Record 2000 - 1st:0 2nd:0 3rd:0 Ran:2
Pre2000 - 1st:0 2nd:0 3rd:0 Ran:3
2000 Turf 0-2: (8f, 12f) (gd, g-f)
Scopey, very moderate gelding. **Mrs M Reveley [0-5] Skeltools Ltd.*

GREAT WHITE BHB 56f61a **RR 56df 61a** 760[6]
3 gr g Marju (IRE) 9.2f **(76)** - Galava (CAN) (Graustark) 10.1f **(70)**
Form - 006
Record 2000 - 1st:0 2nd:0 3rd:0 Ran:2
Pre2000 - 1st:0 2nd:0 3rd:2 Ran:7
Win Prizemoney £0 *Total Prizemoney* £1,413
2000 Turf 0-2: (5f, 6f) (g-s, frm)
Light-framed, fair gelding, effective 5f, acts on g-f to frm. Turf high 29. Becoming disappointing. **R Hannon [0-9] I A N Wight.*

GRECIAN HALO (USA) BHB 52f **RR 52f** 4820[18]
2 b f Southern Halo (USA) - Modern Grecian (USA) (Mr Leader (USA)) 9.8f **(66)**
Form - 680
Record 2000 - 1st:0 2nd:0 3rd:0 Ran:3
2000 Turf 0-3: (6f, 7f 2) (gd, g-f, frm)
Currently fair filly. Turf high 52 (began Jly).
**M L W Bell [0-3] D M Littlejohn & W J P Jackson.*

GREEK DANCE (IRE) BHB 122f **RR 124f** 4989[10]
5 b h Sadler's Wells (USA) 11.3f **(87)** - Hellenic (Darshaan) 9.9f **(84)**
Form - 225120
Record 2000 - 1st:1 2nd:3 3rd:0 Ran:6
Pre2000 - 1st:3 2nd:2 3rd:0 Ran:10
Win Prizemoney £92,936 *Total Prizemoney* £364,466
Wins * **2000** Jly Munich (SFT) G1 10f 120 <
* 1999 Aug Haydoc (SFT) G3 10.5f 114+
* 1998 May York (GD) 10.4f 112++
* 1998 Apr Newmar (G-S) 10f 95+
2000 Turf 1-6: (10f 1-3, 11f 2, 12f) (hvy, sft 1-1, g-s, gd 3)
Very high-class colt, effective 10 to 12f, best at 10f, acts on sft to gd. Turf high 124 - 2nd of 7 giving 7lb to Giant's Causeway (9 Spt Leopardstown 10f gd RF 4355a) - also 1st of 8 from Sumitas (30 Jly Munich RF 3353a). A very useful performer, especially with cut in the ground, he was no match for Montjeu on his second start of the year, but did land a German Group One in July when he had his favoured ground. He was given a lot to do when a fast-finishing second to Giant's Causeway in the Irish Champion, but ran poorly in the Champion Stakes at Newmarket.
**Sir Michael Stoute [4-16] Lord Weinstock.*

Greek Dance ran good races against the best last season

GREEK DREAM (USA) RR 65f 1644[6]
2 ch f Distant View (USA) - Wandesta **(110df)** (Nashwan (USA))
Form - 6
Record 2000 - 1st:0 2nd:0 3rd:0 Ran:1
2000 Turf 0-1: (6f) (gd)
Currently average filly. **B W Hills [0-1] K Abdulla.*

GREENAWAY BAY (USA) BHB 78f **RR 80f** 5316[2]
6 ch g Green Dancer (USA) 11.9f **(77)** - Raise 'n Dance (USA) (Raise A Native) 11.2f **(69)**
Form - 51112
Record 2000 - 1st:3 2nd:1 3rd:0 Ran:5
Pre2000 - 1st:2 2nd:0 3rd:4 Ran:23
Win Prizemoney £51,447 *Total Prizemoney* £58,308
Wins * **2000** Oct Newmar (SFT) H 8f 63 80 <
* **2000** Oct Nottin (SFT) H 8.2f 63 72
* **2000** Oct York (HVY) H 8.9f 57 66
* 1999 Aug Bright (G-F) H 8f 54 56
1997 Mar Kempto (G-F) 7f 80+
2000 Turf 3-5: (8f 2-3, 9f 1-2) (sft 2-2, g-s 1-2, frm)
Decent gelding, effective 8f, acts on sft to g-s, best on g-s. Turf high 80 (began Aug) - 1st of 30 getting 25lb from Atlantic Rhapsody (28 Oct Newmarket RF 5240) - also 1st of 17 giving 4lb to Route Sixty Six (24 Oct Nottingham RF 5159).
**K R Burke [4-10] Asterlane Ltd (from W J Musson [0-13] Jly 1999).*

GREEN BOPPER (USA) BHB 58f70a **RR 64f 70a** 3503[7]
7 b g Green Dancer (USA) 11.9f **(77)** - Wayage (USA) (Mr Prospector (USA)) 8.8f **(78)**
Form - 52342175587
Record 2000 - 1st:1 2nd:2 3rd:1 Ran:11
Pre2000 - 1st:7 2nd:3 3rd:2 Ran:30
Win Prizemoney £27,523 *Total Prizemoney* £35,961
Wins * **2000** *Mar Southw (STD) H 12f 70 72*
* 1999 Jly Haydoc (G-S) H 10.5f 56 62
* 1999 *Mar Southw (STD) H 11f 65 68*
* 1999 *Feb Southw (STD) H 11f 59 61*
* 1998 *Apr Wolver (STD) 8.5f 64*
* 1998 *Mar Wolver (STD) H 8.5f 54 62*
* 1998 *Mar Southw (STD) H 8f 47 56*
1996 Apr Newcas (GD) 8f 80 <
2000 Turf 0-5: (10f, 12f 4) (gd 2, g-f, frm 2) 2000 AW 1-6: (11f 4, 12f 1-2) (Fibr 1-6)
Above-average gelding, effective 10 to 12f, best at 12f, acts on gd to g-f - acts on Fibr, has worn blinkers, prefers left handed tracks, favours tight tracks, excels at Southwell, does well at Haydock. Turf high 64. AW high 72 - 2nd of 10 giving 6lb to Parable (14 Mar Southwell 12f Fibr RF 0441) - also 1st of 7 getting 30lb from Murghem (20 Mar Southwell RF 0468). He is a useful middle-distance handicapper on Fibresand, but races on turf only rarely these days and does not look quite so effective on it.
**G Woodward [7-31] Wetherby Racing Bureau 35 (from C P Morlock [0-6] May 1997).*

GREENBOROUGH (IRE) BHB 69f **RR 45f** 5157[15]
2 b c Dr Devious (IRE) 9.9f **(74)** - Port Isaac (USA) (Seattle Song (USA)) 9f **(77)**
Form - 0
Record 2000 - 1st:0 2nd:0 3rd:0 Ran:1
2000 Turf 0-1: (8f) (sft)
Currently above-average colt. **P F I Cole [0-1] Anthony Speelman.*

GREEN CARD (USA) BHB 86f **RR 89+f** 4370[6]
6 br h Green Dancer (USA) 11.9f **(77)** - Dunkellin (USA) (Irish River (FR)) 8.6f **(78)**
Form - 4630416
Record 2000 - 1st:1 2nd:0 3rd:1 Ran:7
Pre2000 - 1st:3 2nd:2 3rd:6 Ran:25
Win Prizemoney £21,840 *Total Prizemoney* £53,389
Wins * **2000** Spt Doncas (G-F) 10.3f 89+
* 1998 Jly Doncas (G-F) 8f 110 <
* 1998 Jun Nottin (GD) 8.2f 98
* 1997 Apr Ripon (G-F) 8f 81+
2000 Turf 1-7: (7f, 8f 4, 10f 1-1, 12f) (g-s 2, gd 1-3, g-f, frm)
Useful horse, effective 9f, acts on gd, has worn blinkers, likes left handed tracks. Turf high 89. **S P C Woods [6-34] P K L Chu.*

GREEN CASKET (IRE) RR 69f 944[6]
3 b c Green Desert (USA) 7.8f **(78)** - Grecian Urn (Ela-Mana-Mou) 10.1f **(70)**
Form - 6
Record 2000 - 1st:0 2nd:0 3rd:0 Ran:1
Pre2000 - 1st:0 2nd:0 3rd:0 Ran:1
2000 Turf 0-1: (8f) (g-s)
Scopey, currently average colt.
**Sir Michael Stoute [0-2] Lord Weinstock.*

GREEN GINGER BHB 45f **RR 41f** 4217[16]
4 ch g Ardkinglass 5f **(64)** - Bella Maggio (Rakaposhi King)
Form - 00000
Record 2000 - 1st:0 2nd:0 3rd:0 Ran:5
Pre2000 - 1st:1 2nd:0 3rd:1 Ran:10
Win Prizemoney £2,417 *Total Prizemoney* £4,117
Wins * 1999 Aug Nottin (G-F) 6.1f 80 <
2000 Turf 0-5: (6f 4, 7f) (frm 4, hrd)
Small, moderate gelding, effective 6f, acts on g-f, has worn blinkers. Turf high 41. Inconsistent. **A Streeter [1-15] B J Garrett.*

GREEN GOD (IRE) RR 65f 5084[8]
4 b c Common Grounds 8.1f **(66)** - Inanna (Persian Bold) 9.3f **(66)**
Form - 050054008
Record 2000 - 1st:0 2nd:0 3rd:0 Ran:9
Pre2000 - 1st:0 2nd:2 3rd:0 Ran:6
Win Prizemoney £0 *Total Prizemoney* £2,402
2000 Turf 0-9: (7f 5, 8f 4) (hvy, g-s 2, gd, g-f 2, frm 3)
Workmanlike, average colt, effective 7f, acts on g-s to gd, has worn blinkers. Turf high 65 - 5th of 20 getting 1lb from Patsy Stone (8 Jun Chepstow 7f gd RF 1798). Becoming disappointing.
**C G Cox [0-10] Mrs Caroline Parker (from M J Heaton-Ellis [0-5] Jun 1999).*

GREENGROOM (FR) RR 95f 5365a[3]
2 b c Green Tune (USA) - Danagroom (USA) (Groom Dancer (USA))
Form - 53
2000 Turf 0-2: (7f, 8f) (hvy, sft)
Currently very useful colt. Turf high 95 (began Oct) - 3rd of 5 to Amiwain (3 Nov Maisons-laffitte 7f hvy RF 5365a).
**C Laffon-Parias in FR [0-2] Wertheimer et Frere.*

GREENHOPE (IRE) RR 77f 5066[5]
2 b c Definite Article - Unbidden Melody (USA) (Chieftain II) 10.4f **(75)**
Form - 05
Record 2000 - 1st:0 2nd:0 3rd:0 Ran:2
2000 Turf 0-2: (8f 2) (g-s 2)
Currently above-average colt. Turf high 77 (began Spt).
**J A Osborne [0-2] Lynn Wilson.*

GREENLEES RR 2f 4653[14]
2 b f Greensmith - Scawsby Lees (Stanford) 7.9f **(56)**
Form - 00
Record 2000 - 1st:0 2nd:0 3rd:0 Ran:2
2000 Turf 0-1: (8f) (g-f) 2000 AW 0-1: (7f) (Fibr)
Currently very poor filly.
**W G M Turner [0-2] Hawks And Doves Racing Syndicate.*

GREEN MAGICAL (IRE) BHB 43f **RR 53f** 5025[15]
4 ch f Magical Strike (USA) 5.5f **(61)** - Green Legend (IRE) (Montekin) 11.1f **(55)**
Form - 00
Record 2000 - 1st:0 2nd:0 3rd:0 Ran:2
Pre2000 - 1st:0 2nd:1 3rd:0 Ran:11
Win Prizemoney £0 *Total Prizemoney* £519
2000 Turf 0-2: (8f, 11f) (g-s, gd)
Fair filly, effective 10 to 12f, acts on sft to g-f, has worn blinkers, prefers right handed tracks. Turf high 6 (began Spt).
**B J Curley [0-2] Mrs B J Curley (from T Carmody in IRE [0-13] Nov 1999).*

GREEN MINSTREL (FR) RR 96f 4844a[8]
2 b f Green Tune (USA) - Shy Minstrel (USA) (The Minstrel (CAN)) 10f **(72)**
Form - 18
2000 Turf 1-2: (8f 1-2) (gd 1-2)
Currently very useful filly. Turf high 96 (began Spt).
** J M Beguigne in FR [1-2].*

GREEN POWER BHB 40f **RR 52?f** 617[15]
6 b g Green Desert (USA) 7.8f **(78)** - Shaft of Sunlight (Sparkler)
Form - 0
Record 2000 - 1st:0 2nd:0 3rd:0 Ran:1
Pre2000 - 1st:1 2nd:1 3rd:2 Ran:17

Win Prizemoney £3,779 *Total Prizemoney* £6,961
Wins 1997 May Windso (SFT) 8.3f 69 <
2000 Turf 0-1: (12f) (gd)
Fair gelding.
**B J Llewellyn [0-4] Miss Emily Jane Jones (from N P Littmoden [0-8] Oct 1998).*

GREEN PURSUIT BHB 51f60a RR 48f 60a 4176[12]

4 b g Green Desert (USA) 7.8f **(78)** - Vayavaig (Damister (USA)) 9f **(73)**
Form - 7820
Record 2000 - 1st:0 2nd:1 3rd:0 Ran:4
Pre2000 - 1st:1 2nd:0 3rd:2 Ran:8
Win Prizemoney £4,296 *Total Prizemoney* £5,866
Wins 1999 Jun Cork (G-F) 6f 74 <
2000 Turf 0-2: (7f, 8f) (g-f, frm) 2000 AW 0-2: (6f, 7f) (Fibr 2)
Moderate gelding, effective 6f, acts on g-f, has worn blinkers. Turf high 48. AW high 39. Inconsistent.
**J A Osborne [0-4] The Woolfie and Tom Partnership (from N Meade in IRE [1-8] Aug 1999).*

GREEN TAMBOURINE RR 80+f 3201[6]

2 b f Green Desert (USA) 7.8f **(78)** - Maid For The Hills **(84f)** (Indian Ridge)
Form - 16
Record 2000 - 1st:1 2nd:0 3rd:0 Ran:2
Win Prizemoney £3,841 *Total Prizemoney* £3,841
Wins * 2000 Jly Haydoc (G-F) 6f 80+ <
2000 Turf 1-2: (6f 1-2) (gd 1-2)
Currently decent filly. Turf high 80 (1st run) (began Jly) - 1st of 8 getting 11lb from Proud Boast (8 Jly Haydock RF 2631). Easy winner at Haydock on her debut. **R Charlton [1-2] Mountgrange Stud.*

GREEN TURTLE CAY (IRE) BHB 40f RR 44f 2940[11]

4 b g Turtle Island (IRE) - Pinta (IRE) (Ahonoora) 8.1f **(73)**
Form - 0000
Record 2000 - 1st:0 2nd:0 3rd:0 Ran:4
Pre2000 - 1st:0 2nd:0 3rd:0 Ran:3
2000 Turf 0-3: (6f, 8f, 9f) (gd 2, frm) 2000 AW 0-1: (7f) (Equi)
Scopey, moderate gelding.
**T E Powell [0-4] Lawrence Pratt (from J Noseda [0-3] Aug 1999).*

GREEN WILDERNESS (USA) BHB 72f RR 75f 5101[19]

3 b f Green Dancer (USA) 11.9f **(77)** - Wild Vintage (USA) (Alysheba (USA)) 9f **(84)**
Form - 6260
Record 2000 - 1st:0 2nd:1 3rd:0 Ran:4
Win Prizemoney £0 *Total Prizemoney* £1,130
2000 Turf 0-4: (10f 3, 11f) (gd 2, frm 2)
Unfurnished, above-average filly. Turf high 70 - 2nd of 8 getting 5lb from Krispin (11 Jly Pontefract 10f frm RF 2695).
**J R Fanshawe [0-4] Car Colston Hall Stud.*

GREENWOOD BHB 92f RR 89f 5107[12]

2 ch c Emarati (USA) 6.6f **(63)** - Charnwood Queen **(57f 42a)** (Cadeaux Genereux)
Form - 120
Record 2000 - 1st:1 2nd:1 3rd:0 Ran:3
Win Prizemoney £4,049 *Total Prizemoney* £6,216
Wins * 2000 Jly Windso (G-F) 6f 74 <
2000 Turf 1-3: (5f, 6f 1-2) (gd, g-f, frm 1-1)
Currently useful colt. Turf high 89 (began Jly) - 2nd of 7 giving 9lb to Sonatina (14 Spt Yarmouth 6f g-f RF 4397). Made a winning debut at Windsor and probably ran into a decent sort when beaten at Yarmouth next time. **J M P Eustace [1-3] J C Smith.*

GREGORIAN (IRE) RR 96f 3648a[4]

3 b c Foxhound (USA) - East River (FR) (Arctic Tern (USA)) 8.9f **(69)**
Form - 0854
2000 Turf 0-4: (6f 2, 7f, 8f) (g-s 2, gd, frm)
Very useful colt, has worn blinkers. Turf high 96.
**Patrick Flynn in IRE [0-4] A G Moylan (from P J Flynn in IRE [0-1] Apr 1999).*

GREMLIN ONE BHB 36f RR 37f 3427[6]

3 ch g Democratic (USA) - Calcutta Queen (Night Shift (USA)) 7.2f **(69)**
Form - 76
Record 2000 - 1st:0 2nd:0 3rd:0 Ran:2
2000 Turf 0-2: (6f, 7f) (g-f, frm)
Rangy, currently very moderate gelding. Turf high 37 (began Aug).
**W Storey [0-2] Gremlin Racing.*

GRENADIER (IRE) RR 77f 1539[12]

3 b c Sadler's Wells (USA) 11.3f **(87)** - Sandhurst Goddess (Sandhurst Prince) 7.9f **(63)**
Form - 540
Record 2000 - 1st:0 2nd:0 3rd:0 Ran:3
Pre2000 - 1st:0 2nd:0 3rd:0 Ran:1
Win Prizemoney £0 *Total Prizemoney* £840
2000 Turf 0-3: (7f, 8f, 9f) (sft 2, g-s)
Scopey, above-average colt. Turf high 77.
**W R Muir [0-4] Song And Dance Partnership.*

GREY BIRD (IRE) RR 31f 414[12]

3 ro f Prince of Birds (USA) - Ganador **(42f 41a)** (Weldnaas (USA))
Form - 0
Record 2000 - 1st:0 2nd:0 3rd:0 Ran:1
Pre2000 - 1st:0 2nd:0 3rd:0 Ran:2
2000 AW 0-1: (12f) (Fibr)
Unfurnished, currently very moderate filly.
**Martyn Wane [0-3] J P Slattery.*

GREY BUTTONS BHB 22f RR 1f 1649[12]

5 gr m Norton Challenger 10f **(41)** - Albury Grey (Petong) 6.6f **(58)**
Form - 0000
Record 2000 - 1st:0 2nd:0 3rd:0 Ran:4
Pre2000 - 1st:0 2nd:0 3rd:0 Ran:5
2000 Turf 0-4: (12f 3, 15f) (g-s, gd, g-f, frm)
Very poor filly.
**Derrick Morris [0-4] K Powell (from D G Bridgwater [0-2] Jly 1999).*

GREYCOAT BHB 52f RR 35f 5319[17]

2 ch g Lion Cavern (USA) 7.5f **(74)** - It's Academic **(64f)** (Royal Academy (USA))
Form - 00
Record 2000 - 1st:0 2nd:0 3rd:0 Ran:2
2000 Turf 0-2: (5f, 6f) (sft, g-s)
Currently moderate gelding. Turf high 35 (began Oct).
**J J Quinn [0-2] Mrs Jane Dwyer.*

GREY COSSACK BHB 75f RR 63f 1598[12]

3 gr g Kasakov - Royal Rebeka **(24f)** (Grey Desire) 8.7f **(50)**
Form - 63410
Record 2000 - 1st:1 2nd:0 3rd:1 Ran:5
Pre2000 - 1st:0 2nd:0 3rd:0 Ran:1
Win Prizemoney £2,800 *Total Prizemoney* £3,780
Wins * 2000 May Redcar (G-S) 6f 63 <
2000 Turf 1-5: (5f, 6f 1-4) (gd 1-3, g-f 2)
Leggy, average gelding, effective 5 to 6f, best at 6f, acts on gd to g-f, best on gd, has worn blinkers. Turf high 63 - 1st of 8 from Pretrail (29 May Redcar RF 1532). **M Brittain [1-6] Robert Cook.*

GREY EMINENCE (FR) BHB 100f RR 96f 5228[1]

3 gr c Indian Ridge 7.6f **(74)** - Rahaam (USA) (Secreto (USA)) 8.7f **(72)**
Form - 22212021
Record 2000 - 1st:2 2nd:5 3rd:0 Ran:8
Pre2000 - 1st:0 2nd:0 3rd:0 Ran:1
Win Prizemoney £13,051 *Total Prizemoney* £22,976
Wins * 2000 Oct Newmar (SFT) 6f 96 <
*** 2000** Aug Ascot (G-F) 7f 79
2000 Turf 2-8: (6f 1-3, 7f 1-2, 8f 3) (g-s 3, gd 1-4, g-f 1-1)
Well made, very useful colt, effective 6f, acts on g-s to gd, best on gd. Turf high 96 - 1st of 11 giving 5lb to Molly Brown (27 Oct Newmarket RF 5228). Consistent. He found one too good on each of his first three starts this term before scoring at Ascot. Seven furlongs looks his trip. **R Hannon [2-9] Jeffen Racing.*

GREYFIELD (IRE) BHB 70f RR 72f 5168[2]

4 b g Persian Bold 10f **(69)** - Noble Dust (USA) (Dust Commander (USA)) 10.3f **(77)**
Form - 4574544012
Record 2000 - 1st:1 2nd:1 3rd:0 Ran:10
Pre2000 - 1st:3 2nd:5 3rd:4 Ran:22
Win Prizemoney £14,938 *Total Prizemoney* £27,956
Wins * 2000 Oct Bath (GD) H 10.2f 64 72

* 1999	Aug	Cheste	(G-S)	H	10.3f	71	75 <
* 1999	Jly	Beverl	(G-F)		9.9f		69
* 1999	Jly	Folkes	(G-F)		9.7f		67

2000 Turf 1-10: (10f 1-2, 11f, 12f 4, 13f, 14f, 16f) (g-s 1-1, gd, g-f 7, frm)
Leggy, above-average gelding, effective 10 to 13f, best at 10f, acts on g-s to frm, likes right handed tracks, likes tight tracks, excels at Chester. Turf high 72 - 4th of 11 getting 13lb from Flossy (6 Aug Chester 12f g-f RF 3416) - also 1st of 20 giving 11lb to Wilemmgeo (19 Oct Bath RF 5072). Consistent.
**M R Channon [5-39] Paulton Bloodstock.*

GREY FLYER BHB 60f58a **RR 55f 58a** 2467[1]

3 gr g Factual (USA) - Faraway Grey (Absalom) 7.2f **(58)**
Form - 4212850301

Record	**2000 -**	1st:2	2nd:1	3rd:1	Ran:8
	Pre2000 -	1st:1	2nd:1	3rd:0	Ran:6

Win Prizemoney £7,316 *Total Prizemoney* £9,183

Wins	* **2000**	Jly	Mussel	(FRM)	SH	5f	55	55
	* **2000**	*Jan*	*Lingfi*	*(STD)*	*H*	*6f*	*55*	*56*
	* 1999	Spt	Mussel	(G-F)	C	5f		63 <

2000 Turf 1-4: (5f 1-3, 6f) (g-f, frm 1-3) 2000 AW 1-4: (5f 2, 6f 1-2) (Equi 1-4)
Leggy, fair gelding, effective 5 to 6f, best at 5f, acts on g-f to frm - acts on Equi. Turf high 55 - 1st of 14 from Branston Lucy (3 Jly Musselburgh RF 2467). AW high 64 - 2nd of 7 getting 6lb from Castle Sempill (5 Jan Lingfield 5f Equi RF 0030) - also 1st of 10 giving 6lb to Toldya (2 Jan Lingfield RF 0003). In good form on the equitrack during the winter. **Mrs L Stubbs [3-14] D M Smith.*

GREY IMPERIAL (IRE) **RR 65f** 4218[11]

2 gr c Imperial Frontier (USA) 7f **(65)** - Petrel **(60f)** (Petong) 6.6f **(58)**
Form - 00

Record	**2000 -**	1st:0	2nd:0	3rd:0	Ran:2

2000 Turf 0-2: (7f 2) (frm 2)
Currently average colt. Turf high 65 (began Aug).
**P W Harris [0-2] The Border Team.*

GREY PRINCESS (IRE) BHB 69f **RR 60f** 2081[11]

4 gr f Common Grounds 8.1f **(66)** - Miss Goodbody (Castle Keep) 8.3f **(57)**
Form - 00

Record	**2000 -**	1st:0	2nd:0	3rd:0	Ran:2
	Pre2000 -	1st:4	2nd:2	3rd:1	Ran:14

Win Prizemoney £11,523 *Total Prizemoney* £15,442

Wins	* 1998	Oct	Bright	(GD)	H	5.3f	85	92+ <
	* 1998	Spt	Bright	(FRM)	H	5.3f	80	82
	* 1998	Jly	Salisb	(FRM)		6f		78
	* 1998	Jun	Windso	(G-F)		6f		75

2000 Turf 0-2: (5f 2) (frm 2)
Neat, average filly, effective 6f, acts on gd. Turf high 29. Inconsistent. **P W Harris [4-16] The Commitments.*

GREY STRIKE (IRE) BHB 35f35a **RR 45f 35a** 1005[19]

4 gr g Magical Strike (USA) 5.5f **(61)** - Narrow Band (IRE) (Standaan (FR)) 7f **(55)**
Form - 0

Record	**2000 -**	1st:0	2nd:0	3rd:0	Ran:1
	Pre2000 -	1st:0	2nd:1	3rd:0	Ran:11

Win Prizemoney £0 *Total Prizemoney* £530
2000 Turf 0-1: (8f) (gd)
Scopey, moderate gelding, has worn blinkers. Inconsistent.
**R J Hodges [0-1] R J Hodges (from J Berry [0-11] Mar 1999).*

GRIEF (IRE) BHB 55f **RR 41f** 1015[11]

7 ch g Broken Hearted 10.1f **(65)** - Crecora (Royal Captive) 10f **(50)**
Form - 0080

Record	**2000 -**	1st:0	2nd:0	3rd:0	Ran:4
	Pre2000 -	1st:3	2nd:4	3rd:2	Ran:21

Win Prizemoney £10,308 *Total Prizemoney* £16,777

Wins	1999	Oct	Bright	(G-S)	C	11.9f		70
	1997	Aug	Epsom	(GD)	H	12f	82	87 <
	1996	Aug	Roscom	(GD)		10f		79

2000 Turf 0-4: (10f, 12f 3) (sft, g-s, gd, frm)
Moderate gelding, has worn blinkers, favours tight tracks. Turf high 41. Becoming disappointing.
**Miss A M Newton-Smith [0-4] Mike Balcomb (from D R C Elsworth [2-16] Oct 1999).*

GRINKOV (IRE) BHB 92f **RR 96f** 3471a[1]

5 b br g Soviet Lad (USA) 9.4f **(63)** - Tallow Hill (Dunphy) 9.4f **(57)**
Form - 31631
2000 Turf 2-5: (8f, 9f 1-2, 12f 1-2) (sft, gd 2-3, frm)
Very useful gelding, effective 10 to 12f, acts on gd. Turf high 96 - 1st of 14 giving 12lb to McCracken (4 Aug Galway RF 3471a). Effective between nine and 12 furlongs, he scored twice last season, including a valuable handicap at Galway. Has since transferred successfully to hurdles.
**P Hughes in IRE [2-9] Anns Backer Syndicate (from H Morrison [4-13] Oct 1999).*

GROESFAEN LAD BHB 63f60a **RR 65f 60a** 5245[9]

3 b g Casteddu 7.4f **(54)** - Curious Feeling (Nishapour (FR)) 9.1f **(61)**
Form - 0470635310

Record	**2000 -**	1st:1	2nd:0	3rd:2	Ran:10
	Pre2000 -	1st:0	2nd:3	3rd:0	Ran:10

Win Prizemoney £1,792 *Total Prizemoney* £5,741

Wins	* **2000**	*Oct*	*Wolver*	*(STD)*	*H*	*8.5f*	*58*	*65* <

2000 Turf 0-4: (7f 2, 8f 2) (g-f 2, frm 2) 2000 AW 1-6: (6f, 7f, 8f 1-3, 9f) (Fibr 1-6)
Workmanlike, average gelding, effective 5 to 7f, best at 7f, acts on gd to hrd, has worn blinkers, likes tight tracks. Turf high 65. AW high 65 (began Jly).
**P S McEntee [1-5] John Harris and Mrs Sian Harris (from B Palling [0-15] Aug 2000).*

GROOMS GOLD (IRE) BHB 22f29a **RR 33f 20a** 3213[6]

8 ch g Groom Dancer (USA) 9.5f **(75)** - Gortynia (FR) (My Swallow) 9.2f **(71)**
Form - 00422008204066

Record	**2000 -**	1st:0	2nd:3	3rd:0	Ran:13
	Pre2000 -	1st:1	2nd:4	3rd:6	Ran:35

Win Prizemoney £3,280 *Total Prizemoney* £9,510
2000 Turf 0-6: (12f 3, 14f, 16f 2) (gd 2, g-f, frm 3) 2000 AW 0-7: (11f 2, 13f 2, 16f 3) (Equi 2, Fibr 5)
Very moderate gelding, effective 10 to 12f, - acts on AW, best on Equi, has worn blinkers, favours left handed tracks. Turf high 33. AW high 35. He has finished runner-up often enough, but winning seems to be beyond him at present.
**J Pearce [0-27] Mrs Anne Holman-Chappell (from P W Harris [1-20] Oct 1998).*

GROSVENOR FLYER (IRE) BHB 54f **RR 39f** 5069[17]

4 ch g Dolphin Street (FR) - Kilcsem Eile (IRE) (Commanche Run) 8.5f **(58)**
Form - 070

Record	**2000 -**	1st:0	2nd:0	3rd:0	Ran:3
	Pre2000 -	1st:0	2nd:3	3rd:3	Ran:13

Win Prizemoney £0 *Total Prizemoney* £5,282
2000 Turf 0-3: (12f 2, 14f) (sft, g-s, gd)
Very moderate gelding, effective 9 to 15f, acts on g-s to g-f, has worn blinkers, excels at Lingfield. Turf high 32. Becoming disappointing.
**T D McCarthy [0-7] A D Spence (from A G Foster [0-2] Oct 1999).*

GROVE DANCER BHB 57f **RR 70f** 5237[11]

2 b f Reprimand 8.2f **(63)** - Brisighella (IRE) (Al Hareb (USA))
Form - 1340780

Record	**2000 -**	1st:1	2nd:0	3rd:1	Ran:7

Win Prizemoney £3,282 *Total Prizemoney* £4,103

Wins	* **2000**	May	Yarmou	(GD)	6f	70 <

2000 Turf 1-7: (6f 1-2, 7f 2, 8f 3) (g-s 2, gd 1-1, g-f 2, frm 2)
Above-average filly, effective 6f, acts on gd, has worn blinkers. Turf high 70 (1st run) - 1st of 6 getting 5lb from Carnival Lad (31 May Yarmouth RF 1610). **M H Tompkins [1-7] P H Betts.*

GROVE LODGE BHB 44f **RR 50f** 5200[3]

3 b c Donna's Red - Shanuke (IRE) **(12f 20a)** (Contract Law (USA))
Form - 00878006003

Record	**2000 -**	1st:0	2nd:0	3rd:1	Ran:11
	Pre2000 -	1st:0	2nd:0	3rd:0	Ran:3

Win Prizemoney £0 *Total Prizemoney* £272
2000 Turf 0-11: (6f 2, 7f 3, 8f 4, 10f 2) (sft, g-s 3, gd 3, g-f, frm 3)
Workmanlike, fair colt. Turf high 64.
**S Woodman [0-14] R Howitt.*

GRUB STREET BHB 54f **RR 54+f** 1728[1]

4 b c Barathea (IRE) - Broadmara (IRE) (Thatching) 8f **(66)**
Form - 01
Record 2000 - 1st:1 2nd:0 3rd:0 Ran:2
Pre2000 - 1st:0 2nd:0 3rd:0 Ran:2
Win Prizemoney £3,425 *Total Prizemoney* £3,425
Wins * **2000** Jun Thirsk (SFT) H 8f 50 54 <
2000 Turf 1-2: (7f, 8f 1-1) (gd 1-2)
Scopey, fair colt. Turf high 54 - 1st of 10 giving 10lb to Best Ever (5 Jun Thirsk RF 1728).
**M Brittain [1-2] Mel Brittain (from J H M Gosden [0-2] Oct 1999).*

GRUINART (IRE) BHB 66f **RR 76f** 5316[10]

3 br g Elbio 9f **(62)** - Doppio Filo (Vision (USA)) 9f **(64)**
Form - 80431407040
Record 2000 - 1st:1 2nd:0 3rd:1 Ran:11
Pre2000 - 1st:0 2nd:0 3rd:0 Ran:1
Win Prizemoney £2,884 *Total Prizemoney* £4,277
Wins * **2000** Jun Salisb (G-F) H 8f 66 76 <
2000 Turf 1-11: (6f, 8f 1-8, 10f 2) (g-s, gd 5, g-f 3, frm 1-2)
Leggy, above-average gelding, effective 8f, acts on g-f to frm, best on g-f, likes tight tracks. Turf high 76 - 1st of 16 getting 4lb from Cowboys And Angels (18 Jun Salisbury RF 2084).
**H Morrison [1-12] The Gruinart Partnership.*

GRYFFINDOR BHB 89f **RR 80f** 3166[2]

2 b c Marju (IRE) 9.2f **(76)** - Hard Task (Formidable (USA)) 9.2f **(63)**
Form - 372
Record 2000 - 1st:0 2nd:1 3rd:1 Ran:3
Win Prizemoney £0 *Total Prizemoney* £2,892
2000 Turf 0-3: (7f 3) (gd, g-f, frm)
Currently decent colt. Turf high 80 (began Jly). Stayed on nicely in a decent maiden on his debut, and should make a decent handicapper. **B J Meehan [0-3] Mrs Susan Roy.*

GUARANDA RR 75f 4472[2]

2 b f Acatenango (GER) - Gryada **(83df)** (Shirley Heights) 10.3f **(74)**
Form - 52
Record 2000 - 1st:0 2nd:1 3rd:0 Ran:2
Win Prizemoney £0 *Total Prizemoney* £1,700
2000 Turf 0-2: (7f, 8f) (g-f, frm)
Currently above-average filly. Turf high 75 (began Spt) - 2nd of 5 to Branicki (16 Spt Newmarket 8f g-f RF 4472).
**W Jarvis [0-2] Exors of the late Lord Howard de Walden.*

GUARD DUTY BHB 75f **RR 80df** 5104[3]

3 b g Deploy 11.4f **(67)** - Hymne D'Amour (USA) (Dixieland Band (USA)) 7f **(74)**
Form - 62453
Record 2000 - 1st:0 2nd:1 3rd:1 Ran:5
Pre2000 - 1st:0 2nd:0 3rd:2 Ran:2
Win Prizemoney £0 *Total Prizemoney* £3,092
2000 Turf 0-5: (10f, 12f 2, 13f, 15f) (sft, g-s, gd, frm 2)
Neat, decent gelding, effective 8 to 15f, acts on sft to gd, has worn blinkers. Turf high 80 - 2nd of 11 getting 1lb from Pompeii (1 May Warwick 12f sft RF 0956). **M P Tregoning [0-7] The Earl Cadogan.*

GUARDED SECRET BHB 75f72a **RR 74f 72a** 5220[2]

3 ch g Mystiko (USA) 7.7f **(59)** - Fen Dance (IRE) (Trojan Fen) 8.1f **(62)**
Form - 022172
Record 2000 - 1st:1 2nd:3 3rd:0 Ran:6
Pre2000 - 1st:0 2nd:0 3rd:1 Ran:1
Win Prizemoney £3,058 *Total Prizemoney* £6,184
Wins * **2000** Aug Salisb (GD) H 9.9f 69 74 <
2000 Turf 1-5: (8f, 9f, 10f 1-3) (sft, gd 2, frm 1-2) 2000 AW 0-1: (8f) (Fibr)
Workmanlike, above-average gelding, effective 8 to 10f, best at 10f, acts on sft to frm - acts on Fibr, prefers tight tracks. Turf high 74 - 2nd of 4 giving 3lb to Such Flair (27 Oct Brighton 10f sft RF 5220) - also 1st of 16 giving 4lb to Browning (16 Aug Salisbury RF 3705). (1st run) - 2nd of 7 giving 5lb to Belinda (16 Jun Southwell 8f Fibr RF 2029). **P J Makin [1-7] D M Ahier.*

GUARDIA RR 73f 4214[2]

2 ch f Grand Lodge (USA) - Gisarne (USA) (Diesis) 9.3f **(69)**
Form - 72
Record 2000 - 1st:0 2nd:1 3rd:0 Ran:2
Win Prizemoney £0 *Total Prizemoney* £1,196
2000 Turf 0-2: (6f, 8f) (frm 2)
Currently above-average filly. Turf high 73 - 2nd of 6 to Baranova (5 Spt Leicester 8f frm RF 4214).
**J L Dunlop [0-2] Exors of the late Lord Howard de Walden.*

GUDLAGE (USA) BHB 82f **RR 93f** 2658[18]

4 b g Gulch (USA) 9.6f **(79)** - Triple Kiss (Shareef Dancer (USA)) 9.9f **(73)**
Form - 00
Record 2000 - 1st:0 2nd:0 3rd:0 Ran:2
Pre2000 - 1st:1 2nd:1 3rd:1 Ran:6
Win Prizemoney £4,659 *Total Prizemoney* £10,637
Wins * 1998 Jly Newmar (G-F) 7f 81 <
2000 Turf 0-2: (7f, 8f) (g-f, frm)
Scopey, useful gelding. Turf high 72. **B Hanbury [1-8] Hilal Salem.*

GUEST ENVOY (IRE) BHB 40f47a **RR 37f 47a** 4024[5]

5 b m Paris House 5.9f **(64)** -Peace Mission (Dunbeath (USA)) 7.8f **(70)**
Form - 832214411267555054607 5
Record 2000 - 1st:3 2nd:3 3rd:1 Ran:22
Pre2000 - 1st:2 2nd:1 3rd:1 Ran:30
Win Prizemoney £16,743 *Total Prizemoney* £20,815
Wins * **2000** Apr Haydoc (GD) H 7.1f 36 51
* **2000** *Mar Southw (STD) H 7f 49 52* <
* **2000** *Feb Southw (STD) H 6f 43 48*
* 1999 *Aug Wolver (STD) H 8.5f 42 50+*
* 1998 Aug Hamilt (SFT) H 6f 40 46
2000 Turf 1-9: (6f 2, 7f 1-5, 8f 2) (sft, gd 1-5, g-f 2, frm) 2000 AW 2-13: (6f 1-3, 7f 1-8, 8f 2) (Fibr 2-13)
Fair filly, effective 6 to 8f, best at 7f, acts on gd - acts on Fibr, has worn blinkers, likes left handed tracks, likes tight tracks, does well at Southwell. Turf high 51 (1st run) - 1st of 16 getting 19lb from My Tess (1 Apr Haydock RF 0591). AW high 52 - 1st of 7 getting 7lb from My Alibi (27 Mar Southwell RF 0512) - also 1st of 8 getting 18lb from Muja's Magic (21 Feb Southwell RF 0326).
**C N Allen [5-52] ShadowfaxRacing Com.*

GUEST OF HONOUR BHB 63a **RR 52f** 591[16]

4 gr f Petong 7.6f **(58)** - Special Guest (Be My Guest (USA)) 9.3f **(67)**
Form - 0
Record 2000 - 1st:0 2nd:0 3rd:0 Ran:1
Pre2000 - 1st:1 2nd:1 3rd:0 Ran:8
Win Prizemoney £2,206 *Total Prizemoney* £3,334
Wins * 1999 Mar Catter (G-S) 5f 60 <
2000 Turf 0-1: (7f) (gd)
Workmanlike, average filly, effective 5 to 6f, acts on gd - acts on Fibr. **B W Hills [1-9] Major Christopher Hanbury.*

GUIDED TOUR (USA) RR 5332a[12]

4 b c Hansel (USA) 12.6f **(78)** - Dancing Mahmoud (USA) (Topsider (USA)) 8.3f **(71)**
Form - 0
2000 AW 0-1: (10f) (Dirt)
Currently Pattern-class colt, always wears blinkers.
**N M O'Callaghan in USA [0-1] M Fink.*

GUILLAMOU CITY (FR) RR 110f 3943a[3]

3 b c Lesotho (USA) 6f **(53)**
Form - 63
2000 Turf 0-2: (10f 2) (g-s, gd)
Currently Group-class colt. Turf high 110.
**J-C Rouget in FR [0-2] G Tanaka.*

GUILSBOROUGH BHB 51f82a **RR 49f 82a** 4823[14]

5 br g Northern Score (USA) - Super Sisters (AUS) (Call Report (USA))
Form - 681110
Record 2000 - 1st:3 2nd:0 3rd:0 Ran:4
Pre2000 - 1st:1 2nd:3 3rd:0 Ran:17
Win Prizemoney £9,641 *Total Prizemoney* £12,323
Wins * **2000** *Jly Southw (STD) H 8f 75 82* <
* **2000** *Jun Southw (STD) H 8f 65 76*
* **2000** *Jun Southw (STD) H 8f 65 69*
1999 *Jun Southw (STD) H 7f 56 67+*
2000 Turf 0-1: (10f) (g-f) 2000 AW 3-3: (8f 3-3) (Fibr 3-3)
Decent gelding, effective 8f, - acts on Fibr, has worn blinkers, prefers left handed tracks, prefers tight tracks. AW high 82 - 1st of

13 giving 31lb to Robbies Dream (14 Jly Southwell RF 2816) - also 1st of 9 giving 22lb to Hoh Gem (30 Jun Southwell RF 2420). Inconsistent.
**J G Smyth-Osbourne [3-4] P A Mason (from D Morris [1-17] Dec 1999).*

GUINEA HUNTER (IRE) BHB 98f RR 99f 5127[15]

4 b g Pips Pride 6.7f **(70)** - Preponderance (IRE) (Cyrano de Bergerac) 6f **(68)**
Form - 7107100503580
Record 2000 - 1st:2 2nd:0 3rd:1 Ran:13
Pre2000 - 1st:2 2nd:2 3rd:1 Ran:9
Win Prizemoney £22,441 *Total Prizemoney* £39,857
Wins * 2000 Jly Newmar (G-F) H 5f 96 97
*** 2000** May Haydoc (GD) 6f 95
* 1999 May Haydoc (GD) 6f 101 <
* 1998 Jun Carlis (G-S) 5.9f 80+
2000 Turf 2-13: (5f 1-6, 6f 1-7) (g-s 3, gd 1-6, g-f 1-3, frm)
Strong, very useful gelding, effective 5 to 6f, best at 6f, acts on g-s to g-f, has worn blinkers (effectively), likes Haydock. Turf high 99 - 3rd of 28 giving 13lb to Bahamian Pirate (16 Spt Ayr 6f gd RF 4451) - also 1st of 6 giving 15lb to Annette Vallon (22 Jly Newmarket RF 3033). He goes especially well at Haydock and scored again there on his second start of this season. He scraped home over the minimum trip at Newmarket in July, but is probably better at six furlongs, as he showed when third in the Ayr Gold Cup.
**T D Easterby [1-22] M P Burke.*

GULCHIE BHB 85f RR 75f 3842[4]

2 ch c Thunder Gulch (USA) - Asterita **(99f)** (Rainbow Quest (USA)) 10.4f **(75)**
Form - 14
Record 2000 - 1st:1 2nd:0 3rd:0 Ran:2
Win Prizemoney £3,003 *Total Prizemoney* £3,271
Wins * 2000 Jly Redcar (G-F) 7f 69+ <
2000 Turf 1-2: (7f 1-1, 8f) (gd, g-f 1-1)
Currently above-average colt. Turf high 75 (began Jly) - also 1st of 10 from Eddys Lad (23 Jly Redcar RF 3055).
**H R A Cecil [1-2] The Thoroughbred Corporation.*

GULF SHAADI BHB 64f73a RR 70df 73a 4619[10]

8 b g Shaadi (USA) 8.1f **(75)** Ela Meem (USA) (Kris) 9.5f **(73)**
Form - 008475405360
Record 2000 - 1st:0 2nd:0 3rd:1 Ran:10
Pre2000 - 1st:13 2nd:8 3rd:7 Ran:90
Win Prizemoney £104,604 *Total Prizemoney* £140,129
Wins 1998 *Mar Wolver (STD) H 9.4f 85 90* <
1997 Oct Newmar (GD) H 8f 82 90 <
1997 Spt Ascot (G-F) H 8f 74 81
1997 Aug Sandow (G-F) H 7.1f 66 71
1997 Apr Beverl (G-F) H 7.5f 59 62
1997 *Jan Southw (STD) H 8f 51 67*
1997 *Jan Southw (STD) H 8f 55 60*
2000 Turf 0-9: (7f 2, 8f 6, 10f) (sft, gd 2, g-f 2, frm 4) 2000 AW 0-1: (9f) (Fibr)
Above-average gelding, effective 8f, acts on g-f to frm, best on g-f, has worn blinkers. Turf high 81. He showed something of a revival last summer when making the frame in some decent events, but his form then tailed off again.
**Miss Gay Kelleway [0-24] Wetherby Racing Bureau 40 (from E J Alston [7-55] Nov 1998).*

GUMPTION RR 68+f 5312[4]

2 b g Muhtarram (USA) - Dancing Spirit (IRE) (Ahonoora) 8.1f **(73)**
Form - 4
Record 2000 - 1st:0 2nd:0 3rd:0 Ran:1
Win Prizemoney £0 *Total Prizemoney* £307
2000 Turf 0-1: (8f) (g-s)
Currently average gelding. **J L Dunlop [0-1] Sir David Sieff.*

GUNBOAT DIPLOMACY RR 39f 3999[10]

5 b br g Mtoto 11.5f **(71)** - Pepper Star (IRE) (Salt Dome (USA))
Form - 001570
Record 2000 - 1st:1 2nd:0 3rd:0 Ran:6
Pre2000 - 1st:0 2nd:0 3rd:0 Ran:8
Win Prizemoney £2,373 *Total Prizemoney* £2,373
Wins * 2000 Jun Redcar (FRM) C 10f 39 <
2000 Turf 1-6: (10f 1-3, 11f, 12f, 13f) (gd, g-f 2, frm 1-3)
Very moderate gelding, effective 10 to 12f, acts on g-f to frm, has worn blinkers, prefers left handed tracks. Turf high 39 - 1st of 9 getting 10lb from Night City (23 Jun Redcar RF 2231). Inconsistent.
**Mrs M Reveley [1-10] A Sharratt (from M J Fetherston-Godley [0-5] Jun 1998).*

GUNNER SAM BHB 40f38a RR 35f 38a 4811[10]

4 ch g Emarati (USA) 6.6f **(63)** - Minne Love (Homeric) 9.8f **(67)**
Form - 60650780000
Record 2000 - 1st:0 2nd:0 3rd:0 Ran:7
Pre2000 - 1st:1 2nd:1 3rd:1 Ran:12
Win Prizemoney £2,722 *Total Prizemoney* £3,963
Wins 1999 Apr Catter (SFT) 7f 69 <
2000 Turf 0-3: (6f 2, 7f) (gd 2, frm) 2000 AW 0-4: (5f, 6f, 7f, 8f) (Equi, Fibr 3)
Scopey, very moderate gelding, effective 6 to 7f, acts on gd, has worn blinkers, likes left handed tracks, likes tight tracks. Turf high 32. AW high 34.
**B R Johnson [0-1] Peter Crate (from J L Harris [0-10] Jun 2000).*

GURU RR 41f 5099[17]

2 b c Slip Anchor 12.7f **(75)** - Ower (IRE) (Lomond (USA)) 8.8f **(65)**
Form - 0
Record 2000 - 1st:0 2nd:0 3rd:0 Ran:1
2000 Turf 0-1: (7f) (gd)
Currently moderate colt. **I A Balding [0-1] Dr J A E Hobby.*

GWENDOLINE RR 84f 3767[7]

3 b f Polar Falcon (USA) 9f **(74)** - Merlins Charm (USA) (Bold Bidder) 8.8f **(67)**
Form - 2127
Record 2000 - 1st:1 2nd:2 3rd:0 Ran:4
Win Prizemoney £3,672 *Total Prizemoney* £6,322
Wins * 2000 Jun Salisb (G-F) 7f 78 <
2000 Turf 1-4: (7f 1-3, 8f) (g-s, g-f 2, frm 1-1)
Light-framed, decent filly. Turf high 84 - 2nd of 14 getting 4lb from Smooth Sailing (4 Aug Newmarket 8f g-f RF 3368) - also 1st of 14 from Harmonic (28 Jun Salisbury RF 2353). Won a Salisbury maiden in fine style on her second start and ran very well against older rivals in a handicap at Newmarket next time. There should be more improvement in her. **J R Fanshawe [1-4] Mrs M Slater.*

GWENEIRA BHB 82f RR 82+f 5314[5]

3 gr f Machiavellian (USA) 9.8f **(83)** - English Spring (USA) (Grey Dawn II) 11.1f **(72)**
Form - 15
Record 2000 - 1st:1 2nd:0 3rd:0 Ran:2
Win Prizemoney £4,309 *Total Prizemoney* £4,309
Wins * 2000 Aug Sandow (G-F) 10f 82+ <
2000 Turf 1-2: (10f 1-2) (sft, frm 1-1)
Leggy, currently decent filly. Turf high 82 (1st run) (began Aug) - 1st of 6 from Summer Dreams (18 Aug Sandown RF 3770).
**J H M Gosden [1-2] Sheikh Mohammed.*

GYMCRAK FIREBIRD (IRE) BHB 34f43a RR 42f 43a 4649[9]

3 ch f Petardia 8.2f **(58)** - Fiery Song (Ballad Rock) 7.8f **(63)**
Form - 4600000
Record 2000 - 1st:0 2nd:0 3rd:0 Ran:5
Pre2000 - 1st:0 2nd:1 3rd:0 Ran:7
Win Prizemoney £0 *Total Prizemoney* £578
2000 Turf 0-3: (8f, 12f 2) (sft, frm 2) 2000 AW 0-2: (7f, 11f) (Fibr 2)
Scopey, fair filly, effective 7f, - acts on Fibr, has worn blinkers, likes left handed tracks, likes tight tracks. Turf high 42. AW high 13. Inconsistent.
**G Holmes [0-12] The Gymcrak Thoroughbred Racing Club.*

GYMCRAK FLYER BHB 36f65a RR 39f 65a 4123[10]

9 b m Aragon 7.7f **(58)** - Intellect (Frimley Park) 6.5f **(67)**
Form - 0000050
Record 2000 - 1st:0 2nd:0 3rd:0 Ran:7
Pre2000 - 1st:12 2nd:5 3rd:5 Ran:66
Win Prizemoney £40,448 *Total Prizemoney* £51,215
Wins * 1999 Spt Mussel (G-F) H 8f 44 52
* 1999 Aug Carlis (G-F) H 8f 44 46
* 1997 Spt Yarmou (FRM) H 8f 62 68
* 1997 May Redcar (GD) H 7f 60 63
* 1997 Apr Pontef (GD) H 8f 62

* 1996	Jly	Yarmou	(FRM)	H	7f	63	66
* 1996	Jly	Redcar	(G-F)	H	7f	58	60
* 1996	Jun	Carlis	(FRM)		8f		61

2000 Turf 0-7: (7f, 8f 6) (g-s, frm 4, hrd 2)

Moderate mare, effective 8f, acts on frm, has worn blinkers (effectively), likes right handed tracks, likes tight tracks. Turf high 39.

**G Holmes [12-73] The Gymcrak Thoroughbred Racing Club.*

GYPSY (IRE) BHB 62f60a **RR 64f 60a** 4645[6]

4 b g Distinctly North (USA) 7.4f **(63)** - Winscarlet North (Garland Knight)

Form - 35443756

Record 2000 - 1st:0 2nd:0 3rd:2 Ran:8
Pre2000 - 1st:2 2nd:1 3rd:1 Ran:13

Win Prizemoney £9,698 *Total Prizemoney* £12,981

Wins 1999 May Lingfi (G-F) H 9f 67 72 <
* 1998 Jly Yarmou (G-F) 7f 68

2000 Turf 0-4: (10f 4) (g-s, gd 2, g-f) 2000 AW 0-4: (9f, 10f, 12f 2) (Equi, Fibr 3)

Workmanlike, average gelding, effective 9 to 11f, best at 10f, acts on g-s to frm - acts on Fibr, has worn blinkers, likes tight tracks, excels at Yarmouth. Turf high 69 (1st run) - 3rd of 18 giving 18lb to Smarter Charter (11 Apr Pontefract 10f g-s RF 0658). AW high 65 (1st run) - 3rd of 9 giving 9lb to Al Mabrook (6 Jan Wolverhampton 9f Fibr RF 0031).

**M H Tompkins [2-21] Richard Flatt.*

GYPSY SONG (IRE) BHB 39f42a **RR 38f 42a** 5059[2]

3 b g Turtle Island (IRE) - Kate Labelle (Teenoso (USA)) 9.9f **(72)**

Form - 0057052

Record 2000 - 1st:0 2nd:1 3rd:0 Ran:7

Win Prizemoney £0 *Total Prizemoney* £519

2000 Turf 0-4: (6f 2, 11f, 14f) (sft, gd, frm 2) 2000 AW 0-3: (7f, 8f, 12f) (Fibr 3)

Light-framed, moderate gelding, effective 14f, acts on sft, likes left handed tracks, likes tight tracks. Turf high 38 - 2nd of 6 getting 18lb from Dangerous Deploy (18 Oct Nottingham 14f sft RF 5059). AW high 40 (began Jly). **J A Glover [0-7] Boston S.*

HAAFEL (USA) **RR 40f** 1349[8]

3 ch c Diesis 9f **(80)** - Dish Dash (Bustino) 10.4f **(64)**

Form - 8

Record 2000 - 1st:0 2nd:0 3rd:0 Ran:1

2000 Turf 0-1: (12f) (gd)

Scopey, currently moderate colt.

**R W Armstrong [0-1] Hamdan Al Maktoum.*

HAASIL (IRE) **RR 73f** 5099[4]

2 b c Machiavellian (USA) 9.8f **(83)** - Mahasin (USA) (Danzig (USA)) 8.4f **(76)**

Form - 34

Record 2000 - 1st:0 2nd:0 3rd:1 Ran:2

Win Prizemoney £0 *Total Prizemoney* £839

2000 Turf 0-2: (7f 2) (gd 2)

Currently above-average colt. Turf high 73 (began Spt).

**J L Dunlop [0-2] Hamdan Al Maktoum.*

HABIBA BHB 37f **RR 40f** 1995[11]

3 b f Charmer 9f **(59)** - Run for Love (Runnett) 7f **(59)**

Form - 000

Record 2000 - 1st:0 2nd:0 3rd:0 Ran:3

2000 Turf 0-3: (7f, 10f 2) (g-f 2, frm)

Currently moderate filly, often wears blinkers. Turf high 40.

**S C Williams [0-3] The No Hassle Partnership.*

HADATH (IRE) BHB 82f **RR 83f** 4449[23]

3 br g Mujtahid (USA) 7.4f **(69)** - Al Sylah (Nureyev (USA)) 8.7f **(78)**

Form - 07561212300

Record 2000 - 1st:2 2nd:2 3rd:1 Ran:11
Pre2000 - 1st:0 2nd:1 3rd:0 Ran:4

Win Prizemoney £11,680 *Total Prizemoney* £18,352

Wins * 2000 Jly Beverl (G-F) H 7.5f 77 81 <
* 2000 Jun Thirsk (FRM) 7f 77

2000 Turf 2-11: (6f, 7f 2-3, 8f 6, 11f) (hvy 2, gd 3, g-f 2, frm 2-4)

Scopey, decent gelding, effective 7 to 8f, best at 8f, acts on g-s to frm, best on frm, has worn blinkers, prefers tight tracks. Turf high 83 - 2nd of 8 giving 5lb to Triccolo (29 Jly Nottingham 8f frm RF 3216) - also 1st of 9 giving 18lb to Stormville (18 Jly Beverley RF 2884). Inconsistent.

**M A Buckley [2-11] Mrs D J Buckley (from M P Tregoning [0-4] Oct 1999).*

HADEQA BHB 38f **RR 27f** 4544[15]

4 ch g Hadeer 8.9f **(58)** - Heavenly Queen (Scottish Reel) 7f **(61)**

Form - 00000

Record 2000 - 1st:0 2nd:0 3rd:0 Ran:5
Pre2000 - 1st:4 2nd:2 3rd:2 Ran:25

Win Prizemoney £13,370 *Total Prizemoney* £17,337

Wins	1999	Jly	Carlis	(GD)	C	6.9f		59	
	1999	Jun	Pontef	(GD)	S	8f		63+	
	1999	Apr	Catter	(SFT)	H	7f	66	74+	<
	1998	Aug	Redcar	(G-F)	H	6f	61	63	

2000 Turf 0-5: (8f 3, 9f, 10f) (gd, g-f 2, frm, hrd)

Light-framed, moderate gelding, effective 7 to 8f, acts on gd, mostly wears blinkers (effectively), favours tight tracks. Turf high 39 (began Jly). Inconsistent.

**F Jordan [1-11] The French Connection (from P D Evans [4-23] Jly 1999).*

HADLEIGH (IRE) BHB 57f53a **RR 59f 53a** 4304[8]

4 b c Perugino (USA) - Risacca (ITY) (Sir Gaylord) 10.6f **(64)**

Form - 0000288

Record 2000 - 1st:0 2nd:1 3rd:0 Ran:7
Pre2000 - 1st:1 2nd:0 3rd:1 Ran:10

Win Prizemoney £3,728 *Total Prizemoney* £5,425

Wins 1998 Aug Kempto (G-F) 6f 83 <

2000 Turf 0-7: (7f, 8f 3, 10f 3) (gd 5, g-f, frm)

Workmanlike, fair colt, has worn blinkers. Turf high 66.

**H J Collingridge [0-7] C G Donovan (from R W Armstrong [1-10] Oct 1999).*

HAIKAL **RR 63f** 5054[16]

3 b g Owington - Magic Milly (Simply Great (FR)) 8.2f **(65)**

Form - 884600

Record 2000 - 1st:0 2nd:0 3rd:0 Ran:6
Pre2000 - 1st:0 2nd:0 3rd:0 Ran:1

Win Prizemoney £0 *Total Prizemoney* £240

2000 Turf 0-6: (6f, 7f, 8f 2, 10f 2) (sft, g-s, gd 3, frm)

Scopey, average gelding, effective 8f, acts on gd to frm, has worn blinkers. Turf high 63 - 4th of 20 getting 3lb from Sign of The Tiger (25 May Newcastle 8f gd RF 1441).

**E W Tuer [0-2] E Tuer (from N A Graham [0-5] Jun 2000).*

HAIL SHEEVA **RR 26f** 3783[11]

3 ch f Democratic (USA) - Sun Storm (Sunyboy)

Form - 0

Record 2000 - 1st:0 2nd:0 3rd:0 Ran:1
Pre2000 - 1st:0 2nd:0 3rd:0 Ran:1

2000 Turf 0-1: (10f) (frm)

Leggy, currently little account filly.

**Miss K M George [0-2] R J Matthews.*

HAIL THE CHIEF BHB 85f107a **RR 72f 107a** 4924[2]

3 b c Be My Chief (USA) 10.2f **(62)** - Jade Pet **(84df)** (Petong) 6.6f **(58)**

Form - 426011262

Record 2000 - 1st:2 2nd:3 3rd:0 Ran:9
Pre2000 - 1st:0 2nd:0 3rd:0 Ran:1

Win Prizemoney £9,928 *Total Prizemoney* £14,021

Wins * **2000** Aug Bright (G-F) 7f 70
* **2000** Jly Folkes (GD-) H 7f 68 72 <

2000 Turf 2-8: (7f 2-6, 8f 2) (gd 2, g-f 1-5, frm 1-1) 2000 AW 0-1: (8f) (Equi)

Workmanlike, very useful colt, effective 7 to 8f, best at 7f, acts on g-f to frm - acts on Equi. Turf high 72 - 1st of 8 getting 7lb from Aretino (31 Jly Folkestone RF 3246) - also 1st of 9 getting 3lb from Butrinto (10 Aug Brighton RF 3519). (1st run) - 2nd of 12 giving 10lb to Tapage (11 Oct Lingfield 8f Equi RF 4924). Found his form in the late summer and scored at Folkestone and Brighton. Suited by seven furlongs. Has taken well to the All-Weather this winter.

**R Hannon [2-10] Peter Crane.*

HAITHEM (IRE) BHB 56f **RR 57f** 5007[12]

3 b g Mtoto 11.5f **(71)** - Wukk (IRE) (Glow (USA)) 6.7f **(71)**

Form - 0600

Record 2000 - 1st:0 2nd:0 3rd:0 Ran:4

Pre2000 - 1st:0 2nd:1 3rd:0 Ran:3
Win Prizemoney £0 *Total Prizemoney* £1,392
2000 Turf 0-3: (7f, 10f 2) (gd, g-f, frm) 2000 AW 0-1: (12f) (Fibr)
Fair gelding, effective 7f, acts on frm. Turf high 46. He showed some ability at two, but also looked headstrong and a difficult ride. Better will be seen of him once he matures.
**D Shaw [0-1] Century Racing (from M Johnston [0-6] Jly 2000).*

HAKEEM (IRE) BHB 58f **RR 63f** 4492[10]
5 ch g Kefaah (USA) 11.2f **(64)** -Masarrah (Formidable (USA)) 9.2f **(63)**
Form - 022033000
Record 2000 - 1st:0 2nd:2 3rd:2 Ran:9
Pre2000 - 1st:2 2nd:1 3rd:1 Ran:19
Win Prizemoney £5,656 *Total Prizemoney* £13,339
Wins * 1999 May Thirsk (G-F) H 8f 53 56
1997 Spt Folkes (GD) 6f 78 <
2000 Turf 0-9: (6f, 7f 3, 8f 5) (gd 3, g-f 4, frm 2)
Average gelding, effective 7 to 8f, best at 7f, acts on gd to frm, best on frm, has worn blinkers, prefers left handed tracks, prefers tight tracks. Turf high 63 - 2nd of 16 giving 1lb to Tornado Prince (20 Jun Thirsk 7f frm RF 2121). Becoming disappointing. He has a modest strike-rate, but was running well during the summer without quite managing to force his head in front. Best on fast ground.
**M Brittain [1-18] Mel Brittain (from R W Armstrong [1-10] Spt 1998).*

HALAWAN (IRE) RR 84+f 4466[2]
2 b c Muhtarram (USA) - Haladiya (IRE) (Darshaan) 9.9f **(84)**
Form - 2
Record 2000 - 1st:0 2nd:1 3rd:0 Ran:1
Win Prizemoney £0 *Total Prizemoney* £1,666
2000 Turf 0-1: (7f) (g-f)
Currently decent colt. (1st run) - 2nd of 22 to West Order (16 Spt Newbury 7f g-f RF 4466). **Sir Michael Stoute [0-1] H H Aga Khan.*

HALCYON DAZE BHB 84f **RR 77f** 4876[2]
2 ch f Halling (USA) - Ardisia (USA) (Affirmed (USA)) 9.3f **(79)**
Form - 842
Record 2000 - 1st:0 2nd:1 3rd:0 Ran:3
Win Prizemoney £0 *Total Prizemoney* £1,230
2000 Turf 0-3: (7f 3) (g-s, gd, g-f)
Currently above-average filly. Turf high 77 (began Aug) - 2nd of 10 to Pearl Bright (9 Oct Leicester 7f g-s RF 4876).
**L M Cumani [0-3] Christopher Wright.*

HALCYON MAGIC BHB 72f **RR 73f** 4998[7]
2 b g Magic Ring (IRE) 6.5f **(64)** - Consistent Queen (Queen's Hussar) 11.6f **(58)**
Form - 0045526227
Record 2000 - 1st:0 2nd:3 3rd:0 Ran:10
Win Prizemoney £0 *Total Prizemoney* £3,462
2000 Turf 0-9: (5f 3, 6f 6) (g-s, g-f 5, frm 3) 2000 AW 0-1: (5f) (Fibr)
Above-average gelding, effective 6f, acts on g-f. Turf high 73 - 2nd of 16 getting 9lb from Flint River (11 Spt Warwick 6f g-f RF 4323). Inconsistent. **Pat Mitchell [0-10] The Magic Partnership.*

HALE BOPP (GER) RR 94f 1454a[5]
3 f
Form - 5
2000 Turf 0-1: (10f) (sft)
Currently useful, always wears blinkers.
**M Hofer in GER [0-1].*

HALF MOON BAY RR 65f 4832[23]
3 b g Cyrano de Bergerac 7.3f **(58)** - Tarnside Rosal **(56f)** (Mummy's Game) 8.2f **(60)**
Form - 6000
Record 2000 - 1st:0 2nd:0 3rd:0 Ran:4
Pre2000 - 1st:3 2nd:0 3rd:0 Ran:5
Win Prizemoney £10,467 *Total Prizemoney* £10,467
Wins * 1999 Jly Thirsk (FRM) H 5f 88+ <
* 1999 Jly Doncas (G-F) H 5f 86
* 1999 May Thirsk (GD) 5f 80+
2000 Turf 0-4: (5f 4) (g-s, g-f 2, frm)
Strong, average gelding, effective 5f, acts on g-f to frm, best on g-f. Turf high 65 (began Jly). Consistent.
**T D Barron [3-9] Mrs Ann Lockhart.*

HALF TIDE BHB 47f42a **RR 50f 42a** 5012[1]
6 ch g Nashwan (USA) 10.3f **(79)** - Double River (USA) (Irish River (FR)) 8.6f **(78)**
Form - 38621058571
Record 2000 - 1st:2 2nd:1 3rd:0 Ran:10
Pre2000 - 1st:1 2nd:3 3rd:2 Ran:11
Win Prizemoney £8,409 *Total Prizemoney* £12,497
Wins * **2000** *Oct Southw (STD) H 14f 43 46*
* **2000** Jly Epsom (G-S) H 12f 39 47
* 1999 *Feb Lingfi (STD) H 12f 48 48* <
2000 Turf 1-8: (9f, 10f, 12f 1-6) (g-s, gd 1-3, g-f 4) 2000 AW 1-2: (12f, 14f 1-1) (Equi, Fibr 1-1)
Fair gelding, effective 10f, - acts on Equi, prefers left handed tracks. Turf high 50. AW high 46. Consistent.
**P Mitchell [3-21] The Fruit Cake Partnership.*

HALF TONE BHB 34f45a **RR 39f 45a** 3485[10]
8 gr h Touch of Grey 8.1f **(47)** - Demilinga (Nishapour (FR)) 9.1f **(61)**
Form - 00530385080
Record 2000 - 1st:0 2nd:0 3rd:2 Ran:11
Pre2000 - 1st:10 2nd:15 3rd:18 Ran:100
Win Prizemoney £30,680 *Total Prizemoney* £56,295
Wins * 1999 *Jan Lingfi (STD) H 5f 53 56*
* 1998 Oct Bath (HVY) H 5.1f 54 60
* 1998 Aug Sandow (G-F) H 5f 51 56
* 1997 Aug Sandow (GD) H 5f 56 60
* 1997 May Goodwo (G-S) H 5f 52 53
* 1996 Aug Sandow (G-F) H 5f 50 51
* 1996 *Feb Lingfi (STD) H 5f 64 65* <
2000 Turf 0-10: (5f 4, 6f 4, 7f 2) (g-s 2, gd 4, g-f 3, frm) 2000 AW 0-1: (5f) (Fibr)
Average horse, effective 5f, - acts on Equi, mostly wears blinkers, prefers left handed tracks, prefers tight tracks, excels at Lingfield. Turf high 40. **R M Flower [10-111] M G Rogers.*

HALHOO LAMMTARRA BHB 67f **RR 70f** 2263[5]
3 ch c Lammtarra (USA) - Shadha (USA) (Devil's Bag (USA)) 12.4f **(78)**
Form - 0055
Record 2000 - 1st:0 2nd:0 3rd:0 Ran:4
Pre2000 - 1st:0 2nd:1 3rd:0 Ran:1
Win Prizemoney £0 *Total Prizemoney* £1,326
2000 Turf 0-4: (8f 2, 10f 2) (g-s, gd, g-f, frm)
Scopey, above-average colt. Turf high 70.
**M R Channon [0-5] Sheikh Ahmed Al Maktoum.*

HAL HOO YAROOM BHB 60f65a **RR 59f 65a** 2041[2]
7 b h Belmez (USA) 11.4f **(65)** - Princess Nawaal (USA) (Seattle Slew (USA)) 9.4f **(76)**
Form - 32
Record 2000 - 1st:0 2nd:1 3rd:1 Ran:2
Pre2000 - 1st:4 2nd:2 3rd:3 Ran:24
Win Prizemoney £13,738 *Total Prizemoney* £19,487
Wins * 1999 Jly Warwic (G-F) H 15.8f 52 59
* 1999 Jun Bath (GD) H 17.2f 50 51
1996 Jly Folkes (FRM) H 15.4f 67 82 <
1996 Jun Yarmou (FRM) 14.1f 67
2000 Turf 0-2: (16f, 17f) (gd, hrd)
Average horse, effective 16 to 17f, best at 16f, acts on gd to hrd - acts on Equi, favours left handed tracks. Turf high 59 - 2nd of 13 giving 12lb to Sheriff (17 Jun Bath 17f hrd RF 2041).
**J R Jenkins [6-34] R M Ellis (from R Akehurst [0-4] Oct 1997).*

HALLAND BHB 85f **RR 85f** 5186[1]
2 ch c Halling (USA) - Northshiel (Northfields (USA)) 9f **(72)**
Form - 661
Record 2000 - 1st:1 2nd:0 3rd:0 Ran:3
Win Prizemoney £4,160 *Total Prizemoney* £4,160
Wins * **2000** Oct Yarmou (SFT) 7f 85 <
2000 Turf 1-3: (6f, 7f 1-2) (g-s 1-1, g-f, frm)
Currently useful colt. Turf high 85 (began Aug) - 1st of 16 from Continuation (25 Oct Yarmouth RF 5186).
**G Wragg [1-3] Mollers Racing.*

HALLAND PARK GIRL (IRE) BHB 98f **RR 103df** 3398[7]
3 b f Primo Dominie 7.2f **(67)** - Katsina (USA) (Cox's Ridge (USA)) 8f **(68)**

Form - 602087
Record 2000 - 1st:0 2nd:1 3rd:0 Ran:6
Pre2000 - 1st:5 2nd:2 3rd:0 Ran:8
Win Prizemoney £101,393 *Total Prizemoney* £135,667
Wins * 1999 Oct Doncas (SFT) L 6f 106 <
* 1999 Aug Currag (G-S) 6f 96+
* 1999 Jly Salisb (FRM) 6f 96
* 1999 Jly Ascot (G-F) H 6f 86+
* 1999 May Lingfi (G-F) 5f 75
2000 Turf 0-6: (6f 3, 7f 2, 8f) (gd 2, g-f 2, frm, hrd)
Workmanlike, very useful filly, effective 6f, acts on g-s to frm, has worn blinkers. Turf high 103. The winner of four of her seven starts at two, including the valuable Tattersalls Breeders Stakes in Ireland, she was not disgraced in the Nell Gwyn or the Guineas this year, but looked more at home for a return to sprinting when chasing home the older Hot Tin Roof at Nottingham. Held since, however. **R Hannon [5-14] Mrs B Burchett.*

HALLIANA RR 1f 2277[6]

2 b f Turtle Island (IRE) - Princess Dechtra (IRE) (Bellypha) 9.8f **(73)**
Form - 6
Record 2000 - 1st:0 2nd:0 3rd:0 Ran:1
2000 Turf 0-1: (6f) (frm)
Currently very poor filly. **D HaydnJones [0-1] Mrs E M HaydnJones.*

HALMAHERA (IRE) BHB 102f RR 105f 3840[3]

5 b g Petardia 8.2f **(58)** - Champagne Girl (Robellino (USA)) 7.6f **(80)**
Form - 5285560403
Record 2000 - 1st:0 2nd:1 3rd:1 Ran:10
Pre2000 - 1st:5 2nd:7 3rd:1 Ran:26
Win Prizemoney £56,673 *Total Prizemoney* £118,789
Wins * 1999 Jun Newcas (G-F) L 6f 110
* 1997 Oct Ascot (HVY) G3 5f 111? <
* 1997 Spt Ayr (G-S) L 5f 96
* 1997 Jly Goodwo (G-F) H 6f 89
* 1997 Jly Chepst (G-S) 6.1f 71
2000 Turf 0-9: (5f 3, 6f 6) (hvy, g-s, gd 4, g-f 2, hrd) 2000 AW 0-1: (5f) (Dirt)
Pattern-class gelding, effective 5 to 6f, best at 6f, acts on hvy to frm, best on g-f, has worn blinkers, does well at Newmarket and Ascot. Turf high 108 - 2nd of 11 giving 4lb to Dananeyev (4 Apr Maisons-laffitte 6f hvy RF 0704a). A useful sprinter, he ran a series of good races last term but could not get his head in front.
**I A Balding [5-36] Robert Hitchins.*

HALMANERROR BHB 56f50a RR 64f 50a 4277[8]

10 gr g Lochnager 6.9f **(50)** - Counter Coup (Busted) 10.2f **(61)**
Form - 65332468
Record 2000 - 1st:0 2nd:1 3rd:2 Ran:8
Pre2000 - 1st:10 2nd:5 3rd:5 Ran:71
Win Prizemoney £46,325 *Total Prizemoney* £58,362
Wins * 1999 Jun Chepst (GD) H 7.1f 63 64
* 1999 May Chepst (GD) H 7.1f 60 62
* 1998 Jun Salisb (G-S) CH 7f 53 59
* 1998 Apr Bright (GD) C 6f 51
1997 May Doncas (G-S) H 6f 57 60
1996 Aug Doncas (G-F) 6f 65
2000 Turf 0-8: (6f 3, 7f 5) (hvy, gd 5, g-f 2)
Average gelding, effective 6 to 7f, best at 7f, acts on sft to g-f, best on gd, excels at Goodwood, does well at Chepstow. Turf high 64.
**G M McCourt [4-35] Caulkheads Racing (from Mrs J R Ramsden [6-48] Oct 1997).*

HAMADEENAH BHB 83f RR 78f 4599[11]

2 ch f Alhijaz 7.7f **(57)** - Mahbob Dancer (FR) (Groom Dancer (USA))
Form - 150
Record 2000 - 1st:1 2nd:0 3rd:0 Ran:3
Win Prizemoney £4,810 *Total Prizemoney* £5,227
Wins * **2000** Aug Newmar (G-F) 6f 74 <
2000 Turf 1-3: (6f 1-1, 7f 2) (gd, g-f 1-1, frm)
Currently above-average filly. Turf high 78 (began Aug) - also 1st of 8 from Lunevision (26 Aug Newmarket RF 3990).
**K Mahdi [1-3] Miss Debbie Mountain.*

HAMASKING (IRE) BHB 56f RR 47f 2694[11]

2 b f Hamas (IRE) 8f **(72)** - Sialia (IRE) (Bluebird (USA)) 7.5f **(69)**
Form - 6610
Record 2000 - 1st:1 2nd:0 3rd:0 Ran:4
Win Prizemoney £2,299 *Total Prizemoney* £2,299
Wins * **2000** Jun Catter (SFT) S 6f 47 <
2000 Turf 1-4: (5f 2, 6f 1-2) (g-s 1-1, gd, frm 2)
Moderate filly. Turf high 47 - 1st of 11 getting 11lb from Sand Bankes (3 Jun Catterick RF 1669).
**T D Easterby [1-4] Ryedale Partners No 3.*

HAMATARA (IRE) BHB 75f RR 73f 3838[6]

2 ch g Tagula (IRE) - Arctic Poppy (USA) **(55f 39a)** (Arctic Tern (USA)) 8.9f **(69)**
Form - 404126
Record 2000 - 1st:1 2nd:1 3rd:0 Ran:6
Win Prizemoney £2,925 *Total Prizemoney* £5,941
Wins * **2000** Jly Leices (G-F) H 5f 67 <
2000 Turf 1-6: (5f 1-4, 6f 2) (g-s, gd 3, g-f, frm 1-1)
Above-average gelding, effective 5f, acts on gd to frm. Turf high 73 - 2nd of 8 giving 1lb to Soldier On (3 Aug Goodwood 5f gd RF 3345) - also 1st of 7 giving 5lb to Ticcatoo (26 Jly Leicester RF 3134). **I A Balding [1-6] Robert Hitchins.*

HAMBLEDEN BHB 82f80a RR 84f 80a 5104[4]

3 b g Vettori (IRE) - Dalu (IRE) **(69f)** (Dancing Brave (USA)) 8.4f **(76)**
Form - 0318320104
Record 2000 - 1st:2 2nd:1 3rd:2 Ran:10
Pre2000 - 1st:0 2nd:0 3rd:0 Ran:2
Win Prizemoney £6,853 *Total Prizemoney* £9,110
Wins * **2000** Spt Sandow (G-F) H 14f 80 83 <
* **2000** *May Wolver (STD) H 12f 65 78+*
2000 Turf 1-9: (8f, 11f, 12f, 14f 1-4, 15f 2) (hvy, gd 3, g-f 3, frm 1-2)
2000 AW 1-1: (12f 1-1) (Fibr 1-1)
Scopey, decent gelding, effective 12 to 15f, best at 14f, acts on gd to frm - acts on Fibr, best on frm, likes tight tracks. Turf high 84 - 4th of 17 getting 10lb from Loop The Loup (20 Oct Doncaster 15f gd RF 5104) - also 1st of 13 giving 3lb to Fletcher (13 Spt Sandown RF 4373). (1st run) - 1st of 8 giving 9lb to Tufty Hopper (11 May Wolverhampton RF 1151). Inconsistent. Absolutely bolted up in a maiden on the Wolverhampton Fibresand in May and has run with credit on turf since, winning at Sandown. May still have some improvement in him. **M A Jarvis [2-12] Stag and Huntsman.*

HAMBLETON HIGHLITE (IRE) BHB 74f69a RR 77+f 69a 4778[3]

2 ch g Paris House 5.9f **(64)** - Sempreverde (USA) (Lear Fan (USA)) 8.5f **(73)**
Form - 1374473
Record 2000 - 1st:1 2nd:0 3rd:2 Ran:7
Win Prizemoney £2,821 *Total Prizemoney* £4,496
Wins * **2000** May Hamilt (FRM) 5f 77+ <
2000 Turf 1-6: (5f 1-5, 6f) (gd 3, g-f 2, frm 1-1) 2000 AW 0-1: (6f) (Fibr)
Above-average gelding, effective 5f, acts on gd to frm, often wears blinkers. Turf high 83 - 4th of 6 giving 9lb to Laurel Dawn (15 Jly York 5f gd RF 2856) - also 1st of 6 giving 5lb to Shatin Dollybird (11 May Hamilton RF 1141). **K A Ryan [1-7] Mrs C M Barlow.*

HAMERKOP BHB 20f RR 40f 4470[10]

5 br m Damister (USA) 9.1f **(66)** - Royal Scene (NZ) (Sovereign Edition)
Form - 7400
Record 2000 - 1st:0 2nd:0 3rd:0 Ran:4
Pre2000 - 1st:0 2nd:0 3rd:0 Ran:11
Win Prizemoney £0 *Total Prizemoney* £236
2000 Turf 0-3: (8f, 10f, 14f) (g-f 3) 2000 AW 0-1: (13f) (Equi)
Moderate filly, effective 8f, acts on gd, has worn blinkers. Turf high 40. Inconsistent. **John Berry [0-25] John Berry.*

HAMISH G RR 34f 3831[12]

3 ch g Sure Blade (USA) 10.6f **(66)** - Horton Line (High Line) 10.3f **(70)**
Form - 00
Record 2000 - 1st:0 2nd:0 3rd:0 Ran:2
2000 Turf 0-2: (8f, 9f) (frm, hrd)
Tall, currently very moderate gelding. Turf high 12 (began Aug).
**Mrs M Reveley [0-2] W Ginzel.*

HAMLYN (IRE) BHB 70f RR 84f 4755[14]

3 br g Lure (USA) - Passamaquoddy (USA) (Drone) 10.3f **(74)**
Form - 646470
Record 2000 - 1st:0 2nd:0 3rd:0 Ran:6
Pre2000 - 1st:0 2nd:0 3rd:0 Ran:2

Win Prizemoney £0 *Total Prizemoney* £1,215
2000 Turf 0-6: (7f 3, 8f 3) (g-s 2, gd, g-f 3)
Scopey, decent gelding, has worn blinkers. Turf high 84.
**D R C Elsworth [0-8] M Tabor.*

HAMMER AND SICKLE (IRE) BHB 80f **RR 90df** 5127[17]

3 b c Soviet Lad (USA) 9.4f **(63)** - Preponderance (IRE) (Cyrano de Bergerac) 6f **(68)**
Form - 000
Record 2000 - 1st:0 2nd:0 3rd:0 Ran:3
Pre2000 - 1st:2 2nd:1 3rd:0 Ran:5
Win Prizemoney £6,043 *Total Prizemoney* £6,964
Wins * 1999 May Redcar (FRM) 5f 78+
* 1999 Apr Ripon (G-S) 5f 82 <
2000 Turf 0-3: (5f 3) (g-s 2, gd)
Strong, useful colt, effective 5f, acts on gd. Turf high 79 (began Spt). A robust individual, he looked a useful sprinting juvenile in the first half of '99, but was off the track for 15 months before reappearing at Ascot in September.
**M Johnston [2-8] The 4th Middleham Partnership.*

HAMMOCK (IRE) BHB 58f49a **RR 58f 49a** 4728[18]

2 b br c Hamas (IRE) 8f **(72)** - Sure Victory (IRE) (Stalker)
Form - 0550
Record 2000 - 1st:0 2nd:0 3rd:0 Ran:4
2000 Turf 0-4: (6f, 7f 3) (gd 2, g-f 2)
Fair colt, has worn blinkers. Turf high 58.
**R M Beckett [0-4] Mrs P T Walwyn.*

HAMOND (GER) **RR 112+f** 1634a[1]

5 h Acatenango (GER) - Happy Gini (USA) (Ginistrelli (USA)) 5.6f **(66)**
Form - 1
2000 Turf 1-1: (12f 1-1) (g-f 1-1)
Group-class colt. (1st run) - 1st of 9 from Noel (28 May Capannelle RF 1634a). Made all to win an Italian Group Two in May.
**A Wohler in GER [1-4] Gestut Fahrhof.*

HANA'S PRIDE (IRE) BHB 30f **RR 42f** 3019[8]

4 gr f Pips Pride 6.7f **(70)** - Singhana (IRE) (Mouktar)
Form - 8
Record 2000 - 1st:0 2nd:0 3rd:0 Ran:1
Pre2000 - 1st:0 2nd:0 3rd:0 Ran:3
2000 AW 0-1: (6f) (Fibr)
Tall, moderate filly. **Mrs A Duffield [0-4] Bill Martin.*

HAND CHIME BHB 85f **RR 84+f** 4177[1]

3 ch g Clantime 6.6f **(57)** - Warning Bell (Bustino) 10.4f **(64)**
Form - 01123111
Record 2000 - 1st:5 2nd:1 3rd:1 Ran:8
Win Prizemoney £20,917 *Total Prizemoney* £22,126
Wins * **2000** *Spt Wolver (STD) H* 7f 80 86+ <
* **2000** Aug Pontef (G-F) 6f 84+
* **2000** Aug Kempto (G-F) H 7f 70 83
* **2000** Jun Carlis (G-F) H 8f 62 67+
* **2000** Jun Catter (SFT) 7f 59+
2000 Turf 4-7: (6f 1-2, 7f 2-2, 8f 1-3) (g-s 1-1, gd 2, g-f 2-2, frm 1-2)
2000 AW 1-1: (7f 1-1) (Fibr 1-1)
Leggy, useful gelding, effective 6 to 7f, best at 7f, acts on g-f to frm - acts on Fibr. Turf high 84 - 1st of 7 giving 6lb to Garth Pool (9 Aug Pontefract RF 3504) - also 1st of 12 getting 4lb from Cowboys And Angels (2 Aug Kempton RF 3325). (1st run) - 1st of 10 giving 6lb to Oscar Pepper (2 Spt Wolverhampton RF 4177). Improving.
**W J Haggas [5-8] Mrs M M Haggas.*

HANDSOME BADSHA (IRE) BHB 62f **RR 38f** 5217[4]

2 b c Petardia 8.2f **(58)** - Cape Shirley (Head for Heights) 9.6f **(55)**
Form - 64
Record 2000 - 1st:0 2nd:0 3rd:0 Ran:2
Win Prizemoney £0 *Total Prizemoney* £284
2000 Turf 0-1: (6f) (sft) 2000 AW 0-1: (6f) (Fibr)
Currently average colt. **J A Osborne [0-2] Aziz-Ur Rahman.*

HANDSOME BEAU BHB 25f **RR 38f** 35[7]

5 ch g Handsome Sailor 6.6f **(53)** - Chester Belle (Ballacashtal (CAN)) 5.3f **(50)**
Form - 07
Record 2000 - 1st:0 2nd:0 3rd:0 Ran:1
Pre2000 - 1st:0 2nd:0 3rd:0 Ran:4
2000 AW 0-1: (7f) (Fibr)
Very moderate gelding, often wears blinkers.
**A Bailey [0-5] Sandybrow Stables Ltd.*

HANDSOME LAD (IRE) RR 2167[10]

2 b c Inzar (USA) - Elite Exhibition (Exhibitioner) 8.7f **(61)**
Form - 60
Record 2000 - 1st:0 2nd:0 3rd:0 Ran:2
2000 Turf 0-2: (5f 2) (sft, g-f)
Currently very poor colt. **A Scott [0-2] Andy Scott.*

HANDSOME RIDGE BHB 116f **RR 117f** 895[6]

6 ch h Indian Ridge 7.6f **(74)** - Red Rose Garden (Electric) 10.1f **(61)**
Form - 26
Record 2000 - 1st:0 2nd:0 3rd:0 Ran:1
Pre2000 - 1st:7 2nd:5 3rd:3 Ran:26
Win Prizemoney £170,805 *Total Prizemoney* £252,802
Wins * 1999 May Goodwo (GD) 9.9f 121+ <
* 1999 Apr Sandow (G-S) G2 8.1f 113
* 1998 Nov Saint- (HLD) G3 8f 118+
* 1998 Spt Doncas (GD) G3 8f 116
* 1997 Jly Maison (SFT) G3 9f 101
* 1997 Jun Goodwo (G-S) 9f 104
* 1996 Nov Doncas (SFT) 7f 91+
2000 Turf 0-1: (8f) (sft)
High-class horse, effective 8 to 10f, best at 10f, acts on hvy to g-f, best on gd, prefers right handed tracks. Consistent. A high class miler who did connections proud over the years, he finished last on his only start of 2001 and has been retired to stud.
**J H M Gosden [7-27] Platt Promotions Ltd.*

HANGOVER SQUARE (IRE) BHB 83f **RR 110f** 4131a[2]

6 ch h Jareer (USA) 10.2f **(54)** - Dancing Line (High Line) 10.3f **(70)**
Form - 32
2000 Turf 0-1: (10f) (gd) 2000 AW 0-1: (9f) (Dirt)
Group-class horse. (1st run) - 2nd of 10 getting 4lb from Elle Danzig (25 Aug Baden-Baden 10f gd RF 4131a).
**L Reuterskjold in SWE [1-3] Castle Stables.*

HANNAH BURDETT **RR 70f** 3408[5]

3 ch f Kris 10f **(75)** - Polka Dancer **(95f)** (Dancing Brave (USA)) 8.4f **(76)**
Form - 35
Record 2000 - 1st:0 2nd:0 3rd:1 Ran:2
Win Prizemoney £0 *Total Prizemoney* £680
2000 Turf 0-2: (7f 2) (g-f, frm)
Strong, currently above-average filly. Turf high 70 (1st run) (began Jly) - 3rd of 8 to Sea Drift (22 Jly Newmarket 7f g-f RF 3034).
**R M H Cowell [0-2] G B Strahan & Partners.*

HANNIBAL LAD BHB 81f81a **RR 84f 81a** 4892[5]

4 ch g Rock City 8.8f **(62)** - Appealing (Star Appeal) 9.6f **(65)**
Form - 2152311350421144135565
Record 2000 - 1st:6 2nd:2 3rd:3 Ran:21
Pre2000 - 1st:2 2nd:1 3rd:1 Ran:10
Win Prizemoney £43,763 *Total Prizemoney* £53,571
Wins * **2000** Jly Ascot (GD) H 12f 76 81 <
* **2000** Jun Doncas (G-F) H 12f 67 73
* **2000** May Southw (HVY) H 12f 64 67
* **2000** *Feb Southw (STD) H 11f 74 78*
* **2000** *Feb Southw (STD) H 11f 70 72*
* **2000** *Jan Wolver (STD) H 9.4f 62 66*
1999 *Apr Wolver (STD) S 9.4f 64*
1998 *Spt Southw (STD) S 7f 68*
2000 Turf 3-13: (10f, 12f 3-10, 13f 2) (hvy, gd 3-5, g-f 5, frm 2) 2000 AW 3-8: (8f, 9f 1-3, 11f 2-2, 12f 2) (Fibr 3-8)
Leggy, decent gelding, effective 11 to 12f, best at 12f, acts on gd to frm - acts on Fibr, and excels at Southwell and Doncaster. Turf high 84 - 5th of 11 to Flossy (6 Aug Chester 12f g-f RF 3416) - also 1st of 14 getting 3lb from St Helensfield (15 Jly Ascot RF 2826). AW high 79 - 3rd of 10 giving 12lb to Parable (14 Mar Southwell 12f Fibr RF 0441) - also 1st of 9 getting 13lb from China Castle (28 Feb Southwell RF 0375). Consistent. He had previously just looked to be a Fibresand plater, albeit an effective one, but improved out of all recognition on turf last season, gaining victories at Southwell in May and Doncaster in June and winning a decent handicap at Ascot in July. Suited by 12 furlongs.

**W M Brisbourne [6-22] John Pugh (from P D Evans [2-9] Jun 1999).*

HANOI BHB 26f **RR 20f** 3968[15]
3 b f Deploy 11.4f **(67)** - A Nymph Too Far (IRE) (Precocious) 8.6f **(62)**
Form - 850070
Record 2000 - 1st:0 2nd:0 3rd:0 Ran:6
2000 Turf 0-6: (7f, 8f 3, 10f 2) (gd, g-f 5)
Light-framed, little account filly, mostly wears blinkers. Turf high 33. **Dr J D Scargill [0-6] Mrs Susan Scargill.*

HAP (USA) RR 117f 5327a[9]
4 ch c Theatrical 11.5f **(78)** - Committed (USA) (Hagley (USA))
Form - 20
2000 Turf 0-1: (8f) (frm)
High-class colt. **W Mott in USA [0-2] Allen Paulson Living Trust.*

HAPPYANUNOIT (NZ) RR 119f 3941a[2]
5 br m Yachtie (AUS) - Easter Queen (Prefairy)
Form - 12
2000 Turf 0-1: (10f) (g-s)
Currently high-class filly, often wears blinkers.
**R Frankel in USA [1-2] Amerman Racing Stables.*

HAPPY CHANGE (GER) BHB 109f **RR 110f** 5130[6]
6 ch g Surumu (GER) - Happy Gini (USA) (Ginistrelli (USA)) 5.6f **(66)**
Form - 3815326
Record 2000 - 1st:1 2nd:1 3rd:2 Ran:7
Pre2000 - 1st:2 2nd:2 3rd:2 Ran:12
Win Prizemoney £37,822 *Total Prizemoney* £121,635
Wins * **2000** Aug Windso (G-F) 11.6f 110 <
* 1999 Aug Epsom (GD) 10.1f 110 <
1998 Aug Baden- (SFT) G3 10f 108+
2000 Turf 1-7: (10f, 11f 2, 12f 1-4) (sft, gd 1-4, g-f)
Group-class gelding, effective 10 to 12f, best at 12f, acts on g-f, best on gd. Turf high 110 - 2nd of 6 getting 3lb from Mutamam (23 Spt Ascot 12f gd RF 4594) - also 1st of 6 giving 13lb to Blue Gold (26 Aug Windsor RF 4003). Consistent. A Group Three winner in Germany, he landed a decent race at Windsor in August. Found wanting in a Group Three next time, he only went down in a three-way photo in the Blandford Stakes at the Curragh and ran another good race in Ascot's Cumberland Lodge Stakes. He appreciates some cut in the ground.
**M Johnston [2-9] The Winning Line (from Miss Venetia Williams [0-1] Spt 1998).*

HAPPY DAYS BHB 28f **RR 42f** 5193[7]
5 b g Primitive Rising (USA) 8.1f **(48)** -Miami Dolphin (Derrylin) 8.8f **(54)**
Form - 7084262524407
Record 2000 - 1st:0 2nd:3 3rd:0 Ran:13
Pre2000 - 1st:1 2nd:3 3rd:1 Ran:22
Win Prizemoney £3,663 *Total Prizemoney* £11,742
Wins * 1999 May Ripon (G-F) H 16f 38 44 <
2000 Turf 0-12: (13f 6, 14f 2, 15f, 16f 2, 17f) (g-s 2, gd 2, g-f 5, frm 3)
2000 AW 0-1: (16f) (Fibr)
Moderate gelding, effective 13 to 16f, best at 13f, acts on g-f to frm, best on g-f, has worn blinkers, prefers right handed tracks, favours tight tracks, excels at Hamilton. Turf high 42 - 2nd of 9 getting 23lb from Swagger (19 May Hamilton 13f g-f RF 1301).
**D Moffatt [1-43] J W Barrett (from J Berry [0-2] Spt 1998).*

HAPPY DIAMOND (USA) BHB 108f **RR 105+f** 3361[1]
3 b c Diesis 9f **(80)** - Urus (USA) (Kris S (USA)) 7.9f **(71)**
Form - 3024111
Record 2000 - 1st:3 2nd:1 3rd:1 Ran:7
Pre2000 - 1st:1 2nd:1 3rd:0 Ran:2
Win Prizemoney £59,157 *Total Prizemoney* £64,859
Wins * **2000** Aug Goodwo (GD) H 9.9f 94 105 <
* **2000** Jly Ascot (G-F) H 10f 94 101
* **2000** Jly Doncas (GD) H 10.3f 89 98+
* 1999 Jly Thirsk (FRM) 5f 83+
2000 Turf 3-7: (6f 2, 10f 3-5) (gd 1-3, g-f 1-2, frm 1-2)
Scopey, Pattern-class colt, effective 10f, acts on gd to frm. Turf high 105 - 1st of 11 giving 11lb to Starlyte Girl (4 Aug Goodwood RF 3361) - also 1st of 9 getting 7lb from Westender (29 Jly Ascot RF 3200). Very unfortunate to be the victim of Royston Ffrench's ghastly aberration at Doncaster in July, he then managed to get disqualified from second place at Newcastle a week later. He then really found his form, completing a hat-trick in a valuable handicap at Glorious Goodwood. He was progressing well, but was not seen out again. **M Johnston [4-9] Jaber Abdullah.*

HAPPY GO LUCKY BHB 63f **RR 65f** 4539[12]
6 ch m Teamster 11.4f **(22)** - Meritsu (IRE) (Lyphard's Special (USA)) 10.3f **(72)**
Form - 06230
Record 2000 - 1st:0 2nd:1 3rd:1 Ran:5
Pre2000 - 1st:3 2nd:1 3rd:4 Ran:20
Win Prizemoney £10,149 *Total Prizemoney* £17,636
Wins * 1998 Spt Folkes (G-F) 12f 68
1997 Jun Warwic (FRM) 10.8f 78 <
1996 Aug Sandow (G-F) 8.1f 78 <
2000 Turf 0-5: (12f 3, 13f, 14f) (gd, g-f, frm 3)
Average mare. Turf high 65 - 3rd of 9 giving 6lb to Alnajashee (29 Jun Salisbury 14f frm RF 2378).
**M J Weeden [1-14] M J Weeden (from R J O'Sullivan [2-13] Oct 1997).*

HAPPY HOOLIGAN BHB 72f **RR 75f** 1143[3]
3 b c Ezzoud (IRE) - Continual (USA) (Damascus (USA)) 8.9f **(71)**
Form - 0533
Record 2000 - 1st:0 2nd:0 3rd:2 Ran:4
Pre2000 - 1st:0 2nd:1 3rd:0 Ran:1
Win Prizemoney £0 *Total Prizemoney* £1,812
2000 Turf 0-4: (7f 2, 8f, 9f) (g-s, gd 2, frm)
Above-average colt. Turf high 75 - 3rd of 7 to Barton Sands (11 May Hamilton 9f frm RF 1143). (DEAD)
**M Johnston [0-5] Maktoum Al Maktoum.*

HAPPY LADY (FR) BHB 62f45a **RR 60f 45a** 347[6]
4 b f Cadeaux Genereux 7.9f **(76)** - Siwaayib (Green Desert (USA)) 8.6f **(78)**
Form - 36
Record 2000 - 1st:0 2nd:0 3rd:1 Ran:2
Pre2000 - 1st:0 2nd:0 3rd:1 Ran:6
Win Prizemoney £0 *Total Prizemoney* £886
2000 AW 0-2: (9f 2) (Fibr 2)
Scopey, average filly, effective 8f, acts on g-f. AW high 40.
**B W Hills [0-8] R A N Bonnycastle.*

HARD DAYS NIGHT (IRE) BHB 43f33a **RR 45f 33a** 4583[9]
3 b g Mujtahid (USA) 7.4f **(69)** - Oiche Mhaith (Night Shift (USA)) 7.2f **(69)**
Form - 00064620240
Record 2000 - 1st:0 2nd:2 3rd:0 Ran:11
Pre2000 - 1st:0 2nd:0 3rd:0 Ran:7
Win Prizemoney £0 *Total Prizemoney* £1,612
2000 Turf 0-10: (8f 2, 10f, 11f, 12f, 14f, 16f 4) (g-s, gd 3, g-f 5, frm)
2000 AW 0-1: (16f) (Equi)
Moderate gelding. Turf high 45. **M Blanshard [0-18] David Sykes.*

HARD LINES (USA) BHB 60f55a **RR 62f 55a** 4875[3]
4 b g Silver Hawk (USA) 11.2f **(85)** - Arctic Eclipse (USA) (Northern Dancer) 9.6f **(80)**
Form - 00804133
Record 2000 - 1st:1 2nd:0 3rd:2 Ran:8
Pre2000 - 1st:1 2nd:0 3rd:0 Ran:2
Win Prizemoney £6,387 *Total Prizemoney* £7,258
Wins * **2000** Spt Bath (GD) SH 8f 55 60
* 1998 May Newbur (G-F) 6f 83+ <
2000 Turf 1-7: (7f, 8f 1-6) (g-s, gd, g-f, frm 1-3, hrd) 2000 AW 0-1: (9f) (Fibr)
Scopey, average gelding. Turf high 62.
**I A Balding [2-10] C H Bothway.*

HARD TO CASH (IRE) BHB 45f **RR 34f** 4930[23]
2 b c Distinctly North (USA) 7.4f **(63)** - Zertxuna (Averof) 8.2f **(62)**
Form - 740
Record 2000 - 1st:0 2nd:0 3rd:0 Ran:3
2000 Turf 0-3: (6f, 7f 2) (gd 2, frm)
Currently very moderate colt. Turf high 34 (began Jly).
**D J S Cosgrove [0-3] Ms C Hehir.*

HARD TO CATCH (IRE) BHB 76a **RR 73f** 4926[6]
2 b g Namaqualand (USA) - Brook's Dilemma (Known Fact (USA)) 7.4f **(67)**

Form - 534671706
Record 2000 - 1st:1 2nd:0 3rd:1 Ran:9
Win Prizemoney £3,640 *Total Prizemoney* £4,167
Wins * 2000 Aug Lingfi (G-F) 5f 71 <
2000 Turf 1-8: (5f 1-6, 6f 2) (sft, g-s, gd 3, g-f, frm 1-2) 2000 AW 0-1: (6f) (Equi)
Above-average gelding, effective 5 to 6f, acts on gd to frm, often wears blinkers. Turf high 73 - also 1st of 8 giving 5lb to Unparalleled (23 Aug Lingfield RF 3906).
**K T Ivory [1-7] E H Maloney (from M R Channon [0-2] Apr 2000).*

HARD TO FOLLOW RR 27f 3184^{7}
5 b m Dilum (USA) 7.1f **(56)** - Cedar Lady (Telsmoss)
Form - 007
Record 2000 - 1st:0 2nd:0 3rd:0 Ran:3
Pre2000 - 1st:0 2nd:0 3rd:0 Ran:3
2000 Turf 0-3: (8f, 10f, 12f) (frm 2, hrd)
Little account filly. Turf high 27 (began Jly).
**R J Hodges [0-6] J W Mursell.*

HARD TO KNOW (IRE) BHB 69f RR 68f 3990^{4}
2 b c Common Grounds 8.1f **(66)** - Lady Fern (Old Vic)
Form - 404
Record 2000 - 1st:0 2nd:0 3rd:0 Ran:3
Win Prizemoney £0 *Total Prizemoney* £647
2000 Turf 0-3: (6f 3) (g-f, frm 2)
Currently average colt. Turf high 68 (began Jly). Showed ability first time, and raced alone on his second run. Can do better in handicaps. **D J S Cosgrove [0-3] Ms C Hehir.*

HARD TO LAY (IRE) BHB 58f RR 61f 3919^{3}
2 br f Dolphin Street (FR) - Yavarro (Raga Navarro (ITY)) 8f **(64)**
Form - 257823
Record 2000 - 1st:0 2nd:2 3rd:1 Ran:6
Win Prizemoney £0 *Total Prizemoney* £1,930
2000 Turf 0-6: (5f 2, 6f, 7f 3) (gd 2, g-f 2, frm 2)
Average filly, effective 7f, acts on gd to g-f. Turf high 61 - 3rd of 14 getting 5lb from Sawbo Lad (24 Aug Folkestone 7f gd RF 3919).
**D J S Cosgrove [0-6] Liam Mulryan.*

HARDY (USA) RR 95f $4805a^{6}$
3 b c Mr Prospector (USA) 8.6f **(88)** - Korveya (USA) (Riverman (USA)) 9.1f **(76)**
Form - 16
2000 Turf 1-2: (7f, 8f 1-1) (sft 1-2)
Currently very useful colt. Turf high 95 - also 1st of 14 from Pine Dance (1 May Curragh RF 1120a). A half brother to Bosra Sham and Hector Protector among others, he whizzed home in a maiden on his belated debut, but was not particularly fancied when sixth in a Group Three on his only other run. He looks unlikely to reach the heights of his illustrious relatives.
**A P O'Brien in IRE [1-2] Mrs John Magnier.*

HAREEBA BHB 65f RR 65f 3731^{10}
3 ch f Hernando (FR) - La Nureyeva (USA) (Nureyev (USA)) 8.7f **(78)**
Form - 400
Record 2000 - 1st:0 2nd:0 3rd:0 Ran:3
Win Prizemoney £0 *Total Prizemoney* £432
2000 Turf 0-3: (7f 3) (g-s, gd, frm)
Scopey, currently average filly. Turf high 65.
**P J Makin [0-3] Mrs D Joly.*

HARIK BHB 55f77a RR 28f 77a 436^{2}
6 ch g Persian Bold 10f **(69)** - Yaqut (USA) (Northern Dancer) 9.6f **(80)**
Form - 3112
Record 2000 - 1st:2 2nd:1 3rd:1 Ran:4
Pre2000 - 1st:3 2nd:3 3rd:1 Ran:14
Win Prizemoney £15,444 *Total Prizemoney* £20,043
Wins * 2000 *Feb Lingfi (STD) H 16f 78 80* <
*** 2000** *Jan Lingfi (STD) H 16f 70 75*
* 1999 *Feb Lingfi (STD) H 16f 65 70*
* 1998 *Mar Lingfi (SLW) H 13f 65 73*
* 1998 *Feb Lingfi (SLW) 12f 65*
2000 AW 2-4: (12f, 16f 2-3) (Equi 2-3, Fibr)
Decent gelding, effective 16f, - acts on AW, best on Equi, favours left handed tracks, favours tight tracks. AW high 81 - 2nd of 7 giving 17lb to Maknaas (11 Mar Wolverhampton 16f Fibr RF 0436) - also 1st of 7 giving 8lb to Alhesn (19 Feb Lingfield RF 0317). He seems to show his best form in staying events on Equitrack.
**G L Moore [6-30] The Best Beech Partnership (from B Hanbury [0-1] Oct 1996).*

HARISHON (IRE) RR 105f $4722a^{3}$
4 b c Waajib 8.9f **(67)** - Chenya (Beldale Flutter (USA)) 9.7f **(71)**
Form - 233
2000 Turf 0-3: (12f 2, 16f) (gd 3)
Currently Pattern-class colt. Turf high 105 (1st run) - 2nd of 6 to Akbar (12 Jun Frauenfeld 12f gd RF 2197a). **M Weiss in SWI [0-3] .*

HARIYMI (IRE) BHB 76f RR 79f 1274^{12}
5 gr g Woodman (USA) 9.7f **(77)** - Harouniya (Siberian Express (USA)) 8.8f **(65)**
Form - 0
Record 2000 - 1st:0 2nd:0 3rd:0 Ran:1
Pre2000 - 1st:1 2nd:1 3rd:0 Ran:3
Win Prizemoney £2,406 *Total Prizemoney* £3,612
Wins 1999 May Dundal (GD) 9f 74+ <
2000 Turf 0-1: (12f) (gd)
Above-average gelding.
**R Rowe [1-6] Mrs Jean Bishop (from J Oxx in IRE [1-3] Jun 1999).*

HARLEQUIN BHB 80f RR 74f 5309^{6}
2 b c Halling (USA) - Russian Grace (IRE) (Soviet Star (USA))
Form - 066
Record 2000 - 1st:0 2nd:0 3rd:0 Ran:3
2000 Turf 0-3: (7f 3) (g-s 2, g-f)
Currently above-average colt. Turf high 74 (began Spt).
**Sir Michael Stoute [0-3] Highclere Thoroughbred Racing Ltd.*

HARLEQUIN DANCER BHB 50f RR 52f 4538^{14}
4 b g Distant Relative 7f **(69)** - Proudfoot (IRE) (Shareef Dancer (USA)) 9.9f **(73)**
Form - 07800
Record 2000 - 1st:0 2nd:0 3rd:0 Ran:5
Pre2000 - 1st:1 2nd:0 3rd:1 Ran:8
Win Prizemoney £2,448 *Total Prizemoney* £8,338
Wins 1999 May Leices (GD) 8f 83 <
2000 Turf 0-5: (8f 3, 10f, 11f) (g-s, gd, g-f, frm, hrd)
Strong, fair gelding, effective 8f, acts on g-f, has worn blinkers. Turf high 52.
**J G FitzGerald [0-5] C T S Racing Partnership (from J H M Gosden [1-8] Oct 1999).*

HARMONIC (USA) BHB 72f RR 73f 5229^{2}
3 b f Shadeed (USA) 7.7f **(72)** - Running Melody (Rheingold) 10.4f **(62)**
Form - 602220242
Record 2000 - 1st:0 2nd:5 3rd:0 Ran:9
Pre2000 - 1st:0 2nd:1 3rd:0 Ran:4
Win Prizemoney £0 *Total Prizemoney* £8,031
2000 Turf 0-9: (7f 7, 8f, 9f) (g-s, gd 3, g-f 4, frm)
Workmanlike, above-average filly, effective 6 to 9f, acts on gd to frm, best on frm. Turf high 73 - 2nd of 24 to Eve (27 Oct Newmarket 8f gd RF 5229). **D R C Elsworth [0-13] Mrs P J Sheen.*

HARMONIC WAY BHB 112f RR 113f 4966^{10}
5 ch h Lion Cavern (USA) 7.5f **(74)** - Pineapple (Superlative) 7.2f **(56)**
Form - 6421620460
Record 2000 - 1st:1 2nd:2 3rd:0 Ran:10
Pre2000 - 1st:2 2nd:5 3rd:3 Ran:22
Win Prizemoney £112,694 *Total Prizemoney* £168,187
Wins * 2000 Jun Ascot (G-F) H 6f 102 113 <
* 1999 Jly Goodwo (G-F) H 6f 92 99
* 1997 Aug Salisb (G-F) 6f 80
2000 Turf 1-10: (5f, 6f 1-9) (g-s 3, gd 1-4, frm 2, hrd)
Group-class colt, effective 6f, acts on g-s to gd. Turf high 113 - 1st of 29 giving 13lb to Tussle (23 Jun Ascot RF 2209). Consistent. Winner of the Stewards' Cup in '99 and the Wokingham at Ascot last term, he benefits from exaggerated waiting tactics and goes well for Richard Hughes. A strongly-run six furlongs obviously suits him ideally, conditions he is more likely to find in the big handicaps than in Pattern races, but having finished fourth in the Group One Haydock Sprint Cup he is likely to be ineligible for handicaps now. **R Charlton [3-32] Mrs Alexandra Chandris.*

HARMONIZE BHB 48f **RR 49f** 2407[4]
3 b f Emperor Jones (USA) - Hemline (Sharpo) 7.7f **(59)**
Form - 4
Record 2000 - 1st:0 2nd:0 3rd:0 Ran:1
Pre2000 - 1st:0 2nd:0 3rd:0 Ran:3
Win Prizemoney £0 *Total Prizemoney* £392
2000 Turf 0-1: (6f) (g-f)
Scopey, moderate filly, has broken blood-vessels.
**Martyn Wane [0-4] J P Slattery.*

HARMONY HALL BHB 58f **RR 61f** 5072[16]
6 ch g Music Boy 6.5f **(56)** - Fleeting Affair (Hotfoot) 10.5f **(59)**
Form - 4422278300
Record 2000 - 1st:0 2nd:3 3rd:1 Ran:10
Pre2000 - 1st:1 2nd:6 3rd:3 Ran:33
Win Prizemoney £5,247 *Total Prizemoney* £25,099
Wins 1998 Jly Nottin (G-F) H 10f 64 69 <
2000 Turf 0-10: (8f 7, 9f, 10f 2) (g-s, gd, g-f 4, frm 4)
Average gelding, effective 8 to 9f, best at 8f, acts on gd to frm, best on g-f, has worn blinkers. Turf high 68 - 2nd of 6 getting 1lb from Goodenough Mover (8 Jly Chepstow 8f frm RF 2629). He is on a long losing run on the Flat, but was running particularly well during the summer. Effective from between a mile and ten furlongs, he needs fast ground.
**J M Bradley [1-29] E A Hayward (from J R Fanshawe [1-21] Aug 1998).*

HARMONY ROW RR 88f 5099[1]
2 ch c Barathea (IRE) - Little Change (Grundy) 10.3f **(65)**
Form - 31
Record 2000 - 1st:1 2nd:0 3rd:1 Ran:2
Win Prizemoney £3,477 *Total Prizemoney* £4,260
Wins * **2000** Oct Doncas (GD) 7f 88 <
2000 Turf 1-2: (7f 1-2) (gd 1-1, g-f)
Currently useful colt. Turf high 88 (began Spt) - 1st of 22 from Tramway (20 Oct Doncaster RF 5099).
**E A L Dunlop [1-2] The Right Angle Club.*

HARNAGE (IRE) BHB 22f **RR 25f** 1522[14]
5 b g Mujadil (USA) 7.7f **(70)** - Wilderness (Martinmas) 7.6f **(59)**
Form - 0
Record 2000 - 1st:0 2nd:0 3rd:0 Ran:1
Pre2000 - 1st:0 2nd:0 3rd:1 Ran:12
Win Prizemoney £0 *Total Prizemoney* £259
2000 Turf 0-1: (10f) (gd)
Little account gelding.
**P Burgoyne [0-8] Philip Saunders (from M R Channon [0-5] Jly 1997).*

HAROLDON (IRE) BHB 34f37a **RR 42f 37a** 1512[6]
11 ch g Heraldiste (USA) 8.9f **(54)** - Cordon (Morston (FR)) 9.4f **(55)**
Form - 06
Record 2000 - 1st:0 2nd:0 3rd:0 Ran:2
Pre2000 - 1st:7 2nd:6 3rd:8 Ran:84
Win Prizemoney £24,629 *Total Prizemoney* £35,582
Wins * 1998 May Nottin (FRM) SH 10f 52 57
* 1997 Jly Windso (GD) H 10f 65 68
2000 Turf 0-2: (11f 2) (hvy 2)
Moderate gelding, effective 8 to 11f, acts on sft to frm, has worn blinkers. Turf high 32. **B Palling [8-91] Lamb Brook Associates.*

HARRIER (IRE) BHB 100f **RR 99f** 4447[1]
2 b br g Prince of Birds (USA) - Casaveha (IRE) (Persian Bold) 9.3f **(66)**
Form - 330111
Record 2000 - 1st:3 2nd:0 3rd:2 Ran:6
Win Prizemoney £9,493 *Total Prizemoney* £10,568
Wins * **2000** Spt Ayr (SFT) 8f 99 <
* **2000** Aug Beverl (G-F) 7.5f 84+
* **2000** Aug Thirsk (GD) C 7f 84+
2000 Turf 3-6: (5f 3, 7f 2-2, 8f 1-1) (gd 1-3, frm 2-3)
Very useful gelding, effective 8f, acts on gd. Turf high 99 - 1st of 6 giving 11lb to Zulfaa (16 Spt Ayr RF 4447). Appreciated the step up in trip and drop in class when winning a claimer at Thirsk in August, and by the middle of the following month had completed the hat-trick. Ground does not appear to be a problem, and there may be more to come. **T D Easterby [3-6] The Rumpole Partnership.*

HARRYANA BHB 68f **RR 79f** 5313[21]
3 b f Efisio 7.7f **(69)** - Allyana (IRE) **(62df)** (Thatching) 8f **(66)**
Form - 00
Record 2000 - 1st:0 2nd:0 3rd:0 Ran:2
Pre2000 - 1st:2 2nd:2 3rd:0 Ran:9
Win Prizemoney £9,796 *Total Prizemoney* £11,846
Wins * 1999 Aug Redcar (G-F) 5f 79+ <
* 1999 May Cheste (G-F) 5.1f 79+ <
2000 Turf 0-2: (5f 2) (g-s 2)
Strong, above-average filly, effective 5 to 6f, best at 5f, acts on sft to frm. Turf high 20 (began Oct). Inconsistent. **M Johnston [2-11] S Kimberley.*

HARRY JUNIOR BHB 45f **RR 60f** 3489[11]
2 b c River Falls 8.2f **(56)** - Badger Bay (IRE) **(34f 46a)** (Salt Dome (USA))
Form - 675280
Record 2000 - 1st:0 2nd:1 3rd:0 Ran:6
Win Prizemoney £0 *Total Prizemoney* £524
2000 Turf 0-6: (5f 2, 6f 2, 7f 2) (gd 2, g-f 2, frm 2)
Average colt, has worn blinkers. Turf high 60.
**C A Dwyer [0-6] M E Hall.*

HARRY TASTERS BHB 56f **RR 46f** 1594[10]
3 ch c Efisio 7.7f **(69)** - Laugharne (Known Fact (USA)) 7.4f **(67)**
Form - 000
Record 2000 - 1st:0 2nd:0 3rd:0 Ran:3
Pre2000 - 1st:0 2nd:0 3rd:0 Ran:2
2000 Turf 0-3: (6f, 7f, 8f) (gd, g-f 2)
Scopey, moderate colt. Turf high 46.
**D R C Elsworth [0-5] Sir Stanley and Lady Grinstead.*

HARVEY LEADER BHB 65f **RR 61f** 4812[10]
5 b g Prince Sabo 6.6f **(64)** - Mrs Leader (USA) (Mr Leader (USA)) 9.8f **(66)**
Form - 300
Record 2000 - 1st:0 2nd:0 3rd:1 Ran:3
Win Prizemoney £0 *Total Prizemoney* £372
2000 Turf 0-2: (8f 2) (g-s, gd) 2000 AW 0-1: (8f) (Fibr)
Average gelding. Turf high 61.
**Miss D A McHale [0-1] C Murhead (from J R Fanshawe [0-4] Jun 2000).*

HARVEY'S FUTURE BHB 50f52a **RR 45f 52a** 5112[7]
6 b g Never so Bold 7.1f **(62)** - Orba Gold (USA) (Gold Crest (USA))
Form - 320627
Record 2000 - 1st:0 2nd:2 3rd:1 Ran:6
Pre2000 - 1st:1 2nd:3 3rd:1 Ran:18
Win Prizemoney £2,920 *Total Prizemoney* £8,303
Wins * 1999 Apr Bath (SFT) H 5.1f 36 42 <
2000 Turf 0-6: (5f 5, 6f) (g-s, gd, g-f 3, frm)
Fair gelding, effective 5 to 6f, best at 5f, acts on g-s to frm, best on g-f, has worn blinkers. Turf high 45 - 2nd of 25 getting 13lb from Square Dancer (6 Oct Windsor 6f g-f RF 4826).
**P L Gilligan [1-20] Treasure Seekers Partnership (from T T Clement [0-4] Aug 1997).*

HARVEY WHITE (IRE) BHB 31f37a **RR 30f 37a** 163[3]
8 b or br g Petorius 8f **(66)** - Walkyria (Lord Gayle (USA)) 8.8f **(62)**
Form - 023
Record 2000 - 1st:0 2nd:1 3rd:1 Ran:3
Pre2000 - 1st:4 2nd:6 3rd:11 Ran:62
Win Prizemoney £13,357 *Total Prizemoney* £26,414
Wins * 1997 Jun Lingfi (GD) H 9f 52 55
* 1996 Spt Kempto (GD) H 10f 56 62
* 1996 May Warwic (FRM) H 10.8f 53 62
2000 AW 0-3: (12f, 16f 2) (Equi, Fibr 2)
Very moderate gelding, effective 10 to 16f, best at 12f, - acts on AW, best on Equi, has worn blinkers, prefers left handed tracks, favours tight tracks, excels at Lingfield. AW high 37 - 2nd of 12 giving 3lb to Medelai (13 Jan Wolverhampton 16f Fibr RF 0079).
**J Pearce [4-65] B & G Racing.*

HARVY BHB 30f **RR** 3180[12]
3 ch c Beveled (USA) 6.9f **(64)** - Miss Copyforce (Aragon) 8.1f **(60)**
Form - 000
Record 2000 - 1st:0 2nd:0 3rd:0 Ran:3

2000 Turf 0-3: (6f, 7f 2) (gd, g-f, frm)
Leggy, currently very poor colt. **M Madgwick [0-3] Mrs H Veal.*

HASENE (FR) RR 107f 4419a[3]
5 b m Akarad (FR) 9.7f **(73)** - She's My Lovely (Sharpo) 7.7f **(59)**
Form - 63
2000 Turf 0-2: (8f, 10f) (g-s, gd)
Currently Pattern-class filly. Turf high 107 (began Jly).
**D Smaga in FR [0-2].*

HASTA LA VISTA BHB 40f31a **RR 51f 31a** 4777[8]
10 b g Superlative 8.8f **(57)** - Falcon Berry (FR) (Bustino) 10.4f **(64)**
Form - 102143508738
Record 2000 - 1st:2 2nd:1 3rd:2 Ran:12
Pre2000 - 1st:14 2nd:10 3rd:10 Ran:94
Win Prizemoney £53,174 *Total Prizemoney* £74,214
Wins * **2000** Jun Catter (G-S) H 12f 47 50
* **2000** Apr Mussel (G-S) H 14f 43 47
* 1998 Jly Beverl (GD) H 12f 52 55
* 1998 May Catter (G-S) H 13.8f 47 51
* 1998 May Mussel (G-F) H 12f 44 47
* 1997 Aug Ripon (GD) H 12.3f 55 60
* 1997 Aug Catter (G-F) H 13.8f 50 55
* 1997 Jly Catter (SFT) H 15.8f 52 55
* 1997 Jun Hamilt (G-S) H 13f 47 54
* 1997 May Mussel (G-F) H 16f 48 53
* 1996 Apr Catter (GD) H 12f 50 54
2000 Turf 2-11: (12f 1-4, 13f, 14f 1-4, 16f 2) (g-s 3, gd 2-4, g-f, frm 3)
2000 AW 0-1: (16f) (Fibr)
Fair gelding, effective 12 to 14f, acts on g-s to frm, mostly wears blinkers, prefers right handed tracks, favours tight tracks, and excels at Hamilton. Turf high 51 - 2nd of 14 giving 6lb to Elsie Bamford (3 Jun Catterick 14f g-s RF 1673) - also 1st of 13 giving 2lb to Evening Scent (9 Jun Catterick RF 1839).
**M W Easterby [16-109] K Hodgson & Mrs J Hodgson.*

HASTY PRINCE RR 65f 3608[6]
2 ch c Halling (USA) - Sister Sophie (USA) (Effervescing (USA)) 8.1f **(79)**
Form - 6
Record 2000 - 1st:0 2nd:0 3rd:0 Ran:1
2000 Turf 0-1: (7f) (frm)
Currently average colt. **B Hanbury [0-1] Ahmed Ali.*

HASTY WORDS (IRE) BHB 104f **RR 104f** 5239[5]
4 b f Polish Patriot (USA) 7.8f **(70)** - Park Elect (Ahonoora) 8.1f **(73)**
Form - 1640485
Record 2000 - 1st:1 2nd:0 3rd:0 Ran:7
Pre2000 - 1st:1 2nd:1 3rd:2 Ran:8
Win Prizemoney £18,171 *Total Prizemoney* £33,151
Wins * **2000** Mar Doncas (G-F) L 8f 94+ <
* 1998 May Sandow (G-F) 5f 78+
2000 Turf 1-7: (8f 1-4, 9f 3) (g-s, gd 3, g-f 2, frm 1-1)
Scopey, very useful filly, effective 8 to 9f, best at 9f, acts on gd to g-f, best on g-f. Turf high 105 - 6th of 11 getting 3lb from Indian Lodge (19 Apr Newmarket 9f gd RF 0795). Consistent. Tough and consistent as a juvenile, she ran just twice at three. Presumably her trainer would not have held on to her if she did not retain some ability, and she proved him right by winning a Listed event at the Doncaster Lincoln meeting. Her best effort since was when fourth in the Sun Chariot after a break. Obviously goes well fresh.
**B W Hills [2-15] W J Gredley.*

HATA (IRE) RR 73tf 1332[4]
2 ch f Hamas (IRE) 8f **(72)** - Enaya (Caerleon (USA)) 8.6f **(71)**
Form - 4
Record 2000 - 1st:0 2nd:0 3rd:0 Ran:1
Win Prizemoney £0 *Total Prizemoney* £352
2000 Turf 0-1: (6f) (g-f)
Currently above-average filly. (1st run) - 4th of 13 getting 5lb from Patsy's Double (20 May Newbury 6f g-f RF 1332).
**R W Armstrong [0-1] Hamdan Al Maktoum.*

HATAAB (USA) BHB 112f **RR 115+f** 4731[4]
3 ch c Woodman (USA) 9.7f **(77)** - Miss Mistletoes (IRE) (The Minstrel (CAN)) 10f **(72)**
Form - 1274
Record 2000 - 1st:1 2nd:1 3rd:0 Ran:4
Pre2000 - 1st:2 2nd:1 3rd:0 Ran:3
Win Prizemoney £35,573 *Total Prizemoney* £43,144
Wins * **2000** May York (FRM) L 10.4f 115 <
* 1999 Oct Pontef (GD) L 8f 101
* 1999 Jly Ascot (G-F) 7f 73+
2000 Turf 1-4: (10f 1-2, 12f 2) (gd 1-2, g-f, frm)
Scopey, high-class colt, effective 10f, acts on gd to frm. Turf high 115 (1st run) - 1st of 6 giving 6lb to Sandmason (18 May York RF 1278). He looks flashy, but is a tough sort who stayed on well to beat Sandmason in York's Michael Seely Glasgow Stakes. Ran a game race at Kempton next time, but appeared not to stay a mile and a half on his final two runs.
**E A L Dunlop [3-7] Hamdan Al Maktoum.*

HATCHED BLADE (GER) RR 94f 1824a[5]
4 m
Form - 5
2000 Turf 0-1: (11f) (sft)
Currently useful. **W Hefter in GER [0-1].*

HATHA ANNA (IRE) BHB 105f **RR 110f** 2206[7]
3 b c Sadler's Wells (USA) 11.3f **(87)** - Moon Cactus (Kris) 9.5f **(73)**
Form - 567
Record 2000 - 1st:0 2nd:0 3rd:0 Ran:3
Win Prizemoney £0 *Total Prizemoney* £16,420
2000 Turf 0-3: (10f, 12f 2) (gd 3)
Well made, currently Group-class colt. Turf high 110. Won a trial in Dubai, and finished fifth to Hataab at York on his first run under Rules. Ran above himself when sixth in the Derby, but put in an inexplicably poor showing at Royal Ascot and was not seen again.
**S bin Suroor [0-3] Godolphin.*

HATHEETHAH (IRE) BHB 72f **RR 84f** 3564[4]
3 b br f Machiavellian (USA) 9.8f **(83)** - Ishtiyak **(72f)** (Green Desert (USA)) 8.6f **(78)**
Form - 0554
Record 2000 - 1st:0 2nd:0 3rd:0 Ran:4
Win Prizemoney £0 *Total Prizemoney* £280
2000 Turf 0-4: (7f, 8f 2, 10f) (g-f 2, frm 2)
Scopey, decent filly. Turf high 84 - 5th of 9 to Mynah (11 Jun Newmarket 10f frm RF 1885).
**L M Cumani [0-4] Sheikh Mohammed Obaid Al Maktoum.*

HATHNI KHOUND BHB 34f28a **RR 45df 28a** 4694[15]
4 b f Reprimand 8.2f **(63)** - Rattle Along (Tap On Wood) 10.3f **(65)**
Form - 067000
Record 2000 - 1st:0 2nd:0 3rd:0 Ran:5
Pre2000 - 1st:0 2nd:1 3rd:1 Ran:8
Win Prizemoney £0 *Total Prizemoney* £1,161
2000 Turf 0-4: (10f, 11f 3) (hvy, sft, gd, g-f) 2000 AW 0-1: (16f) (Fibr)
Unfurnished, moderate filly, effective 10 to 11f, acts on sft to gd, likes left handed tracks. Turf high 48. Becoming disappointing.
**D Marks [0-16] G J King.*

HATTAB (IRE) BHB 103f **RR 104f** 577a[7]
6 b h Marju (IRE) 9.2f **(76)** - Funun (USA) (Fappiano (USA)) 8.7f **(77)**
Form - 7
2000 AW 0-1: (6f) (Dirt)
Very useful horse. Consistent.
**K McLaughlin in USA [0-1] (from P T Walwyn [4-12] Spt 1997).*

HAULAGE MAN RR 57f 1141[6]
2 ch g Komaite (USA) 6.9f **(61)** - Texita (Young Generation) 7.7f **(63)**
Form - 66
Record 2000 - 1st:0 2nd:0 3rd:0 Ran:2
2000 Turf 0-2: (5f 2) (gd, frm)
Currently fair gelding. Turf high 57. **D Eddy [0-2] James Adams.*

HAUNT THE ZOO BHB 39f62a **RR 34f 62a** 5006[2]
5 b m Komaite (USA) 6.9f **(61)** - Merryhill Maid (IRE) (M Double M (USA)) 14.1f **(52)**
Form - 117377078103032
Record 2000 - 1st:1 2nd:1 3rd:3 Ran:12
Pre2000 - 1st:2 2nd:0 3rd:1 Ran:13
Win Prizemoney £6,943 *Total Prizemoney* £9,638
Wins * **2000** *May Southw (STD) H 7f 49 58+* <

* 1999 Dec Lingfi (STD) H 6f 47 54
* 1999 Nov Southw (STD) H 6f 40 45
2000 Turf 0-5: (5f, 6f 2, 7f 2) (gd 2, g-f, frm, hrd) 2000 AW 1-7: (6f 3, 7f 1-3, 8f) (Fibr 1-7)
Average filly, effective 6 to 8f, best at 7f, - acts on AW, best on Fibr, prefers left handed tracks, prefers tight tracks, excels at Southwell. Turf high 34. AW high 62 - 3rd of 15 to Moonlight Song (26 Spt Southwell 7f Fibr RF 4652) - also 1st of 12 giving 11lb to Oare Kite (26 May Southwell RF 1481). Inconsistent.
**J L Harris [3-25] R Atkinson.*

HAVANA (IRE) BHB 56f **RR 72f** 5063[4]

4 b f Dolphin Street (FR) - Royaltess (Royal And Regal (USA)) 9.5f **(60)**
Form - 4233074
Record 2000 - 1st:0 2nd:1 3rd:2 Ran:7
Pre2000 - 1st:0 2nd:0 3rd:2 Ran:2
Win Prizemoney £0 *Total Prizemoney* £3,815
2000 Turf 0-7: (10f 4, 12f 2, 13f) (sft, gd 3, frm 3)
Workmanlike, above-average filly, effective 10f, acts on gd, has worn blinkers. Turf high 72 (1st run) - 4th of 13 giving 14lb to Revival (18 May Salisbury 10f gd RF 1267).
**Mrs A J Perrett [0-7] Usk Valley Stud (from J E Banks [0-2] Jly 1999).*

HAVENT MADE IT YET BHB 28f **RR 40f** 2305[10]

3 ch f Be My Guest (USA) 10.2f **(66)** - Onika (Great Nephew) 9.9f **(64)**
Form - 000
Record 2000 - 1st:0 2nd:0 3rd:0 Ran:3
Pre2000 - 1st:0 2nd:0 3rd:0 Ran:3
2000 Turf 0-1: (8f) (gd) 2000 AW 0-2: (8f, 12f) (Equi, Fibr)
Neat, moderate filly, has worn blinkers. **J R Jenkins [0-6] T J Bird.*

HAWK BHB 85f **RR 76f** 3255[3]

2 b c A P Jet (USA) - Miss Enjoleur (USA) (L'Enjoleur (CAN)) 8f **(65)**
Form - 333
Record 2000 - 1st:0 2nd:0 3rd:3 Ran:3
Win Prizemoney £0 *Total Prizemoney* £2,058
2000 Turf 0-3: (5f 3) (g-s, gd, frm)
Currently above-average colt. Turf high 76.
**R Hannon [0-3] Highclere Thoroughbred Racing Ltd.*

HAWKES RUN BHB 73f75a **RR 84f 75a** 4784[2]

2 b g Hernando (FR) - Wise Speculation (USA) (Mr Prospector (USA)) 8.8f **(78)**
Form - 66452
Record 2000 - 1st:0 2nd:1 3rd:0 Ran:5
Win Prizemoney £0 *Total Prizemoney* £484
2000 Turf 0-4: (6f, 7f 2, 8f) (g-s, gd, g-f, frm) 2000 AW 0-1: (8f) (Fibr)
Decent gelding. Turf high 77 - 4th of 10 giving 3lb to Carnot (9 Aug Brighton 7f g-f RF 3481). (1st run) - 2nd of 9 giving 3lb to El Hamra (3 Oct Wolverhampton 8f Fibr RF 4784).
**B J Meehan [0-5] Family Amusements Ltd.*

HAWKSBILL HENRY (USA) BHB 37f58a **RR 48f 58a** 1880[22]

6 ch g Known Fact (USA) 8.3f **(72)** - Novel Approach (USA) (Codex (USA)) 8.6f **(73)**
Form - 7071317360
Record 2000 - 1st:2 2nd:0 3rd:2 Ran:8
Pre2000 - 1st:1 2nd:6 3rd:3 Ran:27
Win Prizemoney £9,085 *Total Prizemoney* £16,063
Wins * **2000** *Feb Lingfi (STD) H 12f 53 58* <
* **2000** *Jan Lingfi (STD) H 12f 49 56*
* 1998 *Jly Lingfi (STD) H 10f 48 54*
2000 Turf 0-2: (12f 2) (frm 2) 2000 AW 2-6: (12f 2-6) (Equi 2-6)
Fair gelding, effective 10 to 12f, best at 10f, - acts on Equi, has worn blinkers, favours left handed tracks, favours tight tracks, excels at Lingfield. Turf high 41. AW high 58 - 1st of 7 getting 27lb from Space Race (9 Feb Lingfield RF 0250) - also 1st of 11 getting 29lb from Fahs (15 Jan Lingfield RF 0093). A fair sort over ten furlongs on Equitrack and turf, but he does not appear to put it all in at the finish. **Mrs A J Perrett [3-35] Miss G Harwood.*

HAYAAIN BHB 62f **RR 74f** 1707[16]

7 b h Shirley Heights 12.1f **(76)** - Littlefield (Bay Express) 7.1f **(60)**
Form - 300
Record 2000 - 1st:0 2nd:0 3rd:1 Ran:3
Pre2000 - 1st:1 2nd:0 3rd:2 Ran:9
Win Prizemoney £3,780 *Total Prizemoney* £5,389
Wins 1996 Jun Bath (FRM) 11.7f 81 <
2000 Turf 0-3: (16f 2, 17f) (g-s 2, hrd)
Above-average horse, has broken blood-vessels. Turf high 74 (1st run) - 3rd of 15 giving 17lb to Charming Admiral (11 Apr Pontefract 17f g-s RF 0663). He still shows the odd piece of form in staying handicaps, but has been rather more successful over hurdles of late.
**K C Bailey [3-16] Quicksilver Racing Partnership (from Major W R Hern [1-7] Jly 1996).*

HAYA YA KEFAAH BHB 42f47a **RR 33f 47a** 3044[11]

8 b g Kefaah (USA) 11.2f **(64)** - Hayat (IRE) (Sadler's Wells (USA)) 10f **(76)**
Form - 8010000
Record 2000 - 1st:1 2nd:0 3rd:0 Ran:7
Pre2000 - 1st:3 2nd:2 3rd:0 Ran:16
Win Prizemoney £15,979 *Total Prizemoney* £18,462
Wins * **2000** Apr Ripon (SFT) SH 12.3f 47 53
* 1996 Spt Haydoc (GD) H 11.9f 63 66 <
* 1996 May Doncas (G-F) H 12f 55 60
* 1996 Mar Doncas (GD) H 12f 33 55+
2000 Turf 1-6: (11f, 12f 1-3, 13f, 14f) (gd 1-2, g-f 3, frm) 2000 AW 0-1: (12f) (Fibr)
Very moderate gelding, effective 12f, acts on gd, has worn blinkers. Turf high 53 - 1st of 18 giving 4lb to Skyers A Kite (5 Apr Ripon RF 0617). Inconsistent.
**N M Babbage [4-22] Alan Craddock (from Sir Mark Prescott [0-4] Feb 1995).*

HAYDN JAMES (USA) BHB 49f60a **RR 43f 60a** 3168[4]

6 ch g Danzig Connection (USA) 8.2f **(75)** - Royal Fi Fi (USA) (Conquistador Cielo (USA)) 8.8f **(69)**
Form - 64
Record 2000 - 1st:0 2nd:0 3rd:0 Ran:1
Pre2000 - 1st:3 2nd:7 3rd:4 Ran:35
Win Prizemoney £8,094 *Total Prizemoney* £14,712
Wins 1998 *Nov Wolver (STD) H 9.4f 57 58* <
1998 Aug Windso (G-F) H 10f 54 57
1998 May Nottin (FRM) H 10f 51 53
2000 Turf 0-1: (12f) (frm)
Average gelding, effective 12f, - acts on Equi, often wears blinkers (extremely effectively), prefers left handed tracks.
**P J Hobbs [2-6] Mrs Ann Painter (from P W Harris [3-35] Nov 1999).*

HAYLEY'S AFFAIR (IRE) **RR 69f** 4806[5]

2 b f Night Shift (USA) 8.1f **(73)** - Sea Mistress (Habitat) 9.4f **(70)**
Form - 5
Record 2000 - 1st:0 2nd:0 3rd:0 Ran:1
2000 Turf 0-1: (7f) (g-s)
Currently average filly.
**P W Harris [0-1] Graham & Lynn Knight.*

HAYSTACKS (IRE) BHB 51f **RR 54f** 3497[5]

4 b g Contract Law (USA) 8.9f **(54)** - Florissa (FR) (Persepolis (FR)) 6.4f **(67)**
Form - 0425
Record 2000 - 1st:0 2nd:1 3rd:0 Ran:4
Pre2000 - 1st:0 2nd:2 3rd:3 Ran:17
Win Prizemoney £0 *Total Prizemoney* £4,109
2000 Turf 0-4: (8f, 12f 2, 14f) (g-f 4)
Leggy, fair gelding, effective 11 to 12f, best at 11f, acts on g-s to g-f, often wears blinkers (very effectively), prefers left handed tracks. Turf high 54 - 2nd of 7 giving 13lb to Chaka Zulu (31 Jly Newcastle 12f g-f RF 3253). Consistent. He is a winner over hurdles, but seems to lack pace on the Flat and does not seem the heartiest of battlers either. **D Moffatt [2-30] & Mrs A G Milligan.*

HAZIRAAN (IRE) BHB 52f **RR 74f** 4474[7]

3 b c Primo Dominie 7.2f **(67)** - Hazaradjat (IRE) (Darshaan) 9.9f **(84)**
Form - 73707
Record 2000 - 1st:0 2nd:0 3rd:1 Ran:5
Win Prizemoney £0 *Total Prizemoney* £518
2000 Turf 0-4: (7f, 8f 3) (g-s 2, g-f 2) 2000 AW 0-1: (8f) (Fibr)
Scopey, above-average colt. Turf high 74.
**R A Fahey [0-3] D A Read (from Sir Michael Stoute [0-2] Jly 2000).*

HAZY HEIGHTS BHB 52f **RR 51f** 3898[1]
3 b f Shirley Heights 12.1f **(76)** - Dancing Spirit (IRE) (Ahonoora) 8.1f **(73)**
Form - 68088431
Record 2000 - 1st:1 2nd:0 3rd:1 Ran:8
Win Prizemoney £2,830 *Total Prizemoney* £3,183
Wins * **2000** Aug Bright (FRM) H 8f 45 51 <
2000 Turf 1-8: (7f 3, 8f 1-4, 10f) (g-s 2, g-f 4, frm, hrd 1-1)
Workmanlike, fair filly. Turf high 69. Consistent.
**B J Meehan [1-8] Wyck Hall Stud.*

HEAD IN THE CLOUDS (IRE) RR 87f 4599[3]
2 b f Rainbow Quest (USA) 11.2f **(81)** - Ballerina (IRE) **(77f)** (Dancing Brave (USA)) 8.4f **(76)**
Form - 53
Record 2000 - 1st:0 2nd:0 3rd:1 Ran:2
Win Prizemoney £0 *Total Prizemoney* £2,310
2000 Turf 0-2: (7f 2) (gd, frm)
Currently useful filly. Turf high 87 (began Aug) - 3rd of 11 to Small Change (23 Spt Ascot 7f gd RF 4599). **J L Dunlop [0-2] Neil Jones.*

HEADLAND (USA) RR 77f 5140[4]
2 b br c Distant View (USA) - Fijar Echo (USA) (In Fijar (USA)) 7.5f **(70)**
Form - 4
Record 2000 - 1st:0 2nd:0 3rd:0 Ran:1
Win Prizemoney £0 *Total Prizemoney* £325
2000 Turf 0-1: (6f) (g-s)
Currently above-average colt.
**J M P Eustace [0-1] The MacDougall Partnership.*

HEAD SCRATCHER BHB 56f **RR 63f** 4382[10]
2 ch g Alhijaz 7.7f **(57)** - Sabrata (IRE) (Zino) 12.9f **(54)**
Form - 30
Record 2000 - 1st:0 2nd:0 3rd:1 Ran:2
Win Prizemoney £0 *Total Prizemoney* £388
2000 Turf 0-2: (5f, 6f) (gd, g-f)
Currently average gelding. Turf high 63 (1st run) (began Aug) - 3rd of 10 giving 5lb to White Star Lady (24 Aug Musselburgh 5f g-f RF 3926).
**A Bailey [0-1] Sandybrow Stables Ltd (from W W Haigh [0-1] Aug 2000).*

HEALEY (IRE) BHB 92f **RR 96+f** 4862[3]
2 ch c Dr Devious (IRE) 9.9f **(74)** - Bean Siamsa (Solinus) 9f **(71)**
Form - 1143
Record 2000 - 1st:2 2nd:0 3rd:1 Ran:4
Win Prizemoney £9,267 *Total Prizemoney* £12,353
Wins * **2000** Aug Ripon (G-F) 6f 96+ <
* **2000** Aug Ripon (GD) 6f 69+
2000 Turf 2-4: (6f 2-3, 7f) (sft, gd, g-f 1-1, frm 1-1)
Very useful colt. Turf high 96 (began Aug) - 1st of 5 giving 5lb to Petongski (19 Aug Ripon RF 3795). Won his first two starts at Ripon, but was very disappointing when stepped up to seven furlongs at Doncaster, and found the ground against him in listed company next time. Will not be easy to place next season.
**J D Bethell [2-4] WWW Clarendon Racing Com.*

HEATHERHILL LASS (IRE) RR 4893[4]
5 b m Tout Ensemble - Ballydiddle (Abednego)
Form - 4
Record 2000 - 1st:0 2nd:0 3rd:0 Ran:1
Win Prizemoney £0 *Total Prizemoney* £307
2000 Turf 0-1: (10f) (hvy)
Currently very poor filly. **Miss L A Perratt [0-1] R D Lennox.*

HEATHER VALLEY BHB 40f37a **RR 40f 37a** 3834[14]
4 ch f Clantime 6.6f **(57)** - Sannavally (Sagaro) 9.7f **(55)**
Form - 05540
Record 2000 - 1st:0 2nd:0 3rd:0 Ran:5
Pre2000 - 1st:0 2nd:0 3rd:0 Ran:3
Win Prizemoney £0 *Total Prizemoney* £216
2000 Turf 0-3: (7f 2, 8f) (g-f 2, frm) 2000 AW 0-2: (6f, 8f) (Fibr 2)
Workmanlike, moderate filly, effective 7f, acts on g-f. Turf high 40 (1st run) (began Jly) - 5th of 16 getting 20lb from Peter's Imp (22 Jly Warwick 7f g-f RF 3041). AW high 30 (began Jun).
**W J Haggas [0-5] Miss Vivian Pratt (from C F Wall [0-3] Oct 1999).*

HEATHYARDSBLESSING (IRE) BHB 101f **RR 103f** 2597[8]
3 b c Unblest - Noble Nadia (Thatching) 8f **(66)**
Form - 8
Record 2000 - 1st:0 2nd:0 3rd:0 Ran:1
Pre2000 - 1st:3 2nd:2 3rd:1 Ran:10
Win Prizemoney £8,946 *Total Prizemoney* £50,352
Wins * 1999 Oct Nottin (FRM) 6.1f 103 <
* 1999 Jly Cheste (G-F) H 5.1f 83+
* 1999 May Haydoc (GD) 5f 75
2000 Turf 0-1: (6f) (g-f)
Light-framed, very useful colt, effective 5 to 6f, best at 6f, acts on g-f to frm, best on g-f. **R Hollinshead [3-11] L A Morgan.*

HEATHYARDS GUEST (IRE) BHB 72f67a **RR 70f 67a** 5167[6]
2 ch c Be My Guest (USA) 10.2f **(66)** - Noble Nadia (Thatching) 8f **(66)**
Form - 7246
Record 2000 - 1st:0 2nd:1 3rd:0 Ran:4
Win Prizemoney £0 *Total Prizemoney* £1,233
2000 Turf 0-4: (7f 3, 10f) (g-s, gd, g-f, frm)
Above-average colt. Turf high 70 (began Jly) - 2nd of 9 giving 9lb to Wondergreen (13 Spt Beverley 7f g-f RF 4359).
**R Hollinshead [0-4] L A Morgan.*

HEATHYARDS JAKE BHB 45f43a **RR 45f 43a** 5113[5]
4 b c Nomination 7.3f **(57)** - Safe Bid (Sure Blade (USA)) 11.3f **(67)**
Form - ?62214547866570540477I5
Record 2000 - 1st:1 2nd:0 3rd:0 Ran:18
Pre2000 - 1st:1 2nd:10 3rd:7 Ran:36
Win Prizemoney £4,878 *Total Prizemoney* £15,904
Wins * **2000** Spt Bright (SFT) S 8f 45
* 1999 *Dec Wolver (STD) 8.5f 49* <
2000 Turf 1-6: (8f 1-5, 11f) (gd 1-4, g-f, frm) 2000 AW 0-12: (8f 6, 9f 6) (Fibr 12)
Unfurnished, fair colt, effective 7 to 9f, - acts on Fibr, likes left handed tracks, likes tight tracks, and does well at Wolverhampton. Turf high 45 (began Jly). AW high 60 (1st run) - 4th of 9 giving 4lb to Al Mabrook (6 Jan Wolverhampton 9f Fibr RF 0031). Acts on Fibresand, but must have now found every conceivable method of getting himself beaten. **R Hollinshead [2-54] L A Morgan.*

HEATHYARDS LAD (IRE) BHB 51f60a **RR 55f 60a** 5063[10]
3 b c Petardia 8.2f **(58)** - Maiden's Dance (Hotfoot) 10.5f **(59)**
Form - 547632565500345040
Record 2000 - 1st:0 2nd:1 3rd:2 Ran:18
Pre2000 1st:1 2nd:0 3rd:2 Ran:15
Win Prizemoney £2,199 *Total Prizemoney* £6,812
Wins * 1999 *Spt Wolver (STD) 8.5f* 62 <
2000 Turf 0-14: (7f 5, 8f 8, 10f) (sft, g-s 3, gd 4, g-f 3, frm 3) 2000 AW 0-4: (7f, 8f, 9f 2) (Fibr 4)
Light-framed, fair colt, effective 5 to 8f, acts on g-s to gd - acts on Fibr. Turf high 62 - 2nd of 16 giving 3lb to Nod's Nephew (19 Apr Beverley 7f g-s RF 0791). AW high 59.
**R Hollinshead [1-33] L A Morgan.*

HEATHYARDS MATE BHB 50f67a **RR 46f 67a** 3330[3]
3 b g Timeless Times (USA) 6.1f **(56)** - Quenlyn (Welsh Pageant) 10f **(65)**
Form - 21143842100663
Record 2000 - 1st:1 2nd:1 3rd:1 Ran:9
Pre2000 - 1st:2 2nd:2 3rd:2 Ran:15
Win Prizemoney £6,629 *Total Prizemoney* £10,061
Wins * **2000** *Mar Southw (STD)* S *7f* 64
* 1999 *Nov Southw (STD)* H *8f* 65 71 <
* 1999 *Nov Southw (STD) 8f* 61
2000 Turf 0-4: (8f 3, 10f) (gd, g-f 2, frm) 2000 AW 1-5: (7f 1-2, 8f, 9f, 11f) (Fibr 1-5)
Unfurnished, average gelding, effective 8f, - acts on Fibr, likes left handed tracks, likes tight tracks. Turf high 46. AW high 64.
**R Hollinshead [3-24] L A Morgan.*

HEATHYARDS SIGNET RR 32f 3627[13]
2 b g King's Signet (USA) 7f **(51)** - Heathyards Gem **(43f 45a)** (Governor General)
Form - 560
Record 2000 - 1st:0 2nd:0 3rd:0 Ran:3
2000 Turf 0-3: (5f 3) (g-f 2, frm)

Currently very moderate gelding. Turf high 32 (began Jly).
**D McCain [0-3] L A Morgan.*

HEAVENLY MISS (IRE) BHB 49f43a **RR 53f 43a** 4487[12]

6 b m Anita's Prince 6f **(62)** - Heavenly Blessed (Monseigneur (USA)) 7.7f **(63)**
Form - 5450414000080
Record 2000 - 1st:1 2nd:0 3rd:0 Ran:9
Pre2000 - 1st:6 2nd:8 3rd:6 Ran:67
Win Prizemoney £20,052 *Total Prizemoney* £30,921
Wins * 2000 May Hamilt (FRM) H 5f 49 53
1999 Oct Bath (SFT) H 5.1f 45 49
1999 Apr Wolver (STD) H 5f 42 52
1999 Apr Thirsk (GD) H 6f 45 49
1996 Dec Lingfi (STD) C 5f 71
1996 Spt Nottin (FRM) H 6.1f 64 77 <
1996 Aug Leices (G-F) S 6f 63+
2000 Turf 1-7: (5f 1-2, 6f 5) (gd 2, g-f, frm 1-4) 2000 AW 0-2: (5f, 6f) (Fibr 2)
Fair mare, effective 5 to 6f, best at 5f, acts on gd to frm - acts on Fibr, has worn blinkers (very effectively), does well at Wolverhampton. Turf high 53 - 1st of 18 giving 10lb to Sunset Harbour (11 May Hamilton RF 1145). AW high 44 (1st run) - 4th of 13 giving 8lb to Whizz Kid (20 May Wolverhampton 6f Fibr RF 1354). **D Carroll [1-9] E Gray (from D Shaw [3-16] Dec 1999).*

HEAVENLY WHISPER (IRE) RR 84+f 5136[1]

2 b f Halling (USA) - Rock the Boat (Slip Anchor) 9.8f **(73)**
Form - 01
Record 2000 - 1st:1 2nd:0 3rd:0 Ran:2
Win Prizemoney £3,233 *Total Prizemoney* £3,233
Wins * 2000 Oct Yarmou (HVY) 8f 84+ <
2000 Turf 1-2: (7f, 8f 1-1) (g-s 1-1, g-f)
Currently decent filly. Turf high 84 (began Spt) - 1st of 11 from Ranin (22 Oct Yarmouth RF 5136).
**M L W Bell [1-2] DGH Partnership.*

HEFIN BHB 50f **RR 49f** 3922[4]

3 ch c Red Rainbow - Summer Impressions (USA) (Lyphard (USA)) 9.9f **(72)**
Form - 0074
Record 2000 - 1st:0 2nd:0 3rd:0 Ran:4
Win Prizemoney £0 *Total Prizemoney* £310
2000 Turf 0-4: (8f 2, 9f, 10f) (g-s, gd, g-f, frm)
Scopey, moderate colt. Turf high 49. **S C Williams [0-4] Tyrnest Ltd.*

HEIRESS OF MEATH (IRE) BHB 27f25a **RR 31f 25a** 3938a[2]

5 ch m Imperial Frontier (USA) 7f **(65)** - Rich Heiress (IRE) (Last Tycoon) 8.5f **(62)**
Form - 3004072
Record 2000 - 1st:0 2nd:1 3rd:1 Ran:7
Pre2000 - 1st:0 2nd:0 3rd:0 Ran:11
Win Prizemoney £0 *Total Prizemoney* £829
2000 Turf 0-5: (8f 2, 10f 2, 12f) (gd 2, g-f, frm, hrd) 2000 AW 0-2: (7f, 10f) (Equi 2)
Very moderate filly, effective 8 to 12f, acts on gd to frm, prefers left handed tracks. Turf high 31 - 4th of 7 getting 28lb from Twenty First (19 Jun Brighton 8f frm RF 2089). AW high 32. Inconsistent.
**M J Weeden [0-7] (from E J Creighton in IRE [0-2] Nov 1998).*

HEJAZIAH (USA) BHB 99f **RR 82f** 2786a[1]

2 b f Gone West (USA) 7.8f **(82)** - Top Trestle (USA) (Nijinsky (CAN)) 10.3f **(77)**
Form - 2311
Record 2000 - 1st:2 2nd:1 3rd:1 Ran:4
Win Prizemoney £29,613 *Total Prizemoney* £32,628
Wins * 2000 Jly San Si (G-F) L 7.5f 82+ <
*** 2000** Jun Ascot (G-F) 6f 82
2000 Turf 2-4: (5f, 6f 1-2, 8f 1-1) (g-s, gd 1-2, g-f 1-1)
Decent filly. Turf high 82 - 1st of 7 from Secret Valley (6 Jly San Siro RF 2786a) - also 1st of 6 getting 7lb from Millenium Princess (24 Jun Ascot RF 2241). **P F I Cole [2-4] H R H Prince Fahd Salman.*

HELALI MANOR BHB 35f **RR 22f** 4771[11]

2 b f Muhtarram (USA) - Royal Mazi **(25f)** (Kings Lake (USA)) 10.8f **(67)**
Form - 060
Record 2000 - 1st:0 2nd:0 3rd:0 Ran:3
2000 Turf 0-3: (5f 2, 7f) (gd 2, frm)
Currently little account filly. Turf high 22 (began Aug).
**G P Kelly [0-3] A M McArdle.*

HELEN ALBADOU (USA) BHB 73f **RR 70f** 1909[8]

3 b f Sheikh Albadou 9.2f **(75)** - Sister Troy (USA) (Far North (CAN)) 9.7f **(75)**
Form - 18
Record 2000 - 1st:1 2nd:0 3rd:0 Ran:2
Pre2000 - 1st:0 2nd:0 3rd:1 Ran:1
Win Prizemoney £2,352 *Total Prizemoney* £2,784
Wins * 2000 Apr Nottin (HVY) 5.1f 67 <
2000 Turf 1-2: (5f 1-2) (sft 1-1, frm)
Leggy, currently above-average filly. Turf high 67 (1st run) - 1st of 11 getting 5lb from Budelli (24 Apr Nottingham RF 0849).
**J M P Eustace [1-3] J C Smith.*

HELEN'S DAY BHB 85f **RR 87f** 5226[P]

4 ch f Grand Lodge (USA) - Swordlestown Miss (USA) (Apalachee (USA)) 9.4f **(71)**
Form - 221014P
Record 2000 - 1st:2 2nd:2 3rd:0 Ran:7
Win Prizemoney £10,037 *Total Prizemoney* £13,808
Wins * 2000 Spt Ayr (SFT) H 13.1f 78 86 <
*** 2000** Jly Newcas (GD) 12.4f 51++
2000 Turf 2-7: (10f, 11f, 12f 1-3, 13f 1-1, 16f) (gd 1-3, g-f 1-3, frm)
Well made, useful filly, effective 10 to 13f, acted on gd to g-f, best on gd. Turf high 87 (1st run) - 2nd of 6 giving 12lb to Bella Lambada (16 Jun York 10f g-f RF 2037) - also 1st of 9 getting 9lb from Raise A Prince (16 Spt Ayr RF 4453). (DEAD)
**W Jarvis [2-7] Mrs M Dearman.*

HELLOFABUNDLE BHB 53f **RR 32f** 3720[9]

2 b g Phountzi (USA) 9.6f **(60)** - Helleborus (King of Spain) 7.8f **(52)**
Form - 030
Record 2000 - 1st:0 2nd:0 3rd:1 Ran:3
Win Prizemoney £0 *Total Prizemoney* £596
2000 Turf 0-3: (6f, 7f 2) (g-f, frm 2)
Currently very moderate gelding. Turf high 32 (began Jly).
**S Dow [0-3] Ken Butler.*

HELLO HOLLY BHB 44f **RR 48f** 4275[14]

3 b f Lake Coniston (IRE) - Amandine (IRE) (Darshaan) 9.9f **(84)**
Form - 60300
Record 2000 - 1st:0 2nd:0 3rd:1 Ran:5
Pre2000 - 1st:0 2nd:0 3rd:0 Ran:3
Win Prizemoney £0 *Total Prizemoney* £351
2000 Turf 0-5: (7f 2, 8f 3) (g-f, frm 4)
Workmanlike, moderate filly. Turf high 48.
**Mrs A L M King [0-8] Mrs Bettina Melliger.*

HELLO SAILOR BHB 20f **RR** 2407[5]

3 ch f Handsome Sailor 6.6f **(53)** - Miss Marjorie (Swing Easy (USA)) 6.5f **(55)**
Form - 85
Record 2000 - 1st:0 2nd:0 3rd:0 Ran:2
Pre2000 - 1st:0 2nd:0 3rd:0 Ran:2
2000 Turf 0-2: (6f, 7f) (g-f, frm)
Workmanlike, formerly very poor filly.
**Mrs D Thomson [0-4] Mrs Dorothy Thomson.*

HELLO VEGAS BHB 69f **RR 66f** 2190[P]

3 b c First Trump - Meet Again (Lomond (USA)) 8.8f **(65)**
Form - 04P
Record 2000 - 1st:0 2nd:0 3rd:0 Ran:3
Pre2000 - 1st:0 2nd:0 3rd:0 Ran:1
Win Prizemoney £0 *Total Prizemoney* £306
2000 Turf 0-3: (8f 2, 10f) (g-s, gd, frm)
Lengthy, average colt. Turf high 66.
**J H M Gosden [0-4] D H Armitage.*

HELVETIUS BHB 80f **RR 91df** 3510[6]

4 b g In The Wings 11.2f **(77)** - Hejraan (USA) (Alydar (USA)) 9.1f **(76)**
Form - 546
Record 2000 - 1st:0 2nd:0 3rd:0 Ran:3
Pre2000 - 1st:1 2nd:1 3rd:3 Ran:10
Win Prizemoney £4,380 *Total Prizemoney* £13,702

Wins 1999 May Bright (FRM) 11.9f 55+ <
2000 Turf 0-3: (10f, 12f, 14f) (gd, g-f, hrd)
Workmanlike, useful gelding, effective 12f, acts on gd to g-f, has worn blinkers, likes tight tracks. Turf high 83.
**P C Ritchens [0-3] John Pearl (from C E Brittain [1-10] Oct 1999).*

HEMINGWAY (IRE) RR 110+f 3850[1]
2 b c Spectrum (IRE) - Welsh Love (Ela-Mana-Mou) 10.1f **(70)**
Form - 11
2000 Turf 2-2: (7f 2-2) (gd 2-2)
Currently Group-class colt. Turf high 110 (began Jly) - 1st of 5 giving 5lb to Eminence (22 Aug York RF 3850). Gained an easy win on his Galway debut and was impressive when following up in the Acomb at York. He should stay further and is another intriguing prospect from his yard.
**A P O'Brien in IRE [2-2] M Tabor & Mrs John Magnier.*

Hemingway won both his starts as a two-year-old

HENRIETTA HOLMES (IRE) BHB 53f50a RR 56+f 50a 2378[9]
4 gr f Persian Bold 10f **(69)** - Faakirah (Dragonara Palace (USA)) 6.1f **(55)**
Form - 4650

Record	**2000** -	1st:0	2nd:0	3rd:0	Ran:1
	Pre2000 -	1st:1	2nd:2	3rd:1	Ran:13

Win Prizemoney £2,469 *Total Prizemoney* £4,080
Wins 1999 Spt Yarmou (G-F) C 11.5f 56 <
2000 Turf 0-1: (14f) (frm)
Scopey, fair filly, effective 10 to 11f, best at 11f, acts on gd to g-f - acts on Equi, has worn blinkers, prefers left handed tracks, prefers tight tracks.
**Mrs L Richards [0-8] The Henrietta Partnership (from J R Fanshawe [1-10] Spt 1999).*

HENRY HALL (IRE) BHB 91f RR 98f 4258[22]
4 b c Common Grounds 8.1f **(66)** - Sovereign Grace (IRE) (Standaan (FR)) 7f **(55)**
Form - 606003110000

Record	**2000** -	1st:2	2nd:0	3rd:1	Ran:12
	Pre2000 -	1st:3	2nd:5	3rd:1	Ran:21

Win Prizemoney £34,807 *Total Prizemoney* £51,580

Wins	* **2000**	Jun	Newcas (FRM)	H	5f	90	98	<
	* **2000**	Jun	York (GD)	H	5f	85	93	
	* 1998	Jly	Doncas (G-F)		5f		90	
	* 1998	Jly	Beverl (GD)		5f		90	
	* 1998	May	Thirsk (G-F)	C	5f		79	

2000 Turf 2-12: (5f 2-11, 6f) (g-s, gd 3, g-f 2-6, frm 2)
Very useful colt, effective 5f, acts on gd to frm, best on g-f, has worn blinkers. Turf high 98 - 1st of 18 getting 10lb from Indian Spark (30 Jun Newcastle RF 2404) - also 1st of 22 giving 18lb to Double Oscar (16 Jun York RF 2032). Effective when held up or ridden positively, he ended a long losing run at York in June and followed up in the Gosforth Park Cup at Newcastle. Held off higher marks afterwards. **N Tinkler [5-33] Mike Gosse.*

HENRY HEALD BHB 35f RR 19f 4033[15]
5 b br g Anshan 8.2f **(63)** - Zalfa (Luthior) 9.8f **(71)**
Form - 0000

Record	**2000** -	1st:0	2nd:0	3rd:0	Ran:4
	Pre2000 -	1st:1	2nd:2	3rd:1	Ran:4

Win Prizemoney £2,211 *Total Prizemoney* £4,963
Wins 1998 Aug Bright (G-F) 7f 67 <
2000 Turf 0-3: (8f, 9f, 10f) (gd, g-f, frm) 2000 AW 0-1: (7f) (Equi)
Poor gelding, has worn blinkers. Turf high 19 (began Jly). Becoming disappointing.
**J A B Old [0-9] W E Sturt (from P J Makin [1-4] Aug 1998).*

HENRY ISLAND (IRE) BHB 75f RR 70f 5111[10]
7 ch g Sharp Victor (USA) 10f **(56)** - Monterana (Sallust) 8.4f **(63)**
Form - 00

Record	**2000** -	1st:0	2nd:0	3rd:0	Ran:1
	Pre2000 -	1st:3	2nd:2	3rd:2	Ran:19

Win Prizemoney £24,464 *Total Prizemoney* £31,632

Wins	1998	May	Goodwo (G-F)	H	14f	90	93	<
	1996	Oct	Doncas (GD)	H	12f	88	93	<
	1996	May	Leices (G-S)		8f		73++	

2000 Turf 0-1: (16f) (gd)
Above-average gelding.
**Mrs A J Bowlby [2-7] J G Hickford (from M Pitman [0-7] Nov 1999).*

HENRY PEARSON (USA) BHB 69f RR 66f 4554[10]
2 ch c Distant View (USA) - Lady Ellen (USA) (Explosive Bid (USA))
Form - 850

Record	**2000** -	1st:0	2nd:0	3rd:0	Ran:3

2000 Turf 0-3: (6f 3) (gd 3)
Currently average colt. Turf high 66 (began Aug).
**T H Caldwell [0-3] Hogarth Racing.*

HENRY THE HAWK BHB 45f39a RR 43f 39a 3406[11]
9 b g Doulab (USA) 7.4f **(61)** - Plum Blossom (USA) (Gallant Romeo (USA)) 8.4f **(64)**
Form - 4005020

Record	**2000** -	1st:0	2nd:1	3rd:0	Ran:7
	Pre2000 -	1st:5	2nd:7	3rd:9	Ran:76

Win Prizemoney £13,040 *Total Prizemoney* £23,645

Wins	* 1998	May	Hamilt (SFT)	H	5f	40	47	
	* 1997	Jun	Hamilt (G-F)	H	6f	42	46	
	* 1996	May	Hamilt (SFT)	H	5f	47	51	<
	* 1996	Apr	Carlis (G-S)	H	5.9f	43	47	

2000 Turf 0-7: (5f 3, 6f 4) (sft, gd, g-f 2, frm, hrd 2)
Moderate gelding, effective 5 to 6f, best at 6f, acts on g-f to frm, best on g-f, often wears blinkers (effectively). Turf high 43 - 2nd of 12 giving 5lb to Theo's Lad (21 Jly Hamilton 6f g-f RF 2992).
**M Dods [5-83] S Barras.*

HENRY TUN BHB 51f RR 61f 1873[8]
2 b g Chaddleworth (IRE) - B Grade (Lucky Wednesday) 8f **(50)**
Form - 68

Record	**2000** -	1st:0	2nd:0	3rd:0	Ran:2

2000 Turf 0-2: (5f, 6f) (frm 2)
Currently average gelding. Turf high 61.
**Miss J F Craze [0-2] Mrs O Tunstall.*

HERACLES BHB 70f RR 72f 4892[4]
4 b g Unfuwain (USA) 11.4f **(74)** - La Masse (High Top) 10.2f **(67)**
Form - 634100624

Record	**2000** -	1st:1	2nd:1	3rd:1	Ran:9

Win Prizemoney £2,769 *Total Prizemoney* £6,808

Wins * **2000** Jly Catter (G-F) 13.8f 72 <
2000 Turf 1-9: (11f 3, 12f 2, 13f, 14f 1-2, 16f) (hvy, sft, gd 2, g-f 2, frm 1-3)
Workmanlike, above-average gelding, effective 11 to 16f, acts on gd to frm, best on frm. Turf high 79 - 4th of 9 giving 11lb to Stage Direction (16 Jly Haydock 11f frm RF 2861) - also 1st of 5 giving 19lb to Bayswater (26 Jly Catterick RF 3130). Inconsistent.
**A Berry [1-12] Exors of the late Lord Mostyn.*

HERBSHAN DANCER BHB 44f48a RR 47f 48a 3577[P]

6 b g Warrshan (USA) 9.7f **(59)** - Herbary (USA) (Herbager) 13f **(65)**
Form - 56025P
Record 2000 - 1st:0 2nd:1 3rd:0 Ran:6
Pre2000 - 1st:0 2nd:2 3rd:5 Ran:24
Win Prizemoney £0 *Total Prizemoney* £5,355
2000 Turf 0-6: (10f 2, 12f, 14f 2, 16f) (sft, g-s, gd, frm 3)
Moderate gelding, effective 14f, acts on frm, has worn blinkers. Turf high 48 - 2nd of 9 getting 12lb from Alnajashee (29 Jun Salisbury 14f frm RF 2378). Inconsistent.
**V Soane [0-6] The Kingtroll Racing Partnership (from S Earle [0-9] Oct 1998).*

HERCULANO (FR) RR 106f 2982a[2]

3 b c Subotica (FR) - Hokey Pokey (FR) (Lead on Time (USA)) 8f **(65)**
Form - 32
2000 Turf 0-2: (12f, 13f) (sft, g-s)
Currently Pattern-class colt. Turf high 106 - 2nd of 5 getting 10lb from War Game (16 Jly Maisons-laffitte 13f sft RF 2982a).
**Mme M Bollack-Badel in FR [0-2] C Motschmann.*

HERETIC RR 89f 5223[1]

2 b c Bishop of Cashel - Barford Lady (Stanford) 7.9f **(56)**
Form - 61
Record 2000 - 1st:1 2nd:0 3rd:0 Ran:2
Win Prizemoney £4,589 *Total Prizemoney* £4,589
Wins * **2000** Oct Newmar (SFT) 6f 89 <
2000 Turf 1-2: (6f 1-1, 7f) (g-s, gd 1-1)
Currently useful colt. Turf high 89 (began Oct) - 1st of 21 giving 5lb to Future Flight (27 Oct Newmarket RF 5223).
**J R Fanshawe [1-2] Barford Bloodstock.*

HERITAGE BHB 68f RR 73f 3669a[8]

6 b g Danehill (USA) 9.1f **(79)** - Misty Halo (High Top) 10.2f **(67)**
Form - 60628
Record 2000 - 1st:0 2nd:1 3rd:0 Ran:5
Pre2000 - 1st:2 2nd:0 3rd:1 Ran:11
Win Prizemoney £32,795 *Total Prizemoney* £35,318
Wins 1997 Jun Ascot (GD) H 12f 82 90 <
1997 May Haydoc (G-S) 10.5f 71++
2000 Turf 0-5: (10f, 12f, 13f 2, 14f) (g-s, gd, g-f, frm 2)
Above-average gelding, has worn blinkers. Turf high 73. Consistent.
**Mrs S A Bramall in IRE [2-22] Mrs S A Bramall (from D Nicholls [0-4] Jly 2000).*

HERITAGE OF GOLD (USA) RR 5325a[3]

5 m Gold Legend (USA) 8f **(76)** - Lyphard Gal (USA) (Lyphard (USA)) 9.9f **(72)**
Form - 3
2000 AW 0-1: (9f) (Dirt)
Currently Group-class. (1st run) - 3rd of 9 giving 3lb to Spain (4 Nov Churchill Downs 9f Dirt RF 5325a).
**T Amoss in USA [0-2] J Garey.*

HERITAGE PARK (IRE) BHB 76f RR 78f 1962[9]

3 gr g Paris House 5.9f **(64)** - Caradene (IRE) (Ballad Rock) 7.8f **(63)**
Form - 50
Record 2000 - 1st:0 2nd:0 3rd:0 Ran:2
Pre2000 - 1st:1 2nd:1 3rd:2 Ran:6
Win Prizemoney £3,615 *Total Prizemoney* £5,755
Wins * 1999 Jly Sandow (G-F) 5f 80 <
2000 Turf 0-2: (6f 2) (g-f 2)
Workmanlike, above-average gelding, effective 5 to 6f, acted on frm. Turf high 72. (DEAD) **R Hannon [1-8] R V Lewis.*

HERMIT'S HIDEAWAY BHB 51f RR 51f 3194[3]

3 b g Rock City 8.8f **(62)** - Adriya (Vayrann) 9.7f **(74)**
Form - 533
Record 2000 - 1st:0 2nd:0 3rd:2 Ran:3
Win Prizemoney £0 *Total Prizemoney* £1,129
2000 Turf 0-3: (6f 2, 7f) (g-f, frm, hrd)
Lengthy, currently fair gelding. Turf high 51 (began Jly).
**T D Barron [0-3] Harrowgate Bloodstock Ltd.*

HERNANDITA RR 75f 4873[2]

2 b f Hernando (FR) - Dara Dee (Dara Monarch) 8.8f **(59)**
Form - 82
Record 2000 - 1st:0 2nd:1 3rd:0 Ran:2
Win Prizemoney £0 *Total Prizemoney* £992
2000 Turf 0-2: (7f 2) (g-s, g-f)
Currently above-average filly. Turf high 75 (began Spt) - 2nd of 11 to Goncharova (9 Oct Leicester 7f g-s RF 4873).
**J L Dunlop [0-2] R N Khan.*

HEROS FATAL (FR) BHB 93f RR 91f 4987[1]

6 ch g Hero's Honor (USA) 9.2f **(76)** - Femme Fatale (FR) (Garde Royale)
Form - 301
Record 2000 - 1st:1 2nd:0 3rd:1 Ran:3
Pre2000 - 1st:1 2nd:1 3rd:1 Ran:6
Win Prizemoney £98,202 *Total Prizemoney* £113,714
Wins * **2000** Oct Newmar (G-S) H 18f 83 91 <
1998 Spt Toulou () L 8f
2000 Turf 1-3: (16f, 18f 1-1, 20f) (gd 1-2, frm)
Useful gelding, effective 17 to 20f, acts on gd. Turf high 91 - 1st of 33 giving 1lb to Wave of Optimism (14 Oct Newmarket RF 4987). Inconsistent. He was a big gamble for the Ascot Stakes on his return to the Flat, but in the event could only manage third. Never a factor in the Northumberland Plate, he ended the season with victory in the Cesarewitch.
**M C Pipe [5-18] Frank Farrant (from H-A Pantall in FR [1-2] Spt 1998).*

HER OWN WAY (USA) RR 87f 1083[3]

3 b f Danzig (USA) 8.1f **(88)** - Formidable Lady (USA) (Silver Hawk (USA)) 8.6f **(70)**
Form - 3
Record 2000 - 1st:0 2nd:0 3rd:1 Ran:1
Pre2000 - 1st:0 2nd:0 3rd:0 Ran:1
Win Prizemoney £0 *Total Prizemoney* £1,337
2000 Turf 0-1: (8f) (frm)
Strong, currently useful filly. (1st run) - 3rd of 19 getting 5lb from Champion Lodge (7 May Newmarket 8f frm RF 1083).
**J H M Gosden [0-2] George Strawbridge.*

HERRING GREEN BHB 40f RR 19f 5198[9]

3 b g Greensmith - Jane Herring (Nishapour (FR)) 9.1f **(61)**
Form - 00700
Record 2000 - 1st:0 2nd:0 3rd:0 Ran:5
2000 Turf 0-5: (6f, 7f, 8f, 10f 2) (gd, g-f 2, frm 2)
Workmanlike, poor gelding. Turf high 19.
**E A Wheeler [0-5] Four Of A Kind Racing.*

HERR TRIGGER BHB 45f60a RR 53f 60a 2738[9]

9 gr g Sharrood (USA) 11.1f **(67)** - Four-Legged Friend (Aragon) 8.1f **(60)**
Form - 5870
Record 2000 - 1st:0 2nd:0 3rd:0 Ran:3
Pre2000 - 1st:8 2nd:4 3rd:6 Ran:41
Win Prizemoney £30,736 *Total Prizemoney* £43,885
Wins * 1999 *May Lingfi (STD) 10f 68*
* 1998 *Mar Lingfi (SLW) H 10f 75 81* <
2000 Turf 0-2: (10f 2) (g-f 2) 2000 AW 0-1: (10f) (Equi)
Average gelding, effective 10f, - acts on Equi, mostly wears blinkers, likes left handed tracks, likes tight tracks. Turf high 44. Becoming disappointing. **Dr J D Scargill [8-44] The Inn Crowd.*

HERSELF BHB 43f RR 50f 4766[11]

3 b f Hernando (FR) - Kirsten (Kris) 9.5f **(73)**
Form - 87683560
Record 2000 - 1st:0 2nd:0 3rd:1 Ran:8
Win Prizemoney £0 *Total Prizemoney* £331
2000 Turf 0-8: (10f 2, 12f, 14f, 16f, 17f 2, 18f) (sft 2, g-s, g-f 2, frm 3)
Scopey, fair filly, effective 17f, acts on frm. Turf high 50.
**J Mackie [0-2] Ms Caroline Breay (from R Guest [0-6] Jly 2000).*

HESIODE (FR) RR 112f 4846a[9]
3 gr c Highest Honor (FR) 10.9f **(72)** - Elite Guest (IRE) (Be My Guest (USA)) 9.3f **(67)**
Form - 30330
2000 Turf 0-5: (10f 2, 11f, 12f 2) (hvy 2, gd 2, g-f)
Group-class colt, has worn blinkers. Turf high 112. In the frame in Group Two company in France, but was beaten out of sight in the French Derby and when partnered by Frankie Dettori in the Arc. **J-C Rouget in FR [0-5].*

HETRA HAWK BHB 36f **RR 47f** 262[9]
4 ch g Be My Guest (USA) 10.2f **(66)** - Silver Ore (FR) (Silver Hawk (USA)) 8.6f **(70)**
Form - 0
Record 2000 - 1st:0 2nd:0 3rd:0 Ran:1
Pre2000 - 1st:0 2nd:0 3rd:0 Ran:4
2000 AW 0-1: (8f) (Fibr)
Leggy, moderate gelding. **W J Musson [0-5] B N Fulton.*

HETRA HEIGHTS (USA) BHB 29f52a **RR 31f 52a** 3245[1]
5 b m Cox's Ridge (USA) 9.4f **(72)** - Top Hope (High Top) 10.2f **(67)**
Form - 61103051
Record 2000 - 1st:3 2nd:0 3rd:1 Ran:8
Pre2000 - 1st:0 2nd:1 3rd:0 Ran:9
Win Prizemoney £7,164 *Total Prizemoney* £8,936
Wins * **2000** Jly Folkes (GD-) H 15.4f 28 31
* **2000** *Mar Southw (STD) H 16f 44 54+* <
* **2000** *Feb Wolver (STD) H 16.2f 37 44*
2000 Turf 1-4: (15f 1-1, 16f, 17f, 22f) (sft, gd, frm 1-2) 2000 AW 2-4: (16f 2-4) (Fibr 2-4)
Fair filly, effective 16f, - acts on Fibr, favours tight tracks. Turf high 31. AW high 54 - 1st of 14 getting 11lb from Sposa (6 Mar Southwell RF 0415). **W J Musson [3-17] K L West.*

HETRA REEF BHB 46f **RR 45f** 4930[16]
2 b c First Trump - Cuban Reef **(49f 30a)** (Dowsing (USA))
Form - 000
Record 2000 - 1st:0 2nd:0 3rd:0 Ran:3
2000 Turf 0-3: (6f, 7f 2) (gd 2, g-f)
Currently moderate colt. Turf high 45 (began Jly). **W J Musson [0-3] K L West.*

HEVER GOLF GLORY BHB 30f42a **RR 31f 42a** 5116[5]
6 b g Efisio 7.7f **(69)** - Zaius (Artaius (USA)) 9f **(69)**
Form - 08774503038056000335
Record 2000 - 1st:0 2nd:0 3rd:4 Ran:17
Pre2000 - 1st:3 2nd:2 3rd:1 Ran:41
Win Prizemoney £27,397 *Total Prizemoney* £36,871
Wins * 1999 *May Wolver (Std) H 8.5f 62 72*
* 1999 *Feb Wolver (STD) H 8.5f 53 68*
1997 Jun Taby (GD) 8f 81 <
2000 Turf 0-10: (8f 3, 9f 2, 10f 5) (gd 5, g-f 2, frm, hrd 2) 2000 AW 0-7: (8f 4, 9f 2, 10f) (Equi 2, Fibr 5)
Moderate gelding, effective 8f, - acts on Fibr, has worn blinkers. Turf high 33. AW high 53.
**C N Kellett [2-37] The Muir/Waters Partnership (from N P Littmoden [0-9] Oct 1998).*

HIBAAT BHB 43f25a **RR 34f 25a** 748[P]
4 ch g Zafonic (USA) 9f **(83)** - Realisatrice (USA) (Raja Baba (USA)) 10f **(64)**
Form - 000070400P
Record 2000 - 1st:0 2nd:0 3rd:0 Ran:9
Pre2000 - 1st:0 2nd:0 3rd:0 Ran:5
2000 Turf 0-2: (12f, 22f) (sft, frm) 2000 AW 0-7: (7f, 8f 2, 12f 2, 16f 2) (Fibr 7)
Scopey, very moderate gelding. AW high 27. Becoming disappointing.
**M C Chapman [0-10] Barry Brown (from P T Walwyn [0-4] Jun 1999).*

HIBERNATE (IRE) BHB 57f54a **RR 76f 54a** 4814[10]
6 ch g Lahib (USA) 8f **(69)** - Ministra (USA) (Deputy Minister (CAN)) 7.4f **(80)**
Form - 780000427S00880
Record 2000 - 1st:0 2nd:1 3rd:0 Ran:15
Pre2000 - 1st:4 2nd:5 3rd:1 Ran:17
Win Prizemoney £33,036 *Total Prizemoney* £48,649
Wins * 1999 Jly Bright (FRM) H 11.9f 76 83 <
* 1999 Jun Carlis (G-F) H 12f 68 76
* 1999 Jun Mussel (GD) H 12f 68 73
* 1999 *Feb Lingfi (STD) 12f 68*
2000 Turf 0-13: (9f 2, 10f 3, 12f 7, 13f) (hvy, g-s 2, gd 6, g-f 2, frm 2) 2000 AW 0-2: (12f 2) (Equi 2)
Above-average gelding, effective 9 to 12f, best at 12f, acts on g-s to hrd, best on hrd, has worn blinkers, likes right handed tracks, likes tight tracks. Turf high 76 - 2nd of 14 getting 7lb from Prince Slayer (9 Jun Epsom 9f g-s RF 1833). AW high 50. Becoming disappointing. Does not have anything in the way of a turn of foot and is at his best when able to dominate from the front.
**K R Burke [4-31] Nigel Shields (from R Charlton [0-1] Spt 1996).*

HICKLETON DANCER RR 5009[9]
3 b g Rambo Dancer (CAN) 8.4f **(59)** - Honest Opinion (Free State) 8.7f **(61)**
Form - 60
Record 2000 - 1st:0 2nd:0 3rd:0 Ran:2
2000 Turf 0-1: (7f) (g-s) 2000 AW 0-1: (6f) (Fibr)
Unfurnished, currently very poor gelding. **G Woodward [0-2] D Leech.*

HICKLETON DREAM BHB 35f **RR 24f** 4769[6]
3 b f Rambo Dancer (CAN) 8.4f **(59)** - Elegant Approach (Prince Ragusa)
Form - 056
Record 2000 - 1st:0 2nd:0 3rd:0 Ran:3
2000 Turf 0-3: (8f 2, 10f) (g-s, frm, hrd)
Leggy, currently little account filly. Turf high 24 (began Aug). **G Woodward [0-3] D Leech.*

HIDALGUIA (IRE) RR 113f 4847a[4]
3 b f Barathea (IRE) - Halesia (USA) (Chief's Crown (USA)) 9.8f **(72)**
Form - 23014
2000 Turf 1-5: (9f, 10f 1-3, 11f) (hvy, g-s, gd 1-3)
Group-class filly. Turf high 113 - 4th of 13 to Petrushka (1 Oct Longchamp 10f gd RF 4847a) - also 1st of 12 from Fall Habit (5 Aug Deauville RF 3540a). Useful middle-distance filly, in the frame in Group Ones. **J deRoualle in FR [1-5].*

HIDDEN BRAVE BHB 88f **RR 90f** 2080[2]
3 b c Bin Ajwaad (IRE) - Fire Lily **(48df)** (Unfuwain (USA))
Form - 162
Record 2000 - 1st:1 2nd:1 3rd:0 Ran:3
Pre2000 - 1st:0 2nd:1 3rd:0 Ran:1
Win Prizemoney £2,821 *Total Prizemoney* £5,893
Wins * **2000** Apr Hamilt (GD) 11.1f 41 <
2000 Turf 1-3: (11f 1-1, 12f, 14f) (gd 1-1, frm 2)
Scopey, useful colt. Turf high 90 - 2nd of 3 giving 11lb to Fait Le Jojo (18 Jun Salisbury 14f frm RF 2080). Showed ability on his only start at two and made a winning reappearance at Hamilton, but was unable to build on that. **M Johnston [1-4] Salem Suhail.*

HIDDEN ENEMY BHB 60f54a **RR 67f 54a** 908[16]
4 b c Meqdaam (USA) - Orchard Bay (Formidable (USA)) 9.2f **(63)**
Form - 680
Record 2000 - 1st:0 2nd:0 3rd:0 Ran:2
Pre2000 - 1st:0 2nd:0 3rd:0 Ran:3
Win Prizemoney £0 *Total Prizemoney* £177
2000 Turf 0-2: (10f, 11f) (hvy, gd)
Average colt. Turf high 10. **R Hollinshead [0-5] J Holcombe.*

HIDDEN FORT BHB 76f **RR 78df** 5061[11]
3 ch c Mujtahid (USA) 7.4f **(69)** - Temple Fortune (USA) (Ziggy's Boy (USA))
Form - 0
Record 2000 - 1st:0 2nd:0 3rd:0 Ran:1
Pre2000 - 1st:1 2nd:0 3rd:0 Ran:6
Win Prizemoney £5,154 *Total Prizemoney* £5,154
Wins 1999 Jun Windso (G-F) 5f 85 <
2000 Turf 0-1: (6f) (sft)
Strong, above-average colt, effective 5f, acts on frm. Scored in good style at Windsor on his second start at two, but was very disappointing afterwards.
**Mrs A J Perrett [0-1] A N Solomons (from S Dow [1-6] Spt 1999).*

HIDDEN LAKE (IRE) RR 56f 5217[6]

2 b g Lake Coniston (IRE) - Valmarana (USA) (Danzig Connection (USA)) 8f **(68)**
Form - 506
Record 2000 - 1st:0 2nd:0 3rd:0 Ran:3
2000 Turf 0-3: (6f 3) (sft, g-f, frm)
Currently fair gelding. Turf high 56.
**Mrs A J Bowlby [0-3] The North and South Partnership.*

HIDDEN MEANING RR 66f 4437[8]

2 ch f Cadeaux Genereux 7.9f **(76)** - Cubby Hole (Town And Country) 8.1f **(68)**
Form - 38
Record 2000 - 1st:0 2nd:0 3rd:1 Ran:2
Win Prizemoney £0 *Total Prizemoney* £645
2000 Turf 0-2: (6f, 7f) (g-f, frm)
Currently average filly. Turf high 66 (began Aug).
**R Hannon [0-2] Lord Carnarvon.*

HIDDNAH (USA) BHB 102f RR 106f 4953a[6]

3 ch f Affirmed (USA) 10.3f **(75)** - L'Extra Honor (USA) (Hero's Honor (USA)) 8.2f **(86)**
Form - 23636
Record 2000 - 1st:0 2nd:1 3rd:2 Ran:5
Pre2000 - 1st:1 2nd:1 3rd:1 Ran:4
Win Prizemoney £3,663 *Total Prizemoney* £18,648
Wins * 1999 Jly Newcas (FRM) 7f 82 <
2000 Turf 0-5: (10f, 12f 3, 15f) (sft, gd 2, g-f 2)
Pattern-class filly, effective 10 to 15f, acts on gd to g-f, best on g-f. Turf high 106 (began Jly) - 6th of 11 getting 5lb from Miletrian (6 Spt Doncaster 15f gd RF 4260). She ran respectably in listed races last season, but was well held on her final two starts. Does not stay two miles. **M Johnston [1-9].*

HI-FALUTIN BHB 30f RR 11f 5126[10]

4 b f Lugana Beach 7f **(63)** - Hitravelscene (Mansingh (USA)) 7.4f **(55)**
Form - 0
Record 2000 - 1st:0 2nd:0 3rd:0 Ran:1
Pre2000 - 1st:0 2nd:0 3rd:0 Ran:1
2000 Turf 0-1: (7f) (g-s)
Currently poor filly.
**J Pearce [0-1] Clayfields Racing (from A T Murphy [0-1] Oct 1999).*

HIGH BARN RR 72+f 5070[3]

3 b f Shirley Heights 12.1f **(76)** - Mountain Lodge (Blakeney) 10.5f **(64)**
Form - 043
Record 2000 - 1st:0 2nd:0 3rd:1 Ran:3
Win Prizemoney £0 *Total Prizemoney* £942
2000 Turf 0-3: (10f, 12f 2) (g-s 3)
Scopey, currently above-average filly. Turf high 72 (began Spt).
**J R Fanshawe [0-3] Lord Halifax.*

HIGH BEAUTY BHB 27f39a RR 36f 39a 5182[3]

3 br f High Kicker (USA) 8.4f **(52)** - Tendresse (IRE) **(21f)** (Tender King) 6.8f **(54)**
Form - 04848050070653
Record 2000 - 1st:0 2nd:0 3rd:1 Ran:14
Pre2000 - 1st:0 2nd:0 3rd:0 Ran:3
Win Prizemoney £0 *Total Prizemoney* £327
2000 Turf 0-13: (8f, 10f 5, 11f, 12f 4, 14f 2) (sft 2, g-s 2, gd 3, g-f 3, frm 3) 2000 AW 0-1: (12f) (Fibr)
Leggy, very moderate filly, has worn blinkers. Turf high 45. Consistent. **M J Ryan [0-18] M J Ryan.*

HIGHCAL BHB 48f RR 49+f 4499[11]

3 gr g King's Signet (USA) 7f **(51)** - Guarded Expression **(45f)** (Siberian Express (USA)) 8.8f **(65)**
Form - 0087110
Record 2000 - 1st:2 2nd:0 3rd:0 Ran:7
Pre2000 - 1st:0 2nd:0 3rd:0 Ran:3
Win Prizemoney £5,240 *Total Prizemoney* £5,240
Wins * **2000** Aug Bright (FRM) H 10f 40 49+ <
* **2000** Jly Ripon (G-F) SH 10f 36 42
2000 Turf 2-7: (10f 2-5, 12f 2) (g-s, gd, g-f 1-1, frm 1-3, hrd)
Scopey, moderate gelding, effective 10f, acts on g-f, likes tight tracks. Turf high 49 - 1st of 14 getting 23lb from Shaman (21 Aug Brighton RF 3837). Inconsistent.
**Ronald Thompson [2-7] J Bradwell (from D R C Elsworth [0-3] Aug 1999).*

HIGH CAPACITY (IRE) BHB 36f RR 46f 1029[12]

3 b f Dolphin Street (FR) - Foresta Verde (USA) **(24f 42a)** (Green Forest (USA)) 9.9f **(68)**
Form - 060
Record 2000 - 1st:0 2nd:0 3rd:0 Ran:3
Pre2000 - 1st:0 2nd:0 3rd:1 Ran:7
Win Prizemoney £0 *Total Prizemoney* £502
2000 Turf 0-2: (10f, 12f) (g-s, gd) 2000 AW 0-1: (12f) (Fibr)
Scopey, moderate filly, has worn blinkers. Turf high 36. Inconsistent. **T D Easterby [0-10] Edmolift UK Ltd.*

HIGH CARRY BHB 51f RR 49f 1443[4]

5 b m Forzando 7.2f **(63)** - Carn Maire (Northern Prospect (USA)) 9.5f **(71)**
Form - 34
Record 2000 - 1st:0 2nd:0 3rd:1 Ran:2
Pre2000 - 1st:2 2nd:6 3rd:3 Ran:38
Win Prizemoney £6,388 *Total Prizemoney* £18,482
Wins * 1997 Aug Sandow (G-S) H 5f 71 87 <
1997 Jly Beverl (G-F) C 5f 71
2000 Turf 0-2: (5f 2) (gd, frm)
Moderate filly, effective 5 to 6f, best at 5f, acted on g-f to frm, best on frm, had worn blinkers. Turf high 49. (DEAD)
**N Tinkler [1-37] James Marshall & Mrs Susan Marshall (from J E Banks [1-3] Jly 1997).*

HIGH DRAMA RR 67f 2614[15]

3 b c In The Wings 11.2f **(77)** - Maestrale (Top Ville) 11.7f **(68)**
Form - 80080
Record 2000 - 1st:0 2nd:0 3rd:0 Ran:5
2000 Turf 0-5: (10f 4, 11f) (gd, g-f 2, frm 2)
Scopey, average colt, has worn blinkers. Turf high 67.
**W R Muir [0-5] C L A Edginton.*

HIGH ESTEEM BHB 44f57a RR 48f 57a 5083[6]

4 b g Common Grounds 8.1f **(66)** - Whittle Woods Girl **(74f 60a)** (Emarati (USA))
Form - 1000506
Record 2000 - 1st:1 2nd:0 3rd:0 Ran:7
Pre2000 - 1st:0 2nd:0 3rd:0 Ran:10
Win Prizemoney £2,261 *Total Prizemoney* £2,703
Wins * **2000** *May Southw (STD) H 6f 53 58* <
2000 Turf 0-5: (5f, 6f 4) (hvy, sft, gd, g-f, frm) 2000 AW 1-2: (5f, 6f 1-1) (Fibr 1-2)
Workmanlike, fair gelding, effective 5 to 6f, acts on sft - acts on Fibr. Turf high 39. AW high 58 (1st run) - 1st of 14 giving 16lb to Superfrills (22 May Southwell RF 1377).
**M A Buckley [1-17] C C Buckley.*

HIGHFIELDER (IRE) BHB 47f39a RR 49f 39a 313[4]

4 br g Unblest - River Low (IRE) (Lafontaine (USA)) 8.7f **(49)**
Form - 040306554
Record 2000 - 1st:0 2nd:0 3rd:0 Ran:3
Pre2000 - 1st:0 2nd:0 3rd:3 Ran:17
Win Prizemoney £0 *Total Prizemoney* £1,448
2000 AW 0-3: (8f, 9f, 12f) (Equi, Fibr 2)
Neat, moderate gelding, effective 7 to 12f, acts on gd - acts on Equi, has worn blinkers. AW high 36. Inconsistent.
**J S Moore [0-20] J S Moore.*

HIGHFIELD FIZZ BHB 33f44a RR 44f 44a 4750[7]

8 b m Efisio 7.7f **(69)** - Jendor (Condorcet (FR)) 12.3f **(62)**
Form - 00P0016763413077
Record 2000 - 1st:2 2nd:0 3rd:2 Ran:16
Pre2000 - 1st:5 2nd:9 3rd:8 Ran:58
Win Prizemoney £23,109 *Total Prizemoney* £37,664
Wins * **2000** Aug Ayr (GD) H 15f 37 38
* **2000** May Redcar (G-S) H 14.1f 35 44
* 1999 May Mussel (FRM) H 16f 41 44
* 1998 Jun Mussel (G-F) H 16f 50 53
* 1998 Apr Pontef (G-S) H 17.1f 45 50
* 1996 Oct Redcar (G-F) H 14.1f 36 44
2000 Turf 2-16: (14f 1-4, 15f 1-1, 16f 9, 17f, 22f) (sft, g-s 3, gd 1-4, g-f

2, frm 1-5, hrd)
Moderate mare, effective 14 to 17f, best at 16f, acts on gd to hrd, likes right handed tracks, prefers tight tracks, excels at Redcar, likes Musselburgh. Turf high 44 - 1st of 8 getting 10lb from Simple Ideals (29 May Redcar RF 1533) - also 1st of 7 from Smudger Smith (15 Aug Ayr RF 3642). Consistent.
**C W Fairhurst [7-74] Mrs P J Taylor-Garthwaite.*

HIGHLAND FLIGHT BHB 57f **RR 58f** 4965[29]
2 gr f Missed Flight - In The Highlands **(38f)** (Petong) 6.6f **(58)**
Form - 0470
Record 2000 - 1st:0 2nd:0 3rd:0 Ran:4
Win Prizemoney £0 *Total Prizemoney* £237
2000 Turf 0-4: (5f 2, 6f 2) (gd, g-f, frm 2)
Fair filly. Turf high 58 (began Jly).
**Bob Jones [0-4] Matthew Sharkey.*

HIGHLAND GOLD (IRE) RR 67tf 4893[2]
3 ch c Indian Ridge 7.6f **(74)** - Anjuli (Northfields (USA)) 9f **(72)**
Form - 35788402
Record 2000 - 1st:0 2nd:1 3rd:1 Ran:8
Pre2000 - 1st:0 2nd:0 3rd:0 Ran:2
Win Prizemoney £0 *Total Prizemoney* £2,641
2000 Turf 0-8: (8f 4, 9f, 10f, 11f 2) (hvy 2, g-s, gd 2, g-f 2, frm)
Strong, average colt. Turf high 67.
**Miss L A Perratt [0-10] Miss L A Perratt.*

HIGHLAND REEL BHB 92f **RR 92f** 5133[2]
3 ch c Selkirk (USA) 7.9f **(76)** - Taj Victory (Final Straw) 7.9f **(64)**
Form - 3733172
Record 2000 - 1st:1 2nd:1 3rd:3 Ran:7
Win Prizemoney £4,218 *Total Prizemoney* £10,223
Wins * 2000 Jly Windso (G-F) 8.3f 73+ <
2000 Turf 1-7: (8f 1-4, 9f, 10f 2) (sft 2, g-s, gd 2, g-f, frm 1-1)
Scopey, useful colt, effective 9f, acts on sft. Turf high 92 - 2nd of 11 getting 7lb from Cornelius (21 Oct Newbury 9f sft RF 5133).
**D R C Elsworth [1-7] Sir Gordon Brunton.*

HIGHLY FANCIED BHB 35f **RR 17f** 1615[0]
4 b f High Kicker (USA) 8.4f **(52)** - Angie's Darling (Milford) 9f **(61)**
Form - 000
Record 2000 - 1st:0 2nd:0 3rd:0 Ran:3
Pre2000 - 1st:0 2nd:3 3rd:2 Ran:16
Win Prizemoney £0 *Total Prizemoney* £4,415
2000 Turf 0-3: (5f, 6f 2) (g-s, g-f, frm)
Workmanlike, poor filly, effective 6f, acts on g-f. Turf high 17. Becoming disappointing.
**Miss L A Perratt [0-13] T P Finch (from S E Kettlewell [0-6] Jly 1999).*

HIGHLY PLEASED (USA) RR 49f 4304[10]
5 b g Hansel (USA) 12.6f **(78)** - Bint Alfalla (USA) (Nureyev (USA)) 8.7f **(78)**
Form - 00
Record 2000 - 1st:0 2nd:0 3rd:0 Ran:2
Pre2000 - 1st:0 2nd:1 3rd:2 Ran:10
Win Prizemoney £0 *Total Prizemoney* £1,751
2000 Turf 0-2: (8f 2) (gd, frm)
Moderate gelding. Turf high 49. Consistent.
**P Burgoyne [0-8] Philip Saunders (from E A L Dunlop [0-4] May 1998).*

HIGHLY PRIZED BHB 55f50a **RR 58f 50a** 4928[7]
6 b g Shirley Heights 12.1f **(76)** - On The Tiles (Thatch (USA)) 9.8f **(62)**
Form - 54316700107
Record 2000 - 1st:2 2nd:0 3rd:0 Ran:8
Pre2000 - 1st:1 2nd:3 3rd:3 Ran:22
Win Prizemoney £7,835 *Total Prizemoney* £13,512
Wins * 2000 Aug Chepst (G-F) C 12.1f 55
*** 2000** *Jan Wolver (STD) H 14.8f 57 61*
***** 1998 Jly Salisb (G-F) H 14.1f 70 77 <
2000 Turf 1-4: (12f 1-1, 14f 3) (frm 1-4) 2000 AW 1-4: (12f, 15f 1-1, 16f 2) (Equi 2, Fibr 1-2)
Average gelding, effective 12 to 15f, best at 14f, acts on g-f to frm - acts on Fibr, best on frm. Turf high 58 (began Jly). AW high 61 (1st run) - 1st of 11 getting 8lb from Count de Money (6 Jan Wolverhampton RF 0038).
**J S King [3-31] Mrs Marygold O'Kelly (from I A Balding [0-5] Jun 1997).*

HIGHLY SOCIABLE BHB 46f **RR 19f** 5105[18]
3 b f Puissance 7.1f **(60)** - Come To Tea (IRE) (Be My Guest (USA)) 9.3f **(67)**
Form - 00
Record 2000 - 1st:0 2nd:0 3rd:0 Ran:2
Pre2000 - 1st:0 2nd:0 3rd:1 Ran:4
Win Prizemoney £0 *Total Prizemoney* £420
2000 Turf 0-2: (7f 2) (g-s, gd)
Neat, poor filly. Turf high 19 (began Spt).
**A Bailey [0-2] The Highly Sociable Syndicate (from S A Brookshaw [0-4] Spt 1999).*

HIGH PASTURE (USA) RR 54f 5132[13]
2 b br f El Gran Senor (USA) 8.9f **(85)** - Summer Retreat (USA) **(77f)** (Gone West (USA)) 6.5f **(75)**
Form - 60
Record 2000 - 1st:0 2nd:0 3rd:0 Ran:2
2000 Turf 0-2: (6f 2) (sft, gd)
Currently fair filly. Turf high 54 (began Spt).
**R Charlton [0-2] K Abdulla.*

HIGH POLICY (IRE) BHB 60f **RR 66df** 5012[3]
4 ch g Machiavellian (USA) 9.8f **(83)** - Road To The Top (Shirley Heights) 10.3f **(74)**
Form - 106023
Record 2000 - 1st:1 2nd:1 3rd:1 Ran:6
Pre2000 - 1st:0 2nd:0 3rd:1 Ran:3
Win Prizemoney £2,613 *Total Prizemoney* £4,134
Wins * 2000 *Feb Wolver (STD) 12f 52+* <
2000 Turf 0-2: (12f, 14f) (gd, g-f) 2000 AW 1-4: (12f 1-3, 14f) (Equi, Fibr 1-3)
Workmanlike, average gelding, effective 12f, acts on frm, has worn blinkers, prefers left handed tracks, favours tight tracks. Turf high 52. AW high 60.
**D J G MurraySmith [1-6] D MurraySmith (from Sir Michael Stoute [0-3] May 1999).*

HIGH-RISE (IRE) BHB 119f **RR 119f** 578a[3]
5 b h High Estate 10.5f **(66)** - High Tern (High Line) 10.3f **(70)**
Form - 313
2000 Turf 1-2: (12f 1-2) (gd)
High-class colt, effective 10 to 12f, best at 12f, acts on gd to frm, best on gd. Turf high 118 - 3rd of 16 giving 2lb to Fantastic Light (25 Mar Nad Al Sheba 12f gd RF 0578a). Consistent. Winner of the 1998 Derby, he finished third to Fantastic Light in Dubai in March before continuing his career in America. Retired after sustaining an injury at Belmont Park, he becomes the seventh Derby winner of the 90s to stand at stud in Japan.
**S bin Suroor in UAE [1-3] (from S bin Suroor [0-3] Nov 1999).*

HIGH SHOT BHB 51f52a **RR 51f 52a** 4499[8]
10 b g Darshaan 11.9f **(81)** - Nollet (High Top) 10.2f **(67)**
Form - 22331408
Record 2000 - 1st:1 2nd:0 3rd:2 Ran:6
Pre2000 - 1st:0 2nd:3 3rd:1 Ran:10
Win Prizemoney £1,986 *Total Prizemoney* £5,686
Wins 2000 *Feb Lingfi (STD) S 8f 41* <
2000 Turf 0-2: (10f, 11f) (g-s, g-f) 2000 AW 1-4: (8f 1-2, 10f 2) (Equi 1-4)
Fair gelding, likes left handed tracks. Turf high 44 (began Spt). AW high 49.
**A L Forbes [0-3] Tony Forbes (from G L Moore [1-7] Feb 2000).*

HIGH SOCIETY LADY (IRE) BHB 47f **RR 55f** 5053[13]
2 ch f General Monash (USA) - Bardia **(43f 22a)** (Jalmood (USA)) 10.1f **(52)**
Form - 0007087000
Record 2000 - 1st:0 2nd:0 3rd:0 Ran:10
2000 Turf 0-8: (5f, 6f, 7f 4, 8f 2) (sft, g-s, g-f 3, frm 3) 2000 AW 0-2: (5f, 6f) (Fibr 2)
Fair filly, has worn blinkers. Turf high 55. AW high 24. Inconsistent. **N Bycroft [0-10] The Country Stayers.*

HIGH SPOT RR 70f 5309[5]
2 b f Shirley Heights 12.1f **(76)** - Rash Gift **(56f 54a)** (Cadeaux Genereux)
Form - 05

Record 2000 - 1st:0 2nd:0 3rd:0 Ran:2
2000 Turf 0-2: (7f, 8f) (g-s, gd)
Currently above-average filly. Turf high 70 (began Oct).
**R Charlton [0-2] The Queen.*

HIGH SUN BHB 44f **RR 56df** 4814^{16}

4 b g High Estate 10.5f **(66)** - Clyde Goddess (IRE) **(69df)** (Scottish Reel) 7f **(61)**
Form - 470078507550
Record 2000 - 1st:0 2nd:0 3rd:0 Ran:12
Pre2000 - 1st:3 2nd:0 3rd:1 Ran:15
Win Prizemoney £9,287 *Total Prizemoney* £9,937
Wins * 1999 Oct Newmar (G-S) H 8f 48 61 <
* 1999 Oct Doncas (G-S) H 7f 48 54
* 1999 Aug Leices (G-F) C 8f 50
2000 Turf 0-12: (7f 2, 8f 7, 10f 3) (sft 2, g-s 2, gd 2, g-f, frm 4, hrd)
Unfurnished, fair gelding, effective 7 to 8f, acts on gd, has worn blinkers. Turf high 46. **S Gollings [3-27] R L Houlton.*

HIGH TEMPO BHB 40f **RR 37f** 5184^{16}

2 b g Piccolo - Reem Fever (IRE) **(46f 31a)** (Fairy King (USA)) 7.7f **(59)**
Form - 000
Record 2000 - 1st:0 2nd:0 3rd:0 Ran:3
2000 Turf 0-3: (7f, 8f 2) (g-s, gd 2)
Currently very moderate gelding. Turf high 37 (began Spt).
**K R Burke [0-3] Haven Partnership.*

HIGH TOPPER (FR) BHB 74f **RR 83f** 4431^{6}

3 b c Wolfhound (USA) 7.3f **(71)** - Blushing Barada (USA) (Blushing Groom (FR)) 10.3f **(76)**
Form - 25244116456
Record 2000 - 1st:2 2nd:2 3rd:0 Ran:11
Pre2000 - 1st:0 2nd:0 3rd:0 Ran:1
Win Prizemoney £19,253 *Total Prizemoney* £22,565
Wins * 2000 Jly Chepst (FRM) H 16.2f 78 84 <
*** 2000** Jly Cheste (G-S) H 15.9f 73 76
2000 Turf 2-11: (9f, 11f, 12f 3, 14f 2, 16f 2-3, 17f) (g-s 2, gd 2, g-f 1-2, frm 1-4, hrd)
Scopey, decent colt, effective 12 to 16f, acts on g-f to hrd, has worn blinkers, prefers tight tracks. Turf high 84 - 1st of 4 giving 16lb to Jack Dawson (28 Jly Chepstow RF 3170) - also 1st of 7 getting 23lb from Renzo (15 Jly Chester RF 2836). He gradually improved when stepped up in trip and got off the mark when making all over two miles at Chester in July, though it was a race which lacked strength in depth for the money on offer. Nevertheless, he followed up at Chepstow on much faster ground. **M Johnston [2-12] Maktoum Al Maktoum.*

HIGHTORI (FR) **RR 119f** $4846a^{5}$

3 c Vettori (IRE) - High Mecene (FR) (Highest Honor (FR))
Form - 115
2000 Turf 1-2: (10f 1-1, 12f) (gd 1-2)
High-class colt. Turf high 119 (began Spt) - also 1st of 7 from Bleu D'Altair (16 Spt Longchamp RF 4565a). A decent juvenile, he was absent from the track from November '99 until making a winning reappearance in a Group Three at Longchamp in September. Finished a respectable fifth in the Arc, in which he was sent off at 50/1. **P Demercastel in FR [2-5].*

HIGH TOWER **RR 77f** 5070^{9}

3 b c Lycius (USA) 8.8f **(71)** - Sedova (USA) (Nijinsky (CAN)) 10.3f **(77)**
Form - 440
Record 2000 - 1st:0 2nd:0 3rd:0 Ran:3
Win Prizemoney £0 *Total Prizemoney* £712
2000 Turf 0-3: (10f, 12f 2) (g-s, gd, g-f)
Scopey, currently above-average colt. Turf high 77 (began Jly).
**Mrs A J Perrett [0-3] K Abdulla.*

HIGH WALDEN (USA) BHB 110f **RR 111f** 3394^{4}

3 b f El Gran Senor (USA) 8.9f **(85)** - Modena (USA) (Roberto (USA)) 10f **(76)**
Form - 5324
Record 2000 - 1st:0 2nd:1 3rd:1 Ran:4
Pre2000 - 1st:1 2nd:1 3rd:0 Ran:3
Win Prizemoney £4,110 *Total Prizemoney* £34,977
Wins * 1999 Spt Leices (FRM) 8f 82 <
2000 Turf 0-4: (8f, 9f, 10f 2) (g-s, g-f 2, frm)
Scopey, Group-class filly, effective 9 to 10f, best at 10f, acts on g-s to g-f, best on g-f. Turf high 111 - 4th of 7 to Crimplene (5 Aug Goodwood 10f g-f RF 3394). She has always had a big reputation, and was fifth in the Guineas on her seasonal bow. Stayed on into third in the Musidora next time, and it was surprising to see her dropped in trip at Epsom, where she was just touched off. She ended her campaign with an excellent fourth in the Group One Nassau Stakes. **H R A Cecil [1-7] K Abdulla.*

HILL COUNTRY (IRE) BHB 100f **RR 99f** 4853^{2}

2 b c Danehill (USA) 9.1f **(79)** - Rose of Jericho (USA) (Alleged (USA)) 10f **(76)**
Form - 0132
Record 2000 - 1st:1 2nd:1 3rd:1 Ran:4
Win Prizemoney £4,348 *Total Prizemoney* £22,298
Wins * 2000 Spt Kempto (GD) 8f 91+ <
2000 Turf 1-4: (7f, 8f 1-3) (sft, g-s, g-f 1-2)
Very useful colt. Turf high 99 (began Jly) - also 1st of 15 from Border Comet (3 Spt Kempton RF 4191). A half-brother to Dr Devious among others, he stepped up on his debut effort to score at Kempton and ran very well to finish third in the Royal Lodge. Was a distant second to Nayef next time, but that colt looks top notch. He should be able to win good races next term, but may have to avoid the top colts to do so.
**J H M Gosden [1-4] R E Sangster & Mrs J Magnier.*

HILL FARM BLUES BHB 60f55a **RR 62f 55a** 3558^{4}

7 b m Mon Tresor 7.9f **(60)** - Loadplan Lass (Nicholas Bill) 10.1f **(56)**
Form - 4508824
Record 2000 - 1st:0 2nd:1 3rd:0 Ran:7
Pre2000 - 1st:5 2nd:3 3rd:2 Ran:32
Win Prizemoney £19,680 *Total Prizemoney* £40,595
Wins 1999 Jun Haydoc (G-S) H 16.2f 54 70 <
1999 May Haydoc (GD) H 14f 54 58
1998 Oct Nottin (SFT) H 16f 51 56
1997 Jly Bath (GD) H 10.2f 58 63
1997 May Nottin (GD) SH 10f 49 57
2000 Turf 0-7: (12f 3, 15f, 16f 2, 17f) (hvy, gd 2, g-f, frm 2, hrd)
Average mare, effective 12 to 19f, acts on gd to g-f, best on g-f, prefers left handed tracks, likes tight tracks. Turf high 71. Consistent.
**Miss S E Baxter [0-7] Dennis Newton (from W M Brisbourne [6-29] Oct 1999).*

HILL FARM DANCER BHB 38f31a **RR 36f 31a** 2096^{2}

9 ch m Gunner B 11.2f **(45)** - Loadplan Lass (Nicholas Bill) 10.1f **(56)**
Form - R4035523143511452
Record 2000 - 1st:3 2nd:2 3rd:2 Ran:13
Pre2000 - 1st:10 2nd:9 3rd:12 Ran:85
Win Prizemoney £33,782 *Total Prizemoney* £51,033
Wins * 2000 May Hamilt (FRM) SH 12.1f 33 35
*** 2000** *Apr Wolver (STD) S 12f 48*
*** 2000** *Feb Wolver (STD) H 12f 30 32*
* 1999 *Apr Southw (STD) S 12f 54*
* 1998 Jly Mussel (GD) H 12f 45 49
* 1997 *Jan Wolver (STD) H 12f 68 76* <
* 1996 *Nov Wolver (STD) 12f 70*
* 1996 *Nov Wolver (STD) H 12f 53 62*
* 1996 *Mar Wolver (STD) C 12f 57*
* 1996 *Feb Wolver (STD) H 12f 47 53*
2000 Turf 1-4: (12f 1-1, 13f, 14f 2) (gd, frm 1-3) 2000 AW 2-9: (12f 2-7, 16f 2) (Fibr 2-9)
Moderate mare, effective 11 to 12f, best at 12f, - acts on Fibr, likes left handed tracks, and excels at Southwell. Turf high 36. AW high 48 - 1st of 12 getting 5lb from Banneret (28 Apr Wolverhampton RF 0904). Consistent.
**W M Brisbourne [13-95] M E Hughes (from P D Evans [0-3] Jly 1993).*

HILL MAGIC BHB 74f **RR 79f** 4433^{7}

5 br g Magic Ring (IRE) 6.5f **(64)** -Stock Hill Lass (Air Trooper) 9.1f **(63)**
Form - 0000027
Record 2000 - 1st:0 2nd:1 3rd:0 Ran:7
Pre2000 - 1st:3 2nd:2 3rd:1 Ran:19
Win Prizemoney £45,663 *Total Prizemoney* £57,858
Wins 1999 Apr Kempto (GD) 6f 100 <
1998 May Lingfi (GD) H 6f 89 94
1997 Jly Bath (GD) 5.7f 77
2000 Turf 0-7: (6f 5, 7f 2) (g-s, gd 3, g-f, frm 2)

Above-average gelding, effective 6f, acts on g-f. Turf high 79.
*L G Cottrell [0-7] E Gadsden (from D R C Elsworth [3-19] Oct 1999).

HILL STORM (IRE) BHB 40f30a **RR 19f 30a** 483[10]
4 b g Mukaddamah (USA) 7.6f **(74)** - Brockley Hill Lass (IRE) (Alzao (USA)) 7.1f **(68)**
Form - 30
Record 2000 - 1st:0 2nd:0 3rd:1 Ran:2
Pre2000 - 1st:0 2nd:0 3rd:0 Ran:7
Win Prizemoney £0 _Total Prizemoney_ £210
2000 AW 0-2: (12f, 15f) (Fibr 2)
Workmanlike, little account gelding, has worn blinkers. AW high 26. _*K McAuliffe [0-9] K W J McAuliffe._

HILLSWICK BHB 33f **RR 35df** 4630[5]
9 ch g Norwick (USA) 9.4f **(51)** - Quite Lucky (Precipice Wood) 17.2f **(38)**
Form - 5
Record 2000 - 1st:0 2nd:0 3rd:0 Ran:1
Pre2000 - 1st:1 2nd:5 3rd:2 Ran:23
Win Prizemoney £3,533 _Total Prizemoney_ £9,286
Wins * 1997 Aug Bath (GD) H 17.2f 37 40 <
2000 Turf 0-1: (17f) (g-s)
Very moderate gelding. Consistent. _*J S King [4-33] M G A Court._

HILLTOP WARNING BHB 75f **RR 70f** 4743[3]
3 b c Reprimand 8.2f **(63)** - Just Irene (Sagaro) 9.7f **(55)**
Form - 015483
Record 2000 - 1st:1 2nd:0 3rd:1 Ran:6
Pre2000 - 1st:0 2nd:2 3rd:1 Ran:3
Win Prizemoney £4,342 _Total Prizemoney_ £8,797
Wins * **2000** Jun Newbur (G-F) 7f 77 <
2000 Turf 1-6: (6f, 7f 1-4, 8f) (gd 2, g-f 1-3, frm)
Workmanlike, above-average colt, effective 6 to 7f, best at 7f, acts on g-f to frm, best on g-f, has worn blinkers. Turf high 79 - 5th of 12 to Rushmore (26 Jly Sandown 7f g-f RF 3141) - also 1st of 8 from Fool On The Hill (15 Jun Newbury RF 1991). Scraped home in a Newbury maiden, after hanging, and has run well in decent handicaps since. _*S P C Woods [1-9] G Noble._

HILL WELCOME BHB 62f57a **RR 59f 57a** 4760[11]
2 ch f Most Welcome 8.6f **(66)** - Tarvie (Swing Easy (USA)) 6.5f **(55)**
Form - 340
Record 2000 - 1st:0 2nd:0 3rd:1 Ran:3
Win Prizemoney £0 _Total Prizemoney_ £793
2000 Turf 0-2: (6f 2) (gd, frm) 2000 AW 0-1: (6f) (Fibr)
Currently fair filly. Turf high 59 (began Jly).
*B W Hills [0-3] P Fetherston-Godley.

HILTON HEAD **RR 78f** 4772[1]
2 b f Primo Dominie 7.2f **(67)** - Low Hill (Rousillon (USA)) 8.2f **(74)**
Form - 1
Record 2000 - 1st:1 2nd:0 3rd:0 Ran:1
Win Prizemoney £2,730 _Total Prizemoney_ £2,730
Wins * **2000** Oct Catter (SFT) 5f 78 <
2000 Turf 1-1: (5f 1-1) (gd 1-1)
Currently above-average filly. (1st run) - 1st of 12 from Lady Lenor (3 Oct Catterick RF 4772).
*T D Easterby [1-1] & Mrs John Poynton.

HIMSELF (USA) **RR 96f** 3912[4]
5 b h El Gran Senor (USA) 8.9f **(85)** - Celtic Loot (USA) (Irish River (FR)) 8.6f **(78)**
Form - 434
Record 2000 - 1st:0 2nd:0 3rd:1 Ran:3
Pre2000 - 1st:3 2nd:0 3rd:0 Ran:6
Win Prizemoney £35,371 _Total Prizemoney_ £42,362
Wins * 1998 Spt Doncas (GD) H 10.3f 91 95 <
* 1998 Aug Newcas (GD) H 10.1f 87 90
* 1997 Oct Leices (GD) 8f 81+
2000 Turf 0-3: (10f 3) (gd 2, frm)
Very useful colt. Turf high 96 - 3rd of 9 giving 7lb to Happy Diamond (29 Jly Ascot 10f gd RF 3200). Rejoined Henry Cecil last term after a season in France. He ran well in a light campaign, but looks to need 12 furlongs now.
*H R A Cecil [3-9] Scrope, Scott Partners.

HI MUJTAHID (IRE) BHB 32f48a **RR 29f 48a** 4925[4]
6 ch g Mujtahid (USA) 7.4f **(69)** - High Tern (High Line) 10.3f **(70)**
Form - 00820884
Record 2000 - 1st:0 2nd:1 3rd:0 Ran:8
Pre2000 - 1st:2 2nd:4 3rd:3 Ran:38
Win Prizemoney £4,828 _Total Prizemoney_ £10,415
Wins 1998 _Dec Wolver (STD) H 8.5f 34 41_
1997 Jly Ayr (G-F) H 7f 44 50 <
2000 Turf 0-6: (7f 3, 8f 3) (gd 2, g-f 2, frm, hrd) 2000 AW 0-2: (6f, 7f) (Equi, Fibr)
Moderate gelding, effective 7f, acts on frm, has worn blinkers. Turf high 29 - 2nd of 11 getting 4lb from Celtic Venture (25 Jly Brighton 7f frm RF 3088). AW high 27.
*J M Bradley [0-11] J M Bradley (from Mrs H L Walton [1-16] Aug 1999).

HINDAAM (USA) BHB 76f **RR 72+f** 5139[3]
3 b c Thunder Gulch (USA) - Party Cited (USA) (Alleged (USA)) 10f **(76)**
Form - 513
Record 2000 - 1st:1 2nd:0 3rd:1 Ran:3
Win Prizemoney £2,561 _Total Prizemoney_ £3,176
Wins * **2000** Oct Lingfi (SFT) 7.6f 72+ <
2000 Turf 1-3: (8f 1-3) (g-s 1-2, gd)
Strong, currently above-average colt. Turf high 72 (began Spt) - 1st of 18 from Mac Be Lucky (4 Oct Lingfield RF 4813).
*F A I Dunlop [1-3] Hamdan Al Maktoum.

HINDI BHB 63f **RR 66f** 1309[8]
4 b g Indian Ridge 7.6f **(74)** - Tootsiepop (USA) (Robellino (USA)) 7.6f **(80)**
Form - 8208
Record 2000 - 1st:0 2nd:1 3rd:0 Ran:4
Pre2000 - 1st:0 2nd:0 3rd:0 Ran:5
Win Prizemoney £0 _Total Prizemoney_ £1,256
2000 Turf 0-4: (10f 4) (g-s, gd 3)
Lengthy, average gelding, effective 8 to 10f, acts on g-s to frm, has worn blinkers. Turf high 66 - 2nd of 15 getting 1lb from Admirals Place (18 Apr Folkestone 10f g-s RF 0765).
*N A Graham [0-9] Douglas Guyer, Norman Fish & Paul Jacobs.

HI NICKY BHB 44f **RR 47df** 4626[8]
4 ch f High Kicker (USA) 8.4f **(52)** - Sharp Top (Sharpo) 7.7f **(59)**
Form - 00070748
Record 2000 - 1st:0 2nd:0 3rd:0 Ran:8
Pre2000 - 1st:1 2nd:0 3rd:1 Ran:6
Win Prizemoney £4,503 _Total Prizemoney_ £5,791
Wins 1998 May Newmar (G-F) 6f 60 <
2000 Turf 0-8: (5f, 7f 2, 8f 4, 10f) (g-s, gd 2, g-f 3, frm 2)
Workmanlike, moderate filly. Turf high 48. Inconsistent.
*W Storey [0-8] Dr P and Mrs D M Johnson (from M J Ryan [1-6] Jly 1999).

HINT OF MAGIC BHB 60f **RR 57f** 5229[19]
3 b g Magic Ring (IRE) 6.5f **(64)** - Thames Glow (Kalaglow) 9.8f **(67)**
Form - 440070
Record 2000 - 1st:0 2nd:0 3rd:0 Ran:6
Pre2000 - 1st:0 2nd:1 3rd:0 Ran:2
Win Prizemoney £0 _Total Prizemoney_ £1,702
2000 Turf 0-6: (8f 3, 10f 3) (g-s 2, gd 3, g-f)
Scopey, fair gelding, effective 8 to 10f, acts on g-s. Turf high 79. Becoming disappointing. _*J G Portman [0-8] Madhatter Racing._

HIRAETH BHB 73f **RR 79f** 5131[3]
2 b f Petong 7.6f **(58)** - Floppie (FR) (Law Society (USA)) 9.9f **(70)**
Form - 323
Record 2000 - 1st:0 2nd:1 3rd:2 Ran:3
Win Prizemoney £0 _Total Prizemoney_ £2,314
2000 Turf 0-3: (5f, 6f 2) (sft, gd, hrd)
Currently above-average filly. Turf high 79 (began Aug).
*B Palling [0-3] Derek D & Mrs Jean P Clee.

HIRAPOUR (IRE) **RR 96f** 5180a[10]
4 b g Kahyasi 12.9f **(74)** - Himaya (IRE) (Mouktar)
Form - 0130000
2000 Turf 1-7: (11f, 12f 1-3, 14f 2, 16f) (sft, g-s, gd 4)
Very useful gelding, effective 10 to 14f, acts on gd, has worn blink-

ers. Turf high 96 - 3rd of 5 getting 4lb from Royal Rebel (24 May Leopardstown 14f gd RF 1565a) - also 1st of 8 giving 5lb to Morning Breeze (15 Apr Listowel RF 0780a). Inconsistent. A decent Irish stayer, he ran his best race of last term when third to Royal Rebel and Enzeli at Leopardstown. Struggled in handicaps under welter weights afterwards.
**D K Weld in IRE [1-7] Michael Watt (from J Oxx in IRE [1-2] Aug 1999).*

HISAR (IRE) BHB 60f **RR 4f** 3705[16]

7 br g Doyoun 10.7f **(69)** - Himaya (IRE) (Mouktar)
Form - 0
Record 2000 - 1st:0 2nd:0 3rd:0 Ran:1
Pre2000 - 1st:1 2nd:2 3rd:0 Ran:7
Win Prizemoney £3,425 *Total Prizemoney* £5,395
Wins 1996 Oct Leopar (G-S) 10f 70 <
2000 Turf 0-1: (10f) (frm)
Very poor gelding. Inconsistent.
**P C Ritchens [3-20] R Catton (from C P E Brooks [0-8] Spt 1997).*

HISTORIC (IRE) BHB 73f **RR 77f** 2153[8]

4 b c Sadler's Wells (USA) 11.3f **(87)** - Urjwan (USA) (Seattle Slew (USA)) 9.4f **(76)**
Form - 8308
Record 2000 - 1st:0 2nd:0 3rd:1 Ran:4
Pre2000 - 1st:0 2nd:2 3rd:0 Ran:3
Win Prizemoney £0 *Total Prizemoney* £3,520
2000 Turf 0-4: (14f, 16f 2, 20f) (g-s 2, gd 2)
Scopey, above-average colt, effective 12f, acts on sft to g-s, has worn blinkers. Turf high 77.
**W J Haggas [0-7] Highclere Thoroughbred Racing Ltd.*

HIT THE TRAIL (IRE) **RR 49f** 746[4]

2 b f Treasure Kay 6.5f **(53)** - Shoot The Dealer (IRE) (Common Grounds)
Form - 4
Record 2000 - 1st:0 2nd:0 3rd:0 Ran:1
Win Prizemoney £0 *Total Prizemoney* £242
2000 Turf 0-1: (5f) (sft)
Currently moderate filly. **D Carroll [0-1] Sam Murphy.*

HOBART JUNCTION (IRE) BHB 60f **RR 52f** 3322[9]

5 ch g Classic Secret (USA) 8.8f **(56)** - Art Duo (Artaius (USA)) 9f **(69)**
Form - 0
Record 2000 - 1st:0 2nd:0 3rd:0 Ran:1
Pre2000 - 1st:1 2nd:1 3rd:1 Ran:10
Win Prizemoney £2,248 *Total Prizemoney* £3,617
Wins 1998 Jly Hamilt (FRM) C 9.2f 69 <
2000 Turf 0-1: (12f) (g-f)
Fair gelding, has worn blinkers. Consistent.
**J A T de Giles [0-11] Gavin MacEchern (from S C Williams [1-10] Jly 1998).*

HOBB ALWAHTAN **RR 79f** 1307[5]

3 ch c Machiavellian (USA) 9.8f **(83)** - Colorado Dancer (Shareef Dancer (USA)) 9.9f **(73)**
Form - 5
Record 2000 - 1st:0 2nd:0 3rd:0 Ran:1
2000 Turf 0-1: (8f) (gd)
Scopey, currently above-average colt. (1st run) - 5th of 15 to Takrir (19 May Newbury 8f gd RF 1307). **S bin Suroor [0-1] Godolphin.*

HOBO **RR 65f** 4362[4]

2 b g Timeless Times (USA) 6.1f **(56)** - Skiddaw Bird (Bold Owl) 8.5f **(45)**
Form - 0704
Record 2000 - 1st:0 2nd:0 3rd:0 Ran:4
Win Prizemoney £0 *Total Prizemoney* £234
2000 Turf 0-4: (5f, 7f 2, 8f) (gd, g-f, frm 2)
Average gelding. Turf high 64.
**D W Barker [0-4] Alba Racing Syndicate.*

HOH GEM BHB 42f48a **RR 47f 48a** 4875[7]

4 b g Be My Chief (USA) 10.2f **(62)** - Jennies' Gem (Sayf El Arab (USA)) 7.1f **(54)**
Form - 01410204607
Record 2000 - 1st:2 2nd:1 3rd:0 Ran:11
Pre2000 - 1st:0 2nd:0 3rd:0 Ran:4
Win Prizemoney £4,075 *Total Prizemoney* £4,849
Wins * 2000 May Warwic (HVY) H 7.7f 44 47
* 2000 *May Southw (STD) H 8f 40 49* <
2000 Turf 1-8: (8f 1-4, 10f 2, 11f, 12f) (hvy 1-2, g-s, gd 2, g-f 2, frm)
2000 AW 1-3: (8f 1-3) (Fibr 1-3)
Fair gelding, effective 8 to 10f, best at 8f, acts on hvy to g-f - acts on Fibr, prefers left handed tracks, prefers tight tracks. Turf high 47 - 1st of 16 getting 15lb from Swing Along (27 May Warwick RF 1509). AW high 53 - 2nd of 9 getting 22lb from Guilsborough (30 Jun Southwell 8f Fibr RF 2420) - also 1st of 16 getting 5lb from Midnight Watch (8 May Southwell RF 1096).
**B R Millman [2-14] Brian Lovrey (from Miss Gay Kelleway [0-1] Jun 1999).*

HOH HOH SEVEN (IRE) BHB 48f **RR 55f** 4923[12]

4 b g College Chapel - Fighting Run (Runnett) 7f **(59)**
Form - 035700
Record 2000 - 1st:0 2nd:0 3rd:1 Ran:6
Pre2000 - 1st:0 2nd:0 3rd:1 Ran:10
Win Prizemoney £0 *Total Prizemoney* £1,584
2000 Turf 0-5: (7f 4, 8f) (sft, gd 3, g-f) 2000 AW 0-1: (16f) (Equi)
Rangy, fair gelding, effective 8f, acts on frm, has worn blinkers. Turf high 55. Inconsistent.
**P Mitchell [0-2] D W Smith (from N E Berry [0-10] Jun 2000).*

HOLBECK (IRE) BHB 30f **RR 26f** 2290[5]

2 b f Efisio 7.7f **(69)** - Autumn Fall (USA) (Sanglamore (USA))
Form - 655
Record 2000 - 1st:0 2nd:0 3rd:0 Ran:3
2000 Turf 0-3: (5f 2, 6f) (g-s, g-f 2)
Currently little account filly. Turf high 26.
**N Tinkler [0-3] & Mrs G Middlebrook.*

HOLDING COURT BHB 124f **RR 123f** 5094a[5]

3 b c Hernando (FR) - Indian Love Song (Be My Guest (USA)) 9.3f **(67)**
Form - 111655
Record 2000 - 1st:3 2nd:0 3rd:0 Ran:6
Pre2000 - 1st:1 2nd:1 3rd:0 Ran:4
Win Prizemoney £273,489 *Total Prizemoney* £294,438
Wins * 2000 Jun Chanti (HVY) G1 12f 123+ <
* 2000 May Longch (GD) G3 12f 104
* 2000 Apr Haydoc (HVY) H 10.5f 97 104+
1999 Oct Haydoc (HVY) 8.1f 89++
2000 Turf 3-6: (11f 1-1, 12f 2-5) (hvy 1-2, sft, g-s 1-1, gd 1-2)
Very high-class colt, effective 12f, acts on gd. Turf high 123 - 1st of 14 from Lord Flasheart (4 Jun Chantilly RF 1825a). Inconsistent. Trained by Brian Meehan as a juvenile, he showed useful form but disappointed in the Racing Post Trophy. He landed a Haydock handicap on his first start for Michael Jarvis before running away with a Longchamp Group Three. His win in the Prix du Jockey-Club next time was a revelation, as he made all the running to slam his field by six lengths. Well beaten in the Irish Derby after being supplemented for £85,000, he did not seem to handle the track in the Grosser Preis von Baden, and flopped in a Group Two at Longchamp. His best form was shown with plenty of cut in the ground. **M A Jarvis [3-6] (from B J Meehan [1-4] Oct 1999).*

HO LENG (IRE) BHB 107f **RR 108f** 4698[10]

5 ch g Statoblest 6.4f **(63)** - Indigo Blue (IRE) (Bluebird (USA)) 7.5f **(69)**
Form - 3030233450
Record 2000 - 1st:0 2nd:1 3rd:4 Ran:10
Pre2000 - 1st:4 2nd:3 3rd:1 Ran:20
Win Prizemoney £68,126 *Total Prizemoney* £106,083
Wins * 1999 Spt York (G-F) H 6f 101 103
* 1998 Jly Newmar (FRM) H 7f 102 105 <
* 1998 May York (GD) H 7f 95 100
* 1997 Aug Hamilt (G-F) 6f 88+
2000 Turf 0-10: (6f 5, 7f 3, 8f 2) (gd, g-f 7, frm 2)
Pattern-class gelding, effective 6 to 8f, best at 6f, acts on gd to frm, best on g-f, excels at Newbury and does well at Newmarket. Turf high 108 - 4th of 22 giving 20lb to Compton Banker (6 Spt Doncaster 6f gd RF 4258). Effective from six furlongs to a mile, this former front-runner now goes well when held-up behind a fast pace but needs the race to go his way. Always one to reckon with in handicap company, but not quite up to Pattern class. Best on firm ground. **Miss L A Perratt [4-30] Alan Guthrie.*

HOLLY BLUE BHB 92f **RR 97df** 2151[30]
4 ch f Bluebird (USA) 7.9f **(71)** - Nettle (Kris) 9.5f **(73)**
Form - 00
Record 2000 - 1st:0 2nd:0 3rd:0 Ran:2
Pre2000 - 1st:2 2nd:2 3rd:0 Ran:11
Win Prizemoney £16,904 *Total Prizemoney* £24,322
Wins * 1999 Jun Ascot (G-F) LH 8f 84 87 <
* 1999 Jun Bath (GD) H 8f 75 81+
2000 Turf 0-2: (7f, 8f) (gd 2)
Scopey, very useful filly, effective 7 to 8f, best at 7f, acts on gd to frm. Turf high 49. **R Charlton [2-13] The Queen.*

HOLY ISLAND RR 66+f 5058[7]
3 b f Deploy 11.4f **(67)** - Bells **(57f)** (Sadler's Wells (USA)) 10f **(76)**
Form - 37
Record 2000 - 1st:0 2nd:0 3rd:1 Ran:2
Win Prizemoney £0 *Total Prizemoney* £608
2000 Turf 0-2: (10f 2) (sft, g-s)
Scopey, currently average filly. Turf high 66 (began Spt).
**L M Cumani [0-2] G Shiel.*

HOMBRE RR 44f 3314[9]
5 ch g Shernazar 11.8f **(71)** - Delray Jet (USA) (Northjet) 10.3f **(74)**
Form - 460
Record 2000 - 1st:0 2nd:0 3rd:0 Ran:3
Pre2000 - 1st:0 2nd:0 3rd:0 Ran:3
Win Prizemoney £0 *Total Prizemoney* £319
2000 Turf 0-3: (11f, 14f 2) (g-f 3)
Moderate gelding. Turf high 44.
**M D Hammond [0-9] R D Bickenson (from J W Watts [0-3] Spt 1997).*

HOME COUNTIES (IRE) BHB 36f **RR 45f** 4431[4]
11 ch g Ela-Mana-Mou 12.7f **(72)** - Safe Home (Home Guard (USA)) 9.3f **(66)**
Form - 077064
Record 2000 - 1st:0 2nd:0 3rd:0 Ran:6
Pre2000 - 1st:1 2nd:2 3rd:2 Ran:23
Win Prizemoney £3,468 *Total Prizemoney* £10,741
2000 Turf 0-6: (12f, 13f, 14f, 16f, 17f 2) (gd 5, frm)
Moderate gelding, effective 14 to 17f, best at 14f, acts on g-s to gd, best on gd, has worn blinkers, prefers left handed tracks. Turf high 45. Consistent.
**J Hetherton [0-18] Ms A Hartley (from D Moffatt [6-47] Spt 1997).*

HOME FORCE BHB 63f **RR 54f** 2356[1]
3 b g Chaddleworth (IRE) - Breed Reference (Reference Point) 6.8f **(70)**
Form - 0061
Record 2000 - 1st:1 2nd:0 3rd:0 Ran:4
Pre2000 - 1st:0 2nd:0 3rd:0 Ran:2
Win Prizemoney £1,951 *Total Prizemoney* £2,215
Wins * **2000** Jun Warwic (G-F) S 10.5f 54 <
2000 Turf 1-4: (7f, 11f 1-2, 12f) (gd 2, g-f 1-2)
Lengthy, fair gelding. Turf high 54.
**C F Wall [1-6] Induna Racing Partners.*

HOMELIFE (IRE) BHB 74f **RR 84f** 5157[4]
2 b g Persian Bold 10f **(69)** - Share The Vision (Vision (USA)) 9f **(64)**
Form - 64766284
Record 2000 - 1st:0 2nd:1 3rd:0 Ran:8
Win Prizemoney £0 *Total Prizemoney* £1,199
2000 Turf 0-8: (5f, 6f, 7f 3, 8f 2, 10f) (sft, gd 4, g-f 3)
Decent gelding. Turf high 84.
**P W D'Arcy [0-4] Mrs Jean Mitchell (from D Sasse [0-4] Jly 2000).*

HOMESTEAD BHB 58f54a **RR 39f 54a** 4658a[8]
6 ch g Indian Ridge 7.6f **(74)** - Bertrade (Homeboy) 6.6f **(55)**
Form - 148
Record 2000 - 1st:0 2nd:0 3rd:0 Ran:2
Pre2000 - 1st:6 2nd:5 3rd:3 Ran:41
Win Prizemoney £15,841 *Total Prizemoney* £21,721
Wins 1999 *Nov Southw (STD) H 12f 52 54*
1999 *May Wolver (STD) H 9.4f 48 54*
1999 Apr Leices (HVY) H 10f 53 65+ <
1999 Apr Pontef (Sft) H 10f 50 61
1997 Aug Bright (FRM) 8f 57
1997 Aug Bright (GD) H 7f 45 51
2000 Turf 0-1: (16f) (sft) 2000 AW 0-1: (12f) (Equi)
Fair gelding, effective 10f, acts on sft to frm, best on frm, has worn blinkers, favours tight tracks, excels at Sandown.
**E McNamara in IRE [0-6] E McNamara (from R Hannon [6-43] Jan 2000).*

HONEST BORDERER BHB 79f **RR 84f** 4934[29]
5 b g Selkirk (USA) 7.9f **(76)** - Tell No Lies (High Line) 10.3f **(70)**
Form - 614340
Record 2000 - 1st:1 2nd:0 3rd:1 Ran:6
Pre2000 - 1st:1 2nd:1 3rd:3 Ran:14
Win Prizemoney £13,632 *Total Prizemoney* £21,924
Wins * **2000** Jun Lingfi (G-F) H 7.6f 77 84 <
* 1998 Aug Ripon (G-F) H 9f 78 81
2000 Turf 1-6: (7f, 8f 1-5) (g-s, gd 2, g-f, frm 1-2)
Decent gelding, effective 8 to 10f, best at 8f, acts on gd to frm, best on frm, has worn blinkers. Turf high 84 - 1st of 11 getting 3lb from Rich In Love (25 Jun Lingfield RF 2260). Consistent. Returned to winning form in quite a decent Lingfield handicap in June. Best on fast ground, he is suited by hold-up tactics.
**J L Dunlop [2-20] Mrs A Johnstone.*

HONEST LADY (USA) RR 5328a[2]
4 br f Seattle Slew (USA) 7.8f **(64)** - Toussaud (USA) (El Gran Senor (USA)) 9.6f **(76)**
Form - 2
2000 AW 0-1: (6f) (Dirt)
Strong, currently high-class filly. (1st run) - 2nd of 14 getting 5lb from Kona Gold (4 Nov Churchill Downs 6f Dirt RF 5328a).
**R Frankel in USA [0-1] Juddmonte Farms.*

HONEST OBSESSION (IRE) RR 33f 5309[15]
2 b c Sadler's Wells (USA) 11.3f **(87)** - Valley of Gold (FR) **(102f)** (Shirley Heights) 10.3f **(74)**
Form - 0
Record 2000 - 1st:0 2nd:0 3rd:0 Ran:1
2000 Turf 0-1: (7f) (g-s)
Currently very moderate colt. **B W Hills [0-1] Maktoum Al Maktoum.*

HONEST VILLAIN (USA) BHB 54f **RR 37f** 4205[14]
3 b g St Jovite (USA) 11.8f **(75)** - Villandry (USA) (Lyphard's Wish (FR)) 9f **(74)**
Form - 0
Record 2000 - 1st:0 2nd:0 3rd:0 Ran:1
Pre2000 - 1st:0 2nd:0 3rd:1 Ran:3
Win Prizemoney £0 *Total Prizemoney* £499
2000 Turf 0-1: (13f) (frm)
Leggy, very moderate gelding. **P D Evans [0-4] Colin Booth.*

HONEST WARNING BHB 70f **RR 74f** 4812[12]
3 b c Mtoto 11.5f **(71)** - Peryllys **(62f)** (Warning)
Form - 42450
Record 2000 - 1st:0 2nd:1 3rd:0 Ran:5
Win Prizemoney £0 *Total Prizemoney* £1,723
2000 Turf 0-5: (6f 2, 7f 2, 8f) (g-s, frm 3, hrd)
Unfurnished, above-average colt. Turf high 74 (1st run) - 4th of 16 to Mister Superb (25 Jun Lingfield 6f frm RF 2258).
**B Smart [0-5] Lacey/Buckham.*

HONESTY FAIR BHB 95f **RR 97+f** 4735[1]
3 b f Reprimand 8.2f **(63)** - Truthful Image **(68df 70a)** (Reesh)
Form - 41180046611
Record 2000 - 1st:4 2nd:0 3rd:0 Ran:11
Pre2000 - 1st:0 2nd:0 3rd:1 Ran:4
Win Prizemoney £37,024 *Total Prizemoney* £38,801
Wins * **2000** Spt Newmar (GD) H 6f 84 97 <
* **2000** Aug York (GD) H 5f 80 86
* **2000** May Thirsk (GD) H 5f 72 87+
* **2000** May Beverl (G-F) 5f 74
2000 Turf 4-11: (5f 3-9, 6f 1-2) (gd 2-6, g-f, frm 1-3, hrd 1-1)
Strong, very useful filly, effective 5 to 6f, acts on gd. Turf high 97 - 1st of 11 getting 9lb from Areydha (29 Spt Newmarket RF 4735). Showed progressive form to win twice in May and was not disgraced from a higher mark afterwards, ultimately scoring in a decent handicap at the York Ebor meeting, and showing six furlongs was within his capabilities at Newmarket the following month. **J A Glover [4-15] P and S Partnership.*

HONEY HOUSE (IRE) BHB 30a **RR 5f** 3187[11]
4 gr f Paris House 5.9f **(64)** - Heather Honey (Insan (USA))
Form - 7070
Record 2000 - 1st:0 2nd:0 3rd:0 Ran:3
Pre2000 - 1st:0 2nd:0 3rd:0 Ran:2
2000 AW 0-3: (6f, 8f, 12f) (Fibr 3)
Neat, poor filly. AW high 17. **A W Carroll [0-5] R T C Racing.*

HONG KONG BHB 41f **RR 51f** 1601[10]
3 b g Sri Pekan (USA) - Sheryl Lynn (Miller's Mate) 7f **(63)**
Form - 0000
Record 2000 - 1st:0 2nd:0 3rd:0 Ran:4
Pre2000 - 1st:0 2nd:1 3rd:0 Ran:6
Win Prizemoney £0 *Total Prizemoney* £811
2000 Turf 0-4: (7f, 8f 3) (gd 3, frm)
Fair gelding, effective 8f, acts on frm, has worn blinkers. Turf high 37. **M W Easterby [0-10] Guy Reed.*

HONOURS LIST (IRE) RR 110f 4952a[3]
2 b c Danehill (USA) 9.1f **(79)** - Gold Script (FR) (Script Ohio (USA))
Form - 1123
2000 Turf 2-4: (6f 1-1, 7f 1-2, 8f) (sft, g-s 1-1, gd 1-2)
Group-class colt. Turf high 110 - 3rd of 7 to Okawango (8 Oct Longchamp 8f sft RF 4952a). Winner of his first two starts, he stepped down in trip to take the Railway Stakes at the Curragh. Runner-up to Tobougg in the Salamandre, before finishing third in the Grand Criterium. **A P O'Brien in IRE [2-4] Mrs John Magnier.*

HO PANG YAU BHB 68f **RR 63f** 4447[6]
2 b gr c Pivotal - La Cabrilla (Carwhite) 7.2f **(61)**
Form - 7526
Record 2000 - 1st:0 2nd:1 3rd:0 Ran:4
Win Prizemoney £0 *Total Prizemoney* £1,055
2000 Turf 0-4: (6f, 7f, 8f 2) (gd, frm 3)
Average colt. Turf high 63 (began Jly).
**Miss L A Perratt [0-4] Alan Guthrie.*

HOPEFUL RR 41f 2108[8]
3 b f Elmaamul (USA) 8.1f **(70)** - Quaver (USA) (The Minstrel (CAN)) 10f **(72)**
Form - 8
Record 2000 - 1st:0 2nd:0 3rd:0 Ran:1
2000 Turf 0-1: (10f) (frm)
Neat, currently moderate filly. **H Candy [0-1] Girsonfield Ltd.*

HOPEFUL HENRY BHB 45f41a **RR 44f 41a** 4825[14]
4 ch g Cadeaux Genereux 7.9f **(76)** - Fernlea (USA) (Sir Ivor) 10.2f **(70)**
Form - 06080
Record 2000 - 1st:0 2nd:0 3rd:0 Ran:4
Pre2000 - 1st:0 2nd:0 3rd:0 Ran:1
2000 Turf 0-4: (5f 2, 6f 2) (gd, g-f, frm 2)
Unfurnished, moderate gelding. Turf high 44 (began Aug).
**G L Moore [0-5] Danny Bloor.*

HOPEFUL LIGHT BHB 111f **RR 110f** 4698[1]
3 b g Warning 8.1f **(77)** - Hope (IRE) (Dancing Brave (USA)) 8.4f **(76)**
Form - 481141
Record 2000 - 1st:3 2nd:0 3rd:0 Ran:6
Pre2000 - 1st:1 2nd:0 3rd:0 Ran:1
Win Prizemoney £40,104 *Total Prizemoney* £42,562

Wins								
*** 2000**	Spt	Newmar	(GD)	L	8f		110	<
*** 2000**	Aug	Salisb	(G-F)	L	8f		103	
*** 2000**	Jun	Salisb	(G-F)		7f		103	
* 1999	Nov	Doncas	(SFT)		7f		81+	

2000 Turf 3-6: (6f, 7f 1-2, 8f 2-2, 9f) (g-s, gd 2, g-f 2-2, frm 1-1)
Scopey, Group-class gelding, effective 6 to 8f, best at 8f, acts on gd to frm, best on g-f. Turf high 110 - 1st of 12 from On The Ridge (28 Spt Newmarket RF 4698) - also 1st of 4 getting 7lb from Late Night Out (11 Aug Salisbury RF 3566). Developed into a useful performer at a mile, successful in listed races at Salisbury and Newmarket. He is a front runner. **J H M Gosden [4-7] K Abdulla.*

HOPGROVE BHB 50f **RR 49f** 2033[9]
2 b br f So Factual (USA) - Awham (USA) (Lear Fan (USA)) 8.5f **(73)**
Form - 660350
Record 2000 - 1st:0 2nd:0 3rd:1 Ran:6
Win Prizemoney £0 *Total Prizemoney* £445
2000 Turf 0-5: (5f 3, 6f 2) (gd 3, g-f, hrd) 2000 AW 0-1: (5f) (Fibr)
Moderate filly. Turf high 49. **M Brittain [0-6] Mel Brittain.*

HORMUZ (IRE) BHB 56f67a **RR 60f 67a** 4272[6]
4 b g Hamas (IRE) 8f **(72)** - Balqis (USA) (Advocator) 10.9f **(80)**
Form - 000087185526
Record 2000 - 1st:1 2nd:1 3rd:0 Ran:12
Pre2000 - 1st:4 2nd:2 3rd:0 Ran:12
Win Prizemoney £18,279 *Total Prizemoney* £22,202

Wins								
*** 2000**	Jly	Ripon	(G-F)	S	8f		61	
1999	Jly	Beverl	(SFT)	H	8.5f	81	86	<
1999	Jun	Ripon	(G-F)		10f		79	
1999	*Mar*	*Lingfi*	*(STD)*	*H*	*10f*	*78*	*84*	
1999	*Jan*	*Lingfi*	*(STD)*		*10f*		*72*	

2000 Turf 1-12: (8f 1-7, 9f, 10f 4) (gd 2, g-f 1-7, frm, hrd 2)
Rangy, decent gelding, effective 8 to 10f, best at 10f, acts on gd to hrd - acts on Equi, likes right handed tracks, likes tight tracks, excels at Lingfield, does well at Ripon. Turf high 61.
**J M Bradley [1-12] E A Hayward (from M Johnston [4-12] Oct 1999).*

HORNBEAM RR 96f 2151[27]
6 b h Rich Charlie 5.9f **(50)** - Thinkluckybelucky (Maystreak) 8.7f **(53)**
Form - 022410
Record 2000 - 1st:1 2nd:2 3rd:0 Ran:6
Pre2000 - 1st:2 2nd:0 3rd:2 Ran:22
Win Prizemoney £22,532 *Total Prizemoney* £46,560

Wins								
*** 2000**	Jun	Pontef	(SFT)	H	6f	93	90	
* 1998	Mar	Doncas	(GD)	L	8f		107	<
* 1997	May	Newbur	(SFT)		7.3f		86	

2000 Turf 1-6: (6f 1-2, 7f, 8f 3) (g-s, gd 1-5)
Very useful horse, effective 6 to 8f, acts on g-s to frm. Turf high 96 - 2nd of 22 giving 4lb to Bold King (3 May Ascot 7f gd RF 1001) - also 1st of 5 giving 13lb to Easter Ogil (4 Jun Pontefract RF 1698). Inconsistent. He was only just touched off when stepped back to six furlongs in soft ground at Windsor on his second start of the season, but landed a five-runner event under similar conditions at Pontefract in June. Clearly useful, but a bit frustrating and difficult to win with. **J R Jenkins [3-28] K C Payne.*

HORNBY BOY RR 33f 5319[15]
2 b g Dolphin Street (FR) - Miss Walsh **(38f)** (Distant Relative)
Form - 0
Record 2000 - 1st:0 2nd:0 3rd:0 Ran:1
2000 Turf 0-1: (6f) (sft)
Currently very moderate gelding. **J Hetherton [0-1] Mrs C A Brown.*

HORTA (IRE) BHB 56f **RR 67f** 3490[14]
3 b g Distinctly North (USA) 7.4f **(63)** - Roouan Girl (IRE) (Tremblant)
Form - 0
Record 2000 - 1st:0 2nd:0 3rd:0 Ran:1
Pre2000 - 1st:0 2nd:0 3rd:0 Ran:5
2000 Turf 0-1: (10f) (frm)
Workmanlike, average gelding.
**B I Case [0-1] Mrs Betty Barrett & Mrs Anne Charlton (from G C Bravery [0-5] Spt 1999).*

HORTON DANCER BHB 34f **RR 48f** 4000[5]
3 b g Rambo Dancer (CAN) 8.4f **(59)** - Horton Lady **(43+f)** (Midyan (USA)) 6f **(60)**
Form - 6704803035
Record 2000 - 1st:0 2nd:0 3rd:2 Ran:10
Pre2000 - 1st:0 2nd:0 3rd:0 Ran:1
Win Prizemoney £0 *Total Prizemoney* £816
2000 Turf 0-8: (10f 2, 12f 3, 14f 2, 16f) (g-s, gd, g-f 5, hrd) 2000 AW 0-2: (12f 2) (Fibr 2)
Leggy, moderate gelding, effective 12 to 14f, acts on g-f, has worn blinkers, favours tight tracks. Turf high 48. AW high 44.
**M Brittain [0-11] Robert Cook.*

HOSSRUM (IRE) BHB 77f **RR 68f** 3268[3]
2 br c Definite Article - Petite Maxine **(63f)** (Sharpo) 7.7f **(59)**
Form - 673
Record 2000 - 1st:0 2nd:0 3rd:1 Ran:3
Win Prizemoney £0 *Total Prizemoney* £505
2000 Turf 0-3: (6f, 7f 2) (gd 2, frm)
Currently average colt. Turf high 68. **E A L Dunlop [0-3] Ahmed Ali.*

HOTELGENIE DOT COM BHB 100f **RR 95+f** 4595[3]

2 gr ch f Selkirk (USA) 7.9f **(76)** - Birch Creek (Carwhite) 7.2f **(61)**
Form - 1223
Record 2000 - 1st:1 2nd:2 3rd:1 Ran:4
Win Prizemoney £6,955 *Total Prizemoney* £66,795
Wins * 2000 Jly Sandow (GD) 7.1f 79+ <
2000 Turf 1-4: (7f 1-3, 8f) (gd 1-3, g-f)
Very useful filly. Turf high 95 (began Jly) - 2nd of 12 to Silver Jorden (27 Jly Sandown 7f g-f RF 3153). She put up a fine performance to beat some previous winners in a Sandown novice stakes on her debut and has finished runner-up in a listed race at Sandown and the Group One Moyglare Stud Stakes. A third in the Fillies' Mile when not getting the best of runs suggests she may be a lively outsider for the 1000 Guineas.
**M R Channon [1-4] Derek D & Mrs Jean P Clee.*

HOTELIERS PRIDE BHB 50f **RR 58f** 3575[5]

3 b g Lugana Beach 7f **(63)** - Pride of Britain (CAN) **(64f 53a)** (Linkage (USA)) 9.1f **(82)**
Form - 0505
Record 2000 - 1st:0 2nd:0 3rd:0 Ran:4
Pre2000 - 1st:0 2nd:0 3rd:0 Ran:2
2000 Turf 0-3: (8f, 12f 2) (gd, g-f, hrd) 2000 AW 0-1: (15f) (Fibr)
Fair gelding. Turf high 58. **L G Cottrell [0-6] Pride of Britain Ltd.*

HOT ICE (IRE) BHB 49f43a **RR 52f 43a** 1258[12]

3 b f Petardia 8.2f **(58)** - Blackpool Belle (The Brianstan) 5.9f **(55)**
Form - 000
Record 2000 - 1st:0 2nd:0 3rd:0 Ran:3
Pre2000 - 1st:1 2nd:0 3rd:1 Ran:6
Win Prizemoney £4,260 *Total Prizemoney* £4,772
Wins 1999 Spt Mussel (G-F) H 5f 53 52 <
2000 Turf 0-1: (5f) (g-f) 2000 AW 0-2: (5f, 7f) (Fibr 2)
Light-framed, fair filly, effective 5f, acts on frm. AW high 29. Becoming disappointing.
**P W D'Arcy [0-3] Mrs Jean Mitchell (from H Morrison [1-6] Spt 1999).*

HOT LEGS BHB 32f30a **RR 31f 30a** 2195[16]

4 b f Sizzling Melody 6.3f **(49)** - Ra Ra Girl (Shack (USA)) 5.8f **(53)**
Form - 00545583000
Record 2000 - 1st:0 2nd:0 3rd:1 Ran:9
Pre2000 - 1st:0 2nd:0 3rd:0 Ran:12
Win Prizemoney £0 *Total Prizemoney* £364
2000 Turf 0-1: (6f) (g-s) 2000 AW 0-8: (5f 2, 6f 4, 7f 2) (Fibr 8)
Scopey, very moderate filly, has worn blinkers. AW high 35.
**B A McMahon [0-21] D J Allen.*

HOT OPINION RR 93f 1455a[16]

3 b f Salse (USA) 10.9f **(71)** - Tudorealm (USA) (Palace Music (USA))
Form - 0
2000 Turf 0-1: (11f) (gd)
Useful filly. **M Guarnieri in ITY [0-2].*

HOT PANTS BHB 70f **RR 70f** 3552[4]

2 ch f Rudimentary (USA) 8.2f **(66)** - True Precision **(61f 59a)** (Presidium)
Form - 053064
Record 2000 - 1st:0 2nd:0 3rd:1 Ran:6
Win Prizemoney £0 *Total Prizemoney* £816
2000 Turf 0-6: (5f 6) (gd, g-f 2, frm 3)
Above-average filly, effective 5f, acts on g-f. Turf high 70 - 3rd of 8 getting 5lb from Warlingham (19 Jly Yarmouth 5f g-f RF 2947).
**K T Ivory [0-6] K T Ivory.*

HOT POTATO BHB 27a **RR 43f** 5126[9]

4 b c Roman Warrior - My Song of Songs **(7f)** (Norwick (USA)) 7.2f **(56)**
Form - 50468757206050
Record 2000 - 1st:0 2nd:1 3rd:0 Ran:13
Pre2000 - 1st:0 2nd:0 3rd:0 Ran:12
Win Prizemoney £0 *Total Prizemoney* £1,260
2000 Turf 0-9: (7f 2, 8f 2, 9f 3, 10f, 11f) (hvy, g-s 2, gd 3, g-f 3) 2000 AW 0-4: (8f, 9f, 11f, 12f) (Fibr 4)
Moderate colt, effective 6 to 10f, acts on gd - acts on Fibr, has worn blinkers, likes left handed tracks, likes tight tracks. Turf high 43 - 2nd of 13 giving 18lb to Floating Ember (4 Jun Pontefract 10f gd RF 1695). AW high 29.
**J S Wainwright [0-17] Mrs S A Donald (from C Smith [0-8] Jan 1999).*

HOTSPUR STREET BHB 30f47a **RR 47a** 175[10]

8 b g Cadeaux Genereux 7.9f **(76)** - Excellent Alibi (USA) (Exceller (USA)) 12.5f **(74)**
Form - 0
Record 2000 - 1st:0 2nd:0 3rd:0 Ran:1
Pre2000 - 1st:0 2nd:2 3rd:3 Ran:17
Win Prizemoney £0 *Total Prizemoney* £4,452
2000 AW 0-1: (12f) (Fibr)
Very poor gelding, has worn blinkers.
**E L James [1-21] Mrs D C Samworth (from M W Easterby [0-7] Jun 1996).*

HOT TIN ROOF (IRE) BHB 110f **RR 109f** 3828[8]

4 b f Thatching 7.8f **(69)** - No Reservations (IRE) (Commanche Run) 8.5f **(58)**
Form - 211236148
Record 2000 - 1st:3 2nd:2 3rd:1 Ran:9
Pre2000 - 1st:1 2nd:1 3rd:2 Ran:5
Win Prizemoney £48,447 *Total Prizemoney* £70,196
Wins * 2000 Jly York (GD) L 6f 109 <
*** 2000** May Nottin (GD) L 6.1f 105
*** 2000** May Lingfi (G-S) L 7f 102
1999 Jun Newcas (GD) 6f 74+
2000 Turf 3-9: (6f 2-5, 7f 1-4) (g-s 1-2, gd 1-3, g-f 1-2, frm, hrd)
Unfurnished, Pattern-class filly, effective 6 to 7f, best at 6f, acts on g-s to frm, best on gd, excels at Lingfield. Turf high 100 4th of 11 getting 5lb from Bold Edge (6 Aug Deauville 7f gd RF 3542a) - also 1st of 9 from Cassandra Go (14 Jly York RF 2822). Consistent. Progressed into a useful sprinter, successful three times at listed level and beaten under two lengths in the Group One Prix Maurice de Gheest.
**T D Easterby [3-9] Giles Pritchard-Gordon (from J E Banks [1-5] Spt 1999).*

HOUNDS OF LOVE (IRE) BHB 50f45a **RR 57f 45a** 4788a[14]

3 b f Foxhound (USA) - Foolish Lady (USA) (Foolish Pleasure (USA)) 8.9f **(72)**
Form - 033370
Record 2000 - 1st:0 2nd:0 3rd:3 Ran:6
Pre2000 - 1st:0 2nd:0 3rd:0 Ran:1
Win Prizemoney £0 *Total Prizemoney* £843
2000 Turf 0-3: (7f, 9f, 16f) (hvy, sft, gd) 2000 AW 0-3: (8f, 11f, 12f) (Equi, Fibr 2)
Light-framed, fair filly, effective 11f, - acts on Fibr. Turf high 57. AW high 48 - 3rd of 11 getting 12lb from Pickens (22 May Southwell 11f Fibr RF 1371).
**A Slattery in IRE [0-2] John Bernard O'Connor (from R Guest [0-5] May 2000).*

HOUSEMASTER (IRE) BHB 117f **RR 121df** 815a[3]

4 b c Rudimentary (USA) 8.2f **(66)** - Glenarff (USA) (Irish River (FR)) 8.6f **(78)**
Form - 3
2000 Turf 0-1: (10f) (gd)
Scopey, very high-class colt, effective 10 to 12f, acts on gd. (1st run) - 3rd of 13 to Industrialist (15 Apr Sha Tin 10f gd RF 0815a).
**I Allan in HK [0-1] (from M L W Bell [1-10] Jly 1999).*

HOUSE OF DREAMS BHB 48f41a **RR 53f 41a** 4750[3]

8 b g Darshaan 11.9f **(81)** -Helens Dreamgirl (Caerleon (USA)) 8.6f **(71)**
Form - 0123
Record 2000 - 1st:1 2nd:1 3rd:1 Ran:4
Pre2000 - 1st:3 2nd:2 3rd:3 Ran:26
Win Prizemoney £16,133 *Total Prizemoney* £22,709
Wins * 2000 Aug Redcar (FRM) S 14.1f 42
1998 Spt Thirsk (GD) H 12f 62 65 <
1998 Jly Carlis (G-F) H 14.1f 59 63
1998 Jun Catter (G-S) H 12f 54 56
2000 Turf 1-4: (12f, 14f 1-2, 16f) (g-s, gd, g-f 1-2)
Fair gelding, effective 12 to 16f, best at 12f, acts on g-s to hrd, best on gd, favours left handed tracks, prefers tight tracks. Turf high 51 (began Aug) - 3rd of 16 getting 11lb from Mr Fortywinks (30 Spt Redcar 14f gd RF 4750). Consistent.
**Mrs M Reveley [2-10] J & M Leisure / Unos Restaurant (from G M Moore [7-42] Oct 1999).*

HOUSEPARTY (IRE) RR 56f 5023[3]
2 b br c Grand Lodge (USA) - Special Display (Welsh Pageant) 10f **(65)**
Form - 3
Record 2000 - 1st:0 2nd:0 3rd:1 Ran:1
Win Prizemoney £0 *Total Prizemoney* £582
2000 Turf 0-1: (7f) (g-s)
Currently fair colt.
**Sir Michael Stoute [0-1] Highclere Thoroughbred Racing Ltd.*

HOUT BAY BHB 56f52a **RR 64f 52a** 5248[7]
3 ch c Komaite (USA) 6.9f **(61)** - Maiden Pool (Sharpen Up) 8.3f **(67)**
Form - 6453805477
Record 2000 - 1st:0 2nd:0 3rd:1 Ran:10
Pre2000 - 1st:0 2nd:0 3rd:0 Ran:4
Win Prizemoney £0 *Total Prizemoney* £1,551
2000 Turf 0-7: (5f 2, 6f 3, 7f 2) (sft, gd 3, g-f, frm 2) 2000 AW 0-3: (5f, 6f 2) (Fibr 3)
Workmanlike, average colt, effective 6f, acts on gd. Turf high 64 - 3rd of 12 getting 4lb from Morgan Le Fay (19 May Thirsk 6f gd RF 1319). AW high 49. Inconsistent.
**S E Kettlewell [0-14] Hout's Partnership.*

HOWABOYS QUEST (USA) BHB 44f **RR 58f** 2216[6]
3 b g Quest for Fame 12.8f **(75)** - Doctor Black (USA) (Family Doctor (USA))
Form - 886
Record 2000 - 1st:0 2nd:0 3rd:0 Ran:3
Pre2000 - 1st:0 2nd:0 3rd:0 Ran:3
Win Prizemoney £0 *Total Prizemoney* £523
2000 Turf 0-3: (7f 2, 12f) (gd 2, frm)
Leggy, fair gelding. Turf high 29.
**Ferdy Murphy [0-6] Winlow Brothers.*

HOWARDS DREAM (IRE) RR 47f 5298[6]
2 b c King's Theatre (IRE) - Keiko **(65f)** (Generous (IRE))
Form - 6
Record 2000 - 1st:0 2nd:0 3rd:0 Ran:1
2000 Turf 0-1: (8f) (g-s)
Currently moderate colt. **I Semple [0-1] Gordon McDowall.*

HOWARD'S LAD (IRE) BHB 57a **RR 58f** 5294[16]
3 b g Reprimand 8.2f **(63)** - Port Isaac (USA) (Seattle Song (USA)) 9f **(77)**
Form - 0000510200884O
Record 2000 - 1st:1 2nd:1 3rd:0 Ran:14
Pre2000 - 1st:1 2nd:0 3rd:1 Ran:6
Win Prizemoney £5,850 *Total Prizemoney* £7,882
Wins * 2000 Jly Hamilt (G-F) 6f 58
1999 Jly Ayr (GD) 6f 73 <
2000 Turf 1-13: (5f, 6f 1-9, 7f, 9f, 12f) (g-s, gd 2, g-f 1-5, frm 5) 2000 AW 0-1: (8f) (Fibr)
Strong, fair gelding, effective 6f, acts on gd to g-f, often wears blinkers. Turf high 58.
**I Semple [1-16] Gordon McDowall (from Miss L A Perratt [1-4] Aug 1999).*

HOW DO I KNOW BHB 80f **RR 82f** 5163[1]
2 gr f Petong 7.6f **(58)** - Glenfield Portion (Mummy's Pet) 7.7f **(60)**
Form - 8221
Record 2000 - 1st:1 2nd:2 3rd:0 Ran:4
Win Prizemoney £2,404 *Total Prizemoney* £3,866
Wins * 2000 Oct Redcar (SFT) 5f 82 <
2000 Turf 1-4: (5f 1-2, 6f 2) (gd 1-3, g-f)
Decent filly. Turf high 82 (began Aug) - 1st of 12 from Sophielu (24 Oct Redcar RF 5163). **G A Butler [1-4] Manny Bernstein (Racing) Ltd.*

HOW HIGH BHB 35f **RR 8f** 4695[16]
5 b g Puissance 7.1f **(60)** - Lucky Starkist (Lucky Wednesday) 8f **(50)**
Form - 0
Record 2000 - 1st:0 2nd:0 3rd:0 Ran:1
Pre2000 - 1st:0 2nd:0 3rd:1 Ran:5
Win Prizemoney £0 *Total Prizemoney* £327
2000 Turf 0-1: (10f) (gd)
Very poor gelding, has worn blinkers.
**J Neville [0-4] James Bradley (from R Simpson [0-2] Jly 1998).*

HOXTON SQUARE (IRE) BHB 47f58a **RR 62df 58a** 4652[15]
3 ch f Case Law 6f **(64)** - Guv's Joy (IRE) (Thatching) 8f **(66)**
Form - 7200800
Record 2000 - 1st:0 2nd:1 3rd:0 Ran:7
Pre2000 - 1st:0 2nd:2 3rd:1 Ran:4
Win Prizemoney £0 *Total Prizemoney* £2,401
2000 Turf 0-3: (6f 2, 7f) (gd 2, frm) 2000 AW 0-4: (6f 2, 7f 2) (Fibr 4)
Unfurnished, average filly, effective 5f, acts on frm - acts on Fibr. Turf high 30 (began Aug). AW high 62. Becoming disappointing.
**N P Littmoden [0-11] J G B Elliott.*

HTTP FLYER BHB 36f **RR 47f** 5025[13]
3 b f Priolo (USA) 10.9f **(71)** - Cox's Pippin (USA) (Cox's Ridge (USA)) 8f **(68)**
Form - 07700
Record 2000 - 1st:0 2nd:0 3rd:0 Ran:5
2000 Turf 0-5: (8f 3, 11f, 12f) (g-s 2, g-f, frm 2)
Leggy, moderate filly, has worn blinkers. Turf high 47.
**W J Musson [0-5] HTTP Partnership Ltd.*

HUAMBO (USA) RR 108f 4411a[1]
3 b c Green Dancer (USA) 11.9f **(77)** - Hard Knocker (USA) (Raja Baba (USA)) 10f **(64)**
Form - 431
2000 Turf 1-3: (8f 1-1, 9f, 10f) (sft, gd 1-2)
Strong, currently Pattern-class colt. Turf high 108 - 1st of 8 getting 8lb from Bosporus (9 Spt Veliefendi RF 4411a).
**A Schutz in GER [1-3] H von Finck.*

HUDOOD (USA) BHB 91f **RR 95f** 3991[3]
5 ch h Gone West (USA) 7.8f **(82)** - Fife (IRE) (Lomond (USA)) 8.8f **(65)**
Form - 500D053
Record 2000 - 1st:0 2nd:0 3rd:1 Ran:7
Win Prizemoney £0 *Total Prizemoney* £3,292
2000 Turf 0-7: (10f 6, 12f) (gd 4, g-f 3)
Very useful colt, effective 10 to 12f, best at 10f, acts on gd to g-f, best on g-f. Turf high 95 - disqualified behind Baileys Prize (21 Jly Newmarket 10f gd RF 3006). A winner in France and Dubai, he is a decent handicapper who was disqualified after finishing first at Newmarket in July. He was unable to gain compensation despite running well afterwards.
**C E Brittain [0-7] H E Sheikh Rashid Bin Mohammed.*

HUGS DANCER (FR) BHB 63f **RR 59f** 5229[16]
3 b g Cadeaux Genereux 7.9f **(76)** - Embracing **(93f)** (Reference Point) 6.8f **(70)**
Form - 3340370
Record 2000 - 1st:0 2nd:0 3rd:3 Ran:7
Win Prizemoney £0 *Total Prizemoney* £2,642
2000 Turf 0-7: (7f, 8f 4, 10f 2) (sft, gd 2, g-f 3, hrd)
Scopey, fair gelding. Turf high 70 (began Aug).
**J G Given [0-7] J G White.*

HUGWITY BHB 60f80a **RR 74f 80a** 4061[6]
8 ch g Cadeaux Genereux 7.9f **(76)** - Nuit D'Ete (USA) (Super Concorde (USA)) 10.9f **(66)**
Form - 6811244387336214015366
Record 2000 - 1st:4 2nd:2 3rd:4 Ran:21
Pre2000 - 1st:7 2nd:5 3rd:0 Ran:31
Win Prizemoney £46,545 *Total Prizemoney* £60,295

Wins * 2000	Jly	Yarmou	(G-F)	C	8f		55
*** 2000**	May	Nottin	(GD)		8.2f		74
*** 2000**	*Jan*	*Lingfi*	*(STD)*	*C*	*10f*		*64*
*** 2000**	*Jan*	*Lingfi*	*(STD)*	*C*	*10f*		*63*
* 1999	*Jan*	*Lingfi*	*(STD)*	*H*	*7f*	*79*	*83* <
* 1998	*Dec*	*Lingfi*	*(STD)*	*H*	*8f*	*67*	*74*
* 1998	*Dec*	*Southw*	*(STD)*	*C*	*8f*		*66*
* 1998	Jly	Yarmou	(GD)	H	8f	75	80
1996	May	Goodwo	(GD)	H	8f	79	83 <
1996	May	Cheste	(GD)	H	10.3f	75	80
1996	Apr	Leices	(GD)		10f		73

2000 Turf 2-12: (7f, 8f 2-7, 9f, 10f 2, 12f) (gd 1-2, g-f 5, frm 1-3, hrd 2)
2000 AW 2-9: (9f, 10f 2-7, 12f) (Equi 2-8, Fibr)
Decent gelding, effective 7 to 12f, - acts on AW, best on Equi, likes left handed tracks, likes Lingfield. Turf high 74. AW high 88 - 4th of 4 to Adelphi Boy (8 Feb Wolverhampton 9f Fibr RF 0244).
**G C Bravery [8-44] Sawyer Whatley Partnership (from B Hanbury [3-8]*

Jun 1996).

HULLBANK BHB 57f54a RR 60f 54a 5012^{2}

10 b g Uncle Pokey 10f **(43)** - Dubavarna (Dubassoff (USA)) 14.2f **(55)**
Form - 14512
Record 2000 - 1st:2 2nd:1 3rd:0 Ran:5
Pre2000 - 1st:6 2nd:9 3rd:5 Ran:36
Win Prizemoney £25,129 *Total Prizemoney* £39,141
Wins * **2000** Aug Redcar (FRM) C 14.1f 49++
* **2000** Jun Catter (GD) S 13.8f 45+
* 1999 May Redcar (FRM) H 14.1f 65 67
1998 Jly Redcar (G-F) H 16f 68 71 <
1998 *Jly Southw (STD) H 14f 55 58*
* 1997 Jun Beverl (G-F) H 16.2f 63 68
* 1996 Jly Beverl (G-F) H 16.2f 55 60
2000 Turf 2-4: (14f 2-2, 16f 2) (g-f 2, frm 1-1, hrd 1-1) 2000 AW 0-1: (14f) (Fibr)
Average gelding, effective 14 to 16f, best at 14f, acts on gd to frm, best on frm, has worn blinkers, and excels at Redcar. Turf high 60 - 4th of 9 giving 3lb to Fujiyama Crest (26 Jun Nottingham 16f g-f RF 2279).
**W W Haigh [7-37] Mrs V Haigh (from J M Jefferson [0-3] Oct 1998).*

HUME'S LAW BHB 65f RR 74f 4965^{18}

2 b c Puissance 7.1f **(60)** - Will Be Bold (Bold Lad (IRE)) 8.4f **(68)**
Form - 74610700
Record 2000 - 1st:1 2nd:0 3rd:0 Ran:8
Win Prizemoney £3,107 *Total Prizemoney* £3,485
Wins * **2000** Jly Beverl (G-F) 5f 74 <
2000 Turf 1-8: (5f 1-5, 6f 3) (hvy, gd 2, frm 4, hrd 1-1)
Above-average colt, effective 5f, acts on frm to hrd. Turf high 74 - 1st of 17 giving 5lb to Once Removed (18 Jly Beverley RF 2881).
**A Berry [1-8] T Herbert-Jackson.*

HUNAN SCHOLAR (IRE) BHB 24f36a RR 15f 36a 4272^{16}

5 b g Royal Academy (USA) 7.8f **(77)** - Decadence (Vaigly Great) 7f **(58)**
Form - 000000080
Record 2000 - 1st:0 2nd:0 3rd:0 Ran:8
Pre2000 - 1st:0 2nd:0 3rd:0 Ran:13
Win Prizemoney £0 *Total Prizemoney* £225
2000 Turf 0-6: (6f, 7f, 8f 4) (gd, g-f 2, frm, hrd 2) 2000 AW 0-2: (7f 2) (Fibr 2)
Poor gelding, effective 7f, acts on g-f, has worn blinkers. Turf high 15. AW high 13.
**P Burgoyne [0-9] Philip Saunders (from K Prendergast in IRE [0-12] Jun 1999).*

HUNTERS TWEED BHB 63f RR 72f 5323^{9}

4 ch g Nashwan (USA) 10.3f **(79)** - Zorette (USA) **(60f)** (Zilzal (USA))
Form - 028276660
Record 2000 - 1st:0 2nd:2 3rd:0 Ran:9
Pre2000 - 1st:1 2nd:0 3rd:1 Ran:8
Win Prizemoney £4,123 *Total Prizemoney* £8,002
Wins * 1999 Jly Doncas (G-F) 12f 74+ <
2000 Turf 0-9: (11f, 12f 6, 13f, 15f) (sft, g-s, gd 4, g-f 2, frm)
Rangy, above-average gelding, effective 12 to 13f, best at 12f, acts on gd to g-f, best on g-f, has worn blinkers, likes left handed tracks. Turf high 76 - 2nd of 7 getting 4lb from Captain's Log (9 Jly Newcastle 12f gd RF 2653). **J D Bethell [1-17] Robert Gibbons.*

HUNT HILL (IRE) BHB 55f65a RR 70f 65a 663^{15}

5 b g High Estate 10.5f **(66)** - Royaltess (Royal And Regal (USA)) 9.5f **(60)**
Form - 0
Record 2000 - 1st:0 2nd:0 3rd:0 Ran:1
Pre2000 - 1st:3 2nd:0 3rd:1 Ran:9
Win Prizemoney £8,559 *Total Prizemoney* £9,087
Wins 1998 Aug Leices (GD) H 10f 62 66 <
1998 Jun Bright (GD) 10f 64
1998 *Jun Southw (STD) H 8f 54 58*
2000 Turf 0-1: (17f) (g-s)
Above-average gelding.
**J J O'Neill [3-13] P Byrne (from Sir Mark Prescott [3-8] Aug 1998).*

HUNTING LION (IRE) BHB 108f RR 110+f 2148^{3}

3 b c Piccolo - Jalopy (Jalmood (USA)) 10.1f **(52)**
Form - 8713
Record 2000 - 1st:1 2nd:0 3rd:1 Ran:4
Pre2000 - 1st:1 2nd:1 3rd:1 Ran:4
Win Prizemoney £29,533 *Total Prizemoney* £54,141
Wins * **2000** Jun Newmar (G-F) H 6f 104 108 <
* 1999 Jly Bath (G-F) 5.7f 76
2000 Turf 1-4: (6f 1-2, 7f 2) (gd 3, frm 1-1)
Scopey, Group-class colt, effective 6 to 7f, acts on gd to frm. Turf high 110 - 3rd of 19 to Observatory (21 Jun Ascot 7f gd RF 2148) - also 1st of 30 giving 17lb to Peruvian Chief (3 Jun Newmarket RF 1690). He showed little sparkle early on this season, but popped up at 50/1 in a valuable sprint handicap at Newmarket before finishing a fine third in the Jersey Stakes. Not seen out again.
**M R Channon [2-8] Jaber Abdullah.*

HUNTING TIGER BHB 69f RR 71f 3177^{10}

3 ch g Pursuit of Love 9.5f **(69)** - Pernilla (IRE) (Tate Gallery (USA)) 7.4f **(67)**
Form - 7000805270
Record 2000 - 1st:0 2nd:1 3rd:0 Ran:10
Pre2000 - 1st:1 2nd:1 3rd:0 Ran:5
Win Prizemoney £3,902 *Total Prizemoney* £8,268
Wins * 1999 Spt Haydoc (G-F) 7.1f 76 <
2000 Turf 0-10: (5f 2, 6f 7, 7f) (gd 2, g-f 7, frm)
Neat, above-average gelding, effective 6 to 7f, acts on gd to frm. Turf high 71. **M R Channon [1-15] Mohammed Jaber.*

HUREYA (USA) RR 72f 0020^{4}

2 b f Woodman (USA) 9.7f **(77)** - Istiqlal (USA) (Diesis) 9.3f **(69)**
Form - 54
Record 2000 - 1st:0 2nd:0 3rd:0 Ran:2
Win Prizemoney £0 *Total Prizemoney* £348
2000 Turf 0-2: (7f 2) (g-f 2)
Currently above-average filly. Turf high 72 (began Jly).
**J L Dunlop [0-2] Hamdan Al Maktoum.*

HURGILL DANCER BHB 36f46a RR 35f 46a 2891^{6}

6 b g Rambo Dancer (CAN) 8.4f **(59)** - Try Vickers (USA) (Fuzzbuster (USA)) 6.3f **(63)**
Form - 3434766
Record 2000 - 1st:0 2nd:0 3rd:1 Ran:5
Pre2000 - 1st:2 2nd:1 3rd:4 Ran:26
Win Prizemoney £6,517 *Total Prizemoney* £9,248
Wins * 1999 *Feb Lingfi (STD) H 12f 36 43*
1997 Apr Ripon (G-F) H 12.3f 65 68 <
2000 Turf 0-2: (10f, 12f) (frm 2) 2000 AW 0-3: (12f 3) (Equi, Fibr 2)
Moderate gelding, effective 10 to 12f, best at 12f, acts on frm - acts on AW, best on Equi, has worn blinkers, and likes Brighton. Turf high 35. AW high 40 (1st run) - 3rd of 14 getting 2lb from Lost Spirit (8 Jan Lingfield 12f Equi RF 0051). Consistent.
**R J O'Sullivan [1-19] Never Ever Bet Partnership (from J A R Toller [0-4] Aug 1998).*

HURLINGHAM STAR (IRE) BHB 45f55a RR 11f 55a 5013^{7}

2 b g Distinctly North (USA) 7.4f **(63)** - Charrua (Sharpo) 7.7f **(59)**
Form - 70667
Record 2000 - 1st:0 2nd:0 3rd:0 Ran:5
2000 Turf 0-4: (5f 2, 7f, 9f) (gd, g-f 2, frm) 2000 AW 0-1: (6f) (Fibr)
Fair gelding, has worn blinkers. Turf high 11.
**P Mitchell [0-5] Mrs Patricia Mitchell.*

HURRICANE FLOYD (IRE) BHB 100f RR 91+f 4463^{7}

2 ch c Pennekamp (USA) - Mood Swings (IRE) **(72+f)** (Shirley Heights) 10.3f **(74)**
Form - 2147
Record 2000 - 1st:1 2nd:1 3rd:0 Ran:4
Win Prizemoney £4,426 *Total Prizemoney* £12,856
Wins * **2000** Aug Newmar (GD) 6f 84 <
2000 Turf 1-4: (6f 1-3, 7f) (gd, g-f, frm 1-2)
Useful colt. Turf high 91 (began Jly) - 4th of 10 to Bannister (23 Aug York 6f frm RF 3915) - also 1st of 17 from Bannister (5 Aug Newmarket RF 3399). He raced too freely over seven on his debut, but was a ready winner next time when dropped back a furlong. He had no luck in running when favourite for the Gimcrack and was then found to be lame after disappointing in the Mill Reef. Could well put those unfortunate experiences behind him in the new season. **J Noseda [1-4] Lucayan Stud.*

HURRICANE LOUIS (IRE) RR 95f 1456a[6]
4 br c Fabulous Dancer (USA) 10.6f **(81)** - Lobmille (Mill Reef (USA)) 10.5f **(78)**
Form - 26
2000 Turf 0-2: (8f 2) (hvy, g-s)
Very useful colt, effective 8f, acts on hvy to gd. Turf high 95 (1st run) - 2nd of 9 to Embody (7 May San Siro 8f hvy RF 1160a).
**B Grizzetti in ITY [0-2] (from J Noseda [2-4] Jly 1999).*

HURRICANE STORM BHB 55f **RR 57f** 1991[8]
3 b g Runnett 6.7f **(56)** - Polar Storm (IRE) **(69f)** (Law Society (USA)) 9.9f **(70)**
Form - 8
Record 2000 - 1st:0 2nd:0 3rd:0 Ran:1
Pre2000 - 1st:0 2nd:0 3rd:0 Ran:2
2000 Turf 0-1: (7f) (g-f)
Leggy, currently fair gelding. **B J Meehan [0-3] Miss Howard Evans.*

HUTCHIES LADY BHB 35f33a **RR 37f 33a** 5193[4]
8 b m Efisio 7.7f **(69)** - Keep Mum (Mummy's Pet) 7.7f **(60)**
Form - 3100254
Record 2000 - 1st:1 2nd:1 3rd:1 Ran:7
Pre2000 - 1st:1 2nd:3 3rd:0 Ran:43
Win Prizemoney £6,521 *Total Prizemoney* £11,078
Wins * 2000 Spt Hamilt (SFT) H 11.1f 32 37
1996 May Hamilt (HVY) H 8.3f 30 41 <
2000 Turf 1-7: (8f, 9f, 10f, 11f 1-1, 12f, 13f, 16f) (hvy 2, g-s 1-3, gd, frm)
Very moderate mare, effective 8 to 11f, acts on hvy to frm, best on frm, has worn blinkers, prefers tight tracks. Turf high 37 (began Aug) - also 1st of 7 getting 22lb from Perpetuo (3 Spt Hamilton RF 4185). **J S Goldie [1-7] Magteam (from M A Peill [0-5] Aug 1999).*

HUTOON BHB 56f **RR 53f** 4676[12]
3 b c Mizoram (USA) - Mey Madam (Song) 7.2f **(61)**
Form - 6000
Record 2000 - 1st:0 2nd:0 3rd:0 Ran:4
Pre2000 - 1st:0 2nd:0 3rd:1 Ran:3
Win Prizemoney £0 *Total Prizemoney* £449
2000 Turf 0-4: (8f 2, 10f, 12f) (g-s, g-f 2, frm)
Scopey, fair colt, effective 8 to 9f, acts on frm. Turf high 53.
**J W Hills [0-7] Ziad Galadari.*

HWISPRIAN RR 63f 4466[10]
2 b f Definite Article - No Islands (Lomond (USA)) 8.8f **(65)**
Form - 80
Record 2000 - 1st:0 2nd:0 3rd:0 Ran:2
2000 Turf 0-2: (7f, 8f) (g-f, frm)
Currently average filly. Turf high 63 (began Aug).
**V Soane [0-2] Acorns To Oaks Racing.*

HYDE HALL RR 55f 5098[21]
2 b f Barathea (IRE) - Catawba (Mill Reef (USA)) 10.5f **(78)**
Form - 0
Record 2000 - 1st:0 2nd:0 3rd:0 Ran:1
2000 Turf 0-1: (8f) (gd)
Currently fair filly.
**H R A Cecil [0-1] Exors of the late Lord Howard de Walden.*

HYDE PARK (IRE) BHB 50f58a **RR 54df 58a** 4378[11]
6 b g Alzao (USA) 9.8f **(73)** - Park Elect (Ahonoora) 8.1f **(73)**
Form - 0000180
Record 2000 - 1st:1 2nd:0 3rd:0 Ran:7
Pre2000 - 1st:4 2nd:4 3rd:4 Ran:28
Win Prizemoney £21,187 *Total Prizemoney* £28,358
Wins * 2000 Aug Carlis (FRM) H 8f 48 50
1998 Oct Bright (GD) H 8f 67 70
1998 Aug Cheste (G-S) H 7.6f 60 62
1998 Jly Pontef (G-F) H 8f 55 59
1996 *Nov Lingfi (STD) 5f 71* <
2000 Turf 1-6: (7f 4, 8f 1-2) (g-s 2, g-f, frm 1-3) 2000 AW 0-1: (7f) (Fibr)
Average gelding, effective 7 to 8f, best at 7f, acts on frm - acts on AW, has worn blinkers. Turf high 50. Inconsistent.
**D Nicholls [1-15] Ian Hewitson (from Sir Mark Prescott [4-20] Mar 1999).*

HYDERABAD RR 31f 5309[17]
2 ch c Deploy 11.4f **(67)** - Ajuga (USA) (The Minstrel (CAN)) 10f **(72)**
Form - 0
Record 2000 - 1st:0 2nd:0 3rd:0 Ran:1
2000 Turf 0-1: (7f) (g-s)
Currently very moderate colt. **B W Hills [0-1] K Abdulla.*

HYMN (IRE) BHB 102f **RR 106f** 3159a[2]
3 b c Fairy King (USA) 7.7f **(75)** - Handsewn (USA) (Sir Ivor) 10.2f **(70)**
Form - 2112
Record 2000 - 1st:2 2nd:2 3rd:0 Ran:4
Win Prizemoney £12,791 *Total Prizemoney* £39,029
Wins * 2000 Jun Ascot (G-F) 8f 103 <
*** 2000** May Sandow (HVY) 8.1f 84
2000 Turf 2-4: (8f 2-3, 10f) (g-s 1-1, gd 1-1, frm 2)
Scopey, Pattern-class colt. Turf high 106 - 2nd of 4 to Pine Dance (23 Jly Arlington Park 10f frm RF 3159a) - also 1st of 6 from Modern British (24 Jun Ascot RF 2240). Beaten only a head on his Newmarket debut, he came on for the run and went one better with a narrow victory in a four-runner Sandown maiden next time. Gained a similarly brave victory in an Ascot classified stakes before a good effort in a Group Two at Arlington Park. He obviously knows how to battle. **J H M Gosden [2-4] R Nip & S Goldsher.*

HYPERACTIVE (IRE) BHB 64f62a **RR 69f 62a** 4992[12]
4 b c Perugino (USA) - Hyannis (FR) (Esprit du Nord (USA))
Form - 02780040
Record 2000 - 1st:0 2nd:1 3rd:0 Ran:8
Pre2000 - 1st:1 2nd:1 3rd:0 Ran:4
Win Prizemoney £4,306 *Total Prizemoney* £7,094
Wins 1999 Oct Yarmou (G-F) 7f 70 <
2000 Turf 0-6: (6f, 7f 5) (g-s, g-f 2, frm 3) 2000 AW 0-2: (6f 2) (Fibr 2)
Scopey, average colt, effective 7f, acts on g-f to frm, has worn blinkers. Turf high 69 - 2nd of 22 getting 7lb from I Cried For You (10 Jun Doncaster 7f frm RF 1869). AW high 61 (began Spt).
**B Ellison [0-1] Philip Serbert (from A C Stewart [1-11] Spt 2000).*

HYPERSONIC BHB 73f **RR 76f** 1962[12]
3 b c Marju (IRE) 9.2f **(76)** - Hi-Li (High Top) 10.2f **(67)**
Form - 000
Record 2000 - 1st:0 2nd:0 3rd:0 Ran:3
Pre2000 - 1st:0 2nd:1 3rd:1 Ran:4
Win Prizemoney £0 *Total Prizemoney* £2,065
2000 Turf 0-3: (6f, 8f 2) (hvy, g-f, frm)
Light-framed, above-average colt, effective 7f, acts on g-s. Turf high 52. Showed plenty in four runs as a juvenile, and needed his reappearance. From a shrewd yard, and one to watch in a handicap. **G Wragg [0-7] Katsumi Yoshida.*

HYPNOTIZE BHB 100f **RR 106?f** 3340[10]
3 b f Machiavellian (USA) 9.8f **(83)** - Belle et Deluree (USA) (The Minstrel (CAN)) 10f **(72)**
Form - 67270
Record 2000 - 1st:0 2nd:1 3rd:0 Ran:5
Pre2000 - 1st:2 2nd:0 3rd:0 Ran:4
Win Prizemoney £15,798 *Total Prizemoney* £21,938
Wins * 1999 Jly Sandow (G-F) L 7.1f 93 <
* 1999 Jly Yarmou (GD) 7f 85+
2000 Turf 0-5: (7f, 8f 2, 9f, 10f) (g-s, gd 2, frm 2)
Scopey, Pattern-class filly, effective 8f, acts on frm. Turf high 106 - 2nd of 4 giving 10lb to My Hansel (29 Jun Newcastle 8f frm RF 2371). **Sir Michael Stoute [2-9] Cheveley Park Stud.*

IAMATMEWHITZEND RR 5191[6]
3 ch f Whittingham (IRE) - The Fernhill Flyer (IRE) **(21f 65a)** (Red Sunset) 8.2f **(63)**
Form - 6
Record 2000 - 1st:0 2nd:0 3rd:0 Ran:1
2000 Turf 0-1: (8f) (gd)
Unfurnished, currently very poor filly. **Martyn Wane [0-1] B Batey.*

I BITE RR 5135[12]
3 b c Domitor (USA) 7.6f **(56)** - Sardine (Saritamer (USA)) 9.5f **(63)**
Form - 0
Record 2000 - 1st:0 2nd:0 3rd:0 Ran:1
2000 Turf 0-1: (10f) (sft)
Unfurnished, currently very poor colt.
**R J Price [0-1] M Jenkins.*

I CAN'T REMEMBER BHB 41f25a **RR 48f 25a** 5164[2]

6 br g Petong 7.6f **(58)** - Glenfield Portion (Mummy's Pet) 7.7f **(60)**

Form - 6624540506734002

Record	**2000 -**	1st:0	2nd:2	3rd:1	Ran:16
	Pre2000 -	1st:9	2nd:4	3rd:1	Ran:53

Win Prizemoney £32,015 *Total Prizemoney* £40,438

Wins								
* 1999	Aug	Nottin	(G-F)	H	14.1f	58	61	
* 1999	Aug	Ripon	(G-F)	H	12.3f	60	64	
* 1999	Jun	Pontef	(G-S)	H	8f	59	64	
1999	May	Nottin	(FRM)	S	10f		53	
1998	Jun	Cheste	(G-S)	C	10.3f		59	
1996	Oct	Doncas	(GD)	H	8f	77	80	<
1996	Aug	Cheste	(G-S)	H	7f	74	79	
1996	Aug	Cheste	(G-F)	H	6.1f	70	67	
1996	Jly	Catter	(G-S)	S	5f		46	

2000 Turf 0-12: (8f, 10f, 11f, 12f 6, 14f 2, 16f) (sft, g-s 2, gd 3, g-f 2, frm 4) 2000 AW 0-4: (12f 2, 16f 2) (Fibr 4)

Moderate gelding, effective 8 to 14f, acts on gd to frm, has worn blinkers, likes tight tracks. Turf high 57. AW high 51.

**S R Bowring [3-26] J Doxey (from M C Pipe [1-5] May 1999).*

ICE BHB 91f **RR 96f** 4452[10]

4 b g Polar Falcon (USA) 9f **(74)** - Sarabah (IRE) (Ela-Mana-Mou) 10.1f **(70)**

Form - 516144070

Record	**2000 -**	1st:2	2nd:0	3rd:0	Ran:9
	Pre2000 -	1st:5	2nd:2	3rd:1	Ran:16

Win Prizemoney £58,094 *Total Prizemoney* £63,461

Wins								
* **2000**	Jun	York	(G-F)	H	8.9f	90	95	
* **2000**	Jun	Lingfi	(GD)	H	9f	88	89	
* 1999	May	York	(SFT)	H	7.9f	92	98	<
* 1999	Apr	Dielsd	(HVY)	L	8f		95	
* 1998	Oct	York	(GD)	H	7.9f	83	95	
* 1998	Spt	York	(GD)	H	7.9f	69	80	
* 1998	Aug	Mussel	(GD)	H	7.1f	69	74	

2000 Turf 2-9: (8f 5, 9f 2-2, 10f 2) (g-s, gd 1-4, g-f 1-3, frm)

Scopey, very useful gelding, effective 8 to 10f, best at 8f, acts on hvy to frm, mostly wears blinkers (extremely effectively), prefers left handed tracks. Turf high 96 - 4th of 7 giving 6lb to Arabian Moon (25 Jun Pontefract 10f frm RF 2266) - also 1st of 16 giving 4lb to Jedi Knight (17 Jun York RF 2060). He scored twice in June last year, but struggled in the second half of the campaign. Managed to win from the front and also when held up, but is not entirely consistent and looks a far-from-easy ride.

**M Johnston [7-25] David Abell.*

ICE AGE BHB 42f40a **RR 33f 40a** 299[11]

6 gr h Chilibang 7f **(55)** - Mazarine Blue (Bellypha) 9.8f **(73)**

Form - 8850700

Record	**2000 -**	1st:0	2nd:0	3rd:0	Ran:6
	Pre2000 -	1st:5	2nd:3	3rd:3	Ran:41

Win Prizemoney £11,981 *Total Prizemoney* £15,144

Wins								
1999	*Mar*	*Southw*	*(SLW)*	*S*	*6f*		*65*	
1998	Jly	Yarmou	(GD)	H	6f	44	49	
1998	*May*	*Southw*	*(STD)*	*S*	*6f*		*61*	
1998	*Jan*	*Southw*	*(STD)*	*H*	*6f*	*54*	*59*	
1996	May	Doncas	(G-F)		5f		80+	<

2000 AW 0-6: (5f 2, 6f 4) (Fibr 6)

Moderate horse, effective 6f, - acts on Fibr, mostly wears blinkers, likes left handed tracks, likes tight tracks. AW high 40. Inconsistent.

**M J Polglase [0-7] W P Smith (from R J R Williams [5-39] Jun 1999).*

ICEALION **RR 14f** 906[11]

2 b g Lion Cavern (USA) 7.5f **(74)** - Icecapped (Caerleon (USA)) 8.6f **(71)**

Form - 0

Record	**2000 -**	1st:0	2nd:0	3rd:0	Ran:1

2000 Turf 0-1: (5f) (gd)

Currently poor gelding.

**M W Easterby [0-1] J W P Curtis.*

ICE CRYSTAL BHB 54f **RR 75f** 5063[8]

3 b g Slip Anchor 12.7f **(75)** - Crystal Fountain (Great Nephew) 9.9f **(64)**

Form - 87480678

Record	**2000 -**	1st:0	2nd:0	3rd:0	Ran:8

Win Prizemoney £0 *Total Prizemoney* £273

2000 Turf 0-8: (10f 2, 11f, 12f 4, 14f) (sft 2, gd 2, g-f 3, frm)

Lengthy, above-average gelding Turf high 75.

**H Candy [0-8] David Clark & Partners.*

ICE MAIDEN BHB 79f **RR 80f** 4257[21]

2 b f Polar Falcon (USA) 9f **(74)** - Affair of State (IRE) (Tate Gallery (USA)) 7.4f **(67)**

Form - 1340

Record	**2000 -**	1st:1	2nd:0	3rd:1	Ran:4

Win Prizemoney £4,810 *Total Prizemoney* £6,083

Wins								
* **2000**	Apr	Newmar	(G-S)		5f		75	<

2000 Turf 1-4: (5f 1-2, 7f 2) (gd 1-3, frm)

Decent filly. Turf high 80 - also 1st of 10 from Pashmeena (19 Apr Newmarket RF 0798). She made a winning debut at Newmarket, but was then sidelined for four months and has been held in small fields since.

**M R Channon [1-4] Stephen Crown & Brook Land.*

ICEMOON (GER) **RR 108f** 4572a[3]

6 ch h Monsagem (USA) - Icena (Jimmy Reppin) 8.8f **(64)**

Form - 63

2000 Turf 0-2: (10f 2) (sft, gd)

Pattern-class horse, has worn blinkers. Turf high 108 (began Jly) - 3rd of 8 giving 3lb to Elle Danzig (17 Spt Frankfurt 10f gd RF 4572a).

**P Remmert in GER [0-6].*

ICE PACK BHB 29f45a **RR 36f 45a** 5011[10]

4 gr f Mukaddamah (USA) 7.6f **(74)** - Mrs Gray (Red Sunset) 8.2f **(63)**

Form - 6008343600

Record	**2000 -**	1st:0	2nd:0	3rd:2	Ran:10
	Pre2000 -	1st:0	2nd:3	3rd:1	Ran:10

Win Prizemoney £0 *Total Prizemoney* £2,830

2000 Turf 0-7: (12f, 13f, 14f, 16f 2, 17f 2) (g-s, g-f, frm 5) 2000 AW 0-3: (12f, 14f 2) (Fibr 3)

Very moderate filly, effective 11 to 12f, - acts on Fibr, likes left handed tracks, favours tight tracks. Turf high 36. AW high 14.

**Don Enrico Incisa [0-8] Don Enrico Incisa (from N Tinkler [0-3] Mar 2000).*

ICE PRINCE BHB 66f **RR 72f** 4475[6]

2 b c Polar Falcon (USA) 9f **(74)** - The Jotter **(88f)** (Night Shift (USA)) 7.2f **(69)**

Form - 006

Record	**2000 -**	1st:0	2nd:0	3rd:0	Ran:3

2000 Turf 0-2: (7f, 8f) (g-s, g-f) 2000 AW 0-1: (8f) (Fibr)

Currently above-average colt. Turf high 72 (began Spt).

**J A Osborne [0-3] Martyn Booth.*

ICHI BEAU (IRE) BHB 53f **RR 45f** 509[8]

6 b g Convinced - May As Well (Kemal (FR))

Form - 41138

Record	**2000 -**	1st:2	2nd:0	3rd:1	Ran:5
	Pre2000 -	1st:0	2nd:0	3rd:1	Ran:4

Win Prizemoney £4,333 *Total Prizemoney* £4,904

Wins								
* **2000**	*Mar*	*Southw*	*(STD)*	*H*	*12f*	*47*	*53*	<
* **2000**	*Feb*	*Wolver*	*(STD)*	*H*	*12f*	*40*	*46*	

2000 AW 2-5: (12f 2-5) (Fibr 2-5)

Fair gelding, effective 10 to 12f, best at 12f, acts on sft - acts on Fibr. AW high 53 - 1st of 10 giving 9lb to Tempramental (6 Mar Southwell RF 0412) - also 1st of 8 getting 10lb from Western Rainbow (19 Feb Wolverhampton RF 0323).

**Ferdy Murphy [2-5] Mrs Fiona Butterly (from A J Martin in IRE [0-10] Nov 1999).*

ICICLE **RR 107f** 4282[9]

3 br f Polar Falcon (USA) 9f **(74)** - Blessed Honour (Ahonoora) 8.1f **(73)**

Form - 03540

Record	**2000 -**	1st:0	2nd:0	3rd:1	Ran:5
	Pre2000 -	1st:2	2nd:1	3rd:0	Ran:5

Win Prizemoney £26,360 *Total Prizemoney* £38,089

Wins								
* 1999	Aug	Goodwo	(GD)	G3	7f		98	<
* 1999	May	Folkes	(G-F)		6f		74+	

2000 Turf 0-5: (6f, 7f 2, 8f, 9f) (g-s, gd, frm 3)

Strong, Pattern-class filly, effective 6 to 7f, best at 7f, acts on gd to frm, best on gd. Turf high 107.

**J R Fanshawe [2-10] Cheveley Park Stud.*

ICICLE QUEEN BHB 25f **RR 31f** 217[9]
3 ch f Aragon 7.7f **(58)** - Kristal Diva **(55df 43a)** (Kris) 9.5f **(73)**
Form - 0
Record 2000 - 1st:0 2nd:0 3rd:0 Ran:1
Pre2000 - 1st:0 2nd:0 3rd:0 Ran:2
2000 AW 0-1: (8f) (Fibr)
Light-framed, currently very moderate filly.
**A G Newcombe [0-1] A G Newcombe (from S C Williams [0-2] Oct 1999).*

ICON BHB 35f50a **RR 60f 50a** 4928[18]
3 b f Warning 8.1f **(77)** - Blessed Event (Kings Lake (USA)) 10.8f **(67)**
Form - 00080
Record 2000 - 1st:0 2nd:0 3rd:0 Ran:5
2000 Turf 0-3: (5f, 7f, 10f) (g-s, gd, g-f) 2000 AW 0-2: (9f, 12f) (Equi, Fibr)
Unfurnished, average filly. Turf high 60. AW high 19 (began Oct).
**D W P Arbuthnot [0-3] Eastwind Racing Ltd (from G A Butler [0-2] May 2000).*

I CRIED FOR YOU (IRE) BHB 87f61a **RR 87f 61a** 5240[23]
5 b g Statoblest 6.4f **(63)** - Fall of The Hammer (IRE) (Auction Ring (USA)) 8.6f **(65)**
Form - 1321207410
Record 2000 - 1st:3 2nd:2 3rd:1 Ran:10
Pre2000 - 1st:3 2nd:1 3rd:4 Ran:28
Win Prizemoney £31,855 *Total Prizemoney* £45,196

Wins								
* **2000**	Oct	York	(HVY)	H	7f	82	87	<
* **2000**	Jun	Doncas	(G-F)	H	7f	75	78	
* **2000**	Apr	Lingfi	(G-S)		7f		74	
* 1999	Jun	Windso	(G-F)	H	6f	67	71	
* 1999	May	Nottin	(FRM)		6.1f		65	
1998	May	Bright	(FRM)	H	5.3f	68	72	

2000 Turf 3-10: (6f, 7f 3-5, 8f 4) (sft 1-2, g-s, gd 1-4, g-f 2, frm 1-1)
Useful gelding, effective 6 to 8f, best at 7f, acts on sft to frm, best on gd, has worn blinkers, does well at Windsor. Turf high 87 - 1st of 22 giving 12lb to Melodian (7 Oct York RF 4866) - also 1st of 22 giving 7lb to Hyperactive (10 Jun Doncaster RF 1869). In fine form last term, winning twice in the spring, and returning to form in the autumn when a close fourth in a valuable Ascot handicap before taking a competitive race at York. He does most of his racing at seven furlongs, has won on fast ground, but looks better suited by some cut.
**J G Given [5-21] One Stop Partnership (from R Hannon [1-17] Oct 1998).*

IDLE POWER (IRE) BHB 88f **RR 89f** 5129[12]
2 b br g Common Grounds 8.1f **(66)** - Idle Fancy **(79f)** (Mujtahid (USA))
Form - 2516610
Record 2000 - 1st:2 2nd:1 3rd:0 Ran:7
Win Prizemoney £10,803 *Total Prizemoney* £12,025

Wins								
* **2000**	Oct	Newmar	(SFT)	H	6f	84	89	<
* **2000**	Jun	Kempto	(G-F)		5f		78	

2000 Turf 2-7: (5f 1-3, 6f 1-4) (sft, gd 1-3, g-f, frm 1-2)
Useful gelding, effective 6f, acts on gd. Turf high 89 - 1st of 22 getting 4lb from Blue Reigns (12 Oct Newmarket RF 4932). Suited by fast ground, he pulled too hard when beaten at Yarmouth in September. Won a competitive race next time.
**P W Harris [2-7] The Dreamers.*

IDOLIZE BHB 90f **RR 96f** 4931[10]
3 ch f Polish Precedent (USA) 9f **(73)** - Knight's Baroness (Rainbow Quest (USA)) 10.4f **(75)**
Form - 01870
Record 2000 - 1st:1 2nd:0 3rd:0 Ran:5
Pre2000 - 1st:1 2nd:1 3rd:0 Ran:3
Win Prizemoney £9,942 *Total Prizemoney* £11,152

Wins							
* **2000**	Jun	Chepst	(GD)	10.2f		96	<
* 1999	Aug	Chepst	(G-S)	8.1f		78+	

2000 Turf 1-5: (9f, 10f 1-4) (g-s, gd 1-3, g-f)
Neat, very useful filly, effective 10f, acts on gd. Turf high 96 - 1st of 5 getting 18lb from Komistar (8 Jun Chepstow RF 1801).
**P F I Cole [2-8] H R H Prince Fahd Salman.*

IF BY CHANCE BHB 60f66a **RR 61f 66a** 3784[5]
2 ch c Risk Me (FR) 8f **(53)** - Out of Harmony (Song) 7.2f **(61)**
Form - 042855
Record 2000 - 1st:0 2nd:1 3rd:0 Ran:6
Win Prizemoney £0 *Total Prizemoney* £913
2000 Turf 0-5: (5f 5) (sft 2, gd, frm 2) 2000 AW 0-1: (5f) (Fibr)
Average colt, effective 5f, - acts on Fibr. Turf high 61. (1st run) - 2nd of 12 to Sandles (11 May Wolverhampton 5f Fibr RF 1149).
**D W P Arbuthnot [0-6] G S Thompson & P Banfield.*

IFFAH (IRE) **RR 71f** 3980[2]
2 ch f Halling (USA) - Taroob (IRE) (Roberto (USA)) 10f **(76)**
Form - 62
Record 2000 - 1st:0 2nd:1 3rd:0 Ran:2
Win Prizemoney £0 *Total Prizemoney* £1,140
2000 Turf 0-2: (7f 2) (gd, frm)
Currently above-average filly. Turf high 71 (began Aug).
**J L Dunlop [0-2] Hamdan Al Maktoum.*

IFTIRAAS BHB 111f **RR 113f** 4254a[1]
3 b f Distant Relative 7f **(69)** - Ideal Home (Home Guard (USA)) 9.3f **(66)**
Form - 156031
Record 2000 - 1st:2 2nd:0 3rd:1 Ran:6
Pre2000 - 1st:1 2nd:2 3rd:0 Ran:4
Win Prizemoney £51,740 *Total Prizemoney* £67,001

Wins							
* **2000**	Spt	Currag	(GD)	G3	8f	113	<
* **2000**	Apr	Newbur	(SFT)	G3	7f	104	
* 1999	Spt	Lingfi	(G-F)		6f	83	

2000 Turf 2-6: (7f 1-1, 8f 1-5) (g-s 1-2, gd 1-4)
Scopey, Group-class filly, effective 7 to 8f, best at 8f, acts on g-s to gd, best on gd. Turf high 113 - 1st of 11 giving 4lb to Danceabout (3 Spt Curragh RF 4254a) - also 1st of 9 from Glen Rosie (14 Apr Newbury RF 0713). Slightly disappointing after taking Newbury's Fred Darling Stakes on her reappearance, when subsequent Classic winners Crimplene and Lahan were behind, she came back to form when getting up to win a Group Three at the Curragh in September. Suited by testing ground, she is notably game. **J L Dunlop [3-10] Kuwait Racing Syndicate II.*

IFTITAH (USA) BHB 100f105a **RR 91f 105a** 2501[3]
4 ch c Gone West (USA) 7.8f **(82)** - Mur Taasha (USA) **(103f)** (Riverman (USA)) 9.1f **(76)**
Form - 243
Record 2000 - 1st:0 2nd:1 3rd:1 Ran:3
Pre2000 - 1st:1 2nd:0 3rd:0 Ran:2
Win Prizemoney £6,326 *Total Prizemoney* £39,169

Wins						
* 1998	Oct	Newmar	(GD)	7f	91++	<

2000 Turf 0-2: (7f, 8f) (g-f, frm) 2000 AW 0-1: (8f) (Dirt)
Strong, Pattern-class colt. Turf high 91. (1st run) - 2nd of 13 to Conflict (25 Mar Nad Al Sheba 8f Dirt RF 0575a).
**S bin Suroor [1-4] Godolphin (from S bin Suroor in UAE [0-1] Mar 2000).*

IGMAN (USA) **RR 96f** 4290a[8]
3 b c Mt Livermore (USA) 7.7f **(90)** - Tidal Treasure (USA) (Crafty Prospector (USA)) 8.2f **(104)**
Form - 18
2000 Turf 1-2: (7f 1-1, 8f) (hvy 1-1, sft)
Currently very useful colt. Turf high 96 (1st run) - 1st of 7 from Contexte (7 Mar Maisons-laffitte RF 0452a). **A Fabre in FR [1-2].*

IGNITE (IRE) BHB 60f **RR 66f** 5069[12]
3 b g Bluebird (USA) 7.9f **(71)** - Save Me The Waltz (Kings Lake (USA)) 10.8f **(67)**
Form - 0680
Record 2000 - 1st:0 2nd:0 3rd:0 Ran:4
Pre2000 - 1st:0 2nd:0 3rd:4 Ran:10
Win Prizemoney £0 *Total Prizemoney* £2,816
2000 Turf 0-4: (10f, 12f 3) (g-s, g-f 2, frm)
Scopey, average gelding, effective 5 to 6f, best at 6f, acts on gd to frm, best on frm, has worn blinkers. Turf high 66 (began Jly). Consistent.
**R T Phillips [0-4] Ellangowan Racing Partners (from M L W Bell [0-4] Oct 1999).*

I GOT RHYTHM BHB 46f46a **RR 50f 46a** 5247[5]
2 gr f Lycius (USA) 8.8f **(71)** - Eurythmic **(57?f)** (Pharly (FR)) 9.8f **(68)**
Form - 004005
Record 2000 - 1st:0 2nd:0 3rd:0 Ran:6

2000 Turf 0-5: (5f 2, 6f 2, 8f) (gd, frm 4) 2000 AW 0-1: (8f) (Fibr)
Fair filly. Turf high 50. **Mrs M Reveley [0-6] J Shack.*

IHTIMAAM (FR) BHB 26f40a **RR 26f 40a** 4723[12]

8 b g Polish Precedent (USA) 9f **(73)** - Haebeh (USA) (Alydar (USA)) 9.1f **(76)**
Form - 00
Record 2000 - 1st:0 2nd:0 3rd:0 Ran:2
Pre2000 - 1st:2 2nd:1 3rd:4 Ran:27
Win Prizemoney £4,116 *Total Prizemoney* £6,801
Wins 1996 *Nov Southw (STD) S 11f 63 <*
1996 *Jly Southw (STD) C 11f 53*
2000 AW 0-2: (10f, 12f) (Equi 2)
Little account gelding, has worn blinkers. AW high 17.
**H E Haynes [0 10] Mrs H E Haynes (from Mrs A Duffield [2-24] Aug 1997).*

IKBAL **RR 57+f** 5132[8]

2 ch c Indian Ridge 7.6f **(74)** - Amaniy (USA) **(73f)** (Dayjur (USA))
Form - 8
Record 2000 - 1st:0 2nd:0 3rd:0 Ran:1
2000 Turf 0-1: (6f) (sft)
Currently fair colt. **M P Tregoning [0-1] Hamdan Al Maktoum.*

IL CAPITANO BHB 80f **RR 94f** 4385[5]

3 ch c Be My Chief (USA) 10.2f **(62)** - Taza **(40f)** (Persian Bold) 9.3f **(66)**
Form - 75075
Record 2000 - 1st:0 2nd:0 3rd:0 Ran:5
Pre2000 - 1st:1 2nd:2 3rd:0 Ran:5
Win Prizemoney £3,649 *Total Prizemoney* £7,639
Wins * 1999 Jly Ayr (SFT) 7f 93+ <
2000 Turf 0-5: (12f 2, 14f, 15f, 16f) (gd 3, g-f 2)
Scopey, useful colt, effective 7 to 8f, acts on g-s, has worn blinkers. Turf high 94. A winner on soft ground as a juvenile, he was not beaten too far in the two-mile Queen's Vase, despite giving the impression that the trip stretched his stamina, but was well held subsequently, and was sold in the autumn to go hurdling.
**B W Hills [1-10] Guy Reed.*

IL CAVALIERE BHB 72f **RR 82+f** 4624[3]

5 b g Mtoto 11.5f **(71)** - Kalmia (Miller's Mate) 7f **(63)**
Form - 37473
Record 2000 - 1st:0 2nd:0 3rd:2 Ran:5
Win Prizemoney £0 *Total Prizemoney* £1,194
2000 Turf 0-5: (8f 2, 10f, 12f, 14f) (gd, g-f, frm 3)
Decent gelding. Turf high 82.
**Mrs M Reveley [2-10] The Thoughtful Partnership.*

IL DESTINO BHB 56f65a **RR 58f 65a** 5072[4]

5 b g Casteddu 7.4f **(54)** - At First Sight (He Loves Me) 7.9f **(55)**
Form - 65883034
Record 2000 - 1st:0 2nd:0 3rd:2 Ran:8
Pre2000 - 1st:2 2nd:4 3rd:2 Ran:18
Win Prizemoney £9,491 *Total Prizemoney* £15,219
Wins 1999 Jly Bath (G-F) H 10.2f 56 55
1997 *Nov Lingfi (STD) 7f 62 <*
2000 Turf 0-8: (10f 5, 12f 3) (g-s, gd 3, g-f 3, frm)
Average gelding, effective 10f, acts on frm - acts on Equi, has worn blinkers, likes left handed tracks. Turf high 58.
**B W Hills [0-8] Mrs B W Hills (from P J Makin [2-18] Spt 1999).*

ILE DISTINCT (IRE) BHB 52f **RR 62f** 4649[8]

6 b g Dancing Dissident (USA) 6.8f **(65)** - Golden Sunlight (Ile de Bourbon (USA)) 10.1f **(67)**
Form - 2048
Record 2000 - 1st:0 2nd:1 3rd:0 Ran:4
Pre2000 - 1st:2 2nd:1 3rd:3 Ran:15
Win Prizemoney £5,030 *Total Prizemoney* £9,001
Wins * 1997 Spt Nottin (G-F) 10f 69 <
* 1997 Aug Mussel (G-F) 8f 54
2000 Turf 0-3: (10f, 11f, 12f) (g-f, frm 2) 2000 AW 0-1: (11f) (Fibr)
Average gelding, effective 9 to 12f, best at 9f, acts on g-f to frm, best on frm, has worn blinkers. Turf high 62 (1st run) - 2nd of 5 getting 2lb from Fatehalkhair (20 Jun Thirsk 12f frm RF 2119). Becoming disappointing.
**Mrs A Duffield [2-21] Windsor Room Syndicate.*

ILE MICHEL BHB 85f **RR 88df** 4968[13]

3 b g Machiavellian (USA) 9.8f **(83)** - Circe's Isle (Be My Guest (USA)) 9.3f **(67)**
Form - 0
Record 2000 - 1st:0 2nd:0 3rd:0 Ran:1
Pre2000 - 1st:1 2nd:1 3rd:0 Ran:3
Win Prizemoney £3,057 *Total Prizemoney* £4,593
Wins * 1999 Spt Catter (G-F) 6f 76++ <
2000 Turf 0-1: (8f) (gd)
Well made, useful gelding. **G Wragg [1-4] A E Oppenheimer.*

ILEWIN JANINE (IRE) **RR 44f** 264[10]

9 b m Soughaan (USA) 8f **(42)** - Mystery Queen (Martinmas) 7.6f **(59)**
Form - 0
Record 2000 - 1st:0 2nd:0 3rd:0 Ran:1
Pre2000 - 1st:0 2nd:0 3rd:0 Ran:1
2000 AW 0-1: (12f) (Fibr)
Moderate mare.
**P Eccles [0-2] Tom Segrue (from P D Evans [0-1] Oct 1999).*

ILISSUS (USA) BHB 48f54a **RR 17f 54a** 4813[16]

4 b g Alleged (USA) 11.8f **(81)** - Reine des Iles (USA) (Nureyev (USA)) 8.7f **(78)**
Form - 00000
Record 2000 - 1st:0 2nd:0 3rd:0 Ran:4
Pre2000 - 1st:0 2nd:1 3rd:1 Ran:4
Win Prizemoney £0 *Total Prizemoney* £1,667
2000 Turf 0-3: (8f 2, 10f) (sft, g-s, gd) 2000 AW 0-1: (10f) (Equi)
Scopey, poor gelding, effective 7 to 8f, acts on gd, has worn blinkers, favours tight tracks. Turf high 17.
**P Mitchell [0-5] Crossbar Racing Partnership (from M P Tregoning [0-3] May 1999).*

ILJASOOR (USA) **RR 76f** 964[6]

3 b c Rainbow Quest (USA) 11.2f **(81)** - Jasoorah (IRE) (Sadler's Wells (USA)) 10f **(76)**
Form - 6
Record 2000 - 1st:0 2nd:0 3rd:0 Ran:1
Pre2000 - 1st:0 2nd:0 3rd:0 Ran:1
2000 Turf 0-1: (10f) (gd)
Light-framed, currently above-average colt.
**M P Tregoning [0-2] Sheikh Ahmed Al Maktoum.*

ILLUSIONIST BHB 68f **RR 65f** 5223[8]

2 b c Mujtahid (USA) 7.4f **(69)** - Merlin's Fancy **(64f)** (Caerleon (USA)) 8.6f **(71)**
Form - 408
Record 2000 - 1st:0 2nd:0 3rd:0 Ran:3
Win Prizemoney £0 *Total Prizemoney* £260
2000 Turf 0-3: (6f 3) (gd 3)
Currently average colt. Turf high 65.
**E A L Dunlop [0-3] Meg Dennis,Michael B Brown.*

ILLUSIVE (IRE) BHB 70f83a **RR 71f 83a** 4207[17]

3 b g Night Shift (USA) 8.1f **(73)** - Mirage (Red Sunset) 8.2f **(63)**
Form - 2141120355332000
Record 2000 - 1st:2 2nd:2 3rd:3 Ran:14
Pre2000 - 1st:2 2nd:1 3rd:0 Ran:8
Win Prizemoney £14,232 *Total Prizemoney* £21,208
Wins * **2000** *Feb Lingfi (STD) H 6f 75 83 <*
2000 *Feb Lingfi (STD) H 6f 71 78*
1999 *Nov Southw (STD) H 5f 65 70*
1999 *Oct Lingfi (STD) H 6f 56 64*
2000 Turf 0-10: (5f 4, 6f 6) (gd, g-f 6, frm 2, hrd) 2000 AW 2-4: (5f, 6f 2-3) (Equi 2-3, Fibr)
Strong, decent gelding, effective 5 to 6f, best at 6f, - acts on Equi, mostly wears blinkers (very effectively), prefers left handed tracks, prefers tight tracks. Turf high 71. AW high 83 - 1st of 6 giving 1lb to Otime (26 Feb Lingfield RF 0362) - also 1st of 5 giving 1lb to Castle Sempill (2 Feb Lingfield RF 0207). Becoming disappointing. He is an effective sort in sprint company on sand and acts on both types of surface. Suited by five and six furlongs.
**M Wigham [1-12] Danny Bloor (from H J Collingridge [2-4] Feb 2000).*

ILLUSTRIOUS DUKE BHB 48f58a **RR 40f 58a** 5157[16]

2 b c Dancing Spree (USA) 8f **(59)** - Killick **(64f 55a)** (Slip Anchor) 9.8f

(73)
Form - 000
Record 2000 - 1st:0 2nd:0 3rd:0 Ran:3
2000 Turf 0-3: (6f, 7f, 8f) (sft, g-s, g-f)
Currently average colt. Turf high 40 (began Spt).
**M Mullineaux [0-3] Esprit de Corps Racing.*

IL PRINCIPE (IRE) BHB 34f65a RR 56f 65a 4459[9]

6 b g Ela-Mana-Mou 12.7f **(72)** - Seattle Siren (USA) (Seattle Slew (USA)) 9.4f **(76)**
Form - 240070080840
Record 2000 - 1st:0 2nd:0 3rd:0 Ran:10
Pre2000 - 1st:10 2nd:5 3rd:6 Ran:41
Win Prizemoney £43,635 *Total Prizemoney* £51,899

Wins								
* 1999	Nov	Doncas	(SFT)	H	16.5f	75	77	<
* 1999	Oct	York	(SFT)	H	13.9f	69	72	
* 1999	Aug	Mussel	(G-S)	H	16f	63	69	
* 1999	Aug	Haydoc	(SFT)	H	14f	57	63	
* 1998	Oct	Redcar	(G-S)	H	14.1f	58	60	
* 1997	Spt	Catter	(G-F)	H	15.8f	54	65	
* 1997	Spt	Mussel	(G-F)	H	16f	46	61	
* 1997	*Spt*	*Southw*	*(STD)*	*H*	*14f*	*50*	*59*	
* 1997	Aug	Mussel	(G-F)	H	12f	35	48	
* 1997	Aug	Hamilt	(GD)	H	11.1f	35	40	

2000 Turf 0-10: (10f, 12f, 13f 2, 14f 3, 15f, 16f 2) (g-s 3, gd 2, g-f 4, frm)
Above-average gelding, effective 14 to 17f, best at 14f, acts on sft to frm - acts on Fibr, has worn blinkers, likes tight tracks, excels at Haydock. Turf high 67. An effective stayer in modest company, he tries his hardest and is well handled by his underrated trainer. He is best suited by soft ground.
**John Berry [10-51] The 1997 Partnership.*

I'M A CHARACTER RR 43f 3190[5]

2 br f Tragic Role (USA) 9.4f **(63)** - Lizzie Bee (Kind of Hush) 10.1f **(62)**
Form - 785
Record 2000 - 1st:0 2nd:0 3rd:0 Ran:3
2000 Turf 0-2: (7f 2) (gd, frm) 2000 AW 0-1: (7f) (Fibr)
Currently moderate filly. Turf high 43.
**M Blanshard [0-3] Aykroyd and Sons Ltd.*

IMAD (USA) BHB 50f45a RR 54f 45a 1901[10]

10 b or br g Al Nasr (FR) 9.9f **(72)** - Blue Grass Field (Top Ville) 11.7f **(68)**
Form - 3410
Record 2000 - 1st:1 2nd:0 3rd:1 Ran:4
Pre2000 - 1st:2 2nd:1 3rd:0 Ran:10
Win Prizemoney £20,014 *Total Prizemoney* £20,989

Wins							
* 2000	Apr	Pontef	(HVY)	H	21.6f	46	54
* 1999	Apr	Pontef	(G-S)	H	21.6f	41	44

2000 Turf 1-3: (16f, 17f, 22f 1-1) (sft 1-1, g-s, frm) 2000 AW 0-1: (16f) (Fibr)
Fair gelding, effective 22f, acts on sft to gd, has worn blinkers. Turf high 54 - 1st of 17 getting 7lb from Charming Admiral (17 Apr Pontefract RF 0748). A real stayer on the Flat and over hurdles, he appreciated the test of stamina when winning over the extended two miles five at Pontefract in April.
**K C Comerford [3-19] Alan Brackley (from J White [3-19] Jun 1996).*

IMAGINE (IRE) RR 95f 4990[2]

2 b f Sadler's Wells (USA) 11.3f **(87)** - Doff the Derby (USA) (Master Derby (USA)) 9.5f **(69)**
Form - 361412
2000 Turf 2-6: (7f 1-4, 8f 1-2) (sft 1-1, gd 1-5)
Very useful filly, effective 7 to 8f, best at 7f, acts on sft to gd, best on gd. Turf high 95 (began Aug) - 1st of 12 from Katherine Seymour (30 Spt Curragh RF 4793a) - also 1st of 12 from Dance Till Dawn (14 Spt Gowran Park RF 4513a). A half-sister to Generous, she tackled high-class company on her first two starts and was found wanting. Landed the odds in a maiden before finishing a fair fourth in the Fillies' Mile, back at the top level.
**A P O'Brien in IRE [2-6] Mrs John Magnier & John T L Jones Jr.*

IMARI BHB 63f52a RR 69df 52a 4695[13]

3 b f Rock City 8.8f **(62)** - Misty Goddess (IRE) **(51df 37a)** (Godswalk (USA)) 7.3f **(58)**
Form - 02501326310
Record 2000 - 1st:2 2nd:2 3rd:2 Ran:10
Pre2000 - 1st:0 2nd:0 3rd:0 Ran:6
Win Prizemoney £4,259 *Total Prizemoney* £7,010

Wins								
2000	Aug	Yarmou	(G-F)	C	10.1f	60+		<
2000	Jun	Yarmou	(GD)	SH	8f	55	58	

2000 Turf 2-8: (7f, 8f 1-2, 10f 1-5) (gd 1-2, g-f 1-5, frm) 2000 AW 0-2: (8f 2) (Fibr 2)
Light-framed, average filly, effective 10f, acts on g-f. Turf high 69 - 3rd of 17 giving 9lb to Alexandrine (15 Jun Yarmouth 10f g-f RF 1999) - also 1st of 7 giving 6lb to Ede'iff (16 Aug Yarmouth RF 3709). AW high 43.
**R G Frost [0-1] J F O'Donovan (from N P Littmoden [2-7] Aug 2000).*

IMBACKAGAIN (IRE) BHB 47f38a RR 48f 38a 2538[6]

5 b g Mujadil (USA) 7.7f **(70)** - Ballinclogher (IRE) (Creative Plan (USA)) 7.5f **(67)**
Form - 0063080202146
Record 2000 - 1st:1 2nd:2 3rd:1 Ran:11
Pre2000 - 1st:1 2nd:2 3rd:2 Ran:23
Win Prizemoney £3,915 *Total Prizemoney* £8,144

Wins								
* **2000**	*Jun*	*Southw*	*(STD)*	*SH*	*7f*	*30*	*42*	
* 1998	*Jan*	*Southw*	*(STD)*	*H*	*6f*	*60*	*64*	<

2000 Turf 0-5: (7f 5) (gd 2, g-f, frm 2) 2000 AW 1-6: (7f 1-1, 8f 3, 9f, 11f) (Fibr 1-6)
Moderate gelding, effective 7f, acts on g-f - acts on AW, favours left handed tracks, favours tight tracks. Turf high 48 (1st run) - 2nd of 16 giving 8lb to Mr Cube (17 May Brighton 7f g-f RF 1260). AW high 42. He won on Fibresand at the start of last year, and though he has not won since, his best form since has been on that surface.
**N P Littmoden [2-31] Turf 2000 Ltd (from P C Haslam [0-3] Aug 1997).*

I'M LULU BHB 60f52a RR 60f 52a 4820[12]

2 b f Piccolo - Everdene (Bustino) 10.4f **(64)**
Form - 060
Record 2000 - 1st:0 2nd:0 3rd:0 Ran:3
2000 Turf 0-3: (6f 2, 7f) (g-s, g-f, frm)
Currently average filly. Turf high 60 (began Spt).
**Mrs A J Perrett [0-3] S P Tindall.*

IMMACULATE CHARLIE (IRE) BHB 46f RR 50f 4264[7]

2 ch f Rich Charlie 5.9f **(50)** - Miner's Society (Miner's Lamp)
Form - 32047
Record 2000 - 1st:0 2nd:1 3rd:1 Ran:5
Win Prizemoney £0 *Total Prizemoney* £1,321
2000 Turf 0-5: (6f 3, 8f, 9f) (g-s, gd, g-f, frm 2)
Fair filly. Turf high 50 - 2nd of 8 to Forest Moon (19 Jun Windsor 6f frm RF 2104). **A T Murphy [0-5] Mrs Ann Fortune.*

IMPALDI (IRE) BHB 46f RR 45f 4173[3]

5 b m Imp Society (USA) 7.1f **(63)** - Jaldi (IRE) (Nordico (USA)) 6.5f **(62)**
Form - 80507023373
Record 2000 - 1st:0 2nd:1 3rd:3 Ran:11
Pre2000 - 1st:0 2nd:1 3rd:0 Ran:21
Win Prizemoney £0 *Total Prizemoney* £3,620
2000 Turf 0-10: (5f 6, 6f 4) (g-f 2, frm 7, hrd) 2000 AW 0-1: (5f) (Fibr)
Moderate filly, effective 5 to 6f, acts on frm to hrd, has worn blinkers. Turf high 45.
**B Ellison [0-23] Mrs Susan Ellison (from M J Grassick in IRE [0-9] Spt 1998).*

IMPEACHMENT (USA) RR 1449a[3]

3 b c Deputy Minister (CAN) 9.2f **(71)** - Misconduct (Criminal Type (USA))
Form - 33
2000 AW 0-2: (10f 2) (Dirt 2)
Currently high-class colt. AW high 117 - 3rd of 8 to Red Bullet (20 May Pimlico 10f Dirt RF 1449a). One of the leading colts in America last year, he finished strongly to grab third place in both the Preakness and Kentucky Derby.
**T Pletcher in USA [0-2] Dogwood Stable.*

IMPERIAL BEAUTY (USA) BHB 113f RR 117f 2110[4]

4 b f Imperial Ballet (IRE) - Multimara (USA) (Arctic Tern (USA)) 8.9f **(69)**
Form - 44
Record 2000 - 1st:0 2nd:0 3rd:0 Ran:2
Pre2000 - 1st:3 2nd:4 3rd:0 Ran:9

Win Prizemoney £50,381 *Total Prizemoney* £129,355

Wins * 1999 Spt Newbur (G-S) L 5.2f 104+ <
* 1999 Jly York (G-F) L 6f 104
* 1998 Spt Salisb (GD) 6f 90+

2000 Turf 0-2: (5f 2) (g-s, gd)

Scopey, high-class filly, effective 5f, acts on sft to gd. Turf high 108 - 4th of 23 getting 3lb from Nuclear Debate (20 Jun Ascot 5f gd RF 2110). She developed into a high-class sprinter in soft ground in 1999, cruising home in a Newbury Listed event before failing narrowly to beat the Japanese colt Agnes World in the Prix de l'Abbaye. She had no chance from her draw in the Group Two Temple Stakes on her return and was unlucky in running at Royal Ascot next time. Was subsequently bought by Michael Tabor for 950,000gns, and be trained next season by John Hammond in France. **P J Makin [3-11] Dr Carlos Stelling.*

Imperial Beauty will be trained by John Hammond next season

IMPERIAL DANCER RR 95f 5108[8]

2 b c Primo Dominie 7.2f **(67)** - Gorgeous Dancer (IRE) (Nordico (USA)) 6.5f **(62)**

Form - 4213024513258

Record 2000 - 1st:2 2nd:3 3rd:2 Ran:13

Win Prizemoney £14,705 *Total Prizemoney* £32,958

Wins * **2000** Aug York (GD) H 7f 95 95 <
* **2000** Apr Warwic (HVY) 5f 79

2000 Turf 2-13: (5f 1-4, 6f 3, 7f 1-5, 8f) (hvy 1-1, g-s, gd 1-6, frm 2, hrd 2)

Very useful colt, effective 6 to 7f, best at 7f, acts on frm, best on gd. Turf high 95 - 5th of 13 to King Charlemagne (29 Spt Newmarket 7f gd RF 4733) - also 1st of 13 giving 19lb to Dominaite (22 Aug York RF 3855). **M R Channon [2-13] Imperial Racing.*

IMPERIALIST (IRE) RR 78df 4809[9]

3 b f Imperial Frontier (USA) 7f **(65)** - Petrine (IRE) (Petorius) 7.3f **(61)**

Form - 5007280040

Record 2000 - 1st:0 2nd:1 3rd:0 Ran:10
Pre2000 - 1st:2 2nd:0 3rd:2 Ran:8

Win Prizemoney £6,760 *Total Prizemoney* £25,037

Wins * 1999 Jun Salisb (GD) 5f 99 <
* 1999 May Sandow (GD) 5f 80

2000 Turf 0-10: (5f 4, 6f 5, 7f) (g-s 3, g-f 4, frm 2, hrd)

Scopey, above-average filly, effective 5f, acts on g-f, has worn blinkers. Turf high 81. **R Hannon [2-18] Taylor Homer Racing*

IMPERIAL MEASURE BHB 96f **RR 89f** 5108[9]

2 b c Inchinor 8.9f **(64)** - Fair Eleanor (Saritamer (USA)) 9.5f **(63)**

Form - 1502130

Record 2000 - 1st:2 2nd:1 3rd:1 Ran:7

Win Prizemoney £6,389 *Total Prizemoney* £39,165

Wins * **2000** Aug Nottin (GD) H 6.1f 82 89 <
* **2000** May Windso (G-S) 5f 69

2000 Turf 2-7: (5f 1-2, 6f 1-4, 7f) (gd 1-4, g-f 1-1, frm, hrd)

Useful colt, effective 6f, acts on gd to frm. Turf high 89 - 3rd of 22 to Goggles (6 Spt Doncaster 6f gd RF 4259) - also 1st of 7 giving 2lb to Injaaz (21 Aug Nottingham RF 3838). He made a winning debut at Windsor in May despite not getting the clearest of runs, but raced too freely next time. Ran well in nurseries, including winning under top weight at Nottingham.
**B R Millman [2-7] Southern Cross Racing.*

IMPERIAL ROCKET (USA) BHB 83f **RR 90f** 5134[13]

3 b br g Northern Flagship (USA) 12.2f **(72)** - Starsawhirl (USA) (Star de Naskra (USA)) 9.7f **(65)**

Form - 46702280

Record 2000 - 1st:0 2nd:2 3rd:0 Ran:8
Pre2000 - 1st:2 2nd:0 3rd:0 Ran:4

Win Prizemoney £10,714 *Total Prizemoney* £16,264

Wins * 1999 Nov Windso (G-S) H 8.3f 83 96 <
* 1999 Oct Leices (GD) 8f 83+

2000 Turf 0-8: (8f, 10f 7) (sft, g-s 2, gd, g-f 3, frm)

Scopey, useful gelding, effective 8 to 10f, best at 10f, acts on gd to frm. Turf high 90. Ended 1999 with victories in a Leicester maiden and a Windsor nursery. Mixed form in 2000, but in good heart in July, twice second over ten furlongs on fast ground.
**R Hannon [2-12] The Royal Ascot Racing Club.*

IMPERIOSO (GER) RR 102f 2981a[1]

4 ch c Royal Academy (USA) - Ilana (GER)

Form - 51

2000 Turf 1-2: (10f 1-1, 11f) (hvy, gd 1-1)

Currently very useful. Turf high 116 - 1st of 9 getting 6lb from Kalatos (16 Jly Frankfurt RF 2981a). A tough sort, he has won Group 3s at Frankfurt in each of the past two seasons. He is capable of scoring in that grade again next term.
**P Schiergen in GER [1-2] Gestut Schlenderhan.*

IMPERO BHB 63f **RR 66f** 5066[13]

2 b c Emperor Jones (USA) - Fight Right (FR) (Crystal Glitters (USA)) 11.3f **(79)**

Form - 5700

Record 2000 - 1st:0 2nd:0 3rd:0 Ran:4

2000 Turf 0-4: (7f 2, 8f 2) (g-s, gd, g-f, frm)

Average colt. Turf high 66. **B Smart [0-4] R Lamb.*

IMPISH LAD BHB 57f55a **RR 56f 55a** 3383[9]

2 b g Imp Society (USA) 7.1f **(63)** - Madonna da Rossi **(42f 25a)** (Mtoto)

Form - 052363230

Record 2000 - 1st:0 2nd:2 3rd:3 Ran:9

Win Prizemoney £0 *Total Prizemoney* £1,974

2000 Turf 0-7: (5f 2, 7f 5) (g-s, g-f, frm 5) 2000 AW 0-2: (6f, 7f) (Fibr 2)

Fair gelding, effective 6 to 7f, best at 7f, acts on frm - acts on Fibr, often wears blinkers (effectively). Turf high 56 - 3rd of 10 giving 5lb to Windchill (13 Jun Redcar 7f frm RF 1910). AW high 56. Consistent. **B S Rothwell [0-9] Mrs L Beharrell.*

IMPREVUE (IRE) BHB 59f55a **RR 62f 55a** 4616[15]

6 ch m Priolo (USA) 10.9f **(71)** - Las Bela (Welsh Pageant) 10f **(65)**

Form - 146310

Record 2000 - 1st:1 2nd:0 3rd:1 Ran:4
Pre2000 - 1st:5 2nd:4 3rd:4 Ran:29

Win Prizemoney £15,988 *Total Prizemoney* £24,170

Wins * **2000** Aug Yarmou (G-F) 10.1f 62
* 1999 *Nov Lingfi (STD) 10f 61*
* 1999 Oct Nottin (FRM) 10f 62
* 1999 Spt Bright (G-F) H 10f 44 55
* 1999 *Jly Lingfi (STD) H 10f 47 53*
1997 Oct Currag (SFT) 12f 85 <

2000 Turf 1-4: (10f 1-2, 12f 2) (gd, g-f 1-2, frm)

Average mare, effective 9 to 12f, best at 10f, acts on g-s to frm - acts on Equi, often wears blinkers, likes left handed tracks, favours tight tracks, likes Lingfield. Turf high 62 (began Jly) - 1st of 12 getting 3lb from Mawingo (16 Aug Yarmouth RF 3710). Consistent.

**R J O'Sullivan [5-19] Mrs Barbara Marchant (from D P Kelly in IRE [1-8] Oct 1998).*

IMPREZA BHB 31f **RR 13f** 4996[11]

2 b f Mistertopogigo (IRE) - Little Redwing **(34f)** (Be My Chief (USA))

Form - 847000

Record 2000 - 1st:0 2nd:0 3rd:0 Ran:6

Win Prizemoney £0 *Total Prizemoney* £222

2000 Turf 0-5: (5f, 6f 2, 7f 2) (g-s, gd 3, frm) 2000 AW 0-1: (8f) (Fibr)

Poor filly, often wears blinkers. Turf high 13. **Miss A Stokell [0-6] Ms Caron Stokell.*

IMPULSIVE AIR (IRE) BHB 39f44a **RR 45f 44a** 4745[19]

8 b g Try My Best (USA) 7.8f **(68)** - Tracy's Sundown (Red Sunset) 8.2f **(63)**

Form - 5072784377070

Record 2000 - 1st:0 2nd:1 3rd:1 Ran:13
Pre2000 - 1st:8 2nd:8 3rd:4 Ran:65

Win Prizemoney £30,972 *Total Prizemoney* £53,538

Wins 1999 Jun Hamilt (GD) H 9.2f 47 48
1998 Jun Carlis (G-S) H 8f 65 68 <
1998 May Ripon (GD) H 8f 59 65
1997 Aug Mussel (G-F) 7.1f 62
1997 Aug Redcar (FRM) 8f 63
1996 Aug Newcas (G-F) H 8f 60 64
1996 Jun Carlis (FRM) H 6.9f 58 57

2000 Turf 0-12: (8f 3, 9f 7, 10f, 11f) (gd 4, g-f 5, frm 3) 2000 AW 0-1: (9f) (Fibr)

Moderate gelding, effective 8 to 10f, best at 9f, acts on gd to frm, has worn blinkers, likes left handed tracks, likes tight tracks, and excels at Ayr. Turf high 45 - 2nd of 10 getting 6lb from Adobe (19 May Hamilton 8f g-f RF 1298).

**J R Weymes [0-13] T A Scothern (from E Weymes [8-65] Oct 1999).*

I'M SOPHIE (IRE) BHB 57f40a **RR 63f 40a** 5118[10]

3 ch f Shalford (IRE) 7.8f **(63)** - Caisson **(67f)** (Shaadi (USA))

Form - 450

Record 2000 - 1st:0 2nd:0 3rd:0 Ran:3
Pre2000 - 1st:0 2nd:1 3rd:0 Ran:1

Win Prizemoney £0 *Total Prizemoney* £1,059

2000 Turf 0-1: (6f) (g-s) 2000 AW 0-2: (5f, 6f) (Fibr 2)

Workmanlike, average filly. AW high 48.

**D Burchell [0-1] Three Acres Racing (from T D Barron [0-3] Apr 2000).*

INAAQ **RR 109f** 4963[3]

3 ch f Lammtarra (USA) - Elfaslah (IRE) (Green Desert (USA)) 8.6f **(78)**

Form - 143

Record 2000 - 1st:1 2nd:0 3rd:1 Ran:3

Win Prizemoney £5,655 *Total Prizemoney* £11,642

Wins * **2000** Jly Newmar (G-S) 10f 85+ <

2000 Turf 1-3: (10f 1-1, 12f, 13f) (gd 1-3)

Currently Pattern-class filly. Turf high 109 (began Jly) - 4th of 11 to Mouramara (30 Spt Longchamp 13f gd RF 4837a). A half-sister to Almutawakel, she made a belated winning debut at Newmarket. Did not do too badly on her next run in a Group Two at the Arc meeting, and in the rescheduled Princess Royal at Newmarket. However, it is possible that she does not quite get a mile and a half, and a drop back in trip may prove worthwhile. **S bin Suroor [1-3] Godolphin.*

IN A TWINKLING (IRE) BHB 56f **RR 59f** 4616[18]

3 b f Brief Truce (USA) 9.1f **(73)** - Glim (USA) (Damascus (USA)) 8.9f **(71)**

Form - 0060

Record 2000 - 1st:0 2nd:0 3rd:0 Ran:4
Pre2000 - 1st:0 2nd:0 3rd:1 Ran:7

Win Prizemoney £0 *Total Prizemoney* £2,088

2000 Turf 0-4: (7f, 10f 3) (gd 2, g-f, frm)

Fair filly. Turf high 59.

**Major D N Chappell [0-4] The Star Racing Partnership (from W M Roper in IRE [0-7] Oct 1999).*

INCA STAR (USA) BHB 85f **RR 85f** 2182[P]

3 b c Trempolino (USA) 11.9f **(77)** - Inca Empress (USA) (Sovereign Dancer (USA)) 11.2f **(68)**

Form - 56121P

Record 2000 - 1st:2 2nd:1 3rd:0 Ran:6
Pre2000 - 1st:0 2nd:0 3rd:1 Ran:1

Win Prizemoney £7,904 *Total Prizemoney* £9,601

Wins * **2000** Jun Ripon (G-S) H 12.3f 82 85 <
* **2000** May Hamilt (G-F) 12.1f 76+

2000 Turf 2-6: (8f, 10f, 12f 2-4) (gd 2, g-f 2-4)

Scopey, useful colt, effective 12f, acted on g-f. Turf high 85 - 1st of 7 giving 14lb to Under The Sand (11 Jun Ripon RF 1890) - also 1st of 8 from Full Ahead (19 May Hamilton RF 1300). (DEAD)

**M Johnston [2-7] Jaber Abdullah.*

INCEPTA BHB 45f48a **RR 39f 48a** 5077[19]

5 b g Selkirk (USA) 7.9f **(76)** - Ringlet (USA) **(53f 54a)** (Secreto (USA)) 8.7f **(72)**

Form - 0

Record 2000 - 1st:0 2nd:0 3rd:0 Ran:1
Pre2000 - 1st:1 2nd:1 3rd:1 Ran:13

Win Prizemoney £2,814 *Total Prizemoney* £4,248

Wins 1998 *Dec Wolver (STD) 8.5f 61* <

2000 Turf 0-1: (10f) (g-s)

Average gelding, has worn blinkers. Becoming disappointing.

**Miss Z C Davison [0-1] Miss Z C Davison (from P S McEntee [1-9] Apr 1999).*

INCHALONG BHB 57f47a **RR 62df 47a** 4442[11]

5 b m Inchinor 8.9f **(64)** - Reshift (Night Shift (USA)) 7.2f **(69)**

Form - 06000

Record 2000 - 1st:0 2nd:0 3rd:0 Ran:3
Pre2000 - 1st:5 2nd:9 3rd:9 Ran:55

Win Prizemoney £25,045 *Total Prizemoney* £44,941

Wins * 1999 Spt Pontef (G-F) H 6f 59 61
* 1998 Aug Ripon (G-F) H 6f 72 75 <
* 1998 Jly Windso (GD) H 6f 69 72
* 1997 Aug Mussel (GD) H 7.1f 64 70
* 1997 Jun Newcas (GD) S 6f 61

2000 Turf 0-3: (6f, 7f 2) (gd 2, frm)

Average filly, effective 6 to 7f, best at 6f, acts on gd to frm, often wears blinkers (effectively). Turf high 43.

**M Brittain [5-58] Northgate Lodge Partnerships.*

INCHCAPE **RR 77+f** 5318[3]

2 b c Indian Ridge 7.6f **(74)** - Inchmurrin (Lomond (USA)) 8.8f **(65)**

Form - 3

Record 2000 - 1st:0 2nd:0 3rd:1 Ran:1

Win Prizemoney £0 *Total Prizemoney* £517

2000 Turf 0-1: (6f) (sft)

Currently above-average colt. **R Charlton [0-1] A E Oppenheimer.*

INCHDURA RR 57f 5310[9]

2 ch c Inchinor 8.9f **(64)** - Sunshine Coast (Posse (USA)) 8.9f **(61)**
Form - 0
Record 2000 - 1st:0 2nd:0 3rd:0 Ran:1
2000 Turf 0-1: (7f) (g-s)
Currently fair colt. *R Charlton [0-1] S M De Zoete.*

INCHING CLOSER BHB 82f **RR 84f** 3471a[3]

3 b g Inchinor 8.9f **(64)** - Maiyaasah (Kris) 9.5f **(73)**
Form - 8013333
Record 2000 - 1st:1 2nd:0 3rd:4 Ran:7
Pre2000 - 1st:0 2nd:1 3rd:0 Ran:3
Win Prizemoney £3,770 *Total Prizemoney* £10,338
Wins * **2000** Jun Ayr (G-F) 10f 81 <
2000 Turf 1-7: (8f, 9f, 10f 1-2, 12f 3) (g-s, gd, g-f, frm 1-3, hrd)
Scopey, decent gelding, effective 6 to 12f, best at 12f, acts on gd to hrd. Turf high 84 - 3rd of 14 getting 18lb from Grinkov (4 Aug Galway 12f gd RF 3471a) - also 1st of 8 from Takamaka Bay (2 Jun Ayr RF 1639). *N A Callaghan [1-10] Gallagher Equine Ltd.*

INCHINNAN BHB 70f **RR 74f** 3346[6]

3 b f Inchinor 8.9f **(64)** - Westering **(29f 38a)** (Auction Ring (USA)) 8.6f **(65)**
Form - 21326
Record 2000 - 1st:1 2nd:2 3rd:1 Ran:5
Pre2000 - 1st:0 2nd:3 3rd:1 Ran:8
Win Prizemoney £4,309 *Total Prizemoney* £10,310
Wins * **2000** Apr Epsom (HVY) 8.5f 61 <
2000 Turf 1-5: (8f 2, 9f 1-2, 10f) (sft 1-1, gd 2, g-f, frm)
Light-framed, above-average filly, effective 7 to 10f, best at 7f, acts on gd to frm, best on g-f. Turf high 74 - 3rd of 19 giving 9lb to Tempramental (26 May Pontefract 10f g-f RF 1471). Consistent.
C Weedon [1-5] C Rosbottom (from D Morris [0-8] Oct 1999).

INCHIRI RR 85f 5241[4]

2 b f Sadler's Wells (USA) 11.3f **(87)** - Inchyre **(100f)** (Shirley Heights) 10.3f **(74)**
Form - 54
Record 2000 - 1st:0 2nd:0 3rd:0 Ran:2
Win Prizemoney £0 *Total Prizemoney* £1,590
2000 Turf 0-2: (7f, 8f) (g-s, gd)
Currently useful filly. Turf high 85 (began Spt). Ran on in the closing stages on her Ascot debut and ran a similar race in a listed event next time. She should find a race over middle distances if not aimed too high. *G A Butler [0-2] Woodcote Stud Ltd.*

INCHLONAIG RR 102f 1863[11]

3 ch c Nashwan (USA) 10.3f **(79)** - Inchmurrin (Lomond (USA)) 8.8f **(65)**
Form - 40
Record 2000 - 1st:0 2nd:0 3rd:0 Ran:2
Pre2000 - 1st:1 2nd:0 3rd:0 Ran:1
Win Prizemoney £166,850 *Total Prizemoney* £182,094
Wins 1999 Spt Newmar (G-S) 7f 98+ <
2000 Turf 0-1: (12f) (gd) 2000 AW 0-1: (9f) (Dirt)
Scopey, currently Group-class colt. He reportedly cost £1m after winning a valuable sales race in 1999, but has yet to live up to that price tag. Not seen out after running poorly in the Derby, he should stay middle-distances and remains unexposed. It will be interesting to see if Godolphin include him in their European squad for 2001.
S bin Suroor [0-1] Godolphin (from S bin Suroor in UAE [0-1] Mar 2000).

INCH PERFECT BHB 84f76a **RR 89+f 76a** 4197[8]

5 b g Inchinor 8.9f **(64)** - Scarlet Veil (Tyrnavos) 10.1f **(55)**
Form - 113131008
Record 2000 - 1st:3 2nd:0 3rd:2 Ran:8
Pre2000 - 1st:6 2nd:0 3rd:4 Ran:14
Win Prizemoney £41,425 *Total Prizemoney* £46,504

Wins * **2000** Jun York (GD) H 13.9f 80 89 <
* **2000** May York (G-F) H 11.9f 73 79
* **2000** Apr Thirsk (SFT) H 8f 65 74
* 1999 *Nov Wolver (STD) H 12f 57 64*
* 1999 Oct Bath (SFT) H 10.2f 47 61++
* 1999 Oct Newcas (G-S) H 10.1f 47 59+
* 1999 Oct Pontef (GD) H 10f 47 52
1999 Spt Redcar (G-F) SH 10f 42 43
1999 *Mar Southw (STD) S 8f 54*

2000 Turf 3-8: (8f 1-1, 10f 3, 12f 1-1, 14f 1-3) (g-s 1-1, gd 2, g-f 2-4, frm)
Useful gelding, effective 10 to 14f, best at 10f, acts on gd to g-f, best on g-f, and excels at Redcar. Turf high 89 - 1st of 10 getting 11lb from Eminence Grise (16 Jun York RF 2034). Effective on both sand and turf, he had a blinding time in '99, winning six times. He started off last season in the same vein with three victories so far of which two were at York. He has the speed to win at a mile, but his second victory at York came over 14 furlongs. Versatile as well as progressive.
R A Fahey [7-13] Tommy Staunton (from J Hetherton [2-7] Spt 1999).

INCH PINCHER BHB 60f54a **RR 59f 54a** 293[5]

3 ch c Inchinor 8.9f **(64)** - Cutpurse Moll **(71f)** (Green Desert (USA)) 8.6f **(78)**
Form - 025755
Record 2000 - 1st:0 2nd:0 3rd:0 Ran:3
Pre2000 - 1st:1 2nd:3 3rd:1 Ran:15
Win Prizemoney £3,225 *Total Prizemoney* £5,771
Wins 1999 Aug Sandow (GD) SH 7.1f 58 66 <
2000 AW 0-3: (6f, 7f 2) (Equi 2, Fibr)
Unfurnished, fair colt, effective 6 to 7f, best at 7f, acted on g-f to frm - acted on Equi, best on g-f, had worn blinkers, liked tight tracks. AW high 52. (DEAD)
P Howling [0-6] Paul Howling (from M R Channon [1-12] Oct 1999).

INCHRORY BHB 108f **RR 104f** 4141a[3]

7 b h Midyan (USA) 9.9f **(64)** - Applecross (Glint of Gold) 9.3f **(66)**
Form - 23
2000 Turf 0-2: (9f, 12f) (sft, gd)
Very useful horse. Turf high 104 (began Aug) - 3rd of 14 to Valley Chapel (27 Aug Ovrevoll 9f sft RF 4141a). Consistent.
A Hyldmo in NOR [1-7].

INCLINATION BHB 57a **RR 15f** 527[15]

6 b m Beveled (USA) 6.9f **(64)** - Pallomere (Blue Cashmere) 6.4f **(54)**
Form - 0
Record 2000 - 1st:0 2nd:0 3rd:0 Ran:1
Pre2000 - 1st:1 2nd:6 3rd:8 Ran:31
Win Prizemoney £2,083 *Total Prizemoney* £11,045
Wins 1998 *Feb Southw (STD) H 8f 56 57* <
2000 Turf 0-1: (16f) (g-s)
Little account mare.
L R Lloyd-James [0-1] L R Lloyd-James (from Mrs L C Jewell [0-1] Oct 1998).

INCREDULOUS (FR) BHB 98f **RR 102f** 4145[8]

3 ch f Indian Ridge 7.6f **(74)** - Fetlar (Pharly (FR)) 9.8f **(68)**
Form - 241748
Record 2000 - 1st:1 2nd:1 3rd:0 Ran:6
Pre2000 - 1st:0 2nd:0 3rd:0 Ran:1
Win Prizemoney £3,672 *Total Prizemoney* £6,925
Wins * **2000** Jun Nottin (G-F) 8.2f 83 <
2000 Turf 1-6: (7f 5, 8f 1-1) (gd 3, g-f 1-3)
Scopey, very useful filly, effective 7f, acts on gd. Turf high 102 - 4th of 11 to Danceabout (3 Aug Goodwood 7f gd RF 3340). Took a Nottingham maiden by eight lengths and her running at Newmarket next time can be disregarded, as she raced on the unfavoured side. Good effort at Goodwood, where the seven furlongs looked too sharp. *J R Fanshawe [1-7] Dr Catherine Wills.*

INDEFINITE STAY RR 63f 5065[7]

2 b g Beveled (USA) 6.9f **(64)** - Wassl's Sister (Troy) 10.4f **(68)**
Form - 07
Record 2000 - 1st:0 2nd:0 3rd:0 Ran:2
2000 Turf 0-2: (8f 2) (g-s, gd)
Currently average gelding. Turf high 63 (began Spt).
W R Muir [0-2] The Four Willies Partnership.

INDEPENDENCE RR 77f 4599[7]

2 b f Selkirk (USA) 7.9f **(76)** - Yukon Hope (USA) **(71f)** (Forty Niner (USA))
Form - 37
Record 2000 - 1st:0 2nd:0 3rd:1 Ran:2

Win Prizemoney £0 *Total Prizemoney* £470
2000 Turf 0-2: (7f 2) (gd, frm)
Currently above-average filly. Turf high 77 (1st run) (began Spt) - 3rd of 12 to Lyonette (5 Spt Lingfield 7f frm RF 4222).
**E A L Dunlop [0-2] Cliveden Stud.*

INDIANA JONES (IRE) BHB 44f **RR 49f** 4655[16]

3 b g Emperor Jones (USA) - Broadway Rosie (Absalom) 7.2f **(58)**
Form - 0700

Record	**2000 -**	1st:0	2nd:0	3rd:0	Ran:4

2000 Turf 0-3: (7f 3) (g-s, gd, g-f) 2000 AW 0-1: (6f) (Fibr)
Scopey, moderate gelding. Turf high 49.
**D W Chapman [0-1] Michael Hill (from P F I Cole [0-3] May 2000).*

INDIANA PRINCESS BHB 64f **RR 68f** 1682[5]

7 b m Warrshan (USA) 9.7f **(59)** - Lovely Greek Lady (Ela-Mana-Mou) 10.1f **(70)**
Form - 2635

Record	**2000 -**	1st:0	2nd:1	3rd:1	Ran:4
	Pre2000 -	1st:5	2nd:1	3rd:4	Ran:22

Win Prizemoney £14,704 *Total Prizemoney* £19,726

Wins								
* 1999	Aug	Redcar	(GD)	H	16f	62	65	<
* 1999	Jun	Mussel	(G-S)	H	16f	59	65	<
* 1999	Jun	Mussel	(GD)	H	14f	54	57	
* 1998	Jly	Pontef	(G-F)	H	12f	49	59	
* 1998	May	Pontef	(G-F)	H	12f	46	47	

2000 Turf 0-4: (14f, 16f 3) (gd 3, frm)
Average mare, effective 12 to 16f, best at 16f, acts on gd to frm, best on frm, excels at Musselburgh. Turf high 68 (1st run) - 2nd of 11 giving 23lb to Batoutoftheblue (30 Mar Musselburgh 16f gd RF 0570). Consistent. **Mrs M Reveley [9-38] The Phoenix Racing C O.*

INDIANA SPRINGS (IRE) BHB 36f30a **RR 46f 30a** 5200[10]

3 b g Foxhound (USA) - Moss Agate (Alias Smith (USA)) 9.8f **(58)**
Form - 0754876035380

Record	**2000 -**	1st:0	2nd:0	3rd:2	Ran:13
	Pre2000 -	1st:0	2nd:0	3rd:0	Ran:3

Win Prizemoney £0 *Total Prizemoney* £562
2000 Turf 0-9: (10f 4, 11f 3, 12f 2) (g-s 2, gd 3, g-f 2, frm, hrd) 2000 AW 0-4: (7f, 8f, 11f, 12f) (Fibr 4)
Scopey, moderate gelding, effective 11f, acts on frm, has worn blinkers (effectively), likes left handed tracks. Turf high 46. AW high 31.
**J G Given [0-6] Plyvine, Guy, Howles & Slater (from N P Littmoden [0-10] Jun 2000).*

INDIAN BAZAAR (IRE) BHB 43f **RR 42f** 4276[7]

4 ch g Indian Ridge 7.6f **(74)** - Bazaar Promise (Native Bazaar) 6.9f **(62)**
Form - 03201705607

Record	**2000 -**	1st:1	2nd:1	3rd:1	Ran:11
	Pre2000 -	1st:0	2nd:1	3rd:1	Ran:7

Win Prizemoney £2,194 *Total Prizemoney* £4,522

Wins								
* **2000**	Jun	Beverl	(G-F)	H	5f	42	42	<

2000 Turf 1-11: (5f 1-7, 6f 3, 8f) (gd 3, g-f 4, frm 1-3, hrd)
Tall, moderate gelding, effective 5 to 6f, best at 5f, acts on g-f to hrd, best on frm. Turf high 42 - 5th of 17 getting 4lb from Off Hire (18 Jly Beverley 5f hrd RF 2883) - also 1st of 20 getting 4lb from Shady Deal (27 Jun Beverley RF 2299). Consistent.
**J M Bradley [1-11] Leeway (Wholesale) Meats Ltd (from Sir Mark Prescott [0-7] Spt 1999).*

INDIAN BLAZE BHB 70f65a **RR 82df 65a** 4934[16]

6 ch g Indian Ridge 7.6f **(74)** - Odile (Green Dancer (USA)) 10.3f **(74)**
Form - 34700000

Record	**2000 -**	1st:0	2nd:0	3rd:0	Ran:6
	Pre2000 -	1st:6	2nd:6	3rd:3	Ran:42

Win Prizemoney £20,153 *Total Prizemoney* £29,709

Wins								
* 1999	Oct	Newmar	(GD)	H	8f	80	84	<
* 1999	Aug	Kempto	(G-F)	H	8f	74	76+	
* 1999	Jly	Kempto	(G-F)	H	7f	69	71	
* 1999	Mar	Folkes	(SFT)	H	7f	61	64	
* 1998	*Dec*	*Wolver*	*(SLW)*	*H*	*7f*	*58*	*63*	
* 1998	Nov	Bright	(SFT)	H	6f	55	62	

2000 Turf 0-6: (6f, 7f, 8f 4) (sft, g-s, gd 3, g-f)
Decent gelding, effective 7 to 8f, best at 8f, acts on gd to frm, best on gd, has worn blinkers, likes right handed tracks. Turf high 85. A winner four times during a busy 1999, he ran very well to finish seventh in the Lincoln on his return but has cut no ice since, including on his return from a four-month break.
**D R C Elsworth [6-35] The Braves (from P W Harris [0-13] Apr 1998).*

INDIAN DANCE BHB 54f70a **RR 48f 70a** 5122[15]

4 ch g Indian Ridge 7.6f **(74)** - Petronella (USA) (Nureyev (USA)) 8.7f **(78)**
Form - 00007300

Record	**2000 -**	1st:0	2nd:0	3rd:1	Ran:8
	Pre2000 -	1st:0	2nd:0	3rd:1	Ran:7

Win Prizemoney £0 *Total Prizemoney* £940
2000 Turf 0-7: (6f 4, 7f 2, 8f) (g-s, g-f 2, frm 4) 2000 AW 0-1: (8f) (Fibr)
Workmanlike, above-average gelding. Turf high 48.
**M C Chapman [0-9] Twinacre Nurseries Ltd (from J W Hills [0-7] Spt 1999).*

INDIAN DANEHILL (IRE) **RR 118f** 4989[5]

4 b c Danehill (USA) 9.1f **(79)** - Danse Indienne (USA) (Green Dancer (USA)) 10.3f **(74)**
Form - 11245
2000 Turf 2-5: (9f, 10f 1-3, 11f 1-1) (hvy 1-1, g-s 1-2, gd 2)
Well made, high-class colt, effective 8 to 10f, best at 10f, acts on g-s to gd, best on g-s, prefers right handed tracks, likes Longchamp. Turf high 118 - also 1st of 5 from Chelsea Manor (2 Apr Longchamp RF 0630a). Improving. Top-class horse who put up an excellent display to beat Greek Dance in the Prix Ganay. A shade below that form subsequently, he pulled hard but stayed a mile and a quarter and had a smart turn-of-foot. He has been retired to the Irish National Stud.
**A Fabre in FR [3-10] Baron Edouard de Rothschild.*

INDIAN DRIVE (IRE) **RR 69f** 1991[5]

3 b c Indian Ridge 7.6f **(74)** - Daniella Drive (USA) (Shelter Half (USA)) 7.9f **(79)**
Form - 65

Record	**2000 -**	1st:0	2nd:0	3rd:0	Ran:2

2000 Turf 0-2: (6f, 7f) (g-f 2)
Currently average colt. Turf high 69.
**R Hannon [0-2] Mrs Chris Harrington.*

INDIAN FILE **RR 38f** 4466[19]

2 ch c Indian Ridge 7.6f **(74)** - Shining Water (Kalaglow) 9.8f **(67)**
Form - 0

Record	**2000 -**	1st:0	2nd:0	3rd:0	Ran:1

2000 Turf 0-1: (7f) (g-f)
Currently very moderate colt. **B W Hills [0-1] K Abdulla.*

INDIAN GIVER **RR 60f** 4820[11]

2 ch f Cadeaux Genereux 7.9f **(76)** - About Face (Midyan (USA)) 6f **(60)**
Form - 00

Record	**2000 -**	1st:0	2nd:0	3rd:0	Ran:2

2000 Turf 0-2: (5f, 6f) (g-f, frm)
Currently average filly. Turf high 60 (began Spt).
**R Hannon [0-2] Geoff Howard-Spink & Lindy Regis.*

INDIAN LODGE (IRE) BHB 123f **RR 124f** 5327a[13]

4 b c Grand Lodge (USA) - Repetitious (Northfields (USA)) 9f **(72)**
Form - 11371710

Record	**2000 -**	1st:4	2nd:0	3rd:1	Ran:8
	Pre2000 -	1st:4	2nd:1	3rd:2	Ran:11

Win Prizemoney £227,561 *Total Prizemoney* £257,213

Wins							
* **2000**	Oct	Longch	(SFT)	G1	7f	124	<
* **2000**	Spt	Longch	(SFT)	G1	8f	122	
* **2000**	Apr	Sandow	(SFT)	G2	8.1f	120	
* **2000**	Apr	Newmar	(G-S)	G3	9f	116	
* 1999	Oct	Newmar	(GD)	L	8.5f	100	
* 1999	Spt	Newmar	(G-S)	L	8f	108	
* 1999	May	Yarmou	(FRM)		8f	89+	
* 1999	May	Newbur	(Sft)		8f	85+	

2000 Turf 4-8: (7f 1-1, 8f 2-6, 9f 1-1) (sft 3-3, gd 1-3, g-f, frm)
Scopey, very high-class colt, effective 7 to 9f, best at 8f, acts on sft to g-f, best on sft, excels at Longchamp and Newbury and Newmarket. Turf high 124 - 1st of 11 from Dansili (15 Oct Longchamp RF 5095a) - also 1st of 8 from Kingsalsa (3 Spt Longchamp RF 4290a). Consistent. He showed himself to be a progressive sort by ending 1999 with victories in a couple of Newmarket Listed events. He continued to progress last year, tak-

ing the Earl Of Sefton Stakes at Newmarket and Sandown's KLM Mile in the spring and gaining Group One glory in the Prix du Moulin at Longchamp. He disappointed in the QEII but bounced back on his favoured soft ground in the Prix de la Foret. The Breeders' Cup Mile on firm ground was never going to be his cup of tea and he duly performed below par.

**Mrs A J Perrett [8-19] Seymour Cohn.*

Indian Lodge had no reservations at Longchamp

INDIAN MUSIC BHB 63f **RR 67f** 4449^{19}

3 b g Indian Ridge 7.6f **(74)** - Dagny Juel (USA) (Danzig (USA)) 8.4f **(76)**

Form - 004555326040

Record				
2000 -	1st:0	2nd:1	3rd:1	Ran:12
Pre2000 -	1st:1	2nd:0	3rd:0	Ran:6

Win Prizemoney £3,468 *Total Prizemoney* £5,550

Wins								
1999	Nov	Doncas	(SFT)	H	5f	72	74	<

2000 Turf 0-12: (5f 3, 6f 8, 7f) (hvy, gd 4, g-f 3, frm 3, hrd)

Scopey, average gelding, effective 5 to 6f, best at 5f, acts on g-s to frm, has worn blinkers. Turf high 68 - 5th of 12 getting 10lb from Molly Brown (12 Jly Doncaster 6f frm RF 2728).

**A Berry [0-12] Robert Aird (from J Berry [1-6] Nov 1999).*

INDIAN NECTAR BHB 59f51a **RR 59f 51a** 4269^{13}

7 b m Indian Ridge 7.6f **(74)** - Sheer Nectar (Piaffer (USA))

Form - 84205236410

Record				
2000 -	1st:1	2nd:2	3rd:1	Ran:11
Pre2000 -	1st:3	2nd:0	3rd:2	Ran:20

Win Prizemoney £11,751 *Total Prizemoney* £15,471

Wins								
*** 2000**	Aug	Chepst	(G-F)	H	10.2f	54	59	<
* 1999	Aug	Chepst	(G-S)	H	10.2f	46	54	
* 1999	Aug	Lingfi	(G-F)	H	10f	46	49	
* 1999	Aug	Nottin	(G-F)	H	10f	40	43	

2000 Turf 1-11: (10f 1-7, 11f, 12f 3) (gd, g-f 4, frm 1-5, hrd)

Fair mare, effective 10 to 11f, best at 10f, acts on g-f to hrd, best on frm, has worn blinkers, prefers left handed tracks, favours tight tracks, excels at Lingfield and Chepstow, likes Nottingham. Turf high 59 - 1st of 15 getting 6lb from Sheer Face (28 Aug Chepstow RF 4033).

**R Brotherton [6-43] Mrs Carol Newman (from G B Balding [0-8] Mar 1997).*

INDIAN PLUME BHB 85f **RR 83f** 4627^{7}

4 b c Efisio 7.7f **(69)** - Boo Hoo (Mummy's Pet) 7.7f **(60)**

Form - 01001703527

Record				
2000 -	1st:2	2nd:1	3rd:1	Ran:11
Pre2000 -	1st:1	2nd:0	3rd:1	Ran:7

Win Prizemoney £12,668 *Total Prizemoney* £17,698

Wins								
*** 2000**	May	Ripon	(GD)	H	8f	76	81	
*** 2000**	Apr	Mussel	(G-S)		7.1f		82	<
* 1998	Aug	Pontef	(G-F)		6f		77	

2000 Turf 2-11: (7f 1-4, 8f 1-6, 9f) (gd 1-8, g-f 1-2, frm)

Scopey, decent colt, effective 7 to 8f, best at 8f, acts on gd to frm, best on gd, prefers right handed tracks, prefers tight tracks. Turf high 83 - 2nd of 12 giving 6lb to Strong Presence (28 Aug Ripon 8f frm RF 4050) - also 1st of 6 from Robzelda (13 Apr Musselburgh RF 0700). He loves to bowl along in front on a turning track.

**C W Thornton [3-18] Guy Reed.*

INDIAN PROSPECTOR (FR) **RR 109f** $2004a^{2}$

3 b c Machiavellian (USA) 9.8f **(83)** - Danse Indienne (USA) (Green Dancer (USA)) 10.3f **(74)**

Form - 2

2000 Turf 0-1: (8f) (gd)

Currently Pattern-class colt. (1st run) - 2nd of 8 to Cayoke (11 Jun Chantilly 8f gd RF 2004a).

**A Fabre in FR [0-1] Baron Edouard de Rothschild.*

INDIAN ROPE TRICK BHB 40f **RR 40f** 3270^{10}

4 ch g Kris 10f **(75)** - Lassoo (Caerleon (USA)) 8.6f **(71)**

Form - 000

Record				
2000 -	1st:0	2nd:0	3rd:0	Ran:3
Pre2000 -	1st:0	2nd:0	3rd:0	Ran:3

2000 Turf 0-3: (12f 2, 13f) (gd, g-f, frm)

Workmanlike, moderate gelding. Turf high 35.

**C W Thornton [0-6] Guy Reed.*

INDIAN RUBY (GER) **RR 110f** $4136a^{2}$

3 ch c Selkirk (USA) 7.9f **(76)** - Indian Night (GER) (Windwurf (GER)) 12.7f **(72)**

Form - 262622

2000 Turf 0-6: (8f, 9f, 11f 2, 12f 2) (hvy, sft 2, gd 3)

Group-class colt, effective 11 to 12f, best at 11f, acts on sft to gd, best on gd. Turf high 110 - 2nd of 5 to Sword Local (27 Aug Baden-Baden 11f sft RF 4136a). He ran consistently in some hot German Group races, but lacked the turn-of-foot required to win at that level. He might be worth a try over extended distances in 2001.

**P Schiergen in GER [0-6] Gestut Schlenderhan.*

INDIAN SPARK BHB 111f **RR 106f** 4157^{13}

6 ch g Indian Ridge 7.6f **(74)** - Annes Gift (Ballymoss) 8.5f **(55)**

Form - 841501182710

Record				
2000 -	1st:4	2nd:1	3rd:0	Ran:12
Pre2000 -	1st:6	2nd:5	3rd:2	Ran:50

Win Prizemoney £84,687 *Total Prizemoney* £104,384

Wins								
*** 2000**	Jly	Cheste	(G-S)	L	5.1f		106	<
*** 2000**	Jun	York	(GD)	H	6f	91	100	
*** 2000**	May	Haydoc	(SFT)	H	5f	85	93	
*** 2000**	Apr	Newcas	(SFT)	H	5f	78	87	
* 1999	Jun	York	(G-S)	H	6f	84	87	
* 1998	Oct	Doncas	(HVY)	H	5f	84	87	
* 1998	Spt	Doncas	(GD)	H	5f	80	84	
* 1998	Jly	Thirsk	(FRM)	H	6f	76	82	
1997	May	Salisb	(G-F)	H	6f	98	99	
1996	Mar	Doncas	(GD)		5f		85+	

2000 Turf 4-12: (5f 3-6, 6f 1-6) (sft 1-1, g-s 1-3, gd 2, g-f 2-4, frm 2)

Pattern-class gelding, effective 5 to 6f, best at 5f, acts on g-f, excels at Newcastle, likes York. Turf high 106 - 1st of 8 from Rosselli (15 Jly Chester RF 2833) - also 1st of 14 getting 2lb from Kayo (16 Jun York RF 2035). He was gelded before the start of the season and was in fine form with four victories, the last of which came in a competitive Chester Listed race. He is obviously improving, even at the age of six.

**J S Goldie [8-51] Frank Brady (from W G M Turner [2-11] Spt 1997).*

INDIAN SUN BHB 74f **RR 76f** 4484^{15}

3 ch g Indian Ridge 7.6f **(74)** - Star Tulip **(91f)** (Night Shift (USA)) 7.2f **(69)**

Form - 460720

Record				
2000 -	1st:0	2nd:1	3rd:0	Ran:6
Pre2000 -	1st:1	2nd:0	3rd:0	Ran:4

Win Prizemoney £3,492 *Total Prizemoney* £5,210

Wins								
* 1999	Oct	Lingfi	(HVY)		6f		73+	<

2000 Turf 0-6: (6f, 7f, 8f 4) (sft 2, g-s, gd 2, frm)
Scopey, above-average gelding, effective 6 to 8f, acts on sft to g-s, has worn blinkers. Turf high 77. *J L Dunlop [1-10] James Flower.*

INDIAN SWINGER (IRE) BHB 36f40a **RR 22f 40a** 5113[9]

4 ch c Up and At 'em - Seanee Squaw (Indian Ridge)
Form - 00522073377030

Record	**2000 -**	1st:0	2nd:2	3rd:3	Ran:14
	Pre2000 -	1st:1	2nd:1	3rd:2	Ran:10

Win Prizemoney £3,099 *Total Prizemoney* £7,410

Wins	1998	*Oct Southw (STD) H*	*6f*	*62*	*69*	<

2000 Turf 0-2: (8f, 10f) (gd, g-f) 2000 AW 0-12: (7f 2, 8f 8, 9f, 11f) (Equi, Fibr 11)
Workmanlike, moderate colt, effective 7f, - acts on Equi. Turf high 22 (began Jly). AW high 52.
**P Howling [0-14] Richard Berenson (from J M P Eustace [1-10] Aug 1999).*

INDIAN WARRIOR BHB 43f48a **RR 42f 48a** 4826[6]

4 b g Be My Chief (USA) 10.2f **(62)** - Wanton (Kris) 9.5f **(73)**
Form - 76660700602806

Record	**2000 -**	1st:0	2nd:1	3rd:0	Ran:14
	Pre2000 -	1st:2	2nd:2	3rd:1	Ran:11

Win Prizemoney £6,077 *Total Prizemoney* £10,280

Wins	1999	Oct Lingfi (G-F) S	7f		55+	
	1998	Aug Warwic (G-F)	7f		81	<

2000 Turf 0-10: (6f 3, 7f 3, 8f 2, 9f, 10f) (sft, gd 2, g-f 4, frm 3) 2000 AW 0-4: (7f 3, 8f) (Equi 3, Fibr)
Scopey, fair gelding, has worn blinkers. Turf high 42. AW high 54.
**W J Musson [0-15] Broughton Thermal Insulation (from J Noseda [2-10] Oct 1999).*

INDIGENOUS (IRE) RR 119f 580a[8]

7 br g Marju (IRE) 9.2f **(76)** - Sea Port (Averof) 8.2f **(62)**
Form - 2408
2000 Turf 0-1: (5f) (g-f) 2000 AW 0-1: (10f) (Dirt)
High-class gelding, effective 10 to 12f, acts on g-f to frm. Inconsistent. He originally raced in Ireland under the name Qualtron (IRE), but the name was amended under Rule 31 with effect from 3rd June 1999. Remains a force to reckon having finished second in the 1999 Japan Cup. Usually held up, he has worn a tongue strap. **I Allan in HK [1-7].*

INDIGO BAY (IRE) BHB 44f48a **RR 44f 48a** 4649[2]

4 b g Royal Academy (USA) 7.8f **(77)** - Cape Heights (Shirley Heights) 10.3f **(74)**
Form - 208451080077517302

Record	**2000 -**	1st:2	2nd:1	3rd:1	Ran:15
	Pre2000 -	1st:2	2nd:3	3rd:2	Ran:17

Win Prizemoney £10,297 *Total Prizemoney* £15,435

Wins	*** 2000**	Aug Mussel (GD) H	12f	38	41	
	2000	*Feb Lingfi (STD) C*	*13f*		*56*	
	1999	Jly Lingfi (G-F) H	11.5f	66	72	<
	1999	May Bright (FRM) SH	11.9f	55	59	

2000 Turf 1-11: (11f 2, 12f 1-7, 14f 2) (g-s, gd 2, g-f 4, frm 1-4) 2000 AW 1-4: (11f, 12f, 13f 1-1, 16f) (Equi 1-3, Fibr)
Workmanlike, fair gelding, effective 11 to 12f, best at 12f, acts on g-f to frm - acts on Equi, best on frm, has worn blinkers, favours tight tracks, excels at Brighton, likes Lingfield. Turf high 47. AW high 56.
**R Bastiman [1-11] Robin Bastiman (from P D Evans [0-1] Mar 2000).*

INDIUM BHB 76f66a **RR 78f 66a** 4375[8]

6 b g Groom Dancer (USA) 9.5f **(75)** - Gold Bracelet (Golden Fleece (USA)) 7.9f **(74)**
Form - 404010500008

Record	**2000 -**	1st:1	2nd:0	3rd:0	Ran:12
	Pre2000 -	1st:2	2nd:3	3rd:3	Ran:33

Win Prizemoney £54,990 *Total Prizemoney* £63,190

Wins	*** 2000**	May Newbur (G-F) H	10f	76	78	<
	* 1999	Spt Ascot (HVY) H	8f	74	78	<
	* 1998	Spt Newbur (GD) H	8f	71	77	

2000 Turf 1-11: (8f 7, 9f, 10f 1-3) (g-s 2, gd 1-4, g-f 3, frm 2) 2000 AW 0-1: (8f) (Fibr)
Above-average gelding, effective 7 to 10f, best at 8f, acts on sft to frm, likes left handed trackslikes right handed tracks, excels at Newbury, likes Kempton. Turf high 78 - 1st of 22 giving 9lb to Admirals Place (19 May Newbury RF 1306). Winner of the Mail On Sunday Series Final in heavy ground at Ascot in 1999, he returned to winning ways at Newbury in May when stepped up to ten furlongs. Banned from running for 40 days after being found not to have run on his merits at Yarmouth in September. Suited by coming late off a fast pace.
**W J Musson [3-40] Magnificent Seven (from J H M Gosden [0-5] Jun 1997).*

INDUCEMENT BHB 85f **RR 86f** 4556[3]

4 ch g Sabrehill (USA) 8.5f **(64)** - Verchinina (Star Appeal) 9.6f **(65)**
Form - 4153

Record	**2000 -**	1st:1	2nd:0	3rd:1	Ran:4
	Pre2000 -	1st:2	2nd:0	3rd:2	Ran:12

Win Prizemoney £14,592 *Total Prizemoney* £20,497

Wins	*** 2000**	Aug Leices (G-F) H	10f	81	83	
	1999	Jun Sandow (GD) H	9f	82	85	<
	1998	Aug Beverl (G-F)	8.5f		81	

2000 Turf 1-4: (10f 1-4) (gd 1-3, g-f)
Leggy, useful gelding, effective 9 to 10f, best at 10f, acts on gd to g-f, best on g-f, likes right handed tracks, likes tight tracks. Turf high 85 (began Jly) - 3rd of 10 giving 7lb to Annadawi (21 Spt Pontefract 10f gd RF 4556) - also 1st of 9 giving 26lb to Trois (13 Aug Leicester RF 3612). Consistent.
**Mrs A J Perrett [1-8] J B Dale (from B W Hills [2-9] Jly 1999).*

INDUSTRIALIST RR 117f 815a[1]

4 gh g Rudimentary (USA) 8.2f **(66)** - Musianica (Music Boy) 6.8f **(57)**
Form - 1
2000 Turf 1-1: (10f 1-1) (gd 1-1)
Currently high-class gelding. (1st run) - 1st of 13 getting 3lb from Jim And Tonic (15 Apr Sha Tin RF 0815a). He raced under the name Mensa for Mark Tompkins in 1998 and 1999, winning twice and running Kalanisi to a head in a Listed event at Kempton. Transferred to Hong Kong, he was in excellent form during the spring, winning the Hong Kong Gold Cup and Queen Elizabeth II Cup at Sha Tin. He will remain a major player in big races in his adopted home. **P C Kan in HK [1-1] Peter Wong Yau Ming.*

INDY CARR BHB 35f49a **RR 59f 49a** 5200[8]

3 b f Pyramus (USA) - Miss Adventure (Adonijah) 10f **(61)**
Form - 6046688801068

Record	**2000 -**	1st:1	2nd:0	3rd:0	Ran:13
	Pre2000 -	1st:1	2nd:0	3rd:0	Ran:1

Win Prizemoney £6,048 *Total Prizemoney* £6,341

Wins	*** 2000**	Spt Catter (SFT) S	13.8f		42+	
	1999	Oct Newmar (SFT) S	8f		71+	<

2000 Turf 1-12: (7f 4, 8f 3, 10f 2, 11f, 14f 1-2) (hvy, sft, g-s 1-1, gd 5, g-f, frm 3) 2000 AW 0-1: (6f) (Fibr)
Scopey, fair filly, effective 8f, acts on gd. Turf high 59.
**M Dods [1-13] N A Riddell (from H J Collingridge [1-1] Oct 1999).*

INFORAPENNY BHB 105f **RR 111df** 4260[10]

3 b f Deploy 11.4f **(67)** - Morina (USA) (Lyphard (USA)) 9.9f **(72)**
Form - 1235370

Record	**2000 -**	1st:1	2nd:1	3rd:2	Ran:7
	Pre2000 -	1st:0	2nd:0	3rd:0	Ran:2

Win Prizemoney £2,899 *Total Prizemoney* £33,364

Wins	*** 2000**	Apr Pontef (G-S)	10f		79	<

2000 Turf 1-7: (10f 1-3, 11f, 12f, 14f, 15f) (g-s 1-2, gd 2, g-f 3)
Group-class filly. Turf high 111. A useful filly, she was a good third in the Irish Oaks but was well beaten at Deauville next time. She does not want the ground too soft.
**R A Fahey [1-7] Colm McEvoy (from K Prendergast in IRE [0-2] Spt 1999).*

INFOTEC (IRE) BHB 67f **RR 80f** 5185[17]

3 b br g Shalford (IRE) 7.8f **(63)** - Tomona (Linacre) 6.7f **(40)**
Form - 71053000

Record	**2000 -**	1st:1	2nd:0	3rd:1	Ran:8
	Pre2000 -	1st:0	2nd:2	3rd:0	Ran:3

Win Prizemoney £4,277 *Total Prizemoney* £6,541

Wins	*** 2000**	May Warwic (SFT) H	6.8f	72	80	<

2000 Turf 1-8: (6f, 7f 1-5, 8f 2) (sft 1-2, g-s 2, gd 3, frm)
Decent gelding, effective 7f, acts on sft to gd. Turf high 80 - 1st of 20 giving 7lb to Blackpool Mamma's (1 May Warwick RF 0953). Inconsistent. **H Akbary [1-11] Michael Whatley.*

INGLEMOTTE MISS RR 1208[5]
2 ch f Hatim (USA) 7.8f **(56)** - Phantom Singer (Relkino) 8.9f **(65)**
Form - 5
Record 2000 - 1st:0 2nd:0 3rd:0 Ran:1
2000 Turf 0-1: (8f) (gd)
Currently very poor filly. **Miss J F Craze [0-1] J P R Deans & Co.*

INGLENOOK (IRE) BHB 110f **RR 116+f** 5209a[1]
3 b c Cadeaux Genereux 7.9f **(76)** - Spring (Sadler's Wells (USA)) 10f **(76)**
Form - 5117441
Record 2000 - 1st:3 2nd:0 3rd:0 Ran:7
Win Prizemoney £33,092 *Total Prizemoney* £36,462
Wins * **2000** Oct Saint- (HVY) L 10f 116+ <
* **2000** May Kempto (SFT) L 8f 115
* **2000** May Kempto (G-S) 8f 100+
2000 Turf 3-7: (8f 2-4, 9f, 10f 1-1, 11f) (hvy 1-1, g-s 2-2, gd 4)
Workmanlike, high-class colt, effective 8 to 11f, best at 8f, acts on hvy to gd. Turf high 116 - 1st of 9 giving 5lb to Cazoullas (21 Oct Saint-Cloud RF 5209a) - also 1st of 5 from Sir Ninja (27 May Kempton RF 1500). Unraced at two, he made rapid progress and was contesting the Group One St James's Palace Stakes by June. Disappointing on good to firm ground there, he appreciates some give underfoot and ran out the cheeky winner of a Listed event at Saint-Cloud in October. Probably suited by a mile and a quarter, he is lightly raced and can land a Group race under suitable conditions in 2001. **J L Dunlop [3-7] Seymour Cohn.*

IN GOOD FAITH BHB 37f42a **RR 52f 42a** 4559[11]
8 b g Beveled (USA) 6.9f **(64)** - Dulcidene (Behistoun) 14.1f **(45)**
Form - 0
Record 2000 - 1st:0 2nd:0 3rd:0 Ran:1
Pre2000 - 1st:3 2nd:1 3rd:3 Ran:27
Win Prizemoney £14,226 *Total Prizemoney* £16,448
2000 Turf 0-1: (10f) (gd)
Fair gelding, has worn blinkers.
**R E Barr [9-35] P Cartmell (from J J Quinn [3-33] Jan 1998).*

INHERIT THE EARTH RR 2672[8]
6 b m Silver Season - Balayer (Balidar) 7.9f **(63)**
Form - 8
Record 2000 - 1st:0 2nd:0 3rd:0 Ran:1
2000 Turf 0-1. (10f) (gd)
Currently very poor mare. **I Semple [0-1] Mrs Mary Meek.*

INIGO JONES (IRE) BHB 93f **RR 100f** 3914[17]
4 b g Alzao (USA) 9.8f **(73)** - Kindjal (Kris) 9.5f **(73)**
Form - 14560
Record 2000 - 1st:1 2nd:0 3rd:0 Ran:5
Pre2000 - 1st:1 2nd:3 3rd:3 Ran:7
Win Prizemoney £10,728 *Total Prizemoney* £21,631
Wins * **2000** Apr Haydoc (GD) H 11.9f 88 100 <
* 1999 Aug Nottin (G-F) 14.1f 73
2000 Turf 1-5: (12f 1-3, 14f, 16f) (hvy, gd 1-1, g-f, frm 2)
Workmanlike, very useful gelding, effective 12 to 16f, best at 12f, acts on gd to frm, favours left handed tracks. Turf high 100 (1st run) - 1st of 11 giving 20lb to Quedex (1 Apr Haydock RF 0589). Quite a headstrong sort, he is probably best when making the running. Two miles is stretching his stamina, and he relishes fast ground. **P W Harris [2-12] Mrs P W Harris.*

INITIATIVE BHB 35f **RR 36f** 5166[15]
4 ch g Arazi (USA) 9.2f **(74)** - Dance Quest (FR) (Green Dancer (USA)) 10.3f **(74)**
Form - 00730
Record 2000 - 1st:0 2nd:0 3rd:1 Ran:5
Pre2000 - 1st:1 2nd:0 3rd:1 Ran:3
Win Prizemoney £3,873 *Total Prizemoney* £5,837
Wins 1999 May Thirsk (G-F) 8f 73++ <
2000 Turf 0-5: (8f 3, 9f, 10f) (g-s, gd 2, g-f, frm)
Scopey, very moderate gelding, effective 8f, acts on g-f, has worn blinkers, likes left handed tracks. Turf high 36. Becoming disappointing.
**B W Murray [0-5] Frank Reay (from H R A Cecil [1-3] Aug 1999).*

INJAAZ BHB 82f **RR 83f** 4642[11]
2 ch f Sheikh Albadou 9.2f **(75)** - Ferber's Follies (USA) (Saratoga Six (USA)) 7f **(73)**
Form - 01270
Record 2000 - 1st:1 2nd:1 3rd:0 Ran:5
Win Prizemoney £2,925 *Total Prizemoney* £3,821
Wins * **2000** Aug Leices (G-F) 6f 67 <
2000 Turf 1-5: (6f 1-3, 7f 2) (gd 2, g-f 1-3)
Decent filly. Turf high 83 (began Jly) - 2nd of 7 getting 2lb from Imperial Measure (21 Aug Nottingham 6f g-f RF 3838). Won an ordinary maiden in good style before finishing runner-up in a nursery. **J L Dunlop [1-5] Kuwait Racing Syndicate II.*

INKWELL BHB 28f33a **RR 15f 33a** 1643[13]
6 b g Relief Pitcher 7.6f **(47)** - Fragrant Hackette (Simply Great (FR)) 8.2f **(65)**
Form - 45250000
Record 2000 - 1st:0 2nd:1 3rd:0 Ran:7
Pre2000 - 1st:3 2nd:3 3rd:5 Ran:35
Win Prizemoney £12,478 *Total Prizemoney* £16,956
Wins * 1998 Nov Bright (SFT) C 7f 57 <
* 1998 Aug Bath (GD) H 8f 38 41
* 1998 Apr Bright (GD) H 8f 34 43
2000 Turf 0-3: (10f, 11f, 12f) (sft, gd 2) 2000 AW 0-4: (10f, 12f 3) (Equi, Fibr 3)
Very moderate gelding, effective 10 to 12f, acts on sft to g-s - acts on Fibr, often wears blinkers (extremely effectively), favours tight tracks. AW high 34 (1st run) - 5th of 11 giving 8lb to Manful (4 Jan Wolverhampton 12f Fibr RF 0021). Becoming disappointing.
**G L Moore [3-33] Phil Collins (from R P C Hoad [0-1] Mar 1999).*

INNES BHB 51f **RR 55f** 62[4]
4 b f Inchinor 8.9f **(64)** - Trachelium **(44df)** (Formidable (USA)) 9.2f **(63)**
Form - 4
Record 2000 - 1st:0 2nd:0 3rd:0 Ran:1
Pre2000 - 1st:0 2nd:0 3rd:1 Ran:4
Win Prizemoney £0 *Total Prizemoney* £525
2000 AW 0-1: (12f) (Fibr)
Unfurnished, fair filly. **Miss S E Hall [2-8] C Platts.*

INNIT (IRE) BHB 100f **RR 98f** 4955a[1]
2 b br f Distinctly North (USA) 7.4f **(63)** - Tidal Reach (USA) **(66f 63a)** (Kris S (USA)) 7.9f **(71)**
Form - 321354340821111
Record 2000 - 1st:5 2nd:2 3rd:3 Ran:15
Win Prizemoney £107,803 *Total Prizemoney* £114,991
Wins * **2000** Oct San Si (SFT) G3 8f 98 <
* **2000** Spt San Si (G-S) L 7.5f 93+
* **2000** Spt Maison (GD) L 7f 88+
* **2000** Spt Doncas (GD) H 6.5f 85 87
* **2000** May Hamilt (G-F) 5f 76
2000 Turf 5-15: (5f 1-7, 6f 4, 7f 2-2, 8f 2-2) (hvy, sft 1-1, g-s 1-3, gd 2-6, g-f 1-2, frm, hrd)
Very useful filly, effective 7 to 8f, best at 8f, acts on sft to gd. Turf high 98 - 1st of 12 from Zaza Top (8 Oct San Siro RF 4955a) - also 1st of 6 giving 2lb to Fedina (23 Spt San Siro RF 4714a). Improving. A speedy juvenile who was kept busy, she won five of her 15 races, really hitting form in the autumn when completing a four-timer, culminating in three Pattern events abroad. If she trains on she could well make hay in similar events.
**M R Channon [5-15] Tim Corby.*

INNKEEPER BHB 60f55a **RR 78f 55a** 5150[10]
3 b g Night Shift (USA) 8.1f **(73)** - Riyoom (USA) (Vaguely Noble) 10.1f **(72)**
Form - 520066400
Record 2000 - 1st:0 2nd:1 3rd:0 Ran:9
Pre2000 - 1st:0 2nd:1 3rd:0 Ran:6
Win Prizemoney £0 *Total Prizemoney* £3,698
2000 Turf 0-8: (6f 2, 7f 5, 8f) (hvy, sft, gd 3, g-f, frm 2) 2000 AW 0-1: (10f) (Equi)
Unfurnished, above-average gelding, effective 6 to 7f, best at 6f, acts on gd to frm, best on gd. Turf high 78 - 2nd of 17 to Autumn Rain (12 May Lingfield 7f gd RF 1172). Inconsistent.
**Miss Gay Kelleway [0-9] Chris Wilkinson (from Sir Michael Stoute [0-6] Aug 1999).*

INNUENDO (IRE) BHB 107f **RR 120f** 5096a[3]
5 b m Caerleon (USA) 10.9f **(79)** - Infamy (Shirley Heights) 10.3f **(74)**

Form - 3
2000 Turf 0-1: (10f) (frm)
Very high-class filly. (1st run) - 3rd of 6 to Fly For Avie (15 Oct Woodbine 10f frm RF 5096a).
**C Clement in USA [0-1] (from L M Cumani [4-9] Spt 1999).*

INOURHEARTS (IRE) RR 100+f 4523a[1]

4 b f Pips Pride 6.7f **(70)** - Secret Heart (Vision (USA)) 9f **(64)**
Form - 5721011
2000 Turf 3-7: (5f 3-7) (g-s, gd 2-4, g-f)
Very useful filly, effective 5f, acts on gd. Turf high 100 - 1st of 8 giving 2lb to Tiger Royal (16 Spt Curragh RF 4523a) - also 1st of 12 giving 32lb to Polish Legion (3 Spt Curragh RF 4251a). Progressed rapidly in the second half of last season, making all to win three five-furlong events at the Curragh. She may be up to winning in Pattern company if kept in training.
**F Ennis in IRE [4-14] Mrs S Lenehan.*

INSENOR (USA) RR 97f 4354a[5]

3 ch f El Gran Senor (USA) 8.9f **(85)** - Informatrice (USA) (Trempolino (USA)) 12f **(71)**
Form - 23125
2000 Turf 1-5: (10f 1-3, 12f 2) (gd 2, g-f, frm 1-2)
Very useful filly, effective 12f, acts on frm. Turf high 97 - 2nd of 3 getting 3lb from Palace Royale (21 Aug Roscommon 12f frm RF 4068a). **J Oxx in IRE [1-7] Sheikh Mohammed.*

IN SEQUENCE (USA) BHB 48f RR 43f 4442[18]

3 gr f Robyn Dancer (USA) - What Option (USA) (Star de Naskra (USA)) 9.7f **(65)**
Form - 700
Record 2000 - 1st:0 2nd:0 3rd:0 Ran:3
Pre2000 - 1st:0 2nd:0 3rd:0 Ran:2
Win Prizemoney £0 *Total Prizemoney* £247
2000 Turf 0-3: (5f, 6f, 7f) (gd, frm 2)
Scopey, moderate filly. Turf high 43 (began Jly).
**D W Chapman [0-2] Michael Hill (from J A R Toller [0-3] Jly 2000).*

INSHEEN (IRE) RR 44f 1904[19]

2 b g Inzar (USA) - Moonshine Lady (Ballad Rock) 7.8f **(63)**
Form - 050
Record 2000 - 1st:0 2nd:0 3rd:0 Ran:3
2000 Turf 0-3: (5f, 6f 2) (gd, g-f, frm)
Currently moderate gelding. Turf high 44.
**J S Moore [0-3] Alan Speyer.*

INSIGHTFUL (IRE) BHB 62f80a RR 78f 80a 4877[P]

3 b g Desert Style (IRE) - Insight (Ballad Rock) 7.8f **(63)**
Form - 1250264406400P
Record 2000 - 1st:0 2nd:1 3rd:0 Ran:12
Pre2000 - 1st:2 2nd:2 3rd:1 Ran:8
Win Prizemoney £8,651 *Total Prizemoney* £14,785
Wins * 1999 *Nov Lingfi (STD)* 7f 89+ <
1999 Jly Newmar (GD) S 7f 75
2000 Turf 0-12: (7f 4, 8f 6, 10f 2) (g-s 2, gd 3, g-f 4, frm 3)
Useful gelding, effective 7f, - acted on Equi, had worn blinkers. Turf high 78. (DEAD)
**R Hannon [1-18] Mrs B Burchett (from B J Meehan [1-2] Jly 1999).*

INSPECTOR BLUE RR 36f 5131[14]

2 ch c Royal Academy (USA) 7.8f **(77)** - Blue Siren **(110f)** (Bluebird (USA)) 7.5f **(69)**
Form - 0
Record 2000 - 1st:0 2nd:0 3rd:0 Ran:1
2000 Turf 0-1: (6f) (sft)
Currently very moderate colt. **I A Balding [0-1] J C Smith.*

INSPECTOR GENERAL (IRE) BHB 100f RR 101f 4965[12]

2 b c Dilum (USA) 7.1f **(56)** - New Generation (Young Generation) 7.7f **(63)**
Form - 1110
Record 2000 - 1st:3 2nd:0 3rd:0 Ran:4
Win Prizemoney £14,848 *Total Prizemoney* £14,848
Wins * **2000** Spt Salisb (SFT) 6f 101+ <
* **2000** May Thirsk (GD) 5f 82+
* **2000** Apr Newbur (SFT) 5.2f 86+
2000 Turf 3-4: (5f 2-2, 6f 1-2) (g-s 1-1, gd 2-3)
Very useful colt. Turf high 101 - 1st of 6 giving 11lb to Delta Song (27 Spt Salisbury RF 4690). A winner at Newbury and Thirsk early in the season, he came back from a five-month break to complete the hat-trick at Salisbury. Acts well on soft ground.
**P F I Cole [3-4] The Blenheim Partnership.*

IN SPIRIT (IRE) BHB 75a RR 39f 75a 5243[2]

2 b c Distinctly North (USA) 7.4f **(63)** - June Goddess (Junius (USA)) 7.7f **(65)**
Form - 82
Record 2000 - 1st:0 2nd:1 3rd:0 Ran:2
Win Prizemoney £0 *Total Prizemoney* £646
2000 Turf 0-1: (6f) (gd) 2000 AW 0-1: (6f) (Fibr)
Currently decent colt. (1st run) - 2nd of 12 to Travel Tardia (28 Oct Wolverhampton 6f Fibr RF 5243).
**D J S Cosgrove [0-2] Crown Pkg & Mailing Svs Ltd.*

INTENSITY BHB 75f RR 79f 5287a[10]

4 b g Bigstone (IRE) - Brillante (FR) (Green Dancer (USA)) 10.3f **(74)**
Form - 53700
Record 2000 - 1st:0 2nd:0 3rd:1 Ran:5
Pre2000 - 1st:2 2nd:0 3rd:0 Ran:6
Win Prizemoney £8,223 *Total Prizemoney* £9,415
Wins 1999 Oct Doncas (G-S) H 10.3f 72 79 <
1999 Aug Newcas (FRM) 9f 70
2000 Turf 0-5: (9f, 10f 3, 12f) (hvy, gd 4)
Workmanlike, above-average gelding, effective 9 to 12f, best at 10f, acts on gd to frm, best on gd. Turf high 79 - 3rd of 14 getting 4lb from Carlys Quest (19 May Newbury 12f gd RF 1304). Inconsistent. Landed a Doncaster handicap in good style on his final run of 1999, his first outing for Mark Tompkins. His efforts last term would suggest that 12 furlongs may suit him best now.
**Robert John Osborne in IRE [0-1] D Cox (from M H Tompkins [1-6] Jun 2000).*

INTERLUDE BHB 109f RR 111f 4260[9]

3 b f Sadler's Wells (USA) 11.3f **(87)** - Starlet (Teenoso (USA)) 9.9f **(72)**
Form - 34160
Record 2000 - 1st:1 2nd:0 3rd:1 Ran:5
Pre2000 - 1st:1 2nd:0 3rd:0 Ran:1
Win Prizemoney £32,676 *Total Prizemoney* £53,701
Wins * **2000** Jly Deauvi (G-S) G2 13.5f 110 <
* 1999 Oct Doncas (G-S) 8f 73++
2000 Turf 1-5: (12f 3, 14f 1-1, 15f) (g-s 1-1, gd 2, g-f, frm)
Leggy, Group-class filly, effective 12 to 14f, best at 12f, acts on g-s to g-f. Turf high 111 (1st run) - 3rd of 9 to Miletrian (22 Jun Ascot 12f g-f RF 2178) - also 1st of 8 from Sadler's Flag (30 Jly Deauville RF 3352a). She was hindered by poor tactical rides on her first two starts last year and ridden much closer to the pace when digging deep to win a Group Three at Deauville in July. Disappointing thereafter, she lacks scope and does not look the sort to improve from three to four.
**Sir Michael Stoute [2-6] The Queen.*

INTERNAL AFFAIR (USA) BHB 68a RR 54f 902[6]

5 b g Nicholas (USA) 6.1f **(63)** - Gdynia (USA) (Sir Ivor) 10.2f **(70)**
Form - 62818141351566
Record 2000 - 1st:4 2nd:0 3rd:1 Ran:11
Pre2000 - 1st:2 2nd:3 3rd:0 Ran:23
Win Prizemoney £14,526 *Total Prizemoney* £18,300
Wins * **2000** *Mar Southw (STD) H* 8f 64 65 <
* **2000** *Feb Wolver (STD) H* 8.5f 62 65 <
* **2000** *Jan Wolver (STD) C* 8.5f 62
* **2000** *Jan Wolver (STD) C* 8.5f 61
* 1999 *Oct Wolver (STD) H* 8.5f 60 63
1998 *Jun Wolver (STD)* 5f 62
2000 Turf 0-1: (8f) (g-s) 2000 AW 4-10: (8f 4-9, 9f) (Fibr 4-10)
Average gelding, effective 8 to 9f, best at 8f, acts on hvy to gd - acts on Fibr, likes left handed tracks, likes tight tracks, excels at Southwell, likes Wolverhampton. AW high 65 - 1st of 15 giving 26lb to Erupt (6 Mar Southwell RF 0418) - also 1st of 8 giving 3lb to Aberkeen (15 Feb Wolverhampton RF 0287). Consistent. His optimum conditions are a strongly-run mile over the Wolverhampton Fibresand.
**T D Barron [5-21] Stephen Woodall (from W J Haggas [1-13] Jun 1999).*

INTERROGATE (USA) RR 353a[2]

3 b c
Form - 2
2000 AW 0-1: (8f) (Dirt)
Currently very useful colt. (1st run) - 2nd of 11 getting 6lb from Bachir (20 Feb Nad Al Sheba 8f Dirt RF 0353a).
**S bin Suroor in UAE [0-1] (from FR [0-1] Spt 1999).*

IN THE ARENA (USA) BHB 77f72a RR 79+f 72a 5021[1]
3 ch g Cadeaux Genereux 7.9f **(76)** - Tajfah (USA) (Shadeed (USA)) 8.2f **(70)**
Form - 434801
Record 2000 - 1st:1 2nd:0 3rd:1 Ran:6
Pre2000 - 1st:0 2nd:0 3rd:0 Ran:2
Win Prizemoney £3,360 *Total Prizemoney* £4,666
Wins * 2000 Oct Yarmou (SFT) 7f 79+ <
2000 Turf 1-6: (6f, 7f 1-3, 8f 2) (sft, g-s 1-1, gd 2, g-f, frm)
Scopey, above-average gelding, effective 7f, acts on g-s. Turf high 79 - 1st of 11 giving 5lb to Akhira (17 Oct Yarmouth RF 5021). Inconsistent. **B W Hills [1-8] Maktoum Al Maktoum.*

IN THE NIGHT (ITY) RR 97f 5090a[7]
3 f
Form - 07
2000 Turf 0-2: (10f, 11f) (hvy, gd)
Currently very useful filly. Turf high 97 (1st run) - 9th of 18 to Timi (21 May San Siro 11f gd RF 1455a). **B Grizzetti in ITY [0-2].*

IN THE STOCKS BHB 50f RR 47f 4694[5]
6 b m Reprimand 8.2f **(63)** - Stock Hill Lass (Air Trooper) 9.1f **(63)**
Form - 0062015
Record 2000 - 1st:1 2nd:1 3rd:0 Ran:7
Pre2000 - 1st:2 2nd:0 3rd:0 Ran:16
Win Prizemoney £7,818 *Total Prizemoney* £8,874
Wins * 2000 Spt Warwic (G-F) CH 10.9f 45 47
***** 1999 Oct Lingfi (G-F) H 11.5f 47 49
***** 1998 Spt Bath (GD) SH 8f 47 52 <
2000 Turf 1-7: (10f 3, 11f 1-1, 12f 3) (gd 3, g-f 1-2, frm 2)
Moderate mare, effective 8 to 12f, acts on sft to frm, likes left handed tracks, and likes Bath and Warwick. Turf high 47 - 1st of 20 getting 2lb from Arbenig (11 Spt Warwick RF 4327). Consistent.
**L G Cottrell [3-23] E Gadsden.*

IN THE WOODS BHB 99f RR 88f 3201[8]
2 br f You and I (USA) 8.5f **(78)** - Silent Indulgence (USA) (Woodman (USA)) 9f **(74)**
Form - 118
Record 2000 - 1st:2 2nd:0 3rd:0 Ran:3
Win Prizemoney £15,452 *Total Prizemoney* £15,452
Wins * 2000 Jly Newmar (G-F) L 6f 88 <
*** 2000** Jun Salisb (G-F) 6f 78+
2000 Turf 2-3: (6f 2-3) (gd, g-f 1-1, frm 1-1)
Currently useful filly. Turf high 88 - 1st of 10 from Santolina (1 Jly Newmarket RF 2450). Won on her Salisbury debut despite running green before making all to land a Newmarket Listed event next time. Outclassed in the Princess Margaret, she missed the remainder of the season. **D J S Cosgrove [2-3] Global Racing Club.*

INTO THE CLOUDS RR 16f 2108[11]
4 br f Rock Hopper 10.6f **(54)** - Kaasiha (Kings Lake (USA)) 10.8f **(67)**
Form - 0
Record 2000 - 1st:0 2nd:0 3rd:0 Ran:1
2000 Turf 0-1: (10f) (frm)
Workmanlike, currently poor filly. **T M Jones [0-1] Richard Page.*

IN TOUCH BHB 40f RR 20f 5228[10]
2 ch f Inchinor 8.9f **(64)** - Nitouche (Scottish Reel) 7f **(61)**
Form - 000
Record 2000 - 1st:0 2nd:0 3rd:0 Ran:3
2000 Turf 0-2: (6f 2) (gd 2) 2000 AW 0-1: (6f) (Fibr)
Currently very moderate filly. Turf high 20 (began Spt).
**S C Williams [0-3] D A Shekells.*

INTRICATE WEB (IRE) BHB 67f69a RR 73f 69a 5242[6]
4 b g Warning 8.1f **(77)** - In Anticipation (IRE) (Sadler's Wells (USA)) 10f **(76)**
Form - 60061337530006
Record 2000 - 1st:1 2nd:0 3rd:3 Ran:14
Pre2000 - 1st:1 2nd:0 3rd:1 Ran:7
Win Prizemoney £8,897 *Total Prizemoney* £11,801
Wins * 2000 Jun Carlis (G-F) H 6.9f 66 72 <
***** 1999 Oct Redcar (GD) H 7f 63 68
2000 Turf 1-13: (7f 1-6, 8f 7) (sft 2, g-s 2, gd, g-f 3, frm 1-5) 2000 AW 0-1: (7f) (Fibr)
Above-average gelding, effective 7 to 8f, best at 8f, acts on g-f to frm, best on frm, has worn blinkers. Turf high 73 - 3rd of 8 getting 1lb from Riberac (15 Aug Ayr 8f frm RF 3640) - also 1st of 9 giving 9lb to Only For Gold (28 Jun Carlisle RF 2326). Formerly with Dermot Weld, he scored at Carlisle in June, but has looked held by the Handicapper since.
**E J Alston [2-19] Morris, Oliver, Pierce (from D K Weld in IRE [0-2] Jun 1999).*

INTRUM MORSHAAN (IRE) BHB 81f RR 88+f 4603[6]
3 b br f Darshaan 11.0f **(81)** - Auntie Maureen (IRE) **(65f)** (Roi Danzig (USA))
Form - 02176
Record 2000 - 1st:1 2nd:1 3rd:0 Ran:5
Pre2000 - 1st:0 2nd:0 3rd:1 Ran:3
Win Prizemoney £2,800 *Total Prizemoney* £4,625
Wins * 2000 Aug Haydoc (G-S) H 16.2f 71 88 <
2000 Turf 1-5: (10f, 12f, 14f 2, 16f 1-1) (sft, gd 1-3, frm)
Scopey, useful filly, effective 14 to 16f, acts on sft to gd, favours tight tracks. Turf high 88 - 1st of 10 giving 17lb to Furness (19 Aug Haydock RF 3776). Gradually found her form once stepped up in trip and got off the mark with an easy win in a two-mile Haydock handicap in August. **J L Dunlop [1-8] Mrs Maria Mai Goransson.*

INVADER BHB 82f90a RR 80f 90a 4370[5]
4 b c Danehill (USA) 9.1f **(79)** - Donya (Mill Reef (USA)) 10.5f **(78)**
Form - 55002175
Record 2000 - 1st:1 2nd:1 3rd:0 Ran:8
Pre2000 - 1st:0 2nd:0 3rd:0 Ran:6
Win Prizemoney £4,231 *Total Prizemoney* £7,560
Wins * 2000 Jly Sandow (G-F) 8.1f 80 <
2000 Turf 1-6: (8f 1-4, 9f, 10f) (sft, gd, g-f 1-2, frm 2) 2000 AW 0-2: (8f, 10f) (Equi, Fibr)
Scopey, very useful colt, effective 8 to 10f, - acts on AW, has worn blinkers. Turf high 80. AW high 99 - 5th of 14 to Zanay (18 Mar Lingfield 10f Equi RF 0463). He was highly-tried in his early starts and ran some creditable races, but needed a drop in class and finally got off the mark in a maiden at Sandown in July.
**C E Brittain [1-14] R J Swinbourne.*

INVER GOLD BHB 71f72a RR 79f 72a 4949a[14]
3 ch c Arazi (USA) 9.2f **(74)** - Mary Martin (Be My Guest (USA)) 9.3f **(67)**
Form - 241308430170
Record 2000 - 1st:2 2nd:0 3rd:2 Ran:10
Pre2000 - 1st:0 2nd:1 3rd:0 Ran:3
Win Prizemoney £6,636 *Total Prizemoney* £10,551
Wins * 2000 *Aug Wolver (STD) H* *8.5f* *73* *76* <
*** 2000** *Jan Southw (STD)* *7f* *69*
2000 Turf 0-5: (8f, 9f, 10f 3) (g-s, gd 2, g-f 2) 2000 AW 2-5: (7f 1-2, 8f 1-2, 12f) (Fibr 2-4, Dirt)
Above-average colt, effective 7 to 8f, best at 8f, - acts on Fibr, prefers left handed tracks, prefers tight tracks. Turf high 79. AW high 76 - 1st of 7 giving 3lb to Manxwood (11 Aug Wolverhampton RF 3573). Inconsistent.
**A G Newcombe [2-11] (from M Johnston [0-2] Nov 1999).*

INVESTMENT FORCE (IRE) BHB 69f RR 73f 4623[12]
2 b c Imperial Frontier (USA) 7f **(65)** - Superb Investment (IRE) (Hatim (USA))
Form - 805280
Record 2000 - 1st:0 2nd:1 3rd:0 Ran:6
Win Prizemoney £0 *Total Prizemoney* £1,004
2000 Turf 0-5: (6f 2, 7f, 8f 2) (gd 3, g-f, frm) 2000 AW 0-1: (5f) (Equi)
Above-average colt, effective 7f, acts on gd. Turf high 73 - 2nd of 9 to Port Moresby (1 Aug Beverley 7f gd RF 3274).
**M Johnston [0-6] Markus Graff.*

INVESTOR RELATIONS (IRE) BHB 61f RR 69f 4441[9]
2 b g Goldmark (USA) - Debach Delight (Great Nephew) 9.9f **(64)**
Form - 600
Record 2000 - 1st:0 2nd:0 3rd:0 Ran:3

2000 Turf 0-3: (6f 3) (gd, g-f, frm)
Currently average gelding. Turf high 66 (began Aug).
**B J Meehan [0-3] Citigate Partnership.*

INVINCIBLE RR 71f 5065[4]

2 b f Slip Anchor 12.7f **(75)** - Blessed Honour (Ahonoora) 8.1f **(73)**
Form - 4
Record 2000 - 1st:0 2nd:0 3rd:0 Ran:1
Win Prizemoney £0 *Total Prizemoney* £178
2000 Turf 0-1: (8f) (g-s)
Currently above-average filly.
**J R Fanshawe [0-1] Cheveley Park Stud.*

INVINCIBLE SPIRIT (IRE) BHB 106f RR 107f 4986[6]

3 b c Green Desert (USA) 7.8f **(78)** - Rafha (Kris) 9.5f **(73)**
Form - 46
Record 2000 - 1st:0 2nd:0 3rd:0 Ran:2
Pre2000 - 1st:2 2nd:0 3rd:1 Ran:4
Win Prizemoney £20,376 *Total Prizemoney* £25,218
Wins * 1999 Aug Ripon (GD) L 6f 106+ <
* 1999 Jly Goodwo (G-F) 6f 85+
2000 Turf 0-2: (7f 2) (gd, g-f)
Scopey, Pattern-class colt, effective 6 to 7f, acts on g-f. Turf high 107 (1st run) (began Spt) - 4th of 9 getting 3lb from Warningford (16 Spt Newbury 7f g-f RF 4462). He was a decent two-year-old, including winning a Ripon Listed event with the minimum of fuss, but had been off the track for a year with a cracked pelvis before running creditably in a Newbury Listed event on his return. Another decent effort in the Challenge Stakes at Newmarket.
**J L Dunlop [2-6] Prince A A Faisal.*

INVIRAMENTAL BHB 38f40a RR 44f 40a 5155[14]

4 b g Pursuit of Love 9.5f **(69)** - Corn Futures (Nomination) 7f **(60)**
Form - 42500
Record 2000 - 1st:0 2nd:1 3rd:0 Ran:4
Pre2000 - 1st:0 2nd:0 3rd:0 Ran:4
Win Prizemoney £0 *Total Prizemoney* £551
2000 Turf 0-1: (8f) (g-s) 2000 AW 0-3: (6f, 7f 2) (Equi 2, Fibr)
Moderate gelding, has worn blinkers. AW high 46.
**Mrs L C Jewell [0-2] Robert Clark (from D HaydnJones [0-6] Jan 2000).*

INVISIBLE FORCE (IRE) BHB 44f36a RR 48f 36a 4185[3]

3 b c Imperial Frontier (USA) 7f **(65)** - Virginia Cottage (Lomond (USA)) 8.8f **(65)**
Form - 60466134443
Record 2000 - 1st:1 2nd:0 3rd:2 Ran:11
Pre2000 - 1st:0 2nd:0 3rd:0 Ran:2
Win Prizemoney £2,977 *Total Prizemoney* £5,428
Wins * 2000 Jly Carlis (FM) H 9.3f 38 50 <
2000 Turf 1-8: (5f 2, 7f, 9f 1-1, 10f 2, 11f, 12f) (hvy, g-s, gd, g-f 2, frm 2, hrd 1-1) 2000 AW 0-3: (6f, 9f, 11f) (Equi, Fibr 2)
Well made, moderate colt, effective 9 to 10f, best at 10f, acts on g-f to hrd, best on g-f, often wears blinkers (extremely effectively), prefers tight tracks. Turf high 50 - 1st of 8 getting 10lb from Woodwind Down (21 Jly Carlisle RF 2987). AW high 33.
**M Johnston [1-11] Jim Browne (from B S Rothwell [0-2] Spt 1999).*

INVITATION RR 57f 5110[7]

2 b c Bin Ajwaad (IRE) - On Request (IRE) (Be My Guest (USA)) 9.3f **(67)**
Form - 7
Record 2000 - 1st:0 2nd:0 3rd:0 Ran:1
2000 Turf 0-1: (8f) (gd)
Currently fair colt.
**D R C Elsworth [0-1] Woodhaven Racing Syndicate.*

INVOQUE (IRE) RR 98f 1586a[13]

3 ch f Nashwan (USA) 10.3f **(79)** - Gharam (USA) (Green Dancer (USA)) 10.3f **(74)**
Form - 4660
2000 Turf 0-3: (7f, 8f, 12f) (sft, g-s, g-f)
Very useful filly. Turf high 98 - 6th of 9 getting 7lb from Preseli (14 May Leopardstown 8f g-f RF 1250a).
**J S Bolger in IRE [1-5] Mrs J M Ryan.*

INZACURE (IRE) BHB 81f RR 61f 4673[1]

2 b g Inzar (USA) - Whittingham Girl **(23f 58a)** (Primo Dominie) 6.2f **(80)**
Form - 8051
Record 2000 - 1st:1 2nd:0 3rd:0 Ran:4
Win Prizemoney £3,636 *Total Prizemoney* £3,636
Wins * 2000 Spt Bright (SFT) H 6f 55 61 <
2000 Turf 1-3: (5f, 6f 1-1, 7f) (g-s 1-1, frm 2) 2000 AW 0-1: (5f) (Fibr)
Above-average gelding. Turf high 61 - 1st of 9 getting 2lb from Bee King (27 Spt Brighton RF 4673).
**R M Beckett [1-4] The Inzacure Partnership.*

INZARMOOD (IRE) BHB 40f RR 32f 5237[15]

2 b f Inzar (USA) - Pepilin (Coquelin (USA)) 8.4f **(58)**
Form - 000
Record 2000 - 1st:0 2nd:0 3rd:0 Ran:3
2000 Turf 0-2: (7f, 8f) (g-s, gd) 2000 AW 0-1: (6f) (Fibr)
Currently very moderate filly. Turf high 32 (began Oct).
**K R Burke [0-3] Mrs Elaine Burke.*

IONIAN SPRING (IRE) BHB 72f81a RR 71f 81a 4196[7]

5 b g Ela-Mana-Mou 12.7f **(72)** - Well Head (IRE) (Sadler's Wells (USA)) 10f **(76)**
Form - 007
Record 2000 - 1st:0 2nd:0 3rd:0 Ran:3
Pre2000 - 1st:1 2nd:2 3rd:1 Ran:4
Win Prizemoney £2,872 *Total Prizemoney* £5,587
Wins 1998 *Aug Wolver (STD) 9.4f 83+* <
2000 Turf 0-3: (7f, 8f, 10f) (g-f 2, frm)
Decent gelding. Turf high 71. Missed the whole of '99 and has not much since returning.
**C R Egerton [0-3] Elite Racing Club (from Lord Huntingdon [1-4] Aug 1998).*

IORANA (FR) RR 76f 3782[2]

4 ch g Marignan (USA) - Fareham (FR) (Fast Topaze (USA))
Form - 22
Record 2000 - 1st:0 2nd:2 3rd:0 Ran:2
Win Prizemoney £0 *Total Prizemoney* £1,580
2000 Turf 0-2: (10f, 14f) (frm 2)
Above-average gelding. Turf high 76 (1st run) (began Jly) - 2nd of 12 giving 5lb to Willie Conquer (28 Jly Salisbury 10f frm RF 3184).
**M C Pipe [2-7] Mrs Alison Farrant.*

IPANEMA BEACH BHB 66f RR 62f 5246[1]

3 ch f Lion Cavern (USA) 7.5f **(74)** - Girl From Ipanema **(102df)** (Salse (USA)) 7.5f **(66)**
Form - 83601
Record 2000 - 1st:1 2nd:0 3rd:1 Ran:5
Pre2000 - 1st:0 2nd:0 3rd:0 Ran:1
Win Prizemoney £2,899 *Total Prizemoney* £3,499
Wins * 2000 *Oct Wolver (STD) 8.5f 58+* <
2000 Turf 0-4: (7f, 8f 3) (g-s, g-f 3) 2000 AW 1-1: (8f 1-1) (Fibr 1-1)
Lengthy, average filly, effective 8f, - acts on Fibr. Turf high 62. (1st run) - 1st of 12 from Summer Jazz (28 Oct Wolverhampton RF 5246). **J W Hills [1-6] Christopher Wright.*

IPLEDGEALLEGIANCE (USA) BHB 88f RR 98f 4311[19]

4 b g Alleged (USA) 11.8f **(81)** - Yafill (USA) (Nureyev (USA)) 8.7f **(78)**
Form - 307080
Record 2000 - 1st:0 2nd:0 3rd:1 Ran:6
Pre2000 - 1st:3 2nd:1 3rd:1 Ran:12
Win Prizemoney £17,421 *Total Prizemoney* £21,147
Wins * 1999 Aug Newbur (GD) H 10f 91 93 <
* 1999 Jly Sandow (G-F) H 10f 86 89
* 1999 Jun Pontef (GD) 10f 85
2000 Turf 0-6: (10f 6) (sft, g-s, gd 2, g-f, frm)
Light-framed, very useful gelding, effective 10f, acts on g-s to frm. Turf high 99 (1st run) - 3rd of 18 giving 18lb to Milligan (28 Mar Newcastle 10f g-s RF 0524). He won three times over ten furlongs in 1999, each time with Kieren Fallon aboard. Failed to add to that last season, but ran better than his form figures would suggest. Was subsequently sold to go hurdling.
**E A L Dunlop [3-18] Maktoum Al Maktoum.*

I PROMISE YOU BHB 71f RR 71f 2437[5]

3 b g Shareef Dancer (USA) 10.1f **(67)** - Abuzz (Absalom) 7.2f **(58)**
Form - 100035

Record 2000 - 1st:1 2nd:0 3rd:1 Ran:8
Pre2000 - 1st:0 2nd:0 3rd:1 Ran:6
Win Prizemoney £7,124 *Total Prizemoney* £8,679
Wins * 2000 Mar Leices (GD) H 7f 70 75 <
2000 Turf 1-6: (7f 1-5, 8f) (g-s, gd 1-2, frm 3)
Neat, above-average gelding, effective 7 to 8f, best at 7f, acts on gd to frm. Turf high 75 (1st run) - 1st of 7 getting 6lb from Proud Chief (30 Mar Leicester RF 0565). Consistent. Showed bits and pieces of form at two, and got off the mark in a Leicester handicap on his reappearance. Held since, he lacks a turn of foot.
**C E Brittain [1-12] Mrs C E Brittain.*

IRANOO (IRE) BHB 21f **RR 34f** 4455^{8}

3 b g Persian Bold 10f **(69)** - Rose of Summer (IRE) (Taufan (USA)) 7f **(57)**
Form - 8074588
Record 2000 - 1st:0 2nd:0 3rd:0 Ran:7
Pre2000 - 1st:0 2nd:1 3rd:0 Ran:7
Win Prizemoney £0 *Total Prizemoney* £760
2000 Turf 0-7: (8f, 9f 2, 11f, 12f, 14f, 16f) (g-s, gd, g-f, frm 4)
Workmanlike, very moderate gelding, effective 8f, acts on g-f. Turf high 34.
**R Allan [0-7] The Banana Bunch (from S C Williams [0-7] Aug 1999).*

I RECALL (IRE) BHB 38f44a **RR 47f 44a** 690^{9}

9 b g Don't Forget Me 9.5f **(66)** - Sable Lake (Thatching) 8f **(66)**
Form - 0
Record 2000 - 1st:0 2nd:0 3rd:0 Ran:1
Pre2000 - 1st:0 2nd:2 3rd:2 Ran:16
Win Prizemoney £0 *Total Prizemoney* £3,399
2000 Turf 0-1: (11f) (hvy)
Moderate gelding, often wore blinkers (effectively). (DEAD)
**P Hayward [0-41] P Hayward (from P Hayward [0-1] May 1995).*

IRELAND'S EYE (IRE) BHB 35f29a **RR 55f 29a** 5161^{15}

5 b g Shareef Dancer (USA) 10.1f **(67)** - So Romantic (IRE) (Teenoso (USA)) 9.9f **(72)**
Form - 83328668360
Record 2000 - 1st:0 2nd:1 3rd:3 Ran:10
Pre2000 - 1st:0 2nd:1 3rd:1 Ran:8
Win Prizemoney £0 *Total Prizemoney* £3,484
2000 Turf 0-10: (14f, 16f 5, 17f 3, 18f) (sft, g-s 4, gd, g-f, frm, hrd 2)
Fair gelding, effective 14 to 16f, acts on gd, has worn blinkers, likes left handed tracks, favours tight tracks. Turf high 55.
**J Norton [2-22] Ejam Connection.*

IRIDANOS (FR) **RR 111f** $1152a^{4}$

4 ch c Sabrehill (USA) 8.5f **(64)** - Loxandra **(74f)** (Last Tycoon) 8.5f **(62)**
Form - 24
2000 Turf 0-2: (8f 2) (g-s 2)
Group-class colt, effective 8f, acts on g-s. Turf high 111 - 4th of 5 to Dansili (1 May Saint-cloud 8f g-s RF 1152a). He ran a couple of decent races behind Dansili over a mile in the spring and may benefit from a step up in trip. **C Laffon-Parias in FR [1-6].*

IRIDESCENT **RR 51f** 3549^{4}

2 b f Spectrum (IRE) - Ingenuity (Clever Trick (USA)) 6.6f **(77)**
Form - 4
Record 2000 - 1st:0 2nd:0 3rd:0 Ran:1
Win Prizemoney £0 *Total Prizemoney* £510
2000 Turf 0-1: (6f) (g-f)
Currently fair filly. **W M Brisbourne [0-1] J Sankey.*

IRISH CREAM (IRE) BHB 28f41a **RR 44f 41a** 4179^{2}

4 b f Petong 7.6f **(58)** - Another Baileys **(49f 55a)** (Deploy)
Form - 2710626202
Record 2000 - 1st:1 2nd:4 3rd:0 Ran:10
Pre2000 - 1st:5 2nd:0 3rd:4 Ran:30
Win Prizemoney £13,258 *Total Prizemoney* £18,046
Wins * 2000 *Mar Southw (STD) C 14f 47*
1999 *Mar Southw (STD) C 8f 66*
1999 *Feb Southw (STD) S 7f 75* <
1999 *Feb Southw (STD) S 7f 64*
1998 *Jly Southw (STD) C 6f 67*
1998 Mar Hamilt (HVY) 5f 55
2000 Turf 0-2: (12f, 14f) (gd 2) 2000 AW 1-8: (12f 5, 14f 1-1, 15f, 16f) (Fibr 1-8)
Strong, moderate filly, effective 7 to 8f, - acts on Fibr, often wears blinkers, likes left handed tracks, likes tight tracks. Turf high 32. AW high 47.
**Andrew Reid [1-24] A S Reid (from P D Evans [5-16] Mar 1999).*

IRISH DANCER (IRE) BHB 56f46a **RR 57f 46a** 4053^{7}

3 ch f Lahib (USA) 8f **(69)** - Mazarine Blue (USA) (Chief's Crown (USA)) 9.8f **(72)**
Form - 40731107
Record 2000 - 1st:2 2nd:0 3rd:1 Ran:7
Pre2000 - 1st:0 2nd:0 3rd:0 Ran:7
Win Prizemoney £7,209 *Total Prizemoney* £7,763
Wins * 2000 Jly Ripon (G-S) H 12.3f 45 56
2000 Jly Pontef (GD) SH 12f 45 57 <
2000 Turf 2-6: (7f, 10f, 11f, 12f 2-3) (g-s 1-1, gd, frm 1-4) 2000 AW 0-1: (9f) (Fibr)
Workmanlike, fair filly, effective 12f, acted on g-s to frm, had worn blinkers, liked tight tracks. Turf high 57 - 1st of 14 getting 3lb from Unicorn Star (3 Jly Pontefract RF 2474) - also 1st of 6 getting 25lb from Sudden Flight (10 Jly Ripon RF 2676). (DEAD)
**Ronald Thompson [1-3] B Bruce (from Miss Gay Kelleway [1-11] Jly 2000).*

IRISH DISTINCTION (IRE) **RR 69f** 1637^{5}

2 b c Distinctly North (USA) 7.4f **(63)** - Shane's Girl (IRE) (Marktingo)
Form - 5
Record 2000 - 1st:0 2nd:0 3rd:0 Ran:1
2000 Turf 0-1: (8f) (g-f)
Currently average colt. **A P Jarvis [0-1] Ambrose Turnbull.*

IRISH MELODY (IRE) BHB 25f19a **RR 26f 19a** 313^{7}

4 ch f Mac's Imp (USA) 5.6f **(54)** - Musical Gem (USA) (The Minstrel (CAN)) 10f **(72)**
Form - 0607
Record 2000 - 1st:0 2nd:0 3rd:0 Ran:1
Pre2000 - 1st:0 2nd:0 3rd:0 Ran:12
2000 AW 0-1: (8f) (Equi)
Leggy, little account filly, has worn blinkers.
**A J McNae [0-9] Mrs Ruth Egan (from B J Meehan [0-4] Jly 1998).*

IRISH STREAM (USA) BHB 80f **RR 88f** 5099^{6}

2 ch c Irish River (FR) 9f **(77)** - Euphonic (USA) (The Minstrel (CAN)) 10f **(72)**
Form - 326
Record 2000 - 1st:0 2nd:1 3rd:1 Ran:3
Win Prizemoney £0 *Total Prizemoney* £2,110
2000 Turf 0-3: (7f 3) (gd 2, g-f)
Currently useful colt. Turf high 88 (1st run) (began Aug) - 3rd of 10 to Fair Question (25 Aug Newmarket 7f g-f RF 3964).
**R Charlton [0-3] K Abdulla.*

IRISH VERSE (IRE) **RR 72+f** 5075^{9}

2 ch f Indian Ridge 7.6f **(74)** - Limerick Belle (IRE) **(92f)** (Roi Danzig (USA))
Form - 60
Record 2000 - 1st:0 2nd:0 3rd:0 Ran:2
Win Prizemoney £0 *Total Prizemoney* £250
2000 Turf 0-2: (7f, 8f) (g-s, frm)
Currently above-average filly. Turf high 72 (began Spt).
**J H M Gosden [0-2] Sheikh Mohammed.*

IRON DRAGON (IRE) BHB 70f **RR 65f** 2810^{6}

2 b c Royal Academy (USA) 7.8f **(77)** - Kerry Project (IRE) **(39f)** (Project Manager)
Form - 646
Record 2000 - 1st:0 2nd:0 3rd:0 Ran:3
Win Prizemoney £0 *Total Prizemoney* £270
2000 Turf 0-3: (6f 3) (g-f, frm 2)
Currently average colt. Turf high 65. **J Noseda [0-3] Lucayan Stud.*

IRON HORSE (AUS) **RR 99f** $428a^{3}$

8 b g Zephyr Zip (NZ) - Spyglass (NZ) (Sir Sian (NZ))
Form - 3
2000 Turf 0-1: (10f) (gd)
Currently very useful gelding. (1st run) - 3rd of 14 to Timahs (5 Mar Kranji 10f gd RF 0428a). **J Morish in AUS [0-1].*

IRON MAN (IRE) BHB 41f60a **RR 56?f 60a** 419[8]
8 b g Conquering Hero (USA) 10.6f **(50)** - Doppio Filo (Vision (USA)) 9f **(64)**
Form - 708
Record 2000 - 1st:0 2nd:0 3rd:0 Ran:3
Pre2000 - 1st:2 2nd:2 3rd:1 Ran:10
Win Prizemoney £5,271 *Total Prizemoney* £7,544
2000 AW 0-3: (7f, 8f 2) (Fibr 3)
Fair gelding, often wears blinkers. AW high 44. Inconsistent.
**R F Marvin [0-3] Mrs E M Welch (from M Johnston [0-1] Feb 1995).*

IRON MASK (USA) RR 103f 4845a[5]
2 b c Danzig - Raise A Beauty (FR) (Alydar (USA)) 9.1f **(76)**
Form - 2215
2000 Turf 1-4: (5f 2, 6f 1-2) (hvy, g-s, gd 1-2)
Very useful colt. Turf high 103 (began Jly) - also 1st of 6 giving 3lb to Season's Greetings (30 Aug Chantilly RF 4287a). A speedy French juvenile, he finished fifth against his elders in the Prix de l'Abbaye. **Mme C Head in FR [1-4] Wertheimer Brothers.*

IRON MOUNTAIN (IRE) BHB 78f **RR 78+f** 5026[1]
5 b g Scenic 10.6f **(66)** - Merlannah (IRE) (Shy Groom (USA)) 10f **(66)**
Form - 3534014385371
Record 2000 - 1st:2 2nd:0 3rd:4 Ran:13
Pre2000 - 1st:5 2nd:6 3rd:2 Ran:37
Win Prizemoney £39,342 *Total Prizemoney* £54,220

Wins								
* 2000	Oct	Yarmou	(SFT)	H	10.1f	70	78+	<
* 2000	Jly	Newmar	(G-S)	H	8f	68	73	
* 1999	Jun	Goodwo	(G-S)	H	9f	66	74	
* 1998	Oct	Leices	(G-S)	H	10f	67	69	
* 1998	Jly	Beverl	(GD)	H	9.9f	65	64	
* 1998	Jly	Bright	(GD)	H	10f	63	67	
* 1998	Jun	Yarmou	(GD)	H	10.1f	58	61	

2000 Turf 2-13: (8f 1-7, 9f 3, 10f 1-3) (g-s 1-2, gd 1-7, g-f, frm 3)
Above-average gelding, effective 8 to 10f, best at 10f, acts on g-s to frm, best on frm, has worn blinkers, likes Goodwood and Newmarket. Turf high 78 - 1st of 16 from Generous Diana (17 Oct Yarmouth RF 5026) - also 1st of 18 getting 11lb from I Cried For You (11 Jly Newmarket RF 2687). Won at Nwmarket and on his last turf start at Yarmouth. Appreciates cut in the ground.
**N A Callaghan [7-51] Gallagher Equine Ltd.*

Iron Mountain peaked at Newmarket and Yarmouth

IRSAL BHB 18f23a **RR 15f 23a** 1685[16]
6 ch g Nashwan (USA) 10.3f **(79)** - Amwag (USA) (El Gran Senor (USA)) 9.6f **(76)**
Form - 503028000
Record 2000 - 1st:0 2nd:1 3rd:1 Ran:7
Pre2000 - 1st:1 2nd:1 3rd:3 Ran:18
Win Prizemoney £3,730 *Total Prizemoney* £9,219
Wins 1997 Jly Salisb (FRM) H 12f 75 73 <
2000 Turf 0-3: (9f, 11f, 12f) (g-s, gd, frm) 2000 AW 0-4: (11f 3, 12f) (Fibr 4)
Very moderate gelding, effective 12f, acts on g-f, has worn blinkers. Turf high 15. AW high 32.
**D W Chapman [0-17] Michael Hill (from M C Pipe [1-3] Aug 1997).*

ISADORA RR 85++f 4273[1]
3 b f Sadler's Wells (USA) 11.3f **(87)** - Ahead (Shirley Heights) 10.3f **(74)**
Form - 1
Record 2000 - 1st:1 2nd:0 3rd:0 Ran:1
Win Prizemoney £4,182 *Total Prizemoney* £4,182
Wins * 2000 Spt Chepst (G-S) 12.1f 85 <
2000 Turf 1-1: (12f 1-1) (gd 1-1)
Lengthy, currently useful filly. (1st run) - 1st of 7 getting 5lb from Shair (7 Spt Chepstow RF 4273). **L M Cumani [1-1] Gerald Leigh.*

ISHAAM RR 56f 5236[11]
2 ch f Selkirk (USA) 7.9f **(76)** - Elaine's Honor (USA) (Chief's Crown (USA)) 9.8f **(72)**
Form - 0
Record 2000 - 1st:0 2nd:0 3rd:0 Ran:1
2000 Turf 0-1: (7f) (g-s)
Currently fair filly. **Sir Michael Stoute [0-1] Hamdan Al Maktoum.*

ISHIGURU (USA) RR 89+f 5177a[1]
2 b c Danzig (USA) 8.1f **(88)** - Strategic Maneuver (USA) (Cryptoclearance (USA))
Form - 21
2000 Turf 1-2: (6f 1-2) (g-s 1-1, gd)
Well made, currently very useful colt. Turf high 89+ (began Oct) - 1st of 23 from Faolchu (22 Oct Naas RF 5177a). Cost over $1m as a yearling. Second on his first outing in the Snailwell Maiden at Newmarket to Ajwaa, beaten just a neck, he went one better when scoring at Naas in October. Should make a cracking three-year-old. **A P O'Brien in IRE [1-2] Mrs John Magnier.*

Ishiguru, an exciting prospect as a three-year-old

ISIT IZZY BHB 33f35a **RR 35f 35a** 2792[9]
8 b m Crofthall 8.6f **(54)** - Angie's Girl (Dubassoff (USA)) 14.2f **(55)**
Form - 0300
Record 2000 - 1st:0 2nd:0 3rd:1 Ran:4

Pre2000 - 1st:0 2nd:0 3rd:1 Ran:0
Win Prizemoney £0 *Total Prizemoney* £1,034
2000 Turf 0-4: (6f, 8f 3) (g-f, frm 3)
Very moderate mare, has worn blinkers. Turf high 35 - 3rd of 20 giving 1lb to Kierchem (21 Jun Ripon 8f g-f RF 2166).
**A Streeter [0-4] Mrs Angela Beard (from B A McMahon [0-9] Jly 1998).*

ISLA (IRE) BHB 38f RR 39f 2482[8]

3 b f Turtle Island (IRE) - State Treasure (USA) (Secretariat (USA)) 9f **(79)**
Form - 708
Record 2000 - 1st:0 2nd:0 3rd:0 Ran:3
Pre2000 - 1st:0 2nd:0 3rd:0 Ran:1
2000 Turf 0-2: (8f, 10f) (g-s, gd) 2000 AW 0-1: (12f) (Fibr)
Light-framed, very moderate filly. Turf high 39.
**T R Watson [0-4] Countess of Lonsdale.*

ISLANDAGORE (IRE) RR 96f 3645a[2]

3 ch f Indian Ridge 7.6f **(74)** - Dancing Sunset (IRE) **(106f)** (Red Sunset) 8.2f **(63)**
Form - 12
2000 Turf 1-2: (7f 1-1, 9f) (gd 1-2)
Currently very useful filly. Turf high 96 - 2nd of 6 getting 3lb from Shakespeare (7 Aug Cork 9f gd RF 3645a). Unraced as a juvenile, won his maiden first time up, but was then not seen for three months. Beaten by a useful sort on his return, he is highly regarded, but has obviously had his problems.
**J Oxx in IRE [1-2] Mrs P H Burns.*

ISLAND ESCAPE (IRE) BHB 43f RR 48f 3256[21]

4 b f Turtle Island (IRE) - Clear Procedure (USA) (The Minstrel (CAN)) 10f **(72)**
Form - 00
Record 2000 - 1st:0 2nd:0 3rd:0 Ran:2
Pre2000 - 1st:0 2nd:0 3rd:1 Ran:8
Win Prizemoney £0 *Total Prizemoney* £385
2000 Turf 0-2: (8f, 10f) (frm 2)
Moderate filly, effective 9f, acts on sft, often wears blinkers (very effectively). Turf high 20 (began Jly). Becoming disappointing.
**M P Muggeridge [0-2] Shefford Valley Stud (from D K Weld in IRE [0-8] Oct 1999).*

ISLAND HOUSE (IRE) BHB 114f RR 117f 5130[4]

4 ch c Grand Lodge (USA) - Fortitude (IRE) (Last Tycoon) 8.5f **(62)**
Form - 1115414
Record 2000 - 1st:4 2nd:0 3rd:0 Ran:7
Pre2000 - 1st:2 2nd:2 3rd:0 Ran:9
Win Prizemoney £71,024 *Total Prizemoney* £82,852

Wins							
*** 2000**	Spt	Ayr	(SFT)	L	10.9f	117	<
*** 2000**	Jun	Kempto	(G-F)	L	10f	115+	
*** 2000**	May	Goodwo	(SFT)	L	9.9f	114	
*** 2000**	May	Newmar	(GD)		10f	117	<
* 1999	Oct	Ayr	(SFT)		8f	93	
* 1999	Spt	Pontef	(G-F)		8f	82	

2000 Turf 4-7: (10f 3-5, 11f 1-1, 12f) (sft, g-s 1-1, gd 2-3, frm 1-2)
Well made, high-class colt, effective 10 to 11f, best at 10f, acts on g-s to frm, best on gd, prefers tight tracks, excels at Ayr. Turf high 117 (1st run) - 1st of 6 giving 11lb to Mutamam (6 May Newmarket RF 1063) - also 1st of 6 giving 11lb to Forbearing (16 Spt Ayr RF 4450). Consistent. He made great strides from three to four, winning competitive Listed races at Goodwood, Kempton and Ayr. Well beaten when tried in Group company, he prefers give underfoot and seems best around a mile and a quarter.
**G Wragg [6-16] Mollers Racing.*

ISLAND PRINCESS (IRE) BHB 62f49a RR 72f 49a 5135[9]

3 b f Turtle Island (IRE) - Classic Dilemma (Sandhurst Prince) 7.9f **(63)**
Form - 50400
Record 2000 - 1st:0 2nd:0 3rd:0 Ran:5
Pre2000 - 1st:0 2nd:1 3rd:0 Ran:5
Win Prizemoney £0 *Total Prizemoney* £1,412
2000 Turf 0-5: (10f 4, 12f) (sft 2, g-s 2, g-f)
Scopey, above-average filly, effective 7 to 12f, acts on g-s. Turf high 77.
**D R C Elsworth [0-10] Philip J Costello & John F Costello.*

ISLAND QUEEN (IRE) BHB 76f RR 78f 5066[6]

2 b f Turtle Island (IRE) - Holy Devotion (Commanche Run) 8.5f **(58)**
Form - 43256
Record 2000 - 1st:0 2nd:1 3rd:1 Ran:5
Win Prizemoney £0 *Total Prizemoney* £1,651
2000 Turf 0-5: (5f, 7f 2, 8f 2) (g-s 4, frm)
Above-average filly. Turf high 78 - 2nd of 15 to Lipica (18 Spt Kempton 7f g-s RF 4480). **R Hannon [0-5] R A Bernard.*

ISLAND SANDS (IRE) BHB 114f RR 118f 4133a[2]

4 b br c Turtle Island (IRE) - Tiavanita (USA) (J O Tobin (USA)) 9.4f **(67)**
Form - 2
Record 2000 - 1st:0 2nd:1 3rd:0 Ran:1
Pre2000 - 1st:3 2nd:0 3rd:0 Ran:4
Win Prizemoney £180,209 *Total Prizemoney* £187,894

Wins							
* 1999	May	Newmar	(G-F)	G1	8f	118	<
1998	Spt	Salisb	(HVY)		6f	102+	
1998	Aug	Salisb	(G-F)		6f	102+	

2000 Turf 0-1: (8f) (g-f)
Workmanlike, high-class colt. (1st run) - 2nd of 6 giving 9lb to Penny's Gold (25 Aug Deauville 8f g-f RF 4133a). Trained to the minute when winning the 2000 Guineas in 1999, he suffered a foot problem in the second half of his three-year-old campaign. A respectable second on his return at Deauville in August, he promises to stay a mile and a quarter and could bounce back in 2001, when he will no longer be burdened by a Group One penalty.
**S bin Suroor [1-3] Godolphin (from D R C Elsworth [2-2] Spt 1998).*

ISLAND SOUND BHB 112f RR 114f 5225[1]

3 b g Turtle Island (IRE) - Ballet (Sharrood (USA)) 10.5f **(72)**
Form - 253441
Record 2000 - 1st:1 2nd:1 3rd:1 Ran:6
Pre2000 - 1st:2 2nd:0 3rd:0 Ran:3
Win Prizemoney £22,794 *Total Prizemoney* £32,553

Wins							
*** 2000**	Oct	Newmar	(SFT)	L	10f	114	<
* 1999	Oct	Newbur	(G-S)		8f	95+	
* 1999	Spt	Salisb	(HVY)		8f	98+	

2000 Turf 1-6: (8f, 9f 2, 10f 1-3) (hvy, g-s, gd 1-2, g-f 2)
Scopey, Group-class gelding, effective 9 to 10f, acts on gd. Turf high 114 - 1st of 11 from Man O'Mystery (27 Oct Newmarket RF 5225). Best when able to dictate the running, he ran pretty well when runner-up to his stablemate in the Feilden Stakes in the spring and bounced back to form at Newmarket in the autumn. He goes well in soft ground and ten furlongs has seemed as far as he wants. **D R C Elsworth [3-9] Mrs Michael Meredith.*

ISLAND THYMES BHB 52f RR 54f 978[18]

3 br g Alhijaz 7.7f **(57)** - Harmonious Sound (Auction Ring (USA)) 8.6f **(65)**
Form - 370
Record 2000 - 1st:0 2nd:0 3rd:1 Ran:3
Pre2000 - 1st:0 2nd:0 3rd:0 Ran:3
Win Prizemoney £0 *Total Prizemoney* £763
2000 Turf 0-3: (7f 2, 10f) (hvy, sft, gd)
Leggy, fair gelding. Turf high 54.
**R Dickin [0-3] Double Eight Ltd (from B J Meehan [0-3] Jun 1999).*

ISLE OF SODOR BHB 34f50a RR 38f 50a 1983[12]

4 b f Cyrano de Bergerac 7.3f **(58)** - Costa Verde **(40df)** (King of Spain) 7.8f **(52)**
Form - 08500
Record 2000 - 1st:0 2nd:0 3rd:0 Ran:5
Pre2000 - 1st:1 2nd:0 3rd:2 Ran:11
Win Prizemoney £3,687 *Total Prizemoney* £4,645
Wins * 1998 Spt Leices (G-F) H 6f 58 68 <
2000 Turf 0-5: (7f 2, 8f 2, 9f) (gd 2, frm 3)
Scopey, very moderate filly. Turf high 38. Becoming disappointing.
**K W Hogg [1-16] Auldyn Stud Ltd.*

ISSARA (IRE) BHB 25f RR 20f 1967[12]

3 b g Puissance 7.1f **(60)** - Hollia (Touch Boy) 5f **(66)**
Form - 00
Record 2000 - 1st:0 2nd:0 3rd:0 Ran:2
Pre2000 - 1st:0 2nd:0 3rd:0 Ran:6
2000 Turf 0-2: (8f, 11f) (gd, frm)
Workmanlike, little account gelding, often wears blinkers.

*B A Pearce [0-8] J Salter.

ISSEY ROSE (IRE) BHB 87f **RR 99f** 5133[7]
3 b f Bigstone (IRE) - Aneeda (Rainbow Quest (USA)) 10.4f **(75)**
Form - 07007
Record 2000 - 1st:0 2nd:0 3rd:0 Ran:5
Pre2000 - 1st:1 2nd:1 3rd:1 Ran:5
Win Prizemoney £4,495 *Total Prizemoney* £14,929
Wins * 1999 Jly Folkes (G-F) 7f 71+ <
2000 Turf 0-5: (8f 2, 9f 2, 10f) (sft, gd 3, frm)
Workmanlike, very useful filly, effective 8f, acts on sft. Turf high 99. Inconsistent. Fourth in the Fillies' Mile at Ascot at two, she was not entirely disgraced in the 1000 Guineas first time out. Off the course for three months subsequently, she ran only creditably afterwards, and gave the impression of not having trained on.
T G Mills [1-10] Mrs T G Mills.

ISTIHSAAN (IRE) RR 68f 4853[6]
2 b c Barathea (IRE) - Ghazwat (USA) (Riverman (USA)) 9.1f **(76)**
Form - 56
Record 2000 - 1st:0 2nd:0 3rd:0 Ran:2
2000 Turf 0-2: (7f, 8f) (sft, g-f)
Currently average colt. Turf high 68 (began Spt).
M P Tregoning [0-2] Hamdan Al Maktoum.

ISTINTAJ (USA) BHB 83f **RR 87f** 5367a[2]
4 b br h Nureyev (USA) 8.4f **(84)** - Mathkurh (USA) (Riverman (USA)) 9.1f **(76)**
Form - 2
2000 AW 0-1: (7f) (Dirt)
Unfurnished, very useful colt. (1st run) - 2nd of 6 to Stalwart Member (4 Nov Aqueduct 7f Dirt RF 5367a).
K McLaughlin in USA [0-1] (from M P Tregoning [1-4] Oct 1999).

IS WONDERFUL (USA) RR 48f 4969[26]
2 ch c Diesis 9f **(80)** - Falling In Love (IRE) (Sadler's Wells (USA)) 10f **(76)**
Form - 0
Record 2000 - 1st:0 2nd:0 3rd:0 Ran:1
2000 Turf 0-1: (8f) (gd)
Currently moderate colt. *Mrs A J Perrett [0-1] Seymour Cohn.*

ITALIAN AFFAIR RR 58f 3926[10]
2 ch f Fumo Di Londra (IRE) - Sergentti (IRE) **(67f)** (Common Grounds)
Form - 727217504670
Record 2000 - 1st:1 2nd:2 3rd:0 Ran:12
Win Prizemoney £1,897 *Total Prizemoney* £3,711
Wins * **2000** Jly Yarmou (FRM) S 6f 55 <
2000 Turf 1-12: (5f 7, 6f 1-4, 7f) (g-f 1-5, frm 7)
Fair filly, effective 5 to 6f, best at 5f, acts on g-f to frm, best on frm. Turf high 58 - 4th of 10 getting 20lb from Candothat (2 Aug Musselburgh 5f frm RF 3337) - also 1st of 8 getting 5lb from John Foley (4 Jly Yarmouth RF 2500). *A Bailey [1-12] John Duffy.*

ITALIAN ROSE BHB 28f30a **RR 30f 30a** 5182[13]
5 ch m Aragon 7.7f **(58)** - Cayla (Tumble Wind (USA)) 7.5f **(57)**
Form - 06100
Record 2000 - 1st:1 2nd:0 3rd:0 Ran:5
Pre2000 - 1st:0 2nd:2 3rd:2 Ran:22
Win Prizemoney £2,035 *Total Prizemoney* £4,292
Wins * **2000** Jly Nottin (G-F) SH 14.1f 28 30 <
2000 Turf 1-5: (8f, 13f, 14f 1-2, 16f) (sft, g-f, frm 1-3)
Very moderate filly, effective 14f, acts on frm, has worn blinkers, likes left handed tracks, likes tight tracks. Turf high 30 - 1st of 15 getting 1lb from Best Port (29 Jly Nottingham RF 3213).
A W Carroll [1-25] Serafino Agodino (from W J Musson [0-7] Nov 1997).

ITALIAN SYMPHONY (IRE) BHB 54f85a **RR 58f 85a** 5166[13]
6 b g Royal Academy (USA) 7.8f **(77)** - Terracotta Hut (Habitat) 9.4f **(70)**
Form - 854344150505774557563516578 70
Record 2000 - 1st:1 2nd:0 3rd:1 Ran:21
Pre2000 - 1st:18 2nd:12 3rd:13 Ran:93
Win Prizemoney £61,272 *Total Prizemoney* £87,593
Wins * **2000** Aug Yarmou (GD) H 7f 52 55
* 1999 *Dec Southw (SLW) H 7f 88 94*
* 1999 Nov Mussel (GD) H 8f 53 57
* 1999 Aug Catter (FRM) H 7f 45 48
* 1999 Jly Warwic (G-F) H 6.8f 41 45
* 1999 Jun Newmar (G-F) H 7f 37 41
* 1999 *Feb Wolver (STD) H 7f 90 95*
* 1999 *Feb Lingfi (STD) 8f 96* <
* 1998 *Nov Lingfi (STD) 7f 84*
* 1998 *Oct Wolver (sta) C 7f 74*
* 1998 *Spt Wolver (STD) H 6f 69 74*
* 1998 *Jly Southw (STD) C 7f 73*
* 1998 *May Southw (STD) C 7f 73*
* 1998 *Apr Wolver (STD) C 6f 60*
* 1998 *Feb Wolver (STD) C 7f 67*
* 1998 *Feb Lingfi (SLW) H 7f 63 72*
* 1998 *Feb Wolver (STD) C 6f 61*
* 1997 *Dec Lingfi (STD) H 7f 59 63*
* 1997 *Nov Wolver (STD) H 6f 55 60*
2000 Turf 1-15: (7f 1-7, 8f 8) (gd 2, g-f 1-4, frm 8, hrd) 2000 AW 0-6: (7f 2, 8f 3, 10f) (Equi 3, Fibr 3)
Useful gelding, effective 7 to 8f, best at 8f, - acts on AW, best on Equi, mostly wears blinkers (effectively). Turf high 58. AW high 90. Amazingly tough and genuine, he is no better than fair on the turf and capable of much better form on sand.
P D Evans [19-104] J E Abbey (from M Johnston [0-10] May 1997).

IT CAN BE DONE (IRE) BHB 58f **RR 79f** 3823[10]
3 ch g Case Law 6f **(64)** - Breeze Away **(40f 48a)** (Prince Sabo) 7.2f **(62)**
Form - 00321600600
Record 2000 - 1st:1 2nd:1 3rd:1 Ran:11
Pre2000 - 1st:0 2nd:0 3rd:0 Ran:4
Win Prizemoney £4,290 *Total Prizemoney* £5,575
Wins * **2000** Jun Nottin (SFT) H 8.2f 57 66 <
2000 Turf 1-11: (6f, 7f 2, 8f 1-5, 10f, 11f, 16f) (g-s 1-1, gd 5, g-f 4, frm)
Light-framed, above-average gelding, effective 7f, acts on gd, likes left handed tracks. Turf high 79.
R Hollinshead [1-15] Michael Oliver.

ITCH BHB 35f47a **RR 29f 47a** 667[8]
5 b h Puissance 7.1f **(60)** - Panienka (POL) (Dom Racine (FR)) 9.2f **(62)**
Form - 21314208
Record 2000 - 1st:2 2nd:2 3rd:1 Ran:8
Pre2000 - 1st:1 2nd:0 3rd:0 Ran:10
Win Prizemoney £6,657 *Total Prizemoney* £8,713
Wins * **2000** *Feb Southw (STD) H 7f 43 53*
* **2000** *Jan Southw (STD) H 7f 35 42*
* 1997 Oct Pontef (G-S) 6f 75 <
2000 AW 2-8: (6f, 7f 2-6, 8f) (Fibr 2-8)
Fair colt, effective 7f, - acts on Fibr, has worn blinkers, prefers left handed tracks, likes tight tracks. AW high 57 - 2nd of 10 getting 21lb from Palawan (28 Feb Southwell 7f Fibr RF 0369) - also 1st of 11 giving 3lb to Utah (7 Feb Southwell RF 0235). Showed decent form on Fibresand at the start of the year, winning twice over seven furlongs at Southwell, before going off the boil.
R Bastiman [3-18] Chris Mills.

I T CONSULTANT BHB 63f **RR 36f** 4200[9]
2 b c Rock City 8.8f **(62)** - Game Germaine (Mummy's Game) 8.2f **(60)**
Form - 0
Record 2000 - 1st:0 2nd:0 3rd:0 Ran:1
2000 Turf 0-1: (6f) (g-f)
Currently fair colt. *A G Newcombe [0-1] Cedar Tree IT Ltd.*

IT GIRL BHB 64f **RR 70f** 4555[8]
2 b f Robellino (USA) 9.5f **(68)** - On The Tiles (Thatch (USA)) 9.8f **(62)**
Form - 24658
Record 2000 - 1st:0 2nd:1 3rd:0 Ran:5
Win Prizemoney £0 *Total Prizemoney* £1,578
2000 Turf 0-5: (6f, 7f 3, 8f) (gd 2, g-f 2, frm)
Above-average filly. Turf high 70 (1st run) (began Jun) - 2nd of 6 to Rizerie (30 Jun Goodwood 7f gd RF 2400).
I A Balding [0-5] J C Smith.

ITHADTOBEYOU BHB 44f49a **RR 40f 49a** 4180[9]
5 b g Prince Sabo 6.6f **(64)** - Secret Valentine (Wollow) 8.2f **(61)**
Form - 2238050

Record 2000 - 1st:0 2nd:2 3rd:1 Ran:7
Pre2000 - 1st:1 2nd:0 3rd:1 Ran:13
Win Prizemoney £3,420 *Total Prizemoney* £6,097
Wins 1998 *Feb Lingfi (SLW) 5f* 75+ <
2000 Turf 0-3: (6f 2, 7f) (gd, g-f, frm) 2000 AW 0-4: (6f 2, 7f, 8f) (Equi 2, Fibr 2)
Fair gelding, has worn blinkers. Turf high 40. AW high 51. Inconsistent. Got off the mark on his debut over the minimum on the Lingfield Equitrack in February 1998, but did not seem to stay the extra two furlongs in a hot race at Wolverhampton next time. Tailed off in a decent race in soft on his turf debut and no form since.
**D J Murphy [0-2] Willie McKay (from G L Moore [0-14] Jun 2000).*

I TINA BHB 58f59a RR 60df 59a 4987[30]
4 b f Lycius (USA) 8.8f **(71)** - Tintomara (IRE) (Niniski (USA)) 10.6f **(65)**
Form - 604050
Record 2000 - 1st:0 2nd:0 3rd:0 Ran:6
Pre2000 - 1st:0 2nd:1 3rd:1 Ran:4
Win Prizemoney £0 *Total Prizemoney* £2,789
2000 Turf 0-6: (10f, 12f 3, 14f, 18f) (gd 3, frm 3)
Leggy, average filly, effective 12f, acts on gd to frm, has worn blinkers, prefers left handed tracks, favours tight tracks. Turf high 60. **M P Tregoning [0-10] R Axford.*

ITIS ITIS (IRE) RR 31f 4108[19]
2 b g Nicolotte - Infra Blue (IRE) **(35f)** (Bluebird (USA)) 7.5f **(69)**
Form - 70
Record 2000 - 1st:0 2nd:0 3rd:0 Ran:2
2000 Turf 0-2: (5f, 8f) (gd 2)
Currently very moderate gelding. Turf high 31.
**T D Easterby [0-2] A Arton.*

ITSAKINDOFMAGIC RR 20f 3971[12]
2 b f Presidium 7.5f **(56)** - Hivally (High Line) 10.3f **(70)**
Form - 80
Record 2000 - 1st:0 2nd:0 3rd:0 Ran:2
2000 Turf 0-2: (7f 2) (frm 2)
Currently little account filly. Turf high 20.
**B W Murray [0-2] Mrs M Lingwood.*

IT'S ALLOWED BHB 66f RR 72f 4442[12]
3 b f Piccolo - Double Flutter **(68df)** (Beldale Flutter (USA)) 9.7f **(71)**
Form - 0750700
Record 2000 - 1st:0 2nd:0 3rd:0 Ran:7
Pre2000 - 1st:3 2nd:3 3rd:4 Ran:16
Win Prizemoney £9,976 *Total Prizemoney* £22,546
Wins * 1999 Oct Catter (GD,) H 7f 77 81 <
1999 Aug Lingfi (GD) S 6f 78+
1999 Jly Thirsk (FRM) C 7f 71
2000 Turf 0-7: (6f 3, 7f 4) (gd 2, g-f 4, frm)
Workmanlike, above-average filly, effective 6 to 7f, best at 7f, acts on gd to frm, best on gd, likes tight tracks. Turf high 72. Consistent.
**T D Easterby [1-13] Ian Armitage (from M R Channon [2-10] Aug 1999).*

ITS ANOTHER GIFT BHB 57f58a RR 53f 58a 1319[5]
3 b f Primo Dominie 7.2f **(67)** - Margaret's Gift **(92f)** (Beveled (USA)) 9f **(59)**
Form - 83055
Record 2000 - 1st:0 2nd:0 3rd:1 Ran:5
Pre2000 - 1st:0 2nd:1 3rd:2 Ran:7
Win Prizemoney £0 *Total Prizemoney* £2,565
2000 Turf 0-4: (5f 2, 6f 2) (gd 2, frm 2) 2000 AW 0-1: (6f) (Fibr)
Scopey, fair filly, effective 5f, acts on gd to frm, has worn blinkers. Turf high 53.
**A Berry [0-5] Margaret's Partnership (from J Berry [0-7] Oct 1999).*

ITSANOTHERGIRL BHB 70f62a RR 70f 62a 1216[9]
4 b f Reprimand 8.2f **(63)** - Tasmim (Be My Guest (USA)) 9.3f **(67)**
Form - 001220
Record 2000 - 1st:1 2nd:2 3rd:0 Ran:6
Pre2000 - 1st:1 2nd:1 3rd:3 Ran:12
Win Prizemoney £7,750 *Total Prizemoney* £13,011
Wins * 2000 Apr Thirsk (G-S) H 8f 65 72
* 1998 Oct Catter (SFT) H 7f 68 74 <
2000 Turf 1-5: (7f, 8f 1-2, 10f, 12f) (sft, gd 1-3, g-f) 2000 AW 0-1: (8f) (Fibr)
Above-average filly, effective 8 to 10f, acts on gd to frm, best on gd, prefers tight tracks. Turf high 72 - 1st of 16 giving 18lb to Falls O'Moness (15 Apr Thirsk RF 0739).
**M W Easterby [2-23] Miss V Foster.*

ITS ECCO BOY BHB 73f RR 77f 4830[4]
2 ch c Clantime 6.6f **(57)** - Laena (Roman Warrior) 5.6f **(57)**
Form - 744
Record 2000 - 1st:0 2nd:0 3rd:0 Ran:3
Win Prizemoney £0 *Total Prizemoney* £506
2000 Turf 0-3: (6f 3) (g-s, g-f 2)
Currently above-average colt. Turf high 77 (began Aug) - 4th of 16 getting 3lb from Flint River (11 Spt Warwick 6f g-f RF 4323).
**K R Burke [0-3] Cowan Wahlman.*

ITSGOTTABDUN (IRE) BHB 51f51a RR 58f 51a 2940[2]
3 b g Foxhound (USA) - Lady Ingrid (Taufan (USA)) 7f **(57)**
Form - 3447614236643002
Record 2000 - 1st:1 2nd:2 3rd:2 Ran:15
Pre2000 - 1st:0 2nd:1 3rd:1 Ran:9
Win Prizemoney £1,867 *Total Prizemoney* £5,417
Wins 2000 *Feb Lingfi (STD) S 6f 58* <
2000 Turf 0-5: (5f, 6f 3, 7f) (gd 3, g-f 2) 2000 AW 1-10: (5f 2, 6f 1-5, 7f 2, 8f) (Equi 1-9, Fibr)
Workmanlike, fair gelding, effective 6f, acts on Equi, often wears blinkers. Turf high 58. AW high 58.
**B A Pearce [0-1] J Salter (from K T Ivory [1-23] Jly 2000).*

IT'S MAGIC BHB 58f57a RR 66f 57a 5026[11]
4 b g Magic Ring (IRE) 6.5f **(64)** - Ryewater Dream (Touching Wood (USA)) 8.2f **(55)**
Form - 06206600
Record 2000 - 1st:0 2nd:1 3rd:0 Ran:8
Pre2000 - 1st:3 2nd:0 3rd:0 Ran:12
Win Prizemoney £10,259 *Total Prizemoney* £12,611
Wins * 1999 Aug Leices (GD) H 8f 62 73+ <
* 1999 Aug Leices (GD) H 8f 62 69
* 1999 May Newcas (G-F) H 8f 55 69
2000 Turf 0-8: (8f 7, 10f) (g-s 2, gd, g-f 2, frm 3)
Scopey, average gelding, effective 8f, acts on g-f to hrd, best on g-f, often wears blinkers (very effectively). Turf high 73 - 2nd of 15 getting 10lb from Salty Jack (30 Jly Ascot 8f g-f RF 3229). Not the easiest of rides, he is a capable handicapper at around a mile.
**B Hanbury [3-20] Mrs Hazel Barber.*

IT'S OUR SECRET (IRE) BHB 55f58a RR 67f 58a 4929[4]
4 ch g Be My Guest (USA) 10.2f **(66)** - Lady Dulcinea (ARG) (General (FR))
Form - 24005004
Record 2000 - 1st:0 2nd:1 3rd:0 Ran:8
Pre2000 - 1st:1 2nd:1 3rd:0 Ran:13
Win Prizemoney £2,966 *Total Prizemoney* £5,048
Wins * 1999 May Nottin (FRM) 8.2f 70 <
2000 Turf 0-7: (7f, 8f 6) (gd, g-f 2, frm 3, hrd) 2000 AW 0-1: (8f) (Equi)
Scopey, average gelding, effective 8f, acts on gd to hrd, has worn blinkers, likes left handed tracks, prefers tight tracks. Turf high 67 (1st run) - 2nd of 16 getting 12lb from Court Express (13 May Beverley 8f hrd RF 1188). **M H Tompkins [1-21] Mrs M Barwell.*

IT'S SMEE AGAIN BHB 59f50a RR 62+f 50a 4460[16]
2 ch f Mizoram (USA) - Mountain Dew (Pharly (FR)) 9.8f **(68)**
Form - 444610
Record 2000 - 1st:1 2nd:0 3rd:0 Ran:6
Win Prizemoney £2,282 *Total Prizemoney* £2,789
Wins 2000 Aug Ripon (GD) S 6f 62+ <
2000 Turf 1-6: (5f 2, 6f 1-2, 7f 2) (g-s, gd 2, g-f, frm 1-1, hrd)
Average filly, effective 5 to 6f, acts on gd to frm. Turf high 62 - 1st of 16 getting 5lb from Miss Equinox (28 Aug Ripon RF 4048).
**Ronald Thompson [0-1] B Bruce (from B W Hills [1-5] Aug 2000).*

ITS YOUR BID RR 5152[13]
2 b f Dilum (USA) 7.1f **(56)** - By Arrangement (IRE) **(47f 30a)** (Bold Arrangement)
Form - 0

Record 2000 - 1st:0 2nd:0 3rd:0 Ran:1
2000 Turf 0-1: (7f) (g-s)
Currently very poor filly.
**S Woodman [0-1] John Nicholson Auctioneers.*

IVANS BRIDE (IRE) BHB 56f50a RR 60f 50a 5160[5]
2 b f Inzar (USA) - Sweet Nature (IRE) **(66f 68a)** (Classic Secret (USA))
Form - 86486240015
Record 2000 - 1st:1 2nd:1 3rd:0 Ran:11
Win Prizemoney £1,911 *Total Prizemoney* £3,141
Wins * 2000 Oct Bath (GD) S 5.7f 60 <
2000 Turf 1-10: (5f, 6f 1-4, 7f 4, 8f) (sft, g-s 1-2, g-f 5, frm 2) 2000 AW 0-1: (7f) (Fibr)
Average filly, effective 6 to 7f, acts on g-s to g-f. Turf high 60 - 2nd of 7 giving 5lb to Miss Progressive (19 Aug Sandown 7f g-f RF 3800) - also 1st of 18 from Miss Inform (19 Oct Bath RF 5067).
**G G Margarson [1-11] K Reveley.*

IVOR'S INVESTMENT BHB 35f RR 40f 4759[12]
4 ch f Forzando 7.2f **(63)** - Abbotswood (Ahonoora) 8.1f **(73)**
Form - 7000
Record 2000 - 1st:0 2nd:0 3rd:0 Ran:4
Pre2000 - 1st:2 2nd:4 3rd:1 Ran:19
Win Prizemoney £5,268 *Total Prizemoney* £9,476
Wins 1999 Jun Epsom (GD) C 8.5f 58 <
1999 Jun Chepst (GD) C 7.1f 58+
2000 Turf 0-3: (6f, 7f, 8f) (g-f 2, frm) 2000 AW 0-1: (7f) (Fibr)
Scopey, moderate filly, effective 6 to 8f, acts on g-f to hrd, best on frm, excels at Lingfield and Salisbury. Turf high 40 (began Jly). Becoming disappointing.
**B D Leavy [0-9] R Brown (from D R C Elsworth [2-14] Jly 1999).*

IVORY DAWN RR 78f 5141[10]
6 b m Batshoof 9.5f **(66)** - Cradle of Love (USA) (Roberto (USA)) 10f **(76)**
Form - 0722403015773028780
Record 2000 - 1st:1 2nd:3 3rd:2 Ran:19
Pre2000 - 1st:5 2nd:5 3rd:9 Ran:56
Win Prizemoney £20,571 *Total Prizemoney* £47,527

Wins									
* 2000	Jly	Lingfi	(G-F)	H	6f	72	78	<
* 1999	Jly	Lingfi	(G-F)	H	6f	64	76	
* 1999	Jun	Bright	(GD)	H	6f	65	67	
* 1998	Jly	Lingfi	(G-F)	H	6f	60	72	
* 1998	Jly	Bright	(GD)	H	6f	60	64	
* 1997	Jun	Goodwo	(GD)	H	6f	65	70	

2000 Turf 1-19: (5f 2, 6f 1-16, 7f) (sft, g-s, gd 6, g-f 6, frm 1-5)
Above-average mare, effective 6f, acts on gd to frm, best on frm, has worn blinkers, excels at Lingfield, does well at Newmarket, likes Goodwood. Turf high 78 - 1st of 11 giving 2lb to Bahamian Pirate (19 Jly Lingfield RF 2942). Suited by six furlongs and fast ground on a downhill track, she snatched victory at Lingfield in July, and has held her form well since. **K T Ivory [6-75] Dean Ivory.*

IVORY'S JOY BHB 112f89a RR 106f 89a 4700[9]
5 b m Tina's Pet 7.4f **(56)** - Jacqui Joy (Music Boy) 6.8f **(57)**
Form - 1056031604571210
Record 2000 - 1st:3 2nd:1 3rd:1 Ran:14
Pre2000 - 1st:6 2nd:7 3rd:8 Ran:49
Win Prizemoney £81,022 *Total Prizemoney* £109,099

Wins									
* 2000	Spt	Newbur	(G-F)	L	5.2f		106	<
* 2000	Aug	Haydoc	(GD)	H	5f	86	92	
* 2000	Jun	Bright	(G-F)	H	5.3f	77	83	
* 1999	*Nov*	*Wolver*	*(STD)*	*H*	*5f*	*80*	*85*	
* 1999	Spt	Haydoc	(SFT)	H	5f	74	76	
* 1999	May	Thirsk	(Sft)	H	5f	69	74	
* 1997	Spt	Newbur	(G-S)	H	5.2f	70	73	
* 1997	Jun	Goodwo	(SFT)	S	6f		73	
* 1997	Jun	Goodwo	(GD)	S	5f		65	

2000 Turf 3-14: (5f 3-14) (g-s, gd 1-5, g-f 5, frm 2-3)
Pattern-class filly, effective 5f, acts on frm, has worn blinkers, excels at Haydock. Turf high 106 - 1st of 11 getting 8lb from Eastern Purple (15 Spt Newbury RF 4434). A speedy five-furlong specialist, she ran a career best to win a listed race at Newbury.
**K T Ivory [9-63] K T Ivory.*

IYAVAYA (USA) BHB 85f RR 80df 3045[R]
3 b f Valiant Nature (USA) - Odori (USA) (The Minstrel (CAN)) 10f **(72)**
Form - 707R
Record 2000 - 1st:0 2nd:0 3rd:0 Ran:4
Pre2000 - 1st:2 2nd:0 3rd:0 Ran:7
Win Prizemoney £7,169 *Total Prizemoney* £7,551
Wins * 1999 Jly Chepst (G-F) 5.1f 85
* 1999 Jun Warwic (HVY) 5f 87? <
2000 Turf 0-4: (6f, 7f, 8f 2) (g-s, gd 2, g-f)
Unfurnished, decent filly, effective 5f, acts on g-s to frm. Turf high 80. **M R Channon [2-11] Mrs Claire Smith.*

IZZET MUZZY (FR) BHB 57f63a RR 62f 63a 5115[7]
2 ch c Piccolo - Texanne (BEL) **(45f)** (Efisio)
Form - 585546007
Record 2000 - 1st:0 2nd:0 3rd:0 Ran:9
2000 Turf 0-7: (5f 2, 6f 2, 7f 2, 8f) (gd 4, frm 3) 2000 AW 0-2: (6f, 8f) (Fibr 2)
Above-average colt, has worn blinkers. Turf high 62. AW high 41. Becoming disappointing.
**C N Kellett [0-9] Sean Taylor.*

JABUKA BHB 70f RR 75f 4121[1]
3 b f Shareef Dancer (USA) 10.1f **(67)** - Neptunalia **(66f)** (Slip Anchor) 9.8f **(73)**
Form 4321
Record 2000 - 1st:1 2nd:1 3rd:1 Ran:4
Win Prizemoney £2,576 *Total Prizemoney* £4,654
Wins * 2000 Aug Mussel (G-F) 7.1f 46 <
2000 Turf 1-4: (6f, 7f 1-3) (g-f 2, frm 1-2)
Light-framed, above-average filly. Turf high 75.
**J A R Toller [1-4] Mrs J Toller.*

JACANA (USA) RR 76f 4737[5]
2 ch f Woodman (USA) 9.7f **(77)** - Storm Teal (USA) (Storm Bird (CAN)) 10.3f **(74)**
Form - 25
Record 2000 - 1st:0 2nd:1 3rd:0 Ran:2
Win Prizemoney £0 *Total Prizemoney* £1,570
2000 Turf 0-2: (6f 2) (g-f, frm)
Currently above-average filly. Turf high 76 (began Aug).
**J H M Gosden [0-2] R E Sangster & Mrs J Magnier.*

JACK DAWSON (IRE) BHB 68f RR 74f 4741[12]
3 b g Persian Bold 10f **(69)** - Dream of Jenny (Caerleon (USA)) 8.6f **(71)**
Form - 88025012231200
Record 2000 - 1st:2 2nd:4 3rd:1 Ran:14
Pre2000 - 1st:0 2nd:0 3rd:0 Ran:3
Win Prizemoney £7,016 *Total Prizemoney* £11,306
Wins * 2000 Aug Redcar (FRM) H 14.1f 63 70 <
* 2000 Jly Chepst (G-F) H 16.2f 54 66+
2000 Turf 2-14: (6f, 7f, 8f, 10f 2, 12f, 14f 1-2, 16f 1-6) (g-s, gd 2, g-f 1-4, frm 1-7)
Light-framed, above-average gelding, effective 14 to 16f, best at 16f, acts on g-f to frm, best on g-f, prefers left handed tracks. Turf high 74 - 2nd of 16 giving 4lb to Lord Alaska (11 Spt Warwick 16f g-f RF 4328) - also 1st of 10 getting 2lb from Vanishing Dancer (26 Aug Redcar RF 4000). An effective staying handicapper, he does not want the ground too soft.
**John Berry [2-14] The Premier Cru (from J Noseda [0-3] Oct 1999).*

JACKERIN (IRE) BHB 41f44a RR 50f 44a 5057[4]
5 b g Don't Forget Me 9.5f **(66)** - Meanz Beanz (High Top) 10.2f **(67)**
Form - 655447664880204
Record 2000 - 1st:0 2nd:1 3rd:0 Ran:15
Pre2000 - 1st:3 2nd:4 3rd:2 Ran:32
Win Prizemoney £8,828 *Total Prizemoney* £17,358
Wins 1998 Oct Ayr (G-S) H 5f 61 66
1997 May Doncas (GD) 5f 79 <
1997 Mar Doncas (G-F) S 5f 63
2000 Turf 0-14: (5f 7, 6f 6, 7f) (hvy, sft 3, gd 4, g-f 2, frm 3, hrd) 2000 AW 0-1: (5f) (Fibr)
Fair gelding, effective 5 to 6f, acts on frm, often wears blinkers. Turf high 50 - 4th of 21 getting 12lb from Fire Dome (15 May Redcar 6f frm RF 1201).
**Miss J F Craze [0-5] Holgate Racing Club (from B S Rothwell [3-42] Jun 2000).*

JACKIE'S BABY BHB 77f70a **RR 85f 70a** 3840[12]

4 b g Then Again 7.4f **(52)** - Guarded Expression **(45f)** (Siberian Express (USA)) 8.8f **(65)**

Form - 0400845400400

Record 2000 - 1st:0 2nd:0 3rd:0 Ran:13
Pre2000 - 1st:4 2nd:3 3rd:4 Ran:19

Win Prizemoney £15,683 *Total Prizemoney* £31,819

Wins * 1999 Jly Bath (FRM) H 5.1f 82 84 <
* 1998 Aug Folkes (G-F) H 5f 77 84 <
* 1998 *Jly Southw (STD) H 5f 76*
* 1998 *May Southw (STD) 5f 68*

2000 Turf 0-8: (5f 7, 6f) (gd 2, g-f, frm 4, hrd) 2000 AW 0-5: (5f 5) (Equi, Fibr 4)

Leggy, useful gelding, effective 5f, acts on g-f to frm, best on g-f, excels at Chester. Turf high 85 - 4th of 14 giving 20lb to Xanadu (3 Jun Musselburgh 5f frm RF 1683). AW high 73.

**W G M Turner [4-32] D & J Racing.*

JACKS BIRTHDAY (IRE) RR 69f 2739[13]

2 b c Mukaddamah (USA) 7.6f **(74)** - High Concept (IRE) (Thatching) 8f **(66)**

Form - 8500

Record 2000 - 1st:0 2nd:0 3rd:0 Ran:4

2000 Turf 0-4: (5f 2, 6f 2) (sft, g-s, g-f 2)

Average colt. Turf high 69. **R J O'Sullivan [0 4] Jack Joseph.*

JACK SPRATT (IRE) BHB 103f **RR 97f** 5107[6]

2 b c So Factual (USA) - Raindancing (IRE) **(64f)** (Tirol)

Form - 033181126

Record 2000 - 1st:3 2nd:1 3rd:2 Ran:9

Win Prizemoney £9,756 *Total Prizemoney* £16,022

Wins * **2000** Aug Chepst (G-F) H 5.1f 84 91 <
* **2000** Aug Lingfi (G-F) H 5f 78 81
* **2000** Jly Chepst (G-F) 5.1f 74

2000 Turf 3-9: (5f 3-9) (gd 5, frm 3-4)

Very useful colt, effective 5f, acts on gd to frm. Turf high 97 - 2nd of 9 giving 3lb to Season's Greetings (15 Spt Chantilly 5f gd RF 4563a) - also 1st of 6 giving 9lb to Milly's Lass (28 Aug Chepstow RF 4029). He was successful twice at Chepstow and once at Lingfield last season before running second in a listed event in France. Likes to make the running, and is suited by fast ground and the minimum trip. **R Hannon [3-9] Lady Davis.*

JACK THE KNIFE RR 21f 5122[19]

4 b g Nawwar - Rudda Flash (General David)

Form - 0

Record 2000 - 1st:0 2nd:0 3rd:0 Ran:1

2000 Turf 0-1: (7f) (g-s)

Currently little account gelding. **N Wilson [0-1] J D and J R Evans.*

JACK TO A KING BHB 33f52a **RR 31f 52a** 4992[11]

5 b g Nawwar - Rudda Flash (General David)

Form - 76152721200000800

Record 2000 - 1st:2 2nd:3 3rd:0 Ran:15
Pre2000 - 1st:0 2nd:0 3rd:0 Ran:8

Win Prizemoney £4,386 *Total Prizemoney* £6,220

Wins **2000** *Feb Wolver (STD) H 5f 51 54* <
2000 *Jan Wolver (STD) H 5f 46 49*

2000 Turf 0-5: (5f 4, 6f) (gd 3, frm 2) 2000 AW 2-10: (5f 2-8, 6f 2) (Equi, Fibr 2-9)

Fair gelding, effective 5f, - acts on Fibr, has worn blinkers (very effectively), likes left handed tracks, likes tight tracks. Turf high 31. AW high 57 - 2nd of 12 getting 2lb from Supreme Angel (14 Mar Southwell 5f Fibr RF 0444) - also 1st of 8 getting 16lb from Ashover Amber (29 Feb Wolverhampton RF 0378).

**N Wilson [0-8] J D and J R Evans (from J Balding [2-15] Mar 2000).*

JACMAR (IRE) BHB 43f **RR 51f** 5190[5]

5 br g High Estate 10.5f **(66)** - Inseyab (Persian Bold) 9.3f **(66)**

Form - 2641052103700005

Record 2000 - 1st:2 2nd:2 3rd:1 Ran:16
Pre2000 - 1st:4 2nd:4 3rd:3 Ran:40

Win Prizemoney £23,539 *Total Prizemoney* £41,538

Wins * **2000** Jun Hamilt (G-F) H 6f 48 48
* **2000** May Hamilt (G-F) H 5f 44 47
* 1999 Jun Hamilt (G-S) H 5f 55 60
* 1997 Spt Hamilt (GD) H 6f 90 93+ <
* 1997 Aug Hamilt (GD) H 6f 80 81
* 1997 Jun Hamilt (G-F) 6f 79

2000 Turf 2-16: (5f 1-4, 6f 1-8, 7f 4) (sft, gd 4, g-f 1-7, frm 1-4)

Fair gelding, effective 5 to 6f, best at 6f, acts on g-f to frm, best on g-f, excels at Hamilton. Turf high 51.

**Miss L A Perratt [6-56] Marett-Sutherland-Hay.*

JACOBINA BHB 42f **RR 32f** 3978[16]

5 b m Magic Ring (IRE) 6.5f **(64)** - Mistitled (USA) (Miswaki (USA)) 9f **(81)**

Form - 000

Record 2000 - 1st:0 2nd:0 3rd:0 Ran:3
Pre2000 - 1st:1 2nd:2 3rd:2 Ran:18

Win Prizemoney £3,160 *Total Prizemoney* £5,675

Wins 1998 Aug Haydoc (G-S) H 7.1f 59 63 <

2000 Turf 0-3: (6f, 6f 2) (g-f, frm, hrd)

Very moderate filly. Turf high 32 (began Jly).

**D Nicholls [0-4] J M Ranson (from B S Rothwell [1-13] Jly 1999).*

JADE TIGER BHB 62f44a **RR 69f 44a** 376[6]

4 ch g Lion Cavern (USA) 7.5f **(74)** - Precious Jade (Northfields (USA)) 9f **(72)**

Form - 8406

Record 2000 - 1st:0 2nd:0 3rd:0 Ran:4
Pre2000 - 1st:1 2nd:3 3rd:3 Ran:17

Win Prizemoney £2,574 *Total Prizemoney* £7,260

Wins 1999 Jun Leices (GD) C 8f 58+ <

2000 AW 0-4: (9f 2, 12f 2) (Fibr 4)

Workmanlike, average gelding, effective 8f, acts on gd to frm, has worn blinkers. AW high 45. Inconsistent.

**F Jordan [0-16] Graham Brown (from B J Meehan [1-9] Jun 1999).*

JAHMHOOR BHB 66f **RR 77f** 3731[5]

3 b g Cadeaux Genereux 7.9f **(76)** - Alyka (USA) (Riverman (USA)) 9.1f **(76)**

Form - 06575

Record 2000 - 1st:0 2nd:0 3rd:0 Ran:5

2000 Turf 0-5: (7f 3, 8f 2) (gd 2, g-f 2, frm)

Above-average gelding. Turf high 77.

**E A L Dunlop [0-5] Mohammed Jaber.*

JAILHOUSE ROCKET BHB 59f **RR 74f** 5057[8]

3 gr g Petong 7.6f **(58)** - Selvi (Mummy's Pet) 7.7f **(60)**

Form - 0000008

Record 2000 - 1st:0 2nd:0 3rd:0 Ran:7
Pre2000 - 1st:2 2nd:1 3rd:2 Ran:7

Win Prizemoney £6,103 *Total Prizemoney* £9,100

Wins * 1999 Spt Beverl (SFT) 5f 100 <
* 1999 Aug Carlis (G-F) 5f 76+

2000 Turf 0-7: (5f 4, 6f 3) (sft, gd 2, g-f 2, frm 2)

Light-framed, above-average gelding, effective 5f, acts on g-s to g-f. Turf high 74. **Sir Mark Prescott [2-14] The Speculators.*

JALAD (IRE) BHB 97f **RR 100f** 4968[8]

3 b c Marju (IRE) 9.2f **(76)** - Hamsaat (IRE) **(82+f)** (Sadler's Wells (USA)) 10f **(76)**

Form - 20408

Record 2000 - 1st:0 2nd:1 3rd:0 Ran:5
Pre2000 - 1st:1 2nd:1 3rd:0 Ran:3

Win Prizemoney £3,241 *Total Prizemoney* £7,557

Wins * 1999 Aug Leices (G-F) 7f 91 <

2000 Turf 0-5: (8f 4, 10f) (g-s, gd 3, g-f)

Scopey, very useful colt, effective 7 to 8f, best at 8f, acts on gd to frm. Turf high 100 (1st run) - 2nd of 8 giving 3lb to Sobriety (1 May Doncaster 8f gd RF 0933). Decent at two, he pulls hard and wears a tongue strap, and has been unable to fulfill his potential.

**B Hanbury [1-8] Hamdan Al Maktoum.*

JALISCO (IRE) BHB 97f **RR 103f** 4963[14]

3 b f Machiavellian (USA) 9.8f **(83)** - Las Flores (IRE) **(96f)** (Sadler's Wells (USA)) 10f **(76)**

Form - 120

Record 2000 - 1st:1 2nd:1 3rd:0 Ran:3

Win Prizemoney £4,173 *Total Prizemoney* £11,373

Wins * **2000** Spt Leices (G-F) 10f 85 <

2000 Turf 1-3: (10f 1-1, 12f 2) (g-s, gd, frm 1-1)

Strong, currently very useful filly. Turf high 103 (began Spt) - 2nd

of 11 to Riyafa (24 Spt Ascot 12f g-s RF 4613). She made a winning debut in a Leicester maiden and ran very well to finish runner-up in an Ascot Listed event next time.

**J H M Gosden [1-3] George Strawbridge.*

JALONS STAR (IRE) BHB 60f **RR 57f** 4999[6]

2 b g Eagle Eyed (USA) - Regina St Cyr (IRE) (Doulab (USA)) 9.8f **(65)**

Form - 5066

Record 2000 - 1st:0 2nd:0 3rd:0 Ran:4

Win Prizemoney £0 *Total Prizemoney* £200

2000 Turf 0-4: (6f, 7f 3) (g-s 2, gd, frm)

Fair gelding. Turf high 57 (began Spt).

**M C Chapman [0-4] Jalons Partnership.*

JALOUSIE (IRE) RR 67f 4643[16]

2 b f Barathea (IRE) - Duende (High Top) 10.2f **(67)**

Form - 0

Record 2000 - 1st:0 2nd:0 3rd:0 Ran:1

2000 Turf 0-1: (7f) (g-f)

Currently average filly. **S P C Woods [0-1] Dennis Yardy.*

JAM (IRE) RR 5070[18]

3 b f Arazi (USA) 9.2f **(74)** - Jezebel Monroe (USA) (Lyphard (USA)) 9.9f **(72)**

Form - 0

Record 2000 - 1st:0 2nd:0 3rd:0 Ran:1

2000 Turf 0-1: (12f) (g-s)

Scopey, currently very poor filly.

**J G Smyth-Osbourne [0-1] Lady Rothschild.*

JAMADYAN (IRE) BHB 68f **RR 60f** 4814[19]

3 b c Mujadil (USA) 7.7f **(70)** - Truly Flattering (Hard Fought) 8.8f **(62)**

Form - 646400

Record 2000 - 1st:0 2nd:0 3rd:0 Ran:6
Pre2000 - 1st:1 2nd:0 3rd:0 Ran:1

Win Prizemoney £9,113 *Total Prizemoney* £10,143

Wins * 1999 Oct San Si (GD) 8f

2000 Turf 0-6: (6f, 7f, 8f 2, 10f 2) (sft, g-s, gd, frm 2, hrd)

Average colt. Turf high 79.

**H Akbary [1-7] Cristiano Leonardi.*

JAMAICAN FLIGHT (USA) BHB 58f65a **RR 68f 65a** 3974[3]

7 b h Sunshine Forever (USA) 13.2f **(76)** - Kalamona (USA) (Hawaii) 9.4f **(66)**

Form - 533443204876554423

Record 2000 - 1st:0 2nd:2 3rd:4 Ran:17
Pre2000 - 1st:6 2nd:12 3rd:6 Ran:48

Win Prizemoney £27,234 *Total Prizemoney* £54,093

Wins * 1999 Jly Doncas (G-F) H 16.5f 72 76
* 1999 Jly Carlis (FRM) H 14.1f 67 71
* 1999 May Pontef (GD) 18f 72
* 1998 Aug Pontef (G-F) 18f 78
* 1998 *Feb Wolver (STD) H 12f 72 79* <
1996 Jly Beverl (G-F) 16.2f 57

2000 Turf 0-13: (12f 3, 14f 2, 15f 2, 16f 3, 17f, 18f 2) (hvy, sft, gd 4, g-f 4, frm 3) 2000 AW 0-4: (16f 4) (Fibr 4)

Average horse, effective 12 to 20f, acts on sft to frm - acts on Fibr, has worn blinkers, likes right handed tracks, excels at Southwell, likes Pontefract and Doncaster. Turf high 78 (1st run) - 3rd of 12 giving 5lb to Royal Expression (24 Mar Doncaster 18f gd RF 0487). AW high 69 (1st run) - 3rd of 10 giving 19lb to Aboo Hom (3 Jan Southwell 16f Fibr RF 0014). This front-running stayer is a thorough professional under both codes. He is most effective when able to gain an uncontested early lead.

**Mrs S Lamyman [12-81] P Lamyman (from C Smith [0-2] May 1997).*

JAMAIEL (IRE) BHB 71f **RR 70f** 2498[3]

3 b f Polish Precedent (USA) 9f **(73)** - Avice Caro (USA) (Caro)

Form - 363

Record 2000 - 1st:0 2nd:0 3rd:2 Ran:3
Pre2000 - 1st:0 2nd:0 3rd:0 Ran:1

Win Prizemoney £0 *Total Prizemoney* £1,205

2000 Turf 0-3: (10f, 11f, 12f) (gd, g-f, frm)

Unfurnished, above-average filly. Turf high 70.

**C E Brittain [0-4] Saeed Manana.*

JAMES DEE (IRE) BHB 61f76a **RR 64f 76a** 3485[4]

4 b g Shalford (IRE) 7.8f **(63)** - Glendale Joy (IRE) (Glenstal (USA)) 10.1f **(64)**

Form - 022262004

Record 2000 - 1st:0 2nd:4 3rd:0 Ran:9
Pre2000 - 1st:2 2nd:4 3rd:2 Ran:20

Win Prizemoney £6,556 *Total Prizemoney* £15,992

Wins * 1999 *Spt Wolver (STD) H 7f 68 76* <
* 1999 May Bright (FRM) C 7f 62

2000 Turf 0-6: (6f 3, 7f 3) (gd 3, g-f 3) 2000 AW 0-3: (6f 2, 7f) (Equi, Fibr 2)

Scopey, decent gelding, effective 6 to 7f, best at 6f, - acts on Fibr, prefers left handed tracks, prefers tight tracks. Turf high 65. AW high 80 - 2nd of 16 to Blue Kite (6 Mar Southwell 6f Fibr RF 0416).

**A P Jarvis [2-29] Mrs Ann Jarvis.*

JAMES STARK (IRE) BHB 87f83a **RR 84f 83a** 5199[8]

3 b g Up and At 'em - June Maid (Junius (USA)) 7.7f **(65)**

Form - 116008027342445615318

Record 2000 - 1st:2 2nd:2 3rd:2 Ran:18
Pre2000 - 1st:2 2nd:0 3rd:0 Ran:5

Win Prizemoney £16,636 *Total Prizemoney* £21,843

Wins * **2000** Oct Pontef (HVY) H 5f 79 84 <
* **2000** Spt Goodwo (GD) H 5f 71 76
* 1999 *Nov Lingfi (STD) H 6f 80 83*
* 1999 *Nov Southw (STD) 5f 80*

2000 Turf 2-17: (5f 2-12, 6f 5) (g-s 1-2, gd 1-6, g-f 4, frm 4, hrd) 2000 AW 0-1: (6f) (Fibr)

Light-framed, decent gelding, effective 5 to 6f, best at 5f, acts on g-s to g-f - acts on AW, mostly wears blinkers (extremely effectively), prefers left handed tracks. Turf high 84 - 1st of 18 giving 23lb to Bowlers Boy (16 Oct Pontefract RF 5003) - also 1st of 16 giving 12lb to Branston Pickle (9 Spt Goodwood RF 4320).

**N P Littmoden [4-23] Paul Dixon.*

JAMESTOWN BHB 68f74a **RR 71f 74a** 5122[4]

3 b g Merdon Melody 6.8f **(56)** - Thabeh (Shareef Dancer (USA)) 9.9f **(73)**

Form - 0461484

Record 2000 - 1st:1 2nd:0 3rd:0 Ran:7
Pre2000 - 1st:1 2nd:1 3rd:0 Ran:7

Win Prizemoney £5,219 *Total Prizemoney* £9,685

Wins * **2000** Aug Beverl (G-F) C 7.5f 61
* 1999 Spt Warwic (SFT) 6.8f 74 <

2000 Turf 1-7: (7f 1-5, 8f 2) (g-s 2, gd, g-f, frm 1-2, hrd)

Workmanlike, above-average gelding, effective 5 to 7f, best at 7f, acts on sft to hrd. Turf high 71 - 4th of 18 getting 3lb from Social Contract (18 Jun Leicester 7f hrd RF 2072).

**C Smith [2-14] A E Needham.*

JAMIE MY BOY (IRE) BHB 65f **RR 63f** 5186[9]

2 b g Common Grounds 8.1f **(66)** - House of Fame (USA) (Trempolino (USA)) 12f **(71)**

Form - 480

Record 2000 - 1st:0 2nd:0 3rd:0 Ran:3

Win Prizemoney £0 *Total Prizemoney* £327

2000 Turf 0-3: (7f 3) (g-s 2, gd)

Currently average gelding. Turf high 63 (began Aug).

**K R Burke [0-3] Select Racing Partnership.*

JAMILA (IRE) BHB 75a **RR 69f** 4747[14]

2 b br f Green Desert (USA) 7.8f **(78)** - Virelai (Kris) 9.5f **(73)**

Form - 022020

Record 2000 - 1st:0 2nd:3 3rd:0 Ran:6

Win Prizemoney £0 *Total Prizemoney* £2,750

2000 Turf 0-4: (6f 3, 7f) (gd 2, g-f, frm) 2000 AW 0-2: (6f, 7f) (Fibr 2)

Above-average filly, effective 6 to 7f, best at 7f, acts on g-f - acts on Fibr, has worn blinkers. Turf high 69 - 2nd of 7 getting 3lb from Silk Law (28 Jun Warwick 7f g-f RF 2354). AW high 78 - 2nd of 9 getting 5lb from Act of Reform (19 Aug Wolverhampton 7f Fibr RF 3810). Ordinary placed form in maidens, including on the All-Weather. **E J O'Neill [0-6] M S Fakhry.*

JAMMAAL RR 113+f 5355a[1]

3 b c Robellino (USA) 9.5f **(68)** - Navajo Love Song (IRE) **(43f 37a)** (Dancing Brave (USA)) 8.4f **(76)**

Form - 212124321

2000 Turf 3-9: (7f, 8f, 9f 1-2, 10f 2-4, 12f) (hvy 1-1, sft, g-s 2-2, gd 3, g-f 2)

Group-class colt, effective 7 to 12f, best at 10f, acts on hvy to gd, often wears blinkers (effectively), likes right handed tracks, and likes Leopardstown. Turf high 113 - 1st of 12 giving 7lb to Golovin (30 Oct Leopardstown RF 5355a) - also 1st of 8 from Korasoun (28 May Curragh RF 1585a). Consistent. He stood up well to a busy campaign, winning Listed events at The Curragh and Leopardstown. Exposed in Group races between those victories, he enjoys soft ground, which helps offset his lack of acceleration.

**D K Weld in IRE [4-12] Hamdan Al Maktoum.*

JAMMIE DODGER BHB 37f32a **RR 39f 32a** 4194[15]

4 b g Ardkinglass 5f **(64)** - Ling Lane (Slip Anchor) 9.8f **(73)**
Form - 000201U0680
Record 2000 - 1st:1 2nd:1 3rd:0 Ran:11
Pre2000 - 1st:0 2nd:0 3rd:0 Ran:7
Win Prizemoney £2,660 *Total Prizemoney* £3,544
Wins * 2000 Jly Mussel (G-S) SH 8f 35 36 <
2000 Turf 1-11: (8f 1-6, 9f 3, 10f, 12f) (gd 1-4, g-f 5, frm 2)

Neat, very moderate gelding, effective 7 to 8f, acts on gd to frm, favours tight tracks. Turf high 39. Consistent.

**R M Whitaker [1-18] R M Whitaker.*

JAMORIN DANCER BHB 51f47a **RR 55f 47a** 171[8]

5 b g Charmer 9f **(59)** - Geryea (USA) (Desert Wine (USA)) 9.7f **(80)**
Form - 08188
Record 2000 - 1st:1 2nd:0 3rd:0 Ran:3
Pre2000 - 1st:1 2nd:1 3rd:3 Ran:17
Win Prizemoney £3,974 *Total Prizemoney* £6,823
Wins * 2000 *Jan Southw (STD) H 11f 46 47*
1998 Jun Lingfi (GD) 9f 72 <
2000 AW 1-3: (11f 1-1, 12f 2) (Fibr 1-3)

Fair gelding, effective 14f, acts on gd, has worn blinkers, likes left handed tracks. AW high 47 (1st run).

**D Nicholls [1-5] Miss Karen Shine (from W Jarvis [0-6] Spt 1999).*

JAMPET BHB 26f **RR ?f** 3184[12]

4 b g No Big Deal - Jealous Lover (Alias Smith (USA)) 9.8f **(58)**
Form - 00
Record 2000 - 1st:0 2nd:0 3rd:0 Ran:2
Pre2000 - 1st:0 2nd:0 3rd:0 Ran:9
2000 Turf 0-2: (7f, 10f) (frm 2)

Very poor gelding, has worn blinkers. (began Jly).

**A Barrow [0-14] Don Hazzard.*

JANE ANN (IRE) BHB 30f45a **RR 40df 45a** 3512[9]

4 ch f Perugino (USA) - Height of Elegance (Shirley Heights) 10.3f **(74)**
Form - 0R0
Record 2000 - 1st:0 2nd:0 3rd:0 Ran:3
Pre2000 - 1st:1 2nd:1 3rd:2 Ran:18
Win Prizemoney £2,507 *Total Prizemoney* £3,881
Wins 1999 *Mar Lingfi (STD) 13f 48+* <
2000 Turf 0-3: (12f, 14f 2) (sft, g-f, frm)

Moderate filly, effective 10 to 13f, acts on gd - acts on Equi. Becoming disappointing. Winner of an awful maiden on the Lingfield Equitrack in March, she has not shown much on turf this season.

**M Pitman [0-7] Just Good Fun Club (from A P Jarvis [1-18] Spt 1999).*

JANET BHB 78f **RR 78f** 2108[1]

3 b f Emperor Jones (USA) - Bid Dancer (Spectacular Bid (USA)) 11.2f **(76)**
Form - 1
Record 2000 - 1st:1 2nd:0 3rd:0 Ran:1
Pre2000 - 1st:0 2nd:1 3rd:0 Ran:2
Win Prizemoney £2,951 *Total Prizemoney* £4,011
Wins * 2000 Jun Windso (G-F) 10f 78 <
2000 Turf 1-1: (10f 1-1) (frm 1-1)

Scopey, currently above-average filly. (1st run) - 1st of 13 getting 12lb from Spellbinder (19 Jun Windsor RF 2108).

**G C H Chung [1-1] Osvaldo Pedroni (from A Kelleway [0-2] May 1999).*

JANETTE PARKES **RR 29f** 1672[4]

3 ch f Pursuit of Love 9.5f **(69)** - Summerhill Spruce (Windjammer (USA)) 7f **(59)**
Form - 4
Record 2000 - 1st:0 2nd:0 3rd:0 Ran:1
2000 Turf 0-1: (7f) (g-s)

Leggy, currently little account filly. **A Berry [0-1] Joseph Heler.*

JANICELAND (IRE) BHB 61f62a **RR 65f 62a** 5248[4]

3 b f Foxhound (USA) - Rebecca's Girl (IRE) (Nashamaa) 7.1f **(66)**
Form - 5411755334
Record 2000 - 1st:1 2nd:0 3rd:2 Ran:7
Pre2000 - 1st:1 2nd:4 3rd:1 Ran:14
Win Prizemoney £3,646 *Total Prizemoney* £8,790
Wins 2000 *Feb Lingfi (STD) S 6f 52*
1999 *Nov Wolver (STD) S 5f 66* <
2000 Turf 0-1: (6f) (g-f) 2000 AW 1-6: (5f 2, 6f 1-4) (Equi 1-3, Fibr 3)

Scopey, average filly, effective 5 to 6f, best at 5f, acts on gd to frm - acts on Fibr, has worn blinkers. AW high 52 (1st run). She is only plating class and has been successful on both Fibresand and Equitrack at that level.

**M Wigham [0-3] Cable Media Consultancy Ltd (from S E Kettlewell [2-18] Mar 2000).*

JANMO **RR 29f** 1342[10]

2 ch f Wolfhound (USA) 7.3f **(71)** - Runelia (Runnett) 7f **(59)**
Form - 0
Record 2000 - 1st:0 2nd:0 3rd:0 Ran:1
2000 Turf 0-1: (6f) (g-f)

Currently little account filly. **C A Dwyer [0-1] Mrs J Parvizi.*

JAR (IRE) **RR 102f** 5215a[9]

5 b h Niniski (USA) 13.2f **(67)** - Mistral's Collette (Simply Great (FR)) 8.2f **(65)**
Form - 220
2000 Turf 0-3: (11f, 12f, 16f) (hvy 2, gd)

Very useful colt, effective 11 to 16f, acts on hvy to gd, best on hvy. Turf high 102 - 2nd of 5 to Poseidon (1 Oct San Siro 11f hvy RF 4852a). **B Grizzetti in ITY [1-10].*

JARDINES LOOKOUT (IRE) BHB 104f **RR 104+f** 5311[1]

3 b g Fourstars Allstar (USA) - Foolish Flight (IRE) (Fools Holme (USA))
Form - 536212D151
Record 2000 - 1st:3 2nd:2 3rd:1 Ran:10
Win Prizemoney £26,022 *Total Prizemoney* £38,618
Wins * 2000 Nov Doncas (HVY) 14.6f 85+
*** 2000** Spt Newmar (SFT) H 14f 100 104+ <
*** 2000** Jly Salisb (GD) 14.1f 90
2000 Turf 3-10: 12f, 14f 2-7, 15f 1-1, 16f)(sft 1-1, g-s, gd 2, g-f 2-5, frm)

Light-framed, very useful gelding, effective 14f, acts on g-f. Turf high 104 - 1st of 6 giving 5lb to Mardani (16 Spt Newmarket RF 4469). Unraced at two, he won well at Salisbury in July but was unfortunate to be thrown out after winning the Melrose at the Ebor meeting. He gained compensation with victories at Newmarket and Doncaster and is worth another try in Pattern company.

**A P Jarvis [3-10] Ambrose Turnbull.*

JARN BHB 107f **RR 107+f** 4145[6]

3 b c Green Desert (USA) 7.8f **(78)** - Alkariyh (USA) (Alydar (USA)) 9.1f **(76)**
Form - 1826
Record 2000 - 1st:1 2nd:1 3rd:0 Ran:4
Pre2000 - 1st:1 2nd:0 3rd:0 Ran:2
Win Prizemoney £13,991 *Total Prizemoney* £16,411
Wins * 2000 May Newbur (G-F) 6f 107 <
* 1999 Spt Newbur (G-F) 6f 97+
2000 Turf 1-4: (6f 1-1, 7f 3) (gd 1-1, g-f 2, frm)

Scopey, Pattern-class colt, effective 6 to 7f, best at 6f, acts on gd to frm. Turf high 107 (1st run) - 1st of 9 getting 2lb from Winning Venture (19 May Newbury RF 1302). Campaigned at seven furlongs following his winning reappearance at Newbury, he ran well subsequently but is likely to continue to prove hard to place.

**B Hanbury [2-6] Hamdan Al Maktoum.*

JARV (IRE) BHB 59f55a **RR 58f 55a** 5218[4]

2 b f Inzar (USA) - Conditional Sale (IRE) (Petorius) 7.3f **(61)**
Form - 07024
Record 2000 - 1st:0 2nd:1 3rd:0 Ran:5
Win Prizemoney £0 *Total Prizemoney* £1,138

2000 Turf 0-5: (5f, 6f, 7f 2, 8f) (sft, g-s, gd, g-f 2)
Fair filly. Turf high 58 - 2nd of 17 giving 4lb to Saorsie (19 Oct Brighton 7f g-s RF 5074). **J Akehurst [0-5] C Jarvis.*

JASEUR (USA) BHB 67f **RR 87f** 5322[5]
7 b g Lear Fan (USA) 10.4f **(80)** - Spur Wing (USA) (Storm Bird (CAN)) 10.3f **(74)**
Form - 07760245
Record 2000 - 1st:0 2nd:1 3rd:0 Ran:8
Pre2000 - 1st:3 2nd:4 3rd:1 Ran:19
Win Prizemoney £27,339 *Total Prizemoney* £58,391
Wins 1997 Oct Ascot (HVY) H 16.2f 82 87+ <
1997 Spt Ascot (GD) H 16.2f 74 82+
1997 Spt Bath (GD) H 13.1f 69 77
2000 Turf 0-8: (14f 2, 16f 5, 17f) (sft, g-s 2, gd 3, g-f 2)
Useful gelding, effective 14 to 22f, acts on gd to frm, mostly wears blinkers (effectively), likes tight tracks. Turf high 87.
**G Barnett [0-9] J C Bradbury (from J H M Gosden [3-19] Spt 1999).*

JASHIN (IRE) RR 106f 1152a[5]
7 h
Form - 5
2000 Turf 0-1: (8f) (g-s)
Pattern-class horse. **A Lowe in GER [0-6].*

JASMICK (IRE) RR 54f 2038[7]
2 ch f Definite Article - Glass Minnow (IRE) (Alzao (USA)) 7.1f **(68)**
Form - 7
Record 2000 - 1st:0 2nd:0 3rd:0 Ran:1
2000 Turf 0-1: (5f) (hrd)
Currently fair filly. **H Morrison [0-1] Melksham Craic.*

JATHAAB (USA) RR 82f 1100[8]
3 b br c Silver Hawk (USA) 11.2f **(85)** - Best Of Memories (USA) (Halo (USA)) 10.6f **(75)**
Form - 58
Record 2000 - 1st:0 2nd:0 3rd:0 Ran:2
Pre2000 - 1st:1 2nd:0 3rd:1 Ran:4
Win Prizemoney £3,826 *Total Prizemoney* £4,622
Wins * 1999 Spt Haydoc (SFT) 7.1f 74 <
2000 Turf 0-2: (10f, 12f) (g-f, frm)
Scopey, decent colt, effective 7 to 10f, acts on g-s to frm. Turf high 82 (1st run) - 5th of 17 giving 12lb to Kaiapoi (23 Mar Doncaster 10f frm RF 0474). **J L Dunlop [1-6] Hamdan Al Maktoum.*

JATHAABEH BHB 93f **RR 94f** 4740[18]
3 ch f Nashwan (USA) 10.3f **(79)** - Pastorale (Nureyev (USA)) 8.7f **(78)**
Form - 1010
Record 2000 - 1st:2 2nd:0 3rd:0 Ran:4
Pre2000 - 1st:0 2nd:0 3rd:0 Ran:1
Win Prizemoney £22,600 *Total Prizemoney* £22,600
Wins *** 2000** Jly Newmar (G-F) H 8f 89 94 <
*** 2000** Jun Newmar (G-F) 8f 91
2000 Turf 2-4: (7f, 8f 2-2, 9f) (gd, g-f 1-2, frm 1-1)
Neat, useful filly. Turf high 94 - 1st of 13 giving 4lb to Blue Sugar (22 Jly Newmarket RF 3032) - also 1st of 13 getting 5lb from Asly (3 Jun Newmarket RF 1688). Landed a Newmarket maiden over a mile on her reappearance, but never figured in the Jersey Stakes. Bounced back to land a valuable Newmarket handicap but was below par in the Cambridgeshire. Looks capable of winning in Pattern company next season.
**M A Jarvis [2-5] Sheikh Ahmed Al Maktoum.*

JATO DANCER (IRE) BHB 20f26a **RR 39f 26a** 3451[6]
5 b m Mukaddamah (USA) 7.6f **(74)** - Que Tranquila (Dominion) 8.5f **(63)**
Form - 000570875406086
Record 2000 - 1st:0 2nd:0 3rd:0 Ran:12
Pre2000 - 1st:2 2nd:1 3rd:1 Ran:24
Win Prizemoney £4,750 *Total Prizemoney* £6,341
Wins 1998 May Windso (G-F) C 8.3f 49 <
1997 Jly Bright (FRM) S 7f 49 <
2000 Turf 0-4: (7f, 12f 3) (gd 2, frm 2) 2000 AW 0-8: (8f 2, 9f 3, 11f 2, 12f) (Fibr 8)
Very moderate filly, effective 12f, acts on gd, has worn blinkers. Turf high 39. AW high 24. Inconsistent.
**R Hollinshead [0-15] Mrs Norman Hill (from J R Arnold [1-18] Jun 1999).*

JAVA SHRINE (USA) BHB 48f62a **RR 37f 62a** 108[6]
9 b g Java Gold (USA) 9.3f **(67)** - Ivory Idol (USA) (Alydar (USA)) 9.1f **(76)**
Form - 326716
Record 2000 - 1st:1 2nd:0 3rd:0 Ran:2
Pre2000 - 1st:6 2nd:3 3rd:5 Ran:35
Win Prizemoney £18,124 *Total Prizemoney* £22,070
Wins *** 2000** *Jan Wolver (STD) C 12f 57*
1999 *Jan Lingfi (STD) C 10f 75+* <
1999 *Jan Lingfi (STD) 10f 72*
1999 *Jan Lingfi (STD) C 10f 71+*
1998 *Spt Lingfi (STA) SH 10f 60 68*
1998 Jly Warwic (G-F) SH 10.8f 50 56
2000 AW 1-2: (12f 1-2) (Fibr 1-2)
Fair gelding, effective 10f, - acts on Equi, often wears blinkers (very effectively), favours left handed tracks, excels at Lingfield. AW high 57 (1st run). An effective sort in modest company, though he is not an easy ride and needs plenty of driving along to keep in touch. He goes particularly well over ten furlongs on the Lingfield Equitrack.
**D J Wintle [1-6] Plough Twenty (Ashto Keynes) (from P Eccles [3-14] May 1999).*

JAVELIN BHB 51a **RR 62?f** 4474[13]
4 ch g Generous (IRE) 11.5f **(82)** - Moss (Alzao (USA)) 7.1f **(68)**
Form - 540600
Record 2000 - 1st:0 2nd:0 3rd:0 Ran:6
2000 Turf 0-3: (8f 2, 10f) (sft, gd 2) 2000 AW 0-3: (8f 2, 9f) (Fibr 3)
Average gelding. Turf high 62. AW high 52.
**Ian Williams [0-6] Cockbury Court Partnership.*

JAWAH (IRE) BHB 53f **RR 65f** 3315[8]
6 br g In The Wings 11.2f **(77)** - Saving Mercy (Lord Gayle (USA)) 8.8f **(62)**
Form - 8078
Record 2000 - 1st:0 2nd:0 3rd:0 Ran:4
Pre2000 - 1st:4 2nd:3 3rd:1 Ran:26
Win Prizemoney £15,688 *Total Prizemoney* £21,418
Wins 1999 Oct Doncas (G-S) H 14.6f 74 79
1997 Oct Nottin (GD) H 14.1f 70 81+ <
1997 Oct Doncas (GD) H 14.6f 70 75
1997 Jly Bellew (G-S) H 14f 66 62
2000 Turf 0-4: (14f, 16f, 18f, 20f) (g-s, gd 2, g-f)
Average gelding, effective 14 to 15f, best at 14f, acts on g-s to frm, has worn blinkers, prefers left handed tracks. Turf high 65.
**J R Jenkins [0-10] R M Ellis (from K Mahdi [3-19] Oct 1999).*

JAWHARI BHB 62f68a **RR 45f 68a** 525[9]
6 b g Lahib (USA) 8f **(69)** - Lady of the Land (Wollow) 8.2f **(61)**
Form - 7170
Record 2000 - 1st:1 2nd:0 3rd:0 Ran:4
Pre2000 - 1st:2 2nd:2 3rd:0 Ran:19
Win Prizemoney £11,840 *Total Prizemoney* £13,862
Wins ** 2000 Feb Wolver (STD) H 5f 63 68*
* 1999 Jly Catter (GD) H 5f 62 63
1997 Jly Lingfi (G-F) 7.6f 80 <
2000 Turf 0-1: (5f) (gd) 2000 AW 1-3: (5f 1-3) (Fibr 1-3)
Average gelding, effective 5f, acts on g-f - acts on Fibr, has worn blinkers. AW high 68 - 1st of 11 getting 6lb from Samwar (15 Feb Wolverhampton RF 0284).
**D Nicholls [2-17] Geoffrey Thompson (from J L Dunlop [1-6] Oct 1997).*

JAWLA BHB 93f **RR 91+f** 5366a[5]
3 ch f Wolfhound (USA) 7.3f **(71)** -Majmu (USA) (Al Nasr (FR)) 9.3f **(68)**
Form - 32110515
Record 2000 - 1st:3 2nd:1 3rd:1 Ran:8
Pre2000 - 1st:0 2nd:0 3rd:0 Ran:1
Win Prizemoney £10,627 *Total Prizemoney* £13,988
Wins *** 2000** Oct Yarmou (HVY) H 8f 83 91+ <
*** 2000** Aug Doncas (G-F) H 8f 80 82
*** 2000** Jly Catter (G-F) 7f 68+
2000 Turf 3-8: (7f 1-4, 8f 2-4) (hvy, g-s 1-2, gd 2, g-f 1-2, frm 1-1)
Leggy, useful filly, effective 8f, acts on g-s to g-f. Turf high 91 - 1st of 8 giving 17lb to Catalonia (22 Oct Yarmouth RF 5139) - also 1st of 9 giving 17lb to Diamond Rachael (5 Aug Doncaster RF 3390).
**J H M Gosden [3-9].*

JAWRJIK (IRE) RR 38f 4828[19]
2 b c Blues Traveller (IRE) - Eva Fay (IRE) (Fayruz)
Form - 00
Record 2000 - 1st:0 2nd:0 3rd:0 Ran:2
2000 Turf 0-2: (8f 2) (g-s, gd)
Currently very moderate colt. Turf high 38 (began Spt).
**B S Rothwell [0-2] Richard Brown.*

JAYCAT (IRE) RR 36f 5319[10]
2 ch f Catrail (USA) - Improviste (CAN) (The Minstrel (CAN)) 10f **(72)**
Form - 00
Record 2000 - 1st:0 2nd:0 3rd:0 Ran:2
2000 Turf 0-2: (6f 2) (sft 2)
Currently very moderate filly. Turf high 38 (began Oct).
**G A Butler [0-2] Terry Barwick.*

JAY-DEES-GIRL RR 3811[11]
3 ch f Wing Park - Nanny Margaret (IRE) (Prince Rupert (FR))
Form - 0
Record 2000 - 1st:0 2nd:0 3rd:0 Ran:1
2000 AW 0-1: (9f) (Fibr)
Unfurnished, currently very poor filly.
**P S McEntee [0-1] D Donovan.*

JAYNE'S PRINCESS (IRE) RR 30f 1357[8]
3 b f College Chapel - Water Spirit (USA) (Riverman (USA)) 9.1f **(76)**
Form - 8
Record 2000 - 1st:0 2nd:0 3rd:0 Ran:1
Pre2000 - 1st:0 2nd:0 3rd:0 Ran:1
2000 Turf 0-1: (8f) (frm)
Scopey, currently very moderate filly. **B Palling [0-2] Glyn and Albert Yemm.*

JAY-OWE-TWO (IRE) BHB 70f72a **RR 75df 72a** 1886[16]
6 b g Distinctly North (USA) 7.4f **(63)** - Fiery Song (Ballad Rock) 7.8f **(63)**
Form - 0
Record 2000 - 1st:0 2nd:0 3rd:0 Ran:1
Pre2000 - 1st:6 2nd:4 3rd:2 Ran:41
Win Prizemoney £31,945 *Total Prizemoney* £48,268

Wins								
	* 1998	*Dec Wolver*	*(STD)*	*H*	*8.5f*	*76*	*78*	
	* 1998	Spt Ayr	(G-S)	H	7f	66	70+	
	* 1997	Oct Newmar	(G-S)	H	8f	71	81	<
	* 1997	Oct Pontef	(G-F)	H	8f	71	77	
	* 1997	Apr Beverl	(G-F)	H	7.5f	75	81	<
	* 1996	*Dec Southw*	*(SLW)*		*6f*		*79+*	

2000 Turf 0-1: (8f) (g-f)
Above-average gelding, effective 8f, acts on g-f - acts on Fibr, often wears blinkers (effectively), prefers left handed tracks, favours tight tracks. **R M Whitaker [6-42] Country Lane Partnership.*

JAYPEECEE BHB 43f **RR 41f** 3698[15]
4 b g Never so Bold 7.1f **(62)** - Treeline (High Top) 10.2f **(67)**
Form - 0004580
Record 2000 - 1st:0 2nd:0 3rd:0 Ran:7
Pre2000 - 1st:1 2nd:0 3rd:0 Ran:4
Win Prizemoney £4,100 *Total Prizemoney* £4,100
Wins * 1999 Apr Beverl (GD) 5f 72 <
2000 Turf 0-7: (6f 4, 7f 3) (gd 5, frm 2)
Workmanlike, moderate gelding, effective 5f, acts on gd, has worn blinkers. Turf high 41. Unraced at two, he made a winning debut in a Beverley maiden last season but did not go on from there.
**J L Eyre [1-11] Billy Parker.*

JAZZNIC BHB 43f58a **RR 58a** 2039[19]
4 b f Alhijaz 7.7f **(57)** - Irenic (Mummy's Pet) 7.7f **(60)**
Form - 5601000
Record 2000 - 1st:1 2nd:0 3rd:0 Ran:6
Pre2000 - 1st:0 2nd:2 3rd:0 Ran:7
Win Prizemoney £2,743 *Total Prizemoney* £3,913
Wins * **2000** *Apr Lingfi (STD) 5f* 50 <
2000 Turf 0-2: (5f, 6f) (sft, hrd) 2000 AW 1-4: (5f 1-1, 6f, 7f, 8f) (Equi 1-3, Fibr)
Light-framed, fair filly, has worn blinkers, likes left handed tracks. AW high 50. Becoming disappointing.
**W G M Turner [1-4] O J Stokes (from P J Makin [0-9] Feb 2000).*

JAZZ NIGHT BHB 37f **RR 41f** 4995[5]
3 b g Alhijaz 7.7f **(57)** - Hen Night (Mummy's Game) 8.2f **(60)**
Form - 85
Record 2000 - 1st:0 2nd:0 3rd:0 Ran:2
Pre2000 - 1st:0 2nd:0 3rd:0 Ran:1
2000 Turf 0-1: (9f) (frm) 2000 AW 0-1: (7f) (Fibr)
Leggy, currently moderate gelding, has worn blinkers.
**J Balding [0-2] J M Lacey (from G Woodward [0-1] Spt 1999).*

JAZZ TRACK (IRE) BHB 40f50a **RR 73f 50a** 663[10]
6 b g Sadler's Wells (USA) 11.3f **(87)** - Minnie Hauk (USA) (Sir Ivor) 10.2f **(70)**
Form - 600
Record 2000 - 1st:0 2nd:0 3rd:0 Ran:3
Pre2000 - 1st:1 2nd:1 3rd:2 Ran:8
Win Prizemoney £3,717 *Total Prizemoney* £5,883
Wins 1997 Oct Catter (SFT) H 15.8f 78 80 <
2000 Turf 0-1: (17f) (g-s) 2000 AW 0-2: (16f 2) (Fibr 2)
Above-average gelding, has worn blinkers. AW high 40. Becoming disappointing.
**M A Peill [0-3] O R Dukes (from M C Pipe [0-10] May 1999).*

JAZZY MILLENNIUM BHB 59f **RR 67f** 5064[13]
3 ch c Lion Cavern (USA) 7.5f **(74)** - Woodcrest **(82f)** (Niniski (USA)) 10.6f **(65)**
Form - 835000
Record 2000 - 1st:0 2nd:0 3rd:1 Ran:6
Pre2000 - 1st:0 2nd:2 3rd:0 Ran:4
Win Prizemoney £0 *Total Prizemoney* £3,345
2000 Turf 0-6: (6f 2, 7f, 8f 3) (sft, g-s, gd, g-f 3)
Workmanlike, average colt, effective 6 to 7f, best at 7f, acts on gd to g-f, best on gd. Turf high 67. Becoming disappointing.
**B R Millman [0-3] Millennium Millionaires Partnership (from Miss Gay Kelleway [0-7] Jun 2000).*

JEANNIE'S GIRL BHB 35f **RR 52f** 4215[13]
2 b f Superlative 8.8f **(57)** - One for Jeannie **(50f 66a)** (Clantime)
Form - 007800
Record 2000 - 1st:0 2nd:0 3rd:0 Ran:6
2000 Turf 0-6: (5f 2, 6f 2, 7f, 8f) (gd, g-f 3, frm 2)
Fair filly, has worn blinkers. Turf high 52.
**A Bailey [0-6] Mrs Jean Jones.*

JEDEYDD RR 56f 5142[8]
3 b g Shareef Dancer (USA) 10.1f **(67)** - Bilad (USA) (Riverman (USA)) 9.1f **(76)**
Form - 8
Record 2000 - 1st:0 2nd:0 3rd:0 Ran:1
2000 Turf 0-1: (11f) (g-s)
Unfurnished, currently fair gelding. **B Hanbury [0-1] A Merza.*

JEDI KNIGHT BHB 87f **RR 90f** 2854[18]
6 b g Emarati (USA) 6.6f **(63)** - Hannie Caulder (Workboy) 7.3f **(46)**
Form - 020
Record 2000 - 1st:0 2nd:1 3rd:0 Ran:3
Pre2000 - 1st:7 2nd:7 3rd:2 Ran:47
Win Prizemoney £36,249 *Total Prizemoney* £60,973

Wins								
	* 1999	Aug Hamilt	(G-F)	H	9.2f	84	87	<
	* 1999	Jly York	(G-F)	H	7.9f	80	84	
	* 1999	May Beverl	(GD)	H	8.5f	70	84+	
	* 1997	Nov Redcar	(GD)	H	10f	69	74	
	* 1997	Aug Thirsk	(G-F)	H	8f	67	70	
	* 1997	Jun Carlis	(FRM)	H	8f	55	62++	
	* 1997	Jun Doncas	(GD)	H	7f	55	62	

2000 Turf 0-3: (8f, 9f, 10f) (gd 2, g-f)
Useful gelding, effective 8 to 9f, best at 9f, acts on gd to frm, best on frm, has worn blinkers, likes left handed tracks. Turf high 90 - 2nd of 16 getting 4lb from Ice (17 Jun York 9f g-f RF 2060). Lightly raced last season, he showed the ability is still there with a fine effort at York in June.
**M W Easterby [7-50] K Hodgson & Mrs J Hodgson.*

JEED (IRE) BHB 89f **RR 89f** 2414[4]
3 b f Mujtahid (USA) 7.4f **(69)** - Secretary Bird (IRE) (Kris) 9.5f **(73)**
Form - 84
Record 2000 - 1st:0 2nd:0 3rd:0 Ran:2

Pre2000 - 1st:1 2nd:0 3rd:0 Ran:1
Win Prizemoney £4,272 *Total Prizemoney* £4,805
Wins * 1999 Jun Newmar (G-F) 6f 80+ <
2000 Turf 0-2: (6f, 7f) (g-s, g-f)
Workmanlike, currently useful filly. Turf high 89.
**E A L Dunlop [1-3] Hamdan Al Maktoum.*

JEFFREY ANOTHERRED BHB 63f73a **RR 65f 73a** 5299[6]

6 b g Emarati (USA) 6.6f **(63)** - First Pleasure (Dominion) 8.5f **(63)**
Form - 00060420446
Record 2000 - 1st:0 2nd:1 3rd:0 Ran:11
Pre2000 - 1st:7 2nd:4 3rd:6 Ran:50
Win Prizemoney £33,240 *Total Prizemoney* £54,377

Wins								
* 1999	Jly	Ayr	(SFT)	H	7f	71	75	
* 1999	Jun	Ayr	(G-S)	H	7f	68	71	
* 1998	Jly	Ayr	(SFT)	H	6f	70	84	
* 1998	Jly	Carlis	(G-F)		5.9f		70	
1996	Nov	Doncas	(SFT)	H	7f	86	96	<
1996	Spt	Kempto	(GD)	H	6f	78	74	
1996	Aug	Hamilt	(G-F)		5f		69	

2000 Turf 0-11: (6f 2, 7f 7, 8f 2) (g-s 3, gd 3, g-f 3, frm 2)
Average gelding, has broken blood-vessels, effective 7 to 8f, best at 7f, acts on g-s to g-f, has worn blinkers, prefers left handed tracks, prefers tight tracks. Turf high 67. Consistent.
**M Dods [4-43] N A Riddell (from K McAuliffe [3-18] Oct 1997).*

JELBA BHB 85f **RR 81f** 4737[4]

2 b f Pursuit of Love 9.5f **(69)** - Gold Bracelet (Golden Fleece (USA)) 7.9f **(74)**
Form - 535054
Record 2000 - 1st:0 2nd:0 3rd:1 Ran:6
Win Prizemoney £0 *Total Prizemoney* £1,740
2000 Turf 0-6: (6f 5, 8f) (gd, g-f, frm 4)
Decent filly, effective 6f, acts on frm. Turf high 81.
**N P Littmoden [0-6] Wilwyn Racing (WWW Wilwyn Com).*

JELLYBEEN (IRE) BHB 52f32a **RR 50f 32a** 224[9]

4 ch f Petardia 8.2f **(58)** - Lux Aeterna (Sandhurst Prince) 7.9f **(63)**
Form - 0
Record 2000 - 1st:0 2nd:0 3rd:0 Ran:1
Pre2000 - 1st:1 2nd:1 3rd:1 Ran:12
Win Prizemoney £2,179 *Total Prizemoney* £3,341
Wins * 1998 *Nov Wolver (STD) 9.4f 65* <
2000 AW 0-1: (13f) (Equi)
Lengthy, fair filly, effective 14f, acts on g-f, has worn blinkers, likes left handed tracks. Becoming disappointing.
**Miss Gay Kelleway [1-13] N Parker.*

JEMIMA BHB 101f **RR 98f** 3937[6]

3 b f Owington - Poyle Fizz (Damister (USA)) 9f **(73)**
Form - 00006036
Record 2000 - 1st:0 2nd:0 3rd:1 Ran:8
Pre2000 - 1st:3 2nd:2 3rd:0 Ran:8
Win Prizemoney £55,244 *Total Prizemoney* £63,980

Wins							
* 1999	Aug	York	(GD)	G2	6f	100	<
* 1999	Aug	Ripon	(G-F)		6f	95+	
* 1999	Jun	York	(G-S)		5f	72	

2000 Turf 0-8: (5f, 6f 5, 7f 2) (gd 2, g-f 3, frm 2, hrd)
Unfurnished, very useful filly, effective 6f, acts on gd to hrd, has worn blinkers. Turf high 98 - 3rd of 13 to Arabesque (20 Aug Pontefract 6f hrd RF 3828). Consistent. She won three times at two including a substandard renewal of the Lowther Stakes, but showed little in the Nell Gwyn on her return last season and was found wanting in handicaps, despite running with credit on several occasions.
**T D Easterby [3-16] Mrs Jean Connew.*

JEMINAR BHB 42f **RR ?f** 5057[19]

3 b f Clantime 6.6f **(57)** - Bad Payer (Tanfirion) 7f **(61)**
Form - 00
Record 2000 - 1st:0 2nd:0 3rd:0 Ran:2
Pre2000 - 1st:0 2nd:0 3rd:0 Ran:3
Win Prizemoney £0 *Total Prizemoney* £201
2000 Turf 0-2: (5f, 6f) (sft, g-s)
Leggy, very poor filly. (began Oct).
**M W Easterby [0-5] Bernard Bargh & Garry & Linda Owen.*

JENIN RR 4f 2467[13]

3 b f Rambo Dancer (CAN) 8.4f **(59)** - Rich Lass (Broxted) 6.7f **(65)**
Form - 000
Record 2000 - 1st:0 2nd:0 3rd:0 Ran:3
Pre2000 - 1st:0 2nd:0 3rd:0 Ran:2
2000 Turf 0-3: (5f, 6f, 7f) (g-f, frm 2)
Very poor filly. Turf high 4. **J W Payne [0-5] Sir Simon Lycett Green.*

JENKO (IRE) BHB 37f **RR 44f** 3232[14]

3 b g College Chapel - Flicker of Hope (IRE) (Baillamont (USA)) 7f **(78)**
Form - 000
Record 2000 - 1st:0 2nd:0 3rd:0 Ran:3
Pre2000 - 1st:0 2nd:0 3rd:0 Ran:4
Win Prizemoney £0 *Total Prizemoney* £230
2000 Turf 0-3: (7f 2, 10f) (g-f 2, hrd)
Scopey, moderate gelding, has worn blinkers. Turf high 15.
**H J Collingridge [0-7] J W Jenkins.*

JENNASH RR 48f 5138[11]

2 b f Sabrehill (USA) 8.5f **(64)** - Kayartis **(3f)** (Kaytu)
Form - 00
Record 2000 - 1st:0 2nd:0 3rd:0 Ran:2
2000 Turf 0-2: (7f, 8f) (g-s, g-f)
Currently moderate filly. Turf high 48 (began Spt).
**C A Dwyer [0-2] Mrs J A Cornwell.*

JENNIFER JENKINS RR 53f 5066[14]

2 b f Komaite (USA) 6.9f **(61)** - Joemlujen (Forzando) 7.6f **(59)**
Form - 0
Record 2000 - 1st:0 2nd:0 3rd:0 Ran:1
2000 Turf 0-1: (8f) (g-s)
Currently fair filly. **A P Jarvis [0-1] J Powell-Tuck.*

JENNY WEST BHB 20a **RR 20a** 189[12]

3 ch f Handsome Sailor 6.6f **(53)** - Malindi (Mansingh (USA)) 7.4f **(55)**
Form - 000
Record 2000 - 1st:0 2nd:0 3rd:0 Ran:1
Pre2000 - 1st:0 2nd:0 3rd:0 Ran:2
2000 AW 0-1: (6f) (Fibr)
Neat, currently very poor filly.
**M E Sowersby [0-3] The Southwold Set.*

JENSENS TALE (IRE) BHB 25f41a **RR 28f 41a** 3981[12]

3 b g Mukaddamah (USA) 7.6f **(74)** - Miss Tagalie (IRE) (Cyrano de Bergerac) 6f **(68)**
Form - 7000070
Record 2000 - 1st:0 2nd:0 3rd:0 Ran:7
Pre2000 - 1st:0 2nd:1 3rd:1 Ran:13
Win Prizemoney £0 *Total Prizemoney* £914
2000 Turf 0-7: (6f 2, 8f 3, 10f, 11f) (gd 3, g-f 2, frm 2)
Light-framed, little account gelding, has worn blinkers. Turf high 39. **Mrs A L M King [0-20] All The Kings Horses.*

JENTZEN (USA) RR 82+f 3702[1]

2 b c Miswaki (USA) 8.1f **(81)** - Bold Jessie (Never so Bold) 6.3f **(66)**
Form - 41
Record 2000 - 1st:1 2nd:0 3rd:0 Ran:2
Win Prizemoney £3,601 *Total Prizemoney* £4,117
Wins *** 2000** Aug Salisb (GD) 6f 82+ <
2000 Turf 1-2: (6f 1-2) (gd, frm 1-1)
Currently decent colt. Turf high 82 (began Jly) - 1st of 13 from Aintnecessarilyso (16 Aug Salisbury RF 3702). Ran in a very hot Ascot maiden on his debut and went on to win a Salisbury maiden in good style on his second start. **R Hannon [1-2] Jeffen Racing.*

JEPAJE BHB 49f44a **RR 46f 44a** 4577[5]

3 b g Rambo Dancer (CAN) 8.4f **(59)** - Hi-Hunsley (Swing Easy (USA)) 6.5f **(55)**
Form - 470006445825
Record 2000 - 1st:0 2nd:1 3rd:0 Ran:10
Pre2000 - 1st:0 2nd:1 3rd:0 Ran:7
Win Prizemoney £0 *Total Prizemoney* £2,215
2000 Turf 0-9: (6f 5, 7f 4) (sft, gd, g-f 3, frm 3, hrd) 2000 AW 0-1: (6f) (Fibr)
Fair gelding, effective 5f, acts on gd, has worn blinkers, likes left handed tracks, likes tight tracks. Turf high 46.

**A Bailey [0-17] Mrs V Farrington.*

JESSINCA BHB 45f48a **RR 47f 48a** 4130[8]
4 b f Minshaanshu Amad (USA) 11.3f **(53)** - Noble Soul (Sayf El Arab (USA)) 7.1f **(54)**
Form - 3151087142208
Record 2000 - 1st:3 2nd:2 3rd:1 Ran:13
Pre2000 - 1st:0 2nd:0 3rd:0 Ran:13
Win Prizemoney £7,214 *Total Prizemoney* £10,073
Wins 2000 May Bright (SFT) H 8f 38 47
2000 *Mar Wolver (STD) H 8.5f 48 52* <
2000 *Feb Southw (STD) H 8f 44 52* <
2000 Turf 1-7: (8f 1-5, 10f 2) (gd 1-3, g-f, frm 2, hrd) 2000 AW 2-6: (7f, 8f 2-4, 9f) (Fibr 2-6)
Leggy, fair filly, effective 8f, acts on gd to frm - acts on Fibr. Turf high 47 - 1st of 13 getting 18lb from Carinthia (26 May Brighton RF 1461). AW high 52 - 1st of 10 getting 26lb from My Tess (14 Feb Southwell RF 0279) - also 1st of 12 getting 9lb from Bread Winner (16 Mar Wolverhampton RF 0445).
**A P Jones [0-15] The Lambourn Racing Club (from Derrick Morris [3-9] Jun 2000).*

JE'THAME (IRE) BHB 63f **RR 69f** 5320[14]
2 ch f Definite Article - Victorian Flower (Tate Gallery (USA)) 7.4f **(67)**
Form - 77353320
Record 2000 - 1st:0 2nd:1 3rd:3 Ran:8
Win Prizemoney £0 *Total Prizemoney* £3,312
2000 Turf 0-8: (5f 2, 6f 2, 7f 4) (sft, g-s, gd 4, g-f, frm)
Average filly, effective 7f, acts on gd to frm, best on gd, has worn blinkers. Turf high 69 - 2nd of 29 getting 5lb from Nose The Trade (12 Oct Newmarket 7f gd RF 4930).
**B J Meehan [0-8] Thame Partnership.*

JETSTREAM FLYER RR 27f 4726[11]
2 b f Distant Relative 7f **(69)** - Persian Air (Persian Bold) 9.3f **(66)**
Form - 0
Record 2000 - 1st:0 2nd:0 3rd:0 Ran:1
2000 Turf 0-1: (6f) (gd)
Currently little account filly.
**J M P Eustace [0-1] Guy and James Carstairs.*

JEUNE PREMIER (FR) BHB 41f **RR 55f** 4374[6]
3 ch g Jeune Homme (USA) - Misaine (FR) (Saint Cyrien (FR)) 8.4f **(80)**
Form - 500500006
Record 2000 - 1st:0 2nd:0 3rd:0 Ran:9
Pre2000 - 1st:0 2nd:0 3rd:0 Ran:1
2000 Turf 0-9: (10f 3, 11f 2, 12f 3, 16f) (sft, g-s 2, gd, g-f 3, frm 2)
Workmanlike, fair gelding, has worn blinkers. Turf high 61.
**B J Meehan [0-10] Mrs E A Lerpiniere.*

JEWEL FIGHTER BHB 33f **RR 47df** 4695[10]
6 br m Good Times (ITY) 8.7f **(53)** - Duellist (Town Crier) 10.2f **(55)**
Form - 800
Record 2000 - 1st:0 2nd:0 3rd:0 Ran:3
Pre2000 - 1st:0 2nd:0 3rd:1 Ran:7
Win Prizemoney £0 *Total Prizemoney* £698
2000 Turf 0-2: (10f 2) (gd, frm) 2000 AW 0-1: (11f) (Fibr)
Moderate mare. Turf high 20 (began Aug). Becoming disappointing.
**J M Bradley [0-3] Weir Investments (from P D Evans [0-3] Oct 1999).*

JEWELLERY BOX BHB 20f **RR 22f** 1680[6]
2 b f King's Signet (USA) 7f **(51)** - Diamond Time (Clantime)
Form - 5056
Record 2000 - 1st:0 2nd:0 3rd:0 Ran:4
2000 Turf 0-3: (5f 3) (sft, gd, frm) 2000 AW 0-1: (5f) (Fibr)
Little account filly. Turf high 22. **W G M Turner [0-4] Arthur Bevan.*

JEZADIL (IRE) BHB 58f65a **RR 64f 65a** 5247[1]
2 b f Mujadil (USA) 7.7f **(70)** - Tender Time (Tender King) 6.8f **(54)**
Form - 764434011
Record 2000 - 1st:2 2nd:0 3rd:1 Ran:9
Win Prizemoney £3,745 *Total Prizemoney* £4,786
Wins * **2000** *Oct Wolver (STD) SH 8.5f 59 66+* <
2000 *Oct Wolver (STD) S 8.5f 63*
2000 Turf 0-7: (5f, 6f 2, 7f, 8f 2, 10f) (g-s, gd 3, g-f 2, frm) 2000 AW 2-2: (8f 2-2) (Fibr 2-2)
Average filly, effective 6 to 8f, best at 8f, acts on g-s to frm - acts on Fibr, prefers left handed tracks, excels at Wolverhampton. Turf high 64 - 4th of 11 giving 2lb to Fazzani (4 Aug Thirsk 7f frm RF 3384). AW high 66 (began Oct) - 1st of 10 from Finn McCool (28 Oct Wolverhampton RF 5247) - also 1st of 12 from Mrs Tiggywinkle (14 Oct Wolverhampton RF 4996).
**P S McEntee [1-1] John Harris and Mrs Sian Harris (from M Dods [1-8] Oct 2000).*

JEZEBEL RR 107f 4564a[3]
3 b f Owington - Just Ice **(81f)** (Polar Falcon (USA))
Form - 253223
Record 2000 - 1st:0 2nd:3 3rd:2 Ran:6
Pre2000 - 1st:2 2nd:0 3rd:0 Ran:2
Win Prizemoney £29,251 *Total Prizemoney* £46,613
Wins * 1999 Jun San Si (FRM) L 6f
* 1999 Jun San Si (GD) 5f
2000 Turf 0-6: (6f 6) (g-s, gd 2, g-f 2, hrd)
Pattern-class filly, effective 6f, acts on g-s to hrd, likes San Siro. Turf high 107 - 3rd of 7 getting 3lb from Danger Over (15 Spt Chantilly 6f gd RF 4564a). She ran well without reward in listed races and a Group Three. **C F Wall [2-8] Ettore Landi.*

JIBEREEN BHB 44f50a **RR 49f 50a** 4650[8]
8 b g Lugana Beach 7f **(63)** - Fashion Lover (Shiny Tenth) 9.2f **(56)**
Form - 8042743108848
Record 2000 - 1st:1 2nd:1 3rd:1 Ran:12
Pre2000 - 1st:11 2nd:5 3rd:2 Ran:56
Win Prizemoney £34,471 *Total Prizemoney* £44,735
Wins * **2000** *Apr Southw (STD) C 11f 52*
* 1999 *Jan Southw (STD) C 8f 86* <
* 1998 *Jan Southw (STD) H 8f 72 78*
* 1997 Jly Newmar (GD) H 8f 56 62
* 1997 Jun Newmar (SFT) H 7f 53 56
* 1997 *Apr Southw (STD) H 8f 70 75*
* 1997 *Jan Wolver (STD) C 7f 73*
* 1997 *Jan Southw (STD) C 7f 73*
* 1996 *Dec Southw (SLW) H 6f 67 67*
2000 Turf 0-2: (8f 2) (frm 2) 2000 AW 1-10: (8f 3, 11f 1-4, 12f 3) (Fibr 1-10)
Average gelding, effective 8 to 9f, best at 8f, - acts on Fibr, likes left handed tracks, likes tight tracks. Turf high 49. AW high 70. A fair handicapper on his day, his best recent form has been on Fibresand. A mile at Southwell looks to be his ideal conditions.
**P Howling [9-55] Liam Sheridan (from G Lewis [3-13] Apr 1996).*

JIEMCE (FR) BHB 48f **RR** 4267[12]
3 b g Cardoun (FR) - Fidavi (Northern Baby (CAN)) 11.6f **(71)**
Form - 0
Record 2000 - 1st:0 2nd:0 3rd:0 Ran:1
2000 Turf 0-1: (9f) (g-f)
Currently very poor gelding. **G L Moore [0-1] Phil Collins.*

JILA (IRE) BHB 101f **RR 101f** 454a[3]
5 ch h Kris 10f **(75)** - Enaya (Caerleon (USA)) 8.6f **(71)**
Form - 3
2000 AW 0-1: (8f) (Dirt)
Very useful colt. (1st run) - 3rd of 5 to Blue Snake (12 Mar Nad Al Sheba 8f Dirt RF 0454a).
**in UAE [0-1] (from R W Armstrong [3-6] May 1998).*

JIMAL BHB 65f **RR 66f** 2736[6]
3 b c Reprimand 8.2f **(63)** - Into the Fire (Dominion) 8.5f **(63)**
Form - 056
Record 2000 - 1st:0 2nd:0 3rd:0 Ran:3
2000 Turf 0-3: (7f, 8f 2) (g-s, g-f 2)
Workmanlike, currently average colt. Turf high 66.
**V Soane [0-3] Paint Art International.*

JIM AND TONIC (FR) RR 124f 5369a[1]
6 g g Double Bed (FR) 13.9f **(54)** - Jimka (FR) (Jim French (USA)) 10.3f **(71)**
Form - 1221
2000 Turf 1-3: (8f 1-1, 10f 2) (hvy 1-1, gd 2)
Very high-class gelding, effective 8 to 10f, best at 10f, acts on hvy to frm, does well at Sha Tin and Saint-cloud. Turf high 121 - 1st of

9 giving 3lb to Memory Maker (4 Nov Saint-cloud RF 5369a). Consistent. Something of a globetrotter, he showed near top-class form in Europe, Singapore and Hong Kong last season. Effective between eight and ten furlongs, he picked up a Group Three at home, and was placed in three of the biggest races in the Far East.
**F Doumen in FR [6-17] J D Martin.*

JIMGAREEN (IRE) BHB 45f **RR 56f** 3357[6]
3 b br f Lahib (USA) 8f **(69)** - Sharp Circle (IRE) (Sure Blade (USA)) 11.3f **(67)**
Form - 7645006
Record 2000 - 1st:0 2nd:0 3rd:0 Ran:7
Pre2000 - 1st:0 2nd:1 3rd:0 Ran:5
Win Prizemoney £0 *Total Prizemoney* £1,362
2000 Turf 0-7: (8f, 9f 4, 11f 2) (g-f 2, frm 5)
Workmanlike, fair filly, has worn blinkers. Turf high 56. Becoming disappointing. **Miss L A Perratt [0-12] Dr J Walker.*

JIMMY SWIFT (IRE) BHB 46f **RR 38f** 1908[7]
5 b g Petardia 8.2f **(58)** - Grade A Star (IRE) (Alzao (USA)) 7.1f **(68)**
Form - 47
Record 2000 - 1st:0 2nd:0 3rd:0 Ran:2
Pre2000 - 1st:1 2nd:2 3rd:3 Ran:17
Win Prizemoney £2,234 *Total Prizemoney* £5,511
Wins 1998 Aug Roscom (G-S) 10f 88 <
2000 Turf 0-2: (11f, 12f) (hvy, frm)
Very moderate gelding. Turf high 38. Becoming disappointing.
**P R Hedger [0-10] P R Hedger (from N Meade in IRE [1-21] Oct 1999).*

JINAAN (USA) **RR 68f** 4187[6]
2 ch f Mr Prospector (USA) 8.6f **(88)** - Firdous (Nashwan (USA))
Form - 6
Record 2000 - 1st:0 2nd:0 3rd:0 Ran:1
2000 Turf 0-1: (6f) (g-f)
Currently average filly. **J L Dunlop [0-1] Hamdan Al Maktoum.*

JOCKO GLASSES BHB 85f **RR 83+f** 3043[1]
3 ch g Inchinor 8.9f **(64)** - Corinthia (USA) (Empery (USA)) 11.2f **(69)**
Form - 0511
Record 2000 - 1st:2 2nd:0 3rd:0 Ran:4
Pre2000 - 1st:0 2nd:0 3rd:0 Ran:1
Win Prizemoney £8,446 *Total Prizemoney* £8,446
Wins * 2000 Jly Warwic (G-F) H 10.9f 74 83 <
*** 2000** Jun Pontef (G-F) H 10f 67 76
2000 Turf 2-4: (6f, 10f 1-2, 11f 1-1) (g-f 1-2, frm 1-2)
Scopey, decent gelding. Turf high 83 - 1st of 9 giving 12lb to Rapid Deployment (22 Jly Warwick RF 3043) - also 1st of 10 getting 5lb from Amritsar (25 Jun Pontefract RF 2263). He showed some ability in maiden company, but has improved since being stepped up to ten furlongs on fast ground, winning in good style at both Pontefract and Warwick during the summer. Now hurdling with Nicky Henderson. **C F Wall [2-5] Jocko Partnership.*

JODEEKA BHB 72f **RR 76f** 2413[7]
3 ch f Fraam - Gold And Blue (IRE) (Bluebird (USA)) 7.5f **(69)**
Form - 5157
Record 2000 - 1st:1 2nd:0 3rd:0 Ran:4
Win Prizemoney £2,899 *Total Prizemoney* £2,899
Wins * 2000 May Doncas (G-S) 5f 76 <
2000 Turf 1-4: (5f 1-3, 6f) (g-s, gd 1-1, g-f, frm)
Above-average filly. Turf high 76 - 1st of 9 from Fly Like The Wind (27 May Doncaster RF 1485). **J A Glover [1-4] S J Beard.*

JOEBERTEDY (IRE) BHB 36f30a **RR 23f 30a** 3188[11]
3 b c Tirol 8.1f **(64)** - Hinari Disk Deck (Indian King (USA)) 7.4f **(64)**
Form - 0000
Record 2000 - 1st:0 2nd:0 3rd:0 Ran:4
Pre2000 - 1st:0 2nd:0 3rd:0 Ran:1
2000 Turf 0-3: (6f 2, 8f) (hvy, gd, g-f) 2000 AW 0-1: (6f) (Fibr)
Workmanlike, little account colt. Turf high 22.
**Ronald Thompson [0-5] B Bruce.*

JOELY GREEN BHB 60f57a **RR 60f 57a** 2793[6]
3 b g Binary Star (USA) - Comedy Lady (Comedy Star (USA)) 7.5f **(50)**
Form - 102345807016
Record 2000 - 1st:1 2nd:1 3rd:1 Ran:10
Pre2000 - 1st:1 2nd:1 3rd:1 Ran:8
Win Prizemoney £5,591 *Total Prizemoney* £8,821
Wins * 2000 Jly Lingfi (G-F) H 11.5f 57 60
* 1999 *Nov Wolver (STD)* *7f* 67 <
2000 Turf 1-5: (8f, 10f, 11f 1-2, 16f) (g-f, frm 1-4) 2000 AW 0-5: (7f 2, 8f 2, 10f) (Equi 3, Fibr 2)
Leggy, average gelding, effective 7 to 11f, acts on frm - acts on AW, has worn blinkers (effectively), likes left handed tracks, likes tight tracks. Turf high 60 - 1st of 7 getting 9lb from Exile (1 Jly Lingfield RF 2433). AW high 66 (1st run) - 2nd of 4 giving 5lb to Shamsan (5 Jan Lingfield 8f Equi RF 0027). A winner on Fibresand last year, he got off the mark on turf at Lingfield in July when blinkered for the first time.
**N P Littmoden [2-16] Paul Dixon (from W G M Turner [0-2] Apr 1999).*

JOE TAYLOR (CAN) **RR 45f** 4367[11]
2 b c Known Fact (USA) 8.3f **(72)** - Shore Mist (USA) (Coastal (USA)) 11.5f **(72)**
Form - 0
Record 2000 - 1st:0 2nd:0 3rd:0 Ran:1
2000 Turf 0-1: (5f) (frm)
Currently moderate colt. **D W P Arbuthnot [0-1] Sean Taylor.*

JOEY TRIBBIANI (IRE) BHB 49f67a **RR 45f 67a** 5142[10]
3 b g Foxhound (USA) - Mardi Gras Belle (USA) (Masked Dancer (USA))
Form - 0000
Record 2000 - 1st:0 2nd:0 3rd:0 Ran:4
Pre2000 - 1st:0 2nd:0 3rd:1 Ran:6
Win Prizemoney £0 *Total Prizemoney* £657
2000 Turf 0-4: (7f, 8f, 10f, 11f) (g-s, gd 2, frm)
Scopey, average gelding. Turf high 45. Becoming disappointing.
**C N Allen [0-10] NewmarketConnections com.*

JOHAYRO BHB 56f60a **RR 59f 60a** 5188[12]
7 ch g Clantime 6.6f **(57)** - Arroganza (Crofthall) 6.3f **(59)**
Form - 04050078024300712200
Record 2000 - 1st:1 2nd:3 3rd:1 Ran:20
Pre2000 - 1st:10 2nd:10 3rd:2 Ran:79
Win Prizemoney £39,426 *Total Prizemoney* £61,734
Wins * 2000 Aug Redcar (FRM) H 6f 53 56
* 1999 Jly Thirsk (FRM) H 6f 68 72
* 1999 May Mussel (FRM) H 5f 52 62+
* 1999 May Ayr (GD) H 5f 52 58
* 1999 May Mussel (G-F) H 7.1f 52 56
* 1998 Jly Ayr (GD) H 5f 60 65
* 1997 Spt Redcar (FRM) H 6f 60 63
* 1997 Apr Catter (GD) 6f 54
* 1997 Apr Ripon (G-F) H 5f 51 61
* 1997 Apr Mussel (G-F) 5f 59
2000 Turf 1-20: (5f 9, 6f 1-8, 7f 3) (sft, g-s, gd 4, g-f 6, frm 7, hrd 1-1)
Average gelding, effective 5 to 6f, best at 5f, acts on g-f to frm, best on g-f, has worn blinkers, likes tight tracks. Turf high 57. Inconsistent.
**J S Goldie [10-85] Frank Brady (from W G M Turner [1-14] Jly 1996).*

JOHN COMPANY (IRE) BHB 65f57a **RR 64f 57a** 223[2]
3 ch c Indian Ridge 7.6f **(74)** - Good Policy (IRE) (Thatching) 8f **(66)**
Form - 5732
Record 2000 - 1st:0 2nd:1 3rd:1 Ran:3
Pre2000 - 1st:0 2nd:1 3rd:0 Ran:4
Win Prizemoney £0 *Total Prizemoney* £1,354
2000 AW 0-3: (6f, 7f 2) (Equi, Fibr 2)
Workmanlike, average colt, effective 7f, acts on gd - acts on Equi. AW high 60 - 2nd of 9 giving 3lb to Damasquiner (5 Feb Lingfield 7f Equi RF 0223).
**R M Beckett [0-4] Alan Lillingston (from P T Walwyn [0-3] Oct 1999).*

JOHN FERNELEY BHB 100f97a **RR 105f 97a** 4968[3]
5 b g Polar Falcon (USA) 9f **(74)** - I'll Try (Try My Best (USA)) 7.6f **(67)**
Form - 312443
Record 2000 - 1st:1 2nd:1 3rd:2 Ran:6
Pre2000 - 1st:4 2nd:0 3rd:2 Ran:10
Win Prizemoney £65,086 *Total Prizemoney* £111,747
Wins * 2000 Mar Doncas () H 8f 90 98 <
* 1999 Oct York (G-S) H 7.9f 82 86
* 1998 Jly Sandow (G-F) H 7.1f 78 81+
* 1998 Jun Thirsk (GD) 7f 81
* 1998 Apr Folkes (SFT) 7f 75

2000 Turf 1-5: (8f 1-5) (gd 1-4, g-f) 2000 AW 0-1: (8f) (Fibr)
Pattern-class gelding, effective 8f, acts on gd to g-f, best on gd, has worn blinkers, excels at York. Turf high 105 - 2nd of 32 getting 1lb from Caribbean Monarch (21 Jun Ascot 8f gd RF 2151) - also 1st of 24 giving 1lb to King Priam (25 Mar Doncaster RF 0494). Consistent. He ran very well when a very close third in Wolverhampton's Lincoln Trial on his reappearance and showed the benefit when landing the Lincoln itself. Beaten a neck in the Hunt Cup on his next start, he ran well at both Glorious Goodwood and York, but the handicapper might just have him now. He goes well fresh. Has now moved to be trained by Lynda Ramsden in 2001. **P F I Cole [5-16] Richard Green (Fine Paintings).*

JOHN FOLEY (IRE) BHB 59f55a **RR 55f 55a** 2663[6]
2 b g Petardia 8.2f **(58)** - Fast Bay (Bay Express) 7.1f **(60)**
Form - 802524226
Record 2000 - 1st:0 2nd:4 3rd:0 Ran:9
Win Prizemoney £0 *Total Prizemoney* £2,564
2000 Turf 0-4: (5f 3, 6f) (sft, gd 2, g-f) 2000 AW 0-5: (5f 3, 6f, 7f) (Equi, Fibr 4)
Fair gelding, effective 6f, acts on g-f, has worn blinkers. Turf high 55 - 2nd of 8 giving 5lb to Italian Affair (4 Jly Yarmouth 6f g-f RF 2500). AW high 56. **W G M Turner [0-9] Foley Steelstock.*

JOHNNY DOLLAR (USA) RR 114f 4950a[3]
4 b g Olympic (USA) - Java Drums (USA) (Java Gold (USA))
Form - 3
2000 Turf 0-1: (8f) (frm)
Currently Group-class gelding. (1st run) - 3rd of 9 getting 3lb from Forbidden Apple (8 Oct Belmont Park 8f frm RF 4950a). **A Borosh in USA [0-1].*

JOHNNY OSCAR BHB 75f **RR 74f** 4603[10]
3 b g Belmez (USA) 11.4f **(65)** - Short Rations (Lorenzaccio) 10f **(64)**
Form - 4330
Record 2000 - 1st:0 2nd:0 3rd:2 Ran:4
Win Prizemoney £0 *Total Prizemoney* £1,559
2000 Turf 0-4: (10f 2, 12f, 14f) (gd 2, g-f, frm)
Scopey, above-average gelding. Turf high 74 - 3rd of 6 giving 5lb to Frangy (13 Jly Doncaster 12f frm RF 2754). Placed in maidens at up to a mile and a half. **J R Fanshawe [0-4] J M Greetham.*

JOHNNY REB BHB 74f **RR 86f** 5320[13]
2 b c Danehill (USA) 9.1f **(79)** - Dixie Eyes Blazing (USA) (Gone West (USA)) 6.5f **(75)**
Form - 260500
Record 2000 - 1st:0 2nd:1 3rd:0 Ran:6
Win Prizemoney £0 *Total Prizemoney* £2,772
2000 Turf 0-6: (5f 2, 6f 3, 7f) (sft, gd 2, g-f 2, frm)
Useful colt, effective 5f, acts on g-f. Turf high 86. **R Hannon [0-6] Lindy Regis & Geoff Howard-Spink.*

JOHNNY STACCATO BHB 32f30a **RR 28f 30a** 3546[12]
6 b g Statoblest 6.4f **(63)** - Frasquita (Song) 7.2f **(61)**
Form - 000070
Record 2000 - 1st:0 2nd:0 3rd:0 Ran:6
Pre2000 - 1st:2 2nd:2 3rd:3 Ran:41
Win Prizemoney £7,734 *Total Prizemoney* £12,460
Wins 1997 Jun Sandow (G-F) 5f 88
1996 Aug Windso (G-F) 6f 89+ <
2000 Turf 0-6: (5f, 6f 5) (gd 2, g-f 2, frm 2)
Moderate gelding, effective 5 to 6f, best at 6f, acts on gd to frm, has worn blinkers, prefers left handed tracks, likes tight tracks. Turf high 28. **M Quinn [0-19] W Trezise (from R J O'Sullivan [0-15] Dec 1998).*

JOHN O'GROATS (IRE) RR 52f 2368[4]
2 b c Distinctly North (USA) 7.4f **(63)** - Bannons Dream (IRE) **(31f)** (Thatching) 8f **(66)**
Form - 4
Record 2000 - 1st:0 2nd:0 3rd:0 Ran:1
Win Prizemoney £0 *Total Prizemoney* £275
2000 Turf 0-1: (7f) (frm)
Currently fair colt. **T D Easterby [0-1] Bernard Hathaway.*

JOHN'S CALL (USA) RR 124f 5331a[3]
9 ch h Lord At War (ARG) 6.6f **(67)** - Calling Guest (IRE) (Be My Guest (USA)) 9.3f **(67)**
Form - 13
2000 Turf 1-2: (12f 1-2) (frm 1-2)
Currently very high-class horse. Turf high 124 (began Oct) - 3rd of 13 to Kalanisi (4 Nov Churchill Downs 12f frm RF 5331a) - also 1st of 12 from Craigsteel (7 Oct Belmont Park RF 4948a). **T Voss in USA [1-2] Trillium Stable Inc.*

JOHNSON'S POINT BHB 79f **RR 76f** 5103[4]
2 ch f Sabrehill (USA) 8.5f **(64)** - Watership (USA) (Foolish Pleasure (USA)) 8.9f **(72)**
Form - 2184
Record 2000 - 1st:1 2nd:1 3rd:0 Ran:4
Win Prizemoney £4,212 *Total Prizemoney* £5,992
Wins * 2000 Aug Epsom (G-F) 7f 72 <
2000 Turf 1-4: (7f 1-3, 8f) (gd 2, g-f, frm 1-1)
Above-average filly. Turf high 70 (began Aug) - 4th of 12 giving 8lb to Borders Belle (20 Oct Doncaster 8f gd RF 5103) - also 1st of 10 getting 5lb from Spy Master (17 Aug Epsom RF 3720). **B W Hills [1-4] W J Gredley.*

JOHN STEED (IRE) BHB 37f **RR 42f** 5200[6]
3 b g Thatching 7.8f **(69)** - Trinity Hall **(62f)** (Hallgate)
Form - 040006
Record 2000 - 1st:0 2nd:0 3rd:0 Ran:6
Pre2000 - 1st:0 2nd:0 3rd:0 Ran:3
Win Prizemoney £0 *Total Prizemoney* £222
2000 Turf 0-6: (8f 2, 10f 3, 12f) (g-s, gd 2, g-f, frm 2)
Scopey, moderate gelding. Turf high 41. Consistent. **C A Horgan [0-9] Stephen Starkey.*

JOHNSTON'S DIAMOND (IRE) BHB 58f **RR 58f** 4532[6]
2 b g Tagula (IRE) - Toshair Flyer (Ballad Rock) 7.8f **(63)**
Form - 486
Record 2000 - 1st:0 2nd:0 3rd:0 Ran:3
Win Prizemoney £0 *Total Prizemoney* £266
2000 Turf 0-3: (5f, 6f, 7f) (gd, frm 2)
Currently fair gelding. Turf high 58 (began Aug). **E J Alston [0-3] F McKevitt.*

JOHNSTON'S FANFAN (IRE) RR 4168[16]
4 b g Persian Bold 10f **(69)** - Dabtiya (IRE) (Shirley Heights) 10.3f **(74)**
Form - 0
Record 2000 - 1st:0 2nd:0 3rd:0 Ran:1
2000 Turf 0-1: (8f) (gd)
Formerly very poor gelding. **E J Alston [0-1] F McKevitt.*

JOH'S BROTHER BHB 24f **RR 23df** 3429[19]
4 ch g Clantime 6.6f **(57)** - Arroganza (Crofthall) 6.3f **(59)**
Form - 0000
Record 2000 - 1st:0 2nd:0 3rd:0 Ran:4
Pre2000 - 1st:0 2nd:0 3rd:0 Ran:7
2000 Turf 0-4: (5f 2, 6f, 7f) (gd, g-f, frm 2)
Unfurnished, little account gelding. Turf high 3 (began Jly). **J S Goldie [0-11] Frank Brady.*

JOIN THE PARADE BHB 49f36a **RR 58f 36a** 4373[7]
4 b f Elmaamul (USA) 8.1f **(70)** - Summer Pageant (Chief's Crown (USA)) 9.8f **(72)**
Form - 07382007
Record 2000 - 1st:0 2nd:1 3rd:1 Ran:7
Pre2000 - 1st:1 2nd:1 3rd:1 Ran:9
Win Prizemoney £3,243 *Total Prizemoney* £5,945
Wins * 1999 Spt Leices (FRM) H 10f 54 58 <
2000 Turf 0-7: (10f 4, 11f, 12f, 14f) (gd, g-f 2, frm 3, hrd)
Leggy, fair filly, effective 10f, acts on gd to g-f, favours tight tracks. Turf high 58 - 2nd of 15 giving 10lb to City Gambler (31 Jly Yarmouth 10f gd RF 3266). **H J Collingridge [1-16] L Westbury.*

JOINT INSTRUCTION (IRE) BHB 72f **RR 75f** 5129[7]
2 b g Forzando 7.2f **(63)** - Edge of Darkness **(52f)** (Vaigly Great) 7f **(58)**
Form - 45215282011707
Record 2000 - 1st:3 2nd:3 3rd:0 Ran:14
Win Prizemoney £7,960 *Total Prizemoney* £12,264
Wins * 2000 Spt Hamilt (SFT) H 6f 65 75 <
*** 2000** Aug Warwic (GD) H 6.1f 65 75 <
*** 2000** May Bright (SFT) 6f 75 <

2000 Turf 3-14: (5f 3, 6f 3-9, 7f 2) (hvy, sft 2, g-s, gd 3-6, g-f 3, frm)
Above-average gelding, effective 5 to 6f, best at 6f, acts on gd to frm, best on gd. Turf high 75 - 1st of 7 giving 2lb to Classy Act (4 Spt Hamilton RF 4210) - also 1st of 8 getting 24lb from Sir Francis (28 Aug Warwick RF 4056). Inconsistent. He paid his way in a busy season, successful three times on ground with some cut in it.
**M R Channon [3-14] Ridgeway Downs Racing.*

JOKEL RR 450^{13}

5 ch m Finalto - Over My Head (Bay Express) 7.1f **(60)**
Form - 0
Record 2000 - 1st:0 2nd:0 3rd:0 Ran:1
2000 AW 0-1: (6f) (Fibr)
Currently very poor filly. **J M Bradley [0-1] E J Pearse.*

JOLI ECLIPSE BHB 24f RR 5f 4769^{8}

3 b f Romany Rye - Bali Sunset (Balidar) 7.9f **(63)**
Form - 008
Record 2000 - 1st:0 2nd:0 3rd:0 Ran:3
2000 Turf 0-3: (8f 2, 12f) (g-s, frm 2)
Unfurnished, currently very poor filly. Turf high 5 (began Jly).
**R J Hodges [0-3] Joli Racing.*

JOLI FLYERS BHB 39f35a RR 39f 35a 1922^{11}

6 gr g Joli Wasfi (USA) 11.7f **(57)** - Hagen's Bargain (Mount Hagen (FR)) 8.4f **(70)**
Form - 0010
Record 2000 - 1st:1 2nd:0 3rd:0 Ran:4
Pre2000 - 1st:1 2nd:2 3rd:1 Ran:19
Win Prizemoney £6,946 *Total Prizemoney* £11,003
Wins * **2000** May Leices (SFT) H 11.8f 37 39
1998 Jun Kempto (HVY) H 12f 44 47 <
2000 Turf 1-4: (10f, 12f 1-2, 15f) (g-s, gd 1-2, g-f)
Very moderate gelding, effective 12f, acts on gd. Turf high 39 - 1st of 8 getting 27lb from Legend (29 May Leicester RF 1527).
**R J Hodges [1-4] Joli Racing (from V Soane [0-7] Oct 1999).*

JOLI SADDLERS BHB 33f RR 37f 2546^{9}

4 b f Saddlers' Hall (IRE) 10.5f **(65)** - Vitality (Young Generation) 7.7f **(63)**
Form - 8000
Record 2000 - 1st:0 2nd:0 3rd:0 Ran:4
Pre2000 - 1st:0 2nd:0 3rd:0 Ran:8
Win Prizemoney £0 *Total Prizemoney* £291
2000 Turf 0-4: (12f 2, 14f, 16f) (gd 3, frm)
Leggy, very moderate filly, has worn blinkers. Turf high 37.
**M J Haynes [0-12] Joli Racing.*

JOLLANDS BHB 64f RR 74f 4218^{17}

2 b c Ezzoud (IRE) - Rainbow Fleet (Nomination) 7f **(60)**
Form - 830
Record 2000 - 1st:0 2nd:0 3rd:1 Ran:3
Win Prizemoney £0 *Total Prizemoney* £321
2000 Turf 0-3: (6f, 7f 2) (frm 3)
Currently above-average colt. Turf high 74 (began Jly) - 3rd of 12 giving 13lb to Zando's Charm (16 Aug Salisbury 7f frm RF 3703).
**D Marks [0-3] D Marks.*

JOLLY SHARP (USA) BHB 95f RR 100f 5311^{6}

3 ch c Diesis 9f **(80)** - Milly Ha Ha **(101f)** (Dancing Brave (USA)) 8.4f **(76)**
Form - 166
Record 2000 - 1st:1 2nd:0 3rd:0 Ran:3
Pre2000 - 1st:0 2nd:0 3rd:0 Ran:1
Win Prizemoney £4,387 *Total Prizemoney* £4,625
Wins * **2000** Apr Kempto (SFT) 11.1f 89 <
2000 Turf 1-3: (11f 1-1, 12f, 15f) (sft 1-2, g-f)
Rangy, very useful colt. Turf high 100 - 6th of 8 to Millenary (9 May Chester 12f g-f RF 1111). He looked suited by the step up in trip when winning over 12 furlongs on his Kempton reappearance. A close sixth in the Chester Vase next time, he was then off the track nearly six months before his final run. He looks a stayer.
**H R A Cecil [1-4] Cliveden Stud.*

JO MELL BHB 95f84a RR 97f 84a 2444^{10}

7 b g Efisio 7.7f **(69)** - Militia Girl (Rarity) 10.1f **(60)**
Form - 0101200
Record 2000 - 1st:2 2nd:1 3rd:0 Ran:7
Pre2000 - 1st:8 2nd:4 3rd:5 Ran:46
Win Prizemoney £197,676 *Total Prizemoney* £232,789
Wins * **2000** May Beverl (GD) H 8.5f 91 95
* **2000** Apr Beverl (HVY) 7.5f 91
* 1999 Spt Newcas (SFT) 7f 86+
* 1998 Aug Ascot (G-F) H 7f 98 106 <
* 1997 Oct Doncas (GD) 7f 104
* 1997 Spt Ascot (G-F) H 7f 93 103
* 1997 Jly York (GD) H 7.9f 80 92
* 1997 Jly Haydoc (GD) H 7.1f 73 85
* 1997 Jun Newcas (HVY) H 7f 73 80
2000 Turf 2-6: (7f 1-3, 8f 1-3) (g-s 1-2, gd 1-3, frm) 2000 AW 0-1: (7f) (Fibr)
Very useful gelding, effective 7 to 8f, best at 8f, acts on g-s to gd, best on g-s, likes tight tracks. Turf high 97 - 2nd of 9 getting 14lb from Swallow Flight (29 May Sandown 8f g-s RF 1537) - also 1st of 7 giving 14lb to Duraid (23 May Beverley RF 1387). Inconsistent. A tough and genuine front-running handicapper, he was given a good ride in order to win a Beverley classified event on his second start of last season, and again made all to win a rated stakes at the same track in May. He obviously likes it there. His best effort was in defeat when a close second in a Sandown rated stakes.
**T D Easterby [9-49] C H Newton Jnr Ltd (from M H Easterby [1-4] Oct 1995).*

JONA HOLLEY BHB 47f47a RR 42f 47a 750^{6}

7 b g Sharpo 7.5f **(68)** - Spurned (USA) (Robellino (USA)) 7.6f **(80)**
Form - 06
Record 2000 - 1st:0 2nd:0 3rd:0 Ran:2
Pre2000 - 1st:3 2nd:5 3rd:0 Ran:30
Win Prizemoney £7,768 *Total Prizemoney* £13,906
Wins * 1999 Oct Ayr (SFT) S 9.1f 51
1997 *Oct Southw (STD) H 8f 47 52* <
1997 Jly Folkes (SFT) H 9.7f 43 50
2000 Turf 0-2: (8f, 9f) (sft, gd)
Moderate gelding, effective 8 to 9f, acts on sft to g-f, has worn blinkers. Turf high 26.
**A Streeter [2-8] Malt 'N' Hops (from M D Hammond [0-16] Jun 1999).*

JONATHAN'S GIRL BHB 28f29a RR 31f 29a 2892^{13}

5 b m Thowra (FR) 11.2f **(47)** - Sicilian Vespers (Mummy's Game) 8.2f **(60)**
Form - 57404000680
Record 2000 - 1st:0 2nd:0 3rd:0 Ran:11
Pre2000 - 1st:0 2nd:1 3rd:2 Ran:18
Win Prizemoney £0 *Total Prizemoney* £2,618
2000 Turf 0-6: (5f, 6f 3, 7f 2) (g-f 3, frm 3) 2000 AW 0-5: (5f 2, 6f 2, 7f) (Equi 3, Fibr 2)
Very moderate filly, effective 6f, acted on hrd. Turf high 31. AW high 38. (DEAD) **J J Bridger [0-29] J J Bridger.*

JONLOZ BHB 48f43a RR 52f 43a 4764^{16}

3 ch g Presidium 7.5f **(56)** - Stratford Lady (Touching Wood (USA)) 8.2f **(55)**
Form - 40545668120
Record 2000 - 1st:1 2nd:1 3rd:0 Ran:9
Pre2000 - 1st:0 2nd:0 3rd:0 Ran:6
Win Prizemoney £2,310 *Total Prizemoney* £3,215
Wins * **2000** Aug Beverl (GD) SH 12f 37 47 <
2000 Turf 1-7: (8f 2, 10f, 12f 1-4) (sft, g-s 2, gd 1-2, frm 2) 2000 AW 0-2: (7f, 8f) (Fibr 2)
Fair gelding, effective 12f, acts on gd to frm, likes tight tracks. Turf high 52 - 2nd of 12 getting 20lb from Dark Shadows (7 Aug Ripon 12f frm RF 3430) - also 1st of 13 getting 11lb from Unicorn Star (1 Aug Beverley RF 3267). AW high 11. Inconsistent.
**G Woodward [1-15] P Appleyard.*

JOONDEY BHB 77f81a RR 75f 81a 3808^{2}

3 b c Pursuit of Love 9.5f **(69)** - Blueberry Walk (Green Desert (USA)) 8.6f **(78)**
Form - 0325212
Record 2000 - 1st:1 2nd:3 3rd:1 Ran:7
Win Prizemoney £2,834 *Total Prizemoney* £6,476
Wins * **2000** *Aug Wolver (STD) 9.4f 77+* <
2000 Turf 0-5: (8f 2, 9f, 10f 2) (g-s, g-f 3, frm) 2000 AW 1-2: (9f 1-2) (Fibr 1-2)
Workmanlike, decent colt, effective 9 to 10f, best at 9f, acts on g-f -

acts on Fibr. Turf high 75 - 2nd of 15 to Ragdale Hall (5 Jun Windsor 10f g-f RF 1729). AW high 82 (began Aug) - 2nd of 13 giving 3lb to Trois (19 Aug Wolverhampton 9f Fibr RF 3808) - also 1st of 10 giving 5lb to Peaches (11 Aug Wolverhampton RF 3571).

**M A Jarvis [1-7] Sheikh Ahmed Al Maktoum.*

JOPLIN (USA) RR 92f 4699[8]

2 ch c Nureyev (USA) 8.4f **(84)** - Pi Phi Hi D (USA) (Sauce Boat (USA)) 8.3f **(79)**

Form - 1668

2000 Turf 1-4: (5f 2, 6f 1-2) (gd 1-1, g-f, frm 2)

Useful colt. Turf high 92. Narrow winner of a fair race at Navan on his debut, he seemed to find the minimum trip inadequate when well beaten in a York Listed event and was found wanting against the top sprint juveniles at Doncaster.

**A P O'Brien in IRE [1-3] M Tabor & Mrs John Magnier (from A P O'Brien [0-1] Spt 2000).*

JORDAN'S RIDGE (IRE) BHB 52f RR 58f 3905[2]

4 br g Indian Ridge 7.6f **(74)** - Sadie Jordan (USA) (Hail the Pirates (USA)) 11f **(78)**

Form - 072

Record					
2000 -		1st:0	2nd:1	3rd:0	Ran:3
	Pre2000 -	1st:0	2nd:1	3rd:0	Ran:8

Win Prizemoney £0 *Total Prizemoney* £867

2000 Turf 0-3: (12f, 15f, 17f) (g-s, frm 2)

Fair gelding, effective 12f, acts on g f, has worn blinkers, likes right handed tracks. Turf high 56.

**P Monteith [0-2] P Monteith (from D P Kelly in IRE [0-3] May 2000).*

JORROCKS (USA) RR 72df 5086[11]

6 b g Rubiano (USA) 7.1f **(87)** - Perla Fina (USA) (Gallant Man) 10.2f **(68)**

Form - 26700

Record					
2000 -		1st:0	2nd:1	3rd:0	Ran:5
	Pre2000 -	1st:4	2nd:2	3rd:4	Ran:27

Win Prizemoney £34,471 *Total Prizemoney* £43,620

Wins								
* 1999	Spt	Beverl	(SFT)	H	7.5f	51	59+	
1997	Spt	Newbur	(SFT)	H	7.3f	87	94	<
1997	Aug	Goodwo	(G-F)	H	7f	74	85	
1997	Jly	Sandow	(G-F)	H	7.1f	74	77	

2000 Turf 0-5: (7f 4, 9f) (hvy, sft, g-f 3)

Decent gelding, effective 7f, acts on g-s to g-f, best on g-f, has worn blinkers. Turf high 62 (1st run) (began Jly) - 2nd of 16 giving 21lb to Wilemmgeo (24 Jly Beverley 7f g-f RF 3069). Inconsistent.

**M W Easterby [1-14] Stephen Curtis (from I A Balding [3-18] Spt 1998).*

JOSEPH VERNET (IRE) BHB 57f RR 52f 5000[17]

3 b br g Owington - Pizziri (Artaius (USA)) 9f **(69)**

Form - 60

Record					
2000 -		1st:0	2nd:0	3rd:0	Ran:2
	Pre2000 -	1st:0	2nd:0	3rd:0	Ran:2

2000 Turf 0-2: (10f 2) (g-s, frm)

Workmanlike, fair gelding. Turf high 52 (began Jly).

**Mrs V C Ward [0-2] Joseph Vernet Partnership (from P F I Cole [0-2] Spt 1999).*

JOSH MOR RR 55f 5237[3]

2 b g Chaddleworth (IRE) - Little Morston (Morston (FR)) 9.4f **(55)**

Form - 3

Record				
2000 -	1st:0	2nd:0	3rd:1	Ran:1

Win Prizemoney £0 *Total Prizemoney* £550

2000 Turf 0-1: (8f) (g-s)

Currently fair gelding. **G L Moore [0-1] Exors of the late A Moore.*

JOSR ALGARHOUD (IRE) BHB 113f RR 116f 3317[8]

4 b c Darshaan 11.9f **(81)** - Pont-Aven (Try My Best (USA)) 7.6f **(67)**

Form - 18

Record					
2000 -		1st:1	2nd:0	3rd:0	Ran:2
	Pre2000 -	1st:2	2nd:1	3rd:2	Ran:5

Win Prizemoney £111,863 *Total Prizemoney* £138,013

Wins							
* 2000	Jun	Longch	(GD)	G3	7f	115	
* 1999	Jly	Newcas	(G-F)	G3	7f	113	
1998	Aug	York	(G-F)	G2	6f	117+	<

2000 Turf 1-2: (7f 1-1, 8f) (gd 1-2)

Scopey, high-class colt. Turf high 115 (1st run) - 1st of 9 giving 12lb to Cap Coz (25 Jun Longchamp RF 2388a). Successful in Group company at two, three and four, he took after his speedy dam rather than staying sire and was best at distances short of a mile. Retired to the Lavington Stud at a fee of £4,000, he only finished out of the frame once in seven starts and was genuine.

**S bin Suroor [2-5] Godolphin (from M R Channon [1-2] Aug 1998).*

JOSTLE (USA) RR 5325a[9]

3 br f Brocco (USA) - Moon Drone (USA) (Drone (USA))

Form - 0

2000 AW 0-1: (9f) (Dirt)

Currently useful, always wears blinkers.

**J C Servis in USA [0-1] Fox Hill Farms.*

JOURNALIST (IRE) BHB 94f RR 89f 2950[6]

3 b f Night Shift (USA) 8.1f **(73)** - Schlefalora (Mas Media)

Form - 6

Record					
2000 -		1st:0	2nd:0	3rd:0	Ran:1
	Pre2000 -	1st:1	2nd:1	3rd:0	Ran:3

Win Prizemoney £6,004 *Total Prizemoney* £15,161

Wins						
1999	Jly	Newmar	(G-F)	6f	82+	<

2000 Turf 0-1: (7f) (g-f)

Workmanlike, useful filly.

**S bin Suroor [0-1] Godolphin (from B W Hills [1-3] Aug 1999).*

J R STEVENSON (USA) BHB 86f RR 94f 4302[13]

4 ch g Lyphard (USA) 10.6f **(75)** - While it Lasts (USA) (Foolish Pleasure (USA)) 8.9f **(72)**

Form - 0706500

Record					
2000 -		1st:0	2nd:0	3rd:0	Ran:7
	Pre2000 -	1st:2	2nd:0	3rd:1	Ran:7

Win Prizemoney £7,390 *Total Prizemoney* £9,083

Wins						
1999	Jun	Goodwo	(G-S)	9.9f	97	<
1998	Spt	Cheste	(GD)	7f	87+	

2000 Turf 0-7: (9f, 10f 5, 12f) (gd 5, g-f 2)

Light-framed, useful gelding, effective 10f, acts on g-s, has worn blinkers (very effectively), likes right handed tracks. Turf high 94.

**D Nicholls [0-7] Claret & Blue Army (from P W Chapple-Hyam [2-7] Spt 1999).*

JUBILEE SCHOLAR (IRE) BHB 28f37a RR 22f 37a 387[12]

7 b g Royal Academy (USA) 7.8f **(77)** - Jaljuli (Jalmood (USA)) 10.1f **(52)**

Form - 0P00

Record					
2000 -		1st:0	2nd:0	3rd:0	Ran:2
	Pre2000 -	1st:3	2nd:4	3rd:4	Ran:48

Win Prizemoney £6,192 *Total Prizemoney* £9,695

Wins								
* 1998	*Nov*	*Lingfi*	*(STD)*	*H*	*10f*	*54*	*56*	<
* 1998	*Apr*	*Lingfi*	*(STD)*	*H*	*8f*	*45*	*51*	
* 1997	*Nov*	*Lingfi*	*(STD)*	*H*	*10f*	*36*	*39?*	

2000 AW 0-2: (10f 2) (Equi 2)

Little account gelding, effective 8 to 10f, best at 8f, - acts on Equi, mostly wears blinkers (effectively). Becoming disappointing.

**G L Moore [3-40] M V Johnston (from K McAuliffe [0-7] Apr 1997).*

JUDIAM BHB 64f72a RR 63f 72a 4703[24]

3 b f Primo Dominie 7.2f **(67)** - Hoist (IRE) **(72df 63a)** (Bluebird (USA)) 7.5f **(69)**

Form - 45080518000

Record					
2000 -		1st:1	2nd:0	3rd:0	Ran:11
	Pre2000 -	1st:1	2nd:1	3rd:2	Ran:8

Win Prizemoney £7,235 *Total Prizemoney* £9,773

Wins								
* 2000	Jly	Kempto	(G-S)	H	5f	62	63+	
* 1999	Oct	Yarmou	(G-S)	H	5.2f	62	74	<

2000 Turf 1-10: (5f 1-9, 6f) (g-s, gd, g-f 1-7, frm) 2000 AW 0-1: (5f) (Equi)

Light-framed, average filly, effective 5f, acts on gd. Turf high 63.

**C A Dwyer [2-19] R West.*

JUDICIOUS (IRE) BHB 80f RR 86+f 4934[2]

3 b c Fairy King (USA) 7.7f **(75)** - Kama Tashoof **(68f)** (Mtoto)

Form - 8381622

Record					
2000 -		1st:1	2nd:2	3rd:1	Ran:7
	Pre2000 -	1st:0	2nd:0	3rd:0	Ran:2

Win Prizemoney £3,623 *Total Prizemoney* £9,077

Wins								
* 2000	Aug	Leices	(G-F)	H	8f	70	76	<

2000 Turf 1-7: (8f 1-4, 10f 3) (g-s 2, gd, g-f 1-1, frm 3)

Well made, useful colt, effective 8f, acts on g-s to g-f. Turf high 86 - 2nd of 18 giving 25lb to Wilemmgeo (2 Oct Pontefract 8f g-s RF 4767). Inconsistent. **G Wragg [1-9] Mollers Racing.*

JULIA TITUS (IRE) BHB 54f **RR 45f** 4645[18]

3 ch f Perugino (USA) - Blue Vista (IRE) (Pennine Walk) 8.5f **(61)**
Form - 800
Record 2000 - 1st:0 2nd:0 3rd:0 Ran:3
Pre2000 - 1st:0 2nd:0 3rd:0 Ran:2
2000 Turf 0-3: (8f, 10f, 12f) (g-s, g-f, frm)
Scopey, moderate filly. Turf high 45 (began Jly).
**W R Muir [0-5] Aster Partnership.*

JULIE'S GIFT RR 4199[14]

3 ch f Presidium 7.5f **(56)** - Far Dara (Pharly (FR)) 9.8f **(68)**
Form - 80
Record 2000 - 1st:0 2nd:0 3rd:0 Ran:2
2000 Turf 0-2: (10f 2) (g-f, frm)
Small, currently very poor filly. (began Aug).
**N Bycroft [0-2] G J Allison.*

JULIUS (IRE) BHB 90f **RR 89f** 4815[7]

3 b f Persian Bold 10f **(69)** - Babushka (IRE) (Dance of Life (USA)) 7f **(66)**
Form - 121111740517
Record 2000 - 1st:6 2nd:1 3rd:0 Ran:12
Pre2000 - 1st:0 2nd:0 3rd:2 Ran:4
Win Prizemoney £28,117 *Total Prizemoney* £31,139

Wins								
*** 2000**	Spt	Newmar	(G-S)	H	10f	85	88	
*** 2000**	Jun	Newcas	(FRM)		10.1f		79+	
*** 2000**	Jun	Cheste	(G-F)	H	12.3f	74	91	<
*** 2000**	Jun	Ripon	(G-F)		10f		82	
*** 2000**	Jun	Mussel	(FRM)	H	12f	70	82	
*** 2000**	Jun	Nottin	(G-F)		10f		64+	

2000 Turf 6-12: (10f 4-8, 12f 2-4) (g-s, gd 1-2, g-f 2-4, frm 3-5)
Useful filly, effective 10 to 12f, best at 12f, acts on gd to frm, prefers tight tracks. Turf high 91 - 1st of 5 giving 14lb to Crystal Flite (28 Jun Chester RF 2331) - also 1st of 19 giving 7lb to Forest Heath (26 Spt Newmarket RF 4645). Consistent. She became the archetypal filly in form during the summer, well placed to win five times within the month of June. Suited by fast ground and trips of between ten and 12 furlongs, she appeared to be in the Handicapper's grip until battling home in brave fashion in a Newmarket apprentice event.
**M Johnston [6-12] Mrs K E Daley (from D K Weld in IRE [0-4] Oct 1999).*

JUMAIREYAH RR 75+f 5196[1]

2 b f Fairy King (USA) 7.7f **(75)** - Donya (Mill Reef (USA)) 10.5f **(78)**
Form - 1
Record 2000 - 1st:1 2nd:0 3rd:0 Ran:1
Win Prizemoney £4,166 *Total Prizemoney* £4,166
Wins * 2000 Oct Windso (HVY) 8.3f 75+ <
2000 Turf 1-1: (8f 1-1) (gd 1-1)
Currently above-average filly. (1st run) - 1st of 16 from Carioca Dream (26 Oct Windsor RF 5196).
**L M Cumani [1-1] Sheikh Mohammed Obaid Al Maktoum.*

JUMBO JET BHB 69f **RR 78f** 3078[13]

3 b c Emarati (USA) 6.6f **(63)** - Mithi Al Gamar (USA) **(60f)** (Blushing Groom (FR)) 10.3f **(76)**
Form - 48550
Record 2000 - 1st:0 2nd:0 3rd:0 Ran:5
Win Prizemoney £0 *Total Prizemoney* £207
2000 Turf 0-5: (6f, 7f 2, 8f, 10f) (gd 3, frm 2)
Scopey, above-average colt. Turf high 78.
**G A Butler [0-5] Mrs A K H Ooi.*

JUMBO'S FLYER BHB 56f46a **RR 60f 46a** 3312[7]

3 ch c Jumbo Hirt (USA) 15.8f **(44)** - Fragrant Princess (Germont)
Form - 8524628037
Record 2000 - 1st:0 2nd:2 3rd:1 Ran:10
Pre2000 - 1st:0 2nd:0 3rd:0 Ran:3
Win Prizemoney £0 *Total Prizemoney* £2,772
2000 Turf 0-9: (7f, 8f 6, 9f, 12f) (gd, g-f 4, frm 3, hrd) 2000 AW 0-1: (8f) (Fibr)
Scopey, average colt, effective 8f, acts on g-f, likes right handed tracks. Turf high 63 - 2nd of 13 getting 3lb from Hand Chime (29 Jun Carlisle 8f g-f RF 2365). Consistent.
**J L Eyre [0-13] T H Littleton.*

JUMP (USA) BHB 55a **RR 51f** 3490[13]

3 b g Trempolino (USA) 11.9f **(77)** - Professional Dance (USA) (Nijinsky (CAN)) 10.3f **(77)**
Form - 260047700
Record 2000 - 1st:0 2nd:1 3rd:0 Ran:9
Pre2000 - 1st:0 2nd:0 3rd:0 Ran:2
Win Prizemoney £0 *Total Prizemoney* £876
2000 Turf 0-5: (8f 2, 10f 2, 12f) (gd, frm 4) 2000 AW 0-4: (8f 3, 9f) (Equi, Fibr 3)
Scopey, fair gelding, effective 8f, - acts on Fibr, has worn blinkers, likes left handed tracks, likes tight tracks. Turf high 51. AW high 59 (1st run) - 2nd of 13 to National Dance (14 Jan Southwell 8f Fibr RF 0089). Becoming disappointing.
**J A Osborne [0-9] Godiva (from D Marks [0-2] Oct 1999).*

JUNGLE LION RR 91+f 5309[1]

2 ch c Lion Cavern (USA) 7.5f **(74)** - Star Ridge (USA) (Storm Bird (CAN)) 10.3f **(74)**
Form - 1
Record 2000 - 1st:1 2nd:0 3rd:0 Ran:1
Win Prizemoney £3,331 *Total Prizemoney* £3,331
Wins * 2000 Nov Doncas (HVY) 7f 91+ <
2000 Turf 1-1: (7f 1-1) (g-s 1-1)
Currently useful colt. (1st run) - 1st of 18 giving 5lb to Lurina (3 Nov Doncaster RF 5309). A decisive winner of his only outing, in a backend maiden, could be useful. He wore a tongue tie on that occasion. **H R A Cecil [1-1] Buckram Oak Holdings.*

JUNIKAY (IRE) BHB 72f52a **RR 77f 52a** 4464[10]

6 b g Treasure Kay 6.5f **(53)** - Junijo (Junius (USA)) 7.7f **(65)**
Form - 021132841430
Record 2000 - 1st:3 2nd:2 3rd:2 Ran:12
Pre2000 - 1st:3 2nd:4 3rd:3 Ran:46
Win Prizemoney £24,158 *Total Prizemoney* £36,002

Wins								
*** 2000**	Aug	Goodwo	(GD)	H	9f	65	72	
*** 2000**	May	Lingfi	(G-S)	H	9f	57	61+	
*** 2000**	May	Nottin	(G-F)	H	10f	51	56+	
* 1999	May	Nottin	(GD)	H	10f	52	54	
* 1998	May	Bright	(G-F)	H	7f	53	58	
1996	Jly	Ballin	(GD)		6f		73	<

2000 Turf 3-12: (8f, 9f 2-4, 10f 1-5, 11f 2) (hvy, gd 2-4, g-f 1-6, frm)
Above-average gelding, effective 9 to 10f, best at 9f, acts on gd to g-f, best on g-f, has worn blinkers, excels at Nottingham. Turf high 77 - 10th of 17 getting 10lb from Komistar (16 Spt Newbury 10f g-f RF 4464) - also 1st of 20 getting 11lb from Roman King (3 Aug Goodwood RF 3346). Consistent. Nine furlongs looks his trip, and he landed a well contested handicap over that distance at Glorious Goodwood. Decent efforts since, looking just held by the handicapper.
**R Ingram [5-50] Ellangowan Racing Partners (from J S Bolger in IRE [1-9] Jun 1997).*

JUNIOR BRIEF (IRE) BHB 47f **RR 53f** 5160[10]

2 b g Case Law 6f **(64)** - Sharpnkeen (Keen)
Form - 00780070
Record 2000 - 1st:0 2nd:0 3rd:0 Ran:8
2000 Turf 0-6: (5f, 6f 2, 7f 2, 8f) (sft, g-s, gd, g-f 3) 2000 AW 0-2: (6f, 7f) (Fibr 2)
Fair gelding, has worn blinkers. Turf high 53. AW high 22 (began Jly). **K McAuliffe [0-8] Alhambra.*

JUNIPER (USA) RR 94f 4524a[1]

2 b c Danzig (USA) 8.1f **(88)** - Montage (USA) (Alydar (USA)) 9.1f **(76)**
Form - 31
2000 Turf 1-2: (6f 1-2) (frm)
Currently useful colt. Turf high 94 (began Aug) - 1st of 17 from Dr Dignity (17 Spt Curragh RF 4524a). Made his debut in the Group Two Gimcrack Stakes and was beaten only half a length into third. Made no mistake next time. **A P O'Brien in IRE [1-2] Michael Tabor.*

JUNO BEACH BHB 60f **RR 72f** 4730[7]

4 ch f Jupiter Island 10.4f **(57)** - Kovalevskia (Ardross) 10.6f **(68)**
Form - 347

Record 2000 - 1st:0 2nd:0 3rd:1 Ran:3
Win Prizemoney £0 *Total Prizemoney* £949
2000 Turf 0-2: (12f 2) (g-f, frm) 2000 AW 0-1: (13f) (Equi)
Above-average filly. Turf high 72 (began Aug).
**D Morris [1-6] Bloomsbury Stud.*

JUNO MARLOWE (IRE) BHB 92f **RR 95f** 3432[9]

4 b f Danehill (USA) 9.1f **(79)** - Why so Silent (Mill Reef (USA)) 10.5f **(78)**
Form - 0782000
Record 2000 - 1st:0 2nd:1 3rd:0 Ran:7
Pre2000 - 1st:2 2nd:0 3rd:1 Ran:9
Win Prizemoney £12,828 *Total Prizemoney* £17,545
Wins * 1999 Jly Newmar (GD) H 7f 94 96 <
* 1998 Aug Kempto (G-F) 7f 86
2000 Turf 0-7: (6f, 7f 3, 8f 2, 9f) (g-s 2, gd 2, g-f, frm 2)
Scopey, very useful filly, effective 7f, acts on frm. Turf high 95 - 2nd of 18 giving 19lb to Second Wind (23 Jun Newmarket 7f frm RF 2227). **P W Harris [2-16] Mrs P W Harris.*

JUSTALORD BHB 65f63a **RR 66f 63a** 4762[2]

2 b g King's Signet (USA) 7f **(51)** - Just Lady **(44f 50a)** (Emarati (USA))
Form - 61615242
Record 2000 - 1st:2 2nd:2 3rd:0 Ran:8
Win Prizemoney £6,478 *Total Prizemoney* £7,891
Wins * **2000** May Thirsk (GD) C 5f 66 <
* **2000** *Apr Lingfi (STD)* 5f 66 <
2000 Turf 1-6: (5f 1-6) (g-s, gd 1-2, g-f, frm, hrd) 2000 AW 1-2: (5f 1-2) (Equi 1-1, Fibr)
Average gelding, effective 5f, acts on gd to frm - acts on AW. Turf high 66 - 2nd of 6 giving 5lb to Screamin' Georgina (31 Jly Folkestone 5f frm RF 3243) - also 1st of 15 giving 3lb to Waterpark (20 May Thirsk RF 1344). AW high 66 - 2nd of 12 giving 5lb to Acorn Catcher (30 Spt Wolverhampton 5f Fibr RF 4762) - also 1st of 3 from Mamore Gap (12 Apr Lingfield RF 0678). Consistent.
**W G M Turner [2-8] Mrs M S Teversham.*

JUST A STROLL BHB 18f25a **RR 25a** 3524[13]

5 ch g Clantimo 6.6f **(57)** - Willow Walk (Farm Walk) 11.6f **(55)**
Form - 000
Record 2000 - 1st:0 2nd:0 3rd:0 Ran:3
Pre2000 - 1st:0 2nd:1 3rd:0 Ran:4
Win Prizemoney £0 *Total Prizemoney* £570
2000 Turf 0-1: (8f) (frm) 2000 AW 0-2: (9f, 16f) (Fibr 2)
Very poor gelding, has worn blinkers.
**A W Carroll [0-5] Simon Lewis (from D Burchell [0-4] Feb 2000).*

JUST AS YOU ARE (IRE) BHB 50f **RR 49f** 4182[10]

2 b f Common Grounds 8.1f **(66)** - Henrietta Street (IRE) **(53f)** (Royal Academy (USA))
Form - 0700
Record 2000 - 1st:0 2nd:0 3rd:0 Ran:4
2000 Turf 0-4: (5f 3, 6f) (g-s 2, gd, frm)
Moderate filly, has worn blinkers. Turf high 49 (began Jly).
**T D Easterby [0-4] Jim McGrath and Reg Griffin.*

JUST BREMNER BHB 54f62a **RR 41f 62a** 3505[11]

3 b g Rudimentary (USA) 8.2f **(66)** - Legal Precedent (Star Appeal) 9.6f **(65)**
Form - 400
Record 2000 - 1st:0 2nd:0 3rd:0 Ran:2
Pre2000 - 1st:1 2nd:0 3rd:1 Ran:8
Win Prizemoney £2,710 *Total Prizemoney* £3,180
Wins * 1999 Aug Newcas (GD) C 8f 72 <
2000 Turf 0-2: (8f 2) (g-s, frm)
Scopey, average gelding, effective 8f, acts on g-f, likes left handed tracks. Turf high 35 (began Jly).
**T D Easterby [1-10] Leeds United Racing Club Ltd.*

JUST DISSIDENT (IRE) BHB 40f40a **RR 49f 40a** 3131[5]

8 b g Dancing Dissident (USA) 6.8f **(65)** - Betty Bun (St Chad) 6.7f **(67)**
Form - 044454780550045
Record 2000 - 1st:0 2nd:0 3rd:0 Ran:10
Pre2000 - 1st:6 2nd:5 3rd:7 Ran:84
Win Prizemoney £22,875 *Total Prizemoney* £32,144
Wins * 1999 *Aug Lingfi (STD) H* 7f 51 54
* 1997 *Dec Lingfi (STD) H* 5f 52 56
* 1997 Jly Pontef (G-F) H 5f 57 58
* 1996 Aug Carlis (FRM) H 5f 57 58
* 1996 Jly Pontef (G-F) H 5f 55 56
2000 Turf 0-7: (5f 3, 6f 4) (gd, frm 5, hrd) 2000 AW 0-3: (5f 2, 6f) (Equi, Fibr 2)
Moderate gelding, effective 5 to 7f, - acts on Equi, has worn blinkers, likes left handed tracks, likes tight tracks. Turf high 49. AW high 51. **R M Whitaker [6-94] Mrs C A Hodgetts.*

JUSTELLA (IRE) RR 61f 1620[1]

2 b f Hollow Hand - Willabelle (Will Somers) 5.9f **(59)**
Form - 6671
Record 2000 - 1st:1 2nd:0 3rd:0 Ran:4
Win Prizemoney £3,412 *Total Prizemoney* £3,412
Wins * **2000** Jun Goodwo (G-S) S 6f 61 <
2000 Turf 1-4: (5f 3, 6f 1-1) (gd 1-2, frm 2)
Average filly. Turf high 61 - 1st of 7 from Myhat (1 Jun Goodwood RF 1620). **W G M Turner [1-4] Darren Coombes.*

JUST FOR YOU BHB 34f **RR** 54[6]

4 b c Hamas (IRE) 8f **(72)** - Millie's Lady (IRE) (Common Grounds)
Form - 866
Record 2000 - 1st:0 2nd:0 3rd:0 Ran:2
Pre2000 - 1st:0 2nd:0 3rd:0 Ran:1
2000 AW 0-2: (6f, 7f) (Fibr 2)
Workmanlike, currently little account colt. AW high 19.
**K Mahdi [0-3] Hamad Al-Mutawa.*

JUST FOR YOU JANE (IRE) BHB 36f49a **RR 38f 49a** 4100[7]

4 b f Petardia 8.2f **(58)** - Steffi (Precocious) 8.6f **(62)**
Form - 0004377
Record 2000 - 1st:0 2nd:0 3rd:1 Ran:7
Pre2000 - 1st:0 2nd:2 3rd:5 Ran:14
Win Prizemoney £0 *Total Prizemoney* £3,640
2000 Turf 0-6: (6f 3, 7f, 8f, 9f) (sft, g-f 3, frm 2) 2000 AW 0-1: (6f) (Fibr)
Unfurnished, fair filly, effective 6f, - acts on Fibr, often wears blinkers, likes left handed tracks, likes tight tracks. Turf high 38.
**T J Naughton [0-21] G Stupple.*

JUST GIFTED BHB 60f **RR 69f** 5000[11]

4 b g Rudimentary (USA) 8.2f **(66)** - Parfait Amour **(48f)** (Clantime)
Form - 28622273640
Record 2000 - 1st:0 2nd:4 3rd:1 Ran:11
Pre2000 - 1st:0 2nd:0 3rd:3 Ran:10
Win Prizemoney £0 *Total Prizemoney* £10,608
2000 Turf 0-11: (10f, 11f, 12f 8, 14f) (g-s 2, gd 2, g-f 5, frm, hrd)
Workmanlike, average gelding, effective 10 to 12f, best at 12f, acts on g-f to hrd, best on g-f, likes tight tracks, excels at Newmarket, does well at Pontefract. Turf high 69 - 3rd of 5 getting 15lb from Lidakiya (20 Aug Pontefract 12f hrd RF 3829). Consistent.
**R M Whitaker [0-21] Racing Gifts Ltd.*

JUST GOOD FRIENDS (IRE) BHB 25f **RR 25f** 3193[13]

3 b g Shalford (IRE) 7.8f **(63)** - Sinfonietta (Foolish Pleasure (USA)) 8.9f **(72)**
Form - 006600
Record 2000 - 1st:0 2nd:0 3rd:0 Ran:6
2000 Turf 0-6: (7f 3, 8f 2, 10f) (gd 2, g-f, frm 2, hrd)
Little account gelding, has worn blinkers. Turf high 25.
**B Ellison [0-6] B Batey.*

JUST GRAND (IRE) BHB 65f **RR 47f** 2378[8]

6 b g Green Desert (USA) 7.8f **(78)** - Aljood (Kris) 9.5f **(73)**
Form - 8
Record 2000 - 1st:0 2nd:0 3rd:0 Ran:1
Pre2000 - 1st:1 2nd:0 3rd:1 Ran:7
Win Prizemoney £7,002 *Total Prizemoney* £8,627
Wins 1997 Jun Carlis (GD) H 12f 76 80 <
2000 Turf 0-1: (14f) (frm)
Moderate gelding. Consistent.
**Mrs Merrita Jones [0-4] F J Sainsbury (from M Johnston [1-7] Jly 1997).*

JUSTINIA BHB 55f **RR 65f** 4334[8]

2 b f Inchinor 8.9f **(64)** - Just Julia (Natroun (FR))
Form - 73578
Record 2000 - 1st:0 2nd:0 3rd:1 Ran:5

Win Prizemoney £0 *Total Prizemoney* £550
2000 Turf 0-5: (5f, 7f 4) (gd 2, g-f, frm 2)
Average filly. Turf high 65 - 3rd of 4 to Caspian (1 Jly Doncaster 7f frm RF 2428). **E J O'Neill [0-5] Mrs Rosemary Moszkowicz.*

JUST IN TIME BHB 87f93a **RR 95f 93a** 4485[4]

5 b g Night Shift (USA) 8.1f **(73)** - Future Past (USA) (Super Concorde (USA)) 10.9f **(66)**
Form - 14140305744

Record					
2000 -	1st:2	2nd:0	3rd:1	Ran:11
Pre2000 -	1st:1	2nd:3	3rd:2	Ran:13

Win Prizemoney £16,917 *Total Prizemoney* £36,433

Wins							
*** 2000**	Apr	Pontef	(G-S)		10f		90
*** 2000**	*Feb*	*Lingfi*	*(STD)*	*H*	*10f*	*88*	*93* <
* 1998	Aug	Goodwo	(G-F)		9.9f		85+

2000 Turf 1-9: (10f 1-7, 12f 2) (g-s 1-2, gd 4, g-f 2, frm) 2000 AW 1-2: (10f 1-2) (Equi 1-2)
Very useful gelding, effective 10 to 12f, best at 10f, acts on g-s to frm - acts on Equi, prefers left handed tracks, likes tight tracks, excels at Lingfield and Pontefract. Turf high 95 - 5th of 7 getting 14lb from Murghem (4 Aug Goodwood 12f g-f RF 3364) - also 1st of 7 giving 4lb to Seek (11 Apr Pontefract RF 0661). AW high 99 - 4th of 14 to Zanay (18 Mar Lingfield 10f Equi RF 0463) - also 1st of 6 giving 17lb to Forty Forte (19 Feb Lingfield RF 0315). Put up a fine performance to win a decent handicap under top weight on his Equitrack debut at the start of the year and seemed to have no problem with the soft ground when winning back on turf at Pontefract. Mixed form since. **T G Mills [3-24] Mrs Pauline Merrick.*

JUST MAC (USA) BHB 41f52a **RR 35f 52a** 2554[7]

3 br g Dayjur (USA) 6.8f **(79)** - Play On And On (USA) (Stop The Music (USA)) 9.2f **(71)**
Form - 30676707

Record					
2000 -	1st:0	2nd:0	3rd:0	Ran:7
Pre2000 -	1st:0	2nd:0	3rd:1	Ran:2

Win Prizemoney £0 *Total Prizemoney* £370
2000 Turf 0-4: (5f, 7f 2, 8f) (sft, g-s, g-f, frm) 2000 AW 0-3: (6f 2, 7f) (Equi, Fibr 2)
Moderate gelding, has worn blinkers. Turf high 35. AW high 42.
**Mrs L Stubbs [0-8] O J Williams (from J Noseda [0-1] Oct 1999).*

JUST MIDAS BHB 64f **RR 72f** 4675[8]

2 b c Merdon Melody 6.8f **(56)** - Thabeh (Shareef Dancer (USA)) 9.9f **(73)**
Form - 808

Record					
2000 -	1st:0	2nd:0	3rd:0	Ran:3

2000 Turf 0-2: (7f 2) (g-s, g-f) 2000 AW 0-1: (7f) (Fibr)
Currently above-average colt. Turf high 72 (began Spt).
**K R Burke [0-3] D G & D J Robinson.*

JUST MISSED BHB 55f **RR 60f** 4381[3]

2 b f Inchinor 8.9f **(64)** - Lucky Round (Auction Ring (USA)) 8.6f **(65)**
Form - 705053

Record					
2000 -	1st:0	2nd:0	3rd:1	Ran:6

Win Prizemoney £0 *Total Prizemoney* £500
2000 Turf 0-6: (5f, 6f 2, 7f, 8f 2) (g-s, gd 2, g-f 2, frm)
Average filly, effective 8f, acts on gd. Turf high 60 - 3rd of 14 getting 5lb from Rathkenny (14 Spt Ayr 8f gd RF 4381).
**M W Easterby [0-6] Guy Reed.*

JUST MURPHY (IRE) BHB 68f **RR 62+f** 4200[3]

2 b g Namaqualand (USA) - Bui-Doi (IRE) (Dance of Life (USA)) 7f **(66)**
Form - 603

Record					
2000 -	1st:0	2nd:0	3rd:1	Ran:3

Win Prizemoney £0 *Total Prizemoney* £806
2000 Turf 0-3: (5f 2, 6f) (g-f, frm 2)
Currently average gelding. Turf high 62.
**W W Haigh [0-3] Alan Swinbank.*

JUST NICK BHB 72f **RR 73f** 5240[9]

6 b g Nicholas (USA) 6.1f **(63)** - Just Never Know (USA) (Riverman (USA)) 9.1f **(76)**
Form - 36521100

Record					
2000 -	1st:2	2nd:1	3rd:1	Ran:8
Pre2000 -	1st:1	2nd:4	3rd:5	Ran:21

Win Prizemoney £24,282 *Total Prizemoney* £44,473

Wins							
*** 2000**	Jly	Newbur	(G-F)	H	8f	68	73
*** 2000**	Jly	Goodwo	(G-F)	H	8f	62	68
* 1996	Nov	Folkes	(SFT)		6f		74 <

2000 Turf 2-8: (7f 3, 8f 2-5) (g-s 3, gd 2, g-f 2-2, frm)
Above-average gelding, effective 8f, acts on g-f to frm, best on g-f. Turf high 73 - 1st of 8 getting 7lb from Bound For Pleasure (16 Jly Newbury RF 2865) - also 1st of 13 getting 20lb from Volontiers (2 Jly Goodwood RF 2462). Consistent. He has put up some good efforts in recent seasons, but his victory at Goodwood in July was his first since he was a two-year-old. Followed up in good style at Newbury and looks best over a mile these days.
**W R Muir [3-27] D G Clarke (from M McCormack [0-2] Jun 1996).*

JUST ON THE MARKET (IRE) BHB 53f47a **RR 57f 47a** 2814[15]

3 ch f Shalford - Evanna's Pride (Main Reef) 9.6f **(57)**
Form - 0000

Record					
2000 -	1st:0	2nd:0	3rd:0	Ran:4
Pre2000 -	1st:0	2nd:1	3rd:0	Ran:6

Win Prizemoney £0 *Total Prizemoney* £560
2000 Turf 0-1: (5f) (gd) 2000 AW 0-3: (5f 2, 8f) (Fibr 3)
Fair filly, effective 7f, acts on g-s, has worn blinkers. AW high 22.
**D Carroll [0-4] Bloomsville Racing Syndicate (from J G Coogan in IRE [0-6] Spt 1999).*

JUST THE JOB TOO (IRE) BHB 45f48a **RR 41f 48a** 3186[8]

3 b br g Prince of Birds (USA) - Bold Encounter (IRE) (Persian Bold) 9.3f **(66)**
Form - 086410688

Record					
2000 -	1st:1	2nd:0	3rd:0	Ran:7
Pre2000 -	1st:0	2nd:0	3rd:0	Ran:2

Win Prizemoney £2,362 *Total Prizemoney* £2,362

Wins							
*** 2000**	*Feb*	*Southw*	*(STD)*	*H*	*8f*	*52*	*56* <

2000 Turf 0-2: (7f, 10f) (g-s, gd) 2000 AW 1-5: (7f, 8f 1-3, 11f) (Equi, Fibr 1-4)
Scopey, fair gelding, effective 8f, - acts on Fibr, likes left handed tracks, favours tight tracks. Turf high 41. AW high 56 - 1st of 14 getting 4lb from The Sheikh (21 Feb Southwell RF 0324).
**P C Haslam [1-9] A Stancliffe & J Trevillion.*

JUST TRY ME (IRE) BHB 30f **RR** 2086[13]

6 b g Darshaan 11.9f **(81)** - Just Society (USA) (Devil's Bag (USA)) 12.4f **(78)**
Form - 0

Record					
2000 -	1st:0	2nd:0	3rd:0	Ran:1
Pre2000 -	1st:1	2nd:1	3rd:0	Ran:8

Win Prizemoney £2,911 *Total Prizemoney* £3,996

Wins						
1997	Jun	Navan	(G-S)		8f	79 <

2000 Turf 0-1: (8f) (frm)
Very poor gelding, has worn blinkers.
**G L Moore [0-3] John Patty (from P Cluskey in IRE [0-4] Spt 1998).*

JUST WHATEVER RR 3356[6]

3 ch f Major Jacko - Manx Monarch **(35f)** (Dara Monarch) 8.8f **(59)**
Form - 6

Record					
2000 -	1st:0	2nd:0	3rd:0	Ran:1

2000 Turf 0-1: (8f) (frm)
Leggy, currently very poor filly. **F P Murtagh [0-1] F P Murtagh.*

JUST WIZ BHB 51f72a **RR 50f 72a** 4763[1]

4 b g Efisio 7.7f **(69)** - Jade Pet **(84df)** (Petong) 6.6f **(58)**
Form - 1310553002221

Record					
2000 -	1st:1	2nd:3	3rd:1	Ran:10
Pre2000 -	1st:3	2nd:3	3rd:3	Ran:21

Win Prizemoney £10,353 *Total Prizemoney* £17,679

Wins							
*** 2000**	*Spt*	*Wolver*	*(STD)*	*H*	*9.4f*	*66*	*72*
1999	*Dec*	*Lingfi*	*(STD)*	*H*	*10f*	*79*	*83* <
1999	*Nov*	*Lingfi*	*(STD)*	*H*	*10f*	*73*	*77*
1999	*Jan*	*Southw*	*(STD)*	*H*	*7f*	*59*	*72*

2000 Turf 0-5: (10f 3, 11f, 12f) (hvy, gd, g-f, frm 2) 2000 AW 1-5: (8f, 9f 1-1, 10f 3) (Equi 3, Fibr 1-2)
Workmanlike, above-average gelding, effective 9 to 10f, best at 10f, - acts on AW, best on Equi, often wears blinkers, prefers left handed tracks, likes tight tracks. Turf high 50. AW high 72. Has ability on turf, but looks better on sand and has won on both types of surface. Probably best over ten furlongs on Equitrack.
**N P Littmoden [1-1] Turf 2000 Ltd (from Andrew Reid [0-2] Jun 2000).*

JUST WOODY (IRE) RR 81f 4382[16]
2 br g Charnwood Forest (IRE) - Zalamera **(44f 39a)** (Rambo Dancer (CAN))
Form - 30
Record 2000 - 1st:0 2nd:0 3rd:1 Ran:2
Win Prizemoney £0 *Total Prizemoney* £1,045
2000 Turf 0-2: (6f 2) (gd 2)
Currently decent gelding. Turf high 81 (1st run) (began Aug) - 3rd of 4 getting 6lb from Silca Legend (20 Aug Chester 6f gd RF 3819).
**A Berry [0-2] David Brown.*

JUWWI BHB 83f83a **RR 99f 83a** 5317[11]
6 ch g Mujtahid (USA) 7.4f **(69)** - Nouvelle Star (AUS) (Luskin Star (AUS)) 6.3f **(71)**
Form - 322860151441585007707070040050
Record 2000 - 1st:3 2nd:2 3rd:3 Ran:33
Pre2000 - 1st:6 2nd:9 3rd:4 Ran:51
Win Prizemoney £56,771 *Total Prizemoney* £90,275

Wins							
*** 2000**	May	York	(FRM)	H	6f	90	94 <
*** 2000**	Apr	Thirsk	(G-S)	H	5f	82	91
*** 2000**	Mar	Windso	(G-F)	H	6f	77	83
* 1999	*Nov*	*Southw*	*(STD)*	*H*	*6f*	*79*	*83*
* 1999	Spt	Chepst	(GD)	H	5.1f	67	72
* 1999	May	Carlis	(FRM)	H	5.9f	63	70
* 1998	*Apr*	*Lingfi*	*(STD)*	*H*	*5f*	*70*	*80+*
* 1998	*Mar*	*Wolver*	*(STD)*	*C*	*5f*		*64+*
1996	Jun	Newbur	(G-F)		6f		79+

2000 Turf 3-25: (5f 1-6, 6f 2-18, 7f) (sft 4, g-s, gd 2-10, g-f 1-6, frm 4)
2000 AW 0-8: (5f, 6f 5, 7f 2) (Equi 2, Fibr 6)
Very useful gelding, has broken blood-vessels, effective 5 to 6f, best at 6f, acts on gd, excels at Thirsk. Turf high 99 - 5th of 20 giving 14lb to Manorbier (20 May Thirsk 6f gd RF 1346) - also 1st of 15 getting 11lb from Harmonic Way (18 May York RF 1275). AW high 85. In fine form on turf earlier in the year, he likes to come late off a strong pace and goes particularly well for an inexperienced rider. Often runs twice in quick succession, and seems to run better on the second occasion.
**J M Bradley [8-79] J M Bradley (from Major W R Hern [1-5] Jly 1997).*

Juwwi was kept busy

KAAPSTAD WAY (NZ) RR 118f 5207a[2]
5 br g Kaapstad - Crysell Way (NZ) (Star Way)
Form - 2
2000 Turf 0-1: (12f) (gd)
Currently high-class gelding. (1st run) - 2nd of 18 getting 1lb from Diatribe (21 Oct Caulfield 12f gd RF 5207a). **C Wood in AUS [0-1].*

KABOOL BHB 116f **RR 119f** 4986[9]
5 b h Groom Dancer (USA) 9.5f **(75)** - Sheroog (USA) (Shareef Dancer (USA)) 9.9f **(73)**
Form - 444310
Record 2000 - 1st:1 2nd:0 3rd:1 Ran:5
Pre2000 - 1st:2 2nd:2 3rd:2 Ran:9
Win Prizemoney £90,950 *Total Prizemoney* £261,322

Wins							
*** 2000**	Oct	Longch	(GD)	G2	8f	118	<
1998	Aug	Deauvi	(SFT)	G2	10f	112	
1998	Jly	Maison	(GD)	G3	9f	106	

2000 Turf 1-4: (7f, 8f 1-1, 10f, 11f) (hvy, gd 1-3) 2000 AW 0-1: (12f) (Dirt)
High-class colt, effective 8 to 12f, acts on hvy to g-f - acts on Dirt, best on gd, prefers right handed tracks, does well at Longchamp. Turf high 118 - 1st of 8 from Kingsalsa (1 Oct Longchamp RF 4843a). (1st run) - 4th of 11 to Rhythm Band (25 Mar Nad Al Sheba 12f Dirt RF 0579a). He never quite fulfilled the promise of his exciting three-year-old campaign in 1998, but was a consistent performer at the highest level. Given a masterly ride when winning the Prix du Rond-Point at Longchamp in October, he stayed a mile and a quarter and has been retired to the Haras d'Etreham at 25,000 FF.
**S bin Suroor [1-9] Godolphin (from S bin Suroor in UAE [0-3] Mar 2000).*

K-ACE THE JOINT BHB 51f35a **RR 54f 35a** 1310[11]
3 ch g Savahra Sound 7.8f **(55)** - Be My Sweet (Galivanter) 7.8f **(56)**
Form - 000630
Record 2000 - 1st:0 2nd:0 3rd:1 Ran:4
Pre2000 - 1st:0 2nd:0 3rd:0 Ran:3
Win Prizemoney £0 *Total Prizemoney* £286
2000 Turf 0-2: (6f, 8f) (gd 2) 2000 AW 0-2: (5f, 7f) (Fibr 2)
Leggy, fair gelding, has worn blinkers. Turf high 54. AW high 38.
**S R Bowring [0-7] Ace Racing One.*

KACHINA DOLL (IRE) BHB 100f **RR 94f** 5107[4]
2 b br f Mujadil (USA) 7.7f **(70)** - Betelgeuse (Kalaglow) 9.8f **(67)**
Form - 37811852733047344
Record 2000 - 1st:2 2nd:1 3rd:4 Ran:17
Win Prizemoney £6,194 *Total Prizemoney* £22,985

Wins						
*** 2000**	May	Bath	(G-F)	5.1f	83+	<
*** 2000**	May	Windso	(GD)	5f	69	

2000 Turf 2-17: (5f 2-12, 6f 5) (sft 2, g-s 2, gd 5, g-f 1-4, frm 1-3, hrd)
Useful filly, effective 5 to 6f, best at 5f, acts on g-s to g-f. Turf high 94 - 4th of 7 getting 3lb from Sign Of Nike (23 Spt San Siro 6f g-s RF 4715a). Kept busy, she has not been disgraced in decent company after winning minor events at Windsor and Bath in May. Six furlongs just stretches her stamina.
**M R Channon [2-17] Ridgeway Downs Racing.*

KADINSKY (IRE) BHB 59f **RR 49f** 4444[11]
3 b g Sri Pekan (USA) - Daymer Bay (Lomond (USA)) 8.8f **(65)**
Form - 050
Record 2000 - 1st:0 2nd:0 3rd:0 Ran:3
2000 Turf 0-3: (8f 2, 10f) (gd, g-f 2)
Scopey, currently moderate gelding. Turf high 52 (began Aug).
**M L W Bell [0-3] Thurloe Finsbury.*

KADOUN (IRE) BHB 78f **RR 81f** 5079[2]
3 b c Doyoun 10.7f **(69)** - Kumta (IRE) (Priolo (USA))
Form - 244322
Record 2000 - 1st:0 2nd:3 3rd:1 Ran:6
Win Prizemoney £0 *Total Prizemoney* £5,774
2000 Turf 0-6: (12f 4, 14f, 15f) (sft, g-s 2, g-f 2, frm)
Lengthy, decent colt, effective 12 to 15f, best at 12f, acts on sft to frm, best on g-s. Turf high 81 - 2nd of 14 giving 2lb to Distant Prospect (7 Oct York 14f sft RF 4863).
**L M Cumani [0-6] Mrs V Shelton.*

KAFEZAH (FR) RR 83f 4377[4]
2 br f Pennekamp (USA) - Yakin (USA) (Nureyev (USA)) 8.7f **(78)**
Form - 44
Record 2000 - 1st:0 2nd:0 3rd:0 Ran:2
Win Prizemoney £0 *Total Prizemoney* £816
2000 Turf 0-2: (6f, 7f) (g-f, frm)
Currently decent filly. Turf high 83 (began Spt) - 4th of 9 to Nasmatt (13 Spt Yarmouth 6f frm RF 4377).

**B Hanbury [0-2] Hamdan Al Maktoum.*

KAFI (USA) BHB 40f **RR 38f** 2627[13]
4 b c Gulch (USA) 9.6f **(79)** - Nonoalca (FR) (Nonoalco (USA)) 8.5f **(66)**
Form - 0060
Record 2000 - 1st:0 2nd:0 3rd:0 Ran:4
Pre2000 - 1st:0 2nd:0 3rd:0 Ran:5
2000 Turf 0-4: (8f, 10f, 12f, 18f) (g-s, g-f 2, frm)
Rangy, very moderate colt, has worn blinkers. Turf high 38. Inconsistent.
**A Streeter [0-7] Racing For You (from M P Tregoning [0-5] Jun 1999).*

KAFIL (USA) BHB 41f45a **RR 51tf 45a** 5078[12]
6 b br g Housebuster (USA) 7f **(81)** - Alchaasibiyeh (USA) (Seattle Slew (USA)) 9.4f **(76)**
Form - 3656026700030683767O
Record 2000 - 1st:0 2nd:1 3rd:2 Ran:15
Pre2000 - 1st:2 2nd:8 3rd:4 Ran:50
Win Prizemoney £5,408 *Total Prizemoney* £14,348
Wins * 1998 *Oct Lingfi (STD) 7f 59*
1997 Nov Lingfi (STD) 8f 68 <
2000 Turf 0-10: (7f 2, 8f 5, 9f 2, 10f) (g-s 2, gd 2, g-f 4, frm 2) 2000 AW 0-5: (8f 3, 9f, 10f) (Equi 2, Fibr 3)
Fair gelding, effective 8 to 10f, best at 8f, - acts on AW, best on Equi, has worn blinkers, likes left handed tracks, favours tight tracks. Turf high 51. AW high 47.
**J J Bridger [1-54] J J Bridger (from G L Moore [1-8] Dec 1997).*

KAGOSHIMA (IRE) BHB 60f **RR 58f** 3163[12]
5 b g Shirley Heights 12.1f **(76)** - Kashteh (IRE) (Green Desert (USA)) 8.6f **(78)**
Form - 0231210
Record 2000 - 1st:2 2nd:2 3rd:1 Ran:7
Pre2000 - 1st:0 2nd:0 3rd:0 Ran:3
Win Prizemoney £7,098 *Total Prizemoney* £10,910
Wins * 2000 Jly Beverl (G-F) H 16.2f 58 58 <
*** 2000** Jun Pontef (G-F) H 17.1f 45 48
2000 Turf 2-7: (14f, 16f 1-4, 17f 1-1, 18f) (gd 2, g-f, frm 2-3, hrd)
Fair gelding, effective 16f, acts on frm, often wears blinkers (extremely effectively), likes tight tracks. Turf high 58. Consistent. He stays very well but is rather one-paced. In good form in the summer.
**J Norton [2-9] Keep On Running (from L M Cumani [0-1] Jly 1998).*

KAHTAN BHB 107f **RR 115f** 4092a[4]
5 b h Nashwan (USA) 10.3f **(79)** - Harmless Albatross (Pas de Seul) 9.1f **(67)**
Form - 4464
Record 2000 - 1st:0 2nd:0 3rd:0 Ran:4
Pre2000 - 1st:4 2nd:1 3rd:4 Ran:13
Win Prizemoney £43,563 *Total Prizemoney* £69,239
Wins * 1999 Oct Newmar (G-S) L 12f 107 <
* 1999 Jly Cheste (G-F) H 18.7f 105 104
* 1998 Jly Newmar (FRM) L 14.8f 103
* 1997 Oct Newcas (G-F) 8f 80+
2000 Turf 0-4: (12f, 14f 2, 22f) (gd 3, g-f)
High-class colt, effective 12 to 14f, best at 12f, acts on gd to g-f, best on gd, excels at Newmarket. Turf high 115 (1st run) - 4th of 11 to Blueprint (5 May Newmarket 12f g-f RF 1047). He failed to build on a promising fourth in the Jockey Club Stakes and proved difficult to place. Effective at a mile and a half, he stays long distances but looks one-paced against top-class opposition.
**J L Dunlop [4-17] Hamdan Al Maktoum.*

KAHYASI MOLL (IRE) BHB 41f29a **RR 44f 29a** 221[9]
3 b f Brief Truce (USA) 9.1f **(73)** - Deydarika (IRE) (Kahyasi)
Form - 860
Record 2000 - 1st:0 2nd:0 3rd:0 Ran:1
Pre2000 - 1st:0 2nd:0 3rd:0 Ran:7
2000 AW 0-1: (12f) (Equi)
Neat, moderate filly. Inconsistent. **J S Moore [0-8] Mick Green.*

KAIAPOI BHB 77f **RR 85f** 5101[11]
3 ch c Elmaamul (USA) 8.1f **(70)** - Salanka (IRE) **(65df 56a)** (Persian Heights)
Form - 11U3502860
Record 2000 - 1st:2 2nd:1 3rd:1 Ran:10
Pre2000 - 1st:1 2nd:0 3rd:0 Ran:6
Win Prizemoney £16,410 *Total Prizemoney* £19,242
Wins * 2000 May Cheste (GD) H 12.3f 73 81 <
*** 2000** Mar Doncas (G-F) H 10.3f 67 74
* 1999 Spt Cheste (SFT) 7f 75
2000 Turf 2-10: (10f 1-4, 12f 1-3, 14f 3) (sft, g-s, gd, g-f 1-4, frm 1-3)
Light-framed, useful colt, effective 7 to 12f, best at 12f, acts on g-s to frm, best on g-f, likes tight tracks. Turf high 85 - 2nd of 7 giving 9lb to Sporting Gesture (18 Aug Chester 10f g-f RF 3745) - also 1st of 10 getting 2lb from Mickley (10 May Chester RF 1132). Inconsistent. Began the season in good style, but has been held by the Handicapper since. **R Hollinshead [3-16] J D Graham.*

KAID (IRE) BHB 32f **RR 51f** 420[7]
5 b g Alzao (USA) 9.8f **(73)** - Very Charming (USA) (Vaguely Noble) 10.1f **(72)**
Form - 5467
Record 2000 - 1st:0 2nd:0 3rd:0 Ran:3
Pre2000 - 1st:0 2nd:0 3rd:1 Ran:10
Win Prizemoney £0 *Total Prizemoney* £752
2000 AW 0-3: (12f, 15f, 16f) (Equi, Fibr 2)
Fair gelding, effective 14f, acts on g-f, has worn blinkers, likes left handed tracks. AW high 41.
**N P Littmoden [0-7] Joy and Valentine Feerick (from Mrs Barbara Waring [0-7] Aug 1999).*

KAILAN SCAMP BHB 18f **RR 16f** 4814[14]
7 gr m Palm Track - Noble Scamp (Scallywag)
Form - 050
Record 2000 - 1st:0 2nd:0 3rd:0 Ran:3
2000 Turf 0-3: (10f 2, 12f) (g-s 2, frm)
Poor mare. Turf high 16 (began Aug).
**J Parkes [0-5] Mrs G M Z Spink.*

KAI ONE BHB 82f **RR 81f** 5073[3]
2 b c Puissance 7.1f **(60)** - Kind of Shy (Kind of Hush) 10.1f **(62)**
Form - 32333
Record 2000 - 1st:0 2nd:1 3rd:4 Ran:5
Win Prizemoney £0 *Total Prizemoney* £4,668
2000 Turf 0-5: (6f 3, 7f 2) (g-s, gd, g-f, frm 2)
Decent colt. Turf high 81 (began Aug).
**R Hannon [0-5] The Cayman 'A' Team.*

KAKA RR 107f 4286a[2]
5 b h Sharpo 7.5f **(68)** - Key Generation (Young Generation) 7.7f **(63)**
Form - 32
2000 Turf 0-2: (5f, 6f) (gd, g-f)
Currently Pattern-class colt. Turf high 107 (began Jly) - 2nd of 9 to Barrow Creek (30 Aug Baden-Baden 6f gd RF 4286a).
**M Hofer in GER [0-2].*

KALAHARI FERRARI BHB 40f **RR 44f** 2611[17]
4 ch g Clantime 6.6f **(57)** - Royal Agnes (Royal Palace) 9f **(56)**
Form - 00
Record 2000 - 1st:0 2nd:0 3rd:0 Ran:2
Pre2000 - 1st:0 2nd:2 3rd:5 Ran:17
Win Prizemoney £0 *Total Prizemoney* £3,743
2000 Turf 0-2: (8f 2) (gd 2)
Moderate gelding, effective 8 to 9f, best at 8f, acts on g-f to frm, best on g-f. Turf high 12. Becoming disappointing.
**A G Hobbs [0-8] Furnish With Abbey (from J Berry [0-16] Jly 1999).*

KALANISI (IRE) BHB 126f **RR 129f** 5331a[1]
4 b c Doyoun 10.7f **(69)** - Kalamba (IRE) (Green Dancer (USA)) 10.3f **(74)**
Form - 212211
Record 2000 - 1st:3 2nd:3 3rd:0 Ran:6
Pre2000 - 1st:3 2nd:0 3rd:0 Ran:3
Win Prizemoney £1,113,708 *Total Prizemoney* £1,300,088
Wins * 2000 Nov Church (FRM) G1 12f 125+
*** 2000** Oct Newmar (G-S) G1 10f 128 <
*** 2000** Jun Ascot (G-F) G2 8f 123+
1999 May Kempto (G-F) L 8f 109
1999 May Newmar (G-F) 7f 112
1999 Apr Folkes (SFT) 7f 87+
2000 Turf 3-6: (8f 1-2, 10f 1-3, 12f 1-1) (gd 2-3, frm 1-3)
Workmanlike, top-class colt, effective 8 to 12f, best at 10f, acts on

gd to frm, best on gd, likes Newmarket. Turf high 129 - 2nd of 6 giving 8lb to Giant's Causeway (22 Aug York 10f gd RF 3852) - also 1st of 15 from Montjeu (14 Oct Newmarket RF 4989). Just beaten by Swallow Flight in a Listed race on his reappearance before running out a game winner of the Queen Anne at Ascot, he was not inconvenienced by the step up to ten furlongs when just edged out by Giant's Causeway after a thrilling battle in the Eclipse and was once again outbattled by the same horse in the Juddmonte International. He gained ample compensation for those two defeats, and at the same time showed his toughness by beating Montjeu in the Dubai Champion Stakes and then crowning his season by taking the Breeders' Cup Turf on his first attempt at a mile and a half. He reportedly remains in training, with connections believing the best is yet to come.
**Sir Michael Stoute [3-6] Aga Khan (from L M Cumani [3-3] May 1999).*

KALAR BHB 41f26a **RR 44df 26a** 3849[17]
11 b g Kabour 6.1f **(36)** - Wind And Reign (Tumble Wind (USA)) 7.5f **(57)**
Form - 00500410000
Record 2000 - 1st:1 2nd:0 3rd:0 Ran:11
Pre2000 - 1st:15 2nd:26 3rd:14 Ran:162
Win Prizemoney £44,449 *Total Prizemoney* £75,066
Wins * 2000 Jun Hamilt (G-F) H 5f 39 45
* 1999 Aug Ripon (G-F) SH 5f 37 42
* 1997 *Feb Lingfi (STD) C 6f 67*
* 1997 *Jan Wolver (STD) C 5f 00*
* 1996 *Dec Southw (SLW) H 6f 70 69* <
* 1996 *Nov Lingfi (STD) H 5f 61 63*
* 1996 Aug Catter (G-F) H 5f 48 49
2000 Turf 1-7: (5f 1-6, 6f) (gd 2, g-f 1-2, frm 2, hrd) 2000 AW 0-4: (5f 4) (Equi, Fibr 3)
Moderate gelding, effective 5 to 6f, best at 5f, acts on gd to frm - acts on AW, mostly wears blinkers, likes left handed tracks, likes tight tracks, excels at Hamilton. Turf high 45 - 1st of 11 giving 2lb to Biff-Em (28 Jun Hamilton RF 2336). AW high 15. Becoming disappointing. A very fast starter when on-song, but he does not win very often these days. **D W Chapman [16-173] David Chapman.*

KALA SUNRISE BHB 78f **RR 73f** 3311[1]
7 ch h Kalaglow 11.2f **(67)** - Belle of the Dawn (Bellypha) 9.8f **(73)**
Form - 0733501
Record 2000 - 1st:1 2nd:0 3rd:2 Ran:7
Pre2000 - 1st:3 2nd:4 3rd:2 Ran:47
Win Prizemoney £19,858 *Total Prizemoney* £37,860
Wins * 2000 Aug Carlis (FRM) 8f 59
* 1999 Apr Leices (GD) H 7f 79 83
* 1996 Oct York (GD) H 7.9f 83 86 <
2000 Turf 1-7: (8f 1-7) (g-s, gd 3, g-f 1-3)
Above-average horse, effective 7 to 8f, best at 8f, acts on gd to frm, best on frm. Turf high 73. **C Smith [4-54] A E Needham.*

KALATOS (GER) **RR 116f** 4713a[8]
8 ch h Big Shuffle (USA) - Kardia (GER) (Mister Rock's (GER))
Form - 2128
2000 Turf 1-4: (8f 1-2, 10f 2) (sft 2, gd 1-2)
High-class horse, effective 8 to 10f, best at 10f, acts on sft to gd, best on gd. Turf high 116 - 2nd of 9 giving 6lb to Imperioso (16 Jly Frankfurt 10f gd RF 2981a) - also 1st of 9 from Bernardon (28 May Baden-Baden RF 1633a). Consistent. He is a grand campaigner and maintained a high level of performance last season, gaining a well deserved Group 3 success at Baden-Baden.
**H Remmert in GER [1-3] (from H Jentzsch in GER [0-4] Apr 2000).*

KALEMAAT BHB 77f **RR 78?f** 4052[2]
3 ch f Unfuwain (USA) 11.4f **(74)** - Ardassine (Ahonoora) 8.1f **(73)**
Form - 542
Record 2000 - 1st:0 2nd:1 3rd:0 Ran:3
Win Prizemoney £0 *Total Prizemoney* £1,615
2000 Turf 0-3: (10f 2, 12f) (frm 3)
Rangy, currently above-average filly. Turf high 78 (began Jly) - 4th of 6 to Gweneira (18 Aug Sandown 10f frm RF 3770).
**R W Armstrong [0-3] Hamdan Al Maktoum.*

KALINDI BHB 100f **RR 98f** 4608[10]
3 ch f Efisio 7.7f **(69)** - Rohita (IRE) **(83df)** (Waajib)
Form - 0760180
Record 2000 - 1st:1 2nd:0 3rd:0 Ran:7
Pre2000 - 1st:1 2nd:2 3rd:0 Ran:7
Win Prizemoney £35,301 *Total Prizemoney* £40,077
Wins * 2000 Spt Doncas (G-F) L 7f 98 <
* 1999 Jun Ascot (G-F) 5f 98 <
2000 Turf 1-7: (5f 2, 6f 3, 7f 1-2) (hvy, g-s 2, gd, g-f 2, frm 1-1)
Workmanlike, very useful filly, effective 5 to 7f, best at 5f, acts on gd to frm. Turf high 98 - 1st of 11 from Veil of Avalon (7 Spt Doncaster RF 4282). She took advantage of favourable conditions to win the Windsor Castle Stakes at Royal Ascot at two, but did not make the grade in Group and Listed races thereafter. After some modest efforts in 2000, she caught the eye at York in August and duly landed a Listed event at Doncaster. Beaten in decent company since. **M R Channon [2-14] Barry Taylor.*

KALLISTO (GER) **RR 113f** 2581a[4]
3 b c Sternkonig (IRE) - Kalinikta (GER) (Konigsstuhl (GER)) 11.2f **(76)**
Form - 114
2000 Turf 2-3: (10f 1-1, 12f 1-2) (sft, gd 1-1, g-f 1-1)
Currently Group-class colt. Turf high 113 - 1st of 20 from Windsor Boy (28 May Capannelle RF 1636a). He ran right away from a respectable field on good-firm ground in the Italian Derby, but could not reproduce that performance on a softer surface in the German equivalent. He should win another top prize on the continent. **H Blume in GER [2-3].*

KALUANA COURT BHB 30f **RR 38f** 4695[14]
4 b f Batshoof 9.5f **(66)** - Fairfields Cone (Celtic Cone) 9.8f **(43)**
Form - 0
Record 2000 - 1st:0 2nd:0 3rd:0 Ran:1
Pre2000 - 1st:0 2nd:0 3rd:0 Ran:4
2000 Turf 0-1: (10f) (gd)
Leggy, very moderate filly.
**R J Price [0-1] Derek & Cheryl Holder (from R Dickin [0-4] Oct 1999).*

KALUGA (IRE) **RR 48f** 1898[11]
2 ch f Tagula (IRE) - Another Baileys **(49f 55a)** (Deploy)
Form - 80
Record 2000 - 1st:0 2nd:0 3rd:0 Ran:2
2000 Turf 0-2: (5f, 6f) (gd, frm)
Currently moderate filly. Turf high 48.
**I A Balding [0-2] Robinski Bloodstock Ltd & M Rabone.*

KALUKI BHB 65f60a **RR 74f 60a** 5017[7]
2 ch c First Trump - Wild Humour (IRE) **(47f)** (Fayruz)
Form - 633420332277
Record 2000 - 1st:0 2nd:3 3rd:4 Ran:12
Win Prizemoney £0 *Total Prizemoney* £4,124
2000 Turf 0-11: (5f 4, 6f 3, 7f 4) (gd 5, g-f, frm 4, hrd) 2000 AW 0-1: (7f) (Fibr)
Above-average colt, effective 6 to 7f, best at 7f, acts on gd to frm, prefers tight tracks. Turf high 74 - 3rd of 7 giving 23lb to Miss Progressive (19 Aug Sandown 7f g-f RF 3800).
**Mrs L Stubbs [0-3] D R Richards (from W R Muir [0-9] Aug 2000).*

KALYPSO KATIE (IRE) BHB 114f **RR 115f** 2918a[5]
3 gr f Fairy King (USA) 7.7f **(75)** - Miss Toot (Ardross) 10.6f **(68)**
Form - 125
Record 2000 - 1st:1 2nd:1 3rd:0 Ran:3
Pre2000 - 1st:1 2nd:0 3rd:0 Ran:1
Win Prizemoney £29,178 *Total Prizemoney* £106,203
Wins * 2000 May York (G-F) G3 10.4f 106 <
* 1999 Oct Windso (SFT) 8.3f 100++
2000 Turf 1-3: (10f 1-1, 12f 2) (g-s, g-f 1-2)
Scopey, high-class filly. Turf high 115 - 2nd of 16 to Love Divine (9 Jun Epsom 12f g-s RF 1832) - also 1st of 9 from Lady Upstage (16 May York RF 1218). She was made joint-favourite for the Oaks after winning York's Musidora Stakes on her reappearance, and beat all bar Love Divine at Epsom. Below par when a disappointing fifth in the Irish Oaks, she is talented but probably needs easy ground when competing at the highest level.
**J Noseda [2-4] M Tabor.*

KAMARAZI (IRE) BHB 59f65a **RR 60f 65a** 2086[4]
3 ch c Arazi (USA) 9.2f **(74)** - Marie D'Argonne (FR) (Jefferson) 7.9f **(89)**
Form - 15078804
Record 2000 - 1st:1 2nd:0 3rd:0 Ran:8

Pre2000 - 1st:0 2nd:0 3rd:0 Ran:2
Win Prizemoney £5,764 *Total Prizemoney* £6,581
Wins * **2000** *Jan Cagnes (STD) 8f 54* <
2000 Turf 0-5: (8f 4, 10f) (g-s, gd 2, g-f, frm) 2000 AW 1-3: (7f, 8f 1-2) (Equi 2, Fibr 1-1)
Workmanlike, average colt, has worn blinkers. Turf high 60. AW high 65. Scored at Cagnes-Sur-Mer in January but looks moderate.
**S Dow [1-8] Byerley Bloodstock (from P F I Cole [0-2] Oct 1999).*

Kalypso Katie led her rivals a merry dance in the Musidora

KAMAREYAH (IRE) BHB 69f **RR 77f** 5185[16]
3 b f Hamas (IRE) 8f **(72)** - Nur (USA) (Diesis) 9.3f **(69)**
Form - 07700
Record 2000 - 1st:0 2nd:0 3rd:0 Ran:5
Pre2000 - 1st:1 2nd:0 3rd:1 Ran:4
Win Prizemoney £3,655 *Total Prizemoney* £5,309
Wins * 1999 Spt Yarmou (G-S) 6f 77 <
2000 Turf 0-5: (6f, 7f 4) (g-s, g-f, frm 3)
Neat, above-average filly, effective 6 to 7f, acts on g-s to frm. Turf high 77 - 7th of 14 giving 8lb to Shadow Prince (28 Jun Kempton 7f frm RF 2345). **R W Armstrong [1-9] Hamdan Al Maktoum.*

KAMA SUTRA RR 89+f 4935[4]
2 b c Pursuit of Love 9.5f **(69)** - Note Book (Mummy's Pet) 7.7f **(60)**
Form - 4
Record 2000 - 1st:0 2nd:0 3rd:0 Ran:1
Win Prizemoney £0 *Total Prizemoney* £569
2000 Turf 0-1: (6f) (gd)
Currently useful colt. (1st run) - 4th of 29 to Ajwaa (12 Oct Newmarket 6f gd RF 4935). **W Jarvis [0-1] W J Simms.*

KANAKA CREEK (USA) BHB 74f **RR 83?f** 1616[6]
3 ch f Thunder Gulch (USA) - Book Collector (USA) (Irish River (FR)) 8.6f **(78)**
Form - 216
Record 2000 - 1st:1 2nd:1 3rd:0 Ran:3
Pre2000 - 1st:0 2nd:1 3rd:3 Ran:8
Win Prizemoney £2,913 *Total Prizemoney* £7,881
Wins * **2000** May Warwic (SFT) 7.7f 71 <
2000 Turf 1-3: (6f, 8f 1-2) (sft 1-1, g-s, frm)
Decent filly, likes left handed tracks, likes tight tracks. Turf high 83. Improving.
**A Berry [1-3] Mrs John Magnier (from J Berry [0-8] Nov 1999).*

KANDYMAL (IRE) BHB 52f45a **RR 52f 45a** 5004[19]
2 ch f Prince of Birds (USA) - Gentle Papoose (Commanche Run) 8.5f **(58)**
Form - 768660
Record 2000 - 1st:0 2nd:0 3rd:0 Ran:6
2000 Turf 0-6: (5f 3, 6f, 7f, 8f) (g-s 2, gd, g-f, frm 2)
Fair filly, effective 7f, acts on g-s. Turf high 52 - 6th of 14 getting 19lb from Classy Act (3 Oct Catterick 7f g-s RF 4773).
**R A Fahey [0-6] Mrs Andrea Mallinson.*

KANZ WOOD (USA) BHB 65f66a **RR 65f 66a** 2629[4]
4 ch g Woodman (USA) 9.7f **(77)** - Kanz (USA) (The Minstrel (CAN)) 10f **(72)**
Form - 1874
Record 2000 - 1st:1 2nd:0 3rd:0 Ran:4
Pre2000 - 1st:0 2nd:0 3rd:1 Ran:8
Win Prizemoney £6,012 *Total Prizemoney* £7,216
Wins * **2000** May Goodwo (SFT) H 8f 62 65 <
2000 Turf 1-4: (8f 1-3, 9f) (g-s 1-1, gd, g-f, frm)
Scopey, above-average gelding, effective 8f, acts on g-s, likes tight tracks. Turf high 65 (1st run). Last of five on his debut but stayed on nicely in a decent maiden next time. Rather disappointing since. **W R Muir [1-12] D J Deer.*

KAPITOL (GER) RR 110f 5211a[1]
3 br f Winged Love (IRE) - Kaiserreich (GER) (Deep Roots)
Form - 41
2000 Turf 1-2: (11f, 12f 1-1) (sft 1-1, gd)
Currently Group-class filly. Turf high 110 - 1st of 12 getting 9lb from Laveron (22 Oct Dusseldorf RF 5211a).
**A Schutz in GER [1-2] Gestut Karlshof.*

KARAJAN (IRE) BHB 65a **RR 72f** 4923[9]
3 b c Fairy King (USA) 7.7f **(75)** - Dernier Cri **(64df)** (Slip Anchor) 9.8f **(73)**
Form - 7470
Record 2000 - 1st:0 2nd:0 3rd:0 Ran:4
Pre2000 - 1st:0 2nd:0 3rd:1 Ran:1
Win Prizemoney £0 *Total Prizemoney* £1,448
2000 Turf 0-2: (10f 2) (gd, frm) 2000 AW 0-2: (9f, 16f) (Equi, Fibr)
Workmanlike, above-average colt. Turf high 72 (began Jly). AW high 58 (began Aug). **J W Hills [0-5] Ken Lim & Chris Wright.*

KARAKAL (GER) RR 114f 4131a[3]
4 bl h Dashing Blade 7.9f **(80)** - Kardia (GER) (Mister Rock's (GER))
Form - 33
2000 Turf 0-2: (10f 2) (gd 2)
Group-class colt, effective 10 to 11f, best at 10f, acts on gd. Turf high 114 (1st run) (began Jly) - 3rd of 9 giving 4lb to Imperioso (16 Jly Frankfurt 10f gd RF 2981a). He is a useful middle-distance performer, but looks a shade one-paced in Group company.
**Dr A Bolte in GER [0-1] Frau U Herberts & Frau R Von Mitzlaff (from A Wohler in GER [0-5] Jly 2000).*

KARAKUL (IRE) BHB 44f34a **RR 20f 34a** 5227[11]
4 ch f Persian Bold 10f **(69)** - Cindy's Baby (Bairn (USA)) 7.7f **(59)**
Form - 0000000
Record 2000 - 1st:0 2nd:0 3rd:0 Ran:6
Pre2000 - 1st:4 2nd:1 3rd:1 Ran:18
Win Prizemoney £12,100 *Total Prizemoney* £13,764
Wins 1999 Aug Beverl (GD) H 9.9f 56 67 <
1999 Aug Leices (G-F) H 10f 56 63+
1999 Jun Windso (G-F) H 10f 50 55
1998 Jly Bright (GD) C 7f 62
2000 Turf 0-4: (8f 3, 12f) (gd, g-f, frm 2) 2000 AW 0-2: (8f 2) (Fibr 2)
Neat, little account filly, effective 10f, acts on g-f, likes right handed tracks, likes tight tracks. Turf high 20 (began Jly).
**C A Dwyer [0-2] Larkwood Stud (from R Brotherton [0-5] Aug 2000).*

KARALIYFA (IRE) BHB 84f **RR 91f** 3389[7]
3 gr f Kahyasi 12.9f **(74)** - Karliyka (IRE) **(97f)** (Last Tycoon) 8.5f **(62)**
Form - 617

Record 2000 - 1st:1 2nd:0 3rd:0 Ran:3
Pre2000 - 1st:0 2nd:0 3rd:1 Ran:1
Win Prizemoney £3,500 *Total Prizemoney* £5,678
Wins * 2000 Jly Ripon (G-F) 9f 64+ <
2000 Turf 1-3: (9f 1-1, 10f, 11f) (gd, g-f 1-2)
Scopey, useful filly. Turf high 91. A good third in a decent race on her only start at two, she disappointed in the Lingfield Oaks Trial and was dropped in trip to land long odds-on in a three-runner Ripon maiden, though she made hard work of it.
**Sir Michael Stoute [1-4] H H Aga Khan.*

KARAMEG (IRE) BHB 80f RR 81f 4865[16]

4 b f Danehill (USA) 9.1f **(79)** - House of Queens (IRE) (King of Clubs) 7.1f **(57)**
Form - 04220500
Record 2000 - 1st:0 2nd:2 3rd:0 Ran:8
Pre2000 - 1st:2 2nd:1 3rd:2 Ran:14
Win Prizemoney £11,600 *Total Prizemoney* £21,186
Wins * 1999 Oct Newmar (SFT) H 7f 74 78 <
* 1999 Jun Doncas (G-F) H 7f 67 72
2000 Turf 0-8: (6f, 7f 7) (sft, g-s, gd 2, g-f, frm 3)
Light-framed, decent filly, effective 7f, acts on gd to frm, best on gd. Turf high 85 - 2nd of 11 getting 1lb from Tony Tie (29 Jly Newcastle 7f g-f RF 3210). **P W Harris [2-22] Graham & Lynn Knight.*

KARA SEA (USA) BHB 57f63a RR 57f 63a 4994[7]

3 ch f River Special (USA) - Arctic Interlude (CAN) (Woodman (USA)) 9f **(74)**
Form - 184207
Record 2000 - 1st:1 2nd:1 3rd:0 Ran:6
Win Prizemoney £2,743 *Total Prizemoney* £3,624
Wins * 2000 *Feb Southw (STD) 8f* *66* <
2000 Turf 0-1: (10f) (frm) 2000 AW 1-5: (7f, 8f 1-1, 11f, 12f 2) (Equi, Fibr 1-4)
Neat, average filly, effective 8 to 11f, - acts on Fibr, has worn blinkers. AW high 69 - 2nd of 11 getting 2lb from Bahamas (28 Jly Southwell 11f Fibr RF 3186) - also 1st of 7 getting 24lb from Kustom Kit Kevin (11 Feb Southwell RF 0266).
**D J G MurraySmith [1-6] D MurraySmith.*

KARASTA (IRE) RR 101f 4844a[2]

2 b f Lake Coniston (IRE) - Karliyka (IRE) **(97f)** (Last Tycoon) 8.5f **(62)**
Form - 112
Record 2000 - 1st:2 2nd:1 3rd:0 Ran:3
Win Prizemoney £28,875 *Total Prizemoney* £59,615
Wins * 2000 Spt Doncas (G-F) G3 8f 99+ <
*** 2000** Aug Newmar (G-F) 7f 87++
2000 Turf 2-3: (7f 1-1, 8f 1-2) (gd, g-f 1-1, frm 1-1)
Currently very useful filly. Turf high 101 (began Aug) - 2nd of 10 to Amonita (1 Oct Longchamp 8f gd RF 4844a) - also 1st of 12 from Ameerat (7 Spt Doncaster RF 4280). An impressive filly who won really well on her debut, she confirmed the promise by taking the May Hill despite running green once in front. Was beaten in the Marcel Boussac, but the winner broke the race record. She is full of potential, and the Guineas is an obvious target, although her breeding suggests she will not want much further.
**Sir Michael Stoute [2-3] H H Aga Khan.*

KAREEB (FR) BHB 80f RR 84f 5240[20]

3 b g Green Desert (USA) 7.8f **(78)** - Braari (USA) **(100f)** (Gulch (USA)) 8f **(81)**
Form - 650834361030
Record 2000 - 1st:1 2nd:0 3rd:3 Ran:12
Pre2000 - 1st:0 2nd:3 3rd:1 Ran:5
Win Prizemoney £9,165 *Total Prizemoney* £15,366
Wins * 2000 Spt Newbur (G-F) H 8f 76 79 <
2000 Turf 1-12: (6f 2, 7f 4, 8f 1-6) (g-s 3, gd, g-f 1-4, frm 4)
Scopey, decent gelding, effective 6 to 8f, acts on g-s to frm, has worn blinkers. Turf high 84 - 5th of 17 giving 4lb to Rendition (16 May York 7f g-f RF 1217) - also 1st of 16 getting 2lb from Shadow Prince (16 Spt Newbury RF 4465). Despite running well in varied company, he did not win a race until landing a handicap at Newbury in September.
**W R Muir [1-13] J Bernstein (from B W Hills [0-4] Oct 1999).*

KARIN'S LAD (IRE) BHB 25f RR 3f 4216[16]

3 b g Up and At 'em - Sharp Goodbye (Sharpo) 7.7f **(59)**
Form - 50
Record 2000 - 1st:0 2nd:0 3rd:0 Ran:2
2000 Turf 0-2: (10f 2) (frm 2)
Currently very poor gelding. Turf high 3 (began Jly).
**R Hollinshead [0-2] C Forster.*

KARITSA BHB 66f RR 70f 5081[5]

2 b f Rudimentary (USA) 8.2f **(66)** - Desert Ditty (Green Desert (USA)) 8.6f **(78)**
Form - 2518345
Record 2000 - 1st:1 2nd:1 3rd:1 Ran:7
Win Prizemoney £4,212 *Total Prizemoney* £6,386
Wins * 2000 Jly Cheste (G-S) 5.1f 70 <
2000 Turf 1-7: (5f 1-6, 6f) (hvy, g-s, gd 3, g-f 1-1, frm)
Above-average filly, effective 5 to 6f, acts on g-f to frm. Turf high 70 - also 1st of 5 getting 5lb from Smirfys Party (15 Jly Chester RF 2832). **M R Channon [1-7] Colin Brown Racing III.*

KARMINIYA (IRE) RR 63f 5152[5]

2 b f Primo Dominie 7.2f **(67)** - Karamiyna (IRE) **(92f)** (Shernazar) 10.2f **(73)**
Form - 5
Record 2000 - 1st:0 2nd:0 3rd:0 Ran:1
2000 Turf 0-1: (7f) (g-s)
Currently average filly. **Sir Michael Stoute [0-1] H H Aga Khan.*

KAROWNA BHB 67f62a RR 68f 62a 3454a[12]

4 ch f Karinga Bay - Misowni (Niniski (USA)) 10.6f **(65)**
Form - 400
Record 2000 - 1st:0 2nd:0 3rd:0 Ran:3
Pre2000 - 1st:0 2nd:0 3rd:2 Ran:10
Win Prizemoney £0 *Total Prizemoney* £2,152
2000 Turf 0-3: (16f 3) (gd 2, frm)
Light-framed, average filly, effective 7 to 16f, best at 7f, acts on gd to frm. Turf high 68. Consistent.
**S A Brookshaw [0-8] M Twenty-Eight Partnership (from B A McMahon [0-10] Aug 1999).*

KARPASIANA (USA) RR 73f 5138[8]

2 ch f Woodman (USA) 9.7f **(77)** - Redwood Falls (IRE) (Dancing Brave (USA)) 8.4f **(76)**
Form - 8
Record 2000 - 1st:0 2nd:0 3rd:0 Ran:1
2000 Turf 0-1: (8f) (g-s)
Currently above-average filly. **M A Jarvis [0-1] Tigerland Ltd.*

KASHRA (IRE) BHB 90f RR 95f 4258[6]

3 b f Dancing Dissident (USA) 6.8f **(65)** - Tudor Loom (Sallust) 8.4f **(63)**
Form - 48002066
Record 2000 - 1st:0 2nd:1 3rd:0 Ran:8
Pre2000 - 1st:3 2nd:2 3rd:0 Ran:9
Win Prizemoney £27,170 *Total Prizemoney* £35,877
Wins * 1999 Aug Newmar (G-F) H 6f 81 87+ <
* 1999 Jly Goodwo (G-F) H 6f 72
* 1999 Jly Pontef (G-S) H 6f 58
2000 Turf 0-8: (5f, 6f 5, 7f 2) (g-s, gd 3, g-f 3, hrd)
Scopey, very useful filly, effective 6 to 7f, acts on g-f to frm. Turf high 96 - 2nd of 9 to Veil of Avalon (5 Aug Goodwood 7f g-f RF 3398). **M Johnston [3-17] K Towey.*

KASS ALHAWA BHB 65f56a RR 70f 56a 4824[9]

7 b g Shirley Heights 12.1f **(76)** - Silver Braid (USA) (Miswaki (USA)) 9f **(81)**
Form - 1820624754244225840
Record 2000 - 1st:0 2nd:5 3rd:0 Ran:17
Pre2000 - 1st:7 2nd:14 3rd:7 Ran:71
Win Prizemoney £23,015 *Total Prizemoney* £48,106
Wins * 1999 *Nov Wolver (STD) H 8.5f 50 55*
* 1999 Jly Beverl (G-F) H 8.5f 68 71+ <
* 1998 Aug Beverl (G-F) H 7.5f 63 66
* 1998 Jun Beverl (G-S) H 7.5f 63 68
* 1998 *Feb Southw (STD) H 6f 31 38*
* 1997 Aug Catter (G-F) H 7f 59 63
* 1997 Jun Redcar (GD) H 8f 53 58
2000 Turf 0-14: (7f 8, 8f 5, 9f) (g-s 2, gd 2, g-f 4, frm 5, hrd) 2000 AW 0-3: (8f 2, 9f) (Fibr 3)
Above-average gelding, effective 6 to 10f, best at 8f, acts on g-s to hrd, best on frm, has worn blinkers, and excels at Catterick. Turf

high 70 - 4th of 8 giving 16lb to Lady of Windsor (5 May Musselburgh 8f frm RF 1039). AW high 53.
**D W Chapman [7-85] J B Wilcox (from Sir Michael Stoute [0-3] May 1996).*

KASTAWAY BHB 90f **RR 90+f** 1864[6]

4 b f Distant Relative 7f **(69)** - Flourishing (IRE) (Trojan Fen) 8.1f **(62)**
Form - 76

Record					
2000 -	1st:0	2nd:0	3rd:0	Ran:2
Pre2000 -	1st:4	2nd:2	3rd:0	Ran:9

Win Prizemoney £14,937 *Total Prizemoney* £22,287

Wins						
1998	Jun	Windso	(SFT)	5f	88	<
1998	May	Doncas	(G-F)	5f	86	
1998	Apr	Thirsk	(G-S)	5f	86	
1998	*Mar*	*Lingfi*	*(STD)*	*5f*	*86*	

2000 Turf 0-2: (5f 2) (gd 2)
Neat, useful filly. Turf high 90.
**D R C Elsworth [0-3] C J Harper (from J Berry [4-8] Spt 1998).*

KATHAKALI (IRE) BHB 60f80a **RR 61f 80a** 4033[13]

3 b c Dancing Dissident (USA) 6.8f **(65)** - Shes A Dancer (IRE) (Alzao (USA)) 7.1f **(68)**
Form - 2111007005000

Record					
2000 -	1st:3	2nd:1	3rd:0	Ran:13
Pre2000 -	1st:0	2nd:0	3rd:0	Ran:7

Win Prizemoney £11,690 *Total Prizemoney* £12,583

Wins								
*** 2000**	*Apr*	*Lingfi*	*(STD)*	*H*	*10f*	*73*	*75*	<
*** 2000**	*Jan*	*Lingfi*	*(STD)*		*10f*		*75*	<
*** 2000**	*Jan*	*Lingfi*	*(STD)*		*8f*		*64+*	

2000 Turf 0-8: (9f, 10f 4, 12f 3) (g-s, g-f 3, frm 4) 2000 AW 3-5: (8f 1-1, 10f 2-3, 12f) (Equi 3-5)
Scopey, useful colt, effective 6 to 10f, best at 10f, acts on frm - acts on Equi, has worn blinkers, prefers left handed tracks, likes tight tracks. Turf high 61. AW high 75 - 1st of 5 getting 2lb from Thats All Folks (29 Jan Lingfield RF 0183) - also 1st of 8 giving 4lb to Thatcham (12 Apr Lingfield RF 0680). He showed little on turf at two, but was in brilliant form on Equitrack earlier in the year, winning three at up to ten furlongs. Not so effective back on turf.
**V Soane [3-20] M B N Clements.*

KATHANN BHB 48f **RR 50f** 4362[7]

2 ch f Presidium 7.5f **(56)** - Travel Mystery (Godswalk (USA)) 7.3f **(58)**
Form - 007

Record					
2000 -	1st:0	2nd:0	3rd:0	Ran:3

2000 Turf 0-3: (6f, 7f 2) (g-f, frm 2)
Currently fair filly. Turf high 50 (began Jly).
**J A Glover [0-3] Kenneth Paul Beecroft.*

KATHERINE SEYMOUR **RR 94f** 4990[3]

2 b f Green Desert (USA) 7.8f **(78)** - Sudeley (Dancing Brave (USA)) 8.4f **(76)**
Form - 123
2000 Turf 1-3: (7f 1-3) (sft, gd)
Currently useful filly. Turf high 94 (began Spt) - 2nd of 12 to Imagine (30 Spt Curragh 7f sft RF 4793a). Made a winning debut at the Curragh, and then ran well in a Group Three and the Rockfel Stakes at Newmarket. Not that big, she should nevertheless make a high-class three-year-old.
**M J Grassick in IRE [1-3] Miss P F O'Kelly.*

KATHIR (USA) BHB 85f **RR 89f** 4609[19]

3 ch c Woodman (USA) 9.7f **(77)** - Alcando (Alzao (USA)) 7.1f **(68)**
Form - 03215250

Record					
2000 -	1st:1	2nd:2	3rd:1	Ran:8
Pre2000 -	1st:1	2nd:1	3rd:0	Ran:2

Win Prizemoney £10,985 *Total Prizemoney* £20,357

Wins						
*** 2000**	Jly	Warwic	(G-F)	8.1f	81	<
* 1999	Aug	Nottin	(G-F)	8.2f	72+	

2000 Turf 1-8: (8f 1-6, 9f 2) (sft, g-s, gd 2, g-f 1-3, frm)
Strong, useful colt, effective 8 to 9f, best at 9f, acts on gd to g-f, best on g-f, prefers tight tracks. Turf high 89 - 2nd of 11 to Everest (27 Aug Goodwood 9f g-f RF 4016) - also 1st of 7 getting 12lb from Culzean (22 Jly Warwick RF 3045). A front-runner, he progressed steadily before winning a classified stakes at Warwick in July. Has a pronounced knee action, but did not seem particularly suited by the soft ground at Newcastle in June.
**A C Stewart [2-10] Hamdan Al Maktoum.*

KATHMANDU (FR) **RR 114f** 4418a[4]

3 br c Kaldounevees (FR) - Midnight Lady (FR) (Mill Reef (USA)) 10.5f **(78)**
Form - 34
2000 Turf 0-2: (12f 2) (gd 2)
Currently Group-class colt, often wears blinkers. Turf high 111 (began Aug). He was way out of his depth behind Sinndar in the Prix Niel and will be better employed in Listed races.
**D Sepulchre in FR [0-2].*

KATHOLOGY (IRE) BHB 92f82a **RR 96f 82a** 5109[11]

3 b c College Chapel - Wicken Wonder (IRE) **(56f)** (Distant Relative)
Form - 232114002000

Record					
2000 -	1st:2	2nd:2	3rd:0	Ran:10
Pre2000 -	1st:0	2nd:3	3rd:1	Ran:6

Win Prizemoney £18,136 *Total Prizemoney* £30,800

Wins								
*** 2000**	May	Cheste	(GD)	H	5.1f	89	93	<
*** 2000**	Apr	Sandow	(SFT)	H	5f	84	87	

2000 Turf 2-10: (5f 2-7, 6f 3) (g-s 1-2, gd 3, g-f 1-2, frm 3)
Scopey, very useful colt, effective 5 to 6f, best at 5f, acts on g-s to frm, best on frm. Turf high 96 - 2nd of 17 giving 11lb to Honesty Fair (23 Aug York 5f frm RF 3918) - also 1st of 12 giving 9lb to Nifty Major (9 May Chester RF 1114). Inconsistent. He won twice in the spring and showed a return to form in August when going down narrowly in a valuable York handicap.
**D R C Elsworth [2-16] McDowell Racing.*

KATHRYN'S PET BHB 82f **RR 84f** 5323[19]

7 b m Blakeney 11.9f **(53)** - Starky's Pet (Mummy's Pet) 7.7f **(60)**
Form - 61200

Record					
2000 -	1st:1	2nd:1	3rd:0	Ran:5
Pre2000 -	1st:5	2nd:2	3rd:2	Ran:26

Win Prizemoney £26,935 *Total Prizemoney* £32,158

Wins								
*** 2000**	May	Nottin	(GD)	H	14.1f	73	76	<
* 1999	Oct	Newmar	(G-S)	H	12f	66	70	
* 1999	Mar	Catter	(G-S)	H	13.8f	66	68	
* 1998	Apr	Catter	(GD)	H	13.8f	61	67	
* 1997	Jun	Cheste	(SFT)	H	12.3f	60	64	
* 1997	Mar	Mussel	(SFT)		12f		56	

2000 Turf 1-5: (10f, 12f 3, 14f 1-1) (sft, g-s, gd 1-3)
Decent mare, effective 10 to 14f, acts on gd, likes tight tracks. Turf high 84 - 2nd of 15 giving 7lb to Nowell House (30 Spt Redcar 10f gd RF 4749) - also 1st of 15 giving 25lb to Mental Pressure (20 May Nottingham RF 1340). Inconsistent. A useful dual-purpose mare, she seems best when held up and is still capable of winning races under both codes. Fourteen furlongs looks her best trip on the level.
**Mrs M Reveley [11-46] Bill Brown.*

KATIE HAWK BHB 18f **RR 13df** 3385[12]

6 b m Buzzards Bay 8.9f **(44)** - Rayne Park (Julio Mariner) 7.2f **(57)**
Form - 0

Record					
2000 -	1st:0	2nd:0	3rd:0	Ran:1
Pre2000 -	1st:0	2nd:0	3rd:0	Ran:4

2000 Turf 0-1: (7f) (frm)
Poor mare. **J M Bradley [0-5] Mrs T D Watts.*

KATIE KING BHB 25f **RR 18f** 3237[9]

3 ch f River Falls 8.2f **(56)** - Lady Kate (USA) **(7f)** (Trempolino (USA)) 12f **(71)**
Form - 68080

Record					
2000 -	1st:0	2nd:0	3rd:0	Ran:5

2000 Turf 0-3: (8f, 10f, 12f) (frm 3) 2000 AW 0-2: (6f 2) (Equi 2)
Light-framed, poor filly, has worn blinkers. Turf high 18. AW high 4. **W J Musson [0-5] Broughton Thermal Insulation.*

KATIE KOMAITE BHB 34f34a **RR 41f 34a** 5085[8]

7 b m Komaite (USA) 6.9f **(61)** - City to City (Windjammer (USA)) 7f **(59)**
Form - 40772352208

Record					
2000 -	1st:0	2nd:3	3rd:1	Ran:11
Pre2000 -	1st:3	2nd:5	3rd:4	Ran:52

Win Prizemoney £8,677 *Total Prizemoney* £17,925

Wins								
* 1999	Oct	Newcas	(G-S)	H	10.1f	35	36	
* 1998	Jun	Pontef	(SFT)	H	8f	39	43	
1997	Oct	Nottin	(GD)	H	8.2f	39	45	<

2000 Turf 0-11: (10f 2, 11f 5, 12f 4) (hvy 2, sft, gd 4, g-f 2, frm 2)
Moderate mare, effective 8 to 12f, acts on hvy to g-f, often wears

blinkers (extremely effectively), likes left handed tracks, and excels at Haydock. Turf high 41 - 2nd of 8 giving 11lb to Notation (22 Aug Hamilton 12f gd RF 3844). She is a difficult type to win with, but often runs with credit. She does not want the ground fast.
**Mrs G S Rees [2-31] Red Rose Partnership (from Capt J Wilson [1-32] Nov 1997).*

KATIE'S CRACKER BHB 14f19a **RR 12f 19a** 5182[9]
5 b m Rambo Dancer (CAN) 8.4f **(59)** - Tea-Pot (Ragstone) 9.6f **(59)**
Form - 60700746400
Record 2000 - 1st:0 2nd:0 3rd:0 Ran:7
Pre2000 - 1st:4 2nd:7 3rd:6 Ran:49
Win Prizemoney £9,180 *Total Prizemoney* £15,990
Wins * 1999 *Mar Southw (STD) C 14f 36*
* 1999 *Feb Lingfi (STD) SH 13f 36 41*
* 1998 Oct Nottin (SFT) SH 14.1f 37 46
* 1998 *Mar Southw (STD) H 11f 53 56+* <
2000 Turf 0-2: (12f, 14f) (sft, g-f) 2000 AW 0-5: (13f, 14f, 15f, 16f 2) (Equi 2, Fibr 3)
Little account filly, effective 12 to 16f, best at 13f, - acts on AW, best on Equi, favours left handed tracks, favours tight tracks, does well at Lingfield. Turf high 11 (began Spt). AW high 23.
**M Quinn [4-56] Mrs S G Davies (from M R Channon [0-7] Spt 1997).*

KATIES DOLPHIN (IRE) BHB 57f54a **RR 64f 54a** 4770[9]
2 ch f Dolphin Street (FR) - Kuwah (IRE) (Be My Guest (USA)) 9.3f **(67)**
Form - 6237560
Record 2000 - 1st:0 2nd:1 3rd:1 Ran:7
Win Prizemoney £0 *Total Prizemoney* £1,543
2000 Turf 0-7: (5f, 6f 5, 7f) (g-s, gd 2, g-f 4)
Average filly, effective 5 to 6f, acts on g-f, has worn blinkers. Turf high 64 - 3rd of 15 to Bijan (29 Jun Carlisle 5f g-f RF 2361).
**J L Eyre [0-7] W P Burnell.*

KATIE'S VALENTINE BHB 51f50a **RR 55f 50a** 2777[10]
3 b f Balnibarbi - Ring Side (IRE) (Alzao (USA)) 7.1f **(68)**
Form - 4532800
Record 2000 - 1st:0 2nd:1 3rd:1 Ran:5
Pre2000 - 1st:0 2nd:0 3rd:0 Ran:3
Win Prizemoney £0 *Total Prizemoney* £1,388
2000 Turf 0-4: (6f 3, 8f) (gd, g-f, frm 2) 2000 AW 0-1: (8f) (Fibr)
Scopey, fair filly, effective 6f, acts on gd to g-f, has worn blinkers. Turf high 55 (1st run) - 3rd of 15 getting 7lb from The Prosecutor (26 May Haydock 6f gd RF 1469). **R A Fahey [0-8] G Shiel.*

KATIYKHA (IRE) BHB 105f **RR 111f** 4520a[7]
4 b f Darshaan 11.9f **(81)** - Katiyfa (Auction Ring (USA)) 8.6f **(65)**
Form - 241117
2000 Turf 3-6: (12f 2-2, 14f 1-4) (hvy, g-s 1-2, gd 2-3)
Well made, Group-class filly, effective 12 to 14f, best at 12f, acts on gd, prefers right handed tracks, excels at Newmarket. Turf high 111 - 1st of 8 giving 14lb to Chimes At Midnight (26 Aug Curragh RF 4092a) - also 1st of 20 giving 14lb to Gallery God (20 Jun Ascot RF 2114). She won Listed events either side of a game victory in the Duke Of Edinburgh Handicap at Royal Ascot. Well backed there, she finished distressed when unplaced in the Irish St Leger and was not seen out again.
**J Oxx in IRE [3-6] H H Aga Khan (from L M Cumani [3-8] Oct 1999).*

KATIYMANN (IRE) BHB 40f **RR 26f** 2094[P]
8 ch g Persian Bold 10f **(69)** - Katiyfa (Auction Ring (USA)) 8.6f **(65)**
Form - 00P
Record 2000 - 1st:0 2nd:0 3rd:0 Ran:3
Pre2000 - 1st:2 2nd:0 3rd:0 Ran:7
Win Prizemoney £4,446 *Total Prizemoney* £4,446
Wins * 1999 May Leices (GD) SH 10f 40 42
1997 Jun Clonme (GD) 10f 66 <
2000 Turf 0-3: (10f, 12f 2) (gd, frm 2)
Little account gelding, had broken blood-vessels, liked right handed tracks, liked tight tracks. Turf high 26. (DEAD)
**B Ellison [1-19] C P Lowther (from T J Taaffe in IRE [4-17] Aug 1997).*

KATIYPOUR (IRE) BHB 73f **RR 73f** 4754[14]
3 ch c Be My Guest (USA) 10.2f **(66)** - Katiyfa (Auction Ring (USA)) 8.6f **(65)**
Form - 82300
Record 2000 - 1st:0 2nd:1 3rd:1 Ran:5
Win Prizemoney £0 *Total Prizemoney* £1,879
2000 Turf 0-5: (8f, 9f, 10f 3) (g-s, gd, g-f, frm 2)
Well made, above-average colt. Turf high 73 - 2nd of 6 to Tarboush (17 Jun Sandown 10f g-f RF 2058).
**Sir Michael Stoute [0-5] H H Aga Khan.*

KATTEGAT BHB 90f **RR 90f** 4987[32]
4 b g Slip Anchor 12.7f **(75)** - Kirsten (Kris) 9.5f **(73)**
Form - 30
Record 2000 - 1st:0 2nd:0 3rd:1 Ran:2
Pre2000 - 1st:2 2nd:1 3rd:1 Ran:5
Win Prizemoney £10,241 *Total Prizemoney* £14,240
Wins 1999 Oct Ayr (SFT) H 13.1f 88 90 <
1998 Oct Nottin (SFT) 8.2f 81
2000 Turf 0-2: (16f, 18f) (g-s, gd)
Workmanlike, useful gelding. Turf high 80.
**J A B Old [0-7] W E Sturt (from W Jarvis [2-5] Oct 1999).*

KATUN (FR) **RR 110f** 4848a[9]
7 b h Saumarez 15.1f **(87)** - All Found (USA) (Alleged (USA)) 10f **(76)**
Form - 260
2000 Turf 0-3: (16f 2, 20f) (hvy, g-s, gd)
Group-class horse, effective 16f, acts on hvy to gd. Turf high 103 (1st run) - 2nd of 7 getting 7lb from Amilynx (30 Apr Longchamp 16f hvy RF 1037a). A useful French stayer, he is unlikely to improve at this stage of his career. **X Nakkachdji in FR [1-7].*

KATY IVORY (IRE) BHB 65f60a **RR 63f 60a** 422[5]
3 b f Night Shift (USA) 8.1f **(73)** - Echo Cove (Slip Anchor) 9.8f **(73)**
Form - 5
Record 2000 - 1st:0 2nd:0 3rd:0 Ran:1
Pre2000 - 1st:0 2nd:1 3rd:0 Ran:6
Win Prizemoney £0 *Total Prizemoney* £976
2000 AW 0-1: (7f) (Equi)
Neat, average filly, effective 8f, acts on g-f.
**K T Ivory [0-1] K T Ivory Ltd (from P W Harris [0-6] Oct 1999).*

Katy Nowaitee didn't hang around

KATY NOWAITEE BHB 104f **RR 107+f** 4931[1]
4 b f Komaite (USA) 6.9f **(61)** - Cold Blow (Posse (USA)) 8.9f **(61)**
Form - 111
Record 2000 - 1st:3 2nd:0 3rd:0 Ran:3
Pre2000 - 1st:2 2nd:1 3rd:0 Ran:4
Win Prizemoney £109,816 *Total Prizemoney* £112,186
Wins * **2000** Oct Newmar (SFT) L 10f 104+
* **2000** Spt Newmar (GD) H 9f 92 107+ <
* **2000** Mar Doncas (GD) H 8f 84 92
* 1999 Oct Redcar (GD) H 8f 77 82
* 1999 Aug Newmar (G-F) 8f 75
2000 Turf 3-3: (8f 1-1, 9f 1-1, 10f 1-1) (gd 2-2, g-f 1-1)
Scopey, Pattern-class filly, effective 9 to 10f, acts on gd to g-f. Turf high 107 - 1st of 35 getting 2lb from Nooshman (30 Spt Newmarket RF 4740) - also 1st of 12 giving 5lb to Salee (12 Oct Newmarket RF 4931). Lightly raced, she landed the Spring Mile at Doncaster in March in fluent style but was then sidelined for six months. Returned to land an ante-post gamble in the Cambridgeshire

before taking a step up to listed company in her stride.
**P W Harris [5-7] The Stable Maites.*

KAURI (USA) RR 35f 2753[11]
2 b f Woodman (USA) 9.7f **(77)** - No Ordinary Storm (USA) (Storm Bird (CAN)) 10.3f **(74)**
Form - 0
Record 2000 - 1st:0 2nd:0 3rd:0 Ran:1
2000 Turf 0-1: (6f) (frm)
Currently fair filly. **M Johnston [0-1] David Abell.*

KAYF TARA BHB 122f **RR 123f** 2180[1]
6 b h Sadler's Wells (USA) 11.3f **(87)** - Colorspin (FR) (High Top) 10.2f **(67)**
Form - 11

Record	**2000** -	1st:2	2nd:0	3rd:0	Ran:2
	Pre2000 -	1st:8	2nd:1	3rd:2	Ran:13

Win Prizemoney £627,696 *Total Prizemoney* £659,351

Wins	*** 2000**	Jun	Ascot	(G-F)	G1	20f	119	
	*** 2000**	May	York	(FRM)	G2	13.9f	123+	<
	* 1999	Spt	Currag	(SFT)	G1	14f	123+	<
	* 1999	Aug	Deauvi	(HVY)	G2	15f	123	
	* 1999	Jly	Goodwo	(G-F)	G2	16f	113+	
	* 1999	May	Longch	(HVY)	G2	15.5f	121	
	* 1998	Spt	Currag	(SFT)	G1	14f	123	
	* 1998	Jun	Ascot	(SFT)	G1	20f	118	
	* 1998	May	Haydoc	(GD)		11.9f	95+	
	1997	Jly	Ascot	(GD)		10f	91	

2000 Turf 2-2: (14f 1-1, 20f 1-1) (gd 1-1, g-f 1-1)
Very high-class horse, effective 14 to 20f, best at 14f, acts on g-s to frm, best on gd. Turf high 123 (1st run) - 1st of 8 giving 5lb to Rainbow Ways (18 May York RF 1277) - also 1st of 11 from Far Cry (22 Jun Ascot RF 2180). Consistent. A brilliant stayer, he landed a hat-trick in the Goodwood Cup, the Prix Kergorlay at Deauville and the Irish St Leger in '99, but sustained a serious leg injury when being prepared for the Melbourne Cup. He fortunately came back fit and well to win the Yorkshire Cup easily on his return before landing his second Gold Cup. He was not seen again, but retires to stud as one of the greatest stayers of recent times.
**S bin Suroor [9-13] Godolphin (from Sir Michael Stoute [1-2] Jly 1997).*

KAYO BHB 96f72a **RR 98f 72a** 5006[12]
5 b g Superpower 6.6f **(58)** - Shiny Kay (Star Appeal) 9.6f **(65)**
Form - 308802312203504070

Record	**2000** -	1st:1	2nd:3	3rd:2	Ran:16
	Pre2000 -	1st:9	2nd:2	3rd:3	Ran:37

Win Prizemoney £68,152 *Total Prizemoney* £95,813

Wins	*** 2000**	Jly	Newcas	(FRM)	H	7f	94	102	<
	* 1999	Oct	Newcas	(G-S)	H	6f	79	93	
	* 1999	Oct	Newmar	(GD)	H	7f	79	92	
	* 1999	Oct	Redcar	(GD)	H	7f	80	83	
	1998	Oct	Warwic	(GD)	H	8f	91	92	
	1998	Jun	Newbur	(HVY)		7f		86	
	1998	*May*	*Southw*	*(STD)*	*H*	*7f*	*73*	*78*	
	1998	*Apr*	*Southw*	*(STD)*	*H*	*6f*	*67*	*72*	
	1997	Oct	Ayr	(SFT)	H	8f	67	71	
	1997	Spt	Mussel	(G-F)	C	8f		66	

2000 Turf 1-12: (6f 5, 7f 1-7) (sft, gd 3, g-f 5, frm 1-3) 2000 AW 0-4: (6f, 7f 2, 8f) (Equi, Fibr 3)
Very useful gelding, effective 6 to 7f, best at 6f, acts on gd to frm, has worn blinkers, and excels at Newcastle. Turf high 102 - 1st of 10 giving 20lb to Royal Artist (1 Jly Newcastle RF 2444). AW high 68. Becoming disappointing. A decent performer at six or seven furlongs, he was in good form during the summer and made all to win on very fast ground at Newcastle in July. In the handicapper's grip latterly.
**M Johnston [4-23] David Abell (from T J Etherington [6-30] Jly 1999).*

KAYO GEE BHB 46f53a **RR 59f 53a** 5155[2]
4 b f Komaite (USA) 6.9f **(61)** - Darling Miss Daisy (Tina's Pet) 6.8f **(59)**
Form - 08673700002

Record	**2000** -	1st:0	2nd:1	3rd:1	Ran:9
	Pre2000 -	1st:3	2nd:0	3rd:0	Ran:12

Win Prizemoney £10,690 *Total Prizemoney* £11,954

Wins	1999	*Feb*	*Lingfi*	*(STD)*	*H*	*5f*	*73*	*80*	
	1999	*Jan*	*Lingfi*	*(STD)*	*H*	*5f*	*60*	*81*	<
	1998	*Dec*	*Lingfi*	*(STD)*		*5f*		*72?*	

2000 Turf 0-6: (5f 2, 6f 3, 7f) (g-s, gd, g-f 2, frm 2) 2000 AW 0-3: (5f 2, 7f) (Equi 3)
Light-framed, average filly, effective 5f, - acts on Equi, mostly wears blinkers (effectively), likes left handed tracks, likes tight tracks. Turf high 59. AW high 62. Inconsistent.
**L MontagueHall [0-9] Mrs E N Nield (from A J McNae [3-12] Dec 1999).*

KAZANA RR 77f 5098[2]
2 b f Salse (USA) 10.9f **(71)** - Sea Ballad (USA) (Bering) 7.4f **(61)**
Form - 42
Record 2000 - 1st:0 2nd:1 3rd:0 Ran:2
Win Prizemoney £0 *Total Prizemoney* £1,644
2000 Turf 0-2: (8f 2) (gd, frm)
Currently above-average filly. Turf high 77 (began Spt).
**S P C Woods [0-2] Leydens Farm Stud.*

KAZEEM RR 74f 5098[6]
2 b f Darshaan 11.9f **(81)** - Kanz (USA) (The Minstrel (CAN)) 10f **(72)**
Form - 66
Record 2000 - 1st:0 2nd:0 3rd:0 Ran:2
2000 Turf 0-2: (7f, 8f) (gd, frm)
Currently above-average filly. Turf high 74 (began Aug).
**B W Hills [0-2] D J Deer.*

KEALAKEKUA BAY (IRE) RR 30f 5200[9]
3 ch g Shalford (IRE) 7.8f **(63)** - Sonbere (Electric) 10.1f **(61)**
Form - 0
Record 2000 - 1st:0 2nd:0 3rd:0 Ran:1
2000 Turf 0-1: (10f) (gd)
Workmanlike, currently very moderate gelding.
**G L Moore [0-1] Mrs J Moore.*

KEBABS (IRE) BHB 51f49a **RR 61f 49a** 5105[16]
3 b f Catrail (USA) - Common Rumpus (IRE) **(81f)** (Common Grounds)
Form - 550703058400

Record	**2000** -	1st:0	2nd:0	3rd:1	Ran:12
	Pre2000 -	1st:1	2nd:0	3rd:0	Ran:4

Win Prizemoney £4,485 *Total Prizemoney* £5,476
Wins 1999 Aug Currag (GD) 6f 68 <
2000 Turf 0-11: (5f, 6f 6, 7f 4) (gd 5, g-f 3, frm 3) 2000 AW 0-1: (6f) (Fibr)
Above-average filly, effective 6f, acts on frm, has worn blinkers. Turf high 72.
**J A Osborne [0-12] L Queally (from N Meade in IRE [1-4] Oct 1999).*

KEEN DANCER BHB 52f58a **RR 49f 58a** 3149[6]
6 ch g Keen 11.1f **(58)** - Royal Shoe (Hotfoot) 10.5f **(59)**
Form - 66

Record	**2000** -	1st:0	2nd:0	3rd:0	Ran:2
	Pre2000 -	1st:0	2nd:0	3rd:0	Ran:13

Win Prizemoney £0 *Total Prizemoney* £449
2000 Turf 0-2: (12f 2) (g-f, frm)
Moderate gelding, had worn blinkers. Turf high 45 (began Jly). (DEAD)
**M C Pipe [1-17] Mrs Alison Farrant (from M L W Bell [0-7] Jun 1997).*

KEEN HANDS BHB 52f67a **RR 54f 67a** 4825[22]
4 ch g Keen 11.1f **(58)** - Broken Vow (IRE) (Local Suitor (USA)) 8.4f **(67)**
Form - 48241041758551847060

Record	**2000** -	1st:3	2nd:0	3rd:0	Ran:16
	Pre2000 -	1st:4	2nd:4	3rd:1	Ran:23

Win Prizemoney £24,751 *Total Prizemoney* £28,331

Wins	*** 2000**	*May*	*Southw*	*(STD)*	*H*	*6f*	*72*	*78*	<
	*** 2000**	*Feb*	*Southw*	*(STD)*	*H*	*6f*	*74*	*78*	<
	*** 2000**	*Jan*	*Southw*	*(STD)*	*H*	*6f*	*68*	*71*	
	* 1999	*Apr*	*Southw*	*(STD)*	*H*	*6f*	*68*	*72*	
	* 1999	*Mar*	*Southw*	*(STD)*	*S*	*5f*		*71*	
	* 1999	*Mar*	*Southw*	*(STD)*	*S*	*7f*		*61*	
	* 1999	*Jan*	*Wolver*	*(STD)*	*S*	*5f*		*55*	

2000 Turf 0-5: (5f, 6f 3, 7f) (gd, g-f, frm 3) 2000 AW 3-11: (5f 2, 6f 3-6, 7f 3) (Equi, Fibr 3-10)
Average gelding, effective 5 to 6f, best at 6f, - acts on Fibr, mostly wears blinkers (very effectively), likes left handed tracks, likes tight tracks, and excels at Southwell. Turf high 60 (began Jly). AW high 78 - 1st of 10 giving 15lb to Pleading (4 Feb Southwell RF 0218) - also 1st of 14 giving 1lb to Teyaar (26 May Southwell RF

1479). Becoming disappointing. Apparently resents being hit with the whip, but has been successful on Fibresand in the past couple of years. Six furlongs at Southwell seem to be his ideal conditions.
Mrs N Macauley [7-39] Andy Peake.

KEEN WATERS BHB 32f25a **RR 31f 25a** 138[9]
6 b m Keen 11.1f **(58)** - Miss Oasis (Green Desert (USA)) 8.6f **(78)**
Form - 80
Record 2000 - 1st:0 2nd:0 3rd:0 Ran:2
Pre2000 - 1st:1 2nd:2 3rd:2 Ran:19
Win Prizemoney £2,219 *Total Prizemoney* £4,583
Wins 1997 Aug Bright (G-F) SH 11.9f 35 40 <
2000 AW 0-2: (12f, 16f) (Equi 2)
Very moderate mare, has worn blinkers. AW high 8.
B R Johnson [0-2] Mrs K Oseman (from Mrs S D Williams [0-4] Oct 1997).

KEEP DREAMING RR 18f 2590[6]
2 b f Mistertopogigo (IRE) - Ominous (Dominion) 8.5f **(63)**
Form - 8876
Record 2000 - 1st:0 2nd:0 3rd:0 Ran:4
2000 Turf 0-3: (5f 2, 7f) (g-f, frm 2) 2000 AW 0-1: (5f) (Fibr)
Little account filly. Turf high 18. *S Gollings [0-4] S Harris.*

KEEP IKIS BHB 63f **RR 63+f** 3826[1]
6 ch m Anshan 8.2f **(63)** Santee Sioux (Dancing Brave (USA)) 8.4f **(76)**
Form - 143151
Record 2000 - 1st:3 2nd:0 3rd:1 Ran:6
Pre2000 - 1st:0 2nd:1 3rd:1 Ran:8
Win Prizemoney £10,845 *Total Prizemoney* £13,613
Wins * **2000** Aug Pontef (G-F) H 17.1f 56 63 <
* **2000** Jly Catter (G-F) H 15.8f 50 51
* **2000** May Ripon (GD) H 16f 40 45
2000 Turf 3-6: (16f 2-3, 17f 1-2, 18f) (g-f 2-2, frm 3, hrd 1-1)
Average mare, effective 16 to 17f, acts on frm to hrd. Turf high 63 - 1st of 14 getting 1lb from Chief Wallah (20 Aug Pontefract RF 3826). Improving. A thorough stayer, she enjoyed a good season. Particularly effective on fast ground.
Mrs M Reveley [3-7] T McGoran (from S Gollings [0-11] Spt 1999).

KEEPSAKE (IRE) BHB 30f **RR 25f** 345[9]
6 b m Distinctly North (USA) 7.4f **(63)** - Souveniers (Relko) 9.9f **(59)**
Form - 0
Record 2000 - 1st:0 2nd:0 3rd:0 Ran:1
Pre2000 - 1st:1 2nd:4 3rd:3 Ran:38
Win Prizemoney £3,073 *Total Prizemoney* £8,946
Wins * 1997 Aug Salisb (G-F) H 12f 49 54 <
2000 AW 0-1: (16f) (Fibr)
Little account mare, effective 16f, - acts on AW, has worn blinkers, favours left handed tracks. *M D I Usher [1-44] B Duke.*

KEEP TAPPING (IRE) RR 80f 688[3]
3 b g Mac's Imp (USA) 5.6f **(54)** - Mystery Bid (Auction Ring (USA)) 8.6f **(65)**
Form - 3
Record 2000 - 1st:0 2nd:0 3rd:1 Ran:1
Pre2000 - 1st:1 2nd:1 3rd:1 Ran:11
Win Prizemoney £3,403 *Total Prizemoney* £7,153
Wins 1999 Jun Sandow (GD) 5f 80 <
2000 Turf 0-1: (6f) (hvy)
Scopey, decent gelding, effective 5 to 6f, best at 5f, acts on hvy to frm, has worn blinkers. (1st run) - 3rd of 15 giving 3lb to Footprints (12 Apr Warwick 6f hvy RF 0688).
J A Osborne [0-1] Mrs Julie Mitchell (from A P Jarvis [1-11] Aug 1999).

KEEP THE PEACE (IRE) RR 66tf 1961[19]
2 br c Petardia 8.2f **(58)** - Eiras Mood (Jalmood (USA)) 10.1f **(52)**
Form - 00
Record 2000 - 1st:0 2nd:0 3rd:0 Ran:2
2000 Turf 0-2: (6f 2) (g-f 2)
Currently average colt. Turf high 66. *I A Balding [0-2] Miss A V Hill.*

KEE RING BHB 44f **RR 67f** 3077[9]
4 ch g Keen 11.1f **(58)** - Rose And The Ring (Welsh Pageant) 10f **(65)**
Form - 6760670
Record 2000 - 1st:0 2nd:0 3rd:0 Ran:7
Pre2000 - 1st:0 2nd:1 3rd:1 Ran:9
Win Prizemoney £0 *Total Prizemoney* £1,377
2000 Turf 0-7: (6f 6, 7f) (gd 2, g-f, frm 4)
Leggy, average gelding, has worn blinkers. Turf high 67.
P R Chamings [0-16] Mrs J E L Wright.

KELBURNE (USA) BHB 48f **RR 46f** 5064[6]
3 b c Red Ransom (USA) 8.6f **(83)** - Golden Klair (Damister (USA)) 9f **(73)**
Form - 54480806
Record 2000 - 1st:0 2nd:0 3rd:0 Ran:8
Win Prizemoney £0 *Total Prizemoney* £643
2000 Turf 0-8: (8f, 9f, 10f 5, 12f) (sft, g-s, g-f 2, frm 3, hrd)
Scopey, moderate colt. Turf high 53.
J M Jefferson [0-8] Kelburne Construction Ltd.

KELETI RR 57f 2230[6]
2 b c Efisio 7.7f **(69)** - Perioscope (Legend of France (USA)) 9.5f **(61)**
Form - 56
Record 2000 - 1st:0 2nd:0 3rd:0 Ran:2
2000 Turf 0-2: (5f 2) (frm 2)
Currently fair colt. Turf high 57. *M Johnston [0-2] B E P Partnership.*

KELLING HALL BHB 40f **RR 28f** 2611[12]
3 b g Distant Relative 7f **(69)** - Naulakha **(55f)** (Bustino) 10.4f **(64)**
Form - 000
Record 2000 - 1st:0 2nd:0 3rd:0 Ran:3
Pre2000 - 1st:0 2nd:0 3rd:0 Ran:2
2000 Turf 0-3: (8f 2, 10f) (gd 3)
Workmanlike, little account gelding. Turf high 28.
D J S ffrenchDavis [0-5] Miss Henrietta Senn.

KELLS (IRE) BHB 67f58a **RR 70f 58a** 5073[5]
2 b c Dilum (USA) 7.1f **(56)** - Elizabethan Air **(30f)** (Elegant Air) 13.2f **(61)**
Form - 005
Record 2000 - 1st:0 2nd:0 3rd:0 Ran:3
2000 Turf 0-3: (7f 3) (g-s 2, g-f)
Currently above-average colt. Turf high 70 (began Jly).
M Blanshard [0 3] The Kells Partnership.

KELSO MAGIC (USA) BHB 80f **RR 57f** 3610[7]
3 ch f Distant View (USA) - Bowl of Honey (USA) (Lyphard (USA)) 9.9f **(72)**
Form - 0807
Record 2000 - 1st:0 2nd:0 3rd:0 Ran:4
Pre2000 - 1st:2 2nd:2 3rd:0 Ran:10
Win Prizemoney £6,831 *Total Prizemoney* £11,389
Wins * 1999 Spt Bright (G-F) H 5.3f 79 89 <
* 1999 Jun Salisb (G-F) 5f 89 <
2000 Turf 0-4: (5f, 6f 3) (hvy, g-s, gd, frm)
Scopey, fair filly, effective 5f, acts on gd to frm, has worn blinkers. Turf high 57. Becoming disappointing.
B J Meehan [2-14] F C T Wilson.

KELTECH GOLD (IRE) BHB 76f **RR 74f** 4166[17]
3 b c Petorius 8f **(66)** - Creggan Vale Lass (Simply Great (FR)) 8.2f **(65)**
Form - 821510
Record 2000 - 1st:2 2nd:1 3rd:0 Ran:6
Pre2000 - 1st:0 2nd:0 3rd:0 Ran:2
Win Prizemoney £9,332 *Total Prizemoney* £10,760
Wins * **2000** Aug Chepst (G-F) H 8.1f 71 74 <
* **2000** Jun Bath (G-S) H 8f 65 74 <
2000 Turf 2-6: (8f 2-6) (hvy, gd 1-2, g-f, frm 1-2)
Above-average colt, effective 8f, acts on gd to frm, best on gd. Turf high 74 - 1st of 16 giving 3lb to Bold Raider (2 Jun Bath RF 1648) - also 1st of 8 getting 16lb from Flamenco Red (10 Aug Chepstow RF 3527). Has improved with experience, winning two handicaps over a mile. Seems to handle any ground, and is best when racing prominently. *B Palling [2-8] D Brennan.*

KELTECH STAR (IRE) BHB 38f **RR 42f** 3074[5]
4 b f Bigstone (IRE) - Coryana (Sassafras (FR)) 9.6f **(69)**
Form - 6705
Record 2000 - 1st:0 2nd:0 3rd:0 Ran:4
Pre2000 - 1st:0 2nd:0 3rd:1 Ran:4
Win Prizemoney £0 *Total Prizemoney* £280

2000 Turf 0-4: (10f 2, 12f, 13f) (g-f 2, frm 2)
Moderate filly, has worn blinkers. Turf high 42.
**E J O'Neill [0-4] D Brennan (from N Meade in IRE [0-4] Nov 1999).*

KELTIC BARD BHB 79f82a **RR 79f 82a** 4761[10]
3 b g Emperor Jones (USA) - Broughton Singer (IRE) **(49f)** (Common Grounds)
Form - 00751210
Record 2000 - 1st:2 2nd:1 3rd:0 Ran:8
Pre2000 - 1st:1 2nd:2 3rd:0 Ran:4
Win Prizemoney £9,678 *Total Prizemoney* £12,663
Wins * 2000 Aug Folkes (G-F) H 9.7f 75 79
*** 2000** Jly Folkes (FRM) H 9.7f 68 73
* 1999 *Spt Wolver (STD) 8.5f 89 <*
2000 Turf 2-7: (8f 3, 10f 2-4) (g-f 1-2, frm 1-5) 2000 AW 0-1: (12f) (Fibr)
Scopey, useful gelding, effective 8 to 10f, acts on g-f - acts on Fibr, prefers tight tracks. Turf high 79. Got off the mark on Fibresand at Wolverhampton at the end 1999, but has shown himself to be at least as effective on turf with two wins on fast ground at Folkestone during the summer. Suited by ten furlongs.
**S P C Woods [3-12] G A Roberts.*

KENNET BHB 70f53a **RR 73f 53a** 5125[7]
5 b g Kylian (USA) 8.1f **(66)** - Marwell Mitzi **(29f)** (Interrex (CAN))
Form - 56007820223113657
Record 2000 - 1st:2 2nd:3 3rd:2 Ran:17
Pre2000 - 1st:3 2nd:7 3rd:5 Ran:32
Win Prizemoney £16,457 *Total Prizemoney* £32,825
Wins * 2000 Aug Bath (GD) H 13.1f 62 71
*** 2000** Aug Windso (GD) H 11.6f 62 70
* 1999 Oct Bright (G-S) 11.9f 71
* 1999 May Windso (GD) 10f 72
* 1999 *Feb Lingfi (STD) 10f 73 <*
2000 Turf 2-14: (8f, 9f, 10f 4, 12f 1-5, 13f 1-1, 15f, 16f) (g-s, gd 3, g-f 2-6, frm 4) 2000 AW 0-3: (10f, 11f 2) (Equi, Fibr 2)
Above-average gelding, effective 8 to 16f, acts on gd to frm - acts on Equi, has worn blinkers, likes tight tracks, excels at Leicester, does well at Windsor. Turf high 73 - 5th of 9 getting 18lb from Bangalore (15 Spt Newbury 16f frm RF 4438) - also 1st of 13 giving 23lb to Kirisnippa (20 Aug Bath RF 3818). AW high 62. Consistent. He hit form in August, winning a brace of ordinary races at Windsor and Bath and finishing third in an amateurs' race at Epsom.
**P D Cundell [5-49] Miss M C Fraser.*

KENNYTHORPE BOPPY (IRE) BHB 56f **RR 59f** 5103[12]
2 ch g Aragon 7.7f **(58)** - Spark (IRE) **(62df 47a)** (Flash of Steel) 7.2f **(53)**
Form - 5850
Record 2000 - 1st:0 2nd:0 3rd:0 Ran:4
2000 Turf 0-4: (7f 2, 8f 2) (gd, g-f, frm 2)
Fair gelding. Turf high 59 (began Aug).
**J S Wainwright [0-4] R Bond.*

KENT BHB 51a **RR 36f** 763[7]
5 b g Kylian (USA) 8.1f **(66)** - Precious Caroline (IRE) **(26a)** (The Noble Player (USA)) 6.5f **(67)**
Form - 5121647
Record 2000 - 1st:2 2nd:1 3rd:0 Ran:6
Pre2000 - 1st:0 2nd:0 3rd:1 Ran:8
Win Prizemoney £5,194 *Total Prizemoney* £6,760
Wins * 2000 *Feb Southw (STD) H 16f 45 53 <*
*** 2000** *Jan Southw (STD) H 16f 39 44*
2000 Turf 0-1: (15f) (g-s) 2000 AW 2-5: (16f 2-5) (Fibr 2-5)
Moderate gelding, effective 16f, - acts on Fibr, has worn blinkers, prefers left handed tracks, likes tight tracks. AW high 53 - 1st of 11 getting 13lb from Cresset (11 Feb Southwell RF 0268).
**P D Cundell [2-14] P D Cundell.*

KENTISH ROCK BHB 23f **RR** 4723[15]
5 b g Rock Hopper 10.6f **(54)** - Capel Lass (The Brianstan) 5.9f **(55)**
Form - 0450
Record 2000 - 1st:0 2nd:0 3rd:0 Ran:4
2000 Turf 0-1: (14f) (frm) 2000 AW 0-3: (7f, 10f, 12f) (Equi 3)
Formerly very poor gelding, has worn blinkers.
**D C O'Brien [0-6] The Lively Lads.*

KENTUCKY BOUND (IRE) BHB 57f **RR 58f** 5140[11]
2 b c Charnwood Forest (IRE) - Blown-Over **(37f)** (Ron's Victory (USA))
Form - 780
Record 2000 - 1st:0 2nd:0 3rd:0 Ran:3
2000 Turf 0-3: (5f 2, 6f) (g-s 2, frm)
Currently fair colt. Turf high 58. **J W Payne [0-3] C Cotran.*

KERATAKA (IRE) RR 93f 4796a[9]
3 bb f Doyoun 10.7f **(69)** - Kerita (Formidable (USA)) 9.2f **(63)**
Form - 3135320
2000 Turf 1-7: (7f 2, 8f 1-4, 10f) (g-s 2, gd 1-4)
Useful filly, effective 8f, acts on g-s. Turf high 93 - 2nd of 18 giving 1lb to Creux Noir (16 Spt Curragh 8f RF 4522a).
**J Oxx in IRE [1-7] H H Aga Khan.*

KERMIYANA (IRE) RR 100f 5048a[10]
3 b f Green Desert (USA) 7.8f **(78)** - Keraka (USA) (Storm Bird (CAN)) 10.3f **(74)**
Form - 115860
2000 Turf 2-6: (6f, 7f 1-2, 8f 1-3) (g-s 1-2, gd 1-2, g-f)
Very useful filly, effective 7 to 8f, acts on g-s to gd, has worn blinkers. Turf high 100 - 1st of 10 from Sand Partridge (8 Jly Leopardstown RF 2722a) - also 1st of 8 from Air Of Approval (7 Jun Gowran Park RF 1932a). **J Oxx in IRE [2-6] H H Aga Khan.*

KERRICH BHB 34f **RR 24f** 4206[10]
3 ch f Presidium 7.5f **(56)** - Miss Realm (Realm) 8.1f **(65)**
Form - 000
Record 2000 - 1st:0 2nd:0 3rd:0 Ran:3
2000 Turf 0-3: (6f, 7f 2) (gd, frm 2)
Neat, currently little account filly. Turf high 24.
**B N Doran [0-3] B N Doran.*

KERRIDGE CHAPEL (IRE) BHB 32f35a **RR 30f 35a** 5018[7]
3 b f College Chapel - Crimson Ring (Persian Bold) 9.3f **(66)**
Form - 0006086077
Record 2000 - 1st:0 2nd:0 3rd:0 Ran:9
Pre2000 - 1st:0 2nd:0 3rd:0 Ran:9
2000 Turf 0-7: (5f 5, 7f, 8f) (gd, g-f 3, frm 3) 2000 AW 0-2: (7f 2) (Fibr 2)
Very moderate filly, often wears blinkers. Turf high 30. AW high 14 (began Oct). **A Senior [0-18] A Senior.*

KERRYGOLD (FR) RR 113f 3157a[1]
4 ch c Tel Quel (FR) - Star System
Form - 31
2000 Turf 1-2: (10f 1-2) (sft 1-1, gd)
Currently Group-class colt. Turf high 113 (1st run) - 3rd of 8 to Slickly (15 Jun Longchamp 10f gd RF 2200a) - also 1st of 11 from Tijiyr (19 Jly Vichy RF 3157a). He produced an impressive burst of speed to win a Group 3 at Vichy during July and can score again at that level. **P Bary in FR [1-2] Mme H Devin.*

KESTLE IMP (IRE) BHB 45a **RR 45a** 5114[2]
2 b f Imp Society (USA) 7.1f **(63)** - Dark Truffle **(49f)** (Deploy)
Form - 2
Record 2000 - 1st:0 2nd:1 3rd:0 Ran:1
Win Prizemoney £0 *Total Prizemoney* £782
2000 AW 0-1: (9f) (Fibr)
Currently moderate filly. **R M H Cowell [0-1] & Mrs D A Gamble.*

KESTRAL BHB 55f37a **RR 58f 37a** 5294[8]
4 ch g Ardkinglass 5f **(64)** - Shiny Kay (Star Appeal) 9.6f **(65)**
Form - 506062321238
Record 2000 - 1st:1 2nd:3 3rd:2 Ran:12
Pre2000 - 1st:0 2nd:0 3rd:0 Ran:15
Win Prizemoney £2,989 *Total Prizemoney* £8,143
Wins * 2000 Aug Newcas (FRM) H 9f 42 54 <
2000 Turf 1-10: (6f, 7f 2, 8f 3, 9f 1-2, 10f, 12f) (g-s, gd, g-f 2, frm 1-6) 2000 AW 0-2: (7f, 9f) (Fibr 2)
Scopey, fair gelding, effective 6 to 10f, acts on gd to frm. Turf high 58 - 3rd of 15 giving 3lb to Thihn (13 Spt Beverley 8f g-f RF 4361) - also 1st of 18 giving 4lb to Ambushed (25 Aug Newcastle RF 3959). AW high 31.
**T J Etherington [1-27] The R and R Partnership.*

KEWARRA BHB 65f **RR 65f** 2790[3]
6 b g Distant Relative 7f **(69)** - Shalati (FR) (High Line) 10.3f **(70)**
Form - 773
Record 2000 - 1st:0 2nd:0 3rd:1 Ran:3
Pre2000 - 1st:4 2nd:2 3rd:6 Ran:31
Win Prizemoney £26,186 *Total Prizemoney* £35,850
Wins 1998 Apr Epsom (SFT) H 10.1f 85 90 <
1997 Oct Newmar (G-F) H 10f 78 84
1997 Spt Chepst (GD) H 10.2f 74 78
1997 Aug Chepst (G-F) H 10.2f 70 75
2000 Turf 0-3: (10f, 12f 2) (g-f 2, frm)
Average gelding, has worn blinkers. Turf high 59.
**A Streeter [0-3] Dr C V MacPhail (from B R Millman [4-31] Aug 1999).*

KEW GARDENS BHB 83f **RR 90f** 4936[17]
3 ch g Arazi (USA) 9.2f **(74)** - Hatton Gardens (Auction Ring (USA)) 8.6f **(65)**
Form - 23000
Record 2000 - 1st:0 2nd:1 3rd:1 Ran:5
Pre2000 - 1st:1 2nd:0 3rd:0 Ran:4
Win Prizemoney £3,857 *Total Prizemoney* £8,015
Wins * 1999 Oct Pontef (SFT) 10f 80 <
2000 Turf 0-5: (10f, 12f 2, 14f, 16f) (sft, gd 2, g-f 2)
Useful gelding, effective 10 to 12f, best at 10f, acts on sft to g-f. Turf high 90 - 3rd of 8 giving 3lb to Cephalonia (20 May Newbury 12f g-f RF 1320). He was well beaten when tackling two miles in the Queen's Vase at Royal Ascot.
**Mrs A J Perrett [1-9] Sir Eric Parker.*

KEY BHB 48f **RR 44f** 4266[9]
4 b f Midyan (USA) 9.9f **(64)** - Diamond Park (IRE) **(60f)** (Alzao (USA)) 7.1f **(68)**
Form - 00
Record 2000 - 1st:0 2nd:0 3rd:0 Ran:2
Pre2000 - 1st:1 2nd:2 3rd:1 Ran:17
Win Prizemoney £3,371 *Total Prizemoney* £7,851
Wins 1998 Aug Bright (FRM) H 5.3f 70 78 <
2000 Turf 0-2: (5f, 6f) (g-f, hrd)
Moderate filly, effective 6 to 7f, best at 7f, acts on g-f to frm, best on frm. Turf high 44 (began Aug). Becoming disappointing.
**Mrs A Duffield [0-2] Wyck Hall Stud (from C E Brittain [0-2] Oct 1999).*

KEZ BHB 51f50a **RR 57f 50a** 2889[4]
4 b g Polar Falcon (USA) 9f **(74)** - Briggsmaid (Elegant Air) 13.2f **(61)**
Form - 07204
Record 2000 - 1st:0 2nd:1 3rd:0 Ran:5
Pre2000 - 1st:1 2nd:1 3rd:3 Ran:9
Win Prizemoney £2,684 *Total Prizemoney* £6,415
Wins * 1999 Aug Bright (FRM) 11.9f 63+ <
2000 Turf 0-4: (8f, 12f 3) (gd 2, frm 2) 2000 AW 0-1: (10f) (Equi)
Lengthy, fair gelding, effective 10f, acts on frm, has worn blinkers. Turf high 57. **S P C Woods [1-14] Dennis Yardy.*

KHABAR BHB 45f35a **RR 34f 35a** 547[10]
7 b g Forzando 7.2f **(63)** - Ella Mon Amour (Ela-Mana-Mou) 10.1f **(70)**
Form - 0
Record 2000 - 1st:0 2nd:0 3rd:0 Ran:1
Pre2000 - 1st:0 2nd:4 3rd:3 Ran:25
Win Prizemoney £0 *Total Prizemoney* £6,878
2000 Turf 0-1: (7f) (frm)
Very moderate gelding, has broken blood-vessels, effective 8 to 9f, best at 8f, acts on g-s to frm, best on frm, prefers tight tracks. Becoming disappointing.
**R Bastiman [0-22] Mrs P Bastiman (from D Morley [0-4] Spt 1995).*

KHALED (IRE) BHB 65a **RR 68df** 4924[12]
5 b g Petorius 8f **(66)** - Felin Special (Lyphard's Special (USA)) 10.3f **(72)**
Form - 03000
Record 2000 - 1st:0 2nd:0 3rd:1 Ran:5
Pre2000 - 1st:1 2nd:0 3rd:1 Ran:5
Win Prizemoney £3,980 *Total Prizemoney* £5,555
Wins * 1998 Aug Warwic (G-F) 8f 75 <
2000 Turf 0-3: (8f 3) (g-f 2, frm) 2000 AW 0-2: (8f, 9f) (Equi, Fibr)
Above-average gelding, effective 8f, acts on g-f. Turf high 68 (1st run) (began Aug) - 3rd of 14 getting 11lb from Smooth Sailing (4 Aug Newmarket 8f g-f RF 3368). AW high 11. Becoming disappointing.
**K Mahdi [1-9] Prospect Estates Ltd (from D Nicholls [0-1] Jan 2000).*

KHALIK (IRE) BHB 69f59a **RR 70f 59a** 5141[3]
6 br g Lear Fan (USA) 10.4f **(80)** - Silver Dollar (Shirley Heights) 10.3f **(74)**
Form - 031477363
Record 2000 - 1st:1 2nd:0 3rd:3 Ran:8
Pre2000 - 1st:2 2nd:2 3rd:2 Ran:18
Win Prizemoney £8,299 *Total Prizemoney* £14,168
Wins * 2000 May Bath (G-S) H 5.1f 64 67 <
* 1999 Aug Lingfi (GD) H 6f 58 63+
* 1999 Aug Salisb (SFT) H 6f 58 58
2000 Turf 1-8: (5f 1-4, 6f 4) (g-s 2, gd 1-3, g-f, frm 2)
Above-average gelding, effective 5 to 6f, best at 6f, acts on g-s to frm, has worn blinkers, excels at Windsor, likes Lingfield. Turf high 70 - 3rd of 13 giving 6lb to Bintang Timor (22 Oct Yarmouth 6f g-s RF 5141) - also 1st of 20 giving 15lb to Bowlers Boy (2 May Bath RF 0963). Consistent. Suited by six furlongs or a stiff five, over which he won at Bath in May.
**Miss Gay Kelleway [3-15] A P Griffin (from Mrs L Stubbs [0-8] Spt 1998).*

KHASAYL (IRE) BHB 100f **RR 108f** 4845a[8]
3 b f Lycius (USA) 8.8f **(71)** - Maraatib (IRE) (Green Desert (USA)) 8.6f **(78)**
Form - 28
2000 Turf 0-2: (5f, 6f) (gd 2)
Scopey, Pattern-class filly, effective 5 to 6f, best at 6f, acts on g-s to g-f. Turf high 108 (1st run) (began Spt) - 2nd of 7 getting 3lb from Danger Over (15 Spt Chantilly 6f gd RF 4564a).
**J E Hammond in FR [0-2] Hamdan Al Maktoum (from P T Walwyn [4-7] Oct 1999).*

KHATANI (IRE) BHB 92f **RR 93f** 3414[6]
5 b g Kahyasi 12.9f **(74)** - Khanata (USA) (Riverman (USA)) 9.1f **(76)**
Form - 6
Record 2000 - 1st:0 2nd:0 3rd:0 Ran:1
Pre2000 - 1st:3 2nd:0 3rd:1 Ran:7
Win Prizemoney £17,860 *Total Prizemoney* £19,796
Wins 1999 Jly Currag (G-F) H 16f 92 93 <
1999 Jun Gowran (GD) H 14f 86 93 <
1998 Jun Roscom (G-F) 10f 93 <
2000 Turf 0-1: (19f) (g-f)
Useful gelding. Inconsistent. A winner at up to two miles on the Flat in Ireland, he has since become a very decent hurdler. Suited by a sound surface.
**D R Gandolfo [5-10] R E Brinkworth (from J Oxx in IRE [3-7] Jly 1999).*

KHAYYAM (USA) RR 60f 4601[4]
2 b c Affirmed (USA) 10.3f **(75)** - True Celebrity (USA) (Lyphard (USA)) 9.9f **(72)**
Form - 84
Record 2000 - 1st:0 2nd:0 3rd:0 Ran:2
Win Prizemoney £0 *Total Prizemoney* £308
2000 Turf 0-2: (6f, 7f) (gd, frm)
Currently average colt. Turf high 60.
**P F I Cole [0-2] H R H Prince Fahd Salman.*

KHITAAM (IRE) RR 86f 4109[4]
2 b c Charnwood Forest (IRE) - Queen's Ransom (IRE) **(66f)** (Last Tycoon) 8.5f **(62)**
Form - 24
Record 2000 - 1st:0 2nd:1 3rd:0 Ran:2
Win Prizemoney £0 *Total Prizemoney* £2,608
2000 Turf 0-2: (7f 2) (gd, frm)
Currently useful colt. Turf high 86 (began Aug) - 4th of 9 to Tobougg (30 Aug York 7f gd RF 4109). Showed plenty of promise on his debut, and should have no difficulty getting off the mark.
**B Hanbury [0-2] Hamdan Al Maktoum.*

KHUCHN (IRE) BHB 48f **RR 52f** 3270[P]
4 b c Unfuwain (USA) 11.4f **(74)** - Stay Sharpe (USA) (Sharpen Up) 8.3f **(67)**
Form - 00505265422P
Record 2000 - 1st:0 2nd:3 3rd:0 Ran:12
Pre2000 - 1st:1 2nd:0 3rd:0 Ran:5

Win Prizemoney £2,652 *Total Prizemoney* £6,684
Wins 1999 Jly Nottin (GD) 10f 63 <
2000 Turf 0-12: (8f 2, 10f 8, 12f 2) (sft, g-s 2, gd 4, g-f 4, frm)
Scopey, fair colt, effective 10f, acts on g-f. Turf high 52. Consistent.
**M Brittain [0-12] Mel Brittain (from R W Armstrong [1-5] Aug 1999).*

KHULAN (USA) BHB 100f **RR 96f** 4644[13]
2 b f Bahri (USA) - Jawlaat (USA) **(90f)** (Dayjur (USA))
Form - 120
Record 2000 - 1st:1 2nd:1 3rd:0 Ran:3
Win Prizemoney £5,785 *Total Prizemoney* £23,385
Wins * 2000 Jly Newmar (G-S) 6f 95++ <
2000 Turf 1-3: (6f 1-3) (gd 1-2, g-f)
Currently very useful filly. Turf high 96 (began Jly) - 2nd of 7 getting 3lb from Enthused (24 Aug York 6f gd RF 3933) - also 1st of 9 from Mujado (13 Jly Newmarket RF 2776). She was highly impressive in a maiden at the Newmarket July meeting, but still looked green when beaten by Enthused in the Lowther. Finished last in the Cheveley Park, but was not beaten all that far and ran better than her final position suggests. Looks up to winning a Pattern race. **J L Dunlop [1-3] Hamdan Al Maktoum.*

KI CHI SAGA (USA) BHB 19f25a **RR 9f 25a** 2738[11]
8 ch g Miswaki (USA) 8.1f **(81)** - Cedilla (USA) (Caro)
Form - 04402060744006030
Record 2000 - 1st:0 2nd:0 3rd:1 Ran:11
Pre2000 - 1st:5 2nd:6 3rd:7 Ran:62
Win Prizemoney £9,550 *Total Prizemoney* £16,431
Wins * 1999 *Aug Lingfi (STD) S 12f 54*
1998 *Apr Lingfi (STD) S 10f 64* <
1998 *Mar Lingfi (STD) H 8f* 52 *57*
1998 *Feb Lingfi (SLW) S 8f 51*
1997 *Mar Lingfi (STD) 8f 61*
2000 Turf 0-1: (12f) (frm) 2000 AW 0-10: (10f 2, 11f, 12f, 13f 4, 14f, 16f) (Equi 8, Fibr 2)
Poor gelding, effective 8 to 12f, - acts on Equi, often wears blinkers (effectively), favours left handed tracks. AW high 32.
**P Burgoyne [1-34] Philip Saunders (from G L Moore [3-19] Oct 1998).*

KIDNAPPED BHB 43f38a **RR 29?f 38a** 1106[18]
4 b g Emarati (USA) 6.6f **(63)** - Haddon Anna (Dragonara Palace (USA)) 6.1f **(55)**
Form - 0700
Record 2000 - 1st:0 2nd:0 3rd:0 Ran:2
Pre2000 - 1st:0 2nd:0 3rd:0 Ran:7
2000 Turf 0-1: (6f) (frm) 2000 AW 0-1: (8f) (Fibr)
Unfurnished, little account gelding, has worn blinkers. Inconsistent.
**A J McNae [0-5] L R Gotch (from Mrs A L M King [0-4] Jun 1999).*

KIDOLOGY (IRE) BHB 34f **RR 22f** 1791[9]
4 b g Petardia 8.2f **(58)** - Loveville (USA) (Assert) 10.6f **(85)**
Form - 0
Record 2000 - 1st:0 2nd:0 3rd:0 Ran:1
Pre2000 - 1st:0 2nd:0 3rd:0 Ran:3
2000 Turf 0-1: (10f) (sft)
Leggy, little account gelding. **W Storey [0-4] Foster Watson.*

KID'Z'PLAY (IRE) BHB 57f **RR 58f** 5316[7]
4 b g Rudimentary (USA) 8.2f **(66)** - Saka Saka (Camden Town) 9.3f **(53)**
Form - 714040014P327
Record 2000 - 1st:2 2nd:1 3rd:1 Ran:13
Pre2000 - 1st:1 2nd:1 3rd:0 Ran:9
Win Prizemoney £8,110 *Total Prizemoney* £10,510
Wins * 2000 Spt Ayr (SFT) H 10.9f 51 57 <
*** 2000** Jun Mussel (FRM) H 9f 53 57 <
* 1999 Aug Hamilt (G-F) H 8.3f 40 50
2000 Turf 2-13: (7f, 8f 3, 9f 1-2, 10f 4, 11f 1-1, 12f, 13f) (hvy 2, g-s 2, gd 1-3, g-f 2, frm 1-4)
Fair gelding, effective 8 to 11f, acts on g-s to frm, best on gd, prefers tight tracks, and excels at Musselburgh. Turf high 58 - 3rd of 18 getting 4lb from Such Flair (16 Oct Pontefract 10f g-s RF 5000) - also 1st of 18 getting 1lb from Strictly Speaking (14 Spt Ayr RF 4387). Inconsistent.
**J S Goldie [3-20] Liam McGuigan (from M Johnston [0-2] Spt 1998).*

KIERCHEM (IRE) BHB 37f **RR 38f** 5166[11]
9 b g Mazaad 8.5f **(53)** - Smashing Gale (Lord Gayle (USA)) 8.8f **(62)**
Form - 26014600430360
Record 2000 - 1st:1 2nd:1 3rd:2 Ran:14
Pre2000 - 1st:1 2nd:1 3rd:1 Ran:12
Win Prizemoney £5,524 *Total Prizemoney* £8,493
Wins * 2000 Jun Ripon (G-F) SH 8f 34 35
2000 Turf 1-14: (7f, 8f 1-6, 10f 4, 11f, 12f, 16f) (sft, g-s 4, gd, g-f 1-4, frm 4)
Fair gelding, effective 8 to 12f, acts on g-f, has worn blinkers, likes tight tracks. Turf high 44 - 3rd of 11 getting 6lb from Nosey Native (18 Aug Catterick 12f g-f RF 3738) - also 1st of 20 getting 11lb from Danzas (21 Jun Ripon RF 2166).
**C Grant [6-51] Mrs M Hunter (from R F Fisher [1-12] May 1996).*

KIER PARK (IRE) BHB 112f **RR 111f** 1061[2]
3 b c Foxhound (USA) - Merlannah (IRE) (Shy Groom (USA)) 10f **(66)**
Form - 2
Record 2000 - 1st:0 2nd:1 3rd:0 Ran:1
Pre2000 - 1st:2 2nd:1 3rd:0 Ran:4
Win Prizemoney £27,935 *Total Prizemoney* £39,775
Wins * 1999 Oct Ascot (G-S) G3 5f 101 <
* 1999 Oct Lingfi (HVY) 5f 86+
2000 Turf 0-1: (5f) (gd)
Well made, Group-class colt. (1st run) - 2nd of 21 getting 3lb from Pipalong (6 May Newmarket 5f gd RF 1061). Probably the pick of the sprinting juveniles in 1999, he ran a tremendous race when caught close home by Pipalong in the Palace House Stakes at Newmarket during May. Injured shortly afterwards, he remains a sprinter of real potential and should land a major prize in 2001 if all is well. Despite a promising run on good to firm, he may need give underfoot. **M A Jarvis [2-5] H R H Sultan Ahmad Shah.*

KIFTSGATE BHB 93f **RR 97+f** 4107[2]
3 ch c Kris 10f **(75)** - Blush Rambler (IRE) (Blushing Groom (FR)) 10.3f **(76)**
Form - 6122
Record 2000 - 1st:1 2nd:2 3rd:0 Ran:4
Win Prizemoney £4,426 *Total Prizemoney* £11,852
Wins * 2000 Jly Sandow (G-S) 10f 81+ <
2000 Turf 1-4: (10f 1-2, 12f 2) (gd, g-f 1-1, frm 2)
Scopey, very useful colt. Turf high 96 - 2nd of 4 giving 5lb to Cracow (30 Aug York 12f gd RF 4107).
**Sir Michael Stoute [1-4] Sir Evelyn De Rothschild.*

KIGEMA (IRE) BHB 57f55a **RR 58f 55a** 459[6]
3 ch f Case Law 6f **(64)** - Grace de Bois (Tap On Wood) 10.3f **(65)**
Form - 576146226
Record 2000 - 1st:1 2nd:2 3rd:0 Ran:6
Pre2000 - 1st:1 2nd:0 3rd:0 Ran:9
Win Prizemoney £4,076 *Total Prizemoney* £6,038
Wins * 2000 *Jan Lingfi (STD) C 8f 56*
* 1999 Jun Bright (G-F) S 6f 58 <
2000 AW 1-6: (7f, 8f 1-4, 10f) (Equi 1-4, Fibr 2)
Neat, fair filly, effective 6 to 8f, acts on g-f to frm - acts on Equi. AW high 57 - 2nd of 10 giving 3lb to Paddywack (8 Mar Lingfield 7f Equi RF 0425) - also 1st of 7 getting 9lb from Master Jones (2 Jan Lingfield RF 0002). **C N Allen [2-15] Green Square Racing.*

KILBARCHAN BHB 62f **RR 52f** 5298[5]
2 ch f Selkirk (USA) 7.9f **(76)** - Haitienne (FR) (Green Dancer (USA)) 10.3f **(74)**
Form - 355
Record 2000 - 1st:0 2nd:0 3rd:1 Ran:3
Win Prizemoney £0 *Total Prizemoney* £583
2000 Turf 0-3: (5f, 6f, 8f) (g-s, g-f 2)
Currently fair filly. Turf high 52 (1st run) - 3rd of 4 getting 5lb from Blue Planet (28 Jun Hamilton 6f g-f RF 2337).
**Miss L A Perratt [0-3] Dr J Walker.*

KILBRANNAN SOUND BHB 44f **RR 73f** 5120[7]
3 b f Makbul - Highland Rowena (Roybens) 7.3f **(60)**
Form - 450000007
Record 2000 - 1st:0 2nd:0 3rd:0 Ran:9
Pre2000 - 1st:1 2nd:3 3rd:1 Ran:8
Win Prizemoney £25,000 *Total Prizemoney* £29,159
Wins * 1999 Spt Doncas (G-F) 6f 77 <

2000 Turf 0-8: (5f 3, 6f 4, 7f) (gd 2, g-f 4, frm, hrd) 2000 AW 0-1: (6f) (Fibr)
Leggy, above-average filly, effective 5 to 6f, best at 5f, acts on gd to frm. Turf high 73. **B A McMahon [1-17] Michael Stokes.*

KILCREGGAN BHB 45f43a RR 56f 43a 5294[6]

6 b g Landyap (USA) - Lehmans Lot (Oats) 8.9f **(46)**
Form - 833606
Record 2000 - 1st:0 2nd:0 3rd:2 Ran:6
Pre2000 - 1st:1 2nd:0 3rd:1 Ran:11
Win Prizemoney £3,315 *Total Prizemoney* £5,254
Wins * 1999 Oct Redcar (GD) H 14.1f 58 60 <
2000 Turf 0-5: (10f, 12f, 13f, 14f 2) (g-s, gd, g-f, frm 2) 2000 AW 0-1: (14f) (Fibr)
Fair gelding, effective 10 to 14f, acts on g-f to frm, best on frm. Turf high 56 - 3rd of 5 giving 23lb to Alpha Rose (22 May Musselburgh 14f frm RF 1369). **Mrs M Reveley [1-20] C Anderson.*

KILCULLEN LAD (IRE) BHB 60f64a RR 73f 64a 5112[13]

6 b g Fayruz 6.6f **(63)** - Royal Home (Royal Palace) 9f **(56)**
Form - 05230060350500
Record 2000 - 1st:0 2nd:1 3rd:2 Ran:14
Pre2000 - 1st:7 2nd:7 3rd:0 Ran:46
Win Prizemoney £35,783 *Total Prizemoney* £49,026

Wins									
	1999	Aug	Bright	(SFT)	H	5.3f	65	74	
	1998	May	Redcar	(G-F)	H	5f	75	81	<
	1997	May	Lingfi	(G-F)	H	6f	67	74	
	1996	*Dec*	*Lingfi*	*(STD)*	*H*	*6f*	*70*	*75*	
	1996	*Nov*	*Lingfi*	*(STD)*	*H*	*5f*	*61*	*77*	
	1996	Spt	Redcar	(FRM)	H	5f	56	53	
	1996	Jun	Lingfi	(FRM)	S	6f		48	

2000 Turf 0-14: (5f 7, 6f 7) (gd 5, g-f 3, frm 5, hrd)
Above-average gelding, effective 5 to 6f, best at 6f, acts on g-s to hrd, mostly wears blinkers (effectively), prefers left handed tracks, excels at Salisbury and Bath. Turf high 73 - 2nd of 19 getting 6lb from Bold Effort (13 Jun Salisbury 6f g-f RF 1921).
**Lady Herries [0-14] George Tobitt (from R Ingram [1-14] Oct 1999).*

KILDARE CHILLER (IRE) BHB 52f RR 54f 4304[18]

6 b g Shahrastani (USA) 11.5f **(69)** - Ballycuirke (Taufan (USA)) 7f **(57)**
Form - 0
Record 2000 - 1st:0 2nd:0 3rd:0 Ran:1
Pre2000 - 1st:3 2nd:1 3rd:0 Ran:19
Win Prizemoney £10,497 *Total Prizemoney* £11,285

Wins									
	1999	Oct	Currag	(SFT)	H	9f	51	54	
	1998	Nov	Currag	(SFT)	H	9f	54	54+	
	1998	Jly	Killar	(G-S)	H	11f	51	65	<

2000 Turf 0-1: (8f) (gd)
Fair gelding, effective 9 to 11f, acts on sft to g-s, likes right handed tracks.
**P R Hedger [0-1] P R Hedger (from F Flood in IRE [5-29] Oct 1999).*

KILLARNEY RR 17f 5223[20]

2 gr f Pursuit of Love 9.5f **(69)** - Laune (AUS) **(50f)** (Kenmare (FR)) 6.5f **(72)**
Form - 0
Record 2000 - 1st:0 2nd:0 3rd:0 Ran:1
2000 Turf 0-1: (6f) (gd)
Currently poor filly.
**R Hannon [0-1] Exors of the late Lord Howard de Walden.*

KILLARNEY JAZZ BHB 49f56a RR 49f 56a 2819[8]

5 b g Alhijaz 7.7f **(57)** - Killarney Belle (USA) (Irish Castle (USA)) 11.2f **(75)**
Form - 48838150258
Record 2000 - 1st:1 2nd:1 3rd:1 Ran:10
Pre2000 - 1st:3 2nd:2 3rd:2 Ran:21
Win Prizemoney £8,203 *Total Prizemoney* £11,886

Wins									
	* **2000**	*Apr*	*Southw*	*(STD)*	*S*	*8f*		*54+*	
	1998	*May*	*Southw*	*(STD)*	*C*	*8f*		*71+*	<
	1998	*Mar*	*Southw*	*(STD)*	*C*	*8f*		*69*	
	1998	*Feb*	*Southw*	*(STD)*	*H*	*8f*	*59*	*62*	

2000 Turf 0-1: (7f) (gd) 2000 AW 1-9: (7f 2, 8f 1-6, 11f) (Fibr 1-9)
Average gelding, effective 7 to 9f, best at 8f, - acts on Fibr, often wears blinkers, favours tight tracks. AW high 62 - 2nd of 16 giving 25lb to Imbackagain (22 Jun Southwell 7f Fibr RF 2195) - also 1st of 16 from Waiting Knight (11 Apr Southwell RF 0669).
**G C H Chung [1-16] G C H Chung (from N P Littmoden [1-8] Feb 1999).*

KILMEENA LAD BHB 55f76a RR 60f 76a 4826[12]

4 b g Minshaanshu Amad (USA) 11.3f **(53)** - Kilmeena Glen (Beveled (USA)) 9f **(59)**
Form - 7441000500772O
Record 2000 - 1st:1 2nd:1 3rd:0 Ran:12
Pre2000 - 1st:3 2nd:0 3rd:1 Ran:16
Win Prizemoney £17,590 *Total Prizemoney* £19,894

Wins									
	* **2000**	*Feb*	*Lingfi*	*(STD)*	*H*	*7f*	*76*	*80*	<
	* *1999*	*Oct*	*Lingfi*	*(STD)*	*H*	*6f*	*72*	*75*	
	* 1999	Aug	Newmar	(G-F)	H	6f	69	70	
	* 1998	Oct	Newbur	(HVY)		6f		80	<

2000 Turf 0-10: (6f 7, 7f 2, 8f) (gd 4, g-f 3, frm 2, hrd) 2000 AW 1-2: (7f 1-1, 8f) (Equi 1-2)
Workmanlike, decent gelding, effective 6 to 8f, best at 6f, acts on frm - acts on Equi, has worn blinkers, prefers left handed tracks. Turf high 60. AW high 80 - 1st of 11 getting 7lb from Juwwi (5 Feb Lingfield RF 0226). Inconsistent. **E A Wheeler [4-28] Mrs J A Cleary.*

KILMEENA STAR RR 33f 5217[5]

2 b c So Factual (USA) - Kilmeena Glen (Beveled (USA)) 9f **(59)**
Form - 05
Record 2000 - 1st:0 2nd:0 3rd:0 Ran:2
2000 Turf 0-2: (5f, 6f) (sft, gd)
Currently very moderate colt. Turf high 33 (began Spt).
**E A Wheeler [0-2] Mrs J A Cleary.*

KIMOE WARRIOR BHB 48f RR 50f 4828[10]

2 ch c Royal Abjar (USA) - Thewaari (USA) (Eskimo (USA))
Form - 50050
Record 2000 - 1st:0 2nd:0 3rd:0 Ran:5
2000 Turf 0-5: (6f 3, 7f, 8f) (g-s 2, gd 3)
Fair colt. Turf high 50. **M Mullineaux [0-5] Birch Vale Racing.*

KINAN (USA) BHB 80f RR 86f 5165[17]

4 b c Dixieland Band (USA) 10.1f **(80)** - Alsharta (USA) (Mr Prospector (USA)) 8.8f **(78)**
Form - 010036060
Record 2000 - 1st:1 2nd:0 3rd:1 Ran:9
Pre2000 - 1st:1 2nd:1 3rd:0 Ran:8
Win Prizemoney £10,584 *Total Prizemoney* £12,712

Wins									
	* **2000**	Jly	Epsom	(G-S)	H	7f	81	85	<
	1998	Spt	Nottin	(GD)		6.1f		85	<

2000 Turf 1-9: (6f 2, 7f 1-7) (sft, g-s, gd 1-5, g-f, frm)
Workmanlike, useful colt, effective 7f, acts on sft to gd, prefers tight tracks. Turf high 86 - also 1st of 12 giving 23lb to Contrary Mary (5 Jly Epsom RF 2548). Inconsistent. He landed a competitive handicap at Epsom in July and ran a good race in heavy ground at Haydock in September. Seven furlongs is his trip.
**G C Bravery [1-9] Sawyer Whatley Partnership (from R W Armstrong [1-8] May 1999).*

KIND EMPEROR BHB 53f67a RR 56f 67a 4825[21]

3 br g Emperor Jones (USA) - Kind Lady (Kind of Hush) 10.1f **(62)**
Form - 3442537004R0280
Record 2000 - 1st:0 2nd:2 3rd:1 Ran:14
Pre2000 - 1st:0 2nd:5 3rd:2 Ran:14
Win Prizemoney £0 *Total Prizemoney* £11,755
2000 Turf 0-11: (5f 2, 6f 7, 7f, 9f) (sft, g-s, gd 3, g-f 3, frm 3) 2000 AW 0-3: (5f, 6f 2) (Fibr 3)
Light-framed, average gelding, effective 5 to 6f, best at 6f, acts on gd to frm, best on gd, has worn blinkers. Turf high 74 (1st run) - 2nd of 13 to Look Here Now (25 Mar Doncaster 6f gd RF 0492). AW high 61. **M J Polglase [0-28] Emperor Alliance.*

KIND REGARDS (IRE) BHB 110f RR 111+f 5094a[4]

3 b f Unfuwain (USA) 11.4f **(74)** - Barari (USA) (Blushing Groom (FR)) 10.3f **(76)**
Form - 052545111514
Record 2000 - 1st:4 2nd:1 3rd:0 Ran:12
Pre2000 - 1st:1 2nd:1 3rd:0 Ran:5
Win Prizemoney £75,375 *Total Prizemoney* £83,669

Wins									
	* **2000**	Spt	Ascot	(SFT)	H	12f	88	111+	<
	* **2000**	Aug	Newcas	(G-S)	LH	10.1f	88	101+	
	* **2000**	Aug	Hamilt	(SFT)	H	9.2f	82	94	
	* **2000**	Aug	Beverl	(G-F)	H	9.9f	82	89	

* 1999 Spt Beverl (GD) 7.5f 78
2000 Turf 4-12: (7f 2, 8f 3, 9f 1-2, 10f 2-3, 12f 1-2) (sft, g-s 2-2, gd 1-4, g-f 3, frm 1-2)
Leggy, Group-class filly, effective 10 to 12f, acts on g-s, prefers right handed tracks. Turf high 111 - 1st of 11 getting 6lb from Romantic Affair (24 Spt Ascot RF 4611). On a roll in August, winning at Hamilton and completing a hat-trick in a Listed fillies' handicap at Newcastle, but was well and truly found out in Group Three company at Goodwood, before scoring back in handicap company at Ascot. **M Johnston [5-17].*

KIND SIR BHB 69f70a **RR 68?f 70a** 595[8]
4 b g Generous (IRE) 11.5f **(82)** - Noble Conquest (USA) (Vaguely Noble) 10.1f **(72)**
Form - 8
Record 2000 - 1st:0 2nd:0 3rd:0 Ran:1
Pre2000 - 1st:1 2nd:0 3rd:0 Ran:4
Win Prizemoney £3,538 *Total Prizemoney* £3,788
Wins 1999 *Feb Lingfi (STD) 10f 80+* <
2000 Turf 0-1: (12f) (sft)
Scopey, decent gelding.
**R Dickin [0-6] B K Smith (from B W Hills [1-4] Mar 1999).*

KING ADAM (IRE) BHB 113f **RR 115+f** 4967[6]
4 b c Fairy King (USA) 7.7f **(75)** - Sailor's Mate (Shirley Heights) 10.3f **(74)**
Form - 1546
Record 2000 - 1st:1 2nd:0 3rd:0 Ran:4
Pre2000 - 1st:2 2nd:2 3rd:0 Ran:5
Win Prizemoney £24,913 *Total Prizemoney* £36,982
Wins * **2000** Jun Doncas (G-F) 10.3f 115+ <
* 1999 Jun Kempto (G-F) L 10f 115+ <
* 1998 Spt Goodwo (G-S) 8f 104+
2000 Turf 1-4: (9f 2, 10f 1-2) (gd 1-4)
Scopey, high-class colt, effective 10 to 12f, best at 10f, acts on gd to frm, best on frm. Turf high 115 - also 1st of 6 giving 7lb to Tissifer (10 Jun Doncaster RF 1870). He has always been held in high regard, but proved slightly disappointing after a smooth win on his belated reappearance. Still lightly raced, he goes well when fresh and is one to note if not too highly tried on his seasonal bow in 2001. **Sir Michael Stoute [3-9] Lord Weinstock.*

KING CAREW (IRE) **RR 84f** 4853[5]
2 b c Fairy King (USA) 7.7f **(75)** - Kareena (Riverman (USA)) 9.1f **(76)**
Form - 25
Record 2000 - 1st:0 2nd:1 3rd:0 Ran:2
Win Prizemoney £0 *Total Prizemoney* £4,565
2000 Turf 0-2: (7f, 8f) (sft, g-s)
Currently decent colt. Turf high 84 (began Spt).
**M R Channon [0-2] John Carey.*

KING CHARLEMAGNE (USA) **RR 98+f** 4733[1]
2 b c Nureyev (USA) 8.4f **(84)** - Race The Wild Wind (USA) (Sunny's Halo (CAN)) 6.7f **(70)**
Form - 211
2000 Turf 2-3: (6f 1-2, 7f 1-1) (gd 2-2, frm)
Currently very useful colt. Turf high 98 (began Aug) - 1st of 13 from Grandera (29 Spt Newmarket RF 4733) - also 1st of 12 from Dr Dignity (9 Spt Leopardstown RF 4351a). Runner-up on his debut at York, he made no mistake at prohibitive odds at Leopardstown. Followed up with a battling success in the Somerville Tattersall Stakes at Newmarket.
**A P O'Brien in IRE [2-3] M Tabor & Mrs John Magnier.*

KINGCHIP BOY BHB 36f36a **RR 20f 36a** 417[10]
11 b g Petong 7.6f **(58)** - Silk St James (Pas de Seul) 9.1f **(67)**
Form - 70037705600
Record 2000 - 1st:0 2nd:0 3rd:1 Ran:8
Pre2000 - 1st:25 2nd:16 3rd:8 Ran:147
Win Prizemoney £70,983 *Total Prizemoney* £96,646
Wins * 1999 *May Wolver (Std) C 9.4f 59*
* 1999 *Mar Southw (STD) C 8f 64*
* 1999 *Feb Wolver (STD) S 8.5f 67*
* 1999 *Feb Southw (STD) H 7f 55 63*
* 1999 *Jan Southw (STD) H 8f 50 57*
* 1998 *Feb Southw (STD) C 7f 68+*
* 1998 *Feb Southw (STD) H 7f 65 71*
* 1998 *Jan Southw (STD) H 8f 56 61*
* 1997 *Feb Southw (STD) H 8f 71 79* <
* 1997 *Feb Southw (STD) H 8f 71 75*
* 1997 *Jan Southw (STD) H 7f 68 68*
* 1996 *Apr Southw (STD) H 8f 64 69*
* 1996 *Jan Southw (STD) H 8f 46 66+*
* 1996 *Jan Southw (STD) H 8f 46 67*
* 1996 *Jan Southw (STD) H 8f 49 57*
2000 AW 0-8: (7f, 8f 6, 9f) (Fibr 8)
Very moderate gelding, effective 7 to 9f, best at 8f, - acts on Fibr, often wears blinkers, and excels at Wolverhampton. AW high 46.
**M J Ryan [25-156] Doug Fleet.*

KING CUGAT (USA) **RR 120f** 5327a[11]
3 b c Kingmambo (USA) 10.9f **(85)** - Tricky Game (USA) (Majestic Light (USA)) 10.6f **(75)**
Form - 20
2000 Turf 0-2: (8f, 10f) (g-s, frm)
Currently very high-class colt. Turf high 120 (1st run) (began Aug) - 2nd of 8 giving 3lb to Ciro (19 Aug Arlington Park 10f g-s RF 3943a). Runner-up to Ciro in the Secretariat, he was well supported for tthe Breeders' Cup Mile, but did not get the best of runs and was unable to make an impression.
**W Mott in USA [0-2] Centennial Farms.*

KINGDOM OF GOLD (USA) BHB 81f **RR 84f** 2649[4]
3 b c Gone West (USA) 7.8f **(82)** - Aviara (USA) (Cox's Ridge (USA)) 8f **(68)**
Form - 044
Record 2000 - 1st:0 2nd:0 3rd:0 Ran:3
Pre2000 - 1st:1 2nd:0 3rd:0 Ran:3
Win Prizemoney £3,420 *Total Prizemoney* £5,075
Wins * 1999 Aug Hamilt (G-F) 8.3f 73+ <
2000 Turf 0-3: (8f, 10f 2) (gd, g-f, frm)
Workmanlike, decent colt. Turf high 84.
**Sir Mark Prescott [1-6] Faisal Salman.*

KINGFISHER EVE (IRE) RR 4012[13]
2 b f Hamas (IRE) 8f **(72)** - Houwara (IRE) (Darshaan) 9.9f **(84)**
Form - 0
Record 2000 - 1st:0 2nd:0 3rd:0 Ran:1
2000 Turf 0-1: (8f) (frm)
Currently very poor filly. **C Grant [0-1] C E Whiteley.*

KINGFISHER GOLD (IRE) BHB 40f **RR 41f** 1203[26]
4 b g Perugino (USA) - Cerosia (Pitskelly) 8.5f **(53)**
Form - 0
Record 2000 - 1st:0 2nd:0 3rd:0 Ran:1
Pre2000 - 1st:0 2nd:0 3rd:0 Ran:8
2000 Turf 0-1: (8f) (frm)
Scopey, moderate gelding.
**N Wilson [0-1] Goaled Fish (from T P Tate [0-8] Oct 1999).*

KINGFISHERS BONNET BHB 41f36a **RR 55f 36a** 3329[7]
4 b f Hamas (IRE) 8f **(72)** - Mainmast (Bustino) 10.4f **(64)**
Form - 713540387
Record 2000 - 1st:1 2nd:0 3rd:2 Ran:9
Pre2000 - 1st:0 2nd:3 3rd:2 Ran:19
Win Prizemoney £2,478 *Total Prizemoney* £7,159
Wins * **2000** Apr Warwic (HVY) H 10.5f 42 55 <
2000 Turf 1-8: (10f 5, 11f 1-2, 12f) (hvy 1-1, sft, gd 2, g-f 3, frm) 2000 AW 0-1: (8f) (Fibr)
Leggy, fair filly, effective 10 to 12f, best at 11f, acts on hvy to frm, favours tight tracks. Turf high 55 (1st run) - 1st of 18 giving 3lb to Rock Scene (12 Apr Warwick RF 0689). Becoming disappointing.
**S G Knight [1-28] P J Wightman.*

KING FLYER (IRE) BHB 73f63a **RR 73f 63a** 4399[1]
4 b g Ezzoud (IRE) - Al Guswa (Shernazar) 10.2f **(73)**
Form - 605211221
Record 2000 - 1st:3 2nd:3 3rd:0 Ran:9
Pre2000 - 1st:1 2nd:3 3rd:3 Ran:13
Win Prizemoney £24,065 *Total Prizemoney* £33,987
Wins * **2000** Spt Yarmou (G-F) H 18.2f 70 73 <
* **2000** Aug Sandow (GD) H 14f 65 67
* **2000** Jly Newmar (GD) H 14.8f 60 65
* 1999 Jun Newmar (G-F) C 10f 56
2000 Turf 3-8: (12f 2, 14f 1-3, 15f 1-1, 16f, 18f 1-1) (gd 1-3, g-f 2-3, frm

2) 2000 AW 0-1: (13f) (Equi)

Small, above-average gelding, effective 12 to 18f, acts on gd to frm, best on g-f, has worn blinkers, prefers right handed tracks, and excels at Sandown. Turf high 73 - 1st of 4 getting 14lb from Eastwell Hall (14 Spt Yarmouth RF 4399) - also 1st of 6 giving 3lb to Copyforce Girl (9 Aug Sandown RF 3510). Improving.

**H J Collingridge [4-18] In The Know (2) (from B Hanbury [0-4] Oct 1998).*

KING FOR A DAY BHB 37f **RR 43f** 4445[12]

4 b g Machiavellian (USA) 9.8f **(83)** - Dizzy Heights (USA) (Danzig (USA)) 8.4f **(76)**

Form - 0041440

Record 2000 - 1st:1 2nd:0 3rd:0 Ran:7
Pre2000 - 1st:0 2nd:0 3rd:1 Ran:9

Win Prizemoney £2,873 *Total Prizemoney* £3,775

Wins * **2000** Jly Yarmou (G-F) H 14.1f 38 41 <

2000 Turf 1-7: (12f, 14f 1-3, 16f 3) (gd 2, g-f, frm 1-4)

Well made, moderate gelding, often wears blinkers (effectively), likes left handed tracks. Turf high 43.

**Bob Jones [1-14] Mrs Joan Marioni (from B W Hills [0-8] Jun 1999).*

KING HALO (JPN) RR 115f 1828a[3]

5 b h Dancing Bravo (USA) 10.4f **(78)** - Goodbye Halo (USA) (Halo (USA)) 10.6f **(75)**

Form - 3

2000 Turf 0-1: (8f) (frm)

Currently high-class colt. - 3rd of 18 to Fairy King Prawn (4 Jun Fuchu 8f frm RF 1828a). **M Sakaguchi in JPN [0-1].*

KING OF INDIA (IRE) RR 47f 3048[8]

2 ch g Indian Ridge 7.6f **(74)** - Total Chic (USA) (Far North (CAN)) 9.7f **(75)**

Form - 8

Record 2000 - 1st:0 2nd:0 3rd:0 Ran:1

2000 Turf 0-1: (7f) (frm)

Currently moderate gelding. **E A L Dunlop [0-1] Mohammed Jaber.*

KING OF MOMMUR (IRE) BHB 47f **RR 53f** 2242[4]

5 b g Fairy King (USA) 7.7f **(75)** - Monoglow (Kalaglow) 9.8f **(67)**

Form - 31

Record 2000 - 1st:0 2nd:0 3rd:1 Ran:2
Pre2000 - 1st:0 2nd:0 3rd:3 Ran:15

Win Prizemoney £0 *Total Prizemoney* £2,712

2000 Turf 0-2: (13f, 16f) (g-s, gd)

Fair gelding, effective 12f, acts on g-f, has worn blinkers, likes right handed tracks, likes tight tracks. Turf high 53. Consistent.

**B R Millman [1-6] The Three Bears Racing (from B J Meehan [0-15] Spt 1999).*

KING OF PERU BHB 70f80a **RR 70f 80a** 4039[4]

7 b g Inca Chief (USA) 5.6f **(45)** - Julie's Star (IRE) (Thatching) 8f **(66)**

Form - 5564422011424

Record 2000 - 1st:2 2nd:3 3rd:0 Ran:13
Pre2000 - 1st:5 2nd:7 3rd:8 Ran:59

Win Prizemoney £37,226 *Total Prizemoney* £62,524

Wins * **2000** Aug Kempto (G-F) C 5f 63
* **2000** Jly Catter (G-F) C 5f 61
1999 May Bright (FRM) H 6f 60 61
1996 May Goodwo (GD) H 7f 100 97 <

2000 Turf 2-11: (5f 2-7, 6f 4) (gd 3, g-f 3, frm 2-5) 2000 AW 0-2: (5f, 6f) (Fibr 2)

Decent gelding, effective 6f, - acts on Fibr, has worn blinkers, likes left handed tracks, likes tight tracks. Turf high 70. AW high 81 (1st run) - 5th of 13 getting 1lb from Blue Star (11 Mar Wolverhampton 6f Fibr RF 0432).

**D Nicholls [2-5] The Gardening Partnership (from N P Littmoden [1-45] Jly 2000).*

KING OF RUSSIA RR 92f 3657a[3]

3 b c Common Grounds 8.1f **(66)** - Heart of India (IRE) (Try My Best (USA)) 7.6f **(67)**

Form - 413863

2000 Turf 1-6: (5f 2, 6f 1-3, 7f) (sft, gd, g-f 1-3, frm)

Useful colt, effective 6f, acts on frm. Turf high 92 - 3rd of 9 giving 15lb to Reptar (9 Aug Fairyhouse 6f frm RF 3657a).

**E Lynam in IRE [3-9] R P Behan.*

KING OF SPAIN (USA) RR 54f 3777[3]

3 ch c Rahy (USA) 9.1f **(80)** - Royal Fandango (USA) **(92f)** (Slew O' Gold (USA)) 8f **(75)**

Form - 3

Record 2000 - 1st:0 2nd:0 3rd:1 Ran:1

Win Prizemoney £0 *Total Prizemoney* £595

2000 Turf 0-1: (8f) (gd)

Well made, currently fair colt.

**M Johnston [0-1] Maktoum Al Maktoum.*

KING OF THE WEST (USA) RR 36f 2608[7]

4 ch g St Jovite (USA) 11.8f **(75)** - Espuela (USA) (Gone West (USA)) 6.5f **(75)**

Form - 07

Record 2000 - 1st:0 2nd:0 3rd:0 Ran:2

2000 Turf 0-2: (10f, 14f) (g-s, gd)

Workmanlike, currently very moderate gelding.

**J J Sheehan [0-2] Mrs Eileen Sheehan.*

KING OF TRUTH RR 3018[6]

2 b g King's Signet (USA) 7f **(51)** - Total Truth (Reesh)

Form - 6

Record 2000 - 1st:0 2nd:0 3rd:0 Ran:1

2000 AW 0-1: (5f) (Fibr)

Little account gelding. (DEAD)

**T T Clement [0-1] Whitwell Bloodstock.*

KING O' THE MANA (IRE) BHB 108f **RR 110f** 5130[7]

3 b c Turtle Island (IRE) - Olivia Jane (IRE) (Ela-Mana-Mou) 10.1f **(70)**

Form - 84132347

Record 2000 - 1st:1 2nd:1 3rd:2 Ran:8
Pre2000 - 1st:2 2nd:1 3rd:0 Ran:5

Win Prizemoney £43,148 *Total Prizemoney* £66,451

Wins * **2000** May Bath (G-S) 10.2f 102 <
* 1999 Aug Newcas (GD) H 8f 90 100+
* 1999 Jly Warwic (G-F) 6.8f 84

2000 Turf 1-8: (8f 2, 10f 1-1, 11f, 12f 3, 15f) (sft, g-s, gd 1-5, g-f)

Workmanlike, Group-class colt, effective 8 to 15f, best at 12f, acts on g-s to g-f, best on gd. Turf high 110 - 4th of 7 to Epitre (30 Spt Longchamp 15f gd RF 4840a) - also 1st of 9 giving 2lb to Riddlesdown (2 May Bath RF 0960). A useful nursery performer in '99, he disappointed in his first couple of starts last term but found a winning opportunity in a Bath classified stakes. Put in a fair run in the Lingfield Derby Trial next time, and ran well in the autumn after more than four months off. Did not seem to stay when tried at a mile and seven. **R Hannon [3-13] D Boocock.*

KING PRIAM (IRE) BHB 90f93a **RR 99df 93a** 2151[13]

5 b g Priolo (USA) 10.9f **(71)** - Barinia (Corvaro (USA)) 9f **(53)**

Form - 1115231362008500

Record 2000 - 1st:1 2nd:1 3rd:2 Ran:11
Pre2000 - 1st:8 2nd:7 3rd:6 Ran:47

Win Prizemoney £49,032 *Total Prizemoney* £82,079

Wins * **2000** *Feb Wolver (STD) 8.5f 97* <
* 1999 *Dec Wolver (STD) H 9.4f 86 91*
* 1999 *Dec Wolver (STD) H 8.5f 80 89*
* 1999 *Nov Southw (STD) H 8f 74 79*
* 1999 Oct York (G-S) H 10.4f 70 75
* 1999 Spt Haydoc (SFT) H 8.1f 57 69+
* 1999 Spt Leices (GD) 8f 66
* 1999 *Mar Southw (STD) H 8f 68 72*
1998 Oct Newmar (gd) C 12f 66

2000 Turf 0-6: (8f 4, 9f, 10f) (sft 2, g-s, gd 3) 2000 AW 1-5: (8f 1-3, 9f 2) (Fibr 1-4, Dirt)

Very useful gelding, effective 8 to 9f, best at 8f, acts on gd - acts on Fibr, mostly wears blinkers (very effectively), likes left handed tracks, likes tight tracks, and excels at Wolverhampton. Turf high 101. AW high 97 - 1st of 7 from Weet-A-Minute (3 Feb Wolverhampton RF 0211). Becoming disappointing. Kept very busy, he was in fine form on the All-Weather before finishing a close second in the Lincoln, but was well beaten when tried in Group company and in some warm handicaps. Absent after June, he needs a strongly-run race and is suited by trips just in excess of a mile.

**M J Polglase [8-50] Ian Puddle (from M C Pipe [1-5] Oct 1998).*

KING ROLLER (USA) RR 1822a^1
9 ch g Silent King (USA) - Native Roller (USA) (Native Cadet (USA))
Form - 1
2000 AW 1-1: (6f 1-1) (Dirt 1-1)
Currently useful gelding. (1st run) - 1st of 9 giving 3lb to Balancethebudget (3 Jun Suffolk Downs RF 1822a).
**P Bazeos in USA [1-1] A Pyliotis.*

KINGSALSA (USA) RR 118f 4843a^2
4 br c Kingmambo (USA) 10.9f **(85)** - Caretta (Caro)
Form - 3213322
2000 Turf 1-6: (8f 1-6) (hvy, sft 1-2, g-s, gd, g-f) 2000 AW 0-1: (12f) (Dirt)
High-class colt, effective 8 to 12f, best at 8f, acts on hvy to gd - acts on Dirt. Turf high 118 - 2nd of 8 to Kabool (1 Oct Longchamp 8f gd RF 4843a) - also 1st of 7 from Banyumanik (30 May Chantilly RF 1818a). (1st run) - 3rd of 11 to Rhythm Band (25 Mar Nad Al Sheba 12f Dirt RF 0579a). Consistent. He returned in good form after an injury-curtailed campaign in 1999, running his best race when chasing Indian Lodge home in the Prix du Moulin. Often given too much to do (certainly the case behind Kabool in the Prix du Rond-Point), he is worth another try beyond a mile and can add to his sole Group race success.
**A Fabre in FR [1-9] D Wildenstein (from P Demercastel in FR [0-1] Spt 1998).*

Record	**2000 -**	1st:1	2nd:1	3rd:0	Ran:3
	Pre2000 -	1st:2	2nd:0	3rd:0	Ran:3

Win Prizemoney £199,048 *Total Prizemoney* £210,348

Wins						
*** 2000**	May	Newmar (GD)	G1	8f	127	<
* 1999	Aug	York (GD)	L	7f	111+	
* 1999	Aug	Newmar (GD)		7f	88++	

2000 Turf 1-3: (8f 1-2, 12f) (gd 1-3)
Top-class colt, effective 8f, acts on gd. Turf high 127 - 1st of 27 from Giant's Causeway (6 May Newmarket RF 1060). He hardly put a foot wrong on his first two starts at two in 1999, but got his tongue over the bit and pulled like a train when running poorly in the Dewhurst Stakes. Went some way to redeeming his reputation when second in the Craven on his seasonal bow, settling better, before producing a stunning display in the Guineas, showing great acceleration to win going away. That was to be the highlight, for he was forced to miss the Derby, and then pulled up in the Irish Derby with a fractured off-fore cannon bone, prematurely ending his career. He was however, rated second only to Sinndar among the three-year-olds in the International Classifications, and represents an interesting stud prospect who will stand at Kildangan Stud at a fee of IR£25,000. **Sir Michael Stoute [3-6] Saeed Suhail.*

KING'S BOY (GER) RR 114f 4412a^2
3 ch c Platini (GER)
Form - 02

Kingsalsa was placed in some hot races

2000 Turf 0-2: (12f 2) (sft, gd)
Currently Group-class colt. Turf high 114 (began Jly) - 2nd of 8 to Caitano (9 Spt Veliefendi 12f gd RF 4412a). **A Wohler in GER [0-2].*

KING'S BALLET (USA) BHB 92f **RR 90f** 5107^{10}
2 b c Imperial Ballet (IRE) - Multimara (USA) (Arctic Tern (USA)) 8.9f **(69)**
Form - 810

Record	**2000 -**	1st:1	2nd:0	3rd:0	Ran:3

Win Prizemoney £4,634 *Total Prizemoney* £4,634

Wins					
*** 2000**	Spt	Haydoc (SFT)	5f	90	<

2000 Turf 1-3: (5f 1-3) (gd 1-2, frm)
Currently useful colt. Turf high 90 - 1st of 14 from Benedictine (1 Spt Haydock RF 4149). Handled the soft ground well when getting off the mark at Haydock on his second start and should win more races under those conditions.
**P J Makin [1-3] Admin of the late C Stelling.*

KING'S BEST (USA) BHB 125f **RR 127f** 2530a^P
3 b c Kingmambo (USA) 10.9f **(85)** - Allegretta (Lombard (GER)) 10.5f **(66)**
Form - 21P

KINGS CAY (IRE) BHB 22f **RR 27f** 376^{12}
9 b g Taufan (USA) 8.3f **(65)** - Provocation (Kings Lake (USA)) 10.8f **(67)**
Form - 740

Record	**2000 -**	1st:0	2nd:0	3rd:0	Ran:3
	Pre2000 -	1st:5	2nd:4	3rd:4	Ran:40

Win Prizemoney £17,405 *Total Prizemoney* £24,348

Wins						
* 1996	Jly	Hamilt (GD)	H	11.1f	51	59
* 1996	Jun	Carlis (FRM)		12f		62
* 1996	Jun	Ripon (G-F)	H	12.3f	46	55

2000 AW 0-3: (12f 2, 15f) (Fibr 3)
Little account gelding, has worn blinkers. AW high 22.
**T H Caldwell [3-42] T H Caldwell (from D R Loder [2-6] Jun 1994).*

KING'S CHAMBERS BHB 29f **RR 32f** 4494^{2}

4 ch g Sabrehill (USA) 8.5f **(64)** - Flower Girl (Pharly (FR)) 9.8f **(68)**

Form - 00000552

Record 2000 - 1st:0 2nd:1 3rd:0 Ran:6
Pre2000 - 1st:0 2nd:0 3rd:0 Ran:3

Win Prizemoney £0 *Total Prizemoney* £587

2000 Turf 0-4: (6f, 12f 2, 14f) (g-s, g-f 3) 2000 AW 0-2: (7f, 8f) (Fibr 2)

Light-framed, very moderate gelding, effective 12f, acts on g-s, often wears blinkers, favours tight tracks. Turf high 32 - 2nd of 14 getting 5lb from Field of Vision (19 Spt Beverley 12f g-s RF 4494). Improving.

**J Parkes [0-3] P J Cronin (from R F Marvin [0-6] May 2000).*

KINGSCLERE BHB 105f **RR 110df** 4004^{9}

3 b g Fairy King (USA) 7.7f **(75)** - Spurned (USA) (Robellino (USA)) 7.6f **(80)**

Form - 15050

Record 2000 - 1st:1 2nd:0 3rd:0 Ran:5
Pre2000 - 1st:2 2nd:1 3rd:2 Ran:6

Win Prizemoney £29,428 *Total Prizemoney* £56,530

Wins * 2000 Apr Kempto (SFT) L 8f 110 <
* 1999 Jly York (G-F) 7f 93+
* 1999 Jun Newbur (GD) 6f 85+

2000 Turf 1-5: (8f 1-1, 10f, 12f 3) (sft 1-1, gd 3, g-f)

Leggy, Group-class colt, effective 7 to 12f, best at 8f, acts on sft to g-f, best on g-f. Turf high 110 (1st run) - 1st of 6 from Safarando (22 Apr Kempton RF 0830). Becoming disappointing. He won a Listed event at Kempton in April and looked unlucky when fifth in the Chester Vase. Virtually unsteerable in the Derby, he pulled far too hard on his last two starts and has reportedly been gelded. He has a stack of ability but cannot be supported until learning to settle.

**I A Balding [3-11] M Tabor.*

KING'S COUNTY (IRE) RR 116f $5214a^{2}$

2 b c Fairy King (USA) 7.7f **(75)** - Kardelle **(31f)** (Kalaglow) 9.8f **(67)**

Form - 1222

2000 Turf 1-4: (6f 1-1, 7f, 8f 2) (hvy, sft, g-f 1-1)

High-class colt. Turf high 116 (began Jly) - 2nd of 7 to Okawango (8 Oct Longchamp 8f sft RF 4952a). Scrambled home in a Leopardstown maiden on his debut, but ran well to finish runner-up to stable-companion Beckett in the National Stakes, and was subsequently a good second in Gran Criteriums in France and Italy. A high-class colt who is likely to appreciate further in 2001.

**A P O'Brien in IRE [1-4] M Tabor & Mrs John Magnier.*

KING'S CREST BHB 66f61a **RR 64f 61a** 5103^{2}

2 b g Deploy 11.4f **(67)** - Classic Beauty (IRE) **(48f 54a)** (Fairy King (USA)) 7.7f **(59)**

Form - 06641452

Record 2000 - 1st:1 2nd:1 3rd:0 Ran:8

Win Prizemoney £5,232 *Total Prizemoney* £7,019

Wins * 2000 Spt Mussel (G-S) H 8f 49 56+ <

2000 Turf 1-7: (5f 2, 8f 1-4, 10f) (g-s, gd 1-4, g-f 2) 2000 AW 0-1: (6f) (Fibr)

Average gelding, effective 8 to 10f, best at 8f, acts on gd to g-f, best on gd. Turf high 64 - 2nd of 12 getting 10lb from Borders Belle (20 Oct Doncaster 8f gd RF 5103) - also 1st of 13 getting 18lb from Lady Bear (24 Spt Musselburgh RF 4623). Inconsistent.

**S C Williams [1-8] Ivyclose.*

KINGSCROSS RR 73f 5102^{7}

2 ch c King's Signet (USA) 7f **(51)** - Calamanco **(65f 66a)** (Clantime)

Form - 07

Record 2000 - 1st:0 2nd:0 3rd:0 Ran:2

2000 Turf 0-2: (5f, 6f) (gd 2)

Currently above-average colt. Turf high 73 (began Spt).

**Major D N Chappell [0-2] Mrs D Ellis.*

KINGSDON (IRE) BHB 84f **RR 93f** 4934^{5}

3 b c Brief Truce (USA) 9.1f **(73)** - Richly Deserved (IRE) (Kings Lake (USA)) 10.8f **(67)**

Form - 6300654405

Record 2000 - 1st:0 2nd:0 3rd:1 Ran:10
Pre2000 - 1st:2 2nd:2 3rd:1 Ran:5

Win Prizemoney £7,936 *Total Prizemoney* £13,863

Wins * 1999 Spt Salisb (HVY) 7f 93 +
* 1999 Aug Kempto (G-S) 6f 81

2000 Turf 0-10: (8f 8, 10f, 11f) (sft 2, g-s, gd 6, frm)

Scopey, useful colt, effective 7 to 11f, best at 7f, acts on sft to g-f, prefers tight tracks, excels at Sandown. Turf high 96. Fair efforts this term and is capable of winning again when conditions are in his favour, but needs some leniency from the Handicapper.

**R Hannon [2-15] Fieldspring Racing.*

KING'S GINGER BHB 43f44a **RR 62f 44a** 2275^{16}

3 ch g King's Signet (USA) 7f **(51)** - Cosset (Comedy Star (USA)) 7.5f **(50)**

Form - 073403800

Record 2000 - 1st:0 2nd:0 3rd:2 Ran:9
Pre2000 - 1st:0 2nd:0 3rd:2 Ran:6

Win Prizemoney £0 *Total Prizemoney* £1,969

2000 Turf 0-3: (8f 3) (g-s, gd, g-f) 2000 AW 0-6: (7f, 8f 2, 9f 2, 11f) (Fibr 6)

Strong, average gelding, effective 7 to 8f, acts on gd to g-f, has worn blinkers. Turf high 21. AW high 58. Inconsistent.

**Mrs N Macauley [0-2] Ralph Peters Wiltshire (from D J Wintle [0-7] May 2000).*

KING SILCA BHB 76f **RR 76f** 4265^{3}

3 b g Emarati (USA) 6.6f **(63)** - Silca-Cisa (Hallgate)

Form - 213803

Record 2000 - 1st:1 2nd:1 3rd:2 Ran:6

Win Prizemoney £4,030 *Total Prizemoney* £6,922

Wins * 2000 Jun Warwic (G-S) 6.8f 76 <

2000 Turf 1-6: (6f, 7f 1-5) (hvy, g-s 1-1, g-f 2, frm 2)

Above-average gelding, effective 7f, acts on g-s to g-f, best on g-f. Turf high 76 - 1st of 12 giving 5lb to Gwendoline (4 Jun Warwick RF 1704). Unraced at two, he has progressed well this term and seems to act on any ground. **M R Channon [1-6] Tim Corby.*

KING'S IRONBRIDGE (IRE) BHB 100f **RR 99f** 4988^{8}

2 b c King's Theatre (IRE) - Dream Chaser (Record Token) 6.3f **(53)**

Form - 21518

Record 2000 - 1st:2 2nd:1 3rd:0 Ran:5

Win Prizemoney £23,148 *Total Prizemoney* £25,116

Wins * 2000 Aug Sandow (GD) G3 7.1f 99 <
*** 2000** Jly Newmar (G-F) 7f 87+

2000 Turf 2-5: (6f, 7f 2-4) (gd 2, g-f 1-2, frm 1-1)

Very useful colt. Turf high 99 - 1st of 7 from Storming Home (19 Aug Sandown RF 3802). Was touched off on his debut in a hot maiden, but gained compensation when making all at Newmarket. Disappointed next time though there were excuses, and ran out a game winner of the Solario Stakes at Sandown. Out of his depth in the Dewhurst, he is likely to be avoiding the big guns in 2001.

**R Hannon [2-5] T A Johnsey.*

KING'S MILL (IRE) BHB 105f **RR 106f** 3583^{5}

3 b c Doyoun 10.7f **(69)** - Adarika (Kings Lake (USA)) 10.8f **(67)**

Form - 111855

Record 2000 - 1st:3 2nd:0 3rd:0 Ran:6
Pre2000 - 1st:0 2nd:2 3rd:1 Ran:4

Win Prizemoney £26,539 *Total Prizemoney* £33,116

Wins * 2000 May York (G-F) H 10.4f 92 99 <
*** 2000** Apr Newmar (SFT) H 10f 81 94
*** 2000** Apr Southw (G-S) 10f 93

2000 Turf 3-6: (10f 3-4, 11f, 12f) (g-s 1-1, gd 1-3, g-f 1-2)

Workmanlike, Pattern-class colt, effective 10 to 11f, best at 10f, acts on gd to g-f, best on gd. Turf high 106 - 5th of 9 to Ekraar (12 Aug Haydock 11f gd RF 3583) - also 1st of 15 getting 2lb from Secret Agent (16 May York RF 1219). Improving. Best over ten furlongs, he completed an early-season hat-trick in the style of a progressive performer and put in a very decent effort in a Group Three on his final start. **N A Graham [3-10] First Millennium Racing.*

KINGS OF EUROPE (USA) BHB 87f **RR 85f** 5238^{9}

2 b c Rainbow Quest (USA) 11.2f **(81)** - Bemissed (USA) (Nijinsky (CAN)) 10.3f **(77)**

Form - 420

Record 2000 - 1st:0 2nd:1 3rd:0 Ran:3

Win Prizemoney £0 *Total Prizemoney* £1,395

2000 Turf 0-3: (7f, 8f, 10f) (g-s, frm 2)

Currently useful colt. Turf high 85 (began Aug) - 2nd of 9 to Steel Band (28 Aug Chepstow 8f frm RF 4030). A half-brother to Jet Ski Lady, he looks a stayer in the making.

**B W Hills [0-3] Manchester United Racing Club.*

KING SPINNER (IRE) BHB 77f **RR 80f** 5101[3]
3 b g Mujadil (USA) 7.7f **(70)** - Money Spinner (USA) (Teenoso (USA)) 9.9f **(72)**
Form - 803
Record 2000 - 1st:0 2nd:0 3rd:1 Ran:3
Pre2000 - 1st:1 2nd:0 3rd:1 Ran:4
Win Prizemoney £3,297 *Total Prizemoney* £5,030
Wins * 1999 Oct Yarmou (G-S) 8f 72 <
2000 Turf 0-3: (8f, 10f 2) (gd 3)
Scopey, decent gelding, effective 7 to 8f, best at 7f, acts on gd. Turf high 74.
**A P Jarvis [1-7] Grant & Bowman Ltd.*

KING'S SECRET (USA) RR 98f 4482[2]
2 ch c Kingmambo (USA) 10.9f **(85)** - Mystery Rays (USA) (Nijinsky (CAN)) 10.3f **(77)**
Form - 32
Record 2000 - 1st:0 2nd:1 3rd:1 Ran:2
Win Prizemoney £0 *Total Prizemoney* £1,751
2000 Turf 0-2: (7f, 8f) (g-s, frm)
Currently very useful colt. Turf high 98 (began Spt) - 2nd of 10 to Worthily (18 Spt Kempton 8f g-s RF 4482).
**Sir Michael Stoute [0-2] Saeed Suhail.*

KINGS SIGNAL (USA) RR 53f 4689[8]
2 b c Red Ransom (USA) 8.6f **(83)** - Star of Albion (Ajdal (USA)) 9.2f **(89)**
Form - 8
Record 2000 - 1st:0 2nd:0 3rd:0 Ran:1
2000 Turf 0-1: (8f) (gd)
Currently fair colt.
**J J Sheehan [0-1] P J Sheehan.*

KINGSTON VENTURE BHB 89f **RR 97f** 1497[7]
4 b g Interrex (CAN) 7.7f **(51)** - Tricata (Electric) 10.1f **(61)**
Form - 7
Record 2000 - 1st:0 2nd:0 3rd:0 Ran:1
Pre2000 - 1st:3 2nd:1 3rd:0 Ran:10
Win Prizemoney £13,537 *Total Prizemoney* £16,498
Wins * 1999 May Lingfi (G-F) 11.5f 97 <
* 1999 Mar Doncas (GD) H 10.3f 74 78
* 1998 Jun Salisb (G-F) 7f 66
2000 Turf 0-1: (16f) (g-s)
Leggy, very useful gelding, effective 11 to 12f, acts on frm.
**W G M Turner [4-17] Miss Corinne Overton.*

KINGS TO OPEN BHB 40f49a **RR 46f 49a** 4327[13]
3 b g First Trump - Shadiyama (Nishapour (FR)) 9.1f **(61)**
Form - 76700
Record 2000 - 1st:0 2nd:0 3rd:0 Ran:5
Pre2000 - 1st:0 2nd:0 3rd:0 Ran:1
2000 Turf 0-4: (7f, 11f 3) (gd 2, g-f, frm) 2000 AW 0-1: (7f) (Fibr)
Light-framed, moderate gelding, has worn blinkers. Turf high 46.
**J A Osborne [0-5] Godiva (from D Marks [0-1] Spt 1999).*

KING'S VIEW BHB 61f **RR 64f** 3492[7]
3 b g Distant View (USA) - Migiyas (Kings Lake (USA)) 10.8f **(67)**
Form - 047
Record 2000 - 1st:0 2nd:0 3rd:0 Ran:3
Pre2000 - 1st:0 2nd:0 3rd:0 Ran:2
2000 Turf 0-3: (8f, 11f, 12f) (gd, g-f, frm)
Scopey, average gelding. Turf high 64 - 4th of 9 getting 16lb from Fahs (19 Jly Yarmouth 11f g-f RF 2952).
**E A L Dunlop [0-5] The Serendipity Partnership.*

KING'S WELCOME BHB 90f **RR 88f** 4160[3]
2 b c Most Welcome 8.6f **(66)** - Reine de Thebes (FR) (Darshaan) 9.9f **(84)**
Form - 313
Record 2000 - 1st:1 2nd:0 3rd:2 Ran:3
Win Prizemoney £3,103 *Total Prizemoney* £5,006
Wins * **2000** Aug Thirsk (GD) 7f 77+ <
2000 Turf 1-3: (7f 1-2, 8f) (sft, g-f, frm 1-1)
Currently useful colt. Turf high 88 (began Jly) - 3rd of 4 getting 4lb from Spettro (2 Spt Haydock 8f sft RF 4160).
**C W Fairhurst [1-3] G H & S Leggott.*

KING TUT BHB 49f36a **RR 51df 36a** 5056[2]
4 ch g Anshan 8.2f **(63)** - Fahrenheit (Mount Hagen (FR)) 8.4f **(70)**
Form - 2204782
Record 2000 - 1st:0 2nd:3 3rd:0 Ran:7
Pre2000 - 1st:0 2nd:0 3rd:0 Ran:4
Win Prizemoney £0 *Total Prizemoney* £2,563
2000 Turf 0-6: (7f, 8f 3, 10f, 11f) (sft, gd 2, g-f, frm 2) 2000 AW 0-1: (8f) (Fibr)
Fair gelding, effective 7 to 8f, best at 8f, acts on sft to frm, likes left handed tracks. Turf high 51 (1st run) - 2nd of 11 giving 10lb to Ever Revie (31 May Southwell 7f gd RF 1601).
**J G Given [0-6] A Clarke (from W Jarvis [0-5] May 2000).*

KING UNO BHB 52f60a **RR 48f 60a** 644[9]
6 b g Be My Chief (USA) 10.2f **(62)** - The Kings Daughter (Indian King (USA)) 7.4f **(64)**
Form - 00
Record 2000 - 1st:0 2nd:0 3rd:0 Ran:2
Pre2000 - 1st:5 2nd:2 3rd:3 Ran:38
Win Prizemoney £16,139 *Total Prizemoney* £22,676
Wins * 1998 Spt Leices (G-S) H 7f 59 62 <
* 1998 Aug Pontef (G-F) H 6f 54 58
1998 Jun Nottin (GD) H 6.1f 49 52
1997 Spt Haydoc (G-S) SH 6f 47 50
1997 Jun Pontef (GD) H 6f 43 46
2000 Turf 0-2: (6f, 8f) (gd, g-f)
Fair gelding, has worn blinkers. Turf high 48.
**E J Alston [2-16] The Pain And Heartache Partnership (from Mrs J R Ramsden [3-24] Jun 1998).*

KINNESCASH (IRE) BHB 77f65a **RR 79f 65a** 2863[2]
7 ch g Persian Heights 10.5f **(61)** - Gayla Orchestra (Lord Gayle (USA)) 8.8f **(62)**
Form - 702
Record 2000 - 1st:0 2nd:1 3rd:0 Ran:3
Pre2000 - 1st:6 2nd:4 3rd:3 Ran:34
Win Prizemoney £32,439 *Total Prizemoney* £42,925
Wins * 1999 Spt Epsom (GD) H 12f 74 79 <
* 1999 Apr Epsom (SFT) H 12f 73 76
* 1997 Jun Windso (G-S) H 11.6f 59 67
* 1997 Apr Leices (G-S) H 10f 53 62
2000 Turf 0-3: (12f, 16f, 18f) (sft, gd, g-f)
Above-average gelding, effective 12 to 16f, best at 12f, acts on g-s to frm. Turf high 76 - 2nd of 4 getting 19lb from Knockholt (16 Jly Newbury 16f g-f RF 2863). Inconsistent.
**P Bowen [12-58] D R James (from M S Saunders [1-12] Jun 1996).*

KINNINO BHB 41f40a **RR 43f 40a** 5077[8]
6 b g Polish Precedent (USA) 9f **(73)** - On Tiptoes (Shareef Dancer (USA)) 9.9f **(73)**
Form - 28134032144668
Record 2000 - 1st:2 2nd:1 3rd:2 Ran:12
Pre2000 - 1st:0 2nd:1 3rd:1 Ran:20
Win Prizemoney £4,887 *Total Prizemoney* £7,255
Wins * **2000** Aug Nottin (G-F) H 10f 39 45 <
* **2000** *Jan Wolver (STD) H 8.5f 35 41*
2000 Turf 1-7: (8f, 10f 1-6) (g-s 2, gd, g-f 1-3, frm) 2000 AW 1-5: (8f 1-3, 9f, 10f) (Equi 2, Fibr 1-3)
Moderate gelding, effective 10f, acts on g-f to frm, best on g-f, has worn blinkers, favours tight tracks. Turf high 45 (began Jly) - 1st of 12 getting 18lb from Rare Talent (4 Aug Nottingham RF 3373). AW high 41 (1st run). Consistent.
**G L Moore [2-32] Exors of the late A Moore.*

KINSAILE BHB 50f **RR 52f** 2609[13]
3 ro f Robellino (USA) 9.5f **(68)** - Snowing **(87f)** (Tate Gallery (USA)) 7.4f **(67)**
Form - 800
Record 2000 - 1st:0 2nd:0 3rd:0 Ran:3
Pre2000 - 1st:0 2nd:0 3rd:0 Ran:1
2000 Turf 0-3: (5f, 6f 2) (gd, g-f, frm)
Workmanlike, fair filly. Turf high 52.
**P L Gilligan [0-3] Lady Bland (from R Charlton [0-1] Apr 1999).*

KINSMAN (IRE) BHB 75f82a **RR 69f 82a** 4809[19]
3 b g Distant Relative 7f **(69)** - Besito (Wassl) 9.7f **(62)**
Form - 370623160170

Record 2000 - 1st:2 2nd:1 3rd:2 Ran:12
Pre2000 - 1st:1 2nd:1 3rd:0 Ran:8
Win Prizemoney £10,573 *Total Prizemoney* £13,357
Wins 2000 Aug Epsom (GD) H 6f 66 69 <
2000 Jun Bright (FRM) H 6f 63 69 <
1999 Spt Bright (SFT) H 6f 63 69 <
2000 Turf 2-10: (6f 2-6, 7f 4) (sft, g-s, gd 3, g-f 1-3, frm 1-2) 2000 AW 0-2: (7f 2) (Equi, Fibr)
Above-average gelding, effective 6 to 7f, best at 6f, acts on g-s to frm, often wears blinkers (very effectively), prefers left handed tracks, prefers tight tracks. Turf high 69 - 2nd of 8 getting 10lb from Compradore (24 May Brighton 7f gd RF 1424) - also 1st of 11 getting 4lb from Trajan (16 Aug Epsom RF 3695). AW high 74.
**Andrew Reid [0-1] A S Reid (from I A Balding [3-19] Aug 2000).*

KIPPANOUR (USA) BHB 22f **RR 23f** 5002[10]

8 b g Alleged (USA) 11.8f **(81)** - Innsbruck (General Assembly (USA)) 10f **(68)**
Form - 050
Record 2000 - 1st:0 2nd:0 3rd:0 Ran:3
Pre2000 - 1st:0 2nd:0 3rd:0 Ran:2
2000 Turf 0-2: (18f, 22f) (sft, g-s) 2000 AW 0-1: (16f) (Fibr)
Very moderate gelding, has worn blinkers. Turf high 23.
**A G Hobbs [2-10] Furnish With Abbey (from Mrs N Macauley [0-5] Jun 1998).*

KIRISNIPPA BHB 49f53a **RR 54f 53a** 4192[12]

5 b g Beveled (USA) 6.9f **(64)** - Kiri Te (Liboi (USA))
Form - 60513160532740350420
Record 2000 - 1st:2 2nd:2 3rd:3 Ran:18
Pre2000 - 1st:0 2nd:0 3rd:1 Ran:8
Win Prizemoney £5,759 *Total Prizemoney* £10,837
Wins * 2000 *Feb Southw (STD) H 11f 51 53* <
*** 2000** *Jan Southw (STD) H 11f 42 46*
2000 Turf 0-11: (11f, 12f 7, 13f 2, 14f) (gd, g-f 5, frm 5) 2000 AW 2-7: (11f 2-5, 12f 2) (Fibr 2-7)
Fair gelding, has broken blood-vessels, effective 11 to 13f, best at 11f, acts on gd to frm - acts on Fibr, has worn blinkers, likes left handed tracks, likes tight tracks, excels at Brighton, likes Southwell. Turf high 54 - 4th of 15 getting 9lb from Ravenswood (8 Jun Newbury 13f g-f RF 1813). AW high 53 - 1st of 10 getting 19lb from Green Bopper (7 Feb Southwell RF 0230).
**Derrick Morris [2-27] Mrs Lisa Morris.*

KIRIWINA (IRE) BHB 40f **RR 38f** 4581[14]

2 ch f Tagula (IRE) - Dancing Sensation (USA) **(72f 51a)** (Faliraki)
Form - 06000
Record 2000 - 1st:0 2nd:0 3rd:0 Ran:5
2000 Turf 0-5: (5f, 6f 2, 7f 2) (g-s, gd, g-f 2, frm)
Very moderate filly. Turf high 38.
**Mrs A J Bowlby [0-2] Robert Hitchins (from Miss Gay Kelleway [0-3] Jun 2000).*

KIRKBY'S TREASURE BHB 64f **RR 68f** 4869[9]

2 br c Mind Games - Gem of Gold (Jellaby) 6.4f **(58)**
Form - 836650
Record 2000 - 1st:0 2nd:0 3rd:1 Ran:6
Win Prizemoney £0 *Total Prizemoney* £537
2000 Turf 0-6: (5f 4, 6f 2) (sft, g-s, g-f 3, frm)
Average colt. Turf high 66. **A Berry [0-6] Kirkby Lonsdale Racing.*

KIRONA RR 99f 5368a[3]

3 b f Robellino (USA) 9.5f **(68)** - Kingston Avenue (USA) (Crusader Sword (USA))
Form - 13
2000 Turf 1-2: (8f 1-2) (hvy 1-2)
Currently very useful filly. Turf high 99 (1st run) (began Jun) - 1st of 16 getting 1lb from Turning Leaf (30 Jun Hamburg RF 2579a).
**P Rau in GER [1-2].*

KIROVSKI (IRE) BHB 90f **RR 90f** 4609[3]

3 b g Common Grounds 8.1f **(66)** - Nordic Doll (IRE) **(71f 59a)** (Royal Academy (USA))
Form - 21113
Record 2000 - 1st:3 2nd:1 3rd:1 Ran:5
Pre2000 - 1st:0 2nd:0 3rd:0 Ran:3
Win Prizemoney £34,664 *Total Prizemoney* £42,454
Wins * 2000 Aug Ascot (G-F) H 8f 04 00 <
*** 2000** Jly Newmar (GD) H 8f 76 82+
*** 2000** Jun Carlis (G-F) H 8f 70 78
2000 Turf 3-5: (8f 3-5) (g-s, g-f 2-2, frm 1-2)
Light-framed, useful gelding, effective 8f, acts on g-f. Turf high 90 - also 1st of 12 getting 22lb from Mayaro Bay (13 Aug Ascot RF 3601). Improving. Showed little in three outings at two, but has done well in handicap company this term. Beaten by the minimum margin at Sandown on his return, he won a valuable handicap at Carlisle in clear-cut fashion before following up in impressive fashion at Newmarket. Completed the hat trick in fine style at Ascot in August, and ran well off a higher mark despite probably finding the easy ground against him at the same track on his last run. There could be more to come.
**P W Harris [3-8] Batten, Bowstead, Gregory & Manning.*

KIRSCH BHB 46f66a **RR 58f 66a** 4871[18]

3 ch f Wolfhound (USA) 7.3f **(71)** - Pondicherry (USA) (Sir Wimborne (USA)) 10f **(73)**
Form - 23315608537600
Record 2000 - 1st:1 2nd:0 3rd:2 Ran:12
Pre2000 - 1st:1 2nd:2 3rd:5 Ran:14
Win Prizemoney £6,246 *Total Prizemoney* £11,383
Wins * 2000 *Jan Wolver (STD) H 5f 66 71* <
* 1999 Aug Lingfi (G-F) C 6f 69
2000 Turf 0-8: (5f 2, 6f 4, 7f 2) (sft, gd, g-f 3, frm 3) 2000 AW 1-4: (5f 1-3, 6f) (Equi 3, Fibr 1-1)
Neat, above-average filly, effective 5f, acts on g-f, often wears blinkers. Turf high 58. AW high 71. Becoming disappointing.
**C A Dwyer [2-26] Cedar Lodge Syndicate.*

KIRTHAR (USA) RR 81f 4300[6]

2 b c Mt Livermore (USA) 7.7f **(90)** - Kazadancoa (FR) (Green Dancer (USA)) 10.3f **(74)**
Form - 26
Record 2000 - 1st:0 2nd:1 3rd:0 Ran:2
Win Prizemoney £0 *Total Prizemoney* £900
2000 Turf 0-2: (6f 2) (gd, frm)
Currently decent colt. Turf high 81 (began Aug).
**M A Jarvis [0-2] Mohammed Al Khalifa.*

KISS CURL RR 1f 4821[19]

2 ch f Beveled (USA) 6.9f **(64)** - Laquetto **(33f)** (Bairn (USA)) 7.7f **(59)**
Form - 00
Record 2000 - 1st:0 2nd:0 3rd:0 Ran:2
2000 Turf 0-2: (6f, 7f) (g-s, g-f)
Currently very poor filly. Turf high 1 (began Spt).
**M Madgwick [0-2] Miss D M Green.*

KISSED BY MOONLITE BHB 28f **RR 39f** 4649[12]

4 gr f Petong 7.6f **(58)** - Rose Bouquet (General Assembly (USA)) 10f **(68)**
Form - 060
Record 2000 - 1st:0 2nd:0 3rd:0 Ran:3
Pre2000 - 1st:0 2nd:1 3rd:0 Ran:10
Win Prizemoney £0 *Total Prizemoney* £1,216
2000 Turf 0-2: (7f, 16f) (gd, frm) 2000 AW 0-1: (11f) (Fibr)
Lengthy, very moderate filly, effective 8f, acts on g-f. (began Jly). Becoming disappointing.
**K C Comerford [0-3] A Fairfield (from P W Harris [0-10] Spt 1999).*

KISSING TIME BHB 66f **RR 72f** 5313[20]

3 b f Lugana Beach 7f **(63)** - Princess Athena (Ahonoora) 8.1f **(73)**
Form - 05000
Record 2000 - 1st:0 2nd:0 3rd:0 Ran:5
Pre2000 - 1st:1 2nd:0 3rd:0 Ran:5
Win Prizemoney £4,318 *Total Prizemoney* £4,318
Wins * 1999 Aug Bath (GD) 5.1f 80 <
2000 Turf 0-5: (5f 2, 6f 2, 7f) (g-s 2, g-f, frm 2)
Scopey, above-average filly, effective 5f, acts on frm, has worn blinkers. Turf high 68. **P F I Cole [1-10] W H Ponsonby.*

KISS ME KATE BHB 65f **RR 64f** 1306[16]

4 b f Aragon 7.7f **(58)** - Ingerence (FR) (Akarad (FR)) 9f **(76)**
Form - 0
Record 2000 - 1st:0 2nd:0 3rd:0 Ran:1
Pre2000 - 1st:2 2nd:1 3rd:2 Ran:19

Win Prizemoney £5,484 *Total Prizemoney* £8,165
Wins 1999 Oct Redcar (SFT) 10f 64
1999 Jun Ripon (G-F) 10f 67 <
2000 Turf 0-1: (10f) (gd)
Leggy, average filly, effective 10f, acts on gd to hrd, likes tight tracks. Consistent.
**S E H Sherwood [2-7] Richard Green (Fine Paintings) (from J W Hills [2-19] Oct 1999).*

KISTY (IRE) BHB 60f RR 73f 5229[15]
3 b f Kris 10f **(75)** - Pine Ridge (High Top) 10.2f **(67)**
Form - 83336660
Record 2000 - 1st:0 2nd:0 3rd:3 Ran:8
Pre2000 - 1st:0 2nd:0 3rd:0 Ran:3
Win Prizemoney £0 *Total Prizemoney* £2,009
2000 Turf 0-8: (8f, 10f 2, 12f 4, 14f) (g-s, gd 4, g-f, frm, hrd)
Scopey, above-average filly, effective 12f, acts on hrd, likes tight tracks. Turf high 73 - 3rd of 9 getting 10lb from El Zito (14 Jun Beverley 12f hrd RF 1950). Inconsistent.
**H Candy [0-11] Capt J Macdonald-Buchanan.*

KITTY BANKES RR 29f 5066[15]
2 b f Forzando 7.2f **(63)** - St Kitts **(45f)** (Tragic Role (USA))
Form - 0
Record 2000 - 1st:0 2nd:0 3rd:0 Ran:1
2000 Turf 0-1: (8f) (g-s)
Currently little account filly. **W G M Turner [0-1] Mrs J Lightbowne.*

KIVOTOS (USA) RR 63f 4614[4]
2 gr c Trempolino (USA) 11.9f **(77)** - Authorized Staff (USA) (Relaunch (USA)) 6f **(92)**
Form - 64
Record 2000 - 1st:0 2nd:0 3rd:0 Ran:2
2000 Turf 0-2: (8f 2) (gd 2)
Currently average colt. Turf high 63 (began Spt).
**E J O'Neill [0-2] J D Martin.*

KLEOMENIS (GER) RR 96f 707a[5]
3 f
Form - 5
2000 Turf 0-1: (11f) (hvy)
Currently very useful. **A Fabre in FR [0-1].*

KNAVE'S ASH (USA) BHB 38f RR 34f 3551[6]
9 ch g Miswaki (USA) 8.1f **(81)** - Quiet Rendezvous (USA) (Nureyev (USA)) 8.7f **(78)**
Form - 00003678606
Record 2000 - 1st:0 2nd:0 3rd:1 Ran:11
Pre2000 - 1st:7 2nd:4 3rd:6 Ran:50
Win Prizemoney £51,852 *Total Prizemoney* £70,564
Wins 1999 Jly Redcar (FRM) H 8f 51 53
1998 Spt Newcas (GD) H 8f 64 68
1998 Jly Thirsk (FRM) H 8f 60 61
2000 Turf 0-11: (7f 2, 8f 5, 9f, 10f, 11f 2) (sft, g-s, gd, g-f 4, frm 4)
Very moderate gelding, effective 8 to 10f, best at 8f, acts on gd to hrd. Turf high 43. Consistent.
**M Todhunter [0-12] Steve Baron (from D Nicholls [3-34] Aug 1999).*

KNIGHT CROSSING (IRE) RR 52f 5052[10]
2 b c Doyoun 10.7f **(69)** - Princess Sarara (USA) **(42a)** (Trempolino (USA)) 12f **(71)**
Form - 50
Record 2000 - 1st:0 2nd:0 3rd:0 Ran:2
2000 Turf 0-2: (6f 2) (sft, g-s)
Currently fair colt. Turf high 52 (began Oct).
**Mrs A Duffield [0-2] Miss Betty Duxbury.*

KNIGHT'S EMPEROR (IRE) BHB 62f RR 70f 4216[13]
3 b g Grand Lodge (USA) - So Kind (Kind of Hush) 10.1f **(62)**
Form - 40060
Record 2000 - 1st:0 2nd:0 3rd:0 Ran:5
Pre2000 - 1st:0 2nd:0 3rd:0 Ran:1
Win Prizemoney £0 *Total Prizemoney* £308
2000 Turf 0-5: (7f, 8f 2, 10f, 11f) (gd 3, g-f, frm)
Scopey, above-average gelding, has worn blinkers. Turf high 75.
**J L Spearing [0-2] M Olden (from J Noseda [0-4] May 2000).*

KNIGHT'S RETURN BHB 30f RR 23f 2356[5]
3 ch g Never so Bold 7.1f **(62)** - Return to Romance (Trojan Fen) 8.1f **(62)**
Form - 005
Record 2000 - 1st:0 2nd:0 3rd:0 Ran:3
Pre2000 - 1st:0 2nd:0 3rd:0 Ran:3
2000 Turf 0-2: (11f, 14f) (g-f 2) 2000 AW 0-1: (9f) (Fibr)
Light-framed, little account gelding. Turf high 23.
**F Jordan [0-3] D Pugh (from P D Evans [0-3] Aug 1999).*

KNOBBLEENEEZE BHB 40f47a RR 43f 47a 5086[4]
10 ch g Aragon 7.7f **(58)** - Proud Miss (USA) (Semi-Pro) 7.5f **(70)**
Form - 0883705241670004
Record 2000 - 1st:1 2nd:1 3rd:1 Ran:16
Pre2000 - 1st:11 2nd:11 3rd:12 Ran:111
Win Prizemoney £51,987 *Total Prizemoney* £80,428
Wins * 2000 Aug Salisb (G-F) H 7f 41 42
* 1998 May Newbur (GD) H 7.3f 62 67
* 1997 Spt Ayr (G-S) H 7f 65 65
* 1997 Apr Ripon (GD) H 8f 65 78 <
* 1996 Jun Cheste (G-F) H 7f 67 73
2000 Turf 1-16: (7f 1-11, 8f 5) (hvy, g-s, gd 4, g-f 1-3, frm 5, hrd 2)
Moderate gelding, effective 8f, acts on gd, mostly wears blinkers. Turf high 43. **M R Channon [12-127] Anthony Andrews.*

KNOCK (IRE) BHB 74f RR 79f 4673[4]
2 b c Mujadil (USA) 7.7f **(70)** - Beechwood (USA) (Blushing Groom (FR)) 10.3f **(76)**
Form - 41524304
Record 2000 - 1st:1 2nd:1 3rd:1 Ran:8
Win Prizemoney £2,886 *Total Prizemoney* £7,274
Wins * 2000 Jun Bright (G-F) 6f 74 <
2000 Turf 1-8: (6f 1-6, 7f 2) (g-s, gd, g-f 3, frm 1-3)
Above-average colt, effective 6 to 7f, best at 6f, acts on g-f to frm, best on g-f. Turf high 79 - also 1st of 7 from Thomas Smythe (2 Jun Brighton RF 1650).
**R Hannon [1-8] Mrs Suzanne Costello-Haloute.*

KNOCKEMBACK NELLIE BHB 52f51a RR 66f 51a 5112[15]
4 b f Forzando 7.2f **(63)** - Sea Clover (IRE) (Ela-Mana-Mou) 10.1f **(70)**
Form - 00712100500570
Record 2000 - 1st:2 2nd:1 3rd:0 Ran:14
Pre2000 - 1st:0 2nd:2 3rd:0 Ran:14
Win Prizemoney £6,405 *Total Prizemoney* £9,102
Wins 2000 Jun Sandow (G-F) C 5f 66 <
2000 May Lingfi (HVY) H 5f 60 65
2000 Turf 2-14: (5f 2-12, 6f 2) (g-s 1-1, gd 6, g-f 4, frm 1-2, hrd)
Unfurnished, average filly, effective 5 to 6f, best at 5f, acts on g-s to frm, best on frm, often wears blinkers. Turf high 66 - 1st of 6 getting 6lb from King of Peru (16 Jun Sandown RF 2024) - also 1st of 8 getting 6lb from Whizz Kid (27 May Lingfield RF 1507).
**P W Harris [0-8] Resplendent Racing Ltd (from D R C Elsworth [2-20] Jun 2000).*

KNOCKHOLT BHB 96f RR 97f 4295[12]
4 b g Be My Chief (USA) 10.2f **(62)** - Saffron Crocus (Shareef Dancer (USA)) 9.9f **(73)**
Form - 008170
Record 2000 - 1st:1 2nd:0 3rd:0 Ran:6
Pre2000 - 1st:3 2nd:1 3rd:0 Ran:8
Win Prizemoney £44,366 *Total Prizemoney* £47,247
Wins * 2000 Jly Newbur (G-F) H 16f 95 95
* 1999 Spt Doncas (G-F) H 14.6f 95 97 <
* 1999 Jly Goodwo (FRM) H 14f 87 91
* 1999 May Salisb (G-F) 12f 83
2000 Turf 1-6: (12f, 15f, 16f 1-3, 22f) (gd 3, g-f 1-2, frm)
Leggy, very useful gelding, effective 14 to 16f, best at 16f, acts on gd to frm, best on g-f, likes right handed tracks. Turf high 96 - 7th of 9 giving 5lb to Dominant Duchess (12 Aug Ascot 16f gd RF 3577) - also 1st of 4 giving 19lb to Kinnescash (16 Jly Newbury RF 2863). Inconsistent. Apart from winning a win a four-runner handicap at Newbury in July, his form last season was moderate. Goes well on fast ground. **S P C Woods [4-14] Crawley Racing.*

KNOCKTOPHER ABBEY BHB 71f RR 81f 5064[10]
3 ch g Pursuit of Love 9.5f **(69)** - Kukri (Kris) 9.5f **(73)**
Form - 50536500

Record 2000 - 1st:0 2nd:0 3rd:1 Ran:8
Pre2000 - 1st:1 2nd:1 3rd:2 Ran:9
Win Prizemoney £2,794 *Total Prizemoney* £6,577
Wins * 1999 Jly Chepst (G-F) 6.1f 70 <
2000 Turf 0-8: (7f 3, 8f 5) (sft, g-s 2, g-f 2, frm 3)
Workmanlike, decent gelding, effective 5 to 8f, acts on g-s to frm. Turf high 81 (1st run) - 5th of 16 giving 5lb to Peacock Alley (9 Jun Epsom 7f g-s RF 1830). **B R Millman [1-17] Seasons Holidays.*

KNOTTY HILL BHB 45f50a RR 23f 50a 3961[19]
8 b g Green Ruby (USA) 6.9f **(47)** - Esilam (Frimley Park) 6.5f **(67)**
Form - 0
Record 2000 - 1st:0 2nd:0 3rd:0 Ran:1
Pre2000 - 1st:2 2nd:5 3rd:3 Ran:31
Win Prizemoney £6,665 *Total Prizemoney* £14,664
Wins * 1999 May Hamilt (SFT) 6f 59
* 1997 *Feb Southw (STD) 7f 79+* <
2000 Turf 0-1: (6f) (hrd)
Little account gelding. Becoming disappointing.
**R Craggs [2-32] Ray Craggs.*

KOCAL BHB 36f37a RR 34f 37a 2479[16]
4 b g Warrshan (USA) 9.7f **(59)** - Jeethgaya (USA) (Critique (USA))
Form - 2508000
Record 2000 - 1st:0 2nd:1 3rd:0 Ran:7
Pre2000 - 1st:0 2nd:0 3rd:0 Ran:4
Win Prizemoney £0 *Total Prizemoney* £516
2000 Turf 0-3: (7f, 8f, 10f) (gd 2, frm) 2000 AW 0-4: (8f 4) (Fibr 4)
Leggy, moderate gelding, effective 8f, - acts on Fibr, has worn blinkers, likes left handed tracks, likes tight tracks. Turf high 34. AW high 46 (1st run) - 2nd of 12 getting 8lb from Kustom Kit Kevin (25 Feb Southwell 8f Fibr RF 0354). Becoming disappointing.
**D W Barker [0-11] T Calver.*

KOINCIDENTAL (IRE) BHB 45f RR 49f 4677[12]
3 b f Mtoto 11.5f **(71)** - Floris (Master Willie) 7f **(70)**
Form - 7000550
Record 2000 - 1st:0 2nd:0 3rd:0 Ran:7
2000 Turf 0-7: (7f, 8f 4, 10f 2) (g-s, gd, g-f 5)
Small, moderate filly. Turf high 50. **M Kettle [0-7] J M Ainsworth.*

KOMALUNA BHB 46f RR 51df 5169[10]
2 ch c Komaite (USA) 6.9f **(61)** - Sugar Token (Record Token) 6.3f **(53)**
Form - 70080
Record 2000 - 1st:0 2nd:0 3rd:0 Ran:5
2000 Turf 0-5: (5f 2, 6f 3) (gd, g-f, frm 3)
Fair colt. Turf high 51. **S R Bowring [0-5] Mrs P A Barratt.*

KOMASEPH BHB 30f42a RR 15f 42a 4333[17]
8 b g Komaite (USA) 6.9f **(61)** - Starkist (So Blessed) 8.7f **(67)**
Form - 360640070
Record 2000 - 1st:0 2nd:0 3rd:1 Ran:9
Pre2000 - 1st:2 2nd:2 3rd:0 Ran:22
Win Prizemoney £4,806 *Total Prizemoney* £6,400
Wins * 1998 *Aug Southw (STD) H 6f 53 58* <
* 1998 *Jan Southw (STD) 6f 51*
2000 Turf 0-3: (6f, 7f, 8f) (gd, frm 2) 2000 AW 0-6: (5f, 6f 4, 7f) (Fibr 6)
Very moderate gelding, effective 6f, - acts on Fibr, has worn blinkers (very effectively), likes left handed tracks, likes tight tracks. Turf high 15. AW high 40. He seems to show his best form after a substantial layoff. That looks to be the key to him.
**R F Marvin [2-31] Mrs M A Marvin.*

KOMENA BHB 86f RR 86f 4642[22]
2 b f Komaite (USA) 6.9f **(61)** - Mena **(33f)** (Blakeney) 10.5f **(64)**
Form - 42140
Record 2000 - 1st:1 2nd:1 3rd:0 Ran:5
Win Prizemoney £2,341 *Total Prizemoney* £5,208
Wins * **2000** Aug Bright (FRM) 6f 86+ <
2000 Turf 1-5: (5f, 6f 1-2, 7f 2) (gd, g-f 1-3, frm)
Useful filly. Turf high 86 (began Jly) - 1st of 8 from Regal Air (21 Aug Brighton RF 3832). Hacked up in a weak maiden at Brighton, and ran well in a valuable nursery at Doncaster.
**J W Payne [1-5] The Frankland Lodgers.*

KOMISTAR BHB 87f RR 89f 5134[9]
5 ch g Komaite (USA) 6.9f **(61)** - Rosie's Gold (Glint of Gold) 9.3f **(66)**

Form - 02807310
Record 2000 - 1st:1 2nd:1 3rd:1 Ran:8
Pre2000 - 1st:3 2nd:1 3rd:3 Ran:14
Win Prizemoney £100,725 *Total Prizemoney* £109,500
Wins * **2000** Spt Newbur (G-F) H 10f 83 88
* 1999 Spt Newbur (G-F) H 10f 82 87
* 1999 Jun Doncas (Gd) H 10.3f 82 85
* 1997 Oct Warwic (G-F) 7f 93+ <
2000 Turf 1-8: (10f 1-7, 12f) (sft 2, gd 3, g-f 1-2, frm)
Useful gelding, effective 10 to 12f, best at 10f, acts on gd to frm, likes left handed tracks. Turf high 89 - 8th of 14 getting 2lb from Blue (24 Jun Ascot 10f gd RF 2239) - also 1st of 17 giving 2lb to Bonaguil (16 Spt Newbury RF 4464). A useful handicapper, he is not particularly consistent. Usually makes the running.
**P W Harris [4-22] Class Act.*

KOMPLIMENT BHB 86f RR 88f 2179[11]
2 ch c Komaite (USA) 6.9f **(61)** - Eladale (IRE) (Ela-Mana-Mou) 10.1f **(70)**
Form - 5130
Record 2000 - 1st:1 2nd:0 3rd:1 Ran:4
Win Prizemoney £7,085 *Total Prizemoney* £8,711
Wins * **2000** May Cheste (GD) 5.1f 79+ <
2000 Turf 1-4: (5f 1-4) (gd 2, g-f 1-2)
Useful colt. Turf high 88 - 3rd of 6 giving 8lb to Rare Old Times (22 May Windsor 5f g-f RF 1382) - also 1st of 9 from Ragamuffin (10 May Chester RF 1128). **A Bailey [1-4] Ray Bailey.*

KONA GOLD (USA) RR 5328a[1]
6 b h Java Gold (USA) 9.3f **(67)** - Double Sunrise (USA) (Slew O' Gold (USA)) 8f **(75)**
Form - 1
2000 AW 1-1: (6f 1-1) (Dirt 1-1)
Currently very high-class horse. (1st run) - 1st of 14 giving 5lb to Honest Lady (4 Nov Churchill Downs RF 5328a). Having finished third and second in previous runnings of the Breeders' Cup Sprint, he claimed the prize in authoritative style in 2000.
**B Headley in CAN [1-3] Headley, Molasky, Molasky & High Tech St.*

KONKER BHB 58f RR 56f 5054[1]
5 ch g Selkirk (USA) 7.9f **(76)** - Helens Dreamgirl (Caerleon (USA)) 8.6f **(71)**
Form - 0031
Record 2000 - 1st:1 2nd:0 3rd:1 Ran:4
Pre2000 - 1st:1 2nd:0 3rd:2 Ran:12
Win Prizemoney £6,258 *Total Prizemoney* £8,163
Wins * **2000** Oct Newcas (HVY) H 10.1f 52 56
1998 May Newbur (GD) C 10f 69 <
2000 Turf 1-4: (9f, 10f 1-3) (sft 1-1, gd, frm 2)
Fair gelding. Turf high 56 (began Aug). Showed little in three starts at two, but ran quite well in a handicap on heavy ground at Kempton on his reappearance. Looked a tricky ride in a maiden next time.
**Mrs M Reveley [1-4] J & M Leisure / Unos Restaurant (from G M Moore [0-8] Apr 1999).*

KOOKABURRA (FR) BHB 104f RR 102f 4294[2]
3 b c Zafonic (USA) 9f **(83)** - Annoconnor (USA) (Nureyev (USA)) 8.7f **(78)**
Form - 10463412
Record 2000 - 1st:2 2nd:1 3rd:1 Ran:8
Pre2000 - 1st:0 2nd:2 3rd:2 Ran:6
Win Prizemoney £11,472 *Total Prizemoney* £28,682
Wins * **2000** Aug Newbur (G-F) H 10f 97 102 <
* **2000** Mar Doncas (G-F) 8f 89
2000 Turf 2-8: (7f, 8f 1-4, 10f 1-3) (g-s, gd 2, g-f 1-3, frm 1-2)
Very useful colt, effective 8 to 10f, best at 10f, acts on gd to g-f, best on g-f. Turf high 102 - 1st of 6 giving 22lb to After The Blue (18 Aug Newbury RF 3760). Got off the mark in a Doncaster maiden on his reappearance, and put in some excellent efforts in decent handicap company in the summer. Just found wanting in listed races. **B J Meehan [2-14] Mrs Susan Roy.*

KOOL JULES BHB 21f25a RR 4f 25a 1794[9]
4 b f Sabrehill (USA) 8.5f **(64)** - Carrie Kool **(61df)** (Prince Sabo) 7.2f **(62)**
Form - 00600
Record 2000 - 1st:0 2nd:0 3rd:0 Ran:5

2000 Turf 0-1: (8f) (gd) 2000 AW 0-4: (7f, 8f 2, 11f) (Fibr 4)
Very poor filly, has worn blinkers. AW high 2.
**S C Williams [0-5] D A Shekells.*

KOORI RR 4300[12]

2 b f Komaite (USA) 6.9f **(61)** - Unadorned (Never so Bold) 6.3f **(66)**
Form - 0
Record 2000 - 1st:0 2nd:0 3rd:0 Ran:1
2000 Turf 0-1: (6f) (gd)
Currently very poor filly. **B A Pearce [0-1] Richard Gray.*

KORASOUN (IRE) RR 110f 2530a[10]

3 b c Darshaan 11.9f **(81)** - Kozana (Kris) 9.5f **(73)**
Form - 1250
2000 Turf 1-4: (10f 1-2, 12f 2) (g-s, gd, g-f 1-2)
Group-class colt, has worn blinkers. Turf high 110 - 2nd of 8 to Jammaal (28 May Curragh 10f g-s RF 1585a). Unraced at two, he was impressive in a minor heat at Navan on his debut and ran well in Listed company on his next start. Outclassed in the Irish Derby, he made 100,000gns at Newmarket in October and will continue his career with Bobby Frankel in California.
**J Oxx in IRE [1-4] H H Aga Khan.*

KOSEVO (IRE) BHB 41f48a RR 44f 48a 4654[15]

6 b g Shareef Dancer (USA) 10.1f **(67)** - Kallista (Zeddaan) 9f **(76)**
Form - 0700052000000003000610

Record	**2000** -	1st:1	2nd:1	3rd:1	Ran:21
	Pre2000 -	1st:3	2nd:9	3rd:3	Ran:52

Win Prizemoney £15,267 *Total Prizemoney* £24,728

Wins								
	* **2000**	Spt	Yarmou	(G-F)	H	6f	38	40
	* 1999	Jly	Haydoc	(FRM)	H	5f	55	58 <
	* 1998	*Jly*	*Southw*	*(STD)*	*H*	*7f*	*50*	*54*
	1998	*Jly*	*Southw*	*(STD)*	*S*	*7f*		*58* <

2000 Turf 1-15: (5f 8, 6f 1-6, 7f) (g-s, gd 3, g-f 1-3, frm 8) 2000 AW 0-6: (5f 2, 6f 4) (Fibr 6)
Moderate gelding, effective 5 to 7f, best at 5f, acts on g-f to frm - acts on Fibr, mostly wears blinkers (effectively), likes left handed tracks, likes tight tracks, and excels at Wolverhampton. Turf high 44. AW high 47.
**D Shaw [3-60] K Nicholls (from A Kelleway [1-4] Jly 1998).*

KOSMIC LADY BHB 50f45a RR 51f 45a 5071[3]

3 b f Cosmonaut - Ktolo (Tolomeo) 5.6f **(60)**
Form - 00703
Record 2000 - 1st:0 2nd:0 3rd:1 Ran:5
Win Prizemoney £0 *Total Prizemoney* £327
2000 Turf 0-5: (7f, 8f 2, 10f 2) (sft, g-s 3, g-f)
Workmanlike, fair filly. Turf high 55. **G A Butler [0-5] R K Bids Ltd.*

KRANTOR BHB 90f RR 97+f 4470[5]

3 ch c Arazi (USA) 9.2f **(74)** - Epagris **(101f)** (Zalazl (USA))
Form - 62155
Record 2000 - 1st:1 2nd:1 3rd:0 Ran:5
Win Prizemoney £4,389 *Total Prizemoney* £5,970
Wins * **2000** Jly Epsom (G-S) 10.1f 97 <
2000 Turf 1-5: (8f 2, 10f 1-3) (g-s, gd 1-1, g-f 3)
Scopey, very useful colt. Turf high 97 - 1st of 3 giving 5lb to Clog Dance (5 Jly Epsom RF 2551). (DEAD)
**H R A Cecil [1-5] L Marinopoulos.*

KRISPIN BHB 85f RR 91f 4829[12]

3 ch c Kris 10f **(75)** - Mariakova (USA) (The Minstrel (CAN)) 10f **(72)**
Form - 60331020
Record 2000 - 1st:1 2nd:1 3rd:2 Ran:8
Win Prizemoney £3,672 *Total Prizemoney* £7,252
Wins * **2000** Jly Pontef (GD) 10f 76 <
2000 Turf 1-8: (7f, 8f 3, 10f 1-4) (g-s, gd 3, g-f 2, frm 1-2)
Leggy, useful colt, effective 10f, acts on frm. Turf high 91 - 2nd of 15 giving 18lb to Lycian (13 Spt Yarmouth 10f frm RF 4380). A keen type, he landed a Pontefract maiden in July and looks best suited by a truly-run race. **G Wragg [1-8] John Pearce Racing Ltd.*

KRISTINEAU RR 53f 5236[13]

2 ch f Cadeaux Genereux 7.9f **(76)** - Kantikoy (Alzao (USA)) 7.1f **(68)**
Form - 00
Record 2000 - 1st:0 2nd:0 3rd:0 Ran:2
2000 Turf 0-2: (7f 2) (g-s 2)
Currently fair filly. Turf high 53 (began Oct).
**C F Wall [0-2] Kieran Scott.*

KRYSTAL MAX (IRE) BHB 68f74a RR 69f 74a 2940[1]

7 b g Classic Music (USA) 7.2f **(57)** - Lake Isle (IRE) (Caerleon (USA)) 8.6f **(71)**
Form - 42025111

Record	**2000** -	1st:3	2nd:1	3rd:0	Ran:5
	Pre2000 -	1st:13	2nd:6	3rd:4	Ran:43

Win Prizemoney £47,531 *Total Prizemoney* £56,784

Wins								
	* **2000**	*Jly*	*Lingfi*	*(STD)*	*C*	*7f*		*74*
	* **2000**	*Jly*	*Lingfi*	*(STD)*	*C*	*5f*		*59*
	* **2000**	*Jan*	*Lingfi*	*(STD)*	*C*	*6f*		*67*
	* 1999	*Feb*	*Wolver*	*(STD)*	*C*	*6f*		*78*
	1999	*Jan*	*Lingfi*	*(STD)*	*C*	*5f*		*70*
	1999	*Jan*	*Lingfi*	*(STD)*	*C*	*5f*		*70+*
	1999	*Jan*	*Lingfi*	*(STD)*	*C*	*6f*		*66*
	1998	*Mar*	*Lingfi*	*(STD)*	*H*	*5f*	*70*	*79*
	1998	*Mar*	*Southw*	*(STD)*	*H*	*5f*	*70*	*75*
	1998	*Feb*	*Lingfi*	*(SLW)*	*H*	*6f*	*60*	*65*
	1997	*Jan*	*Lingfi*	*(STD)*	*C*	*5f*		*67*
	1996	*Feb*	*Lingfi*	*(STD)*	*C*	*7f*		*82*
	1996	*Jan*	*Lingfi*	*(STD)*	*H*	*5f*	*83*	*82*

2000 AW 3-5: (5f 1-2, 6f 1-2, 7f 1-1) (Equi 3-3, Fibr 2)
Above-average gelding, effective 5 to 7f, best at 6f, - acts on AW, best on Fibr, has worn blinkers, favours left handed tracks, favours tight tracks, and excels at Lingfield. AW high 74 - 1st of 11 giving 11lb to Itsgottabdun (19 Jly Lingfield RF 2940). He is an effective sprinter on sand, especially in claiming company. He responds best if left alone and not bullied. He has been particularly well ridden by two female jockeys in recent seasons.
**T G Mills [4-13] Shipman Racing Ltd (from T D Barron [12-29] Jan 1999).*

KUMAIT (USA) BHB 81f RR 85f 3746[6]

6 b br g Danzig (USA) 8.1f **(88)** - Colour Chart (USA) (Mr Prospector (USA)) 8.8f **(78)**
Form - 47606

Record	**2000** -	1st:0	2nd:0	3rd:0	Ran:5
	Pre2000 -	1st:3	2nd:6	3rd:6	Ran:29

Win Prizemoney £15,957 *Total Prizemoney* £47,098

Wins						
	* 1999	Oct	Redcar	(GD)	7f	97
	* 1998	Spt	Yarmou	(G-S)	6f	102 <
	1996	Nov	Newmar	(GD)	6f	94

2000 Turf 0-5: (6f, 7f 4) (g-f 5)
Useful gelding, effective 7f, acts on gd to g-f, best on gd. Turf high 85. Consistent. He usually looks well and is at his best when allowed to dominate a small field. Suited by six or seven furlongs on fast ground, he races with tremendous enthusiasm.
**E A L Dunlop [2-23] Maktoum Al Maktoum (from D R Loder [0-3] Spt 1997).*

KUMAKAWA BHB 70f82a RR 52f 82a 5115[3]

2 ch g Dancing Spree (USA) 8f **(59)** - Maria Cappuccini (Siberian Express (USA)) 8.8f **(65)**
Form - 000013
Record 2000 - 1st:1 2nd:0 3rd:1 Ran:6
Win Prizemoney £1,939 *Total Prizemoney* £2,335
Wins 2000 Spt Leices (G-F) SH 8f 47 52 <
2000 Turf 1-5: (5f, 6f 2, 7f, 8f 1-1) (g-f, frm 1-4) 2000 AW 0-1: (8f) (Fibr)
Decent gelding, effective 8f, acts on frm - acts on Fibr, has worn blinkers. Turf high 52 - 1st of 19 giving 1lb to Eastern Red (5 Spt Leicester RF 4215). (1st run) - 3rd of 13 getting 10lb from Forum Finale (20 Oct Wolverhampton 8f Fibr RF 5115).
**M J Polglase [0-1] Nilesh Unadkat (from J G Given [1-5] Spt 2000).*

KUMATOUR BHB 100f RR 103f 3581[6]

5 b h Batshoof 9.5f **(66)** - Runelia (Runnett) 7f **(59)**
Form - 306

Record	**2000** -	1st:0	2nd:0	3rd:1	Ran:3
	Pre2000 -	1st:2	2nd:4	3rd:0	Ran:7

Win Prizemoney £13,328 *Total Prizemoney* £33,436

Wins						
	1998	Jun	San Si	(G-F)	10f	93 <
	1998	May	Windso	(G-F)	10f	86

2000 Turf 0-3: (12f 2, 16f) (gd 2, frm)
Very useful colt. Turf high 103 (1st run) - 3rd of 8 giving 20lb to Gallery God (5 Jun Thirsk 12f gd RF 1725). A dual winner for Luca Cumani in 1998, he was then sent to race in Dubai, but returned to

join Clive Brittain and ran really well to finish third under a welter burden at Thirsk on his return. Seemed not to get two miles next time, and will remain difficult to place.

**C E Brittain [0-3] H E Sheikh Rashid Bin Mohammed (from L M Cumani [2-7] Jly 1998).*

KUMHAR (USA) RR 101f 2205a[6]

3 f

Form - 06

2000 Turf 0-2: (12f 2) (g-f 2)

Very useful, often wears blinkers. Turf high 101.

**L Brogi in ITY [0-2].*

KUMON EILEEN BHB 45f30a **RR 46f 30a** 138[7]

4 ch f Anshan 8.2f **(63)** - Katie Eileen (USA) (Bering) 7.4f **(61)**

Form - 07

Record 2000 - 1st:0 2nd:0 3rd:0 Ran:2

Pre2000 - 1st:0 2nd:0 3rd:0 Ran:2

2000 AW 0-2: (10f, 12f) (Equi 2)

Scopey, moderate filly. AW high 14.

**J R Jenkins [0-6] The Royston Raiders.*

KUNDALILA BHB 56f **RR 63f** 4773[14]

2 b f River Falls 8.2f **(56)** - Kalou **(64f)** (K-Battery)

Form - 0480

Record 2000 - 1st:0 2nd:0 3rd:0 Ran:4

Win Prizemoney £0 *Total Prizemoney* £287

2000 Turf 0-4: (6f, 7f 2, 8f) (g-s, g-f 2, frm)

Average filly. Turf high 63 (began Aug).

**J Hetherton [0-4] R N Cardwell.*

KURANDA RR 55f 4023[6]

2 gr f Environment Friend 7.5f **(67)** - Lady Barkley (Habitat) 9.4f **(70)**

Form - 6

Record 2000 - 1st:0 2nd:0 3rd:0 Ran:1

2000 Turf 0-1: (8f) (gd)

Currently fair filly. **M Johnston [0-1] David Abell.*

KUSTER BHB 85f **RR 91f** 5323[5]

4 b c Indian Ridge 7.6f **(74)** - Ustka (Lomond (USA)) 8.0f **(65)**

Form - 42475

Record 2000 - 1st:0 2nd:1 3rd:0 Ran:5

Pre2000 - 1st:1 2nd:1 3rd:0 Ran:4

Win Prizemoney £4,279 *Total Prizemoney* £9,150

Wins * 1999 Apr Epsom (SFT) 8.5f 86 <

2000 Turf 0-5: (8f, 10f, 12f 3) (sft, g-s, gd, g-f, frm)

Scopey, useful colt, effective 8 to 12f, acts on sft to frm. Turf high 91 - 2nd of 5 giving 12lb to Ferzao (8 May Windsor 10f g-f RF 1099). Consistent. **L M Cumani [1-9] Lord Vestey.*

KUSTOM KIT KEVIN BHB 35f58a **RR 40f 58a** 4493[17]

4 b g Local Suitor (USA) 9.7f **(58)** - Sweet Revival (Claude Monet (USA))

Form - 322018007300000

Record 2000 - 1st:1 2nd:2 3rd:2 Ran:15

Pre2000 - 1st:0 2nd:0 3rd:0 Ran:2

Win Prizemoney £1,806 *Total Prizemoney* £4,138

Wins * 2000 *Feb Southw (STD) H 8f 53 59* **<**

2000 Turf 0-9: (7f, 8f 6, 10f, 11f) (sft, gd, g-f 3, frm 3, hrd) 2000 AW 1-6: (8f 1-4, 11f, 12f) (Fibr 1-6)

Workmanlike, average gelding, effective 8f, - acts on Fibr, has worn blinkers, likes tight tracks. Turf high 40. AW high 61 - also 1st of 12 giving 8lb to Kocal (25 Feb Southwell RF 0354).

**S R Bowring [1-17] Charterhouse Holdings Plc.*

KUT O ISLAND (USA) RR 61f 4643[24]

2 br c Woodman (USA) 9.7f **(77)** - Cherry Jubilee (USA) (Coastal (USA)) 11.5f **(72)**

Form - 00

Record 2000 - 1st:0 2nd:0 3rd:0 Ran:2

2000 Turf 0-2: (7f, 8f) (g-f 2)

Currently average colt. Turf high 61 (began Spt).

**G A Butler [0-2] Mrs A K H Ooi.*

KUTUB (IRE) RR 119f 4562a[3]

3 b c In The Wings 11.2f **(77)** - Minnie Habit (Habitat) 9.4f **(70)**

Form - 12423

2000 Turf 1-5: (10f 2, 11f 1-2, 12f) (hvy 1-1, gd 3, g-f)

High-class colt, has worn blinkers. Turf high 119 - 3rd of 8 getting 4lb from Agol Lack (13 Spt Maisons-laffitte 10f gd RF 4562a) - also 1st of 9 from Lord Flasheart (9 Apr Longchamp RF 0707a). He had a big reputation during the spring, but proved below Classic standard and did not always impress with his attitude. Tried in blinkers when flopping in the French Derby, he probably needs soft ground and is worth another try over a mile and a half.

**F Head in FR [1-5] Hamdan Al Maktoum.*

KUUIPO BHB 40f47a **RR 56f 47a** 3780[4]

3 b f Puissance 7.1f **(60)** - Yankee Special (Bold Lad (IRE)) 8.4f **(68)**

Form - 7006726574

Record 2000 - 1st:0 2nd:1 3rd:0 Ran:10

Pre2000 - 1st:0 2nd:0 3rd:1 Ran:8

Win Prizemoney £0 *Total Prizemoney* £2,143

2000 Turf 0-9: (7f, 8f 2, 10f 3, 11f, 12f 2) (gd 4, g-f, frm 4) 2000 AW 0-1: (7f) (Fibr)

Light-framed, fair filly, has worn blinkers. Turf high 56.

**B S Rothwell [0-18] S P Hudson.*

KUWAIT DAWN (IRE) BHB 69f **RR 59f** 5239[10]

4 b f Pips Pride 6.7f **(70)** - Red Note (Rusticaro (FR)) 8.2f **(65)**

Form - 00068000

Record 2000 - 1st:0 2nd:0 3rd:0 Ran:8

Pre2000 - 1st:1 2nd:1 3rd:0 Ran:17

Win Prizemoney £6,776 *Total Prizemoney* £13,351

Wins * 1999 Mar Doncas (G-S) 8f 90 **<**

2000 Turf 0-8: (7f 2, 8f 2, 9f 2, 10f, 12f) (sft, g-s 2, gd 2, g-f 2, frm)

Lengthy, fair filly, effective 7 to 8f, acts on gd to frm, has worn blinkers. Turf high 73. Becoming disappointing.

**K Mahdi [1-25] John Lund.*

KUWAIT FLAVOUR (IRE) BHB 65f **RR 67?f** 4216[8]

4 b c Bluebird (USA) 7.9f **(71)** - Plume Magique (Kenmare (FR)) 6.5f **(72)**

Form - 68458

Record 2000 - 1st:0 2nd:0 3rd:0 Ran:5

Pre2000 - 1st:0 2nd:0 3rd:1 Ran:2

Win Prizemoney £0 *Total Prizemoney* £1,181

2000 Turf 0-4: (7f, 8f 2, 10f) (gd, g-f 2, frm) 2000 AW 0-1: (7f) (Fibr)

Workmanlike, average colt. Turf high 67 (began Aug).

**K Mahdi [0-7] Greenfield Stud.*

KUWAIT MILLENNIUM BHB 72f **RR 69f** 2058[5]

3 b c Salse (USA) 10.9f **(71)** - Lypharitissima (FR) (Lightning (FR)) 7.9f **(74)**

Form - 545

Record 2000 - 1st:0 2nd:0 3rd:0 Ran:3

Win Prizemoney £0 *Total Prizemoney* £293

2000 Turf 0-3: (10f, 12f 2) (g-s, gd, g-f)

Rangy, currently average colt. Turf high 69.

**H R A Cecil [0-3] Greenfield Stud.*

KUWAIT ROSE BHB 68f65a **RR 76f 65a** 4619[13]

4 b c Inchinor 8.9f **(64)** - Black Ivor (USA) (Sir Ivor) 10.2f **(70)**

Form - 6264540258100

Record 2000 - 1st:1 2nd:1 3rd:0 Ran:10

Pre2000 - 1st:0 2nd:1 3rd:1 Ran:5

Win Prizemoney £4,225 *Total Prizemoney* £6,519

Wins * 2000 Aug Warwic (GD) 7.1f 70 **<**

2000 Turf 1-10: (6f 4, 7f 1-5, 8f) (sft, gd 1-4, g-f 3, frm 2)

Neat, above-average colt, effective 6 to 7f, acts on gd, likes left handed tracks, likes tight tracks. Turf high 76 - also 1st of 14 giving 5lb to Faraway Look (28 Aug Warwick RF 4059). Inconsistent. He got off the mark at Warwick in August, and seems suited by seven furlongs and easy ground. **K Mahdi [1-15] Greenfield Stud.*

KUWAIT THUNDER (IRE) BHB 33f35a **RR 38f 35a** 3847[6]

4 ch c Mac's Imp (USA) 5.6f **(54)** - Romangoddess (IRE) (Rhoman Rule (USA))

Form - 07440607505726

Record 2000 - 1st:0 2nd:1 3rd:0 Ran:14

Pre2000 - 1st:0 2nd:0 3rd:3 Ran:14

Win Prizemoney £0 *Total Prizemoney* £3,206

2000 Turf 0-10: (7f, 8f 8, 10f) (gd 4, g-f 2, frm 3, hrd) 2000 AW 0-4: (7f, 8f, 12f 2) (Fibr 4)

Workmanlike, very moderate colt, has worn blinkers. Turf high 38. AW high 31.
**J L Eyre [0-15] The Flowerpot Men (from K Mahdi [0-13] Oct 1999).*

KUWAIT TROOPER (USA) BHB 107f59a **RR 110f 59a**
4310[11]
3 b br c Cozzene (USA) 10.1f **(87)** - Super Fan (USA) (Lear Fan (USA)) 8.5f **(73)**
Form - 684103185220

Record	**2000 -**	1st:2	2nd:2	3rd:1	Ran:10
	Pre2000 -	1st:0	2nd:0	3rd:0	Ran:2

Win Prizemoney £11,798 *Total Prizemoney* £28,289

Wins	*** 2000**	May York	(G-F)	13.9f	96	<
	*** 2000**	Mar Mussel	(GD)	12f	65	

2000 Turf 2-9: (12f 1-5, 14f 1-2, 15f, 16f) (g-s, gd 1-3, g-f 1-4, frm) 2000 AW 0-1: (10f) (Equi)
Unfurnished, Group-class colt, effective 12 to 14f, acts on gd to g-f, has worn blinkers. Turf high 110. Inconsistent. An improving performer, best over fourteen furlongs, he finished runner-up in the March Stakes at Goodwood and Kempton's September Stakes before finishing down the field in the St Leger.
**G A Butler [2-12] Sheikh Khaled Duaij Al Sabah.*

KWAHERI BHB 70f **RR 74f**
3567[11]
2 b f Efisio 7.7f **(69)** - Fleeting Affair (Hotfoot) 10.5f **(59)**
Form - 040

Record	**2000 -**	1st:0	2nd:0	3rd:0	Ran:3

Win Prizemoney £0 *Total Prizemoney* £342
2000 Turf 0-3: (6f, 7f 2) (g-f 2, frm)
Currently above-average filly. Turf high 74 - 4th of 11 giving 6lb to Trumpington (21 Jly Newbury 7f frm RF 2998).
**Mrs P N Dutfield [0-3] Simon Dutfield.*

KYLKENNY BHB 50f **RR 54f**
5069[9]
5 b g Kylian (USA) 8.1f **(66)** - Fashion Flow (Balidar) 7.9f **(63)**
Form - 00

Record	**2000 -**	1st:0	2nd:0	3rd:0	Ran:2
	Pre2000 -	1st:0	2nd:0	3rd:0	Ran:3

2000 Turf 0-2: (10f, 12f) (g-s 2)
Fair gelding. Turf high 49 (began Spt).
**H Morrison [0-5] H Morrison.*

KYLLACHY BHB 89f **RR 92f**
4751[2]
2 b c Pivotal - Pretty Poppy (Song) 7.2f **(61)**
Form - 122

Record	**2000 -**	1st:1	2nd:2	3rd:0	Ran:3

Win Prizemoney £2,800 *Total Prizemoney* £5,366

Wins	*** 2000**	Aug Chepst	(G-F)	5.1f	83	<

2000 Turf 1-3: (5f 1-3) (g-s 2, frm 1-1)
Currently useful colt. Turf high 92 (began Aug) - 2nd of 10 giving 25lb to Adweb (30 Spt Sandown 5f g-s RF 4751) - also 1st of 11 from Attorney (10 Aug Chepstow RF 3525).
**H Candy [1-3] Thurloe Thoroughbreds V.*

LAA JADEED (IRE) BHB 24f22a **RR 26f 22a**
3213[14]
5 b g Petorius 8f **(66)** - Sea Mistress (Habitat) 9.4f **(70)**
Form - 77576000

Record	**2000 -**	1st:0	2nd:0	3rd:0	Ran:8
	Pre2000 -	1st:1	2nd:0	3rd:1	Ran:23

Win Prizemoney £2,126 *Total Prizemoney* £2,544

Wins	***** 1999	*Jan Southw*	*(STD)*	*11f*	*48*	<

2000 Turf 0-3: (7f, 10f, 14f) (g-f, frm 2) 2000 AW 0-5: (7f, 9f 2, 12f 2) (Fibr 5)
Very moderate gelding, effective 11f, - acts on Fibr, has worn blinkers. Turf high 26. AW high 31.
**M J Polglase [1-24] T A Farrin (from J A Glover [0-9] Nov 1998).*

LA BIRBA (IRE) BHB 42f **RR 49f**
966[11]
3 b f Prince of Birds (USA) - Ariadne (Bustino) 10.4f **(64)**
Form - 80

Record	**2000 -**	1st:0	2nd:0	3rd:0	Ran:2
	Pre2000 -	1st:0	2nd:0	3rd:0	Ran:4

2000 Turf 0-2: (6f, 7f) (sft, gd)
Workmanlike, moderate filly, has worn blinkers. Turf high 28.
**B J Meehan [0-6] G Battocchi.*

LABRETT BHB 71f **RR 77f**
4809[7]
3 b g Tragic Role (USA) 9.4f **(63)** - Play the Game (Mummy's Game) 8.2f **(60)**
Form - 70004481140807

Record	**2000 -**	1st:2	2nd:0	3rd:0	Ran:14
	Pre2000 -	1st:2	2nd:0	3rd:1	Ran:11

Win Prizemoney £11,354 *Total Prizemoney* £15,138

Wins	*** 2000**	Aug Bath	(G-F)	C	5.7f	60	
	*** 2000**	Jly Kempto	(G-F)	C	6f	75+	
	* 1999	Jun Cheste	(G-F)		5.1f	82	<
	* 1999	May Redcar	(SFT)		5f	72	

2000 Turf 2-14: (5f 5, 6f 2-8, 7f) (hvy, g-s 3, gd, g-f 6, frm 2-3)
Leggy, above-average gelding, effective 5 to 6f, best at 5f, acts on gd to frm, best on frm, mostly wears blinkers. Turf high 77.
**B J Meehan [4-25] Mrs E A Lerpiniere.*

LA CAPRICE (USA) BHB 77f **RR 77f**
5228[6]
3 ch f Housebuster (USA) 7f **(81)** - Shicklah (USA) (The Minstrel (CAN)) 10f **(72)**
Form - 0320271706

Record	**2000 -**	1st:1	2nd:2	3rd:1	Ran:10
	Pre2000 -	1st:1	2nd:2	3rd:0	Ran:6

Win Prizemoney £7,470 *Total Prizemoney* £14,616

Wins	*** 2000**	Jly Sandow	(G-F)	H	5f	76	77	<
	1999	Aug Lingfi	(G-F)		5f		73	

2000 Turf 1-10: (5f 1-5, 6f 5) (g-s, gd 4, g-f 1-4, frm)
Above-average filly, effective 5 to 6f, best at 5f, acts on gd to frm, best on g-f. Turf high 77 - 1st of 11 giving 6lb to Illusive (27 Jly Sandown RF 3152). Suited by fast ground and the minimum trip, she scored at Sandown in July and was not disgraced at York next time. **A Berry [1-10] Slatch Farm Stud (from J Berry [1-6] Aug 1999).*

LACE WING BHB 89f **RR 89f**
1989[6]
3 ch f Caerleon (USA) 10.9f **(79)** -Capo Di Monte (Final Straw) 7.9f **(64)**
Form - 16

Record	**2000 -**	1st:1	2nd:0	3rd:0	Ran:2
	Pre2000 -	1st:0	2nd:0	3rd:0	Ran:1

Win Prizemoney £3,243 *Total Prizemoney* £3,243

Wins	*** 2000**	May Salisb	(GD)	9.9f	84	<

2000 Turf 1-2: (10f 1-2) (gd 1-1, g-f)
Scopey, currently useful filly. Turf high 87 - also 1st of 13 from Riyafa (18 May Salisbury RF 1268).
**B W Hills [1-3] Maktoum Al Maktoum.*

LA CHATELAINE BHB 32a **RR 28f**
693[11]
6 b m Then Again 7.4f **(52)** - La Domaine (Dominion) 8.5f **(63)**
Form - 0

Record	**2000 -**	1st:0	2nd:0	3rd:0	Ran:1
	Pre2000 -	1st:2	2nd:2	3rd:1	Ran:30

Win Prizemoney £7,271 *Total Prizemoney* £10,202

Wins	1998	Jun Epsom	(GD)	H	12f	39	45	
	1997	Aug Bright	(G-F)	H	7f	43	48	<

2000 Turf 0-1: (12f) (gd)
Little account mare, has worn blinkers.
**Miss Z C Davison [0-6] The Secret Circle (1) (from Miss B Sanders [1-19] Jun 1999).*

LA CINECITTA (FR) BHB 25f **RR 33f**
3996[10]
4 ch f Dancing Spree (USA) 8f **(59)** - Cox's Feather (USA) (Cox's Ridge (USA)) 8f **(68)**
Form - 006050

Record	**2000 -**	1st:0	2nd:0	3rd:0	Ran:6
	Pre2000 -	1st:0	2nd:0	3rd:0	Ran:7

2000 Turf 0-5: (8f, 9f, 11f, 12f, 14f) (g-s, gd, g-f 2, frm) 2000 AW 0-1: (11f) (Fibr)
Workmanlike, very moderate filly, effective 12f, acts on frm, has worn blinkers, likes left handed tracks, likes tight tracks. Turf high 33 - 5th of 11 getting 7lb from Wrangel (8 Aug Catterick 12f frm RF 3451). **C B B Booth [0-13] C B B Booth.*

LADIES DIN (USA) **RR 123f**
5327a[8]
5 b g Din's Dancer (USA) - Ladies Double (USA) (Kris S (USA)) 7.9f **(71)**
Form - 58
2000 Turf 0-1: (8f) (frm) 2000 AW 0-1: (12f) (Dirt)
Currently very high-class gelding, has worn blinkers. (1st run) -

8th of 14 giving 3lb to War Chant (4 Nov Churchill Downs 8f frm RF 5327a). (1st run) - 5th of 11 to Rhythm Band (25 Mar Nad Al Sheba 12f Dirt RF 0579a). **J Canani in USA [1-3] Lanni & Schiappa & Sloan.*

LADY ABAI BHB 37f **RR 55f** 4204[12]

3 b f Bin Ajwaad (IRE) - Charmed I'M Sure (Nicholas Bill) 10.1f **(56)**
Form - 800
Record 2000 - 1st:0 2nd:0 3rd:0 Ran:3
2000 Turf 0-3: (10f 2, 12f) (gd, frm 2)
Leggy, currently fair filly. Turf high 55.
**A W Carroll [0-3] Nigel Coulson-Stevens.*

LADY AMBITION **RR 55f** 3697[6]

2 b f Emarati (USA) 6.6f **(63)** - Forest Song (Forzando) 7.6f **(59)**
Form - 0506
Record 2000 - 1st:0 2nd:0 3rd:0 Ran:4
2000 Turf 0-4: (5f 3, 7f) (gd, g-f, frm 2)
Fair filly. Turf high 55. **M W Easterby [0-4] E J Mangan.*

LADY ANGHARAD (IRE) BHB 87f **RR 88f** 4740[20]

4 b f Tenby 10.4f **(76)** - Lavezzola (IRE) (Salmon Leap (USA)) 11f **(61)**
Form - 11100

Record	**2000** -	1st:3	2nd:0	3rd:0	Ran:5		
	Pre2000 -	1st:2	2nd:1	3rd:0	Ran:16		

Win Prizemoney £95,292 *Total Prizemoney* £97,905

Wins	*** 2000**	Jly	Sandow	(GD)	H	10f	80	88	<
	*** 2000**	Jun	Leices	(G-F)		10f		87	
	*** 2000**	May	Nottin	(G-F)		10f		79	
	1998	Jun	Salisb	(G-F)		7f		88	<
	1998	Jun	Epsom	(GD)	L	6f		88	<

2000 Turf 3-5: (9f, 10f 3-4) (g-s, gd 1-1, g-f 1-2, hrd 1-1)
Workmanlike, useful filly, effective 10f, acts on gd to hrd, has worn blinkers, prefers tight tracks. Turf high 88 - 1st of 20 getting 23lb from Albarahin (7 Jly Sandown RF 2606) - also 1st of 6 from St Helensfield (18 Jun Leicester RF 2076). Consistent. She was in fine form in the summer, completing a hat-trick in an ultra-competitive Sandown handicap. Ran poorly in a listed race in rain-softened ground. Ten furlongs and fast ground suit.
**J R Fanshawe [3-5] Ian Deane (from A P Jarvis [2-16] Spt 1999).*

Lady Angharad (right), scored a hat-trick in the summer

LADY ANGOLA (USA) BHB 76f **RR 73f** 5196[7]

2 ch f Lord At War (ARG) 6.6f **(67)** - Benguela (USA) (Little Current (USA)) 9.6f **(75)**
Form - 407
Record 2000 - 1st:0 2nd:0 3rd:0 Ran:3
Win Prizemoney £0 *Total Prizemoney* £375
2000 Turf 0-3: (7f 2, 8f) (g-s, gd, g-f)
Currently above-average filly. Turf high 73 (began Aug).

**J L Dunlop [0-3] Ricketts (Susan Abbo Racing).*

LADY BALLA CALM (IRE) BHB 18f **RR** 202[11]

4 b f Balla Cove - Across The Ring (IRE) (Auction Ring (USA)) 8.6f **(65)**
Form - 00880

Record 2000 -	1st:0	2nd:0	3rd:0	Ran:3
Pre2000 -	1st:0	2nd:0	3rd:0	Ran:6

2000 AW 0-3: (5f, 6f, 7f) (Equi 3)
Very poor filly.
**J J Bridger [0-6] T S D (from M J Byrne in IRE [0-3] Oct 1998).*

LADY BEAR (IRE) BHB 79f **RR 79f** 4818[1]

2 b f Grand Lodge (USA) - Boristova (IRE) (Royal Academy (USA))
Form - 633441021
Record 2000 - 1st:2 2nd:1 3rd:2 Ran:9
Win Prizemoney £11,147 *Total Prizemoney* £14,329

Wins	*** 2000**	Oct	York	(SFT)	H	7.9f	76	79	<
	*** 2000**	Aug	Mussel	(G-F)	H	7.1f	64	69	

2000 Turf 2-8: (6f 2, 7f 1-3, 8f 1-3) (g-s 1-1, gd, frm 1-6) 2000 AW 0-1: (7f) (Fibr)
Above-average filly, effective 7 to 8f, best at 8f, acts on g-s to frm, has worn blinkers. Turf high 79 - 1st of 11 giving 3lb to Fazzani (5 Oct York RF 4818). **R A Fahey [2-9] A & K Lingerie.*

LADY BENSON (IRE) BHB 32f24a **RR 28f 24a** 764[7]

7 h m Pennine Walk 8.9f **(64)** - Sit Elnaas (USA) (Sir Ivor) 10.2f **(70)**
Form - 47

Record 2000 -	1st:0	2nd:0	3rd:0	Ran:2
Pre2000 -	1st:0	2nd:2	3rd:0	Ran:21

Win Prizemoney £0 *Total Prizemoney* £2,331
2000 Turf 0-2: (11f, 12f) (g-s, gd)
Little account mare, effective 9 to 10f, acts on gd to g-f, prefers right handed tracks. Turf high 28.
**W M Brisbourne [0-22] B L Benson (from D J S Cosgrove [0-3] Aug 1996).*

LADY BOXER BHB 86f **RR 90f** 5239[11]

4 b f Komaite (USA) 6.9f **(61)** - Lady Broker **(44a)** (Petorius) 7.3f **(61)**
Form - 00P081011000

Record 2000 -	1st:3	2nd:0	3rd:0	Ran:12
Pre2000 -	1st:2	2nd:0	3rd:1	Ran:10

Win Prizemoney £38,206 *Total Prizemoney* £39,704

Wins	*** 2000**	Spt	Cheste	(SFT)		6.1f		86+	<
	*** 2000**	Spt	Ayr	(SFT)	H	6f	74	81	
	*** 2000**	Aug	Cheste	(GD)	H	7.6f	56	75	
	* 1999	Spt	Cheste	(SFT)		6.1f		75	
	* 1998	Jun	Leices	(SFT)		6f		74+	

2000 Turf 3-12: (6f 2-7, 7f, 8f 1-4) (sft, g-s 1-2, gd 2-5, g-f 3, frm)
Leggy, useful filly, effective 6f, acts on g-s to gd, prefers left handed tracks, prefers tight tracks. Turf high 90 - also 1st of 15 giving 3lb to Downland (20 Spt Chester RF 4533). Inconsistent. She caused a 50/1 shock when winning at Chester in August having shown very little previously in 2000. Gained a last-gasp victory in the Ayr Silver Cup before winning again at her beloved Chester. Has gone up in the weights as a result and beaten in consequence. Very much suited by soft ground.
**M Mullineaux [5-22] Esprit de Corps Racing.*

LADY BREANNE (IRE) BHB 47f44a **RR 51df 44a** 2948[9]

4 b f Woods of Windsor (USA) - Tootsie Roll (Comedy Star (USA)) 7.5f **(50)**
Form - 636000

Record 2000 -	1st:0	2nd:0	3rd:0	Ran:3
Pre2000 -	1st:0	2nd:1	3rd:2	Ran:10

Win Prizemoney £0 *Total Prizemoney* £2,345
2000 Turf 0-3: (6f, 7f, 8f) (g-f 3)
Fair filly, effective 7f, acts on frm. Turf high 41. Consistent.
**G L Moore [0-10] Brian Palmer (from B Lawlor in IRE [0-3] Oct 1998).*

LADYCAKE (IRE) BHB 34f45a **RR 18f 45a** 4057[14]

4 gr f Perugino (USA) - Olivia's Pride (IRE) (Digamist (USA))
Form - 8800

Record 2000 -	1st:0	2nd:0	3rd:0	Ran:4
Pre2000 -	1st:2	2nd:2	3rd:2	Ran:19

Win Prizemoney £5,392 *Total Prizemoney* £7,635

Wins	1998	Aug	Mussel	(GD)	S	5f		67	<

1998 May Mussel (GD) 5f 65+
2000 Turf 0-4: (5f 4) (gd 2, frm, hrd)
Workmanlike, fair filly, has worn blinkers. Turf high 18.
**R J Hodges [0-4] Footsteps Flyers (from J Berry [2-19] Jun 1999).*

LADY CARLINA (IRE) RR 102f 1455a[7]
3 f
Form - 47
2000 Turf 0-2: (8f, 11f) (sft, gd)
Currently very useful filly. Turf high 102 (1st run) - 4th of 18 to Xua (30 Apr Capannelle 8f sft RF 1031a). **J Heloury in ITY [0-2].*

LADY CAROLINE (IRE) BHB 47a RR 37f 2792[15]
4 b f Hamas (IRE) 8f **(72)** - Pericolo (IRE) (Kris) 9.5f **(73)**
Form - 00
Record 2000 - 1st:0 2nd:0 3rd:0 Ran:1
Pre2000 - 1st:1 2nd:3 3rd:2 Ran:22
Win Prizemoney £2,832 *Total Prizemoney* £5,873
Wins 1998 *Dec Lingfi (STD) H 6f 65 69* <
2000 Turf 0-1: (8f) (frm)
Scopey, very moderate filly, effective 6f, acts on gd, has worn blinkers. Inconsistent.
**A T Murphy [0-7] Hertford Offset Ltd (from M Johnston [1-17] Apr 1999).*

LADY COLDUNELL BHB 57f59a RR 58f 59a 4047[2]
4 b f Deploy 11.4f **(67)** - Beau's Delight (USA) (Lypheor) 12f **(71)**
Form - 032
Record 2000 - 1st:0 2nd:1 3rd:1 Ran:3
Pre2000 - 1st:2 2nd:4 3rd:1 Ran:18
Win Prizemoney £7,557 *Total Prizemoney* £14,057
Wins * 1999 Aug Epsom (GD) H 12f 55 55
* 1999 *Jly Lingfi (STD) H 12f 52 62* <
2000 Turf 0-3: (12f, 13f, 14f) (g-s, gd, g-f)
Scopey, average filly, effective 12 to 16f, acts on g-s to frm - acts on Equi, has worn blinkers, likes tight tracks, does well at Epsom. Turf high 56 - 2nd of 5 getting 12lb from Barcelona (28 Aug Newcastle 14f g-s RF 4047). **N A Callaghan [3-24] Peter Crane.*

LADY CYRANO BHB 32f44a RR 49f 44a 5009[8]
3 b f Cyrano de Bergerac 7.3f **(58)** - Hazy Kay (IRE) (Treasure Kay)
Form - 362060200008
Record 2000 - 1st:0 2nd:2 3rd:1 Ran:12
Pre2000 - 1st:0 2nd:0 3rd:3 Ran:10
Win Prizemoney £0 *Total Prizemoney* £2,328
2000 Turf 0-6: (6f, 7f 3, 8f 2) (gd, g-f 2, frm 3) 2000 AW 0-6: (6f, 7f 3, 8f 2) (Fibr 6)
Scopey, moderate filly, effective 6f, acts on g-f, has worn blinkers. Turf high 49. AW high 45. **Mrs N Macauley [0-22] J Teasdale.*

LADY DEALER BHB 25f RR 6f 4925[15]
5 b m No Big Deal - Our Horizon (Skyliner) 7.3f **(53)**
Form - 08U000
Record 2000 - 1st:0 2nd:0 3rd:0 Ran:6
Pre2000 - 1st:0 2nd:0 3rd:0 Ran:3
2000 Turf 0-5: (5f, 6f, 7f, 8f 2) (g-s 3, g-f 2) 2000 AW 0-1: (7f) (Equi)
Very poor filly. Turf high 6. **M D I Usher [0-9] Mrs J Gawthorpe.*

LADY DONATELLA BHB 48f45a RR 60f 45a 4364[7]
3 b f Last Tycoon 9.4f **(73)** - Nekhbet (Artaius (USA)) 9f **(69)**
Form - 627
Record 2000 - 1st:0 2nd:1 3rd:0 Ran:3
Pre2000 - 1st:0 2nd:0 3rd:0 Ran:3
Win Prizemoney £0 *Total Prizemoney* £660
2000 Turf 0-3: (10f, 12f 2) (gd, g-f 2)
Leggy, average filly. Turf high 52 (began Jly).
**M L W Bell [0-6] Mrs M Swinburn.*

LADY EBERSPACHER (IRE) BHB 67f RR 68f 4724[15]
2 b f Royal Abjar (USA) - Samriah (IRE) (Wassl) 9.7f **(62)**
Form - 042440
Record 2000 - 1st:0 2nd:1 3rd:0 Ran:6
Win Prizemoney £0 *Total Prizemoney* £1,866
2000 Turf 0-6: (5f 6) (g-s, gd, frm 4)
Average filly, effective 5f, acts on frm. Turf high 68 - 2nd of 11 to Strumpet (28 Jun Salisbury 5f frm RF 2348).
**Mrs P N Dutfield [0-6] The Two Legs Partnership.*

LADY FEARLESS BHB 36f RR 28f 4766[14]
3 b f Cosmonaut - Lady Broker **(44a)** (Petorius) 7.3f **(61)**
Form - 8060
Record 2000 - 1st:0 2nd:0 3rd:0 Ran:4
Pre2000 - 1st:0 2nd:0 3rd:0 Ran:2
2000 Turf 0-3: (7f, 9f, 17f) (g-s, gd, g-f) 2000 AW 0-1: (6f) (Fibr)
Light-framed, little account filly. Turf high 25 (began Spt).
**M Mullineaux [0-6] Esprit de Corps Racing.*

LADY FLORA RR ?f 4209[9]
4 b f Alflora (IRE) - Lady Marguerrite **(57f)** (Blakeney) 10.5f **(64)**
Form - 00
Record 2000 - 1st:0 2nd:0 3rd:0 Ran:2
Pre2000 - 1st:0 2nd:0 3rd:0 Ran:1
2000 Turf 0-2: (8f, 9f) (gd, hrd)
Lengthy, very poor filly. Turf high 4 (began Aug).
**D McCain [0-3] Mrs D McCain.*

LADY GLITTERS (FR) RR 98f 1445a[3]
3 f
Form - 3
2000 Turf 0-1: (8f) (gd)
Currently very useful. **P Demercastel in FR [0-2] Jly 1999).*

LADY HELEN (IRE) RR 75f 3745[7]
3 b f Salse (USA) 10.9f **(71)** - Old Domesday Book (High Top) 10.2f **(67)**
Form - 05101707
Record 2000 - 1st:2 2nd:0 3rd:0 Ran:8
Pre2000 - 1st:1 2nd:0 3rd:0 Ran:5
Win Prizemoney £12,191 *Total Prizemoney* £12,191
Wins *** 2000** Jly Newcas (FRM) H 9f 70 75 <
*** 2000** Jly Haydoc (G-F) H 8.1f 62 69
* 1999 Jly Beverl (G-F) 7.5f 63
2000 Turf 2-8: (7f 2, 8f 1-4, 9f 1-1, 10f) (gd, g-f 1-4, frm 1-3)
Light-framed, above-average filly, effective 8 to 9f, acts on g-f to frm, likes left handed tracks. Turf high 75 (began Jly) - 1st of 5 getting 5lb from Sea Squirt (29 Jly Newcastle RF 3212) - also 1st of 9 getting 4lb from Cibenze (16 Jly Haydock RF 2857). She looked suited by being ridden closer to the pace when winning over a mile at Haydock in July and the same tactics were successfully employed when she won over a bit further at Newcastle later the same month. Suited by fast ground. **T D Easterby [3-13] M P Burke.*

LADY INCH RR 53f 5136[10]
2 b f Inchinor 8.9f **(64)** - Head Turner **(43f 52a)** (My Dad Tom (USA))
Form - 0
Record 2000 - 1st:0 2nd:0 3rd:0 Ran:1
2000 Turf 0-1: (8f) (g-s)
Currently fair filly. **B Smart [0-1] The Dyball Partnership.*

LADY IN LOVE RR 39f 3209[11]
2 b f Robellino (USA) 9.5f **(68)** - Lets Fall In Love (USA) (Northern Baby (CAN)) 11.6f **(71)**
Form - 00
Record 2000 - 1st:0 2nd:0 3rd:0 Ran:2
2000 Turf 0-2: (6f, 7f) (g-f, frm)
Currently very moderate filly, often wears blinkers. Turf high 39.
**R A Fahey [0-2] Lets Go Racing 1.*

LADY IN THE NIGHT (IRE) BHB 50f RR 50f 4300[11]
2 ch f Royal Academy (USA) 7.8f **(77)** - Pig Tail (Habitat) 9.4f **(70)**
Form - 400
Record 2000 - 1st:0 2nd:0 3rd:0 Ran:3
Win Prizemoney £0 *Total Prizemoney* £258
2000 Turf 0-3: (5f, 6f 2) (gd, g-f, frm)
Currently fair filly. Turf high 50. **I A Balding [0-3] M E Wates.*

LADY IN WAITING BHB 108f RR 109f 2522a[5]
5 b m Kylian (USA) 8.1f **(66)** - High Savannah (Rousillon (USA)) 8.2f **(74)**
Form - 55
Record 2000 - 1st:0 2nd:0 3rd:0 Ran:2
Pre2000 - 1st:6 2nd:4 3rd:0 Ran:17
Win Prizemoney £76,240 *Total Prizemoney* £143,240
Wins * 1999 Oct Newmar (SFT) G2 10f 109 <

* 1999	May	York	(SFT)	L	10.4f	102	
* 1998	Oct	Newmar	(GD)	L	10f	97	
* 1998	Spt	Chepst	(G-S)		10.2f	109+	
* 1997	Jun	Newmar	(SFT)	L	6f	92	
* 1997	Jun	Leices	(G-F)		5f	86	

2000 Turf 0-2: (10f 2) (g-s 2)

Pattern-class filly, effective 10f, acts on g-s to g-f, best on g-f. Turf high 107 - 5th of 10 giving 14lb to Lady Upstage (1 Jly Curragh 10f g-s RF 2522a). Consistent. She showed high-class form at three, but ran just twice in 2000 when she attempted to make the running each time. **P F I Cole [6-19] Pegasus Racing Ltd.*

LADY IONA BHB 28f **RR 27f** 100[7]

4 ch f Weldnaas (USA) 8.4f **(55)** - Shadha (Shirley Heights) 10.3f **(74)**

Form - 7

Record 2000 - 1st:0 2nd:0 3rd:0 Ran:1
Pre2000 - 1st:0 2nd:1 3rd:0 Ran:13

Win Prizemoney £0 *Total Prizemoney* £720

2000 AW 0-1: (12f) (Fibr)

Light-framed, little account filly, effective 8f, acts on g-f, likes left handed tracks. **Martyn Wane [0-15] Mrs C M Barlow.*

LADY IRENE (IRE) BHB 37f23a **RR 41f 23a** 1720[11]

4 br f Tirol 8.1f **(64)** - Felsen (IRE) (Ballad Rock) 7.8f **(63)**

Form - 800

Record 2000 - 1st:0 2nd:0 3rd:0 Ran:2
Pre2000 - 1st:0 2nd:2 3rd:0 Ran:11

Win Prizemoney £0 *Total Prizemoney* £1,693

2000 Turf 0-1: (12f) (gd) 2000 AW 0-1: (11f) (Fibr)

Neat, moderate filly, effective 10 to 12f, acts on g-s to gd, has worn blinkers. Inconsistent. **T J Naughton [0-16] T J Naughton.*

LADY JAZZ BHB 50f53a **RR 22f 53a** 3181[10]

5 b m Night Shift (USA) 8.1f **(73)** - Penamint (Siberian Express (USA)) 8.8f **(65)**

Form - 0

Record 2000 - 1st:0 2nd:0 3rd:0 Ran:1
Pre2000 - 1st:0 2nd:2 3rd:0 Ran:7

Win Prizemoney £0 *Total Prizemoney* £2,184

2000 Turf 0-1: (7f) (frm)

Little account filly. **T J Naughton [0-8] Miss L A Elliott.*

LADY JEANNIE BHB 40f **RR 30f** 5198[8]

3 b f Emarati (USA) 6.6f **(63)** - Cottonwood (Teenoso (USA)) 9.9f **(72)**

Form - 06008

Record 2000 - 1st:0 2nd:0 3rd:0 Ran:5

2000 Turf 0-5: (6f 3, 7f 2) (gd 3, g-f, frm)

Unfurnished, very moderate filly. Turf high 30. **M J Haynes [0-5] G R Sanford & Partners.*

LADY JO BHB 55f50a **RR 58f 50a** 4928[10]

4 ch f Phountzi (USA) 9.6f **(60)** - Lady Kalliste (Another Realm) 6.6f **(55)**

Form - 66676751600

Record 2000 - 1st:1 2nd:0 3rd:0 Ran:11
Pre2000 - 1st:2 2nd:0 3rd:2 Ran:13

Win Prizemoney £9,212 *Total Prizemoney* £9,989

Wins	* 2000	Aug	Lingfi	(G-F)	H	11.5f	54	58	
	* 1999	Jun	Lingfi	(G-F)	H	10f	64	66+	<
	* 1999	Jun	Yarmou	(GD)	H	10.1f	58	65	

2000 Turf 1-8: (9f 2, 10f 3, 11f 1-1, 12f 2) (gd, g-f 5, frm 1-2) 2000 AW 0-3: (10f, 12f 2) (Equi 3)

Workmanlike, fair filly, effective 10 to 12f, best at 10f, acts on gd to frm - acts on Equi, best on g-f, likes left handed tracks, prefers tight tracks, excels at Lingfield. Turf high 58 - 1st of 9 giving 9lb to Forest Dream (11 Aug Lingfield RF 3557). AW high 59 (1st run) - 6th of 14 giving 17lb to Lost Spirit (8 Jan Lingfield 12f Equi RF 0051). **S Dow [3-24] Ken Butler.*

LADY JONES BHB 59f **RR 59f** 5162[1]

3 b f Emperor Jones (USA) - So Beguiling (USA) (Woodman (USA)) 9f **(74)**

Form - 013005671

Record 2000 - 1st:2 2nd:0 3rd:1 Ran:9
Pre2000 - 1st:1 2nd:0 3rd:0 Ran:6

Win Prizemoney £8,291 *Total Prizemoney* £8,717

Wins	* 2000	Oct	Nottin	(SFT)	H	10f	51	58+	
	* 2000	Jun	Haydoc	(G-S)	H	8.1f	50	59	<
	* 1999	Spt	Bright	(G-F)	S	7f		57	

2000 Turf 2-9: (8f 1-5, 9f, 10f 1-3) (sft 1-1, g-s 1-3, gd, g-f, frm 3)

Workmanlike, fair filly, effective 7 to 10f, best at 8f, acts on sft to frm, prefers left handed tracks, prefers tight tracks. Turf high 59 - 1st of 10 getting 10lb from Pix Me Up (9 Jun Haydock RF 1851) - also 1st of 14 giving 11lb to Satire (24 Oct Nottingham RF 5162). **J Pearce [3-15] Mrs Jean Routledge.*

LADY KINVARRAH (IRE) BHB 72f **RR 75f** 5074[9]

2 b f Brief Truce (USA) 9.1f **(73)** - Al Corniche (IRE) **(45f 37a)** (Bluebird (USA)) 7.5f **(69)**

Form - 067310

Record 2000 - 1st:1 2nd:0 3rd:1 Ran:6

Win Prizemoney £2,990 *Total Prizemoney* £3,244

Wins	* 2000	Spt	Leices	(G-S)	H	6f	69	75	<

2000 Turf 1-6: (5f 2, 6f 1-2, 7f 2) (g-s, gd 2, g-f 1-0)

Above-average filly, effective 6f, acts on g-f. Turf high 75 - 1st of 19 giving 4lb to Divine Wind (18 Spt Leicester RF 4490).
**P J Makin [1-2] John Gale & George Darling (from J R Arnold [0-4] Jly 2000).*

LADY LAHAR BHB 109f **RR 97f** 5203a[4]

2 b f Fraam - Brigadiers Bird (IRE) (Mujadil (USA))

Form - 134104

Record 2000 - 1st:2 2nd:0 3rd:1 Ran:6

Win Prizemoney £35,919 *Total Prizemoney* £44,799

Wins	* 2000	Aug	Currag	(G-S)	G3	7f	98	<
	* 2000	Jun	Chepst	(FRM)		6.1f	77	

2000 Turf 2-6: (6f 1-3, 7f 1-2, 8f) (hvy, g-s 1-1, gd, g-f 1-2, frm)

Very useful filly, effective 6 to 8f, acts on hvy to frm. Turf high 98 - 1st of 7 getting 3lb from Bonnard (26 Aug Curragh RF 4089a). She surprised a better fancied stable-mate on her debut, but proved that was no fluke when winning a Group 3 at The Curragh in August. Unlikely to stay beyond a mile, she is tough and consistent. **M R Channon [2-6].*

LADY LAUREATE BHB 55f55a **RR 57?f 55a** 4965[20]

2 b f Sir Harry Lewis (USA) - Cyrillic **(86f)** (Rock City)

Form - 0560

Record 2000 - 1st:0 2nd:0 3rd:0 Ran:4

2000 Turf 0-3: (6f 2, 8f) (gd 2, g-f) 2000 AW 0-1: (8f) (Fibr)

Fair filly. Turf high 57 (began Spt). **C C Bravery [0-4] Blackfoot Bloodstock.*

LADY LAZARUS BHB 40f **RR 33f** 739[16]

4 ch f Beveled (USA) 6.9f **(64)** - Swilly Express (Ballacashtal (CAN)) 5.3f **(50)**

Form - 0

Record 2000 - 1st:0 2nd:0 3rd:0 Ran:1
Pre2000 - 1st:0 2nd:0 3rd:1 Ran:9

Win Prizemoney £0 *Total Prizemoney* £772

2000 Turf 0-1: (8f) (gd)

Scopey, very moderate filly. Becoming disappointing. **M Blanshard [0-10] P J Doherty.*

LADY LENOR BHB 73f70a **RR 72f 70a** 5243[3]

2 b f Presidium 7.5f **(56)** - Sparkling Roberta **(39f 33a)** (Kind of Hush) 10.1f **(62)**

Form - 023

Record 2000 - 1st:0 2nd:1 3rd:1 Ran:3

Win Prizemoney £0 *Total Prizemoney* £1,163

2000 Turf 0-2: (5f 2) (gd, frm) 2000 AW 0-1: (6f) (Fibr)

Currently above-average filly. Turf high 72 (began Aug) - 2nd of 12 to Hilton Head (3 Oct Catterick 5f gd RF 4772).
**Mrs G S Rees [0-2] Longlands Racing (from J R Weymes [0-1] Aug 2000).*

LADY LIFFEY (IRE) **RR 37f** 3441[14]

2 ch f Case Law 6f **(64)** - Grace de Bois (Tap On Wood) 10.3f **(65)**

Form - 80

Record 2000 - 1st:0 2nd:0 3rd:0 Ran:2

2000 Turf 0-2: (5f 2) (g-f, frm)

Currently very moderate filly. Turf high 37 (began Jly). **Mrs P N Dutfield [0-2] John Hudson.*

LADY-LOVE BHB 60f56a **RR 65f 56a** 3961[2]
3 b f Pursuit of Love 9.5f **(69)** - Lady Day (FR) (Lightning (FR)) 7.9f **(74)**
Form - 502002
Record 2000 - 1st:0 2nd:2 3rd:0 Ran:6
Pre2000 - 1st:1 2nd:0 3rd:0 Ran:4
Win Prizemoney £2,801 *Total Prizemoney* £4,421
Wins * 1999 Jun Mussel (GD) 5f 64+ <
2000 Turf 0-6: (6f, 7f 3, 8f 2) (g-f 2, frm 3, hrd)
Scopey, average filly, effective 5 to 8f, acts on g-f to hrd, best on g-f, has worn blinkers. Turf high 65 (1st run) - 5th of 8 to Lady of Windsor (5 May Musselburgh 8f frm RF 1039). Inconsistent.
**Denys Smith [1-10] Duke of Sutherland.*

LADY LUCHA (USA) BHB 72f **RR 73f** 2489[4]
3 ch f Lord Avie (USA) - Sin Lucha (USA) (Northfields (USA)) 9f **(72)**
Form - 0214
Record 2000 - 1st:1 2nd:1 3rd:0 Ran:4
Win Prizemoney £2,824 *Total Prizemoney* £3,358
Wins * **2000** Jun Ripon (G-F) 10f 73 <
2000 Turf 1-4: (8f 2, 10f 1-1, 12f) (gd, frm 1-3)
Above-average filly. Turf high 73 - also 1st of 9 getting 5lb from Lanntansa (22 Jun Ripon RF 2184). **B W Hills [1-4] K Abdulla.*

LADY MILETRIAN (IRE) BHB 77f **RR 79f** 3436[8]
2 b f Barathea (IRE) - Local Custom (IRE) (Be My Native (USA)) 10.2f **(71)**
Form - 528
Record 2000 - 1st:0 2nd:1 3rd:0 Ran:3
Win Prizemoney £0 *Total Prizemoney* £1,320
2000 Turf 0-3: (6f 3) (gd, g-f 2)
Currently above-average filly. Turf high 79 (began Jly) - 2nd of 11 to Foodbroker Fancy (22 Jly Newmarket 6f g-f RF 3028).
**M R Channon [0-3] Miletrian Plc.*

LADY MUCK (IRE) BHB 40f **RR 29f** 5025[7]
4 b f Shalford (IRE) 7.8f **(63)** - Kept in Style (Castle Keep) 8.3f **(57)**
Form - 007
Record 2000 - 1st:0 2nd:0 3rd:0 Ran:3
Pre2000 - 1st:1 2nd:2 3rd:0 Ran:13
Win Prizemoney £3,647 *Total Prizemoney* £5,617
Wins * 1998 Jly Epsom (G-F) 7f 72 <
2000 Turf 0-3: (8f 2, 11f) (g-s, g-f 2)
Light-framed, little account filly, has worn blinkers. Turf high 29 (began Spt). **D J S ffrenchDavis [1-17] Mrs Patrick McCarthy.*

LADY NAIRN BHB 30f **RR 37f** 152[9]
4 b f Mujadil (USA) 7.7f **(70)** - Animate (IRE) (Tate Gallery (USA)) 7.4f **(67)**
Form - 000
Record 2000 - 1st:0 2nd:0 3rd:0 Ran:2
Pre2000 - 1st:0 2nd:0 3rd:1 Ran:4
Win Prizemoney £0 *Total Prizemoney* £444
2000 AW 0-2: (6f, 7f) (Fibr 2)
Unfurnished, very moderate filly. AW high 8.
**A Berry [0-2] Murray Grubb (from J Berry [0-1] Nov 1999).*

LADY NOOR BHB 47f **RR 45f** 4826[17]
3 b f Lugana Beach 7f **(63)** - Noor El Houdah (IRE) **(49f 48a)** (Fayruz)
Form - 0000500
Record 2000 - 1st:0 2nd:0 3rd:0 Ran:7
Pre2000 - 1st:0 2nd:0 3rd:2 Ran:6
Win Prizemoney £0 *Total Prizemoney* £1,515
2000 Turf 0-7: (6f 5, 7f 2) (gd 3, g-f 3, frm)
Leggy, moderate filly. Turf high 45.
**Mrs P N Dutfield [0-13] Mrs Margaret Sinanan.*

LADY OF BILSTON (IRE) RR 231[4]
3 b f Bin Ajwaad (IRE) - Takeshi (IRE) **(62f 51a)** (Cadeaux Genereux)
Form - 34
Record 2000 - 1st:0 2nd:0 3rd:1 Ran:2
Win Prizemoney £0 *Total Prizemoney* £430
2000 AW 0-2: (7f, 9f) (Fibr 2)
Unfurnished, currently fair filly. AW high 54.
**D R C Elsworth [0-2] James Bell.*

LADY OF CHAD (IRE) RR 118?f 4739[6]
3 b f Last Tycoon 9.4f **(73)** - Sahara Breeze (Ela-Mana-Mou) 10.1f **(70)**
Form - 187106
2000 Turf 2-6: (8f 2-5, 11f) (hvy 1-1, g-s 1-1, gd 2, g-f 2)
High-class filly, effective 8f, acts on sft to g-s, favours right handed tracks. Turf high 118 - 1st of 13 getting 8lb from Danzigaway (30 Jly Deauville RF 3351a). She looked an excellent prospect when making all to win the Prix Marcel Boussac in 1999, but failed to live up to expectations last year. Probably best when able to dominate, she benefited from an aggressive ride when winning the Prix d'Astarte at Deauville in July, but had no excuse for tame efforts on her last two starts. **R Gibson in FR [4-8] Teruya Yoshida.*

LADY OF THE NIGHT (IRE) BHB 47a **RR 56?f** 201[10]
5 b m Night Shift (USA) 8.1f **(73)** - Joma Kaanem (Double Form) 7.3f **(58)**
Form - 200
Record 2000 - 1st:0 2nd:0 3rd:0 Ran:2
Pre2000 - 1st:0 2nd:1 3rd:0 Ran:3
Win Prizemoney £0 *Total Prizemoney* £1,092
2000 AW 0-2: (7f, 12f) (Equi 2)
Fair filly. AW high 11.
**Mrs L Stubbs [0-3] D R Richards (from P W Harris [0-2] Oct 1999).*

LADY OF WINDSOR (IRE) BHB 64f **RR 73f** 5190[1]
3 ch f Woods of Windsor (USA) - North Lady (Northfields (USA)) 9f **(72)**
Form - 5102380674041
Record 2000 - 1st:2 2nd:1 3rd:1 Ran:13
Pre2000 - 1st:0 2nd:2 3rd:1 Ran:11
Win Prizemoney £5,349 *Total Prizemoney* £11,482
Wins * **2000** Oct Mussel (SFT) H 7.1f 58 64
* **2000** May Mussel (FRM) 8f 73 <
2000 Turf 2-12: (6f 2, 7f 1-7, 8f 1-3) (gd 1-5, g-f 2, frm 1-5) 2000 AW 0-1: (6f) (Fibr)
Above-average filly, effective 6 to 8f, best at 7f, acts on gd to frm, best on g-f, mostly wears blinkers (extremely effectively), prefers right handed tracks, likes tight tracks, does well at Musselburgh and Carlisle. Turf high 73 - 1st of 8 getting 19lb from Royal Artist (5 May Musselburgh RF 1039) - also 1st of 8 giving 4lb to Encounter (26 Oct Musselburgh RF 5190).
**I Semple [2-24] Raeburn Brick Ltd.*

LADY PAHIA (IRE) RR 73f 3621[4]
2 ch f Pivotal - Appledorn (Doulab (USA)) 9.8f **(65)**
Form - 4
Record 2000 - 1st:0 2nd:0 3rd:0 Ran:1
Win Prizemoney £0 *Total Prizemoney* £336
2000 Turf 0-1: (7f) (frm)
Currently above-average filly. (1st run) - 4th of 9 to Shahirah (14 Aug Kempton 7f frm RF 3621). **A P Jarvis [0-1] Ambrose Turnbull.*

LADY RACHEL (IRE) BHB 40f47a **RR 43f 47a** 851[7]
5 b m Priolo (USA) 10.9f **(71)** - Alpine Spring (Head for Heights) 9.6f **(55)**
Form - 37257
Record 2000 - 1st:0 2nd:1 3rd:1 Ran:5
Pre2000 - 1st:2 2nd:4 3rd:7 Ran:28
Win Prizemoney £6,607 *Total Prizemoney* £18,640
Wins 1998 Aug Carlis (G-S) H 12f 64 69 <
1998 May Pontef (G-F) H 10f 60 66
2000 Turf 0-2: (14f, 16f) (sft, g-s) 2000 AW 0-3: (16f 3) (Fibr 3)
Moderate filly, effective 13 to 14f, best at 14f, acts on g-s to gd, best on gd, has worn blinkers, likes tight tracks. Turf high 37. AW high 46. Consistent.
**M W Easterby [0-7] Steve Macdonald (from J L Eyre [2-28] Nov 1999).*

LADY ROCK RR 66f 5183[6]
2 b f Mistertopogigo (IRE) - Bollin Victoria (Jalmood (USA)) 10.1f **(52)**
Form - 7846366
Record 2000 - 1st:0 2nd:0 3rd:1 Ran:7
Win Prizemoney £0 *Total Prizemoney* £1,187
2000 Turf 0-7: (5f 7) (g-s, gd, g-f, frm 3, hrd)
Average filly, effective 5f, acts on g-f to hrd. Turf high 66 - 3rd of 13 to Ami's Angel (20 Aug Pontefract 5f hrd RF 3825).
**R Bastiman [0-7] New Kids on the Rock Ltd.*

LADY ROCKSTAR BHB 66f **RR 67f** 5026[10]
5 b m Rock Hopper 10.6f **(54)** - Silk St James (Pas de Seul) 9.1f **(67)**

Form - 727070
Record 2000 - 1st:0 2nd:1 3rd:0 Ran:6
Pre2000 - 1st:9 2nd:2 3rd:1 Ran:33
Win Prizemoney £28,631 *Total Prizemoney* £38,598
Wins * 1999 May Newbur (G-S) H 10f 76 80
* 1998 Jun Windso (GD) 10f 86+ <
* 1998 Jun Folkes (G-F) H 9.7f 65 76+
* 1998 Jun Windso (GD) H 10f 65 78
* 1998 Jun Nottin (G-S) H 8.2f 56 75
* 1998 Jun Yarmou (SFT) H 10.1f 47 61+
* 1998 Jun Haydoc (GD) H 8.1f 40 55
* 1998 Jun Folkes (GD) H 9.7f 40 53+
* 1998 May Ayr (G-F) H 9.1f 40 48
2000 Turf 0-6: (10f 6) (g-s 2, gd, g-f 2, frm)
Average filly, effective 10 to 11f, best at 10f, acts on g-s to frm, has worn blinkers, likes left handed tracks, likes tight tracks. Turf high 69.
**M J Ryan [9-39] The Five Star Partnership.*

LADY SANDROVITCH (IRE) BHB 38f42a **RR 28f 42a** 3600[14]
3 b f Desert Style (IRE) - Mauras Pride (IRE) (Cadeaux Genereux)
Form - 437600
Record 2000 - 1st:0 2nd:0 3rd:0 Ran:4
Pre2000 - 1st:0 2nd:0 3rd:1 Ran:4
Win Prizemoney £0 *Total Prizemoney* £250
2000 Turf 0-2: (5f, 6f) (frm, hrd) 2000 AW 0-2: (6f, 7f) (Fibr 2)
Workmanlike, very moderate filly. Turf high 28 (began Aug). AW high 30. Consistent. **R A Fahey [0-8] J M Flynn.*

LADY SANTANA (IRE) BHB 60f **RR 66f** 521[5]
3 b f Doyoun 10.7f **(69)** - Santana Lady (IRE) **(64df 60a)** (Blakeney) 10.5f **(64)**
Form - 5
Record 2000 - 1st:0 2nd:0 3rd:0 Ran:1
Pre2000 - 1st:0 2nd:0 3rd:0 Ran:3
2000 Turf 0-1: (12f) (frm)
Leggy, average filly. (1st run) - 5th of 20 getting 7lb from Zorro (27 Mar Windsor 12f frm RF 0521).
**Mrs Merrita Jones [0-2] F J Sainsbury (from C G Cox [0-1] Aug 1999).*

LADY SHARP SHOT (IRE) **RR 78f** 5065[13]
2 b f Son of Sharp Shot (IRE) - Ski For Gold **(69f)** (Shirley Heights) 10.3f **(74)**
Form - 50
Record 2000 - 1st:0 2nd:0 3rd:0 Ran:2
2000 Turf 0-2: (8f 2) (g-s 2)
Currently above-average filly. Turf high 78 (began Spt).
**J L Dunlop [0-2] Windflower Overseas Holdings Inc.*

LADY STALKER BHB 46f **RR 47f** 4320[15]
3 b f Primo Dominie 7.2f **(67)** - Tarvie (Swing Easy (USA)) 6.5f **(55)**
Form - 000300
Record 2000 - 1st:0 2nd:0 3rd:1 Ran:6
Pre2000 - 1st:0 2nd:0 3rd:0 Ran:5
Win Prizemoney £0 *Total Prizemoney* £914
2000 Turf 0-6: (5f 2, 6f 4) (gd, g-f, frm 4)
Small, moderate filly. Turf high 47.
**Andrew Reid [0-6] P Fetherston-Godley (from M J Fetherston-Godley [0-5] Oct 1999).*

LADY TILLY BHB 38f40a **RR 39f 40a** 3930[10]
3 b f Puissance 7.1f **(60)** - Lady of Itatiba (BEL) (King Of Macedon) 8.1f **(59)**
Form - 0544000
Record 2000 - 1st:0 2nd:0 3rd:0 Ran:7
Pre2000 - 1st:0 2nd:0 3rd:1 Ran:8
Win Prizemoney £0 *Total Prizemoney* £550
2000 Turf 0-6: (7f 4, 8f 2) (gd 2, g-f, frm 2, hrd) 2000 AW 0-1: (7f) (Fibr)
Leggy, very moderate filly, has worn blinkers. Turf high 39. Inconsistent.
**B Ellison [0-7] James S Kennerley and Miss Jenny Hall (from Martyn Wane [0-8] Nov 1999).*

LADY TWO K (IRE) BHB 73f **RR 74f** 5069[1]
3 b f Grand Lodge (USA) - Princess Pavlova (IRE) (Sadler's Wells (USA)) 10f **(76)**
Form - 84601
Record 2000 - 1st:1 2nd:0 3rd:0 Ran:5
Win Prizemoney £3,669 *Total Prizemoney* £0,900
Wins * 2000 Oct Bath (GD) H 11.7f 67 74 <
2000 Turf 1-5: (8f 3, 11f, 12f 1-1) (g-s 1-3, g-f, frm)
Strong, above-average filly. Turf high 74 - 1st of 20 giving 2lb to Gemini Guest (19 Oct Bath RF 5069). **J Mackie [1-5] Gwen Dot Com.*

LADY UPSTAGE (IRE) **RR 119f** 5096a[2]
3 b f Alzao (USA) 9.8f **(73)** - She's the Tops (Shernazar) 10.2f **(73)**
Form - 1251732
Record 2000 - 1st:2 2nd:2 3rd:1 Ran:7
Pre2000 - 1st:1 2nd:0 3rd:1 Ran:4
Win Prizemoney £66,695 *Total Prizemoney* £141,850
Wins * 2000 Jly Currag (G-S) G2 10f 110 <
*** 2000** Apr Kempto (SFT) L 8f 103+
* 1999 Spt Bright (SFT) 7f 86+
2000 Turf 2-7: (8f 1-1, 10f 1-5, 12f) (sft 1-1, g-s 1-2, gd, g-f 2, frm)
Well made, high-class filly, effective 10f, acts on g-s to frm. Turf high 119 - 2nd of 6 getting 6lb from Fly For Avie (15 Oct Woodbine 10f frm RF 5096a) - also 1st of 10 getting 5lb from Preseli (1 Jly Curragh RF 2522a). Improving. A thoroughly likeable filly who raced gamely in the face of some stiff tasks. Edged out in close finishes to the Musidora Stakes and Grade 1 EP Taylor Stakes, she is worth another try over a mile and a half and acts on any ground.
**B W Hills [3-11].*

Lady Upstage ran some fine races in defeat

LADY VIENNA BHB 36f **RR 36f** 3133[7]
3 ch f Weldnaas (USA) 8.4f **(55)** - Fresh Lady (IRE) (Fresh Breeze (USA))
Form - 58387
Record 2000 - 1st:0 2nd:0 3rd:1 Ran:5
Pre2000 - 1st:0 2nd:0 3rd:0 Ran:4
Win Prizemoney £0 *Total Prizemoney* £278
2000 Turf 0-5: (8f, 10f 3, 11f) (g-s, g-f, frm 3)
Leggy, very moderate filly, has worn blinkers. Turf high 36.
**W G M Turner [0-9] D & J Racing.*

LADY WARD (IRE) BHB 59f54a **RR 70df 54a** 4257[17]
2 b f Mujadil (USA) 7.7f **(70)** - Sans Ceriph (IRE) (Thatching) 8f **(66)**
Form - 83650
Record 2000 - 1st:0 2nd:0 3rd:1 Ran:5
Win Prizemoney £0 *Total Prizemoney* £593
2000 Turf 0-5: (6f 4, 7f) (gd 2, g-f 2, frm)
Above-average filly. Turf high 70 (began Jly).
**M H Tompkins [0-5] Lillypop Racing Club.*

LADYWELL BLAISE (IRE) BHB 50f60a **RR 43f 60a** 4633[8]
3 b f Turtle Island (IRE) - Duly Elected (Persian Bold) 9.3f **(66)**
Form - 53146406012007000008
Record 2000 - 1st:2 2nd:1 3rd:1 Ran:19

Pre2000 - 1st:0 2nd:0 3rd:0 Ran:1
Win Prizemoney £5,193 *Total Prizemoney* £6,939
Wins 2000 Jly Doncas (G-F) H 7f 53 55
2000 *Jan Lingfi (STD) 6f 61* <
2000 Turf 1-14: (5f, 6f 2, 7f 1-9, 8f, 11f) (sft, g-s 2, gd 2, g-f 4, frm 1-5)
2000 AW 1-5: (6f 1-2, 7f 3) (Equi 1-3, Fibr 2)
Workmanlike, average filly, effective 6 to 7f, best at 7f, acts on g-f to frm - acts on AW. Turf high 60 - 2nd of 7 getting 16lb from Night Empress (4 Jly Yarmouth 7f g-f RF 2503) - also 1st of 14 getting 5lb from Unchain My Heart (1 Jly Doncaster RF 2432). AW high 61 - also 1st of 9 getting 5lb from Lusong (15 Jan Lingfield RF 0095).
**J J Bridger [0-9] W Wood (from M L W Bell [2-11] Jly 2000).*

LADY WYN BHB 20f RR 1703[13]
5 ch m Mac's Fighter - Wanracine (Dom Racine (FR)) 9.2f **(62)**
Form - 000
Record 2000 - 1st:0 2nd:0 3rd:0 Ran:3
Pre2000 - 1st:0 2nd:0 3rd:0 Ran:3
2000 Turf 0-3: (10f, 11f, 12f) (g-s, frm 2)
Very poor filly. **J M Bradley [0-6] Philip Davies.*

LA FAY BHB 57f RR 64f 5069[10]
3 b f Caerleon (USA) 10.9f **(79)** - Fayrooz (USA) **(81df)** (Gulch (USA)) 8f **(81)**
Form - 07800
Record 2000 - 1st:0 2nd:0 3rd:0 Ran:5
Pre2000 - 1st:0 2nd:1 3rd:0 Ran:2
Win Prizemoney £0 *Total Prizemoney* £2,160
2000 Turf 0-5: (10f 2, 12f 3) (g-s, g-f 2, frm 2)
Scopey, average filly, effective 7f, acts on frm. Turf high 64.
**J L Dunlop [0-7] Capt J Macdonald-Buchanan.*

LAFAYETTE (IRE) RR 57f 5312[11]
2 b c General Monash (USA) - Bezee (Belmez (USA))
Form - 00
Record 2000 - 1st:0 2nd:0 3rd:0 Ran:2
2000 Turf 0-2: (7f, 8f) (g-s, gd)
Currently fair colt. Turf high 57 (began Oct).
**A C Stewart [0-2] Racing For Gold.*

LAFFAH (USA) BHB 68f RR 69f 4987[29]
5 b g Silver Hawk (USA) 11.2f **(85)** - Sakiyah (USA) (Secretariat (USA)) 9f **(79)**
Form - 13411810
Record 2000 - 1st:4 2nd:0 3rd:1 Ran:8
Pre2000 - 1st:0 2nd:0 3rd:0 Ran:8
Win Prizemoney £30,052 *Total Prizemoney* £30,968
Wins * 2000 Spt Goodwo (GD) H 16f 66 69 <
*** 2000** Aug Goodwo (G-F) H 20f 58 68
*** 2000** Jly Bath (FRM) H 17.2f 60 64
*** 2000** Jly Chepst (G-F) H 18f 54 52
2000 Turf 4-8: (15f, 16f 1-3, 17f 1-1, 18f 1-2, 20f 1-1) (gd 2-4, g-f, frm 2-3)
Average gelding, effective 16 to 20f, acts on gd to frm, best on gd, has worn blinkers. Turf high 69 (began Jly) - 1st of 8 getting 4lb from King Flyer (9 Spt Goodwood RF 4317) - also 1st of 8 getting 15lb from Seliana (2 Aug Goodwood RF 3315). He has enjoyed a fine season, with victory in the Goodwood Stakes the highlight. He is suited by marathon trips and fast ground.
**G L Moore [5-14] Richard Green (Fine Paintings) (from M C Pipe [0-1] Oct 1998).*

LAFITE BHB 90f RR 102f 1860[11]
4 b f Robellino (USA) 9.5f **(68)** - Gorgeous Dancer (IRE) (Nordico (USA)) 6.5f **(62)**
Form - 010
Record 2000 - 1st:1 2nd:0 3rd:0 Ran:3
Pre2000 - 1st:3 2nd:0 3rd:3 Ran:11
Win Prizemoney £34,195 *Total Prizemoney* £36,518
Wins * 2000 May York (FRM) L 10.4f 102 <
* 1999 Oct Bright (G-S) H 10f 79 83
* 1999 Spt Newbur (G-S) H 10f 75 78+
* 1999 Jly Chepst (G-F) H 8.1f 74 75
2000 Turf 1-3: (10f 1-3) (gd 2, g-f 1-1)
Strong, very useful filly, effective 10f, acts on g-f, prefers left handed tracks. Turf high 102 - 1st of 8 from Fantazia (17 May York RF 1262). She caused something of a surprise when just getting up to land a Listed event on very fast ground at York on her second start of the season, but was well held in a handicap next time and did not reappear. **J W Hills [4-14] Wood Hall Stud Ltd.*

LAFLEUR (IRE) BHB 58f RR 61f 1895[9]
3 ch f Grand Lodge (USA) - Russian Countess (USA) (Nureyev (USA)) 8.7f **(78)**
Form - 00070
Record 2000 - 1st:0 2nd:0 3rd:0 Ran:5
Pre2000 - 1st:0 2nd:0 3rd:0 Ran:1
2000 Turf 0-5: (8f, 10f, 11f, 12f 2) (sft, gd, g-f 2, frm)
Light-framed, average filly, has worn blinkers. Turf high 64.
**M R Channon [0-6] Wood Hall Stud Ltd.*

LA FOSCARINA RR 823[12]
2 ch f Rudimentary (USA) 8.2f **(66)** - Tea and Scandals (USA) (Key to the Kingdom (USA)) 8.3f **(65)**
Form - 0
Record 2000 - 1st:0 2nd:0 3rd:0 Ran:1
2000 Turf 0-1: (5f) (hvy)
Currently very poor filly. **B J Meehan [0-1] Mario Lanfranchi.*

LA GANDILIE (FR) RR 96f 2578a[3]
3 gr f Highest Honor (FR) 10.9f **(72)** - Prospector's Star (USA) (Mr Prospector (USA)) 8.8f **(78)**
Form - 3
2000 Turf 0-1: (9f) (gd)
Currently very useful filly. (1st run) - 3rd of 11 to Di Moi Oui (30 Jun Chantilly 9f gd RF 2578a). **R Gibson in FR [0-1] J D Martin.*

LAGER (USA) RR 2003a[2]
6 ch g Pleasant Tap (USA) 13.1f **(71)** - Lady Ghislaine (FR) (Lydian (FR))
Form - 2
2000 AW 0-1: (9f) (Dirt)
Currently very useful gelding. **H A Jerkens in USA [0-1].*

LAGGAN MINSTREL (IRE) BHB 70f RR 62f 4532[11]
2 b c Mark of Esteem (IRE) - Next Episode (USA) (Nijinsky (CAN)) 10.3f **(77)**
Form - 80
Record 2000 - 1st:0 2nd:0 3rd:0 Ran:2
2000 Turf 0-2: (7f 2) (gd, g-f)
Currently above-average colt. Turf high 62 (began Jly).
**R Hannon [0-2] Stonethorn Stud Farms Ltd.*

LAGO RR 53f 4030[8]
2 b c Maelstrom Lake 8.8f **(53)** - Jugendliebe (IRE) (Persian Bold) 9.3f **(66)**
Form - 8
Record 2000 - 1st:0 2nd:0 3rd:0 Ran:1
2000 Turf 0-1: (8f) (frm)
Currently fair colt. **I A Balding [0-1] N C Kersey.*

LAGO DI COMO BHB 58f55a RR 60f 55a 4035[12]
3 b c Piccolo - Farmer's Pet (Sharrood (USA)) 10.5f **(72)**
Form - 304100
Record 2000 - 1st:1 2nd:0 3rd:1 Ran:6
Pre2000 - 1st:0 2nd:0 3rd:0 Ran:4
Win Prizemoney £2,324 *Total Prizemoney* £2,756
Wins * 2000 Jly Lingfi (G-F) 9f 60 <
2000 Turf 1-4: (9f 1-2, 10f, 11f) (gd, g-f, frm 1-2) 2000 AW 0-2: (10f 2) (Equi 2)
Scopey, average colt, effective 9 to 11f, acts on frm - acts on Equi, prefers left handed tracks, favours tight tracks. Turf high 60 - 1st of 8 from Guarded Secret (1 Jly Lingfield RF 2434). AW high 57 (1st run) - 3rd of 13 giving 5lb to Bluebell Wood (2 Jan Lingfield 10f Equi RF 0001). Inconsistent.
**T J Naughton [1-10] Exors of the late E J Fenaroli.*

LAGO DI LEVICO BHB 44f39a RR 51f 39a 4277[15]
3 ch g Pelder (IRE) - Langton Herring (Nearly A Hand) 5.6f **(48)**
Form - 1546880
Record 2000 - 1st:1 2nd:0 3rd:0 Ran:7
Pre2000 - 1st:0 2nd:0 3rd:0 Ran:1
Win Prizemoney £1,939 *Total Prizemoney* £1,939
Wins 2000 Mar Nottin (GD) S 8.2f 66 <
2000 Turf 1-7: (7f, 8f 1-4, 10f 2) (gd 1-3, g-f, frm 3)

Unfurnished, fair gelding, effective 8f, acts on gd. Turf high 66 (1st run) - 1st of 10 giving 5lb to Bondi Bay (29 Mar Nottingham RF 0556). Becoming disappointing.

**Derrick Morris [0-3] The Unpronounceable Partners (from A P Jarvis [1-5] Jun 2000).*

LAGO DI VARANO BHB 86f RR 88f 5127[8]

8 b g Clantime 6.6f **(57)** - On the Record (Record Token) 6.3f **(53)**

Form - 066835315053071200265 8

Record	**2000 -**	1st:2	2nd:2	3rd:3	Ran:22
	Pre2000 -	1st:9	2nd:11	3rd:7	Ran:90

Win Prizemoney £57,972 *Total Prizemoney* £137,769

Wins							
* **2000**	Aug	Ripon	(GD)	H	6f	82	84
* **2000**	Jun	Haydoc	(G-S)	H	5f	75	79
* 1999	Aug	Sandow	(GD)	H	5f	80	86
* 1999	Jun	York	(G-S)	H	5f	77	80
* 1998	Jun	Ripon	(SFT)	H	5f	80	84
* 1997	Jly	Newcas	(GD)	H	5f	79	80
* 1996	Jun	Doncas	(G-F)	H	5f	83	84
1996	Apr	Ripon	(G-F)	C	5f		73

2000 Turf 2-22: (5f 1-13, 6f 1-8, 7f) (sft, g-s 3, gd 1-12, g-f 4, frm 1-2)

Useful gelding, effective 5 to 6f, best at 5f, acts on g-s to frm, best on gd, mostly wears blinkers (effectively), excels at Ayr and Sandown, does well at Ripon. Turf high 88 - 2nd of 28 to Bahamian Pirate (16 Spt Ayr 6f gd RF 4451) - also 1st of 13 from Emerging Market (7 Aug Ripon RF 3432). Consistent. A veteran sprint handicapper, he is usually good for a couple of wins each season. Won at Haydock in June and has been running well since, adding another victory at Ripon in August. Acts well with cut.

**R M Whitaker [7-92] The PBT Group (from J Berry [4-20] Apr 1996).*

LAGOON (IRE) BHB 93f RR 98f 5240[5]

3 ch c Common Grounds 8.1f **(66)** - Secret Hideaway (USA) (Key To The Mint (USA)) 9.4f **(75)**

Form - 847083145

Record	**2000 -**	1st:1	2nd:0	3rd:1	Ran:9
	Pre2000 -	1st:1	2nd:0	3rd:2	Ran:5

Win Prizemoney £11,129 *Total Prizemoney* £17,809

Wins						
* **2000**	Spt	Newmar	(GD)	8f	93	<
* 1999	Spt	Pontef	(CD)	6f	80	

2000 Turf 1-9: (7f 5, 8f 1-4) (g-s, gd 1-4, g-f 2, frm 2)

Scopey, very useful colt, effective 6 to 8f, best at 8f, acted on gd to g-f, best on gd, excelled at Newmarket. Turf high 98 - 4th of 18 giving 7lb to Camberley (24 May Goodwood 7f gd RF 1427) - also 1st of 11 getting 4lb from Prairie Wolf (29 Spt Newmarket RF 4736). (DEAD) **B W Hills [2-14] Guy Reed.*

LAGUDIN (IRE) RR 88f 5023[1]

2 b c Eagle Eyed (USA) - Liaison (USA) (Blushing Groom (FR)) 10.3f **(76)**

Form - 121

Record	**2000 -**	1st:2	2nd:1	3rd:0	Ran:3

Win Prizemoney £9,376 *Total Prizemoney* £19,396

Wins						
* **2000**	Oct	Yarmou	(SFT)	7f	88	<
* **2000**	Spt	Newmar	(SFT)	7f	80+	

2000 Turf 2-3: (7f 2-2, 8f) (hvy, g-s 1-1, g-f 1-1)

Currently useful colt. Turf high 88 (began Spt) - 1st of 7 giving 7lb to Muthaaber (17 Oct Yarmouth RF 5023) - also 1st of 5 from Albuhera (16 Spt Newmarket RF 4473).

**L M Cumani [2-3] Miss Gatto Roissard.*

LAGUNA BAY (IRE) BHB 30f24a RR 40df 24a 4112[17]

6 b m Arcane (USA) 11.6f **(66)** - Meg Daughter (IRE) (Doulab (USA)) 9.8f **(65)**

Form - 0

Record	**2000 -**	1st:0	2nd:0	3rd:0	Ran:1
	Pre2000 -	1st:2	2nd:3	3rd:0	Ran:24

Win Prizemoney £4,969 *Total Prizemoney* £8,266

Wins							
* 1999	Jun	Bath	(FRM)	SH	17.2f	44	46
1997	Aug	Yarmou	(G-F)	C	10.1f		54 <

2000 Turf 0-1: (16f) (frm)

Moderate mare, effective 16 to 17f, best at 17f, acts on g-f to hrd, favours left handed tracks.

**G M McCourt [4-31] Christopher Shankland (from A P Jarvis [1-13] Oct 1997).*

LAHAAY BHB 68f RR 72f 4498[16]

3 ch g Lahib (USA) 8f **(69)** - Jasarah (IRE) (Green Desert (USA)) 8.6f **(78)**

Form - 0745360

Record	**2000 -**	1st:0	2nd:0	3rd:1	Ran:7
	Pre2000 -	1st:0	2nd:0	3rd:0	Ran:2

Win Prizemoney £0 *Total Prizemoney* £1,091

2000 Turf 0-7: (7f 2, 8f 4, 10f) (hvy, g-s, g-f 2, frm 3)

Scopey, above-average gelding, effective 7 to 10f, acts on frm, prefers tight tracks. Turf high 72 - 3rd of 14 giving 1lb to Bandler Ching (9 Aug Leicester 10f frm RF 3490).

**M P Tregoning [0-9] Hamdan Al Maktoum.*

LAHAN BHB 117f RR 122f 1080[1]

3 b f Unfuwain (USA) 11.4f **(74)** - Amanah (USA) **(96f)** (Mr Prospector (USA)) 8.8f **(78)**

Form - 41

Record	**2000 -**	1st:1	2nd:0	3rd:0	Ran:2
	Pre2000 -	1st:2	2nd:0	3rd:0	Ran:2

Win Prizemoney £171,143 *Total Prizemoney* £173,068

Wins						
* **2000**	May	Newmar (GD)	G1	8f	122	<
* 1999	Oct	Newmar (GD)	G2	7f	100+	
* 1999	Oct	Redcar (GD)		7f	83+	

2000 Turf 1-2: (7f, 8f 1-1) (g-s, frm 1-1)

Rangy, very high-class filly. Turf high 122 - 1st of 18 from Princess Ellen (7 May Newmarket RF 1080). She may not have coped with the soft ground on her return in the Fred Darling, but better ground saw her in a much better light as she scored a famous victory in the 1000 Guineas. With some of the fancied fillies running below their best, the form may have been suspect, but we never had the chance to find out, as she suffered an injury to her off-fore, and that proved to be the end of her season.

**J H M Gosden [3-4] Hamdan Al Maktoum.*

LAILANI RR 70f 5236[7]

2 b f Unfuwain (USA) 11.4f **(74)** - Lailati (USA) (Mr Prospector (USA)) 8.8f **(78)**

Form - 07

Record	**2000 -**	1st:0	2nd:0	3rd:0	Ran:2

2000 Turf 0-2: (7f, 8f) (g-s, gd)

Currently above-average filly. Turf high 70 (began Oct).

**E A L Dunlop [0-2] Maktoum Al Maktoum.*

LAI SEE (IRE) BHB 69f64a RR 71f 64a 6015[7]

2 b c Tagula (IRE) - Sevens Are Wild (Petorius) 7.3f **(61)**

Form - 0082225557

Record	**2000 -**	1st:0	2nd:3	3rd:0	Ran:10

Win Prizemoney £0 *Total Prizemoney* £3,716

2000 Turf 0-9: (5f 6, 6f 3) (gd 3, g-f 3, frm 3) 2000 AW 0-1: (6f) (Fibr)

Above-average colt, effective 5f, acts on g-f to frm, best on frm, has worn blinkers. Turf high 71 - 2nd of 11 giving 3lb to Samadilla (3 Jly Pontefract 5f frm RF 2472). Consistent.

**A P Jarvis [0-10] St Davids Racing Syndicate 2.*

LAJADHAL (FR) BHB 10f15a RR ?f 15a 3956[7]

11 gr g Bellypha 11.9f **(66)** - Rose d'Amour (USA) (Lines of Power (USA))

Form - 07

Record	**2000 -**	1st:0	2nd:0	3rd:0	Ran:2
	Pre2000 -	1st:0	2nd:0	3rd:0	Ran:32

Win Prizemoney £0 *Total Prizemoney* £174

2000 Turf 0-2: (16f, 17f) (gd, hrd)

Very poor gelding, has worn blinkers. (began Jly).

**P D Purdy [0-16] P D Purdy (from K Bishop [0-12] Aug 1995).*

LA JURISTE (FR) RR 106f 5306a[3]

6 m Homme de Loi (IRE) - Sponte Sua (FR) (Spoleto (IRE))

Form - 3

2000 Turf 0-1: (11f) (g-s)

Currently Pattern-class. (1st run) - 3rd of 8 giving 4lb to Audacieuse (24 Oct Saint-cloud 11f g-s RF 5306a).

**M Prod'homme in FR [0-2] .*

LAKE ARIA BHB 16f19a RR 24df 19a 62[12]

7 b m Rambo Dancer (CAN) 8.4f **(59)** - Hinge (Import) 6.6f **(68)**

Form - 800

Record	**2000 -**	1st:0	2nd:0	3rd:0	Ran:1
	Pre2000 -	1st:0	2nd:1	3rd:0	Ran:21

Win Prizemoney £0 *Total Prizemoney* £585

2000 AW 0-1: (12f) (Fibr)
Little account mare, has worn blinkers.
**J Balding [0-4] Mrs M P Neatby (from J L Eyre [0-7] Mar 1999).*

LAKE DOMINION BHB 24f29a **RR 25f 29a** 46[7]

11 b g Primo Dominie 7.2f **(67)** - Piney Lake (Sassafras (FR)) 9.6f **(69)**
Form - 67
Record 2000 - 1st:0 2nd:0 3rd:0 Ran:1
Pre2000 - 1st:1 2nd:1 3rd:4 Ran:29
Win Prizemoney £1,984 *Total Prizemoney* £4,512
Wins * 1997 *Jly Wolver (STD) H 16.2f 37 36* <
2000 AW 0-1: (16f) (Equi)
Little account gelding, has worn blinkers.
**K C Comerford [1-16] Mrs Betty Bate and Mark Campbell (from J White [1-3] Jun 1994).*

LAKE KINNERET (IRE) **RR 65f** 5236[10]

2 b f Danehill (USA) 9.1f **(79)** - Dancing Shadow (Dancers Image (USA)) 9.3f **(71)**
Form - 0
Record 2000 - 1st:0 2nd:0 3rd:0 Ran:1
2000 Turf 0-1: (7f) (g-s)
Currently average filly. **Sir Michael Stoute [0-1] Lord Weinstock.*

LAKELAND PADDY (IRE) BHB 69f **RR 74f** 4809[12]

3 b c Lake Coniston (IRE) - Inshad (Indian King (USA)) 7.4f **(64)**
Form - 336417000
Record 2000 - 1st:1 2nd:0 3rd:2 Ran:9
Pre2000 - 1st:0 2nd:1 3rd:0 Ran:7
Win Prizemoney £4,498 *Total Prizemoney* £9,079
Wins * **2000** Jun Newbur (G-F) 6f 74 <
2000 Turf 1-9: (6f 1-7, 7f, 8f) (sft, g-s 3, gd, g-f, frm 1-3)
Scopey, above-average colt, effective 6f, acts on gd to frm, best on frm. Turf high 78 (1st run) - 3rd of 21 to Castle Sempill (10 Apr Windsor 6f frm RF 0655). He took a long time in getting off the mark, despite consistent efforts in maiden and handicap company, but managed to do so in a Newbury maiden in June. Well beaten since, however. **M Blanshard [1-16] Mrs R G Wellman.*

LAKESIDE LADY BHB 27f **RR 8f** 5246[9]

3 b f Handsome Sailor 6.6f **(53)** - Collison Lane (Reesh)
Form - 070
Record 2000 - 1st:0 2nd:0 3rd:0 Ran:3
2000 Turf 0-2: (5f, 6f) (g-s, g-f) 2000 AW 0-1: (8f) (Fibr)
Unfurnished, currently poor filly. Turf high 8 (began Spt).
**T D Easterby [0-3] A D Bottomley.*

LAKE SUNBEAM BHB 68f64a **RR 72f 64a** 4194[9]

4 b g Nashwan (USA) 10.3f **(79)** - Moon Drop (Dominion) 8.5f **(63)**
Form - 455611320
Record 2000 - 1st:2 2nd:1 3rd:1 Ran:7
Pre2000 - 1st:1 2nd:0 3rd:2 Ran:10
Win Prizemoney £11,386 *Total Prizemoney* £16,547
Wins * **2000** Jly Sandow (G-F) C 8.1f 71
* **2000** Jly Epsom (G-S) C 8.5f 43+
1999 Jun Salisb (G-F) 7f 86 <
2000 Turf 2-7: (8f 1-2, 9f 1-3, 10f 2) (gd 1-2, g-f 1-3, frm, hrd)
Scopey, above-average gelding, effective 7 to 8f, best at 7f, acts on gd to frm. Turf high 72.
**W R Muir [2-9] Percipacious Punters Racing Club (from G L Moore [0-1] Nov 1999).*

LAKOTA BRAVE BHB 57a **RR 57f** 4304[6]

6 ch g Anshan 8.2f **(63)** - Pushkinia (FR) (Pharly (FR)) 9.8f **(68)**
Form - 6416
Record 2000 - 1st:1 2nd:0 3rd:0 Ran:4
Pre2000 - 1st:0 2nd:0 3rd:0 Ran:1
Win Prizemoney £2,786 *Total Prizemoney* £3,060
Wins * **2000** *Aug Lingfi (STD) 8f 60* <
2000 Turf 0-3: (7f, 8f 2) (gd, g-f, frm) 2000 AW 1-1: (8f 1-1) (Equi 1-1)
Average gelding. Turf high 57 (began Jly). (1st run) - 1st of 8 giving 9lb to Verdura (31 Aug Lingfield RF 4113).
**C N Allen [1-5] Newmarket Connections Ltd.*

LALA SALAMA (IRE) BHB 43f **RR 48df** 4650[10]

4 br f College Chapel - Sally St Clair (Sallust) 8.4f **(63)**
Form - 00040
Record 2000 - 1st:0 2nd:0 3rd:0 Ran:5
Pre2000 - 1st:0 2nd:0 3rd:0 Ran:3
2000 Turf 0-4: (8f, 9f, 10f, 11f) (gd, g-f 2, frm) 2000 AW 0-1: (11f) (Fibr)
Leggy, moderate filly. Turf high 42. **Lady Herries [0-8] R Bremner.*

LAMBAY RULES (IRE) **RR 61f** 4646[9]

2 b c Dr Devious (IRE) 9.9f **(74)** - Socialite (IRE) (Alzao (USA)) 7.1f **(68)**
Form - 70
Record 2000 - 1st:0 2nd:0 3rd:0 Ran:2
2000 Turf 0-2: (7f, 8f) (g-f, frm)
Currently average colt. Turf high 61 (began Aug).
**N A Callaghan [0-2] M Tabor.*

LAMBRINI LAD (IRE) BHB 30f **RR 56f** 175[9]

5 b g Shalford (IRE) 7.8f **(63)** - Swift Reply (He Loves Me) 7.9f **(55)**
Form - 0
Record 2000 - 1st:0 2nd:0 3rd:0 Ran:1
Pre2000 - 1st:0 2nd:0 3rd:1 Ran:6
Win Prizemoney £0 *Total Prizemoney* £310
2000 AW 0-1: (12f) (Fibr)
Fair gelding, has worn blinkers.
**Mrs L Williamson [0-5] Halewood International Ltd (from A Bailey [0-6] Aug 1998).*

LAMEH BHB 80f **RR 79f** 1050[3]

3 ch f Mujtahid (USA) 7.4f **(69)** - Tablah (USA) **(77f)** (Silver Hawk (USA)) 8.6f **(70)**
Form - 3
Record 2000 - 1st:0 2nd:0 3rd:1 Ran:1
Pre2000 - 1st:0 2nd:0 3rd:0 Ran:3
Win Prizemoney £0 *Total Prizemoney* £1,064
2000 Turf 0-1: (7f) (g-f)
Scopey, above-average filly. Third in a decent Newmarket maiden on her reappearance, when she swished her tail.
**R W Armstrong [0-1] Hamdan Al Maktoum (from P T Walwyn [0-3] Oct 1999).*

LAMENT BHB 50a **RR 48f** 1379[4]

4 b f Phountzi (USA) 9.6f **(60)** - Devils Dirge (Song) 7.2f **(61)**
Form - 8804
Record 2000 - 1st:0 2nd:0 3rd:0 Ran:2
Pre2000 - 1st:2 2nd:3 3rd:1 Ran:17
Win Prizemoney £4,959 *Total Prizemoney* £6,915
Wins * 1999 Oct Pontef (SFT) C 6f 48
1998 Aug Lingfi (GD) C 6f 65 <
2000 Turf 0-2: (6f, 8f) (sft, g-f)
Workmanlike, moderate filly, effective 6f, acts on gd, has worn blinkers. Turf high 43.
**Miss Gay Kelleway [1-7] A P Griffin (from Mrs L Stubbs [1-8] Apr 1999).*

LAMMOSKI (IRE) BHB 27f32a **RR 46f 32a** 4455[3]

3 ch g Hamas (IRE) 8f **(72)** - Penny In My Shoe (USA) (Sir Ivor) 10.2f **(70)**
Form - 00058005005000403
Record 2000 - 1st:0 2nd:0 3rd:1 Ran:13
Pre2000 - 1st:0 2nd:0 3rd:0 Ran:14
Win Prizemoney £0 *Total Prizemoney* £263
2000 Turf 0-9: (5f 3, 6f 2, 10f, 12f, 14f, 16f) (g-s, gd 3, frm 5) 2000 AW 0-4: (5f, 6f 3) (Fibr 4)
Scopey, moderate gelding, has worn blinkers. Turf high 49. AW high 43. **M C Chapman [0-28] Gordon & Julie Lamming.*

LA MONDOTTE (IRE) **RR 66f** 4631[5]

2 b f Alzao (USA) 9.8f **(73)** - Saucy Maid (IRE) **(67f)** (Sure Blade (USA)) 11.3f **(67)**
Form - 5
Record 2000 - 1st:0 2nd:0 3rd:0 Ran:1
2000 Turf 0-1: (10f) (g-s)
Currently average filly. **J A Osborne [0-1] Wood Hall Stud Ltd.*

LANCE FEATHER (IRE) BHB 53f **RR 58+f** 4557[12]

2 b c Petardia 8.2f **(58)** - Fantasticus (IRE) **(67f)** (Lycius (USA))
Form - 680
Record 2000 - 1st:0 2nd:0 3rd:0 Ran:3
2000 Turf 0-3: (7f 2, 8f) (gd, frm 2)
Currently fair colt. Turf high 58 (began Aug).

J L Eyre [0-3] Tony Fawcett.

LANCER (USA) BHB 53f43a **RR 56f 43a** 5294[4]
8 ch g Diesis 9f **(80)** - Last Bird (USA) (Sea Bird II) 9f **(71)**
Form - 8616606583261534
Record 2000 - 1st:2 2nd:1 3rd:2 Ran:15
Pre2000 - 1st:5 2nd:9 3rd:3 Ran:43
Win Prizemoney £27,937 *Total Prizemoney* £45,255
Wins * **2000** Oct Pontef (HVY) H 12f 49 56
* **2000** Apr Warwic (SFT) H 12.3f 63 65
* 1999 May Folkes (G-F) 12f 70
* 1998 Oct York (GD) H 11.9f 66 71 <
* 1998 Jun Folkes (G-F) H 12f 59 63
* 1998 May Leices (GD) H 11.8f 53 60
2000 Turf 2-15: (12f 2-13, 13f, 16f) (sft 1-1, g-s 1 6, gd, g-f 3, frm 4)
Fair gelding, effective 12f, acts on sft to frm, best on gd, often wears blinkers (very effectively), likes right handed tracks, excels at Pontefract, does well at Newmarket. Turf high 67 - 6th of 21 getting 27lb from Mowelga (19 Apr Newmarket 12f gd RF 0796) - also 1st of 10 getting 4lb from Legal Lunch (3 Apr Warwick RF 0595). Consistent. An able performer at around a mile and a half, he is best held up for a late run, but is not one to rely too much on.
J Pearce [6-49] Chris Marsh (from R T Juckes [1-16] Feb 1998).

LANCIANA (GER) RR 92f 2199a[8]
3 f
Form - 8
2000 Turf 0-1: (11f) (gd)
Currently useful filly. *in GER [0-1].*

L'ANCRESS PRINCESS RR 231[5]
3 b f Rock City 8.8f **(62)** - Premier Princess (Hard Fought) 8.8f **(62)**
Form - 05
Record 2000 - 1st:0 2nd:0 3rd:0 Ran:1
Pre2000 - 1st:0 2nd:0 3rd:0 Ran:1
2000 AW 0-1: (9f) (Fibr)
Workmanlike, currently very poor filly. *G A Ham [0-2] D M Drury.*

LAND AHEAD (USA) BHB 80f **RR 85+f** 4369[12]
3 ch f Distant View (USA) - Nimble Folly (USA) (Cyane) 8.8f **(67)**
Form - 322320
Record 2000 - 1st:0 2nd:3 3rd:2 Ran:6
Pre2000 - 1st:0 2nd:0 3rd:0 Ran:1
Win Prizemoney £0 *Total Prizemoney* £5,037
2000 Turf 0-6: (7f, 8f 2, 10f 3) (g-s, g-f 2, frm 3)
Scopey, useful filly, effective 8 to 10f, best at 10f, acts on g-s to frm, best on frm. Turf high 85 - 2nd of 9 to Amelinaa (29 Jly Nottingham 10f frm RF 3217). *H R A Cecil [0-7] K Abdulla.*

LANDFALL LIL (IRE) BHB 42f44a **RR 43f 44a** 3355[13]
3 b f Mujadil (USA) 7.7f **(70)** - Local Belle (Ballymore) 7.3f **(64)**
Form - 8000
Record 2000 - 1st:0 2nd:0 3rd:0 Ran:2
Pre2000 - 1st:0 2nd:1 3rd:0 Ran:6
Win Prizemoney £0 *Total Prizemoney* £744
2000 Turf 0-2: (6f, 7f) (g-f, frm)
Neat, moderate filly, effective 5f, acts on g-f. Turf high 18 (began Jly). Becoming disappointing. *I Semple [0-8] Raeburn Brick Ltd.*

LAND GIRL RR 19f 2570[8]
2 b f General Monash (USA) - Charming Madam (General Holme (USA)) 5.7f **(63)**
Form - 8
Record 2000 - 1st:0 2nd:0 3rd:0 Ran:1
2000 Turf 0-1: (6f) (frm)
Currently poor filly. *Miss S E Hall [0-1] C Platts.*

LANDICAN LAD BHB 44f **RR 59f** 5192[7]
3 b c Petong 7.6f **(58)** - Dancing Daughter (Dance In Time (CAN)) 8.9f **(59)**
Form - 0750007
Record 2000 - 1st:0 2nd:0 3rd:0 Ran:7
2000 Turf 0-7: (5f, 6f 3, 7f, 9f, 10f) (sft, gd 3, g-f 2, frm)
Unfurnished, fair colt. Turf high 59.
A C Whillans [0-2] I Campbell (from R F JohnsonHoughton [0-5] Aug 2000).

LANDICAN LANE BHB 26f29a **RR 15f 29a** 3982[U]
4 b g Handsome Sailor 6.6f **(53)** - Harifa (Local Suitor (USA)) 8.4f **(67)**
Form - 000000000U
Record 2000 - 1st:0 2nd:0 3rd:0 Ran:9
Pre2000 - 1st:1 2nd:2 3rd:1 Ran:18
Win Prizemoney £1,955 *Total Prizemoney* £3,855
Wins 1998 Spt Bright (GD) S 5.3f 58 <
2000 Turf 0-7: (7f 2, 9f 2, 10f, 11f, 12f) (sft, gd 3, frm 3) 2000 AW 0-2: (6f, 12f) (Equi 2)
Leggy, poor gelding, effective 5f, acts on sft to g-s, often wears blinkers (effectively). Turf high 24. AW high 7.
T M Jones [0-10] Mrs J A Radford (from G L Moore [0-11] Oct 1999).

LANDING CRAFT BHB 49f49a **RR 56f 49a** 5086[5]
6 ch g Zilzal (USA) 8.5f **(79)** - Dockage (CAN) (Riverman (USA)) 9.1f **(76)**
Form - 0032070005
Record 2000 - 1st:0 2nd:1 3rd:1 Ran:10
Pre2000 - 1st:1 2nd:2 3rd:3 Ran:21
Win Prizemoney £2,750 *Total Prizemoney* £7,208
Wins 1998 Oct Fairyh (G-S) H 7f 60 <
2000 Turf 0-9: (6f 3, 7f 2, 8f 4) (hvy, sft 2, g-s 2, gd 2, g-f, frm) 2000 AW 0-1: (8f) (Fibr)
Fair gelding, effective 8 to 9f, best at 8f, acts on sft to g-f, has worn blinkers, prefers right handed tracks. Turf high 56 - 2nd of 19 giving 11lb to Piccolo Cativo (1 May Warwick 8f sft RF 0958).
D Carroll [0-10] The Green Army (from V Kennedy in IRE [1-21] Aug 1999).

LANELLE (USA) BHB 70f **RR 66f** 1267[9]
3 b f Trempolino (USA) 11.9f **(77)** - Laluche (USA) (Alleged (USA)) 10f **(76)**
Form - 80
Record 2000 - 1st:0 2nd:0 3rd:0 Ran:2
Pre2000 - 1st:0 2nd:0 3rd:0 Ran:1
2000 Turf 0-2: (10f, 12f) (gd, g-f)
Unfurnished, currently average filly. Turf high 66.
J H M Gosden [0-3] Sheikh Mohammed.

LANESBOROUGH (USA) RR 84+f 5167[1]
2 ch c Irish River (FR) 9f **(77)** - Hot Option (USA) (Explodent (USA)) 9.4f **(87)**
Form - 51
Record 2000 - 1st:1 2nd:0 3rd:0 Ran:2
Win Prizemoney £3,510 *Total Prizemoney* £4,020
Wins * **2000** Oct Redcar (SFT) 7f 84+ <
2000 Turf 1-2: (7f 1-2) (g-s, gd 1-1)
Currently decent colt. Turf high 84 (began Spt) - 1st of 7 getting 7lb from Mutarased (24 Oct Redcar RF 5167).
G A Butler [1-2] & Mrs J Amerman.

LANNTANSA (IRE) BHB 70f **RR 72f** 2184[2]
3 b c Dolphin Street (FR) - Antakiya (IRE) (Ela-Mana-Mou) 10.1f **(70)**
Form - 762
Record 2000 - 1st:0 2nd:1 3rd:0 Ran:3
Win Prizemoney £0 *Total Prizemoney* £869
2000 Turf 0-3: (10f 2, 12f) (sft, g-s, frm)
Tall, above-average colt. Turf high 72 - 2nd of 9 giving 5lb to Lady Lucha (22 Jun Ripon 10f frm RF 2184). (DEAD)
E A L Dunlop [0-3] Mohammed Jaber.

LANOSO (IRE) RR 5151[15]
2 b c Charnwood Forest (IRE) - Silver Spark (USA) (Silver Hawk (USA)) 8.6f **(70)**
Form - 0
Record 2000 - 1st:0 2nd:0 3rd:0 Ran:1
2000 Turf 0-1: (7f) (g-s)
Currently moderate colt. *C R Egerton [0-1] Ian Hogg.*

LA NOTTE BHB 83f **RR 80f** 5121[3]
2 b f Factual (USA) - Miss Mirror (Magic Mirror)
Form - 3133
Record 2000 - 1st:1 2nd:0 3rd:3 Ran:4
Win Prizemoney £2,593 *Total Prizemoney* £5,209
Wins * **2000** Spt Lingfi (G-F) 6f 69+ <
2000 Turf 1-4: (6f 1-2, 7f 2) (g-s 2, g-f, frm 1-1)
Decent filly. Turf high 80 (began Aug) - 3rd of 14 getting 5lb from

Modrik (21 Oct Doncaster 7f g-s RF 5121).
**W Jarvis [1-4] A L Harrison.*

LANTIC BAY BHB 27f **RR 30f** 4489[9]
3 b f Afzal - Silent Dancer (Quiet Fling (USA)) 11.8f **(36)**
Form - 740
Record 2000 - 1st:0 2nd:0 3rd:0 Ran:3
2000 Turf 0-3: (10f, 12f 2) (g-f 2, hrd)
Light-framed, currently very moderate filly. Turf high 30 (began Aug). **J C Tuck [0-3] J C Tuck.*

LANZLO (FR) BHB 68f **RR 63f** 2876[5]
3 b br g Le Balafre (FR) - L'eternite (FR) (Cariellor (FR))
Form - 25
Record 2000 - 1st:0 2nd:1 3rd:0 Ran:2
Pre2000 - 1st:0 2nd:0 3rd:0 Ran:5
Win Prizemoney £0 *Total Prizemoney* £888
2000 Turf 0-2: (12f 2) (gd, frm)
Leggy, average gelding, effective 12f, acts on gd. Turf high 63 (1st run) (began Jly) - 2nd of 18 giving 1lb to Brisbane Road (10 Jly Bath 12f gd RF 2666). **P J Hobbs [0-7] Winton Bloodstock Ltd.*

LA PASSIONE (USA) RR 77+f 5318[2]
2 ch f Gulch (USA) 9.6f **(79)** - Larking (USA) **(83df)** (Green Forest (USA)) 9.9f **(68)**
Form - 2
Record 2000 - 1st:0 2nd:1 3rd:0 Ran:1
Win Prizemoney £0 *Total Prizemoney* £1,035
2000 Turf 0-1: (6f) (sft)
Currently above-average filly. (1st run) - 2nd of 22 getting 5lb from Zilch (4 Nov Doncaster 6f sft RF 5318).
**H R A Cecil [0-1] M Tabor & Mrs John Magnier.*

LA PETITE FLAMECHE BHB 38f33a **RR 26f 33a** 1703[15]
5 b m Cigar 6.3f **(43)** - Little Missile (Ile de Bourbon (USA)) 10.1f **(67)**
Form - 0
Record 2000 - 1st:0 2nd:0 3rd:0 Ran:1
Pre2000 - 1st:0 2nd:0 3rd:1 Ran:11
Win Prizemoney £0 *Total Prizemoney* £575
2000 Turf 0-1: (11f) (g-s)
Very moderate filly, has worn blinkers.
**G A Ham [0-1] Mrs S Hutchings (from R J O'Sullivan [0-14] Jun 1999).*

LA PIAZZA (IRE) BHB 70f60a **RR 68f 60a** 5245[12]
4 ch f Polish Patriot (USA) 7.8f **(70)** - Blazing Glory (IRE) (Glow (USA)) 6.7f **(71)**
Form - 00702336600
Record 2000 - 1st:0 2nd:1 3rd:2 Ran:11
Pre2000 - 1st:3 2nd:4 3rd:1 Ran:12
Win Prizemoney £12,094 *Total Prizemoney* £19,219

Wins	1999	Aug	Lingfi	(GD)	H	6f	72	79+	<
	1999	Jly	Lingfi	(FRM)	H	6f	60	70	
	1999	*Jun*	*Wolver*	*(STD)*		*5f*		*66*	

2000 Turf 0-9: (5f 2, 6f 7) (g-s, gd 3, g-f 2, frm 3) 2000 AW 0-2: (6f, 7f) (Fibr 2)
Workmanlike, average filly, effective 5 to 6f, best at 6f, acts on gd to frm, best on gd, excels at Lingfield. Turf high 76 - 3rd of 8 giving 2lb to Glowing (21 Jly Newmarket 6f gd RF 3005). AW high 56.
**A Berry [0-4] S F DeMartino (from W J Haggas [3-19] Jly 2000).*

LAPWING (IRE) RR 77f 4534[6]
2 b c Tagula (IRE) - Wasaif (IRE) (Lomond (USA)) 8.8f **(65)**
Form - 4116
Record 2000 - 1st:2 2nd:0 3rd:0 Ran:4
Win Prizemoney £10,712 *Total Prizemoney* £10,988

Wins	*** 2000**	Spt	Warwic	(G-F)	H	7.1f	78	77	<
	*** 2000**	Aug	Ayr	(G-F)		6f		71	

2000 Turf 2-4: (6f 1-2, 7f 1-2) (g-s, g-f 1-1, frm 1-2)
Above-average colt. Turf high 77 (began Jly) - 1st of 10 giving 1lb to Nun Left (11 Spt Warwick RF 4325) - also 1st of 5 from Little Task (4 Aug Ayr RF 3354). Found out by the soft ground when attempting a hat-trick.
**B W Hills [2-4] The Hon Mrs J M Corbett & C Wright.*

LARA FALANA RR 18f 5152[12]
2 b f Tagula (IRE) - Victoria Mill (Free State) 8.7f **(61)**
Form - 0
Record 2000 - 1st:0 2nd:0 3rd:0 Ran:1
2000 Turf 0-1: (7f) (g-s)
Currently poor filly. **J A Osborne [0-1] Mrs C A Waters.*

LARA'S DELIGHT BHB 40f **RR 42f** 2954[6]
5 b m Then Again 7.4f **(52)** - Sarah Dream (IRE) (Strong Gale) 5.6f **(66)**
Form - 776
Record 2000 - 1st:0 2nd:0 3rd:0 Ran:3
2000 Turf 0-3: (12f 3) (gd, frm, hrd)
Moderate filly. Turf high 42.
**M J Weeden [0-5] C Thistlethwaite & S Frost.*

LARAZA BHB 60f **RR 65f** 4729[3]
3 ch f Arazi (USA) 9.2f **(74)** - Queen Midas (Glint of Gold) 9.3f **(66)**
Form - 5507523
Record 2000 - 1st:0 2nd:1 3rd:1 Ran:7
Pre2000 - 1st:0 2nd:0 3rd:1 Ran:2
Win Prizemoney £0 *Total Prizemoney* £2,208
2000 Turf 0-7: (7f, 8f 4, 10f, 11f) (gd 2, g-f 3, frm 2)
Scopey, average filly, effective 8 to 10f, best at 8f, acts on g-f to frm, best on frm, has worn blinkers. Turf high 65 - 5th of 11 getting 8lb from Omniheat (2 Jun Brighton 10f frm RF 1651). Consistent.
**Miss I Foustok [0-9] R & M Fustok.*

LARGESSE BHB 110f97a **RR 115f 97a** 1277[5]
6 b h Cadeaux Genereux 7.9f **(76)** - Vilanika (FR) (Top Ville) 11.7f **(68)**
Form - 1035
Record 2000 - 1st:1 2nd:0 3rd:1 Ran:4
Pre2000 - 1st:7 2nd:3 3rd:2 Ran:28
Win Prizemoney £55,547 *Total Prizemoney* £110,883

Wins	*** 2000**	Mar	Doncas	()		12f		115	<
	* 1999	Mar	Doncas	(G-S)		12f		102+	
	* 1998	Spt	Ayr	(G-S)	L	10.9f		107	
	* 1998	May	York	(GD)	H	11.9f	94	98	
	* 1998	Mar	Nottin	(G-S)	H	10f	82	87	
	* 1997	Spt	Haydoc	(GD)	H	11.9f	73	77	
	* 1997	Spt	Haydoc	(G-S)	H	10.5f	67	71	
	* 1996	Jly	Pontef	(G-F)		5f		84+	

2000 Turf 1-4: (12f 1-3, 14f) (hvy, gd 1-2, g-f)
High-class horse, effective 12 to 15f, acts on gd to g-f, best on gd, has worn blinkers. Turf high 115 - 3rd of 11 to Blueprint (5 May Newmarket 12f g-f RF 1047) - also 1st of 10 giving 4lb to Murghem (25 Mar Doncaster RF 0493). Inconsistent. The star of John Berry's small yard, he disappointed over hurdles, but bounced back to form when winning the Listed Doncaster Shield in March (his second success in the race). Not seen out after mid-May, he has done most of his winning during spring and autumn and does not want the ground too firm. **John Berry [8-32] Mrs Rosemary Moszkowicz.*

LARIMAR BAY BHB 34f **RR 10f** 2039[15]
4 b g Puissance 7.1f **(60)** - Aryaf (CAN) (Vice Regent (CAN)) 8.7f **(74)**
Form - 00
Record 2000 - 1st:0 2nd:0 3rd:0 Ran:2
Pre2000 - 1st:0 2nd:0 3rd:0 Ran:6
Win Prizemoney £0 *Total Prizemoney* £739
2000 Turf 0-2: (6f, 7f) (g-s, hrd)
Scopey, poor gelding. Turf high 10. Becoming disappointing.
**W M Brisbourne [0-6] John Oldknow (from B J Meehan [0-2] Oct 1998).*

L'ARITA (FR) BHB 82f **RR 85f** 2846[7]
3 ch f Arazi (USA) 9.2f **(74)** - Lypharita (FR) (Lightning (FR)) 7.9f **(74)**
Form - D47
Record 2000 - 1st:0 2nd:0 3rd:0 Ran:3
Pre2000 - 1st:1 2nd:0 3rd:1 Ran:3
Win Prizemoney £3,925 *Total Prizemoney* £5,067

Wins	* 1999	Oct	Redcar	(GD)	6f	75+	<

2000 Turf 0-3: (7f, 8f 2) (g-f 2, frm)
Neat, useful filly, effective 6 to 8f, acts on g-f to frm. Turf high 85.
**J H M Gosden [1-6] Sheikh Mohammed.*

LAROUSSE RR 75f 5310[13]
2 ch f Unfuwain (USA) 11.4f **(74)** - Allespagne (USA) (Trempolino (USA)) 12f **(71)**
Form - 60
Record 2000 - 1st:0 2nd:0 3rd:0 Ran:2
2000 Turf 0-2: (7f, 8f) (g-s 2)

Currently above-average filly. Turf high 75 (began Oct).
**S C Williams [0-2] Alasdair Simpson.*

LA-SAYIDA (IRE) RR 5128[11]

2 b f Fairy King (USA) 7.7f **(75)** - Sil Sila (IRE) **(111f)** (Marju (IRE))
Form - 0
Record 2000 - 1st:0 2nd:0 3rd:0 Ran:1
2000 Turf 0-1: (7f) (sft)
Currently very poor filly. **B Smart [0-1] Alvarez Cervera.*

LAS LLANADAS RR 49f 3926[6]

2 b f Minshaanshu Amad (USA) 11.3f **(53)** - A Sharp (Sharpo) 7.7f **(59)**
Form - 56
Record 2000 - 1st:0 2nd:0 3rd:0 Ran:2
2000 Turf 0-2: (5f, 6f) (g-f, hrd)
Moderate filly. Turf high 49 (began Jly). (DEAD)
**T D Barron [0-2] J G Brown.*

LA SPEZIANA (IRE) BHB 80f RR 91f 1648[3]

3 b f Perugino (USA) - Election Special **(62f)** (Chief Singer) 8.9f **(66)**
Form - 113
Record 2000 - 1st:2 2nd:0 3rd:1 Ran:3
Pre2000 - 1st:0 2nd:0 3rd:0 Ran:3
Win Prizemoney £11,713 *Total Prizemoney* £12,391
Wins * 2000 May Sandow (HVY) H 7.1f 68 91 <
*** 2000** May Newbur (G-F) H 7f 62 69
2000 Turf 2-3: (7f 2-2, 8f) (g-s 1-1, gd, g-f 1-1)
Workmanlike, useful filly, effective 7f, acts on g-s. Turf high 91 - 1st of 7 getting 12lb from Serra Negra (29 May Sandown RF 1534). She stepped up considerably on her two-year-old form, almost completing a quick-fire hat-trick during a 13 day period in the summer. Likely to stay beyond a mile, she remains open to further improvement. **D R C Elsworth [2-6] Pampas Partnership.*

LAS RAMBLAS (IRE) BHB 70f RR 82f 4991[27]

3 b c Thatching 7.8f **(69)** - Raise a Warning **(43+f)** (Warning)
Form - 000742305000
Record 2000 - 1st:0 2nd:1 3rd:1 Ran:12
Pre2000 - 1st:1 2nd:1 3rd:2 Ran:7
Win Prizemoney £4,581 *Total Prizemoney* £10,266
Wins * 1999 Aug Newmar (G-F) 6f 92 <
2000 Turf 0-12: (5f, 6f 9, 7f 2) (g-s 2, gd 2, g-f 5, frm 3)
Unfurnished, decent colt, effective 6f, acts on g-f to frm, has worn blinkers. Turf high 82. Probably best suited by fast ground, he has run some good races this year and might be suited by seven furlongs. **R F JohnsonHoughton [1-19] C W Sumner.*

LAST IMPRESSION BHB 76f RR 73f 2340[2]

2 b f Imp Society (USA) 7.1f **(63)** - Figment (Posse (USA)) 8.9f **(61)**
Form - 142
Record 2000 - 1st:1 2nd:1 3rd:0 Ran:3
Win Prizemoney £2,730 *Total Prizemoney* £3,582
Wins 2000 Jun Hamilt (GD) C 5f 59+ <
2000 Turf 1-3: (5f 1-2, 6f) (gd, g-f 1-2)
Currently above-average filly. Turf high 73 - 2nd of 4 giving 1lb to Wilson Blyth (28 Jun Hamilton 6f g-f RF 2340).
**J S Goldie [0-2] W M Johnstone (from A P Jarvis [1-1] Jun 2000).*

LASTMAN (USA) BHB 58f RR 61f 4535[2]

5 b br g Fabulous Dancer (USA) 10.6f **(81)** - Rivala (USA) (Riverman (USA)) 9.1f **(76)**
Form - 52202
Record 2000 - 1st:0 2nd:3 3rd:0 Ran:5
Pre2000 - 1st:0 2nd:0 3rd:0 Ran:2
Win Prizemoney £0 *Total Prizemoney* £4,032
2000 Turf 0-5: (11f, 12f, 16f 2, 17f) (sft, g-s, gd, g-f, frm)
Average gelding, effective 12 to 17f, acts on sft to frm. Turf high 61 - 2nd of 15 getting 23lb from Prairie Falcon (20 Spt Chester 16f g-s RF 4535).
**J J O'Neill [1-15] Darren Mercer (from D Nicholson [0-6] Apr 1999).*

LASTOFTHECASH RR 297[6]

4 b g Ballacashtal (CAN) 7.9f **(51)** - Blue Empress (Blue Cashmere) 6.4f **(54)**
Form - 86
Record 2000 - 1st:0 2nd:0 3rd:0 Ran:2
2000 AW 0-2: (7f 2) (Fibr 2)
Currently poor gelding. AW high 19
**N P Littmoden [0-2] Three Of A Kind Racing.*

LAST OF THE MICE RR 64f 4012[6]

2 b c Deploy 11.4f **(67)** - Top Mouse (High Top) 10.2f **(67)**
Form - 6
Record 2000 - 1st:0 2nd:0 3rd:0 Ran:1
2000 Turf 0-1: (8f) (frm)
Currently average colt. **J A Osborne [0-1] Lady Vestey.*

LASTOFTHEWHALLEYS BHB 49f44a RR 45f 44a 3971[9]

2 b f Noble Patriarch 12.2f **(43)** - Pride of Whalley (IRE) **(48f)** (Fayruz)
Form - 701600
Record 2000 - 1st:1 2nd:0 3rd:0 Ran:6
Win Prizemoney £2,892 *Total Prizemoney* £2,892
Wins * 2000 Jun Thirsk (SFT) S 6f 45 <
2000 Turf 1-4: (5f, 6f 1-1, 7f 2) (gd 1-2, frm 2) 2000 AW 0-2: (5f, 7f) (Fibr 2)
Moderate filly, effective 6f, acts on gd. Turf high 45 - 1st of 8 from Windchill (5 Jun Thirsk RF 1723). AW high 21.
**K A Ryan [1-6] Mrs C M Barlow.*

LAST RESORT BHB 111f RR 115f 4986[1]

3 ch f Lahib (USA) 8f **(69)** - Breadcrumb (Final Straw) 7.9f **(64)**
Form - 413634331
Record 2000 - 1st:2 2nd:0 3rd:4 Ran:9
Win Prizemoney £64,857 *Total Prizemoney* £80,909
Wins * 2000 Oct Newmar (G-S) G2 7f 115 <
*** 2000** May Cheste (GD) 7f 90
2000 Turf 2-9: (7f 2-7, 8f 2) (g-s 2, gd 1-4, g-f 1-2, frm)
Unfurnished, high-class filly, effective 7f, acts on g-s to gd. Turf high 115 - 1st of 9 getting 5lb from Maidaan (14 Oct Newmarket RF 4986). She ran a series of good races in listed company at around seven furlongs and stepped up on that form to win the Challenge Stakes at Newmarket, although the leaders went off too fast in that Group Two event. **B W Hills [2-9] H R H Prince Fahd Salman.*

LAST SYMPHONY BHB 75f RR 78f 1493[1]

3 b c Last Tycoon 9.4f **(73)** - Dancing Heights (IRE) **(80f)** (High Estate)
Form - 061
Record 2000 - 1st:1 2nd:0 3rd:0 Ran:3
Win Prizemoney £4,004 *Total Prizemoney* £4,004
Wins * 2000 May Haydoc (SFT) 7.1f 77 <
2000 Turf 1-3: (7f 1-2, 8f) (g-s 1-1, gd 2)
Scopey, currently above-average colt. Turf high 78 - also 1st of 8 from Capricho (27 May Haydock RF 1493). **M A Jarvis [1-3] R Leah.*

LAST TIME BHB 35f RR 25f 5163[10]

2 b f So Factual (USA) - Times (Junius (USA)) 7.7f **(65)**
Form - 00
Record 2000 - 1st:0 2nd:0 3rd:0 Ran:2
2000 Turf 0-2: (5f 2) (gd 2)
Currently little account filly. Turf high 25 (began Oct).
**T D Easterby [0-2] Times of Wigan.*

LA SYLPHIDE RR 51?f 3831[14]

3 ch f Rudimentary (USA) 8.2f **(66)** - Primitive Gift (Primitive Rising (USA))
Form - 360
Record 2000 - 1st:0 2nd:0 3rd:1 Ran:3
Win Prizemoney £0 *Total Prizemoney* £798
2000 Turf 0-3: (8f 2, 10f) (gd, frm, hrd)
Lengthy, currently fair filly. Turf high 51 (1st run) (began Jly) - 3rd of 6 getting 5lb from Riparian (9 Jly Newcastle 8f gd RF 2650).
**Mrs A Duffield [0-3] Mrs S E Turnbull.*

LATALOMNE (USA) BHB 82f86a RR 90df 86a 2444[7]

6 ch g Zilzal (USA) 8.5f **(79)** - Sanctuary (Welsh Pageant) 10f **(65)**
Form - 08507
Record 2000 - 1st:0 2nd:0 3rd:0 Ran:5
Pre2000 - 1st:2 2nd:3 3rd:0 Ran:11
Win Prizemoney £15,688 *Total Prizemoney* £22,432
Wins * 1999 May Thirsk (G-F) H 8f 88 92 <
1997 Apr Nottin (G-F) 8.2f 88
2000 Turf 0-4: (7f, 8f 2, 10f) (gd 2, frm 2) 2000 AW 0-1: (8f) (Fibr)
Useful gelding, effective 7 to 8f, acts on g-f to frm, has worn blinkers. Turf high 91. Inconsistent. A shade disappointing on the Flat

last term, he has developed into a useful novice chaser and is better employed over obstacles nowadays.
**B Ellison [2-13] Everaldo Partnership (from E A L Dunlop [1-6] Jun 1998).*

LATE ARRIVAL BHB 56f **RR 58f** 4402[3]
3 b g Emperor Jones (USA) - Try Vickers (USA) (Fuzzbuster (USA)) 6.3f **(63)**
Form - 4280023
Record 2000 - 1st:0 2nd:2 3rd:1 Ran:7
Pre2000 - 1st:0 2nd:0 3rd:0 Ran:3
Win Prizemoney £0 *Total Prizemoney* £2,494
2000 Turf 0-7: (7f, 8f, 10f 4, 11f) (sft, gd, g-f 4, frm)
Leggy, fair gelding, effective 7 to 10f, acts on g-f to frm, has worn blinkers. Turf high 58 - 2nd of 16 giving 3lb to Pinheiros Dream (25 Aug Newmarket 7f g-f RF 3968).
**D Morris [0-7] Meadowcrest Ltd (from J J O'Neill [0-3] Aug 1999).*

LATE AT NIGHT (USA) BHB 55f50a **RR 54f 50a** 4762[12]
2 b g Twilight Agenda (USA) - Full O Cherries (USA) (Full Out (USA)) 8f **(46)**
Form - 8084250
Record 2000 - 1st:0 2nd:1 3rd:0 Ran:7
Win Prizemoney £0 *Total Prizemoney* £660
2000 Turf 0-5: (5f, 6f 3, 7f) (g-f 3, frm, hrd) 2000 AW 0-2: (5f, 6f) (Fibr 2)
Fair gelding, effective 6f, acts on hrd, often wears blinkers (very effectively). Turf high 54. AW high 27 (began Jly).
**T D Barron [0-7] Harrowgate Bloodstock Ltd.*

LATE NIGHT OUT BHB 107f **RR 109f** 4805a[7]
5 b g Lahib (USA) 8f **(69)** - Chain Dance (Shareef Dancer (USA)) 9.9f **(73)**
Form - 012177
Record 2000 - 1st:2 2nd:1 3rd:0 Ran:6
Pre2000 - 1st:3 2nd:1 3rd:3 Ran:17
Win Prizemoney £53,218 *Total Prizemoney* £74,261
Wins * **2000** Aug York (GD) L 7f 109 <
* **2000** Jly Cheste (G-S) 7f 97
* 1999 May Haydoc (GD) LH 7.1f 99 99
* 1998 Oct Redcar (G-S) 7f 94
* 1997 Oct Nottin (GD) 6.1f 88+
2000 Turf 2-5: (7f 2-4, 8f) (sft, g-f 2-4) 2000 AW 0-1: (8f) (Dirt)
Pattern-class gelding, effective 6 to 8f, best at 7f, acts on sft to frm. Turf high 109 (began Jly) - 1st of 11 giving 5lb to Mahfooth (24 Aug York RF 3937). A decent seven-furlong performer, he was in action in Dubai in the spring and was having his first run since when inching home at Chester in July. He was stepped up to a mile next time, and just edged out in a conditions race, before landing a York listed race back at seven.
**W Jarvis [5-23] J M Greetham.*

LATENSAANI RR 27f 5140[14]
2 b c Shaamit (IRE) - Intoxication (Great Nephew) 9.9f **(64)**
Form - 0
Record 2000 - 1st:0 2nd:0 3rd:0 Ran:1
2000 Turf 0-1: (6f) (g-s)
Currently little account colt. **W J Haggas [0-1] Khalifa Dasmal.*

LATE PARADE (IRE) RR 110f 2980a[1]
9 b h Astronef 7.9f **(59)** - Skisette (Malinowski (USA)) 10f **(56)**
Form - 1
2000 Turf 1-1: (5f 1-1) (g-f 1-1)
Group-class horse. (1st run) - 1st of 11 from Development (16 Jly Agnano RF 2980a).
**A Renzoni in ITY [4-6] Scuderia Jerome (from A Spanu in FR [0-1] Oct 1995).*

LATE SUMMER (USA) RR 64f 5136[6]
2 b f Gone West (USA) 7.8f **(82)** - Sun and Shade (Ajdal (USA)) 9.2f **(89)**
Form - 6
Record 2000 - 1st:0 2nd:0 3rd:0 Ran:1
2000 Turf 0-1: (8f) (g-s)
Currently average filly. **H R A Cecil [0-1] Cliveden Stud.*

LATIN BAY BHB 33f43a **RR 42f 43a** 2256[2]
5 b g Superlative 8.8f **(57)** - Hugging (Beveled (USA)) 9f **(59)**
Form - 002
Record 2000 - 1st:0 2nd:1 3rd:0 Ran:3
Pre2000 - 1st:3 2nd:0 3rd:2 Ran:24
Win Prizemoney £6,580 *Total Prizemoney* £8,111
Wins 1999 *Jan Lingfi (STD) SH 12f 38 54*
1999 *Jan Lingfi (STD) SH 13f 42 56* <
1998 Aug Kempto (G-F) H 9f 42 45
2000 Turf 0-2: (12f, 14f) (g-f 2) 2000 AW 0-1: (12f) (Equi)
Moderate gelding, effective 12 to 13f, - acts on Equi, likes left handed tracks. Turf high 29.
**P G Murphy [0-3] Mrs J Whitburn (from D J Wintle [0-4] Oct 1999).*

LATINO BAY (IRE) BHB 42f45a **RR 51f 45a** 4995[1]
3 ch g Perugino (USA) - Slightly Latin (Ahonoora) 8.1f **(73)**
Form - 768081
Record 2000 - 1st:1 2nd:0 3rd:0 Ran:6
Pre2000 - 1st:0 2nd:0 3rd:0 Ran:3
Win Prizemoney £2,233 *Total Prizemoney* £2,233
Wins * **2000** *Oct Wolver (STD) 7f 48* <
2000 Turf 0-3: (7f 3) (g-f 2, hrd) 2000 AW 1-3: (7f 1-1, 9f, 12f) (Fibr 1-3)
Workmanlike, fair gelding. Turf high 51. AW high 48 (began Aug). Inconsistent. **N P Littmoden [1-9] The Southgate Seven.*

LA TORTUGA BHB 55f65a **RR 60f 65a** 5083[19]
3 b g Turtle Island (IRE) - Ville Sainte (FR) (Saint Estephe (FR)) 16.4f **(79)**
Form - 45807660
Record 2000 - 1st:0 2nd:0 3rd:0 Ran:5
Pre2000 - 1st:1 2nd:0 3rd:0 Ran:8
Win Prizemoney £3,260 *Total Prizemoney* £4,387
Wins 1999 Aug Carlis (FRM) 5f 76 <
2000 Turf 0-5: (6f 3, 7f, 11f) (hvy, sft, gd 2, frm)
Leggy, above-average gelding, effective 5f, acts on frm, has worn blinkers. Turf high 60. Becoming disappointing.
**A Berry [0-1] Muckleton Racing Partnership (from W M Brisbourne [0-4] Jun 2000).*

L A TOUCH BHB 47f52a **RR 46f 52a** 3961[20]
7 b m Tina's Pet 7.4f **(56)** - Silvers Era (Balidar) 7.9f **(63)**
Form - 0368600
Record 2000 - 1st:0 2nd:0 3rd:1 Ran:7
Pre2000 - 1st:4 2nd:5 3rd:3 Ran:39
Win Prizemoney £11,755 *Total Prizemoney* £17,816
Wins 1999 Jly Cheste (G-F) H 7.6f 41 48
1999 Jun Yarmou (GD) H 6f 41 44
1998 Aug Yarmou (FRM) H 6f 33 42
2000 Turf 0-7: (5f, 6f 2, 7f 4) (g-f 2, frm 3, hrd 2)
Moderate mare, effective 6 to 8f, best at 7f, acts on gd to frm, best on g-f. Turf high 47 (began Jly) - 3rd of 16 getting 15lb from Peter's Imp (22 Jly Warwick 7f g-f RF 3041). Inconsistent.
**C A Dwyer [1-18] H M de B Lipscomb (from M A Peill [2-8] Aug 1999).*

LATOUR RR 81f 4632[11]
3 b br f Sri Pekan (USA) - Fenny Rough (Home Guard (USA)) 9.3f **(66)**
Form - 232000
Record 2000 - 1st:0 2nd:2 3rd:1 Ran:6
Pre2000 - 1st:0 2nd:0 3rd:0 Ran:3
Win Prizemoney £0 *Total Prizemoney* £3,667
2000 Turf 0-6: (8f 3, 10f 2, 11f) (g-s 2, gd, g-f 3)
Scopey, decent filly, has worn blinkers. Turf high 81. Becoming disappointing. **J W Hills [0-9] Wood Hall Stud Ltd.*

LA TRAVIATA BHB 46f **RR 41f** 5053[8]
2 b f Spectrum (IRE) - Opera Lover (IRE) **(97f)** (Sadler's Wells (USA)) 10f **(76)**
Form - 008
Record 2000 - 1st:0 2nd:0 3rd:0 Ran:3
2000 Turf 0-3: (7f 3) (sft, g-s 2)
Currently moderate filly. Turf high 41 (began Spt).
**Sir Mark Prescott [0-3] Cheveley Park Stud.*

LAUDABLE LAD BHB 30f **RR 23f** 4930[27]
2 b g Most Welcome 8.6f **(66)** - Santarem (USA) (El Gran Senor (USA)) 9.6f **(76)**
Form - 000
Record 2000 - 1st:0 2nd:0 3rd:0 Ran:3
2000 Turf 0-3: (5f, 7f, 8f) (gd 2, frm)

Currently little account gelding, has worn blinkers. Turf high 23 (began Spt). **G L Moore [0-3] Joe Bates (Bloodstock) Ltd.*

LAUND VIEW LADY BHB 36f40a RR 36df 40a 5314[8]

3 ch f Presidium 7.5f **(56)** - Vickenda (Giacometti) 11.2f **(56)**
Form - 8600088
Record 2000 - 1st:0 2nd:0 3rd:0 Ran:7
Pre2000 - 1st:1 2nd:0 3rd:0 Ran:5
Win Prizemoney £4,435 *Total Prizemoney* £4,435
Wins * 1999 Aug Ripon (GD) 6f 78 <
2000 Turf 0-6: (6f, 7f 2, 8f, 9f, 10f) (sft, gd 2, g-f, frm 2) 2000 AW 0-1: (6f) (Fibr)
Strong, very moderate filly, effective 6f, acts on gd. Turf high 36. Becoming disappointing. **Mrs S J Smith [1-13] Laund View Racing.*

LAUND VIEW LEONA BHB 30f RR 5019[21]

2 ch f Piccolo - Punta Leona (IRE) (Shernazar) 10.2f **(73)**
Form - 0
Record 2000 - 1st:0 2nd:0 3rd:0 Ran:1
2000 Turf 0-1: (6f) (sft)
Currently poor filly. **R Bastiman [0-1] Laund View Racing.*

LAUNFAL BHB 89f RR 87f 1427[11]

3 gr c Rudimentary (USA) 8.2f **(66)** - Laune (AUS) **(50f)** (Kenmare (FR)) 6.5f **(72)**
Form - 040
Record 2000 - 1st:0 2nd:0 3rd:0 Ran:3
Pre2000 - 1st:1 2nd:1 3rd:4 Ran:8
Win Prizemoney £3,403 *Total Prizemoney* £18,335
Wins * 1999 Apr Windso (G-F) 5f 76 <
2000 Turf 0-3: (6f 2, 7f) (gd 2, g-f)
Workmanlike, useful colt, effective 6 to 7f, acts on g-s to frm. Turf high 87. **R Hannon [1-11] J A Lazzari.*

LAUREL DAWN BHB 82f78a RR 80f 78a 5102[5]

2 gr c Paris House 5.9f **(64)** - Madrina **(61f)** (Waajib)
Form - 48121345
Record 2000 - 1st:2 2nd:1 3rd:1 Ran:8
Win Prizemoney £11,042 *Total Prizemoney* £14,855
Wins * **2000** Jly York (GD) H 5f 79 <
* **2000** *Jun Lingfi (STD) 5f 69+*
2000 Turf 1-7: (5f 1-6, 6f) (gd 1-3, frm 3, hrd) 2000 AW 1-1: (5f 1-1) (Equi 1-1)
Decent colt, effective 5f, acts on gd to hrd. Turf high 80 - also 1st of 6 getting 11lb from Silca Legend (15 Jly York RF 2856). (1st run). Improving. **A Berry [2-8] Laurel (Leisure) Ltd.*

LAURIESTON FLO (IRE) RR 46f 5196[11]

2 b f Nicolotte - Brown Foam (Horage) 10.3f **(61)**
Form - 0
Record 2000 - 1st:0 2nd:0 3rd:0 Ran:1
2000 Turf 0-1: (8f) (gd)
Currently moderate filly. **B J Meehan [0-1] L A Warren.*

LAUTREC BHB 45a RR 54f 377[9]

4 b g Shareef Dancer (USA) 10.1f **(67)** - Pride of Paris (Troy) 10.4f **(68)**
Form - 050
Record 2000 - 1st:0 2nd:0 3rd:0 Ran:2
Pre2000 - 1st:0 2nd:0 3rd:3 Ran:8
Win Prizemoney £0 *Total Prizemoney* £1,705
2000 AW 0-2: (8f, 12f) (Equi, Fibr)
Neat, fair gelding, has worn blinkers. AW high 20. Becoming disappointing.
**G M McCourt [0-6] G Redford (from R J R Williams [0-7] Jly 1999).*

LAVANTER RR 42f 4702[14]

2 b c Green Desert (USA) 7.8f **(78)** - Gussy Marlowe (Final Straw) 7.9f **(64)**
Form - 0
Record 2000 - 1st:0 2nd:0 3rd:0 Ran:1
2000 Turf 0-1: (7f) (g-f)
Currently moderate colt. **E A L Dunlop [0-1] Mrs John Van Geest.*

LAVERON RR 110f 5211a[2]

6 b h Konigsstuhl (GER) 9f **(115)** - La Virginia (GER) (Surumu (GER)) 10f **(83)**
Form - 34662
2000 Turf 0-5: (11f, 12f 4) (sft 3, gd 2)
Group-class horse, effective 12f, acts on sft to gd, best on sft. Turf high 110 - 2nd of 12 giving 9lb to Kapitol (22 Oct Dusseldorf 12f sft RF 5211a). Consistent. **P Rau in GER [2-8] Spt 2000).*

LA VIDA LOCA (IRE) RR 97f 4844a[4]

2 ch f Caerleon (USA) 10.9f **(79)** - Sharata (IRE) (Darshaan) 9.9f **(84)**
Form - 521544
2000 Turf 1-6: (5f 1-1, 6f 3, 7f, 8f) (g-s, gd 3, g-f 1-2)
Very useful filly, effective 5 to 8f, acts on gd to g-f. Turf high 97 - 4th of 10 to Amonita (1 Oct Longchamp 8f gd RF 4844a) - also 1st of 6 from Patinham (29 Jly Curragh RF 3302a). She raced exclusively in Group 1 company after winning a maiden at The Curragh, running her best race when finishing fourth in the Prix Marcel Boussac. A mile looks the limit of her stamina at present.
**A P O'Brien in IRE [1-6].*

LA VITA E BELLA (IRE) BHB 100f RR 93f 5241[1]

2 b f Definite Article - Coolrain Lady (IRE) (Common Grounds)
Form - 7211
Record 2000 - 1st:2 2nd:1 3rd:0 Ran:4
Win Prizemoney £16,806 *Total Prizemoney* £17,682
Wins * **2000** Oct Newmar (SFT) L 8f 93 <
* **2000** Spt Haydoc (HVY) 8.1f 75+
2000 Turf 2-4: (7f, 8f 2-3) (g-s 1-2, gd 1-1, g-f)
Useful filly. Turf high 93 (began Jly) - 1st of 9 from Esyoueffcee (28 Oct Newmarket RF 5241). Has progressed with her racing, and handles soft ground well. **C F Wall [2-4] Ettore Landi.*

LAW BREAKER (IRE) BHB 49a RR 64f 5197[3]

2 ch c Case Law 6f **(64)** - Revelette (Runnett) 7f **(59)**
Form - 7405303
Record 2000 - 1st:0 2nd:0 3rd:2 Ran:7
Win Prizemoney £0 *Total Prizemoney* £1,913
2000 Turf 0-6: (5f, 6f 5) (g-s, gd, g-f 3, frm) 2000 AW 0-1: (6f) (Fibr)
Average colt, effective 6f, acts on gd. Turf high 64 - 3rd of 8 getting 17lb from Barathiki (26 Oct Windsor 6f gd RF 5197).
**J Cullinan [0-7] Alan Spargo Ltd Toolmakers.*

LAW COMMISSION BHB 65f RR 66f 4224[7]

10 ch g Ela-Mana-Mou 12.7f **(72)** - Adjala (Northfields (USA)) 9f **(72)**
Form - 6014277
Record 2000 - 1st:1 2nd:1 3rd:0 Ran:7
Pre2000 - 1st:7 2nd:5 3rd:2 Ran:66
Win Prizemoney £44,088 *Total Prizemoney* £80,301
Wins * **2000** Jly Bath (FRM) 5.7f 61
* 1999 May Newbur (G-F) H 7f 81 85
* 1997 Spt Goodwo (G-S) H 7f 91 93 <
* 1996 Aug Ascot (G-F) H 7f 88 91
* 1996 Jly Kempto (GD) C 6f 81
* 1996 Jun Folkes (G-F) H 6f 79 81
2000 Turf 1-7: (6f 1-4, 7f 2, 8f) (g-f 2, frm 1-5)
Average gelding, effective 7f, acts on g-f. Turf high 66. Consistent.
**D R C Elsworth [8-73] Raymond Tooth.*

LAWNETT BHB 35f50a RR 47f 50a 3450[9]

4 b f Runnett 6.7f **(56)** - Polar Storm (IRE) **(69f)** (Law Society (USA)) 9.9f **(70)**
Form - 85670500
Record 2000 - 1st:0 2nd:0 3rd:0 Ran:8
Pre2000 - 1st:1 2nd:0 3rd:2 Ran:14
Win Prizemoney £3,265 *Total Prizemoney* £3,755
Wins 1999 Jly Dundal (G-F) H 9f 52+ <
2000 Turf 0-6: (9f, 10f, 12f, 13f, 14f 2) (sft, g-f 3, frm 2) 2000 AW 0-2: (9f, 12f) (Fibr 2)
Scopey, moderate filly, effective 8 to 14f, acts on hvy to frm, best on gd, has worn blinkers, likes left handed tracks. Turf high 55 (1st run) - 6th of 15 getting 16lb from Noukari (29 Mar Catterick 14f frm RF 0546). AW high 41.
**M Todhunter [2-16] Andrew Gorton (from D Gillespie in IRE [1-12] Jly 1999).*

LAYAN BHB 54f47a RR 60f 47a 5005[3]

3 b f Puissance 7.1f **(60)** - Most Uppitty **(47f 49a)** (Absalom) 7.2f **(58)**
Form - 5660342030343
Record 2000 - 1st:0 2nd:1 3rd:4 Ran:13
Pre2000 - 1st:0 2nd:1 3rd:0 Ran:6

Win Prizemoney £0 *Total Prizemoney* £3,418
2000 Turf 0-11: (5f 8, 6f 3) (g-s, gd 4, g-f 2, frm 4) 2000 AW 0-2: (6f 2) (Fibr 2)
Light-framed, average filly, effective 5 to 6f, acts on gd - acts on Fibr. Turf high 60. AW high 66 (1st run) (began Jly) - 2nd of 11 to Branston Fizz (28 Jly Southwell 6f Fibr RF 3188).
**J Balding [0-13] Rowley Racing (from J Berry [0-6] Spt 1999).*

LAY DOWN SALLY (IRE) BHB 58f54a **RR 55f 54a** 5008[4]
2 ch f General Monash (USA) - Sally Fay (IRE) (Fayruz)
Form - 7084
Record 2000 - 1st:0 2nd:0 3rd:0 Ran:4
Win Prizemoney £0 *Total Prizemoney* £218
2000 Turf 0-3: (6f 2, 7f) (g-s, gd, g-f) 2000 AW 0-1: (6f) (Fibr)
Fair filly. Turf high 55 (began Jly). **J G Portman [0-4] Nick Quesnel.*

LAZEEM (USA) RR 71f 5184[7]
2 b c Tabasco Cat (USA) - Sea Ditty (CAN) (Afleet (CAN))
Form - 77
Record 2000 - 1st:0 2nd:0 3rd:0 Ran:2
2000 Turf 0-2: (8f 2) (g-s, g-f)
Currently above-average colt. Turf high 71 (began Spt).
**E A L Dunlop [0-2] Mohammed Rashid.*

LAZZAZ BHB 75f70a **RR 79f 70a** 4030[4]
2 b c Muhtarram (USA) - Astern (USA) (Polish Navy (USA)) 8f **(67)**
Form - 74
Record 2000 - 1st:0 2nd:0 3rd:0 Ran:2
Win Prizemoney £0 *Total Prizemoney* £268
2000 Turf 0-2: (7f, 8f) (frm 2)
Currently above-average colt. Turf high 79 (began Aug) - 4th of 9 to Steel Band (28 Aug Chepstow 8f frm RF 4030).
**M P Tregoning [0-2] Khalid Khalifa Al Nabooda.*

LEADING SPIRIT (IRE) BHB 60f63a **RR 29f 63a** 4692[17]
8 b g Fairy King (USA) 7.7f **(75)** - Shopping (FR) (Sheshoon) 11.9f **(69)**
Form - R0
Record 2000 - 1st:0 2nd:0 3rd:0 Ran:2
Pre2000 - 1st:5 2nd:3 3rd:3 Ran:30
Win Prizemoney £22,873 *Total Prizemoney* £31,526
Wins 1997 *Feb Wolver (STD) H* 12f 71 79+
1996 Spt Kempto (GD) H 12f 83 87 <
1996 Jun Kempto (G-F) H 12f 73 83+
2000 Turf 0-1: (14f) (gd) 2000 AW 0-1: (12f) (Fibr)
Little account gelding, has worn blinkers. Inconsistent.
**A D Smith [1-5] Miss K Smith (from D Sasse [0-3] Jun 1999).*

LEANADIS ROSE BHB 39f **RR 29f** 4772[9]
2 b f Namaqualand (USA) - Fiorini (Formidable (USA)) 9.2f **(63)**
Form - 560
Record 2000 - 1st:0 2nd:0 3rd:0 Ran:3
2000 Turf 0-3: (5f, 7f, 8f) (gd, frm 2)
Currently little account filly. Turf high 29 (began Aug).
**J M Jefferson [0-3] J M Jefferson.*

LEAPING CHARLIE BHB 54f53a **RR 57f 53a** 5003[8]
4 b g Puissance 7.1f **(60)** - Impala Lass (Kampala) 8.4f **(56)**
Form - 058
Record 2000 - 1st:0 2nd:0 3rd:0 Ran:3
Pre2000 - 1st:1 2nd:1 3rd:1 Ran:15
Win Prizemoney £2,388 *Total Prizemoney* £3,562
Wins * 1999 Jun Hamilt (GD) H 5f 57 58 <
2000 Turf 0-2: (5f 2) (g-s, gd) 2000 AW 0-1: (6f) (Fibr)
Leggy, fair gelding, effective 5f, acts on sft to g-f, best on g-f. Turf high 34 (began Spt).
**Mrs A Duffield [1-18] Starnotes Racing.*

LEARNED LAD (FR) RR 71+f 5110[5]
2 ch c Royal Academy (USA) 7.8f **(77)** - Blushing Storm (USA) (Blushing Groom (FR)) 10.3f **(76)**
Form - 75
Record 2000 - 1st:0 2nd:0 3rd:0 Ran:2
Win Prizemoney £0 *Total Prizemoney* £285
2000 Turf 0-2: (7f, 8f) (gd, g-f)
Currently above-average colt. Turf high 71 (began Spt).
**D R C Elsworth [0-2] J C Smith.*

LEAR SPEAR (USA) BHB 118f **RR 120f** 4297[1]
5 b h Lear Fan (USA) 10.4f **(80)** - Golden Gorse (USA) (His Majesty (USA)) 10.9f **(82)**
Form - 32031
Record 2000 - 1st:1 2nd:1 3rd:1 Ran:4
Pre2000 - 1st:5 2nd:1 3rd:6 Ran:22
Win Prizemoney £213,045 *Total Prizemoney* £371,150
Wins * 2000 Spt Doncas (G-F) L 12f 108+
* 1999 Spt Goodwo (G-F) G3 9.9f 118
* 1999 Jun Ascot (G-F) G2 10f 120 <
* 1999 Jun Epsom (GD,) G3 8.5f 110
* 1998 Oct Newmar () H 9f 90 96
* 1998 Aug Sandow (GD) 8.1f 75
2000 Turf 1-2: (10f, 12f 1-1) (gd, g-f 1-1) 2000 AW 0-2: (10f 2) (Dirt 2)
Very high-class colt, effective 9 to 10f, best at 10f, acts on gd to g-f - acts on Dirt, best on g-f. Turf high 118 (began Aug). AW high 118 (1st run) - 2nd of 6 to Dubai Millennium (2 Mar Nad Al Sheba 10f Dirt RF 0427a). Successful in the Prince Of Wales's Stakes at Royal Ascot in 1999, he went missing for five months after finishing unplaced in the Dubai World Cup. A promising third in the Juddmonte International on his comeback, he was tried over a mile and a half at Doncaster in September and got the trip well enough to break the course record. While likely to be found out in the very top class, he should win another Group race in 2001.
**D R C Elsworth [6-26] Raymond Tooth.*

Lear Spear broke the course record at Doncaster

LEATHERBACK (IRE) BHB 74f **RR 75f** 5320[1]
2 b g Turtle Island (IRE) - Phyllode **(53f)** (Pharly (FR)) 9.8f **(68)**
Form - 8000111
Record 2000 - 1st:3 2nd:0 3rd:0 Ran:7
Win Prizemoney £11,511 *Total Prizemoney* £11,511
Wins * 2000 Nov Doncas (HVY) H 7f 68 75 <
*** 2000** Oct Bright (SFT) H 8f 53 67
*** 2000** Oct Pontef (HVY) H 8f 53 58
2000 Turf 3-7: (6f 3, 7f 1-1, 8f 2-3) (sft 2-2, g-s 1-1, g-f, frm 3)
Above-average gelding, effective 7 to 8f, acts on sft. Turf high 75 - 1st of 22 getting 8lb from Church Mice (4 Nov Doncaster RF 5320) - also 1st of 11 getting 13lb from Meriden Mist (27 Oct Brighton RF 5218).
**N A Callaghan [3-7] M Tabor.*

LEA VALLEY EXPRESS (IRE) BHB 29f44a RR 3f 44a
3133[15]
3 b f Fayruz 6.6f **(63)** - Fenland Express (IRE) (Reasonable (FR))
Form - 5000000
Record 2000 - 1st:0 2nd:0 3rd:0 Ran:6
Pre2000 - 1st:0 2nd:0 3rd:1 Ran:8
Win Prizemoney £0 *Total Prizemoney* £501
2000 Turf 0-4: (6f, 7f, 8f, 12f) (hvy, gd, frm 2) 2000 AW 0-2: (6f, 8f) (Equi, Fibr)
Unfurnished, fair filly, often wears blinkers. Turf high 3. AW high 11. **J R Jenkins [0-14] Lea Valley.*

LEAVE US LEAP (USA) RR 113f
4133a[3]
4 b c Summer Squall (USA) 7f **(80)** - Sporades (USA) (Vaguely Noble) 10.1f **(72)**
Form - 23
2000 Turf 0-1: (8f) (g-f)
Currently Group-class colt. (1st run) - 3rd of 6 giving 7lb to Penny's Gold (25 Aug Deauville 8f g-f RF 4133a).
**A Fabre in FR [0-3] B Lalemant.*

LE CAVALIER (USA) BHB 44f51a RR 59f 51a
5246[4]
3 b g Mister Baileys - Secret Deed (USA) (Shadeed (USA)) 8.2f **(70)**
Form - 4777222226500074
Record 2000 - 1st:0 2nd:5 3rd:0 Ran:14
Pre2000 - 1st:0 2nd:0 3rd:1 Ran:7
Win Prizemoney £0 *Total Prizemoney* £5,221
2000 Turf 0-2: (10f, 12f) (gd, frm) 2000 AW 0-12: (8f, 9f, 10f 2, 12f 7, 16f) (Equi 4, Fibr 8)
Scopey, fair gelding, effective 9 to 12f, best at 12f, - acts on Fibr, has worn blinkers, likes left handed tracks, likes tight tracks. Turf high 36. AW high 66 - 2nd of 8 to Spanish Star (22 Feb Wolverhampton 12f Fibr RF 0334). Inconsistent.
**C N Allen [0-21] Mrs K A Hyytiainen.*

LEDGENDRY LINE BHB 53f RR 55f
5104[11]
7 b g Mtoto 11.5f **(71)** - Eider (Niniski (USA)) 10.6f **(65)**
Form - 5641570
Record 2000 - 1st:1 2nd:0 3rd:0 Ran:7
Pre2000 - 1st:1 2nd:4 3rd:5 Ran:25
Win Prizemoney £5,528 *Total Prizemoney* £16,690
Wins * **2000** Jun Pontef (SFT) H 17.1f 55 54
* 1997 Jun Ayr (GD) H 13.1f 70 77 <
2000 Turf 1-7: (14f, 15f, 16f 2, 17f 1-2, 18f) (g-s, gd 1-4, frm 2)
Fair gelding, effective 14 to 17f, acts on g-s to frm, and excels at Haydock and Newcastle. Turf high 59 (1st run) - 5th of 15 giving 16lb to Swiftway (28 Mar Newcastle 16f g-s RF 0527). Consistent.
**Mrs M Reveley [6-42] The Home & Away Partnership.*

LEEN BHB 28f57a RR 47f 57a
5162[4]
3 b f Distant Relative 7f **(69)** - St James's Antigua (IRE) (Law Society (USA)) 9.9f **(70)**
Form - 8000760274
Record 2000 - 1st:0 2nd:1 3rd:0 Ran:10
Pre2000 - 1st:1 2nd:1 3rd:0 Ran:5
Win Prizemoney £3,571 *Total Prizemoney* £5,576
Wins 1999 Spt Bath (FRM) 5.1f 73 <
2000 Turf 0-8: (6f, 7f 4, 8f 2, 10f) (sft, gd, g-f 3, frm 3) 2000 AW 0-2: (6f, 7f) (Fibr 2)
Neat, moderate filly, effective 5 to 6f, acts on frm, has worn blinkers. Turf high 49. AW high 50.
**M J Polglase [0-1] R D Letby (from C G Cox [1-12] Aug 2000).*

LEEROY (IRE) BHB 52f RR 60f
4471[12]
3 b g Dancing Dissident (USA) 6.8f **(65)** - Birdhill (IRE) (Petorius) 7.3f **(61)**
Form - 28750
Record 2000 - 1st:0 2nd:1 3rd:0 Ran:5
Pre2000 - 1st:0 2nd:2 3rd:1 Ran:5
Win Prizemoney £0 *Total Prizemoney* £4,113
2000 Turf 0-5: (7f 5) (sft, gd 2, g-f, frm)
Scopey, average gelding, effective 6 to 7f, best at 6f, acts on gd to g-f, best on g-f. Turf high 80 (1st run) - 2nd of 16 to Grand Bahamian (7 Apr Lingfield 7f gd RF 0637). Becoming disappointing.
**R Hannon [0-10] Mrs Barrie Gallop.*

LEES FIRST STEP BHB 41f RR 50f
5116[7]
3 b f Reprimand 8.2f **(63)** - Classic Coral (USA) (Seattle Dancer (USA))
Form - 0707
Record 2000 - 1st:0 2nd:0 3rd:0 Ran:4
Pre2000 - 1st:0 2nd:1 3rd:0 Ran:4
Win Prizemoney £0 *Total Prizemoney* £892
2000 Turf 0-3: (12f 3) (gd, g-f, frm) 2000 AW 0-1: (8f) (Fibr)
Scopey, fair filly, has broken blood-vessels, effective 7f, acts on g-f, likes left handed tracks, likes tight tracks. Turf high 50. Inconsistent. **P G Murphy [0-9] Second Step.*

LE FANTASME RR 29f
4482[8]
2 b c Fairy King (USA) 7.7f **(75)** - La Splendide (FR) (Slip Anchor) 9.8f **(73)**
Form - 8
Record 2000 - 1st:0 2nd:0 3rd:0 Ran:1
2000 Turf 0-1: (8f) (g-s)
Currently little account colt. **S Dow [0-1] D G Churston.*

LE FOLLIE (CHI) RR 45f
3439[7]
3 ch f Hussonet (USA) - Whisper Loud (CHI) (Worldwatch (USA))
Form - 77
Record 2000 - 1st:0 2nd:0 3rd:0 Ran:2
2000 Turf 0-2: (6f, 8f) (gd, g-f)
Leggy, currently moderate filly. Turf high 45 (began Jly).
**B W Hills [0-2] Wafic Said.*

LEGACY OF LOVE BHB 50f RR 55f
3900[6]
4 b f Distant Relative 7f **(69)** - May Hills Legacy (IRE) (Be My Guest (USA)) 9.3f **(67)**
Form - 02046
Record 2000 - 1st:0 2nd:1 3rd:0 Ran:5
Pre2000 - 1st:1 2nd:1 3rd:0 Ran:6
Win Prizemoney £2,476 *Total Prizemoney* £4,259
Wins 1999 Jly Lingfi (G-F) 7.6f 64 <
2000 Turf 0-5: (8f 2, 9f, 12f 2) (g-f 2, frm 3)
Neat, fair filly, effective 8 to 10f, best at 8f, acts on gd to hrd, has worn blinkers. Turf high 55.
**Miss S E Hall [0-5] J Hanson (from B W Hills [1-6] Oct 1999).*

LEGAL ISSUE (IRE) BHB 66f62a RR 66f 62a
751[P]
8 b h Contract Law (USA) 8.9f **(54)** - Natuschka (Authi) 8.9f **(89)**
Form - 43184P
Record 2000 - 1st:0 2nd:0 3rd:0 Ran:1
Pre2000 - 1st:11 2nd:13 3rd:7 Ran:80
Win Prizemoney £33,444 *Total Prizemoney* £51,968

Wins	* 1999	*Nov*	*Southw*	*(STD)*	*H*	*11f*	*55*	*62*	
	* 1999	Jun	Beverl	(GD)	H	8.5f	67	81+	<
	* 1999	Apr	Thirsk	(GD)	H	8f	62	67	
	1998	Jun	Beverl	(G-S)	H	8.5f	67	68	
	1998	Apr	Pontef	(G-S)		8f		67	
	1997	*Dec*	*Lingfi*	*(STD)*	*H*	*10f*	*55*	*59*	
	1997	*Aug*	*Wolver*	*(STD)*	*H*	*8.5f*	*51*	*52*	
	1996	Jly	Catter	(G-S)		7f		68	
	1996	Jun	Doncas	(GD)	H	7f	56	59	

2000 Turf 0-1: (10f) (sft)
Average horse, effective 8f, acted on gd, had worn blinkers, liked tight tracks. (DEAD)
**B S Rothwell [3-21] B Valentine (from J M Jefferson [0-4] Nov 1998).*

LEGAL JOUSTING (IRE) RR 108f
1576a[6]
3 b c Indian Ridge 7.6f **(74)** - In Anticipation (IRE) (Sadler's Wells (USA)) 10f **(76)**
Form - 1226
2000 Turf 1-4: (7f, 8f 1-3) (sft 1-3, g-s)
Pattern-class colt, has worn blinkers. Turf high 108. Not seen out after finishing sixth to Bachir in the Irish Guineas.
**D K Weld in IRE [1-5] Moyglare Stud Farm.*

LEGAL LUNCH (USA) BHB 69f RR 71f
5069[8]
5 b g Alleged (USA) 11.8f **(81)** - Dinner Surprise (USA) (Lyphard (USA)) 9.9f **(72)**
Form - 33420531356158
Record 2000 - 1st:2 2nd:1 3rd:2 Ran:12
Pre2000 - 1st:1 2nd:4 3rd:4 Ran:25
Win Prizemoney £13,144 *Total Prizemoney* £28,504
Wins * **2000** Jly Epsom (GD) H 12f 69 70

* **2000**	May Doncas (G-S)	H	12f	68	69	
* 1998	May Haydoc (G-S)		10.5f		90	<

2000 Turf 2-12: (12f 2-10, 14f, 15f) (sft, g-s 2, gd 1-4, g-f 1-3, frm 2)
Above-average gelding, effective 12 to 16f, best at 16f, acts on gd to frm, best on frm, often wears blinkers, likes Doncaster. Turf high 71. He is rather one-paced and had been on a very long losing run, but having blinkers fitted rather than a visor seemed to do the trick when he scored at Doncaster in May. He is effective from 12 to 16 furlongs. **P W Harris [3-37] The Alleged Partnership.*

LEGAL SET (IRE) BHB 73f69a RR 75f 69a 4924[10]

4 b br g Second Set (IRE) 9.2f **(67)** - Tiffany's Case (IRE) **(58f)** (Thatching) 8f **(66)**
Form - 20033672300

Record	**2000 -**	1st:0	2nd:2	3rd:3	Ran:11
	Pre2000 -	1st:0	2nd:0	3rd:1	Ran:6

Win Prizemoney £0 *Total Prizemoney* £6,874
2000 Turf 0-10: (8f 9, 9f) (gd 3, g-f 3, frm 4) 2000 AW 0-1: (8f) (Equi)
Workmanlike, above-average gelding, effective 7 to 8f, best at 8f, acts on gd to frm, has worn blinkers, prefers right handed tracks, prefers tight tracks, excels at Windsor. Turf high 75 - 3rd of 9 getting 7lb from Border Subject (26 Aug Windsor 8f gd RF 4005). Consistent.
**K R Burke [0-11] John Kelsey-Fry (from C A Horgan [0-6] Jun 1999).*

LEGAL TENDER RR 21f 1519[8]

3 b g Contract Law (USA) 8.9f **(54)** - Slip a Coin **(48f 55a)** (Slip Anchor) 9.8f **(73)**
Form - 008

Record	**2000 -**	1st:0	2nd:0	3rd:0	Ran:3

2000 Turf 0-3: (6f, 8f 2) (g-s, frm 2)
Unfurnished, currently little account gelding. Turf high 13.
**D Burchell [0-3] Tycroes Five Star Racing.*

LEGAL VENTURE (IRE) BHB 38f42a RR 36f 42a 3899[7]

4 ch g Case Law 6f **(64)** - We Two (Glenstal (USA)) 10.1f **(64)**
Form - 00U0034027467

Record	**2000 -**	1st:0	2nd:1	3rd:1	Ran:10
	Pre2000 -	1st:2	2nd:5	3rd:4	Ran:33

Win Prizemoney £3,565 *Total Prizemoney* £9,733

Wins	1999	*May Wolver (STD)*	*S*	*5f*	*60*	
	1998	Jly Lingfi (G-F)	S	5f	64+	<

2000 Turf 0-3: (5f 3) (frm 2, hrd) 2000 AW 0-7: (5f 6, 6f) (Equi, Fibr 6)
Moderate gelding, effective 5f, - acts on Fibr, often wears blinkers, likes tight tracks. Turf high 36 (began Aug). AW high 48.
**J C Poulton [0-5] The Three Bears Go Racing (from N P Littmoden [1-27] Feb 2000).*

LEGAL WORD RR 30f 3048[14]

2 b c Nashwan (USA) 10.3f **(79)** - Miznah (IRE) (Sadler's Wells (USA)) 10f **(76)**
Form - 0

Record	**2000 -**	1st:0	2nd:0	3rd:0	Ran:1

2000 Turf 0-1: (7f) (frm)
Currently very moderate colt. **Sir Michael Stoute [0-1] Abdullah Ali.*

LEGEND BHB 65f RR 65f 1896[12]

4 b f Belmez (USA) 11.4f **(65)** - Once Upon a Time (Teenoso (USA)) 9.9f **(72)**
Form - 20

Record	**2000 -**	1st:0	2nd:1	3rd:0	Ran:2
	Pre2000 -	1st:0	2nd:0	3rd:2	Ran:4

Win Prizemoney £0 *Total Prizemoney* £2,260
2000 Turf 0-2: (12f, 14f) (gd 2)
Scopey, average filly. Turf high 65 (1st run) - 2nd of 8 giving 27lb to Joli Flyers (29 May Leicester 12f gd RF 1527).
**R Hannon [0-2] The Queen (from I A Balding [0-2] Jly 1999).*

LEGENDAIRE (USA) BHB 57f60a RR 61f 60a 3034[8]

3 gr c Fly Till Dawn (USA) - Iolani **(49f)** (Alzao (USA)) 7.1f **(68)**
Form - 2243668

Record	**2000 -**	1st:0	2nd:2	3rd:1	Ran:7
	Pre2000 -	1st:0	2nd:1	3rd:0	Ran:7

Win Prizemoney £0 *Total Prizemoney* £3,384
2000 Turf 0-3: (7f 3) (g-f 2, frm) 2000 AW 0-4: (7f, 8f 2, 10f) (Equi 4)
Scopey, average colt, effective 7f, acts on g-f - acts on Equi, likes left handed tracks, likes tight tracks. Turf high 61 (1st run) - 3rd of 9 to Mister Clinton (17 May Brighton 7f g-f RF 1257). AW high 62 - 2nd of 11 getting 11lb from Direct Reaction (9 Feb Lingfield 7f Equi RF 0252).
**Miss Gay Kelleway [0-4] Legend Racing (from C A Dwyer [0-10] Feb 2000).*

LEGENDARY LOVER (IRE) BHB 60a RR 54f 4692[14]

6 b g Fairy King (USA) 7.7f **(75)** - Broken Romance (IRE) (Ela-Mana-Mou) 10.1f **(70)**
Form - 530

Record	**2000 -**	1st:0	2nd:0	3rd:1	Ran:3
	Pre2000 -	1st:0	2nd:1	3rd:1	Ran:11

Win Prizemoney £0 *Total Prizemoney* £2,461
2000 Turf 0-3: (11f, 12f, 14f) (hvy, gd, g-f)
Fair gelding, effective 11f, acts on frm, has worn blinkers, likes right handed tracks, favours tight tracks. Turf high 54.
**J R Jenkins [1-18] Southern Counties Finance & Leasing (from R Charlton [0-5] Spt 1997).*

LEGGIT (IRE) BHB 59f58a RR 66f 58a 4114[2]

2 b f Night Shift (USA) 8.1f **(73)** - Scales of Justice (Final Straw) 7.9f **(64)**
Form - 07052

Record	**2000 -**	1st:0	2nd:1	3rd:0	Ran:5

Win Prizemoney £0 *Total Prizemoney* £560
2000 Turf 0-5: (5f 2, 6f 2, 7f) (g-f, frm 4)
Average filly. Turf high 66 (began Jly).
**M R Channon [0-5] Tim Corby.*

LEGGY LADY BHB 36f RR 50df 4923[8]

4 b f Sir Harry Lewis (USA) - Lady Minstrel (Tudor Music) 6.8f **(59)**
Form - 48538

Record	**2000 -**	1st:0	2nd:0	3rd:1	Ran:4
	Pre2000 -	1st:0	2nd:0	3rd:0	Ran:4

Win Prizemoney £0 *Total Prizemoney* £436
2000 Turf 0-3: (13f, 16f, 17f) (frm 2, hrd) 2000 AW 0-1: (16f) (Equi)
Scopey, fair filly. Turf high 46. **J A R Toller [0-8] M E Wates.*

LE GRAND GOUSIER (USA) BHB 40f46a RR 46a 4327[17]

6 ch g Strawberry Road (AUS) 14.5f **(57)** - Sandy Baby (USA) (Al Hattab (USA)) 9.3f **(74)**
Form - 0

Record	**2000 -**	1st:0	2nd:0	3rd:0	Ran:1
	Pre2000 -	1st:1	2nd:2	3rd:0	Ran:15

Win Prizemoney £1,984 *Total Prizemoney* £3,415

Wins	1997	Jly Warwic (G-F)	SH	12.5f	52	57	<

2000 Turf 0-1: (11f) (g-f)
Very poor gelding, has worn blinkers.
**R J Price [2-24] Mrs S G Davies (from R J R Williams [2-16] Spt 1997).*

LEGS BE FRENDLY (IRE) BHB 62f60a RR 66f 60a 4758[4]

5 b g Fayruz 6.6f **(63)** - Thalssa (Rusticaro (FR)) 8.2f **(65)**
Form - 35004

Record	**2000 -**	1st:0	2nd:0	3rd:1	Ran:5
	Pre2000 -	1st:1	2nd:7	3rd:1	Ran:20

Win Prizemoney £4,653 *Total Prizemoney* £16,225

Wins	1997	Oct Lingfi (GD)		5f	64	<

2000 Turf 0-4: (5f 4) (gd 2, frm 2) 2000 AW 0-1: (6f) (Fibr)
Average gelding, effective 5f, acts on gd to frm, best on frm, often wears blinkers (extremely effectively). Turf high 66 (1st run) - 3rd of 16 giving 18lb to Cool Prospect (5 May Musselburgh 5f frm RF 1038). **D Nicholls [0-5] V Greaves (from K McAuliffe [1-20] Spt 1999).*

LEILA RR 26tf 4204[8]

5 b m Aragon 7.7f **(58)** - Carpe Diem (Good Times (ITY)) 6.6f **(54)**
Form - 848

Record	**2000 -**	1st:0	2nd:0	3rd:0	Ran:3

Win Prizemoney £0 *Total Prizemoney* £218
2000 Turf 0-3: (10f, 12f, 14f) (g-f, frm 2)
Little account filly. Turf high 26 (began Aug).
**J S King [0-3] D F Jordan.*

LE KHOUMF (FR) BHB 55f RR 51f 1089[12]

9 ch g Son of Silver - Bentry (FR) (Ben Trovato (FR))
Form - 10

Record	**2000 -**	1st:1	2nd:0	3rd:0	Ran:2
	Pre2000 -	1st:0	2nd:0	3rd:0	Ran:7

Win Prizemoney £2,446 *Total Prizemoney* £2,715
Wins * **2000** Apr Southw (G-S) H 16f 50 50 <
2000 Turf 1-2: (14f, 16f 1-1) (g-s 1-1, g-f)
Fair gelding. Turf high 51. Consistent.
**J Neville [2-10] George Moore (from J M Bradley [0-9] Jun 1996).*

LE LOUP BHB 48f43a **RR 61f 43a** 4221[14]

3 b g Wolfhound (USA) 7.3f **(71)** - Chandni (IRE) (Ahonoora) 8.1f **(73)**
Form - 0043840
Record 2000 - 1st:0 2nd:0 3rd:1 Ran:7
Pre2000 - 1st:0 2nd:0 3rd:1 Ran:6
Win Prizemoney £0 *Total Prizemoney* £896
2000 Turf 0-6: (6f, 7f, 8f 4) (gd 2, g-f 3, frm) 2000 AW 0-1: (10f) (Equi)
Workmanlike, average gelding, effective 5f, acts on g-s. Turf high 61. **Miss E C Lavelle [0-13] The 1st Little Hatherden Partnership.*

LEMARATE (USA) RR 58f 4754[12]

3 b c Gulch (USA) 9.6f **(79)** - Sayyedati **(119f)** (Shadeed (USA)) 8.2f **(70)**
Form - 00
Record 2000 - 1st:0 2nd:0 3rd:0 Ran:2
2000 Turf 0-2: (8f, 10f) (g-s, g-f)
Workmanlike, currently fair colt. Turf high 58 (began Aug).
**C E Brittain [0-2] Mohamed Obaida.*

LE MERIDIEN (IRE) BHB 58f **RR 65f** 4490[14]

2 ch f Magical Wonder (USA) 7.2f **(60)** - Dutch Queen (Ahonoora) 8.1f **(73)**
Form - 844040
Record 2000 - 1st:0 2nd:0 3rd:0 Ran:6
Win Prizemoney £0 *Total Prizemoney* £788
2000 Turf 0-6: (5f, 6f 5) (gd, g-f, frm 4)
Average filly, effective 6f, acts on frm. Turf high 65 - 4th of 9 getting 5lb from Xipe Totec (16 Jly Haydock 6f frm RF 2858).
**J S Wainwright [0-6] J S Wainwright.*

LEMON BRIDGE (IRE) BHB 73f **RR 76f** 4190[5]

5 b g Shalford (IRE) 7.8f **(63)** - Sharply (Sharpman) 11.3f **(66)**
Form - 55
Record 2000 - 1st:0 2nd:0 3rd:0 Ran:2
Pre2000 - 1st:1 2nd:3 3rd:3 Ran:13
Win Prizemoney £3,850 *Total Prizemoney* £10,282
Wins 1998 Jun Goodwo (G-F) 9.9f 79 <
2000 Turf 0-2: (12f 2) (sft, g-f)
Above-average gelding. Turf high 75 - 5th of 7 getting 17lb from Ulundi (3 Spt Kempton 12f g-f RF 4190).
**R T Phillips [0-6] Lemon Connections (from J W Hills [1-10] Spt 1998).*

LEMON DROP KID (USA) RR 5332a[5]

4 b c Kingmambo (USA) 10.9f **(85)** - Charming Lassie (USA) (Seattle Slew (USA)) 9.4f **(76)**
Form - 115
2000 AW 2-3: (9f 2-2, 10f) (Dirt 2-3)
Top-class colt, has worn blinkers. AW high 127 - 1st of 6 giving 6lb to Cat Thief (6 Aug Saratoga RF 3545a) - also 1st of 7 giving 6lb to Lager (11 Jun Belmont Park RF 2003a). He has been one of the top dirt horses in the US in recent years, but for the second year running did not show his very best in the Breeders' Cup Classic.
**F Schulhofer in USA [3-6] Jeanne Vance.*

LEMON STRIP BHB 34f35a **RR 10f 35a** 1718[21]

4 ch f Emarati (USA) 6.6f **(63)** - Lon Isa **(39f 47a)** (Grey Desire) 8.7f **(50)**
Form - 42440600
Record 2000 - 1st:0 2nd:0 3rd:0 Ran:3
Pre2000 - 1st:0 2nd:2 3rd:1 Ran:17
Win Prizemoney £0 *Total Prizemoney* £1,790
2000 Turf 0-1: (6f) (gd) 2000 AW 0-2: (5f, 6f) (Fibr 2)
Unfurnished, poor filly, has worn blinkers. AW high 5. Becoming disappointing.
**A G Juckes [0-3] H Weeks (from B Palling [0-17] Dec 1999).*

LEND A HAND BHB 116f **RR 122f** 3542a[2]

5 b h Great Commotion (USA) 9.2f **(80)** - Janaat (Kris) 9.5f **(73)**
Form - 61352
Record 2000 - 1st:1 2nd:1 3rd:1 Ran:5
Pre2000 - 1st:7 2nd:4 3rd:1 Ran:15
Win Prizemoney £186,823 *Total Prizemoney* £404,362

Wins	* **2000**	May	York	(FRM)	G3	6f		118
	* 1999	Aug	Newbur	(GD)	G3	7.3f		118+
	1999	*Mar*	*Nad Al*	*(FST)*	*L*	*8f*		*123* <
	1997	Oct	San Si	(GD)	G1	8f		115+
	1997	Spt	Doncas	(G-F)	H	8f	94	103+
	1997	Jly	Beverl	(G-F)		7.5f		90
	1997	Jly	Catter	(G-F)		7f		94+
	1997	Jly	Epsom	(G-S)		6f		75

2000 Turf 1-4: (6f 1-3, 7f) (gd 1-4) 2000 AW 0-1: (6f) (Dirt)
Very high-class colt, effective 6 to 8f, best at 8f, acts on gd to frm - acts on Dirt, excels at Newmarket. Turf high 118 (1st run) - 1st of 10 giving 3lb to Pipalong (18 May York RF 1276). Consistent. He raced exclusively around six furlongs last year, looking a potential champion sprinter when beating Pipalong in the Group Three Duke Of York Stakes in May. Heavily backed when third in the Cork And Orrery Stakes at Royal Ascot, he was hampered in the July Cup and failed by a neck to collar Bold Edge in the Group One Prix Maurice de Gheest at Deauville in August. Thoroughly genuine, he stayed a mile and has been retired to the Kildangan Stud, Kildare, at IR£5,000.
**S bin Suroor [2-8] Godolphin (from S bin Suroor in UAE [1-2] Mar 2000).*

LENNEL BHB 69f **RR 72f** 4869[5]

2 b g Presidium 7.5f **(56)** - Ladykirk **(60f)** (Slip Anchor) 9.8f **(73)**
Form - 63555
Record 2000 - 1st:0 2nd:0 3rd:1 Ran:5
Win Prizemoney £0 *Total Prizemoney* £566
2000 Turf 0-5: (6f 4, 7f) (sft, gd, frm 3)
Above-average gelding. Turf high 72 - 5th of 11 getting 12lb from Soldier On (15 Spt Ayr 6f gd RF 4425).
**Denys Smith [0-5] Exors of The Duke of Sutherland.*

LENNOX RR 51f 2975[7]

4 b g Bustino 11f **(64)** - Ivory Gull (USA) (Storm Bird (CAN)) 10.3f **(74)**
Form - 7
Record 2000 - 1st:0 2nd:0 3rd:0 Ran:1
Pre2000 - 1st:0 2nd:0 3rd:1 Ran:7
Win Prizemoney £0 *Total Prizemoney* £618
2000 Turf 0-1: (12f) (frm)
Scopey, fair gelding.
**C Weedon [0-2] Alf Chadwick (from P F I Cole [0-7] Oct 1999).*

Lemon Drop Kid, one of the top American dirt horses

LENNY THE LION BHB 46f **RR 49f** 5193[10]

3 b g Bin Ajwaad (IRE) - Patriotic (Hotfoot) 10.5f **(59)**
Form - 05538070
Record 2000 - 1st:0 2nd:0 3rd:1 Ran:8
Pre2000 - 1st:0 2nd:0 3rd:0 Ran:4
Win Prizemoney £0 *Total Prizemoney* £348
2000 Turf 0-8: (10f 3, 12f 4, 13f) (g-s, gd 4, g-f 2, frm)
Scopey, moderate gelding, effective 10 to 12f, acts on g-f to frm, has worn blinkers, likes tight tracks. Turf high 55 - 3rd of 16 giving 14lb to Chaka Zulu (1 Jly Bath 10f frm RF 2426).
**Mrs M Reveley [0-3] A D Simmons (from R Hannon [0-9] Jly 2000).*

LE NOMADE (IRE) RR 99f 3348a[3]
3 b c Nashwan (USA) 10.3f **(79)** - La Splendide (FR) (Slip Anchor) 9.8f **(73)**
Form - 3
2000 Turf 0-1: (15f) (sft)
Currently very useful colt. (1st run) - 3rd of 9 to Samsaam (28 Jly Chantilly 15f sft RF 3348a). **P Bary in FR [0-1] Mlle C Jacob.*

LEOFRIC BHB 37f34a **RR 41f 34a** 2550[7]
5 b g Alhijaz 7.7f **(57)** - Wandering Stranger (Petong) 6.6f **(58)**
Form - 4035833730630007
Record 2000 - 1st:0 2nd:0 3rd:5 Ran:14
Pre2000 - 1st:2 2nd:0 3rd:6 Ran:52
Win Prizemoney £4,489 *Total Prizemoney* £11,377
Wins * 1999 Aug Sandow (G-S) H 8.1f 39 44?
* 1999 *Jan Southw (STD) C 7f 65 <*
2000 Turf 0-11: (7f 2, 8f 5, 9f 2, 10f 2) (sft 2, g-s 2, gd 3, g-f 2, frm, hrd)
2000 AW 0-3: (7f 2, 8f) (Fibr 3)
Moderate gelding, effective 7f, - acts on Fibr, often wears blinkers (effectively), likes right handed tracks. Turf high 41. AW high 36. Becoming disappointing. **M J Polglase [2-66] Southwell Racing Club.*

LEONATO (FR) BHB 75f **RR 71f** 4469[5]
8 b g Law Society (USA) 11.6f **(71)** - Gala Parade (Alydar (USA)) 9.1f **(76)**
Form - 05
Record 2000 - 1st:0 2nd:0 3rd:0 Ran:2
Pre2000 - 1st:0 2nd:4 3rd:1 Ran:14
Win Prizemoney £0 *Total Prizemoney* £21,341
2000 Turf 0-2: (14f 2) (g-f 2)
Above-average gelding. Turf high 71 (began Spt). Consistent. Lightly raced and obviously difficult to train, he stays well and appreciates some give underfoot.
**I A Balding [0-2] Colin Booth (from P D Evans [0-14] Jun 1999).*

LEONIE SAMUAL BHB 42f **RR 43f** 5077[13]
5 b m Safawan 6.6f **(60)** - Hy Wilma (Jalmood (USA)) 10.1f **(52)**
Form - 431800
Record 2000 - 1st:1 2nd:0 3rd:1 Ran:6
Pre2000 - 1st:0 2nd:0 3rd:0 Ran:2
Win Prizemoney £2,488 *Total Prizemoney* £2,757
Wins * **2000** May Pontef (SFT) SH 8f 42 43 <
2000 Turf 1-6: (6f, 7f, 8f 1-2, 10f 2) (g-s 2, gd 1-3, frm)
Moderate filly, effective 7 to 8f, acts on gd. Turf high 43 - 1st of 20 from Special-K (3 May Pontefract RF 1005).
**R J Hodges [1-8] Mrs Carol Taylor.*

LEOPARDSTOWN (GER) RR 98f 2581a[13]
3 f
Form - 00
2000 Turf 0-2: (8f, 12f) (sft, gd)
Currently very useful. Turf high 98. **M Hofer in GER [0-2].*

LEOZIAN BHB 85f **RR 83f** 4926[7]
2 b c Lion Cavern (USA) 7.5f **(74)** - Alzianah **(102f)** (Alzao (USA)) 7.1f **(68)**
Form - 20417
Record 2000 - 1st:1 2nd:1 3rd:0 Ran:5
Win Prizemoney £3,909 *Total Prizemoney* £5,063
Wins * **2000** Spt Lingfi (SFT) 5f 72 <
2000 Turf 1-4: (5f 1-4) (gd 1-2, frm 2) 2000 AW 0-1: (6f) (Equi)
Decent colt. Turf high 83 (1st run) (began Aug) - 2nd of 10 to Senior Minister (11 Aug Lingfield 5f frm RF 3552).
**Miss Gay Kelleway [1-5] & Mrs Gary Pinchen.*

LE PIN BHB 57f **RR 63f** 793[9]
3 ch f Persian Bold 10f **(69)** - Red Rose Garden (Electric) 10.1f **(61)**
Form - 0
Record 2000 - 1st:0 2nd:0 3rd:0 Ran:1
Pre2000 - 1st:0 2nd:0 3rd:0 Ran:4
2000 Turf 0-1: (12f) (g-s)
Scopey, average filly. **M R Channon [0-5] Wood Hall Stud Ltd.*

LERMONTOV (USA) RR 113f 4989[12]
3 br c Alleged (USA) 11.8f **(81)** - Prospect Dalia (USA) (Mr Prospector (USA)) 8.8f **(78)**
Form - 4800
2000 Turf 0-4: (8f, 10f 2, 14f) (g-s, gd 3)
Group-class colt, effective 8f, acts on g-s. Turf high 95 (began Spt). Second in the Group 1 Racing Post Trophy in 1999, he proved bitterly disappointing last year and was used as a pace-maker in the autumn.
**A P O'Brien in IRE [2-7] M Tabor & Mrs John Magnier.*

LE ROI CHIC (FR) RR 111f 1818a[3]
4 m Balleroy (USA) - Chic Emilie (FR) (Policeman (FR)) 9.8f **(80)**
Form - 3
2000 Turf 0-1: (8f) (sft)
Group-class. (1st run) - 3rd of 7 to Kingsalsa (30 May Chantilly 8f sft RF 1818a).
**N Clement in FR [1-5] Investment Tandem (from J P Despeyroux in FR [1-1] Apr 1998).*

LE SAUVAGE (IRE) BHB 23f33a **RR 28f 33a** 4119[8]
5 b g Tirol 8.1f **(64)** - Cistus (Sun Prince) 12.4f **(52)**
Form - 08
Record 2000 - 1st:0 2nd:0 3rd:0 Ran:1
Pre2000 - 1st:0 2nd:1 3rd:1 Ran:13
Win Prizemoney £0 *Total Prizemoney* £860
2000 Turf 0-1: (16f) (frm)
Very moderate gelding, effective 12f, - acts on Fibr, likes left handed tracks, favours tight tracks.
**D W Barker [0-17] The Ebor Partnership (from M R Channon [0-3] Oct 1998).*

LES GIRLS RR 35f 5073[U]
2 b f Dilum (USA) 7.1f **(56)** - Diamond Bebe (Sparkling Boy) 5f **(36)**
Form - 00U
Record 2000 - 1st:0 2nd:0 3rd:0 Ran:3
2000 Turf 0-3: (5f, 6f, 7f) (g-s, gd, frm)
Currently very moderate filly. Turf high 35 (began Spt).
**Mrs A J Bowlby [0-3] Cliff Basson.*

LET ALONE BHB 72f **RR 78f** 3165[10]
3 b br f Warning 8.1f **(77)** - Mettlesome (Lomond (USA)) 8.8f **(65)**
Form - 7100
Record 2000 - 1st:1 2nd:0 3rd:0 Ran:4
Win Prizemoney £6,955 *Total Prizemoney* £6,955
Wins * **2000** Jun Bath (G-S) 8f 78 <
2000 Turf 1-4: (7f, 8f 1-1, 10f 2) (g-s, gd 1-1, g-f 2)
Scopey, above-average filly. Turf high 78 - 1st of 10 from Seeking Success (2 Jun Bath RF 1646). Appreciated the step up to a mile when getting off the mark in a Bath maiden, but has been found out in decent handicap company on faster ground since then.
**B W Hills [1-4] K Abdulla.*

LE TETEU (FR) BHB 53f **RR 49f** 1323[7]
7 b g Saint Andrews (FR) - Nouvelle Star (USA) (Star de Naskra (USA)) 9.7f **(65)**
Form - 7
Record 2000 - 1st:0 2nd:0 3rd:0 Ran:1
Pre2000 - 1st:1 2nd:0 3rd:1 Ran:8
Win Prizemoney £3,241 *Total Prizemoney* £4,103
Wins * 1996 Jun Haydoc (GD) H 8.1f 55 61 <
2000 Turf 0-1: (16f) (gd)
Moderate gelding. Consistent.
**Bob Jones [3-18] The Le Teteu Partnership.*

LETHAL AGENDA (USA) RR 90f 5352a[4]
2 ch c Twilight Agenda (USA) - Mrs K (USA) 00
Form - 14
2000 Turf 1-2: (7f 1-2) (hvy, sft 1-1)
Currently useful colt. Turf high 90 (1st run) (began Oct) - 1st of 12 from Frosty Wind (1 Oct Cork RF 4804a).
**D K Weld in IRE [1-2] Kenneth Ramsey.*

LE TINTORET (FR) RR 115f 4848a[7]
7 Goldneyev (USA) - Abariya (FR) (Akarad (FR)) 9f **(76)**
Form - 257
2000 Turf 0-3: (15f, 16f, 20f) (g-s 2, gd)
High-class. Turf high 115 - 7th of 9 to San Sebastian (1 Oct Longchamp 20f gd RF 4848a). **Y de Nicolay in FR [2-6].*

LETS REFLECT BHB 52f **RR 62f** 4769[7]
3 b f Mtoto 11.5f **(71)** - Lets Fall In Love (USA) (Northern Baby (CAN)) 11.6f **(71)**
Form - 54757
Record 2000 - 1st:0 2nd:0 3rd:0 Ran:5
Win Prizemoney £0 *Total Prizemoney* £275
2000 Turf 0-5: (7f, 8f, 10f 3) (g-s 2, frm 3)
Light-framed, average filly. Turf high 62 (began Jly).
**J R Turner [0-5] Hilton Cox.*

LEVEL BEST RR 27f 3702[12]
2 ch g Beveled (USA) 6.9f **(64)** - Rhythmical (Swing Easy (USA)) 6.5f **(55)**
Form - 0
Record 2000 - 1st:0 2nd:0 3rd:0 Ran:1
2000 Turf 0-1: (6f) (frm)
Currently little account gelding. **M Blanshard [0-1] D A Poole.*

LEVEL HEADED BHB 58f45a **RR 60?f 45a** 4749[8]
5 b m Beveled (USA) 6.9f **(64)** - Snowline (Bay Express) 7.1f **(60)**
Form - 5083504413410118
Record 2000 - 1st:4 2nd:0 3rd:2 Ran:14
Pre2000 - 1st:0 2nd:0 3rd:0 Ran:10
Win Prizemoney £12,230 *Total Prizemoney* £13,104
Wins * 2000 Spt Bright (G-S) H 10f 44 57+
*** 2000** Spt Beverl (HVY) H 9.9f 44 60? <
*** 2000** Aug Lingfi (G-F) H 10f 40 43
*** 2000** Jly Bath (FRM) H 10.2f 36 38
2000 Turf 4-13: (7f, 8f, 10f 4-11) (g-s 1-3, gd 1-3, g-f 3, frm 1-2, hrd 1-2)
2000 AW 0-1: (10f) (Equi)
Average filly, has broken blood-vessels, effective 10f, acts on g-s to gd, has worn blinkers, favours tight tracks. Turf high 60 - 1st of 17 getting 4lb from Ratified (19 Spt Beverley RF 4499) - also 1st of 18 getting 22lb from Nouf (24 Spt Brighton RF 4616).
**P W Hiatt [4-14] Anthony Harrison (from E A Wheeler [0-10] Dec 1999).*

LEVENDI (IRE) BHB 44f **RR** 4872[7]
3 ch g Mukaddamah (USA) 7.6f **(74)** - Christle Mill (Pas de Seul) 9.1f **(67)**
Form - 807
Record 2000 - 1st:0 2nd:0 3rd:0 Ran:3
2000 Turf 0-3: (5f, 7f, 8f) (hvy, g-s, gd)
Leggy, currently very poor gelding. (began Spt).
**I S Wainwright [0-3] P Charalambous.*

LIBERTY BOUND BHB 58f **RR 60f** 4747[21]
2 b f Primo Dominie 7.2f **(67)** - Tshusick **(77f)** (Dancing Brave (USA)) 8.4f **(76)**
Form - 480
Record 2000 - 1st:0 2nd:0 3rd:0 Ran:3
Win Prizemoney £0 *Total Prizemoney* £247
2000 Turf 0-3: (5f, 6f 2) (gd 3)
Currently average filly. Turf high 60 (began Spt).
**D Shaw [0-3] J C Fretwell.*

LICENCE TO THRILL BHB 75f77a **RR 82f 77a** 3365[7]
3 ch f Wolfhound (USA) 7.3f **(71)** - Crime of Passion (Dragonara Palace (USA)) 6.1f **(55)**
Form - 25110207
Record 2000 - 1st:2 2nd:1 3rd:0 Ran:6
Pre2000 - 1st:0 2nd:1 3rd:0 Ran:3
Win Prizemoney £6,760 *Total Prizemoney* £13,260
Wins * 2000 *Mar Lingfi (STD) H 5f 70 76* <
*** 2000** *Feb Lingfi (STD) 5f 69*
2000 Turf 0-4: (5f 4) (gd 2, g-f, frm) 2000 AW 2-2: (5f 2-2) (Equi 2-2)
Decent filly, effective 5 to 6f, best at 5f, acts on gd - acts on Equi. Turf high 82 - 2nd of 18 getting 2lb from Compton Banker (24 Jun Ascot 5f gd RF 2237). AW high 76 - 1st of 6 getting 11lb from Illusive (8 Mar Lingfield RF 0423). She is very effective over the minimum distance on the Lingfield Equitrack and scored twice under those conditions. Obviously suited by a turning left-handed track, but handled Ascot's stiff five well when second in June.
**D W P Arbuthnot [2-9] Christopher Wright.*

LIDAKIYA (IRE) BHB 101f **RR 101+f** 4041[12]
3 b f Kahyasi 12.9f **(74)** - Lilissa (IRE) (Doyoun) 9f **(69)**
Form - 411210
Record 2000 - 1st:3 2nd:1 3rd:0 Ran:6
Win Prizemoney £18,499 *Total Prizemoney* £22,052
Wins * 2000 Aug Pontef (G-F) H 12f 92 101 <
*** 2000** Jun Newbur (G-F) H 10f 79 83++
*** 2000** May Thirsk (GD) 12f 72+
2000 Turf 3-6: (10f 1-3, 12f 2-3) (g-s, gd 1-2, g-f 1-2, hrd 1-1)
Light-framed, very useful filly, effective 12f, acts on g-f to hrd. Turf high 101 - 1st of 5 getting 4lb from Three Green Leaves (20 Aug Pontefract RF 3829). A useful middle-distance handicapper, she had earned her crack at some black type on her final start but unfortunately her saddle slipped.
**Sir Michael Stoute [3-6] H H Aga Khan.*

L'IDEA GENIALE (ITY) RR 96f 1455a[13]
3 f
Form - 0
2000 Turf 0-1: (11f) (gd)
Currently very useful filly. (1st run) - 13th of 18 to Timi (21 May San Siro 11f gd RF 1455a). **F Camici in ITY [0-1].*

LIDIO (GER) RR 113f 4956a[5]
4 b c Alzao (USA) 9.8f **(73)** - Ligona (Aragon) 8.1f **(60)**
Form - 345
2000 Turf 0-3: (8f 3) (hvy, sft 2)
Currently Group-class colt. Turf high 113 (began Jly) - 5th of 9 to Faberger (8 Oct San Siro 8f sft RF 4956a). **H Steguweit in GER [0-3].*

LIFE IS LIFE (FR) BHB 108f **RR 113f** 3031[8]
4 b f Mansonnien (FR) 12f **(91)** - La Vie Immobile (USA) (Alleged (USA)) 10f **(76)**
Form - 3258
Record 2000 - 1st:0 2nd:1 3rd:1 Ran:4
Pre2000 - 1st:1 2nd:1 3rd:0 Ran:3
Win Prizemoney £4,070 *Total Prizemoney* £29,105
Wins * 1999 Spt Kempto (HVY) 12f 84++ <
2000 Turf 0-4: (12f 2, 13f, 20f) (hvy, g-f 3)
Scopey, Group-class filly, effective 12 to 20f, acts on hvy to g-f, best on g-f. Turf high 113 - 5th of 11 getting 5lb from Kayf Tara (22 Jun Ascot 20f g-f RF 2180). She ran the race of her life behind Daliapour in Chester's Ormonde Stakes, but failed to stay in the Gold Cup and appeared unsuited by front-running tactics when dropped into Listed company at Newmarket in July. Best on easy ground, she made a successful debut over hurdles in November and will find more opportunities in that sphere than on the Flat.
**M A Jarvis [1-7] & Mrs Raymond Anderson Green.*

LIFE OF RILEY BHB 97f **RR 100f** 2442[18]
6 ch g Caerleon (USA) 10.9f **(79)** - Catina (Nureyev (USA)) 8.7f **(78)**
Form - 0
Record 2000 - 1st:0 2nd:0 3rd:0 Ran:1
Pre2000 - 1st:5 2nd:2 3rd:2 Ran:18
Win Prizemoney £27,324 *Total Prizemoney* £33,522
Wins 1999 Aug Newmar (G-F) H 14.8f 94 100 <
1999 Jun Goodwo (G-F) H 14f 86 90
1998 Jly Sandow (GD) H 16.4f 85 89
1998 May Kempto (G-F) H 14.4f 76 81
1997 Jun Pontef (G-F) 10f 74
2000 Turf 0-1: (16f) (frm)
Very useful gelding, effective 14 to 16f, acts on frm, has worn blinkers.
**C J Mann [2-3] Stanley Clarke (from B J Meehan [4-13] Oct 1999).*

LIFFORD LADY BHB 45f **RR 49f** 5243[7]
2 b f Syrtos 8.1f **(57)** - Sally Maxwell (Roscoe Blake) 11f **(66)**
Form - 80067
Record 2000 - 1st:0 2nd:0 3rd:0 Ran:5
2000 Turf 0-4: (6f 2, 7f 2) (gd, g-f 2, frm) 2000 AW 0-1: (6f) (Fibr)
Moderate filly. Turf high 49 (began Aug).
**B N Doran [0-5] The Lifford Lady Partnership.*

LIFT THE OFFER (IRE) BHB 44f54a **RR 41f 54a** 129[12]
5 ch g Ballad Rock 7.2f **(63)** - Timissara (USA) (Shahrastani (USA)) 8.8f **(72)**
Form - 700
Record 2000 - 1st:0 2nd:0 3rd:0 Ran:2
Pre2000 - 1st:2 2nd:2 3rd:3 Ran:27

Win Prizemoney £6,272 *Total Prizemoney* £10,200
Wins 1997 *Nov Lingfi (STD)* 7f 67+
1997 *Nov Lingfi (STD) H* 8f 68 77 <
2000 AW 0-2: (7f 2) (Fibr 2)
Moderate gelding, effective 6 to 8f, acts on g-f, has worn blinkers. AW high 30.
**J J Quinn [0-12] Bowlers Racing (from R Hannon [2-17] Oct 1998).*

LIGHT EVIDENCE BHB 52f60a RR 54f 60a 4927[6]

2 ch f Factual (USA) - Blazing Sunset (Blazing Saddles (AUS)) 6.7f **(46)**
Form - 8586
Record 2000 - 1st:0 2nd:0 3rd:0 Ran:4
2000 Turf 0-3: (5f, 6f 2) (gd 2, g-f) 2000 AW 0-1: (5f) (Equi)
Average filly. Turf high 54 - 5th of 20 getting 8lb from Piccolo Rose (22 Spt Lingfield 6f gd RF 4581).
**S C Williams [0-4] Bainey Racing Partnership.*

LIGHTNING ARROW (USA) BHB 109f RR 111f 4128[2]

4 br g Silver Hawk (USA) 11.2f **(85)** - Strait Lane (USA) (Chieftain II) 10.4f **(75)**
Form - 0241222
Record 2000 - 1st:1 2nd:4 3rd:0 Ran:7
Pre2000 - 1st:1 2nd:4 3rd:1 Ran:10
Win Prizemoney £12,215 *Total Prizemoney* £61,409
Wins * 2000 Jly Newmar (G-F) 12f 109 <
* 1998 Oct Newmar (G-S) 8f 90
2000 Turf 1-7: (12f 1-4, 13f 2, 14f) (hvy, gd 1-2, g-f 2, frm, hrd)
Neat, Group-class gelding, effective 10 to 14f, acts on g-s to frm, has worn blinkers, excels at Chester and Newmarket. Turf high 111 - 2nd of 4 getting 1lb from Zaajer (20 Aug Chester 13f gd RF 3821) - also 1st of 4 from Rain In Spain (21 Jly Newmarket RF 3004). Gelded after his three-year-old campaign, he raced more genuinely last season. Unplaced when sent for an ambitious tilt at the Melbourne Cup, he is worth another try over two miles and goes well on turning tracks. **J L Dunlop [2-17] Wafic Said.*

LIGHTNING STAR (USA) BHB 72f RR 74f 5079[7]

5 b g El Gran Senor (USA) 8.9f **(85)** - Cuz's Star (USA) (Galaxy Libra) 8.1f **(82)**
Form - 47
Record 2000 - 1st:0 2nd:0 3rd:0 Ran:2
Pre2000 - 1st:1 2nd:0 3rd:1 Ran:6
Win Prizemoney £5,480 *Total Prizemoney* £6,731
Wins 1997 Aug Galway (G-S) 8.5f 81 <
2000 Turf 0-2: (12f 2) (sft, g-s)
Above-average gelding, has worn blinkers. Turf high 74. Consistent.
**T P McGovern [0-6] Ashley Carr Racing (5) (from A P O'Brien in IRE [1-6] May 1998).*

LIGHT OF ARAGON BHB 33f RR 42f 4996[9]

2 b f Aragon 7.7f **(58)** - Light the Way (Nicholas Bill) 10.1f **(56)**
Form - 000760
Record 2000 - 1st:0 2nd:0 3rd:0 Ran:6
2000 Turf 0-5: (6f 2, 7f 3) (g-f, frm 4) 2000 AW 0-1: (8f) (Fibr)
Moderate filly. Turf high 42. **J L Eyre [0-6] J L Eyre.*

LIGHT OF FASHION BHB 50f RR 46f 5060[5]

2 b f Common Grounds 8.1f **(66)** - May Light **(60df)** (Midyan (USA)) 6f **(60)**
Form - 805
Record 2000 - 1st:0 2nd:0 3rd:0 Ran:3
2000 Turf 0-3: (6f 3) (sft, g-f, hrd)
Currently moderate filly. Turf high 46 (began Aug).
**B Smart [0-3] Dr J A E Hobby.*

LIGHT PROGRAMME BHB 60f RR 62f 934[12]

6 b g El Gran Senor (USA) 8.9f **(85)** - Nashmeel (USA) (Blushing Groom (FR)) 10.3f **(76)**
Form - 00
Record 2000 - 1st:0 2nd:0 3rd:0 Ran:2
Pre2000 - 1st:1 2nd:1 3rd:0 Ran:4
Win Prizemoney £5,481 *Total Prizemoney* £6,790
Wins 1997 Jly Newmar (G-F) 10f 87 <
2000 Turf 0-1: (10f) (gd) 2000 AW 0-1: (8f) (Fibr)
Average gelding.
**J G Smyth-Osbourne [0-5] G F T Agricultural Products Ltd (from H R A Cecil [1-2] Jly 1997).*

LIGHT THE ROCKET (IRE) BHB 90f RR 102?f 5127[12]

4 ch g Pips Pride 6.7f **(70)** - Coolrain Lady (IRE) (Common Grounds)
Form - 0
Record 2000 - 1st:0 2nd:0 3rd:0 Ran:1
Pre2000 - 1st:2 2nd:5 3rd:0 Ran:17
Win Prizemoney £10,457 *Total Prizemoney* £25,566
Wins 1998 Aug Ascot (G-F) 5f 90 <
1998 Aug Sandow (GD) 5f 83+
2000 Turf 0-1: (5f) (g-s)
Leggy, very useful gelding, effective 5 to 6f, best at 6f, acts on g-s to frm, best on frm.
**W J Musson [0-1] HTTP Partnership Ltd (from R Hannon [2-17] Oct 1999).*

LIGNE GAGNANTE (IRE) BHB 94f RR 96f 3914[9]

4 b g Turtle Island (IRE) - Lightino (Bustino) 10.4f **(64)**
Form - 602230
Record 2000 - 1st:0 2nd:2 3rd:1 Ran:6
Pre2000 - 1st:3 2nd:1 3rd:2 Ran:11
Win Prizemoney £19,938 *Total Prizemoney* £59,155
Wins * 1999 Jun Newcas (GD) H 12.4f 79 83
* 1999 Jun Goodwo (GD) H 12f 77 85 <
* 1999 May Ayr (GD) 9.1f 72
2000 Turf 0-6: (12f 5, 14f) (hvy, gd 2, g-f 2, frm)
Scopey, very useful gelding, effective 12 to 14f, best at 12f, acts on sft to frm. Turf high 96 - 9th of 22 giving 5lb to Give The Slip (23 Aug York 14f frm RF 3914). He threatened to win a decent handicap but lacks a telling turn-of-foot and was left playing bridesmaid. Effective over an easy mile and three-quarters, he handles any ground and is genuine. **W J Haggas [3-17] The Winning Line.*

LIKE BLAZES RR 48f 4480[11]

2 ch f Halling (USA) - Derniere Danse (Gay Mecene (USA)) 8.6f **(69)**
Form - 0
Record 2000 - 1st:0 2nd:0 3rd:0 Ran:1
2000 Turf 0-1: (7f) (g-s)
Currently moderate filly. **C E Brittain [0-1] Alessandro Gaucci.*

LILANITA BHB 38f35a RR 36f 35a 4194[6]

5 b m Anita's Prince 6f **(62)** - Jimlil (Nicholas Bill) 10.1f **(56)**
Form - 32732880006
Record 2000 - 1st:0 2nd:1 3rd:0 Ran:7
Pre2000 - 1st:1 2nd:4 3rd:4 Ran:28
Win Prizemoney £2,374 *Total Prizemoney* £6,459
Wins 1998 Jun Chepst (G-S) S 8.1f 53 <
2000 Turf 0-2: (8f, 9f) (g-f 2) 2000 AW 0-5: (7f, 8f 2, 9f 2) (Fibr 5)
Very moderate filly, effective 8 to 10f, best at 8f, - acts on AW, best on Fibr, has worn blinkers, likes left handed tracks, likes tight tracks. Turf high 36 (began Aug). AW high 44. Inconsistent.
**P D Evans [0-9] J E Potter (from B Palling [1-26] Dec 1999).*

LILIUM RR 93f 4990[15]

2 b f Nashwan (USA) 10.3f **(79)** - Satin Flower (USA) (Shadeed (USA)) 8.2f **(70)**
Form - 110
Record 2000 - 1st:2 2nd:0 3rd:0 Ran:3
Win Prizemoney £16,330 *Total Prizemoney* £16,330
Wins * 2000 Spt Newmar (GD) L 7f 93 <
*** 2000** Spt Warwic (G-F) 7.1f 80+
2000 Turf 2-3: (7f 2-3) (gd, g-f 2-2)
Currently useful filly. Turf high 93 (began Spt) - 1st of 11 from Nafisah (30 Spt Newmarket RF 4738). Out of a very useful race-mare, she made a winning debut at Warwick before handling the step up in class in the Oh So Sharp Stakes at Newmarket.
**Sir Michael Stoute [2-3] Sheikh Mohammed.*

LILLAN BHB 60f RR 38tf 4810[6]

3 b f Hernando (FR) - Lillemor (Connaught) 7.7f **(63)**
Form - 644436
Record 2000 - 1st:0 2nd:0 3rd:1 Ran:6
Win Prizemoney £0 *Total Prizemoney* £1,082
2000 Turf 0-3: (8f, 10f 2) (gd 3) 2000 AW 0-3: (8f, 12f 2) (Equi 2, Fibr)
Scopey, average filly, effective 12f, - acts on Equi. Turf high 38. AW high 62 (began Spt) - 3rd of 18 getting 13lb from The Green

Grey (22 Spt Lingfield 12f Equi RF 4585). *G A Butler [0-6] M Berger.*

LILLEMAN BHB 82f82a **RR 78f 82a** 5129[9]
2 b c Distant Relative 7f **(69)** - Lillemor (Connaught) 7.7f **(63)**
Form - 572230
Record 2000 - 1st:0 2nd:2 3rd:1 Ran:6
Win Prizemoney £0 *Total Prizemoney* £2,300
2000 Turf 0-4: (6f 4) (sft, gd, g-f, frm) 2000 AW 0-2: (6f 2) (Equi, Fibr)
Above-average colt, effective 6f, acts on gd to g-f - acts on Fibr, has worn blinkers. Turf high 78 (1st run) (began Aug) - 5th of 7 to Goggles (1 Aug Goodwood 6f g-f RF 3281). AW high 78 (began Spt). Showed ability in a very warm maiden at the York Ebor meeting, but has spurned some good opportunities since. **G A Butler [0-6] M Berger.*

LIL'S JESSY (IRE) BHB 95f **RR 90f** 4990[12]
2 b f Kris 10f **(75)** - Lobmille (Mill Reef (USA)) 10.5f **(78)**
Form - 5101130
Record 2000 - 1st:3 2nd:0 3rd:1 Ran:7
Win Prizemoney £17,985 *Total Prizemoney* £20,330
Wins * **2000** Spt Doncas (G-F) H 7f 85 90 <
* **2000** Aug Cheste (GD) H 7f 78 87
* **2000** Jly Yarmou (FRM) 7f 75
2000 Turf 3-7: (6f, 7f 3-6) (gd, g-f 2-4, frm 1-2)
Useful filly, effective 7f, acts on g-f to frm, best on g-f. Turf high 90 - 3rd of 11 to Lilium (30 Spt Newmarket 7f g-f RF 4738) - also 1st of 22 giving 2lb to Whale Beach (9 Spt Doncaster RF 4313). She tries hard and developed into a useful juvenile. Unlikely to improve enough to make a mark in Group company at home, she may have to be campaigned on the continent. **J Noseda [3-7] Razza Pallorsi.*

LIMBO DANCER BHB 30f **RR 13f** 4778[11]
2 ch f Superlative 8.8f **(57)** - Marcroft (Crofthall) 6.3f **(59)**
Form - 60000
Record 2000 - 1st:0 2nd:0 3rd:0 Ran:5
2000 Turf 0-3: (5f 2, 7f) (gd, frm 2) 2000 AW 0-2: (6f 2) (Fibr 2)
Poor filly. Turf high 13. AW high 7.
**A Bailey [0-1] Mrs M A Clayton (from R M Whitaker [0-4] Jly 2000).*

LIMBURG (IRE) RR 54f 3535[13]
2 b br c Hamas (IRE) 8f **(72)** - Tambora (Darshaan) 9.9f **(84)**
Form - 070
Record 2000 - 1st:0 2nd:0 3rd:0 Ran:3
2000 Turf 0-3: (6f 2, 7f) (gd, g-f 2)
Currently fair colt. Turf high 54. **W R Muir [0-3] Dulverton Equine.*

LIME GARDENS RR 90f 5351a[1]
2 b f Sadler's Wells (USA) 11.3f **(87)** - Hatton Gardens (Auction Ring (USA)) 8.6f **(65)**
Form - 1
2000 Turf 1-1: (7f 1-1) (hvy 1-1)
Currently useful filly. (1st run) - 1st of 18 from Madamaa (30 Oct Leopardstown RF 5351a). **M J Grassick in IRE [1-1] J Higgins.*

LIMELIGHTING (USA) BHB 104f **RR 105f** 4837a[9]
4 b f Alleged (USA) 11.8f **(81)** - Steal The Thunder (CAN) (Lyphard (USA)) 9.9f **(72)**
Form - 2454140
Record 2000 - 1st:1 2nd:0 3rd:0 Ran:6
Pre2000 - 1st:2 2nd:4 3rd:0 Ran:7
Win Prizemoney £51,665 *Total Prizemoney* £72,123
Wins * **2000** Aug Deauvi (G-F) L 10f 105 <
* 1999 Nov Doncas (SFT) 10.3f 96
* 1999 Spt York (G-F) 10.4f 79
2000 Turf 1-6: (10f 1-3, 12f 2, 13f) (gd 3, g-f 1-3)
Lengthy, Pattern-class filly, effective 10 to 12f, best at 12f, acts on hvy to g-f, best on g-f, excels at York. Turf high 105 - 1st of 10 from Star Of Akkar (19 Aug Deauville RF 3946a). Consistent. Camapigned abroad in the second half of the season, she took a listed race at Deauville. A front-runner, she appreciates a bit of cut in the ground. **J H M Gosden [3-13].*

LINCOLN DANCER (IRE) BHB 116f **RR 121f** 5213a[2]
3 b c Turtle Island (IRE) - Double Grange (IRE) (Double Schwartz) 7.9f **(55)**
Form - 4012702
Record 2000 - 1st:1 2nd:2 3rd:0 Ran:7
Pre2000 - 1st:2 2nd:0 3rd:1 Ran:4
Win Prizemoney £25,682 *Total Prizemoney* £71,405
Wins * **2000** May Haydoc (SFT) LH 6f 105 115+ <
1999 May York (SFT) 6f 100
1999 Apr Warwic (GD) 5f 82
2000 Turf 1-7: (5f, 6f 1-4, 8f 2) (hvy, sft, g-s 1-3, gd 2)
Workmanlike, very high-class colt, effective 6f, acts on g-s to gd. Turf high 121 - 2nd of 11 getting 6lb from Agnes World (13 Jly Newmarket 6f gd RF 2773) - also 1st of 12 giving 9lb to Presentation (27 May Haydock RF 1490). Finished fourth in a Listed race on his reappearance and was not totally disgraced in the 2000 Guineas but, brought back to six furlongs, absolutely bolted up in a decent Listed handicap at Haydock. He probably ran his best ever race when just beaten by Agnes World in the July Cup, but was rather disappointing back at Haydock before chasing home Repertory at Longchamp. Needs six furlongs and easy ground. **M A Jarvis [1-7] Michael Baker (from G Lewis [2-4] Jun 1999).*

LINCOLN DEAN BHB 42f60a **RR 45f 60a** 3959[4]
4 b g Mtoto 11.5f **(71)** - Play With Me (IRE) (Alzao (USA)) 7.1f **(68)**
Form - 7803204
Record 2000 - 1st:0 2nd:1 3rd:1 Ran:7
Pre2000 - 1st:1 2nd:1 3rd:0 Ran:11
Win Prizemoney £3,543 *Total Prizemoney* £8,829
Wins 1999 *Jan Lingfi (STD) H 8f 61 70* <
2000 Turf 0-7: (8f 2, 9f 5) (g-f 2, frm 5)
Scopey, above-average gelding, effective 8f, - acts on Equi, likes left handed tracks, likes tight tracks. Turf high 45.
**J S Goldie [0-12] L H Gilmurray & T J Docherty (from Sir Mark Prescott [1-6] Feb 1999).*

L'INCONNU RR 1196[12]
5 ch g Groom Dancer (USA) 9.5f **(75)** - Love Potion (Rio Bravo (USA))
Form - 0
Record 2000 - 1st:0 2nd:0 3rd:0 Ran:1
2000 Turf 0-1: (10f) (sft)
Currently very poor gelding, always wears blinkers.
**Miss A M Newton-Smith [0-2] Ian Moody.*

LINDEN GRACE (USA) BHB 84f **RR 87f** 2620[P]
3 b f Mister Baileys - Gracefully Bold (USA) (Nasty And Bold (USA))
Form - 1P
Record 2000 - 1st:1 2nd:0 3rd:0 Ran:2
Pre2000 - 1st:1 2nd:1 3rd:0 Ran:4
Win Prizemoney £10,423 *Total Prizemoney* £12,882
Wins * **2000** Jun Newcas (FRM) H 8f 80 84 <
* 1999 Jly Epsom (G-F) 7f 76+
2000 Turf 1-2: (8f 1-2) (g-f 1-2)
Scopey, useful filly, effective 6 to 8f, acts on g-f. Turf high 84 (1st run) (began Jun) - 1st of 7 getting 15lb from Tony Tie (30 Jun Newcastle RF 2405). **M Johnston [2-6] R C Moules.*

LINEA D'OMBRA (USA) RR 93f 5203a[3]
2 ch f Zafonic (USA) 9f **(83)** -Canaletto (USA) (Iron Duke (FR)) 8.8f **(60)**
Form - 3
2000 Turf 0-1: (8f) (hvy)
Currently useful filly. (1st run) - 3rd of 8 to Perfect Plum (17 Oct Deauville 8f hvy RF 5203a). **D Smaga in FR [0-1] Haras d'Etreham.*

LINEA-G BHB 60f65a **RR 60f 65a** 5007[5]
6 ch m Keen 11.1f **(58)** - Horton Line (High Line) 10.3f **(70)**
Form - 605
Record 2000 - 1st:0 2nd:0 3rd:0 Ran:3
Pre2000 - 1st:3 2nd:3 3rd:1 Ran:16
Win Prizemoney £7,095 *Total Prizemoney* £9,605
Wins * 1999 Aug Beverl (GD) 12f 66 <
* 1999 May Newcas (G-F) H 12.4f 49 54
* 1999 *Mar Southw (STD) 12f 57*
2000 Turf 0-2: (12f, 14f) (gd, frm) 2000 AW 0-1: (12f) (Fibr)
Average mare, effective 12 to 13f, best at 12f, acts on gd to frm - acts on Fibr. Turf high 47 (began Jly). Consistent.
**Mrs M Reveley [6-32] W Ginzel.*

LINGUISTIC DANCER BHB 34f46a **RR 27f 46a** 1174[1]
5 ch m Aragon 7.7f **(58)** - Linguistic (Porto Bello) 8.9f **(43)**
Form - 1
Record 2000 - 1st:1 2nd:0 3rd:0 Ran:1

Pre2000 - 1st:0 2nd:0 3rd:1 Ran:10
Win Prizemoney £2,758 *Total Prizemoney* £2,984
Wins * **2000** *May Lingfi (STD) H 10f 28 52* <
2000 AW 1-1: (10f 1-1) (Equi 1-1)
Fair filly. (1st run) - 1st of 10 getting 22lb from Paperweight (12 May Lingfield RF 1174). Inconsistent.
**G L Moore [1-1] Mrs J Moore (from A G Newcombe [0-10] Mar 1999).*

LINIRISO (FR) RR 102f 1281a[5]
99 f Mt Livermore (USA) 7.7f **(90)** - **(37f 25a)** 00
Form - 5
2000 Turf 0-1: (11f) (hvy)
Currently very useful. (1st run) - 5th of 6 to Lord Flasheart (8 May Chantilly 11f hvy RF 1281a). **Mme C Head in FR [0-1].*

LIONEL ANDROS RR 62f 2422[5]
2 b c Lion Cavern (USA) 7.5f **(74)** - Guyum (Rousillon (USA)) 8.2f **(74)**
Form - 05
Record 2000 - 1st:0 2nd:0 3rd:0 Ran:2
2000 Turf 0-2: (6f 2) (gd, frm)
Currently average colt. Turf high 62.
**R J Hodges [0-2] Miss R Dobson.*

LIONESS BHB 28f **RR 19f** 3406[22]
4 b f Lion Cavern (USA) 7.5f **(74)** - Pidona (Baillamont (USA)) 7f **(78)**
Form - 0007000
Record 2000 - 1st:0 2nd:0 3rd:0 Ran:7
Pre2000 - 1st:0 2nd:0 3rd:1 Ran:4
Win Prizemoney £0 *Total Prizemoney* £603
2000 Turf 0-7: (6f 2, 8f 2, 10f 3) (sft, g-s, g-f, frm 3, hrd)
Workmanlike, poor filly, effective 8 to 9f, acts on g-f to frm, has worn blinkers. Turf high 19.
**J M Bradley [0-7] Martyn James (from J R Fanshawe [0-4] Jly 1999).*

LION GUEST (IRE) BHB 48f **RR 55f** 5071[7]
3 ch c Lion Cavern (USA) 7.5f **(74)** - Decrescendo (IRE) (Polish Precedent (USA)) 10.2f **(60)**
Form - 405007
Record 2000 - 1st:0 2nd:0 3rd:0 Ran:6
Pre2000 - 1st:0 2nd:0 3rd:0 Ran:2
2000 Turf 0-6: (7f, 8f 3, 10f 2) (g-s, gd, g-f 3, frm)
Workmanlike, fair colt, has worn blinkers. Turf high 55. Becoming disappointing. **G G Margarson [0-8] John Guest.*

LION IN THE COURSE (USA) BHB 75f **RR 75f** 4293[7]
2 b c Chimes Band (USA) - Late Flight (FR) (Caracolero (USA)) 8.2f **(57)**
Form - 437
Record 2000 - 1st:0 2nd:0 3rd:1 Ran:3
Win Prizemoney £0 *Total Prizemoney* £903
2000 Turf 0-3: (6f 2, 7f) (gd, g-f, frm)
Currently above-average colt. Turf high 75 (began Aug).
**M Johnston [0-3] Jaber Abdullah.*

LION OF JUDAH RR 52f 1519[5]
3 b c Caerleon (USA) 10.9f **(79)** - Lyndonville (IRE) (Top Ville) 11.7f **(68)**
Form - 5
Record 2000 - 1st:0 2nd:0 3rd:0 Ran:1
2000 Turf 0-1: (8f) (g-s)
Workmanlike, currently fair colt.
**L M Cumani [0-1] G Howard-Spink.*

LION'S DOMANE BHB 49f47a **RR 47+f 47a** 3569[11]
3 b g Lion Cavern (USA) 7.5f **(74)** - Vilany (Never so Bold) 6.3f **(66)**
Form - 8268610
Record 2000 - 1st:1 2nd:1 3rd:0 Ran:6
Pre2000 - 1st:0 2nd:0 3rd:0 Ran:3
Win Prizemoney £2,814 *Total Prizemoney* £3,471
Wins * **2000** Aug Thirsk (GD) H 7f 41 47+ <
2000 Turf 1-4: (6f, 7f 1-2, 8f) (g-f, frm 1-3) 2000 AW 0-2: (7f 2) (Fibr 2)
Scopey, moderate gelding, effective 7f, acts on frm - acts on Fibr. Turf high 47 - 1st of 15 giving 6lb to Royal Reprimand (4 Aug Thirsk RF 3385). AW high 48 (1st run) - 2nd of 12 giving 5lb to Croeso Adref (4 Jan Wolverhampton 7f Fibr RF 0018).
**P C Haslam [1-9] Mrs C Barclay.*

LION SONG RR 26f 592[12]
2 b c Savahra Sound 7.8f **(55)** - Lucky Candy (Lucky Wednesday) 8f **(50)**
Form - 00
Record 2000 - 1st:0 2nd:0 3rd:0 Ran:2
2000 Turf 0-2: (5f 2) (sft, gd)
Currently little account colt. Turf high 26.
**D Nicholls [0-2] Paul Dixon.*

LIPICA (IRE) BHB 100f **RR 89f** 5128[3]
2 b f Night Shift (USA) 8.1f **(73)** - Top Knot (High Top) 10.2f **(67)**
Form - 313
Record 2000 - 1st:1 2nd:0 3rd:2 Ran:3
Win Prizemoney £3,038 *Total Prizemoney* £6,117
Wins * **2000** Spt Kempto (SFT) 7f 82+ <
2000 Turf 1-3: (7f 1-3) (sft, g-s 1-1, gd)
Currently useful filly. Turf high 89 (began Aug) - 3rd of 11 to Relish The Thought (21 Oct Newbury 7f sft RF 5128) - also 1st of 15 from Island Queen (18 Spt Kempton RF 4480). Third to Tobougg on her debut, she scored nicely on her second run.
**K R Burke [1-3] Paul Green.*

LISA-B (IRE) BHB 45f46a **RR 41f 46a** 1738[9]
3 b f Case Law 6f **(64)** - Nishiki (USA) (Brogan (USA))
Form - 77270800
Record 2000 - 1st:0 2nd:1 3rd:0 Ran:6
Pre2000 - 1st:2 2nd:0 3rd:2 Ran:16
Win Prizemoney £3,743 *Total Prizemoney* £5,323
Wins 1999 *Jun Wolver (STD) S 6f 64+* <
1999 *Jun Southw (STD) S 6f 62*
2000 Turf 0-3: (5f, 6f, 7f) (gd 2, g-f) 2000 AW 0-3: (5f 2, 6f) (Equi, Fibr 2)
Scopey, moderate filly, effective 6f, acts on frm - acts on Fibr, mostly wears blinkers, likes left handed tracks, likes tight tracks. Turf high 36. AW high 45.
**D L Williams [0-6] D L Williams (from J A Glover [2-16] Nov 1999).*

LISA'S PRINCESS (IRE) BHB 30a **RR 46f 30a** 269[10]
7 b m Dancing Dissident (USA) 6.8f **(65)** - Arabian Princess (Taufan (USA)) 7f **(57)**
Form - 000
Record 2000 - 1st:0 2nd:0 3rd:0 Ran:3
Pre2000 - 1st:0 2nd:0 3rd:1 Ran:17
Win Prizemoney £0 *Total Prizemoney* £707
2000 AW 0-3: (5f, 6f, 7f) (Equi, Fibr 2)
Moderate mare. AW high 19. Inconsistent.
**D J Wintle [0-3] D J Wintle (from M McElhone in IRE [0-2] Oct 1999).*

LITE A CANDLE BHB 46f **RR 51f** 2743[12]
3 b f Komaite (USA) 6.9f **(61)** - Hound Song (Jukebox) 8.2f **(49)**
Form - 0000
Record 2000 - 1st:0 2nd:0 3rd:0 Ran:4
2000 Turf 0-4: (6f, 7f 2, 8f) (gd 2, g-f 2)
Workmanlike, fair filly. Turf high 51. (DEAD)
**R Ingram [0-4] Luke Devine.*

LITERARY SOCIETY (USA) BHB 87f **RR 85f** 4164[4]
7 ch h Runaway Groom (CAN) 8.1f **(69)** - Dancing Gull (USA) (Northern Dancer) 9.6f **(80)**
Form - 0074
Record 2000 - 1st:0 2nd:0 3rd:0 Ran:4
Pre2000 - 1st:7 2nd:4 3rd:6 Ran:34
Win Prizemoney £48,171 *Total Prizemoney* £69,273
Wins * 1998 Aug York (G-F) H 6f 90 94 <
* 1998 Jun Yarmou (GD) 6f 91
* 1998 May Newmar (G-F) H 5f 83 86
* 1997 Jly Newbur (G-F) H 6f 77 77
* 1997 May Newmar (G-F) H 5f 71 74
* 1996 Aug Thirsk (GD) H 5f 66 67+
* 1996 Jly Bright (FRM) 5.3f 61
2000 Turf 0-4: (6f 4) (gd 2, g-f 2)
Useful horse, effective 6f, acts on g-f to frm, best on frm. Turf high 85. No show in three runs early in 2000, but ran really well on his return to action in the autumn. He must have fast ground, and is on a reasonable mark now.
**J A R Toller [7-38] Lady Celina Carter.*

LITIGIOUS BHB 35f **RR 42f** 4925[14]
3 b f Mtoto 11.5f **(71)** - Kiomi **(64f)** (Niniski (USA)) 10.6f **(65)**
Form - 220040
Record 2000 - 1st:0 2nd:2 3rd:0 Ran:6
Win Prizemoney £0 *Total Prizemoney* £2,351
2000 Turf 0-5: (8f 5) (gd, g-f 3, hrd) 2000 AW 0-1: (7f) (Equi)
Unfurnished, moderate filly, effective 8f, acts on g-f, has worn blinkers. Turf high 42. **K R Burke [0-6] Leydens Farm Stud.*

LITTLE AMIN BHB 76f **RR 79f** 4740[14]
4 b g Unfuwain (USA) 11.4f **(74)** - Ghassanah (Pas de Seul) 9.1f **(67)**
Form - 00016326650
Record 2000 - 1st:1 2nd:1 3rd:1 Ran:11
Pre2000 - 1st:2 2nd:1 3rd:2 Ran:11
Win Prizemoney £12,116 *Total Prizemoney* £19,122
Wins * **2000** Jun Beverl (G-S) H 8.5f 70 75
* 1999 Aug Haydoc (G-S) H 11.9f 72 78 <
1999 Mar Newcas (G-S) 7f 73
2000 Turf 1-11: (8f 1-2, 9f 3, 10f 3, 12f 3) (hvy, sft, gd 1-6, g-f 2, frm)
Above-average gelding, effective 7 to 12f, acts on gd to hrd, best on gd, prefers right handed tracks, likes tight tracks, excels at Beverley and Goodwood. Turf high 79 - 2nd of 7 giving 3lb to Kind Regards (17 Aug Beverley 10f frm RF 3718) - also 1st of 7 from Gralmano (7 Jun Beverley RF 1778). Consistent. Likes cut in the ground and scored under those conditions at Haydock in August of last year. Rather disappointing afterwards until winning a falsely-run event at Beverley in June and has run well on fast ground since.
**W R Muir [2-14] Sheikh Amin Dahlawi (from J D Bethell [1-8] Jun 1999).*

LITTLE BRAVE BHB 57f75a **RR 64f 75a** 4058[6]
5 b g Kahyasi 12.9f **(74)** - Littlemisstrouble (USA) (My Gallant (USA)) 9f **(71)**
Form - 244605143336
Record 2000 - 1st:1 2nd:0 3rd:3 Ran:10
Pre2000 - 1st:4 2nd:3 3rd:1 Ran:22
Win Prizemoney £20,628 *Total Prizemoney* £28,387
Wins * **2000** Jly Lingfi (G-F) H 16f 54 67+
* 1999 Spt Yarmou (SFT) H 18.2f 57 60
* 1999 Aug Warwic (GD) H 15.8f 55 57
* 1999 *Jly Lingfi (STD) 16f 78* <
* 1998 *Mar Southw (STD) 8f 68*
2000 Turf 1-10: (14f, 16f 1-6, 17f, 18f, 22f) (sft, g-s, gd 2, g-f 3, frm 1-3)
Above-average gelding, effective 16f, - acts on AW, prefers left handed tracks, prefers tight tracks. Turf high 67. A fair stayer on both turf and sand, he seems to go best in small fields.
**J M P Eustace [5-32] Brave Maple Partnership.*

LITTLE CALLIAN BHB 62f **RR 67f** 5102[10]
2 ch f Charmer 9f **(59)** - Eucharis (Tickled Pink) 6.5f **(59)**
Form - 60436250
Record 2000 - 1st:0 2nd:1 3rd:1 Ran:8
Win Prizemoney £0 *Total Prizemoney* £1,843
2000 Turf 0-8: (5f 2, 6f 5, 7f) (gd 3, g-f 2, frm 3)
Average filly, effective 5f, acts on frm. Turf high 67 (began Jun).
**T M Jones [0-8] Richard Page.*

LITTLE CHAPEL (IRE) BHB 39f **RR 31f** 4492[18]
4 b f College Chapel - Istaraka (IRE) (Darshaan) 9.9f **(84)**
Form - 40000
Record 2000 - 1st:0 2nd:0 3rd:0 Ran:5
Pre2000 - 1st:0 2nd:1 3rd:1 Ran:11
Win Prizemoney £0 *Total Prizemoney* £2,120
2000 Turf 0-5: (6f 2, 7f, 8f 2) (g-s, gd, g-f, frm 2)
Scopey, very moderate filly, effective 6f, acts on hrd. Turf high 31. Becoming disappointing.
**G H Yardley [0-5] Philip Jones (from D J S ffrenchDavis [0-11] Spt 1999).*

LITTLE CHRISTIAN (IRE) BHB 51f40a **RR 56f 40a** 146[7]
3 b g Common Grounds 8.1f **(66)** - Alexanders Way (FR) (Persian Heights)
Form - 507
Record 2000 - 1st:0 2nd:0 3rd:0 Ran:3
Pre2000 - 1st:0 2nd:1 3rd:2 Ran:12
Win Prizemoney £0 *Total Prizemoney* £1,280
2000 AW 0-3: (7f, 8f 2) (Fibr 3)
Leggy, fair gelding, effective 6 to 7f, best at 6f, acts on gd to g-f, best on g-f. AW high 33. **N Tinkler [0-15] Mike Gosse.*

LITTLE DOCKER (IRE) BHB 70f **RR 71f** 2370[2]
3 b g Vettori (IRE) - Fair Maid of Kent (USA) (Diesis) 9.3f **(69)**
Form - 3542
Record 2000 - 1st:0 2nd:1 3rd:1 Ran:4
Pre2000 - 1st:0 2nd:0 3rd:0 Ran:1
Win Prizemoney £0 *Total Prizemoney* £2,118
2000 Turf 0-4: (10f 2, 12f, 16f) (gd, frm 2, hrd)
Workmanlike, above-average gelding. Turf high 71 - 2nd of 6 giving 4lb to Barrow (29 Jun Newcastle 16f frm RF 2370).
**T D Easterby [0-5] C H Stevens.*

LITTLEFEATHER (IRE) BHB 105f **RR 110f** 4549[8]
3 b f Indian Ridge 7.6f **(74)** - Marwell (Habitat) 9.4f **(70)**
Form - 510278
Record 2000 - 1st:1 2nd:1 3rd:0 Ran:6
Pre2000 - 1st:3 2nd:1 3rd:1 Ran:7
Win Prizemoney £34,293 *Total Prizemoney* £57,570
Wins * **2000** Aug Newmar (GD) 6f 110 <
* 1999 Aug Cheste (G-S) 6.1f 103+
* 1999 Jly Newmar (G-F) H 6f 89
* 1999 Jly Ripon (G-F) 5f 86+
2000 Turf 1-6: (6f 1-4, 7f 2) (g-s, gd, g-f 1-2, frm 2)
Leggy, Group-class filly, effective 6 to 7f, best at 6f, acts on gd to g-f, best on g-f, excels at Newmarket. Turf high 110 (began Jly) - 1st of 10 giving 5lb to Jezebel (4 Aug Newmarket RF 3370). A useful juvenile in 1999, she failed to progress last year and struggles to stay seven furlongs. From an excellent family, she has a bright future at stud. **Sir Mark Prescott [4-13] Sir Edmund Loder.*

LITTLE FINTLOCH RR 285[8]
7 b m Roscoe Blake 7.4f **(51)** - Darling Eve (Darling Boy)
Form - 8
Record 2000 - 1st:0 2nd:0 3rd:0 Ran:1
2000 AW 0-1: (12f) (Fibr)
Formerly very poor mare.
**C N Kollett [0-3] The Muir/Waters Partnership.*

LITTLE FIREFLY (IRE) RR 90f 4793a[6]
2 b f Danehill (USA) 9.1f **(79)** - Tootling (IRE) (Pennine Walk) 8.5f **(61)**
Form - 1356
2000 Turf 1-4: (5f, 6f 1-1, 7f 2) (sft, gd 1-3)
Useful filly. Turf high 90. She disappointed after finishing third in the Group 3 Queen Mary Stakes at Royal Ascot. Possibly best over six furlongs, she may have peaked early.
**A P O'Brien in IRE [1-4] Michael Tabor.*

LITTLE IBNR BHB 46f50a **RR 48f 50a** 450[11]
9 b g Formidable (USA) 7.8f **(60)** - Zalatia (Music Boy) 6.8f **(57)**
Form - 8430620
Record 2000 - 1st:0 2nd:1 3rd:1 Ran:7
Pre2000 - 1st:12 2nd:12 3rd:13 Ran:103
Win Prizemoney £35,504 *Total Prizemoney* £52,947
Wins * 1997 *Mar Wolver (STD) S 5f 58*
* 1997 *Jan Wolver (STD) 7f 63*
* 1996 *Apr Wolver (STD) H 6f 68 66*
2000 AW 0-7: (5f, 6f 5, 7f) (Fibr 7)
Fair gelding, effective 5 to 6f, best at 6f, - acts on Fibr, has worn blinkers (effectively). AW high 51 - 2nd of 11 giving 15lb to Petite Danseuse (28 Feb Southwell 6f Fibr RF 0374).
**P D Evans [10-88] Swinnerton Transport Ltd (from P D Cundell [0-9] Feb 1998).*

LITTLE JOHN BHB 57f **RR 60f** 5195[5]
4 b g Warrshan (USA) 9.7f **(59)** - Silver Venture (USA) (Silver Hawk (USA)) 8.6f **(70)**
Form - 3432524235
Record 2000 - 1st:0 2nd:3 3rd:3 Ran:10
Pre2000 - 1st:0 2nd:1 3rd:1 Ran:12
Win Prizemoney £0 *Total Prizemoney* £7,725
2000 Turf 0-10: (8f, 9f 3, 10f, 11f, 12f 4) (gd, g-f 4, frm 5)
Lengthy, average gelding, effective 12f, acts on frm, has worn blinkers. Turf high 60. Despite numerous placings, he remains a maiden and has looked unco-operative on many occasions. One

to treat with caution. **Miss L A Perratt [0-23] T P Finch.*

LITTLE LES BHB 26f **RR 34f** 4122[6]
4 b g Jumbo Hirt (USA) 15.8f **(44)** - Hand on Heart (IRE) (Taufan (USA)) 7f **(57)**
Form - 676406
Record 2000 - 1st:0 2nd:0 3rd:0 Ran:6
Win Prizemoney £0 *Total Prizemoney* £262
2000 Turf 0-6: (5f, 7f, 8f 3, 10f) (gd, frm 5)
Very moderate gelding. Turf high 34. **P Monteith [0-7] L Irvine.*

LITTLE LOTTIE BHB 20f **RR** 1695[12]
4 gr f Nalchik (USA) 12.6f **(44)** - Grey Runner (Crofthall) 6.3f **(59)**
Form - 000
Record 2000 - 1st:0 2nd:0 3rd:0 Ran:2
Pre2000 - 1st:0 2nd:0 3rd:0 Ran:1
2000 Turf 0-1: (10f) (gd) 2000 AW 0-1: (12f) (Fibr)
Light-framed, currently very poor filly.
**W M Brisbourne [0-1] Mrs V Fortune (from M Mullineaux [0-2] Jan 2000).*

LITTLE MOUSE BHB 42f **RR 37f** 2290[4]
2 b f Mistertopogigo (IRE) - Caribbee Beach (IRE) **(6f)** (Magical Strike (USA))
Form - 0004
Record 2000 - 1st:0 2nd:0 3rd:0 Ran:4
2000 Turf 0-4: (5f 3, 6f) (g-f 4)
Very moderate filly. Turf high 37.
**G G Margarson [0-4] Mrs S E A Burton.*

LITTLEPACEPADDOCKS (IRE) BHB 108f **RR 110+f** 4963[2]
3 b f Accordion 11.3f **(75)** - Lady in Pace (Burslem) 8.8f **(53)**
Form - 314282
Record 2000 - 1st:1 2nd:2 3rd:1 Ran:6
Pre2000 - 1st:1 2nd:0 3rd:0 Ran:1
Win Prizemoney £18,045 *Total Prizemoney* £41,121
Wins *** 2000** Jun Newbur (G-F) L 10f 110+ <
* 1999 Nov Mussel (GD) 8f 78+
2000 Turf 1-6: (8f, 10f 1-1, 12f 3, 15f) (gd 2, g-f 1-2, frm 2)
Scopey, Group-class filly, effective 10 to 12f, best at 12f, acts on gd to g-f, best on gd. Turf high 110 - also 1st of 9 from Eurolink Raindance (15 Jun Newbury RF 1989). She stayed on bravely when winning a Listed event at Newbury in June and went on to take part in two Classics, running well to finish fourth in the Irish Oaks. Still lightly raced, she is a sister to Yavana's Pace and, like him, should improve with age and win in Group company.
**M Johnston [2-7] Mrs Joan Keaney.*

LITTLE PIPPIN BHB 85f **RR 87f** 1435[9]
4 ch f Rudimentary (USA) 8.2f **(66)** - Accuracy (Gunner B) 11.2f **(58)**
Form - 40
Record 2000 - 1st:0 2nd:0 3rd:0 Ran:2
Pre2000 - 1st:2 2nd:0 3rd:3 Ran:12
Win Prizemoney £8,013 *Total Prizemoney* £11,494
Wins * 1999 Aug Kempto (SFT) H 12f 73 80 <
* 1999 Aug Salisb (G-S) H 12f 73 75
2000 Turf 0-2: (12f, 14f) (g-s, gd)
Neat, useful filly, effective 12 to 13f, best at 12f, acts on g-s to gd, best on gd. Turf high 87 (1st run) - 4th of 21 getting 9lb from Mowelga (19 Apr Newmarket 12f gd RF 0796).
**G B Balding [2-14] Miss B Swire.*

LITTLE PIXIE (USA) RR 4816[10]
2 ch f Woodman (USA) 9.7f **(77)** - Tryarra (IRE) (Persian Heights)
Form - 0
Record 2000 - 1st:0 2nd:0 3rd:0 Ran:1
2000 Turf 0-1: (7f) (g-s)
Currently very poor filly.
**N Tinkler [0-1] James Marshall & Mrs Susan Marshall.*

LITTLE ROCK RR 117f 4520a[5]
4 b c Warning 8.1f **(77)** - Much Too Risky (Bustino) 10.4f **(64)**
Form - 161345
Record 2000 - 1st:2 2nd:0 3rd:1 Ran:6
Pre2000 - 1st:3 2nd:1 3rd:0 Ran:6
Win Prizemoney £81,404 *Total Prizemoney* £109,582
Wins *** 2000** Jly Newmar (G-S) G2 12f 117 <
*** 2000** Apr Sandow (SFT) G3 10f 112
* 1999 Oct Newmar (G-S) L 10f 112
* 1999 Apr Sandow (G-S) 8.1f 91+
* 1998 Oct Leices (G-S) 7f 86+
2000 Turf 2-6: (10f 1-1, 12f 1-3, 13f, 14f) (sft 1-1, g-s 2, gd 1-3)
Light-framed, high-class colt, effective 10 to 13f, best at 12f, acts on sft to gd, best on gd, prefers right handed tracks, and excels at Sandown. Turf high 117 - 1st of 6 from Yavana's Pace (11 Jly Newmarket RF 2689) - also 1st of 8 getting 2lb from Diamond White (29 Apr Sandown RF 0929). Consistent. He goes well fresh and was making a successful reappearance for the third consecutive season when landing the Group 3 Marriott Hotels Stakes at Sandown in April. Consistent until failing to stay a mile and three-quarters on his final start, he revels in soft ground and can win another decent prize under suitable conditions.
**Sir Michael Stoute [5-12] J M Greetham.*

Little Rock made a successful reappearance at Sandown

LITTLE TARA BHB 25f **RR 20f** 3524[11]
3 b f Pyramus (USA) - Eastwood Heiress (Known Fact (USA)) 7.4f **(67)**
Form - 800000
Record 2000 - 1st:0 2nd:0 3rd:0 Ran:6
Pre2000 - 1st:0 2nd:0 3rd:0 Ran:2
2000 Turf 0-5: (7f, 8f 2, 10f, 12f) (sft, g-f, frm 3) 2000 AW 0-1: (10f) (Equi)
Unfurnished, little account filly. Turf high 47. Becoming disappointing. **J C Fox [0-8] Mrs J A Cleary.*

LITTLE TASK BHB 59f56a **RR 66f 56a** 5010[1]
2 b c Environment Friend 7.5f **(67)** - Lucky Thing (Green Desert (USA)) 8.6f **(78)**
Form - 3824260681
Record 2000 - 1st:1 2nd:2 3rd:1 Ran:10
Win Prizemoney £1,967 *Total Prizemoney* £5,057
Wins *** 2000** *Oct Southw (STD) S 7f 62* <
2000 Turf 0-9: (6f 3, 7f 4, 8f 2) (g-s, gd 3, g-f, frm 4) 2000 AW 1-1: (7f 1-1) (Fibr 1-1)
Average colt, effective 6 to 7f, best at 6f, acts on frm - acts on Fibr, has worn blinkers. Turf high 66 - 2nd of 5 to Lapwing (4 Aug Ayr 6f frm RF 3354). (1st run) - 1st of 16 getting 6lb from Co Dot Uk (16 Oct Southwell RF 5010). **A Berry [1-10] Keith Jackson.*

LITTLE TUMBLER (IRE) BHB 47f42a **RR 47f 42a** 4101[2]
5 b m Cyrano de Bergerac 7.3f **(58)** - Glass Minnow (IRE) (Alzao (USA)) 7.1f **(68)**
Form - 0565022
Record 2000 - 1st:0 2nd:2 3rd:0 Ran:6
Pre2000 - 1st:2 2nd:2 3rd:0 Ran:20
Win Prizemoney £5,326 *Total Prizemoney* £8,956
Wins * 1999 Aug Bright (FRM) H 10f 47 49
* 1998 May Lingfi (G-F) H 6f 55 61 <
2000 Turf 0-6: (8f, 9f 2, 10f 3) (gd, g-f, frm 3, hrd)
Moderate filly, effective 8 to 10f, best at 10f, acts on gd to hrd, best on frm, excels at Brighton, likes Goodwood. Turf high 47 - 2nd of 20 giving 9lb to Beckon (30 Aug Brighton 10f frm RF 4101).

Inconsistent. *S Woodman [2-26] Mrs W Edgar.*

LITZINSKY RR 59f 5312[10]
2 b g Muhtarram (USA) - Boulevard Girl (Nicholas Bill) 10.1f **(56)**
Form - 0
Record 2000 - 1st:0 2nd:0 3rd:0 Ran:1
2000 Turf 0-1: (8f) (g-s)
Currently fair gelding.
**C B B Booth [0-1] Mrs A M Lyons.*

LIVADIYA (IRE) RR 99f 4254a[5]
4 f Shernazar - Lilissa
Form - 8521310455
2000 Turf 2-10: (8f 3, 9f 2-4, 10f 3) (hvy, sft, g-s, gd 1-4, g-f 1-2, frm)
Very useful. Turf high 99. Improving. A French import, he did well last season, running away with a valuable Listed handicap at Leopardstown in July. Shown no mercy by the handicapper thereafter, he is not Group class and looks difficult to place at present.
**H Rogers in IRE [2-10] Gerard McStay (from A deRoyerDupre in FR [0-1] May 1999).*

LIVE IN LOVER (IRE) BHB 30f RR 9f 4999[7]
2 b g Up and At 'em - Inesse (Simply Great (FR)) 8.2f **(65)**
Form - 007
Record 2000 - 1st:0 2nd:0 3rd:0 Ran:3
2000 Turf 0-3: (6f 2, 8f) (g-s, gd, g-f)
Currently very poor gelding. Turf high 9 (began Aug).
**P C Haslam [0-3] Mrs B M Hawkins.*

LIVELY FELIX BHB 48f RR 56f 5071[6]
3 b g Presidium 7.5f **(56)** - Full of Life (Wolverlife) 9.3f **(54)**
Form - 004056
Record 2000 - 1st:0 2nd:0 3rd:0 Ran:6
Win Prizemoney £0 *Total Prizemoney* £325
2000 Turf 0-6: (7f, 8f 5) (g-s 2, gd, g-f 2, frm)
Workmanlike, fair gelding. Turf high 56 (began Jly).
**S Mellor [0-6] The Felix Bowness Partnership.*

LIVELY JACQ (IRE) BHB 60f43a RR 54f 43a 35[4]
4 ch f Case Law 6f **(64)** - Nordic Living (IRE) (Nordico (USA)) 6.5f **(62)**
Form - 04664
Record 2000 - 1st:0 2nd:0 3rd:0 Ran:1
Pre2000 - 1st:2 2nd:3 3rd:2 Ran:22
Win Prizemoney £5,171 *Total Prizemoney* £14,836
Wins * 1998 Aug Yarmou (G-F) H 6f 62 60 <
* 1998 Jly Yarmou (G-F) S 6f 60 <
2000 AW 0-1: (7f) (Fibr)
Lengthy, fair filly, effective 5 to 6f, best at 6f, acts on g-f to frm, best on g-f, has worn blinkers. **C N Allen [2-23] J T B Racing.*

LIVELY LADY BHB 85f70a RR 91f 70a 5199[3]
4 b f Beveled (USA) 6.9f **(64)** - In the Papers (Aragon) 8.1f **(60)**
Form - 4103300083
Record 2000 - 1st:1 2nd:0 3rd:3 Ran:10
Pre2000 - 1st:4 2nd:4 3rd:1 Ran:19
Win Prizemoney £23,569 *Total Prizemoney* £32,139
Wins * **2000** Apr Kempto (SFT) H 5f 81 89 <
* 1999 Nov Doncas (SFT) H 5f 76 78
* 1999 Jun Kempto (GD) H 6f 71 75
* 1999 Mar Nottin (G-S) H 6.1f 66 71
* 1998 Apr Folkes (SFT) S 5f 67+
2000 Turf 1-10: (5f 1-4, 6f 6) (g-s 1-2, gd 6, g-f 2)
Light-framed, useful filly, effective 5 to 6f, best at 5f, acts on g-s to g-f, best on g-s, mostly wears blinkers (extremely effectively), excels at Kempton and Windsor. Turf high 91 - 3rd of 13 getting 3lb from Danielle's Lad (27 May Kempton 6f g-s RF 1501) - also 1st of 15 getting 2lb from Paradise Lane (24 Apr Kempton RF 0835). She goes well on soft ground and comes to hand early. Effective over five and six furlongs, she is one to look out for at Kempton this spring. **J R Jenkins [5-29] Mrs Jean Powell.*

LIVELY MILLIE BHB 40f35a RR 48f 35a 4007[5]
3 b f Ridgewood Ben - Sweet Pleasure (Sweet Revenge) 7.2f **(54)**
Form - 07045
Record 2000 - 1st:0 2nd:0 3rd:0 Ran:5
Pre2000 - 1st:0 2nd:0 3rd:0 Ran:5
Win Prizemoney £0 *Total Prizemoney* £271
2000 Turf 0 6: (6f, 7f 2, 8f 2) (g-f 3, frm 2)
Leggy, moderate filly, has worn blinkers. Turf high 48. Consistent.
**R M Beckett [0-5] John Guest (from P T Walwyn [0-5] Oct 1999).*

LIVE THE DREAM BHB 56f RR 50f 3336[4]
2 b f Exit To Nowhere (USA) 8.7f **(77)** - Inveraven (Alias Smith (USA)) 9.8f **(58)**
Form - 874
Record 2000 - 1st:0 2nd:0 3rd:0 Ran:3
2000 Turf 0-3: (6f, 7f 2) (frm 3)
Currently fair filly. Turf high 50 (began Jly).
**J Hetherton [0-3] D Gladwin.*

LIVIUS (IRE) BHB 87f RR 89f 4936[18]
6 b g Alzao (USA) 9.8f **(73)** - Marie de Beaujeu (FR) (Kenmare (FR)) 6.5f **(72)**
Form - 34160
Record 2000 - 1st:1 2nd:0 3rd:1 Ran:5
Pre2000 - 1st:1 2nd:4 3rd:1 Ran:11
Win Prizemoney £20,877 *Total Prizemoney* £29,177
Wins * **2000** Aug Goodwo (GD) H 12f 83 89 <
* 1999 Aug Ascot (GD) H 12f 77 82
2000 Turf 1-5: (12f 1-4, 14f) (g-s, gd, g-f 1-2, frm)
Useful gelding, effective 12f, acts on gd to frm, has worn blinkers, favours right handed tracks. Turf high 89 - also 1st of 13 giving 1lb to Veridian (27 Aug Goodwood RF 4015). Difficult to train, he returned to his best with a fine victory in quite a valuable handicap at Goodwood. A fast-run mile and a half seems to suit him best.
**Major D N Chappell [2-16] Mrs G McClintock and Miss E Kilfeather.*

LIZZEY LETTI BHB 64a RR 41f 64a 2502[7]
2 ch f Grand Lodge (USA) - Crystal Ring (IRE) (Kris) 9.5f **(73)**
Form - 7
Record 2000 - 1st:0 2nd:0 3rd:0 Ran:1
2000 Turf 0-1: (7f) (g-f)
Currently above-average filly. **T G Mills [0-1] Mrs T G Mills.*

LIZZIE SIMMONDS (IRE) BHB 53f RR 54f 4871[14]
3 b f Common Grounds 8.1f **(66)** - Able Susan (Formidable (USA)) 9.2f **(63)**
Form - 455016530500
Record 2000 - 1st:1 2nd:0 3rd:1 Ran:12
Pre2000 - 1st:0 2nd:0 3rd:1 Ran:5
Win Prizemoney £2,478 *Total Prizemoney* £3,580
Wins * **2000** Jun Catter (G-S) H 5f 53 54 <
2000 Turf 1-12: (5f 1-11, 6f) (sft, gd 1-5, g-f 2, frm, hrd 3)
Scopey, fair filly, effective 5f, acts on gd to hrd, best on gd, excels at Catterick, likes Beverley. Turf high 55 - 3rd of 17 giving 2lb to Off Hire (18 Jly Beverley 5f hrd RF 2883) - also 1st of 14 getting 9lb from College Maid (9 Jun Catterick RF 1840).
**N Tinkler [1-17] Mike Gosse.*

LOBLITE LEADER (IRE) BHB 30f RR 35f 3015[10]
3 b g Tirol 8.1f **(64)** - Cyrano Beauty (IRE) (Cyrano de Bergerac) 6f **(68)**
Form - 00040
Record 2000 - 1st:0 2nd:0 3rd:0 Ran:5
Pre2000 - 1st:0 2nd:0 3rd:0 Ran:7
Win Prizemoney £0 *Total Prizemoney* £447
2000 Turf 0-4: (10f 2, 12f, 14f) (sft, gd, g-f, frm) 2000 AW 0-1: (12f) (Fibr)
Leggy, very moderate gelding. Turf high 35. Inconsistent.
**G M Moore [0-12] Montagu Bloodstock Ltd.*

LOBUCHE (IRE) BHB 26f30a RR 26f 30a 1318[10]
5 b g Petardia 8.2f **(58)** - Lhotse (IRE) (Shernazar) 10.2f **(73)**
Form - 00
Record 2000 - 1st:0 2nd:0 3rd:0 Ran:1
Pre2000 - 1st:1 2nd:3 3rd:1 Ran:31
Win Prizemoney £3,054 *Total Prizemoney* £5,386
Wins * 1998 Jun Yarmou (SFT) H 6f 58 67 <
2000 Turf 0-1: (12f) (gd)
Very moderate gelding, has worn blinkers.
**M C Chapman [2-36] K D Blanch (from R Hannon [0-13] Apr 1998).*

LOCH AILORT BHB 39f RR 38f 5122[10]
4 b f Be My Chief (USA) 10.2f **(62)** - Lochbelle **(63f)** (Robellino (USA)) 7.6f **(80)**

Form - 0
Record 2000 - 1st:0 2nd:0 3rd:0 Ran:1
2000 Turf 0-1: (7f) (g-s)
Currently very moderate filly, always wears blinkers.
**J A Glover [0-1] Miss V Haigh.*

LOCHARATI BHB 72f RR 84f 5141[11]
3 ch c Emarati (USA) 6.6f **(63)** - Lochspring (IRE) (Precocious) 8.6f **(62)**
Form - 18200000
Record 2000 - 1st:1 2nd:1 3rd:0 Ran:8
Win Prizemoney £2,492 *Total Prizemoney* £5,120
Wins * 2000 Apr Lingfi (G-S) 6f 84 <
2000 Turf 1-8: (6f 1-5, 7f 2, 8f) (g-s, gd 1-3, g-f 2, frm 2)
Scopey, decent colt, effective 6f, acts on gd to g-f. Turf high 84 - 2nd of 6 getting 3lb from San Salvador (20 May Nottingham 6f g-f RF 1338) - also 1st of 18 giving 5lb to Diver's Pearl (7 Apr Lingfield RF 0634). **J M P Eustace [1-8] J C Smith.*

LOCH DIAMOND RR 40f 1708[9]
3 ch f Cadeaux Genereux 7.9f **(76)** - Lochsong **(126f)** (Song) 7.2f **(61)**
Form - 00
Record 2000 - 1st:0 2nd:0 3rd:0 Ran:2
2000 Turf 0-2: (5f 2) (g-s, hrd)
Unfurnished, currently moderate filly. Turf high 40.
**I A Balding [0-2] J C Smith.*

LOCH INCH BHB 78f82a RR 75f 82a 5127[18]
3 ch c Inchinor 8.9f **(64)** - Carrie Kool **(61df)** (Prince Sabo) 7.2f **(62)**
Form - 000
Record 2000 - 1st:0 2nd:0 3rd:0 Ran:3
Pre2000 - 1st:2 2nd:0 3rd:1 Ran:10
Win Prizemoney £7,253 *Total Prizemoney* £8,145
Wins * 1999 Oct Windso (SFT) H 6f 85 87 <
* 1999 Aug Nottin (G-F) 6.1f 78
2000 Turf 0-3: (5f, 6f, 8f) (sft, g-s, frm)
Lengthy, above-average colt, effective 6f, acts on gd to frm, has worn blinkers. Turf high 68. Inconsistent.
**K McAuliffe [2-13] Folly Road Racing Partners (1996).*

LOCH LAIRD BHB 66f RR 75f 3727[6]
5 b g Beveled (USA) 6.9f **(64)** - Daisy Loch (Lochnager) 6f **(59)**
Form - 5070006
Record 2000 - 1st:0 2nd:0 3rd:0 Ran:7
Pre2000 - 1st:2 2nd:4 3rd:2 Ran:15
Win Prizemoney £7,444 *Total Prizemoney* £12,244
Wins * 1999 Jun Goodwo (SFT) H 6f 78 79
* 1999 May Salisb (G-F) 6f 81 <
2000 Turf 0-7: (6f 6, 8f) (gd, g-f 4, frm 2)
Above-average gelding, effective 6f, acts on g-s to frm, has worn blinkers. Turf high 75. **M Madgwick [2-22] Miss E M L Coller.*

LOCHLASS (IRE) BHB 18f33a RR 23f 33a 66[13]
6 b m Distinctly North (USA) 7.4f **(63)** - Littleton Song (Song) 7.2f **(61)**
Form - 0
Record 2000 - 1st:0 2nd:0 3rd:0 Ran:1
Pre2000 - 1st:0 2nd:0 3rd:4 Ran:21
Win Prizemoney £0 *Total Prizemoney* £1,564
2000 AW 0-1: (9f) (Fibr)
Little account mare, has worn blinkers.
**R J Price [0-13] My Left Foot Racing Syndicate (from S P C Woods [0-15] Oct 1997).*

LOCH SOUND BHB 29f RR 34f 3981[13]
4 b g Primitive Rising (USA) 8.1f **(48)** - Lochcross (Lochnager) 6f **(59)**
Form - 0
Record 2000 - 1st:0 2nd:0 3rd:0 Ran:1
Pre2000 - 1st:0 2nd:0 3rd:0 Ran:5
2000 Turf 0-1: (10f) (frm)
Workmanlike, very moderate gelding.
**C W Thornton [0-6] Mrs Jill Murphy.*

LOCHSPRITE BHB 75f RR 69f 4772[3]
2 ch f So Factual (USA) - Lochspring (IRE) (Precocious) 8.6f **(62)**
Form - 823
Record 2000 - 1st:0 2nd:1 3rd:1 Ran:3
Win Prizemoney £0 *Total Prizemoney* £1,318
2000 Turf 0-3: (5f, 6f 2) (gd 2, frm)
Currently average filly. Turf high 69 (began Spt) - 2nd of 15 to Canterloupe (25 Spt Bath 6f gd RF 4628).
**I A Balding [0-3] J C Smith.*

LOCOMBE HILL (IRE) BHB 74f RR 82f 4753[9]
4 b c Barathea (IRE) - Roberts Pride (Roberto (USA)) 10f **(76)**
Form - 3030840
Record 2000 - 1st:0 2nd:0 3rd:2 Ran:7
Pre2000 - 1st:3 2nd:1 3rd:1 Ran:11
Win Prizemoney £14,358 *Total Prizemoney* £22,101
Wins * 1999 Spt Kempto (HVY) 12f 95 <
* 1998 Jly Newbur (G-F) 6f 95+
* 1998 Jun Newbur (SFT) 6f 85+
2000 Turf 0-7: (7f, 8f, 10f 3, 12f, 14f) (g-s 4, g-f 3)
Decent colt, effective 12f, acts on g-s, likes right handed tracks, likes tight tracks. Turf high 82. A very useful sort at two, he has not lived up to that early promise.
**M Blanshard [3-18] Stanley Hinton.*

LOCOMOTION (IRE) BHB 50f44a RR 53f 44a 370[10]
4 ch g Seattle Dancer (USA) 10.1f **(74)** - Pipe Opener (Prince Sabo) 7.2f **(62)**
Form - 0007350
Record 2000 - 1st:0 2nd:0 3rd:1 Ran:5
Pre2000 - 1st:1 2nd:3 3rd:2 Ran:11
Win Prizemoney £2,640 *Total Prizemoney* £6,836
Wins 1999 *Jun Southw (STD) 8f* 67 <
2000 AW 0-5: (7f 3, 8f, 9f) (Fibr 5)
Strong, fair gelding, effective 6 to 8f, acts on frm - acts on Fibr. AW high 43. Inconsistent.
**S Dow [0-7] Byerley Bloodstock (from W J Haggas [1-9] Oct 1999).*

LODEN BLUE BHB 38f RR 34f 622[24]
3 b f Anshan 8.2f **(63)** - Dolly Bevan (Another Realm) 6.6f **(55)**
Form - 0
Record 2000 - 1st:0 2nd:0 3rd:0 Ran:1
Pre2000 - 1st:0 2nd:0 3rd:0 Ran:4
2000 Turf 0-1: (10f) (gd)
Very moderate filly.
**R C Spicer [0-1] John Purcell (from C A Dwyer [0-1] Nov 1999).*

LODGE HILL (USA) RR 97f 4835a[3]
3 ch c Cozzene (USA) 10.1f **(87)** - L'Insatiable (USA) (Caveat (USA))
Form - 3
2000 Turf 0-1: (12f) (frm)
Currently very useful colt. **in USA [0-1].*

LOGANLEA (IRE) BHB 49f40a RR 52f 40a 419[10]
6 br m Petong 7.6f **(58)** - White's Pet (Mummy's Pet) 7.7f **(60)**
Form - 0
Record 2000 - 1st:0 2nd:0 3rd:0 Ran:1
Pre2000 - 1st:1 2nd:0 3rd:1 Ran:15
Win Prizemoney £2,455 *Total Prizemoney* £2,831
Wins 1998 Spt Yarmou (G-S) H 6f 48 52 <
2000 AW 0-1: (8f) (Fibr)
Fair mare. Becoming disappointing.
**M J Polglase [0-4] Roger Langley (from W J Musson [1-15] Apr 1999).*

LOGIC LANE (IRE) BHB 86f RR 79f 3392[8]
2 ch c Lahib (USA) 8f **(69)** - Reflection (Mill Reef (USA)) 10.5f **(78)**
Form - 0128
Record 2000 - 1st:1 2nd:1 3rd:0 Ran:4
Win Prizemoney £6,890 *Total Prizemoney* £8,798
Wins * 2000 Jun Goodwo (GD) 6f 77 <
2000 Turf 1-4: (6f 1-3, 7f) (gd 1-1, g-f 2, frm)
Above-average colt. Turf high 79 - also 1st of 4 getting 7lb from Where's Jasper (30 Jun Goodwood RF 2401). Made his debut in a warm maiden, and won a small race at Goodwood next time.
**R Charlton [1-4] Michael Pescod.*

LOKOMOTIV BHB 52f40a RR 49f 40a 4649[10]
4 b g Salse (USA) 10.9f **(71)** - Rainbow's End (My Swallow) 9.2f **(71)**
Form - 60771052610
Record 2000 - 1st:2 2nd:1 3rd:0 Ran:11
Pre2000 - 1st:1 2nd:1 3rd:1 Ran:13
Win Prizemoney £6,334 *Total Prizemoney* £8,312
Wins * 2000 Spt Yarmou (G-F) S 10.1f 45

* 2000	Jly	Ayr	(FRM)	S	10.9f	39	
1998	Jly	Yarmou	(G-F)	S	7f	67+	<

2000 Turf 2-9: (10f 1-6, 11f 1-1, 12f 2) (gd, g-f 2, frm 2-4, hrd 2) 2000 AW 0-2: (11f, 12f) (Fibr 2)

Scopey, moderate gelding, effective 7 to 10f, best at 8f, acts on gd to hrd, best on g-f, often wears blinkers. Turf high 49 (1st run) - 6th of 18 giving 11lb to Mice Ideas (14 Jun Beverley 10f hrd RF 1952). AW high 27 (began Spt).

**J M Bradley [2-11] Mrs H Raw (from P D Evans [0-10] Oct 1999).*

LOMOND DANCER (IRE) BHB 38f RR 63f 4583[8]

3 b g Common Grounds 8.1f **(66)** - Lomond's Breeze (Lomond (USA)) 8.8f **(65)**

Form - 85700008

Record 2000 - 1st:0 2nd:0 3rd:0 Ran:8
Pre2000 - 1st:0 2nd:0 3rd:0 Ran:4

Win Prizemoney £0 *Total Prizemoney* £250

2000 Turf 0-7: (8f, 10f 4, 11f, 12f) (g-f 3, frm 4) 2000 AW 0-1: (16f) (Equi)

Neat, average gelding, effective 7 to 11f, acts on frm. Turf high 63 - 5th of 11 giving 21lb to Adriana (14 Jun Lingfield 11f frm RF 1970).

**P W Harris [0-12] Friends of Lomond.*

LONDON BANK RR 98f 4852a[3]

4 h Bigstone (IRE) - Bourbon Queen (Ile de Bourbon (USA)) 10.1f **(67)**

Form - 83

2000 Turf 0-2: (11f, 12f) (hvy, g-f)

Very useful colt. Turf high 98 - 3rd of 5 to Poseidon (1 Oct San Siro 11f hvy RF 4852a). **B Grizzetti in ITY [0-4] Scuderia Belforte.*

LONDONER (USA) BHB 100f RR 93f 4301[4]

2 ch c Sky Classic (CAN) 10f **(83)** - Love And Affection (USA) (Exclusive Era (USA))

Form - 114

Record 2000 - 1st:2 2nd:0 3rd:0 Ran:3

Win Prizemoney £10,341 *Total Prizemoney* £11,334

Wins	*** 2000**	Aug	Yarmou	(GD)	7f	86+	<
	*** 2000**	Jly	Newmar	(G-S)	7f	86+	<

2000 Turf 2-3: (7f 2-2, 8f) (gd 1-2, g-f 1-1)

Currently useful colt. Turf high 93 (began Jly) - 4th of 8 to Atlantic Prince (8 Spt Goodwood 8f gd RF 4301) - also 1st of 4 giving 11lb to Referral (9 Aug Yarmouth RF 3516). A rangy individual, he showed a grand attitude when winning a maiden and minor event during the summer. Touched off in a four-way photo to a Listed heat at Goodwood in September, he will stay a mile and a quarter and is open to improvement.

**H R A Cecil [2-3] H R H Prince Fahd Salman.*

Londoner showed a capital attitude

LONDON EYE BHB 57f50a RR 57f 50a 4673[5]

2 b f Distinctly North (USA) 7.4f **(63)** - Clonavon Girl (IRE) **(50f)** (Be My Guest (USA)) 9.3f **(67)**

Form - 76033277164405

Record 2000 - 1st:1 2nd:1 3rd:2 Ran:14

Win Prizemoney £2,236 *Total Prizemoney* £4,080

Wins * 2000 Jly Bright (FRM) 5.3f 57 <

2000 Turf 1-12: (5f 1-6, 6f 5, 7f) (g-s 2, gd 2, g-f 3, frm 1-5) 2000 AW 0-2: (5f 2) (Fibr 2)

Fair filly, effective 5f, acts on frm, mostly wears blinkers (very effectively), prefers left handed tracks, prefers tight tracks. Turf high 57 - also 1st of 5 from Queen's College (24 Jly Brighton RF 3072). AW high 39. **K T Ivory [1-14] J B Waterfall.*

LONDONNET (IRE) RR 69f 5236[8]

2 b f Catrail (USA) - Society Ball (Law Society (USA)) 9.9f **(70)**

Form - 8

Record 2000 - 1st:0 2nd:0 3rd:0 Ran:1

2000 Turf 0-1: (7f) (g-s)

Currently average filly. **H R A Cecil [0-1] Derek D & Mrs Jean P Clee.*

LONE PIPER BHB 74f95a RR 74f 95a 4834[18]

5 b h Warning 8.1f **(77)** - Shamisen (Diesis) 9.3f **(69)**

Form - 40000000300

Record 2000 - 1st:0 2nd:0 3rd:1 Ran:11
Pre2000 - 1st:2 2nd:1 3rd:1 Ran:13

Win Prizemoney £24,284 *Total Prizemoney* £30,405

Wins	* 1998	Spt	York	(GD)	H	6f	96	101	<
	* 1998	May	Newmar	(GD)		7f		99	

2000 Turf 0-10: (5f 3, 6f 6, 7f) (g-s, gd 3, g-f 5, frm) 2000 AW 0-1: (6f) (Fibr)

Very useful colt, effective 6f, - acts on Fibr, has worn blinkers. Turf high 74. (1st run) - 4th of 13 giving 12lb to Blue Star (11 Mar Wolverhampton 6f Fibr RF 0432). He is on a long losing run but retains plenty of ability despite being thoroughly inconsistent. Probably best on an easy surface, he stays seven furlongs.

**C E Brittain [2-24] Saeed Manana.*

LONER BHB 73f RR 80f 4932[19]

2 b g Magic Ring (IRE) 6.5f **(64)** - Jolis Absent **(25f 41a)** (Primo Dominio) 6.2f **(80)**

Form - 8462158400

Record 2000 - 1st:1 2nd:1 3rd:0 Ran:10

Win Prizemoney £7,020 *Total Prizemoney* £9,781

Wins * 2000 Aug Goodwo (GD) H 7f 72 73 <

2000 Turf 1-10: (5f 2, 6f 4, 7f 1-3, 8f) (gd 4, g-f 1-3, frm 3)

Decent gelding, effective 6 to 7f, best at 7f, acts on gd to g-f, best on g-f. Turf high 80 (began Jly) - 4th of 11 getting 4lb from Soldier On (15 Spt Ayr 6f gd RF 4425) - also 1st of 6 getting 7lb from Foodbroker Fancy (27 Aug Goodwood RF 4018).

**N A Callaghan [1-10] N A Callaghan.*

LONGCHAMP DU LAC RR 33f 3778[11]

2 b c Lake Coniston (IRE) - Kaprisky (IRE) (Red Sunset) 8.2f **(63)**

Form - 80

Record 2000 - 1st:0 2nd:0 3rd:0 Ran:2

2000 Turf 0-2: (6f 2) (gd, frm)

Currently very moderate colt. Turf high 33 (began Jly).

**A Berry [0-2] The Property Racing Partnership.*

LONG DAY (IRE) RR 53f 5076[7]

2 b f Muhtarram (USA) - Well Proud (IRE) (Sadler's Wells (USA)) 10f **(76)**

Form - 07

Record 2000 - 1st:0 2nd:0 3rd:0 Ran:2

2000 Turf 0-2: (6f, 8f) (g-s, g-f)

Currently fair filly. Turf high 53 (began Spt).

**R Hannon [0-2] W J Gredley.*

LONGUEVILLE LEGEND (IRE) RR 96f 4249a[4]

2 bb f Cajun Cadet - Media Legend (NOR) 00

Form - 244

2000 Turf 0-3: (6f 2, 7f) (gd 3)

Currently very useful filly. Turf high 96 (began Jly). She ran three excellent races in defeat, only being beaten six and a quarter lengths in the Group 1 Heinz 57 at Leopardstown. A maiden is surely there for the taking next spring.

**C Collins in IRE [0-3] A Stang.*

LONG WEEKEND (IRE) BHB 62f **RR 65f** 4728[14]
2 b c Flying Spur (AUS) - Friday Night (USA) **(24f)** (Trempolino (USA)) 12f **(71)**
Form - 7540
Record 2000 - 1st:0 2nd:0 3rd:0 Ran:4
Win Prizemoney £0 *Total Prizemoney* £296
2000 Turf 0-4: (6f 2, 7f 2) (gd, g-f, frm 2)
Average colt. Turf high 65 (began Jly).
**J L Dunlop [0-4] The Earl Cadogan.*

LOOK FIRST (IRE) BHB 65f60a **RR 68f 60a** 5237[2]
2 b c Namaqualand (USA) - Be Prepared (IRE) (Be My Guest (USA)) 9.3f **(67)**
Form - 23182
Record 2000 - 1st:1 2nd:2 3rd:1 Ran:5
Win Prizemoney £2,194 *Total Prizemoney* £4,138
Wins * 2000 Aug Bright (GD) S 7f 68 <
2000 Turf 1-5: (7f 1-3, 8f, 10f) (g-s, gd, g-f 1-2, frm)
Average colt. Turf high 68 (began Jly) - 2nd of 16 giving 3lb to Polish Paddy (28 Oct Newmarket 8f g-s RF 5237) - also 1st of 4 giving 5lb to Hard To Lay (9 Aug Brighton RF 3482).
**A P Jarvis [1-5] Mrs Ann Jarvis.*

LOOK HERE NOW BHB 75f **RR 77f** 5317[15]
3 gr c Ardkinglass 5f **(64)** - Where's Carol (Anfield) 8.5f **(59)**
Form - 150000160
Record 2000 - 1st:2 2nd:0 3rd:0 Ran:9
Win Prizemoney £12,402 *Total Prizemoney* £12,655
Wins * 2000 Oct York (SFT) 6f 75
*** 2000** Mar Doncas (GD) 6f 77 <
2000 Turf 2-9: (5f, 6f 2-5, 7f 3) (sft, g-s 1-3, gd 1-3, frm 2)
Leggy, above-average colt, effective 6f, acts on g-s to gd. Turf high 77 (1st run) - 1st of 13 from Kind Emperor (25 Mar Doncaster RF 0492) - also 1st of 23 getting 1lb from Mantles Pride (6 Oct York RF 4834). Unraced at two, he made a winning debut in a Doncaster maiden, but faced some stiff tasks afterwards and did not show much until scoring a 33/1 surprise at York in October.
**B A McMahon [2-9] S L Edwards.*

LOOKING FOR LOVE (IRE) BHB 77f **RR 80f** 5106[1]
2 b f Tagula (IRE) - Mousseux (IRE) (Jareer (USA)) 5.9f **(75)**
Form - 83332321
Record 2000 - 1st:1 2nd:2 3rd:4 Ran:8
Win Prizemoney £4,602 *Total Prizemoney* £8,145
Wins * 2000 Oct Newbur (SFT) H 7f 73 80 <
2000 Turf 1-8: (6f 3, 7f 1-4, 8f) (gd 1-4, g-f 3, frm)
Decent filly, effective 6 to 7f, best at 7f, acts on gd to frm, best on gd. Turf high 80 - 1st of 15 getting 4lb from Pasithea (20 Oct Newbury RF 5106). Consistent.
**J G Portman [1-8] Out To Grass Partnership.*

LOOP THE LOUP BHB 87f **RR 88f** 5104[1]
4 b g Petit Loup (USA) - Mithi Al Gamar (USA) **(60f)** (Blushing Groom (FR)) 10.3f **(76)**
Form - 508001
Record 2000 - 1st:1 2nd:0 3rd:0 Ran:6
Pre2000 - 1st:3 2nd:3 3rd:1 Ran:10
Win Prizemoney £31,003 *Total Prizemoney* £39,517
Wins * 2000 Oct Doncas (GD) H 14.6f 83 88
1999 Aug York (GD) H 13.9f 89 95 <
1999 Jly Salisb (G-S) H 12f 83 84
1999 Jun Lingfi (G-S) 11.5f 84
2000 Turf 1-6: (12f 3, 14f 2, 15f 1-1) (hvy, gd 1-3, g-f, frm)
Scopey, useful gelding, effective 14 to 15f, best at 15f, acts on gd to frm, best on gd, likes left handed tracks. Turf high 88 - 1st of 17 giving 16lb to Palua (20 Oct Doncaster RF 5104). Consistent. He made 70,000 guineas at Newmarket following a successful three-year-old campaign, but failed to find his form for his new connections until scoring at Doncaster in October.
**Mrs M Reveley [1-6] and Mrs J D Cotton (from J L Dunlop [3-10] Spt 1999).*

LOOSE CHIPPINS (IRE) RR 59f 5152[7]
2 b f Bigstone (IRE) - Fortune Teller (Troy) 10.4f **(68)**
Form - 07
Record 2000 - 1st:0 2nd:0 3rd:0 Ran:2
2000 Turf 0-2: (7f 2) (g-s, g-f)
Currently fair filly. Turf high 59 (began Spt).
**G L Moore [0-2] Mrs J Moore.*

LORD ADVOCATE BHB 16f38a **RR 34f 38a** 4450[6]
12 br g Law Society (USA) 11.6f **(71)** - Kereolle (Riverman (USA)) 9.1f **(76)**
Form - 0006066856
Record 2000 - 1st:0 2nd:0 3rd:0 Ran:10
Pre2000 - 1st:12 2nd:18 3rd:14 Ran:145
Win Prizemoney £36,549 *Total Prizemoney* £61,160
Wins * 1998 Jun Hamilt (GD) H 13f 40 44
* 1997 Jun Hamilt (GD) H 13f 46 57
* 1996 Jun Hamilt (GD) H 13f 45 53
* 1996 May Mussel (GD) H 11.1f 42 47
* 1996 May Hamilt (SFT) H 13f 32 43
2000 Turf 0-10: (9f, 11f, 12f 3, 13f 5) (gd 3, g-f 2, frm 5)
Very moderate gelding, effective 11 to 14f, best at 13f, acts on gd to frm, best on frm, mostly wears blinkers, favours right handed tracks, likes Hamilton. Turf high 34. Inconsistent. A real old character who has won a multitude of modest races in Scotland over the years, but is now at the veteran stage.
**D A Nolan [8-110] Mrs J McFadyen-Murray (from T Craig [1-5] Jly 1993).*

LORD ALASKA (IRE) BHB 76f **RR 76+f** 4741[2]
3 b g Sir Harry Lewis (USA) - Anchorage (IRE) (Slip Anchor) 9.8f **(73)**
Form - 00501112
Record 2000 - 1st:3 2nd:1 3rd:0 Ran:8
Win Prizemoney £7,608 *Total Prizemoney* £11,930
Wins * 2000 Spt Warwic (G-F) H 16.2f 64 74 <
*** 2000** Aug Mussel (G-F) H 16f 55 69
*** 2000** Aug Folkes (G-F) H 16.4f 55 59+
2000 Turf 3-8: (10f 3, 12f, 14f, 16f 3-3) (gd 2, g-f 2-4, frm 1-2)
Unfurnished, above-average gelding, effective 14 to 16f, best at 16f, acts on g-f to frm, best on g-f. Turf high 76 - 2nd of 17 getting 25lb from Thari (30 Spt Newmarket 14f g-f RF 4741) - also 1st of 16 getting 4lb from Jack Dawson (11 Spt Warwick RF 4328). Improving nicely, completing a hat-trick in two-mile events on fast ground. **J A R Toller [3-8] Mrs Claire Smith.*

LORD BERGERAC BHB 44f56a **RR 32f 56a** 3896[10]
4 b g Cyrano de Bergerac 7.3f **(58)** - Vax Lady (Millfontaine)
Form - 00
Record 2000 - 1st:0 2nd:0 3rd:0 Ran:2
Pre2000 - 1st:1 2nd:0 3rd:1 Ran:11
Win Prizemoney £3,582 *Total Prizemoney* £3,987
Wins * 1998 Aug Hamilt (SFT) 6f 78+ <
2000 Turf 0-1: (7f) (hrd) 2000 AW 0-1: (6f) (Fibr)
Strong, moderate gelding, often wears blinkers.
**J L Spearing [1-13] J Spearing.*

LORD EFISIO RR 2064[9]
2 b c Efisio 7.7f **(69)** - Vax Lady (Millfontaine)
Form - 0
Record 2000 - 1st:0 2nd:0 3rd:0 Ran:1
2000 Turf 0-1: (6f) (frm)
Currently very poor colt. **D Nicholls [0-1] A J & Mrs L Brazier.*

LORD EUROLINK (IRE) BHB 68f67a **RR 68f 67a** 4870[6]
6 b g Danehill (USA) 9.1f **(79)** - Lady Eurolink (Kala Shikari) 8.4f **(54)**
Form - 7305311174464501236
Record 2000 - 1st:4 2nd:1 3rd:3 Ran:19
Pre2000 - 1st:1 2nd:0 3rd:3 Ran:10
Win Prizemoney £17,079 *Total Prizemoney* £23,700
Wins * 2000 Spt York (GD) C 8.9f 61+
*** 2000** *Mar Wolver (STD) H 8.5f 62 67*
*** 2000** *Mar Southw (STD) C 8f 65*
*** 2000** *Feb Wolver (STD) S 8.5f 48*
1997 May Doncas (GD) 8f 83 <
2000 Turf 1-8: (8f, 9f 1-2, 10f 5) (hvy, sft, g-s, gd 2, g-f 1-2, frm) 2000 AW 3-11: (8f 3-6, 9f, 10f 2, 12f 2) (Equi 4, Fibr 3-7)
Average gelding, effective 8 to 10f, best at 10f, acts on gd to g-f - acts on Fibr, has worn blinkers. Turf high 68 - 4th of 17 giving 20lb to A Day On The Dub (19 May Nottingham 10f gd RF 1309). AW high 67 - 1st of 6 getting 1lb from Mellors (25 Mar Wolverhampton RF 0504).

**C A Dwyer [4-25] Roalco Ltd (from J L Dunlop [1-6] May 1998).*

LORD FLASHEART (USA) RR 115f 1825a[2]

3 b c Blush Rambler (USA) - Miss Henderson Co (USA) (Silver Hawk (USA)) 8.6f **(70)**

Form - 212

2000 Turf 1-3: (11f 1-2, 12f) (hvy 1-2, gd)

High-class colt, has worn blinkers. Turf high 115 - 2nd of 14 to Holding Court (4 Jun Chantilly 12f gd RF 1825a) - also 1st of 6 from Crimson Quest (8 May Chantilly RF 1281a). He lacks scope, but is tough and confirmed the promise of his juvenile campaign with some smart performances last year. Given too much to do when second behind Holding Court in the French Derby, he has reportedly been sold to race in America.

**A deRoyerDupre in FR [2-5] E Gann.*

LORD GIZZMO BHB 40f50a RR 33f 50a 4677[15]

3 ch c Democratic (USA) - Figrant (USA) (L'Emigrant (USA)) 10.5f **(62)**

Form - 0670

Record 2000 - 1st:0 2nd:0 3rd:0 Ran:4

2000 Turf 0-4: (8f, 10f 2, 12f) (g-s, g-f 2, frm)

Scopey, very moderate colt. Turf high 33 (began Jly).

**V Soane [0-4] The Paddy Pipers.*

LORD HARLEY BHB 59f70a RR 55f 70a 1364[5]

3 b g Formidable (USA) 7.8f **(60)** - Nanny Doon (Dominion) 8.5f **(63)**

Form - 422115

Record 2000 - 1st:2 2nd:2 3rd:0 Ran:5
Pre2000 - 1st:0 2nd:0 3rd:0 Ran:4

Win Prizemoney £6,056 *Total Prizemoney* £7,317

Wins * 2000 *Apr Wolver (STD) H 9.4f 60 71+*
*** 2000** *Feb Wolver (STD) H 8.5f 56 76 <*

2000 Turf 0-1: (8f) (frm) 2000 AW 2-4: (7f, 8f 1-2, 9f 1-1)(Equi, Fibr 2-3)

Neat, above-average gelding, effective 8 to 9f, - acted on Fibr, liked left handed tracks, preferred tight tracks. AW high 76 - 1st of 8 getting 29lb from Safarando (29 Feb Wolverhampton RF 0382) - also 1st of 13 giving 15lb to Cyber Babe (28 Apr Wolverhampton RF 0905). (DEAD)

**B R Millman [2-9] H Gooding.*

LORD HIGH ADMIRAL (CAN) BHB 47f56a RR 41f 56a 3546[8]

12 b g Bering 9.6f **(80)** - Baltic Sea (CAN) (Danzig (USA)) 8.4f **(76)**

Form - 41400400

Record 2000 - 1st:1 2nd:0 3rd:0 Ran:7
Pre2000 - 1st:11 2nd:10 3rd:6 Ran:79

Win Prizemoney £51,791 *Total Prizemoney* £74,974

Wins * 2000 *Mar Southw (STD) H 5f 50 56*
1999 May Doncas (G-F) C 6f 55
1997 Spt Salisb (G-S) H 5f 75 85+
1996 Spt Haydoc (GD) H 5f 82 87
1996 Jly Sandow (G-S) H 5f 82 86
1996 Jun Sandow (G-F) C 5f 70

2000 Turf 0-5: (5f 3, 6f 2) (gd, g-f 4) 2000 AW 1-2: (5f 1-2) (Fibr 1-2)

Fair gelding, effective 5 to 6f, best at 5f, acts on gd to hrd - acts on Fibr, has worn blinkers (very effectively). Turf high 56 (1st run) - 4th of 16 getting 15lb from Fearby Cross (28 Mar Sandown 5f g-f RF 0530). AW high 56 (1st run) - 1st of 12 giving 2lb to Ready To Rock (14 Mar Southwell RF 0443). A veteran, he has been a credit to his connections over the years and is still capable when able to dominate over a stiff five with cut in the ground.

**C G Cox [1-13] Elite Racing Club (from M J Heaton-Ellis [11-62] Aug 1999).*

LORD JIM (IRE) BHB 90f93a RR 89f 93a 1590[5]

8 b g Kahyasi 12.9f **(74)** - Sarah Georgina (Persian Bold) 9.3f **(66)**

Form - 5

Record 2000 - 1st:0 2nd:0 3rd:0 Ran:1
Pre2000 - 1st:3 2nd:3 3rd:4 Ran:27

Win Prizemoney £18,172 *Total Prizemoney* £49,580

Wins 1996 Aug Leopar (GD) L 14f 97 <
1996 Jun Salisb (G-F) 14f 90

2000 Turf 0-1: (10f) (g-s)

Useful gelding, has worn blinkers. Consistent.

**G A Butler [0-1] Mrs S Y Thomas (from Lord Huntingdon [2-14] Jly 1998).*

LORD JOSHUA (IRE) RR 49+f 5315[3]

2 b c King's Theatre (IRE) - Lady Joshua (IRE) **(69f)** (Royal Academy (USA))

Form - 3

Record 2000 - 1st:0 2nd:0 3rd:1 Ran:1

Win Prizemoney £0 *Total Prizemoney* £936

2000 Turf 0-1: (8f) (g-s)

Currently moderate colt. **G A Butler [0-1] Mrs A E Butler.*

LORD KINTYRE BHB 112f RR 107f 4434[5]

5 b g Makbul - Highland Rowena (Royben) 7.3f **(60)**

Form - 244821115

Record 2000 - 1st:3 2nd:2 3rd:0 Ran:9
Pre2000 - 1st:2 2nd:4 3rd:2 Ran:16

Win Prizemoney £105,214 *Total Prizemoney* £164,146

Wins * 2000 Spt Doncas (G-F) L 5f 105 <
*** 2000** Aug Nottin (GD) 5.1f 105 <
*** 2000** Jly Newmar (GD) 5f 103
* 1997 Jly Newbur (G-F) 5.2f 98
* 1997 Jun Windso (G-F) 6f 80

2000 Turf 3-9: (5f 3-9) (g-s 2, gd 2, g-f 2-2, frm 1-3)

Pattern-class gelding, effective 5f, acts on g-s to frm, excels at Newmarket. Turf high 107 - also 1st of 8 giving 6lb to See You Later (7 Spt Doncaster RF 4278). Consistent. He hit a rich vein of form in the late summer and is a very able sprinter when on song.

**B R Millman [5-25] M Calvert.*

Lord Kintyre hit a purple patch in the summer

LORD LAMB BHB 92f RR 91f 825[2]

8 gr g Dunbeath (USA) 9.9f **(53)** - Caroline Lamb (Hotfoot) 10.5f **(59)**

Form - 2

Record 2000 - 1st:0 2nd:1 3rd:0 Ran:1
Pre2000 - 1st:1 2nd:1 3rd:3 Ran:9

Win Prizemoney £7,262 *Total Prizemoney* £18,087

Wins * 1998 Spt Haydoc (G-F) H 14f 69 69+ <

2000 Turf 0-1: (12f) (hvy)

Useful gelding. (1st run) - 2nd of 15 giving 11lb to Spring Pursuit (22 Apr Haydock 12f hvy RF 0825). Inconsistent.

**Mrs M Reveley [8-21] A Sharratt & J Renton.*

LORD LIAM (USA) BHB 73f63a RR 71f 63a 5013[8]

2 b c Foxhound (USA) - Crackling Sike **(71df)** (Salse (USA)) 7.5f **(66)**

Form - 534568

Record 2000 - 1st:0 2nd:0 3rd:1 Ran:6

Win Prizemoney £0 *Total Prizemoney* £819

2000 Turf 0-4: (5f, 6f, 7f 2) (gd, g-f, frm 2) 2000 AW 0-2: (6f 2) (Fibr 2)

Above-average colt. Turf high 71 (began Aug). AW high 54 (began Spt).

**N P Littmoden [0-6] Mrs Julie Mitchell.*

LORDOFENCHANTMENT (IRE) BHB 52f **RR 60f** 4768[13]
3 ch g Soviet Lad (USA) 9.4f **(63)** - Sauvignon (IRE) (Alzao (USA)) 7.1f **(68)**
Form - 0522755240
Record 2000 - 1st:0 2nd:3 3rd:0 Ran:10
Pre2000 - 1st:1 2nd:0 3rd:0 Ran:8
Win Prizemoney £2,253 *Total Prizemoney* £5,179
Wins * 1999 Aug Ripon (GD) S 6f 67+ <
2000 Turf 0-10: (6f 6, 7f 4) (sft, g-s 3, gd, g-f 2, frm 3)
Strong, average gelding, effective 6f, acts on sft to g-f, best on g-f, has worn blinkers (very effectively). Turf high 60 - 2nd of 21 giving 5lb to College Maid (31 May Ripon 6f g-f RF 1598).
**N Tinkler [1-18] David Scott.*

LORD OMNI (USA) BHB 71f **RR 72f** 2884[5]
3 ch c El Prado (IRE) 8f **(74)** - Muskoka Ice (USA) (It's Freezing (USA)) 10f **(83)**
Form - 615
Record 2000 - 1st:1 2nd:0 3rd:0 Ran:3
Pre2000 - 1st:0 2nd:0 3rd:0 Ran:3
Win Prizemoney £2,827 *Total Prizemoney* £3,073
Wins * **2000** Jun Thirsk (FRM) H 6f 67 72 <
2000 Turf 1-3: (6f 1-2, 7f) (sft, frm 1-2)
Tall, above-average colt, effective 6f, acts on g-f to frm. Turf high 72 - 1st of 13 giving 13lb to Desraya (20 Jun Thirsk RF 2118).
**T D Barron [1-6] Peter Jones.*

LORD PACAL (IRE) BHB 89f **RR 91f** 4991[2]
3 b g Indian Ridge 7.6f **(74)** - Please Believe Me (Try My Best (USA)) 7.6f **(67)**
Form - 00082214102
Record 2000 - 1st:2 2nd:3 3rd:0 Ran:11
Pre2000 - 1st:1 2nd:1 3rd:1 Ran:8
Win Prizemoney £18,400 *Total Prizemoney* £36,657
Wins * **2000** Aug Newmar (G-F) H 7f 83 86
* **2000** Jly Yarmou (G-F) H 6f 80 81
* 1999 May Newbur (G-F) 5.2f 95+ <
2000 Turf 2-11: (6f 1-5, 7f 1-6) (g-s, gd 5, g-f 1-3, frm 1-2)
Leggy, useful gelding, effective 5 to 7f, best at 5f, acts on gd to g-f, best on g-f, excels at Ascot, likes Newmarket. Turf high 91 - 2nd of 29 giving 9lb to Social Contract (14 Oct Newmarket 7f gd RF 4991) - also 1st of 15 giving 11lb to Shather (26 Aug Newmarket RF 3992). Improving. **N A Callaghan [3-19] Paul & Jenny Green.*

LORD PROTECTOR (IRE) BHB 81f **RR 79f** 5100[5]
2 b c Nicolotte - Scared (Royal Academy (USA))
Form - 425
Record 2000 - 1st:0 2nd:1 3rd:0 Ran:3
Win Prizemoney £0 *Total Prizemoney* £2,693
2000 Turf 0-3: (7f 2, 8f) (g-s, gd, g-f)
Currently above-average colt. Turf high 79 (began Spt).
**D W P Arbuthnot [0-3] Derrick Broomfield.*

LORD YASMIN (IRE) BHB 73f73a **RR 69f 73a** 2418[8]
3 b c Lahib (USA) 8f **(69)** - Adieu Cherie (IRE) (Bustino) 10.4f **(64)**
Form - 10318
Record 2000 - 1st:2 2nd:0 3rd:1 Ran:5
Pre2000 - 1st:0 2nd:1 3rd:0 Ran:2
Win Prizemoney £5,575 *Total Prizemoney* £7,303
Wins * **2000** Jun Bright (G-F) 6f 69
* **2000** *Mar Southw (STD) 6f 71* <
2000 Turf 1-3: (5f, 6f 1-2) (g-f 2, frm 1-1) 2000 AW 1-2: (6f 1-1, 7f) (Fibr 1-2)
Workmanlike, above-average colt, effective 5 to 6f, best at 6f, acts on gd to frm - acts on Fibr. Turf high 69 - 1st of 8 giving 3lb to Stoney Garnett (2 Jun Brighton RF 1653). AW high 71 (1st run) - 1st of 14 giving 5lb to Welsh Valley (17 Mar Southwell RF 0458).
**J Noseda [2-7] L P Calvente.*

LOST AT SEA (IRE) BHB 89f **RR 85f** 4325[5]
2 b c Exit To Nowhere (USA) 8.7f **(77)** - Night At Sea (Night Shift (USA)) 7.2f **(69)**
Form - 827175
Record 2000 - 1st:1 2nd:1 3rd:0 Ran:6
Win Prizemoney £2,821 *Total Prizemoney* £4,533
Wins * **2000** Jly Yarmou (GD) 7f 80 <
2000 Turf 1-6: (6f 4, 7f 1-2) (gd 1-1, g-f 2, frm 3)
Useful colt, effective 6 to 7f, best at 7f, acts on gd to frm. Turf high 85 - 5th of 10 giving 12lb to Lapwing (11 Spt Warwick 7f g-f RF 4325) - also 1st of 10 giving 8lb to April Lee (31 Jly Yarmouth RF 3264). All out to win an ordianry race on his fourth start.
**K R Burke [1-6] David Morgan.*

LOST IN HOOK (IRE) BHB 62f78a **RR 69f 78a** 4756[11]
3 b f Dancing Dissident (USA) 6.8f **(65)** - Rathbawn Realm (Doulab (USA)) 9.8f **(65)**
Form - 307000
Record 2000 - 1st:0 2nd:0 3rd:1 Ran:6
Pre2000 - 1st:1 2nd:1 3rd:0 Ran:5
Win Prizemoney £2,762 *Total Prizemoney* £5,266
Wins * 1999 Jly Ripon (GD) 5f 94+ <
2000 Turf 0-5: (5f 5) (g-s 2, gd, g-f 2) 2000 AW 0-1: (5f) (Equi)
Scopey, decent filly, effective 5f, acts on gd, has worn blinkers. Turf high 69. Becoming disappointing.
**A P Jarvis [1-11] A L R Morton.*

LOST SPIRIT BHB 40f38a **RR 47f 38a** 4723[9]
4 b g Strolling Along (USA) - Shoag (USA) (Affirmed (USA)) 9.3f **(79)**
Form - 766012025067035064011352100
Record 2000 - 1st:4 2nd:3 3rd:2 Ran:23
Pre2000 - 1st:2 2nd:1 3rd:2 Ran:18
Win Prizemoney £18,409 *Total Prizemoney* £23,819
Wins * **2000** Aug Folkes (G-F) H 12f 38 41
* **2000** Aug Beverl (GD) H 12f 32 37
* **2000** Jly Warwic (G-F) SH 12.6f 30 31
* **2000** *Jan Lingfi (STD) H 12f 45 47*
* 1999 *Mar Wolver (SLW) H 12f 54 63*
* 1999 *Feb Southw (STD) C 12f 73+* <
2000 Turf 3-12: (11f 2, 12f 2-8, 13f 1-2) (hvy 2, gd 1-3, g-f 2-5, frm 2)
2000 AW 1-11: (12f 1-9, 13f 2) (Equi 1-7, Fibr 4)
Light-framed, moderate gelding, effective 12f, - acts on Fibr, has worn blinkers. Turf high 47. AW high 52.
**P W Hiatt [6-41] P W Hiatt (from B Hanbury [0-3] Aug 1998).*

LOST THE PLOT **RR 51f** 2849[7]
5 b m Lyphento (USA) - La Comedienne (Comedy Star (USA)) 7.5f **(50)**
Form - 7
Record 2000 - 1st:0 2nd:0 3rd:0 Ran:1
2000 Turf 0-1: (14f) (g-f)
Fair filly. **D W P Arbuthnot [2-7] The Kennet Partnership.*

LOTS OF LOVE (USA) **RR 101f** 4488[4]
2 b c Woodman (USA) 9.7f **(77)** - Accountable Lady (USA) (The Minstrel (CAN)) 10f **(72)**
Form - 14
Record 2000 - 1st:1 2nd:0 3rd:0 Ran:2
Win Prizemoney £2,814 *Total Prizemoney* £3,137
Wins * **2000** Aug Newcas (G-S) 7f 101+ <
2000 Turf 1-2: (7f 1-2) (g-s 1-1, g-f)
Currently very useful colt. Turf high 101 (1st run) (began Aug) - 1st of 12 from Lucefer (28 Aug Newcastle RF 4043). Won a maiden in good style, but gurgled next time. **M Johnston [1-2] M Doyle.*

LOTS OF MAGIC BHB 106f **RR 104f** 2997[7]
4 b c Magic Ring (IRE) 6.5f **(64)** - Pounelta (Tachypous) 8.6f **(55)**
Form - 6887
Record 2000 - 1st:0 2nd:0 3rd:0 Ran:4
Pre2000 - 1st:3 2nd:2 3rd:0 Ran:10
Win Prizemoney £49,121 *Total Prizemoney* £56,192
Wins * 1999 Jun Ascot (G-F) G3 7f 115 <
* 1999 May Lingfi (G-F) 7f 97
* 1998 Spt Epsom (GD) 7f 85
2000 Turf 0-4: (6f 2, 7f 2) (gd 2, frm 2)
Leggy, very useful colt, effective 7f, acts on gd to g-f. Turf high 104. Consistent. He made all for a shock victory in the Jersey Stakes at Royal Ascot in 1999, but was off the track for three months afterwards due to a lung infection. He has been lightly-raced since but the ability remains. Suited by fast ground, he finds six furlongs too sharp. **R Hannon [3-14] Peter Valentine.*

L'OUEST (USA) **RR 44f** 5158[3]
3 br c Gone West (USA) 7.8f **(82)** - La Carene (FR) (Kenmare (FR)) 6.5f **(72)**
Form - 73

Record 2000 - 1st:0 2nd:0 3rd:1 Ran:2
Win Prizemoney £0 *Total Prizemoney* £710
2000 Turf 0-2: (7f, 8f) (sft, g-s)
Workmanlike, currently moderate colt. Turf high 44 (began Oct).
**G Wragg [0-2] Baron G Von Ullmann.*

LOUGH BOW (IRE) RR 53f 4012[10]

2 b g Nicolotte - Gale Force Seven (Strong Gale) 5.6f **(66)**
Form - 70
Record 2000 - 1st:0 2nd:0 3rd:0 Ran:2
2000 Turf 0-2: (7f, 8f) (g-f, frm)
Currently fair gelding. Turf high 53 (began Aug).
**M W Easterby [0-2] Mrs Anne Jarvis.*

LOUGH SWILLY (IRE) BHB 42f RR 48f 2848[13]

4 b g Mukaddamah (USA) 7.6f **(74)** - Flooding (USA) (Irish River (FR)) 8.6f **(78)**
Form - 00070
Record 2000 - 1st:0 2nd:0 3rd:0 Ran:5
Pre2000 - 1st:2 2nd:0 3rd:1 Ran:14
Win Prizemoney £8,935 *Total Prizemoney* £10,326
Wins 1998 Spt Goodwo (G-F) 7f 93 <
1998 Aug Nottin (G-F) 6.1f 93+
2000 Turf 0-5: (6f, 7f, 8f 3) (gd 2, g-f 2, frm)
Workmanlike, moderate gelding. Turf high 48. Inconsistent.
**V Soane [0-5] Trevor Sharman (from B W Hills [2-14] Spt 1999).*

LOUP CERVIER (IRE) BHB 35f46a RR 54f 46a 4583[12]

3 b g Wolfhound (USA) 7.3f **(71)** - Luth D'Or (FR) (Noir Et Or) 10f **(38)**
Form - 0000003448000
Record 2000 - 1st:0 2nd:0 3rd:1 Ran:13
Win Prizemoney £0 *Total Prizemoney* £487
2000 Turf 0-11: (6f 2, 7f 2, 8f 2, 10f 4, 12f) (gd 2, g-f 3, frm 6) 2000 AW 0-2: (6f, 16f) (Equi, Fibr)
Scopey, fair gelding, effective 10f, acts on frm, likes left handed tracks, likes tight tracks. Turf high 57. AW high 9. Becoming disappointing. **S Dow [0-13] D G Churston.*

LOU'S WISH BHB 46f53a RR 29f 53a 5006[14]

3 b g Thatching 7.8f **(60)** - Shamaka **(57df 41a)** (Kris) 9.5f **(73)**
Form - 31263670008000
Record 2000 - 1st:1 2nd:1 3rd:2 Ran:14
Pre2000 - 1st:0 2nd:0 3rd:0 Ran:8
Win Prizemoney £1,904 *Total Prizemoney* £4,440
Wins * 2000 *Jan Wolver (STD) H 7f 54 65* <
2000 Turf 0-4: (7f, 8f 3) (gd, g-f 2, frm) 2000 AW 1-10: (6f, 7f 1-4, 8f 5) (Fibr 1-10)
Light-framed, moderate gelding, effective 6 to 8f, best at 7f, - acts on Fibr, often wears blinkers (extremely effectively), likes left handed tracks, likes tight tracks. Turf high 29. AW high 66 - 2nd of 11 giving 3lb to Sign of The Tiger (28 Jan Southwell 7f Fibr RF 0179) - also 1st of 10 giving 5lb to Baytown Rhapsody (18 Jan Wolverhampton RF 0107).
**M J Polglase [1-22] Ian Puddle.*

LOVE (IRE) BHB 67f RR 71f 4622[5]

2 b c Royal Academy (USA) 7.8f **(77)** - Kentmere (FR) (Galetto (FR)) 13.1f **(60)**
Form - 505
Record 2000 - 1st:0 2nd:0 3rd:0 Ran:3
2000 Turf 0-3: (5f 2, 6f) (gd, g-f 2)
Currently above-average colt. Turf high 71.
**M Johnston [0-3] M Doyle.*

LOVE BITTEN (IRE) BHB 67f RR 69f 2589[11]

3 b g Darshaan 11.9f **(81)** - Kentmere (FR) (Galetto (FR)) 13.1f **(60)**
Form - 0084521340
Record 2000 - 1st:1 2nd:1 3rd:1 Ran:10
Win Prizemoney £2,786 *Total Prizemoney* £5,516
Wins * 2000 Jun Ayr (GD) H 13.1f 67 69 <
2000 Turf 1-10: (7f, 8f, 10f, 11f, 12f 3, 13f 1-1, 14f 2) (gd 4, g-f 3, frm 1-3)
Light-framed, average gelding, effective 11 to 14f, acts on gd to frm, best on frm, prefers tight tracks. Turf high 69 - 1st of 6 giving 15lb to William The Lion (23 Jun Ayr RF 2217). Consistent.
**M Johnston [1-10] M Doyle.*

LOVE DIAMONDS (IRE) BHB 42f61a RR 41f 61a 5007[2]

4 b g Royal Academy (USA) 7.8f **(77)** - Baby Diamonds (Habitat) 9.4f **(70)**
Form - 0206000332
Record 2000 - 1st:0 2nd:2 3rd:2 Ran:9
Pre2000 - 1st:2 2nd:5 3rd:2 Ran:23
Win Prizemoney £5,635 *Total Prizemoney* £14,260
Wins 1999 *Jan Lingfi (STD) H 8f 62 76+* <
1998 *Dec Lingfi (STD) H 8f 56 58*
2000 Turf 0-4: (8f, 10f 2, 11f) (g-f 3, frm) 2000 AW 0-5: (11f 3, 12f 2) (Fibr 5)
Scopey, average gelding, effective 8f, - acts on AW, best on Equi, has worn blinkers, likes left handed tracks, favours tight tracks. Turf high 41 (began Jly). AW high 64. Inconsistent.
**N P Littmoden [0-11] P L Williams (from M Johnston [2-21] Jly 1999).*

LOVE DIVINE BHB 120f RR 120f 4989[4]

3 b f Diesis 9f **(80)** - La Sky (IRE) (Law Society (USA)) 9.9f **(70)**
Form - 11244
Record 2000 - 1st:2 2nd:1 3rd:0 Ran:5
Pre2000 - 1st:0 2nd:1 3rd:0 Ran:1
Win Prizemoney £210,900 *Total Prizemoney* £287,995
Wins * 2000 Jun Epsom (G-S) G1 12f 118+ <
*** 2000** May Goodwo (SFT) L 9.9f 107+
2000 Turf 2-5: (10f 1-2, 12f 1-3) (g-s 1-1, gd 1-3, frm)
Rangy, very high-class filly, effective 10 to 12f, best at 12f, acts on g s to frm. Turf high 120 - 2nd of 6 to Petrushka (23 Aug York 12f frm RF 3913) - also 1st of 10 from Kalypso Katie (9 Jun Epsom RF 1832). She looked to have improved a good deal from two to three when taking the Lupe Stakes in impressive fashion on her return. Became Oaks favourite after that and ran out a most impressive winner at Epsom. She found Petrushka too strong in the Yorkshire Oaks and ran pretty well to finish fourth in the Prix Vermeille and again when filling the same position behind Kalanisi in the Champion Stakes. Her best form has been with give in the ground.
**H R A Cecil [2-6] Lordship Stud.*

Love Divine is all heart

LOVE EVERLASTING BHB 91f RR 91f 5241[5]

2 b f Pursuit of Love 9.5f **(69)** - In Perpetuity (Great Nephew) 9.9f **(64)**
Form - 342125
Record 2000 - 1st:1 2nd:2 3rd:1 Ran:6
Win Prizemoney £3,705 *Total Prizemoney* £14,370
Wins * 2000 Spt Beverl (G-F) 7.5f 70+ <
2000 Turf 1-6: (6f 2, 7f 1-3, 8f) (g-s, gd, g-f 1-2, frm 2)

Useful filly, effective 7f, acts on gd to g-f. Turf high 91 (began Jly) - 2nd of 22 getting 1lb from Palatial (26 Spt Newmarket 7f g-f RF 4642). Seemed to appreciate the step up to the extended seven furlongs when overcoming trouble in running to win a Beverley maiden in September then ran another good race when second in a valuable Newmarket nursery. Looks to be improving.
**M Johnston [1-6] & Mrs G Middlebrook.*

LOVE IN VAIN (IRE) BHB 43a **RR 43a** 682[3]
3 b f Lahib (USA) 8f **(69)** - Little America (Belmez (USA))
Form - 733
Record 2000 - 1st:0 2nd:0 3rd:2 Ran:3
Win Prizemoney £0 *Total Prizemoney* £532
2000 AW 0-3: (7f, 9f, 10f) (Equi, Fibr 2)
Leggy, currently moderate filly. AW high 40.
**M L W Bell [0-3] The Aldwych Partnership.*

LOVE KISS (IRE) BHB 51f **RR 60?f** 5195[6]
5 b g Brief Truce (USA) 9.1f **(73)** - Pendulina (Prince Tenderfoot (USA)) 9f **(61)**
Form - 0020064146
Record 2000 - 1st:1 2nd:1 3rd:0 Ran:10
Pre2000 - 1st:0 2nd:0 3rd:1 Ran:7
Win Prizemoney £4,013 *Total Prizemoney* £6,188
Wins * 2000 Oct Ayr (HVY) H 10f 45 60? <
2000 Turf 1-10: (6f, 7f 3, 8f, 9f 3, 10f 1-2) (hvy 1-1, sft, g-s 2, gd, g-f, frm 3, hrd)
Average gelding, has broken blood-vessels, effective 10f, acts on hvy, likes left handed tracks, likes tight tracks. Turf high 60 - 1st of 15 getting 4lb from Spree Vision (9 Oct Ayr RF 4870).
**W Storey [1-13] K Knox (from M Johnston [0-4] May 1998).*

LOVE LADY (USA) BHB 64f **RR 67f** 4143[7]
2 b br f Woodman (USA) 9.7f **(77)** - Franziska (IRE) **(53f)** (Sadler's Wells (USA)) 10f **(76)**
Form - 4437
Record 2000 - 1st:0 2nd:0 3rd:1 Ran:4
Win Prizemoney £0 *Total Prizemoney* £1,015
2000 Turf 0-4: (6f 4) (g-f, frm 3)
Average filly. Turf high 67. (DEAD) **M Johnston [0-4] M Doyle.*

LOVE LANE (IRE) BHB 80f **RR 82f** 565[3]
3 b g Mujtahid (USA) 7.4f **(69)** - Ibda (Mtoto)
Form - 3
Record 2000 - 1st:0 2nd:0 3rd:1 Ran:1
Pre2000 - 1st:1 2nd:0 3rd:1 Ran:6
Win Prizemoney £3,624 *Total Prizemoney* £5,275
Wins * 1999 Aug Beverl (GD) H 7.5f 79 82 <
2000 Turf 0-1: (7f) (gd)
Scopey, decent gelding, effective 7f, acts on gd to g-f, has worn blinkers. (1st run) - 3rd of 7 giving 10lb to I Promise You (30 Mar Leicester 7f gd RF 0565). **M Johnston [1-7] M Doyle.*

LOVE LETTERS BHB 80f **RR 70f** 1048[15]
3 ch f Pursuit of Love 9.5f **(69)** - Pinkie Rose (FR) (Kenmare (FR)) 6.5f **(72)**
Form - 0
Record 2000 - 1st:0 2nd:0 3rd:0 Ran:1
Pre2000 - 1st:1 2nd:1 3rd:1 Ran:5
Win Prizemoney £2,613 *Total Prizemoney* £4,258
Wins 1999 Jly Warwic (G-F) 6.8f 91+ <
2000 Turf 0-1: (7f) (g-f)
Light-framed, above-average filly, effective 7f, acts on g-f.
**T D Easterby [0-1] Giles Pritchard-Gordon (from J E Banks [1-5] Aug 1999).*

LOVER'S LEAP BHB 62f **RR 78f** 5072[14]
4 b g Pursuit of Love 9.5f **(69)** - Anna Karietta (Precocious) 8.6f **(62)**
Form - 07607800
Record 2000 - 1st:0 2nd:0 3rd:0 Ran:8
Pre2000 - 1st:1 2nd:2 3rd:1 Ran:8
Win Prizemoney £4,380 *Total Prizemoney* £8,245
Wins * 1999 Jun Newbur (GD) 7f 78 <
2000 Turf 0-8: (7f 2, 8f 2, 10f 4) (sft, g-s, gd 2, g-f 3, frm)
Leggy, above-average gelding, effective 7 to 8f, best at 7f, acts on gd to frm, best on g-f, has worn blinkers. Turf high 78 - 6th of 14 giving 16lb to Dolphinelle (31 May Newbury 7f gd RF 1588). Becoming disappointing. **H Candy [1-16] The Earl Cadogan.*

LOVE'S DESIGN (IRE) BHB 68f **RR 72f** 1790[9]
3 b br g Pursuit of Love 9.5f **(69)** - Cephista **(56f 50a)** (Shirley Heights) 10.3f **(74)**
Form - 30800
Record 2000 - 1st:0 2nd:0 3rd:1 Ran:5
Pre2000 - 1st:1 2nd:0 3rd:1 Ran:4
Win Prizemoney £3,225 *Total Prizemoney* £4,391
Wins * 1999 Nov Mussel (GD) 7.1f 67 <
2000 Turf 0-5: (6f 4, 7f) (sft, gd 2, g-f, frm)
Workmanlike, above-average gelding, effective 7f, acts on g-s to g-f, often wears blinkers. Turf high 73.
**J Noseda [1-9] Mrs Caroline Parker.*

LOVE THING BHB 70f **RR 75?f** 4965[9]
2 b f Phountzi (USA) 9.6f **(60)** - Devils Dirge (Song) 7.2f **(61)**
Form - 60100
Record 2000 - 1st:1 2nd:0 3rd:0 Ran:5
Win Prizemoney £4,371 *Total Prizemoney* £4,371
Wins * 2000 Aug Ripon (G-F) 6f 65 <
2000 Turf 1-5: (5f 2, 6f 1-3) (g-s, gd 2, g-f 1-2)
Above-average filly, often wears blinkers. Turf high 75. A full-sister to Superior Premium, she improved for the application of a visor when taking a Beverley maiden auction.
**R A Fahey [1-5] Giles Pritchard-Gordon.*

LOVE TUNE BHB 68f **RR 71f** 4965[16]
2 b f Alhijaz 7.7f **(57)** - Heights of Love **(22f)** (Persian Heights)
Form - 53622200
Record 2000 - 1st:0 2nd:3 3rd:1 Ran:8
Win Prizemoney £0 *Total Prizemoney* £4,046
2000 Turf 0-7: (5f 4, 6f 3) (gd 3, g-f 4) 2000 AW 0-1: (5f) (Fibr)
Above-average filly, effective 5f, acts on gd. Turf high 71 - 2nd of 9 to Effervesce (10 Aug Haydock 5f gd RF 3531).
**K R Burke [0-8] Mrs Elaine Burke.*

LOVE YOU TOO BHB 70f **RR 84f** 4645[14]
3 ch f Be My Chief (USA) 10.2f **(62)** - Nagida **(69f)** (Skyliner) 7.3f **(53)**
Form - 040580
Record 2000 - 1st:0 2nd:0 3rd:0 Ran:6
Pre2000 - 1st:1 2nd:0 3rd:0 Ran:8
Win Prizemoney £3,777 *Total Prizemoney* £5,739
Wins 1999 Jun Doncas (GD) 6f 64 <
2000 Turf 0-6: (7f 2, 8f 3, 10f) (gd 3, g-f, frm, hrd)
Scopey, decent filly. Turf high 84. Inconsistent.
**S P C Woods [0-6] Mike Perkins (from A Kelleway [1-8] Oct 1999).*

LOW PIVOT **RR 99f** 5364a[1]
2 ch c Pivotal - Stay Low (Tina's Pet) 6.8f **(59)**
Form - 31
2000 Turf 1-2: (6f, 7f 1-1) (hvy 1-1, g-s)
Currently very useful colt. Turf high 99 (began Spt) - 1st of 11 getting 23lb from Xua (1 Nov San Siro RF 5364a).
**G Colleo in ITY [1-2] Scuderia Andy Capp.*

LOYAL TARTARE (FR) RR 100f 1826a[5]
3 f
Form - 5
2000 Turf 0-1: (9f) (gd)
Currently very useful. **E Lellouche in FR [0-1].*

LOYAL TOAST (USA) BHB 23f33a **RR 44f 33a** 4648[15]
5 b g Lyphard (USA) 10.6f **(75)** - Lisieux (USA) (Steady Growth (CAN)) 9.9f **(78)**
Form - 2703858533670
Record 2000 - 1st:0 2nd:1 3rd:3 Ran:13
Pre2000 - 1st:1 2nd:0 3rd:0 Ran:16
Win Prizemoney £4,854 *Total Prizemoney* £6,801
Wins 1998 Jun Goodwo (G-F) H 9.9f 73 78 <
2000 Turf 0-10: (9f, 10f, 12f 5, 13f, 14f, 16f) (gd 4, g-f 2, frm 2, hrd 2)
2000 AW 0-3: (11f 2, 16f) (Fibr 3)
Moderate gelding. Turf high 44. AW high 38. Inconsistent.
**N Tinkler [0-21] W F Burton (from L M Cumani [1-9] Jun 1999).*

LOYAL TYCOON (IRE) BHB 90f **RR 80f** 4816[9]
2 br c Royal Abjar (USA) - Rosy Lydgate **(45f 45a)** (Last Tycoon) 8.5f

(62)
Form - 31620
Record 2000 - 1st:1 2nd:1 3rd:1 Ran:5
Win Prizemoney £3,055 *Total Prizemoney* £6,345
Wins * **2000** Jly Leices (G-F) 7f 77+ <
2000 Turf 1-5: (6f, 7f 1-4) (g-s, gd 2, g-f, frm 1-1)
Decent colt. Turf high 80 (began Jly) - 2nd of 9 giving 5lb to Blushing Bride (20 Spt Goodwood 7f gd RF 4541) - also 1st of 12 giving 6lb to Soona (26 Jly Leicester RF 3135). Appreciated the step up to seven furlongs when bolting up in a Leicester maiden auction event on his second start, but was found out when tried in Pattern company. **S Dow [1-5] Michael A J Hall & Miss M Shields.*

L S LOWRY (USA) BHB 72f67a RR 74f 67a 4810[12]
4 b g Thorn Dance (USA) 8.2f **(77)** - Queluz (USA) (Saratoga Six (USA)) 7f **(73)**
Form - 0
Record 2000 - 1st:0 2nd:0 3rd:0 Ran:1
Pre2000 - 1st:5 2nd:2 3rd:0 Ran:10
Win Prizemoney £22,717 *Total Prizemoney* £24,305

Wins	1999	Aug	Yarmou	(FRM)	C	10.1f		70	
	1999	Jly	Newmar	(G-F)	C	10f		74	
	1999	Jly	Lingfi	(G-F)	H	11.5f	70	72	
	1999	May	Newbur	(G-F)	C	10f		73	
	1998	Oct	Newmar	(GD)	S	7f		78	<

2000 AW 0-1: (12f) (Equi)
Strong, above-average gelding, effective 10 to 12f, best at 10f, acts on g-f to frm, best on frm, has worn blinkers.
**Miss K M George [2-14] Exterior Profiles Ltd (from P F I Cole [5-10] Aug 1999).*

LUANSHYA BHB 65f RR 67f 3560[P]
4 b f First Trump - Blues Indigo (Music Boy) 6.8f **(57)**
Form - 45400034P
Record 2000 - 1st:0 2nd:0 3rd:1 Ran:9
Pre2000 - 1st:1 2nd:3 3rd:2 Ran:14
Win Prizemoney £2,882 *Total Prizemoney* £11,157
Wins * 1999 May Catter (FRM) 6f 79 <
2000 Turf 0-9: (6f 5, 7f 4) (g-s, gd, g-f, frm 5, hrd)
Scopey, average filly, effective 6f, acts on g-f to frm, best on frm. Turf high 67. Inconsistent. **R M Whitaker [1-23] The PBT Group.*

LUBOHENRIK (IRE) BHB 30f RR ?f 5191[5]
3 b f Perugino (USA) - Febian John (FR) (Shafaraz (FR))
Form - 005
Record 2000 - 1st:0 2nd:0 3rd:0 Ran:3
Pre2000 - 1st:0 2nd:0 3rd:0 Ran:4
2000 Turf 0-3: (8f 2, 12f) (gd 2, frm)
Leggy, very poor filly, has worn blinkers. (began Aug).
**I Semple [0-7] The Friar Tuck Racing Club.*

LUCAYAN BEACH BHB 45f49a RR 28f 49a 2934[8]
6 gr g Cyrano de Bergerac 7.3f **(58)** - Mrs Gray (Red Sunset) 8.2f **(63)**
Form - 030008
Record 2000 - 1st:0 2nd:0 3rd:0 Ran:4
Pre2000 - 1st:1 2nd:1 3rd:2 Ran:15
Win Prizemoney £2,866 *Total Prizemoney* £5,045
Wins 1998 Jly Kempto (G-F) C 6f 68 <
2000 Turf 0-4: (6f, 8f 2, 10f) (gd 2, frm, hrd)
Fair gelding, effective 8f, - acts on Equi, has worn blinkers. Turf high 28.
**J W Mullins [0-4] Don Hazzard (from B Gubby [1-15] Nov 1999).*

LUCAYAN CHIEF (IRE) BHB 100f RR 91f 4712a[3]
2 b c With Approval (CAN) 8.7f **(80)** - Little Lady Leah (USA) (Shareef Dancer (USA)) 9.9f **(73)**
Form - 51323
Record 2000 - 1st:1 2nd:1 3rd:2 Ran:5
Win Prizemoney £3,285 *Total Prizemoney* £11,908
Wins * **2000** Aug Beverl (GD) 7.5f 83 <
2000 Turf 1-5: (7f 1-3, 8f 2) (sft 2, gd 1-1, frm 2)
Useful colt. Turf high 91 (began Jly) - 3rd of 6 to Okawango (20 Spt Chantilly 8f sft RF 4712a) - also 1st of 9 from Wainak (1 Aug Beverley RF 3268). He developed into a smart juvenile, running his best race when third behind Okawango in the Group 3 Prix la Rochette at Chantilly in September. Likely to stay beyond a mile, he handles any ground and is game.
**S P C Woods [1-5] Lucayan Stud.*

LUCEFER (IRE) BHB 83f RR 96f 5073[2]
2 b g Lycius (USA) 8.8f **(71)** - Maharani (USA) (Red Ransom (USA))
Form - 02022
Record 2000 - 1st:0 2nd:3 3rd:0 Ran:5
Win Prizemoney £0 *Total Prizemoney* £2,877
2000 Turf 0-5: (7f 5) (g-s 3, g-f, frm)
Very useful gelding. Turf high 96 (began Aug) - 2nd of 12 to Lots of Love (28 Aug Newcastle 7f g-s RF 4043).
**G C H Chung [0-5] M O'Leary.*

LUCIDO (IRE) BHB 111f RR 118f 2689[6]
4 b c Royal Academy (USA) 7.8f **(77)** - Lady Ambassador (General Assembly (USA)) 10f **(68)**
Form - 546
Record 2000 - 1st:0 2nd:0 3rd:0 Ran:3
Pre2000 - 1st:3 2nd:0 3rd:2 Ran:8
Win Prizemoney £44,547 *Total Prizemoney* £70,585

Wins	* 1999	May	Lingfi	(G-F)	G3	11.5f	120	<
	* 1999	Apr	Newbur	(G-F)		10f	105+	
	* 1998	Spt	Salisb	(HVY)		8f	82	

2000 Turf 0-3: (12f 3) (gd 2, g-f)
Light-framed, high-class colt, effective 11 to 12f, best at 12f, acts on g-f, best on gd. Turf high 115 (1st run) - 5th of 11 to Blueprint (5 May Newmarket 12f g-f RF 1047). Inconsistent. Injured in the 1999 Derby (started second favourite), he has struggled to rediscover his form and ran poorly when last seen at Newmarket in July. He is one to watch until showing definite signs of a recovery.
**J L Dunlop [3-11] Mrs H Focke.*

LUCILLE (IRE) RR 63f 5098[16]
2 b f Sadler's Wells (USA) 11.3f **(87)** - Lady Ambassador (General Assembly (USA)) 10f **(68)**
Form - 0
Record 2000 - 1st:0 2nd:0 3rd:0 Ran:1
2000 Turf 0-1: (8f) (gd)
Currently average filly. **J L Dunlop [0-1] Mrs H Focke.*

LUCKS LUVLY RR 4149[14]
2 ch f Clantime 6.6f **(57)** - Blueit (FR) (Bold Lad (IRE)) 8.4f **(68)**
Form - 0
Record 2000 - 1st:0 2nd:0 3rd:0 Ran:1
2000 Turf 0-1: (5f) (gd)
Currently very poor filly. **N Tinkler [0-1] Philip Grundy.*

LUCKY ARCHER BHB 67f RR 64df 2260[9]
7 b g North Briton 8.2f **(53)** - Preobrajenska (Double Form) 7.3f **(58)**
Form - 80
Record 2000 - 1st:0 2nd:0 3rd:0 Ran:2
Pre2000 - 1st:5 2nd:4 3rd:3 Ran:36
Win Prizemoney £25,451 *Total Prizemoney* £32,733

Wins	* 1999	Aug	Bath	(HRD)	H	8f	71	73	<
	* 1999	Jun	Yarmou	(GD)	H	8f	70	71	
	* 1998	Jun	Carlis	(G-S)	H	8f	64	71	
	* 1998	May	Yarmou	(FRM)	H	7f	55	67	
	1998	May	Nottin	(FRM)	H	8.2f	55	59	

2000 Turf 0-2: (7f, 8f) (g-f, frm)
Average gelding, effective 7 to 8f, best at 8f, acts on gd to frm, best on frm, has worn blinkers. Turf high 60. Consistent.
**J M Bradley [5-24] The Parishioners (from C E Brittain [0-14] Oct 1996).*

LUCKY ARROW RR 65f 1333[10]
3 b f Indian Ridge 7.6f **(74)** - Tide of Fortune (Soviet Star (USA))
Form - 0
Record 2000 - 1st:0 2nd:0 3rd:0 Ran:1
2000 Turf 0-1: (10f) (g-f)
Scopey, currently average filly.
**A C Stewart [0-1] Paterson, Costain & Woodward.*

LUCKY BEA BHB 28f RR 4922[11]
7 b g Lochnager 6.9f **(50)** - Knocksharry (Palm Track) 9.8f **(50)**
Form - 0
Record 2000 - 1st:0 2nd:0 3rd:0 Ran:1
Pre2000 - 1st:1 2nd:3 3rd:5 Ran:30
Win Prizemoney £3,631 *Total Prizemoney* £8,297
Wins 1996 May Newcas (GD) H 8f 54 56 <

2000 AW 0-1: (7f) (Equi)
Little account gelding, has worn blinkers.
**K A Ryan [0-1] Steve Ryan (from G Holmes [0-2] Spt 1998).*

LUCKY BREAK (IRE) BHB 67f RR 62+f 4432[13]

2 ch c Brief Truce (USA) 9.1f **(73)** - Paradise Forum (Prince Sabo) 7.2f **(62)**
Form - 070
Record 2000 - 1st:0 2nd:0 3rd:0 Ran:3
2000 Turf 0-3: (6f 3) (frm 3)
Currently average colt. Turf high 62 (began Jly).
**C A Horgan [0-3] Mrs B Sumner.*

LUCKY CHRYSTAL (IRE) RR 65f 3264[5]

2 b c Lucky Guest - Chrysilia (USA) (Tilt Up (USA)) 9.8f **(55)**
Form - 5
Record 2000 - 1st:0 2nd:0 3rd:0 Ran:1
2000 Turf 0-1: (7f) (gd)
Currently average colt. **E A L Dunlop [0-1] Anamoine Ltd.*

LUCKY COVE BHB 47f50a RR 50f 50a 5057[7]

4 gr g Lugana Beach 7f **(63)** - Port Na Blath (On Your Mark) 7.7f **(58)**
Form - 0700000047
Record 2000 - 1st:0 2nd:0 3rd:0 Ran:10
Pre2000 - 1st:0 2nd:1 3rd:4 Ran:11
Win Prizemoney £0 *Total Prizemoney* £2,788
2000 Turf 0-9: (5f 7, 6f 2) (sft, gd 4, g-f, frm 3) 2000 AW 0-1: (6f) (Fibr)
Leggy, fair gelding, effective 5f, acts on gd, has worn blinkers. Turf high 50. Inconsistent.
**N Tinkler [0-2] Mrs Christine Cawley (from Don Enrico Incisa [0-8] Aug 2000).*

LUCKY DREAM (FR) RR 116f 2982a[3]

6 b h Homme de Loi (IRE) - Lady Of The House (Habitat) 9.4f **(70)**
Form - 553
2000 Turf 0-3: (12f, 13f, 16f) (sft, g-s, gd)
High-class horse, effective 12 to 15f, acts on sft to gd, best on gd. Turf high 116 - 5th of 6 giving 8lb to Daring Miss (11 Jun Chantilly 12f gd RF 2006a). Consistent. He is tough and durable, but needs to be ridden patiently and probably hit the front too soon when third in a Group Two at Maisons-Laffitte during July.
**H-A Pantall in FR [2-11] Mme C Dutertre-Hallope.*

LUCKY GITANO (IRE) BHB 85f RR 87+f 5317[1]

4 b br g Lucky Guest - April Wind (Windjammer (USA)) 7f **(59)**
Form - 00246411
Record 2000 - 1st:2 2nd:1 3rd:0 Ran:8
Pre2000 - 1st:0 2nd:2 3rd:2 Ran:5
Win Prizemoney £7,946 *Total Prizemoney* £12,419
Wins * 2000 Nov Doncas (HVY) H 7f 77 87+ <
*** 2000** Oct Redcar (SFT) H 8f 70 75+
2000 Turf 2-8: (7f 1-1, 8f 1-3, 10f 4) (sft 1-1, g-s, gd 1-2, g-f 2, frm 2)
Workmanlike, useful gelding, effective 7 to 9f, acts on sft to g-f. Turf high 87 - 1st of 22 giving 5lb to Topton (4 Nov Doncaster RF 5317). Still a maiden, he showed ability early on in '99, but was off the track for over a year until reappearing in May. Gradually found his form, taking handicaps at Redcar and Doncaster late in the season. **J L Dunlop [2-13] Anamoine Ltd.*

LUCKY HETTIE RR 38f 5131[11]

2 b f Alzao (USA) 9.8f **(73)** - Halo's Charm (USA) (Halo (USA)) 10.6f **(75)**
Form - 0
Record 2000 - 1st:0 2nd:0 3rd:0 Ran:1
2000 Turf 0-1: (6f) (sft)
Currently moderate filly. **C R Egerton [0-1] Alan Stubbs.*

LUCKY JUDGE BHB 63f58a RR 63f 58a 5082[3]

3 b g Saddlers' Hall (IRE) 10.5f **(65)** - Lady Lydia (Ela-Mana-Mou) 10.1f **(70)**
Form - 57464233
Record 2000 - 1st:0 2nd:1 3rd:2 Ran:8
Pre2000 - 1st:0 2nd:0 3rd:0 Ran:1
Win Prizemoney £0 *Total Prizemoney* £2,136
2000 Turf 0-8: (9f, 11f 2, 12f, 14f, 16f 3) (hvy, gd, g-f 3, frm 3)
Small, average gelding, effective 12 to 16f, best at 16f, acts on g-f to frm, best on frm, prefers tight tracks. Turf high 63. Consistent.
**W W Haigh [0-9] Mrs I Gibson.*

LUCKY LADY BHB 90f RR 90f 2683[2]

3 ch f Nashwan (USA) 10.3f **(79)** - Jet Ski Lady (USA) (Vaguely Noble) 10.1f **(72)**
Form - 212
Record 2000 - 1st:1 2nd:2 3rd:0 Ran:3
Win Prizemoney £3,737 *Total Prizemoney* £7,079
Wins * 2000 Jun Chepst (FRM) 12.1f 88 <
2000 Turf 1-3: (11f, 12f 1-2) (gd 2, g-f 1-1)
Lengthy, currently useful filly. Turf high 90 - 2nd of 6 giving 1lb to Cool Investment (10 Jly Windsor 12f gd RF 2683) - also 1st of 4 from Metronome (16 Jun Chepstow RF 2010). Out of a mare that ran away with the Oaks in 1991, she shapes like a thorough stayer and is worth a try beyond middle-distances.
**Sir Michael Stoute [1-3] Maktoum Al Maktoum.*

LUCKY MELODY BHB 30f30a RR 41f 30a 461[8]

3 b c Suluk (USA) - Impromptu Melody (IRE) **(46f)** (Mac's Imp (USA))
Form - 0888
Record 2000 - 1st:0 2nd:0 3rd:0 Ran:4
Pre2000 - 1st:0 2nd:0 3rd:2 Ran:4
Win Prizemoney £0 *Total Prizemoney* £504
2000 AW 0-4: (7f, 8f 3) (Equi, Fibr 3)
Moderate colt, has worn blinkers. AW high 26. Inconsistent.
**B S Rothwell [0-8] S P Hudson.*

LUCKY RASCAL (IRE) BHB 59a RR 59f 197[6]

4 b g Indian Ridge 7.6f **(74)** - Chesnut Tree (USA) (Shadeed (USA)) 8.2f **(70)**
Form - 6
Record 2000 - 1st:0 2nd:0 3rd:0 Ran:1
Pre2000 - 1st:0 2nd:0 3rd:0 Ran:7
Win Prizemoney £0 *Total Prizemoney* £214
2000 AW 0-1: (6f) (Fibr)
Unfurnished, fair gelding, has worn blinkers. Becoming disappointing. **D Nicholls [0-1] V Greaves (from B Hanbury [0-7] Jly 1999).*

LUCKY'S SON (IRE) BHB 46f37a RR 44f 37a 4116[16]

3 gr g Lucky Guest - April Wind (Windjammer (USA)) 7f **(59)**
Form - 00802160
Record 2000 - 1st:1 2nd:1 3rd:0 Ran:8
Win Prizemoney £4,137 *Total Prizemoney* £4,818
Wins 2000 Aug Thirsk (GD) H 6f 42 43 <
2000 Turf 1-8: (6f 1-4, 7f, 8f 2, 10f) (gd 2, g-f, frm 1-5)
Scopey, moderate gelding, effective 6f, acts on g-f to frm, best on frm. Turf high 44 - 6th of 11 getting 18lb from Kinsman (16 Aug Epsom 6f g-f RF 3695) - also 1st of 19 getting 3lb from Megs Pearl (4 Aug Thirsk RF 3380).
**P Howling [0-2] Arkland International (UK) Ltd (from J L Dunlop [1-6] Aug 2000).*

LUCKY STAR BHB 50f60a RR 58df 60a 2637[10]

3 b f Emarati (USA) 6.6f **(63)** - Child Star (FR) **(32f 39a)** (Bellypha) 9.8f **(73)**
Form - 6131470
Record 2000 - 1st:2 2nd:0 3rd:1 Ran:6
Pre2000 - 1st:0 2nd:0 3rd:0 Ran:4
Win Prizemoney £4,992 *Total Prizemoney* £5,365
Wins * 2000 *Mar Wolver (STD) 8.5f 58*
*** 2000** *Jan Lingfi (STD) H 7f 57 61* <
2000 Turf 0-2: (8f, 12f) (frm, hrd) 2000 AW 2-4: (7f 1-3, 8f 1-1) (Equi 1-2, Fibr 1-2)
Unfurnished, average filly, effective 7 to 8f, - acts on AW, has worn blinkers, likes left handed tracks, likes tight tracks. Turf high 45. AW high 61 (1st run) - 1st of 9 giving 9lb to Croeso Adref (8 Jan Lingfield RF 0048) - also 1st of 9 getting 1lb from For Heavens Sake (4 Mar Wolverhampton RF 0407). Becoming disappointing.
**D Marks [2-10] D Marks.*

LUCKY SWEEP BHB 69f RR 71f 1350[8]

3 ch c Cadeaux Genereux 7.9f **(76)** - Phantom Gold **(115f)** (Machiavellian (USA))
Form - 58
Record 2000 - 1st:0 2nd:0 3rd:0 Ran:2
Pre2000 - 1st:0 2nd:0 3rd:0 Ran:2
Win Prizemoney £0 *Total Prizemoney* £237

2000 Turf 0-2: (7f, 8f) (sft, gd)
Workmanlike, above-average colt. Turf high 71.
R Hannon [0-4] The Queen.

LUCKY UNO BHB 33f **RR 29f** 5311[8]
4 b g Rock City 8.8f **(62)** - Free Skip (Free State) 8.7f **(61)**
Form - 00608
Record 2000 - 1st:0 2nd:0 3rd:0 Ran:5
Pre2000 - 1st:0 2nd:0 3rd:1 Ran:9
Win Prizemoney £0 *Total Prizemoney* £533
2000 Turf 0-5: (5f, 6f, 10f 2, 15f) (sft, gd, frm 3)
Scopey, little account gelding, has worn blinkers. Turf high 29.
C Smith [0-14] H G Norman.

LUCY MARIELLA BHB 61f **RR 62f** 1588[14]
4 b f Mystiko (USA) 7.7f **(59)** - Deanta in Eirinn (Red Sunset) 8.2f **(63)**
Form - 00
Record 2000 - 1st:0 2nd:0 3rd:0 Ran:2
Pre2000 - 1st:1 2nd:3 3rd:1 Ran:12
Win Prizemoney £3,184 *Total Prizemoney* £6,797
Wins * 1999 May Bright (FRM) H 6f 64 67 <
2000 Turf 0-2: (6f, 7f) (gd, frm)
Average filly, effective 5 to 6f, best at 6f, acts on g-f to hrd, best on g-f, has worn blinkers. Turf high 43.
G A Butler [1-9] Terry Barwick (from J R Arnold [0-5] Oct 1998).

LUCY TUFTY BHB 29f24a **RR 32f 24a** 1880[34]
9 b m Vin St Benet 11.4f **(48)** - Manor Farm Toots (Royalty) 11.4f **(49)**
Form - 0
Record 2000 - 1st:0 2nd:0 3rd:0 Ran:1
Pre2000 - 1st:2 2nd:0 3rd:1 Ran:18
Win Prizemoney £4,974 *Total Prizemoney* £5,448
Wins 1998 Apr Ripon (SFT) SH 12.3f 33 44 <
1996 Nov Folkes (SFT) SH 12f 35 44 <
2000 Turf 0-1: (12f) (frm)
Very moderate mare. Consistent.
G Prodromou [0-18] George Prodromou (from J Pearce [4-47] Jun 1998).

LUDERE (IRE) BHB 37f37a **RR 40f 37a** 3448[1]
5 ch g Desse Zenny (USA) 12f **(53)** - White Jasmin (Jalmood (USA)) 10.1f **(52)**
Form - 41
Record 2000 - 1st:1 2nd:0 3rd:0 Ran:2
Pre2000 - 1st:1 2nd:3 3rd:2 Ran:23
Win Prizemoney £4,178 *Total Prizemoney* £9,946
Wins * 2000 Aug Catter (G-F) S 15.8f 40 <
1998 May Mussel (GD) C 12f 40 <
2000 Turf 1-2: (12f, 16f 1-1) (frm 1-2)
Moderate gelding, effective 12 to 16f, acts on gd to frm, has worn blinkers. Turf high 40 (began Jly) - 1st of 7 giving 5lb to Syrah (8 Aug Catterick RF 3448). Consistent.
B J Llewellyn [1-2] The Trade Import Agency Ltd (from P Monteith [0-14] Jly 1999).

LULLABY BHB 63f **RR 67f** 3616[5]
3 b f Unfuwain (USA) 11.4f **(74)** - Heart's Harmony (Blushing Groom (FR)) 10.3f **(76)**
Form - 3401205
Record 2000 - 1st:1 2nd:1 3rd:1 Ran:7
Pre2000 - 1st:0 2nd:0 3rd:0 Ran:1
Win Prizemoney £3,581 *Total Prizemoney* £5,710
Wins 2000 Jun Newmar (G-F) C 10f 53 <
2000 Turf 1-7: (8f 3, 10f 1-1, 11f, 12f 2) (sft, g-s, gd, g-f 1-2, frm 2)
Neat, average filly, effective 8f, acted on g-s. Turf high 69 (1st run) - 3rd of 15 to Claranet (17 Apr Windsor 8f g-s RF 0754). (DEAD)
Jedd O'Keeffe [0-1] Jonathan Ramsden (from J O'Keeffe [0-2] Jly 2000).

LUMIERE D'ESPOIR (FR) RR 53f 5219[4]
2 br f Saumarez 15.1f **(87)** - Light of Hope (USA) (Lyphard (USA)) 9.9f **(72)**
Form - 04
Record 2000 - 1st:0 2nd:0 3rd:0 Ran:2
Win Prizemoney £0 *Total Prizemoney* £221
2000 Turf 0-2: (7f, 10f) (sft, gd)
Currently fair filly. Turf high 53 (began Spt).
S Dow [0-2] Byerley Bloodstock.

LUMIERE DU SOLEIL BHB 60f **RR 58f** 4386[6]
2 b f Tragic Role (USA) 9.4f **(63)** - Pounelta (Tachypous) 8.6f **(55)**
Form - 576
Record 2000 - 1st:0 2nd:0 3rd:0 Ran:3
2000 Turf 0-3: (6f, 7f 2) (g-s, gd, g-f)
Currently fair filly. Turf high 58 (began Aug).
K A Ryan [0-3] Tony Fawcett.

LUNA FLIGHT BHB 51f45a **RR 56f 45a** 5154[8]
3 b f Ela-Mana-Mou 12.7f **(72)** - Lotus Moon (Shareef Dancer (USA)) 9.9f **(73)**
Form - 55618
Record 2000 - 1st:1 2nd:0 3rd:0 Ran:5
Win Prizemoney £2,716 *Total Prizemoney* £2,716
Wins * 2000 Oct Wolver (STD) H 12f 45 53 <
2000 Turf 0-2: (10f, 12f) (gd, g-f) 2000 AW 1-3: (10f, 12f 1-2) (Equi 2, Fibr 1-1)
Scopey, fair filly. Turf high 56 (began Aug). AW high 53 (began Spt) - 1st of 12 getting 18lb from Tufty Hopper (20 Oct Wolverhampton RF 5119).
M Johnston [1-5] J Godfrey.

LUNAJAZ BHB 30f35a **RR 35df 35a** 1977[12]
3 ch g Alhijaz 7.7f **(57)** -Lunagraphe (USA) (Time For A Change (USA))
Form - 57700
Record 2000 - 1st:0 2nd:0 3rd:0 Ran:5
Pre2000 - 1st:0 2nd:0 3rd:0 Ran:3
2000 Turf 0-2: (7f, 10f) (frm 2) 2000 AW 0-3: (7f, 8f 2) (Equi 3)
Leggy, moderate gelding, has worn blinkers. Turf high 1. AW high 44. Becoming disappointing.
T M Jones [0-8] T M Jones.

LUNALUX BHB 46f **RR 49f** 4768[6]
3 b f Emarati (USA) 6.6f **(63)** - Ragged Moon (Raga Navarro (ITY)) 8f **(64)**
Form - 82470526
Record 2000 - 1st:0 2nd:2 3rd:0 Ran:8
Pre2000 - 1st:0 2nd:0 3rd:1 Ran:10
Win Prizemoney £0 *Total Prizemoney* £1,909
2000 Turf 0-8: (5f 5, 6f 3) (g-s, gd 2, g-f 2, frm 3)
Strong, moderate filly, effective 5f, acts on frm, has worn blinkers (effectively). Turf high 49. Consistent.
C Smith [0-18] Anne Lady Scott.

LUNAR CRYSTAL (IRE) BHB 100f **RR 96f** 5238[8]
2 b c Shirley Heights 12.1f **(76)** - Solar Crystal (IRE) **(97f)** (Alzao (USA)) 7.1f **(68)**
Form - 148
Record 2000 - 1st:1 2nd:0 3rd:0 Ran:3
Win Prizemoney £12,035 *Total Prizemoney* £13,072
Wins * 2000 Spt Ascot (SFT) 7f 85+ <
2000 Turf 1-3: (7f 1-1, 8f, 10f) (sft, g-s 1-2)
Currently very useful colt. Turf high 96 (began Spt). Made a winning debut in soft ground at Ascot and ran respectably in a listed race there next time.
D R C Elsworth [1-3] Michael Poland.

LUNAR LEO BHB 84f **RR 84f** 4965[5]
2 b g Muhtarram (USA) - Moon Mistress **(84f)** (Storm Cat (USA))
Form - 413635
Record 2000 - 1st:1 2nd:0 3rd:2 Ran:6
Win Prizemoney £3,568 *Total Prizemoney* £9,358
Wins * 2000 Jly Warwic (GD) 6.8f 83+ <
2000 Turf 1-6: (6f 3, 7f 1-3) (gd 1-4, g-f, frm)
Decent gelding, effective 6 to 7f, best at 6f, acts on gd to g-f, best on gd. Turf high 84 - 5th of 30 to Goodie Twosues (13 Oct Newmarket 6f gd RF 4965) - also 1st of 12 giving 5lb to April Lee (7 Jly Warwick RF 2610). Made all on his second start at Warwick.
S C Williams [1-6] Bruce Wyatt.

LUNAR LORD BHB 31f27a **RR 37f 27a** 5244[7]
4 b g Elmaamul (USA) 8.1f **(70)** - Cache (Bustino) 10.4f **(64)**
Form - 0042022448337
Record 2000 - 1st:0 2nd:3 3rd:2 Ran:13
Pre2000 - 1st:0 2nd:0 3rd:0 Ran:7
Win Prizemoney £0 *Total Prizemoney* £2,750
2000 Turf 0-11: (10f, 11f, 12f 8, 14f) (g-s 2, gd 4, g-f 2, frm 3) 2000 AW 0-2: (12f 2) (Fibr 2)

Small, very moderate gelding, effective 10 to 12f, best at 12f, acts on g-s to frm. Turf high 37 - 4th of 10 giving 13lb to Beauchamp Magic (25 Jly Brighton 12f frm RF 3085). AW high 6. Consistent.
**J S Moore [0-20] Alex Gorrie.*

LUNASALT (IRE) RR 91f
4132a[1]
2 b c Salse (USA) 10.9f **(71)** -Lunafairy (FR) **(107f)** (Always Fair (USA))
Form - 31
2000 Turf 1-2: (6f, 7f 1-1) (g-f 1-2)
Currently useful colt. Turf high 91 (began Aug) - 1st of 5 from Dayglow Dancer (25 Aug Deauville RF 4132a). He seemed to appreciate a step-up to seven furlongs when winning a Listed heat at Deauville in August and is a useful prospect.
**A Fabre in FR [1-2] J-L Lagardere.*

LUNCH PARTY BHB 59f57a RR 63f 57a
4627[9]
8 b g Beveled (USA) 6.9f **(64)** - Crystal Sprite (Crystal Glitters (USA)) 11.3f **(79)**
Form - 40610
Record 2000 - 1st:1 2nd:0 3rd:0 Ran:5
Pre2000 - 1st:8 2nd:3 3rd:1 Ran:33
Win Prizemoney £27,613 *Total Prizemoney* £31,826

Wins								
* 2000	Aug	Catter	(G-F)	H	7f	54	58	
1999	Jun	Thirsk	(G-F)	H	7f	62	64	<
1999	May	Catter	(FRM)		7f		62	
1998	Aug	Catter	(G-F)	H	7f	60	63	
1998	May	Catter	(G-S)	H	7f	52	57	
1998	May	Mussel	(G-F)	H	7.1f	47	49	
1997	Nov	Mussel	(G-S)	H	8f	40	49	
1997	Spt	Yarmou	(FRM)	H	7f	38	42	
1996	May	Thirsk	(G-F)	S	7f		57+	

2000 Turf 1-5: (7f 1-4, 8f) (gd 2, frm 1-3)
Average gelding, effective 7f, acts on gd to frm, best on frm, prefers left handed tracks, favours tight tracks, excels at Thirsk and Catterick. Turf high 58 - 1st of 18 giving 11lb to Thatched (8 Aug Catterick RF 3449). Inconsistent.
**A Berry [1-5] S Aitken (from J Berry [5-20] Oct 1999).*

LUNEVISION (FR) BHB 70f RR 69f
5203a[8]
2 b f Solid Illusion (USA) - Lumiere Celeste (FR) (Always Fair (USA))
Form - 3238
Record 2000 - 1st:0 2nd:1 3rd:2 Ran:4
Win Prizemoney £0 *Total Prizemoney* £2,446
2000 Turf 0-4: (5f, 6f 2, 8f) (hvy, gd, g-f, frm)
Average filly. Turf high 69 (began Aug). **H J Collingridge [0-4].*

LU RAVI (USA) RR
5325a[5]
5 b m A P Indy (USA) - At The Half (USA) (Seeking the Gold (USA))
Form - 5
2000 AW 0-1: (9f) (Dirt)
Currently very useful. **C Bowman in USA [0-1] Yoshio Fujita.*

LURINA (IRE) RR 78+f
5309[2]
2 b f Lure (USA) - Alligatrix (USA) (Alleged (USA)) 10f **(76)**
Form - 2
Record 2000 - 1st:0 2nd:1 3rd:0 Ran:1
Win Prizemoney £0 *Total Prizemoney* £1,025
2000 Turf 0-1: (7f) (g-s)
Currently above-average filly. (1st run) - 2nd of 18 getting 5lb from Jungle Lion (3 Nov Doncaster 7f g-s RF 5309).
**J H M Gosden [0-1] Mrs Shirley Taylor.*

LUSONG (IRE) BHB 55f54a RR 52f 54a
3171[15]
3 ch c Fayruz 6.6f **(63)** - Mildred Anne (IRE) (Thatching) 8f **(66)**
Form - 226340550
Record 2000 - 1st:0 2nd:2 3rd:1 Ran:9
Win Prizemoney £0 *Total Prizemoney* £2,691
2000 Turf 0-6: (6f 5, 7f) (g-f 2, frm 4) 2000 AW 0-3: (5f, 6f 2) (Equi 2, Fibr)
Unfurnished, fair colt, effective 6f, acts on frm. Turf high 66 - 4th of 21 getting 11lb from Castle Sempill (10 Apr Windsor 6f frm RF 0655). AW high 57. Consistent.
**R Hannon [0-9] Taylor Homer Racing.*

LUTINE BELL BHB 20f RR
224[10]
5 b g Fairy King (USA) 7.7f **(75)** - Bell Toll (High Line) 10.3f **(70)**
Form - 70
Record 2000 - 1st:0 2nd:0 3rd:0 Ran:2
Pre2000 - 1st:0 2nd:0 3rd:0 Ran:3
2000 AW 0-2: (13f, 15f) (Equi, Fibr)
Very poor gelding.
**D T Thom [0-2] D T Thom (from J E Banks [0-3] Oct 1998).*

LUVADUCK BHB 56f RR 3f
2103[13]
4 b f Pursuit of Love 9.5f **(69)** - Pillowing (Good Times (ITY)) 6.6f **(54)**
Form - 000
Record 2000 - 1st:0 2nd:0 3rd:0 Ran:3
Pre2000 - 1st:0 2nd:0 3rd:0 Ran:4
Win Prizemoney £0 *Total Prizemoney* £204
2000 Turf 0-3: (7f, 8f, 10f) (gd 2, frm)
Workmanlike, very poor filly, effective 8f, acts on frm, has worn blinkers.
**C G Cox [0-4] Mrs Zara Campbell Harris & TH Luckock (from M J Heaton-Ellis [0-3] May 1999).*

LUVLY TIMES RR 27f
847[9]
2 ch g Timeless Times (USA) 6.1f **(56)** - Merry Molly **(22f)** (Deploy)
Form - 00
Record 2000 - 1st:0 2nd:0 3rd:0 Ran:2
2000 Turf 0-2: (5f 2) (sft, gd)
Currently little account gelding. Turf high 27.
**M W Easterby [0-2] T R Beston.*

LUXOR BHB 85f RR 89f
5133[10]
3 ch c Grand Lodge (USA) - Escrime (USA) (Sharpen Up) 8.3f **(67)**
Form - 421870
Record 2000 - 1st:1 2nd:1 3rd:0 Ran:6
Win Prizemoney £5,050 *Total Prizemoney* £6,263

Wins						
* 2000	Jun	Newmar	(G-F)	10f	89	<

2000 Turf 1-6: (9f, 10f 1-4, 12f) (sft, gd 2, frm 1-3)
Leggy, useful colt, effective 10f, acts on frm. Turf high 89 - 1st of 9 from Executive Order (23 Jun Newmarket RF 2229). Unraced at two, he got off the mark in a Newmarket maiden in June, but finished last on his handicap debut at the same track next time, though he did meet a bit of interference. Suited by forcing tactics.
**H R A Cecil [1-6] Exors of the late Lord Howard de Walden.*

LV GIRL (IRE) BHB 49f42a RR 49f 42a
465[12]
4 ch f Mukaddamah (USA) 7.6f **(74)** - Penny Fan **(34f)** (Nomination) 7f **(60)**
Form - 70
Record 2000 - 1st:0 2nd:0 3rd:0 Ran:2
Pre2000 - 1st:0 2nd:1 3rd:0 Ran:15
Win Prizemoney £0 *Total Prizemoney* £1,617
2000 AW 0-2: (7f, 8f) (Fibr 2)
Light-framed, moderate filly, effective 6 to 8f, acts on sft to frm, has worn blinkers. AW high 40. She showed promise on her hurdling debut, but looks as if she will need a sound surface to show her best. **G B Balding [0-20] Mrs C A Richardson.*

LYCHEEL RR 70f
5066[10]
2 ch c Lycius (USA) 8.8f **(71)** - Talon D'Aiguille (USA) (Big Spruce (USA)) 11f **(71)**
Form - 0
Record 2000 - 1st:0 2nd:0 3rd:0 Ran:1
2000 Turf 0-1: (8f) (g-s)
Currently above-average colt.
**W R Muir [0-1] Mrs E Clowes And Mrs D Edginton.*

LYCIAN (IRE) BHB 64f70a RR 66f 70a
4645[4]
5 b g Lycius (USA) 8.8f **(71)** - Perfect Time (IRE) (Dance of Life (USA)) 7f **(66)**
Form - 67347114
Record 2000 - 1st:2 2nd:0 3rd:1 Ran:8
Pre2000 - 1st:5 2nd:4 3rd:2 Ran:22
Win Prizemoney £28,143 *Total Prizemoney* £35,064

Wins								
* 2000	Spt	Yarmou	(G-F)	H	10.1f	56	66	
* 2000	Spt	Leices	(G-F)	H	10f	56	66	
* 1999	Jun	Goodwo	(G-F)	H	9f	56	60	
* 1999	*Jan*	*Lingfi*	*(STD)*	*H*	*8f*	*63*	*70*	<
* 1998	*Dec*	*Lingfi*	*(STD)*	*H*	*8f*	*58*	*63*	
* 1998	Jly	Bright	(G-F)	H	8f	52	57	
* 1998	May	Bath	(G-F)	H	8f	47	48	

2000 Turf 2-8: (8f 3, 10f 2-5) (g-f 3, frm 2-5)

Above-average gelding, effective 8 to 10f, best at 8f, acts on g-f to frm - acts on Equi, likes tight tracks, excels at Lingfield. Turf high 66 - 1st of 15 getting 18lb from Krispin (13 Spt Yarmouth RF 4380) - also 1st of 18 getting 17lb from Amrak Ajeeb (5 Spt Leicester RF 4220).
**J A R Toller [7-26] A Ilsley (from Sir Mark Prescott [0-4] Oct 1997).*

LYCIAT SPARKLE (IRE) BHB 25f **RR** 4998[10]
2 b g Lycius (USA) 8.8f **(71)** - Benguiat (FR) (Exceller (USA)) 12.5f **(74)**
Form - 0
Record 2000 - 1st:0 2nd:0 3rd:0 Ran:1
2000 Turf 0-1: (6f) (g-s)
Currently little account gelding.
**Mrs G S Rees [0-1] The Most Wanted Partnership.*

LYCITUS (IRE) RR 113f 4418a[5]
3 b c Lycius (USA) 8.8f **(71)** - Royal Lorna (USA) (Val de L'Orne (FR)) 12f **(75)**
Form - 15
2000 Turf 1-2: (12f, 13f 1-1) (gd 1-2)
Currently Group-class colt, always wears blinkers. Turf high 110 - also 1st of 5 from Epitre (28 Jun Chantilly RF 2577a). He looked to have a bright future when winning a Group 3 at Chantilly during June, but was found out when only fifth in the Prix Niel. An imposing individual, he could improve in 2001 and may stay beyond middle-distances. **F Doumen in FR [1-2].*

LYDIA'S LOOK (IRE) BHB 47f55a **RR 37f 55a** 4276[15]
3 b f Distant View (USA) - Mrs Croesus (USA) (Key To The Mint (USA)) 9.4f **(75)**
Form - 54108000
Record 2000 - 1st:1 2nd:0 3rd:0 Ran:8
Win Prizemoney £2,743 *Total Prizemoney* £2,958
Wins * 2000 *Mar Southw (STD) 5f 54* <
2000 Turf 0-2: (5f 2)(g-f, frm) 2000 AW 1-6: (5f 1-2, 6f 2, 7f, 8f)(Fibr 1-6)
Rangy, fair filly, effective 5f, - acts on Fibr. Turf high 37 (began Aug). AW high 54 - 1st of 8 from United Passion (27 Mar Southwell RF 0513). **T J Etherington [1-8] Callers And Clerks.*

LYMOND (GER) RR 107f 4951a[3]
5 b h Bakharoff (USA) - La Lyra (Slip Anchor) 9.8f **(73)**
Form - 33
2000 Turf 0-2: (8f, 9f) (sft, gd)
Currently Pattern-class colt. Turf high 107 (began Jly) - 3rd of 11 giving 6lb to Peppercorn (8 Oct Dusseldorf 9f sft RF 4951a).
**H Remmert in GER [0-2] Gestut Simmenach.*

LYNA RR 57f 3621[7]
2 b f Slip Anchor 12.7f **(75)** - Sarmatia (USA) (Danzig (USA)) 8.4f **(76)**
Form - 7
Record 2000 - 1st:0 2nd:0 3rd:0 Ran:1
2000 Turf 0-1: (7f) (frm)
Currently fair filly.
**J L Dunlop [0-1] Exors of the late Lord Howard de Walden.*

LYNTON LAD BHB 54f44a **RR 53f 44a** 5086[9]
8 b g Superpower 6.6f **(58)** - House Maid (Habitat) 9.4f **(70)**
Form - 6600100500
Record 2000 - 1st:1 2nd:0 3rd:0 Ran:10
Pre2000 - 1st:3 2nd:5 3rd:2 Ran:29
Win Prizemoney £14,335 *Total Prizemoney* £26,367
Wins * 2000 Jly Pontef (G-F) H 8f 55 56
* 1999 May Ayr (GD) H 8f 57 56
2000 Turf 1-10: (7f 5, 8f 1-5) (hvy, sft 2, gd 2, g-f 2, frm 1-2, hrd)
Fair gelding, effective 8f, acts on gd to frm, best on gd, has worn blinkers, likes left handed tracks, prefers tight tracks. Turf high 56 - 1st of 13 giving 19lb to Kestral (21 Jly Pontefract RF 3012).
**E J Alston [2-16] Miss Kim Jones (from C P E Brooks [0-20] Jly 1997).*

LYONETTE (IRE) RR 4222[1]
2 br f Royal Academy (USA) 7.8f **(77)** - Inanna (Persian Bold) 9.3f **(66)**
Form - 1
Record 2000 - 1st:1 2nd:0 3rd:0 Ran:1
Win Prizemoney £3,055 *Total Prizemoney* £3,055
Wins * 2000 Spt Lingfi (G-F) 7f 82+ <
2000 Turf 1-1: (7f 1-1) (frm 1-1)
Currently very poor filly. (1st run) - 1st of 12 from Annatto (5 Spt Lingfield RF 4222). **J Noseda [1-1] Dr T A Ryan.*

LYRICAL LEGACY (IRE) BHB 37f **RR 38f** 1960[16]
3 ch f Common Grounds 8.1f **(66)** - Lyric Junction (IRE) (Classic Secret (USA))
Form - 000
Record 2000 - 1st:0 2nd:0 3rd:0 Ran:3
Pre2000 - 1st:0 2nd:0 3rd:0 Ran:3
2000 Turf 0-3: (5f, 6f, 7f) (gd 2, frm)
Neat, very moderate filly, has worn blinkers. Turf high 38.
**A P Jarvis [0-6] Mrs Ann Jarvis.*

LYSANDER'S QUEST (IRE) BHB 80f **RR 74f** 4752[6]
2 br c King's Theatre (IRE) - Haramayda (FR) (Doyoun) 9f **(69)**
Form - 456
Record 2000 - 1st:0 2nd:0 3rd:0 Ran:3
Win Prizemoney £0 *Total Prizemoney* £506
2000 Turf 0-3: (7f 2, 8f) (g-s, g-f, frm)
Currently above-average colt. Turf high 74 (began Aug).
**L MontagueHall [0-3] Mrs E N Nield.*

LYSANDROS (IRE) BHB 70f73a **RR 72f 73a** 168[5]
6 b g Lycius (USA) 8.8f **(71)** - Trojan Relation (Trojan Fen) 8.1f **(62)**
Form - 5
Record 2000 - 1st:0 2nd:0 3rd:0 Ran:1
Pre2000 - 1st:1 2nd:3 3rd:1 Ran:8
Win Prizemoney £3,606 *Total Prizemoney* £8,122
Wins * 1999 *Feb Wolver (STD) H 12f 67 70* <
2000 AW 0-1: (12f) (Fibr)
Above-average gelding. Consistent.
**Noel Chance [1-8] Premier Chance Racing (from J H M Gosden [0-4] Oct 1997).*

MABROOKAH BHB 50f55a **RR 59f 55a** 4812[15]
4 b f Deploy 11.4f **(67)** - Adorable Cherub (USA) (Halo (USA)) 10.6f **(75)**
Form - 50600
Record 2000 - 1st:0 2nd:0 3rd:0 Ran:4
Pre2000 - 1st:0 2nd:1 3rd:0 Ran:6
Win Prizemoney £0 *Total Prizemoney* £1,251
2000 Turf 0-4: (7f, 8f 2, 10f) (g-s, gd, g-f, frm)
Workmanlike, fair filly, effective 8 to 9f, acts on g-s, prefers left handed tracks, prefers tight tracks. Turf high 53 (began Aug).
**K Mahdi [0-10] Hamad Al-Mutawa.*

MABSHUSH (IRE) RR 2231[9]
4 b g Mujtahid (USA) 7.4f **(69)** - Just a Mirage (Green Desert (USA)) 8.6f **(78)**
Form - 80
Record 2000 - 1st:0 2nd:0 3rd:0 Ran:2
2000 Turf 0-2: (10f 2) (frm 2)
Leggy, currently very poor gelding. **J Norton [0-2] J B Thomson.*

MACARA (GER) RR 93f 4955a[3]
2 b f Acatenango (GER) - Midnight Society (USA) (Imp Society (USA))
Form - 3
2000 Turf 0-1: (8f) (sft)
Currently useful filly. (1st run) - 3rd of 12 to Innit (8 Oct San Siro 8f sft RF 4955a). **P Schiergen in GER [0-1] Gestut Fahrhof Stiftung.*

MAC BE LUCKY BHB 73f **RR 77f** 5022[3]
3 b c Magic Ring (IRE) 6.5f **(64)** - Take Heart (Electric) 10.1f **(61)**
Form - 072023
Record 2000 - 1st:0 2nd:2 3rd:1 Ran:6
Pre2000 - 1st:0 2nd:1 3rd:1 Ran:3
Win Prizemoney £0 *Total Prizemoney* £4,155
2000 Turf 0-6: (7f, 8f 3, 10f 2) (g-s 2, gd 3, frm)
Lengthy, above-average colt, effective 7 to 8f, best at 8f, acts on sft to gd, best on g-s. Turf high 77.
**J Noseda [0-9] Michael McDonnell.*

MAC BOBO RR 4568a[3]
2 b c Barathea (IRE) - Almela (IRE) (Akarad (FR)) 9f **(76)**
Form - 3
Record 2000 - 1st:0 2nd:0 3rd:1 Ran:1
Win Prizemoney £0 *Total Prizemoney* £1,562
2000 Turf 0-1: (8f) (gd)

Currently very poor colt - 3rd of 8 to Scabiun (16 Spt San Siro 8f gd RF 4568a). **M Quinlan [0-1].*

MACDUNE (FR) RR 78f 5099[9]
2 b c Machiavellian (USA) 9.8f **(83)** - Sandhill (IRE) **(93f)** (Danehill (USA)) 10f **(72)**
Form - 80
Record 2000 - 1st:0 2nd:0 3rd:0 Ran:2
2000 Turf 0-2: (7f 2) (gd, g-f)
Currently above-average colt. Turf high 78 (began Spt).
**E A L Dunlop [0-2] Patrick Milmo.*

MACHALINI BHB 50f **RR** 3575[10]
7 b g Machiavellian (USA) 9.8f **(83)** - Trescalini (IRE) (Sadler's Wells (USA)) 10f **(76)**
Form - 50
Record 2000 - 1st:0 2nd:0 3rd:0 Ran:2
Pre2000 - 1st:2 2nd:1 3rd:2 Ran:14
Win Prizemoney £10,275 *Total Prizemoney* £12,417
Wins 1997 Apr Listow (G-S) 8f 74
1996 Aug Tralee (Y-S) 7f 76 <
2000 AW 0-2: (15f, 16f) (Fibr 2)
Fair gelding, has worn blinkers. AW high 52 (began Jly). Becoming disappointing.
**R M H Cowell [0-2] & Mrs D A Gamble (from J S Bolger in IRE [2-14] Jun 1997).*

MAC HALL RR 75f 1294a[2]
3 b c Saddlers' Hall (IRE) 10.5f **(65)** - Irish Impulse (USA) (Irish River (FR)) 8.6f **(78)**
Form - 62
Record 2000 - 1st:0 2nd:1 3rd:0 Ran:2
Pre2000 - 1st:0 2nd:0 3rd:1 Ran:1
Win Prizemoney £0 *Total Prizemoney* £4,175
2000 Turf 0-2: (10f, 12f) (hvy, gd)
Currently above-average colt. Turf high 75.
**M Quinlan [0-2] (from M G Quinlan [0-1] Apr 2000).*

MACHE BHB 32f **RR 44f** 3714[8]
3 b g Noble Patriarch 12.2f **(43)** - Shalta (FR) (Targowice (USA)) 11.4f **(70)**
Form - 08
Record 2000 - 1st:0 2nd:0 3rd:0 Ran:2
Pre2000 - 1st:0 2nd:0 3rd:0 Ran:3
2000 Turf 0-2: (10f, 16f) (g-f, frm)
Strong, moderate gelding. Turf high 15.
**R D E Woodhouse [0-4] R D E Woodhouse (from J J Quinn [0-1] Jun 2000).*

MACHIAVELLI BHB 50f **RR 39f** 290[8]
6 b g Machiavellian (USA) 9.8f **(83)** - Forest Blossom (USA) (Green Forest (USA)) 9.9f **(68)**
Form - 588
Record 2000 - 1st:0 2nd:0 3rd:0 Ran:3
Pre2000 - 1st:1 2nd:0 3rd:1 Ran:10
Win Prizemoney £3,615 *Total Prizemoney* £5,118
Wins 1997 Jly Pontef (GD) 12f 87 <
2000 AW 0-3: (13f, 16f 2) (Equi 2, Fibr)
Fair gelding, has worn blinkers. AW high 51. Inconsistent.
**G L Moore [4-20] B V & C J Pennick II (from H R A Cecil [1-6] Spt 1997).*

MACHO UNO (USA) RR 5330a[1]
2 gr f Holy Bull (USA) - Primal Force (USA) (Blushing Groom (USA))
Form - 1
2000 AW 1-1: (9f 1-1) (Dirt 1-1)
High-class colt - 1st of 14 from Point Given (4 Nov Churchill Downs RF 5330a). **J Orseno in USA [1-1] Stronach Stables.*

MACHRIE BAY BHB 77f **RR 88f** 5142[3]
3 b c Emarati (USA) 6.6f **(63)** - Fleeting Rainbow (Rainbow Quest (USA)) 10.4f **(75)**
Form - 32523
Record 2000 - 1st:0 2nd:2 3rd:2 Ran:5
Pre2000 - 1st:0 2nd:0 3rd:1 Ran:3
Win Prizemoney £0 *Total Prizemoney* £3,538
2000 Turf 0-5: (10f, 11f, 12f 3) (sft, g-s 2, gd 2)
Neat, useful colt, effective 8 to 12f, acts on sft to gd. Turf high 88 - 2nd of 7 to Almost Free (24 Apr Newcastle 12f sft RF 0844).
**J L Dunlop [0-8] Mrs Simon Boscawen.*

MACHUDI BHB 52f47a **RR 55f 47a** 1353[10]
3 b f Bluebird (USA) 7.9f **(71)** - Machaera (Machiavellian (USA))
Form - 6060
Record 2000 - 1st:0 2nd:0 3rd:0 Ran:4
Pre2000 - 1st:0 2nd:0 3rd:0 Ran:1
2000 Turf 0-2: (7f, 8f) (hvy, frm) 2000 AW 0-2: (7f 2) (Fibr 2)
Lengthy, fair filly. Turf high 55. AW high 41.
**B A McMahon [0-5] Barouche Stud Ltd.*

MACKEM BEAT RR 26f 3244[7]
2 ch f Aragon 7.7f **(58)** - Fancy Flight (FR) (Arctic Tern (USA)) 8.9f **(69)**
Form - 05587
Record 2000 - 1st:0 2nd:0 3rd:0 Ran:5
2000 Turf 0-3: (5f, 6f, 7f) (gd 2, frm) 2000 AW 0-2: (5f, 6f) (Fibr 2)
Little account filly. Turf high 26. AW high 1.
**A J McNae [0-5] The Country Life Partnership.*

MAC'S DREAM (USA) BHB 44f42a **RR 46f 42a** 4925[9]
5 b g Mister Frisky (USA) - Annie's Dream (USA) (Droll Role (USA))
Form - 0005750
Record 2000 - 1st:0 2nd:0 3rd:0 Ran:7
Pre2000 - 1st:0 2nd:1 3rd:1 Ran:17
Win Prizemoney £0 *Total Prizemoney* £1,249
2000 Turf 0-6: (7f 4, 8f, 10f) (gd 3, g-f, frm 2) 2000 AW 0-1: (7f) (Equi)
Moderate gelding, effective 8f, acts on g-f to frm. Turf high 46 (began Jly).
**A W Carroll [0-18] J R Barr (from W Jarvis [0-2] Spt 1999).*

MADAM ALISON BHB 82f **RR 84f** 5133[8]
4 b f Puissance 7.1f **(60)** - Copper Burn (Electric) 10.1f **(61)**
Form - 313150308
Record 2000 - 1st:2 2nd:0 3rd:3 Ran:9
Pre2000 - 1st:2 2nd:2 3rd:1 Ran:13
Win Prizemoney £17,865 *Total Prizemoney* £25,337
Wins * **2000** Jly Windso (G-F) H 8.3f 80 82 <
* **2000** Jun Windso (G-F) 8.3f 81
* 1999 Jun Newmar (G-F) H 8f 72 76
* 1998 Oct Leices (HVY) 6f 71
2000 Turf 2-9: (7f 2, 8f 2-5, 9f, 10f) (sft, g-s, gd, g-f, frm 2-5)
Strong, decent filly, effective 8 to 10f, best at 8f, acts on gd to frm, excels at Windsor and Newmarket. Turf high 83 - 3rd of 19 giving 3lb to Julius (26 Spt Newmarket 10f g-f RF 4645) - also 1st of 10 giving 12lb to Patsy Stone (24 Jly Windsor RF 3083). Returned to form when winning a Windsor classified event in June with a good deal in hand. After a good effort a Newmarket next time, she narrowly took a handicap on the Berkshire track.
**R Hannon [4-22] William Kelly.*

MADAME BUTTERFLY BHB 58f **RR 39f** 3258[14]
2 b f Reprimand 8.2f **(63)** - Mill D'Art (Artaius (USA)) 9f **(69)**
Form - 0
Record 2000 - 1st:0 2nd:0 3rd:0 Ran:1
2000 Turf 0-1: (6f) (frm)
Currently moderate filly. **A J McNae [0-1] Eridge Lodge Racing.*

MADAME GENEREUX BHB 47f **RR 55f** 3380[16]
3 ch f Cadeaux Genereux 7.9f **(76)** - Bright Spells (Salse (USA)) 7.5f **(66)**
Form - 45600
Record 2000 - 1st:0 2nd:0 3rd:0 Ran:5
Pre2000 - 1st:0 2nd:0 3rd:0 Ran:1
Win Prizemoney £0 *Total Prizemoney* £272
2000 Turf 0-5: (6f 4, 7f) (hvy, g-s, g-f, frm 2)
Workmanlike, fair filly. Turf high 55.
**N A Graham [0-6] Association Des Hommes Genereux.*

MADAME JONES (IRE) BHB 43f38a **RR 50f 38a** 5112[18]
5 ch m Lycius (USA) 8.8f **(71)** - Gold Braisim (IRE) (Jareer (USA)) 5.9f **(75)**
Form - 8000050070
Record 2000 - 1st:0 2nd:0 3rd:0 Ran:7
Pre2000 - 1st:3 2nd:1 3rd:3 Ran:21
Win Prizemoney £12,033 *Total Prizemoney* £15,126

Wins * 1998 Spt Cheste (GD) 6.1f 68 <
1998 Jun Goodwo (GD) H 6f 68 68 <
1998 May Nottin (FRM) 6.1f 64
2000 Turf 0-7: (5f 4, 6f, 7f 2) (g-s, gd 2, g-f, frm 2, hrd)
Fair filly, has worn blinkers. Turf high 50 (began Aug).
**A T Murphy [1-13] E H Jones (Paints) Ltd (from M A Buckley [2-11] Spt 1998).*

MADAME ROUX BHB 59f **RR 56f** 4367[9]

2 b f Rudimentary (USA) 8.2f **(66)** - Foreign Mistress (Darshaan) 9.9f **(84)**
Form - 400
Record 2000 - 1st:0 2nd:0 3rd:0 Ran:3
2000 Turf 0-3: (5f 2, 6f) (frm 3)
Currently fair filly. Turf high 56.
**J O Smyth Osbourne [0-3] Ashley Carr Racing (6).*

MADELINE BASSETT (IRE) RR 69f 5098[12]

2 b f Kahyasi 12.9f **(74)** - Impressive Lady (Mr Fluorocarbon) 6f **(55)**
Form - 0
Record 2000 - 1st:0 2nd:0 3rd:0 Ran:1
2000 Turf 0-1: (8f) (gd)
Currently average filly.
**G A Butler [0-1] The Blewbury Hill Partnership.*

MADEMOISELLE PARIS BHB 28f36a **RR 41df 36a** 5077[16]

3 gr f Paris House 5.9f **(64)** - Heather Honey (Insan (USA))
Form - 0400050000
Record 2000 - 1st:0 2nd:0 3rd:0 Ran:6
Pre2000 - 1st:0 2nd:0 3rd:1 Ran:9
Win Prizemoney £0 *Total Prizemoney* £512
2000 Turf 0-3: (6f, 8f, 10f) (g-s, gd 2) 2000 AW 0-3: (6f, 7f, 8f) (Fibr 3)
Light-framed, moderate filly, has worn blinkers. Turf high 8. AW high 33. **A W Carroll [0-15] R T C Racing.*

MAD HABIT BHB 40f **RR 36f** 4631[8]

2 b c Minshaanshu Amad (USA) 11.3f **(53)** - Shady Habitat (Sharpo) 7.7f **(59)**
Form - 008
Record 2000 - 1st:0 2nd:0 3rd:0 Ran:3
2000 Turf 0-3: (7f, 8f, 10f) (g-s, g-f, frm)
Currently very moderate colt. Turf high 36 (began Jly).
**W R Muir [0-3] F Hope.*

MADIES PRIDE (IRE) BHB 51f **RR 56f** 4060[10]

2 b f Fayruz 6.6f **(63)** - June Lady (Junius (USA)) 7.7f **(65)**
Form - 470
Record 2000 - 1st:0 2nd:0 3rd:0 Ran:3
Win Prizemoney £0 *Total Prizemoney* £217
2000 Turf 0-3: (5f 3) (g-s, frm, hrd)
Currently fair filly. Turf high 56 (began Jly).
**J J Quinn [0-3] Pride Of Yorkshire Racing Club.*

MADMUN (IRE) BHB 74f **RR 74f** 2731[5]

6 ch g Cadeaux Genereux 7.9f **(76)** - Kates Cabin (Habitat) 9.4f **(70)**
Form - 55
Record 2000 - 1st:0 2nd:0 3rd:0 Ran:2
Pre2000 - 1st:1 2nd:2 3rd:2 Ran:10
Win Prizemoney £2,918 *Total Prizemoney* £7,132
Wins * 1999 Oct Windso (SFT) 6f 74 <
2000 Turf 0-2: (6f 2) (frm 2)
Above-average gelding, effective 6f, acts on gd to frm, best on frm, has worn blinkers. Turf high 73 (began Jly) - 5th of 14 to Pips Magic (12 Jly Doncaster 6f frm RF 2731). Consistent.
**M P Tregoning [1-12] Hamdan Al Maktoum.*

MADRASEE BHB 70f **RR 71f** 4808[5]

2 b f Beveled (USA) 6.9f **(64)** - Pendona (Blue Cashmere) 6.4f **(54)**
Form - 363832045
Record 2000 - 1st:0 2nd:1 3rd:3 Ran:9
Win Prizemoney £0 *Total Prizemoney* £2,796
2000 Turf 0-9: (5f 5, 6f 4) (g-s, gd 2, g-f, frm 5)
Above-average filly, effective 5f, acts on frm. Turf high 71.
**M Blanshard [0-9] Mrs H Chakko & H C Promotions Ltd.*

MADURESE BHB 64f **RR 66f** 4498[12]

3 b c Machiavellian (USA) 9.8f **(83)** - Luana **(94f)** (Shaadi (USA))
Form - 4730
Record 2000 - 1st:0 2nd:0 3rd:1 Ran:4
Win Prizemoney £0 *Total Prizemoney* £938
2000 Turf 0-4: (7f, 8f 2, 9f) (g-s, gd, g-f 2)
Scopey, average colt. Turf high 66.
**C E Brittain [0-4] Saeed Manana.*

MAEANDER (FR) RR 95f 1821a[3]

3 ch f Nashwan (USA) 10.3f **(79)** - Massaraat (USA) (Nureyev (USA)) 8.7f **(78)**
Form - 3
2000 Turf 0-1: (12f) (gd)
Currently very useful filly. (1st run) - 3rd of 6 to Sadler's Flag (3 Jun Chantilly 12f gd RF 1821a).
**A Fabre in FR [0-1] Sheikh Mohammed.*

MAGDALEON RR 35f 5319[17]

2 b f Lion Cavern (USA) 7.5f **(74)** - Magdala (IRE) (Sadler's Wells (USA)) 10f **(76)**
Form - 0
Record 2000 - 1st:0 2nd:0 3rd:0 Ran:1
2000 Turf 0-1: (6f) (sft)
Currently very moderate filly.
**R Charlton [0-1] Golden Arrow S A & Geoff Howard-Spink.*

MAGELTA BHB 72f76a **RR 73f 76a** 3325[9]

3 b c Magic Ring (IRE) 6.5f **(64)** - Pounelta (Tachypous) 8.6f **(55)**
Form - 002070
Record 2000 - 1st:0 2nd:1 3rd:0 Ran:6
Pre2000 - 1st:0 2nd:0 3rd:1 Ran:3
Win Prizemoney £0 *Total Prizemoney* £2,254
2000 Turf 0-6: (6f 2, 7f 4) (sft, gd, g-f 4)
Leggy, above-average colt. Turf high 73.
**R Hannon [0-9] Peter Valentine.*

MAGENKO (IRE) BHB 45f **RR 48f** 2329[10]

3 ch g Forest Wind (USA) - Bebe Auction (IRE) (Auction Ring (USA)) 8.6f **(65)**
Form - 260
Record 2000 - 1st:0 2nd:1 3rd:0 Ran:3
Pre2000 - 1st:0 2nd:0 3rd:0 Ran:3
Win Prizemoney £0 *Total Prizemoney* £630
2000 Turf 0-2: (16f, 17f) (g-f, frm) 2000 AW 0-1: (14f) (Fibr)
Lengthy, moderate gelding, effective 16f, acts on g-f. Turf high 39 (1st run) - 2nd of 7 getting 4lb from Open Ground (31 May Yarmouth 16f g-f RF 1611).
**M H Tompkins [0-6] Flint Fairyhouse Partnership.*

MAGGIE FLYNN RR 4760[9]

2 b f Imp Society (USA) 7.1f **(63)** - Lonely Street (Frimley Park) 6.5f **(67)**
Form - 0
Record 2000 - 1st:0 2nd:0 3rd:0 Ran:1
2000 AW 0-1: (6f) (Fibr)
Currently very moderate filly. **A P Jarvis [0-1] Terence Lyons II.*

MAGIC AIR RR 38f 3907[16]

2 b f Magic Ring (IRE) 6.5f **(64)** - Exhibit Air (IRE) **(48f 58a)** (Exhibitioner) 8.7f **(61)**
Form - 0
Record 2000 - 1st:0 2nd:0 3rd:0 Ran:1
2000 Turf 0-1: (8f) (frm)
Currently very moderate filly. **N Hamilton [0-1] Derek Theobald.*

MAGICAL BAILIWICK (IRE) BHB 56f **RR 51f** 4824[6]

4 ch g Magical Wonder (USA) 7.2f **(60)** - Alpine Dance (USA) (Apalachee (USA)) 9.4f **(71)**
Form - 000087216
Record 2000 - 1st:1 2nd:1 3rd:0 Ran:9
Pre2000 - 1st:0 2nd:0 3rd:1 Ran:4
Win Prizemoney £2,695 *Total Prizemoney* £4,690
Wins * **2000** Spt Bath (SFT) H 8f 46 51 <
2000 Turf 1-9: (7f, 8f 1-5, 10f 2, 12f) (g-s 1-1, gd, g-f 4, frm 3)
Workmanlike, fair gelding, effective 8f, acts on g-f, has worn blinkers. Turf high 51.
**R J Baker [1-13] Islands Racing Connection.*

MAGICAL FLUTE BHB 75f82a **RR 76f 82a** 5106[8]
2 ch f Piccolo - Stride Home (Absalom) 7.2f **(58)**
Form - 731328
Record 2000 - 1st:1 2nd:1 3rd:2 Ran:6
Win Prizemoney £2,464 *Total Prizemoney* £5,385
Wins * 2000 Jly Bath (FRM) 5.7f 67 <
2000 Turf 1-5: (5f 2, 6f 1-1, 7f 2) (gd, g-f, frm, hrd 1-2) 2000 AW 0-1: (6f) (Equi)
Above-average filly, effective 6 to 7f, acts on hrd - acts on Equi. Turf high 76 - 3rd of 7 getting 10lb from Barking Mad (28 Jly Thirsk 7f hrd RF 3195). (1st run) - 2nd of 13 getting 2lb from Nearctic Lady (11 Oct Lingfield 6f Equi RF 4926). Got off the mark on very fast ground at Bath on her third start and was unlucky not to follow up at Thirsk. Useful if not top class. **M R Channon [1-6] Peter Taplin.*

MAGICAL JACK BHB 36f **RR** 39[13]
3 b c Belfort (FR) 6.7f **(53)** - Gavea (African Sky) 7.7f **(50)**
Form - 000
Record 2000 - 1st:0 2nd:0 3rd:0 Ran:1
Pre2000 - 1st:0 2nd:0 3rd:0 Ran:3
2000 AW 0-1: (7f) (Fibr)
Unfurnished, poor colt. **G Woodward [0-4] David Chamley.*

MAGICAL RIVER BHB 38f52a **RR 36f 52a** 4275[17]
3 ch f Lahib (USA) 8f **(69)** - Awtaar (USA) **(35df)** (Lyphard (USA)) 9.9f **(72)**
Form - 070
Record 2000 - 1st:0 2nd:0 3rd:0 Ran:3
Pre2000 - 1st:0 2nd:0 3rd:1 Ran:6
Win Prizemoney £0 *Total Prizemoney* £510
2000 Turf 0-3: (7f 2, 8f) (g-f 2, hrd)
Leggy, very moderate filly. Turf high 36 (began Aug). Inconsistent. **C E Brittain [0-9] W H Carson.*

MAGIC BABE BHB 56f48a **RR 59f 48a** 4551[11]
3 b f Magic Ring (IRE) 6.5f **(64)** - Head Turner **(43f 52a)** (My Dad Tom (USA))
Form - 8241245000
Record 2000 - 1st:1 2nd:2 3rd:0 Ran:10
Pre2000 - 1st:0 2nd:0 3rd:0 Ran:8
Win Prizemoney £3,302 *Total Prizemoney* £6,287
Wins * 2000 Jun Newbur (G-F) H 7f 55 59 <
2000 Turf 1-9: (6f, 7f 1-6, 8f 2) (g-s, gd 2, g-f 2, frm 1-4) 2000 AW 0-1: (6f) (Equi)
Light-framed, fair filly, effective 7f, acts on g-f to frm. Turf high 59 - 1st of 21 getting 10lb from Cibenze (8 Jun Newbury RF 1816). Becoming disappointing.
**J R Poulton [1-10] Mrs J Wotherspoon (from D R C Elsworth [0-8] Aug 1999).*

MAGIC BOX BHB 81f **RR 80f** 4023[1]
2 b c Magic Ring (IRE) 6.5f **(64)** - Princess Poquito (Hard Fought) 8.8f **(62)**
Form - 644341
Record 2000 - 1st:1 2nd:0 3rd:1 Ran:6
Win Prizemoney £3,510 *Total Prizemoney* £5,062
Wins * 2000 Aug Yarmou (G-F) 8f 75 <
2000 Turf 1-6: (5f 2, 6f 2, 7f, 8f 1-1) (gd 1-2, g-f, frm 3)
Decent colt, effective 6 to 8f, acts on gd to g-f. Turf high 80 - 4th of 21 getting 3lb from Man of Distinction (14 Jun Kempton 6f g-f RF 1961) - also 1st of 8 from Regatta Point (27 Aug Yarmouth RF 4023). **A P Jarvis [1-6] Quadrillian Partnership.*

MAGIC COMBINATION (IRE) BHB 68f **RR 73+f** 4863[13]
7 b g Scenic 10.6f **(66)** - Etage (Ile de Bourbon (USA)) 10.1f **(67)**
Form - 451580
Record 2000 - 1st:1 2nd:0 3rd:0 Ran:6
Pre2000 - 1st:5 2nd:2 3rd:2 Ran:25
Win Prizemoney £22,739 *Total Prizemoney* £29,636

Wins								
* 2000	Aug	Sandow (GD)	H	14f	65	73	
* 1999	Jly	Galway (G-F)	H	12f	44	68	
* 1997	Jly	Sandow (G-S)	H	11.4f	69	72	
1996	Aug	Roscom (GD)	H	12f	84	77+	<
1996	Jly	Bellew (GD)	H	14f	79	73	
1996	Jun	Leopar (GD)	H	9f	75	65	

2000 Turf 1-6: (12f, 14f 1-4, 15f) (sft 2, gd 2, g-f 1-2)
Above-average gelding, effective 12 to 15f, best at 14f, acts on sft to g-f, has worn blinkers. Turf high 73 (began Jly) - 1st of 9 getting 4lb from King Flyer (19 Aug Sandown RF 3804). Better known as a hurdler these days, though he did win on the Flat at Sandown in August.
**B J Curley [6-32] Mrs B J Curley (from K Prendergast in IRE [3-10] Nov 1996).*

MAGIC EAGLE BHB 48f52a **RR 57f 52a** 5150[7]
3 b g Magic Ring (IRE) 6.5f **(64)** - Shadow Bird (Martinmas) 7.6f **(59)**
Form - 6700007
Record 2000 - 1st:0 2nd:0 3rd:0 Ran:7
2000 Turf 0-6: (6f 3, 7f 2, 8f) (g-s, gd 2, g-f 2, frm) 2000 AW 0-1: (10f) (Equi)
Fair gelding. Turf high 64.
**G L Moore [0-7] The Straight Forward Partnership II.*

MAGIC FLUTE RR 67f 3705[13]
4 ch f Magic Ring (IRE) 6.5f **(64)** - Megan's Flight (Welsh Pageant) 10f **(65)**
Form - 206800
Record 2000 - 1st:0 2nd:1 3rd:0 Ran:6
Pre2000 - 1st:0 2nd:1 3rd:0 Ran:6
Win Prizemoney £0 *Total Prizemoney* £2,203
2000 Turf 0-6: (7f 2, 8f 3, 10f) (gd, g-f, frm 4)
Scopey, average filly, effective 8f, acts on gd to frm. Turf high 67 (1st run) - 2nd of 11 getting 3lb from Hugwity (20 May Nottingham 8f gd RF 1336). Becoming disappointing.
**Lady Herries [0-12] Angmering Park Stud.*

MAGIC GEM (IRE) BHB 58f50a **RR 62f 50a** 4143[9]
2 gr c Petong 7.6f **(58)** - Fairy Magic (IRE) (Fairy King (USA)) 7.7f **(59)**
Form - 0550
Record 2000 - 1st:0 2nd:0 3rd:0 Ran:4
2000 Turf 0-4: (5f 2, 6f 2) (gd, g-f 2, frm)
Above-average colt. Turf high 62. **J A Osborne [0-4] A Edward.*

MAGIC HARP (IRE) RR 59f 4820[13]
2 b f Common Grounds 8.1f **(66)** - Princess of Zurich (IRE) (Law Society (USA)) 9.9f **(70)**
Form - 0
Record 2000 - 1st:0 2nd:0 3rd:0 Ran:1
2000 Turf 0-1: (6f) (g-f)
Currently fair filly. **M A Jarvis [0-1] Gary Seidler & Andy J Smith.*

MAGIC LAWYER RR 4778[7]
2 b f Magic Ring (IRE) 6.5f **(64)** - Miss Lawsuit (Neltino) 7.6f **(54)**
Form - 07
Record 2000 - 1st:0 2nd:0 3rd:0 Ran:2
2000 Turf 0-1: (6f) (gd) 2000 AW 0-1: (6f) (Fibr)
Currently poor filly. **B J Meehan [0-2] Vintage Services Ltd.*

MAGIC MILL (IRE) BHB 55f72a **RR 53f 72a** 5084[5]
7 b g Simply Great (FR) 11.9f **(61)** - Rosy O'Leary (Majetta) 6.5f **(58)**
Form - 408005
Record 2000 - 1st:0 2nd:0 3rd:0 Ran:6
Pre2000 - 1st:2 2nd:2 3rd:2 Ran:22
Win Prizemoney £7,543 *Total Prizemoney* £13,795
Wins 1998 Apr Newcas (SFT) H 7f 73 87? <
2000 Turf 0-6: (6f 3, 7f 3) (hvy, sft 2, gd 2, g-f)
Above-average gelding, has worn blinkers. Turf high 66.
**J S Goldie [0-12] A S Scott (from J L Eyre [1-14] Jun 1998).*

MAGIC OF LOVE BHB 96f **RR 98f** 4735[10]
3 b f Magic Ring (IRE) 6.5f **(64)** - Mistitled (USA) (Miswaki (USA)) 9f **(81)**
Form - 3304600
Record 2000 - 1st:0 2nd:0 3rd:2 Ran:7
Pre2000 - 1st:3 2nd:0 3rd:1 Ran:4
Win Prizemoney £54,027 *Total Prizemoney* £68,374

Wins						
* 1999	Oct	Newmar (GD)	6f	82	
* 1999	Aug	Lingfi (GD)	6f	86+	<
* 1999	Jly	Beverl (G-F)	5f	86+	<

2000 Turf 0-7: (6f 6, 7f) (g-s, gd 4, g-f, hrd)
Scopey, very useful filly, effective 5 to 6f, best at 6f, acts on gd to frm. Turf high 98 - 4th of 9 getting 10lb from Hot Tin Roof (14 Jly York 6f gd RF 2822). Consistent. Third in the Group 2 Flying Childers Stakes in 1999, she disappointed last year. Still at the

wrong end of the handicap, she is difficult to place.
**M L W Bell [3-11] Mrs Maureen Buckley.*

MAGIC OF YOU BHB 65f **RR 70f** 4334[13]
2 b f Magic Ring (IRE) 6.5f **(64)** - Daarat Alayaam (IRE) (Reference Point) 6.8f **(70)**
Form - 1300
Record 2000 - 1st:1 2nd:0 3rd:1 Ran:4
Win Prizemoney £2,604 *Total Prizemoney* £2,931
Wins * 2000 Jly Mussel (FRM) 7.1f 66+ <
2000 Turf 1-4: (7f 1-4) (g-f, frm 1-3)
Above-average filly, has worn blinkers. Turf high 70 (began Jly) - also 1st of 7 getting 1lb from Tefi (3 Jly Musselburgh RF 2470).
**M L W Bell [1-4] Mrs Maureen Buckley.*

MAGIC POWERS BHB 48f **RR 46f** 2598[15]
5 ch g Magical Wonder (USA) 7.2f **(60)** - Kissin' Cousin (Be Friendly) 9.3f **(53)**
Form - 000
Record 2000 - 1st:0 2nd:0 3rd:0 Ran:3
Pre2000 - 1st:0 2nd:0 3rd:1 Ran:7
Win Prizemoney £0 *Total Prizemoney* £633
2000 Turf 0-3: (7f 2, 8f) (gd 2, frm)
Moderate gelding, has worn blinkers. Turf high 46. Inconsistent.
**G B Balding [0-10] The Wizards.*

MAGIC RAINBOW BHB 86f92a **RR 85f 92a** 4258[7]
5 b g Magic Ring (IRE) 6.5f **(64)** - Blues Indigo (Music Boy) 6.8f **(57)**
Form - 1060065157
Record 2000 - 1st:2 2nd:0 3rd:0 Ran:10
Pre2000 - 1st:5 2nd:1 3rd:1 Ran:23
Win Prizemoney £95,464 *Total Prizemoney* £107,155

Wins								
* **2000**	Jly	Ascot	(G-F)	H	5f	81	85	
* **2000**	*Mar*	*Lingfi*	*(STD)*		*7f*		*82*	
* 1999	May	Kempto	(G-F)	H	6f	81	85	
* 1999	*Mar*	*Lingfi*	*(STD)*	*H*	*6f*	*81*	*94*	<
* 1998	May	Newmar	(G-F)	H	6f	77	84	
* 1998	*Mar*	*Southw*	*(STD)*	*H*	*6f*	*76*	*80+*	
* 1997	Jun	Leicos	(GD)		5f		76	

2000 Turf 1-8: (5f 1-3, 6f 4, 7f) (gd 5, g-f 1-3) 2000 AW 1-2: (6f, 7f 1-1) (Equi 1-1, Fibr)
Useful gelding, effective 5 to 6f, best at 6f, acts on g-f to frm - acts on AW, excels at Lingfield, likes Ascot. Turf high 85 - 1st of 20 from Compton Banker (30 Jly Ascot RF 3227). AW high 82 (1st run). An effective if not altogether consistent sprinter on turf and sand, he successfully returned from a six-month break over seven furlongs on the Lingfield Equitrack in March, but that trip seems to be right on the limit of his stamina. Landed a valuable Ascot handicap in July when dropped back to the minimum trip.
**M L W Bell [7-33] P T Fenwick.*

MAGIC SISTER BHB 55f56a **RR 56f 56a** 1713[8]
3 ch f Cadeaux Genereux 7.9f **(76)** - Gunner's Belle (Gunner B) 11.2f **(58)**
Form - 7378
Record 2000 - 1st:0 2nd:0 3rd:1 Ran:4
Pre2000 - 1st:0 2nd:0 3rd:0 Ran:2
Win Prizemoney £0 *Total Prizemoney* £395
2000 Turf 0-3: (6f 2, 7f) (gd, g-f, frm) 2000 AW 0-1: (7f) (Fibr)
Scopey, fair filly, effective 7f, acts on gd. Turf high 51 - 3rd of 9 to Alpathar (15 Apr Thirsk 7f gd RF 0738).
**M L W Bell [0-6] M Dawson & Usk Valley Stud.*

MAGIC SUNSET BHB 55f **RR 62f** 2778[1]
3 b f Magic Ring (IRE) 6.5f **(64)** - Run To The Sun (Run The Gantlet (USA)) 12.1f **(59)**
Form - 0001
Record 2000 - 1st:1 2nd:0 3rd:0 Ran:4
Pre2000 - 1st:0 2nd:0 3rd:0 Ran:2
Win Prizemoney £2,198 *Total Prizemoney* £2,198
Wins * 2000 *Jly Wolver (STD) C 9.4f 49* <
2000 Turf 0-3: (10f 2, 12f) (gd, g-f 2) 2000 AW 1-1: (9f 1-1) (Fibr 1-1)
Scopey, average filly, has worn blinkers. Turf high 62. (1st run).
**I A Balding [1-6] M E Wates.*

MAGIC SYMBOL BHB 43f **RR 40f** 4677[16]
3 gr f Be My Chief (USA) 10.2f **(62)** - Moon Magic **(59f)** (Polish Precedent (USA)) 10.2f **(60)**
Form - 085600
Record 2000 - 1st:0 2nd:0 3rd:0 Ran:6
2000 Turf 0-6: (8f 2, 10f 4) (g-s, gd 3, frm 2)
Workmanlike, moderate filly, has worn blinkers. Turf high 64.
**Lady Herries [0-6] Angmering Park Stud.*

MAGIC TO DO (IRE) RR 66f 5100[9]
2 b c Spectrum (IRE) - Smouldering (IRE) (Caerleon (USA)) 8.6f **(71)**
Form - 0
Record 2000 - 1st:0 2nd:0 3rd:0 Ran:1
2000 Turf 0-1: (7f) (gd)
Currently average colt.
**R F JohnsonHoughton [0-1] Anthony Pye-Jeary.*

MAGIC WATERS RR 60f 1265[7]
2 b g Ezzoud (IRE) - Paradise Waters **(68f)** (Celestial Storm (USA))
Form - 7
Record 2000 - 1st:0 2nd:0 3rd:0 Ran:1
2000 Turf 0-1: (6f) (frm)
Currently average gelding.
**T D Easterby [0-1] D F Sills.*

MAGIQUE ETOILE (IRE) BHB 50f45a **RR 57f 45a** 4021[4]
4 b f Magical Wonder (USA) 7.2f **(60)** - Shes A Dancer (IRE) (Alzao (USA)) 7.1f **(68)**
Form - 32706226684
Record 2000 - 1st:0 2nd:2 3rd:0 Ran:9
Pre2000 - 1st:0 2nd:2 3rd:5 Ran:21
Win Prizemoney £0 *Total Prizemoney* £5,427
2000 Turf 0-6: (6f 4, 7f, 10f) (g-f 4, frm 2) 2000 AW 0-3: (7f 3) (Equi 2, Fibr)
Workmanlike, fair filly, effective 6 to 10f, best at 6f, acts on gd to frm - acts on Equi, best on frm, has worn blinkers, likes tight tracks. Turf high 57 - 2nd of 17 getting 3lb from Contrary Mary (28 Jun Salisbury 6f frm RF 2351). AW high 38.
**M P Muggeridge [0-32] Gallery Racing.*

MAGNANIMOUS RR 52f 5081[3]
2 ch g Presidium 7.5f **(56)** - Mayor (Laxton)
Form - 000073
Record 2000 - 1st:0 2nd:0 3rd:1 Ran:6
Win Prizemoney £0 *Total Prizemoney* £393
2000 Turf 0-6: (5f 4, 6f 2) (hvy, gd 2, g-f 3)
Fair gelding, has worn blinkers. Turf high 52.
**N Tinkler [0-6] The Penniless Partnership.*

MAGNI MOMENTI BHB 25f38a **RR 38a** 2954[14]
5 b m King's Signet (USA) 7f **(51)** - Halka (Daring March) 7.1f **(61)**
Form - 0
Record 2000 - 1st:0 2nd:0 3rd:0 Ran:1
Pre2000 - 1st:0 2nd:2 3rd:1 Ran:14
Win Prizemoney £0 *Total Prizemoney* £2,238
2000 Turf 0-1: (12f) (hrd)
Very poor filly.
**Mrs P Ford [0-5] G W D'Arcy (from J S Moore [0-13] Nov 1998).*

MAGNUS (FR) RR 103f 1037a[3]
4 b g Saumarez 15.1f **(87)** - All Found (USA) (Alleged (USA)) 10f **(76)**
Form - 3
2000 Turf 0-1: (16f) (hvy)
Currently very useful gelding. (1st run) - 3rd of 7 getting 9lb from Amilynx (30 Apr Longchamp 16f hvy RF 1037a).
**J M Beguigne in FR [0-1] N Pharaon.*

MAGNUSSON RR 74f 3638[2]
2 b c Primo Dominie 7.2f **(67)** - Nunsharpa **(81f)** (Sharpo) 7.7f **(59)**
Form - 32
Record 2000 - 1st:0 2nd:1 3rd:1 Ran:2
Win Prizemoney £0 *Total Prizemoney* £1,982
2000 Turf 0-2: (6f, 7f) (gd, frm)
Currently above-average colt. Turf high 74 (began Jly) - 2nd of 12 giving 5lb to Baileys Cream (15 Aug Ayr 7f frm RF 3638).
**J H M Gosden [0-2] P D Savill.*

MAGZAA (IRE) BHB 76f **RR 85f** 5157^{3}

2 gr c Marju (IRE) 9.2f **(76)** - Labibeh (USA) **(105?f)** (Lyphard (USA)) 9.9f **(72)**

Form - 003

Record 2000 - 1st:0 2nd:0 3rd:1 Ran:3

Win Prizemoney £0 *Total Prizemoney* £806

2000 Turf 0-3: (7f, 8f 2) (sft, gd, g-f)

Currently useful colt. Turf high 85 (began Spt).

**J L Dunlop [0-3] Hamdan Al Maktoum.*

MAHFOOTH (USA) BHB 105f **RR 107f** 3937^{2}

3 ch c Diesis 9f **(80)** - I Certainly Am (USA) (Affirmed (USA)) 9.3f **(79)**

Form - 0212

Record 2000 - 1st:1 2nd:2 3rd:0 Ran:4

Pre2000 - 1st:0 2nd:0 3rd:1 Ran:1

Win Prizemoney £4,101 *Total Prizemoney* £16,082

Wins * 2000 Jly Haydoc (G-F) 7.1f 104 <

2000 Turf 1-3: (7f 1-2, 8f) (g-s, g-f, frm 1-1) 2000 AW 0-1: (9f) (Dirt)

Pattern-class colt. Turf high 107 - 2nd of 11 getting 5lb from Late Night Out (24 Aug York 7f g-f RF 3937) - also 1st of 6 from All The Gears (6 Jly Haydock RF 2572). Sent off at 1/10 when winning his maiden, he was just caught on his final run in a listed race.

**S bin Suroor [1-3] Godolphin (from S bin Suroor in UAE [0-1] Mar 2000).*

MAHLSTICK (IRE) BHB 45f **RR 33f** 4725^{12}

2 b c Tagula (IRE) - Guv's Joy (IRE) (Thatching) 8f **(66)**

Form - 000

Record 2000 - 1st:0 2nd:0 3rd:0 Ran:3

2000 Turf 0-3: (5f, 6f 2) (gd 3)

Currently very moderate colt. Turf high 33 (began Spt).

**D W P Arbuthnot [0-3] The Chelsea Arts Racing Club.*

MAIDAAN BHB 109f **RR 112f** 4986^{2}

4 b c Midyan (USA) 9.9f **(64)** - Panache Arabelle **(66f)** (Nashwan (USA))

Form - 32

Record 2000 - 1st:0 2nd:1 3rd:1 Ran:2

Pre2000 - 1st:1 2nd:1 3rd:1 Ran:4

Win Prizemoney £24,759 *Total Prizemoney* £55,961

Wins 1998 Spt Newmar (GD) 7f 104+ <

2000 Turf 0-2: (7f 2) (gd)

Scopey, Group-class colt. Turf high 112 (began Spt) - 2nd of 9 giving 5lb to Last Resort (14 Oct Newmarket 7f gd RF 4986). Lightly-raced, he was in action in Dubai in the spring and ran pretty well at the Curragh in September.

**S bin Suroor [0-4] Godolphin (from M R Channon [1-2] Spt 1998).*

MAIDEN AUNT (IRE) BHB 49f **RR 59f** 4994^{2}

3 b f Distant Relative 7f **(69)** - Lady Kris (IRE) (Kris) 9.5f **(73)**

Form - 500002

Record 2000 - 1st:0 2nd:1 3rd:0 Ran:6

Win Prizemoney £0 *Total Prizemoney* £838

2000 Turf 0-5: (8f 3, 10f 2) (gd 2, g-f, frm 2) 2000 AW 0-1: (12f) (Fibr)

Scopey, fair filly, effective 12f, - acts on Fibr. Turf high 59. (1st run) - 2nd of 12 giving 1lb to Town Gossip (14 Oct Wolverhampton 12f Fibr RF 4994). **W R Muir [0-6] J Bernstein.*

MAID FOR FREEDOM (USA) **RR 54f** 5132^{6}

2 gr f Trempolino (USA) 11.9f **(77)** - Spectacular Native (USA) (Spectacular Bid (USA)) 11.2f **(76)**

Form - 6

Record 2000 - 1st:0 2nd:0 3rd:0 Ran:1

2000 Turf 0-1: (6f) (sft)

Currently fair filly. **G A Butler [0-1] Chris Brasher.*

MAID OF ARC (USA) BHB 60f55a **RR 67f 55a** 4550^{5}

2 b f Patton (USA) - Holy Speed (CAN) (Afleet (CAN))

Form - 022446315

Record 2000 - 1st:1 2nd:2 3rd:1 Ran:9

Win Prizemoney £1,960 *Total Prizemoney* £4,118

Wins 2000 Aug Lingfi (G-F) S 6f 66 <

2000 Turf 1-8: (6f 1-3, 7f 5) (g-s, gd, frm 1-6) 2000 AW 0-1: (6f) (Fibr)

Average filly, effective 6 to 7f, best at 7f, acts on frm. Turf high 66 - 1st of 12 from Leggit (31 Aug Lingfield RF 4114).

**Lady Herries [0-1] Chris Hardy (from M L W Bell [1-8] Aug 2000).*

MAID PLANS (IRE) BHB 30f20a **RR 4f 20a** 288^{9}

4 br f Petardia 8.2f **(58)** - Ballerina Anna (IRE) (Dance of Life (USA)) 7f **(66)**

Form - 05000

Record 2000 - 1st:0 2nd:0 3rd:0 Ran:5

Pre2000 - 1st:0 2nd:0 3rd:0 Ran:8

2000 AW 0-5: (7f 3, 8f, 12f) (Fibr 5)

Light-framed, little account filly. AW high 20. Becoming disappointing.

**C N Kellett [0-5] J W C Coxon (from N P Littmoden [0-4] Feb 1999).*

MAID TO DANCE BHB 55f **RR 60f** 4744^{13}

2 b f Pyramus (USA) - Sari Habit (Saritamer (USA)) 9.5f **(63)**

Form - 500

Record 2000 - 1st:0 2nd:0 3rd:0 Ran:3

2000 Turf 0-3: (6f 2, 7f) (gd, frm 2)

Currently average filly. Turf high 60 (began Jly).

**T D Easterby [0-3] M Woodall.*

MAID TO LOVE (IRE) BHB 52f52a **RR 49f 52a** 2177^{12}

3 ch f Petardia 8.2f **(58)** - Lomond Heights (IRE) (Lomond (USA)) 8.8f **(65)**

Form - 234225000

Record 2000 - 1st:0 2nd:2 3rd:0 Ran:7

Pre2000 - 1st:0 2nd:2 3rd:3 Ran:7

Win Prizemoney £0 *Total Prizemoney* £3,974

2000 Turf 0-1: (7f) (frm) 2000 AW 0-6: (6f, 8f 3, 9f, 10f) (Equi 2, Fibr 4)

Fair filly, effective 6 to 8f, best at 8f, acts on g-f - acts on AW, has worn blinkers. AW high 69 - 2nd of 8 giving 3lb to Calko (24 Jan Southwell 8f Fibr RF 0146). Becoming disappointing.

**T D Barron [0-5] Nigel Shields (from G A Butler [0-9] Jan 2000).*

MAINE LOBSTER (USA) BHB 73f **RR 75f** 5106^{12}

2 ch f Woodman (USA) 9.7f **(77)** - Capades (USA) (Overskate (CAN))

Form - 03250

Record 2000 - 1st:0 2nd:1 3rd:1 Ran:5

Win Prizemoney £0 *Total Prizemoney* £1,891

2000 Turf 0-5: (6f 3, 7f 2) (gd, g-f 2, frm 2)

Above-average filly. Turf high 75 - 2nd of 12 to Galapagos Girl (24 Jly Windsor 6f frm RF 3079). **J L Dunlop [0-5] Robin Scully.*

MAI TAI (IRE) BHB 38f54a **RR 40f 54a** 5084^{10}

5 b m Scenic 10.6f **(66)** - Oystons Propweekly (Swing Easy (USA)) 6.5f **(55)**

Form - 74314254010256662588O

Record 2000 - 1st:1 2nd:3 3rd:0 Ran:16

Pre2000 - 1st:3 2nd:1 3rd:7 Ran:35

Win Prizemoney £14,189 *Total Prizemoney* £21,012

Wins * 2000 *Apr Southw (STD) H 7f 52 54*

* 1999 *Dec Lingfi (STD) H 8f 50 52*

* 1999 May Redcar (SFT) H 7f 48 54

* 1999 *Feb Southw (STD) 7f 56* <

2000 Turf 0-5: (7f, 8f 4) (hvy, g-s 2, frm 2) 2000 AW 1-11: (7f 1-3, 8f 7, 9f) (Fibr 1-11)

Fair filly, effective 7 to 8f, best at 7f, acts on gd - acts on AW, best on Fibr, has worn blinkers, likes left handed tracks, excels at Lingfield, likes Southwell. Turf high 40. AW high 57 - 2nd of 15 getting 9lb from Guilsborough (22 Jun Southwell 8f Fibr RF 2194) - also 1st of 16 from Guest Envoy (11 Apr Southwell RF 0667).

**D W Barker [4-37] Keith Middleton (from Mrs P N Dutfield [0-14] Oct 1998).*

MAITEAMIA BHB 64f75a **RR 68f 75a** 3574^{5}

7 ch g Komaite (USA) 6.9f **(61)** - Mia Scintilla (Blazing Saddles (AUS)) 6.7f **(46)**

Form - 55

Record 2000 - 1st:0 2nd:0 3rd:0 Ran:2

Pre2000 - 1st:7 2nd:12 3rd:8 Ran:57

Win Prizemoney £20,513 *Total Prizemoney* £39,387

Wins * 1999 Spt Redcar (G-F) H 6f 55 67

* 1999 *Mar Southw (STD) H 6f 69 70*

* 1999 *Feb Southw (STD) H 6f 63 67*

* 1996 May Catter (GD) H 5f 63 61

* 1996 May Hamilt (HVY) H 5f 50 68

* 1996 *Apr Southw (STD) H 6f 61 73+* <

* 1996 *Mar Southw (STD) H 6f 50 51*

2000 Turf 0-1: (6f) (frm) 2000 AW 0-1: (6f) (Fibr)

Above-average gelding, effective 5 to 8f, best at 6f, acts on g-f to frm - acts on Fibr, mostly wears blinkers (effectively), excels at Southwell, likes Redcar. **S R Bowring [7-59] Mrs Zoe Grant.*

MAIYSHA BHB 40f **RR 31f** 1612[16]
3 b f Contract Law (USA) 8.9f **(54)** - Bint Al Arab (Ahonoora) 8.1f **(73)**
Form - 0000
Record 2000 - 1st:0 2nd:0 3rd:0 Ran:4
Pre2000 - 1st:0 2nd:0 3rd:0 Ran:2
2000 Turf 0-4: (7f, 11f, 12f 2) (g-s, gd, g-f, frm)
Leggy, very moderate filly, has worn blinkers. Turf high 31. **R M Flower [0-6] Graham Dutnall.*

MAJESTIC (IRE) BHB 67f67a **RR 78f 67a** 321[3]
5 b g Belmez (USA) 11.4f **(65)** - Noble Lily (USA) (Vaguely Noble) 10.1f **(72)**
Form - 3
Record 2000 - 1st:0 2nd:0 3rd:1 Ran:1
Pre2000 - 1st:1 2nd:1 3rd:2 Ran:11
Win Prizemoney £2,762 *Total Prizemoney* £6,379
Wins * 1999 *Apr Wolver (STD) 12f* 75 <
2000 AW 0-1: (16f) (Fibr)
Above-average gelding, has worn blinkers. **Ian Williams [4-16] Patrick Kelly.*

MAJESTIC BAY (IRE) RR 85f 4863[11]
4 b g Unfuwain (USA) 11.4f **(74)** - That'll Be the Day (IRE) (Thatching) 8f **(66)**
Form - 381314100
Record 2000 - 1st:3 2nd:0 3rd:2 Ran:9
Pre2000 - 1st:0 2nd:2 3rd:1 Ran:5
Win Prizemoney £28,999 *Total Prizemoney* £33,973
Wins * 2000 Spt Haydoc (HVY) H 14f 80 85 <
*** 2000** Jly Redcar (G-F) H 16f 75 79
*** 2000** Jun Yarmou (FRM) 14.1f 74
2000 Turf 3-9: (12f, 13f, 14f 2-6, 16f 1-1) (sft 1-3, gd, g-f 1-4, frm 1-1)
Unfurnished, useful gelding, effective 10 to 16f, acts on sft to frm, has worn blinkers, prefers tight tracks, excels at Haydock, likes Kempton. Turf high 85 - 1st of 14 giving 7lb to Sudden Flight (2 Spt Haydock RF 4156) - also 1st of 5 giving 13lb to Pleasant Mount (29 Jly Redcar RF 3223). A front-running stayer, he has won three times last term on varying types of ground. **P W Harris [3-14] The Quiot Ones.*

MAJESTIC PREMIUM (IRE) RR 15f 4602[8]
2 b f Distinctly North (USA) 7.4f **(63)** - Star Of Aran (Artaius (USA)) 9f **(69)**
Form - 8
Record 2000 - 1st:0 2nd:0 3rd:0 Ran:1
2000 Turf 0-1: (8f) (gd)
Currently poor filly. **R A Fahey [0-1] J C Parsons.*

MAJESTIC QUEST (IRE) BHB 65f **RR 69f** 5102[21]
2 b g Piccolo - Teanarco (IRE) **(53df)** (Kafu) 6f **(47)**
Form - 421000
Record 2000 - 1st:1 2nd:1 3rd:0 Ran:6
Win Prizemoney £3,367 *Total Prizemoney* £4,705
Wins * 2000 Jly Ripon (G-F) 5f 69 <
2000 Turf 1-6: (5f 1-3, 6f 3) (gd 4, g-f 1-2)
Average gelding, effective 5f, acts on gd to g-f. Turf high 69 - 1st of 6 from Albaneck (22 Jly Ripon RF 3036). Won at Ripon in July, but hung next time. **J Neville [1-6] Brian Symonds.*

MA JOLIE BHB 76f **RR 74f** 5184[4]
2 ch f Shalford (IRE) 7.8f **(63)** - Scalford Brook (Handsome Sailor)
Form - 834
Record 2000 - 1st:0 2nd:0 3rd:1 Ran:3
Win Prizemoney £0 *Total Prizemoney* £1,441
2000 Turf 0-3: (6f, 8f 2) (g-s 2, gd)
Currently above-average filly. Turf high 74 (began Spt) - 4th of 17 getting 5lb from Caughnawaga (25 Oct Yarmouth 8f g-s RF 5184). **H Akbary [0-3] Charles Alan McKechnie.*

MAJOR ATTRACTION BHB 44f38a **RR 46f 38a** 2596[1]
5 gr g Major Jacko - My Friend Melody (Sizzling Melody)
Form - 0007677017081
Record 2000 - 1st:2 2nd:0 3rd:0 Ran:12
Pre2000 - 1st:0 2nd:0 3rd:1 Ran:7
Win Prizemoney £5,782 *Total Prizemoney* £6,067
Wins * 2000 Jly Haydoc (G-F) C 11.9f 46 <
*** 2000** May Hamilt (G-F) SH 11.1f 29 35+
2000 Turf 2-7: (10f, 11f 1-2, 12f 1-2, 13f, 15f) (g-s, gd 2, g-f 2-2, frm 2)
2000 AW 0-5: (8f, 9f 2, 12f 2) (Fibr 5)
Moderate gelding, effective 11 to 12f, acts on g-f - acts on Fibr, has worn blinkers. Turf high 46 - 1st of 10 getting 10lb from Desert Fighter (7 Jly Haydock RF 2596). AW high 26.
**W M Brisbourne [2-7] Positive Partners (from P Eccles [0-11] Mar 2000).*

MAJOR BART (IRE) BHB 45f47a **RR 40df 47a** 2815[7]
3 gr g Paris House 5.9f **(64)** - Kilnoe (IRE) (Rhoman Rule (USA))
Form - 05007
Record 2000 - 1st:0 2nd:0 3rd:0 Ran:5
Pre2000 - 1st:0 2nd:0 3rd:0 Ran:2
2000 Turf 0-2: (6f 2) (gd, frm) 2000 AW 0-3: (6f 2, 7f) (Fibr 3)
Scopey, moderate gelding. Turf high 9. AW high 44.
**R A Fahey [0-5] Mrs Linda Miller (from N P Littmoden [0-2] Aug 1999).*

MAJOR FORCE (USA) RR 113f 5283a[1]
4 b c Woodman (USA) 9.7f **(77)** - Ready For Action (USA) (Riverman (USA)) 9.1f **(76)**
Form - 3651
2000 Turf 1-3: (7f 2, 8f 1-1) (hvy 1-1, sft, g-f)
Group-class colt, effective 7 to 8f, best at 7f, acts on g-s, has worn blinkers, and excels at Curragh. Turf high 111 - 1st of 11 giving 3lb to Cois Cuain (28 Oct Leopardstown RF 5283a). A useful Irish performer, he had a limited season in 2000 but scored at Leopardstown at the back-end in his favoured heavy ground. **D K Weld in IRE [4-9] Moyglare Stud Farm.*

MAJOR MORRIS (IRE) BHB 30a **RR 30a** 151[13]
5 br g New Express 6.8f **(54)** - Saul Flower (Saulingo) 6.2f **(53)**
Form - 000
Record 2000 - 1st:0 2nd:0 3rd:0 Ran:2
Pre2000 - 1st:0 2nd:0 3rd:0 Ran:2
2000 AW 0-2: (6f, 11f) (Fibr 2)
Little account gelding. AW high 21. **J Mackie [0-5] N J Sessions.*

MAJOR REBUKE BHB 55f **RR 63f** 4103[9]
3 b g Reprimand 8.2f **(63)** - Ackcontent (USA) (Key To Content (USA)) 8f **(54)**
Form - 0002070
Record 2000 - 1st:0 2nd:1 3rd:0 Ran:7
Pre2000 - 1st:1 2nd:0 3rd:0 Ran:3
Win Prizemoney £4,955 *Total Prizemoney* £6,390
Wins * 1999 Spt Goodwo (G-F) 6f 81 <
2000 Turf 0-7: (6f, 7f 3, 8f 3) (gd, g-f 3, frm 2, hrd)
Workmanlike, average gelding, effective 6f, acts on g-f, has worn blinkers. Turf high 63. Consistent. **S P C Woods [1-10] N A D Thomas.*

MAJOR REVIEW (IRE) RR 57f 3344[9]
2 b f Definite Article - Fresh Look (IRE) **(45f 38a)** (Alzao (USA)) 7.1f **(68)**
Form - 0
Record 2000 - 1st:0 2nd:0 3rd:0 Ran:1
2000 Turf 0-1: (7f) (gd)
Currently fair filly. **M L W Bell [0-1] W H Ponsonby.*

MAKAAREM (USA) RR 103f 2148[15]
3 gr c Danzig (USA) 8.1f **(88)** - Sierra Madre (FR) **(111+f)** (Baillamont (USA)) 7f **(78)**
Form - 40
Record 2000 - 1st:0 2nd:0 3rd:0 Ran:2
Win Prizemoney £0 *Total Prizemoney* £1,260
2000 Turf 0-2: (7f 2) (gd, frm)
Currently very useful colt. Turf high 103 (1st run) - 4th of 9 to Shibboleth (3 Jun Newmarket 7f frm RF 1689). Fourth in a listed race at Newmarket on his debut before finishing down the field at Royal Ascot. **S bin Suroor [0-2] Godolphin.*

MAKARIM (IRE) BHB 57a **RR 61df** 5007[4]
4 ch g Generous (IRE) 11.5f **(82)** - Emmaline (USA) (Affirmed (USA)) 9.3f **(79)**

Form - 650504
Record 2000 - 1st:0 2nd:0 3rd:0 Ran:4
Pre2000 - 1st:1 2nd:0 3rd:0 Ran:7
Win Prizemoney £5,836 *Total Prizemoney* £6,112
Wins 1999 Aug Bath (GD) 11.7f 79 <
2000 Turf 0-1: (10f) (frm) 2000 AW 0-3: (10f, 12f, 16f) (Equi, Fibr 2)
Scopey, above-average gelding, effective 11 to 12f, acts on g-f to frm, has worn blinkers, likes left handed tracks, likes tight tracks. AW high 60.
**M R Bosley [0-1] Mrs Jean O'Connor (from P Eccles [0-9] Jun 2000).*

MAKASSEB BHB 71f66a **RR 80f 66a** 4863[14]

3 ch g Kris 10f **(75)** - Shefoog **(89f)** (Kefaah (USA))
Form - 150767448100
Record 2000 - 1st:1 2nd:0 3rd:0 Ran:10
Pre2000 - 1st:1 2nd:2 3rd:1 Ran:6
Win Prizemoney £13,146 *Total Prizemoney* £17,503
Wins * **2000** Aug Ripon (GD) H 16f 72 75
* 1999 Nov Maison (HVY) 9f 83 <
2000 Turf 1-10: (8f 2, 10f 2, 12f 2, 14f 2, 16f 1-1, 17f) (sft, gd 5, g-f 3, frm 1-1)
Scopey, decent gelding, effective 8 to 16f, acts on hvy to frm, best on g-f, prefers right handed tracks, does well at York. Turf high 80 - 6th of 6 getting 12lb from Alva Glen (17 Jun York 10f g-f RF 2063) - also 1st of 7 giving 20lb to Best Port (29 Aug Ripon RF 4065). Inconsistent. **M R Channon [2-16] Ahmed Al Shafar.*

MAKATI BHB 37f46a **RR 34f 46a** 4477[4]

6 b g Efisio 7.7f **(69)** - Seleter (Hotfoot) 10.5f **(59)**
Form - 4
Record 2000 - 1st:0 2nd:0 3rd:0 Ran:1
Pre2000 - 1st:3 2nd:5 3rd:1 Ran:21
Win Prizemoney £7,081 *Total Prizemoney* £10,516
Wins 1999 *Oct Southw (STD) H 14f 43 52* <
1998 *Jly Wolver (STD) H 16.2f 30 41+*
1998 *Jly Southw (STD) H 14f 33 36+*
2000 AW 0-1: (15f) (Fibr)
Fair gelding, effective 14 to 16f, - acted on Fibr, favoured tight tracks. (DEAD)
**J G M O'Shea [0-2] Mrs Ruth Nelmes (from Miss J A Camacho [3-17] Oct 1999).*

MAKBOOLA (IRE) BHB 90f **RR 82f** 2488[2]

2 b f Mujtahid (USA) 7.4f **(69)** - Haddeyah (USA) **(71f)** (Dayjur (USA))
Form - 312
Record 2000 - 1st:1 2nd:1 3rd:1 Ran:3
Win Prizemoney £2,887 *Total Prizemoney* £5,535
Wins * **2000** Jun Redcar (G-F) 6f 68 <
2000 Turf 1-3: (6f 1-3) (g-s, frm 1-2)
Currently decent filly. Turf high 82 - 2nd of 5 getting 6lb from Freefourracing (3 Jly Windsor 6f frm RF 2488).
**J L Dunlop [1-3] Khalil Alsayegh.*

MAKE A WISH (IRE) RR 2390[11]

2 ch c Magical Wonder (USA) 7.2f **(60)** - Jenny Jingle (IRE) (Digamist (USA))
Form - 0
Record 2000 - 1st:0 2nd:0 3rd:0 Ran:1
2000 Turf 0-1: (7f) (g-f)
Currently very poor colt. **M S Saunders [0-1] D Naylor.*

MAKE WAY (USA) BHB 80f **RR 85f** 5078[2]

4 b g Red Ransom (USA) 8.6f **(83)** - Way of The World (USA) (Dance of Life (USA)) 7f **(66)**
Form - 6032255032
Record 2000 - 1st:0 2nd:3 3rd:2 Ran:10
Pre2000 - 1st:1 2nd:1 3rd:2 Ran:7
Win Prizemoney £3,870 *Total Prizemoney* £16,005
Wins * 1999 Jun Windso (G-F) 8.3f 85 <
2000 Turf 0-10: (8f 2, 9f 2, 10f 5, 11f) (hvy, g-s 2, gd 4, g-f 2, frm)
Scopey, useful gelding, effective 7 to 10f, best at 10f, acted on g-s to frm, had worn blinkers, preferred right handed tracks, preferred tight tracks, excelled at Windsor and Ascot and Sandown. Turf high 85 - 3rd of 11 giving 20lb to Pipssalio (27 May Kempton 10f g-s RF 1498). Consistent. (DEAD)
**B J Meehan [1-16] Miss J Semple (from I A Balding [0-1] Jly 1998).*

MAKNAAS BHB 50f80a **RR 50f 80a** 1707[13]

4 ch c Wolfhound (USA) 7.3f **(71)** - White-Wash (Final Straw) 7.9f **(64)**
Form - 31415111100
Record 2000 - 1st:5 2nd:0 3rd:0 Ran:9
Pre2000 - 1st:1 2nd:0 3rd:2 Ran:10
Win Prizemoney £16,296 *Total Prizemoney* £17,313
Wins * **2000** *Mar Wolver (STD) H 16.2f 69 77+* <
* **2000** *Mar Lingfi (STD) H 16f 61 75*
* **2000** *Mar Wolver (STD) H 16.2f 61 65*
* **2000** *Feb Wolver (STD) H 16.2f 53 61*
* **2000** *Jan Lingfi (STD) H 16f 52 53*
* 1999 *Dec Wolver (STD) H 16.2f 47 49*
2000 Turf 0-2: (16f, 17f) (g-s 2) 2000 AW 5-7: (16f 5-7) (Equi 2-3, Fibr 3-4)
Strong, above-average colt, effective 16f, - acts on AW, has worn blinkers, prefers left handed tracks, prefers tight tracks, and excels at Wolverhampton. Turf high 31. AW high 77 - 1st of 7 getting 17lb from Harik (11 Mar Wolverhampton RF 0436) - also 1st of 10 giving 28lb to Mischief (8 Mar Lingfield RF 0420). He showed bits and pieces of form on turf last season, but proved a real star on sand during the winter, winning six times over two miles and proving impossible to catch when able to enjoy an uncontested early lead. Well beaten back on turf since.
**T G Mills [6-11] Travel Spot Ltd (from R W Armstrong [0-8] Oct 1999).*

MALAAH (IRE) BHB 45f44a **RR 49f 44a** 4756[8]

4 gr g Pips Pride 6.7f **(70)** - Lingdale Lass (Petong) 6.6f **(58)**
Form - 0085005608
Record 2000 - 1st:0 2nd:0 3rd:0 Ran:10
Pre2000 - 1st:0 2nd:0 3rd:0 Ran:6
2000 Turf 0-10: (5f 5, 6f 4, 7f) (g-s, gd 2, g-f 2, frm 5)
Strong, moderate gelding, mostly wears blinkers. Turf high 49.
**J C Poulton [0-10] Mrs Elizabeth Reed (from R W Armstrong [0-6] Jun 1999).*

MALADERIE (IRE) BHB 46f56a **RR 57f 56a** 4827[11]

6 b g Thatching 7.8f **(69)** - Native Melody (Tudor Music) 6.8f **(59)**
Form - 700027000007400
Record 2000 - 1st:0 2nd:1 3rd:0 Ran:14
Pre2000 - 1st:5 2nd:10 3rd:7 Ran:66
Win Prizemoney £23,388 *Total Prizemoney* £44,568
Wins * 1999 Jun Bath (GD) H 5.7f 66 69
1998 Oct York (GD) H 5f 69 70
1998 Spt Haydoc (GD) H 5f 64 68
1998 Aug Windso (G-F) H 5f 58 60
1996 Jun Windso (G-F) 6f 76 <
2000 Turf 0-14: (5f 8, 6f 4, 7f 2) (g-s, gd 2, g-f 3, frm 4, hrd 4)
Fair gelding, effective 5 to 7f, best at 5f, acts on g-f to frm, best on frm, often wears blinkers (very effectively), excels at Haydock and Carlisle. Turf high 57. A busy sprinter, he is suited by fast ground and the minimum trip, although he was stepped up to seven furlongs in April.
**M Dods [1-39] N A Riddell (from M R Channon [4-41] Oct 1998).*

MALAKAL (IRE) BHB 40f28a **RR 32f 28a** 2480[13]

4 b c Shernazar 11.8f **(71)** - Malmada (USA) (Fappiano (USA)) 8.7f **(77)**
Form - 08000000
Record 2000 - 1st:0 2nd:0 3rd:0 Ran:6
Pre2000 - 1st:0 2nd:1 3rd:0 Ran:5
Win Prizemoney £0 *Total Prizemoney* £1,470
2000 Turf 0-4: (8f, 10f 2, 13f) (g-s, gd, g-f, frm) 2000 AW 0-2: (8f 2) (Fibr 2)
Very moderate colt, effective 9 to 10f, best at 10f, acts on g-s to frm. Turf high 32. AW high 2. Inconsistent.
**B J Curley [0-8] Mrs B J Curley (from J Oxx in IRE [0-3] Jly 1999).*

MALA MALA (IRE) RR 97f 4644[3]

2 b f Brief Truce (USA) 9.1f **(73)** - Breyani (Commanche Run) 8.5f **(58)**
Form - 533
2000 Turf 0-3: (6f, 7f 2) (gd 2, g-f)
Currently very useful filly. Turf high 97 (began Aug) - 3rd of 13 to Regal Rose (26 Spt Newmarket 6f g-f RF 4644). She kept hot company on all her starts, finishing third in the Moyglare Stud Stakes and the Cheveley Park Stakes. Expected to improve once given the chance to tackle distances around a mile, she is an extremely promising individual and ought to win a Group race this year.
**T Stack in IRE [0-3] Mrs David Nagle.*

MALARKEY BHB 64f **RR 67f** 3725[5]
3 b g Mukaddamah (USA) 7.6f **(74)** - Malwiya (USA) (Shahrastani (USA)) 8.8f **(72)**
Form - 75545325
Record 2000 - 1st:0 2nd:1 3rd:1 Ran:8
Win Prizemoney £0 *Total Prizemoney* £1,545
2000 Turf 0-8: (6f 3, 7f, 8f, 10f, 12f 2) (gd, g-f 2, frm 5)
Lengthy, average gelding, effective 10 to 12f, acts on frm. Turf high 67. Consistent. **J A Osborne [0-8] Godiva.*

MALCHIK BHB 30f42a **RR 41f 42a** 4479[8]
4 ch c Absalom 7.1f **(56)** - Very Good (Noalto) 5.7f **(49)**
Form - 785755560828733312726 0008
Record 2000 - 1st:1 2nd:3 3rd:3 Ran:20
Pre2000 - 1st:1 2nd:2 3rd:6 Ran:37
Win Prizemoney £3,993 *Total Prizemoney* £10,778
Wins * 2000 *Apr Wolver (STD) S 9.4f 55*
* 1998 Spt Leices (G-S) SH 8f 52 59 <
2000 Turf 0-2: (11f, 12f) (g-f, frm) 2000 AW 1-18: (7f 2, 8f 7, 9f 1-1, 10f 4, 12f 3, 15f) (Equi 11, Fibr 1-7)
Scopey, fair colt, effective 8 to 10f, best at 8f, - acts on AW, best on Fibr, has worn blinkers, likes left handed tracks, favours tight tracks. Turf high 20. AW high 56 - 2nd of 13 giving 1lb to Champagne (20 May Wolverhampton 8f Fibr RF 1356) - also 1st of 13 giving 5lb to The Wild Widow (15 Apr Wolverhampton RF 0744). Inconsistent. Some ability on turf and sand, but one win from umpteen starts says plenty. **P Howling [2-57] I G Mirzoian.*

MALHUB (USA) RR 88+f 4702[1]
2 b br c Kingmambo (USA) 10.9f **(85)** - Arjuzah (IRE) **(108f)** (Ahonoora) 8.1f **(73)**
Form - 1
Record 2000 - 1st:1 2nd:0 3rd:0 Ran:1
Win Prizemoney £5,086 *Total Prizemoney* £5,086
Wins * 2000 Spt Newmar (GD) 7f 88+ <
2000 Turf 1-1: (7f 1-1) (g-f 1-1)
Currently useful colt. (1st run) - 1st of 16 from Amicable (28 Spt Newmarket RF 4702). Narrow winner of the second division of a Newmarket maiden that has produced good horses in the past, he looks sure to come on from the run and may well be very useful at around a mile. **J H M Gosden [1-1] Hamdan Al Maktoum.*

MALI (ITY) RR 91f 1636a[10]
3 f
Form - 0
2000 Turf 0-1: (12f) (g-f)
Currently useful. **L Brogi in ITY [0-1].*

MALIAN (IRE) BHB 45f **RR 25f** 2879[5]
4 b br g Arcane (USA) 11.6f **(66)** - Rhein Valley (IRE) (Kings Lake (USA)) 10.8f **(67)**
Form - 0005
Record 2000 - 1st:0 2nd:0 3rd:0 Ran:4
Pre2000 - 1st:0 2nd:0 3rd:0 Ran:5
2000 Turf 0-4: (12f, 14f 2, 22f) (sft, gd 2, frm)
Workmanlike, little account gelding, has worn blinkers. Turf high 40. Becoming disappointing.
**Derrick Morris [0-3] Christopher Shankland (from A P Jarvis [0-8] May 2000).*

MALLEUS BHB 87f **RR 90f** 2183[15]
3 ch g Hamas (IRE) 8f **(72)** - Queen Warrior (Daring March) 7.1f **(61)**
Form - 210
Record 2000 - 1st:1 2nd:1 3rd:0 Ran:3
Pre2000 - 1st:0 2nd:1 3rd:1 Ran:4
Win Prizemoney £8,352 *Total Prizemoney* £12,012
Wins * 2000 May York (FRM) H 7.9f 83 90 <
2000 Turf 1-3: (8f 1-2, 9f) (g-s, gd 1-2)
Workmanlike, useful gelding, effective 8 to 9f, acts on g-s to gd. Turf high 90 - 1st of 21 giving 10lb to Zibeline (18 May York RF 1279). A keen sort, he was given a strong ride from Mick Kinane when winning at York in May. Not seen out after finishing mid-division in the Britannia Handicap at Royal Ascot, he is lightly raced and can pick-up another decent prize around a mile.
**R M Beckett [1-3] S W E J Slack (from P T Walwyn [0-4] Spt 1999).*

MALLIA BHB 64f64a **RR 69f 64a** 2573[17]
7 b g Statoblest 6.4f **(63)** - Pronetta (USA) (Mr Prospector (USA)) 8.8f **(78)**
Form - 604055164140444400
Record 2000 - 1st:2 2nd:0 3rd:0 Ran:16
Pre2000 - 1st:9 2nd:8 3rd:4 Ran:60
Win Prizemoney £67,631 *Total Prizemoney* £90,241
Wins * 2000 *Mar Wolver (STD) C 6f 68*
*** 2000** *Feb Wolver (STD) C 6f 62*
* 1999 Jly Haydoc (G-S) H 6f 70 74
* 1999 *May Wolver (Std) H 6f 70 74*
* 1999 *Mar Wolver (STD) C 6f 69*
* 1998 *Dec Wolver (STD) C 6f 63*
* 1998 Apr Ripon (SFT) H 6f 65 70
* 1997 *Dec Wolver (STD) H 6f 72 77*
* 1997 *Nov Southw (STD) H 6f 64 70+*
* 1996 Jun York (GD) H 6f 76 84 <
2000 Turf 0-7: (6f 7) (gd, g-f 2, frm 4) 2000 AW 2-9: (6f 2-9) (Fibr 2-9)
Average gelding, effective 6f, acts on sft to frm - acts on Fibr, best on g-f, often wears blinkers (extremely effectively), likes left handed tracks, likes tight tracks, excels at Wolverhampton and likes York. Turf high 65. AW high 68 - 6th of 13 getting 7lb from Daawe (17 Feb Wolverhampton 6f Fibr RF 0298) - also 1st of 6 giving 4lb to Russian Romeo (25 Mar Wolverhampton RF 0505). Effective on turf and Fibresand, he is a bit of a character and needs plenty of stoking. Capable of running well in decent company, but his recent victories have been in claimers.
**T D Barron [11-76] H T Duddin.*

MALWINA (IRE) BHB 40f42a **RR 42a** 904[3]
4 ch f Greinton 15.8f **(75)** - Micky's Pleasure (USA) (Foolish Pleasure (USA)) 8.9f **(72)**
Form - 7751253
Record 2000 - 1st:1 2nd:1 3rd:1 Ran:7
Win Prizemoney £1,949 *Total Prizemoney* £2,765
Wins * 2000 *Feb Southw (STD) H 11f 44 46 <*
2000 AW 1-7: (9f 2, 11f 1-2, 12f 2, 16f) (Fibr 1-7)
Moderate filly, effective 9 to 12f, - acts on Fibr. AW high 46 - 1st of 13 giving 6lb to Genuine John (21 Feb Southwell RF 0330).
**M G Quinlan [1-7] D Donovan.*

MAMCAZMA BHB 60f66a **RR 50f 66a** 5100[14]
2 b gr c Terimon 8.7f **(58)** - Merryhill Maid (IRE) (M Double M (USA)) 14.1f **(52)**
Form - 060
Record 2000 - 1st:0 2nd:0 3rd:0 Ran:3
2000 Turf 0-3: (5f, 6f, 7f) (gd 3)
Currently average colt. Turf high 50 (began Spt).
**A Smith [0-3] Alfred Smith.*

MAMEHA BHB 99f **RR 82f** 4595[5]
2 b f Rainbow Quest (USA) 11.2f **(81)** - Musetta (IRE) **(101f)** (Cadeaux Genereux)
Form - 735
Record 2000 - 1st:0 2nd:0 3rd:1 Ran:3
Win Prizemoney £0 *Total Prizemoney* £5,610
2000 Turf 0-3: (6f, 7f, 8f) (gd, g-f 2)
Currently decent filly. Turf high 82 (began Jly). She has shown ability in maidens but is a keen sort who does need to settle.
**C E Brittain [0-3] B H Voak.*

MAMMA'S BOY BHB 50f66a **RR 54f 66a** 5299[12]
5 b g Rock City 8.8f **(62)** - Henpot (IRE) (Alzao (USA)) 7.1f **(68)**
Form - 004111004671670
Record 2000 - 1st:4 2nd:0 3rd:0 Ran:15
Pre2000 - 1st:4 2nd:3 3rd:8 Ran:39
Win Prizemoney £21,879 *Total Prizemoney* £28,522
Wins * 2000 Aug Mussel (G-F) H 8f 49 52
*** 2000** Jun Mussel (FRM) C 7.1f 54
*** 2000** Jun Mussel (FRM) C 7.1f 52
*** 2000** May Redcar (G-S) S 7f 54
1999 May Mussel (FRM) C 7.1f 61
1999 May Thirsk (G-S) S 7f 55
1998 Spt Sandow (G-S) C 5f 63+
1998 Jun Doncas (GD) H 6f 69 72 <
2000 Turf 4-15: (6f, 7f 3-12, 8f 1-2) (g-s 2, gd 1-5, g-f, frm 3-6, hrd)
Fair gelding, effective 6 to 8f, best at 7f, acts on gd to frm, best on g-f, has worn blinkers, prefers right handed tracks, likes tight

tracks, excels at Musselburgh. Turf high 54 - 1st of 13 giving 8lb to Detroit City (19 Jun Musselburgh RF 2092) - also 1st of 19 giving 5lb to Oakwell Ace (29 May Redcar RF 1529). Had a good season again in 2000, winning three times at Musselburgh, where he is becoming a specialist, but once on soft ground at Redcar, showing that easy ground is not necessarily a disadvantage.
**A Berry [4-15] Mrs J M Berry (from J Berry [4-39] Oct 1999).*

MAMMAS F-C (IRE) BHB 57f43a RR 58f 43a 519[F]

4 ch f Case Law 6f **(64)** - Wasaif (IRE) (Lomond (USA)) 8.8f **(65)**
Form - 8055F
Record 2000 - 1st:0 2nd:0 3rd:0 Ran:5
Pre2000 - 1st:6 2nd:7 3rd:1 Ran:29
Win Prizemoney £17,813 *Total Prizemoney* £24,222
Wins * 1999 Aug Ripon (GD) H 6f 55 58
* 1999 Aug Bath (HRD) C 5.7f 49
* 1999 Jly Folkes (G-F) C 7f 46
1998 Spt Haydoc (GD) C 6f 65
1998 Jun Mussel (G-F) C 5f 60+
1998 Jun Southw (STD) 5f 66 <
2000 Turf 0-1: (6f) (g-f) 2000 AW 0-4: (5f 2, 6f 2) (Equi, Fibr 3)
Neat, fair filly, effective 5 to 7f, best at 6f, acts on gd to frm, best on gd, excels at Bath. AW high 34.
**J M Bradley [3-21] J M Kearney (from J Berry [3-13] Oct 1998).*

MAMMA'S TONIGHT BHB 95f RR 94f 5102[15]

2 ch g Timeless Times (USA) 6.1f **(56)** - Miss Merlin (Manacle) 7.8f **(56)**
Form - 133315480440
Record 2000 - 1st:2 2nd:0 3rd:3 Ran:12
Win Prizemoney £10,957 *Total Prizemoney* £15,780
Wins *** 2000** Jun Beverl (G-S) 5f 86 <
*** 2000** *Mar Southw (STD) 5f 75*
2000 Turf 1-11: (5f 1-6, 6f 5) (sft 2, gd 1-6, g-f 2, frm) 2000 AW 1-1: (5f 1-1) (Fibr 1-1)
Useful gelding, effective 5f, acts on gd, has worn blinkers. Turf high 94 - 4th of 12 giving 5lb to Vicious Dancer (14 Spt Ayr 5f gd RF 4383) - also 1st of 8 getting 4lb from Bouncing Bowdler (7 Jun Beverley RF 1777). (1st run). He did well for a colt who began life on the all-weather, running his best race when a close fourth in the Listed Harry Roseberry Stakes at Ayr in September. Seemingly helped by blinkers there, he ran poorly on his last two starts and is going to be difficult to place. **A Berry [2-12] J K Brown.*

MAMORE GAP (IRE) BHB 86f RR 82f 3418[1]

2 b c General Monash (USA) - Ravensdale Rose (IRE) (Henbit (USA)) 9f **(61)**
Form - 22311
Record 2000 - 1st:2 2nd:2 3rd:1 Ran:5
Win Prizemoney £7,071 *Total Prizemoney* £9,531
Wins *** 2000** Aug Newbur (G-F) H 7f 77 82 <
*** 2000** Jly Bright (FRM) 7f 76+
2000 Turf 2-4: (5f, 6f, 7f 2-2) (gd, g-f 1-2, frm 1-1) 2000 AW 0-1: (5f) (Equi)
Decent colt. Turf high 82 - 1st of 11 giving 7lb to Paso Doble (6 Aug Newbury RF 3418) - also 1st of 4 from Chauntry Gold (25 Jly Brighton RF 3084). Placed in maidens in his first three starts and got off the mark in a four-runner Brighton maiden. His form is very modest though. **R Hannon [2-5] The South-Western Partnership II.*

MAMZUG (IRE) BHB 79f RR 81f 3527[5]

3 b c Hamas (IRE) 8f **(72)** - Bellissi (IRE) (Bluebird (USA)) 7.5f **(69)**
Form - 414235
Record 2000 - 1st:1 2nd:1 3rd:1 Ran:6
Pre2000 - 1st:0 2nd:0 3rd:0 Ran:1
Win Prizemoney £1,876 *Total Prizemoney* £5,456
Wins *** 2000** May Bath (G-F) 8f 77+ <
2000 Turf 1-6: (7f, 8f 1-4, 10f) (g-f, frm 1-5)
Unfurnished, decent colt, effective 7 to 8f, best at 8f, acts on frm. Turf high 81 - 2nd of 9 giving 2lb to Granted (12 Jly Doncaster 8f frm RF 2730) - also 1st of 9 from Chris's Little Lad (22 May Bath RF 1357). Dropped back to a mile to win a Bath maiden in May, having run a fair race over ten furlongs at Chester. He has not run badly since being tried in handicap company and should improve with experience. **B Hanbury [1-7] Christopher Cooke.*

MANA D'ARGENT (IRE) BHB 83f RR 91+f 4453[6]

3 b c Ela-Mana-Mou 12.7f **(72)** - Petite-D-Argent **(52f)** (Noalto) 5.7f **(49)**
Form - 27456303132346
Record 2000 - 1st:1 2nd:2 3rd:4 Ran:14
Pre2000 - 1st:0 2nd:0 3rd:2 Ran:3
Win Prizemoney £6,890 *Total Prizemoney* £19,893
Wins *** 2000** Jly Ascot (G-F) H 12f 72 80 <
2000 Turf 1-14:(6f 2, 7f 4, 8f 2, 12f 1-4, 13f, 14f)(sft, gd 5, g-f 1-5, frm 3)
Useful colt, effective 12 to 14f, acts on g-f, has worn blinkers. Turf high 91 - 2nd of 9 getting 4lb from Gentleman Venture (16 Aug Epsom 12f g-f RF 3692). He proved suited by a step-up to middle-distances, but took a hike in the ratings after winning at Ascot in July. Possibly unsuited by soft ground, he stays a mile and three-quarters and seems best when ridden close to the pace.
**M Johnston [1-17] Daniel Couper.*

MANAGERIAL RR 1196[9]

3 b c Afzal - Manageress (Mandamus) 12.6f **(56)**
Form - 0
Record 2000 - 1st:0 2nd:0 3rd:0 Ran:1
2000 Turf 0-1: (10f) (sft)
Workmanlike, currently very poor colt.
**N Hamilton [0-1] The Management.*

MANA-MOU BAY (IRE) BHB 96f RR 97f 4817[9]

3 b g Ela-Mana-Mou 12.7f **(72)** - Summerhill (Habitat) 9.4f **(70)**
Form - 024500
Record 2000 - 1st:0 2nd:1 3rd:0 Ran:6
Pre2000 - 1st:1 2nd:1 3rd:0 Ran:2
Win Prizemoney £11,795 *Total Prizemoney* £17,548
Wins * 1999 Aug Newbur (GD) L 7f 93+ <
2000 Turf 0-6: (7f 2, 8f 3, 10f) (g-s 2, gd, g-f 2, frm)
Scopey, very useful gelding, effective 7f, acts on frm. Turf high 106 - 2nd of 4 giving 4lb to Hopeful Light (28 Jun Salisbury 7f frm RF 2349). He has ability, but has had his problems and so far failed to deliver. Should have won at Salisbury in June, when Richard Hughes was guilty of over-confience, but disappointed latterly and seemed not to stay beyond a mile.
**R Hannon [1-8] N A Woodcock.*

MANDOOB BHB 72f RR 75f 2649[6]

3 b c Zafonic (USA) 9f **(83)** - Thaidah (CAN) (Vice Regent (CAN)) 8.7f **(74)**
Form - 0456
Record 2000 - 1st:0 2nd:0 3rd:0 Ran:4
Pre2000 - 1st:0 2nd:0 3rd:0 Ran:1
Win Prizemoney £0 *Total Prizemoney* £269
2000 Turf 0-4: (8f, 10f 3) (g-f, frm 2, hrd)
Leggy, above-average colt. Turf high 75 - 4th of 8 to Flitwick (31 May Ripon 10f g-f RF 1597). **A C Stewart [0-5] Hamdan Al Maktoum.*

MANE FRAME BHB 71f RR 72f 5297[2]

5 b g Unfuwain (USA) 11.4f **(74)** - Moviegoer (Pharly (FR)) 9.8f **(68)**
Form - 002106622
Record 2000 - 1st:1 2nd:3 3rd:0 Ran:9
Pre2000 - 1st:3 2nd:3 3rd:2 Ran:17
Win Prizemoney £13,243 *Total Prizemoney* £29,742
Wins *** 2000** Jun Warwic (G-S) H 15.8f 65 71+ <
* 1999 Jly Sandow (G-F) H 14f 62 66
* 1999 Jun Warwic (HVY) H 12.3f 60 64
* 1999 Apr Windso (G-S) 11.6f 58
2000 Turf 1-9: (14f 3, 15f, 16f 1-4, 20f) (hvy, g-s 1-2, gd 4, g-f, frm)
Above-average gelding, effective 12 to 17f, best at 16f, acts on hvy to frm, best on g-s, prefers tight tracks, excels at Sandown and Warwick. Turf high 72 - 2nd of 10 giving 11lb to You're Special (1 Nov Musselburgh 16f g-s RF 5297) - also 1st of 18 giving 11lb to Ireland's Eye (4 Jun Warwick RF 1707). Consistent. He bolted up at Warwick but seemed not to stay in the marathon Ascot Stakes. Ideally needs some cut, and ran a cracker at Newbury in October.
**H Morrison [4-26] Rory Sweet.*

MANFUL BHB 34f25a RR 53f 25a 2027[4]

8 b g Efisio 7.7f **(69)** - Mandrian (Mandamus) 12.6f **(56)**
Form - 77188302364
Record 2000 - 1st:1 2nd:1 3rd:2 Ran:9
Pre2000 - 1st:11 2nd:12 3rd:12 Ran:94
Win Prizemoney £41,677 *Total Prizemoney* £63,470
Wins * 2000 *Jan Wolver (STD)* H *12f* 27 33
1999 Jun Ayr (SFT) H 10.9f 59 64
1998 Aug Ayr (G-S) H 10f 60 62
1997 May Hamilt (SFT) H 11.1f 72 76

1997 Apr Hamilt (SFT) H 11.1f 68 73
1996 *Dec Southw (SLW) H 11f 62 68*
1996 *Oct Lingfi (STD) H 12f 54 58*
1996 Spt Hamilt (G-S) C 11.1f 69
1996 May Ayr (G-S) H 10.9f 62 67
1996 Mar Doncas (GD) H 10.3f 54 63
2000 Turf 0-2: (16f 2)(g-s 2) 2000 AW 1-7: (12f 1-3, 14f 3, 16f)(Fibr 1-7)
Fair gelding, effective 10 to 11f, best at 11f, acts on g-s to frm, often wears blinkers, likes left handed tracks. Turf high 34. AW high 33.
**R Brotherton [1-11] Ms Gerardine O'Rellly (from Miss L A Perratt [4-43] Oct 1999).*

MANGUS (IRE) BHB 46f61a **RR 49f 61a** 4124[16]
6 b g Mac's Imp (USA) 5.6f **(54)** - Holly Bird (Runnett) 7f **(59)**
Form - 014650805000
Record 2000 - 1st:0 2nd:0 3rd:0 Ran:9
Pre2000 - 1st:4 2nd:6 3rd:4 Ran:42
Win Prizemoney £13,175 *Total Prizemoney* £23,857
Wins * 1999 *Dec Wolver (STD) H 5f 74 77* <
* 1998 *Jun Wolver (STD) H 5f 72 74*
* 1998 May Lingfi (G-F) H 5f 67 72
* 1997 Apr Warwic (G-F) H 5f 70 72
2000 Turf 0-7: (5f 7) (gd 3, frm 3, hrd) 2000 AW 0-2: (5f 2) (Equi, Fibr)
Above-average gelding, effective 5f, - acts on Fibr, likes left handed tracks, likes tight tracks. Turf high 49. AW high 71.
**K O Cunningham-Brown [4-51] Danebury Racing Stables Ltd.*

MANIATIS BHB 92f **RR 92f** 5070[1]
3 b c Slip Anchor 12.7f **(75)** - Tamassos (Dance In Time (CAN)) 8.9f **(59)**
Form - 0321
Record 2000 - 1st:1 2nd:1 3rd:1 Ran:4
Win Prizemoney £4,033 *Total Prizemoney* £5,758
Wins * 2000 Oct Bath (GD) 11.7f 92 <
2000 Turf 1-4: (10f, 11f, 12f 1-2) (sft, g-s 1-2, gd)
Scopey, useful colt. Turf high 92 - 1st of 20 giving 5lb to Flame of Truth (19 Oct Bath RF 5070). **P F I Cole [1-4] Athos Christodoulou.*

MANICANI (IRE) RR 54f 3917[11]
2 ch c Tagula (IRE) - Pluvia (USA) (Raise A Native) 11.2f **(69)**
Form - 0
Record 2000 - 1st:0 2nd:0 3rd:0 Ran:1
2000 Turf 0-1: (6f) (frm)
Currently fair colt.
**I A Balding [0-1] Robert Hitchins.*

MANIKATO (USA) BHB 38f38a **RR 38f 38a** 4101[5]
6 b g Clever Trick (USA) 7.6f **(69)** - Pasampsi (USA) (Crow (FR)) 7.4f **(75)**
Form - 4615
Record 2000 - 1st:1 2nd:0 3rd:0 Ran:4
Pre2000 - 1st:0 2nd:4 3rd:2 Ran:33
Win Prizemoney £2,814 *Total Prizemoney* £11,516
Wins * 2000 Aug Chepst (G-F) H 8.1f 26 37 <
2000 Turf 1-2: (8f 1-1, 10f) (frm 1-2) 2000 AW 0-2: (7f, 9f) (Fibr 2)
Very moderate gelding, effective 8 to 10f, acts on frm, has worn blinkers. Turf high 38 (began Aug) - 5th of 20 giving 2lb to Beckon (30 Aug Brighton 10f frm RF 4101) - also 1st of 15 getting 19lb from Doberman (10 Aug Chepstow RF 3524). AW high 28.
**R Curtis [1-3] The Popsi Partners (from R M Beckett [0-2] Mar 2000).*

MANNDAR (IRE) BHB 110f **RR 121f** 5331a[8]
4 b c Doyoun 10.7f **(69)** - Madiriya (Diesis) 9.3f **(69)**
Form - 128
2000 Turf 1-3: (9f 1-1, 10f, 12f) (g-s, frm)
Well made, very high-class colt, effective 9 to 12f, acts on frm, excels at Churchill Downs. Turf high 121 - 2nd of 7 to Chester House (19 Aug Arlington Park 10f g-s RF 3942a) - also 1st of 8 getting 4lb from Falcon Flight (6 May Churchill Downs RF 1153a). Formerly trained in Britain, he is now trained in the USA and gained his biggest victory when winning the Turf Classic at Churchill Downs in the spring, but was well beaten behind Kalanisi in the Breeders' Cup Turf.
**C B Greely in USA [1-3] Columbine Stables (from L M Cumani [2-7] Spt 1999).*

MAN OF DISTINCTION BHB 88f **RR 87f** 2996[2]
2 b c Spectrum (IRE) - Air Of Distinction (IRE) **(93f)** (Distinctly North (USA))
Form - 512
Record 2000 - 1st:1 2nd:1 3rd:0 Ran:3
Win Prizemoney £3,883 *Total Prizemoney* £5,419
Wins * 2000 Jun Kempto (G-F) 6f 87 <
2000 Turf 1-3: (5f, 6f 1-2) (gd, g-f 1-1, frm)
Currently useful colt. Turf high 87 - 1st of 21 giving 3lb to Moonlight Dancer (14 Jun Kempton RF 1961).
**D R C Elsworth [1-3] Nicholas Cooper.*

MANOLO (FR) BHB 48f48a **RR 38f 48a** 1145[14]
7 b g Cricket Ball (USA) 7.9f **(75)** - Malouna (FR) (General Holme (USA)) 5.7f **(63)**
Form - 07600
Record 2000 - 1st:0 2nd:0 3rd:0 Ran:5
Pre2000 - 1st:4 2nd:4 3rd:1 Ran:28
Win Prizemoney £12,231 *Total Prizemoney* £18,296
Wins 1998 *Feb Lingfi (SLW) H 5f 56 66* <
1998 *Feb Lingfi (SLW) H 6f 58 65*
1997 Apr Pontef (G-F) H 5f 62 64
1996 Spt Beverl (G-F) 5f 62
2000 Turf 0-1: (5f) (frm) 2000 AW 0-4: (6f 4) (Fibr 4)
Very moderate gelding, often wears blinkers. AW high 34.
**D Nicholls [0-6] Lucayan Stud (from D R Loder [2-5] Apr 1998).*

MAN O'MYSTERY (USA) BHB 105f **RR 108f** 5225[2]
3 b c Diesis 9f **(80)** - Eurostorm (USA) (Storm Bird (CAN)) 10.3f **(74)**
Form - 1242642
Record 2000 - 1st:1 2nd:3 3rd:0 Ran:7
Pre2000 - 1st:0 2nd:0 3rd:0 Ran:1
Win Prizemoney £4,004 *Total Prizemoney* £47,102
Wins * 2000 Mar Leices (GD) 8f 86 <
2000 Turf 1-7: (8f 1-3, 9f, 10f 3) (sft, gd 1-5, g-f)
Well made, Pattern-class colt, effective 10f, acts on gd. Turf high 108. Got off the mark in a Leicester maiden on his reappearance despite still running green, and was only caught on the post by Medicean at Sandown next time. He reached the frame in the Britannia Handicap, John Smith's Cup and the Cambridgeshire, and was runner-up in a listed race on his final start. He deserves to find a decent race. **J Noseda [1-8] Ecurie Pharos.*

MANORBIER BHB 104f90a **RR 104f 90a** 3935[10]
4 ch g Shalford (IRE) 7.8f **(63)** - La Pirouette (USA) (Kennedy Road (CAN)) 10f **(66)**
Form - 0141120414050
Record 2000 - 1st:4 2nd:1 3rd:0 Ran:13
Pre2000 - 1st:1 2nd:1 3rd:0 Ran:5
Win Prizemoney £23,068 *Total Prizemoney* £30,011
Wins * 2000 May Thirsk (GD) H 6f 82 86 <
*** 2000** Mar Doncas (GD) H 6f 59 75
*** 2000** *Mar Wolver (STD) S 6f 61*
*** 2000** *Feb Wolver (STD) S 5f 51*
1998 Aug Chepst (G-F) 5.1f 79
2000 Turf 2-9: (5f, 6f 2-7, 7f) (g-s 2, gd 2-6, g-f) 2000 AW 2-4: (5f 1-2, 6f 1-2) (Fibr 2-4)
Leggy, very useful gelding, effective 6f, acts on g-s. Turf high 104 - 4th of 9 to Namid (27 May Curragh 6f g-s RF 1575a). AW high 61. He has progressed from Fibresand sellers to Pattern sprints and is probably capable of winning in Listed company over six furlongs on ground with some cut.
**K A Ryan [4-13] Uncle Jacks Pub (from D W P Arbuthnot [1-5] Oct 1998).*

MANOR LAKE RR 56f 4628[5]
2 b f Puissance 7.1f **(60)** - Harifa (Local Suitor (USA)) 8.4f **(67)**
Form - 5
Record 2000 - 1st:0 2nd:0 3rd:0 Ran:1
2000 Turf 0-1: (6f) (gd)
Currently fair filly.
**R F JohnsonHoughton [0-1] Exors of the late Lord Leverhulme.*

MANSA MUSA (IRE) BHB 68f70a **RR 62df 70a** 1016[9]
5 br g Hamas (IRE) 8f **(72)** - Marton Maid (Silly Season) 9.7f **(56)**
Form - 0020
Record 2000 - 1st:0 2nd:1 3rd:0 Ran:4

Pre2000 - 1st:1 2nd:2 3rd:3 Ran:16
Win Prizemoney £3,745 *Total Prizemoney* £15,436
Wins * 1999 Apr Bright (G-F) 8f 75 <
2000 Turf 0-4: (8f 2, 9f, 10f) (sft, gd, frm 2)
Average gelding, effective 8 to 9f, acts on gd to frm, likes left handed tracks, likes tight tracks. Turf high 62. He has run some good races in varied company, and got off the mark in a weak affair at Brighton. **M R Channon [1-20] Surrey Laminators Ltd.*

MANSTAR (IRE) BHB 39f30a **RR 55f 30a** 5164[11]
3 b g In The Wings 11.2f **(77)** - Model Village (Habitat) 9.4f **(70)**
Form - 58057808630
Record 2000 - 1st:0 2nd:0 3rd:1 Ran:11
Pre2000 - 1st:0 2nd:0 3rd:1 Ran:5
Win Prizemoney £0 *Total Prizemoney* £1,218
2000 Turf 0-11: (8f 2, 10f 2, 11f 5, 12f 2) (hvy, sft, gd 5, g-f 2, frm 2)
Workmanlike, fair gelding, has worn blinkers. Turf high 55.
**C W Fairhurst [0-16] C D Barber-Lomax.*

MANTILLA BHB 70a **RR 74f** 231[3]
3 b f Son Pardo - Well Tried (IRE) (Thatching) 8f **(66)**
Form - 4823
Record 2000 - 1st:0 2nd:1 3rd:1 Ran:3
Pre2000 - 1st:0 2nd:0 3rd:1 Ran:3
Win Prizemoney £0 *Total Prizemoney* £1,998
2000 AW 0-3: (8f 2, 9f) (Fibr 3)
Scopey, above-average filly, effective 5 to 9f, acts on g-s - acts on Fibr. AW high 68 - 3rd of 5 to Fair Lady (5 Feb Wolverhampton 9f Fibr RF 0231). **R Hollinshead [0-6] Exors of the late Mrs J P Bissill.*

MANTLES PRIDE BHB 71f80a **RR 84f 80a** 5242[7]
5 b g Petong 7.6f **(58)** - State Romance (Free State) 8.7f **(61)**
Form - 07418600500022017
Record 2000 - 1st:2 2nd:2 3rd:0 Ran:17
Pre2000 - 1st:4 2nd:2 3rd:6 Ran:28
Win Prizemoney £29,735 *Total Prizemoney* £44,839

Wins								
* **2000**	Oct	Doncas	(SFT)	C	7f		74	
* **2000**	May	Doncas	(G-S)	H	7f	82	84	<
1999	Spt	Haydoc	(G-F)	H	7.1f	76	79+	
1999	Aug	Redcar	(GD)	H	7f	71	76	
1999	Jly	Carlis	(FRM)	H	6.9f	66	69	
1997	Spt	Folkes	(FRM)	H	5f	78	83	

2000 Turf 2-16: (6f 2, 7f 2-12, 8f 2) (sft, g-s 1-4, gd 1-5, g-f 2, frm 4)
2000 AW 0-1: (7f) (Fibr)
Decent gelding, effective 6 to 7f, best at 7f, acts on g-s to frm, best on gd, mostly wears blinkers (very effectively), likes tight tracks. Turf high 84 - 1st of 11 getting 15lb from Adjutant (27 May Doncaster RF 1483).
**J A Glover [2-17] Mrs Janis MacPherson (from P Calver [3-22] Oct 1999).*

MANTUSIS (IRE) BHB 89f **RR 93f** 4647[14]
5 ch g Pursuit of Love 9.5f **(69)** - Mana (GER) (Windwurf (GER)) 12.7f **(72)**
Form - 321401600
Record 2000 - 1st:2 2nd:1 3rd:1 Ran:9
Pre2000 - 1st:2 2nd:3 3rd:3 Ran:17
Win Prizemoney £23,090 *Total Prizemoney* £37,669

Wins								
* **2000**	Jly	Leices	(G-F)	H	11.8f	88	93	<
* **2000**	Jun	Haydoc	(G-S)	H	10.5f	86	90	
* 1999	Oct	Yarmou	(G-F)	H	10.1f	80	83	
* 1997	Oct	Leices	(G-S)		8f		87	

2000 Turf 2-9: (10f 4, 11f 1-3, 12f 1-2) (hvy, gd 1-3, g-f 3, frm 1-2)
Useful gelding, effective 10 to 12f, acts on hvy to frm, best on gd, likes left handed tracks, prefers tight tracks. Turf high 93 - 1st of 5 giving 11lb to Court Shareef (26 Jly Leicester RF 3136) - also 1st of 7 giving 16lb to Mcgillycuddy Reeks (8 Jun Haydock RF 1807). He had a hard race when winning at Leicester in July and proved disappointing thereafter. He probably acts on any ground and has run poorly when sweating. **P W Harris [4-26] The Romantics.*

MANUFAN BHB 42f **RR 42f** 5316[20]
5 b g Sabrehill (USA) 8.5f **(64)** - The Last Empress (IRE) (Last Tycoon) 8.5f **(62)**
Form - 0
Record 2000 - 1st:0 2nd:0 3rd:0 Ran:1
Pre2000 - 1st:0 2nd:2 3rd:4 Ran:19
Win Prizemoney £0 *Total Prizemoney* £4,812
2000 Turf 0-1: (8f) (g-s)
Moderate gelding, effective 7 to 8f, acts on g-f to frm, has worn blinkers.
**G Woodward [0-1] Andrew Lloyd (from W R Muir [0-10] Oct 1999).*

MANUKA TOO (IRE) BHB 60f **RR 59f** 4728[13]
2 ch f First Trump - Kukri (Kris) 9.5f **(73)**
Form - 0500
Record 2000 - 1st:0 2nd:0 3rd:0 Ran:4
2000 Turf 0-4: (6f 3, 7f) (gd, g-f 2, frm)
Fair filly. Turf high 59 (began Aug).
**C F Wall [0-4] The Lively Partners.*

MANX GYPSY BHB 36f **RR 28f** 2668[8]
2 b f Puissance 7.1f **(60)** - Najariya (Northfields (USA)) 9f **(72)**
Form - 408
Record 2000 - 1st:0 2nd:0 3rd:0 Ran:3
Win Prizemoney £0 *Total Prizemoney* £213
2000 Turf 0-3: (5f 3) (gd 3)
Currently little account filly. Turf high 28.
**K W Hogg [0-3] Auldyn Stud Ltd.*

MANX SHADOW BHB 35f **RR 39f** 5164[14]
3 b br f Contract Law (USA) 8.9f **(54)** - Inbisat (Beldale Flutter (USA)) 9.7f **(71)**
Form - 800
Record 2000 - 1st:0 2nd:0 3rd:0 Ran:3
Pre2000 - 1st:0 2nd:0 3rd:0 Ran:6
2000 Turf 0-3: (11f 2, 12f) (gd 3)
Light-framed, very moderate filly. Becoming disappointing.
**K W Hogg [0-9] K W Hogg.*

MANXWOOD (IRE) BHB 63f72a **RR 64f 72a** 4177[4]
3 b g Petorius 8f **(66)** - Eliza Wooding **(24f)** (Faustus (USA)) 10f **(58)**
Form - 0142100284
Record 2000 - 1st:2 2nd:2 3rd:0 Ran:10
Pre2000 - 1st:0 2nd:0 3rd:0 Ran:5
Win Prizemoney £5,442 *Total Prizemoney* £9,439

Wins								
* **2000**	Jun	Windso	(GD)	H	8.3f	60	64	
* ***2000***	*Apr*	*Wolver*	*(STD)*		*7f*		*65*	<

2000 Turf 1-4: (7f, 8f 1-3) (gd, g-f 1-1, frm 2) 2000 AW 1-6: (7f 1-4, 8f, 9f) (Fibr 1-6)
Workmanlike, above-average gelding, effective 7 to 8f, best at 7f, acts on g-f - acts on Fibr, likes left handed tracks, prefers tight tracks. Turf high 64 - 1st of 18 getting 15lb from Eastern Spice (5 Jun Windsor RF 1730). AW high 72 - 2nd of 7 getting 3lb from Inver Gold (11 Aug Wolverhampton 8f Fibr RF 3573) - also 1st of 12 getting 13lb from Top of The Pops (28 Apr Wolverhampton RF 0903). Had shown only bits of form before bolting up on Wolverhampton's All-Weather track in April.
**D J S Cosgrove [2-13] Global Racing Club (from R Ingram [0-2] Jly 1999).*

MANY HAPPY RETURNS BHB 40f **RR 40f** 4695[12]
3 br f Bin Ajwaad (IRE) - Daarat Alayaam (IRE) (Reference Point) 6.8f **(70)**
Form - 0500
Record 2000 - 1st:0 2nd:0 3rd:0 Ran:4
Pre2000 - 1st:0 2nd:0 3rd:0 Ran:2
2000 Turf 0-4: (6f, 8f, 10f 2) (g-s, gd, g-f, frm)
Light-framed, moderate filly. Turf high 40.
**G B Balding [0-6] Rex L Mead & S McQueen.*

MANZONI BHB 49a **RR 47f** 4535[9]
4 b g Warrshan (USA) 9.7f **(59)** - Arc Empress Jane (IRE) (Rainbow Quest (USA)) 10.4f **(75)**
Form - 0060010
Record 2000 - 1st:1 2nd:0 3rd:0 Ran:7
Pre2000 - 1st:1 2nd:2 3rd:1 Ran:11
Win Prizemoney £5,708 *Total Prizemoney* £8,298

Wins								
* **2000**	Aug	Mussel	(G-F)	H	14f	43	46	
* *1999*	*Jly*	*Southw*	*(STD)*	*H*	*12f*	*49*	*50*	<

2000 Turf 1-7: (10f, 12f 4, 14f 1-1, 16f) (g-s, gd 3, g-f 2, frm 1-1)
Fair gelding, effective 9 to 14f, best at 12f, acts on g-f to frm - acts on Fibr, has worn blinkers, likes right handed tracks. Turf high 47 - also 1st of 6 getting 27lb from Bhutan (24 Aug Musselburgh RF 3927). Inconsistent.

**M W Easterby [2-14] Bodfari Stud Ltd (from G Lewis [0-4] Oct 1998).*

MAP BOY RR 4725[15]
2 b g Chaddleworth (IRE) - Chaconia Girl (Bay Express) 7.1f **(60)**
Form - 0
Record 2000 - 1st:0 2nd:0 3rd:0 Ran:1
2000 Turf 0-1: (6f) (gd)
Currently very poor gelding. **B R Johnson [0-1] P Grimes.*

MAPLE (IRE) BHB 60f46a **RR 62f 46a** 424[3]
4 ch g Soviet Lad (USA) 9.4f **(63)** - Little Red Rose (Precocious) 8.6f **(62)**
Form - 7636763
Record 2000 - 1st:0 2nd:0 3rd:1 Ran:4
Pre2000 - 1st:1 2nd:3 3rd:3 Ran:22
Win Prizemoney £3,980 *Total Prizemoney* £10,743
Wins 1998 Spt Newbur (GD) 6f 80 <
2000 AW 0-4: (6f, 7f, 9f, 10f) (Equi 3, Fibr)
Workmanlike, average gelding, effective 6f, acts on frm, has worn blinkers. AW high 46.
**S Dow [0-7] G Steinberg (from D R C Elsworth [1-19] Oct 1999).*

MARABAR RR 71f 4629[3]
2 b f Sri Pekan (USA) - Erbaya (IRE) (El Gran Senor (USA)) 9.6f **(76)**
Form - 63
Record 2000 - 1st:0 2nd:0 3rd:1 Ran:2
Win Prizemoney £0 *Total Prizemoney* £447
2000 Turf 0-2: (6f, 7f) (gd, frm)
Currently above-average filly. Turf high 71 (began Jly).
**P J Makin [0-1] Prof Green (from J R Arnold [0-1] Jly 2000).*

MARAH BHB 82f **RR 83f** 2464[9]
3 ch f Machiavellian (USA) 9.8f **(83)** - Samheh (USA) **(60f)** (Private Account (USA)) 8.5f **(74)**
Form - 660
Record 2000 - 1st:0 2nd:0 3rd:0 Ran:3
Pre2000 - 1st:1 2nd:0 3rd:1 Ran:4
Win Prizemoney £3,403 *Total Prizemoney* £5,154
Wins * 1999 Jun Doncas (G-F) 7f 73+ <
2000 Turf 0-3: (7f, 9f, 10f) (g-f 2, frm)
Workmanlike, decent filly, effective 7f, acts on frm, has worn blinkers. Turf high 75. **J L Dunlop [1-7] Hamdan Al Maktoum.*

MARAHA BHB 70f **RR 81f** 4156[10]
3 ch f Lammtarra (USA) - Taroob (IRE) (Roberto (USA)) 10f **(76)**
Form - 43250
Record 2000 - 1st:0 2nd:1 3rd:1 Ran:5
Pre2000 - 1st:1 2nd:0 3rd:0 Ran:3
Win Prizemoney £3,501 *Total Prizemoney* £6,489
Wins * 1999 Spt Haydoc (SFT) 8.1f 72 <
2000 Turf 0-5: (10f, 12f, 14f 3) (sft, g-f 3, frm)
Rangy, decent filly, effective 8 to 14f, acts on g-s to frm, has worn blinkers. Turf high 81. **J L Dunlop [1-8] Hamdan Al Maktoum.*

MARANI RR 74f 5098[5]
2 ch f Ashkalani (IRE) - Aquamarine (Shardari) 11f **(46)**
Form - 5
Record 2000 - 1st:0 2nd:0 3rd:0 Ran:1
2000 Turf 0-1: (8f) (gd)
Currently above-average filly. **J H M Gosden [0-1] K Abdulla.*

MARCH GROOM (USA) RR 115f 5215a[7]
6 ro h Runaway Groom (CAN) 8.1f **(69)** - Marfa's Alibi (USA) (Marfa (USA)) 14.9f **(73)**
Form - 8077
2000 Turf 0-4: (12f 4) (hvy 2, sft, gd)
High-class horse, effective 12f, acts on g-f, has worn blinkers. Turf high 108 (began Aug).
**E Pils in GER [0-4] (from O Gervai in GER [1-7] Jun 1999).*

MARCHING ORDERS (IRE) BHB 52f **RR 53f** 3715[10]
4 b g Nashwan (USA) 10.3f **(79)** - Minstrels Folly (USA) (The Minstrel (CAN)) 10f **(72)**
Form - 000600
Record 2000 - 1st:0 2nd:0 3rd:0 Ran:6
Pre2000 - 1st:2 2nd:1 3rd:1 Ran:8
Win Prizemoney £8,901 *Total Prizemoney* £10,435
Wins 1999 Oct Cork (SFT) H 8f 85 86 <
1999 Aug Fairyh (GD) 9f 86 <
2000 Turf 0-6: (7f, 8f 2, 10f 2, 11f) (sft, g-s, gd, g-f, frm 2)
Fair gelding, effective 8 to 9f, best at 9f, acts on sft to gd, often wears blinkers (very effectively), prefers right handed tracks. Turf high 53.
**T H Caldwell [0-6] R S G Jones & Hogarth Racing (from D K Weld in IRE [2-8] Oct 1999).*

MARCH KING (IRE) RR 98f 4527a[3]
2 b c Caerleon (USA) 10.9f **(79)** - Porphyrine (FR) (Habitat) 9.4f **(70)**
Form - 423
2000 Turf 0-3: (7f, 8f 2) (sft, gd)
Currently very useful colt. Turf high 98 (began Aug). In the frame in maidens at a mile. **T Stack in IRE [0-3] Mrs John Magnier.*

MARCIANO BHB 30f **RR 51f** 748[13]
4 b g Rock Hopper 10.6f **(54)** - Raintree Venture (Good Times (ITY)) 6.6f **(54)**
Form - 80
Record 2000 - 1st:0 2nd:0 3rd:0 Ran:2
Pre2000 - 1st:0 2nd:0 3rd:0 Ran:5
2000 Turf 0-1: (22f) (sft) 2000 AW 0-1: (13f) (Equi)
Workmanlike, fair gelding.
**R C Spicer [0-4] A J Coupland (from C W Thornton [0-5] Jly 1999).*

MARCUS MAXIMUS (USA) BHB 95f85a **RR 115?f 85a** 4003[6]
5 ch g Woodman (USA) 9.7f **(77)** - Star Pastures (Northfields (USA)) 9f **(72)**
Form - 6
Record 2000 - 1st:0 2nd:0 3rd:0 Ran:1
Pre2000 - 1st:3 2nd:0 3rd:0 Ran:5
Win Prizemoney £18,815 *Total Prizemoney* £19,341
Wins * 1999 May Newcas (FRM) 12.4f 119 <
* 1998 Spt Doncas (GD) 10.3f 105
* 1998 Jly Yarmou (G-F) 11.5f 77
2000 Turf 0-1: (12f) (gd)
High-class gelding. **H R A Cecil [3-6] Wafic Said.*

MARDANI (IRE) BHB 86f92a **RR 89f 92a** 5125[9]
5 b g Fairy King (USA) 7.7f **(75)** - Marmana (USA) (Blushing Groom (FR)) 10.3f **(76)**
Form - 80002662630
Record 2000 - 1st:0 2nd:2 3rd:1 Ran:11
Pre2000 - 1st:4 2nd:4 3rd:1 Ran:14
Win Prizemoney £24,832 *Total Prizemoney* £57,145
Wins * 1999 Jly York (G-F) H 11.9f 93 94 <
* 1999 Jun Beverl (G-F) H 12f 90 91
1998 Aug Leopar (GD) 12f 92+
1998 Jly Dundal (G-F) 12f 82+
2000 Turf 0-10: (12f 8, 14f 2) (g-s, gd 5, g-f 3, frm) 2000 AW 0-1: (12f) (Equi)
Useful gelding, effective 12 to 15f, best at 12f, acts on g-s to frm, best on g-f, likes right handed tracks, does well at York. Turf high 89 - 3rd of 20 giving 4lb to Seren Hill (12 Oct Newmarket 12f gd RF 4936). He is possibly happiest in small fields, goes well on fast ground and is best ridden close to the pace.
**M Johnston [2-19] Markus Graff (from J Oxx in IRE [2-6] Spt 1998).*

MAREMMA BHB 22f34a **RR 32f 34a** 1837[6]
6 b m Robellino (USA) 9.5f **(68)** - Maiden Way (Shareef Dancer (USA)) 9.9f **(73)**
Form - 86
Record 2000 - 1st:0 2nd:0 3rd:0 Ran:2
Pre2000 - 1st:2 2nd:0 3rd:2 Ran:33
Win Prizemoney £5,071 *Total Prizemoney* £6,173
Wins 1998 Jly Doncas (G-F) S 12f 37
1997 Jly Redcar (G-S) S 11f 46 <
2000 Turf 0-2: (14f 2) (gd, frm)
Very moderate mare. Turf high 32 (1st run) - 8th of 8 getting 5lb from Hullbank (2 Jun Catterick 14f frm RF 1656). Consistent.
**Miss Kate Milligan [2-13] A F Monk & Associates (from Don Enrico Incisa [2-33] Jly 1998).*

MARENGO BHB 56a **RR 64f** 5120[5]
6 b g Never so Bold 7.1f **(62)** - Born to Dance (Dancing Brave (USA))

8.4f **(76)**
Form - 083762232150402480006365700105
Record 2000 - 1st:2 2nd:4 3rd:3 Ran:30
Pre2000 - 1st:4 2nd:3 3rd:6 Ran:41
Win Prizemoney £22,589 *Total Prizemoney* £33,890
Wins * **2000** *Spt Southw (STD) H 6f 52 56*
* **2000** May Doncas (G-S) C 6f 63
* 1999 *Dec Southw (STD) H 6f 50 56*
1998 Apr Epsom (SFT) H 6f 62 65
1998 *Apr Wolver (STD) H 6f 57 66* <
1998 *Mar Southw (STD) H 6f 53 53*
2000 Turf 1-16: (5f 5, 6f 1-10, 7f) (g-s 2, gd 5, g-f 1-5, frm 3, hrd) 2000 AW 1-14: (5f, 6f 1-12, 7f) (Fibr 1-14)
Average gelding, effective 6f, acts on g-s to g-f, best on gd, has worn blinkers. Turf high 64 - 4th of 12 giving 3lb to Beyond Calculation (19 May Nottingham 6f gd RF 1313) - also 1st of 14 getting 8lb from Russian Romeo (1 May Doncaster RF 0937). AW high 57. A quirky customer, he is a useful tool on his day and is quite capable of winning races on turf and Fibresand should he wish to. Best over six furlongs.
**M J Polglase [3-38] Brian Androlia (from J Berry [0-13] Oct 1999).*

MARENKA BHB 69f RR 73f 5101[9]
3 b f Mtoto 11.5f **(71)** - Sliprail (USA) (Our Native (USA)) 11.2f **(63)**
Form - 42350
Record 2000 - 1st:0 2nd:1 3rd:1 Ran:5
Win Prizemoney £0 *Total Prizemoney* £1,759
2000 Turf 0-5: (10f 5) (gd 3, frm 2)
Lengthy, above-average filly. Turf high 73 - 2nd of 15 to Eurolink Artemis (20 Jly Leicester 10f frm RF 2973).
**H Candy [0-5] Major M G Wyatt.*

MARE OF WETWANG BHB 42f RR 56f 5102[12]
2 ch f River Falls 8.2f **(56)** - Kudos Blue **(36f)** (Elmaamul (USA))
Form - 608700
Record 2000 - 1st:0 2nd:0 3rd:0 Ran:6
2000 Turf 0-6: (5f 2, 6f 2, 7f 2) (g-s, gd, g-f, frm 3)
Fair filly. Turf high 56 (began Jly).
**J D Bethell [0-6] Richard Whiteley.*

MARGARET'S DANCER BHB 47f44a RR 48f 44a 5316[16]
5 b g Rambo Dancer (CAN) 8.4f **(59)** - Cateryne (Ballymoss) 8.5f **(55)**
Form - 77761030
Record 2000 - 1st:1 2nd:0 3rd:1 Ran:7
Pre2000 - 1st:3 2nd:2 3rd:2 Ran:30
Win Prizemoney £12,026 *Total Prizemoney* £15,171
Wins * **2000** Aug Thirsk (GD) SH 8f 44 46
* 1998 Spt Beverl (G-F) H 8.5f 57 62 <
* 1998 Spt Thirsk (GD) S 8f 57
* 1998 Jun Pontef (SFT) S 8f 49
2000 Turf 1-7: (8f 1-3, 9f, 10f 3) (g-s 2, gd 2, frm 1-3)
Moderate gelding, effective 8f, acts on gd, has worn blinkers, likes tight tracks. Turf high 48 (began Jly).
**J L Eyre [4-29] J Bladen (from C Smith [0-8] Spt 1997).*

MARGARITA (IRE) BHB 50f RR 52f 4114[8]
2 b f Turtle Island (IRE) - Shimeoni (IRE) (Auction Ring (USA)) 8.6f **(65)**
Form - 07058
Record 2000 - 1st:0 2nd:0 3rd:0 Ran:5
2000 Turf 0-5: (5f, 6f 3, 7f) (hvy, gd, frm 3)
Fair filly, had worn blinkers. Turf high 52. (DEAD)
**C Weedon [0-4] Atlantic Foods Ltd (from M Blanshard [0-1] Apr 2000).*

MARGAY (IRE) RR 97f 2722a[6]
3 b f Marju - Almarai (USA) (Vaguely Noble) 10.1f **(72)**
Form - 3226
2000 Turf 0-4: (7f, 8f 3) (sft, g-s, gd 2)
Very useful filly, effective 7 to 8f, best at 8f, acts on sft to gd. Turf high 97. Consistent. She chased Crimplene home at a respectful distance in the German 1000 Guineas but was not seen out after July. **M J Grassick in IRE [1-8] Mrs C Grassick.*

MARIA FROM CAPLAW BHB 34f RR ?f 5188[10]
3 ch f Clantime 6.6f **(57)** - Mary From Dunlow (Nicholas Bill) 10.1f **(56)**
Form - 00
Record 2000 - 1st:0 2nd:0 3rd:0 Ran:2
Pre2000 - 1st:0 2nd:0 3rd:0 Ran:3
2000 Turf 0-2: (5f 2) (sft, gd)
Workmanlike, very poor filly. (began Oct).
**J S Goldie [0-2] Charles Johnston (from J J O'Neill [0-3] Spt 1999).*

MARIANA BHB 30a RR 29f 5182[8]
5 ch m Anshan 8.2f **(63)** - Maria Cappuccini (Siberian Express (USA)) 8.8f **(65)**
Form - 7505000373708
Record 2000 - 1st:0 2nd:0 3rd:2 Ran:12
Pre2000 - 1st:0 2nd:2 3rd:3 Ran:28
Win Prizemoney £0 *Total Prizemoney* £3,346
2000 Turf 0-5: (7f, 8f, 12f 2, 14f) (sft, gd, g-f 2, frm) 2000 AW 0-7: (7f 3, 8f, 11f 2, 16f) (Equi 2, Fibr 5)
Little account filly, effective 12f, acts on g-f, has worn blinkers. Turf high 29 - 3rd of 14 getting 5lb from Mithraic (9 Aug Newcastle 12f g-f RF 3495). AW high 27.
**T T Clement [0-24] C Holcroft (from R M Whitaker [0-16] Oct 1998).*

MARIENBARD (IRE) BHB 111f RR 116+f 5130[2]
3 b c Caerleon (USA) 10.9f **(79)** - Marienbad (FR) (Darshaan) 9.9f **(84)**
Form - 111262
Record 2000 - 1st:3 2nd:2 3rd:0 Ran:6
Win Prizemoney £26,565 *Total Prizemoney* £67,615
Wins * **2000** Jly Haydoc (G-F) L 11.9f 109+ <
* **2000** Jun Windso (G-F) 11.6f 93+
* **2000** Jun Leices (G-S) 11.8f 70+
2000 Turf 3-6: (12f 3-5, 15f) (sft, gd 2-3, g-f 1-1, frm)
Workmanlike, high-class colt, effective 12 to 15f, best at 12f, acts on sft to frm. Turf high 116 - 2nd of 7 to Wellbeing (21 Oct Newbury 12f sft RF 5130) - also 1st of 5 from Air Marshall (8 Jly Haydock RF 2634). Unraced at two, he quickly developed into a smart performer and put up a game effort when beating Air Marshall in a Listed race at Haydock during July. Unable to confirm that form in the Gordon Stakes or St Leger, he made Wellbeing pull out all the stops on his final start and remains an interesting prospect. Probably best on easy ground, he could develop into a Cup horse in 2001. **M A Jarvis [3-6] Saif Ali.*

MARIGLIANO (USA) BHB 55f64a RR 57f 64a 4875[8]
7 b g Riverman (USA) 9.7f **(78)** - Mount Holyoke (Golden Fleece (USA)) 7.9f **(74)**
Form - 8
Record 2000 - 1st:0 2nd:0 3rd:0 Ran:1
Pre2000 - 1st:3 2nd:1 3rd:5 Ran:18
Win Prizemoney £7,940 *Total Prizemoney* £12,098
Wins * 1998 *Jly Southw (STD) C 7f 69*
* 1998 Jun Mussel (SFT) C 7.1f 73+ <
1996 May Beverl (G-F) 7.5f 69+
2000 Turf 0-1: (8f) (g-s)
Average gelding.
**K A Morgan [8-38] Pryke,A Roche,B Jone Scaife (from Sir Michael Stoute [1-4] Jun 1996).*

MARIKA RR 47f 3436[5]
2 b f Marju (IRE) 9.2f **(76)** - Nordica (Northfields (USA)) 9f **(72)**
Form - 5
Record 2000 - 1st:0 2nd:0 3rd:0 Ran:1
2000 Turf 0-1: (6f) (g-f)
Currently moderate filly. **B W Hills [0-1] O F Waller.*

MARINE RR 93f 5001[3]
2 b c Marju (IRE) 9.2f **(76)** - Ivorine (USA) (Blushing Groom (FR)) 10.3f **(76)**
Form - 5115533
Record 2000 - 1st:2 2nd:0 3rd:2 Ran:7
Win Prizemoney £11,812 *Total Prizemoney* £17,521
Wins * **2000** Jun Newbur (G-F) 6f 87 <
* **2000** Jun Goodwo (GD) 6f 80
2000 Turf 2-7: (6f 2-4, 7f, 8f 2) (g-s, gd 3, g-f 2-2, hrd)
Useful colt, effective 6 to 8f, best at 8f, acts on g-s to g-f, best on gd, has worn blinkers. Turf high 93 - 3rd of 9 giving 3lb to Worthily (16 Oct Pontefract 8f g-s RF 5001) - also 1st of 5 from Blueberry Forest (15 Jun Newbury RF 1988). He caught the eye after a tardy start on his debut and developed into a useful performer despite showing signs of temperament. He can improve when tried beyond a mile but looks too high in the handicap at present.
**R Charlton [2-7] K Abdulla.*

MARINO STREET BHB 60f44a **RR 59f 44a** 4487[11]
7 b m Totem (USA) 5f **(38)** - Demerger (Dominion) 8.5f **(63)**
Form - 21156620
Record 2000 - 1st:2 2nd:2 3rd:0 Ran:8
Pre2000 - 1st:3 2nd:8 3rd:10 Ran:60
Win Prizemoney £13,963 *Total Prizemoney* £26,360
Wins * 2000 Jun Warwic (G-F) H 5f 48 54 <
*** 2000** Jun Nottin (G-F) H 6.1f 48 51
* 1999 Jly Haydoc (G-S) H 5f 34 43+
* 1999 Jun Warwic (G-F) H 5f 34 37
1996 Jly Leices (G-F) 5f 48
2000 Turf 2-8: (5f 1-6, 6f 1-2) (gd, g-f 1-3, frm 1-3, hrd)
Fair mare, effective 5 to 6f, best at 5f, acts on gd to frm, best on frm, often wears blinkers (extremely effectively), does well at Warwick and Nottingham. Turf high 59 - 2nd of 18 getting 10lb from Premium Princess (15 Spt Nottingham 6f gd RF 4442) - also 1st of 20 getting 9lb from Poppy's Song (28 Jun Warwick RF 2355). Consistent. She shows only modest form on turf and sand these days.
**B A McMahon [4-16] Roy Penton (from P D Evans [1-52] Aug 1998).*

MARITUN LAD BHB 51f60a **RR 54df 60a** 4992[6]
3 b g Presidium 7.5t **(56)** - Girl Next Door **(35df 36a)** (Local Suitor (USA)) 8.4f **(67)**
Form - 6543164086
Record 2000 - 1st:1 2nd:0 3rd:1 Ran:8
Pre2000 - 1st:0 2nd:0 3rd:0 Ran:3
Win Prizemoney £2,704 *Total Prizemoney* £3,229
Wins * 2000 *Mar Wolver (STD) 5f 60 <*
2000 Turf 0-3: (5f 3) (gd 2, frm) 2000 AW 1-5: (5f 1-2, 6f 3) (Equi, Fibr 1-4)
Average gelding, effective 5 to 6f, best at 6f, - acts on AW, best on Fibr, often wears blinkers. Turf high 56. AW high 60 - 1st of 8 from Tropical King (2 Mar Wolverhampton RF 0393).
**D Shaw [1-11] M G Vines.*

MARJAANA (IRE) BHB 40f **RR 19f** 545[13]
7 b m Shaadi (USA) 8.1f **(75)** - Funun (USA) (Fappiano (USA)) 8.7f **(77)**
Form - 00
Record 2000 - 1st:0 2nd:0 3rd:0 Ran:1
Pre2000 - 1st:4 2nd:6 3rd:1 Ran:27
Win Prizemoney £11,762 *Total Prizemoney* £23,431
Wins 1997 Aug Beverl (G-S) H 7.5f 70 78
1997 Jun Folkes (G-F) 6.9f 74
1997 May Warwic (G-F) H 8f 62 70
2000 Turf 0-1: (7f) (frm)
Little account mare, has worn blinkers. Becoming disappointing. She has enjoyed a good season in '97, often in amateurs' races. Her regular partner Susie Samworth is one of our better lady riders.
**C Smith [0-4] Mrs Julia Scott (from P T Walwyn [4-24] Oct 1997).*

MARJEUNE BHB 63f **RR 69f** 4692[11]
3 b f Marju (IRE) 9.2f **(76)** - Ann Veronica (IRE) (Sadler's Wells (USA)) 10f **(76)**
Form - 72330
Record 2000 - 1st:0 2nd:1 3rd:2 Ran:5
Pre2000 - 1st:1 2nd:0 3rd:0 Ran:5
Win Prizemoney £3,139 *Total Prizemoney* £5,962
Wins * 1999 Oct Nottin (SFT) H 10f 62 65 <
2000 Turf 0-5: (12f 3, 14f, 15f) (gd 2, g-f, frm 2)
Unfurnished, average filly, effective 10 to 12f, acts on g-s to frm, likes tight tracks. Turf high 69 (began Jly) - 2nd of 11 giving 7lb to Sweet Angeline (4 Aug Thirsk 12f frm RF 3381).
**P W Harris [1-10] The Lords Of The Ring.*

MARJORY POLLEY BHB 48f41a **RR 32f 41a** 2485[16]
3 ch f Timeless Times (USA) 6.1f **(56)** - Rubylee **(59f 63a)** (Persian Bold) 9.3f **(66)**
Form - 800
Record 2000 - 1st:0 2nd:0 3rd:0 Ran:3
Pre2000 - 1st:0 2nd:0 3rd:0 Ran:3
2000 Turf 0-2: (7f, 9f) (g-s, gd) 2000 AW 0-1: (6f) (Fibr)
Leggy, very moderate filly, has worn blinkers. Turf high 5.
**Miss A M Newton-Smith [0-3] John Grist (from P T Walwyn [0-3] Spt 1999).*

MARJU GUEST (IRE) BHB 61f60a **RR 00f 60a** 2084[9]
3 b f Marju (IRE) 9.2f **(76)** - Dance Ahead (Shareef Dancer (USA)) 9.9f **(73)**
Form - 2300
Record 2000 - 1st:0 2nd:1 3rd:1 Ran:4
Pre2000 - 1st:0 2nd:0 3rd:0 Ran:3
Win Prizemoney £0 *Total Prizemoney* £1,759
2000 Turf 0-2: (8f, 11f) (hvy, frm) 2000 AW 0-2: (8f, 9f) (Fibr 2)
Leggy, average filly, effective 8f, - acts on Fibr. Turf high 50. AW high 62 (1st run) - 2nd of 9 getting 23lb from Welody (11 Mar Wolverhampton 8f Fibr RF 0430).
**M R Channon [0-7] John Guest.*

MARKELLIS (USA) BHB 28f30a **RR 35f 30a** 510[P]
4 b g Housebuster (USA) 7f **(81)** - Crimsons Contender (USA) (Monsieur Champlain (USA))
Form - 86084184505675P
Record 2000 - 1st:0 2nd:0 3rd:0 Ran:9
Pre2000 - 1st:1 2nd:0 3rd:0 Ran:12
Win Prizemoney £1,861 *Total Prizemoney* £1,861
Wins * 1999 *Dec Southw (SLW) H 12f 36 29 <*
2000 AW 0-9: (11f, 12f 4, 14f, 16f 3) (Fibr 9)
Very moderate gelding, effective 12f, - acted on Fibr, had worn blinkers, favoured left handed tracks, liked tight tracks. AW high 40 - 4th of 10 giving 10lb to Dream On Me (8 Jan Wolverhampton 12f Fibr RF 0056). (DEAD)
**D Carroll [1-18] Mark Barrett (from Patrick Prendergast in IRE [0-4] Jly 1999).*

MARKHAN (UAE) RR 576a[5]
3 f
Form - 5
2000 AW 0-1: (9f) (Dirt)
Currently Group-class.
**J Hennessy in SAR [0-1].*

MARKING TIME (IRE) RR 1205[8]
2 b g Goldmark (USA) - Tamarsiya (USA) (Shahrastani (USA)) 8.8f **(72)**
Form - 8
Record 2000 - 1st:0 2nd:0 3rd:0 Ran:1
2000 AW 0-1: (5f) (Fibr)
Currently very poor gelding.
**K R Burke [0-1] Mrs Elaine Burke.*

MARK OF PROPHET (IRE) BHB 70f **RR 75f** 1082[4]
5 b g Scenic 10.6f **(66)** - Sure Flyer (IRE) (Sure Blade (USA)) 11.3f **(67)**
Form - 4
Record 2000 - 1st:0 2nd:0 3rd:0 Ran:1
Pre2000 - 1st:2 2nd:2 3rd:0 Ran:10
Win Prizemoney £10,505 *Total Prizemoney* £13,698
Wins 1998 Oct Newmar (GD) H 14f 70 75 <
1998 Aug Leices (GD) 11.8f 72
2000 Turf 0-1: (12f) (frm)
Above-average gelding. (1st run) - 4th of 18 getting 28lb from Rainbow Ways (7 May Newmarket 12f frm RF 1082).
**N A Callaghan [0-1] P Cunningham (from J E Banks [2-10] Oct 1998).*

MARK ONE BHB 85f **RR 79f** 4028[5]
2 b f Mark of Esteem (IRE) - One Wild Oat **(53f 43a)** (Shareef Dancer (USA)) 9.9f **(73)**
Form - 325
Record 2000 - 1st:0 2nd:1 3rd:1 Ran:3
Win Prizemoney £0 *Total Prizemoney* £1,571
2000 Turf 0-3: (7f 2, 8f) (g-f, frm 2)
Currently above-average filly. Turf high 79 (began Jly) - 2nd of 4 getting 5lb from Spettro (8 Aug Catterick 7f frm RF 3447).
**B W Hills [0-3] E D Kessly.*

MARKUSHA BHB 70f **RR 72f** 4425[3]
2 b g Alhijaz 7.7f **(57)** - Shafir (IRE) **(61f)** (Shaadi (USA))
Form - 4373
Record 2000 - 1st:0 2nd:0 3rd:2 Ran:4
Win Prizemoney £0 *Total Prizemoney* £1,870
2000 Turf 0-3: (5f, 6f 2) (gd 2, frm) 2000 AW 0-1: (6f) (Fibr)
Above-average gelding. Turf high 72 - 3rd of 11 getting 13lb from Soldier On (15 Spt Ayr 6f gd RF 4425). **D Nicholls [0-4] Nigel Munton.*

MARLATARA (IRE) RR 49f 2334[2]
3 br f Marju (IRE) 9.2f **(76)** - Khalatara (IRE) (Kalaglow) 9.8f **(67)**
Form - 2
Record 2000 - 1st:0 2nd:1 3rd:0 Ran:1
Win Prizemoney £0 *Total Prizemoney* £1,154
2000 Turf 0-1: (13f) (frm)
Light-framed, currently moderate filly. (1st run) - 2nd of 4 to Darariyna (28 Jun Chester 13f frm RF 2334).
**P F I Cole [0-1] Elite Racing Club.*

MARMADUKE (IRE) BHB 65a **RR 66f** 3755[10]
4 ch g Perugino (USA) - Sympathy (Precocious) 8.6f **(62)**
Form - 8703667340
Record 2000 - 1st:0 2nd:0 3rd:2 Ran:8
Pre2000 - 1st:1 2nd:0 3rd:1 Ran:10
Win Prizemoney £8,596 *Total Prizemoney* £11,579
Wins 1998 Oct San Si (SFT) 7.5f
2000 Turf 0-6: (8f, 10f, 12f 2, 14f, 16f) (g-s, gd, g-f 2, frm, hrd) 2000 AW 0-2: (8f 2) (Equi 2)
Average gelding, effective 6 to 7f, acts on gd to frm, has worn blinkers. Turf high 66. AW high 54.
**Miss Gay Kelleway [0-13] Martin Butler (from L M Cumani [1-5] Jly 1999).*

MARNIE BHB 58f59a **RR 57f 59a** 4809[10]
3 ch f First Trump - Miss Aboyne (Lochnager) 6f **(59)**
Form - 006822100
Record 2000 - 1st:1 2nd:2 3rd:0 Ran:9
Pre2000 - 1st:0 2nd:0 3rd:1 Ran:4
Win Prizemoney £2,383 *Total Prizemoney* £5,400
Wins * 2000 Jly Bright (FRM) H 6f 52 57 <
2000 Turf 1-8: (6f 1-6, 7f, 8f) (g-s, gd, g-f 3, frm 1-3) 2000 AW 0-1: (8f) (Fibr)
Scopey, fair filly, effective 6 to 7f, acts on g-f to frm, prefers left handed tracks, prefers tight tracks. Turf high 57 - 1st of 11 giving 10lb to Lucky's Son (24 Jly Brighton RF 3077).
**J Akehurst [1-5] The Grass is Greener Partnership (from J S Moore [0-4] Jun 2000).*

MAROMA BHB 70f **RR 63f** 4142[7]
2 b f First Trump - Madurai **(63f)** (Chilibang)
Form - 547
Record 2000 - 1st:0 2nd:0 3rd:0 Ran:3
Win Prizemoney £0 *Total Prizemoney* £292
2000 Turf 0-3: (6f 2, 7f) (g-s, g-f 2)
Currently average filly. Turf high 63. **J L Dunlop [0-3] J L Dunlop.*

MAROMITO (IRE) BHB 62f **RR 64f** 5083[12]
3 b c Up and At 'em - Amtico (Bairn (USA)) 7.7f **(59)**
Form - 00000200
Record 2000 - 1st:0 2nd:1 3rd:0 Ran:8
Pre2000 - 1st:1 2nd:0 3rd:0 Ran:2
Win Prizemoney £3,817 *Total Prizemoney* £4,797
Wins * 1999 Jun Lingfi (GD) 5f 80+ <
2000 Turf 0-8: (5f 7, 6f) (hvy, sft, gd 2, g-f 2, frm 2)
Strong, average colt, effective 5f, acts on frm. Turf high 64 (began Jly). **R Bastiman [1-10] Peter Beaton-Brown.*

MARON BHB 44f60a **RR 46f 60a** 5018[5]
3 b g Puissance 7.1f **(60)** - Will Be Bold (Bold Lad (IRE)) 8.4f **(68)**
Form - 0032170075
Record 2000 - 1st:1 2nd:1 3rd:1 Ran:10
Pre2000 - 1st:1 2nd:1 3rd:3 Ran:12
Win Prizemoney £5,973 *Total Prizemoney* £10,215
Wins * 2000 Jly Catter (G-F) H 6f 56 58
1999 Jly Hamilt (G-F) 5f 71 <
2000 Turf 1-9: (5f 4, 6f 1-5) (g-s, gd 3, g-f 1-2, frm 3) 2000 AW 0-1: (7f) (Fibr)
Workmanlike, moderate gelding, effective 5f, acts on g-f to frm, best on g-f. Turf high 59. Consistent.
**A Berry [1-10] A S Kelvin (from J Berry [1-12] Oct 1999).*

MARRAKECH (IRE) RR 84+f 4330[13]
3 ch f Barathea (IRE) - Nashkara (Shirley Heights) 10.3f **(74)**
Form - 410
Record 2000 - 1st:1 2nd:0 3rd:0 Ran:3
Win Prizemoney £3,900 *Total Prizemoney* £4,237
Wins * 2000 Aug Sandow (GD) 8.1f 84+ <
2000 Turf 1-3: (8f 1-1, 9f, 10f) (gd, g-f 1-2)
Workmanlike, currently decent filly. Turf high 84 (began Aug) - 1st of 7 from Woolfe (19 Aug Sandown RF 3806).
**P W Harris [1-3] Millennium Crossing.*

MARREL BHB 60f **RR 71f** 5114[3]
2 b g Shareef Dancer (USA) 10.1f **(67)** - Upper Caen (High Top) 10.2f **(67)**
Form - 003
Record 2000 - 1st:0 2nd:0 3rd:1 Ran:3
Win Prizemoney £0 *Total Prizemoney* £391
2000 Turf 0-2: (7f, 8f) (g-s, g-f) 2000 AW 0-1: (9f) (Fibr)
Currently above-average gelding. Turf high 71 (began Spt).
**B Hanbury [0-3] H B E Van Cutsem.*

MARSAD (IRE) BHB 86f **RR 88f** 4865[12]
6 ch g Fayruz 6.6f **(63)** - Broad Haven (IRE) (Be My Guest (USA)) 9.3f **(67)**
Form - 50072000
Record 2000 - 1st:0 2nd:1 3rd:0 Ran:8
Pre2000 - 1st:2 2nd:2 3rd:6 Ran:21
Win Prizemoney £10,671 *Total Prizemoney* £34,871
Wins * 1999 Mar Doncas (G-S) H 6f 82 91+ <
*** 1998** Apr Kempto (SFT) H 6f 69 79?
2000 Turf 0-8: (6f 7, 7f) (sft, gd 6, g-f)
Useful gelding, effective 6f, acts on g-s to gd, best on gd, does well at Goodwood. Turf high 91 (1st run) - 5th of 18 giving 9lb to Passion For Life (25 Mar Kempton 6f gd RF 0502). A soft ground specialist, he is on a long losing run but seems to retain all his ability. Best around six furlongs, he is genuine.
**J Akehurst [2-19] Canisbay Bloodstock Ltd (from R Akehurst [0-3] Jly 1997).*

MARSHAL BOND BHB 65f **RR 69f** 5312[13]
2 b c Celtic Swing - Arminda (Blakeney) 10.5f **(64)**
Form - 6270
Record 2000 - 1st:0 2nd:1 3rd:0 Ran:4
Win Prizemoney £0 *Total Prizemoney* £939
2000 Turf 0-4: (7f 2, 8f 2) (g-s, gd 2, g-f)
Average colt. Turf high 69 (began Aug) - 2nd of 10 giving 3lb to Sister Celestine (13 Spt Beverley 7f g-f RF 4362).
**B Smart [0-4] R C Bond.*

MARSHALL ST CYR BHB 57f **RR 60f** 3057[11]
3 ch g Emarati (USA) 6.6f **(63)** - St Helena (Monsanto (FR)) 6.5f **(59)**
Form - 500564280
Record 2000 - 1st:0 2nd:1 3rd:0 Ran:8
Pre2000 - 1st:0 2nd:1 3rd:0 Ran:3
Win Prizemoney £0 *Total Prizemoney* £1,574
2000 Turf 0-8: (5f 6, 6f, 7f) (g-s, gd 3, g-f, frm 3)
Lengthy, average gelding, effective 5f, acted on gd, had worn blinkers. Turf high 60. (DEAD)
**J G Given [0-4] D Maloney (from P D Evans [0-7] May 2000).*

MARSH MARIGOLD BHB 42f55a **RR 34f 55a** 2359[8]
6 br m Tina's Pet 7.4f **(56)** - Pulga (Blakeney) 10.5f **(64)**
Form - 8
Record 2000 - 1st:0 2nd:0 3rd:0 Ran:1
Pre2000 - 1st:2 2nd:3 3rd:3 Ran:28
Win Prizemoney £4,885 *Total Prizemoney* £9,218
Wins 1997 Jun Pontef (G-F) H 10f 57 65 <
1996 Oct Haydoc (SFT) SH 6f 60 61
2000 Turf 0-1: (16f) (g-f)
Very moderate mare. Inconsistent.
**G Fierro [4-35] G Fierro (from J Hetherton [1-11] Jly 1997).*

MARTELLIAN (SWE) RR 105f 4141a[2]
4 b g Desert Sport (FR) - Martelli (Pitskelly) 8.5f **(53)**
Form - 2
2000 Turf 0-1: (9f) (sft)
Currently Pattern-class gelding. (1st run) - 2nd of 14 to Valley Chapel (27 Aug Ovrevoll 9f sft RF 4141a). **in NOR [0-1].*

MARTELLO BHB 60f **RR 65f** 5063[11]
4 b g Polish Precedent (USA) 9f **(73)** - Round Tower (High Top) 10.2f

(67)
Form - 420
Record 2000 - 1st:0 2nd:1 3rd:0 Ran:3
Pre2000 - 1st:0 2nd:0 3rd:0 Ran:7
Win Prizemoney £0 *Total Prizemoney* £1,240
2000 Turf 0-3: (8f 2, 10f) (sft, g-s 2)
Scopey, average gelding, effective 8f, acts on g-s, has worn blinkers. Turf high 65 (began Spt) - 2nd of 18 giving 4lb to Cautious Joe (9 Oct Leicester 8f g-s RF 4875).
**R Charlton [0-10] Beckhampton Stables Ltd.*

MARTHA P PERKINS (IRE) BHB 62f RR 66f 4580[14]
2 b f Fayruz 6.6f **(63)** - Cake Contract (IRE) (Contract Law (USA))
Form - 850
Record 2000 - 1st:0 2nd:0 3rd:0 Ran:3
2000 Turf 0-3: (5f 3) (gd, frm 2)
Currently average filly. Turf high 66 (began Aug).
**T G Mills [0-3] Mrs Byron Paterson.*

MARTHA REILLY (IRE) BHB 41f39a RR 48f 39a 5161[5]
4 ch f Rainbows For Life (CAN) 9.3f **(64)** - Debach Delight (Great Nephew) 9.9f **(64)**
Form - 03462703155
Record 2000 - 1st:1 2nd:1 3rd:1 Ran:7
Pre2000 - 1st:1 2nd:0 3rd:2 Ran:21
Win Prizemoney £5,567 *Total Prizemoney* £7,546
Wins * **2000** Oct Pontef (HVY) H 17.1f 40 48
* 1999 *Feb Southw (STD) S 8f 59* <
2000 Turf 1-7: (16f 5, 17f 1-1, 18f) (sft, g-s 1-3, frm 3)
Leggy, moderate filly, effective 8f, - acts on Fibr, has worn blinkers, likes left handed tracks. Turf high 48 (began Jly).
**Mrs Barbara Waring [2-28] J McDonnell, H Shapter & P Haggarty.*

MARTIAL EAGLE (IRE) BHB 60f RR 12f 5311[10]
4 b g Sadler's Wells (USA) 11.3f **(87)** - Twine (Thatching) 8f **(66)**
Form - 00
Record 2000 - 1st:0 2nd:0 3rd:0 Ran:2
Pre2000 - 1st:1 2nd:0 3rd:0 Ran:2
Win Prizemoney £3,437 *Total Prizemoney* £3,437
Wins 1999 Jun Cork (G-F) 14f 70 <
2000 Turf 0-2: (10f, 15f) (sft, g-s)
Very moderate gelding. Turf high 12 (began Oct).
**N Tinkler [0-2] The Izz That Right Partnership (from A P O'Brien in IRE [1-2] Jun 1999).*

MARTIN (IRE) BHB 44f RR 49f 3057[15]
3 b g Dancing Dissident (USA) 6.8f **(65)** - Martin's Princess (Martin John) 13.1f **(62)**
Form - 700
Record 2000 - 1st:0 2nd:0 3rd:0 Ran:3
Pre2000 - 1st:0 2nd:0 3rd:0 Ran:4
2000 Turf 0-3: (5f 2, 8f) (gd, g-f, frm)
Small, moderate gelding. Turf high 40.
**Martyn Wane [0-7] J P Slattery.*

MARTINEZ (IRE) BHB 43f RR 30f 5246[10]
4 b g Tirol 8.1f **(64)** - Elka (USA) (Val de L'Orne (FR)) 12f **(75)**
Form - 0
Record 2000 - 1st:0 2nd:0 3rd:0 Ran:1
Pre2000 - 1st:0 2nd:0 3rd:0 Ran:1
2000 AW 0-1: (8f) (Fibr)
Lengthy, currently very moderate gelding.
**C W Thornton [0-2] Guy Reed.*

MARTINO ALONSO (IRE) RR 102f 1160a[3]
6 h Marju (IRE) 9.2f **(76)** - Cheerful Note (Cure The Blues (USA)) 9.5f **(63)**
Form - 3
2000 Turf 0-1: (8f) (hvy)
Very useful horse. Tough and genuine, he struggles to stay a mile and a quarter. **A Botti in ITY [0-3] (from G Botti in ITY [0-2] Nov 1998).*

MARTIN'S PEARL (IRE) RR 36f 1812[8]
3 gr c Petong 7.6f **(58)** - Mainly Dry (The Brianstan) 5.9f **(55)**
Form - 08
Record 2000 - 1st:0 2nd:0 3rd:0 Ran:2
2000 Turf 0-2: (6f, 7f) (gd, frm)
Workmanlike, currently very moderate colt. Turf high 36.
**W R Muir [0-2] Mrs Barbara Jean Martin.*

MARTIN'S SUNSET BHB 82f RR 77f 4540[3]
2 ch c Royal Academy (USA) 7.8f **(77)** - Mainly Sunset (Red Sunset) 8.2f **(63)**
Form - 003
Record 2000 - 1st:0 2nd:0 3rd:1 Ran:3
Win Prizemoney £0 *Total Prizemoney* £500
2000 Turf 0-3: (7f 2, 8f) (gd, frm 2)
Currently above-average colt. Turf high 77 (began Aug) - 3rd of 6 to Northfields Dancer (20 Spt Goodwood 8f gd RF 4540).
**W R Muir [0-3] Mrs Barbara Jean Martin.*

MARTON MERE BHB 57f30a RR 59f 36a 4499[16]
4 ch g Cadeaux Genereux 7.9f **(76)** - Hyatti (Habitat) 9.4f **(70)**
Form - 0810051000
Record 2000 - 1st:2 2nd:0 3rd:0 Ran:10
Pre2000 - 1st:0 2nd:1 3rd:0 Ran:7
Win Prizemoney £5,638 *Total Prizemoney* £6,744
Wins * **2000** Aug Beverl (G-F) C 8.5f 59 <
* **2000** Jly Beverl (GD) SH 7.5f 47 50
2000 Turf 2-8: (7f 1-2, 8f 1-4, 9f, 10f) (g-s, g-f 1-4, frm 1-3) 2000 AW 0-2: (7f, 8f) (Fibr 2)
Leggy, fair gelding, effective 8f, acts on g-f, prefers right handed tracks, likes tight tracks. Turf high 59 (began Jly) - 1st of 15 giving 6lb to Dihatjum (16 Aug Beverley RF 3683). AW high 8.
**A J Lockwood [2-10] A J Lockwood (from T D Easterby [0-7] Jly 1999).*

MARVEL BHB 53f RR 59f 4767[6]
3 b f Rudimentary (USA) 8.2f **(66)** -Maravilla (Mandrake Major) 7.6f **(53)**
Form - 000203606
Record 2000 - 1st:0 2nd:1 3rd:1 Ran:9
Pre2000 - 1st:1 2nd:0 3rd:0 Ran:3
Win Prizemoney £3,652 *Total Prizemoney* £5,400
Wins * 1999 Oct Ayr (SFT) 7f 63 <
2000 Turf 0-9: (7f, 8f 6, 9f, 10f) (g-s 2, gd 3, g-f 3, frm)
Fair filly, effective 7 to 8f, best at 8f, acts on sft to g-f, likes left handed tracks. Turf high 59 - 3rd of 5 getting 15lb from Granted (28 Jun Hamilton 8f g-f RF 2338). Inconsistent.
**Don Enrico Incisa [1-11] Don Enrico Incisa (from N Tinkler [0-1] Apr 2000).*

MARWELL MAGNUS BHB 43f RR 4f 3183[13]
3 b c Beveled (USA) 6.9f **(64)** - Lily of France (Monsanto (FR)) 6.5f **(59)**
Form - 080
Record 2000 - 1st:0 2nd:0 3rd:0 Ran:3
Pre2000 - 1st:0 2nd:0 3rd:0 Ran:1
2000 Turf 0-3: (5f, 6f, 8f) (g-f 2, frm)
Workmanlike, very poor colt. Turf high 1.
**M Madgwick [0-4] Dorothea Viscountess Kelburn.*

MARY HAYDEN RR 34f 2535[5]
2 ch f Imp Society (USA) 7.1f **(63)** - Tricata (Electric) 10.1f **(61)**
Form - 005
Record 2000 - 1st:0 2nd:0 3rd:0 Ran:3
2000 Turf 0-3: (5f, 7f 2) (gd, frm 2)
Currently very moderate filly. Turf high 34.
**W G M Turner [0-3] Miss Corinne Overton.*

MARY JANE BHB 48f65a RR 45f 65a 5112[5]
5 b m Tina's Pet 7.4f **(56)** - Fair Attempt (IRE) (Try My Best (USA)) 7.6f **(67)**
Form - 08000065
Record 2000 - 1st:0 2nd:0 3rd:0 Ran:8
Pre2000 - 1st:8 2nd:3 3rd:4 Ran:36
Win Prizemoney £21,193 *Total Prizemoney* £25,539

Wins								
	1999	Spt	Leices	(GD)	H	5f	57	59
	1999	Jly	Chepst	(G-F)	H	5.1f	48	54
	1999	*Jly*	*Wolver*	*(STD)*	*H*	*5f*	*64*	*66*
	1999	*Jan*	*Wolver*	*(STD)*	*H*	*5f*	*58*	*62+*
	1998	*Dec*	*Southw*	*(STD)*	*C*	*5f*		*57+*
	1998	*Nov*	*Southw*	*(STD)*	*C*	*6f*		*57*
	1998	*Feb*	*Wolver*	*(STD)*	*C*	*5f*		*54+*
	1997	Oct	Redcar	(G-F)		5f		68 <

2000 Turf 0-8: (5f 4, 6f 3, 7f) (sft, g-s, gd 4, g-f, frm)
Average filly, effective 5f, acts on g-f - acts on Fibr, has worn

blinkers, prefers left handed tracks, prefers tight tracks, excels at Wolverhampton. Turf high 45.
**N Tinkler [0-8] Executive Network (P Group) (from R M H Cowell [3-12] Oct 1999).*

MASAKIRA (IRE) RR 64f
5196[13]
2 b f Royal Academy (USA) 7.8f **(77)** - Masafiya (IRE) **(70f)** (Shernazar) 10.2f **(73)**
Form - 40
Record 2000 - 1st:0 2nd:0 3rd:0 Ran:2
Win Prizemoney £0 *Total Prizemoney* £285
2000 Turf 0-2: (7f, 8f) (gd, g-f)
Currently average filly. Turf high 64 (1st run) (began Spt) - 4th of 12 to Love Everlasting (13 Spt Beverley 7f g-f RF 4363).
**Sir Michael Stoute [0-2] H H Aga Khan.*

MASAMADAS BHB 91f83a RR 91f 83a
4461[2]
5 ch g Elmaamul (USA) 8.1f **(70)** - Beau's Delight (USA) (Lypheor) 12f **(71)**
Form - 212
Record 2000 - 1st:1 2nd:2 3rd:0 Ran:3
Pre2000 - 1st:1 2nd:3 3rd:2 Ran:10
Win Prizemoney £10,389 *Total Prizemoney* £23,454
Wins * **2000** Aug Newbur (G-F) H 13.3f 84 87 <
1998 May Windso (G-F) H 11.6f 72 81+
2000 Turf 1-3: (13f 1-3) (g-f 1-3)
Useful gelding. Turf high 91 (began Jly) - 2nd of 15 getting 7lb from Afterjacko (16 Spt Newbury 13f g-f RF 4461) - also 1st of 5 getting 2lb from St Helensfield (18 Aug Newbury RF 3761). A useful dual-purpose horse, he finished strongly when a close second in a valuable handicap at Newbury in September. Worth a try over two miles, he is probably best on fast ground.
**N J Henderson [4-18] Thurloe Thoroughbreds IV (from C F Wall [1-10] Spt 1998).*

MASANIELLA (ITY) RR 100f
5090a[4]
3 b f Masad (IRE)
Form - 0524
2000 Turf 0-4: (8f, 9f, 10f, 11f) (hvy 2, sft, gd)
Very useful filly. Turf high 105 - 4th of 13 getting 4lb from Claxon (15 Oct Capannelle 10f hvy RF 5090a).
**G Botti in ITY [0-1] (from A Botti in ITY [0-3] Oct 2000).*

MASNADA (IRE) RR 97f
5286a[1]
3 b f Erins Isle 8.3f **(76)** - Pecarelli **00**
Form - 161231441
2000 Turf 4-9: (8f 2-4, 9f 2-3, 10f, 12f) (hvy 1-1, sft 3, g-s 1-1, gd 1-2, g-f 1-1)
Very useful filly, effective 8 to 9f, acts on hvy to g-s. Turf high 92 - 1st of 15 getting 10lb from Creux Noir (28 Oct Leopardstown RF 5286a). **J S Bolger in IRE [4-12] F Wall.*

MASQUE TONNERRE (USA) RR 59f
5184[15]
2 b c Thunder Gulch (USA) - Veiled Lady (USA) (Professor Blue (USA))
Form - 00
Record 2000 - 1st:0 2nd:0 3rd:0 Ran:2
2000 Turf 0-2: (7f, 8f) (g-s, g-f)
Currently fair colt. Turf high 59 (began Spt).
**M A Jarvis [0-2] R Meredith.*

MASRORA (USA) BHB 65f RR 71df
3047[5]
3 br f Woodman (USA) 9.7f **(77)** - Overseas Romance (USA) (Assert) 10.6f **(85)**
Form - 453705
Record 2000 - 1st:0 2nd:0 3rd:1 Ran:6
Win Prizemoney £0 *Total Prizemoney* £824
2000 Turf 0-6: (8f 2, 10f 2, 12f 2) (gd 3, g-f 2, frm)
Leggy, above-average filly, effective 8f, acts on gd. Turf high 71 - 5th of 10 to Let Alone (2 Jun Bath 8f gd RF 1646).
**M R Channon [0-6] Sheikh Ahmed Al Maktoum.*

MASSEY BHB 47f58a RR 71f 58a
5077[17]
4 br g Machiavellian (USA) 9.8f **(83)** - Massaraat (USA) (Nureyev (USA)) 8.7f **(78)**
Form - 1600070000000
Record 2000 - 1st:1 2nd:0 3rd:0 Ran:13
Win Prizemoney £2,730 *Total Prizemoney* £2,730
Wins * **2000** *Mar Wolver (STD)* *12f* *66 <*
2000 Turf 0-10: (6f, 7f, 8f 4, 10f 4) (g-s, gd 2, g-f 3, frm 3, hrd) 2000 AW 1-3: (10f, 12f 1-2) (Equi 2, Fibr 1-1)
Leggy, above-average gelding, effective 12f, - acts on Fibr, has worn blinkers, likes left handed tracks, likes tight tracks. Turf high 71. AW high 66 (1st run) - 1st of 9 giving 20lb to Le Cavalier (28 Mar Wolverhampton RF 0534). Becoming disappointing.
**J Pearce [1-14] Saracen Racing.*

MASS MARKET (USA) RR
4406a[2]
3 ch c Marquetry (USA) 10f **(88)** - Dear Guinevere (USA) (Fearless Knight)
Form - 2
2000 AW 0-1: (9f) (Dirt)
Currently Pattern-class colt. (1st run) - 2nd of 10 to Pine Dance (4 Spt Philadelphia Park 9f Dirt RF 4406a). **B Perkins in USA [0-1].*

MASTER BEVELED BHB 56f65a RR 60f 65a
4764[8]
10 b g Beveled (USA) 6.9f **(64)** - Miss Anniversary (Tachypous) 8.6f **(55)**
Form - 30348
Record 2000 - 1st:0 2nd:0 3rd:2 Ran:5
Pre2000 - 1st:11 2nd:8 3rd:9 Ran:94
Win Prizemoney £64,597 *Total Prizemoney* £87,384
Wins * 1998 Spt Ayr (g-s) H 10.9f 69 72
* 1996 Oct Warwic (FRM) 8f 67
* 1996 Oct Haydoc (SFT) 10.5f 74
2000 Turf 0-5: (10f, 11f 2, 12f 2) (sft, g-s 2, gd 2)
Average gelding, has worn blinkers. Turf high 62. A one-time useful handicapper, he is best known as a hurdler these days.
**P D Evans [15-123] Mrs E J Williams (from A P Jones [0-9] Aug 1993).*

MASTER COOL BHB 45f RR 50f
5160[7]
2 br g Cool Jazz - Karen's Lady Luck (Primitive Rising (USA))
Form - 445587
Record 2000 - 1st:0 2nd:0 3rd:0 Ran:6
2000 Turf 0-5: (6f, 7f 3, 8f) (sft, g-s, g-f 2, frm) 2000 AW 0-1: (7f) (Fibr)
Fair gelding. Turf high 50. **G M Moore [0-6] Geoffrey Clarkson.*

MASTER FELLOW BHB 70f RR 62f
5312[8]
2 ch c First Trump - Take Charge (Last Tycoon) 8.5f **(62)**
Form - 648
Record 2000 - 1st:0 2nd:0 3rd:0 Ran:3
Win Prizemoney £0 *Total Prizemoney* £256
2000 Turf 0-3: (6f 2, 8f) (sft, g-s, gd)
Currently average colt. Turf high 62 (began Spt).
**J G Given [0-3] R H Jennings.*

MASTERFUL (USA) RR 71+f
2753[4]
2 b c Danzig (USA) 8.1f **(88)** - Moonlight Serenade (FR) (Dictus (FR))
Form - 4
Record 2000 - 1st:0 2nd:0 3rd:0 Ran:1
Win Prizemoney £0 *Total Prizemoney* £288
2000 Turf 0-1: (6f) (frm)
Currently above-average colt.
**J H M Gosden [0-1] Sheikh Mohammed.*

MASTER GATEMAKER RR 50f
4651[3]
2 b c Tragic Role (USA) 9.4f **(63)** - Girl At the Gate **(47f)** (Formidable (USA)) 9.2f **(63)**
Form - 73
Record 2000 - 1st:0 2nd:0 3rd:1 Ran:2
Win Prizemoney £0 *Total Prizemoney* £444
2000 Turf 0-1: (8f) (g-f) 2000 AW 0-1: (8f) (Fibr)
Currently fair colt. **P W Harris [0-2] John Morley.*

MASTER GEORGE BHB 82f RR 86f
4741[3]
3 b g Mtoto 11.5f **(71)** - Topwinder (USA) (Topsider (USA)) 8.3f **(71)**
Form - 1625743
Record 2000 - 1st:1 2nd:1 3rd:1 Ran:7
Pre2000 - 1st:0 2nd:1 3rd:0 Ran:1
Win Prizemoney £4,043 *Total Prizemoney* £12,441
Wins * **2000** Apr Windso (HVY) 10f 72 <
2000 Turf 1-7: (10f 1-1, 12f 4, 13f, 14f) (g-s 1-2, g-f 5)
Lengthy, useful gelding, effective 12 to 14f, acts on g-f, has worn blinkers. Turf high 86. Consistent. He is a decent middle-distance

handicapper, a never-nearer seventh in the King George V Handicap at Royal Ascot and fourth at Newbury next time.
**I A Balding [1-8] David R Watson & Duncan Lofts.*

MASTER HENRY (GER) BHB 65f RR 67f 2588[5]
6 b g Mille Balles (FR) - Maribelle (GER) (Windwurf (GER)) 12.7f **(72)**
Form - 6667165
Record 2000 - 1st:1 2nd:0 3rd:0 Ran:7
Win Prizemoney £3,094 *Total Prizemoney* £3,601
Wins * 2000 Jly Mussel (FRM) 9f 63 <
2000 Turf 1-7: (6f, 6f, 7f 2, 8f 2, 9f 1-1) (g-s 2, gd, g-f, frm 1-2, hrd)
Average gelding, effective 9f, acts on frm. Turf high 67 - also 1st of 6 giving 3lb to Woore Lass (3 Jly Musselburgh RF 2469).
**M Johnston [1-7] The Winning Line.*

MASTER HYDE (USA) BHB 37f54a RR 40f 54a 1142[9]
11 gr g Trempolino (USA) 11.9f **(77)** - Sandspur (USA) (Al Hattab (USA)) 9.3f **(74)**
Form - 0
Record 2000 - 1st:0 2nd:0 3rd:0 Ran:1
Pre2000 - 1st:5 2nd:6 3rd:6 Ran:54
Win Prizemoney £14,681 *Total Prizemoney* £23,077
2000 Turf 0-1: (12f) (frm)
Average gelding, has worn blinkers (extremely effectively).
**J S Goldie [2-27] J S Goldie (from W Storey [5-25] Oct 1906).*

MASTER JONES BHB 47f49a RR 68f 49a 638[12]
3 b g Emperor Jones (USA) - Tight Spin (High Top) 10.2f **(67)**
Form - 40233253650
Record 2000 - 1st:0 2nd:2 3rd:3 Ran:9
Pre2000 - 1st:0 2nd:0 3rd:0 Ran:6
Win Prizemoney £0 *Total Prizemoney* £1,884
2000 Turf 0-1: (7f) (gd) 2000 AW 0-8: (5f 2, 6f 2, 7f 2, 8f 2) (Equi 6, Fibr 2)
Light-framed, average gelding, effective 8f, - acts on Equi, has worn blinkers. AW high 60 (1st run) - 2nd of 7 giving 9lb to Kigema (2 Jan Lingfield 8f Equi RF 0002).
**Mrs L Stubbs [0-15] Maurice Parker.*

MASTER LUKE BHB 50f62a RR 51f 62a 5198[3]
3 b g Contract Law (USA) 8.9f **(54)** - Flying Wind **(33f 41a)** (Forzando) 7.6f **(59)**
Form - 7802023
Record 2000 - 1st:0 2nd:2 3rd:1 Ran:7
Win Prizemoney £0 *Total Prizemoney* £1,701
2000 Turf 0-6: (5f, 6f 3, 7f, 8f) (gd, g-f 4, frm) 2000 AW 0-1: (7f) (Equi)
Scopey, average gelding, effective 6 to 7f, best at 6f, acts on gd to g-f, best on g-f, often wears blinkers (extremely effectively). Turf high 51 (began Jly) - 2nd of 25 getting 1lb from Bound To Please (6 Oct Windsor 6f g-f RF 4825). **G L Moore [0-7] Bryan Pennick.*

MASTER MAC (USA) BHB 49f41a RR 43f 41a 1016[10]
5 br g Exbourne (USA) - Kentucky Blonde (USA) (General Assembly (USA)) 10f **(68)**
Form - 000
Record 2000 - 1st:0 2nd:0 3rd:0 Ran:3
Pre2000 - 1st:2 2nd:1 3rd:0 Ran:19
Win Prizemoney £9,498 *Total Prizemoney* £12,533
Wins 1997 Jly Lingfi (G-F) H 6f 81 <
1997 Jun Goodwo (G-S) 7f 75
2000 Turf 0-1: (8f) (frm) 2000 AW 0-2: (7f, 10f) (Equi 2)
Moderate gelding. AW high 10. Inconsistent.
**R J O'Sullivan [0-3] Normandy Developments (London) (from N Hamilton [0-6] Oct 1999).*

MASTER MILLFIELD (IRE) BHB 43f52a RR 18?f 52a 1254[P]
8 b g Prince Rupert (FR) 10.4f **(60)** - Calash (Indian King (USA)) 7.4f **(64)**
Form - P
Record 2000 - 1st:0 2nd:0 3rd:0 Ran:1
Pre2000 - 1st:8 2nd:5 3rd:9 Ran:58
Win Prizemoney £24,282 *Total Prizemoney* £35,661
Wins 1998 Spt Goodwo (G-S) H 8f 49 58
1998 Spt Salisb (GD) H 8f 49 53
1997 Spt Folkes (FRM) H 6.9f 47 54
2000 Turf 0-1: (8f) (g-f)
Moderate gelding, has worn blinkers. Becoming disappointing.

**R J Baker [0-9] P Slade (from R J Hodges [5-22] Aug 1999).*

MASTERMIND (IRE) RR 104f 3912[3]
3 ch c Dolphin Street (FR) - Glenarff (USA) (Irish River (FR)) 8.6f **(78)**
Form - 04023
Record 2000 - 1st:0 2nd:1 3rd:1 Ran:5
Pre2000 - 1st:1 2nd:1 3rd:0 Ran:2
Win Prizemoney £4,386 *Total Prizemoney* £12,838
Wins * 1999 Jly Newmar (G-F) 6f 86 <
2000 Turf 0-5: (8f, 10f 3, 12f) (gd 3, frm 2)
Scopey, very useful colt, effective 10f, acts on gd to frm, best on frm. Turf high 104 - 3rd of 17 getting 1lb from Prince Alex (23 Aug York 10f frm RF 3912). He is a useful colt at around ten furlongs, but bit off more than he could chew in the 2000 Guineas and the French Derby. Decent effort in a York handicap on his final run, and there could be a nice race for him in that sphere.
**P F I Cole [1-7] Highclere Thoroughbred Racing Ltd.*

MASTERPIECE (USA) RR 82f 3216[4]
3 b br c Nureyev (USA) 8.4f **(84)** - Lovely Gemstone (USA) (Alydar (USA)) 9.1f **(76)**
Form - 0444
Record 2000 - 1st:0 2nd:0 3rd:0 Ran:4
Pre2000 - 1st:1 2nd:0 3rd:0 Ran:2
Win Prizemoney £4,760 *Total Prizemoney* £6,340
Wins * 1999 Oct Lingfi (HVY) 7f 78+ <
2000 Turf 0-4: (7f, 8f 3) (g-s, g-f, frm 2)
Scopey, decent colt, effective 7 to 8f, best at 8f, acts on g-s to frm. Turf high 82 - 4th of 11 giving 21lb to Flying Carpet (8 Jly Beverley 8f g-f RF 2620). **Sir Michael Stoute [1-6] M Tabor & Mrs John Magnier.*

MASTER SODEN (USA) BHB 60f RR 59f 1202[5]
3 b c Pembroke (USA) - Lady Member (FR) (Saint Estephe (FR)) 16.4f **(79)**
Form - 5
Record 2000 - 1st:0 2nd:0 3rd:0 Ran:1
Pre2000 - 1st:1 2nd:0 3rd:0 Ran:4
Win Prizemoney £3,640 *Total Prizemoney* £3,640
Wins * 1999 Nov Redcar (G-S) H 8f 48 59 <
2000 Turf 0-1: (10f) (frm)
Strong, fair colt. (1st run) - 5th of 16 getting 9lb from Baileys Prize (15 May Redcar 10f frm RF 1202). **T G Mills [1-5] Albert Soden Ltd.*

MATADI (USA) BHB 75f RR 67f 3917[9]
2 b c Dynaformer (USA) 12f **(82)** - Mata Cara (Storm Bird (CAN)) 10.3f **(74)**
Form - 450
Record 2000 - 1st:0 2nd:0 3rd:0 Ran:3
Win Prizemoney £0 *Total Prizemoney* £477
2000 Turf 0-3: (6f 2, 7f) (gd, frm 2)
Currently average colt. Turf high 67 (began Jly). Showed promise first time, but the ground may have been against him on his next run. **C E Brittain [0-3] Madhad Ali.*

MATASHAWAQ (USA) RR 49f 4227[13]
3 gr c Storm Cat (USA) 7f **(86)** - Futuh (USA) (Diesis) 9.3f **(69)**
Form - 0
Record 2000 - 1st:0 2nd:0 3rd:0 Ran:1
2000 Turf 0-1: (7f) (frm)
Scopey, currently moderate colt, always wears blinkers.
**M P Tregoning [0-1] Hamdan Al Maktoum.*

MATERIAL WITNESS (IRE) BHB 88f RR 94f 4458[1]
3 b c Barathea (IRE) - Dial Dream (Gay Mecene (USA)) 8.6f **(69)**
Form - 223021
Record 2000 - 1st:1 2nd:3 3rd:1 Ran:6
Pre2000 - 1st:0 2nd:1 3rd:1 Ran:2
Win Prizemoney £2,860 *Total Prizemoney* £16,455
Wins * 2000 Spt Catter (SFT) 7f 77 <
2000 Turf 1-6: (7f 1-2, 8f 4) (g-s 1-3, gd 2, frm)
Rangy, useful colt, effective 8f, acts on g-s. Turf high 94 - 3rd of 16 giving 2lb to Atlantic Rhapsody (27 May Haydock 8f g-s RF 1491). He chased some good horses home in the spring, but failed to progress and looked ungenuine when winning a weak maiden at Catterick in September.

**W R Muir [1-8] M J Caddy.*

MATLOCK (IRE) BHB 87f82a **RR 85f 82a** 5167[4]
2 b c Barathea (IRE) - Palio Flyer (Slip Anchor) 9.8f **(73)**
Form - 1434
Record 2000 - 1st:1 2nd:0 3rd:1 Ran:4
Win Prizemoney £4,309 *Total Prizemoney* £6,223
Wins * **2000** Jly Sandow (G-F) 7.1f 85+ <
2000 Turf 1-4: (6f, 7f 1-2, 8f) (g-s 2, gd, g-f 1-1)
Useful colt. Turf high 85 (began Jly) - 4th of 7 giving 7lb to Lanesborough (24 Oct Redcar 7f gd RF 5167) - also 1st of 11 from Northfields Dancer (26 Jly Sandown RF 3140). Made all in a Sandown maiden. **P F I Cole [1-4] W J Smith and M D Dudley.*

MATOAKA (USA) RR 84f 4599[4]
2 b f A P Indy (USA) - Appointed One (USA) (Danzig (USA)) 8.4f **(76)**
Form - 24
Record 2000 - 1st:0 2nd:1 3rd:0 Ran:2
Win Prizemoney £0 *Total Prizemoney* £3,437
2000 Turf 0-2: (7f 2) (gd, g-f)
Currently decent filly. Turf high 84 (began Spt) - 4th of 11 to Small Change (23 Spt Ascot 7f gd RF 4599).
**Sir Michael Stoute [0-2] Cheveley Park Stud.*

MATRON (IRE) RR 88f 5319[2]
2 b f Dr Devious (IRE) 9.9f **(74)** - Matrona (USA) (Woodman (USA)) 9f **(74)**
Form - 22
Record 2000 - 1st:0 2nd:2 3rd:0 Ran:2
Win Prizemoney £0 *Total Prizemoney* £2,330
2000 Turf 0-2: (6f 2) (sft, g-s)
Currently useful filly. Turf high 88 (1st run) (began Oct) - 2nd of 15 getting 5lb from Suave Native (22 Oct Yarmouth 6f g-s RF 5140).
**L M Cumani [0-2] Fittocks Stud.*

MATTHIOLA (IRE) RR 67f 5098[13]
2 b f Ela-Mana-Mou 12.7f **(72)** - Maysoura (Nishapour (FR)) 9.1f **(61)**
Form - 0
Record 2000 - 1st:0 2nd:0 3rd:0 Ran:1
2000 Turf 0-1: (8f) (gd)
Currently average filly. **L M Cumani [0-1] Mrs Luca Cumani.*

MAUERSCHWALBE (GER) RR 163[8]
5 b m Acatenango (GER) - Maxi's Dream (Coquelin (USA)) 8.4f **(58)**
Form - 78
Record 2000 - 1st:0 2nd:0 3rd:0 Ran:2
2000 AW 0-2: (10f, 16f) (Equi 2)
Currently poor filly. AW high 14. **J J Bridger [0-2] W Wood.*

M'AULD SEGOISHA (IRE) BHB 80f **RR 78f** 4257[2]
2 br f Dolphin Street (FR) - September Tide (IRE) (Thatching) 8f **(66)**
Form - 0022
Record 2000 - 1st:0 2nd:2 3rd:0 Ran:4
Win Prizemoney £0 *Total Prizemoney* £8,204
2000 Turf 0-4: (6f 3, 7f) (gd 4)
Above-average filly. Turf high 78 (began Jly) - 2nd of 21 getting 8lb from Innit (6 Spt Doncaster 7f gd RF 4257). Showed little on her first two starts, but ran much better at Haydock in August.
**J G FitzGerald [0-4] Tim Kilroe.*

MAURI MOON BHB 97f **RR 87f** 3744[1]
2 b f Green Desert (USA) 7.8f **(78)** - Dazzling Heights (Shirley Heights) 10.3f **(74)**
Form - 511
Record 2000 - 1st:2 2nd:0 3rd:0 Ran:3
Win Prizemoney £12,995 *Total Prizemoney* £12,995
Wins * **2000** Aug Cheste (GD) 6.1f 87 <
* **2000** Jly Nottin (G-F) 6.1f 80
2000 Turf 2-3: (5f, 6f 2-2) (g-f 1-2, frm 1-1)
Currently useful filly. Turf high 87 - 1st of 5 from Millenium Princess (18 Aug Chester RF 3744) - also 1st of 9 from Palatial (15 Jly Nottingham RF 2841). **G Wragg [2-3] Peter Pritchard.*

MA VIE BHB 60f **RR 62f** 5227[5]
3 b f Salse (USA) 10.9f **(71)** - One Life (USA) (L'Emigrant (USA)) 10.5f **(62)**
Form - 827225
Record 2000 - 1st:0 2nd:3 3rd:0 Ran:6
Pre2000 - 1st:0 2nd:0 3rd:0 Ran:3
Win Prizemoney £0 *Total Prizemoney* £3,306
2000 Turf 0-6: (8f, 10f 3, 11f, 12f) (gd 4, g-f, frm)
Workmanlike, average filly, effective 10 to 11f, best at 10f, acts on gd to g-f, best on gd, has worn blinkers. Turf high 62 - 2nd of 15 getting 10lb from Calldat Seventeen (15 Spt Nottingham 10f gd RF 4446). Needed the run on her debut.
**J R Fanshawe [0-9] The Earl Of Lonsdale.*

MAVIS BHB 45f **RR 15f** 2957[12]
3 ch f Prince Sabo 6.6f **(64)** - Eluned May **(42df)** (Clantime)
Form - 070
Record 2000 - 1st:0 2nd:0 3rd:0 Ran:3
2000 Turf 0-3: (5f 3) (g-s, g-f, hrd)
Lengthy, currently poor filly. Turf high 15.
**B Palling [0-3] Derek D & Mrs Jean P Clee.*

MAVURA RR 29f 5135[8]
3 b f Bering 9.6f **(80)** - Mystery Play (IRE) (Sadler's Wells (USA)) 10f **(76)**
Form - 8
Record 2000 - 1st:0 2nd:0 3rd:0 Ran:1
2000 Turf 0-1: (10f) (sft)
Unfurnished, currently very moderate filly.
**M P Tregoning [0-1] Sheikh Mohammed.*

MAWDSLEY BHB 29f **RR 12f** 3408[6]
3 b f Piccolo - Legendary Dancer (Shareef Dancer (USA)) 9.9f **(73)**
Form - 06
Record 2000 - 1st:0 2nd:0 3rd:0 Ran:2
Pre2000 - 1st:0 2nd:0 3rd:0 Ran:1
2000 Turf 0-2: (6f, 7f) (gd, frm)
Unfurnished, currently poor filly.
**G Woodward [0-3] Exors of the late Mrs H M Carr.*

MAWHOOB (USA) BHB 79f **RR 80f** 3970[3]
2 gr c Dayjur (USA) 6.8f **(79)** - Asl (USA) (Caro)
Form - 643
Record 2000 - 1st:0 2nd:0 3rd:1 Ran:3
Win Prizemoney £0 *Total Prizemoney* £945
2000 Turf 0-3: (6f, 7f 2) (gd, frm 2)
Currently decent colt. Turf high 80 (began Jly).
**J L Dunlop [0-3] Hamdan Al Maktoum.*

MAWINGO (IRE) BHB 58f55a **RR 65f 55a** 4875[9]
7 b g Taufan (USA) 8.3f **(65)** - Tappen Zee (Sandhurst Prince) 7.9f **(63)**
Form - 40720
Record 2000 - 1st:0 2nd:1 3rd:0 Ran:4
Pre2000 - 1st:3 2nd:2 3rd:4 Ran:26
Win Prizemoney £18,412 *Total Prizemoney* £28,113
Wins * 1996 Jun Newmar (G-F) H 8f 75 80 <
* 1996 Jun Newmar (G-F) H 8f 69 74
* 1996 May Warwic (FRM) H 7f 64 65
2000 Turf 0-4: (8f 3, 10f) (g-s, gd, g-f 2)
Average gelding, effective 8 to 10f, acts on sft to frm, has worn blinkers, prefers left handed tracks, prefers tight tracks. Turf high 65 (began Jly) - 2nd of 12 giving 3lb to Imprevue (16 Aug Yarmouth 10f g-f RF 3710). He is an able handicapper, but is without a win since June '96. **G Wragg [3-30] Mrs Claude Lilley.*

MAX (FR) BHB 34f34a **RR 48?f 34a** 5078[13]
5 gr g L'Emigrant (USA) - Miss Mendez (FR) (Bellypha) 9.8f **(73)**
Form - 860000300878050
Record 2000 - 1st:0 2nd:0 3rd:1 Ran:14
Pre2000 - 1st:0 2nd:0 3rd:0 Ran:1
Win Prizemoney £0 *Total Prizemoney* £428
2000 Turf 0-12: (7f, 8f, 9f 3, 10f 4, 11f, 12f 2) (g-s 2, gd 4, g-f 5, frm)
2000 AW 0-2: (8f, 10f) (Equi, Fibr)
Moderate gelding, has worn blinkers. Turf high 48. AW high 17.
**J J Bridger [0-15] J J Bridger.*

MAX THE MAN RR 762[10]
3 b g Bold Arrangement 8.7f **(57)** - Hot Feet (Marching On) 6f **(60)**
Form - 0
Record 2000 - 1st:0 2nd:0 3rd:0 Ran:1
2000 Turf 0-1: (7f) (g-s)
Scopey, currently very poor gelding. **J M Bradley [0-1] C P Howells.*

MAYARO (FR) RR 95f
2982a[4]

4 br c Saumarez 15.1f **(87)** - Milesime (USA) (Riverman (USA)) 9.1f **(76)**

Form - 4

2000 Turf 0-1: (13f) (sft)

Currently very useful colt. **Mme C Head in FR [0-2].*

MAYARO BAY BHB 102f RR 103f
4739[5]

4 b f Robellino (USA) 9.5f **(68)** - Down the Valley (Kampala) 8.4f **(56)**

Form - 001603023105

Record 2000 - 1st:2 2nd:1 3rd:2 Ran:12
Pre2000 - 1st:2 2nd:4 3rd:2 Ran:15

Win Prizemoney £69,632 *Total Prizemoney* £103,056

Wins * **2000** Spt Doncas (G-F) H 8f 99 103 <
* **2000** May York (FRM) LH 7.9f 94 99
* 1999 May Goodwo (GD) H 7f 85 90
* 1998 Oct Warwic (GD) 6f 76+

2000 Turf 2-12: (7f, 8f 2-11) (sft, g-s 2, gd 3, g-f 1-5, frm 1-1)

Workmanlike, very useful filly, effective 8f, acts on gd to frm, best on g-f, and excels at York. Turf high 103 - 1st of 10 giving 9lb to Atlantic Rhapsody (9 Spt Doncaster RF 4309) - also 1st of 13 giving 1lb to Caribbean Monarch (17 May York RF 1264). A likeable individual, she is a little in and out, but is capable of very useful form in mile handicaps on fast ground and put up a respectable showing in a Group Two on her final start.

**R Hannon [4-27] J R Shannon.*

MAY BALL BHB 104f RR 104f
5202a[6]

3 b f Cadeaux Genereux 7.9f **(76)** - Minute Waltz (Sadler's Wells (USA)) 10f **(76)**

Form - 1241136

Record 2000 - 1st:3 2nd:1 3rd:1 Ran:7

Win Prizemoney £18,831 *Total Prizemoney* £27,505

Wins * **2000** Aug Deauvi (G-S) L 8f 102 <
* **2000** Jly Ascot (GD) 8f 78
* **2000** May Newmar (GD) 8f 24t

2000 Turf 3-7: (7f, 8f 3-4, 9f, 10f) (hvy, g-s 1-2, gd 1-1, g-f 1-3)

Workmanlike, very useful filly, effective 8f, acts on g-s to g-f. Turf high 104 - 3rd of 9 to Danceabout (30 Spt Newmarket 8f g-f RF 4739) - also 1st of 9 getting 4lb from Peony (20 Aug Deauville RF 3948a). A listed winner and third in the Sun Chariot Stakes over a mile, she failed to stay when tried over ten furlongs.

**J H M Gosden [3-7].*

MAYBEE BHB 38f RR 52f
4650[14]

4 b f Then Again 7.4f **(52)** - Miss Ritz **(59f)** (Robellino (USA)) 7.6f **(80)**

Form - 3700

Record 2000 - 1st:0 2nd:0 3rd:1 Ran:4

Win Prizemoney £0 *Total Prizemoney* £617

2000 Turf 0-3: (8f 2, 10f) (frm 2, hrd) 2000 AW 0-1: (11f) (Fibr)

Rangy, fair filly. Turf high 52 (began Aug).

**J G Given [0-4] Mrs D R Schreiber.*

MAYBE'N BHB 41f RR 47f
5002[8]

3 ch g Deploy 11.4f **(67)** - Travel Mystery (Godswalk (USA)) 7.3f **(58)**

Form - 5678

Record 2000 - 1st:0 2nd:0 3rd:0 Ran:4
Pre2000 - 1st:0 2nd:0 3rd:0 Ran:3

2000 Turf 0-4: (10f, 12f 2, 18f) (g-s 2, gd 2)

Leggy, moderate gelding. Turf high 47.

**Mrs P Sly [0-4] P J Turner (from C Smith [0-3] Jly 1999).*

MAYCOCKS BAY RR 65f
4935[14]

2 b f Muhtarram (USA) - Beacon (High Top) 10.2f **(67)**

Form - 0

Record 2000 - 1st:0 2nd:0 3rd:0 Ran:1

2000 Turf 0-1: (6f) (gd)

Currently average filly. **J A Glover [0-1] Lady Bamford.*

MAY CONTESSA (USA) BHB 98f RR 105f
3828[13]

3 b f Bahri (USA) - Copper Creek (Habitat) 9.4f **(70)**

Form - 11380

Record 2000 - 1st:2 2nd:0 3rd:1 Ran:5
Pre2000 - 1st:0 2nd:0 3rd:1 Ran:2

Win Prizemoney £11,160 *Total Prizemoney* £14,310

Wins * **2000** May Kempto (G-S) 6f 105+ <
* **2000** Apr Newmar (G-S) 6f 85

2000 Turf 2-5: (5f, 6f 2-3, 7f) (g-s 1-2, gd 1-1, g-f, hrd)

Leggy, Pattern-class filly, effective 6 to 7f, acts on g-s. Turf high 105 - 1st of 8 getting 8lb from Jezebel (1 May Kempton RF 0942). Showed some ability at two and made a winning reappearance in a Newmarket maiden. She followed up in good style in a Kempton conditions event, but has just found Listed company a bit tough since. **D R C Elsworth [2-7] DGH Partnership.*

MAYDORO BHB 32f31a RR 33f 31a
3019[5]

7 b m Dominion Royale 7.8f **(63)** - Bamdoro (Cavo Doro) 10.6f **(57)**

Form - 78624005

Record 2000 - 1st:0 2nd:1 3rd:0 Ran:8
Pre2000 - 1st:2 2nd:1 3rd:0 Ran:26

Win Prizemoney £3,998 *Total Prizemoney* £5,396

Wins 1998 Jun Newcas (SFT) S 5f 55 <
1998 Jan Wolver (STD) C 6f 51

2000 Turf 0-4: (7f 2, 9f, 10f) (gd, g-f, frm 2) 2000 AW 0-4: (6f 4) (Fibr 4)

Very moderate mare, effective 7f, acts on gd, likes left handed tracks. Turf high 33 (1st run) - 2nd of 12 getting 17lb from Erupt (31 May Southwell 7f gd RF 1599). AW high 32. Consistent.

**W M Brisbourne [0-13] Manton Hire Ltd (from M Dods [2-21] Jan 1999).*

MAY KING MAYHEM BHB 49f39a RR 55f 39a
2847[8]

7 ch g Great Commotion (USA) 9.2f **(80)** - Queen Ranavalona (Sure Blade (USA)) 11.3f **(67)**

Form - 65111128

Record 2000 - 1st:4 2nd:1 3rd:0 Ran:8
Pre2000 - 1st:5 2nd:1 3rd:0 Ran:46

Win Prizemoney £31,342 *Total Prizemoney* £35,369

Wins * **2000** Jun Newmar (G-F) H 12f 47 48
* **2000** Jun Kempto (G-F) H 12f 47 55 <
* **2000** Jun Newmar (G-F) H 12f 35 50+
* **2000** Jun Lingfi (GD) H 11.5f 39 47
* 1999 Jun Newmar (GD) H 12f 34 40
* 1999 May Leices (GD) H 11.8f 37 39
* 1998 Oct Pontef (GD) H 12f 37 42
* 1998 Aug Haydoc (GD) H 11.9f 31 34
* 1997 Jly Carlis (GD) H 12f 36 47

2000 Turf 4-8: (11f 1-2, 12f 3-6) (gd 1-2, g-f 2-5, frm 1-1)

Fair gelding, effective 11 to 12f, best at 12f, acts on gd to frm, best on g-f, often wears blinkers (very effectively), prefers right handed tracks, excels at Newmarket. Turf high 55 - 1st of 9 getting 10lb from Smarter Charter (21 Jun Kempton RF 2160) - also 1st of 34 getting 14lb from Fletcher (11 Jun Newmarket RF 1880).

**Mrs A L M King [9-52] S J Harrison (from W R Muir [0-2] Spt 1995).*

MAYLAN (IRE) BHB 25f RR 28f
635[15]

5 br m Lashkari 13.1f **(52)** - Miysam (Supreme Sovereign) 9.5f **(53)**

Form - 080

Record 2000 - 1st:0 2nd:0 3rd:0 Ran:1
Pre2000 - 1st:0 2nd:0 3rd:0 Ran:10

2000 Turf 0-1: (7f) (gd)

Little account filly, has worn blinkers. Becoming disappointing.

**W de Best-Turner [0-7] The Spanish Connection (from D M Hyde [0-4] Nov 1997).*

MAYLANE BHB 107f RR 111f
4297[5]

6 b g Mtoto 11.5f **(71)** - Possessive Dancer (Shareef Dancer (USA)) 9.9f **(73)**

Form - 846335

Record 2000 - 1st:0 2nd:0 3rd:2 Ran:6
Pre2000 - 1st:6 2nd:2 3rd:1 Ran:17

Win Prizemoney £84,493 *Total Prizemoney* £101,253

Wins * 1999 Nov Doncas (SFT) L 12f 107+
* 1999 Oct Haydoc (HVY) 11.9f 102
* 1997 Spt Epsom (GD) G3 12f 112 <
* 1997 Jly Goodwo (G-F) H 12f 99 102
* 1997 Jun Goodwo (GD) 9f 93+
* 1996 Oct Lingfi (G-S) 7f 83+

2000 Turf 0-6: (12f 5, 13f) (hvy, gd, g-f 2, frm, hrd)

Group-class gelding, effective 12 to 13f, best at 12f, acts on sft to frm, has worn blinkers, prefers left handed tracks, and excels at Doncaster. Turf high 111 - 3rd of 4 giving 3lb to Monsajem (19 Aug Haydock 12f gd RF 3779). A talented but temperamental performer, he usually gives problems at the start and has dumped his jockey on more than one occasion. Not at his best in 2000, he was often awash with sweat in the preliminaries and is one to avoid for bet-

ting purposes.
**A C Stewart [6-21] Sheikh Ahmed Al Maktoum (from S bin Suroor [0-1] Jun 1998).*

MA YORAM (USA) BHB 106f **RR 106f** 1575a[8]

3 gr c Dayjur (USA) 6.8f **(79)** - Quelle Affaire (USA) (Riverman (USA)) 9.1f **(76)**
Form - 548
Record 2000 - 1st:0 2nd:0 3rd:0 Ran:3
Pre2000 - 1st:1 2nd:1 3rd:1 Ran:3
Win Prizemoney £3,468 *Total Prizemoney* £37,108
Wins * 1999 Apr Kempto (GD) 5f 87+ <
2000 Turf 0-3: (6f 2, 7f) (g-s, gd 2)
Workmanlike, Pattern-class colt, effective 6 to 7f, best at 6f, acts on gd to frm, best on gd. Turf high 106 - 4th of 8 to Mount Abu (3 May Ascot 6f gd RF 1002). Useful as a juvenile, he ran pretty well in the Greenham on his return, but reverted to six furlongs subsequently. Difficult to place.
**M R Channon [1-6] Sheikh Ahmed Al Maktoum.*

MAY PRINCESS BHB 64f **RR 62f** 5183[5]

2 ch f Prince Sabo 6.6f **(64)** - Mim **(10f)** (Midyan (USA)) 6f **(60)**
Form - 8005
Record 2000 - 1st:0 2nd:0 3rd:0 Ran:4
2000 Turf 0-4: (5f, 6f, 7f 2) (g-s, g-f 3)
Average filly. Turf high 62 (began Aug). **D Morris [0-4] P J Turner.*

MAY QUEEN MEGAN BHB 35f38a **RR 42f 38a** 2698[5]

7 gr m Petorius 8f **(66)** - Siva (FR) (Bellypha) 9.8f **(73)**
Form - 465
Record 2000 - 1st:0 2nd:0 3rd:0 Ran:3
Pre2000 - 1st:3 2nd:5 3rd:5 Ran:51
Win Prizemoney £10,023 *Total Prizemoney* £17,494
Wins * 1998 Jly Lingfi (G-F) H 9f 49 52 <
* 1998 Jun Nottin (GD) H 8.2f 38 48
* 1996 Jly Lingfi (G-F) H 6f 52 52 <
2000 Turf 0-3: (8f 2, 10f) (g-f, frm, hrd)
Moderate mare, effective 9 to 10f, best at 10f, acts on g-f to frm, best on frm, has worn blinkers, prefers left handed tracks, prefers tight tracks. Turf high 42. Consistent.
**Mrs A L M King [3-54] All The Kings Horses.*

MAYSBOYO BHB 45f **RR 25f** 3572[10]

2 b g Makbul - Maysimp (IRE) **(19f 20a)** (Mac's Imp (USA))
Form - 38880
Record 2000 - 1st:0 2nd:0 3rd:1 Ran:5
Win Prizemoney £0 *Total Prizemoney* £406
2000 Turf 0-4: (5f 2, 6f 2) (sft, g-s, g-f, frm) 2000 AW 0-1: (7f) (Fibr)
Little account gelding. Turf high 25.
**B P J Baugh [0-5] Mrs Joan Chrimes.*

MAYTIME BHB 60f **RR 69f** 4490[17]

2 ch f Pivotal - May Hinton (Main Reef) 9.6f **(57)**
Form - 08500
Record 2000 - 1st:0 2nd:0 3rd:0 Ran:5
2000 Turf 0-5: (6f 4, 7f) (g-f, frm 3, hrd)
Average filly. Turf high 69. **M L W Bell [0-5] Sir Thomas Pilkington.*

MAYVILLE THUNDER BHB 85f **RR 80f** 5296[1]

2 ch c Zilzal (USA) 8.5f **(79)** - Mountain Lodge (Blakeney) 10.5f **(64)**
Form - 31
Record 2000 - 1st:1 2nd:0 3rd:1 Ran:2
Win Prizemoney £2,307 *Total Prizemoney* £3,140
Wins * **2000** Nov Mussel (G-S) 7.1f 80 <
2000 Turf 1-2: (7f 1-2) (g-s 1-1, g-f)
Currently decent colt. Turf high 80 (began Spt) - 1st of 8 from So Tempting (1 Nov Musselburgh RF 5296).
**G A Butler [1-2] Jan Stenbeck.*

MAZAARR (IRE) BHB 68f **RR 76f** 3170[3]

3 ch c Woodman (USA) 9.7f **(77)** - River Missy (USA) (Riverman (USA)) 9.1f **(76)**
Form - 6700143
Record 2000 - 1st:1 2nd:0 3rd:1 Ran:7
Win Prizemoney £4,241 *Total Prizemoney* £5,336
Wins * **2000** Jun Ripon (G-F) H 12.3f 67 68 <
2000 Turf 1-7: (10f 2, 11f 2, 12f 1-1, 14f, 16f) (g-s, gd 2, g-f, frm 1-3)
Scopey, above-average colt, effective 12 to 16f, acts on frm. Turf high 76 - also 1st of 6 giving 4lb to Red Canyon (22 Jun Ripon RF 2189). **M R Channon [1-7] Sheikh Ahmed Al Maktoum.*

MAZEED (IRE) BHB 47f47a **RR 35f 47a** 2693[14]

7 ch g Lycius (USA) 8.8f **(71)** - Maraatib (IRE) (Green Desert (USA)) 8.6f **(78)**
Form - 0
Record 2000 - 1st:0 2nd:0 3rd:0 Ran:1
Pre2000 - 1st:8 2nd:3 3rd:4 Ran:35
Win Prizemoney £23,075 *Total Prizemoney* £30,851
Wins 1998 Jly Beverl (GD) H 9.9f 71 73
1998 Jun Yarmou (G-F) H 10.1f 58 71
1998 May Yarmou (FRM) H 10.1f 58 68
1998 *Jan Lingfi (STD) 10f 69+*
1997 *Dec Wolver (STD) H 9.4f 57 64+*
1997 *Dec Wolver (STD) H 9.4f 43 56+*
2000 Turf 0-1: (10f) (frm)
Fair gelding, often wears blinkers.
**Miss K M George [0-15] P Dugmore (from P D Evans [6-23] Jan 1999).*

MAZILLA BHB 28f24a **RR 4f 24a** 3528[14]

8 b m Mazilier (USA) 8.5f **(56)** - Mo Ceri (Kampala) 8.4f **(56)**
Form - 0
Record 2000 - 1st:0 2nd:0 3rd:0 Ran:1
Pre2000 - 1st:8 2nd:5 3rd:5 Ran:56
Win Prizemoney £20,386 *Total Prizemoney* £26,528
Wins * 1996 Aug Yarmou (GD) H 10.1f 52 59
* 1996 Jly Nottin (G-F) H 10f 46 53+
* 1996 Jly Warwic (G-F) SH 10.8f 40 52
* 1996 Jun Nottin (G-F) SH 10f 37 42
* 1996 *Feb Southw (STD) H 11f 47 51*
* 1996 *Feb Southw (STD) SH 11f 42 45*
2000 Turf 0-1: (12f) (frm)
Moderate mare, has worn blinkers. Becoming disappointing.
**A Streeter [7-52] M Rhodes (from A L Forbes [0-1] Jun 1995).*

MAZZELMO BHB 58f46a **RR 70f 46a** 3558[7]

7 gr m Thethingaboutitis (USA) 16f **(44)** - Nattfari (Tyrnavos) 10.1f **(55)**
Form - 0507
Record 2000 - 1st:0 2nd:0 3rd:0 Ran:4
Pre2000 - 1st:4 2nd:0 3rd:6 Ran:29
Win Prizemoney £16,232 *Total Prizemoney* £20,949
Wins * 1999 Spt Cheste (HVY) H 15.9f 58 58+
* 1999 Jun Chepst (G-F) H 18f 56 60
* 1998 Aug Cheste (GD) H 15.9f 52 59
* 1998 *Jun Wolver (STD) C 16.2f 64 <*
2000 Turf 0-4: (16f, 17f, 18f, 19f) (g-s, gd, g-f, frm)
Above-average mare, effective 17 to 18f, acts on g-s to g-f, has worn blinkers, likes left handed tracks. Turf high 70 - 5th of 15 giving 15lb to Charming Admiral (11 Apr Pontefract 17f g-s RF 0663).
**A Bailey [6-46] Miss E Oats.*

MBELE BHB 101f **RR 103f** 5226[2]

3 b c Mtoto 11.5f **(71)** - Majestic Image (Niniski (USA)) 10.6f **(65)**
Form - 321612
Record 2000 - 1st:2 2nd:2 3rd:1 Ran:6
Pre2000 - 1st:0 2nd:1 3rd:0 Ran:1
Win Prizemoney £17,426 *Total Prizemoney* £24,920
Wins * **2000** Spt Ascot (G-S) H 16.2f 92 96 <
* **2000** May Nottin (G-S) 14.1f 75
2000 Turf 2-6: (11f, 12f, 14f 1-1, 16f 1-3) (sft, gd 2-4, g-f)
Scopey, very useful colt, effective 16f, acts on gd. Turf high 103 - 2nd of 12 getting 5lb from Romantic Affair (27 Oct Newmarket 16f gd RF 5226) - also 1st of 15 getting 15lb from Montalcino (23 Spt Ascot RF 4600). A thorough stayer, he was in good form in the autumn and is clearly suited by easy ground. Open to improvement, he should do well this year granted suitable conditions.
**W R Muir [2-7] Dr & Mrs John Wilson.*

MCDAB (USA) **RR 104f** 4253a[19]

3 b c Mr. Greeley (USA) - Country Queen (USA) 00
Form - 5224120
2000 Turf 1-8: (7f 1-3, 8f 5) (sft, g-s, gd 1-3, g-f 3)
Very useful colt, effective 8f, acts on g-f, has worn blinkers. Turf high 104 - 2nd of 6 to Shibl (16 Jly Curragh 8f g-f RF 2921a).
**D Hanley in IRE [1-10] McLoughlin Family Syndicate.*

MCGILLYCUDDY REEKS (IRE) BHB 66f74a RR 73f 74a

5323[8]
9 b m Kefaah (USA) 11.2f **(64)** - Kilvarnet (Furry Glen) 8.9f **(63)**
Form - 3252318564558
Record 2000 - 1st:1 2nd:2 3rd:2 Ran:13
Pre2000 - 1st:10 2nd:5 3rd:11 Ran:76
Win Prizemoney £50,343 *Total Prizemoney* £71,035

Wins * 2000 Jly Doncas (GD) H 10.3f 71 77 <
* 1999 Jly Doncas (G-F) H 10.3f 69 73
* 1999 Jun Beverl (G-F) H 9.9f 65 70
* 1998 Aug Thirsk (GD) H 12f 73 77 <
* 1998 Jun Newcas (SFT) H 10.1f 70 73
* 1997 Oct York (GD) H 10.4f 68 71
* 1997 Aug Nottin (G-F) H 10f 53 65
* 1997 Jly Beverl (GD) H 9.9f 46 59
* 1997 Jly Beverl (G-F) H 9.9f 46 51
* 1997 Jly Pontef (GD) H 8f 38 45

2000 Turf 1-13: (10f 1-7, 11f, 12f 5) (sft, g-s 2, gd 5, g-f 1-3, frm 2)
Above-average mare, effective 10 to 12f, best at 10f, acts on gd to frm, prefers right handed tracks, likes tight tracks, and excels at Beverley. Turf high 77 - 1st of 6 giving 1lb to Happy Diamond (2 Jly Doncaster RF 2456). Consistent. She has been a fine servant to connections over the years and capitalised on the unfortunate Royston Ffrench's nightmare aboard Happy Diamond at Doncaster in July. She is probably best over ten furlongs these days and is suited by coming late off a fast pace.
**Don Enrico Incisa [10-66] Don Enrico Incisa (from N Tinkler [0-12] Nov 1996).*

MCQUILLAN BHB 38f34a RR 49f 34a

4366[16]
3 b g Maledetto (IRE) - Macs Maharanee **(71f 70a)** (Indian King (USA)) 7.4f **(64)**
Form - 0800
Record 2000 - 1st:0 2nd:0 3rd:0 Ran:4
Pre2000 - 1st:0 2nd:0 3rd:0 Ran:2
2000 Turf 0-2: (5f, 7f) (g-f, frm) 2000 AW 0-2: (6f, 9f) (Fibr 2)
Moderate gelding. Turf high 47. AW high 13.
**P S Felgate [0-6] P S Felgate.*

MEA CULPA (IRE) RR 50f

3272[11]
2 b f Blues Traveller (IRE) - Tolomena (Tolomeo) 5.6f **(60)**
Form - 500
Record 2000 - 1st:0 2nd:0 3rd:0 Ran:3
2000 Turf 0-3: (5f, 6f 2) (gd, g-f, frm)
Currently fair filly. Turf high 50. **T D Easterby [0-3] Mrs Sue Tindall.*

MEADAAAR (USA) BHB 104f RR 103f

4966[5]
3 ch c Diesis 9f **(80)** - Katiba (USA) (Gulch (USA)) 8f **(81)**
Form - 72535
Record 2000 - 1st:0 2nd:1 3rd:1 Ran:5
Pre2000 - 1st:1 2nd:1 3rd:1 Ran:3
Win Prizemoney £4,560 *Total Prizemoney* £13,364

Wins * 1999 Aug Yarmou (FRM) 7f 84+ <

2000 Turf 0-5: (6f, 7f 3, 8f) (gd 2, g-f, frm 2)
Scopey, very useful colt, effective 6 to 7f, best at 7f, acts on gd to g-f, best on gd. Turf high 103 - 5th of 11 getting 5lb from Late Night Out (24 Aug York 7f g-f RF 3937). Consistent. A decent performer over seven, though he does not look up to Listed class and does not seem to stay a mile. A front-runner.
**J L Dunlop [1-8] Hamdan Al Maktoum.*

MEADOW SONG BHB 30f RR 21f

4581[18]
2 b f Rock City 8.8f **(62)** - Island Mead (Pharly (FR)) 9.8f **(68)**
Form - 480
Record 2000 - 1st:0 2nd:0 3rd:0 Ran:3
2000 Turf 0-3: (6f, 7f 2) (gd, g-f, frm)
Currently little account filly. Turf high 21 (began Aug).
**J A Osborne [0-3] The Hennessy Partnership.*

MEADOWSWEET (IRE) RR 38f

4993[9]
2 b f Fumo Di Londra (IRE) - Make Hay (Nomination) 7f **(60)**
Form - 00
Record 2000 - 1st:0 2nd:0 3rd:0 Ran:2
2000 Turf 0-1: (6f) (gd) 2000 AW 0-1: (6f) (Fibr)
Currently very moderate filly.
**R Charlton [0-2] Beckhampton Partnership.*

MEDAILLE MILITAIRE BHB 83f RR

4696[16]
8 gr h Highest Honor (FR) 10.9f **(72)** - Lovely Noor (USA) (Fappiano (USA)) 8.7f **(77)**
Form - 0
Record 2000 - 1st:0 2nd:0 3rd:0 Ran:1
Pre2000 - 1st:5 2nd:1 3rd:3 Ran:20
Win Prizemoney £57,019 *Total Prizemoney* £64,238

Wins 1996 Nov Doncas (SFT) L 12f 114 <
1996 Oct Yarmou (GD) 10.1f 90

2000 Turf 0-1: (12f) (g-f)
Very poor horse, has worn blinkers.
**Mrs A J Perrett [0-1] James Hartnett (from M C Pipe [0-4] May 1998).*

MEDELAI BHB 31f41a RR 35f 41a

2782[12]
4 b f Marju (IRE) 9.2f **(76)** - No Islands (Lomond (USA)) 8.8f **(65)**
Form - 271740
Record 2000 - 1st:1 2nd:0 3rd:0 Ran:5
Pre2000 - 1st:1 2nd:2 3rd:1 Ran:16
Win Prizemoney £4,518 *Total Prizemoney* £6,509

Wins * 2000 *Jan Wolver (STD) H 16.2f 41 42*
1998 Oct Nottin (SFT) S 8.2f 56 <

2000 Turf 0-1: (22f) (sft) 2000 AW 1-4: (16f 1-4) (Fibr 1-4)
Unfurnished, moderate filly, effective 12 to 16f, acts on gd - acts on Fibr. AW high 42 - 1st of 12 getting 3lb from Harvey White (13 Jan Wolverhampton RF 0079).
**Mrs A E Johnson [1-6] Chasers IV (from J D Bethell [1-15] Oct 1999).*

MEDIA BUYER (USA) BHB 59f54a RR 73f 54a

5160[3]
2 b g Green Dancer (USA) 11.9f **(77)** - California Rush (USA) (Forty Niner (USA))
Form - 08032073
Record 2000 - 1st:0 2nd:1 3rd:2 Ran:8
Win Prizemoney £0 *Total Prizemoney* £2,215
2000 Turf 0-8: (5f, 6f, 7f 5, 8f) (sft, gd 4, g-f 3)
Above-average gelding, effective 7f, acts on gd to g-f, often wears blinkers (extremely effectively). Turf high 73 - 2nd of 7 to Atlantis Prince (20 Jly Epsom 7f g-f RF 2960).
**B J Meehan [0-8] Citigate Partnership.*

MEDIA MOGUL BHB 100f RR 101f

3915[6]
2 b g First Trump - White Heat **(41f 46a)** (Last Tycoon) 8.5f **(62)**
Form - 13126
Record 2000 - 1st:2 2nd:1 3rd:1 Ran:5
Win Prizemoney £6,507 *Total Prizemoney* £17,700

Wins * 2000 May Newcas (GD) 5f 85 <
*** 2000** Apr Beverl (HVY) 5f 77

2000 Turf 2-5: (5f 2-3, 6f 2) (g-s 1-1, gd 1-3, frm)
Very useful gelding. Turf high 101 - 2nd of 6 getting 3lb from Noverre (12 Jly Newmarket 6f gd RF 2746). He ran a cracker when upped in class and trip in the July Stakes at Newmarket, just inched out by Noverre. Sixth in the Gimcrack - it was later announced that he failed the post-race drugs test - he has been sold to continue his career in the United States.
**T D Barron [2-5] Mrs J Hazell.*

MEDIA PUZZLE (USA) RR 115f

4310[4]
3 ch c Theatrical 11.5f **(78)** - Market Slide (USA) (Gulch (USA)) 8f **(81)**
Form - 1137134
2000 Turf 3-7: (10f 1-2, 12f 2-3, 14f, 15f) (g-s 2-3, gd 2, frm 1-2)
High-class colt, effective 10 to 15f, acts on g-s to frm, best on frm, has worn blinkers. Turf high 115 - 4th of 11 to Millenary (9 Spt Doncaster 15f frm RF 4310) - also 1st of 13 from Common Kris (13 Jly Down Royal RF 2905a). Improving. He is a progressive individual and ended the season on a high when finishing fourth in the St Leger. Open to further improvement over long distances, he does not appeal as a Group 1 winner but should pick up another decent prize. **D K Weld in IRE [3-8] Moyglare Stud Farms Ltd.*

MEDICEAN BHB 119f RR 123f

4596[4]
3 ch c Machiavellian (USA) 9.8f **(83)** - Mystic Goddess (USA) (Storm Bird (CAN)) 10.3f **(74)**
Form - 31130314
Record 2000 - 1st:3 2nd:0 3rd:3 Ran:8
Win Prizemoney £60,305 *Total Prizemoney* £138,455

Wins * 2000 Aug Goodwo (GD) G2 8f 123 <
*** 2000** Jun Ayr (G-F) 8f 105+
*** 2000** Apr Sandow (SFT) 8.1f 91

2000 Turf 3-8: (8f 3-7, 10f) (sft 1-1, gd 1-6, frm 1-1)
Well made, very high-class colt, effective 8f, acts on gd. Turf high 123 - 1st of 6 from Observatory (26 Aug Goodwood RF 3985). Inconsistent. A high-class miler, he ran an absolute blinder when a fast-finishing third behind Giant's Causeway in the St James's Palace Stakes at Royal Ascot. He seemed a handicap good thing for York's John Smith's Cup, but the reality was that he faced an impossible task from his draw. Restored his reputation with an excellent effort in the Sussex Stakes before returning to Goodwood to take the Celebration Mile and was far from disgraced when fourth behind Observatory in the Queen Elizabeth II Stakes. He reportedly stays in training.
**Sir Michael Stoute [3-8] Cheveley Park Stud.*

MEDOOZA BHB 37f42a RR 35f 42a 3484[14]
3 b f Night Shift (USA) 8.1f **(73)** - Seastream (USA) (Alleged (USA)) 10f **(76)**
Form - 880000
Record 2000 - 1st:0 2nd:0 3rd:0 Ran:6
2000 Turf 0-5: (7f, 8f, 10f 2, 12f) (sft, g-s, gd, g-f 2) 2000 AW 0-1: (10f) (Equi)
Neat, very moderate filly. Turf high 35.
**G C Bravery [0-6] G C Bravery & The Dove Partnership.*

MEDRAAR RR 18f 5151[9]
2 b c Machiavellian (USA) 9.8f **(83)** - Saleemah (USA) **(92f)** (Storm Bird (CAN)) 10.3f **(74)**
Form - 0
Record 2000 - 1st:0 2nd:0 3rd:0 Ran:1
2000 Turf 0-1: (7f) (g-s)
Currently poor colt. **J L Dunlop [0-1] Hamdan Al Maktoum.*

MEGA (IRE) BHB 37f RR 59f 279[8]
4 b f Petardia 8.2f **(58)** - Gobolino (Don) 7.7f **(64)**
Form - 548
Record 2000 - 1st:0 2nd:0 3rd:0 Ran:3
Pre2000 - 1st:0 2nd:0 3rd:0 Ran:6
2000 AW 0-3: (8f 2, 12f) (Fibr 3)
Leggy, fair filly, has worn blinkers. AW high 31. Inconsistent.
**M H Tompkins [0-10] Mystic Meg Ltd.*

MEGABYTE (IRE) BHB 30f RR 31f 4123[12]
6 b m Glacial Storm (USA) - Panalpina (Petorius) 7.3f **(61)**
Form - 0
Record 2000 - 1st:0 2nd:0 3rd:0 Ran:1
Pre2000 - 1st:1 2nd:0 3rd:2 Ran:19
Win Prizemoney £2,475 *Total Prizemoney* £3,143
Wins 1999 May Dundal (GD) H 9f 24 41 <
2000 Turf 0-1: (8f) (frm)
Very moderate mare, effective 9f, acts on gd, has worn blinkers. Inconsistent.
**Miss Lucinda Russell [0-11] The Gypsy King Partnership (from M Cunningham in IRE [2-33] Spt 1999).*

MEGS PEARL BHB 43f41a RR 41f 41a 4894[18]
4 gr f Petong 7.6f **(58)** - Heaven-Liegh-Grey (Grey Desire) 8.7f **(50)**
Form - 0R250
Record 2000 - 1st:0 2nd:1 3rd:0 Ran:5
Pre2000 - 1st:0 2nd:0 3rd:0 Ran:6
Win Prizemoney £0 *Total Prizemoney* £1,273
2000 Turf 0-4: (6f 2, 7f, 8f) (sft, g-f, frm 2) 2000 AW 0-1: (6f) (Fibr)
Scopey, moderate filly, effective 6f, acts on frm, often wears blinkers (very effectively). Turf high 41 (began Jly) - 2nd of 19 giving 3lb to Lucky's Son (4 Aug Thirsk 6f frm RF 3380). Inconsistent.
**W M Brisbourne [0-5] John Pugh (from P D Evans [0-6] May 1999).*

MEHMAAS BHB 49f RR 62f 5166[6]
4 b g Distant Relative 7f **(69)** - Guest List (Be My Guest (USA)) 9.3f **(67)**
Form - 034100000530406
Record 2000 - 1st:1 2nd:0 3rd:2 Ran:15
Pre2000 - 1st:1 2nd:2 3rd:0 Ran:11
Win Prizemoney £7,126 *Total Prizemoney* £11,637
Wins * 2000 Jun Beverl (G-F) H 7.5f 60 62
1999 Aug Bright (G-F) 7f 75 <
2000 Turf 1-15: (7f 1-7, 8f 8) (gd 5, g-f 4, frm 4, hrd 1-2)
Workmanlike, above-average gelding, effective 7f, acts on frm, often wears blinkers, likes tight tracks. Turf high 62.
**R E Barr [1-15] J C Garbutt (from M R Channon [1-6] Spt 1999).*

MEIKLE PRINCE BHB 46f RR 30f 5293[8]
2 b gr c Contract Law (USA) 8.9f **(54)** - Dunston Princess (Cyrano de Bergerac) 6f **(68)**
Form - 038
Record 2000 - 1st:0 2nd:0 3rd:1 Ran:3
Win Prizemoney £0 *Total Prizemoney* £581
2000 Turf 0-3: (5f, 7f 2) (hvy, g-s, gd)
Currently moderate colt. Turf high 30 (began Aug).
**Miss L A Perratt [0-3] B & J Racing and Breeding Syndicate.*

MEILLEUR (IRE) BHB 54f55a RR 57f 55a 4648[3]
6 b g Nordico (USA) 8.2f **(59)** - Lucy Limelight (Hot Spark) 7.6f **(62)**
Form - 2423606302643
Record 2000 - 1st:0 2nd:2 3rd:3 Ran:11
Pre2000 - 1st:2 2nd:4 3rd:2 Ran:24
Win Prizemoney £5,126 *Total Prizemoney* £12,139
Wins * 1999 Spt Newbur (G-F) H 12f 52 54 <
* 1998 Aug Hamilt (SFT) H 11.1f 51 52
2000 Turf 0-7: (11f, 12f 4, 14f, 16f) (sft, gd 2, g-f 3, frm) 2000 AW 0-4: (12f, 16f 3) (Fibr 4)
Average gelding, effective 11 to 16f, best at 16f, acts on sft to frm - acts on Fibr, has worn blinkers, prefers left handed tracks, likes tight tracks, excels at Southwell. Turf high 57 - 3rd of 16 giving 10lb to Admirals Secret (31 May Yarmouth 11f g-f RF 1612). AW high 60 (1st run) - 2nd of 11 giving 17lb to Kent (7 Jan Southwell 16f Fibr RF 0045). Consistent. **Lady Herries [2-36] Lady Herries.*

MEIOSIS (USA) RR 97f 2822[5]
3 b f Danzig (USA) 8.1f **(88)** - Golden Opinion (USA) 00
Form - 105
Record 2000 - 1st:1 2nd:0 3rd:0 Ran:3
Win Prizemoney £5,226 *Total Prizemoney* £5,226
Wins * 2000 May Newmar (GD) 7f 96 <
2000 Turf 1-3: (6f, 7f 1-1, 8f) (g-s, gd, g-f 1-1)
Scopey, currently very useful filly. Turf high 97 - also 1st of 10 from Papabile (5 May Newmarket RF 1050). A free-going filly, she proved disappointing after an impressive reappearance at Newmarket in May. A beaten favourite in the Irish 1000 Guineas, she should stay a mile but clearly has limitations.
**S bin Suroor [1-3] Godolphin.*

MELANZANA BHB 77f RR 83df 4743[24]
3 b f Alzao (USA) 9.8f **(73)** - Melody Park (Music Boy) 6.8f **(57)**
Form - 4256070
Record 2000 - 1st:0 2nd:1 3rd:0 Ran:7
Pre2000 - 1st:1 2nd:0 3rd:1 Ran:2
Win Prizemoney £3,270 *Total Prizemoney* £7,227
Wins * 1999 Spt Redcar (G-F) 6f 85+ <
2000 Turf 0-7: (5f 2, 6f 4, 7f) (g-s, gd 2, g-f 4)
Scopey, decent filly, effective 6f, acts on gd to frm. Turf high 88 - 2nd of 11 giving 9lb to Corunna (27 Jun Lingfield 6f g-f RF 2304). Becoming disappointing.
**E A L Dunlop [1-9] The Serendipity Partnership.*

MELBA (IRE) BHB 58f RR 60df 897[13]
3 b f Namaqualand (USA) - Priyanka (Last Tycoon) 8.5f **(62)**
Form - 0
Record 2000 - 1st:0 2nd:0 3rd:0 Ran:1
Pre2000 - 1st:0 2nd:0 3rd:0 Ran:2
2000 Turf 0-1: (10f) (sft)
Scopey, currently average filly. **A P Jarvis [0-3] Mrs D B Brazier.*

MELIKAH (IRE) RR 117f 4417a[5]
3 ch f Lammtarra (USA) - Urban Sea (USA) **(119f)** (Miswaki (USA)) 9f **(81)**
Form - 1325
Record 2000 - 1st:1 2nd:1 3rd:1 Ran:4
Win Prizemoney £16,240 *Total Prizemoney* £90,965
Wins * 2000 May Newmar (GD) L 10f 102 <
2000 Turf 1-4: (10f 1-1, 12f 3) (g-s, gd, g-f, frm 1-1)
Well made, high-class filly. Turf high 117 - 5th of 11 to Volvoreta (10 Spt Longchamp 12f gd RF 4417a). Beautifully bred, she overcame obvious inexperience to win the Pretty Polly Stakes on her debut and went on to make the frame in both the English and Irish

Oaks. Outpaced in the Prix Vermeille, she will stay beyond a mile and a half and could do well over long distances if kept in training. A poor mover, she appeared unsuited by the undulations at Epsom and might be best served by a galloping track.
**S bin Suroor [1-4] Godolphin.*

MELLEDGAN (IRE) BHB 49f **RR 41f** 4813[13]
3 b f Catrail (USA) - Dark Hyacinth (IRE) (Darshaan) 9.9f **(84)**
Form - 6400
Record 2000 - 1st:0 2nd:0 3rd:0 Ran:4
Win Prizemoney £0 *Total Prizemoney* £338
2000 Turf 0-4: (5f 2, 6f, 8f) (g-s, gd, g-f 2)
Workmanlike, moderate filly. Turf high 41 (began Aug).
**R Guest [0-4] Bradmill Ltd.*

MELLORS (IRE) BHB 58f64a **RR 62f 64a** 504[2]
7 b g Common Grounds 8.1f **(66)** - Simply Beautiful (IRE) (Simply Great (FR)) 8.2f **(65)**
Form - 32
Record 2000 - 1st:0 2nd:1 3rd:1 Ran:2
Pre2000 - 1st:8 2nd:6 3rd:3 Ran:45
Win Prizemoney £21,027 *Total Prizemoney* £28,879

Wins									
1999	May	Bright	(FRM)	H	10f	57	62	
1999	Apr	Bright	(G-F)	H	8f	53	56	
1998	May	Bright	(FRM)	H	8f	46	52	
1998	Apr	Bright	(GD)	H	8f	41	50	
1998	*Feb*	*Lingfi*	*(SLW)*	*H*	*8f*	*51*	*68*	<
1998	*Feb*	*Lingfi*	*(SLW)*	*H*	*8f*	*51*	*56*	
1997	*Jan*	*Lingfi*	*(STD)*	*H*	*6f*	*57*	*60*	
1996	Jun	Catter	(GD)		6f		52	

2000 AW 0-2: (8f 2) (Equi, Fibr)
Average gelding, effective 8 to 10f, best at 8f, acts on g-f to frm - acts on AW, has worn blinkers, favours left handed tracks, excels at Brighton. AW high 64 - 2nd of 6 giving 1lb to Lord Eurolink (25 Mar Wolverhampton 8f Fibr RF 0504).
**John Berry [0-2] Miss J V May (from M J Heaton-Ellis [7-36] Jly 1999).*

MELLOW JAZZ BHB 72f73a **RR 80df 73a** 1549[3]
3 b f Lycius (USA) 8.8f **(71)** - Slow Jazz (USA) (Chief's Crown (USA)) 9.8f **(72)**
Form - 83
Record 2000 - 1st:0 2nd:0 3rd:1 Ran:2
Pre2000 - 1st:1 2nd:0 3rd:0 Ran:1
Win Prizemoney £3,947 *Total Prizemoney* £4,393
Wins * 1999 Spt Nottin (GD) 6.1f 81 <
2000 Turf 0-2: (6f, 7f) (hvy, g-f)
Lengthy, currently decent filly. Turf high 67. Cosy winner of an ordinary maiden on his debut.
**E A L Dunlop [1-3] Saeed Abdullah Humaid.*

MELLOW MISS BHB 44f44a **RR 51f 44a** 2770[6]
4 b f Danehill (USA) 9.1f **(79)** - Like the Sun (USA) (Woodman (USA)) 9f **(74)**
Form - 448568330876
Record 2000 - 1st:0 2nd:0 3rd:2 Ran:9
Pre2000 - 1st:0 2nd:0 3rd:0 Ran:9
Win Prizemoney £0 *Total Prizemoney* £869
2000 Turf 0-6: (7f, 9f, 10f 4) (gd 4, g-f 2) 2000 AW 0-3: (8f 2, 12f) (Equi 2, Fibr)
Scopey, fair filly, effective 7 to 10f, acts on gd - acts on Equi, has worn blinkers, likes tight tracks. Turf high 53 (1st run) - 3rd of 18 giving 12lb to Danzas (13 Apr Brighton 7f gd RF 0696). AW high 50. **R M Flower [0-16] Trevor Lowe (from E A L Dunlop [0-2] Oct 1998).*

MELODIAN BHB 72f55a **RR 75f 55a** 5240[13]
5 b h Grey Desire 9.3f **(49)** - Mere Melody (Dunphy) 9.4f **(57)**
Form - 82317410000132270
Record 2000 - 1st:3 2nd:3 3rd:2 Ran:17
Pre2000 - 1st:4 2nd:1 3rd:3 Ran:20
Win Prizemoney £26,188 *Total Prizemoney* £37,139

Wins									
* **2000**	Spt	Beverl	(HVY)	H	7.5f	64	69	<
* **2000**	Jun	Beverl	(G-S)	H	7.5f	62	69	<
* **2000**	Apr	Newcas	(SFT)	H	7f	56	65	
* 1999	Aug	Catter	(G-F)	H	7f	51	53	
* 1999	Jly	Doncas	(G-F)	H	7f	42	52	
* 1999	Jly	Beverl	(G-F)	H	7.5f	41	48	
* 1998	Jly	Newcas	(GD)	H	7f	38	41	

2000 Turf 3-16: (7f 3-9, 8f 7) (sft 1-3, g-s 1-3, gd 1-5, g-f, frm 3, hrd) 2000 AW 0-1: (7f) (Fibr)
Above-average colt, effective 7 to 8f, best at 7f, acts on sft to gd, best on gd, mostly wears blinkers (very effectively), does well at Beverley. Turf high 75 - 2nd of 21 getting 17lb from Elghani (13 Oct Newmarket 8f gd RF 4968) - also 1st of 16 giving 14lb to Naissant (7 Jun Beverley RF 1776). He acts on any ground and all of his wins in recent seasons have been at around seven furlongs.
**M Brittain [7-37] Mel Brittain.*

MELODY LADY BHB 60f **RR 52f** 4994[8]
4 ch f Dilum (USA) 7.1f **(56)** - Ansellady **(62f 60a)** (Absalom) 7.2f **(58)**
Form - 00220358
Record 2000 - 1st:0 2nd:2 3rd:1 Ran:8
Pre2000 - 1st:0 2nd:2 3rd:1 Ran:11
Win Prizemoney £0 *Total Prizemoney* £4,435
2000 Turf 0-7: (10f 3, 11f, 12f 3) (gd, g-f 5, frm) 2000 AW 0-1: (12f) (Fibr)
Unfurnished, fair filly, effective 10 to 12f, best at 12f, acts on g-f to frm, best on frm, has worn blinkers, favours left handed tracks. Turf high 52 - 2nd of 12 giving 3lb to Missile Toe (30 Jun Newcastle 10f g-f RF 2403).
**Ferdy Murphy [1-15] R Sunter (from Mrs L Stubbs [0-6] Nov 1998).*

MELOMANIA (USA) BHB 22f35a **RR 5f 35a** 166[9]
8 b g Shadeed (USA) 7.7f **(72)** - Medley of Song (USA) (Secretariat (USA)) 9f **(79)**
Form - 00
Record 2000 - 1st:0 2nd:0 3rd:0 Ran:2
Pre2000 - 1st:1 2nd:0 3rd:1 Ran:18
Win Prizemoney £2,220 *Total Prizemoney* £2,705
Wins *1999 Feb Lingfi (STD) H 8f 40 43* <
2000 AW 0-2: (8f, 9f) (Fibr 2)
Fair gelding, effective 7 to 8f, - acts on AW, likes left handed tracks, likes tight tracks. AW high 11.
**T T Clement [0-2] Mrs P Haddow (from P Howling [1-14] Oct 1999).*

MELON PLACE (IRE) BHB 84f **RR 88df** 5109[13]
3 b c Dancing Dissident (USA) 6.8f **(65)** - Shikari Rose (Kala Shikari) 8.4f **(54)**
Form - 7U0
Record 2000 - 1st:0 2nd:0 3rd:0 Ran:3
Pre2000 - 1st:1 2nd:1 3rd:1 Ran:3
Win Prizemoney £3,761 *Total Prizemoney* £7,366
Wins * 1999 Aug Goodwo (GD) 5f 82+ <
2000 Turf 0-3: (5f 2, 6f) (g-s, gd 2)
Scopey, useful colt, effective 5f, acts on gd. (began Spt). Showed decent form at two, but was off the track for more than a year and showed little on his return. **K R Burke [1-6] Michael Wilson.*

MELS BABY (IRE) BHB 44f41a **RR 42f 41a** 790[11]
7 br g Contract Law (USA) 8.9f **(54)** - Launch The Raft (Home Guard (USA)) 9.3f **(66)**
Form - 70
Record 2000 - 1st:0 2nd:0 3rd:0 Ran:2
Pre2000 - 1st:4 2nd:7 3rd:2 Ran:38
Win Prizemoney £20,523 *Total Prizemoney* £26,562

Wins									
* 1997	May	Beverl	(HVY)	H	9.9f	71	76	<
* 1996	Nov	Doncas	(SFT)	H	8f	61	68	
* 1996	Oct	Pontef	(GD)	H	8f	58	62	
* 1996	Spt	Redcar	(FRM)	H	8f	56	63	

2000 Turf 0-2: (10f, 12f) (g-s, gd)
Fair gelding, has worn blinkers. Turf high 37. Inconsistent.
**J L Eyre [4-40] John Roberts (Wakefield).*

MELVELLA BHB 35f29a **RR 23df 29a** 3236[8]
4 b f Mtoto 11.5f **(71)** - Trojan Desert (Troy) 10.4f **(68)**
Form - 687008
Record 2000 - 1st:0 2nd:0 3rd:0 Ran:6
Pre2000 - 1st:0 2nd:0 3rd:1 Ran:8
Win Prizemoney £0 *Total Prizemoney* £293
2000 Turf 0-3: (10f, 12f, 15f) (gd, g-f, frm) 2000 AW 0-3: (12f 3) (Equi, Fibr 2)
Unfurnished, little account filly. Turf high 12. AW high 23.
**J L Harris [0-6] Paddy Barrett (from M L W Bell [0-8] Oct 1999).*

MEMAMEDA RR 5246[6]
4 b f Cigar 6.3f **(43)** - Mamzooj (IRE) (Shareef Dancer (USA)) 9.9f **(73)**

Form - 6
Record 2000 - 1st:0 2nd:0 3rd:0 Ran:1
2000 AW 0-1: (8f) (Fibr)
Currently little account filly. **K A Ryan [0-1] Frankie Murphy.*

MEMBERS WELCOME (IRE) BHB 26f30a **RR 39f 30a** 1372[13]

7 b g Eve's Error - Manuale Del Utente (Montekin) 11.1f **(55)**
Form - 0
Record 2000 - 1st:0 2nd:0 3rd:0 Ran:1
Pre2000 - 1st:0 2nd:1 3rd:1 Ran:21
Win Prizemoney £0 *Total Prizemoney* £1,312
2000 AW 0-1: (16f) (Fibr)
Very moderate gelding, has worn blinkers. Becoming disappointing. **Miss A Stokell [0-2] T J Ford (from W G M Turner [0-2] Mar 1997).*

MEMORY MAKER (IRE) RR 119f 5369a[2]

3 b c Lure (USA) - Moonlight Dance (USA) **(107f)** (Alysheba (USA)) 9f **(84)**
Form - 2
2000 Turf 0-1: (8f) (hvy)
Currently high-class colt. (1st run) - 2nd of 9 getting 3lb from Jim And Tonic (4 Nov Saint-cloud 8f hvy RF 5369a).
**A Fabre in FR [0-1] D Wildenstein.*

MEMPHIS TEENS BHB 58f **RR 66f** 5162[5]

3 b c Rock City 8.8f **(62)** - Minteen (Teenoso (USA)) 9.9f **(72)**
Form - 37305
Record 2000 - 1st:0 2nd:0 3rd:2 Ran:5
Win Prizemoney £0 *Total Prizemoney* £1,101
2000 Turf 0-5: (10f 3, 12f, 13f) (sft, g-f 2, frm 2)
Average colt. Turf high 66. **J R Jenkins [0-5] Mrs Stella Peirce.*

MEMSAHIB RR 25f 5196[15]

2 b f Alzao (USA) 9.8f **(73)** - Indian Queen (Electric) 10.1f **(61)**
Form - 0
Record 2000 - 1st:0 2nd:0 3rd:0 Ran:1
2000 Turf 0-1: (8f) (gd)
Currently little account filly.
**D R C Elsworth [0-1] Sir Gordon Brunton.*

MENAS ERN BHB 48f52a **RR 52f 52a** 5247[4]

2 b g Young Ern - Menas Gold **(73f)** (Heights of Gold)
Form - 000404
Record 2000 - 1st:0 2nd:0 3rd:0 Ran:6
2000 Turf 0-4: (6f, 7f 3) (g-s, gd 2, frm) 2000 AW 0-2: (7f, 8f) (Fibr 2)
Fair gelding. Turf high 52. AW high 59 (began Spt).
**S Dow [0-6] Mrs Anne Gurney.*

MEN OF WICKENBY BHB 28f **RR 27f** 2339[8]

6 b g Shirley Heights 12.1f **(76)** - Radiant Bride (USA) (Blushing Groom (FR)) 10.3f **(76)**
Form - 8
Record 2000 - 1st:0 2nd:0 3rd:0 Ran:1
Pre2000 - 1st:1 2nd:0 3rd:0 Ran:14
Win Prizemoney £2,853 *Total Prizemoney* £2,853
Wins * 1999 Jun Hamilt (G-S) S 9.2f 39? <
2000 Turf 0-1: (9f) (g-f)
Little account gelding, effective 9 to 11f, acts on g-s to gd, likes right handed tracks. Becoming disappointing.
**Martyn Wane [1-11] J P Slattery (from R M McKellar [0-4] May 1997).*

MENTAL PRESSURE BHB 59f **RR 62f** 4625[3]

7 ch g Polar Falcon (USA) 9f **(74)** - Hysterical (High Top) 10.2f **(67)**
Form - 32521343
Record 2000 - 1st:1 2nd:2 3rd:3 Ran:8
Pre2000 - 1st:0 2nd:4 3rd:3 Ran:13
Win Prizemoney £2,886 *Total Prizemoney* £19,778
Wins * 2000 Aug Redcar (FRM) H 16f 57 62 <
2000 Turf 1-8: (14f 3, 16f 1-5) (gd 5, g-f, frm 1-2)
Average gelding, effective 16f, acts on gd to frm, best on frm. Turf high 62 - 3rd of 7 giving 2lb to Makasseb (29 Aug Ripon 16f frm RF 4065) - also 1st of 10 giving 1lb to Generous Ways (13 Aug Redcar RF 3618). Consistent.
**Mrs M Reveley [1-19] The Mary Reveley Racing Club (from M R Channon [0-2] Spt 1995).*

MENTEITH (USA) BHB 37f30a **RR 30f 30a** 851[16]

4 b g Dehere (USA) - Bunka Bunka (USA) (Raja Baba (USA)) 10f **(64)**
Form - 00
Record 2000 - 1st:0 2nd:0 3rd:0 Ran:2
Pre2000 - 1st:0 2nd:0 3rd:0 Ran:2
2000 Turf 0-1: (14f) (sft) 2000 AW 0-1: (11f) (Fibr)
Workmanlike, very moderate gelding.
**B P J Baugh [0-3] Messrs Chrimes, Winn & Wilson (from P F I Cole [0-1] Apr 1999).*

MENTIGA (IRE) BHB 60f55a **RR 70f 55a** 4545[10]

3 b g Dancing Dissident (USA) 6.8f **(65)** - Lowtown (Camden Town) 9.3f **(53)**
Form - 05067680
Record 2000 - 1st:0 2nd:0 3rd:0 Ran:8
Pre2000 - 1st:1 2nd:3 3rd:2 Ran:8
Win Prizemoney £4,000 *Total Prizemoney* £7,593
Wins * 1999 Oct Newbur (HVY) H 7.3f 77 84 <
2000 Turf 0-8: (8f 5, 9f, 10f 2) (g-s 2, gd 2, g-f 4)
Unfurnished, above-average gelding, effective 5 to 7f, best at 7f, acts on hvy to sft, best on sft, likes left handed tracks. Turf high 78. **B R Millman [1-16] J A Pickford.*

MEPHITIS (IRE) RR 506[7]

6 gr g Ela-Mana-Mou 12.7f **(72)** - Maysoura (Nishapour (FR)) 9.1f **(61)**
Form - 7
Record 2000 - 1st:0 2nd:0 3rd:0 Ran:1
2000 AW 0-1: (9f) (Fibr)
Very poor gelding. (DEAD) **R Ford [0-6] David Bostock.*

MERANTI BHB 36f62a **RR 38f 62a** 1167[9]

7 b g Puissance 7.1f **(60)** - Sorrowful (Moorestyle) 6.9f **(64)**
Form - 070
Record 2000 - 1st:0 2nd:0 3rd:0 Ran:3
Pre2000 - 1st:5 2nd:2 3rd:1 Ran:51
Win Prizemoney £17,359 *Total Prizemoney* £21,460
Wins * 1998 Jly Thirsk (GD) H 6f 56 66 <
* 1998 Jly Salisb (FRM) H 6f 51 54
* 1997 Jly Salisb (G-F) H 6f 56 60
* 1997 Apr Thirsk (G-F) H 7f 43 55
* 1997 Apr Nottin (G-F) H 6.1f 43 57
2000 Turf 0-3: (6f 3) (frm 3)
Very moderate gelding, effective 6f, acts on gd. Turf high 38. Inconsistent.
**J M Bradley [5-39] John Wallis (from S Dow [0-8] Jly 1996).*

MERCEDE (IRE) BHB 32f **RR 29f** 5077[14]

3 b f Perugino (USA) - Miss Busybody (IRE) (Phardante (FR))
Form - 0000
Record 2000 - 1st:0 2nd:0 3rd:0 Ran:3
Pre2000 - 1st:0 2nd:0 3rd:0 Ran:3
2000 Turf 0-3: (8f 2, 10f) (g-s 2, g-f)
Light-framed, little account filly. Turf high 24 (began Spt).
**N P Littmoden [0-6] Josef Fusenich.*

MERCHANT PRINCE BHB 33f36a **RR 40f 36a** 5246[7]

4 b g Flying Tyke 7.2f **(42)** - Bellinote (FR) (Noir Et Or) 10f **(38)**
Form - 500807
Record 2000 - 1st:0 2nd:0 3rd:0 Ran:6
Pre2000 - 1st:0 2nd:0 3rd:0 Ran:6
2000 Turf 0-2: (6f, 10f) (gd 2) 2000 AW 0-4: (5f, 8f 3) (Fibr 4)
Scopey, moderate gelding, has worn blinkers. Turf high 40. AW high 31. **A Smith [0-12] Park Racing Partnership.*

MERIDEN MIST BHB 74f72a **RR 72f 72a** 5218[2]

2 b f Distinctly North (USA) 7.4f **(63)** - Bring on the Choir **(75f)** (Chief Singer) 8.9f **(66)**
Form - 5254148542
Record 2000 - 1st:1 2nd:2 3rd:0 Ran:10
Win Prizemoney £3,523 *Total Prizemoney* £6,831
Wins * 2000 Jly Bright (FRM) H 7f 68 <
2000 Turf 1-10: (6f 4, 7f 1-5, 8f) (sft, g-f 4, frm 1-5)
Above-average filly, effective 6 to 8f, best at 7f, acts on sft to frm. Turf high 72 - 2nd of 11 giving 13lb to Leatherback (27 Oct Brighton 8f sft RF 5218) - also 1st of 8 giving 8lb to Violent (24 Jly Brighton RF 3075). Improving. Showed some form early on, but it was not until she tackled seven furlongs for the first time that she

got off the mark in a Brighton nursery.
**P W Harris [1-10] G E Williams & B Lawrence.*

MERIDIANA (FR) BHB 50f RR 1977[14]
4 gr f Kaldoun (FR) 9.9f **(84)** - Incroyable (FR) (Lead on Time (USA)) 8f **(65)**
Form - 00
Record 2000 - 1st:0 2nd:0 3rd:0 Ran:2
2000 Turf 0-2: (10f 2) (gd, frm)
Currently very poor filly. **J M Bradley [0-2] John Williams.*

MER LOCK RR 14f 3785[8]
2 b f Piccolo - Sojourn (Be My Guest (USA)) 9.3f **(67)**
Form - 8
Record 2000 - 1st:0 2nd:0 3rd:0 Ran:1
2000 Turf 0-1: (6f) (frm)
Currently poor filly. **T J Naughton [0-1] Bonus Partnership.*

MERLY NOTTY BHB 32f RR 47f 1673[6]
4 ch f Inchinor 8.9f **(64)** - Rambadale (Vaigly Great) 7f **(58)**
Form - 246
Record 2000 - 1st:0 2nd:1 3rd:0 Ran:3
Pre2000 - 1st:0 2nd:0 3rd:0 Ran:7
Win Prizemoney £0 *Total Prizemoney* £752
2000 Turf 0-3: (9f, 11f, 14f) (g-s, g-f 2)
Neat, moderate filly, effective 9f, acts on g-f. Turf high 47 (1st run) - 2nd of 10 giving 3lb to Will Iveson (7 May Hamilton 9f g-f RF 1072). Inconsistent.
**W Storey [0-3] Tony Stafford (from J S Haldane [0-7] Aug 1999).*

MER MADE BHB 44f RR 34f 2257[17]
2 b f Prince Sabo 6.6f **(64)** - Blue Zulu (IRE) **(84f)** (Don't Forget Me) 8.3f **(74)**
Form - 580
Record 2000 - 1st:0 2nd:0 3rd:0 Ran:3
2000 Turf 0-2: (5f, 7f) (gd, frm) 2000 AW 0-1: (5f) (Fibr)
Currently very moderate filly. Turf high 34.
**T J Naughton [0-3] & Mrs D J Flahive.*

MERRY (IRE) BHB 30f RR 12f 549[10]
3 ch f Ridgewood Ben - Speedy Action (Horage) 10.3f **(61)**
Form - 0
Record 2000 - 1st:0 2nd:0 3rd:0 Ran:1
Pre2000 - 1st:0 2nd:0 3rd:0 Ran:3
2000 Turf 0-1: (12f) (frm)
Poor filly.
**N Tinkler [0-4] Mrs L Dales.*

MERRY DANCE BHB 56f RR 65f 4615[7]
2 ch f Suave Dancer (USA) 10.7f **(68)** - Sarah Byrne (NZ) (Star Way)
Form - 03007
Record 2000 - 1st:0 2nd:0 3rd:1 Ran:5
Win Prizemoney £0 *Total Prizemoney* £427
2000 Turf 0-5: (6f, 7f 2, 8f 2) (gd 2, g-f 2, hrd)
Average filly. Turf high 65 (began Jly) - 3rd of 5 giving 5lb to Billie H (23 Aug Brighton 7f hrd RF 3895).
**A P Jarvis [0-5] Christopher Shankland.*

MERRY MERLIN BHB 110f RR 110f 4004[6]
3 b c Polar Falcon (USA) 9f **(74)** - Bronzewing (Beldale Flutter (USA)) 9.7f **(71)**
Form - 0175636
Record 2000 - 1st:1 2nd:0 3rd:1 Ran:7
Pre2000 - 1st:1 2nd:0 3rd:0 Ran:2
Win Prizemoney £33,652 *Total Prizemoney* £37,910
Wins * 2000 May Cheste (GD) L 10.3f 108 <
* 1999 Aug Newmar (G-F) 7f 85+
2000 Turf 1-7: (7f, 8f, 10f 1-5) (g-s, gd 3, g-f 1-2, frm)
Scopey, Group-class colt, effective 8 to 10f, best at 10f, acts on gd to g-f, best on g-f. Turf high 110 - 3rd of 5 giving 4lb to Adilabad (5 Aug Goodwood 8f g-f RF 3393) - also 1st of 8 from Three Points (11 May Chester RF 1134). A fractious individual, he came from behind a suicidal pace to win the Dee Stakes, but proved difficult to settle thereafter. Sold for 66,000gns at Newmarket in October, he will reportedly continue his career in America.
**M L W Bell [2-9] Sir Thomas Pilkington.*

MERRY PRINCE (IRE) BHB 43f46a RR 36f 46a 2680[12]
5 b g Roi Danzig (USA) 10.5f **(62)** - Queen of the Brush (Averof) 8.2f **(62)**
Form - 0
Record 2000 - 1st:0 2nd:0 3rd:0 Ran:1
Pre2000 - 1st:0 2nd:0 3rd:1 Ran:17
Win Prizemoney £0 *Total Prizemoney* £277
2000 Turf 0-1: (10f) (gd)
Moderate gelding, effective 10f, acts on g-f, often wears blinkers (effectively), likes left handed tracks.
**P R Hedger [1-17] J J Whelan (from M A Jarvis [0-7] Oct 1998).*

MERRYVALE MAN BHB 65f70a RR 82df 70a 5101[5]
3 b c Rudimentary (USA) 8.2f **(66)** - Salu **(58f)** (Ardross) 10.6f **(68)**
Form - 2053121827505
Record 2000 - 1st:2 2nd:2 3rd:1 Ran:12
Pre2000 - 1st:0 2nd:1 3rd:1 Ran:7
Win Prizemoney £5,427 *Total Prizemoney* £9,103
Wins 2000 Mar Catter (GD) H 12f 65 72 <
2000 *Feb Southw (STD) C 11f 60*
2000 Turf 1-7: (10f, 12f 1-3, 14f 2, 15f) (g-s 3, gd 2, g-f, frm 1-1) 2000 AW 1-5: (7f, 8f, 11f 1-2, 12f) (Fibr 1-5)
Unfurnished, decent colt, effective 12 to 15f, acts on gd to frm, likes left handed tracks. Turf high 82 - 2nd of 10 getting 5lb from Samsaam (1 May Doncaster 15f gd RF 0935). AW high 72.
**R A Fahey [0-2] Arthur Symons Key (from J G Given [2-17] Jun 2000).*

MERSEY MIRAGE BHB 87f83a RR 88f 83a 5317[19]
3 b c King's Signet (USA) 7f **(51)** - Kirriemuir (Lochnager) 6f **(59)**
Form - 71430
Record 2000 - 1st:1 2nd:0 3rd:1 Ran:5
Pre2000 - 1st:1 2nd:1 3rd:1 Ran:7
Win Prizemoney £13,417 *Total Prizemoney* £18,560
Wins * 2000 Aug Leices (G-F) H 6f 85 86 <
* 1999 Jly Bright (FRM) 6f 74+
2000 Turf 1-5: (6f 1-2, 7f 3) (sft, gd, g-f 2, frm 1-1)
Useful colt, effective 6 to 7f, best at 6f, acts on gd to frm. Turf high 88 (began Aug) - 3rd of 17 getting 2lb from Fire Dome (27 Spt Salisbury 6f gd RF 4691) - also 1st of 8 giving 3lb to Pedro Jack (13 Aug Leicester RF 3610). Scored at Brighton and ran well at Goodwood as a juvenile, and clearly handles downhill tracks. Tried unsuccessfully at seven, he returned to winning form when dropped back in trip on fast ground.
**R Hannon [2-12] Speedlith Group.*

MERSEY SOUND (IRE) RR 87f 4435[3]
2 b c Ela-Mana-Mou 12.7f **(72)** - Coral Sound (IRE) (Glow (USA)) 6.7f **(71)**
Form - 3
Record 2000 - 1st:0 2nd:0 3rd:1 Ran:1
Win Prizemoney £0 *Total Prizemoney* £1,790
2000 Turf 0-1: (8f) (frm)
Currently useful colt. (1st run) - 3rd of 7 to Nayef (15 Spt Newbury 8f frm RF 4435). **D R C Elsworth [0-1] A Heaney.*

METEOR STRIKE (USA) BHB 44f45a RR 48f 45a 4221[13]
6 ch g Lomond (USA) 9.9f **(74)** - Meteoric (High Line) 10.3f **(70)**
Form - 62160354U0
Record 2000 - 1st:1 2nd:1 3rd:1 Ran:10
Pre2000 - 1st:2 2nd:2 3rd:1 Ran:14
Win Prizemoney £11,883 *Total Prizemoney* £15,567
Wins 2000 *Jan Southw (STD) S 11f 33*
1998 *Dec Lingfi (STD) H* 12f 75 82 <
1997 Jly Bath (GD) 10.2f 75
2000 Turf 0-5: (10f 2, 12f 3) (g-f, frm 4) 2000 AW 1-5: (10f, 11f 1-1, 12f 3) (Equi 2, Fibr 1-3)
Fair gelding, effective 9 to 12f, acts on gd to frm, has worn blinkers. Turf high 48 (began Jun). AW high 55. Inconsistent. Formerly with Amanda Perret, he showed very decent form on Equitrack in 1998, but has had his problems since and moved to Dandy Nicholls. He managed to will a Southwell seller in January, but he looks a light of former days and still looks to have a problem.
**K C Comerford [0-2] Alan Brackley (from D Nicholls [1-12] Aug 2000).*

METRONOME BHB 95f RR 97f 4613[7]
3 b f Salse (USA) 10.9f **(71)** - Rapid Repeat (IRE) (Exactly Sharp (USA))

Form - 822157
Record 2000 - 1st:1 2nd:2 3rd:0 Ran:6
Win Prizemoney £7,182 *Total Prizemoney* £9,565
Wins * **2000** Jly Leices (G-F) H 11.8f 82 88 <
2000 Turf 1-6: (8f, 10f, 12f 1-4) (g-s, gd, g-f 2, frm 1-2)
Very useful filly, effective 12f, acts on g-f to frm. Turf high 97 - 5th of 13 to Firecrest (24 Aug York 12f g-f RF 3932) - also 1st of 9 getting 2lb from Red Empress (8 Jly Leicester RF 2640). She failed to make a mark in Listed company after winning a fillies' handicap in July. Unlikely to stay beyond a mile and a half, she is not open to significant improvement. **L M Cumani [1-6] Lord Hartington.*

MEXICAN ROCK BHB 66f RR 66f 4991[28]
4 b c Rock City 8.8f **(62)** - Pink Mex (Tickled Pink) 6.5f **(59)**
Form - 7000
Record 2000 - 1st:0 2nd:0 3rd:0 Ran:4
Pre2000 - 1st:1 2nd:0 3rd:0 Ran:3
Win Prizemoney £2,351 *Total Prizemoney* £2,761
Wins 1999 Apr Folkes (SFT) 6f 95 <
2000 Turf 0-4: (7f 3, 8f) (sft, gd 3)
Workmanlike, average colt, effective 6f, acts on sft. Turf high 66 (began Spt).
**Dr J R J Naylor [0-4] Magno-Pulse Ltd (from J A R Toller [1-3] May 1999).*

MEZZORAMIO BHB 46f30a RR 47f 30a 3711[4]
8 ch g Cadeaux Genereux 7.9f **(76)** - Hopeful Search (USA) (Vaguely Noble) 10.1f **(72)**
Form - 00350284
Record 2000 - 1st:0 2nd:1 3rd:1 Ran:8
Pre2000 - 1st:6 2nd:5 3rd:7 Ran:53
Win Prizemoney £20,020 *Total Prizemoney* £30,098
Wins * 1999 Jly Yarmou (FRM) H 7f 43 46?
* 1999 Jly Warwic (G-F) SH 7.7f 41 41
* 1997 Jly Yarmou (G-F) H 7f 47 51 <
* 1996 Aug Newmar (G-F) H 8f 46 49
* 1996 Jly Leices (G-F) H 7f 40 45
* 1996 *Feb Southw (STD) H 8f 39 44*
2000 Turf 0-8: (7f 5, 8f 2, 10f) (gd, g-f 3, frm 3, hrd)
Moderate gelding, effective 7 to 8f, best at 7f, acts on g-f to hrd, best on frm, mostly wears blinkers (very effectively), likes Yarmouth. Turf high 47 - 4th of 10 getting 3lb from Daryabad (16 Aug Yarmouth 7f g-f RF 3711).
**K A Morgan [6-61] T R Pryke (from Sir Mark Prescott [0-2] May 1995).*

MI AMIGO BHB 69f RR 70f 4618[3]
3 b c Primo Dominie 7.2f **(67)** - Third Movement (Music Boy) 6.8f **(57)**
Form - 243103
Record 2000 - 1st:1 2nd:1 3rd:2 Ran:6
Pre2000 - 1st:0 2nd:0 3rd:0 Ran:1
Win Prizemoney £3,445 *Total Prizemoney* £5,450
Wins * **2000** Jly Hamilt (G-F) 6f 64 <
2000 Turf 1-6: (6f 1-5, 8f) (g-s, gd 2, g-f 1-1, frm 2)
Above-average colt, effective 6f, acts on g-f. Turf high 74. Had to be shaken up to win a Hamilton maiden at 2/5.
**L M Cumani [1-7] M J Dawson.*

MICE DESIGN (IRE) BHB 43f37a RR 54df 37a 1979[3]
3 b g Presidium 7.5f **(56)** - Diplomatist **(55f)** (Dominion) 8.5f **(63)**
Form - 0543
Record 2000 - 1st:0 2nd:0 3rd:1 Ran:4
Win Prizemoney £0 *Total Prizemoney* £418
2000 Turf 0-4: (12f 3, 16f) (gd, g-f 2, frm)
Rangy, fair gelding. Turf high 54.
**N P Littmoden [0-4] Mice Group Plc.*

MICE IDEAS (IRE) BHB 41f49a RR 45f 49a 2617[9]
4 ch g Fayruz 6.6f **(63)** - Tender Encounter (Prince Tenderfoot (USA)) 9f **(61)**
Form - 16751236160
Record 2000 - 1st:3 2nd:1 3rd:1 Ran:11
Pre2000 - 1st:0 2nd:1 3rd:0 Ran:12
Win Prizemoney £8,296 *Total Prizemoney* £10,575
Wins * **2000** Jun Beverl (G-F) H 9.9f 43 45
* **2000** *Mar Southw (STD) S 11f 45*
* **2000** *Jan Southw (STD) 11f 49* <
2000 Turf 1-5: (10f 1-2, 11f 2, 12f) (g-s, gd, g-f 2, hrd 1-1) 2000 AW 2-6: (11f 2-3, 12f 2, 16f) (Fibr 2-6)
Leggy, moderate gelding, favours tight tracks. Turf high 45. AW high 49 (1st run).
**N P Littmoden [3-11] Mice Group Plc (from S Mellor [0-12] Spt 1999).*

MICHELE MARIESCHI BHB 82f RR 79f 5125[3]
3 b g Alzao (USA) 9.8f **(73)** - Escape Path (Wolver Hollow) 8f **(56)**
Form - 50003
Record 2000 - 1st:0 2nd:0 3rd:1 Ran:5
Pre2000 - 1st:1 2nd:2 3rd:0 Ran:4
Win Prizemoney £4,425 *Total Prizemoney* £12,134
Wins * 1999 Jun Newmar (G-F) 7f 85+ <
2000 Turf 0-5: (8f 2, 10f, 12f 2) (g-s 2, gd, g-f, frm)
Rangy, above-average gelding, effective 7 to 8f, best at 8f, acts on g-s to frm, has worn blinkers. Turf high 79.
**P F I Cole [1-9] Richard Green (Fine Paintings).*

MICKLEY (IRE) BHB 80f RR 82f 4576[8]
3 b g Ezzoud (IRE) - Dawsha (IRE) **(69f)** (Slip Anchor) 9.8f **(73)**
Form - 25453631108
Record 2000 - 1st:2 2nd:1 3rd:2 Ran:11
Pre2000 - 1st:2 2nd:0 3rd:0 Ran:8
Win Prizemoney £17,469 *Total Prizemoney* £24,538
Wins * **2000** Aug Ripon (G-F) H 12.3f 76 82 <
* **2000** Jly Thirsk (FRM) H 12f 70 77
* 1999 Jly Cheste (G-F) H 7f 82 <
* 1999 Jun Mussel (SFT) 7.1f 76
2000 Turf 2-11: (10f, 11f, 12f 2-8, 14f) (sft, g-s, g-f 5, frm 1-3, hrd 1-1)
Scopey, decent gelding, effective 7 to 12f, best at 12f, acts on gd to hrd, best on frm, has worn blinkers (effectively), likes left handed tracks, likes tight tracks, excels at Chester. Turf high 82 - 1st of 5 getting 9lb from Original Spin (19 Aug Ripon RF 3799) - also 1st of 6 giving 8lb to Twist (28 Jly Thirsk RF 3196).
**J D Bethell [4-19] WWW Clarendon Racing Co UK.*

MICKLOW MAGIC BHB 67f RR 76f 5053[5]
2 b f Farfelu - Scotto's Regret (Celtic Cone) 9.8f **(43)**
Form - 225
Record 2000 - 1st:0 2nd:2 3rd:0 Ran:3
Win Prizemoney £0 *Total Prizemoney* £1,924
2000 Turf 0-3: (5f, 6f, 7f) (sft, gd, frm)
Currently above-average filly. Turf high 76 (began Jly) - 2nd of 14 getting 5lb from Ynysmon (24 Spt Musselburgh 5f gd RF 4622).
**C Grant [0-3] F Taylor.*

MICK MY MONGRELLO (IRE) RR 80f 4525a[R]
3 b g Blues Traveller (IRE) - Comfrey Glen (Glenstal (USA)) 10.1f **(64)**
Form - 14UR
2000 Turf 1-4: (8f 1-1, 10f, 11f, 12f) (gd 1-2, g-f)
Decent gelding, has worn blinkers. Turf high 91 (began Jun) - 4th of 5 giving 5lb to Fantasia Girl (29 Jly Curragh 10f g-f RF 3308a). He is temperamental and one to avoid.
**Edward Butler in IRE [1-4] Mrs S C Butler.*

MICKY DEE BHB 30a RR 22f 30a 424[6]
4 ch g Lion Cavern (USA) 7.5f **(74)** - Bellagio (Busted) 10.2f **(61)**
Form - 00077606
Record 2000 - 1st:0 2nd:0 3rd:0 Ran:6
Pre2000 - 1st:0 2nd:0 3rd:0 Ran:3
2000 AW 0-6: (5f 2, 6f 3, 8f) (Equi 5, Fibr)
Scopey, very moderate gelding. AW high 35.
**P W Hiatt [0-8] P W Hiatt (from A P Jarvis [0-1] Spt 1998).*

MIDDAY COWBOY (USA) BHB 10f RR 34tf 1710[6]
7 b g Houston (USA) 7.7f **(65)** - Perfect Isn't Easy (USA) (Saratoga Six (USA)) 7f **(73)**
Form - 006
Record 2000 - 1st:0 2nd:0 3rd:0 Ran:3
Pre2000 - 1st:0 2nd:1 3rd:1 Ran:23
Win Prizemoney £0 *Total Prizemoney* £1,849
2000 Turf 0-2: (12f, 16f) (gd, g-f) 2000 AW 0-1: (14f) (Fibr)
Very moderate gelding, has worn blinkers.
**Miss Lucinda Russell [0-19] Stuart Watson (from G Woodward [0-3] Jan 1998).*

MIDDLEHAMPARKFLYER RR 37f 3384[11]
2 b f Missed Flight - Ma Rivale (Last Tycoon) 8.5f **(62)**
Form - 00

Record 2000 - 1st:0 2nd:0 3rd:0 Ran:2
2000 Turf 0-2: (5f, 7f) (gd, frm)
Currently very moderate filly. Turf high 37 (began Aug).
**P C Haslam [0-2] D Frame & Middleham Park Racing.*

MIDDLETHORPE BHB 65f60a RR 70f 60a 5000[6]

3 b g Noble Patriarch 12.2f **(43)** - Prime Property (IRE) **(24f 28a)** (Tirol)
Form - 05173713136
Record 2000 - 1st:3 2nd:0 3rd:3 Ran:11
Pre2000 - 1st:0 2nd:0 3rd:2 Ran:8
Win Prizemoney £14,508 *Total Prizemoney* £18,504
Wins * 2000 Spt Chepst (G-S) H 10.2f 55 61
*** 2000** Aug York (GD) H 10.4f 55 66 <
*** 2000** Jun Beverl (G-S) H 12f 51 56
2000 Turf 3-10: (8f, 10f 2-4, 12f 1-5) (g-s 3, gd 3-5, g-f, hrd) 2000 AW 0-1: (12f) (Fibr)
Unfurnished, above-average gelding, effective 7 to 12f, acts on g-s to g-f, has worn blinkers (extremely effectively), likes right handed tracks. Turf high 70 - 3rd of 19 giving 2lb to Evening Scent (5 Oct York 12f g-s RF 4819) - also 1st of 20 getting 1lb from Kestral (30 Aug York RF 4110). **M W Easterby [3-19] J H Quickfall & A G Black.*

MIDEFIX (ITY) RR 100f 5216a[3]

4 br f Night Shift (USA) 8.1f **(73)** - Malafirst (Malacate (USA)) 8.8f **(63)**
Form - 3
2000 Turf 0-1: (8f) (hvy)
Currently very useful filly. **in ITY [0-1].*

MIDHISH TWO (IRE) BHB 50f RR 67f 4922[6]

4 b g Midhish - Tudor Loom (Sallust) 8.4f **(63)**
Form - 00808800606
Record 2000 - 1st:0 2nd:0 3rd:0 Ran:11
Pre2000 - 1st:2 2nd:0 3rd:1 Ran:12
Win Prizemoney £39,830 *Total Prizemoney* £41,828
Wins * 1999 May Lingfi (G-F) H 6f 81 84 <
1998 Jun Newcas (SFT) 6f 71+
2000 Turf 0-10: (5f, 6f 5, 7f 3, 9f) (sft, g-s, gd 3, g-f 3, frm 2) 2000 AW 0-1: (7f) (Equi)
Workmanlike, average gelding, effective 5 to 6f, acts on g-s to g-f, has worn blinkers. Turf high 67.
**P Mitchell [1-19] Morton,Mrs Cowley,Murray (from Sir Michael Stoute [1-4] Spt 1998).*

MIDNIGHT ALLURE BHB 85f RR 94?f 4598[13]

3 b f Aragon 7.7f **(58)** - Executive Lady (Night Shift (USA)) 7.2f **(69)**
Form - 211623450
Record 2000 - 1st:2 2nd:2 3rd:1 Ran:9
Pre2000 - 1st:0 2nd:0 3rd:0 Ran:3
Win Prizemoney £7,036 *Total Prizemoney* £9,961
Wins * 2000 Jun Nottin (G-F) H 8.2f 67 78 <
*** 2000** May Yarmou (GD) H 8f 59 65+
2000 Turf 2-9: (7f, 8f 2-8) (sft, gd 2-4, g-f 2, frm 2)
Workmanlike, useful filly, effective 7f, acts on frm. Turf high 94 - 5th of 11 to Kalindi (7 Spt Doncaster 7f frm RF 4282). She improved throughout the season and ran a cracker when fifth in a Listed heat at Doncaster in September. Raced almost exclusively around a mile, she is genuine. **C F Wall [2-12] Mervyn Ayers.*

MIDNIGHT ARROW BHB 76f RR 79f 4642[15]

2 b f Robellino (USA) 9.5f **(68)** - Princess Oberon (IRE) **(85f)** (Fairy King (USA)) 7.7f **(59)**
Form - 1508400
Record 2000 - 1st:1 2nd:0 3rd:0 Ran:7
Win Prizemoney £5,525 *Total Prizemoney* £6,011
Wins * 2000 May Newmar (GD) 5f 77+ <
2000 Turf 1-7: (5f 1-3, 6f 3, 7f) (g-s, gd 1-2, g-f 3, frm)
Above-average filly, effective 5f, acts on gd. Turf high 79 - also 1st of 6 getting 5lb from Firework (6 May Newmarket RF 1058). Won at Newmarket first time, but has struggled in pattern-class events since. She needs to drop a level or two.
**I A Balding [1-7] R P B Michaelson & Wafic Said.*

MIDNIGHT CREEK BHB 73f RR 61f 5075[3]

2 b c Tragic Role (USA) 9.4f **(63)** - Greek Night Out (IRE) **(48f 44a)** (Ela-Mana-Mou) 10.1f **(70)**
Form - 523
Record 2000 - 1st:0 2nd:1 3rd:1 Ran:3
Win Prizemoney £0 *Total Prizemoney* £949
2000 Turf 0-3: (8f 3) (g-s, gd 2)
Currently average colt. Turf high 61 (began Spt).
**Mrs A J Perrett [0-3] Fred Cotton.*

MIDNIGHT ESCAPE BHB 79f RR 82f 4691[15]

7 b g Aragon 7.7f **(58)** - Executive Lady (Night Shift (USA)) 7.2f **(69)**
Form - 704561700
Record 2000 - 1st:1 2nd:0 3rd:0 Ran:9
Pre2000 - 1st:6 2nd:1 3rd:3 Ran:32
Win Prizemoney £68,756 *Total Prizemoney* £82,417
Wins * 2000 Jly Kempto (G-F) 6f 82
* 1998 May Kempto (GD) L 5f 110 <
* 1997 Spt Leopar (GD) G3 5f 99+
* 1996 Oct Newmar (GD) H 5f 91 89
* 1996 Jun Ascot (G-F) H 5f 89 91
* 1996 May Windso (GD) H 5f 82 87
2000 Turf 1-9: (5f 4, 6f 1-5) (g-s 2, gd 2, g-f 3, frm 1-2)
Decent gelding, effective 5f, acts on gd. Turf high 82. He still has a race or two in him, probably over six furlongs, but competitive handicaps might be beyond him nowadays.
**C F Wall [7-41] Mervyn Ayers.*

MIDNIGHT MAX BHB 34f35a RR 39f 35a 2643[13]

3 b g Sure Blade (USA) 10.6f **(66)** - Carpadia (Icecapade (USA)) 11f **(62)**
Form - 800
Record 2000 - 1st:0 2nd:0 3rd:0 Ran:3
Pre2000 - 1st:0 2nd:0 3rd:0 Ran:3
2000 Turf 0-2: (8f 2) (g-f, frm) 2000 AW 0-1: (10f) (Equi)
Light-framed, very moderate gelding. Turf high 32.
**C A Dwyer [0-6] Mrs Deborah Crowley.*

MIDNIGHT VENTURE BHB 77f RR 79f 4305[10]

2 b c Night Shift (USA) 8.1f **(73)** - Front Line Romance (Caerleon (USA)) 8.6f **(71)**
Form - 0302210
Record 2000 - 1st:1 2nd:2 3rd:1 Ran:7
Win Prizemoney £4,290 *Total Prizemoney* £6,546
Wins * 2000 Aug Goodwo (GD) 6f 79 <
2000 Turf 1-7: (5f 4, 6f 1-3) (sft, gd 1 3, g-f, frm 2)
Above-average colt, effective 5 to 6f, best at 6f, acts on sft to frm. Turf high 79 - 1st of 9 giving 2lb to Aunt Ruby (26 Aug Goodwood RF 3987). **Mrs L Stubbs [1-7] The Midnight Venture Partnership.*

MIDNIGHT WATCH (USA) BHB 35f40a RR 30f 40a 2420[5]

6 b g Capote (USA) 9.1f **(84)** - Midnight Air (USA) (Green Dancer (USA)) 10.3f **(74)**
Form - 07813220225
Record 2000 - 1st:1 2nd:4 3rd:1 Ran:11
Pre2000 - 1st:0 2nd:1 3rd:1 Ran:8
Win Prizemoney £1,551 *Total Prizemoney* £6,621
Wins * 2000 *Feb Wolver (STD) H 8.5f 30 36* <
2000 Turf 0-1: (9f) (gd) 2000 AW 1-10: (7f, 8f 1-5, 9f, 10f, 12f, 16f) (Equi 3, Fibr 1-7)
Moderate gelding, effective 7 to 9f, - acts on Fibr, prefers left handed tracks. AW high 45 - 2nd of 11 giving 7lb to Wellcome Inn (28 Mar Wolverhampton 9f Fibr RF 0531) - also 1st of 11 getting 8lb from Mustang (1 Feb Wolverhampton RF 0194).
**A G Newcombe [1-8] M B Clemence (from P Winkworth [0-14] Jan 2000).*

MIDSHIPMAN BHB 82f RR 75f 4441[1]

2 b c Executive Man 8.9f **(52)** - Midler (Comedy Star (USA)) 7.5f **(50)**
Form - 051
Record 2000 - 1st:1 2nd:0 3rd:0 Ran:3
Win Prizemoney £3,217 *Total Prizemoney* £3,217
Wins * 2000 Spt Nottin (G-S) 6.1f 75 <
2000 Turf 1-3: (6f 1-3) (gd 1-1, g-f, frm)
Currently above-average colt. Turf high 75 (began Aug) - 1st of 11 from Arjay (15 Spt Nottingham RF 4441).
**Mrs D Haine [1-3] Mrs V Bayley.*

MIDYAN BLUE (IRE) BHB 42f65a RR 57f 65a 2096[P]

10 ch g Midyan (USA) 9.9f **(64)** - Jarretiere (Star Appeal) 9.6f **(65)**
Form - 143P
Record 2000 - 1st:1 2nd:0 3rd:1 Ran:4

Pre2000 - 1st:4 2nd:8 3rd:6 Ran:64
Win Prizemoney £25,291 *Total Prizemoney* £74,974
Wins *** 2000** May Mussel (FRM) C 16f 46
2000 Turf 1-4: (12f, 14f 2, 16f 1-1) (g-f, frm 1-3)
Fair gelding, had worn blinkers. Turf high 57 - 4th of 5 giving 25lb to Alpha Rose (22 May Musselburgh 14f frm RF 1369). Inconsistent. (DEAD)
**P Monteith [1-4] Mrs June Brown (from I Semple [0-6] Nov 1998).*

MI FAVORITA RR 49f 1884[10]
2 b f Piccolo - Mistook (USA) (Phone Trick (USA))
Form - 0
Record 2000 - 1st:0 2nd:0 3rd:0 Ran:1
2000 Turf 0-1: (6f) (frm)
Currently moderate filly. **C E Brittain [0-1] Wyck Hall Stud.*

MIGHTY MAGIC BHB 36f **RR 45f** 4692[16]
5 b m Magic Ring (IRE) 6.5f **(64)** - Mighty Flash (Rolfe (USA)) 12.1f **(65)**
Form - 0
Record 2000 - 1st:0 2nd:0 3rd:0 Ran:1
Pre2000 - 1st:0 2nd:4 3rd:3 Ran:24
Win Prizemoney £0 *Total Prizemoney* £5,898
2000 Turf 0-1: (14f) (gd)
Moderate filly, effective 6f, acts on frm, has worn blinkers.
**Mrs P N Dutfield [0-14] Mrs V A Tory (from D R C Elsworth [0-11] Oct 1998).*

MIGWAR BHB 25f30a **RR 20f 30a** 4479[10]
7 b g Unfuwain (USA) 11.4f **(74)** - Pick of the Pops (High Top) 10.2f **(67)**
Form - 84010673000
Record 2000 - 1st:0 2nd:0 3rd:1 Ran:7
Pre2000 - 1st:5 2nd:2 3rd:0 Ran:25
Win Prizemoney £26,740 *Total Prizemoney* £29,590
Wins 1999 *Dec Lingfi (STD) H 10f 54 55*
1999 *Jan Southw (STD) S 12f 64+*
1999 *Jan Southw (STD) S 11f 65+*
1996 May Redcar (G-F) H 10f 89 95 <
1996 May Doncas (G-F) H 10.3f 83 85+
2000 Turf 0-1: (10f) (frm) 2000 AW 0-6: (9f, 10f 3, 11f, 12f) (Equi 3, Fibr 3)
Moderate gelding, effective 10 to 12f, best at 11f, - acts on AW, best on Fibr, has worn blinkers, favours left handed tracks, favours tight tracks. AW high 49. Becoming disappointing.
**J M Bradley [0-3] Avon & West Racing Club Ltd (from N P Littmoden [3-21] Feb 2000).*

MIKE'S DOUBLE (IRE) BHB 27f34a **RR 25f 34a** 4650[12]
6 br g Cyrano de Bergerac 7.3f **(58)** - Glass Minnow (IRE) (Alzao (USA)) 7.1f **(68)**
Form - 5U60523758000000
Record 2000 - 1st:0 2nd:1 3rd:1 Ran:12
Pre2000 - 1st:4 2nd:6 3rd:10 Ran:71
Win Prizemoney £14,547 *Total Prizemoney* £23,589
Wins * 1998 *Dec Wolver (STD) H 6f 50 60*
* 1998 May Thirsk (GD) H 6f 57 61
* 1998 *Apr Wolver (STD) H 7f 55 62 <*
1997 *Jly Wolver (STD) 6f 62 <*
2000 Turf 0-4: (6f, 7f 2, 8f) (sft, gd 2, g-f) 2000 AW 0-8: (6f 2, 7f 4, 8f, 11f) (Fibr 8)
Very moderate gelding, effective 6f, - acts on Fibr, mostly wears blinkers. Turf high 25. AW high 48. Becoming disappointing. He runs a lot, but his recent strike-rate hardly sets the pulse racing. Effective on soft ground and on Fibresand.
**Mrs N Macauley [3-60] D S Allan (from Miss Gay Kelleway [1-15] Feb 1998).*

MIKE SIMMONS BHB 28f40a **RR 33f 40a** 4630[4]
4 b g Ballacashtal (CAN) 7.9f **(51)** - Lady Crusty (Golden Dipper) 6.5f **(42)**
Form - 74
Record 2000 - 1st:0 2nd:0 3rd:0 Ran:2
Pre2000 - 1st:0 2nd:0 3rd:0 Ran:5
Win Prizemoney £0 *Total Prizemoney* £317
2000 Turf 0-2: (16f, 17f) (g-s, g-f)
Scopey, very moderate gelding. Turf high 33 (began Spt). He got off the mark in a moderate maiden hurdle at Taunton last term, and ran well in much better company at Chepstow. Good effort at Exeter in November. **L P Grassick [1-11] L P Grassick.*

MIKES WIFE BHB 25f28a **RR 3f 28a** 3193[16]
3 b f Tragic Role (USA) 9.4f **(63)** - Grecian Belle (Ilium)
Form - 000
Record 2000 - 1st:0 2nd:0 3rd:0 Ran:2
Pre2000 - 1st:0 2nd:0 3rd:0 Ran:2
2000 Turf 0-1: (8f) (hrd) 2000 AW 0-1: (7f) (Fibr)
Lengthy, very poor filly.
**A Dickman [0-2] Mike Smallman (from N Bycroft [0-2] Nov 1999).*

MILA RR 10f 1692[6]
3 b f Tirol 8.1f **(64)** - Pushkinia (FR) (Pharly (FR)) 9.8f **(68)**
Form - 6
Record 2000 - 1st:0 2nd:0 3rd:0 Ran:1
2000 Turf 0-1: (12f) (frm)
Scopey, currently poor filly.
**Miss I Foustok [0-1] Buckram Oak Holdings.*

MILAD (IRE) BHB 54f48a **RR 64f 48a** 669[16]
5 b g Green Desert (USA) 7.8f **(78)** - Arctic Winter (CAN) (Briartic (CAN)) 9.5f **(84)**
Form - 0
Record 2000 - 1st:0 2nd:0 3rd:0 Ran:1
Pre2000 - 1st:0 2nd:0 3rd:1 Ran:10
Win Prizemoney £0 *Total Prizemoney* £708
2000 AW 0-1: (8f) (Fibr)
Average gelding.
**I A Wood [0-1] Neardown Stables (from K Bell [0-4] Apr 1999).*

MILADY LILLIE (IRE) BHB 42f46a **RR 53f 46a** 4398[6]
4 b f Distinctly North (USA) 7.4f **(63)** - Millingdale Lillie (Tumble Wind (USA)) 7.5f **(57)**
Form - 6007204766006
Record 2000 - 1st:0 2nd:1 3rd:0 Ran:13
Pre2000 - 1st:1 2nd:0 3rd:2 Ran:14
Win Prizemoney £2,859 *Total Prizemoney* £6,086
Wins * 1999 May Bright (FRM) 7f 59 <
2000 Turf 0-13: (6f 4, 7f 9) (g-s, gd, g-f 4, frm 7)
Neat, fair filly, effective 7f, acts on g-f to hrd, has worn blinkers, likes left handed tracks, likes tight tracks. Turf high 56.
**K T Ivory [1-27] K T Ivory.*

MILDON (IRE) BHB 30f **RR 28f** 4168[9]
4 ch g Dolphin Street (FR) - Lycia (Targowice (USA)) 11.4f **(70)**
Form - 0060
Record 2000 - 1st:0 2nd:0 3rd:0 Ran:4
Pre2000 - 1st:0 2nd:0 3rd:0 Ran:4
2000 Turf 0-4: (8f, 9f, 13f, 16f) (gd, g-f 2, frm)
Unfurnished, little account gelding, has worn blinkers. Turf high 28. **J R Weymes [0-4] Don Raper (from E Weymes [0-4] Jly 1999).*

MILETRIAN (IRE) BHB 112f **RR 113f** 4260[1]
3 b f Marju (IRE) 9.2f **(76)** - Warg (Dancing Brave (USA)) 8.4f **(76)**
Form - 04016441
Record 2000 - 1st:2 2nd:0 3rd:0 Ran:8
Pre2000 - 1st:1 2nd:1 3rd:0 Ran:5
Win Prizemoney £108,111 *Total Prizemoney* £137,727
Wins *** 2000** Spt Doncas (G-F) G3 14.6f 113 <
*** 2000** Jun Ascot (G-F) G2 12f 111
* 1999 Spt Redcar (G-F) 9f 78+
2000 Turf 2-8: (8f, 10f, 12f 1-5, 15f 1-1) (g-s, gd 1-2, g-f 1-3, frm 2)
Workmanlike, Group-class filly, effective 12 to 15f, acts on gd to g-f. Turf high 113 - 1st of 11 getting 7lb from Rada's Daughter (6 Spt Doncaster RF 4260) - also 1st of 9 from Teggiano (22 Jun Ascot RF 2178). She kept smart company last season and, while capable of throwing in the odd poor performance, proved herself a smart filly by winning the Ribblesdale and Park Hill Stakes. Suited by an extended mile and three-quarters in the latter contest, she enjoys firm ground and has a useful turn-of-foot.
**M R Channon [3-13] Miletrian Plc.*

MILL AFRIQUE BHB 32f **RR 42f** 4891[12]
4 b f Mtoto 11.5f **(71)** - Milinetta (Milford) 9f **(61)**
Form - 870
Record 2000 - 1st:0 2nd:0 3rd:0 Ran:3

Pre2000 - 1st:0 2nd:1 3rd:0 Ran:11
Win Prizemoney £0 *Total Prizemoney* £1,037
2000 Turf 0-3: (9f, 10f, 12f) (hvy, g-f, frm)
Workmanlike, moderate filly, effective 10f, acts on g-f to frm, has worn blinkers, likes left handed tracks, likes tight tracks. Turf high 33. **Mrs M Reveley [0-10] R Meredith (from C E Brittain [0-8] Jly 1999).*

MILL EMERALD BHB 46f **RR 55f** 3219[8]
3 b f Old Vic 12.8f **(72)** - Milinetta (Milford) 9f **(61)**
Form - 64608
Record 2000 - 1st:0 2nd:0 3rd:0 Ran:5
Pre2000 - 1st:0 2nd:0 3rd:0 Ran:1
Win Prizemoney £0 *Total Prizemoney* £322
2000 Turf 0-5: (11f, 12f 2, 14f, 16f) (g-s, gd, frm 3)
Light-framed, fair filly, has worn blinkers. Turf high 55.
**R A Fahey [0-6] R Meredith.*

MILLENARY BHB 116f **RR 120+f** 4310[1]
3 b c Rainbow Quest (USA) 11.2f **(81)** - Ballerina (IRE) **(77f)** (Dancing Brave (USA)) 8.4f **(76)**
Form - 11811
Record 2000 - 1st:4 2nd:0 3rd:0 Ran:5
Pre2000 - 1st:0 2nd:0 3rd:1 Ran:2
Win Prizemoney £292,200 *Total Prizemoney* £294,253
Wins * **2000** Spt Doncas (G-F) G1 14.6f 120+ <
* **2000** Aug Goodwo (G-F) G3 12f 116+
* **2000** May Cheste (GD) G3 12.3f 105+
* **2000** Apr Newbur (SFT) 11f 83
2000 Turf 4-5: (11f 1-1, 12f 2-3, 15f 1-1) (g-s 1-1, gd, g-f 2-2, frm 1-1)
Scopey, very high-class colt, effective 12 to 15f, acts on g-f to frm. Turf high 120 - 1st of 11 from Air Marshall (9 Spt Doncaster RF 4310) - also 1st of 11 giving 3lb to Air Marshall (1 Aug Goodwood RF 3278). Made a winning reappearance in a Newbury maiden and although following up in the Chester Vase, may have had the run of the race. Well beaten in the French Derby, he came from way back to pip Air Marshall in the Gordon Stakes at Goodwood and confirmed the form with that horse when battling on to gain a famous victory in the St Leger. That proved to be it for the season and, although he obviously has plenty of stamina in his pedigree, it may be that he will revert to 12 furlongs rather than tackle the Cup races. **J L Dunlop [4-7] Neil Jones.*

MILL END QUEST BHB 54f **RR 55+f** 4497[5]
5 b m King's Signet (USA) 7f **(51)** - Milva (Jellaby) 6.4f **(58)**
Form - 01005
Record 2000 - 1st:1 2nd:0 3rd:0 Ran:5
Pre2000 - 1st:2 2nd:0 3rd:2 Ran:25
Win Prizemoney £14,689 *Total Prizemoney* £16,180
Wins * **2000** Aug Thirsk (GD) H 6f 48 55+
* 1999 Jun Pontef (GD) H 6f 50 56
* 1997 Jly Mussel (GD) 5f 66 <
2000 Turf 1-5: (5f 2, 6f 1-2, 7f) (g-s, gd, g-f, frm 1-2)
Fair filly, effective 5 to 6f, best at 6f, acts on gd to frm, best on frm, has worn blinkers. Turf high 55 - 1st of 21 getting 20lb from William's Well (4 Aug Thirsk RF 3379).
**M W Easterby [3-30] W T Allgood.*

MILLENIUM MOONBEAM (USA) BHB 103f **RR 105f** 2148[17]
3 ch c Phone Trick (USA) 7f **(62)** - Shywing (USA) (Wing Out (USA))
Form - 060
Record 2000 - 1st:0 2nd:0 3rd:0 Ran:3
Pre2000 - 1st:1 2nd:0 3rd:0 Ran:3
Win Prizemoney £3,844 *Total Prizemoney* £11,639
Wins * 1999 Aug Salisb (G-S) 6f 86+ <
2000 Turf 0-3: (7f, 8f, 10f) (g-s, gd 2)
Scopey, Pattern-class colt, effective 6f, acts on g-f. Turf high 105. He was found wanting in pattern events, including the 2000 Guineas, and connections seemed unsure as to his best trip.
**M Pitman [1-6] & Mrs John Harris.*

MILLENIUM PRINCESS (IRE) BHB 95f **RR 86f** 4126[4]
2 b f Eagle Eyed (USA) - Sopran Marida (IRE) (Darshaan) 9.9f **(84)**
Form - 12624
Record 2000 - 1st:1 2nd:2 3rd:0 Ran:5
Win Prizemoney £5,164 *Total Prizemoney* £11,511
Wins * **2000** Jun Newmar (G-F) 6f 86 <
2000 Turf 1-5: (5f, 6f 1-4) (gd, g-f 2, frm 1-2)
Useful filly. Turf high 86 - 2nd of 6 giving 7lb to Hejaziah (24 Jun Ascot 6f gd RF 2241) - also 1st of 10 from Rasha's Realm (11 Jun Newmarket RF 1884). She knew her job before making a winning debut at Newmarket, but was just found out under her penalty in an Ascot novice stakes next time.
**R Hannon [1-5] Major A M Everett.*

MILLENNIUM BUG BHB 33f28a **RR 40f 28a** 4584[12]
4 b f Rock Hopper 10.6f **(54)** - So Precise (FR) (Balidar) 7.9f **(63)**
Form - 0
Record 2000 - 1st:0 2nd:0 3rd:0 Ran:1
Pre2000 - 1st:0 2nd:0 3rd:0 Ran:3
2000 AW 0-1: (10f) (Equi)
Scopey, moderate filly.
**M Madgwick [0-1] Carrington Network Services Ltd (from A Streeter [0-3] Jly 1999).*

MILLENNIUM CADEAUX (IRE) RR 72f 4646[3]
2 ch g Cadeaux Genereux 7.9f **(76)** - Quest of Fire (FR) (Rainbow Quest (USA)) 10.4f **(75)**
Form - 5
Record 2000 - 1st:0 2nd:0 3rd:0 Ran:1
2000 Turf 0-1: (8f) (g-f)
Currently above-average gelding. **E A L Dunlop [0-1] Khalifa Sultan.*

MILLENNIUM DASH BHB 95f **RR 97f** 4963[9]
3 ch f Nashwan (USA) 10.3f **(79)** - Milligram (Mill Reef (USA)) 10.5f **(78)**
Form - 410
Record 2000 - 1st:1 2nd:0 3rd:0 Ran:3
Win Prizemoney £3,955 *Total Prizemoney* £4,276
Wins * **2000** Spt Bath (SFT) 10.2f 91+ <
2000 Turf 1-3: (10f 1-2, 12f) (g-s 1-1, gd, frm)
Lengthy, currently very useful filly. Turf high 97 (began Spt) - also 1st of 13 from Flame of Truth (25 Spt Bath RF 4632). From a superb family, she bolted up in a soft-ground Bath maiden on her second start and looks useful.
**L M Cumani [1-3] Helena Springfield Ltd.*

MILLENNIUM DREAM BHB 40f **RR 30f** 636[15]
3 h c Puissance 7.1f **(60)** - Silent Sun (Blakeney) 10.5f **(64)**
Form - 860
Record 2000 - 1st:0 2nd:0 3rd:0 Ran:3
2000 Turf 0-1: (7f) (gd) 2000 AW 0-2: (7f, 8f) (Equi 2)
Leggy, currently very moderate colt. AW high 23.
**T J Naughton [0-3] The New Millennium Partnership.*

MILLENNIUM LADY (USA) BHB 71f **RR 70f** 4532[3]
2 ch f Woodman (USA) 9.7f **(77)** - Salina Cookie (USA) (Seattle Dancer (USA))
Form - 753
Record 2000 - 1st:0 2nd:0 3rd:1 Ran:3
Win Prizemoney £0 *Total Prizemoney* £565
2000 Turf 0-3: (6f, 7f 2) (gd 2, frm)
Currently above-average filly. Turf high 70 (began Aug).
**B W Hills [0-3] C Wright & The Hon Mrs J M Corbett.*

MILLENNIUM MAGIC BHB 70f70a **RR 77f 70a** 4808[10]
2 b f Magic Ring (IRE) 6.5f **(64)** - Country Spirit (Sayf El Arab (USA)) 7.1f **(54)**
Form - 134280800
Record 2000 - 1st:1 2nd:1 3rd:1 Ran:9
Win Prizemoney £3,428 *Total Prizemoney* £5,450
Wins * **2000** Mar Sandow (G-F) 5f 77 <
2000 Turf 1-9: (5f 1-6, 6f 3) (g-s, gd 3, g-f 1-3, frm, hrd)
Above-average filly, effective 5f, acts on g-f to frm. Turf high 77 - 2nd of 4 giving 7lb to Aziz Presenting (18 Jun Salisbury 5f frm RF 2079) - also 1st of 6 from Celtic Island (28 Mar Sandown RF 0529). A cheap foal, she caused a bit of a surprise when making a winning debut in a Sandown maiden in March. She has run well in defeat since then, though she did not perform so well when tried on soft ground. **J G Portman [1-9] Madhatter Racing.*

MILLENNIUM MINX RR 19f 4227[S]
3 b f Red Rainbow - Lassitter (Damister (USA)) 9f **(73)**
Form - S
Record 2000 - 1st:0 2nd:0 3rd:0 Ran:1
2000 Turf 0-1: (7f) (frm)

Currently poor filly. **A J McNae [0-1] D Tye.*

MILLENNIUM SUMMIT (IRE) BHB 62f **RR 72f** 4696^{11}

3 b c Apple Tree (FR) - Word of Honor (FR) (Highest Honor (FR))
Form - 46470
Record 2000 - 1st:0 2nd:0 3rd:0 Ran:5
Win Prizemoney £0 *Total Prizemoney* £217
2000 Turf 0-5: (9f, 10f 2, 12f, 14f) (gd, g-f, frm 3)
Workmanlike, above-average colt. Turf high 72 - 4th of 15 giving 5lb to Eurolink Artemis (20 Jly Leicester 10f frm RF 2973).
**J R Fanshawe [0-5] Ryoki Tanaka.*

MILLER TIME BHB 36f42a **RR 38f 42a** 1201^{18}

3 b g Timeless Times (USA) 6.1f **(56)** - Mashin Time (Palm Track) 9.8f **(50)**
Form - 500400
Record 2000 - 1st:0 2nd:0 3rd:0 Ran:6
2000 Turf 0-2: (6f, 8f) (gd, frm) 2000 AW 0-4: (6f 2, 7f, 8f) (Fibr 4)
Workmanlike, very moderate gelding, has worn blinkers. Turf high 38. AW high 35. **T D Easterby [0-6] P Baillie.*

MILLIGAN (FR) RR 90+f 4740^{32}

5 b g Exit To Nowhere (USA) 8.7f **(77)** - Madigan Mill (Mill Reef (USA)) 10.5f **(78)**
Form - 1020
Record 2000 - 1st:1 2nd:1 3rd:0 Ran:4
Pre2000 - 1st:0 2nd:1 3rd:0 Ran:5
Win Prizemoney £6,857 *Total Prizemoney* £26,536
Wins 2000 Mar Newcas (G-S) H 10.1f 75 88+ <
2000 Turf 1-4: (9f, 10f 1-3) (g-s 1-1, gd, g-f 2)
Useful gelding, effective 10f, acts on g-s to g-f. Turf high 90 - 2nd of 19 giving 6lb to Elmhurst Boy (2 Spt Kempton 10f g-f RF 4167) - also 1st of 18 giving 5lb to Chief Monarch (28 Mar Newcastle RF 0524). Inconsistent. He was given a shrewd tactical ride when winning at Newcastle in March, but proved inconsistent in the second half of the season and looked unco-operative in the Cambridgeshire. Successful over hurdles since then, he has a turn-of-foot.
**Miss Venetia Williams [1-6] G H Leatham (from D Nicholls [1-4] Mar 2000).*

MILLIKEN PARK (IRE) BHB 63f **RR 71f** 5081^{12}

2 ch f Fumo Di Londra (IRE) - Miss Ironwood (Junius (USA)) 7.7f **(65)**
Form - 6123000
Record 2000 - 1st:1 2nd:1 3rd:1 Ran:7
Win Prizemoney £2,808 *Total Prizemoney* £5,705
Wins * 2000 Jly Hamilt (G-F) 6f 69 <
2000 Turf 1-7: (5f 2, 6f 1-5) (hvy, gd 2, g-f 1-2, frm 2)
Above-average filly, effective 6f, acts on g-f to frm. Turf high 71 - also 1st of 7 from Sharp Secret (20 Jly Hamilton RF 2965).
**Miss L A Perratt [1-7] Dr J Walker.*

MILLIONFORMERTHYR BHB 30f30a **RR 29f 30a** 5155^{12}

4 b f Mon Tresor 7.9f **(60)** - Regal Salute (Dara Monarch) 8.8f **(59)**
Form - 0
Record 2000 - 1st:0 2nd:0 3rd:0 Ran:1
Pre2000 - 1st:0 2nd:1 3rd:2 Ran:15
Win Prizemoney £0 *Total Prizemoney* £1,127
2000 AW 0-1: (7f) (Equi)
Leggy, very moderate filly, has worn blinkers. Inconsistent.
**P M Rich [0-1] Brian Henderson (from B Palling [0-15] Aug 1999).*

MILLIONS BHB 64f **RR 66df** 1792^{11}

3 b g Bering 9.6f **(80)** - Miznah (IRE) (Sadler's Wells (USA)) 10f **(76)**
Form - 5200
Record 2000 - 1st:0 2nd:1 3rd:0 Ran:4
Pre2000 - 1st:0 2nd:0 3rd:0 Ran:3
Win Prizemoney £0 *Total Prizemoney* £925
2000 Turf 0-4: (10f 2, 11f, 12f) (g-s, gd 2, frm)
Well made, average gelding, effective 10 to 12f, acts on gd to frm, has worn blinkers. Turf high 66 - 2nd of 20 getting 2lb from Fanfare (15 May Windsor 12f frm RF 1214).
**Sir Michael Stoute [0-7] Abdullah Ali.*

MILLSEC BHB 43f **RR 56f** 5086^{8}

3 b f Petong 7.6f **(58)** - Harmony Park (Music Boy) 6.8f **(57)**
Form - 008
Record 2000 - 1st:0 2nd:0 3rd:0 Ran:3
Pre2000 - 1st:0 2nd:1 3rd:0 Ran:4
Win Prizemoney £0 *Total Prizemoney* £768
2000 Turf 0-3: (5f, 7f 2) (hvy, g-s, gd)
Workmanlike, fair filly, effective 5f, acts on gd. Turf high 18 (began Spt). **R Bastiman [0-7] Robin Bastiman.*

MILLTIDE BHB 61f **RR 62+f** 2406^{6}

2 b f Pyramus (USA) - Sea Farer Lake (Gairloch) 7f **(63)**
Form - 416
Record 2000 - 1st:1 2nd:0 3rd:0 Ran:3
Win Prizemoney £2,702 *Total Prizemoney* £2,702
Wins 2000 Jun Thirsk (FRM) S 6f 62+ <
2000 Turf 1-3: (6f 1-3) (g-f, frm 1-2)
Currently average filly. Turf high 62 - 1st of 9 from Miss Equinox (20 Jun Thirsk RF 2117).
**J L Eyre [0-1] Billy Parker (from R Guest [1-2] Jun 2000).*

MILLY'S LASS BHB 77f **RR 78f** 5153^{2}

2 b f Mind Games - Millie's Lady (IRE) (Common Grounds)
Form - 3121320372572
Record 2000 - 1st:2 2nd:4 3rd:3 Ran:13
Win Prizemoney £4,795 *Total Prizemoney* £13,052
Wins * 2000 May Nottin (G-S) 5.1f 69 <
*** 2000** Apr Leices (G-S) 5f 69 <
2000 Turf 2-13: (5f 2-11, 6f 2) (g-s 2, gd 2-2, g-f 5, frm 3, hrd)
Above-average filly, effective 5f, acts on g-s to frm, excels at Chepstow. Turf high 78 - 2nd of 5 getting 10lb from Clarion (23 Oct Lingfield 5f g-s RF 5153) - also 1st of 6 giving 4lb to Eastern Promise (2 May Nottingham RF 0968). Paying her way in ordinary company. **M R Channon [2-13] Ken Lock Racing Ltd.*

MILORD FONTENAILLE (FR) RR 106f 3157a^{3}

6 ch g Nashamaa 8.1f **(58)** - Miss Fontenailles (Kautokeino (FR))
Form - 3
2000 Turf 0-1: (10f) (sft)
Currently Pattern-class gelding. (1st run) - 3rd of 11 to Kerrygold (19 Jly Vichy 10f sft RF 3157a).
**R Collet in FR [0-1] J-B Andreani (from J E Hammond in FR [1-1] May 1999).*

MIMANDI (IRE) BHB 32f **RR 33f** 4871^{19}

3 b f Pips Pride 6.7f **(70)** - Glass Minnow (IRE) (Alzao (USA)) 7.1f **(68)**
Form - 06060
Record 2000 - 1st:0 2nd:0 3rd:0 Ran:5
Pre2000 - 1st:0 2nd:0 3rd:0 Ran:2
2000 Turf 0-5: (5f 3, 6f 2) (sft, gd 2, frm 2)
Neat, very moderate filly, has worn blinkers. Turf high 33.
**I Semple [0-7] Raeburn Brick Ltd.*

MINALCO BHB 14f **RR 24f** 3996^{8}

4 ch f Minster Son 10.9f **(56)** - La Millie (Nonoalco (USA)) 8.5f **(66)**
Form - 07008
Record 2000 - 1st:0 2nd:0 3rd:0 Ran:5
Pre2000 - 1st:0 2nd:0 3rd:0 Ran:4
2000 Turf 0-5: (14f 3, 16f 2) (g-s, g-f 3, frm)
Workmanlike, little account filly. Turf high 24.
**R E Barr [0-9] Mrs M J Schoenberg.*

MINARDI (USA) RR 120+f 4699^{1}

2 br c Boundary (USA) - Yarn (USA) (Mr Prospector (USA)) 8.8f **(78)**
Form - 211
2000 Turf 2-3: (6f 2-3) (gd 1-2, g-f 1-1)
Currently very high-class colt. Turf high 118 (began Jly) - 1st of 10 from Endless Summer (28 Spt Newmarket RF 4699) - also 1st of 10 giving 3lb to Superstar Leo (13 Aug Leopardstown RF 3674a). Surprisingly beaten on his debut, he quickened five lengths clear of Superstar Leo in the Heinz 57 Phoenix Stakes and produced a good turn-of-foot to take care of Endless Summer in the Middle Park Stakes. Those Group One successes granted him top spot in the European Classifications, although Nayef is preferred in the ante-post market for the 2000 Guineas. An entry in the Kentucky Derby hints connections believe Minardi may stay beyond a mile, but his pedigree and style of racing suggest otherwise. Whatever his fate later in the season, a high cruising speed and ability to quicken should ensure a bold show at Newmarket on May 5.
**A P O'Brien in IRE [2-3] M Tabor & Mrs John Magnier.*

MINDAHRA RR 4149[13]
2 b f Mind Games - Indiahra **(51f 48a)** (Indian Ridge)
Form - 0
Record 2000 - 1st:0 2nd:0 3rd:0 Ran:1
2000 Turf 0-1: (5f) (gd)
Currently very poor filly. *M Mullineaux [0-1] P J Lawton.

MINDANAO BHB 83f RR 90f 934[2]
4 b f Most Welcome 8.6f **(66)** - Salala (Connaught) 7.7f **(63)**
Form - 42
Record 2000 - 1st:0 2nd:1 3rd:0 Ran:2
Pre2000 - 1st:3 2nd:3 3rd:0 Ran:9
Win Prizemoney £18,963 Total Prizemoney £26,280
Wins * 1999 Oct Ayr (SFT) H 10f 75 90 <
* 1999 Aug Ripon (GD) H 10f 65 69
* 1999 Jun Newcas (GD) H 9f 53 58
2000 Turf 0-2: (10f 2) (g-s, gd)
Neat, useful filly, effective 10f, acts on sft to gd, likes left handed tracks. Turf high 85 - 2nd of 15 to Yarob (1 May Doncaster 10f gd RF 0934). *Miss J A Camacho [3-11] Mrs S Camacho.

MIND OVER MATTER RR 37f 2844[11]
2 b g Muhtarram (USA) - Veuve (Tirol)
Form - 00
Record 2000 - 1st:0 2nd:0 3rd:0 Ran:2
2000 Turf 0-1: (7f) (g-f) 2000 AW 0-1: (7f) (Fibr)
Currently very moderate gelding. *C A Cyzer [0-2] Mrs E A Cyzer.

MIND THE SILVER BHB 56f42a RR 55f 42a 4403[1]
3 gr g Petong 7.6f **(58)** - Marjorie's Memory (IRE) **(61df)** (Fairy King (USA)) 7.7f **(59)**
Form - 006004001
Record 2000 - 1st:1 2nd:0 3rd:0 Ran:9
Pre2000 - 1st:0 2nd:0 3rd:0 Ran:3
Win Prizemoney £2,198 Total Prizemoney £2,476
Wins * 2000 Spt Yarmou (G-F) H 8f 52 55 <
2000 Turf 1-9: (6f 3, 7f 2, 8f 1-4) (gd, g-f 1-5, frm 3)
Strong, fair gelding, has worn blinkers. Turf high 58.
*V Soane [1-12] The Soane Rangers.

MINE (IRE) RR 73f 4379[9]
2 b c Primo Dominie 7.2f **(67)** - Ellebanna (Tina's Pet) 6.8f **(59)**
Form - 30
Record 2000 - 1st:0 2nd:0 3rd:1 Ran:2
Win Prizemoney £0 Total Prizemoney £740
2000 Turf 0-2: (6f, 7f) (g-f, frm)
Currently above-average colt. Turf high 73 (1st run) (began Aug) - 3rd of 8 giving 5lb to Hamadeenah (26 Aug Newmarket 6f g-f RF 3990). *L M Cumani [0-2] M J Dawson.

MINETTA RR 75f 4375[13]
5 ch m Mujtahid (USA) 7.4f **(69)** - Minwah (USA) (Diesis) 9.3f **(69)**
Form - 6508170
Record 2000 - 1st:1 2nd:0 3rd:0 Ran:7
Pre2000 - 1st:6 2nd:3 3rd:2 Ran:28
Win Prizemoney £35,919 Total Prizemoney £42,165
Wins * 2000 Aug Bath (G-F) H 8f 69 75
* 1999 Spt Thirsk (FRM) H 8f 73 76+ <
* 1999 Aug Windso (GD) H 8.3f 71 73
* 1999 Jly Windso (G-F) H 8.3f 69 69
* 1998 Jly Bath (GD) 8f 75
* 1998 Jly Newmar (FRM) H 8f 68 74
* 1997 May Carlis (FRM) 5.9f 66
2000 Turf 1-7: (8f 1-7) (gd, g-f, frm 1-5)
Above-average filly, effective 8f, acts on g-f to hrd, best on frm, has worn blinkers, prefers tight tracks, and excels at Bath. Turf high 75 - 1st of 8 giving 8lb to Tapage (8 Aug Bath RF 3444). Consistent. Suited by a mile and fast ground, she should find a race or two. *M L W Bell [7-35] Mrs G Rowland-Clark.

MINETTE BHB 62f RR 56f 4821[15]
2 br f Bishop of Cashel - Creeking **(53f 60a)** (Persian Bold) 9.3f **(66)**
Form - 660
Record 2000 - 1st:0 2nd:0 3rd:0 Ran:3
2000 Turf 0-3: (6f 3) (gd, g-f, frm)
Currently fair filly. Turf high 56 (began Spt).

*E A L Dunlop [0-3] Lucayan Stud.

MINGLING BHB 75f RR 81f 2620[5]
3 b c Wolfhound (USA) 7.3f **(71)** - On the Tide **(67f)** (Slip Anchor) 9.8f **(73)**
Form - 352365
Record 2000 - 1st:0 2nd:1 3rd:2 Ran:6
Pre2000 - 1st:0 2nd:0 3rd:0 Ran:3
Win Prizemoney £0 Total Prizemoney £3,229
2000 Turf 0-6: (8f, 10f 4, 12f) (g-s, g-f 3, frm 2)
Scopey, decent colt, effective 10 to 12f, best at 10f, acts on g-s to frm, has worn blinkers, prefers tight tracks. Turf high 81 (1st run) - 3rd of 8 giving 5lb to Inforapenny (11 Apr Pontefract 10f g-s RF 0660). Consistent. Often placed but is finding it hard to win and looks devoid of pace. A step up in trip may be what is required.
*M H Tompkins [0-9] Mrs Beryl Lockey.

MINIHAHA RR 57f 4969[15]
2 ch f First Trump - Indian Lament **(34df)** (Indian Ridge)
Form - 0
Record 2000 - 1st:0 2nd:0 3rd:0 Ran:1
2000 Turf 0-1: (8f) (gd)
Currently fair filly. *Mrs A J Perrett [0-1] J H Richmond-Watson.

MINI LODGE (IRE) BHB 73f RR 76f 4576[2]
4 ch g Grand Lodge (USA) - Mirea (USA) (The Minstrel (CAN)) 10f **(72)**
Form - 812232
Record 2000 - 1st:1 2nd:3 3rd:1 Ran:6
Pre2000 - 1st:1 2nd:2 3rd:0 Ran:9
Win Prizemoney £8,083 Total Prizemoney £21,238
Wins * 2000 Jly Ripon (G-F) H 10f 60 64
* 1998 Jly Newcas (G-F) 7f 78+ <
2000 Turf 1-6: (8f, 10f 1-3, 11f, 12f) (sft, g-f 1-2, frm 3)
Tall, above-average gelding, effective 10 to 12f, best at 10f, acts on sft to frm, best on frm, has worn blinkers, likes left handed tracks, prefers tight tracks. Turf high 76 (began Jly) - 2nd of 8 giving 3lb to Apple Town (22 Spt Haydock 12f sft RF 4576). Inconsistent. Showed his first form for some time when landing a gamble at Ripon in July and has continued to run well since.
*J G FitzGerald [2-15] Marquesa de Moratalla.

MINIME (IRE) RR 21f 2176[4]
2 b c Mujtahid (USA) 7.4f **(69)** - Mrs Ting (USA) (Lyphard (USA)) 9.9f **(72)**
Form - 84
Record 2000 - 1st:0 2nd:0 3rd:0 Ran:2
2000 Turf 0-1: (5f) (gd) 2000 AW 0-1: (6f) (Fibr)
Currently little account colt.
*N P Littmoden [0-2] Joy and Valentine Feerick.

MINIMUS TIME BHB 30f42a RR 31df 42a 4372[14]
3 ch f Timeless Times (USA) 6.1f **(56)** - Glenfield Greta **(46f 43a)** (Gabitat) 5f **(44)**
Form - 8146406700
Record 2000 - 1st:1 2nd:0 3rd:0 Ran:10
Pre2000 - 1st:0 2nd:0 3rd:1 Ran:4
Win Prizemoney £1,800 Total Prizemoney £2,052
Wins * 2000 Jan Lingfi (STD) S 5f 54 <
2000 Turf 0-5: (5f 5) (g-s, gd, frm 3) 2000 AW 1-5: (5f 1-4, 6f) (Equi 1-5)
Workmanlike, moderate filly, effective 5f, - acts on Equi, often wears blinkers (effectively), likes left handed tracks, likes tight tracks. Turf high 40. AW high 54 - 1st of 6 getting 6lb from Diamond Promise (19 Jan Lingfield RF 0118). Becoming disappointing. *T M Jones [1-14] Mervyn Evans.

MINJARA BHB 37f RR 48f 3598[5]
5 b g Beveled (USA) 6.9f **(64)** - Honey Mill (Milford) 9f **(61)**
Form - 550845
Record 2000 - 1st:0 2nd:0 3rd:0 Ran:6
Pre2000 - 1st:0 2nd:0 3rd:0 Ran:12
Win Prizemoney £0 Total Prizemoney £564
2000 Turf 0-6: (9f, 10f 5) (g-f 3, frm 2, hrd)
Moderate gelding, effective 10f, acted on g-f, had worn blinkers, liked left handed tracks, liked tight tracks. Turf high 48 (1st run) - 5th of 19 giving 6lb to Sheer Face (17 May Brighton 10f g-f RF 1255). (DEAD)
*Derrick Morris [0-11] M L Shone (from J G Smyth-Osbourne [0-4] Apr

1999).

MINKASH (IRE) BHB 85f **RR 94f** 4311[5]
3 b g Caerleon (USA) 10.9f **(79)** - Ingabelle (Taufan (USA)) 7f **(57)**
Form - 7644385
Record 2000 - 1st:0 2nd:0 3rd:1 Ran:7
Pre2000 - 1st:1 2nd:2 3rd:0 Ran:5
Win Prizemoney £5,952 *Total Prizemoney* £15,616
Wins * 1999 Jly York (G-F) 7f 81 <
2000 Turf 0-7: (8f 2, 9f, 10f 3, 12f) (gd, g-f 2, frm 4)
Scopey, useful gelding, effective 8 to 10f, best at 10f, acts on g-f to frm, best on g-f, has worn blinkers, prefers left handed tracks. Turf high 96 - 4th of 11 giving 3lb to Happy Diamond (13 Jly Doncaster 10f frm RF 2755). **B Hanbury [1-12] Hamdan Al Maktoum.*

MIN MIRRI BHB 82f **RR 78f** 4428[9]
2 b f Selkirk (USA) 7.9f **(76)** - Sulitelma (USA) (The Minstrel (CAN)) 10f **(72)**
Form - 45310
Record 2000 - 1st:1 2nd:0 3rd:1 Ran:5
Win Prizemoney £3,939 *Total Prizemoney* £4,864
Wins * **2000** Spt Thirsk (GD) 8f 78 <
2000 Turf 1-5: (6f 2, 7f, 8f 1-2) (gd 1-3, g-f 2)
Above-average filly. Turf high 78 - 1st of 7 getting 5lb from Wainak (2 Spt Thirsk RF 4172). **M R Channon [1-5] Dominion Partners.*

MINNESOTA BHB 43f43a **RR 43df 43a** 3783[4]
4 b g Danehill (USA) 9.1f **(79)** -Santi Sana (Formidable (USA)) 9.2f **(63)**
Form - 4
Record 2000 - 1st:0 2nd:0 3rd:0 Ran:1
Pre2000 - 1st:2 2nd:1 3rd:1 Ran:17
Win Prizemoney £7,605 *Total Prizemoney* £9,318
Wins 1998 Jly Newmar (G-F) H 7f 83 <
1998 *Jun Southw (STD) 7f 78*
2000 Turf 0-1: (10f) (frm)
Light-framed, fair gelding, had worn blinkers. (DEAD)
**M C Pipe [1-7] G-Force Partnership (from N A Callaghan [2-17] Oct 1999).*

MINNIE'S MYSTERY (FR) BHB 42f **RR 25f** 5319[16]
2 gr f Highest Honor (FR) 10.9f **(72)** - Madary (CAN) **(89f)** (Green Desert (USA)) 8.6f **(78)**
Form - 000
Record 2000 - 1st:0 2nd:0 3rd:0 Ran:3
2000 Turf 0-3: (5f, 6f 2) (sft, gd, frm)
Currently little account filly. Turf high 25 (began Spt).
**John Berry [0-3] R A Racing.*

MINNISAM BHB 39f **RR 30f** 2381a[5]
7 ch g Niniski (USA) 13.2f **(67)** - Wise Speculation (USA) (Mr Prospector (USA)) 8.8f **(78)**
Form - 5
Record 2000 - 1st:0 2nd:0 3rd:0 Ran:1
Pre2000 - 1st:1 2nd:1 3rd:2 Ran:15
Win Prizemoney £2,381 *Total Prizemoney* £4,492
Wins 1996 Jly Folkes (FRM) H 12f 65 71 <
2000 Turf 0-1: (14f) (g-f)
Very moderate gelding, has broken blood-vessels, has worn blinkers. Becoming disappointing.
**G A Ham [3-23] (from J L Dunlop [1-10] Aug 1996).*

MINSTREL GEM BHB 30f41a **RR 25f 41a** 4489[16]
3 b g Mon Tresor 7.9f **(60)** - My Serenade (USA) (Sensitive Prince (USA)) 9.1f **(60)**
Form - 00000
Record 2000 - 1st:0 2nd:0 3rd:0 Ran:5
2000 Turf 0-4: (6f, 8f, 10f 2) (gd, g-f 2, frm) 2000 AW 0-1: (7f) (Fibr)
Light-framed, little account gelding. Turf high 25.
**B D Leavy [0-5] D B Holmes.*

MINT LEAF (IRE) BHB 30f25a **RR 44f 25a** 4925[12]
3 b f Sri Pekan (USA) - Suaad (IRE) **(69f)** (Fools Holme (USA))
Form - 00080000
Record 2000 - 1st:0 2nd:0 3rd:0 Ran:8
Pre2000 - 1st:0 2nd:2 3rd:0 Ran:7
Win Prizemoney £0 *Total Prizemoney* £2,790
2000 Turf 0-7: (5f 2, 6f, 7f 2, 8f, 10f) (g-s, gd, g-f 2, frm 3) 2000 AW 0-1: (7f) (Equi)
Moderate filly, effective 5f, acts on g-s to g-f. Turf high 44. Becoming disappointing.
**J R Poulton [0-6] A D Shaw (from Mrs L Richards [0-2] May 2000).*

MINT ROYALE (IRE) RR 56f 3582[8]
2 ch f Cadeaux Genereux 7.9f **(76)** - Clarentia (Ballad Rock) 7.8f **(63)**
Form - 8
Record 2000 - 1st:0 2nd:0 3rd:0 Ran:1
2000 Turf 0-1: (6f) (gd)
Currently fair filly. **T D Easterby [0-1] R J Cornelius.*

MINTY BHB 35f46a **RR 15f 46a** 4426[11]
4 b g Be My Chief (USA) 10.2f **(62)** - Mindomica (Dominion) 8.5f **(63)**
Form - 00
Record 2000 - 1st:0 2nd:0 3rd:0 Ran:2
Pre2000 - 1st:0 2nd:1 3rd:0 Ran:10
Win Prizemoney £0 *Total Prizemoney* £739
2000 Turf 0-2: (8f, 9f) (gd 2)
Workmanlike, very moderate gelding, has worn blinkers. (began Spt). Becoming disappointing.
**A Dickman [0-3] Mike Smallman (from N Bycroft [0-2] Oct 1999).*

MINUSCOLO BHB 63f **RR 67f** 4490[5]
2 b f Piccolo - Wrangbrook (Shirley Heights) 10.3f **(74)**
Form - 08635
Record 2000 - 1st:0 2nd:0 3rd:1 Ran:5
Win Prizemoney £0 *Total Prizemoney* £567
2000 Turf 0-5: (5f 2, 6f 3) (g-f, frm 4)
Average filly. Turf high 67 (began Jly) - 3rd of 16 to Fiamma Royale (13 Spt Sandown 5f frm RF 4367).
**J A Osborne [0-5] Harry Sibley.*

MINUS FOUR (IRE) BHB 37f **RR 31f** 5237[8]
2 b c Standiford (USA) - Minibar (Dominion) 8.5f **(63)**
Form - 078
Record 2000 - 1st:0 2nd:0 3rd:0 Ran:3
2000 Turf 0-2: (5f, 8f) (g-s, gd) 2000 AW 0-1: (7f) (Fibr)
Currently very moderate colt. Turf high 31 (began Spt).
**J G Given [0-3] Ray Monaghan.*

MI ODDS BHB 50f66a **RR 43f 66a** 4730[11]
4 b g Sure Blade (USA) 10.6f **(66)** - Vado Via (Ardross) 10.6f **(68)**
Form - 3758600
Record 2000 - 1st:0 2nd:0 3rd:1 Ran:7
Win Prizemoney £0 *Total Prizemoney* £428
2000 Turf 0-3: (12f, 14f, 16f) (gd 2, g-f) 2000 AW 0-4: (12f 3, 13f) (Equi, Fibr 3)
Leggy, fair gelding. Turf high 43 (began Aug). AW high 50.
**Mrs N Macauley [0-7] G Wiltshire.*

MIRACLE RIDGE (IRE) RR 94f 5350a[1]
5 ch g Indian Ridge 7.6f **(74)** - Highly Delighted (USA) (Verbatim (USA)) 8.5f **(64)**
Form - 8151807541
2000 Turf 3-10: (5f 3-8, 6f 2) (hvy 1-2, sft, g-s 1-2, gd 1-4)
Useful gelding, effective 5f, acts on hvy. Turf high 94 - also 1st of 11 giving 2lb to Jacks Estate (30 Oct Leopardstown RF 5350a). He enjoyed a successful campaign in sprint handicaps. Probably best over five furlongs, he has form on all types of ground.
**J T Gorman in IRE [6-31] Miss Maria McKinney.*

MIRAGGIO BHB 34f29a **RR 50f 29a** 651[15]
4 b g Alhijaz 7.7f **(57)** - Doppio (Dublin Taxi) 6.4f **(55)**
Form - 00
Record 2000 - 1st:0 2nd:0 3rd:0 Ran:2
Pre2000 - 1st:0 2nd:0 3rd:1 Ran:14
Win Prizemoney £0 *Total Prizemoney* £258
2000 Turf 0-1: (16f) (g-s) 2000 AW 0-1: (12f) (Fibr)
Light-framed, fair gelding, effective 10 to 17f, best at 10f, acts on gd to hrd, best on gd, has worn blinkers, prefers tight tracks. Becoming disappointing.
**B J Llewellyn [0-5] Mrs Vicki Guy (from H Morrison [0-13] Oct 1999).*

MIRIO (FR) RR 108f 5209a[3]
3 ch c Priolo (USA) 10.9f **(71)** - Mira Monte (Baillamont (USA)) 7f **(78)**
Form - 3

2000 Turf 0-1: (10f) (hvy)
Currently Pattern-class colt. (1st run) - 3rd of 9 getting 7lb from Inglenook (21 Oct Saint-cloud 10f hvy RF 5209a). *in FR [0-1].

MISALLIANCE BHB 40a **RR 35f** 2416[7]

5 ch m Elmaamul (USA) 8.1f **(70)** - Cabaret Artiste (Shareef Dancer (USA)) 9.9f **(73)**
Form - 07337
Record 2000 - 1st:0 2nd:0 3rd:2 Ran:5
Pre2000 - 1st:1 2nd:0 3rd:1 Ran:16
Win Prizemoney £2,239 *Total Prizemoney* £3,626
Wins 1997 Oct Newcas (G-F) 7f 71+ <
2000 Turf 0-1: (7f) (hrd) 2000 AW 0-4: (11f, 12f, 16f 2) (Fibr 4)
Very moderate filly, effective 8f, acts on gd, has worn blinkers, favours tight tracks. AW high 35.
**M E Sowersby [0-16] The Southwold Set (from C F Wall [1-16] Spt 1999).*

MISBEHAVE BHB 80f **RR 65f** 3232[2]

3 b f Reprimand 8.2f **(63)** - Princess Moodyshoe (Jalmood (USA)) 10.1f **(52)**
Form - 8442
Record 2000 - 1st:0 2nd:1 3rd:0 Ran:4
Pre2000 - 1st:3 2nd:2 3rd:0 Ran:8
Win Prizemoney £13,572 *Total Prizemoney* £18,187
Wins * 1999 Oct Newmar (GD) H 8f 06 92 <
* 1999 Jly Windso (G-F) 6f 85
* 1999 May Warwic (SFT) 5f 75
2000 Turf 0-4: (8f, 10f 2, 11f) (hvy 2, gd, g-f)
Light-framed, average filly, effective 6 to 8f, acts on gd to frm. Turf high 65. Consistent. **M L W Bell [3-12] Frank Farrant.*

MISCHIEF BHB 33f43a **RR 39f 43a** 5182[10]

4 ch g Generous (IRE) 11.5f **(82)** - Knight's Baroness (Rainbow Quest (USA)) 10.4f **(75)**
Form - 0556203080506165000
Record 2000 - 1st:1 2nd:1 3rd:1 Ran:19
Pre2000 - 1st:0 2nd:0 3rd:2 Ran:4
Win Prizemoney £2,758 *Total Prizemoney* £5,897
Wins * 2000 Jly Carlis (FM) H 14.1f 30 33 <
2000 Turf 1-12: (12f 5, 14f 1-4, 15f, 16f, 18f) (hvy, sft 3, g-s, gd 2, g-f 2, frm 2, hrd 1-1) 2000 AW 0-7: (12f 3, 13f, 16f 3) (Equi 3, Fibr 4)
Scopey, very moderate gelding, often wears blinkers, likes right handed tracks. Turf high 51. AW high 41. Bred to win a Classic, he has spent most of his career on the All-Weather, but has also run well on soft ground on Turf. He is still a maiden.
**M Quinn [1-19] Mrs Angela Ellis (from P F I Cole [0-4] Apr 1999).*

MISCONDUCT BHB 50f49a **RR 56f 49a** 4546[11]

6 gr m Risk Me (FR) 8f **(53)** - Grey Cree (Creetown) 6.9f **(50)**
Form - 23240
Record 2000 - 1st:0 2nd:2 3rd:1 Ran:5
Pre2000 - 1st:3 2nd:3 3rd:2 Ran:19
Win Prizemoney £7,640 *Total Prizemoney* £14,710
Wins 1998 *Aug Lingfi* *(STD)* H *10f* 42 48+ <
1998 Jly Bath (GD) H 10.2f 44 47+
1998 Jun Salisb (G-F) H 9.9f 39 42
2000 Turf 0-5: (12f 2, 14f 2, 16f) (g-s, g-f 2, frm 2)
Fair mare, effective 12 to 14f, best at 14f, acts on sft to frm. Turf high 56 (began Jly) - 4th of 12 getting 4lb from Three Lions (3 Spt Kempton 14f g-f RF 4192).
**J G Portman [0-5] The Playmates (from Mrs Merrita Jones [3-9] May 1999).*

MISDEMEANOR BHB 53f44a **RR 55f 44a** 5024[6]

2 b f Presidium 7.5f **(56)** - Fair Madame (Monseigneur (USA)) 7.7f **(63)**
Form - 056
Record 2000 - 1st:0 2nd:0 3rd:0 Ran:3
Win Prizemoney £0 *Total Prizemoney* £149
2000 Turf 0-3: (6f 3) (g-s, g-f, frm)
Currently fair filly. Turf high 55 (began Aug).
**J S Wainwright [0-3] J S Wainwright.*

MISE EN SCENE BHB 73f **RR 81f** 4751[10]

2 b f Lugana Beach 7f **(63)** - Meeson Times **(21f 46a)** (Enchantment) 5.4f **(52)**
Form - 810570
Record 2000 - 1st:1 2nd:0 3rd:0 Ran:6
Win Prizemoney £3,542 *Total Prizemoney* £3,780
Wins * 2000 Jun Sandow (G-F) 5f 81 <
2000 Turf 1-6: (5f 1-5, 6f) (g-s, gd 2, g-f 1-2, hrd)
Decent filly, effective 5f, acts on g-f. Turf high 81 - 1st of 7 from Foodbroker Fancy (17 Jun Sandown RF 2052). Stepped up on her debut to score at Sandown, despite hanging right.
**P Howling [1-6] J J Amass.*

MISHKA BHB 70f **RR 65f** 3987[5]

2 b g Mistertopogigo (IRE) - Walsham Witch (Music Maestro) 7.7f **(66)**
Form - 7835
Record 2000 - 1st:0 2nd:0 3rd:1 Ran:4
Win Prizemoney £0 *Total Prizemoney* £438
2000 Turf 0-4: (5f 2, 6f 2) (gd 2, frm 2)
Average gelding. Turf high 65 (began Jly).
**J C Poulton [0-4] The Three Bears Go Racing.*

MISRAAH (IRE) BHB 108f **RR 108f** 4986[4]

3 ch c Lure (USA) - Dwell (USA) (Habitat) 9.4f **(70)**
Form - 1044
Record 2000 - 1st:1 2nd:0 3rd:0 Ran:4
Pre2000 - 1st:1 2nd:0 3rd:0 Ran:2
Win Prizemoney £10,635 *Total Prizemoney* £17,948
Wins * 2000 Apr Newmar (G-S) 7f 104 <
* 1999 Oct Leices (GD) 7f 92++
2000 Turf 1-4: (7f 1-3, 8f) (gd 1-3, frm)
Scopey, Pattern-class colt, effective 7f, acts on gd to frm. Turf high 108 - also 1st of 13 from Free Rider (18 Apr Newmarket RF 0771). He made a winning reappearance at Newmarket by the minimum margin, but ran poorly in the Guineas. Better efforts over seven furlongs at Newmarket, although looking like a drop to sprint distances would suit.
**Sir Michael Stoute [2-6] Hamdan Al Maktoum.*

MISS ALL ALONE BHB 40f44a **RR 35f 44a** 5168[7]

5 ch m Crofthall 8.6f **(54)** - Uninvited (Be My Guest (USA)) 9.3f **(67)**
Form - 7
Record 2000 - 1st:0 2nd:0 3rd:0 Ran:1
Pre2000 - 1st:0 2nd:6 3rd:4 Ran:19
Win Prizemoney £0 *Total Prizemoney* £8,215
2000 Turf 0-1: (10f) (gd)
Fair filly, effective 7 to 8f, best at 8f, - acts on Fibr, often wears blinkers (extremely effectively), prefers left handed tracks, prefers tight tracks. **J A Glover [0-21] Countrywide Classics Ltd.*

MISS AMBER NECTAR BHB 33f **RR 44f** 4273[7]

3 b f Theatrical Charmer 10.9f **(63)** - Avenmore Star (Comedy Star (USA)) 7.5f **(50)**
Form - 0007
Record 2000 - 1st:0 2nd:0 3rd:0 Ran:4
2000 Turf 0-4: (8f, 10f 2, 12f) (gd 2, g-f 2)
Scopey, moderate filly. Turf high 44. **E A Wheeler [0-4] M V Kirby.*

MISS ARCH (IRE) BHB 16f **RR 31f** 4650[15]

4 ch f Archway (IRE) 8.5f **(60)** - Zanskar (Godswalk (USA)) 7.3f **(58)**
Form - 503700
Record 2000 - 1st:0 2nd:0 3rd:1 Ran:6
Pre2000 - 1st:0 2nd:1 3rd:1 Ran:11
Win Prizemoney £0 *Total Prizemoney* £1,437
2000 Turf 0-5: (12f 4, 16f) (g-s, gd, frm 3) 2000 AW 0-1: (11f) (Fibr)
Leggy, very moderate filly, effective 10 to 12f, best at 10f, acts on g-f to frm, best on frm, has worn blinkers, favours tight tracks. Turf high 31 - 3rd of 10 getting 12lb from Righty Ho (23 Aug Carlisle 12f frm RF 3900). Becoming disappointing.
**M A Buckley [0-15] Will Racing Partnership (from Miss J F Craze [0-1] Oct 1998).*

MISS ASIA QUEST BHB 75f **RR 79f** 3082[8]

3 ch f Rainbow Quest (USA) 11.2f **(81)** - Miss Kuta Beach (Bold Lad (IRE)) 8.4f **(68)**
Form - 8
Record 2000 - 1st:0 2nd:0 3rd:0 Ran:1
Pre2000 - 1st:0 2nd:0 3rd:1 Ran:3
Win Prizemoney £0 *Total Prizemoney* £565
2000 Turf 0-1: (10f) (frm)
Scopey, above-average filly. **G Wragg [0-4] J L C Pearce.*

MISS BANANAS BHB 43f36a **RR 39f 36a** 4487[17]
5 b m Risk Me (FR) 8f **(53)** - Astrid Gilberto (Runnett) 7f **(59)**
Form - 000760015704770001000
Record 2000 - 1st:2 2nd:0 3rd:0 Ran:17
Pre2000 - 1st:2 2nd:4 3rd:3 Ran:38
Win Prizemoney £11,770 *Total Prizemoney* £15,894
Wins * **2000** Aug Leices (G-F) H 5f 39 39
* **2000** Apr Pontef (G-S) S 6f 55
* 1999 Aug Leices (GD) H 5f 29 40
1998 *Feb Lingfi (SLW) H 5f 58 63* <
2000 Turf 2-14: (5f 1-7, 6f 1-7) (hvy, g-s 1-2, gd 2, g-f 3, frm 1-4, hrd 2)
2000 AW 0-3: (5f, 6f 2) (Fibr 3)
Very moderate filly, effective 6f, acts on g-s - acts on AW. Turf high 55 - 1st of 16 from Tancred Arms (11 Apr Pontefract RF 0659). AW high 36.
**C N Kellett [3-43] W Meah (from T T Bill [1-12] Aug 1998).*

MISS BEADY (IRE) BHB 58f **RR 60f** 5169[4]
2 b f Eagle Eyed (USA) - Regal Fanfare (IRE) **(56f 40a)** (Taufan (USA)) 7f **(57)**
Form - 0055084
Record 2000 - 1st:0 2nd:0 3rd:0 Ran:7
Win Prizemoney £0 *Total Prizemoney* £225
2000 Turf 0-7: (5f 4, 6f 3) (g-s, gd 2, g-f, frm 3)
Average filly, effective 5f, acts on frm, has worn blinkers. Turf high 60.
**Don Enrico Incisa [0-2] Don Enrico Incisa (from T D Easterby [0-5] Jly 2000).*

MISS BEETEE (IRE) BHB 62f **RR 68f** 5106[14]
2 b f Brief Truce (USA) 9.1f **(73)** - Majestic Amber (USA) (Majestic Light (USA)) 10.6f **(75)**
Form - 4440
Record 2000 - 1st:0 2nd:0 3rd:0 Ran:4
Win Prizemoney £0 *Total Prizemoney* £868
2000 Turf 0-4: (6f 3, 7f) (g-s, gd, g-f 2)
Average filly. Turf high 68 (began Aug).
**J J Bridger [0-4] The Hop-Pickers Partnership.*

MISS BRIEF (IRE) BHB 67f **RR 77f** 4120[7]
2 b f Brief Truce (USA) 9.1f **(73)** - Preponderance (IRE) (Cyrano de Bergerac) 6f **(68)**
Form - 02442807
Record 2000 - 1st:0 2nd:2 3rd:0 Ran:8
Win Prizemoney £0 *Total Prizemoney* £4,614
2000 Turf 0-8: (5f 7, 6f) (hvy, gd, g-f, frm 4, hrd)
Above-average filly, effective 5f, acts on frm to hrd. Turf high 77 - 2nd of 11 to Dress Code (11 May Chester 5f frm RF 1137). Becoming disappointing.
**P D Evans [0-8] Crewe And Nantwich Racing Club.*

MISS CASH BHB 36f **RR 33f** 4014[4]
3 b f Rock Hopper 10.6f **(54)** - Miss Cashtal (IRE) **(40a)** (Ballacashtal (CAN)) 5.3f **(50)**
Form - 424
Record 2000 - 1st:0 2nd:1 3rd:0 Ran:3
Win Prizemoney £0 *Total Prizemoney* £1,135
2000 Turf 0-3: (10f 2, 11f) (gd, frm 2)
Very moderate filly. Turf high 33 - 2nd of 8 getting 5lb from Wishful Thinker (29 Jly Redcar 11f frm RF 3219).
**M E Sowersby [0-1] R D Seldon (from J R Turner [0-2] Jly 2000).*

MISS DAMINA BHB 54f49a **RR 59f 49a** 5247[7]
2 b f Primo Dominie 7.2f **(67)** - So Beguiling (USA) (Woodman (USA)) 9f **(74)**
Form - 07040407
Record 2000 - 1st:0 2nd:0 3rd:0 Ran:8
Win Prizemoney £0 *Total Prizemoney* £264
2000 Turf 0-7: (5f 3, 6f 2, 7f, 8f) (gd 2, g-f 3, frm 2) 2000 AW 0-1: (8f) (Fibr)
Fair filly, effective 6f, acts on gd. Turf high 59 - 4th of 20 getting 4lb from Piccolo Rose (22 Spt Lingfield 6f gd RF 4581).
**J Pearce [0-8] Mrs Jean Routledge.*

MISS DANGEROUS BHB 35f43a **RR 30f 43a** 4211[7]
5 b m Komaite (USA) 6.9f **(61)** - Khadine (Astec) 8.6f **(66)**
Form - 08613035580807
Record 2000 - 1st:1 2nd:0 3rd:2 Ran:11
Pre2000 - 1st:5 2nd:3 3rd:0 Ran:38
Win Prizemoney £20,560 *Total Prizemoney* £23,517
Wins * **2000** *Jan Lingfi (STD) 7f 59*
* 1999 *Jan Lingfi (STD) H 7f 56 58*
* 1998 Jun Warwic (G-S) H 5f 57 60
* 1998 *Apr Wolver (STD) H 6f 55 67+* <
* 1998 Apr Folkes (SFT) C 5f 56
* 1998 *Jan Wolver (STD) S 5f 54*
2000 Turf 0-4: (5f 2, 6f, 7f) (hvy, g-s, gd, g-f) 2000 AW 1-7: (6f 4, 7f 1-3) (Equi 1-6, Fibr)
Moderate filly, effective 7f, - acts on Equi, has worn blinkers, likes tight tracks. Turf high 30. AW high 59 (1st run) - 1st of 10 getting 2lb from Days of Grace (2 Jan Lingfield RF 0004). She pops up from time to time, both on turf and sand, but is basically inconsistent. Seven furlongs looks the very limit of her stamina, even on a fast track.
**M Quinn [6-44] M Quinn (from M R Channon [0-5] Oct 1997).*

MISS DEVIOUS (IRE) BHB 42f **RR 43f** 5310[16]
2 ch f Dr Devious (IRE) 9.9f **(74)** - Lothlorien (USA) **(80f)** (Woodman (USA)) 9f **(74)**
Form - 000
Record 2000 - 1st:0 2nd:0 3rd:0 Ran:3
2000 Turf 0-3: (6f, 7f 2) (g-s, gd, g-f)
Currently moderate filly. Turf high 43 (began Spt).
**R Guest [0-3] Matthews Breeding and Racing.*

MISS DOMUCH (IRE) BHB 90f **RR 78f** 4091a[3]
2 ch f Definite Article - Eliza Orzeszkowa (IRE) **(56f)** (Polish Patriot (USA))
Form - 23123
Record 2000 - 1st:1 2nd:2 3rd:2 Ran:5
Win Prizemoney £3,474 *Total Prizemoney* £28,729
Wins * **2000** Jly Bath (FRM) 5.7f 76+ <
2000 Turf 1-5: (5f 2, 6f 1-3) (g-s, gd, g-f 2, frm 1-1)
Above-average filly. Turf high 78 - 3rd of 24 to Blue Goddess (26 Aug Curragh 6f g-s RF 4091a) - also 1st of 8 from Be My Tinker (27 Jly Bath RF 3145). Won an ordinary event at Bath and was third to a stablemate in a valuable sales race at the Curragh.
**R Hannon [1-5] E K Cleveland.*

MISS DORDOGNE BHB 86f **RR 90f** 3948a[9]
3 b br f Brief Truce (USA) 9.1f **(73)** - Miss Bergerac (Bold Lad (IRE)) 8.4f **(68)**
Form - 25210
Record 2000 - 1st:1 2nd:2 3rd:0 Ran:5
Win Prizemoney £4,082 *Total Prizemoney* £7,080
Wins * **2000** Jly Cheste (SFT) 7.6f 53++ <
2000 Turf 1-5: (7f, 8f 1-4) (g-s, gd 2, g-f 1-2)
Scopey, useful filly. Turf high 90 (1st run) - 2nd of 18 to Alshakr (19 Apr Newmarket 7f gd RF 0799). She had a simple task when winning at Chester in July but is a useful filly. Suited by easy ground, she is worth another try in Listed company.
**G Wragg [1-5] J L C Pearce.*

MISSED THE BOAT (IRE) BHB 40f31a **RR 31a** 166[11]
10 b g Cyrano de Bergerac 7.3f **(58)** - Lady Portobello (Porto Bello) 8.9f **(43)**
Form - 0
Record 2000 - 1st:0 2nd:0 3rd:0 Ran:1
Pre2000 - 1st:1 2nd:2 3rd:6 Ran:32
Win Prizemoney £3,181 *Total Prizemoney* £6,986
2000 AW 0-1: (9f) (Fibr)
Very poor gelding, has worn blinkers.
**G A Ham [0-1] Mike Cornish (from A G Newcombe [2-12] Feb 1997).*

MISS EQUINOX BHB 53f **RR 58f** 4770[14]
2 b f Presidium 7.5f **(56)** - Miss Nelski (Most Secret) 7.1f **(58)**
Form - 57223132050
Record 2000 - 1st:1 2nd:3 3rd:2 Ran:11
Win Prizemoney £1,869 *Total Prizemoney* £4,451
Wins * **2000** Jly Newcas (G-F) S 6f 58 <
2000 Turf 1-11: (5f 2, 6f 1-7, 7f 2) (g-s 2, gd 2, g-f 1-2, frm 5)
Fair filly, effective 5 to 6f, best at 6f, acts on g-f to frm, best on frm. Turf high 58 - 1st of 10 getting 4lb from Dancing Penney (29 Jly Newcastle RF 3207). **N Tinkler [1-11] Contract Natural Gas Ltd.*

MISS FARA (FR) BHB 71f **RR 74f** 1210[9]

5 ch m Galetto (FR) 11.7f **(86)** - Faracha (FR) (Kenmare (FR)) 6.5f **(72)**
Form - 0
Record 2000 - 1st:0 2nd:0 3rd:0 Ran:1
Pre2000 - 1st:0 2nd:3 3rd:1 Ran:6
Win Prizemoney £0 *Total Prizemoney* £3,706
2000 Turf 0-1: (10f) (frm)
Above-average filly. **M C Pipe [4-20] Mrs Christine Painting.*

MISS FIT (IRE) BHB 57f **RR 59f** 3824[10]

4 b f Hamas (IRE) 8f **(72)** - Soucaro (Rusticaro (FR)) 8.2f **(65)**
Form - 0500805570
Record 2000 - 1st:0 2nd:0 3rd:0 Ran:10
Pre2000 - 1st:4 2nd:2 3rd:? Ran:20
Win Prizemoney £15,934 *Total Prizemoney* £21,307
Wins * 1999 Jly Cheste (G-F) H 5.1f 79 82 <
* 1998 Aug Redcar (G-F) 5f 76
* 1998 Jly Carlis (G-F) 5.9f 77+
* 1998 *Jun Southw (STD) 5f 70+*
2000 Turf 0-10: (5f 7, 6f 3) (gd 4, g-f 3, frm 3)
Scopey, above-average filly, effective 5 to 6f, best at 6f, acts on gd to frm. Turf high 68. **Mrs G S Rees [4-30] Mrs G S Rees.*

MISS FLIRTATIOUS BHB 39f **RR 46f** 5071[15]

3 b f Piccolo - By Candlelight (IRE) **(80f)** (Roi Danzig (USA))
Form - 000030
Record 2000 - 1st:0 2nd:0 3rd:1 Ran:6
Pre2000 - 1st:0 2nd:1 3rd:0 Ran:8
Win Prizemoney £0 *Total Prizemoney* £1,550
2000 Turf 0-5: (6f 2, 7f 2, 8f) (g-s, g-f 2, frm, hrd) 2000 AW 0-1: (6f) (Fibr)
Scopey, moderate filly, effective 6f, acts on g-f, has worn blinkers (very effectively). Turf high 46. Inconsistent.
**D HaydnJones [0-14] Jack Brown (Bookmaker) Ltd.*

MISS GRAPETTE (IRE) BHB 32f33a **RR 26f 33a** 4491[17]

4 b f Brief Truce (USA) 9.1f **(73)** - Grapette (Nebbiolo) 8.1f **(75)**
Form - 0005027000
Record 2000 - 1st:0 2nd:1 3rd:0 Ran:10
Pre2000 - 1st:1 2nd:2 3rd:3 Ran:16
Win Prizemoney £2,901 *Total Prizemoney* £7,417
Wins 1999 Mar Catter (G-S) 6f 69 <
2000 Turf 0-9: (5f 2, 6f 3, 7f 2, 8f 2) (g-s, gd 3, g-f, frm 4) 2000 AW 0-1: (6f) (Fibr)
Workmanlike, little account filly, effective 6f, acts on gd, likes left handed tracks, likes tight tracks. Turf high 33. Inconsistent.
**A Berry [0-10] Mrs A E Robertson (from J Berry [1-16] Oct 1999).*

MISS HIT BHB 68f73a **RR 71f 73a** 5003[12]

5 b m Efisio 7.7f **(69)** - Jennies' Gem (Sayf El Arab (USA)) 7.1f **(54)**
Form - 172050
Record 2000 - 1st:1 2nd:1 3rd:0 Ran:6
Pre2000 - 1st:4 2nd:3 3rd:1 Ran:24
Win Prizemoney £17,362 *Total Prizemoney* £23,373
Wins * 2000 Apr Bright (G-S) H 5.3f 64 69
1999 Aug Salisb (GD) H 6f 64 68
1999 *Jan Lingfi (STD) H 5f 70 71* <
1998 *Dec Wolver (STD) H 5f 65 71* <
1998 Oct Newmar () H 5f 60 63
2000 Turf 1-6: (5f 1-3, 6f 3) (g-s, gd 1-2, g-f 2, frm)
Above-average filly, effective 5 to 6f, best at 5f, acts on gd to frm - acts on Equi, excels at Lingfield. Turf high 71 - 2nd of 13 getting 11lb from Dancing Mystery (13 Aug Ascot 5f g-f RF 3604) - also 1st of 12 from Forgotten Times (13 Apr Brighton RF 0697). She has been successful on both turf and sand in the last couple of seasons and is an effective sort in modest handicap company.
**G A Butler [1-7] D R Windebank (from D R C Elsworth [1-7] Spt 1999).*

MISSILE TOE (IRE) BHB 50f42a **RR 54f 42a** 4110[19]

7 b g Exactly Sharp (USA) 8.4f **(66)** - Debach Dust (Indian King (USA)) 7.4f **(64)**
Form - 0554116530
Record 2000 - 1st:2 2nd:0 3rd:1 Ran:9
Pre2000 - 1st:2 2nd:6 3rd:3 Ran:44
Win Prizemoney £15,044 *Total Prizemoney* £24,129
Wins * 2000 Jun Newcas (FRM) H 10.1f 45 54
* 2000 Jun Newmar (G-F) H 8f 45 49
* 1999 Jly Newmar (G-F) H 10f 41 46
2000 Turf 2-9: (8f 1-5, 9f, 10f 1-3) (sft, gd 2, g-f 1-2, frm 1-4)
Fair gelding, effective 8 to 10f, best at 10f, acts on sft to frm, best on g-f, has worn blinkers, likes left handed tracks, excels at Newmarket. Turf high 57 (1st run) - 5th of 10 giving 18lb to Inchinnan (26 Apr Epsom 9f sft RF 0882) - also 1st of 12 getting 3lb from Melody Lady (30 Jun Newcastle RF 2403). Consistent.
**D Morris [3-32] Stag and Huntsman (from J E Banks [1-21] Oct 1996).*

MISS INFORM BHB 54f **RR 70f** 5067[2]

2 b f So Factual (USA) - As Sharp as **(61f)** (Handsome Sailor)
Form - 3577002
Record 2000 - 1st:0 2nd:1 3rd:1 Ran:7
Win Prizemoney £0 *Total Prizemoney* £1,143
2000 Turf 0-7: (5f 3, 6f 4) (g-s, gd 2, g-f 3, frm)
Above-average filly, effective 5f, acts on gd. Turf high 70 (1st run) - 3rd of 6 getting 5lb from Piccled (1 Jun Goodwood 5f gd RF 1625).
**D R C Elsworth [0-7] Woodhaven Racing Syndicate.*

MISSING A BIT (IRE) BHB 43f **RR 50f** 3800[4]

2 b g Petorius 8f **(66)** - Haysong (IRE) **(28f)** (Ballad Rock) 7.8f **(63)**
Form - 44554
Record 2000 - 1st:0 2nd:0 3rd:0 Ran:5
Win Prizemoney £0 *Total Prizemoney* £250
2000 Turf 0-5: (6f 4, 7f) (g-s, g-f, frm 3)
Fair gelding, has worn blinkers. Turf high 50.
**J A Osborne [0-5] Durkan Ltd.*

MISSING DRINK (IRE) BHB 53f44a **RR 59f 44a** 3264[9]

2 ch g Idris (IRE) - Miss Tuko (Good Times (ITY)) 6.6f **(54)**
Form - 050500
Record 2000 - 1st:0 2nd:0 3rd:0 Ran:6
Win Prizemoney £0 *Total Prizemoney* £220
2000 Turf 0-6: (5f 2, 6f 2, 7f 2) (gd, g-f, frm 3, hrd)
Fair gelding. Turf high 59. **M C Chapman [0-6] R J Hayward.*

MISSING YOU TOO (IRE) RR 60f 4903a[7]

2 b f Goldmark (USA) - Missing You (Ahonoora) 8.1f **(73)**
Form - 687
Record 2000 - 1st:0 2nd:0 3rd:0 Ran:3
2000 Turf 0-3: (6f, 7f 2) (sft, frm 2)
Currently average filly. Turf high 60.
**N Meade in IRE [0-1] L Queally (from P J Makin [0-2] Jun 2000).*

MISS KIRSTY (USA) BHB 84f **RR 83f** 4991[26]

3 ch f Miswaki (USA) 8.1f **(81)** - Spit Curl (USA) (Northern Dancer) 9.6f **(80)**
Form - 60180
Record 2000 - 1st:1 2nd:0 3rd:0 Ran:5
Pre2000 - 1st:0 2nd:0 3rd:1 Ran:1
Win Prizemoney £4,465 *Total Prizemoney* £5,103
Wins 2000 Jun Goodwo (GD) 8f 80 <
2000 Turf 1-5: (7f 2, 8f 1-3) (g-s, gd 1-4)
Leggy, decent filly, effective 7 to 8f, acts on gd. Turf high 83 - also 1st of 18 from Miss Dordogne (9 Jun Goodwood RF 1846). Showed promise on her debut at Newmarket last season, and was not beaten far on her seasonal bow on the same track. Ran respectably in a listed race before landing a Goodwood maiden.
**Mrs A J Perrett [0-1] D R Windebank (from G A Butler [1-5] Jun 2000).*

MISS LACROIX BHB 20f27a **RR 19f 27a** 3743[7]

5 b m Picea 12.7f **(43)** - Smartie Lee (Dominion) 8.5f **(63)**
Form - 7
Record 2000 - 1st:0 2nd:0 3rd:0 Ran:1
Pre2000 - 1st:0 2nd:0 3rd:0 Ran:12
2000 Turf 0-1: (16f) (g-f)
Little account filly. **R Hollinshead [2-26] Mrs Norma Harris.*

MISS LORILAW (FR) BHB 102f **RR 103f** 4963[8]

3 b f Homme de Loi (IRE) - Miss Lorika (FR) (Bikala) 10.1f **(49)**
Form - 3360108
Record 2000 - 1st:1 2nd:0 3rd:2 Ran:7
Pre2000 - 1st:1 2nd:0 3rd:0 Ran:1
Win Prizemoney £21,328 *Total Prizemoney* £23,557
Wins * 2000 Aug Newbur (G-F) L 12f 103 <
* 1999 Oct York (G-S) 7.9f 75

2000 Turf 1-7: (10f, 11f, 12f 1-4, 16f) (sft, gd 4, g-f 1-2)
Scopey, very useful filly, effective 11 to 12f, acts on gd to g-f. Turf high 103 - 1st of 8 getting 11lb from Farfala (6 Aug Newbury RF 3420). After decent runs in conditions events on her first two starts, she put in a fair effort in the Italian Oaks, but did not seem to stay when tried over two miles in the Queen's Vase. Appreciated the drop back in trip when winning at Newbury.
**J W Hills [2-8] David Caruth.*

MISS MANETTE BHB 46f RR 44?f 4634^{10}

3 br f Dilum (USA) 7.1f **(56)** - Lucy Manette (Final Straw) 7.9f **(64)**
Form - 6000
Record 2000 - 1st:0 2nd:0 3rd:0 Ran:4
2000 Turf 0-4: (8f 2, 9f, 10f) (g-s, gd 2, frm)
Leggy, moderate filly. Turf high 44.
**R Curtis [0-4] Mrs E McLoughlin.*

MISS MARPLE RR 65f 2613^{3}

3 b f Puissance 7.1f **(60)** - Juliet Bravo (Glow (USA)) 6.7f **(71)**
Form - 73
Record 2000 - 1st:0 2nd:0 3rd:1 Ran:2
Win Prizemoney £0 *Total Prizemoney* £565
2000 Turf 0-2: (6f 2) (gd, frm)
Currently average filly. Turf high 65 - 3rd of 7 to Eman's Joy (7 Jly Warwick 6f gd RF 2613). **J R Fanshawe [0-2] Peters Friends Two.*

MISS MONEY SPIDER (IRE) BHB 42f47a RR 39f 47a 3908^{2}

5 b m Statoblest 6.4f **(63)** - Dream of Jenny (Caerleon (USA)) 8.6f **(71)**
Form - 00008442
Record 2000 - 1st:0 2nd:1 3rd:0 Ran:8
Pre2000 - 1st:4 2nd:0 3rd:3 Ran:24
Win Prizemoney £9,232 *Total Prizemoney* £11,304
Wins * 1999 Aug Lingfi (GD) H 7f 48 51
* 1999 Jly Folkes (G-F) C 7f 45
* 1999 May Folkes (G-F) C 7f 45
1998 Spt Yarmou (G-S) S 7f 55 <
2000 Turf 0-8: (6f, 7f 6, 8f) (hvy, gd 2, g-f, frm 4)
Above-average filly, effective 7f, acts on g-f to frm, best on frm, has worn blinkers. Turf high 39.
**J M Bradley [3-21] E A Hayward (from N A Callaghan [1-9] Oct 1998).*

MISS MOSELLE (IRE) BHB 76f RR 71f 4969^{7}

2 b f Zieten (USA) - Topseys Tipple (IRE) (Hatim (USA))
Form - 307
Record 2000 - 1st:0 2nd:0 3rd:1 Ran:3
Win Prizemoney £0 *Total Prizemoney* £678
2000 Turf 0-3: (7f 2, 8f) (g-s, gd 2)
Currently above-average filly. Turf high 71 (began Aug).
**P W Harris [0-3] P A Deal.*

MISS ORAH BHB 87f RR 91f 2950^{3}

3 b f Unfuwain (USA) 11.4f **(74)** - Massorah (FR) (Habitat) 9.4f **(70)**
Form - 073
Record 2000 - 1st:0 2nd:0 3rd:1 Ran:3
Pre2000 - 1st:1 2nd:1 3rd:0 Ran:3
Win Prizemoney £5,225 *Total Prizemoney* £10,946
Wins * 1999 Spt Salisb (G-F) 7f 85+ <
2000 Turf 0-3: (6f, 7f 2) (g-s, g-f 2)
Scopey, useful filly, effective 7f, acts on g-f to frm, best on frm. Turf high 91 - 3rd of 6 getting 4lb from Rosse (19 Jly Yarmouth 7f g-f RF 2950). She almost pinched a conditions race at Yarmouth in July. Effective up to seven furlongs, she is genuine but not good enough to win a Listed heat at home. **J Noseda [1-6] G J Beck.*

MISSOURI RR 68f 3766^{6}

2 b f Charnwood Forest (IRE) - Medway (IRE) **(66df)** (Shernazar) 10.2f **(73)**
Form - 6
Record 2000 - 1st:0 2nd:0 3rd:0 Ran:1
2000 Turf 0-1: (7f) (g-f)
Currently average filly. **M H Tompkins [0-1] Pollards Stables.*

MISS PHANTINE (IRE) RR 45f 4481^{15}

2 ch f Be My Guest (USA) 10.2f **(66)** - Rosananti (Blushing Groom (FR)) 10.3f **(76)**
Form - 00
Record 2000 - 1st:0 2nd:0 3rd:0 Ran:2
2000 Turf 0-2: (7f 2) (g-s, frm)
Currently moderate filly. Turf high 45 (began Aug).
**R Hollinshead [0-2] Geoff Lloyd.*

MISS PIPPIN BHB 48f45a RR 52f 45a 3976^{9}

4 ch f Rudimentary (USA) 8.2f **(66)** - Appledorn (Doulab (USA)) 9.8f **(65)**
Form - 580
Record 2000 - 1st:0 2nd:0 3rd:0 Ran:1
Pre2000 - 1st:0 2nd:0 3rd:0 Ran:5
Win Prizemoney £0 *Total Prizemoney* £269
2000 Turf 0-1: (5f) (frm)
Light-framed, fair filly. **B A McMahon [0-6] Michael Sturgess.*

MISS PITZ BHB 68f RR 69f 4226^{9}

2 b f Cadeaux Genereux 7.9f **(76)** - Catch The Sun (Kalaglow) 9.8f **(67)**
Form - 660
Record 2000 - 1st:0 2nd:0 3rd:0 Ran:3
2000 Turf 0-3: (7f 3) (g-f, frm 2)
Currently average filly. Turf high 69 (began Jly).
**E A L Dunlop [0-3] John Pitt.*

MISS POLLY BHB 50f RR 51f 5217^{7}

2 b f Democratic (USA) - My Pretty Niece (Great Nephew) 9.9f **(64)**
Form - 007
Record 2000 - 1st:0 2nd:0 3rd:0 Ran:3
2000 Turf 0-3: (6f, 7f 2) (sft, g-s 2)
Currently fair filly. Turf high 51 (began Spt).
**J R Best [0-3] Edward Charles Brooke.*

MISS PROGRESSIVE (IRE) BHB 55f55a RR 58f 55a 4773^{11}

2 b f Common Grounds 8.1f **(66)** - Kaweah Maid (General Assembly (USA)) 10f **(68)**
Form - 6700825130
Record 2000 - 1st:1 2nd:1 3rd:1 Ran:10
Win Prizemoney £3,250 *Total Prizemoney* £4,224
Wins * **2000** Aug Sandow (GD) SH 7.1f 49 58 <
2000 Turf 1-8: (5f 3, 6f 2, 7f 1-3) (g-s 2, gd 2, g-f 1-2, frm, hrd) 2000 AW 0-2: (5f, 7f) (Fibr 2)
Fair filly, effective 7f, acts on g-s to g-f - acts on Fibr. Turf high 58 - 3rd of 17 giving 4lb to Aporto (16 Spt Catterick 7f g-s RF 4460) - also 1st of 7 getting 5lb from Ivans Bride (19 Aug Sandown RF 3800). AW high 51 - 2nd of 11 to Visitation (28 Jly Southwell 7f Fibr RF 3190). **N Tinkler [1-10] J P Hardiman.*

MISS REBECCA RR 24f 4553^{15}

2 b f Prince Sabo 6.6f **(64)** - Bint Baddi (FR) (Shareef Dancer (USA)) 9.9f **(73)**
Form - 0
Record 2000 - 1st:0 2nd:0 3rd:0 Ran:1
2000 Turf 0-1: (6f) (gd)
Currently little account filly. **N Tinkler [0-1] R Midgley.*

MISS RIMEX (IRE) BHB 72f RR 73f 2350^{8}

4 b f Ezzoud (IRE) - Blue Guitar (Cure The Blues (USA)) 9.5f **(63)**
Form - 508
Record 2000 - 1st:0 2nd:0 3rd:0 Ran:3
Pre2000 - 1st:3 2nd:2 3rd:3 Ran:19
Win Prizemoney £11,679 *Total Prizemoney* £16,448
Wins * 1999 Oct Leices (SFT) C 8f 73
* 1999 Jly Newmar (G-F) H 8f 72 78
* 1998 Aug Kempto (G-F) H 6f 75 79 <
2000 Turf 0-3: (8f 3) (g-s, g-f, frm)
Workmanlike, above-average filly, effective 7 to 10f, acts on gd to frm, best on frm. Turf high 68. Consistent.
**D R C Elsworth [3-22] Park Farm Racing.*

MISS RIVIERA GOLF BHB 103f RR 102f $5366a^{1}$

3 b f Hernando (FR) - Miss Beaulieu (Northfields (USA)) 9f **(72)**
Form - 72811
Record 2000 - 1st:2 2nd:1 3rd:0 Ran:5
Win Prizemoney £17,332 *Total Prizemoney* £18,552
Wins * **2000** Nov Maison (HVY) L 8f 102 <
* **2000** Spt Nottin (SFT) 8.2f 83
2000 Turf 2-5: (7f, 8f 2-2, 10f 2) (hvy 1-1, gd 1-2, frm 2)
Scopey, very useful filly. Turf high 102 - 1st of 16 from Serene View (3 Nov Maisons-laffitte RF 5366a). Unraced at two, she got off

the mark in a Nottingham maiden, before earning black type in a listed event in France. **G Wragg [2-5] J L C Pearce.*

MISS ROXANNE BHB 40f35a **RR 41f 35a** 966[18]
3 b f Cyrano de Bergerac 7.3f **(58)** - Conquista (Aragon) 8.1f **(60)**
Form - 000
Record 2000 - 1st:0 2nd:0 3rd:0 Ran:1
Pre2000 - 1st:0 2nd:0 3rd:0 Ran:6
2000 Turf 0-1: (6f) (gd)
Light-framed, moderate filly. **K W Hogg [0-7] Michael Burley.*

MISS SCARLETT RR 3073[5]
7 ch m Lyphento (USA) - Thank Yourself (Le Bavard (FR))
Form - 05
Record 2000 - 1st:0 2nd:0 3rd:0 Ran:2
2000 Turf 0-1: (8f) (frm) 2000 AW 0-1: (10f) (Equi)
Formerly very poor mare. **Mrs P Townsley [0-2] Brian Tetley.*

MISS SINCERE (IRE) BHB 48f42a **RR 41f 42a** 1684[7]
3 b f Imperial Frontier (USA) 7f **(65)** - Brite Mist (IRE) (Shy Groom (USA)) 10f **(66)**
Form - 044847
Record 2000 - 1st:0 2nd:0 3rd:0 Ran:6
Pre2000 - 1st:0 2nd:0 3rd:0 Ran:4
Win Prizemoney £0 *Total Prizemoney £675*
2000 Turf 0-2: (5f 2) (gd, frm) 2000 AW 0-4: (5f 3, 6f) (Equi, Fibr 3)
Scopey, moderate filly, has worn blinkers. Turf high 41. AW high 42. Inconsistent. **B S Rothwell [0-10] Brian Rothwell.*

MISS SKICAP BHB 61f66a **RR 17f 66a** 970[15]
3 b f Welsh Captain 7.2f **(54)** - Miss Nelski (Most Secret) 7.1f **(58)**
Form - 421480
Record 2000 - 1st:0 2nd:0 3rd:0 Ran:3
Pre2000 - 1st:1 2nd:1 3rd:0 Ran:3
Win Prizemoney £2,284 *Total Prizemoney £3,176*
Wins 1999 *Dec Wolver (STD) C* *6f* *74* <
2000 Turf 0-1: (8f) (gd) 2000 AW 0-2: (5f, 6f) (Fibr 2)
Light-framed, above-average filly, effective 5 to 6f, - acts on Fibr, has worn blinkers. AW high 50.
**Miss S J Wilton [0-3] John Pointon and Sons (from T D Barron [1-3] Dec 1999).*

MISS SPRINGFIELD BHB 40f **RR 43df** 2815[10]
3 b f Environment Friend 7.5f **(67)** - Esilam (Frimley Park) 6.5f **(67)**
Form - 30450
Record 2000 - 1st:0 2nd:0 3rd:1 Ran:5
Pre2000 - 1st:0 2nd:0 3rd:0 Ran:3
Win Prizemoney £0 *Total Prizemoney £275*
2000 Turf 0-4: (7f 2, 8f 2) (gd 2, g-f, frm) 2000 AW 0-1: (7f) (Fibr)
Scopey, moderate filly, effective 7f, acts on gd to g-f, has worn blinkers. Turf high 43 (1st run) - 3rd of 13 getting 19lb from Northern Times (7 Apr Lingfield 7f gd RF 0638). Inconsistent. **D Morris [0-8] Wacky Racing.*

MISS SUTTON BHB 47f **RR 47f** 4478[4]
2 b f Formidable (USA) 7.8f **(60)** - Saysana (Sayf El Arab (USA)) 7.1f **(54)**
Form - 544
Record 2000 - 1st:0 2nd:0 3rd:0 Ran:3
2000 Turf 0-2: (5f, 6f) (g-f, frm) 2000 AW 0-1: (7f) (Fibr)
Currently fair filly. Turf high 47 (began Aug). **T G Mills [0-3] M J Joyce.*

MISS SWIFT RR 1729[15]
3 b f Son Pardo - Lindfield Belle (IRE) (Fairy King (USA)) 7.7f **(59)**
Form - 00
Record 2000 - 1st:0 2nd:0 3rd:0 Ran:2
2000 Turf 0-2: (6f, 10f) (gd, g-f)
Workmanlike, currently very poor filly. **S Dow [0-2] A Guinea A Minute Partnership.*

MISS TAKE (IRE) BHB 32f38a **RR 36f 38a** 1422[7]
4 ch f Red Sunset 9f **(57)** - Grave Error (Northern Treat (USA)) 6f **(50)**
Form - 08440057
Record 2000 - 1st:0 2nd:0 3rd:0 Ran:8
Pre2000 - 1st:4 2nd:5 3rd:6 Ran:37
Win Prizemoney £8,465 *Total Prizemoney £14,301*
Wins 1999 *Jun Wolver (STD) H* *9.4f* *53* *61+*
1998 *Dec Wolver (SLW) S* *7f* *70+* <
1998 *Dec Wolver (STD)* *8.5f* *69?*
1998 *Jun Wolver (STD) S* *6f* *63*
2000 Turf 0-2: (12f 2) (gd, g-f) 2000 AW 0-6: (8f 2, 9f 3, 11f) (Fibr 6)
Light-framed, moderate filly, effective 8 to 10f, - acts on AW, best on Fibr, mostly wears blinkers, favours left handed tracks. Turf high 35. AW high 42. She has shown her best form in modest company on the Wolverhampton Fibresand, all of her wins to date have been on that track.
**A G Newcombe [0-8] Ms Renee Wheeler (from P D Evans [4-37] Aug 1999).*

MISS TEAK (USA) RR 81f 4437[4]
2 b f Woodman (USA) 9.7f **(77)** - Miss Profile (IRE) (Sadler's Wells (USA)) 10f **(76)**
Form - 4
Record 2000 - 1st:0 2nd:0 3rd:0 Ran:1
Win Prizemoney £0 *Total Prizemoney £834*
2000 Turf 0-1: (7f) (frm)
Currently decent filly. (1st run) - 4th of 8 to Palatial (15 Spt Newbury 7f frm RF 4437). **G A Butler [0-1] Beetle N Wedge Partnership.*

MISS TOPOGINO RR 30f 2971[7]
2 b f Mistertopogigo (IRE) - Bitch **(37f 32a)** (Risk Me (FR)) 5.9f **(53)**
Form - 8507
Record 2000 - 1st:0 2nd:0 3rd:0 Ran:4
2000 Turf 0-2: (5f, 6f) (gd, frm) 2000 AW 0-2: (5f 2) (Fibr 2)
Moderate filly. Turf high 30. AW high 42. **Miss J F Craze [0-4] R Naylor.*

MISS TRESS (IRE) BHB 67f **RR 66f** 5074[13]
2 b f Salse (USA) 10.9f **(71)** - Circulate (High Top) 10.2f **(67)**
Form - 46400
Record 2000 - 1st:0 2nd:0 3rd:0 Ran:5
Win Prizemoney £0 *Total Prizemoney £654*
2000 Turf 0-5: (7f 4, 8f) (sft, g-s, gd, frm 2)
Average filly. Turf high 64. **P W Harris [0-5] Michael Smith & Chris Murphy.*

MISS VERITY BHB 76f71a **RR 80?f 71a** 4965[2]
2 ch f Factual (USA) - Ansellady **(62f 60a)** (Absalom) 7.2f **(58)**
Form - 621242
Record 2000 - 1st:1 2nd:3 3rd:0 Ran:6
Win Prizemoney £2,261 *Total Prizemoney £24,412*
Wins * 2000 *Jun Southw (STD)* *5f* *77* <
2000 Turf 0-4: (5f 2, 6f 2) (g-s, gd, g-f 2) 2000 AW 1-2: (5f 1-2)(Fibr 1-2)
Decent filly, effective 5 to 6f, acts on gd - acts on Fibr. Turf high 80 - 2nd of 30 getting 5lb from Goodie Twosues (13 Oct Newmarket 6f gd RF 4965). AW high 77 - 1st of 12 getting 2lb from Tupgill Tipple (22 Jun Southwell RF 2193).
**H Akbary [1-4] Charles Alan McKechnie (from J S Wainwright [0-2] May 2000).*

MISS WORLD (IRE) BHB 32f35a **RR 47f 35a** 5016[10]
3 b f Mujadil (USA) 7.7f **(70)** - Great Land (USA) (Friend's Choice (USA)) 8.6f **(57)**
Form - 232154750000
Record 2000 - 1st:0 2nd:0 3rd:0 Ran:8
Pre2000 - 1st:2 2nd:2 3rd:1 Ran:15
Win Prizemoney £4,734 *Total Prizemoney £7,677*
Wins 1999 *Dec Southw (SLW) H* *8f* *64* *77* <
1999 *Spt Wolver (STD) S* *7f* *69+*
2000 Turf 0-2: (10f 2) (sft, gd) 2000 AW 0-6: (7f, 8f 2, 9f 3) (Equi 2, Fibr 4)
Scopey, moderate filly, effective 7 to 8f, best at 8f, - acts on AW, best on Fibr, likes left handed tracks, likes tight tracks. Turf high 28. AW high 66. Becoming disappointing.
**P Howling [0-2] Bernard Butt (from C N Allen [2-21] Apr 2000).*

MISTER BUCKET (IRE) RR 61f 2764[4]
2 ch c Superlative 8.8f **(57)** - Rose Bouquet (General Assembly (USA)) 10f **(68)**
Form - 4
Record 2000 - 1st:0 2nd:0 3rd:0 Ran:1
2000 Turf 0-1: (7f) (gd)

Currently average colt.
**P W Harris [0-1] R Dagg, S Williams & Mrs P W Harris.*

MISTER CLINTON (IRE) BHB 62f **RR 67f** 3141[4]
3 ch g Lion Cavern (USA) 7.5f **(74)** - Thewaari (USA) (Eskimo (USA))
Form - 41031674
Record 2000 - 1st:2 2nd:0 3rd:1 Ran:8
Pre2000 - 1st:0 2nd:0 3rd:0 Ran:3
Win Prizemoney £6,604 *Total Prizemoney* £7,677
Wins * 2000 Jun Salisb (G-F) H 7f 57 67 <
*** 2000** May Bright (FRM) 7f 67 <
2000 Turf 2-8: (6f, 7f 2-6, 8f) (gd, g-f 2-5, frm, hrd)
Scopey, average gelding, effective 7f, acts on g-f to frm, best on g-f. Turf high 67 - 1st of 19 getting 8lb from Otime (13 Jun Salisbury RF 1923) - also 1st of 9 from The Robster (17 May Brighton RF 1257). He has a high cruising speed and is definitely capable of adding to his victory at Salisbury in June.
**K T Ivory [2-11] Miss Lilo Blum.*

MISTER DOC RR 10f 3638[12]
2 ch g Most Welcome 8.6f **(66)** - Red Poppy (IRE) (Coquelin (USA)) 8.4f **(58)**
Form - 0
Record 2000 - 1st:0 2nd:0 3rd:0 Ran:1
2000 Turf 0-1: (7f) (frm)
Currently poor gelding.
**D W Barker [0-1] L H Gilmurray & T J Docherty.*

MISTER ERMYN RR 42f 2849[13]
7 ch g Minster Son 10.9f **(56)** - Rosana Park (Music Boy) 6.8f **(57)**
Form - 0
Record 2000 - 1st:0 2nd:0 3rd:0 Ran:1
2000 Turf 0-1: (14f) (g-f)
Moderate gelding, always wears blinkers.
**L MontagueHall [2-9] J Daniels.*

MISTER GILL BHB 48f47a **RR 36f 47a** 1915[12]
3 ch g Suave Dancer (USA) 10.7f **(68)** - Bundled Up (USA) (Sharpen Up) 8.3f **(67)**
Form - 0000
Record 2000 - 1st:0 2nd:0 3rd:0 Ran:4
Pre2000 - 1st:0 2nd:0 3rd:1 Ran:7
Win Prizemoney £0 *Total Prizemoney* £620
2000 Turf 0-3: (10f, 12f, 13f) (gd, frm 2) 2000 AW 0-1: (6f) (Fibr)
Moderate gelding, effective 6f, acts on hrd, likes left handed tracks. Turf high 36. Becoming disappointing.
**J J O'Neill [0-3] Miss G C Young (from A T Murphy [0-8] Jan 2000).*

MISTER HAVANA RR 35tf 1968[8]
3 br g Pelder (IRE) - Cee Beat (Bairn (USA)) 7.7f **(59)**
Form - 08
Record 2000 - 1st:0 2nd:0 3rd:0 Ran:2
2000 Turf 0-1: (9f) (frm) 2000 AW 0-1: (7f) (Equi)
Light-framed, currently very moderate gelding.
**E A Wheeler [0-2] Austin Stroud & Co Ltd.*

MISTER JOLSON BHB 49f78a **RR 57f 78a** 4276[17]
11 br g Latest Model 5.4f **(48)** - Impromptu (My Swanee) 7.6f **(52)**
Form - 45040
Record 2000 - 1st:0 2nd:0 3rd:0 Ran:5
Pre2000 - 1st:12 2nd:10 3rd:12 Ran:97
Win Prizemoney £50,558 *Total Prizemoney* £77,096
Wins * 1998 May Bath (FRM) 5.1f 78
* 1997 May Kempto (GD) H 6f 74 76
* 1996 Jun Salisb (G-F) H 5f 75 78
* 1996 Apr Sandow (GD) H 5f 70 73
2000 Turf 0-5: (5f 2, 6f 3) (g-f, frm 4)
Fair gelding, effective 5f, acts on gd to frm, best on gd, has worn blinkers. Turf high 57.
**R J Hodges [12-102] Exors of the late B Froome.*

MISTER KICK (IRE) RR 103f 4291a[2]
3 gr c Linamix (FR) 8.2f **(64)** - Mrs Arkada (FR) **(101f)** (Akarad (FR)) 9f **(76)**
Form - 22
2000 Turf 0-2: (15f 2) (sft 2)
Currently very useful colt. Turf high 103 (began Jly) - 2nd of 5 to Epitre (3 Spt Longchamp 15f sft RF 4291a).
**A Fabre in FR [0-2] J-L Lagadere.*

MISTER MAL (IRE) BHB 73f69a **RR 79f 69a** 5317[8]
4 b g Scenic 10.6f **(66)** - Fashion Parade (Mount Hagen (FR)) 8.4f **(70)**
Form - 050010206588
Record 2000 - 1st:1 2nd:1 3rd:0 Ran:12
Pre2000 - 1st:3 2nd:2 3rd:4 Ran:13
Win Prizemoney £14,030 *Total Prizemoney* £20,887
Wins * 2000 Aug Newcas (GD) H 7f 71 76 <
* 1999 Oct Redcar (SFT) H 7f 70 72
* 1999 Jun Leices (G-S) H 7f 61 70+
* 1999 Jun Catter (GD) 7f 61
2000 Turf 1-12: (6f 5, 7f 1-5, 8f 2) (sft 6, gd 2, g-f 1-2, frm 2)
Strong, above-average gelding, effective 6 to 7f, best at 7f, acts on sft to g-f - acts on Fibr, likes Catterick. Turf high 79 - 2nd of 13 getting 2lb from Prince Babar (2 Spt Haydock 7f sft RF 4158) - also 1st of 6 giving 13lb to Welcome To Unos (9 Aug Newcastle RF 3498). Scored three times in 1999, all of which were over seven furlongs, and he regained winning form over that trip at Newcastle in August. Has form on fast ground, but goes particularly well on soft.
**J A Glover [4-25] Mrs Andrea Mallinson.*

MISTER MCGOLDRICK BHB 67f **RR 70f** 4819[14]
3 b g Sabrehill (USA) 8.5f **(64)** - Anchor Inn (Be My Guest (USA)) 9.3f **(67)**
Form - 710
Record 2000 - 1st:1 2nd:0 3rd:0 Ran:3
Win Prizemoney £4,374 *Total Prizemoney* £4,374
Wins * 2000 Spt Haydoc (HVY) 10.5f 70 <
2000 Turf 1-3: (10f, 11f 1-1, 12f) (sft 1-1, g-s, g-f)
Workmanlike, currently above-average gelding. Turf high 70 (began Aug) - 1st of 5 giving 5lb to Precious Poppy (22 Spt Haydock RF 4573).
**J G Given [1-3] Richard Longley.*

MISTER MIND BHB 48f **RR 38f** 4965[30]
2 b c Mind Games - Madam Bold (Never so Bold) 6.3f **(66)**
Form - 700
Record 2000 - 1st:0 2nd:0 3rd:0 Ran:3
2000 Turf 0-3: (5f 2, 6f) (gd, g-f 2)
Currently very moderate colt. Turf high 38.
**M Brittain [0-3] Northgate Millennium.*

MISTER PQ BHB 30f22a **RR 28f 22a** 3192[12]
4 ch g Ardkinglass 5f **(64)** - Well Off (Welsh Pageant) 10f **(65)**
Form - 6000
Record 2000 - 1st:0 2nd:0 3rd:0 Ran:4
Pre2000 - 1st:1 2nd:0 3rd:0 Ran:12
Win Prizemoney £4,900 *Total Prizemoney* £4,900
Wins * 1999 Aug Bright (G-S) H 11.9f 42 51 <
2000 Turf 0-3: (12f 2, 15f) (g-s, frm 2) 2000 AW 0-1: (16f) (Fibr)
Light-framed, little account gelding, effective 12f, acts on gd, likes left handed tracks, likes tight tracks. Turf high 28. Becoming disappointing. **J G Smyth-Osbourne [1-16] PQ International/Euromedia.*

MISTER RAIDER BHB 32f37a **RR 21f 37a** 3440[8]
8 ch g Ballacashtal (CAN) 7.9f **(51)** - Martian Melody (Enchantment) 5.4f **(52)**
Form - 50080008
Record 2000 - 1st:0 2nd:0 3rd:0 Ran:5
Pre2000 - 1st:4 2nd:4 3rd:3 Ran:66
Win Prizemoney £9,920 *Total Prizemoney* £13,924
Wins * 1997 Jun Leices (G-F) SH 6f 44 46
* 1996 *Dec Lingfi (STD) H 5f 50 51* <
* 1996 *Nov Lingfi (STD) H 5f 48 51* <
1996 *Feb Lingfi (STD) 6f 48*
2000 Turf 0-3: (5f 2, 7f) (g-f, frm 2) 2000 AW 0-2: (6f, 7f) (Equi 2)
Very moderate gelding, effective 5 to 8f, acts on gd - acts on Equi, mostly wears blinkers, likes left handed tracks, prefers tight tracks. Turf high 17. AW high 27.
**E A Wheeler [3-50] Raiders Partnership (from S Mellor [1-21] Feb 1996).*

MISTER RAMBO BHB 72f **RR 83f** 4619[8]
5 b g Rambo Dancer (CAN) 8.4f **(59)** - Ozra (Red Alert) 7.6f **(66)**
Form - 0185286055868
Record 2000 - 1st:1 2nd:1 3rd:0 Ran:13

Pre2000 - 1st:3 2nd:2 3rd:1 Ran:23
Win Prizemoney £22,696 *Total Prizemoney* £33,775
Wins * **2000** Apr Warwic (SFT) H 7.7f 78 81
* 1999 Jly Ascot (G-F) H 7f 82 84
* 1998 Jun Frankf (GD) L 7.8f 91 <
* 1997 Oct Newbur (GD) 6f 87
2000 Turf 1-13: (6f, 7f 7, 8f 1-4, 9f) (sft 1-3, g-s 2, gd 4, g-f 2, frm 2)
Decent gelding, effective 6 to 8f, best at 7f, acts on sft to g-f, has worn blinkers, likes tight tracks. Turf high 83 - 2nd of 11 getting 12lb from Adjutant (13 May Lingfield 7f sft RF 1195) - also 1st of 13 giving 32lb to Trump Street (3 Apr Warwick RF 0597).
**B J Meehan [4-36] Abbott Racing Ltd.*

MISTER SANDERS BHB 59f **RR 61f** 4460[14]
2 ch g Cosmonaut - Arroganza (Crofthall) 6.3f **(59)**
Form - 86000
Record 2000 - 1st:0 2nd:0 3rd:0 Ran:5
2000 Turf 0-5: (5f 2, 6f, 7f 2) (g-s, gd, frm 3)
Average gelding. Turf high 61.
**R M Whitaker [0-5] Paul & Justine Rhodes.*

MISTER SUPERB BHB 78f **RR 89?f** 4991[14]
3 ch c Superlative 8.8f **(57)** - Kiveton Komet (Precocious) 8.6f **(62)**
Form - 30218636070
Record 2000 - 1st:1 2nd:1 3rd:2 Ran:11
Pre2000 - 1st:0 2nd:0 3rd:0 Ran:4
Win Prizemoney £3,818 *Total Prizemoney* £12,422
Wins * **2000** Jun Lingfi (G-F) 6f 79 <
2000 Turf 1-11: (6f 1-8, 7f 3) (gd 3, g-f 4, frm 1-4)
Workmanlike, useful colt, effective 6f, acts on frm. Turf high 89. Consistent. He won a weak Lingfield maiden in June and found life tougher in handicaps thereafter. Invariably held-up, he is worth another try over seven furlongs. **V Soane [1-15] Gordon Weston.*

MISTER TRICKY BHB 61f77a **RR 66f 77a** 5367a[3]
5 ch g Magic Ring (IRE) 6.5f **(64)** - Splintering (Sharpo) 7.7f **(59)**
Form - 112010400023
Record 2000 - 1st:1 2nd:2 3rd:1 Ran:10
Pre2000 - 1st:9 2nd:1 3rd:3 Ran:26
Win Prizemoney £47,580 *Total Prizemoney* £59,629
Wins * **2000** *Apr Lingfi (STD) H 6f 70 77* <
* 1999 *Dec Lingfl (STD) H 6f 67 69*
* 1999 *Nov Lingfi (STD) H 7f 62 65*
* 1999 Oct Bright (G-S) 7f 66
* 1999 Jun Goodwo (G-F) H 6f 60 63
* 1999 May Lingfi (G-F) H 6f 56 58
* 1999 Apr Windso (G-S) H 5f 53 54
* 1999 *Mar Lingfi (STD) 7f 62*
* 1998 *Apr Lingfi (STD) H 7f 53 62*
* 1998 *Mar Lingfi (STD) H 8f 53 56*
2000 Turf 0-3: (6f 2, 7f) (g-f 2, frm) 2000 AW 1-7: (6f 1-5, 7f 2) (Equi 1-3, Fibr, Dirt 3)
Useful gelding, has broken blood-vessels, effective 6 to 7f, best at 6f, - acts on Equi to Dirt, best on Dirt, likes left handed tracks, likes Lingfield. Turf high 38. AW high 86 - 3rd of 6 getting 5lb from Stalwart Member (4 Nov Aqueduct 7f Dirt RF 5367a) - also 1st of 9 giving 3lb to Diamond Geezer (12 Apr Lingfield RF 0681). Inconsistent. He had a very successful 1999, winning four on turf and three on Equitrack, and won on the latter surface last year. Suited by six and seven furlongs, he earned some place money in an ambitious trip Statesidelater in the year. **P Mitchell [10-36].*

MISTER WEBB BHB 54f **RR 64f** 5011[7]
3 b g Whittingham (IRE) - Ruda (FR) (Free Round (USA)) 11.7f **(70)**
Form - 500477
Record 2000 - 1st:0 2nd:0 3rd:0 Ran:6
Pre2000 - 1st:0 2nd:0 3rd:0 Ran:2
Win Prizemoney £0 *Total Prizemoney* £450
2000 Turf 0-5: (10f 2, 12f, 13f, 16f) (g-s 2, g-f, frm 2) 2000 AW 0-1: (14f) (Fibr)
Scopey, average gelding, effective 13f, acts on frm, likes tight tracks. Turf high 64. **B Smart [0-8] Norman Webb.*

MISTER WESTSOUND BHB 36f48a **RR 57f 48a** 5194[3]
8 b g Cyrano de Bergerac 7.3f **(58)** - Captivate (Mansingh (USA)) 7.4f **(55)**
Form - 400008000633
Record 2000 - 1st:0 2nd:0 3rd:2 Ran:12

Pre2000 - 1st:7 2nd:10 3rd:10 Ran:77
Win Prizemoney £23,904 *Total Prizemoney* £43,741
Wins * 1999 May Ayr (GD) H 6f 51 57
* 1998 Oct Ayr (HVY) H 6f 46 50
* 1997 Jun Ayr (GD) H 7f 36 49+
* 1997 Jun Hamilt (G-S) H 6f 37 49
2000 Turf 0-12: (6f 8, 7f 3, 8f) (hvy, sft, gd 2, g-f 4, frm 4)
Fair gelding, effective 6f, acts on g-s to g-f, mostly wears blinkers. Turf high 57 (1st run) - 4th of 15 getting 18lb from Amaranth (2 Jun Ayr 6f g-f RF 1638). Inconsistent.
**Miss L A Perratt [7-89] David Sutherland-Ian Hay.*

MIST OVER MEUGHER BHB 29f **RR 18f** 2274[9]
3 gr f Thowra (FR) 11.2f **(47)** - Misty View **(12f)** (Absalom) 7.2f **(58)**
Form - 0000
Record 2000 - 1st:0 2nd:0 3rd:0 Ran:3
Pre2000 - 1st:0 2nd:0 3rd:0 Ran:5
2000 Turf 0-2: (8f 2) (g-f, frm) 2000 AW 0-1: (8f) (Fibr)
Neat, poor filly. Turf high 18. **C W Fairhurst [0-8] Mrs A M Leggett.*

MISTRESS BANKES (IRE) RR 3833[7]
4 b f Petardia 8.2f **(58)** - Zestino (Shack (USA)) 5.8f **(53)**
Form - 07
Record 2000 - 1st:0 2nd:0 3rd:0 Ran:2
2000 Turf 0-2: (10f 2) (g-f 2)
Currently very poor filly. (began Aug).
**W G M Turner [0-2] T Lightbowne.*

MISTY BELLE **RR 74df** 5067[14]
2 gr f Petong 7.6f **(58)** - La Belle Dominique **(53f 45a)** (Dominion) 8.5f **(63)**
Form - 0323D000
Record 2000 - 1st:0 2nd:1 3rd:2 Ran:8
Win Prizemoney £0 *Total Prizemoney* £1,836
2000 Turf 0-8: (5f 6, 6f 2) (g-s 2, gd, g-f 2, frm 2, hrd)
Above-average filly, effective 5f, acts on hrd. Turf high 74 - 2nd of 10 getting 2lb from Nashira (17 Jun Bath 5f hrd RF 2038). Becoming disappointing. **B R Millman [0-8] J A Pickford.*

MISTY BOY BHB 46f **RR 38f** 5083[5]
3 br g Polar Falcon (USA) 9f **(74)** - Misty Silks **(77f 70a)** (Scottish Reel) 7f **(61)**
Form - 0005
Record 2000 - 1st:0 2nd:0 3rd:0 Ran:4
Pre2000 - 1st:0 2nd:0 3rd:0 Ran:3
2000 Turf 0-4: (6f 2, 7f 2) (hvy, g-s, gd, g-f)
Scopey, very moderate gelding, has worn blinkers. Turf high 38.
**M J Ryan [0-7] M J Baxter.*

MISTY DIAMOND **RR 55f** 2419[8]
2 b f Missed Flight - Corallia (IRE) (Alzao (USA)) 7.1f **(68)**
Form - 008
Record 2000 - 1st:0 2nd:0 3rd:0 Ran:3
2000 Turf 0-2: (6f 2) (frm 2) 2000 AW 0-1: (7f) (Fibr)
Currently fair filly. Turf high 55.
**P S McEntee [0-3] Clearview Partnership.*

MISTY EYED (IRE) BHB 100f **RR 103+f** 4463[5]
2 gr f Paris House 5.9f **(64)** - Bold As Love (Lomond (USA)) 8.8f **(65)**
Form - 51711125
Record 2000 - 1st:4 2nd:1 3rd:0 Ran:8
Win Prizemoney £46,389 *Total Prizemoney* £56,739
Wins * **2000** Aug Goodwo (GD) G3 5f 99 <
* **2000** Jly Sandow (GD) L 5f 90
* **2000** Jly Windso (GD) 5f 89+
* **2000** Jun Windso (GD) 5f 77+
2000 Turf 4-8: (5f 4-7, 6f) (gd, g-f 3-5, frm 1-2)
Very useful filly, effective 5 to 6f, best at 5f, acts on g-f to frm, best on g-f. Turf high 103 - 2nd of 11 to Superstar Leo (9 Spt Doncaster 5f frm RF 4312) - also 1st of 10 getting 2lb from Bouncing Bowdler (4 Aug Goodwood RF 3363). A very speedy and thoroughly likeable juvenile, her wins include the Molecomb at Goodwood. Lost nothing in defeat in the Flying Childers next time but appeared to find six furlongs a shade far on her final start. For all her qualities she does not impress as the type to improve at three, however.
**Mrs P N Dutfield [4-8] Mrs Jan Fuller.*

MISTY MAGIC BHB 53f38a **RR 56f 38a** 5116[6]
3 b f Distinctly North (USA) 7.4f **(63)** - Meadmore Magic (Mansingh (USA)) 7.4f **(55)**
Form - 7043263006
Record 2000 - 1st:0 2nd:1 3rd:2 Ran:10
Pre2000 - 1st:0 2nd:0 3rd:1 Ran:3
Win Prizemoney £0 *Total Prizemoney* £2,475
2000 Turf 0-9: (7f 2, 8f 5, 9f, 10f) (g-s 2, gd, g-f 4, frm 2) 2000 AW 0-1: (8f) (Fibr)
Unfurnished, fair filly, effective 6 to 9f, acts on g-s to frm, best on frm, likes left handed tracks, likes tight tracks. Turf high 56 - 3rd of 13 getting 2lb from Altay (6 Spt Epsom 9f g-f RF 4267). Becoming disappointing. **P W Harris [0-13] Grover, Hartshorn, Williams & Willis.*

MISTY MISS BHB 102f **RR 94f** 961[P]
3 b f Distant Relative 7f **(69)** - Baino Clinic (USA) (Sovereign Dancer (USA)) 11.2f **(68)**
Form - 0P
Record 2000 - 1st:0 2nd:0 3rd:0 Ran:2
Pre2000 - 1st:3 2nd:1 3rd:1 Ran:6
Win Prizemoney £45,011 *Total Prizemoney* £48,459
Wins * 1999 *Aug Wolver (STD) 6f 87+*
* 1999 Jly Goodwo (G-F) G3 5f 93 <
* 1999 Jly Bath (G-F) S 5.1f 58
2000 Turf 0-2: (5f, 7f) (gd 2)
Light-framed, useful filly, effective 5 to 6f, best at 5f, acts on g-f to frm - acts on Fibr. Turf high 94. She was pulled-up at Bath in May and did not run again. **P D Evans [3-8] Stott-Richmond.*

MITCHAM (IRE) BHB 97f **RR 94f** 4434[11]
4 br c Hamas (IRE) 8f **(72)** - Arab Scimetar (IRE) (Sure Blade (USA)) 11.3f **(67)**
Form - 040770
Record 2000 - 1st:0 2nd:0 3rd:0 Ran:6
Pre2000 - 1st:3 2nd:2 3rd:1 Ran:11
Win Prizemoney £105,359 *Total Prizemoney* £116,464
Wins * 1999 Jun Ascot (G-F) G2 5f 118 <
* 1999 May Newmar (GD) H 6f 98 106
* 1998 Spt Warwic (G-F) 6f 81
2000 Turf 0-6: (5f 2, 6f 2, 7f 2) (gd 2, g-f 3, frm)
Workmanlike, useful colt, effective 5f, acts on g-f, has worn blinkers. Turf high 100. He came fast and late to land the King's Stand Stakes at Ascot in '99, but has not reached those heights since. Seemed to stay seven furlongs when fourth at Leopardstown in June but is best suited by a fast-run five. **T G Mills [3-17] T G Mills.*

MITCHELLS MAYHEM BHB 31f **RR 23f** 3057[14]
3 b f Mistertopogigo (IRE) - Mayday Kitty **(51f 40a)** (Interrex (CAN))
Form - 580
Record 2000 - 1st:0 2nd:0 3rd:0 Ran:3
Pre2000 - 1st:0 2nd:0 3rd:0 Ran:1
2000 Turf 0-2: (5f 2) (g-f, frm) 2000 AW 0-1: (5f) (Equi)
Small, little account filly. Turf high 23.
**W G M Turner [0-4] T Lightbowne.*

MITHRAIC (IRE) BHB 31f **RR 35f** 5164[9]
8 b g Kefaah (USA) 11.2f **(64)** - Persian's Glory (Prince Tenderfoot (USA)) 9f **(61)**
Form - 5610
Record 2000 - 1st:1 2nd:0 3rd:0 Ran:4
Pre2000 - 1st:3 2nd:4 3rd:4 Ran:17
Win Prizemoney £8,915 *Total Prizemoney* £13,626
Wins * **2000** Aug Newcas (GD) S 12.4f 35
* 1999 Aug Newcas (FRM) S 12.4f 46
* 1996 Jly Mussel (G-F) 11.1f 59 <
* 1996 Jly Hamilt (G-F) C 11.1f 59 <
2000 Turf 1-4: (10f, 11f, 12f 1-2) (gd, g-f 1-1, frm 2)
Very moderate gelding, effective 11 to 12f, best at 12f, acts on g-f to frm, best on g-f, has worn blinkers. Turf high 35. Consistent.
**W S Cunningham [8-44] A R Boocock (from J W Watts [0-5] Aug 1995).*

MITIE ACCESS (IRE) BHB 25f **RR 7f** 2552[11]
4 ch f Mujtahid (USA) 7.4f **(69)** - Simply Marilyn (IRE) (Simply Great (FR)) 8.2f **(65)**
Form - 00
Record 2000 - 1st:0 2nd:0 3rd:0 Ran:2
Pre2000 - 1st:0 2nd:0 3rd:1 Ran:7
Win Prizemoney £0 *Total Prizemoney* £530
2000 Turf 0-2: (7f, 8f) (g-f, frm)
Light-framed, very poor filly, has worn blinkers. Turf high 7.
**C A Dwyer [0-10] David Bowkett.*

MIZHAR (USA) BHB 77f **RR 78f** 4266[4]
4 b br g Dayjur (USA) 6.8f **(79)** - Futuh (USA) (Diesis) 9.3f **(69)**
Form - 008080224
Record 2000 - 1st:0 2nd:2 3rd:0 Ran:9
Pre2000 - 1st:2 2nd:0 3rd:0 Ran:7
Win Prizemoney £9,310 *Total Prizemoney* £14,730
Wins 1998 Oct Newmar () H 6f 91 94 <
1998 Spt Nottin (GD) 6.1f 82
2000 Turf 0-9: (5f 7, 6f 2) (gd 2, g-f 5, frm 2)
Scopey, above-average gelding, effective 5f, acts on gd to g-f, best on g-f, has worn blinkers (extremely effectively). Turf high 78 - 4th of 13 giving 5lb to Forgotten Times (6 Spt Epsom 5f g-f RF 4266). Consistent.
**D Nicholls [0-9] J H Knight (from E A L Dunlop [2-7] May 1999).*

MIZOG RR 17f 28[11]
5 b m Selkirk (USA) 7.9f **(76)** - Embroideress (Stanford) 7.9f **(56)**
Form - 0
Record 2000 - 1st:0 2nd:0 3rd:0 Ran:1
Pre2000 - 1st:0 2nd:0 3rd:0 Ran:1
2000 AW 0-1: (12f) (Equi)
Currently poor filly.
**B A Pearce [0-1] Custom Racing (from J E Long [0-1] Spt 1997).*

MIZZEN MAST (USA) RR 95f 4952a[6]
2 gr c Cozzene (USA) 10.1f **(87)** - Kinema (USA) (Graustark) 10.1f **(70)**
Form - 26
2000 Turf 0-2: (8f 2) (sft, gd)
Currently very useful colt. Turf high 95 (began Spt).
**Mme C Head in FR [0-2].*

MJOLNIR RR 28f 584[10]
3 gr g Casteddu 7.4f **(54)** - Myjinka **(23f 47a)** (Myjinski (USA)) 9.5f **(54)**
Form - 60
Record 2000 - 1st:0 2nd:0 3rd:0 Ran:2
2000 Turf 0-1: (7f) (frm) 2000 AW 0-1: (8f) (Fibr)
Unfurnished, currently little account gelding.
**T T Clement [0-2] Ian Watkinson.*

MOBO-BACO BHB 47f **RR 63f** 4768[5]
3 ch g Bandmaster (USA) - Darakah **(37f 46a)** (Doulab (USA)) 9.8f **(65)**
Form - 040600005
Record 2000 - 1st:0 2nd:0 3rd:0 Ran:9
2000 Turf 0-9: (6f 3, 7f 3, 8f 3) (g-s 2, gd 4, g-f 2, frm)
Strong, average gelding. Turf high 63.
**R J Hodges [0-9] Frome Racing.*

MOBTAKER (IRE) RR 66f 3397[8]
2 b c Marju (IRE) 9.2f **(76)** - Absaar (USA) (Alleged (USA)) 10f **(76)**
Form - 8
Record 2000 - 1st:0 2nd:0 3rd:0 Ran:1
2000 Turf 0-1: (7f) (g-f)
Currently average colt. **B W Hills [0-1] Hamdan Al Maktoum.*

MODEL GROOM (USA) BHB 41f **RR 30f** 4620[4]
4 b c Dayjur (USA) 6.8f **(79)** - Model Bride (USA) (Blushing Groom (FR)) 10.3f **(76)**
Form - 654
Record 2000 - 1st:0 2nd:0 3rd:0 Ran:3
2000 Turf 0-3: (8f 3) (gd, g-f 2)
Very moderate colt. Turf high 30 (began Aug).
**A G Newcombe [0-4] A G Newcombe.*

MODEL QUEEN (USA) RR 67f 5076[3]
2 ch f Kingmambo (USA) 10.9f **(85)** - Model Bride (USA) (Blushing Groom (FR)) 10.3f **(76)**
Form - 3
Record 2000 - 1st:0 2nd:0 3rd:1 Ran:1
Win Prizemoney £0 *Total Prizemoney* £444
2000 Turf 0-1: (8f) (g-s)

Currently average filly. (1st run) - 3rd of 8 to Among Women (19 Oct Brighton 8f g-s RF 5076). **B W Hills [0-1] K Abdulla.*

MODEM (IRE) BHB 47f47a RR 58df 47a 5229[7]

3 b g Midhish - Holy Water (Monseigneur (USA)) 7.7f **(63)**
Form - 136407
Record 2000 - 1st:1 2nd:0 3rd:1 Ran:6
Pre2000 - 1st:0 2nd:0 3rd:0 Ran:3
Win Prizemoney £1,500 *Total Prizemoney* £2,249
Wins 2000 *Jan Southw (STD) S 7f 64 <*
2000 Turf 0-2: (7f, 8f) (gd 2) 2000 AW 1-4: (7f 1-1, 8f 3) (Fibr 1-4)
Scopey, fair gelding, effective 7f, - acts on Fibr, has worn blinkers. Turf high 48 (began Oct). AW high 64 (1st run) - 1st of 10 from Priceless Second (7 Jan Southwell RF 0042).
**D Shaw [0-5] J C Fretwell (from M H Tompkins [1-4] Jan 2000).*

MODERN BRITISH (IRE) RR 102f 2607[5]

3 ch g Indian Ridge 7.6f **(74)** - Touraya (Tap On Wood) 10.3f **(65)**
Form - 125
Record 2000 - 1st:1 2nd:1 3rd:0 Ran:3
Win Prizemoney £3,900 *Total Prizemoney* £7,384
Wins * 2000 Jun Goodwo (GD) 7f 84+ <
2000 Turf 1-3: (7f 1-1, 8f 2) (gd 1-3)
Workmanlike, currently very useful gelding. Turf high 102 - 2nd of 6 to Hymn (24 Jun Ascot 8f gd RF 2240). Unraced at two, he scored on his Goodwood debut and put up a good effort at Ascot on his second start. Held in decent company at Sandown on his third run. **G L Moore [1-3] Richard Green (Fine Paintings).*

MODEST HOPE (USA) BHB 11f15a RR 9f 15a 264[9]

13 b g Blushing Groom (FR) 10.2f **(80)** - Key Dancer (USA) (Nijinsky (CAN)) 10.3f **(77)**
Form - 0770
Record 2000 - 1st:0 2nd:0 3rd:0 Ran:4
Pre2000 - 1st:11 2nd:9 3rd:19 Ran:111
Win Prizemoney £29,709 *Total Prizemoney* £45,698
Wins * 1998 Aug Bright (FRM) SH 11.9f 26 34
1996 Jan Southw (STD) H 11f 44 48
2000 AW 0-4: (11f 2, 12f 2) (Fibr 4)
Poor gelding, effective 11 to 13f, - acts on AW, has worn blinkers, likes left handed tracks.
**Mrs S Lamyman [1-28] P Lamyman (from B Richmond [5-64] Spt 1996).*

MODESTY BHB 48f RR 47f 4965[28]

2 b f Bin Ajwaad (IRE) - Penny Dip **(86f)** (Cadeaux Genereux)
Form - 000
Record 2000 - 1st:0 2nd:0 3rd:0 Ran:3
2000 Turf 0-3: (6f 3) (gd, g-f, frm)
Currently moderate filly. Turf high 47 (began Jly).
**B N Doran [0-3] R P & M Berrow.*

MODIGLIANI (USA) RR 93f 5179a[5]

2 b c Danzig (USA) 8.1f **(88)** - Hot Princess (Hot Spark) 7.6f **(62)**
Form - 134255
2000 Turf 1-6: (5f 1-1, 6f 4, 7f) (sft 1-1, g-s, gd 2, g-f)
Useful colt, effective 6f, acts on gd, has worn blinkers. Turf high 93 - 3rd of 12 to Cd Europe (20 Jun Ascot 6f gd RF 2112). He failed to progress after finishing third in the Group 3 Coventry Stakes at Royal Ascot. Not an obvious improver, he may have peaked already. **A P O'Brien in IRE [1-6] Mrs John Magnier.*

MODISH (IRE) BHB 96f RR 98f 1220[2]

3 b c Tenby 10.4f **(76)** - Moorfield Daisy (IRE) (Waajib)
Form - 22
Record 2000 - 1st:0 2nd:2 3rd:0 Ran:2
Pre2000 - 1st:2 2nd:0 3rd:0 Ran:4
Win Prizemoney £7,203 *Total Prizemoney* £16,293
Wins * 1999 Spt Ayr (G-S) 8f 89 <
* 1999 Aug Beverl (GD) 7.5f 82+
2000 Turf 0-2: (10f, 14f) (sft, g-f)
Lengthy, very useful colt, effective 8 to 14f, acts on sft to g-f, best on g-f. Turf high 98 (1st run) - 2nd of 5 to Eternal Spring (26 Apr Epsom 10f sft RF 0878). He looked uncomfortable on fast ground at York in May and was not seen out again.
**M H Tompkins [2-6] Mrs Beryl Lockey.*

MODRIK (USA) BHB 90f RR 87f 5121[1]

2 ch c Dixieland Band (USA) 10.1f **(80)** - Seattle Summer (USA) (Seattle Slew (USA)) 9.4f **(76)**
Form - 83421
Record 2000 - 1st:1 2nd:1 3rd:1 Ran:5
Win Prizemoney £6,844 *Total Prizemoney* £8,923
Wins * 2000 Oct Doncas (SFT) H 7f 85 87 <
2000 Turf 1-5: (6f, 7f 1-3, 8f) (g-s 1-2, g-f 3)
Useful colt. Turf high 87 (began Jly) - 1st of 14 giving 6lb to My Lucy Locket (21 Oct Doncaster RF 5121).
**R W Armstrong [1-5] Hamdan Al Maktoum.*

MODUS OPERANDI (USA) BHB 82a RR 71f 3982[12]

4 b g Known Fact (USA) 8.3f **(72)** - Proud Lou (USA) (Proud Clarion) 8.7f **(82)**
Form - 640800
Record 2000 - 1st:0 2nd:0 3rd:0 Ran:6
Pre2000 - 1st:1 2nd:0 3rd:0 Ran:4
Win Prizemoney £2,960 *Total Prizemoney* £4,325
Wins 1999 Jun Redcar (FRM) 10f 79 <
2000 Turf 0-4: (9f 2, 10f 2) (gd, g-f, frm 2) 2000 AW 0-2: (10f, 12f) (Equi 2)
Well made, above-average gelding, effective 10f, acts on frm, likes tight tracks. Turf high 71 (began Jun). AW high 76. Inconsistent.
**K R Burke [0-6] Mrs Julie Mitchell (from H R A Cecil [1-4] Jun 1999).*

MOGIN BHB 25f27a RR 27f 27a 554[5]

7 ch m Komaite (USA) 6.9f **(61)** - Misdevious (USA) (Alleged (USA)) 10f **(76)**
Form - 00445
Record 2000 - 1st:0 2nd:0 3rd:0 Ran:4
Pre2000 - 1st:3 2nd:4 3rd:2 Ran:41
Win Prizemoney £6,463 *Total Prizemoney* £10,651
Wins *1998 Jan Lingfi (STD) H 10f 42 46*
1998 Jan Lingfi (STD) H 8f 38 41
1996 Aug Bright (G-F) 7f 51 <
2000 AW 0-4: (10f, 12f 2, 13f) (Equi 4)
Little account mare, effective 10f, - acts on Equi, has worn blinkers. AW high 29.
**L MontagueHall [0-7] Les Dutton (from A J McNae [0-6] Jly 1999).*

MOGUL BHB 43f49a RR 34f 49a 3526[7]

6 b g Formidable (USA) 7.8f **(60)** - Madiyla (Darshaan) 9.9f **(84)**
Form - 7
Record 2000 - 1st:0 2nd:0 3rd:0 Ran:1
Pre2000 - 1st:0 2nd:2 3rd:0 Ran:10
Win Prizemoney £0 *Total Prizemoney* £1,666
2000 Turf 0-1: (7f) (frm)
Very moderate gelding, has worn blinkers. Consistent. He showed improved form on the All-Weather during the winter, but showed little on turf.
**R J Baker [0-5] R J Baker (from N A Graham [0-9] Jly 1997).*

MOLE CREEK BHB 64f RR 55f 3053[10]

5 gr m Unfuwain (USA) 11.4f **(74)** - Nicholas Grey (Track Spare) 8.8f **(62)**
Form - 0070
Record 2000 - 1st:0 2nd:0 3rd:0 Ran:4
Pre2000 - 1st:1 2nd:6 3rd:0 Ran:11
Win Prizemoney £3,501 *Total Prizemoney* £13,976
Wins 1998 Oct Warwic (GD) 10.8f 83 <
2000 Turf 0-4: (12f 3, 13f) (gd, g-f, frm 2)
Fair filly. Turf high 55. Becoming disappointing.
**Miss H C Knight [0-6] Lord Vestey (from J R Fanshawe [1-11] May 1999).*

MOLLY BROWN BHB 90f RR 93f 5228[2]

3 b f Rudimentary (USA) 8.2f **(66)** - Sinking (Midyan (USA)) 6f **(60)**
Form - 04701220302
Record 2000 - 1st:1 2nd:3 3rd:1 Ran:11
Pre2000 - 1st:1 2nd:0 3rd:0 Ran:3
Win Prizemoney £7,697 *Total Prizemoney* £19,911
Wins * 2000 Jly Doncas (GD) H 6f 80 81
* 1999 Jun Haydoc (GD-) 5f 83+ <
2000 Turf 1-11: (5f, 6f 1-9, 7f) (sft, g-s 2, gd 5, g-f 2, frm 1-1)
Scopey, useful filly, effective 5 to 6f, acts on gd. Turf high 93. Inconsistent. She was kept busy in sprint handicaps and held her

form well. Probably suited by easy ground, she is tough.
**R Hannon [2-14] The Sinking Fast Partnership.*

MOLLY IRWIN (IRE) BHB 39f52a **RR 53f 52a** 4581[15]

2 b f General Monash (USA) - Bunny Run **(21f)** (Dowsing (USA))
Form - 31200070
Record 2000 - 1st:1 2nd:1 3rd:1 Ran:8
Win Prizemoney £1,844 *Total Prizemoney* £2,906
Wins * 2000 *Mar Wolver (STD) S 5f 48+* <
2000 Turf 0-6: (5f 4, 6f 2) (gd 4, g-f, frm) 2000 AW 1-2: (5f 1-2) (Fibr 1-2)
Fair filly, effective 5f, acts on gd - acts on Fibr. Turf high 53 - 2nd of 5 to Nine To Five (7 Apr Lingfield 5f gd RF 0633). AW high 48 (1st run) - 1st of 7 getting 5lb from Deceives The Eye (25 Mar Wolverhampton RF 0508). Landed a seller on the Wolverhampton Fibresand in March having only made her racecourse debut at Doncaster the previous day. **J S Moore [1-8] Alljays Racing.*

MOLLY MALONE RR 54f 4874[19]

3 gr f Formidable (USA) 7.8f **(60)** - Pharland (FR) (Bellypha) 9.8f **(73)**
Form - 6000
Record 2000 - 1st:0 2nd:0 3rd:0 Ran:4
2000 Turf 0-4: (6f, 7f, 8f 2) (g-s, gd 2, frm)
Workmanlike, fair filly. Turf high 56. **J C Tuck [0-4] G S Tuck.*

MOLLY-O (IRE) RR 95f 5181a[1]

4 b f Dolphin Street (FR) - Sweetest Thing **00**
Form - 326137431205171
2000 Turf 4-15: (8f 3-8, 9f 1-7) (hvy 2, sft 1-4, g-s 1-2, gd 3, g-f 1-2, frm 1-2)
Very useful filly, effective 8 to 9f, acts on sft to g-s, likes left handed tracks. Turf high 95 - 1st of 13 giving 3lb to Cakestown Lady (22 Oct Naas RF 5181a) - also 1st of 12 giving 6lb to Tango Pasion (1 Oct Cork RF 4802a). **M Halford in IRE [4-23] S Dalton.*

MOLLYTIME BHB 17f **RR 20f** 465[11]

4 ch f Timeless Times (USA) 6.1f **(56)** - Merry Molly **(22f)** (Deploy)
Form - 7870
Record 2000 - 1st:0 2nd:0 3rd:0 Ran:3
Pre2000 - 1st:0 2nd:0 3rd:0 Ran:9
2000 AW 0-3: (8f 2, 12f) (Fibr 3)
Leggy, little account filly, has worn blinkers. AW high 6.
**N Bycroft [0-13] G W H Burnett.*

MOLOMO RR 106f 4254a[7]

3 b f Barathea (IRE) - Nishan **00**
Form - 3227
2000 Turf 0-4: (8f, 10f 2, 12f) (g-s 2, gd 2)
Pattern-class filly. Turf high 106 - 2nd of 5 getting 3lb from Takali (20 Aug Curragh 10f gd RF 3891a). A maiden, he was beaten just a head in the Group Two Royal Whip at the Curragh.
**N Meade in IRE [0-4] Barouche Stud (Ireland) Ltd.*

MOMENTOUS JONES BHB 52f **RR 65f** 4021[8]

3 b g Emperor Jones (USA) - Ivory Moment (USA) (Sir Ivor) 10.2f **(70)**
Form - 78
Record 2000 - 1st:0 2nd:0 3rd:0 Ran:2
Pre2000 - 1st:0 2nd:1 3rd:0 Ran:4
Win Prizemoney £0 *Total Prizemoney* £654
2000 Turf 0-2: (10f 2) (g-f, frm)
Leggy, average gelding, effective 8f, acts on gd. Turf high 46 (began Aug).
**M Madgwick [0-2] Peter Taplin (from M R Channon [0-4] Nov 1999).*

MOMENTS IN TIME BHB 50f **RR 65f** 4215[19]

2 b f Emperor Jones (USA) - Dame Helene (USA) (Sir Ivor) 10.2f **(70)**
Form - 646570
Record 2000 - 1st:0 2nd:0 3rd:0 Ran:6
Win Prizemoney £0 *Total Prizemoney* £324
2000 Turf 0-6: (5f, 7f 4, 8f) (gd 3, g-f, frm 2)
Average filly. Turf high 65.
**M R Channon [0-6] Four Jays Racing Partnership.*

MONACLE BHB 42f39a **RR 43f 39a** 4648[2]

6 b g Saddlers' Hall (IRE) 10.5f **(65)** - Endless Joy (Law Society (USA)) 9.9f **(70)**
Form - 3412542
Record 2000 - 1st:1 2nd:2 3rd:1 Ran:7
Pre2000 - 1st:1 2nd:0 3rd:2 Ran:18
Win Prizemoney £5,563 *Total Prizemoney* £8,126
Wins * 2000 Jly Yarmou (GD) H 16f 36 41 <
* 1999 May Yarmou (FRM) H 11.5f 32 39
2000 Turf 1-6: (12f, 14f 3, 16f 1-2) (gd 1-3, g-f, frm, hrd) 2000 AW 0-1: (16f) (Fibr)
Moderate gelding, effective 11 to 16f, best at 16f, acts on gd to hrd - acts on Fibr, has worn blinkers, excels at Yarmouth, likes Southwell. Turf high 43 (began Jly) - 5th of 8 giving 13lb to Beauchamp Magic (14 Aug Thirsk 16f frm RF 3629) - also 1st of 7 getting 13lb from Xellance (31 Jly Yarmouth RF 3261). (1st run) - 2nd of 16 getting 16lb from Vincent (26 Spt Southwell 16f Fibr RF 4648). Improving.
**John Berry [2-19] Chris Benest (from D Morris [0-7] Oct 1997).*

MONACO (IRE) BHB 19f **RR 30f** 4184[7]

6 b g Classic Music (USA) 7.2f **(57)** - Larosterna (Busted) 10.2f **(61)**
Form - 0700077
Record 2000 - 1st:0 2nd:0 3rd:0 Ran:7
Pre2000 - 1st:0 2nd:0 3rd:2 Ran:15
Win Prizemoney £0 *Total Prizemoney* £1,359
2000 Turf 0-7: (7f 2, 8f, 9f 2, 11f, 12f) (g-s, g-f 2, frm 4)
Very moderate gelding, effective 9f, acts on frm, has worn blinkers, likes right handed tracks. Turf high 30.
**R Allan [0-25] R Allan (from L M Cumani [0-5] Aug 1997).*

MONASHEE MOUNTAIN (USA) RR 116f 2773[9]

3 b c Danzig (USA) 8.1f **(88)** - Prospectors Delite (USA)
Form - 11500
2000 Turf 2-5: (6f, 7f 2-3, 8f) (sft 2-2, gd 3)
High-class colt, effective 7f, acts on sft, has worn blinkers. Turf high 115 (1st run) - 1st of 6 giving 7lb to Jammaal (26 Mar Curragh RF 0539a). Unbeaten as a juvenile, he maintained that record with two workmanlike performances in the spring. Found wanting when moved up in class, he was not seen out after failing to figure in the six-furlong July Cup. Likely to appreciate further, he clearly has limitations but should win another Group race.
**A P O'Brien in IRE [4-7] M Tabor & Mrs John Magnier.*

MONASH FREEWAY (IRE) BHB 49f **RR 50f** 4270[13]

2 ch c General Monash (USA) - Pennine Pearl (IRE) (Pennine Walk) 8.5f **(61)**
Form - 000
Record 2000 - 1st:0 2nd:0 3rd:0 Ran:3
2000 Turf 0-3: (6f, 7f, 8f) (g-f, frm 2)
Currently fair colt. Turf high 53 (began Aug).
**Miss Jacqueline Doyle [0-3] A W Regan.*

MONASH LADY (IRE) BHB 49f **RR 49f** 4930[6]

2 ch f General Monash (USA) - Don't Be That Way (IRE) (Dance of Life (USA)) 7f **(66)**
Form - 466
Record 2000 - 1st:0 2nd:0 3rd:0 Ran:3
2000 Turf 0-3: (6f 2, 7f) (gd 2, frm)
Currently moderate filly. Turf high 49 (began Aug).
**J S Moore [0-3] G Patterson.*

MONAWARA (IRE) RR 82f 1846[18]

3 b f Namaqualand (USA) - Monus (IRE) (Thatching) 8f **(66)**
Form - 0
Record 2000 - 1st:0 2nd:0 3rd:0 Ran:1
Pre2000 - 1st:0 2nd:0 3rd:1 Ran:1
Win Prizemoney £0 *Total Prizemoney* £492
2000 Turf 0-1: (8f) (gd)
Currently decent filly. **M R Channon [0-2] Ahmed Al Shafar.*

MONDRAGON BHB 48f60a **RR 54f 60a** 2279[3]

10 b g Niniski (USA) 13.2f **(67)** - La Lutine (My Swallow) 9.2f **(71)**
Form - 253
Record 2000 - 1st:0 2nd:1 3rd:1 Ran:3
Pre2000 - 1st:5 2nd:10 3rd:10 Ran:54
Win Prizemoney £15,953 *Total Prizemoney* £38,308
Wins * 1998 Aug Beverl (G-F) H 16.2f 59 62
* 1998 Jly Redcar (G-F) H 16f 55 57
2000 Turf 0-3: (16f 3) (g-f, frm 2)
Average gelding. Turf high 54. **Mrs M Reveley [6-58] D Young.*

MONDURU BHB 50f **RR 66df** 5007^{9}

3 b c Lion Cavern (USA) 7.5f **(74)** - Bint Albadou (IRE) (Green Desert (USA)) 8.6f **(78)**

Form - 7357000

Record	**2000** -	1st:0	2nd:0	3rd:1	Ran:7
	Pre2000 -	1st:0	2nd:0	3rd:0	Ran:1

Win Prizemoney £0 *Total Prizemoney* £605

2000 Turf 0-6: (7f, 8f 3, 10f 2) (sft, g-s, gd 2, g-f, frm) 2000 AW 0-1: (12f) (Fibr)

Scopey, average colt, effective 7f, acts on sft. Turf high 68 - 3rd of 12 giving 5lb to Wildflower (24 Apr Kempton 7f sft RF 0834). Becoming disappointing. **W R Muir [0-8] J Haim.*

MONICA BHB 40f **RR 31f** 3337^{9}

2 ch f Democratic (USA) - Smocking **(37f 25a)** (Night Shift (USA)) 7.2f **(69)**

Form - 0045600

Record	**2000** -	1st:0	2nd:0	3rd:0	Ran:7

2000 Turf 0-7: (5f 6, 7f) (gd, frm 6)

Very moderate filly. Turf high 31. **W T Kemp [0-7] W T Kemp.*

MONICA GELLER BHB 70f62a **RR 71?f 62a** 4818^{6}

2 b f Komaite (USA) 6.9f **(61)** - Rion River (IRE) (Taufan (USA)) 7f **(57)**

Form - 7637362166

Record	**2000** -	1st:1	2nd:1	3rd:2	Ran:10

Win Prizemoney £4,416 *Total Prizemoney* £6,774

Wins	* **2000**	Spt	Goodwo	(SFT)	H	8f	57	61	<

2000 Turf 1-6: (7f 4, 8f 1-2) (g-s 1-2, g-f, frm 3) 2000 AW 0-4: (5f, 6f 2, 7f) (Fibr 4)

Above-average filly, effective 7 to 8f, acts on g-s to g-f. Turf high 71 (began Aug) - 6th of 22 getting 18lb from Palatial (26 Spt Newmarket 7f g-f RF 4642). AW high 53. Consistent in her early starts, but did not get off the mark until tackling a mile at Goodwood in September.

**C N Allen [1-10] Newmarket Connections Ltd.*

MONKEY BUSINESS BHB 59f **RR 68f** 5150^{5}

3 b f Warning 8.1f **(77)** - Rosie Sweetheart (IRE) **(70f)** (Sadler's Wells (USA)) 10f **(76)**

Form - 06005

Record	**2000** -	1st:0	2nd:0	3rd:0	Ran:5
	Pre2000 -	1st:0	2nd:0	3rd:1	Ran:2

Win Prizemoney £0 *Total Prizemoney* £832

2000 Turf 0-4: (8f, 10f 3) (gd, frm 2, hrd) 2000 AW 0-1: (10f) (Equi)

Unfurnished, average filly. Turf high 68.

**N A Callaghan [0-7] Wafic Said.*

MONKSTON POINT (IRE) BHB 103f **RR 108f** 5324^{7}

4 b g Fayruz 6.6f **(63)** - Doon Belle (Ardoon) 7.3f **(53)**

Form - 11713007087

Record	**2000** -	1st:3	2nd:0	3rd:1	Ran:11
	Pre2000 -	1st:3	2nd:1	3rd:4	Ran:17

Win Prizemoney £46,591 *Total Prizemoney* £97,297

Wins	* **2000**	May	Kempto	(SFT)	L	5f		108	
	* **2000**	Apr	Kempto	(SFT)		6f		110+	<
	* **2000**	Apr	Newbur	(SFT)	H	5.2f	95	99	
	* 1998	Spt	Ayr	(G-S)	L	5f		99+	
	* 1998	Jun	Bath	(G-S)		5.1f		93	
	* 1998	Apr	Bath	(SFT)		5.1f		88	

2000 Turf 3-11: (5f 2-4, 6f 1-7) (sft, g-s 3-5, gd 5)

Workmanlike, Pattern-class gelding, effective 5 to 6f, acts on g-s, has worn blinkers (very effectively). Turf high 110 - 1st of 8 giving 13lb to Presentation (24 Apr Kempton RF 0838) - also 1st of 8 giving 9lb to Vita Spericolata (27 May Kempton RF 1499). A smart juvenile in 1998, he bounced back to his best on soft ground in the spring, winning a Listed heat at Kempton. Far from disgraced in Group company thereafter, he is unlikely to improve but could do well in the first half of the season if conditions are favourable.

**D W P Arbuthnot [6-28] Derrick Broomfield.*

MONO LADY (IRE) BHB 70f73a **RR 73f 73a** 4994^{5}

7 b m Polish Patriot (USA) 7.8f **(70)** - Phylella (Persian Bold) 9.3f **(66)**

Form - 0284514435

Record	**2000** -	1st:1	2nd:1	3rd:1	Ran:10
	Pre2000 -	1st:7	2nd:7	3rd:4	Ran:44

Win Prizemoney £31,833 *Total Prizemoney* £45,503

Wins	* **2000**	*Jun*	*Wolver*	*(STD)*	H	*12f*	*65*	*69*	
	* 1999	May	Cheste	(G-F)	H	12.3f	65	68	
	* 1998	Aug	Leices	(GD)	H	11.8f	72	74	<
	* 1997	Spt	Bright	(G-F)	H	11.9f	60	68	
	* 1997	*May*	*Lingfi*	*(STD)*	*H*	*10f*	*63*	*71*	
	* 1997	*Jan*	*Southw*	*(STD)*	*H*	*8f*	*54*	*58*	
	* 1997	*Jan*	*Wolver*	*(SLW)*	*H*	*9.4f*	*48*	*52*	
	* 1996	Oct	Folkes	(G-S)	H	9.7f	51	57	

2000 Turf 0-4: (12f 4) (gd, g-f, frm 2) 2000 AW 1-6: (9f, 12f 1-5) (Equi 3, Fibr 1-3)

Above-average mare, effective 12f, acts on gd to frm - acts on AW, best on g-f, often wears blinkers (extremely effectively), excels at Chester. Turf high 73 - 4th of 5 giving 26lb to May King Mayhem (30 Jun Newmarket 12f g-f RF 2411). AW high 69 - 1st of 5 giving 25lb to Irish Cream (21 Jun Wolverhampton RF 2172). Won at Chester's May meeting in 1999, but is basically very inconsistent. Best on a sharp left-handed track.

**D HaydnJones [8-54] Monolithic Refractories Ltd.*

MONONGAHELA (IRE) BHB 40f **RR 24f** 4477^{10}

6 b g Caerleon (USA) 10.9f **(79)** - Monoglow (Kalaglow) 9.8f **(67)**

Form - 00

Record	**2000** -	1st:0	2nd:0	3rd:0	Ran:2
	Pre2000 -	1st:2	2nd:1	3rd:3	Ran:16

Win Prizemoney £6,507 *Total Prizemoney* £10,136

Wins	1997	Jly	Naas	(GD)	10f	76	
	1997	Apr	Navan	(GD)	8f	77	<

2000 Turf 0-1: (12f) (frm) 2000 AW 0-1: (15f) (Fibr)

Little account gelding, has worn blinkers.

**J G M O'Shea [0-4] W Tyler (from A P O'Brien in IRE [2-16] Oct 1997).*

Monkston Point (far side), has a habit of winning in the spring

MONOS (GER) **RR 93f** $5214a^{6}$

2 f

Form - 6

2000 Turf 0-1: (8f) (hvy)

Currently useful. **A Lowe in GER [0-1].*

MON POTE LE GITAN (FR) **RR 106f** $1290a^{6}$

3 ch c Thunder Gulch (USA) - Firm Friend (IRE) **(100f)** (Affirmed (USA)) 9.3f **(79)**

Form - 6

2000 Turf 0-1: (8f) (gd)

Currently Pattern-class colt. **D Smaga in FR [0-2].*

MON PREFERE (FR) BHB 63f **RR 32f** 5316^{14}

5 ch g Pistolet Bleu (IRE) - Salve (Sallust) 8.4f **(63)**

Form - 0

Record	**2000** -	1st:0	2nd:0	3rd:0	Ran:1

2000 Turf 0-1: (8f) (g-s)

Currently moderate gelding. **I A Wood [0-1] Neardown Stables.*

MONSAJEM (USA) BHB 106f **RR 110f** 4611^{8}

5 ch h Woodman (USA) 9.7f **(77)** - Fairy Dancer (USA) (Nijinsky (CAN)) 10.3f **(77)**

Form - 6043518

Record	**2000** -	1st:1	2nd:0	3rd:1	Ran:7
	Pre2000 -	1st:6	2nd:0	3rd:6	Ran:21

Win Prizemoney £71,529 *Total Prizemoney* £92,708

Wins	Year	Mth	Course	Going		Dist		RR	
Wins	* 2000	Aug	Haydoc	(G-S)		11.9f		110	<
	* 1999	Oct	Ascot	(G-S)	H	10f	105	109	
	* 1999	Aug	Newbur	(GD)	H	11f	103	103	
	* 1999	Jun	Epsom	(GD,)	H	10.1f	98	103	
	* 1998	Oct	Yarmou	(SFT)		10.1f		89+	
	* 1998	Oct	Yarmou	(G-S)	H	10.1f	85	88	
	1997	Aug	Chepst	(GD)		8.1f		76	

2000 Turf 1-6: (10f 4, 12f 1-2) (sft, g-s 2, gd 1-2, g-f) 2000 AW 0-1: (12f) (Dirt)

Group-class colt, effective 10 to 12f, best at 10f, acts on sft to g-f, best on gd, has worn blinkers, likes left handed tracks, excels at Kempton and Epsom. Turf high 110 - 1st of 4 from Capri (19 Aug Haydock RF 3779). He proved difficult to place, but was given a smart tactical ride when winning a conditions race at Haydock in August. Best on easy ground, he was sold for 115,000gns at Newmarket in October and will continue his career with Darrell Vienna in America.

**E A L Dunlop [6-23] Khalifa Sultan (from S bin Suroor [1-5] Oct 1997).*

MON SECRET (IRE) BHB 68f61a **RR 73f 61a** 4932[21]

2 b c General Monash (USA) - Ron's Secret **(70f)** (Efisio)

Form - 832414000

Record 2000 - 1st:1 2nd:1 3rd:1 Ran:9

Win Prizemoney £4,030 *Total Prizemoney* £6,283

Wins * 2000 Jun Carlis (G-F) 5.9f 69 <

2000 Turf 1-9: (5f 4, 6f 1-4, 7f) (gd 4, g-f 3, frm 1-2)

Above-average colt, effective 5 to 6f, acts on g-f to frm. Turf high 73 - also 1st of 10 giving 5lb to Eau Rouge (28 Jun Carlisle RF 2324).

**J L Eyre [1-9] Pinnacle Monash Partnership.*

MONSIEUR LE BLANC (IRE) BHB 80f **RR 78f** 4283[7]

2 b c Alzao (USA) 9.8f **(73)** - Dedara (Head for Heights) 9.6f **(55)**

Form - 63567

Record 2000 - 1st:0 2nd:0 3rd:1 Ran:5

Win Prizemoney £0 *Total Prizemoney* £1,120

2000 Turf 0-5: (6f, 7f 2, 8f 2) (gd, g-f, frm 3)

Above-average colt, has worn blinkers. Turf high 78 - 3rd of 12 to No Excuse Needed (8 Jly Sandown 7f frm RF 2644).

**I A Balding [0-5] Kennet Valley Thoroughbreds IV.*

MONSIEUR RICK BHB 80a **RR 80a** 363[4]

3 b c Sillery (USA) - Movieland (USA) (Nureyev (USA)) 8.7f **(78)**

Form - 3414

Record 2000 - 1st:1 2nd:0 3rd:1 Ran:4

Win Prizemoney £2,782 *Total Prizemoney* £4,006

Wins * 2000 *Feb Lingfi (STD) 10f 71* <

2000 AW 1-4: (8f 2, 10f 1-2) (Equi 1-3, Fibr)

Unfurnished, decent colt. AW high 80 - also 1st of 8 from You da Man (16 Feb Lingfield RF 0289).

**Miss Gay Kelleway [1-4] The Dan Abbott Racing Partnership Two.*

MONTALBAN (GER) RR 115f 5215a[3]

4 ch c Mondrian (GER) - Majestic Image (Niniski (USA)) 10.6f **(65)**

Form - 513

2000 Turf 1-3: (12f 1-3) (hvy, gd 1-2)

High-class colt, effective 11 to 12f, acts on hvy to gd. Turf high 115 - 3rd of 10 to Golden Snake (22 Oct San Siro 12f hvy RF 5215a).

**A Lowe in GER [1-9] Stall Hanse.*

MONTALCINO (IRE) BHB 97f **RR 97f** 4600[2]

4 b g Robellino (USA) 9.5f **(68)** - Only Gossip (USA) (Trempolino (USA)) 12f **(71)**

Form - 5422

Record 2000 - 1st:0 2nd:2 3rd:0 Ran:4

Pre2000 - 1st:1 2nd:2 3rd:1 Ran:8

Win Prizemoney £4,143 *Total Prizemoney* £21,496

Wins 1999 May Goodwo (GD) 12f 78+ <

2000 Turf 0-4: (12f, 14f 2, 16f) (g-s, gd 2, g-f)

Scopey, very useful gelding, effective 12 to 16f, best at 14f, acts on g-s to g-f, excels at Goodwood. Turf high 97 - 2nd of 15 giving 15lb to Mbele (23 Spt Ascot 16f gd RF 4600). Consistent. Improved as went up in trip in '99, and ran a couple of fair races early last term. Capable of winning a decent handicap.

**P J Makin [0-5] The late Dr Carlos E Stelling (from P W Chapple-Hyam [1-7] Spt 1999).*

MONTANA MISS (IRE) BHB 78f **RR 79f** 5106[7]

2 b f Earl of Barking (IRE) - Cupid Miss (Anita's Prince)

Form - 411637

Record 2000 - 1st:2 2nd:0 3rd:1 Ran:6

Win Prizemoney £5,124 *Total Prizemoney* £6,028

Wins	Year	Mth	Course	Going	Dist	RR	
Wins	* 2000	Jly	Catter	(G-F)	7f	83	<
	* 2000	Jun	Beverl	(G-F)	7.5f	58+	

2000 Turf 2-6: (6f, 7f 2-5) (g-s, gd 2, frm 2-3)

Above-average filly, effective 7f, acts on g-s to frm. Turf high 83 - 1st of 6 from Parvenue (19 Jly Catterick RF 2922).

**B Palling [2-6] Mrs A L Stacey.*

MONTE CARLO (IRE) BHB 102f **RR 104f** 928[6]

3 b c Rainbows For Life (CAN) 9.3f **(64)** - Roberts Pride (Roberto (USA)) 10f **(76)**

Form - 86

Record 2000 - 1st:0 2nd:0 3rd:0 Ran:2

Pre2000 - 1st:2 2nd:0 3rd:2 Ran:5

Win Prizemoney £14,674 *Total Prizemoney* £15,816

Wins	Year	Mth	Course	Going		Dist	RR	
Wins	* 1999	Oct	Newmar	(SFT)	L	10f	104	<
	* 1999	Spt	Epsom	(GD)		8.5f	77	

2000 Turf 0-2: (10f, 11f) (hvy, sft)

Strong, very useful colt, effective 10f, acts on gd. Turf high 104. Won twice at two including the Listed Zetland Stakes over ten furlongs, but well beaten in two April outings in 2000.

**R Hannon [2-7] Highclere Thoroughbred Racing Ltd.*

MONTECRISTO BHB 80f90a **RR 90f 90a** 5297[4]

7 br g Warning 8.1f **(77)** - Sutosky (Great Nephew) 9.9f **(64)**

Form - 35545304

Record 2000 - 1st:0 2nd:0 3rd:2 Ran:8

Pre2000 - 1st:14 2nd:2 3rd:7 Ran:45

Win Prizemoney £62,327 *Total Prizemoney* £83,947

Wins	Year	Mth	Course	Going		Dist		RR	
Wins	* 1999	Spt	Hamilt	(SFT)	H	13f	90	90	<
	* 1999	Aug	Newbur	(GD)		12f		90	<
	* 1998	Spt	Epsom	(SFT)	H	12f	83	86	
	* 1998	Jly	Bright	(GD)	H	11.9f	77	82	
	* 1998	Mar	Warwic	(G-S)	H	12.5f	73	77	
	* 1998	*Feb*	*Wolver*	*(STD)*	*H*	*12f*	*72*	*71+*	
	* 1997	*Nov*	*Wolver*	*(STD)*		*12f*		*73+*	
	* 1997	Nov	Nottin	(GD)		14.1f		74	
	* 1997	*Oct*	*Southw*	*(STD)*		*12f*		*51*	
	* 1997	Spt	Newbur	(SFT)	H	12f	66	70	
	* 1997	Aug	Hamilt	(G-F)	H	11.1f	62	65	
	* 1996	Apr	Beverl	(G-F)	C	9.9f		65	
	* 1996	*Feb*	*Lingfi*	*(STD)*	*C*	*12f*		*54*	
	* 1996	*Feb*	*Lingfi*	*(STD)*	*H*	*10f*	*60*	*70*	

2000 Turf 0-8: (12f 6, 16f 2) (sft, g-s 3, gd 3, hrd)

Useful gelding, effective 12 to 16f, best at 12f, acts on sft to gd, likes tight tracks, does well at Epsom. Turf high 92 (1st run) - 3rd of 11 giving 4lb to Zilarator (26 Apr Epsom 12f sft RF 0879). Consistent. Suited by easy ground, he stays a mile and three-quarters but was not at his best last year. **R Guest [14-53] Rae Guest.*

MONTE MAYOR GOLF (IRE) BHB 62f78a **RR 59f 78a** 5019[1]

2 b f Case Law 6f **(64)** - Nishiki (USA) (Brogan (USA))

Form - 0506871

Record 2000 - 1st:1 2nd:0 3rd:0 Ran:7

Win Prizemoney £2,219 *Total Prizemoney* £2,219

Wins * 2000 *Oct Wolver (STD) 7f 69* <

2000 Turf 0-5: (5f, 6f 3, 7f) (gd 2, g-f, frm 2) 2000 AW 1-2: (6f, 7f 1-1) (Fibr 1-2)

Useful filly, effective 7f, - acts on Fibr. Turf high 53. AW high 69 (began Spt) - 1st of 9 getting 6lb from Sylvan Girl (17 Oct Wolverhampton RF 5019).

**D HaydnJones [1-7] Mrs E M HaydnJones.*

MONTENDRE BHB 42f **RR 32f** 2039[9]

13 b g Longleat (USA) 7.2f **(59)** - La Lutine (My Swallow) 9.2f **(71)**

Form - 0000

Record 2000 - 1st:0 2nd:0 3rd:0 Ran:4

Pre2000 - 1st:9 2nd:14 3rd:17 Ran:98

Win Prizemoney £61,552 *Total Prizemoney* £161,082

Wins	Year	Mth	Course	Going		Dist		RR
Wins	* 1999	Jly	Kempto	(G-F)	C	6f		56
	* 1998	Aug	Haydoc	(GD)	C	6f		66
	* 1998	Apr	Nottin	(SFT)	C	5.1f		62
	1997	Spt	Bath	(GD)	H	5.7f	75	78

2000 Turf 0-4: (6f 3, 7f) (sft, g-s, g-f, hrd)

Very moderate gelding, effective 6f, acts on frm. Turf high 32. Inconsistent.
**R J Hodges [3-36] David Mort (from M J Heaton-Ellis [1-5] Oct 1997).*

MONTEV LADY BHB 61f **RR 60f** 4926[8]
2 ch f Greensmith - Flair Lady **(15f 37a)** (Chilibang)
Form - 01408
Record 2000 - 1st:1 2nd:0 3rd:0 Ran:5
Win Prizemoney £2,247 *Total Prizemoney* £2,510
Wins * 2000 Aug Bath (G-F) S 5.1f 60 <
2000 Turf 1-4: (5f 1-2, 6f 2) (gd 2, frm 1-2) 2000 AW 0-1: (6f) (Equi)
Average filly. Turf high 60 (began Jly) - 1st of 18 from Tuscan (8 Aug Bath RF 3441). **W G M Turner [1-5] Mrs M S Teversham.*

MONTICELLO (IRE) RR 18f 4031[6]
8 ch g Accordion 11.3f **(75)** - Erck (Sun Prince) 12.4f **(52)**
Form - 6
Record 2000 - 1st:0 2nd:0 3rd:0 Ran:1
2000 Turf 0-1: (12f) (frm)
Poor gelding.
**M P Muggeridge [0-7] Brian A Lewendon & Mrs Carol Lewendon.*

MONTJEU (IRE) RR 135f 5331a[7]
4 ch c Sadler's Wells (USA) 11.3f **(87)** - Floripedes (FR) (Top Ville) 11.7f **(68)**
Form - 41111127
2000 Turf 4-7: (10f, 11f 1-1, 12f 3-5) (g-s 1-1, gd 3-5, frm)
Exceptional colt, effective 10 to 12f, best at 12f, acts on sft to gd, best on gd, likes right handed tracks, and excels at Curragh. Turf high 135 - 1st of 4 giving 3lb to Daring Miss (2 Jly Saint-cloud RF 2582a) - also 1st of 7 from Fantastic Light (29 Jly Ascot RF 3203). He returned as good as ever early on last year with Group One victories at Leopardstown and Saint-Cloud in his first two starts before treating his rivals with utter contempt in the King George. He had nothing more than a workout when winning a slowly-run Prix Foy but, for whatever reason, ran below his best in his bid for his second Arc. Unfortunately, the season ended with further disappointment when he finished behind Kalanisi in both the Champion Stakes and Breeders Cup Turf. A magnificent specimen of a thoroughbred, he had a devastating turn of foot when on song. **J E Hammond in FR [9-14] M Tabor.*

MONT ROCHER (FR) RR 115f 4562a[2]
5 b g Caerleon (USA) 10.9f **(79)** - Cuixmala (IRE)
Form - 232
2000 Turf 0-3: (10f, 13f 2) (g-s, gd 2)
High-class gelding, has worn blinkers. Turf high 115 (began Aug) - 2nd of 8 getting 3lb from Agol Lack (13 Spt Maisons-laffitte 10f gd RF 4562a). He is a tricky ride and has been tried in blinkers. Seemingly best when produced late, he is worth a try over extended distances. **J E Hammond in FR [1-4] Tsega Ltd.*

MONUMENT BHB 41f34a **RR 57f 34a** 3260[12]
8 ch g Cadeaux Genereux 7.9f **(76)** - In Perpetuity (Great Nephew) 9.9f **(64)**
Form - 300
Record 2000 - 1st:0 2nd:0 3rd:1 Ran:3
Pre2000 - 1st:6 2nd:1 3rd:3 Ran:32
Win Prizemoney £18,697 *Total Prizemoney* £22,013
Wins * 1999 Jun Bath (FRM) CH 8f 56 62
* 1998 Aug Kempto (G-F) H 12f 56 58
* 1997 Jly Nottin (G-F) 10f 65
* 1996 Jly Windso (G-F) H 10f 65 64
* 1996 Jun Salisb (G-F) C 8f 62
2000 Turf 0-3: (12f 3) (frm 3)
Fair gelding, has broken blood-vessels, effective 8f, acts on hrd. Turf high 55.
**J S King [6-38] V Askew (from R Charlton [1-5] Spt 1995).*

MOO-AZ (USA) RR 85+f 3382[1]
3 b c Red Ransom (USA) 8.6f **(83)** - Fappies Cosy Miss (USA) (Fappiano (USA)) 8.7f **(77)**
Form - 1
Record 2000 - 1st:1 2nd:0 3rd:0 Ran:1
Win Prizemoney £4,319 *Total Prizemoney* £4,319
Wins * 2000 Aug Thirsk (GD) 8f 85 <
2000 Turf 1-1: (8f 1-1) (frm 1-1)
Lengthy, currently useful colt. (1st run) - 1st of 3 giving 5lb to Caballe (4 Aug Thirsk RF 3382).
**M P Tregoning [1-1] Hamdan Al Maktoum.*

MOOCHA CHA MAN BHB 58f60a **RR 57df 60a** 4758[6]
4 b g Sizzling Melody 6.3f **(49)** - Nilu (IRE) (Ballad Rock) 7.8f **(63)**
Form - 705000516
Record 2000 - 1st:1 2nd:0 3rd:0 Ran:9
Pre2000 - 1st:2 2nd:2 3rd:2 Ran:18
Win Prizemoney £7,604 *Total Prizemoney* £10,667
Wins * 2000 *Spt Wolver (STD) H 6f 57 62*
* 1999 Aug Pontef (G-F) C 5f 65 <
* 1998 *Jly Wolver (STD) 5f 65* <
2000 Turf 0-4: (5f 2, 6f 2) (gd, frm, hrd 2) 2000 AW 1-5: (6f 1-5) (Fibr 1-5)
Workmanlike, average gelding, effective 5 to 6f, best at 6f, acts on sft to frm - acts on Fibr, has worn blinkers (effectively), likes left handed tracks, likes tight tracks, does well at Nottingham. Turf high 49. AW high 62 - 1st of 13 getting 5lb from Carols Choice (16 Spt Wolverhampton RF 4476).
**B A McMahon [3-27] Michael Sturgess.*

MOON AT NIGHT BHB 65f60a **RR 69f 60a** 4929[12]
5 gr g Pursuit of Love 9.5f **(69)** - La Nureyeva (USA) (Nureyev (USA)) 8.7f **(78)**
Form - 1030700
Record 2000 - 1st:1 2nd:0 3rd:1 Ran:7
Pre2000 - 1st:3 2nd:0 3rd:1 Ran:13
Win Prizemoney £13,176 *Total Prizemoney* £14,014
Wins * 2000 May Bright (G-F) H 8f 64 69 <
* 1999 Aug Bright (G-S) H 8f 59 60
* 1999 Jly Chepst (G-F) H 7.1f 56 60
* 1998 Spt Goodwo (G-F) CH 8f 50 55
2000 Turf 1-6: (7f 2, 8f 1-4) (g-s, g-f 2, frm 1-2, hrd) 2000 AW 0-1: (8f) (Equi)
Average gelding, effective 7 to 8f, best at 8f, acts on gd to frm, best on frm, likes left handed tracks. Turf high 69 (1st run) - 1st of 14 giving 13lb to Junikay (4 May Brighton RF 1016).
**L G Cottrell [4-17] H C Seymour (from I A Balding [0-3] Jun 1998).*

MOON COLONY BHB 44f50a **RR 53f 50a** 4404[6]
7 b g Top Ville 11f **(71)** - Honeymooning (USA) (Blushing Groom (FR)) 10.3f **(76)**
Form - 006
Record 2000 - 1st:0 2nd:0 3rd:0 Ran:2
Pre2000 - 1st:3 2nd:4 3rd:3 Ran:26
Win Prizemoney £13,837 *Total Prizemoney* £21,609
Wins 1998 Jly Newmar (G-F) H 12f 76 79
1998 Jly Doncas (G-F) H 12f 73 74
1997 Oct Nottin (SFT) 14.1f 81 <
2000 Turf 0-2: (12f, 16f) (g-s, g-f)
Fair gelding, effective 12f, acts on frm, likes tight tracks. Turf high 53 (began Spt). Inconsistent.
**A L Forbes [0-5] Tony Forbes (from Lady Herries [3-26] Nov 1999).*

MOON DREAM BHB 27f **RR 30f** 3449[17]
4 gr f Interrex (CAN) 7.7f **(51)** - Zamoon (Zambrano) 6.1f **(37)**
Form - 080
Record 2000 - 1st:0 2nd:0 3rd:0 Ran:3
Pre2000 - 1st:0 2nd:0 3rd:0 Ran:3
2000 Turf 0-3: (7f 2, 8f) (gd, g-f, frm)
Leggy, very moderate filly.
**J G Smyth-Osbourne [0-6] Edenwood Partnership.*

MOON EMPEROR BHB 93f **RR 95f** 4309[7]
3 b c Emperor Jones (USA) - Sir Hollow (USA) (Sir Ivor) 10.2f **(70)**
Form - 1857
Record 2000 - 1st:1 2nd:0 3rd:0 Ran:4
Pre2000 - 1st:0 2nd:0 3rd:1 Ran:4
Win Prizemoney £3,588 *Total Prizemoney* £4,671
Wins * 2000 Apr Ripon (SFT) 8f 84 <
2000 Turf 1-4: (7f, 8f 1-3) (gd 1-3, frm)
Scopey, very useful colt, effective 8f, acts on g-f. Turf high 95. He ran out the decisive winner of a Ripon maiden in the spring and was sold for 22,000gns at Newmarket in October. Already successful over hurdles and on the All-Weather for his new connections, he is a versatile individual.
**H Akbary [1-8] Egerton Stud Farm Ltd.*

MOON GLOW (IRE) RR 75f
4194[24]

4 b g Fayruz 6.6f **(63)** - Jarmar Moon **(55f)** (Unfuwain (USA))
Form - 4270
Record 2000 - 1st:0 2nd:1 3rd:0 Ran:4
Pre2000 - 1st:0 2nd:1 3rd:2 Ran:9
Win Prizemoney £0 *Total Prizemoney* £4,155
2000 Turf 0-4: (7f, 8f, 9f, 10f) (g-f, frm, hrd 2)
Scopey, above-average gelding, effective 8 to 9f, acts on gd to frm, prefers tight tracks. Turf high 75. **Miss S E Hall [1-17] C Platts.*

MOON GOD (USA) BHB 80f RR 89df
1677[3]

3 b c Thunder Gulch (USA) - Lyric Fantasy (IRE) (Tate Gallery (USA)) 7.4f **(67)**
Form - 3
Record 2000 - 1st:0 2nd:0 3rd:1 Ran:1
Pre2000 - 1st:0 2nd:2 3rd:1 Ran:4
Win Prizemoney £0 *Total Prizemoney* £3,154
2000 Turf 0-1: (7f) (g-f)
Useful colt.
**E A L Dunlop [0-1] Manchester United Racing Club (from A P O'Brien in IRE [0-4] Oct 1999).*

MOONJAZ RR 87+f
4754[3]

3 ch c Nashwan (USA) 10.3f **(79)** - Harayir (USA) **(116f)** (Gulch (USA)) 8f **(81)**
Form - 3
Record 2000 - 1st:0 2nd:0 3rd:1 Ran:1
Win Prizemoney £0 *Total Prizemoney* £643
2000 Turf 0-1: (10f) (g-s)
Scopey, currently useful colt. (1st run) - 3rd of 17 giving 5lb to Return (30 Spt Sandown 10f g-s RF 4754).
**S bin Suroor [0-1] Godolphin.*

MOONLADY (GER) RR 110+f
5212a[7]

3 b f Platini (GER) - Midnight Fever (GER) (Sure Blade (USA)) 11.3f **(67)**
Form - 1117
2000 Turf 3-4: (11f 1-1, 12f 1-1, 14f 1-1, 16f) (hvy 1-2, sft 1-1, gd 1-1)
Group-class filly. Turf high 110 - 1st of 8 getting 4lb from Aeskulap (1 Oct Dortmund RF 4842a) - also 1st of 8 from Well Minded (10 Spt Hanover RF 4414a). **H Remmert in GER [3-4].*

MOONLIGHT DANCER BHB 68f66a RR 82f 66a
4808[17]

2 b c Polar Falcon (USA) 9f **(74)** - Guanhumara (Caerleon (USA)) 8.6f **(71)**
Form - 422725750
Record 2000 - 1st:0 2nd:3 3rd:0 Ran:9
Win Prizemoney £0 *Total Prizemoney* £3,603
2000 Turf 0-9: (5f 4, 6f 3, 7f 2) (g-s, gd 3, g-f 2, frm 3)
Decent colt, effective 5 to 7f, acts on gd to g-f, best on g-f. Turf high 82 - 2nd of 21 getting 3lb from Man of Distinction (14 Jun Kempton 6f g-f RF 1961).
**R Hannon [0-9] The Mystery Partnership.*

MOONLIGHT FLIT BHB 42a RR 38f
15[5]

5 b m Presidium 7.5f **(56)** - Moonwalker (Night Shift (USA)) 7.2f **(69)**
Form - 7505
Record 2000 - 1st:0 2nd:0 3rd:0 Ran:1
Pre2000 - 1st:3 2nd:0 3rd:5 Ran:25
Win Prizemoney £7,629 *Total Prizemoney* £9,598

Wins							
* 1999	*Mar Southw*	*(STD)*	*H*	*8f*	*41*	*50*	
1998	Aug Pontef	(G-F)	S	10f		38	
1997	Spt Beverl	(G-F)	SH	7.5f	54	63	<

2000 AW 0-1: (8f) (Fibr)
Very moderate filly, effective 8f, - acts on Fibr, has worn blinkers, prefers left handed tracks.
**J L Eyre [1-17] The Claire King Partnership (from J G FitzGerald [2-9] Aug 1998).*

MOONLIGHT MONTY BHB 49f RR 58df
5020[12]

4 ch g Elmaamul (USA) 8.1f **(70)** - Lovers Light (Grundy) 10.3f **(65)**
Form - 300
Record 2000 - 1st:0 2nd:0 3rd:1 Ran:3
Pre2000 - 1st:0 2nd:0 3rd:1 Ran:6
Win Prizemoney £0 *Total Prizemoney* £1,159
2000 Turf 0-2: (14f, 16f) (g-s, frm) 2000 AW 0-1: (12f) (Fibr)
Scopey, fair gelding. Turf high 58 (1st run) - 3rd of 15 getting 21lb from Noukari (29 Mar Catterick 14f frm RF 0546). Inconsistent.
**B Ellison [0-3] Three Muskateers (2) (from J L Dunlop [0-6] Spt 1999).*

MOONLIGHT SONG (IRE) BHB 63f65a RR 60f 65a
5245[4]

3 b f Mujadil (USA) 7.7f **(70)** - Model Show (IRE) **(80?f)** (Dominion) 8.5f **(63)**
Form - 0081222814
Record 2000 - 1st:2 2nd:3 3rd:0 Ran:10
Win Prizemoney £5,201 *Total Prizemoney* £8,841

Wins							
* 2000	*Spt Southw*	*(STD)*	*H*	*7f*	*63*	*68*	*<*
* 2000	*Jly Southw*	*(STD)*	*C*	*7f*		*61*	

2000 Turf 0-7: (6f 3, 7f 4) (gd 3, g-f 2, frm, hrd) 2000 AW 2-3: (7f 2-3) (Fibr 2-3)
Average filly, effective 7f, acts on gd to g-f - acts on Fibr. Turf high 60 - 2nd of 8 getting 10lb from Ravine (18 Aug Newmarket 7f g-f RF 3767). AW high 68 (began Jly) - 1st of 15 giving 11lb to Puppet Play (26 Spt Southwell RF 4652) - also 1st of 13 giving 10lb to Presidents Lady (14 Jly Southwell RF 2815). Fair placed form on turf, but both of her victories so far have come on the Southwell Fibresand. **W Jarvis [2-10] Rams Racing Club.*

MOON MASTER RR 73f
5151[7]

2 b c Primo Dominie 7.2f **(67)** - Sickle Moon (Shirley Heights) 10.3f **(74)**
Form - 47
Record 2000 - 1st:0 2nd:0 3rd:0 Ran:2
Win Prizemoney £0 *Total Prizemoney* £283
2000 Turf 0-2: (6f, 7f) (g-s, gd)
Currently above-average colt. Turf high 73 (1st run) - 4th of 5 to Earl Grey (30 May Leicester 6f gd RF 1543).
**J A Osborne [0-2] Thehasbeens Com.*

MOON OF ALABAMA BHB 40f RR 21f
4677[19]

3 b f Sadler's Wells (USA) 11.3f **(87)** - Military Tune (IRE) (Nashwan (USA))
Form - 0000
Record 2000 - 1st:0 2nd:0 3rd:0 Ran:4
Pre2000 - 1st:0 2nd:0 3rd:0 Ran:2
2000 Turf 0-4: (7f, 8f 2, 10f) (g-s 2, g-f, frm)
Workmanlike, little account filly. Turf high 21 (began Jly).
**B J Meehan [0-4] Geoff Howard-Spink & Lindy Regis (from J W Hills [0-2] Oct 1999).*

MOONRAKING BHB 35f49a RR 25f 49a
5244[3]

7 gr g Rusticaro (FR) 11.3f **(45)** - Lunaire (Try My Best (USA)) 7.6f **(67)**
Form - 3
Record 2000 - 1st:0 2nd:0 3rd:1 Ran:1
Pre2000 - 1st:6 2nd:7 3rd:5 Ran:34
Win Prizemoney £13,685 *Total Prizemoney* £21,928

Wins							
* 1999	*Feb Southw*	*(STD)*	*C*	*12f*		*68+*	*<*
1999	*Feb Southw*	*(STD)*	*C*	*8f*		*57*	
1998	*Mar Southw*	*(STD)*	*H*	*8f*	*58*	*68*	
1998	*Feb Southw*	*(STD)*	*H*	*11f*	*58*	*60*	
1997	*Dec Southw*	*(STD)*	*H*	*11f*	*50*	*54*	
1997	*Mar Southw*	*(STD)*	*H*	*12f*	*50*	*56*	

2000 AW 0-1: (12f) (Fibr)
Moderate gelding, effective 12f, - acts on Fibr, often wears blinkers (very effectively), favours left handed tracks. Inconsistent.
**Miss S J Wilton [3-21] John Pointon and Sons (from T J Etherington [5-27] Feb 1999).*

MOONRIDGE (IRE) BHB 52f RR 72f
2028[11]

3 b f Common Grounds 8.1f **(66)** - Concave (Connaught) 7.7f **(63)**
Form - 000
Record 2000 - 1st:0 2nd:0 3rd:0 Ran:3
Pre2000 - 1st:0 2nd:0 3rd:1 Ran:5
Win Prizemoney £0 *Total Prizemoney* £270
2000 Turf 0-1: (5f) (g-s) 2000 AW 0-2: (5f, 7f) (Fibr 2)
Above-average filly, effective 6f, acts on gd, has worn blinkers. AW high 2. Inconsistent.
**D Carroll [0-2] G O'Leary (from G O'Leary in IRE [0-6] May 2000).*

MOON ROYALE RR 63f
4454[10]

2 ch f Royal Abjar (USA) - Ragged Moon (Raga Navarro (ITY)) 8f **(64)**
Form - 50
Record 2000 - 1st:0 2nd:0 3rd:0 Ran:2
2000 Turf 0-2: (6f, 7f) (g-s, gd)

Currently average filly. Turf high 63 (began Spt).
**Martyn Wane [0-2] B Batey.*

MOONSHIFT BHB 33f40a **RR 34f 40a** 3843[6]
6 b g Cadeaux Genereux 7.9f **(76)** - Thewaari (USA) (Eskimo (USA))
Form - 05866
Record 2000 - 1st:0 2nd:0 3rd:0 Ran:2
Pre2000 - 1st:1 2nd:0 3rd:0 Ran:14
Win Prizemoney £1,986 *Total Prizemoney* £2,244
Wins * 1999 May Yarmou (FRM) H 10.1f 24 28 <
2000 Turf 0-2: (10f 2) (gd, g-f)
Very moderate gelding, effective 10f, acts on gd, has worn blinkers. Turf high 34 (began Aug) - 6th of 13 getting 17lb from Paarl Rock (21 Aug Nottingham 10f gd RF 3843). Inconsistent.
**H J Collingridge [1-15] C V Lines (from Sir Michael Stoute [0-2] May 1997).*

MOON SOLITAIRE (IRE) BHB 98f **RR 102f** 4734[11]
3 b c Night Shift (USA) 8.1f **(73)** - Gay Fantastic (Ela-Mana-Mou) 10.1f **(70)**
Form - 4131301330
Record 2000 - 1st:3 2nd:0 3rd:4 Ran:10
Pre2000 - 1st:0 2nd:0 3rd:0 Ran:1
Win Prizemoney £61,132 *Total Prizemoney* £77,382
Wins * **2000** Jly Newmar (GD) H 10f 91 100 <
* **2000** May Goodwo (GD) H 9f 78 94
* **2000** Apr Folkes (SFT) 7f 76
2000 Turf 3-10: (7f 1-2, 8f 2, 9f 1-1, 10f 1-4, 11f) (sft, g-s 2-3, gd 1-4, g-f, frm)
Scopey, very useful colt, effective 9 to 11f, best at 10f, acts on sft to g-f, has worn blinkers. Turf high 102 - 3rd of 9 getting 3lb from Polar Red (2 Spt Haydock 11f sft RF 4155) - also 1st of 13 getting 14lb from Forbearing (12 Jly Newmarket RF 2747). Consistent. He got off the mark in a soft-ground Folkestone maiden in April and has become a very useful handicapper at around ten furlongs. Landed a very valuable Goodwood handicap in May and had the draw on his side when scoring at Newmarket's July meeting.
**E A L Dunlop [3-11] Maktoum Al Maktoum.*

MOORLANDS AGAIN BHB 65f **RR 76?f** 5072[3]
5 b g Then Again 7.4f **(52)** - Sandford Springs (USA) (Robellino (USA)) 7.6f **(80)**
Form - 6574543
Record 2000 - 1st:0 2nd:0 3rd:1 Ran:7
Win Prizemoney £0 *Total Prizemoney* £1,664
2000 Turf 0-7: (7f 2, 8f 2, 10f 3) (g-s 2, gd, g-f 2, frm 2)
Above-average gelding, effective 10f, acts on g-s. Turf high 76 (began Jly). **D Burchell [0-9] Mrs Lynda Williams.*

MOOSE MALLOY BHB 41f **RR 43f** 3989[16]
3 ch g Formidable (USA) 7.8f **(60)** - Jolimo (Fortissimo) 11.8f **(61)**
Form - 00000
Record 2000 - 1st:0 2nd:0 3rd:0 Ran:5
Pre2000 - 1st:0 2nd:0 3rd:0 Ran:3
Win Prizemoney £0 *Total Prizemoney* £99
2000 Turf 0-5: (7f, 8f, 10f 2, 12f) (gd, g-f 4)
Workmanlike, moderate gelding. Turf high 40. Inconsistent.
**M J Ryan [0-8] Extraman Ltd.*

MOOTAFAYILL (USA) BHB 91f **RR 96f** 4629[2]
2 b c Danzig (USA) 8.1f **(88)** - Ruznama (USA) **(100f)** (Forty Niner (USA))
Form - 222
Record 2000 - 1st:0 2nd:3 3rd:0 Ran:3
Win Prizemoney £0 *Total Prizemoney* £4,793
2000 Turf 0-3: (6f 3) (gd, g-f, frm)
Currently very useful colt. Turf high 96 (began Aug) - 2nd of 21 to Palanzo (15 Spt Newbury 6f frm RF 4432). He was well touted before hitting the racecourse but had to settle for second spot on all his starts. Likely to stay beyond six furlongs, he should win a maiden at the very least. **B W Hills [0-3] Hamdan Al Maktoum.*

MORE MODERN (USA) RR 77f 5223[4]
2 ch c Mt Livermore (USA) 7.7f **(90)** - A la Mode (USA) **(64+f)** (Known Fact (USA)) 7.4f **(67)**
Form - 4
Record 2000 - 1st:0 2nd:0 3rd:0 Ran:1
Win Prizemoney £0 *Total Prizemoney* £353
2000 Turf 0-1: (6f) (gd)
Currently above-average colt. **R Charlton [0-1] K Abdulla.*

MOREOVER (IRE) BHB 62f57a **RR 66f 57a** 5309[13]
2 b f Caerleon (USA) 10.9f **(79)** - Overcall (Bustino) 10.4f **(64)**
Form - 40
Record 2000 - 1st:0 2nd:0 3rd:0 Ran:2
Win Prizemoney £0 *Total Prizemoney* £270
2000 Turf 0-2: (7f 2) (g-s 2)
Currently average filly. Turf high 66 (began Oct).
**Sir Mark Prescott [0-2] Sir Edmund Loder.*

MORE THAN READY (USA) RR 5328a[5]
3 br c Southern Halo (USA) - Woodman's Girl (USA) (Woodman (USA)) 9f **(74)**
Form - 5
2000 AW 0-1: (6f) (Dirt)
Currently Group-class colt. **T Pletcher in USA [0-1] J T Scatuorchio.*

MORGAN LE FAY BHB 55f52a **RR 60f 52a** 4654[4]
5 b m Magic Ring (IRE) 6.5f **(64)** - Melody Park (Music Boy) 6.8f **(57)**
Form - 10054
Record 2000 - 1st:1 2nd:0 3rd:0 Ran:5
Pre2000 - 1st:0 2nd:4 3rd:3 Ran:15
Win Prizemoney £3,737 *Total Prizemoney* £9,445
Wins 2000 May Thirsk (GD) 6f 60 <
2000 Turf 1-4: (6f 1-3, 7f) (gd 1-2, g-f 2) 2000 AW 0-1: (6f) (Fibr)
Average filly, effective 6 to 8f, best at 6f, acts on gd to frm - acts on Fibr, best on frm. Turf high 60 (1st run) - 1st of 12 giving 9lb to Star Princess (19 May Thirsk RF 1319). (1st run) - 4th of 15 giving 5lb to Marengo (26 Spt Southwell 6f Fibr RF 4654).
**Don Enrico Incisa [0-5] Don Enrico Incisa (from N Tinkler [1-3] Spt 2000).*

MORGANS ORCHARD (IRE) BHB 56f64a **RR 64f 64a** 5069[7]
4 ch g Forest Wind (USA) - Regina St Cyr (IRE) (Doulab (USA)) 9.8f **(65)**
Form - 3152155202326877
Record 2000 - 1st:2 2nd:4 3rd:1 Ran:15
Pre2000 - 1st:0 2nd:0 3rd:1 Ran:3
Win Prizemoney £3,262 *Total Prizemoney* £16,069
Wins * **2000** *Feb Wolver (STD) H 12f 60 65* <
* **2000** *Jan Southw (STD) H 12f 57 61*
2000 Turf 0-10: (12f 7, 13f 2, 14f) (sft, g-s 2, gd 3, g-f 4) 2000 AW 2-5: (12f 2-4, 16f) (Fibr 2-5)
Strong, average gelding, effective 12 to 14f, best at 12f, acts on sft to g-f - acts on Fibr, does well at Wolverhampton. Turf high 66 - 2nd of 18 getting 25lb from Seek (22 Aug York 12f gd RF 3854). AW high 65 - 2nd of 6 giving 11lb to Evezio Rufo (22 Feb Wolverhampton 12f Fibr RF 0331) - also 1st of 12 giving 22lb to Our People (29 Feb Wolverhampton RF 0376). He is a fair sort in middle-distance handicaps on Fibresand and scored twice over a mile and a half on that surface earlier this year. Also has ability on turf and ran a couple of decent races on that surface last season, especially when runner up in a competitive handicap at the Ebor meeting. Very much suited by a sharp left-handed track.
**A G Newcombe [2-18] After Hours Partnership.*

MORNING BREEZE (IRE) RR 94f 4092a[6]
4 b f Bigstone (IRE) - Eyeliner (USA) (Raise A Native) 11.2f **(69)**
Form - 0626U4236
2000 Turf 0-8: (8f, 10f, 12f 3, 14f 3) (sft, g-s 2, gd 3, frm)
Useful filly, effective 12 to 14f, best at 12f, acts on frm. Turf high 94 - 4th of 11 getting 3lb from Pairumani Star (22 Jly Leopardstown 14f gd RF 3118a). Raised 10lb after finishing fourth in a Listed race at Leopardstown in July, she is difficult to place on the Flat and better employed over obstacles.
**T Doyle in IRE [0-9] Mrs P O'Connor (from P J Flynn in IRE [1-8] Oct 1999).*

MORNING LOVER (IRE) BHB 73f **RR 80f** 2860[3]
3 b c Ela-Mana-Mou 12.7f **(72)** - The Dawn Trader (USA) (Naskra (USA)) 8.8f **(69)**
Form - 5143
Record 2000 - 1st:1 2nd:0 3rd:1 Ran:4
Pre2000 - 1st:0 2nd:0 3rd:0 Ran:1

Win Prizemoney £2,772 *Total Prizemoney* £4,197
Wins * 2000 Jun Catter (GD) 12f 80 <
2000 Turf 1-4: (12f 1-4) (gd, g-f, frm 1-2)
Workmanlike, decent colt. Turf high 80 - also 1st of 7 giving 5lb to Apple Town (2 Jun Catterick RF 1657).
**K R Burke [1-5] D & M Cased Hole.*

MORNINGSIDE (IRE) BHB 60f **RR 68f** 4823[13]

3 b f Night Shift (USA) 8.1f **(73)** - Recipe (Bustino) 10.4f **(64)**
Form - 6460
Record 2000 - 1st:0 2nd:0 3rd:0 Ran:4
Pre2000 - 1st:0 2nd:0 3rd:0 Ran:1
Win Prizemoney £0 *Total Prizemoney* £322
2000 Turf 0-4: (10f, 12f 3) (g-s, g-f 2, frm)
Lengthy, average filly. Turf high 68.
**D R C Elsworth [0-5] Mrs Michael Meredith.*

MORNINGS MINION BHB 82f **RR 86f** 4991[16]

3 b g Polar Falcon (USA) 9f **(74)** - Fair Dominion (Dominion) 8.5f **(63)**
Form - 441530
Record 2000 - 1st:1 2nd:0 3rd:1 Ran:6
Win Prizemoney £3,006 *Total Prizemoney* £6,117
Wins * 2000 Jly Warwic (GD) 7.7f 86 <
2000 Turf 1-6: (7f 4, 8f 1-2) (hvy, gd 1-4, g-f)
Strong, useful gelding, effective 7 to 8f, best at 8f, acts on gd to g-f, best on gd. Turf high 86 - 1st of 13 giving 5lb to Sincerity (7 Jly Warwick RF 2615). Unraced at two, he got off the mark with a narrow success in a Warwick maiden in July and probably still has some improvement in him.
**R Charlton [1-6] Exors of the Late D A Shirley.*

MORNING SUIT RR 2173[5]

6 b g Reprimand 8.2f **(63)** - Morica (Moorestyle) 6.9f **(64)**
Form - 5
Record 2000 - 1st:0 2nd:0 3rd:0 Ran:1
2000 AW 0-1: (16f) (Fibr)
Very poor gelding. **S Mellor [0-9] Mrs S C Haine.*

MOROCCO (IRE) BHB 44f **RR 41f** 5056[16]

11 b g Cyrano de Bergerac 7.3f **(58)** - Lightning Laser (Monseigneur (USA)) 7.7f **(63)**
Form - 030
Record 2000 - 1st:0 2nd:0 3rd:1 Ran:3
Pre2000 - 1st:9 2nd:6 3rd:10 Ran:85
Win Prizemoney £31,748 *Total Prizemoney* £44,132
Wins 1998 Jly Leices (GD) H 7f 58 58
1996 Spt Lingfi (FRM) H 7f 54 56
1996 May Salisb (G-F) H 7f 56 52
2000 Turf 0-3: (7f 2, 8f) (sft, gd, g-f)
Moderate gelding, has worn blinkers. Turf high 41 (began Aug).
**J A Osborne [0-3] Martin Myers (from M R Channon [6-67] Jun 1999).*

MORSHDI BHB 94f **RR 92+f** 5238[7]

2 b c Slip Anchor 12.7f **(75)** - Reem Albaraari (Sadler's Wells (USA)) 10f **(76)**
Form - 517
Record 2000 - 1st:1 2nd:0 3rd:0 Ran:3
Win Prizemoney £3,066 *Total Prizemoney* £3,066
Wins * 2000 Spt Haydoc (SFT) 8.1f 92+ <
2000 Turf 1-3: (7f, 8f 1-1, 10f) (g-s 1-2, g-f)
Currently useful colt. Turf high 92 (began Jly) - 1st of 15 giving 5lb to La Vita E Bella (1 Spt Haydock RF 4148). He held some fancy entries and had no trouble winning a maiden at Haydock in September. Below par when beaten in a Listed event on his only subsequent start, he deserves another chance and may develop into a useful middle-distance stayer.
**M A Jarvis [1-3] Sheikh Ahmed Al Maktoum.*

MORSHID (USA) BHB 79f **RR 80f** 5080[3]

2 b c Gulch (USA) 9.6f **(79)** - Possessive Dancer (Shareef Dancer (USA)) 9.9f **(73)**
Form - 733
Record 2000 - 1st:0 2nd:0 3rd:2 Ran:3
Win Prizemoney £0 *Total Prizemoney* £1,187
2000 Turf 0-3: (8f 3) (hvy, gd, frm)
Currently decent colt. Turf high 80 (began Aug) - 3rd of 8 to Elmonjed (9 Spt Goodwood 8f gd RF 4318).
**M R Channon [0-3] Sheikh Ahmed Al Maktoum.*

MOSAAHIM (IRE) RR 74f 4261[5]

2 b c Nashwan (USA) 10.3f **(79)** - Azdihaar (USA) **(84f)** (Mr Prospector (USA)) 8.8f **(78)**
Form - 25
Record 2000 - 1st:0 2nd:1 3rd:0 Ran:2
Win Prizemoney £0 *Total Prizemoney* £1,368
2000 Turf 0-2: (7f, 8f) (gd, g-f)
Currently above-average colt. Turf high 74 (began Aug).
**J L Dunlop [0-2] Hamdan Al Maktoum.*

MOSAIC TIMES BHB 41a **RR 41a** 61[9]

3 ch c Timeless Times (USA) 6.1f **(56)** - Pastelle **(57a)** (Tate Gallery (USA)) 7.4f **(67)**
Form - 760
Record 2000 - 1st:0 2nd:0 3rd:0 Ran:1
Pre2000 - 1st:0 2nd:1 3rd:0 Ran:3
Win Prizemoney £0 *Total Prizemoney* £521
2000 AW 0-1: (6f) (Fibr)
Neat, moderate colt. **Mrs G S Rees [0-4] David Morley.*

MOSAYTER (USA) RR 86f 4701[4]

2 b c Storm Cat (USA) 7f **(86)** - Bashayer (USA) (Mr Prospector (USA)) 8.8f **(78)**
Form - 4
Record 2000 - 1st:0 2nd:0 3rd:0 Ran:1
Win Prizemoney £0 *Total Prizemoney* £392
2000 Turf 0-1: (7f) (g-f)
Currently useful colt. (1st run) - 4th of 17 to Demophilos (28 Spt Newmarket 7f g-f RF 4701).
**M P Tregoning [0-1] Hamdan Al Maktoum.*

MOSCA RR 71f 5066[7]

2 ch f Most Welcome 8.6f **(66)** - Moidart **(88f)** (Electric) 10.1f **(61)**
Form - 7
Record 2000 - 1st:0 2nd:0 3rd:0 Ran:1
2000 Turf 0-1: (8f) (g-s)
Currently above-average filly.
**J R Fanshawe [0-1] Dr Catherine Wills.*

MOSELLE BHB 100f **RR 106f** 4739[9]

3 b f Mtoto 11.5f **(71)** - Miquette (FR) (Fabulous Dancer (USA)) 9.4f **(70)**
Form - 201362530
Record 2000 - 1st:1 2nd:2 3rd:2 Ran:9
Pre2000 - 1st:0 2nd:0 3rd:1 Ran:1
Win Prizemoney £3,558 *Total Prizemoney* £16,698
Wins * 2000 Jun Yarmou (FRM) 8f 88+ <
2000 Turf 1-9: (7f, 8f 1-4, 9f, 10f 3) (g-s, gd 3, g-f 1-3, frm 2)
Pattern-class filly, effective 7 to 10f, best at 10f, acts on gd to frm, best on gd. Turf high 106. Consistent. She ran a series of respectable races in listed company after landing her maiden.
**W J Haggas [1-10] & Mrs G Middlebrook/& Mrs P Brain.*

MOSQUERA (GER) RR 102f 5368a[1]

3 ch f Acatenango (GER) - Midnight Society (USA) (Imp Society (USA))
Form - 6331
2000 Turf 1-4: (8f 1-2, 10f, 11f) (hvy 1-2, gd 2)
Very useful filly. Turf high 102 - 1st of 15 giving 3lb to Granted (4 Nov Cologne RF 5368a).
**P Schiergen in GER [1-4] Stiftung Gestut Fahrhof.*

MOSSY MOOR BHB 91f **RR 92f** 4598[7]

3 ch f Sanglamore (USA) 12.9f **(67)** - Moss (Alzao (USA)) 7.1f **(68)**
Form - 53174267
Record 2000 - 1st:1 2nd:1 3rd:1 Ran:8
Pre2000 - 1st:0 2nd:0 3rd:0 Ran:1
Win Prizemoney £7,020 *Total Prizemoney* £11,053
Wins * 2000 Jun Kempto (G-F) H 8f 83 90 <
2000 Turf 1-8: (8f 1-7, 9f) (g-s, gd 3, g-f 1-1, frm 3)
Scopey, useful filly, effective 8f, acts on gd to frm. Turf high 92 - 7th of 14 getting 1lb from Riberac (23 Spt Ascot 8f gd RF 4598) - also 1st of 9 giving 10lb to Granted (21 Jun Kempton RF 2163). She confirmed the promise shown in maidens when winning a mile handicap at Kempton in June. Consistent on fast ground for

the remainder of the campaign, she can score again in run-of-the-mill company. **Mrs A J Perrett [1-9] K Abdulla.*

MOSTABSHIR (IRE) RR 32f 5309[16]
2 b c Unfuwain (USA) 11.4f **(74)** - Istibshar (USA) **(70f)** (Mr Prospector (USA)) 8.8f **(78)**
Form - 0
Record 2000 - 1st:0 2nd:0 3rd:0 Ran:1
2000 Turf 0-1: (7f) (g-s)
Currently very moderate colt.
**J H M Gosden [0-1] Hamdan Al Maktoum.*

MOST RESPECTFUL BHB 47f45a **RR 47f 45a** 240[8]
7 ch g Respect 5.7f **(44)** - Active Movement (Music Boy) 6.8f **(57)**
Form - 4308
Record 2000 - 1st:0 2nd:0 3rd:1 Ran:4
Pre2000 - 1st:3 2nd:2 3rd:2 Ran:33
Win Prizemoney £7,642 *Total Prizemoney* £10,175
Wins ** 1999 Jun Southw (STD) SH* 7f 50 54 <
** 1998 Spt Southw (STD) H* 6f 50 54 <
* 1998 Aug Beverl (G-F) 5f 54 <
2000 AW 0-4: (7f 4) (Fibr 4)
Moderate gelding, effective 6 to 7f, best at 6f, acts on g-f - acts on Fibr. AW high 44.
**N Tinkler [3-32] Mrs Lisa Olley (from Denys Smith [0-7] May 1997).*

MOST-SAUCY BHB 76f73a **RR 78f 73a** 4866[20]
4 br f Most Welcome 8.6f **(66)** - So Saucy **(35f 41a)** (Teenoso (USA)) 9.9f **(72)**
Form - 300
Record 2000 - 1st:0 2nd:0 3rd:1 Ran:3
Pre2000 - 1st:2 2nd:1 3rd:1 Ran:9
Win Prizemoney £8,114 *Total Prizemoney* £11,559
Wins 1999 Aug Lingfi (G-F) H 7.6f 72 76 <
1999 Jly Leices (G-F) H 7f 68 72
2000 Turf 0-3: (7f 2, 8f) (sft, g-s, g-f)
Unfurnished, above-average filly, effective 7 to 8f, best at 8f, acts on gd to frm, best on g-f. Turf high 76 (1st run) (began Aug) - 3rd of 9 giving 15lb to Silk Daisy (4 Aug Nottingham 8f g-f RF 3377). Inconsistent.
**I A Wood [0-3] Averagemanracing com (from B J Meehan [2-9] Spt 1999).*

MOST STYLISH BHB 60f58a **RR 72f 58a** 5000[15]
3 ch f Most Welcome 8.6f **(66)** - Corman-Style (Ahonoora) 8.1f **(73)**
Form - 52344640
Record 2000 - 1st:0 2nd:1 3rd:1 Ran:8
Win Prizemoney £0 *Total Prizemoney* £1,428
2000 Turf 0-6: (7f, 8f, 10f 4) (g-s 2, gd 2, g-f, frm) 2000 AW 0-2: (8f, 11f) (Fibr 2)
Scopey, above-average filly, effective 7 to 10f, acts on gd to g-f. Turf high 72 - 3rd of 11 getting 5lb from Sahara Spirit (31 May Southwell 7f gd RF 1605). AW high 60.
**C G Cox [0-8] Elite Racing Club.*

MOTET BHB 70f **RR 83df** 2242[10]
6 b g Mtoto 11.5f **(71)** - Guest Artiste (Be My Guest (USA)) 9.3f **(67)**
Form - 0
Record 2000 - 1st:0 2nd:0 3rd:0 Ran:1
Pre2000 - 1st:3 2nd:2 3rd:4 Ran:16
Win Prizemoney £14,042 *Total Prizemoney* £21,755
Wins 1997 Spt Yarmou (FRM) H 18.2f 85 90 <
1997 Aug Newcas (GD) H 16.1f 82 84
1997 *Mar Lingfi (STD)* *10f* 66+
2000 Turf 0-1: (16f) (gd)
Decent gelding, has worn blinkers (extremely effectively).
**M Pitman [2-15] H J Jarvis (from G Wragg [3-15] Spt 1998).*

MOTHER CORRIGAN (IRE) BHB 48f43a **RR 58f 43a** 4652[12]
4 gr f Paris House 5.9f **(64)** - Missed Opportunity (IRE) (Exhibitioner) 8.7f **(61)**
Form - 01000080000
Record 2000 - 1st:1 2nd:0 3rd:0 Ran:11
Pre2000 - 1st:0 2nd:0 3rd:0 Ran:5
Win Prizemoney £7,702 *Total Prizemoney* £7,999
Wins *** **2000** May Redcar (G-F) H 7f 54 58 <
2000 Turf 1-10: (6f 5, 7f 1-4, 8f) (gd 2, g-f 2, frm 1-6) 2000 AW 0-1: (7f) (Fibr)
Fair filly, effective 7f, acts on frm, often wears blinkers (effectively). Turf high 58 - 1st of 21 getting 6lb from Tous Les Jours (15 May Redcar RF 1200).
**M Brittain [1-11] Mel Brittain (from L M Cumani [0-5] Aug 1999).*

MOTHER MOLLY (USA) BHB 60f55a **RR 72f 55a** 4458[3]
3 b br f Irish River (FR) 9f **(77)** - Charming Molly (USA) (Diesis) 9.3f **(69)**
Form - 3
Record 2000 - 1st:0 2nd:0 3rd:1 Ran:1
Pre2000 - 1st:0 2nd:1 3rd:0 Ran:1
Win Prizemoney £0 *Total Prizemoney* £1,720
2000 Turf 0-1: (7f) (g-s)
Scopey, currently above-average filly. (1st run) - 3rd of 8 getting 5lb from Material Witness (16 Spt Catterick 7f g-s RF 4458).
**R Guest [0-2] Matthews Breeding and Racing*

MOT JUSTE RR 76+f 4401[1]
2 b f Mtoto 11.5f **(71)** - Bunting **(90f)** (Shaadi (USA))
Form - 1
Record 2000 - 1st:1 2nd:0 3rd:0 Ran:1
Win Prizemoney £3,620 *Total Prizemoney* £3,620
Wins *** **2000** Spt Yarmou (G-F) 8f 76+ <
2000 Turf 1-1: (8f 1-1) (g-f 1-1)
Currently above-average filly. (1st run) - 1st of 8 getting 5lb from Roferral (14 Spt Yarmouth RF 4401).
**E A L Dunlop [1-1] Mohammed Al Nahouda.*

MOTTO (FR) RR 52f 5319[6]
2 b f Mtoto 11.5f **(71)** - Coigach **(97f)** (Niniski (USA)) 10.6f **(65)**
Form - 6
Record 2000 - 1st:0 2nd:0 3rd:0 Ran:1
2000 Turf 0-1: (6f) (sft)
Currently fair filly. **H R A Cecil [0-1] Dr Catherine Wills.*

MOUJEEDA BHB 68f **RR 69f** 4111[3]
3 ch f Zafonic (USA) 9f **(83)** - Dafinah (USA) (Graustark) 10.1f **(70)**
Form - 60433
Record 2000 - 1st:0 2nd:0 3rd:2 Ran:5
Pre2000 - 1st:0 2nd:0 3rd:0 Ran:1
Win Prizemoney £0 *Total Prizemoney* £1,300
2000 Turf 0-5: (10f 3, 11f, 12f) (gd, frm 4)
Leggy, average filly, effective 10 to 12f, acts on frm. Turf high 69 - 3rd of 11 giving 8lb to Sweet Angeline (4 Aug Thirsk 12f frm RF 3381).
**W Jarvis [0-5] Mitaab Abdullah (from Sir Michael Stoute [0-1] Oct 1999).*

MOULOUYA (FR) RR 64f 1262[8]
5 gr m Turgeon (USA) - Charabia (A.ARAB) (FR) (Bazin)
Form - 8
Record 2000 - 1st:0 2nd:0 3rd:0 Ran:1
2000 Turf 0-1: (10f) (g-f)
Average filly. **J R Best [1-6] Mercato Ltd.*

MOUNT ABU (IRE) BHB 113f **RR 113f** 4986[7]
3 b c Foxhound (USA) - Twany Angel (Double Form) 7.3f **(58)**
Form - 4116317
Record 2000 - 1st:3 2nd:0 3rd:1 Ran:7
Pre2000 - 1st:1 2nd:1 3rd:0 Ran:5
Win Prizemoney £58,953 *Total Prizemoney* £72,235
Wins *** **2000** Spt Goodwo (SFT) G3 7f 113 <
*** **2000** Jun Lingfi (G-S) L 6f 112
*** **2000** May Ascot (G-S) L 6f 113 <
1999 May Newbur (SFT) 6f 70
2000 Turf 3-7: (6f 2-3, 7f 1-4) (g-s 1-2, gd 1-4, g-f 1-1)
Light-framed, Group-class colt, effective 6 to 7f, best at 6f, acts on g-s to g-f. Turf high 113 - 1st of 8 getting 3lb from One Won One (21 Spt Goodwood RF 4549) - also 1st of 8 from Sir Nicholas (3 May Ascot RF 1002). A soft ground specialist, he was well placed by John Gosden and gained a deserved Group 3 success at Goodwood in September. Probably over the top when unplaced on his final start, he stays seven furlongs and looks an ideal type for the Leicestershire Stakes at Leicester on April 28.
**J H M Gosden [3-7] Gary Seidler & Andy J Smith (from P W Chapple-Hyam [1-5] Aug 1999).*

MOUNTAIN DANCER (IRE) BHB 74f **RR 73f** 2459[1]
3 b f Rainbow Quest (USA) 11.2f **(81)** - Jammaayil (IRE) (Lomond (USA)) 8.8f **(65)**
Form - 631
Record 2000 - 1st:1 2nd:0 3rd:1 Ran:3
Win Prizemoney £4,134 *Total Prizemoney* £4,785
Wins * 2000 Jly Doncas (GD) 12f 69 <
2000 Turf 1-3: (9f, 10f, 12f 1-1) (gd, g-f 1-2)
Leggy, currently above-average filly. Turf high 73 - also 1st of 4 from Five of Wands (2 Jly Doncaster RF 2459).
**M Johnston [1-3] Maktoum Al Maktoum.*

MOUNTAIN MAGIC BHB 46f35a **RR 42f 35a** 166[13]
5 b m Magic Ring (IRE) 6.5f **(64)** - Nevis (Connaught) 7.7f **(63)**
Form - 0
Record 2000 - 1st:0 2nd:0 3rd:0 Ran:1
Pre2000 - 1st:1 2nd:0 3rd:1 Ran:21
Win Prizemoney £4,042 *Total Prizemoney* £4,447
Wins 1998 May Newbur (G-F) H 7.3f 54 61 <
2000 AW 0-1: (9f) (Fibr)
Moderate filly, effective 8f, acts on frm, has worn blinkers. Inconsistent.
**A G Juckes [0-3] A C W Price (from D J S ffrenchDavis [1-22] Oct 1999).*

MOUNT LOGAN RR 4730[8]
5 b h Shareef Dancer (USA) 10.1f **(67)** - Double Entendre (Dominion) 8.5f **(63)**
Form - 8
Record 2000 - 1st:0 2nd:0 3rd:0 Ran:1
2000 AW 0-1: (13f) (Equi)
Currently very moderate colt. **P W Harris [0-1] Ken Blake.*

MOUNT MCKINLEY (USA) RR 61f 4577[6]
3 ch c Mr Prospector (USA) 8.6f **(88)** - Julie's Jazz (USA) (Nureyev (USA)) 8.7f **(78)**
Form - 76
Record 2000 - 1st:0 2nd:0 3rd:0 Ran:2
2000 Turf 0-2: (7f 2) (sft, frm)
Scopey, currently average colt. Turf high 61 (began Spt).
**J Noseda [0-2] Mrs John Magnier & M Tabor.*

MOUNT PARK (IRE) BHB 44f43a **RR 37f 43a** 4825[24]
3 b f Colonel Collins (USA) - Make Hay (Nomination) 7f **(60)**
Form - 800006000000185000
Record 2000 - 1st:1 2nd:0 3rd:0 Ran:18
Pre2000 - 1st:0 2nd:1 3rd:1 Ran:5
Win Prizemoney £2,404 *Total Prizemoney* £4,092
Wins * 2000 Jly Redcar (G-F) SH 5f 44 49 <
2000 Turf 1-12: (5f 1-3, 6f 5, 7f 3, 8f) (g-s, gd, g-f 1-3, frm 6, hrd) 2000 AW 0-6: (6f 3, 7f, 8f 2) (Fibr 6)
Scopey, very moderate filly, effective 5 to 6f, best at 6f, acts on gd to frm, best on gd, often wears blinkers. Turf high 49. AW high 36. Becoming disappointing.
**D W Chapman [1-18] David Chapman (from H S Howe [0-5] Oct 1999).*

MOUNTRATH ROCK BHB 42f **RR 53f** 4329[5]
3 b f Rock Hopper 10.6f **(54)** - Point of Law (Law Society (USA)) 9.9f **(70)**
Form - 00044015665
Record 2000 - 1st:1 2nd:0 3rd:0 Ran:11
Pre2000 - 1st:0 2nd:2 3rd:0 Ran:4
Win Prizemoney £2,094 *Total Prizemoney* £3,245
Wins * 2000 Jun Nottin (G-F) SH 8.2f 47 49 <
2000 Turf 1-11: (8f 1-7, 10f 2, 11f, 12f) (g-s, gd 3, g-f 1-3, frm 3, hrd)
Neat, fair filly, effective 6 to 8f, best at 6f, acts on g-f to frm, best on g-f, often wears blinkers. Turf high 53 - also 1st of 17 giving 1lb to Red Sonny (26 Jun Nottingham RF 2275).
**N Tinkler [1-15] Racingclub co uk.*

MOUNT ROYALE (IRE) BHB 57f **RR 64f** 4443[10]
2 ch c Wolfhound (USA) 7.3f **(71)** - Mahabba (USA) (Elocutionist (USA)) 8f **(77)**
Form - 7000
Record 2000 - 1st:0 2nd:0 3rd:0 Ran:4
2000 Turf 0-4: (5f, 6f, 7f, 8f) (g-s, gd 2, frm)
Average colt. Turf high 64. **N Tinkler [0-4] Langton Partnership.*

MOURAMARA (IRE) RR 112+f 4837a[1]
3 b f Kahyasi 12.9f **(74)** - Mamoura (IRE) (Lomond (USA)) 8.8f **(65)**
Form - 3111
2000 Turf 3-4: (8f, 12f 2-2, 13f 1-1) (sft, gd 1-1, g-f 1-1)
Scopey, Group-class filly. Turf high 112 - 1st of 11 from Beyond The Waves (30 Spt Longchamp RF 4837a). Landed a maiden at Roscommon in June, and improved steadily to win the Prix Royallieu at the Arc meeting. Looks capable of winning more good races in 2001.
**J Oxx in IRE [3-4] H H Aga Khan (from L M Cumani [0-1] Nov 1999).*

MOUSEHOLE BHB 67f **RR 66f** 5068[12]
8 b g Statoblest 6.4f **(63)** - Alo Ez (Alzao (USA)) 7.1f **(68)**
Form - 0000828218800
Record 2000 - 1st:1 2nd:2 3rd:0 Ran:13
Pre2000 - 1st:10 2nd:12 3rd:7 Ran:65
Win Prizemoney £33,783 *Total Prizemoney* £54,531
Wins * 2000 Jly Sandow (G-F) H 5f 66 71
* 1999 Aug Windso (G-F) H 5f 69 71
* 1999 Jly Nottin (G-F) 5.1f 66
* 1999 Jly Windso (G-F) H 5f 63 65
* 1999 May Nottin (FRM) H 5.1f 57 61
* 1998 Aug Bath (FRM) 5.1f 77 <
* 1998 Jly Carlis (G-F) 5f 70
* 1997 Aug Bath (GD) 5.1f 72
* 1997 Jly Warwic (G-F) 5f 63
* 1996 Jun Windso (G-F) 5f 63
2000 Turf 1-13: (5f 1-13) (g-s 2, gd 5, g-f 1-2, frm 4)
Average gelding, effective 5f, acts on g-f to frm, best on frm, has worn blinkers, excels at Nottingham and Windsor. Turf high 71 - 2nd of 13 giving 11lb to Beyond The Clouds (17 Jly Windsor 5f frm RF 2880) - also 1st of 12 getting 1lb from Diamond Geezer (26 Jly Sandown RF 3144). **R Guest [11-78] Mrs Janet Linskey.*

MOUTON (IRE) BHB 30f37a **RR 29f 37a** 2397[8]
4 b f Dolphin Street (FR) - The Queen of Soul (Chief Singer) 8.9f **(66)**
Form - 50500006008
Record 2000 - 1st:0 2nd:0 3rd:0 Ran:11
Pre2000 - 1st:0 2nd:3 3rd:1 Ran:6
Win Prizemoney £0 *Total Prizemoney* £3,131
2000 Turf 0-7: (5f, 6f 2, 7f 2, 8f, 10f) (g-s, gd 3, g-f 2, frm) 2000 AW 0-4: (6f, 7f, 8f, 10f) (Equi 4)
Workmanlike, little account filly, effective 8 to 9f, best at 9f, acts on g-f to frm, best on frm, likes left handed tracks, likes tight tracks. Turf high 29. AW high 29.
**J J Bridger [0-11] W Wood (from J W Hills [0-6] Aug 1999).*

MOVING EXPERIENCE (IRE) BHB 52f **RR 60f** 4634[7]
3 b f Nicolotte - Sound Performance (IRE) (Ahonoora) 8.1f **(73)**
Form - 74767
Record 2000 - 1st:0 2nd:0 3rd:0 Ran:5
Pre2000 - 1st:0 2nd:0 3rd:0 Ran:2
Win Prizemoney £0 *Total Prizemoney* £408
2000 Turf 0-5: (7f, 8f 3, 10f) (g-s, gd 2, g-f 2)
Average filly. Turf high 60.
**D W P Arbuthnot [0-5] The Moving Partnership (from M J Fetherston-Godley [0-2] Oct 1999).*

MOVING ON UP RR 102f 5173a[1]
6 b g Salse (USA) 10.9f **(71)** - Thundercloud (Electric) 10.1f **(61)**
Form - 15821
2000 Turf 1-4: (9f, 10f 1-3) (hvy 1-2, sft)
Very useful gelding, effective 10f, acts on hvy to g-s, best on hvy, often wears blinkers (extremely effectively). Turf high 98 - 1st of 7 giving 8lb to Benovia (18 Oct Navan RF 5173a). A useful dual-purpose horse, he goes well under testing conditions but struggles in Listed company nowadays.
**D K Weld in IRE [8-30] Michael Hilary Burke.*

MOWASSEL (IRE) RR 91f 5170a[6]
2 b c General Monash (USA) - Dublah (USA) (Private Account (USA)) 8.5f **(74)**
Form - 1626
2000 Turf 1-4: (5f 1-3, 6f) (hvy, sft 1-1, g-s, gd)

Useful colt. Turf high 91 - 2nd of 11 to Berlin (30 Jun Curragh 6f gd RF 2515a). Speedily bred, he made a winning debut in April but will struggle for openings this term.
**K Prendergast in IRE [1-4] Hamdan Al Maktoum.*

MOWBRAY (USA) BHB 95f RR 99f 4936[11]

5 b br g Opening Verse (USA) 11.8f **(70)** - Peppy Raja (USA) (Raja Baba (USA)) 10f **(64)**
Form - 5604403050
Record 2000 - 1st:0 2nd:0 3rd:1 Ran:10
Pre2000 - 1st:4 2nd:4 3rd:1 Ran:20
Win Prizemoney £45,646 *Total Prizemoney* £139,849
Wins * 1999 Jly Goodwo (G-F) H 14f 89 94
* 1998 Oct Leices (HVY) 11.8f 100 <
' 1997 Aug Kempto (GD) 7f 97
* 1997 Aug Catter (G-F) 7f 77
2000 Turf 0-10: (12f 3, 13f, 14f 5, 15f) (sft, gd 4, g-f 3, frm 2)
Very useful gelding, effective 12 to 14f, best at 14f, acts on sft to frm, best on gd, has worn blinkers (extremely effectively), prefers tight tracks, excels at Salisbury, does well at York and Goodwood. Turf high 99 - 3rd of 8 getting 6lb from Churlish Charm (31 Aug Salisbury 14f frm RF 4128). Consistent. He is capable of useful form but must be regarded as unreliable for betting purposes. Sold for 10,000gns at Newmarket in October, he disappointed on his first two starts over hurdles.
**P F I Cole [4-30] Sir George Meyrick.*

MOWELGA BHB 103f RR 104f 4611[9]

6 ch g Most Welcome 8.6f **(66)** - Galactic Miss (Damister (USA)) 9f **(73)**
Form - 1720
Record 2000 - 1st:1 2nd:1 3rd:0 Ran:4
Pre2000 - 1st:4 2nd:1 3rd:2 Ran:9
Win Prizemoney £34,845 *Total Prizemoney* £47,525
Wins * **2000** Apr Newmar (G-S) H 12f 93 98 <
* 1998 Aug Newbur (GD) 12f 92
* 1998 Aug Pontef (G-F) H 12f 88 92
* 1998 May Doncas (G-F) H 10.3f 77 81
* 1997 Oct Newbur (GD) 10f 61
2000 Turf 1-4: (12f 1-3, 13f) (g-s, gd 1-1, g f, frm)
Very useful gelding. Turf high 104 - 2nd of 15 giving 16lb to Takwin (9 Spt Doncaster 12f frm RF 4308) - also 1st of 21 giving 14lb to Alhawa (19 Apr Newmarket RF 0796). A very useful middle-distance handicapper at his best, he missed the whole of 1999 but came back to win a decent Newmarket handicap in April. That effort may have taken the edge off him as he was well beaten next time, but a four-month break saw him run a much better race at Doncaster in September. Obviously goes well fresh.
**Lady Herries [5-13] L G Lazarus.*

MOY (IRE) BHB 32f38a RR 38f 38a 1684[5]

5 ch m Beveled (USA) 6.9f **(64)** - Exceptional Beauty (Sallust) 8.4f **(63)**
Form - 268530020505
Record 2000 - 1st:0 2nd:2 3rd:1 Ran:12
Pre2000 - 1st:0 2nd:1 3rd:2 Ran:27
Win Prizemoney £0 *Total Prizemoney* £4,246
2000 Turf 0-3: (5f 2, 6f) (gd, g-f, frm) 2000 AW 0-9: (5f, 6f 5, 7f 3) (Fibr 9)
Moderate filly, effective 6 to 7f, best at 7f, - acts on Fibr, has worn blinkers, likes left handed tracks, likes tight tracks. Turf high 38. AW high 43 - 3rd of 12 getting 4lb from Beguile (4 Mar Wolverhampton 7f Fibr RF 0406).
**W M Brisbourne [0-27] Christopher Chell (from M Brittain [0-12] Jun 1998).*

MOYNE PLEASURE (IRE) BHB 78f RR 18f 5013[1]

2 b c Exit To Nowhere (USA) 8.7f **(77)** - Ilanga (IRE) **(81f)** (Common Grounds)
Form - 051
Record 2000 - 1st:1 2nd:0 3rd:0 Ran:3
Win Prizemoney £1,757 *Total Prizemoney* £1,757
Wins * **2000** *Oct Wolver (STD) 6f 69* <
2000 Turf 0-1: (6f) (gd) 2000 AW 1-2: (6f 1-2) (Fibr 1-2)
Currently decent colt. AW high 69 (began Oct) - 1st of 9 from African Czar (17 Oct Wolverhampton RF 5013).
**J A Osborne [1-3] Berkeley Land Ltd.*

MOZART (IRE) RR 111f 4988[4]

2 b c Danehill (USA) 9.1f **(79)** - Victoria Cross (USA) (Spectacular Bid (USA)) 11.2f **(76)**
Form - 114
2000 Turf 2-3: (7f 2-3) (gd 1-2, g-f 1-1)
Currently Group-class colt. Turf high 111 (began Jly) - 4th of 10 to Tobougg (14 Oct Newmarket 7f gd RF 4988) - also 1st of 27 giving 5lb to Pretty Girl (26 Spt Newmarket RF 4643). Hit the right note when landing long odds-on on his Curragh debut, and followed up in the valuable Houghton Sales Stakes at Newmarket. Had his limitations exposed when only fourth in the Dewhurst.
**A P O'Brien in IRE [2-3] M Tabor & Mrs John Magnier.*

Mozart was chased home by a Pretty Girl at Newmarket

MR ACADEMY (IRE) RR 107f 2000a[2]

4 b c Royal Academy (USA) 7.8f **(77)** - Miss d'Ouilly (FR) (Bikala) 10.1f **(49)**
Form - 2
2000 Turf 0-1: (15f) (sft)
Currently Pattern-class colt. (1st run) - 2nd of 5 getting 6lb from Three Cheers (9 Jun Maisons-Laffitte 15f sft RF 2000a). **in FR [0-1].*

MR BERGERAC (IRE) BHB 62f64a RR 64f 64a 1430[11]

9 b g Cyrano de Bergerac 7.3f **(58)** - Makalu (Godswalk (USA)) 7.3f **(58)**
Form - 556B0
Record 2000 - 1st:0 2nd:0 3rd:0 Ran:2
Pre2000 - 1st:9 2nd:10 3rd:10 Ran:88
Win Prizemoney £41,034 *Total Prizemoney* £77,350
Wins * 1999 Aug Bath (GD) H 8f 60 62
* 1997 Aug Newmar (G-F) H 6f 80 84
* 1997 May Leices (GD) H 6f 80 82
* 1996 Jly Newmar (GD) H 6f 79 83
2000 Turf 0-2: (8f 2) (g-s, frm)
Average gelding, effective 6 to 8f, best at 8f, acts on gd to frm, best on frm, has worn blinkers (extremely effectively), likes tight tracks. Turf high 14. Becoming disappointing.
**B Palling [9-90] P R John.*

MR BOUNTIFUL (IRE) BHB 57f54a RR 63f 54a 3493[8]

2 b c Mukaddamah (USA) 7.6f **(74)** - Nawadder (Kris) 9.5f **(73)**
Form - 708
Record 2000 - 1st:0 2nd:0 3rd:0 Ran:3
2000 Turf 0-3: (5f, 6f 2) (gd, g-f 2)
Currently average colt. Turf high 62.
**Andrew Turnell [0-3] Mrs Claire Hollowood.*

MR CHRISBI RR 1524[10]

3 b g Mistertopogigo (IRE) - Whispering Sea (Bustino) 10.4f **(64)**
Form - 00
Record 2000 - 1st:0 2nd:0 3rd:0 Ran:2
2000 Turf 0-2: (6f, 8f) (gd, frm)
Scopey, currently very poor gelding.
**S R Bowring [0-2] D H Bowring.*

MR COMBUSTIBLE (IRE) RR 84+f 4557[2]

2 b c Hernando (FR) - Warg (Dancing Brave (USA)) 8.4f **(76)**

Form - 72
Record 2000 - 1st:0 2nd:1 3rd:0 Ran:2
Win Prizemoney £0 *Total Prizemoney* £1,220
2000 Turf 0-2: (7f, 8f) (gd 2)
Currently decent colt. Turf high 84 (began Jly) - 2nd of 12 to Tiyoun (21 Spt Pontefract 8f gd RF 4557).
**B W Hills [0-2] R A N Bonnycastle.*

MR COSPECTOR BHB 60f RR 62f 5000[18]

3 b g Cosmonaut - L'Ancressaan (Dalsaan) 9.8f **(64)**
Form - 108400
Record 2000 - 1st:1 2nd:0 3rd:0 Ran:6
Pre2000 - 1st:0 2nd:0 3rd:0 Ran:4
Win Prizemoney £4,043 *Total Prizemoney* £4,280
Wins * **2000** Apr Haydoc (HVY) 7.1f 80 <
2000 Turf 1-6: (7f 1-1, 8f, 9f, 10f 2, 11f) (hvy 1-1, g-s 2, gd, g-f, frm)
Average gelding, effective 7f, acts on hvy, likes left handed tracks, likes tight tracks. Turf high 80 (1st run) - 1st of 7 from Criss Cross (22 Apr Haydock RF 0826). Inconsistent.
**T H Caldwell [1-10] R Cabrera-Vargas.*

MR CUBE (IRE) BHB 34f32a RR 44f 32a 4620[9]

10 ch g Tate Gallery (USA) 8.2f **(63)** - Truly Thankful (CAN) (Graustark) 10.1f **(70)**
Form - 808671743552478000
Record 2000 - 1st:1 2nd:1 3rd:1 Ran:18
Pre2000 - 1st:8 2nd:10 3rd:14 Ran:107
Win Prizemoney £27,100 *Total Prizemoney* £44,163
Wins * **2000** May Bright (FRM) H 7f 39 44
* 1997 Jly Epsom (G-S) H 7f 49 59
* 1996 Spt Folkes (G-F) H 6.9f 50 54
2000 Turf 1-13: (6f 2, 7f 1-5, 8f 6) (hvy, gd 3, g-f 1-5, frm 2, hrd 2) 2000 AW 0-5: (6f, 7f 3, 8f) (Equi 2, Fibr 3)
Moderate gelding, effective 6 to 8f, best at 7f, acts on g-s to frm, best on g-f, mostly wears blinkers. Turf high 44 (1st run) - 1st of 16 getting 8lb from Imbackagain (17 May Brighton RF 1260). AW high 26. Becoming disappointing.
**J M Bradley [7-109] R Miles (from P F I Cole [2-18] Nov 1993).*

MR ED (IRE) RR 23f 1904[20]

2 ch c In The Wings 11.2f **(77)** - Center Moriches (IRE) (Magical Wonder (USA))
Form - 0
Record 2000 - 1st:0 2nd:0 3rd:0 Ran:1
2000 Turf 0-1: (6f) (frm)
Currently little account colt.
**D R C Elsworth [0-1] Del & Jake Partnership.*

MR FORTYWINKS (IRE) BHB 62f65a RR 63f 65a 5322[2]

6 ch g Fools Holme (USA) 10.3f **(64)** - Dream on (Absalom) 7.2f **(58)**
Form - 2041341482
Record 2000 - 1st:2 2nd:2 3rd:1 Ran:10
Pre2000 - 1st:7 2nd:9 3rd:5 Ran:39
Win Prizemoney £23,396 *Total Prizemoney* £45,267
Wins * **2000** Spt Redcar (SFT) H 14.1f 59 63 <
* **2000** Jun Newcas (SFT) 12.4f 61
* 1999 Jly Carlis (GD) H 12f 61 62
* 1999 Jun Ripon (G-F) H 12.3f 58 61
* 1999 May Hamilt (Sft) H 13f 57 57
* 1998 Apr Nottin (SFT) H 10f 53 58
* 1998 *Jan Southw (STD) H 11f 61 61+*
* 1997 *Nov Wolver (STD) H 12f 49 63* <
* 1997 Aug Hamilt (GD) S 9.2f 44
2000 Turf 2-9: (12f 1-2, 13f 3, 14f 1-1, 15f 2, 17f) (sft 1-2, gd 1-3, g-f 2, frm 2) 2000 AW 0-1: (14f) (Fibr)
Above-average gelding, effective 12 to 17f, acts on sft to hrd - acts on Fibr, and likes Doncaster. Turf high 63 - 1st of 16 giving 22lb to Aldwych Arrow (30 Spt Redcar RF 4750) - also 1st of 5 from Lastman (7 Jun Newcastle RF 1789). Consistent. An able if modest middle-distance performer, he goes particularly well for Diana Jones. **J L Eyre [9-49] Miss Nuala Cassidy.*

MR GEORGE SMITH BHB 55f62a RR 59f 62a 753[15]

3 b g Prince Sabo 6.6f **(64)** - Nellie's Gamble **(36f 59a)** (Mummy's Game) 8.2f **(60)**
Form - 3130
Record 2000 - 1st:0 2nd:0 3rd:1 Ran:2
Pre2000 - 1st:1 2nd:0 3rd:1 Ran:6
Win Prizemoney £2,791 *Total Prizemoney* £3,582
Wins * 1999 *Dec Lingfi (STD) H 7f 54 56* <
2000 Turf 0-1: (8f) (g-s) 2000 AW 0-1: (6f) (Equi)
Fair gelding, effective 6 to 7f, - acts on Equi, prefers tight tracks. (1st run) - 3rd of 10 giving 5lb to Grey Flyer (2 Jan Lingfield 6f Equi RF 0003). **G L Moore [1-8] George Smith Ltd.*

MR KIPLING (USA) RR 44f 4270[12]

2 ch c Mr. Greeley (USA) - Exceedingly Bold (USA) (Exceedingly)
Form - 0
Record 2000 - 1st:0 2nd:0 3rd:0 Ran:1
2000 Turf 0-1: (7f) (g-f)
Currently moderate colt. **J W Hills [0-1] N N Browne.*

MR MAHOOSE (USA) RR 66f 5156[3]

2 b c Rakeen (USA) - Golden Hen (USA) (Native Prospector (USA))
Form - 3
Record 2000 - 1st:0 2nd:0 3rd:1 Ran:1
Win Prizemoney £0 *Total Prizemoney* £702
2000 Turf 0-1: (5f) (g-s)
Currently average colt. (1st run) - 3rd of 17 giving 5lb to Night Gypsy (24 Oct Nottingham 5f g-s RF 5156).
**W J Haggas [0-1] Wentworth Racing (Pty) Ltd.*

MR MAJICA BHB 51f41a RR 41f 41a 669[9]

6 b h Rudimentary (USA) 8.2f **(66)** - Pellinora (USA) (King Pellinore (USA)) 8.2f **(68)**
Form - 80
Record 2000 - 1st:0 2nd:0 3rd:0 Ran:2
Pre2000 - 1st:2 2nd:3 3rd:1 Ran:27
Win Prizemoney £6,271 *Total Prizemoney* £12,041
Wins 1998 Jun Salisb (G-F) C 8f 69
1997 Spt Yarmou (G-F) 6f 80 <
2000 AW 0-2: (8f 2) (Fibr 2)
Fair horse, effective 8f, acts on frm, often wears blinkers. AW high 26. Becoming disappointing.
**A J McNae [0-9] A J McNae (from B J Meehan [2-20] Jly 1998).*

MR MORIARTY (IRE) BHB 27f24a RR 25f 24a 2188[6]

9 ch g Tate Gallery (USA) 8.2f **(63)** - Bernica (FR) (Caro)
Form - 76
Record 2000 - 1st:0 2nd:0 3rd:0 Ran:2
Pre2000 - 1st:3 2nd:4 3rd:3 Ran:50
Win Prizemoney £11,736 *Total Prizemoney* £15,577
Wins * 1998 Jun Newmar (GD) H 12f 27 36
* 1996 *Feb Southw (STD) H 12f 36 41* <
* 1996 *Jan Southw (STD) H 12f 24 40*
2000 Turf 0-1: (12f) (frm) 2000 AW 0-1: (16f) (Fibr)
Little account gelding, has worn blinkers.
**S R Bowring [10-65] D H Bowring (from A L Forbes [0-7] Jly 1994).*

MR NEVERMIND (IRE) BHB 34f40a RR 40a 5316[17]

10 b g The Noble Player (USA) 7.7f **(58)** - Salacia (Seaepic (USA)) 9f **(56)**
Form - 0
Record 2000 - 1st:0 2nd:0 3rd:0 Ran:1
Pre2000 - 1st:13 2nd:15 3rd:13 Ran:78
Win Prizemoney £42,414 *Total Prizemoney* £62,232
Wins 1997 *Feb Wolver (STD) H 7f 85 85* <
1997 *Feb Lingfi (STD) H 7f 80 83*
1997 *Jan Lingfi (STD) H 8f 76 80*
1996 *Dec Lingfi (STD) C 8f 62+*
1996 *Nov Lingfi (STD) H 7f 73 74*
1996 Spt Bright (FRM) C 8f 67
1996 *Mar Lingfi (STD) C 7f 75*
2000 Turf 0-1: (8f) (g-s)
Little account gelding, has worn blinkers.
**J E Long [0-1] John Nicholson (from G L Moore [12-68] Oct 1998).*

MR PERRY (IRE) BHB 37f48a RR 42f 48a 5316[6]

4 br g Perugino (USA) - Elegant Tune (USA) (Alysheba (USA)) 9f **(84)**
Form - 0723000600886
Record 2000 - 1st:0 2nd:1 3rd:1 Ran:13
Pre2000 - 1st:1 2nd:2 3rd:0 Ran:11
Win Prizemoney £2,967 *Total Prizemoney* £6,158
Wins 1999 *Spt Wolver (STD) H 8.5f 65 66* <
2000 Turf 0-13: (7f 5, 8f 5, 9f 2, 10f) (g-s 2, gd 4, g-f 2, frm 5)

Workmanlike, moderate gelding, effective 7f, acts on g-s, has worn blinkers. Turf high 54.
**M D Hammond [0-16] Steve Semple (from J S Moore [1-11] Oct 1999).*

MR PERTEMPS BHB 49f50a **RR 51f 50a** 4182[2]
2 b c Primo Dominie 7.2f **(67)** - Amber Mill (Doulab (USA)) 9.8f **(65)**
Form - 0602
Record 2000 - 1st:0 2nd:1 3rd:0 Ran:4
Win Prizemoney £0 *Total Prizemoney* £1,156
2000 Turf 0-3: (5f 2, 7f) (g-s, gd 2) 2000 AW 0-1: (6f) (Fibr)
Fair colt. Turf high 51 - 2nd of 12 getting 25lb from Da Vinci (3 Spt Hamilton 5f g-s RF 4182).
**S C Williams [0-4] Pertemps Flexipeople Owners Syndicate.*

MR PIANO MAN (IRE) BHB 70f **RR 68f** 3825[9]
2 gr g Paris House 5.9f **(64)** - Winter March (Ballad Rock) 7.8f **(63)**
Form - 3050
Record 2000 - 1st:0 2nd:0 3rd:1 Ran:4
Win Prizemoney £0 *Total Prizemoney* £450
2000 Turf 0-4: (5f 2, 6f 2) (frm 3, hrd)
Average gelding. Turf high 68 (began Jly) - 5th of 9 to Times Square (26 Jly Catterick 6f frm RF 3126).
**J L Eyre [0-4] Mrs S J Yates.*

MR ROUGH BHB 38f36a **RR 41f 36a** 83[9]
9 b g Fayruz 6.6f **(63)** - Rheinbloom (Rheingold) 10.4f **(62)**
Form - 75200
Record 2000 - 1st:0 2nd:0 3rd:0 Ran:2
Pre2000 - 1st:5 2nd:8 3rd:15 Ran:81
Win Prizemoney £15,954 *Total Prizemoney* £30,357
Wins * 1998 Jly Bright (GD) S 8f 39
* 1997 Jun Yarmou (FRM) SH 8f 50 57
2000 AW 0-2: (8f 2) (Fibr 2)
Moderate gelding, effective 8f, acts on gd - acts on AW, has worn blinkers (effectively). AW high 12. **D Morris [5-84] D Morris.*

MRS JODI BHB 39f **RR 27f** 5082[10]
4 b f Yaheeb (USA) - Knayton Lass **(56f)** (Presidium)
Form - 00
Record 2000 - 1st:0 2nd:0 3rd:0 Ran:2
Pre2000 - 1st:0 2nd:0 3rd:1 Ran:5
Win Prizemoney £0 *Total Prizemoney* £594
2000 Turf 0-2: (10f 2) (hvy, g-s)
Little account filly. Turf high 27 (began Oct).
**J M Jefferson [3-13] & Mrs J M Davenport.*

MRS MITCHELL BHB 45f39a **RR 47f 39a** 5010[9]
2 ch f River Falls 8.2f **(56)** - White Hare **(32f)** (Indian Ridge)
Form - 6700
Record 2000 - 1st:0 2nd:0 3rd:0 Ran:4
2000 Turf 0-2: (5f, 6f) (gd, g-f) 2000 AW 0-2: (5f, 7f) (Fibr 2)
Moderate filly. Turf high 47 (began Jly). AW high 32 (began Spt).
**D Nicholls [0-4] Robert Macgregor.*

MRS P BHB 95f **RR 87f** 4700[18]
3 b f First Trump - Zinzi (Song) 7.2f **(61)**
Form - 000
Record 2000 - 1st:0 2nd:0 3rd:0 Ran:3
Pre2000 - 1st:2 2nd:4 3rd:1 Ran:8
Win Prizemoney £30,233 *Total Prizemoney* £36,212
Wins * 1999 Spt Doncas (G-F) G2 5f 94 <
* 1999 Aug Sandow (GD) H 5f 75 73
2000 Turf 0-3: (5f 3) (g-s, gd, g-f)
Workmanlike, useful filly, effective 5f, acts on frm. Turf high 87. Consistent. She caused a real surprise when winning the 1999 Flying Childers at 33/1. However, in a light season last year, failed to build on that, and probably failed to train on.
**Mrs L Stubbs [2-11] Sir Stephen Hastings.*

MR SPEAKER (IRE) BHB 49f40a **RR 18f 40a** 5316[11]
7 ch g Statoblest 6.4f **(63)** - Casting Vote (USA) (Monteverdi) 6.5f **(61)**
Form - 508000
Record 2000 - 1st:0 2nd:0 3rd:0 Ran:6
Pre2000 - 1st:3 2nd:2 3rd:3 Ran:31
Win Prizemoney £9,078 *Total Prizemoney* £12,981
Wins * 1999 Oct Bright (G-S) H 8f 54 56
* 1998 Spt Beverl (G-F) H 7.5f 55 60 <
* 1996 Jly Chepst (G-F) H 8.1f 60 60 <
2000 Turf 0-3: (7f, 8f, 10f) (g-s 2, frm) 2000 AW 0-3: (8f 2, 10f) (Equi, Fibr 2)
Little account gelding, effective 8 to 9f, acts on gd to frm, likes tight tracks. Turf high 18 (began Spt). AW high 28. Inconsistent.
**C F Wall [3-36] David Allan (from G C Bravery [0-2] Jan 1998).*

MR SPECULATOR BHB 45f40a **RR 14f 40a** 171[6]
7 ch g Kefaah (USA) 11.2f **(64)** - Humanity (Ahonoora) 8.1f **(73)**
Form - 305346
Record 2000 - 1st:0 2nd:0 3rd:1 Ran:5
Pre2000 - 1st:3 2nd:1 3rd:5 Ran:24
Win Prizemoney £9,155 *Total Prizemoney* £11,597
Wins *1997 Feb Wolver (STD) H 12f 51 52*
1996 Dec Wolver (STD) H 12f 48 49
1996 Jly Warwic (G-F) H 14.9f 56 60 <
2000 AW 0-5: (12f 4, 15f) (Fibr 5)
Moderate gelding, effective 12f, - acts on Fibr, often wears blinkers. AW high 45 - 3rd of 7 getting 8lb from Java Shrine (11 Jan Wolverhampton 12f Fibr RF 0068). Is rather one-paced, but has run some genuine races at Wolverhampton.
**J L Spearing [4-27] North Kilworth Racing (from J E Banks [2-14] Oct 1997).*

MRS PERTEMPS BHB 73f **RR 73f** 3442[4]
2 ch f Ashkalani (IRE) - Allepolina (USA) (Trempolino (USA)) 12f **(71)**
Form - 031
Record 2000 - 1st:0 2nd:0 3rd:1 Ran:3
Win Prizemoney £0 *Total Prizemoney* £642
2000 Turf 0-3: (5f 2, 6f) (frm 2, hrd)
Currently above-average filly. Turf high 73 (began Jly).
**J R Fanshawe [0-3] Pertemps Flexipeople Owners Syndicate.*

MR SQUIGGLE (IRE) BHB 50f **RR 57f** 4172[6]
2 b c Persian Bold 10f **(69)** - Soul Fire (IRE) (Exactly Sharp (USA))
Form - 866
Record 2000 - 1st:0 2nd:0 3rd:0 Ran:3
2000 Turf 0-2: (6f, 8f) (gd, g-f) 2000 AW 0-1: (6f) (Fibr)
Currently fair colt. Turf high 57. **A Dickman [0-3] Damian McGuigan.*

MR STICKYWICKET BHB 27f32a **RR 25f 32a** 3968[13]
3 b g Mistertopogigo (IRE) - Low Road (Lomond (USA)) 8.8f **(65)**
Form - 0080670600
Record 2000 - 1st:0 2nd:0 3rd:0 Ran:9
Pre2000 - 1st:0 2nd:0 3rd:0 Ran:1
2000 Turf 0-4: (7f 4) (g-s, gd, g-f, frm) 2000 AW 0-5: (5f 2, 6f 2, 7f) (Fibr 5)
Little account gelding, has worn blinkers. Turf high 25. AW high 23. **M J Polglase [0-10] M J Polglase.*

MRS TIGGYWINKLE BHB 50a **RR 54f** 5243[6]
2 b f Magic Ring (IRE) 6.5f **(64)** - Upper Sister (Upper Case (USA)) 8.2f **(55)**
Form - 640706026
Record 2000 - 1st:0 2nd:1 3rd:0 Ran:9
Win Prizemoney £0 *Total Prizemoney* £542
2000 Turf 0-4: (5f 2, 6f 2) (gd, frm 3) 2000 AW 0-5: (5f 2, 6f 2, 8f) (Fibr 5)
Fair filly, effective 5f, - acts on Fibr, has worn blinkers. Turf high 54. AW high 57 - 4th of 14 giving 2lb to Broughtons Motto (15 May Southwell 5f Fibr RF 1207). Consistent.
**N P Littmoden [0-9] Wilwyn Racing (WWW Wilwyn Com).*

MR STYLISH BHB 76f76a **RR 76f 76a** 5068[1]
4 b g Mazilier (USA) 8.5f **(56)** - Moore Stylish (Moorestyle) 6.9f **(64)**
Form - 02330505330171
Record 2000 - 1st:2 2nd:1 3rd:4 Ran:14
Pre2000 - 1st:0 2nd:3 3rd:2 Ran:11
Win Prizemoney £7,842 *Total Prizemoney* £15,626
Wins * 2000 Oct Bath (GD) H 5.1f 70 76 <
*** 2000** Spt Beverl (G-F) 5f 65+
2000 Turf 2-14: (5f 2-2, 6f 11, 7f) (g-s 1-2, gd, g-f 1-7, frm 4)
Unfurnished, decent gelding, effective 5 to 6f, best at 6f, acts on g-s to frm, has worn blinkers, prefers left handed tracks, excels at Bath and Goodwood. Turf high 76 - 1st of 20 getting 2lb from Ulysses Daughter (19 Oct Bath RF 5068).
**I A Balding [2-25] T J W Burton.*

MR TOD BHB 44f44a **RR 48f 44a** 5102[17]

2 b g Mistertopogigo (IRE) - Pillow Talk (IRE) **(40df 47a)** (Taufan (USA)) 7f **(57)**
Form - 06080
Record 2000 - 1st:0 2nd:0 3rd:0 Ran:5
2000 Turf 0-1: (6f) (gd) 2000 AW 0-4: (6f 2, 7f 2) (Fibr 4)
Fair gelding. AW high 51 (began Aug).
**J G Given [0-5] Wilwyn Racing (WWW Wilwyn Com).*

MR UPHILL RR 45f 4653[6]

2 b g Tragic Role (USA) 9.4f **(63)** - Kumzar (Hotfoot) 10.5f **(59)**
Form - 06
Record 2000 - 1st:0 2nd:0 3rd:0 Ran:2
2000 Turf 0-1: (6f) (g-f) 2000 AW 0-1: (7f) (Fibr)
Currently moderate gelding, often wears blinkers.
**R M Beckett [0-2] The Inzacure Partnership.*

MUAKAAD RR 108+f 4354a[1]

3 b c Muhtarram (USA) - Forest Lair (Habitat) 9.4f **(70)**
Form - 130131
2000 Turf 3-6: (8f, 10f 3-4, 12f) (sft 1-1, gd 1-3, g-f 1-2)
Pattern-class colt, effective 8 to 10f, best at 10f, acts on gd to g-f, best on gd. Turf high 108 - 1st of 8 getting 11lb from Dolydille (9 Spt Leopardstown RF 4354a) - also 1st of 5 from Polish Panache (19 Jly Leopardstown RF 3109a). Finished third of four to Sinndar at Leopardstown before finishing last in the French Derby. Landed a listed event at Leopardstown in September and should be up to winning a pattern event on the continent.
**D K Weld in IRE [3-6] Hamdan Al Maktoum.*

MUBTAKER (USA) RR 102++f 5321[3]

3 ch c Silver Hawk (USA) 11.2f **(85)** - Gazayil (USA) (Irish River (FR)) 8.6f **(78)**
Form - 13
Record 2000 - 1st:1 2nd:0 3rd:1 Ran:2
Win Prizemoney £5,174 *Total Prizemoney* £7,364
Wins * 2000 Oct Newbur (HVY) 10f 102++ <
2000 Turf 1-2: (10f 1-1, 12f) (sft 1-2)
Currently very useful colt. Turf high 102 (1st run) (began Oct) - 1st of 12 from Petersham (21 Oct Newbury RF 5135). Landed a Newbury maiden on his belated reappearance.
**M P Tregoning [1-2] Hamdan Al Maktoum.*

MUCH ADO BHB 60f **RR 60f** 5022[6]

3 b f Mujtahid (USA) 7.4f **(69)** - Lamu Lady (IRE) (Lomond (USA)) 8.8f **(65)**
Form - 06
Record 2000 - 1st:0 2nd:0 3rd:0 Ran:2
2000 Turf 0-2: (7f, 8f) (g-s 2)
Scopey, currently average filly. Turf high 60 (began Oct).
**J H M Gosden [0-2] David Simpson.*

MUCHANA YETU BHB 45f **RR 64f** 4634[6]

3 b f Mtoto 11.5f **(71)** - Bobbie Dee **(74f)** (Blakeney) 10.5f **(64)**
Form - 86065856
Record 2000 - 1st:0 2nd:0 3rd:0 Ran:8
Pre2000 - 1st:0 2nd:0 3rd:1 Ran:4
Win Prizemoney £0 *Total Prizemoney* £1,123
2000 Turf 0-8: (8f, 10f 2, 12f 4, 16f) (g-s 2, gd 2, g-f 4)
Neat, average filly, effective 6f, acts on frm, has worn blinkers. Turf high 64. **Mrs P N Dutfield [0-12] Mrs Nerys Dutfield.*

MUCHEA BHB 98f **RR 104f** 4991[8]

6 ch h Shalford (IRE) 7.8f **(63)** - Bargouzine (Hotfoot) 10.5f **(59)**
Form - 022754004125058
Record 2000 - 1st:1 2nd:3 3rd:0 Ran:15
Pre2000 - 1st:5 2nd:3 3rd:5 Ran:24
Win Prizemoney £102,811 *Total Prizemoney* £223,901
Wins * 2000 Aug Goodwo (GD) H 7f 96 99
* 1998 Jun Newmar (GD) G3 7f 115 <
* 1998 Apr Currag (HVY) G3 7f 111
* 1996 Aug Baden- (GD) G2 6f 104
* 1996 Apr Newmar (G-F) 5f 84+
* 1996 Mar Catter (G-S) 5f 93
2000 Turf 1-15: (7f 1-13, 8f 2) (hvy, g-s 2, gd 1-11, g-f)
Very useful horse, effective 7f, acts on g-s to g-f, best on gd, has worn blinkers (very effectively), excels at Newmarket and Goodwood. Turf high 104 - 2nd of 21 giving 15lb to Present Laughter (19 Apr Newmarket 7f gd RF 0794) - also 1st of 8 giving 1lb to Omaha City (26 Aug Goodwood RF 3986). A winner twice at Group Three level in 1998, he raced in Hong Kong in 1999, but did not take to the conditions there. Mixed form in varied company last term before taking a rated stakes at Goodwood in August.
**M R Channon [6-39] Andy Smith.*

MUCHO GUSTO RR 53f 2564[5]

2 b c Casteddu 7.4f **(54)** - Heather Honey (Insan (USA))
Form - 05
Record 2000 - 1st:0 2nd:0 3rd:0 Ran:2
2000 Turf 0-2: (6f, 7f) (g-f, frm)
Currently fair colt. Turf high 53. **J L Dunlop [0-2] J L Dunlop.*

MUDAA-EB RR 106f 4798a[3]

4 br c Machiavellian (USA) 9.8f **(83)** - Alkaffeyeh (IRE) (Sadler's Wells (USA)) 10f **(76)**
Form - 47043284723
2000 Turf 0-11: (8f 2, 9f 4, 11f, 12f 4) (hvy, gd 6, g-f 2)
Pattern-class colt, effective 9 to 12f, acts on g-f, has worn blinkers, likes right handed tracks. Turf high 106 - 2nd of 13 giving 5lb to Shoal Creek (17 Spt Curragh 9f RF 4528a). Tried in the Irish Derby in 1999, he ran well in Listed heats last year but does not seem to have a trip. **K Prendergast in IRE [2-19] Hamdan Al Maktoum.*

MUDDY WATER BHB 56f40a **RR 61f 40a** 2819[7]

4 b f Salse (USA) 10.9f **(71)** - Rainbow Fleet (Nomination) 7f **(60)**
Form - 017732507
Record 2000 - 1st:1 2nd:1 3rd:1 Ran:9
Pre2000 - 1st:0 2nd:2 3rd:1 Ran:10
Win Prizemoney £1,879 *Total Prizemoney* £5,547
Wins * 2000 Apr Folkes (SFT) H 6f 52 61+ <
2000 Turf 1-4: (6f 1-1, 8f 2, 10f) (sft, g-s 1-2, frm) 2000 AW 0-5: (7f 2, 8f 3) (Equi, Fibr 4)
Unfurnished, average filly, effective 6f, acts on g-s. Turf high 61 (1st run) - 1st of 15 giving 1lb to Marengo (18 Apr Folkestone RF 0758). AW high 48. **D Marks [1-19] C R Buttery.*

MUD'N'BERT BHB 30f **RR 29f** 5053[11]

2 b f Lightning Dealer - Ardleigh Venture (Daring March) 7.1f **(61)**
Form - 000
Record 2000 - 1st:0 2nd:0 3rd:0 Ran:3
2000 Turf 0-3: (7f 2, 8f) (sft, gd, frm)
Currently little account filly. Turf high 29 (began Aug).
**D Moffatt [0-3] Mrs Maureen Pickering.*

MUFFIN MAN BHB 47f **RR 44f** 4147[12]

3 b c Timeless Times (USA) 6.1f **(56)** - Allesca **(68f)** (Alleging (USA))
Form - 00046740
Record 2000 - 1st:0 2nd:0 3rd:0 Ran:8
Pre2000 - 1st:0 2nd:1 3rd:0 Ran:13
Win Prizemoney £0 *Total Prizemoney* £3,072
2000 Turf 0-8: (6f 3, 7f 4, 8f) (g-f 3, frm 5)
Workmanlike, moderate colt, effective 7f, acts on g-f, likes left handed tracks. Turf high 44. **M D I Usher [0-21] Miss D G Kerr.*

MUFFLED (USA) BHB 62f56a **RR 64f 56a** 4173[1]

3 ch f Mizaaya - Sound It (USA) (Believe It (USA)) 9.4f **(70)**
Form - 702081
Record 2000 - 1st:1 2nd:1 3rd:0 Ran:6
Pre2000 - 1st:0 2nd:0 3rd:0 Ran:2
Win Prizemoney £4,394 *Total Prizemoney* £5,906
Wins * 2000 Spt Thirsk (GD) 6f 54 <
2000 Turf 1-5: (6f 1-4, 7f) (gd, g-f 1-2, frm 2) 2000 AW 0-1: (9f) (Fibr)
Workmanlike, average filly, effective 6f, acts on frm. Turf high 64 - 2nd of 14 giving 1lb to Water Babe (8 Jly Leicester 6f frm RF 2642).
**J L Dunlop [1-8] P D Player.*

MUGHARREB (USA) RR 89+f 4935[3]

2 b c Gone West (USA) 7.8f **(82)** - Marling (IRE) (Lomond (USA)) 8.8f **(65)**
Form - 3
Record 2000 - 1st:0 2nd:0 3rd:1 Ran:1
Win Prizemoney £0 *Total Prizemoney* £1,138
2000 Turf 0-1: (6f) (gd)

Currently useful colt. (1st run) - 3rd of 29 to Ajwaa (12 Oct Newmarket 6f gd RF 4935). Out of a high-class mare, he should make a name for himself at three.
**B Hanbury [0-1] Hamdan Al Maktoum.*

MUHTATHIR BHB 124f **RR 124f** 5327a[5]
5 ch h Elmaamul (USA) 8.1f **(70)** - Majmu (USA) (Al Nasr (FR)) 9.3f **(68)**
Form - 4316155
Record 2000 - 1st:2 2nd:0 3rd:1 Ran:6
Pre2000 - 1st:6 2nd:3 3rd:1 Ran:17
Win Prizemoney £271,168 *Total Prizemoney* £411,629
Wins * **2000** Aug Deauvi (G-F) G1 8f 124+ <
* **2000** May San Si (G-S) G2 8f 120
* 1999 Oct San Si (GD) G1 8f 107+
1998 Aug Goodwo (G-F) G2 8f 121
1998 Aug Newbur (G-F) G3 7.3f 118
1998 Jly Doncas (G-F) 8f 109+
1997 Jly Sandow (G-S) 7.1f 105+
1997 Jun Sandow (G-F) 7.1f 90
2000 Turf 2-5: (8f 2-5) (g-s 1-1, gd, g-f 1-1, frm 2) 2000 AW 0-1: (8f) (Dirt)
Very high-class colt, effective 8f, acts on g-s to frm - acts on Dirt, excels at San Siro. Turf high 124 - 1st of 11 from Sendawar (13 Aug Deauville RF 3735a) - also 1st of 8 giving 4lb to Embody (21 May San Siro RF 1466a). (1st run) - 3rd of 13 giving 11lb to Conflict (25 Mar Nad Al Sheba 8f Dirt RF 0575a). One of Godolphin's clutch of high-class milers, he scored at San Siro on his second run of last year, but gained a somewhat surprising win in the Prix Jacques Le Marois at Deauville which had been seen as a match between Sendawar and Crimplene. Besides that, his globetrotting did not pay many dividends in 2000. Suited by making the running.
**S bin Suroor [3-8] Godolphin (from S bin Suroor in UAE [0-3] Mar 2000).*

MUJAALED (IRE) RR 4329[10]
3 b g Elmaamul (USA) 8.1f **(70)** - Balaabel (USA) **(76f)** (Sadler's Wells (USA)) 10f **(76)**
Form - 00
Record 2000 - 1st:0 2nd:0 3rd:0 Ran:2
2000 Turf 0-2: (7f, 11f) (gd, frm)
Rangy, currently very poor gelding. (began Aug) - 10th of 10 giving 15lb to Chez Bonito (12 Spt Yarmouth 11f gd RF 4329).
**D W Chapman [0-2] Michael Hill*

MUJADO (IRE) BHB 97f **RR 86f** 4259[11]
2 b f Mujadil (USA) 7.7f **(70)** - Unaria (Prince Tenderfoot (USA)) 9f **(61)**
Form - 2210
Record 2000 - 1st:1 2nd:2 3rd:0 Ran:4
Win Prizemoney £3,854 *Total Prizemoney* £8,130
Wins * **2000** Aug Windso (G-F) 6f 85+ <
2000 Turf 1-4: (6f 1-4) (gd 2, g-f 1-2)
Useful filly. Turf high 86 (began Jly) - also 1st of 17 from Tickle (7 Aug Windsor RF 3436). Came up against high-class fillies in Khulan and Regal Rose on her first two starts before bolting up at Windsor. **B J Meehan [1-4] Total (Bloodstock) Ltd.*

MUJA FAREWELL BHB 86f **RR 83f** 4697[1]
2 ch f Mujtahid (USA) 7.4f **(69)** - Highland Rhapsody (IRE) **(76f)** (Kris) 9.5f **(73)**
Form - 122101
Record 2000 - 1st:3 2nd:2 3rd:0 Ran:6
Win Prizemoney £15,042 *Total Prizemoney* £17,196
Wins * **2000** Spt Newmar (GD) H 5f 81 83 <
* **2000** Jun Windso (G-F) 5f 74
* **2000** May Redcar (G-S) 5f 62+
2000 Turf 3-6: (5f 3-6) (gd 1-4, g-f 1-1, frm 1-1)
Decent filly, effective 5f, acts on gd to frm. Turf high 83 - 1st of 14 giving 3lb to Amelia (28 Spt Newmarket RF 4697) - also 1st of 5 getting 3lb from Fantasy Believer (19 Jun Windsor RF 2107). A pacey sort with the right attitude, she should continue to pay her way if not over-faced. **T D Barron [3-6] Hollins Huntbach Rut Carson.*

MUJAGEM (IRE) BHB 40f51a **RR 36f 51a** 4652[5]
4 br f Mujadil (USA) 7.7f **(70)** - Lili Bengam (Welsh Saint) 7.6f **(64)**
Form - 0146027035
Record 2000 - 1st:1 2nd:1 3rd:1 Ran:10
Pre2000 - 1st:0 2nd:0 3rd:0 Ran:7
Win Prizemoney £2,756 *Total Prizemoney* £4,297
Wins * **2000** *May Southw (STD) H 8f 44 46* <
2000 Turf 0-5: (5f 2, 6f 2, 7f) (gd 4, hrd) 2000 AW 1-5: (5f, 7f, 8f 1-3) (Fibr 1-5)
Workmanlike, moderate filly, has broken blood-vessels, effective 5 to 8f, - acts on Fibr, has worn blinkers. Turf high 36. AW high 47 - also 1st of 11 getting 8lb from Stravsea (15 May Southwell RF 1206). She has not shown much on turf and missed all of last season, but she looked a natural when winning at Southwell on her Fibresand debut and definitely has a future on that surface.
**M W Easterby [1-17] C F Spence.*

MUJAHID (USA) BHB 110f **RR 111f** 895[5]
4 b c Danzig (USA) 8.1f **(88)** - Elrafa Ah (USA) **(101f)** (Storm Cat (USA))
Form - 35
Record 2000 - 1st:0 2nd:0 3rd:1 Ran:2
Pre2000 - 1st:3 2nd:1 3rd:1 Ran:10
Win Prizemoney £142,822 *Total Prizemoney* £189,133
Wins * 1998 Oct Newmar (GD) G1 7f 118 <
* 1998 Jly Salisb (G-F) 6f 95+
* 1998 Jly Newmar (G-F) 6f 98+
2000 Turf 0-2: (8f, 9f) (sft, gd)
Scopey, Group-class colt, effective 8 to 10f, acts on gd to frm, best on gd, has worn blinkers. Turf high 111 (1st run) - 3rd of 11 to Indian Lodge (19 Apr Newmarket 9f gd RF 0795). Consistent. He won the Dewhurst back in 1998 and went on to finish third in the following year's 2000 Guineas. However, he was disappointing in two starts last spring and has been retired to the Beech House Stud, Newmarket, at £4,000 plus VAT.
**J L Dunlop [3-12] Hamdan Al Maktoum.*

MUJALIA (IRE) BHB 48f **RR 58f** 4725[14]
2 b g Mujtahid (USA) 7.4f **(69)** - Danalia (IRE) **(51f)** (Danehill (USA)) 10f **(72)**
Form - 00000
Record 2000 - 1st:0 2nd:0 3rd:0 Ran:5
2000 Turf 0-5: (5f, 6f, 7f 2, 8f) (g-s 2, gd, g-f, frm)
Fair gelding. Turf high 58. **S Dow [0-5] Byerley Bloodstock.*

MUJALINA (IRE) BHB 80f79a **RR 78f 79a** 5320[6]
2 b c Mujadil (USA) 7.7f **(70)** - Talina's Law (IRE) **(69f)** (Law Society (USA)) 9.9f **(70)**
Form - 02187006
Record 2000 - 1st:1 2nd:1 3rd:0 Ran:8
Win Prizemoney £2,775 *Total Prizemoney* £3,615
Wins * **2000** *Jly Southw (STD) 7f 79* <
2000 Turf 0-7: (6f, 7f 6) (sft, gd, g-f, frm 4) 2000 AW 1-1: (7f 1-1) (Fibr 1-1)
Above-average colt, effective 7f, - acts on Fibr, has worn blinkers. Turf high 79. (1st run) - 1st of 10 from Blushing Spur (3 Jly Southwell RF 2483). Got off the mark with a fluent victory on the Southwell Fibresand in July and should find another race or two..
**E J O'Neill [1-8] M Donovan.*

MUJA'S MAGIC (IRE) BHB 49f60a **RR 49f 60a** 3994[8]
5 b m Mujadil (USA) 7.7f **(70)** - Grave Error (Northern Treat (USA)) 6f **(50)**
Form - 71244727508501702008
Record 2000 - 1st:1 2nd:3 3rd:0 Ran:18
Pre2000 - 1st:4 2nd:5 3rd:6 Ran:51
Win Prizemoney £19,745 *Total Prizemoney* £29,729
Wins * **2000** Jly Yarmou (G-F) H 6f 48 52
* 1999 *Dec Wolver (STD) H 7f 58 64* <
1999 Aug Beverl (GD) H 5f 39 45
1998 Jun Bright (GD) H 6f 53 59
1997 *Dec Lingfi (STD) H 6f 54 58*
2000 Turf 1-10: (5f 2, 6f 1-6, 7f, 8f) (g-f 3, frm 1-5, hrd 2) 2000 AW 0-8: (6f 4, 7f 3, 8f) (Fibr 8)
Moderate filly, effective 6 to 7f, best at 6f, - acts on Fibr, mostly wears blinkers (effectively), likes tight tracks, excels at Wolverhampton, likes Southwell. Turf high 52. AW high 63 (1st run) - 2nd of 9 giving 2lb to Days of Grace (7 Jan Southwell 6f Fibr RF 0041).
**Mrs N Macauley [2-21] T J Bird (from K T Ivory [3-48] Spt 1999).*

MUJKARI (IRE) BHB 34f37a **RR 37f 37a** 4147[11]
4 ch g Mujtahid (USA) 7.4f **(69)** - Hot Curry (USA) (Sharpen Up) 8.3f

(67)
Form - 080084702370
Record 2000 - 1st:0 2nd:1 3rd:1 Ran:12
Pre2000 - 1st:1 2nd:1 3rd:0 Ran:15
Win Prizemoney £3,273 *Total Prizemoney* £5,113
Wins * 1999 Aug Bright (FRM) H 7f 38 41 <
2000 Turf 0-9: (7f 6, 8f 3) (gd, g-f 3, frm 5) 2000 AW 0-3: (7f 2, 8f) (Equi, Fibr 2)
Very moderate gelding, effective 7f, acts on frm, often wears blinkers (effectively). Turf high 37 - 2nd of 18 getting 10lb from Who Goes There (28 Jly Chepstow 7f frm RF 3171). AW high 23.
**J M Bradley [1-21] Robert Bailey (from R Hannon [0-6] Oct 1998).*

MUJODA BHB 33f RR 19f 966[17]
3 b f Mizoram (USA) - Titian Beauty (Auction Ring (USA)) 8.6f **(65)**
Form - 0
Record 2000 - 1st:0 2nd:0 3rd:0 Ran:1
Pre2000 - 1st:0 2nd:0 3rd:0 Ran:3
2000 Turf 0-1: (6f) (gd)
Light-framed, poor filly. **R Brotherton [0-4] Mrs Sandra Hall.*

MUKAABED (USA) BHB 77f RR 82f 3008[3]
3 ch c Phone Trick (USA) 7f **(62)** - Slick Delivery (USA) (Topsider (USA)) 8.3f **(71)**
Form - 23
Record 2000 - 1st:0 2nd:1 3rd:1 Ran:2
Pre2000 - 1st:0 2nd:0 3rd:1 Ran:2
Win Prizemoney £0 *Total Prizemoney* £2,283
2000 Turf 0-2: (5f, 6f) (gd, g-f)
Scopey, decent colt. Turf high 78 (1st run) (began Jun) - 2nd of 9 giving 5lb to Annette Vallon (30 Jun Folkestone 5f g-f RF 2394).
**M P Tregoning [0-4] Hamdan Al Maktoum.*

MUKARRAB (USA) BHB 49f67a RR 51f 67a 5057[2]
6 b br g Dayjur (USA) 6.8f **(79)** - Mahassin (NZ) (Biscay (AUS)) 6.5f **(51)**
Form - 006043601004445082
Record 2000 - 1st:1 2nd:1 3rd:1 Ran:15
Pre2000 - 1st:7 2nd:7 3rd:11 Ran:61
Win Prizemoney £24,536 *Total Prizemoney* £42,899
Wins * 2000 Jun Thirsk (SFT) H 5f 48 51
* 1999 *Feb Lingfi (STD) H 6f 76 85* <
* 1999 *Feb Lingfi (STD) H 5f 76 78*
* 1999 *Jan Lingfi (STD) H 6f 67 74*
* 1999 *Jan Lingfi (STD) H 6f 49 74*
* 1998 *Dec Lingfi (STD) H 5f 49 55*
* 1998 *Dec Lingfi (STD) H 6f 42 51*
* 1998 Spt Thirsk (GD) H 5f 47 56
2000 Turf 1-11: (5f 1-9, 6f, 7f) (sft, gd 1-2, g-f 3, frm 5) 2000 AW 0-4: (5f 3, 6f) (Equi, Fibr 3)
Above-average gelding, effective 5 to 6f, best at 5f, - acts on AW, best on Equi, has worn blinkers, likes left handed tracks, likes tight tracks, and excels at Lingfield. Turf high 52. AW high 73.
**D W Chapman [8-70] Ian Armitage (from D K Weld in IRE [0-6] Jly 1997).*

MUKHALIF (IRE) BHB 110f RR 105f 3581[4]
4 ch c Caerleon (USA) 10.9f **(79)** - Potri Pe (ARG) (Potrillazo (ARG))
Form - 04
Record 2000 - 1st:0 2nd:0 3rd:0 Ran:2
Pre2000 - 1st:3 2nd:2 3rd:0 Ran:6
Win Prizemoney £164,451 *Total Prizemoney* £181,045
Wins * 1999 May Capann (G-F) G1 12f 105 <
1998 Spt Ascot (SFT) 7f 102+
1998 Spt Leices (G-S) 7f 97+
2000 Turf 0-2: (10f, 12f) (gd 2)
Scopey, Pattern-class colt, effective 10 to 12f, best at 10f, acts on gd to frm. Turf high 105. Improving. Winner of the Italian Derby in '99, he was well held in just two European starts last season.
**S bin Suroor [1-6] Godolphin (from D R Loder [2-2] Spt 1998).*

MUKHLLES (USA) BHB 47f48a RR 45f 48a 2160[P]
7 b g Diesis 9f **(80)** - Serenely (USA) (Alydar (USA)) 9.1f **(76)**
Form - 07P
Record 2000 - 1st:0 2nd:0 3rd:0 Ran:3
Pre2000 - 1st:1 2nd:0 3rd:3 Ran:24
Win Prizemoney £3,272 *Total Prizemoney* £5,177
Wins * 1999 Jun Lingfi (GD) H 10f 43 52 <
2000 Turf 0-3: (11f, 12f 2) (gd, g-f, frm)
Moderate gelding, effective 10 to 11f, acted on gd to g-f, preferred tight tracks. Turf high 45. (DEAD)
**Bob Jones [1-25] Mrs Daphne Downey (from Major W R Hern [0-2] Apr 1996).*

MULA GULA (USA) RR 120f 3942a[3]
4 b c Lil E.Tee (USA) - Night Tan (USA) (Ascot Knight (CAN))
Form - 3
2000 Turf 0-1: (10f) (g-s)
Currently very high-class colt, always wears blinkers. (1st run) - 3rd of 7 to Chester House (19 Aug Arlington Park 10f g-s RF 3942a). He finished third behind Chester House in the Arlington Million. **J Hollendorfer in USA [0-1] S Gula.*

MULLAGH HILL LAD (IRE) BHB 48f31a RR 59?f 31a 381[7]
7 b g Cyrano de Bergerac 7.3f **(58)** - Fantasise (FR) (General Assembly (USA)) 10f **(68)**
Form - 7
Record 2000 - 1st:0 2nd:0 3rd:0 Ran:1
Pre2000 - 1st:1 2nd:2 3rd:2 Ran:33
Win Prizemoney £2,085 *Total Prizemoney* £5,181
2000 AW 0-1: (8f) (Fibr)
Fair gelding, has worn blinkers.
**N P Littmoden [0-15] Nick Littmoden (from B A McMahon [1-19] Jly 1997).*

MULLAGHMORE (IRE) BHB 52f72a RR 51f 72a 4361[8]
4 b g Petardia 8.2f **(58)** - Comfrey Glen (Glenstal (USA)) 10.1f **(64)**
Form - 151550005138
Record 2000 - 1st:3 2nd:0 3rd:1 Ran:12
Pre2000 - 1st:0 2nd:0 3rd:2 Ran:11
Win Prizemoney £7,776 *Total Prizemoney* £9,363
Wins * 2000 Aug Bath (FRM) H 8f 46 49
* 2000 *Mar Lingfi (STD) H 10f 63 67* <
* 2000 *Jan Lingfi (STD) 8f 61*
2000 Turf 1-8: (8f 1-6, 9f, 10f) (gd, g-f 3, frm 3, hrd 1-1) 2000 AW 2-4: (8f 1-1, 10f 1-3) (Equi 2-4)
Scopey, average gelding, effective 8 to 10f, best at 8f, acts on g-f - acts on Equi, often wears blinkers, likes left handed tracks, excels at Bath and Leicester, likes Lingfield. Turf high 51. AW high 67 - 1st of 13 giving 5lb to Bonds Gully (1 Mar Lingfield RF 0389) - also 1st of 12 giving 5lb to Springtime Lady (19 Jan Lingfield RF 0114). Found his form when tried on Equitrack and has won twice on it early last year. Acted well on the firm surface when scoring his first Turf win at Bath in the summer, and currently racing off a much lower mark on grass. **M Kettle [3-23] Greenacres.*

MULLING IT OVER (IRE) BHB 52f RR 62f 4869[3]
2 b f Blues Traveller (IRE) - Wonderment (Mummy's Pet) 7.7f **(60)**
Form - 37703
Record 2000 - 1st:0 2nd:0 3rd:2 Ran:5
Win Prizemoney £0 *Total Prizemoney* £1,146
2000 Turf 0-5: (5f, 6f 2, 7f 2) (sft, gd, frm 3)
Average filly. Turf high 62.
**T D Easterby [0-5] Anglia Bloodstock Syndicate 1999.*

MULSANNE BHB 30f RR 40f 5060[12]
2 b c Clantime 6.6f **(57)** - Prim Lass **(39f 37a)** (Reprimand)
Form - 70080
Record 2000 - 1st:0 2nd:0 3rd:0 Ran:5
2000 Turf 0-5: (5f 2, 6f 2, 7f) (sft, g-f 2, frm 2)
Moderate colt. Turf high 40 (began Jly).
**P A Pritchard [0-1] P A Pritchard (from M Quinn [0-4] Aug 2000).*

MULTI FRANCHISE BHB 26f27a RR 27f 27a 1908[11]
7 ch g Gabitat 8.5f **(44)** - Gabibti (IRE) (Dara Monarch) 8.8f **(59)**
Form - 80
Record 2000 - 1st:0 2nd:0 3rd:0 Ran:2
Pre2000 - 1st:4 2nd:2 3rd:3 Ran:48
Win Prizemoney £10,045 *Total Prizemoney* £13,730
Wins 1997 *Nov Lingfi (STD) H 10f 39 46*
1996 Aug Bright (FRM) C 8f 54
1996 *Feb Lingfi (STD) C 10f 57*
2000 Turf 0-2: (12f 2) (g-f, frm)
Little account gelding, has worn blinkers. Turf high 27.
**Mrs L C Jewell [0-29] Mrs A Emanuel (from R M Flower [1-29] Spt*

1998).

MUMBAI BHB 25f RR 26f 1373[10]

4 b g Theatrical Charmer 10.9f **(63)** - Lehzen (Posse (USA)) 8.9f **(61)**
Form - 0
Record 2000 - 1st:0 2nd:0 3rd:0 Ran:1
Pre2000 - 1st:0 2nd:0 3rd:0 Ran:3
2000 AW 0-1: (11f) (Fibr)
Light-framed, little account gelding.
**D J Wintle [0-5] Lavender Hill Stud L L C.*

MUMBLING (IRE) RR 71f 4969[18]

2 ch c Dr Devious (IRE) 9.9f **(74)** - Valley Lights (IRE) (Dance of Life (USA)) 7f **(66)**
Form - 00
Record 2000 - 1st:0 2nd:0 3rd:0 Ran:2
2000 Turf 0-2: (7f, 8f) (gd, g-f)
Currently above-average colt. Turf high 71 (began Spt).
**M H Tompkins [0-2] Mrs Beryl Lockey.*

MUMMY NOSE BEST BHB 34f RR 30f 4[10]

4 b f Cyrano de Bergerac 7.3f **(58)** - Wendy's Way **(44f 41a)** (Merdon Melody)
Form - 0
Record 2000 - 1st:0 2nd:0 3rd:0 Ran:1
Pre2000 - 1st:0 2nd:0 3rd:0 Ran:8
2000 AW 0-1: (7f) (Equi)
Light-framed, very moderate filly.
**V Soane [0-9] The Fillies Fanciers.*

MUNADIL RR 83f 4969[3]

2 ch c Nashwan (USA) 10.3f **(79)** - Bintalshaati **(91f)** (Kris) 9.5f **(73)**
Form - 63
Record 2000 - 1st:0 2nd:0 3rd:1 Ran:2
Win Prizemoney £0 *Total Prizemoney* £1,200
2000 Turf 0-2: (8f 2) (gd, g-f)
Currently decent colt. Turf high 83 (began Spt) - 3rd of 29 to Terrestrial (13 Oct Newmarket 8f gd RF 4969).
**M P Tregoning [0-2] Hamdan Al Maktoum.*

MUNEEFA (USA) BHB 79f RR 79+f 4331[1]

3 b br f Storm Cat (USA) 7f **(86)** - By Land By Sea (USA) (Sauce Boat (USA)) 8.3f **(79)**
Form - 221
Record 2000 - 1st:1 2nd:2 3rd:0 Ran:3
Win Prizemoney £4,368 *Total Prizemoney* £6,608
Wins * 2000 Spt Yarmou (G-F) 6f 75 <
2000 Turf 1-3: (6f 1-2, 7f) (g-f, frm 1-2)
Light-framed, currently above-average filly. Turf high 79 - also 1st of 6 getting 5lb from Wind Chime (12 Spt Yarmouth RF 4331).
**E A L Dunlop [1-1] Maktoum Al Maktoum (from S bin Suroor [0-2] Jly 2000).*

MUNGO DUFF (IRE) BHB 58f RR 67f 1545[9]

5 b g Priolo (USA) 10.9f **(71)** - Noble Dust (USA) (Dust Commander (USA)) 10.3f **(77)**
Form - 0
Record 2000 - 1st:0 2nd:0 3rd:0 Ran:1
Pre2000 - 1st:0 2nd:0 3rd:0 Ran:4
2000 Turf 0-1: (10f) (gd)
Average gelding.
**Mrs V C Ward [0-1] & Mrs Jonathan Jay (from J R Fanshawe [0-2] Aug 1999).*

MUNGO PARK BHB 79f RR 84f 5055[12]

6 b g Selkirk (USA) 7.9f **(76)** - River Dove (USA) (Riverman (USA)) 9.1f **(76)**
Form - 20202222510000
Record 2000 - 1st:1 2nd:6 3rd:0 Ran:14
Pre2000 - 1st:7 2nd:5 3rd:4 Ran:52
Win Prizemoney £34,874 *Total Prizemoney* £59,545

Wins	*** 2000**	Aug	Beverl	(G-F)	H	5f	77	83 <
	* 1999	Apr	Thirsk	(GD)		5f		82+
	1998	Jly	Newcas	(G-F)	H	5f	77	80
	1998	Jun	Nottin	(G-F)	H	5.1f	75	76
	1998	May	Beverl	(GD)	H	5f	70	75
	1998	Apr	Newcas	(SFT)	H	5f	64	70
	1997	Oct	Newcas	(G-F)	H	5f	53	60
	1997	May	Carlis	(FRM)		5f		51

2000 Turf 1-14: (5f 1-9, 6f 5) (sft, gd 5, g-f 1-3, frm 5)
Decent gelding, effective 5 to 6f, best at 5f, acts on gd to frm, has worn blinkers, and excels at Bath. Turf high 83 - 1st of 19 giving 5lb to Mizhar (16 Aug Beverley RF 3688). He is a useful come-from-behind sprinter when in the mood, but does not have a great wins-to-runs ratio. Did win at Beverley in August when the blinkers were left off.
**M Dods [2-32] Exors of the late Mrs H M Carr (from Mrs J R Ramsden [6-34] Oct 1998).*

MUNIR RR 94+f 5131[1]

2 ch c Indian Ridge 7.6f **(74)** - Al Bahathri (USA) (Blushing Groom (FR)) 10.3f **(76)**
Form - 31
Record 2000 - 1st:1 2nd:0 3rd:1 Ran:2
Win Prizemoney £5,102 *Total Prizemoney* £5,551
Wins * 2000 Oct Newbur (HVY) 6f 94+ <
2000 Turf 1-2: (6f 1-2) (sft 1-1, gd)
Currently useful colt. Turf high 94 (began Spt) - 1st of 18 from Funny Valentine (21 Oct Newbury RF 5131).
**B W Hills [1-2] Hamdan Al Maktoum.*

MUNJIZ (IRE) BHB 110f RR 114f 2773[10]

4 b br h Marju (IRE) 9.2f **(76)** - Absaar (USA) (Alleged (USA)) 10f **(76)**
Form - 00
Record 2000 - 1st:0 2nd:0 3rd:0 Ran:2
Pre2000 - 1st:2 2nd:4 3rd:1 Ran:11
Win Prizemoney £12,597 *Total Prizemoney* £49,479
Wins * 1999 Apr Newmar (GD) H 6f 90 94 <
* 1998 Spt Goodwo (G-S) 6f 88
2000 Turf 0-1: (6f) (gd) 2000 AW 0-1: (6f) (Dirt)
Scopey, Group-class colt, effective 6f, acts on sft.
**B W Hills [2-12] Hamdan Al Maktoum (from K McLaughlin in USA [0-1] Mar 2000).*

MUQTADI (IRE) RR 83f 3988[1]

2 b c Marju (IRE) 9.2f **(76)** - Kadwah (USA) (Mr Prospector (USA)) 8.8f **(78)**
Form - 21
Record 2000 - 1st:1 2nd:1 3rd:0 Ran:2
Win Prizemoney £4,251 *Total Prizemoney* £5,532
Wins * 2000 Aug Goodwo (GD) 7f 83 <
2000 Turf 1-2: (7f 1-2) (gd 1-1, frm)
Currently decent colt. Turf high 83 (began Aug) - 1st of 4 from Elmonjed (26 Aug Goodwood RF 3988). Made heavy weather of landing the odds at Goodwood.
**J H M Gosden [1-2] Hamdan Al Maktoum.*

MUQTARB (IRE) BHB 80f RR 87df 1893[8]

4 ch g Cadeaux Genereux 7.9f **(76)** - Jasarah (IRE) (Green Desert (USA)) 8.6f **(78)**
Form - 08
Record 2000 - 1st:0 2nd:0 3rd:0 Ran:2
Pre2000 - 1st:1 2nd:0 3rd:0 Ran:4
Win Prizemoney £6,775 *Total Prizemoney* £7,796
Wins 1998 Jly Ascot (G-F) 6f 89+ <
2000 Turf 0-2: (5f, 6f) (gd 2)
Scopey, useful gelding. Turf high 71. Lightly raced since beating a field of fellow debutants at Ascot as a juvenile.
**W J Musson [0-2] Mrs Rita Brown (from M P Tregoning [1-4] Oct 1999).*

MUQTARIB (USA) BHB 107f RR 100f 577a[5]

4 b c Gone West (USA) 7.8f **(82)** - Shicklah (USA) (The Minstrel (CAN)) 10f **(72)**
Form - 5
2000 AW 0-1: (6f) (Dirt)
Neat, very useful colt.
**K McLaughlin in USA [0-1] (from J L Dunlop [2-5] Nov 1999).*

MURAWWI (IRE) RR 105f 4353a[5]

3 bb c Perugino (USA) - Pheopotstown (Henbit (USA)) 9f **(61)**
Form - 21075
2000 Turf 1-5: (7f 1-3, 8f, 10f) (g-s 1-2, gd 2, g-f)
Pattern-class colt, effective 7f, acts on g-s to gd, often wears blink-

ers. Turf high 105 - 1st of 6 giving 5lb to Sand Partridge (3 Jun Naas RF 1762a). Inconsistent.

**D K Weld in IRE [2-10] Hamdan Al Maktoum.*

MURCHAN TYNE (IRE) BHB 42f36a **RR 51f 36a** 3547^{14}

7 ch m Good Thyne (USA) 11.8f **(60)** - Ardnamurchan (Ardross) 10.6f **(68)**

Form - 075743760

Record	**2000 -**	1st:0	2nd:0	3rd:1	Ran:9
	Pre2000 -	1st:2	2nd:3	3rd:2	Ran:20

Win Prizemoney £6,251 *Total Prizemoney* £13,429

Wins								
	1999	Aug	Ripon (GD)	H	16f	53	56	
	1998	Jun	Leices (GD)	H	11.8f	53	57	<

2000 Turf 0-7: (10f, 12f 2, 14f, 15f 3) (hvy, gd 4, g-f, frm) 2000 AW 0-2: (11f, 16f) (Fibr 2)

Fair mare, effective 12 to 16f, best at 16f, acts on hvy to frm, prefers tight tracks. Turf high 51 - 4th of 12 giving 11lb to Elsie Bamford (27 May Warwick 15f hvy RF 1513). AW high 37.

**B A McMahon [0-9] J F Harrington (from E J Alston [3-23] Oct 1999).*

MURGHEM (IRE) BHB 114f **RR 117f** $5097a^{6}$

5 b h Common Grounds 8.1f **(66)** - Fabulous Pet (Somethingfabulous (USA)) 9.5f **(75)**

Form - 224211112146

Record	**2000 -**	1st:5	2nd:4	3rd:0	Ran:12
	Pre2000 -	1st:2	2nd:7	3rd:4	Ran:21

Win Prizemoney £130,740 *Total Prizemoney* £200,670

Wins								
	*** 2000**	Aug	Newbur (G-F)	G2	13.3f		117+	<
	*** 2000**	Aug	Goodwo (GD)	LH	12f	110	112	
	*** 2000**	Jly	Newmar (G-F)	L	12f		113	
	*** 2000**	Jun	Leices (G-F)	L	11.8f		111	
	*** 2000**	Jun	Epsom (GD)	H	12f	104	107	
	1999	Aug	Sandow (G-S)	H	14f	90	93	
	1998	Jly	Kempto (G-F)		12f		80	

2000 Turf 5-11: (12f 4-8, 13f 1-1, 14f, 16f) (g-s 2, gd 1-4, g-f 1-1, frm 2-3, hrd 1-1) 2000 AW 0-1: (12f) (Fibr)

High-class colt, effective 12 to 13f, best at 12f, acts on gd to hrd, best on frm, has worn blinkers, prefers right handed tracks, likes tight tracks. Turf high 117 - 2nd of 6 to Arctic Owl (12 Aug Ascot 12f gd RF 3581) - also 1st of 6 giving 11lb to Savoire Vivre (19 Aug Newbury RF 3789). Consistent. He was a revelation last year, winning five times including the Group 2 Geoffrey Freer Stakes. Probably best up to a mile and three-quarters, he is best when dictating the pace and hard to pass. Proven on everything bar heavy ground, he is notably game but may be difficult to place in 2001.

**M Johnston [5-15] (from B Hanbury [2-18] Spt 1999).*

Murghem gained a quintet of victories last season

MURJAN (FR) BHB 67f **RR 70f** 3557^{7}

3 ch g Lycius (USA) 8.8f **(71)** - Raknah (IRE) **(85df)** (Night Shift (USA)) 7.2f **(69)**

Form - 5747

Record	**2000 -**	1st:0	2nd:0	3rd:0	Ran:4
	Pre2000 -	1st:0	2nd:0	3rd:1	Ran:3

Win Prizemoney £0 *Total Prizemoney* £1,332

2000 Turf 0-4: (10f, 11f, 12f 2) (gd 2, frm 2)

Workmanlike, above-average gelding, effective 8 to 9f, acts on frm, prefers tight tracks. Turf high 70.

**E A L Dunlop [0-4] Mohammed Jaber (from M Johnston [0-3] Spt 1999).*

MURRENDI (IRE) BHB 80f **RR 80f** 4557^{3}

2 b c Ashkalani (IRE) - Formaestre (IRE) **(26f 31a)** (Formidable (USA)) 9.2f **(63)**

Form - 585423

Record	**2000 -**	1st:0	2nd:1	3rd:1	Ran:6

Win Prizemoney £0 *Total Prizemoney* £3,069

2000 Turf 0-6: (7f 4, 8f 2) (gd, g-f 3, frm 2)

Decent colt, effective 7 to 8f, best at 8f, acts on gd to frm, best on frm. Turf high 80 (began Jly) - 3rd of 12 to Tiyoun (21 Spt Pontefract 8f gd RF 4557). **M R Channon [0-6] The Dapper Boys.*

MURRON WALLACE BHB 34f28a **RR 16f 28a** 4492^{14}

6 gr m Reprimand 8.2f **(63)** - Fair Eleanor (Saritamer (USA)) 9.5f **(63)**

Form - 70080

Record	**2000 -**	1st:0	2nd:0	3rd:0	Ran:5
	Pre2000 -	1st:2	2nd:1	3rd:1	Ran:12

Win Prizemoney £5,084 *Total Prizemoney* £6,178

Wins								
	* 1997	Spt	Bath (GD)	SH	8f	44	50	<
	* 1997	Aug	Hamilt (GD)	H	8.3f	41	44	

2000 Turf 0-2: (8f, 11f) (gd, g-f) 2000 AW 0-3: (8f, 9f 2) (Fibr 3)

Little account mare. Turf high 16 (began Aug). AW high 17.

**D HaydnJones [2-11] Barry Adams (from R M Whitaker [0-6] Apr 1997).*

MUSADIF (USA) RR 4172^{R}

2 ch c Shadeed (USA) 7.7f **(72)** - Tadwin (Never so Bold) 6.3f **(66)**

Form - R

Record	**2000 -**	1st:0	2nd:0	3rd:0	Ran:1

2000 Turf 0-1: (8f) (gd)

Currently very poor colt. **B Hanbury [0-1] Hamdan Al Maktoum.*

MUSALLIAH (USA) BHB 62f **RR 66f** 3705^{15}

3 ch f Nureyev (USA) 8.4f **(84)** - Grand Falls (USA) (Ogygian (USA))

Form - 7480

Record	**2000 -**	1st:0	2nd:0	3rd:0	Ran:4

Win Prizemoney £0 *Total Prizemoney* £273

2000 Turf 0-4: (8f 2, 10f 2) (gd, g-f, frm 2)

Leggy, average filly, has worn blinkers. Turf high 66.

**J L Dunlop [0-4] Hamdan Al Maktoum.*

MUSALLY BHB 74f **RR 85f** 4556^{7}

3 ch c Muhtarram (USA) - Flourishing (IRE) (Trojan Fen) 8.1f **(62)**

Form - 41807

Record	**2000 -**	1st:1	2nd:0	3rd:0	Ran:5

Win Prizemoney £2,847 *Total Prizemoney* £3,142

Wins								
	*** 2000**	May	Newcas (GD)		10.1f		85	<

2000 Turf 1-5: (8f, 10f 1-4) (gd 1-3, g-f 2)

Workmanlike, useful colt. Turf high 85 - 1st of 11 from Gimco (25 May Newcastle RF 1444). He won a maiden very easily but was well beaten on his handicap bow.

**N A Graham [1-5] Hamdan Al Maktoum.*

MUSALSE BHB 35f40a **RR 35f 40a** 527^{14}

5 b g Salse (USA) 10.9f **(71)** - Musical Sally (USA) (The Minstrel (CAN)) 10f **(72)**

Form - 870

Record	**2000 -**	1st:0	2nd:0	3rd:0	Ran:2
	Pre2000 -	1st:4	2nd:2	3rd:5	Ran:27

Win Prizemoney £9,912 *Total Prizemoney* £13,137

Wins								
	* 1998	Spt	Warwic (G-F)	H	16.1f	47	57+	<
	* 1998	Spt	Catter (G-F)	H	15.8f	47	54	
	* 1998	*Aug*	*Lingfi (STD)*	*H*	*16f*	*42*	*51*	
	* 1998	May	Redcar (G-F)	H	14.1f	35	41	

2000 Turf 0-1: (16f) (g-s) 2000 AW 0-1: (16f) (Fibr)
Very moderate gelding, effective 16f, - acts on AW, has worn blinkers, likes left handed tracks, favours tight tracks.
**P C Haslam [4-31] Mrs Barclay/Mid'ham Park Racing/DJones.*

MUSCHANA BHB 96f RR 89f 5205a[2]

3 ch f Deploy 11.4f **(67)** - Youthful (FR) (Green Dancer (USA)) 10.3f **(74)**
Form - 3173152
Record 2000 - 1st:2 2nd:1 3rd:2 Ran:7
Pre2000 - 1st:0 2nd:1 3rd:1 Ran:3
Win Prizemoney £9,184 *Total Prizemoney* £17,123
Wins * 2000 Aug Epsom (G-F) H 10.1f 82 88 <
*** 2000** Jun Windso (G-F) H 10f 73 81+
2000 Turf 2-7: (9f 2, 10f 2-5) (hvy, gd 3, frm 2-3)
Neat, useful filly, effective 9 to 10f, best at 10f, acts on hvy to frm. Turf high 89 - 2nd of 11 to Terre Vierge (19 Oct Longchamp 9f hvy RF 5205a) - also 1st of 7 giving 10lb to Santiburi Girl (17 Aug Epsom RF 3723). A winner at Windsor in June, she still looked a fast-improving filly when scoring at Epsom in August. Decent effort next time. **J L Dunlop [2-10].*

MUSH (IRE) RR 76f 4934[25]

3 b c Thatching 7.8f **(69)** - Petite Jameel (IRE) (Ahonoora) 8.1f **(73)**
Form - 210
Record 2000 1st:1 2nd:1 3rd:0 Ran:3
Pre2000 - 1st:0 2nd:0 3rd:1 Ran:2
Win Prizemoney £2,488 *Total Prizemoney* £4,421
Wins * 2000 Spt Warwic (G-F) 8.1f 76 <
2000 Turf 1-3: (8f 1-3) (gd, g-f 1-1, hrd)
Scopey, above-average colt. Turf high 76 (began Aug) - 1st of 18 from Parker (11 Spt Warwick RF 4326). Lightly raced, he confirmed the promise of his belated reappearance when landing a gamble at Warwick in August.
**N P Littmoden [1-3] Turf 2000 Ltd (from P W Harris [0-2] Spt 1999).*

MUSICAL FRUITS BHB 25f RR 32f 1665[14]

3 b f Tuam - Golden Apple (Athens Wood) 19.6f **(38)**
Form - 00
Record 2000 - 1st:0 2nd:0 3rd:0 Ran:2
Pre2000 - 1st:0 2nd:0 3rd:0 Ran:3
2000 Turf 0-2: (7f, 10f) (g-s, gd)
Unfurnished, very moderate filly.
**Mrs P N Dutfield [0-4] Edwin Phillips (from R T Phillips [0 1] Jly 1999).*

MUSICAL HEATH (IRE) BHB 76f RR 80f 4452[8]

3 b c Common Grounds 8.1f **(66)** - Song of The Glens (Horage) 10.3f **(61)**
Form - 42218
Record 2000 - 1st:1 2nd:2 3rd:0 Ran:5
Win Prizemoney £4,192 *Total Prizemoney* £6,723
Wins * 2000 Spt Epsom (GD) 8.5f 78+ <
2000 Turf 1-5: (8f 3, 9f 1-2) (gd, g-f 1-2, frm 2)
Well made, decent colt. Turf high 80 (began Jly) - 2nd of 6 to Finished Article (17 Aug Epsom 9f frm RF 3721) - also 1st of 7 giving 5lb to Russian Rhapsody (1 Spt Epsom RF 4146). Gradually improving and got off the mark when making all to win very easily at Epsom in September. There should be more to come.
**P W Harris [1-5] The Highlanders.*

MUSICIAN BHB 94f RR 95f 2853[2]

4 b f Shirley Heights 12.1f **(76)** - Rose Alto (Adonijah) 10f **(61)**
Form - 02
Record 2000 - 1st:0 2nd:1 3rd:0 Ran:2
Pre2000 - 1st:4 2nd:0 3rd:2 Ran:8
Win Prizemoney £30,509 *Total Prizemoney* £38,999
Wins * 1999 Spt Doncas (G-F) H 12f 88 93 <
* 1999 Jun Newmar (G-F) H 12f 79 84
* 1999 Jun Thirsk (G-F) H 12f 79 83+
* 1999 May Warwic (SFT) H 10.5f 78 79
2000 Turf 0-2: (12f, 14f) (gd, frm)
Leggy, very useful filly, effective 12 to 14f, best at 12f, acts on sft to frm. Turf high 95 - 2nd of 9 getting 1lb from Eminence Grise (15 Jly York 14f gd RF 2853). Touched off in a Listed handicap at York in July, she went missing in the second half of the season. Bred to improve, she stays a mile and three-quarters and remains relatively unexposed. **J R Fanshawe [4-10] T & J Vestey.*

MUSIC MAID (IRE) BHB 82f RR 79f 5128[10]

2 b f Inzar (USA) - Richardstown Lass (IRE) (Muscatite) 5f **(51)**
Form - 61300100
Record 2000 - 1st:2 2nd:0 3rd:1 Ran:8
Win Prizemoney £7,936 *Total Prizemoney* £9,185
Wins * 2000 Aug Epsom (GD) 7f 79 <
*** 2000** Jun Lingfi (G-F) 7f 76
2000 Turf 2-8: (6f 3, 7f 2-4, 8f) (sft, gd 1-4, g-f 2, frm 1-1)
Above-average filly, effective 7f, acts on gd to frm. Turf high 79 - 1st of 4 getting 8lb from Count Dubois (28 Aug Epsom RF 4038) - also 1st of 18 from Trustthunder (25 Jun Lingfield RF 2257). Inconsistent. She has faced some stiff tasks, but was successful when outsider of four at Epsom in August.
**H S Howe [2-8] R J Parish.*

MUSIC PARK (IRE) RR 95f 2386a[5]

3 f
Form - 5
2000 Turf 0-1: (12f) (gd)
Currently very useful filly, always wears blinkers.
**Mme M Bollack-Badel in FR [0-1].*

MUSKETRY BHB 32f19a RR 39f 19a 130[6]

4 b c Terimon 8.7f **(58)** - Mousquetade (Moulton)
Form - 066
Record 2000 - 1st:0 2nd:0 3rd:0 Ran:2
Pre2000 - 1st:0 2nd:0 3rd:0 Ran:5
2000 AW 0-2: (11f, 12f) (Equi, Fibr)
Leggy, very moderate colt, often wears blinkers. AW high 10.
**N A Graham [0-7] R E S Greenwood.*

MUSTANG BHB 38f37a RR 40f 37a 3896[9]

7 ch g Thatching 7.8f **(69)** - Lassoo (Caerleon (USA)) 8.6f **(71)**
Form - 4543002503061054500
Record 2000 - 1st:1 2nd:1 3rd:2 Ran:16
Pre2000 - 1st:2 2nd:8 3rd:0 Ran:39
Win Prizemoney £6,842 *Total Prizemoney* £15,193
Wins * 2000 Jun Bright (FRM) S 8f 40
1997 *Nov Lingfi (STD) H 7f 33 45* <
1997 *Mar Wolver (STD) H 7f 27 32*
2000 Turf 1-9: (7f, 8f 1-8) (gd 3, frm 1-5, hrd) 2000 AW 0-7: (8f 4, 9f 2, 10f) (Equi 2, Fibr 5)
Moderate gelding, effective 7 to 10f, best at 8f, acts on gd to frm - acts on Equi, often wears blinkers (effectively), likes left handed tracks, likes tight tracks. Turf high 40 - also 1st of 14 from Dovebrace (19 Jun Brighton RF 2086). AW high 36.
**J Pearce [1-22] Chris Marsh (from C W Thornton [2-33] Nov 1998).*

MUST BE MAGIC BHB 61a RR 64f 5229[6]

3 b g Magic Ring (IRE) 6.5f **(64)** - Sequin Lady (Star Appeal) 9.6f **(65)**
Form - 063431006
Record 2000 - 1st:1 2nd:0 3rd:2 Ran:9
Pre2000 - 1st:0 2nd:0 3rd:1 Ran:5
Win Prizemoney £3,656 *Total Prizemoney* £5,479
Wins * 2000 Jly Epsom (GD) H 8.5f 61 64 <
2000 Turf 1-7: (7f, 8f 4, 9f 1-1, 10f) (g-s, gd, g-f 1-3, frm 2) 2000 AW 0-2: (9f, 10f) (Equi, Fibr)
Workmanlike, average gelding, effective 8 to 9f, acts on g-s to g-f, has worn blinkers, likes tight tracks. Turf high 64 - also 1st of 13 getting 6lb from Evergreen (20 Jly Epsom RF 2964). AW high 60. He had made the frame in varied company, but did not get off the mark until winning an Epsom handicap in good style in July. Best over a mile. **H J Collingridge [1-14] The Headquarters Partnership III.*

MUTABARI (USA) BHB 37f52a RR 38f 52a 3092[8]

6 ch g Seeking the Gold (USA) 7.4f **(80)** - Cagey Exuberance (USA) (Exuberant (USA)) 7.8f **(84)**
Form - 8034253040047650068
Record 2000 - 1st:0 2nd:1 3rd:2 Ran:17
Pre2000 - 1st:3 2nd:2 3rd:2 Ran:40
Win Prizemoney £7,107 *Total Prizemoney* £12,685
Wins * 1999 *Mar Wolver (STD) H 7f 57 61* <
* 1999 *Feb Lingfi (STD) H 7f 50 55*
* 1999 *Jan Southw (STD) H 7f 46 54*
2000 Turf 0-8: (6f, 7f 3, 8f 3, 10f) (g-s, gd 4, frm 3) 2000 AW 0-9: (6f, 7f 4, 8f 3, 16f) (Fibr 9)
Average gelding, effective 7f, - acts on AW, best on Fibr, has worn

blinkers, likes left handed tracks, likes tight tracks. Turf high 38. AW high 58 - 2nd of 12 to Aberkeen (21 Jan Southwell 7f Fibr RF 0129).

**Mrs S Lamyman [3-43] P Lamyman (from K Mahdi [0-12] Nov 1998).*

MUTABASSIR (IRE) BHB 63f56a **RR 65f 56a** 4619^{9}

6 ch g Soviet Star (USA) 8.6f **(74)** - Anghaam (USA) (Diesis) 9.3f **(69)**

Form - 6543825150

Record					
2000 -	1st:1	2nd:1	3rd:1	Ran:10
Pre2000 -	1st:6	2nd:5	3rd:2	Ran:22

Win Prizemoney £19,818 *Total Prizemoney* £29,418

Wins								
*** 2000**	Aug	Bright	(FRM)	H	8f	60	62	
* 1999	Apr	Bright	(G-F)	H	8f	60	73+	<
* 1998	*Nov*	*Southw*	*(STD)*	*H*	*7f*	*44*	*53*	
* 1998	*Nov*	*Lingfi*	*(STD)*	*H*	*7f*	*44*	*53+*	
* 1998	Spt	Folkes	(G-F)	H	7f	53	57	
* 1998	Spt	Epsom	(GD)	H	7f	47	52	
* 1998	Aug	Bright	(FRM)	H	7f	40	50	

2000 Turf 1-10: (7f 3, 8f 1-7) (gd 5, g-f 1-3, frm 2)

Average gelding, effective 7 to 8f, best at 7f, acts on g-f to hrd, prefers left handed tracks, excels at Brighton. Turf high 65 - 2nd of 9 giving 4lb to Tapage (18 Jly Brighton 8f frm RF 2890). Consistent.

**G L Moore [7-31] Stanley Clarke (from A C Stewart [0-1] Aug 1997).*

MUTADARRA (IRE) BHB 53f39a **RR 56f 39a** 4327^{7}

7 ch g Mujtahid (USA) 7.4f **(69)** - Silver Echo (Caerleon (USA)) 8.6f **(71)**

Form - 400802510207

Record				
2000 -	1st:1	2nd:2	3rd:0	Ran:12
Pre2000 -	1st:3	2nd:6	3rd:1	Ran:32

Win Prizemoney £19,330 *Total Prizemoney* £31,804

Wins								
*** 2000**	Jly	Windso	(SFT)	H	10f	52	60	
1999	Jun	Sandow	(GD)	H	10f	63	66	
1997	Jly	Newmar	(G-F)	H	10f	62	69	
1996	May	Pontef	(GD)		6f		80	<

2000 Turf 1-8: (10f 1-3, 11f, 12f 4) (gd 1-2, g-f 3, frm 2, hrd) 2000 AW 0-4: (8f, 9f 2, 16f) (Fibr 4)

Fair gelding, has broken blood-vessels, effective 10f, acts on frm, has worn blinkers, likes right handed tracks, likes tight tracks. Turf high 60. AW high 41.

**G M McCourt [2-16] McCourt Fine Meats Ltd (from W J Musson [2-26] Oct 1999).*

Record				
2000 -	1st:0	2nd:0	3rd:0	Ran:9
Pre2000 -	1st:0	2nd:2	3rd:3	Ran:21

Win Prizemoney £0 *Total Prizemoney* £3,590

2000 Turf 0-7: (14f, 16f, 17f 3, 18f 2) (g-s, gd 2, g-f, frm 2, hrd) 2000 AW 0-2: (14f, 15f) (Fibr 2)

Moderate gelding, effective 16 to 18f, best at 17f, acts on g-f to frm, best on g-f, has worn blinkers. Turf high 43. AW high 27 (began Aug). **J Gallagher [0-2] Mrs V W Jones (from R Dickin [0-2] Aug 2000).*

MUTAFAWEQ (USA) BHB 120f **RR 126f** $5097a^{1}$

4 b c Silver Hawk (USA) 11.2f **(85)** - The Caretaker (Caerleon (USA)) 8.6f **(71)**

Form - 371831

Record				
2000 -	1st:2	2nd:0	3rd:2	Ran:6
Pre2000 -	1st:4	2nd:1	3rd:0	Ran:7

Win Prizemoney £756,148 *Total Prizemoney* £786,302

Wins							
*** 2000**	Oct	Woodbi	(FRM)	G1	12f	125	
*** 2000**	Jly	Dussel	(GD)	G1	12f	113+	
* 1999	Spt	Doncas	(G-F)	G1	14.6f	126	<
* 1999	Jun	Ascot	(G-F)	G2	12f	112	
* 1999	May	Doncas	(G-F)		10.3f	104+	
* 1998	Oct	Newmar	(GD)		8f	87	

2000 Turf 2-6: (11f, 12f 2-4, 14f) (hvy, g-s 2, gd 1-2, frm 1-1)

Scopey, top-class colt, effective 11 to 15f, best at 12f, acts on g-s to frm, best on frm, excels at Doncaster. Turf high 125 - 1st of 12 from Williams News (15 Oct Woodbine RF 5097a). He showed admirable battling qualities when winning the 1999 St Leger and was equally game when landing Group Ones in Germany and Canada (the Canadian International) last year. Unsuited by soft ground, he should stay beyond a mile and three-quarters and could be an able deputy for the recently retired Kayf Tara.

**S bin Suroor [6-13] Godolphin.*

MUTAHADETH BHB 39f47a **RR 29f 47a** 1356^{7}

6 ch g Rudimentary (USA) 8.2f **(66)** - Music in My Life (IRE) (Law Society (USA)) 9.9f **(70)**

Form - 4032567344460447

Record				
2000 -	1st:0	2nd:1	3rd:2	Ran:14
Pre2000 -	1st:4	2nd:5	3rd:6	Ran:46

Win Prizemoney £8,541 *Total Prizemoney* £16,808

Wins								
* 1999	*Mar*	*Southw*	*(STD)*	*H*	*8f*	*57*	*60*	
* 1999	*Feb*	*Wolver*	*(STD)*	*C*	*8.5f*		*60*	
* 1998	*Jan*	*Southw*	*(STD)*	*C*	*7f*		*68*	<
* 1997	*Feb*	*Southw*	*(STD)*	*H*	*8f*	*58*	*60+*	

2000 Turf 0-1: (7f) (frm) 2000 AW 0-13: (7f 6, 8f 7) (Equi, Fibr 12)

Moderate gelding, effective 8f, - acts on Fibr, mostly wears blinkers (effectively), favours tight tracks. AW high 57 - 2nd of 12 giving

Mutafaweq, an able substitute for the since-retired Kayf Tara

MU-TADIL BHB 25f **RR 43f** 5012^{11}

8 ch g Be My Chief (USA) 10.2f **(62)** - Inveraven (Alias Smith (USA)) 9.8f **(58)**

Form - 000067480

19lb to Shontaine (10 Jan Southwell 8f Fibr RF 0058).
**D Shaw [4-56] K G Radford (from N A Graham [0-4] Spt 1996).*

MUTAMADEE (USA) RR 54f
5073[10]
2 ch c Beau Genius (CAN) - Tied To Time (USA) (Poleax (USA))
Form - 00
Record 2000 - 1st:0 2nd:0 3rd:0 Ran:2
2000 Turf 0-2: (6f, 7f) (g-s, g-f)
Currently fair colt. Turf high 54.
**E A L Dunlop [0-2] Mohammed Jaber.*

MUTAMAM BHB 119f RR 124+f
5331a[4]
5 b h Darshaan 11.9f **(81)** - Petal Girl (Caerleon (USA)) 8.6f **(71)**
Form - 214114
Record 2000 - 1st:3 2nd:1 3rd:0 Ran:6
Pre2000 - 1st:5 2nd:1 3rd:1 Ran:10
Win Prizemoney £119,646 *Total Prizemoney* £256,388

Wins							
* 2000	Spt	Ascot	(G-S)	G3	12f	120+	
* 2000	Spt	Kempto	(GD)	G3	12f	124	<
* 2000	May	Goodwo	(SFT)		12f	106	
* 1998	Spt	Goodwo	(G-S)	G3	9.9f	118+	
* 1998	Aug	Haydoc	(GD)	G3	10.5f	113+	
* 1998	Jly	Sandow	(GD)		10f	116+	
* 1997	Spt	Cheste	(GD)		7.6f	102++	
* 1997	Aug	Lingfi	(G-S)		7.6f	86+	

2000 Turf 3-6: (10f, 12f 3-5) (g-s 1-1, gd 1-3, g-f 1-1, frm)
Very high-class colt, effective 12f, acts on gd to frm. Turf high 124 - 4th of 13 to Kalanisi (4 Nov Churchill Downs 12f frm RF 5331a) - also 1st of 7 giving 9lb to Kuwait Trooper (2 Spt Kempton RF 4165). He disappointed for Saeed bin Suroor in 1999, but bounced back better than ever when returned to Alec Stewart last year. Impressive when making all to win the September Stakes and Cumberland Lodge Stakes, he ran the race of his life when only beaten three-parts of a length by Kalanisi in the Breeders' Cup Turf. Thoroughly genuine, he handles any ground nowadays and deserves to win a Group 1 this term.
**A C Stewart [8-15] Hamdan Al Maktoum (from S bin Suroor in UAE [0-1] Mar 1999).*

Mutamam bounced back to form when returning to Alec Stewart

MUTARASED (USA) BHB 92f RR 89f
5167[2]
2 b c Storm Cat (USA) 7f **(86)** - Sajjaya (USA) (Blushing Groom (FR)) 10.3f **(76)**
Form - 812
Record 2000 - 1st:1 2nd:1 3rd:0 Ran:3
Win Prizemoney £3,807 *Total Prizemoney* £4,887
Wins * **2000** Spt Bright (SFT) 7f 94+ <
2000 Turf 1-3: (7f 1-3) (g-s 1-1, gd, frm)
Currently useful colt. Turf high 94 (began Spt) - 1st of 18 from Lucefer (27 Spt Brighton RF 4675).
**J L Dunlop [1-3] Hamdan Al Maktoum.*

MUTASADER (IRE) BHB 68f RR 77f
4632[6]
3 b f Unfuwain (USA) 11.4f **(74)** - Bawaeth (USA) (Blushing Groom (FR)) 10.3f **(76)**
Form - 506
Record 2000 - 1st:0 2nd:0 3rd:0 Ran:3
Pre2000 - 1st:0 2nd:0 3rd:0 Ran:1
2000 Turf 0-3: (10f 3) (g-s, gd 2)
Scopey, above-average filly. Turf high 77 (1st run) - 5th of 10 to Abscond (23 May Beverley 10f gd RF 1389).
**B W Hills [0-4] Hamdan Al Maktoum.*

MUTASAWWAR BHB 46f64a RR 49tf 64a
5112[14]
6 ch g Clantime 6.6f **(57)** - Keen Melody (USA) (Sharpen Up) 8.3f **(67)**
Form - 5780480222000
Record 2000 - 1st:0 2nd:3 3rd:0 Ran:13
Pre2000 - 1st:2 2nd:4 3rd:1 Ran:32
Win Prizemoney £5,486 *Total Prizemoney* £12,123
Wins 1998 Spt Chepst (G-S) H 5.1f 51 55
1998 *Jan Lingfi (STD) H 6f 00 61* <
2000 Turf 0-12: (5f 8, 6f 4) (sft, gd 4, g-f 4, frm 2, hrd) 2000 AW 0-1: (6f) (Fibr)
Average gelding, effective 6f, - acts on AW, has worn blinkers, likes left handed tracks, prefers tight tracks. Turf high 55. (1st run) - 2nd of 15 giving 3lb to Marengo (26 Spt Southwell 6f Fibr RF 4654). Becoming disappointing.
**J M Bradley [0-6] Clifton Hunt (from M S Saunders [2-34] Aug 2000).*

MUTAWAQED (IRE) RR 22f
5099[20]
2 ch c Zafonic (USA) 9f **(83)** - Waqood (USA) **(63f)** (Riverman (USA)) 9.1f **(76)**
Form - 0
Record 2000 - 1st:0 2nd:0 3rd:0 Ran:1
2000 Turf 0-1: (7f) (gd)
Currently little account colt.
**M P Tregoning [0-1] Hamdan Al Maktoum.*

MUTED GIFT RR
4225[17]
2 ch f King's Signet (USA) 7f **(51)** - Ballet on Ice (FR) **(44f)** (Fijar Tango (FR))
Form - 0
Record 2000 - 1st:0 2nd:0 3rd:0 Ran:1
2000 Turf 0-1: (6f) (frm)
Currently very poor filly. **W G M Turner [0-1] Darren Coombes.*

MUTHAABER RR 79f
5023[2]
2 br c Machiavellian (USA) 9.8f **(83)** - Raheefa (USA) **(72f)** (Riverman (USA)) 9.1f **(76)**
Form - 52
Record 2000 - 1st:0 2nd:1 3rd:0 Ran:2
Win Prizemoney £0 *Total Prizemoney* £1,165
2000 Turf 0-2: (7f 2) (g-s, g-f)
Currently above-average colt. Turf high 79 (began Spt) - 2nd of 7 getting 7lb from Lagudin (17 Oct Yarmouth 7f g-s RF 5023).
**J H M Gosden [0-2] Hamdan Al Maktoum.*

MUWAKALL (IRE) BHB 80f78a RR 82f 78a
2551[3]
3 b c Doyoun 10.7f **(69)** - Sabayik (IRE) **(84f)** (Unfuwain (USA))
Form - 3245345533
Record 2000 - 1st:0 2nd:1 3rd:4 Ran:10
Pre2000 - 1st:0 2nd:0 3rd:1 Ran:4
Win Prizemoney £0 *Total Prizemoney* £8,534
2000 Turf 0-8: (10f 6, 12f, 14f) (g-s, gd 5, frm 2) 2000 AW 0-2: (8f, 10f) (Equi, Dirt)
Scopey, decent colt, effective 10 to 12f, acts on frm, has worn blinkers, likes tight tracks. Turf high 82 - 3rd of 6 giving 10lb to My Pledge (28 Jun Kempton 12f frm RF 2347). AW high 63. He has made the frame a few times, including at Cagnes-Sur-Mer, but looks moderate.
**R W Armstrong [0-14] Mrs M Parker & Sir Eric Parker.*

MUYASSIR (IRE) BHB 82f75a **RR 83f 75a** 4035^{5}
5 b h Brief Truce (USA) 9.1f **(73)** - Twine (Thatching) 8f **(66)**
Form - 811355
Record 2000 - 1st:2 2nd:0 3rd:1 Ran:6
Pre2000 - 1st:2 2nd:2 3rd:2 Ran:17
Win Prizemoney £27,478 *Total Prizemoney* £33,678
Wins * 2000 Jun Goodwo (G-F) H 9f 79 83 <
*** 2000** Jun Kempto (G-F) H 8f 74 79
* 1999 Jly Newmar (GD) H 8f 69 72
* 1998 *Oct Lingfi (STD) H 10f 67 69*
2000 Turf 2-6: (8f 1-2, 9f 1-3, 10f) (gd 1-2, g-f 1-3, frm)
Decent colt, effective 8 to 9f, best at 9f, acts on gd to frm, best on g-f, likes right handed tracks. Turf high 83 - 1st of 9 giving 7lb to Kathir (30 Jun Goodwood RF 2398) - also 1st of 18 giving 3lb to Sky Dome (14 Jun Kempton RF 1963). Consistent. Got the run of the race when winning over a mile at Kempton on his second start of the season, and was produced just at the right time to follow up over a furlong further at Goodwood. He has continued to run well since despite a rise in the weights and is suited by a fast surface.
**P J Makin [4-19] William Otley (from C J Benstead [0-4] Oct 1997).*

MYAHSMONT RR 1351^{11}
5 ch g Nicholas Bill 9.8f **(56)** - My Ducats (IRE) (Red Sunset) 8.2f **(63)**
Form - 0
Record 2000 - 1st:0 2nd:0 3rd:0 Ran:1
2000 AW 0-1: (9f) (Fibr)
Little account gelding. **J Neville [0-7] Mrs Andrea Aldridge.*

MY ALIBI (USA) BHB 61a **RR 58f** 5093a^{3}
4 b f Sheikh Albadou 9.2f **(75)** - Fellwaati (USA) (Alydar (USA)) 9.1f **(76)**
Form - 126121263
Record 2000 - 1st:3 2nd:3 3rd:1 Ran:9
Pre2000 - 1st:0 2nd:0 3rd:0 Ran:5
Win Prizemoney £7,189 *Total Prizemoney* £24,793
Wins * 2000 *Jly Southw (STD) H 6f 61 71* <
*** 2000** *Jun Southw (STD) 6f 60*
*** 2000** *Mar Southw (STD) H 8f 56 58*
2000 Turf 0-1: (8f) (gd) 2000 AW 3-8: (6f 2-3, 7f 3, 8f 1-1, 9f) (Fibr 3-5, Dirt 3)
Scopey, above-average filly, effective 6 to 7f, - acts on Fibr, prefers left handed tracks, prefers tight tracks. AW high 71 - 1st of 14 getting 4lb from Russian Romeo (21 Jly Southwell RF 3020). Becoming disappointing.
**K R Burke [3-9] (from E A L Dunlop [0-5] Spt 1999).*

MY AMERICAN BEAUTY BHB 67f **RR 68f** 4742^{12}
2 ch f Wolfhound (USA) 7.3f **(71)** - Hooray Lady (Ahonoora) 8.1f **(73)**
Form - 683170
Record 2000 - 1st:1 2nd:0 3rd:1 Ran:6
Win Prizemoney £8,079 *Total Prizemoney* £8,597
Wins * 2000 Spt York (GD) H 6f 65 68 <
2000 Turf 1-6: (5f, 6f 1-5) (gd, g-f 1-3, frm 2)
Average filly, effective 5 to 6f, acts on g-f. Turf high 68 (began Jly) - 1st of 11 getting 16lb from Wally McArthur (3 Spt York RF 4193). Won at York but was beaten in soft ground at Ayr.
**T D Easterby [1-6] Peter Gorvin.*

MY BOLD BOYO BHB 41f50a **RR 41f 50a** 3954^{14}
5 b g Never so Bold 7.1f **(62)** - My Rosie (Forzando) 7.6f **(59)**
Form - 04405000
Record 2000 - 1st:0 2nd:0 3rd:0 Ran:7
Pre2000 - 1st:1 2nd:0 3rd:2 Ran:15
Win Prizemoney £2,070 *Total Prizemoney* £3,714
Wins 1998 Aug Lingfi (GD) 7.6f 76 <
2000 Turf 0-4: (7f, 8f 2, 10f) (g-s, g-f, frm, hrd) 2000 AW 0-3: (10f 2, 12f) (Equi 3)
Moderate gelding, effective 7 to 8f, acts on frm, has worn blinkers. Turf high 41. AW high 48.
**J R Poulton [0-9] Mrs M J Taylor (from D R C Elsworth [1-13] Aug 1999).*

MYBOTYE BHB 54f43a **RR 54f 43a** 5084^{7}
7 br g Rambo Dancer (CAN) 8.4f **(59)** - Sigh (Highland Melody) 6.3f **(55)**
Form - 004101007
Record 2000 - 1st:2 2nd:0 3rd:0 Ran:7
Pre2000 - 1st:4 2nd:1 3rd:5 Ran:37
Win Prizemoney £20,813 *Total Prizemoney* £25,667
Wins * 2000 Jun Catter (SFT) 7f 54
*** 2000** May Redcar (G-S) S 7f 54
1997 Spt Chepst (GD) H 7.1f 58 64
1996 Jun Redcar (FRM) H 7f 76 77 <
2000 Turf 2-7: (6f, 7f 2-6) (hvy, g-s 1-1, gd 1-1, frm 4)
Fair gelding, effective 7f, acts on g-s to gd, has worn blinkers. Turf high 54 - 1st of 23 from Up in Flames (4 May Redcar RF 1019) - also 1st of 10 giving 3lb to Prix Star (3 Jun Catterick RF 1671). He was disqualified after passing the post in front at Catterick in August '97, but managed to win at Chepstow the following month. He has run well on occasions since then but does not look an easy ride.
**A B Mulholland [2-12] J F Wright (from R Bastiman [1-20] Jly 1998).*

MY BROADSTAIRS JOY BHB 42f **RR 46f** 102^{11}
4 b g Terimon 8.7f **(58)** - Al Raja (Kings Lake (USA)) 10.8f **(67)**
Form - 0
Record 2000 - 1st:0 2nd:0 3rd:0 Ran:1
Pre2000 - 1st:0 2nd:0 3rd:0 Ran:4
2000 AW 0-1: (7f) (Fibr)
Unfurnished, moderate gelding.
**D Shaw [0-1] Mrs Judy Hunt (from J J O'Neill [0-4] Oct 1999).*

MY BROTHER BHB 40f **RR 44f** 2453^{5}
6 b g Lugana Beach 7f **(63)** - Lucky Love (Mummy's Pet) 7.7f **(60)**
Form - 15
Record 2000 - 1st:1 2nd:0 3rd:0 Ran:2
Pre2000 - 1st:0 2nd:0 3rd:0 Ran:8
Win Prizemoney £3,250 *Total Prizemoney* £3,250
Wins * 2000 Jun Goodwo (GD) H 6f 34 39 <
2000 Turf 1-2: (6f 1-1, 7f) (g-f 1-1, frm)
Moderate gelding, has worn blinkers. Turf high 39 (1st run). Inconsistent.
**Dr J R J Naylor [1-2] Robert & Cora Till (from P Eccles [0-5] Spt 1999).*

MY DARLING DODO (IRE) BHB 48f31a **RR 50f 31a** 56^{7}
4 b f Anita's Prince 6f **(62)** - Seldovia (Charlottown) 10.9f **(57)**
Form - 087
Record 2000 - 1st:0 2nd:0 3rd:0 Ran:1
Pre2000 - 1st:0 2nd:0 3rd:0 Ran:5
2000 AW 0-1: (12f) (Fibr)
Leggy, fair filly. **B Palling [0-6] Mrs Anita Quinn.*

MY DESPERADO (IRE) BHB 66f62a **RR 70f 62a** 104^{6}
7 b m Un Desperado (FR) 9.3f **(42)** - Lady Kasbah (Lord Gayle (USA)) 8.8f **(62)**
Form - 6
Record 2000 - 1st:0 2nd:0 3rd:0 Ran:1
Pre2000 - 1st:3 2nd:0 3rd:2 Ran:18
Win Prizemoney £10,527 *Total Prizemoney* £11,786
Wins 1998 Oct Redcar (SFT) 10f 65
1998 Oct Pontef (SFT) H 10f 66 69
1998 Jly Thirsk (GD) 8f 73 <
2000 AW 0-1: (11f) (Fibr)
Above-average mare.
**M A Peill [0-7] Willie Smith (from L R Lloyd-James [3-16] Nov 1998).*

MY DILEMMA BHB 35f28a **RR 25f 28a** 172^{10}
4 b f Pursuit of Love 9.5f **(69)** - Butosky (Busted) 10.2f **(61)**
Form - 0
Record 2000 - 1st:0 2nd:0 3rd:0 Ran:1
Pre2000 - 1st:0 2nd:0 3rd:1 Ran:9
Win Prizemoney £0 *Total Prizemoney* £833
2000 AW 0-1: (8f) (Fibr)
Leggy, moderate filly, has worn blinkers. Inconsistent.
**M J Ryan [0-11] Peter Scott (from K G Wingrove [0-3] Spt 1998).*

MY DREAM CASTLES (USA) RR 102f 4408a^{3}
3 b f Woodman (USA) 9.7f **(77)** - My Sea Castles (USA) (Polish Navy (USA)) 8f **(67)**
Form - 3
2000 Turf 0-1: (8f) (sft)
Currently very useful filly. (1st run) - 3rd of 13 to Airline (6 Spt Chantilly 8f sft RF 4408a). **in FR [0-1].*

MY EMILY BHB 66f63a **RR 68f 63a** 4922[2]
4 b f King's Signet (USA) 7f **(51)** - Flying Wind **(33f 41a)** (Forzando) 7.6f **(59)**
Form - 2167022602
Record 2000 - 1st:1 2nd:4 3rd:0 Ran:10
Pre2000 - 1st:1 2nd:2 3rd:1 Ran:10
Win Prizemoney £5,744 *Total Prizemoney* £11,451
Wins * **2000** Jun Salisb (G-F) C 7f 61
* 1999 Jun Bright (G-F) H 7f 63 65+ <
2000 Turf 1-9: (5f, 6f 3, 7f 1-5) (gd 4, g-f 1-2, frm 3) 2000 AW 0-1: (7f) (Equi)
Neat, average filly, effective 6 to 7f, best at 6f, acts on g-f to frm, best on frm, likes Lingfield. Turf high 69 - 6th of 14 giving 9lb to Shadow Prince (28 Jun Kempton 7f frm RF 2345).
**G L Moore [2-20] B V and C J Pennick.*

MY FRIEND JACK BHB 58f **RR 57f** 4927[3]
2 b g Petong 7.6f **(58)** - Spring Collection (Tina's Pet) 6.8f **(59)**
Form - 50603
Record 2000 - 1st:0 2nd:0 3rd:1 Ran:5
Win Prizemoney £0 *Total Prizemoney* £265
2000 Turf 0-4: (5f 4) (sft, gd, g-f 2) 2000 AW 0-1: (5f) (Equi)
Fair gelding. Turf high 57. (1st run) - 3rd of 10 to Pat The Builder (11 Oct Lingfield 5f Equi RF 4927).
**J Akehurst [0-5] The Grass Is Greener Partnership II.*

MY HANSEL (USA) RR 98f 3801[9]
3 b br f Hansel (USA) 12.6f **(78)** - My Shafy (Rousillon (USA)) 8.2f **(74)**
Form - 0100
Record 2000 - 1st:1 2nd:0 3rd:0 Ran:4
Pre2000 - 1st:1 2nd:0 3rd:1 Ran:2
Win Prizemoney £19,905 *Total Prizemoney* £40,380
Wins * **2000** Jun Newcas (FRM) 8f 98 <
* 1999 Aug Newmar (G-F) 7f 97+
2000 Turf 1-4: (7f, 8f 1-2, 10f) (gd, g-f 2, frm 1-1)
Scopey, very useful filly, effective 7 to 8f, best at 8f, acts on sft to frm, best on frm. Turf high 98 - 1st of 4 getting 10lb from Hypnotize (29 Jun Newcastle RF 2371). Third in the Group One Fillies' Mile in 1999, she was a shade disappointing last year and is not expected to improve. **B Hanbury [2-6] Hilal Salem.*

MYHAT BHB 65f **RR 73f** 4820[10]
2 ch f Factual (USA) - Rose Elegance **(56df 48a)** (Bairn (USA)) 7.7f **(59)**
Form - 223265000
Record 2000 - 1st:0 2nd:3 3rd:1 Ran:9
Win Prizemoney £0 *Total Prizemoney* £5,561
2000 Turf 0-9: (6f 7, 7f 2) (g-s, gd 2, g-f 3, frm 3)
Above-average filly, effective 6f, acts on g-f, has worn blinkers. Turf high 73.
**K T Ivory [0-8] Dean Ivory (from M Blanshard [0-1] Jun 2000).*

MYLANIA BHB 57f **RR 61f** 2049[7]
4 b f Midyan (USA) 9.9f **(64)** - Appelania (Star Appeal) 9.6f **(65)**
Form - 67
Record 2000 - 1st:0 2nd:0 3rd:0 Ran:2
Pre2000 - 1st:0 2nd:1 3rd:0 Ran:6
Win Prizemoney £0 *Total Prizemoney* £908
2000 Turf 0-2: (7f, 10f) (gd, g-f)
Workmanlike, average filly, effective 8f, acts on g-s to gd. Turf high 52. Consistent.
**J G Given [0-2] J Ellis (from M H Tompkins [0-6] Oct 1999).*

MY LAST BEAN (IRE) RR 79f 5070[4]
3 gr g Soviet Lad (USA) 9.4f **(63)** - Meanz Beanz (High Top) 10.2f **(67)**
Form - 54
Record 2000 - 1st:0 2nd:0 3rd:0 Ran:2
Win Prizemoney £0 *Total Prizemoney* £310
2000 Turf 0-2: (10f, 12f) (g-s, gd)
Currently above-average gelding. Turf high 79 (1st run) - 5th of 15 to Fantasy Park (2 May Bath 10f gd RF 0964).
**B Smart [0-2] B Smart.*

MY LEGAL EAGLE (IRE) BHB 36f40a **RR 62f 40a** 5161[8]
6 b g Law Society (USA) 11.6f **(71)** - Majestic Nurse (On Your Mark) 7.7f **(58)**
Form - 7532740322222136060840648
Record 2000 - 1st:1 2nd:5 3rd:2 Ran:19
Pre2000 - 1st:2 2nd:3 3rd:7 Ran:37
Win Prizemoney £8,415 *Total Prizemoney* £21,457
Wins * **2000** Apr Nottin (HVY) H 14.1f 57 59 <
* 1999 Spt Salisb (HVY) H 9.9f 42 49+
1998 Jly Thirsk (GD) H 7f 45 47
2000 Turf 1-14: (12f, 14f 1-3, 15f 2, 16f 7, 17f) (hvy 2, sft 1-3, g-s 3, gd 3, g-f 3) 2000 AW 0-5: (12f, 16f 4) (Fibr 5)
Average gelding, effective 12 to 16f, acts on hvy to g-f, best on sft, has worn blinkers, favours tight tracks, does well at Nottingham. Turf high 62 - 6th of 12 getting 11lb from Veridian (11 May Chester 12f g-f RF 1139) - also 1st of 17 giving 16lb to Nosey Native (24 Apr Nottingham RF 0851). AW high 41. Becoming disappointing. Had been runner-up on five successive occasions in '99 and the early part of 2000, before getting his well-deserved reward at Nottingham over Easter.
**R J Price [2-43] E G Bevan (from J W Hills [1-11] Dec 1998).*

MY LINE BHB 40f **RR 34f** 4775[14]
3 b c Perpendicular - My Desire **(84f)** (Grey Desire) 8.7f **(50)**
Form - 0000
Record 2000 - 1st:0 2nd:0 3rd:0 Ran:4
2000 Turf 0-4: (8f, 9f, 10f, 12f) (g-s, frm 2, hrd)
Workmanlike, very moderate colt. Turf high 16 (began Jly).
**Mrs M Reveley [0-4] Mrs M A Spensley.*

MY LITTLE MAN BHB 30f **RR ?f** 4130[18]
5 b g Lugana Beach 7f **(63)** - Gay Ming (Gay Meadow)
Form - 00
Record 2000 - 1st:0 2nd:0 3rd:0 Ran:2
Pre2000 - 1st:0 2nd:1 3rd:1 Ran:9
Win Prizemoney £0 *Total Prizemoney* £1,453
2000 Turf 0-2: (8f, 10f) (g-f, frm)
Fair gelding, has worn blinkers. Turf high 2 (began Aug). Inconsistent.
**Dr J R J Naylor [0-2] W Clifford (from B Smart [0-9] Mar 1999).*

MY LOVELY BHB 85f **RR 84?f** 4495[1]
2 b f Dolphin Street (FR) - My Bonus **(50df 42a)** (Cyrano de Bergerac) 6f **(68)**
Form - 11
Record 2000 - 1st:2 2nd:0 3rd:0 Ran:2
Win Prizemoney £6,059 *Total Prizemoney* £6,059
Wins * **2000** Spt Beverl (HVY) 5f 84? <
* **2000** Aug Windso (G-F) S 5f 58
2000 Turf 2-2: (5f 2-2) (g-s 1-1, g-f 1-1)
Currently decent filly. Turf high 84 (began Aug) - 1st of 8 getting 7lb from Kyllachy (19 Spt Beverley RF 4495). She made a winning debut in a Windsor seller, but showed herself to be better than that when winning a Beverley novice stakes on heavy ground.
**D J S Cosgrove [2-2] Mrs Jean McGinn.*

MY LUCY LOCKET (IRE) BHB 82f **RR 79f** 5121[2]
2 b f Mujadil (USA) 7.7f **(70)** - First Nadia (Auction Ring (USA)) 8.6f **(65)**
Form - 33217502
Record 2000 - 1st:1 2nd:2 3rd:2 Ran:8
Win Prizemoney £5,586 *Total Prizemoney* £9,902
Wins * **2000** Jly Cheste (SFT) H 5.1f 80 <
2000 Turf 1-8: (5f 1-6, 6f, 7f) (hvy, g-s, g-f 1-4, frm, hrd)
Above-average filly, effective 5 to 7f, acts on g-s to g-f. Turf high 80 - 1st of 8 giving 18lb to Love Tune (14 Jly Chester RF 2799). Consistent.
**R Hannon [1-8] Mrs H F Prendergast.*

MY MAN FRIDAY BHB 34f44a **RR 34f 44a** 3569[6]
4 b g Lugana Beach 7f **(63)** - My Ruby Ring **(61df 50a)** (Blushing Scribe (USA)) 6f **(45)**
Form - 076
Record 2000 - 1st:0 2nd:0 3rd:0 Ran:3
Pre2000 - 1st:0 2nd:0 3rd:1 Ran:11
Win Prizemoney £0 *Total Prizemoney* £890
2000 Turf 0-3: (7f 2, 8f) (g-f, frm 2)
Leggy, very moderate gelding, effective 7f, acts on frm. Turf high 33 (began Jly). Consistent.
**W R Muir [0-14] Mrs Marion Wickham.*

MYNAH BHB 92f **RR 95f** 4041[5]
3 b f Selkirk (USA) 7.9f **(76)** - Reyah (Young Generation) 7.7f **(63)**
Form - 012215
Record 2000 - 1st:2 2nd:2 3rd:0 Ran:6
Win Prizemoney £13,198 *Total Prizemoney* £18,503
Wins * **2000** Aug Ascot (G-F) H 10f 89 95 <
* **2000** Jun Newmar (G-F) 10f 89
2000 Turf 2-6: (8f, 10f 2-5) (g-s, gd, g-f 1-1, frm 1-3)
Leggy, very useful filly, effective 10f, acts on gd to frm. Turf high 95 - 1st of 11 giving 11lb to The Green Grey (13 Aug Ascot RF 3602) - also 1st of 9 from Zibilene (11 Jun Newmarket RF 1885). She sprang a 33-1 shock at Newmarket in June, but proved that was no fluke when stringing together four creditable efforts. Probably best on a fast surface, she has a useful turn-of-foot and should improve again in 2001.
**A C Stewart [2-6] Hamish Leslie-Melville & Lord Hartington.*

MY PETAL BHB 58f **RR 63f** 1360[15]
4 gr f Petong 7.6f **(58)** - Najariya (Northfields (USA)) 9f **(72)**
Form - 00
Record 2000 - 1st:0 2nd:0 3rd:0 Ran:2
Pre2000 - 1st:2 2nd:1 3rd:0 Ran:8
Win Prizemoney £11,039 *Total Prizemoney* £12,074
Wins * 1998 Jly Goodwo (GD) H 6f 85 <
* 1998 Jly Newbur (G-F) 5.2f 67
2000 Turf 0-2: (6f, 7f) (gd, frm)
Scopey, average filly, has worn blinkers. Turf high 40.
**R Hannon [2-10] Jubert Family.*

MY PLACE BHB 70f **RR 72f** 5065[6]
2 b f Environment Friend 7.5f **(67)** - Verchinina (Star Appeal) 9.6f **(65)**
Form - 3846
Record 2000 - 1st:0 2nd:0 3rd:1 Ran:4
Win Prizemoney £0 *Total Prizemoney* £1,244
2000 Turf 0-4: (7f 2, 8f 2) (g-s 2, g-f, frm)
Above-average filly. Turf high 72 (began Jly) - 4th of 22 to The Bystander (6 Oct York 8f g-s RF 4828). **B W Hills [0-4] W J Gredley.*

MY PLEDGE (IRE) BHB 56f **RR 61f** 4192[9]
5 b g Waajib 8.9f **(67)** - Pollys Glow (IRE) (Glow (USA)) 6.7f **(71)**
Form - 2103440
Record 2000 - 1st:1 2nd:1 3rd:1 Ran:7
Pre2000 - 1st:1 2nd:0 3rd:0 Ran:11
Win Prizemoney £7,822 *Total Prizemoney* £10,238
Wins * **2000** Jun Kempto (G-F) H 12f 56 59
* 1998 Jun Windso (SFT) H 10f 69 71 <
2000 Turf 1-7: (11f, 12f 1-5, 14f) (g-f 5, frm 1-2)
Average gelding, effective 12f, acts on g-f to frm, best on frm, has worn blinkers, prefers tight tracks. Turf high 61 - 3rd of 19 giving 13lb to Mysterium (31 Jly Windsor 12f frm RF 3260) - also 1st of 6 getting 13lb from First Impression (28 Jun Kempton RF 2347). Consistent. He had a fruitless campaign last season, but has been returning to form this summer and won in game style at Kempton in June. Suited by 12 furlongs. **C A Horgan [2-18] Mrs B Sumner.*

MY RETREAT (USA) BHB 80f **RR 76f** 5299[1]
3 b c Hermitage (USA) 8.6f **(84)** - My Jessica Ann (USA) (Native Rythm)
Form - 10050521
Record 2000 - 1st:2 2nd:1 3rd:0 Ran:8
Pre2000 - 1st:0 2nd:1 3rd:0 Ran:2
Win Prizemoney £7,000 *Total Prizemoney* £8,814
Wins * **2000** Nov Mussel (G-S) H 8f 70 76
* **2000** Apr Warwic (HVY) 7.7f 80 <
2000 Turf 2-8: (8f 2-5, 9f, 10f, 11f) (hvy 1-1, sft, g-s 1-2, g-f, frm 3)
Well made, decent colt, effective 7 to 8f, best at 8f, acts on hvy to gd, has worn blinkers, prefers tight tracks. Turf high 80 (1st run) - 1st of 19 from Criss Cross (12 Apr Warwick RF 0684) - also 1st of 14 giving 4lb to Thihn (1 Nov Musselburgh RF 5299). Inconsistent.
**B W Hills [2-8] Ms A Soltesova (from L M Cumani [0-2] Oct 1999).*

MYSTERI DANCER BHB 80f75a **RR 74f 75a** 5015[3]
2 b g Rudimentary (USA) 8.2f **(66)** - Mystery Ship (Decoy Boy) 6.7f **(56)**
Form - 7223
Record 2000 - 1st:0 2nd:2 3rd:1 Ran:4
Win Prizemoney £0 *Total Prizemoney* £2,063
2000 Turf 0-3: (6f 3) (gd, g-f, frm) 2000 AW 0-1: (6f) (Fibr)
Above-average gelding. Turf high 74 (began Aug) - 2nd of 15 giving 5lb to Trustthunder (29 Spt Lingfield 6f gd RF 4725). (1st run) - 3rd of 9 to Tumbleweed Tenor (17 Oct Wolverhampton 6f Fibr RF 5015). **R J O'Sullivan [0-4] Jack Joseph.*

MYSTERIUM BHB 55f63a **RR 57f 63a** 5020[1]
6 gr g Mystiko (USA) 7.7f **(59)** - Way to Go (Troy) 10.4f **(68)**
Form - 12402124708251178031
Record 2000 - 1st:4 2nd:3 3rd:1 Ran:16
Pre2000 - 1st:3 2nd:2 3rd:5 Ran:29
Win Prizemoney £20,998 *Total Prizemoney* £26,035
Wins * **2000** *Oct Wolver (STD) H 12f 50 57*
* **2000** Aug Newmar (G-F) H 10f 52 57
* **2000** Jly Windso (G-F) H 11.6f 45 51
* **2000** *Jan Wolver (STD) H 9.4f 49 50*
* 1999 *Nov Wolver (STD) H 9.4f 41 49*
1999 Jly Yarmou (G-F) H 11.5f 40 43
* 1997 *Feb Wolver (STD) 7f 59 <*
2000 Turf 2-7: (10f 1-3, 11f 2, 12f 1-2) (gd, g-f 4, frm 2-2) 2000 AW 2-9: (9f 1-6, 10f, 12f 1-2) (Equi, Fibr 2-8)
Average gelding, effective 9 to 12f, best at 12f, acts on frm - acts on AW, has worn blinkers. Turf high 57 - 1st of 12 giving 13lb to Dande's Rambo (12 Aug Newmarket RF 3589) - also 1st of 19 getting 15lb from Kennet (31 Jly Windsor RF 3260). AW high 57 - 1st of 12 giving 5lb to Sharp Belline (17 Oct Wolverhampton RF 5020) - also 1st of 10 giving 14lb to Ocean Line (22 Jan Wolverhampton RF 0144). A multiple winner on the Wolverhampton Fibresand, he can win on turf too. Suited by around ten furlongs and by coming late off a strong pace.
**N P Littmoden [6-42] Alcester Associates (from J G Given [1-3] Aug 1999).*

MYSTICAL STAR (FR) RR 70f 2661[6]
3 b g Nicolotte - Addaya (IRE) **(39f)** (Persian Bold) 9.3f **(66)**
Form - 6
Record 2000 - 1st:0 2nd:0 3rd:0 Ran:1
2000 Turf 0-1: (10f) (g-f)
Scopey, currently above-average gelding.
**J J Sheehan [0-1] Mrs T L Harman.*

MYSTICAL WISDOM BHB 50f45a **RR 46df 45a** 2012[17]
3 b f Mystiko (USA) 7.7f **(59)** - Surprise Surprise (Robellino (USA)) 7.6f **(80)**
Form - 070
Record 2000 - 1st:0 2nd:0 3rd:0 Ran:3
Pre2000 - 1st:0 2nd:0 3rd:0 Ran:6
2000 Turf 0-1: (7f) (g-f) 2000 AW 0-2: (8f, 11f) (Fibr 2)
Light-framed, moderate filly. AW high 8. Becoming disappointing.
**P R Chamings [0-9] Mrs J E L Wright.*

MYSTIC-GEM BHB 30f **RR 16f** 744[10]
4 ch g Mystiko (USA) 7.7f **(59)** - Ela-Yianni-Mou (Anfield) 8.5f **(59)**
Form - 800
Record 2000 - 1st:0 2nd:0 3rd:0 Ran:3
2000 Turf 0-1: (7f) (gd) 2000 AW 0-2: (9f, 12f) (Fibr 2)
Unfurnished, poor gelding. **J S Wainwright [0-4] Mrs J R Bamforth.*

MYSTIC RIDGE BHB 57f62a **RR 64f 62a** 4782[4]
6 ch g Mystiko (USA) 7.7f **(59)** - Vallauris (Faustus (USA)) 10f **(58)**
Form - 0041004086004
Record 2000 - 1st:1 2nd:0 3rd:0 Ran:11
Pre2000 - 1st:4 2nd:2 3rd:5 Ran:28
Win Prizemoney £21,863 *Total Prizemoney* £26,633
Wins * **2000** *Feb Southw (STD) H 7f 58 73 <*
* 1999 Spt Lingfi (G-F) H 7f 68 71+
* 1999 Jly Galway (G-F) H 7f 68
* 1999 Jly Leopar (G-F) H 8f 58
* 1999 May Bright (FRM) H 8f 42 50+
2000 Turf 0-8: (6f, 7f 4, 8f 3) (g-s, gd 4, frm 3) 2000 AW 1-3: (7f 1-1, 8f 2) (Fibr 1-3)
Above-average gelding, effective 7f, acts on g-f to frm - acts on Fibr, has worn blinkers. Turf high 64. AW high 73 - 1st of 11 getting 1lb from Aberkeen (7 Feb Southwell RF 0240).
**B J Curley [5-38] P Byrne (from D R C Elsworth [0-5] Jun 1997).*

MYSTIFY BHB 96f **RR 99f** 4598[2]
3 b f Batshoof 9.5f **(66)** - Santa Linda (USA) (Sir Ivor) 10.2f **(70)**

Form - 15262
Record 2000 - 1st:1 2nd:2 3rd:0 Ran:5
Pre2000 - 1st:0 2nd:0 3rd:0 Ran:2
Win Prizemoney £2,496 *Total Prizemoney* £15,572
Wins * **2000** May Redcar (G-S) 7f 64++ <
2000 Turf 1-5: (7f 1-1, 8f 4) (sft, g-s, gd 1-3)
Scopey, very useful filly, effective 8f, acts on gd. Turf high 99 - 2nd of 14 giving 2lb to Riberac (23 Spt Ascot 8f gd RF 4598). She wears a Monty Roberts rug for stalls entry and ran well in Listed company after winning a weak Redcar maiden in the spring. A scopey individual, she is likely to improve.
**J H M Gosden [1-7] Lord Hartington.*

MY TESS BHB 65f79a RR 68f 79a 4874[14]

4 br f Lugana Beach 7f **(63)** - Barachois Princess (USA) (Barachois (CAN)) 8.3f **(63)**
Form - 1445221324250
Record **2000** - 1st:1 2nd:4 3rd:1 Ran:11
Pre2000 - 1st:2 2nd:0 3rd:3 Ran:15
Win Prizemoney £16,201 *Total Prizemoney* £23,133
Wins * **2000** *Feb Southw (STD) H 7f 70 77* <
* 1999 *Nov Wolver (STD) H 8.5f 64 66*
* 1999 Apr Nottin (HVY) 8.2f 77 <
2000 Turf 0-5: (6f, 7f 2, 8f 2) (g-s, gd 3, frm) 2000 AW 1-6: (7f 1-3, 8f 2, 9f) (Fibr 1-6)
Light-framed, decent filly, effective 6 to 10f, best at 8f, acts on sft to gd - acts on Fibr, likes left handed tracks, prefers tight tracks, excels at Southwell and Nottingham, likes Wolverhampton. Turf high 68 - 2nd of 20 giving 1lb to Talaria (2 May Nottingham 6f gd RF 0967). AW high 77 - 2nd of 10 giving 26lb to Jessinca (14 Feb Southwell 8f Fibr RF 0279) - also 1st of 8 giving 32lb to Oare Kite (25 Feb Southwell RF 0358). S **B A McMahon [3-26] J D Graham.*

MYTHICAL JINKS (USA) BHB 78f RR 77f 4313[8]

2 b br c Miswaki (USA) 8.1f **(81)** - Avarice (USA) (Manila (USA)) 9.3f **(71)**
Form - 5668
Record **2000** - 1st:0 2nd:0 3rd:0 Ran:4
2000 Turf 0-4: (6f, 7f 3) (g-f, frm 3)
Above-average colt. Turf high 77 (began Jly).
**E A L Dunlop [0-4] Saeed Suhail.*

MYTHICAL KING (IRE) RR 83f 4262[10]

3 b c Fairy King (USA) 7.7f **(75)** - Whatcombe (USA) **(75df)** (Alleged (USA)) 10f **(76)**
Form - 3314200
Record **2000** - 1st:1 2nd:1 3rd:2 Ran:7
Pre2000 - 1st:0 2nd:0 3rd:1 Ran:3
Win Prizemoney £4,387 *Total Prizemoney* £9,414
Wins * **2000** Jun Goodwo (GD) H 9.9f 78 83 <
2000 Turf 1-7: (10f 1-7) (gd 1-3, g-f 2, frm, hrd)
Scopey, decent colt, effective 10f, acts on gd to hrd, prefers tight tracks. Turf high 83 - 1st of 11 giving 2lb to Baileys Prize (9 Jun Goodwood RF 1847). Inconsistent.
**B Palling [1-10] Glyn and Albert Yemm.*

MYTHOLOGICAL (USA) RR 90f 3673a[11]

3 b c El Gran Senor (USA) 8.9f **(85)** - Finance Charge (USA) **00**
Form - 5720
2000 Turf 0-4: (10f 2, 12f, 14f) (g-s 2, gd, g-f)
Useful colt. Turf high 90 - 2nd of 5 giving 1lb to Fantasia Girl (29 Jly Curragh 10f g-f RF 3308a). He was very disappointing bar one creditable effort at The Curragh in July.
**A P O'Brien in IRE [1-5] Mrs John Magnier.*

MYTTON'S AGAIN BHB 65f56a RR 73f 56a 5316[12]

3 b g Rambo Dancer (CAN) 8.4f **(59)** - Sigh (Highland Melody) 6.3f **(55)**
Form - 604702665076311647800
Record **2000** - 1st:2 2nd:1 3rd:1 Ran:19
Pre2000 - 1st:1 2nd:2 3rd:0 Ran:14
Win Prizemoney £11,696 *Total Prizemoney* £15,568
Wins * **2000** Aug Mussel (G-F) H 7.1f 59 64
* **2000** Aug Ayr (GD) S 7f 48
* 1999 Spt Cheste (HVY) H 7f 65 72 <
2000 Turf 2-16: (6f 2, 7f 2-10, 8f 4) (g-s, gd 5, g-f 5, frm 2-5) 2000 AW 0-3: (6f, 7f, 8f) (Fibr 3)
Unfurnished, above-average gelding, effective 7 to 8f, best at 7f, acts on g-s to frm, often wears blinkers, likes tight tracks, excels at Musselburgh. Turf high 71 - also 1st of 11 giving 9lb to For Heavens Sake (24 Aug Musselburgh RF 3930). AW high 52. Becoming disappointing. No great shakes, but found his form in August when winning at Ayr and Musselburgh and suffered slipping blinkers in his hat-trick bid at Brighton.
**A Bailey [3-33] Gordon Mytton.*

MYTTONS MISTAKE BHB 53f50a RR 53f 50a 4277[6]

7 b g Rambo Dancer (CAN) 8.4f **(59)** - Hi-Hunsley (Swing Easy (USA)) 6.5f **(55)**
Form - 80224213666
Record **2000** - 1st:1 2nd:3 3rd:1 Ran:10
Pre2000 - 1st:9 2nd:7 3rd:13 Ran:81
Win Prizemoney £35,237 *Total Prizemoney* £58,046
Wins * **2000** Jun Warwic (G-F) H 7.7f 51 60
1999 Aug Bright (G-S) S 6f 44
1998 Aug Kempto (G-F) H 7f 68 70
1998 Jly Bath (GD) H 5.7f 64 67
1997 Oct Leices (GD) CH 8f 62 . 78?
1997 Spt Sandow (G-F) H 7.1f 59 64
1997 Aug Beverl (GD) H 7.5f 57 60
1997 Jly Cheste (G-F) H 7.6f 53 58
2000 Turf 1-10: (6f, 7f 6, 8f 1-3) (sft, gd 2, g-f 1-3, frm 4)
Fair gelding, effective 6 to 8f, acts on g-f to hrd, has worn blinkers, prefers left handed tracks, prefers tight tracks. Turf high 60 - 1st of 10 getting 6lb from White Emir (28 Jun Warwick RF 2360). Consistent.
**R J Baker [1-14] P Clado (from R J Hodges [3-32] Spt 1999).*

MYTTON'S MOMENT (IRE) BHB 46f40a RR 56f 40a 2693[16]

4 b g Waajib 8.9f **(67)** - Late Swallow (My Swallow) 9.2f **(71)**
Form - 344550
Record **2000** - 1st:0 2nd:0 3rd:0 Ran:5
Pre2000 - 1st:1 2nd:0 3rd:2 Ran:18
Win Prizemoney £3,622 *Total Prizemoney* £5,633
Wins * 1999 Jun Newmar (GD) S 8f 69 <
2000 Turf 0-1: (10f) (frm) 2000 AW 0-4: (8f, 11f, 12f, 16f) (Fibr 4)
Light-framed, fair gelding, effective 8f, acts on gd, often wears blinkers. AW high 44. **A Bailey [3-30] Gordon Mytton.*

MY TYSON (IRE) BHB 31f48a RR 25f 48a 3406[21]

5 b g Don't Forget Me 9.5f **(66)** - Shuckran Habibi (Thatching) 8f **(66)**
Form - 6008713600000
Record **2000** - 1st:1 2nd:0 3rd:1 Ran:11
Pre2000 - 1st:1 2nd:0 3rd:0 Ran:14
Win Prizemoney £4,489 *Total Prizemoney* £4,887
Wins * **2000** *Mar Wolver (STD) H 8.5f 44 52*
1997 *Nov Lingfi (STD) 5f 66* <
2000 Turf 0-5: (6f 2, 8f 2, 9f) (gd 2, frm 2, hrd) 2000 AW 1-6: (7f 2, 8f 1-3, 10f) (Equi, Fibr 1-5)
Fair gelding, effective 8f, - acts on Fibr, has worn blinkers, likes left handed tracks, likes tight tracks. Turf high 29. AW high 52 - 1st of 12 giving 4lb to Midnight Watch (16 Mar Wolverhampton RF 0446).
**K A Ryan [1-13] Mrs Candice Reilly (from K Mahdi [1-12] Jly 1998).*

MY VERY OWN (IRE) BHB 75f75a RR 68f 75a 4970[15]

2 ch c Persian Bold 10f **(69)** - Cossack Princess (IRE) (Lomond (USA)) 8.8f **(65)**
Form - 06220
Record **2000** - 1st:0 2nd:2 3rd:0 Ran:5
Win Prizemoney £0 *Total Prizemoney* £2,545
2000 Turf 0-3: (6f, 8f 2) (gd 2, g-f) 2000 AW 0-2: (7f, 8f) (Fibr 2)
Average colt. Turf high 68 - 2nd of 19 giving 8lb to Princess Emily (30 Aug York 8f gd RF 4108). AW high 68 (began Aug) - 2nd of 9 getting 1lb from Browser (3 Oct Wolverhampton 8f Fibr RF 4783).
**N P Littmoden [0-5] Mrs Mike Curley.*

NABADHAAT (USA) BHB 72f RR 80f 4617[4]

3 b f Mr Prospector (USA) 8.6f **(88)** - Roseate Tern (Blakeney) 10.5f **(64)**
Form - 404
Record **2000** - 1st:0 2nd:0 3rd:0 Ran:3
Pre2000 - 1st:0 2nd:0 3rd:0 Ran:2
Win Prizemoney £0 *Total Prizemoney* £748
2000 Turf 0-3: (8f, 10f, 12f) (gd, g-f, frm)
Decent filly. Turf high 80. **E A L Dunlop [0-5] Hamdan Al Maktoum.*

NADDER BHB 30f42a **RR 17f 42a** 4814[18]
5 ch g Lion Cavern (USA) 7.5f **(74)** - Nadia Nerina (CAN) (Northern Dancer) 9.6f **(80)**
Form - 782503020700
Record 2000 - 1st:0 2nd:2 3rd:1 Ran:10
Pre2000 - 1st:0 2nd:0 3rd:0 Ran:11
Win Prizemoney £0 *Total Prizemoney* £1,295
2000 Turf 0-4: (6f 3, 10f) (g-s, g-f, frm 2) 2000 AW 0-6: (6f 3, 7f 3) (Fibr 6)
Moderate gelding, effective 6 to 7f, - acted on Fibr, had worn blinkers (effectively), liked left handed tracks, liked tight tracks. Turf high 17. AW high 44 - 2nd of 16 getting 3lb from Petite Danseuse (22 May Southwell 6f Fibr RF 1378). (DEAD)
**W M Brisbourne [0-21] Mrs N J Roberts.*

NADOUR AL BAHR (IRE) BHB 98f93a **RR 101f 93a** 5130[5]
5 b h Be My Guest (USA) 10.2f **(66)** - Nona (GER) (Cortez (GER)) 8.6f **(75)**
Form - 65
Record 2000 - 1st:0 2nd:0 3rd:0 Ran:2
Pre2000 - 1st:1 2nd:2 3rd:1 Ran:5
Win Prizemoney £15,202 *Total Prizemoney* £149,708
Wins 1998 Apr Frankf (GD) G3 10f 96 <
2000 Turf 0-2: (12f 2) (sft, gd)
Very useful colt. Turf high 101 (began Spt). Showed high-class form in '98 when German-trained.
**T G Mills [0-2] T G Mills (from M Hofer in GER [1-5] Spt 1998).*

NAFISAH (IRE) BHB 97f **RR 92f** 5128[5]
2 ch f Lahib (USA) 8f **(69)** - Alyakkh (IRE) (Sadler's Wells (USA)) 10f **(76)**
Form - 22125
Record 2000 - 1st:1 2nd:3 3rd:0 Ran:5
Win Prizemoney £3,038 *Total Prizemoney* £10,526
Wins * 2000 Spt Kempto (SFT) 7f 83 <
2000 Turf 1-5: (7f 1-5) (sft, g-s 1-1, g-f 2, frm)
Useful filly. Turf high 92 (began Aug) - 2nd of 11 to Lilium (30 Spt Newmarket 7f g-f RF 4738) - also 1st of 15 from Pearl Bright (18 Spt Kempton RF 4481). Decisive winner of a maiden, she was just caught in a competitive Group Three at Newmarket. She ought to stay a mile plus. **B Hanbury [1-5] Hamdan Al Maktoum.*

NAFITH BHB 43f45a **RR 47f 45a** 1309[12]
4 ch g Elmaamul (USA) 8.1f **(70)** - Wanisa (USA) (Topsider (USA)) 8.3f **(71)**
Form - 3213760
Record 2000 - 1st:1 2nd:1 3rd:2 Ran:7
Pre2000 - 1st:0 2nd:0 3rd:0 Ran:7
Win Prizemoney £2,730 *Total Prizemoney* £4,291
Wins * 2000 *Feb Wolver (STD) 9.4f 51* <
2000 Turf 0-3: (8f, 10f 2) (gd 2, frm) 2000 AW 1-4: (8f, 9f 1-3) (Fibr 1-4)
Scopey, fair gelding, likes left handed tracks, likes tight tracks. Turf high 47. AW high 52.
**E L James [1-11] Nicholas Cowan (from M P Tregoning [0-7] Jun 1999).*

NAILER (IRE) BHB 40f **RR 63f** 1527[8]
4 b g Darshaan 11.9f **(81)** - Raysiya (Cure The Blues (USA)) 9.5f **(63)**
Form - 608
Record 2000 - 1st:0 2nd:0 3rd:0 Ran:3
Pre2000 - 1st:0 2nd:0 3rd:0 Ran:2
2000 Turf 0-3: (12f 2, 16f) (gd 2, hrd)
Tall, average gelding. Turf high 63.
**E J O'Neill [0-5] Mrs Patrick O'Neill.*

NAISSANT BHB 50f48a **RR 46f 48a** 3849[14]
7 b m Shaadi (USA) 8.1f **(75)** - Nophe (USA) (Super Concorde (USA)) 10.9f **(66)**
Form - 5086304253531207300
Record 2000 - 1st:1 2nd:2 3rd:4 Ran:19
Pre2000 - 1st:6 2nd:5 3rd:4 Ran:64
Win Prizemoney £26,257 *Total Prizemoney* £45,383
Wins * 2000 Jly Hamilt (G-F) H 6f 48 54
* 1999 Aug Carlis (G-F) 6.9f 58
* 1999 May Hamilt (Sft) H 5f 63 66
1998 Aug Hamilt (SFT) H 6f 55 61
1998 Jun Hamilt (SFT) H 6f 51 53
1996 Aug Carlis (FRM) 6.9f 61
1996 Aug Ripon (G-S) H 6f 60 71 <
2000 Turf 1-19: (5f 4, 6f 1-9, 7f 6) (gd 5, g-f 1-7, frm 5, hrd 2)
Moderate mare, effective 5 to 7f, best at 5f, acts on hvy to frm, best on gd, likes Ayr and Hamilton. Turf high 54. Inconsistent.
**J S Goldie [3-37] William Graham (from Martyn Wane [2-18] Oct 1998).*

NAJ-DE RR 81f 4300[5]
2 ch c Zafonic (USA) 9f **(83)** -River Jig (USA) (Irish River (FR)) 8.6f **(78)**
Form - 5
Record 2000 - 1st:0 2nd:0 3rd:0 Ran:1
2000 Turf 0-1: (6f) (gd)
Currently decent colt. **P F I Cole [0-1] H R H Prince Fahd Salman.*

NAJEYBA BHB 70f **RR 77f** 5003[15]
3 ch f Indian Ridge 7.6f **(74)** - Innocence **(68df)** (Unfuwain (USA))
Form - 1340800
Record 2000 - 1st:1 2nd:0 3rd:1 Ran:7
Win Prizemoney £3,848 *Total Prizemoney* £5,075
Wins * 2000 May Southw (HVY) 6f 64+ <
2000 Turf 1-7: (5f, 6f 1-4, 7f 2) (g-s 2, gd 1-1, frm 4)
Scopey, above-average filly, effective 6f, acts on frm. Turf high 77 - 3rd of 6 to Nisr (25 Jun Pontefract 6f frm RF 2265).
**A C Stewart [1-7] Sheikh Ahmed Al Maktoum.*

NAJJAR (USA) BHB 50f **RR 57?f** 1071[15]
5 gr g El Prado (IRE) 8f **(74)** - With Strawberries (USA) (Maudlin (USA)) 8f **(74)**
Form - 0
Record 2000 - 1st:0 2nd:0 3rd:0 Ran:1
Pre2000 - 1st:2 2nd:0 3rd:1 Ran:12
Win Prizemoney £6,658 *Total Prizemoney* £7,145
Wins 1998 Aug Leices (GD) H 8f 59 66 <
1998 Aug Newcas (GD) H 8f 57 58
2000 Turf 0-1: (8f) (g-f)
Fair gelding, has worn blinkers. Inconsistent.
**C Grant [0-1] John Smith's Ltd (from J G FitzGerald [2-9] Oct 1998).*

NAJJM (USA) BHB 80f **RR 81f** 4317[5]
3 br c Dynaformer (USA) 12f **(82)** - Azusa (USA) (Flying Paster (USA))
Form - 65145
Record 2000 - 1st:1 2nd:0 3rd:0 Ran:5
Pre2000 - 1st:0 2nd:2 3rd:2 Ran:4
Win Prizemoney £5,307 *Total Prizemoney* £9,376
Wins * 2000 Jly Ripon (G-F) H 12.3f 73 81 <
2000 Turf 1-5: (12f 1-3, 13f, 16f) (sft, gd, g-f 2, frm 1-1)
Scopey, decent colt, effective 7 to 16f, acts on gd to hrd, likes tight tracks. Turf high 81 - 5th of 8 giving 2lb to Laffah (9 Spt Goodwood 16f gd RF 4317) - also 1st of 9 giving 6lb to Westgate Run (30 Jly Ripon RF 3242). Consistent. Consistent early on, but took time in getting off the mark. Scored in good style at Ripon in July, but rose sharply in the handicap and it seems to have found him out.
**J L Dunlop [1-9] Hamdan Al Maktoum.*

NAJMAT JUMAIRAH (USA) BHB 53f **RR 54f** 3089[13]
3 b f Mr Prospector (USA) 8.6f **(88)** - Sheroog (USA) (Shareef Dancer (USA)) 9.9f **(73)**
Form - 6500
Record 2000 - 1st:0 2nd:0 3rd:0 Ran:4
2000 Turf 0-4: (9f, 10f, 11f, 12f) (g-f, frm 3)
Leggy, fair filly. Turf high 54.
**M R Channon [0-4] Sheikh Ahmed Al Maktoum.*

NAKED OAT BHB 44f41a **RR 44f 41a** 4620[6]
5 b g Imp Society (USA) 7.1f **(63)** - Bajina (Dancing Brave (USA)) 8.4f **(76)**
Form - 80787001608066
Record 2000 - 1st:1 2nd:0 3rd:0 Ran:14
Pre2000 - 1st:2 2nd:3 3rd:4 Ran:28
Win Prizemoney £6,599 *Total Prizemoney* £11,133
Wins * 2000 Jun Bright (FRM) S 10f 40
* 1999 May Warwic (GD) H 8f 50 56
* 1999 *Feb Wolver (STD) 9.4f 69+* <
2000 Turf 1-9: (8f 5, 10f 1-4) (sft 2, gd 3, g-f, frm 1-3) 2000 AW 0-5: (8f 2, 9f 2, 11f) (Fibr 5)

Moderate gelding, effective 9f, - acts on Fibr, has worn blinkers, likes left handed tracks. Turf high 44. AW high 43.
**B Smart [3-42] The Dyball Partnership.*

NAKWA (IRE) RR 18f 3412[9]
2 b g Namaqualand (USA) - Cajo (IRE) (Tirol)
Form - 00
Record 2000 - 1st:0 2nd:0 3rd:0 Ran:2
2000 Turf 0-2: (5f, 7f) (hvy, g-f)
Currently poor gelding. Turf high 18. **E J Alston [0-2] Alan Dick.*

NAMID RR 122+f 4845a[1]
4 b c Indian Ridge 7.6f **(74)** - Dawnsio (IRE) (Tate Gallery (USA)) 7.4f **(67)**
Form - 31111
2000 Turf 4-5: (5f 2-2, 6f 2-2, 7f) (g-s 1-2, gd 0-0)
Very high-class colt, effective 5f, acts on gd. Turf high 122 - 1st of 11 giving 21lb to Superstar Leo (1 Oct Longchamp RF 4845a) - also 1st of 9 giving 3lb to Tedburrow (9 Spt Leopardstown RF 4352a). Improving. He failed to stay seven furlongs on his reappearance and proved a revelation when dropped back to sprint distances. Outpaced in the early stages, he pounced late to win the Prix de l'Abbaye at Longchamp, thereby earning himself top-spot among European speed horses on the International Classifications. He has retired to Rathbarry Stud in Ireland at a fee of IR£7,000. **J Oxx in IRE [5-9] Lady Clague.*

NAMLLAMS RR 70f 2850[5]
2 b c Magic Ring (IRE) 6.5f **(64)** - White Flash **(54df)** (Sure Blade (USA)) 11.3f **(67)**
Form - 775
Record 2000 - 1st:0 2nd:0 3rd:0 Ran:3
2000 Turf 0-3: (5f, 6f 2) (gd, g-f 2)
Currently above-average colt. Turf high 70.
**A Dickman [0-3] Mike Smallman.*

NANCY'S BOY RR 71?f 5293[4]
2 b g Perpendicular - Derry's Delight (Mufrij)
Form - 804
Record 2000 - 1st:0 2nd:0 3rd:0 Ran:3
Win Prizemoney £0 *Total Prizemoney* £178
2000 Turf 0-3: (6f, 7f 2) (sft, g-s, gd)
Currently above-average gelding. Turf high 71 (began Oct).
**J Hetherton [0-3] R G Fell.*

NAPIER STAR BHB 31f38a **RR 33f 38a** 3449[16]
7 b m Inca Chief (USA) 5.6f **(45)** - America Star (Norwick (USA)) 7.2f **(56)**
Form - 260400
Record 2000 - 1st:0 2nd:1 3rd:0 Ran:6
Pre2000 - 1st:4 2nd:8 3rd:8 Ran:53
Win Prizemoney £9,262 *Total Prizemoney* £19,360
Wins 1997 *May Wolver (STD) H 5f 63 63* <
1996 *Nov Wolver (STD) H 5f 60 61*
1996 *Jly Wolver (STD) H 5f 51 51*
1996 *Apr Southw (STD) 6f 57*
2000 Turf 0-4: (5f, 6f 2, 7f) (g-f, frm 2, hrd) 2000 AW 0-2: (6f 2) (Fibr 2)
Moderate mare, often wears blinkers. Turf high 33. AW high 40. Inconsistent.
**A B Mulholland [0-8] P M Heaton (from Mrs N Macauley [4-51] Jan 1998).*

NAPPER BLOSSOM (IRE) BHB 30f **RR 30tf** 4101[18]
3 b f Petardia 8.2f **(58)** - Pass No Problem (Pas de Seul) 9.1f **(67)**
Form - 00000
Record 2000 - 1st:0 2nd:0 3rd:0 Ran:5
2000 Turf 0-5: (6f, 7f, 8f, 10f, 12f) (g-s, g-f 2, frm 2)
Very moderate filly. Turf high 30.
**Mrs P N Dutfield [0-5] Mrs Linda Salter.*

NARJIS FLOWER (USA) RR 5114[6]
2 b f Pleasant Colony (USA) 12.4f **(88)** - Flowing (USA) (El Gran Senor (USA)) 9.6f **(76)**
Form - 86
Record 2000 - 1st:0 2nd:0 3rd:0 Ran:2
2000 Turf 0-1: (10f) (g-s) 2000 AW 0-1: (9f) (Fibr)
Currently very moderate filly. **M Johnston [0-2] Jaber Abdullah.*

NARRATEUR (IRE) RR 95f 3673a[8]
3 b c Polish Precedent (USA) 9f **(73)** - Narwala (Darshaan) 9.9f **(84)**
Form - 421608
2000 Turf 1-6: (10f 2, 12f 1-3, 14f) (g-s 1-3, gd 3)
Very useful colt, effective 10 to 12f, acts on g-s, has worn blinkers. Turf high 95 - also 1st of 10 giving 5lb to Molomo (10 Jun Curragh RF 1945a). He fell short when stepped-up to Listed company.
**J Oxx in IRE [1-6] Sheikh Mohammed.*

NASHAAB (USA) RR 72f 3500[3]
3 b c Zafonic (USA) 9f **(83)** - Tajannub (USA) **(103f)** (Dixieland Band (USA)) 7f **(74)**
Form - 553
Record 2000 - 1st:0 2nd:0 3rd:1 Ran:3
Win Prizemoney £0 *Total Prizemoney* £525
2000 Turf 0-3: (7f, 8f 2) (g-f, frm 2)
Light-framed, currently above-average colt. Turf high 72 (began Jly) - 3rd of 4 giving 5lb to Seeking Success (9 Aug Pontefract 8f frm RF 3500). **R W Armstrong [0-3] Hamdan Al Maktoum.*

NASHIRA BHB 80f **RR 76f** 4747[15]
2 ch f Prince Sabo 6.6f **(64)** - Aldevonie **(75f)** (Green Desert (USA)) 8.6f **(78)**
Form - 310
Record 2000 - 1st:1 2nd:0 3rd:1 Ran:3
Win Prizemoney £2,828 *Total Prizemoney* £3,376
Wins * 2000 Jun Bath (G-F) 5.1f **76** <
2000 Turf 1-3: (5f 1-1, 6f 2) (gd 2, hrd 1-1)
Currently above-average filly. Turf high 76 - 1st of 10 giving 2lb to Misty Belle (17 Jun Bath RF 2038). Ran at Bath on her first two starts, a narrow winner when dropped slightly in trip on the second of them. **C R Egerton [1-3] Mrs R F Lowe.*

NASMATT BHB 93f **RR 88f** 5204a[2]
2 b f Danehill (USA) 9.1f **(79)** - Society Lady (USA) (Mr Prospector (USA)) 8.8f **(78)**
Form - 33142
Record 2000 - 1st:1 2nd:1 3rd:2 Ran:5
Win Prizemoney £3,558 *Total Prizemoney* £12,590
Wins * 2000 Spt Yarmou (G-F) 6f 88 <
2000 Turf 1-5: (6f 1-4, 7f) (hvy, gd, g-f, frm 1-2)
Useful filly. Turf high 88 (began Aug) - 2nd of 5 getting 8lb from Sign Of Nike (18 Oct Deauville 6f hvy RF 5204a) - also 1st of 9 from Rockerlong (13 Spt Yarmouth RF 4377). **M R Channon [1-5].*

NATALIE JAY BHB 82f73a **RR 80f 73a** 5316[1]
4 b f Ballacashtal (CAN) 7.9f **(51)** - Falls of Lora (Scottish Rifle) 10f **(55)**
Form - 3043017633131
Record 2000 - 1st:3 2nd:0 3rd:5 Ran:13
Pre2000 - 1st:1 2nd:2 3rd:3 Ran:16
Win Prizemoney £16,055 *Total Prizemoney* £23,417
Wins * 2000 Nov Doncas (HVY) H 8f 71 80 <
*** 2000** Oct Leices (HVY) H 8f 67 73
*** 2000** Aug Salisb (G-F) H 8f 62 66
* 1999 Aug Salisb (SFT) H 8f 63 67
2000 Turf 3-13: (7f 2, 8f 3-7, 9f 2, 10f 2) (g-s 2-2, gd 7, g-f, frm 1-3)
Lengthy, decent filly, effective 7 to 8f, best at 8f, acts on g-s to gd, best on g-s. Turf high 80 - 1st of 20 giving 3lb to Greenaway Bay (3 Nov Doncaster RF 5316) - also 1st of 20 giving 6lb to Eve (9 Oct Leicester RF 4874). **M R Channon [4-29] Peter Jolliffe.*

NATION (USA) RR 89f 4321[3]
2 b c Miesque's Son (USA) - Erica's Fault (USA) (Muttering (USA)) 9.2f **(89)**
Form - 23
Record 2000 - 1st:0 2nd:1 3rd:1 Ran:2
Win Prizemoney £0 *Total Prizemoney* £2,086
2000 Turf 0-2: (7f 2) (g-f 2)
Currently useful colt. Turf high 89 (began Aug).
**Sir Michael Stoute [0-2] Highclere Thoroughbred Racing Ltd.*

NATIONAL ACADEMY (GER) RR 100f 4722a[2]
5 b h Royal Academy (USA) 7.8f **(77)** - Narola (GER) (Nebos (GER)) 9f **(78)**
Form - 2
2000 Turf 0-1: (12f) (gd)

Very useful colt. (1st run) - 2nd of 8 giving 2lb to Akbar (24 Spt Dielsdorf 12f gd RF 4722a).

**H Remmert in GER [0-4] Jly 1998).*

NATIONAL ANTHEM BHB 106f RR 109f 4315[2]

4 b c Royal Academy (USA) 7.8f **(77)** - Heart's Harmony (Blushing Groom (FR)) 10.3f **(76)**

Form - 14412

Record 2000 - 1st:2 2nd:1 3rd:0 Ran:5
Pre2000 - 1st:1 2nd:2 3rd:1 Ran:8

Win Prizemoney £20,285 *Total Prizemoney* £47,738

Wins * **2000** Aug Epsom (GD) 10.1f 101+
* **2000** May Newmar (GD) H 10f 96 105 <
* 1999 Aug Sandow (G-S) 10f 80+

2000 Turf 2-5: (10f 2-3, 12f 2) (gd 2-4, frm)

Light-framed, Pattern-class colt, effective 10 to 12f, best at 12f, acts on gd to frm, best on gd, likes Newmarket. Turf high 109 - 2nd of 5 giving 4lb to Ekraar (9 Spt Goodwood 10f gd RF 4315) - also 1st of 16 giving 10lb to Supply And Demand (6 May Newmarket RF 1059). An imposing individual, he won well at Newmarket before finishing fourth in the Duke of Edinburgh handicap at Ascot, for which he started a warm favourite. Beaten again over that trip next time, he reverted to ten furlongs to score at Epsom, despite struggling to handle the track. Finished second in a Group Three on his final run, albeit no match for Ekraar.

**Sir Michael Stoute [3-13] Mrs Denis Haynes.*

NATIONAL DANCE BHB 75f68a RR 68a 309[2]

3 b g Deploy 11.4f **(67)** - Fairy Flax (IRE) (Dancing Brave (USA)) 8.4f **(76)**

Form - 142

Record 2000 - 1st:1 2nd:1 3rd:0 Ran:3

Win Prizemoney £2,847 *Total Prizemoney* £4,629

Wins * **2000** *Jan Southw (STD) 8f 60* <

2000 AW 1-3: (8f 1-2, 10f) (Equi, Fibr 1-2)

Strong, currently above-average gelding. AW high 70 - 2nd of 7 giving 5lb to Calko (18 Feb Southwell 8f Fibr RF 0309).

**J G Given [1-3] Michael Payton.*

NATIONAL PRINCESS RR 68f 1524[6]

3 br f Bin Ajwaad (IRE) - Griddle Cake (IRE) **(65df)** (Be My Guest (USA)) 9.3f **(67)**

Form - 06

Record 2000 - 1st:0 2nd:0 3rd:0 Ran:2

2000 Turf 0-2: (8f 2) (gd, frm)

Light-framed, currently average filly. Turf high 68.

**W Jarvis [0-2] N S Yong.*

NATIVE FORCE (IRE) RR 69f 5098[11]

2 b f Indian Ridge 7.6f **(74)** - La Pellegrina (IRE) **(63f 59a)** (Be My Guest (USA)) 9.3f **(67)**

Form - 0

Record 2000 - 1st:0 2nd:0 3rd:0 Ran:1

2000 Turf 0-1: (8f) (gd)

Currently average filly.

**J H M Gosden [0-1] R E Sangster.*

NATIVE TITLE RR 84f 3706[4]

2 b c Pivotal - Bermuda Lily (Dunbeath (USA)) 7.8f **(70)**

Form - 54

Record 2000 - 1st:0 2nd:0 3rd:0 Ran:2

Win Prizemoney £0 *Total Prizemoney* £268

2000 Turf 0-2: (7f 2) (g-f, frm)

Currently decent colt. Turf high 84 (began Aug) - 4th of 7 getting 2lb from Trillie (16 Aug Salisbury 7f frm RF 3706).

**M Blanshard [0-2] C McKenna.*

NATSMAGIRL (IRE) BHB 44f41a RR 44f 41a 3898[6]

3 b f Blues Traveller (IRE) - Top The Rest (Top Ville) 11.7f **(68)**

Form - 585056246

Record 2000 - 1st:0 2nd:1 3rd:0 Ran:7
Pre2000 - 1st:1 2nd:2 3rd:2 Ran:17

Win Prizemoney £2,722 *Total Prizemoney* £7,285

Wins * 1999 Jun Thirsk (G-F) S 6f 63 <

2000 Turf 0-6: (6f 3, 7f 2, 8f) (g-f, frm 4, hrd) 2000 AW 0-1: (6f) (Fibr)

Light-framed, moderate filly, effective 5 to 7f, best at 6f, acts on g-f to hrd, best on frm, has worn blinkers, excels at Thirsk. Turf high 44.

**Martyn Wane [1-24] Darren & Annaley Yates.*

NATURAL (IRE) BHB 64f RR 67f 2843[7]

3 b g Bigstone (IRE) - You Make Me Real (USA) (Give Me Strength (USA))

Form - 0627

Record 2000 - 1st:0 2nd:1 3rd:0 Ran:4
Pre2000 - 1st:0 2nd:0 3rd:0 Ran:1

Win Prizemoney £0 *Total Prizemoney* £972

2000 Turf 0-4: (6f, 7f, 8f, 10f) (hvy, g-f 2, frm)

Scopey, average gelding. Turf high 67 - 2nd of 11 getting 1lb from Bold State (17 Jun Nottingham 8f g-f RF 2051).

**John Berry [0-4] Mrs Mrs Dinham, Veale, Berry (from J Noseda [0-1] Spt 1999).*

NATURAL EIGHT (IRE) BHB 56f51a RR 54f 51a 2153[B]

6 b g In The Wings 11.2f **(77)** - Fenny Rough (Home Guard (USA)) 9.3f **(66)**

Form - 6163335B

Record 2000 - 1st:0 2nd:0 3rd:3 Ran:6
Pre2000 - 1st:2 2nd:2 3rd:3 Ran:20

Win Prizemoney £5,362 *Total Prizemoney* £12,261

Wins * 1999 *Dec Lingfi (STD) H 13f 42 51* <
* 1999 Spt Bath (FRM) H 13.1f 43 45+

2000 Turf 0-5: (13f, 14f 2, 15f, 20f) (g-s 2, gd 3) 2000 AW 0-1: (16f) (Equi)

Fair gelding, effective 13 to 16f, best at 14f, acted on g-s to frm - acted on Equi, best on gd, had worn blinkers, preferred left handed tracks, excelled at Nottingham. Turf high 54 - 5th of 13 getting 16lb from Turtle Soup (31 May Newbury 13f g-s RF 1592). (DEAD)

**J R Poulton [2-18] Michael Siu (from R W Armstrong [0-4] Spt 1998).*

NAUGHTY KNIGHT BHB 45f50a RR 51f 50a 5081[13]

2 ch g King's Signet (USA) 7f **(51)** - Maid of Mischief (Be My Chief (USA))

Form - 0571135000

Record 2000 - 1st:2 2nd:0 3rd:1 Ran:10

Win Prizemoney £4,553 *Total Prizemoney* £5,093

Wins 2000 May Leices (SFT) C 5f 51 <
2000 May Beverl (GD) S 5f 51 <

2000 Turf 2-9: (5f 2-6, 6f 3) (hvy, sft, g-s, gd 2-2, g-f, frm 3) 2000 AW 0-1: (5f) (Fibr)

Fair gelding, effective 5f, acts on gd. Turf high 51 - 1st of 5 giving 1lb to Amelia (29 May Leicester RF 1525) - also 1st of 11 giving 5lb to Windchill (23 May Beverley RF 1385). Becoming disappointing.

**A Berry [0-2] Walt Sylvester (from G B Balding [2-8] Aug 2000).*

NAUTICAL LIGHT RR 25f 653[16]

3 b f Slip Anchor 12.7f **(75)** - Lighted Glitter (FR) (Crystal Glitters (USA)) 11.3f **(79)**

Form - 0

Record 2000 - 1st:0 2nd:0 3rd:0 Ran:1

2000 Turf 0-1: (10f) (frm)

Unfurnished, currently little account filly.

**T R Watson [0-1] Alan Wright.*

NAUTICAL STAR BHB 75f RR 78f 4696[9]

5 b g Slip Anchor 12.7f **(75)** - Comic Talent (Pharly (FR)) 9.8f **(68)**

Form - 000700

Record 2000 - 1st:0 2nd:0 3rd:0 Ran:6
Pre2000 - 1st:3 2nd:3 3rd:2 Ran:15

Win Prizemoney £20,257 *Total Prizemoney* £38,399

Wins * 1998 Aug Epsom (G-F) H 12f 89 **94** <
* 1998 Apr Newmar (SFT) H 10f 83 91
* 1997 Aug Ayr (G-F) 7f 80+

2000 Turf 0-6: (12f 6) (gd 3, g-f 2, frm)

Above-average gelding, effective 12f, acts on g-s to gd, best on gd, has worn blinkers, prefers tight tracks. Turf high 87. Becoming disappointing.

**J W Hills [3-21] Wauchope,Sir Simon D Cottam.*

NAUTICAL WARNING BHB 54f75a RR 53f 75a 4825[16]

5 b g Warning 8.1f **(77)** - Night At Sea (Night Shift (USA)) 7.2f **(69)**

Form - 121400

Record 2000 - 1st:1 2nd:0 3rd:0 Ran:4
Pre2000 - 1st:5 2nd:2 3rd:1 Ran:21

Win Prizemoney £24,887 *Total Prizemoney* £29,059

Wins * **2000** *Jan Lingfi (STD) H* *7f* *77* *80* <
* 1999 *Nov Lingfi (STD) H* *8f* *69* *75*
* 1999 *Jly Lingfi* (FRM) H 7.6f 51 53
* 1999 *Jun Lingfi (STD)* *8f* *71*
* 1999 *Feb Lingfi (STD) H* *8f* *58* *71*
1998 *Jan Lingfi (STD) H* *7f* *57* *63*
2000 Turf 0-1: (6f) (g-f) 2000 AW 1-3: (7f 1-2, 10f) (Equi 1-3)
Above-average gelding, effective 7 to 8f, best at 7f, - acts on AW, best on Equi, prefers left handed tracks, likes tight tracks, excels at Lingfield. AW high 80 (1st run) - 1st of 15 getting 7lb from Topton (15 Jan Lingfield RF 0098). Inconsistent.
**B R Johnson [5-15] The Twenty Five Club (from J Noseda [1-6] Oct 1998).*

NAVAL AFFAIR (IRE) BHB 98f **RR 98f** 4330[4]
3 b f Last Tycoon 9.4f **(73)** - Sailor's Mate (Shirley Heights) 10.3f **(71)**
Form - 4004
Record 2000 - 1st:0 2nd:0 3rd:0 Ran:4
Pre2000 - 1st:1 2nd:0 3rd:1 Ran:2
Win Prizemoney £3,631 *Total Prizemoney* £6,812
Wins * 1999 Aug Kempto (G-S) 7f 79 <
2000 Turf 0-4: (10f 3, 11f) (gd 3, frm)
Scopey, very useful filly, effective 10 to 11f, best at 10f, acts on gd to frm, best on gd. Turf high 98 - 4th of 15 getting 4lb from Courting (12 Spt Yarmouth 10f gd RF 4330).
**Sir Michael Stoute [1-6] Lord Weinstock.*

NAVAN PROJECT (IRE) BHB 25f **RR 29f** 2994[6]
6 gr g Project Manager 7.2f **(47)** - Just Possible (Kalaglow) 9.8f **(67)**
Form - 086
Record 2000 - 1st:0 2nd:0 3rd:0 Ran:3
Pre2000 - 1st:1 2nd:0 3rd:1 Ran:15
Win Prizemoney £2,911 *Total Prizemoney* £3,667
Wins 1997 Aug Tipper (GD) H 9f 69 79 <
2000 Turf 0-3: (9f, 10f, 11f) (gd 2, g-f)
Little account gelding, has worn blinkers. Turf high 29. Becoming disappointing.
**A R Dicken [1-20] Got To Be In It To Win It Partnership (from J S Bolger in IRE [1-11] Oct 1997).*

NAVARRE SAMSON (FR) RR 59f 4036[4]
5 b br g Ganges (USA) - L'eternite (FR) (Cariellor (FR))
Form - 4
Record 2000 - 1st:0 2nd:0 3rd:0 Ran:1
Win Prizemoney £0 *Total Prizemoney* £802
2000 Turf 0-1: (12f) (gd)
Currently fair gelding. **P J Hobbs [0-1] Winton Bloodstock Ltd.*

NAVIASKY (IRE) BHB 77f **RR 80f** 3601[9]
5 b br g Scenic 10.6f **(66)** - Black Molly (IRE) (High Top) 10.2f **(67)**
Form - 00040466340
Record 2000 - 1st:0 2nd:0 3rd:1 Ran:11
Pre2000 - 1st:5 2nd:1 3rd:4 Ran:27
Win Prizemoney £41,595 *Total Prizemoney* £54,077
Wins * 1999 Aug Leices (G-F) H 8f 77 81 <
* 1999 Jly Goodwo (G-F) H 8f 69 73
* 1999 Jun Goodwo (G-F) H 8f 66 69
1998 Jun Carlis (G-S) H 8f 60 66
1997 Aug Thirsk (G-F) 5f 79+
2000 Turf 0-11: (7f, 8f 9, 9f) (sft, g-s 2, gd 2, g-f 5, frm)
Decent gelding, effective 7 to 8f, best at 8f, acts on g-s to frm, best on frm, prefers right handed tracks, prefers tight tracks, excels at Goodwood. Turf high 80 - 4th of 16 getting 8lb from Persiano (23 May Goodwood 8f g-s RF 1392).
**W R Muir [3-21] Percipacious Punters Racing Club (from Mrs J R Ramsden [2-19] Aug 1998).*

NAYEF (USA) RR 120++f 4853[1]
2 b c Gulch (USA) 9.6f **(79)** -Height of Fashion (FR) (Bustino) 10.4f **(64)**
Form - 11
Record 2000 - 1st:2 2nd:0 3rd:0 Ran:2
Win Prizemoney £22,926 *Total Prizemoney* £22,926
Wins * **2000** Oct Ascot (HVY) L 8f 120++ <
* **2000** Spt Newbur (G-F) 8f 94+
2000 Turf 2-2: (8f 2-2) (sft 1-1, frm 1-1)
Currently very high-class colt. Turf high 120 (began Spt) - 1st of 6 from Hill Country (7 Oct Ascot RF 4853). He has the same imposing presence as his half-brother Nashwan and gained a host of admirers when going unbeaten in two starts last year. An excellent mover, he floated over heavy ground when routing a strong field in the Listed Autumn Stakes at Ascot in October and is rated below only Minardi, Okawango and Tobougg among European colts on the International Classification. Currently ante-post favourite for the 2000 Guineas and Derby, he is reported to be wintering well and is clearly an outstanding prospect. Likely to stay at least a mile and a quarter, his reappearance is eagerly awaited.
**M P Tregoning [2-2] Hamdan Al Maktoum.*

NEARCTIC LADY (USA) BHB 92f **RR 90+f** 4926[1]
2 gr ro f Night Shift (USA) 8.1f **(73)** - Snowing (USA) (Icecapade (USA)) 11f **(62)**
Form - 4011
Record 2000 - 1st:2 2nd:0 3rd:0 Ran:4
Win Prizemoney £7,114 *Total Prizemoney* £7,354
Wins * **2000** *Oct Lingfi (STD)* *6f* *89+*
* **2000** Spt Bath (GD) 5.1f 90+ <
2000 Turf 1-3: (5f 1-2, 6f) (gd, frm 1-2) 2000 AW 1-1: (6f 1-1) (Equi 1-1)
Useful filly. Turf high 90 - 1st of 9 from Bee One (4 Spt Bath RF 4201). (1st run) - 1st of 13 giving 2lb to Magical Flute (11 Oct Lingfield RF 4926). She looked useful under forcing tactics in the autumn and could develop into a decent sprint handicapper this year. **R Hannon [2-4] D Boocock.*

NEARLY A FOOL BHB 96f **RR 90f** 4862[2]
2 b g Komaite (USA) 6.9f **(61)** - Greenway Lady **(53f)** (Prince Daniel (USA))
Form - 14331333302
Record 2000 - 1st:2 2nd:1 3rd:6 Ran:11
Win Prizemoney £9,070 *Total Prizemoney* £21,898
Wins * **2000** Jun Bath (G-F) 5.1f 81 <
* **2000** Mar Doncas (G-F) 5f 81 <
2000 Turf 2-11: (5f 2-8, 6f 3) (sft, gd 2, g-f 3, frm 1-4, hrd 1-1)
Useful gelding, effective 5 to 6f, best at 5f, acts on sft to hrd. Turf high 89 - 2nd of 4 getting 5lb from Atmospheric (7 Oct York 6f sft RF 4862) - also 1st of 7 giving 12lb to My Lucy Locket (17 Jun Bath RF 2040). Consistent. Landed the Brocklesby in good style on his debut and has run some good races since in decent company since, adding another victory at Bath in June.
**B A McMahon [2-11] Nearly A Fool Partnership.*

NEEDWOOD BLADE RR 53f 4440[10]
2 ch c Pivotal - Finlaggan **(81f 69a)** (Be My Chief (USA))
Form - 70
Record 2000 - 1st:0 2nd:0 3rd:0 Ran:2
2000 Turf 0-2: (5f, 6f) (gd 2)
Currently fair colt. Turf high 53 (began Spt).
**B C Morgan [0-2] Needwood Racing Ltd.*

NEEDWOOD BRAVE BHB 66f **RR 74f** 4646[14]
2 b c Lion Cavern (USA) 7.5f **(74)** - Woodcrest **(82f)** (Niniski (USA)) 10.6f **(65)**
Form - 080
Record 2000 - 1st:0 2nd:0 3rd:0 Ran:3
2000 Turf 0-3: (7f, 8f 2) (g-s, g-f 2)
Currently above-average colt. Turf high 74 (began Spt).
**B C Morgan [0-3] Needwood Racing Ltd.*

NEEDWOOD MAESTRO BHB 39f30a **RR 37f 30a** 4184[1]
4 b g Sizzling Melody 6.3f **(49)** - Needwood Poppy **(25f 39a)** (Rolfe (USA)) 12.1f **(65)**
Form - 57031
Record 2000 - 1st:1 2nd:0 3rd:1 Ran:5
Pre2000 - 1st:0 2nd:0 3rd:2 Ran:10
Win Prizemoney £2,834 *Total Prizemoney* £3,715
Wins * **2000** Spt Hamilt (SFT) S 12.1f 37 <
2000 Turf 1-4: (11f, 12f 1-3) (hvy, g-s 1-1, gd 2) 2000 AW 0-1: (12f) (Fibr)
Light-framed, very moderate gelding, effective 8f, acts on g-s, has worn blinkers. Turf high 37. Consistent.
**B C Morgan [1-15] Needwood Racing Ltd.*

NEEDWOOD MINSTREL BHB 45f30a **RR 46f 30a** 152[8]
4 b g Clantime 6.6f **(57)** - Azubah **(29a)** (Castle Keep) 8.3f **(57)**
Form - 08
Record 2000 - 1st:0 2nd:0 3rd:0 Ran:1

Pre2000 - 1st:0 2nd:0 3rd:0 Ran:13
2000 AW 0-1: (7f) (Fibr)
Small, moderate gelding, effective 5f, acts on g-f. Becoming disappointing. **B C Morgan [0-14] Needwood Racing Ltd.*

NEEDWOOD MYSTIC BHB 42f32a RR 52f 32a 3923[10]
5 b m Rolfe (USA) 11.2f **(46)** - Enchanting Kate (Enchantment) 5.4f **(52)**
Form - 04001850
Record 2000 - 1st:1 2nd:0 3rd:0 Ran:7
Pre2000 - 1st:2 2nd:1 3rd:2 Ran:20
Win Prizemoney £8,403 *Total Prizemoney* £10,341
Wins * **2000** Jly Catter (G-F) H 12f 42 53+ <
* 1999 Aug Warwic (GD) H 12.3f 43 48
* 1999 Jun Warwic (G-F) H 12.3f 38 40
2000 Turf 1-7: (12f 1-5, 13f, 14f) (g-f 4, frm 1-3)
Fair filly, effective 12 to 14f, best at 12f, acts on gd to frm, best on gd, prefers tight tracks, excels at Catterick and Warwick. Turf high 53 - 1st of 7 giving 2lb to Rayware Boy (5 Jly Catterick RF 2545).
**B C Morgan [3-27] Needwood Racing Ltd.*

NEEDWOOD SPIRIT BHB 56f50a RR 62f 50a 1707[9]
5 b g Rolfe (USA) 11.2f **(46)** - Needwood Nymph (Bold Owl) 8.5f **(45)**
Form - 02070
Record 2000 - 1st:0 2nd:1 3rd:0 Ran:5
Pre2000 - 1st:2 2nd:1 3rd:2 Ran:22
Win Prizemoney £5,750 *Total Prizemoney* £14,166
Wins * 1999 Apr Folkes (SFT) H 15.4f 61 66 <
* 1998 Oct Catter (SFT) 13.8f 61
2000 Turf 0-5: (14f 2, 15f, 16f 2) (hvy, sft, g-s, gd 2)
Average gelding, effective 13 to 15f, best at 14f, acts on hvy to gd, best on g-s, has worn blinkers, likes tight tracks, excels at Catterick. Turf high 62 - 2nd of 16 getting 11lb from Quedex (6 May Haydock 14f gd RF 1056). Consistent. A modest staying handicapper who goes well in soft ground, he ran well on soft ground in autumn 1999, but has been well beaten over hurdles since.
**B C Morgan [2-29] Needwood Racing Ltd.*

NEEDWOOD TRIBESMAN BHB 31f48a RR 46f 48a 4403[20]
3 gr c Clantime 6.6f **(57)** - Strawberry Pink (Absalom) 7.2f **(58)**
Form - 0000000
Record 2000 - 1st:0 2nd:0 3rd:0 Ran:7
2000 Turf 0-6: (5f, 6f 4, 8f) (g-s, g-f 2, frm 2, hrd) 2000 AW 0-1: (7f) (Fibr)
Unfurnished, moderate colt. Turf high 46.
**B C Morgan [0-7] Needwood Racing Ltd.*

NEEDWOOD TRICKSTER (IRE) BHB 55f55a RR 74f 55a 4558[6]
3 gr g Fayruz 6.6f **(63)** - Istaraka (IRE) (Darshaan) 9.9f **(84)**
Form - 83367006
Record 2000 - 1st:0 2nd:0 3rd:2 Ran:8
Win Prizemoney £0 *Total Prizemoney* £779
2000 Turf 0-8: (5f 5, 6f 3) (sft, gd 3, g-f, frm 3)
Light-framed, above-average gelding, effective 5f, acts on sft. Turf high 74. **B C Morgan [0-8] Needwood Racing Ltd.*

NEEDWOOD TRIDENT BHB 35f34a RR 42f 34a 5082[7]
3 b f Minshaanshu Amad (USA) 11.3f **(53)** - Needwood Nymph (Bold Owl) 8.5f **(45)**
Form - 050742047
Record 2000 - 1st:0 2nd:1 3rd:0 Ran:9
Pre2000 - 1st:0 2nd:0 3rd:0 Ran:2
Win Prizemoney £0 *Total Prizemoney* £845
2000 Turf 0-8: (7f, 10f 3, 16f 3, 17f) (hvy, sft, gd, g-f 2, frm 2, hrd) 2000 AW 0-1: (16f) (Equi)
Unfurnished, moderate filly, effective 16f, acts on g-f to frm. Turf high 42 - 2nd of 8 getting 6lb from Beauchamp Magic (14 Aug Thirsk 16f frm RF 3629).
**J Pearce [0-6] Miss Sarah Diane Warren (from B C Morgan [0-5] May 2000).*

NEEDWOOD TROOPER BHB 62f RR 60f 3508[3]
3 br c Puissance 7.1f **(60)** - Blueit (FR) (Bold Lad (IRE)) 8.4f **(68)**
Form - 443
Record 2000 - 1st:0 2nd:0 3rd:1 Ran:3
Pre2000 - 1st:0 2nd:0 3rd:0 Ran:1
Win Prizemoney £0 *Total Prizemoney* £1,289
2000 Turf 0-3: (5f 3) (gd, frm, hrd)
Unfurnished, average colt. Turf high 60.
**B C Morgan [0-4] Needwood Racing Ltd.*

NEEDWOOD TRUFFLE (IRE) BHB 62f RR 53f 4049[16]
3 ch f Brief Truce (USA) 9.1f **(73)** - Green Wings (General Assembly (USA)) 10f **(68)**
Form - 000
Record 2000 - 1st:0 2nd:0 3rd:0 Ran:3
Pre2000 - 1st:1 2nd:0 3rd:2 Ran:7
Win Prizemoney £7,107 *Total Prizemoney* £8,337
Wins * 1999 Jly Goodwo (G-F) H 5f 76 <
2000 Turf 0-3: (5f 2, 6f) (g-f 2, frm)
Unfurnished, fair filly, effective 5f, acts on g-f. Turf high 53. Inconsistent. **B C Morgan [1-10] Needwood Racing Ltd.*

NEEDWOOD TRUMP (IRE) BHB 39f RR 33f 42[10]
3 br g Marju (IRE) 9.2f **(76)** - Play The Queen (IRE) (King of Clubs) 7.1f **(57)**
Form - 0
Record 2000 - 1st:0 2nd:0 3rd:0 Ran:1
Pre2000 - 1st:0 2nd:0 3rd:0 Ran:3
2000 AW 0-1: (7f) (Fibr)
Light-framed, very moderate gelding.
**B C Morgan [0-4] Needwood Racing Ltd.*

NEELA (IRE) BHB 47f48a RR 61df 48a 2222[11]
4 ch f Bluebird (USA) 7.9f **(71)** - Scammony (IRE) (Persian Bold) 9.3f **(66)**
Form - 7000
Record 2000 - 1st:0 2nd:0 3rd:0 Ran:3
Pre2000 - 1st:0 2nd:0 3rd:0 Ran:3
Win Prizemoney £0 *Total Prizemoney* £206
2000 Turf 0-2: (7f 2) (g-s, g-f) 2000 AW 0-1: (7f) (Fibr)
Lengthy, average filly, effective 6f, acts on gd. Turf high 33.
**R Hannon [0-6] Ananda Krishnan.*

NEERUAM STAR RR 45tf 2803[P]
2 b c Cool Jazz - Bay Meadows Star (Sharpo) 7.7f **(59)**
Form - 3P
Record 2000 - 1st:0 2nd:0 3rd:1 Ran:2
Win Prizemoney £0 *Total Prizemoney* £436
2000 Turf 0-2: (5f 2) (g-f 2)
Moderate colt. Turf high 45. (DEAD)
**D Moffatt [0-2] Mrs Maureen Pickering.*

NEGATIVE EQUITY BHB 33f47a RR 46?f 47a 345[10]
8 ch g Be My Chief (USA) 10.2f **(62)** - Rather Romantic (CAN) (Verbatim (USA)) 8.5f **(64)**
Form - 140
Record 2000 - 1st:1 2nd:0 3rd:0 Ran:3
Pre2000 - 1st:0 2nd:2 3rd:0 Ran:10
Win Prizemoney £1,517 *Total Prizemoney* £3,705
Wins * **2000** *Feb Lingfi (STD) SH 13f 30 34* <
2000 AW 1-3: (13f 1-2, 16f) (Equi 1-2, Fibr)
Moderate gelding, often wears blinkers (effectively). AW high 34 (1st run).
**D G Bridgwater [1-5] D E McDowell (from K R Burke [0-10] Aug 1995).*

NEGRONI RR 69f 3709[6]
3 br f Mtoto 11.5f **(71)** - Carousel Music **(36f)** (On Your Mark) 7.7f **(58)**
Form - 336
Record 2000 - 1st:0 2nd:0 3rd:2 Ran:3
Pre2000 - 1st:0 2nd:0 3rd:0 Ran:1
Win Prizemoney £0 *Total Prizemoney* £1,130
2000 Turf 0-3: (8f 2, 10f) (g-f 3)
Average filly. Turf high 69 (began Jly) - 3rd of 7 to Ellway Queen (4 Aug Nottingham 8f g-f RF 3378).
**J W Hills [0-4] Scott Hardy Partnership.*

NEIGES ETERNELLES (FR) BHB 70f RR 52f 57[7]
5 b m Exit To Nowhere (USA) 8.7f **(77)** - Nabita (FR) (Akarad (FR)) 9f **(76)**
Form - 7
Record 2000 - 1st:0 2nd:0 3rd:0 Ran:1
Pre2000 - 1st:0 2nd:0 3rd:1 Ran:5
Win Prizemoney £0 *Total Prizemoney* £3,828

2000 AW 0-1: (16f) (Fibr)
Fair filly.
**D J Wintle [0-1] Mrs Joan Egan (from P R Webber [0-3] Nov 1999).*

NELSONS FLAGSHIP BHB 58f **RR 54f** 3620^{10}
2 b c Petong 7.6f **(58)** - Marie's Crusader (IRE) (Last Tycoon) 8.5f **(62)**
Form - 080
Record 2000 - 1st:0 2nd:0 3rd:0 Ran:3
2000 Turf 0-3: (6f 2, 7f) (g-f, frm 2)
Currently fair colt. Turf high 51. **J Akehurst [0-3] Fraser Miller.*

NEPTUNE BHB 32f **RR 34f** 232^{2}
4 b g Dolphin Street (FR) - Seal Indigo (IRE) (Glenstal (USA)) 10.1f **(64)**
Form - 8332
Record 2000 - 1st:0 2nd:1 3rd:2 Ran:3
Pre2000 - 1st:0 2nd:0 3rd:0 Ran:8
Win Prizemoney £0 *Total Prizemoney* £898
2000 AW 0-3: (12f 2, 15f) (Fibr 3)
Scopey, very moderate gelding. AW high 34.
**K C Comerford [0-4] The Old Style Partnership (from W J Haggas [0-1] Spt 1999).*

NERA ZILZAL (IRE) **RR 56f** 3552^{6}
2 b f Zilzal (USA) 8.5f **(79)** - Lady President (IRE) (Dominion) 8.5f **(63)**
Form - 6
Record 2000 - 1st:0 2nd:0 3rd:0 Ran:1
2000 Turf 0-1: (5f) (frm)
Currently fair filly. **G C H Chung [0-1] Osvaldo Pedroni.*

NERONIAN (IRE) BHB 34f34a **RR 33f 34a** 4811^{5}
6 ch g Mujtahid (USA) 7.4f **(69)** - Nimieza (USA) (Nijinsky (CAN)) 10.3f **(77)**
Form - 6056430500103005
Record 2000 - 1st:1 2nd:0 3rd:2 Ran:12
Pre2000 - 1st:1 2nd:2 3rd:1 Ran:18
Win Prizemoney £5,689 *Total Prizemoney* £9,289
Wins * 2000 Jun Bright (FRM) H 7f 33 33
1997 Jun Beverl (SFT) 8.5f 71 <
2000 Turf 1-7: (7f 1-5, 8f 2) (gd, g-f 2, frm 1-4) 2000 AW 0-5: (6f, 8f 2, 9f, 12f) (Equi, Fibr 4)
Moderate gelding, has worn blinkers. Turf high 33. AW high 41.
**Miss D A McHale [1-12] Mrs Susan Mountain (from K R Burke [0-12] Dec 1999).*

NESYRED (IRE) BHB 70f57a **RR 76f 57a** 416^{12}
4 b f Paris House 5.9f **(64)** - Abrika (Dominion) 8.5f **(63)**
Form - 800
Record 2000 - 1st:0 2nd:0 3rd:0 Ran:3
Pre2000 - 1st:1 2nd:0 3rd:0 Ran:3
Win Prizemoney £3,315 *Total Prizemoney* £3,315
Wins 1999 Aug Folkes (GD) 6f 76 <
2000 AW 0-3: (6f 3) (Fibr 3)
Unfurnished, above-average filly, effective 6f, acts on gd. AW high 54.
**M J Ryan [0-3] The Matches Group (from Mrs D Haine [1-3] Oct 1999).*

NETTLES BHB 57f52a **RR 62f 52a** 5298^{7}
2 br g Cyrano de Bergerac 7.3f **(58)** - Sylvandra **(60f)** (Mazilier (USA))
Form - 00776287
Record 2000 - 1st:0 2nd:1 3rd:0 Ran:8
Win Prizemoney £0 *Total Prizemoney* £548
2000 Turf 0-8: (5f 4, 6f, 7f, 8f 2) (g-s 2, gd 2, g-f 3, frm)
Average gelding, effective 7f, acts on g-f, has worn blinkers. Turf high 62 - 2nd of 14 giving 5lb to Petit Tor (18 Aug Catterick 7f g-f RF 3739). Inconsistent. **Denys Smith [0-8] Denys Smith.*

NETWORK (GER) **RR 111f** $2581a^{9}$
3 bl c Monsun (GER) - Note (GER) (Reliance (GER))
Form - 10
2000 Turf 1-2: (11f 1-1, 12f) (sft, gd 1-1)
Currently Group-class colt. Turf high 111 (1st run) - 1st of 7 from Indian Ruby (11 Jun Cologne RF 2007a). **A Schutz in GER [1-2].*

NEVER DISS MISS BHB 71f **RR 77f** 5201^{3}
3 b f Owington - Pennine Pink (IRE) **(75f 60a)** (Pennine Walk) 8.5f **(61)**
Form - 5132503
Record 2000 - 1st:1 2nd:1 3rd:2 Ran:7
Pre2000 - 1st:1 2nd:0 3rd:1 Ran:7
Win Prizemoney £7,869 *Total Prizemoney* £12,472
Wins * 2000 May Beverl (GD) H 9.9f 71 77
1999 Apr Sandow (G-S) 5f 79 <
2000 Turf 1-7: (7f, 10f 1-5, 12f) (sft, g-s, gd 1-3, g-f 2)
Neat, above-average filly, effective 5 to 12f, best at 5f, acts on g-s to frm, excels at Sandown. Turf high 77 - 2nd of 6 getting 1lb from El Zito (7 Jun Chester 10f gd RF 1783) - also 1st of 17 from Romantic Affair (23 May Beverley RF 1390). Inconsistent. Stepped up to a mile to win at Beverley in May, and has appeared to require even further since.
**W Jarvis [1-7] Tim Fenner (from R J R Williams [1-7] Oct 1999).*

NEVER END **RR 80+f** 5152^{1}
2 b f Alzao (USA) 9.8f **(73)** - Eternal (Kris) 9.5f **(73)**
Form - 1
Record 2000 - 1st:1 2nd:0 3rd:0 Ran:1
Win Prizemoney £3,510 *Total Prizemoney* £3,510
Wins * 2000 Oct Lingfi (HVY) 7f 80+ <
2000 Turf 1-1: (7f 1-1) (g-s 1-1)
Currently decent filly. (1st run) - 1st of 14 from Golden Sparrow (23 Oct Lingfield RF 5152). **B W Hills [1-1] K Abdulla.*

NEVER FEAR BHB 35f **RR** 1892^{10}
2 b f Mistertopogigo (IRE) - Never Say so **(8f 50a)** (Prince Sabo) 7.2f **(62)**
Form - 70
Record 2000 - 1st:0 2nd:0 3rd:0 Ran:2
2000 Turf 0-2: (5f 2) (gd 2)
Currently very moderate filly. **Mrs S Lamyman [0-2] P Lamyman.*

NEVER PROMISE (FR) **RR 72f** 5186^{8}
2 b f Cadeaux Genereux 7.9f **(76)** - Yazeanhaa (USA) (Zilzal (USA))
Form - 78
Record 2000 - 1st:0 2nd:0 3rd:0 Ran:2
2000 Turf 0-2: (7f 2) (g-s, frm)
Currently above-average filly. Turf high 72 (began Spt).
**B W Hills [0-2] Maktoum Al Maktoum.*

NEW ASSEMBLY (IRE) BHB 96f **RR 100f** 4931^{4}
3 b f Machiavellian (USA) 9.8f **(83)** - Abbey Strand (USA) (Shadeed (USA)) 8.2f **(70)**
Form - 211644
Record 2000 - 1st:2 2nd:1 3rd:0 Ran:6
Pre2000 - 1st:0 2nd:0 3rd:0 Ran:2
Win Prizemoney £11,251 *Total Prizemoney* £17,776
Wins * 2000 Jun Nottin (G-F) H 10f 82 90 <
*** 2000** Jun Lingfi (FRM) 9f 80
2000 Turf 2-6: (8f, 9f 1-1, 10f 1-3, 12f) (gd, g-f 1-4, frm 1-1)
Scopey, very useful filly, effective 10 to 12f, best at 10f, acts on gd to g-f, best on g-f. Turf high 100. Showed progressive form in handicaps, and was not disgraced in the Group One Nassau Stakes despite the big rise in class. Fourth in listed races subsequently, she lacks a turn of foot.
**Sir Michael Stoute [2-8] The Queen.*

NEW EARTH MAIDEN BHB 25f **RR 19f** 2474^{14}
3 b f Ezzoud (IRE) - Susie's Baby (Balidar) 7.9f **(63)**
Form - 00
Record 2000 - 1st:0 2nd:0 3rd:0 Ran:2
Pre2000 - 1st:0 2nd:0 3rd:0 Ran:4
2000 Turf 0-2: (11f, 12f) (frm 2)
Unfurnished, poor filly.
**J G Smyth-Osbourne [0-2] Mrs A C Hudson (from J Cullinan [0-4] Jly 1999).*

NEW FORTUNE (FR) BHB 50f **RR 64f** 4819^{19}
3 ch f Exit To Nowhere (USA) 8.7f **(77)** - Fortuna Redux (Primo Dominie) 6.2f **(80)**
Form - 84000
Record 2000 - 1st:0 2nd:0 3rd:0 Ran:5
Pre2000 - 1st:0 2nd:0 3rd:0 Ran:1
2000 Turf 0-5: (10f 4, 12f) (g-s, gd, g-f 3)
Neat, average filly. Turf high 64.
**W R Muir [0-6] J Bernstein.*

NEW IBERIA (USA) BHB 77f **RR 70f** 3013[2]
3 gr c Tabasco Cat (USA) - Carolina Saga (USA) (Caro)
Form - 002
Record 2000 - 1st:0 2nd:1 3rd:0 Ran:3
Win Prizemoney £0 *Total Prizemoney* £1,145
2000 Turf 0-3: (8f, 10f 2) (frm 3)
Scopey, currently above-average colt. Turf high 70. **Sir Michael Stoute [0-3] Maktoum Al Maktoum.*

NEWPARK LADY (IRE) RR 97f 3875a[4]
3 b f Foxhound (USA) - Toledana 00
Form - 74443764
2000 Turf 0-7: (5f, 6f 4, 7f, 8f) (g-s, gd 5, frm)
Very useful filly, effective 6f, acts on gd. Turf high 97 - 3rd of 12 getting 6lb from Conormara (2 Jly Curragh 6f gd RF 2529a). Effective from six furlongs to a mile, she is genuine but may be unsuited by soft ground. **K F O'Brien in IRE [1-13] Sax Syndicate.*

NEWRYMAN BHB 30f **RR** 2481[12]
5 ch g Statoblest 6.4f **(63)** - With Love (Be My Guest (USA)) 9.3f **(67)**
Form - 080
Record 2000 - 1st:0 2nd:0 3rd:0 Ran:3
2000 Turf 0-2: (5f, 7f) (gd, frm) 2000 AW 0-1: (11f) (Fibr)
Formerly very poor gelding. **G P Kelly [0-8] A M McArdle.*

NEW STORY (USA) RR 109f 3735a[6]
3 f Dynaformer (USA) 12f **(82)** - Dancey Kate (USA)
Form - 606
2000 Turf 0-3: (8f 2, 11f) (g-s, gd, g-f)
Pattern-class filly. Turf high 109. **R Collet in FR [0-5].*

NEW WONDER BHB 59f **RR 59f** 3595[3]
2 b f Presidium 7.5f **(56)** - Miss Tri Colour **(20f 32a)** (Shavian)
Form - 304273
Record 2000 - 1st:0 2nd:1 3rd:2 Ran:6
Win Prizemoney £0 *Total Prizemoney* £1,518
2000 Turf 0-5: (5f 3, 6f 2) (g-s, gd, frm, hrd 2) 2000 AW 0-1: (5f) (Fibr)
Fair filly, effective 5f, - acts on Fibr. Turf high 59. (1st run) - 3rd of 12 getting 8lb from Sandles (11 May Wolverhampton 5f Fibr RF 1149). **J G Given [0-6] D Morrison.*

NEXT CHAPTER (IRE) RR 39f 3323[7]
2 b br f Cois Na Tine (IRE) - Book Choice (North Summit)
Form - 7
Record 2000 - 1st:0 2nd:0 3rd:0 Ran:1
2000 Turf 0-1: (7f) (g-f)
Currently very moderate filly. **A P Jarvis [0-1] Mrs Ann Jarvis.*

NIAGARA (IRE) BHB 66f **RR 71f** 4053[10]
3 b c Rainbows For Life (CAN) 9.3f **(64)** - Highbrook (USA) **(74f)** (Alphabatim (USA))
Form - 00360
Record 2000 - 1st:0 2nd:0 3rd:1 Ran:5
Pre2000 - 1st:1 2nd:1 3rd:0 Ran:6
Win Prizemoney £2,940 *Total Prizemoney* £5,228
Wins * 1999 May Ayr (GD) 6f 84 <
2000 Turf 0-5: (7f, 8f, 10f 3) (gd, g-f, frm 3)
Workmanlike, above-average colt, effective 5 to 6f, acts on g-s to frm. Turf high 71. **M H Tompkins [1-11] Pollards Stables.*

NICANDER (USA) RR 64f 4969[12]
2 b c Rahy (USA) 9.1f **(80)** - Night Secret (Nijinsky (CAN)) 10.3f **(77)**
Form - 0
Record 2000 - 1st:0 2nd:0 3rd:0 Ran:1
2000 Turf 0-1: (8f) (gd)
Currently average colt. **M P Tregoning [0-1] Sheikh Mohammed.*

NICE BALANCE (USA) BHB 26f29a **RR 53f 29a** 2481[8]
5 b g Shadeed (USA) 7.7f **(72)** - Fellwaati (USA) (Alydar (USA)) 9.1f **(76)**
Form - 061431565300008
Record 2000 - 1st:2 2nd:0 3rd:2 Ran:14
Pre2000 - 1st:0 2nd:0 3rd:0 Ran:8
Win Prizemoney £4,158 *Total Prizemoney* £5,002
Wins * **2000** *Jan Southw (STD) H 8f 39 43* <
* **2000** *Jan Southw (STD) H 8f 35 30*
2000 Turf 0-2: (8f, 11f) (g-f, frm) 2000 AW 2-12: (7f, 8f 2-8, 11f 3) (Fibr 2-12)
Fair gelding, effective 8f, - acts on Fibr, has worn blinkers, likes left handed tracks, likes tight tracks. Turf high 10. AW high 43. Becoming disappointing. **M C Chapman [2-29] R J Hayward.*

NICELY (IRE) BHB 59f **RR 73f** 5226[10]
4 gr f Bustino 11f **(64)** - Nichodoula (Doulab (USA)) 9.8f **(65)**
Form - 05070770
Record 2000 - 1st:0 2nd:0 3rd:0 Ran:8
Pre2000 - 1st:2 2nd:0 3rd:0 Ran:11
Win Prizemoney £9,752 *Total Prizemoney* £10,528
Wins * 1999 Oct Newbur (G-S) H 16f 73 80+ <
* 1998 Oct Bath (SFT) 8f 73
2000 Turf 0-8: (14f, 16f 7) (sft, g-s 2, gd 3, g-f, frm)
Lengthy, above-average filly, effective 11 to 16f, acts on g-s to g-f, has worn blinkers, likes left handed tracks. Turf high 73. Inconsistent. **J W Hills [2-19] Mrs Claire Smith.*

NICE ONE CLARE (IRE) BHB 94f **RR 96+f** 4597[2]
4 b f Mukaddamah (USA) 7.6f **(74)** - Sarah-Clare (Reach) 7f **(83)**
Form - 53202
Record 2000 - 1st:0 2nd:2 3rd:1 Ran:5
Pre2000 - 1st:3 2nd:1 3rd:1 Ran:5
Win Prizemoney £17,333 *Total Prizemoney* £44,801
Wins * 1999 Aug Newmar (G-F) H 7f 85 87+ <
* 1999 Aug Kempto (G-F) H 7f 82 86
* 1999 May Folkes (G-F) 7f 78
2000 Turf 0-5: (6f, 7f 3, 8f) (gd 4, frm)
Leggy, very useful filly, effective 7 to 8f, best at 7f, acts on gd to frm, best on gd, excels at Newmarket. Turf high 96 - 2nd of 26 getting 2lb from Duke of Modena (23 Spt Ascot 7f gd RF 4597). Well backed when fifth in the Wokingham on her reappearance, she is a classy hold-up handicapper. Effective up to seven furlongs, she is still fairly treated and deserves to win a valuable prize. **J W Payne [3-10] Oremsa Partnership.*

NICHOLAS MISTRESS BHB 27f27a **RR 28f 27a** 446[11]
4 b f Beveled (USA) 6.9f **(64)** - Foreign Mistress (Darshaan) 9.9f **(84)**
Form - 05070
Record 2000 - 1st:0 2nd:0 3rd:0 Ran:5
Pre2000 - 1st:1 2nd:4 3rd:3 Ran:25
Win Prizemoney £2,558 *Total Prizemoney* £6,489
Wins * 1999 *Feb Lingfi (STD) H 6f 43 52* <
2000 AW 0-5: (7f 2, 8f 3) (Equi, Fibr 4)
Light-framed, little account filly, effective 6f, - acts on AW, has worn blinkers, favours left handed tracks. AW high 23. **P D Evans [1-30] J E Abbey.*

NICHOL FIFTY BHB 68f **RR 73f** 5104[17]
6 b g Old Vic 12.8f **(72)** - Jawaher (IRE) (Dancing Brave (USA)) 8.4f **(76)**
Form - 40
Record 2000 - 1st:0 2nd:0 3rd:0 Ran:2
Pre2000 - 1st:4 2nd:3 3rd:1 Ran:21
Win Prizemoney £18,574 *Total Prizemoney* £24,233
Wins * 1999 Jun Kempto (GD) 14.4f 77 <
* 1999 Apr Nottin (SFT) H 14.1f 71 75
* 1997 Oct Leices (GD) 11.8f 73
* 1997 Jly Cheste (G-F) 12.3f 67
2000 Turf 0-2: (12f, 15f) (gd 2)
Above-average gelding, effective 12 to 17f, best at 14f, acts on g-s to frm, best on gd, prefers tight tracks, excels at Haydock. Turf high 73 (1st run) (began Aug) - 4th of 11 giving 5lb to Capriolo (30 Aug York 12f gd RF 4104). **M H Tompkins [5-28] Lloyd Bedack.*

NICIARA (IRE) BHB 38f44a **RR 38f 44a** 5002[7]
3 b g Soviet Lad (USA) 9.4f **(63)** - Verusa (IRE) (Petorius) 7.3f **(61)**
Form - 033P8753246057040332322477 7
Record 2000 - 1st:0 2nd:4 3rd:4 Ran:22
Pre2000 - 1st:0 2nd:0 3rd:2 Ran:8
Win Prizemoney £0 *Total Prizemoney* £5,985
2000 Turf 0-12: (10f 2, 12f, 14f, 16f 6, 17f, 18f) (sft, g-s 2, gd 3, g-f 4, frm 2) 2000 AW 0-10: (8f 7, 11f, 12f 2) (Fibr 10)
Workmanlike, fair gelding, effective 8 to 17f, best at 8f, acts on g-f to frm - acts on Fibr, has worn blinkers (very effectively). Turf high 48 - 2nd of 17 giving 6lb to Turned Out Well (24 Jly Beverley 16f g-f RF 3066). AW high 57 - 2nd of 5 getting 16lb from Special Promise

(4 Feb Southwell 8f Fibr RF 0215). **M C Chapman [2-32] W P Gaff.*

NICKLES BHB 54f **RR 52f** 4748[11]

5 b g Lugana Beach 7f **(63)** - Instinction (Never so Bold) 6.3f **(66)**
Form - 06481080
Record 2000 - 1st:1 2nd:0 3rd:0 Ran:8
Pre2000 - 1st:1 2nd:0 3rd:4 Ran:14
Win Prizemoney £5,434 *Total Prizemoney* £7,544
Wins 2000 Aug Warwic (GD) C 5f 51
1999 Aug Lingfi (GD) C 5f 57 <
2000 Turf 1-8: (5f 1-8) (gd 1-4, frm 3, hrd)
Fair gelding, effective 5f, acts on gd to frm, best on frm. Turf high 52.
**S R Bowring [0-3] Roland Wheatley (from L G Cottrell [2-19] Aug 2000).*

NICK'S JULE (IRE) BHB 38f **RR 26f** 4877[16]

3 ch f Perugino (USA) - Miss Lee Ann (Tumble Wind (USA)) 7.5f **(57)**
Form - 700
Record 2000 - 1st:0 2nd:0 3rd:0 Ran:3
Pre2000 - 1st:0 2nd:0 3rd:0 Ran:2
2000 Turf 0-3: (6f, 10f 2) (g-s, gd, g-f)
Leggy, little account filly. Turf high 26.
**C F Wall [0-1] Mrs Julie Mitchell (from J A Osborne [0-2] Jun 2000).*

NICOBAR BHB 109f **RR 115f** 4462[9]

3 b c Indian Ridge 7.6f **(74)** - Duchess of Alba **(74f)** (Belmez (USA))
Form - 316185010
Record 2000 - 1st:3 2nd:0 3rd:1 Ran:9
Pre2000 - 1st:1 2nd:1 3rd:1 Ran:5
Win Prizemoney £60,920 *Total Prizemoney* £66,768
Wins * 2000 Spt Epsom (GD) L 7f 110
*** 2000** Jun Epsom (G-S) L 7f 115 <
*** 2000** May Cheste (GD) H 7.6f 100 105
* 1999 Aug Haydoc (G-S) 7.1f 94+
2000 Turf 3-9: (7f 2-5, 8f 1-3, 9f) (g-s 1-2, gd 4, g-f 2-3)
Scopey, high-class colt, effective 7 to 8f, best at 7f, acts on g-s to g-f, prefers left handed tracks, prefers tight tracks. Turf high 115 - 1st of 9 from Smart Ridge (9 Jun Epsom RF 1834) - also 1st of 9 giving 8lb to Veil of Avalon (1 Spt Epsom RF 4145). A keen individual, he failed to stay nine furlongs in the spring and gained all his wins over the specialist seven furlong trip. Successful at Epsom and Chester, he operates well on turning tracks and may not be at his best on fast ground. **I A Balding [4-14] Robert Hitchins.*

NICOL (IRE) RR 3809[9]

2 b f Nicolotte - Frensham Manor (Le Johnstan) 7.4f **(55)**
Form - 0
Record 2000 - 1st:0 2nd:0 3rd:0 Ran:1
2000 AW 0-1: (6f) (Fibr)
Currently very poor filly. **K McAuliffe [0-1] Mrs J A Hall.*

NICOLAI BHB 52f **RR 52f** 4499[15]

3 b g Piccolo - Fair Eleanor (Saritamer (USA)) 9.5f **(63)**
Form - 0080410
Record 2000 - 1st:1 2nd:0 3rd:0 Ran:7
Win Prizemoney £2,236 *Total Prizemoney* £2,448
Wins * 2000 Aug Beverl (FRM) H 9.9f 45 52 <
2000 Turf 1-7: (5f, 6f 2, 8f, 9f, 10f 1-2) (sft, g-s 2, gd, g-f, frm 1-2)
Strong, fair gelding, effective 10f, acts on frm. Turf high 52 - 1st of 14 giving 6lb to Silver Socks (26 Aug Beverley RF 3981).
**M L W Bell [1-7] Mrs Anne Yearley.*

NICOLE DILLON RR 97f 1455a[11]

3 f
Form - 0
2000 Turf 0-1: (11f) (gd)
Currently very useful filly. (1st run) - 11th of 18 to Timi (21 May San Siro 11f gd RF 1455a). **E Borromeo in ITY [0-1].*

NIFTY ALICE BHB 81f **RR 83f** 5102[3]

2 ch f First Trump - Nifty Fifty (IRE) (Runnett) 7f **(59)**
Form - 1244180183
Record 2000 - 1st:3 2nd:1 3rd:1 Ran:10
Win Prizemoney £11,762 *Total Prizemoney* £17,254
Wins * 2000 Aug Mussel (G-F) H 5f 79 83 <
*** 2000** Jun Ayr (GD) 5f 70
*** 2000** Mar Mussel (GD) 5f 64
2000 Turf 3-10: (5f 3-9, 6f) (gd 2-7, frm 1-2, hrd)
Decent filly, effective 5 to 6f, acts on gd to frm. Turf high 83 - 1st of 9 getting 1lb from Vendome (31 Aug Musselburgh RF 4120).
**A Berry [3-10] Mrs Norma Peebles.*

NIFTY MAJOR BHB 70f **RR 83f** 5313[12]

3 b g Be My Chief (USA) 10.2f **(62)** - Nifty Fifty (IRE) (Runnett) 7f **(59)**
Form - 02000705R300
Record 2000 - 1st:0 2nd:1 3rd:1 Ran:12
Pre2000 - 1st:2 2nd:1 3rd:0 Ran:9
Win Prizemoney £5,809 *Total Prizemoney* £10,604
Wins 1999 Aug Mussel (G-S) H 5f 73 84 <
1999 Apr Mussel (G-F) 5f 71
2000 Turf 0-12: (5f 12) (g-s 3, gd 5, g-f 3, frm)
Light-framed, decent gelding, effective 5f, acts on gd to g-f, best on g-f. Turf high 83 - 2nd of 12 getting 9lb from Kathology (0 May Chester 5f g-f RF 1114).
**A Berry [0-12] Roy Peebles (from J Berry [2-9] Spt 1999).*

NIFTY NORMAN BHB 61f70a **RR 66f 70a** 5003[14]

6 b g Rock City 8.8f **(62)** - Nifty Fifty (IRE) (Runnett) 7f **(59)**
Form - 665132363463861315300
Record 2000 - 1st:3 2nd:1 3rd:6 Ran:18
Pre2000 - 1st:5 2nd:6 3rd:4 Ran:46
Win Prizemoney £25,754 *Total Prizemoney* £36,648
Wins * 2000 Jly Folkes (GD) H 5f 59 66
*** 2000** *Jun Southw (STD) H 6f 52 65*
*** 2000** *Jan Wolver (STD) C 5f 59*
* 1999 Jun Cheste (SFT) H 5.1f 57 67
* 1999 *Mar Southw (STD) H 5f 62 69*
* 1999 *Feb Southw (STD) H 6f 52 58*
1997 Jun Ayr (GD) H 5f 72 73
1997 May Beverl (HVY) 5f 82? <
2000 Turf 1-8: (5f 1-8) (sft 2, g-s, gd 1-3, g-f, frm) 2000 AW 2-10: (5f 1-6, 6f 1-4) (Equi, Fibr 2-9)
Above-average gelding, effective 5 to 6f, best at 6f, acts on g-s to gd - acts on Fibr, has worn blinkers, likes left handed tracks, likes tight tracks, excels at Southwell. Turf high 66 - 1st of 9 getting 1lb from Clan Chief (13 Jly Folkestone RF 2768). AW high 71 - 3rd of 14 giving 9lb to My Alibi (21 Jly Southwell 6f Fibr RF 3020) - also 1st of 15 giving 4lb to Petite Danseuse (30 Jun Southwell RF 2415). He is pretty inconsistent these days, but capable of winning modest events on turf or sand as long as he hits the traps running, something he does not always do.
**D Nicholls [6-44] The David Nicholls Racing Club (from J Berry [2-20] Spt 1998).*

NIGELS CHOICE BHB 30f **RR 35f** 151[7]

8 gr g Teenoso (USA) 10.5f **(62)** - Warm Winter (Kalaglow) 9.8f **(67)**
Form - 07
Record 2000 - 1st:0 2nd:0 3rd:0 Ran:2
Pre2000 - 1st:0 2nd:0 3rd:1 Ran:3
Win Prizemoney £0 *Total Prizemoney* £311
2000 AW 0-2: (11f, 16f) (Fibr 2)
Very moderate gelding. AW high 6. Now trained by A. D. Smith.
**A D Smith [0-5] Duckhaven Stud (from C J Hill [0-2] May 1997).*

NIGHT ADVENTURE (IRE) BHB 29f **RR 29f** 3896[13]

4 ch g Night Shift (USA) 8.1f **(73)** - Mary Hinge **(96f)** (Dowsing (USA))
Form - 0000500
Record 2000 - 1st:0 2nd:0 3rd:0 Ran:7
Pre2000 - 1st:0 2nd:0 3rd:1 Ran:3
Win Prizemoney £0 *Total Prizemoney* £529
2000 Turf 0-7: (6f 2, 7f 4, 8f) (frm 6, hrd)
Workmanlike, little account gelding, effective 7f, acts on frm. Turf high 29.
**J M Bradley [0-7] E A Hayward (from J L Dunlop [0-3] Spt 1999).*

NIGHT AND DAY BHB 54a **RR 51f** 4785[6]

3 ch f Anshan 8.2f **(63)** - Midnight Break **(62f)** (Night Shift (USA)) 7.2f **(69)**
Form - 32230540456
Record 2000 - 1st:0 2nd:2 3rd:1 Ran:10
Pre2000 - 1st:0 2nd:0 3rd:1 Ran:1
Win Prizemoney £0 *Total Prizemoney* £2,485
2000 Turf 0-4: (6f, 8f, 10f 2) (g-f, frm 2, hrd) 2000 AW 0-6: (6f, 7f 3, 9f, 11f) (Fibr 6)

Unfurnished, fair filly, effective 7f, - acts on Fibr, has worn blinkers, favours left handed tracks, favours tight tracks. Turf high 51 (began Aug). AW high 61 (1st run) - 2nd of 14 getting 5lb from Inver Gold (7 Jan Southwell 7f Fibr RF 0039).

**P S McEntee [0-7] Miss C Cherry (from W Jarvis [0-4] Jan 2000).*

NIGHT CITY BHB 56f49a **RR 60f 49a** 3637[2]

9 b g Kris 10f **(75)** - Night Secret (Nijinsky (CAN)) 10.3f **(77)**

Form - 1032652267214764415 2252

Record 2000 - 1st:2 2nd:6 3rd:0 Ran:19
Pre2000 - 1st:18 2nd:10 3rd:7 Ran:67

Win Prizemoney £86,961 *Total Prizemoney* £108,354

Wins * **2000** Jun Catter (G-S) C 13.8f 51
* **2000** *Mar Lingfi (STD) C 12f 59*
* 1999 *Nov Lingfi (STD) C 8f 70*
* 1999 Oct Bright (G-S) H 10f 65 74
* 1999 Oct York (G-S) C 10.4f 69
* 1999 Jun Hamilt (GD) C 11.1f 67+
* 1998 *Dec Lingfi (STD) H 12f 77 84*
* 1998 Oct York (GD) C 10.4f 77
* 1998 Oct Bright (GD) C 11.9f 75
* 1998 Aug Lingfi (FRM) H 11.5f 70 77
* 1998 Aug Catter (GD) C 12f 66
* 1998 Jly Hamilt (FRM) C 12.1f 55
* 1998 May Thirsk (GD) C 12f 71
* 1998 Mar Hamilt (HVY) H 11.1f 65 75
* 1998 *Feb Lingfi (SLW) C 12f 75+*
* 1998 *Jan Lingfi (STD) C 12f 83+*
* 1997 *Dec Lingfi (STD) H 13f 70 73*
* 1997 *Nov Lingfi (STD) C 12f 68*
1996 May Newbur (SFT) H 9f 96 102 <

2000 Turf 1-8: (10f 3, 12f 3, 14f 1-1, 16f) (gd 1-3, g-f, frm 4) 2000 AW 1-11: (8f, 10f 2, 11f, 12f 1-6, 13f) (Equi 1-6, Fibr 5)

Average gelding, effective 10 to 12f, acts on gd - acts on Equi, has worn blinkers. Turf high 57. AW high 65. He has been a real moneyspinner for connections in recent seasons in middle-distance events on both turf and sand. Kept very busy, he seems as good as ever just now and remains a difficult horse to pass if allowed an uncontested early lead.

**K R Burke [18-71] Nigel Shields (from Lady Herries [2-16] May 1997).*

NIGHT DIAMOND BHB 57f **RR 61f** 4677[3]

3 b g Night Shift (USA) 8.1f **(73)** - Dashing Water **(84f)** (Dashing Blade)

Form - 000404241043

Record 2000 - 1st:1 2nd:1 3rd:1 Ran:12
Pre2000 - 1st:0 2nd:0 3rd:1 Ran:4

Win Prizemoney £4,875 *Total Prizemoney* £6,609

Wins * **2000** Aug Goodwo (GD) H 9.9f 54 56 <

2000 Turf 1-12: (6f 5, 7f, 8f 2, 10f 1-4) (g-s 2, gd 2, g-f 1-4, frm 4)

Unfurnished, average gelding, likes right handed tracks, likes tight tracks. Turf high 61. **I A Balding [1-16] J C Smith.*

NIGHT EMPRESS BHB 79f74a **RR 86f 74a** 5078[1]

3 br f Emperor Jones (USA) - Night Trader (USA) (Melyno) 10.4f **(55)**

Form - 2451501

Record 2000 - 1st:2 2nd:1 3rd:0 Ran:7
Pre2000 - 1st:0 2nd:1 3rd:1 Ran:4

Win Prizemoney £8,216 *Total Prizemoney* £12,075

Wins * **2000** Oct Bright (SFT) 8f 80 <
* **2000** Jly Yarmou (FRM) H 7f 75 79+

2000 Turf 2-7: (7f 1-6, 8f 1-1) (g-s 1-2, gd, g-f 1-4)

Light-framed, useful filly, effective 7 to 8f, best at 7f, acts on g-s to g-f, best on g-f. Turf high 86 - 5th of 6 getting 4lb from Rosse (19 Jly Yarmouth 7f g-f RF 2950) - also 1st of 15 getting 6lb from Make Way (19 Oct Brighton RF 5078).

**J R Fanshawe [2-11] The Woodman Racing Syndicate.*

NIGHT FALL (IRE) BHB 72f65a **RR 76f 65a** 3792[6]

2 ch f Night Shift (USA) 8.1f **(73)** - Tumble (Mtoto)

Form - 561406

Record 2000 - 1st:1 2nd:0 3rd:0 Ran:6

Win Prizemoney £4,056 *Total Prizemoney* £4,591

Wins * **2000** Jun Goodwo (GD) 7f 76 <

2000 Turf 1-6: (5f 2, 7f 1-4) (gd 2, g-f 1-3, frm)

Above-average filly, effective 7f, acts on g-f. Turf high 76 - 1st of 5 from Queen Spain (23 Jun Goodwood RF 2219). Improved for the step up to seven furlongs when winning at Goodwood.

**R Hannon [1-6] Jubert Family.*

NIGHT FLIGHT BHB 91f82a **RR 93f 82a** 5127[7]

6 gr g Night Shift (USA) 8.1f **(73)** - Ancestry (Persepolis (FR)) 6.4f **(67)**

Form - 00200608012037

Record 2000 - 1st:1 2nd:2 3rd:1 Ran:14
Pre2000 - 1st:5 2nd:4 3rd:7 Ran:41

Win Prizemoney £85,180 *Total Prizemoney* £117,544

Wins * **2000** Aug York (GD) H 6f 86 90
* 1999 Jly Ascot (G-F) H 5f 94 100 <
* 1999 May Haydoc (GD) H 5f 86 91
* 1999 May York (SFT) H 5f 81 85
* 1998 Jun Newcas (GD) H 6f 71 80+
1997 Apr Pontef (GD) H 6f 72 82

2000 Turf 1-13: (5f 9, 6f 1-4) (g-s 2, gd 1-6, g-f 3, frm 2) 2000 AW 0-1: (6f) (Fibr)

Useful gelding, effective 5 to 6f, best at 5f, acts on gd to frm, best on gd, likes York. Turf high 93 - 3rd of 20 getting 5lb from Dancing Mystery (12 Oct Newmarket 5f gd RF 4933). He only managed one win last season, but remains a consistent and useful sprint handicapper. Probably not at his best on fast ground, he is genuine.

**R A Fahey [5-41] C H Stevens (from J J O'Neill [1-14] Spt 1997).*

NIGHTGLADE (IRE) BHB 32f31a **RR 37f 31a** 617[10]

4 b c Night Shift (USA) 8.1f **(73)** - Woodland Garden (Godswalk (USA)) 7.3f **(58)**

Form - 0

Record 2000 - 1st:0 2nd:0 3rd:0 Ran:1
Pre2000 - 1st:0 2nd:0 3rd:1 Ran:13

Win Prizemoney £0 *Total Prizemoney* £668

2000 Turf 0-1: (12f) (gd)

Unfurnished, very moderate colt, effective 12f, acts on gd, likes right handed tracks, favours tight tracks.

**M Brittain [0-14] Northgate Lodge Racing Club.*

NIGHT GYPSY BHB 78f **RR 69f** 5156[1]

2 b f Mind Games - Ocean Grove (IRE) **(78f)** (Fairy King (USA)) 7.7f **(59)**

Form - 3201

Record 2000 - 1st:1 2nd:1 3rd:1 Ran:4

Win Prizemoney £4,563 *Total Prizemoney* £6,222

Wins * **2000** Oct Nottin (G-S) 5.1f 69 <

2000 Turf 1-4: (5f 1-2, 6f 2) (g-s 1-2, gd, g-f)

Average filly. Turf high 69 (began Spt) - 1st of 17 from Pride In Me (24 Oct Nottingham RF 5156). **T D Easterby [1-4] T G Holdcroft.*

NIGHT HAVEN BHB 80f **RR 81f** 4932[5]

2 gr f Night Shift (USA) 8.1f **(73)** - Noble Haven (Indian King (USA)) 7.4f **(64)**

Form - 22145

Record 2000 - 1st:1 2nd:2 3rd:0 Ran:5

Win Prizemoney £3,386 *Total Prizemoney* £6,435

Wins * **2000** Aug Newcas (G-F) 5f 76 <

2000 Turf 1-5: (5f 1-3, 6f 2) (gd, g-f, frm 2, hrd 1-1)

Decent filly. Turf high 81 (began Jly) - 5th of 22 getting 4lb from Idle Power (12 Oct Newmarket 6f gd RF 4932) - also 1st of 4 getting 7lb from Wilson Blyth (25 Aug Newcastle RF 3958).

**M L W Bell [1-5] B H Farr.*

NIGHTINGALE SONG BHB 41f54a **RR 42f 54a** 4543[9]

6 b m Tina's Pet 7.4f **(56)** - Songlines (Night Shift (USA)) 7.2f **(69)**

Form - 774000

Record 2000 - 1st:0 2nd:0 3rd:0 Ran:5
Pre2000 - 1st:4 2nd:1 3rd:6 Ran:32

Win Prizemoney £12,680 *Total Prizemoney* £16,815

Wins * 1999 Aug Sandow (GD) H 5f 47 47
* 1999 Jun Leices (G-S) H 6f 41 47
* 1999 Jun Lingfi (GD) H 6f 38 41
1996 Jly Windso (GD) S 6f 63 <

2000 Turf 0-5: (5f 3, 6f 2) (g-s 2, gd, g-f, frm)

Moderate mare, effective 5 to 6f, best at 6f, acts on gd to g-f, best on gd. Turf high 42.

**L MontagueHall [3-16] Stephen & Michelle Bayless (from M Meade [1-21] Jly 1998).*

NIGHT MUSIC BHB 52f **RR 56df** 4328[8]

3 br f Piccolo - Oribi (Top Ville) 11.7f **(68)**

Form - 7538368

Record 2000 - 1st:0 2nd:0 3rd:2 Ran:7
Pre2000 - 1st:0 2nd:0 3rd:0 Ran:3
Win Prizemoney £0 *Total Prizemoney* £1,093
2000 Turf 0-7: (10f, 12f 3, 14f 2, 16f) (g-s, gd, g-f 3, frm 2)
Neat, fair filly, effective 12 to 14f, best at 14f, acts on g-f to frm, best on frm, prefers tight tracks. Turf high 56 - 3rd of 12 getting 1lb from Sea Danzig (28 Jly Salisbury 14f frm RF 3185). Consistent. **Major D N Chappell [0-10] Super Sprinters.*

NIGHT OF GLASS BHB 86f **RR 85f** 1067[13]

7 b g Mazilier (USA) 8.5f **(56)** - Donna Elvira (Chief Singer) 8.9f **(66)**
Form - 740
Record 2000 - 1st:0 2nd:0 3rd:0 Ran:3
Pre2000 - 1st:9 2nd:4 3rd:12 Ran:56
Win Prizemoney £40,061 *Total Prizemoney* £74,055
Wins 1999 May Beverl (GD) H 8.5f 90 92 <
1998 Spt Mussel (GD) H 7.1f 85 88
1998 May Beverl (GD) H 8.5f 84 87
1998 May Thirsk (GD) H 7f 78 85
1998 Apr Carlis (G-S) H 8f 68 79
1998 Apr Thirsk (G-S) H 7f 68 74
1998 Apr Catter (GD) H 7f 64 68
1997 Oct Catter (SFT) H 7f 61 65
1996 Spt Yarmou (G-F) H 8f 55 58
2000 Turf 0-3: (7f, 8f 2) (g-s, gd, frm)
Useful gelding, effective 7 to 8f, best at 8f, acts on g-s to frm, best on gd, mostly wears blinkers (effectively). Turf high 81. Consistent.
**N Tinkler [0-3] K Silvester and B Silvester (from J L Eyre [8-44] Oct 1999).*

NIGHT OF GLORY BHB 19f **RR 21f** 4494[10]

5 b m Perpendicular - Donna Elvira (Chief Singer) 8.9f **(66)**
Form - 000
Record 2000 - 1st:0 2nd:0 3rd:0 Ran:3
Pre2000 - 1st:0 2nd:0 3rd:0 Ran:2
2000 Turf 0-3: (8f, 9f, 12f) (g-s, g-f 2)
Little account filly, has worn blinkers. Turf high 21 (began Aug).
**N Tinkler [0-3] K Silvester and B Silvester (from J L Eyre [0-2] Aug 1999).*

NIGHT OF NIGHTS RR 59f 5243[9]

2 b br f Never so Bold 7.1f **(62)** - Shamasiya (FR) (Vayrann) 9.7f **(74)**
Form - 00
Record 2000 - 1st:0 2nd:0 3rd:0 Ran:2
2000 Turf 0-1: (5f) (gd) 2000 AW 0-1: (6f) (Fibr)
Currently fair filly. **M Dods [0-2] D B Stanley.*

NIGHT OMEN (IRE) BHB 58f **RR 59df** 628[13]

3 ch g Night Shift (USA) 8.1f **(73)** - Propitious (IRE) (Doyoun) 9f **(69)**
Form - 0
Record 2000 - 1st:0 2nd:0 3rd:0 Ran:1
Pre2000 - 1st:0 2nd:0 3rd:0 Ran:2
2000 Turf 0-1: (10f) (gd)
Strong, currently fair gelding. **S C Williams [0-3] D G Burge.*

NIGHT ON THE TOWN BHB 63f **RR 56f** 5065[10]

2 b g Dancing Spree (USA) 8f **(59)** - Ling Lane (Slip Anchor) 9.8f **(73)**
Form - 00
Record 2000 - 1st:0 2nd:0 3rd:0 Ran:2
2000 Turf 0-2: (7f, 8f) (g-s, g-f)
Currently average gelding. Turf high 56 (began Spt).
**B Smart [0-2] Anglia Bloodstock Syndicate 1999.*

NIGHT SHIFTER (IRE) BHB 45f **RR 51f** 4826[24]

3 b f Night Shift (USA) 8.1f **(73)** - Atsuko (IRE) (Mtoto)
Form - 0070000
Record 2000 - 1st:0 2nd:0 3rd:0 Ran:7
Pre2000 - 1st:1 2nd:1 3rd:1 Ran:8
Win Prizemoney £2,912 *Total Prizemoney* £5,344
Wins 1999 Aug Lingfi (GD) H 5f 63 69 <
2000 Turf 0-7: (6f 3, 7f, 8f 2, 9f) (sft, gd, g-f, frm 4)
Workmanlike, fair filly, effective 5 to 6f, acts on g-f to hrd. Turf high 51. Inconsistent.
**J R Poulton [0-7] Glendale Partnership Ltd (from M R Channon [1-8] Spt 1999).*

NIGHT SIGHT (USA) BHB 80f **RR 80df** 2736[2]

3 b c Eagle Eyed (USA) - El Hamo (USA) (Search For Gold (USA))
Form - 8022322
Record 2000 - 1st:0 2nd:4 3rd:1 Ran:7
Win Prizemoney £0 *Total Prizemoney* £6,325
2000 Turf 0-7: (7f 3, 8f 3, 9f) (g-s 2, gd, g-f, frm 3)
Strong, useful colt, effective 8 to 9f, best at 8f, acts on g-s to frm, best on frm. Turf high 88 - 2nd of 7 to Reach The Top (23 May Goodwood 8f g-s RF 1391). **G Wragg [0-7] Mollers Racing.*

NIGHT STYLE (FR) BHB 104f **RR 108f** 2872[7]

3 b c Night Shift (USA) 8.1f **(73)** - Style For Life (IRE) (Law Society (USA)) 9.9f **(70)**
Form - 60407
Record 2000 - 1st:0 2nd:0 3rd:0 Ran:5
Pre2000 - 1st:3 2nd:2 3rd:1 Ran:8
Win Prizemoney £52,369 *Total Prizemoney* £59,197
Wins * 1999 Oct San Si (G-F) G1 8f 106 <
* 1999 Spt Leices (GD) 7f 98
* 1999 Jun Ripon (G-F) 6f 80+
2000 Turf 0-4: (10f 2, 12f 2) (gd, g-f 2, frm) 2000 AW 0-1: (9f) (Dirt)
Scopey, Pattern-class colt, effective 7 to 12f, acts on g-f, has worn blinkers. Turf high 108. Saddled with a Group One penalty, he was difficult to place in 2000. **E A L Dunlop [3-13] Mohammed Jaber.*

NIGHT SUN (GER) RR 103f 5216a[2]

4 ch f Big Shuffle (USA) - Never Mind (High Line) 10.3f **(70)**
Form - 2
2000 Turf 0-1: (8f) (hvy)
Currently very useful filly. (1st run) - 2nd of 10 to Proudwings (22 Oct San Siro 8f hvy RF 5216a). **in ITY [0-1].*

NIGHT VENTURE (USA) BHB 84f **RR 87f** 5111[4]

4 b c Dynaformer (USA) 12f **(82)** - Charming Ballerina (Caerleon (USA)) 8.6f **(71)**
Form - 1080030444
Record 2000 - 1st:1 2nd:0 3rd:1 Ran:10
Pre2000 - 1st:2 2nd:0 3rd:1 Ran:8
Win Prizemoney £25,258 *Total Prizemoney* £30,217
Wins * 2000 Apr Epsom (HVY) H 10.1f 83 89 <
* 1999 Jun Newcas (G-F) H 10.1f 89 89 <
* 1999 May Ripon (G-F) 10f 84
2000 Turf 1-10. (10f 1-3, 12f 3, 13f 2, 14f, 16f) (sft 1-2, gd 5, g-f 3)
Workmanlike, useful colt, effective 10 to 16f, best at 10f, acts on sft to frm, likes left handed tracks, prefers tight tracks, excels at Chester. Turf high 89 (1st run) - 1st of 20 giving 11lb to Captain's Log (26 Apr Epsom RF 0880). **B W Hills [3-18] Maktoum Al Maktoum.*

NIGRASINE BHB 89f100a **RR 101f 100a** 4732[8]

6 b h Mon Tresor 7.9f **(60)** - Early Gales (Precocious) 8.6f **(62)**
Form - 73045104008
Record 2000 - 1st:1 2nd:0 3rd:1 Ran:11
Pre2000 - 1st:6 2nd:6 3rd:4 Ran:41
Win Prizemoney £44,237 *Total Prizemoney* £107,931
Wins * 2000 Jun Yarmou (G-F) 6f 101
* 1999 Jun Yarmou (GD) 6f 114 <
* 1999 Apr Thirsk (GD) 6f 113
* 1998 Jun Haydoc (GD) L 7.1f 107
* 1997 Jly Haydoc (GD) H 6f 99 103
* 1996 Jly Pontef (G-F) 6f 101
* 1996 Jun Redcar (G-F) 6f 73
2000 Turf 1-11: (6f 1-6, 7f 5) (gd 9, g-f 1-2)
Very useful horse, effective 6 to 7f, best at 6f, acts on gd to frm, often wears blinkers (effectively). Turf high 103. He is the veteran of many tough battles, but retains his enthusiasm and will to win. Unfortunately that also means he remains high in the handicap, and his only win of the season came when winning a Yarmouth conditions event in June for the second year in succession. Best over six and seven furlongs. **J L Eyre [7-52] Sunpak Potatoes.*

NILOUPHAR BHB 25f **RR 19f** 5164[8]

3 b f Pharly (FR) 11.5f **(64)** - White African (Carwhite) 7.2f **(61)**
Form - 08708
Record 2000 - 1st:0 2nd:0 3rd:0 Ran:5
Pre2000 - 1st:0 2nd:0 3rd:0 Ran:3
2000 Turf 0-3: (8f, 10f, 11f) (gd, frm 2) 2000 AW 0-2: (7f 2) (Fibr 2)
Leggy, poor filly, has worn blinkers. Turf high 19 (began Jly). AW

high 14.
**R Hollinshead [0-3] Richard Underwood (from J A Glover [0-2] May 2000).*

NIMELLO (USA) BHB 84f **RR 88f** 5240[3]

4 b c Kingmambo (USA) 10.9f **(85)** - Zakota (IRE) (Polish Precedent (USA)) 10.2f **(60)**
Form - 0100743
Record 2000 - 1st:1 2nd:0 3rd:1 Ran:7
Pre2000 - 1st:1 2nd:1 3rd:0 Ran:4
Win Prizemoney £15,182 *Total Prizemoney* £22,469
Wins * **2000** Apr Sandow (SFT) H 8.1f 85 89 <
* 1998 Jly Newmar (G-F) 7f 87+
2000 Turf 1-7: (8f 1-7) (sft 1-1, g-s, gd 2, g-f 2, frm)
Useful colt, effective 8f, acts on sft to g-s, best on sft, has worn blinkers. Turf high 89 - 1st of 10 getting 3lb from Regal Philosopher (28 Apr Sandown RF 0894).
**P F I Cole [2-11] C Shiacolas.*

NINEACRES BHB 91f85a **RR 92f 85a** 5317[10]

9 b g Sayf El Arab (USA) 8.2f **(57)** - Mayor (Laxton)
Form - 22614401375221011038413022101O
Record 2000 - 1st:8 2nd:6 3rd:4 Ran:31
Pre2000 - 1st:4 2nd:8 3rd:6 Ran:50
Win Prizemoney £45,788 *Total Prizemoney* £72,938
Wins * **2000** Oct Windso (HVY) H 5f 87 92 <
* **2000** Oct York (SFT) H 5f 78 85
* **2000** Aug Chepst (G-F) H 6.1f 70 73
* **2000** Jun Windso (G-F) H 6f 59 65
* **2000** Jun Bath (G-F) H 5.7f 59 65
* **2000** May Bath (G-F) H 5.7f 56 59
* **2000** Mar Southw (GD) H 6f 43 53
* **2000** *Feb Wolver (STD) H 5f 53 56*
* 1999 *Dec Wolver (STD) C 6f 50*
2000 Turf 7-23: (5f 2-5, 6f 5-17, 7f) (sft, g-s 1-3, gd 1-6, g-f 4, frm 4-8, hrd 1-1) 2000 AW 1-8: (5f 1-1, 6f 5, 7f 2) (Equi 4, Fibr 1-4)
Useful gelding, effective 5f, acts on g-s to gd, mostly wears blinkers (effectively), excels at Windsor and Bath and Wolverhampton. Turf high 92 - 1st of 20 giving 8lb to Carlton (26 Oct Windsor RF 5199) - also 1st of 23 giving 7lb to Premium Princess (6 Oct York RF 4832). AW high 58. Seems equally effective on turf and sand these days and does not let the grass grow under his hooves. Already victorious eight times last season, he remains a useful sort in modest sprint handicaps. Suited by fast ground.
**J M Bradley [9-39] J M Bradley (from N M Babbage [0-12] Nov 1997).*

NINETEENNINETYNINE BHB 46f58a **RR 58f 58a** 3015[8]

3 b g Warning 8.1f **(77)** - Flower Girl (Pharly (FR)) 9.8f **(68)**
Form - 7058
Record 2000 - 1st:0 2nd:0 3rd:0 Ran:4
Pre2000 - 1st:0 2nd:0 3rd:0 Ran:3
Win Prizemoney £0 *Total Prizemoney* £79
2000 Turf 0-2: (7f, 8f) (gd, hrd) 2000 AW 0-2: (8f, 12f) (Fibr 2)
Light-framed, fair gelding, has worn blinkers. Turf high 33. AW high 25.
**Mrs N Macauley [0-4] Shirebrook Park Management Ltd (from R W Armstrong [0-3] Oct 1999).*

NINE TO FIVE BHB 49f44a **RR 59f 44a** 4674[7]

2 b f Imp Society (USA) 7.1f **(63)** - Queen And Country (Town And Country) 8.1f **(68)**
Form - 1133445607
Record 2000 - 1st:2 2nd:0 3rd:2 Ran:10
Win Prizemoney £4,995 *Total Prizemoney* £5,903
Wins 2000 Apr Lingfi (G-S) C 5f 59 <
2000 Mar Doncas (GD) S 5f 59 <
2000 Turf 2-9: (5f 2-8, 6f) (g-s, gd 2-4, g-f, frm 3) 2000 AW 0-1: (5f) (Equi)
Fair filly, effective 5f, acts on gd. Turf high 59 - also 1st of 5 from Molly Irwin (7 Apr Lingfield RF 0633). Becoming disappointing.
**R Brotherton [0-8] Ms Gerardine O'Reilly (from W G M Turner [2-2] Apr 2000).*

NINNOLO (IRE) BHB 65f60a **RR 71f 60a** 3725[3]

3 b c Perugino (USA) - Primo Stampari **(78?f)** (Primo Dominie) 6.2f **(80)**
Form - 5370523
Record 2000 - 1st:0 2nd:1 3rd:2 Ran:7
Win Prizemoney £0 *Total Prizemoney* £2,749
2000 Turf 0-6: (10f 2, 12f 3, 14f) (gd, g-f, frm 4) 2000 AW 0-1: (10f) (Equi)
Above-average colt, effective 10 to 12f, best at 12f, acts on g-f to frm, best on frm. Turf high 71 - 3rd of 15 to Ragdale Hall (5 Jun Windsor 10f g-f RF 1729). Unraced as a juvenile, he has shown enough in maidens and handicaps to suggest a win is not too far away. **C N Allen [0-7] Newmarket Connections Ltd.*

NIP IN SHARP BHB 43f **RR 41f** 4361[15]

7 b h Sharpo 7.5f **(68)** - Nip In The Air (USA) (Northern Dancer) 9.6f **(80)**
Form - 000
Record 2000 - 1st:0 2nd:0 3rd:0 Ran:3
Pre2000 - 1st:0 2nd:0 3rd:0 Ran:2
Win Prizemoney £0 *Total Prizemoney* £275
2000 Turf 0-3: (8f 3) (g-f, frm, hrd)
Moderate horse. Turf high 41 (began Jly).
**J L Eyre [0-5] Peter Watson.*

NISAN BIR BHB 55f **RR 62f** 4360[12]

2 b g First Trump - Al Raja (Kings Lake (USA)) 10.8f **(67)**
Form - 0475080
Record 2000 - 1st:0 2nd:0 3rd:0 Ran:7
Win Prizemoney £0 *Total Prizemoney* £241
2000 Turf 0-7: (6f 3, 7f 4) (gd 2, g-f 2, frm 3)
Average gelding, effective 6f, acts on frm. Turf high 62.
**T D Easterby [0-7] April Fools.*

NISR BHB 78f **RR 78f** 4265[8]

3 b g Grand Lodge (USA) - Tharwa (IRE) **(60f)** (Last Tycoon) 8.5f **(62)**
Form - 6018
Record 2000 - 1st:1 2nd:0 3rd:0 Ran:4
Pre2000 - 1st:0 2nd:1 3rd:0 Ran:3
Win Prizemoney £5,772 *Total Prizemoney* £7,038
Wins * **2000** Jun Pontef (G-F) 6f 78 <
2000 Turf 1-4: (5f, 6f 1-2, 7f) (g-s 2, g-f, frm 1-1)
Scopey, above-average gelding, effective 6f, acts on g-f to frm. Turf high 78 - 1st of 6 from Sumthinelse (25 Jun Pontefract RF 2265). Appreciated the fast ground when landing a minor event at Pontefract in June. **J W Payne [1-7] C Cotran.*

NITE OWLER BHB 31f47a **RR 45f 47a** 536[7]

6 b g Saddlers' Hall (IRE) 10.5f **(65)** - Lorne Lady (Local Suitor (USA)) 8.4f **(67)**
Form - 02607
Record 2000 - 1st:0 2nd:1 3rd:0 Ran:4
Pre2000 - 1st:4 2nd:2 3rd:1 Ran:23
Win Prizemoney £9,164 *Total Prizemoney* £11,208
Wins * 1999 *Jly Wolver (STD) H 7f 54 56* <
* 1999 *Jun Southw (STD) H 7f 50 52*
* 1999 *Mar Southw (STD) SH 6f 41 47*
* 1998 *Jun Southw (STD) H 6f 34 41*
2000 AW 0-4: (7f 4) (Fibr 4)
Fair gelding, effective 6 to 7f, best at 6f, - acts on Fibr. AW high 50. He is an effective sort in modest handicap company on Fibresand at between six and seven furlongs.
**J Balding [4-24] Steer Arms Belton Racing Club (from J O'Reilly [0-2] Spt 1997).*

NITE-OWL MATE BHB 50f68a **RR 33f 68a** 4476[13]

3 b c Komaite (USA) 6.9f **(61)** - Nite-Owl Dancer **(63f 61a)** (Robellino (USA)) 7.6f **(80)**
Form - 33700170000
Record 2000 - 1st:1 2nd:0 3rd:2 Ran:11
Win Prizemoney £2,785 *Total Prizemoney* £3,647
Wins 2000 *Jly Wolver (STD) H 6f 62 71* <
2000 Turf 0-5: (6f 4, 7f) (gd, frm 4) 2000 AW 1-6: (6f 1-5, 7f) (Fibr 1-6)
Unfurnished, above-average colt, effective 6f, - acts on Fibr, likes left handed tracks, likes tight tracks. Turf high 50. AW high 71 - 1st of 8 getting 4lb from Doctor Dennis (13 Jly Wolverhampton RF 2779). **D Shaw [0-3] J Saul (from G Woodward [1-8] Aug 2000).*

NITWITTY BHB 45f42a **RR 45f 42a** 2039[18]

6 b g Nomination 7.3f **(57)** - Dawn Ditty (Song) 7.2f **(61)**
Form - 0
Record 2000 - 1st:0 2nd:0 3rd:0 Ran:1

Pre2000 - 1st:1 2nd:1 3rd:1 Ran:22
Win Prizemoney £2,668 *Total Prizemoney* £4,326
Wins 1999 Jly Salisb (G-S) CH 6f 48 51 <
2000 Turf 0-1: (6f) (hrd)
Moderate gelding, effective 6 to 7f, best at 6f, acts on gd to frm, best on frm, likes left handed tracks.
**A G Juckes [0-1] A C W Price (from R J Hodges [1-21] Oct 1999).*

NIYABAH (IRE) RR 63f 5186[6]

2 ch f Nashwan (USA) 10.3f **(79)** - Gharam (USA) (Green Dancer (USA)) 10.3f **(74)**
Form - 6
Record 2000 - 1st:0 2nd:0 3rd:0 Ran:1
2000 Turf 0-1: (7f) (g-s)
Currently average filly. **A C Stewart [0-1] Hamdan Al Maktoum.*

NIZAAL (USA) BHB 30f70a RR 34f 70a 644[10]

9 ch g Diesis 9f **(80)** - Shicklah (USA) (The Minstrel (CAN)) 10f **(72)**
Form - 0
Record 2000 - 1st:0 2nd:0 3rd:0 Ran:1
Pre2000 - 1st:2 2nd:1 3rd:0 Ran:19
Win Prizemoney £11,107 *Total Prizemoney* £13,587
2000 Turf 0-1: (8f) (gd)
Very moderate gelding, has worn blinkers. Consistent.
**T A K Cuthbert [0-3] J J H Walker (from R Allan [0-4] Oct 1996).*

NOBALINO BHB 57f67a RR 56f 67a 1009[8]

6 ch h Sharpo 7.5f **(68)** - Zipperti Do (Precocious) 8.6f **(62)**
Form - 3135058
Record 2000 - 1st:0 2nd:0 3rd:0 Ran:3
Pre2000 - 1st:2 2nd:7 3rd:5 Ran:33
Win Prizemoney £4,420 *Total Prizemoney* £14,528
Wins 1999 *Nov Lingfi (STD) H 7f 60 64*
1997 *Dec Southw (STD) H 5f 59 67 <*
2000 Turf 0-3: (7f 3) (sft, gd, frm)
Average horse, effective 7f, acts on gd - acts on Equi, often wears blinkers (extremely effectively), likes left handed tracks, likes tight tracks. Turf high 52.
**C Smith [0-3] Two Out & Hard Held (from Mrs V C Ward [1-9] Dec 1999)*

NOBBY BARNES BHB 32f32a RR 38f 32a 4209[5]

11 b g Nordance (USA) 7.4f **(69)** - Loving Doll (Godswalk (USA)) 7.3f **(58)**
Form - 823826705
Record 2000 - 1st:0 2nd:2 3rd:1 Ran:9
Pre2000 - 1st:7 2nd:15 3rd:18 Ran:157
Win Prizemoney £23,137 *Total Prizemoney* £56,379
Wins * 1998 Jun Hamilt (SFT) H 9.2f 38 45
2000 Turf 0-9: (8f 4, 9f 5) (gd, g-f 6, frm 2)
Very moderate gelding, effective 8f, acts on g-f. Turf high 38.
**Don Enrico Incisa [1-103] Don Enrico Incisa (from D A Wilson [6-51] Jly 1994).*

NOBELIST BHB 94f RR 102+f 4936[9]

5 b g Bering 9.6f **(80)** - Noble Peregrine (Lomond (USA)) 8.8f **(65)**
Form - 61008860
Record 2000 - 1st:1 2nd:0 3rd:0 Ran:8
Pre2000 - 1st:0 2nd:0 3rd:1 Ran:1
Win Prizemoney £11,066 *Total Prizemoney* £15,106
Wins * 2000 May Redcar (G-S) H 10f 95 102+ <
2000 Turf 1-8: (8f, 9f, 10f 1-5, 12f) (gd 1-6, frm 2)
Very useful gelding, effective 10f, acts on gd, has worn blinkers. Turf high 102 - 1st of 13 giving 27lb to Star Dynasty (29 May Redcar RF 1531). A useful performer in France at three, he missed the following season and did not shape badly on his British debut at Windsor. Gained the big payday when landing the Zetland Gold Cup next time in the style of a useful performer, but was never a threat in well-contested races on his next few starts.
**C E Brittain [1-8] H E Sheikh Rashid Bin Mohammed (from A Fabre in FR [0-1] Jun 1998).*

NOBLE ARC RR 5312[22]

2 b c Noble Patriarch 12.2f **(43)** - Time for Joy (Good Times (ITY)) 6.6f **(54)**
Form - 0
Record 2000 - 1st:0 2nd:0 3rd:0 Ran:1
2000 Turf 0-1: (8f) (g-s)
Currently very poor colt. **B S Rothwell [0-1] Peter Bailey.*

NOBLE CALLING (FR) BHB 62f65a RR 67f 65a 4810[2]

3 b c Caller I D (USA) - Specificity (USA) (Alleged (USA)) 10f **(76)**
Form - 372062322
Record 2000 - 1st:0 2nd:4 3rd:2 Ran:9
Pre2000 - 1st:0 2nd:0 3rd:0 Ran:4
Win Prizemoney £0 *Total Prizemoney* £6,541
2000 Turf 0-7: (10f 3, 11f 2, 12f, 14f) (gd 3, g-f 2, frm 2) 2000 AW 0-2: (10f, 12f) (Equi 2)
Neat, average colt, effective 10 to 12f, best at 10f, acts on gd to frm - acts on Equi, often wears blinkers (extremely effectively), likes left handed tracks, prefers tight tracks, excels at Lingfield and Beverley. Turf high 67 (1st run) - 3rd of 17 getting 8lb from Never Diss Miss (23 May Beverley 10f gd RF 1390). AW high 67 (began Spt) - 2nd of 13 getting 14lb from The Green Grey (4 Oct Lingfield 12f Equi RF 4810). **N A Graham [0-13] Fieldspring Racing.*

NOBLE CHARGER (IRE) BHB 40f35a RR 31f 35a 4649[11]

5 ch g Cadeaux Genereux 7.9f **(76)** - Shawgatny (USA) (Danzig Connection (USA)) 8f **(68)**
Form - 0860
Record 2000 - 1st:0 2nd:0 3rd:0 Ran:4
Pre2000 - 1st:0 2nd:0 3rd:0 Ran:9
2000 Turf 0-3: (5f, 6f, 8f) (gd, g-f, frm) 2000 AW 0-1: (11f) (Fibr)
Very moderate gelding, has worn blinkers. Turf high 31.
**R F Marvin [0-12] R A B Saville (from E A L Dunlop [0 1] May 1998)*

NOBLE CYRANO BHB 46f55a RR 54f 55a 5166[16]

5 ch g Generous (IRE) 11.5f **(82)** - Miss Bergerac (Bold Lad (IRE)) 8.4f **(68)**
Form - 21080400
Record 2000 - 1st:1 2nd:0 3rd:0 Ran:7
Pre2000 - 1st:1 2nd:1 3rd:1 Ran:8
Win Prizemoney £10,135 *Total Prizemoney* £11,469
Wins 2000 *Jan Southw (STD) H 8f 58 68 <*
1999 Aug Haydoc (G-S) H 8.1f 55 58
2000 Turf 0-4: (8f 3, 10f) (gd 2, g-f 2) 2000 AW 1-3: (8f 1-2, 9f)(Fibr 1-3)
Average gelding, effective 8f, acts on g-f - acts on Fibr, prefers left handed tracks, likes tight tracks. Turf high 54. AW high 68 (1st run) - 1st of 16 getting 20lb from Almazhar (3 Jan Southwell RF 0012). Inconsistent.
**M D Hammond [0-4] Wetherby Racing Bureau 38 (from G Woodward [2-9] Feb 2000).*

NOBLE DOBLE BHB 71f RR 74f 4822[5]

2 b c Shareef Dancer (USA) 10.1f **(67)** - Kshessinskaya **(86f)** (Hadeer)
Form - 4523405
Record 2000 - 1st:0 2nd:1 3rd:1 Ran:7
Win Prizemoney £0 *Total Prizemoney* £4,632
2000 Turf 0-7: (6f, 7f 3, 8f 2, 10f) (g-s, gd, g-f, frm 4)
Above-average colt, effective 7 to 10f, acts on gd to g-f. Turf high 74. **B W Hills [0-7] W J Gredley.*

NOBLE INVESTMENT BHB 34f65a RR 24f 65a 1703[16]

6 b g Shirley Heights 12.1f **(76)** - Noble Destiny (Dancing Brave (USA)) 8.4f **(76)**
Form - 3016F0000
Record 2000 - 1st:1 2nd:0 3rd:1 Ran:9
Pre2000 - 1st:0 2nd:0 3rd:0 Ran:8
Win Prizemoney £2,002 *Total Prizemoney* £2,780
Wins * 2000 *Feb Southw (STD) C 8f 44 <*
2000 Turf 0-2: (11f 2) (sft, g-s) 2000 AW 1-7: (7f, 8f 1-4, 9f 2) (Fibr 1-7)
Little account gelding, effective 8f, - acts on Fibr, has worn blinkers. Turf high 24. AW high 44 - 1st of 12 from Celestial Key (4 Feb Southwell RF 0216).
**J Neville [1-10] Mrs P K Chick (from J M P Eustace [0-8] Jun 1997).*

NOBLENOR BHB 76f RR 79f 4934[24]

3 ch c Inchinor 8.9f **(64)** - Noble Flutter (IRE) (The Noble Player (USA)) 6.5f **(67)**
Form - 8160
Record 2000 - 1st:1 2nd:0 3rd:0 Ran:4
Win Prizemoney £2,496 *Total Prizemoney* £2,496
Wins * 2000 May Redcar (G-S) 7f 79 <
2000 Turf 1-4: (7f 1-1, 8f 2, 9f) (hvy, gd 1-3)

Above-average colt. Turf high 79 - 1st of 6 giving 5lb to Still In Love (4 May Redcar RF 1022). **L M Cumani [1-4] Il Paralupo.*

NOBLE PASAO (IRE) BHB 67f70a **RR 67f 70a** 5299[11]

3 b g Alzao (USA) 9.8f **(73)** -Belle Passe (Be My Guest (USA)) 9.3f **(67)**

Form - 26883055313370

Record 2000 - 1st:1 2nd:1 3rd:4 Ran:14
Pre2000 - 1st:1 2nd:0 3rd:0 Ran:6

Win Prizemoney £7,198 *Total Prizemoney* £10,429

Wins * 2000 Jly Thirsk (FRM) H 8f 65 67
* 1999 Spt Mussel (G-S) H 8f 67 71 <

2000 Turf 1-11: (7f 6, 8f 1-5) (g-s, gd 2, g-f 3, frm 3, hrd 1-2) 2000 AW 0-3: (8f 2, 9f) (Fibr 3)

Scopey, above-average gelding, effective 8f, acts on gd to hrd - acts on Fibr, has worn blinkers, likes left handed tracks, prefers tight tracks. Turf high 67 - 1st of 11 giving 18lb to Taker Chance (28 Jly Thirsk RF 3199). AW high 75 (1st run) - 2nd of 9 getting 3lb from Special Promise (10 Feb Wolverhampton 8f Fibr RF 0259). Won a one-mile Musselburgh nursery at two, but did not build on that and looks moderate.

**Andrew Turnell [2-20] Mrs Claire Hollowood.*

NOBLE PATRIOT BHB 48f42a **RR 49f 42a** 3931[4]

5 b g Polish Patriot (USA) 7.8f **(70)** - Noble Form (Double Form) 7.3f **(58)**

Form - 2834575007255341114

Record 2000 - 1st:3 2nd:1 3rd:1 Ran:16
Pre2000 - 1st:0 2nd:2 3rd:4 Ran:29

Win Prizemoney £8,024 *Total Prizemoney* £11,751

Wins * 2000 Aug Catter (G-F) H 5f 44 47 <
*** 2000** Jly Doncas (G-F) H 5f 39 44
*** 2000** Jly Doncas (G-F) H 6f 33 42

2000 Turf 3-5: (5f 2-4, 6f 1-1) (g-f, frm 3-4) 2000 AW 0-11: (5f 3, 7f 5, 8f, 9f, 12f) (Fibr 11)

Moderate gelding, effective 5 to 7f, best at 5f, acts on frm - acts on Fibr, has worn blinkers. Turf high 47 - 1st of 13 getting 7lb from Tancred Times (8 Aug Catterick RF 3452) - also 1st of 14 getting 23lb from Flak Jacket (19 Jly Doncaster RF 2928). AW high 40.

**R Hollinshead [3-45] The Four Dreamers.*

NOBLE PURSUIT BHB 88f **RR 90f** 3233[8]

3 b c Pursuit of Love 9.5f **(69)** - Noble Peregrine (Lomond (USA)) 8.8f **(65)**

Form - 4041038

Record 2000 - 1st:1 2nd:0 3rd:1 Ran:7
Pre2000 - 1st:1 2nd:1 3rd:0 Ran:3

Win Prizemoney £10,337 *Total Prizemoney* £14,685

Wins * 2000 Jun Ripon (G-F) H 8f 83 85 <
* 1999 Aug Salisb (SFT) 7f 76+

2000 Turf 1-7: (7f, 8f 1-5, 9f) (g-s 2, g-f 2, frm 1-3)

Unfurnished, useful colt, effective 7 to 8f, acts on g-f to frm. Turf high 90 - also 1st of 6 getting 5lb from Strasbourg (22 Jun Ripon RF 2187). Consistent. He can take a good hold and was suited by aggressive tactics when winning at Ripon in June. Unlikely to stay beyond a mile, he was sold for 6,500gns at Newmarket in October.

**T G Mills [2-10] Mrs Stephanie Merrydew.*

NOBLE REEF BHB 58f52a **RR 62f 52a** 5007[15]

3 b c Deploy 11.4f **(67)** - Penny Mint (Mummy's Game) 8.2f **(60)**

Form - 03300

Record 2000 - 1st:0 2nd:0 3rd:2 Ran:5
Pre2000 - 1st:0 2nd:0 3rd:1 Ran:8

Win Prizemoney £0 *Total Prizemoney* £1,258

2000 Turf 0-4: (8f, 10f 2, 12f) (gd, g-f 2, frm) 2000 AW 0-1: (12f) (Fibr)

Leggy, average colt, effective 7 to 12f, acts on g-f to frm, best on frm, prefers left handed tracks, prefers tight tracks. Turf high 62 - 3rd of 12 to After The Blue (17 Jun Nottingham 10f g-f RF 2050). Inconsistent. **Mrs G S Rees [0-13] Lady Lilford.*

NOBLE SPLENDOUR BHB 60f57a **RR 70f 57a** 5016[8]

3 ch g Grand Lodge (USA) - Haskeir (Final Straw) 7.9f **(64)**

Form - 582334508

Record 2000 - 1st:0 2nd:1 3rd:2 Ran:9
Pre2000 - 1st:0 2nd:0 3rd:1 Ran:5

Win Prizemoney £0 *Total Prizemoney* £3,273

2000 Turf 0-8: (7f, 8f 5, 9f, 10f) (g-s, gd 2, g-f, frm 4) 2000 AW 0-1: (9f) (Fibr)

Scopey, above-average gelding, effective 7 to 10f, acts on gd to frm, best on frm, likes left handed tracks. Turf high 70. Becoming disappointing.

**J D Bethell [0-4] M J Dawson (from L M Cumani [0-10] Jly 2000).*

NOCCIOLA BHB 48f50a **RR 52f 50a** 3554[17]

4 ch f Cadeaux Genereux 7.9f **(76)** - Norpella (Northfields (USA)) 9f **(72)**

Form - 0600

Record 2000 - 1st:0 2nd:0 3rd:0 Ran:4
Pre2000 - 1st:0 2nd:0 3rd:0 Ran:1

2000 Turf 0-3: (6f, 7f 2) (gd 2, frm) 2000 AW 0-1: (7f) (Fibr)

Neat, fair filly. Turf high 52. **Sir Mark Prescott [0-5] William Fox.*

NO DISS GRACE BHB 40f **RR 39f** 3433[5]

2 b g Cigar 6.3f **(43)** - Llanelly (FR) (Kenmare (FR)) 6.5f **(72)**

Form - 5

Record 2000 - 1st:0 2nd:0 3rd:0 Ran:1

2000 Turf 0-1: (6f) (frm)

Currently very moderate gelding.

**P C Haslam [0-1] Kary-On Racing Partnership.*

NOD'S NEPHEW BHB 62f55a **RR 64f 55a** 4497[10]

3 b g Efisio 7.7f **(69)** - Nordan Raider **(58f 67a)** (Domynsky) 8f **(82)**

Form - 418470100

Record 2000 - 1st:2 2nd:0 3rd:0 Ran:9
Pre2000 - 1st:0 2nd:0 3rd:0 Ran:2

Win Prizemoney £5,618 *Total Prizemoney* £5,830

Wins * 2000 Aug Beverl (G-F) C 7.5f 64 <
*** 2000** Apr Beverl (HVY) H 7.5f 59 63

2000 Turf 2-6: (6f, 7f 2-4, 8f) (g-s 1-2, g-f 2, frm 1-2) 2000 AW 0-3: (7f 3) (Fibr 3)

Workmanlike, average gelding, effective 6 to 7f, best at 7f, acts on g-s to frm, best on frm, prefers tight tracks. Turf high 64 - 1st of 12 giving 9lb to Lordofenchantment (27 Aug Beverley RF 4007) - also 1st of 16 getting 3lb from Heathyards Lad (19 Apr Beverley RF 0791). AW high 48. Inconsistent.

**Miss J A Camacho [2-11] Brian Nordan.*

NOEL (GER) **RR 113f** 2205a[5]

5

Form - 025

2000 Turf 0-3: (12f 3) (gd, g-f 2)

Group-class, effective 11 to 12f, best at 12f, acts on g-f. Turf high 108. **H Blume in GER [1-7].*

NO EXCUSE NEEDED BHB 100f **RR 104f** 4610[5]

2 ch c Machiavellian (USA) 9.8f **(83)** - Nawaiet (USA) (Zilzal (USA))

Form - 115

Record 2000 - 1st:2 2nd:0 3rd:0 Ran:3

Win Prizemoney £37,280 *Total Prizemoney* £37,280

Wins * 2000 Aug Goodwo (G-F) G3 7f 104 <
*** 2000** Jly Sandow (GD) 7.1f 80+

2000 Turf 2-3: (7f 2-2, 8f) (g-s, gd 1-1, frm 1-1)

Currently very useful colt. Turf high 104 (began Jly) - 1st of 10 from Bonnard (2 Aug Goodwood RF 3316). He showed the right attitude on his winning debut at Sandown and battled on well to land Goodwood's Group Three Vintage Stakes next time. Failed to handle the soft ground on his final run.

**Sir Michael Stoute [2-3] Maktoum Al Maktoum.*

NO EXTRAS (IRE) BHB 70f90a **RR 75df 90a** 4102[7]

10 b g Efisio 7.7f **(69)** - Parkland Rose (Sweet Candy (VEN)) 6.4f **(103)**

Form - 116827

Record 2000 - 1st:2 2nd:1 3rd:0 Ran:6
Pre2000 - 1st:10 2nd:13 3rd:10 Ran:94

Win Prizemoney £77,243 *Total Prizemoney* £144,729

Wins * 2000 Jun Newmar (G-F) H 8f 70 73
*** 2000** May Bright (FRM) H 8f 67 69
* 1999 Jun Windso (SFT) 8.3f 78
* 1998 Jun Newmar (GD) H 7f 87 92
* 1997 Jly Goodwo (G-F) H 8f 72 78
* 1997 Jun Goodwo (G-S) H 8f 62 67

2000 Turf 2-6: (8f 2-3, 9f 2, 10f) (gd, g-f 1-3, frm 1-2)

Above-average gelding, effective 8 to 10f, best at 8f, acts on gd to frm, has worn blinkers, likes left handed tracks, likes tight tracks, likes Brighton. Turf high 73 - 1st of 27 giving 16lb to Rambo Waltzer (3 Jun Newmarket RF 1686) - also 1st of 15 getting 7lb

from Copplestone (17 May Brighton RF 1254).
**G L Moore [11-90] K Higson (from J Sutcliffe [1-10] Nov 1992).*

NO FRILLS (IRE) RR 62f 1891[3]

3 b f Darshaan 11.9f **(81)** - Bubbling Danseuse (USA) (Arctic Tern (USA)) 8.9f **(69)**
Form - 63
Record 2000 - 1st:0 2nd:0 3rd:1 Ran:2
Win Prizemoney £0 *Total Prizemoney* £655
2000 Turf 0-2: (9f, 10f) (gd, g-f)
Scopey, currently average filly. Turf high 62.
**Sir Michael Stoute [0-2] Mrs Doreen Swinburn.*

NOIRIE BHB 25f29a RR 39f 29a 5012[14]

6 br g Warning 8.1f **(77)** - Callipoli (USA) (Green Dancer (USA)) 10.3f **(74)**
Form - 238208000
Record 2000 - 1st:0 2nd:2 3rd:1 Ran:9
Pre2000 - 1st:1 2nd:0 3rd:1 Ran:25
Win Prizemoney £2,237 *Total Prizemoney* £6,472
Wins * 1998 Jun Pontef (HVY) H 10f 38 40 <
2000 Turf 0-7: (10f 3, 11f, 12f, 14f 2) (hvy, sft 2, gd 2, g-f, hrd) 2000 AW 0-2: (11f, 14f) (Fibr 2)
Very moderate gelding, effective 10f, acts on sft, has worn blinkers. Turf high 40 (1st run) - 2nd of 18 getting 25lb from Wilton (17 Apr Pontefract 10f sft RF 0751). AW high 24.
**M Brittain [1-24] Miss Debi Woods.*

NO LANGUAGE PLEASE (IRE) BHB 52f RR 56f 5020[10]

6 ch g Arapahos (FR) - Strong Language (Formidable (USA)) 9.2f **(63)**
Form - 130
Record 2000 - 1st:1 2nd:0 3rd:1 Ran:3
Win Prizemoney £2,289 *Total Prizemoney* £2,685
Wins * **2000** Jun Bright (G-F) C 11.9f 42 <
2000 Turf 1-2: (12f 1-2) (frm 1-2) 2000 AW 0-1: (12f) (Fibr)
Fair gelding. Turf high 56 - 3rd of 7 giving 6lb to Copyforce Girl (15 Jun Brighton 12f frm RF 1978). **R Curtis [1-9] Mrs G Fletcher.*

NO MATTER WHAT (USA) RR 110f 4140a[1]

3 ch f Nureyev (USA) 8.4f **(84)**
Form - 01
2000 Turf 1-2: (8f, 9f 1-1) (g-s, frm 1-1)
Currently Group-class filly. Turf high 110 (began Jly) - 1st of 9 from Theoretically (27 Aug Del Mar RF 4140a).
**N Drysdale in USA [1-1] Augustin Stables (from J E Pease in FR [0-1] Jly 2000).*

NO MERCY BHB 76a RR 69f 5072[12]

4 ch g Faustus (USA) 9.1f **(54)** - Nashville Blues (IRE) **(74f)** (Try My Best (USA)) 7.6f **(67)**
Form - 502750
Record 2000 - 1st:0 2nd:1 3rd:0 Ran:6
Pre2000 - 1st:1 2nd:0 3rd:3 Ran:9
Win Prizemoney £2,558 *Total Prizemoney* £7,349
Wins * 1999 *Apr Lingfi (STD) 10f 73* <
2000 Turf 0-6: (8f 2, 10f 4) (g-s, g-f, frm 4)
Workmanlike, above-average gelding, effective 8 to 10f, best at 10f, acts on g-f to hrd - acts on Equi, best on frm, has worn blinkers, excels at Windsor. Turf high 69 - 2nd of 9 to The Green Grey (24 Jly Windsor 10f frm RF 3081). **J W Hills [1-16] Freddy Bienstock.*

NOMINATOR LAD BHB 72f66a RR 76f 66a 4864[11]

6 b g Nomination 7.3f **(57)** - Ankara's Princess (USA) (Ankara (USA)) 8f **(71)**
Form - 0004416060
Record 2000 - 1st:1 2nd:0 3rd:0 Ran:10
Pre2000 - 1st:5 2nd:3 3rd:1 Ran:34
Win Prizemoney £41,079 *Total Prizemoney* £49,533

Wins								
* **2000**	Aug	Haydoc	(GD)	H	10.5f	72	76	
* 1999	Apr	Pontef	(SFT)	H	8f	76	82	<
* 1998	Spt	Ayr	(G-S)	H	8f	75	79	
* 1998	*Jun*	*Wolver*	*(STD)*	*H*	*8.5f*	*70*	*70*	
* 1997	Spt	Haydoc	(GD)	H	7.1f	67	71	
* 1997	Jly	Nottin	(G-F)		8.2f		72	

2000 Turf 1-7: (8f 4, 9f, 10f, 11f 1-1) (sft, g-s, gd 2, g-f 1-3) 2000 AW 0-3: (8f 2, 9f) (Fibr 3)
Above-average gelding, effective 8 to 11f, best at 8f, acts on sft to g-f, has worn blinkers (effectively), likes left handed tracks, likes tight tracks. Turf high 76 - 1st of 11 giving 8lb to Mini Lodge (11 Aug Haydock RF 3548). AW high 70 (began Jly). An inconsistent sort, first-time blinkers did the trick at Haydock in August, but the novelty did not last for long. **B A McMahon [6-44] J D Graham.*

NOMORE MR NICEGUY BHB 68f80a RR 78f 80a 4991[19]

6 b h Rambo Dancer (CAN) 8.4f **(59)** - Lariston Gale (Pas de Seul) 9.1f **(67)**
Form - 0078727400664603500
Record 2000 - 1st:0 2nd:1 3rd:1 Ran:19
Pre2000 - 1st:7 2nd:9 3rd:10 Ran:67
Win Prizemoney £43,972 *Total Prizemoney* £109,905

Wins								
* 1999	Jun	Cheste	(G-F)	H	6.1f	83	86	
* 1998	*Dec*	*Lingfi*	*(STD)*		*8f*		*94*	<
* 1998	*Nov*	*Wolver*	*(STD)*	*H*	*7f*	*90*	*94*	<
* 1998	Jun	Cheste	(GD)	H	7f	79	90+	
* 1997	*Mar*	*Wolver*	*(STD)*	*H*	*7f*	*84*	*88*	
* 1996	*Dec*	*Wolver*	*(STD)*	*H*	*7f*	*78*	*84*	
* 1996	Jly	Hamilt	(GD)		5f		67	

2000 Turf 0-18: (5f, 6f 4, 7f 6, 8f 7) (sft, g-s 3, gd 8, g-f 3, frm 3) 2000 AW 0-1: (8f) (Fibr)
Above-average horse, effective 8f, - acts on Fibr, has worn blinkers. Turf high 78. **E J Alston [7-86] Mrs Carol McPhail.*

NO NAME CITY (IRE) BHB 62f61a RR 54f 61a 5115[8]

2 ch c Royal Abjar (USA) - Broadway Gal (USA) (Foolish Pleasure (USA)) 8.9f **(72)**
Form - 0038
Record 2000 - 1st:0 2nd:0 3rd:1 Ran:4
Win Prizemoney £0 *Total Prizemoney* £242
2000 Turf 0-2: (6f, 7f) (gd, frm) 2000 AW 0-2: (8f 2) (Fibr 2)
Fair colt. Turf high 54. AW high 51 (began Oct).
**J W Hills [0-4] The Wandering Stars.*

NO NO NORA BHB 20f RR 58f 354[12]

5 ch m Inchinor 8.9f **(64)** - Lucky Fingers (Hotfoot) 10.5f **(59)**
Form - 00
Record 2000 - 1st:0 2nd:0 3rd:0 Ran:2
Pre2000 - 1st:0 2nd:0 3rd:0 Ran:5
Win Prizemoney £0 *Total Prizemoney* £194
2000 AW 0-2: (8f, 9f) (Fibr 2)
Fair filly, has worn blinkers.
**A G Newcombe [0-2] Miss D S Jackson (from S C Williams [0-5] Spt 1998).*

NON VINTAGE (IRE) BHB 33f30a RR 30f 30a 663[12]

9 ch g Shy Groom (USA) 8.2f **(59)** - Great Alexandra (Runnett) 7f **(59)**
Form - 00
Record 2000 - 1st:0 2nd:0 3rd:0 Ran:2
Pre2000 - 1st:2 2nd:5 3rd:7 Ran:47
Win Prizemoney £9,212 *Total Prizemoney* £21,408
2000 Turf 0-1: (17f) (g-s) 2000 AW 0-1: (12f) (Fibr)
Very moderate gelding, has worn blinkers.
**M C Chapman [6-107] Alan Mann (from M H Easterby [1-17] Aug 1994).*

NOON GUN RR 61f 5017[4]

2 ch c Ashkalani (IRE) - Lady Kris (IRE) (Kris) 9.5f **(73)**
Form - 44
Record 2000 - 1st:0 2nd:0 3rd:0 Ran:2
Win Prizemoney £0 *Total Prizemoney* £224
2000 Turf 0-1: (6f) (gd) 2000 AW 0-1: (7f) (Fibr)
Currently average colt. **W R Muir [0-2] J Bernstein.*

NOOSHMAN (USA) BHB 107f RR 111+f 4740[2]

3 ch g Woodman (USA) 9.7f **(77)** - Knoosh (USA) (Storm Bird (CAN)) 10.3f **(74)**
Form - 15813202
Record 2000 - 1st:2 2nd:2 3rd:1 Ran:8
Pre2000 - 1st:0 2nd:2 3rd:0 Ran:3
Win Prizemoney £16,510 *Total Prizemoney* £65,023

Wins								
* **2000**	Jly	Goodwo	(G-F)	H	9.9f	85	97+	<
* **2000**	May	Thirsk	(GD)	H	7f	81	84+	

2000 Turf 2-8: (7f 1-1, 8f 2, 9f, 10f 1-4) (g-s, gd 1-3, g-f 1-3, frm)
Scopey, Group-class gelding, effective 9 to 10f, acts on g-f to frm. Turf high 111 - 2nd of 35 giving 2lb to Katy Nowaitee (30 Spt

Newmarket 9f g-f RF 4740). Improving. Showed a good turn of foot to win a Thirsk handicap on his reappearance. He appreciated the step up to ten furlongs when bolting up at Goodwood in July and was a staying-on third in the John Smith's Cup at York. Ran another good race at York in August and ended his season with a fine second in the Cambridgeshire. He deserves to pick up a decent prize. **Sir Michael Stoute [2-11] Maktoum Al Maktoum.*

NO PASS NO HONOR (FR) BHB 46f **RR 46f** 5201[7]

3 b g Highest Honor (FR) 10.9f **(72)** - Marzipan (IRE) **(61f)** (Green Desert (USA)) 8.6f **(78)**

Form - 657

Record 2000 - 1st:0 2nd:0 3rd:0 Ran:3
Pre2000 - 1st:0 2nd:0 3rd:0 Ran:2

2000 Turf 0-3: (10f 2, 12f) (sft, gd 2)

Scopey, moderate gelding. Turf high 41. **S Dow [0-5] D G Churston.*

NORCROFT JOY BHB 77f **RR 77f** 5125[1]

5 b m Rock Hopper 10.6f **(54)** - Greenhills Joy (Radetzky) 9.8f **(56)**

Form - 50333174551

Record 2000 - 1st:2 2nd:0 3rd:3 Ran:11
Pre2000 - 1st:6 2nd:2 3rd:1 Ran:25

Win Prizemoney £42,350 *Total Prizemoney* £47,283

Wins	Year	Month	Course	Going	Type	Dist			
	*** 2000**	Oct	Doncas	(SFT)	H	12f	70	77	<
	*** 2000**	Jly	Beverl	(GD)	H	12f	69	73	
	1999	Jun	Doncas	(GD)	H	12f	73	74	
	1999	Mar	Warwic	(G-S)	H	12.5f	70	73	
	1998	Spt	Haydoc	(GD)	H	11.9f	61	70	
	1998	Aug	Beverl	(G-F)	H	12f	54	57	
	1998	Aug	Hamilt	(SFT)	H	12.1f	54	61	
	1998	Jun	Yarmou	(SFT)	H	14.1f	52	60	

2000 Turf 2-11: (10f 3, 12f 2-6, 14f 2) (g-s 1-1, gd 2, g-f 5, frm 1-3)

Above-average filly, effective 10 to 14f, best at 12f, acts on sft to frm, likes right handed tracks, does well at Doncaster and Newmarket and likes Nottingham. Turf high 77 - 1st of 19 getting 5lb from Capriolo (21 Oct Doncaster RF 5125) - also 1st of 12 giving 26lb to Spa Lane (7 Jly Beverley RF 2589). Consistent. A very tough filly, she looks to need at least a mile and a half these days.
**N A Callaghan [2-13] Norcroft Park Stud (from M J Ryan [6-23] Spt 1999).*

NORCROFT LADY BHB 87f **RR 83f** 4325[6]

2 b f Mujtahid (USA) 7.4f **(69)** - Polytess (IRE) (Polish Patriot (USA))

Form - 141606

Record 2000 - 1st:2 2nd:0 3rd:0 Ran:6

Win Prizemoney £7,172 *Total Prizemoney* £7,814

Wins	Year	Month	Course	Going	Type	Dist			
	*** 2000**	Jly	Lingfi	(GD)	H	6f		83	<
	*** 2000**	Jun	Yarmou	(GD)		6f		70	

2000 Turf 2-6: (6f 2-5, 7f) (gd 1-1, g-f 1-3, frm, hrd)

Decent filly, effective 6 to 7f, acts on g-f. Turf high 83 - 6th of 10 giving 11lb to Lapwing (11 Spt Warwick 7f g-f RF 4325) - also 1st of 10 giving 9lb to Ebullience (12 Jly Lingfield RF 2740). Landed a nursery, but was found wanting in a listed race at Newbury.
**N A Callaghan [2-6] Norcroft Park Stud.*

NORDIC SABRE BHB 75f **RR 74f** 3958[4]

2 b f Sabrehill (USA) 8.5f **(64)** - Nordico Princess **(52f 67a)** (Nordico (USA)) 6.5f **(62)**

Form - 614

Record 2000 - 1st:1 2nd:0 3rd:0 Ran:3

Win Prizemoney £2,795 *Total Prizemoney* £3,055

Wins	Year	Month	Course	Going	Type	Dist			
	*** 2000**	Aug	Mussel	(GD)		5f		74	<

2000 Turf 1-3: (5f 1-3) (g-f, frm 1-1, hrd)

Currently above-average filly. Turf high 74 (began Jly) - 1st of 9 from Extra Guest (2 Aug Musselburgh RF 3334).
**Mrs L Stubbs [1-3] K F F Potatoes Ltd.*

NO REGRETS BHB 41f49a **RR 46f 49a** 4144[14]

3 b c Bin Ajwaad (IRE) - Marton Maid (Silly Season) 9.7f **(56)**

Form - 0570050072650

Record 2000 - 1st:0 2nd:1 3rd:0 Ran:12
Pre2000 - 1st:0 2nd:0 3rd:1 Ran:6

Win Prizemoney £0 *Total Prizemoney* £1,646

2000 Turf 0-10: (7f, 8f 3, 10f 5, 12f) (g-s, g-f 5, frm 4) 2000 AW 0-2: (8f, 10f) (Equi 2)

Scopey, moderate colt, has worn blinkers. Turf high 46. AW high 33. **M Quinn [0-18] Mrs J M Ferguson.*

NORFOLK REED (IRE) **RR 86f** 5242[21]

3 b g Thatching 7.8f **(69)** - Sawaki (Song) 7.2f **(61)**

Form - 45808031000

Record 2000 - 1st:1 2nd:0 3rd:1 Ran:11
Pre2000 - 1st:1 2nd:1 3rd:0 Ran:4

Win Prizemoney £10,719 *Total Prizemoney* £15,040

Wins	Year	Month	Course	Going	Type	Dist			
	*** 2000**	Spt	Doncas	(G-F)	H	7f	79	84	<
	* 1999	May	Lingfi	(G-F)		5f		69+	

2000 Turf 1-11: (6f 3, 7f 1-8) (g-s 2, gd, g-f 5, frm 1-3)

Leggy, useful gelding, effective 6 to 7f, best at 6f, acts on g-f to frm, best on frm, has worn blinkers. Turf high 86 - 8th of 30 getting 18lb from Hunting Lion (3 Jun Newmarket 6f frm RF 1690) - also 1st of 21 getting 9lb from Peacock Alley (7 Spt Doncaster RF 4284). Best on a sound surface, he was unlucky in a claimer before landing a Doncaster handicap.
**R Hannon [2-15] The South-Western Partnership.*

NORTH ARDAR BHB 42f29a **RR 43f 29a** 2738[12]

10 b g Ardar 9.5f **(63)** - Langwaite (Seaepic (USA)) 9f **(56)**

Form - 00246570073350

Record 2000 - 1st:0 2nd:0 3rd:2 Ran:9
Pre2000 - 1st:15 2nd:12 3rd:10 Ran:90

Win Prizemoney £41,230 *Total Prizemoney* £56,906

Wins	Year	Month	Course	Going	Type	Dist			
	* 1999	*Jun*	*Southw*	*(STD)*	*S*	*11f*		*50*	
	1998	*Feb*	*Lingfi*	*(STD)*	*H*	*12f*	*40*	*46*	
	1998	*Jan*	*Lingfi*	*(STD)*	*H*	*10f*	*35*	*41*	
	1996	*Spt*	*Southw*	*(STD)*	*H*	*8f*	*52*	*57*	
	1996	Aug	Hamilt	(G-F)	S	8.3f		60	
	1996	Jly	Ripon	(GD)	S	10f		57	
	1996	Jun	Redcar	(FRM)	C	10f		60	
	1996	Jun	Pontef	(G-F)	S	10f		53	
	1996	May	Catter	(GD)	S	10.2f		60	

2000 Turf 0-2: (10f, 11f) (g-s, gd) 2000 AW 0-7: (8f, 10f, 11f 3, 12f 2) (Equi, Fibr 6)

Moderate gelding, effective 11 to 13f, best at 11f, acts on g-s to frm - acts on AW, best on Fibr, has worn blinkers. Turf high 43 - 3rd of 20 giving 9lb to Vanborough Lad (4 Jun Warwick 11f g-s RF 1703). AW high 39. Inconsistent.
**R Brotherton [1-26] Roy Brotherton (from N P Littmoden [2-7] Feb 1998).*

NORTH BY NORTH (IRE) **RR 40f** 4930[14]

2 b g Distinctly North (USA) 7.4f **(63)** - Winscarlet North (Garland Knight)

Form - 70

Record 2000 - 1st:0 2nd:0 3rd:0 Ran:2

2000 Turf 0-2: (5f, 7f) (gd, frm)

Currently moderate gelding. Turf high 40 (began Jly).
**M H Tompkins [0-2] Flint Fairyhouse Partnership.*

NORTH EAST BOUND (USA) **RR 125f** 5327a[2]

4 br h D'Accord (USA) - North East Dancer (USA) (Far North (USA))

Form - 2

2000 Turf 0-1: (8f) (frm)

Strong, currently top-class colt, always wears blinkers. - 2nd of 14 giving 3lb to War Chant (4 Nov Churchill Downs 8f frm RF 5327a). Was an outsider when running a close second in the Breeders' Cup Mile. **W Perry in USA [0-1] Julian DeMarco & Richard J DiSano.*

NORTHERN ACCORD BHB 34f **RR 36f** 1952[11]

6 b g Akarad (FR) 9.7f **(73)** - Sioux City (Simply Great (FR)) 8.2f **(65)**

Form - 6040

Record 2000 - 1st:0 2nd:0 3rd:0 Ran:4
Pre2000 - 1st:2 2nd:0 3rd:0 Ran:10

Win Prizemoney £5,222 *Total Prizemoney* £5,735

Wins	Year	Month	Course	Going	Type	Dist			
	1998	Spt	Beverl	(G-F)	H	9.9f	41	45	<
	1998	Aug	Hamilt	(SFT)	H	8.3f	37	39	

2000 Turf 0-4: (10f 3, 12f) (sft 2, g-f, hrd)

Very moderate gelding, has worn blinkers. Turf high 36.
**M Dods [0-8] Mrs R Olivier (from Mrs J R Ramsden [2-10] Oct 1998).*

NORTHERN CASTLE (IRE) BHB 30f **RR 23f** 4784[8]

2 b g Distinctly North (USA) 7.4f **(63)** - Dunbally (Dunphy) 9.4f **(57)**

Form - 008

Record 2000 - 1st:0 2nd:0 3rd:0 Ran:3

2000 Turf 0-2: (5f, 8f) (gd, hrd) 2000 AW 0-1: (8f) (Fibr)

Currently little account gelding. Turf high 23 (began Aug).

**P C Haslam [0-3] Northern Lights Racing.*

NORTHERN ECHO BHB 49f44a **RR 53f 44a** 5119[8]
3 b g Pursuit of Love 9.5f **(69)** - Stop Press (USA) (Sharpen Up) 8.3f **(67)**
Form - 770532086208
Record 2000 - 1st:0 2nd:2 3rd:1 Ran:12
Pre2000 - 1st:0 2nd:0 3rd:0 Ran:1
Win Prizemoney £0 *Total Prizemoney* £2,057
2000 Turf 0-11: (6f 3, 7f 2, 8f 3, 10f, 12f 2) (g-s 2, gd 3, g-f 3, frm 2, hrd)
2000 AW 0-1: (12f) (Fibr)
Leggy, fair gelding, effective 7 to 12f, acts on frm, has worn blinkers. Turf high 53. **M Dods [0-13] The Northern Echo Partnership.*

NORTHERN FLEET BHB 57f **RR 65f** 3755[12]
7 b g Slip Anchor 12.7f **(75)** - Kamkova (USA) (Northern Dancer) 9.6f **(80)**
Form - 4500
Record 2000 - 1st:0 2nd:0 3rd:0 Ran:4
Pre2000 - 1st:2 2nd:2 3rd:1 Ran:15
Win Prizemoney £7,153 *Total Prizemoney* £14,568
Wins 1999 Jly Salisb (FRM) H 14.1f 65 69
1996 Aug Beverl (G-F) H 16.2f 72 <
2000 Turf 0-4; (14f 3, 16f) (g-f 2, frm 2)
Average gelding, effective 14 to 16f, best at 14f, acts on gd to frm, best on frm, has worn blinkers. Turf high 65 - 5th of 9 giving 8lb to Alnajashee (29 Jun Salisbury 14f frm RF 2378).
**Mark Campion [0-4] Mrs J Howell (from Mrs A J Perrett [2-19] Spt 1999).*

NORTHERN LIFE (IRE) BHB 30f **RR 42f** 3330[12]
3 b f Distinctly North (USA) 7.4f **(63)** - Another Way (Wolverlife) 9.3f **(54)**
Form - 0060060
Record 2000 - 1st:0 2nd:0 3rd:0 Ran:7
Pre2000 - 1st:0 2nd:0 3rd:0 Ran:3
2000 Turf 0-7: (7f 4, 8f 2, 10f) (gd, g-f 4, frm 2)
Workmanlike, moderate filly, has worn blinkers. Turf high 42.
**J S Moore [0-7] Midas Touch (from P Shakespeare [0-3] Oct 1999).*

NORTHERN MOTTO BHB 40f35a **RR 54f 35a** 5297[9]
7 b g Mtoto 11.5f **(71)** - Soulful (FR) (Zino) 12.9f **(54)**
Form - 507033344367820
Record 2000 - 1st:0 2nd:1 3rd:4 Ran:15
Pre2000 - 1st:8 2nd:3 3rd:4 Ran:50
Win Prizemoney £44,263 *Total Prizemoney* £56,913
Wins * 1999 Jly Cheste (G-F) H 15.9f 52 54
* 1999 Jun Mussel (G-F) H 16f 50 53
* 1998 Jly Cheste (G-F) H 15.9f 56 60 <
* 1998 May Mussel (G-S) H 16f 55 58
* 1998 Apr Mussel (G-S) H 16f 48 59
* 1997 Jun Doncas (G-F) H 12f 50 55
* 1997 *Feb Wolver (STD) H 12f 52 57*
* 1996 Nov Mussel (G-S) H 15.1f 47 54
2000 Turf 0-15: (13f, 14f 2, 16f 10, 17f 2) (g-s 2, gd 6, g-f, frm 5, hrd)
Fair gelding, effective 14 to 18f, best at 16f, acts on gd to hrd, best on frm, has worn blinkers, likes right handed tracks, likes Musselburgh. Turf high 54 - 3rd of 6 getting 27lb from Christiansted (3 Jun Musselburgh 16f frm RF 1682). Despite several placings, he has been on a long losing run since and can be a very difficult ride.
**J S Goldie [8-67] Alf Chadwick (from W Storey [0-3] Oct 1996).*

NORTHERN SVENGALI (IRE) BHB 67f70a **RR 70f 70a** 4487[7]
4 b g Distinctly North (USA) 7.4f **(63)** - Trilby's Dream (IRE) (Mansooj)
Form - 30470006004050302157
Record 2000 - 1st:1 2nd:1 3rd:2 Ran:20
Pre2000 - 1st:2 2nd:6 3rd:2 Ran:20
Win Prizemoney £10,564 *Total Prizemoney* £23,309
Wins * 2000 Aug Thirsk (G-F) H 5f 61 66
* 1998 Oct Catter (G-S) H 5f 79 82 <
* 1998 Spt Catter (G-F) 6f 80
2000 Turf 1-19: (5f 1-8, 6f 6, 7f 5) (sft, gd 4, g-f 5, frm 1-9) 2000 AW 0-1: (5f) (Equi)
Unfurnished, above-average gelding, effective 6f, acts on hvy to frm. Turf high 75. **T D Barron [3-40] Timothy Cox.*

NORTHERN TIMES (USA) BHB 39f **RR 54f** 5071[14]
3 ch g Cahill Road (USA) 8.5f **(82)** - Northern Nation (USA) (Northrop (USA))
Form - 51710800
Record 2000 - 1st:2 2nd:0 3rd:0 Ran:8
Pre2000 - 1st:0 2nd:0 3rd:0 Ran:1
Win Prizemoney £3,768 *Total Prizemoney* £3,768
Wins * 2000 Apr Lingfi (G-S) SH 7f 58 64 <
2000 *Feb Southw (STD) S 7f 54*
2000 Turf 1-5: (7f 1-1, 8f 2, 12f 2) (g-s 2, gd 1-2, frm) 2000 AW 1-3: (6f, 7f 1-1, 8f) (Fibr 1-3)
Scopey, fair gelding, effective 7f, acts on gd - acts on Fibr. Turf high 64 (1st run) - 1st of 13 giving 23lb to Tabbetinna Blue (7 Apr Lingfield RF 0638). AW high 54.
**R Brotherton [1-6] Ms Gerardine O'Reilly (from T D Easterby [1-3] Feb 2000).*

NORTHERN TRIO (FR) BHB 26f50a **RR 44f 50a** 5162[13]
3 b g Aragon 7.7f **(58)** - Northern Notion (USA) (Northern Baby (CAN)) 11.6f **(71)**
Form - 778006040
Record 2000 - 1st:0 2nd:0 3rd:0 Ran:9
Pre2000 - 1st:0 2nd:0 3rd:0 Ran:3
2000 Turf 0-7: (6f 3, 7f, 8f, 10f, 12f) (sft, g-s 2, gd, g-f 2, frm) 2000 AW 0-2: (7f 2) (Fibr 2)
Workmanlike, moderate gelding. Turf high 44. AW high 31.
**Mrs Barbara Waring [0-6] T McCullough & W C Anthony (from D Carroll [0-6] Apr 2000).*

NORTHFIELDS DANCER (IRE) BHB 93f **RR 89f** 5001[5]
2 ch c Dr Devious (IRE) 9.9f **(74)** - Heartland (Northfields (USA)) 9f **(72)**
Form - 722822125
Record 2000 - 1st:1 2nd:5 3rd:0 Ran:9
Win Prizemoney £3,250 *Total Prizemoney* £16,249
Wins * 2000 Spt Goodwo (HVY) 8f 79 <
2000 Turf 1-9: (7f 4, 8f 1-5) (g-s 2, gd 1-2, g-f 3, frm 2)
Useful colt, effective 7 to 8f, best at 8f, acts on g-s to frm. Turf high 89 (began Jly) - 2nd of 15 getting 3lb from Snowstorm (7 Spt Doncaster 8f frm RF 4283). Consistent. Ran well in nurseries before taking his maiden. Seems to handle both fast and soft ground. **R Hannon [1-9] John Michael.*

NORTHGATE (IRE) BHB 46f40a **RR 49f 40a** 5166[19]
4 b c Thatching 7.8f **(69)** - Tender Time (Tender King) 6.8f **(54)**
Form - 85421420060
Record 2000 - 1st:1 2nd:2 3rd:0 Ran:11
Pre2000 - 1st:0 2nd:1 3rd:0 Ran:14
Win Prizemoney £3,818 *Total Prizemoney* £7,705
Wins * 2000 Jun Beverl (G-F) H 7.5f 46 48 <
2000 Turf 1-10: (7f 1-5, 8f 5) (g-s, gd 2, g-f 2, frm 1-4, hrd) 2000 AW 0-1: (7f) (Fibr)
Leggy, moderate colt, effective 7 to 8f, best at 7f, acts on g-s to frm, best on frm, mostly wears blinkers (extremely effectively), prefers tight tracks. Turf high 49 - also 1st of 16 getting 21lb from Kass Alhawa (27 Jun Beverley RF 2297). Becoming disappointing.
**M Brittain [1-25] Mel Brittain.*

NORTH OF KALA (IRE) BHB 40f32a **RR 44f 32a** 4306[10]
7 b g Distinctly North (USA) 7.4f **(63)** - Hi Kala (Kampala) 8.4f **(56)**
Form - 13380
Record 2000 - 1st:1 2nd:0 3rd:2 Ran:5
Pre2000 - 1st:0 2nd:0 3rd:0 Ran:10
Win Prizemoney £2,989 *Total Prizemoney* £3,874
Wins * 2000 Jun Salisb (G-F) H 12f 24 42 <
2000 Turf 1-5: (12f 1-4, 14f) (gd, g-f 1-3, frm)
Moderate gelding, effective 12f, acts on g-f, has worn blinkers. Turf high 44 - 3rd of 10 getting 10lb from Wadi (30 Jun Folkestone 12f g-f RF 2395) - also 1st of 11 getting 20lb from Tommy Carson (13 Jun Salisbury RF 1922).
**G L Moore [4-22] B Lennard (from S J Treacy in IRE [0-15] Jun 1998).*

NORTH POINT (IRE) BHB 79f **RR 69f** 5099[5]
2 b c Definite Article - Friendly Song (Song) 7.2f **(61)**
Form - 805
Record 2000 - 1st:0 2nd:0 3rd:0 Ran:3
2000 Turf 0-3: (7f, 8f 2) (gd 3)
Currently average colt. Turf high 69 (began Spt).

**A P Jarvis [0-3] Ambrose Turnbull.*

NORTON (IRE) BHB 88f **RR 89f** 2412[7]
3 ch c Barathea (IRE) - Primrose Valley (Mill Reef (USA)) 10.5f **(78)**
Form - 837
Record 2000 - 1st:0 2nd:0 3rd:1 Ran:3
Pre2000 - 1st:1 2nd:0 3rd:0 Ran:3
Win Prizemoney £3,452 *Total Prizemoney* £5,193
Wins * 1999 Nov Redcar (G-S) 7f 84+ <
2000 Turf 0-3: (10f 2, 12f) (g-s 2, g-f)
Scopey, useful colt, effective 7 to 12f, acts on g-s to frm. Turf high 89 - 3rd of 8 getting 6lb from Riddlesdown (10 Jun Haydock 12f g-s RF 1874). Finished last in a Derby trial on his reappearance, but ran better in a handicap and there are more races to be won with him at a realistic level. **T G Mills [1-6] T G Mills.*

NO SAM NO **RR 48f** 4554[9]
2 b f Reprimand 8.2f **(63)** - Samjamalifran (Blakeney) 10.5f **(64)**
Form - 0
Record 2000 - 1st:0 2nd:0 3rd:0 Ran:1
2000 Turf 0-1: (6f) (gd)
Currently moderate filly. **J A Osborne [0-1] Mrs Alison Farrant.*

NOSE THE TRADE BHB 72f **RR 80f** 5121[4]
2 b g Cyrano de Bergerac 7.3f **(58)** - Iolite (Forzando) 7.6f **(59)**
Form - 514
Record 2000 - 1st:1 2nd:0 3rd:0 Ran:3
Win Prizemoney £6,097 *Total Prizemoney* £6,623
Wins * **2000** Oct Newmar (SFT) S 7f 80 <
2000 Turf 1-3: (5f, 7f 1-2) (g-s, gd 1-2)
Currently decent gelding. Turf high 80 (began Spt) - 1st of 29 giving 5lb to Je'thame (12 Oct Newmarket RF 4930).
**J A Osborne [1-3] Martyn Booth.*

NOSEY NATIVE BHB 52f38a **RR 47f 38a** 3738[1]
7 b g Cyrano de Bergerac 7.3f **(58)** - Native Flair (Be My Native (USA)) 10.2f **(71)**
Form - 0032262411
Record 2000 - 1st:2 2nd:3 3rd:1 Ran:10
Pre2000 - 1st:5 2nd:3 3rd:6 Ran:55
Win Prizemoney £20,792 *Total Prizemoney* £29,154
Wins * **2000** Aug Catter (G-S) H 12f 44 47
* **2000** Aug Yarmou (GD) H 14.1f 44 47
* 1998 Aug Catter (G-F) H 12f 44 46
* 1998 Jun Ripon (SFT) H 12.3f 40 41
* 1997 Jun Ripon (GD) H 12.3f 61 58
* 1996 Oct Haydoc (SFT) H 10.5f 51 71
2000 Turf 2-8: (11f, 12f 1-4, 14f 1-2, 17f) (sft, g-f 2-4, frm 3) 2000 AW 0-2: (12f, 16f) (Fibr 2)
Moderate gelding, effective 11 to 14f, best at 12f, acts on sft to frm, best on g-f, has worn blinkers, likes left handed tracks, prefers tight tracks, excels at Yarmouth. Turf high 47 - 1st of 9 giving 3lb to Monacle (9 Aug Yarmouth RF 3512) - also 1st of 11 giving 6lb to Lost Spirit (18 Aug Catterick RF 3738). AW high 12. Consistent. **J Pearce [7-65] Jeff Pearce.*

NOSMOKEWITHOUTFIRE **RR 18f** 5196[16]
2 ch f Dancing Spree (USA) 8f **(59)** - Djanila (Fabulous Dancer (USA)) 9.4f **(70)**
Form - 00
Record 2000 - 1st:0 2nd:0 3rd:0 Ran:2
2000 Turf 0-2: (8f 2) (g-s, gd)
Currently poor filly. Turf high 18 (began Oct).
**D J S ffrenchDavis [0-2] Mrs N A Madsen.*

NO SURRENDER BHB 45f39a **RR 50f 39a** 5247[9]
2 ch f Brief Truce (USA) 9.1f **(73)** - Furry Dance (USA) (Nureyev (USA)) 8.7f **(78)**
Form - 60800
Record 2000 - 1st:0 2nd:0 3rd:0 Ran:5
2000 Turf 0-2: (7f, 8f) (gd, frm) 2000 AW 0-3: (5f, 8f 2) (Fibr 3)
Fair filly. Turf high 50. AW high 35 (began Spt).
**D W Chapman [0-3] David Chapman (from T D Easterby [0-2] Spt 2000).*

NOSY BE BHB 73f **RR 68f** 5013[3]
2 b c Cyrano de Bergerac 7.3f **(58)** - Blossomville **(48f)** (Petong) 6.6f **(58)**
Form - 5323
Record 2000 - 1st:0 2nd:1 3rd:2 Ran:4
Win Prizemoney £0 *Total Prizemoney* £1,369
2000 Turf 0-3: (5f, 6f 2) (gd, frm 2) 2000 AW 0-1: (6f) (Fibr)
Average colt. Turf high 68 (began Jly) - 2nd of 16 to Baron Crocodile (22 Spt Lingfield 5f gd RF 4580). (1st run) - 3rd of 9 to Moyne Pleasure (17 Oct Wolverhampton 6f Fibr RF 5013).
**P J Makin [0-4] Ten of Hearts.*

NOTABLE CAREER (USA) **RR** 5326a[5]
2 br f Avenue Of Flags (USA) - Excellent Lady (USA) (Smarten (USA))
Form - 5
2000 AW 0-1: (9f) (Dirt)
Currently useful filly. **B Baffert in USA [0-1] Golden Eagle Farm.*

NOTAGAINTHEN BHB 30f **RR 22f** 3818[11]
4 b f Then Again 7.4f **(52)** - Fairy Ballerina (Fairy King (USA)) 7.7f **(59)**
Form - 00
Record 2000 - 1st:0 2nd:0 3rd:0 Ran:2
Pre2000 - 1st:0 2nd:0 3rd:0 Ran:7
2000 Turf 0-2: (12f, 13f) (g-f, frm)
Lengthy, very moderate filly. Turf high 22 (began Aug). Consistent.
**S G Knight [0-11] J F Jones.*

NOTATION (IRE) BHB 26f22a **RR 32f 22a** 5011[9]
6 b g Arazi (USA) 9.2f **(74)** - Grace Note (FR) (Top Ville) 11.7f **(68)**
Form - 8804000040850114000
Record 2000 - 1st:2 2nd:0 3rd:0 Ran:19
Pre2000 - 1st:2 2nd:2 3rd:2 Ran:31
Win Prizemoney £10,481 *Total Prizemoney* £13,159
Wins * **2000** Aug Beverl (G-F) H 12f 18 28
* **2000** Aug Hamilt (SFT) H 12.1f 18 32
* 1997 *Dec Southw (STD) H 14f 45 51* <
* 1997 *Nov Southw (STD) H 14f 29 43*
2000 Turf 2-10: (9f, 12f 2-3, 13f, 16f 4, 17f) (gd 1-3, g-f, frm 1-5, hrd)
2000 AW 0-9: (11f, 12f 2, 14f 2, 16f 4) (Fibr 9)
Very moderate gelding, effective 11 to 12f, best at 12f, acts on gd to frm - acts on Fibr, has worn blinkers, likes right handed tracks. Turf high 32 - 1st of 8 getting 11lb from Katie Komaite (22 Aug Hamilton RF 3844) - also 1st of 14 getting 20lb from Yes Keemo Sabee (27 Aug Beverley RF 4011). AW high 23 - 4th of 13 getting 13lb from Malwina (21 Feb Southwell 11f Fibr RF 0330).
**D W Chapman [4-50] J M Chapman.*

NOTEWORTHY BHB 22f **RR 46f** 4269[20]
4 br m Saddlers' Hall (IRE) 10.5f **(65)** - Rushing River (USA) (Irish River (FR)) 8.6f **(78)**
Form - 0700000
Record 2000 - 1st:0 2nd:0 3rd:0 Ran:7
Pre2000 - 1st:0 2nd:0 3rd:1 Ran:6
Win Prizemoney £0 *Total Prizemoney* £972
2000 Turf 0-7: (12f 2, 13f, 14f, 16f, 17f 2) (g-s, g-f 2, frm 3, hrd)
Scopey, moderate filly, effective 14f, acts on g-f, has worn blinkers. Turf high 46. Becoming disappointing.
**J Neville [0-7] T Jones (from J Noseda [0-6] Aug 1999).*

NOT FADE AWAY **RR 34f** 5157[17]
2 b c Ezzoud (IRE) - Green Flower (USA) (Fappiano (USA)) 8.7f **(77)**
Form - 0
Record 2000 - 1st:0 2nd:0 3rd:0 Ran:1
2000 Turf 0-1: (8f) (sft)
Currently very moderate colt.
**M Johnston [0-1] Maktoum Al Maktoum.*

NOTHING DAUNTED BHB 96f **RR 97f** 1032a[13]
3 ch c Selkirk (USA) 7.9f **(76)** - Khubza (Green Desert (USA)) 8.6f **(78)**
Form - 30
Record 2000 - 1st:0 2nd:0 3rd:1 Ran:2
Pre2000 - 1st:1 2nd:2 3rd:1 Ran:5
Win Prizemoney £4,440 *Total Prizemoney* £11,016
Wins * 1999 Aug Goodwo (GD) 7f 85 <
2000 Turf 0-2: (6f, 8f) (sft, gd)
Leggy, very useful colt, effective 6 to 8f, best at 6f, acts on gd to g-f, best on gd. Turf high 97 (1st run) - 3rd of 19 giving 6lb to Strahan (20 Apr Newmarket 6f gd RF 0804). He caught the eye when finishing fast to snatch third spot at Newmarket in April, but went miss-

ing after disappointing in the Italian 2000 Guineas later that month. Proven over a mile, he is a useful performer. **E A L Dunlop [1-7].*

NOT JUST A DREAM BHB 58f **RR 59f** 4443[13]
2 b f Mujadil (USA) 7.7f **(70)** - Red Cloud (IRE) **(35df)** (Taufan (USA)) 7f **(57)**
Form - 430460
Record 2000 - 1st:0 2nd:0 3rd:1 Ran:6
Win Prizemoney £0 *Total Prizemoney* £560
2000 Turf 0-6: (5f, 6f 3, 7f 2) (gd 2, frm 4)
Fair filly, effective 5 to 6f, acts on frm. Turf high 59 - 4th of 9 to Berezina (29 Jly Redcar 6f frm RF 3220).
**A Berry [0-6] Norman Jackson.*

NO TOMORROW (IRE) BHB 49f **RR 52f** 4994[12]
3 b f Night Shift (USA) 8.1f **(73)** - Fancy Boots (IRE) (Salt Dome (USA))
Form - 6000
Record 2000 - 1st:0 2nd:0 3rd:0 Ran:4
2000 Turf 0-3: (7f 2, 8f) (gd, frm 2) 2000 AW 0-1: (12f) (Fibr)
Fair filly. Turf high 52. **C R Egerton [0-4] Austin Allison.*

NOUF BHB 72f80a **RR 76f 80a** 4934[20]
4 b f Efisio 7.7f **(69)** - Miss Witch (High Line) 10.3f **(70)**
Form - 08206600512050
Record 2000 - 1st:1 2nd:2 3rd:0 Ran:14
Pre2000 - 1st:1 2nd:0 3rd:0 Ran:3
Win Prizemoney £9,427 *Total Prizemoney* £12,620

Wins								
* **2000**	Spt	Haydoc	(HVY)	H	8.1f	66	76	
* 1999	Mar	Doncas	(G-S)		7f		93++	<

2000 Turf 1-13: (7f 3, 8f 1-6, 9f, 10f 2, 12f) (sft 1-3, gd 6, g-f 3, frm)
2000 AW 0-1: (8f) (Fibr)
Scopey, above-average filly, effective 7f, acts on g-s. Turf high 78.
**K Mahdi [2-17] Solaiman Alsaiary.*

NOUFARI (FR) BHB 70f70a **RR 76f 70a** 2173[1]
9 b g Kahyasi 12.9f **(74)** - Noufiyla (Top Ville) 11.7f **(68)**
Form - 1151211
Record 2000 - 1st:3 2nd:1 3rd:0 Ran:5
Pre2000 - 1st:16 2nd:15 3rd:16 Ran:86
Win Prizemoney £57,000 *Total Prizemoney* £94,907

Wins								
* **2000**	*Jun*	*Wolver*	*(STD)*	*C*	*10.2f*		*56*	
* **2000**	Jun	Redcar	(G-F)	C	16f		46	
* **2000**	*Jan*	*Southw*	*(STD)*	*C*	*16f*		*60*	
* 1999	*Dec*	*Wolver*	*(STD)*	*S*	*14.8f*		*68*	
* 1999	*Nov*	*Wolver*	*(STD)*	*C*	*14.8f*		*65*	
* 1999	Aug	Thirsk	(G-F)	H	16f	70	75	
* 1999	Aug	Nottin	(G-F)	H	16f	64	69	
* 1998	*Dec*	*Wolver*	*(STD)*	*S*	*14.8f*		*51+*	
* 1998	Aug	Newcas	(GD)	H	16.1f	64	67	
* 1998	*Apr*	*Wolver*	*(STD)*	*H*	*14.8f*	*78*	*82*	<
* 1998	*Mar*	*Wolver*	*(STD)*	*H*	*14.8f*	*74*	*69*	
* 1998	*Feb*	*Southw*	*(STD)*	*H*	*16f*	*70*	*74*	
* 1998	*Jan*	*Southw*	*(STD)*	*H*	*16f*	*60*	*66*	
* 1997	Jly	Ayr	(G-F)		13.1f		74	

2000 Turf 1-1: (16f 1-1) (frm 1-1) 2000 AW 2-4: (16f 2-4) (Fibr 2-4)
Above-average gelding, effective 15 to 16f, - acts on Fibr, favours left handed tracks, favours tight tracks, likes Wolverhampton. (1st run). AW high 72. A useful stayer on turf, and an especially successful one on Fibresand, he is getting on a bit now but wins more than his share of staying events at a modest level.
**R Hollinshead [19-91] Ed Weetman.*

NOUKARI (IRE) BHB 75f76a **RR 78f 76a** 2835[5]
7 b g Darshaan 11.9f **(81)** - Noufiyla (Top Ville) 11.7f **(68)**
Form - 3111427544532140102005
Record 2000 - 1st:2 2nd:3 3rd:1 Ran:17
Pre2000 - 1st:11 2nd:10 3rd:9 Ran:51
Win Prizemoney £43,751 *Total Prizemoney* £62,631

Wins							
* **2000**	May	Cheste	(GD)	H	10.3f	74	78
* **2000**	Mar	Catter	(GD)	H	13.8f	70	75
* 1999	*Dec*	*Lingfi*	*(STD)*	*H*	*12f*	*77*	*79* <
* 1999	*Nov*	*Lingfi*	*(STD)*	*H*	*12f*	*67*	*76*
* 1999	*Nov*	*Lingfi*	*(STD)*	*H*	*12f*	*68*	*72*
* 1999	*Oct*	*Lingfi*	*(STD)*		*12f*		*69*
* 1999	Aug	Pontef	(GD)		12f		69
* 1999	Aug	Catter	(G-F)	H	12f	62	68
* 1999	Jly	Newmar	(G-F)	H	10f	57	63
* 1999	Jun	Cheste	(G-F)	C	10.3f		45
* 1999	*Jan*	*Lingfi*	*(STD)*	*H*	*13f*	*62*	*66*
* 1998	*Dec*	*Lingfi*	*(STD)*	*H*	*13f*	*58*	*63*
* 1998	*Nov*	*Southw*	*(STD)*	*H*	*12f*	*53*	*61*

2000 Turf 2-10: (10f 1-4, 12f 5, 14f 1-1) (hvy, gd, g-f 1-5, frm 1-3) 2000 AW 0-7: (11f, 12f 5, 16f) (Equi 5, Fibr 2)
Above-average gelding, effective 10 to 14f, best at 12f, acts on gd to frm - acts on Equi, likes left handed tracks, excels at Catterick and Chester, does well at Lingfield. Turf high 78 - 1st of 13 getting 14lb from Yarob (9 May Chester RF 1112) - also 1st of 15 giving 13lb to Prince Nicholas (29 Mar Catterick RF 0546). AW high 80 (1st run) - 2nd of 9 giving 5lb to Space Race (2 Jan Lingfield 12f Equi RF 0006).
**P D Evans [17-76] J E Abbey (from J Oxx in IRE [0-3] May 1997).*

NOVELLINI STAR RR 35f 2421[8]
3 ch g My Generation 6.5f **(68)** - Ramas Silk (Amber Rama (USA)) 10.2f **(45)**
Form - 78
Record 2000 - 1st:0 2nd:0 3rd:0 Ran:2
2000 Turf 0-1: (12f) (frm) 2000 AW 0-1: (12f) (Equi)
Workmanlike, currently very moderate gelding.
**N M Babbage [0-2] Provex Products Ltd.*

NOVELTY BHB 25f **RR 23f** 2796[3]
5 b m Primo Dominie 7.2f **(67)** - Nophe (USA) (Super Concorde (USA)) 10.9f **(66)**
Form - 003
Record 2000 - 1st:0 2nd:0 3rd:1 Ran:3
Pre2000 - 1st:0 2nd:0 3rd:0 Ran:4
Win Prizemoney £0 *Total Prizemoney* £628
2000 Turf 0-3: (7f 2, 8f) (gd, g-f, frm)
Little account filly. Turf high 13.
**N P Littmoden [0-2] Mrs H F Mahr (from Miss J F Craze [0-1] Apr 2000).*

NOVERRE (USA) RR 112f 5330a[11]
2 b c Rahy (USA) 9.1f **(80)** - Danseur Fabuleux (USA) (Northern Dancer) 9.6f **(80)**
Form - 13120
2000 Turf 2-4: (6f 1-2, 7f 1-2) (g-s, gd 1-2, g-f 1-1) 2000 AW 0-1: (9f) (Dirt)
Group-class colt. Turf high 112 (began Jly) - 2nd of 10 to Tobougg (14 Oct Newmarket 7f gd RF 4988) - also 1st of 8 from Cd Europe (8 Spt Doncaster RF 4296). Won his first two starts in France before gaining a battling victory in the July Stakes at Newmarket. Only third in a Deauville Group One, he bounced back by winning Doncaster's Champagne Stakes, getting the seventh furlong well. Unsurprisingly found wanting in the Breeders' Cup Juvenile, he has the scope to do well as a three-year-old.
**D R Loder in FR [2-5] Godolphin.*

NOWELL HOUSE BHB 78f **RR 79f** 5323[4]
4 ch g Polar Falcon (USA) 9f **(74)** - Langtry Lady (Pas de Seul) 9.1f **(67)**
Form - 080071104
Record 2000 - 1st:2 2nd:0 3rd:0 Ran:9
Pre2000 - 1st:3 2nd:1 3rd:3 Ran:15
Win Prizemoney £20,201 *Total Prizemoney* £24,379

Wins								
* **2000**	Spt	Redcar	(SFT)	H	10f	72	77	<
* **2000**	Spt	Catter	(SFT)	H	12f	60	71	
* 1999	Oct	Redcar	(GD)	H	10f	60	63	
* 1999	Oct	Pontef	(SFT)	H	12f	60	64+	
* 1999	Spt	Beverl	(GD)	H	12f	51	55	

2000 Turf 2-9: (9f 2, 10f 1-3, 12f 1-3, 14f) (sft 3, g-s 1-1, gd 1-3, g-f 2)
Light-framed, above-average gelding, effective 10 to 12f, best at 12f, acts on sft to gd, prefers left handed tracks, likes tight tracks, excels at Redcar. Turf high 79 - 4th of 20 getting 2lb from Batswing (4 Nov Doncaster 12f sft RF 5323) - also 1st of 15 getting 7lb from Kathryn's Pet (30 Spt Redcar RF 4749). Inconsistent. A winner three times in the autumn of 1999, having taken a big step-up in distance, he may be a back-end type and bolted up at Catterick in September. Followed up with a battling victory at Redcar even though the ten-furlong trip looked inadequate, but disappointed at York. **M W Easterby [5-24] Bernard Bargh & John Walsh.*

NOWHERE TO EXIT BHB 116f **RR 119f** 3789[5]
4 b c Exit To Nowhere (USA) 8.7f **(77)** - Tromond **(92f)** (Lomond (USA)) 8.8f **(65)**

Form - 5
Record 2000 - 1st:0 2nd:0 3rd:0 Ran:1
Pre2000 - 1st:4 2nd:2 3rd:0 Ran:8
Win Prizemoney £48,518 *Total Prizemoney* £157,690
Wins 1999 May Longch (HVY) G3 12f 108 <
1999 Apr Chanti (SFT) L 12f 90
1999 Apr Haydoc (SFT) H 10.5f 91 96
1998 Oct Bright (G-S) 8f 83
2000 Turf 0-1: (13f) (frm)
Light-framed, high-class colt, effective 12f, acts on gd. Inconsistent. Runner-up in the French Derby at three, he was well held on his only start for Godolphin in 2000.
**S bin Suroor [0-1] Godolphin (from J L Dunlop [4-8] Aug 1999).*

NOW IS THE HOUR BHB 35f46a RR 34f 46a 4366[6]

4 ch g Timeless Times (USA) 6.1f **(56)** - Macs Maharanee **(71f 70a)** (Indian King (USA)) 7.4f **(64)**
Form - 662073656
Record 2000 - 1st:0 2nd:1 3rd:1 Ran:9
Pre2000 - 1st:0 2nd:0 3rd:0 Ran:13
Win Prizemoney £0 *Total Prizemoney* £1,322
2000 Turf 0-4: (5f 3, 6f)(g-f 2, frm 2) 2000 AW 0-5: (5f 2, 6f 2, 7f)(Fibr 5)
Neat, moderate gelding, effective 5f, - acts on Fibr, has worn blinkers, likes left handed tracks, likes tight tracks. Turf high 34. AW high 43 - 2nd of 13 to Samwar (11 May Wolverhampton 5f Fibr RF 1150). **P S Felgate [0-22] John Martin.*

NOW LOOK HERE BHB 93f RR 105f 5324[4]

4 b g Reprimand 8.2f **(63)** - Where's Carol (Anfield) 8.5f **(59)**
Form - 23334502705024
Record 2000 - 1st:0 2nd:3 3rd:3 Ran:14
Pre2000 - 1st:1 2nd:0 3rd:5 Ran:13
Win Prizemoney £3,598 *Total Prizemoney* £36,718
Wins * 1999 Apr Haydoc (SFT) 7.1f 83 <
2000 Turf 0-14: (5f 3, 6f 8, 7f 3) (sft, g-s 4, gd 6, g-f, frm, hrd)
Pattern-class gelding, effective 5 to 7f, best at 6f, acts on g-s to gd, best on gd, has worn blinkers, excels at Haydock. Turf high 105 (1st run) - 2nd of 14 to Andreyev (25 Mar Doncaster 6f gd RF 0495). Ran a number of good races in decent company without getting his head in front. He stays seven furlongs, but is probably better over shorter. **B A McMahon [1-27] S L Edwards.*

NOWT BUT TROUBLE (IRE) BHB 60f RR 65f 4313[21]

2 ch g Midhish - Shinadeosee (IRE) (Adonijah) 10f **(61)**
Form - 63500
Record 2000 - 1st:0 2nd:0 3rd:1 Ran:5
Win Prizemoney £0 *Total Prizemoney* £404
2000 Turf 0-5: (5f 3, 6f, 7f) (gd, frm 4)
Average gelding. Turf high 65 - 3rd of 14 giving 5lb to Franica (22 May Musselburgh 5f frm RF 1365). **D Nicholls [0-5] Neil Smith.*

NOWT FLASH (IRE) BHB 48f50a RR 64f 50a 5007[14]

3 ch g Petardia 8.2f **(58)** - Mantlepiece (IRE) (Common Grounds)
Form - 2018761752250040400
Record 2000 - 1st:2 2nd:2 3rd:0 Ran:18
Pre2000 - 1st:0 2nd:1 3rd:0 Ran:6
Win Prizemoney £3,936 *Total Prizemoney* £7,107
Wins *** 2000** *Feb Southw (STD) S 7f 66*
*** 2000** *Jan Southw (STD) C 6f 68* <
2000 Turf 0-10: (6f, 7f 5, 8f 4) (g-s 4, gd 3, g-f, frm 2) 2000 AW 2-8: (6f 1-4, 7f 1-2, 8f, 12f) (Fibr 2-8)
Average gelding, effective 6 to 8f, acts on gd - acts on Fibr, has worn blinkers. Turf high 64 - 2nd of 16 getting 16lb from Sovereign State (20 May Thirsk 8f gd RF 1350). AW high 68 - 1st of 11 getting 7lb from Sirene (10 Jan Southwell RF 0061) - also 1st of 7 giving 12lb to Dulzie (25 Feb Southwell RF 0359).
**B S Rothwell [2-24] B Valentine.*

NUBILE BHB 27f28a RR 37f 28a 3497[10]

6 b m Pursuit of Love 9.5f **(69)** - Trojan Lady (USA) (Irish River (FR)) 8.6f **(78)**
Form - 76002550
Record 2000 - 1st:0 2nd:1 3rd:0 Ran:7
Pre2000 - 1st:2 2nd:0 3rd:1 Ran:20
Win Prizemoney £4,546 *Total Prizemoney* £6,085
Wins ***** 1999 *Jly Southw (STD) H 12f 25 31*
1997 *Jly Windso (G-F) S 11.6f 46* <
2000 Turf 0-4: (14f 2, 16f 2) (gd 2, g-f 2) 2000 AW 0-3: (12f, 14f, 16f) (Fibr 3)
Very moderate mare, effective 12 to 16f, acts on gd to g-f - acts on Fibr, has worn blinkers, favours left handed tracks, favours tight tracks. Turf high 37 (1st run) - 2nd of 15 getting 19lb from Zincalo (12 Jun Nottingham 14f gd RF 1896). AW high 2. Inconsistent.
**W J Musson [1-29] Broughton Bloodstock (from B W Hills [1-5] Jly 1997).*

NUCLEAR DEBATE (USA) BHB 98f RR 123+f 3935[1]

5 b g Geiger Counter (USA) 7.8f **(85)** - I'm An Issue (USA) (Cox's Ridge (USA)) 8f **(68)**
Form - 0111
2000 Turf 3-3: (5f 3-3) (gd 3-3)
Very high-class gelding, effective 5f, acts on hvy to gd, best on gd. Turf high 123 - 1st of 13 from Bertolini (24 Aug York RF 3935) - also 1st of 23 getting 3lb from Agnes World (20 Jun Ascot RF 2110). A useful sprint handicapper when trained by Lynda Ramsden, he showed his wellbeing with a game victory in a Group Two at Chantilly in June before beating Agnes World in the King's Stand at Ascot. Particularly impressive when winning the Nunthorpe to complete the hat trick, he looked the best sprinter around last summer. A stiff five furlongs clearly suits him.
**J E Hammond in FR [5-9] J R Chester (from Mrs J R Ramsden [2-15] Spt 1998).*

NUGGET (IRE) RR 52f 5019[5]

2 b g Goldmark (USA) - Folly Vision (IRE) (Vision (USA)) 9f **(64)**
Form - 05
Record 2000 - 1st:0 2nd:0 3rd:0 Ran:2
2000 Turf 0-1: (7f) (g-f) 2000 AW 0-1: (7f) (Fibr)
Currently average gelding. **P Mitchell [0-2] Christopher Ransom.*

NUMERATE RR 70+f 5121[12]

2 b f Bishop of Cashel - Half a Dozen (USA) (Saratoga Six (USA)) 7f **(73)**
Form - 3100
Record 2000 - 1st:1 2nd:0 3rd:1 Ran:4
Win Prizemoney £2,990 *Total Prizemoney* £3,366
Wins * 2000 May Redcar (G-S) 6f 70+ <
2000 Turf 1-4: (6f 1-2, 7f 2) (g-s, gd, g-f 1-2)
Above-average filly. Turf high 70 - 1st of 14 from Classy Act (30 May Redcar RF 1547). **M L W Bell [1-4] Cheveley Park Stud.*

NUNKIE GIRL (IRE) BHB 38f RR 51f 4100[3]

3 ch f Thatching 7.8f **(69)** - Ecco Mi (IRE) (Priolo (USA))
Form - 086083
Record 2000 - 1st:0 2nd:0 3rd:1 Ran:6
Win Prizemoney £0 *Total Prizemoney* £354
2000 Turf 0-6: (7f 2, 8f 2, 9f, 10f) (sft, g-s 2, frm 3)
Scopey, fair filly, often wears blinkers. Turf high 59.
**R Hannon [0-6] Royce Communications Ltd.*

NUN LEFT (IRE) BHB 79f RR 76f 4642[14]

2 b f Bishop of Cashel - Salsita (Salse (USA)) 7.5f **(66)**
Form - 3242120
Record 2000 - 1st:1 2nd:3 3rd:1 Ran:7
Win Prizemoney £2,446 *Total Prizemoney* £7,753
Wins * 2000 Aug Warwic (GD) 7.1f 75 <
2000 Turf 1-7: (5f, 6f 2, 7f 1-4) (gd 1-1, g-f 3, frm 2, hrd)
Above-average filly, effective 6 to 7f, best at 7f, acts on gd to hrd. Turf high 76 - 2nd of 10 getting 1lb from Lapwing (11 Spt Warwick 7f g-f RF 4325) - also 1st of 12 giving 5lb to Looking For Love (28 Aug Warwick RF 4055). Consistent, her only victory so far came in a Warwick maiden, but she has run well otherwise and should continue to make her mark in nursery company.
**R M Beckett [1-7] The Millennium Madness Partnership.*

NUTMEG (IRE) BHB 37f RR 56f 5229[9]

3 ch f Lake Coniston (IRE) - Overdue Reaction (Be My Guest (USA)) 9.3f **(67)**
Form - 4706600
Record 2000 - 1st:0 2nd:0 3rd:0 Ran:7
Pre2000 - 1st:0 2nd:0 3rd:0 Ran:6
Win Prizemoney £0 *Total Prizemoney* £233
2000 Turf 0-6: (6f, 8f 3, 10f, 12f) (gd 3, g-f 3) 2000 AW 0-1: (12f) (Equi)
Workmanlike, fair filly, effective 7f, acts on g-f. Turf high 57. Becoming disappointing. Disappointing so far in maidens over

sprint distances. **M H Tompkins [0-13] Mystic Meg Ltd.*

NUTS IN MAY (USA) BHB 62f **RR 64df** 1269[17]
3 b f A P Indy (USA) - Regal State (USA) (Affirmed (USA)) 9.3f **(79)**
Form - 0
Record 2000 - 1st:0 2nd:0 3rd:0 Ran:1
Pre2000 - 1st:0 2nd:1 3rd:0 Ran:3
Win Prizemoney £0 *Total Prizemoney* £1,240
2000 Turf 0-1: (8f) (gd)
Scopey, average filly. **J L Dunlop [0-4] Robin Scully.*

NZAME (IRE) RR 64f 4702[11]
2 b c Darshaan 11.0f **(81)** -Dawnsio (IRE)(Tate Gallery (USA)) 7.4f **(67)**
Form - 50
Record 2000 - 1st:0 2nd:0 3rd:0 Ran:2
Win Prizemoney £0 *Total Prizemoney* £273
2000 Turf 0-2: (7f 2) (g-f 2)
Currently average colt. Turf high 64 (began Spt).
**J L Dunlop [0-2] Lady Clague.*

OAKWELL ACE BHB 38f36a **RR 49f 36a** 3313[5]
4 b f Clantime 6.6f **(57)** - Fardella (ITY) (Molvedo)
Form - 0580525045
Record 2000 - 1st:0 2nd:1 3rd:0 Ran:9
Pre2000 - 1st:1 2nd:0 3rd:1 Ran:10
Win Prizemoney £2,521 *Total Prizemoney* £0,902
Wins * 1999 Jun Warwic (HVY) C 6.8f 59 <
2000 Turf 0-9: (6f, 7f 4, 8f 4) (sft, g-s, gd 3, g-f 2, frm 2)
Neat, moderate filly, effective 7f, acts on g-s, has worn blinkers, likes left handed tracks. Turf high 49. **J A Glover [1-19] J A Bower.*

OARE KITE BHB 46f38a **RR 48f 38a** 4457[5]
5 b m Batshoof 9.5f **(66)** - Portvasco (Sharpo) 7.7f **(59)**
Form - 6354246320100075
Record 2000 - 1st:1 2nd:2 3rd:2 Ran:15
Pre2000 - 1st:2 2nd:3 3rd:3 Ran:30
Win Prizemoney £7,920 *Total Prizemoney* £13,609
Wins * 2000 Jun Leices (G-F) H 6f 46 48
1999 Aug Leices (G-F) S 7f 48
1998 Oct Leices (G-S) 7f 62 <
2000 Turf 1-7: (6f 1-4, 7f 3) (g-s, gd 2, frm 3, hrd 1-1) 2000 AW 0-8: (6f, 7f 3, 8f 4) (Fibr 8)
Moderate filly, effective 6 to 8f, best at 7f, acts on frm to hrd - acts on Fibr, best on frm, mostly wears blinkers (effectively). Turf high 48 - 1st of 13 getting 13lb from Santiburi Girl (18 Jun Leicester RF 2077). AW high 43 - 2nd of 8 getting 32lb from My Tess (25 Feb Southwell 7f Fibr RF 0358).
**P S Felgate [1-15] Foreneish Racing (from G L Moore [2-19] Dec 1999).*

OARE PINTAIL BHB 57f **RR 59f** 4320[12]
3 b f Distant Relative 7f **(69)** - Oare Sparrow **(71f 61a)** (Night Shift (USA)) 7.2f **(69)**
Form - 0040
Record 2000 - 1st:0 2nd:0 3rd:0 Ran:4
Pre2000 - 1st:0 2nd:0 3rd:0 Ran:4
Win Prizemoney £0 *Total Prizemoney* £217
2000 Turf 0-4: (5f 2, 6f, 8f) (gd 2, frm 2)
Scopey, fair filly, effective 5f, acts on frm. Turf high 59 - 4th of 17 giving 9lb to American Cousin (31 Aug Salisbury 5f frm RF 4124).
**R M Beckett [0-2] Geoffrey Pooley (from R Charlton [0-2] Jun 2000).*

OBSERVATORY (USA) BHB 127f **RR 128f** 4596[1]
3 ch c Distant View (USA) - Stellaria (USA) (Roberto (USA)) 10f **(76)**
Form - 21121
Record 2000 - 1st:3 2nd:2 3rd:0 Ran:5
Pre2000 - 1st:2 2nd:0 3rd:0 Ran:3
Win Prizemoney £282,419 *Total Prizemoney* £308,148
Wins * 2000 Spt Ascot (G-S) G1 8f 128 <
*** 2000** Aug Goodwo (GD) G3 7f 119
*** 2000** Jun Ascot (G-F) G3 7f 115
* 1999 Oct Yarmou (G-F) 6f 91
* 1999 Jun Yarmou (GD) 6f 82++
2000 Turf 3-5: (7f 2-3, 8f 1-2) (gd 2-3, g-f 1-1, frm)
Top-class colt, effective 7 to 8f, best at 8f, acts on gd to g-f, best on gd, excels at Ascot and Goodwood and Yarmouth. Turf high 128 - 1st of 12 from Giant's Causeway (23 Spt Ascot RF 4596) - also 1st of 8 giving 4lb to Three Points (4 Aug Goodwood RF 3362). Improving. Runner-up to Shibboleth on his reappearance, he stepped up on that to win the competitive Jersey Stakes at Royal Ascot. Followed up over seven at Glorious Goodwood and showed he stayed a mile when runner-up to Medicean at the same track. He gained his biggest victory when ending Giant's Causeway's winning run in the Queen Elizabeth II Stakes at Ascot, and while many believed it was a tactical victory, it is more likely that it was just a measure of how fast he was improving.
**J H M Gosden [5-8] K Abdulla.*

OCEAN DRIVE (IRE) BHB 45f **RR 50f** 5294[2]
4 b br g Dolphin Street (FR) - Blonde Goddess (IRE) (Godswalk (USA)) 7.3f **(58)**
Form - U56543422454217052
Record 2000 - 1st:0 2nd:4 3rd:1 Ran:18
Pre2000 - 1st:1 2nd:0 3rd:3 Ran:19
Win Prizemoney £2,621 *Total Prizemoney* £10,739
Wins * 1999 Jun Hamilt (GD) H 12.1f 58 59 <
2000 Turf 0-18: (9f, 10f 3, 11f 5, 12f 5, 13f 4) (hvy, g-s, gd 5, g-f 6, frm 5)
Workmanlike, fair gelding, effective 11 to 13f, best at 12f, acts on gd to frm, best on g-f, favours tight tracks, likes Ayr and Hamilton. Turf high 54 - 2nd of 9 getting 5lb from Captain Brady (16 Aug Hamilton 11f gd RF 3700).
**Miss L A Perratt [1-37] Sutherland Marett Hay.*

OCEAN LINE (IRE) BHB 37f42a **RR 47f 42a** 0761[3]
5 b g Kefaah (USA) 11.2f **(64)** - Tropic Sea (IRE) (Sure Blade (USA)) 11.3f **(67)**
Form - 232274001203
Record 2000 - 1st:1 2nd:4 3rd:2 Ran:12
Pre2000 - 1st:2 2nd:1 3rd:2 Ran:22
Win Prizemoney £6,709 *Total Prizemoney* £12,087
Wins * 2000 *Jly Lingfi (STD) S 10f 38*
* 1999 Aug Bright (G-F) C 10f 50 <
* 1999 Jly Windso (G-F) SH 11.6f 34 39
2000 Turf 0-6: (10f 2, 12f 3, 14f) (g-f 3, frm 3) 2000 AW 1-6: (8f, 9f, 10f 1-1, 12f 3) (Equi 1-2, Fibr 4)
Moderate gelding, effective 8 to 12f, best at 10f, acts on g-f to frm, best on frm, excels at Windsor. Turf high 47 - 2nd of 11 giving 16lb to Titus Bramble (19 Jly Yarmouth 10f g-f RF 2946). AW high 38.
**G M McCourt [3-25] Christopher Shankland (from K Bell [0-2] Apr 1999).*

OCEAN LOVE (IRE) BHB 66f **RR 66f** 4023[3]
2 b f Dolphin Street (FR) - Scuba Diver (Kings Lake (USA)) 10.8f **(67)**
Form - 523
Record 2000 - 1st:0 2nd:1 3rd:1 Ran:3
Win Prizemoney £0 *Total Prizemoney* £1,284
2000 Turf 0-3: (7f 2, 8f) (gd, g-f, frm)
Currently average filly. Turf high 61 (began Jly) - 3rd of 8 getting 7lb from Magic Box (27 Aug Yarmouth 8f gd RF 4023).
**M L W Bell [0-3] J M Ratcliffe.*

OCEAN OF WISDOM (USA) RR 92f 1289a[7]
3 b c Mr Prospector (USA) 8.6f **(88)** - Coup de Folie (USA) (Halo (USA)) 10.6f **(75)**
Form - 7
2000 Turf 0-1: (11f) (gd)
Currently useful colt. **P Bary in FR [1-3].*

OCEAN RAIN (IRE) BHB 66f **RR 70f** 5105[10]
3 ch c Lake Coniston (IRE) - Alicedale (USA) (Trempolino (USA)) 12f **(71)**
Form - 0507473460
Record 2000 - 1st:0 2nd:0 3rd:1 Ran:10
Pre2000 - 1st:1 2nd:1 3rd:0 Ran:5
Win Prizemoney £3,060 *Total Prizemoney* £5,645
Wins 1999 Aug Haydoc (G-S) 6f 76+ <
2000 Turf 0-10: (6f, 7f 5, 8f 3, 9f) (g-s, gd 3, g-f 2, frm 4)
Strong, above-average colt, effective 6 to 9f, best at 6f, acts on gd to frm, best on frm, has worn blinkers, prefers left handed tracks. Turf high 76.
**C G Cox [0-12] Stephen Barrow (from M J Heaton-Ellis [1-3] Aug 1999).*

OCEAN ROAD BHB 69f **RR 76f** 5099[11]
2 ch c Inchinor 8.9f **(64)** - Executive Lady (Night Shift (USA)) 7.2f **(69)**
Form - 860
Record 2000 - 1st:0 2nd:0 3rd:0 Ran:3
2000 Turf 0-3: (7f 3) (gd, g-f 2)
Currently above-average colt. Turf high 76 (began Spt).
**Mrs A J Perrett [0-3] Bernard Keay.*

OCEAN SONG BHB 57a **RR 55f** 3374[12]
3 b f Savahra Sound 7.8f **(55)** - Marina Plata (Julio Mariner) 7.2f **(57)**
Form - 2460037730
Record 2000 - 1st:0 2nd:1 3rd:2 Ran:10
Win Prizemoney £0 *Total Prizemoney* £1,842
2000 Turf 0-7: (7f 3, 8f, 10f 2, 16f) (gd 2, g-f 3, frm 2) 2000 AW 0-3: (7f, 8f, 12f) (Fibr 3)
Unfurnished, fair filly, has worn blinkers. Turf high 56. AW high 51.
**S R Bowring [0-10] Simon Mapletoft.*

OCEAN TIDE RR 77f 4754[15]
3 b g Deploy 11.4f **(67)** - Dancing Tide (Pharly (FR)) 9.8f **(68)**
Form - 480
Record 2000 - 1st:0 2nd:0 3rd:0 Ran:3
2000 Turf 0-3: (10f 2, 12f) (hvy, g-s 2)
Currently above-average gelding. Turf high 77.
**L M Cumani [0-3] Mrs E H Vestey.*

OCEAN VIEW RR 47f 1597[8]
4 ch f Rope Trick - Nashya (Rousillon (USA)) 8.2f **(74)**
Form - 88
Record 2000 - 1st:0 2nd:0 3rd:0 Ran:2
Pre2000 - 1st:0 2nd:0 3rd:0 Ran:1
2000 Turf 0-2: (10f 2) (g-f 2)
Leggy, currently moderate filly. Turf high 28.
**W T Kemp [0-3] Terry Anthony.*

OCHOS RIOS (IRE) BHB 37f33a **RR 28f 33a** 235[6]
9 br g Horage 11.4f **(58)** - Morgiana (Godswalk (USA)) 7.3f **(58)**
Form - 6
Record 2000 - 1st:0 2nd:0 3rd:0 Ran:1
Pre2000 - 1st:6 2nd:5 3rd:9 Ran:74
Win Prizemoney £27,019 *Total Prizemoney* £40,062
Wins * 1998 Jun Thirsk (SFT) H 7f 40 50
* 1998 Jun Beverl (GD) H 7.5f 40 43
* 1996 Spt York (GD) H 7f 56 59
2000 AW 0-1: (7f) (Fibr)
Little account gelding, has worn blinkers.
**B S Rothwell [6-75] J B Young.*

OCKER (IRE) BHB 84f72a **RR 86?f 72a** 4150[3]
6 br g Astronef 7.9f **(59)** - Violet Somers (Will Somers) 5.9f **(59)**
Form - 460800860455003
Record 2000 - 1st:0 2nd:0 3rd:1 Ran:11
Pre2000 - 1st:7 2nd:10 3rd:10 Ran:69
Win Prizemoney £41,752 *Total Prizemoney* £71,510
Wins * 1999 Spt Haydoc (G-F) 6f 92
* 1999 Aug Nottin (G-F) 5.1f 100 <
* 1999 Apr Thirsk (GD) H 5f 80 84
* 1998 Nov Doncas (SFT) H 5f 74 78
* 1998 Aug Newbur (GD) H 5.2f 74 77
* 1998 Jly Haydoc (G-F) H 5f 68 71
1998 Mar Nottin (G-S) H 6.1f 53 76
2000 Turf 0-11: (5f 5, 6f 6) (g-s 2, gd, g-f 5, frm 3)
Useful gelding, effective 5 to 6f, acts on g-f, has worn blinkers. Turf high 85. Becoming disappointing.
**Mrs N Macauley [6-61] J Teasdale (from M H Tompkins [1-19] Apr 1998).*

OCTANE (USA) BHB 70f **RR 72f** 3389[5]
4 b g Cryptoclearance (USA) - Something True (USA) (Sir Ivor) 10.2f **(70)**
Form - 003132721145
Record 2000 - 1st:3 2nd:2 3rd:2 Ran:12
Pre2000 - 1st:0 2nd:0 3rd:0 Ran:5
Win Prizemoney £15,521 *Total Prizemoney* £23,749
Wins * **2000** Jly Sandow (GD) H 10f 59 71 <
* **2000** Jly Haydoc (G-F) H 10.5f 54 57+
* **2000** May Mussel (FRM) H 12f 46 47
2000 Turf 3-12: (8f, 9f, 10f 1-3, 11f 1-1, 12f 1-5, 13f) (g-s, gd 2, g-f 2-4, frm 1-5)
Light-framed, above-average gelding, effective 10 to 12f, best at 10f, acts on gd to g-f, best on g-f, has worn blinkers. Turf high 72 - 5th of 12 getting 10lb from Gralmano (5 Aug Doncaster 10f g-f RF 3389) - also 1st of 15 getting 8lb from Stromsholm (9 Jly Sandown RF 2657).
**W M Brisbourne [3-12] Christopher Chell (from H R A Cecil [0-5] Jly 1999).*

OCTAVIUS CAESAR (USA) BHB 82f **RR 80f** 4461[6]
3 ch c Affirmed (USA) 10.3f **(75)** - Secret Imperatrice (USA) (Secretariat (USA)) 9f **(79)**
Form - 3126
Record 2000 - 1st:1 2nd:1 3rd:1 Ran:4
Pre2000 - 1st:0 2nd:1 3rd:0 Ran:2
Win Prizemoney £5,499 *Total Prizemoney* £8,563
Wins * 2000 Aug Bath (GD) 11.7f 80 <
2000 Turf 1-4: (10f, 12f 1-2, 13f) (gd, g-f 1-2, frm)
Scopey, decent colt, effective 9 to 12f, best at 12f, acts on g-f to frm, best on frm. Turf high 80 (began Aug) - 2nd of 10 giving 3lb to Darariyna (26 Aug Beverley 12f frm RF 3979) - also 1st of 11 giving 5lb to Saluem (20 Aug Bath RF 3817). An impressive winner at Bath in August, he was beaten at odds-on next time. Finished sixth in Newbury's Autumn Cup after going off far too fast.
**P F I Cole [1-6] Sir George Meyrick.*

ODDSANENDS BHB 48f60a **RR 40f 60a** 1316[7]
4 b g Alhijaz 7.7f **(57)** - Jans Contessa (Rabdan) 5.9f **(53)**
Form - 02285100057
Record 2000 - 1st:1 2nd:0 3rd:0 Ran:8
Pre2000 - 1st:1 2nd:2 3rd:1 Ran:10
Win Prizemoney £7,828 *Total Prizemoney* £12,737
Wins * 2000 *Mar Southw (STD) 7f 56*
1998 Aug Ascot (G-F) H 7f 63 73? <
2000 Turf 0-4: (7f 4) (g-s, gd 2, frm) 2000 AW 1-4: (7f 1-4) (Fibr 1-4)
Scopey, average gelding, has worn blinkers. Turf high 40. AW high 56.
**T D Barron [1-8] Harrowgate Bloodstock Ltd (from C N Allen [1-10] Dec 1999).*

ODYN DANCER BHB 28f38a **RR 22f 38a** 4648[12]
3 b f Minshaanshu Amad (USA) 11.3f **(53)** - Themeda (Sure Blade (USA)) 11.3f **(67)**
Form - 7036662067470310
Record 2000 - 1st:1 2nd:1 3rd:1 Ran:13
Pre2000 - 1st:0 2nd:1 3rd:1 Ran:9
Win Prizemoney £1,897 *Total Prizemoney* £3,877
Wins * 2000 *Spt Wolver (STD) SH 12f 35 39* <
2000 Turf 0-2: (12f, 16f) (g-s, g-f) 2000 AW 1-11: (8f, 10f 2, 11f, 12f 1-5, 16f 2) (Equi 4, Fibr 1-7)
Leggy, moderate filly, effective 11f, - acts on Fibr, favours left handed tracks. Turf high 22. AW high 45 - 2nd of 9 getting 16lb from Chief of Justice (18 Feb Southwell 11f Fibr RF 0306).
**M D I Usher [1-22] Kinsmen Racing.*

OFFENBURG BHB 40f **RR 32f** 314[6]
3 b g Petong 7.6f **(58)** - Bold County (Never so Bold) 6.3f **(66)**
Form - 566
Record 2000 - 1st:0 2nd:0 3rd:0 Ran:3
Pre2000 - 1st:0 2nd:0 3rd:0 Ran:4
2000 AW 0-3: (8f, 10f, 12f) (Equi 3)
Scopey, very moderate gelding, has worn blinkers. AW high 37.
**J S Moore [0-7] Chris Bradbury.*

OFF HIRE BHB 52f55a **RR 56f 55a** 5112[16]
4 b g Clantime 6.6f **(57)** - Lady Pennington (Blue Cashmere) 6.4f **(54)**
Form - 7314218674415670
Record 2000 - 1st:3 2nd:1 3rd:0 Ran:14
Pre2000 - 1st:1 2nd:1 3rd:3 Ran:16
Win Prizemoney £10,364 *Total Prizemoney* £12,662
Wins * 2000 Jly Beverl (G-F) H 5f 51 51
* **2000** *Feb Wolver (STD) H 5f 54 58* <
* **2000** *Jan Wolver (STD) C 5f 50*
* 1998 Nov Mussel (SFT) SH 5f 35 48
2000 Turf 1-6: (5f 1-6) (gd 3, g-f, frm, hrd 1-1) 2000 AW 2-8: (5f 2-7, 6f) (Fibr 2-8)
Unfurnished, fair gelding, effective 5 to 6f, best at 5f, acts on gd to

g-f - acts on Fibr, often wears blinkers, and does well at Wolverhampton. Turf high 56 - 5th of 12 getting 9lb from Mousehole (26 Jly Sandown 5f g-f RF 3144). AW high 58 - 1st of 8 getting 13lb from Bedevilled (29 Feb Wolverhampton RF 0383). Consistent. **C Smith [4-30] John Martin-Hoyes.*

OGGI BHB 70f **RR 37f** 2490[14]

9 gr g Efisio 7.7f **(69)** - Dolly Bevan (Another Realm) 6.6f **(55)**
Form - 00
Record 2000 - 1st:0 2nd:0 3rd:0 Ran:2
Pre2000 - 1st:6 2nd:1 3rd:3 Ran:35
Win Prizemoney £27,667 *Total Prizemoney* £38,756

Wins	* 1997	May	Goodwo	(G-S)	H	6f	79	81	<
	* 1997	Apr	Leices	(G-S)	H	6f	72	78	
	* 1996	Oct	Leices	(G-F)	H	6f	65	71	
	* 1996	Spt	Haydoc	(G-F)	H	6f	59	65	

2000 Turf 0-2: (6f 2) (gd, frm)
Very moderate gelding, has worn blinkers. Turf high 37. Becoming disappointing.
**P J Makin [5-34] Mrs P J Makin (from A G Foster [1-3] Apr 1994).*

OGILIA BHB 80f **RR 79f** 4369[2]

3 b f Bin Ajwaad (IRE) - Littlemisstrouble (USA) (My Gallant (USA)) 9f **(71)**
Form - 07461802
Record 2000 - 1st:1 2nd:1 3rd:0 Ran:8
Pre2000 - 1st:1 2nd:1 3rd:3 Ran:7
Win Prizemoney £9,964 *Total Prizemoney* £22,211

Wins	* 2000	Aug	Sandow	(G-F)	H	8.1f	75	77	
	* 1999	Aug	Bath	(HRD)		5.7f		83+	<

2000 Turf 1-8: (7f, 8f 1-6, 9f) (g-s, g-f 5, frm 1-2)
Unfurnished, above-average filly, effective 6 to 8f, best at 6f, acts on gd to frm, best on gd, excels at Sandown. Turf high 79 - 2nd of 12 giving 12lb to Colne Valley Amy (13 Spt Sandown 8f frm RF 4369). Consistent. She landed a Sandown handicap over a mile in August, but gives the impression that a longer trip would suit her even better. **I A Balding [2-15] Exors of the late G M Smart.*

OH JAMILA RR 5066[16]

2 b f Ezzoud (IRE) - True Bird (IRE) **(63f)** (In The Wings)
Form - 0
Record 2000 - 1st:0 2nd:0 3rd:0 Ran:1
2000 Turf 0-1: (8f) (g-s)
Currently very poor filly. **W R Muir [0-1] Wooburn Racing.*

OH NO NOT HIM BHB 30f **RR 8f** 4870[12]

4 b g Reprimand 8.2f **(63)** - Lucky Mill **(23f)** (Midyan (USA)) 6f **(60)**
Form - 0
Record 2000 - 1st:0 2nd:0 3rd:0 Ran:1
Pre2000 - 1st:0 2nd:0 3rd:0 Ran:6
2000 Turf 0-1: (10f) (hvy)
Workmanlike, very poor gelding, has worn blinkers.
**W M Brisbourne [0-1] Mugs Inc (from M Mullineaux [0-3] Spt 1999).*

OH SO DUSTY BHB 87f **RR 87f** 3262[6]

2 b f Piccolo - Dark Eyed Lady (IRE) **(42f 58a)** (Exhibitioner) 8.7f **(61)**
Form - 6104446
Record 2000 - 1st:1 2nd:0 3rd:0 Ran:7
Win Prizemoney £3,776 *Total Prizemoney* £5,063
Wins * 2000 Jun Newbur (G-F) 5.2f 74 <
2000 Turf 1-7: (5f 1-6, 6f) (hvy, gd 2, frm 1-4)
Useful filly, effective 5f, acts on frm, has worn blinkers. Turf high 79 - also 1st of 18 getting 5lb from Zilch (8 Jun Newbury RF 1811).
**B J Meehan [1-7] J S Gutkin.*

OKAWANGO (USA) RR 118+f 4952a[1]

2 b c Kingmambo (USA) 10.9f **(85)** - Krissante (USA) **(96f)** (Kris) 9.5f **(73)**
Form - 11
2000 Turf 2-2: (8f 2-2) (sft 2-2)
Currently high-class colt. Turf high 118 (began Spt) - 1st of 7 from King's County (8 Oct Longchamp RF 4952a). Unbeaten in three races, he took the step up to Group One company in his stride when winning the Gran Criterium. He is bred to be a top-class miler, and is likely to attempt to emulate his sire by winning the Poule d'Essai des Poulains in 2001.
**Mme C Head in FR [2-2] Wertheimer et Frere.*

OK BABE BHB 28f36a **RR 23f 36a** 4396[11]

5 b m Bold Arrangement 8.7f **(57)** - Celtic Bird (Celtic Cone) 9.8f **(43)**
Form - 0800
Record 2000 - 1st:0 2nd:0 3rd:0 Ran:2
Pre2000 - 1st:2 2nd:1 3rd:1 Ran:19
Win Prizemoney £4,786 *Total Prizemoney* £6,144

Wins	1998	*Feb*	*Southw*	*(STD)*	*H*	*6f*	*65*	*73*	<
	1997	*Nov*	*Wolver*	*(STD)*	*S*	*6f*		*67*	

2000 Turf 0-2: (6f, 7f) (g-f, frm)
Little account filly, has worn blinkers. Turf high 13 (began Jly). She improved towards the end of '97, especially when tried on Fibresand.
**G L Moore [0-2] Mrs J Moore (from G P Enright [0-6] Dec 1999).*

OK JOHN (IRE) BHB 12f16a **RR 40df 45a** 202[7]

5 b g Mac's Imp (USA) 5.6f **(54)** - Ching A Ling (Pampapaul) 10.9f **(63)**
Form - 383867
Record 2000 - 1st:0 2nd:0 3rd:0 Ran:3
Pre2000 - 1st:0 2nd:4 3rd:4 Ran:25
Win Prizemoney £0 *Total Prizemoney* £3,803
2000 AW 0-3: (5f, 6f, 7f) (Equi 2, Fibr)
Moderate gelding, effective 5 to 6f, best at 6f, - acts on AW, best on Equi, has worn blinkers, likes left handed tracks, prefers tight tracks. AW high 33. Inconsistent.
**G P Enright [0-6] OK Partnership (from L T Reilly in IRE [0-4] Oct 1999)*

OK TWIGGY RR 30f 5200[7]

3 b f Kylian (USA) 8.1f **(66)** - B B Glen **(52f)** (Hadeer)
Form - 67
Record 2000 - 1st:0 2nd:0 3rd:0 Ran:2
2000 Turf 0-2: (10f 2) (g-s, gd)
Strong, currently very moderate filly. Turf high 30 (began Oct).
**G P Enright [0-2] OK Partnership.*

OLDEN TIMES RR 81+f 2825[4]

2 b c Darshaan 11.9f **(81)** - Garah (Ajdal (USA)) 9.2f **(89)**
Form - 4
Record 2000 - 1st:0 2nd:0 3rd:0 Ran:1
Win Prizemoney £0 *Total Prizemoney* £545
2000 Turf 0-1: (7f) (gd)
Currently decent colt. (1st run) - 4th of 11 to Saratov (14 Jly York 7f gd RF 2825). He did not enjoy the run of the race on his York debut, but nevertheless ran a race full of promise. One to watch out for. **J L Dunlop [0-1] Prince A A Faisal.*

OLD FEATHERS (IRE) BHB 52f **RR 59f** 4119[3]

3 b g Hernando (FR) - Undiscovered (Tap On Wood) 10.3f **(65)**
Form - 0760813
Record 2000 - 1st:1 2nd:0 3rd:1 Ran:7
Pre2000 - 1st:0 2nd:0 3rd:0 Ran:3
Win Prizemoney £2,884 *Total Prizemoney* £3,326
Wins * 2000 Aug Catter (G-S) H 15.8f 46 55 <
2000 Turf 1-7: (7f, 10f, 12f 2, 16f 1-3) (g-s, gd, g-f 1-2, frm 2, hrd)
Scopey, fair gelding. Turf high 59. Inconsistent.
**J G FitzGerald [1-10] Marquesa de Moratalla.*

OLD HUSH WING (IRE) BHB 35f38a **RR 40f 38a** 4777[11]

7 b g Tirol 8.1f **(64)** - Saneena (Kris) 9.5f **(73)**
Form - 56000700
Record 2000 - 1st:0 2nd:0 3rd:0 Ran:8
Pre2000 - 1st:3 2nd:3 3rd:3 Ran:22
Win Prizemoney £8,717 *Total Prizemoney* £11,782

Wins	* 1999	Apr	Pontef	(SFT)	H	17.1f	50	53	<
	* 1999	Mar	Newcas	(G-S)	H	16.1f	43	49	
	1997	Jly	Hamilt	(G-F)	H	13f	40	44	

2000 Turf 0-8: (14f, 16f 5, 17f, 18f) (g-s 2, gd 3, g-f, frm, hrd)
Moderate gelding, effective 16 to 18f, acts on sft to gd, best on gd, has worn blinkers, likes left handed tracks. Turf high 52 (1st run) - 5th of 12 getting 15lb from Royal Expression (24 Mar Doncaster 18f gd RF 0487).
**Mrs M Reveley [4-23] Mark Barrett Racing (from P C Haslam [3-24] Jly 1998).*

OLD IRISH BHB 60f **RR 44f** 1804[13]

7 gr g Old Vic 12.8f **(72)** - Dunoof (Shirley Heights) 10.3f **(74)**

Form - 0
Record 2000 - 1st:0 2nd:0 3rd:0 Ran:1
Pre2000 - 1st:1 2nd:2 3rd:0 Ran:7
Win Prizemoney £3,850 *Total Prizemoney* £7,070
Wins 1996 May Salisb (G-F) H 12f 75 86 <
2000 Turf 0-1: (18f) (gd)
Moderate gelding. Inconsistent.
**O O'Neill [0-1] AAS Contracts Ltd (from L M Cumani [1-7] Jly 1996).*

OLD SCHOOL HOUSE BHB 29f50a **RR 32f 50a** 4112[13]
7 ch g Polar Falcon (USA) 9f **(74)** - Farewell Letter (USA) (Arts And Letters (USA)) 12.7f **(68)**
Form - 050
Record 2000 - 1st:0 2nd:0 3rd:0 Ran:3
Pre2000 - 1st:4 2nd:3 3rd:1 Ran:17
Win Prizemoney £11,102 *Total Prizemoney* £14,131
Wins * 1996 *Aug Lingfi (STD) 16f 73 <*
* 1996 Aug Bath (G-F) H 17.2f 50 56+
* 1996 Aug Doncas (G-F) H 16.5f 50 62
* 1996 *Jun Wolver (STD) H 14.8f 45 56*
2000 Turf 0-3: (10f, 12f, 16f) (gd, g-f, frm)
Very moderate gelding. Turf high 32. Inconsistent.
**T J Naughton [4-16] The New Millennium Partnership (from C N Allen [0-4] Oct 1995).*

OLENKA RR 78+f 2542[1]
2 gr f Grand Lodge (USA) - Sarouel (IRE) (Kendor (FR))
Form - 1
Record 2000 - 1st:1 2nd:0 3rd:0 Ran:1
Win Prizemoney £2,782 *Total Prizemoney* £2,782
Wins * 2000 Jly Catter (G-F) 6f 78+ <
2000 Turf 1-1: (6f 1-1) (frm 1-1)
Currently above-average filly. (1st run) - 1st of 6 from Queen Spain (5 Jly Catterick RF 2542). **J G Given [1-1] Nigel Munton.*

OLIVERS TRAIL RR 37f 5309[14]
2 ch c Catrail (USA) - Carmenoura (IRE) **(6f 20a)** (Carmelite House (USA))
Form - 0
Record 2000 - 1st:0 2nd:0 3rd:0 Ran:1
2000 Turf 0-1: (7f) (g-s)
Currently very moderate colt. **A Smith [0-1] Alfred Smith.*

OLLIE'S CHUCKLE (IRE) BHB 36f42a **RR 35f 42a** 3959[8]
5 b g Mac's Imp (USA) 5.6f **(54)** - Chenya (Beldale Flutter (USA)) 9.7f **(71)**
Form - 6006676038
Record 2000 - 1st:0 2nd:0 3rd:1 Ran:10
Pre2000 - 1st:1 2nd:2 3rd:4 Ran:23
Win Prizemoney £1,881 *Total Prizemoney* £5,890
Wins * 1999 Apr Redcar (G-S) H 9f 55 56 <
2000 Turf 0-10: (7f, 8f 5, 9f 2, 10f 2) (sft, g-s, gd, g-f, frm 6)
Very moderate gelding, effective 8 to 9f, best at 8f, acted on gd, liked right handed tracks, liked tight tracks. Turf high 40. Consistent. (DEAD)
**J J Quinn [1-31] Mrs S Quinn (from J A Glover [0-2] Aug 1997).*

OLLY MAY BHB 24f **RR 22f** 4694[16]
5 b m Silver Owl - Chevitino (Rugantino)
Form - 0000
Record 2000 - 1st:0 2nd:0 3rd:0 Ran:4
2000 Turf 0-4: (7f, 8f, 10f 2) (gd 2, g-f, frm)
Little account filly. Turf high 22.
**R J Hodges [0-4] V R V Partnership.*

OLOROSO RR 25f 5158[7]
3 b g Piccolo - Saunders Lass (Hillandale) 8f **(60)**
Form - 07
Record 2000 - 1st:0 2nd:0 3rd:0 Ran:2
2000 Turf 0-2: (8f, 12f) (sft, g-s)
Workmanlike, currently little account gelding. Turf high 25 (began Oct). **J Neville [0-2] Charles Saunders Ltd.*

OLYMPIC PRIDE (IRE) RR 56f 5136[9]
2 b f Up and At 'em - So Far Away (Robellino (USA)) 7.6f **(80)**
Form - 00
Record 2000 - 1st:0 2nd:0 3rd:0 Ran:2
2000 Turf 0-2: (7f, 8f) (g-s, frm)
Currently fair filly. Turf high 56 (began Spt).
**C N Allen [0-2] Robert McLachlan.*

OLY'S DREAM BHB 49f44a **RR 47f 44a** 5010[11]
2 ch f Whittingham (IRE) - Miss Derby (USA) (Master Derby (USA)) 9.5f **(69)**
Form - 5868870
Record 2000 - 1st:0 2nd:0 3rd:0 Ran:7
2000 Turf 0-6: (5f 4, 6f 2) (sft, gd, g-f 2, frm 2) 2000 AW 0-1: (7f) (Fibr)
Moderate filly. Turf high 61.
**N Tinkler [0-5] W F Burton (from J J O'Neill [0-2] Aug 2000).*

OLY'S GILL (IRE) BHB 35f37a **RR 28f 37a** 5295[5]
2 b f Eagle Eyed (USA) - Jealous One (USA) (Raise A Native) 11.2f **(69)**
Form - 40770775
Record 2000 - 1st:0 2nd:0 3rd:0 Ran:8
Win Prizemoney £0 *Total Prizemoney* £268
2000 Turf 0-4: (5f 3, 7f) (sft, g-s 2, frm) 2000 AW 0-4: (5f, 6f 2, 7f) (Fibr 4)
Moderate filly. Turf high 28. AW high 44.
**A Berry [0-5] A B Parr (from J J O'Neill [0-3] Jun 2000).*

OLY'S WHIT RR 45f 3309[6]
2 ch g Whittingham (IRE) - Nellie O'Dowd (USA) (Diesis) 9.3f **(69)**
Form - 46
Record 2000 - 1st:0 2nd:0 3rd:0 Ran:2
Win Prizemoney £0 *Total Prizemoney* £218
2000 Turf 0-2: (5f, 6f) (g-f 2)
Currently moderate gelding, often wears blinkers. Turf high 45.
**J J O'Neill [0-2] A J Oliver.*

OMAHA CITY (IRE) BHB 98f **RR 100f** 4732[13]
6 b g Night Shift (USA) 8.1f **(73)** - Be Discreet (Junius (USA)) 7.7f **(65)**
Form - 00750352170
Record 2000 - 1st:1 2nd:1 3rd:1 Ran:11
Pre2000 - 1st:4 2nd:3 3rd:6 Ran:44
Win Prizemoney £38,072 *Total Prizemoney* £101,199
Wins * 2000 Spt Goodwo (GD) H 7f 96 100 <
* 1999 Oct York (G-S) H 7f 90 94
* 1999 Jun Goodwo (G-F) H 8f 82 87
* 1997 Aug Goodwo (G-F) H 7f 100 100 <
* 1996 Jun Cheste (G-F) 5.1f 73
2000 Turf 1-11: (7f 1-7, 8f 4) (g-s 2, gd 1-6, g-f, frm 2)
Very useful gelding, effective 7 to 8f, best at 7f, acts on gd, likes right handed tracks, likes tight tracks. Turf high 106 - also 1st of 7 getting 2lb from Muchea (9 Spt Goodwood RF 4314). Consistent. He is very difficult to win with these days, but he is a different horse at Goodwood and has scored there yet again last term.
**B Gubby [5-55] Brian Gubby Ltd.*

OMNIHEAT BHB 70f67a **RR 80f 67a** 5185[3]
3 b f Ezzoud (IRE) - Lady Bequick (Sharpen Up) 8.3f **(67)**
Form - 32316540775043
Record 2000 - 1st:1 2nd:1 3rd:3 Ran:14
Pre2000 - 1st:1 2nd:0 3rd:0 Ran:7
Win Prizemoney £7,419 *Total Prizemoney* £12,532
Wins * 2000 Jun Bright (G-F) H 10f 74 80 <
* 1999 Nov Doncas (SFT) H 7f 66 67
2000 Turf 1-14: (7f 3, 8f 9, 9f, 10f 1-1) (sft, g-s 3, g-f 4, frm 1-6)
Workmanlike, decent filly, effective 7 to 10f, acts on g-s to frm, best on frm, has worn blinkers, likes tight tracks, and excels at Windsor. Turf high 80 - 1st of 11 giving 6lb to Able Native (2 Jun Brighton RF 1651). Scored over ten furlongs at Brighton in June, but has struggled a bit since over shorter trips from a higher mark.
**M J Ryan [2-21] Mrs E Delaney.*

ONCE MORE FOR LUCK (IRE) BHB 61f62a **RR 67f 62a** 4819[17]
9 b g Petorius 8f **(66)** - Mrs Lucky (Royal Match) 11.8f **(54)**
Form - 06031252300
Record 2000 - 1st:1 2nd:2 3rd:2 Ran:11
Pre2000 - 1st:8 2nd:8 3rd:9 Ran:51
Win Prizemoney £31,769 *Total Prizemoney* £55,104
Wins * 2000 Jun Hamilt (G-F) H 13f 60 63
* 1998 Oct Catter (SFT) C 12f 78 <

* 1998 Spt Mussel (GD) H 12f 65 67
* 1998 Spt York (GD) H 10.4f 60 67
* 1997 Oct Ayr (SFT) S 13.1f 53+
* 1996 Oct Redcar (G-F) C 11f 67

2000 Turf 1-11: (10f, 11f, 12f 3, 13f 1-4, 14f 2) (g-s 3, gd 2, g-f 3, frm 1-3)
Average gelding, effective 13 to 15f, best at 14f, acts on g-s to g-f, best on gd, likes tight tracks. Turf high 67 - 2nd of 6 giving 24lb to Papi Special (21 Jly Hamilton 13f g-f RF 2995). Consistent.
**Mrs M Reveley [20-92] The Mary Reveley Racing Club (from M Johnston [0-8] Spt 1994).*

ONCE REMOVED BHB 60f **RR 68f** 4820[20]

2 b f Distant Relative 7f **(69)** - Hakone (IRE) **(72df)** (Alzao (USA)) 7.1f **(68)**
Form - 8447234850
Record 2000 - 1st:0 2nd:1 3rd:1 Ran:10
Win Prizemoney £0 *Total Prizemoney* £2,209
2000 Turf 0-10: (5f 6, 6f 3, 7f) (gd 2, g-f 5, frm, hrd 2)
Average filly, effective 5 to 7f, best at 5f, acts on g-f to hrd, best on hrd. Turf high 68 - 2nd of 17 getting 5lb from Hume's Law (18 Jly Beverley 5f hrd RF 2881). **S Dow [0-10] Mrs A M Upsdell.*

ONE BELOVED BHB 54f **RR 60f** 3067[5]

2 b f Piccolo - Eternal Flame (Primo Dominie) 6.2f **(80)**
Form - 703245
Record 2000 - 1st:0 2nd:1 3rd:1 Ran:6
Win Prizemoney £0 *Total Prizemoney* £1,036
2000 Turf 0-6: (5f 2, 6f 3, 7f) (g-s, gd, g-f 2, frm 2)
Average filly, effective 5f, acts on gd. Turf high 60.
**M R Channon [0-6] Miss Bridget Coyle.*

ONE CHARMER BHB 49f41a **RR 45f 41a** 5010[13]

2 b bl g Charmer 9f **(59)** - One Sharper (Dublin Taxi) 6.4f **(55)**
Form - 00000
Record 2000 - 1st:0 2nd:0 3rd:0 Ran:5
2000 Turf 0-3: (5f 3) (gd, g-f, frm) 2000 AW 0-2: (5f, 7f) (Fibr 2)
Moderate gelding. Turf high 45 (began Aug). AW high 28 (began Spt). **P S McEntee [0-5] N F Tebbutt.*

ONE DINAR (FR) BHB 61f77a **RR 62f 77a** 5242[9]

5 b h Generous (IRE) 11.5f **(82)** - Lypharitissima (FR) (Lightning (FR)) 7.9f **(74)**
Form - 212850360320
Record 2000 - 1st:1 2nd:3 3rd:2 Ran:12
Pre2000 - 1st:1 2nd:2 3rd:1 Ran:20
Win Prizemoney £10,439 *Total Prizemoney* £18,321
Wins * 2000 *Feb Wolver (STD) H 8.5f 64 75* <
* 1999 Spt Lingfi (G-F) 7f 72
2000 Turf 0-7: (7f, 8f 6) (sft, g-s, gd 3, frm 2) 2000 AW 1-5: (8f 1-4, 9f) (Fibr 1-5)
Above-average colt, effective 7 to 9f, best at 8f, acts on frm - acts on Fibr, has worn blinkers, prefers left handed tracks, likes tight tracks. Turf high 62. AW high 79 - 3rd of 13 giving 8lb to Trois (19 Aug Wolverhampton 9f Fibr RF 3808) - also 1st of 11 getting 10lb from Floating Charge (24 Feb Wolverhampton RF 0349).
**K Mahdi [2-30] Mrs T L Lund (from J H M Gosden [0-2] Spt 1997).*

ONE DOMINO BHB 55f **RR 62f** 3066[5]

3 ch g Efisio 7.7f **(69)** - Dom One **(85f)** (Dominion) 8.5f **(63)**
Form - 30832485
Record 2000 - 1st:0 2nd:1 3rd:2 Ran:8
Pre2000 - 1st:0 2nd:0 3rd:1 Ran:5
Win Prizemoney £0 *Total Prizemoney* £3,344
2000 Turf 0-8: (7f, 8f 2, 11f, 12f 3, 16f) (gd 3, g-f 2, frm 3)
Scopey, average gelding, effective 11 to 12f, acts on gd to frm, has worn blinkers (extremely effectively), likes tight tracks. Turf high 64. Consistent.
**M Dods [0-8] Bernard Hathaway (from J Berry [0-5] Spt 1999).*

ONEFOURSEVEN BHB 40f64a **RR 42f 64a** 2264[10]

7 b g Jumbo Hirt (USA) 15.8f **(44)** - Dominance (Dominion) 8.5f **(63)**
Form - 00730
Record 2000 - 1st:0 2nd:0 3rd:1 Ran:5
Pre2000 - 1st:6 2nd:3 3rd:3 Ran:28
Win Prizemoney £22,177 *Total Prizemoney* £40,725
Wins 1997 *Spt Wolver (STD) H 14.8f 57 64*
1997 May Thirsk (GD) H 10f 68 72 <
1997 Mar Doncas (G-F) H 18f 57 65
1996 *Nov Southw (STD) H 16f 52 58*
1996 *Nov Southw (STD) H 14f 45 46*
1996 Spt Catter (G-F) H 15.8f 36 47
2000 Turf 0-2: (16f, 18f) (g-s, frm) 2000 AW 0-3: (16f 3) (Fibr 3)
Moderate gelding, has worn blinkers. Turf high 42. AW high 41.
**D Shaw [0-5] J Roundtree (from J L Eyre [6-20] Jun 1998).*

ONE IN THE EYE BHB 21f31a **RR 41df 31a** 1739[12]

7 br g Arrasas (USA) 14.4f **(37)** - Mingalles (Prince de Galles)
Form - 0
Record 2000 - 1st:0 2nd:0 3rd:0 Ran:1
Pre2000 - 1st:0 2nd:0 3rd:4 Ran:24
Win Prizemoney £0 *Total Prizemoney* £1,672
2000 Turf 0-1: (11f) (gd)
Moderate gelding, has worn blinkers. **J R Poulton [1-38] F Willson.*

ONE LIFE TO LIVE (IRE) BHB 27f43a **RR 27f 43a** 5193[6]

7 gr g Classic Music (USA) 7.2f **(57)** - Fine Flame (Le Prince) 5.8f **(49)**
Form - 056
Record 2000 - 1st:0 2nd:0 3rd:0 Ran:3
Pre2000 - 1st:0 2nd:1 3rd:0 Ran:15
Win Prizemoney £0 *Total Prizemoney* £1,759
2000 Turf 0-2: (13f, 16f) (g-s, gd) 2000 AW 0-1: (14f) (Fibr)
Little account gelding, has worn blinkers. Turf high 27 (began Oct).
**D W Barker [0-5] Mrs S J Barker (from S E Kettlewell [0-5] Jly 1997).*

ONE MIND RR 22f 5223[19]

2 b c Mind Games - Cafe Solo **(38f)** (Nomination) 7f **(60)**
Form - 0
Record 2000 - 1st:0 2nd:0 3rd:0 Ran:1
2000 Turf 0-1: (6f) (gd)
Currently little account colt. **R Hannon [0-1] Mrs D M Wight.*

ONE QUICK LION BHB 64f50a **RR 73f 50a** 3017[8]

4 b c Lion Cavern (USA) 7.5f **(74)** - One Quick Bid (USA) (Commemorate (USA))
Form - 7488
Record 2000 - 1st:0 2nd:0 3rd:0 Ran:4
Pre2000 - 1st:0 2nd:0 3rd:0 Ran:3
Win Prizemoney £0 *Total Prizemoney* £216
2000 AW 0-4: (8f 3, 9f) (Equi, Fibr 3)
Leggy, above-average colt, effective 8f, acts on g-f, likes tight tracks. AW high 52.
**R W Armstrong [0-7] R J Arculli.*

ONES ENOUGH BHB 47f **RR 46f** 4491[15]

4 b g Reprimand 8.2f **(63)** - Sea Fairy (Wollow) 8.2f **(61)**
Form - 000100400
Record 2000 - 1st:1 2nd:0 3rd:0 Ran:9
Pre2000 - 1st:2 2nd:0 3rd:2 Ran:15
Win Prizemoney £8,414 *Total Prizemoney* £9,856
Wins * 2000 Jun Bath (G-F) SH 5.7f 47 46
* 1998 Oct Lingfi (HVY) 5f 88 <
* 1998 Spt Folkes (G-F) 5f 70
2000 Turf 1-9: (6f 1-4, 7f 4, 8f) (sft, gd 2, g-f 2, frm 2, hrd 1-2)
Leggy, moderate gelding, has worn blinkers, likes left handed tracks. Turf high 46. Inconsistent.
**G L Moore [3-24] Heart Of The South Racing (3).*

ONE WON ONE (USA) RR 115f 4549[2]

6 b g Naevus (USA) 7.2f **(86)** - Harvard's Bay (ARG) (Halpern Bay (USA))
Form - 55337D203242
2000 Turf 1-12: (6f 5, 7f 1-5, 8f 2) (g-s 1-5, gd 4, g-f 2)
High-class gelding, effective 6 to 7f, best at 7f, acts on g-s to g-f, best on g-s, has worn blinkers. Turf high 115 - 2nd of 12 giving 18lb to Conormara (2 Jly Curragh 6f gd RF 2529a) - also 1st of 10 giving 5lb to Pulau Tioman (10 Jun Haydock RF 1876). Consistent. He was better than ever last season, but lost his sole victory (a Listed event at Haydock) after testing positive for phenylbutazone and oxyphenbutazone. A mile stretches his stamina to breaking point and easy ground suits.
**Ms J Morgan in IRE [8-42] Heavenly Syndicate.*

ON GUARD RR 71f 5223^{6}
2 b c Sabrehill (USA) 8.5f **(64)** - With Care **(72f)** (Warning)
Form - 6
Record 2000 - 1st:0 2nd:0 3rd:0 Ran:1
2000 Turf 0-1: (6f) (gd)
Currently above-average colt. **W Jarvis [0-1] J M Greetham.*

ONICE NERO RR 109f $5089a^{2}$
4 b c Primo Dominie 7.2f **(67)** - Nord's Lucy (IRE) (Nordico (USA)) 6.5f **(62)**
Form - 362
2000 Turf 0-2: (5f, 8f) (hvy, sft)
Pattern-class colt, effective 7f, acts on g-s. Turf high 99 (began Oct). **B Grizzetti in ITY [2-7] Scuderia Blueberry.*

ONKAPARINGA RR 1650^{6}
2 b f Timeless Times (USA) 6.1f **(56)** - Marfen (Lochnager) 6f **(59)**
Form - 6
Record 2000 - 1st:0 2nd:0 3rd:0 Ran:1
2000 Turf 0-1: (6f) (frm)
Very poor filly. (DEAD) **S Dow [0-1] J & S Kelly.*

ONLY FOR GOLD BHB 57f50a **RR 57f 50a** 5190^{4}
5 b g Presidium 7.5f **(56)** - Calvanne Miss (Martinmas) 7.6f **(59)**
Form - 6662302005614
Record 2000 - 1st:1 2nd:2 3rd:1 Ran:12
Pre2000 - 1st:2 2nd:4 3rd:2 Ran:29
Win Prizemoney £17,494 *Total Prizemoney* £32,043
Wins * 2000 Oct Newcas (HVY) H 7f 51 56
1997 Jun Beverl (G-F) 5f 84 <
1997 May Cheste (SFT) 5.1f 84 <
2000 Turf 1-12: (7f 1-9, 8f 3) (hvy 1-1, gd 4, g-f, frm 6)
Fair gelding, effective 6 to 8f, acts on g-f to frm, has worn blinkers. Turf high 58.
**A Berry [1-12] John Milner & Stephen Milner (from J Berry [2-29] Nov 1999).*

ONLYMAN (USA) RR 98f 1060^{14}
3 ch c Woodman (USA) 9.7f **(77)** - Only Seule (Lyphard (USA)) 9.9f **(72)**
Form - 20
2000 Turf 0-2: (7f, 8f) (gd)
Currently very useful colt. Turf high 98. A half-brother to Occupandiste, he failed to quicken with the winner when runner-up in the Djebel. Unplaced in the 2000 Guineas, he missed the remainder of the season.
**Mme C Head in FR [0-2] Wertheimer et Frere.*

ONLY ONE LEGEND (IRE) BHB 82f **RR 81f** 3995^{2}
2 b g Eagle Eyed (USA) - Afifah **(51f)** (Nashwan (USA))
Form - 0331052
Record 2000 - 1st:1 2nd:1 3rd:2 Ran:7
Win Prizemoney £3,510 *Total Prizemoney* £5,415
Wins * 2000 Jly Doncas (GD) H 5f 72 <
2000 Turf 1-7: (5f 1-5, 6f 2) (hvy, gd, g-f 2, frm 1-3)
Decent gelding, effective 5f, acts on g-f to frm, best on frm. Turf high 81 - 2nd of 10 giving 2lb to Tomthevic (26 Aug Redcar 5f g-f RF 3995) - also 1st of 7 giving 1lb to Fenwicks Pride (12 Jly Doncaster RF 2726). Made all on his nursery debut at Doncaster. Fair efforts since, but does not appear to stay six furlongs.
**T D Easterby [1-7] The Four Ball Partnership.*

ONLYONEUNITED BHB 66f **RR 73df** 1383^{15}
3 b f Pelder (IRE) - Supreme Rose (Frimley Park) 6.5f **(67)**
Form - 00
Record 2000 - 1st:0 2nd:0 3rd:0 Ran:2
Pre2000 - 1st:0 2nd:1 3rd:0 Ran:3
Win Prizemoney £0 *Total Prizemoney* £1,230
2000 Turf 0-2: (5f 2) (sft, g-f)
Lengthy, above-average filly. Turf high 13.
**M Blanshard [0-5] Aykroyd and Sons Ltd.*

ONLYTIME WILL TELL BHB 68f64a **RR 75f 64a** 5224^{6}
2 ch g Efisio 7.7f **(69)** - Prejudice (Young Generation) 7.7f **(63)**
Form - 06
Record 2000 - 1st:0 2nd:0 3rd:0 Ran:2
Win Prizemoney £0 *Total Prizemoney* £147
2000 Turf 0-2: (8f 2) (gd 2)
Currently above-average gelding. Turf high 75 (began Oct).
**C A Dwyer [0-2] Miss Lilo Blum.*

ONLY WHEN PROVOKED (IRE) BHB 25f **RR 36f** 5160^{12}
2 b g General Monash (USA) - Lyzia (IRE) **(64f)** (Lycius (USA))
Form - 07000
Record 2000 - 1st:0 2nd:0 3rd:0 Ran:5
2000 Turf 0-4: (6f 2, 7f, 8f) (sft, gd, g-f, frm) 2000 AW 0-1: (7f) (Fibr)
Very moderate gelding, has worn blinkers. Turf high 36.
**A Streeter [0-5] The Saturday Lunchtime Syndicate.*

ONLY WORDS (USA) BHB 54f **RR 56f** 2730^{6}
3 ch c Shuailaan (USA) - Conversation Piece (USA) (Seeking the Gold (USA))
Form - 6086
Record 2000 - 1st:0 2nd:0 3rd:0 Ran:4
2000 Turf 0-4: (8f 2, 10f 2) (gd, g-f, frm 2)
Workmanlike, fair colt. Turf high 56.
**A C Stewart [0-4] Mrs B Berrick, R Clemons & R Collins.*

ON MY HONOUR RR 44f 4725^{11}
2 b f Pyramus (USA) - Princess Matilda (Habitat) 9.4f **(70)**
Form - 00
Record 2000 - 1st:0 2nd:0 3rd:0 Ran:2
2000 Turf 0-2: (6f, 7f) (g-s, gd)
Currently moderate filly. Turf high 44 (began Spt).
**J C Fox [0-2] The Slaney Partnership.*

ON PORPOISE BHB 44f **RR 41f** 3954^{7}
4 b g Dolphin Street (FR) - Floppie (FR) (Law Society (USA)) 9.9f **(70)**
Form - 080017
Record 2000 - 1st:1 2nd:0 3rd:0 Ran:6
Pre2000 - 1st:0 2nd:0 3rd:0 Ran:3
Win Prizemoney £2,044 *Total Prizemoney* £2,044
Wins * 2000 Aug Yarmou (GD) SH 8f 38 41 <
2000 Turf 1-5: (8f 1-4, 11f) (hvy, g-s, g-f 1-1, frm, hrd) 2000 AW 0-1: (11f) (Fibr)
Moderate gelding. Turf high 41. Inconsistent.
**P W D'Arcy [1-9] & Mrs G M Vergette.*

ON SHADE BHB 40f **RR 47?f** 1851^{6}
3 ch f Polar Falcon (USA) 9f **(74)** - Vagrant Maid (USA) (Honest Pleasure (USA)) 10.4f **(73)**
Form - 006
Record 2000 - 1st:0 2nd:0 3rd:0 Ran:3
Pre2000 - 1st:0 2nd:0 3rd:0 Ran:2
2000 Turf 0-3: (7f, 8f 2) (g-s, gd, g-f)
Workmanlike, moderate filly. Turf high 47.
**N Tinkler [0-5] Philip Grundy.*

ON THE RIDGE (IRE) BHB 106f **RR 108f** 4967^{5}
5 ch h Risk Me (FR) 8f **(53)** - Star Ridge (USA) (Storm Bird (CAN)) 10.3f **(74)**
Form - 25
Record 2000 - 1st:0 2nd:1 3rd:0 Ran:2
Pre2000 - 1st:1 2nd:2 3rd:2 Ran:6
Win Prizemoney £7,440 *Total Prizemoney* £32,052
Wins * 1998 Jun York (G-S) 7.9f 98+ <
2000 Turf 0-2: (8f, 9f) (gd, g-f)
Pattern-class colt. Turf high 105 (1st run) (began Spt) - 2nd of 12 to Hopeful Light (28 Spt Newmarket 8f g-f RF 4698). Obviously unhappy when unplaced on a fast surface at Royal Ascot in 1999, he was off the track for 15 months before going down narrowly in a Newmarket listed event in September.
**H R A Cecil [1-8] Buckram Oak Holdings.*

ON THE TRAIL RR 27f 5112^{17}
3 ch g Catrail (USA) - From The Rooftops (IRE) (Thatching) 8f **(66)**
Form - 0070
Record 2000 - 1st:0 2nd:0 3rd:0 Ran:4
Pre2000 - 1st:0 2nd:0 3rd:0 Ran:2
2000 Turf 0-4: (5f, 6f 3) (gd 2, g-f, frm)
Scopey, very moderate gelding. Turf high 27.
**S Dow [0-6] A N Solomons.*

ON TILL MORNING (IRE) BHB 47f **RR 55f** 4123[11]
4 ch f Never so Bold 7.1f **(62)** - Shamasiya (FR) (Vayrann) 9.7f **(74)**
Form - 00074080
Record 2000 - 1st:0 2nd:0 3rd:0 Ran:8
Pre2000 - 1st:3 2nd:1 3rd:3 Ran:13
Win Prizemoney £9,083 *Total Prizemoney* £12,417
Wins 1999 Jly Ayr (GD) H 7f 65 67 <
1999 Jly Pontef (G-F) 6f 61
1998 Spt Mussel (GD) 5f 66
2000 Turf 0-8: (6f 2, 7f 5, 8f) (sft, g-s, g-f 2, frm 4)
Light-framed, fair filly, effective 6 to 7f, best at 6f, acts on gd to frm, likes tight tracks. Turf high 55.
**M Dods [0-8] D B Stanley (from P Calver [3-13] Spt 1999).*

ON TIME (IRE) BHB 87f **RR 96f** 4548[4]
3 b c Blues Traveller (IRE) - Go Flightline (IRE) (Common Grounds)
Form - 354
Record 2000 - 1st:0 2nd:0 3rd:1 Ran:3
Pre2000 - 1st:2 2nd:0 3rd:1 Ran:3
Win Prizemoney £7,856 *Total Prizemoney* £11,075
Wins * 1999 Spt Goodwo (SFT) 7f 93+ <
* 1999 Aug Warwic (GD) 6.8f 72+
2000 Turf 0-3: (7f, 8f 2) (g-s, gd, frm)
Scopey, very useful colt, effective 7f, acts on sft to gd, best on gd. Turf high 96 (1st run) - 3rd of 3 getting 13lb from Granny's Pet (30 May Leicester 7f gd RF 1544). He held Group entries in the spring, but did not prove up to that class and is difficult to place.
**J R Fanshawe [2-6] Mrs David Russell.*

OOMPH BHB 82f **RR 83f** 5073[6]
2 b f Shareef Dancer (USA) 10.1f **(67)** - Seductress (Known Fact (USA)) 7.4f **(67)**
Form - 4366
Record 2000 - 1st:0 2nd:0 3rd:1 Ran:4
Win Prizemoney £0 *Total Prizemoney* £3,311
2000 Turf 0-4: (6f 3, 7f) (g-s, gd, g-f, frm)
Decent filly. Turf high 83 (began Spt) - 3rd of 9 to Nasmatt (13 Spt Yarmouth 6f frm RF 4377). **W Jarvis [0-4] J M Greetham.*

OPEN ARMS BHB 65f **RR 65f** 4645[16]
4 ch g Most Welcome 8.6f **(66)** - Amber Fizz (USA) (Effervescing (USA)) 8.1f **(79)**
Form - 0771300
Record 2000 - 1st:1 2nd:0 3rd:1 Ran:7
Pre2000 - 1st:0 2nd:1 3rd:2 Ran:7
Win Prizemoney £2,873 *Total Prizemoney* £5,474
Wins *** 2000** Aug Beverl (G-F) H 8.5f 65 65 <
2000 Turf 1-7: (8f 1-4, 9f, 10f 2) (g-s, gd 2, g-f 2, frm 1-2)
Scopey, average gelding, effective 7f, acts on frm, prefers tight tracks. Turf high 65. Inconsistent. Gained a narrow victory in an amateur riders' event at Beverley in August and ran well in a similar race at Goodwood next time. Obviously goes well for an inexperienced rider.
**Mrs A L M King [1-8] Aiden Murphy (from C E Brittain [0-6] Oct 1998).*

OPEN GROUND (IRE) BHB 48f49a **RR 51f 49a** 5002[4]
3 ch g Common Grounds 8.1f **(66)** - Poplina (USA) (Roberto (USA)) 10f **(76)**
Form - 7630816104
Record 2000 - 1st:2 2nd:0 3rd:0 Ran:7
Pre2000 - 1st:0 2nd:0 3rd:1 Ran:4
Win Prizemoney £4,452 *Total Prizemoney* £5,090
Wins **2000** May Yarmou (GD) C 16f 46
2000 Apr Pontef (HVY) S 12f 58 <
2000 Turf 2-6: (10f, 12f 1-1, 15f, 16f 1-2, 18f) (sft 1-1, g-s, gd 2, g-f 1-2)
2000 AW 0-1: (10f) (Equi)
Fair gelding, effective 12f, acts on sft, likes left handed tracks, likes tight tracks. Turf high 58 - 1st of 9 giving 5lb to Dame Fonteyn (17 Apr Pontefract RF 0747).
**Ian Williams [0-2] The Net Partnership (from P Howling [2-8] May 2000).*

OPEN WARFARE (IRE) BHB 77f **RR 64f** 5320[18]
2 b br f General Monash (USA) - Pipe Opener (Prince Sabo) 7.2f **(62)**
Form - 3341353335803010
Record 2000 - 1st:2 2nd:0 3rd:7 Ran:16
Win Prizemoney £6,745 *Total Prizemoney* £11,184
Wins *** 2000** Oct Nottin (SFT) 6.1f 64 <
*** 2000** May Haydoc (GD) 5f 63
2000 Turf 2-16: (5f 1-10, 6f 1-5, 7f) (hvy, sft 1-2, g-s 3, gd 1-3, g-f 2, frm 4, hrd)
Average filly, effective 5f, acts on frm. Turf high 78 - 3rd of 6 getting 2lb from Byo (7 Jly Beverley 5f frm RF 2590).
**M Quinn [2-16] Open Warfare Partners.*

OPERATION ENVY BHB 45f **RR 62f** 3255[14]
2 b c Makbul - Safe Bid (Sure Blade (USA)) 11.3f **(67)**
Form - 46840080
Record 2000 - 1st:0 2nd:0 3rd:0 Ran:8
Win Prizemoney £0 *Total Prizemoney* £211
2000 Turf 0-7: (5f 4, 6f, 7f 2)(gd 2, g-f 2, frm 3) 2000 AW 0-1: (5f) (Equi)
Average colt. Turf high 62. **R M Flower [0-8] M Lickert.*

OPPORTUNE (GER) BHB 48a **RR 32f** 3547[11]
5 br g Shirley Heights 12.1f **(76)** - On The Tiles (Thatch (USA)) 9.8f **(62)**
Form - 50
Record 2000 - 1st:0 2nd:0 3rd:0 Ran:2
Pre2000 - 1st:1 2nd:0 3rd:1 Ran:12
Win Prizemoney £2,425 *Total Prizemoney* £2,740
Wins 1998 May Beverl (GD) S 9.9f 49 <
2000 Turf 0-2: (12f, 14f) (g-f 2)
Very moderate gelding. Turf high 32 (began Aug).
**W M Brisbourne [0-2] The Ox Hill Flyers (from C A Smith [1-7] May 1998).*

OPTIMAITE BHB 85f **RR 103f** 4647[6]
3 b c Komaite (USA) 6.9f **(61)** - Leprechaun Lady (Royal Blend) 11.9f **(58)**
Form - 310505706
Record 2000 - 1st:1 2nd:0 3rd:1 Ran:9
Pre2000 - 1st:2 2nd:1 3rd:0 Ran:8
Win Prizemoney £18,757 *Total Prizemoney* £23,969
Wins *** 2000** May Salisb (GD) 12f 103 <
* 1999 Apr Ascot (GD) 5f 94+
* 1999 Apr Windso (G-F) 5f 81+
2000 Turf 1-9: (10f 2, 11f, 12f 1-4, 13f, 16f) (sft, gd 1-4, g-f 4)
Workmanlike, very useful colt, effective 5 to 12f, acts on gd to g-f, best on gd, prefers right handed tracks. Turf high 103 - 1st of 5 giving 2lb to Riddlesdown (18 May Salisbury RF 1271). He proved more than just an early-season juvenile and scored over a mile and a half in a Salisbury Listed event in May, but continues to find Pattern company too much.
**B R Millman [3-17] Always Hopeful Partnership.*

OPTION (IRE) BHB 42f **RR 45tf** 3900[10]
3 b f Red Ransom (USA) 8.6f **(83)** - Familiar (USA) (Diesis) 9.3f **(69)**
Form - 577500
Record 2000 - 1st:0 2nd:0 3rd:0 Ran:6
2000 Turf 0-6: (8f, 9f, 10f, 12f 3) (gd, g-f 2, frm 3)
Unfurnished, moderate filly, has worn blinkers. Turf high 52.
**J A Osborne [0-6] Old Road Securities Plc.*

ORANGERIE (IRE) RR 65f 2941[7]
2 b c Darshaan 11.9f **(81)** - Fleur D'Oranger (Northfields (USA)) 9f **(72)**
Form - 757
Record 2000 - 1st:0 2nd:0 3rd:0 Ran:3
2000 Turf 0-2: (6f 2) (g-f, frm) 2000 AW 0-1: (7f) (Fibr)
Currently average colt. Turf high 65 (began Jly).
**Sir Mark Prescott [0-3] Sturt Osborne House.*

ORANGETREE COUNTY (IRE) RR 4f 1505[6]
2 b f Dolphin Street (FR) - Empress Kim (Formidable (USA)) 9.2f **(63)**
Form - 6
Record 2000 - 1st:0 2nd:0 3rd:0 Ran:1
2000 Turf 0-1: (6f) (g-s)
Currently very poor filly. **C A Dwyer [0-1] Yusuf Baig.*

ORANGE TREE LAD BHB 62f70a **RR 64f 70a** 3494[11]
2 b g Tragic Role (USA) 9.4f **(63)** - Adorable Cherub (USA) (Halo (USA)) 10.6f **(75)**
Form - 0232770
Record 2000 - 1st:0 2nd:2 3rd:1 Ran:7
Win Prizemoney £0 *Total Prizemoney* £2,282
2000 Turf 0-6: (5f 5, 7f) (gd 3, g-f 2, frm) 2000 AW 0-1: (5f) (Fibr)

Average gelding, effective 5f, acts on gd - acts on Fibr. Turf high 64. (1st run) - 2nd of 9 to Uhoomagoo (15 May Southwell 5f Fibr RF 1205).
**M D Hammond [0-3] Jay Dee Bloodstock Ltd (from A Berry [0-4] May 2000).*

ORANGEVILLE (USA) BHB 78f RR 80+f 2429[3]

3 b br c Dynaformer (USA) 12f **(82)** - Orange Sickle (USA) (Rich Cream (USA))
Form - 43
Record 2000 - 1st:0 2nd:0 3rd:1 Ran:2
Pre2000 - 1st:0 2nd:1 3rd:0 Ran:1
Win Prizemoney £0 *Total Prizemoney* £2,010
2000 Turf 0-2: (9f, 10f) (g-f, frm)
Workmanlike, currently decent colt. Turf high 74.
**J H M Gosden [0-3] Sheikh Mohammed.*

ORANGINO RR 42f 4772[7]

2 b c Primo Dominie 7.2f **(67)** - Sweet Jaffa (Never so Bold) 6.3f **(66)**
Form - 07
Record 2000 - 1st:0 2nd:0 3rd:0 Ran:2
2000 Turf 0-2: (5f 2) (gd 2)
Currently moderate colt. Turf high 42 (began Spt).
**C W Thornton [0-2] Guy Reed.*

ORCHARD RAIDER (IRE) BHB 57f65a RR 61f 65a 3572[9]

2 b c Mujadil (USA) 7.7f **(70)** - Apple Brandy (USA) (Cox's Ridge (USA)) 8f **(68)**
Form - 82412020
Record 2000 - 1st:1 2nd:3 3rd:0 Ran:8
Win Prizemoney £1,834 *Total Prizemoney* £5,375
Wins * 2000 *Jun Southw (STD) S 6f 68+* <
2000 Turf 0-4: (5f, 6f 2, 7f) (sft, gd 2, g-f) 2000 AW 1-4: (5f, 6f 1-2, 7f) (Fibr 1-4)
Average colt, effective 5 to 6f, best at 6f, acts on g-f - acts on Fibr. Turf high 61 - 2nd of 12 giving 5lb to Windchill (30 Jun Newcastle 6f g-f RF 2406). AW high 68 - 1st of 5 getting 1lb from Running For Me (9 Jun Southwell RF 1858). Inconsistent.
**C A Dwyer [1-8] Cedar Lodge 2000 Syndicate.*

ORCHESTRA STALL BHB 117f RR 116f 5212a[8]

8 b g Old Vic 12.8f **(72)** - Blue Brocade (Reform) 8.9f **(62)**
Form - 6118
Record 2000 - 1st:2 2nd:0 3rd:0 Ran:4
Pre2000 - 1st:6 2nd:3 3rd:2 Ran:15
Win Prizemoney £131,468 *Total Prizemoney* £150,952

Wins								
* 2000	Spt	Longch	(G-S)	G3	15.5f		112+	
* 2000	May	Ascot	(G-S)	G3	16.2f		114	
* 1997	Spt	Longch	(GD)	G3	15.5f		116+	<
* 1997	Jun	Currag	(G-S)	G3	14f		107+	
* 1997	Apr	Ascot	(G-F)	G3	16.2f		111	
* 1996	Nov	Newmar	(GD)	LH	16f	89	96+	
* 1996	Aug	Newcas	(GD)	H	16.1f	80	87+	
* 1996	Apr	Ripon	(GD)	H	16f	75	82	

2000 Turf 2-4: (12f, 16f 2-3) (hvy 2, g-s 2-2)
High-class gelding. Turf high 114 - 1st of 9 from Persian Punch (3 May Ascot RF 1000) - also 1st of 5 giving 6lb to Wajina (5 Spt Longchamp RF 4407a). Consistent. Absent since winning three Group races in 1997, he came back in great form last year, putting-up a tremendous effort to short-head Persian Punch in the Sagaro Stakes (his second victory in the race). Not risked on fast ground nowadays, he may stay beyond two miles and could go well in the Ascot Gold Cup granted a wet summer. **J L Dunlop [8-19].*

ORDAINED BHB 39f30a RR 47f 30a 5227[7]

7 b m Mtoto 11.5f **(71)** - In the Habit (USA) (Lyphard (USA)) 9.9f **(72)**
Form - 460423074122680677
Record 2000 - 1st:1 2nd:3 3rd:1 Ran:18
Pre2000 - 1st:3 2nd:7 3rd:5 Ran:44
Win Prizemoney £13,880 *Total Prizemoney* £29,477

Wins								
* 2000	Jly	Pontef	(G-F)	H	12f	38	44	
1997	Oct	Newmar	(G-F)	H	12f	52	60	
1996	Aug	Redcar	(FRM)	H	11f	54	61	<
1996	Jun	Redcar	(G-F)	H	10f	50	54	

2000 Turf 1-13: (11f, 12f 1-9, 14f 2, 15f) (gd 3, g-f 7, frm 1-3) 2000 AW 0-5: (10f, 12f 4) (Equi 5)
Moderate mare, effective 11 to 14f, acts on g-f to frm, best on frm, likes right handed tracks, excels at Brighton. Turf high 47 (1st run) - 2nd of 18 giving 3lb to Evezio Rufo (4 May Brighton 12f frm RF 1015) - also 1st of 10 getting 25lb from Cashmere Lady (21 Jly Pontefract RF 3010). AW high 30.
**Miss Gay Kelleway [1-18] Peter Ebdon Racing (from E J Alston [3-41] Oct 1999).*

OREANA (FR) BHB 95f RR 95f 5319[1]

2 b f Anabaa (USA) - Lavinia Fontana (IRE) **(107f)** (Sharpo) 7.7f **(59)**
Form - 051
Record 2000 - 1st:1 2nd:0 3rd:0 Ran:3
Win Prizemoney £3,347 *Total Prizemoney* £3,347
Wins * 2000 Nov Doncas (HVY) 6f 95 <
2000 Turf 1-3: (6f 1-3) (sft 1-1, g-f, frm)
Currently very useful filly. Turf high 95 (began Spt) - 1st of 21 from Matron (4 Nov Doncaster RF 5319).
**J L Dunlop [1-3] Cyril Humphris.*

OREGON FLIGHT RR 640[8]

2 ch f Hatim (USA) 7.8f **(56)** - Glenrock Dancer (IRE) **(32f)** (Glenstal (USA)) 10.1f **(64)**
Form - 78
Record 2000 - 1st:0 2nd:0 3rd:0 Ran:2
2000 Turf 0-2: (5f 2) (gd 2)
Very poor filly. Turf high 19. (DEAD) **W T Kemp [0-2] Realm (UK).*

ORIEL STAR BHB 39f42a RR 47f 42a 5057[17]

4 b f Safawan 6.6f **(60)** - Silvers Era (Balidar) 7.9f **(63)**
Form - 076300680070580
Record 2000 - 1st:0 2nd:0 3rd:1 Ran:15
Pre2000 - 1st:2 2nd:0 3rd:4 Ran:28
Win Prizemoney £10,043 *Total Prizemoney* £12,753

Wins								
1999	May	Windso	(GD)	H	5f	59	63	
1998	Spt	Ripon	(SFT)		5f		74	<

2000 Turf 0-13: (5f 10, 6f 3) (sft 2, gd 4, g-f 3, frm 4) 2000 AW 0-2: (5f 2) (Equi, Fibr)
Unfurnished, moderate filly, effective 5f, acts on gd, mostly wears blinkers. Turf high 47. AW high 17.
**N Bycroft [0-4] D Maloney (from P D Evans [2-39] Aug 2000).*

ORIENTAL MIST (IRE) BHB 70f RR 73f 5103[11]

2 gr c Balla Cove - Donna Katrina (Kings Lake (USA)) 10.8f **(67)**
Form - 54337446010
Record 2000 - 1st:1 2nd:0 3rd:2 Ran:11
Win Prizemoney £3,672 *Total Prizemoney* £5,435
Wins * 2000 Oct Ayr (HVY) H 8f 68 73 <
2000 Turf 1-11: (5f 2, 6f 3, 7f 2, 8f 1-4) (hvy 1-1, gd 4, g-f 2, frm 4)
Above-average colt, effective 5 to 8f, acts on hvy to frm, best on frm. Turf high 73 - also 1st of 10 giving 8lb to Thorntoun Dancer (10 Oct Ayr RF 4890).
**Miss L A Perratt [1-11] Oriental Mist Partnership.*

ORIENTAL PRIDE (IRE) BHB 45f RR 32f 1908[12]

4 ch g Indian Ridge 7.6f **(74)** - Mercy Bien (IRE) (Be My Guest (USA)) 9.3f **(67)**
Form - 50
Record 2000 - 1st:0 2nd:0 3rd:0 Ran:2
Pre2000 - 1st:0 2nd:0 3rd:0 Ran:5
2000 Turf 0-2: (12f 2) (gd, frm)
Tall, very moderate gelding, has worn blinkers. Turf high 31.
**J Cullinan [0-3] Mrs E Reid (from E A L Dunlop [0-5] May 1999).*

ORIENT EXPRESS (IRE) BHB 60f56a RR 74f 56a 4924[9]

3 b g Blues Traveller (IRE) - Oriental Splendour (Runnett) 7f **(59)**
Form - 070303000
Record 2000 - 1st:0 2nd:0 3rd:2 Ran:9
Win Prizemoney £0 *Total Prizemoney* £894
2000 Turf 0-8: (7f, 8f 4, 9f 2, 10f) (g-s, gd 3, g-f 2, frm 2) 2000 AW 0-1: (8f) (Equi)
Leggy, above-average gelding. Turf high 74.
**B J Meehan [0-9] Miss J Semple.*

ORIENTOR BHB 88f RR 85f 5319[3]

2 b c Inchinor 8.9f **(64)** - Orient (Bay Express) 7.1f **(60)**
Form - 3203
Record 2000 - 1st:0 2nd:1 3rd:2 Ran:4
Win Prizemoney £0 *Total Prizemoney* £3,139
2000 Turf 0-4: (6f 4) (sft, g-s 2, gd)

Useful colt. Turf high 85 (began Spt). **J S Goldie [0-4] S Bruce.*

ORIGINAL SINNER BHB 62f **RR 69f** 5027[7]

2 b g Rudimentary (USA) 8.2f **(66)** - Coryana Dancer (IRE) **(74df 51a)** (Waajib)
Form - 64657
Record 2000 - 1st:0 2nd:0 3rd:0 Ran:5
2000 Turf 0-5: (7f 4, 8f) (g-s, gd, g-f, frm 2)
Average gelding. Turf high 69 (began Jly) - 4th of 11 giving 2lb to Specific Sorceror (22 Jly Warwick 7f g-f RF 3042).
**W J Haggas [0-5] Ali K Al Jafleh and Mrs P Deal.*

ORIGINAL SPIN (IRE) BHB 85f **RR 86f** 5314[10]

3 b f Machiavellian (USA) 9.8f **(83)** - Not Before Time (IRE) (Polish Precedent (USA)) 10.2f **(60)**
Form - 2112200
Record 2000 - 1st:2 2nd:3 3rd:0 Ran:7
Pre2000 - 1st:0 2nd:1 3rd:0 Ran:2
Win Prizemoney £10,026 *Total Prizemoney* £16,821
Wins * 2000 Jun Newcas (FRM) H 12.4f 81 86 <
*** 2000** Jun Leices (G-S) H 10f 77 83
2000 Turf 2-7: (8f, 10f 1-2, 12f 1-3, 13f) (sft, g-s, gd 1-2, g-f, frm 1-2)
Lengthy, useful filly, effective 10 to 12f, best at 12f, acts on gd to frm, best on frm, has worn blinkers, likes tight tracks. Turf high 86 - 2nd of 5 getting 9lb from St Helensfield (22 Jly Ripon 12f g-f RF 3038) - also 1st of 4 giving 10lb to After The Blue (29 Jun Newcastle RF 2369). **J L Dunlop [2-9] R Barnett.*

ORIOLE BHB 41f50a **RR 46f 50a** 5165[12]

7 b g Mazilier (USA) 8.5f **(56)** - Odilese (Mummy's Pet) 7.7f **(60)**
Form - 50000048010
Record 2000 - 1st:1 2nd:0 3rd:0 Ran:10
Pre2000 - 1st:6 2nd:5 3rd:4 Ran:67
Win Prizemoney £21,458 *Total Prizemoney* £30,405
Wins * 2000 Oct Newcas (HVY) H 7f 43 46
* 1998 Aug Redcar (G-F) H 7f 47 49
* 1998 Jun Carlis (G-S) H 6.9f 46 50
* 1997 Aug Redcar (FRM) H 7f 48 52
* 1997 May Redcar (GD) H 8f 33 39
1996 Jly Ayr (G-S) H 7f 46 49
2000 Turf 1-10: (7f 1-6, 8f 4) (hvy 1-1, sft, gd 2, g-f, frm 5)
Moderate gelding, effective 7 to 8f, best at 7f, acts on hvy to frm, has worn blinkers. Turf high 46 - 1st of 14 getting 6lb from Sand Hawk (19 Oct Newcastle RF 5086).
**Don Enrico Incisa [5-50] Don Enrico Incisa (from N Tinkler [2-27] Oct 1996).*

ORLANDO SUNRISE (IRE) BHB 59f **RR 65f** 2374[5]

3 ch f Dolphin Street (FR) - Miss Belgravia (USA) (Smarten (USA))
Form - 06745
Record 2000 - 1st:0 2nd:0 3rd:0 Ran:5
2000 Turf 0-5: (7f, 8f 3, 10f) (g-s, gd, g-f, frm 2)
Unfurnished, average filly. Turf high 65.
**J L Spearing [0-5] Charles Eden.*

ORLANDO SUNSHINE BHB 46f **RR 43f** 3445[6]

3 ch g Beveled (USA) 6.9f **(64)** - Harvest Rose **(51f 47a)** (Bairn (USA)) 7.7f **(59)**
Form - 0776
Record 2000 - 1st:0 2nd:0 3rd:0 Ran:4
Pre2000 - 1st:0 2nd:1 3rd:0 Ran:5
Win Prizemoney £0 *Total Prizemoney* £788
2000 Turf 0-4: (6f 4) (frm 3, hrd)
Moderate gelding, effective 6f, acts on hrd, has worn blinkers, likes left handed tracks. Turf high 43.
**J L Spearing [0-9] Charles Eden.*

ORMELIE (IRE) BHB 91f **RR 96f** 4647[2]

5 b h Jade Hunter (USA) 10.4f **(72)** - Trolley Song (USA) (Caro)
Form - 753302
Record 2000 - 1st:0 2nd:1 3rd:2 Ran:6
Pre2000 - 1st:3 2nd:0 3rd:2 Ran:11
Win Prizemoney £44,357 *Total Prizemoney* £53,803
Wins 1999 Jly Goodwo (G-F) H 9.9f 90 93 <
1998 Aug Newbur (G-F) H 13.3f 83 88
1998 May Ayr (GD) 10f 74
2000 Turf 0-6: (8f, 10f 2, 11f, 12f 2) (gd, g-f 4, frm)
Very useful colt, effective 10 to 12f, acts on gd to frm, best on g-f, has worn blinkers. Turf high 96 (began Jly) - 2nd of 18 giving 2lb to Flossy (26 Spt Newmarket 12f g-f RF 4647). Consistent. A lazy individual, he looked much sharper when fitted with blinkers at Newmarket in September, rallying strongly and only just failing to collar Flossy. Sold to Chris Dwyer for 12,000gns in the autumn, he is capable of winning a decent middle-distance handicap.
**J H M Gosden [0-6] K Doyle (from P W Chapple-Hyam [3-11] Jly 1999).*

ORO STREET (IRE) BHB 72f **RR 69f** 595[6]

4 b g Dolphin Street (FR) - Love Unlimited (Dominion) 8.5f **(63)**
Form - 216
Record 2000 - 1st:1 2nd:1 3rd:0 Ran:3
Pre2000 - 1st:0 2nd:0 3rd:0 Ran:5
Win Prizemoney £2,613 *Total Prizemoney* £4,051
Wins * 2000 *Jan Southw (STD) 12f 61+* <
2000 Turf 0-1: (12f) (sft) 2000 AW 1-2: (12f 1-2) (Fibr 1-2)
Workmanlike, above-average gelding, effective 12f, - acts on Fibr. AW high 72 (1st run) - 2nd of 15 to Wood Pound (10 Jan Southwell 12f Fibr RF 0062).
**D G Bridgwater [2-6] Led Astray Again Partnership (from G C H Chung [0-1] Aug 1999).*

OSCAR PEPPER (USA) BHB 60f85a **RR 58f 85a** 5105[6]

3 b g Brunswick (USA) - Princess Baja (USA) (Conquistador Cielo (USA)) 8.8f **(69)**
Form - 11220373626
Record 2000 - 1st:2 2nd:3 3rd:2 Ran:11
Pre2000 - 1st:0 2nd:0 3rd:0 Ran:5
Win Prizemoney £5,113 *Total Prizemoney* £10,079
Wins * 2000 *Jan Southw (STD) H 6f 53 67+* <
*** 2000** *Jan Southw (STD) H 6f 53 66+*
2000 Turf 0-6: (6f 2, 7f 4) (gd, g-f 3, frm 2) 2000 AW 2-5: (6f 2-3, 7f 2) (Fibr 2-5)
Tall, useful gelding, effective 6 to 7f, best at 7f, - acts on Fibr, has worn blinkers, prefers left handed tracks, prefers tight tracks. Turf high 58 (began Jly). AW high 78 - 2nd of 10 getting 6lb from Hand Chime (2 Spt Wolverhampton 7f Fibr RF 4177).
**T D Barron [2-16] Ian Armitage.*

OSCIETRA BHB 41f **RR 49f** 5077[6]

4 b f Robellino (USA) 9.5f **(68)** - Top Treat (USA) (Topsider (USA)) 8.3f **(71)**
Form - 0555678306
Record 2000 - 1st:0 2nd:0 3rd:1 Ran:10
Pre2000 - 1st:1 2nd:0 3rd:0 Ran:9
Win Prizemoney £2,739 *Total Prizemoney* £3,662
Wins * 1999 Aug Kempto (G-S) H 9f 63 67 <
2000 Turf 0-10: (8f, 9f, 10f 7, 12f) (g-s 2, gd 4, g-f 3, frm)
Workmanlike, moderate filly, effective 8 to 10f, acts on g-s to g-f, has worn blinkers, likes right handed tracks. Turf high 52.
**G B Balding [1-19] Mrs B T Attenborough.*

O'SO NEET BHB 42f **RR 57f** 5219[6]

2 b c Teenoso (USA) 10.5f **(62)** - Unveiled **(54f 48a)** (Sayf El Arab (USA)) 7.1f **(54)**
Form - 7680006
Record 2000 - 1st:0 2nd:0 3rd:0 Ran:7
2000 Turf 0-7: (5f 2, 6f 3, 8f, 10f) (sft 2, gd 4, frm)
Fair colt, has worn blinkers. Turf high 57.
**J C Fox [0-7] Lord Mutton Racing Partnership.*

OSOOD (IRE) BHB 82f **RR 94f** 2755[10]

3 b c Caerleon (USA) 10.9f **(79)** - Ozette (Dancing Brave (USA)) 8.4f **(76)**
Form - 660
Record 2000 - 1st:0 2nd:0 3rd:0 Ran:3
Pre2000 - 1st:2 2nd:0 3rd:0 Ran:3
Win Prizemoney £6,872 *Total Prizemoney* £6,959
Wins * 1999 Oct Redcar (SFT) 7f 94 <
* 1999 Spt Salisb (HVY) 8f 82
2000 Turf 0-3: (10f 2, 12f) (gd, g-f, frm)
Workmanlike, useful colt, effective 7f, acts on gd. Turf high 88. He has put in a couple of fair efforts this term and a mile and a half would seem to be his trip.
**M P Tregoning [2-6] Sheikh Ahmed Al Maktoum.*

OSPREY RIDGE (IRE) RR 98f 5355a[4]
7 b h Polish Patriot (USA) 7.8f **(70)** - Joshua's Daughter 00
Form - 615160702464
2000 Turf 2-11: (8f 2, 9f 1-3, 10f 1-3, 11f 2, 12f) (hvy 1-2, g-s 1-3, gd 4, g-f)
Very useful horse, effective 8 to 10f, acts on g-s to gd, best on g-s, likes right handed tracks. Turf high 98 - also 1st of 10 giving 21lb to Royal Dane (27 May Curragh RF 1578a). Consistent. He won a couple of handicaps in the spring but was found out when tried in Listed and Group company.
**K Prendergast in IRE [7-27] Mrs Anne Coughlan.*

OSTARA (IRE) BHB 64f **RR 64f** 4749[11]
3 b g Petorius 8f **(66)** - Onde de Choc (USA) (L'Enjoleur (CAN)) 8f **(65)**
Form - 038051100
Record 2000 - 1st:2 2nd:0 3rd:1 Ran:9
Pre2000 - 1st:0 2nd:1 3rd:0 Ran:6
Win Prizemoney £6,613 *Total Prizemoney* £8,004
Wins * 2000 Aug Thirsk (GD) H 8f 53 64 <
*** 2000** Aug Haydoc (G-S) C 8.1f 55
2000 Turf 2-9: (6f, 7f 3, 8f 2-3, 10f 2) (gd 1-4, g-f 2, frm 1-3)
Scopey, average gelding, effective 6 to 8f, acts on gd to frm, best on frm, has worn blinkers. Turf high 64 - 1st of 8 giving 5lb to Yenaled (14 Aug Thirsk RF 3626) - also 1st of 15 giving 4lb to Night Diamond (10 Aug Haydock RF 3533). A bit of a character, but has ability too as he showed when gaining back-to-back victories at Haydock and Thirsk in August. Suited by a mile.
**K A Ryan [2-15] J Nixon.*

OSWALD BHB 38f34a **RR 33f 34a** 106[9]
4 b g Distant Relative 7f **(69)** - River Dove (USA) (Riverman (USA)) 9.1f **(76)**
Form - 0
Record 2000 - 1st:0 2nd:0 3rd:0 Ran:1
Pre2000 - 1st:0 2nd:0 3rd:0 Ran:3
2000 AW 0-1: (8f) (Fibr)
Workmanlike, very moderate gelding.
**C W Thornton [0-4] Guy Reed.*

OTAHUNA BHB 60f **RR 60f** 908[18]
4 b g Selkirk (USA) 7.9f **(76)** - Stara (Star Appeal) 9.6f **(65)**
Form - 30
Record 2000 - 1st:0 2nd:0 3rd:1 Ran:2
Pre2000 - 1st:1 2nd:1 3rd:1 Ran:15
Win Prizemoney £3,315 *Total Prizemoney* £6,303
Wins 1999 Spt Nottin (G-F) 10f 63 <
2000 Turf 0-2: (10f, 12f) (gd 2)
Lengthy, average gelding, effective 8f, acts on g-f, likes tight tracks. Turf high 60. Inconsistent.
**M D Hammond [0-3] The Otahuna Partnership (from R Hollinshead [1-15] Oct 1999).*

OTIME (IRE) BHB 62f62a **RR 72f 62a** 4922[10]
3 b g Mujadil (USA) 7.7f **(70)** - Kick the Habit (Habitat) 9.4f **(70)**
Form - 1371467206625000
Record 2000 - 1st:0 2nd:2 3rd:0 Ran:11
Pre2000 - 1st:3 2nd:0 3rd:1 Ran:11
Win Prizemoney £7,028 *Total Prizemoney* £9,755
Wins 1999 *Dec Lingfi* *(STD)* H *6f* 73 76 <
1999 *Nov Lingfi* *(STD)* C *6f* *66*
1999 Aug Bath (HRD) S 5.1f 66
2000 Turf 0-5: (6f, 7f 4) (g-f 4, hrd) 2000 AW 0-6: (6f 3, 7f 2, 8f) (Equi 4, Fibr 2)
Workmanlike, above-average gelding, effective 6 to 7f, best at 6f, acts on g-f - acts on Equi, often wears blinkers, likes left handed tracks. Turf high 72 - 2nd of 19 giving 8lb to Mister Clinton (13 Jun Salisbury 7f g-f RF 1923). AW high 79 - 2nd of 6 getting 1lb from Illusive (26 Feb Lingfield 6f Equi RF 0362). Inconsistent.
**M Wigham [0-5] Miss F V Cove (from Mrs N Macauley [1-10] May 2000).*

OTTERINGTON GIRL BHB 25f **RR 25f** 2235[13]
4 b f Noble Patriarch 12.2f **(43)** - Bidweaya (USA) (Lear Fan (USA)) 8.5f **(73)**
Form - 80
Record 2000 - 1st:0 2nd:0 3rd:0 Ran:2
Pre2000 - 1st:0 2nd:0 3rd:0 Ran:10
2000 Turf 0-2: (8f 2) (g-f, frm)
Neat, little account filly, has worn blinkers. Turf high 25.
**Mrs A Duffield [0-2] Mrs D S Wilkinson (from Miss S E Hall [0-10] Jly 1999).*

OUDALMUTEENA (IRE) BHB 48f44a **RR 45f 44a** 689[6]
5 b g Lahib (USA) 8f **(69)** - Roxy Music (IRE) (Song) 7.2f **(61)**
Form - 706
Record 2000 - 1st:0 2nd:0 3rd:0 Ran:3
Pre2000 - 1st:0 2nd:1 3rd:2 Ran:15
Win Prizemoney £0 *Total Prizemoney* £3,087
2000 Turf 0-2: (7f, 11f) (hvy, gd) 2000 AW 0-1: (8f) (Equi)
Moderate gelding, effective 7 to 10f, acts on sft to frm, has worn blinkers. Turf high 45. Consistent.
**V Soane [0-19] Abdallah,D Harris,J Parslow (from A C Stewart [0-2] Oct 1998).*

OUR DESTINY BHB 72f **RR 81f** 5129[21]
2 b c Mujadil (USA) 7.7f **(70)** - Superspring (Superlative) 7.2f **(56)**
Form - 0136300
Record 2000 - 1st:1 2nd:0 3rd:2 Ran:7
Win Prizemoney £3,038 *Total Prizemoney* £4,327
Wins * 2000 Jly Haydoc (G-F) 6f 81 <
2000 Turf 1-7: (5f, 6f 1-6) (sft, g-f 1-2, frm 2, hrd 2)
Decent colt, effective 6f, acts on g-f. Turf high 81 - also 1st of 14 giving 2lb to Totally Committed (7 Jly Haydock RF 2593).
**A P Jarvis [1-7] Quadrillian Partnership.*

OUR EMILY (IRE) RR 62f 5136[7]
2 b f Charnwood Forest (IRE). - Lacinia **(100f)** (Groom Dancer (USA))
Form - 07
Record 2000 - 1st:0 2nd:0 3rd:0 Ran:2
2000 Turf 0-2: (7f, 8f) (g-s, gd)
Currently average filly. Turf high 62 (began Spt).
**K R Burke [0-2] Mrs Julie Mitchell.*

OUR FIRST LADY BHB 70f68a **RR 74f 68a** 4929[11]
3 b f Alzao (USA) 9.8f **(73)** - Eclipsing (IRE) (Baillamont (USA)) 7f **(78)**
Form - 0220
Record 2000 - 1st:0 2nd:2 3rd:0 Ran:4
Pre2000 - 1st:0 2nd:0 3rd:0 Ran:1
Win Prizemoney £0 *Total Prizemoney* £2,339
2000 Turf 0-3: (6f 2, 8f) (g-s, gd, frm) 2000 AW 0-1: (8f) (Equi)
Light-framed, above-average filly. Turf high 74 - 2nd of 8 to Pageant (7 Jun Yarmouth 6f gd RF 1795).
**D W P Arbuthnot [0-5] Derrick Broomfield.*

OUR FRED BHB 83f78a **RR 82f 78a** 4332[14]
3 ch g Prince Sabo 6.6f **(64)** - Sheila's Secret (IRE) **(92f)** (Bluebird (USA)) 7.5f **(69)**
Form - 44021120
Record 2000 - 1st:2 2nd:2 3rd:0 Ran:8
Pre2000 - 1st:0 2nd:0 3rd:3 Ran:4
Win Prizemoney £6,669 *Total Prizemoney* £10,931
Wins * 2000 Aug Thirsk (GD) H 5f 75 80 <
*** 2000** Jly Leices (G-F) 5f 70
2000 Turf 2-8: (5f 2-7, 6f) (gd, g-f 4, frm 2-3)
Workmanlike, decent gelding, effective 5 to 6f, best at 5f, acts on g-s to frm, often wears blinkers (effectively). Turf high 82 - 2nd of 12 getting 2lb from Amaranth (26 Aug Newmarket 5f g-f RF 3994) - also 1st of 17 giving 17lb to Pips Star (14 Aug Thirsk RF 3630).
**T G Mills [2-12] Sherwoods Transport Ltd.*

OUR INDULGENCE (IRE) BHB 50f **RR 52f** 4362[9]
2 ch g Prince of Birds (USA) - Megan's Dream (IRE) **(38f)** (Fayruz)
Form - 070
Record 2000 - 1st:0 2nd:0 3rd:0 Ran:3
2000 Turf 0-3: (6f 2, 7f) (g-f 3)
Currently fair gelding. Turf high 52 (began Aug).
**T D Easterby [0-3] Mrs Barbara Woodworth.*

OUR JACK BHB 30f **RR** 105[7]
5 ch g Rock City 8.8f **(62)** - Queen Canute (IRE) (Ahonoora) 8.1f **(73)**
Form - 47
Record 2000 - 1st:0 2nd:0 3rd:0 Ran:2
Pre2000 - 1st:0 2nd:0 3rd:0 Ran:1
2000 AW 0-2: (9f, 12f) (Fibr 2)

Currently very moderate gelding. AW high 25.

**C N Kellett [0-3] Mrs J Salt.*

OUR LITTLE CRACKER BHB 42f RR 47f 2535[4]

2 b f Petong 7.6f **(58)** - Pattis Pet (Mummy's Pet) 7.7f **(60)**

Form - 744

Record 2000 - 1st:0 2nd:0 3rd:0 Ran:3

2000 Turf 0-2: (6f, 7f) (gd, frm) 2000 AW 0-1: (5f) (Equi)

Currently moderate filly. Turf high 47.

**M Quinn [0-3] Ms H Rees & J Marks.*

OUR MEMOIRS BHB 48f RR 43f 1812[12]

3 ch g Lake Coniston (IRE) - Julip (Track Spare) 8.8f **(62)**

Form - 00

Record 2000 - 1st:0 2nd:0 3rd:0 Ran:2
Pre2000 - 1st:0 2nd:0 3rd:0 Ran:1

2000 Turf 0-2: (6f 2) (gd, frm)

Scopey, moderate gelding. Turf high 43.

**P R Chamings [0-3] Amity Finance Ltd.*

OUR MONOGRAM BHB 51f RR 54f 4630[8]

4 b g Deploy 11.4f **(67)** - Darling Splodge (Elegant Air) 13.2f **(61)**

Form - 08731158

Record 2000 - 1st:2 2nd:0 3rd:1 Ran:8
Pre2000 - 1st:0 2nd:0 3rd:0 Ran:5

Win Prizemoney £6,712 *Total Prizemoney* £7,428

Wins * **2000** Aug Bath (FRM) H 17.2f 43 53+ <
* **2000** Aug Sandow (G-F) H 16.4f 43 48

2000 Turf 2-8: (12f, 16f 1-5, 17f 1-2) (g-s, gd 2, g-f 2, frm 1-2, hrd 1-1)

Workmanlike, fair gelding, effective 16f, acts on frm, prefers tight tracks. Turf high 54.

**A C Stewart [2-13] The Foxons Fillies Partnership.*

OUR PEOPLE BHB 52f39a RR 50f 39a 415[9]

6 ch g Indian Ridge 7.6f **(74)** - Fair and Wise (High Line) 10.3f **(70)**

Form - 0550353313220

Record 2000 - 1st:1 2nd:2 3rd:4 Ran:9
Pre2000 - 1st:3 2nd:1 3rd:4 Ran:32

Win Prizemoney £12,241 *Total Prizemoney* £18,998

Wins * **2000** *Feb Wolver (STD) H 12f 30 35*
* 1998 Aug Redcar (G-F) H 11f 56 60
* 1998 Jly Carlis (G-F) H 8f 49 53
* 1996 Oct Leices (G-F) 8f 84 <

2000 AW 1-9: (9f, 12f 1-5, 13f, 16f 2) (Equi, Fibr 1-8)

Fair gelding, effective 10f, acts on g-f, has worn blinkers. AW high 39.

**M Johnston [4-41] Mark Johnston Racing Ltd.*

OUR SHELLBY (IRE) BHB 35f RR 18f 4765[7]

2 b br f Petardia 8.2f **(58)** - Davenport Goddess (IRE) (Classic Secret (USA))

Form - 07

Record 2000 - 1st:0 2nd:0 3rd:0 Ran:2

2000 Turf 0-2: (7f, 10f) (g-s, g-f)

Currently poor filly. Turf high 18 (began Spt).

**J L Eyre [0-2] Billy Parker.*

OUR SOUSY (USA) RR 92f 4009[1]

3 b f Silver Hawk (USA) 11.2f **(85)** - Sous Entendu (USA) (Shadeed (USA)) 8.2f **(70)**

Form - 1

Record 2000 - 1st:1 2nd:0 3rd:0 Ran:1

Win Prizemoney £4,117 *Total Prizemoney* £4,117

Wins * **2000** Aug Beverl (G-F) 9.9f 84 <

2000 Turf 1-1: (10f 1-1) (frm 1-1)

Workmanlike, currently useful filly. (1st run) - 1st of 10 from Gledswood (27 Aug Beverley RF 4009).

**E A L Dunlop [1-1] Maktoum Al Maktoum.*

OUT OF AFRICA (IRE) BHB 85f RR 92df 4735[11]

3 b f Common Grounds 8.1f **(66)** - Limpopo (Green Desert (USA)) 8.6f **(78)**

Form - 0060

Record 2000 - 1st:0 2nd:0 3rd:0 Ran:4
Pre2000 - 1st:3 2nd:4 3rd:2 Ran:10

Win Prizemoney £55,253 *Total Prizemoney* £62,385

Wins 1999 Oct York (SFT) L 6f 92 <
1999 Spt Newmar (G-S) H 7f 86 90
1999 Spt Doncas (G-F) H 6.5f 81 85

2000 Turf 0-4: (6f 2, 7f 2) (g-s 2, gd 2)

Workmanlike, useful filly, effective 5 to 7f, best at 7f, acts on g-s to g-f, best on gd. Turf high 80. A useful juvenile, she pulled far too hard and finished tailed off on her reappearance in the 1000 Guineas, and subsequent runs suggested she failed to train on.

**T D Easterby [0-1] Cathal Ryan (from R Hannon [0-3] Jun 2000).*

OUT OF MIND (BRA) RR 1823a[2]

1805 br h Sestero (BRA) - Optativa (BRA) (Janus II)

Form - 2

2000 AW 0-1: (9f) (Dirt)

Currently high-class horse. (1st run) - 2nd of 8 to Running Stag (3 Jun Suffolk Downs 9f Dirt RF 1823a).

**R Mandella in USA [0-1].*

OUT OF REACH BHB 110f RR 110f 4254a[3]

3 b f Warning 8.1f **(77)** - Well Beyond (IRE) (Don't Forget Me) 8.3f **(74)**

Form - 521413

Record 2000 - 1st:2 2nd:1 3rd:1 Ran:6
Pre2000 - 1st:1 2nd:0 3rd:0 Ran:1

Win Prizemoney £29,133 *Total Prizemoney* £36,760

Wins * **2000** Aug Sandow (GD) L 8.1f 110 <
* **2000** Jly Newmar (G-S) H 7f 90 98
* 1999 Oct Newbur (HVY) 6f 81

2000 Turf 2-6: (7f 1-3, 8f 1-3) (g-s, gd 1-3, g-f 1-1, frm)

Scopey, Group-class filly, effective 7 to 8f, best at 8f, acts on gd to g-f, best on gd. Turf high 110 - 1st of 10 from Moselle (19 Aug Sandown RF 3801). She progressed steadily last year, putting up a smart effort to win a Listed event at Sandown in August. Third in the Group 3 Matron Stakes at The Curragh on her only subsequent start, she enjoys forcing the pace and may improve again.

**B W Hills [3-7] K Abdullah.*

OUT OF SIGHT (IRE) BHB 59f75a RR 59f 75a 4609[22]

6 ch g Salse (USA) 10.9f **(71)** - Starr Danias (USA) (Sensitive Prince (USA)) 9.1f **(60)**

Form - 121730007143480

Record 2000 - 1st:2 2nd:1 3rd:2 Ran:14
Pre2000 - 1st:2 2nd:0 3rd:0 Ran:20

Win Prizemoney £19,705 *Total Prizemoney* £27,184

Wins * **2000** Jly Nottin (G-F) 8.2f 51
* **2000** *Feb Southw (STD) H 7f 68 71*
* 1999 *Nov Southw (STD) H 7f 60 67*
* 1997 May York (GD) H 7.9f 75 79 <

2000 Turf 1-10: (7f 2, 8f 1-8) (hvy, g-s 2, g-f 4, frm 1-3) 2000 AW 1-4: (7f 1-2, 8f 2) (Fibr 1-4)

Above-average gelding, effective 7 to 8f, best at 7f, acts on gd to frm - acts on Fibr, prefers left handed tracks, prefers tight tracks, excels at Southwell. Turf high 59. AW high 74 - 1st of 8 giving 2lb to Sand Hawk (18 Feb Southwell RF 0308). More successful on sand than on turf so far, he scored twice over seven furlongs at Southwell during the winter, but won a Nottingham classified event in July when apparently badly in at the weights.

**B A McMahon [4-34] D J Allen.*

OUT ON A PROMISE (IRE) BHB 43f60a RR 44f 60a 4112[9]

8 b g Night Shift (USA) 8.1f **(73)** - Lovers' Parlour (Beldale Flutter (USA)) 9.7f **(71)**

Form - 871740

Record 2000 - 1st:1 2nd:0 3rd:0 Ran:6
Pre2000 - 1st:2 2nd:3 3rd:5 Ran:24

Win Prizemoney £10,582 *Total Prizemoney* £19,436

Wins * **2000** Jly Chepst (FRM) H 12.1f 41 44

2000 Turf 1-6: (10f, 12f 1-3, 14f, 16f) (g-f, frm 1-5)

Moderate gelding, has worn blinkers. Turf high 44 (began Jun). Consistent.

**B J Meehan [1-4] Mrs Lynsey Le Cornu (from C J Mann [3-13] Jly 2000).*

OUTPLACEMENT (USA) BHB 28f RR 21f 415[12]

5 b g Mountain Cat (USA) - Coolernearthelake (USA) (Hail the Pirates (USA)) 11f **(78)**

Form - 810

Record 2000 - 1st:1 2nd:0 3rd:0 Ran:3
Pre2000 - 1st:0 2nd:0 3rd:0 Ran:2

Win Prizemoney £1,907 *Total Prizemoney* £1,907

Wins * **2000** *Feb Southw (STD) H 16f 25 27* <

2000 AW 1-3: (11f, 16f 1-2) (Fibr 1-3)

Little account gelding. AW high 27 - 1st of 9 getting 17lb from Silver Gyre (18 Feb Southwell RF 0304).
**S R Bowring [1-4] The Royal George Racing Partnership (from C R Egerton [0-2] Apr 1998).*

OUTRAGEOUSE RR 62f
4023[4]

2 b g Be My Chief (USA) 10.2f **(62)** - Pink Brief (IRE) **(63f 45a)** (Ela-Mana-Mou) 10.1f **(70)**
Form - 04
Record 2000 - 1st:0 2nd:0 3rd:0 Ran:2
Win Prizemoney £0 *Total Prizemoney* £270
2000 Turf 0-2: (7f, 8f) (gd, g-f)
Currently average gelding. Turf high 62 (began Aug).
**Andrew Reid [0-2] A S Reid.*

OUT RANKING (FR) BHB 64f RR 60f
3147[5]

8 b m Le Glorieux - Restless Nell (Northern Baby (CAN)) 11.6f **(71)**
Form - 25
Record 2000 - 1st:0 2nd:1 3rd:0 Ran:2
Win Prizemoney £0 *Total Prizemoney* £846
2000 Turf 0-2: (17f, 18f) (frm 2)
Average mare. Turf high 60 (began Jly). Tremendously game, she is effective between two and three miles on any ground. She jumps to her right, but that does not seem to hinder her performance. Virtually unbeatable in claimers though she can win handicaps, she will win again at the right level.
**M C Pipe [18-42] Knight Hawks Partnership.*

OUTSTANDING TALENT BHB 40f RR 52f
4877[8]

3 gr f Environment Friend 7.5f **(67)** -Chaleureuse (Final Straw) 7.9f **(64)**
Form - 6072478
Record 2000 - 1st:0 2nd:1 3rd:0 Ran:7
Pre2000 - 1st:0 2nd:0 3rd:1 Ran:5
Win Prizemoney £0 *Total Prizemoney* £1,259
2000 Turf 0-7: (6f 2, 7f 3, 8f, 10f) (g-s, gd, g-f 3, frm 2)
Light-framed, fair filly, effective 6f, acts on g-f. Turf high 52.
**A W Carroll [0-7] Talent Entertainment (from V Soane [0-3] Oct 1999).*

OUZO (NZ) RR 120f
575a[7]

7 ch g Interrex (CAN) 7.7f **(51)** - Ville Air (Town Crier) 10.2f **(55)**
Form - 17
2000 Turf 1-1: (10f 1-1) (gd 1-1) 2000 AW 0-1: (8f) (Dirt)
Currently very high-class gelding. (1st run) - 1st of 14 from Jim And Tonic (5 Mar Kranji RF 0429a). Landed the hugely valuable Singapore Airlines International in March. **M Thwaites in SIN [1-3].*

OVAMBO (IRE) RR 80f
5065[3]

2 b c Namaqualand (USA) - Razana (IRE) **(77f)** (Kahyasi)
Form - 33
Record 2000 - 1st:0 2nd:0 3rd:2 Ran:2
Win Prizemoney £0 *Total Prizemoney* £995
2000 Turf 0-2: (8f 2) (g-s, gd)
Currently decent colt. Turf high 80 (began Spt) - 3rd of 15 to Prince Shaamaal (19 Oct Bath 8f g-s RF 5065).
**P J Makin [0-2] R A Henley.*

OVERSLEPT BHB 30a RR 30a
3571[9]

3 br c Missed Flight - Own Free Will (Nicholas Bill) 10.1f **(56)**
Form - 880
Record 2000 - 1st:0 2nd:0 3rd:0 Ran:3
2000 AW 0-3: (6f 2, 9f) (Fibr 3)
Rangy, currently poor colt. AW high 10 (began Jun).
**C F Wall [0-3] Mrs Noreen Callan.*

OVERSMAN BHB 48f55a RR 48f 55a
1373[8]

7 b g Keen 11.1f **(58)** - Jamaican Punch (IRE) (Shareef Dancer (USA)) 9.9f **(73)**
Form - 28
Record 2000 - 1st:0 2nd:1 3rd:0 Ran:2
Pre2000 - 1st:1 2nd:2 3rd:5 Ran:14
Win Prizemoney £2,900 *Total Prizemoney* £7,748
Wins * 1996 *Feb Southw (STD) 12f 46+* <
2000 Turf 0-1: (12f) (frm) 2000 AW 0-1: (11f) (Fibr)
Moderate gelding. Inconsistent.
**J G FitzGerald [5-44] Marquesa de Moratalla.*

OVERSPECT BHB 100f RR 93f
4536[6]

2 b c Spectrum (IRE) - Portelet **(87f 72a)** (Night Shift (USA)) 7.2f **(69)**
Form - 1316
Record 2000 - 1st:2 2nd:0 3rd:1 Ran:4
Win Prizemoney £12,713 *Total Prizemoney* £13,392
Wins * **2000** Spt Doncas (GD) 7f 93 <
* **2000** May San Si (GD) 6f
2000 Turf 2-4: (6f 1-1, 7f 1-2, 8f) (g-s, gd 2-2, frm)
Useful colt. Turf high 93 - 1st of 6 from Tempest (6 Spt Doncaster RF 4256). He claimed a decent scalp when beating Tempest at Doncaster in September, and can be excused a poor effort at Chester later that month as the ground was unsuitably soft. Already a winner at San Siro, he looks a likely type for the Italian 2000 Guineas. **P F I Cole [2-4] Luciano Gaucci.*

OVER THE MOON BHB 29f37a RR 44f 37a
3187[7]

6 ch m Beveled (USA) 6.9f **(64)** - Beyond the Moon (IRE) (Ballad Rock) 7.8f **(63)**
Form - 567181014707043667
Record 2000 - 1st:3 2nd:0 3rd:1 Ran:15
Pre2000 - 1st:4 2nd:0 3rd:3 Ran:31
Win Prizemoney £14,524 *Total Prizemoney* £16,057

Wins					
2000	*Mar Southw (STD) S*	*11f*	*50*		
2000	*Feb Southw (STD) C*	*8f*	*55*		
2000	*Jan Wolver (STD) S*	*9.4f*	*50*		
1999	*Apr Wolver (STD) C*	*8.5f*	*55*		
1998	*Spt Wolver (STD) C*	*7f*	*59*		
1998	*Jly Wolver (STD) C*	*8.5f*	*56*		
1998	*Jun Wolver (STD) C*	*7f*	*60*	<	

2000 Turf 0-3: (10f 2, 12f) (gd 2, frm) 2000 AW 3-12: (8f 1-4, 9f 1-3, 11f 1-3, 12f, 16f) (Fibr 3-12)
Moderate mare, effective 7 to 11f, best at 8f, - acts on Fibr, has worn blinkers, favours left handed tracks, favours tight tracks. Turf high 37. AW high 55 - 1st of 16 getting 7lb from Saguaro (28 Feb Southwell RF 0370) - also 1st of 9 getting 4lb from Royal Partnership (14 Mar Southwell RF 0442). She took her time in getting off the mark, but has been very successful in modest events on the Wolverhampton Fibresand. She does not seem to run two consecutive races alike, however.
**Mrs N Macauley [0-6] The Lovatt Partnership (from M J Polglase [1-6] May 2000).*

OZAWA (IRE) BHB 41f RR 40f
3515[13]

3 gr g Brief Truce (USA) 9.1f **(73)** - Classy **(52f 43a)** (Kalaglow) 9.8f **(67)**
Form - 0000
Record 2000 - 1st:0 2nd:0 3rd:0 Ran:4
Pre2000 - 1st:0 2nd:0 3rd:0 Ran:1
2000 Turf 0-4: (6f 2, 8f 2) (g-s, gd, g-f, frm)
Workmanlike, moderate gelding. Turf high 40.
**J W Payne [0-5] G Jabre.*

OZONE LAYER RR 90f
3349a[5]

2 b c Zafonic (USA) 9f **(83)** - Ozone Friendly (USA) (Green Forest (USA)) 9.9f **(68)**
Form - 15
2000 Turf 1-2: (5f 1-1, 6f) (hvy, g-s 1-1)
Currently useful colt. Turf high 90 (began Jly). A game winner of the Group 3 Prix du Bois, he ran below that form when fifth in the Prix Robert Papin. Worth another chance, he may stay beyond sprint distances.
**A Fabre in FR [1-2].*

PAARL ROCK BHB 56f47a RR 58f 47a
5020[5]

5 ch g Common Grounds 8.1f **(66)** - Markievicz (IRE) (Doyoun) 9f **(69)**
Form - 800321441605
Record 2000 - 1st:2 2nd:1 3rd:1 Ran:12
Pre2000 - 1st:0 2nd:0 3rd:1 Ran:11
Win Prizemoney £7,013 *Total Prizemoney* £10,220
Wins * **2000** Aug Nottin (GD) H 10f 55 58 <
* **2000** Aug Leices (G-F) H 10f 50 54
2000 Turf 2-9: (8f, 10f 2-6, 11f 2) (sft, g-s, gd 1-2, g-f 1-4, frm) 2000 AW 0-3: (8f 2, 12f) (Fibr 3)
Fair gelding, effective 8 to 11f, best at 10f, acts on gd to frm, often wears blinkers (extremely effectively), favours tight tracks, excels at Leicester, likes Haydock. Turf high 58 - 1st of 13 getting 5lb from Sheer Face (21 Aug Nottingham RF 3843) - also 1st of 7 getting 3lb from Shamsan (2 Aug Leicester RF 3329). AW high 33.
**G Barnett [2-20] J C Bradbury (from D R Loder [0-3] Spt 1997).*

PACHINCO RR 5184[17]

2 ch c Bluebird (USA) 7.9f **(71)** - Lady Philippa (IRE) (Taufan (USA)) 7f **(57)**
Form - 0
Record 2000 - 1st:0 2nd:0 3rd:0 Ran:1
2000 Turf 0-1: (8f) (g-s)
Currently very poor colt.
**P Mitchell [0-1] Gordon Li.*

PACIFIC ALLIANCE (IRE) BHB 78f75a RR 80+f 75a 5242[12]

4 b g Fayruz 6.6f **(63)** - La Gravotte (FR) (Habitat) 9.4f **(70)**
Form - 34407311100
Record 2000 - 1st:3 2nd:0 3rd:2 Ran:11
Pre2000 - 1st:2 2nd:0 3rd:1 Ran:9
Win Prizemoney £25,485 *Total Prizemoney* £27,885
Wins * **2000** Spt Mussel (G-S) 8f 80+ <
* **2000** Spt York (GD) H 7.9f 61 74
* **2000** Aug Mussel (G-F) H 8f 59 69
1999 Jun Sandow (GD) H 8.1f 60 63
1999 *Feb Lingfi (STD) 8f 68*
2000 Turf 3-8: (7f 2, 8f 3-6) (g-s, gd 1-2, g-f 1-4, frm 1-1) 2000 AW 0-3: (8f 2, 10f) (Equi 3)
Decent gelding, effective 8f, acts on gd to g-f, has worn blinkers (effectively). Turf high 80 (began Jly) - 1st of 14 giving 13lb to Fair Lady (24 Spt Musselburgh RF 4626) - also 1st of 24 getting 2lb from Donna's Double (3 Spt York RF 4196). AW high 62. In fine form in the autumn, winning at Musselburgh and York, making all on both occasions.
**M Wigham [3-10] Mrs D E Armitage (from P S McEntee [0-1] Feb 2000).*

PACIFIC PLACE (IRE) BHB 53f RR 53f 4809[16]

3 gr c College Chapel - Kaitlin (IRE) (Salmon Leap (USA)) 11f **(61)**
Form - 024232280800
Record 2000 - 1st:0 2nd:4 3rd:1 Ran:12
Pre2000 - 1st:0 2nd:0 3rd:0 Ran:2
Win Prizemoney £0 *Total Prizemoney* £4,406
2000 Turf 0-12: (5f 6, 6f 6) (g-s, gd 3, g-f 3, frm 5)
Workmanlike, fair colt, effective 5 to 6f, acts on g-f to frm. Turf high 60 - 2nd of 11 getting 2lb from Cryfield (28 Jun Carlisle 6f frm RF 2328).
**M Quinn [0-14] John Breslin.*

PACINO RR 108f 4713a[9]

3 b c Zafonic (USA) 9f **(83)** - June Moon (IRE) (Sadler's Wells (USA)) 10f **(76)**
Form - 0130
Record 2000 - 1st:1 2nd:0 3rd:1 Ran:4
Pre2000 - 1st:1 2nd:1 3rd:0 Ran:2
Win Prizemoney £65,017 *Total Prizemoney* £74,046
Wins * **2000** May Cologn (GD) G2 8f 100 <
1999 Jly Salisb (G-F) 7f 80
2000 Turf 1-3: (8f 1-2, 9f) (sft, gd 1-2) 2000 AW 0-1: (9f) (Dirt)
Scopey, Pattern-class colt, effective 8f, acts on gd. Turf high 108 - also 1st of 11 from Djibouti (14 May Cologne RF 1285a). He landed the Group Two German 2000 Guineas in May and was not totally disgraced, if well held, in the Prix Jean Prat. A mile looks as far as he wants.
**S bin Suroor [1-3] Godolphin (from S bin Suroor in UAE [0-1] Mar 2000).*

PACK-A-PUNCH (IRE) BHB 38f47a RR 35f 47a 2093[13]

3 b f Up and At 'em - Soul Fire (IRE) (Exactly Sharp (USA))
Form - 46700
Record 2000 - 1st:0 2nd:0 3rd:0 Ran:3
Pre2000 - 1st:0 2nd:0 3rd:0 Ran:2
2000 Turf 0-3: (5f 3) (gd, frm 2)
Leggy, moderate filly. Turf high 35.
**Miss L A Perratt [0-5] Clayton Bigley Partnership Ltd.*

PACKIN EM IN BHB 58f RR 65f 5197[8]

2 b c Young Ern - Wendy's Way **(44f 41a)** (Merdon Melody)
Form - 08448
Record 2000 - 1st:0 2nd:0 3rd:0 Ran:5
Win Prizemoney £0 *Total Prizemoney* £247
2000 Turf 0-5: (5f, 6f 3, 7f) (g-s, gd 3, frm)
Average colt. Turf high 65 (began Jly).
**N Hamilton [0-5] John Hopkins (T/A So Racing).*

PADAUK BHB 34f50a RR 31f 50a 187[8]

6 b h Warrshan (USA) 9.7f **(59)** - Free on Board (Free State) 8.7f **(61)**
Form - 08
Record 2000 - 1st:0 2nd:0 3rd:0 Ran:1
Pre2000 - 1st:1 2nd:6 3rd:6 Ran:35
Win Prizemoney £2,772 *Total Prizemoney* £11,256
Wins * 1999 *Jan Lingfi (STD) H 16f 51 56* <
2000 AW 0-1: (16f) (Equi)
Fair horse, effective 16f, - acts on Equi, has worn blinkers (extremely effectively), prefers left handed tracks, favours tight tracks.
**M J Haynes [1-36] Butler, Bob Pettis, Haynes.*

PADDY MCGOON (USA) BHB 48f45a RR 53f 45a 1978[4]

5 ch g Irish River (FR) 9f **(77)** - Flame McGoon (USA) (Staff Writer (USA)) 10f **(54)**
Form - 604
Record 2000 - 1st:0 2nd:0 3rd:0 Ran:3
Pre2000 - 1st:0 2nd:0 3rd:1 Ran:8
Win Prizemoney £0 *Total Prizemoney* £840
2000 Turf 0-3: (10f 2, 12f) (gd, g-f, frm)
Fair gelding. Turf high 53. **D R C Elsworth [0-11] Mrs Ann Shaw.*

PADDY MUL BHB 26f RR 33f 4868[10]

3 ch c Democratic (USA) - My Pretty Niece (Great Nephew) 9.9f **(64)**
Form - 003040
Record 2000 - 1st:0 2nd:0 3rd:1 Ran:6
Pre2000 - 1st:0 2nd:0 3rd:0 Ran:4
Win Prizemoney £0 *Total Prizemoney* £530
2000 Turf 0-6: (8f, 9f 2, 10f, 11f, 14f) (hvy, g-s, gd, g-f, frm 2)
Unfurnished, very moderate colt, has worn blinkers. Turf high 33.
**W Storey [0-10] Gremlin Racing.*

PADDY'S RICE BHB 31f RR 25f 4101[14]

9 ch g Hadeer 8.9f **(58)** - Requiem (Song) 7.2f **(61)**
Form - 0060
Record 2000 - 1st:0 2nd:0 3rd:0 Ran:4
Pre2000 - 1st:5 2nd:3 3rd:3 Ran:45
Win Prizemoney £16,402 *Total Prizemoney* £20,826
Wins 1998 Jun Bath (G-S) CH 8f 49 54
1997 May Bright (FRM) H 8f 53 52
1996 Jun Warwic (FRM) 7f 60 <
2000 Turf 0-4: (10f 3, 12f) (g-f 2, frm 2)
Little account gelding, has worn blinkers. Turf high 25 (began Jly). He managed a Brighton fast-ground win in May, but did not sparkle otherwise, and was not seen out after July.
**K Bell [0-4] Mrs L L Edwards (from M Blanshard [2-16] Spt 1998).*

PADDYWACK (IRE) BHB 55f62a RR 56f 62a 4992[13]

3 b g Bigstone (IRE) - Millie's Return (IRE) (Ballad Rock) 7.8f **(63)**
Form - 600524112220020U0050
Record 2000 - 1st:2 2nd:5 3rd:0 Ran:18
Pre2000 - 1st:1 2nd:0 3rd:1 Ran:11
Win Prizemoney £8,855 *Total Prizemoney* £13,002
Wins * **2000** *Mar Lingfi (STD) H 7f 42 54*
* **2000** *Mar Wolver (STD) H 6f 42 48+*
* 1999 Oct Redcar (SFT) H 6f 55 57 <
2000 Turf 0-4: (6f 4) (g-f 2, frm 2) 2000 AW 2-14: (5f 2, 6f 1-9, 7f 1-3) (Equi 1-3, Fibr 1-11)
Neat, average gelding, effective 5 to 7f, best at 6f, acts on gd to g-f - acts on AW, mostly wears blinkers (extremely effectively), and excels at Lingfield. Turf high 56 (1st run) - 2nd of 16 giving 10lb to Tondyne (29 Mar Nottingham 6f g-f RF 0558). AW high 61 - 2nd of 14 giving 15lb to French Fancy (6 Jun Lingfield 6f Equi RF 1738) - also 1st of 10 getting 3lb from Kigema (8 Mar Lingfield RF 0425). Inconsistent.
**D W Chapman [3-24] J B Wilcox (from G Lewis [0-5] Aug 1999).*

PADHAMS GREEN BHB 72f80a RR 72f 80a 4929[1]

4 b g Aragon 7.7f **(58)** - Double Dutch (Nicholas Bill) 10.1f **(56)**
Form - 36215211
Record 2000 - 1st:3 2nd:2 3rd:1 Ran:8
Pre2000 - 1st:1 2nd:0 3rd:2 Ran:13
Win Prizemoney £11,423 *Total Prizemoney* £16,592
Wins * **2000** *Oct Lingfi (STD) H 8f 67 85+* <
* **2000** *Oct Wolver (STD) H 8.5f 67 82+*

*** 2000** Jly Newmar (G-F) H 8f 65 68
1999 Aug Salisb (GD) H 7f 62 64

2000 Turf 1-6: (7f 2, 8f 1-3, 10f) (gd 1-2, g-f, frm 3) 2000 AW 2-2: (8f 2-2) (Equi 1-1, Fibr 1-1)

Workmanlike, useful gelding, effective 8f, - acts on AW, likes left handed tracks. Turf high 72. AW high 85 (began Oct) - 1st of 12 giving 18lb to Don Bosco (11 Oct Lingfield RF 4929) - also 1st of 13 giving 5lb to Teofilio (3 Oct Wolverhampton RF 4782).

**B W Hills [3-8] Mrs B W Hills (from M H Tompkins [1-13] Oct 1999).*

PAGAN KING (IRE) BHB 69f68a **RR 72f 68a** 4745[22]

4 b g Unblest - Starinka (Risen Star (USA))
Form - 56084320
Record 2000 - 1st:0 2nd:1 3rd:1 Ran:6
Pre2000 - 1st:2 2nd:0 3rd:1 Ran:12
Win Prizemoney £7,142 *Total Prizemoney* £10,624
Wins * 1999 Aug Bright (SFT) H 7f 71 76
* 1998 Oct Bright (G-S) 7f 78 <

2000 Turf 0-6: (7f 2, 8f 4) (g-s, gd 3, g-f 2)

Leggy, above-average gelding, effective 7 to 8f, best at 8f, acts on g-s to frm, best on g-s, likes left handed tracks, likes tight tracks. Turf high 72 - 2nd of 19 giving 2lb to Sweet Reward (18 Spt Kempton 8f g-s RF 4484). Both of his wins to date have come over seven furlongs at Brighton with give in the ground.

**J A R Toller [2-18] The Gap Partnership.*

PAGAN PRINCE BHB 66f **RR 64f** 4227[6]

3 br c Primo Dominie 7.2f **(67)** - Mory Kante (USA) (Icecapade (USA)) 11f **(62)**
Form - 056
Record 2000 - 1st:0 2nd:0 3rd:0 Ran:3

2000 Turf 0-3: (7f, 8f 2) (g-f 2, frm)

Leggy, currently average colt. Turf high 64.

**J A R Toller [0-3] The Gap Partnership.*

PAGEANT BHB 70f54a **RR 82f 54a** 4925[8]

3 br f Inchinor 8.9f **(64)** - Positive Attitude (Red Sunset) 8.2f **(63)**
Form - 512625558
Record 2000 - 1st:1 2nd:2 3rd:0 Ran:9
Pre2000 - 1st:0 2nd:0 3rd:1 Ran:3
Win Prizemoney £3,802 *Total Prizemoney* £7,175
Wins * 2000 Jun Yarmou (GD) 6f 75 <

2000 Turf 1-8: (6f 1-2, 7f 5, 8f) (g-s, gd 1-1, g-f 3, frm 2, hrd) 2000 AW 0-1: (7f) (Equi)

Workmanlike, decent filly, effective 6 to 8f, acts on gd to hrd. Turf high 82 - 2nd of 13 giving 1lb to Capricho (22 Jly Newmarket 7f g-f RF 3029) - also 1st of 8 from Our First Lady (7 Jun Yarmouth RF 1795). Becoming disappointing. She showed ability in three starts at two and got off the mark in a six-furlong Yarmouth maiden in June. Has run well over seven furlongs since and that may turn out to be her best trip.

**W Jarvis [1-9] R J R Williams (from R J R Williams [0-3] Oct 1999).*

PAGEBOY BHB 40f37a **RR 38f 37a** 545[3]

11 b g Tina's Pet 7.4f **(56)** - Edwin's Princess (Owen Dudley) 8.3f **(61)**
Form - 664453
Record 2000 - 1st:0 2nd:0 3rd:1 Ran:4
Pre2000 - 1st:11 2nd:14 3rd:6 Ran:109
Win Prizemoney £35,667 *Total Prizemoney* £59,478
Wins * 1998 *Jan Lingfi (STD) H 6f 70 75* <
* 1997 *Jan Lingfi (STD) H 6f 73 75* <
* 1996 *Spt Wolver (STD) H 6f 67 65*
* 1996 Aug Hamilt (G-F) H 6f 58 66+
* 1996 *Jan Lingfi (STD) H 6f 61 63*

2000 Turf 0-1: (7f) (frm) 2000 AW 0-3: (6f 2, 7f) (Equi, Fibr 2)

Very moderate gelding, effective 6 to 7f, - acts on Equi, has worn blinkers (effectively), favours left handed tracks, favours tight tracks. AW high 39.

**P C Haslam [11-113] Mrs A Haslam.*

PAGE NOUVELLE (FR) BHB 89f **RR 79f** 4595[7]

2 b f Spectrum (IRE) - Page Bleue (Sadler's Wells (USA)) 10f **(76)**
Form - 317
Record 2000 - 1st:1 2nd:0 3rd:1 Ran:3
Win Prizemoney £4,121 *Total Prizemoney* £5,801
Wins * 2000 Aug Beverl (G-F) 7.5f 75 <

2000 Turf 1-3: (7f 1-2, 8f) (gd 2, g-f 1-1)

Currently above-average filly. Turf high 79 (began Aug) - also 1st of 8 from Esyoueffcee (16 Aug Beverley RF 3687). Scraped home in a Beverley maiden.

**B W Hills [1-3] E D Kessly.*

PAGLIACCI **RR 87f** 2210[5]

2 ch c Gone West (USA) 7.8f **(82)** - Applaud (USA) **(100f)** (Rahy (USA))
Form - 45
Record 2000 - 1st:0 2nd:0 3rd:0 Ran:2
Win Prizemoney £0 *Total Prizemoney* £1,279

2000 Turf 0-2: (5f, 6f) (gd, frm)

Currently useful colt. Turf high 87 (1st run) - 4th of 17 to Volata (3 Jun Newmarket 6f frm RF 1687).

**Sir Michael Stoute [0-2] Faisal Salman.*

PAID UP BHB 64f **RR 62f** 3627[8]

2 b g Mind Games - Indian Summer (Young Generation) 7.7f **(63)**
Form - 468
Record 2000 - 1st:0 2nd:0 3rd:0 Ran:3
Win Prizemoney £0 *Total Prizemoney* £225

2000 Turf 0-3: (5f 3) (frm 2, hrd)

Currently average gelding. Turf high 62 (began Jly).

**M W Easterby [0-3] G H Sparkes.*

PAINTED ROOM (USA) **RR 84f** 4969[2]

2 ch c Woodman (USA) 9.7f **(77)** - All At Sea (USA) (Riverman (USA)) 9.1f **(76)**
Form - 22
Record 2000 - 1st:0 2nd:2 3rd:0 Ran:2
Win Prizemoney £0 *Total Prizemoney* £4,156

2000 Turf 0-2: (8f 2) (gd, g-f)

Currently decent colt. Turf high 84 (began Spt) - 2nd of 29 to Terrestrial (13 Oct Newmarket 8f gd RF 4969). Out of a high-class mare, came up against potentially useful sorts in backend maidens at Newmarket, and should have no trouble breaking his duck in 2001.

**H R A Cecil [0-2] K Abdulla.*

PAIRING (IRE) BHB 80f **RR 89f** 5129[23]

2 ch g Rudimentary (USA) 8.2f **(66)** - Splicing **(68f 75a)** (Sharpo) 7.7f **(59)**
Form - 4100
Record 2000 - 1st:1 2nd:0 3rd:0 Ran:4
Win Prizemoney £3,185 *Total Prizemoney* £3,447
Wins * 2000 Jly Lingfi (GD) 6f 89 <

2000 Turf 1-4: (5f, 6f 1-2, 7f) (sft, g-f 1-2, frm)

Useful gelding. Turf high 89 - 1st of 18 giving 8lb to That's Jazz (12 Jly Lingfield RF 2739). Beat a big field in a Lingfield maiden auction event.

**H Morrison [1-4] The Beach Club.*

PAIRUMANI STAR (IRE) BHB 105f **RR 105f** 4985[9]

5 ch h Caerleon (USA) 10.9f **(79)** - Dawn Star (High Line) 10.3f **(70)**
Form - 01140
Record 2000 - 1st:2 2nd:0 3rd:0 Ran:5
Pre2000 - 1st:6 2nd:4 3rd:2 Ran:20
Win Prizemoney £67,110 *Total Prizemoney* £90,220
Wins * 2000 Jly Leopar (GD) L 14f 103 <
*** 2000** May Goodwo (SFT) H 14f 95 103 <
* 1999 Jly Newbur (G-F) H 16f 90 90
* 1999 Jun Salisb (FRM) 14.1f 92+
* 1999 Jun York (G-S) H 13.9f 87 90
* 1998 Aug Goodwo (G-F) H 12f 85 87
* 1998 Jly Salisb (GD) H 12f 80 86
* 1998 Jun Haydoc (GD) H 14f 78 80

2000 Turf 2-5: (12f, 14f 2-2, 15f, 16f) (g-s 1-2, gd 1-2, frm)

Pattern-class colt, effective 14 to 15f, best at 14f, acts on g-s to gd, best on g-s, has worn blinkers. Turf high 105 - 4th of 7 to Persian Punch (20 Aug Deauville 15f g-s RF 3949a) - also 1st of 11 getting 4lb from Murghem (25 May Goodwood RF 1435). Inconsistent. Probably best when forcing the pace, he looks suited by 14 furlongs, but does not quite look up to winning in Group company at this stage.

**J L Dunlop [8-25] Windflower Overseas Holdings Inc.*

PAIYDA **RR 82+f** 4807[1]

2 b f Danehill (USA) 9.1f **(79)** - Meadow Pipit (CAN) **(103f)** (Meadowlake (USA))
Form - 1
Record 2000 - 1st:1 2nd:0 3rd:0 Ran:1
Win Prizemoney £3,542 *Total Prizemoney* £3,542
Wins * 2000 Oct Lingfi (SFT) 7f 82+ <

2000 Turf 1-1: (7f 1-1) (g-s 1-1)

Currently decent filly. (1st run) - 1st of 18 from Yorkshire Rose (4 Oct Lingfield RF 4807). **E A L Dunlop [1-1] Mohammed Ali.*

PALACE AFFAIR BHB 100f RR 92+f 5107[16]

2 ch f Pursuit of Love 9.5f **(69)** - Palace Street (USA) (Secreto (USA)) 8.7f **(72)**
Form - 510
Record 2000 - 1st:1 2nd:0 3rd:0 Ran:3
Win Prizemoney £4,602 *Total Prizemoney* £4,830
Wins * 2000 Spt Kempto (GD) 6f 92+ <
2000 Turf 1-3: (5f, 6f 1-2) (gd, g-f 1-2)
Currently useful filly, always wears blinkers. Turf high 92 (began Aug) - 1st of 12 from Ghazal (3 Spt Kempton RF 4187). Withdrawn after failing to enter the stalls on her intended debut, she ran away with a Kempton maiden in September. Never a threat when unplaced in the Cornwallis Stakes on her only subsequent start, she deserves another chance on decent ground.
**G B Balding [1-3] Miss B Swire.*

PALACEGATE JACK (IRE) BHB 65f55a RR 55tf 55a 4748[7]

9 gr g Neshad (USA) 5.5f **(59)** -Pasadena Lady (Captain James) 5f **(59)**
Form - 5225323803054560547
Record 2000 - 1st:0 2nd:2 3rd:3 Ran:17
Pre2000 - 1st:15 2nd:13 3rd:11 Ran:99
Win Prizemoney £129,138 *Total Prizemoney* £153,357

Wins							
	1999	Jun Newcas	(G-F)	C	5f		49
	1998	May Catter	(SFT)	C	5f		56
	1997	*Nov Lingfi*	*(STD)*	*H*	*5f*	*68*	*72*
	1997	*Spt Southw*	*(STD)*	*C*	*5f*		*67*
	1997	Jly Mussel	(G-F)	H	5f	65	67
	1997	Jun Hamilt	(G-S)	S	5f		55
	1997	Jun Newcas	(FRM)	S	5f		49
	1996	Nov Redcar	(G-F)		5f		75
	1996	*Spt Southw*	*(STD)*	*C*	*5f*		*75*

2000 Turf 0-11: (5f 10, 6f) (sft, g-s, gd 3, g-f 2, frm 3, hrd) 2000 AW 0-6: (5f 6) (Equi 3, Fibr 3)
Fair gelding, effective 5f, acted on gd - acted on Equi to Fibr, often wore blinkers. Turf high 55. AW high 53. (DEAD)
**A Berry [0-17] Alan Berry (from J Berry [14-89] Dec 1999).*

PALACEGATE TOUCH BHB 50f60a RR 46?f 60a 5248[1]

10 gr g Petong 7.6f **(58)** - Dancing Chimes (London Bells (CAN)) 5.8f **(53)**
Form - 3253427571307303658048700341
Record 2000 - 1st:2 2nd:1 3rd:6 Ran:26
Pre2000 - 1st:27 2nd:13 3rd:17 Ran:130
Win Prizemoney £91,185 *Total Prizemoney* £119,705

Wins							
	*** 2000**	*Oct Wolver*	*(STD)*	*H*	*6f*	*55*	*59*
	*** 2000**	*May Wolver*	*(STD)*	*C*	*6f*		*57*
	1999	*Mar Lingfi*	*(STD)*	*C*	*6f*		*67*
	1999	*Jan Lingfi*	*(STD)*	*C*	*6f*		*63*
	1998	Jly Catter	(GD)	C	6f		58
	1998	Jly Catter	(FRM)	S	6f		55
	1998	Jly Hamilt	(FRM)	S	6f		60
	1998	Jun Warwic	(GD)	C	6f		64
	1998	*Jan Lingfi*	*(STD)*	*C*	*6f*		*72*
	1997	*Nov Lingfi*	*(STD)*	*H*	*7f*	*72*	*76*
	1997	Aug Haydoc	(G-F)	C	6f		72
	1997	Jly Hamilt	(G-S)	H	6f	77	78
	1997	May Catter	(G-F)	C	5f		64
	1997	May Doncas	(GD)	C	5f		75
	1996	Oct Catter	(GD)	H	5f	74	78
	1996	Spt Sandow	(G-F)	C	5f		75
	1996	Aug Catter	(G-F)	C	5f		65
	1996	Jly Warwic	(FRM)		5f		72
	1996	*Jly Lingfi*	*(STD)*	*C*	*5f*		*66*
	1996	Apr Carlis	(G-S)	C	6.9f		65

2000 Turf 0-18: (5f 5, 6f 11, 7f 2) (g-s 3, gd 5, g-f 3, frm 6, hrd) 2000 AW 2-8: (6f 2-6, 7f 2) (Equi 4, Fibr 2-4)
Average gelding, mostly wears blinkers, likes left handed tracks, likes tight tracks. Turf high 46. AW high 59. He can still win in claiming company, either on turf or on Equitrack.
**A Berry [2-26] A B Parr (from J Berry [27-130] Nov 1999).*

PALACE GREEN (IRE) BHB 58f43a RR 67f 43a 112[12]

4 ch f Rudimentary (USA) 8.2f **(66)** -Show Home (Music Boy) 6.8f **(57)**
Form - 070800
Record 2000 - 1st:0 2nd:0 3rd:0 Ran:2
Pre2000 - 1st:3 2nd:5 3rd:3 Ran:24
Win Prizemoney £6,840 *Total Prizemoney* £12,836

Wins							
	*** 1999**	*Jan Southw*	*(STD)*	*H*	*6f*	*65*	*75* <
	1998	*May Southw*	*(STD)*	*S*	*6f*		*60*
	1998	*May Southw*	*(STD)*	*S*	*5f*		*60*

2000 AW 0-2: (6f 2) (Fibr 2)
Scopey, average filly, effective 6f, - acts on Fibr, favours left handed tracks, favours tight tracks. AW high 1.
**D W Chapman [1-21] J M Chapman (from M R Channon [2-5] May 1998).*

PALACE ROYALE (IRE) RR 97f 4339a[4]

4 b f Perugino (USA) - Trojan Tale (USA) 00
Form - 28214
2000 Turf 1-5: (12f 1-5) (g-s, gd 3, frm 1-1)
Very useful filly, effective 9 to 12f, best at 12f, acts on g-s to frm, best on gd, prefers right handed tracks. Turf high 97 (1st run) - 2nd of 9 to Katiykha (7 Jun Gowran Park 12f g-s RF 1934a) - also 1st of 3 giving 3lb to Insenor (21 Aug Roscommon RF 4068a). She is a solid performer in Listed races but lacks a turn-of-foot.
**M J Grassick in IRE [2-9] J F O'Malley.*

PALAIS (IRE) BHB 27f32a RR 28f 32a 1896[13]

5 b g Darshaan 11.9f **(81)** - Dance Festival (Nureyev (USA)) 8.7f **(78)**
Form - 780800
Record 2000 - 1st:0 2nd:0 3rd:0 Ran:5
Pre2000 - 1st:1 2nd:1 3rd:1 Ran:17
Win Prizemoney £2,892 *Total Prizemoney* £6,796
Wins * 1999 *Jan Southw (STD) 11f 65* <
2000 Turf 0-2: (11f, 14f) (g-s, gd) 2000 AW 0-3: (11f 2, 16f) (Fibr 3)
Fair gelding, effective 11f, - acts on Fibr, has worn blinkers. Turf high 28. AW high 13.
**J L Harris [1-23] J South (from Sir Michael Stoute [0-5] Jly 1998).*

PALANZO (IRE) BHB 100f RR 96f 4733[8]

2 b c Green Desert (USA) 7.8f **(78)** - Karpacka (IRE) **(100f)** (Rousillon (USA)) 8.2f **(74)**
Form - 218
Record 2000 - 1st:1 2nd:1 3rd:0 Ran:3
Win Prizemoney £5,486 *Total Prizemoney* £6,991
Wins * 2000 Spt Newbur (G-F) 6f 96 <
2000 Turf 1-3: (6f 1-2, 7f) (gd, frm 1-2)
Currently very useful colt. Turf high 96 - 1st of 21 from Mootafayill (15 Spt Newbury RF 4432). Strongly fancied when narrowly beaten on his debut, he made no mistake at Newbury in September and was not disgraced in the Somerville Tattersall Stakes on his final start. Likely to stay a mile, he is open to improvement but may struggle to win a Group race. **P W Harris [1-3] Mrs P W Harris.*

PALATIAL RR 93+f 4642[1]

2 b f Green Desert (USA) 7.8f **(78)** - White Palace **(81f)** (Shirley Heights) 10.3f **(74)**
Form - 222111
Record 2000 - 1st:3 2nd:3 3rd:0 Ran:6
Win Prizemoney £34,618 *Total Prizemoney* £37,908

Wins							
	*** 2000**	Spt Newmar	(G-S)	H	7f	89	93+ <
	*** 2000**	Spt Newbur	(G-F)		7f		86
	*** 2000**	Aug Newmar	(G-F)	H	7f	82	84

2000 Turf 3-6: (6f 3, 7f 3-3) (gd, g-f 1-1, frm 2-4)
Useful filly, effective 7f, acts on g-f to frm, best on frm. Turf high 93 - 1st of 22 giving 1lb to Love Everlasting (26 Spt Newmarket RF 4642) - also 1st of 8 from Sayedah (15 Spt Newbury RF 4437). Runner-up in ordinary maidens before landing a Newmarket nursery on her first run over seven furlongs, but improved to win a Newbury maiden and a Newmarket nursery the following month.
**J R Fanshawe [3-6] Cheveley Park Stud.*

PALAWAN BHB 76f73a RR 76f 73a 4832[5]

4 br g Polar Falcon (USA) 9f **(74)** - Krameria (Kris) 9.5f **(73)**
Form - 211203017625385
Record 2000 - 1st:3 2nd:3 3rd:2 Ran:15
Pre2000 - 1st:0 2nd:3 3rd:0 Ran:7
Win Prizemoney £8,032 *Total Prizemoney* £17,521

Wins							
	*** 2000**	Jun Windso	(G-F)		5f		69
	*** 2000**	*Feb Southw*	*(STD)*	*H*	*7f*	*71*	*78* <
	*** 2000**	*Feb Wolver*	*(STD)*		*7f*		*55+*

2000 Turf 1-12: (5f 1-8, 6f 4) (g-s 2, gd 2, g-f 5, frm 1-3) 2000 AW 2-3: (7f 2-3) (Fibr 2-3)

Scopey, above-average gelding, effective 5 to 7f, acts on gd to frm - acts on Fibr, and excels at Windsor. Turf high 76 - 3rd of 25 giving 7lb to At Large (8 May Windsor 6f g-f RF 1097) - also 1st of 8 from King of Peru (12 Jun Windsor RF 1909). AW high 78 - 1st of 10 giving 21lb to Itch (28 Feb Southwell RF 0369). Consistent.
**I A Balding [3-22] Westenders.*

PALLIUM (IRE) BHB 25f59a **RR 28f 59a** 5188[13]
12 b g Try My Best (USA) 7.8f **(68)** - Jungle Gardenia (Nonoalco (USA)) 8.5f **(66)**
Form - 0070000
Record 2000 - 1st:0 2nd:0 3rd:0 Ran:7
Pre2000 - 1st:7 2nd:14 3rd:13 Ran:139
Win Prizemoney £21,855 *Total Prizemoney* £46,469
Wins * 1997 Jly Hamilt (G-F) H 5f 45 47
2000 Turf 0-7: (5f 6, 6f) (sft, gd 2, g-f 2, frm 2)
Moderate gelding, has worn blinkers. Turf high 28.
**D A Nolan [1-53] Mrs J McFadyen-Murray (from Mrs A M Naughton [2-31] Spt 1996).*

PALMSTEAD BELLE (IRE) BHB 52f **RR 57f** 3630[15]
3 b f Wolfhound (USA) 7.3f **(71)** - Fiction (Dominion) 8.5f **(63)**
Form - 8000
Record 2000 - 1st:0 2nd:0 3rd:0 Ran:4
Pre2000 - 1st:1 2nd:0 3rd:1 Ran:6
Win Prizemoney £2,637 *Total Prizemoney* £3,200
Wins * 1999 May Nottin (FRM) 5.1f 80 <
2000 Turf 0-4: (5f 4) (gd, g-f 2, frm)
Scopey, fair filly, effective 5f, acts on g-f. Turf high 57.
**C B B Booth [1-10] The Palmstead Partnership.*

PALO BLANCO BHB 54f67a **RR 55f 67a** 5248[8]
9 b m Precocious 7.2f **(54)** - Linpac Mapleleaf (Dominion) 8.5f **(63)**
Form - 03342233246204401638
Record 2000 - 1st:1 2nd:4 3rd:5 Ran:19
Pre2000 - 1st:4 2nd:8 3rd:7 Ran:53
Win Prizemoney £15,510 *Total Prizemoney* £37,161
Wins *** 2000** *Spt Southw (STD) H 6f 47 53*
1997 Spt Sandow (G-F) C 5f 58
1996 May Ayr (GD) H 6f 71 73 <
2000 Turf 0-7: (6f 7) (g-s, g-f 5, frm) 2000 AW 1-12: (6f 1-12) (Equi 2, Fibr 1-10)
Average mare, effective 6f, acts on g-f to frm - acts on Fibr, and likes Wolverhampton. Turf high 55 - 6th of 25 giving 9lb to Bound To Please (6 Oct Windsor 6f g-f RF 4825). AW high 54 - 3rd of 13 giving 13lb to Whizz Kid (20 May Wolverhampton 6f Fibr RF 1354) - also 1st of 16 giving 2lb to Bangled (26 Spt Southwell RF 4655).
**Andrew Reid [1-20] A S Reid (from M J Ryan [0-9] Spt 1998).*

PALUA BHB 77f **RR 80f** 5104[2]
3 b c Sri Pekan (USA) - Reticent Bride (IRE) (Shy Groom (USA)) 10f **(66)**
Form - 34320332432
Record 2000 - 1st:0 2nd:3 3rd:5 Ran:11
Pre2000 - 1st:0 2nd:0 3rd:1 Ran:4
Win Prizemoney £0 *Total Prizemoney* £8,683
2000 Turf 0-11: (10f 3, 12f 4, 14f, 15f, 16f, 17f) (g-s, gd 4, g-f 2, frm 4)
Unfurnished, decent colt, effective 7 to 17f, acts on g-s to frm, best on gd, has worn blinkers (very effectively), prefers left handed tracks, prefers tight tracks. Turf high 80 - 2nd of 17 getting 16lb from Loop The Loup (20 Oct Doncaster 15f gd RF 5104). Consistent.
**Mrs A J Bowlby [0-15] Robert Hitchins.*

PALVIC LADY BHB 42f45a **RR 54df 45a** 4655[7]
4 b f Cotation 5f **(52)** - Palvic Grey (Kampala) 8.4f **(56)**
Form - 0087
Record 2000 - 1st:0 2nd:0 3rd:0 Ran:4
Pre2000 - 1st:1 2nd:0 3rd:2 Ran:13
Win Prizemoney £3,923 *Total Prizemoney* £5,070
Wins * 1999 Spt Beverl (GD) 5f 61 <
2000 Turf 0-2: (5f 2) (hrd 2) 2000 AW 0-2: (5f, 6f) (Fibr 2)
Leggy, fair filly, effective 5f, acts on gd. Turf high 35. AW high 39 (began Aug).
**C Smith [1-17] Alan Pickard.*

PAMELA ANSHAN BHB 40f **RR 38f** 4812[14]
3 b f Anshan 8.2f **(63)** - Have Form (Haveroid) 6f **(48)**
Form - 0087600
Record 2000 - 1st:0 2nd:0 3rd:0 Ran:7
Pre2000 - 1st:0 2nd:0 3rd:0 Ran:3
2000 Turf 0-7: (6f 2, 7f 2, 8f, 10f 2) (g-s 2, g-f 3, frm 2)
Workmanlike, very moderate filly, has worn blinkers. Turf high 38.
**J Cullinan [0-10] Alan Spargo Ltd Toolmakers.*

PAMIR (SWI) RR 92f 1155a[2]
3 b c Komtur (USA)
Form - 2
2000 Turf 0-1: (8f) (gd)
Currently useful colt. (1st run) - 2nd of 10 to Etbash (7 May Dielsdorf 8f gd RF 1155a). **K Schafflutzel in SWI [0-1].*

PAMPERED QUEEN (USA) RR 3438[12]
6 b m Red Ransom (USA) 8.6f **(83)** - Quadratic Queen (USA) (Quadratic (USA)) 7f **(75)**
Form - 0
Record 2000 - 1st:0 2nd:0 3rd:0 Ran:1
2000 Turf 0-1: (10f) (g-f)
Currently very poor mare.
**J R Best [0-1] K Woodhouse & Mrs A Woodhouse.*

PANDJOJOE (IRE) BHB 55f54a **RR 56f 54a** 5083[13]
4 b g Archway (IRE) 8.5f **(60)** - Vital Princess (Prince Sabo) 7.2f **(62)**
Form - 0556860030
Record 2000 - 1st:0 2nd:0 3rd:1 Ran:10
Pre2000 - 1st:3 2nd:0 3rd:0 Ran:15
Win Prizemoney £10,195 *Total Prizemoney* £10,983
Wins * 1999 May Haydoc (GD) H 6f 70 73
* 1999 May Windso (GD) H 6f 56 74+ <
* 1999 May Newcas (G-F) H 6f 56 64+
2000 Turf 0-10: (5f 4, 6f 5, 7f) (hvy, sft 2, gd 4, g-f 2, frm)
Tall, fair gelding, effective 6f, acts on g-f to frm, best on g-f, has worn blinkers. Turf high 56. **R A Fahey [3-25] J Dixon.*

PANG VALLEY GIRL RR 53f 3323[6]
2 ch f Rock Hopper 10.6f **(54)** - Riverine **(20f)** (Risk Me (FR)) 5.9f **(53)**
Form - 6
Record 2000 - 1st:0 2nd:0 3rd:0 Ran:1
2000 Turf 0-1: (7f) (g-f)
Currently fair filly. **H Morrison [0-1] Pangfield Partners.*

PANIS (USA) RR 90f 4838a[1]
2 b c Miswaki (USA) 8.1f **(81)** - Political Parody (FR) (Doonesbury (USA)) 7.7f **(99)**
Form - 31
2000 Turf 1-2: (8f, 9f 1-1) (gd 1-2)
Currently useful colt. Turf high 90 (began Spt) - 1st of 7 from Dayglow Dancer (30 Spt Longchamp RF 4838a).
**P Bary in FR [1-2] Ecurie Jean-Louis Bouchard.*

PAN JAMMER BHB 100f **RR 94f** 4463[6]
2 b c Piccolo - Ingerence (FR) (Akarad (FR)) 9f **(76)**
Form - 41231406
Record 2000 - 1st:2 2nd:1 3rd:1 Ran:8
Win Prizemoney £30,842 *Total Prizemoney* £44,842
Wins *** 2000** Jly Currag (GD) G3 6.3f 91+ <
*** 2000** May Salisb (GD) 5f 69
2000 Turf 2-8: (5f 1-3, 6f 1-5) (g-s, gd 2-6, g-f)
Useful colt, effective 5 to 6f, acts on gd. Turf high 94 - also 1st of 5 from Pirate Of Penzance (16 Jly Curragh RF 2916a). Inconsistent. A tough individual, he was a cosy winner of the Group 3 Anglesey Stakes at The Curragh in July and ran creditably thereafter. Thoroughly exposed, he will struggle to win another Group race in 2001. **M R Channon [2-8] Ms Lynn Bell.*

PANNA RR 76f 5236[4]
2 b f Polish Precedent (USA) 9f **(73)** - Gull Nook (Mill Reef (USA)) 10.5f **(78)**
Form - 4
Record 2000 - 1st:0 2nd:0 3rd:0 Ran:1
Win Prizemoney £0 *Total Prizemoney* £374
2000 Turf 0-1: (7f) (g-s)
Currently above-average filly. (1st run) - 4th of 22 to Good Standing (28 Oct Newmarket 7f g-s RF 5236).

**G Wragg [0-1] Lord Halifax.*

PANOORAS LORD (IRE) BHB 20f28a **RR 19f 28a** 1075[12]

6 b g Topanoora 8.3f **(67)** - Ladyship (Windjammer (USA)) 7f **(59)**
Form - 0
Record 2000 - 1st:0 2nd:0 3rd:0 Ran:1
Pre2000 - 1st:0 2nd:0 3rd:0 Ran:4
2000 Turf 0-1: (13f) (g-f)
Poor gelding. **J S Wainwright [1-20] J S Wainwright.*

PANSY BHB 53f48a **RR 54f 48a** 369[10]

4 br m Lugana Beach 7f **(63)** - Smah (Mtoto)
Form - 0
Record 2000 - 1st:0 2nd:0 3rd:0 Ran:1
Pre2000 - 1st:0 2nd:0 3rd:0 Ran:9
Win Prizemoney £0 *Total Prizemoney £423*
2000 AW 0-1: (7f) (Fibr)
Neat, fair filly, has worn blinkers.
**J A Pickering [0-1] Mrs Leesa Dennis (from H Morrison [0-6] Jly 1999).*

PANTAR (IRE) BHB 97f90a **RR 96f 90a** 4740[22]

5 b g Shirley Heights 12.1f **(76)** - Spring Daffodil (Pharly (FR)) 9.8f **(68)**
Form - 732143630023610
Record 2000 - 1st:2 2nd:2 3rd:4 Ran:15
Pre2000 - 1st:1 2nd:1 3rd:5 Ran:22
Win Prizemoney £33,320 *Total Prizemoney £82,288*

Wins	*** 2000**	Spt	Goodwo	(GD)	H	9f	93	96 <
	*** 2000**	*Mar*	*Wolver*	*(STD)*		*9.4f*		*86*
	* 1998	Jun	Goodwo	(GD)	H	8f	90	96 <

2000 Turf 1-10: (8f 5, 9f 1-3, 10f 2) (sft, g-s 2, gd 1-3, g-f 2, frm 2) 2000 AW 1-5: (8f 2, 9f 1-3) (Fibr 1-4, Dirt)
Very useful gelding, effective 8 to 10f, best at 8f, acts on sft to frm, best on g-f, has worn blinkers (very effectively), prefers right handed tracks, likes tight tracks, excels at Kempton and Sandown and Goodwood. Turf high 96 (1st run) - 4th of 24 giving 4lb to John Ferneley (25 Mar Doncaster 8f gd RF 0494) - also 1st of 15 giving 3lb to Welsh Wind (8 Spt Goodwood RF 4302). AW high 86. He raced with greater consistency last term and is always one to consider in smart handicap company around a mile. Seemingly effective on any ground, he is suited by a fast run race.
**I A Balding [3-37] Robert Hitchins.*

PANTHER (IRE) BHB 28f37a **RR 13f 37a** 4272[11]

10 ch g Primo Dominie 7.2f **(67)** - High Profile (High Top) 10.2f **(67)**
Form - 000
Record 2000 - 1st:0 2nd:0 3rd:0 Ran:3
Pre2000 - 1st:7 2nd:8 3rd:14 Ran:95
Win Prizemoney £24,288 *Total Prizemoney £38,151*

Wins	1996	Aug	Cheste	(G-S)	H	5.1f	68	69 <
	1996	Jun	Warwic	(FRM)	C	6f		57
	1996	May	Redcar	(G-F)	C	6f		63
	1996	Apr	Catter	(GD)		6f		57

2000 Turf 0-3: (5f, 6f, 8f) (gd, g-f 2)
Poor gelding, has worn blinkers. Turf high 13 (began Aug).
**J Pearce [0-3] Treble Chance Partnership (from P D Evans [1-21] Dec 1998).*

PAOLINI (GER) **RR 117f** 4289a[7]

3 b c Lando (GER) - Prairie Darling (Stanford) 7.9f **(56)**
Form - 3027
2000 Turf 0-4: (12f 4) (hvy, sft, gd, g-f)
High-class colt. Turf high 117 - 2nd of 9 getting 9lb from Catella (13 Aug Gelsenkirchen-horst 12f gd RF 3736a). He was touched off by the smart Catella in a Group 1 at Gelsenkirchen in August, but failed to reproduce that form in the Grosser Preis Von Baden. Inconsistent but talented, he should pick up a Group race in 2001.
**A Wohler in GER [0-4].*

PAPABILE (USA) BHB 103f **RR 104f** 4739[8]

3 b f Chief's Crown (USA) 10.2f **(75)** - La Papagena (Habitat) 9.4f **(70)**
Form - 2411148
Record 2000 - 1st:3 2nd:1 3rd:0 Ran:7
Pre2000 - 1st:0 2nd:1 3rd:0 Ran:2
Win Prizemoney £40,582 *Total Prizemoney £48,191*

Wins	*** 2000**	Aug	Ascot	(G-F)	L	8f		102 <
	*** 2000**	Jun	Ascot	(G-F)	LH	8f	89	95
	*** 2000**	Jun	Yarmou	(GD)		8f		88

2000 Turf 3-7: (7f, 8f 3-6) (g-s, gd 2-3, g-f 1-3)
Scopey, very useful filly, effective 8f, acts on gd to g-f, best on gd. Turf high 104 - 4th of 11 getting 4lb from Iftiraas (3 Spt Curragh 8f gd RF 4254a) - also 1st of 6 from Courting (13 Aug Ascot RF 3603). Got off the mark at Yarmouth after a string of good efforts in maiden and handicap company and followed up with two victories in Listed events at Ascot. Ran pretty well when stepped up to Group Three company at the Curragh.
**W Jarvis [3-9] Exors of the late Lord Howard de Walden.*

PAPAGENA (USA) BHB 44f50a **RR 53f 50a** 1183[10]

3 b br f Robellino (USA) 9.5f **(68)** - Morning Crown (USA) (Chief's Crown (USA)) 9.8f **(72)**
Form - 5646243070
Record 2000 - 1st:0 2nd:1 3rd:1 Ran:7
Pre2000 - 1st:0 2nd:1 3rd:1 Ran:10
Win Prizemoney £0 *Total Prizemoney £3,838*
2000 Turf 0-2: (8f, 10f) (gd, hrd) 2000 AW 0-5: (6f, 9f 3, 11f) (Fibr 5)
Neat, fair filly, effective 9f, - acts on Fibr, often wears blinkers (effectively), likes left handed tracks, likes tight tracks. Turf high 31. AW high 50 - 3rd of 9 getting 21lb from Favorisio (23 Mar Wolverhampton 9f Fibr RF 0482).
**C W Thornton [0-17] Simon Brown.*

PAPARAZZA (IRE) BHB 42f **RR 49f** 4764[14]

3 b f Arazi (USA) 9.2f **(74)** - Marie de Flandre (FR) (Crystal Palace (FR)) 12.5f **(76)**
Form - 5000
Record 2000 - 1st:0 2nd:0 3rd:0 Ran:4
2000 Turf 0-4: (8f 2, 10f, 12f) (g-s, g-f 2, frm)
Neat, moderate filly. Turf high 49 (began Aug).
**P W Harris [0-4] Godfrey, Kirkland, Willett & Winter.*

PAPE DIOUF BHB 36f53a **RR 32f 53a** 4871[17]

3 b g Prince Sabo 6.6f **(64)** - Born to Dance (Dancing Brave (USA)) 8.4f **(76)**
Form - 0141060000700
Record 2000 - 1st:2 2nd:0 3rd:0 Ran:13
Pre2000 - 1st:0 2nd:2 3rd:0 Ran:8
Win Prizemoney £3,642 *Total Prizemoney £5,214*

Wins	**2000**	*Mar*	*Lingfi*	*(STD)*	*S*	*5f*		*56 <*
	2000	*Feb*	*Lingfi*	*(STD)*	*S*	*5f*		*55*

2000 Turf 0-8: (5f 7, 6f) (sft, g-s, gd, g-f 2, frm 3) 2000 AW 2-5: (5f 2-2, 6f 3) (Equi 2-3, Fibr 2)
Light-framed, fair gelding, effective 5f, acts on g-f to frm - acts on AW, has worn blinkers (very effectively), likes left handed tracks. Turf high 44. AW high 56 - 1st of 6 from Itsgottabdun (1 Mar Lingfield RF 0388) - also 1st of 8 from Power And Demand (9 Feb Lingfield RF 0251).
**Mrs D Thomson [0-7] Willie McKay (from B Smart [2-7] Apr 2000).*

PAPER MOON (IRE) **RR 96f** 1584a[11]

3 b f Lake Coniston (IRE) - Marie Noelle (FR) (Brigadier Gerard) 9.3f **(58)**
Form - 170
2000 Turf 1-3: (8f 1-3) (sft 1-1, g-s, g-f)
Currently very useful filly. Turf high 96 - also 1st of 15 from Yara (22 Apr Cork RF 0866a). She went missing after being outclassed in the Irish 1000 Guineas. **A P O'Brien in IRE [1-3] Michael Tabor.*

PAPERWEIGHT BHB 60f68a **RR 71f 68a** 3438[9]

4 b m In The Wings 11.2f **(77)** - Crystal Reay (Sovereign Dancer (USA)) 11.2f **(68)**
Form - 42303440
Record 2000 - 1st:0 2nd:1 3rd:2 Ran:8
Pre2000 - 1st:0 2nd:2 3rd:1 Ran:5
Win Prizemoney £0 *Total Prizemoney £5,310*
2000 Turf 0-3: (10f 2, 11f) (gd 2, g-f) 2000 AW 0-5: (9f, 10f 3, 12f) (Equi 3, Fibr 2)
Rangy, above-average filly, effective 10f, acts on g-s to frm, has worn blinkers. Turf high 56. AW high 65. Inconsistent.
**Miss K M George [0-13] Exterior Profiles Ltd (from L M Cumani [0-5] Oct 1999).*

PAPI SPECIAL (IRE) BHB 47f **RR 57f** 4868[11]

3 b g Tragic Role (USA) 9.4f **(63)** - Practical (Ballymore) 7.3f **(64)**
Form - 002401D2000

Record 2000 - 1st:1 2nd:2 3rd:0 Ran:11
Pre2000 - 1st:0 2nd:2 3rd:0 Ran:4
Win Prizemoney £3,087 *Total Prizemoney* £7,777
Wins * **2000** Jly Hamilt (G-F) H 13f 54 56 <
2000 Turf 1-11: (10f, 11f 2, 12f 3, 13f 1-4, 14f) (hvy, gd 4, g-f 1-4, frm 2)
Scopey, fair gelding, effective 8f, acts on sft to gd, mostly wears blinkers, likes tight tracks. Turf high 57.
**I Semple [1-15] Mrs E Chung.*

PAPPUS (GER) RR 99f 2581a[12]

3 b c Acatenango (GER) - **(87f 72a)** 00
Form - 630
2000 Turf 0-3: (10f, 11f, 12f) (sft 2, gd)
Currently very useful colt. Turf high 99. **M Hofer in GER [0-3].*

PARABLE BHB 54f70a RR 60f 70a 2215[5]

4 b c Midyan (USA) 9.9f **(64)** - Top Table (Shirley Heights) 10.3f **(74)**
Form - 5130085
Record 2000 - 1st:1 2nd:0 3rd:1 Ran:7
Pre2000 - 1st:0 2nd:0 3rd:0 Ran:3
Win Prizemoney £4,173 *Total Prizemoney* £5,168
Wins * **2000** *Mar Southw (STD) H 12f 66 68* <
2000 Turf 0-4: (10f, 11f, 14f 2) (g-s, gd, g-f, frm) 2000 AW 1-3: (12f 1-3) (Fibr 1-3)
Strong, above-average colt, effective 8 to 12f, best at 12f, acts on g-f - acts on Fibr, has worn blinkers, prefers tight tracks. Turf high 60. AW high 74 - 3rd of 7 to Green Bopper (20 Mar Southwell 12f Fibr RF 0468) - also 1st of 10 getting 6lb from Green Bopper (14 Mar Southwell RF 0441).
**D W Barker [1-7] Triple G DA Racing Syndicate (from L M Cumani [0-3] Oct 1999).*

PARADISE (IRE) RR 36f 723[16]

3 b g Distinctly North (USA) 7.4f **(63)** - Why Not Glow (IRE) (Glow (USA)) 6.7f **(71)**
Form - 0
Record 2000 - 1st:0 2nd:0 3rd:0 Ran:1
Pre2000 - 1st:0 2nd:0 3rd:0 Ran:1
2000 Turf 0-1: (6f) (g-s)
Workmanlike, currently very moderate gelding.
**J J O'Neill [0-2] Carlton Appointments (Aberdeen) Ltd.*

PARADISE GARDEN (USA) BHB 79f RR 87f 4829[14]

3 b c Septieme Ciel (USA) - Water Course (USA) (Irish River (FR)) 8.6f **(78)**
Form - 0384070
Record 2000 - 1st:0 2nd:0 3rd:1 Ran:7
Pre2000 - 1st:1 2nd:2 3rd:1 Ran:5
Win Prizemoney £2,253 *Total Prizemoney* £13,864
Wins * 1999 Aug Newcas (GD) 8f 68+ <
2000 Turf 0-6: (8f 3, 10f 2, 12f) (g-s, gd 2, g-f 3) 2000 AW 0-1: (9f) (Dirt)
Unfurnished, useful colt, effective 8f, acts on g-f to frm. Turf high 87. **M Johnston [1-12] David Abell.*

PARADISE LANE BHB 70f RR 61f 4487[13]

4 ch g Alnasr Alwasheek 9.4f **(62)** - La Belle Vie (Indian King (USA)) 7.4f **(64)**
Form - 200000
Record 2000 - 1st:0 2nd:1 3rd:0 Ran:6
Pre2000 - 1st:2 2nd:1 3rd:0 Ran:9
Win Prizemoney £11,597 *Total Prizemoney* £14,647
Wins * 1999 May Cheste (G-F) H 5.1f 84 91 <
* 1999 Apr Nottin (SFT) 5.1f 88
2000 Turf 0-6: (5f 5, 6f) (g-s 2, gd 2, g-f 2)
Neat, average gelding, effective 5f, acts on sft to g-f. Turf high 81. He looked to be improving when winning in good style over the minimum at Nottingham and Chester in the spring of 1999 before the Handicapper caught up with him, but ran very well on his Kempton reappearance. A speedy front-runner, he has won on fast ground but goes very well on soft, and is now back to his winning mark.
**B R Millman [2-15] Robin Lawson.*

PARADISE NAVY BHB 40f50a RR 49df 50a 4648[9]

11 b g Slip Anchor 12.7f **(75)** - Ivory Waltz (USA) (Sir Ivor) 10.2f **(70)**
Form - 0083670
Record 2000 - 1st:0 2nd:0 3rd:1 Ran:7
Pre2000 - 1st:12 2nd:9 3rd:14 Ran:94
Win Prizemoney £38,091 *Total Prizemoney* £63,274
Wins * 1999 *Jan Lingfi (STD) H 16f 61 64*
* 1998 *Dec Wolver (STD) H 16.2f 50 60*
* 1998 *Nov Southw (STD) H 14f 52 55*
* 1998 Aug Salisb (G-F) H 14.1f 67 71
* 1998 May Nottin (FRM) H 16f 63 65
* 1997 Oct Yarmou (FRM) C 14.1f 56
* 1997 Aug Yarmou (G-F) H 14.1f 70 74 <
* 1997 Jly Doncas (GD) H 16.5f 64 66
* 1997 Apr Folkes (G-F) H 15.4f 65 71
* 1996 *Aug Lingfi (STD) H 16f 65 66*
* 1996 Jly Bath (FRM) H 17.2f 64 69+
2000 Turf 0-6: (12f, 13f 2, 16f 2, 17f) (gd 3, g-f 2, hrd) 2000 AW 0-1: (16f) (Fibr)
Average gelding, effective 14 to 16f, best at 14f, acts on gd to frm - acts on Equi, mostly wears blinkers, favours tight tracks. Turf high 45. Kept on the go, he pays his way in minor company on turf and sand. He is a very difficult ride who needs to be left to do it his way, and when he is likely to show his best is very difficult to predict.
**C R Egerton [11-97] Elite Racing Club (from M C Pipe [2-7] Apr 1994).*

PARADISE YANGSHUO BHB 42f RR 47f 4491[10]

3 b f Whittingham (IRE) - Poly Static (IRE) **(37f)** (Statoblest)
Form - 004153000
Record 2000 - 1st:1 2nd:0 3rd:1 Ran:9
Pre2000 - 1st:0 2nd:3 3rd:0 Ran:10
Win Prizemoney £2,744 *Total Prizemoney* £5,841
Wins * **2000** Jun Mussel (FRM) 5f 49 <
2000 Turf 1-9: (5f 1-6, 6f 3) (gd 2, g-f 3, frm 1-3, hrd)
Scopey, moderate filly, effective 5f, acts on sft to frm. Turf high 49 - 1st of 6 getting 5lb from Tartan Island (26 Jun Musselburgh RF 2273).
**E J Alston [1-16] Valley Paddocks Racing Ltd (from M R Channon [0-3] Apr 1999).*

PARA GLIDER (FR) RR 85f 4965[11]

2 b c Jeune Homme (USA) - Idee Folle (FR) (Crystal Palace (FR)) 12.5f **(76)**
Form - 50
Record 2000 - 1st:0 2nd:0 3rd:0 Ran:2
2000 Turf 0-2: (6f, 7f) (g-s, gd)
Currently useful colt. Turf high 85 (began Oct).
**G C Bravery [0-2] Khalifa Dasmal.*

PARAGON OF VIRTUE BHB 83f RR 88f 2755[3]

3 ch c Cadeaux Genereux 7.9f **(76)** - Madame Dubois (Legend of France (USA)) 9.5f **(61)**
Form - 7233
Record 2000 - 1st:0 2nd:1 3rd:2 Ran:4
Win Prizemoney £0 *Total Prizemoney* £3,089
2000 Turf 0-4: (7f, 8f 2, 10f) (g-s, gd 2, frm)
Well made, useful colt. Turf high 88 - 3rd of 11 getting 6lb from Happy Diamond (13 Jly Doncaster 10f frm RF 2755).
**Sir Michael Stoute [0-4] Abdullah Ali.*

PARDAN BHB 36f24a RR 27f 24a 345[7]

6 b g Pharly (FR) 11.5f **(64)** - Silent Pool (Relkino) 8.9f **(65)**
Form - 657
Record 2000 - 1st:0 2nd:0 3rd:0 Ran:3
Pre2000 - 1st:1 2nd:1 3rd:3 Ran:23
Win Prizemoney £2,215 *Total Prizemoney* £3,865
Wins * 1999 Jly Nottin (GD) SH 14.1f 33 35 <
2000 AW 0-3: (12f, 13f, 16f) (Equi, Fibr 2)
Little account gelding, effective 14f, acts on g-f, has worn blinkers. AW high 11. Becoming disappointing.
**B Palling [1-35] Mrs M M Palling.*

PARDY PET (IRE) BHB 33f RR 43f 4320[14]

3 ch f Petardia 8.2f **(58)** - Elite Exhibition (Exhibitioner) 8.7f **(61)**
Form - 60080500
Record 2000 - 1st:0 2nd:0 3rd:0 Ran:7
Pre2000 - 1st:1 2nd:0 3rd:0 Ran:8
Win Prizemoney £1,912 *Total Prizemoney* £1,912
Wins 1999 Jly Leices (G-F) S 5f 55 <
2000 Turf 0-7: (5f 3, 6f 3, 7f) (gd 4, g-f, frm 2)
Moderate filly, effective 5f, acts on g-f, has worn blinkers. Turf

high 51.
**C G Cox [0-10] Mel Davies & Partners (from M J Heaton-Ellis [1-5] Aug 1999).*

PARES (IRE) RR 95f 3944a[2]
2 ch c Catrail (USA) - Mamoura (IRE) (Lomond (USA)) 8.8f **(65)**
Form - 2
2000 Turf 0-1: (8f) (g-f)
Currently very useful colt. (1st run) - 2nd of 10 to Equerry (19 Aug Deauville 8f g-f RF 3944a). **in FR [0-1].*

PARISIAN LADY (IRE) BHB 43f50a RR 50f 50a 4757[8]
5 b m Paris House 5.9f **(64)** - Mia Gigi (Hard Fought) 8.8f **(62)**
Form - 81066344282U40
Record 2000 - 1st:0 2nd:2 3rd:1 Ran:10
Pre2000 - 1st:3 2nd:1 3rd:1 Ran:23
Win Prizemoney £7,752 *Total Prizemoney* £20,241
Wins * 1999 *Dec Lingfi (STD) H 8f 53 55*
* 1997 Jly Salisb (G-F) 6f 93+ <
* 1997 Jun Salisb (G-F) 6f 80
2000 Turf 0-7: (8f, 10f 5, 12f) (g-s, gd, g-f, frm 2, hrd 2) 2000 AW 0-3: (9f, 12f 2) (Equi 2, Fibr)
Fair filly, effective 8 to 12f, best at 12f, acts on frm - acts on Equi, has worn blinkers, likes left handed tracks, likes tight tracks. Turf high 50 - 2nd of 6 giving 1lb to Alpha Rose (24 Jly Brighton 12f frm RF 3074). AW high 50 - 3rd of 5 giving 5lb to Sleave Silk (16 Feb Lingfield 12f Equi RF 0294). Consistent. She ran her best race of the season when third in an Epsom Listed event in June, but faced stiff tasks throughout the campaign and was not up to it.
**A G Newcombe [3-33] Advanced Marketing Services Ltd.*

PARISIENNE HILL BHB 25f RR 22f 5314[9]
4 b f Lapierre - Snarry Hill (Vitiges (FR)) 8.2f **(59)**
Form - 0870700
Record 2000 - 1st:0 2nd:0 3rd:0 Ran:7
Pre2000 - 1st:0 2nd:0 3rd:0 Ran:13
2000 Turf 0-7: (9f, 10f 3, 12f 2, 16f) (sft, g-f 2, frm 4)
Light-framed, little account filly. Turf high 22.
**B W Murray [0-18] B Murray (from R A Fahey [0-3] Oct 1998).*

PARISIEN STAR (IRE) BHB 86f RR 89f 4302[8]
4 ch g Paris House 5.9f **(64)** - Auction Maid (IRE) (Auction Ring (USA)) 8.6f **(65)**
Form - 48451248
Record 2000 - 1st:1 2nd:1 3rd:0 Ran:8
Pre2000 - 1st:2 2nd:3 3rd:1 Ran:18
Win Prizemoney £20,855 *Total Prizemoney* £52,805
Wins * **2000** Aug Goodwo (G-F) H 8f 79 84 <
1998 Spt Newbur (gd) H 7.3f 80 82
1998 Spt Epsom (GD) H 6f 74 76
2000 Turf 1-8: (7f 3, 8f 1-4, 9f) (sft, g-s, gd 4, g-f 1-1, frm)
Workmanlike, useful gelding, effective 7 to 9f, best at 8f, acts on sft to frm, best on gd, prefers right handed tracks, excels at Lingfield and Goodwood. Turf high 89 - 2nd of 22 getting 13lb from Persiano (3 Aug Goodwood 8f gd RF 3343) - also 1st of 12 giving 1lb to Elmhurst Boy (1 Aug Goodwood RF 3280). He ended a long losing run when winning at Goodwood in August and failed by the minimum margin to follow-up over the same course and distance just two days later. Paid for that with a rise in the handicap though. **N Hamilton [1-9] P Elliott (from G Lewis [2-17] Aug 1999).*

PARKER BHB 72f RR 78f 4326[2]
3 b c Magic Ring (IRE) 6.5f **(64)** - Miss Loving (Northfields (USA)) 9f **(72)**
Form - 2463532
Record 2000 - 1st:0 2nd:2 3rd:2 Ran:7
Pre2000 - 1st:0 2nd:0 3rd:1 Ran:3
Win Prizemoney £0 *Total Prizemoney* £3,303
2000 Turf 0-7: (6f 2, 7f 3, 8f 2) (gd, g-f 2, frm 4)
Scopey, above-average colt, effective 6 to 8f, best at 7f, acts on sft to frm. Turf high 78. Consistent.
**B Palling [0-10] Mrs J Hamilton-Jones.*

PARKER'S PEACE (IRE) BHB 50f RR 49f 2357[5]
3 b g Common Grounds 8.1f **(66)** - Harmer (IRE) (Alzao (USA)) 7.1f **(68)**
Form - 075
Record 2000 - 1st:0 2nd:0 3rd:0 Ran:3
Pre2000 - 1st:0 2nd:0 3rd:0 Ran:3
2000 Turf 0-3: (8f, 10f, 12f) (gd, g-f, frm)
Scopey, moderate gelding. Turf high 47.
**M L W Bell [0-6] Mrs Mary Watt.*

PARK HALL RR 79f 5238[6]
2 b c Saddlers' Hall (IRE) 10.5f **(65)** - Diamond Park (IRE) **(60f)** (Alzao (USA)) 7.1f **(68)**
Form - 46
Record 2000 - 1st:0 2nd:0 3rd:0 Ran:2
Win Prizemoney £0 *Total Prizemoney* £596
2000 Turf 0-2: (7f, 10f) (g-s 2)
Currently above-average colt. Turf high 79 (began Oct). Showed promise on his Lingfield debut, and looks sure to progress with experience. **C E Brittain [0-2] Wyck Hall Stud.*

PARK ROYAL BHB 21f RR 22f 4539[13]
5 b g Secret Appeal - Mohibbah (USA) (Conquistador Cielo (USA)) 8.8f **(69)**
Form - 8680
Record 2000 - 1st:0 2nd:0 3rd:0 Ran:3
Pre2000 - 1st:0 2nd:0 3rd:0 Ran:8
2000 Turf 0-1: (12f) (gd) 2000 AW 0-2: (11f, 12f) (Fibr 2)
Little account gelding. AW high 15. **P Butler [2-26] Mrs P A Wood.*

PARKSIDE (IRE) BHB 64f RR 71f 3643[9]
4 b g Common Grounds 8.1f **(66)** - Warg (Dancing Brave (USA)) 8.4f **(76)**
Form - 05037000
Record 2000 - 1st:0 2nd:0 3rd:1 Ran:8
Pre2000 - 1st:1 2nd:0 3rd:1 Ran:5
Win Prizemoney £4,334 *Total Prizemoney* £7,632
Wins * 1999 Aug Warwic (GD) 7.7f 85 <
2000 Turf 0-8: (7f, 8f 6, 10f) (sft, g-s, gd 4, frm 2)
Scopey, above-average gelding, effective 8f, acts on sft to gd. Turf high 76 - 5th of 10 getting 7lb from Nimello (28 Apr Sandown 8f sft RF 0894). Inconsistent. **W R Muir [1-13] The Parkside Partnership.*

PARKSIDE PROPHECY BHB 53f RR 47+f 2662[6]
2 ch g Aragon 7.7f **(58)** - Fairgroundprincess (Kalaglow) 9.8f **(67)**
Form - 6
Record 2000 - 1st:0 2nd:0 3rd:0 Ran:1
2000 Turf 0-1: (6f) (gd)
Currently moderate gelding. **M R Channon [0-1] Mrs Jean Keegan.*

PARKSIDE PROSPECT BHB 46f44a RR 50f 44a 4116[19]
3 b f Piccolo - Banner (USA) **(75f)** (Known Fact (USA)) 7.4f **(67)**
Form - 2314577700
Record 2000 - 1st:0 2nd:0 3rd:0 Ran:7
Pre2000 - 1st:3 2nd:2 3rd:4 Ran:16
Win Prizemoney £10,027 *Total Prizemoney* £13,672
Wins 1999 *Dec Lingfi (STD) C 6f 59*
1999 Nov Mussel (GD) SH 5f 46 50
1999 Jun Newcas (GD) S 6f 60 <
2000 Turf 0-2: (6f, 7f) (frm 2) 2000 AW 0-5: (5f, 6f 3, 7f) (Equi 4, Fibr)
Neat, fair filly, effective 6f, acts on g-f to frm - acts on Equi, best on g-f, has worn blinkers. Turf high 16 (began Jly). AW high 48. Inconsistent.
**T D McCarthy [0-7] R Gurney (from M R Channon [3-16] Dec 1999).*

PARKSIDE PURSUIT BHB 81f RR 68f 2230[1]
2 b c Pursuit of Love 9.5f **(69)** - Ivory Bride (Domynsky) 8f **(82)**
Form - 701
Record 2000 - 1st:1 2nd:0 3rd:0 Ran:3
Win Prizemoney £2,860 *Total Prizemoney* £2,860
Wins * **2000** Jun Redcar (FRM) 5f 68 <
2000 Turf 1-3: (5f 1-2, 6f) (g-f, frm 1-2)
Currently average colt. Turf high 68 - 1st of 9 from Baccura (23 Jun Redcar RF 2230).
**M R Channon [1-3] John Livock & Mrs Jean Keegan.*

PARTE PRIMA BHB 38f45a RR 36f 45a 2818[6]
4 b g Perpendicular - Pendle's Secret (Le Johnstan) 7.4f **(55)**
Form - 46
Record 2000 - 1st:0 2nd:0 3rd:0 Ran:2
Pre2000 - 1st:0 2nd:0 3rd:4 Ran:9

Win Prizemoney £0 *Total Prizemoney* £1,117
2000 Turf 0-1: (10f) (gd) 2000 AW 0-1: (12f) (Fibr)
Neat, very moderate gelding, effective 7f, - acts on Fibr, has worn blinkers, likes left handed tracks.
**C L Popham [0-4] C L Popham (from S E Kettlewell [0-9] Spt 1999).*

PARTING SHOT RR 59f 1265[9]
2 b c Young Ern - Tribal Lady (Absalom) 7.2f **(58)**
Form - 0
Record 2000 - 1st:0 2nd:0 3rd:0 Ran:1
2000 Turf 0-1: (6f) (frm)
Currently fair colt. **T D Easterby [0-1] C H Stevens.*

PARTY CHARMER BHB 90f **RR 86?f** 4448[9]
2 b f Charmer 9f **(59)** - Party Game (Red Alert) 7.6f **(66)**
Form - 140650
Record 2000 - 1st:1 2nd:0 3rd:0 Ran:6
Win Prizemoney £3,556 *Total Prizemoney* £6,350
Wins * **2000** May Warwic (SFT) 5f 76+ <
2000 Turf 1-6: (5f 1-3, 6f 2, 7f) (sft 1-1, gd 3, frm 2)
Useful filly, effective 5f, acts on sft. Turf high 86. A winner at Warwick on her debut, she has been hopelessly outclassed in decent company since. **C E Brittain [1-6] Michael Clarke.*

PARTY PLOY BHB 66f62a **RR 72f 62a** 4475[8]
2 b g Deploy 11.4f **(67)** - Party Treat (IRE) (Millfontaine)
Form - 788
Record 2000 - 1st:0 2nd:0 3rd:0 Ran:3
2000 Turf 0-2: (6f, 7f) (g-f, frm) 2000 AW 0-1: (8f) (Fibr)
Currently above-average gelding. Turf high 72 (began Jly).
**K R Burke [0-3] Clive Batt.*

PARVENUE (FR) BHB 80f **RR 80f** 3401[4]
2 b f Ezzoud (IRE) - Patria (USA) **(72+f)** (Mr Prospector (USA)) 8.8f **(78)**
Form - 124
Record 2000 - 1st:1 2nd:1 3rd:0 Ran:3
Win Prizemoney £2,646 *Total Prizemoney* £3,845
Wins * **2000** May Nottin (GD) 6.1f 64+ <
2000 Turf 1-3: (6f 1-1, 7f 2) (g-f 1-1, frm 2)
Currently decent filly. Turf high 80 - 4th of 6 getting 5lb from Atlantis Prince (5 Aug Newmarket 7f frm RF 3401). Showed a turn of foot to win at Nottingham, but disappointed next time on fast ground. **E A L Dunlop [1-3] Hesmonds Stud.*

PASADENA BHB 52f **RR 38f** 2565[9]
3 b f Emarati (USA) 6.6f **(63)** - Eccolina (Formidable (USA)) 9.2f **(63)**
Form - 040000
Record 2000 - 1st:0 2nd:0 3rd:0 Ran:6
Win Prizemoney £0 *Total Prizemoney* £343
2000 Turf 0-6: (7f, 8f 4, 10f) (g-s, gd 3, g-f 2)
Workmanlike, very moderate filly, has worn blinkers. Turf high 66.
**H Morrison [0-6] Mrs Sally Faber.*

PAS DE PROBLEME (IRE) RR 68f 4829[9]
4 ch g Ela-Mana-Mou 12.7f **(72)** - Torriglia (USA) (Nijinsky (CAN)) 10.3f **(77)**
Form - 8153146080
Record 2000 - 1st:2 2nd:0 3rd:1 Ran:10
Pre2000 - 1st:0 2nd:1 3rd:0 Ran:9
Win Prizemoney £9,435 *Total Prizemoney* £12,174
Wins * **2000** May Sandow (HVY) H 10f 63 68 <
* **2000** Apr Warwic (HVY) H 10.5f 56 64
2000 Turf 2-10: (10f 1-4, 11f 1-4, 12f, 13f) (hvy 1-2, sft, g-s 1-3, gd, g-f 3)
Neat, average gelding, effective 9 to 12f, acts on hvy to g-f, best on g-f, likes tight tracks, and does well at Kempton. Turf high 68 - 1st of 8 giving 6lb to Generate (29 May Sandown RF 1540) - also 1st of 9 giving 19lb to Annadawi (24 Apr Warwick RF 0856). Becoming disappointing. Both of his wins last season have come over ten furlongs on heavy ground and he should be kept in mind for when those conditions prevail again.
**M Blanshard [2-19] Capt Francis Burne.*

PAS DE SURPRISE RR 8f 4807[18]
2 b c Dancing Spree (USA) 8f **(59)** - Supreme Rose (Frimley Park) 6.5f **(67)**
Form - 0
Record 2000 - 1st:0 2nd:0 3rd:0 Ran:1
2000 Turf 0-1: (7f) (g-s)
Currently very poor colt. **M Blanshard [0-1] Capt Francis Burne.*

PAS FARIBOLE (IRE) RR 35f 4813[14]
3 b f Last Tycoon 9.4f **(73)** - Faribole (IRE) (Esprit du Nord (USA))
Form - 80
Record 2000 - 1st:0 2nd:0 3rd:0 Ran:2
2000 Turf 0-2: (8f, 10f) (g-s, g-f)
Leggy, currently very moderate filly. Turf high 35 (began Aug).
**Dr J D Scargill [0-2] W J de Ruiter.*

PASHMEENA (IRE) BHB 77f **RR 77f** 5129[18]
2 b f Barathea (IRE) - Auriga **(75df)** (Belmez (USA))
Form - 2635770
Record 2000 - 1st:0 2nd:1 3rd:1 Ran:7
Win Prizemoney £0 *Total Prizemoney* £2,295
2000 Turf 0-7: (5f 2, 6f 2, 7f 3) (sft, g-s, gd 2, g-f 2, frm)
Above-average filly, effective 5 to 7f, best at 7f, acts on gd to frm, best on gd. Turf high 77 - 5th of 21 getting 5lb from Innit (6 Spt Doncaster 7f gd RF 4257). She was only just beaten on her Newmarket debut and was third at Kempton in August after an absence of over three months. Decent efforts in nurseries since.
**R Hannon [0-7] Thurloe Thoroughbreds II.*

PASITHEA (IRE) BHB 79f **RR 82f** 5106[2]
2 b f Celtic Swing - Midnight's Reward (Night Shift (USA)) 7.2f **(69)**
Form - 453310222
Record 2000 - 1st:1 2nd:3 3rd:2 Ran:9
Win Prizemoney £3,818 *Total Prizemoney* £10,911
Wins * **2000** Aug Beverl (G-F) H 7.5f 69 74 <
2000 Turf 1-9: (5f 2, 6f 2, 7f 1-4, 8f) (g-s 2, gd 2, g-f 2, frm 1-3)
Decent filly, effective 7f, acts on g-s to frm, best on g-s. Turf high 82 - 2nd of 15 giving 4lb to Looking For Love (20 Oct Newbury 7f gd RF 5106) - also 1st of 9 getting 4lb from Siena Star (17 Aug Beverley RF 3719). **T D Easterby [1-9] Lady Legard.*

PASO DOBLE BHB 76f **RR 76f** 4223[2]
2 b c Dancing Spree (USA) 8f **(59)** - Delta Tempo (IRE) (Bluebird (USA)) 7.5f **(69)**
Form - 734222
Record 2000 - 1st:0 2nd:3 3rd:1 Ran:6
Win Prizemoney £0 *Total Prizemoney* £3,844
2000 Turf 0-6: (5f, 6f, 7f 4) (gd 2, g-f, frm 3)
Above-average colt, effective 7f, acts on g-f to frm, best on frm. Turf high 76 - 2nd of 16 giving 13lb to Chaweng Beach (5 Spt Lingfield 7f frm RF 4223). **B R Millman [0-6] J A Pickford.*

PASSION FOR LIFE BHB 82f **RR 75f** 4691[8]
7 br g Charmer 9f **(59)** - Party Game (Red Alert) 7.6f **(66)**
Form - 180008
Record 2000 - 1st:1 2nd:0 3rd:0 Ran:6
Pre2000 - 1st:7 2nd:3 3rd:3 Ran:34
Win Prizemoney £83,741 *Total Prizemoney* £94,638
Wins * **2000** Mar Kempto (GD) H 6f 83 89
* 1999 Spt Salisb (HVY) H 6f 78 82
* 1999 Apr Kempto (GD) H 6f 79 85
1996 Jun Baden- (GD) G3 6f 112
1996 Apr Newmar (G-F) L 6f 115+ <
1996 Apr Kempto (GD) H 6f 86 103+
2000 Turf 1-6: (5f, 6f 1-5) (g-s 2, gd 1-4)
Above-average gelding, effective 6f, acts on g-s to g-f, has worn blinkers. Turf high 89 (1st run) - 1st of 18 giving 12lb to Palawan (25 Mar Kempton RF 0502). Useful on his day, he won at Kempton first time out, repeating his victory of twelve months earlier in the same event. Obviously goes well fresh.
**J Akehurst [3-15] Canisbay Bloodstock Ltd (from W Jarvis [0-4] Jun 1998).*

PASSIONS PLAYTHING BHB 56f **RR 69f** 1906[13]
4 ch g Pursuit of Love 9.5f **(69)** - Maiyaasah (Kris) 9.5f **(73)**
Form - 6000
Record 2000 - 1st:0 2nd:0 3rd:0 Ran:4
Pre2000 - 1st:0 2nd:0 3rd:0 Ran:3
Win Prizemoney £0 *Total Prizemoney* £558
2000 Turf 0-3: (10f 2, 12f) (g-s, frm 2) 2000 AW 0-1: (12f) (Equi)

Workmanlike, average gelding, has worn blinkers. Turf high 30.
**W R Muir [0-7] Delamere Partnership.*

PASS THE REST (IRE) BHB 60f62a **RR 63f 62a** 1442[6]

5 b g Shalford (IRE) 7.8f **(63)** - Brown Foam (Horage) 10.3f **(61)**
Form - 6
Record 2000 - 1st:0 2nd:0 3rd:0 Ran:1
Pre2000 - 1st:2 2nd:3 3rd:1 Ran:19
Win Prizemoney £9,556 *Total Prizemoney* £13,441
Wins 1998 *Aug Wolver (STD) H 8.5f 79 85* <
1998 Jun Ripon (SFT) H 8f 76 79
2000 Turf 0-1: (16f) (gd)
Average gelding, has worn blinkers.
**D Shaw [0-13] J Roundtree (from J Noseda [2-7] Spt 1998).*

PATACAKE PATACAKE (USA) BHB 65f **RR 62f** 732[6]

3 b f Bahri (USA) - Chaleur (CAN) (Rouge Sang (USA)) 7f **(118)**
Form - 76
Record 2000 - 1st:0 2nd:0 3rd:0 Ran:2
Pre2000 - 1st:0 2nd:0 3rd:0 Ran:3
Win Prizemoney £0 *Total Prizemoney* £494
2000 Turf 0-2: (10f, 12f) (gd 2)
Leggy, average filly. Turf high 62.
**M Johnston [0-5] Lightbody Celebration Cakes Ltd.*

PATHAN BHB 81f83a **RR 77f 83a** 4178[1]

2 b c Pyramus (USA) - Langton Herring (Nearly A Hand) 5.0f **(40)**
Form - 75142321
Record 2000 - 1st:2 2nd:2 3rd:1 Ran:8
Win Prizemoney £5,229 *Total Prizemoney* £7,994
Wins * 2000 *Spt Wolver (STD) 8.5f 76+* <
*** 2000** Jly Lingfi (GD) 7f 70
2000 Turf 1-7: (6f, 7f 1-5, 8f) (g-f 1-2, frm 4, hrd) 2000 AW 1-1: (8f 1-1) (Fibr 1-1)
Above-average colt, effective 7 to 8f, best at 7f, acts on g-f to hrd - acts on Fibr, best on frm. Turf high 77 - 2nd of 6 getting 6lb from Palatial (11 Aug Newmarket 7f frm RF 3562) - also 1st of 14 getting 4lb from Eagles Cache (14 Jly Lingfield RF 2811). (1st run) - 1st of 4 giving 4lb to El Hamra (2 Spt Wolverhampton RF 4178). Consistent. **S P C Woods [2-8] S P C Woods.*

PAT PINKNEY BHB 48f **RR 50f** 3697[11]

2 b f Imp Society (USA) 7.1f **(63)** - Fran Godfrey **(59f 58a)** (Taufan (USA)) 7f **(57)**
Form - 7545460
Record 2000 - 1st:0 2nd:0 3rd:0 Ran:7
Win Prizemoney £0 *Total Prizemoney* £324
2000 Turf 0-7: (5f 5, 6f, 7f) (gd 2, g-f 3, frm 2)
Fair filly. Turf high 50. **E J Alston [0-7] Peter Onslow.*

PATRICIAN FOX (IRE) BHB 57f53a **RR 57f 53a** 5295[7]

2 b f Nicolotte - Peace Mission (Dunbeath (USA)) 7.8f **(70)**
Form - 7834326027
Record 2000 - 1st:0 2nd:2 3rd:2 Ran:10
Win Prizemoney £0 *Total Prizemoney* £2,390
2000 Turf 0-9: (5f 6, 6f 3) (hvy, g-s 2, gd 2, g-f 3, frm) 2000 AW 0-1: (5f) (Fibr)
Fair filly, effective 5f, acts on hvy to g-f. Turf high 57 - 2nd of 16 getting 13lb from Time Maite (19 Oct Newcastle 5f hvy RF 5081).
**J J Quinn [0-10] C R Galloway.*

PATRINIA BHB 30f **RR 32f** 417[16]

4 ch f Superlative 8.8f **(57)** - Dame du Moulin (Shiny Tenth) 9.2f **(56)**
Form - 80
Record 2000 - 1st:0 2nd:0 3rd:0 Ran:2
Pre2000 - 1st:0 2nd:0 3rd:0 Ran:7
2000 AW 0-2: (6f, 8f) (Fibr 2)
Scopey, very moderate filly. AW high 9. Inconsistent.
**M J Ryan [0-9] P E Axon.*

PATRITA PARK BHB 40f43a **RR 41f 43a** 1720[6]

6 br m Flying Tyke 7.2f **(42)** - Bellinote (FR) (Noir Et Or) 10f **(38)**
Form - 06
Record 2000 - 1st:0 2nd:0 3rd:0 Ran:2
Pre2000 - 1st:1 2nd:4 3rd:3 Ran:26
Win Prizemoney £2,473 *Total Prizemoney* £7,436
Wins 1998 Spt Bright (FRM) H 10f 26 33+ <
2000 Turf 0-2. (10f, 12f) (gd, g-f)
Moderate mare, effective 10 to 14f, best at 10f, acts on frm. Turf high 40.
**Mrs M Reveley [0-2] Park Racing Partnership (from Mrs P N Dutfield [0-8] Spt 1999).*

PATSY CULSYTH BHB 43f **RR 43f** 5122[16]

5 b m Tragic Role (USA) 9.4f **(63)** - Regal Salute (Dara Monarch) 8.8f **(59)**
Form - 107368300
Record 2000 - 1st:1 2nd:0 3rd:2 Ran:9
Pre2000 - 1st:2 2nd:5 3rd:1 Ran:26
Win Prizemoney £6,825 *Total Prizemoney* £12,654
Wins * 2000 Mar Newcas (GD) S 6f 50
1998 Aug Ayr (G-S) SH 7f 45 50
1997 Aug Beverl (G-S) C 5f 62 <
2000 Turf 1-9: (5f 2, 6f 1-3, 7f 4) (g-s 2, gd 1-4, frm 2, hrd)
Moderate filly, effective 6 to 7f, best at 6f, acts on gd to frm, best on gd, has worn blinkers. Turf high 50 (1st run) - 1st of 12 getting 4lb from Tancred Arms (28 Mar Newcastle RF 0523).
**Don Enrico Incisa [1-16] Don Enrico Incisa (from N Tinkler [1-10] Spt 1998).*

PATSY'S DOUBLE BHB 100f **RR 97f** 4733[3]

2 b c Emarati (USA) 6.6f **(63)** - Jungle Rose (Shirley Heights) 10.3f **(74)**
Form - 11153
Record 2000 - 1st:3 2nd:0 3rd:1 Ran:5
Win Prizemoney £22,404 *Total Prizemoney* £26,254
Wins * 2000 Jly Newbur (G-F) 7f 92+ <
*** 2000** Jly Salisb (G-S) 6f 92
*** 2000** May Newbur (G-F) 6f 84t
2000 Turf 3-5: (6f 2-2, 7f 1-3) (gd 1-2, g-f 1-2, hrd 1-1)
Very useful colt. Turf high 97 - 3rd of 13 to King Charlemagne (29 Spt Newmarket 7f gd RF 4733) - also 1st of 5 giving 5lb to Blueberry Forest (22 Jly Newbury RF 3022). A powerful individual, he won his first three starts in good style. Upped in class during the autumn, he was beaten less then two lengths in the Champagne Stakes and only half a length in a three-way photo for the Group 3 Somerville Tattersalls Stakes at Newmarket in September. A late foal, he is open to improvement and could pick up a Group race around a mile this year.
**M Blanshard [3-5] Mrs Patricia Buckley.*

PATSY STONE BHB 70f53a **RR 69f 53a** 3229[10]

4 b f Jester 8.5f **(43)** - Third Dam **(47f 45a)** (Slip Anchor) 9.8f **(73)**
Form - 5811445320
Record 2000 - 1st:2 2nd:1 3rd:1 Ran:10
Pre2000 - 1st:1 2nd:2 3rd:4 Ran:24
Win Prizemoney £14,405 *Total Prizemoney* £20,211
Wins * 2000 Jun Chepst (GD) H 7.1f 60 69 <
*** 2000** May Leices (SFT) H 8f 60 69 <
1999 Spt Yarmou (SFT) H 8f 59 63
2000 Turf 2-10: (7f 1-1, 8f 1-9) (gd 2-4, g-f 2, frm 4)
Unfurnished, average filly, effective 7 to 8f, best at 8f, acts on g-s to frm, best on gd, likes right handed tracks, excels at Windsor. Turf high 69 - 1st of 20 giving 24lb to Who Goes There (8 Jun Chepstow RF 1798) - also 1st of 9 from Tipperary Sunset (29 May Leicester RF 1523). Consistent.
**M Kettle [2-30] Fraser, Butt, Goldsmith (from W J Musson [1-4] Oct 1999).*

PAT THE BUILDER (IRE) BHB 54f54a **RR 62f 54a** 5081[7]

2 b c Common Grounds 8.1f **(66)** - Demoiselle **(30+f)** (Midyan (USA)) 6f **(60)**
Form - 5484617
Record 2000 - 1st:1 2nd:0 3rd:0 Ran:7
Win Prizemoney £1,855 *Total Prizemoney* £1,855
Wins * 2000 *Oct Lingfi (STD) S 5f 63* <
2000 Turf 0-6: (5f 6) (hvy, g-f, frm 4) 2000 AW 1-1: (5f 1-1) (Equi 1-1)
Average colt, effective 5f, acts on frm - acts on Equi. Turf high 62 - 4th of 7 giving 7lb to Deceitful (19 Jun Brighton 5f frm RF 2085). (1st run) - 1st of 10 giving 5lb to Branston Gem (11 Oct Lingfield RF 4927). **K R Burke [1-7] James Ryan.*

PAULA'S PRIDE **RR 83?f** 5121[7]

2 ch f Pivotal - Sharp Top (Sharpo) 7.7f **(59)**
Form - 706167
Record 2000 - 1st:1 2nd:0 3rd:0 Ran:6

Win Prizemoney £1,767 *Total Prizemoney* £3,800
Wins * **2000** Spt Bright (G-S) 8f 73 <
2000 Turf 1-6: (5f, 6f 2, 7f 2, 8f 1-1) (g-s, gd 1-2, g-f, frm 2)
Decent filly, effective 6 to 8f, acts on gd. Turf high 83 - 6th of 30 giving 1lb to Goodie Twosues (13 Oct Newmarket 6f gd RF 4965).
**J R Best [1-5] Thomas Tanton & Frederick French (from M J Ryan [0-1] May 2000).*

PAWN BROKER BHB 114f RR 116f 4731[2]

3 ch c Selkirk (USA) 7.9f **(76)** - Dime Bag (High Line) 10.3f **(70)**
Form - 1220312
Record 2000 - 1st:2 2nd:3 3rd:1 Ran:7
Pre2000 - 1st:1 2nd:0 3rd:0 Ran:2
Win Prizemoney £51,325 *Total Prizemoney* £107,056
Wins * **2000** Spt Newbur (G-F) L 11f 114 <
* **2000** Apr Newmar (SFT) L 9f 106
* 1999 Oct Newmar (GD) 8f 87
2000 Turf 2-7: (9f 1-1, 10f 2, 11f 1-1, 12f 3) (sft, gd 1-3, g-f 2, frm 1-1)
Scopey, high-class colt, effective 9 to 12f, best at 10f, acts on sft to frm, likes Newmarket. Turf high 116 - 2nd of 6 to Sakhee (29 Apr Sandown 10f sft RF 0928) - also 1st of 7 from Francesco Guardi (15 Spt Newbury RF 4436). A very big individual, he landed the Feilden Stakes at the Craven Meeting before finishing second to Sakhee in two Derby trials. Took his chance in the Prix du Jockey-Club, but was well beaten in the heavy ground. Having his first run for three months when third in the Group Three September Stakes and regained winning form in a Newbury Listed event.
**D R C Elsworth [3-9] Raymond Tooth.*

PAWN IN LIFE (IRE) BHB 52f RR 22f 5163[11]

2 b g Midhish - Lady-Mumtaz (Martin John) 13.1f **(62)**
Form - 0
Record 2000 - 1st:0 2nd:0 3rd:0 Ran:1
2000 Turf 0-1: (5f) (gd)
Currently fair gelding. **T D Barron [0-1] Laurence O'Kane.*

PAWSIBLE (IRE) BHB 40f43a RR 42f 43a 79[9]

4 b f Mujadil (USA) 7.7f **(70)** - Kentucky Wildcat (Be My Guest (USA)) 9.3f **(67)**
Form - 30
Record 2000 - 1st:0 2nd:0 3rd:0 Ran:1
Pre2000 - 1st:1 2nd:0 3rd:2 Ran:10
Win Prizemoney £1,955 *Total Prizemoney* £2,590
Wins * 1999 *Aug Wolver (STD) H 14.8f 44 45* <
2000 AW 0-1: (16f) (Fibr)
Light-framed, moderate filly.
**D W P Arbuthnot [1-11] The Pawsible Partnership.*

PAX RR 85f 1062[26]

3 ch c Brief Truce (USA) 9.1f **(73)** - Child's Play (USA) (Sharpen Up) 8.3f **(67)**
Form - 400
Record 2000 - 1st:0 2nd:0 3rd:0 Ran:3
Pre2000 - 1st:1 2nd:0 3rd:0 Ran:1
Win Prizemoney £4,695 *Total Prizemoney* £5,242
Wins * 1999 Oct Newmar (G-S) 6f 79+ <
2000 Turf 0-3: (6f 3) (g-s, gd 2)
Light-framed, useful colt. Turf high 85. **J W Payne [1-4] C Cotran.*

PAY HOMAGE BHB 32f RR 34f 3435[7]

12 ch g Primo Dominie 7.2f **(67)** - Embraceable Slew (USA) (Seattle Slew (USA)) 9.4f **(76)**
Form - 057
Record 2000 - 1st:0 2nd:0 3rd:0 Ran:3
Pre2000 - 1st:11 2nd:13 3rd:15 Ran:114
Win Prizemoney £94,677 *Total Prizemoney* £130,051
Wins * 1998 May Warwic (GD) H 10.8f 64 67
* 1997 Jly Bath (FRM) 11.7f 69
2000 Turf 0-3: (12f 3) (g-f 3)
Very moderate gelding, effective 9 to 12f, best at 12f, acts on hvy to frm, best on frm, has worn blinkers, likes left handed tracks, excels at Brighton, does well at Kempton. Turf high 34 (began Jly).
**I A Balding [11-120] I A Balding.*

PAYS D'AMOUR (IRE) BHB 88f RR 90f 4991[3]

3 b c Pursuit of Love 9.5f **(69)** - Lady of the Land (Wollow) 8.2f **(61)**
Form - 72001213023
Record 2000 - 1st:2 2nd:3 3rd:2 Ran:11
Pre2000 - 1st:1 2nd:0 3rd:0 Ran:5
Win Prizemoney £19,876 *Total Prizemoney* £27,069
Wins * **2000** Jly Epsom (GD) 7f 82 <
* **2000** Jly Haydoc (G-F) H 6f 75 78
* 1999 Spt Epsom (GD) H 6f 65 61
2000 Turf 2-11: (6f 1-4, 7f 1-6, 8f) (sft, g-s, gd 1-3, g-f 1-2, frm 4)
Scopey, useful colt, effective 6 to 7f, best at 7f, acts on gd to frm, does well at Newmarket and Epsom. Turf high 90 - 3rd of 29 giving 9lb to Social Contract (14 Oct Newmarket 7f gd RF 4991) - also 1st of 7 giving 2lb to Lord Pacal (20 Jly Epsom RF 2961). Improving.
**R Hannon [3-16] Mrs M W Bird.*

PAY THE SILVER BHB 69f RR 70f 4040[4]

2 gr c Petong 7.6f **(58)** - Marjorie's Memory (IRE) **(61df)** (Fairy King (USA)) 7.7f **(59)**
Form - 043554
Record 2000 - 1st:0 2nd:0 3rd:1 Ran:6
Win Prizemoney £0 *Total Prizemoney* £1,521
2000 Turf 0-6: (5f, 6f 2, 7f 3) (gd, g-f 3, frm 2)
Above-average colt, effective 7f, acts on g-f. Turf high 70.
**A P Jarvis [0-6] Jalal Harake.*

PC'S EUROCRUISER (IRE) BHB 37f38a RR 23f 38a 1695[9]

4 b g Fayruz 6.6f **(63)** - Kuwait Night (Morston (FR)) 9.4f **(55)**
Form - 0
Record 2000 - 1st:0 2nd:0 3rd:0 Ran:1
Pre2000 - 1st:0 2nd:0 3rd:0 Ran:13
2000 Turf 0-1: (10f) (gd)
Workmanlike, very moderate gelding.
**G Woodward [0-10] P C Smith (from N P Littmoden [0-7] Nov 1998).*

PEACE BAND (IRE) BHB 70f RR 67f 4697[8]

2 b c Desert Style (IRE) - Anita's Love (IRE) (Anita's Prince)
Form - 5438
Record 2000 - 1st:0 2nd:0 3rd:1 Ran:4
Win Prizemoney £0 *Total Prizemoney* £826
2000 Turf 0-4: (5f 2, 6f 2) (g-f 2, frm 2)
Average colt. Turf high 67 (began Jly) - 8th of 14 getting 10lb from Muja Farewell (28 Spt Newmarket 5f g-f RF 4697).
**M H Tompkins [0-4] Ian Lochhead.*

PEACEFUL PARADISE BHB 104f RR 98f 4137a[3]

2 b f Turtle Island (IRE) - Megdale (IRE) **(41f)** (Waajib)
Form - 31513
Record 2000 - 1st:2 2nd:0 3rd:2 Ran:5
Win Prizemoney £16,740 *Total Prizemoney* £21,005
Wins * **2000** Aug Newmar (G-F) L 7f 98 <
* **2000** Jun Kempto (G-F) 7f 73
2000 Turf 2-5: (6f, 7f 2-4) (g-s, gd, g-f, frm 2-2)
Very useful filly. Turf high 98 - 3rd of 7 to Ascension (27 Aug Deauville 7f g-s RF 4137a) - also 1st of 7 from Bring Plenty (12 Aug Newmarket RF 3591). She ran on strongly to win a Listed race at Newmarket in August and probably improved again when third in the Group 3 Prix du Calvados at Deauville later that month. Very genuine, she will stay a mile.
**J W Hills [2-5] Karen Scott Barrett (Abbott Racing Ptnrs.*

PEACEFUL PROMISE BHB 86f RR 89f 936[1]

3 b c Cadeaux Genereux 7.9f **(76)** - Island Wedding (USA) (Blushing Groom (FR)) 10.3f **(76)**
Form - 31
Record 2000 - 1st:1 2nd:0 3rd:1 Ran:2
Pre2000 - 1st:0 2nd:0 3rd:0 Ran:1
Win Prizemoney £4,335 *Total Prizemoney* £5,163
Wins * **2000** May Doncas (G-S) 7f 82+ <
2000 Turf 1-2: (7f 1-2) (gd, g-f 1-1)
Scopey, currently useful colt. Turf high 89 - also 1st of 15 from Take Flite (1 May Doncaster RF 0936). (DEAD)
**E A L Dunlop [1-3] Maktoum Al Maktoum.*

PEACE PACT BHB 25f RR 6f 328[7]

4 b f Brief Truce (USA) 9.1f **(73)** - Royal Mazi **(25f)** (Kings Lake (USA)) 10.8f **(67)**
Form - 7
Record 2000 - 1st:0 2nd:0 3rd:0 Ran:1
Pre2000 - 1st:0 2nd:0 3rd:0 Ran:8

2000 AW 0-1: (6f) (Fibr)
Unfurnished, very poor filly, effective 5 to 12f, acts on g-s to frm - acts on Fibr, best on frm, has worn blinkers.
**G P Kelly [0-10] A M McArdle.*

PEACHES BHB 40f41a **RR 56f 41a** 4175[9]
3 b f Selkirk (USA) 7.9f **(76)** - Off The Blocks **(50f)** (Salse (USA)) 7.5f **(66)**
Form - 0020
Record 2000 - 1st:0 2nd:1 3rd:0 Ran:4
Win Prizemoney £0 *Total Prizemoney* £872
2000 Turf 0-2: (7f, 8f) (gd, g-f) 2000 AW 0-2: (8f, 9f) (Fibr 2)
Fair filly. Turf high 56. AW high 58 (began Aug).
**C A Cyzer [0-4] R M Cyzer.*

PEACOCK ALLEY (IRE) BHB 92f **RR 97f** 4598[3]
3 gr f Salse (USA) 10.9f **(71)** - Tagiki (IRE) (Doyoun) 9f **(69)**
Form - 51113623
Record 2000 - 1st:3 2nd:1 3rd:2 Ran:8
Pre2000 - 1st:0 2nd:1 3rd:1 Ran:4
Win Prizemoney £36,968 *Total Prizemoney* £48,918
Wins * **2000** Jun Ayr (GD) H 7f 83 92 <
* **2000** Jun Epsom (G-S) H 7f 77 83
* **2000** May Warwic (HVY) 6.8f 82
2000 Turf 3-8: (7f 3-6, 8f 2) (hvy 1-2, g-s 1-1, gd, g-f 1-2, frm 2)
Neat, very useful filly, effective 7 to 8f, best at 7f, acts on gd to frm, best on frm, prefers tight tracks. Turf high 97 - 3rd of 14 getting 3lb from Riberac (23 Spt Ascot 8f gd RF 4598) - also 1st of 13 getting 12lb from Peartree House (24 Jun Ayr RF 2245). She improved rapidly in the summer and came back to run a couple of solid races in defeat during September. Effective up to a mile, she goes well on easy ground and can win again.
**W J Haggas [3-12] & Mrs G Middlebrook.*

PEACOCK JEWEL BHB 102f **RR 102?f** 2867[2]
3 ch c Rainbow Quest (USA) 11.2f **(81)** - Dafrah (USA) (Danzig (USA)) 8.4f **(76)**
Form - 2
Record 2000 - 1st:0 2nd:0 3rd:0 Ran:1
Pre2000 - 1st:1 2nd:1 3rd:0 Ran:2
Win Prizemoney £5,208 *Total Prizemoney* £8,794
Wins * 1999 Spt Newmar (G-S) 8f 84+ <
2000 Turf 0-1: (10f) (g-f)
Light-framed, currently very useful colt. (1st run) - 2nd of 7 getting 3lb from Ekraar (16 Jly Newbury 10f g-f RF 2867). Runner-up to Ekraar on his only start, he is a colt of considerable potential.
**E A L Dunlop [1-3] Maktoum Al Maktoum.*

PEARL BRIGHT (FR) BHB 87f **RR 78f** 5241[9]
2 gr f Kaldoun (FR) 9.9f **(84)** - Coastal Jewel (IRE) (Kris) 9.5f **(73)**
Form - 210
Record 2000 - 1st:1 2nd:1 3rd:0 Ran:3
Win Prizemoney £3,211 *Total Prizemoney* £4,146
Wins * **2000** Oct Leices (HVY) 7f 78 <
2000 Turf 1-3: (7f 1-2, 8f) (g-s 1-3)
Currently above-average filly. Turf high 78 (began Spt) - 1st of 10 from Halcyon Daze (9 Oct Leicester RF 4876). Followed up a promising debut by taking a Leicester maiden, and can go on to better things. **J L Dunlop [1-3] Pearl Bright Partnership.*

PEARL BUTTON (IRE) BHB 41f **RR 48f** 138[11]
4 b f Seattle Dancer (USA) 10.1f **(74)** - Riflelina (Mill Reef (USA)) 10.5f **(78)**
Form - 0020
Record 2000 - 1st:0 2nd:1 3rd:0 Ran:2
Pre2000 - 1st:0 2nd:0 3rd:0 Ran:6
Win Prizemoney £0 *Total Prizemoney* £860
2000 AW 0-2: (12f 2) (Equi 2)
Leggy, moderate filly, effective 12f, - acted on Equi, liked left handed tracks. AW high 41 (1st run) - 2nd of 14 getting 5lb from Fusul (5 Jan Lingfield 12f Equi RF 0028). (DEAD)
**C A Cyzer [0-8] R M Cyzer.*

PEARLY BROOKS **RR 65f** 4724[3]
2 b f Efisio 7.7f **(69)** - Elkie Brooks (Relkino) 8.9f **(65)**
Form - 53
Record 2000 - 1st:0 2nd:0 3rd:1 Ran:2
Win Prizemoney £0 *Total Prizemoney* £601
2000 Turf 0-2: (5f, 6f) (gd, frm)
Currently average filly. Turf high 65 (began Aug).
**T J Naughton [0-2] R A Popely.*

PEARTREE HOUSE (IRE) BHB 94f82a **RR 96f 82a** 4609[16]
6 b g Simply Majestic (USA) 7.8f **(72)** - Fashion Front (Habitat) 9.4f **(70)**
Form - 076031244866 1000
Record 2000 - 1st:2 2nd:1 3rd:1 Ran:16
Pre2000 - 1st:4 2nd:2 3rd:1 Ran:27
Win Prizemoney £48,539 *Total Prizemoney* £72,696
Wins * **2000** Aug York (GD) H 7.9f 87 96
* **2000** Jun Ayr (GD) 8f 80+
1998 May Lingfi (GD) 7.6f 92
1997 May Doncas (G-S) 8f 97 <
1996 Aug Catter (G-F) 7f 89
1996 Jun Ayr (G-F) 6f 60+
2000 Turf 2-15: (7f 7, 8f 2-7, 9f) (g-s 2, gd 7, g-f 1-4, frm 1-2) 2000 AW 0-1: (7f) (Fibr)
Very useful gelding, effective 7 to 8f, best at 8f, acts on gd to frm, best on g-f, has worn blinkers, prefers left handed tracks, likes tight tracks, excels at Ayr, likes Goodwood. Turf high 96 - 1st of 16 from Tony Tie (24 Aug York RF 3934). He did well during a hectic campaign, showing his form on most types of ground and under a variety of tactics. A shade high in the weights at present, he will win again when the handicapper relents.
**D Nicholls [2-16] G Vettraino & Fayzad Thoroughbreds I (from W R Muir [2-22] Oct 1999).*

PEDRO JACK (IRE) BHB 81f **RR 83f** 4483[6]
3 b g Mujadil (USA) 7.7f **(70)** - Festival of Light (High Top) 10.2f **(67)**
Form - 317603522066
Record 2000 - 1st:1 2nd:2 3rd:2 Ran:12
Pre2000 - 1st:2 2nd:0 3rd:0 Ran:4
Win Prizemoney £11,609 *Total Prizemoney* £18,684
Wins * **2000** May Windso (G-F) H 6f 74 78 <
* 1999 Spt Nottin (G-F) H 6.1f 70 75
* 1999 Aug Nottin (G-F) 6.1f 63
2000 Turf 1-12: (5f 2, 6f 1-9, 7f) (g-s, gd 2, g-f 3, frm 1-5, hrd)
Scopey, decent gelding, effective 6f, acts on g-f to frm, best on frm, has worn blinkers, excels at Nottingham, likes Kempton. Turf high 83 - 2nd of 8 getting 3lb from Mersey Mirage (13 Aug Leicester 6f frm RF 3610) - also 1st of 19 giving 2lb to Pays d'Amour (15 May Windsor RF 1211). Battled on well to narrowly win a Windsor handicap on his second start of the season and has a commendable attitude. Best on fast ground, he is due another success. **B J Meehan [3-16] Michael Peart.*

PEDRO PETE BHB 78f70a **RR 79f 70a** 4829[1]
3 ch g Fraam - Stride Home (Absalom) 7.2f **(58)**
Form - 41433118501
Record 2000 - 1st:4 2nd:0 3rd:2 Ran:11
Pre2000 - 1st:0 2nd:0 3rd:0 Ran:2
Win Prizemoney £26,951 *Total Prizemoney* £28,712
Wins * **2000** Oct York (SFT) H 10.4f 75 77
* **2000** Jly Ascot (G-F) H 10f 73 79 <
* **2000** Jly Cheste (SFT) H 10.3f 68 71
* **2000** *Feb Lingfi (STD) H 10f 59 68*
2000 Turf 3-8: (8f, 10f 3-7) (g-s 1-1, g-f 2-7) 2000 AW 1-3: (8f 2, 10f 1-1) (Equi 1-2, Fibr)
Scopey, above-average gelding, effective 10f, acts on g-s to g-f, best on g-f, likes left handed tracks. Turf high 79 - 1st of 10 getting 11lb from Imperial Rocket (28 Jly Ascot RF 3165) - also 1st of 14 giving 2lb to Admirals Place (6 Oct York RF 4829). AW high 68. Consistent. A decent ten-furlong handicapper, he is a promising hurdler with Nicky Henderson.
**M R Channon [4-13] Peter Taplin.*

PEEJAY HOBBS **RR 26f** 789[8]
2 ch g Alhijaz 7.7f **(57)** - Hicklam Millie (Absalom) 7.2f **(58)**
Form - 08
Record 2000 - 1st:0 2nd:0 3rd:0 Ran:2
2000 Turf 0-2: (5f 2) (g-s, gd)
Currently little account gelding. Turf high 26.
**M W Easterby [0-2] Winton Bloodstock Ltd.*

PEEP O DAY BHB 27f41a **RR 41a** 3826[13]
9 b m Domynsky 7.8f **(58)** - Betrothed (Aglojo)

Form - 0
Record 2000 - 1st:0 2nd:0 3rd:0 Ran:1
Pre2000 - 1st:2 2nd:0 3rd:0 Ran:13
Win Prizemoney £5,379 *Total Prizemoney* £5,596
Wins 1996 Nov Mussel (G-S) H 12.1f 35 42
2000 Turf 0-1: (17f) (hrd)
Very poor mare, has worn blinkers.
**A J Lockwood [2-28] A J Lockwood (from J L Eyre [2-17] Nov 1997).*

PEGASUS BAY BHB 53f46a RR 59f 46a 4723[6]

9 b g Tina's Pet 7.4f **(56)** - Mossberry Fair (Mossberry) 7.4f **(51)**
Form - 1176
Record 2000 - 1st:2 2nd:0 3rd:0 Ran:4
Pre2000 - 1st:5 2nd:6 3rd:3 Ran:21
Win Prizemoney £19,440 *Total Prizemoney* £24,284
Wins * 2000 Jly Hamilt (G-F) C 9.2f 51
* 2000 Jun Hamilt (G-F) S 9.2f 42
* 1999 Aug Hamilt (G-F) SH 8.3f 52 56+
* 1999 Aug Hamilt (G-F) C 9.2f 51
* 1999 Jly Newmar (G-F) S 8f 62
1997 *Oct Lingfi (STD) 7f 64* <
1997 Spt Yarmou (FRM) S 10.1f 56+
2000 Turf 2-3: (9f 2-3) (gd, g-f 2-2) 2000 AW 0-1: (12f) (Equi)
Fair gelding, effective 8f, acts on frm, has worn blinkers, prefers right handed tracks. Turf high 51.
**D E Cantillon [8-32] Don Cantillon (from Mrs A E Johnson [2-7] Nov 1997).*

PEGGYS ROSE (IRE) BHB 53f45a RR 46df 45a 4768[17]

3 b f Shalford (IRE) 7.8f **(63)** - Afrique Noir (IRE) (Gallic League)
Form - 1400200
Record 2000 - 1st:1 2nd:1 3rd:0 Ran:7
Win Prizemoney £1,991 *Total Prizemoney* £3,467
Wins * 2000 Apr Leices (G-S) S 6f 70 <
2000 Turf 1-6: (6f 1-3, 7f 2, 9f) (sft, g-s, gd 1-2, g-f, frm) 2000 AW 0-1: (6f) (Fibr)
Unfurnished, moderate filly, effective 6f, acts on gd. Turf high 70 (1st run) - 1st of 9 getting 10lb from Mytton's Again (6 Apr Leicester RF 0625).
**P D Evans [1-7] Global Racing Club.*

PEGGY'S SONG BHB 32f RR 27f 4744[14]

2 b f Mind Games - Miss Whittingham (IRE) **(53f 55a)** (Fayruz)
Form - 870
Record 2000 - 1st:0 2nd:0 3rd:0 Ran:3
2000 Turf 0-3: (5f, 6f, 7f) (gd, frm 2)
Currently little account filly. Turf high 27 (began Jly).
**A Berry [0-3] G L Tanner.*

PEGNITZ (USA) BHB 104f RR 108f 3563[4]

5 b h Lear Fan (USA) 10.4f **(80)** - Likely Split (USA) (Little Current (USA)) 9.6f **(75)**
Form - 04434
Record 2000 - 1st:0 2nd:0 3rd:1 Ran:5
Pre2000 - 1st:2 2nd:4 3rd:2 Ran:17
Win Prizemoney £9,301 *Total Prizemoney* £40,467
Wins * 1999 Jly Epsom (G-F) 10.1f 93 <
* 1998 Aug Windso () 10f 80
2000 Turf 0-5: (10f 4, 12f) (g-s, gd 2, g-f, frm)
Pattern-class colt, effective 10 to 12f, best at 10f, acts on gd to frm, best on g-f, has worn blinkers. Turf high 108. Consistent. He continues to run bravely, often in the face of stiff tasks, and seems best around ten furlongs. At his most dangerous when ridden forcefully, he acts well on undulating tracks.
**C E Brittain [2-22] B H Voak.*

PEKANESE (IRE) BHB 70f RR 71f 5021[6]

3 b c Sri Pekan (USA) - Tootle (Main Reef) 9.6f **(57)**
Form - 6206
Record 2000 - 1st:0 2nd:1 3rd:0 Ran:4
Win Prizemoney £0 *Total Prizemoney* £1,210
2000 Turf 0-4: (7f 4) (sft, g-s, gd 2)
Workmanlike, above-average colt. Turf high 71.
**A C Stewart [0-4] Racing For Gold.*

PEKAN HEIGHTS (USA) BHB 62f RR 66f 3416[9]

4 b g Green Dancer (USA) 11.9f **(77)** - Battle Drum (USA) (Alydar (USA)) 9.1f **(76)**
Form - 1740
Record 2000 - 1st:1 2nd:0 3rd:0 Ran:4
Pre2000 - 1st:1 2nd:0 3rd:1 Ran:8
Win Prizemoney £7,646 *Total Prizemoney* £8,508
Wins * **2000** Jun Cheste (G-F) C 10.3f 52
1999 Apr Nottin (G-S) H 10f 77 83 <
2000 Turf 1-4: (10f 1-2, 12f, 17f) (g-f, frm 1-3)
Rangy, average gelding, effective 10f, acts on gd, often wears blinkers, prefers left handed tracks, favours tight tracks. Turf high 66. Consistent. He made a successful reappearance in a Nottingham handicap, but has been rather disappointing since, though he did not seem to stay twelve furlongs when tried over it.
**P D Evans [1-4] Mrs Claire Massey (from E A L Dunlop [1-8] Oct 1999).*

PEKANOORA (IRE) BHB 50f RR 40f 4689[17]

2 b c Sri Pekan (USA) - Shanoora (IRE) **(51f 29a)** (Don't Forget Me) 8.3f **(74)**
Form - 050
Record 2000 - 1st:0 2nd:0 3rd:0 Ran:3
2000 Turf 0-3: (7f, 8f 2) (gd 2, frm)
Currently moderate colt. Turf high 40 (began Aug).
**P W Harris [0-3] J Cowan & Mrs P W Harris.*

PEKANSKI (IRE) BHB 90f RR 93f 3773[6]

3 b f Sri Pekan (USA) - Karinski (USA) (Palace Music (USA))
Form - 76
Record 2000 - 1st:0 2nd:0 3rd:0 Ran:2
Pre2000 - 1st:1 2nd:0 3rd:0 Ran:2
Win Prizemoney £3,988 *Total Prizemoney* £4,136
Wins 1999 Aug Goodwo (GD) 6f 83+ <
2000 Turf 0-2: (7f, 8f) (g-s, frm)
Scopey, useful filly. Turf high 93. She showed little last year, starting slowly on both her runs.
**J H M Gosden [0-2] R E Sangster (from P W Chapple-Hyam [1-2] Oct 1999).*

PEKAY BHB 53f60a RR 58f 60a 2847[16]

7 b g Puissance 7.1f **(60)** - K-Sera (Lord Gayle (USA)) 8.8f **(62)**
Form - 7035300
Record 2000 - 1st:0 2nd:0 3rd:2 Ran:7
Pre2000 - 1st:3 2nd:5 3rd:5 Ran:21
Win Prizemoney £10,637 *Total Prizemoney* £23,877
Wins 1998 Jun Salisb (G-S) H 12f 70 66
1997 Oct Ayr (SFT) H 10.9f 64 69 <
1997 Jun Hamilt (G-F) H 9.2f 60 64
2000 Turf 0-6: (10f, 12f 3, 13f, 14f) (sft, g-s, gd 3, g-f) 2000 AW 0-1: (12f) (Fibr)
Fair gelding, has worn blinkers. Turf high 59.
**B Smart [0-7] Nelson, Newman, Fletcher & Smart (from M C Pipe [3-8] Jun 1998).*

PELAGIA (IRE) RR 80f 4129[4]

2 b f Lycius (USA) 8.8f **(71)** - Sahara Breeze (Ela-Mana-Mou) 10.1f **(70)**
Form - 4
Record 2000 - 1st:0 2nd:0 3rd:0 Ran:1
Win Prizemoney £0 *Total Prizemoney* £386
2000 Turf 0-1: (7f) (frm)
Currently decent filly. (1st run) - 4th of 11 to Up On Points (31 Aug Salisbury 7f frm RF 4129).
**R Hannon [0-1] Repard,G Doran,M Nic Witten.*

PELIGRO (IRE) RR 322[9]

5 b g Petorius 8f **(66)** - Royal Recreation (USA) (His Majesty (USA)) 10.9f **(82)**
Form - 0
Record 2000 - 1st:0 2nd:0 3rd:0 Ran:1
2000 AW 0-1: (9f) (Fibr)
Currently very poor gelding. **G M Moore [0-3] Mrs Susan Moore.*

PELLI BHB 43f38a RR 46f 38a 4653[7]

2 b f Saddlers' Hall (IRE) 10.5f **(65)** - Pellinora (USA) (King Pellinore (USA)) 8.2f **(68)**
Form - 003787
Record 2000 - 1st:0 2nd:0 3rd:1 Ran:6
Win Prizemoney £0 *Total Prizemoney* £266

2000 Turf 0-5: (5f, 7f 3, 8f) (gd, frm 4) 2000 AW 0-1: (7f) (Fibr)
Moderate filly. Turf high 46.
**P Howling [0-6] Mrs P Reditt.*

PEMBROKE STAR BHB 20f **RR 27tf** 3989[17]
4 b f Warshan (USA) 9.7f **(59)** - Gay Princess (Lord Gayle (USA)) 8.8f **(62)**
Form - 000
Record 2000 - 1st:0 2nd:0 3rd:0 Ran:3
2000 Turf 0-3: (7f, 8f, 10f) (gd, g-f 2)
Scopey, currently little account filly.
**J E Long [0-3] Come Racing Ltd.*

PENALTA BHB 46f **RR 47f** 5137[2]
4 ch g Cosmonaut - Targuette (Targowice (USA)) 11.4f **(70)**
Form - 8873102
Record 2000 - 1st:1 2nd:1 3rd:1 Ran:7
Win Prizemoney £2,873 *Total Prizemoney* £4,022
Wins * **2000** Spt Bright (SFT) H 11.9f 37 45 <
2000 Turf 1-5: (7f, 10f 2, 12f 1-1, 14f) (g-s 1-2, frm 3) 2000 AW 0-2: (8f, 12f) (Equi, Fibr)
Moderate gelding, effective 12 to 14f, acts on g-s, prefers tight tracks. Turf high 47 (began Jly) - 2nd of 11 getting 8lb from Coco Loco (22 Oct Yarmouth 14f g-s RF 5137) - also 1st of 13 giving 1lb to Stitch In Time (27 Spt Brighton RF 4679). AW high 31.
**M Wigham [1-7] John Smallman.*

PENANG PEARL (FR) BHB 90f **RR 83f** 5181a[9]
4 b f Bering 9.6f **(80)** - Guapa (Shareef Dancer (USA)) 9.9f **(73)**
Form - 020
Record 2000 - 1st:0 2nd:1 3rd:0 Ran:3
Pre2000 - 1st:3 2nd:4 3rd:1 Ran:13
Win Prizemoney £23,887 *Total Prizemoney* £36,100
Wins 1999 Oct Ascot (G-S) L 8f 104 <
1999 Jun Kempto (G-F) H 9f 79 81
1999 May Windso (G-F) H 8.3f 68 72
2000 Turf 0-3: (8f 3) (g-s 2, g-f)
Neat, decent filly, effective 8f, acts on gd. Turf high 83 (began Aug). Consistent. **G A Butlor [3-11] Mrs A K H Ooi.*

PENDULUM RR 72f 4370[7]
2 ro f Pursuit of Love 9.5f **(69)** - Brilliant Timing (USA) (The Minstrel (CAN)) 10f **(72)**
Form - 7
Record 2000 - 1st:0 2nd:0 3rd:0 Ran:1
2000 Turf 0-1: (7f) (frm)
Currently above-average filly. (1st run) - 7th of 17 getting 5lb from Rebel Storm (13 Spt Yarmouth 7f frm RF 4379).
**W J Haggas [0-1] Cheveley Park Stud.*

PEN FRIEND BHB 53a **RR 58f** 487[2]
6 b g Robellino (USA) 9.5f **(68)** - Nibbs Point (IRE) (Sure Blade (USA)) 11.3f **(67)**
Form - 522
Record 2000 - 1st:0 2nd:2 3rd:0 Ran:3
Pre2000 - 1st:2 2nd:2 3rd:1 Ran:11
Win Prizemoney £5,941 *Total Prizemoney* £11,471
Wins * 1997 Aug Thirsk (G-F) H 16f 47 53 <
* 1997 Jly Beverl (G-F) H 16.2f 43 48
2000 Turf 0-1: (18f) (gd) 2000 AW 0-2: (14f, 16f) (Fibr 2)
Fair gelding. (1st run) - 2nd of 12 getting 16lb from Royal Expression (24 Mar Doncaster 18f gd RF 0487). AW high 55 (1st run) - 5th of 10 giving 2lb to Fearsome Factor (24 Feb Wolverhampton 16f Fibr RF 0346). Consistent.
**W J Haggas [2-14] W J Haggas.*

PENG (IRE) BHB 35f **RR 53f** 5084[13]
3 ch g Case Law 6f **(64)** - Real Bold (Never so Bold) 6.3f **(66)**
Form - 007000700
Record 2000 - 1st:0 2nd:0 3rd:0 Ran:9
2000 Turf 0-8: (7f 2, 8f 5, 10f) (hvy, g-s, gd 3, g-f 2, frm) 2000 AW 0-1: (6f) (Fibr)
Fair gelding. Turf high 53. Inconsistent.
**R Bastiman [0-9] Peter Beaton-Brown.*

PENGAMON BHB 67f74a **RR 67f 74a** 5155[1]
8 b g Efisio 7.7f **(69)** - Dolly Bevan (Another Realm) 6.6f **(55)**
Form - 22123021241
Record 2000 - 1st:2 2nd:2 3rd:1 Ran:7
Pre2000 - 1st:5 2nd:5 3rd:3 Ran:35
Win Prizemoney £26,787 *Total Prizemoney* £40,061
Wins * **2000** *Oct Lingfi (STD)* 7f 68+
* **2000** Jly Doncas (GD) H 7f 54 63
1999 *Nov Lingfi (STD) H* 7f 52 58
1997 *May Lingfi (STD) H* 8f 74 78
1996 *Mar Lingfi (STD) H* 8f 74 79
2000 Turf 1-4: (7f 1-3, 8f) (g-f, frm 1-3) 2000 AW 1-3: (7f 1-1, 8f 2) (Equi 1-2, Fibr)
Above-average gelding, effective 7 to 8f, best at 7f, acts on frm - acts on AW, does well at Lingfield. Turf high 67 - 2nd of 16 giving 3lb to White Emir (19 Jly Kempton 7f frm RF 2936) - also 1st of 21 giving 5lb to Northgate (13 Jly Doncaster RF 2757). AW high 68 - 1st of 15 giving 3lb to Kayo Gee (23 Oct Lingfield RF 5155).
**M Wigham [2-7] Miss Arabella Smallman (from D T Thom [1-4] Dec 1999).*

PENMAR BHB 45f50a **RR 54f 50a** 3979[6]
8 b g Reprimand 8.2f **(63)** - Latakia (Morston (FR)) 9.4f **(55)**
Form - 6
Record 2000 - 1st:0 2nd:0 3rd:0 Ran:1
Pre2000 - 1st:2 2nd:3 3rd:4 Ran:24
Win Prizemoney £6,196 *Total Prizemoney* £10,599
Wins 1998 Nov Mussel (SFT) H 8f 49 56
1996 *May Wolver (STD) H* *9.4f 56 60* <
2000 Turf 0-1. (12f) (frm)
Fair gelding, has worn blinkers.
**A B Mulholland [0-2] J F Wright (from M A Peill [1-3] Nov 1998).*

PENNY FARTHING BHB 70f **RR 60f** 4481[10]
2 b f Mind Games - Souveniers (Relko) 9.9f **(59)**
Form - 770
Record 2000 - 1st:0 2nd:0 3rd:0 Ran:3
2000 Turf 0-3: (7f 3) (g-s, frm 2)
Currently average filly. Turf high 60 (began Aug).
**H Candy [0-3] Mrs George Tricks.*

PENNY LASS RR 70f 4198[3]
2 b f Alhijaz 7.7f **(57)** - Strapped **(55f)** (Reprimand)
Form - 63
Record 2000 - 1st:0 2nd:0 3rd:1 Ran:2
Win Prizemoney £0 *Total Prizemoney* £806
2000 Turf 0-2: (6f 2) (g-f 2)
Above-average filly. Turf high 70 - 3rd of 15 giving 3lb to Tickle (3 Spt York 6f g-f RF 4198). (DEAD)
**J R Fanshawe [0-2] Gay Lass Partnership.*

PENNY MUIR RR 33f 2938[9]
3 b f Presidium 7.5f **(56)** - Miss Muire (Scallywag)
Form - 80
Record 2000 - 1st:0 2nd:0 3rd:0 Ran:2
2000 Turf 0-2: (10f, 12f) (g-s, frm)
Workmanlike, currently very moderate filly.
**R Curtis [0-2] H J S Racing.*

PENNYS FROM HEAVEN BHB 73f **RR 62f** 5244[4]
6 gr g Generous (IRE) 11.5f **(82)** - Heavenly Cause (USA) (Grey Dawn II) 11.1f **(72)**
Form - 7302412457464304044
Record 2000 - 1st:1 2nd:2 3rd:2 Ran:19
Pre2000 - 1st:1 2nd:1 3rd:4 Ran:16
Win Prizemoney £7,570 *Total Prizemoney* £15,470
Wins * **2000** Jun Ayr (GD) H 10.9f 53 56
1997 Aug Bath (GD) H 11.7f 75 77 <
2000 Turf 1-16: (10f 3, 11f 1-2, 12f 7, 13f, 14f 3) (g-s, gd 7, g-f 3, frm 1-5) 2000 AW 0-3: (12f, 14f, 16f) (Fibr 3)
Average gelding, effective 10 to 16f, acts on gd to frm - acts on Fibr, best on frm, has worn blinkers, prefers left handed tracks. Turf high 62 - also 1st of 12 giving 5lb to Melody Lady (23 Jun Ayr RF 2215). AW high 55 (1st run) (began Spt) - 4th of 16 getting 3lb from Vincent (26 Spt Southwell 16f Fibr RF 4648).
**D Nicholls [1-19] T Cooper, P Kent & R Stevenson (from L M Cumani [0-3] Aug 1998).*

PENNY'S GOLD (USA) RR 115+f 4843a[5]

3 b f Kingmambo (USA) 10.9f **(85)** - Penny's Valentine (USA) (Storm Cat (USA))
Form - 215
2000 Turf 1-3: (8f 1-3) (gd 2, g-f 1-1)
Currently high-class filly. Turf high 115 - 1st of 6 getting 9lb from Island Sands (25 Aug Deauville RF 4133a). She clocked a fast time when beating Island Sands in the Group 3 Prix Quincy at Deauville in August, and was unsuited by a muddling pace when fifth in the Prix de Rond-Point five weeks later. Effective on all types of ground, she remains an interesting prospect. **P Bary in FR [1-3].*

PENNYS PRIDE (IRE) BHB 65f **RR 73f** 5316[8]

5 b m Pips Pride 6.7f **(70)** - Mursuma (Rarity) 10.1f **(60)**
Form - 372303008
Record 2000 - 1st:0 2nd:1 3rd:3 Ran:9
Win Prizemoney £0 *Total Prizemoney* £2,832
2000 Turf 0-9: (7f, 8f 7, 10f) (sft 2, g-s 2, gd 4, frm)
Above-average filly, effective 8f, acts on sft to frm. Turf high 74 - 2nd of 4 giving 14lb to Roshani (24 Apr Newcastle 8f sft RF 0845). **Mrs M Reveley [2-12] J Good.*

PENSHIEL (USA) BHB 77f **RR 81f** 3223[3]

3 b g Mtoto 11.5f **(71)** - Highland Ceilidh (IRE) (Scottish Reel) 7f **(61)**
Form - 11233
Record 2000 - 1st:2 2nd:1 3rd:2 Ran:5
Pre2000 - 1st:0 2nd:0 3rd:0 Ran:3
Win Prizemoney £5,411 *Total Prizemoney* £7,689

Wins								
*** 2000**	Jun	Lingfi	(FRM)	H	11.5f	60	67	<
*** 2000**	May	Beverl	(GD)	H	12f	56	59	

2000 Turf 2-5: (11f 1-1, 12f 1-1, 14f, 16f 2) (gd 1-1, g-f, frm 1-3)
Scopey, decent gelding, effective 14 to 16f, best at 16f, acts on g-f to frm, best on frm. Turf high 81 - 2nd of 7 giving 17lb to Typhoon Tilly (26 Jun Yarmouth 14f g-f RF 2289). Inconsistent. Won first time in a handicap on his three-year-old debut at Beverley, and followed up at Lingfield. Upped in trip, he has continued to run well despite a hike in the weights. **J L Dunlop [2-8] Cyril Humphris.*

PENSION FUND BHB 74f **RR 81df** 4050[11]

6 b g Emperor Fountain 10f **(82)** - Navarino Bay (Averof) 8.2f **(62)**
Form - 37000
Record 2000 - 1st:0 2nd:0 3rd:1 Ran:5
Pre2000 - 1st:5 2nd:5 3rd:2 Ran:30
Win Prizemoney £34,078 *Total Prizemoney* £50,702

Wins								
*** 1999**	Spt	York	(G-F)	H	7.9f	78	81	
*** 1998**	Spt	Ripon	(HVY)	H	10f	77	82	<
*** 1997**	Aug	Beverl	(G-S)	H	9.9f	69	70	
*** 1996**	Aug	York	(GD)	H	7f	75	72	
*** 1996**	Jly	Redcar	(G-F)		5f		63	

2000 Turf 0-5: (8f 2, 9f, 10f 2) (gd 2, g-f 2, frm)
Decent gelding, effective 8 to 10f, acts on g-f to frm, has worn blinkers, prefers left handed tracks. Turf high 81 (1st run) - 3rd of 13 giving 6lb to Noukari (9 May Chester 10f g-f RF 1112). **M W Easterby [5-35] Stephen Curtis.*

PENTAGONAL (USA) BHB 87f **RR 89+f** 2061[1]

3 b c Dynaformer (USA) 12f **(82)** - Pent (USA) (Mr Prospector (USA)) 8.8f **(78)**
Form - 0131
Record 2000 - 1st:2 2nd:0 3rd:1 Ran:4
Pre2000 - 1st:0 2nd:0 3rd:0 Ran:1
Win Prizemoney £14,075 *Total Prizemoney* £15,359

Wins								
*** 2000**	Jun	York	(G-F)	H	11.9f	82	89	<
*** 2000**	May	Lingfi	(G-S)		10f		78	

2000 Turf 2-4: (10f 1-2, 12f 1-2) (gd 1-3, g-f 1-1)
Scopey, useful colt, has worn blinkers. Turf high 89 - 1st of 17 getting 5lb from Batswing (17 Jun York RF 2061). Got off the mark in a Lingfield maiden on easy ground on his second start of the season, and stepped up in trip and equipped with a visor won a valuable ladies' event at York from the front. He has a high knee action and the ground was fast there, so it is debatable whether he will go as well on it in the future. **Sir Michael Stoute [2-5] Sheikh Mohammed.*

PENTAGON LAD BHB 70f66a **RR 75f 66a** 5240[21]

4 ch g Secret Appeal - Gilboa (Shirley Heights) 10.3f **(74)**
Form - 0514862514260300
Record 2000 - 1st:2 2nd:2 3rd:1 Ran:16
Pre2000 - 1st:4 2nd:0 3rd:0 Ran:15
Win Prizemoney £38,309 *Total Prizemoney* £42,609

Wins								
*** 2000**	Jly	Hamilt	(G-F)	H	9.2f	67	70	
*** 2000**	May	Hamilt	(FRM)	H	8.3f	63	69	
*** 1999**	Jly	Cheste	(G-F)	H	10.3f	69	71	<
*** 1999**	Jun	Ripon	(G-F)	H	8f	65	69	
*** 1999**	May	Thirsk	(G-S)	H	8f	61	64	
*** 1999**	May	Carlis	(FRM)	H	8f	55	60	

2000 Turf 2-16: (8f 1-12, 9f 1-2, 10f 2) (g-s, gd 5, g-f 1-4, frm 1-4, hrd 2)
Scopey, above-average gelding, effective 8 to 10f, best at 8f, acted on gd to hrd, preferred right handed tracks, preferred tight tracks, did well at Hamilton and Ripon. Turf high 75 - 2nd of 6 giving 20lb to Thwaab (12 Aug Redcar 8f hrd RF 3597) - also 1st of 16 giving 27lb to Lincoln Dean (21 Jly Hamilton RF 2993). (DEAD) **J L Eyre [6-31] Creskeld Racing.*

PENTAGON LADY BHB 51f **RR 56f** 5102[19]

2 ch f Secret Appeal - Gilboa (Shirley Heights) 10.3f **(74)**
Form - 0005400
Record 2000 - 1st:0 2nd:0 3rd:0 Ran:7
Win Prizemoney £0 *Total Prizemoney* £218
2000 Turf 0-7: (5f 2, 6f, 7f 3, 8f) (gd 2, g-f, frm 3, hrd)
Fair filly. Turf high 56. **J L Eyre [0-7] Creskeld Racing.*

PENTLAND (JPN) BHB 74f **RR 73f** 4643[23]

2 br c Pentire - Lay Claim (USA) (Mr Prospector (USA)) 8.8f **(78)**
Form - 0580
Record 2000 - 1st:0 2nd:0 3rd:0 Ran:4
2000 Turf 0-4: (6f 2, 7f 2) (g-f 2, frm 2)
Above-average colt. Turf high 73 (began Aug). **G Wragg [0-4] Mollers Racing.*

PEONY **RR 115f** 4836a[2]

3 ch f Lion Cavern (USA) 7.5f **(74)** - Persiandale (Persian Bold) 9.3f **(66)**
Form - 2522
2000 Turf 0-4: (8f 4) (g-s 2, gd 2)
Strong, high-class filly. Turf high 115 (1st run) - 2nd of 11 to Bluemamba (14 May Longchamp 8f gd RF 1291a). She finished fast when touched off in a blanket finish to the French 1000 Guineas, but failed to reproduce that form in the second half of the season and is unlikely to progress. **D Sepulchre in FR [0-4] Jly 2000).*

PEPE GALVEZ (SWE) BHB 85f **RR 82df** 2385a[6]

3 br c Mango Express - Mango Sampaquita (SWE) (Colombian Friend (USA)) 8.5f **(64)**
Form - 7326
Record 2000 - 1st:0 2nd:1 3rd:1 Ran:4
Win Prizemoney £0 *Total Prizemoney* £1,871
2000 Turf 0-4: (10f, 12f 3) (g-s, gd 2, g-f)
Lengthy, decent colt. Turf high 82 - 3rd of 5 to Entisar (23 May Goodwood 12f g-s RF 1397). **B Hanbury [0-4].*

PEPETA BHB 63f **RR 67f** 1895[4]

3 b f Presidium 7.5f **(56)** - Mighty Flash (Rolfe (USA)) 12.1f **(65)**
Form - 6004
Record 2000 - 1st:0 2nd:0 3rd:0 Ran:4
Pre2000 - 1st:0 2nd:0 3rd:0 Ran:3
Win Prizemoney £0 *Total Prizemoney* £306
2000 Turf 0-4: (7f 2, 8f 2) (gd 2, g-f 2)
Scopey, average filly, effective 8f, acts on g-f. Turf high 66 (1st run) - 6th of 18 getting 7lb from Danakil (8 May Windsor 8f g-f RF 1102). **I A Balding [0-7] Robert Hitchins.*

PEPPERCORN BHB 36f32a **RR 32f 32a** 4694[10]

3 b f Totem (USA) 5f **(38)** - Sparkling Roberta **(39f 33a)** (Kind of Hush) 10.1f **(62)**
Form - 00680360640
Record 2000 - 1st:0 2nd:0 3rd:1 Ran:9
Pre2000 - 1st:0 2nd:0 3rd:0 Ran:6
Win Prizemoney £0 *Total Prizemoney* £292
2000 Turf 0-7: (8f 2, 9f, 10f 3, 11f) (gd 2, g-f 2, frm 3) 2000 AW 0-2: (8f 2) (Fibr 2)
Very moderate filly. Turf high 43 (began Jly). AW high 35. Consistent. **M D I Usher [0-15] Miss D G Kerr.*

PEPPERCORN (GER) **RR 109f** 4951a[1]

3 b c Big Shuffle (USA) - Pasca (GER) (Lagunas)
Form - 61
2000 Turf 1-2: (8f, 9f 1-1) (sft 1-2)
Currently Pattern-class colt. Turf high 109 (began Spt) - 1st of 11 getting 10lb from Banyumanik (8 Oct Dusseldorf RF 4951a).
**U Ostmann in GER [1-2] Stall Biovita.*

PEPPERDINE (IRE) BHB 92f RR 99df 4451[28]

4 b g Indian Ridge 7.6f **(74)** - Rahwah (Northern Baby (CAN)) 11.6f **(71)**
Form - 35000
Record 2000 - 1st:0 2nd:0 3rd:1 Ran:5
Pre2000 - 1st:2 2nd:5 3rd:0 Ran:13
Win Prizemoney £42,329 *Total Prizemoney* £58,551
Wins * 1999 Jun York (G-S) H 6f 85 93+ <
1998 Oct Warwic (GD) H 7f 78 83
2000 Turf 0-5: (5f, 6f 4) (g-s, gd 4)
Lengthy, very useful gelding, effective 6f, acts on gd, has worn blinkers. Turf high 98. Something of a hype horse, he usually attracts plenty of support but failed to deliver last year. Reportedly suffering from a physical problem when tailed off in the Ayr Gold Cup, he is one to treat with caution at present.
**D Nicholls [1-12] P D Savill (from W Jarvis [1-6] Oct 1998).*

PEPPIATT BHB 55f55a RR 62f 55a 5055[16]

6 ch g Efisio 7.7f **(69)** - Fleur du Val (Valiyar) 8.5f **(73)**
Form - 73483508263500000
Record 2000 - 1st:0 2nd:1 3rd:3 Ran:17
Pre2000 - 1st:4 2nd:2 3rd:4 Ran:37
Win Prizemoney £29,589 *Total Prizemoney* £42,895
Wins * 1999 Jly Ayr (SFT) H 6f 68 70
1998 Spt Goodwo (SFT) H 6f 71 77
1997 Jly Lingfi (G-F) H 7f 80 79 <
1997 Apr Folkes (G-F) 6f 75
2000 Turf 0-16: (5f, 6f 9, 7f 6) (sft 3, g-s 2, gd 3, g-f 6, frm 2) 2000 AW 0-1: (7f) (Fibr)
Average gelding, effective 6f, acts on g-s to g-f, best on g-s, has worn blinkers. Turf high 62 - 3rd of 10 getting 19lb from Point of Dispute (4 Aug Newmarket 6f g-f RF 3369).
**N Bycroft [1-37] Swinburne/Moore Partnership (from D Nicholls [1-14] Oct 1998).*

PERADVENTURE (IRE) BHB 72f RR 79df 1602[6]

5 b g Persian Bold 10f **(69)** - Missed Opportunity (IRE) (Exhibitioner) 8.7f **(61)**
Form - 6
Record 2000 - 1st:0 2nd:0 3rd:0 Ran:1
Pre2000 - 1st:1 2nd:1 3rd:2 Ran:11
Win Prizemoney £6,290 *Total Prizemoney* £9,428
Wins 1998 Spt York (GD) 10.4f 79 <
2000 Turf 0-1: (12f) (gd)
Above-average gelding. Becoming disappointing.
**M D Hammond [2-7] Shirebrook Park Management Ltd (from R Hannon [1-10] Oct 1998).*

PERCHANCER (IRE) BHB 54f58a RR 57f 58a 2993[3]

4 ch g Perugino (USA) - Irish Hope (Nishapour (FR)) 9.1f **(61)**
Form - 06321100134483
Record 2000 - 1st:3 2nd:1 3rd:3 Ran:12
Pre2000 - 1st:1 2nd:2 3rd:4 Ran:19
Win Prizemoney £11,114 *Total Prizemoney* £17,657
Wins * **2000** Apr Hamilt (GD) H 9.2f 51 61 <
* **2000** *Feb Southw (STD) H 8f 48 61* <
* **2000** *Feb Wolver (STD) H 8.5f 48 55*
* 1999 Jly Thirsk (FRM) H 7f 51 53
2000 Turf 1-7: (8f, 9f 1-5, 10f) (gd 1-2, g-f 3, frm 2) 2000 AW 2-5: (8f 2-2, 9f 3) (Fibr 2-5)
Scopey, average gelding, effective 7 to 9f, best at 8f, acts on gd to frm - acts on AW, best on gd, has worn blinkers, favours tight tracks, and excels at Lingfield. Turf high 61 - 1st of 18 getting 23lb from Tony Tie (8 Apr Hamilton RF 0643). AW high 61 - 1st of 13 getting 4lb from Sea Ya Maite (11 Feb Southwell RF 0262) - also 1st of 11 getting 6lb from Etisalat (1 Feb Wolverhampton RF 0195). Inconsistent. **P C Haslam [4-31] N P Green.*

PERCHINO RR 123[8]

3 b g Wolfhound (USA) 7.3f **(71)** - Last Request (Dancers Image (USA)) 9.3f **(71)**
Form - 8
Record 2000 - 1st:0 2nd:0 3rd:0 Ran:1
2000 AW 0-1: (7f) (Fibr)
Light-framed, currently very moderate gelding.
**J R Fanshawe [0-1] Mrs M Slater.*

PERCUSSION BHB 47f RR 54f 4814[12]

3 ch c Alhijaz 7.7f **(57)** - Blue Brocade (Reform) 8.9f **(62)**
Form - 0064700
Record 2000 - 1st:0 2nd:0 3rd:0 Ran:7
Win Prizemoney £0 *Total Prizemoney* £348
2000 Turf 0-7: (7f 2, 8f, 10f, 11f, 12f, 14f) (g-s, gd, g-f 3, frm 2)
Lengthy, fair colt, effective 11f, acts on frm. Turf high 54 - 4th of 11 getting 19lb from Romantic Affair (16 Jun Sandown 11f frm RF 2025). **J A R Toller [0-7] Alan Gibson.*

PERCY-VERANCE (IRE) BHB 45f RR 34f 4044[10]

2 ch g Dolphin Street (FR) - Sinology (Rainbow Quest (USA)) 10.1f **(75)**
Form - 000
Record 2000 - 1st:0 2nd:0 3rd:0 Ran:3
2000 Turf 0-2: (5f, 8f) (g-s, gd) 2000 AW 0-1: (5f) (Fibr)
Currently very moderate gelding. Turf high 44.
**A Dickman [0-3] Mike Smallman.*

PEREGIAN (IRE) BHB 88f RR 85f 5121[11]

2 b c Eagle Eyed (USA) - Mo Pheata (Petorius) 7.3f **(61)**
Form - 5371110350
Record 2000 - 1st:3 2nd:0 3rd:2 Ran:10
Win Prizemoney £9,149 *Total Prizemoney* £11,482
Wins * **2000** Jly Catter (G-F) H 7f 83+ <
* **2000** Jly Ayr (G-F) H 7f 83
* **2000** Jly Catter (G-F) 7f 74
2000 Turf 3-10: (5f, 6f 2, 7f 3-6, 8f) (g-s 2, gd 3, g-f, frm 3-4)
Useful colt, effective 6 to 8f, best at 7f, acts on gd to frm, best on frm, and excels at Catterick. Turf high 85 - 5th of 15 getting 3lb from Snowstorm (7 Spt Doncaster 8f frm RF 4283) - also 1st of 7 getting 12lb from Tortuguero (17 Jly Ayr RF 2870). Progressing well, he won three times in July, a maiden and two nurseries, each time over seven. **M Johnston [3-10] David Abell.*

PERESTROIKA (IRE) RR 44f 5100[16]

2 ch c Ashkalani (IRE) - Licentious **(32f)** (Reprimand)
Form - 0
Record 2000 - 1st:0 2nd:0 3rd:0 Ran:1
2000 Turf 0-1: (7f) (gd)
Currently moderate colt. **E A L Dunlop [0-1] Stars And Stripes II.*

PERFECT LOVER (IRE) BHB 40f RR 4999[0]

2 ch c Pursuit of Love 9.5f **(69)** - Elabella (Ela-Mana-Mou) 10.1f **(70)**
Form - 0
Record 2000 - 1st:0 2nd:0 3rd:0 Ran:1
2000 Turf 0-1: (6f) (g-s)
Currently little account colt.
**D J S ffrenchDavis [0-1] Mrs Rolanda Hyams.*

PERFECTLY HONEST RR 5312[19]

2 b f Charnwood Forest (IRE) - Carina Clare (Slip Anchor) 9.8f **(73)**
Form - 0
Record 2000 - 1st:0 2nd:0 3rd:0 Ran:1
2000 Turf 0-1: (8f) (g-s)
Currently very poor filly. **B Smart [0-1] The Winfield Partnership.*

PERFECT MOMENT (IRE) BHB 78f66a RR 77f 66a 4621[1]

3 b f Mujadil (USA) 7.7f **(70)** - Flashing Raven (IRE) (Maelstrom Lake)
Form - 04211161001
Record 2000 - 1st:5 2nd:1 3rd:0 Ran:11
Pre2000 - 1st:1 2nd:0 3rd:0 Ran:6
Win Prizemoney £15,635 *Total Prizemoney* £16,200
Wins * **2000** Spt Bright (SFT) H 11.9f 68 77 <
* **2000** Aug Bright (G-F) H 10f 65 67
* **2000** *Jun Wolver (STD) H 9.4f 49 56*
2000 Jun Pontef (G-F) S 8f 63
2000 Jun Nottin (SFT) SH 10f 53 65
1999 Jly Leices (G-F) 7f 73
2000 Turf 4-9: (6f, 8f 1-2, 9f, 10f 2-3, 12f 1-2) (g-s 1-1, gd 1-3, g-f 1-2, frm 1-3) 2000 AW 1-2: (9f 1-2) (Fibr 1-2)
Leggy, above-average filly, effective 7 to 12f, acts on gd to frm, prefers left handed tracks, likes tight tracks, excels at Brighton.

Turf high 77 - 1st of 8 getting 1lb from Welsh Dream (24 Spt Brighton RF 4621). AW high 56. She landed a brace of sellers for Graham McCourt's yard, and has landed handicaps on sand and turf for her new trainer.
**C A Dwyer [3-6] Casino Racing Partnership (from G M McCourt [2-5] Jun 2000).*

PERFECT PEACH BHB 92f **RR 96?f** 4966[6]

5 b m Lycius (USA) 8.8f **(71)** - Perfect Timing (Comedy Star (USA)) 7.5f **(50)**
Form - 00804346276406
Record 2000 - 1st:0 2nd:1 3rd:1 Ran:14
Pre2000 - 1st:3 2nd:2 3rd:1 Ran:22
Win Prizemoney £13,151 *Total Prizemoney* £21,514
Wins * 1999 Spt Mussel (G-S) H 7.1f 65 68
1997 Aug Beverl (G-S) H 5f 75 78 <
1997 Aug Thirsk (GD) 5f 78 <
2000 Turf 0-14: (5f 2, 6f 3, 7f 7, 8f 2) (gd 3, g-f 3, frm 7, hrd)
Very useful filly, effective 6f, acts on hrd, has worn blinkers, likes tight tracks. Turf high 96. Inconsistent.
**C W Fairhurst [1-29] Mrs Ann Morris (from D W Chapman [0-2] Jun 1998).*

PERFECT PIROUETTE (JPN) **RR 88f** 5138[2]

2 b f Warning 8.1f **(77)** - Prancing Ballerina (USA) (Nijinsky (CAN)) 10.3f **(77)**
Form - 2
Record 2000 - 1st:0 2nd:1 3rd:0 Ran:1
Win Prizemoney £0 *Total Prizemoney* £995
2000 Turf 0-1: (8f) (g-s)
Currently useful filly. **M L W Bell [0-1] Richard Colton Jr.*

PERFECT PLUM (IRE) BHB 111f **RR 102f** 5203a[1]

2 b f Darshaan 11.9f **(81)** - Damascene (IRE) (Scenic)
Form - 52321011
Record 2000 - 1st:3 2nd:2 3rd:1 Ran:8
Win Prizemoney £54,706 *Total Prizemoney* £57,352
Wins * 2000 Oct Deauvi (HVY) G3 8f 96 <
*** 2000** Spt Ayr (SFT) H 8f 85 95
*** 2000** Aug Newcas (G-S) H 8f 76 78
2000 Turf 3-8: (6f, 7f 3, 8f 3-4) (hvy 1-1, g-s 1-1, gd 1-1, g-f 3, frm 2)
Very useful filly, effective 8f, acts on hvy to gd. Turf high 96 - 1st of 8 getting 4lb from Ascension (17 Oct Deauville RF 5203a) - also 1st of 10 giving 17lb to Fazzani (15 Spt Ayr RF 4428). She has a pronounced knee action and came into her own when tackling soft ground in the second half of the season. Ridden forcefully when winning two Group 3 races in France, she will stay beyond a mile and should do well on the continent granted testing conditions.
**Sir Mark Prescott [3-8] Sir Edmund Loder.*

PERFECT STING (USA) **RR 119f** 5329a[1]

4 b f Red Ransom (USA) 8.6f **(83)** - Valid Victress (USA) (Valid Appeal (USA)) 8.9f **(78)**
Form - 1
2000 Turf 1-1: (11f 1-1) (frm 1-1)
Currently high-class filly. (1st run) - 1st of 14 from Tout Charmant (4 Nov Churchill Downs RF 5329a).
**J Orseno in USA [2-3] Stronach Stables.*

PERFECT SUNDAY (USA) BHB 99f **RR 95f** 4261[3]

2 b br c Quest for Fame 12.8f **(75)** - Sunday Bazaar (USA) (Nureyev (USA)) 8.7f **(78)**
Form - 323
Record 2000 - 1st:0 2nd:1 3rd:2 Ran:3
Win Prizemoney £0 *Total Prizemoney* £5,032
2000 Turf 0-3: (7f 2, 8f) (gd, frm 2)
Currently very useful colt. Turf high 95 (began Aug) - 2nd of 5 to Prizeman (18 Aug Newbury 7f frm RF 3757). He ran creditably on all his starts, notably when beaten half a length by Prizeman in a Listed event at Newbury. His pronounced knee-action suggests soft ground would help, and an ordinary maiden is there for the taking. **B W Hills [0-3] K Abdulla.*

PERFIDIOUS (USA) BHB 72f50a **RR 56f 50a** 5318[15]

2 b c Lear Fan (USA) 10.4f **(80)** - Perfolia (USA) (Nodouble (USA)) 8.8f **(68)**
Form - 00
Record 2000 - 1st:0 2nd:0 3rd:0 Ran:2
2000 Turf 0-2: (6f 2) (sft 2)
Currently fair colt. Turf high 56 (began Oct).
**Sir Mark Prescott [0-2] Eclipse Thoroughbreds - Osborne House II.*

PERICLES BHB 45f46a **RR 46f 46a** 696[13]

6 b g Primo Dominie 7.2f **(67)** - Egalite (FR) (Luthier) 9.8f **(71)**
Form - 0
Record 2000 - 1st:0 2nd:0 3rd:0 Ran:1
Pre2000 - 1st:5 2nd:6 3rd:7 Ran:53
Win Prizemoney £17,104 *Total Prizemoney* £26,431
Wins * 1998 Jun Folkes (GD) 7f 67
1997 Oct Wolver (STD) C 7f 85 <
1997 Jun Wolver (STD) H 7f 80 80
1997 Jun Leices (GD) H 7f 70 74
1996 Spt Wolver (STD) 6f 77+
2000 Turf 0-1: (7f) (gd)
Moderate gelding, effective 7 to 8f, best at 7f, acts on g-f - acts on Equi, has worn blinkers.
**Miss Gay Kelleway [1-36] K & W Racing Partnership (from M Johnston [4-20] Oct 1997).*

PERIGEE MOON (USA) **RR 91+f** 5352a[1]

2 ch c Hennessy (USA) - Lovlier Linda (USA) (Vigors (USA)) 10f **(72)**
Form - 11
2000 Turf 2-2: (6f 1-1, 7f 1-1) (hvy 1-1, sft 1-1)
Currently useful colt. Turf high 91 (began Spt) - 1st of 12 from Dr Brendler (30 Oct Leopardstown RF 5352a) - also 1st of 18 giving 5lb to America Calling (30 Spt Curragh RF 4791a). Bolted up in a Curragh maiden on his debut and was confidently ridden to take a Leopardstown Group Three on his only other appearance. Could be anything.
**A P O'Brien in IRE [2-2] Mrs John Magnier.*

PERIGEUX (IRE) BHB 53f64a **RR 59df 64a** 5112[11]

4 b g Perugino (USA) - Rock On (IRE) (Ballad Rock) 7.8f **(63)**
Form - 55075100030040
Record 2000 - 1st:1 2nd:0 3rd:1 Ran:14
Pre2000 - 1st:3 2nd:4 3rd:1 Ran:18
Win Prizemoney £14,237 *Total Prizemoney* £17,712
Wins * 2000 Jly Bright (SFT) H 5.3f 59 60
1998 Jly Wolver (STD) 6f 86 <
1998 *Jly* Ayr (GD) H 6f 79
1998 Jly Southw (STD) 6f 79
2000 Turf 1-13: (5f 1-9, 6f 4) (g-s, gd 1-5, g-f 3, frm 4) 2000 AW 0-1: (6f) (Fibr)
Strong, average gelding, effective 5 to 7f, acts on gd to frm, has worn blinkers, likes tight tracks. Turf high 60 - 1st of 11 giving 11lb to Absolute Fantasy (5 Jly Brighton RF 2539).
**K T Ivory [1-14] Mrs Valerie Hubbard (from J Berry [3-18] Aug 1999).*

PERLE DE SAGESSE BHB 56f50a **RR 57f 50a** 4618[11]

3 b f Namaqualand (USA) - Pearl of Dubai (USA) (Red Ransom (USA))
Form - 217175453821080
Record 2000 - 1st:1 2nd:1 3rd:1 Ran:11
Pre2000 - 1st:3 2nd:1 3rd:2 Ran:11
Win Prizemoney £9,644 *Total Prizemoney* £12,117
Wins * 2000 Jun Windso (G-F) H 6f 53 57
** 1999 Dec Lingfi (STD) C 7f 66*
** 1999 Nov Lingfi (STD) S 7f 68*
1999 Aug Windso (GD) S 5f 69 <
2000 Turf 1-6: (6f 1-4, 7f 2) (gd 3, frm 1-3) 2000 AW 0-5: (7f 4, 8f) (Equi 4, Fibr)
Leggy, fair filly, effective 5 to 7f, best at 7f, acts on frm - acts on Equi. Turf high 57. AW high 54. She won twice during the winter of 1999 on the Equitrack, and stepped up in class to win a Windsor handicap in the summer.
**J C Poulton [3-15] Russell Reed & Gerald West (from P F I Cole [1-7] Spt 1999).*

PERPETUAL PRIDE (IRE) BHB 40f **RR 4f** 356[7]

3 b c Pips Pride 6.7f **(70)** - Miss Springtime **(32f 55a)** (Bluebird (USA)) 7.5f **(69)**
Form - 7
Record 2000 - 1st:0 2nd:0 3rd:0 Ran:1
Pre2000 - 1st:0 2nd:0 3rd:0 Ran:2
2000 AW 0-1: (11f) (Fibr)
Leggy, very moderate colt. (DEAD)

**Mrs N Macauley [0-1] J Teasdale (from E J Alston [0-2] Jun 1999).*

PERPETUITY RR 4970[11]
2 ch c Timeless Times (USA) 6.1f **(56)** - Boadicea's Chariot (Commanche Run) 8.5f **(58)**
Form -
Record 2000 - 1st:0 2nd:0 3rd:1 Ran:6
Win Prizemoney £0 *Total Prizemoney* £937
2000 Turf 0-6: (gd, g-f 2, frm 3)
Above-average colt. Turf high 77.
**R Hannon [0-6] Major A M Everett.*

PERPETUO BHB 65f **RR 65f** 5000[10]
3 b f Mtoto 11.5f **(71)** - Persian Fountain (IRE) (Persian Heights)
Form - 3362100
Record 2000 - 1st:1 2nd:1 3rd:2 Ran:7
Win Prizemoney £3,243 *Total Prizemoney* £5,073
Wins * 2000 Spt Beverl (G-F) H 12f 62 65 <
2000 Turf 1-7: (10f 3, 11f, 12f 1-2, 14f) (g-s 2, g-f 1-3, frm 2)
Unfurnished, average filly, effective 11 to 12f, best at 12f, acts on g-s to frm, prefers tight tracks. Turf high 65 - 1st of 14 getting 3lb from Tufty Hopper (13 Spt Beverley RF 4364). Ran green when taking a Beverley maiden. **R A Fahey [1-7] A N Barrett.*

PERRYSTON VIEW BHB 115f **RR 117?f** 5213a[6]
8 b h Primo Dominie 7.2f **(67)** - Eastern Ember (Indian King (USA)) 7.4f **(64)**
Form - 1001055646
Record 2000 - 1st:2 2nd:0 3rd:0 Ran:10
Pre2000 - 1st:11 2nd:1 3rd:3 Ran:43
Win Prizemoney £182,727 *Total Prizemoney* £208,460

Wins	*** 2000**	May	Sandow	(HVY)	G2	5f		117?	<
	*** 2000**	Mar	Doncas	(G-F)	H	5f	98	109	
	1999	Oct	Doncas	(SFT)	H	5f	93	98	
	1999	May	Newmar	(G-F)	H	6f	89	96	
	1998	Aug	Ripon	(GD)	H	6f	86	92	
	1997	Spt	Ayr	(GD)	H	6f	81	92	
	1997	May	Newmar	(GD)	H	6f	78	80	

2000 Turf 2-10: (5f 2-9, 6f) (hvy, g-s 1-2, gd 4, frm 1-3)
High-class horse, effective 5f, acts on g-s to frm, mostly wears blinkers (effectively). Turf high 117 - 1st of 9 from Proud Native (29 May Sandown RF 1536) - also 1st of 21 giving 8lb to Sheer Viking (23 Mar Doncaster RF 0475). A grand campaigner, he won his first Group race when capitalising on a plum draw in the Temple Stakes at Sandown in May. Fourth in the Prix de l'Abbaye in October, he is a fast starter and goes particularly well when fresh (successful on his seasonal debut four times).
**J A Glover [2-10] (from P Calver [11-43] Oct 1999).*

PERSEUS WAY RR 31f 4806[12]
2 b c Bering 9.6f **(80)** - Petronella (USA) (Nureyev (USA)) 8.7f **(78)**
Form - 0
Record 2000 - 1st:0 2nd:0 3rd:0 Ran:1
2000 Turf 0-1: (7f) (g-s)
Currently very moderate colt.
**P R Chamings [0-1] Mrs Alexandra Chandris.*

PERSIAN CAT BHB 72f **RR 65f** 2270[4]
2 b f Persian Bold 10f **(69)** - Echo Cove (Slip Anchor) 9.8f **(73)**
Form - 514
Record 2000 - 1st:1 2nd:0 3rd:0 Ran:3
Win Prizemoney £3,006 *Total Prizemoney* £3,216
Wins * 2000 Jun Thirsk (FRM) 7f 65 <
2000 Turf 1-3: (6f, 7f 1-2) (g-f, frm 1-2)
Currently average filly. Turf high 65 - 1st of 13 from Maid of Arc (20 Jun Thirsk RF 2115). **Sir Mark Prescott [1-3] Mrs C R Philipson.*

PERSIAN FAYRE BHB 61f56a **RR 67f 56a** 5245[11]
8 b g Persian Heights 10.5f **(61)** - Dominion Fayre (Dominion) 8.5f **(63)**
Form - 010882800
Record 2000 - 1st:1 2nd:1 3rd:0 Ran:9
Pre2000 - 1st:9 2nd:9 3rd:4 Ran:64
Win Prizemoney £50,237 *Total Prizemoney* £72,940

Wins	*** 2000**	Jun	Ayr	(G-F)	H	7f	59	65	
	1999	May	Ayr	(GD)	H	7f	70	80	
	1999	May	Carlis	(FRM)	C	6.9f		57	
	1999	Apr	Redcar	(G-S)	S	7f		66	
	1998	Jun	Haydoc	(GD)		7.1f		86+	<
	1996	Nov	Newmar	(GD)	H	7f	79	83	
	1996	Oct	York	(GD)	H	7f	75	78	
	1996	Aug	Newcas	(GD)	H	7f	67	77	

2000 Turf 1-8: (6f, 7f 1-7) (sft, gd, g-f 3, frm 1-3) 2000 AW 0-1: (7f) (Fibr)
Average gelding, effective 7f, acts on gd, likes left handed tracks, likes tight tracks. Turf high 67. A veteran handicapper, he completed a hat-trick in the spring of 1999, but lost his form in the second half of the campaign. Returned to winning form on his second start of last season when able to dominate from the front. Seven furlongs is his trip.
**A Berry [1-9] Murray Grubb (from J Berry [9-66] Nov 1999).*

PERSIAN FILLY (IRE) RR 97f 3352a[6]
3 b f Persian Bold 10f **(69)** - Kafayef (USA) **(44tf)** (Secreto (USA)) 8.7f **(72)**
Form - 26
2000 Turf 0-2: (10f, 14f) (hvy, g-s)
Currently very useful filly. Turf high 97. **B Grizzetti in ITY [0-3].*

PERSIANO BHB 100f **RR 102f** 3934[14]
5 ch g Efisio 7.7f **(69)** - Persiandale (Persian Bold) 9.3f **(66)**
Form - 83132510
Record 2000 - 1st:2 2nd:1 3rd:2 Ran:8
Pre2000 - 1st:3 2nd:0 3rd:2 Ran:16
Win Prizemoney £92,743 *Total Prizemoney* £124,197

Wins	*** 2000**	Aug	Goodwo	(GD)	H	8f	97	102	<
	*** 2000**	May	Goodwo	(GD)	H	8f	88	92	
	* 1998	May	Doncas	(GD)	H	7f	90	99+	
	* 1998	May	Salisb	(FRM)	H	7f	75	89+	
	* 1998	May	Warwic	(GD)	H	7f	75	83	

2000 Turf 2-8: (7f 3, 8f 2-5) (g-s 1-1, gd 1-6, g-f)
Very useful gelding, effective 7 to 8f, best at 8f, acts on g-s to frm, best on gd, has worn blinkers, excels at Goodwood. Turf high 102 - 1st of 22 giving 13lb to Parisien Star (3 Aug Goodwood RF 3343). Consistent. He is a very useful handicapper when everything slots into pace as it did in the William Hill Mile at Glorious Goodwood, a victory he thoroughly deserved after some good efforts in competitive handicaps. He is game and genuine.
**J R Fanshawe [5-24] Miss A Church.*

PERSIAN POINT BHB 29f **RR 19f** 2468[6]
4 ch g Persian Bold 10f **(69)** - Kind Thoughts (Kashmir II) 11.7f **(48)**
Form - 006
Record 2000 - 1st:0 2nd:0 3rd:0 Ran:3
Pre2000 - 1st:0 2nd:0 3rd:0 Ran:4
2000 Turf 0-3: (7f, 8f, 14f) (frm 3)
Leggy, poor gelding. Turf high 19.
**Mrs A Duffield [0-7] A C & A D Partners.*

PERSIAN PRIDE (IRE) BHB 90f **RR 82f** 4643[17]
2 ch c Barathea (IRE) - Glenarff (USA) (Irish River (FR)) 8.6f **(78)**
Form - 0420
Record 2000 - 1st:0 2nd:1 3rd:0 Ran:4
Win Prizemoney £0 *Total Prizemoney* £1,604
2000 Turf 0-4: (7f 3, 8f) (gd, g-f, frm 2)
Decent colt. Turf high 82 (began Jly) - 2nd of 10 to Theatre Script (6 Spt Doncaster 8f gd RF 4261).
**P W Harris [0-4] Dr Jamal Ahmadzadeh.*

PERSIAN PUNCH (IRE) BHB 122f **RR 122f** 4985[1]
7 ch g Persian Heights 10.5f **(61)** - Rum Cay (USA) (Our Native (USA)) 11.2f **(63)**
Form - 281651321
Record 2000 - 1st:3 2nd:2 3rd:1 Ran:9
Pre2000 - 1st:9 2nd:2 3rd:6 Ran:27
Win Prizemoney £221,485 *Total Prizemoney* £420,693

Wins	*** 2000**	Oct	Newmar	(G-S)	G3	16f	122	<
	*** 2000**	Aug	Deauvi	(G-S)	G2	15f	111+	
	*** 2000**	May	Sandow	(HVY)	G3	16.4f	114	
	* 1999	Nov	Doncas	(SFT)		14.6f	99	
	* 1998	Aug	York	(G-F)	G3	15.9f	115	
	* 1998	May	Sandow	(GD)	G3	16.4f	119	
	* 1998	May	Newmar	(G-S)	G3	16f	120	
	* 1997	May	Sandow	(G-F)	G3	16.4f	115	
	* 1997	May	Newbur	(SFT)	L	13.3f	116	
	* 1996	Jly	Newmar	(GD)	L	14.8f	106	

* 1996	Jun	Salisb	(GD)	14f	90
* 1996	May	Windso	(G-F)	10f	79+

2000 Turf 3-9: (14f, 15f 1-1, 16f 2-4, 18f, 20f 2) (g-s 2-3, gd 1-4, g-f, frm)

Very high-class gelding, effective 12 to 20f, best at 20f, acts on g-s to frm, best on gd, likes right handed tracks, and excels at Doncaster and Sandown. Turf high 122 - 1st of 9 from Royal Rebel (14 Oct Newmarket RF 4985) - also 1st of 7 getting 5lb from Churlish Charm (29 May Sandown RF 1535). Consistent. A huge individual, he became the first horse to win the Group 3 Henry II Stakes three times when fending off Churlish Charm at Sandown in May. He struck up a good understanding with Richard Hughes in the second half of the campaign, making all to win the Prix Kergorlay and Jockey Club Cup (impressive). Possibly best with some cut in the ground nowadays, he will be a tough nut to crack at around two miles next term. **D R C Elsworth [12-36] J C Smith.*

PERSIAN SPIRIT BHB 60f **RR 67f** 4108[11]

2 b f Persian Bold 10f **(69)** - Big Story (Cadeaux Genereux)

Form - 860

Record 2000 - 1st:0 2nd:0 3rd:0 Ran:3

Persian Punch, narrowly beaten on his reappearance at Ascot

2000 Turf 0-3: (7f 2, 8f) (gd, frm 2)

Currently average filly. Turf high 67 (began Jly). **R Hannon [0-3] R Gander.*

PERSIAN WATERS (IRE) BHB 67f **RR 68f** 4546[2]

4 b g Persian Bold 10f **(69)** - Emerald Waters (Kings Lake (USA)) 10.8f **(67)**

Form - 12

Record 2000 - 1st:1 2nd:1 3rd:0 Ran:2
Pre2000 - 1st:1 2nd:0 3rd:1 Ran:9

Win Prizemoney £6,401 *Total Prizemoney* £8,377

Wins								
* 2000	Spt	Nottin	(SFT)	H	16f	62	68	<
1998	Oct	Pontef	(SFT)	H	8f	64	68	<

2000 Turf 1-2: (16f 1-2) (g-s, gd 1-1)

Scopey, average gelding, effective 16f, acts on g-s to gd. Turf high 68 (1st run) (began Spt) - 1st of 14 giving 24lb to Righty Ho (15 Spt Nottingham RF 4445). Consistent. A winner on soft ground at Pontefract at two, he has had a few trainers in his time and has been hurdling, but showed he still has what it takes on the level when winning at Nottingham in September.
**J R Fanshawe [2-8] Paul & Jenny Green (from M C Pipe [0-2] Jly 1999).*

PERSUADE BHB 79f **RR 76f** 3706[6]

2 ch c Lure (USA) - Shapely (USA) **(74+f)** (Alleged (USA)) 10f **(76)**

Form - 446

Record 2000 - 1st:0 2nd:0 3rd:0 Ran:3

Win Prizemoney £0 *Total Prizemoney* £872

2000 Turf 0-3: (7f 3) (g-f, frm 2)

Currently above-average colt. Turf high 76 - 4th of 12 to No Excuse Needed (8 Jly Sandown 7f frm RF 2644). Misbehaved beforehand and missed the break when favourite on his debut. Better effort next time. **J H M Gosden [0-3] K Abdulla.*

PERTEMPS BOYCOTT (IRE) BHB 35f **RR 32f** 5318[21]

2 b g Indian Ridge 7.6f **(74)** - Coupe D'Hebe (Ile de Bourbon (USA)) 10.1f **(67)**

Form - 000

Record 2000 - 1st:0 2nd:0 3rd:0 Ran:3

2000 Turf 0-3: (6f 3) (sft 2, g-f)

Currently very moderate gelding. Turf high 32 (began Spt). **W J Haggas [0-3] Pertemps Network Owners Syndicate.*

PERTEMPS FC BHB 45f43a **RR 51f 43a** 3849[12]

3 b g Prince Sabo 6.6f **(64)** - Top Mouse (High Top) 10.2f **(67)**

Form - 0800080

Record 2000 - 1st:0 2nd:0 3rd:0 Ran:7
Pre2000 - 1st:2 2nd:1 3rd:0 Ran:8

Win Prizemoney £9,068 *Total Prizemoney* £10,074

Wins								
* 1999	Aug	Beverl	(GD)	H	5f	65	67	<
* 1999	Jly	Newcas	(G-F)	S	6f	62		

2000 Turf 0-7: (5f 3, 6f 3, 7f) (gd, g-f 3, frm 3)

Small, fair gelding, effective 5 to 6f, acts on g-f to frm, has worn blinkers. Turf high 51. **T D Easterby [2-15] The Pertemps Professionals.*

PERTEMPS GILL BHB 43f **RR 40f** 3072[4]

2 b f Silca Blanka (IRE) - Royal Celerity (USA) (Riverman (USA)) 9.1f **(76)**

Form - 703054

Record 2000 - 1st:0 2nd:0 3rd:1 Ran:6

Win Prizemoney £0 *Total Prizemoney* £263

2000 Turf 0-5: (5f 4, 7f) (sft, gd, g-f, frm 2) 2000 AW 0-1: (5f) (Equi)

Moderate filly. Turf high 40. **A D Smith [0-6] Pertemps Group Ltd.*

PERTEMPS JACK BHB 27f **RR 20f** 4097[3]

2 br g Silca Blanka (IRE) - Stella Royale (Astronef)

Form - 663

Record 2000 - 1st:0 2nd:0 3rd:1 Ran:3

Win Prizemoney £0 *Total Prizemoney* £315

2000 Turf 0-2: (6f, 7f) (frm 2) 2000 AW 0-1: (6f) (Fibr)

Currently little account gelding. Turf high 20. **A D Smith [0-3] Pertemps Group Ltd.*

PERTEMPS JARDINE (IRE) BHB 62f **RR 74f** 3407[9]

2 b br c General Monash (USA) - Indescent Blue **(43f)** (Bluebird (USA)) 7.5f **(69)**

Form - 3450

Record 2000 - 1st:0 2nd:0 3rd:1 Ran:4

Win Prizemoney £0 *Total Prizemoney* £764

2000 Turf 0-4: (5f 4) (gd 2, g-f, hrd)

Above-average colt. Turf high 74. **R A Fahey [0-4] Pertemps Network Owners Syndicate.*

PERTEMPS REVEREND (IRE) **RR 37f** 5160[6]

2 b g Spectrum (IRE) - Young Isabel (IRE) (Last Tycoon) 8.5f **(62)**

Form - 06

Record 2000 - 1st:0 2nd:0 3rd:0 Ran:2

2000 Turf 0-2: (5f, 8f) (sft, gd)

Currently very moderate gelding. Turf high 37 (began Spt). **S C Williams [0-2] Pertemps Flexipeople Owners Syndicate.*

PERTEMPS STAR BHB 37f **RR 23f** 4756[17]

3 b g Imperial Frontier (USA) 7f **(65)** - Stella Royale (Astronef)

Form - 7000

Record 2000 - 1st:0 2nd:0 3rd:0 Ran:2
Pre2000 - 1st:0 2nd:0 3rd:0 Ran:6

2000 Turf 0-2: (5f 2) (g-s, gd)

Neat, fair gelding. Turf high 23 (began Spt).
**A D Smith [0-6] Duckhaven Stud (from A G Newcombe [0-2] Jun 1999).*

PERTEMPS THATCHER BHB 67f **RR 60f** 2765[2]

2 b br f Petong 7.6f **(58)** - Nadema (Artaius (USA)) 9f **(69)**
Form - 402
Record 2000 - 1st:0 2nd:1 3rd:0 Ran:3
Win Prizemoney £0 *Total Prizemoney* £836
2000 Turf 0-3: (6f, 7f 2) (gd, g-f, frm)
Currently average filly. Turf high 74 - 2nd of 9 getting 5lb from El Maximo (13 Jly Folkestone 7f gd RF 2765).
**S C Williams [0-3] Pertemps Flexipeople Owners Syndicate.*

PERUGIA (IRE) BHB 82f RR 87f 5324[11]

3 gr f Perugino (USA) - Lightning Bug (Prince Bee) 12f **(46)**
Form - 8480
Record 2000 - 1st:0 2nd:0 3rd:0 Ran:4
Pre2000 - 1st:1 2nd:1 3rd:0 Ran:4
Win Prizemoney £4,204 *Total Prizemoney* £8,669
Wins 1999 May Goodwo (GD) 6f 90+ <
2000 Turf 0-4: (6f 2, 7f 2) (sft, gd, g-f, frm)
Scopey, useful filly, effective 6 to 7f, acts on gd to frm. Turf high 87. Inconsistent.
**K McAuliffe [0-2] Mrs Mary O'Connor (from B W Hills [1-6] Jly 2000).*

PERUGINA (FR) RR 99f 3542a[10]

3 b f Highest Honor (FR) 10.9f **(72)** - Piacenza (FR) (Darshaan) 9.9f **(84)**
Form - 10
2000 Turf 1-2: (7f 1-2) (hvy 1-1, gd)
Very useful filly. Turf high 99 (1st run) (began Jly) - 1st of 9 from Castiya (14 Jly Deauville RF 2978a). She produced a sharp burst of speed to win a Group Three at Saint-Cloud in October and is a useful prospect. Likely to stay a mile or beyond, she goes well on easy ground. **Mme C Head in FR [2-5].*

PERUGINO PEARL (IRE) BHB 35f32a RR 25f 32a 901[12]

3 b f Perugino (USA) - Farnacliffe (Taufan (USA)) 7f **(57)**
Form - 00
Record 2000 - 1st:0 2nd:0 3rd:0 Ran:2
Pre2000 - 1st:0 2nd:0 3rd:0 Ran:2
2000 Turf 0-1: (6f) (g-s) 2000 AW 0-1: (5f) (Fibr)
Leggy, little account filly. (DEAD)
**M Brittain [0-4] Northgate Lodge Racing Club.*

PERUGINO'S MALT (IRE) BHB 53f50a RR 28f 50a 1364[12]

4 ch f Perugino (USA) - Malt Leaf (IRE) (Nearly a Nose (USA))
Form - 60
Record 2000 - 1st:0 2nd:0 3rd:0 Ran:1
Pre2000 - 1st:1 2nd:0 3rd:1 Ran:7
Win Prizemoney £3,953 *Total Prizemoney* £4,809
Wins 1999 Jly Naas (G-F) 8f 70 <
2000 Turf 0-1: (8f) (frm)
Little account filly, effective 8 to 10f, acts on g-s to g-f, best on g-f. Becoming disappointing.
**A T Murphy [0-3] R W Savery (from A P O'Brien in IRE [1-5] Spt 1999).*

PERUVIAN CHIEF (IRE) BHB 86f RR 90f 4150[9]

3 b c Foxhound (USA) - John's Ballad (IRE) (Ballad Rock) 7.8f **(63)**
Form - 1305204336800
Record 2000 - 1st:0 2nd:1 3rd:2 Ran:11
Pre2000 - 1st:2 2nd:1 3rd:1 Ran:6
Win Prizemoney £5,214 *Total Prizemoney* £20,288
Wins * 1999 *Nov Lingfi (STD) H 7f 76 87* <
* 1999 *Oct Wolver (STD) 6f 80*
2000 Turf 0-11: (5f, 6f 8, 7f 2) (g-s 2, gd 3, g-f 2, frm 4)
Scopey, useful colt, effective 6 to 7f, best at 6f, acts on gd to frm - acts on AW, best on frm, excels at Newmarket. Turf high 90 - 2nd of 30 getting 17lb from Hunting Lion (3 Jun Newmarket 6f frm RF 1690). Consistent. Usually held-up, he looked unlucky on occasions last year. Unlikely to stay beyond seven furlongs, he might benefit from more enterprising tactics.
**N P Littmoden [2-17] M C S D Racing Ltd.*

PERUVIAN JADE BHB 73f69a RR 77f 69a 770[8]

3 gr f Petong 7.6f **(58)** - Rion River (IRE) (Taufan (USA)) 7f **(57)**
Form - 648
Record 2000 - 1st:0 2nd:0 3rd:0 Ran:3
Pre2000 - 1st:2 2nd:1 3rd:1 Ran:9
Win Prizemoney £7,532 *Total Prizemoney* £20,578
Wins * 1999 Spt Leices (GD) H 6f 73 74 <
* 1999 Spt Goodwo (G-F) H 6f 70 74 <
2000 Turf 0-2: (6f, 7f) (hvy, gd) 2000 AW 0-1: (5f) (Equi)
Neat, above-average filly, effective 6f, acts on hvy to g-f. Turf high 77 (1st run) - 4th of 15 to Footprints (12 Apr Warwick 6f hvy RF 0688). Consistent. **N P Littmoden [2-12] M C S D Racing Ltd.*

PERUVIAN STAR BHB 41f65a RR 28f 65a 2491[11]

4 b g Emarati (USA) 6.6f **(63)** - Julie's Star (IRE) (Thatching) 8f **(66)**
Form - 850005060
Record 2000 - 1st:0 2nd:0 3rd:0 Ran:9
Pre2000 - 1st:1 2nd:1 3rd:1 Ran:6
Win Prizemoney £2,853 *Total Prizemoney* £3,771
Wins 1998 *Dec Wolver (SLW) 6f 84+* <
2000 Turf 0-6: (7f 3, 8f 2, 10f) (sft, gd 2, frm 2, hrd) 2000 AW 0-3: (6f, 7f, 8f) (Fibr 3)
Moderate gelding. Turf high 55. AW high 41.
**L A Dace [0-9] M C S D Racing Ltd (from N P Littmoden [1-6] Jun 1999).*

PETALITE RR 55f 2935[8]

2 gr f Petong 7.6f **(58)** - Veuve Hoornaert (IRE) **(76f)** (Standaan (FR)) 7f **(55)**
Form - 68
Record 2000 - 1st:0 2nd:0 3rd:0 Ran:2
2000 Turf 0-2: (5f, 6f) (g-f, frm)
Currently fair filly. Turf high 55 (began Jly).
**M A Jarvis [0-2] T G Warner.*

PETANE (IRE) BHB 22f RR 25f 1739[14]

5 b g Petardia 8.2f **(58)** - Senane (Vitiges (FR)) 8.2f **(59)**
Form - 0
Record 2000 - 1st:0 2nd:0 3rd:0 Ran:1
Pre2000 - 1st:1 2nd:0 3rd:1 Ran:18
Win Prizemoney £1,725 *Total Prizemoney* £2,256
Wins 1998 Aug Folkes (G-F) S 12f 47 <
2000 Turf 0-1: (11f) (gd)
Little account gelding, often wears blinkers. Becoming disappointing.
**T J Arnold [0-1] Steppey Lane Bloodstock (from John Harris [0-4] Spt 1999).*

PETARA (IRE) BHB 35f RR 37f 5056[20]

5 ch g Petardia 8.2f **(58)** - Romangoddess (IRE) (Rhoman Rule (USA))
Form - 5080
Record 2000 - 1st:0 2nd:0 3rd:0 Ran:4
Pre2000 - 1st:2 2nd:1 3rd:3 Ran:30
Win Prizemoney £5,796 *Total Prizemoney* £8,871
Wins * 1999 Spt Lingfi (FRM) SH 10f 38 40
* 1997 Spt Catter (G-F) H 7f 60 65 <
2000 Turf 0-4: (8f, 10f, 11f, 12f) (sft, g-s, g-f, frm)
Very moderate gelding, effective 10f, acts on frm, mostly wears blinkers, favours left handed tracks, likes tight tracks. Turf high 31 (began Aug). Inconsistent.
**J S Wainwright [2-35] Wisma Partnership.*

PETARGA BHB 77f RR 76f 4832[17]

5 b m Petong 7.6f **(58)** - One Half Silver (CAN) (Plugged Nickle (USA)) 7.8f **(68)**
Form - 0850110
Record 2000 - 1st:2 2nd:0 3rd:0 Ran:7
Pre2000 - 1st:2 2nd:2 3rd:4 Ran:20
Win Prizemoney £15,173 *Total Prizemoney* £21,247
Wins * **2000** Spt Leices (G-S) H 5f 73 76
* **2000** Spt Bath (GD) H 5.7f 68 78 <
* 1999 Jly Folkes (G-F) H 6f 73 75
* 1997 Jun Bath (G-F) 5.1f 72
2000 Turf 2-7: (5f 1-2, 6f 1-5) (g-s, g-f 1-3, frm 1-2, hrd)
Above-average filly, effective 5 to 6f, best at 6f, acts on g-f to frm, best on frm. Turf high 78 - 1st of 18 getting 3lb from Rule of Thumb (4 Spt Bath RF 4207) - also 1st of 20 giving 26lb to Mutasawwar (18 Spt Leicester RF 4487).
**J A R Toller [4-27] Mrs R W Gore-Andrews.*

PETER PERFECT BHB 20f46a RR 46a 4679[7]

6 gr g Chilibang 7f **(55)** - Misdevious (USA) (Alleged (USA)) 10f **(76)**
Form - 07
Record 2000 - 1st:0 2nd:0 3rd:0 Ran:2

Pre2000 - 1st:0 2nd:3 3rd:1 Ran:19
Win Prizemoney £0 *Total Prizemoney* £3,186
2000 Turf 0-2: (12f 2) (g-s 2)
Little account gelding, often wears blinkers. (began Spt).
**Mrs S Lamyman [0-14] P Lamyman (from R Curtis [0-2] Spt 1997).*

PETERSHAM RR 89+f 5135[2]
3 b c Petardia 8.2f **(58)** - Hayhurst (Sandhurst Prince) 7.9f **(63)**
Form - 2
Record 2000 - 1st:0 2nd:1 3rd:0 Ran:1
Win Prizemoney £0 *Total Prizemoney* £1,592
2000 Turf 0-1: (10f) (sft)
Workmanlike, currently useful colt. **L M Cumani [0-1] J Camuda.*

PETER'S IMP (IRE) BHB 71f59a RR 77f 59a 5165[10]
5 b g Imp Society (USA) 7.1f **(63)** - Catherine Clare (Sallust) 8.4f **(63)**
Form - 58253011433600
Record 2000 - 1st:2 2nd:1 3rd:3 Ran:14
Pre2000 - 1st:4 2nd:3 3rd:4 Ran:29
Win Prizemoney £23,671 *Total Prizemoney* £35,400

Wins								
	* **2000**	Jly	Ascot	(G-F)	H	7f	67	78
	* **2000**	Jly	Warwic	(G-F)	H	7.1f	64	63
	1999	Jun	Redcar	(FRM)		7f		80
	1999	May	Hamilt	(G-F)		6f		67
	1998	Jly	Haydoc	(G-F)		7.1f		68
	1997	Aug	Newcas	(G-F)	H	6f	77	81 <

2000 Turf 2-13: (6f, 7f 2-8, 8f 4) (sft 2, g-s 2, gd 1-4, g-f 1-2, frm 3) 2000 AW 0-1: (7f) (Fibr)
Above-average gelding, effective 6 to 8f, best at 7f, acts on gd to frm, best on gd, has worn blinkers, likes left handed tracks. Turf high 78 - 1st of 28 giving 2lb to Tornado Prince (29 Jly Ascot RF 3204).
**A Berry [2-14] & Mrs Peter Foden (from J Berry [4-29] Oct 1999).*

PETER'S PRINCESS (IRE) BHB 30f RR 13f 4174[20]
3 ch f Lycius (USA) 8.8f **(71)** - Regal Scintilla (King of Spain) 7.8f **(52)**
Form - 600
Record 2000 - 1st:0 2nd:0 3rd:0 Ran:3
Pre2000 - 1st:0 2nd:0 3rd:0 Ran:4
2000 Turf 0-3: (5f 2, 6f) (g-s, g-f 2)
Workmanlike, poor filly. Turf high 13.
**A Berry [0-3] & Mrs Peter Foden (from J Berry [0-4] Nov 1999).*

PETEURESQUE (USA) BHB 75f RR 73f 4274[14]
3 ch g Peteski (CAN) - Miss Ultimo (USA) (Screen King (USA))
Form - 62002810
Record 2000 - 1st:1 2nd:2 3rd:0 Ran:8
Pre2000 - 1st:0 2nd:1 3rd:0 Ran:2
Win Prizemoney £4,111 *Total Prizemoney* £8,450
Wins * **2000** Aug Redcar (FRM) H 10f 69 73 <
2000 Turf 1-8: (6f, 7f, 8f, 10f 1-4, 12f) (gd 4, g-f, frm 2, hrd 1-1)
Scopey, above-average gelding, effective 7 to 10f, best at 10f, acts on frm to hrd, best on frm, prefers left handed tracks. Turf high 73 - 1st of 14 giving 25lb to Glen Vale Walk (12 Aug Redcar RF 3598). Inconsistent. Broke his duck at Redcar in August, having failed to stay twelve furlongs the time before. **T D Barron [1-10] J Baggott.*

PETITE DANSEUSE BHB 37f39a RR 36f 39a 5118[9]
6 b m Aragon 7.7f **(58)** - Let Her Dance (USA) (Sovereign Dancer (USA)) 11.2f **(68)**
Form - 755801461160525467 00
Record 2000 - 1st:3 2nd:1 3rd:0 Ran:19
Pre2000 - 1st:4 2nd:7 3rd:8 Ran:60
Win Prizemoney £19,563 *Total Prizemoney* £33,430

Wins								
	* **2000**	*May*	*Southw*	*(STD)*	*H*	*6f*	*43*	*48*
	* **2000**	*May*	*Wolver*	*(STD)*	*H*	*6f*	*38*	*41*
	* **2000**	*Feb*	*Southw*	*(STD)*	*SH*	*6f*	*33*	*37*
	1997	Spt	Leices	(G-F)	C	6f		61
	1997	Aug	Leices	(GD)	C	7f		59+
	1996	May	Windso	(GD)		5f		75 <
	1996	May	Bath	(G-F)		5.1f		72

2000 Turf 0-4: (6f 4) (frm 2, hrd 2) 2000 AW 3-15: (6f 3-13, 7f 2) (Fibr 3-15)
Moderate mare, effective 6f, acts on g-f - acts on Fibr, has worn blinkers, likes left handed tracks, likes tight tracks. Turf high 36. AW high 48 - 1st of 16 giving 3lb to Nadder (22 May Southwell RF 1378) - also 1st of 13 getting 9lb from Palo Blanco (11 May Wolverhampton RF 1146). Consistent. She is a capable performer on Fibresand when in the mood and has done well on that surface last year, winning three times over six furlongs. She does stay further and likes to come late.
**D W Chapman [3-53] David Chapman (from C A Dwyer [2-14] Spt 1997).*

PETITE GALERIE (IRE) BHB 35a RR 6f 35a 5021[10]
3 b f Pips Pride 6.7f **(70)** - Tizzy (Formidable (USA)) 9.2f **(63)**
Form - 0
Record 2000 - 1st:0 2nd:0 3rd:0 Ran:1
2000 Turf 0-1: (7f) (g-s)
Rangy, currently poor filly. **T G Mills [0-1] T G Mills.*

PETIT MARQUIS (FR) BHB 87f RR 93f 2747[13]
3 b c Lost World (IRE) - Ephemeride (USA) (Al Nasr (FR)) 9.3f **(68)**
Form - 1200
Record 2000 - 1st:1 2nd:1 3rd:0 Ran:4
Pre2000 - 1st:0 2nd:1 3rd:0 Ran:1
Win Prizemoney £2,278 *Total Prizemoney* £5,074
Wins * **2000** *Mar Wolver (STD) 8.5f 87* <
2000 Turf 0-3: (7f, 9f, 10f) (g-s 2, gd) 2000 AW 1-1: (8f 1-1) (Fibr 1-1)
Strong, useful colt. Turf high 93 (1st run) - 2nd of 7 getting 11lb from Jo Mell (19 Apr Beverley 7f g-s RF 0792). (1st run) - 1st of 5 from Sir Ferbet (23 Mar Wolverhampton RF 0481). He lost his way after a promising start to the campaign.
**J R Fanshawe [1-5] Miss A Church.*

PETIT TOR BHB 59f RR 60f 4773[4]
2 b f Rock City 8.8f **(62)** - Kinoora (Kind of Hush) 10.1f **(62)**
Form - 84252641224
Record 2000 - 1st:1 2nd:4 3rd:0 Ran:11
Win Prizemoney £1,918 *Total Prizemoney* £5,648
Wins * **2000** Aug Catter (G-S) S 7f 58 <
2000 Turf 1-11: (5f 2, 6f 3, 7f 1-6) (g-s, gd 3, g-f 1-2, frm 4, hrd)
Average filly, effective 5 to 7f, best at 7f, acted on g-s to frm. Turf high 60 - 2nd of 16 getting 1lb from The Fancy Man (13 Spt Beverley 7f g-f RF 4360) - also 1st of 14 getting 5lb from Nettles (18 Aug Catterick RF 3739). (DEAD) **J Norton [1-11] J Wightman.*

PETONGSKI BHB 85f RR 88f 4747[13]
2 b g Petong 7.6f **(58)** - Madam Petoski (Petoski) 5.7f **(62)**
Form - 21280
Record 2000 - 1st:1 2nd:2 3rd:0 Ran:5
Win Prizemoney £2,709 *Total Prizemoney* £7,157
Wins * **2000** Aug Newcas (GD) 6f 84+ <
2000 Turf 1-5: (6f 1-5) (gd 2, g-f 1-3)
Useful gelding. Turf high 88 (began Jly) - 2nd of 5 getting 5lb from Healey (19 Aug Ripon 6f g-f RF 3795) - also 1st of 16 from Stretton (9 Aug Newcastle RF 3493). He has plenty of pace but is rather headstrong. **D W Barker [1-5] P Asquith.*

PETOSKIN BHB 36f40a RR 47f 40a 38[10]
8 b g Petoski 10.4f **(56)** - Farcical (Pharly (FR)) 9.8f **(68)**
Form - 0
Record 2000 - 1st:0 2nd:0 3rd:0 Ran:1
Pre2000 - 1st:10 2nd:2 3rd:7 Ran:51
Win Prizemoney £24,562 *Total Prizemoney* £31,864

Wins								
	* 1998	*Jan*	*Wolver*	*(STD)*	*H*	*14.8f*	*62*	*66*
	* 1997	Jly	Bath	(G-F)	S	11.7f		52
	* 1997	*Jun*	*Wolver*	*(STD)*	*C*	*16.2f*		*63*
	* 1997	*May*	*Lingfi*	*(STD)*	*C*	*16f*		*68* <
	* 1997	Apr	Bright	(FRM)	C	11.9f		55
	* 1997	*Feb*	*Wolver*	*(STD)*	*C*	*14.8f*		*68* <
	* 1996	*Dec*	*Wolver*	*(STD)*	*S*	*14.8f*		*66*
	* 1996	*Nov*	*Wolver*	*(STD)*	*C*	*14.8f*		*67*
	* 1996	Oct	Yarmou	(G-F)	SH	11.5f	50	58

2000 AW 0-1: (15f) (Fibr)
Average gelding, has worn blinkers.
**J Pearce [9-43] Mrs Jean Routledge (from R Hannon [1-9] Oct 1994).*

PETRAIL (IRE) BHB 65f RR 58f 3272[4]
2 b f Catrail (USA) - Smart Pet **(68f)** (Petong) 6.6f **(58)**
Form - 074
Record 2000 - 1st:0 2nd:0 3rd:0 Ran:3
2000 Turf 0-3: (5f 3) (g-s, gd, hrd)
Currently fair filly. Turf high 58 (began Jly).
**D Nicholls [0-3] N Phillips-Hill.*

PETRA NOVA BHB 34f **RR 37f** 4748[8]
4 ch f First Trump - Spinner (Blue Cashmere) 6.4f **(54)**
Form - 00608
Record 2000 - 1st:0 2nd:0 3rd:0 Ran:5
Pre2000 - 1st:0 2nd:1 3rd:0 Ran:13
Win Prizemoney £0 *Total Prizemoney* £1,493
2000 Turf 0-5: (5f, 6f 2, 7f, 8f) (gd 2, g-f, frm 2)
Strong, very moderate filly, has worn blinkers. Turf high 37 (began Jly). **R M Whitaker [0-18] R M Whitaker.*

PETRIE BHB 35f38a **RR 56f 38a** 5018[8]
3 ch g Fraam - Canadian Capers (Ballacashtal (CAN)) 5.3f **(50)**
Form - 32256035030806008
Record 2000 - 1st:0 2nd:0 3rd:2 Ran:12
Pre2000 - 1st:0 2nd:3 3rd:1 Ran:10
Win Prizemoney £0 *Total Prizemoney* £2,727
2000 Turf 0-11: (5f, 6f 4, 7f 3, 8f 2, 12f) (g-s, gd 4, g-f 3, frm 3) 2000 AW 0-1: (7f) (Fibr)
Workmanlike, fair gelding, effective 6 to 7f, - acts on Fibr, likes left handed tracks, likes tight tracks. Turf high 56.
**D Burchell [0-5] D N Carey (from M R Channon [0-17] Jly 2000).*

PETRISK BHB 25f **RR 4f** 1255[19]
3 b f Risk Me (FR) 8f **(53)** - Bernstein Bette **(35f 44a)** (Petong) 6.6f **(58)**
Form - 0
Record 2000 - 1st:0 2nd:0 3rd:0 Ran:1
Pre2000 - 1st:0 2nd:0 3rd:0 Ran:3
2000 Turf 0-1: (10f) (g-f)
Unfurnished, very poor filly. **T E Powell [0-4] Lawrence Pratt.*

PETROSELLI (IRE) RR 102f 1825a[11]
3 b c Grand Lodge (USA) - Will Be Blue (Darshaan) 9.9f **(84)**
Form - 40
2000 Turf 0-2: (11f, 12f) (hvy, gd)
Very useful colt. Turf high 102 (1st run) - 4th of 9 to Kutub (9 Apr Longchamp 11f hvy RF 0707a). **Mme C Head in FR [0-5].*

PETROV BHB 68f **RR 72f** 4675[14]
2 b c Cadeaux Genereux 7.9f **(76)** - Anna Petrovna (FR) (Wassl) 9.7f **(62)**
Form - 040
Record 2000 - 1st:0 2nd:0 3rd:0 Ran:3
Win Prizemoney £0 *Total Prizemoney* £300
2000 Turf 0-3: (7f 2, 8f) (g-s, gd, frm)
Currently above-average colt. Turf high 72 (began Spt).
**E A L Dunlop [0-3] Maktoum Al Maktoum.*

PETRUS (IRE) BHB 65f **RR 69f** 4224[4]
4 b c Perugino (USA) - Love With Honey (USA) (Full Pocket (USA)) 14.1f **(61)**
Form - 0000508804
Record 2000 - 1st:0 2nd:0 3rd:0 Ran:10
Pre2000 - 1st:3 2nd:0 3rd:1 Ran:15
Win Prizemoney £29,819 *Total Prizemoney* £33,008
Wins * 1999 Jly Goodwo (FRM) H 7f 79 88 <
* 1999 Jly Yarmou (G-F) H 7f 73 80
* 1999 May Kempto (G-F) H 7f 68 73
2000 Turf 0-10: (6f, 7f 5, 8f 4) (sft, gd 2, g-f 3, frm 4)
Scopey, average colt, effective 7f, acts on g-f. Turf high 72.
**C E Brittain [3-25] C E Brittain.*

PETRUSHKA (IRE) BHB 122f **RR 124+f** 5329a[5]
3 ch f Unfuwain (USA) 11.4f **(74)** - Ballet Shoes (IRE) (Ela-Mana-Mou) 10.1f **(70)**
Form - 1341115
Record 2000 - 1st:4 2nd:0 3rd:1 Ran:7
Pre2000 - 1st:1 2nd:0 3rd:0 Ran:1
Win Prizemoney £331,353 *Total Prizemoney* £390,109
Wins *** 2000** Oct Longch (GD) G1 10f 121+
*** 2000** Aug York (GD) G1 11.9f 122+ <
*** 2000** Jly Currag (G-F) G1 12f 122+ <
*** 2000** Apr Newmar (G-S) G3 7f 119
* 1999 Oct Leices (G-S) 7f 89++
2000 Turf 4-7: (7f 1-1, 8f, 10f 1-1, 11f, 12f 2-3) (g-s, gd 2-2, g-f 1-1, frm 1-3)
Scopey, very high-class filly, effective 7 to 12f, best at 12f, acts on g-s to frm. Turf high 122 - 1st of 10 from Melikah (16 Jly Curragh RF 2918a) - also 1st of 6 from Love Divine (23 Aug York RF 3913). Consistent. She bolted up in the Nell Gwyn on her reappearance, but ran a bit flat when third in the 1000 Guineas and was later found to have a slight potassium imbalance. She ran well in the Oaks without ever being a threat to the winner, but showed her true colours when running way with the Irish version. Put the last two Epsom Oaks winners firmly in their place in the Yorkshire version and gained a comfortable victory in the Prix l'Opera. She started favourite for the Breeders' Cup Filly and Mare Turf, but was not at her best and could only manage fifth.
**Sir Michael Stoute [5-8] Highclere Thoroughbred Racing Ltd.*

PETURA (IRE) BHB 40f **RR 39f** 568[16]
4 br g Petardia 8.2f **(58)** - Roman Heights (IRE) (Head for Heights) 9.6f **(55)**
Form - 0
Record 2000 - 1st:0 2nd:0 3rd:0 Ran:1
Pre2000 - 1st:0 2nd:0 3rd:0 Ran:7
Win Prizemoney £0 *Total Prizemoney* £598
2000 Turf 0-1: (9f) (gd)
Scopey, very moderate gelding, has worn blinkers. Inconsistent.
**J S Wainwright [0-8] Mrs Mary Moloney.*

PEYTO PRINCESS BHB 71f **RR 73f** 4120[3]
2 b br f Bold Arrangement 8.7f **(57)** -Bo' Babbity (Strong Gale) 5.6f **(66)**
Form - 32243
Record 2000 - 1st:0 2nd:2 3rd:2 Ran:5
Win Prizemoney £0 *Total Prizemoney* £3,142
2000 Turf 0-5: (5f 5) (gd 2, g-f, frm 2)
Above-average filly. Turf high 73 - 3rd of 9 getting 9lb from Nifty Alice (31 Aug Musselburgh 5f frm RF 4120).
**C W Fairhurst [0-5] North Cheshire Trading & Storage Ltd.*

PHANTOM FOOTSTEPS RR 2267[8]
3 gr g Komaite (USA) 6.9f **(61)** - Hyperion Palace (Dragonara Palace (USA)) 6.1f **(55)**
Form - 8
Record 2000 - 1st:0 2nd:0 3rd:0 Ran:1
2000 Turf 0-1: (12f) (frm)
Rangy, currently very poor gelding. **C N Kellett [0-1] B G Peacock.*

PHANTOM RAIN BHB 75f **RR 75f** 3922[9]
3 b f Rainbow Quest (USA) 11.2f **(81)** - Illusory (Kings Lake (USA)) 10.8f **(67)**
Form - 02510
Record 2000 - 1st:1 2nd:1 3rd:0 Ran:5
Win Prizemoney £3,510 *Total Prizemoney* £4,667
Wins *** 2000** Aug Ripon (GD) 10f 75 <
2000 Turf 1-5: (10f 1-5) (gd 2, g-f 2, frm 1-1)
Workmanlike, above-average filly. Turf high 76 - 2nd of 9 to Drama Class (10 Jly Bath 10f gd RF 2665) - also 1st of 6 from South Sea Pearl (7 Aug Ripon RF 3434). **B W Hills [1-5] K Abdulla.*

PHANTOM STAR (IRE) BHB 41f **RR 38f** 586[12]
3 b g Foxhound (USA) - Une Parisienne (FR) (Bolkonski) 7.6f **(64)**
Form - 850
Record 2000 - 1st:0 2nd:0 3rd:0 Ran:3
Pre2000 - 1st:0 2nd:0 3rd:0 Ran:8
2000 Turf 0-1: (10f) (gd) 2000 AW 0-2: (7f, 10f) (Equi 2)
Unfurnished, very moderate gelding, has worn blinkers. AW high 39. **Mrs A E Johnson [0-4] Chasers III (from N Tinkler [0-7] Aug 1999).*

PHARAOH HATSHEPSUT (IRE) BHB 61f **RR 55f** 5081[8]
2 b f Definite Article - Maid of Mourne (Fairy King (USA)) 7.7f **(59)**
Form - 407045818
Record 2000 - 1st:1 2nd:0 3rd:0 Ran:9
Win Prizemoney £3,656 *Total Prizemoney* £3,973
Wins *** 2000** Oct Ayr (HVY) H 6f 55 55 <
2000 Turf 1-9: (5f 5, 6f 1-2, 7f, 8f) (hvy, sft 1-1, gd 3, g-f, frm 3)
Fair filly, effective 6f, acts on sft. Turf high 55 - 1st of 12 getting 20lb from Galy Bay (9 Oct Ayr RF 4869).
**J S Goldie [1-9] Mike Flynn.*

PHARAOH'S HOUSE (IRE) BHB 34f **RR 43f** 3448[5]
3 b g Desert Style (IRE) - Cellatica (USA) (Sir Ivor) 10.2f **(70)**
Form - 800555

Record 2000 - 1st:0 2nd:0 3rd:0 Ran:6
Pre2000 - 1st:0 2nd:0 3rd:2 Ran:6
Win Prizemoney £0 *Total Prizemoney* £1,124
2000 Turf 0-6: (7f, 8f, 11f, 12f 2, 16f) (g-s, gd, frm 4)
Workmanlike, moderate gelding, often wears blinkers. Turf high 43. **T D Easterby [0-12] P England.*

PHARMACY'S PET (IRE) BHB 58f52a **RR 59f 52a** 5017[9]

2 b f Petardia 8.2f **(58)** - Pharmacy **(74f)** (Mtoto)
Form - 70760
Record 2000 - 1st:0 2nd:0 3rd:0 Ran:5
Win Prizemoney £0 *Total Prizemoney* £161
2000 Turf 0-4: (6f 3, 7f) (gd, g-f 3) 2000 AW 0-1: (7f) (Fibr)
Fair filly. Turf high 59 (began Jly).
**H S Howe [0-5] I Forster,A Roxburgh/Exe River Racing.*

PHAROAH'S GOLD (IRE) BHB 78f **RR 71f** 2515a[7]

2 b c Namaqualand (USA) - Queen Nefertiti (IRE) **(48f)** (Fairy King (USA)) 7.7f **(59)**
Form - 4417
Record 2000 - 1st:1 2nd:0 3rd:0 Ran:4
Win Prizemoney £2,632 *Total Prizemoney* £3,143
Wins * 2000 May Nottin (GD) 6.1f 67 <
2000 Turf 1-4: (5f 2, 6f 1-2) (gd 2, g-f 1-1, frm)
Above-average colt. Turf high 71 - 4th of 15 to The Names Bond (12 May Carlisle 5f frm RF 1161) - also 1st of 12 giving 5lb to Extra Guest (20 May Nottingham RF 1342).
**W Jarvis [1-4] Sales Race 2000 Syndicate.*

PHASE EIGHT GIRL BHB 16f **RR 28f** 4119[10]

4 b f Warrshan (USA) 9.7f **(59)** - Bugsy's Sister (Aragon) 8.1f **(60)**
Form - 07760
Record 2000 - 1st:0 2nd:0 3rd:0 Ran:5
Pre2000 - 1st:1 2nd:0 3rd:2 Ran:10
Win Prizemoney £2,460 *Total Prizemoney* £3,362
Wins * 1999 Jly Beverl (G-F) SH 12f 25 33 <
2000 Turf 0-5: (12f 3, 16f 2) (gd 2, frm 3)
Little account filly, effective 12 to 16f, best at 16f, acts on gd to frm. Turf high 28. Becoming disappointing.
**J Hetherton [1-15] Peter Urquhart.*

PHEISTY BHB 71f **RR 76f** 4539[1]

3 b f Faustus (USA) 9.1f **(54)** - Phlirty (Pharly (FR)) 9.8f **(68)**
Form - 541652661
Record 2000 - 1st:2 2nd:1 3rd:0 Ran:9
Pre2000 - 1st:1 2nd:0 3rd:1 Ran:5
Win Prizemoney £8,063 *Total Prizemoney* £10,028
Wins * 2000 Spt Goodwo (HVY) 12f 74 <
*** 2000** Jly Yarmou (FRM) H 10.1f 72 71
* 1999 Apr Leices (GD) 5f 70
2000 Turf 2-9: (8f, 9f 2, 10f 1-4, 12f 1-2) (gd 1-3, g-f 1-5, frm)
Neat, above-average filly, effective 5 to 12f, best at 12f, acts on gd to frm, best on g-f, has worn blinkers, likes right handed tracks, likes tight tracks. Turf high 76 - 2nd of 9 getting 6lb from Flight Sequence (16 Aug Epsom 10f g-f RF 3693) - also 1st of 13 getting 9lb from Sovereigns Court (20 Spt Goodwood RF 4539). Consistent. Stepping up to twelve furlongs when winning in heavy ground at Goodwood.
**R F JohnsonHoughton [3-14] Mrs R F JohnsonHoughton.*

PHILAGAIN BHB 40f **RR 39f** 5190[3]

3 b f Ardkinglass 5f **(64)** - Andalucia (Rheingold) 10.4f **(62)**
Form - 4016304003
Record 2000 - 1st:1 2nd:0 3rd:2 Ran:10
Pre2000 - 1st:0 2nd:0 3rd:0 Ran:3
Win Prizemoney £2,744 *Total Prizemoney* £3,815
Wins * 2000 Jun Mussel (FRM) H 8f 37 40 <
2000 Turf 1-10: (7f 3, 8f 1-2, 9f 4, 10f) (hvy, gd 2, g-f 2, frm 1-5)
Neat, very moderate filly, effective 7 to 8f, acts on frm, likes tight tracks. Turf high 44 - 3rd of 10 getting 25lb from Cowboys And Angels (17 Jly Ayr 7f frm RF 2871) - also 1st of 9 getting 20lb from Absinther (26 Jun Musselburgh RF 2274). Inconsistent.
**Miss L A Perratt [1-10] C D Barber-Lomax (from J Hetherton [0-3] Oct 1999).*

PHILANTHA (USA) **RR 99f** 4836a[4]

3 b f Woodman (USA) 9.7f **(77)** - Tiger Flower (Sadler's Wells (USA)) 10f **(76)**
Form - 4
Record 2000 - 1st:0 2nd:0 3rd:0 Ran:1
Pre2000 - 1st:1 2nd:0 3rd:0 Ran:1
Win Prizemoney £5,390 *Total Prizemoney* £7,695
Wins * 1999 Oct Newmar (SFT) 6f 80 <
2000 Turf 0-1: (8f) (gd)
Strong, currently very useful filly. (1st run) - 4th of 10 to Terre A Terre (27 Spt Saint-cloud 8f gd RF 4836a). **J H M Gosden [1-2].*

PHILATELIC LADY (IRE) BHB 80f78a **RR 87f 78a** 4034[4]

4 ch f Pips Pride 6.7f **(70)** - Gold Stamp (Golden Act (USA)) 8.8f **(67)**
Form - 5337314
Record 2000 - 1st:1 2nd:0 3rd:3 Ran:7
Pre2000 - 1st:3 2nd:3 3rd:0 Ran:12
Win Prizemoney £17,457 *Total Prizemoney* £25,668
Wins * 2000 Aug Lingfi (G-F) H 9f 78 81 <
* 1999 Nov Windso (G-S) H 10f 74 79
* 1999 Jun Lingfi (G-S) H 10f 70 73
* 1998 *Nov Lingfi (STD) 8f 74*
2000 Turf 1-6: (8f, 9f 1-1, 10f 4) (sft, g-s, gd 2, frm 1-2) 2000 AW 0-1: (10f) (Equi)
Neat, useful filly, effective 8 to 10f, best at 10f, acts on sft to frm, best on frm, likes left handed tracks, favours tight tracks, and likes Lingfield. Turf high 87 - also 1st of 5 giving 7lb to Copplestone (19 Aug Lingfield RF 3781). **M J Haynes [4-19] G B Farmer.*

PHILIPPI **RR 66f** 4673[9]

2 b c Alzao (USA) 9.8f **(73)** - Lighted Glitter (FR) (Crystal Glitters (USA)) 11.3f **(79)**
Form - 8300
Record 2000 - 1st:0 2nd:0 3rd:1 Ran:4
Win Prizemoney £0 *Total Prizemoney* £528
2000 Turf 0-4: (5f, 6f 2, 7f) (g-s, g-f, frm 2)
Average colt, often wears blinkers. Turf high 66 (began Aug) - 3rd of 6 to Statue Gallery (30 Aug Brighton 6f frm RF 4096).
**J A Osborne [0-4] J D Martin.*

PHILISTAR BHB 35f50a **RR 37f 50a** 3834[12]

7 ch h Bairn (USA) 9.4f **(55)** - Philgwyn (Milford) 9f **(61)**
Form - 2653360050360700
Record 2000 - 1st:0 2nd:0 3rd:3 Ran:13
Pre2000 - 1st:9 2nd:6 3rd:10 Ran:73
Win Prizemoney £59,121 - *Total Prizemoney* £82,086
Wins 1999 *Jan Lingfi (STD) H 10f 70 75*
1998 Jun Epsom (GD) H 8.5f 75 81 <
1998 *Apr Lingfi (STD) H 7f 67 71*
1998 *Feb Lingfi (SLW) 7f 70*
1997 Jun Bright (FRM) 10f 70
1997 Jun Hamilt (GD) H 8.3f 60 70
1997 Jun Epsom (GD) H 8.5f 65 77
1997 Jun Newcas (FRM) 9f 61
1996 *Jly Lingfi (STD) H 10f 60 65*
2000 Turf 0-8: (8f 7, 10f) (gd 2, g-f 5, frm) 2000 AW 0-5: (8f 3, 10f 2) (Equi 2, Fibr 3)
Fair horse, effective 8 to 10f, best at 10f, acts on frm - acts on Equi, has worn blinkers, likes tight tracks. Turf high 41. AW high 67. Becoming disappointing.
**D Shaw [0-7] Paul Dixon (from N P Littmoden [0-4] Jun 2000).*

PHILMIST BHB 24f42a **RR 24f 42a** 5193[11]

8 b m Hard Fought 8.9f **(51)** - Andalucia (Rheingold) 10.4f **(62)**
Form - 00070
Record 2000 - 1st:0 2nd:0 3rd:0 Ran:5
Pre2000 - 1st:8 2nd:7 3rd:7 Ran:59
Win Prizemoney £21,668 *Total Prizemoney* £31,993
Wins * 1999 Jun Hamilt (GD) H 13f 46 48
* 1999 May Hamilt (G-F) SH 12.1f 37 40
* 1998 Aug Hamilt (SFT) S 12.1f 47+
* 1997 Spt Ayr (G-S) H 10.9f 45 50 <
* 1997 Aug Hamilt (GD) H 11.1f 40 48
* 1997 Jly Hamilt (G-S) H 11.1f 40 40
1996 *May Southw (STD) H 11f 48 50* <
2000 Turf 0-5: (9f 2, 11f, 13f 2) (hvy, gd 2, g-f, frm)
Fair mare, effective 11 to 13f, best at 13f, acts on g-s to g-f, best on gd, mostly wears blinkers (effectively), favours right handed tracks, excels at Hamilton. Turf high 24. Becoming disappointing.
**Miss L A Perratt [6-34] T P Finch (from J Hetherton [0-9] Feb 1997).*

PHOEBE BUFFAY (IRE) BHB 60f63a **RR 58f 63a** 3319[8]
3 b f Petardia 8.2f **(58)** - Art Duo (Artaius (USA)) 9f **(69)**
Form - 008
Record 2000 - 1st:0 2nd:0 3rd:0 Ran:3
Pre2000 - 1st:1 2nd:3 3rd:0 Ran:6
Win Prizemoney £2,262 *Total Prizemoney* £8,466
Wins * 1999 *Jly Southw (STD) 6f 72* **<**
2000 Turf 0-3: (7f, 8f, 9f) (gd 2, g-f)
Lengthy, average filly, effective 6f, acts on frm - acts on Fibr, has worn blinkers. Turf high 58 (began Jly). Becoming disappointing. She showed ability at two but has been well beaten in handicap company this year. **C N Allen [1-9] Newmarket Connections Ltd.*

PHOEBE ROBINSON (IRE) BHB 78f **RR 72f** 4889[2]
2 b f Alzao (USA) 9.8f **(73)** - Savelli (IRE) (Vision (USA)) 9f **(64)**
Form - 032
Record 2000 - 1st:0 2nd:1 3rd:1 Ran:3
Win Prizemoney £0 *Total Prizemoney* £1,574
2000 Turf 0-3: (7f 2, 8f) (hvy, g-s, gd)
Currently above-average filly. Turf high 72 (began Spt).
**G C Bravery [0-3] OTT Partnership.*

PHOEBUS BHB 43f58a **RR 20f 58a** 4491[18]
3 b c Piccolo - Slava (USA) (Diesis) 9.3f **(69)**
Form - 1500033000
Record 2000 - 1st:0 2nd:0 3rd:2 Ran:8
Pre2000 - 1st:1 2nd:0 3rd:0 Ran:6
Win Prizemoney £2,822 *Total Prizemoney* £3,390
Wins * 1999 *Nov Southw (STD) H 7f 63 68* **<**
2000 Turf 0-4: (6f, 7f 2, 8f) (hvy, g-f, frm 2) 2000 AW 0-4: (6f, 7f 2, 8f) (Fibr 4)
Scopey, average colt, effective 7 to 8f, - acts on Fibr, likes left handed tracks, likes tight tracks. Turf high 20. AW high 63 - 3rd of 11 getting 12lb from Baron de Pichon (28 Jly Southwell 8f Fibr RF 3191). Inconsistent. **W R Muir [1-14] Duncan Wiltshire.*

PHURTIVE BHB 50f **RR 68f** 5237[7]
2 b g Factual (USA) - Phlirty (Pharly (FR)) 9.8f **(68)**
Form - 007
Record 2000 - 1st:0 2nd:0 3rd:0 Ran:3
2000 Turf 0-3: (6f, 7f, 8f) (g-s, gd, g-f)
Currently average gelding. Turf high 68 (began Spt).
**R F JohnsonHoughton [0-3] Mrs R F JohnsonHoughton.*

PHYSICAL FORCE BHB 52f **RR 46f** 5074[14]
2 b g Casteddu 7.4f **(54)** - Kaiserlinde (GER) (Frontal) 6.4f **(64)**
Form - 0080
Record 2000 - 1st:0 2nd:0 3rd:0 Ran:4
2000 Turf 0-4: (6f 3, 7f) (g-s, gd, g-f, frm)
Moderate gelding. Turf high 46.
**J R Best [0-4] Mercato Ltd.*

PIANIST (IRE) BHB 40f **RR 51f** 1372[14]
5 ch g Balla Cove - Hit For Six (Tap On Wood) 10.3f **(65)**
Form - 0
Record 2000 - 1st:0 2nd:0 3rd:0 Ran:1
Pre2000 - 1st:0 2nd:2 3rd:0 Ran:10
Win Prizemoney £0 *Total Prizemoney* £1,414
2000 AW 0-1: (16f) (Fibr)
Fair gelding, has worn blinkers.
**Miss K M George [0-5] Exterior Profiles Ltd (from D L Williams [0-1] Jun 1998).*

PIANO POWER RR 29f 4382[12]
2 b c Cool Jazz - Panayr (Faraway Times (USA)) 7.4f **(52)**
Form - 0
Record 2000 - 1st:0 2nd:0 3rd:0 Ran:1
2000 Turf 0-1: (6f) (gd)
Currently little account colt.
**Miss L A Perratt [0-1] Miss Heather Galbraith.*

PICASSO'S HERITAGE BHB 31f31a **RR 9f 31a** 2925[12]
4 gr g Greensmith - Jane Herring (Nishapour (FR)) 9.1f **(61)**
Form - 0300000
Record 2000 - 1st:0 2nd:0 3rd:1 Ran:7
Pre2000 - 1st:0 2nd:0 3rd:0 Ran:4
Win Prizemoney £0 *Total Prizemoney* £317
2000 Turf 0-3: (6f 2, 7f) (gd, frm 2) 2000 AW 0-4: (5f 2, 7f, 8f) (Fibr 4)
Little account gelding, has worn blinkers. Turf high 9. AW high 23.
**W Clay [0-7] Miss Denise Foode (from M C Pipe [0-4] Spt 1998).*

PICCADILLY BHB 31f **RR 39f** 3335[5]
5 ch m Belmez (USA) 11.4f **(65)** - Polly's Pear (USA) (Sassafras (FR)) 9.6f **(69)**
Form - 208465
Record 2000 - 1st:0 2nd:1 3rd:0 Ran:6
Pre2000 - 1st:1 2nd:0 3rd:2 Ran:17
Win Prizemoney £2,368 *Total Prizemoney* £5,442
Wins * 1999 Apr Ripon (G-F) SH 12.3f 35 39 **<**
2000 Turf 0-6: (12f 5, 16f) (gd, g-f, frm 4)
Very moderate filly, effective 12f, acts on g-f to frm, best on frm, has worn blinkers, prefers right handed tracks. Turf high 39 - 4th of 8 getting 7lb from Alexandrine (26 Jun Musselburgh 12f frm RF 2271).
**Miss Kate Milligan [1-16] S Ward (from T J Etherington [0-13] Oct 1998).*

PICCALILLI RR 25f 3955[7]
3 ch f Piccolo - Hat Hill (Roan Rocket) 7.8f **(57)**
Form - 06060777
Record 2000 - 1st:0 2nd:0 3rd:0 Ran:8
2000 Turf 0-8: (6f, 7f 2, 8f, 9f, 10f, 12f 2) (gd, g-f 6, hrd)
Small, little account filly, has worn blinkers. Turf high 25.
**S Woodman [0-8] Mrs Fiona Gordon.*

PICCATA BHB 45f **RR 29f** 180[4]
3 b g Piccolo - Katya (IRE) **(93f)** (Dancing Dissident (USA))
Form - 74
Record 2000 - 1st:0 2nd:0 3rd:0 Ran:2
Pre2000 - 1st:0 2nd:0 3rd:0 Ran:2
2000 AW 0-2: (7f 2) (Fibr 2)
Neat, moderate gelding. AW high 49.
**M R Channon [0-4] John Mitchell.*

PICCLED BHB 81f **RR 79f** 3363[9]
2 b c Piccolo - Creme de Menthe (IRE) (Green Desert (USA)) 8.6f **(78)**
Form - 610
Record 2000 - 1st:1 2nd:0 3rd:0 Ran:3
Win Prizemoney £3,883 *Total Prizemoney* £3,883
Wins * **2000** Jun Goodwo (G-S) 5f 79 **<**
2000 Turf 1-3: (5f 1-3) (g-s, gd 1-1, g-f)
Currently above-average colt. Turf high 79 - 1st of 6 giving 5lb to Strumpet (1 Jun Goodwood RF 1625). Made all in an ordinary maiden on his second start.
**M R Channon [1-3] Capt J Macdonald-Buchanan.*

PICCOLITIA RR 56f 4187[11]
2 ch f Piccolo - Miss Laetitia (IRE) **(36f)** (Entitled)
Form - 0
Record 2000 - 1st:0 2nd:0 3rd:0 Ran:1
2000 Turf 0-1: (6f) (g-f)
Currently fair filly. **N A Graham [0-1] T H Chadney.*

PICCOLO CATIVO BHB 44f38a **RR 49f 38a** 5194[2]
5 b m Komaite (USA) 6.9f **(61)** - Malcesine (IRE) **(38f 31a)** (Auction Ring (USA)) 8.6f **(65)**
Form - 1040802
Record 2000 - 1st:1 2nd:1 3rd:0 Ran:7
Pre2000 - 1st:4 2nd:3 3rd:0 Ran:36
Win Prizemoney £13,812 *Total Prizemoney* £18,415
Wins * **2000** May Warwic (SFT) H 7.7f 43 49
* 1999 Apr Catter (SFT) 6f 58
* 1998 Jun Carlis (G-S) H 5f 60 64
* 1998 May Hamilt (GD) H 5f 54 55
1997 *May Southw (STD) 5f 68* **<**
2000 Turf 1-7: (5f, 7f 2, 8f 1-4) (sft 1-2, g-s 3, gd, frm)
Moderate filly, effective 6 to 8f, best at 6f, acts on sft to frm, prefers left handed tracks, prefers tight tracks. Turf high 49 (1st run) - 1st of 19 getting 11lb from Landing Craft (1 May Warwick RF 0958).
**Mrs G S Rees [4-38] J W Gittins (from Capt J Wilson [1-5] Jan 1998).*

PICCOLO PLAYER RR 95f 5123[3]

2 b g Piccolo - The Frog Lady (IRE) **(50f 41a)** (Al Hareb (USA))
Form - 2141123
Record 2000 - 1st:3 2nd:2 3rd:1 Ran:7
Win Prizemoney £19,929 *Total Prizemoney* £28,133
Wins * **2000** Aug Windso (GD) 6f 95+ <
* **2000** Aug Goodwo (G-F) H 6f 88+
* **2000** Jun Windso (G-F) 6f 83+
2000 Turf 3-7: (5f, 6f 3-6) (g-s, gd 2, g-f 2-2, frm 1-2)
Very useful gelding, effective 6f, acts on g-f to frm, best on g-f. Turf high 95 - 2nd of 4 giving 3lb to Baaridd (28 Aug Ripon 6f frm RF 4051) - also 1st of 7 getting 2lb from Warden Warren (14 Aug Windsor RF 3633). He showed improved form after being gelded and is capable of winning a Listed race over six or seven furlongs.
**R Hannon [3-7] Park Walk Racing.*

PICCOLO ROSE BHB 62f RR 67f 5129[22]
2 b f Piccolo - Saunders Lass (Hillandale) 8f **(60)**
Form - 500100
Record 2000 - 1st:1 2nd:0 3rd:0 Ran:6
Win Prizemoney £2,548 *Total Prizemoney* £2,548
Wins * **2000** Spt Lingfi (GD) C 6f 67 <
2000 Turf 1-6: (5f 2, 6f 1-3, 7f) (sft, g-s, gd 1-2, g-f, hrd)
Average filly, effective 6f, acts on gd. Turf high 67 (began Aug) - 1st of 20 giving 4lb to Clansinge (22 Spt Lingfield RF 4581).
**M R Channon [1-6] Mrs Pat Scott.*

PICKENS (USA) BHB 43f63a RR 51f 63a 4649[6]
8 b g Theatrical 11.5f **(78)** - Alchi (USA) (Alleged (USA)) 10f **(76)**
Form - 0060146
Record 2000 - 1st:1 2nd:0 3rd:0 Ran:7
Pre2000 - 1st:7 2nd:4 3rd:1 Ran:30
Win Prizemoney £17,028 *Total Prizemoney* £19,899
Wins * **2000** *May Southw (STD) C 11f 46*
* 1999 *Feb Southw (STD) S 11f 62*
* 1998 *Feb Southw (STD) H 12f 54 66+* <
* 1998 *Feb Southw (STD) S 11f 52*
* 1998 *Jan Southw (STD) S 11f 53*
* 1998 *Jan Southw (STD) S 12f 55+*
* 1997 Oct Redcar (G-F) C 11f 41
1996 Jly Beverl (G-F) S 12f 52
2000 AW 1-7: (11f 1-4, 12f 3) (Fibr 1-7)
Fair gelding, effective 11f, - acts on Fibr, has worn blinkers. AW high 46.
**Don Enrico Incisa [7-30] Don Enrico Incisa (from N Tinkler [2-16] Nov 1996).*

PICKETT POINT BHB 40f RR 32f 3907[17]
2 b g Magic Ring (IRE) 6.5f **(64)** - Bay Runner (Bay Express) 7.1f **(60)**
Form - 070
Record 2000 - 1st:0 2nd:0 3rd:0 Ran:3
2000 Turf 0-3: (5f, 7f, 8f) (gd, g-f, frm)
Currently very moderate gelding. Turf high 32 (began Jly).
**J J Bridger [0-3] Mrs Julie Lankshear.*

PICO RR 62f 5140[7]
2 ch f Piccolo - Chatterberry (Aragon) 8.1f **(60)**
Form - 07
Record 2000 - 1st:0 2nd:0 3rd:0 Ran:2
2000 Turf 0-2: (6f 2) (g-s, gd)
Currently average filly. Turf high 62 (began Oct).
**C E Brittain [0-2] High Seas Leisure Ltd.*

PIC OF THE FIELD RR 2488[5]
2 ch f Piccolo - Moorefield Girl (IRE) (Gorytus (USA)) 7.8f **(60)**
Form - 5
Record 2000 - 1st:0 2nd:0 3rd:0 Ran:1
Win Prizemoney £0 *Total Prizemoney* £224
2000 Turf 0-1: (6f) (frm)
Currently very poor filly. **D W P Arbuthnot [0-1] Noel Cronin.*

PICOT BHB 70f RR 22f 4991[29]
3 b br f Piccolo - Special Guest (Be My Guest (USA)) 9.3f **(67)**
Form - 00
Record 2000 - 1st:0 2nd:0 3rd:0 Ran:2
Pre2000 - 1st:1 2nd:0 3rd:1 Ran:3
Win Prizemoney £2,700 *Total Prizemoney* £3,305
Wins * 1999 Oct Leices (SFT) 6f 74 <
2000 Turf 0-2: (7f 2) (gd, g-f)
Little account filly. Turf high 22 (began Spt).
**H Candy [1-5] Major M G Wyatt.*

PICTURE MEE BHB 41f RR 44f 4215[10]
2 b f Aragon 7.7f **(58)** - Heemee (On Your Mark) 7.7f **(58)**
Form - 88770
Record 2000 - 1st:0 2nd:0 3rd:0 Ran:5
2000 Turf 0-5: (6f 2, 7f, 8f 2) (g-s, g-f, frm 3)
Moderate filly. Turf high 44.
**Miss J A Camacho [0-5] Mrs M J Adamson.*

PICTURE PALACE RR 18f 5319[18]
2 ch c Salse (USA) 10.9f **(71)** - Moviegoer (Pharly (FR)) 9.8f **(68)**
Form - 0
Record 2000 - 1st:0 2nd:0 3rd:0 Ran:1
2000 Turf 0-1: (6f) (sft)
Currently little account colt.
**Sir Mark Prescott [0-1] Neil Greig Osborne H IV.*

PICTURE PUZZLE BHB 73f RR 77f 3592[12]
4 b f Royal Academy (USA) 7.8f **(77)** - Cloudslea (USA) (Chief's Crown (USA)) 9.8f **(72)**
Form - 32120
Record 2000 - 1st:1 2nd:2 3rd:1 Ran:5
Pre2000 - 1st:3 2nd:0 3rd:0 Ran:9
Win Prizemoney £16,502 *Total Prizemoney* £20,879
Wins * **2000** Jly Bath (FRM) 8f 68
* 1999 Spt Newcas (G-F) H 8f 68 71
* 1999 May Yarmou (FRM) H 8f 68 72 <
* 1999 May Thirsk (G-F) 7f 59
2000 Turf 1-5: (8f 1-5) (g-f, frm 3, hrd 1-1)
Leggy, above-average filly, effective 8f, acts on g-f to hrd, best on frm, prefers left handed tracks, excels at Thirsk. Turf high 77 - 2nd of 8 getting 1lb from Shalimar (1 Jly Newmarket 8f frm RF 2448) - also 1st of 4 giving 5lb to Major Rebuke (20 Jly Bath RF 2955). She scored three times in 1999, all on firm ground, and she never ran to anything like the same form when there was some cut in the ground. She ran very well on fast ground last term before getting her reward in a small event at Bath. Though she has shown some temperament pre-race, it has yet to affect her performances.
**W J Haggas [4-14] M H Wilson.*

PIDDINGTON FLYER (IRE) RR 5117[7]
2 ch g Case Law 6f **(64)** - Boston View (IRE) (Simply Great (FR)) 8.2f **(65)**
Form - 67
Record 2000 - 1st:0 2nd:0 3rd:0 Ran:2
2000 AW 0-2: (5f 2) (Fibr 2)
Currently moderate gelding. AW high 44 (began Oct).
**B J Meehan [0-2] F C T Wilson.*

PIERPOINT (IRE) BHB 59f63a RR 65f 63a 4468[15]
5 ch g Archway (IRE) 8.5f **(60)** - Lavinia (Habitat) 9.4f **(70)**
Form - 0001075370
Record 2000 - 1st:1 2nd:0 3rd:1 Ran:10
Pre2000 - 1st:5 2nd:5 3rd:3 Ran:33
Win Prizemoney £18,452 *Total Prizemoney* £26,857
Wins * **2000** Jun Pontef (G-F) 5f 65
* 1999 Aug Pontef (GD) H 6f 68 69
* 1999 Aug Redcar (FRM) H 6f 60 65
* 1999 *Jun Southw (STD) H 6f 60 64*
1997 Jly Hamilt (G-F) H 5f 78 <
1997 Jun Hamilt (G-F) C 5f 69+
2000 Turf 1-10: (5f 1-8, 6f 2) (gd 2, g-f 4, frm 1-3, hrd)
Average gelding, effective 5 to 7f, best at 6f, acts on frm - acts on Fibr, has worn blinkers, prefers left handed tracks, prefers tight tracks, excels at Pontefract. Turf high 65 - 1st of 12 giving 3lb to Avondale Girl (12 Jun Pontefract RF 1902).
**D Nicholls [4-31] J H Knight (from R A Fahey [2-12] Jun 1998).*

PIES AR US BHB 52f RR 53?f 3598[12]
3 b g Perpendicular - Jendor (Condorcet (FR)) 12.3f **(62)**
Form - 4640
Record 2000 - 1st:0 2nd:0 3rd:0 Ran:4
Win Prizemoney £0 *Total Prizemoney* £540

2000 Turf 0-4: (9f, 10f 2, 14f) (g-f, frm 2, hrd)
Fair gelding. Turf high 53. **C W Fairhurst [0-4] H Taylor & Sons.*

PIETA (IRE) BHB 45f40a **RR 43f 40a** 3786[16]
3 b f Perugino (USA) - Auction Maid (IRE) (Auction Ring (USA)) 8.6f **(65)**
Form - 00050
Record 2000 - 1st:0 2nd:0 3rd:0 Ran:5
2000 Turf 0-5: (5f, 6f 3, 8f) (g-s, gd 3, frm)
Light-framed, moderate filly. Turf high 43.
**K McAuliffe [0-5] Brown, Czolak & Krosinsky.*

PIETRO SIENA (USA) RR 73+f 5186[4]
2 b br c Gone West (USA) 7.8f **(82)** - Via Borghese (USA) (Seattle Dancer (USA))
Form - 4
Record 2000 - 1st:0 2nd:0 3rd:0 Ran:1
Win Prizemoney £0 *Total Prizemoney* £320
2000 Turf 0-1: (7f) (g-s)
Currently above-average colt.
**E A L Dunlop [0-1] Maktoum Al Maktoum.*

PIGGY BANK BHB 48f57a **RR 37f 57a** 3379[19]
4 b f Emarati (USA) 6.6f **(63)** - Granny's Bank (Music Boy) 6.8f **(57)**
Form - 60080
Record 2000 - 1st:0 2nd:0 3rd:0 Ran:4
Pre2000 - 1st:2 2nd:2 3rd:0 Ran:25
Win Prizemoney £9,483 *Total Prizemoney* £12,871
Wins * 1999 Jly Ripon (GD) H 6f 61 62
* 1998 Oct Haydoc (SFT) H 5f 60 66 <
2000 Turf 0-4: (5f 2, 6f 2) (g-s, gd, frm 2)
Tall, moderate filly, effective 5 to 6f, acts on gd to g-f. Turf high 37. Inconsistent. **M W Easterby [2-29] Stephen Curtis.*

PILGRIM GOOSE (IRE) BHB 47f **RR 52f** 5218[11]
2 ch g Rainbows For Life (CAN) 9.3f **(64)** - Across The Ring (IRE) (Auction Ring (USA)) 8.6f **(65)**
Form - 8700
Record 2000 - 1st:0 2nd:0 3rd:0 Ran:4
2000 Turf 0-4: (6f, 7f, 8f 2) (sft, gd, g-f, frm)
Fair gelding. Turf high 52 (began Jly).
**M H Tompkins [0-4] M P Bowring.*

PILGRIM PRINCESS (IRE) BHB 55f **RR 47f** 2361[13]
2 b f Flying Spur (AUS) - Hasaid Lady (IRE) **(66f)** (Shaadi (USA))
Form - 0750
Record 2000 - 1st:0 2nd:0 3rd:0 Ran:4
2000 Turf 0-4: (5f 4) (g-s, gd, g-f 2)
Moderate filly, has worn blinkers. Turf high 47.
**E J Alston [0-4] Morris, Oliver, Pierce.*

PILLAGER RR 67f 4110[5]
3 b g Reprimand 8.2f **(63)** - Emerald Ring (Auction Ring (USA)) 8.6f **(65)**
Form - 60264575
Record 2000 - 1st:0 2nd:1 3rd:0 Ran:8
Pre2000 - 1st:0 2nd:0 3rd:0 Ran:1
Win Prizemoney £0 *Total Prizemoney* £938
2000 Turf 0-8: (7f, 8f 3, 10f, 11f 2, 12f) (hvy, gd 7)
Strong, average gelding, effective 8f, acts on gd, likes left handed tracks, likes tight tracks. Turf high 67 - 2nd of 17 giving 3lb to Take Manhattan (2 May Nottingham 8f gd RF 0970).
**Mrs A J Bowlby [0-9] J Shaw & Mrs Amanda Bowlby.*

PILLAR ROCK (USA) RR 93+f 4798a[1]
4 b g Alysheba (USA) 12.1f **(78)** - Butterscotch Sauce (USA) 00
Form - 31
2000 Turf 1-2: (12f 1-1, 14f) (gd 1-2)
Useful gelding, effective 7 to 14f, acts on g-s to frm, does well at Curragh. Turf high 93 (began Aug) - 1st of 14 giving 18lb to Veronica Cooper (30 Spt Down Royal RF 4798a). Consistent. He should stay a mile and a half and is tough without possessing much in the way of finishing speed.
**N Meade in IRE [4-16] D P Sharkey.*

PILOT'S HARBOUR BHB 47f37a **RR 33f 37a** 3314[6]
4 b g Distant Relative 7f **(69)** - Lillemor (Connaught) 7.7f **(63)**
Form - 086
Record 2000 - 1st:0 2nd:0 3rd:0 Ran:3
Pre2000 - 1st:2 2nd:1 3rd:1 Ran:13
Win Prizemoney £9,359 *Total Prizemoney* £11,096
Wins 1998 Aug Newmar (G-F) H 8f 83 85 <
1998 Jly Beverl (GD) 7.5f 80
2000 Turf 0-1: (14f) (g-f) 2000 AW 0-2: (8f, 11f) (Fibr 2)
Scopey, very moderate gelding, has worn blinkers. Inconsistent.
**F P Murtagh [1-5] Alex Gorrie (from D W Chapman [0-4] Mar 2000).*

PIMPINELLA (IRE) BHB 36f29a **RR 38f 29a** 13[14]
4 b f Reprimand 8.2f **(63)** - Lady Leman (Pitskelly) 8.5f **(53)**
Form - 00
Record 2000 - 1st:0 2nd:0 3rd:0 Ran:1
Pre2000 - 1st:0 2nd:0 3rd:0 Ran:5
2000 AW 0-1: (8f) (Fibr)
Leggy, very moderate filly, has worn blinkers.
**B S Rothwell [0-6] Brian Rothwell.*

PINCHANINCH BHB 63f53a **RR 66f 53a** 3925[6]
3 ch g Inchinor 8.9f **(64)** - Wollow Maid (Wollow) 8.2f **(61)**
Form - 704212446
Record 2000 - 1st:1 2nd:2 3rd:0 Ran:9
Pre2000 - 1st:0 2nd:0 3rd:0 Ran:3
Win Prizemoney £2,730 *Total Prizemoney* £5,152
Wins * 2000 Jun Bath (G-F) 11.7f 60 <
2000 Turf 1-8: (11f, 12f 1-6, 16f) (hvy, g-s, gd, g-f 4, hrd 1-1) 2000 AW 0-1: (9f) (Fibr)
Workmanlike, average gelding, effective 11 to 12f, best at 12f, acts on hvy to hrd, best on g-f, has worn blinkers, prefers tight tracks. Turf high 66 - 2nd of 10 giving 20lb to Got One Too (13 Jly Folkestone 12f gd RF 2769) - also 1st of 8 giving 3lb to Send Me An Angel (17 Jun Bath RF 2042). Consistent.
**J G Portman [1-12] A S B Portman.*

PINCHINCHA (FR) BHB 82f76a **RR 88f 76a** 5187[3]
6 b g Priolo (USA) 10.9f **(71)** - Western Heights (Shirley Heights) 10.3f **(74)**
Form - 402343421533
Record 2000 - 1st:1 2nd:2 3rd:4 Ran:12
Pre2000 - 1st:4 2nd:7 3rd:3 Ran:35
Win Prizemoney £22,185 *Total Prizemoney* £74,458
Wins * 2000 Aug Newmar (GD) H 10f 78 81 <
* 1997 Jun Pontef (G-F) H 10f 75 78
* 1997 May Doncas (G-S) 10.3f 71
* 1997 Apr Folkes (G-F) H 9.7f 65 67
* 1996 *Nov Southw (STD) S 8f 72*
2000 Turf 1-12: (9f, 10f 1-11) (sft 2, gd 2, g-f 5, frm 1-3)
Useful gelding, effective 10f, acts on sft to frm, best on g-f, has worn blinkers, excels at Nottingham and Newmarket. Turf high 88 - 2nd of 18 giving 18lb to Star Turn (5 May Newmarket 10f g-f RF 1045) - also 1st of 8 giving 4lb to Eastways (5 Aug Newmarket RF 3403). Consistent. He finally got his head in front at Newmarket in August, after a string of placings. Ten furlongs looks his ideal trip.
**D Morris [5-47] T J Wells.*

PINE DANCE (USA) RR 108f 5332a[10]
3 b c Pine Bluff (USA) - Dancing Affair (CAN)
Form - 72117110
2000 Turf 3-6: (8f 1-3, 9f 1-1, 10f 1-2) (sft 1-2, g-s 1-3, frm 1-1) 2000 AW 1-2: (9f 1-1, 10f) (Dirt 1-2)
Group-class colt, effective 9 to 10f, acts on frm - acts on Dirt, often wears blinkers (effectively). Turf high 108 - 1st of 4 from Hymn (23 Jly Arlington Park RF 3159a). AW high 112 (1st run) (began Spt) - 1st of 10 from Mass Market (4 Spt Philadelphia Park RF 4406a). Inconsistent. Only rated 85 when successful in a handicap at The Curragh in May, he went on to win the American Derby and Pennsylvania Derby for his astute handler. Never able to strike a blow in the Breeders' Cup Classic, he is a different horse on the dirt and will continue to earn a good living on that surface.
**D K Weld in IRE [4-9] George Hofmeister.*

PINE RIDGE LAD (IRE) BHB 47f40a **RR 46f 40a** 86[10]
10 gr g Taufan (USA) 8.3f **(65)** - Rosserk (Roan Rocket) 7.8f **(57)**
Form - 000
Record 2000 - 1st:0 2nd:0 3rd:0 Ran:2
Pre2000 - 1st:17 2nd:16 3rd:13 Ran:118
Win Prizemoney £48,254 *Total Prizemoney* £68,864

Wins * 1999 *Apr Southw (STD) H 8f 44 48*
1998 May Redcar (GD) H 8f 57 62
1998 *Jan Southw (STD) S 7f 59+*
1997 Spt Hamilt (GD) H 8.3f 50 54
1996 Jly Cheste (G-F) H 7.6f 57 65
1996 Mar Beverl (GD) H 7.5f 54 63
1996 *Feb Wolver (STD) H 7f 79 79* <
1996 *Feb Southw (STD) H 8f 71 78*
2000 AW 0-2: (8f, 11f) (Fibr 2)
Moderate gelding, had broken blood-vessels, effective 8 to 10f, best at 10f, acted on gd to g-f - acted on Fibr, had worn blinkers (extremely effectively). AW high 14. Becoming disappointing. (DEAD)
**J L Harris [1-18] E Gray (from J L Eyre [11-59] Jun 1998).*

PING ALONG BHB 44f **RR 51f** 3528[16]
3 b f Prince Sabo 6.6f **(64)** - Reel Foyle (USA) (Irish River (FR)) 8.6f **(78)**
Form - 6050
Record 2000 - 1st:0 2nd:0 3rd:0 Ran:4
2000 Turf 0-4: (7f 3, 12f) (g-f, frm 3)
Scopey, fair filly. Turf high 51. **M C Pipe [0-4] W J Gredley.*

PINHEIROS DREAM (IRE) BHB 58f56a **RR 69f 56a** 5006[7]
3 ch f Grand Lodge (USA) - Nikki's Groom (Shy Groom (USA)) 10f **(66)**
Form - 505031046217
Record 2000 - 1st:2 2nd:1 3rd:1 Ran:12
Pre2000 - 1st:0 2nd:0 3rd:1 Ran:4
Win Prizemoney £7,133 *Total Prizemoney* £9,580
Wins 2000 Aug Newmar (G-F) C 7f 58 <
2000 Jly Newmar (G-F) C 8f 56
2000 Turf 2-11: (7f 1-3, 8f 1-6, 10f 2) (g-f 1-7, frm 1-4) 2000 AW 0-1: (8f) (Fibr)
Scopey, average filly, effective 8f, acts on g-f, has worn blinkers. Turf high 69 - 5th of 18 giving 8lb to Manxwood (5 Jun Windsor 8f g-f RF 1730).
**M A Jarvis [0-1] Mohammed Al Khalifa (from B J Meehan [2-15] Aug 2000).*

PINKAI (IRE) **RR 103f** 3945a[5]
3 f **Form** - 5
2000 Turf 0-1: (10f) (g-f)
Currently very useful. **Mme C Head in FR [0-1].*

PINK CHAMPAGNE **RR 24f** 3832[6]
2 ch f Cosmonaut - Riviere Rouge **(15f 40a)** (Forzando) 7.6f **(59)**
Form - 76
Record 2000 - 1st:0 2nd:0 3rd:0 Ran:2
2000 Turf 0-2: (6f 2) (g-f, frm)
Currently little account filly. Turf high 24 (began Jly).
**S G Knight [0-2] Richard Withers.*

PINK MOSAIC BHB 49f **RR 45f** 2812[13]
4 b f Safawan 6.6f **(60)** - Stoneydale (Tickled Pink) 6.5f **(59)**
Form - 00
Record 2000 - 1st:0 2nd:0 3rd:0 Ran:2
Pre2000 - 1st:0 2nd:0 3rd:0 Ran:4
2000 Turf 0-2: (5f, 6f) (g-f 2)
Workmanlike, moderate filly. Turf high 31.
**J G Smyth-Osbourne [0-6] GFT Agricultural Products And Partners.*

PINMOOR HILL BHB 34f **RR 40f** 2478[9]
4 b g Saddlers' Hall (IRE) 10.5f **(65)** - Pennine Pink (IRE) **(75f 60a)** (Pennine Walk) 8.5f **(61)**
Form - 0760
Record 2000 - 1st:0 2nd:0 3rd:0 Ran:4
Pre2000 - 1st:0 2nd:0 3rd:0 Ran:2
2000 Turf 0-4: (8f, 10f, 13f, 22f) (sft, gd, frm 2)
Scopey, moderate gelding. Turf high 40 - 6th of 6 getting 7lb from Love Bitten (23 Jun Ayr 13f frm RF 2217).
**D Nicholls [0-4] J E Swiers (from Mrs J R Ramsden [0-2] Spt 1998).*

PIPADASH (IRE) BHB 72f **RR 78df** 5159[12]
3 b f Pips Pride 6.7f **(70)** - Petite Maxine **(63f)** (Sharpo) 7.7f **(59)**
Form - 270083000010
Record 2000 - 1st:1 2nd:1 3rd:1 Ran:12
Pre2000 - 1st:3 2nd:1 3rd:2 Ran:9
Win Prizemoney £16,958 *Total Prizemoney* £34,875

Wins * 2000 Oct Pontef (HVY) C 6f 59+
* 1999 Aug Ascot (GD) 5f 87 <
* 1999 Apr Pontef (G-S) 5f 75
* 1999 Apr Haydoc (SFT) 5f 73+
2000 Turf 1-12: (5f 5, 6f 1-6, 8f) (hvy, sft, g-s 1-2, gd 3, g-f 2, frm 3)
Light-framed, above-average filly, effective 5 to 6f, best at 5f, acts on g-s to g-f, best on gd, has worn blinkers, excels at Doncaster and Pontefract. Turf high 87.
**T D Easterby [4-21] T H Bennett.*

PIPADOR (IRE) BHB 38f40a **RR 31f 40a** 440[8]
4 ch g Pips Pride 6.7f **(70)** - Dorado Llave (USA) (Well Decorated (USA)) 7.6f **(64)**
Form - 508
Record 2000 - 1st:0 2nd:0 3rd:0 Ran:2
Pre2000 - 1st:0 2nd:0 3rd:0 Ran:9
2000 AW 0-2: (9f, 11f) (Fibr 2)
Well made, very moderate gelding, has worn blinkers. AW high 9. Inconsistent.
**R Guest [0-8] Rae Guest (from R Hannon [0-3] Oct 1998).*

PIPALONG (IRE) BHB 115f **RR 118f** 4845a[3]
4 b f Pips Pride 6.7f **(70)** - Limpopo (Green Desert (USA)) 8.6f **(78)**
Form - 112103313
Record 2000 - 1st:4 2nd:1 3rd:3 Ran:9
Pre2000 - 1st:5 2nd:6 3rd:0 Ran:19
Win Prizemoney £263,091 *Total Prizemoney* £370,499
Wins * 2000 Spt Haydoc (HVY) G1 6f 118 <
*** 2000** Jun Haydoc (G-S) L 6f 108+
*** 2000** May Newmar (GD) G3 5f 106
*** 2000** Apr Thirsk (G-S) 6f 108
* 1999 Nov Doncas (SFT) L 6f 99
* 1999 Aug Ripon (GD) H 6f 101 106
* 1998 Oct Redcar (HVY) 6f 100
* 1998 May York (GD) 5f 95
* 1998 Apr Ripon (SFT) 5f 99+
2000 Turf 4-9: (5f 1-3, 6f 3-6) (g-s 2-2, gd 2-7)
Workmanlike, high-class filly, effective 6f, acts on g-s to gd, best on gd, likes Newmarket and Haydock. Turf high 118 - 3rd of 11 getting 3lb from Agnes World (13 Jly Newmarket 6f gd RF 2773) - also 1st of 13 getting 3lb from Sampower Star (2 Spt Haydock RF 4157). Consistent. She looked removed from the top-class during arduous campaigns at two and three, but defied the sceptics by developing into an outstanding sprinter last year. At her best over six furlongs on soft ground, she found conditions ideal when beating Sampower Star in the Group One Stanley Leisure Sprint Cup at Haydock in September and is a credit to her connections.
**T D Easterby [9-28] T H Bennett.*

PIPED ABOARD (IRE) BHB 65f **RR 78f** 3612[6]
5 b g Pips Pride 6.7f **(70)** - Last Gunboat (Dominion) 8.5f **(63)**
Form - 3500606
Record 2000 - 1st:0 2nd:0 3rd:1 Ran:7
Pre2000 - 1st:1 2nd:4 3rd:0 Ran:12
Win Prizemoney £2,337 *Total Prizemoney* £8,906
Wins 1998 Apr Thirsk (G-S) 7f 71 <
2000 Turf 0-7: (10f 2, 12f 4, 16f) (gd 2, g-f 4, frm)
Above-average gelding, effective 12f, acts on g-f, has worn blinkers (effectively), likes left handed tracks, favours tight tracks. Turf high 78 (1st run) - 3rd of 12 giving 3lb to Veridian (11 May Chester 12f g-f RF 1139).
**T D Barron [0-5] Nigel Shields (from M C Pipe [4-20] Jun 2000).*

PIPE DREAM BHB 40f38a **RR 42f 38a** 3636[5]
4 b g King's Signet (USA) 7f **(51)** - Rather Warm (Tribal Chief) 8.5f **(61)**
Form - 0073368750435
Record 2000 - 1st:0 2nd:0 3rd:3 Ran:10
Pre2000 - 1st:0 2nd:0 3rd:1 Ran:12
Win Prizemoney £0 *Total Prizemoney* £2,317
2000 Turf 0-5: (7f, 8f 4) (gd, g-f 2, frm 2) 2000 AW 0-5: (7f, 8f 4) (Equi 4, Fibr)
Moderate gelding, effective 8 to 9f, acts on gd, likes right handed tracks. Turf high 42. AW high 54.
**P Burgoyne [0-15] The Simpsons Partnership (from K Prendergast in IRE [0-7] Jly 1999).*

PIPE MUSIC (IRE) BHB 44f60a **RR 39f 60a** 3314[1]
5 b g Mujadil (USA) 7.7f **(70)**- Sunset Cafe (IRE) (Red Sunset) 8.2f **(63)**

Form - 36327507221

Record 2000 - 1st:1 2nd:3 3rd:1 Ran:9

Pre2000 - 1st:2 2nd:4 3rd:3 Ran:28

Win Prizemoney £7,261 *Total Prizemoney* £14,600

Wins * 2000 Aug Carlis (GD) H 14.1f 37 39

* 1999 *Feb Southw (STD) H 16f 66 70*

* 1998 *Feb Southw (STD) H 8f 60 71 <*

2000 Turf 1-4: (13f, 14f 1-3) (gd, g-f 1-1, frm 2) 2000 AW 0-5: (16f 5) (Fibr 5)

Average gelding, effective 16f, - acts on AW, best on Fibr, often wears blinkers (effectively), likes left handed tracks, and excels at Wolverhampton. Turf high 39. AW high 61 - 2nd of 9 getting 7lb from Alhesn (18 Jan Wolverhampton 16f Fibr RF 0109).

**P C Haslam [3-40] Lord Scarsdale.*

PIPIJI (IRE) BHB 26f30a RR 15f 30a 3385[8]

5 gr m Pips Pride 6.7f **(70)** - Blue Alicia (Wolver Hollow) 8f **(56)**

Form - 000488

Record 2000 - 1st:0 2nd:0 3rd:0 Ran:6

Pre2000 - 1st:0 2nd:2 3rd:0 Ran:11

Win Prizemoney £0 *Total Prizemoney* £2,024

2000 Turf 0-5: (6f, 7f 2, 8f 2) (g-f, frm 3, hrd) 2000 AW 0-1: (8f) (Fibr)

Little account filly, effective 7 to 8f, best at 8f, acts on gd to frm - acts on Fibr, prefers tight tracks. Turf high 15. (1st run) - 4th of 12 giving 3lb to Bewildered (13 Jly Wolverhampton 8f Fibr RF 2777).

**Mrs G S Rees [0-17] Mrs G S Rees.*

PIPISFLYING (IRE) RR 93f 5171a[7]

3 ch f Pips Pride 6.7f **(70)** - Time Is Flying

Form - 2644457

2000 Turf 0-7: (5f 6, 6f) (hvy, g-s 2, gd 2, frm)

Useful filly, effective 6f, acts on g-s. Turf high 93 (1st run) - 2nd of 15 getting 5lb from Conormara (3 Jun Naas 6f g-s RF 1766a). She has the ability to win a modest sprint, but became frustrating.

**C Collins in IRE [0-7] P M Grace.*

PIPPAS PRIDE (IRE) BHB 39f50a RR 39f 50a 5245[8]

5 ch g Pips Pride 6.7f **(70)** - Al Shany (Burslem) 8.8f **(53)**

Form - 113115435003023608

Record 2000 - 1st:3 2nd:1 3rd:4 Ran:17

Pre2000 - 1st:2 2nd:0 3rd:0 Ran:14

Win Prizemoney £10,169 *Total Prizemoney* £12,451

Wins 2000 *Feb Southw (STD) H 8f 59 66 <*

2000 *Jan Southw (STD) C 8f 65*

2000 *Jan Southw (STD) C 7f 60*

1999 *Dec Southw (STD) C 8f 53*

1999 *Jan Lingfi (STD) H 8f 35 43*

2000 Turf 0-4: (7f, 8f 3) (g-f 2, frm 2) 2000 AW 3-13: (7f 1-3, 8f 2-9, 9f) (Fibr 3-13)

Fair gelding, effective 7 to 8f, best at 8f, - acts on Fibr, prefers left handed tracks, favours tight tracks, excels at Southwell. Turf high 39. AW high 66 - 1st of 9 getting 9lb from Out of Sight (7 Feb Southwell RF 0237) - also 1st of 6 giving 3lb to Rambo Waltzer (21 Jan Southwell RF 0127). Inconsistent.

**A J McNae [0-3] A J McNae (from S R Bowring [4-15] Jly 2000).*

PIP'S BRAVE BHB 34f43a RR 50f 43a 4112[7]

4 b g Be My Chief (USA) 10.2f **(62)** - Pipistrelle (Shareef Dancer (USA)) 9.9f **(73)**

Form - 3672400015767

Record 2000 - 1st:1 2nd:1 3rd:1 Ran:13

Pre2000 - 1st:2 2nd:0 3rd:1 Ran:23

Win Prizemoney £8,861 *Total Prizemoney* £10,962

Wins 2000 *Jly Southw (STD) C 11f 38*

1999 Jly Warwic (G-F) H 10.5f 50 50

1999 *Jan Southw (STD) 8f 56 <*

2000 Turf 0-9: (10f 3, 11f 3, 12f 2, 16f) (hvy, sft, gd 2, g-f 3, frm 2) 2000 AW 1-4: (8f 2, 11f 1-2) (Fibr 1-4)

Fair gelding, effective 8 to 11f, best at 8f, acts on hvy to g-f - acts on Fibr, often wears blinkers (effectively), likes left handed tracks, excels at Warwick, likes Southwell. Turf high 50 - 4th of 19 getting 14lb from Diablo Dancer (1 May Warwick 11f sft RF 0957). AW high 52 (1st run) - 3rd of 9 getting 8lb from Pippas Pride (7 Feb Southwell 8f Fibr RF 0237). A winner on turf and sand in a busy 1999, he caused something of a surprise when winning a claimer on the Southwell Fibresand in July last year, though with the leaders falling in a heap the form may not amount to much.

**L A Dace [0-4] Gerry Boyer (from M J Polglase [3-32] Jly 2000).*

PIPS MAGIC (IRE) BHB 79f RR 87f 5127[14]

4 b g Pips Pride 6.7f **(70)** - Kentucky Starlet (USA) (Cox's Ridge (USA)) 8f **(68)**

Form - 0000081081800700000

Record 2000 - 1st:2 2nd:0 3rd:0 Ran:19

Pre2000 - 1st:3 2nd:2 3rd:2 Ran:26

Win Prizemoney £29,579 *Total Prizemoney* £44,197

Wins * 2000 Jly Newcas (GD) H 6f 78 81

*** 2000** Jly Doncas (GD) 6f 80

* 1999 Jun Ascot (G-F) H 5f 90 94 <

* 1998 May Ayr (G-F) 5f 84

* 1998 May Ripon (G-F) 6f 66

2000 Turf 2-19: (5f 4, 6f 2-13, 7f 2) (sft, g-s, gd 7, g-f 1-3, frm 1-7)

Scopey, useful gelding, effective 5 to 6f, best at 6f, acts on g-f to frm, best on g-f. Turf high 82. Put in a couple of useful placed efforts prior to winning a valuable handicap at the 1999 Ascot Heath Meeting, but showed nothing at all afterwards until winning twice in July. Respectable efforts in defeat since.

**J S Goldie [5-45] Frank Brady.*

PIPSSALIO (SPA) BHB 79f RR 85f 5134[8]

3 b c Pips Pride 6.7f **(70)** - Tesalia (SPA) (Finissimo (SPA))

Form - 2140148

Record 2000 - 1st:2 2nd:1 3rd:0 Ran:7

Pre2000 - 1st:0 2nd:0 3rd:0 Ran:3

Win Prizemoney £22,425 *Total Prizemoney* £24,691

Wins * 2000 May Kempto (SFT) H 10f 70 85 <

*** 2000** Apr Sandow (SFT) H 8.1f 63 77

2000 Turf 2-7: (8f 1-3, 10f 1-4) (sft 1-2, g-s 1-3, gd, g-f)

Workmanlike, useful colt, effective 8 to 10f, acts on sft to g-s, prefers right handed tracks. Turf high 85 - 1st of 11 getting 27lb from Supply And Demand (27 May Kempton RF 1498) - also 1st of 11 getting 9lb from Everest (29 Apr Sandown RF 0927). Landed a valuable handicap at Sandown on his second start of last season and scored again at Kempton in May. Looks a much better horse on soft ground.

**J R Poulton [2-10] Chris Steward & Christina Taylor.*

PIPS SONG (IRE) BHB 77f77a RR 73f 77a 5242[15]

5 ch g Pips Pride 6.7f **(70)** - Friendly Song (Song) 7.2f **(61)**

Form - 02401030000

Record 2000 - 1st:1 2nd:1 3rd:1 Ran:10

Pre2000 - 1st:3 2nd:2 3rd:2 Ran:20

Win Prizemoney £22,567 *Total Prizemoney* £32,787

Wins * 2000 Apr Pontef (HVY) H 6f 74 85 <

* 1999 Apr Leices (HVY) H 6f 69 78

* 1999 *Mar Wolver (STD) H 6f 71 76*

* 1998 *Apr Wolver (STD) 6f 63*

2000 Turf 1-7: (6f 1-5, 7f 2) (sft 1-2, g-s, gd 4) 2000 AW 0-3: (6f 3) (Fibr 3)

Above-average gelding, effective 6f, acts on sft to g-f - acts on Fibr, best on sft, likes left handed tracks, likes tight tracks, excels at Wolverhampton. Turf high 85 - 1st of 17 getting 4lb from Redoubtable (17 Apr Pontefract RF 0749). AW high 78 - 4th of 13 giving 1lb to Daawe (17 Feb Wolverhampton 6f Fibr RF 0298). Becoming disappointing. Returned to form when winning on his favoured heavy ground at Pontefract.

**Dr J D Scargill [4-29] P J Edwards (from I A Balding [0-1] Jly 1997).*

PIPS STAR BHB 62f55a RR 61f 55a 3827[7]

3 b f Pips Pride 6.7f **(70)** - Kentucky Starlet (USA) (Cox's Ridge (USA)) 8f **(68)**

Form - 326240001127

Record 2000 - 1st:2 2nd:3 3rd:1 Ran:12

Pre2000 - 1st:1 2nd:1 3rd:1 Ran:8

Win Prizemoney £8,542 *Total Prizemoney* £13,950

Wins * 2000 Aug Carlis (FRM) H 5.9f 46 54

*** 2000** Aug Doncas (G-F) H 5f 46 47

1999 *Oct Wolver (STD) S 5f 73 <*

2000 Turf 2-7: (5f 1-6, 6f 1-1) (gd, frm 2-5, hrd) 2000 AW 0-5: (5f 5) (Equi 2, Fibr 3)

Workmanlike, average filly, effective 5f, acted on gd - acted on Fibr. Turf high 61 (began Jly). AW high 63. (DEAD)

**J S Goldie [2-7] Colin Barnfather and Frank Steele (from D W P Arbuthnot [1-13] Mar 2000).*

PIPS TANGO (IRE) BHB 30f **RR ?f** 3738^{11}
3 ch f Pips Pride 6.7f **(70)** - Suppression (Kind of Hush) 10.1f **(62)**
Form - 000
Record 2000 - 1st:0 2nd:0 3rd:0 Ran:3
Pre2000 - 1st:0 2nd:0 3rd:0 Ran:3
2000 Turf 0-3: (6f, 8f, 12f) (g-f, frm, hrd)
Light-framed, very poor filly. (began Aug).
**M Mullineaux [0-6] Michael Mullineaux.*

PIPS WAY (IRE) BHB 78f **RR 79f** 5240^{11}
3 ch f Pips Pride 6.7f **(70)** - Algonquin Park (High Line) 10.3f **(70)**
Form - 60414315400
Record 2000 - 1st:2 2nd:0 3rd:1 Ran:11
Pre2000 - 1st:1 2nd:0 3rd:1 Ran:8
Win Prizemoney £12,684 *Total Prizemoney* £15,630
Wins * 2000 Jly Kempto (G-S) H 9f 77 79 <
*** 2000** Jun Newcas (SFT) H 8f 73 77
***** 1999 May Ripon (G-S) 6f 67
2000 Turf 2-11: (8f 1-6, 9f 1-3, 10f, 12f)(sft 1-2, g-s, gd 3, g-f 1-3, frm 2)
Scopey, above-average filly, effective 6 to 10f, acts on sft to frm, best on g-f, has worn blinkers, likes left handed tracks, likes tight tracks. Turf high 79 - 5th of 12 giving 15lb to Pedro Pete (14 Jly Chester 10f g-f RF 2800) - also 1st of 14 giving 8lb to Divine Prospect (12 Jly Kempton RF 2732). Consistent. Held in Listed and nursery company after making a winning debut in a Ripon maiden at two, she returned to form when encountering soft ground at Newcastle in June and there was again cut in the ground when he won at Kempton in July. Yet to prove he stays beyond ten furlongs. **K R Burke [3-19] Paul James McCaughey.*

PIQUET BHB 65f61a **RR 66f 61a** 5129^{5}
2 br f Mind Games - Petonellajill **(57f 50a)** (Petong) 6.6f **(58)**
Form - 8455
Record 2000 - 1st:0 2nd:0 3rd:0 Ran:4
2000 Turf 0-4: (5f, 6f 3) (sft, gd, g-f, frm)
Average filly. Turf high 66 (began Spt).
**R Hannon [0-4] Miss Jane Collier.*

PIRANESI (IRE) RR 92f 3914^{21}
4 ch g Grand Lodge (USA) - Princess Dixieland (USA) (Dixieland Band (USA)) 7f **(74)**
Form - 150050
2000 Turf 1-6: (12f 1-4, 14f 2) (gd 3, g-f 1-1, frm 2)
Useful gelding, effective 10 to 14f, best at 12f, acts on gd to frm. Turf high 92 - 5th of 5 getting 4lb from Royal Rebel (24 May Leopardstown 14f gd RF 1565a) - also 1st of 8 giving 9lb to Forrestfield (14 May Leopardstown RF 1252a).
**D Gillespie in IRE [3-15] Mrs Chryss O'Reilly.*

PISCES LAD BHB 49f60a **RR 60f 60a** 4827^{24}
4 b g Cyrano de Bergerac 7.3f **(58)** - Tarnside Rosal **(56f)** (Mummy's Game) 8.2f **(60)**
Form - 18280082070
Record 2000 - 1st:1 2nd:2 3rd:0 Ran:11
Pre2000 - 1st:0 2nd:3 3rd:2 Ran:19
Win Prizemoney £2,702 *Total Prizemoney* £8,170
Wins * 2000 Mar Catter (GD) 6f 60 <
2000 Turf 1-11: (5f 7, 6f 1-4) (gd, g-f 2, frm 1-7, hrd)
Scopey, average gelding, effective 5 to 6f, best at 5f, acts on frm - acts on Equi, has worn blinkers, likes left handed tracks, likes tight tracks. Turf high 60 - 2nd of 16 giving 5lb to Sue Me (22 May Musselburgh 5f frm RF 1366) - also 1st of 8 giving 13lb to Danakim (29 Mar Catterick RF 0548).
**T D Barron [1-11] J Falvey & G Williamson (from S Dow [0-19] Spt 1999).*

PIVOTABLE BHB 66f **RR 69f** 5106^{15}
2 ch f Pivotal - Lady Dowery (USA) (Manila (USA)) 9.3f **(71)**
Form - 32570
Record 2000 - 1st:0 2nd:1 3rd:1 Ran:5
Win Prizemoney £0 *Total Prizemoney* £1,489
2000 Turf 0-5: (5f, 6f 3, 7f) (g-s 2, gd, frm 2)
Average filly. Turf high 69 - 2nd of 9 to Strange Destiny (4 Jun Warwick 5f g-s RF 1702). **M L W Bell [0-5] The Aldwych Partnership.*

PIX ME UP (IRE) BHB 41f44a **RR 54f 44a** 3928^{4}
3 b f Up and At 'em - Water Pixie (IRE) (Dance of Life (USA)) 7f **(66)**
Form - 8708124005474
Record 2000 - 1st:1 2nd:1 3rd:0 Ran:13
Pre2000 - 1st:0 2nd:1 3rd:1 Ran:5
Win Prizemoney £2,282 *Total Prizemoney* £4,686
Wins * 2000 May Ripon (GD) C 8f 52 <
2000 Turf 1-11: (7f 2, 8f 1-5, 9f, 10f 2, 12f) (g-s 3, gd, g-f 1-1, frm 5, hrd) 2000 AW 0-2: (8f, 9f) (Fibr 2)
Small, fair filly, effective 6 to 8f, acts on g-f to hrd. Turf high 54 - also 1st of 17 getting 2lb from Send It To Penny (31 May Ripon RF 1594). AW high 39. **K A Ryan [1-18] Roses Racing Club.*

PLAIN CHANT RR 43f 4486^{14}
3 b c Doyoun 10.7f **(69)** - Sing Softly (Luthier) 9.8f **(71)**
Form - 000
Record 2000 - 1st:0 2nd:0 3rd:0 Ran:3
2000 Turf 0-3: (10f 2, 12f) (g-s, g-f, frm)
Workmanlike, currently moderate colt. Turf high 62 (began Jly).
**P W Harris [0-3] Mrs P W Harris.*

PLANET GIRL RR 77f 4271^{11}
2 b f Mtoto 11.5f **(71)** - Galactic Miss (Damister (USA)) 9f **(73)**
Form - 30
Record 2000 - 1st:0 2nd:0 3rd:1 Ran:2
Win Prizemoney £0 *Total Prizemoney* £587
2000 Turf 0-2: (7f, 8f) (g-f 2)
Currently above-average filly. Turf high 77 (began Aug).
**J L Dunlop [0-2] Hesmonds Stud.*

PLANTAGEANT RR 39^{8}
3 ch g Superlative 8.8f **(57)** - International Star (IRE) **(70df)** (Astronef)
Form - 8
Record 2000 - 1st:0 2nd:0 3rd:0 Ran:1
2000 AW 0-1: (7f) (Fibr)
Currently little account gelding.
**R W Armstrong [0-1] F J Crouch & D A Morgan.*

PLATINUM TIARA (USA) RR $5326a^{2}$
2 gr f Cozzene (USA) 10.1f **(87)** - Michelle's Monarch (USA) (Wavering Monarch (USA)) 10.4f **(94)**
Form - 2
2000 AW 0-1: (9f) (Dirt)
Currently very useful filly. (1st run) - 2nd of 12 to Caressing (4 Nov Churchill Downs 9f Dirt RF 5326a).
**J Waunsch in USA [0-1] M375 Thoroughbreds Inc.*

PLAYACT (IRE) RR 110f $4837a^{3}$
3 ch f Hernando (FR) - Play or Pay (USA) (Play Fellow (USA))
Form - 23
2000 Turf 0-2: (13f 2) (g-s, gd)
Currently Group-class filly. Turf high 110 (began Jly) - 3rd of 11 to Mouramara (30 Spt Longchamp 13f gd RF 4837a).
**N Clement in FR [0-2] Ecurie Skymarc Farm.*

PLAYINAROUND BHB 37f47a **RR 52df 47a** 2554^{11}
3 ch f Anshan 8.2f **(63)** - Karonga (Main Reef) 9.6f **(57)**
Form - 0000
Record 2000 - 1st:0 2nd:0 3rd:0 Ran:4
Pre2000 - 1st:1 2nd:0 3rd:1 Ran:8
Win Prizemoney £1,819 *Total Prizemoney* £2,089
Wins * 1999 May Bright (FRM) S 6f 45 <
2000 Turf 0-3: (6f, 7f 2) (g-f, frm 2) 2000 AW 0-1: (6f) (Equi)
Workmanlike, fair filly, effective 5 to 7f, acts on g-f to hrd. Turf high 38. Becoming disappointing. **W G M Turner [1-12] Gongolfin.*

PLAYMAKER BHB 25f33a **RR 3f 33a** 2212^{15}
7 b g Primo Dominie 7.2f **(67)** - Salacious (Sallust) 8.4f **(63)**
Form - 0
Record 2000 - 1st:0 2nd:0 3rd:0 Ran:1
Pre2000 - 1st:1 2nd:1 3rd:1 Ran:22
Win Prizemoney £4,240 *Total Prizemoney* £6,767
2000 Turf 0-1: (8f) (frm)
Very poor gelding, has worn blinkers. Inconsistent.
**F P Murtagh [0-6] Mrs Anna Kenny (from D Nicholls [0-14] May 1997).*

PLAYONETOONEDOTCOM (IRE) BHB 40f **RR 29f** 4876^{7}
2 b f Desert Style (IRE) - Reacted (IRE) (Entitled)
Form - 0067

Record 2000 - 1st:0 2nd:0 3rd:0 Ran:4
2000 Turf 0-4: (7f 3, 8f) (g-s 2, g-f 2)
Little account filly. Turf high 29 (began Aug).
**C M Kinane [0-4] Exors of the late G A Hubbard.*

PLAY TIME RR 66f 5196[9]

2 b f Unfuwain (USA) 11.4f **(74)** - Break Point **(41f)** (Reference Point) 6.8f **(70)**
Form - 00
Record 2000 - 1st:0 2nd:0 3rd:0 Ran:2
2000 Turf 0-2: (8f 2) (gd 2)
Currently average filly. Turf high 66 (began Oct).
**D R C Elsworth [0-2] Brian Cooper.*

PIAZZOTTA (IRE) BHB 30f RR 15f 4173[P]

3 b g Sri Pekan (USA) - Porte des Iles (IRE) **(70?f)** (Kris) 9.5f **(73)**
Form - 6P
Record 2000 - 1st:0 2nd:0 3rd:0 Ran:2
Pre2000 - 1st:0 2nd:0 3rd:0 Ran:1
2000 Turf 0-2: (6f, 8f) (gd, g-f)
Scopey, currently poor gelding, has broken blood-vessels. Turf high 15 (began Aug).
**M C Chapman [0-2] Miss C T Hickford (from B J Meehan [0-1] Oct 1999).*

PLEADING BHB 59a RR 60f 4493[18]

7 b g Never so Bold 7.1f **(62)** - Ask Mama (Mummy's Pot) 7.7f **(60)**
Form - 2330050061000
Record 2000 - 1st:1 2nd:1 3rd:2 Ran:13
Pre2000 - 1st:4 2nd:3 3rd:3 Ran:38
Win Prizemoney £21,257 *Total Prizemoney* £39,951
Wins * 2000 Aug Newmar (G-F) C 7f 60
1999 Spt Chepst (GD) H 7.1f 63 73
1998 Apr Pontef (G-S) H 6f 65 70
1996 May Leices (G-S) H 6f 80 91+ <
1996 May Salisb (GD) 6f 77
2000 Turf 1-11: (6f, 7f 1-6, 8f 4) (g-s 2, gd 3, g-f, frm 1-4, hrd) 2000 AW 0-2: (6f 2) (Fibr 2)
Average gelding, effective 6 to 7f, best at 6f, acts on sft to frm, best on frm, has worn blinkers. Turf high 60. AW high 60. Inconsistent.
**M A Buckley [1-13] Stamford Bridge Partnership (from W J Musson [2-25] Oct 1999).*

PLEASANT MOUNT BHB 63f64a RR 64f 64a 3642[3]

4 b g First Trump - Alo Ez (Alzao (USA)) 7.1f **(68)**
Form - 01503023
Record 2000 - 1st:1 2nd:1 3rd:2 Ran:8
Pre2000 - 1st:3 2nd:2 3rd:3 Ran:11
Win Prizemoney £12,565 *Total Prizemoney* £19,832
Wins * 2000 *Apr Wolver (STD) H 16.2f 63 65* <
* 1999 Aug Redcar (G-F) H 14.1f 56 60
* 1999 Aug Thirsk (SFT) H 16f 51 56
* 1999 Jly Beverl (G-F) H 16.2f 48 53
2000 Turf 0-7: (14f, 15f 2, 16f 3, 17f) (g-s 2, gd, g-f 2, frm 2) 2000 AW 1-1: (16f 1-1) (Fibr 1-1)
Tall, average gelding, effective 14 to 17f, best at 16f, acts on g-s to frm - acts on Fibr, prefers left handed tracks, likes tight tracks, and excels at Ayr. Turf high 64 - 5th of 10 getting 13lb from Wave of Optimism (29 Apr Doncaster 17f gd RF 0910). (1st run) - 1st of 9 giving 31lb to Quakeress (15 Apr Wolverhampton RF 0740).
**Miss J A Camacho [4-19] Shangri-La Racing Club.*

PLEASURE BHB 52f52a RR 55f 52a 5057[18]

5 ch m Most Welcome 8.6f **(66)** - Peak Squaw (USA)(Icecapade (USA)) 11f **(62)**
Form - 546410
Record 2000 - 1st:1 2nd:0 3rd:0 Ran:6
Pre2000 - 1st:2 2nd:0 3rd:1 Ran:15
Win Prizemoney £8,544 *Total Prizemoney* £8,839
Wins * 2000 *Jun Southw (STD) H 5f 48 48*
* 1999 Jun Beverl (SFT) H 5f 53 56 <
* 1998 Oct Doncas (SFT) H 7f 51 54
2000 Turf 0-2: (5f, 6f) (sft, g-f) 2000 AW 1-4: (5f 1-1, 6f 2, 7f) (Fibr 1-4)
Fair filly, effective 5f, acts on gd to g-f - acts on Fibr, often wears blinkers (extremely effectively). Turf high 55. AW high 48 - 1st of 17 getting 7lb from Samwar (9 Jun Southwell RF 1859). Inconsistent.

**A Smith [3-20] The Rufus Partnership (from R W Armstrong [0-1] Nov 1997).*

PLEASURE CENTER (USA) BHB 98f RR 100f 3801[5]

3 ch f Diesis 9f **(80)** - Creaking Board (Night Shift (USA)) 7.2f **(69)**
Form - 1405
Record 2000 - 1st:1 2nd:0 3rd:0 Ran:4
Pre2000 - 1st:0 2nd:0 3rd:0 Ran:1
Win Prizemoney £3,488 *Total Prizemoney* £5,527
Wins * 2000 May Nottin (G-F) 8.2f 89+ <
2000 Turf 1-4: (8f 1-3, 9f) (g-s, gd, g-f 1-2)
Light-framed, very useful filly. Turf high 100. She looked to have improved from two to three and won a Nottingham maiden in good style on her return. Stepped up on that form to finish fourth in an Epsom Listed race, but suffered a slipping saddle when down the field in an Ascot Listed handicap.
**J H M Gosden [1-5] George Strawbridge.*

PLEASURE DOME RR 76f 4965[14]

2 b f Most Welcome 8.6f **(66)** - Hickleton Lady (IRE) **(60f 60a)** (Kala Shikari) 8.4f **(54)**
Form - 20
Record 2000 - 1st:0 2nd:1 3rd:0 Ran:2
Win Prizemoney £0 *Total Prizemoney* £714
2000 Turf 0-2: (6f 2) (gd 2)
Currently above-average filly. Turf high 76 (1st run) (began Aug) - 2nd of 12 to Sonatina (18 Aug Folkestone 6f gd RF 3750).
**J M P Eustace [0-2] Park Lane Racing.*

PLEASURE PRINCESS BHB 38f RR 7f 2563[7]

3 b f Presidium 7.5f **(56)** - Harem Queen (Prince Regent (FR)) 9.8f **(54)**
Form - 7
Record 2000 - 1st:0 2nd:0 3rd:0 Ran:1
Pre2000 - 1st:0 2nd:0 3rd:0 Ran:3
2000 Turf 0-1: (6f) (g-f)
Light-framed, very poor filly.
**A Bailey [0-4] WWW Mark-Kilner-Raci (16).*

PLEASURE TIME BHB 64f65a RR 66f 65a 4487[16]

7 ch g Clantime 6.6f **(57)** - First Experience (Le Johnstan) 7.4f **(55)**
Form - 0678160
Record 2000 - 1st:1 2nd:0 3rd:0 Ran:7
Pre2000 - 1st:6 2nd:6 3rd:6 Ran:47
Win Prizemoney £22,022 *Total Prizemoney* £33,102
Wins * 2000 Aug Nottin (G-F) 5.1f 66
* 1999 Jun Bath (FRM) 5.7f 78 <
* 1998 Aug Thirsk (G-F) H 5f 65 70
* 1998 May Nottin (G-F) H 5.1f 60 66
* 1997 May Nottin (GD) H 5.1f 58 63
2000 Turf 1-7: (5f 1-7) (gd 2, g-f 1-3, frm 2)
Average gelding, effective 5 to 6f, best at 5f, acts on g-f to hrd, mostly wears blinkers (effectively). Turf high 66.
**C Smith [7-54] A E Needham.*

PLEASURE TRICK (USA) BHB 32f40a RR 38f 40a 1728[10]

9 br g Clever Trick (USA) 7.6f **(69)** - Pleasure Garden (USA) (Foolish Pleasure (USA)) 8.9f **(72)**
Form - 007580500
Record 2000 - 1st:0 2nd:0 3rd:0 Ran:9
Pre2000 - 1st:9 2nd:4 3rd:5 Ran:79
Win Prizemoney £29,818 *Total Prizemoney* £36,003
Wins * 1998 *Feb Southw (STD) H 7f 55 58*
* 1998 *Jan Southw (STD) H 7f 49 50*
* 1997 Jly Pontef (G-F) H 8f 41 47
* 1997 *Feb Southw (STD) H 8f 49 56*
* 1997 *Jan Southw (STD) H 7f 42 46*
* 1996 *Nov Southw (STD) H 7f 34 43*
2000 Turf 0-5: (7f 3, 8f 2) (g-s, gd 3, frm) 2000 AW 0-4: (7f, 8f 3)(Fibr 4)
Moderate gelding, has worn blinkers. Turf high 38. AW high 44.
**Don Enrico Incisa [6-66] Don Enrico Incisa (from N Tinkler [3-18] Jun 1999).*

PLEINMONT POINT (IRE) BHB 67f RR 73f 5132[11]

2 b g Tagula (IRE) - Cree's Figurine (Creetown) 6.9f **(50)**
Form - 460
Record 2000 - 1st:0 2nd:0 3rd:0 Ran:3
Win Prizemoney £0 *Total Prizemoney* £403

2000 Turf 0-3: (6f 3) (sft, gd, g-f)
Currently above-average gelding. Turf high 73 (1st run) (began Spt) - 4th of 15 giving 8lb to Tickle (3 Spt York 6f g-f RF 4198).
**P D Evans [0-3] Trevor Gallienne.*

PLUM FIRST BHB 45f33a **RR 46f 33a** 5120[12]
10 b g Nomination 7.3f **(57)** - Plum Bold (Be My Guest (USA)) 9.3f **(67)**
Form - 6000

Record	**2000 -**	1st:0	2nd:0	3rd:0	Ran:4
	Pre2000 -	1st:5	2nd:11	3rd:13	Ran:116

Win Prizemoney £18,673 *Total Prizemoney* £43,468
2000 Turf 0-3: (5f 3) (sft, g-s, gd) 2000 AW 0-1: (6f) (Fibr)
Moderate gelding, effective 6f, acts on frm, has worn blinkers. Turf high 15 (began Spt). Becoming disappointing.
**N Wilson [0-4] J B Slatcher (from J S Wainwright [0-15] Jly 1999).*

PLURALIST (IRE) BHB 63f69a **RR 72f 69a** 1964[9]
4 b c Mujadil (USA) 7.7f **(70)** - Encore Une Fois (IRE) **(75f)** (Shirley Heights) 10.3f **(74)**
Form - 124110

Record	**2000 -**	1st:2	2nd:1	3rd:0	Ran:5
	Pre2000 -	1st:1	2nd:4	3rd:0	Ran:12

Win Prizemoney £8,342 *Total Prizemoney* £15,284

Wins								
* **2000**	*Jun*	*Lingfi*	*(STD)*	*H*	*12f*	*70*	*72*	<
2000	May	Warwic	(HVY)	C	10.5f	64		
1999	*Dec*	*Southw*	*(STD)*		*11f*		*47++*	

2000 Turf 1-4: (10f, 11f 1-2, 12f) (hvy 1-1, g-s 2, g-f) 2000 AW 1-1: (12f 1-1) (Equi 1-1)
Strong, above-average colt, effective 9 to 12f, acts on hvy to g-f - acts on Equi, likes left handed tracks, excels at Lingfield and Southwell. Turf high 72 (1st run) - 2nd of 16 giving 14lb to Bachelors Pad (10 Apr Southwell 11f g-s RF 0646) - also 1st of 12 giving 16lb to The Wild Widow (27 May Warwick RF 1512). (1st run) - 1st of 10 giving 22lb to Another Monk (3 Jun Lingfield RF 1679). Consistent.
**Miss K M George [1-2] Exterior Profiles Ltd (from W Jarvis [2-15] May 2000).*

PLUTOCRAT BHB 74f **RR 72f** 1266[8]
4 b g Polar Falcon (USA) 9f **(74)** - Choire Mhor (Dominion) 8.5f **(63)**
Form - 18

Record	**2000 -**	1st:1	2nd:0	3rd:0	Ran:2
	Pre2000 -	1st:1	2nd:2	3rd:1	Ran:5

Win Prizemoney £7,297 *Total Prizemoney* £10,287

Wins								
* **2000**	May	Mussel	(FRM)	H	12f	69	72	<
1999	Aug	Mussel	(G-F)	C	9f		56	

2000 Turf 1-2: (12f 1-1, 14f) (g-f, frm 1-1)
Unfurnished, above-average gelding, effective 7 to 14f, acts on gd to frm, best on frm. Turf high 72 (1st run) - 1st of 8 giving 19lb to Sing And Dance (5 May Musselburgh RF 1042).
**L Lungo [4-8] N A Bulmer (from J Noseda [1-5] Aug 1999).*

POCKET VENUS (IRE) BHB 20f **RR** 4996[12]
2 b f King's Theatre (IRE) - Taidja (IRE) (Shahrastani (USA)) 8.8f **(72)**
Form - 000

Record	**2000 -**	1st:0	2nd:0	3rd:0	Ran:3

2000 Turf 0-2: (7f, 10f) (g-s, frm) 2000 AW 0-1: (8f) (Fibr)
Currently very poor filly. (began Jly).
**M Salaman [0-3] J P M & J W Cook.*

POCO A POCO (IRE) **RR 103f** 4519a[4]
3 b f Imperial Frontier (USA) 7f **(65)** - Cut the Red Tape (IRE) **(63f)** (Sure Blade (USA)) 11.3f **(67)**
Form - 3564
2000 Turf 0-4: (6f 3, 7f) (gd 2, g-f)
Very useful filly, effective 6 to 7f, best at 6f, acts on sft to g-f, best on gd. Turf high 103 - 6th of 8 getting 7lb from Eastern Purple (13 Aug Leopardstown 6f gd RF 3675a).
**E Lynam in IRE [1-8] J Carthy.*

POETIC (USA) BHB 86f **RR 87f** 1727[1]
3 b f Nureyev (USA) 8.4f **(84)** - Draw Straws (USA) (Key To The Mint (USA)) 9.4f **(75)**
Form - 321

Record	**2000 -**	1st:1	2nd:1	3rd:1	Ran:3

Win Prizemoney £4,179 *Total Prizemoney* £6,072

Wins								
* **2000**	Jun	Thirsk	(SFT)		8f		60+	<

2000 Turf 1-3: (7f, 8f 1-2) (g-s, gd 1-1, g-f)
Scopey, currently useful filly. Turf high 87 - 2nd of 11 to Coco (12 May Nottingham 8f g-f RF 1177).
**H R A Cecil [1-3] The Thoroughbred Corporation.*

POETRY IN MOTION (IRE) BHB 63f54a **RR 66f 54a** 2928[11]
5 gr m Ballad Rock 7.2f **(63)** - Nasseem (FR) (Zeddaan) 9f **(76)**
Form - 8500

Record	**2000 -**	1st:0	2nd:0	3rd:0	Ran:4
	Pre2000 -	1st:1	2nd:4	3rd:0	Ran:19

Win Prizemoney £2,612 *Total Prizemoney* £11,541

Wins								
1999	Jun	Mussel	(G-F)		5f		72	<

2000 Turf 0-4: (5f 4) (g-f, frm 3)
Average filly, effective 5f, acts on g-s to g-f, has worn blinkers. Turf high 66 (began Jly). Inconsistent.
**R Guest [0-4] Peter Ebdon Racing (from E J Alston [1-19] Oct 1999).*

POINT GIVEN (USA) **RR** 5330a[2]
2 ch f Thunder Gulch (USA) - Turko's Turn (USA) (Turkoman (USA))
Form - 2
2000 AW 0-1: (9f) (Dirt)
Currently Pattern-class filly, wears blinkers. (1st run) - 2nd of 14 to Macho Uno (4 Nov Churchill Downs 9f Dirt RF 5330a).
**B Baffert in USA [0-1] The Thoroughbred Corporation.*

POINT OF DISPUTE BHB 91f **RR 84f** 4115[3]
5 b g Cyrano de Bergerac 7.3f **(58)** - Opuntia (Rousillon (USA)) 8.2f **(74)**
Form - 4413

Record	**2000 -**	1st:1	2nd:0	3rd:1	Ran:4
	Pre2000 -	1st:3	2nd:0	3rd:0	Ran:11

Win Prizemoney £20,314 *Total Prizemoney* £22,086

Wins								
* **2000**	Aug	Newmar	(GD)	H	6f	80	84	<
* 1999	Oct	Nottin	(FRM)	H	6.1f	72	79	
* 1999	Aug	Lingfi	(GD)	H	7f	69	74+	
* 1998	May	Salisb	(G-S)		6f		82	

2000 Turf 1-4: (6f 1-3, 7f) (g-f 1-2, frm 2)
Useful gelding, effective 6 to 7f, best at 6f, acts on g-f to frm, best on g-f, often wears blinkers (extremely effectively). Turf high 84 - 1st of 10 giving 13lb to Diamond Geezer (4 Aug Newmarket RF 3369). He came good at Newmarket in August, and is most effective over six furlongs on fast ground.
**P J Makin [4-15] Mrs B J Carrington.*

POKER POLKA BHB 69f **RR 69f** 911[24]
3 b f Salse (USA) 10.9f **(71)** - Poker Chip **(97df)** (Bluebird (USA)) 7.5f **(69)**
Form - 0

Record	**2000 -**	1st:0	2nd:0	3rd:0	Ran:1
	Pre2000 -	1st:1	2nd:0	3rd:0	Ran:6

Win Prizemoney £3,915 *Total Prizemoney* £3,915

Wins								
* 1999	Aug	Nottin	(G-F)		5.1f		75	<

2000 Turf 0-1: (8f) (gd)
Workmanlike, average filly, effective 5f, acts on gd.
**J M P Eustace [1-7] J C Smith.*

POLAR CHALLENGE BHB 81f **RR 83f** 4968[5]
3 b c Polar Falcon (USA) 9f **(74)** - Warning Light (High Top) 10.2f **(67)**
Form - 033523105

Record	**2000 -**	1st:1	2nd:1	3rd:3	Ran:9
	Pre2000 -	1st:0	2nd:0	3rd:0	Ran:2

Win Prizemoney £4,062 *Total Prizemoney* £13,060

Wins								
* **2000**	Aug	Windso	(G-F)		8.3f		83+	<

2000 Turf 1-9: (8f 1-7, 9f, 10f) (hvy, gd 2, g-f 1-2, frm 4)
Scopey, decent colt, effective 7 to 10f, best at 8f, acts on gd to frm, excels at Chester. Turf high 83 - 5th of 21 getting 9lb from Elghani (13 Oct Newmarket 8f gd RF 4968) - also 1st of 7 from Finished Article (7 Aug Windsor RF 3439). Consistent. Not winning out of turn when making all at Windsor in August. Suited by a mile and fast ground. **Sir Michael Stoute [1-11] Cheveley Park Stud.*

POLAR CHARGE **RR 103f** 3352a[8]
3 f Polar Falcon (USA) 9f **(74)**
Form - 8238
2000 Turf 0-4: (8f, 11f, 12f, 14f) (sft, g-s, gd 2)
Very useful filly. Turf high 103 - 2nd of 18 to Timi (21 May San Siro

11f gd RF 1455a). **B Grizzetti in ITY [0-4].*

POLAR DIAMOND BHB 60f63a **RR 67f 63a** 2228[13]

3 b f Polar Falcon (USA) 9f **(74)** - Bold Gem **(50f 52a)** (Never so Bold) 6.3f **(66)**

Form - 03000

Record	**2000 -**	1st:0	2nd:0	3rd:1	Ran:5

Win Prizemoney £0 *Total Prizemoney* £448

2000 Turf 0-4: (6f, 7f, 8f 2) (sft, g-s, g-f, frm) 2000 AW 0-1: (8f) (Fibr)

Unfurnished, average filly. Turf high 67 - 3rd of 9 to Kanaka Creek (1 May Warwick 8f sft RF 0955).

**H Morrison [0-5] Alistair Morrison & Partners.*

POLAR ECLIPSE BHB 50f40a **RR 52f 40a** 53[11]

7 ch g Polar Falcon (USA) 9f **(74)** - Princess Zepoll (Persepolis (FR)) 6.4f **(67)**

Form - 600

Record	**2000 -**	1st:0	2nd:0	3rd:0	Ran:1
	Pre2000 -	1st:1	2nd:3	3rd:2	Ran:30

Win Prizemoney £4,320 *Total Prizemoney* £10,556

2000 AW 0-1: (9f) (Fibr)

Fair gelding, effective 8 to 10f, best at 10f, acts on g-f to frm, best on g-f, has worn blinkers, favours tight tracks.

**J G Given [0-7] J R Good (from K R Burke [0-3] May 1999).*

POLAR HAZE BHB 65f **RR 72f** 4626[9]

3 ch g Polar Falcon (USA) 9f **(74)** - Sky Music **(82f)** (Absalom) 7.2f **(58)**

Form - 230360

Record	**2000 -**	1st:0	2nd:1	3rd:2	Ran:6
	Pre2000 -	1st:0	2nd:2	3rd:0	Ran:4

Win Prizemoney £0 *Total Prizemoney* £4,259

2000 Turf 0-6: (5f 2, 6f 2, 7f, 8f) (gd, g-f, frm 4)

Lengthy, above-average gelding, effective 5 to 6f, best at 5f, acts on gd to frm. Turf high 72 - 3rd of 7 getting 6lb from Hand Chime (9 Aug Pontefract 6f frm RF 3504). Inconsistent.

**Miss S E Hall [0-10] Mrs Joan Hodgson.*

POLAR ICE BHB 60a **RR 39f** 3752[13]

4 b c Polar Falcon (USA) 9f **(74)** - Sweet Slew (USA) (Seattle Slew (USA)) 9.4f **(76)**

Form - 70000700

Record	**2000 -**	1st:0	2nd:0	3rd:0	Ran:6
	Pre2000 -	1st:2	2nd:3	3rd:1	Ran:11

Win Prizemoney £6,533 *Total Prizemoney* £10,670

Wins	1999	*Jun*	*Wolver*	*(STD)*	*H*	*7f*	*75*	*79*	<
	1999	*Jun*	*Wolver*	*(STA)*		*7f*		*76*	

2000 Turf 0-1: (7f) (gd) 2000 AW 0-5: (6f, 7f 2, 9f 2) (Equi, Fibr 4)

Workmanlike, very moderate colt, effective 7f, acts on frm - acts on Fibr, prefers left handed tracks, prefers tight tracks. AW high 35.

**D J S Cosgrove [0-6] Colin Davey (from N P Littmoden [0-2] Apr 2000).*

POLAR LADY **RR 66f** 5105[15]

3 ch f Polar Falcon (USA) 9f **(74)** - Soluce (Junius (USA)) 7.7f **(65)**

Form - 3504280

Record	**2000 -**	1st:0	2nd:1	3rd:1	Ran:7
	Pre2000 -	1st:0	2nd:0	3rd:0	Ran:1

Win Prizemoney £0 *Total Prizemoney* £2,133

2000 Turf 0-7: (5f 3, 6f 3, 7f) (g-s, gd 2, g-f 2, frm, hrd)

Scopey, average filly, has worn blinkers. Turf high 66. Inconsistent.

**D Morris [0-4] Colin Davey (from J R Fanshawe [0-4] Jun 2000).*

POLAR MIST BHB 52f57a **RR 55f 57a** 5112[9]

5 b g Polar Falcon (USA) 9f **(74)** - Post Mistress (IRE) **(71f)** (Cyrano de Bergerac) 6f **(68)**

Form - 000186020606030

Record	**2000 -**	1st:1	2nd:1	3rd:1	Ran:15
	Pre2000 -	1st:5	2nd:8	3rd:3	Ran:34

Win Prizemoney £17,647 *Total Prizemoney* £26,512

Wins	*** 2000**	May	Goodwo	(SFT)	H	5f	52	55	
	1999	*Jun*	*Wolver*	*(STD)*	*H*	*5f*	*59*	*61*	
	1999	Apr	Folkes	(HVY)		5f		70	
	1999	*Mar*	*Wolver*	*(STD)*	*S*	*5f*		*56*	
	1999	*Jan*	*Wolver*	*(STD)*	*C*	*6f*		*64*	
	1998	*Jan*	*Wolver*	*(STD)*		*6f*		*73*	<

2000 Turf 1-11: (5f 1 10, 6f) (hvy, g-s 1-1, gd 2, g-f 4, hrd 3) 2000 AW 0-4: (5f, 6f 3) (Fibr 4)

Fair gelding, effective 5 to 6f, best at 5f, acts on g-s to gd - acts on Fibr, has worn blinkers (extremely effectively), and does well at Southwell. Turf high 55. AW high 52. Consistent. He is an effective sort in Fibresand sprint handicaps, though he can win on soft ground on turf. He stays six furlongs, but is probably best over a stiff five. At his best when able to dominate.

**M Wigham [1-12] Stephen Roots (from Mrs N Macauley [4-32] May 2000).*

POLAR PROSPECT BHB 60f **RR 60f** 5069[3]

7 b g Polar Falcon (USA) 9f **(74)** - Littlemisstrouble (USA) (My Gallant (USA)) 9f **(71)**

Form - 3

Record	**2000 -**	1st:0	2nd:0	3rd:1	Ran:1
	Pre2000 -	1st:2	2nd:2	3rd:2	Ran:16

Win Prizemoney £6,881 *Total Prizemoney* £14,968

Wins	1997	Oct	Redcar	(G-F)	H	9f	56	60	
	1996	Jun	Beverl	(G-F)		7.5f		66	<

2000 Turf 0-1: (12f) (g-s)

Average gelding. (1st run) - 3rd of 20 to Lady Two K (19 Oct Bath 12f g-s RF 5069). Consistent.

**P J Hobbs [4-21] & Mrs Don Last and Bill Yates (from B Hanbury [2-15] Oct 1997).*

POLAR RED BHB 105f **RR 108+f** 5225[10]

3 ch g Polar Falcon (USA) 9f **(74)** Sharp Top (Sharpo) 7.7f **(59)**

Form - 312431110

Record	**2000 -**	1st:4	2nd:1	3rd:2	Ran:9
	Pre2000 -	1st:1	2nd:1	3rd:1	Ran:8

Win Prizemoney £32,963 *Total Prizemoney* £40,222

Wins	*** 2000**	Spt	Haydoc	(HVY)	H	10.5f	100	108	<
	*** 2000**	Aug	Haydoc	(G-S)	H	10.5f	91	102	
	*** 2000**	Jly	Kempto	(G-F)	H	10f	85	95	
	*** 2000**	May	Haydoc	(G-S)	H	10.5f	75	85	
	* 1999	Oct	Windso	(G-S)	H	8.3f	66.	73	

2000 Turf 4-9: (9f, 10f 1-4, 11f 3-3, 12f) (sft 1-1, g-s 1-2, gd 1-3, g-f, frm 1-2)

Workmanlike, Pattern-class gelding, effective 11f, acts on sft to gd, has worn blinkers, prefers tight tracks. Turf high 108 - 1st of 9 from Vintage Premium (2 Spt Haydock RF 4155) - also 1st of 7 giving 16lb to Capriccio (10 Aug Haydock RF 3534). Looked a rapidly-improving sort when completing a hat-trick at Haydock in September but was well beaten in a listed race on his final run.

**M J Ryan [5-17] Mrs H J Clarke.*

POLAR ROCK **RR 74f** 5138[7]

2 ch f Polar Falcon (USA) 9f **(74)** - South Rock **(97f)** (Rock City)

Form - 07

Record	**2000 -**	1st:0	2nd:0	3rd:0	Ran:2

2000 Turf 0-2: (7f, 8f) (g-s, g-f)

Currently above-average filly. Turf high 74 (began Spt).

**M L W Bell [0-2] B H Farr.*

POLAR STAR **RR 79f** 5135[7]

3 b c Polar Falcon (USA) 9f **(74)** - Glowing With Pride (Ile de Bourbon (USA)) 10.1f **(67)**

Form - 04577

Record	**2000 -**	1st:0	2nd:0	3rd:0	Ran:5
	Pre2000 -	1st:0	2nd:1	3rd:0	Ran:2

Win Prizemoney £0 *Total Prizemoney* £1,668

2000 Turf 0-5: (8f, 10f 3, 12f) (sft, g-s, g-f 2, frm)

Scopey, above-average colt, effective 6f, acts on g-s. Turf high 79.

**C F Wall [0-7] A E Oppenheimer.*

POLES APART (IRE) BHB 71f **RR 77f** 3688[12]

4 b g Distinctly North (USA) 7.4f **(63)** - Slightly Latin (Ahonoora) 8.1f **(73)**

Form - 00005400

Record	**2000 -**	1st:0	2nd:0	3rd:0	Ran:8
	Pre2000 -	1st:2	2nd:0	3rd:1	Ran:12

Win Prizemoney £7,223 *Total Prizemoney* £17,319

Wins	* 1999	Jly	Doncas	(G-F)	H	6f	83	86	<
	* 1998	Aug	Folkes	(G-F)		6f		84+	

2000 Turf 0-8: (5f, 6f 6, 7f) (gd 3, g-f 4, frm)

Scopey, above-average gelding, effective 6f, acts on g-f to frm, has worn blinkers. Turf high 77.

**M H Tompkins [2-20] Flint Fairyhouse Partnership.*

POLE STAR RR 91f
5312[2]

2 b br c Polar Falcon (USA) 9f **(74)** - Ellie Ardensky **(99f)** (Slip Anchor) 9.8f **(73)**
Form - 32
Record 2000 - 1st:0 2nd:1 3rd:1 Ran:2
Win Prizemoney £0 *Total Prizemoney* £1,680
2000 Turf 0-2: (7f, 8f) (g-s, frm)
Currently useful colt. Turf high 91 (began Aug) - 2nd of 22 giving 5lb to Golden Sparrow (3 Nov Doncaster 8f g-s RF 5312).
**J R Fanshawe [0-2] D I Russell.*

POLICASTRO RR 62f
4300[8]

2 b c Anabaa (USA) - Belle Arrivee (Bustino) 10.4f **(64)**
Form - 8
Record 2000 - 1st:0 2nd:0 3rd:0 Ran:1
2000 Turf 0-1: (6f) (gd)
Currently average colt. **J W Hills [0-1] Roger Paul.*

POLI KNIGHT BHB 60f RR 76f
5135[11]

3 b f Polish Precedent (USA) 9f **(73)** - River Spey (Mill Reef (USA)) 10.5f **(78)**
Form - 55360
Record 2000 - 1st:0 2nd:0 3rd:1 Ran:5
Win Prizemoney £0 *Total Prizemoney* £633
2000 Turf 0-5: (10f 5) (sft, g-s, gd, frm 2)
Light-framed, above-average filly. Turf high 76.
**J W Hills [0-5] Derek D & Mrs Jean P Clee.*

POLISHED UP BHB 46f RR 46f
3911[12]

3 b f Polish Precedent (USA) 9f **(73)** - Smarten Up (Sharpen Up) 8.3f **(67)**
Form - 6030
Record 2000 - 1st:0 2nd:0 3rd:1 Ran:4
Pre2000 - 1st:0 2nd:0 3rd:0 Ran:1
Win Prizemoney £0 *Total Prizemoney* £481
2000 Turf 0-4: (6f 2, 10f 2) (frm 4)
Workmanlike, moderate filly. Turf high 46 - 3rd of 11 getting 17lb from Diva (7 Jly Beverley 10f frm RF 2591).
**R M Beckett [0-4] Major & Mrs Kennard and Partners (from P T Walwyn [0-1] Spt 1999).*

POLISH FLAME RR 66f
5219[3]

2 b c Blushing Flame (USA) - Lady Emm (Emarati (USA))
Form - 3
Record 2000 - 1st:0 2nd:0 3rd:1 Ran:1
Win Prizemoney £0 *Total Prizemoney* £442
2000 Turf 0-1: (10f) (sft)
Currently average colt. **P W Harris [0-1] Skeltools Ltd.*

POLISH GIRL BHB 42f RR 31df
1803[20]

4 b f Polish Precedent (USA) 9f **(73)** - Stack Rock **(105df)** (Ballad Rock) 7.8f **(63)**
Form - 000
Record 2000 - 1st:0 2nd:0 3rd:0 Ran:3
Pre2000 - 1st:0 2nd:0 3rd:0 Ran:1
2000 Turf 0-3: (7f, 10f 2) (sft, gd 2)
Scopey, very moderate filly. Turf high 19.
**B J Meehan [0-4] F C T Wilson.*

POLISH OFF BHB 88f RR 93f
5100[3]

2 b c Polish Precedent (USA) 9f **(73)** - Lovely Lyca **(72f)** (Night Shift (USA)) 7.2f **(69)**
Form - 443
Record 2000 - 1st:0 2nd:0 3rd:1 Ran:3
Win Prizemoney £0 *Total Prizemoney* £1,983
2000 Turf 0-3: (6f, 7f 2) (gd, frm 2)
Currently useful colt. Turf high 93 (began Aug) - 4th of 18 to Sixty Seconds (5 Spt Leicester 7f frm RF 4218). He showed ability on all his starts but appears to lack a turn-of-foot. Softer ground may held, while he should stay beyond a mile.
**B W Hills [0-3] A L R Morton.*

POLISH PADDY (IRE) BHB 65f RR 68f
5237[1]

2 b c Priolo (USA) 10.9f **(71)** - Polish Widow **(70f)** (Polish Precedent (USA)) 10.2f **(60)**
Form - 066446001
Record 2000 - 1st:1 2nd:0 3rd:0 Ran:9
Win Prizemoney £3,575 *Total Prizemoney* £4,272
Wins * 2000 Oct Newmar (SFT) S 8f 68 <
2000 Turf 1-9: (5f, 7f 4, 8f 1-3, 10f) (g-s 1-2, gd 2, g-f 3, frm 2)
Average colt, effective 8f, acts on g-s to frm, has worn blinkers. Turf high 68 - 1st of 16 getting 3lb from Look First (28 Oct Newmarket RF 5237). **R Hannon [1-9] Denis Barry.*

POLISH PANACHE (USA) RR 92f
4528a[13]

3 br g Gone West (USA) 7.8f **(82)** - Polish Style (USA) (Danzig (USA)) 8.4f **(76)**
Form - 220
2000 Turf 0-3: (8f, 9f, 10f) (g-f, frm)
Useful gelding, effective 7f, acts on gd to g-f, has worn blinkers. Turf high 92 (began Jly). Third behind Giant's Causeway in a Group 3 during 1999, he has not progressed and struggles in Listed company.
**J Oxx in IRE [1-8] Sheikh Mohammed.*

POLISH PILOT (IRE) BHB 32f67a RR 32f 67a
1373[6]

5 b g Polish Patriot (USA) 7.8f **(70)** -Va Toujours(Alzao (USA)) 7.1f **(68)**
Form - 86
Record 2000 - 1st:0 2nd:0 3rd:0 Ran:2
Pre2000 - 1st:0 2nd:0 3rd:1 Ran:14
Win Prizemoney £0 *Total Prizemoney* £429
2000 AW 0-2: (11f 2) (Fibr 2)
Very moderate gelding, has worn blinkers. AW high 35.
**W R Muir [1-25] Mrs Barbara Jean Martin.*

POLISH SPIRIT BHB 84f RR 87f
4302[5]

5 b g Emarati (USA) 6.6f **(63)** - Gentle Star (Comedy Star (USA)) 7.5f **(50)**
Form - 11117306815
Record 2000 - 1st:5 2nd:0 3rd:1 Ran:11
Pre2000 - 1st:2 2nd:1 3rd:4 Ran:19
Win Prizemoney £41,114 *Total Prizemoney* £51,143

Wins								
* 2000	Aug	Sandow	(GD)	H	10f	80	87	<
* 2000	May	Ascot	(G-S)	H	8f	68	84	
* 2000	Apr	Sandow	(HVY)	H	8.1f	68	82+	
* 2000	Apr	Pontef	(HVY)		8f		70	
* 2000	Apr	Windso	(GD)	H	8.3f	59	65	
* 1999	Aug	Windso	(HVY)	H	8.3f	58	62	
* 1998	Jly	Warwic	(G-F)		7f		69	

2000 Turf 5-11: (8f 4-7, 9f, 10f 1-3) (sft 2-2, g-s, gd 1-3, g-f 1-3, frm 1-2)
Useful gelding, effective 8 to 10f, best at 10f, acts on sft to frm, best on gd, likes right handed tracks, likes tight tracks, excels at Windsor and does well at Ascot and Sandown. Turf high 87 - 1st of 10 getting 10lb from Ulundi (19 Aug Sandown RF 3803) - also 1st of 30 giving 3lb to Roller (3 May Ascot RF 1004). Consistent. He was in fine form earlier on this season, rattling-up a fine four-timer over a mile before appearing to fall into the Handicapper's grip. Returned to winning ways over ten furlongs at Sandown in August. Suited by cut in the ground.
**B R Millman [7-30] Mrs Izabel Palmer.*

POLIZIANO (USA) BHB 50f72a RR 37f 72a
4327[18]

4 ch g Storm Bird (CAN) 8.5f **(82)** - Polemic (USA) (Roberto (USA)) 10f **(76)**
Form - 6000
Record 2000 - 1st:0 2nd:0 3rd:0 Ran:4
Pre2000 - 1st:0 2nd:1 3rd:2 Ran:3
Win Prizemoney £0 *Total Prizemoney* £2,408
2000 Turf 0-3: (7f, 9f, 11f) (g-f 2, frm) 2000 AW 0-1: (8f) (Fibr)
Scopey, moderate gelding. Turf high 37 (began Aug).
**W W Haigh [0-4] B Williamson (from H R A Cecil [0-3] Aug 1999).*

POLLSTER (IRE) RR 70f
2754[5]

3 b br c Polish Precedent (USA) 9f **(73)** - Trojan Miss (Troy) 10.4f **(68)**
Form - 0045
Record 2000 - 1st:0 2nd:0 3rd:0 Ran:4
Win Prizemoney £0 *Total Prizemoney* £300
2000 Turf 0-4: (8f, 10f, 12f 2) (gd, g-f 2, frm)
Workmanlike, above-average colt, has worn blinkers. Turf high 79.
**Sir Michael Stoute [0-4] Lord Weinstock.*

POLLY GOLIGHTLY BHB 69f50a RR 71f 50a
5313[4]

7 ch m Weldnaas (USA) 8.4f **(55)** - Polly's Teahouse (Shack (USA)) 5.8f **(53)**
Form - 0022064800043811004
Record 2000 - 1st:2 2nd:2 3rd:1 Ran:19
Pre2000 - 1st:8 2nd:4 3rd:7 Ran:74
Win Prizemoney £49,292 *Total Prizemoney* £71,498

Wins								
* 2000	Spt	Haydoc	(HVY)	H	5f	61	71	
* 2000	Spt	Cheste	(SFT)	H	5.1f	61	67	
* 1999	Aug	Cheste	(G-S)	H	5.1f	63	68	
* 1998	Jun	York	(G-S)	H	5f	56	73	
* 1998	Jun	Cheste	(GD)	H	5.1f	56	76?	
* 1997	Oct	Catter	(SFT)	H	5f	54	60	
* 1997	Jun	Goodwo	(G-F)	H	5f	59	64	
* 1997	May	Lingfi	(G-F)	H	5f	54	57	

2000 Turf 2-19: (5f 2-19) (hvy, g-s 1-6, gd 1-9, g-f 3)
Above-average mare, effective 5f, acts on g-s to g-f, best on gd, mostly wears blinkers, likes tight tracks, likes Chester. Turf high 71 - 1st of 17 getting 12lb from Abbajabba (23 Spt Haydock RF 4605) - also 1st of 11 getting 17lb from Bodfari Pride (20 Spt Chester RF 4537). A speedy mare who runs from the front, she ended a long losing run at Chester in September, and followed up at Haydock. She is at her best when racing on easy ground.
**M Blanshard [8-84] David Sykes (from B Smart [2-9] Nov 1995).*

POLLY MILLS BHB 58f62a RR 61f 62a 312^{9}

4 b f Lugana Beach 7f **(63)** - Danseuse Davis (FR) **(46f 42a)** (Glow (USA)) 6.7f **(71)**
Form - 827036570
Record 2000 - 1st:0 2nd:0 3rd:1 Ran:6
Pre2000 - 1st:3 2nd:6 3rd:5 Ran:42
Win Prizemoney £8,848 *Total Prizemoney* £18,661

Wins								
* 1999	*Mar*	*Southw*	*(STD)*	*H*	*6f*	*79*	*83*	<
* 1998	*Nov*	*Southw*	*(STD)*	*H*	*5f*	*72*	*78*	
* 1998	Jun	Windso	(SFT)	S	5f		66	

2000 AW 0-6: (5f, 6f 4, 7f) (Equi 3, Fibr 3)
Light-framed, average filly, effective 6 to 7f, best at 6f, - acts on AW, best on Equi, mostly wears blinkers, likes left handed tracks, likes tight tracks. AW high 57. Consistent.
**P D Evans [3-48] The Dave Evans Racing Club.*

POLLYOLLY (IRE) BHB 39f35a RR 50f 35a 30^{7}

3 b f Emarati (USA) 6.6f **(63)** - Eurolink Virago (Charmer)
Form - 77
Record 2000 - 1st:0 2nd:0 3rd:0 Ran:1
Pre2000 - 1st:0 2nd:0 3rd:0 Ran:5
2000 AW 0-1: (5f) (Equi)
Workmanlike, fair filly.
**M J Haynes [0-6] M J Haynes.*

POLMARA (IRE) RR 68f 800^{19}

3 b f Polish Precedent (USA) 9f **(73)** - Broadmara (IRE) (Thatching) 8f **(66)**
Form - 0
Record 2000 - 1st:0 2nd:0 3rd:0 Ran:1
2000 Turf 0-1: (8f) (gd)
Leggy, currently average filly.
**B W Hills [0-1] Burton Agnes Bloodstock.*

POLONAISE RR 66f 4820^{9}

2 b f Pivotal - Vallauris (Faustus (USA)) 10f **(58)**
Form - 40
Record 2000 - 1st:0 2nd:0 3rd:0 Ran:2
Win Prizemoney £0 *Total Prizemoney* £223
2000 Turf 0-2: (6f 2) (gd, g-f)
Currently average filly. Turf high 66 (began Spt).
**I A Balding [0-2] Mrs Duncan Allen.*

POLO VENTURE BHB 51f68a RR 54f 68a 1533^{6}

5 ch g Polar Falcon (USA) 9f **(74)** - Ceramic (USA) (Raja Baba (USA)) 10f **(64)**
Form - 86
Record 2000 - 1st:0 2nd:0 3rd:0 Ran:2
Pre2000 - 1st:1 2nd:1 3rd:4 Ran:13
Win Prizemoney £2,898 *Total Prizemoney* £5,983

Wins								
1998	*May*	*Lingfi*	*(STD)*		*10f*		*69*	<

2000 Turf 0-2: (13f, 14f) (gd, g-f)
Above-average gelding. Turf high 54. (DEAD)
**M D Hammond [1-17] Mrs Eve Sweetman (from S P C Woods [1-12] Aug 1998).*

POLRUAN BHB 50f RR 56f 4824^{12}

4 ch g Elmaamul (USA) 8.1f **(70)** - Trelissick (Electric) 10.1f **(61)**
Form - 5640
Record 2000 - 1st:0 2nd:0 3rd:0 Ran:4
Pre2000 - 1st:1 2nd:2 3rd:0 Ran:14
Win Prizemoney £3,030 *Total Prizemoney* £6,133

Wins								
1998	Oct	Warwic	(GD)		6f		74+	<

2000 Turf 0-4: (8f 2, 10f, 11f) (hvy, g-f 2, frm)
Leggy, fair gelding. Turf high 56. He had shown some promise before landing a Warwick maiden last October, but has found life tough in handicaps since.
**S G Knight [0-4] Michael WingfieldDigby (from Lady Herries [0-7] Oct 1999).*

POLWHELE BHB 43f RR 45f 3608^{14}

2 ch g Mujtahid (USA) 7.4f **(69)** - Safayn (USA) (Lyphard (USA)) 9.9f **(72)**
Form - 080
Record 2000 - 1st:0 2nd:0 3rd:0 Ran:3
2000 Turf 0-3: (7f 3) (gd, g-f, frm)
Currently moderate gelding. Turf high 45 (began Jly).
**R M H Cowell [0-3] & Mrs D A Gamble.*

POLYPHONIC BHB 51f RR 58f 5102^{18}

2 b f Binary Star (USA) - Plainsong **(51df)** (Ballad Rock) 7.8f **(63)**
Form - 065000
Record 2000 - 1st:0 2nd:0 3rd:0 Ran:6
2000 Turf 0-6: (5f 2, 6f 4) (gd 3, g-f 3)
Fair filly. Turf high 58. **G Woodward [0-6] Mrs Helen Godfrey.*

POMFRET LAD BHB 100f RR 107f 4699^{5}

2 b c Cyrano de Bergerac 7.3f **(58)** - Lucky Flinders (Free State) 8.7f **(61)**
Form - 8125
Record 2000 - 1st:1 2nd:1 3rd:0 Ran:4
Win Prizemoney £4,446 *Total Prizemoney* £19,796

Wins								
* 2000	Aug	Kempto	(G-F)		6f		101+	<

2000 Turf 1-4: (6f 1-4) (gd, g-f 2, frm 1-1)
Pattern-class colt. Turf high 107 (began Jly) - also 1st of 13 giving 5lb to Sister Celestine (14 Aug Kempton RF 3020). A disappointment on his debut, he bolted up by nine lengths at Kempton next time and was just beaten in the Group Two Mill Reef Stakes. Not at all disgraced when fifth in the Middle Park Stakes on his last run, he is tough and genuine.
**P J Makin [1-4] Mrs Pauline Smith & Four Seasons Racing.*

POMPEII (IRE) BHB 80f77a RR 81f 77a 4761^{8}

3 b g Salse (USA) 10.9f **(71)** - Before Dawn (USA) (Raise A Cup (USA)) 7.6f **(74)**
Form - 211608
Record 2000 - 1st:2 2nd:1 3rd:0 Ran:6
Pre2000 - 1st:0 2nd:1 3rd:0 Ran:3
Win Prizemoney £7,974 *Total Prizemoney* £10,714

Wins								
* 2000	May	Warwic	(SFT)	H	12.3f	80	81	<
* 2000	Apr	Leices	(G-S)		11.8f		81+	

2000 Turf 2-5: (10f, 12f 2-3, 14f) (sft 1-1, gd 1-1, g-f 2, frm) 2000 AW 0-1: (12f) (Fibr)
Scopey, decent gelding, effective 8 to 12f, acts on sft to frm. Turf high 82 (1st run) - 2nd of 17 giving 8lb to Kaiapoi (23 Mar Doncaster 10f frm RF 0474) - also 1st of 9 getting 15lb from Seliana (6 Apr Leicester RF 0627). Inconsistent. A progressive sort, he showed the right attitude to land a Warwick handicap when stepped up to 12 furlongs having won his maiden on easy ground the previous month. Subsequent runs suggest he does not want the ground too fast.
**P F I Cole [2-8] Highclere Thoroughbred Racing Ltd (from P W Chapple-Hyam [0-1] Spt 1999).*

PONTIKONISI BHB 36f47a RR 55f 47a 3330^{13}

3 b g Mistertopogigo (IRE) - Anse Chastanet (Cavo Doro) 10.6f **(57)**
Form - 54585000
Record 2000 - 1st:0 2nd:0 3rd:0 Ran:5
Pre2000 - 1st:0 2nd:0 3rd:0 Ran:7
2000 Turf 0-4: (7f, 8f 3) (g-f 4) 2000 AW 0-1: (7f) (Fibr)
Unfurnished, fair gelding, effective 7f, acts on g-f, often wears

blinkers. Turf high 55 (1st run) - 5th of 20 giving 5lb to Bint Habibi (16 Jun Chepstow 7f g-f RF 2012). Becoming disappointing.
**K McAuliffe [0-12] Delamere Cottage Racing Partners (1996).*

POPPADAM BHB 77f **RR 80f** 2120[1]
3 ch f Salse (USA) 10.9f **(71)** - Wanton (Kris) 9.5f **(73)**
Form - 6521
Record 2000 - 1st:1 2nd:1 3rd:0 Ran:4
Pre2000 - 1st:0 2nd:0 3rd:0 Ran:1
Win Prizemoney £6,500 *Total Prizemoney* £7,725
Wins * 2000 Jun Thirsk (FRM) H 8f 73 79 <
2000 Turf 1-4: (8f 1-4) (gd, g-f 2, frm 1-1)
Decent filly. Turf high 80 - 2nd of 12 giving 6lb to Midnight Allure (12 Jun Nottingham 8f gd RF 1895) - also 1st of 8 giving 14lb to Falls O'Moness (20 Jun Thirsk RF 2120).
**J R Fanshawe [1-4] Lady Halifax (from L M Cumani [0-1] Oct 1999).*

POPPAEA (IRE) RR 63f 3436[4]
2 b f Definite Article - Classic Ring (IRE) (Auction Ring (USA)) 8.6f **(65)**
Form - 4
Record 2000 - 1st:0 2nd:0 3rd:0 Ran:1
Win Prizemoney £0 *Total Prizemoney* £296
2000 Turf 0-1: (6f) (g-f)
Currently average filly. **R Hannon [0-1] Thurloe Thoroughbreds V.*

POPPY'S CHOICE RR 36f 2406[12]
2 b f Bin Ajwaad (IRE) - Truthful Image **(68df 70a)** (Reesh)
Form - 0600
Record 2000 - 1st:0 2nd:0 3rd:0 Ran:4
2000 Turf 0-4: (5f 3, 6f) (gd 3, g-f)
Very moderate filly. Turf high 36. **M W Easterby [0-4] E J Mangan.*

POPPY'S SONG BHB 68f **RR 73f** 5199[17]
3 b f Owington - Pretty Poppy (Song) 7.2f **(61)**
Form - 77214000
Record 2000 - 1st:1 2nd:1 3rd:0 Ran:8
Pre2000 - 1st:1 2nd:0 3rd:2 Ran:5
Win Prizemoney £7,358 *Total Prizemoney* £10,767
Wins * 2000 Jly Nottin (G-F) H 5.1f 71 73 <
* 1999 Oct Catter (SFT) 5f 61
2000 Turf 1-8: (5f 1-8) (gd 2, g-f 5, frm 1-1)
Scopey, above-average filly, effective 5f, acts on g-f to frm, best on g-f. Turf high 73 - 1st of 7 getting 8lb from Sharoura (15 Jly Nottingham RF 2842). She has ability but looks a pretty awkward ride. **H Candy [2-13] Thomas Frost & Partners.*

POP SHOP BHB 58f **RR 66f** 4396[9]
3 b c Owington - Diamond Park (IRE) **(60f)** (Alzao (USA)) 7.1f **(68)**
Form - 0077707750
Record 2000 - 1st:0 2nd:0 3rd:0 Ran:10
Pre2000 - 1st:1 2nd:1 3rd:0 Ran:6
Win Prizemoney £3,150 *Total Prizemoney* £4,254
Wins * 1999 Jun Nottin (GD) 5.1f 68 <
2000 Turf 0-10: (5f 2, 6f 5, 7f 3) (g-s, gd, g-f 3, frm 5)
Scopey, average colt, effective 5f, acts on g-f to frm, best on g-f, has worn blinkers. Turf high 66. Consistent.
**J W Payne [1-16] Sir Simon Lycett Green.*

POP THE CORK RR 64f 4299[22]
3 ch g Clantime 6.6f **(57)** - Hyde Princess (Touch Paper) 6.8f **(57)**
Form - 088370170
Record 2000 - 1st:1 2nd:0 3rd:1 Ran:8
Pre2000 - 1st:0 2nd:0 3rd:0 Ran:1
Win Prizemoney £2,938 *Total Prizemoney* £3,582
Wins * 2000 Jun Mussel (FRM) H 5f 60 64 <
2000 Turf 1-6: (5f 1-6) (gd 2, g-f, frm 1-2, hrd) 2000 AW 0-2: (5f, 6f) (Fibr 2)
Strong, average gelding, has broken blood-vessels, effective 5f, acts on frm. Turf high 64 - also 1st of 15 giving 3lb to Marshall St Cyr (19 Jun Musselburgh RF 2093). AW high 39. Inconsistent.
**R M Whitaker [1-9] Country Lane Partnership.*

PORAK (IRE) BHB 60f **RR 56f** 4813[7]
3 ch g Perugino (USA) - Gayla Orchestra (Lord Gayle (USA)) 8.8f **(62)**
Form - 687
Record 2000 - 1st:0 2nd:0 3rd:0 Ran:3
2000 Turf 0-3: (8f 3) (g-s, gd, g-f)
Unfurnished, currently fair gelding. Turf high 59.
**H Akbary [0-3] Egerton Stud Farm Ltd.*

PORTHILLY BUOY BHB 33f30a **RR 21f 30a** 400[10]
5 ch g Keen 11.1f **(58)** - Hissma (Midyan (USA)) 6f **(60)**
Form - 0
Record 2000 - 1st:0 2nd:0 3rd:0 Ran:1
Pre2000 - 1st:0 2nd:0 3rd:0 Ran:7
2000 AW 0-1: (10f) (Equi)
Very moderate gelding. **M J Haynes [0-9] Porthilly Partners.*

PORTIA LADY BHB 44f **RR 48f** 2596[8]
3 b f Noble Patriarch 12.2f **(43)** - Gymcrak Lovebird (Taufan (USA)) 7f **(57)**
Form - 0058
Record 2000 - 1st:0 2nd:0 3rd:0 Ran:4
Pre2000 - 1st:0 2nd:1 3rd:0 Ran:7
Win Prizemoney £0 *Total Prizemoney* £735
2000 Turf 0-4: (8f, 10f, 12f 2) (sft, gd, g-f, hrd)
Neat, moderate filly, effective 7 to 12f, best at 7f, acts on gd to hrd, often wears blinkers (extremely effectively), favours tight tracks. Turf high 48 - 5th of 9 getting 30lb from El Zito (14 Jun Beverley 12f hrd RF 1950). **T D Easterby [0-11] Mrs Sue Tindall.*

PORTITE SOPHIE BHB 35f29a **RR 46f 29a** 438[11]
9 b m Doulab (USA) 7.4f **(61)** - Impropriety (Law Society (USA)) 9.9f **(70)**
Form - 0
Record 2000 - 1st:0 2nd:0 3rd:0 Ran:1
Pre2000 - 1st:3 2nd:11 3rd:9 Ran:79
Win Prizemoney £7,018 *Total Prizemoney* £19,383
Wins * 1998 Spt Hamilt (SFT) S 9.2f 41
* 1997 *Jly Southw (STD) C 11f 45* <
* 1996 *Jly Wolver (STD) H 8.5f 29 32*
2000 AW 0-1: (14f) (Fibr)
Moderate mare, effective 10 to 12f, acts on gd to g-f, best on gd, has worn blinkers. **M Brittain [3-80] Ms Maureen Hanlon.*

PORT MORESBY (IRE) BHB 74f67a **RR 77f 67a** 5027[1]
2 b c Tagula (IRE) - Santana Lady (IRE) **(64df 60a)** (Blakeney) 10.5f **(64)**
Form - 0718001
Record 2000 - 1st:2 2nd:0 3rd:0 Ran:7
Win Prizemoney £6,189 *Total Prizemoney* £6,189
Wins * 2000 Oct Yarmou (SFT) H 8f 70 77 <
*** 2000** Aug Beverl (GD) 7.5f 75
2000 Turf 2-7: (6f 2, 7f 1-4, 8f 1-1) (g-s 1-1, gd 1-3, g-f, frm 2)
Above-average colt, effective 7 to 8f, acts on g-s to gd. Turf high 77 (began Jly) - 1st of 12 from Reviewer (17 Oct Yarmouth RF 5027) - also 1st of 9 from Investment Force (1 Aug Beverley RF 3274). **N A Callaghan [2-7] Martin Moore.*

PORT OF CALL (IRE) BHB 41f41a **RR 39f 41a** 1096[16]
5 ch g Arazi (USA) 9.2f **(74)** - Port Helene (Troy) 10.4f **(68)**
Form - 567000
Record 2000 - 1st:0 2nd:0 3rd:0 Ran:6
2000 Turf 0-3: (8f. 10f, 11f) (g-s, gd 2) 2000 AW 0-3: (6f 2, 8f) (Fibr 3)
Moderate gelding. Turf high 39. AW high 42.
**R F Marvin [0-8] J Shine.*

PORTRACK JUNCTION (IRE) BHB 29f50a **RR 36f 50a** 4455[5]
3 b g Common Grounds 8.1f **(66)** - Boldabsa (Persian Bold) 9.3f **(66)**
Form - 7000880505
Record 2000 - 1st:0 2nd:0 3rd:0 Ran:10
Pre2000 - 1st:0 2nd:0 3rd:0 Ran:4
2000 Turf 0-9: (7f, 8f, 10f 2, 12f 2, 14f, 16f, 17f) (g-s, gd, g-f, frm 5, hrd)
2000 AW 0-1: (7f) (Fibr)
Scopey, very moderate gelding, has worn blinkers. Turf high 38.
**A B Mulholland [0-8] Miss K Watson (from N Tinkler [0-6] Mar 2000).*

PORT ST CHARLES (IRE) BHB 72f **RR 78f** 3594[6]
3 b br c Night Shift (USA) 8.1f **(73)** - Safe Haven (Blakeney) 10.5f **(64)**
Form - 24506
Record 2000 - 1st:0 2nd:1 3rd:0 Ran:5
Pre2000 - 1st:0 2nd:0 3rd:2 Ran:2
Win Prizemoney £0 *Total Prizemoney* £2,859

2000 Turf 0-5: (6f 4, 7f) (gd 2, frm 3)

Strong, above-average colt, effective 5 to 6f, best at 6f, acts on gd to frm, best on gd. Turf high 81 - 4th of 19 getting 9lb from Strahan (20 Apr Newmarket 6f gd RF 0804). Showed ability in both of his starts at two and ran well to finish-runner up on his Kempton reappearance with the rest well beaten. In the frame since, there should be a race for him. **N A Callaghan [0-7] Mrs Doreen Tabor.*

PORT VILA (FR) BHB 108f **RR 113f** 4436[5]

3 b c Barathea (IRE) - Girouette (USA) (Nodouble (USA)) 8.8f **(68)**

Form - 31355

Record 2000 - 1st:1 2nd:0 3rd:2 Ran:5
Pre2000 - 1st:2 2nd:0 3rd:0 Ran:3

Win Prizemoney £31,359 *Total Prizemoney* £48,380

Wins * 2000 Jun Ascot (G-F) L 10f 112 <
* 1999 Spt Kempto (G-F) 7f 92+
* 1999 Aug Newbur (GD) 7f 80+

2000 Turf 1-5: (10f 1-3, 11f, 12f) (gd 1-2, frm 3)

Scopey, Group-class colt, effective 10 to 11f, best at 10f, acts on gd to frm, best on frm, excels at Newbury. Turf high 113 - 3rd of 7 getting 17lb from Endless Hall (17 Jly Ayr 10f frm RF 2872) - also 1st of 8 from Rasm (24 Jun Ascot RF 2238). He overcame a troubled passage to win a Listed event at Ascot in June, but failed to progress (including when tried in a tongue strap). Possibly best over a mile and a quarter, he is one to watch at present. **J H M Gosden [3-8] Hamdan Al Maktoum.*

POSEIDON BHB 99f **RR 113f** 5215a[10]

6 b h Polar Falcon (USA) 9f **(74)** - Nastassia (FR) (Noble Decree (USA)) 10.2f **(76)**

Form - 51810

2000 Turf 2-4: (10f 1-2, 11f 1-1, 12f) (hvy 2-3, gd)

Group-class horse, effective 10 to 12f, acts on hvy to g-f, best on hvy. Turf high 113 (1st run) - 1st of 9 giving 3lb to Forest Buck (16 Apr San Siro RF 0819a). Useful when trained by Mick Channon up to 1998, he has developed into a smart middle-distance performer in Italy and goes well on heavy ground. **L Brogi in ITY [2-7] (from M R Channon [3-17] Aug 1998).*

POSITIVE AIR BHB 39f **RR 42f** 1718[17]

5 b m Puissance 7.1f **(60)** - Breezy Day (Day Is Done) 6.3f **(67)**

Form - 00

Record 2000 - 1st:0 2nd:0 3rd:0 Ran:1
Pre2000 - 1st:1 2nd:3 3rd:2 Ran:27

Win Prizemoney £7,304 *Total Prizemoney* £11,747

Wins 1998 Jun Pontef (GD) H 6f 75 78 <

2000 Turf 0-1: (6f) (gd)

Moderate filly, has worn blinkers. Becoming disappointing. **Mrs A M Naughton [0-2] Mrs C T Woodley (from B A McMahon [1-26] Spt 1999).*

POST BOX (USA) **RR 84f** 5312[5]

2 b c Quest for Fame 12.8f **(75)** - Crowning Ambition (USA) (Chief's Crown (USA)) 9.8f **(72)**

Form - 25

Record 2000 - 1st:0 2nd:1 3rd:0 Ran:2

Win Prizemoney £0 *Total Prizemoney* £714

2000 Turf 0-2: (8f 2) (g-s 2)

Currently decent colt. Turf high 84 (1st run) (began Oct) - 2nd of 15 to Prince Shaamaal (19 Oct Bath 8f g-s RF 5065). **R Charlton [0-2] K Abdulla.*

POTARO (IRE) BHB 100f **RR 98f** 5108[4]

2 b c Catrail (USA) - Bianca Cappello (IRE) **(27f 30a)** (Glenstal (USA)) 10.1f **(64)**

Form - 5353114

Record 2000 - 1st:2 2nd:0 3rd:2 Ran:7

Win Prizemoney £23,549 *Total Prizemoney* £26,706

Wins * 2000 Oct Saint- (G-S) G3 6.5f 90+ <
* 2000 Spt Warwic (G-F) 6.1f 78+

2000 Turf 2-7: (6f 1-2, 7f 1-5) (g-s 1-1, gd, g-f 1-4, frm)

Very useful colt, effective 7f, acts on g-s. Turf high 98 - also 1st of 7 from Inzar's Best (4 Oct Saint-cloud RF 4945a). Did not tackle anything other than fast ground on his first five starts, but handled a yielding surface and step up to Group Three company when successful at Saint-Cloud. **B J Meehan [2-7] Mrs Susan McCarthy.*

POTENTILLE (IRE) **RR 91f** 3647a[6]

3 b f Caerleon (USA) 10.9f **(79)** - Potri Pe (ARG) (Potrillazo (ARG))

Form - 1826

2000 Turf 1-4: (10f, 12f 1-3) (g-s, gd, g-f 1-2)

Useful filly, effective 7 to 12f, best at 7f, acts on g-s to g-f. Turf high 91 (1st run) - 1st of 2 getting 23lb from Catherina (9 May Navan RF 1232a). She had a simple task when winning her maiden and went on to run well for an inexperienced rider. **J Oxx in IRE [1-7] Sheikh Mohammed.*

POT LUCK BHB 65f **RR 70f** 2849[6]

3 b c Be My Guest (USA) 10.2f **(66)** - Cremets (Mummy's Pet) 7.7f **(60)**

Form - 356

Record 2000 - 1st:0 2nd:0 3rd:1 Ran:3

Win Prizemoney £0 *Total Prizemoney* £645

2000 Turf 0-3: (14f 3) (g-s, gd, g-f)

Workmanlike, currently above-average colt. Turf high 70. **H Morrison [0-3] Lord Margadale.*

POUNCE (IRE) BHB 68f **RR 66f** 4821[6]

2 ch f Grand Lodge (USA) - Mary Ellen Best (IRE) (Danehill (USA)) 10f **(72)**

Form - 4446

Record 2000 - 1st:0 2nd:0 3rd:0 Ran:4

Win Prizemoney £0 *Total Prizemoney* £4,615

2000 Turf 0-4: (6f 2, 7f 2) (g-s, gd, g-f 2)

Average filly. Turf high 66. **J A Osborne [0-4] Durkan Ltd.*

POUR NOUS BHB 45f **RR 37f** 4460[11]

2 gr g Petong 7.6f **(58)** - Pour Moi (Bay Express) 7.1f **(60)**

Form - 0700

Record 2000 - 1st:0 2nd:0 3rd:0 Ran:4

2000 Turf 0-4: (6f 2, 7f 2) (g-s, g-f, frm 2)

Very moderate gelding. Turf high 37 (began Jly). **J J Quinn [0-4] Mrs Karan Ridley.*

POWDER (IRE) BHB 41f **RR 35f** 4927[9]

2 gr f Idris (IRE) - Poetry (IRE) **(82df)** (Treasure Kay)

Form - 770

Record 2000 - 1st:0 2nd:0 3rd:0 Ran:3

2000 Turf 0-2: (5f, 6f) (gd, frm) 2000 AW 0-1: (5f) (Equi)

Currently very moderate filly. Turf high 35. **M H Tompkins [0-3] Prof Greer.*

POWDER RIVER BHB 64f67a **RR 61f 67a** 3053[9]

6 b h Alzao (USA) 9.8f **(73)** - Nest (Sharpo) 7.7f **(59)**

Form - 0

Record 2000 - 1st:0 2nd:0 3rd:0 Ran:1
Pre2000 - 1st:3 2nd:1 3rd:4 Ran:20

Win Prizemoney £14,505 *Total Prizemoney* £21,635

Wins * 1999 Aug Redcar (G-F) H 11f 57 58
1999 *Mar Lingfi (STD) H 10f 62 67*
1996 Jly Epsom (G-F) 6f 77 <

2000 Turf 0-1: (12f) (frm)

Average horse, effective 8 to 12f, best at 10f, acts on gd to frm - acts on Equi, has worn blinkers, prefers left handed tracks. **A G Newcombe [1-8] Alex Gorrie (from K R Burke [1-7] Jun 1999).*

POWER AND DEMAND BHB 39f49a **RR 31f 49a** 2299[18]

3 b g Formidable (USA) 7.8f **(60)** - Mazurkanova (Song) 7.2f **(61)**

Form - 472543700500

Record 2000 - 1st:0 2nd:1 3rd:1 Ran:11
Pre2000 - 1st:0 2nd:0 3rd:0 Ran:5

Win Prizemoney £0 *Total Prizemoney* £784

2000 Turf 0-4: (5f 3, 6f) (g-f 2, frm 2) 2000 AW 0-7: (5f 4, 6f 2, 7f) (Equi 4, Fibr 3)

Unfurnished, fair gelding, effective 5f, - acts on Equi, often wears blinkers (very effectively), likes left handed tracks, likes tight tracks. Turf high 31. AW high 56. Inconsistent. **D Shaw [0-16] J C Fretwell.*

POWER FLAME (GER) **RR 116f** 4285a[3]

7 ch g Dashing Blade 7.9f **(80)** -Pikante (GER)(Surumu (GER)) 10f **(83)**

Form - 13

2000 Turf 1-2: (8f 1-2) (hvy 1-1, sft)

High-class gelding. Turf high 113 (1st run) (began Jly) - 1st of 7 getting 5lb from Bernardon (30 Jly Cologne RF 3350a). Consistent.

He retains his form remarkably well and finished powerfully to win a Group 3 at Cologne in July. Campaigned around a mile, he does most of his racing on an easy surface.

**A Wohler in GER [6-9] Rennstall Darboven.*

POWER GAME BHB 26f49a RR 31f 49a 5190[7]

7 b g Puissance 7.1f **(60)** - Play the Game (Mummy's Game) 8.2f **(60)**

Form - 048007

Record 2000 - 1st:0 2nd:0 3rd:0 Ran:6
Pre2000 - 1st:6 2nd:3 3rd:9 Ran:47

Win Prizemoney £16,798 *Total Prizemoney* £25,967

Wins 1997 May Mussel (G-F) H 8f 51 59
1997 May Mussel (G-S) S 8f 54
1996 Oct Leices (GD) C 8f 66 <
1996 Spt Hamilt (GD) C 8.3f 64
1996 Spt Thirsk (G-F) S 8f 59
1996 Aug Haydoc (G-F) S 8.1f 58

2000 Turf 0-6: (6f, 7f 3, 8f, 9f) (gd 2, g-f 2, frm 2)

Very moderate gelding, often wears blinkers. Turf high 31.

**D A Nolan [0-18] Mrs J McFadyen-Murray (from J Berry [6-35] Jly 1997).*

POWER HIT (USA) BHB 48f RR 54f 1422[11]

4 b g Leo Castelli (USA) - Rajana (USA) (Rajab (USA))

Form - 00

Record 2000 - 1st:0 2nd:0 3rd:0 Ran:2
Pre2000 - 1st:0 2nd:1 3rd:1 Ran:8

Win Prizemoney £0 *Total Prizemoney* £1,810

2000 Turf 0-2: (12f 2) (gd, frm)

Fair gelding, effective 12f, acts on gd to frm, often wears blinkers (extremely effectively). Turf high 26. Inconsistent.

**B R Millman [0-10] Avalon Surfacing Ltd.*

POWERLINE BHB 64f RR 73f 5227[12]

3 b f Warning 8.1f **(77)** - Kantikoy (Alzao (USA)) 7.1f **(68)**

Form - 863450

Record 2000 - 1st:0 2nd:0 3rd:1 Ran:6
Pre2000 - 1st:0 2nd:0 3rd:0 Ran:2

Win Prizemoney £0 *Total Prizemoney* £1,137

2000 Turf 0-6: (7f, 8f, 10f 2, 12f 2) (sft, gd 4, frm)

Scopey, above-average filly, effective 10f, acts on gd. Turf high 79.

**R Hannon [0-8] R Hannon.*

POWER PACKED BHB 73f RR 88f 5141[9]

3 b c Puissance 7.1f **(60)** - My First Romance **(64f)** (Danehill (USA)) 10f **(72)**

Form - 56000

Record 2000 - 1st:0 2nd:0 3rd:0 Ran:5
Pre2000 - 1st:1 2nd:2 3rd:0 Ran:4

Win Prizemoney £5,810 *Total Prizemoney* £9,702

Wins * 1999 Aug Pontef (GD) 5f 80 <

2000 Turf 0-5: (5f 4, 6f) (g-s 4, gd)

Light-framed, useful colt, effective 5f, acts on gd to frm, has worn blinkers. Turf high 88. Becoming disappointing.

**M A Jarvis [1-9] Mrs Greta Sarfaty Marchant.*

POYLE PICKLE BHB 52f RR 36f 5318[13]

2 b f Piccolo - Hithermoor Lass (Red Alert) 7.6f **(66)**

Form - 00

Record 2000 - 1st:0 2nd:0 3rd:0 Ran:2

2000 Turf 0-2: (6f 2) (sft, gd)

Currently fair filly. Turf high 36 (began Spt).

**B Smart [0-2] Cecil Wiggins.*

POZARICA BHB 106f RR 108f 578a[6]

5 b h Rainbow Quest (USA) 11.2f **(81)** - Anna Matrushka (Mill Reef (USA)) 10.5f **(78)**

Form - 36

2000 Turf 0-2: (12f 2) (gd)

Pattern-class colt. Turf high 108.

**S bin Suroor in UAE [0-2] (from S bin Suroor [0-3] Spt 1999).*

PRAIRIE FALCON (IRE) BHB 83f RR 86f 5297[5]

6 b g Alzao (USA) 9.8f **(73)** - Sea Harrier (Grundy) 10.3f **(65)**

Form - 604F060408165

Record 2000 - 1st:1 2nd:0 3rd:0 Ran:13
Pre2000 - 1st:3 2nd:3 3rd:2 Ran:19

Win Prizemoney £17,762 *Total Prizemoney* £34,298

Wins * 2000 Spt Cheste (SFT) H 15.9f 78 85 <
* 1998 Spt Goodwo (G-F) H 12f 81 85 <
* 1998 Spt Haydoc (GD) H 10.5f 80 80
* 1997 May Chepst (GD) 12.1f 80

2000 Turf 1-13: (14f 3, 15f, 16f 1-5, 18f, 19f 2, 20f) (sft, g-s 1-3, gd 3, g-f 4, frm 2)

Useful gelding, effective 14 to 19f, best at 19f, acts on g-s to frm, best on g-f, prefers left handed tracks, excels at Chester and York. Turf high 86 - 4th of 6 getting 7lb from Fantasy Hill (6 Aug Chester 19f g-f RF 3414) - also 1st of 15 giving 23lb to Lastman (20 Spt Chester RF 4535). Consistent. He goes well at Chester, finishing fourth in the Chester Cup for the last two seasons, and scored there in September on ground softer than was thought to be ideal. Decent run in the Cesarewitch.

**B W Hills [4-32] Mrs B W Hills.*

PRAIRIE WOLF BHB 90f74a RR 94f 74a 4736[2]

4 ch g Wolfhound (USA) 7.3f **(71)** - Bay Queen **(75f)** (Damister (USA)) 9f **(73)**

Form - 3402082

Record 2000 - 1st:0 2nd:2 3rd:1 Ran:7
Pre2000 - 1st:4 2nd:1 3rd:3 Ran:13

Win Prizemoney £24,972 *Total Prizemoney* £51,869

Wins * 1999 Aug Yarmou (GD) 10.1f 93 <
* 1999 May Nottin (FRM) H 8.2f 78 85+
* 1999 Apr Ripon (G-S) H 8f 73 75
* 1999 *Mar Wolver (STD)* *8.5f* *75*

2000 Turf 0-7: (8f 2, 9f, 10f 4) (gd 4, g-f 2, frm)

Workmanlike, useful gelding, effective 8 to 10f, best at 10f, acts on gd to frm, best on gd, prefers right handed tracks, prefers tight tracks, excels at Goodwood. Turf high 94 - 2nd of 11 getting 7lb from Sharp Play (1 Aug Goodwood 10f g-f RF 3277). He was strongly fancied when touched-off in a valuable handicap at Goodwood in August. Not quite up to that form later in the campaign, he is best around a mile and a quarter and still reasonably treated. **M L W Bell [4-20] B J Warren.*

PRASLIN ISLAND BHB 47f80a RR 51f 80a 5137[9]

4 ch g Be My Chief (USA) 10.2f **(62)** - Hence (USA) (Mr Prospector (USA)) 8.8f **(78)**

Form - 2121230OD5030

Record 2000 - 1st:0 2nd:1 3rd:2 Ran:9
Pre2000 - 1st:2 2nd:5 3rd:0 Ran:15

Win Prizemoney £5,490 *Total Prizemoney* £12,264

Wins 1999 *Dec Southw (STD) H* *14f* *70* *77* <
1999 *Dec Wolver (STD)* *12f* *72*

2000 Turf 0-7: (14f 3, 15f, 16f 3) (g-s 2, gd 3, g-f 2) 2000 AW 0-2: (16f 2) (Fibr 2)

Workmanlike, decent gelding, effective 14 to 16f, best at 16f, - acts on Fibr, has worn blinkers, likes left handed tracks, likes tight tracks. Turf high 51. AW high 83 (1st run) - 2nd of 7 getting 9lb from Be Gone (8 Jan Wolverhampton 16f Fibr RF 0057). A winner twice on Fibresand at the end of last year, he was very unlucky to be disqualified after passing the post in front at Nottingham in June. 14 furlongs looks about as far as he wants.

**Miss Gay Kelleway [0-5] Kevin Hudson (from P W Harris [0-2] Apr 2000).*

PRECIOUS LOVE (IRE) RR 60f 1386[10]

3 ch c Cadeaux Genereux 7.9f **(76)** - Touch and Love (IRE) (Green Desert (USA)) 8.6f **(78)**

Form - 080

Record 2000 - 1st:0 2nd:0 3rd:0 Ran:3

2000 Turf 0-3: (7f 3) (gd 2, g-f)

Scopey, currently average colt. Turf high 60.

**B W Hills [0-3] Maktoum Al Maktoum.*

PRECIOUS PENNY RR 50f 3436[14]

2 b f Persian Bold 10f **(69)** - Illana Bay (USA) (Manila (USA)) 9.3f **(71)**

Form - 70

Record 2000 - 1st:0 2nd:0 3rd:0 Ran:2

2000 Turf 0-2: (6f 2) (g-f, frm)

Currently fair filly. Turf high 51 (began Jly).

**A P Jarvis [0-2] M Woodall.*

PRECIOUS POPPY BHB 72f RR 75f 4573[2]

3 b f Polish Precedent (USA) 9f **(73)** - Benazir (High Top) 10.2f **(67)**

Form - 4332
Record 2000 - 1st:0 2nd:1 3rd:2 Ran:4
Win Prizemoney £0 *Total Prizemoney* £2,908
2000 Turf 0-4: (10f 2, 11f, 12f) (sft, g-f, frm 2)
Light-framed, above-average filly, has worn blinkers. Turf high 75.
**Sir Michael Stoute [0-4] J M Greetham.*

PRECIOUS YEARS BHB 32f RR 13f 105[8]
5 ch g Dilum (USA) 7.1f **(56)** - Tantot (Charlottown) 10.9f **(57)**
Form - 8
Record 2000 - 1st:0 2nd:0 3rd:0 Ran:1
Pre2000 - 1st:0 2nd:0 3rd:0 Ran:4
2000 AW 0-1: (12f) (Fibr)
Poor gelding.
**L R Lloyd-James [0-3] Miss Kate Waddington (from R Simpson [0-2] Oct 1998).*

PRECISION BHB 37f RR 38f 3741[13]
5 b g Kris 10f **(75)** - Sweetly (FR) (Lyphard (USA)) 9.9f **(72)**
Form - 00060800
Record 2000 - 1st:0 2nd:0 3rd:0 Ran:8
Pre2000 - 1st:0 2nd:0 3rd:0 Ran:1
2000 Turf 0-8: (5f 3, 6f, 7f 3, 8f) (gd 4, g-f 3, frm)
Very moderate gelding. Turf high 42.
**C Grant [0-9] D Buckle (from R Charlton [0-1] Jun 1998).*

PRECISO (IRE) BHB 77f RR 78f 5066[3]
2 b c Definite Article - Symphony (IRE) (Cyrano de Bergerac) 6f **(68)**
Form - 283
Record 2000 - 1st:0 2nd:1 3rd:1 Ran:3
Win Prizemoney £0 *Total Prizemoney* £1,357
2000 Turf 0-3: (8f 3) (g-s 2, gd)
Currently above-average colt. Turf high 78 (began Spt).
**Mrs A J Perrett [0-3] John Bodie.*

PREDOMINANT (USA) BHB 44a RR 44a 28[10]
4 ch g Sky Classic (CAN) 10f **(83)** - Hard Knocker (USA) (Raja Baba (USA)) 10f **(64)**
Form - 040
Record 2000 - 1st:0 2nd:0 3rd:0 Ran:1
Pre2000 - 1st:0 2nd:0 3rd:0 Ran:2
2000 AW 0-1: (12f) (Equi)
Workmanlike, currently very moderate gelding.
**W J Haggas [0-3] Philip Ellick.*

PREFERRED (IRE) BHB 93f RR 89f 4747[16]
2 b c Distant Relative 7f **(69)** - Fruhlingserwachen (USA) (Irish River (FR)) 8.6f **(78)**
Form - 711300
Record 2000 - 1st:2 2nd:0 3rd:1 Ran:6
Win Prizemoney £10,205 *Total Prizemoney* £12,284
Wins * 2000 Jly Ascot (GD) H 6f 85+ <
*** 2000** Jun Nottin (G-F) 5.1f 69
2000 Turf 2-6: (5f 1-1, 6f 1-4, 7f) (gd 2-3, g-f 2, hrd)
Useful colt, effective 6 to 7f, acts on gd to hrd. Turf high 85 - 1st of 9 getting 4lb from Silk Law (15 Jly Ascot RF 2830). Stepped up on his debut effort behind Patsy's Double to win his next two starts. Held in better class since.
**R Hannon [2-6] R J Brennan & N J Hemmington.*

PREMIER AMBITIONS BHB 51f RR 58f 5013[9]
2 b c Bin Ajwaad (IRE) - Good Thinking (USA) (Raja Baba (USA)) 10f **(64)**
Form - 080
Record 2000 - 1st:0 2nd:0 3rd:0 Ran:3
2000 Turf 0-2: (6f 2) (g-f 2) 2000 AW 0-1: (6f) (Fibr)
Currently fair colt. Turf high 58 (began Aug).
**W J Haggas [0-3] The First Division Partnership.*

PREMIER BARON BHB 85f66a RR 86f 66a 4991[4]
5 b g Primo Dominie 7.2f **(67)** - Anna Karietta (Precocious) 8.6f **(62)**
Form - 14006444610004
Record 2000 - 1st:2 2nd:0 3rd:0 Ran:14
Pre2000 - 1st:1 2nd:4 3rd:3 Ran:18
Win Prizemoney £41,387 *Total Prizemoney* £55,659
Wins * 2000 Aug Newmar (G-F) H 7f 76 83
*** 2000** Mar Kempto (GD) H 7f 80 85 <
1999 Aug Sandow (G-S) H 7.1f 75 78
2000 Turf 2-14: (6f 2, 7f 2-11, 8f) (g-s 2, gd 1-8, g-f 2, frm 1-2)
Useful gelding, effective 7f, acts on gd to frm, best on gd, has worn blinkers. Turf high 86 - 4th of 29 giving 8lb to Social Contract (14 Oct Newmarket 7f gd RF 4991) - also 1st of 17 getting 15lb from Pulau Tioman (25 Mar Kempton RF 0499). Consistent. A useful handicapper, he returned to form when winning from a good draw at Newmarket in August.
**P S McEntee [2-14] Miss T J Fitzgerald (from Pat Mitchell [1-9] Oct 1999).*

PREMIER BOY (IRE) BHB 53f46a RR 46f 46a 5169[5]
2 b g Blues Traveller (IRE) - Little Min (Nebbiolo) 8.1f **(75)**
Form - 004765
Record 2000 - 1st:0 2nd:0 3rd:0 Ran:6
Win Prizemoney £0 *Total Prizemoney* £234
2000 Turf 0-4: (6f 2, 7f 2) (gd, g-f 2, frm) 2000 AW 0-2: (7f, 8f) (Fibr 2)
Moderate gelding. Turf high 46 (began Jly). AW high 28 (began Oct).
**B S Rothwell [0-6] Premier Protection Services Ltd.*

PREMIERE CREATION (FR) RR 108f 4140a[3]
3 ch f Green Tune (USA) - Allwaki (FR) (Miswaki (USA)) 9f **(81)**
Form - 243
2000 Turf 0-3: (8f, 9f 2) (g-s, gd, frm)
Currently Pattern-class filly. Turf high 108 (began Jun) - 3rd of 9 to No Matter What (27 Aug Del Mar 9f frm RF 4140a).
**In USA [0-1] (from J deRoualle in FR [0-2] Jly 2000).*

PREMIERE FOULEE (FR) BHB 29f27a RR 31f 27a 3085[9]
5 ch m Sillery (USA) - Dee (Caerleon (USA)) 8.6f **(71)**
Form - 08686640
Record 2000 - 1st:0 2nd:0 3rd:0 Ran:7
Pre2000 - 1st:0 2nd:1 3rd:0 Ran:8
Win Prizemoney £0 *Total Prizemoney* £684
2000 Turf 0-4: (10f, 12f 2, 13f) (g-f, frm 3) 2000 AW 0-3: (9f, 12f 2) (Fibr 3)
Very moderate filly, has worn blinkers. Turf high 31. AW high 11.
**F Jordan [0-21] Bill Woodward.*

PREMIERE VALENTINO BHB 43f RR 48f 4489[13]
3 b g Tragic Role (USA) 9.4f **(63)** - Mirkan Honey (Ballymore) 7.3f **(64)**
Form - 5600
Record 2000 - 1st:0 2nd:0 3rd:0 Ran:4
Pre2000 - 1st:0 2nd:0 3rd:0 Ran:1
2000 Turf 0-4: (10f, 12f 2, 13f) (g-s, gd, g-f 2, frm)
Unfurnished, moderate gelding, has worn blinkers. Turf high 48.
**D W P Arbuthnot [0-5] Mrs W A Oram.*

PREMIER FOIS BHB 68f RR 61f 1326[5]
3 b f Pelder (IRE) - Doris Doors **(57f 48a)** (Beveled (USA)) 9f **(59)**
Form - 5
Record 2000 - 1st:0 2nd:0 3rd:0 Ran:1
Pre2000 - 1st:1 2nd:0 3rd:0 Ran:2
Win Prizemoney £2,119 *Total Prizemoney* £2,310
Wins * 1999 Aug Lingfi (GD) 6f 62 <
2000 Turf 0-1: (7f) (gd)
Leggy, currently average filly. **G C H Chung [1-3] Osvaldo Pedroni.*

PREMIER LASS (IRE) BHB 49f RR 54f 3067[6]
2 b f Distinctly North (USA) 7.4f **(63)** - Cuirassier (IRE) (Pennine Walk) 8.5f **(61)**
Form - 7046
Record 2000 - 1st:0 2nd:0 3rd:0 Ran:4
2000 Turf 0-3: (5f 2, 6f) (gd, g-f, frm) 2000 AW 0-1: (5f) (Fibr)
Fair filly. Turf high 54 - 4th of 9 to Milltide (20 Jun Thirsk 6f frm RF 2117). **B S Rothwell [0-4] Premier Protection Services Ltd.*

PREMIER LEAGUE (IRE) BHB 28f35a RR 26f 35a 350[9]
10 gr g Don't Forget Me 9.5f **(66)** - Kilmara (USA) (Caro)
Form - 80
Record 2000 - 1st:0 2nd:0 3rd:0 Ran:1
Pre2000 - 1st:4 2nd:3 3rd:2 Ran:46
Win Prizemoney £13,262 *Total Prizemoney* £16,741
Wins 1998 Aug Windso (G-F) H 11.6f 48 52
1998 Jly Windso (G-F) SH 11.6f 43 48
2000 AW 0-1: (12f) (Fibr)

Very moderate gelding, has broken blood-vessels.
**M Salaman [0-1] The Harkander Partnership (from K O Cunningham-Brown [2-21] Nov 1999).*

PREMIER PAS (FR) RR 116f 2979a[2]

3 b c Sillery (USA) - Passionnee (USA) **(94f)** (Woodman (USA)) 9f **(74)**
Form - 3222
2000 Turf 0-3: (8f, 10f 2) (hvy 2, gd)
High-class colt, often wears blinkers. Turf high 116 - 2nd of 7 to Beat Hollow (25 Jun Longchamp 10f gd RF 2387a). He improved for blinkers when chasing Beat Hollow home in the Grand Prix de Paris, but failed to show the same form at Deauville in August. Usually held-up, he lacks a turn-of-foot in the top-class and could benefit from more enterprising tactics.
**Mme C Head in FR [0-4] Wertheimer et Frere.*

PREMIER PRIZE BHB 93f RR 96f 1832[15]

3 ch f Selkirk (USA) 7.9f **(76)** - Spot Prize (USA) **(96df)** (Seattle Dancer (USA))
Form - 630
Record 2000 - 1st:0 2nd:0 3rd:1 Ran:3
Pre2000 - 1st:1 2nd:0 3rd:0 Ran:2
Win Prizemoney £4,477 *Total Prizemoney* £6,827
Wins * 1999 Oct Newmar (SFT) 7f 85 <
2000 Turf 0-3: (8f, 10f, 12f) (g-s 2, gd)
Scopey, very useful filly. Turf high 96. Comfortably held in listed events before finishing last in the Oaks.
**D R C Elsworth [1-5] J C Smith.*

PREMIUM PRINCESS BHB 72f61a RR 72f 61a 5061[4]

5 b m Distant Relative 7f **(69)** - Solemn Occasion (USA) (Secreto (USA)) 8.7f **(72)**
Form - 00005533624114410234
Record 2000 - 1st:3 2nd:2 3rd:4 Ran:21
Pre2000 - 1st:1 2nd:4 3rd:2 Ran:23
Win Prizemoney £19,534 *Total Prizemoney* £34,984
Wins * **2000** Spt Nottin (SFT) H 6.1f 68 70 <
* **2000** Aug Pontef (G-F) H 5f 55 68
* **2000** Aug Sandow (G-F) H 5f 55 57
* 1999 May Newcas (FRM) H 5f 56 57
2000 Turf 3-20: (5f 2-10, 6f 1-10) (sft, g-s 3, gd 1-6, g-f 1-1, frm 7, hrd 1-2) 2000 AW 0-1: (7f) (Fibr)
Above-average filly, effective 5 to 6f, best at 6f, acts on sft to hrd, excels at Goodwood, likes Nottingham. Turf high 72 - also 1st of 18 giving 10lb to Marino Street (15 Spt Nottingham RF 4442). Consistent. Won twice in three days in August, having had a moderate win-to-run ratio prior to that, then ran well at Goodwood off a higher mark six days later. **J J Quinn [4-44] Derrick Bloy.*

PREPOSITION BHB 37f41a RR 35f 41a 1096[10]

4 b g Then Again 7.4f **(52)** - Little Emmeline **(39df)** (Emarati (USA))
Form - 24524170
Record 2000 - 1st:1 2nd:2 3rd:0 Ran:8
Pre2000 - 1st:0 2nd:0 3rd:0 Ran:4
Win Prizemoney £2,842 *Total Prizemoney* £4,188
Wins * **2000** *Mar Southw (STD) H 11f 37 41* <
2000 Turf 0-1: (12f) (gd) 2000 AW 1-7: (7f, 8f 4, 9f, 11f 1-1) (Equi, Fibr 1-6)
Scopey, moderate gelding, effective 11f, - acts on Fibr, favours left handed tracks. AW high 41 - 1st of 9 getting 9lb from Mice Ideas (27 Mar Southwell RF 0515). Consistent.
**M A Peill [1-11] Ms V B Foster (from Mrs J R Ramsden [0-2] May 1998).*

PRESELI (IRE) RR 115f 2918a[9]

3 b f Caerleon (USA) 10.9f **(79)** - Hill Of Snow 00
Form - 1020
2000 Turf 1-4: (8f 1-2, 10f, 12f) (g-s 2, g-f 1-2)
High-class filly, effective 7 to 10f, acts on g-s to g-f, best on g-f. Turf high 115 - 2nd of 10 giving 5lb to Lady Upstage (1 Jly Curragh 10f g-s RF 2522a) - also 1st of 9 giving 7lb to Storm Dream (14 May Leopardstown RF 1250a). Unbeaten in three starts as a juvenile (including the Group 1 Moyglare Stud Stakes), she scrambled home in a Listed race on her reappearance and was in season when disappointing in the Irish 1000 Guineas. A non-staying ninth in the Irish Oaks, she is game but may struggle if kept in training.
**M J Grassick in IRE [4-7] Neil Jones.*

PRESENTATION (IRE) BHB 94f RR 96f 4612[19]

3 b f Mujadil (USA) 7.7f **(70)** - Beechwood (USA) (Blushing Groom (FR)) 10.3f **(76)**
Form - 2326685220
Record 2000 - 1st:0 2nd:4 3rd:1 Ran:10
Pre2000 - 1st:1 2nd:0 3rd:2 Ran:7
Win Prizemoney £5,243 *Total Prizemoney* £47,356
Wins * 1999 May Windso (GD) 5f 72+ <
2000 Turf 0-10: (5f 3, 6f 7) (g-s 4, gd 2, g-f 3, frm)
Strong, very useful filly, effective 6f, acts on g-s to gd. Turf high 100 (1st run) - 2nd of 8 getting 13lb from Monkston Point (24 Apr Kempton 6f g-s RF 0838). Small but tough, she ran respectably in useful company. She was given a really hard race when narrowly beaten at Ascot in August. **R Hannon [1-17] Dr A Haloute.*

PRESENT CHANCE BHB 52f44a RR 56f 44a 5061[14]

6 ch g Cadeaux Genereux 7.9f **(76)** - Chance All (FR) (Glenstal (USA)) 10.1f **(64)**
Form - 00000005055600
Record 2000 - 1st:0 2nd:0 3rd:0 Ran:14
Pre2000 - 1st:2 2nd:4 3rd:8 Ran:33
Win Prizemoney £9,488 *Total Prizemoney* £22,188
Wins * 1999 *Jun Southw (STD) H 5f 58 65*
1998 *Jly* Goodwo (G-S) 6f 80 <
2000 Turf 0-9: (5f, 6f 6, 7f 2) (sft 2, gd 3, g-f 2, frm 2) 2000 AW 0-5: (5f 2, 6f 3) (Fibr 5)
Fair gelding, effective 5 to 6f, acts on gd - acts on Fibr, has worn blinkers (effectively). Turf high 62. AW high 42. Inconsistent.
**D Shaw [1-22] Ian Guise & Celia M Guise (from B A McMahon [1-25] Oct 1998).*

PRESENT LAUGHTER BHB 88f80a RR 90f 80a 1001[9]

4 b c Cadeaux Genereux 7.9f **(76)** - Ever Genial (Brigadier Gerard) 9.3f **(58)**
Form - 410
Record 2000 - 1st:1 2nd:0 3rd:0 Ran:3
Pre2000 - 1st:1 2nd:2 3rd:0 Ran:7
Win Prizemoney £13,955 *Total Prizemoney* £18,693
Wins * **2000** Apr Newmar (G-S) H 7f 85 90 <
* 1999 Mar Warwic (G-S) 5f 79
2000 Turf 1-3: (7f 1-3) (gd 1-3)
Scopey, useful colt, effective 7f, acted on gd. Turf high 90 - 1st of 21 getting 15lb from Muchea (19 Apr Newmarket RF 0794). (DEAD)
**P F I Cole [2-10] Penelope, Viscountess Portman.*

PRESENTOFAROSE (IRE) BHB 48f44a RR 43f 44a 4581[17]

2 b f Presenting - Little Red Rose (Precocious) 8.6f **(62)**
Form - 5502343170
Record 2000 - 1st:1 2nd:1 3rd:2 Ran:10
Win Prizemoney £1,844 *Total Prizemoney* £3,068
Wins * **2000** Jly Yarmou (GD) S 6f 43 <
2000 Turf 1-10: (5f, 6f 1-7, 7f 2) (g-s, gd 1-4, g-f 3, frm 2)
Moderate filly, effective 6f, acts on gd. Turf high 43 - also 1st of 6 from Banningham Bliz (31 Jly Yarmouth RF 3263). Inconsistent.
**J S Moore [1-10] Chris Bradbury.*

PRESIDENTS LADY BHB 42f48a RR 31f 48a 4677[13]

3 b f Superpower 6.6f **(58)** - Flirty Lady (Never so Bold) 6.3f **(66)**
Form - 0020
Record 2000 - 1st:0 2nd:1 3rd:0 Ran:4
Pre2000 - 1st:0 2nd:0 3rd:0 Ran:1
Win Prizemoney £0 *Total Prizemoney* £642
2000 Turf 0-3: (7f, 8f, 10f) (g-s 2, gd) 2000 AW 0-1: (7f) (Fibr)
Workmanlike, moderate filly. Turf high 31. (1st run) - 2nd of 13 getting 10lb from Moonlight Song (14 Jly Southwell 7f Fibr RF 2815).
**J G Smyth-Osbourne [0-5] Mrs J Harmsworth.*

PRESS AHEAD BHB 35f42a RR 61f 42a 4654[11]

5 b g Precocious 7.2f **(54)** - By Line (High Line) 10.3f **(70)**
Form - 81550160800060000
Record 2000 - 1st:2 2nd:0 3rd:0 Ran:16
Pre2000 - 1st:1 2nd:2 3rd:0 Ran:14
Win Prizemoney £6,785 *Total Prizemoney* £8,449
Wins * **2000** May Doncas (G-S) C 6f 61
2000 *Jan Wolver (STD) H 6f 50 53*
1998 *Jly Wolver (STD) 6f 65* <

2000 Turf 1-10: (5f 4, 6f 1-5, 7f) (gd 2, g-f 1-2, frm 5, hrd) 2000 AW 1-0: (5f, 6f 1-4, 7f) (Fibr 1-6)
Average gelding, effective 5 to 6f, best at 6f, acts on gd to frm - acts on Fibr, has worn blinkers. Turf high 61 (1st run) - 1st of 14 giving 5lb to Palo Blanco (1 May Doncaster RF 0932). AW high 53 (1st run) - 1st of 12 getting 9lb from Xsynna (18 Jan Wolverhampton RF 0112).
**S R Bowring [1-12] Roland Wheatley (from B A McMahon [2-18] Mar 2000).*

PRESTO BHB 57a RR 63f 3329[5]

3 b g Namaqualand (USA) - Polish Dancer (USA) (Malinowski (USA)) 10f **(56)**
Form - 70510175
Record 2000 - 1st:2 2nd:0 3rd:0 Ran:7
Pre2000 - 1st:0 2nd:0 3rd:0 Ran:3
Win Prizemoney £5,185 *Total Prizemoney* £5,185
Wins 2000 Jly Leices (G-F) C 10f 55+ <
2000 May Newbur (SFT) C 10f 51
2000 Turf 2-6: (8f, 10f 2-4, 12f) (sft, g-s 1-1, g-f 2, frm 1-2) 2000 AW 0-1: (12f) (Fibr)
Leggy, average gelding, effective 10 to 12f, acts on g-f to frm. Turf high 63 - 7th of 10 getting 13lb from Legal Lunch (20 Jly Epsom 12f g-f RF 2962) - also 1st of 13 giving 5lb to Unimpeachable (8 Jly Leicester RF 2641).
**Mrs Merrita Jones [0-2] F J Sainsbury (from W J Haggas [2-8] Jly 2000).*

PRETENDING BHB 47f RR 51f 2637[8]

3 b g Primo Dominie 7.2f **(67)** - Red Salute (Soviet Star (USA))
Form - 0653608
Record 2000 - 1st:0 2nd:0 3rd:1 Ran:7
Pre2000 - 1st:0 2nd:1 3rd:0 Ran:6
Win Prizemoney £0 *Total Prizemoney* £1,177
2000 Turf 0-7: (6f 3, 7f, 8f 3) (gd 3, g-f, frm 3)
Light-framed, fair gelding, effective 5f, acts on g-f. Turf high 51.
**J D Bethell [0-13] Mrs John Lee.*

PRETRAIL (IRE) BHB 75f RR 80f 4734[7]

3 b c Catrail (USA) - Pretty Lady (High Top) 10.2f **(67)**
Form - 02100237
Record 2000 - 1st:1 2nd:2 3rd:1 Ran:8
Pre2000 - 1st:0 2nd:1 3rd:0 Ran:2
Win Prizemoney £3,731 *Total Prizemoney* £8,404
Wins * 2000 Jun Lingfi (G-S) 7f 80 <
2000 Turf 1-8: (6f 2, 7f 1-2, 8f 3, 10f) (gd 3, g-f 1-3, frm 2)
Workmanlike, decent colt, effective 7 to 10f, best at 8f, acts on gd to g-f, best on g-f. Turf high 80 - 1st of 6 giving 5lb to Reematna (3 Jun Lingfield RF 1677). Got off the mark in a modest Lingfield maiden in June. Tough tasks afterwards, but ran better in slightly easier company at Salisbury. **A C Stewart [1-10] S J Hammond.*

PRETTY (IRE) RR 109f 4419a[1]

4 b f Darshaan 11.9f **(81)** - Lady Nessa (Al Nasr (FR)) 9.3f **(68)**
Form - 1
2000 Turf 1-1: (10f 1-1) (gd 1-1)
Currently Pattern-class filly. (1st run) - 1st of 8 from Abitara (10 Spt Longchamp RF 4419a).
**J E Hammond in FR [1-1] Mlle L Oung.*

PRETTY FLY GUY (IRE) BHB 24f RR 329[12]

4 ch g Forest Wind (USA) - Achtung Lady (IRE) (Warning)
Form - 0400
Record 2000 - 1st:0 2nd:0 3rd:0 Ran:3
Pre2000 - 1st:0 2nd:0 3rd:0 Ran:3
2000 AW 0-3: (11f 2, 16f) (Fibr 3)
Very moderate gelding. AW high 37.
**J Parkes [0-4] Mrs Lynn Parkes (from J C Harley in IRE [0-2] Spt 1999).*

PRETTY GIRL (IRE) RR 97f 4643[2]

2 ch f Polish Precedent (USA) 9f **(73)** - Petal Girl (Caerleon (USA)) 8.6f **(71)**
Form - 2
2000 Turf 0-1: (7f) (g-f)
Currently very useful filly. (1st run) - 2nd of 27 getting 5lb from Mozart (26 Spt Newmarket 7f g-f RF 4643). A half-sister to Mutamam out of a half-sister to Mtoto, she was a prolific winner in Norway before finishing a good second in a valuable sales race at Newmarket. **W Neuroth in NOR [0-1] Meridian Racing.*

PRETTY OBVIOUS BHB 52f RR 55df 5082[11]

4 ch f Pursuit of Love 9.5f **(69)** - Settlement (USA) (Irish River (FR)) 8.6f **(78)**
Form - 00
Record 2000 - 1st:0 2nd:0 3rd:0 Ran:2
Pre2000 - 1st:3 2nd:1 3rd:0 Ran:13
Win Prizemoney £13,174 *Total Prizemoney* £14,302
Wins * 1999 Oct Nottin (SFT) H 16f 46 61 <
* 1999 Spt Newcas (SFT) H 16.1f 46 55
* 1999 Aug Catter (FRM) S 15.8f 43
2000 Turf 0-2: (14f, 16f) (hvy, gd)
Scopey, fair filly, effective 16f, acts on g-s to gd, has worn blinkers, prefers left handed tracks. Turf high 10 (began Spt).
**Mrs M Reveley [4-9] H Hurst (from R A Fahey [0-8] Jun 1999).*

PRICELESS SECOND BHB 51f52a RR 41f 52a 1208[4]

3 b g Lugana Beach 7f **(63)** - Early Gales (Precocious) 8.6f **(62)**
Form - 5242314322064
Record 2000 - 1st:1 2nd:3 3rd:2 Ran:10
Pre2000 - 1st:0 2nd:1 3rd:0 Ran:6
Win Prizemoney £1,842 *Total Prizemoney* £4,395
Wins * 2000 *Jan Southw (STD) S 7f 63* <
2000 Turf 0-1: (7f) (g-f) 2000 AW 1-9: (6f 2, 7f 1-7) (Fibr 1-9)
Scopey, average gelding, effective 7f, acts on Fibr, often wears blinkers, prefers left handed tracks, prefers tight tracks. AW high 63 (1st run) - 2nd of 10 to Modem (7 Jan Southwell 7f Fibr RF 0042) - also 1st of 8 getting 1lb from Bescaby Blue (28 Jan Southwell RF 0180). **J A Glover [1-13] Vic Atherton (from P Calver [0-3] Spt 1999).*

PRICE OF PASSION BHB 66f RR 68f 4299[19]

4 b f Dolphin Street (FR) - Food of Love (Music Boy) 6.8f **(57)**
Form - 000450
Record 2000 - 1st:0 2nd:0 3rd:0 Ran:6
Pre2000 - 1st:2 2nd:1 3rd:1 Ran:17
Win Prizemoney £7,638 *Total Prizemoney* £9,420
Wins * 1999 Spt Goodwo (G-F) H 5f 67 69
* 1998 Spt Folkes (G-F) H 5f 77 81 <
2000 Turf 0-6: (5f 6) (gd 2, g-f 3, frm)
Workmanlike, average filly, effective 5f, acts on g-f, has worn blinkers (extremely effectively). Turf high 68 - 4th of 10 giving 20lb to Soaked (7 Aug Windsor 5f g-f RF 3440).
**D W P Arbuthnot [2-23] Noel Cronin.*

PRICKLY POPPY RR 62f 4363[5]

2 b f Lear Fan (USA) 10.4f **(80)** - Prickwillow (USA) **(71+f)** (Nureyev (USA)) 8.7f **(78)**
Form - 5
Record 2000 - 1st:0 2nd:0 3rd:0 Ran:1
2000 Turf 0-1: (7f) (g-f)
Currently average filly. **M P Tregoning [0-1] Sheikh Mohammed.*

PRIDDY FAIR BHB 31f51a RR 35f 51a 3314[8]

7 b m North Briton 8.2f **(53)** - Rainbow Ring (Rainbow Quest (USA)) 10.4f **(75)**
Form - 348
Record 2000 - 1st:0 2nd:0 3rd:1 Ran:3
Pre2000 - 1st:0 2nd:0 3rd:0 Ran:8
Win Prizemoney £0 *Total Prizemoney* £879
2000 Turf 0-3: (13f, 14f, 16f) (gd, g-f 2)
Very moderate mare. Turf high 35 (began Jly).
**B Mactaggart [1-17] Play Fair Partnership (from D W Barker [1-10] Jan 1998).*

PRIDE IN ME RR 65f 5156[2]

2 ch f Indian Ridge 7.6f **(74)** - Easy Option (IRE) **(111f)** (Prince Sabo) 7.2f **(62)**
Form - 02
Record 2000 - 1st:0 2nd:1 3rd:0 Ran:2
Win Prizemoney £0 *Total Prizemoney* £1,404
2000 Turf 0-2: (5f, 6f) (g-s, gd)
Currently average filly. Turf high 65 (began Oct) - 2nd of 17 to Night Gypsy (24 Oct Nottingham 5f g-s RF 5156).
**E A L Dunlop [0-2] Maktoum Al Maktoum.*

PRIDE OF BRIXTON BHB 47f71a **RR 46f 71a** 4827[16]

7 b g Dominion 8.9f **(65)** - Caviar Blini (What A Guest) 7f **(62)**
Form - 01112070
Record 2000 - 1st:3 2nd:1 3rd:0 Ran:7
Pre2000 - 1st:6 2nd:5 3rd:3 Ran:49
Win Prizemoney £26,609 *Total Prizemoney* £33,329

Wins							
*** 2000**	*May*	*Wolver*	*(STD)*	*H*	*5f*	*64*	*68*
*** 2000**	*Apr*	*Wolver*	*(STD)*	*C*	*5f*		*54*
*** 2000**	*Mar*	*Wolver*	*(STD)*	*S*	*5f*		*57*
1998	*Dec*	*Wolver*	*(SLW)*	*H*	*5f*	*63*	*73*
1998	*Dec*	*Wolver*	*(STD)*	*H*	*6f*	*63*	*68*
1998	*Nov*	*Wolver*	*(STD)*	*H*	*5f*	*58*	*62*
1998	*Aug*	*Wolver*	*(STD)*	*S*	*5f*		*65*
1998	May	Carlis	(G-S)		5f		64
1996	May	Cheste	(GD)	H	5.1f	78	81 <

2000 Turf 0-3: (5f 3) (gd, g-f 2) 2000 AW 3-4: (5f 3-4) (Fibr 3-4)
Above-average gelding, effective 5f, - acts on Fibr, has worn blinkers, prefers left handed tracks, prefers tight tracks. Turf high 46. AW high 68 - 1st of 12 getting 7lb from Eastern Trumpeter (4 May Wolverhampton RF 1027). Revitalised by a four-month break, he came back to his best last year and chalked up a hat-trick over the minimum at Wolverhampton in progressively better company.
**Andrew Reid [3-18] A S Reid (from P D Evans [3-12] Jan 1999).*

PRIDE OF INDIA (IRE) BHB 63f **RR 58f** 5142[7]

3 b g Ezzoud (IRE) - Indian Queen (Electric) 10.1f **(61)**
Form - 07
Record 2000 - 1st:0 2nd:0 3rd:0 Ran:2
Pre2000 - 1st:0 2nd:0 3rd:0 Ran:1
2000 Turf 0-2: (11f, 12f) (g-s 2)
Scopey, currently fair gelding. Turf high 58 (began Spt).
**J L Dunlop [0-3] Sir Gordon Brunton.*

PRIDE OF PERU (IRE) BHB 43f **RR 37f** 4366[5]

3 b f Perugino (USA) - Nation's Game (Mummy's Game) 8.2f **(60)**
Form - 085505
Record 2000 - 1st:0 2nd:0 3rd:0 Ran:6
Pre2000 - 1st:0 2nd:0 3rd:0 Ran:6
Win Prizemoney £0 *Total Prizemoney* £220
2000 Turf 0-6: (5f, 6f 3, 7f, 8f) (g-f, frm 4, hrd)
Leggy, very moderate filly. Turf high 37. Consistent.
**M Brittain [0-12] Mel Brittain.*

PRIDEWAY (IRE) BHB 49f66a **RR 58f 66a** 3847[13]

4 b f Pips Pride 6.7f **(70)** - Up The Gates (Captain James) 5f **(59)**
Form - 447613765678060
Record 2000 - 1st:1 2nd:0 3rd:1 Ran:15
Pre2000 - 1st:1 2nd:3 3rd:1 Ran:17
Win Prizemoney £5,473 *Total Prizemoney* £10,243

Wins							
*** 2000**	*May*	*Southw*	*(STD)*	*H*	*8f*	*63*	*67*
1999	*Feb*	*Wolver*	*(STD)*	*H*	*7f*	*68*	*80* <

2000 Turf 0-8: (7f, 8f 4, 9f 2, 10f) (gd 3, g-f, frm 4) 2000 AW 1-7: (6f 2, 7f 3, 8f 1-2) (Fibr 1-7)
Light-framed, average filly, effective 7f, acts on gd - acts on Fibr, has worn blinkers, likes left handed tracks, likes tight tracks. Turf high 61. AW high 67.
**W M Brisbourne [1-15] Nev Jones (from A Bailey [1-17] Spt 1999).*

PRIESTLAW (USA) **RR 52f** 4409a[3]

3 ch c El Gran Senor (USA) 8.9f **(85)** - Schwanensee (USA) (Mr Leader (USA)) 9.8f **(66)**
Form - 8253
Record 2000 - 1st:0 2nd:1 3rd:1 Ran:4
Pre2000 - 1st:1 2nd:0 3rd:1 Ran:2
Win Prizemoney £7,290 *Total Prizemoney* £23,199
Wins * 1999 Spt San Si (HVY) 8f
2000 Turf 0-4: (9f, 10f 3) (hvy, gd 2, g-f)
Fair colt. Turf high 52.
**J L Dunlop [1-5] (from M Quinlan [0-1] Oct 1999).*

PRIESTRIG BRAE **RR** 2339[10]

4 ch f Hatim (USA) 7.8f **(56)** - Hare Hill (Lochnager) 6f **(59)**
Form - 00
Record 2000 - 1st:0 2nd:0 3rd:0 Ran:2
2000 Turf 0-2: (7f, 9f) (g-f, frm)
Currently very poor filly. **B Mactaggart [0-2] J W Borthwick.*

PRIMA **RR 82f** 3087[6]

3 b f Primo Dominie 7.2f **(67)** - Phyliel (USA) (Lyphard (USA)) 9.9f **(72)**
Form - 56
Record 2000 - 1st:0 2nd:0 3rd:0 Ran:2
Pre2000 - 1st:0 2nd:1 3rd:1 Ran:3
Win Prizemoney £0 *Total Prizemoney* £1,213
2000 Turf 0-2: (6f, 8f) (g-f, frm)
Lengthy, decent filly. Turf high 56.
**W J Haggas [0-5] Cheveley Park Stud.*

PRIMATICCIO (IRE) BHB 43f46a **RR 49f 46a** 510[13]

5 b g Priolo (USA) 10.9f **(71)** - Martinova (Martinmas) 7.6f **(59)**
Form - 800
Record 2000 - 1st:0 2nd:0 3rd:0 Ran:3
Pre2000 - 1st:2 2nd:1 3rd:0 Ran:10
Win Prizemoney £4,850 *Total Prizemoney* £5,730

Wins							
1998	*Spt*	*Southw*	*(STD)*	*H*	*14f*	*48*	*50+* <
1998	Jly	Folkes	(G-F)	H	15.4f	42	50

2000 AW 0-3: (16f 3) (Equi, Fibr 2)
Moderate gelding, often wears blinkers. AW high 34. Becoming disappointing.
**E J O'Neill [0-3] The Ballybrit Partnership (from Sir Mark Prescott [2-10] Oct 1998).*

PRIMA VENTURE **RR 54f** 1505[4]

2 b f Pursuit of Love 9.5f **(69)** - Prima Cominna **(65f 60a)** (Unfuwain (USA))
Form - 4
Record 2000 - 1st:0 2nd:0 3rd:0 Ran:1
Win Prizemoney £0 *Total Prizemoney* £276
2000 Turf 0-1: (6f) (g-s)
Currently fair filly. **S P C Woods [0-1] Dr Frank Chao.*

PRIME OFFER BHB 64f **RR 67f** 5185[10]

4 b g Primo Dominie 7.2f **(67)** - Single Bid (Auction Ring (USA)) 8.6f **(65)**
Form - 50
Record 2000 - 1st:0 2nd:0 3rd:0 Ran:2
Pre2000 - 1st:1 2nd:0 3rd:2 Ran:7
Win Prizemoney £3,422 *Total Prizemoney* £4,658
Wins 1999 Jly Hamilt (FRM) 6f 67 <
2000 Turf 0-2: (7f 2) (g-s, frm)
Leggy, average gelding, effective 6 to 7f, best at 6f, acts on g-f to frm, best on frm. Turf high 64 (1st run) (began Spt) - 5th of 20 giving 8lb to Unchain My Heart (5 Spt Leicester 7f frm RF 4217).
**D Morris [0-2] Miss K A Bartlett (from K A Morgan [1-7] Jly 1999).*

PRIME RECREATION BHB 64f **RR 60f** 5188[2]

3 b g Primo Dominie 7.2f **(67)** - Night Transaction (Tina's Pet) 6.8f **(59)**
Form - 000370070612
Record 2000 - 1st:1 2nd:1 3rd:1 Ran:12
Pre2000 - 1st:0 2nd:0 3rd:1 Ran:3
Win Prizemoney £3,087 *Total Prizemoney* £4,845
Wins * 2000 Oct Ayr (HVY) H 5f 54 60 <
2000 Turf 1-12: (5f 1-12) (sft 1-1, gd 5, g-f 4, frm, hrd)
Average gelding, effective 5f, acts on sft to gd, best on gd. Turf high 60 - also 1st of 20 getting 10lb from College Maid (9 Oct Ayr RF 4871). **P S Felgate [1-15] Moneyleague Ltd.*

PRIME TRUMP BHB 79f **RR 76f** 3386[8]

2 b c First Trump - Maristax **(67f)** (Reprimand)
Form - 548
Record 2000 - 1st:0 2nd:0 3rd:0 Ran:3
Win Prizemoney £0 *Total Prizemoney* £301
2000 Turf 0-3: (7f 3) (g-f, frm 2)
Currently above-average colt. Turf high 76.
**P W Harris [0-3] The Full Deck.*

PRIMEVAL BHB 50f45a **RR 44f 45a** 3812[12]

6 b g Primo Dominie 7.2f **(67)** - Class Adorns (Sadler's Wells (USA)) 10f **(76)**
Form - 0
Record 2000 - 1st:0 2nd:0 3rd:0 Ran:1
Pre2000 - 1st:1 2nd:1 3rd:1 Ran:10
Win Prizemoney £1,871 *Total Prizemoney* £3,536
Wins * 1999 *Jly Wolver (STD) S 12f 49+* <

2000 AW 0-1: (8f) (Fibr)
Moderate gelding, favours left handed tracks, favours tight tracks.
**K C Comerford [1-8] The Old Style Partnership (from P W Harris [0-3] Apr 1998).*

PRIME VERSION RR 95f 5132[1]
2 b c Primo Dominie 7.2f **(67)** - Cashew **(77f)** (Sharrood (USA)) 10.5f **(72)**
Form - 1
Record 2000 - 1st:1 2nd:0 3rd:0 Ran:1
Win Prizemoney £5,102 *Total Prizemoney* £5,102
Wins * 2000 Oct Newbur (HVY) 6f 95 <
2000 Turf 1-1: (6f 1-1) (sft 1-1)
Currently very useful colt. (1st run) - 1st of 19 from Smirk (21 Oct Newbury RF 5132) **P F I Cole [1-1] Richard Green (Fine Paintings).*

PRIM N PROPER BHB 53f RR 59f 2603[8]
3 b f Tragic Role (USA) 9.4f **(63)** - Charolles (Ajdal (USA)) 9.2f **(89)**
Form - 008
Record 2000 - 1st:0 2nd:0 3rd:0 Ran:3
2000 Turf 0-3: (6f, 7f 2) (g-s, gd, g-f)
Workmanlike, currently fair filly. Turf high 59.
**R Hannon [0-3] T G & Mrs M E Holdcroft.*

PRIMO VALENTINO (IRE) BHB 116f RR 117f 4845a[9]
3 b c Primo Dominie 7.2f **(67)** - Dorothea Brooke (IRE) **(88df)** (Dancing Brave (USA)) 8.4f **(76)**
Form - 7640
Record 2000 - 1st:0 2nd:0 3rd:0 Ran:4
Pre2000 - 1st:5 2nd:1 3rd:0 Ran:7
Win Prizemoney £120,861 *Total Prizemoney* £132,550

Wins						
* 1999	Spt	Newmar (G-S)	G1	6f	108	
* 1999	Spt	Newbur (G-F)	G2	6f	113+	<
* 1999	Spt	Kempto (G-F)	L	6f	104+	
* 1999	Jun	Goodwo (G-F)		6f	85+	
* 1999	Jun	Leices (G-S)		6f	83+	

2000 Turf 0-4: (5f, 6f 2, 8f) (g-s, gd 3)
Scopey, high-class colt, effective 6f, acts on gd to frm, best on gd, likes Newmarket. Turf high 117 - 4th of 11 getting 6lb from Agnes World (13 Jly Newmarket 6f gd RF 2773). Successful in the Mill Reef and Middle Park Stakes as a juvenile in 1999, he failed to stay a mile in the 2000 Guineas and found life tough against the top sprinters. Still, a game fourth in the July Cup proved he had trained on and he must not be written off just yet.
**P W Harris [5-11] Primo Donnas.*

PRIMO VENTURE BHB 47f RR 48f 4482[9]
2 b f Primo Dominie 7.2f **(67)** - Jade Venture **(66f)** (Never so Bold) 6.3f **(66)**
Form - 680
Record 2000 - 1st:0 2nd:0 3rd:0 Ran:3
2000 Turf 0-3: (7f 2, 8f) (g-s, g-f 2)
Currently moderate filly. Turf high 48 (began Jly).
**S P C Woods [0-3] Dr Frank Chao.*

PRINCE ALBERT BHB 55f RR 45f 5224[8]
2 ch g Rock City 8.8f **(62)** - Russell Creek (Sandy Creek) 8.9f **(59)**
Form - 608
Record 2000 - 1st:0 2nd:0 3rd:0 Ran:3
2000 Turf 0-3: (7f 2, 8f) (g-s 2, gd)
Currently moderate gelding. Turf high 45 (began Oct).
**J R Jenkins [0-3] S A Barningham.*

PRINCE ALEX (IRE) BHB 102f RR 102+f 4464[8]
6 b g Night Shift (USA) 8.1f **(73)** - Finalist (Star Appeal) 9.6f **(65)**
Form - 118
Record 2000 - 1st:2 2nd:0 3rd:0 Ran:3
Pre2000 - 1st:4 2nd:1 3rd:1 Ran:11
Win Prizemoney £57,421 *Total Prizemoney* £63,566

Wins							
* 2000	Aug	York (GD)	H	10.4f	93	102+	<
* 2000	Jly	Newmar (GD)	H	10f	87	94	
* 1999	Jly	Ascot (G-F)	H	12f	74	78++	
* 1999	Jun	Kempto (GD)	H	12f	69	71	
* 1999	May	Kempto (G-F)	H	12f	64	69	
1997	Aug	Newmar (GD)	H	12f	63	68	

2000 Turf 2-3: (10f 2-3) (g-f 1-2, frm 1-1)
Very useful gelding, effective 10f, acts on g-f to frm, best on g-f, excels at Kempton. Turf high 102 (began Jly) - 1st of 17 giving 2lb to Nooshman (23 Aug York RF 3912) - also 1st of 10 giving 10lb to Pinchincha (30 Jly Newmarket RF 3235). Inconsistent. Fine effort to win a decent Newmarket handicap on his belated return, and added a valuable handicap at the York Ebor meeting. He is a very useful tool between ten and twelve furlongs.
**Mrs A J Perrett [5-9] Dawson, Mercer, Jones (from A C Stewart [1-5] Spt 1997).*

PRINCE AMONG MEN BHB 79f RR 82f 4814[2]
3 b g Robellino (USA) 9.5f **(68)** - Forelino (USA) (Trempolino (USA)) 12f **(71)**
Form - 333322
Record 2000 - 1st:0 2nd:2 3rd:4 Ran:6
Pre2000 - 1st:0 2nd:0 3rd:4 Ran:7
Win Prizemoney £0 *Total Prizemoney* £9,044
2000 Turf 0-6: (10f, 11f 3, 12f, 14f) (hvy, g-s 2, gd, g-f, frm)
Decent gelding, effective 6 to 14f, acts on sft to frm, has worn blinkers, prefers left handed tracks. Turf high 82 - 3rd of 7 getting 20lb from Mantusis (8 Jun Haydock 11f gd RF 1807). Consistent.
**M C Pipe [1-8] Jim Ennis (from P D Evans [0-1] Oct 1999).*

PRINCE BABAR BHB 80f RR 83f 5240[12]
9 b g Fairy King (USA) 7.7f **(75)** - Bell Toll (High Line) 10.3f **(70)**
Form - 244501650
Record 2000 - 1st:1 2nd:1 3rd:0 Ran:9
Pre2000 - 1st:4 2nd:7 3rd:4 Ran:34
Win Prizemoney £203,873 *Total Prizemoney* £282,305

Wins							
* 2000	Spt	Haydoc (HVY)	H	7.1f	79	83	
1998	Oct	Newmar (GD)	H	7f	85	92	<
1996	Oct	Ascot (GD)		8f		83	

2000 Turf 1-9: (7f 1-4, 8f 5) (sft 1-2, g-s 4, gd 3)
Decent gelding, effective 7 to 8f, best at 7f, acts on sft to gd, best on sft, has worn blinkers, likes left handed tracks. Turf high 83 - 1st of 13 giving 2lb to Mister Mal (2 Spt Haydock RF 4158). A useful handicapper on his day, he ended a long losing run when winning in heavy ground at Haydock in September.
**R A Fahey [1-9] Giles Pritchard-Gordon (from J E Banks [2-28] Spt 1999).*

PRINCE CASPIAN BHB 83f RR 91f 4968[18]
3 ch g Mystiko (USA) 7.7f **(59)** - Real Princess (Aragon) 8.1f **(60)**
Form - 14000
Record 2000 - 1st:1 2nd:0 3rd:0 Ran:5
Win Prizemoney £3,981 *Total Prizemoney* £4,531
Wins * 2000 Jun Nottin (SFT) 8.2f 70 <
2000 Turf 1-5: (7f 3, 8f 1-2) (g-s 1-1, gd, g-f 2, frm)
Workmanlike, useful gelding. Turf high 91. He disappointed in the second half of the campaign and is one to watch at present.
**C E Brittain [1-5] Lady Sieff.*

PRINCE DARKHAN (IRE) BHB 32f RR 51f 4328[12]
4 b g Doyoun 10.7f **(69)** - Sovereign Dona (Sovereign Path) 9.3f **(55)**
Form - 008560
Record 2000 - 1st:0 2nd:0 3rd:0 Ran:6
Pre2000 - 1st:0 2nd:0 3rd:0 Ran:4
Win Prizemoney £0 *Total Prizemoney* £248
2000 Turf 0-6: (10f 2, 12f, 14f, 16f 2) (g-f 4, frm 2)
Leggy, fair gelding. Turf high 55.
**P W Harris [0-10] Daydream Believers.*

PRINCE DU SOLEIL (FR) BHB 63f RR 68f 5159[8]
4 b c Cardoun (FR) - Revelry (FR) (Blakeney) 10.5f **(64)**
Form - 80070048
Record 2000 - 1st:0 2nd:0 3rd:0 Ran:8
2000 Turf 0-8: (8f 7, 10f) (sft 3, g-s, gd, g-f 2, frm)
Average colt. Turf high 68. **J R Jenkins [0-8] R M Ellis.*

PRINCE ELMAR BHB 54f RR 65f 4823[21]
3 b g Elmaamul (USA) 8.1f **(70)** - Dramatic Mood (Jalmood (USA)) 10.1f **(52)**
Form - 000700
Record 2000 - 1st:0 2nd:0 3rd:0 Ran:6
Pre2000 - 1st:0 2nd:0 3rd:1 Ran:2
Win Prizemoney £0 *Total Prizemoney* £700
2000 Turf 0-6: (10f 4, 11f, 12f) (sft, gd, g-f 3, frm)
Light-framed, average gelding, effective 8f, acts on gd. Turf high

67. Inconsistent. **W R Muir [0-8] Mrs Richard Plummer & Partners.*

PRINCE GRIGORI (IRE) BHB 57f **RR 60f** 3249[8]

2 ch g Prince of Birds (USA) - Zinovia (USA) (Ziggy's Boy (USA))
Form - 0478
Record 2000 - 1st:0 2nd:0 3rd:0 Ran:4
Win Prizemoney £0 *Total Prizemoney* £262
2000 Turf 0-4: (5f 3, 6f) (sft 2, g-f 2)
Average gelding. Turf high 60. **E J Alston [0-4] Morris, Oliver, Pierce.*

PRINCE HUSSAR RR 4774[10]

3 b c Emarati (USA) 6.6f **(63)** - Folly Finnesse **(61f 70a)** (Joligeneration)
Form - 0
Record 2000 - 1st:0 2nd:0 3rd:0 Ran:1
2000 Turf 0-1: (6f) (g-s)
Currently very poor colt. **P Howling [0-1] P Gwilliam.*

PRINCE JACK RR 5052[14]

2 b c Puissance 7.1f **(60)** - Sabo Song **(28f)** (Prince Sabo) 7.2f **(62)**
Form - 0
Record 2000 - 1st:0 2nd:0 3rd:0 Ran:1
2000 Turf 0-1: (6f) (sft)
Currently very poor colt. **Martyn Wane [0-1] James Kennerley.*

PRINCE KINSKY BHB 54f79a **RR 58f 79a** 1813[13]

7 ch g Master Willie 9.2f **(67)** - Princess Lieven (Royal Palace) 9f **(56)**
Form - 0
Record 2000 - 1st:0 2nd:0 3rd:0 Ran:1
Pre2000 - 1st:2 2nd:0 3rd:4 Ran:16
Win Prizemoney £8,825 *Total Prizemoney* £12,340
Wins * 1997 Apr Epsom (GD) H 12f 74 80 <
1996 Apr Lingfi (STD) 10f 61
2000 Turf 0-1: (13f) (g-f)
Above-average gelding.
**J A B Old [2-14] J A B Old (from Lord Huntingdon [1-8] Nov 1996).*

PRINCELY DREAM (IRE) BHB 71f **RR 69f** 4834[8]

4 br g Night Shift (USA) 8.1f **(73)** - Princess of Zurich (IRE) (Law Society (USA)) 9.9f **(70)**
Form - 000458
Record 2000 - 1st:0 2nd:0 3rd:0 Ran:6
Pre2000 - 1st:2 2nd:4 3rd:2 Ran:15
Win Prizemoney £9,241 *Total Prizemoney* £22,479
Wins * 1999 Aug Ayr (G-F) 6f 85 <
* 1998 Aug Pontef (G-F) 5f 82
2000 Turf 0-6: (5f, 6f 4, 7f) (g-s 2, gd, g-f, frm 2)
Scopey, average gelding, effective 6f, acts on gd to g-f, best on g-f, has worn blinkers. Turf high 69. **R A Fahey [2-21] I Bray.*

PRINCE MILLENNIUM BHB 75f66a **RR 77f 66a** 4970[11]

2 b c First Trump - Petit Point (IRE) **(70df)** (Petorius) 7.3f **(61)**
Form - 563740
Record 2000 - 1st:0 2nd:0 3rd:1 Ran:6
Win Prizemoney £0 *Total Prizemoney* £937
2000 Turf 0-6: (5f, 6f 3, 8f 2) (gd, g-f 2, frm 3)
Above-average colt, effective 8f, acts on frm. Turf high 77 - 4th of 13 giving 1lb to Flit About (4 Spt Bath 8f frm RF 4203).
**R Hannon [0-6] Major A M Everett.*

PRINCE NICHOLAS BHB 49f **RR 59f** 5193[9]

5 ch g Midyan (USA) 9.9f **(64)** - Its My Turn (Palm Track) 9.8f **(50)**
Form - 0224474060
Record 2000 - 1st:0 2nd:2 3rd:0 Ran:10
Pre2000 - 1st:2 2nd:2 3rd:0 Ran:11
Win Prizemoney £4,944 *Total Prizemoney* £10,275
Wins * 1999 Mar Hamilt (HVY) H 12.1f 40 49++
* 1999 Mar Doncas (GD) H 12f 40 53 <
2000 Turf 0-10: (11f, 12f 3, 13f 3, 14f 2, 17f) (g-s, gd 5, g-f, frm 3)
Fair gelding, effective 12 to 17f, acts on gd to frm, best on gd, and likes Doncaster. Turf high 62 - 4th of 10 getting 12lb from Wave of Optimism (29 Apr Doncaster 17f gd RF 0910). Becoming disappointing. **K W Hogg [2-24] Auldyn Stud Ltd.*

PRINCE NICO (IRE) BHB 43f60a **RR 27f 60a** 2808[4]

3 b g Nicolotte - Chummy's Friend (IRE) (Be My Guest (USA)) 9.3f **(67)**
Form - 0077654
Record 2000 - 1st:0 2nd:0 3rd:0 Ran:7
2000 Turf 0-3: (5f, 6f 2) (gd, g-f, frm) 2000 AW 0-4: (5f 3, 6f) (Equi, Fibr 3)
Unfurnished, fair gelding. Turf high 27. AW high 47.
**R Guest [0-7] Michael Hills.*

PRINCE NOR RR 50f 3067[8]

2 b g Prince Sabo 6.6f **(64)** - Nordesta (IRE) **(64f)** (Nordico (USA)) 6.5f **(62)**
Form - 058
Record 2000 - 1st:0 2nd:0 3rd:0 Ran:3
2000 Turf 0-2: (5f 2) (gd, g-f) 2000 AW 0-1: (6f) (Fibr)
Currently fair gelding. Turf high 50.
**R A Fahey [0-3] Mrs Janis MacPherson.*

PRINCE OF ARAGON BHB 40f55a **RR 37f 55a** 2103[10]

4 b g Aragon 7.7f **(58)** - Queens Welcome (Northfields (USA)) 9f **(72)**
Form - 0
Record 2000 - 1st:0 2nd:0 3rd:0 Ran:1
Pre2000 - 1st:1 2nd:1 3rd:0 Ran:18
Win Prizemoney £2,477 *Total Prizemoney* £3,054
Wins 1999 Apr Thirsk (GD) 7f 56 <
2000 Turf 0-1: (8f) (frm)
Leggy, fair gelding, effective 6 to 7f, acts on gd - acts on Fibr, has worn blinkers, prefers left handed tracks, likes tight tracks.
**R Ingram [0-1] Robin Smith (from K T Ivory [1-18] Oct 1999).*

PRINCE OF BLUES (IRE) BHB 91f86a **RR 88f 86a** 4926[4]

2 b c Prince of Birds (USA) - Reshift (Night Shift (USA)) 7.2f **(69)**
Form - 526587124
Record 2000 - 1st:1 2nd:2 3rd:0 Ran:9
Win Prizemoney £1,974 *Total Prizemoney* £4,961
Wins * 2000 Spt Lingfi (GD) 5f 88 <
2000 Turf 1-7: (5f 1-1, 6f 6) (gd 1-4, frm, hrd 2) 2000 AW 0-2: (5f, 6f) (Equi, Fibr)
Useful colt, effective 5f, acts on gd. Turf high 88 - also 1st of 16 giving 5lb to How Do I Know (22 Spt Lingfield RF 4579). AW high 88 (began Oct). Consistent. A half-brother to Inchalong, it took him a while to get off the mark but he managed to do so over the minimum trip at Lingfield in September. **N P Littmoden [1-9] T Clarke.*

PRINCE OF MY HEART BHB 85f **RR 84f** 1059[6]

7 ch h Prince Daniel (USA) 11.4f **(46)** - Blue Room (Gorytus (USA)) 7.8f **(60)**
Form - 66
Record 2000 - 1st:0 2nd:0 3rd:0 Ran:2
Pre2000 - 1st:3 2nd:1 3rd:5 Ran:31
Win Prizemoney £18,589 *Total Prizemoney* £46,801
Wins 1997 May Newbur (SFT) H 9f 100 108? <
1996 Apr Catter (GD) 12f 87++
2000 Turf 0-2: (10f 2) (sft, gd)
Decent horse, has worn blinkers. Turf high 84. Consistent. A one-time high-class handicapper, he is now with Henry Cecil and has given the impression that he retains some ability. Needs cut in the ground.
**H R A Cecil [0-2] G J Hicks (from D HaydnJones [0-9] Jun 1999).*

PRINCE OF MYSTERY (IRE) BHB 42f42a **RR 38f 42a** 4995[2]

3 b br g Shalford (IRE) 7.8f **(63)** - Mary Kate Danagher (Petoski) 5.7f **(62)**
Form - 8002
Record 2000 - 1st:0 2nd:1 3rd:0 Ran:4
Pre2000 - 1st:0 2nd:0 3rd:1 Ran:3
Win Prizemoney £0 *Total Prizemoney* £1,663
2000 Turf 0-3: (8f, 9f 2) (g-f 2, frm) 2000 AW 0-1: (7f) (Fibr)
Scopey, moderate gelding, has worn blinkers. Turf high 38 (began Aug).
**N P Littmoden [0-4] Select Racing Partnership (from A P Jarvis [0-3] Aug 1999).*

PRINCE OMID (USA) BHB 66f **RR 72df** 4823[7]

3 b g Shuailaan (USA) - Matilda The Hun (USA) (Young Bob (USA))
Form - 3400437
Record 2000 - 1st:0 2nd:0 3rd:2 Ran:7
Pre2000 - 1st:0 2nd:0 3rd:0 Ran:2
Win Prizemoney £0 *Total Prizemoney* £1,227
2000 Turf 0-6: (8f 2, 10f 3, 12f) (g-s, gd 2, g-f 2, frm) 2000 AW 0-1: (8f) (Fibr)

Scopey, above-average gelding, effective 8 to 10f, acts on gd to frm, has worn blinkers. Turf high 72. Consistent.
**J R Fanshawe [0-9] Arashan Ali.*

PRINCE PROSPECT BHB 70f75a RR 75f 75a 4020[6]

4 b g Lycius (USA) 8.8f **(71)** - Princess Dechtra (IRE) (Bellypha) 9.8f **(73)**
Form - 08102207408006
Record 2000 - 1st:1 2nd:2 3rd:0 Ran:13
Pre2000 - 1st:2 2nd:2 3rd:7 Ran:22
Win Prizemoney £12,352 *Total Prizemoney* £24,458
Wins * 2000 *Jan Lingfi (STD) 6f 76*
* 1999 Jly Sandow (G-F) H 5f 73 76
* 1998 *Dec Lingfi (STD) 6f 81* <
2000 Turf 0-9: (5f 6, 6f 2, 7f) (g-f 5, frm 4) 2000 AW 1-4: (6f 1-2, 7f 2) (Equi 1-3, Fibr)
Workmanlike, useful gelding, effective 5 to 7f, acts on g-f - acts on Equi, has worn blinkers, likes left handed tracks, likes tight tracks. Turf high 82 (1st run) - 2nd of 16 giving 7lb to Fearby Cross (28 Mar Sandown 5f g-f RF 0530). AW high 85 - 2nd of 8 giving 6lb to Magic Rainbow (4 Mar Lingfield 7f Equi RF 0401). Becoming disappointing. A fair sprinter, effective on both Equitrack and turf, he is suited by six furlongs or a stiff five. Looks a bit high in the weights these days and needs to drop a bit further yet.
**Mrs L Stubbs [3-29] Maurice Parker (from J Noseda [0-6] Oct 1998).*

PRINCE PYRAMUS BHB 83f RR 78f 5129[2]

2 b c Pyramus (USA) - Rekindled Flame (IRE) (Kings Lake (USA)) 10.8f **(67)**
Form - 44122
Record 2000 - 1st:1 2nd:2 3rd:0 Ran:5
Win Prizemoney £4,091 *Total Prizemoney* £13,593
Wins * 2000 Spt Beverl (G-F) 5f 75 <
2000 Turf 1-5: (5f 1-1, 6f 4) (sft, g-s, g-f 1-2, frm)
Above-average colt. Turf high 78 (began Jly) - also 1st of 19 from Brandon Wizzard (13 Spt Beverley RF 4365). Dropped back to the minimum trip to score at Beverley, and ran a brave race in defeat next time. **C Grant [1-5] Havelock Racing.*

PRINCE SHAAMAAL RR 85f 5065[1]

2 b c Shaamit (IRE) - Princess Alaska (Northern State (USA))
Form - 1
Record 2000 - 1st:1 2nd:0 3rd:0 Ran:1
Win Prizemoney £2,320 *Total Prizemoney* £2,320
Wins * 2000 Oct Bath (GD) 8f 85 <
2000 Turf 1-1: (8f 1-1) (g-s 1-1)
Currently useful colt. (1st run) - 1st of 15 from Post Box (19 Oct Bath RF 5065). **K Bell [1-1] The Upshire Racing Partnership.*

PRINCE SLAYER BHB 74f RR 84df 5078[9]

4 b g Batshoof 9.5f **(66)** - Top Sovereign (High Top) 10.2f **(67)**
Form - 0201008700
Record 2000 - 1st:1 2nd:1 3rd:0 Ran:10
Pre2000 - 1st:0 2nd:2 3rd:1 Ran:5
Win Prizemoney £22,750 *Total Prizemoney* £26,592
Wins * 2000 Jun Epsom (G-S) H 8.5f 76 84 <
2000 Turf 1-10: (8f 4, 9f 1-2, 10f 4) (g-s 1-4, gd, g-f 3, frm 2)
Scopey, decent gelding, effective 9 to 10f, best at 9f, acts on g-s to frm, has worn blinkers, likes tight tracks. Turf high 84 - 1st of 14 giving 7lb to Hibernate (9 Jun Epsom RF 1833). He scored at 33/1 in a valuable handicap on Oaks day, though he has been well beaten since. He can cope with fast ground, but looks better on soft.
**T P McGovern [1-9] Ahmed Abdel-Khaleq (from B Smart [0-6] Apr 2000).*

PRINCESS AURORA BHB 34f RR 30f 4174[19]

3 ch f Prince Sabo 6.6f **(64)** - Made in Heaven **(68f 67a)** (Primo Dominie) 6.2f **(80)**
Form - 06700
Record 2000 - 1st:0 2nd:0 3rd:0 Ran:5
Pre2000 - 1st:0 2nd:1 3rd:0 Ran:5
Win Prizemoney £0 *Total Prizemoney* £1,050
2000 Turf 0-5: (5f 4, 6f) (gd 2, g-f, frm 2)
Very moderate filly. Turf high 30. Becoming disappointing.
**P W Harris [0-10] The Lightning Twelve.*

PRINCESS CARLA (USA) RR 115f 5369a[3]

5 br m Caerleon (USA) 10.9f **(79)** - Dellagrazia (USA) (Trempolino (USA)) 12f **(71)**
Form - 13
2000 Turf 1-2: (8f 1-2) (hvy 1-2)
Currently high-class filly. Turf high 115 (began Oct) - 3rd of 9 getting 4lb from Jim And Tonic (4 Nov Saint-cloud 8f hvy RF 5369a).
**R Gibson in FR [1-2] T Yoshida.*

PRINCESS CHLOE BHB 75f RR 79f 4821[1]

2 br f Primo Dominie 7.2f **(67)** - Louise Moillon (Mansingh (USA)) 7.4f **(55)**
Form - 81
Record 2000 - 1st:1 2nd:0 3rd:0 Ran:2
Win Prizemoney £2,908 *Total Prizemoney* £2,908
Wins * 2000 Oct Windso (G-S) 6f 79 <
2000 Turf 1-2: (6f 1-2) (g-f 1-2)
Currently above-average filly. Turf high 79 (began Spt) - 1st of 19 from Beenaboutabit (6 Oct Windsor RF 4821).
**M A Jarvis [1-2] Mrs Christine Stevenson.*

PRINCESS CLAUDIA (IRE) BHB 60f RR 59f 4555[10]

2 b f Kahyasi 12.9f **(74)** - Shamarra (FR) (Zayyani)
Form - 0340
Record 2000 - 1st:0 2nd:0 3rd:1 Ran:4
Win Prizemoney £0 *Total Prizemoney* £819
2000 Turf 0-4: (7f 3, 8f) (gd 3, g-f)
Fair filly. Turf high 58 (began Jly). **T D Easterby [0-4] Cathal Ryan.*

PRINCESS ELLEN BHB 116f RR 120f 3394[3]

3 br f Tirol 8.1f **(64)** - Celt Song (IRE) (Unfuwain (USA))
Form - 82523
Record 2000 - 1st:0 2nd:2 3rd:1 Ran:5
Pre2000 - 1st:2 2nd:0 3rd:0 Ran:4
Win Prizemoney £20,270 *Total Prizemoney* £150,170
Wins 1999 Aug Newmar (GD) L 7f 88 <
1999 Jly Ascot (G-F) 6f 86+
2000 Turf 0-5: (7f, 8f 3, 10f) (g-s, gd 2, g-f, frm)
Scopey, very high-class filly, effective 8 to 10f, best at 8f, acts on gd to frm. Turf high 120 - 2nd of 18 to Lahan (7 May Newmarket 8f frm RF 1080). She made little show in the Nell Gwyn on her return, but she appeared to run way above herself when chasing home Lahan in the 1000 Guineas. She must have been sick of the sight of Crimplene after that, as she finished behind that filly in the Irish Guineas, Coronation Stakes and Nassau. She can be considered a 'nearly' filly.
**G A Butler [0-6] Mrs S Y Thomas (from P W Chapple-Hyam [2-3] Spt 1999).*

PRINCESS EMERALD RR 13f 4876[9]

2 b f Mtoto 11.5f **(71)** - Diamond Princess (Horage) 10.3f **(61)**
Form - 80
Record 2000 - 1st:0 2nd:0 3rd:0 Ran:2
2000 Turf 0-2: (7f 2) (g-s, gd)
Currently poor filly. Turf high 13 (began Jly).
**D W P Arbuthnot [0-2] Stephen Crown.*

PRINCESS EMILY (IRE) BHB 71f RR 66f 4555[12]

2 b f Dolphin Street (FR) - Partita **(41f)** (Polish Precedent (USA)) 10.2f **(60)**
Form - 03150
Record 2000 - 1st:1 2nd:0 3rd:1 Ran:5
Win Prizemoney £6,698 *Total Prizemoney* £7,146
Wins * 2000 Aug York (GD) 7.9f 60 <
2000 Turf 1-5: (7f 2, 8f 1-3) (gd 1-3, g-f, frm)
Average filly. Turf high 66 (began Jly) - also 1st of 19 getting 8lb from My Very Own (30 Aug York RF 4108).
**B S Rothwell [1-5] Mrs Julie Mitchell.*

PRINCESS MO BHB 22f28a RR 28f 28a 1908[10]

4 b f Prince Sabo 6.6f **(64)** - Morica (Moorestyle) 6.9f **(64)**
Form - 0580060
Record 2000 - 1st:0 2nd:0 3rd:0 Ran:5
Pre2000 - 1st:0 2nd:0 3rd:0 Ran:9
2000 Turf 0-3: (7f, 8f, 12f) (gd, g-f, frm) 2000 AW 0-2: (7f, 10f) (Equi 2)
Unfurnished, little account filly, has worn blinkers. Turf high 28. AW high 21.
**B R Johnson [0-6] Peter Crate (from T E Powell [0-4] Dec 1999).*

PRINCESS OF GARDA BHB 83f RR 83f 5183[2]

2 b f Komaite (USA) 6.9f **(61)** - Malcesine (IRE) **(38f 31a)** (Auction Ring (USA)) 8.6f **(65)**

Form - U43121454002

Record 2000 - 1st:2 2nd:2 3rd:1 Ran:12

Win Prizemoney £6,566 *Total Prizemoney* £10,526

Wins * 2000 Jun Cheste (G-F) 5.1f 77 <

*** 2000** May Haydoc (G-S) 5f 71

2000 Turf 2-12: (5f 2-9, 6f 3) (hvy, g-s, gd 1-6, g-f, frm 1-3)

Decent filly, effective 5 to 6f, acts on frm. Turf high 83 - also 1st of 8 getting 3lb from Laurel Dawn (28 Jun Chester RF 2333). Consistent. She has plenty of pace, and six furlongs is as far as she wants to go.

**Mrs G S Rees [2-12] North West Racing Club - Owners Group.*

PRINCESS PENNY BHB 47a RR 11f 47a 2176[7]

2 ch f King's Signet (USA) 7f **(51)** - Princess Tallulah **(15f 30a)** (Chief Singer) 8.9f **(66)**

Form - R381357

Record 2000 - 1st:1 2nd:0 3rd:2 Ran:7

Win Prizemoney £1,834 *Total Prizemoney* £2,355

Wins * 2000 *May Southw (STD) S 6f 51* <

2000 Turf 0-3: (5f, 6f 2) (sft, gd, frm) 2000 AW 1-4: (5f, 6f 1-3) (Fibr 1-4)

Fair filly, effective 6f, - acts on Fibr. Turf high 11. AW high 52 - also 1st of 7 getting 5lb from Impish Lad (22 May Southwell RF 1376).

**W G M Turner [1-7] Mrs A F Horsington.*

PRINCESS RIA (IRE) BHB 42f RR 50f 5316[19]

3 b f Petong 7.6f **(58)** - Walking Saint (Godswalk (USA)) 7.3f **(58)**

Form - 000

Record 2000 - 1st:0 2nd:0 3rd:0 Ran:3

Pre2000 - 1st:1 2nd:0 3rd:1 Ran:5

Win Prizemoney £3,733 *Total Prizemoney* £4,251

Wins * 1999 Jly Haydoc (G-S) 6f 61 <

2000 Turf 0-3: (7f 2, 8f) (g-s, gd, g-f)

Light-framed, fair filly, effective 6f, acts on gd. Turf high 45.

**A Bailey [1-8] Mrs M M Johnson.*

PRINCESS SENORITA BHB 24f RR 12f 3139[9]

5 gr m Timeless Times (USA) 6.1f **(56)** - Misty Rocket (Roan Rocket) 7.8f **(57)**

Form - 000

Record 2000 - 1st:0 2nd:0 3rd:0 Ran:3

Pre2000 - 1st:0 2nd:0 3rd:0 Ran:1

2000 Turf 0-3: (8f, 10f, 11f) (hvy, g-f, frm)

Poor filly. Turf high 12.

**M P Muggeridge [0-3] Mrs Hilary Jackson (from P Eccles [0-1] Jun 1997).*

PRINCESS SOPHIE RR 4381[14]

2 b f Tragic Role (USA) 9.4f **(63)** - Octavia (Sallust) 8.4f **(63)**

Form - 0

Record 2000 - 1st:0 2nd:0 3rd:0 Ran:1

2000 Turf 0-1: (8f) (gd)

Currently very poor filly. **K W Hogg [0-1] Mrs Thelma White.*

PRINCESS TITANIA (IRE) BHB 72f RR 74f 4208[3]

2 b f Fairy King (USA) 7.7f **(75)** - Chiquelina (FR) (Le Glorieux)

Form - 4723

Record 2000 - 1st:0 2nd:1 3rd:1 Ran:4

Win Prizemoney £0 *Total Prizemoney* £1,683

2000 Turf 0-4: (6f, 7f 2, 8f) (gd, g-f, frm, hrd)

Above-average filly. Turf high 74 (began Jly).

**N A Callaghan [0-4] Norcroft Park Stud.*

PRINCESS TOPAZ BHB 42f RR 53df 3512[8]

6 b m Midyan (USA) 9.9f **(64)** - Diamond Princess (Horage) 10.3f **(61)**

Form - 2678

Record 2000 - 1st:0 2nd:1 3rd:0 Ran:4

Pre2000 - 1st:3 2nd:3 3rd:4 Ran:28

Win Prizemoney £11,834 *Total Prizemoney* £25,489

Wins 1998 Jly Newmar (GD) H 14.8f 75 78 <

1997 Aug Sandow (G-F) H 14f 68 72

1997 Aug Newmar (GD) H 12f 61 65

2000 Turf 0-4: (14f 3, 16f) (g-f 3, frm)

Average mare, effective 12 to 16f, acts on frm, has worn blinkers. Turf high 56. Inconsistent.

**G M McCourt [1-13] Calypso Racing (from C A Cyzer [3-23] Spt 1998).*

PRINCES STREET RR 827[2]

2 b c Sri Pekan (USA) - Abbey Strand (USA) (Shadeed (USA)) 8.2f **(70)**

Form - 2

Record 2000 - 1st:0 2nd:1 3rd:0 Ran:1

Win Prizemoney £0 *Total Prizemoney* £1,100

2000 Turf 0-1: (5f) (sft)

Currently very poor colt. (1st run) - 2nd of 9 to Shush (22 Apr Kempton 5f sft RF 0827). **R Hannon [0-1] The Queen.*

PRINCESS VICTORIA BHB 56f60a RR 59f 60a 1107[9]

3 b f Deploy 11.4f **(67)** - Scierpan (USA) (Sharpen Up) 8.3f **(67)**

Form - 263330

Record 2000 - 1st:0 2nd:0 3rd:3 Ran:4

Pre2000 - 1st:1 2nd:1 3rd:0 Ran:4

Win Prizemoney £2,285 *Total Prizemoney* £3,904

Wins * 1999 May Beverl (GD) S 5f 61 <

2000 Turf 0-4: (5f, 6f, 7f, 8f) (g-s, gd 2, frm)

Unfurnished, average filly, effective 5 to 8f, best at 5f, acts on g-s to gd - acts on Equi, best on gd. Turf high 59 - 3rd of 7 getting 4lb from Breezy Louise (18 Apr Folkestone 5f g-s RF 0759).

**N A Callaghan [1-8] N A Callaghan.*

PRINCES THEATRE RR 87f 4321[4]

2 b c Prince Sabo 6.6f **(64)** - Frisson (Slip Anchor) 9.8f **(73)**

Form - 44

Record 2000 - 1st:0 2nd:0 3rd:0 Ran:2

Win Prizemoney £0 *Total Prizemoney* £669

2000 Turf 0-2: (7f 2) (g-f 2)

Currently useful colt. Turf high 87 (began Aug).

**I A Balding [0-2] T J W Burton.*

PRINCIPAL BOY (IRE) BHB 35f32a RR 40f 32a 4891[11]

7 br g Cyrano de Bergerac 7.3f **(58)** - Shenley Lass (Prince Tenderfoot (USA)) 9f **(61)**

Form - 384600

Record 2000 - 1st:0 2nd:0 3rd:0 Ran:3

Pre2000 - 1st:5 2nd:6 3rd:6 Ran:73

Win Prizemoney £14,319 *Total Prizemoney* £22,978

Wins 1998 *Jan Southw (STD) H 8f 37 40*

1997 Jun Hamilt (G-S) H 9.2f 44 47

1997 May Hamilt (SFT) H 8.3f 35 45

1996 *May Southw (STD) H 7f 52 52* <

1996 *Feb Southw (STD) H 7f 42 45*

2000 Turf 0-1: (9f) (hvy) 2000 AW 0-2: (7f, 8f) (Fibr 2)

Moderate gelding, effective 6 to 8f, best at 7f, acts on gd to frm - acts on Fibr, best on gd, has worn blinkers. AW high 26.

**Miss J F Craze [0-35] Mrs S E Cooper (from J A Glover [1-7] May 1998).*

PRINCIPLE (IRE) BHB 75a RR 85f 3936[12]

3 b c Caerleon (USA) 10.9f **(79)** - Point of Honour (Kris) 9.5f **(73)**

Form - 431410

Record 2000 - 1st:2 2nd:0 3rd:1 Ran:6

Pre2000 - 1st:0 2nd:1 3rd:0 Ran:3

Win Prizemoney £11,264 *Total Prizemoney* £13,978

Wins * 2000 Aug Haydoc (G-S) H 11.9f 78 85 <

*** 2000** Jly Haydoc (G-F) H 11.9f 74 79

2000 Turf 2-5: (10f, 12f 2-3, 14f) (gd 1-2, g-f 2, frm 1-1) 2000 AW 0-1: (10f) (Equi)

Scopey, useful colt, effective 12f, acts on gd to frm. Turf high 85 - 1st of 10 from Sudden Flight (10 Aug Haydock RF 3537) - also 1st of 6 getting 13lb from Bonaguil (16 Jly Haydock RF 2860). Showed the right attitude to land a brace of handicaps at Haydock.

**Sir Mark Prescott [2-9] Sir Edmund Loder.*

PRINCIPLE ACCOUNT BHB 76f RR 77?f 1078[P]

3 b c Rudimentary (USA) 8.2f **(66)** - Fairy Story (IRE) **(75f 64a)** (Persian Bold) 9.3f **(66)**

Form - P

Record 2000 - 1st:0 2nd:0 3rd:0 Ran:1

Pre2000 - 1st:0 2nd:1 3rd:1 Ran:5

Win Prizemoney £0 *Total Prizemoney* £3,133

2000 Turf 0-1: (8f) (frm)

Strong, above-average colt, effective 6 to 7f, acted on gd to g-f.

(DEAD) *C A Dwyer [0-6] The Fairy Story Partnership.*

PRINISHA BHB 45f **RR 60f** 5071[8]
3 gr f Prince Sabo 6.6f **(64)** - Nisha (Nishapour (FR)) 9.1f **(61)**
Form - 828228008
Record 2000 - 1st:0 2nd:3 3rd:0 Ran:9
Win Prizemoney £0 *Total Prizemoney* £2,613
2000 Turf 0-9: (7f 3, 8f 4, 10f 2) (g-s, gd 2, g-f 2, frm 4)
Leggy, average filly, effective 7 to 8f, best at 7f, acts on gd to frm, best on frm. Turf high 63 - 2nd of 5 to Daniysha (8 Jly Chepstow 7f frm RF 2628). Becoming disappointing.
**H Candy [0-9] Girsonfield Ltd.*

PRINTSMITH (IRE) BHB 57f49a **RR 56f 49a** 5105[1]
3 br f Petardia 8.2f **(58)** - Black And Blaze (Taufan (USA)) 7f **(57)**
Form - 010603801
Record 2000 - 1st:2 2nd:0 3rd:1 Ran:9
Pre2000 - 1st:1 2nd:0 3rd:1 Ran:7
Win Prizemoney £8,419 *Total Prizemoney* £9,265
Wins * **2000** Oct Doncas (GD) H 7f 51 56
* **2000** Jun Warwic (G-S) H 6.8f 53 56
* 1999 Jly Catter (GD) S 5f 61 <
2000 Turf 2-8: (6f 3, 7f 2-5) (g-s 1-2, gd 1-1, g-f 2, frm 3) 2000 AW 0-1: (6f) (Fibr)
Unfurnished, fair filly, effective 5 to 7f, best at 5f, acts on g-s to frm. Turf high 56 - 1st of 21 getting 12lb from Cryfield (20 Oct Doncaster RF 5105) - also 1st of 15 getting 20lb from Footprints (4 Jun Warwick RF 1706). **J Norton [3-16] Ecosse Racing.*

PRIOLETTE (IRE) BHB 35f **RR 33f** 1142[R]
5 b m Priolo (USA) 10.9f **(71)** - Celestial Path (Godswalk (USA)) 7.3f **(58)**
Form - R
Record 2000 - 1st:0 2nd:0 3rd:0 Ran:1
Pre2000 - 1st:0 2nd:1 3rd:1 Ran:17
Win Prizemoney £0 *Total Prizemoney* £2,761
2000 Turf 0-1: (12f) (frm)
Very moderate filly. Inconsistent.
**J L Eyre [0-1] K A Ayres (from Don Enrico Incisa [0-5] Jun 1999).*

PRIORS LODGE (IRE) RR 90f 5108[7]
2 br c Grand Lodge (USA) - Addaya (IRE) **(39f)** (Persian Bold) 9.3f **(66)**
Form - 17
Record 2000 - 1st:1 2nd:0 3rd:0 Ran:2
Win Prizemoney £3,640 *Total Prizemoney* £3,640
Wins * **2000** Jun Salisb (G-F) 7f 82+ <
2000 Turf 1-2: (7f 1-2) (gd, frm 1-1)
Currently useful colt. Turf high 90 - also 1st of 10 from Clearing (29 Jun Salisbury RF 2379). Won a Salisbury maiden nicely first time out. **R Hannon [1-2] Lady Tennant.*

PRIORS MOOR BHB 25f34a **RR 24f 34a** 2479[13]
5 br g Petong 7.6f **(58)** - Jaziyah (IRE) (Lead on Time (USA)) 8f **(65)**
Form - 07700
Record 2000 - 1st:0 2nd:0 3rd:0 Ran:5
Pre2000 - 1st:1 2nd:0 3rd:2 Ran:17
Win Prizemoney £2,994 *Total Prizemoney* £3,782
Wins 1998 Spt Yarmou (G-S) H 8f 48 53 <
2000 Turf 0-2: (8f, 10f) (gd, hrd) 2000 AW 0-3: (8f, 9f, 12f) (Fibr 3)
Little account gelding, effective 10f, - acts on Equi, has worn blinkers, likes left handed tracks, likes tight tracks. Turf high 12. AW high 18.
**K Bell [0-5] Mrs L Alexander (from R W Armstrong [1-17] Aug 1999).*

PRIORY GARDENS (IRE) BHB 40f38a **RR 38f 38a** 4620[10]
6 b g Broken Hearted 10.1f **(65)** - Rosy O'Leary (Majetta) 6.5f **(58)**
Form - 3007004407354610360
Record 2000 - 1st:1 2nd:0 3rd:3 Ran:19
Pre2000 - 1st:4 2nd:1 3rd:0 Ran:31
Win Prizemoney £14,863 *Total Prizemoney* £17,346
Wins * **2000** Jly Chepst (G-F) SH 8.1f 38 40
* 1999 May Leices (GD) H 6f 34 43
* 1998 Jun Carlis (G-S) H 6.9f 30 34
* 1998 Jun Goodwo (GD) H 6f 30 36
* 1997 Jun Thirsk (GD) H 6f 40 47 <
2000 Turf 1-14: (6f 5, 7f 5, 8f 1-4) (sft, gd 2, g-f 2, frm 1-8, hrd) 2000 AW 0-5: (6f 3, 7f, 8f) (Equi 3, Fibr 2)
Very moderate gelding, effective 6 to 8f, acts on g-f to hrd, likes left handed tracks, and excels at Catterick. Turf high 40 - 1st of 19 getting 10lb from Arbenig (14 Jly Chepstow RF 2792). AW high 34.
**J M Bradley [5-51] Gwilym Fry.*

PRIVATE SEAL BHB 30f39a **RR 31f 39a** 4102[5]
5 b g King's Signet (USA) 7f **(51)** - Slender (Aragon) 8.1f **(60)**
Form - 566074075
Record 2000 - 1st:0 2nd:0 3rd:0 Ran:9
Pre2000 - 1st:1 2nd:2 3rd:4 Ran:28
Win Prizemoney £1,984 *Total Prizemoney* £4,980
Wins 1997 Oct Bright (FRM) S 5.3f 69 <
2000 Turf 0-6: (7f 2, 8f 2, 10f 2) (g-f 2, frm 4) 2000 AW 0-3: (6f, 8f, 13f) (Equi 3)
Moderate gelding, effective 7f, - acts on Equi, has worn blinkers (effectively). Turf high 31. AW high 31.
**J C Poulton [0-27] Russell Reed & Gerald West (from G L Moore [1-12] Jly 1998).*

PRIX STAR BHB 55f50a **RR 61f 50a** 4627[12]
5 ch g Superpower 6.6f **(58)** - Celestine **(40f 44a)** (Skyliner) 7.3f **(53)**
Form - 4550320407752230
Record 2000 - 1st:0 2nd:3 3rd:2 Ran:13
Pre2000 - 1st:2 2nd:5 3rd:2 Ran:30
Win Prizemoney £7,381 *Total Prizemoney* £22,995
Wins * 1999 Jun Catter (GD) H 6f 60 61
* 1997 Jly Hamilt (G-S) 5f 76 <
2000 Turf 0-13: (6f 7, 7f 6) (g-s, gd, g-f 3, frm 5, hrd 3)
Average gelding, effective 6 to 7f, best at 6f, acts on gd to hrd, best on frm, often wears blinkers, likes right handed tracks, excels at Windsor, does well at Catterick. Turf high 61 - 3rd of 16 getting 4lb from Bahamian Pirate (12 May Carlisle 6f frm RF 1166).
**C W Fairhurst [2-43] M J Grace.*

PRIYA BHB 78f **RR 72f** 4187[10]
2 b f Primo Dominie 7.2f **(67)** - Promissory **(55f)** (Caerleon (USA)) 8.6f **(71)**
Form - 462240
Record 2000 - 1st:0 2nd:2 3rd:0 Ran:6
Win Prizemoney £0 *Total Prizemoney* £3,010
2000 Turf 0-6: (5f 3, 6f 2, 7f) (g-s, g-f 4, frm)
Above-average filly, effective 5 to 7f, acts on g-f to frm, best on g-f. Turf high 72 - 4th of 9 to Ashlinn (18 Aug Newmarket 7f g-f RF 3766). **C E Brittain [0-6] B H Voak.*

PRIZE DANCER (FR) BHB 77f **RR 76f** 5110[6]
2 ch c Suave Dancer (USA) 10.7f **(68)** - Spot Prize (USA) **(96df)** (Seattle Dancer (USA))
Form - 7486
Record 2000 - 1st:0 2nd:0 3rd:0 Ran:4
Win Prizemoney £0 *Total Prizemoney* £500
2000 Turf 0-4: (7f, 8f 3) (gd 2, g-f 2)
Above-average colt. Turf high 76 (began Jly) - 4th of 8 to Elmonjed (9 Spt Goodwood 8f gd RF 4318).
**D R C Elsworth [0-4] J C Smith.*

PRIZEMAN (USA) BHB 100f **RR 96f** 5108[2]
2 b c Prized (USA) - Shuttle (USA) (Conquistador Cielo (USA)) 8.8f **(69)**
Form - 1142
Record 2000 - 1st:2 2nd:1 3rd:0 Ran:4
Win Prizemoney £19,851 *Total Prizemoney* £34,501
Wins * **2000** Aug Newbur (G-F) L 7f 96 <
* **2000** Jly York (GD) 6f 93+
2000 Turf 2-4: (6f 1-1, 7f 1-2, 8f) (g-s, gd 1-2, frm 1-1)
Very useful colt. Turf high 96 (began Jly) - 2nd of 9 to Clearing (20 Oct Newbury 7f gd RF 5108) - also 1st of 5 from Perfect Sunday (18 Aug Newbury RF 3757). An attractive individual, he was well touted before winning a maiden and Listed event on his first two starts. Tried in Group company thereafter, he was hampered when fourth in the Royal Lodge Stakes at Ascot and looked one-paced when second in Newbury's Horris Hill Stakes. Capable of better when tried beyond a mile, he has a good attitude and could make a smart three-year-old.
**R Hannon [2-4] Highclere Thoroughbred Racing Ltd.*

PROCEED WITH CARE BHB 100f **RR 106f** 4833[5]
2 b c Danehill (USA) 9.1f **(79)** - Ultra Finesse (USA) (Rahy (USA))

Form - 51285

Prizeman took the honours at Newbury

Record 2000 - 1st:1 2nd:1 3rd:0 Ran:5
Win Prizemoney £3,601 *Total Prizemoney* £7,407
Wins * **2000** Jun Ripon (G-F) 6f 84 <
2000 Turf 1-5: (5f 2, 6f 1-3) (sft, g-s, g-f, frm 1-2)
Pattern-class colt. Turf high 99 - 2nd of 9 giving 5lb to Santolina (3 Spt Kempton 6f g-f RF 4189). A free-running individual, he is probably best on fast ground and may need to dominate.
**M Johnston [1-5] Maktoum Al Maktoum.*

PRODIGAL SON (IRE) BHB 66f75a **RR 69f 75a** 3372[9]
5 b g Waajib 8.9f **(67)** - Nouveau Lady (IRE) (Taufan (USA)) 7f **(57)**
Form - 2836830
Record 2000 - 1st:0 2nd:0 3rd:2 Ran:5
Pre2000 - 1st:4 2nd:7 3rd:1 Ran:25
Win Prizemoney £10,434 *Total Prizemoney* £20,323
Wins * 1999 Jun Nottin (GD) H 8.2f 62 67 <
* 1999 *Mar Wolver (STD) H 8.5f 65 65*
* 1999 *Feb Lingfi (STD) H 8f 60 67* <
* 1999 *Feb Wolver (STD) H 7f 51 59*
2000 Turf 0-5: (10f 3, 12f 2) (gd, g-f 2, frm 2)
Above-average gelding, effective 8 to 12f, best at 10f, acts on gd to frm - acts on AW, has worn blinkers, likes left handed tracks, favours tight tracks, and excels at Wolverhampton. Turf high 72 (1st run) - 3rd of 20 giving 16lb to Acebo Lyons (23 Mar Doncaster 10f frm RF 0478).
**Mrs V C Ward [4-18] Prodigal Son Partnership (from R J R Williams [0-13] Oct 1998).*

PROFOUND RR 4813[18]
4 b g Zafonic (USA) 9f **(83)** - Houseproud (USA) (Riverman (USA)) 9.1f **(76)**
Form - 00
Record 2000 - 1st:0 2nd:0 3rd:0 Ran:2
2000 Turf 0-2: (7f, 8f) (g-s 2)
Scopey, currently very poor gelding.
**H J Collingridge [0-2] The Headquarters Partnership I.*

PROLETARIAT BHB 85f **RR 90f** 5129[15]
2 gr g Petong 7.6f **(58)** - Primulette (Mummy's Pet) 7.7f **(60)**
Form - 2420
Record 2000 - 1st:0 2nd:2 3rd:0 Ran:4
Win Prizemoney £0 *Total Prizemoney* £2,842
2000 Turf 0-4: (6f 4) (sft, frm 3)
Useful gelding. Turf high 90 (began Jly) - 2nd of 12 to Takaroa (25 Aug Thirsk 6f frm RF 3970). He showed a respectable level of form in maidens, and can be forgiven a poor effort on his final start as he was hampered shortly after leaving the stalls. Worth a try over seven furlongs, he should win a race.
**H Candy [0-4] Simon Broke and Partners.*

PROMISED (IRE) BHB 92f **RR 86f** 5123[7]
2 b f Petardia 8.2f **(58)** - Where's the Money (Lochnager) 6f **(59)**
Form - 13777407
Record 2000 - 1st:1 2nd:0 3rd:1 Ran:8
Win Prizemoney £2,522 *Total Prizemoney* £4,080
Wins * **2000** May Redcar (G-S) 5f 75+ <
2000 Turf 1-8: (5f 1-3, 6f 5) (g-s 2, gd 1-6)
Useful filly, effective 6f, acts on gd, has worn blinkers. Turf high 86 - 4th of 9 to Alshadiyah (16 Spt Ayr 6f gd RF 4448). Put in a good effort to finish fourth in a listed race at Ayr in September.
**J A Glover [1-8] Paul Dixon.*

PROMISING LADY BHB 82f **RR 91f** 5286a[7]
3 b f Thunder Gulch (USA) - Sovinista **(97f)** (Soviet Star (USA))
Form - 76726087
Record 2000 - 1st:0 2nd:1 3rd:0 Ran:8
Pre2000 - 1st:1 2nd:0 3rd:0 Ran:1
Win Prizemoney £5,175 *Total Prizemoney* £7,309
Wins 1999 Aug Tralee (G-S) 8f 78+ <
2000 Turf 0-8: (8f, 9f, 10f 2, 12f 2, 15f, 16f) (hvy, g-s 2, gd 3, g-f 2)
Useful filly, effective 12f, acts on gd to g-f. Turf high 91.
**J G Burns in IRE [0-1] John McKay (from M R Channon [0-7] Spt 2000).*

PROPER GENT BHB 33f **RR 10df** 1143[7]
3 b g Alhijaz 7.7f **(57)** - Proper Madam (Mummy's Pet) 7.7f **(60)**
Form - 007
Record 2000 - 1st:0 2nd:0 3rd:0 Ran:3
Pre2000 - 1st:0 2nd:0 3rd:0 Ran:4
2000 Turf 0-3: (6f, 9f, 10f) (gd 2, frm)
Unfurnished, poor gelding, has worn blinkers.
**D W Barker [0-3] P Asquith (from M Brittain [0-4] Nov 1999).*

PROPER SQUIRE (USA) BHB 70f **RR 79f** 2666[11]
3 b c Bien Bien (USA) - La Cumbre (Sadler's Wells (USA)) 10f **(76)**
Form - 6200
Record 2000 - 1st:0 2nd:1 3rd:0 Ran:4
Pre2000 - 1st:0 2nd:1 3rd:1 Ran:3
Win Prizemoney £0 *Total Prizemoney* £2,518
2000 Turf 0-4: (10f 2, 12f 2) (gd 2, g-f, frm)
Well made, above-average colt, effective 8f, acts on gd to frm. Turf high 79.
**J H M Gosden [0-4] J Toffan & T McCaffery (from A G Foster [0-1] Oct 1999).*

PROPERTY MAN RR 277[8]
8 gr g Clantime 6.6f **(57)** - Cool Number (Swing Easy (USA)) 6.5f **(55)**
Form - 8
Record 2000 - 1st:0 2nd:0 3rd:0 Ran:1
Pre2000 - 1st:0 2nd:1 3rd:1 Ran:2
Win Prizemoney £0 *Total Prizemoney* £2,369
2000 AW 0-1: (7f) (Fibr)
Very poor gelding, has worn blinkers.
**Mrs S C Bradburne [0-4] Mrs S Irwin (from B Hellier in GER [0-1] Spt 1995).*

PROPERTY ZONE RR 42f 2618[7]
2 b g Cool Jazz - Prime Property (IRE) **(24f 28a)** (Tirol)
Form - 087
Record 2000 - 1st:0 2nd:0 3rd:0 Ran:3
2000 Turf 0-3: (6f 2, 7f) (g-s, g-f, frm)
Currently moderate gelding. Turf high 42.
**M W Easterby [0-3] Alan Black & Co.*

PROSPECTOR'S COVE BHB 68f53a **RR 71f 53a** 5299[13]
7 b g Dowsing (USA) 7f **(61)** - Pearl Cove (Town And Country) 8.1f **(68)**
Form - 300808010466236000
Record 2000 - 1st:1 2nd:1 3rd:2 Ran:18
Pre2000 - 1st:6 2nd:7 3rd:8 Ran:55
Win Prizemoney £25,464 *Total Prizemoney* £38,477
Wins * **2000** May Yarmou (GD) H 7f 65 68
* 1999 Spt Yarmou (G-S) H 8f 71 74
* 1999 Aug Newmar (GD) H 8f 64 69+
* 1998 *Dec Lingfi (STD) H 10f 56 61*
* 1998 Aug Bright (FRM) H 8f 56 62
* 1996 Apr Kempto (GD) 10f 86 <
2000 Turf 1-15: (7f 1-6, 8f 9) (sft, g-s 2, gd 1-3, g-f 6, frm 3) 2000 AW 0-3: (8f, 10f 2) (Equi 2, Fibr)
Above-average gelding, effective 7 to 9f, best at 8f, acts on g-s to frm - acts on Fibr, has worn blinkers, excels at Yarmouth. Turf high 71 - 4th of 11 getting 10lb from Rich In Love (5 Jly Yarmouth 8f frm RF 2553) - also 1st of 20 giving 9lb to Samara Song (31 May Yarmouth RF 1609). AW high 59. He is suited by decent ground and a decent pace, and scored at Yarmouth in May when dropped back to seven furlongs. Running with credit since.
**J Pearce [7-76] Saracen Racing.*

PROTARAS BAY BHB 34f36a **RR 37f 36a** 4054[13]
6 b g Superpower 6.6f **(58)** - Vivid Impression (Cure The Blues (USA)) 9.5f **(63)**
Form - 0
Record 2000 - 1st:0 2nd:0 3rd:0 Ran:1
Pre2000 - 1st:1 2nd:4 3rd:2 Ran:24
Win Prizemoney £1,668 *Total Prizemoney* £5,815
Wins * 1998 Oct Newcas (SFT) CH 8f 43 44 <
2000 Turf 0-1: (11f) (gd)
Moderate gelding, often wears blinkers.
**P L Gilligan [1-23] Patrick Gilligan (from T T Clement [0-3] Jly 1996).*

PROTECTOR BHB 65f **RR 65f** 2234[1]
3 b g Be My Chief (USA) 10.2f **(62)** - Clicquot (Bold Lad (IRE)) 8.4f **(68)**
Form - 0481
Record 2000 - 1st:1 2nd:0 3rd:0 Ran:4
Pre2000 - 1st:0 2nd:0 3rd:0 Ran:2
Win Prizemoney £2,268 *Total Prizemoney* £2,460
Wins * **2000** Jun Redcar (FRM) 11f 65 <
2000 Turf 1-4: (6f, 7f, 10f, 11f 1-1) (gd 3, frm 1-1)
Scopey, average gelding, effective 11f, acts on frm. Turf high 65 - 1st of 5 from Noble Calling (23 Jun Redcar RF 2234).
**J W Hills [1-6] Highclere Thoroughbred Racing Ltd.*

PROTOCOL (IRE) BHB 44f31a **RR 48f 31a** 4987[26]
6 ch g Taufan (USA) 8.3f **(65)** - Ukraine's Affair (USA) (The Minstrel (CAN)) 10f **(72)**
Form - 78723558422318350
Record 2000 - 1st:1 2nd:3 3rd:3 Ran:16
Pre2000 - 1st:4 2nd:5 3rd:4 Ran:45
Win Prizemoney £14,840 *Total Prizemoney* £27,816
Wins * **2000** Aug Pontef (G-F) H 10f 40 40
* 1999 Nov Nottin (SFT) 14.1f 57
* 1998 Apr Leices (SFT) H 10f 79 83 <
* 1998 Mar Doncas (GD) H 12f 73 78
1997 May Sandow (G-F) H 11.4f 73 74
2000 Turf 1-16: (10f 1-1, 12f 4, 14f 5, 17f 4, 18f, 22f) (sft, g-s 2, gd 7, g-f, frm 1-3, hrd 2)
Moderate gelding, effective 10 to 17f, acts on g-s to frm, has worn blinkers. Turf high 57 - 2nd of 15 to Charming Admiral (11 Apr Pontefract 17f g-s RF 0663). Improving.
**Mrs S Lamyman [4-59] P Lamyman (from J W Hills [1-12] Oct 1997).*

PROUD BOAST BHB 92f **RR 92f** 4383[6]
2 b f Komaite (USA) 6.9f **(61)** - Red Rosein (Red Sunset) 8.2f **(63)**
Form - 10231526
Record 2000 - 1st:2 2nd:2 3rd:1 Ran:8
Win Prizemoney £10,712 *Total Prizemoney* £14,851
Wins * **2000** Aug Thirsk (G-F) H 5f 85 90+ <
* **2000** Jun Cheste (G-S) 5.1f 79
2000 Turf 2-8: (5f 2-7, 6f) (gd 1-4, g-f, frm 2, hrd 1-1)
Useful filly, effective 5 to 6f, best at 5f, acts on gd to hrd. Turf high 92 - 2nd of 9 getting 5lb from Reel Buddy (29 Aug Ripon 5f frm RF 4064) - also 1st of 11 giving 14lb to Miss Brief (5 Aug Thirsk RF 3407). Out of a Wokingham winner, she developed into a decent two-year-old but falls fractionally short of Listed class. Game and genuine, she should stay six furlongs and has won when sweating.
**Mrs G S Rees [2-8] J W Gittins.*

PROUD CAVALIER BHB 25f33a **RR 33f 33a** 5025[4]
4 b g Pharly (FR) 11.5f **(64)** - Midnight Flit (Bold Lad (IRE)) 8.4f **(68)**
Form - 05004084
Record 2000 - 1st:0 2nd:0 3rd:0 Ran:8
Pre2000 - 1st:0 2nd:0 3rd:0 Ran:3
2000 Turf 0-5: (7f, 10f 2, 11f, 12f) (g-s, gd, g-f 2, hrd) 2000 AW 0-3: (8f, 10f, 12f) (Equi 2, Fibr)
Neat, very moderate gelding, effective 12f, acts on hrd, favours left handed tracks, favours tight tracks. Turf high 33 - 4th of 15 to Duello (20 Jly Bath 12f hrd RF 2954). AW high 33 (began Jly).
**K Bell [0-10] S J Edwards (from M R Bosley [0-1] Nov 1998).*

PROUD CHIEF BHB 62f **RR 58f** 3959[16]
3 ch g Be My Chief (USA) 10.2f **(62)** - Fleur de Foret (USA) (Green Forest (USA)) 9.9f **(68)**
Form - 26000080
Record 2000 - 1st:0 2nd:1 3rd:0 Ran:8
Pre2000 - 1st:1 2nd:0 3rd:0 Ran:6
Win Prizemoney £3,550 *Total Prizemoney* £5,742
Wins * 1999 Jun Goodwo (G-F) 6f 87 <
2000 Turf 0-8: (7f 5, 8f 2, 9f) (g-s 2, gd 2, g-f 2, frm 2)
Workmanlike, fair gelding, effective 6 to 7f, acts on gd, has worn blinkers. Turf high 80 (1st run) - 2nd of 7 giving 6lb to I Promise You (30 Mar Leicester 7f gd RF 0565). Consistent.
**A P Jarvis [1-14] Grant & Bowman Ltd.*

PROUD NATIVE (IRE) BHB 109f **RR 112f** 4700[11]
6 b g Imp Society (USA) 7.1f **(63)** - Karamana (Habitat) 9.4f **(70)**
Form - 00822062230
Record 2000 - 1st:0 2nd:4 3rd:1 Ran:10
Pre2000 - 1st:11 2nd:1 3rd:2 Ran:36
Win Prizemoney £193,872 *Total Prizemoney* £260,895
Wins * 1999 Spt Taby (GD) G3 5.8f 103
* 1999 Jun Leopar (G-S) G3 5f 109 <
* 1999 May Kempto (G-F) L 5f 109 <
* 1998 Aug Nottin (G-F) 5.1f 109 <
* 1998 Aug Haydoc (GD) H 5f 98 103
* 1998 Mar Doncas (GD) H 5f 100 105
1997 Aug Yarmou (G-F) 6f 101
1996 Oct Redcar (G-F) 6f 103
1996 Jun Epsom (GD) L 6f 105
1996 May York (G-F) 6f 84
1996 Apr Ripon (GD) 5f 78
2000 Turf 0-10: (5f 8, 6f 2) (g-s 2, gd 4, g-f 3, frm)
Group-class gelding, effective 5 to 6f, best at 5f, acts on gd to frm, best on gd, has worn blinkers, excels at Doncaster. Turf high 112 - 2nd of 12 giving 1lb to Astonished (10 Jun Epsom 5f gd RF 1864). He ran a string of solid races without winning last year and remains dangerous in Listed events. Probably best over the minimum trip (he stays an easy six), he does not want the ground too soft. **D Nicholls [6-31] P D Savill (from A P Jarvis [5-15] Spt 1997).*

PROUD REFLECTION RR 66f 1396[5]
2 b c Petong 7.6f **(58)** - Fleur de Foret (USA) (Green Forest (USA)) 9.9f **(68)**
Form - 5
Record 2000 - 1st:0 2nd:0 3rd:0 Ran:1
2000 Turf 0-1: (5f) (g-s)
Currently average colt. **A P Jarvis [0-1] Christopher Shankland.*

PROUDWINGS (GER) RR 109f 5216a[1]
4 b f Dashing Blade 7.9f **(80)** - Peraja (GER) (Kaiseradler)
Form - 21
2000 Turf 1-2: (8f 1-2) (hvy 1-1, sft)
Currently Pattern-class filly. Turf high 109 (began Aug) - 1st of 10 from Night Sun (22 Oct San Siro RF 5216a).
**R Suerland in GER [1-2] Hyperion Breeding.*

PROVE RR 91f 4844a[9]
2 f
Form - 0
2000 Turf 0-1: (8f) (gd)

Currently useful. **M Zilber in FR [0-1].*

PROVIDENT (USA) RR 73+f
4628[7]

2 b br c Mt Livermore (USA) 7.7f **(90)** - Seattle Special (USA) **(94f)** (Nureyev (USA)) 8.7f **(78)**

Form - 77

Record 2000 - 1st:0 2nd:0 3rd:0 Ran:2

2000 Turf 0-2: (6f 2) (gd, frm)

Currently above-average colt. Turf high 73 (began Spt).

**J H M Gosden [0-2] Sheikh Mohammed.*

PROVOSKY (IRE) RR 92f
4672a[11]

4 ch g Polish Patriot (USA) 7.8f **(70)** - Sheen Falls (IRE) (Prince Rupert (FR))

Form - 4110000

2000 Turf 2-7: (8f 1-3, 9f 1-3, 10f) (hvy, sft, g-s 1-1, gd 2, g-f 1-1)

Useful gelding, effective 8 to 9f, best at 9f, acts on g-s to g-f, mostly wears blinkers (extremely effectively), prefers left handed tracks. Turf high 92 - also 1st of 9 getting 16lb from Free To Speak (5 Jun Leopardstown RF 1928a). Becoming disappointing. Useful at his best, he was badly out of sorts in the second half of the season and is one to watch until showing a return to form.

**Miss I T Oakes in IRE [4-29] O Brady.*

PRUDENT RR
430[6]

3 b f Caerleon (USA) 10.9f **(79)** - Refinancing (USA) (Forli (ARG)) 9.6f **(67)**

Form - 6

Record 2000 - 1st:0 2nd:0 3rd:0 Ran:1

2000 AW 0-1: (8f) (Fibr)

Scopey, currently very moderate filly.

**J R Fanshawe [0-1] Cheveley Park Stud.*

PSALMIST BHB 50f RR 61f
4616[8]

3 ch f Mystiko (USA) 7.7f **(59)** - Son Et Lumiere (Rainbow Quest (USA)) 10.4f **(75)**

Form - 308708

Record 2000 - 1st:0 2nd:0 3rd:1 Ran:6

Win Prizemoney £0 *Total Prizemoney* £587

2000 Turf 0-5: (6f, 7f, 8f, 9f, 10f) (hvy, gd 2, g-f, frm) 2000 AW 0-1: (12f) (Fibr)

Leggy, average filly. Turf high 61.

**Noel Chance [0-6] R W and J R Fidler.*

PTAH (IRE) BHB 40f39a RR 57f 39a
4923[7]

3 b g Petardia 8.2f **(58)** - Davenport Goddess (IRE) (Classic Secret (USA))

Form - 00432300627

Record 2000 - 1st:0 2nd:2 3rd:2 Ran:11

Pre2000 - 1st:0 2nd:0 3rd:0 Ran:6

Win Prizemoney £0 *Total Prizemoney* £3,212

2000 Turf 0-8: (10f, 12f 3, 14f 3, 16f) (gd 3, g-f 5) 2000 AW 0-3: (8f, 16f 2) (Equi 2, Fibr)

Leggy, fair gelding, effective 12f, acts on g-f. Turf high 57 - 3rd of 7 getting 25lb from Inca Star (11 Jun Ripon 12f g-f RF 1890). AW high 52. Inconsistent. **J L Eyre [0-17] M Ford, M James & N Tritton.*

PTARMIGAN RIDGE BHB 76f RR 80f
5313[7]

4 b c Sea Raven (IRE) - Panayr (Faraway Times (USA)) 7.4f **(52)**

Form - 10007

Record 2000 - 1st:1 2nd:0 3rd:0 Ran:5

Pre2000 - 1st:1 2nd:1 3rd:0 Ran:9

Win Prizemoney £10,126 *Total Prizemoney* £12,515

Wins								
* 2000	Spt	Ayr	(SFT)	H	5f	72	80	<
* 1998	Oct	Catter	(SFT)		5f		80?	

2000 Turf 1-5: (5f 1-4, 6f) (g-s 2, gd 1-3)

Workmanlike, decent colt, effective 5f, acts on g-s to gd. Turf high 80 (1st run) (began Spt) - 1st of 27 from Get Stuck In (14 Spt Ayr RF 4384). Returned from a layoff of a year when scoring at Ayr in September, but finished down the field in the Ayr Silver Cup the following day.

**Miss L A Perratt [2-14] Miss Heather Galbraith.*

PUBLIC PURSE (USA) RR 121f
580a[3]

6 b h Private Account (USA) 10.1f **(80)** - Prodigious (FR) (Pharly (FR)) 9.8f **(68)**

Form - 213

2000 AW 1-2: (10f 1-2) (Dirt 1-2)

Very high-class horse, effective 12 to 13f, best at 12f, acts on sft to gd, best on sft. AW high 118. Formerly trained by Andre Fabre, he did well when transferred to Bobby Frankel's American yard, finishing third to Dubai Millennium in the Dubai Work Cup.

**R Frankel in USA [1-3] (from A Fabre in FR [3-8] Aug 1999).*

PUERTO MADERO (CHI) RR
580a[4]

6 b h Gallantsky (CHI) - Party Game (CHI) (Saratoga Game (USA))

Form - 634

2000 AW 0-3: (9f, 10f 2) (Dirt 3)

Currently high-class horse. AW high 117. **R Mandella in USA [0-3].*

PUFFIN BHB 75f RR 73f
5236[6]

2 b f Pennekamp (USA) - Spring (Sadler's Wells (USA)) 10f **(76)**

Form - 566

Record 2000 - 1st:0 2nd:0 3rd:0 Ran:3

2000 Turf 0-3: (7f 3) (g-s, g-f, frm)

Currently above-average filly. Turf high 73 (began Aug).

**J L Dunlop [0-3] Lord Halifax.*

PUIWEE BHB 14f27a RR 26f 27a
1480[11]

5 b m Puissance 7.1f **(60)** - Glow Again (The Brianstan) 5.9f **(55)**

Form - 0800

Record 2000 - 1st:0 2nd:0 3rd:0 Ran:4

Pre2000 - 1st:0 2nd:1 3rd:2 Ran:22

Win Prizemoney £0 *Total Prizemoney* £1,535

2000 Turf 0-1: (7f) (gd) 2000 AW 0-3: (8f 2, 11f) (Fibr 3)

Little account filly, has worn blinkers. AW high 13.

**P T Dalton [0-26] P T Dalton.*

PULAU PINANG (IRE) BHB 75f RR 79f
5322[12]

4 ch f Dolphin Street (FR) - Inner Pearl (Gulf Pearl) 12f **(54)**

Form - 221870

Record 2000 - 1st:1 2nd:2 3rd:0 Ran:6

Pre2000 - 1st:1 2nd:0 3rd:1 Ran:3

Win Prizemoney £6,040 *Total Prizemoney* £9,745

Wins								
* 2000	May	Bath	(G-F)	H	13.1f	72	76	<
* 1999	Spt	Lingfi	(FRM)		11.5f		64	

2000 Turf 1-5: (12f, 13f 1-1, 15f, 16f, 17f) (sft, gd 2, frm 1-2) 2000 AW 0-1: (12f) (Equi)

Leggy, above-average filly, effective 12 to 16f, acts on gd to frm, best on frm, likes left handed tracks, likes tight tracks, excels at Bath. Turf high 79 - 8th of 12 giving 9lb to Renzo (8 Jly Sandown 16f frm RF 2648) - also 1st of 12 giving 4lb to Fee Mail (22 May Bath RF 1362). Very much suited by fast ground, she looked a real stayer when scoring over 13 furlongs at Bath in May. Held since.

**G A Butler [2-9] Mrs A K H Ooi.*

PULAU TIOMAN BHB 104f RR 108f
4633[3]

4 b c Robellino (USA) 9.5f **(68)** - Ella Mon Amour (Ela-Mana-Mou) 10.1f **(70)**

Form - 2124220333

Record 2000 - 1st:1 2nd:4 3rd:3 Ran:10

Pre2000 - 1st:3 2nd:2 3rd:1 Ran:13

Win Prizemoney £37,661 *Total Prizemoney* £88,882

Wins								
* 2000	Apr	Kempto	(SFT)	H	8f	97	103	<
* 1999	Aug	Sandow	(G-S)		7.1f		102	
* 1999	Jly	Haydoc	(G-S)	H	7.1f	92	98	
* 1998	Aug	Nottin	(G-F)		8.2f		82	

2000 Turf 1-10: (7f 3, 8f 1-6, 9f) (sft 1-1, g-s 3, gd 3, g-f 3)

Scopey, Pattern-class colt, effective 7 to 9f, best at 8f, acts on sft to g-f, best on g-s, likes right handed tracks, excels at Haydock, does well at Kempton. Turf high 108 - 2nd of 9 getting 5lb from Sugarfoot (15 Jly Ascot 8f gd RF 2827) - also 1st of 20 giving 12lb to Espada (24 Apr Kempton RF 0837). He was beaten a whisker on his Kempton reappearance, and gained due compensation when a narrow winner of the Rosebery. He ran well afterwards, including in listed events, and is clearly useful when conditions are right.

**M A Jarvis [4-23] H R H Sultan Ahmad Shah.*

PULSE RR 57f
4300[9]

2 b c Salse (USA) 10.9f **(71)** - French Gift **(92f)** (Cadeaux Genereux)

Form - 0

Record 2000 - 1st:0 2nd:0 3rd:0 Ran:1

2000 Turf 0-1: (6f) (gd)

Currently fair colt. **R Hannon [0-1] Raymond Tooth.*

PUNCHER (USA) RR 1630a[1]
4 gr c Two Punch (USA) - Oystercatcher (USA) (Proud Birdie (USA))
Form - 1
2000 AW 1-1: (6f 1-1) (Dirt 1-1)
Currently very useful colt. (1st run) - 1st of 6 giving 5lb to Unreal Madness (26 May Belmont Park RF 1630a).
**P Johnson in USA [1-1] Sullimar Stable.*

PUNCTUATE BHB 85f **RR 88f** 4150[4]
3 b g Distant Relative 7f **(69)** - Niggle **(69f)** (Night Shift (USA)) 7.2f **(69)**
Form - 808034
Record 2000 - 1st:0 2nd:0 3rd:1 Ran:6
Pre2000 - 1st:2 2nd:0 3rd:0 Ran:2
Win Prizemoney £12,135 *Total Prizemoney* £14,131
Wins * 1999 Aug Ripon (GD) 5f 102 <
* 1999 Aug Sandow (G-S) 5f 72+
2000 Turf 0-6: (5f, 6f 5) (hvy, g-s 3, frm 2)
Scopey, useful gelding, effective 5f, acts on g-f. Turf high 88. Inconsistent. **W J Haggas [2-8] Wentworth Racing (Pty) Ltd.*

PUNISHMENT BHB 70f75a **RR 75f 75a** 3818[7]
9 b h Midyan (USA) 9.9f **(64)** - In the Shade (Bustino) 10.4f **(64)**
Form - 6235507062467
Record 2000 - 1st:0 2nd:2 3rd:1 Ran:12
Pre2000 - 1st:1 2nd:5 3rd:4 Ran:39
Win Prizemoney £7,746 *Total Prizemoney* £87,933
Wins * 1998 Oct Leices (SFT) H 10f 94 98 <
2000 Turf 0-9: (8f 2, 9f, 10f 4, 12f, 13f) (g-s, gd 3, g-f 3, frm 2) 2000 AW 0-3: (10f 2, 12f) (Equi 3)
Decent horse, effective 10 to 12f, acts on gd to g-f, likes right handed tracks. Turf high 75. AW high 82. Consistent.
**K O Cunningham-Brown [1-37] A J Richards (from J E Hammond in FR [0-3] Jly 1998).*

PUNTILLA (GER) RR 106f 4717a[10]
3 br f Acatonango (GER) - Prada (GER) (Lagunas)
Form - 150
2000 Turf 1-3: (11f 1-1, 12f, 14f) (sft, g-s, gd 1-1)
Strong, currently Pattern-class filly. Turf high 106 - 5th of 8 giving 4lb to Interlude (30 Jly Deauville 14f g-s RF 3352a) - also 1st of 8 from Quezon City (12 Jun Mulheim RF 2199a).
**H Remmert in GER [1-3].*

PUPPET PLAY (IRE) BHB 62f57a **RR 61f 57a** 5118[1]
5 ch m Broken Hearted 10.1f **(65)** - Fantoccini (Taufan (USA)) 7f **(57)**
Form - 64223342830413218 21
Record 2000 - 1st:3 2nd:3 3rd:4 Ran:15
Pre2000 - 1st:0 2nd:4 3rd:0 Ran:12
Win Prizemoney £9,638 *Total Prizemoney* £17,051
Wins *** 2000** *Oct Wolver (STD) H 6f 51 53*
*** 2000** Aug Redcar (FRM) H 7f 56 61 <
*** 2000** Jly Pontef (GD) H 8f 47 52
2000 Turf 2-8: (7f 1-4, 8f 1-2, 9f, 12f) (g-s, g-f 3, frm 2-3, hrd) 2000 AW 1-7: (6f 1-1, 7f 4, 8f 2) (Fibr 1-7)
Average filly, effective 6 to 8f, best at 7f, acts on gd to hrd - acts on Fibr, has worn blinkers, excels at Carlisle. Turf high 61 - 1st of 15 getting 10lb from Perfect Peach (13 Aug Redcar RF 3615) - also 1st of 19 getting 5lb from Caution (11 Jly Pontefract RF 2698). AW high 53 - 2nd of 15 getting 11lb from Moonlight Song (26 Spt Southwell 7f Fibr RF 4652) - also 1st of 12 giving 5lb to Aljaz (20 Oct Wolverhampton RF 5118). Consistent.
**E J Alston [3-19] Mrs F D McAuley (from J O'Haire in IRE [0-8] Spt 1999).*

PUP'S PRIDE BHB 43f55a **RR 45f 55a** 5248[2]
3 b g Efisio 7.7f **(69)** - Moogie (Young Generation) 7.7f **(63)**
Form - 5700340012
Record 2000 - 1st:1 2nd:1 3rd:1 Ran:10
Pre2000 - 1st:0 2nd:0 3rd:0 Ran:5
Win Prizemoney £1,799 *Total Prizemoney* £3,087
Wins *** 2000** *Oct Wolver (STD) H 6f 44 53* <
2000 Turf 0-6: (6f, 8f 4, 10f) (hvy, sft, gd 3, frm) 2000 AW 1-4: (6f 1-4) (Fibr 1-4)
Fair gelding, effective 6 to 8f, best at 6f, acts on sft to gd - acts on Fibr, has worn blinkers (very effectively), prefers left handed tracks, prefers tight tracks. Turf high 50 (1st run) - 5th of 14 getting 14lb from Smooth Sand (30 Mar Musselburgh 8f gd RF 0573). AW high 53 (began Jly) - 1st of 12 getting 9lb from Featherstone Lane (20 Oct Wolverhampton RF 5120).
**R A Fahey [1-15] The Slurping Toads.*

PURE BRIEF (IRE) BHB 54f43a **RR 63f 43a** 5119[12]
3 b g Brief Truce (USA) 9.1f **(73)** - Epure (Bellypha) 9.8f **(73)**
Form - 77370
Record 2000 - 1st:0 2nd:0 3rd:1 Ran:3
Pre2000 - 1st:0 2nd:0 3rd:0 Ran:6
Win Prizemoney £0 *Total Prizemoney* £384
2000 AW 0-3: (9f, 11f, 12f) (Fibr 3)
Lengthy, average gelding. AW high 42.
**D J G MurraySmith [0-9] The Joiners Arms Racing Club Quarndon.*

PURE COINCIDENCE BHB 76f79a **RR 75f 79a** 4487[3]
5 b g Lugana Beach 7f **(63)** - Esilam (Frimley Park) 6.5f **(67)**
Form - 0380703733
Record 2000 - 1st:0 2nd:0 3rd:4 Ran:9
Pre2000 - 1st:3 2nd:2 3rd:3 Ran:24
Win Prizemoney £12,819 *Total Prizemoney* £50,828
Wins * 1999 Aug Carlis (G-F) H 5f 77 78 <
1997 Aug Redcar (FRM) H 5f 75+
1997 Jun Southw (STD) 5f 77+
2000 Turf 0-8: (5f 7, 6f) (g-s, gd 3, g-f, frm 3) 2000 AW 0-1: (5f) (Fibr)
Above-average gelding, effective 5f, acts on g-s to frm - acts on Fibr, has worn blinkers. Turf high 75 - 3rd of 20 giving 1lb to Petarga (18 Spt Leicester 5f g-f RF 4487). (1st run) - 3rd of 8 giving 9lb to Eastern Trumpeter (16 Mar Wolverhampton 5f Fibr RF 0448). Consistent.
**K R Burke [1-14] Asterlane Ltd (from W J Musson [0-4] Jly 1999).*

PURE ELEGANCIA BHB 67f **RR 69f** 4098[9]
4 b f Lugana Beach 7f **(63)** - Esilam (Frimley Park) 6.5f **(67)**
Form - 024300
Record 2000 - 1st:0 2nd:1 3rd:1 Ran:6
Pre2000 - 1st:2 2nd:0 3rd:0 Ran:7
Win Prizemoney £11,120 *Total Prizemoney* £13,981
Wins * 1999 Jly Goodwo (G-F) H 5f 58 69 <
* 1999 Jun Catter (GD) H 5f 53 56
2000 Turf 0-6: (5f 6) (gd 3, frm 2, hrd)
Leggy, average filly, effective 5f, acts on g-f. Turf high 69 (began Jly). **D Nicholls [2-13] Mrs Andry Muinos.*

PURE SHORES (USA) BHB 75f **RR 72f** 4382[9]
2 b c Mt Livermore (USA) 7.7f **(90)** - Symphony Lady (USA) (Theatrical)
Form - 430
Record 2000 - 1st:0 2nd:0 3rd:1 Ran:3
Win Prizemoney £0 *Total Prizemoney* £940
2000 Turf 0-3: (6f 3) (gd, g-f, frm)
Currently above-average colt. Turf high 72 (began Aug) - 3rd of 16 giving 14lb to Love Thing (19 Aug Ripon 6f g-f RF 3798).
**M Johnston [0-3] Mrs Margaret Pett.*

PURNADAS ROAD (IRE) BHB 32f **RR 34f** 4922[12]
5 ch m Petardia 8.2f **(58)** - Choral Park (Music Boy) 6.8f **(57)**
Form - 086036300
Record 2000 - 1st:0 2nd:0 3rd:2 Ran:7
Pre2000 - 1st:0 2nd:0 3rd:0 Ran:7
Win Prizemoney £0 *Total Prizemoney* £605
2000 Turf 0-4: (7f, 8f, 10f 2) (g-f, frm 3) 2000 AW 0-3: (7f 3) (Equi, Fibr 2)
Very moderate filly, has worn blinkers. Turf high 34 (began Jly). AW high 13.
**Dr J R J Naylor [0-6] Nick Ridout (from H E Haynes [0-3] Jan 2000).*

PURPLE DAWN (IRE) BHB 24f34a **RR 39df 34a** 2744[8]
4 b f Tirol 8.1f **(64)** - Tuesday Morning (Sadler's Wells (USA)) 10f **(76)**
Form - 08
Record 2000 - 1st:0 2nd:0 3rd:0 Ran:2
Pre2000 - 1st:1 2nd:1 3rd:0 Ran:20
Win Prizemoney £2,285 *Total Prizemoney* £3,045
Wins 1999 Jun Nottin (GD) SH 10f 43 45 <
2000 Turf 0-1: (8f) (hrd) 2000 AW 0-1: (12f) (Equi)
Leggy, very moderate filly, effective 10f, acts on g-f, has worn blinkers, likes left handed tracks, likes tight tracks.
**B A Pearce [0-5] Laurie Yeomans (from J S Moore [1-22] Oct 1999).*

PURPLE FLAME (IRE) BHB 45f **RR 42f** 4304[17]
4 b f Thatching 7.8f **(69)** - Polistatic (Free State) 8.7f **(61)**
Form - 00
Record 2000 - 1st:0 2nd:0 3rd:0 Ran:2
Pre2000 - 1st:0 2nd:0 3rd:0 Ran:6
2000 Turf 0-2: (7f, 8f) (gd, frm)
Workmanlike, moderate filly. Turf high 42 (began Aug). Becoming disappointing. **C A Horgan [0-8] Mrs B Sumner.*

PURPLE FLING BHB 53f55a **RR 50f 55a** 5248[3]
9 ch g Music Boy 6.5f **(56)** - Divine Fling (Imperial Fling (USA)) 7.1f **(58)**
Form - 16002363
Record 2000 - 1st:0 2nd:1 3rd:2 Ran:6
Pre2000 - 1st:10 2nd:5 3rd:5 Ran:60
Win Prizemoney £31,407 *Total Prizemoney* £43,510
Wins * 1999 *Nov Wolver (STD)* *6f* *63*
* 1999 *Spt Southw (STD) H* *6f* *56* *58*
1997 Jly Redcar (G-S) 7f 76 <
1997 Jun Salisb (G-F) H 6f 68 70
1996 Oct Folkes (G-S) 6f 68
2000 Turf 0-2: (5f, 6f) (gd, frm) 2000 AW 0-4: (6f 4) (Fibr 4)
Fair gelding, effective 5 to 6f, best at 6f, acts on gd - acts on Fibr, prefers left handed tracks, prefers tight tracks, excels at Southwell and Wolverhampton. Turf high 29. AW high 55 (1st run) (began Jly) - 2nd of 8 getting 5lb from Garnock Valley (21 Jly Southwell 6f Fibr RF 3019).
**A J McNae [2-24] A J McNae (from D W Chapman [1-6] Mar 1998).*

PURPLE HEATHER (USA) BHB 90f **RR 94f** 4485[2]
3 b f Rahy (USA) 9.1f **(80)** - Clear Attraction (USA) **(38f)** (Lear Fan (USA)) 8.5f **(73)**
Form - 253021482
Record 2000 - 1st:1 2nd:3 3rd:1 Ran:9
Pre2000 - 1st:0 2nd:1 3rd:0 Ran:3
Win Prizemoney £4,082 *Total Prizemoney* £16,209
Wins * 2000 Aug Windso (G-F) 10f 80+ <
2000 Turf 1-9: (10f 1-6, 11f, 12f 2) (g-s, gd 2, g-f 1-3, frm 3)
Scopey, useful filly, effective 10f, acts on frm, often wears blinkers (very effectively). Turf high 94 - 4th of 10 getting 8lb from First Fantasy (16 Aug Salisbury 10f frm RF 3704). Consistent. She failed to live up to her juvenile promise, but did win a maiden at Windsor. One-paced, she is worth a try beyond middle distances.
**R Hannon [1-12] The Queen.*

PURSUIT OF DREAMS BHB 55f59a **RR 50f 59a** 5071[5]
3 ch c Pursuit of Love 9.5f **(69)** - Follow the Stars (Sparkler)
Form - 0005
Record 2000 - 1st:0 2nd:0 3rd:0 Ran:4
2000 Turf 0-4: (7f, 8f 3) (g-s 2, gd, frm)
Scopey, average colt. Turf high 50 (began Spt).
**P W Harris [0-4] Backers Dozen.*

PURSUIVANT BHB 33f45a **RR 46f 45a** 5119[11]
6 b g Pursuit of Love 9.5f **(69)** - Collapse (Busted) 10.2f **(61)**
Form - 734060320470870
Record 2000 - 1st:0 2nd:1 3rd:2 Ran:15
Pre2000 - 1st:0 2nd:4 3rd:5 Ran:16
Win Prizemoney £0 *Total Prizemoney* £8,090
2000 Turf 0-11: (7f, 8f 3, 9f 2, 10f 2, 11f 2, 12f) (gd 5, g-f 5, frm) 2000 AW 0-4: (8f, 9f, 11f, 12f) (Fibr 4)
Moderate gelding, effective 8 to 9f, best at 8f, acts on gd - acts on Fibr, often wears blinkers, favours tight tracks. Turf high 47. AW high 15. Becoming disappointing. He is a versatile sort but has been a disappointment under each code in recent seasons.
**Mrs N Macauley [0-9] Andy Peake (from M D Hammond [0-18] May 2000).*

PUSSIE WILLOW (IRE) BHB 70f **RR 67f** 5022[8]
3 b br f Catrail (USA) - Quiche (Formidable (USA)) 9.2f **(63)**
Form - 8
Record 2000 - 1st:0 2nd:0 3rd:0 Ran:1
Pre2000 - 1st:0 2nd:1 3rd:0 Ran:2
Win Prizemoney £0 *Total Prizemoney* £1,290
2000 Turf 0-1: (7f) (g-s)
Scopey, currently average filly.
**P F I Cole [0-3] Major Christopher Hanbury.*

PUTRA PEKAN BHB 92f **RR 83f** 4435[6]
2 b c Grand Lodge (USA) - Mazarine Blue (Bellypha) 9.8f **(73)**
Form - 0616
Record 2000 - 1st:1 2nd:0 3rd:0 Ran:4
Win Prizemoney £3,503 *Total Prizemoney* £3,747
Wins * 2000 Aug Cheste (GD) 7f 74 <
2000 Turf 1-4: (6f 2, 7f 1-1, 8f) (gd 1-2, g-f, frm)
Decent colt, often wears blinkers. Turf high 83 (began Jly) - also 1st of 8 from Attache (20 Aug Chester RF 3820). Got off the mark at Chepstow when tried in blinkers.
**M A Jarvis [1-4] H R H Sultan Ahmad Shah.*

PUTRA SANDHURST (IRE) RR 81f 5224[5]
2 b c Royal Academy (USA) 7.8f **(77)** - Kharimata (IRE) (Kahyasi)
Form - 5
Record 2000 - 1st:0 2nd:0 3rd:0 Ran:1
Win Prizemoney £0 *Total Prizemoney* £246
2000 Turf 0-1: (8f) (gd)
Currently decent colt. **M A Jarvis [0-1] H R H Sultan Ahmad Shah.*

PUZZLE RR 51f 5184[9]
2 b c First Trump - Eldoret (High Top) 10.2f **(67)**
Form - 00
Record 2000 - 1st:0 2nd:0 3rd:0 Ran:2
2000 Turf 0-2: (6f, 8f) (g-s, gd)
Currently fair colt. Turf high 51 (began Oct).
**Lady Herries [0-2] Angmering Park Stud.*

PUZZLEMENT BHB 65f70a **RR 72f 70a** 4810[5]
6 gr g Mystiko (USA) 7.7f **(59)** - Abuzz (Absalom) 7.2f **(58)**
Form - 333310055065
Record 2000 - 1st:1 2nd:0 3rd:4 Ran:12
Pre2000 - 1st:6 2nd:3 3rd:2 Ran:40
Win Prizemoney £28,883 *Total Prizemoney* £44,962
Wins * 2000 Mar Leices (GD) H 11.8f 70 73 <
* 1998 Aug Beverl (G-F) H 9.9f 63 71+
* 1998 Aug Beverl (G-F) H 9.9f 59 61
* 1997 *Nov Lingfi (STD) H* *8f* *70* *73* <
* 1997 *Nov Lingfi (STD) H* *8f* *63* *66*
* 1997 *Feb Wolver (STD) H* *9.4f* *52* *60*
* 1997 *Feb Lingfi (STD) H* *8f* *57* *59*
2000 Turf 1-7: (10f 3, 12f 1-4) (gd 2, g-f 1-2, frm 3) 2000 AW 0-5: (11f, 12f 4) (Equi 3, Fibr 2)
Above-average gelding, effective 10 to 12f, best at 12f, acts on sft to frm - acts on AW, best on Equi, likes tight tracks, excels at Kempton, likes Lingfield. Turf high 73 (1st run) - 1st of 13 giving 8lb to Rare Genius (30 Mar Leicester RF 0564). AW high 78 - 3rd of 7 getting 10lb from Quintrell Downs (19 Jan Lingfield 12f Equi RF 0117). **C E Brittain [7-52] Mrs C E Brittain.*

PYJAMA GIRL (USA) BHB 48f50a **RR 51f 50a** 2743[9]
3 gr ro f Night Shift (USA) 8.1f **(73)** - Permissible Tender (USA) (Al Hattab (USA)) 9.3f **(74)**
Form - 6380000
Record 2000 - 1st:0 2nd:0 3rd:1 Ran:6
Pre2000 - 1st:0 2nd:0 3rd:0 Ran:7
Win Prizemoney £0 *Total Prizemoney* £606
2000 Turf 0-4: (6f, 7f 2, 8f) (g-f 2, frm 2) 2000 AW 0-2: (7f, 9f) (Fibr 2)
Workmanlike, fair filly, effective 6f, acts on g-f, has worn blinkers. Turf high 51. AW high 56. Inconsistent.
**P R Chamings [0-13] M A Kirby.*

PYRUS (USA) RR 99f 3947a[5]
2 bb c Mr Prospector (USA) 8.6f **(88)** - Most Precious (USA) (Nureyev (USA)) 8.7f **(78)**
Form - 125
2000 Turf 1-3: (5f 1-1, 6f 2) (g-s 1-2, gd)
Currently very useful colt. Turf high 99 - 2nd of 8 to Endless Summer (3 Aug Goodwood 6f gd RF 3341). A powerful individual, he was easy to back when making a winning debut. Ridden aggressively when a creditable length second to Endless Summer in Goodwood's Group Two Richmond Stakes, he failed to handle bad ground in the Prix Morny at Deauville in August. Much better than that effort implies, he should develop into a useful sprinter this year. **A P O'Brien in IRE [1-3].*

PYTHAGORAS BHB 80f **RR 82f** 2443[8]
3 ch c Kris 10f **(75)** - Tricorne **(72f)** (Green Desert (USA)) 8.6f **(78)**
Form - 608
Record 2000 - 1st:0 2nd:0 3rd:0 Ran:3
Pre2000 - 1st:0 2nd:0 3rd:0 Ran:2
Win Prizemoney £0 *Total Prizemoney* £252
2000 Turf 0-3: (8f 3) (gd 2, frm)
Scopey, decent colt. Turf high 82 (1st run) - 6th of 14 to Foreign Secretary (19 May Newbury 8f gd RF 1308). **W R Muir [0-5] R Haim.*

PYTHIOS (IRE) BHB 100f **RR 112+f** 4740[34]
4 b c Danehill (USA) 9.1f **(79)** - Pithara (GR) (Never so Bold) 6.3f **(66)**
Form - 042000
Record 2000 - 1st:0 2nd:1 3rd:0 Ran:6
Pre2000 - 1st:2 2nd:0 3rd:1 Ran:4
Win Prizemoney £39,741 *Total Prizemoney* £49,011
Wins * 1999 Jun Ascot (G-F) H 8f 92 101 <
* 1999 May Doncas (G-F) 7f 79
2000 Turf 0-6: (8f 4, 9f 2) (g-s, gd 2, g-f 2, frm)
Scopey, Group-class colt, effective 8f, acts on gd. Turf high 112 - 4th of 32 giving 4lb to Caribbean Monarch (21 Jun Ascot 8f gd RF 2151). Inconsistent. He looked desperately unlucky when a close fourth in the Royal Hunt Cup, but failed to fulfil the promise of that effort. Given little respite by the handicapper, he may not be easy to place. **H R A Cecil [2-10] Mrs H G Cambanis.*

QAMOUS (USA) BHB 93f **RR 96f** 2183[24]
3 gr c Bahri (USA) - Bel Ray (USA) (Restivo (USA))
Form - 3830
Record 2000 - 1st:0 2nd:0 3rd:2 Ran:4
Pre2000 - 1st:1 2nd:0 3rd:0 Ran:2
Win Prizemoney £4,980 *Total Prizemoney* £10,789
Wins * 1999 Spt Newmar (G-S) 7f 86 <
2000 Turf 0-4: (7f 2, 8f 2) (g-s 2, gd, frm)
Scopey, very useful colt, effective 7f, acts on g-s to frm. Turf high 96 (1st run) - 3rd of 8 to Spencers Wood (7 May Newmarket 7f frm RF 1081). Well regarded by connections, he disappointed at Haydock in May and appreciated more enterprising tactics when third at Epsom the following month. Possibly best around seven furlongs, he may be better than last season's form suggests. **E A L Dunlop [1-6] Hamdan Al Maktoum.*

QUAKERESS (IRE) BHB 25f27a **RR 25f 27a** 2782[P]
5 b m Brief Truce (USA) 9.1f **(73)** - Deer Emily (Alzao (USA)) 7.1f **(68)**
Form - 000604113453200P
Record 2000 - 1st:2 2nd:1 3rd:2 Ran:13
Pre2000 - 1st:0 2nd:1 3rd:2 Ran:13
Win Prizemoney £2,997 *Total Prizemoney* £6,403
Wins * **2000** *Feb Wolver (STD) SH 16.2f 16 27*
2000 *Feb Wolver (STD) S 14.8f 31* <
2000 Turf 0-2: (12f 2) (gd, frm) 2000 AW 2-11: (12f 2, 13f, 15f 1-1, 16f 1-7) (Equi 2, Fibr 2-9)
Little account filly, effective 6f, acts on hrd, has worn blinkers, likes left handed tracks, likes tight tracks. Turf high 21. AW high 31. A speedy filly in 1997, she has developed stamina with age winning twice over a distance of ground at Wolverhampton early last season.
**R Brotherton [1-9] Ms Gerardine O'Reilly (from John Berry [1-17] Feb 2000).*

QUALITAIR PRIDE BHB 36f33a **RR 28f 33a** 4723[13]
8 b m Siberian Express (USA) 9f **(58)** - Qualitairess (Kampala) 8.4f **(56)**
Form - 0180060000
Record 2000 - 1st:1 2nd:0 3rd:0 Ran:10
Pre2000 - 1st:1 2nd:2 3rd:2 Ran:19
Win Prizemoney £5,472 *Total Prizemoney* £8,480
Wins * **2000** Jly Newmar (G-F) H 7f 23 37
1997 *Jan Southw (STD) H 12f 37 47* <
2000 Turf 1-7: (6f, 7f 1-4, 8f 2) (gd 3, g-f 2, frm 1-2) 2000 AW 0-3: (8f, 12f, 14f) (Equi, Fibr 2)
Little account mare, effective 7f, acts on frm, has worn blinkers. Turf high 37 (1st run) (began Jly) - 1st of 19 getting 27lb from Padhams Green (1 Jly Newmarket RF 2453). AW high 12.
**C A Dwyer [1-12] Mrs Shelley Dwyer (from J F Bottomley [1-25] Aug 1997).*

QUALITAIR SURVIVOR BHB 32f32a **RR 41f 32a** 3600[19]
5 gr g Terimon 8.7f **(58)** - Comtec Princess (Gulf Pearl) 12f **(54)**
Form - 45046880040
Record 2000 - 1st:0 2nd:0 3rd:0 Ran:9
Pre2000 - 1st:0 2nd:0 3rd:0 Ran:7
Win Prizemoney £0 *Total Prizemoney* £285
2000 Turf 0-9: (6f, 7f, 8f 3, 9f 2, 10f 2) (gd, g-f, frm 5, hrd 2)
Moderate gelding, has worn blinkers. Turf high 41. Inconsistent.
**J Hetherton [0-15] Qualitair Holdings Ltd (from T J Etherington [0-5] Jly 1999).*

QUALITY (IRE) BHB 60f87a **RR 46f 87a** 4031[2]
7 b g Rock City 8.8f **(62)** - Queens Welcome (Northfields (USA)) 9f **(72)**
Form - 2
Record 2000 - 1st:0 2nd:1 3rd:0 Ran:1
Pre2000 - 1st:5 2nd:3 3rd:4 Ran:25
Win Prizemoney £18,981 *Total Prizemoney* £28,556
Wins 1996 Aug Yarmou (G-F) H 7f 76 78
1996 *Mar Lingfi (STD) 10f 79+* <
2000 Turf 0-1: (12f) (frm)
Moderate gelding, often wears blinkers. Consistent.
**P J Hobbs [3-8] D B O'Connor (from W A O'Gorman [5-25] Spt 1996).*

QUALITY TEAM (USA) RR 110f 2524a[1]
3 b c Diesis 9f **(80)** -Ready For Action (USA)(Riverman (USA)) 9.1f **(76)**
Form - 321711
2000 Turf 3-5: (12f 2-4, 14f 1-1) (g-s 1-2, gd 1-1, g-f 1-2)
Group-class colt, effective 12 to 14f, acts on g-s to g-f, often wears blinkers (extremely effectively). Turf high 110 - 1st of 7 getting 15lb from Royal Rebel (1 Jly Curragh RF 2524a) - also 1st of 7 giving 3lb to Dutch Harrier (14 Jun Leopardstown RF 2133a). Improving. He developed into a useful performer, putting up an improved effort to beat Royal Rebel in the Group 3 Curragh Cup in July. Suited by the step-up to a mile and three-quarters there, he has a bright future in staying events.
**D K Weld in IRE [3-9] Moyglare Stud Farm.*

QUANTUM LADY BHB 79f **RR 76+f** 4490[F]
2 b f Mujadil (USA) 7.7f **(70)** - Folly Finnesse **(61f 70a)** (Joligeneration)
Form - 41223641F
Record 2000 - 1st:2 2nd:2 3rd:1 Ran:9
Win Prizemoney £6,061 *Total Prizemoney* £8,852
Wins * **2000** Spt Nottin (SFT) H 6.1f 68 76+ <
* **2000** May Bath (G-S) 5.1f 68
2000 Turf 2-9: (5f 1-3, 6f 1-5, 7f) (gd 2-3, g-f 5, frm)
Above-average filly, effective 5 to 7f, acts on gd to g-f, best on gd. Turf high 76 - 1st of 14 getting 1lb from Regal Air (15 Spt Nottingham RF 4443) - also 1st of 14 getting 8lb from Piccolo Player (2 May Bath RF 0959). **B R Millman [2-9] N W Lake.*

QUARRELL RR 61f 2868[4]
3 ch f Nashwan (USA) 10.3f **(79)** - Lead Note (USA) (Nijinsky (CAN)) 10.3f **(77)**
Form - 4
Record 2000 - 1st:0 2nd:0 3rd:0 Ran:1
Win Prizemoney £0 *Total Prizemoney* £318
2000 Turf 0-1: (12f) (g-f)
Scopey, currently average filly. (1st run) - 4th of 8 getting 5lb from Talk To Mojo (16 Jly Newbury 12f g-f RF 2868).
**J H M Gosden [0-1] K Abdulla.*

QUATREDIL (IRE) BHB 57f63a **RR 53f 63a** 5067[8]
2 b f Mujadil (USA) 7.7f **(70)** - Quatre Femme (Petorius) 7.3f **(61)**
Form - 04068
Record 2000 - 1st:0 2nd:0 3rd:0 Ran:5
Win Prizemoney £0 *Total Prizemoney* £225
2000 Turf 0-5: (5f, 6f 4) (g-s, gd 2, g-f, frm)
Average filly. Turf high 53 (began Jly).
**R Hannon [0-5] Deauville Daze Partnership.*

QUAZAR (IRE) BHB 65f **RR 71f** 5004[18]
2 b c Inzar (USA) - Evictress (IRE) (Sharp Victor (USA))
Form - 03850
Record 2000 - 1st:0 2nd:0 3rd:1 Ran:5
Win Prizemoney £0 *Total Prizemoney* £575
2000 Turf 0-5: (6f 3, 8f 2) (g-s 2, gd, g-f, frm)
Above-average colt. Turf high 71 (began Aug).
**J J O'Neill [0-5] C D Carr.*

QUEDEX BHB 83f65a **RR 87f 65a** 4987[7]
4 b c Deploy 11.4f **(67)** - Alwal (Pharly (FR)) 9.8f **(68)**
Form - 60281407187
Record 2000 - 1st:2 2nd:1 3rd:0 Ran:11
Pre2000 - 1st:2 2nd:1 3rd:0 Ran:10
Win Prizemoney £20,447 *Total Prizemoney* £24,751
Wins * **2000** Aug Kempto (G-F) H 16f 80 87 <
* **2000** May Haydoc (GD) H 14f 72 79
* 1999 Jun Bath (GD) 11.7f 68
* 1999 Jun Goodwo (G-S) H 9.9f 62 65
2000 Turf 2-9: (12f 2, 14f 1-3, 15f, 16f 1-2, 18f) (hvy, g-s, gd 1-4, g-f, frm 1-2) 2000 AW 0-2: (9f, 12f) (Fibr 2)
Unfurnished, useful colt, effective 12 to 16f, best at 16f, acts on g-s to frm, best on frm, excels at Haydock, likes Goodwood. Turf high 87 - 1st of 7 giving 15lb to Alrisha (14 Aug Kempton RF 3622) - also 1st of 16 giving 11lb to Needwood Spirit (6 May Haydock RF 1056). AW high 56. Consistent. Seemed to run a blinder for a 50/1 shot when runner-up at Haydock on his first turf start of this year, but showed it to be no fluke by winning over 14 furlongs at the same track in May. Added another victory when stepped up to two miles at Kempton in August. **E L James [4-21] L van Hijkoop.*

QUEEN FOR A DAY BHB 45f47a **RR 41f 47a** 5049a[18]
3 b f Emperor Jones (USA) - Could Have Been (Nomination) 7f **(60)**
Form - 750050
Record 2000 - 1st:0 2nd:0 3rd:0 Ran:5
Pre2000 - 1st:0 2nd:1 3rd:1 Ran:7
Win Prizemoney £0 *Total Prizemoney* £1,545
2000 Turf 0-4: (7f 2, 8f, 10f) (hvy, g-s, gd, hrd) 2000 AW 0-1: (10f) (Equi)
Light-framed, moderate filly, effective 6 to 8f, acts on g-s to g-f. Turf high 32.
**Patrick Flynn in IRE [0-3] Mrs Geraldine Reilly-Maloney (from H J Collingridge [0-3] May 2000).*

QUEENIE RR 79f 4643[8]
2 b f Indian Ridge 7.6f **(74)** - Bint Zamayem (IRE) **(74f 82a)** (Rainbow Quest (USA)) 10.4f **(75)**
Form - 8
Record 2000 - 1st:0 2nd:0 3rd:0 Ran:1
2000 Turf 0-1: (7f) (g-f)
Currently above-average filly. **B W Hills [0-1] Maurice Mogg.*

QUEEN MOLLY BHB 52f **RR 46f** 2157[4]
3 b f Emarati (USA) 6.6f **(63)** - Tiszta Sharok (Song) 7.2f **(61)**
Form - 524
Record 2000 - 1st:0 2nd:1 3rd:0 Ran:3
Win Prizemoney £0 *Total Prizemoney* £840
2000 Turf 0-3: (5f, 6f 2) (g-s, gd, frm)
Workmanlike, currently moderate filly. Turf high 45.
**R M H Cowell [0-3] Select Racing Partnership.*

QUEEN OF FASHION (IRE) BHB 54f **RR 60f** 4694[8]
4 b f Barathea (IRE) - Valuewise (IRE) (Ahonoora) 8.1f **(73)**
Form - 7437008
Record 2000 - 1st:0 2nd:0 3rd:1 Ran:7
Win Prizemoney £0 *Total Prizemoney* £956
2000 Turf 0-7: (10f 4, 12f 2, 13f) (gd, g-f 2, frm 4)
Unfurnished, average filly. Turf high 60.
**J J Sheehan [0-7] P J Sheehan.*

QUEEN OF THE KEYS BHB 37f53a **RR 15f 53a** 3218[10]
4 b f Royal Academy (USA) 7.8f **(77)** - Piano Belle (USA) (Fappiano (USA)) 8.7f **(77)**
Form - 73603080032210
Record 2000 - 1st:1 2nd:2 3rd:2 Ran:11
Pre2000 - 1st:0 2nd:0 3rd:1 Ran:8
Win Prizemoney £2,765 *Total Prizemoney* £5,512
Wins * **2000** *Jly Lingfi (STD) 10f 50* <
2000 Turf 0-3: (7f, 8f, 10f) (gd, g-f, frm) 2000 AW 1-8: (7f, 8f 2, 10f 1-4, 12f) (Equi 1-7, Fibr)
Unfurnished, fair filly, effective 10 to 12f, - acts on Equi, has worn blinkers, favours left handed tracks, favours tight tracks. Turf high 15. AW high 50 - 1st of 8 getting 3lb from Kennet (19 Jly Lingfield RF 2945). Inconsistent. **S Dow [1-19] Mrs A M Upsdell.*

QUEEN OF THE MAY (IRE) BHB 75a **RR 80f** 5313[11]
3 b f Nicolotte - Varnish (Final Straw) 7.9f **(64)**
Form - 13165470675800
Record 2000 - 1st:1 2nd:0 3rd:0 Ran:12
Pre2000 - 1st:2 2nd:0 3rd:1 Ran:9
Win Prizemoney £9,653 *Total Prizemoney* £11,645
Wins * **2000** May Windso (G-S) H 5f 75 80 <
* 1999 *Nov Lingfi (STD) H 6f 70 73*
* 1999 May Bright (FRM) 5.3f 66+
2000 Turf 1-12: (5f 1-9, 6f 3) (g-s 4, gd 1-5, g-f 2, hrd)
Unfurnished, decent filly, effective 5 to 6f, best at 6f, acts on gd - acts on Equi, likes left handed tracks, prefers tight tracks. Turf high 80 (1st run) - 1st of 17 giving 10lb to Corblets (2 May Windsor RF 0976).
**M R Channon [3-21] Miss Maggie Worsdell & Mrs Carolyn Wood.*

QUEEN SARABI (IRE) BHB 48f49a **RR 62f 49a** 5171a[15]
5 b m Mujtahid (USA) 7.4f **(69)** - Sharp Slipper (Sharpo) 7.7f **(59)**
Form - 03002180
Record 2000 - 1st:1 2nd:1 3rd:1 Ran:8
Pre2000 - 1st:1 2nd:1 3rd:2 Ran:20
Win Prizemoney £6,190 *Total Prizemoney* £10,266
Wins * **2000** Jly Down R (FRM) H 5f 48 62
1998 Apr Tipper (HVY) 5f 76 <
2000 Turf 1-6: (5f 1-5, 6f) (hvy, g-s, gd 2, g-f, frm 1-1) 2000 AW 0-2: (5f, 6f) (Fibr 2)
Average filly, effective 5f, acts on g-f, has worn blinkers. Turf high 62. AW high 42. Inconsistent.
**P Martin in IRE [1-13] Damien Shine (from D Nicholls [0-4] May 2000).*

QUEENS BENCH (IRE) BHB 69f **RR 80f** 4753[12]
3 ch f Wolfhound (USA) 7.3f **(71)** - Zafaaf **(98df)** (Kris) 9.5f **(73)**
Form - 48586700
Record 2000 - 1st:0 2nd:0 3rd:0 Ran:8
Pre2000 - 1st:2 2nd:1 3rd:2 Ran:6
Win Prizemoney £10,458 *Total Prizemoney* £14,594
Wins * 1999 Aug Epsom (GD) H 7f 81 85 <
* 1999 Aug Beverl (GD) 5f 78
2000 Turf 0-8: (6f, 7f 5, 8f, 10f) (g-s 2, gd 2, g-f 3, frm)
Workmanlike, decent filly, effective 5 to 7f, best at 7f, acts on gd to frm. Turf high 88 (1st run) - 4th of 21 giving 7lb to Rayyaan (18 Apr Newmarket 7f gd RF 0770). **B Hanbury [2-14] Abdullah Ali.*

QUEEN'S COLLEGE (IRE) BHB 60f **RR 59f** 3635[6]
2 b f College Chapel - Fairy Lore (IRE) (Fairy King (USA)) 7.7f **(59)**
Form - 0526
Record 2000 - 1st:0 2nd:1 3rd:0 Ran:4
Win Prizemoney £0 *Total Prizemoney* £639
2000 Turf 0-4: (5f 2, 6f 2) (g-f, frm 3)
Fair filly. Turf high 59. **M L W Bell [0-4] Messrs Hawtin, Green & Holt.*

QUEENSMEAD BHB 49f **RR 57f** 3057[8]
3 b f Rudimentary (USA) 8.2f **(66)** - Shernborne (Kalaglow) 9.8f **(67)**
Form - 078048
Record 2000 - 1st:0 2nd:0 3rd:0 Ran:6
Pre2000 - 1st:0 2nd:2 3rd:0 Ran:8
Win Prizemoney £0 *Total Prizemoney* £2,251
2000 Turf 0-6: (5f 4, 6f 2) (g-s, gd 2, g-f 2, frm)
Unfurnished, fair filly, effective 5f, acts on gd, has worn blinkers. Turf high 57. Inconsistent.
**D Burchell [0-6] Ralph Morgans (from R Hannon [0-8] Oct 1999).*

QUEENS MUSICIAN BHB 72f **RR 75f** 3627[3]
2 b c Piccolo - Queens Welcome (Northfields (USA)) 9f **(72)**
Form - 3373
Record 2000 - 1st:0 2nd:0 3rd:3 Ran:4
Win Prizemoney £0 *Total Prizemoney* £1,480
2000 Turf 0-4: (5f, 6f 3) (g-f, frm 3)
Above-average colt. Turf high 75. **M Dods [0-4] Bernard Hathaway.*

QUEEN'S PAGEANT BHB 67f79a **RR 72f 79a** 5072[10]
6 ch m Risk Me (FR) 8f **(53)** - Mistral's Dancer (Shareef Dancer (USA)) 9.9f **(73)**
Form - 704465178303260
Record 2000 - 1st:1 2nd:1 3rd:2 Ran:14
Pre2000 - 1st:3 2nd:1 3rd:3 Ran:27
Win Prizemoney £22,347 *Total Prizemoney* £31,387

Wins *** 2000** Jly Windso (G-F) H 10f 64 71
* 1999 Apr Thirsk (GD) H 8f 73 75 <
* 1998 Oct York (GD) H 7f 70 73
* 1996 Oct Haydoc (SFT) 5f 68
2000 Turf 1-14: (8f 5, 10f 1-6, 11f, 12f 2) (g-s, gd 7, g-f, frm 1-5)
Above-average mare, effective 8 to 12f, best at 8f, acts on gd to frm, has worn blinkers. Turf high 72 - 3rd of 9 getting 4lb from Summer Song (27 Aug Beverley 10f frm RF 4013) - also 1st of 21 getting 1lb from Barrettstown (31 Jly Windsor RF 3256). She is a fair handicapper when on song, and scored at Windsor in July. Best over a mile on genuinely good ground.
**J L Spearing [4-41] Mrs Robert Heathcote.*

QUEEN SPAIN (USA) BHB 67f **RR 70f** 3169[7]

2 b f Mister Baileys - Excellus (USA) (Exceller (USA)) 12.5f **(74)**
Form - 722227
Record 2000 - 1st:0 2nd:4 3rd:0 Ran:6
Win Prizemoney £0 *Total Prizemoney* £4,525
2000 Turf 0-6: (6f 5, 7f) (g-s, g-f 2, frm 3)
Above-average filly, effective 6 to 7f, best at 6f, acts on g-s to frm, best on g-f. Turf high 70 - 2nd of 10 getting 5lb from Ecology (11 Jun Ripon 6f g-f RF 1887). **M R Channon [0-6] Jaber Abdullah.*

QUEEN'S SONG BHB 44f **RR 60df** 4674[6]

2 ch f King's Signet (USA) 7f **(51)** - Darakah **(37f 46a)** (Doulab (USA)) 9.8f **(65)**
Form - 836566
Record 2000 - 1st:0 2nd:0 3rd:1 Ran:6
Win Prizemoney £0 *Total Prizemoney* £309
2000 Turf 0-5: (5f 5) (g-s, gd, frm 3) 2000 AW 0-1: (5f) (Equi)
Average filly, effective 5f, acts on gd. Turf high 60 (1st run) (began Jly) - 3rd of 6 getting 5lb from Wattno Eljohn (10 Jly Bath 5f gd RF 2663). **R J Hodges [0-6] Footsteps Flyers.*

QUEENS STROLLER (IRE) BHB 20f25a **RR 22f 25a** 3526[9]

9 b m Pennine Walk 8.9f **(64)** - Mount Isa (Miami Springs) 9.9f **(59)**
Form - 0000
Record 2000 - 1st:0 2nd:0 3rd:0 Ran:4
Pre2000 - 1st:6 2nd:9 3rd:4 Ran:64
Win Prizemoney £19,951 *Total Prizemoney* £30,018
Wins * 1997 *May Southw (STD) H 8f 30 38*
2000 Turf 0-3: (7f, 8f, 12f) (frm, hrd 2) 2000 AW 0-1: (10f) (Equi)
Little account mare, has worn blinkers. Turf high 22. Inconsistent.
**R E Peacock [1-25] R E Peacock (from T Wall [0-7] Jun 1996).*

QUERCUS RR 652[15]

2 ch c Lycius (USA) 8.8f **(71)** - Foresta Verde (USA) **(24f 42a)** (Green Forest (USA)) 9.9f **(68)**
Form - 0
Record 2000 - 1st:0 2nd:0 3rd:0 Ran:1
2000 Turf 0-1: (5f) (frm)
Currently very poor colt.
**V Soane [0-1] Mike Beever, Ruth Hatley & Joan Soan.*

QUEZON CITY (GER) RR 106f 4837a[10]

3 br f Law Society (USA) 11.6f **(71)** - Queen Of Love (GER) (Nebos (GER)) 9f **(78)**
Form - 20270
2000 Turf 0-5: (11f, 12f 3, 13f) (sft, gd 4)
Strong, Pattern-class filly. Turf high 106 - 2nd of 8 getting 18lb from Mutafaweq (23 Jly Dusseldorf 12f gd RF 3161a).
**P Schiergen in GER [0-5].*

QUICKTIME BHB 55f47a **RR 60f 47a** 91[9]

3 ch f Timeless Times (USA) 6.1f **(56)** - Sally Weld **(56f 55a)** (Weldnaas (USA))
Form - 80
Record 2000 - 1st:0 2nd:0 3rd:0 Ran:1
Pre2000 - 1st:0 2nd:0 3rd:0 Ran:4
2000 AW 0-1: (7f) (Fibr)
Workmanlike, average filly. **B Smart [0-5] R Lamb.*

QUICK TO PLEASE (USA) RR 87++f 5098[1]

2 b f Danzig (USA) 8.1f **(88)** - Razyana (USA) (His Majesty (USA)) 10.9f **(82)**
Form - 1
Record 2000 - 1st:1 2nd:0 3rd:0 Ran:1
Win Prizemoney £4,371 *Total Prizemoney* £4,371
Wins *** 2000** Oct Doncas (GD) 8f 87++ <
2000 Turf 1-1: (8f 1-1) (gd 1-1)
Currently useful filly. (1st run) - 1st of 25 from Kazana (20 Oct Doncaster RF 5098). A full sister to Danehill and Shibboleth, she won well from a bad draw on her only juvenile run, and could well be in a similar class to her brothers as a three-year-old.
**H R A Cecil [1-1] K Abdulla.*

QUIDS INN BHB 45f42a **RR 52f 42a** 5150[11]

3 br g Timeless Times (USA) 6.1f **(56)** - Waltz on Air (Doc Marten)
Form - 200600
Record 2000 - 1st:0 2nd:1 3rd:0 Ran:6
Pre2000 - 1st:0 2nd:0 3rd:0 Ran:6
Win Prizemoney £0 *Total Prizemoney* £988
2000 Turf 0-5: (7f, 8f 2, 9f, 12f) (frm 4, hrd) 2000 AW 0-1: (10f) (Equi)
Neat, fair gelding, has worn blinkers. Turf high 52.
**M Quinn [0-1] A Arton (from T D Easterby [0-11] Jly 2000).*

QUIESCENT BHB 92f **RR 87f** 3788[6]

2 ch f Primo Dominie 7.2f **(67)** - Tranquillity **(70f)** (Night Shift (USA)) 7.2f **(69)**
Form - 0136
Record 2000 - 1st:1 2nd:0 3rd:1 Ran:4
Win Prizemoney £3,396 *Total Prizemoney* £4,441
Wins *** 2000** Jun Nottin (SFT) 5.1f 81+ <
2000 Turf 1-4: (5f 1-4) (gd 1-2, g-f 2)
Useful filly. Turf high 87 - also 1st of 5 from Ami's Angel (2 Jun Nottingham RF 1663). She easily won a modest Nottingham maiden on her second start, but may just have needed it when third in a Yarmouth conditions event next time.
**R Hannon [1-4] Sir David Sieff.*

QUIET ARCH (IRE) BHB 49f44a **RR 52f 44a** 1958[11]

7 b g Archway (IRE) 8.5f **(60)** - My Natalie (Rheingold) 10.4f **(62)**
Form - 850
Record 2000 - 1st:0 2nd:0 3rd:0 Ran:3
Pre2000 - 1st:6 2nd:8 3rd:7 Ran:43
Win Prizemoney £17,023 *Total Prizemoney* £30,132
Wins 1998 Jun Bright (FRM) C 10f 63
1998 *Mar Lingfi (STD) 12f 73*
1998 *Feb Lingfi (SLW) H 12f 70 75* <
1997 *Jan Lingfi (STD) H 10f 57 67*
1997 *Jan Lingfi (STD) 10f 51*
1996 *Jun Lingfi (STD) 8f 69*
2000 Turf 0-2: (12f 2) (gd, frm) 2000 AW 0-1: (12f) (Fibr)
Fair gelding, has worn blinkers. Turf high 52.
**J G M O'Shea [0-15] Gary Roberts (from W R Muir [5-28] Nov 1998).*

QUIET READING (USA) BHB 45f56a **RR 65f 56a** 4928[4]

3 b g Northern Flagship (USA) 12.2f **(72)** - Forlis Key (USA) (Forli (ARG)) 9.6f **(67)**
Form - 0036405264
Record 2000 - 1st:0 2nd:1 3rd:1 Ran:10
Win Prizemoney £0 *Total Prizemoney* £1,531
2000 Turf 0-5: (7f, 10f 2, 12f 2) (sft, g-s, g-f, frm, hrd) 2000 AW 0-5: (10f, 12f 3, 16f) (Equi 4, Fibr)
Scopey, average gelding, effective 12f, - acts on Equi, prefers left handed tracks, favours tight tracks. Turf high 65. AW high 65 - 2nd of 12 to Exclusion Zone (5 Spt Lingfield 12f Equi RF 4228).
**C A Cyzer [0-10] R M Cyzer.*

QUIET RESOLVE (USA) RR 124f 5331a[2]

5 b h Affirmed (USA) 10.3f **(75)** - Quiet Cleo (USA) (No Louder (USA))
Form - 2
2000 Turf 0-1: (12f) (frm)
Currently very high-class colt. (1st run) - 2nd of 13 to Kalanisi (4 Nov Churchill Downs 12f frm RF 5331a).
**M Frostad in CAN [1-3] Sam-Son Farm.*

QUIET TRAVELLER (IRE) BHB 49f **RR 42f** 4623[13]

2 b c Blues Traveller (IRE) - Quietly Impressive (IRE) (Taufan (USA)) 7f **(57)**
Form - 0080
Record 2000 - 1st:0 2nd:0 3rd:0 Ran:4
2000 Turf 0-4: (6f, 7f, 8f 2) (gd 2, g-f, frm)
Moderate colt. Turf high 42.

Miss L A Perratt [0-4] Jamarc Construction Ltd.

QUIET VENTURE BHB 57f69a **RR 58f 69a** 5014[7]

6 b g Rainbow Quest (USA) 11.2f **(81)** - Jameelaty (USA) (Nureyev (USA)) 8.7f **(78)**

Form - 0007418007

Record 2000 - 1st:1 2nd:0 3rd:0 Ran:10
Pre2000 - 1st:4 2nd:1 3rd:2 Ran:19

Win Prizemoney £17,982 *Total Prizemoney* £21,059

Wins *** 2000** Aug Carlis (FRM) 6.9f 59
* 1998 *Nov Wolver (STD) H 6f 81 88* <
* 1998 Aug Newcas (GD) H 7f 76 78
* 1998 Aug Mussel (G-F) 7.1f 74
* 1998 Aug Redcar (G-F) 8f 65

2000 Turf 1-9: (6f 2, 7f 1-6, 9f) (g-s, gd 3, g-f 2, frm 1-3) 2000 AW 0-1: (6f) (Fibr)

Above-average gelding, effective 7f, acts on hrd. Turf high 59. Inconsistent.

**I Semple [5-25] Gee Kay Gee Gees (from E A L Dunlop [0-4] Oct 1997).*

QUIGLEYS POINT (IRE) BHB 30f **RR 18f** 4535[P]

4 b g Royal Academy (USA) 7.8f **(77)** - Remind Me (USA) (Riverman (USA)) 9.1f **(76)**

Form - 00P

Record 2000 - 1st:0 2nd:0 3rd:0 Ran:3
Pre2000 - 1st:0 2nd:0 3rd:0 Ran:1

2000 Turf 0-3: (8f, 14f, 16f) (g-s, gd 2)

Scopey, poor gelding. Turf high 18.

**M Mullineaux [0-3] I S Ross (from B W Hills [0-1] Nov 1998).*

QUINK BHB 95f **RR 93f** 5001[4]

2 ch g Selkirk (USA) 7.9f **(76)** - Ink Pot (USA) **(77f)** (Green Dancer (USA)) 10.3f **(74)**

Form - 1313514

Record 2000 - 1st:3 2nd:0 3rd:2 Ran:7

Win Prizemoney £14,740 *Total Prizemoney* £17,671

Wins *** 2000** Oct York (SFT) 7f 90
*** 2000** Jly Ayr (FRM) H 6f 93 <
*** 2000** Jly Yarmou (G-F) 6f 75+

2000 Turf 3-7: (6f 2-4, 7f 1-2, 8f) (g-s 1-2, g-f, frm 2-4)

Useful gelding, effective 6 to 7f, best at 6f, acts on g-s to frm, best on frm. Turf high 93 (began Jly) - 3rd of 9 giving 27lb to Theresa Green (2 Aug Kempton 6f frm RF 3324) - also 1st of 5 giving 20lb to Emissary (24 Jly Ayr RF 3061). A round-actioned individual, he was gelded before his first start and has shown signs of character. However, he settled down with racing and did well to win a conditions event at York in October. Likely to stay a mile, he probably acts on any ground but may be difficult to place.

**Sir Mark Prescott [3-7] Cheveley Park Stud.*

QUINTA LAD **RR 53f** 5318[7]

2 b g Alhijaz 7.7f **(57)** - Jersey Belle **(47f 50a)** (Distant Relative)

Form - 7

Record 2000 - 1st:0 2nd:0 3rd:0 Ran:1

2000 Turf 0-1: (6f) (sft)

Currently average gelding.

**J Balding [0-1] J M Lacey.*

QUINTRELL DOWNS BHB 49f93a **RR 42+f 93a** 117[1]

5 b g Efisio 7.7f **(69)** - Nineteenth of May (Homing) 7.8f **(59)**

Form - 3211

Record 2000 - 1st:2 2nd:0 3rd:0 Ran:2
Pre2000 - 1st:3 2nd:1 3rd:1 Ran:16

Win Prizemoney £20,850 *Total Prizemoney* £23,483

Wins *** 2000** *Jan Lingfi (STD) H 12f 79 94* <
*** 2000** *Jan Southw (STD) H 11f 79 83*
* 1999 *Jun Southw (STD) H 12f 62 70+*
* 1999 *Jun Wolver (STD) H 12f 55 59+*
* 1999 *May Southw (STD) H 11f 41 59+*

2000 AW 2-2: (11f 1-1, 12f 1-1) (Equi 1-1, Fibr 1-1)

Useful gelding, effective 12f, - acts on Equi, has worn blinkers, prefers left handed tracks. AW high 94 - 1st of 7 giving 19lb to Rayik (19 Jan Lingfield RF 0117). Inconsistent. He developed into a useful all-weather performer, but was not seen out after scoring decisively in January. Also successful over hurdles, he could stay beyond a mile and a half.

**R M H Cowell [5-10] & Mrs D A Gamble (from M Brassil in IRE [0-9] Oct 1998).*

QUITE HAPPY (IRE) BHB 60f60a **RR 63f 60a** 4543[17]

5 b m Statoblest 6.4f **(63)** - Four-Legged Friend (Aragon) 8.1f **(60)**

Form - 03335364222840

Record 2000 - 1st:0 2nd:4 3rd:4 Ran:15
Pre2000 - 1st:2 2nd:2 3rd:3 Ran:20

Win Prizemoney £5,093 *Total Prizemoney* £14,216

Wins 1999 Aug Catter (GD) C 5f 58
1998 May Folkes (G-F) H 5f 68 76? <

2000 Turf 0-14: (5f 14) (gd 3, frm 9, hrd 2) 2000 AW 0-1: (6f) (Fibr)

Average filly, effective 5f, acts on g-f to hrd, has worn blinkers, likes tight tracks. Turf high 63 - 2nd of 18 getting 3lb from Premium Princess (20 Aug Pontefract 5f hrd RF 3827).

**W J Musson [0-5] Asterlane Ltd (from M H Tompkins [1-22] Aug 2000).*

QUITTE LA FRANCE **RR 87+f** 4744[1]

2 b f Saddlers' Hall (IRE) 10.5f **(65)** - Tafila (Adonijah) 10f **(61)**

Form - 1

Record 2000 - 1st:1 2nd:0 3rd:0 Ran:1

Win Prizemoney £3,146 *Total Prizemoney* £3,146

Wins *** 2000** Spt Redcar (SFT) 7f 87+ <

2000 Turf 1-1: (7f 1-1) (gd 1-1)

Currently useful filly. (1st run) - 1st of 15 from Starry Lady (30 Spt Redcar RF 4744). A late foal out of a mare who won twice over a mile, she was very green when scoring on her debut, and should improve considerably for the experience.

**J G Given [1-1] D Morrison.*

QUI WARRANTO (IRE) BHB 72f **RR 80f** 4557[7]

2 ch c Spectrum (IRE) - Braneakins (Sallust) 8.4f **(63)**

Form - 8477

Record 2000 - 1st:0 2nd:0 3rd:0 Ran:4

Win Prizemoney £0 *Total Prizemoney* £315

2000 Turf 0-4: (6f, 7f 2, 8f) (gd 3, g-f)

Decent colt. Turf high 80 (began Jly).

**J G FitzGerald [0-4] Marquesa de Moratalla.*

QUIZZICAL LADY BHB 54f56a **RR 70f 56a** 5067[9]

2 b f Mind Games - Salacious (Sallust) 8.4f **(63)**

Form - 7516848642883050

Record 2000 - 1st:1 2nd:1 3rd:1 Ran:16

Win Prizemoney £2,917 *Total Prizemoney* £5,506

Wins *** 2000** Apr Warwic (HVY) 5f 70 <

2000 Turf 1-15: (5f 1-9, 6f 6) (hvy 1-1, g-s 2, gd 6, g-f 2, frm 4) 2000 AW 0-1: (5f) (Equi)

Above-average filly, effective 5 to 6f, acts on hvy to gd. Turf high 70 - also 1st of 4 from Beverley Macca (24 Apr Warwick RF 0853).

**M Quinn [1-16] & Mrs Gary Pinchen.*

QUWS **RR 99f** 1586a[10]

6 b h Robellino (USA) 9.5f **(68)** - Fleeting Rainbow (Rainbow Quest (USA)) 10.4f **(75)**

Form - 020

2000 Turf 0-3: (8f, 10f, 12f) (sft 2, g-s)

Very useful horse. Turf high 99.

**K Prendergast in IRE [6-20] Hamdan Al Maktoum (from K P McLaughlin in USA [0-1] Mar 1999).*

RAASED BHB 34f36a **RR 30f 36a** 3625[6]

8 b g Unfuwain (USA) 11.4f **(74)** - Sajjaya (USA) (Blushing Groom (FR)) 10.3f **(76)**

Form - 0006

Record 2000 - 1st:0 2nd:0 3rd:0 Ran:4
Pre2000 - 1st:4 2nd:4 3rd:3 Ran:35

Win Prizemoney £11,058 *Total Prizemoney* £16,683

Wins * 1999 Aug Nottin (G-F) H 8.2f 42 44
* 1999 Jun Carlis (G-F) H 6.9f 38 41
* 1998 *Feb Southw (STD) H 8f 36 43*

2000 Turf 0-4: (8f 4) (g-f, frm 3)

Moderate gelding, effective 7 to 9f, acts on gd to hrd, has worn blinkers, likes right handed tracks, likes tight tracks. Turf high 30.

**F Watson [3-34] F Watson (from J L Dunlop [1-5] Jun 1995).*

RACE LEADER (USA) BHB 112f **RR 106f** 2148[12]

3 b c Gone West (USA) 7.8f **(82)** - Dubian (High Line) 10.3f **(70)**

Form - 100

Record 2000 - 1st:1 2nd:0 3rd:0 Ran:3
Pre2000 - 1st:1 2nd:1 3rd:1 Ran:3
Win Prizemoney £19,902 *Total Prizemoney* £40,686
Wins * 2000 Apr Thirsk (G-S) L 8f 105 <
* 1999 Jly Newmar (GD) 7f 86+
2000 Turf 1-3: (7f, 8f 1-2) (gd 1-3)
Unfurnished, Pattern-class colt, effective 7 to 8f, best at 7f, acts on sft to g-f. Turf high 105 (1st run) - 1st of 6 getting 3lb from French Fellow (15 Apr Thirsk RF 0733). A half-brother to 1000 Guineas winner Sayyedati, he beat French Fellow in the Thirsk Classic Trial on his reappearance but was well beaten in the Guineas and the Jersey Stakes. **B W Hills [2-6] Mohamed Obaida.*

RACHEL GREEN (IRE) BHB 59f RR 66?f 2888[4]
2 b f Case Law 6f **(64)** - Alzeam (IRE) **(51f)** (Alzao (USA)) 7.1f **(68)**
Form - 604
Record 2000 - 1st:0 2nd:0 3rd:0 Ran:3
Win Prizemoney £0 *Total Prizemoney* £260
2000 Turf 0-3: (5f 2, 6f) (g-f 2, frm)
Currently average filly. Turf high 49.
**C N Allen [0-3] Newmarket Connections Ltd.*

RACINA BHB 101f RR 85f 4644[11]
2 ch f Bluebird (USA) 7.9f **(71)** - Swellegant (Midyan (USA)) 6f **(60)**
Form - 2130
Record 2000 - 1st:1 2nd:1 3rd:1 Ran:4
Win Prizemoney £3,727 *Total Prizemoney* £8,624
Wins * 2000 Aug Beverl (G-F) 5f 77+ <
2000 Turf 1-4: (5f 1-2, 6f 2) (gd, g-f 2, frm 1-1)
Useful filly. Turf high 85 (began Jly) - also 1st of 8 from Night Haven (17 Aug Beverley RF 3716). Absolutely bolted up in a Beverley maiden on her second start and did not fare too badly in a Chantilly Group Three next time.
**W J Haggas [1-4] I A Southcott.*

RACINGFORYOU LASS BHB 30f RR 12f 5237[10]
2 b f Moujeeb (USA) - Kentucky Mole VII (Damsire Unregistered)
Form - 00
Record 2000 - 1st:0 2nd:0 3rd:0 Ran:2
2000 Turf 0-2: (7f, 8f) (g-s, gd)
Currently little account filly. Turf high 12 (began Spt).
**A Streeter [0-2] Racing For You.*

RADA'S DAUGHTER BHB 103f RR 108f 5226[1]
4 br m Robellino (USA) 9.5f **(68)** - Drama School (Young Generation) 7.7f **(63)**
Form - 770178274
Record 2000 - 1st:1 2nd:1 3rd:0 Ran:9
Pre2000 - 1st:4 2nd:0 3rd:1 Ran:12
Win Prizemoney £60,424 *Total Prizemoney* £72,346
Wins * 2000 Jly Haydoc (G-F) H 11.9f 91 96 <
* 1999 Spt Newmar (G-S) H 12f 90 92
* 1999 Jly Ascot (FRM) H 12f 81 83
* 1999 May Windso (GD) H 11.6f 75 81
* 1999 Apr Bath (SFT) H 10.2f 70 74
2000 Turf 1-9: (12f 1-6, 14f, 15f, 16f) (gd 1-6, g-f 2, frm)
Workmanlike, Pattern-class filly, effective 14 to 15f, acts on gd to frm, likes left handed tracks. Turf high 108 - 2nd of 11 giving 7lb to Miletrian (6 Spt Doncaster 15f gd RF 4260). She did not show a great deal early on this season, but bounced right back to her best with a clear-cut victory in the Old Newton Cup. Never threatened in a Listed race next time and stayed on late in the Ebor, but probably put up her best performance when going down narrowly in the Park Hill at Doncaster.
**I A Balding [5-21] Mrs Richard Plummer.*

RADICAL JACK BHB 43f RR 39f 1296[10]
3 b g Presidium 7.5f **(56)** - Luckifosome (Smackover) 6f **(52)**
Form - 00
Record 2000 - 1st:0 2nd:0 3rd:0 Ran:2
Pre2000 - 1st:0 2nd:0 3rd:0 Ran:5
2000 Turf 0-2: (5f, 8f) (g-f 2)
Leggy, very moderate gelding, has worn blinkers. Turf high 39.
**Denys Smith [0-7] Lord Durham.*

RADIO STAR (USA) BHB 82f RR 85f 4734[22]
3 b br c Storm Cat (USA) 7f **(86)** - Andover Way (USA) (His Majesty (USA)) 10.9f **(82)**
Form - 130
Record 2000 - 1st:1 2nd:0 3rd:1 Ran:3
Win Prizemoney £4,114 *Total Prizemoney* £5,249
Wins * 2000 Jun Sandow (G-F) 7.1f 80 <
2000 Turf 1-3: (7f 1-1, 10f 2) (gd 2, frm 1-1)
Scopey, currently useful colt. Turf high 85 - also 1st of 4 from Dance West (16 Jun Sandown RF 2021). Unraced at two, he landed a four-runner Sandown maiden on his debut and did not fare badly in a Doncaster conditions event next time.
**J R Fanshawe [1-3] Joseph Allen.*

RAED BHB 39f44a RR 38f 44a 3894[5]
7 b g Nashwan (USA) 10.3f **(79)** - Awayed (USA) (Sir Ivor) 10.2f **(70)**
Form - 0603605
Record 2000 - 1st:0 2nd:0 3rd:1 Ran:4
Pre2000 - 1st:4 2nd:11 3rd:1 Ran:40
Win Prizemoney £11,344 *Total Prizemoney* £25,897
Wins 1999 Aug Windso (HVY) H 10f 60 61
1998 *Feb Southw (STD) H* 11f 62 72 <
1998 *Feb Southw (STD) H* 11f 62 65
1997 *Dec Southw (STD) H* 11f 57 62
2000 Turf 0-2: (10f 2) (g-f, hrd) 2000 AW 0-2: (11f, 12f) (Fibr 2)
Moderate gelding, effective 10 to 11f, best at 10f, acts on gd to frm - acts on Fibr, favours tight tracks. Turf high 38 (began Aug). AW high 7. **A J McNae [0-3] David Young (from J Pearce [1-10] Jan 2000).*

RAFTERS MUSIC (IRE) BHB 56f66a RR 55f 66a 3961[4]
5 b g Thatching 7.8f **(69)** - Princess Dixieland (USA) (Dixieland Band (USA)) 7f **(74)**
Form - 12168331304
Record 2000 - 1st:3 2nd:1 3rd:3 Ran:11
Pre2000 - 1st:1 2nd:0 3rd:0 Ran:14
Win Prizemoney £12,376 *Total Prizemoney* £15,856
Wins * 2000 May Doncas (G-S) H 7f 52 55
* 2000 *Jan Southw (STD) H* 6f 58 65+ <
* 2000 *Jan Southw (STD) H* 6f 48 60
1999 Jly Epsom (G-F) C 6f 52
2000 Turf 1-6: (6f, 7f 1-5) (gd 1-1, g-f, frm 3, hrd) 2000 AW 2-5: (6f 2-5) (Fibr 2-5)
Average gelding, effective 6 to 7f, best at 6f, acts on gd - acts on Fibr, prefers left handed tracks, likes tight tracks. Turf high 55. AW high 65 - 1st of 11 giving 1lb to Telecaster (31 Jan Southwell RF 0188) - also 1st of 9 getting 19lb from Bedevilled (17 Jan Southwell RF 0103).
**D Nicholls [3-11] Miss N F Thesiger (from Mrs A J Perrett [1-14] Oct 1999).*

RAGAMUFFIN BHB 86f RR 78f 1528[1]
2 ch c Prince Sabo 6.6f **(64)** - Valldemosa (Music Boy) 6.8f **(57)**
Form - 4621
Record 2000 - 1st:1 2nd:1 3rd:0 Ran:4
Win Prizemoney £2,847 *Total Prizemoney* £5,290
Wins * 2000 May Redcar (G-S) 5f 78 <
2000 Turf 1-4: (5f 1-4) (hvy, gd 1-2, g-f)
Above-average colt. Turf high 78 - 1st of 9 giving 3lb to Muja Farewell (29 May Redcar RF 1528).
**T D Easterby [1-4] Mrs Jennifer Pallister.*

RAGDALE HALL (USA) BHB 80f RR 83f 4734[21]
3 b c Bien Bien (USA) - Gift of Dance (USA) (Trempolino (USA)) 12f **(71)**
Form - 518370
Record 2000 - 1st:1 2nd:0 3rd:1 Ran:6
Win Prizemoney £2,996 *Total Prizemoney* £3,609
Wins * 2000 Jun Windso (GD) 10f 77 <
2000 Turf 1-6: (10f 1-4, 12f 2) (gd 2, g-f 1-3, frm)
Scopey, decent colt, effective 10 to 12f, best at 10f, acts on gd to g-f, best on g-f, has worn blinkers. Turf high 83 - also 1st of 15 from Joondey (5 Jun Windsor RF 1729). Took a Windsor maiden in fluent style on his second run. **J H M Gosden [1-6] Ragdale Racing.*

RAGING FEVER (USA) RR 5326a[6]
2 br f Storm Cat (USA) 7f **(86)** - Pennant Fever (USA) (Seattle Slew (USA)) 9.4f **(76)**
Form - 6
2000 AW 0-1: (9f) (Dirt)
Currently useful filly. **M Hennig in USA [0-1] E P Evans.*

RAGING TIMES BHB 37f **RR 36f** 4581[11]
2 ch f Timeless Times (USA) 6.1f **(56)** - Naufrage (Main Reef) 9.6f **(57)**
Form - 760
Record 2000 - 1st:0 2nd:0 3rd:0 Ran:3
2000 Turf 0-2: (6f 2) (gd, frm) 2000 AW 0-1: (7f) (Fibr)
Currently very moderate filly. Turf high 36 (began Aug).
**W G M Turner [0-3] Kevin Glastonbury.*

RAGLAN ACCOLADE BHB 32f **RR 36f** 2256[14]
3 b f New Reputation - Ophiuchus (Nader)
Form - 0
Record 2000 - 1st:0 2nd:0 3rd:0 Ran:1
Pre2000 - 1st:0 2nd:0 3rd:0 Ran:3
2000 AW 0-1: (12f) (Equi)
Strong, very moderate filly.
**J W Mullins [0-1] C Munden (from Derrick Morris [0-3] Spt 1999).*

RAHEIBB (IRE) **RR 47f** 5309[10]
2 ch c Lion Cavern (USA) 7.5f **(74)** - Abeyr **(104f)** (Unfuwain (USA))
Form - 00
Record 2000 - 1st:0 2nd:0 3rd:0 Ran:2
2000 Turf 0-2: (7f 2) (g-s, gd)
Currently moderate colt. Turf high 47 (began Oct).
**A C Stewart [0-2] Sheikh Ahmed Al Maktoum.*

RAILROADER BHB 77f **RR 83f** 5199[11]
3 ch g Piccolo - Poyle Amber (Sharrood (USA)) 10.5f **(72)**
Form - 61028000
Record 2000 - 1st:1 2nd:1 3rd:0 Ran:8
Pre2000 - 1st:0 2nd:0 3rd:2 Ran:6
Win Prizemoney £12,506 *Total Prizemoney* £25,895
Wins * 2000 May Cheste (GD) H 6.1f 74 75 <
2000 Turf 1-8: (5f 2, 6f 1-6) (hvy, gd 4, g-f 1-2, frm)
Decent gelding, effective 6f, acts on hvy to frm. Turf high 83 - 2nd of 23 getting 15lb from Cotton House (17 Jun York 6f frm RF 2062) - also 1st of 16 getting 6lb from Charlottevalentina (10 May Chester RF 1127). **G B Balding [1-14] Peter Richardson.*

RAINBOW FRONTIER (IRE) BHB 82f **RR 79f** 2153[12]
6 b g Law Society (USA) 11.6f **(71)** - Tatchers Mate (Thatching) 8f **(66)**
Form - 0
Record 2000 - 1st:0 2nd:0 3rd:0 Ran:1
Pre2000 - 1st:3 2nd:5 3rd:3 Ran:18
Win Prizemoney £10,617 *Total Prizemoney* £49,351
Wins 1997 Jly Killar (G-S) H 14f 79 75+
1997 Jun Currag (G-S) H 11f 75 79 <
1997 May Wexfor (GD) H 13f 79 <
2000 Turf 0-1: (20f) (gd)
Above-average gelding, has broken blood-vessels. Consistent.
**M C Pipe [2-17] Clive Smith (from A P O'Brien in IRE [6-18] Oct 1997).*

RAINBOW HIGH BHB 114f **RR 117f** 4985[3]
5 b h Rainbow Quest (USA) 11.2f **(81)** - Imaginary (IRE) (Dancing Brave (USA)) 8.4f **(76)**
Form - 54243
Record 2000 - 1st:0 2nd:1 3rd:1 Ran:5
Pre2000 - 1st:4 2nd:4 3rd:1 Ran:16
Win Prizemoney £81,437 *Total Prizemoney* £150,943
Wins * 1999 Oct Newmar (SFT) G3 16.1f 114 <
* 1999 May Cheste (G-F) H 18.7f 103 107
* 1999 Apr Newbur (G-F) H 16f 93 103+
* 1998 Jun Ripon (SFT) 12.3f 76
2000 Turf 0-5: (16f 3, 18f, 19f) (gd 3, g-f, frm)
High-class colt, effective 16 to 19f, best at 16f, acts on gd to frm, best on gd, excels at Chester and Newmarket. Turf high 117 - 2nd of 5 getting 2lb from Royal Rebel (22 Aug York 16f gd RF 3851). Consistent. He has bags of talent and is a top-class stayer. However, he finds little off the bridle and wins rarely as a direct result of refusing to relax during the early stages of a race. He made all when gaining his last success (in the 1999 Jockey Club Cup) and those tactics are worth trying again.
**B W Hills [4-21] K Abdulla.*

RAINBOW HILL BHB 84f **RR 86+f** 3233[7]
3 b c Rainbow Quest (USA) 11.2f **(81)** - Hill Hopper (IRE) **(104f)** (Danehill (USA)) 10f **(72)**
Form - 217
Record 2000 - 1st:1 2nd:1 3rd:0 Ran:3
Win Prizemoney £3,458 *Total Prizemoney* £4,688
Wins * **2000** Jun Ripon (G-F) 8f 76 <
2000 Turf 1-3: (8f 1-3) (gd, g-f 1-2)
Light-framed, currently useful colt. Turf high 86 (1st run) - 2nd of 16 giving 5lb to Papabile (7 Jun Yarmouth 8f gd RF 1793). Unraced at two, he landed long odds-on in a Ripon maiden on his second start, but looked an extremely difficult ride. He should improve with time and experience. **Sir Michael Stoute [1-3] N S P C C.*

RAINBOW PRINCESS (IRE) **RR** 2935[P]
2 b f Spectrum (IRE) - Richly Deserved (IRE) (Kings Lake (USA)) 10.8f **(67)**
Form - P
Record 2000 - 1st:0 2nd:0 3rd:0 Ran:1
2000 Turf 0-1: (6f) (frm)
Currently very poor filly.
**P W D'Arcy [0-1] Keith Harrison & Terry Miller.*

RAINBOW RAIN (USA) BHB 60f58a **RR 59f 58a** 4619[7]
6 b g Capote (USA) 9.1f **(84)** - Grana (USA) (Miswaki (USA)) 9f **(81)**
Form - 2375372200020002U7
Record 2000 - 1st:0 2nd:4 3rd:1 Ran:14
Pre2000 - 1st:4 2nd:5 3rd:4 Ran:53
Win Prizemoney £16,349 *Total Prizemoney* £32,563
Wins * 1999 Jly Bright (FRM) 6f 62
* 1999 Jly Bright (FRM) H 7f 58 65
* *1998 Aug Lingfi (STD) H 7f 59 69*
1997 Jun Carlis (FRM) H 8f 73 75 <
2000 Turf 0-10: (5f, 6f 3, 7f 5, 8f) (gd 3, g-f 4, frm 3) 2000 AW 0-4: (7f 4) (Equi 4)
Fair gelding, effective 6 to 8f, best at 7f, acts on gd to frm - acts on Equi, has worn blinkers, likes left handed tracks, likes tight tracks, and excels at Brighton. Turf high 59 - 2nd of 15 getting 1lb from Mutabassir (21 Aug Brighton 8f g-f RF 3834). AW high 57 (1st run) - 3rd of 15 getting 19lb from Nautical Warning (15 Jan Lingfield 7f Equi RF 0098).
**S Dow [3-56] P McCarthy (from M Johnston [1-11] Jly 1997).*

RAINBOW RAVER (IRE) BHB 33f43a **RR 25f 43a** 3070[7]
4 ch f Rainbows For Life (CAN) 9.3f **(64)** - Foolish Passion (USA) (Secretariat (USA)) 9f **(79)**
Form - 0007
Record 2000 - 1st:0 2nd:0 3rd:0 Ran:4
Pre2000 - 1st:0 2nd:2 3rd:1 Ran:17
Win Prizemoney £0 *Total Prizemoney* £2,874
2000 Turf 0-4: (10f 2, 12f 2) (gd, g-f, frm 2)
Workmanlike, little account filly, effective 10 to 12f, best at 12f, acts on frm, has worn blinkers, likes tight tracks. Turf high 25.
**J L Eyre [0-13] Alma & Stewart Pinner (from C Smith [0-10] May 1999).*

RAINBOW RIVER (IRE) BHB 59f **RR 59f** 4215[3]
2 ch g Rainbows For Life (CAN) 9.3f **(64)** - Shrewd Girl (USA) (Sagace (FR)) 8f **(124)**
Form - 0753
Record 2000 - 1st:0 2nd:0 3rd:1 Ran:4
Win Prizemoney £0 *Total Prizemoney* £277
2000 Turf 0-4: (5f, 6f, 7f, 8f) (g-f, frm 2, hrd)
Fair gelding. Turf high 59 - 3rd of 19 giving 11lb to Kumakawa (5 Spt Leicester 8f frm RF 4215). **P C Haslam [0-4] Mrs B M Hawkins.*

RAINBOW SPIRIT (IRE) BHB 59f59a **RR 72f 59a** 5104[16]
3 b g Rainbows For Life (CAN) 9.3f **(64)** - Merrie Moment (IRE) (Taufan (USA)) 7f **(57)**
Form - 57343423330
Record 2000 - 1st:0 2nd:1 3rd:5 Ran:11
Pre2000 - 1st:0 2nd:0 3rd:0 Ran:1
Win Prizemoney £0 *Total Prizemoney* £3,830
2000 Turf 0-10: (11f 2, 12f 4, 14f 2, 15f, 16f) (g-s 2, gd 2, g-f 3, frm 2, hrd) 2000 AW 0-1: (14f) (Fibr)
Workmanlike, above-average gelding, effective 11 to 14f, acts on gd to frm, prefers tight tracks. Turf high 72. Consistent.
**A P Jarvis [0-12] Mrs Rebecca Caudle.*

RAINBOW STAR (FR) **RR 36f** 2847[17]
6 b br g Saumarez 15.1f **(87)** -In the Star (FR) (In Fijar (USA)) 7.5f **(70)**

Form - 0
Record 2000 - 1st:0 2nd:0 3rd:0 Ran:1
2000 Turf 0-1: (12f) (g-f)
Very moderate gelding. **Mrs P Ford [0-1] W E Donohue.*

RAINBOW VIEW (IRE) BHB 52f RR 57f 4875[15]

4 b g Rainbows For Life (CAN) 9.3f **(64)** - L'Anno d'Oro (Habitat) 9.4f **(70)**
Form - 0
Record 2000 - 1st:0 2nd:0 3rd:0 Ran:1
Pre2000 - 1st:1 2nd:0 3rd:1 Ran:8
Win Prizemoney £3,038 *Total Prizemoney* £3,522
Wins 1999 May Redcar (FRM) 6f 52 <
2000 Turf 0-1: (8f) (g-s)
Angular, fair gelding, effective 6 to 8f, acts on gd to frm.
**W M Brisbourne [0-1] Miss Marjorie Thompson (from Mrs G S Rees [1-8] Spt 1999).*

RAINBOW WAYS BHB 111f RR 113f 3789[4]

5 b h Rainbow Quest (USA) 11.2f **(81)** - Siwaayib (Green Desert (USA)) 8.6f **(78)**
Form - 1223484
Record 2000 - 1st:1 2nd:2 3rd:1 Ran:7
Pre2000 - 1st:4 2nd:3 3rd:1 Ran:14
Win Prizemoney £43,312 *Total Prizemoney* £110,017
Wins * 2000 May Newmar (GD) H 12f 98 108 <
* 1999 Jly York (G-F) LH 13.9f 96 101
* 1998 Oct Newmar (GD) H 12f 88 93
* 1998 Spt Haydoc (G-F) H 11.9f 81 84
* 1998 Aug Newmar (G-F) 12f 74
2000 Turf 1-7: (12f 1-3, 13f, 14f, 16f 2) (gd 3, frm 1-3, hrd)
Group-class colt, effective 12 to 16f, acts on gd to hrd, has worn blinkers. Turf high 116 - 3rd of 18 giving 21lb to Bay of Islands (1 Jly Newcastle 16f frm RF 2442) - also 1st of 18 giving 24lb to Captain Miller (7 May Newmarket RF 1082). Consistent. Tough and reliable, he developed into a smart stayer last year, putting up an excellent weight-carrying performance when third under 9st 11lbs in the Northumberland Plate. Effective from a mile and a half to two miles, he is best on fast ground.
**B W Hills [5-21] Maktoum Al Maktoum.*

RAIN IN SPAIN BHB 100f RR 110f 3004[2]

4 b c Unfuwain (USA) 11.4f **(74)** - Maria Isabella (FR) (Young Generation) 7.7f **(63)**
Form - 324882
Record 2000 - 1st:0 2nd:2 3rd:1 Ran:6
Pre2000 - 1st:2 2nd:0 3rd:1 Ran:3
Win Prizemoney £7,579 *Total Prizemoney* £17,407
Wins * 1999 Jly Windso (GD) 11.6f 90+ <
* 1999 Jun Kempto (GD) 12f 75
2000 Turf 0-6: (10f 2, 12f 4) (gd 5, g-f)
Unfurnished, Group-class colt, effective 10 to 12f, best at 12f, acts on gd to g-f, best on gd. Turf high 110 - 2nd of 5 to Sossus Vlei (11 May Chester 10f g-f RF 1136). Consistent. He became headstrong last year and has proved a shade disappointing, including over hurdles. **J Noseda [2-9] Mrs E Schmidt-Bodner.*

RAIN LILY (FR) RR 93f 260a[3]

6 ch m Beaudelaire (USA) - Canadian Express (Siberian Express (USA)) 8.8f **(65)**
Form - 3
2000 Turf 0-1: (13f) (gd)
Currently useful mare. (1st run) - 3rd of 12 getting 8lb from Ben Ewar (2 Feb Cagnes-sur-mer 13f gd RF 0260a).
**H-A Pantall in FR [0-1].*

RAIN RAIN GO AWAY (USA) BHB 58f77a RR 46f 77a 3017[6]

4 ch c Miswaki (USA) 8.1f **(81)** - Stormagain (USA) (Storm Cat (USA))
Form - 8433161431106
Record 2000 - 1st:4 2nd:0 3rd:1 Ran:9
Pre2000 - 1st:0 2nd:0 3rd:3 Ran:8
Win Prizemoney £11,485 *Total Prizemoney* £13,085
Wins * 2000 *Apr Lingfi (STD) H 7f 70 73+* <
* 2000 *Mar Wolver (STD) H 7f 66 72*
* 2000 *Feb Lingfi (STD) 7f 69*
* 2000 *Jan Wolver (STD) 7f 58*
2000 Turf 0-1: (6f) (g-f) 2000 AW 4-8: (7f 4-5, 8f 3) (Equi 2-3, Fibr 2-5)
Workmanlike, above-average colt, effective 7 to 8f, best at 7f, acts on AW, best on Fibr, prefers left handed tracks, prefers tight tracks, excels at Wolverhampton, does well at Lingfield. AW high 73 - 1st of 8 giving 21lb to Ithadtobeyou (12 Apr Lingfield RF 0679) - also 1st of 8 getting 1lb from Risk Free (25 Mar Wolverhampton RF 0507). Some ability on turf, but has become a very decent performer on sand, winning four times last year. Suited by seven furlongs and forcing tactics.
**D J S Cosgrove [4-15] G G Grayson (from E A L Dunlop [0-2] Apr 1999).*

RAINSTORM BHB 74a RR 40f 4101[12]

5 b g Rainbow Quest (USA) 11.2f **(81)** - Katsina (USA) (Cox's Ridge (USA)) 8f **(68)**
Form - 03570
Record 2000 - 1st:0 2nd:0 3rd:1 Ran:5
Pre2000 - 1st:1 2nd:1 3rd:0 Ran:12
Win Prizemoney £2,788 *Total Prizemoney* £4,400
Wins 1998 *Dec Lingfi (STD) 7f 64* <
2000 Turf 0-5: (8f, 10f 3, 12f) (g-f 2, frm 3)
Fair gelding, has worn blinkers. Turf high 40 (began Jly).
**P D Evans [0-5] C M & S J Owen (from E J O'Neill [0-4] Spt 1999).*

RAINWORTH LADY BHB 39f40a RR 47f 40a 4559[8]

3 b f Governor General 6.8f **(45)** - Monongelia (Welsh Pageant) 10f **(65)**
Form - 05000635P8
Record 2000 - 1st:0 2nd:0 3rd:1 Ran:9
Pre2000 - 1st:0 2nd:0 3rd:0 Ran:4
Win Prizemoney £0 *Total Prizemoney* £797
2000 Turf 0-7: (8f 2, 10f 3, 12f 2) (sft, gd 2, g-f 2, frm, hrd) 2000 AW 0-2: (6f, 12f) (Fibr 2)
Rangy, moderate filly, has worn blinkers. Turf high 41. AW high 25. Inconsistent. **M J Polglase [0-13] Southwell Racing Club.*

RAINY RIVER (IRE) RR 66f 5186[5]

2 b f Irish River (FR) 9f **(77)** - Forest Storm (USA) (Woodman (USA)) 9f **(74)**
Form - 5
Record 2000 - 1st:0 2nd:0 3rd:0 Ran:1
2000 Turf 0-1: (7f) (g-s)
Currently average filly. **B W Hills [0-1] R A Scarborough.*

RAISA'S GOLD (IRE) RR 1149[10]

2 b f Goldmark (USA) - Princess Raisa (Indian King (USA)) 7.4f **(64)**
Form - 600
Record 2000 - 1st:0 2nd:0 3rd:0 Ran:3
2000 AW 0-3: (5f 3) (Fibr 3)
Currently little account filly. AW high 21.
**B S Rothwell [0-3] Brian Rothwell.*

RAISE A GLASS RR 21f 4580[15]

2 ch c King's Signet (USA) 7f **(51)** - Anouska (Interrex (CAN))
Form - 0
Record 2000 - 1st:0 2nd:0 3rd:0 Ran:1
2000 Turf 0-1: (5f) (gd)
Currently little account colt. **C G Cox [0-1] T Y Bissett.*

RAISE A PRINCE (FR) BHB 86f98a RR 91f 98a 4892[3]

7 b g Machiavellian (USA) 9.8f **(83)** - Enfant D'Amour (USA) (Lyphard (USA)) 9.9f **(72)**
Form - 56600253
Record 2000 - 1st:0 2nd:1 3rd:1 Ran:8
Pre2000 - 1st:7 2nd:4 3rd:6 Ran:35
Win Prizemoney £76,785 *Total Prizemoney* £108,886
Wins * 1999 Apr Nottin (SFT) 14.1f 106 <
* 1998 Spt Ascot (SFT) H 12f 90 92
* 1998 Spt Ayr (G-S) H 13.1f 89 92
* 1998 Apr Newmar (SFT) H 12f 79 89
* 1997 *Nov Lingfi (STD) 12f 82*
* 1997 Oct Newbur (G-S) C 12f 81+
1997 Jly Nottin (SFT) H 10f 69 69
2000 Turf 0-8: (12f 3, 13f 3, 14f, 16f) (hvy 2, g-s 2, gd 3, g-f)
Useful gelding, effective 12 to 16f, acts on sft to gd, has worn blinkers. Turf high 98. Consistent. He is on a long losing run despite dropping dramatically in the weights. Equally disappointing after a bright start to his hurdling career, he is one to watch at present.
**S P C Woods [6-31] Dr Frank Chao (from J W Hills [1-9] Jly 1997).*

RAJMATA (IRE) BHB 53f50a **RR 42f 50a** 2077^{R}

4 b f Prince Sabo 6.6f **(64)** - Heart of India (IRE) (Try My Best (USA)) 7.6f **(67)**

Form - 76R

Record					
2000 -	1st:0	2nd:0	3rd:0	Ran:3
Pre2000 -	1st:0	2nd:3	3rd:1	Ran:15

Win Prizemoney £0 *Total Prizemoney* £2,919

2000 Turf 0-1: (6f) (hrd) 2000 AW 0-2: (6f 2) (Equi, Fibr)

Scopey, moderate filly, effective 5f, acts on gd - acts on Fibr, often wears blinkers (very effectively). AW high 16. Becoming disappointing.

**Mrs N Macauley [0-10] Mrs N Macauley (from Sir Mark Prescott [0-8] Jan 1999).*

RAKEEB (USA) BHB 67f **RR 59f** 1868^{8}

5 ch g Irish River (FR) 9f **(77)** - Ice House (Northfields (USA)) 9f **(72)**

Form - 148

Record				
2000 -	1st:1	2nd:0	3rd:0	Ran:3
Pre2000 -	1st:2	2nd:0	3rd:2	Ran:14

Win Prizemoney £10,099 *Total Prizemoney* £11,536

Wins								
* **2000**	Mar	Doncas	(G-F)	H	12f	60	66	
1998	Aug	Haydoc	(G-S)	H	11.9f	85	91	
1998	Jly	Ayr	(SFT)		10f		94	<

2000 Turf 1-3: (12f 1-2, 14f) (gd, frm 1-2)

Fair gelding, effective 12f, acts on frm, has worn blinkers (very effectively), likes left handed tracks. Turf high 66 (1st run) - 1st of 24 giving 1lb to Double Blade (23 Mar Doncaster RF 0472).

**M W Easterby [1-16] Lady Manton (from A C Stewart [2-6] Spt 1998).*

RAKE HEY BHB 45f **RR 47f** 2300^{4}

6 gr g Petong 7.6f **(58)** - Dancing Daughter (Dance In Time (CAN)) 8.9f **(59)**

Form - 64

Record				
2000 -	1st:0	2nd:0	3rd:0	Ran:2
Pre2000 -	1st:0	2nd:1	3rd:0	Ran:6

Win Prizemoney £0 *Total Prizemoney* £959

2000 Turf 0-1: (10f) (gd) 2000 AW 0-1: (10f) (Equi)

Moderate gelding, has worn blinkers. Consistent.

**D G Bridgwater [2-11] Terry & Sarah Amos (from R F JohnsonHoughton [0-6] Nov 1996).*

RAMADANZEN **RR 10f** 1800^{13}

3 b f Mizoram (USA) - The Country Dancer **(29f 24a)** (Mashhor Dancer (USA)) 10f **(65)**

Form - 00

Record				
2000 -	1st:0	2nd:0	3rd:0	Ran:2

2000 Turf 0-2: (10f 2) (gd, g-f)

Neat, currently poor filly. Turf high 10. **J Akehurst [0-2] W J Wyatt.*

RAMBAGH BHB 68f **RR 67f** 4547^{4}

2 b f Polish Precedent (USA) 9f **(73)** - My Preference (Reference Point) 6.8f **(70)**

Form - 4254

Record				
2000 -	1st:0	2nd:1	3rd:0	Ran:4

Win Prizemoney £0 *Total Prizemoney* £2,015

2000 Turf 0-4: (7f 3, 8f) (g-s, gd 2, frm)

Average filly. Turf high 67 (1st run) (began Jun) - 4th of 6 to Rizerie (30 Jun Goodwood 7f gd RF 2400).

**J L Dunlop [0-4] The Rajmata of Jaipur.*

RAMBLING BEAR BHB 106f **RR 109f** 4700^{13}

7 ch h Sharrood (USA) 11.1f **(67)** - Supreme Rose (Frimley Park) 6.5f **(67)**

Form - 330756370

Record				
2000 -	1st:0	2nd:0	3rd:3	Ran:9
Pre2000 -	1st:7	2nd:4	3rd:5	Ran:45

Win Prizemoney £88,985 *Total Prizemoney* £129,606

Wins							
* 1999	May	Newmar	(G-F)	G3	5f	110	
* 1998	May	Goodwo	(G-F)		6f	109	
* 1996	Jly	Goodwo	(G-F)	G3	5f	107	
* 1996	Jun	Lingfi	(G-F)	L	6f	114	<
* 1996	May	Newbur	(G-F)		6f	108	

2000 Turf 0-9: (5f 9) (g-s, gd 3, g-f 2, frm 3)

Pattern-class horse, effective 5 to 6f, best at 5f, acts on gd to frm, best on frm, has worn blinkers, excels at Newmarket. Turf high 109 (1st run) - 3rd of 21 giving 6lb to Pipalong (6 May Newmarket 5f gd RF 1061). He invariably looks well and is a very useful sprinter who goes well fresh. Not easy to win with, he usually comes with a late rattle. **M Blanshard [7-54] Mrs Michael Hill.*

RAMBLIN' MAN (IRE) BHB 59f **RR 61f** 4305^{8}

2 b c Blues Traveller (IRE) - Saborinie (Prince Sabo) 7.2f **(62)**

Form - 050388

Record				
2000 -	1st:0	2nd:0	3rd:1	Ran:6

Win Prizemoney £0 *Total Prizemoney* £611

2000 Turf 0-6: (5f 3, 6f 3) (gd, g-f, frm 3, hrd)

Average colt. Turf high 58. **V Soane [0-6] The First Timers.*

RAMBOLD BHB 37f37a **RR 29f 37a** 24^{7}

9 b m Rambo Dancer (CAN) 8.4f **(59)** - Boldie (Bold Lad (IRE)) 8.4f **(68)**

Form - 07

Record				
2000 -	1st:0	2nd:0	3rd:0	Ran:1
Pre2000 -	1st:7	2nd:5	3rd:4	Ran:66

Win Prizemoney £25,076 *Total Prizemoney* £32,509

Wins							
* 1998	Jly	Bright	(G-F)		6f		58
* 1998	May	Chepst	(G-F)	H	6.1f	47	51
* 1996	Aug	Yarmou	(GD)	H	6f	60	65
* 1996	Jun	Hamilt	(GD)		6f		48

2000 AW 0-1: (6f) (Equi)

Little account mare, effective 6f, acts on frm.

**N E Berry [4-46] Ron Collins (from T M Jones [3-21] Jan 1995).*

RAMBO NINE BHB 33f43a **RR 50df 43a** 4875^{17}

3 b g Rambo Dancer (CAN) 8.4f **(59)** - Asmarina **(44f 44a)** (Ascendant)

Form - 00

Record				
2000 -	1st:0	2nd:0	3rd:0	Ran:2
Pre2000 -	1st:0	2nd:0	3rd:0	Ran:4

2000 Turf 0-2: (8f, 12f) (g-s, g-f)

Workmanlike, fair gelding. Turf high 19 (began Spt).

**S R Bowring [0-6] J E Reed & P M Sedgwick.*

RAMBO WALTZER BHB 54f65a **RR 56f 65a** 5006^{6}

8 b g Rambo Dancer (CAN) 8.4f **(59)** - Vindictive Lady (USA) (Foolish Pleasure (USA)) 8.9f **(72)**

Form - 141112126113270246

Record				
2000 -	1st:5	2nd:4	3rd:1	Ran:15
Pre2000 -	1st:20	2nd:11	3rd:9	Ran:84

Win Prizemoney £82,051 *Total Prizemoney* £101,683

Wins								
* **2000**	*Mar*	*Wolver*	*(STD)*	*C*	*8.5f*		*69+*	
* **2000**	*Mar*	*Southw*	*(STD)*	*C*	*7f*		*59+*	
2000	*Feb*	*Wolver*	*(STD)*	*C*	*9.4f*		*59+*	
2000	*Jan*	*Wolver*	*(STD)*	*S*	*7f*		*55+*	
2000	*Jan*	*Southw*	*(STD)*	*S*	*8f*		*63*	
1999	*Dec*	*Southw*	*(STD)*	*C*	*8f*		*56*	
1999	*Nov*	*Southw*	*(STD)*	*S*	*8f*		*56*	
1999	*May*	*Southw*	*(STD)*	*C*	*7f*		*71*	
1999	Apr	Thirsk	(GD)	H	7f	67	69	
1999	Mar	Catter	(G-S)	H	7f	63	67	
1998	*Dec*	*Southw*	*(STD)*	*C*	*8f*		*73*	
1998	*Apr*	*Southw*	*(STD)*	*H*	*8f*	*81*	*87*	<
1998	*Jan*	*Wolver*	*(STD)*	*H*	*9.4f*	*76*	*78*	
1997	Apr	Hamilt	(G-S)	H	8.3f	65	71	
1997	*Mar*	*Wolver*	*(STD)*	*H*	*8.5f*	*78*	*78*	
1997	*Feb*	*Southw*	*(STD)*	*H*	*8f*	*70*	*76*	
1997	*Jan*	*Southw*	*(STD)*	*C*	*7f*		*70+*	
1997	*Jan*	*Southw*	*(STD)*	*C*	*8f*		*81+*	
1996	Apr	Ripon	(GD)	H	8f	61	68	
1996	Apr	Thirsk	(G-F)	H	8f	55	64	
1996	Apr	Hamilt	(G-S)	H	8.3f	55	58	
1996	*Jan*	*Wolver*	*(STD)*	*C*	*7f*		*78*	
1996	*Jan*	*Southw*	*(STD)*	*C*	*8f*		*75+*	

2000 Turf 0-4: (7f, 8f 2, 10f) (hvy, gd, frm 2) 2000 AW 5-11: (7f 2-3, 8f 2-5, 9f 1-3) (Fibr 5-11)

Above-average gelding, effective 7 to 9f, acts on gd - acts on Fibr, has worn blinkers, favours left handed tracks, prefers tight tracks, excels at Wolverhampton, likes Southwell. Turf high 56. AW high 76 - 2nd of 8 giving 8lb to Santandre (2 Mar Wolverhampton 7f Fibr RF 0392) - also 1st of 9 giving 6lb to Bentico (28 Mar Wolverhampton RF 0532). He is a consistent performer, and though most of his wins in recent seasons have been on Fibresand, a surface on which he is particularly effective, he remains perfectly capable of winning on turf. A turning track suits him best, and he seems to need at least a mile now. Now with Sue Wilton, he still keeps on winning.

Miss S J Wilton [2-11] John Pointon and Sons (from D Nicholls [21-73] Feb 2000).

RAMESES BHB 53f **RR 59f** 4930[22]
2 b g Petardia 8.2f **(58)** - Kirkby Belle (Bay Express) 7.1f **(60)**
Form - 0400
Record 2000 - 1st:0 2nd:0 3rd:0 Ran:4
Win Prizemoney £0 *Total Prizemoney* £267
2000 Turf 0-4: (5f 2, 6f, 7f) (gd 2, g-f, frm)
Fair gelding, often wears blinkers. Turf high 59.
**Mrs L Stubbs [0-4] M S & C S Griffiths.*

RAMOOZ (USA) BHB 107f **RR 112f** 2109[9]
7 b h Rambo Dancer (CAN) 8.4f **(59)** - My Shafy (Rousillon (USA)) 8.2f **(74)**
Form - 4530
Record 2000 - 1st:0 2nd:0 3rd:1 Ran:4
Pre2000 - 1st:10 2nd:10 3rd:6 Ran:48
Win Prizemoney £146,497 *Total Prizemoney* £263,041

Wins								
1999	Jly	Currag	(G-F)	G3	8f		113	
1999	Jun	Goodwo	(G-F)	L	8f		113	
1998	Spt	Currag	(SFT)	G3	7f		109+	
1998	May	York	(GD)	LH	7.9f	110	112	
1997	Jly	Currag	(GD)	G3	8f		115	<
1997	Jun	Newmar	(SFT)	G3	7f		108	
1996	Jun	Epsom	(GD)		7f		98	
1996	Apr	Thirsk	(G-F)		8f		94	

2000 Turf 0-4: (7f, 8f 2, 9f) (gd 4)
Group-class horse, effective 7 to 9f, best at 8f, acts on g-s to g-f, best on gd, has worn blinkers, prefers left handed tracks, prefers tight tracks, excels at Epsom. Turf high 112 - 3rd of 5 getting 2lb from Trans Island (10 Jun Epsom 9f gd RF 1862). He was sold cheaply at the end of 1999 (11,500gns), but remains competitive in minor Group races. Effective up to a mile, he may be hard to place.
**J W Hills [0-4] Mrs Julie Mitchell (from B Hanbury [10-48] Spt 1999).*

RAMP AND RAVE (USA) RR 577a[4]
6 ch h Ramplett (USA) - Turbonative (USA) (Sitzmark (USA))
Form - 4
2000 AW 0-1: (6f) (Dirt)
Currently Group-class horse, often wears blinkers.
**D J Selvaratnam in UAE [1-2].*

RAMPANT (IRE) RR 81f 4689[2]
2 b c Pursuit of Love 9.5f **(69)** - Flourishing (IRE) (Trojan Fen) 8.1f **(62)**
Form - 2
Record 2000 - 1st:0 2nd:1 3rd:0 Ran:1
Win Prizemoney £0 *Total Prizemoney* £1,276
2000 Turf 0-1: (8f) (gd)
Currently decent colt. (1st run) - 2nd of 18 to Regatta Point (27 Spt Salisbury 8f gd RF 4689). **R M Beckett [0-1] Mrs Richard Aykroyd.*

RAMPART BHB 44f **RR 67f** 3356[5]
3 b g Kris 10f **(75)** - Balliasta (USA) (Lyphard (USA)) 9.9f **(72)**
Form - 05
Record 2000 - 1st:0 2nd:0 3rd:0 Ran:2
Pre2000 - 1st:0 2nd:0 3rd:1 Ran:2
Win Prizemoney £0 *Total Prizemoney* £492
2000 Turf 0-2: (8f, 10f) (gd, frm)
Scopey, average gelding. Turf high 51. **B W Hills [0-4] K Abdulla.*

RAMRUMA (USA) BHB 117f **RR 118?f** 4613[3]
4 ch f Diesis 9f **(80)** - Princess of Man (Green God) 9.6f **(68)**
Form - 033
Record 2000 - 1st:0 2nd:0 3rd:2 Ran:3
Pre2000 - 1st:5 2nd:2 3rd:1 Ran:8
Win Prizemoney £432,310 *Total Prizemoney* £543,188

Wins							
* 1999	Aug	York	(GD)	G1	11.9f	117	
* 1999	Jly	Currag	(G-F)	G1	12f	118+	
* 1999	Jun	Epsom	(G-S)	G1	12f	120	<
* 1999	May	Lingfi	(G-F)	L	11.5f	104	
* 1999	Apr	Newmar	(GD)		12f	102+	

2000 Turf 0-3: (12f 3) (g-s, g-f, frm)
Leggy, high-class filly, effective 12 to 15f, best at 12f, acts on gd to frm, does well at York. Turf high 118 - 3rd of 6 giving 10lb to Petrushka (23 Aug York 12f frm RF 3913). Successful in the English, Irish and Yorkshire Oaks' as a three-year-old in 1999, she was an outstandingly game performer at her best but failed to fire last term and has been retired.
**H R A Cecil [5-11] H R H Prince Fahd Salman.*

RANDOM KINDNESS BHB 64f75a **RR 72df 75a** 396[7]
7 b g Alzao (USA) 9.8f **(73)** - Lady Tippins (USA) (Star de Naskra (USA)) 9.7f **(65)**
Form - 477
Record 2000 - 1st:0 2nd:0 3rd:0 Ran:3
Pre2000 - 1st:7 2nd:10 3rd:4 Ran:43
Win Prizemoney £23,894 *Total Prizemoney* £40,729

Wins								
1998	*Nov*	*Lingfi*	*(STD)*		*12f*		*94*	<
1998	May	Bright	(FRM)		11.9f		70	
1998	*Apr*	*Lingfi*	*(STD)*		*12f*		*84*	
1997	*Nov*	*Wolver*	*(STD)*	*H*	*12f*	*77*	*82*	
1997	Oct	Lingfi	(FRM)		11.5f		62	
1997	*Apr*	*Wolver*	*(STD)*	*H*	*14.8f*	*66*	*77*	
1997	*Mar*	*Wolver*	*(STD)*		*16.2f*		*77*	

2000 AW 0-3: (12f 2, 16f) (Equi 2, Fibr)
Decent gelding. AW high 82. Inconsistent.
**R Rowe [0-5] 949 Racing (from R Ingram [7-38] Aug 1999).*

RANDOM QUEST RR 95f 5157[1]
2 b c Rainbow Quest (USA) 11.2f **(81)** - Anne Bonny (Ajdal (USA)) 9.2f **(89)**
Form - 01
Record 2000 - 1st:1 2nd:0 3rd:0 Ran:2
Win Prizemoney £5,239 *Total Prizemoney* £5,239
Wins * **2000** Oct Nottin (SFT) 8.2f 95 <
2000 Turf 1-2: (7f, 8f 1-1) (sft 1-1, g-f)
Currently very useful colt. Turf high 95 (began Spt) - 1st of 17 from Staging Post (24 Oct Nottingham RF 5157).
**P F I Cole [1-2] The Blandford Partnership.*

RANDOM TASK (IRE) BHB 77f75a **RR 73f 75a** 4866[18]
3 b c Tirol 8.1f **(64)** - Minami (IRE) (Caerleon (USA)) 8.6f **(71)**
Form - 0610
Record 2000 - 1st:1 2nd:0 3rd:0 Ran:4
Pre2000 - 1st:1 2nd:0 3rd:0 Ran:2
Win Prizemoney £10,731 *Total Prizemoney* £11,163

Wins								
* **2000**	Spt	Kempto	(SFT)	H	6f	70	73	
* *1999*	*May*	*Wolver*	*(Std)*		*6f*		*81+*	<

2000 Turf 1-3: (6f 1-1, 7f 2) (sft, g-s 1-1, g-f) 2000 AW 0-1: (7f) (Fibr)
Leggy, decent colt, effective 6f, acts on g-s - acts on Fibr, has worn blinkers. Turf high 73 (began Aug) - 1st of 23 getting 18lb from Grey Eminence (18 Spt Kempton RF 4483). Landed a surprise 33/1 victory at Kempton in September. Suited by soft ground.
**D Shaw [2-6] J C Fretwell.*

RANEEN NASHWAN BHB 78f **RR 74f** 520[6]
4 b g Nashwan (USA) 10.3f **(79)** - Raneen Alwatar (Sadler's Wells (USA)) 10f **(76)**
Form - 6
Record 2000 - 1st:0 2nd:0 3rd:0 Ran:1
Pre2000 - 1st:1 2nd:0 3rd:0 Ran:6
Win Prizemoney £3,512 *Total Prizemoney* £4,199
Wins * 1998 Nov Mussel (SFT) 8f 77 <
2000 Turf 0-1: (10f) (frm)
Above-average gelding.
**M R Channon [1-7] Sheikh Ahmed Al Maktoum.*

RANIN BHB 81f **RR 79f** 5136[2]
2 b f Unfuwain (USA) 11.4f **(74)** - Nafhaat (USA) (Roberto (USA)) 10f **(76)**
Form - 352
Record 2000 - 1st:0 2nd:1 3rd:1 Ran:3
Win Prizemoney £0 *Total Prizemoney* £1,771
2000 Turf 0-3: (7f 2, 8f) (g-s, g-f, frm)
Currently above-average filly. Turf high 79 (began Aug) - 2nd of 11 to Heavenly Whisper (22 Oct Yarmouth 8f g-s RF 5136).
**E A L Dunlop [0-3] Hamdan Al Maktoum.*

RANVILLE RR 50f 5184[10]
2 ch c Deploy 11.4f **(67)** - Kibitka (FR) (Baby Turk) 11.3f **(90)**
Form - 00
Record 2000 - 1st:0 2nd:0 3rd:0 Ran:2
2000 Turf 0-2: (8f 2) (g-s, g-f)

Currently fair colt. Turf high 50 (began Spt).
**M A Jarvis [0-2] K G Powter.*

RAPIDASH BHB 40f **RR 34f** 3138[11]

3 gr g Petong 7.6f **(58)** - Join the Clan **(91f)** (Clantime)
Form - 0080

Record	2000 -	1st:0	2nd:0	3rd:0	Ran:4
	Pre2000 -	1st:0	2nd:0	3rd:0	Ran:2

2000 Turf 0-4: (5f 4) (sft, g-f, frm, hrd)
Small, very moderate gelding, often wears blinkers. Turf high 34.
**Mrs N Macauley [0-6] Mrs N Macauley.*

RAPID DEPLOYMENT BHB 61f **RR 66f** 4364[4]

3 b g Deploy 11.4f **(67)** - City Times (IRE) (Last Tycoon) 8.5f **(62)**
Form - 70214

Record	2000 -	1st:1	2nd:1	3rd:0	Ran:5
	Pre2000 -	1st:0	2nd:0	3rd:1	Ran:4

Win Prizemoney £4,624 *Total Prizemoney* £6,337

Wins	* 2000	Aug	Carlis	(FRM)	H	12f	60	66	<

2000 Turf 1-5: (8f, 10f, 11f, 12f 1-2) (gd 2, g-f 2, frm 1-1)
Scopey, average gelding, effective 7 to 12f, best at 7f, acts on gd to frm, best on frm, likes tight tracks. Turf high 66 - 1st of 2 getting 17lb from Spectrometer (7 Aug Carlisle RF 3426).
**J G Smyth-Osbourne [1-9] Mrs E T Smyth-Osbourne & Partners.*

RAPIER BHB 78f **RR 81f** 4453[8]

6 b g Sharpo 7.5f **(68)** - Sahara Breeze (Ela-Mana-Mou) 10.1f **(70)**
Form - 401308

Record	2000 -	1st:1	2nd:0	3rd:1	Ran:6
	Pre2000 -	1st:3	2nd:2	3rd:4	Ran:20

Win Prizemoney £28,725 *Total Prizemoney* £41,876

Wins	* 2000	Jun	Haydoc	(G-S)	C	11.9f		71+	
	* 1999	May	Ayr	(GD)	H	10f	83	78	
	* 1998	Jun	York	(G-S)	H	8.9f	82	88	<
	1996	Spt	Bright	(FRM)		8f		77	

2000 Turf 1-6: (10f, 11f, 12f 1-3, 13f) (hvy, gd 1-5)
Decent gelding, has broken blood-vessels, effective 10 to 12f, acts on hvy to gd, best on gd. Turf high 81 - 3rd of 14 giving 2lb to Hannibal Lad (15 Jly Ascot 12f gd RF 2826).
**M D Hammond [4-17] Mrs A Kane (from R Hannon [1-11] Oct 1997).*

RAPT (IRE) **RR 64f** 5296[6]

2 b c Septieme Ciel (USA) - Dream Play (USA) (Blushing Groom (FR)) 10.3f **(76)**
Form - 06

Record	2000 -	1st:0	2nd:0	3rd:0	Ran:2

2000 Turf 0-2: (7f, 8f) (g-s, gd)
Currently average colt. Turf high 64 (began Oct).
**W Jarvis [0-2] Stephen Hobson.*

RAPTOR (IRE) BHB 52f **RR 49f** 5100[15]

2 ch c Eagle Eyed (USA) - Ahakista (IRE) (Persian Bold) 9.3f **(66)**
Form - 000

Record	2000 -	1st:0	2nd:0	3rd:0	Ran:3

2000 Turf 0-3: (6f, 7f 2) (gd 2, g-f)
Currently moderate colt. Turf high 49 (began Aug).
**B W Hills [0-3] R A N Bonnycastle.*

RA RA RASPUTIN BHB 25f25a **RR 19f 25a** 2330[14]

5 b g Petong 7.6f **(58)** - Ra Ra Girl (Shack (USA)) 5.8f **(53)**
Form - 037014100880000

Record	2000 -	1st:2	2nd:0	3rd:0	Ran:12
	Pre2000 -	1st:1	2nd:2	3rd:2	Ran:31

Win Prizemoney £21,987 *Total Prizemoney* £25,064

Wins	2000	*Jan*	*Wolver*	*(STD)*	*S*	*7f*		*53*	
	2000	*Jan*	*Wolver*	*(STD)*	*S*	*7f*		*54*	
	1997	*Aug*	*Wolver*	*(STD)*		*6f*		*82*	<

2000 Turf 0-2: (7f, 10f) (gd, frm) 2000 AW 2-10: (6f, 7f 2-6, 8f 3) (Fibr 2-10)
Little account gelding, effective 7 to 8f, - acts on Fibr, has worn blinkers, favours left handed tracks, favours tight tracks. Turf high 19. AW high 54 (1st run). Scored a 50/1 shock win in the Weatherbys Dash at Wolverhampton in '97 and obviously likes Fibresand. A tight left-handed track suits, as he has run some of his best races on turf at Chester.
**B P J Baugh [0-12] C Harrison (from B A McMahon [3-34] Jan 2000).*

RARE GENIUS (USA) BHB 64f **RR 66f** 2347[6]

4 ch g Beau Genius (CAN) - Aunt Nola (USA) (Olden Times) 11.4f **(67)**
Form - 23576

Record	2000 -	1st:0	2nd:1	3rd:1	Ran:5
	Pre2000 -	1st:0	2nd:1	3rd:1	Ran:7

Win Prizemoney £0 *Total Prizemoney* £3,995
2000 Turf 0-5: (12f 3, 14f 2) (gd, g-f 3, frm)
Leggy, average gelding, effective 10 to 14f, best at 14f, acts on g-s to frm, best on g-f, favours tight tracks. Turf high 66 - 3rd of 17 getting 17lb from Afterjacko (7 May Salisbury 14f g-f RF 1089). Consistent. **P W Harris [0-12] Beever,E Long,R Spen Harris.*

RARE OLD TIMES (IRE) BHB 68f **RR 86f** 4582[8]

2 b f Inzar (USA) - Moona (USA) (Lear Fan (USA)) 8.5f **(73)**
Form - 510608

Record	2000 -	1st:1	2nd:0	3rd:0	Ran:6

Win Prizemoney £7,308 *Total Prizemoney* £7,547

Wins	* 2000	May	Windso	(G-S)	5f	86	<

2000 Turf 1-6: (5f 1-4, 6f 2) (gd 2, g-f 1-4)
Useful filly, effective 5f, acts on g-f. Turf high 86 - 1st of 6 getting 2lb from Johnny Reb (22 May Windsor RF 1382). Showed the benefit of her debut when scoring at rewarding odds at Windsor.
**Mrs P N Dutfield [1-6] Graham Brown.*

RARE TALENT BHB 65f **RR 65f** 4311[11]

6 b g Mtoto 11.5f **(71)** - Bold As Love (Lomond (USA)) 8.8f **(65)**
Form - 00383261522410

Record	2000 -	1st:2	2nd:3	3rd:2	Ran:14
	Pre2000 -	1st:6	2nd:4	3rd:3	Ran:41

Win Prizemoney £35,157 *Total Prizemoney* £45,678

Wins	* 2000	Aug	Epsom	(GD)	H	12f	62	65	<
	* 2000	Jly	Beverl	(G-F)	H	9.9f	53	59	
	* 1999	Aug	Windso	(G-F)	H	11.6f	48	58	
	* 1999	Jly	Beverl	(G-F)	H	9.9f	50	55	
	* 1998	Jly	Cheste	(G-F)	H	10.3f	60	63	
	* 1998	Jun	Doncas	(GD)	H	10.3f	55	59	
	1997	Spt	Leices	(G-F)	S	10f		60	
	1997	Aug	Ripon	(G-F)	SH	10f	60	65	<

2000 Turf 2-14: (10f 1-11, 11f, 12f 1-2) (gd 1-2, g-f 1-6, frm 6)
Average gelding, effective 10 to 12f, best at 10f, acts on gd to frm, has worn blinkers, likes right handed tracks, and likes Newmarket. Turf high 65 - 1st of 9 getting 17lb from Wasp Ranger (28 Aug Epsom RF 4036) - also 1st of 11 giving 5lb to Khuchn (24 Jly Beverley RF 3070). A fair handicapper on his day, he is often there or thereabouts in modest middle-distance events and won twice last season, at Beverley in July and the Moet & Chandon Silver Magnum at Epsom the following month. Goes well for an amateur.
**S Gollings [6-45] John King, Bill Hobs King (from M R Channon [2-11] Spt 1997).*

RASHA'S REALM (USA) BHB 81f **RR 81f** 4726[7]

2 ch f Woodman (USA) 9.7f **(77)** - Performing Arts (The Minstrel (CAN)) 10f **(72)**
Form - 237

Record	2000 -	1st:0	2nd:1	3rd:1	Ran:3

Win Prizemoney £0 *Total Prizemoney* £2,347
2000 Turf 0-3: (6f 3) (gd 2, frm)
Currently decent filly. Turf high 81 - 3rd of 12 getting 5lb from Appellation (8 Spt Goodwood 6f gd RF 4300).
**J L Dunlop [0-3] Wafic Said.*

RASHIK BHB 60f **RR 65f** 4195[13]

6 ch h Cadeaux Genereux 7.9f **(76)** - Ghzaalh (USA) (Northern Dancer) 9.6f **(80)**
Form - 500

Record	2000 -	1st:0	2nd:0	3rd:0	Ran:3
	Pre2000 -	1st:1	2nd:0	3rd:0	Ran:1

Win Prizemoney £3,427 *Total Prizemoney* £3,701

Wins	1997	Apr	Newbur	(G-F)	8f	97	<

2000 Turf 0-3: (7f, 8f, 9f) (gd, g-f 2)
Average horse. Turf high 58 (began Aug).
**A Streeter [0-3] Racing For You (from Major W R Hern [1-1] Apr 1997).*

RASM BHB 107f **RR 109f** 3004[3]

3 b c Darshaan 11.9f **(81)** - Northshiel (Northfields (USA)) 9f **(72)**
Form - 123

Record	2000 -	1st:1	2nd:1	3rd:1	Ran:3

Pre2000 - 1st:0 2nd:0 3rd:1 Ran:1
Win Prizemoney £4,160 *Total Prizemoney* £12,371
Wins * **2000** Jun Newmar (G-F) 10f 91 <
2000 Turf 1-3: (10f 1-2, 12f) (gd 2, frm 1-1)
Scopey, Pattern-class colt. Turf high 109 - 2nd of 8 to Port Vila (24 Jun Ascot 10f gd RF 2238). Ready winner of a Newmarket maiden on his return and was just held in a listed race next time. Seemed not to stay twelve furlongs on his final start.
**A C Stewart [1-4] Hamdan Al Maktoum.*

RASMALAI BHB 65f **RR 71f** 4874[12]
3 b f Sadler's Wells (USA) 11.3f **(87)** - Raymouna (IRE) (High Top) 10.2f **(67)**
Form - 03020
Record 2000 - 1st:0 2nd:1 3rd:1 Ran:5
Win Prizemoney £0 *Total Prizemoney* £1,971
2000 Turf 0-5: (7f, 8f, 9f 2, 10f) (sft, g-s 2, g-f, frm)
Scopey, above-average filly. Turf high 71.
**R Hannon [0-5] J A Lazzari.*

RASOUM (USA) BHB 100f **RR 111+f** 5129[1]
2 gr c Miswaki (USA) 8.1f **(81)** - Bel Ray (USA) (Restivo (USA))
Form - 313081
Record 2000 - 1st:2 2nd:0 3rd:2 Ran:6
Win Prizemoney £26,520 *Total Prizemoney* £28,141
Wins * **2000** Oct Newbur (HVY) H 6f 90 111+ <
* **2000** Jly Newmar (OD) 6f 73+
2000 Turf 2-6: (5f, 6f 2-5) (sft 1-1, gd 2, g-f 1-3)
Group-class colt, effective 6f, acts on sft. Turf high 111 - 1st of 23 giving 9lb to Prince Pyramus (21 Oct Newbury RF 5129).
**E A L Dunlop [2-6] Khalid Ali.*

RASSENDYLL RR 56f 2390[7]
2 b c Rudimentary (USA) 8.2f **(66)** - La Lutine (My Swallow) 9.2f **(71)**
Form - 7
Record 2000 - 1st:0 2nd:0 3rd:0 Ran:1
2000 Turf 0-1: (7f) (g-f)
Currently fair colt. **P W Harris [0-1] Skeltools Ltd.*

RATEEBA (IRE) RR 43f 5186[14]
2 b f Green Desert (USA) 7.8f **(78)** - Wathbat Mtoto **(88f)** (Mtoto)
Form - 00
Record 2000 - 1st:0 2nd:0 3rd:0 Ran:2
2000 Turf 0-2: (6f, 7f) (g-s, gd)
Currently moderate filly. Turf high 43 (began Oct).
**A C Stewart [0-2] Sheikh Ahmed Al Maktoum.*

RATHCLOGHEENDANCER (IRE) BHB 45f42a **RR 45f 42a** 107[10]
3 ch g Colonel Collins (USA) - Fleeting Quest (Rainbow Quest (USA)) 10.4f **(75)**
Form - 0
Record 2000 - 1st:0 2nd:0 3rd:0 Ran:1
Pre2000 - 1st:0 2nd:0 3rd:0 Ran:7
2000 AW 0-1: (7f) (Fibr)
Light-framed, moderate gelding, has worn blinkers. Inconsistent.
**K A Ryan [0-8] The Gloria Darley Racing Partnership.*

RATHER DIZZY BHB 20f **RR** 2616[12]
5 b g Sizzling Melody 6.3f **(49)** - Rather Dark (Nomination) 7f **(60)**
Form - 0
Record 2000 - 1st:0 2nd:0 3rd:0 Ran:1
Pre2000 - 1st:0 2nd:0 3rd:0 Ran:2
2000 Turf 0-1: (8f) (gd)
Currently very poor gelding, has worn blinkers.
**P Butler [0-3] Mrs Gill Oakley.*

RATHKENNY (IRE) BHB 94f **RR 92?f** 5238[4]
2 b c Standiford (USA) - Shine **(47f)** (Sharrood (USA)) 10.5f **(72)**
Form - 5641624
Record 2000 - 1st:1 2nd:1 3rd:0 Ran:7
Win Prizemoney £3,250 *Total Prizemoney* £9,082
Wins * **2000** Spt Ayr (SFT) S 8f 68 <
2000 Turf 1-7: (6f 3, 8f 1-2, 10f 2) (g-s 2, gd 1-1, g-f, frm 3)
Useful colt, effective 8 to 10f, acts on g-s. Turf high 92 (began Jly) - 4th of 9 getting 5lb from Worthily (28 Oct Newmarket 10f g-s RF 5238). He has shown his best form since stepped up to a mile on soft ground. **J G Given [1-7] Ray Monaghan.*

RATHLEA BHB 34f **RR 27f** 4813[17]
6 b h Risk Me (FR) 8f **(53)** - Star of Jupiter (Jupiter Island) 14f **(62)**
Form - 0000
Record 2000 - 1st:0 2nd:0 3rd:0 Ran:4
Pre2000 - 1st:0 2nd:0 3rd:0 Ran:3
2000 Turf 0-4: (5f 2, 8f 2) (sft, g-s, gd, g-f)
Little account horse. Turf high 27.
**R Hollinshead [0-7] Mrs Robert Heathcote.*

RATIFIED BHB 54f52a **RR 59f 52a** 4676[6]
3 b g Not in Doubt (USA) - Festival of Magic (USA) (Clever Trick (USA)) 6.6f **(77)**
Form - 72148526
Record 2000 - 1st:1 2nd:2 3rd:0 Ran:7
Pre2000 - 1st:0 2nd:0 3rd:0 Ran:4
Win Prizemoney £2,562 *Total Prizemoney* £4,162
Wins * **2000** Apr Nottin (HVY) H 10f 51 59 <
2000 Turf 1-6: (8f, 9f, 10f 1-4) (sft 1-1, g-s 2, gd, g-f 2) 2000 AW 0-1: (10f) (Equi)
Unfurnished, fair gelding, effective 10f, acts on sft to gd, likes left handed tracks, likes tight tracks. Turf high 59 - 1st of 13 getting 10lb from Selton Hill (24 Apr Nottingham RF 0850).
**H Candy [1-11] Mrs David Blackburn.*

RATTLE BHB 23f25a **RR ?f 25a** 3701[12]
7 b g Mazilier (USA) 8.5f **(56)** - Snake Song (Mansingh (USA)) 7.4f **(55)**
Form - 0
Record 2000 - 1st:0 2nd:0 3rd:0 Ran:1
Pre2000 - 1st:0 2nd:1 3rd:4 Ran:26
Win Prizemoney £0 *Total Prizemoney* £2,340
2000 Turf 0-1: (8f) (gd)
Very poor gelding, has worn blinkers.
**D A Nolan [0-12] Mrs J McFadyen-Murray (from J J O'Neill [0-16] Jly 1996).*

RAVENSWOOD (IRE) BHB 90f **RR 95f** 4987[21]
3 b c Warning 8.1f **(77)** - Green Lucia (Green Dancer (USA)) 10.3f **(74)**
Form - 421400
Record 2000 - 1st:1 2nd:1 3rd:0 Ran:6
Pre2000 - 1st:1 2nd:0 3rd:0 Ran:4
Win Prizemoney £7,507 *Total Prizemoney* £12,650
Wins * **2000** Jun Newbur (G-F) H 13.3f 78 86 <
* 1999 Aug Bright (FRM) 7f 81
2000 Turf 1-6: (12f 2, 13f 1-1, 14f, 16f, 18f) (gd 3, g-f 1-3)
Scopey, very useful colt, effective 13 to 16f, acts on gd to g-f. Turf high 95 - 4th of 13 to Dalampour (20 Jun Ascot 16f gd RF 2113) - also 1st of 15 getting 14lb from Wait For The Will (8 Jun Newbury RF 1813). Inconsistent. He put up an improved effort to finish fourth in the Queen's Vase at Royal Ascot, but paid the penalty with an eight point rise in the ratings. Soundly beaten in useful handicap company thereafter, he is worth another try over two miles.
**M C Pipe [2-10] Lord Donoughmore.*

RAVINE RR 73f 4020[4]
3 ch f Indian Ridge 7.6f **(74)** - Cubby Hole (Town And Country) 8.1f **(68)**
Form - 04114
Record 2000 - 1st:2 2nd:0 3rd:0 Ran:5
Pre2000 - 1st:0 2nd:0 3rd:0 Ran:1
Win Prizemoney £7,862 *Total Prizemoney* £8,501
Wins * **2000** Aug Newmar (G-F) H 7f 71 73 <
* **2000** Jly Windso (G-F) H 6f 68 67
2000 Turf 2-5: (6f 1-1, 7f 1-3, 8f) (gd, g-f 1-2, frm 1-2)
Lengthy, above-average filly, effective 6 to 7f, acts on g-f to frm. Turf high 73 - 1st of 8 giving 10lb to Moonlight Song (18 Aug Newmarket RF 3767) - also 1st of 13 giving 1lb to Doctor Dennis (24 Jly Windsor RF 3078). Scored on fast ground at Windsor and Newmarket in the summer, but found the rise in the handicap too much in her hat-trick bid at Goodwood.
**R Hannon [2-6] Lord Carnarvon.*

RAVISHING (IRE) RR 79f 5242[19]
3 b f Bigstone (IRE) - Dazzling Maid (IRE) (Tate Gallery (USA)) 7.4f **(67)**
Form - 410000000

Record 2000 - 1st:1 2nd:0 3rd:0 Ran:9
Pre2000 - 1st:1 2nd:0 3rd:0 Ran:1
Win Prizemoney £9,268 *Total Prizemoney* £9,557
Wins *** 2000** May Newbur (G-F) H 6f 77 79 <
* 1999 Oct Pontef (GD) 6f 77+
2000 Turf 1-9: (6f 1-6, 7f 3) (sft, g-s 4, gd, g-f 1-1, frm 2)
Unfurnished, above-average filly, effective 6 to 7f, best at 6f, acts on sft to g-f, best on g-f. Turf high 79 - 1st of 18 getting 8lb from Salviati (20 May Newbury RF 1335). Becoming disappointing.
**W J Haggas [2-10] G C Johnston.*

RAWI BHB 30f34a **RR 33f 34a** 2752[5]

7 ch g Forzando 7.2f **(63)** - Finally (Final Straw) 7.9f **(64)**
Form - 30860025
Record 2000 - 1st:0 2nd:1 3rd:0 Ran:6
Pre2000 - 1st:3 2nd:4 3rd:7 Ran:47
Win Prizemoney £7,381 *Total Prizemoney* £14,411
Wins 1997 Jly Folkes (G-F) C 6.9f 46
1997 *Jan Lingfi (STD) H 7f 53 56* <
1996 *Dec Lingfi (STD) 7f 50*
2000 Turf 0-3: (8f, 12f, 17f) (gd, frm 2) 2000 AW 0-3: (12f 2, 13f) (Equi 2, Fibr)
Very moderate gelding, effective 10f, - acts on Equi, has worn blinkers. Turf high 33. AW high 26. Inconsistent.
**Mrs A J Perrett [0-14] Miss G Harwood (from J I A Charlton [1-9] Feb 1999).*

RAW SILK BHB 59f **RR 58f** 4400[9]

2 b g Rudimentary (USA) 8.2f **(66)** - Misty Silks **(77f 70a)** (Scottish Reel) 7f **(61)**
Form - 8060
Record 2000 - 1st:0 2nd:0 3rd:0 Ran:4
2000 Turf 0-4: (5f, 6f 2, 8f) (gd, g-f 3)
Fair gelding. Turf high 58. **M J Ryan [0-4] Paul Blows.*

RAYIK BHB 48f58a **RR 56+f 58a** 4694[D]

5 br g Marju (IRE) 9.2f **(76)** - Matila (IRE) (Persian Bold) 9.3f **(66)**
Form - 06712141200173D
Record 2000 - 1st:4 2nd:2 3rd:1 Ran:12
Pre2000 - 1st:1 2nd:1 3rd:1 Ran:20
Win Prizemoney £19,428 *Total Prizemoney* £28,437
Wins *** 2000** Aug Windso (G-F) H 11.6f 47 56
*** 2000** *Mar Lingfi (STD) H 12f 70 73* <
*** 2000** *Jan Lingfi (STD) H 12f 67 70*
*** 2000** *Jan Lingfi (STD) H 13f 60 64*
1998 *Dec Lingfi (STD) 10f 69*
2000 Turf 1-6: (10f 2, 12f 1-4) (gd 2, g-f 1-3, frm) 2000 AW 3-6: (12f 2-5, 13f 1-1) (Equi 3-6)
Average gelding, effective 12f, - acts on AW, best on Equi, has worn blinkers, likes left handed tracks, favours tight tracks, excels at Lingfield. Turf high 56 (began Jly). AW high 82 - 2nd of 9 getting 9lb from China Castle (4 Mar Lingfield 12f Equi RF 0404) - also 1st of 6 giving 28lb to Ocean Line (1 Mar Lingfield RF 0390). Inconsistent. He looks much better on Equitrack than anything else and had another successful winter, winning three times and running well in defeat against some decent sorts. Suited by twelve furlongs.
**G L Moore [4-16] Lancing Racing Syndicate (from N E Berry [1-13] Aug 1999).*

RAYPOUR (IRE) RR 115f 4846a[10]

3 ch c Barathea (IRE) - Rayseka
Form - 226246160
2000 Turf 1-9: (8f, 9f, 10f, 11f 1-1, 12f 5) (sft, g-s 2, gd 1-5)
High-class colt, likes right handed tracks. Turf high 115. A useful horse in his own right, he did an admirable job as Sinndar's pace-maker in the Irish Derby, Prix Niel and Arc.
**J Oxx in IRE [1-12] Aga Khan.*

RAYSIZA (IRE) RR 99f 5090a[6]

3 f
Form - 866
2000 Turf 0-3: (10f 2, 11f) (hvy, gd, g-f)
Currently very useful filly. Turf high 99 (1st run) - 8th of 18 to Timi (21 May San Siro 11f gd RF 1455a). **A Peraino in ITY [0-3].*

RAYWARE BOY (IRE) BHB 37f44a **RR 40f 44a** 4179[3]

4 b c Scenic 10.6f **(66)** - Amata (USA) (Nodouble (USA)) 8.8f **(68)**
Form - 0000545277403
Record 2000 - 1st:0 2nd:1 3rd:1 Ran:12
Pre2000 - 1st:2 2nd:1 3rd:0 Ran:14
Win Prizemoney £5,602 *Total Prizemoney* £8,212
Wins * 1999 *Feb Southw (STD) H 8f 60 60* <
* 1999 *Jan Southw (STD) H 8f 48 57*
2000 Turf 0-8: (8f, 10f, 12f 4, 14f, 16f) (gd, g-f 3, frm 4) 2000 AW 0-4: (8f 2, 11f, 12f) (Fibr 4)
Light-framed, moderate colt, effective 8 to 12f, best at 8f, - acts on Fibr, mostly wears blinkers, likes left handed tracks, likes tight tracks. Turf high 42. AW high 40. **D Shaw [2-33] Rayton Racing.*

RAYYAAN (IRE) BHB 88f **RR 90f** 4991[17]

3 ch c Cadeaux Genereux 7.9f **(76)** - Anam **(80df)** (Persian Bold) 9.3f **(66)**
Form - 1116200
Record 2000 - 1st:3 2nd:1 3rd:0 Ran:7
Pre2000 - 1st:0 2nd:2 3rd:0 Ran:4
Win Prizemoney £18,590 *Total Prizemoney* £24,787
Wins *** 2000** May Newmar (GD) H 7f 85 89 <
*** 2000** Apr Newmar (G-S) H 7f 80 88
*** 2000** Mar Southw (GD) 7f 82
2000 Turf 3-7: (7f 3-7) (gd 1-4, g-f 1-2, frm 1-1)
Workmanlike, useful colt, effective 6 to 8f, best at 7f, acts on sft to frm, best on g-f, likes Newmarket. Turf high 90 - 2nd of 7 getting 3lb from Cantina (18 Aug Chester 7f g-f RF 3746) - also 1st of 20 getting 6lb from Strahan (5 May Newmarket RF 1048). Consistent. He was in tremendous form during the spring, gaining short-head victories in a couple of valuable handicaps at Newmarket. A seven furlong specialist, he has reportedly been transferred to Dubai.
**N A Graham [3-7] Hamdan Al Maktoum (from P T Walwyn [0-4] Oct 1999).*

RAZIK (CAN) RR 105f 575a[4]

5 b h Dayjur (USA) 6.8f **(79)** - Sirona (CAN) (Irish Stronghold (USA))
Form - 4
2000 AW 0-1: (8f) (Dirt)
Pattern-class colt, has worn blinkers. (1st run) - 4th of 13 to Conflict (25 Mar Nad Al Sheba 8f Dirt RF 0575a).
**E Charpy in UAE [0-1] (from D K Weld in IRE [1-6] Spt 1998).*

RAZZAMATAZZ RR 33f 5110[9]

2 b c Alhijaz 7.7f **(57)** - Salvezza (IRE) **(83df)** (Superpower)
Form - 0
Record 2000 - 1st:0 2nd:0 3rd:0 Ran:1
2000 Turf 0-1: (8f) (gd)
Currently very moderate colt.
**R Dickin [0-1] Mrs Byrne-Cooper-Mrs Cooper.*

REACHFORYOURPOCKET (IRE) BHB 52f64a **RR 55f 64a** 5112[23]

5 b g Royal Academy (USA) 7.8f **(77)** - Gemaasheh (Habitat) 9.4f **(70)**
Form - 461203660001878250
Record 2000 - 1st:2 2nd:2 3rd:1 Ran:18
Pre2000 - 1st:0 2nd:0 3rd:0 Ran:11
Win Prizemoney £3,832 *Total Prizemoney* £5,549
Wins *** 2000** Jly Bright (FRM) H 7f 42 46 <
*** 2000** *Feb Lingfi (STD) H 7f 40 40*
2000 Turf 1-14: (5f, 6f, 7f 1-9, 8f 2, 10f) (sft, g-s, gd 2, g-f 6, frm 1-3, hrd) 2000 AW 1-4: (7f 1-2, 8f, 10f) (Equi 1-4)
Average gelding, has worn blinkers, likes left handed tracks, likes tight tracks. Turf high 55. AW high 46.
**M D I Usher [2-18] Bryan Fry (from K Mahdi [0-11] Oct 1999).*

REACH THE TOP BHB 106f **RR 110f** 4436[4]

3 b c Zafonic (USA) 9f **(83)** - Andaleeb (USA) (Lyphard (USA)) 9.9f **(72)**
Form - 16144
Record 2000 - 1st:2 2nd:0 3rd:0 Ran:5
Win Prizemoney £11,969 *Total Prizemoney* £16,559
Wins *** 2000** Aug Newmar (G-F) 10f 103 <
*** 2000** May Goodwo (GD) 8f 95
2000 Turf 2-5: (8f 1-2, 10f 1-1, 11f, 12f) (g-s 1-1, gd, g-f, frm 1-2)
Scopey, Group-class colt. Turf high 110 - 4th of 7 to Pawn Broker (15 Spt Newbury 11f frm RF 4436) - also 1st of 6 giving 3lb to Mastermind (11 Aug Newmarket RF 3563). Impressive over a mile on his debut, he often found himself tapped for toe over longer trips as the season progressed. Blinkers may be an option in 2001.

J H M Gosden [2-5] K Abdulla.

READING RHONDA (USA) BHB 27f44a **RR 53f 44a** 4099[6]

4 b f Eastern Echo (USA) 8f **(61)** - Higher Learning (USA) (Fappiano (USA)) 8.7f **(77)**
Form - 5700036706
Record 2000 - 1st:0 2nd:0 3rd:1 Ran:10
Pre2000 - 1st:0 2nd:0 3rd:0 Ran:1
Win Prizemoney £0 *Total Prizemoney* £385
2000 Turf 0-7: (8f, 10f 3, 12f, 14f, 16f) (g-s, g-f 3, frm 3) 2000 AW 0-3: (8f, 10f, 12f) (Equi 2, Fibr)
Scopey, fair filly. Turf high 53. AW high 45. Becoming disappointing.
**P Mitchell [0-10] J Morton & Mrs J Davies (from I A Balding [0-1] Jun 1998).*

READY TO ROCK (IRE) BHB 51f51a **RR 35f 51a** 553[4]

4 b g Up and At 'em - Rocklands Rosie (Muscatile) 5f **(51)**
Form - 3000681224
Record 2000 - 1st:1 2nd:2 3rd:0 Ran:8
Pre2000 - 1st:0 2nd:0 3rd:1 Ran:14
Win Prizemoney £2,769 *Total Prizemoney* £5,081
Wins * **2000** *Feb Lingfi (STD) H 5f 40 49* <
2000 AW 1-8: (5f 1-4, 6f 4) (Equi 1-5, Fibr 3)
Moderate gelding, effective 5f, - acts on AW, often wears blinkers (effectively). AW high 49 - 1st of 6 getting 19lb from Charge (23 Feb Lingfield RF 0342).
**J S Moore [1-10] J P Fitzgerald (from B Lawlor in IRE [0-12] Oct 1999).*

REAL ESTATE BHB 64f **RR 67f** 4823[11]

6 b g High Estate 10.5f **(66)** - Haitienne (FR) (Green Dancer (USA)) 10.3f **(74)**
Form - 32000
Record 2000 - 1st:0 2nd:1 3rd:1 Ran:5
Pre2000 - 1st:2 2nd:1 3rd:1 Ran:7
Win Prizemoney £7,029 *Total Prizemoney* £16,160
Wins 1997 Jly Ripon (GD) H 12.3f 75 77 <
1997 Jun Windso (SFT) H 11.6f 70 74
2000 Turf 0-5: (10f 3, 13f, 14f) (gd, g-f 3, frm)
Average gelding. Turf high 67. Becoming disappointing.
**J S King [0-5] Robert Skillen (from C F Wall [2-7] Jly 1997).*

REAL TING BHB 30f23a **RR 8f 23a** 2485[0]

4 br g Forzando 7.2f **(63)** - St Helena (Monsanto (FR)) 6.5f **(59)**
Form - 580
Record 2000 - 1st:0 2nd:0 3rd:0 Ran:2
Pre2000 - 1st:0 2nd:0 3rd:0 Ran:6
2000 AW 0-2: (6f 2) (Fibr 2)
Little account gelding, often wears blinkers. AW high 14.
**P D Evans [0-6] P D Evans (from P C Haslam [0-2] Aug 1998).*

REAP BHB 59f61a **RR 36tf 61a** 5243[4]

2 b c Emperor Jones (USA) - Corn Futures (Nomination) 7f **(60)**
Form - 064
Record 2000 - 1st:0 2nd:0 3rd:0 Ran:3
2000 Turf 0-2: (6f 2) (gd, g-f) 2000 AW 0-1: (6f) (Fibr)
Currently average colt, has worn blinkers. Turf high 36 (began Jly).
**J Pearce [0-3] Jim Furlong.*

REBEL STORM (USA) **RR 85f** 4379[1]

2 b c Storm Bird (CAN) 8.5f **(82)** - Heavenly Rhythm (USA) (Septieme Ciel (USA))
Form - 01
Record 2000 - 1st:1 2nd:0 3rd:0 Ran:2
Win Prizemoney £3,753 *Total Prizemoney* £3,753
Wins * **2000** Spt Yarmou (G-F) 7f 85 <
2000 Turf 1-2: (6f, 7f 1-1) (frm 1-2)
Currently useful colt. Turf high 85 (began Aug) - 1st of 17 from Albashoosh (13 Spt Yarmouth RF 4379). Came on a great deal from his debut to score with authority at Yarmouth next time and will do even better in due course.
**J H M Gosden [1-2] R Sangster, B Sangster & A Sangster.*

RECIPROCAL (IRE) BHB 74f **RR 74f** 5128[9]

2 gr f Night Shift (USA) 8.1f **(73)** - African Light (Kalaglow) 9.8f **(67)**
Form - 0040
Record 2000 - 1st:0 2nd:0 3rd:0 Ran:4
Win Prizemoney £0 *Total Prizemoney* £233
2000 Turf 0-4: (5f, 7f 3) (sft, g-s, g-f, hrd)
Above-average filly. Turf high 74 (began Jly) - 4th of 15 to Lipica (18 Spt Kempton 7f g-s RF 4480).
**D R C Elsworth [0-4] The Caledonian Racing Society.*

RECOLETA **RR 39f** 1591[6]

3 b f Ezzoud (IRE) - Hug Me (Shareef Dancer (USA)) 9.9f **(73)**
Form - 006
Record 2000 - 1st:0 2nd:0 3rd:0 Ran:2
Pre2000 - 1st:0 2nd:0 3rd:0 Ran:3
2000 Turf 0-2: (10f 2) (g-s, gd)
Leggy, very moderate filly, has worn blinkers. Turf high 39.
**D R C Elsworth [0-5] D R C Elsworth.*

RECORD TIME BHB 60f **RR 59f** 3791[6]

4 ch f Clantime 6.6f **(57)** - On the Record (Record Token) 6.3f **(53)**
Form - 004816
Record 2000 - 1st:1 2nd:0 3rd:0 Ran:6
Pre2000 - 1st:1 2nd:3 3rd:0 Ran:14
Win Prizemoney £11,230 *Total Prizemoney* £14,413
Wins * **2000** Jly Newmar (G-S) H 5f 54 59 <
* 1999 Spt Newmar (G-S) H 5f 53 55
2000 Turf 1-6: (5f 1-5, 6f) (g-s, gd 1-3, g-f, frm)
Scopey, fair filly, effective 5f, acts on gd to g-f, best on gd. Turf high 59 - 1st of 11 getting 20lb from Bahamian Pirate (11 Jly Newmarket RF 2692). **E J Alston [2-20] Peter Onslow.*

RED APOLLO BHB 35f34a **RR 37f 34a** 1005[12]

4 gr g Petong 7.6f **(58)** - Scarlet Veil (Tyrnavos) 10.1f **(55)**
Form - 64000
Record 2000 - 1st:0 2nd:0 3rd:0 Ran:5
Pre2000 - 1st:0 2nd:2 3rd:0 Ran:12
Win Prizemoney £0 *Total Prizemoney* £1,562
2000 Turf 0-2: (8f 2) (sft, gd) 2000 AW 0-3: (7f, 8f 2) (Equi 2, Fibr)
Strong, very moderate gelding, effective 7f, - acts on Fibr, has worn blinkers (very effectively), likes left handed tracks, likes tight tracks. Turf high 8. AW high 18.
**A Streeter [0-2] Malt 'N' Hops (from P Howling [0-8] Feb 2000).*

RED BLAZER (NZ) **RR 31f** 5126[7]

7 ch g Omnicorp (NZ) - Gay Reef (Reform) 8.9f **(62)**
Form - 7
Record 2000 - 1st:0 2nd:0 3rd:0 Ran:1
2000 Turf 0-1: (7f) (g-s)
Very moderate gelding. **A W Carroll [0-4] K Marshall.*

RED BORDEAUX BHB 37f **RR 43f** 4112[11]

5 b g Alzao (USA) 9.8f **(73)** - Marie de Flandre (FR) (Crystal Palace (FR)) 12.5f **(76)**
Form - 005080
Record 2000 - 1st:0 2nd:0 3rd:0 Ran:6
Pre2000 - 1st:1 2nd:0 3rd:1 Ran:9
Win Prizemoney £2,290 *Total Prizemoney* £3,065
Wins 1998 Oct Catter (G-S) 12f 64 <
2000 Turf 0-6: (12f 3, 15f, 16f 2) (g-s, gd 2, frm 3)
Moderate gelding, has worn blinkers. Turf high 45. Inconsistent.
**J Akehurst [1-21] A D Spence (from B W Hills [1-8] Oct 1998).*

RED BULLET (USA) **RR** 1449a[1]

3 ch c Unbridled (USA) - Cargo (USA) (Caro)
Form - 1
2000 AW 1-1: (10f 1-1) (Dirt 1-1)
Currently very high-class colt. (1st run) - 1st of 8 from Fusaichi Pegasus (20 May Pimlico RF 1449a). Enjoyed his moment of fortune when beating Kentucky Derby winner Fusaichi Pegasus in the Preakness Stakes. **J Orseno in USA [1-1] Stronach Stables.*

RED CAFE (IRE) BHB 55f **RR 44f** 5077[1]

4 ch f Perugino (USA) - Test Case (Busted) 10.2f **(61)**
Form - 360004240011
Record 2000 - 1st:2 2nd:1 3rd:1 Ran:12
Pre2000 - 1st:0 2nd:0 3rd:1 Ran:4
Win Prizemoney £4,872 *Total Prizemoney* £6,481
Wins * **2000** Oct Bright (SFT) SH 10f 44 44 <
* **2000** Oct Ayr (HVY) S 9.1f 32
2000 Turf 2-12: (8f 5, 9f 1-3, 10f 1-2, 11f 2) (hvy 1-1, g-s 1-3, gd 3, g-f 2, frm 3)

Light-framed, fair filly, effective 8 to 10f, acts on g-s to frm, has worn blinkers, favours tight tracks. Turf high 50 (1st run) - 3rd of 18 getting 7lb from Polish Spirit (10 Apr Windsor 8f frm RF 0657) - also 1st of 19 getting 16lb from Zidac (19 Oct Brighton RF 5077).
**P D Evans [2-16] J E Abbey.*

RED CANYON (IRE) BHB 57f **RR 64f** 5063[12]
3 b g Zieten (USA) - Bayazida (Bustino) 10.4f **(64)**
Form - 24412340400
Record 2000 - 1st:1 2nd:2 3rd:1 Ran:11
Pre2000 - 1st:0 2nd:0 3rd:0 Ran:5
Win Prizemoney £3,757 *Total Prizemoney* £7,833
Wins * 2000 Jun Ayr (G-F) H 10.9f 62 64 <
2000 Turf 1-11: (8f, 9f, 10f 3, 11f 1-1, 12f 3, 13f, 16f) (sft, g-s 2, gd, g-f 2, frm 1-5)
Scopey, average gelding, effective 8 to 13f, acts on g-s to frm, best on frm, prefers right handed tracks, prefers tight tracks, excels at Ripon. Turf high 64 - 4th of 12 getting 19lb from Bonaguil (1 May Kempton 9f g-s RF 0939) - also 1st of 8 getting 5lb from Love Bitten (1 Jun Ayr RF 1619). **M L W Bell [1-16] Terry Neill.*

RED CARNATION (IRE) RR 82f 5140[3]
2 b f Polar Falcon (USA) 9f **(74)** - Red Bouquet **(40f)** (Reference Point) 6.8f **(70)**
Form - 33
Record 2000 - 1st:0 2nd:0 3rd:2 Ran:2
Win Prizemoney £0 *Total Prizemoney* £1,517
2000 Turf 0-2: (6f 2) (g-s, g-f)
Currently decent filly. Turf high 82 (began Spt).
**M A Jarvis [0-2] Red Carnation Partnership.*

RED CARPET BHB 100f **RR 112?f** 4699[3]
2 ch c Pivotal - Fleur Rouge (Pharly (FR)) 9.8f **(68)**
Form - 25113
Record 2000 - 1st:2 2nd:1 3rd:1 Ran:5
Win Prizemoney £20,569 *Total Prizemoney* £38,589
Wins * 2000 Aug Newmar (G-F) H 6f 84 92 <
*** 2000** Jly Chepst (FRM) 6.1f 79
2000 Turf 2-5: (6f 2-4, 7f) (gd, g-f 1-2, frm 1-2)
Group-class colt. Turf high 112 (began Jly) - 3rd of 10 to Minardi (28 Spt Newmarket 6f g-f RF 4699). Very progressive, he landed some hefty bets in a valuable nursery before chasing Minardi and Endless Summer home in the Group 1 Middle Park Stakes. Open to further improvement, he may struggle to stay a mile but should win a Group race at up to seven furlongs.
**M L W Bell [2-5] Cheveley Park Stud.*

RED CHARGER (IRE) BHB 54f **RR 45f** 4276[12]
4 ch g Up and At 'em - Smashing Pet (Mummy's Pet) 7.7f **(60)**
Form - 070000
Record 2000 - 1st:0 2nd:0 3rd:0 Ran:6
Pre2000 - 1st:4 2nd:1 3rd:2 Ran:20
Win Prizemoney £20,525 *Total Prizemoney* £22,340
Wins * 1999 Aug Thirsk (SFT) H 5f 60 62
1998 Aug York (G-F) S 6f 79
1998 Jly Catter (FRM) 7f 82 <
1998 May Redcar (GD) 5f 67
2000 Turf 0-6: (5f 4, 6f 2) (gd 3, g-f, frm 2)
Scopey, above-average gelding, effective 5 to 6f, best at 5f, acts on gd to frm, best on gd, has worn blinkers. Turf high 45.
**D Nicholls [1-18] Gemini Upholstery/GR 1980 Ltd (from J Berry [3-8] Aug 1998).*

RED CRYSTAL RR 5098[F]
2 b f Presidium 7.5f **(56)** - Crystallography (Primitive Rising (USA))
Form - F
Record 2000 - 1st:0 2nd:0 3rd:0 Ran:1
2000 Turf 0-1: (8f) (gd)
Currently very poor filly. **J Norton [0-1] Mrs V C Sugden.*

RED DEER RR 66f 4172[4]
2 ch c Cadeaux Genereux 7.9f **(76)** - Barboukh (Night Shift (USA)) 7.2f **(69)**
Form - 004
Record 2000 - 1st:0 2nd:0 3rd:0 Ran:3
Win Prizemoney £0 *Total Prizemoney* £303
2000 Turf 0-3: (7f 2, 8f) (gd, g-f 2)
Currently average colt. Turf high 66 (began Jly).
**E A L Dunlop [0-3] Jaber Abdullah.*

RED DELIRIUM BHB 53f63a **RR 62f 63a** 5063[13]
4 b g Robellino (USA) 9.5f **(68)** - Made of Pearl (USA) (Nureyev (USA)) 8.7f **(78)**
Form - 200700057600
Record 2000 - 1st:0 2nd:1 3rd:0 Ran:12
Pre2000 - 1st:1 2nd:2 3rd:0 Ran:20
Win Prizemoney £4,581 *Total Prizemoney* £8,822
Wins 1998 May Goodwo (G-F) 6f 88+ <
2000 Turf 0-12: (5f, 6f 6, 7f 2, 8f, 10f, 11f) (sft, gd 2, g-f 4, frm 5)
Average gelding, effective 6 to 8f, acts on g-f, has worn blinkers. Turf high 69 (1st run) - 2nd of 14 getting 11lb from Juwwi (27 Mar Windsor 6f g-f RF 0519).
**R Brotherton [0-1] Mrs David Hodgkinson (from I A Balding [0-11] Spt 2000).*

RED EMPRESS BHB 85f **RR 87f** 3225[11]
3 b f Nashwan (USA) 10.3f **(79)** - Nearctic Flame (Sadler's Wells (USA)) 10f **(76)**
Form - 26120
Record 2000 - 1st:1 2nd:2 3rd:0 Ran:5
Win Prizemoney £3,716 *Total Prizemoney* £7,414
Wins * 2000 Jun Ripon (G-F) 12.3f 81+ <
2000 Turf 1-5: (10f 2, 12f 1-3) (g-f 1-3, frm 2)
Scopey, useful filly. Turf high 87 - 2nd of 9 giving 2lb to Metronome (8 Jly Leicester 12f frm RF 2640) - also 1st of 4 getting 5lb from Gimco (21 Jun Ripon RF 2170). Beaten by Metronome at Leicester after winning at Ripon.
**Sir Michael Stoute [1-5] Cheveley Park Stud.*

RED FANFARE BHB 55f47a **RR 63f 47a** 5247[10]
2 ch f First Trump - Corman-Style (Ahonoora) 8.1f **(73)**
Form - 7070250
Record 2000 - 1st:0 2nd:1 3rd:0 Ran:7
Win Prizemoney £0 *Total Prizemoney* £563
2000 Turf 0-4: (5f 2, 6f, 7f)(gd, g-f, frm 2) 2000 AW 0-3: (7f, 8f 2)(Fibr 3)
Average filly, effective 7f, - acts on Fibr. Turf high 63. AW high 54 (1st run) (began Spt) - 2nd of 12 getting 5lb from Finn McCool (16 Spt Wolverhampton 7f Fibr RF 4478).
**J A Osborne [0-7] Elite Racing Club.*

REDHILL BHB 36f28a **RR 56f 28a** 3378[7]
3 b f Tragic Role (USA) 9.4f **(63)** - Indivisible (Remainder Man) 11.2f **(45)**
Form - 0657
Record 2000 - 1st:0 2nd:0 3rd:0 Ran:4
2000 Turf 0-4: (7f, 8f 2, 10f)(gd, g-f 2, hrd)
Unfurnished, fair filly. Turf high 56.
**R Hollinshead [0-4] R Hollinshead.*

RED KING BHB 45f38a **RR 44f 38a** 1147[6]
3 b g King Among Kings 7.4f **(49)** - Market Blues (Porto Bello) 8.9f **(43)**
Form - 066
Record 2000 - 1st:0 2nd:0 3rd:0 Ran:2
Pre2000 - 1st:0 2nd:0 3rd:0 Ran:6
2000 Turf 0-1: (10f) (gd) 2000 AW 0-1: (8f) (Fibr)
Moderate gelding, has worn blinkers. Inconsistent.
**A Berry [0-2] The Red Shirt Brigade Ltd (from J Berry [0-6] Nov 1999).*

RED LETTER BHB 80f **RR 87f** 4167[14]
3 b f Sri Pekan (USA) - Never Explain (IRE) **(79f)** (Fairy King (USA)) 7.7f **(59)**
Form - 326730
Record 2000 - 1st:0 2nd:1 3rd:2 Ran:6
Pre2000 - 1st:1 2nd:0 3rd:0 Ran:5
Win Prizemoney £5,680 *Total Prizemoney* £10,687
Wins * 1999 Jun Ascot (G-F) 6f 82 <
2000 Turf 0-6: (8f 4, 9f, 10f) (gd 3, g-f, frm 2)
Scopey, useful filly, effective 6 to 8f, acts on g-f to frm, has worn blinkers. Turf high 87 - 2nd of 14 getting 1lb from Sir Ferbet (11 Jun Newmarket 8f frm RF 1881). **R Hannon [1-11] Terry Neill.*

RED LION BHB 77f **RR 83f** 4468[18]
4 ch g Lion Cavern (USA) 7.5f **(74)** -Fleur Rouge (Pharly (FR)) 9.8f **(68)**
Form - 000000

Record 2000 - 1st:0 2nd:0 3rd:0 Ran:6
Pre2000 - 1st:4 2nd:0 3rd:1 Ran:17
Win Prizemoney £19,383 *Total Prizemoney* £21,413
Wins * 1999 Jly Yarmou (FRM) H 6f 93 95
* 1999 Jun Leices (GD) 6f 101+ <
* 1998 Jun Windso (GD) 5f 83
* 1998 May Redcar (G-F) 5f 89
2000 Turf 0-6: (5f, 6f 4, 7f) (gd 2, g-f 3, frm)
Scopey, decent gelding, effective 6f, acts on g-f, has worn blinkers. Turf high 83. **J W Payne [4-23] R G Gibney.*

RED LION (FR) RR 65f 5101[2]

3 ch g Lion Cavern (USA) 7.5f **(74)** - Mahogany River (Irish River (FR)) 8.6f **(78)**
Form - 008642
Record 2000 - 1st:0 2nd:1 3rd:0 Ran:6
Win Prizemoney £0 *Total Prizemoney* £1,813
2000 Turf 0-6: (8f, 10f 5) (gd 3, g-f 3)
Workmanlike, average gelding, effective 10f, acts on gd to g-f. Turf high 65 - 2nd of 20 getting 4lb from Scheming (20 Oct Doncaster 10f gd RF 5101). **B J Meehan [0-6] W H Ponsonby.*

RED MAGIC (FR) RR 89+f 3947a[6]

2 b br c Grand Lodge (USA) - Ma Priere (FR) (Highest Honor (FR))
Form - 216
Record 2000 - 1st:1 2nd:1 3rd:0 Ran:3
Win Prizemoney £6,825 *Total Prizemoney* £8,675
Wins * 2000 Jly Ascot (G-F) 7f 89+ <
2000 Turf 1-3: (6f 2, 7f 1-1) (g-s, gd, g-f 1-1)
Currently useful colt. Turf high 89 (began Jly) - 1st of 11 from Gryffindor (28 Jly Ascot RF 3166). Landed an Ascot maiden, but ran poorly when pitched into Group One company in the Prix Morny. **R Hannon [1-3].*

RED MILLENNIUM (IRE) BHB 100f RR 96f 5107[3]

2 b f Tagula (IRE) - Lovely Me (IRE) **(56f 57a)** (Vision (USA)) 9f **(64)**
Form - 1212113423
Record 2000 - 1st:4 2nd:3 3rd:2 Ran:10
Win Prizemoney £20,436 *Total Prizemoney* £38,927
Wins * 2000 Jly Cheste (SFT) 5.1f 94 <
*** 2000** Jly Doncas (G-F) 5f 86+
*** 2000** Jun Nottin (SFT) 5.1f 80+
*** 2000** Apr Mussel (G-S) 5f 68
2000 Turf 4-10: (5f 4-9, 6f) (gd 2-6, g-f 1-2, frm 1-2)
Very useful filly, effective 5f, acts on gd to frm. Turf high 96 - also 1st of 6 getting 3lb from Byo (14 Jly Chester RF 2798). Tough and speedy, she held her form remarkably well through a long campaign. Best on an easy surface, she has bags of early pace and is one to look out for in a Listed race this spring. **A Berry [4-10] The Red Shirt Brigade Ltd.*

RED MITTENS BHB 36f RR 37f 4174[15]

3 ch f Wolfhound (USA) 7.3f **(71)** - Red Gloves (Red God) 8.5f **(65)**
Form - 786670
Record 2000 - 1st:0 2nd:0 3rd:0 Ran:6
Pre2000 - 1st:0 2nd:0 3rd:0 Ran:4
2000 Turf 0-6: (5f, 6f 2, 7f 3) (g-f 2, frm 4)
Neat, very moderate filly. Turf high 37. **Martyn Wane [0-10] J P Slattery.*

REDNAP (USA) RR 39f 5023[7]

2 b br c Red Ransom (USA) 8.6f **(83)** - Smooth Asset (IRE) **(62f 61a)** (Fairy King (USA)) 7.7f **(59)**
Form - 7
Record 2000 - 1st:0 2nd:0 3rd:0 Ran:1
2000 Turf 0-1: (7f) (g-s)
Currently very moderate colt.
**M A Jarvis [0-1] Mohammed Al Khalifa.*

RED N' SOCKS (USA) BHB 90f RR 90f 4732[10]

3 ch c Devil's Bag (USA) 9.3f **(73)** - Racing Blue (Reference Point) 6.8f **(70)**
Form - 20717060
Record 2000 - 1st:1 2nd:1 3rd:0 Ran:8
Pre2000 - 1st:1 2nd:0 3rd:0 Ran:5
Win Prizemoney £9,255 *Total Prizemoney* £14,557
Wins * 2000 Jly Lingfi (G-F) 7.6f 93 <
* 1999 Oct Yarmou (G-F) H 8f 76 81+
2000 Turf 1-8: (7f, 8f 1-6, 9f) (g-s, gd 3, g-f 2, frm 1-2)
Workmanlike, useful colt, effective 8f, acts on gd to frm, best on frm. Turf high 95 - also 1st of 7 getting 5lb from Nice One Clare (19 Jly Lingfield RF 2943). Consistent. **J L Dunlop [2-13] Mrs H Focke.*

RED OCARINA RR 7f 3595[7]

2 ch f Piccolo - Morica (Moorestyle) 6.9f **(64)**
Form - 07
Record 2000 - 1st:0 2nd:0 3rd:0 Ran:2
2000 Turf 0-2: (5f, 6f) (g-f, hrd)
Currently very poor filly. Turf high 7 (began Jly).
**A Berry [0-2] The Red Shirt Brigade Ltd.*

REDOUBLE BHB 58f52a RR 62f 52a 4692[2]

4 b g First Trump - Sunflower Seed (Mummy's Pet) 7.7f **(60)**
Form - 07223322
Record 2000 - 1st:0 2nd:4 3rd:2 Ran:7
Pre2000 - 1st:0 2nd:2 3rd:3 Ran:21
Win Prizemoney £0 *Total Prizemoney* £8,823
2000 Turf 0-7: (10f, 12f 2, 13f, 14f 3) (gd, g-f 3, frm 3)
Strong, average gelding, effective 8 to 14f, acts on sft to frm, favours tight tracks. Turf high 62 - 2nd of 15 giving 1lb to Distant Prospect (4 Spt Bath 13f frm RF 4205). Running well in the summer and there could be a race for him over a distance of ground.
**J Akehurst [0-7] Normandy Developments (London) (from R J O'Sullivan [0-1] Dec 1999).*

REDOUBTABLE (USA) BHB 63f73a RR 84f 73a 5165[9]

9 b h Grey Dawn II 6.8f **(76)** - Seattle Rockette (USA) (Seattle Slew (USA)) 9.4f **(76)**
Form - 63641214320100700360041430504 0
Record 2000 - 1st:4 2nd:2 3rd:3 Ran:28
Pre2000 - 1st:7 2nd:8 3rd:8 Ran:63
Win Prizemoney £59,852 *Total Prizemoney* £117,528
Wins * 2000 Jly Redcar (G-F) 7f 47+
*** 2000** May Warwic (SFT) 6.8f 84
*** 2000** *Feb Lingfi (STD) H 7f 77 81*
*** 2000** *Jan Southw (STD) H 6f 70 76*
* 1999 May Thirsk (G-S) H 6f 72 79
* 1998 Jun Newcas (SFT) H 7f 72 77
* 1998 May Ayr (G-F) H 7f 68 69
* 1998 *Jan Lingfi (STD) H 7f 67 73+*
* 1997 *Dec Wolver (STD) H 6f 60 65+*
2000 Turf 2-21: (6f 7, 7f 2-13, 8f) (sft 1-3, g-s, gd 5, g-f 3, frm 1-9) 2000 AW 2-7: (6f 1-3, 7f 1-4) (Equi 1-2, Fibr 1-5)
Decent horse, effective 6 to 7f, best at 7f, acts on sft to frm - acts on AW, has worn blinkers, and excels at Ayr. Turf high 84 - 1st of 6 giving 15lb to Criss Cross (1 May Warwick RF 0952). AW high 81 - 1st of 9 giving 5lb to Ron's Pet (16 Feb Lingfield RF 0291) - also 1st of 8 giving 16lb to Rafters Music (24 Jan Southwell RF 0149). A winner on Equitrack and Fibresand early on this year, he landed a weak soft-ground classified event at Warwick in May. He is not altogether consistent and needs things his own way. Probably best suited by seven furlongs these days.
**D W Chapman [9-79] David Chapman (from R Hannon [2-12] Aug 1994).*

RED RAJA BHB 55f44a RR 59f 44a 740[8]

7 b g Persian Heights 10.5f **(61)** - Jenny Splendid (John Splendid) 8.1f **(62)**
Form - 88
Record 2000 - 1st:0 2nd:0 3rd:0 Ran:1
Pre2000 - 1st:2 2nd:1 3rd:1 Ran:20
Win Prizemoney £4,077 *Total Prizemoney* £4,934
Wins * 1999 Jun Lingfi (G-S) H 16f 55 59
* 1999 *Jan Lingfi (STD) H 16f 52 60* <
2000 AW 0-1: (16f) (Fibr)
Fair gelding, effective 14 to 16f, best at 16f, acts on g-s to frm - acts on Equi, has worn blinkers, favours left handed tracks, favours tight tracks. Becoming disappointing.
**P Mitchell [5-40] Mrs Mitchell,Mrs Gerber, Cohen.*

RED RAMONA BHB 77f RR 85df 4987[18]

5 b g Rudimentary (USA) 8.2f **(66)** -Apply (Kings Lake (USA)) 10.8f **(67)**
Form - 00
Record 2000 - 1st:0 2nd:0 3rd:0 Ran:2
Pre2000 - 1st:1 2nd:1 3rd:1 Ran:12

Win Prizemoney £2,406 *Total Prizemoney* £9,023
Wins 1998 Jun Folkes (GD) 12f 75 <
2000 Turf 0-2: (12f, 18f) (g-s, gd)
Useful gelding, effective 14f, acts on frm. Turf high 63 (began Oct). Becoming disappointing.
**J Akehurst [0-8] A D Spence (from R Charlton [1-6] Oct 1998).*

RED REVOLUTION (USA) BHB 72f **RR 76f** 4332[18]

3 ch g Explosive Red (CAN) - Braided Way (USA) (Mining (USA))
Form - 216800
Record 2000 - 1st:1 2nd:0 3rd:0 Ran:5
Pre2000 - 1st:0 2nd:1 3rd:1 Ran:2
Win Prizemoney £2,691 *Total Prizemoney* £3,849
Wins * 2000 *Jan Lingfi (STD) 5f 70+* <
2000 Turf 0-4: (5f 2, 6f 2) (gd, g-f, frm 2) 2000 AW 1-1: (5f 1-1) (Equi 1-1)
Scopey, above-average gelding, effective 5 to 6f, acts on frm - acts on Equi. Turf high 76 (1st run) - 6th of 23 getting 16lb from Cotton House (17 Jun York 6f frm RF 2062). (1st run) - 1st of 4 from Lusong (8 Jan Lingfield RF 0050). Ran green on both of his juvenile starts, but made no mistake when bolting up in a four-runner maiden on the Lingfield Equitrack in January. He was having his first race since when a fine sixth in the William Hill Trophy at York, but the race may have come too soon when running very poorly at Newmarket next time. **T D Barron [1-7] P D Savill.*

RED RIVER REBEL BHB 62f **RR 59f** 5309[18]

2 b g Inchinor 8.9f **(64)** - Bidweaya (USA) (Lear Fan (USA)) 8.5f **(73)**
Form - 670
Record 2000 - 1st:0 2nd:0 3rd:0 Ran:3
2000 Turf 0-3: (6f, 7f 2) (g-s, gd, g-f)
Currently fair gelding. Turf high 59. **J Norton [0-3] Jeff Slaney.*

RED ROSES (IRE) **RR 37f** 4494[4]

4 b f Mukaddamah (USA) 7.6f **(74)** - Roses Red (IRE) (Exhibitioner) 8.7f **(61)**
Form - 00087407434
Record 2000 - 1st:0 2nd:0 3rd:1 Ran:11
Pre2000 - 1st:0 2nd:1 3rd:1 Ran:10
Win Prizemoney £0 *Total Prizemoney* £2,204
2000 Turf 0-11: (10f 4, 11f 2, 12f 5) (sft, g-s 2, gd 4, g-f 3, frm)
Very moderate filly, effective 8f, acts on sft, has worn blinkers. Turf high 37.
**Don Enrico Incisa [0-14] Don Enrico Incisa (from N Tinkler [0-2] Apr 2000).*

RED ROSIE (USA) **RR 58f** 4969[13]

2 b f Red Ransom (USA) 8.6f **(83)** - Do's Gent (CAN) (Vice Regent (CAN)) 8.7f **(74)**
Form - 0
Record 2000 - 1st:0 2nd:0 3rd:0 Ran:1
2000 Turf 0-1: (8f) (gd)
Currently fair filly. **Mrs A J Perrett [0-1] R C O'Hare.*

RED RYDING HOOD BHB 76f **RR 74f** 5183[4]

2 ch f Wolfhound (USA) 7.3f **(71)** - Downeaster Alexa (USA) (Red Ryder (USA))
Form - 634232054
Record 2000 - 1st:0 2nd:2 3rd:2 Ran:9
Win Prizemoney £0 *Total Prizemoney* £8,031
2000 Turf 0-9: (5f 6, 6f 2, 7f) (g-s, gd, g-f 5, frm 2)
Above-average filly, effective 5 to 6f, best at 5f, acts on g-f to frm, best on g-f. Turf high 74 - 2nd of 11 getting 10lb from Red Carpet (26 Aug Newmarket 6f g-f RF 3993). Consistent. Has been narrowly beaten in maidens, and deserves to pick up a race.
**C A Dwyer [0-9] P Venner.*

REDS DESIRE BHB 22f **RR 19f** 4174[16]

3 ch g Bold Arrangement 8.7f **(57)** - Dreamy Desire (Palm Track) 9.8f **(50)**
Form - 806000
Record 2000 - 1st:0 2nd:0 3rd:0 Ran:6
2000 Turf 0-6: (5f 3, 6f 2, 8f) (sft, gd 2, g-f 2, frm)
Workmanlike, poor gelding. Turf high 19.
**Miss J F Craze [0-6] Des Redhead.*

RED SEPTEMBER BHB 38f **RR 45f** 3497[7]

3 b g Presidium 7.5f **(56)** - Tangalooma (Hotfoot) 10.5f **(59)**
Form - 0607
Record 2000 - 1st:0 2nd:0 3rd:0 Ran:4
Pre2000 - 1st:0 2nd:0 3rd:0 Ran:5
2000 Turf 0-3: (8f, 9f, 14f) (g-f 2, frm) 2000 AW 0-1: (11f) (Fibr)
Leggy, moderate gelding, has worn blinkers. Turf high 32.
**G M Moore [0-9] Dr C I Emmerson.*

RED SONNY (IRE) BHB 47f46a **RR 46f 46a** 2479[10]

3 ch g Foxhound (USA) - Olivia's Pride (IRE) (Digamist (USA))
Form - 8740023620
Record 2000 - 1st:0 2nd:2 3rd:1 Ran:10
Pre2000 - 1st:0 2nd:0 3rd:0 Ran:4
Win Prizemoney £0 *Total Prizemoney* £1,818
2000 Turf 0-6: (6f, 7f, 8f 3, 10f) (g-s, gd 2, g-f, frm 2) 2000 AW 0-4: (5f, 6f, 8f 2) (Fibr 4)
Strong, moderate gelding. Turf high 46. AW high 46. Inconsistent.
**A Berry [0-10] The Red Shirt Brigade Ltd (from J Berry [0-4] Oct 1999).*

REDSWAN BHB 68f68a **RR 70f 68a** 5122[6]

5 ch g Risk Me (FR) 8f **(53)** - Bocas Rose (Jalmood (USA)) 10.1f **(52)**
Form - 0700020331506
Record 2000 - 1st:1 2nd:1 3rd:2 Ran:13
Pre2000 - 1st:3 2nd:1 3rd:2 Ran:17
Win Prizemoney £20,859 *Total Prizemoney* £27,469
Wins * 2000 Spt Newmar (SFT) C 7f 64
* 1999 Spt Doncas (G-F) H 7f 68 71 <
* 1999 Jly Leices (G-F) H 7f 66 67
* 1998 Jun Newmar (GD) C 8f 67+
2000 Turf 1-13: (6f, 7f 1-10, 8f 2) (g-s 2, gd 3, g-f 1-3, frm 5)
Above-average gelding, effective 7 to 8f, best at 7f, acts on g-f to frm, best on g-f, excels at Newmarket and Leicester. Turf high 70 - 5th of 28 getting 11lb from Sea Mark (30 Spt Newmarket 7f g-f RF 4743) - also 1st of 22 getting 4lb from Mantles Pride (16 Spt Newmarket RF 4471). **S C Williams [4-30] P Geoghan.*

RED SYMPHONY BHB 41f48a **RR 47f 48a** 4894[12]

4 b f Merdon Melody 6.8f **(56)** - Woodland Steps (Bold Owl) 8.5f **(45)**
Form - 050081000800
Record 2000 - 1st:1 2nd:0 3rd:0 Ran:11
Pre2000 - 1st:3 2nd:1 3rd:3 Ran:19
Win Prizemoney £9,125 *Total Prizemoney* £11,191
Wins * 2000 Jun Newcas (SFT) S 5f 47
* 1998 Spt Mussel (GD) H 5f 60 72 <
1998 May Mussel (G-S) S 5f 55
1998 Apr Wolver (STD) S 5f 48+
2000 Turf 1-10: (5f 1-7, 6f 3) (sft 1-2, gd 5, frm 3) 2000 AW 0-1: (5f) (Fibr)
Light-framed, moderate filly, effective 5f, acts on sft to gd, best on sft, has worn blinkers. Turf high 47 - 1st of 14 getting 5lb from Souperficial (7 Jun Newcastle RF 1788).
**I Semple [2-25] W Edward (from J Berry [2-5] Jun 1998).*

RED THATCH BHB 30f **RR 54f** 4444[10]

3 ch c Pelder (IRE) - Straw Castle (Final Straw) 7.9f **(64)**
Form - 00
Record 2000 - 1st:0 2nd:0 3rd:0 Ran:2
Pre2000 - 1st:0 2nd:0 3rd:0 Ran:2
2000 Turf 0-2: (8f 2) (gd, g-f)
Fair colt. Turf high 54 (began Aug).
**M P Muggeridge [0-2] The Top Maite Partnership (from G F H Charles-Jones [0-2] Jly 1999).*

RED TYPHOON BHB 68f **RR 70f** 5313[17]

3 ro f Belfort (FR) 6.7f **(53)** - Dash Cascade (Absalom) 7.2f **(58)**
Form - 000028000
Record 2000 - 1st:0 2nd:1 3rd:0 Ran:9
Pre2000 - 1st:2 2nd:0 3rd:2 Ran:11
Win Prizemoney £5,067 *Total Prizemoney* £7,461
Wins 1999 Oct Lingfi (HVY) C 6f 84+ <
1999 Spt Haydoc (G-F) C 6f 67+
2000 Turf 0-9: (5f 5, 6f 4) (g-s, gd 4, g-f 3, frm)
Strong, above-average filly, effective 6f, acts on g-s. Turf high 70. Won twice over six furlongs as a juvenile in 1999 on varying ground. Showed little in her early starts last season, but ran better when just touched off at Kempton in July.
**M Kettle [0-9] Espro Racing (from J Berry [2-11] Oct 1999).*

REDUIT BHB 100f **RR 92f** 5308a[2]
2 ch c Lion Cavern (USA) 7.5f **(74)** - Soolaimon (IRE) **(68f)** (Shareef Dancer (USA)) 9.9f **(73)**
Form - 4412
Record 2000 - 1st:1 2nd:1 3rd:0 Ran:4
Win Prizemoney £2,775 *Total Prizemoney* £20,157
Wins * **2000** Spt Chepst (G-S) 8.1f 85 <
2000 Turf 1-4: (7f 2, 8f 1-1, 10f) (hvy, gd, g-f 1-2)
Useful colt. Turf high 92 (began Jly) - 2nd of 8 to Sagacity (29 Oct Saint-cloud 10f hvy RF 5308a) - also 1st of 16 giving 5lb to Dubai Seven Stars (7 Spt Chepstow RF 4271). Followed an encouraging debut by being outclassed at York, but was suited by a mile on easy ground when coming late to score at Chepstow. Did not appear to quite get home when trying ten furlongs on heavy ground in the Criterium de Saint-Cloud.
**G A Butler [1-4] Five Horses Ltd.*

RED VENUS (IRE) BHB 46f50a **RR 62f 50a** 5049a[4]
4 ch f Perugino (USA) - Reflection Time (IRE) (Fayruz)
Form - 53370530004
Record 2000 - 1st:0 2nd:0 3rd:3 Ran:11
Pre2000 - 1st:2 2nd:1 3rd:3 Ran:23
Win Prizemoney £4,135 *Total Prizemoney* £7,311
Wins 1999 *Apr Southw (STD) H 7f 54 61* <
1999 *Jan Southw (STD) S 7f 50*
2000 Turf 0-5: (7f 4, 10f) (sft, g-s 2, g-f 2) 2000 AW 0-6: (7f 3, 8f 3) (Equi 2, Fibr 4)
Average filly, effective 7 to 8f, best at 7f, acts on g-f - acts on AW, best on Fibr, often wears blinkers, likes tight tracks. Turf high 62 (1st run) (began Jly) - 3rd of 13 giving 5lb to Pearl Barley (3 Jly Sligo 7f g-f RF 2701a). AW high 55 - 3rd of 13 to My Alibi (20 Mar Southwell 8f Fibr RF 0465).
**Ms Caroline Hutchinson in IRE [0-5] Ms Caroline Hutchinson (from Miss Gay Kelleway [1-16] May 2000).*

RED WHITE AND BLUE BHB 25f **RR 30f** 5198[14]
3 b f Zafonic (USA) 9f **(83)** - Malham Tarn (Riverman (USA)) 9.1f **(76)**
Form - 0000
Record 2000 - 1st:0 2nd:0 3rd:0 Ran:4
2000 Turf 0-4: (6f, 7f 2, 8f) (gd 2, frm 2)
Very moderate filly. Turf high 30.
**K O Cunningham-Brown [0-4] A J Richards.*

RED WOLF BHB 39f **RR 38f** 4122[7]
4 ch g Timeless Times (USA) 6.1f **(56)** - Stealthy (Kind of Hush) 10.1f **(62)**
Form - 0083207
Record 2000 - 1st:0 2nd:1 3rd:1 Ran:6
Pre2000 - 1st:0 2nd:0 3rd:0 Ran:4
Win Prizemoney £0 *Total Prizemoney* £1,132
2000 Turf 0-5: (7f 2, 8f 3) (g-f 2, frm 3) 2000 AW 0-1: (8f) (Fibr)
Very moderate gelding. Turf high 38 (began Jly). Inconsistent.
**J G Given [0-10] K H Benson.*

REEDS RAINS BHB 78f **RR 75f** 4259[16]
2 b f Mind Games - Me Spede (Valiyar) 8.5f **(73)**
Form - 1440
Record 2000 - 1st:1 2nd:0 3rd:0 Ran:4
Win Prizemoney £4,049 *Total Prizemoney* £4,915
Wins * **2000** Apr Thirsk (SFT) 5f 75 <
2000 Turf 1-4: (5f 1-2, 6f 2) (g-s 1-1, gd 2, frm)
Above-average filly. Turf high 75 (1st run) - 1st of 5 getting 2lb from Milly's Lass (14 Apr Thirsk RF 0718). Won in soft ground on her debut, but hung on her third start and subsequently sidelined.
**T D Easterby [1-4] Ron George.*

REEL BUDDY (USA) BHB 100f **RR 99f** 5107[14]
2 ch c Mr. Greeley (USA) - Rosebud **(78f)** (Indian Ridge)
Form - 620771120
Record 2000 - 1st:2 2nd:2 3rd:0 Ran:9
Win Prizemoney £9,695 *Total Prizemoney* £73,437
Wins * **2000** Aug Ripon (GD) 5f 99 <
* **2000** Aug Bath (GD) 5.1f 98+
2000 Turf 2-9: (5f 2-6, 6f 3) (gd 3, g-f 1-2, frm 1-3, hrd)
Very useful colt, effective 5 to 6f, best at 5f, acts on gd to frm. Turf high 99 - 1st of 9 giving 5lb to Proud Boast (29 Aug Ripon RF 4064) - also 1st of 10 giving 14lb to Tickle (20 Aug Bath RF 3813). A powerful colt, he kept smart company before winning two minor heats during August. Unlucky in a valuable sales race at Doncaster the following month, he stays six furlongs and is good enough to win a Listed contest. **R Hannon [2-9] Speedlith Group.*

REEMATNA BHB 58f58a **RR 75f 58a** 4616[10]
3 b f Sabrehill (USA) 8.5f **(64)** - Reem Albaraari (Sadler's Wells (USA)) 10f **(76)**
Form - 424630
Record 2000 - 1st:0 2nd:1 3rd:1 Ran:6
Pre2000 - 1st:0 2nd:0 3rd:0 Ran:1
Win Prizemoney £0 *Total Prizemoney* £2,035
2000 Turf 0-5: (7f 2, 8f, 10f, 11f) (sft, gd 2, g-f, frm) 2000 AW 0-1: (8f) (Fibr)
Small, above-average filly, effective 7f, acts on g-f. Turf high 75 - 2nd of 6 getting 5lb from Pretrail (3 Jun Lingfield 7f g-f RF 1677).
**M A Jarvis [0-7] Sheikh Ahmed Al Maktoum.*

REFERENDUM (IRE) BHB 73f83a **RR 75f 83a** 4384[21]
6 b g Common Grounds 8.1f **(66)** - Final Decision (Tap On Wood) 10.3f **(65)**
Form - 0000085266022300
Record 2000 - 1st:0 2nd:3 3rd:1 Ran:16
Pre2000 - 1st:1 2nd:4 3rd:1 Ran:18
Win Prizemoney £4,513 *Total Prizemoney* £72,666
Wins 1996 Aug Goodwo (GD) 6f 94 <
2000 Turf 0-15: (5f 9, 6f 6) (sft, g-s, gd 5, g-f 3, frm 5) 2000 AW 0-1: (6f) (Fibr)
Above-average gelding, effective 6f, acts on frm, has worn blinkers. Turf high 77.
**D Nicholls [0-22] M A Scaife (from G Lewis [1-12] Oct 1990).*

REFERRAL (USA) RR 80f 4401[2]
2 ch c Silver Hawk (USA) 11.2f **(85)** -True Joy (IRE) **(57f)** (Zilzal (USA))
Form - 252
Record 2000 - 1st:0 2nd:2 3rd:0 Ran:3
Win Prizemoney £0 *Total Prizemoney* £3,226
2000 Turf 0-3: (7f 2, 8f) (gd, g-f 2)
Currently decent colt. Turf high 80 (began Aug) - 2nd of 8 giving 5lb to Mot Juste (14 Spt Yarmouth 8f g-f RF 4401).
**K R Burke [0-3] Mrs Julie Mitchell.*

REFLEX BLUE BHB 73f **RR 85f** 5104[5]
3 b g Ezzoud (IRE) - Briggsmaid (Elegant Air) 13.2f **(61)**
Form - 44236405
Record 2000 - 1st:0 2nd:1 3rd:1 Ran:8
Pre2000 - 1st:1 2nd:2 3rd:0 Ran:4
Win Prizemoney £4,503 *Total Prizemoney* £14,821
Wins * 1999 Jly Newmar (G-F) 7f 82 <
2000 Turf 0-8: (10f 3, 12f 3, 15f 2) (gd 2, g-f 5, frm)
Scopey, useful gelding, effective 7 to 10f, acts on g-f to frm, best on frm, has worn blinkers. Turf high 85. Consistent. Winner of a Newmarket maiden last summer, he has run well over middle distances without managing to force his head in front. Best on fast ground. **J W Hills [1-12] The Jonathawn Q Partnership.*

REFRACT RR 75f 4701[11]
2 b c Spectrum (IRE) - Sofala (Home Guard (USA)) 9.3f **(66)**
Form - 0
Record 2000 - 1st:0 2nd:0 3rd:0 Ran:1
2000 Turf 0-1: (7f) (g-f)
Currently above-average colt. **D E Cantillon [0-1] Mickey Brennan.*

REGAL ACADEMY (IRE) BHB 33f **RR 37f** 4099[3]
6 b m Royal Academy (USA) 7.8f **(77)** - Polistatic (Free State) 8.7f **(61)**
Form - 043
Record 2000 - 1st:0 2nd:0 3rd:1 Ran:3
Pre2000 - 1st:0 2nd:0 3rd:1 Ran:13
Win Prizemoney £0 *Total Prizemoney* £1,310
2000 Turf 0-3: (10f, 12f 2) (frm 2, hrd)
Very moderate mare, effective 12f, acts on g-f to frm, has worn blinkers (extremely effectively). Turf high 36 (began Jly). Consistent. **C A Horgan [0-16] Mrs B Sumner.*

REGAL AIR (IRE) BHB 70f **RR 69f** 4443[2]
2 b f Distinctly North (USA) 7.4f **(63)** - Dignified Air (FR) (Wolver Hollow) 8f **(56)**

Form - 35303722
Record 2000 - 1st:0 2nd:2 3rd:3 Ran:8
Win Prizemoney £0 *Total Prizemoney* £2,675
2000 Turf 0-6: (5f 4, 6f 2) (gd 2, g-f 2, frm, hrd) 2000 AW 0-2: (5f 2) (Fibr 2)
Average filly. Turf high 67. AW high 54. **B I Case [0-8] B I Case.*

REGAL CHARM (IRE) BHB 59f **RR 48f** 1517^{6}

3 b f Sadler's Wells (USA) 11.3f **(87)** - Abury (IRE) (Law Society (USA)) 9.9f **(70)**
Form - 06
Record 2000 - 1st:0 2nd:0 3rd:0 Ran:2
Pre2000 - 1st:0 2nd:0 3rd:0 Ran:1
2000 Turf 0-2: (10f, 12f) (g-s, gd)
Currently moderate filly. Turf high 39.
**J H M Gosden [0-2] R E Sangster (from A G Foster [0-1] Oct 1999).*

REGAL HOLLY RR 15f 1314^{10}

5 b m Gildoran 11.6f **(58)** - Pusey Street (Native Bazaar) 6.9f **(62)**
Form - 0
Record 2000 - 1st:0 2nd:0 3rd:0 Ran:1
2000 Turf 0-1: (14f) (gd)
Poor filly, always wears blinkers. **B A McMahon [2-5] M A Wilkins.*

REGAL MISTRESS BHB 35f **RR 21f** 789^{7}

2 b f Tragic Role (USA) 9.4f **(63)** - Regal Salute (Dara Monarch) 8.8f **(59)**
Form - 587
Record 2000 - 1st:0 2nd:0 3rd:0 Ran:3
2000 Turf 0-2: (5f 2) (g-s, gd) 2000 AW 0-1: (5f) (Fibr)
Currently little account filly. Turf high 21.
**D Shaw [0-3] D C G Cooper.*

REGALO BHB 37f **RR ?f** 5112^{25}

5 b h Nalchik (USA) 12.6f **(44)** - Stardrop (Starch Reduced) 11.5f **(52)**
Form - 000
Record 2000 - 1st:0 2nd:0 3rd:0 Ran:3
Pre2000 - 1st:0 2nd:0 3rd:1 Ran:11
Win Prizemoney £0 *Total Prizemoney* £826
2000 Turf 0-3: (5f, 6f, 8f) (g-s, gd, g-f)
Very poor colt, has worn blinkers. (began Oct).
**W de Best-Turner [0-4] The Spanish Connection (from D M Hyde [0-10] May 1998).*

REGAL PHILOSOPHER BHB 90f **RR 93f** 2824^{5}

4 b g Faustus (USA) 9.1f **(54)** - Princess Lucy (Local Suitor (USA)) 8.4f **(67)**
Form - 6224035
Record 2000 - 1st:0 2nd:2 3rd:1 Ran:7
Pre2000 - 1st:2 2nd:4 3rd:1 Ran:12
Win Prizemoney £8,230 *Total Prizemoney* £31,607
Wins * 1999 Jun Newcas (G-F) H 8f 83 88 <
*** 1999** May Bath (GD) 8f 84
2000 Turf 0-7: (8f 6, 9f) (sft, g-s 2, gd, g-f 2, frm)
Well made, useful gelding, effective 8 to 10f, best at 8f, acts on sft to frm, best on g-s, prefers right handed tracks, prefers tight tracks, excels at Sandown and Newcastle. Turf high 93 - 3rd of 18 getting 12lb from Caribbean Monarch (9 Jly Sandown 8f g-f RF 2658). Consistent. Usually held-up (has been left with too much to do), he is on a long losing run and looked jaded on his final start. Effective on most surfaces, he stays a mile and often comes to hand early. **J W Hills [2-19] Trajan Partners.*

REGAL ROSE RR 100+f 4644^{1}

2 b f Danehill (USA) 9.1f **(79)** - Ruthless Rose (USA) (Conquistador Cielo (USA)) 8.8f **(69)**
Form - 11
Record 2000 - 1st:2 2nd:0 3rd:0 Ran:2
Win Prizemoney £83,512 *Total Prizemoney* £83,512
Wins * 2000 Spt Newmar (G-S) G1 6f 100+ <
*** 2000** Jly Ascot (G-F) 6f 88++
2000 Turf 2-2: (6f 2-2) (g-f 2-2)
Currently very useful filly. Turf high 100 (began Jly) - 1st of 13 from Toroca (26 Spt Newmarket RF 4644). Did everything that was required of her when winning on her Ascot debut, and won the Shadwell Stud Cheveley Park despite missing a beat at the start. She is now favourite for the 1000 Guineas, and connections believe she will improve as a three-year-old.
**Sir Michael Stoute [2-2] Cheveley Park Stud.*

REGAL SONG (IRE) BHB 68f54a **RR 67f 54a** 5313^{2}

4 b g Anita's Prince 6f **(62)** - Song Beam (Song) 7.2f **(61)**
Form - 32035030102
Record 2000 - 1st:1 2nd:2 3rd:3 Ran:11
Pre2000 - 1st:1 2nd:0 3rd:3 Ran:11
Win Prizemoney £5,219 *Total Prizemoney* £11,021
Wins * 2000 Oct Newcas (HVY) H 5f 61 67 <
***** 1999 Jun Hamilt (GD) 5f 67 <
2000 Turf 1-7: (5f 1-4, 6f 2, 7f) (sft 1-1, g-s, gd 4, frm) 2000 AW 0-4: (6f 3, 7f) (Fibr 4)
Workmanlike, average gelding, effective 5f, acts on sft to g-f, often wears blinkers. Turf high 67 - also 1st of 20 giving 13lb to Mukarrab (18 Oct Newcastle RF 5057). AW high 50.
**T J Etherington [2-22] Mrs Y Brierley.*

REGAL SPLENDOUR (CAN) BHB 43a **RR 34f** 241^{10}

7 ch g Vice Regent (CAN) 7.3f **(70)** - Seattle Princess (USA) (Seattle Slew (USA)) 9.4f **(76)**
Form - 600
Record 2000 - 1st:0 2nd:0 3rd:0 Ran:1
Pre2000 - 1st:1 2nd:3 3rd:0 Ran:27
Win Prizemoney £2,427 *Total Prizemoney* £5,527
Wins 1997 *Feb Lingfi (STD) H 8f 60 62* <
2000 AW 0-1: (8f) (Fibr)
Very moderate gelding, has broken blood-vessels, effective 8f, acts on frm.
**B A McMahon [0-7] Miss Sarah Jones (from J J Bridger [0-11] Spt 1998).*

REGAL VISION (IRE) BHB 51f **RR 56f** 4677^{5}

3 b g Emperor Jones (USA) - Shining Eyes (USA) (Mr Prospector (USA)) 8.8f **(78)**
Form - 6805
Record 2000 - 1st:0 2nd:0 3rd:0 Ran:4
2000 Turf 0-4: (7f, 8f 2, 10f) (g-s, gd, g-f 2)
Leggy, fair gelding. Turf high 56 (began Aug). **C G Cox [0-4] Axom.*

REGARDEZ-MOI BHB 38f **RR 57f** 5229^{14}

3 b f Distinctly North (USA) 7.4f **(63)** - Tomard (Thatching) 8f **(66)**
Form - 00630000
Record 2000 - 1st:0 2nd:0 3rd:1 Ran:8
Pre2000 - 1st:0 2nd:0 3rd:3 Ran:11
Win Prizemoney £0 *Total Prizemoney* £2,968
2000 Turf 0-8: (7f 3, 8f 4, 10f) (sft, gd, g-f 3, frm 3)
Workmanlike, fair filly, effective 5 to 8f, acts on gd to g-f, best on gd. Turf high 57 - 6th of 18 getting 2lb from Manxwood (5 Jun Windsor 8f g-f RF 1730). Inconsistent.
**A W Carroll [0-19] Mrs Madeleine Gilles.*

REGATTA POINT (IRE) BHB 95f **RR 93f** 5238^{3}

2 b c Goldmark (USA) - Flashing Raven (IRE) (Maelstrom Lake)
Form - 02113
Record 2000 - 1st:2 2nd:1 3rd:1 Ran:5
Win Prizemoney £9,399 *Total Prizemoney* £12,855
Wins * 2000 Oct Newmar (SFT) H 8f 77 82 <
*** 2000** Spt Salisb (SFT) 8f 82 <
2000 Turf 2-5: (7f, 8f 2-3, 10f) (g-s, gd 2-3, frm)
Useful colt. Turf high 93 (began Aug) - 3rd of 9 getting 5lb from Worthily (28 Oct Newmarket 10f g-s RF 5238). Improved from his first two runs to take his next two races on soft ground in the autumn. Looks to be still on the upgrade.
**A P Jarvis [2-5] Grant & Bowman Ltd.*

REGENT BHB 47a **RR 19f** 5198^{7}

5 ch g Zafonic (USA) 9f **(83)** - Queen Midas (Glint of Gold) 9.3f **(66)**
Form - 0000807
Record 2000 - 1st:0 2nd:0 3rd:0 Ran:7
Pre2000 - 1st:0 2nd:0 3rd:0 Ran:11
2000 Turf 0-6: (6f, 7f 2, 8f 2, 11f) (gd 3, g-f 3) 2000 AW 0-1: (8f) (Equi)
Poor gelding, effective 8 to 10f, best at 8f, acts on gd to frm, likes right handed tracks, prefers tight tracks. Turf high 19 (began Aug).
**P W Hiatt [0-7] P J & Mrs K D Morgan (from C P Morlock [0-15] Feb 2000).*

*C Wragg [0-?] The Romney Partnership.

REGENT COURT (IRE) BHB 73f **RR 74f** 4818[10]
2 gr f Marju (IRE) 9.2f **(76)** - Silver Singing (USA) (Topsider (USA)) 8.3f **(71)**
Form - 54530
Record 2000 - 1st:0 2nd:0 3rd:1 Ran:5
Win Prizemoney £0 *Total Prizemoney* £950
2000 Turf 0-5: (7f 3, 8f 2) (g-s, gd 3, frm)
Above-average filly. Turf high 74 (began Aug) - 3rd of 9 to Saltwood (14 Spt Ayr 7f gd RF 4386). **T D Easterby [0-5] M P Burke.*

REGGIE BUCK (USA) BHB 34f46a **RR 32f 46a** 1340[11]
6 b br g Alleged (USA) 11.8f **(81)** - Hello Memphis (USA) (Super Concorde (USA)) 10.9f **(66)**
Form - 60
Record 2000 - 1st:0 2nd:0 3rd:0 Ran:2
Pre2000 - 1st:0 2nd:1 3rd:2 Ran:12
Win Prizemoney £0 *Total Prizemoney* £2,521
2000 Turf 0-2: (14f, 16f) (gd, hrd)
Fair gelding, has worn blinkers. Turf high 32.
**J Mackie [2-8] Fools Who Dream (from J L Harris [1-13] Spt 1999).*

REIMS (IRE) BHB 60f **RR 75+f** 4828[22]
2 b c Topanoora 8.3f **(67)** - Fairy Folk (IRE) (Fairy King (USA)) 7.7f **(59)**
Form - 000
Record 2000 - 1st:0 2nd:0 3rd:0 Ran:3
2000 Turf 0-3: (7f 2, 8f) (g-s, gd, frm)
Currently above-average colt. Turf high 75 (began Aug).
**T D Easterby [0-3] Elite Racing Club.*

REINHARDT (IRE) BHB 33f22a **RR 28f 22a** 288[8]
7 b g Bluebird (USA) 7.9f **(71)** - Rhein Bridge (Rheingold) 10.4f **(62)**
Form - 8
Record 2000 - 1st:0 2nd:0 3rd:0 Ran:1
Pre2000 - 1st:1 2nd:2 3rd:5 Ran:29
Win Prizemoney £2,232 *Total Prizemoney* £9,451
Wins 1997 Jun Beverl (G-F) H 5f 40 44 <
2000 AW 0-1: (12f) (Fibr)
Little account gelding, has worn blinkers.
**L R Lloyd-James [0-13] Nelson Unit Ltd (from D Nicholls [1-11] Spt 1997).*

REKEN BHB 28f **RR 26f** 2086[10]
4 b g Mujtahid (USA) 7.4f **(69)** - Room Albaraari (Sadler's Wells (USA)) 10f **(76)**
Form - 0070
Record 2000 - 1st:0 2nd:0 3rd:0 Ran:4
Pre2000 - 1st:0 2nd:0 3rd:0 Ran:8
2000 Turf 0-4: (7f, 8f 3) (g-s, gd 2, frm)
Unfurnished, little account gelding. Turf high 26.
**P Burgoyne [0-12] Philip Saunders.*

RELATIVE DELIGHT **RR 54f** 5236[17]
2 b f Distant Relative 7f **(69)** - Pasja (IRE) (Posen (USA))
Form - 00
Record 2000 - 1st:0 2nd:0 3rd:0 Ran:2
2000 Turf 0-2: (7f 2) (g-s, g-f)
Currently fair filly. Turf high 54 (began Spt).
**R Hollinshead [0-2] Kieron Grealis.*

RELISH THE THOUGHT (IRE) **RR 93+f** 5128[1]
2 b f Sadler's Wells (USA) 11.3f **(87)** - Viz (USA) (Kris S (USA)) 7.9f **(71)**
Form - 1
Record 2000 - 1st:1 2nd:0 3rd:0 Ran:1
Win Prizemoney £13,520 *Total Prizemoney* £13,520
Wins * 2000 Oct Newbur (HVY) L 7f 93+ <
2000 Turf 1-1: (7f 1-1) (sft 1-1)
Currently useful filly. (1st run) - 1st of 11 from Blushing Bride (21 Oct Newbury RF 5128). A rangy filly, won a listed event at Newbury on her debut and looks to have plenty of potential.
**B W Hills [1-1] Maktoum Al Maktoum.*

REMARKABLE **RR 62f** 5310[11]
2 ch f Wolfhound (USA) 7.3f **(71)** - Valika (Valiyar) 8.5f **(73)**
Form - 60
Record 2000 - 1st:0 2nd:0 3rd:0 Ran:2
2000 Turf 0-2: (7f 2) (g-s 2)
Currently average filly. Turf high 62 (began Oct).

REMEMBER STAR BHB 25f **RR 30f** 4679[4]
7 ch m Don't Forget Me 9.5f **(66)** - Star Girl Gay (Lord Gayle (USA)) 8.8f **(62)**
Form - 432254
Record 2000 - 1st:0 2nd:2 3rd:1 Ran:6
Pre2000 - 1st:0 2nd:0 3rd:0 Ran:6
Win Prizemoney £0 *Total Prizemoney* £2,018
2000 Turf 0-6: (12f 3, 15f, 16f 2) (g-s, g-f 2, frm 3)
Very moderate mare, effective 12 to 16f, acts on g-f to frm, best on g-f, favours tight tracks. Turf high 30 (1st run) - 4th of 13 getting 14lb from Renaissance Lady (19 Jun Warwick 16f g-f RF 2101).
**R J Baker [3-21] Duckhaven Stud (from A G Newcombe [0-5] Feb 1999).*

RENAISSANCE LADY (IRE) BHB 57f **RR 62f** 4317[4]
4 ch f Imp Society (USA) 7.1f **(63)** - Easter Morning (FR) (Nice Havrais (USA))
Form - 0711125334
Record 2000 - 1st:3 2nd:1 3rd:2 Ran:10
Pre2000 - 1st:1 2nd:1 3rd:0 Ran:12
Win Prizemoney £12,727 *Total Prizemoney* £19,156
Wins * 2000 Jly Warwic (GD) H 14.6f 49 54
*** 2000** Jun Warwic (G-F) H 15.8f 42 58 <
*** 2000** Jun Warwic (G-F) H 15.8f 42 49
* 1999 Jun Bright (G-F) 11.9f 54+
2000 Turf 3-10: (12f, 15f 1-2, 16f 2-5, 17f, 20f) (hvy, gd 1-4, g-f 2-3, frm, hrd)
Scopey, average filly, effective 12 to 20f, acts on gd to hrd, likes left handed tracks, likes tight tracks, excels at Goodwood, does well at Warwick. Turf high 62 - 3rd of 8 getting 3lb from Laffah (2 Aug Goodwood 20f gd RF 3315) - also 1st of 8 getting 26lb from Bid Me Welcome (28 Jun Warwick RF 2359). Consistent. Showed progressive form last summer, running up a quick hat-trick at Warwick, and continued to run well afterwards.
**T R Watson [5-30] Alan Wright.*

RENDITA (IRE) BHB 30f42a **RR 33f 42a** 4922[4]
4 b f Waajib 8.9f **(67)** - Rend Rover (FR) (Monseigneur (USA)) 7.7f **(63)**
Form - 0700534
Record 2000 - 1st:0 2nd:0 3rd:1 Ran:7
Pre2000 - 1st:1 2nd:1 3rd:1 Ran:11
Win Prizemoney £2,621 *Total Prizemoney* £4,506
Wins * 1999 *Apr Lingfi (STD) H* 7f 48 59 <
2000 Turf 0-3: (8f, 10f, 11f) (g-f 2, frm) 2000 AW 0-4: (7f 2, 8f 2) (Equi 3, Fibr)
Scopey, moderate filly, effective 7 to 8f, acts on g-f - acts on Equi, has worn blinkers. Turf high 33. AW high 41.
**D HaydnJones [1-18] Mrs William Byrne.*

RENDITION BHB 89f **RR 91f** 4598[6]
3 b f Polish Precedent (USA) 9f **(73)** - Rensaler (USA) (Stop The Music (USA)) 9.2f **(71)**
Form - 1130366
Record 2000 - 1st:2 2nd:0 3rd:2 Ran:7
Pre2000 - 1st:0 2nd:0 3rd:1 Ran:3
Win Prizemoney £26,520 *Total Prizemoney* £35,549
Wins * 2000 May York (G-F) H 7f 79 91 <
*** 2000** May Bright (G-F) 7f 82
2000 Turf 2-7: (6f, 7f 2-5, 8f) (gd, g-f 1-2, frm 1-4)
Scopey, useful filly, effective 6 to 8f, best at 7f, acts on gd to frm, excels at York. Turf high 91 - 1st of 17 getting 1lb from Card Games (16 May York RF 1217) - also 1st of 11 from Omniheat (4 May Brighton RF 1012). Consistent. She created a good impression when winning twice during May and looked unlucky on more than one occasion later in the season. Effective up to a mile, she reportedly needs fast ground and could yet make a mark in Listed events.
**W J Haggas [2-7] Pims UK Ltd (from J H M Gosden [0-3] Oct 1999).*

RENEE BHB 55f **RR 57f** 5081[9]
2 b f Wolfhound (USA) 7.3f **(71)** - Montserrat **(76f)** (Aragon) 8.1f **(60)**
Form - 355060
Record 2000 - 1st:0 2nd:0 3rd:1 Ran:6
Win Prizemoney £0 *Total Prizemoney* £494
2000 Turf 0-6: (5f 5, 6f) (hvy, gd, g-f 3, frm)
Fair filly. Turf high 57. **M L W Bell [0-6] Mrs Anne Yearley.*

RENZO (IRE) BHB 75f **RR 79f** 4987^{10}
7 b g Alzao (USA) 9.8f **(73)** - Watership (USA) (Foolish Pleasure (USA)) 8.9f **(72)**
Form - 113012730
Record 2000 - 1st:3 2nd:1 3rd:2 Ran:9
Pre2000 - 1st:3 2nd:4 3rd:3 Ran:28
Win Prizemoney £43,264 *Total Prizemoney* £59,204
Wins * **2000** Jly Sandow (GD) H 16.4f 71 77
* **2000** May Thirsk (GD) H 16f 67 74
* **2000** Apr Sandow (SFT) H 16.4f 60 62
* 1998 Nov Doncas (SFT) H 16.5f 78 78
1997 Spt Kempto (GD) H 14.4f 79 86 <
1996 Nov Redcar (G-F) H 11f 77 83
2000 Turf 3-9: (16f 3-7, 18f, 20f) (sft 1-1, g-s, gd 1-3, g-f 2, frm 1-2)
Above-average gelding, effective 16f, acts on g-s to frm, best on g-f, has worn blinkers, prefers tight tracks, excels at Sandown. Turf high 79 - 2nd of 7 giving 23lb to High Topper (15 Jly Chester 16f g-f RF 2836) - also 1st of 12 getting 12lb from Virgin Soldier (8 Jly Sandown RF 2648). Consistent. Despite a high head carriage, he has plenty of ability as he has demonstrated by winning at Sandown (twice) and Thirsk, having fallen considerably in the handicap after a fruitless 1999.
**J L Harris [5-30] Cleartherm Ltd (from Mrs A J Perrett [1-13] Oct 1998).*

REPEAT PERFORMANCE (IRE) BHB 59f56a **RR 68f 56a** 3919^{8}
2 b g Mujadil (USA) 7.7f **(70)** - Encore Une Fois (IRE) **(75f)** (Shirley Heights) 10.3f **(74)**
Form - 4244405578
Record 2000 - 1st:0 2nd:1 3rd:0 Ran:10
Win Prizemoney £0 *Total Prizemoney* £1,927
2000 Turf 0-9: (5f 3, 6f 3, 7f 3) (gd 4, g-f, frm 4) 2000 AW 0-1: (7f) (Fibr)
Average gelding, effective 5 to 7f, acts on frm, prefers left handed tracks. Turf high 68. **W G M Turner [0-10] P A N Bailey.*

REPERTORY BHB 109f **RR 105f** $5213a^{1}$
7 b g Anshan 8.2f **(63)** - Susie's Baby (Balidar) 7.9f **(63)**
Form - 703235071801
Record 2000 - 1st:2 2nd:1 3rd:2 Ran:12
Pre2000 - 1st:4 2nd:9 3rd:3 Ran:41
Win Prizemoney £99,603 *Total Prizemoney* £171,812
Wins * **2000** Oct Longch (HVY) G3 5f 105
* **2000** Aug Epsom (GD) H 5f 102 104
* 1998 Aug Epsom (G-F) H 5f 98 106
* 1998 Jly Currag (G-S) LH 5f 107 <
* 1997 Apr Newbur (G-F) H 5.2f 88 88
2000 Turf 2-12: (5f 2-11, 6f) (hvy 1-1, g-s 2, gd 1-3, g-f 4, frm 2)
Pattern-class gelding, effective 5 to 6f, best at 5f, acts on hvy to frm, excels at Sandown, does well at Epsom. Turf high 105 - 1st of 8 from Lincoln Dancer (22 Oct Longchamp RF 5213a) - also 1st of 19 giving 9lb to Ivory's Joy (28 Aug Epsom RF 4037). A real flying machine, he is a bit of a short runner who barely gets five furlongs. If enjoying an uncontested early lead, he can be very difficult to overhaul.
**M S Saunders [5-45] M S Saunders (from M R Channon [1-8] Oct 1996).*

REPLACEMENT PET (IRE) BHB 45f40a **RR 45f 40a** 5246^{8}
3 b f Petardia 8.2f **(58)** - Richardstown Lass (IRE) (Muscatite) 5f **(51)**
Form - 4008
Record 2000 - 1st:0 2nd:0 3rd:0 Ran:4
Win Prizemoney £0 *Total Prizemoney* £307
2000 Turf 0-3: (6f, 7f, 8f) (g-f, frm 2) 2000 AW 0-1: (8f) (Fibr)
Leggy, moderate filly, has worn blinkers. Turf high 45 (began Aug).
**A J McNae [0-4] Mrs Ruth Egan.*

REPTON BHB 30f36a **RR 35f 36a** 3818^{5}
5 ch g Rock City 8.8f **(62)** - Hasty Key (USA) (Key To The Mint (USA)) 9.4f **(75)**
Form - 0700835
Record 2000 - 1st:0 2nd:0 3rd:1 Ran:5
Pre2000 - 1st:2 2nd:0 3rd:4 Ran:20
Win Prizemoney £4,774 *Total Prizemoney* £6,241
Wins 1999 *Mar Southw (STD) H 12f 47 52*
1998 Jly Redcar (G-S) H 10f 50 58+ <
2000 Turf 0-4: (12f, 13f, 14f, 16f) (g-s, g-f 3) 2000 AW 0-1: (12f) (Fibr)
Very moderate gelding, effective 12f, - acts on Fibr, has worn blinkers. Turf high 35.
**B Smart [0-9] Mrs Julie Martin (from Mrs A Duffield [2-16] Jun 1999).*

REPUBLICAN LADY BHB 23f **RR 45f** 4648^{16}
8 b m Battle Hymn - Sweet Helen (No Mercy) 8f **(61)**
Form - 04660
Record 2000 - 1st:0 2nd:0 3rd:0 Ran:5
Win Prizemoney £0 *Total Prizemoney* £239
2000 Turf 0-4: (10f, 12f 3) (g-f 2, frm 2) 2000 AW 0-1: (16f) (Fibr)
Moderate mare. Turf high 45. **C Drew [0-7] C Drew.*

REPULSE BAY (IRE) BHB 88f **RR 87f** $5092a^{8}$
2 b c Barathea (IRE) - Bourbon Topsy (Ile de Bourbon (USA)) 10.1f **(67)**
Form - 4238
Record 2000 - 1st:0 2nd:1 3rd:1 Ran:4
Win Prizemoney £0 *Total Prizemoney* £2,257
2000 Turf 0-4: (7f 2, 8f 2) (sft, gd, g-f, frm)
Useful colt. Turf high 87 (began Aug) - 3rd of 6 getting 8lb from Harrier (16 Spt Ayr 8f gd RF 4447). **M R Channon [0-4].*

REQUEST RR 93+f 1305^{4}
3 b f Rainbow Quest (USA) 11.2f **(81)** - Highbrow (Shirley Heights) 10.3f **(74)**
Form - 24
Record 2000 - 1st:0 2nd:1 3rd:0 Ran:2
Win Prizemoney £0 *Total Prizemoney* £2,567
2000 Turf 0-2: (10f 2) (sft, gd)
Scopey, currently useful filly. Turf high 93. A half-sister to Blueprint, she was touched off in a hot maiden on her debut but faded tamely in a Listed contest on her only subsequent start. Bred to improve, she is one to note if kept in training as a four-year-old. **Sir Michael Stoute [0-2] The Queen.*

REQUESTOR BHB 69f **RR 66f** 3240^{6}
5 br g Distinctly North (USA) 7.4f **(63)** - Bebe Altesse (GER) (Alpenkonig (GER)) 10.8f **(76)**
Form - 0116
Record 2000 - 1st:2 2nd:0 3rd:0 Ran:4
Pre2000 - 1st:0 2nd:3 3rd:3 Ran:14
Win Prizemoney £6,369 *Total Prizemoney* £12,425
Wins * **2000** Jly Hamilt (G-F) 8.3f 66 <
* **2000** Jly Ripon (G-S) H 8f 60 63
2000 Turf 2-4: (8f 2-3, 9f) (g-s 1-2, g-f 1-1, frm)
Average gelding, effective 8 to 9f, best at 8f, acts on g-s to frm, has worn blinkers. Turf high 66 - 1st of 5 giving 5lb to Legacy of Love (20 Jly Hamilton RF 2968) - also 1st of 15 giving 16lb to Love Kiss (10 Jly Ripon RF 2678). Improving.
**J G FitzGerald [2-18] Marquesa de Moratalla.*

RESEARCH MASTER BHB 40f **RR 28f** 2565^{16}
3 br g Primo Dominie 7.2f **(67)** - Nutmeg Point (Nashwan (USA))
Form - 0000
Record 2000 - 1st:0 2nd:0 3rd:0 Ran:4
Pre2000 - 1st:0 2nd:0 3rd:0 Ran:3
Win Prizemoney £0 *Total Prizemoney* £200
2000 Turf 0-3: (8f 2, 11f) (g-f, frm 2) 2000 AW 0-1: (9f) (Fibr)
Workmanlike, little account gelding, has worn blinkers. Turf high 28. **P R Chamings [0-7] Twenty Twenty Research.*

RESILIENT BHB 65f69a **RR 55f 69a** 3400^{10}
3 b c Last Tycoon 9.4f **(73)** - Alilisa (USA) **(14f)** (Alydar (USA)) 9.1f **(76)**
Form - 06520
Record 2000 - 1st:0 2nd:1 3rd:0 Ran:5
Win Prizemoney £0 *Total Prizemoney* £851
2000 Turf 0-3: (7f, 8f 2) (g-s 2, frm) 2000 AW 0-2: (6f 2) (Fibr 2)
Scopey, average colt. Turf high 55. AW high 68 (began Jun) - 2nd of 8 to Geronimo (13 Jly Wolverhampton 6f Fibr RF 2780).
**W J Haggas [0-5] Tyali Partnership.*

RESIST THE FORCE (USA) BHB 80f65a **RR 78f 65a** 1013^{11}
10 br g Shadeed (USA) 7.7f **(72)** - Countess Tully (Hotfoot) 10.5f **(59)**
Form - 178280
Record 2000 - 1st:0 2nd:1 3rd:0 Ran:4
Pre2000 - 1st:6 2nd:4 3rd:3 Ran:29
Win Prizemoney £20,740 *Total Prizemoney* £34,198
Wins * 1999 *Dec Lingfi (STD) H 8f 60 66+*

1998	Aug	Epsom	(G-F)		7f		85 <
1998	Jun	Folkes	(GD)	H	6f	66	74+
1997	Jly	Bright	(FRM)	H	6f	55	68
1997	Jly	Bright	(FRM)		6f		64
1997	*May*	*Lingfi*	*(STD)*	*H*	*8f*	*55*	*60*

2000 Turf 0-3: (6f 2, 8f) (sft, gd, frm) 2000 AW 0-1: (8f) (Equi)
Above-average gelding, has broken blood-vessels, effective 8f, acts on gd. Turf high 78 (1st run) - 2nd of 13 giving 3lb to Silca Blanka (13 Apr Brighton 8f gd RF 0695). Inconsistent. A winner twice on turf in 1998, he came back from a break of 16 months to score on the Lingfield Equitrack in December of 1999. Fair effort back on turf at Brighton in April, he seems to go well on a sharp left-handed track.
**R Rowe [1-6] Mrs Barbara Hogan (from C A Cyzer [5-27] Aug 1998).*

RESOUNDING (IRE) BHB 75f RR 86f 5078[14]

3 b f Elmaamul (USA) 8.1f **(70)** - Echoing (Formidable (USA)) 9.2f **(63)**
Form - 324650

Record					
	2000 -	1st:0	2nd:1	3rd:1	Ran:6
	Pre2000 -	1st:1	2nd:0	3rd:0	Ran:2

Win Prizemoney £4,169 *Total Prizemoney* £7,539
Wins * 1999 Oct Nottin (SFT) 6.1f 78 <
2000 Turf 0-6: (8f 4, 10f 2) (g-s 2, gd 2, g-f, frm)
Scopey, useful filly, effective 6 to 10f, acts on gd to g-f, best on gd, has worn blinkers. Turf high 86 - 2nd of 13 giving 1lb to Chapel Royale (13 Jly Newmarket 8f gd RF 2772).
**A C Stewart [1-8] Racing For Gold.*

RESPLENDENT FLYER (FR) BHB 60f RR 58f 3987[7]

2 b c Danehill (USA) 9.1f **(79)** -Zehoor Alsafa (USA) (Wild Again (USA))
Form - 047
Record 2000 - 1st:0 2nd:0 3rd:0 Ran:3
Win Prizemoney £0 *Total Prizemoney* £305
2000 Turf 0-3: (6f 3) (gd, frm 2)
Currently fair colt. Turf high 58 (began Jly).
**P W Harris [0-3] Resplendent Racing Ltd.*

RESPLENDENT STAR (IRE) BHB 71f85a RR 85f 85a 4819[16]

3 b g Northern Baby (CAN) 10.2f **(74)** - Whitethroat (Artaius (USA)) 9f **(69)**
Form - 400350

Record					
	2000 -	1st:0	2nd:0	3rd:1	Ran:6
	Pre2000 -	1st:2	2nd:1	3rd:1	Ran:8

Win Prizemoney £5,812 *Total Prizemoney* £8,093

Wins								
*	*1999*	*Spt*	*Southw*	*(STD)*		*8f*		*85* <
*	1999	Aug	Newcas	(FRM)	H	7f	80	85 <

2000 Turf 0-6: (8f 3, 10f 2, 12f) (g-s, gd 2, g-f, frm 2)
Unfurnished, useful gelding, effective 7 to 8f, best at 8f, acts on gd to hrd - acts on Fibr, often wears blinkers. Turf high 85 (1st run) - 4th of 21 getting 1lb from Malleus (18 May York 8f gd RF 1279).
**P W Harris [2-14] Resplendent Racing Ltd.*

RETALIATOR BHB 60f51a RR 65f 51a 2834[6]

4 b f Rudimentary (USA) 8.2f **(66)** - Redgrave Design (Nebbiolo) 8.1f **(75)**
Form - 8020706

Record					
	2000 -	1st:0	2nd:1	3rd:0	Ran:7
	Pre2000 -	1st:3	2nd:1	3rd:4	Ran:24

Win Prizemoney £11,388 *Total Prizemoney* £19,211

Wins								
*	1999	Jun	Cheste	(G-F)	H	7f	71	76 <
	1999	Jun	Cheste	(SFT)	C	6.1f		67+
	1998	Jly	Leices	(GD)	H	6f		70

2000 Turf 0-7: (5f 2, 6f 2, 7f 3) (gd 2, g-f 3, frm 2)
Leggy, average filly, effective 6 to 7f, best at 7f, acts on g-s to frm, has worn blinkers. Turf high 65. Inconsistent.
**P D Evans [1-19] Treble Chance Partnership (from M L W Bell [2-12] Jun 1999).*

RETSKI RR 40f 1812[7]

3 b g Gabitat 8.5f **(44)** - Born to Be **(51f 51a)** (Never so Bold) 6.3f **(66)**
Form - 07
Record 2000 - 1st:0 2nd:0 3rd:0 Ran:2
2000 Turf 0-2: (6f 2) (gd, frm)
Workmanlike, currently moderate gelding. Turf high 40.
**S Dow [0-2] J A Redmond.*

RETURN (USA) RR 84+f 4754[1]

3 b f Sadler's Wells (USA) 11.3f **(87)** - Slightly Dangerous (USA) (Roberto (USA)) 10f **(76)**
Form - 1
Record 2000 - 1st:1 2nd:0 3rd:0 Ran:1
Win Prizemoney £4,179 *Total Prizemoney* £4,179
Wins * 2000 Spt Sandow (SFT) 10f 84+ <
2000 Turf 1-1: (10f 1-1) (g-s 1-1)
Scopey, currently decent filly. (1st run) - 1st of 17 getting 5lb from Maniatis (30 Spt Sandown RF 4754). **H R A Cecil [1-1] K Abdulla.*

RETURN OF AMIN BHB 71f61a RR 80f 61a 4865[17]

6 ch h Salse (USA) 10.9f **(71)** - Ghassanah (Pas de Seul) 9.1f **(67)**
Form - 000024000

Record					
	2000 -	1st:0	2nd:1	3rd:0	Ran:9
	Pre2000 -	1st:4	2nd:7	3rd:2	Ran:37

Win Prizemoney £49,114 *Total Prizemoney* £82,732

Wins							
1998	Jun	Pontef	(SFT)	H	6f	85	89 <
1997	Jun	York	(G-S)	H	6f	66	78
1996	*Nov*	*Southw*	*(STD)*	*H*	*7f*	*70*	*82*
1996	Nov	Folkes	(SFT)	H	6.9f	61	68

2000 Turf 0-9: (6f 8, 7f) (sft, g-s, gd 5, g-f 2)
Decent horse, effective 6 to 7f, acts on gd to g-f, has worn blinkers. Turf high 84. On a long losing run and has gradually slipped down the handicap. Best suited by easy ground.
**W R Muir [0-9] Sheikh Amin Dahlawi (from J D Bethell [4-37] Jun 1000).*

REVE D'OSCAR (FR) RR 120f 5215a[2]

3 gr f Highest Honor (FR) 10.9f **(72)** - Numidie (FR) (Baillamont (USA)) 7f **(78)**
Form - 2143222
2000 Turf 1-7: (10f 1-3, 11f 2, 12f 2) (hvy, sft, g-s 1-1, gd 3, g-f)
Very high-class filly, effective 10 to 12f, best at 12f, acts on hvy to gd, best on gd, prefers right handed tracks. Turf high 120 - 2nd of 13 to Petrushka (1 Oct Longchamp 10f gd RF 4847a). She broke her duck in style, winning the Group 1 Prix Saint-Alary at Longchamp in May. Ultra-consistent thereafter, she lacks a telling burst of speed and would be suited by enterprising tactics.
**Mme M Bollack-Badel in FR [1-7] K Yoshida.*

REVENGE BHB 55f RR 58f 5082[8]

4 b g Saddlers' Hall (IRE) 10.5f **(65)** - Classic Heights (Shirley Heights) 10.3f **(74)**
Form - 8028

Record					
	2000 -	1st:0	2nd:1	3rd:0	Ran:4
	Pre2000 -	1st:0	2nd:0	3rd:0	Ran:2

Win Prizemoney £0 *Total Prizemoney* £1,133
2000 Turf 0-4: (13f, 14f, 16f 2) (hvy, g-s 2, frm)
Workmanlike, fair gelding, often wears blinkers. Turf high 58.
**C G Cox [0-4] Axom (from R T Phillips [0-2] Aug 1999).*

REVERIE RR 55f 5132[10]

2 b c Bishop of Cashel - Space Travel (Dancing Dissident (USA))
Form - 000
Record 2000 - 1st:0 2nd:0 3rd:0 Ran:3
2000 Turf 0-3: (6f 2, 7f) (sft, frm 2)
Currently fair colt. Turf high 55 (began Jly).
**R Hannon [0-3] J A Lazzari.*

REVE RUSSE (USA) RR 96f 4339a[3]

3 b f Red Ransom (USA) 8.6f **(83)** - Rose Russe (USA) (Nijinsky (CAN)) 10.3f **(77)**
Form - 0321363
2000 Turf 1-7: (7f 2, 9f 2, 10f 1-1, 12f 2) (sft, g-s, gd 3, g-f, frm 1-1)
Very useful filly, effective 9f, acts on gd, often wears blinkers (very effectively), likes right handed tracks. Turf high 96. She improved once stepped-up in trip but will not be easy to place.
**D Gillespie in IRE [1-13] Mrs Chryss O'Reilly.*

REVIEWER (IRE) RR 77f 5027[2]

2 b c Sadler's Wells (USA) 11.3f **(87)** - Clandestina (USA) (Secretariat (USA)) 9f **(79)**
Form - 60452
Record 2000 - 1st:0 2nd:1 3rd:0 Ran:5
Win Prizemoney £0 *Total Prizemoney* £1,098
2000 Turf 0-5: (7f, 8f 2, 10f 2) (g-s 3, g-f, frm)

Above-average colt, often wears blinkers. Turf high 77 (began Aug). **J H M Gosden [0-5] R E Sangster & A K Collins.*

REVIVAL BHB 81f **RR 81f** 4427[4]

3 b f Sadler's Wells (USA) 11.3f **(87)** - Fearless Revival (Cozzene (USA)) 6f **(93)**
Form - 1274
Record 2000 - 1st:1 2nd:1 3rd:0 Ran:4
Pre2000 - 1st:0 2nd:0 3rd:0 Ran:1
Win Prizemoney £3,243 *Total Prizemoney* £6,106
Wins * 2000 May Salisb (GD) 9.9f 75+ <
2000 Turf 1-4: (10f 1-2, 11f, 12f) (g-s, gd 1-2, g-f)
Scopey, decent filly. Turf high 81 - 2nd of 3 getting 10lb from First Fantasy (4 Jun Warwick 11f g-s RF 1705) - also 1st of 13 from Ardanza (18 May Salisbury RF 1267). Second of three in a conditions race after winning her maiden.
**Sir Michael Stoute [1-5] Cheveley Park Stud.*

REVOLVER (IRE) RR 54f 4581[8]

2 b g Inzar (USA) - Genzyme Gene (Riboboy (USA)) 14f **(54)**
Form - 078
Record 2000 - 1st:0 2nd:0 3rd:0 Ran:3
2000 Turf 0-3: (6f 3) (gd, g-f, frm)
Currently fair gelding. Turf high 54 (began Aug).
**W J Haggas [0-3] A A Goodman.*

REX IS OKAY BHB 67f56a **RR 70f 56a** 5165[2]

4 ch g Mazilier (USA) 8.5f **(56)** - Cocked Hat Girl (Ballacashtal (CAN)) 5.3f **(50)**
Form - 06664002600752
Record 2000 - 1st:0 2nd:2 3rd:0 Ran:14
Pre2000 - 1st:2 2nd:1 3rd:7 Ran:18
Win Prizemoney £12,037 *Total Prizemoney* £20,851
Wins * 1998 Nov Doncas (SFT) H 7f 66 77 <
* 1998 Oct Leices (HVY) H 7f 59 65
2000 Turf 0-9: (6f 4, 7f 3, 8f 2) (sft, g-s, gd 5, g-f, hrd) 2000 AW 0-5: (5f, 6f, 7f 2, 8f) (Fibr 5)
Workmanlike, above-average gelding, effective 6 to 8f, best at 7f, acts on g-s to frm, best on gd, has worn blinkers, excels at Redcar. Turf high 70 - 2nd of 22 getting 1lb from Daawe (1 May Doncaster 6f g-f RF 0938). AW high 62.
**S R Bowring [2-32] The Belfitt Family.*

RHAGAAS BHB 110f **RR 116f** 1047[9]

4 b c Sadler's Wells (USA) 11.3f **(87)** - Darara (Top Ville) 11.7f **(68)**
Form - 40
Record 2000 - 1st:0 2nd:0 3rd:0 Ran:2
Pre2000 - 1st:1 2nd:2 3rd:2 Ran:6
Win Prizemoney £3,900 *Total Prizemoney* £131,575
Wins 1998 Spt Nottin (GD) 8.2f 94+ <
2000 Turf 0-2: (12f 2) (gd, g-f)
Light-framed, high-class colt, often wears blinkers. Turf high 116.
**S bin Suroor [0-6] Godolphin (from S bin Suroor in UAE [0-1] Mar 2000).*

RHENIUM (IRE) RR 115f 4565a[3]

3 ch c Rainbows For Life (CAN) 9.3f **(64)** - Miss Mulaz (FR) (Luthier) 9.8f **(71)**
Form - 1333
2000 Turf 1-4: (10f 2, 11f 1-2) (hvy 1-1, gd 3)
High-class colt. Turf high 115 - 3rd of 7 giving 4lb to Hightori (16 Spt Longchamp 10f gd RF 4565a).
**J-C Rouget in FR [1-4] D Firestone.*

RHIANN BHB 38f32a **RR 37f 32a** 4632[10]

4 b f Anshan 8.2f **(63)** - Nell of The North (USA) (Canadian Gil (CAN)) 9.2f **(77)**
Form - 00
Record 2000 - 1st:0 2nd:0 3rd:0 Ran:2
2000 Turf 0-2: (7f, 10f) (g-s, frm)
Scopey, currently very moderate filly. Turf high 37 (began Spt).
**J M Bradley [0-2] Miss Tammy Armstrong.*

RHODAMINE (IRE) BHB 58f66a **RR 66f 66a** 4387[15]

3 b g Mukaddamah (USA) 7.6f **(74)** - Persian Empress (IRE) (Persian Bold) 9.3f **(66)**
Form - 70842614340440
Record 2000 - 1st:1 2nd:1 3rd:1 Ran:14
Pre2000 - 1st:1 2nd:0 3rd:1 Ran:8
Win Prizemoney £8,561 *Total Prizemoney* £18,577
Wins * 2000 May Redcar (G-S) H 11f 64 66
* 1999 Jly Newcas (G-F) 6f 73 <
2000 Turf 1-13: (9f, 10f 8, 11f 1-3, 12f) (gd 1-8, g-f, frm 4) 2000 AW 0-1: (9f) (Fibr)
Scopey, average gelding, effective 6 to 11f, best at 8f, acts on gd to frm, excels at Newcastle, does well at Pontefract. Turf high 67 - also 1st of 8 getting 3lb from Waseem (29 May Redcar RF 1530). He has been kept busy, but keeps his form well and landed a Redcar handicap in May. Probably best with a bit of cut, he has tended to make life difficult for himself by starting slowly.
**J L Eyre [2-22] M Gleason.*

RHYTHM BAND (USA) BHB 116f **RR 121f** 4004[7]

4 gr c Cozzene (USA) 10.1f **(87)** - Golden Wave Band (USA) (Dixieland Band (USA)) 7f **(74)**
Form - 1467
Record 2000 - 1st:1 2nd:0 3rd:0 Ran:4
Pre2000 - 1st:1 2nd:0 3rd:0 Ran:1
Win Prizemoney £738,677 *Total Prizemoney* £753,413
Wins 2000 *Mar Nad Al (GD) G3 12f 121* <
* 1999 Jly Doncas (G-F) 8f 105
2000 Turf 0-3: (9f, 10f 2) (gd 2) 2000 AW 1-1: (12f 1-1) (Dirt 1-1)
Leggy, very high-class colt. Turf high 121 (1st run) - 4th of 8 giving 9lb to Manndar (6 May Churchill Downs 9f RF 1153a). (1st run) - 1st of 11 from Easaar (25 Mar Nad Al Sheba RF 0579a). Formerly trained in the US, he has been globetrotting for Godolphin in the last couple of years with limited success and was well beaten in two domestic outings last season. Best at around a mile on fast ground.
**S bin Suroor [1-3] Godolphin (from S bin Suroor in UAE [1-2] May 2000).*

RHYTHMICALL (IRE) BHB 87f **RR 90+f** 2266[6]

3 b c In The Wings 11.2f **(77)** - Rhoman Ruby (IRE) (Rhoman Rule (USA))
Form - 016
Record 2000 - 1st:1 2nd:0 3rd:0 Ran:3
Win Prizemoney £3,750 *Total Prizemoney* £3,750
Wins * 2000 Jun Bath (G-S) 10.2f 90+ <
2000 Turf 1-3: (8f, 10f 1-2) (gd 1-1, frm 2)
Workmanlike, currently useful colt. Turf high 90 - 1st of 7 from Proper Squire (2 Jun Bath RF 1645). He looked useful when winning a moderate Bath maiden, but disappointed on firmer ground on his only subsequent start. Unexposed, he is worth another chance on an easy surface. **Mrs A J Perrett [1-3] Sunday School.*

RIBBLE ASSEMBLY BHB 33f **RR 31df** 4061[13]

5 ch g Presidium 7.5f **(56)** - Spring Sparkle (Lord Gayle (USA)) 8.8f **(62)**
Form - 0
Record 2000 - 1st:0 2nd:0 3rd:0 Ran:1
Pre2000 - 1st:2 2nd:3 3rd:1 Ran:26
Win Prizemoney £5,269 *Total Prizemoney* £8,401
Wins * 1999 Mar Hamilt (HVY) 8.3f 62 <
1998 May Carlis (G-S) H 8f 52 60
2000 Turf 0-1: (8f) (frm)
Very moderate gelding, effective 8f, acts on hvy, has worn blinkers, likes tight tracks.
**K A Ryan [1-24] Swan At Whalley Partnership (from R A Fahey [1-8] May 1998).*

RIBBLE PRINCESS BHB 30f **RR 35f** 1886[17]

5 b m Selkirk (USA) 7.9f **(76)** - Ricochet Romance (USA) (Shadeed (USA)) 8.2f **(70)**
Form - 077035000
Record 2000 - 1st:0 2nd:0 3rd:1 Ran:9
Pre2000 - 1st:0 2nd:0 3rd:1 Ran:4
Win Prizemoney £0 *Total Prizemoney* £1,117
2000 Turf 0-5: (8f, 9f 2, 10f, 12f) (g-s, gd, g-f, frm 2) 2000 AW 0-4: (7f, 9f 2, 12f) (Fibr 4)
Very moderate filly, effective 9 to 10f, acts on g-s to gd, has worn blinkers. Turf high 37 (1st run) - 3rd of 16 getting 12lb from Ace of Trumps (30 Mar Musselburgh 9f gd RF 0568). AW high 32.
**K A Ryan [0-13] Swan At Whalley Partnership.*

RIBBON LAKE (IRE) BHB 50f **RR 53f** 5071[11]

3 b f Namaqualand (USA) - Topmost (IRE) (Top Ville) 11.7f **(68)**
Form - 000500
Record 2000 - 1st:0 2nd:0 3rd:0 Ran:6
Pre2000 - 1st:1 2nd:1 3rd:1 Ran:6
Win Prizemoney £2,937 *Total Prizemoney* £4,241
Wins * 1999 Jly Lingfi (G-F) 6f 74 <
2000 Turf 0-6: (6f, 7f, 8f 3, 10f) (g-s, gd, g-f, frm 3)
Leggy, fair filly, effective 6 to 7f, best at 6f, acts on g-f to frm, best on frm. Turf high 53.
**Mrs P N Dutfield [1-12] The Wheelwright Wanderers.*

RIBBON OF LIGHT **RR 52f** 5099[12]

2 b c Spectrum (IRE) - Brush Away (Ahonoora) 8.1f **(73)**
Form - 0
Record 2000 - 1st:0 2nd:0 3rd:0 Ran:1
2000 Turf 0-1: (7f) (gd)
Currently fair colt. **B W Hills [0-1] J Hanson.*

RIBERAC BHB 95f **RR 97f** 5240[26]

4 b f Efisio 7.7f **(69)** - Ciboure (Norwick (USA)) 7.2f **(56)**
Form - 00200711711010
Record 2000 - 1st:5 2nd:1 3rd:0 Ran:14
Pre2000 - 1st:1 2nd:0 3rd:2 Ran:9
Win Prizemoney £44,353 *Total Prizemoney* £49,611

Wins								
* **2000**	Spt	Ascot	(G-S)	LH	8f	89	97+	<
* **2000**	Spt	Epsom	(GD)		10.1f		95+	
* **2000**	Aug	Epsom	(GD)	H	8.5f	79	90+	
* **2000**	Aug	Ayr	(GD)	H	8f	71	82	
* **2000**	Aug	Sandow	(GD)	H	8.1f	71	84	
1998	Jly	Windso	(G-F)		5f		74+	

2000 Turf 5-14: (5f 3, 6f 3, 8f 3-5, 9f 1-2, 10f 1-1) (g-s, gd 3-6, g-f 1-3, frm 1-4)
Workmanlike, very useful filly, effective 8 to 10f, acts on gd to g-f, best on gd, prefers tight tracks. Turf high 97 - 1st of 14 getting 2lb from Mystify (23 Spt Ascot RF 4598) - also 1st of 7 getting 3lb from Captain's Log (6 Spt Epsom RF 4268). She proved a revelation once tried beyond sprint distances, winning five times including a Listed event at Ascot. Best when ridden close to the pace, she has disappointed on soft ground and has given trouble at the stalls.
**M Johnston [5-15] & Mrs G Middlebrook (from W J Haggas [1-8] Aug 1999).*

RIBOLETTA (BRA) **RR** 5325a[7]

5 b m Roi Normand (USA) - Joy Valley (USA) (Ghadeer (FR))
Form - 7
2000 AW 0-1: (9f) (Dirt)
Currently very useful. **E Inda in USA [0-1] Marie & Aaron U Jones.*

RICCARTON BHB 50f **RR 48f** 1315[4]

There was no looking back for Riberac once tried beyond sprint distances

7 b g Nomination 7.3f **(57)** - Legendary Dancer (Shareef Dancer (USA)) 9.9f **(73)**
Form - 4
Record 2000 - 1st:0 2nd:0 3rd:0 Ran:1
Pre2000 - 1st:4 2nd:2 3rd:6 Ran:33
Win Prizemoney £12,681 *Total Prizemoney* £18,986

Wins									
1998	Jly	Doncas	(G-F)	H	10.3f	60	61	<
1998	Jun	Hamilt	(GD)	H	9.2f	56	57	
1998	Apr	Redcar	(SFT)	H	11f	52	55+	
1997	Aug	Beverl	(GD)	H	9.9f	46	52	

2000 Turf 0-1: (10f) (gd)
Moderate gelding, effective 10f, acts on gd to g-f, has worn blinkers. Consistent. Suited by exaggerated hold-up tactics.
**J M Bradley [1-16] Terry Warner (from P Calver [4-26] Oct 1998).*

RICHENDA BHB 73f **RR 74f** 5027[9]

2 b f Mister Baileys - Forget Me (IRE) (Don't Forget Me) 8.3f **(74)**
Form - 0766870
Record 2000 - 1st:0 2nd:0 3rd:0 Ran:7
2000 Turf 0-7: (6f 4, 7f, 8f 2) (g-s, gd 2, g-f, frm 3)
Above-average filly, effective 6 to 8f, acts on gd to frm. Turf high 74 - 6th of 9 to Sheppard's Watch (2 Aug Goodwood 6f gd RF 3320).
**R Hannon [0-7] Mrs W H GibsonFleming.*

RICH GIFT **RR 66f** 4554[1]

2 b f Cadeaux Genereux 7.9f **(76)** - Deep Divide **(74f)** (Nashwan (USA))
Form - 51
Record 2000 - 1st:1 2nd:0 3rd:0 Ran:2
Win Prizemoney £3,347 *Total Prizemoney* £3,347
Wins * **2000** Spt Pontef (G-S) 6f 66 <
2000 Turf 1-2: (6f 1-1, 7f) (g-s, gd 1-1)
Currently average filly. Turf high 66 (began Aug) - 1st of 14 from Night Gypsy (21 Spt Pontefract RF 4554).
**J D Bethell [1-2] Mrs J E Vickers.*

RICH IN LOVE (IRE) BHB 80f **RR 84f** 4732[14]

6 b m Alzao (USA) 9.8f **(73)** - Chief's Quest (USA) (Chief's Crown (USA)) 9.8f **(72)**
Form - 00231805000
Record 2000 - 1st:1 2nd:1 3rd:1 Ran:11
Pre2000 - 1st:4 2nd:7 3rd:1 Ran:42
Win Prizemoney £28,400 *Total Prizemoney* £52,812

Wins									
* **2000**	Jly	Yarmou	(G-F)	H	8f	80	88	<
* 1998	Aug	Yarmou	(G-F)	H	7f	72	78	
* 1998	Jly	Ascot	(G-F)	H	7f	65	71	
* 1997	Aug	Yarmou	(G-F)	H	7f	69	75	
* 1996	Jun	Ripon	(G-F)		6f		73	

2000 Turf 1-11: (7f 7, 8f 1-4) (g-s, gd 3, g-f 4, frm 1-3)
Decent mare, effective 7 to 8f, best at 7f, acts on gd to frm, has worn blinkers. Turf high 88 - 1st of 11 giving 10lb to Topton (5 Jly Yarmouth RF 2553). She is a useful filly when conditions are right, and looked as though seven furlongs was her trip, but she ran on consecutive days at Yarmouth in July and actually managed to score over a mile on the second occasion.
**C A Cyzer [5-53] R M Cyzer.*

RICH VEIN (IRE) BHB 84f85a **RR 90f 85a** 4936[10]

3 b g Up and At 'em - Timissara (USA) (Shahrastani (USA)) 8.8f **(72)**
Form - 42112147840
Record 2000 - 1st:3 2nd:2 3rd:0 Ran:11
Pre2000 - 1st:0 2nd:0 3rd:0 Ran:3
Win Prizemoney £12,124 *Total Prizemoney* £21,615

Wins									
* **2000**	Jly	Sandow	(G-F)	H	10f	74	88	<
* ***2000***	*Jun*	*Lingfi*	*(STD)*	*H*	*10f*	*70*	*81+*	
* ***2000***	*May*	*Lingfi*	*(STD)*	*H*	*10f*	*67*	*74*	

2000 Turf 1-9: (8f 2, 10f 1-3, 12f 4) (g-s, gd 4, g-f 1-2, frm 2) 2000 AW 2-2: (10f 2-2) (Equi 2-2)
Scopey, useful gelding, effective 10 to 12f, best at 10f, acts on gd to g-f - acts on Equi, often wears blinkers (very effectively), prefers tight tracks. Turf high 90 - also 1st of 5 getting 26lb from Ulundi (27 Jly Sandown RF 3155). AW high 81 - 1st of 12 giving 18lb to Queen of The Keys (25 Jun Lingfield RF 2261). Consistent. He took to Equitrack like a duck to water during the summer, winning both his starts over ten furlongs at Lingfield, but is better still on turf and was a facile winner at Sandown in July. The resulting rise in the handicap looks to have found him out, however.
**S P C Woods [3-14] Arashan Ali.*

RIDDLESDOWN (IRE) BHB 107f **RR 113f** 5212a[5]

3 ch c Common Grounds 8.1f **(66)** - Neat Dish (CAN) (Stalwart (USA)) 9.9f **(78)**

Form - 221001125

Record 2000 - 1st:3 2nd:3 3rd:0 Ran:9
Pre2000 - 1st:1 2nd:1 3rd:1 Ran:3

Win Prizemoney £38,664 *Total Prizemoney* £58,065

Wins * **2000** Spt Haydoc (HVY) 14f 104+
* **2000** Aug York (GD) H 13.9f 98 108 <
* **2000** Jun Haydoc (G-S) H 11.9f 96 101
* 1999 Oct Bath (SFT) 8f 85

2000 Turf 3-9: (10f, 12f 1-2, 14f 2-3, 15f, 16f 2) (hvy, sft 1-1, g-s 1-1, gd 4, g-f 1-2)

Workmanlike, Group-class colt, effective 14 to 15f, best at 14f, acts on sft to g-f, likes tight tracks. Turf high 113 - also 1st of 17 giving 7lb to Romantic Affair (24 Aug York RF 3936). Runner-up in his first two starts of the season, he showed battling qualities to win a Haydock rated stakes in June. He was fortunate to get the race in the Stewards' room when second past the post in York's Melrose Handicap, but won on merit when bolting up in a Haydock conditions event. Stepped up on that form with sound efforts in pattern races at Longchamp. **S P C Woods [4-12].*

RIDE THE TIGER (IRE) BHB 54f60a **RR 52f 60a** 2778[2]

3 ch g Imp Society (USA) 7.1f **(63)** - Krisdaline (USA) (Kris S (USA)) 7.9f **(71)**

Form - 1362

Record 2000 - 1st:1 2nd:1 3rd:1 Ran:4
Pre2000 - 1st:0 2nd:0 3rd:0 Ran:3

Win Prizemoney £2,219 *Total Prizemoney* £3,169

Wins * **2000** *May Wolver (STD) C 8.5f 59* <

Riddlesdown, a fortunate winner at York

2000 Turf 0-1: (8f) (frm) 2000 AW 1-3: (8f 1-1, 9f, 10f) (Equi, Fibr 1-2)

Unfurnished, average gelding, effective 8 to 9f, - acts on Fibr. AW high 62 - 2nd of 9 giving 15lb to Magic Sunset (13 Jly Wolverhampton 9f Fibr RF 2778) - also 1st of 13 getting 4lb from Albergo (11 May Wolverhampton RF 1147). **M D I Usher [1-7] G A Summers.*

RIDGE AND FURROW (IRE) BHB 58f **RR 60f** 5298[4]

2 ch g Ridgewood Ben - Ryazana (IRE) **(59f)** (Fairy King (USA)) 7.7f **(59)**

Form - 04

Record 2000 - 1st:0 2nd:0 3rd:0 Ran:2

Win Prizemoney £0 *Total Prizemoney* £271

2000 Turf 0-2: (7f, 8f) (g-s, gd)

Currently average gelding. Turf high 60 (began Oct). **T P Tate [0-2] T P Tate.*

RIDGECREST BHB 47f37a **RR 46f 37a** 5113[7]

3 ch g Anshan 8.2f **(63)** - Lady Sabo **(37?f 42a)** (Prince Sabo) 7.2f **(62)**

Form - 842425450537

Record 2000 - 1st:0 2nd:0 3rd:1 Ran:7
Pre2000 - 1st:0 2nd:2 3rd:1 Ran:8

Win Prizemoney £0 *Total Prizemoney* £1,739

2000 Turf 0-3: (8f 3) (g-s, frm 2) 2000 AW 0-4: (7f, 8f 2, 10f) (Equi, Fibr 3)

Leggy, moderate gelding, effective 8f, - acts on Equi. Turf high 46 (began Aug). AW high 44. Consistent. **P D Evans [0-5] R J Hayward (from R Ingram [0-11] Mar 2000).*

RIDGE RUNNER BHB 84f **RR 84f** 4932[9]

2 b c Indian Ridge 7.6f **(74)** - By Charter (Shirley Heights) 10.3f **(74)**

Form - 2150

Record 2000 - 1st:1 2nd:1 3rd:0 Ran:4

Win Prizemoney £3,900 *Total Prizemoney* £5,055

Wins * **2000** Jly Ripon (G-F) 6f 74+ <

2000 Turf 1-4: (6f 1-4) (gd, frm 1-3)

Decent colt. Turf high 84 (began Jly) - 9th of 22 giving 1lb to Idle Power (12 Oct Newmarket 6f gd RF 4932). Seven furlongs should suit. **J L Dunlop [1-4] Seymour Cohn.*

RIDGEWAY DAWN (IRE) RR 82f 4162[1]

2 ch f Mujtahid (USA) 7.4f **(69)** - Soviet Maid (IRE) (Soviet Star (USA))

Form - 11

Record 2000 - 1st:2 2nd:0 3rd:0 Ran:2

Win Prizemoney £9,231 *Total Prizemoney* £9,231

Wins * **2000** Spt Kempto (GD) 7f 82 <
* **2000** Aug Salisb (G-F) 7f 70+

2000 Turf 2-2: (7f 2-2) (g-f 1-1, frm 1-1)

Currently decent filly. Turf high 82 (began Aug) - 1st of 9 from Matoaka (2 Spt Kempton RF 4162). **M R Channon [2-2] Ridgeway Downs Racing.*

RIDGEWAY LAD RR 75f 1463[3]

2 ch c Primo Dominie 7.2f **(67)** -Phyliel (USA) (Lyphard (USA)) 9.9f **(72)**

Form - 3

Record 2000 - 1st:0 2nd:0 3rd:1 Ran:1

Win Prizemoney £0 *Total Prizemoney* £432

2000 Turf 0-1: (5f) (gd)

Currently above-average colt. (1st run) - 3rd of 15 giving 8lb to Princess of Garda (26 May Haydock 5f gd RF 1463). **T D Easterby [0-1] David & Steven Dudley.*

RIDGEWOOD BAY (IRE) BHB 32f **RR 22f** 2744[7]

3 b f Ridgewood Ben - Another Baileys **(49f 55a)** (Deploy)

Form - 708017

Record 2000 - 1st:1 2nd:0 3rd:0 Ran:6
Pre2000 - 1st:0 2nd:0 3rd:0 Ran:8

Win Prizemoney £1,844 *Total Prizemoney* £1,932

Wins * **2000** *Jly Lingfi (STD) S 13f 32* <

2000 Turf 0-4: (8f, 10f, 11f, 14f) (sft, g-s, gd, g-f) 2000 AW 1-2: (12f, 13f 1-1) (Equi 1-2)

Scopey, very moderate filly, effective 13f, - acts on Equi, likes left handed tracks, likes tight tracks. Turf high 22. AW high 32 (1st run) (began Jly) - 1st of 8 getting 24lb from Full Egalite (1 Jly Lingfield RF 2435). **J C Fox [1-14] Lord Mutton Racing Partnership.*

RIDGEWOOD BELLE (IRE) RR 4821[18]

2 b f Ridgewood Ben - Ring Dem Bells (Simply Great (FR)) 8.2f **(65)**

Form - 0

Record 2000 - 1st:0 2nd:0 3rd:0 Ran:1

2000 Turf 0-1: (6f) (g-f)

Currently very poor filly. **B J Meehan [0-1] O'Reilly Hyland & Pidgley Partnership.*

RIDWAN (GER) RR 113f 3353a[8]

7

Form - 8

2000 Turf 0-1: (10f) (sft)

Currently Group-class. Fourth in a Group 1 during August, he is a

useful gelding.

**Frau J Mayer in GER [0-2].*

RIFIFI BHB 50f53a **RR 27f 53a** 4586[15]

7 ch g Aragon 7.7f **(58)** - Bundled Up (USA) (Sharpen Up) 8.3f **(67)**

Form - 788300000

Record	**2000 -**	1st:0	2nd:0	3rd:1	Ran:9
	Pre2000 -	1st:8	2nd:1	3rd:2	Ran:44

Win Prizemoney £42,107 *Total Prizemoney* £48,068

Wins								
	1998	*Dec Lingfi*	*(STD)*	*H*	*7f*	*73*	*78*	
	1998	Aug Sandow	(G-F)	H	5f	69	72	
	1998	Aug Newbur	(G-F)	H	6f	71	72	
	1997	Aug Goodwo	(G-F)	H	6f	71	80	<
	1997	Aug Newmar	(GD)	H	6f	64	71	
	1997	Jun Windso	(G-F)	H	6f	58	61	
	1997	*Feb Lingfi*	*(STD)*	*H*	*5f*	*60*	*66*	
	1997	*Feb Lingfi*	*(STD)*		*5f*		*66*	

2000 Turf 0-5: (6f 3, 7f, 8f) (gd 2, g-f, frm 2) 2000 AW 0-4: (6f 2, 7f 2) (Equi 3, Fibr)

Average gelding, effective 6 to 7f, acts on g-f - acts on Equi, has worn blinkers. Turf high 27. AW high 69. Becoming disappointing.

**R Ford [0-5] Gary Williams (from R Ingram [8-46] Feb 2000).*

RIGADOON (IRE) BHB 53f **RR 58f** 4119[2]

4 b g Be My Chief (USA) 10.2f **(62)** - Loucoum (FR) (Iron Duke (FR)) 8.8f **(60)**

Form - 450462

Record	**2000 -**	1st:0	2nd:1	3rd:0	Ran:6
	Pre2000 -	1st:3	2nd:0	3rd:1	Ran:12

Win Prizemoney £7,394 *Total Prizemoney* £9,217

Wins								
	* 1999	Spt Catter	(G-F)	H	15.8f	51	55	<
	* 1999	Jly Nottin	(G-F)	H	16f	46	53	
	* 1999	Jun Carlis	(G-F)	H	17.2f	39	45	

2000 Turf 0-6: (16f 6) (gd, g-f 2, frm 2, hrd)

Leggy, fair gelding, effective 16f, acts on gd to hrd, often wears blinkers (extremely effectively), prefers right handed tracks, excels at Musselburgh. Turf high 58 - 2nd of 12 giving 10lb to Lord Alaska (31 Aug Musselburgh 16f frm RF 4119). Consistent.

**M W Easterby [4-21] C Buckton, K Mercer & A Ford.*

RIGHT WING (IRE) BHB 112f **RR 117f** 5206a[1]

6 b h In The Wings 11.2f **(77)** - Nekhbet (Artaius (USA)) 9f **(69)**

Form - 31221321

Record	**2000 -**	1st:3	2nd:3	3rd:2	Ran:8
	Pre2000 -	1st:5	2nd:1	3rd:6	Ran:22

Win Prizemoney £134,368 *Total Prizemoney* £189,863

Wins								
	*** 2000**	Oct Bordea	(HVY)	G3	9.5f		110+	
	*** 2000**	Aug York	(GD)	*L	8.9f		114+	<
	*** 2000**	Apr Kempto	(SFT)	L	10f		110	
	* 1999	Nov Nottin	(SFT)		8.2f		101+	
	* 1999	Mar Doncas	(G-S)	H	8f	100	107	
	* 1998	Spt Doncas	(GD)	H	8f	97	100	
	1997	Oct Ayr	(SFT)		8f		88+	
	1997	Jun Ascot	(SFT)		8f		89	

2000 Turf 3-8: (8f, 9f 1-1, 10f 2-6) (hvy 1-1, sft 1-1, g-s 2, gd 1-4)

High-class horse, effective 8 to 10f, best at 10f, acts on hvy to gd, best on gd, often wears blinkers (extremely effectively), excels at Doncaster, likes Goodwood. Turf high 117 - 2nd of 5 giving 3lb to Island House (25 May Goodwood 10f g-s RF 1433) - also 1st of 9 giving 12lb to Autonomy (30 Aug York RF 4105). Consistent. Better than ever last year, he was badly drawn when third in the Lincoln (a race he won in 1999), but went on to prove himself in better company, winning a Group 3 at Bordeaux in October. Suited by waiting tactics, he goes well on easy ground and should add to his tally in 2001.

**J L Dunlop [6-22] The Earl Cadogan (from Major W R Hern [2-8] Oct 1997).*

RIGHTY HO BHB 39f57a **RR 47f 57a** 4814[U]

6 b g Reprimand 8.2f **(63)** - Challanging (Mill Reef (USA)) 10.5f **(78)**

Form - 78022125U

Record	**2000 -**	1st:1	2nd:3	3rd:0	Ran:9
	Pre2000 -	1st:2	2nd:2	3rd:3	Ran:24

Win Prizemoney £7,906 *Total Prizemoney* £14,464

Wins								
	*** 2000**	Aug Carlis	(GD)	C	12f		45	
	1997	Aug Epsom	(GD)	H	10.1f	58	66	<
	1997	Jun Salisb	(SFT)	H	8f	57	62	

2000 Turf 1-9: (10f 2, 12f 1-3, 13f, 14f 2, 16f) (g-s, gd 2, g-f 2, frm 1-2, hrd 2)

Fair gelding, effective 10 to 12f, acts on gd to frm, has worn blinkers. Turf high 47.

**W H Tinning [1-12] W H Tinning (from C B B Booth [0-8] Oct 1999).*

RIMATARA BHB 33f37a **RR 32f 37a** 5054[15]

4 ch g Selkirk (USA) 7.9f **(76)** - Humble Pie (Known Fact (USA)) 7.4f **(67)**

Form - 00000

Record	**2000 -**	1st:0	2nd:0	3rd:0	Ran:5
	Pre2000 -	1st:0	2nd:0	3rd:0	Ran:1

2000 Turf 0-5: (7f, 8f 2, 10f, 12f) (sft, gd, g-f 2, frm)

Unfurnished, very moderate gelding. Turf high 32.

**M W Easterby [0-3] Winton Bloodstock Ltd (from G P Kelly [0-2] May 2000).*

RIMFAXI RR 33f 3249[7]

2 ch g Risk Me (FR) 8f **(53)** - Legal Sound (Legal Eagle) 7.3f **(54)**

Form - 7

Record	**2000 -**	1st:0	2nd:0	3rd:0	Ran:1

2000 Turf 0-1: (6f) (g-f)

Currently very moderate gelding. **D Nicholls [0-1] J M Ranson.*

RING DANCER BHB 72f **RR 75f** 5014[3]

5 b g Polar Falcon (USA) 9f **(74)** - Ring Cycle (Auction Ring (USA)) 8.6f

Right Wing flew past his rivals at York

(65)

Form - 000173

Record	**2000 -**	1st:1	2nd:0	3rd:1	Ran:6
	Pre2000 -	1st:1	2nd:2	3rd:1	Ran:10

Win Prizemoney £7,042 *Total Prizemoney* £11,979

Wins								
	*** 2000**	Jly Bath	(FRM)	H	5.7f	72	75	
	* 1997	Aug Ripon	(GD)		6f		93+	<

2000 Turf 1-5: (6f 1-5) (gd 2, frm 1-3) 2000 AW 0-1: (6f) (Fibr)

Above-average gelding. Turf high 75.

**P J Makin [2-16] Mrs Tricia Mitchell.*

RING MY MATE BHB 48f50a **RR 52f 50a** 5005[6]

3 ch c Komaite (USA) 6.9f **(61)** - My Ruby Ring **(61df 50a)** (Blushing Scribe (USA)) 6f **(45)**

Form - 3407006

Record	**2000 -**	1st:0	2nd:0	3rd:0	Ran:5
	Pre2000 -	1st:0	2nd:0	3rd:1	Ran:3

Win Prizemoney £0 *Total Prizemoney* £325

2000 Turf 0-3: (7f 2, 8f) (g-f 2, frm) 2000 AW 0-2: (6f, 8f) (Fibr 2)

Unfurnished, fair colt. Turf high 30. AW high 41 (began Spt).

**W R Muir [0-8] Mrs Marion Wickham.*

RING OF LOVE BHB 60f56a **RR 51f 56a** 2814[7]

4 b f Magic Ring (IRE) 6.5f **(64)** - Fine Honey (USA) (Drone) 10.3f **(74)**

Form - 04513653030007

Record	**2000 -**	1st:1	2nd:0	3rd:3	Ran:11
	Pre2000 -	1st:3	2nd:2	3rd:1	Ran:20

Win Prizemoney £12,231 *Total Prizemoney* £16,437

Wins								
	*** 2000**	*Jan Lingfi*	*(STD)*	*H*	*5f*	*56*	*60*	
	1999	Spt Mussel	(G-F)	H	5f	64	67	
	1999	Aug Mussel	(G-F)	H	5f	64	65	

1998 Jly Cheste (G-F) 5.1f 76 <
2000 Turf 0-4: (5f 4) (gd, frm 2, hrd) 2000 AW 1-7: (5f 1-7) (Equi 1-2, Fibr 5)
Neat, fair filly, effective 5f, acts on gd to frm - acts on AW, best on g-f, has worn blinkers, excels at Musselburgh. Turf high 51. AW high 60 (1st run) - 1st of 9 giving 2lb to Boldly Cliff (22 Jan Lingfield RF 0133).
**J L Eyre [1-14] Dab Hand Racing (from M L W Bell [3-17] Oct 1999).*

RINGSIDE JACK BHB 69f **RR 69f** 5026[5]
4 b g Batshoof 9.5f **(66)** - Celestine **(40f 44a)** (Skyliner) 7.3f **(53)**
Form - 1060408105
Record 2000 - 1st:2 2nd:0 3rd:0 Ran:10
Pre2000 - 1st:1 2nd:2 3rd:2 Ran:18
Win Prizemoney £11,723 *Total Prizemoney* £15,819
Wins * **2000** Spt Cheste (SFT) H 10.3f 63 69
* **2000** Apr Beverl (HVY) H 9.9f 64 66
* 1998 Jun Redcar (G-S) 5f 70 <
2000 Turf 2-10: (10f 2-7, 12f 3) (hvy, g-s 2-3, gd 2, g-f 3, frm)
Scopey, average gelding, effective 8f, acts on frm, has worn blinkers. Turf high 69. **C W Fairhurst [3-28] M J G Partnership.*

RING THE CHIEF BHB 35f35a **RR 40f 35a** 3574[9]
8 b g Chief Singer 8.6f **(62)** - Lomond Ring (Lomond (USA)) 8.8f **(65)**
Form - 0
Record 2000 - 1st:0 2nd:0 3rd:0 Ran:1
Pre2000 - 1st:4 2nd:4 3rd:9 Ran:46
Win Prizemoney £7,941 *Total Prizemoney* £14,169
Wins * 1999 *Jan Southw (STD) H 8f 35 42* <
* 1997 Aug Salisb (G-S) H 7f 34 42 <
* 1997 *Jun Southw (STD) SH 7f 33 39*
* 1997 *Feb Southw (STD) H 7f 30 34*
2000 AW 0-1: (6f) (Fibr)
Moderate gelding, effective 8f, - acts on Fibr.
**M D I Usher [4-37] G A Summers (from R Akehurst [0-7] Aug 1995).*

RINGWOOD (USA) BHB 72f **RR 75f** 4540[4]
2 b c Foxhound (USA) - Tewksbury Garden (USA) (Wolf Power (SAF))
Form - 644
Record 2000 - 1st:0 2nd:0 3rd:0 Ran:3
Win Prizemoney £0 *Total Prizemoney* £250
2000 Turf 0-3: (6f 2, 8f) (gd, frm 2)
Currently above-average colt. Turf high 65 (began Jly).
**C F Wall [0-3] Jane Dobie & John Bridge.*

RINKA BLUE RR 5156[17]
2 b f Faustus (USA) 9.1f **(54)** - True Is Blue (Gabitat) 5f **(44)**
Form - 0
Record 2000 - 1st:0 2nd:0 3rd:0 Ran:1
2000 Turf 0-1: (5f) (g-s)
Currently very poor filly. **P S McEntee [0-1] N F Tebbutt.*

RIOJA BHB 51f59a **RR 54f 59a** 4894[11]
5 ch g Anshan 8.2f **(63)** - Executive Flare (Executive Man) 6f **(77)**
Form - 70000
Record 2000 - 1st:0 2nd:0 3rd:0 Ran:5
Pre2000 - 1st:1 2nd:1 3rd:1 Ran:10
Win Prizemoney £8,220 *Total Prizemoney* £9,616
Wins * 1998 Apr Newmar (SFT) H 6f 70 77 <
2000 Turf 0-4: (5f 2, 6f 2) (sft, gd, g-f, frm) 2000 AW 0-1: (6f) (Fibr)
Fair gelding. Turf high 54. **T P Tate [1-15] Mrs Sylvia Clegg.*

RIO NAPO (IRE) RR 107f 3949a[6]
6 b h Law Society (USA) 11.6f **(71)** - My Southern love (ITY) (Southern Arrow (USA))
Form - 5686
2000 Turf 0-4: (10f, 12f 2, 15f) (g-s, gd, g-f 2)
Pattern-class horse, effective 12f, acts on g-f to frm. Turf high 107.
**L Camici in ITY [1-12].*

RIO'S DIAMOND BHB 43f41a **RR 51df 41a** 5229[22]
3 b f Formidable (USA) 7.8f **(60)** - Rio Piedras (Kala Shikari) 8.4f **(54)**
Form - 8720513408300
Record 2000 - 1st:1 2nd:1 3rd:2 Ran:11
Pre2000 - 1st:0 2nd:0 3rd:1 Ran:9
Win Prizemoney £2,436 *Total Prizemoney* £4,332
Wins * **2000** Jun Warwic (G-F) H 6.8f 39 43 <
2000 Turf 1-9: (6f 2, 7f 1-4, 8f 3) (hvy, gd, g-f 1-2, frm 4, hrd) 2000 AW 0-2: (7f, 8f) (Fibr 2)
Light-framed, fair filly, effective 7 to 8f, best at 7f, acts on g-f to frm - acts on Fibr, has worn blinkers, likes left handed tracks, prefers tight tracks. Turf high 51 - 3rd of 9 giving 13lb to Philagain (26 Jun Musselburgh 8f frm RF 2274) - also 1st of 11 getting 8lb from Lady Cyrano (19 Jun Warwick RF 2100). AW high 45 (1st run) - 2nd of 16 getting 15lb from Africa (8 May Southwell 7f Fibr RF 1091).
**M J Ryan [1-20] Mrs Sandie Ross.*

RIPARIAN BHB 70f **RR 69f** 4456[15]
3 b g Last Tycoon 9.4f **(73)** - La Riveraine (USA) **(81f)** (Riverman (USA)) 9.1f **(76)**
Form - 3140
Record 2000 - 1st:1 2nd:0 3rd:1 Ran:4
Pre2000 - 1st:0 2nd:0 3rd:0 Ran:1
Win Prizemoney £5,187 *Total Prizemoney* £6,186
Wins * **2000** Jly Newcas (G-F) 8f 62 <
2000 Turf 1-4: (8f 1-2, 10f, 12f) (g-s 2, gd 1-1, frm)
Average gelding. Turf high 69 - 4th of 5 getting 6lb from Stallone (29 Jly Redcar 10f frm RF 3222) - also 1st of 6 from Fizzle (9 Jly Newcastle RF 2650). **Sir Michael Stoute [1-5] J H Richmond-Watson.*

RIPCORD (IRE) BHB 65f **RR 48+f** 5318[8]
2 b c Diesis 9f **(80)** - Native Twine (Be My Native (USA)) 10.2f **(71)**
Form - 008
Record 2000 - 1st:0 2nd:0 3rd:0 Ran:3
2000 Turf 0-3: (6f, 7f, 8f) (sft, gd, g-f)
Currently moderate colt. Turf high 48 (began Spt).
**J H M Gosden [0-3] Lady Harrison.*

RIPPLE (IRE) RR 15f 1899[12]
3 ch f Bob Back (USA) 11.5f **(71)** - Loshian (IRE) (Montelimar (USA))
Form - 00
Record 2000 - 1st:0 2nd:0 3rd:0 Ran:2
2000 Turf 0-2: (8f, 10f) (gd, frm)
Small, currently poor filly. Turf high 15.
**Mrs M Reveley [0-2] & Mrs W J Williams.*

RIPSNORTER (IRE) BHB 24f20a **RR ?f 20a** 4695[17]
11 ch g Rousillon (USA) 10.4f **(69)** - Formulate (Reform) 8.9f **(62)**
Form - 000
Record 2000 - 1st:0 2nd:0 3rd:0 Ran:3
Pre2000 - 1st:4 2nd:5 3rd:3 Ran:59
Win Prizemoney £9,433 *Total Prizemoney* £15,091
Wins * 1998 *Feb Lingfi (SLW) SH 8f 26 36*
2000 Turf 0-2: (10f 2) (gd, frm) 2000 AW 0-1: (8f) (Fibr)
Very poor gelding, has worn blinkers. (began Jly).
**P D Purdy [1-19] P D Purdy (from K Bishop [0-8] Aug 1996).*

RISING PASSION (IRE) BHB 44f **RR 38f** 3627[12]
2 ch g General Monash (USA) - Brazilian Princess (Absalom) 7.2f **(58)**
Form - 000
Record 2000 - 1st:0 2nd:0 3rd:0 Ran:3
2000 Turf 0-3: (5f 2, 7f) (g-f, frm 2)
Currently very moderate gelding. Turf high 38.
**D Nicholls [0-3] David Waters.*

RISING SPRAY BHB 48f **RR 57f** 4823[17]
9 ch g Waajib 8.9f **(67)** - Rose Bouquet (General Assembly (USA)) 10f **(68)**
Form - 0770600
Record 2000 - 1st:0 2nd:0 3rd:0 Ran:7
Pre2000 - 1st:4 2nd:5 3rd:7 Ran:45
Win Prizemoney £14,201 *Total Prizemoney* £23,753
Wins 1997 May Salisb (G-F) H 14f 67 71 <
1997 Apr Folkes (G-F) H 12f 62 66
1996 Aug Folkes (G-F) H 12f 44 53+
1996 Aug Folkes (G-F) H 12f 44 52
2000 Turf 0-7: (10f 2, 12f 2, 14f 3) (gd 2, g-f 4, frm)
Fair gelding, effective 10 to 14f, acts on gd to frm, has worn blinkers. Turf high 57 (began Jly). Inconsistent.
**Dr J R J Naylor [0-7] Exors of the late J T Heritage (from C A Horgan [4-37] Jun 1999).*

RISK FREE BHB 75f80a **RR 81f 80a** 2437[9]
3 ch g Risk Me (FR) 8f **(53)** - Princess Lily (Blakeney) 10.5f **(64)**

Form - 2421400
Record 2000 - 1st:1 2nd:1 3rd:0 Ran:6
Pre2000 - 1st:1 2nd:2 3rd:0 Ran:7
Win Prizemoney £6,191 *Total Prizemoney* £10,219
Wins * **2000** *Apr Wolver (STD) H 8.5f 85 86* <
* 1999 *May Southw (STD) 5f 78*
2000 Turf 0-3: (7f, 8f 2) (gd, frm 2) 2000 AW 1-3: (7f 2, 8f 1-1) (Equi, Fibr 1-2)
Leggy, useful gelding, effective 5 to 8f, - acts on Fibr, has worn blinkers. Turf high 81. AW high 88 - 2nd of 8 giving 1lb to Rain Rain Go Away (25 Mar Wolverhampton 7f Fibr RF 0507) - also 1st of 12 giving 15lb to Adobe (15 Apr Wolverhampton RF 0743).
**N P Littmoden [2-13] Mrs P J Sheen.*

RISKY DREAM RR 2012[20]

3 ch f Risk Me (FR) 8f **(53)** - Jove's Voodoo (USA) (Northern Jove (CAN)) 9.7f **(66)**
Form - 00
Record 2000 - 1st:0 2nd:0 3rd:0 Ran:2
2000 Turf 0-2: (7f, 10f) (gd, g-f)
Lengthy, currently very poor filly. **D J Wintle [0-2] Dennis Deacon.*

RISKY GEM BHB 53f63a RR 60df 63a 966[15]

3 ch c Risk Me (FR) 8f **(53)** - Dark Kristal (IRE) (Gorytus (USA)) 7.8f **(60)**
Form - 2400
Record 2000 - 1st:0 2nd:1 3rd:0 Ran:4
Pre2000 - 1st:1 2nd:1 3rd:0 Ran:9
Win Prizemoney £2,801 *Total Prizemoney* £4,341
Wins 1999 *Jly Wolver (STD) H 6f 56* <
2000 Turf 0-2: (6f, 7f) (hvy, gd) 2000 AW 0-2: (6f 2) (Fibr 2)
Light-framed, average colt, effective 5 to 6f, acts on frm - acts on Fibr, likes left handed tracks. Turf high 14. AW high 63 (1st run) - 2nd of 12 giving 9lb to Christopherssister (31 Jan Southwell 6f Fibr RF 0189). Inconsistent.
**J Pearce [0-4] Exors of the late G H Tufts (from R Hannon [1-9] Oct 1999).*

RISKY LOVER BHB 26f21a RR 25tf 21a 258[9]

7 b m Risk Me (FR) 8f **(53)** - Dawn Love (He Loves Me) 7.9f **(55)**
Form - 00
Record 2000 - 1st:0 2nd:0 3rd:0 Ran:2
Pre2000 - 1st:0 2nd:0 3rd:0 Ran:6
2000 AW 0-2: (9f, 16f) (Fibr 2)
Little account mare, has worn blinkers. AW high 4.
**C N Kellett [0-4] J A Day (from T T Bill [0-5] Apr 1998).*

RISKY REEF BHB 64f65a RR 64f 65a 5112[10]

3 ch g Risk Me (FR) 8f **(53)** - Pas de Reef (Pas de Seul) 9.1f **(67)**
Form - 455040
Record 2000 - 1st:0 2nd:0 3rd:0 Ran:6
Pre2000 - 1st:0 2nd:1 3rd:0 Ran:2
Win Prizemoney £0 *Total Prizemoney* £766
2000 Turf 0-4: (5f, 6f 3) (g-s 2, gd, frm) 2000 AW 0-2: (6f, 7f) (Fibr 2)
Average gelding, effective 6f, acts on g-s to g-f - acts on Fibr. Turf high 64 (began Spt) - 4th of 19 giving 3lb to Toldya (4 Oct Lingfield 6f g-s RF 4809). AW high 67 (1st run) - 4th of 11 giving 5lb to Diamond Rachael (19 Feb Wolverhampton 6f Fibr RF 0318).
**I A Balding [0-8] Park House Partnership.*

RISQUE SERMON BHB 75f RR 74f 4965[21]

2 b g Risk Me (FR) 8f **(53)** - Sunday Sport Star (Star Appeal) 9.6f **(65)**
Form - 817430
Record 2000 - 1st:1 2nd:0 3rd:1 Ran:6
Win Prizemoney £3,601 *Total Prizemoney* £4,598
Wins * **2000** Jly Lingfi (G-F) 6f 63 <
2000 Turf 1-6: (5f 3, 6f 1-3) (gd 3, g-f 2, frm 1-1)
Above-average gelding, effective 5f, acts on gd to g-f. Turf high 74 (began Jly) - 3rd of 15 giving 5lb to Amelia (22 Spt Lingfield 5f gd RF 4582). **Miss B Sanders [1-6] R Lamb.*

RITA MACKINTOSH (IRE) BHB 46f42a RR 55f 42a 1028[5]

3 b f Port Lucaya - Silver Stream (USA) (Silver Hawk (USA)) 8.6f **(70)**
Form - 0305
Record 2000 - 1st:0 2nd:0 3rd:1 Ran:3
Pre2000 - 1st:0 2nd:0 3rd:2 Ran:7
Win Prizemoney £0 *Total Prizemoney* £789
2000 AW 0-3: (8f 2, 9f) (Fibr 3)
Neat, fair filly, effective 7 to 8f, acts on frm, has worn blinkers. AW high 44. Inconsistent.
**R Brotherton [0-4] Mrs Carol Newman (from M H Tompkins [0-6] Oct 1999).*

RITA'S ROCK APE BHB 79f60a RR 80f 60a 4266[2]

5 b m Mon Tresor 7.9f **(60)** - Failand (Kala Shikari) 8.4f **(54)**
Form - 80600108212
Record 2000 - 1st:2 2nd:2 3rd:0 Ran:11
Pre2000 - 1st:5 2nd:4 3rd:6 Ran:29
Win Prizemoney £19,963 *Total Prizemoney* £31,654
Wins * **2000** Aug Bright (FRM) H 5.3f 70 73
* **2000** Jly Chepst (FRM) H 5.1f 68 69
* 1999 Spt Salisb (G-F) H 5f 72 79 <
* 1999 Jly Bright (FRM) 5.3f 62+
* 1999 Jly Lingfi (G-F) H 5f 50 61
* 1999 Jly Bath (G-F) H 5.1f 50 65
* 1999 Jun Bright (GD) H 5.3f 50 54
2000 Turf 2-11: (5f 2-11) (gd, g-f 3, frm 2-7)
Decent filly, has broken blood-vessels, effective 5f, acts on g-f to frm, best on frm, likes left handed tracks, prefers tight tracks, excels at Brighton. Turf high 80 - 2nd of 13 giving 6lb to Forgotten Times (6 Spt Epsom 5f g-f RF 4266) - also 1st of 9 giving 9lb to Soaked (30 Aug Brighton RF 4098). She has bags of pace and scored five times in 1999 including a sparkling four-timer during the summer. A winner at Chepstow and Brighton so far last term, a sharp five furlongs and fast ground are what she needs.
**R Brotherton [7-40] Mrs Janet Pearce.*

RIVER ALN BHB 64f RR 64f 2618[1]

2 b f Inchinor 8.9f **(64)** - Play With Me (IRE) (Alzao (USA)) 7.1f **(68)**
Form - 851
Record 2000 - 1st:1 2nd:0 3rd:0 Ran:3
Win Prizemoney £2,268 *Total Prizemoney* £2,268
Wins * **2000** Jly Beverl (GD) S 7.5f 64 <
2000 Turf 1-2: (6f, 7f 1-1) (g-f 1-2) 2000 AW 0-1: (6f) (Fibr)
Currently average filly, often wears blinkers. Turf high 64 (began Jly) - 1st of 9 getting 5lb from Impish Lad (8 Jly Beverley RF 2618). **Sir Mark Prescott [1-3] Cyril Humphris.*

RIVER BANN (USA) BHB 89f RR 88f 1623[4]

3 ch c Irish River (FR) 9f **(77)** - Spiritual Star (USA) (Soviet Star (USA))
Form - 2214
Record 2000 - 1st:1 2nd:2 3rd:0 Ran:4
Pre2000 - 1st:0 2nd:1 3rd:0 Ran:1
Win Prizemoney £7,085 *Total Prizemoney* £12,811
Wins * **2000** May Windso (GD) H 11.6f 85 88 <
2000 Turf 1-4: (10f, 12f 1-3) (g-s, gd 2, g-f 1-1)
Scopey, useful colt. Turf high 88 - 4th of 9 giving 16lb to Star Cast (1 Jun Goodwood 12f gd RF 1623) - also 1st of 12 giving 20lb to Box Car (8 May Windsor RF 1100). Probably needed the run when beaten on his Doncaster reappearance, but flashed his tail under pressure when odds-on next time, although he may have had excuses. Made no mistake at Windsor however.
**P F I Cole [1-5] H R H Prince Fahd Salman.*

RIVER BLEST (IRE) BHB 53f48a RR 52f 48a 4174[3]

4 b g Unblest - Vaal Salmon (IRE) (Salmon Leap (USA)) 11f **(61)**
Form - 508203
Record 2000 - 1st:0 2nd:1 3rd:1 Ran:6
Pre2000 - 1st:0 2nd:0 3rd:2 Ran:5
Win Prizemoney £0 *Total Prizemoney* £1,878
2000 Turf 0-5: (5f, 6f, 7f 3) (gd, g-f 2, frm 2) 2000 AW 0-1: (6f) (Fibr)
Workmanlike, fair gelding, effective 5 to 7f, acts on g-f to frm, best on g-f. Turf high 52 - 3rd of 22 giving 17lb to Upper Chamber (2 Spt Thirsk 5f g-f RF 4174). **Mrs A Duffield [0-11] J W Haygarth.*

RIVERBLUE (IRE) BHB 72f61a RR 72f 61a 4578[15]

4 b c Bluebird (USA) 7.9f **(71)** - La Riveraine (USA) **(81f)** (Riverman (USA)) 9.1f **(76)**
Form - 800515340
Record 2000 - 1st:1 2nd:0 3rd:1 Ran:8
Pre2000 - 1st:2 2nd:2 3rd:1 Ran:15
Win Prizemoney £9,635 *Total Prizemoney* £26,779
Wins * **2000** *Feb Wolver (STD) H 9.4f 60 63*
1998 Aug Thirsk (G-F) H 6f 80 91+ <
1998 Aug Catter (GD) 7f 76

2000 Turf 0-2: (8f, 12f) (sft 2) 2000 AW 1-6: (9f 1-5, 12f) (Fibr 1-6)
Scopey, above-average colt, effective 8f, acts on gd to g-f, has worn blinkers, likes left handed tracks, likes tight tracks. Turf high 72. AW high 65.
**D J Wintle [1-11] Mrs Joan Egan (from M R Channon [0-6] Aug 1999).*

RIVER CANYON (IRE) RR 107f 522a[5]

4 b g College Chapel - Na-Ammah (IRE) **(84f)** (Ela-Mana-Mou) 10.1f **(70)**
Form - 85
2000 Turf 0-1: (8f) (sft)
Pattern-class gelding, has worn blinkers.
**D K Weld in IRE [1-5] Michael Smurfit.*

RIVER CAPTAIN (USA) BHB 30f33a RR 29f 33a 1209[13]

7 ch g Riverman (USA) 9.7f **(78)** - Katsura (USA) (Northern Dancer) 9.6f **(80)**
Form - 00600

Record	**2000** -	1st:0	2nd:0	3rd:0	Ran:4
	Pre2000 -	1st:4	2nd:2	3rd:1	Ran:21

Win Prizemoney £9,679 *Total Prizemoney* £11,614

Wins						
* 1999	*Mar Southw (STD) H*	*12f*	*53*	*61+*	
* 1998	*Oct Southw (STD)*	*12f*		*61*	
* 1998	*Mar Southw (STD) H*	*12f*	*54*	*57*	
* 1997	*Mar Southw (STD)*	*11f*		*62*	<

2000 AW 0-4: (11f 4) (Fibr 4)
Little account gelding, effective 12f, - acts on Fibr, favours left handed tracks. AW high 11. Inconsistent. Three times a winner over middle distances at Southwell, he is not particularly consistent, but he may have another race in him under his ideal conditions.
**D J G MurraySmith [4-26] Ms Diana Wilder (from J H M Gosden [0-1] Apr 1996).*

RIVERDANCE (IRE) BHB 39a RR 38f 37[5]

4 ch g College Chapel - Valmarana (USA) (Danzig Connection (USA)) 8f **(68)**
Form - 0865

Record	**2000** -	1st:0	2nd:0	3rd:0	Ran:1
	Pre2000 -	1st:0	2nd:1	3rd:0	Ran:16

Win Prizemoney £0 *Total Prizemoney* £1,257
2000 AW 0-1: (7f) (Fibr)
Leggy, very moderate gelding, effective 8f, acts on g-s, has worn blinkers.
**P D Evans [0-11] Gallagher Equine Ltd (from Mrs L C Jewell [0-3] Jun 1999).*

RIVER ENSIGN BHB 57f52a RR 56f 52a 1781[3]

7 br m River God (USA) 6f **(37)** - Ensigns Kit (Saucy Kit) 6f **(43)**
Form - 406213704168183601

Record	**2000** -	1st:4	2nd:1	3rd:3	Ran:16
	Pre2000 -	1st:5	2nd:7	3rd:8	Ran:60

Win Prizemoney £25,194 *Total Prizemoney* £37,298

Wins					
* **2000**	May Southw (HVY) H	10f	52	56	<
* **2000**	Apr Southw (G-S) H	10f	46	49+	
* **2000**	*Feb Wolver (STD) H*	*9.4f*	*47*	*48*	
* **2000**	*Jan Wolver (STD) C*	*9.4f*		*47*	
* 1999	Spt Cheste (HVY) H	10.3f	41	50	
* 1999	*Apr Wolver (STD) C*	*6f*		*50*	
* 1998	Apr Nottin (SFT) H	6.1f	39	44	
* 1998	*Jan Southw (STD) H*	*6f*	*35*	*36*	
* 1997	Aug Thirsk (GD) H	6f	35	41	

2000 Turf 2-6: (8f, 10f 2-5) (g-s 1-2, gd 1-4) 2000 AW 2-10: (6f, 8f 2, 9f 2-7) (Fibr 2-10)
Fair mare, effective 6 to 10f, best at 10f, acts on g-s to gd - acts on Fibr, best on gd, excels at Chester and likes Southwell. Turf high 56 - 3rd of 9 getting 8lb from Batswing (7 Jun Chester 10f gd RF 1781) - also 1st of 12 getting 6lb from Bachelors Pad (31 May Southwell RF 1606). AW high 51 (1st run) - 2nd of 9 getting 10lb from Al Mabrook (6 Jan Wolverhampton 9f Fibr RF 0031) - also 1st of 7 getting 8lb from Areish (17 Feb Wolverhampton RF 0295). Inconsistent. She enjoyed a good season in 2000, like a number of her stablemates.
**W M Brisbourne [9-76] Crispandave Racing Associates.*

RIVER FRONTIER (IRE) BHB 33f28a RR 33f 28a 2101[8]

5 b m Imperial Frontier (USA) 7f **(65)** - River Low (IRE) (Lafontaine (USA)) 8.7f **(49)**
Form - 8

Record	**2000** -	1st:0	2nd:0	3rd:0	Ran:1
	Pre2000 -	1st:1	2nd:1	3rd:3	Ran:24

Win Prizemoney £2,425 *Total Prizemoney* £4,056

Wins					
* 1998	Aug Ripon (G-F) SH	10f	30	40	<

2000 Turf 0-1: (16f) (g-f)
Very moderate filly. **M D I Usher [4-46] G A Summers.*

RIVER OF FIRE BHB 61f RR 66f 4728[8]

2 ch g Dilum (USA) 7.1f **(56)** - Bracey Brook (Gay Fandango (USA)) 8.5f **(59)**
Form - 81158

Record	**2000** -	1st:2	2nd:0	3rd:0	Ran:5

Win Prizemoney £3,857 *Total Prizemoney* £3,857

Wins					
* **2000**	Aug Leices (G-F) SH	6f	60	66	<
* **2000**	Jly Yarmou (G-F) S	7f		62	

2000 Turf 2-4: (6f 1-1, 7f 1-3) (gd 2, frm 2-2) 2000 AW 0-1: (5f) (Fibr)
Average gelding, has worn blinkers. Turf high 66 (began Jly) - 1st of 11 giving 5lb to Circuit Life (9 Aug Leicester RF 3489) - also 1st of 9 giving 5lb to Banningham Bliz (25 Jly Yarmouth RF 3091).
**J M P Eustace [2-5] J C Smith.*

RIVER RAVEN BHB 94f RR 90f 4747[4]

2 b c Efisio 7.7f **(69)** - River Spey (Mill Reef (USA)) 10.5f **(78)**
Form - 214124

Record	**2000** -	1st:2	2nd:2	3rd:0	Ran:6

Win Prizemoney £6,325 *Total Prizemoney* £17,775

Wins					
* **2000**	*Aug Wolver (STD) H*	*7f*	*88*	*90*	<
* **2000**	Jly Hamilt (G-F)	5f		69+	

2000 Turf 1-5: (5f 1-1, 6f 3, 7f) (gd 2, g-f 1-1, frm, hrd) 2000 AW 1-1: (7f 1-1) (Fibr 1-1)
Useful colt, effective 6 to 7f, best at 7f, acts on gd to hrd - acts on Fibr. Turf high 90. (1st run) - 1st of 11 giving 20lb to Carraban (11 Aug Wolverhampton RF 3572). He is a tricky customer and has a habit of hanging under pressure. Sold for 40,00gns at Newmarket in October, he may not be easy to place.
**Sir Mark Prescott [2-6] Hesmonds Stud.*

RIVER'S CURTAIN (USA) RR 104f 1636a[19]

3 b c Theatrical 11.5f **(78)** - Marshua's River (USA) (Riverman (USA)) 9.1f **(76)**
Form - 60

Record	**2000** -	1st:0	2nd:0	3rd:0	Ran:2

2000 Turf 0-2: (11f, 12f) (gd, g-f)
Currently very useful colt. Turf high 104 (1st run) - 6th of 7 to Ciro (14 May Longchamp 11f gd RF 1289a). **S bin Suroor [0-2] Godolphin.*

RIVERSDALE (IRE) BHB 48f46a RR 52f 46a 5192[6]

4 b g Elbio 9f **(62)** - Embustera (Sparkler)
Form - 086

Record	**2000** -	1st:0	2nd:0	3rd:0	Ran:2
	Pre2000 -	1st:0	2nd:1	3rd:1	Ran:8

Win Prizemoney £0 *Total Prizemoney* £1,901
2000 Turf 0-2: (9f, 10f) (g-s, gd)
Lengthy, fair gelding, effective 8f, acts on g-f to frm. Turf high 29 (began Oct). Becoming disappointing.
**J G FitzGerald [0-10] Mrs R A G Haggie.*

RIVER SOUNDS (IRE) RR 94f 782a[3]

3 b c Shalford - Classical Flair (USA) 00
Form - 053
2000 Turf 0-3: (7f, 8f, 9f) (sft 2, g-s)
Useful colt, effective 7 to 8f, acts on sft to g-s. Turf high 94 - 3rd of 4 getting 3lb from Bach (16 Apr Leopardstown 8f sft RF 0782a). He ran a blinder behind Bach in Listed event at Leopardstown in April but was not seen out again. Raised a harsh 12lb in the ratings, he may be difficult to place. **J G Murphy in IRE [1-7] J G Murphy.*

RIVER TERN BHB 51f63a RR 66f 63a 4487[5]

7 b g Puissance 7.1f **(60)** - Millaine (Formidable (USA)) 9.2f **(63)**
Form - 6060703600000035

Record	**2000** -	1st:0	2nd:0	3rd:2	Ran:16
	Pre2000 -	1st:6	2nd:4	3rd:9	Ran:51

Win Prizemoney £24,397 *Total Prizemoney* £39,205

Wins					
* 1999	Jly York (G-F) H	5f	65	68	<
* 1999	May Thirsk (G-F) H	5f	58	60+	
* 1997	Aug Catter (G-F) C	5f		62	

* 1997	Jly	Warwic	(G-F)	H	5f	63 64
* 1997	May	Redcar	(GD)	C	6f	65
1996	Spt	Thirsk	(G-F)		6f	59

2000 Turf 0-16: (5f 13, 6f 3) (gd 2, g-f 4, frm 10)
Average gelding, effective 5 to 6f, best at 5f, acts on gd to frm, best on frm, has worn blinkers, excels at Bath. Turf high 66 - 6th of 14 giving 5lb to Xanadu (3 Jun Musselburgh 5f frm RF 1683). He won twice in 1999 when given a flat track and fast ground, but apparently has an aversion to being hit by the whip. Despite running some fair races in the last couple of seasons, he is currently on a long losing run.
**J M Bradley [5-55] Martyn James, Pete S Jenkins (from J Berry [1-12] Oct 1996).*

RIVER TIMES (USA) BHB 88f95a **RR 91f 95a** 3343[21]
4 b c Runaway Groom (CAN) 8.1f **(69)** - Miss Riverton (USA) (Fred Astaire (USA))
Form - 204880
Record 2000 - 1st:0 2nd:1 3rd:0 Ran:6
Pre2000 - 1st:3 2nd:1 3rd:1 Ran:13
Win Prizemoney £26,141 *Total Prizemoney* £41,547

Wins						
* 1999	Jly	Newmar	(G-F)	H	8f	91 94 <
* 1999	Apr	Beverl	(G-F)		7.5f	92
* 1998	Spt	Haydoc	(GD)		8.1f	77

2000 Turf 0-5: (7f, 8f 4) (gd 3, g-f 2) 2000 AW 0-1: (8f) (Fibr)
Lengthy, very useful colt, effective 7 to 8f, best at 8f, acts on gd to frm - acts on Fibr, has worn blinkers (effectively), likes tight tracks, excels at Beverley. Turf high 91. (1st run) - 2nd of 13 giving 3lb to The Prince (11 Mar Wolverhampton 8f Fibr RF 0435). Effective with or without blinkers, he failed to build on an encouraging reappearance in the Lincoln Trial at Wolverhampton in March. Probably best on fast ground, he has slipped back to a decent mark and can win a handicap in 2001.
**T D Easterby [3-19] M L Al Basti.*

RIVERTOWN (NZ) BHB 82f **RR 89f** 5187[6]
6 b g Oak Ridge (FR) - Star Habit (NZ) (Habituate)
Form - 435606
Record 2000 - 1st:0 2nd:0 3rd:1 Ran:6
Win Prizemoney £0 *Total Prizemoney* £2,130
2000 Turf 0-6: (8f, 9f, 10f 2, 12f, 16f) (sft, gd 3, g-f 2)
Useful gelding. Turf high 89 (began Jly).
**Mrs A J Perrett [0-6] Michael Watt.*

RIVIERA (FR) **RR 117f** 4424a[1]
6 ch h Kris 10f **(75)** - Manureva (USA) (Nureyev (USA)) 8.7f **(78)**
Form - 1
2000 Turf 1-1: (8f 1-1) (frm 1-1)
Currently high-class horse. (1st run) - 1st of 13 getting 2lb from Arkadian Hero (10 Spt Woodbine RF 4424a).
**R Frankel in USA [1-1] E Gann.*

RIYAFA (IRE) BHB 103f **RR 108+f** 4963[5]
3 b f Kahyasi 12.9f **(74)** - Riyama (IRE) **(63f)** (Doyoun) 9f **(69)**
Form - 2153215
Record 2000 - 1st:2 2nd:2 3rd:1 Ran:7
Win Prizemoney £27,209 *Total Prizemoney* £34,595

Wins						
* **2000**	Spt	Ascot	(SFT)	L	12f	108+ <
* **2000**	May	Haydoc	(SFT)		11.9f	80+

2000 Turf 2-7: (10f 2, 12f 2-5) (g-s 2-2, gd 3, g-f, frm)
Scopey, Pattern-class filly, effective 12f, acts on g-s to gd. Turf high 108 - 1st of 11 from Jalisco (24 Spt Ascot RF 4613). Landed the odds in a maiden, but the drop back to ten furlongs and soft ground were against her next time. Finished third over a more suitable trip at York when she would have finished even closer with a clear run, but made no mistake in an Ascot Listed event. Very much suited by soft ground.
**Sir Michael Stoute [2-7] H H Aga Khan.*

RIZERIE (FR) BHB 98f **RR 93f** 4738[9]
2 gr f Highest Honor (FR) 10.9f **(72)** - Riziere (FR) (Groom Dancer (USA))
Form - 12730
Record 2000 - 1st:1 2nd:1 3rd:1 Ran:5
Win Prizemoney £4,231 *Total Prizemoney* £10,078
Wins * **2000** Jun Goodwo (G-F) 7f 70 <
2000 Turf 1-5: (7f 1-5) (gd 1-2, g-f 2, frm)
Useful filly. Turf high 93 (began Jun) - 3rd of 7 to Peaceful Paradise (12 Aug Newmarket 7f frm RF 3591). She progressed well physically during the summer, but may need to travel to win a Group or Listed race.
**L M Cumani [1-5] Robert Smith.*

ROBBER RED BHB 45f38a **RR 48f 38a** 3834[13]
4 b g Mon Tresor 7.9f **(60)** - Starisk **(33f)** (Risk Me (FR)) 5.9f **(53)**
Form - 08000
Record 2000 - 1st:0 2nd:0 3rd:0 Ran:5
Pre2000 - 1st:1 2nd:6 3rd:0 Ran:24
Win Prizemoney £1,972 *Total Prizemoney* £8,410
Wins 1998 Aug Lingfi (FRM) C 6f 78 <
2000 Turf 0-2: (7f, 8f) (g-f, frm) 2000 AW 0-3: (8f 2, 10f) (Equi 2, Fibr)
Moderate gelding, effective 8f, acts on g-f to frm, has worn blinkers, likes left handed tracks, likes tight tracks. Turf high 36. AW high 26.
**R M Flower [0-17] B C Isitt (from B J Meehan [1-12] Oct 1998).*

ROBBIES DREAM (IRE) BHB 43f52a **RR 41f 52a** 5113[3]
4 ch g Balla Cove - Royal Golden (IRE) (Digamist (USA))
Form - 57012123
Record 2000 - 1st:2 2nd:2 3rd:1 Ran:8
Pre2000 - 1st:0 2nd:0 3rd:0 Ran:7
Win Prizemoney £4,578 *Total Prizemoney* £6,442

Wins						
* **2000**	*Aug*	*Wolver*	*(STD)*	*H*	*8.5f*	*48 53* <
* **2000**	*Jly*	*Southw*	*(STD)*	*H*	*8f*	*38 43*

2000 Turf 0-2: (7f 2) (gd, g-f) 2000 AW 2-6: (6f, 8f 2-5) (Fibr 2-6)
Light-framed, fair gelding, effective 8f, - acts on Fibr, has worn blinkers, prefers left handed tracks, favours tight tracks. Turf high 34. AW high 58 - 2nd of 12 getting 7lb from Burning Truth (14 Oct Wolverhampton 8f Fibr RF 4997) - also 1st of 13 getting 15lb from Air of Esteem (19 Aug Wolverhampton RF 3812). He took a long time in getting off the mark and looked moderate, but has looked a different horse since being tried on Fibresand, winning twice on that surface in the summer.
**R M H Cowell [2-8] James Brown (from D Morris [0-7] Aug 1999).*

ROBBO BHB 50f70a **RR 50f 70a** 5082[4]
6 b g Robellino (USA) 9.5f **(68)** - Basha (USA) (Chief's Crown (USA)) 9.8f **(72)**
Form - 64
Record 2000 - 1st:0 2nd:0 3rd:0 Ran:2
Pre2000 - 1st:3 2nd:2 3rd:4 Ran:18
Win Prizemoney £6,039 *Total Prizemoney* £10,015

Wins						
1997	*Oct*	*Wolver*	*(STD)*	*H*	*14.8f*	*00 70* <
1997	*Spt*	*Wolver*	*(STD)*		*14.8f*	*63+*
1997	*Aug*	*Southw*	*(STD)*	*H*	*14f*	*54 61*

2000 Turf 0-2: (16f 2) (hvy, g-s)
Above-average gelding, often wears blinkers. Turf high 50 (began Oct).
**Mrs M Reveley [8-28] The Scarth Racing Partnership (from C W Thornton [3-14] Nov 1997).*

ROBELLANDO **RR 28f** 5070[12]
3 b g Robellino (USA) 9.5f **(68)** - Drama School (Young Generation) 7.7f **(63)**
Form - 0
Record 2000 - 1st:0 2nd:0 3rd:0 Ran:1
2000 Turf 0-1: (12f) (g-s)
Scopey, currently little account gelding.
**I A Balding [0-1] Ann Plummer & Partners.*

ROBELLION BHB 55f65a **RR 51f 65a** 3908[11]
9 b g Robellino (USA) 9.5f **(68)** - Tickled Trout (Red Alert) 7.6f **(66)**
Form - 513070
Record 2000 - 1st:1 2nd:0 3rd:1 Ran:6
Pre2000 - 1st:11 2nd:12 3rd:11 Ran:94
Win Prizemoney £35,156 *Total Prizemoney* £56,133

Wins						
* **2000**	Jun	Lingfi	(G-S)	H	7f	54 51
* 1999	May	Lingfi	(G-F)	H	7f	60 58
1998	*Mar*	*Southw*	*(STD)*	*H*	*7f*	*62 67*
1998	*Feb*	*Lingfi*	*(SLW)*		*8f*	*62*
1998	*Jan*	*Lingfi*	*(STD)*	*C*	*8f*	*62*
1997	Oct	Salisb	(GD)	H	6f	47 53
1996	Aug	Newmar	(GD)	H	6f	61 69
1996	Jly	Chepst	(G-F)	H	5.1f	61 63
1996	*Feb*	*Lingfi*	*(STD)*	*H*	*10f*	*63 62*
1996	*Jan*	*Lingfi*	*(STD)*	*H*	*8f*	*58 55*

2000 Turf 1-6: (6f, 7f 1-3, 8f 2) (hvy, gd, g-f 1-2, frm 2)

Average gelding, effective 7f, acts on g-f to frm, often wears blinkers. Turf high 51 - 1st of 10 getting 18lb from My Emily (3 Jun Lingfield RF 1674).
**Miss E C Lavelle [2-12] The Forty Ninth Partnership (from Mrs L Stubbs [2-10] Aug 1998).*

ROBELLITA BHB 56f58a **RR 57df 58a** 2612[11]
6 b g Robellino (USA) 9.5f **(68)** - Miellita (King Emperor (USA)) 9.4f **(58)**
Form - 26700
Record 2000 - 1st:0 2nd:0 3rd:0 Ran:3
Pre2000 - 1st:2 2nd:3 3rd:1 Ran:10
Win Prizemoney £6,014 *Total Prizemoney* £9,115
Wins * 1999 Mar Nottin (G-S) H 14.1f 50 57
* 1999 *Mar Southw (STD) 12f 64+* <
2000 Turf 0-1: (15f) (gd) 2000 AW 0-2: (11f, 16f) (Fibr 2)
Average gelding, effective 12f, - acts on AW, best on Fibr. AW high 42. Becoming disappointing.
**B Smart [2-10] Angels Racing Syndicate (from C P Morlock [0-6] Jun 1998).*

ROBERT THE BRUCE BHB 43f **RR 32f** 645[6]
5 ch g Distinct Native - Kawarau Queen (Taufan (USA)) 7f **(57)**
Form - 6
Record 2000 - 1st:0 2nd:0 3rd:0 Ran:1
Pre2000 - 1st:0 2nd:0 3rd:0 Ran:2
2000 Turf 0-1: (11f) (gd)
Very moderate gelding.
**L Lungo [0-4] G G Fraser (from R A Fahey [0-2] Aug 1997).*

ROBIN HOOD RR 51f 5188[4]
3 b g Komaite (USA) 6.9f **(61)** - Plough Hill (North Briton)
Form - 70444761020034
Record 2000 - 1st:1 2nd:1 3rd:1 Ran:14
Pre2000 - 1st:0 2nd:0 3rd:0 Ran:1
Win Prizemoney £2,996 *Total Prizemoney* £4,559
Wins * 2000 Aug Hamilt (SFT) H 5f 46 48 <
2000 Turf 1-14: (5f 1-7, 6f 4, 7f, 9f, 11f) (sft 2, gd 1-5, g-f 5, frm 2)
Lengthy, fair gelding, effective 5 to 6f, best at 5f, acts on sft to gd, best on gd. Turf high 51 - 2nd of 17 getting 8lb from Branston Pickle (4 Spt Hamilton 5f gd RF 4211) - also 1st of 18 getting 5lb from Facile Tigre (22 Aug Hamilton RF 3849).
**Miss L A Perratt [1-15] Cree Lodge Racing Club.*

ROBIN SHARP BHB 70f **RR 73f** 5223[5]
2 ch c First Trump - Mo Stopher **(31f)** (Sharpo) 7.7f **(59)**
Form - 55
Record 2000 - 1st:0 2nd:0 3rd:0 Ran:2
2000 Turf 0-1: (6f) (gd) 2000 AW 0-1: (6f) (Fibr)
Currently above-average colt.
**W Jarvis [0-2] Canisbay Bloodstock Ltd.*

ROB LEACH BHB 74f **RR 76f** 2025[5]
3 b g Robellino (USA) 9.5f **(68)** - Arc Empress Jane (IRE) (Rainbow Quest (USA)) 10.4f **(75)**
Form - 52655
Record 2000 - 1st:0 2nd:1 3rd:0 Ran:5
Win Prizemoney £0 *Total Prizemoney* £956
2000 Turf 0-5: (8f 2, 10f 2, 11f) (g-s 2, gd 2, frm)
Workmanlike, above-average gelding. Turf high 76 - 5th of 11 getting 3lb from Mythical King (9 Jun Goodwood 10f gd RF 1847).
**R W Armstrong [0-5] Paul Locke.*

ROBOASTAR (USA) BHB 72f **RR 76f** 5101[17]
3 b br c Green Dancer (USA) 11.9f **(77)** - Sweet Alabastar (USA) (Gulch (USA)) 8f **(81)**
Form - 50
Record 2000 - 1st:0 2nd:0 3rd:0 Ran:2
Pre2000 - 1st:0 2nd:0 3rd:2 Ran:3
Win Prizemoney £0 *Total Prizemoney* £1,113
2000 Turf 0-2: (10f 2) (g-s, gd)
Workmanlike, above-average colt. Turf high 76 (began Spt).
**W Jarvis [0-5] The Roboastar Partnership.*

ROBZELDA BHB 68f **RR 75f** 3210[11]
4 b g Robellino (USA) 9.5f **(68)** - Zelda (USA) (Sharpen Up) 8.3f **(67)**
Form - 325644000
Record 2000 - 1st:0 2nd:1 3rd:1 Ran:9
Pre2000 - 1st:1 2nd:1 3rd:5 Ran:11
Win Prizemoney £4,140 *Total Prizemoney* £13,442
Wins 1999 Aug Leopar (GD) 6f 79+ <
2000 Turf 0-9: (7f 2, 8f 3, 10f 3, 11f) (g-s, gd 6, g-f 2)
Above-average gelding, effective 6 to 11f, best at 7f, acts on gd to g-f, best on gd, has worn blinkers. Turf high 79 - 2nd of 6 to Indian Plume (13 Apr Musselburgh 7f gd RF 0700). Becoming disappointing.
**K A Ryan [0-9] Tony Fawcett (from E Lynam in IRE [1-11] Aug 1999).*

ROCCIOSO BHB 38f **RR 21f** 3817[8]
3 br c Pelder (IRE) - Priory Bay (Petong) 6.6f **(58)**
Form - 08
Record 2000 - 1st:0 2nd:0 3rd:0 Ran:2
Pre2000 - 1st:0 2nd:0 3rd:0 Ran:2
2000 Turf 0-2: (8f, 12f) (g-f, frm)
Workmanlike, little account colt. Turf high 5.
**J C Fox [0-4] Mrs J A Cleary.*

ROCHAMPBEAU (IRE) RR 1916[11]
2 ch f Rainbows For Life (CAN) 9.3f **(64)** - Brandywell (Skyliner) 7.3f **(53)**
Form - 0
Record 2000 - 1st:0 2nd:0 3rd:0 Ran:1
2000 Turf 0-1: (6f) (g-f)
Currently very poor filly. **N M Babbage [0-1] B Babbage.*

ROCK AND SKIP RR 43f 3488[13]
2 b c Rock City 8.8f **(62)** - Free Skip (Free State) 8.7f **(61)**
Form - 000
Record 2000 - 1st:0 2nd:0 3rd:0 Ran:3
2000 Turf 0-3: (5f, 6f 2) (g-f, frm 2)
Currently moderate colt. Turf high 43 (began Jly).
**V Soane [0-3] Robin Barrs,Mike Clements & Paul McCourt.*

ROCK CONCERT RR 52f 5236[15]
2 b f Bishop of Cashel - Summer Pageant (Chief's Crown (USA)) 9.8f **(72)**
Form - 0
Record 2000 - 1st:0 2nd:0 3rd:0 Ran:1
2000 Turf 0-1: (7f) (g-s)
Currently fair filly. **H Candy [0-1] W M Lidsey.*

ROCKERLONG BHB 95f **RR 87f** 4990[13]
2 b f Deploy 11.4f **(67)** - Dancing Rocks (Green Dancer (USA)) 10.3f **(74)**
Form - 220
Record 2000 - 1st:0 2nd:2 3rd:0 Ran:3
Win Prizemoney £0 *Total Prizemoney* £5,715
2000 Turf 0-3: (6f, 7f 2) (gd 2, frm)
Currently useful filly. Turf high 87 (began Spt) - 2nd of 11 to Small Change (23 Spt Ascot 7f gd RF 4599). Runner-up to useful fillies on her first two starts. **G Wragg [0-3] A E Oppenheimer.*

ROCKETTE BHB 25f32a **RR 32a** 4101[19]
5 ch m Rock Hopper 10.6f **(54)** - Primulette (Mummy's Pet) 7.7f **(60)**
Form - 0
Record 2000 - 1st:0 2nd:0 3rd:0 Ran:1
Pre2000 - 1st:1 2nd:0 3rd:0 Ran:16
Win Prizemoney £1,880 *Total Prizemoney* £1,880
Wins 1998 *Jan Lingfi (STD) S 8f 52* <
2000 Turf 0-1: (10f) (frm)
Very poor filly, has worn blinkers.
**A D Smith [0-1] D F Bassett (from S G Knight [0-2] Jly 1998).*

ROCK FALCON (IRE) BHB 92f85a **RR ?f 85a** 1681[R]
7 ch g Polar Falcon (USA) 9f **(74)** - Rockfest (USA) (Stage Door Johnny) 10.3f **(84)**
Form - 000RR
Record 2000 - 1st:0 2nd:0 3rd:0 Ran:5
Pre2000 - 1st:6 2nd:2 3rd:2 Ran:26
Win Prizemoney £37,892 *Total Prizemoney* £48,794
Wins 1998 Spt Bath (G-S) 8f 97+
1998 Aug Goodwo (G-F) H 7f 97 101 <
1998 May Kempto (G-F) H 8f 85 93
1997 Oct Ascot (HVY) H 8f 80 91
1997 Spt Chepst (GD) S 8.1f 67+

1997 May Lingfi (GD) 7f 80
2000 Turf 0-3: (6f, 7f, 8f) (gd 2, frm) 2000 AW 0-2: (7f, 8f) (Fibr 2)
Moderate gelding, effective 7 to 8f, best at 7f, acts on gd, mostly wears blinkers (effectively). Turf high 67. AW high 48. Becoming disappointing.
**D Nicholls [0-11] V Greaves (from Lady Herries [6-20] Jly 1999).*

ROCK ISLAND LINE (IRE) BHB 53f61a **RR 34f 61a** 3020[5]
6 b g New Express 6.8f **(54)** - Gail's Crystal (Crofter (USA)) 8.4f **(56)**
Form - 202655
Record 2000 - 1st:0 2nd:2 3rd:0 Ran:6
Pre2000 - 1st:7 2nd:3 3rd:7 Ran:31
Win Prizemoney £16,613 *Total Prizemoney* £22,663
Wins * 1999 *Jly Southw (STD) H* *7f* *60* *62* <
* 1999 *Jly Southw (STD) C* *7f* *55*
* 1999 *Feb Southw (STD) S* *6f* *60*
1998 *Feb Southw (STD) C* *8f* *52*
1998 *Jan Southw (STD) C* *7f* *58*
1997 May Newcas (GD) C 7f 62 <
1997 Apr Hamilt (SFT) S 8.3f 53
2000 Turf 0-1: (7f) (g-s) 2000 AW 0-5: (6f 3, 7f, 8f) (Fibr 5)
Average gelding, effective 6 to 7f, best at 7f, - acts on Fibr, prefers left handed tracks, prefers tight tracks, excels at Southwell. AW high 65 - 2nd of 11 giving 14lb to Featherstone Lane (11 May Wolverhampton 7f Fibr RF 1148). He runs infrequently on turf these days, but is a regular on the Southwell Fibresand. He boasts quite a good strike-rate at between six furlongs and a mile at that track and can be relied upon to try his best.
**G Woodward [3-13] Burntwood Sports Ltd (from J Berry [4-24] Aug 1998).*

ROCKLANDS LANE BHB 36f **RR 20f** 1097[19]
4 b g Puissance 7.1f **(60)** - Dancing Daughter (Dance In Time (CAN)) 8.9f **(59)**
Form - 000
Record 2000 - 1st:0 2nd:0 3rd:0 Ran:3
Pre2000 - 1st:0 2nd:1 3rd:0 Ran:10
Win Prizemoney £0 *Total Prizemoney* £1,336
2000 Turf 0-3: (5f, 6f 2) (hvy, g-s, g-f)
Unfurnished, little account gelding, effective 6f, acts on gd. Turf high 18. **R F JohnsonHoughton [0-13] R F JohnsonHoughton.*

ROCK ON ROBIN BHB 30f38a **RR 49f 38a** 5077[15]
3 br g Rock City 8.8f **(62)** - Volcalmeh (Lidhame) 9.2f **(50)**
Form - 80268600
Record 2000 - 1st:0 2nd:1 3rd:0 Ran:7
Pre2000 - 1st:0 2nd:0 3rd:0 Ran:7
Win Prizemoney £0 *Total Prizemoney* £700
2000 Turf 0-7: (10f 3, 11f, 12f 2, 15f) (g-s 3, gd, g-f, hrd 2)
Unfurnished, moderate gelding, effective 10f, acts on g-s to hrd, often wears blinkers, likes tight tracks. Turf high 49 - 2nd of 19 giving 5lb to Bondi Bay (13 May Beverley 10f hrd RF 1183).
**J E Long [0-2] Terry Waters (from C W Fairhurst [0-12] Jun 2000).*

ROCK SCENE (IRE) BHB 39f36a **RR 51f 36a** 5164[6]
8 b g Scenic 10.6f **(66)** - Rockeater (Roan Rocket) 7.8f **(57)**
Form - 2865541006
Record 2000 - 1st:1 2nd:1 3rd:0 Ran:10
Pre2000 - 1st:1 2nd:0 3rd:0 Ran:11
Win Prizemoney £5,311 *Total Prizemoney* £6,296
Wins * **2000** Jly Ripon (G-S) S 10f 51 <
* 1998 Jly Warwic (GD) H 10.8f 42 49
2000 Turf 1-10: (9f, 10f 1-4, 11f 5) (hvy, sft, g-s 1-2, gd 5, frm)
Fair gelding, effective 10 to 11f, best at 11f, acts on hvy to g-s, favours tight tracks. Turf high 51 - 1st of 21 giving 5lb to Time Temptress (10 Jly Ripon RF 2674).
**A Streeter [2-21] Mrs J Hughes (from R Hollinshead [0-3] Aug 1995).*

ROCKY ISLAND BHB 41f **RR 41f** 1551[10]
3 b g Rock Hopper 10.6f **(54)** - Queen's Eyot (Grundy) 10.3f **(65)**
Form - 0
Record 2000 - 1st:0 2nd:0 3rd:0 Ran:1
Pre2000 - 1st:0 2nd:0 3rd:0 Ran:3
2000 Turf 0-1: (14f) (g-f)
Light-framed, moderate gelding. **Mrs M Reveley [0-4] W G McHarg.*

RODOSLOVNAYA **RR 15f** 4807[16]
2 b f Distant Relative 7f **(69)** - Balinsky (IRE) **(52f 42a)** (Skyliner) 7.3f **(53)**
Form - 0
Record 2000 - 1st:0 2nd:0 3rd:0 Ran:1
2000 Turf 0-1: (7f) (g-s)
Currently poor filly. **I A Balding [0-1] Rodoslovnaya Partnership.*

ROFFEY SPINNEY (IRE) BHB 49f43a **RR 47f 43a** 3174[2]
6 ch g Masterclass (USA) 5.9f **(63)** - Crossed Line (Thatching) 8f **(66)**
Form - 702
Record 2000 - 1st:0 2nd:1 3rd:0 Ran:3
Pre2000 - 1st:5 2nd:2 3rd:7 Ran:41
Win Prizemoney £11,603 *Total Prizemoney* £16,922
Wins 1999 *Jan Wolver (STD) S* *9.4f* *65*
1998 Oct Leices (G-S) SH 7f 54 67
1998 Jly Folkes (GD) C 7f 50
1997 *Feb Lingfi (STD) H* *5f* *66* *69* <
1997 *Feb Lingfi (STD)* *6f* *63*
2000 Turf 0-2: (7f, 10f) (gd, g-f) 2000 AW 0-1: (6f) (Fibr)
Moderate gelding, effective 9f, - acts on Fibr, has worn blinkers, likes left handed tracks, likes tight tracks. Turf high 47. He has picked up a few modest events on turf and sand in his time, but is not particularly consistent. Best when able to dominate.
**C Drew [0-3] John Huntridge (from J Cullinan [1-13] Oct 1999).*

ROGER ROSS BHB 35f39a **RR 40f 39a** 3556[7]
5 b g Touch of Grey 8.1f **(47)** - Foggy Dew (Smoggy) 8f **(50)**
Form - 6817050007
Record 2000 - 1st:0 2nd:0 3rd:0 Ran:5
Pre2000 - 1st:5 2nd:2 3rd:3 Ran:32
Win Prizemoney £23,713 *Total Prizemoney* £27,078
Wins * 1999 *Nov Lingfi (STD) H* *10f* *49* *54*
* 1998 Oct Ascot (SFT) H 8f 71 75 <
* 1998 Jly Salisb (FRM) H 8f 62 69
* 1998 Jun Sandow (G-S) H 8.1f 52 64
* 1998 Jun Salisb (G-S) H 8f 52 65
2000 Turf 0-4: (8f 2, 10f 2) (g-s, g-f, frm 2) 2000 AW 0-1: (10f) (Equi)
Moderate gelding, effective 10f, - acts on Equi, has worn blinkers, likes left handed tracks. Turf high 40.
**R M Flower [5-37] H Lawrence.*

ROGHAN JOSH **RR 8f** 4365[18]
2 b g Timeless Times (USA) 6.1f **(56)** - Macs Maharanee **(71f 70a)** (Indian King (USA)) 7.4f **(64)**
Form - 00
Record 2000 - 1st:0 2nd:0 3rd:0 Ran:2
2000 Turf 0-2: (5f 2) (g-f, hrd)
Currently very poor gelding. Turf high 8 (began Aug).
**P S Felgate [0-2] Yorkshire Racing Club Owners Group 1990.*

ROGUE SPIRIT BHB 62f65a **RR 69f 65a** 4928[1]
4 b g Petong 7.6f **(58)** - Quick Profit (Formidable (USA)) 9.2f **(63)**
Form - 807407200001
Record 2000 - 1st:1 2nd:1 3rd:0 Ran:12
Pre2000 - 1st:1 2nd:0 3rd:2 Ran:9
Win Prizemoney £6,814 *Total Prizemoney* £9,977
Wins * **2000** *Oct Lingfi (STD) H* *12f* *60* *67*
* 1999 May Folkes (G-F) 6f 70 <
2000 Turf 0-11: (6f 2, 8f 2, 9f 3, 10f 3, 11f) (sft, gd 3, g-f 4, frm 3) 2000 AW 1-1: (12f 1-1) (Equi 1-1)
Workmanlike, average gelding, effective 5 to 12f, best at 6f, acts on gd to frm - acts on Equi, has worn blinkers. Turf high 69 - 2nd of 10 giving 13lb to Swinging The Blues (26 Jun Yarmouth 10f g-f RF 2293). (1st run).
**P W Harris [2-21] L Grover, P Johns, C Stewart & K Swinden.*

ROI DE DANSE BHB 36f38a **RR 23f 38a** 5116[12]
5 ch g Komaite (USA) 6.9f **(61)** - Princess Lucy (Local Suitor (USA)) 8.4f **(67)**
Form - 06312034225025000
Record 2000 - 1st:0 2nd:3 3rd:1 Ran:12
Pre2000 - 1st:3 2nd:4 3rd:1 Ran:35
Win Prizemoney £7,293 *Total Prizemoney* £17,050
Wins * 1999 *Dec Lingfi (STD) H* *10f* *40* *44*
1998 Spt Bright (GD) 8f 71
1997 Aug Kempto (GD) 6f 72 <
2000 Turf 0-2: (7f 2) (gd, g-f) 2000 AW 0-10: (7f, 8f 3, 9f 3, 10f 2, 12f) (Equi 5, Fibr 5)

Moderate gelding, effective 7 to 9f, best at 9f, - acts on Fibr, has worn blinkers, likes left handed tracks, likes tight tracks. Turf high 23. AW high 48 - 2nd of 9 getting 16lb from Tyler's Toast (15 Feb Wolverhampton 9f Fibr RF 0282). Becoming disappointing.
**M Quinn [1-34] Miss A Jones (from J W Hills [2-14] Oct 1998).*

ROISIN SPLENDOUR (IRE) BHB 60f50a **RR 59f 50a** 98[14]
5 ch m Inchinor 8.9f **(64)** - Oriental Splendour (Runnett) 7f **(59)**
Form - 000
Record 2000 - 1st:0 2nd:0 3rd:0 Ran:1
Pre2000 - 1st:3 2nd:4 3rd:3 Ran:29
Win Prizemoney £8,992 *Total Prizemoney* £16,066
Wins * 1999 Jun Goodwo (G-F) H 7f 64 66
* 1999 *Feb Lingfi (STD) H 7f 67 72*
* 1998 Jly Bright (GD) 7f 77 <
2000 AW 0-1: (7f) (Equi)
Fair filly, effective 7f, acts on frm - acts on Equi, likes tight tracks.
**S Dow [3-30] Byerley Bloodstock.*

ROISTERER BHB 28f **RR 30?f** 4174[11]
4 ch g Rudimentary (USA) 8.2f **(66)** - Raffle (Balidar) 7.9f **(63)**
Form - 08070
Record 2000 - 1st:0 2nd:0 3rd:0 Ran:5
2000 Turf 0-4: (5f 2, 6f, 7f) (sft, g-f 3) 2000 AW 0-1: (6f) (Fibr)
Scopey, very moderate gelding. Turf high 30.
**D W Chapman [0-4] Michael Hill (from M P Tregoning [0-1] Apr 2000).*

ROLE MODEL BHB 36f30a **RR 38f 30a** 1372[9]
4 b f Tragic Role (USA) 9.4f **(63)** - Emerald Gulf (IRE) (Wassl) 9.7f **(62)**
Form - 50
Record 2000 - 1st:0 2nd:0 3rd:0 Ran:2
Pre2000 - 1st:0 2nd:1 3rd:0 Ran:9
Win Prizemoney £0 *Total Prizemoney* £575
2000 AW 0-2: (16f 2) (Fibr 2)
Leggy, very moderate filly, effective 14f, acts on frm. AW high 18. Inconsistent. **R M Whitaker [0-14] The PBT Group.*

ROLLER BHB 70f **RR 80f** 5159[9]
4 b g Bluebird (USA) 7.9f **(71)** - Tight Spin (High Top) 10.2f **(67)**
Form - 32122040360630
Record 2000 - 1st:1 2nd:3 3rd:3 Ran:14
Pre2000 - 1st:1 2nd:0 3rd:2 Ran:11
Win Prizemoney £7,009 *Total Prizemoney* £16,275
Wins * **2000** Apr Newcas (SFT) H 8f 65 81 <
1999 May Warwic (SFT) 6.8f 75
2000 Turf 1-13: (8f 1-10, 9f, 10f 2) (hvy, sft 1-5, g-s 2, gd 4, g-f) 2000 AW 0-1: (7f) (Fibr)
Scopey, decent gelding, effective 7 to 8f, best at 8f, acts on sft to frm, best on sft, has worn blinkers (extremely effectively), excels at Haydock and Chepstow. Turf high 81 - 1st of 19 getting 5lb from Itsanothergirl (24 Apr Newcastle RF 0842).
**J G Given [1-14] Mrs Jo Hardy (from H Candy [1-11] Oct 1999).*

ROLLING HIGH (IRE) BHB 20f **RR** 338[13]
5 ch g Roi Danzig (USA) 10.5f **(62)** - Sally Chase (Sallust) 8.4f **(63)**
Form - 00
Record 2000 - 1st:0 2nd:0 3rd:0 Ran:2
Pre2000 - 1st:0 2nd:0 3rd:0 Ran:2
2000 AW 0-2: (9f, 11f) (Fibr 2)
Formerly very poor gelding. **D J G MurraySmith [0-5] D Twomey.*

ROLLING STONE BHB 90f **RR 82+f** 1059[11]
6 b h Northern Amethyst 10.2f **(81)** - First Sapphire (Simply Great (FR)) 8.2f **(65)**
Form - 0
Record 2000 - 1st:0 2nd:0 3rd:0 Ran:1
Pre2000 - 1st:1 2nd:0 3rd:2 Ran:4
Win Prizemoney £3,460 *Total Prizemoney* £4,876
Wins * 1999 Spt Bath (SFT) 10.2f 82+ <
2000 Turf 0-1: (10f) (gd)
Decent horse. Lightly raced, he won a backend maiden in good style and clearly relishes soft ground.
**Mrs A J Perrett [1-4] Brian Cooper (from Lady Herries [0-1] Jun 1997).*

ROLLY POLLY (IRE) **RR 102f** 3947a[4]
2 b f Mukaddamah (USA) 7.6f **(74)** - Rare Sound (Rarity) 10.1f **(60)**
Form - 114
2000 Turf 2-3: (6f 2-3) (hvy 1-1, g-s, g-f 1-1)
Currently very useful filly. Turf high 102 - 1st of 8 getting 3lb from Iron Mask (29 Jly Maisons-Laffitte RF 3349a). A speedy juvenile in Italy, she is reported to be joining Henry Cecil's yard in 2001.
**B Grizzetti in ITY [2-3].*

ROLO TOMASI (IRE) **RR 106+f** 3539a[1]
4 b g Mujtahid (USA) 7.4f **(69)** - Elegant Bloom (Be My Guest (USA)) 9.3f **(67)**
Form - 11
2000 Turf 1-1: (7f 1-1) (sft 1-1) 2000 AW 1-1: (5f 1-1) (Dirt 1-1)
Pattern-class gelding, effective 5 to 7f, best at 5f, acts on sft to gd - acts on Dirt. (1st run). (1st run) - 1st of 10 from State of Caution (14 May Jagersro RF 1287a). Consistent.
**W Neuroth in NOR [2-2] Stall Zuccini (from E Lynam in IRE [3-13] Oct 1999).*

ROMA BHB 30f25a **RR 23f 25a** 2271[6]
5 b m Second Set (IRE) 9.2f **(67)** - Villasanta (Corvaro (USA)) 9f **(53)**
Form - 08006
Record 2000 - 1st:0 2nd:0 3rd:0 Ran:4
Pre2000 - 1st:1 2nd:2 3rd:1 Ran:14
Win Prizemoney £2,668 *Total Prizemoney* £4,546
Wins * 1999 Jun Mussel (G-F) H 12f 43 45 <
2000 Turf 0-4: (12f 4) (frm 4)
Moderate filly, effective 12f, acts on g-f, has worn blinkers, likes right handed tracks. Turf high 23.
**A R Dicken [1-11] J W D Campbell (from C W Thornton [0-10] May 1999).*

ROMAN CANDLE (IRE) BHB 68a **RR 71+f** 390[5]
4 b c Sabrehill (USA) 8.5f **(64)** - Penny Banger (IRE) (Pennine Walk) 8.5f **(61)**
Form - 85
Record 2000 - 1st:0 2nd:0 3rd:0 Ran:2
Pre2000 - 1st:2 2nd:1 3rd:0 Ran:8
Win Prizemoney £7,865 *Total Prizemoney* £8,697
Wins 1999 Jly Ripon (GD) H 12.3f 70 71+ <
1999 Jun Windso (G-F) H 11.6f 62 68
2000 AW 0-2: (12f 2) (Equi, Fibr)
Scopey, above-average colt, effective 12f, acts on gd to frm, favours tight tracks. AW high 57.
**M Kettle [0-1] Taylor Parker Associates Ltd (from C F Wall [2-9] Jan 2000).*

ROMANECH (IRE) BHB 55f45a **RR 58f 45a** 461[5]
3 b c Nicolotte - O La Bamba (IRE) (Commanche Run) 8.5f **(58)**
Form - 85
Record 2000 - 1st:0 2nd:0 3rd:0 Ran:2
Pre2000 - 1st:0 2nd:0 3rd:0 Ran:4
2000 AW 0-2: (7f, 8f) (Fibr 2)
Scopey, fair colt, has worn blinkers. AW high 33.
**J G Smyth-Osbourne [0-6] Deauville Daze Partnership.*

ROMAN EMPEROR BHB 36f44a **RR 26f 44a** 5054[17]
3 ch g Lycius (USA) 8.8f **(71)** - Subya **(99f)** (Night Shift (USA)) 7.2f **(69)**
Form - 0080
Record 2000 - 1st:0 2nd:0 3rd:0 Ran:4
Pre2000 - 1st:0 2nd:0 3rd:0 Ran:6
2000 Turf 0-3: (5f, 10f, 12f) (hvy, sft, g-s) 2000 AW 0-1: (5f) (Fibr)
Little account gelding, has worn blinkers. Turf high 26.
**M W Easterby [0-8] Bernard Bargh & John Walsh (from G P Kelly [0-2] Apr 2000).*

ROMAN HIDEAWAY (IRE) BHB 54f **RR 50f** 5319[11]
2 b c Hernando (FR) - Vaison la Romaine (Arctic Tern (USA)) 8.9f **(69)**
Form - 00
Record 2000 - 1st:0 2nd:0 3rd:0 Ran:2
2000 Turf 0-2: (6f, 7f) (sft, g-s)
Currently fair colt. Turf high 50 (began Oct).
**Sir Mark Prescott [0-2] Neil Greig Osborne House.*

ROMAN KING (IRE) BHB 80f **RR 80df** 3346[2]
5 b g Sadler's Wells (USA) 11.3f **(87)** - Romantic Feeling (Shirley Heights) 10.3f **(74)**
Form - 60342

Record 2000 - 1st:0 2nd:1 3rd:1 Ran:5
Pre2000 - 1st:1 2nd:0 3rd:0 Ran:3
Win Prizemoney £4,208 *Total Prizemoney* £8,562
Wins 1999 Oct Haydoc (HVY) 11.9f 82 <
2000 Turf 0-5: (9f, 10f, 12f, 13f, 16f) (sft, gd 3, g-f)
Decent gelding, effective 9 to 13f, acts on sft to g-f, best on gd. Turf high 82 (1st run) - 6th of 14 giving 25lb to Exalted (8 Apr Hamilton 13f gd RF 0642). Consistent. He changed stables after his first two runs of the season and has been steadily dropped back in trip.
**M Johnston [0-3] D J & F A Jackson (from M D Hammond [0-2] Apr 2000).*

ROMAN REEL (USA) BHB 29f38a **RR 27f 38a** 3520[11]

9 ch g Sword Dance 9.4f **(67)** - Our Mimi (USA) (Believe It (USA)) 9.4f **(70)**
Form - 080800
Record 2000 - 1st:0 2nd:0 3rd:0 Ran:5
Pre2000 - 1st:11 2nd:9 3rd:10 Ran:84
Win Prizemoney £26,660 *Total Prizemoney* £37,512
Wins * 1998 Aug Bright (FRM) H 10f 55 59
* 1998 *Mar Lingfi (STD) H 8f 56 63*
* 1998 *Jan Lingfi (STD) H 10f 53 65*
* 1997 Spt Bright (G-F) H 10f 47 52
* 1997 Jun Bright (FRM) C 10f 55
* 1997 *Mar Lingfi (STD) H 8f 54 58*
* 1996 Jun Bright (FRM) C 10f 70 <
* 1996 May Bright (FRM) S 10f 61
2000 Turf 0-3: (10f, 12f 2) (g-f 2, frm) 2000 AW 0-2: (12f 2) (Equi, Fibr)
Little account gelding, has worn blinkers. AW high 18. Becoming disappointing. **G L Moore [11-90] Mrs J Moore.*

ROMANTIC AFFAIR (IRE) BHB 112f **RR 117f** 5226[1]

3 ch g Persian Bold 10f **(69)** - Broken Romance (IRE) (Ela-Mana-Mou) 10.1f **(70)**
Form - 821142121
Record 2000 - 1st:4 2nd:3 3rd:0 Ran:9
Pre2000 - 1st:1 2nd:0 3rd:1 Ran:3
Win Prizemoney £45,548 *Total Prizemoney* £72,714
Wins * **2000** Oct Newmar (SFT) LH 16f 104 114+ <
* **2000** Spt Doncas (G-F) H 14.6f 98 105
* **2000** Jly Salisb (G-S) H 12f 82 94
* **2000** Jun Sandow (G-F) H 11.4f 73 81
* 1999 Spt Newcas (SFT) 7f 80+
2000 Turf 4-9: (8f, 10f, 11f 1-1, 12f 1-3, 14f, 15f 1-1, 16f 1-1) (g-s 1-2, gd 1-4, g-f 1-2, frm 1-1)
Lengthy, high-class gelding, effective 15 to 16f, acts on gd to g-f, likes right handed tracks. Turf high 114 - 1st of 12 giving 5lb to Mbele (27 Oct Newmarket RF 5226) - also 1st of 13 getting 5lb from Afterjacko (8 Spt Doncaster RF 4295). He progressed well after being stepped up in trip, and his victory in a back-end listed handicap marked him down as a possible Cup horse for 2001. He had shown good form in handicaps earlier, finishing third, promoted to second, over 14 furlongs at York in August and confirming the promise of that effort by battling on really well to win at Doncaster.
**J L Dunlop [5-12] The Earl Cadogan.*

ROMANTIC MYTH BHB 100f **RR 100df** 5107[17]

2 b f Mind Games - My First Romance **(64f)** (Danehill (USA)) 10f **(72)**
Form - 1116450
Record 2000 - 1st:3 2nd:0 3rd:0 Ran:7
Win Prizemoney £45,136 *Total Prizemoney* £51,011
Wins * **2000** Jun Ascot (G-F) G3 5f 100+ <
* **2000** May Cheste (GD) 5.1f 94+
* **2000** Apr Ripon (SFT) 5f 79+
2000 Turf 3-7: (5f 3-6, 6f) (gd 2-4, g-f 1-1, frm, hrd)
Very useful filly, effective 5 to 6f, best at 5f, acts on gd to g-f, best on gd. Turf high 100 - 1st of 20 from Al Ihsas (21 Jun Ascot RF 2149) - also 1st of 7 getting 2lb from Charlie Parkes (9 May Chester RF 1109). She was a high-class recruit, winner of her first three starts including the Lily Agnes at Chester and Ascot's Queen Mary Stakes, in which she was most impressive. She rather lost her way subsequently, although she did have valid excuses more than once. **T D Easterby [3-7] T G Holdcroft.*

ROMANTIC POET **RR 63f** 1731[5]

2 b g Cyrano de Bergerac 7.3f **(58)** - Lady Quinta (IRE) **(50f 49a)** (Gallic League)
Form - 35
Record 2000 - 1st:0 2nd:0 3rd:1 Ran:2
Win Prizemoney £0 *Total Prizemoney* £535
2000 Turf 0-2: (5f 2) (g-s, g-f)
Currently average gelding. Turf high 63.
**B R Millman [0-2] Ray Gudge, Colin Lew Calvert.*

ROMANYLEI (IRE) **RR 102f** 3576[1]

3 gr f Blues Traveller (IRE) - Krayyalei (IRE) **(73f)** (Krayyan) 8.5f **(49)**
Form - 6201
2000 Turf 1-4: (5f, 6f 1-2, 7f) (sft, g-s, gd 1-2)
Very useful filly, effective 6f, acts on g-s to gd. Turf high 102 - 1st of 10 giving 10lb to Presentation (12 Aug Ascot RF 3576). Runner-up in a Haydock listed event in June, she later landed the Shergar Cup Sprint at Ascot.
**J G Burns in IRE [3-6] Mrs J A Dene.*

ROMERO BHB 60f **RR 58f** 1089[11]

4 b g Robellino (USA) 9.5f **(68)** - Casamurrae (Be My Guest (USA)) 9.3f **(67)**
Form - 0
Record 2000 - 1st:0 2nd:0 3rd:0 Ran:1
Pre2000 - 1st:0 2nd:2 3rd:2 Ran:8
Win Prizemoney £0 *Total Prizemoney* £3,131
2000 Turf 0-1: (14f) (g-f)
Fair gelding, effective 10f, acts on gd. Consistent.
**J Akehurst [3-9] Fraser Miller (from C W Thornton [0-7] May 1999).*

ROMNEY BHB 53f **RR 54f** 2263[8]

3 ch g Timeless Times (USA) 6.1f **(56)** - Ewe Lamb (Free State) 8.7f **(61)**
Form - 58
Record 2000 - 1st:0 2nd:0 3rd:0 Ran:2
Pre2000 - 1st:0 2nd:0 3rd:0 Ran:2
2000 Turf 0-2: (10f, 12f) (gd, frm)
Scopey, fair gelding. Turf high 54.
**Mrs P Sly [0-4] Mrs P M Sly.*

RONNI PANCAKE BHB 46f43a **RR 56f 43a** 4677[17]

3 b f Mujadil (USA) 7.7f **(70)** - Funny Choice (IRE) **(55f)** (Commanche Run) 8.5f **(58)**
Form - 6015760000
Record 2000 - 1st:1 2nd:0 3rd:0 Ran:9
Pre2000 - 1st:0 2nd:1 3rd:0 Ran:7
Win Prizemoney £2,467 *Total Prizemoney* £3,537
Wins * **2000** May Leices (G-S) C 8f 56 <
2000 Turf 1-9: (6f, 8f 1-2, 9f, 10f 2, 12f 2, 13f) (g-s, gd 1-1, g-f 5, frm 2)
Workmanlike, fair filly, effective 6f, acts on frm. Turf high 56. Becoming disappointing.
**J S Moore [1-16] J Laughton.*

RONQUISTA D'OR BHB 42f35a **RR 49f 35a** 4650[6]

6 b g Ron's Victory (USA) 9.2f **(52)** - Gild the Lily (Ile de Bourbon (USA)) 10.1f **(67)**
Form - 604006
Record 2000 - 1st:0 2nd:0 3rd:0 Ran:6
Pre2000 - 1st:3 2nd:5 3rd:5 Ran:32
Win Prizemoney £6,641 *Total Prizemoney* £12,504
Wins * 1998 *Dec Wolver (STD) H 12f 47 51*
* 1998 Jly Warwic (G-F) SH 12.5f 43 52
* 1998 *Jan Southw (STD) H 12f 46 56+* <
2000 Turf 0-2: (12f, 13f) (g-f, frm) 2000 AW 0-4: (11f, 12f 2, 15f) (Equi, Fibr 3)
Moderate gelding, effective 12f, acts on gd to frm - acts on Fibr, often wears blinkers (very effectively), favours tight tracks. Turf high 38. AW high 38. **G A Ham [3-38] Ms J C Hutley.*

RON'S PET BHB 60f64a **RR 61df 64a** 722[8]

5 ch g Ron's Victory (USA) 9.2f **(52)** - Penny Mint (Mummy's Game) 8.2f **(60)**
Form - 2602332235548
Record 2000 - 1st:0 2nd:3 3rd:3 Ran:10
Pre2000 - 1st:3 2nd:5 3rd:1 Ran:27
Win Prizemoney £8,855 *Total Prizemoney* £22,798
Wins 1999 *Mar Wolver (STD) H 7f 68 74*
1999 *Mar Wolver (STD) C 7f 67*
1997 Aug Bright (GD) 7f 79 <

2000 Turf 0-1: (7f) (g-s) 2000 AW 0-9: (6f, 7f 5, 8f 2, 10f)(Equi 5, Fibr 4)
Above-average gelding, effective 7 to 10f, best at 7f, - acts on AW, best on Fibr, has worn blinkers, and excels at Lingfield. AW high 74 - 3rd of 5 giving 20lb to Sammy's Shuffle (23 Feb Lingfield 10f Equi RF 0344). Becoming disappointing.
**T D Barron [0-1] Nigel Shields (from K R Burke [1-19] Mar 2000).*

RON'S ROUND BHB 52f44a **RR 59f 44a** 169[10]

6 ch g Ron's Victory (USA) 9.2f **(52)** - Magical Spirit (Top Ville) 11.7f **(68)**
Form - 540
Record 2000 - 1st:0 2nd:0 3rd:0 Ran:3
Pre2000 - 1st:3 2nd:5 3rd:4 Ran:23
Win Prizemoney £7,736 *Total Prizemoney* £13,423
Wins 1998 *Jly Wolver (STD) H* *9.4f 35 46+*
1998 *Jly Southw (STD) H* *11f 35 49+*
1998 Jun Nottin (G-S) SH 10f 48 56 <
2000 AW 0-3: (9f, 12f 2) (Fibr 3)
Fair gelding. AW high 34. Becoming disappointing.
**J M Bradley [0-3] D M Lloyd (from M C Pipe [2-5] Spt 1998).*

ROO BHB 88f **RR 93f** 4150[11]

3 b f Rudimentary (USA) 8.2f **(66)** - Shall We Run (Hotfoot) 10.5f **(59)**
Form - 765322500
Record 2000 - 1st:0 2nd:2 3rd:1 Ran:9
Pre2000 - 1st:2 2nd:3 3rd:1 Ran:10
Win Prizemoney £6,690 *Total Prizemoney* £22,825
Wins * 1999 Aug Haydoc (SFT) 6f 86 <
* 1999 Apr Bath (SFT) 5.1f 82+
2000 Turf 0-9: (6f 7, 7f, 8f) (g-s 3, gd, g-f 4, frm)
Workmanlike, useful filly, effective 6f, acts on gd to g-f, best on g-f. Turf high 93 - 2nd of 14 giving 16lb to Pays d'Amour (8 Jly Haydock 6f gd RF 2635). She looked unlucky on more than one occasion and is clearly capable of winning a decent six furlong handicap. Probably effective on any ground, she should not be written off. **R F JohnsonHoughton [2-19] Mrs H JohnsonHoughton.*

ROOFER (IRE) BHB 78f **RR 81+f** 4970[12]

2 b f Barathea (IRE) - Castlerahan (IRE) (Thatching) 8f **(66)**
Form - 542450
Record 2000 - 1st:0 2nd:1 3rd:0 Ran:6
Win Prizemoney £0 *Total Prizemoney* £3,547
2000 Turf 0-6: (6f 2, 7f 3, 8f) (g-s, gd, g-f 2, frm 2)
Decent filly, effective 6 to 7f, best at 7f, acts on g-s to g-f, best on g-f. Turf high 81 - 4th of 22 getting 10lb from Palatial (26 Spt Newmarket 7f g-f RF 4642). **M R Channon [0-6] Pine Crest Racing.*

ROOFTOP BHB 37f54a **RR 47f 54a** 4061[12]

4 b g Thatching 7.8f **(69)** - Top Berry (High Top) 10.2f **(67)**
Form - 65088004600
Record 2000 - 1st:0 2nd:0 3rd:0 Ran:11
Pre2000 - 1st:0 2nd:1 3rd:1 Ran:10
Win Prizemoney £0 *Total Prizemoney* £2,625
2000 Turf 0-8: (8f 3, 9f 3, 12f, 17f) (sft, gd, g-f 2, frm 4) 2000 AW 0-3: (8f, 11f, 12f) (Fibr 3)
Fair gelding, effective 7 to 11f, best at 7f, acts on g-f - acts on Fibr, has worn blinkers. Turf high 48. AW high 56 - 5th of 9 getting 14lb from Hannibal Lad (28 Feb Southwell 11f Fibr RF 0375).
**C W Fairhurst [0-13] I Anderson (from D Hanley in IRE [0-12] Aug 1999).*

ROOFTOP PROTEST (IRE) BHB 45f **RR 50f** 3696[2]

3 b g Thatching 7.8f **(69)** - Seattle Siren (USA) (Seattle Slew (USA)) 9.4f **(76)**
Form - 0316232
Record 2000 - 1st:1 2nd:2 3rd:2 Ran:7
Pre2000 - 1st:0 2nd:0 3rd:0 Ran:3
Win Prizemoney £3,445 *Total Prizemoney* £5,503
Wins * 2000 Jun Hamilt (GD) C 11.1f 43 <
2000 Turf 1-7: (8f, 9f 2, 11f 1-2, 14f, 16f) (gd 2, g-f 2, frm 1-3)
Scopey, fair gelding, effective 11f, acts on g-f, has worn blinkers, likes tight tracks. Turf high 50 - 2nd of 5 getting 9lb from Santa Lucia (4 Jly Hamilton 11f g-f RF 2493). Consistent.
**Mrs M Reveley [1-7] P D Savill (from N Tinkler [0-3] Aug 1999).*

ROOKIE BHB 41f39a **RR 47df 39a** 247[4]

4 b g Magic Ring (IRE) 6.5f **(64)** - Shot At Love (IRE) **(83f)** (Last Tycoon) 8.5f **(62)**
Form - 084
Record 2000 - 1st:0 2nd:0 3rd:0 Ran:2
Pre2000 - 1st:0 2nd:3 3rd:0 Ran:9
Win Prizemoney £0 *Total Prizemoney* £2,792
2000 AW 0-2: (8f, 13f) (Equi 2)
Leggy, moderate gelding, effective 10f, - acts on Equi, has worn blinkers. AW high 27. Becoming disappointing.
**Mrs A E Johnson [0-3] A Zafiropulo (from C A Cyzer [0-8] Oct 1999).*

ROOM TO ROOM MAGIC (IRE) BHB 38f34a **RR 42f 34a** 5164[3]

3 ch f Casteddu 7.4f **(54)** - Bellatrix (Persian Bold) 9.3f **(66)**
Form - 456025203
Record 2000 - 1st:0 2nd:2 3rd:1 Ran:9
Win Prizemoney £0 *Total Prizemoney* £1,655
2000 Turf 0-5: (11f 2, 12f 3) (g-s, gd, g-f, frm 2) 2000 AW 0-4: (8f, 9f, 10f, 12f) (Equi, Fibr 3)
Leggy, moderate filly, effective 11f, acts on gd, favours left handed tracks. Turf high 42 - 3rd of 15 getting 5lb from Blenheim Terrace (24 Oct Redcar 11f gd RF 5164). AW high 50.
**B Palling [0-9] D Brennan.*

RORKES DRIFT (IRE) **RR 65f** 2547[5]

2 ch f Royal Abjar (USA) - Scanno's Choice (IRE) (Pennine Walk) 8.5f **(61)**
Form - 35
Record 2000 - 1st:0 2nd:0 3rd:1 Ran:2
Win Prizemoney £0 *Total Prizemoney* £526
2000 Turf 0-2: (6f, 7f) (gd, g-f)
Currently average filly. Turf high 65.
**T J Naughton [0-2] Mrs L Archer.*

ROSAKER (USA) **RR** 4936[9]

3 b c Pleasant Tap (USA) 13.1f **(71)** - Rose Crescent (USA) (Nijinsky (CAN)) 10.3f **(77)**
Form -
Record 2000 - 1st:1 2nd:0 3rd:0 Ran:8
Pre2000 - 1st:0 2nd:0 3rd:1 Ran:1
Win Prizemoney £11,066 *Total Prizemoney* £15,106
Wins * 2000 May Redcar (G-S) H 10f 95 102+ <
2000 Turf 1-8: (gd 1-6, frm 2)
Very useful gelding, acts on gd, has worn blinkers. Turf high 102 - 1st of 13 giving 27lb to Star Dynasty (29 May Redcar RF 1531).
**C E Brittain [1-8] H E Sheikh Rashid Bin Mohammed (from A Fabre in FR [0-1] Jun 1998).*

ROSALIA (USA) **RR 67f** 5052[2]

2 b f Red Ransom (USA) 8.6f **(83)** - Normandy Belle (USA) (Fit To Fight (USA)) 9.7f **(45)**
Form - 46362
Record 2000 - 1st:0 2nd:1 3rd:1 Ran:5
Win Prizemoney £0 *Total Prizemoney* £1,882
2000 Turf 0-5: (5f, 6f 2, 7f 2) (sft, gd, g-f, frm 2)
Average filly. Turf high 67 (began Aug).
**T D Easterby [0-5] Cathal Ryan.*

ROSCIUS (IRE) **RR 109f** 2206[3]

3 b c Sadler's Wells (USA) 11.3f **(87)** - Rosefinch (USA) (Blushing Groom (FR)) 10.3f **(76)**
Form - 173
Record 2000 - 1st:1 2nd:0 3rd:1 Ran:3
Win Prizemoney £22,750 *Total Prizemoney* £38,275
Wins * 2000 May Goodwo (GD) L 9.9f 109 <
2000 Turf 1-3: (10f 1-1, 12f 2) (g-s 1-1, gd 2)
Scopey, currently Pattern-class colt. Turf high 109 - also 1st of 8 from St Expedit (23 May Goodwood RF 1393). A winner of a trial in Dubai, this likeable colt was a game winner of the Predominate Stakes at Goodwood but was found wanting in the French Derby in heavy ground. Ran a better race at Royal Ascot but was not seen again. **S bin Suroor [1-3] Godolphin.*

ROSE ADAGIO BHB 70f64a **RR 75f 64a** 4319[8]

3 b f Sadler's Wells (USA) 11.3f **(87)** - Rose Noble (USA) (Vaguely Noble) 10.1f **(72)**
Form - 58
Record 2000 - 1st:0 2nd:0 3rd:0 Ran:2

2000 Turf 0-2: (10f 2) (gd 2)
Well made, currently above-average filly. Turf high 75 (began Jly).
**H R A Cecil [0-2] Exors of the late Lord Howard de Walden.*

ROSELYN BHB 68f **RR 70f** 4490[4]
2 b f Efisio 7.7f **(69)** - Ciboure (Norwick (USA)) 7.2f **(56)**
Form - 64454
Record 2000 - 1st:0 2nd:0 3rd:0 Ran:5
Win Prizemoney £0 *Total Prizemoney* £817
2000 Turf 0-5: (6f 4, 7f) (gd, g-f 4)
Above-average filly. Turf high 70 (began Jly) - 4th of 19 to Lady Kinvarrah (18 Spt Leicester 6f g-f RF 4490).
**I A Balding [0-5] & Mrs G Middlebrook.*

ROSE OF AMERICA BHB 66f **RR 53f** 5293[6]
2 ch f Brief Truce (USA) 9.1f **(73)** - Kilcoy (USA) (Secreto (USA)) 8.7f **(72)**
Form - 5036
Record 2000 - 1st:0 2nd:0 3rd:1 Ran:4
Win Prizemoney £0 *Total Prizemoney* £406
2000 Turf 0-4: (7f 4) (hvy, sft, g-s, gd)
Fair filly. Turf high 53 (began Oct) - 3rd of 12 getting 5lb from Gem Bien (26 Oct Musselburgh 7f gd RF 5189).
**Miss L A Perratt [0-4] Gordon Cowan.*

ROSE OF HYMUS BHB 42f **RR 60f** 3515[11]
3 ch f Rudimentary (USA) 8.2f **(66)** - Green's Cassatt (USA) (Apalachee (USA)) 9.4f **(71)**
Form - 0000
Record 2000 - 1st:0 2nd:0 3rd:0 Ran:4
Pre2000 - 1st:0 2nd:0 3rd:0 Ran:1
2000 Turf 0-4: (6f, 7f, 8f 2) (gd, g-f 2, frm)
Lengthy, average filly. Turf high 60.
**N A Callaghan [0-4] Mrs P A Ovenden (from J E Banks [0-1] Spt 1999).*

ROSE OF MOONCOIN (IRE) BHB 70f **RR 73f** 2731[13]
4 b f Brief Truce (USA) 9.1f **(73)** - Sharp Deposit (Sharpo) 7.7f **(59)**
Form - 66600
Record 2000 - 1st:0 2nd:0 3rd:0 Ran:5
Pre2000 - 1st:1 2nd:0 3rd:0 Ran:5
Win Prizemoney £4,308 *Total Prizemoney* £6,313
Wins 1998 Jun Newmar (GD) 6f 79 <
2000 Turf 0-5: (6f 2, 7f 2, 9f) (g-s, gd, g-f 2, frm)
Light-framed, above-average filly, has worn blinkers. Turf high 73.
**J M P Eustace [0-5] Cunningham Racing (from J E Banks [1-5] Spt 1999).*

ROSE PEEL RR 72f 5098[9]
2 b f Danehill (USA) 9.1f **(79)** - Why so Silent (Mill Reef (USA)) 10.5f **(78)**
Form - 70
Record 2000 - 1st:0 2nd:0 3rd:0 Ran:2
2000 Turf 0-2: (7f, 8f) (sft, gd)
Currently above-average filly. Turf high 72 (began Spt).
**P W Harris [0-2] Mrs P W Harris.*

ROSE'S TREASURE (IRE) BHB 37f39a **RR 38f 39a** 1788[12]
4 b f Treasure Kay 6.5f **(53)** - Euro Miss (IRE) (Double Schwartz) 7.9f **(55)**
Form - 0000050
Record 2000 - 1st:0 2nd:0 3rd:0 Ran:5
Pre2000 - 1st:1 2nd:4 3rd:0 Ran:21
Win Prizemoney £4,305 *Total Prizemoney* £8,720
Wins * 1998 Mar Doncas (GD) 5f 76 <
2000 Turf 0-5: (5f 4, 8f) (hvy, sft, gd 2, frm)
Lengthy, very moderate filly, effective 5f, acts on gd, often wears blinkers. Turf high 38. **B S Rothwell [1-26] Jack Kee.*

ROSE TINA BHB 39f **RR 31f** 4923[10]
3 b f Tina's Pet 7.4f **(56)** - Rosevear (IRE) **(43f 38a)** (Contract Law (USA))
Form - 7000
Record 2000 - 1st:0 2nd:0 3rd:0 Ran:4
2000 Turf 0-3: (8f 2, 10f) (gd, g-f, frm) 2000 AW 0-1: (16f) (Equi)
Light-framed, very moderate filly. Turf high 31.
**E A Wheeler [0-4] Church Racing Partnership.*

ROSETTA BHB 38f **RR 29f** 2565[13]
3 b f Fraam - Starawak (Star Appeal) 9.6f **(65)**
Form - 000
Record 2000 - 1st:0 2nd:0 3rd:0 Ran:3
Pre2000 - 1st:0 2nd:0 3rd:1 Ran:9
Win Prizemoney £0 *Total Prizemoney* £905
2000 Turf 0-3: (7f, 8f 2) (gd, g-f 2)
Neat, little account filly, effective 5 to 7f, acts on g-f to hrd, best on g-f. Turf high 29. Becoming disappointing.
**R J Hodges [0-12] Unity Farm Holiday Centre Ltd.*

ROSEUM BHB 89f **RR 92f** 4954a[7]
4 b f Lahib (USA) 8f **(69)** - Rose Barton (Pas de Seul) 9.1f **(67)**
Form - 6047
Record 2000 - 1st:0 2nd:0 3rd:0 Ran:4
Pre2000 - 1st:3 2nd:0 3rd:0 Ran:5
Win Prizemoney £17,018 *Total Prizemoney* £18,207
Wins * 1999 Jly Haydoc (G-S) H 6f 85 92 <
* 1999 May Newbur (SFT) H 6f 80 83
* 1999 Apr Pontef (SFT) 6f 68+
2000 Turf 0-4: (6f 3, 7f) (sft, gd 2, g-f)
Scopey, useful filly, effective 6f, acts on gd. Turf high 88 (began Aug). **R Guest [3-9].*

ROSHANI (IRE) BHB 79f **RR 77f** 3319[10]
3 b f Kris 10f **(75)** - Maratona (Be My Guest (USA)) 9.3f **(67)**
Form - 210610
Record 2000 - 1st:2 2nd:1 3rd:0 Ran:6
Pre2000 - 1st:0 2nd:0 3rd:1 Ran:3
Win Prizemoney £8,203 *Total Prizemoney* £10,564
Wins * **2000** Jly Newbur (G-F) H 10f 74 77 <
* **2000** Apr Newcas (SFT) 8f 75
2000 Turf 2-6: (8f 1-3, 9f 2, 10f 1-1) (sft 1-1, gd 2, frm 1-3)
Lengthy, above-average filly, effective 7 to 10f, acts on sft to frm, best on gd. Turf high 80 (1st run) - 2nd of 7 getting 3lb from Common Place (25 Mar Kempton 9f gd RF 0501) - also 1st of 8 getting 2lb from Safari Blues (21 Jly Newbury RF 2999). Inconsistent. She was suited by the step up to ten furlongs when winning at Newbury in July. **M R Channon [2-9] Sheikh Ahmed Al Maktoum.*

ROSIE (FR) RR 74f 5309[8]
2 ch f Bering 9.6f **(80)** - Scarlet Plume **(98f)** (Warning)
Form - 558
Record 2000 - 1st:0 2nd:0 3rd:0 Ran:3
2000 Turf 0-3: (7f 2, 8f) (g-s 2, g-f)
Currently above-average filly. Turf high 74 (began Spt).
**J L Dunlop [0-3] Nigel & Carolyn Elwes.*

ROSIES ALL THE WAY BHB 28f **RR 17f** 1673[12]
4 b f Robellino (USA) 9.5f **(68)** - No More Rosies (Warpath) 12.3f **(52)**
Form - 000
Record 2000 - 1st:0 2nd:0 3rd:0 Ran:3
Pre2000 - 1st:0 2nd:0 3rd:0 Ran:4
Win Prizemoney £0 *Total Prizemoney* £244
2000 Turf 0-2: (12f, 14f) (g-s, g-f) 2000 AW 0-1: (11f) (Fibr)
Light-framed, poor filly. Turf high 17. **C W Thornton [0-7] Guy Reed.*

ROSI'S BOY BHB 87f **RR 86f** 5110[4]
2 b c Caerleon (USA) 10.9f **(79)** - Come on Rosi (Valiyar) 8.5f **(73)**
Form - 214
Record 2000 - 1st:1 2nd:1 3rd:0 Ran:3
Win Prizemoney £4,065 *Total Prizemoney* £6,545
Wins * **2000** Aug Newmar (G-F) 8f 86 <
2000 Turf 1-3: (7f, 8f 1-2) (gd 2, g-f 1-1)
Currently useful colt. Turf high 86 (began Jly) - 1st of 6 from Taabeer (18 Aug Newmarket RF 3765). Split Londoner and Cosi Fan Tutte on his debut at Newmarket, and got off the mark on the same track next time. **J L Dunlop [1-3] Wafic Said.*

ROSOLAW (GER) RR 106f 4944a[2]
3 bl c Law Society (USA) 11.6f **(71)**
Form - 02
2000 Turf 0-2: (10f, 12f) (g-s, g-f)
Currently Pattern-class colt. Turf high 106 - 2nd of 9 getting 6lb from Aboard (3 Oct Hoppegarten 10f g-s RF 4944a).
**A Schutz in GER [0-2] Gestut Rietberg.*

ROSSE BHB 100f **RR 104f** 5239[2]
3 ch f Kris 10f **(75)** - Nuryana (Nureyev (USA)) 8.7f **(78)**
Form - 4151362
Record 2000 - 1st:2 2nd:1 3rd:1 Ran:7
Pre2000 - 1st:0 2nd:0 3rd:0 Ran:1
Win Prizemoney £9,632 *Total Prizemoney* £18,390
Wins * 2000 Jly Yarmou (GD) 7f 97 <
*** 2000** Jun Yarmou (G-F) 7f 92
2000 Turf 2-7: (7f 2-3, 8f 3, 10f) (g-s, gd 2, g-f 2-4)
Small, very useful filly, effective 7 to 8f, acts on g-s to g-f. Turf high 104 - 2nd of 11 getting 11lb from Albarahin (28 Oct Newmarket 8f g-s RF 5239) - also 1st of 6 giving 4lb to Veil of Avalon (19 Jly Yarmouth RF 2950). Both of her victories to date have come over seven furlongs at Yarmouth. Fair efforts when tried in Listed class otherwise, without setting the world alight.
**G Wragg [2-8] A E Oppenheimer.*

ROSSELLI (USA) BHB 108f **RR 104f** 4966[14]
4 b c Puissance 7.1f **(60)** - Miss Rossi (Artaius (USA)) 9f **(69)**
Form - 46702603100
Record 2000 - 1st:1 2nd:1 3rd:1 Ran:11
Pre2000 - 1st:3 2nd:0 3rd:1 Ran:9
Win Prizemoney £48,833 *Total Prizemoney* £63,173
Wins * 2000 Spt Beverl (HVY) 5f 100
1998 Jun Ascot (SFT) G3 5f 102 <
1998 Jun Beverl (G-S) 5f 94
1998 May Newcas (G-F) 5f 78+
2000 Turf 1-11: (5f 1-9, 6f 2) (g-s 1-2, gd 5, g-f 3, frm)
Scopey, very useful colt, effective 5f, acts on g-s to g-f, has worn blinkers. Turf high 104 - 6th of 21 giving 3lb to Pipalong (6 May Newmarket 5f gd RF 1061) - also 1st of 10 giving 6lb to Vita Spericolata (19 Spt Beverley RF 4496). A one-time high-class juvenile, he retains ability but has not been easy to place in the last couple of seasons. Scored in first-time blinkers at Beverley in September. **A Berry [1-11] T G Holdcroft (from J Berry [3-9] Spt 1999).*

ROSSINI (USA) RR 117f 2181[13]
3 b c Miswaki (USA) 8.1f **(81)** - Touch of Greatness (USA) (Hero's Honor (USA)) 8.2f **(86)**
Form - 430
2000 Turf 0-3: (6f 2, 8f) (g-s, gd 2)
High-class colt, effective 6 to 8f, acts on g-s to frm, does well at Curragh. Turf high 113 (1st run) - 4th of 6 giving 3lb to Umistim (20 Apr Newmarket 8f gd RF 0803). Successful in the Prix Robert Papin in 1999, he failed to train on and was not seen out after refusing to enter the stalls at Newmarket in July. Genuine despite his aversion to the stalls, he has been retired to Ballyhane Stud, County Carlow, at IR£3,500.
**A P O'Brien in IRE [3-7] M Tabor & Mrs John Magnier.*

ROSSLYN CHAPEL BHB 39f **RR 26f** 1997[14]
3 b g Petong 7.6f **(58)** - Stoneydale (Tickled Pink) 6.5f **(59)**
Form - 0
Record 2000 - 1st:0 2nd:0 3rd:0 Ran:1
Pre2000 - 1st:0 2nd:0 3rd:0 Ran:4
2000 Turf 0-1: (6f) (g-f)
Leggy, little account gelding.
**Bob Jones [0-5] The Rosslyn Chapel Partnership.*

ROSTROPOVICH (IRE) RR 111f 5051a[1]
3 gr c Sadler's Wells (USA) 11.3f **(87)** - Infamy (Shirley Heights) 10.3f **(74)**
Form - 31357431
2000 Turf 2-8: (12f 2-4, 14f, 15f 2, 16f) (g-s 1-2, gd 1-4, g-f, frm)
Group-class colt, effective 15 to 16f, acts on gd, has worn blinkers. Turf high 111. He was highly tried after winning a Galway maiden, running his best race when third in a Group 3 at Longchamp. Sold for 180,000gns at Newmarket in October, he has joined Mouse Morris and made a winning debut over hurdles at Naas in January.
**A P O'Brien in IRE [2-8] Michael Tabor.*

ROTHERHITHE BHB 30f30a **RR 38f 30a** 3088[11]
4 ch g Lycius (USA) 8.8f **(71)** - Cariellor's Miss (FR) (Cariellor (FR))
Form - 38670070
Record 2000 - 1st:0 2nd:0 3rd:0 Ran:5
Pre2000 - 1st:0 2nd:0 3rd:1 Ran:5
Win Prizemoney £0 *Total Prizemoney* £354
2000 Turf 0-2: (7f 2) (g-f, frm) 2000 AW 0-3: (6f, 7f, 8f) (Equi 3)
Light-framed, very moderate gelding. Turf high 26 (began Jly). AW high 12. Inconsistent. **T J Naughton [0-10] T J Naughton.*

ROTOSTAR BHB 40f35a **RR 38f 35a** 267[7]
4 ch f Aragon 7.7f **(58)** - Davinia (Gold Form) 5.6f **(55)**
Form - 7
Record 2000 - 1st:0 2nd:0 3rd:0 Ran:1
Pre2000 - 1st:0 2nd:0 3rd:0 Ran:9
2000 AW 0-1: (7f) (Fibr)
Light-framed, very moderate filly. Consistent.
**N M Babbage [0-1] S R Carter (from P D Evans [0-9] Jly 1999).*

ROUE RR 52f 5099[10]
2 b c Efisio 7.7f **(69)** - Ideal Home (Home Guard (USA)) 9.3f **(66)**
Form - 0
Record 2000 - 1st:0 2nd:0 3rd:0 Ran:1
2000 Turf 0-1: (7f) (gd)
Currently fair colt. **Sir Michael Stoute [0-1] Sir Evelyn De Rothschild.*

ROUGE BHB 53f76a **RR 53f 76a** 4457[2]
5 gr m Rudimentary (USA) 8.2f **(66)** - Couleur de Rose (Kalaglow) 9.8f **(67)**
Form - 20413161P32
Record 2000 - 1st:3 2nd:1 3rd:2 Ran:8
Pre2000 - 1st:1 2nd:6 3rd:2 Ran:16
Win Prizemoney £11,698 *Total Prizemoney* £20,433
Wins * 2000 Jly Windso (G-F) H 6f 45 49
2000 *Jan Lingfi (STD) C 7f 70+*
2000 *Jan Southw (STD) C 6f 72+* <
1999 Oct Wolver (STD) H 7f 64 69
2000 Turf 1-5: (6f 1-2, 7f 2, 8f) (g-s 2, gd, frm 1-2) 2000 AW 2-3: (6f 1-2, 7f 1-1) (Equi 1-1, Fibr 1-2)
Above-average filly, has broken blood-vessels, effective 6 to 7f, best at 7f, - acts on AW, best on Fibr, likes left handed tracks. Turf high 53 (began Jly). AW high 75 - also 1st of 10 giving 3lb to Elton Ledger (7 Jan Southwell RF 0040). Becoming disappointing.
**K R Burke [1-5] Nigel Shields (from J P Leigh [3-20] Jan 2000).*

ROUGE ETOILE RR 50f 4457[15]
4 b f Most Welcome 8.6f **(66)** - Choral Sundown (Night Shift (USA)) 7.2f **(69)**
Form - 000600520
Record 2000 - 1st:0 2nd:1 3rd:0 Ran:9
Pre2000 - 1st:1 2nd:0 3rd:1 Ran:6
Win Prizemoney £2,763 *Total Prizemoney* £5,768
Wins 1998 Oct Folkes (G-S) 6f 80 <
2000 Turf 0-9: (6f 2, 7f 6, 8f) (g-s 3, gd 3, g-f, frm 2)
Light-framed, fair filly, has broken blood-vessels. Turf high 50.
**E J Alston [0-9] D H A MacNair (from A J McNae [1-6] Aug 1999).*

ROUGH SHOOT BHB 78f78a **RR 75f 78a** 4193[7]
2 ch g King's Signet (USA) 7f **(51)** - Tawny (Grey Ghost) 9.9f **(60)**
Form - 15327
Record 2000 - 1st:1 2nd:1 3rd:1 Ran:5
Win Prizemoney £2,254 *Total Prizemoney* £5,157
Wins * 2000 *May Southw (STD) 5f 73* <
2000 Turf 0-4: (5f 3, 6f) (g-f 2, frm 2) 2000 AW 1-1: (5f 1-1) (Fibr 1-1)
Above-average gelding, mostly wears blinkers (extremely effectively). Turf high 75 - 2nd of 12 to Vendome (27 Aug Beverley 5f frm RF 4010). (1st run) - 1st of 15 giving 5lb to Church Mice (22 May Southwell RF 1374).
**T D Barron [1-5] Harrowgate Bloodstock Ltd.*

ROUSING THUNDER BHB 78f **RR 76f** 3534[5]
3 b c Theatrical 11.5f **(78)** - Moss (USA) (Woodman (USA)) 9f **(74)**
Form - 72815
Record 2000 - 1st:1 2nd:1 3rd:0 Ran:5
Pre2000 - 1st:0 2nd:0 3rd:2 Ran:3
Win Prizemoney £3,721 *Total Prizemoney* £5,996
Wins * 2000 Jly Pontef (G-F) 10f 69 <
2000 Turf 1-5: (10f 1-4, 11f) (gd, g-f 2, frm 1-2)
Scopey, above-average colt, effective 7 to 10f, best at 10f, acts on g-f to frm, best on frm, has worn blinkers, prefers tight tracks. Turf high 76 - 2nd of 5 getting 13lb from Colway Ritz (21 Jun Ripon 10f g-f RF 2169) - also 1st of 7 from New Iberia (21 Jly Pontefract RF

3013). Consistent. His best effort to date was when giving the older Colway Ritz a race at Ripon, and he has since made hard work of landing a maiden. **E A L Dunlop [1-8] Abdullah Ali.*

ROUTE BARREE (FR) RR 71f 5157[8]

2 ch c Exit To Nowhere (USA) 8.7f **(77)** - Star des Evees (FR) (Moulin)
Form - 8
Record 2000 - 1st:0 2nd:0 3rd:0 Ran:1
2000 Turf 0-1: (8f) (sft)
Currently above-average colt. **S Dow [0-1] Byerley Bloodstock.*

ROUTE ONE (IRE) BHB 55f RR 75f 4021[14]

7 br g Welsh Term 10.1f **(63)** - Skylin (Skyliner) 7.3f **(53)**
Form - 64500
Record 2000 - 1st:0 2nd:0 3rd:0 Ran:5
Win Prizemoney £0 *Total Prizemoney* £321
2000 Turf 0-4: (10f, 14f 3) (gd 2, g-f 2) 2000 AW 0-1: (12f) (Fibr)
Above-average gelding. Turf high 75 (began Jly).
**Andrew Reid [0-5] Andrew Cohen.*

ROUTE SIXTY SIX (IRE) BHB 60f RR 64f 5159[2]

4 b f Brief Truce (USA) 9.1f **(73)** - Lyphards Goddess (IRE) (Lyphard's Special (USA)) 10.3f **(72)**
Form - 000232232
Record 2000 - 1st:0 2nd:4 3rd:2 Ran:9
Pre2000 - 1st:2 2nd:2 3rd:0 Ran:18
Win Prizemoney £18,163 *Total Prizemoney* £30,415
Wins 1999 May Newmar (G-F) H 8f 77 82 <
1998 Oct Bright (G-S) H 7f 72 72
2000 Turf 0-9: (8f 6, 9f 3) (sft 3, gd 2, g-f, frm 3)
Scopey, average filly, effective 7 to 8f, best at 8f, acts on g-s to frm, best on frm, has worn blinkers, prefers right handed tracks, likes tight tracks. Turf high 64.
**Jedd O'Keeffe [0-7] Wetherby Racing Bureau 47 (from G L Moore [2-20] Apr 2000).*

ROVERETTO BHB 61f RR 65f 4625[4]

5 b g Robellino (USA) 9.5f **(68)** - Spring Flyer (IRE) **(56f 64a)** (Waajib)
Form - 62434
Record 2000 - 1st:0 2nd:1 3rd:1 Ran:5
Pre2000 - 1st:0 2nd:0 3rd:0 Ran:1
Win Prizemoney £0 *Total Prizemoney* £2,256
2000 Turf 0-5: (12f 2, 14f, 16f 2) (g-s, gd 2, g-f 2)
Average gelding. Turf high 65.
**Mrs M Reveley [2-14] Codan Trust Company Ltd.*

ROWAASI BHB 95f RR 86f 3370[10]

3 gr f Green Desert (USA) 7.8f **(78)** - Pamela Peach (Habitat) 9.4f **(70)**
Form - 0040
Record 2000 - 1st:0 2nd:0 3rd:0 Ran:4
Pre2000 - 1st:1 2nd:2 3rd:0 Ran:4
Win Prizemoney £11,477 *Total Prizemoney* £30,981
Wins * 1999 Jun Sandow (GD) L 5f 102++ <
2000 Turf 0-4: (5f 2, 6f 2) (gd, g-f 2, frm)
Scopey, useful filly, effective 5f, acts on g-f. Turf high 86. Consistent. She evoked memories of her late stablemate Bint Allayl when winning the National Stakes at Sandown as a juvenile, but has failed to fulfil that promise. Frustrating in that she seems to find five furlongs too sharp and six furlongs too far.
**M R Channon [1-8] Sheikh Ahmed Al Maktoum.*

ROWENA'S GIRL RR 1440[12]

2 b f Sabrehill (USA) 8.5f **(64)** - William's Bird (USA) (Master Willie) 7f **(70)**
Form - 0
Record 2000 - 1st:0 2nd:0 3rd:0 Ran:1
2000 Turf 0-1: (6f) (gd)
Currently very poor filly. **M W Easterby [0-1] Guy Reed.*

ROWLANDSONS STUD (IRE) BHB 29f29a RR 17f 29a 2280[16]

7 b br g Distinctly North (USA) 7.4f **(63)** - Be My Million (Taufan (USA)) 7f **(57)**
Form - 0006036700
Record 2000 - 1st:0 2nd:0 3rd:1 Ran:7
Pre2000 - 1st:2 2nd:2 3rd:7 Ran:39
Win Prizemoney £4,320 *Total Prizemoney* £8,991
Wins * 1998 *Jun Lingfi (STD) SH 7f 40 50*
1996 *Mar Lingfi (STD) H 6f 55 61* <
2000 Turf 0-2: (6f, 7f) (gd, frm) 2000 AW 0-5: (6f 4, 7f) (Equi 3, Fibr 2)
Very moderate gelding, effective 6f, - acts on Equi, has worn blinkers, favours left handed tracks, favours tight tracks. Turf high 17. AW high 34.
**K C Comerford [1-26] Trojan Racing 2000 (from P Burgoyne [0-6] Nov 1996).*

ROXANNE MILL BHB 73f RR 71f 5117[1]

2 b f Cyrano de Bergerac 7.3f **(58)** - It Must Be Millie **(58f 61a)** (Reprimand)
Form - 5734631
Record 2000 - 1st:1 2nd:0 3rd:2 Ran:7
Win Prizemoney £2,226 *Total Prizemoney* £3,652
Wins * 2000 *Oct Wolver (STD) 5f 71* <
2000 Turf 0-6: (5f 6) (g-s, gd 2, frm 3) 2000 AW 1-1: (5f 1-1) (Fibr 1-1)
Above-average filly, effective 5f, acts on g-s to frm - acts on Fibr. Turf high 71 - 3rd of 10 giving 9lb to Adweb (30 Spt Sandown 5f g-s RF 4751). (1st run) - 1st of 10 from Gemtastic (20 Oct Wolverhampton RF 5117).
**M D I Usher [1-7] The Goodracing Partnership.*

ROXY LABURNUM BHB 25f RR 3f 1916[10]

2 b f Eagle Eyed (USA) - Happy And Blessed (IRE) (Prince Sabo) 7.2f **(62)**
Form - 0000
Record 2000 - 1st:0 2nd:0 3rd:0 Ran:4
2000 Turf 0-3: (5f 2, 6f) (gd 2, g-f) 2000 AW 0-1: (5f) (Equi)
Very poor filly. Turf high 3.
**R M Flower [0-4] Jenningsbury Court Consultants Ltd.*

ROYAL ALIBI BHB 38f RR 30tf 5011[13]

6 b g Royal Academy (USA) 7.8f **(77)** - Excellent Alibi (USA) (Exceller (USA)) 12.5f **(74)**
Form - 0
Record 2000 - 1st:0 2nd:0 3rd:0 Ran:1
Pre2000 - 1st:0 2nd:0 3rd:0 Ran:3
Win Prizemoney £0 *Total Prizemoney* £240
2000 AW 0-1: (14f) (Fibr)
Very moderate gelding.
**D J G MurraySmith [0-3] D MurraySmith (from H R A Cecil [0-1] Jly 1998).*

ROYAL AMARETTO (IRE) BHB 90f RR 80f 4814[1]

6 b g Fairy King (USA) 7.7f **(75)** - Melbourne Miss (Chaparral (FR)) 13.7f **(90)**
Form - 4
Record 2000 - 1st:0 2nd:0 3rd:0 Ran:1
Pre2000 - 1st:2 2nd:3 3rd:3 Ran:20
Win Prizemoney £11,799 *Total Prizemoney* £30,691
Wins * 1997 Apr Newbur (G-F) 10f 110+ <
* 1996 Spt Chepst (G-F) 7.1f 86
2000 Turf 0-1: (10f) (g-s)
Decent gelding, effective 10 to 11f, acts on g-s to g-f. Becoming disappointing. Remains a useful performer, but despite finishing runner-up on a couple of occasions last season is frustrating and difficult to win with. Often employs front-running tactics.
**B J Meehan [2-21] The Harlequin Partnership.*

ROYAL ARROW (USA) RR 58f 3428[5]

4 b g Dayjur (USA) 6.8f **(79)** - Buy The Firm (USA) (Affirmed (USA)) 9.3f **(79)**
Form - 000055
Record 2000 - 1st:0 2nd:0 3rd:0 Ran:6
Pre2000 - 1st:0 2nd:0 3rd:0 Ran:4
2000 Turf 0-6: (6f 2, 7f, 8f 2, 10f) (g-s 2, gd, frm 3)
Fair gelding, has worn blinkers. Turf high 58.
**E J Alston [0-6] K Lee (from Ferdy Murphy [0-3] Aug 1999).*

ROYAL ARTIST BHB 87f85a RR 87f 85a 4991[7]

4 b g Royal Academy (USA) 7.8f **(77)** - Council Rock (General Assembly (USA)) 10f **(68)**
Form - 121262110087
Record 2000 - 1st:3 2nd:3 3rd:0 Ran:11
Pre2000 - 1st:1 2nd:1 3rd:1 Ran:5
Win Prizemoney £25,403 *Total Prizemoney* £33,521

Wins * **2000** Jly Ascot (G-F) H 6f 75 89 <
* **2000** Jly Leices (G-F) H 7f 75 87
* **2000** *Apr Wolver (STD) H 8.5f 72 78*
* 1999 *Nov Lingfi (STD) 7f 52+*

2000 Turf 2-9: (6f 1-2, 7f 1-5, 8f, 9f) (gd 3, g-f 1-2, frm 1-4) 2000 AW 1-2: (7f, 8f 1-1) (Fibr 1-2)

Workmanlike, useful gelding, effective 6 to 7f, best at 7f, acts on gd to frm. Turf high 89 - 1st of 18 getting 13lb from Cryhavoc (28 Jly Ascot RF 3164) - also 1st of 12 giving 7lb to Redswan (20 Jly Leicester RF 2974). AW high 78. He scored twice on sand over the winter and has been running well on turf. Landed a gamble in good style at Leicester in July and had no problem with the drop to six furlongs when winning a decent handicap at Ascot later the same month. Found wanting from a higher mark since.

**W J Haggas [4-16] and Mrs William Gilbert.*

ROYAL ASSAY (IRE) BHB 75f **RR 79f** 2739[4]

2 ch f Goldmark (USA) - Glenista (IRE) **(57f)**(Glenstal (USA)) 10.1f **(64)**

Form - 374

Record 2000 - 1st:0 2nd:0 3rd:1 Ran:3

Win Prizemoney £0 *Total Prizemoney* £480

2000 Turf 0-3: (5f, 6f, 7f) (gd, g-f, frm)

Currently above-average filly. Turf high 79 - 4th of 18 getting 2lb from Pairing (12 Jly Lingfield 6f g-f RF 2739).

**Mrs P N Dutfield [0-3] The Wheelwright Wanderers.*

ROYAL AXMINSTER BHB 40f **RR 40f** 3168[3]

5 b g Alzao (USA) 9.8f **(73)** - Number One Spot (Reference Point) 6.8f **(70)**

Form - 004703

Record 2000 - 1st:0 2nd:0 3rd:1 Ran:6
Pre2000 - 1st:0 2nd:0 3rd:0 Ran:6

Win Prizemoney £0 *Total Prizemoney* £427

2000 Turf 0-6: (10f, 12f 4, 18f) (gd, g-f 3, frm 2)

Moderate gelding, effective 17f, acts on frm, has worn blinkers, likes tight tracks. Turf high 40.

**Mrs P N Dutfield [0-12] Axminster Carpets Ltd.*

ROYAL CANARY (IRE) BHB 41f **RR 24f** 1684[6]

3 ch g Prince of Birds (USA) - Inesse (Simply Great (FR)) 8.2f **(65)**

Form - 0806

Record 2000 - 1st:0 2nd:0 3rd:0 Ran:4
Pre2000 - 1st:0 2nd:1 3rd:0 Ran:4

Win Prizemoney £0 *Total Prizemoney* £632

2000 Turf 0-4: (5f 2, 7f, 11f) (gd 2, frm 2)

Workmanlike, little account gelding, effective 5f, acts on g-f. Turf high 24. Inconsistent.

**Miss L A Perratt [0-8] Clayton Bigley Partnership Ltd.*

ROYAL CASCADE (IRE) BHB 45f53a **RR 41f 53a** 5245[6]

6 b g River Falls 8.2f **(56)** - Relative Stranger (Cragador) 6f **(67)**

Form - 3500638202015826

Record 2000 - 1st:1 2nd:3 3rd:1 Ran:13
Pre2000 - 1st:8 2nd:4 3rd:1 Ran:35

Win Prizemoney £21,284 *Total Prizemoney* £26,732

Wins * **2000** *Aug Wolver (STD) S 6f 58*
* 1999 *Feb Southw (STD) H 7f 72 81+* <
* 1999 *Feb Wolver (STD) H 6f 66 71*
* 1999 *Jan Southw (STD) C 7f 70*
* 1998 *Dec Wolver (STD) C 6f 57*
* 1998 *Mar Wolver (STD) C 6f 65*
* 1998 *Feb Southw (STD) C 6f 69*
* 1998 *Jan Southw (STD) S 6f 53*
* 1997 *Feb Wolver (STD) S 6f 51*

2000 Turf 0-2: (6f, 7f) (frm, hrd) 2000 AW 1-11: (6f 1-3, 7f 5, 8f 3) (Fibr 1-11)

Fair gelding, effective 7f, - acts on Fibr, often wears blinkers (effectively), favours left handed tracks. Turf high 41. AW high 64.

**B A McMahon [9-48] R L Bedding.*

ROYAL CASTLE (IRE) BHB 70f **RR 72f** 2751[7]

6 b g Caerleon (USA) 10.9f **(79)** - Sun Princess (English Prince) 10.1f **(61)**

Form - 6507

Record 2000 - 1st:0 2nd:0 3rd:0 Ran:4
Pre2000 - 1st:2 2nd:1 3rd:2 Ran:14

Win Prizemoney £7,252 *Total Prizemoney* £11,786

Wins 1997 Oct Redcar (G-F) H 14.1f 74 80 <
1997 Jun Pontef (G-F) H 12f 70 73

2000 Turf 0-4: (14f 2, 16f, 18f) (gd, g-f 2, frm)

Above-average gelding, effective 14 to 16f, best at 14f, acts on g-f to frm, best on g-f, has worn blinkers. Turf high 72 (1st run) - 6th of 16 getting 7lb from Dominant Duchess (17 May York 14f g-f RF 1266). Consistent. Bred to be decent, he is probably better known as a hurdler these days and his form on the Flat is nothing out of the ordinary. Best on fast ground.

**M H Tompkins [2-15] Mrs B Cross & M Sakal (from M P Tregoning [0-3] Oct 1998).*

ROYAL CAVALIER BHB 73f80a **RR 76f 80a** 5299[4]

3 b g Prince of Birds (USA) - Gold Belt (IRE) (Bellypha) 9.8f **(73)**

Form - 27341070627064054

Record 2000 - 1st:1 2nd:1 3rd:1 Ran:16
Pre2000 - 1st:0 2nd:2 3rd:1 Ran:5

Win Prizemoney £2,758 *Total Prizemoney* £8,906

Wins * **2000** *Mar Wolver (STD) 9.4f 76* <

2000 Turf 0-12: (7f 3, 8f 7, 10f 2) (sft, g-s 4, gd 2, g-f 2, frm 3) 2000 AW 1-4: (8f 2, 9f 1-2) (Fibr 1-4)

Scopey, above-average gelding, effective 7 to 9f, best at 8f, acts on g-s to frm - acts on Fibr. Turf high 76. AW high 76 - 1st of 7 from Sea Squirt (25 Mar Wolverhampton RF 0506). Took his time getting off the mark, but did so in a maiden on the Wolverhampton Fibresand in March. That form is nothing special and he also does not look the easiest of rides. **R Hollinshead [1-21] The Three R's.*

ROYAL COMMAND (IRE) **RR 96f** 3675a[7]

4 b c Green Desert (USA) 7.8f **(78)** - Elegance in Design (Habitat) 9.4f **(70)**

Form - 85017

2000 Turf 1-5: (6f 1-3, 7f, 9f) (g-s, gd 2, g-f 1-2)

Very useful colt, effective 6 to 8f, acts on hvy to g-f. Turf high 96 - also 1st of 6 giving 10lb to Regal Ash (22 Jly Leopardstown RF 3117a). He reverted to sprinting in the second half of the season, but struggled when tried in Group company. High in the handicap, he will be difficult to place.

**D K Weld in IRE [2-7] Moyglare Stud Farm.*

ROYAL CZARINA BHB 37f39a **RR 28f 39a** 3921[9]

3 ch f Czaravich (USA) - Sabrata (IRE) (Zino) 12.9f **(54)**

Form - 78700

Record 2000 - 1st:0 2nd:0 3rd:0 Ran:4
Pre2000 - 1st:0 2nd:0 3rd:0 Ran:1

2000 Turf 0-2: (5f, 12f) (gd, g-f) 2000 AW 0-2: (8f, 9f) (Fibr 2)

Leggy, little account filly. Turf high 28 (began Aug). AW high 27.

**M Salaman [0-5] M Salaman.*

ROYAL DOLPHIN (IRE) BHB 27f **RR 29f** 3192[16]

4 b c Dolphin Street (FR) - Diamond Lake (Kings Lake (USA)) 10.8f **(67)**

Form - 007433604000

Record 2000 - 1st:0 2nd:0 3rd:2 Ran:11
Pre2000 - 1st:0 2nd:0 3rd:0 Ran:7

Win Prizemoney £0 *Total Prizemoney* £858

2000 Turf 0-4: (8f, 10f 2, 12f) (g-s, g-f, frm 2) 2000 AW 0-7: (8f 4, 9f, 11f, 16f) (Fibr 7)

Workmanlike, very moderate colt, effective 8f, - acts on Fibr, has worn blinkers. Turf high 29. AW high 51 - 3rd of 9 getting 4lb from Be Warned (17 Mar Southwell 8f Fibr RF 0459). Becoming disappointing.

**A Smith [0-5] B Auchterlounie (from B A McMahon [0-14] Mar 2000).*

ROYAL EAGLE (USA) BHB 89f **RR 95f** 4308[11]

3 b c Eagle Eyed (USA) - Accountinquestion (USA) (Classic Account (USA))

Form - 703870

Record 2000 - 1st:0 2nd:0 3rd:1 Ran:6
Pre2000 - 1st:1 2nd:2 3rd:0 Ran:4

Win Prizemoney £3,501 *Total Prizemoney* £7,972

Wins * 1999 Jly Epsom (G-F) 7f 76+ <

2000 Turf 0-6: (8f, 10f, 12f 3, 15f) (gd 5, frm)

Scopey, very useful colt, effective 7 to 12f, best at 12f, acts on gd. Turf high 95 - 7th of 10 getting 3lb from Blue Gold (2 Aug Goodwood 12f gd RF 3318). He has been ridden in a variety of styles but does not seem to finish his races. Basically disappointing, he is one to watch at present.

**P F I Cole [1-10] Luciano Gaucci.*

ROYAL ENCLOSURE (IRE) BHB 58f **RR 48f** 5132[19]

2 b c Royal Academy (USA) 7.8f **(77)** - Hi Bettina (Henbit (USA)) 9f **(61)**
Form - 000
Record 2000 - 1st:0 2nd:0 3rd:0 Ran:3
2000 Turf 0-3: (6f, 7f 2) (sft, g-f, frm)
Currently moderate colt, has worn blinkers. Turf high 48 (began Aug). **B J Meehan [0-3] Mrs Susan Roy.*

ROYAL EXPOSURE (IRE) RR 32f 4877[2]

3 b g Emperor Jones (USA) - Blue Garter (Targowice (USA)) 11.4f **(70)**
Form - 02
Record 2000 - 1st:0 2nd:1 3rd:0 Ran:2
Win Prizemoney £0 *Total Prizemoney* £564
2000 Turf 0-2: (10f 2) (g-s, g-f)
Workmanlike, currently very moderate gelding. Turf high 32 (began Jly) - 2nd of 17 to Centaur Spirit (9 Oct Leicester 10f g-s RF 4877). **W J Musson [0-2] W J Musson.*

ROYAL EXPRESSION BHB 68f65a **RR 73f 65a** 5322[9]

8 b g Sylvan Express 9.6f **(45)** - Edwin's Princess (Owen Dudley) 8.3f **(61)**
Form - 5201631231630000

Record	**2000** -	1st:2	2nd:1	3rd:3	Ran:12
	Pre2000 -	1st:6	2nd:9	3rd:5	Ran:39

Win Prizemoney £26,003 *Total Prizemoney* £41,965

Wins							
*** 2000**	Mar Doncas	(GD)	H	18f	70	74	<
*** 2000**	*Feb Wolver*	*(STD)*	*H*	*16.2f*	*60*	*64+*	
1999	*Dec Wolver*	*(STD)*	*H*	*16.2f*	*58*	*66*	
1999	Aug Nottin	(G-F)	H	16f	64	71	
1997	Jun Redcar	(FRM)	C	16f		55	
1996	May Carlis	(GD)	H	14.1f	65	72	
1996	May Beverl	(G-F)	H	16.2f	59	67	

2000 Turf 1-7: (12f, 17f 3, 18f 1-2, 19f) (sft, g-s 2, gd 1-3, g-f) 2000 AW 1-5: (16f 1-5) (Fibr 1-5)
Above-average gelding, effective 14 to 18f, best at 17f, acts on gd to frm - acts on Fibr, best on gd, has worn blinkers, favours left handed tracks, likes tight tracks, does well at Doncaster, likes Wolverhampton. Turf high 74 (1st run) - 1st of 12 giving 16lb to Pen Friend (24 Mar Doncaster RF 0487). AW high 66 - 2nd of 7 giving 9lb to Maknaas (2 Mar Wolverhampton 16f Fibr RF 0396). Successful on the Fibresand in February, he scored at the opening Doncaster meeting but has been held since.
**G M Moore [2-11] Mrs A Roddis (from F Jordan [4-19] Jan 2000).*

ROYAL FLAME (IRE) BHB 68f64a **RR 70f 64a** 120[6]

4 b f Royal Academy (USA) 7.8f **(77)** - Samnaun (USA) (Stop The Music (USA)) 9.2f **(71)**
Form - 4316

Record	**2000** -	1st:1	2nd:0	3rd:0	Ran:2
	Pre2000 -	1st:0	2nd:1	3rd:1	Ran:9

Win Prizemoney £2,782 *Total Prizemoney* £5,092
Wins * 2000 *Jan Lingfi (STD) 10f 53+* <
2000 AW 1-2: (9f, 10f 1-1) (Equi 1-1, Fibr)
Workmanlike, above-average filly, effective 8 to 10f, best at 8f, acts on g-s to frm, best on frm, has worn blinkers. AW high 53 (1st run). **J W Hills [1-11] Willy Coleman.*

ROYAL GENT RR 4108[16]

2 b g Presidium 7.5f **(56)** - Harem Queen (Prince Regent (FR)) 9.8f **(54)**
Form - 0
Record 2000 - 1st:0 2nd:0 3rd:0 Ran:1
2000 Turf 0-1: (8f) (gd)
Currently very poor gelding. **L R Lloyd-James [0-1] Mrs M Lingwood.*

ROYAL GLEN (IRE) RR 64f 4198[6]

2 b f Royal Abjar (USA) - Sea Glen (IRE) (Glenstal (USA)) 10.1f **(64)**
Form - 36
Record 2000 - 1st:0 2nd:0 3rd:1 Ran:2
Win Prizemoney £0 *Total Prizemoney* £530
2000 Turf 0-2: (6f 2) (g-f 2)
Currently average filly. Turf high 64 (began Jly).
**Martyn Wane [0-2] James Kennerley.*

ROYAL HIGHLANDER (IRE) RR 98f 797[5]

3 b c Foxhound (USA) - Sky Lover (Ela-Mana-Mou) 10.1f **(70)**
Form - 5

Record	**2000** -	1st:0	2nd:0	3rd:0	Ran:1
	Pre2000 -	1st:1	2nd:0	3rd:0	Ran:1

Win Prizemoney £3,810 *Total Prizemoney* £4,560
Wins 1999 Nov Doncas (SFT) 6f 83++ <
2000 Turf 0-1: (7f) (gd)
Currently very useful colt. Fancied for the 2000 Guineas after winning his only start as a juvenile (form did not work out), he pulled a muscle when unplaced in the Free Handicap and has reportedly been sent to America.
**J W Hills [0-1] Team Valor (from A G Foster [1-1] Nov 1999).*

ROYAL INSULT BHB 76f80a **RR 79f 80a** 4483[9]

3 ch g Lion Cavern (USA) 7.5f **(74)** - Home Truth (Known Fact (USA)) 7.4f **(67)**
Form - 0700

Record	**2000** -	1st:0	2nd:0	3rd:0	Ran:4
	Pre2000 -	1st:1	2nd:1	3rd:0	Ran:2

Win Prizemoney £3,247 *Total Prizemoney* £4,287
Wins * 1999 Oct Redcar (GD) 6f 77 <
2000 Turf 0-4: (6f, 7f, 8f 2) (g-s, gd, g-f, frm)
Scopey, above-average gelding, effective 6f, acts on frm. Turf high 79. **K R Burke [1-6] Mrs Julie Mitchell.*

ROYAL IVY BHB 60f52a **RR 65f 52a** 4729[11]

3 ch f Mujtahid (USA) 7.4f **(69)** - Royal Climber (Kings Lake (USA)) 10.8f **(67)**
Form - 2231005420060

Record	**2000** -	1st:1	2nd:2	3rd:1	Ran:12
	Pre2000 -	1st:0	2nd:1	3rd:1	Ran:8

Win Prizemoney £2,808 *Total Prizemoney* £8,283
Wins * 2000 *Jan Lingfi (STD) 7f 55* <
2000 Turf 0-8: (7f 7, 8f) (gd 3, g-f 3, frm 2) 2000 AW 1-4: (7f 1-2, 8f, 9f) (Equi 1-3, Fibr)
Workmanlike, average filly, effective 6 to 8f, best at 7f, acts on sft to frm - acts on Equi, does well at Lingfield. Turf high 68 - 2nd of 11 getting 13lb from Big Future (1 Jly Lingfield 7f frm RF 2437). AW high 67 (1st run) - 2nd of 10 getting 5lb from Thats All Folks (5 Jan Lingfield 8f Equi RF 0025). Very consistent, but her only win to date came on Equitrack. Looks best over seven furlongs but does stay a mile.
**J Akehurst [1-12] The Goldmine Partnership (from B W Hills [0-8] Dec 1999).*

ROYAL KINGDOM (IRE) RR 111?f 1263[6]

3 b c Fairy King (USA) 7.7f **(75)** - Allicance (USA) (Alleged (USA)) 10f **(76)**
Form - 55
2000 Turf 0-2: (8f, 10f) (hvy, g-f)
Group-class colt, effective 8f, acts on sft. Turf high 98. A game winner of the Group 2 Royal Lodge Stakes in 1999 (beat Best Of The Bests), he moved appallingly when last in the Dante Stakes and was not seen again. Likely to stay beyond a mile and a quarter, he has some questions to answer.
**A P O'Brien in IRE [3-6] M Tabor & Mrs John Magnier.*

ROYAL KISS (IRE) RR 59f 5236[14]

2 b f Royal Academy (USA) 7.8f **(77)** - Hawajiss **(107df)** (Kris) 9.5f **(73)**
Form - 00
Record 2000 - 1st:0 2nd:0 3rd:0 Ran:2
2000 Turf 0-2: (7f, 8f) (g-s, gd)
Currently fair filly. Turf high 59 (began Oct).
**E A L Dunlop [0-2] Maktoum Al Maktoum.*

ROYAL MEASURE BHB 43f38a **RR 52f 38a** 4692[12]

4 b g Inchinor 8.9f **(64)** - Sveltissima (Dunphy) 9.4f **(57)**
Form - 3070

Record	**2000** -	1st:0	2nd:0	3rd:1	Ran:4
	Pre2000 -	1st:0	2nd:0	3rd:0	Ran:8

Win Prizemoney £0 *Total Prizemoney* £907
2000 Turf 0-4: (12f 2, 13f, 14f) (gd 2, g-f, frm)
Leggy, fair gelding. Turf high 52.
**B R Millman [0-12] The Royal Partnership.*

ROYAL MINSTREL (IRE) RR 86f 4815[13]

3 ch c Be My Guest (USA) 10.2f **(66)** - Shanntabariya (IRE) (Shernazar) 10.2f **(73)**
Form - 3145270

Record 2000 - 1st:1 2nd:1 3rd:1 Ran:7
Pre2000 - 1st:0 2nd:0 3rd:0 Ran:3
Win Prizemoney £4,445 *Total Prizemoney* £7,987
Wins * **2000** Apr Thirsk (SFT) 12f 87 <
2000 Turf 1-7: (10f, 12f 1-4, 13f, 15f) (g-s 1-2, gd 3, frm 2)
Scopey, useful colt, effective 10 to 15f, acts on g-s to frm, has worn blinkers, likes left handed tracks. Turf high 87 - 1st of 3 from River Bann (14 Apr Thirsk RF 0720).
**M H Tompkins [1-10] Mrs Debbie Sakal.*

ROYAL MOUNT BHB 36a **RR 72+f 36a** 28[12]

4 ch g Cadeaux Genereux 7.9f **(76)** - Hawait Al Barr (Green Desert (USA)) 8.6f **(78)**
Form - 00
Record 2000 - 1st:0 2nd:0 3rd:0 Ran:1
Pre2000 - 1st:0 2nd:0 3rd:0 Ran:2
2000 AW 0-1: (12f) (Equi)
Workmanlike, currently above-average gelding. Shaped quite well on her debut.
**K T Ivory [0-2] Dean Ivory (from M Johnston [0-1] Jun 1998).*

ROYAL MUSICAL BHB 45f **RR 49f** 5053[14]

2 ch f Royal Abjar (USA) - Musical Sally (USA) (The Minstrel (CAN)) 10f **(72)**
Form - 50070
Record 2000 - 1st:0 2nd:0 3rd:0 Ran:5
2000 Turf 0-5: (5f, 6f 2, 7f 2) (sft, g-f 2, frm 2)
Moderate filly. Turf high 49.
**M Brittain [0-5] Bob Abson BJK Partnership.*

ROYAL ORIGINE (IRE) BHB 49f39a **RR 54f 39a** 199[10]

4 b g Royal Academy (USA) 7.8f **(77)** - Belle Origine (USA) (Exclusive Native (USA)) 9.1f **(81)**
Form - 08070
Record 2000 - 1st:0 2nd:0 3rd:0 Ran:4
Pre2000 1st:0 2nd:0 3rd:2 Ran:9
Win Prizemoney £0 *Total Prizemoney* £1,915
2000 AW 0-4: (6f 3, 7f) (Equi, Fibr 3)
Light-framed, fair gelding. AW high 39.
**J R Jenkins [0-7] R M Ellis (from M Quinn [0-2] Oct 1999).*

ROYAL PARTNERSHIP (IRE) BHB 51f47a **RR 59?f 47a** 1373[1]

4 b g Royal Academy (USA) 7.8f **(77)** - Go Honey Go (General Assembly (USA)) 10f **(68)**
Form - P5140203051
Record 2000 - 1st:2 2nd:1 3rd:1 Ran:11
Pre2000 - 1st:0 2nd:0 3rd:2 Ran:6
Win Prizemoney £3,740 *Total Prizemoney* £5,156
Wins * **2000** *May Southw (STD) C 11f 47* <
* **2000** *Feb Southw (STD) S 11f 45*
2000 Turf 0-1: (9f) (gd) 2000 AW 2-10: (8f 4, 11f 2-5, 12f) (Equi, Fibr 2-9)
Fair gelding, effective 7f, acts on g-f, has worn blinkers. AW high 55. **K R Burke [2-11] Tendorra (from J Oxx in IRE [0-6] Oct 1999).*

ROYAL PASTIMES BHB 25f **RR 37df** 4455[10]

3 b f Ezzoud (IRE) - Royal Recreation (USA) (His Majesty (USA)) 10.9f **(82)**
Form - 60500
Record 2000 - 1st:0 2nd:0 3rd:0 Ran:5
Pre2000 - 1st:0 2nd:0 3rd:0 Ran:5
2000 Turf 0-4: (8f, 11f, 12f, 14f) (sft, g-s, gd, frm) 2000 AW 0-1: (8f) (Fibr)
Light-framed, very moderate filly. Turf high 37.
**Martyn Wane [0-12] J P Slattery.*

ROYAL PATRON BHB 65f **RR 69f** 4192[7]

4 ch f Royal Academy (USA) 7.8f **(77)** - Indian Queen (Electric) 10.1f **(61)**
Form - 235467
Record 2000 - 1st:0 2nd:1 3rd:1 Ran:6
Pre2000 - 1st:1 2nd:1 3rd:0 Ran:7
Win Prizemoney £3,013 *Total Prizemoney* £5,967
Wins * 1999 Aug Lingfi (GD) 14f 75 <
2000 Turf 0-6: (12f, 13f 2, 14f 2, 16f) (g-f 4, frm 2)
Leggy, average filly, effective 12 to 16f, acts on gd to frm, best on gd, likes left handed tracks, favours tight tracks, excels at Redcar. Turf high 70 (1st run) - 2nd of 11 giving 20lb to Sure Quest (10 Apr Windsor 12f frm RF 0656). Consistent. Out of an Ascot Gold Cup winner, she is a rather one-paced stayer.
**J L Dunlop [1-13] Sir Gordon Brunton.*

ROYAL PLUM RR 4624[13]

4 ch g Inchinor 8.9f **(64)** - Miss Plum **(75f)** (Ardross) 10.6f **(68)**
Form - 0
Record 2000 - 1st:0 2nd:0 3rd:0 Ran:1
2000 Turf 0-1: (12f) (gd)
Lengthy, formerly very poor gelding.
**Mrs M Reveley [1-5] Lucayan Stud.*

ROYAL REBEL BHB 116f **RR 119f** 5212a[6]

4 b g Robellino (USA) 9.5f **(68)** - Greenvera (USA) (Riverman (USA)) 9.1f **(76)**
Form - 812211326
Record 2000 - 1st:3 2nd:3 3rd:1 Ran:9
Pre2000 - 1st:2 2nd:1 3rd:2 Ran:11
Win Prizemoney £127,156 *Total Prizemoney* £178,718
Wins * **2000** Aug York (GD) G3 15.9f 119 <
* **2000** Aug Goodwo (GD) G2 16f 119 <
* **2000** May Leopar (GD) L 14f 103
* 1999 Aug Leopar (GD) L 14f 103+
* 1999 Apr Newcas (GD) 8f 82
2000 Turf 3-9: (14f 1-3, 16f 2-5, 20f) (hvy, g-s 2, gd 3-6)
Well made, high-class gelding, effective 11 to 20f, best at 16f, acts on gd, often wears blinkers (extremely effectively), likes left handed tracks. Turf high 119 - 1st of 5 giving 2lb to Rainbow High (22 Aug York RF 3851) - also 1st of 8 from Far Cry (3 Aug Goodwood RF 3342). Consistent. A lazy individual, he responded well to the fitting of blinkers and Mick Kinane's urgings when winning the Goodwood Cup and Lonsdale Stakes. An out-and-out stayer, he continues to improve and should pay a leading role in the Cup races this term. **M Johnston [5-20] P D Savill.*

ROYAL REPRIMAND (IRE) BHB 51f **RR 50f** 5165[6]

5 b g Reprimand 8.2f **(63)** - Lake Ormond (Kings Lake (USA)) 10.8f **(67)**
Form - 700775243236
Record 2000 - 1st:0 2nd:2 3rd:2 Ran:12
Pre2000 - 1st:0 2nd:1 3rd:0 Ran:13
Win Prizemoney £0 *Total Prizemoney* £4,928
2000 Turf 0-12: (7f 6, 8f 3, 10f, 12f, 14f) (sft, g-s, gd 2, g-f, frm 5, hrd 2)
Fair gelding, effective 7 to 9f, acts on gd to hrd, has worn blinkers. Turf high 50 - 2nd of 7 to Sloane (25 Aug Newcastle 7f hrd RF 3960). **R E Barr [0-25] J C Garbutt.*

ROYAL RESULT (USA) BHB 83f **RR 88f** 5317[13]

7 b br g Gone West (USA) 7.8f **(82)** - Norette (Northfields (USA)) 9f **(72)**
Form - 8003644005600
Record 2000 - 1st:0 2nd:0 3rd:1 Ran:13
Pre2000 - 1st:6 2nd:4 3rd:5 Ran:43
Win Prizemoney £63,217 *Total Prizemoney* £95,334
Wins * 1999 Aug Goodwo (GD) H 6f 82 86 <
* 1999 Jly York (G-F) H 6f 75 81
* 1998 Spt Ayr (G-S) H 6f 76 80
* 1998 Spt York (GD) H 7f 70 75
1997 Oct Newmar (G-F) H 7f 65 72
1996 Aug Thirsk (G-F) 8f 56
2000 Turf 0-13: (6f 10, 7f 3) (sft 2, gd 7, g-f 3, frm)
Useful gelding, effective 6f, acts on gd to g-f, best on gd, has worn blinkers, excels at Ayr and Goodwood. Turf high 89 - 4th of 22 giving 5lb to Blue Mountain (2 Jly Goodwood 6f g-f RF 2461). A very useful sprint handicapper, he was very high in the handicap at the start of last season, but has dropped a bit since then and ran a blinder to finish fourth in the Stewards Cup. Suited by patient tactics. **D Nicholls [4-32] Phil Lake (from M W Easterby [1-12] Jly 1998).*

ROYAL ROMEO BHB 70f65a **RR 74f 65a** 5165[7]

3 ch g Timeless Times (USA) 6.1f **(56)** - Farinara (Dragonara Palace (USA)) 6.1f **(55)**
Form - 01638085037
Record 2000 - 1st:1 2nd:0 3rd:2 Ran:11
Pre2000 - 1st:1 2nd:0 3rd:1 Ran:5
Win Prizemoney £7,989 *Total Prizemoney* £10,334

Wins *** 2000** Jun Newcas (SFT) H 6f 70 74 <
* 1999 Spt Beverl (GD) 5f 69
2000 Turf 1-11: (5f 4, 6f 1-5, 7f 2) (sft 1-2, g-s 2, gd 3, g-f, frm 3)
Above-average gelding, effective 5 to 6f, best at 6f, acts on sft to gd, best on sft. Turf high 74 - 1st of 12 giving 12lb to Lordofenchantment (7 Jun Newcastle RF 1790).
**T D Easterby [2-16] Peter Bourke.*

ROYAL SATIN (IRE) BHB 35f **RR 30f** 5219[7]
2 b c Royal Academy (USA) 7.8f **(77)** - Satinette (Shirley Heights) 10.3f **(74)**
Form - 007
Record 2000 - 1st:0 2nd:0 3rd:0 Ran:3
2000 Turf 0-3: (7f 2, 10f) (sft, g-f, frm)
Currently very moderate colt. Turf high 30 (began Aug).
**N A Callaghan [0-3] T Mohan.*

ROYAL SIGNET BHB 30f **RR 35tf** 3818[12]
5 ch m King's Signet (USA) 7f **(51)** - Ladiz (Persian Bold) 9.3f **(66)**
Form - 450
Record 2000 - 1st:0 2nd:0 3rd:0 Ran:3
Pre2000 - 1st:0 2nd:0 3rd:0 Ran:11
Win Prizemoney £0 *Total Prizemoney* £542
2000 Turf 0-3: (12f 2, 13f) (g-f, frm 2)
Very moderate filly, effective 13f, acts on gd, favours left handed tracks. Turf high 35 (began Jly). **M J Weeden [0-14] M J Weeden.*

ROYAL SIX (IRE) BHB 36f **RR 65f** 1208[12]
7 b g Syrtos 8.1f **(57)** - Tumble On (Tumble Wind (USA)) 7.5f **(57)**
Form - 00
Record 2000 - 1st:0 2nd:0 3rd:0 Ran:2
Pre2000 - 1st:0 2nd:0 3rd:0 Ran:3
2000 AW 0-2: (7f, 8f) (Fibr 2)
Average gelding. AW high 26.
**N P Littmoden [0-2] Nick Littmoden (from Cathal McCarthy in IRE [0-4] Oct 1999).*

ROYAL SOUTH (IRE) BHB 33f **RR 81f** 5180a[14]
7 b g Common Grounds 8.1f **(66)** - Arkadina's Million (King of Clubs) 7.1f **(57)**
Form - 103703430000
2000 Turf 0-11: (7f 6, 8f 3, 9f, 11f) (sft 2, g-s 3, gd 4, g-f 2)
Decent gelding, effective 7 to 9f, acts on sft to g-f, best on g-f, does well at Galway, likes Leopardstown. Turf high 90 - 3rd of 17 giving 4lb to Tushna (1 Aug Galway 8f g-s RF 3458a). Inconsistent. He is on a long losing run and looked regressive in the second half of last season.
**D McDonogh in IRE [7-42] Stephen Curran (from P S Felgate [0-9] Aug 1997).*

ROYAL TARRAGON BHB 37f33a **RR 49f 33a** 4059[10]
4 b f Aragon 7.7f **(58)** - Lady Philippa (IRE) (Taufan (USA)) 7f **(57)**
Form - 000000
Record 2000 - 1st:0 2nd:0 3rd:0 Ran:6
Pre2000 - 1st:0 2nd:0 3rd:0 Ran:14
2000 Turf 0-6: (6f 2, 7f 4) (sft, gd 2, frm 3)
Light-framed, moderate filly, has worn blinkers. Turf high 49. Inconsistent.
**W de Best-Turner [0-6] The Crown Racing Club (from J R Arnold [0-14] Aug 1999).*

ROYAL TEMPTATION (USA) RR 62f 5058[8]
3 b g Ghazi (USA) - Heirloom Majesty (USA) (His Majesty (USA)) 10.9f **(82)**
Form - 5748
Record 2000 - 1st:0 2nd:0 3rd:0 Ran:4
Win Prizemoney £0 *Total Prizemoney* £336
2000 Turf 0-4: (9f, 10f 2, 11f) (sft 2, gd, frm)
Average gelding. Turf high 62.
**Jedd O'Keeffe [0-2] Only For Fun Partnership (from D K Weld in IRE [0-2] Jun 2000).*

ROYAL TRYST (USA) RR 87f 4485[3]
3 ch c Kingmambo (USA) 10.9f **(85)** - In On The Secret (USA) (Secretariat (USA)) 9f **(79)**
Form - 213
Record 2000 - 1st:1 2nd:1 3rd:1 Ran:3
Win Prizemoney £6,698 *Total Prizemoney* £9,776
Wins *** 2000** Spt York (GD) 10.4f 68+ <
2000 Turf 1-3: (10f 1-2, 12f) (g-s, gd, g-f 1-1)
Well made, currently useful colt. Turf high 87 (1st run) (began Jly) - 2nd of 9 giving 5lb to Inaaq (13 Jly Newmarket 10f gd RF 2775).
**Sir Michael Stoute [1-3] Sheikh Mohammed.*

ROYAL WANDERER (IRE) BHB 45f **RR 27f** 5114[7]
2 ch c Royal Abjar (USA) - Rose 'n Reason (IRE) (Reasonable (FR))
Form - 707
Record 2000 - 1st:0 2nd:0 3rd:0 Ran:3
2000 Turf 0-2: (6f 2) (gd, frm) 2000 AW 0-1: (9f) (Fibr)
Currently very moderate colt. Turf high 27 (began Aug).
**Mrs A Duffield [0-3] Bill Martin.*

ROYAL WAVE (IRE) BHB 47f47a **RR 40f 47a** 5165[11]
4 b br g Polish Precedent (USA) 9f **(73)** - Mashmoon (USA) (Habitat) 9.4f **(70)**
Form - 0030
Record 2000 - 1st:0 2nd:0 3rd:1 Ran:3
Pre2000 - 1st:1 2nd:0 3rd:0 Ran:7
Win Prizemoney £2,463 *Total Prizemoney* £2,744
Wins 1999 May Pontef (GD) 6f 80 <
2000 Turf 0-2: (7f 2) (gd, g-f) 2000 AW 0-1: (8f) (Fibr)
Scopey, moderate gelding, effective 6f, acts on gd, likes left handed tracks. Turf high 40 (began Aug).
**J L Eyre [0-6] Messrs Cunningham,Hardy,Mason,Jordan (from Mrs A Duffield [1-3] Spt 1999).*

ROYLE FAMILY BHB 44f44a **RR 45f 44a** 4182[12]
2 b c King's Signet (USA) 7f **(51)** - Ichor **(30df)** (Primo Dominie) 6.2f **(80)**
Form - 454540
Record 2000 - 1st:0 2nd:0 3rd:0 Ran:6
2000 Turf 0-2: (5f 2) (g-s, frm) 2000 AW 0-4: (5f 4) (Equi, Fibr 3)
Moderate colt, effective 5f, - acts on Fibr. Turf high 45. AW high 52 (1st run) - 4th of 9 giving 5lb to Countess Bankes (10 Apr Southwell 5f Fibr RF 0647). **A Berry [0-6] Alan Berry.*

ROYMILLON (GER) BHB 79f92a **RR 42f 92a** 4633[9]
6 b g Milesius (USA) - Royal Slope (USA) (His Majesty (USA)) 10.9f **(82)**
Form - 00
Record 2000 - 1st:0 2nd:0 3rd:0 Ran:2
2000 Turf 0-1: (8f) (g-s) 2000 AW 0-1: (10f) (Equi)
Currently above-average gelding.
**D J Wintle [0-1] John Egan (from Mrs A Glodde in GER [0-1] Mar 2000).*

ROZARY RR 3608[15]
2 b f Ezzoud (IRE) - Lady Confess **(41f 36a)** (Backchat (USA))
Form - 70
Record 2000 - 1st:0 2nd:0 3rd:0 Ran:2
2000 Turf 0-2: (5f, 7f) (g-f, frm)
Currently very poor filly. (began Aug).
**B C Morgan [0-2] Mrs R E Tate.*

ROZEL (IRE) BHB 88f **RR 91f** 4716a[2]
3 ch f Wolfhound (USA) 7.3f **(71)** - Noirmant (Dominion) 8.5f **(63)**
Form - 813432
Record 2000 - 1st:1 2nd:1 3rd:2 Ran:6
Win Prizemoney £3,770 *Total Prizemoney* £13,874
Wins *** 2000** May Yarmou (GD) 5.2f 79+ <
2000 Turf 1-6: (5f 1-6) (sft, gd 1-2, g-f, frm, hrd)
Lengthy, useful filly, effective 5f, acts on sft to frm. Turf high 91 - 3rd of 17 giving 6lb to Honesty Fair (23 Aug York 5f frm RF 3918). Unraced as a juvenile, she made great strides last term and was unlucky not to bag a valuable handicap at York in August. Second in a German Listed event on her final start, she has bags of early pace, probably acts on any ground and is still on an upward curve.
**R Guest [1-6].*

RUBY BABE BHB 53f **RR 55f** 4998[9]
2 b f Aragon 7.7f **(58)** - Barrie Baby (Import) 6.6f **(68)**
Form - 680
Record 2000 - 1st:0 2nd:0 3rd:0 Ran:3
2000 Turf 0-2: (5f, 6f) (g-s, frm) 2000 AW 0-1: (5f) (Fibr)

Currently fair filly. Turf high 55 (began Jly).
**J J Quinn [0-3] Rosswood Racing.*

RUBY ESTATE (IRE) BHB 33f35a RR 87f 35a 751^{17}

9 b m High Estate 10.5f **(66)** - Tuesday Morning (Sadler's Wells (USA)) 10f **(76)**
Form - 00
Record 2000 - 1st:0 2nd:0 3rd:0 Ran:2
Pre2000 - 1st:1 2nd:7 3rd:0 Ran:16
Win Prizemoney £2,668 *Total Prizemoney* £9,184
2000 Turf 0-2: (10f, 12f) (sft, g-f)
Very poor mare. Becoming disappointing.
**N A Graham [0-5] Miss H Stratford (from A P James [0-2] Jly 1995).*

RUBY LASER BHB 36f RR 33f 2378^{7}

4 b f Bustino 11f **(64)** - Ower (IRE) (Lomond (USA)) 8.8f **(65)**
Form - 767
Record 2000 - 1st:0 2nd:0 3rd:0 Ran:3
Pre2000 - 1st:0 2nd:0 3rd:1 Ran:5
Win Prizemoney £0 *Total Prizemoney* £733
2000 Turf 0-3: (12f, 14f 2) (gd, frm 2)
Leggy, very moderate filly. Turf high 33. Consistent.
**E L James [0-3] Lady Thompson (from R F JohnsonHoughton [0-5] Spt 1999).*

RUBY RAVEN RR 23tf 4014^{8}

3 b f Sea Raven (IRE) - Give Us a Treat (Cree Song)
Form - 48
Record 2000 - 1st:0 2nd:0 3rd:0 Ran:2
Win Prizemoney £0 *Total Prizemoney* £290
2000 Turf 0-2: (9f, 10f) (g-f, frm)
Leggy, currently little account filly. Turf high 23 (began Aug).
**J R Turner [0-2] Miss S J Turner.*

RUBY SURPRISE (USA) RR $4571a^{2}$

5 br m Farma Way (USA) 12f **(65)** - Santa Rosalia (USA) (Bold Bidder) 8.8f **(67)**
Form - 2
2000 AW 0-1: (9f) (Dirt)
Currently very useful filly. (1st run) - 2nd of 9 to Spain (16 Spt Turfway Park 9f Dirt RF 4571a). **in USA [0-1].*

RUDCROFT BHB 20f RR 24f 3617^{15}

4 ch g Presidium 7.5f **(56)** - Stilvella (Camden Town) 9.3f **(53)**
Form - 00007000
Record 2000 - 1st:0 2nd:0 3rd:0 Ran:8
Pre2000 - 1st:0 2nd:0 3rd:0 Ran:6
2000 Turf 0-8: (5f, 6f 3, 7f, 8f 2, 12f) (gd 3, g-f 2, frm 2, hrd)
Light-framed, little account gelding, has worn blinkers. Turf high 24. **N Bycroft [0-14] M J Bateson.*

RUDDER RR 63f 1852^{2}

2 ch c Deploy 11.4f **(67)** - Wave Dancer (Dance In Time (CAN)) 8.9f **(59)**
Form - 2
Record 2000 - 1st:0 2nd:1 3rd:0 Ran:1
Win Prizemoney £0 *Total Prizemoney* £1,374
2000 Turf 0-1: (6f) (g-s)
Currently average colt. **B W Hills [0-1] R D Hollingsworth.*

RUDE AWAKENING BHB 49f59a RR 49f 59a 4758^{11}

6 b g Rudimentary (USA) 8.2f **(66)** - Final Call (Town Crier) 10.2f **(55)**
Form - 4130310105204030
Record 2000 - 1st:3 2nd:1 3rd:3 Ran:16
Pre2000 - 1st:2 2nd:5 3rd:4 Ran:48
Win Prizemoney £15,804 *Total Prizemoney* £27,630
Wins * 2000 Jly Catter (G-F) H 5f 43 46
*** 2000** *Feb Lingfi (STD) H 6f 56 61*
*** 2000** *Jan Lingfi (STD) H 6f 44 56*
* 1998 *Feb Southw (STD) H 6f 44 49*
1996 Apr Pontef (G-F) 5f 94 <
2000 Turf 1-6: (5f 1-5, 6f) (g-f 2, frm 1-4) 2000 AW 2-10: (5f, 6f 2-8, 7f) (Equi 2-4, Fibr 6)
Average gelding, effective 6 to 7f, best at 6f, - acts on AW, best on Equi, has worn blinkers, likes left handed tracks, likes tight tracks. Turf high 49 (began Jly). AW high 61 - 1st of 14 getting 3lb from Charge (19 Feb Lingfield RF 0312) - also 1st of 12 getting 20lb from Days of Grace (19 Jan Lingfield RF 0119).
**C W Fairhurst [4-58] William Hill (from G Lewis [1-6] Oct 1996).*

RUDETSKI BHB 55f RR 56f 4498^{2}

3 b g Rudimentary (USA) 8.2f **(66)** - Butosky (Busted) 10.2f **(61)**
Form - 0065612
Record 2000 - 1st:1 2nd:1 3rd:0 Ran:7
Win Prizemoney £2,457 *Total Prizemoney* £3,491
Wins * 2000 Aug Pontef (G-F) H 8f 49 56 <
2000 Turf 1-7: (6f 3, 8f 1-3, 11f) (g-s 3, gd, g-f 2, frm 1-1)
Light-framed, fair gelding, effective 8f, acts on frm, likes tight tracks. Turf high 56 - 1st of 14 getting 13lb from Shamsan (9 Aug Pontefract RF 3505). **M Dods [1-7] A F & P Monk.*

RUDIK (USA) BHB 96f RR 97f 3395^{12}

3 b br c Nureyev (USA) 8.4f **(84)** - Nervous Baba (USA) (Raja Baba (USA)) 10f **(64)**
Form - 570
Record 2000 - 1st:0 2nd:0 3rd:0 Ran:3
Pre2000 - 1st:1 2nd:1 3rd:2 Ran:4
Win Prizemoney £3,598 *Total Prizemoney* £7,759
Wins * 1999 Spt Newcas (SFT) 6f 96+ <
2000 Turf 0-3: (6f 3) (gd 2, g-f)
Unfurnished, very useful colt, effective 6f, acts on gd. Turf high 95. He was lightly raced and did not fare too badly when twelfth in the Stewards' Cup. Sold for 18,500gns at Newmarket in October, he has joined David Nicholls and is a name to look out for in sprint handicaps this term.
**Sir Michael Stoute [1-7] Mrs John Magnier & M Tabor.*

RUDI'S PET (IRE) BHB 116f RR 120f 4434^{10}

6 ch g Don't Forget Me 9.5f **(66)** - Pink Fondant (Northfields (USA)) 9f **(72)**
Form - 610370
Record 2000 - 1st:1 2nd:0 3rd:1 Ran:5
Pre2000 - 1st:8 2nd:2 3rd:2 Ran:45
Win Prizemoney £111,514 *Total Prizemoney* £144,045
Wins * 2000 Jun Leopar (G-S) G3 5f 120 <
* 1999 Jly Goodwo (G-F) G3 5f 112+
* 1999 Jly Ascot (GD) H 5f 97 109+
* 1999 Jun Newcas (GD) H 5f 82 90+
* 1999 May Thirsk (GD) H 5f 73 79+
1997 Oct Doncas (GD) H 5f 88 97
1997 Aug Sandow (SFT) H 5f 80 88
1996 Aug Sandow (GD) H 5f 92 99
1996 Jly Windso (GD) 5f 74
2000 Turf 1-5: (5f 1-5) (g-s 1-1, gd 2, g-f, frm)
Very high-class gelding, effective 5f, acts on g-s to frm, often wears blinkers (very effectively), excels at Goodwood. Turf high 120 (1st run) - 1st of 9 giving 6lb to Cassandra Go (5 Jun Leopardstown RF 1926a). Inconsistent. Another example of the training skills of David Nicholls, he improved into a high-class sprinter and things started off well last season when he won a Leoparstown Group Three on his belated return. That was the highlight though, as he was well beaten by the top sprinters afterwards and was very disappointing on his final start. He acts particularly well on fast ground.
**D Nicholls [5-15] G H Leatham (from Mrs J R Ramsden [0-14] Nov 1998).*

RULE OF THUMB BHB 75f RR 75f 4207^{2}

3 ch g Inchinor 8.9f **(64)** - Rockin' Rosie (Song) 7.2f **(61)**
Form - 0005272
Record 2000 - 1st:0 2nd:2 3rd:0 Ran:7
Pre2000 - 1st:1 2nd:0 3rd:0 Ran:2
Win Prizemoney £1,945 *Total Prizemoney* £4,209
Wins * 1999 Oct Pontef (GD) 6f 74+ <
2000 Turf 0-7: (6f, 7f 5, 8f) (gd 3, g-f, frm 3)
Workmanlike, above-average gelding, effective 6 to 7f, best at 6f, acted on gd to frm. Turf high 75 - 2nd of 18 giving 3lb to Petarga (4 Spt Bath 6f frm RF 4207). Consistent. (DEAD)
**G L Moore [1-9] Brighthelm Racing.*

RUM BABA (IRE) BHB 35f RR 35f 3826^{5}

6 b g Tirol 8.1f **(64)** - Rum Cay (USA) (Our Native (USA)) 11.2f **(63)**
Form - 565
Record 2000 - 1st:0 2nd:0 3rd:0 Ran:3
Pre2000 - 1st:1 2nd:2 3rd:6 Ran:27

Win Prizemoney £3,425 *Total Prizemoney* £8,876
Wins 1997 Aug Tralee (HVY) 12f 76 <
2000 Turf 0-3: (16f 2, 17f) (gd, g-f, hrd)
Very moderate gelding, effective 13 to 16f, acts on g-f to frm, has worn blinkers. Turf high 35 (began Jly). Consistent.
**Mrs M Reveley [2-16] P D Savill (from C Collins in IRE [1-22] Oct 1998).*

RUM LAD BHB 54f65a **RR 37f 65a** 3379[20]
6 gr g Efisio 7.7f **(69)** - She's Smart (Absalom) 7.2f **(58)**
Form - 000

Record	**2000** -	1st:0	2nd:0	3rd:0	Ran:3
	Pre2000 -	1st:6	2nd:3	3rd:5	Ran:49

Win Prizemoney £21,663 *Total Prizemoney* £30,879

Wins							
* 1999	Jun	Pontef	(GD)		5f		66
* 1999	Jun	Pontef	(SFT)	H	6f	62	68
* 1998	*Oct*	*Wolver*	*(sta)*	*H*	*6f*	*64*	*66*
* 1997	Jly	Catter	(SFT)	H	6f	55	69 <
* 1997	Jun	Carlis	(GD)	H	5f	56	61
* 1997	May	Catter	(G-F)		6f		53

2000 Turf 0-3: (5f, 6f 2) (g-f, frm 2)
Average gelding, effective 5 to 6f, best at 6f, acts on sft to hrd, best on g-f, likes left handed tracks, likes tight tracks, excels at Pontefract. Turf high 36. Becoming disappointing.
**J J Quinn [6-52] B Shaw.*

RUM LASS BHB 42f **RR 28f** 3429[14]
3 gr f Distant Relative 7f **(69)** - She's Smart (Absalom) 7.2f **(58)**
Form - 0000

Record	**2000** -	1st:0	2nd:0	3rd:0	Ran:4
	Pre2000 -	1st:0	2nd:0	3rd:0	Ran:3

2000 Turf 0-4: (5f 2, 6f, 7f) (g-s, g-f, frm, hrd)
Scopey, little account filly, effective 5f, acts on gd. Turf high 28.
**J J Quinn [0-7] B Shaw.*

RUMORE CASTAGNA (IRE) BHB 84f **RR 85f** 4721a[2]
2 ch g Great Commotion (USA) 9.2f **(80)** - False Spring (IRE) (Petorius) 7.3f **(61)**
Form - 15302

Record	**2000** -	1st:1	2nd:1	3rd:1	Ran:5

Win Prizemoney £3,493 *Total Prizemoney* £10,624
Wins * **2000** Jun Newcas (SFT) 5f 61+ <
2000 Turf 1-5: (5f 1-2, 6f 2, 7f) (sft 1-1, g-s, gd, g-f, frm)
Useful gelding. Turf high 85 - 2nd of 8 giving 4lb to Chiquette (24 Spt Ovrevoll 7f g-s RF 4721a). Made a winning debut in soft ground, but held since. **S E Kettlewell [1-5].*

RUM POINTER (IRE) BHB 95f **RR 93f** 5322[6]
4 b g Turtle Island (IRE) - Osmunda (Mill Reef (USA)) 10.5f **(78)**
Form - 0721005546

Record	**2000** -	1st:1	2nd:1	3rd:0	Ran:10
	Pre2000 -	1st:4	2nd:2	3rd:1	Ran:18

Win Prizemoney £30,432 *Total Prizemoney* £41,048

Wins							
* **2000**	Jun	Haydoc	(G-S)	H	16.2f	87	92 <
* 1999	Spt	Ayr	(G-S)	H	15f	86	90
* 1999	Jun	Haydoc	(GD-)	H	11.9f	80	84
* 1999	May	Ripon	(G-S)	H	12.3f	71	79
* 1999	Mar	Catter	(G-S)	H	12f	64	73

2000 Turf 1-10: (12f 2, 13f, 14f 4, 16f 1-1, 17f, 19f) (hvy, sft 2, gd 1-3, g-f 3, frm)
Scopey, useful gelding, effective 12 to 16f, acts on sft to frm, best on gd, has worn blinkers, likes left handed tracks, prefers tight tracks, excels at Ayr and Haydock. Turf high 93 - 4th of 8 giving 10lb to Riddlesdown (22 Spt Haydock 14f sft RF 4575) - also 1st of 9 giving 14lb to Foundry Lane (8 Jun Haydock RF 1808). An out-and-out stayer, he was inconsistent after making all at Haydock in June. In excellent form over hurdles since then, he could pinch a long distance handicap on the Flat this spring.
**T D Easterby [5-28] M P Burke.*

RUMPOLD **RR 90+f** 3205[1]
2 b c Mister Baileys - Southern Psychic (USA) (Alwasmi (USA))
Form - 1

Record	**2000** -	1st:1	2nd:0	3rd:0	Ran:1

Win Prizemoney £6,711 *Total Prizemoney* £6,711
Wins * **2000** Jly Ascot (G-F) 6f 90+ <
2000 Turf 1-1: (6f 1-1) (gd 1-1)
Currently useful colt. (1st run) - 1st of 9 from Minardi (29 Jly Ascot RF 3205). He caused a stir when beating Minardi by five lengths at Ascot in July and was promptly snapped up by Godolphin. Unraced in the second half of the season, he has the scope to develop into a cracking three-year-old and ought to stay a mile. Quoted around 14-1 for the 2000 Guineas (a race his sire won on his seasonal debut in 1994), his reappearance is eagerly awaited.
**P F I Cole [1-1] Anthony Speelman.*

RUM PUNCH BHB 75f **RR 78+f** 5026[9]
3 b c Shirley Heights 12.1f **(76)** - Gentle Persuasion (Bustino) 10.4f **(64)**
Form - 88200

Record	**2000** -	1st:0	2nd:1	3rd:0	Ran:5
	Pre2000 -	1st:0	2nd:0	3rd:0	Ran:1

Win Prizemoney £0 *Total Prizemoney* £2,260
2000 Turf 0-5: (8f 2, 10f 3) (g-s 2, gd, g-f, frm)
Scopey, above-average colt, effective 10f, acts on frm. Turf high 78 - 2nd of 10 giving 3lb to Waseem (12 Jun Pontefract 10f frm RF 1900). **Sir Michael Stoute [0-6] The Queen.*

RUNAWAY BRIDE **RR 52f** 4360[16]
2 b f Bishop of Cashel - Storm Nymph (USA) **(74f)** (Storm Bird (CAN)) 10.3f **(74)**
Form - 5500

Record	**2000** -	1st:0	2nd:0	3rd:0	Ran:4

2000 Turf 0-4: (5f 2, 6f, 7f) (g-s, gd, g-f 2, hrd)
Fair filly. Turf high 52. **C Smith [0-4] David Thompson.*

RUNAWAY STAR BHB 30f **RR 44f** 5229[10]
3 ch f Superlative 8.8f **(57)** - My Greatest Star (Great Nephew) 9.9f **(64)**
Form - 6657060

Record	**2000** -	1st:0	2nd:0	3rd:0	Ran:7

2000 Turf 0-7: (8f 3, 10f, 11f, 12f 2) (g-s, gd 2, g-f, frm 3)
Leggy, moderate filly. Turf high 44.
**W J Musson [0-7] Mrs N A Ward.*

RUN FOR GLORY (IRE) BHB 44f **RR 33f** 5021[9]
3 ch c Lahib (USA) 8f **(69)** - Blazing Glory (IRE) (Glow (USA)) 6.7f **(71)**
Form - 00

Record	**2000** -	1st:0	2nd:0	3rd:0	Ran:2
	Pre2000 -	1st:0	2nd:0	3rd:0	Ran:1

2000 Turf 0-2: (5f, 7f) (g-s 2)
Scopey, currently very moderate colt. Turf high 17 (began Spt).
**D R C Elsworth [0-3] Everyone's A Winner Partnership.*

RUNIN CIRCLES BHB 52f **RR 51f** 1651[12]
3 b g Presidium 7.5f **(56)** - True Ring (High Top) 10.2f **(67)**
Form - 00

Record	**2000** -	1st:0	2nd:0	3rd:0	Ran:2
	Pre2000 -	1st:0	2nd:0	3rd:0	Ran:3

2000 Turf 0-2: (8f, 14f) (gd, g-f)
Leggy, fair gelding. Turf high 9. **M W Easterby [0-5] T R Beston.*

RUN MACHINE (IRE) BHB 39f **RR 35f** 3487[9]
3 ch g Fayruz 6.6f **(63)** - Anita's Love (IRE) (Anita's Prince)
Form - 00

Record	**2000** -	1st:0	2nd:0	3rd:0	Ran:2
	Pre2000 -	1st:0	2nd:0	3rd:0	Ran:3

2000 Turf 0-2: (5f 2) (g-s, frm)
Scopey, very moderate gelding. Turf high 14.
**Mrs P N Dutfield [0-5] The Two Legs Partnership.*

RUNNING BEAR BHB 25f29a **RR 28f 29a** 20[7]
6 ch g Sylvan Express 9.6f **(45)** - Royal Girl **(55f)** (Kafu) 6f **(47)**
Form - 05507

Record	**2000** -	1st:0	2nd:0	3rd:0	Ran:1
	Pre2000 -	1st:0	2nd:0	3rd:0	Ran:11

Win Prizemoney £0 *Total Prizemoney* £201
2000 AW 0-1: (9f) (Fibr)
Little account gelding, effective 8f, - acted on Fibr, liked left handed tracks, liked tight tracks. (DEAD)
**Miss J F Craze [0-5] Mrs S E Cooper (from Mrs A M Naughton [0-3] Jun 1999).*

RUNNING FOR ME (IRE) BHB 52f60a **RR 37f 60a** 3189[8]
2 ch f Eagle Eyed (USA) - Running For You (FR) (Pampabird) 7.5f **(73)**
Form - 61822518

Record 2000 - 1st:2 2nd:2 3rd:0 Ran:8
Win Prizemoney £3,633 *Total Prizemoney* £4,675
Wins *** 2000** *Jly Wolver (STD) S 5f 64* <
*** 2000** *May Southw (STD) S 5f 62*
2000 Turf 0-2: (5f 2) (gd 2) 2000 AW 2-6: (5f 2-3, 6f 3) (Fibr 2-6)
Average filly, effective 5 to 6f, best at 5f, - acts on Fibr. Turf high 37. AW high 64 - 1st of 6 from Dancing Penney (13 Jly Wolverhampton RF 2781) - also 1st of 9 getting 5lb from Orchard Raider (8 May Southwell RF 1095).
**R Hollinshead [2-8] R Hollinshead.*

RUNNING FREE (IRE) BHB 56a RR 14f 3599[8]

6 b g Waajib 8.9f **(67)** - Selchis (Main Reef) 9.6f **(57)**
Form - 08
Record 2000 - 1st:0 2nd:0 3rd:0 Ran:2
Pre2000 - 1st:2 2nd:0 3rd:2 Ran:17
Win Prizemoney £5,054 *Total Prizemoney* £5,838
Wins 1997 Aug Salisb (G-S) H 12f 45 49
1997 Jly Nottin (G-F) SH 14.1f 49 55 <
2000 Turf 0-2: (14f, 16f) (g-f, hrd)
Poor gelding, has worn blinkers. Turf high 14 (began Jly).
**W S Cunningham [0-2] C P M Racing (from M J Fetherston-Godley [2-17] Oct 1997).*

RUNNING STAG (USA) BHB 115f120a RR 120f 120a 3942a[6]

6 b h Cozzene (USA) 10.1f **(87)** - Fruhlingstag (FR) (Orsini) 10f **(71)**
Form - 222711646
Record 2000 - 1st:2 2nd:1 3rd:0 Ran:7
Pre2000 - 1st:5 2nd:9 3rd:2 Ran:30
Win Prizemoney £560,984 *Total Prizemoney* £998,183
Wins *** 2000** *Jun Suffol (FST) G2H 9f 119*
*** 2000** *May Belmon (FST) 9f 115+*
* 1999 *Aug Sarato (FST) G2H 10f 119*
* 1999 *Jun Belmon (FST) G2H 9f 120* <
* 1998 Aug Deauvi (SFT) G3 10f 115
* 1998 *Mar Lingfi (STD) 10f 104+*
* 1997 *Feb Lingfi (STD) 10f 59++*
2000 Turf 0-1: (10f) (g-s) 2000 AW 2-6: (8f, 9f 2-4, 10f) (Dirt 2-6)
Very high-class horse, effective 9 to 10f, best at 10f, acts on gd to frm - acts on Dirt, excels at Suffolk Downs, does well at Belmont Park. AW high 119 - 1st of 8 from Out Of Mind (3 Jun Suffolk Downs RF 1823a) - also 1st of 6 giving 6lb to Early Warning (24 May Belmont Park RF 1628a). The star of Philip Mitchell's stable, he has become a flagbearer for British racing in the USA over the last couple of seasons. Smart on the turf, he is a top-class performer on dirt and has been a tremendous servant to his small stable. Always prominent when winning the Massachusetts Handicap at Suffolk Downs in June following a win at Belmont the previous month, he stays a mile and a quarter and is thoroughly genuine. He has thoroughly earned his retirement. **P Mitchell [7-37].*

RUNNING TIMES (USA) BHB 61f62a RR 60f 62a 1530[3]

3 b c Brocco (USA) - Concert Peace (USA) (Hold Your Peace (USA)) 9f **(72)**
Form - 503543
Record 2000 - 1st:0 2nd:0 3rd:2 Ran:6
Pre2000 - 1st:0 2nd:0 3rd:1 Ran:5
Win Prizemoney £0 *Total Prizemoney* £2,607
2000 Turf 0-5: (10f, 11f, 12f 2, 15f) (gd 4, frm) 2000 AW 0-1: (9f) (Fibr)
Workmanlike, average colt, effective 7f, acts on gd, has worn blinkers, likes tight tracks. Turf high 60.
**T D Easterby [0-11] Times of Wigan.*

RUNNING WATER (IRE) RR 1314[12]

7 b g Commanche Run 10.3f **(63)** - Paupers Spring (Pauper)
Form - 0
Record 2000 - 1st:0 2nd:0 3rd:0 Ran:1
2000 Turf 0-1: (14f) (gd)
Formerly very poor gelding. **P R Hedger [1-8] Howard Spooner.*

RUN ON BHB 68f RR 54f 4432[18]

2 b c Runnett 6.7f **(56)** - Polar Storm (IRE) **(69f)** (Law Society (USA)) 9.9f **(70)**
Form - 420
Record 2000 - 1st:0 2nd:1 3rd:0 Ran:3
Win Prizemoney £0 *Total Prizemoney* £1,376
2000 Turf 0-3: (5f, 6f 2) (gd, g-f, frm)
Currently fair colt. Turf high 54 (began Jly).

**B J Meehan [0-3] Miss Howard Evans.*

RUSH BROOK (IRE) RR 103+f 4805a[10]

5 ch g Pips Pride 6.7f **(70)** - Mummys Best 00
Form - 5625071100100
2000 Turf 3-12: (6f, 7f 4, 8f 2-5, 9f 1-2) (sft 1-4, g-s 1-4, gd 1-3, g-f)
Very useful gelding, effective 8 to 9f, best at 8f, acts on sft to gd. Turf high 103 - 1st of 20 giving 19lb to Anna Elise (2 Jly Curragh RF 2528a) - also 1st of 10 giving 6lb to Tushna (25 Aug Tralee RF 4086a).
**D Wachman in IRE [6-31] P Fadden (from K Prendergast in IRE [0-1] Oct 1997).*

RUSHBY (IRE) BHB 72f RR 65f 3906[6]

2 b g Fayruz 6.6f **(63)** - Moira My Girl (Henbit (USA)) 9f **(61)**
Form - 636206
Record 2000 1st:0 2nd:1 3rd:1 Ran:6
Win Prizemoney £0 *Total Prizemoney* £1,595
2000 Turf 0-6: (5f 6) (g-s, gd 2, frm 3)
Average gelding, effective 5f, acts on gd to frm. Turf high 65 - 3rd of 11 to Pan Jammer (18 May Salisbury 5f gd RF 1270).
**Mrs P N Dutfield [0-6] The Rushby Partnership.*

RUSHCUTTER BAY BHB 106f RR 104f 4966[3]

7 br g Mon Tresor 7.9f **(60)** - Llwy Bren (Lidhame) 9.2f **(50)**
Form - 2602108213
Record 2000 - 1st:2 2nd:3 3rd:1 Ran:10
Pre2000 - 1st:4 2nd:2 3rd:2 Ran:38
Win Prizemoney £41,711 *Total Prizemoney* £67,951
Wins *** 2000** Spt Newmar (GD) L 5f 104 <
*** 2000** Aug Newmar (G-F) H 6f 77 80
* 1999 May Windso (G-F) 6f 90
* 1998 Jly Newmar (G-F) H 6f 77 81
1996 Jun Nottin (G-F) H 5.1f 79 83
2000 Turf 2-10: (5f 1-4, 6f 1-6) (gd 3, g-f 2-5, frm 2)
Very useful gelding, has broken blood-vessels, effective 5 to 6f, acts on gd to g-f, has worn blinkers. Turf high 104 - 3rd of 15 to Bahamian Pirate (13 Oct Newmarket 6f gd RF 4966) - also 1st of 18 getting 3lb from Astonished (28 Spt Newmarket RF 4700). A decent handicapper, he caused a real surprise when just winning a Newmarket Listed event in October. He goes well fresh and six furlongs and fast ground look to suit him best.
**P L Gilligan [4-30] Treasure Seekers Partnership (from T T Clement [2-18] Jly 1997).*

RUSHED (IRE) BHB 22f27a RR 11f 27a 2261[8]

5 b g Fairy King (USA) 7.7f **(75)** - Exotic Bride (USA) (Blushing Groom (FR)) 10.3f **(76)**
Form - 408
Record 2000 - 1st:0 2nd:0 3rd:0 Ran:3
Pre2000 - 1st:0 2nd:1 3rd:1 Ran:8
Win Prizemoney £0 *Total Prizemoney* £1,175
2000 AW 0-3: (10f, 12f 2) (Equi 3)
Moderate gelding, effective 12f, - acts on Equi, favours left handed tracks. AW high 41. Inconsistent.
**G P Enright [0-14] Anne Ross And The Supremes (from Sir Michael Stoute [0-1] Apr 1998).*

RUSHMORE (USA) BHB 74a RR 86+f 3141[1]

3 ch c Mt Livermore (USA) 7.7f **(90)** - Crafty Nan (USA) (Crafty Prospector (USA)) 8.2f **(104)**
Form - 1001161
Record 2000 - 1st:4 2nd:0 3rd:0 Ran:7
Pre2000 - 1st:0 2nd:0 3rd:1 Ran:1
Win Prizemoney £38,627 *Total Prizemoney* £39,567
Wins *** 2000** Jly Sandow (G-F) H 7.1f 79 86+
*** 2000** Jly Sandow (GD) H 7.1f 74 84+
*** 2000** *Jun Southw (STD) H 7f 74 93* <
*** 2000** Mar Doncas (GD) 7f 83
2000 Turf 3-6: (7f 3-4, 8f, 10f) (gd 1-1, g-f 1-3, frm 1-2) 2000 AW 1-1: (7f 1-1) (Fibr 1-1)
Rangy, useful colt, effective 7f, acts on gd to frm - acts on Fibr. Turf high 86 - 1st of 12 getting 2lb from Falconidae (26 Jly Sandown RF 3141) - also 1st of 16 getting 24lb from Smart Ridge (8 Jly Sandown RF 2645). (1st run) - 1st of 9 getting 2lb from Atylan Boy (30 Jun Southwell RF 2418). Effective when ridden up with the pace or from behind, he was not seen out after July. Bought for only 7,500gns at Newmarket in October, he may have

had a problem. **P F I Cole [4-8] J S Gutkin.*

RUSSIAN FOX (IRE) BHB 74f **RR 86f** 5313[16]
3 ch g Foxhound (USA) - La Petruschka (Ballad Rock) 7.8f **(63)**
Form - 08000000
Record 2000 - 1st:0 2nd:0 3rd:0 Ran:8
Pre2000 - 1st:3 2nd:2 3rd:3 Ran:12
Win Prizemoney £14,497 *Total Prizemoney* £20,679
Wins * 1999 Oct Newmar (GD) H 6f 85 89 <
* 1999 Jly Lingfi (G-F) H 5f 77
* 1999 Jun Lingfi (G-F) 5f 77
2000 Turf 0-8: (5f, 6f 6, 7f) (sft, g-s, gd 4, frm 2)
Useful gelding, effective 5 to 6f, acts on gd to g-f. Turf high 86.
**R Hannon [3-20] Nicholas Hodges.*

RUSSIAN HOPE (IRE) RR 117f 4846a[8]
5 ch h Rock Hopper 10.6f **(54)** - Dievotchka (GER) (Dancing Brave (USA)) 8.4f **(76)**
Form - 1418
2000 Turf 2-4: (10f 1-1, 12f 2, 13f 1-1) (sft, g-s 2-2, gd)
High-class colt. Turf high 117 - also 1st of 6 from Daring Miss (27 Aug Deauville RF 4138a). He cracked a hoof in the spring, but returned better than ever to record a brave win in the Group Two Grand Prix de Deauville. Unplaced in the Arc, he clearly goes well when fresh. **H-A Pantall in FR [3-7].*

RUSSIAN MUSIC BHB 48f100a **RR 26f 100a** 3611[P]
7 b g Forzando 7.2f **(63)** - Sunfleet (Red Sunset) 8.2f **(63)**
Form - 00P
Record 2000 - 1st:0 2nd:0 3rd:0 Ran:3
Pre2000 - 1st:3 2nd:7 3rd:9 Ran:40
Win Prizemoney £21,772 *Total Prizemoney* £72,915
Wins 1997 Spt Doncas (G-F) H 8f 100 105
1997 Mar Warwic (G-F) 7f 108 <
1996 May Lingfi (G-F) 7f 70
2000 Turf 0-3: (7f, 8f, 12f) (gd, hrd 2)
Useful gelding, effective 7f, acted on gd, had worn blinkers. Turf high 20. (DEAD)
**M E Sowersby [0-12] S A Cromie (from Miss Gay Kelleway [3-38] Oct 1999).*

RUSSIAN RHAPSODY BHB 77f **RR 83+f** 5317[5]
3 b f Cosmonaut - Hannah's Music (Music Boy) 6.8f **(57)**
Form - 5422215
Record 2000 - 1st:1 2nd:3 3rd:0 Ran:7
Win Prizemoney £3,341 *Total Prizemoney* £6,980
Wins * 2000 Oct Yarmou (SFT) 7f 83+ <
2000 Turf 1-7: (5f, 7f 1-4, 8f, 9f) (sft 2, g-s 1-2, g-f, frm 2)
Scopey, decent filly, effective 7f, acts on sft to g-s. Turf high 83 (began Jly) - 1st of 11 getting 5lb from Freddy Flintstone (17 Oct Yarmouth RF 5022). **M A Jarvis [1-7] Magno-Pulse Ltd.*

RUSSIAN ROMEO (IRE) BHB 60f68a **RR 70f 68a** 5014[13]
5 b g Soviet Lad (USA) 9.4f **(63)** - Aotearoa (IRE) (Flash of Steel) 7.2f **(53)**
Form - 376055223228823510
Record 2000 - 1st:1 2nd:5 3rd:2 Ran:16
Pre2000 - 1st:5 2nd:3 3rd:2 Ran:35
Win Prizemoney £15,688 *Total Prizemoney* £23,989
Wins * 2000 *Spt Wolver (STD) H* 6f 66 70
* 1999 *Jly Southw (STD)* 6f 70
* 1999 *Jun Wolver (STD) H* 6f 54 57
* 1998 Jun Cheste (GD) C 6.1f 72
* 1997 *Oct Wolver (STD) C* 6f 74 <
* 1997 Aug Leices (GD) S 6f 74 <
2000 Turf 0-7: (5f 2, 6f 4, 7f) (sft, gd, g-f 2, frm 3) 2000 AW 1-9: (6f 1-9) (Fibr 1-9)
Above-average gelding, effective 5 to 6f, best at 6f, acts on g-f to frm - acts on Fibr, mostly wears blinkers (very effectively), likes left handed tracks, likes tight tracks, and does well at Wolverhampton. Turf high 70 - 2nd of 14 giving 8lb to Marengo (1 May Doncaster 6f g-f RF 0937). AW high 70 - 1st of 13 getting 2lb from Days of Grace (2 Spt Wolverhampton RF 4180).
**B A McMahon [6-51] R L Bedding.*

RUSSIAN SILVER (USA) BHB 62f **RR 59f** 2614[3]
3 ch f Red Bishop (USA) - Russian Maid **(81f)** (Cadeaux Genereux)
Form - 843
Record 2000 - 1st:0 2nd:0 3rd:1 Ran:3
Pre2000 - 1st:0 2nd:0 3rd:1 Ran:4
Win Prizemoney £0 *Total Prizemoney* £1,639
2000 Turf 0-3: (9f, 11f, 12f) (sft, gd, frm)
Light-framed, fair filly, effective 7f, acts on gd. Turf high 59.
**C E Brittain [0-7] Ali Saeed.*

RUSSIAN WHISPERS (USA) BHB 90f **RR 84f** 5129[6]
2 b c Red Ransom (USA) 8.6f **(83)** - Idle Gossip (USA) (Lyphard (USA)) 9.9f **(72)**
Form - 3576
Record 2000 - 1st:0 2nd:0 3rd:1 Ran:4
Win Prizemoney £0 *Total Prizemoney* £984
2000 Turf 0-4: (6f 2, 8f 2) (sft, g-s, frm 2)
Useful colt, has worn blinkers. Turf high 84 (began Jly). Obviously has ability, but bit off more than he could chew in the Royal Lodge Stakes. **B J Meehan [0-4] Mrs Susan Roy.*

RUTLAND CHANTRY (USA) BHB 60f69a **RR 62f 69a** 5063[5]
6 b g Dixieland Band (USA) 10.1f **(80)** - Christchurch (FR) (So Blessed) 8.7f **(67)**
Form - 2566053425
Record 2000 - 1st:0 2nd:2 3rd:1 Ran:10
Pre2000 - 1st:3 2nd:5 3rd:0 Ran:20
Win Prizemoney £15,076 *Total Prizemoney* £24,009
Wins * 1999 Jun Beverl (SFT) H 9.9f 71 75 <
1998 Apr Newbur (HVY) H 10f 66 72
1997 Oct Pontef (G-S) H 10f 60 66
2000 Turf 0-8: (10f 7, 12f) (sft, g-s 4, gd, g-f 2) 2000 AW 0-2: (8f 2) (Fibr 2)
Above-average gelding, effective 8 to 12f, best at 10f, acts on g-s to frm - acts on Fibr, best on gd, has worn blinkers. Turf high 65. AW high 74 (1st run) - 2nd of 9 giving 10lb to Davis Rock (28 Feb Southwell 8f Fibr RF 0371).
**S Gollings [1-21] Five Go Racing (from Lord Huntingdon [2-9] Oct 1998).*

RYAN'S GOLD (IRE) BHB 68f **RR 73f** 4970[16]
2 b c Distant View (USA) - Kathleen's Dream (USA) (Last Tycoon) 8.5f **(62)**
Form - 8060
Record 2000 - 1st:0 2nd:0 3rd:0 Ran:4
2000 Turf 0-4: (6f 2, 7f, 8f) (gd, g-f 2, frm)
Above-average colt. Turf high 73 (began Jly).
**Mrs A J Perrett [0-4] John Connolly.*

RYEFIELD BHB 64f **RR 64f** 5299[14]
5 b g Petong 7.6f **(58)** - Octavia (Sallust) 8.4f **(63)**
Form - 0R21426331660
Record 2000 - 1st:2 2nd:2 3rd:2 Ran:13
Pre2000 - 1st:3 2nd:4 3rd:1 Ran:26
Win Prizemoney £28,273 *Total Prizemoney* £38,294
Wins * 2000 Oct Ayr (HVY) H 6f 62 64
*** 2000** Jly Ayr (FRM) H 7f 56 62
* 1999 Aug Ayr (G-F) H 8f 65 66
* 1999 Jly Newcas (G-F) H 8f 62 64
* 1998 Jly Carlis (G-F) 6.9f 76 <
2000 Turf 2-13: (6f 1-2, 7f 1-4, 8f 7) (sft 1-2, g-s, gd 3, g-f 2, frm 1-4, hrd)
Average gelding, effective 6 to 8f, best at 8f, acts on sft to hrd, best on g-f, and does well at Musselburgh. Turf high 64 - 1st of 25 getting 1lb from Gay Breeze (10 Oct Ayr RF 4894) - also 1st of 10 getting 28lb from Tony Tie (24 Jly Ayr RF 3065).
**Miss L A Perratt [5-39] Mrs Elaine Aird.*

RYELAND BHB 55f **RR 53f** 2102[3]
4 b f Presidium 7.5f **(56)** - Ewe Lamb (Free State) 8.7f **(61)**
Form - 3
Record 2000 - 1st:0 2nd:0 3rd:1 Ran:1
Pre2000 - 1st:0 2nd:0 3rd:0 Ran:2
Win Prizemoney £0 *Total Prizemoney* £478
2000 Turf 0-1: (12f) (g-f)
Leggy, currently fair filly. **Mrs P Sly [0-3] Mrs P M Sly.*

RYKA BHB 60f **RR 66f** 702[6]
5 ch g Deploy 11.4f **(67)** - Velda (Thatch (USA)) 9.8f **(62)**
Form - 006

Record 2000 - 1st:0 2nd:0 3rd:0 Ran:3
2000 Turf 0-3: (8f, 9f, 10f) (gd 3)
Average gelding. Turf high 66. **P T Dalton [0-5] S Taberner.*

RYMER'S RASCAL BHB 67f55a **RR 66f 55a** 5166[4]
8 b g Rymer - City Sound (On Your Mark) 7.7f **(58)**
Form - 563425383144
Record 2000 - 1st:1 2nd:1 3rd:3 Ran:12
Pre2000 - 1st:6 2nd:5 3rd:10 Ran:70
Win Prizemoney £42,877 *Total Prizemoney* £62,229
Wins * 2000 Spt Redcar (SFT) H 8f 60 66 <
* 1999 Jly Cheste (G-F) H 7.6f 60 62
* 1998 Oct Redcar (SFT) H 7f 59 61
* 1997 Spt York (SFT) H 7f 60 64
* 1997 Aug Catter (G-F) H 7f 56 61
* 1997 Jly Beverl (G-F) H 7.5f 54 60
2000 Turf 1-12: (7f 7, 8f 1-5) (sft 2, gd 1-2, g-f 4, frm 3, hrd)
Average gelding, effective 7 to 8f, best at 8f, acts on sft to hrd, best on gd, prefers left handed tracks, likes tight tracks, excels at Chester and Ayr and York and likes Catterick. Turf high 66 - 4th of 19 getting 3lb from Lucky Gitano (24 Oct Redcar 8f gd RF 5166) - also 1st of 24 getting 10lb from Bacchus (30 Spt Redcar RF 4745). Consistent. Makes the frame on a regular basis, but does not win very often though he scored in very soft ground at Redcar in September.
**E J Alston [7-78] Brian Chambers (from P C Haslam [0-4] Jun 1994).*

RYTHM N TIME BHB 62f58a **RR 66df 58a** 5245[7]
3 b f Timeless Times (USA) 6.1f **(56)** - Primum Tempus **(42df)** (Primo Dominie) 6.2f **(80)**
Form - 0408144660057
Record 2000 - 1st:1 2nd:0 3rd:0 Ran:13
Pre2000 - 1st:1 2nd:1 3rd:3 Ran:10
Win Prizemoney £6,520 *Total Prizemoney* £13,847
Wins * 2000 Aug Beverl (GD) 5f 55+
1999 Aug Beverl (GD) H 5f 72 80+ <
2000 Turf 1-12: (5f 1-9, 6f 3) (sft, g-s, gd 1-3, g-f 3, frm 4) 2000 AW 0-1: (7f) (Fibr)
Average filly, effective 5f, acts on frm. Turf high 75.
**E J Alston [1-13] Springs Equestrian Ltd (from T D Easterby [1-10] Nov 1999).*

SAAFEND FLYER (IRE) BHB 48f **RR 54f** 4822[20]
2 b c Kahyasi 12.9f **(74)** - Dingle Bay (Petingo) 11f **(72)**
Form - 08000
Record 2000 - 1st:0 2nd:0 3rd:0 Ran:5
2000 Turf 0-5: (6f, 7f 2, 8f, 10f) (g-s, g-f 3, frm)
Fair colt. Turf high 54.
**R Hannon [0-5] J B R Leisure Ltd.*

SAAFEND ROCKET (IRE) BHB 68f60a **RR 68f 60a** 3525[8]
2 b g Distinctly North (USA) 7.4f **(63)** - Simple Annie (Simply Great (FR)) 8.2f **(65)**
Form - 558
Record 2000 - 1st:0 2nd:0 3rd:0 Ran:3
2000 Turf 0-3: (5f 3) (gd, frm 2)
Currently average gelding. Turf high 68.
**R Hannon [0-3] J B R Leisure Ltd.*

SAANEN (IRE) BHB 62f **RR 64f** 2373[3]
3 b g Port Lucaya - Ziffany **(60f)** (Taufan (USA)) 7f **(57)**
Form - 3223
Record 2000 - 1st:0 2nd:2 3rd:2 Ran:4
Pre2000 - 1st:0 2nd:0 3rd:0 Ran:4
Win Prizemoney £0 *Total Prizemoney* £2,491
2000 Turf 0-4: (8f, 9f 2, 10f) (g-f, frm 3)
Workmanlike, average gelding, effective 8 to 10f, acts on frm. Turf high 64 - 2nd of 6 getting 2lb from Bold State (21 Jun Hamilton 8f frm RF 2154).
**Mrs A Duffield [0-8] Miss Betty Duxbury.*

SABANA (IRE) RR 87f 3855[8]
2 b c Sri Pekan (USA) - Atyaaf (USA) (Irish River (FR)) 8.6f **(78)**
Form - 8258
Record 2000 - 1st:0 2nd:1 3rd:0 Ran:4
Win Prizemoney £0 *Total Prizemoney* £1,544
2000 Turf 0-4: (6f, 7f 3) (gd, g-f, frm 2)
Useful colt. Turf high 87 - 2nd of 4 to Vicious Knight (24 Jly Beverley 7f g-f RF 3068).
**N A Callaghan [0-4] M Tabor.*

SABANG BHB 30f43a **RR 21f 43a** 1476[R]
4 ch m Sabrehill (USA) 8.5f **(64)** - Seleter (Hotfoot) 10.5f **(59)**
Form - R
Record 2000 - 1st:0 2nd:0 3rd:0 Ran:1
Pre2000 - 1st:0 2nd:0 3rd:0 Ran:3
2000 AW 0-1: (14f) (Fibr)
Leggy, little account filly.
**Miss J A Camacho [0-4] Stuart Postill.*

SABICA BHB 49f39a **RR 56f 39a** 309[7]
3 b f Prince Sabo 6.6f **(64)** - Mindomica (Dominion) 8.5f **(63)**
Form - 87
Record 2000 - 1st:0 2nd:0 3rd:0 Ran:2
Pre2000 - 1st:0 2nd:0 3rd:0 Ran:2
2000 AW 0-2: (7f, 8f) (Fibr 2)
Leggy, fair filly. AW high 7.
**C W Thornton [0-4] Ailsa Daniels & Guy Reed.*

SABLE CLOAK BHB 20f **RR** 744[12]
5 b m Prince Sabo 6.6f **(64)** - Edge of Darkness **(52f)** (Vaigly Great) 7f **(58)**
Form - 0
Record 2000 - 1st:0 2nd:0 3rd:0 Ran:1
Pre2000 - 1st:0 2nd:0 3rd:0 Ran:3
2000 AW 0-1: (9f) (Fibr)
Formerly very poor filly.
**K A Morgan [0-1] A M Geeson (from J L Harris [0-3] Feb 1998).*

SABO ROSE BHB 81f **RR 83f** 5106[5]
2 b f Prince Sabo 6.6f **(64)** - Crimson Rosella **(53f)** (Polar Falcon (USA))
Form - 3135
Record 2000 - 1st:1 2nd:0 3rd:2 Ran:4
Win Prizemoney £3,363 *Total Prizemoney* £4,680
Wins * 2000 Spt Pontef (G-S) 6f 74 <
2000 Turf 1-4: (6f 1-2, 7f 2) (gd 1-3, frm)
Decent filly. Turf high 83 (began Spt) - 3rd of 22 getting 3lb from Idle Power (12 Oct Newmarket 6f gd RF 4932) - also 1st of 15 getting 5lb from Lilleman (21 Spt Pontefract RF 4553). Won well at Pontefract on her second start and should improve further.
**W J Haggas [1-4] Don Magnifico Partnership.*

SABOT BHB 36f44a **RR 44f 44a** 4101[17]
7 b g Polar Falcon (USA) 9f **(74)** - Power Take Off (Aragon) 8.1f **(60)**
Form - 4040000
Record 2000 - 1st:0 2nd:0 3rd:0 Ran:6
Pre2000 - 1st:1 2nd:7 3rd:0 Ran:28
Win Prizemoney £3,821 *Total Prizemoney* £16,098
Wins 1996 Jun Thirsk (FRM) 7f 65 <
2000 Turf 0-4: (7f, 9f, 10f 2) (gd, g-f 2, frm) 2000 AW 0-2: (8f, 10f) (Equi 2)
Fair gelding, effective 8 to 9f, best at 8f, acts on gd to g-f - acts on Fibr, prefers left handed tracks. Turf high 44. AW high 9. Becoming disappointing. **T J Arnold [0-6] Steppey Lane Bloodstock (from John Harris [0-4] Nov 1999).*

SABRE LADY BHB 65f **RR 84f** 5188[8]
3 ch f Sabrehill (USA) 8.5f **(64)** - Cal Norma's Lady (IRE) (Lyphard's Special (USA)) 10.3f **(72)**
Form - 34080008
Record 2000 - 1st:0 2nd:0 3rd:1 Ran:8

Pre2000 - 1st:1 2nd:1 3rd:1 Ran:4
Win Prizemoney £3,501 *Total Prizemoney* £7,592
Wins * 1999 Jly Hamilt (FRM) 5f 60+ <
2000 Turf 0-8: (5f 5, 6f 3) (g-s, gd 4, g-f 2, frm)
Workmanlike, decent filly, effective 5 to 6f, best at 6f, acts on gd to frm. Turf high 84 (1st run) - 3rd of 12 getting 8lb from Kathology (9 May Chester 5f g-f RF 1114). She ran a cracker on her reappearance at Chester, but has been held since.
**Miss L A Perratt [1-12] David Sutherland.*

SABREON BHB 76f **RR 80f** 5078[7]

3 b f Caerleon (USA) 10.9f **(79)** - Sabria (USA) (Miswaki (USA)) 9f **(81)**
Form - 15067
Record 2000 - 1st:1 2nd:0 3rd:0 Ran:5
Pre2000 - 1st:0 2nd:3 3rd:0 Ran:5
Win Prizemoney £3,913 *Total Prizemoney* £7,560
Wins *** 2000** Jly Chepst (G-F) 10.2f 75 <
2000 Turf 1-5: (8f 2, 9f, 10f 1-2) (g-s 2, gd, g-f 1-2)
Decent filly, effective 7 to 10f, best at 10f, acts on sft to frm, best on g-f. Turf high 80 (began Jly) - 5th of 10 giving 21lb to Santiburi Girl (6 Aug Newbury 10f g-f RF 3421) - also 1st of 5 from Land Ahead (6 Jly Chepstow RF 2566). Short-headed at Chepstow on her reappearance, she was subsequently awarded the race. Held since and looks short of a turn of foot.
**J L Dunlop [1-10] Eurostrait Ltd.*

SACHO (IRE) BHB 106f **RR 72f** 493[9]

7 b h Sadler's Wells (USA) 11.3f **(87)** - Oh So Sharp (Kris) 9.5f **(73)**
Form - 0
Record 2000 - 1st:0 2nd:0 3rd:0 Ran:1
Pre2000 - 1st:1 2nd:4 3rd:0 Ran:8
Win Prizemoney £4,091 *Total Prizemoney* £22,881
Wins 1997 Spt Leices (G-F) 10f 86 <
2000 Turf 0-1: (12f) (gd)
Above-average horse. Consistent. **J L Harris [0-5] J H Henderson (from J H M Gosden [1-4] Spt 1997).*

SACRED HEART (IRE) BHB 33f **RR 32f** 2426[12]

3 b f Catrail (USA) - Merry Devil (IRE) (Sadler's Wells (USA)) 10f **(76)**
Form - 0000
Record 2000 - 1st:0 2nd:0 3rd:0 Ran:4
Pre2000 - 1st:0 2nd:0 3rd:0 Ran:1
2000 Turf 0-4: (7f 2, 8f, 10f) (gd 2, g-f, frm)
Light-framed, very moderate filly. Turf high 32.
**J M Bradley [0-4] Mrs H Raw (from K McAuliffe [0-1] Nov 1999).*

SACRED SONG (USA) BHB 112f **RR 112+f** 4963[1]

3 b f Diesis 9f **(80)** - Ruby Ransom (CAN) (Red Ransom (USA))
Form - 121
Record 2000 - 1st:2 2nd:1 3rd:0 Ran:3
Pre2000 - 1st:1 2nd:0 3rd:0 Ran:1
Win Prizemoney £26,517 *Total Prizemoney* £31,437
Wins *** 2000** Oct Newmar (SFT) G3 12f 112+ <
*** 2000** Jun Nottin (G-F) 8.2f 99+
* 1999 Jly Nottin (FRM) 6.1f 79+
2000 Turf 2-3: (8f 1-1, 10f, 12f 1-1) (gd 2-3)
Scopey, Group-class filly. Turf high 112 - 1st of 15 from Littlepacepaddocks (13 Oct Newmarket RF 4963). Very lightly raced, she appreciated the chance to tackle a mile and a half when winning a Listed race at Newmarket in October. Open to plenty of improvement, she probably acts on any ground and has a grand attitude. **H R A Cecil [3-4] Niarchos Family.*

SACREMENTUM (IRE) BHB 41f44a **RR 54f 44a** 5020[8]

5 b g Night Shift (USA) 8.1f **(73)** - Tantum Ergo (Tanfirion) 7f **(61)**
Form - 6482764024424F68
Record 2000 - 1st:0 2nd:3 3rd:0 Ran:16
Pre2000 - 1st:1 2nd:1 3rd:2 Ran:27
Win Prizemoney £5,843 *Total Prizemoney* £12,014
Wins 1998 Jly Leopar (G-F) H 6f 62 77 <
2000 Turf 0-9: (7f, 8f, 10f 2, 11f, 12f 4) (hvy, gd 2, g-f 2, frm 2, hrd 2)
2000 AW 0-7: (6f, 7f, 8f 3, 9f, 12f) (Equi, Fibr 6)
Fair gelding, effective 7 to 8f, best at 7f, acts on g-s to hrd - acts on Fibr, has worn blinkers. Turf high 54 - 2nd of 18 getting 8lb from The Wild Widow (18 Jun Leicester 8f hrd RF 2078). AW high 56.
**J A Osborne [0-16] S Hussain (from J E Mulhern in IRE [1-27] Oct 1999).*

SACUNDAI (IRE) **RR 94f** 1636a[9]

3 b c
Form - 10
2000 Turf 1-2: (9f 1-1, 12f) (hvy 1-1, g-f)
Currently useful colt. Turf high 94. **P Bary in FR [1-2].*

SADAKA (USA) BHB 69f **RR 70f** 2948[1]

3 ch f Kingmambo (USA) 10.9f **(85)** - Basma (USA) (Grey Dawn II) 11.1f **(72)**
Form - 8341
Record 2000 - 1st:1 2nd:0 3rd:1 Ran:4
Pre2000 - 1st:0 2nd:0 3rd:1 Ran:2
Win Prizemoney £3,071 *Total Prizemoney* £4,343
Wins *** 2000** Jly Yarmou (GD) H 8f 66 70 <
2000 Turf 1-4: (7f, 8f 1-3) (gd 2, g-f 1-2)
Leggy, above-average filly, effective 8f, acts on g-f. Turf high 70 - 1st of 14 giving 15lb to Jessinca (19 Jly Yarmouth RF 2948).
**E A L Dunlop [1-6] Hamdan Al Maktoum.*

SADDLER'S QUEST BHB 108f **RR 110f** 1193[1]

3 b c Saddlers' Hall (IRE) 10.5f **(65)** - Seren Quest **(81f)** (Rainbow Quest (USA)) 10.4f **(75)**
Form - 11
Record 2000 - 1st:2 2nd:0 3rd:0 Ran:2
Pre2000 - 1st:1 2nd:0 3rd:0 Ran:1
Win Prizemoney £44,963 *Total Prizemoney* £44,963
Wins *** 2000** May Lingfi (G-S) G3 11.5f 110 <
*** 2000** Apr Kempto (SFT) 10f 80+
* 1999 Spt Bath (G-S) 10.2f 88+
2000 Turf 2-2: (10f 1-1, 11f 1-1) (sft 1-1, g-s 1-1)
Scopey, currently Group-class colt. Turf high 110 - 1st of 8 from Going Global (13 May Lingfield RF 1193). He developed into a lively Derby outsider after winning the Group 3 Derby Trial at Lingfield in May, but suffered a setback and was not seen out again. Tough and genuine, his form falls some way short of top-class, although he is open to improvement and will stay well.
**G A Butler [3-3] The Fairy Story Partnership.*

Saddler's Quest missed the Derby due to injury

SADLER'S FLAG (IRE) **RR 111f** 4837a[5]

3 b f Sadler's Wells (USA) 11.3f **(87)** - Animatrice (USA) (Alleged (USA)) 10f **(76)**
Form - 312265
2000 Turf 1-6: (11f, 12f 1-3, 13f, 14f) (sft, g-s, gd 1-4)
Group-class filly, effective 12 to 14f, acts on g-s to gd, best on gd.

Turf high 111. **Mme C Head in FR [1-6].*

SADLER'S REALM BHB 67f **RR 70f** 5111[6]

7 b g Sadler's Wells (USA) 11.3f **(87)** - Rensaler (USA) (Stop The Music (USA)) 9.2f **(71)**

Form - 6

Record 2000 - 1st:0 2nd:0 3rd:0 Ran:1
Pre2000 - 1st:1 2nd:1 3rd:1 Ran:7

Win Prizemoney £3,616 *Total Prizemoney* £5,346

Wins * 1999 May Haydoc (GD) H 14f 65 70 <

2000 Turf 0-1: (16f) (gd)

Above-average gelding. **P J Hobbs [6-22] B D Racing (from Sir Michael Stoute [0-5] Aug 1996).*

SADLER'S SECRET (IRE) BHB 69f **RR 64f** 3163[10]

5 b g Sadler's Wells (USA) 11.3f **(87)** - Athyka (USA) (Secretariat (USA)) 9f **(79)**

Form - 30

Record 2000 - 1st:0 2nd:0 3rd:1 Ran:2

Win Prizemoney £0 *Total Prizemoney* £423

2000 Turf 0-2: (16f, 18f) (g-f, frm)

Average gelding, always wears blinkers. Turf high 64 (1st run) (began Jly) - 3rd of 14 giving 16lb to Laffah (8 Jly Chepstow 18f frm RF 2627). Lightly raced on the Flat, he was third in a maiden handicap at Chepstow in July. **M C Pipe [2-14] A S Helaissi.*

SADLER'S SONG BHB 35f **RR 51f** 4775[12]

3 b f Saddlers' Hall (IRE) 10.5f **(65)** - Life Watch (USA) (Highland Park (USA))

Form - 587500

Record 2000 - 1st:0 2nd:0 3rd:0 Ran:6
Pre2000 - 1st:0 2nd:0 3rd:0 Ran:4

2000 Turf 0-6: (10f, 11f, 12f 2, 16f 2) (g-s, gd, g-f 2, frm 2)

Workmanlike, fair filly, effective 12f, acts on gd, likes tight tracks. Turf high 51 (1st run) - 5th of 15 giving 2lb to Middlethorpe (7 Jun Beverley 12f gd RF 1774). **G M Moore [0-1] Mrs Susan Moore (from M R Channon [0-5] Jly 2000).*

SADLERS SWING (USA) BHB 54f **RR 54f** 1559[7]

4 b h Red Ransom (USA) 8.6f **(83)** - Noblissima (IRE) **(77f)** (Sadler's Wells (USA)) 10f **(76)**

Form - 77

Record 2000 - 1st:0 2nd:0 3rd:0 Ran:2
Pre2000 - 1st:0 2nd:0 3rd:0 Ran:1

2000 Turf 0-2: (10f 2) (g-s, gd)

Workmanlike, currently fair colt. Turf high 54. **J J Sheehan [0-3] Mrs Eileen Sheehan.*

SADLERS WALTZ (IRE) RR 46f 5070[8]

3 b g In The Wings 11.2f **(77)** - Fascination Waltz **(52f 51a)** (Shy Groom (USA)) 10f **(66)**

Form - 8

Record 2000 - 1st:0 2nd:0 3rd:0 Ran:1

2000 Turf 0-1: (12f) (g-s)

Scopey, currently moderate gelding. **J J Sheehan [0-1] Mrs Christina Dowling.*

SAFARANDO (IRE) BHB 105f99a **RR 105f 99a** 830[2]

3 b c Turtle Island (IRE) - Hertford Castle **(31f)** (Reference Point) 6.8f **(70)**

Form - 81121162

Record 2000 - 1st:4 2nd:2 3rd:0 Ran:8
Pre2000 - 1st:2 2nd:3 3rd:3 Ran:15

Win Prizemoney £25,052 *Total Prizemoney* £36,357

Wins * **2000** Apr Haydoc (GD) H 8.1f 89 93+ <
* **2000** Mar Doncas () H 7f 77 89
* **2000** *Feb Wolver (STD) H 8.5f 70 82+*
* **2000** *Feb Wolver (STD) H 7f 72 87*
* 1999 Oct Lingfi (HVY) H 7f 65 69
1999 Jun Yarmou (GD) S 7f 64

2000 Turf 2-4: (7f 1-2, 8f 1-2) (sft, gd 2-3) 2000 AW 2-4: (7f 1-2, 8f 1-2) (Equi, Fibr 2-3)

Scopey, Pattern-class colt, effective 7 to 8f, best at 8f, acts on sft to gd - acts on Fibr, excels at Wolverhampton. Turf high 105 - 2nd of 6 to Kingsclere (22 Apr Kempton 8f sft RF 0830). AW high 102 - 2nd of 8 giving 29lb to Lord Harley (29 Feb Wolverhampton 8f Fibr RF 0382). He showed remarkable improvement earlier in the year. Back on turf after winning a couple of Wolverhampton handicaps, he bolted up in a handicap on Lincoln day at Doncaster and added another victory at Haydock. The Greenham was probably a bit too ambitious, but he did not run at all badly when runner-up in a Kempton Listed event next time. **N P Littmoden [5-20] Paul Dixon (from R Hannon [1-3] Jun 1999).*

SAFARI BLUES (IRE) BHB 71f84a **RR 77f 84a** 4616[11]

3 b f Blues Traveller (IRE) - North Hut (Northfields (USA)) 9f **(72)**

Form - 1158526630

Record 2000 - 1st:0 2nd:1 3rd:1 Ran:8
Pre2000 - 1st:2 2nd:2 3rd:1 Ran:10

Win Prizemoney £6,305 *Total Prizemoney* £11,197

Wins * 1999 *Nov Lingfi (STD) H 8f 76 94+* <
* 1999 *Nov Lingfi (STD) 8f 75*

2000 Turf 0-8: (7f, 8f 2, 9f, 10f 4) (gd 2, g-f 4, frm 2)

Unfurnished, useful filly, effective 8f, - acts on Equi, likes left handed tracks, likes tight tracks. Turf high 79. A poor mover, she has shown her best form on the all-weather. Possibly best when ridden from the front over a mile and a quarter, she looks in the handicapper's grasp at present. **R Hannon [2-18] T J Dale.*

SAFE SHARP JO (IRE) BHB 20f **RR 37?f** 1024[12]

5 ch g Case Law 6f **(64)** - Kentucky Wildcat (Be My Guest (USA)) 9.3f **(67)**

Form - 00687000

Record 2000 - 1st:0 2nd:0 3rd:0 Ran:8
Pre2000 - 1st:0 2nd:0 3rd:0 Ran:8

Win Prizemoney £0 *Total Prizemoney* £204

2000 AW 0-8: (6f, 8f 2, 11f, 12f 2, 15f, 16f) (Fibr 8)

Very moderate gelding, has worn blinkers. AW high 17. **G Barnett [0-3] Lee Heath (from W Clay [0-6] Feb 2000).*

SAFFRON BHB 49a **RR 44f** 4375[16]

4 ch m Alhijaz 7.7f **(57)** - Silver Lodge (Homing) 7.8f **(59)**

Form - 0000543640

Record 2000 - 1st:0 2nd:0 3rd:1 Ran:10
Pre2000 - 1st:1 2nd:3 3rd:1 Ran:14

Win Prizemoney £3,246 *Total Prizemoney* £8,180

Wins 1998 Spt Catter (G-F) H 7f 70 74 <

2000 Turf 0-9: (6f 2, 7f 3, 8f 4) (g-f 3, frm 6) 2000 AW 0-1: (6f) (Fibr)

Moderate filly, effective 8f, acts on frm, has worn blinkers, likes left handed tracks. Turf high 44. **D Shaw [0-10] Ernest Bennett (from J A Glover [1-14] Aug 1999).*

SAFFRON WALDEN (FR) RR 115df 2921a[3]

4 b h Sadler's Wells (USA) 11.3f **(87)** - Or Vision (USA) (Irish River (FR)) 8.6f **(78)**

Form - 3

2000 Turf 0-1: (8f) (g-f)

High-class colt, effective 8 to 10f, acts on g-f to frm, has worn blinkers. He never built on his impressive win in the '99 Irish 2000 Guineas, and has been retired to stud in Japan. **A P O'Brien in IRE [3-8] Mrs John Magnier.*

SAFINAZ BHB 51f **RR 59f** 5074[15]

2 gr f Environment Friend 7.5f **(67)** - Safidar (Roan Rocket) 7.8f **(57)**

Form - 86500

Record 2000 - 1st:0 2nd:0 3rd:0 Ran:5

2000 Turf 0-5: (5f, 6f 3, 7f) (g-s, gd 3, g-f)

Fair filly. Turf high 59 (began Jly). **G Brown [0-5] Mark Faulkner.*

SAFRANINE (IRE) BHB 76f85a **RR 76f 85a** 3390[8]

3 b f Dolphin Street (FR) - Webbiana (African Sky) 7.7f **(50)**

Form - 80008

Record 2000 - 1st:0 2nd:0 3rd:0 Ran:5
Pre2000 - 1st:1 2nd:1 3rd:0 Ran:4

Win Prizemoney £2,994 *Total Prizemoney* £3,843

Wins * 1999 Jly Redcar (FRM) 6f 92? <

2000 Turf 0-4: (6f 2, 7f, 8f) (gd, g-f 2, frm) 2000 AW 0-1: (7f) (Equi)

Leggy, above-average filly, effective 6f, acts on g-f to frm. Turf high 76. **J L Eyre [1-9] M Gleason.*

SAGACITY (FR) RR 94f 5308a[1]

2 br c Highest Honor (FR) 10.9f **(72)** - Saganeca (USA) (Sagace (FR)) 8f **(124)**

Form - 1
2000 Turf 1-1: (10f 1-1) (hvy 1-1)
Currently useful colt. (1st run) - 1st of 8 from Reduit (29 Oct Saint-Cloud RF 5308a). Defied trouble in running to land the Criterium de Saint-Cloud and is bred to make a high-class colt over middle distances. **A Fabre in FR [1-1] J-L Lagardere.*

SAGAMIX (FR) RR 122f 2582a[3]
5 br h Linamix (FR) 8.2f **(64)** - Saganeca (USA) (Sagace (FR)) 8f **(124)**
Form - 043
Record 2000 - 1st:0 2nd:0 3rd:1 Ran:3
Pre2000 - 1st:3 2nd:0 3rd:0 Ran:5
Win Prizemoney £453,535 *Total Prizemoney* £508,639
Wins 1998 Oct Longch (SFT) G1 12f 127 <
1998 Spt Longch (SFT) G2 12f 127 <
1998 Apr Longch (HVY) 12f
2000 Turf 0-3: (12f 3) (g-s, gd 2)
Very high-class colt. Turf high 116. His career was anti-climactic after a brave win in the 1998 Arc. One-paced on all his starts last year, he relished soft ground and has been retired to the Haras du Logis at 25,000FF
**S bin Suroor [0-2] Godolphin (from S bin Suroor in UAE [0-1] Mar 2000).*

SAGAPONACK (USA) BHB 71f77a **RR 66f 77a** 5134[5]
4 b g Broad Brush (USA) 9.5f **(51)** - Sharp Dance (USA) (Dancing Czar (USA)) 12f **(51)**
Form - 514005
Record 2000 - 1st:1 2nd:0 3rd:0 Ran:6
Win Prizemoney £2,886 *Total Prizemoney* £3,176
Wins * 2000 *Mar Southw (STD) 12f 79 <*
2000 Turf 0-3: (10f 2, 12f) (sft, g-s 2) 2000 AW 1-3: (9f, 12f 1-1, 14f) (Fibr 1-3)
Above-average gelding, effective 12f, - acts on Fibr. Turf high 66. AW high 79 - 1st of 12 giving 21lb to Le Cavalier (6 Mar Southwell RF 0414). Unraced until last season, he bolted up in a maiden on the Southwell Fibresand in March, but it was a poor race and he was then found out in better company.
**J R Fanshawe [1-6] Joseph Allen.*

SAGAZON (FR) RR 92f 707a[7]
3 f **Form** - 7
2000 Turf 0-1: (11f) (hvy)
Currently useful. **A Fabre in FR [0-1].*

SAGUARO BHB 45f70a **RR 46f 70a** 2974[3]
6 b g Green Desert (USA) 7.8f **(78)** - Badawi (USA) (Diesis) 9.3f **(69)**
Form - 2103
Record 2000 - 1st:1 2nd:1 3rd:1 Ran:4
Pre2000 - 1st:2 2nd:1 3rd:0 Ran:13
Win Prizemoney £7,307 *Total Prizemoney* £10,046
Wins * 2000 May Mussel (FRM) H 7.1f 42 46
* 1999 *Mar Wolver (SLW) H 9.4f 72 75*
* 1999 *Feb Southw (STD) H 8f 54 82 <*
2000 Turf 1-3: (7f 1-3) (gd, frm 1-2) 2000 AW 0-1: (8f) (Fibr)
Average gelding, effective 8 to 9f, - acts on Fibr, has worn blinkers, likes left handed tracks, prefers tight tracks. Turf high 46 (1st run). Inconsistent.
**K A Morgan [3-14] Roemex Ltd (from J H M Gosden [0-5] Jun 1998).*

SAHARA SPIRIT (IRE) BHB 77f **RR 79f** 2183[31]
3 b g College Chapel - Desert Palace (Green Desert (USA)) 8.6f **(78)**
Form - 22410
Record 2000 - 1st:1 2nd:2 3rd:0 Ran:5
Pre2000 - 1st:0 2nd:0 3rd:1 Ran:3
Win Prizemoney £2,268 *Total Prizemoney* £7,028
Wins * 2000 May Southw (HVY) 7f 79 <
2000 Turf 1-5: (7f 1-2, 8f 3) (gd 1-3, g-f 2)
Scopey, above-average gelding, effective 7 to 8f, best at 7f, acts on gd to g-f, best on g-f. Turf high 79 - 1st of 11 from It Can Be Done (31 May Southwell RF 1605). **E A L Dunlop [1-8] Stars And Stripes.*

SAHAYB BHB 62f **RR 57f** 4676[13]
3 b f Green Desert (USA) 7.8f **(78)** - Matila (IRE) (Persian Bold) 9.3f **(66)**
Form - 8010
Record 2000 - 1st:1 2nd:0 3rd:0 Ran:4
Win Prizemoney £3,997 *Total Prizemoney* £3,997
Wins * 2000 Aug Thirsk (G-F) 7f 57 <
2000 Turf 1-4: (7f 1-2, 8f 2) (g-s, gd, g-f, frm 1-1)
Fair filly, often wears blinkers. Turf high 57 - also 1st of 6 from Dianeme (5 Aug Thirsk RF 3408).
**R W Armstrong [1-4] Hamdan Al Maktoum.*

SAHHAR BHB 30f51a **RR 13f 51a** 3780[10]
7 ch g Sayf El Arab (USA) 8.2f **(57)** - Native Magic (Be My Native (USA)) 10.2f **(71)**
Form - 0
Record 2000 - 1st:0 2nd:0 3rd:0 Ran:1
Pre2000 - 1st:0 2nd:1 3rd:1 Ran:10
Win Prizemoney £0 *Total Prizemoney* £1,209
2000 Turf 0-1: (11f) (gd)
Poor gelding. Becoming disappointing.
**B D Leavy [0-4] Mrs Margaret Underwood (from P J Bevan [0-6] Jly 1998).*

SAIFAN BHB 48f65a **RR 49df 65a** 4333[2]
11 ch g Beveled (USA) 6.9f **(64)** - Superfrost (Tickled Pink) 6.5f **(59)**
Form - 08232
Record 2000 - 1st:0 2nd:2 3rd:1 Ran:5
Pre2000 - 1st:12 2nd:5 3rd:11 Ran:89
Win Prizemoney £92,751 *Total Prizemoney* £116,625
Wins * 1999 Jly Yarmou (FRM) H 7f 58 62
* 1000 Jly Yarmou (GD) C 8f 51+
* 1997 Aug Redcar (G-F) H 8f 83 87
* 1996 Nov Newmar (GD) H 8f 83 88 <
* 1996 Jly Yarmou (FRM) H 8f 77 82
* 1996 Jun Newmar (G-F) H 8f 72 77
2000 Turf 0-5: (7f 2, 8f 3) (gd, g-f 2, frm 2)
Fair gelding, has broken blood-vessels, effective 7f, acts on g-f, mostly wears blinkers. Turf high 48. Inconsistent. **D Morris [12-87] D Morris (from J C Fox [0-7] Nov 1991).*

SAILING BHB 104f **RR 107f** 4835a[9]
3 ch f Arazi (USA) 9.2f **(74)** - Up Anchor (IRE) (Slip Anchor) 9.8f **(73)**
Form - 2141710
Record 2000 - 1st:3 2nd:1 3rd:0 Ran:7
Pre2000 - 1st:2 2nd:1 3rd:0 Ran:5
Win Prizemoney £93,627 *Total Prizemoney* £99,815
Wins * 2000 Aug Ascot (G-F) 12f 107 <
*** 2000** Jun San Si (G-F) G3 12f 103
*** 2000** May San Si (HVY) L 10f 88
* 1999 Aug Sandow (GD) 8.1f 84+
* 1999 Jun Goodwo (G-F) 7f 78+
2000 Turf 3-7: (8f, 10f 1-2, 12f 2-4) (hvy 1-1, g-s, gd 1-2, g-f 1-2, frm)
Scopey, Pattern-class filly, effective 12f, acts on gd to g-f, prefers right handed tracks. Turf high 107 - 1st of 5 giving 3lb to Littlepacepaddocks (12 Aug Ascot RF 3580) - also 1st of 11 getting 13lb from Dangerous Mind (18 Jun San Siro RF 2204a). She won twice at San Siro and added a Shergar Cup race at Ascot. Well beaten at Belmont Park on he final start, where the fast ground ought to have suited. **P F I Cole [5-12].*

SAILING SHOES (IRE) BHB 71f **RR 74f** 4537[9]
4 b g Lahib (USA) 8f **(69)** - Born To Glamour (Ajdal (USA)) 9.2f **(89)**
Form - 0006060
Record 2000 - 1st:0 2nd:0 3rd:0 Ran:7
Pre2000 - 1st:1 2nd:2 3rd:1 Ran:13
Win Prizemoney £3,434 *Total Prizemoney* £38,904
Wins * 1998 Jun Cheste (GD) 5.1f 85+ <
2000 Turf 0-7: (5f 5, 6f, 7f) (g-s 2, gd, g-f 2, frm 2)
Scopey, above-average gelding, effective 6f, acts on g-f, has worn blinkers. Turf high 74. **R Hannon [1-20] Hippodrome Racing.*

SAIL-ON BUN BHB 25f **RR ?f** 4777[14]
4 gr m Beveled (USA) 6.9f **(64)** - Sea Farer Lake (Gairloch) 7f **(63)**
Form - 0
Record 2000 - 1st:0 2nd:0 3rd:0 Ran:1
Pre2000 - 1st:0 2nd:0 3rd:0 Ran:6
2000 Turf 0-1: (16f) (g-s)
Leggy, little account filly.
**K McAuliffe [0-7] Mrs S D Fidler.*

SAILORMAITE BHB 45f66a **RR 37?f 66a** 1521[14]
9 ch g Komaite (USA) 6.9f **(61)** - Marina Plata (Julio Mariner) 7.2f **(57)**
Form - 0
Record 2000 - 1st:0 2nd:0 3rd:0 Ran:1
Pre2000 - 1st:9 2nd:5 3rd:3 Ran:49
Win Prizemoney £34,932 *Total Prizemoney* £48,764
Wins * 1996 May Haydoc (G-S) H 5f 78 81
2000 Turf 0-1: (6f) (gd)
Average gelding, has worn blinkers. Inconsistent. He has been reluctant to race on occasions and is not one to rely on.
**S R Bowring [9-49] S R Bowring (from Miss J F Craze [0-3] Aug 1997).*

SAIL WITH THE WIND BHB 41f **RR 51f** 4994[10]
3 b f Saddlers' Hall (IRE) 10.5f **(65)** - Shesadelight (Shirley Heights) 10.3f **(74)**
Form - 0500
Record 2000 - 1st:0 2nd:0 3rd:0 Ran:4
Pre2000 - 1st:0 2nd:0 3rd:0 Ran:2
2000 Turf 0-3: (10f 2, 12f) (g-s, frm 2) 2000 AW 0-1: (12f) (Fibr)
Scopey, fair filly, effective 10f, acts on frm. Turf high 51 (began Jly). **T D McCarthy [0-6] Hesmonds Stud.*

SAINT CRYSTALGLASS RR 4573[5]
3 ch f Ardkinglass 5f **(64)** - Saint Navarro (Raga Navarro (ITY)) 8f **(64)**
Form - 5
Record 2000 - 1st:0 2nd:0 3rd:0 Ran:1
2000 Turf 0-1: (11f) (sft)
Workmanlike, currently very poor filly. **R Bastiman [0-1] E A Brook.*

SAINT GEORGE (IRE) BHB 32f35a **RR 34f 35a** 3807[7]
4 b g Unblest - Jumana (Windjammer (USA)) 7f **(59)**
Form - 0042487
Record 2000 - 1st:0 2nd:1 3rd:0 Ran:7
Pre2000 - 1st:0 2nd:0 3rd:0 Ran:6
Win Prizemoney £0 *Total Prizemoney* £551
2000 Turf 0-4: (8f 2, 10f, 12f) (g-f, frm 3) 2000 AW 0-3: (6f, 10f, 12f) (Equi, Fibr 2)
Unfurnished, very moderate gelding. Turf high 34. AW high 35. Inconsistent.
**B A Pearce [0-1] Miss J Webster (from K R Burke [0-6] Jly 2000).*

SAINTLY THOUGHTS (USA) BHB 64f54a **RR 68f 54a** 1185[17]
5 b br g St Jovite (USA) 11.8f **(75)** - Free Thinker (USA) (Shadeed (USA)) 8.2f **(70)**
Form - 0
Record 2000 - 1st:0 2nd:0 3rd:0 Ran:1
Pre2000 - 1st:1 2nd:3 3rd:1 Ran:17
Win Prizemoney £5,175 *Total Prizemoney* £9,919
Wins 1999 Aug Downpa (G-F) H 17.4f 65 68 <
2000 Turf 0-1: (16f) (hrd)
Average gelding, effective 16 to 17f, best at 16f, acts on g-f, has worn blinkers. **K A Morgan [0-1] Ian Guise & Celia M Guise (from P Hughes in IRE [1-8] Aug 1999).*

SAINT'S HONOR (USA) RR 580a[10]
4 b h St Jovite (USA) 11.8f **(75)** - Luck Too (USA) (What Luck (USA)) 8.1f **(79)**
Form - 320
2000 Turf 0-1: (8f) (g-s) 2000 AW 0-2: (9f, 10f) (Dirt 2)
Currently very useful colt. AW high 101. **C Dollase in USA [0-3].*

SAKAMOTO BHB 50f **RR 29f** 4964[5]
2 b c Celtic Swing - Possessive Lady (Dara Monarch) 8.8f **(59)**
Form - 885
Record 2000 - 1st:0 2nd:0 3rd:0 Ran:3
Win Prizemoney £0 *Total Prizemoney* £326
2000 Turf 0-3: (7f 2, 8f) (g-s 2, gd)
Currently fair colt. Turf high 29 (began Spt).
**C A Dwyer [0-3] John Purcell.*

SAKHAROV BHB 25f30a **RR 15f 30a** 2674[14]
11 b g Bay Express 7.1f **(53)** - Supreme Kingdom (Take A Reef) 7.5f **(59)**
Form - 70
Record 2000 - 1st:0 2nd:0 3rd:0 Ran:2
Pre2000 - 1st:9 2nd:5 3rd:4 Ran:58
Win Prizemoney £25,449 *Total Prizemoney* £32,120
Wins 1998 *Apr Wolver (STD) H* 9.4f 45 47
1998 *Apr Lingfi (STD) H* 10f 35 43
1996 May Redcar (G-F) S 7f 62 <
2000 Turf 0-1: (10f) (g-s) 2000 AW 0-1: (11f) (Fibr)
Poor gelding, has worn blinkers. Becoming disappointing. **J Neville [0-7] Mrs P K Chick (from B Palling [0-7] Jun 1998).*

SAKHEE (USA) BHB 123f **RR 127f** 2647[4]
3 b c Bahri (USA) - Thawakib (IRE) (Sadler's Wells (USA)) 10f **(76)**
Form - 1124
Record 2000 - 1st:2 2nd:1 3rd:0 Ran:4
Pre2000 - 1st:2 2nd:0 3rd:0 Ran:3
Win Prizemoney £132,274 *Total Prizemoney* £383,300
Wins * **2000** May York (FRM) G2 10.4f 118 <
* **2000** Apr Sandow (SFT) G3 10f 118 <
* 1999 Oct Sandow (SFT) 8.1f 101
* 1999 Spt Nottin (G-F) 8.2f 82+
2000 Turf 2-4: (10f 2-3, 12f) (sft 1-1, gd, g-f 1-1, frm)
Scopey, top-class colt, effective 10 to 12f, best at 10f, acts on sft to frm, does well at Sandown. Turf high 127 - 2nd of 15 to Sinndar (10 Jun Epsom 12f gd RF 1863) - also 1st of 5 from Pawn Broker (17 May York RF 1263). An impressive-looking colt, he made all for a game victory in the Thresher Classic Trial on his return and such tactics were similarly successful in the Dante Stakes. He just lost out to Sinndar in the Derby, but did not really perform to his best when fourth in the Eclipse. He was not seen afterwards, but has reportedly joined the Godolphin team for 2001.
**J L Dunlop [4-7] Hamdan Al Maktoum.*

SALABUE (USA) BHB 58f **RR 54f** 912[14]
3 b c Affirmed (USA) 10.3f **(75)** - Parliament House (USA) (General Assembly (USA)) 10f **(68)**
Form - 0
Record 2000 - 1st:0 2nd:0 3rd:0 Ran:1
Pre2000 - 1st:0 2nd:0 3rd:0 Ran:2
2000 Turf 0-1: (10f) (gd)
Lengthy, currently fair colt. **J L Dunlop [0-3] Benny Andersson.*

SALEE (IRE) BHB 99f **RR 101f** 4931[2]
3 b f Caerleon (USA) 10.9f **(79)** - Almaaseh (IRE) (Dancing Brave (USA)) 8.4f **(76)**
Form - 152
Record 2000 - 1st:1 2nd:1 3rd:0 Ran:3
Pre2000 - 1st:0 2nd:0 3rd:0 Ran:1
Win Prizemoney £4,121 *Total Prizemoney* £10,708
Wins * **2000** Spt Goodwo (GD) 9.9f 87 <
2000 Turf 1-3: (10f 1-3) (gd 1-3)
Light-framed, very useful filly. Turf high 101 (began Spt) - 2nd of 12 getting 5lb from Katy Nowaitee (12 Oct Newmarket 10f gd RF 4931). Took a Goodwood maiden on her belated seasonal bow.
**J H M Gosden [1-3] M Stewkesbury & Mrs J Magnier (from A G Foster [0-1] Oct 1999).*

SALEM BHB 65a **RR 72f** 4929[5]
3 b c Sabrehill (USA) 8.5f **(64)** - Fataana (USA) **(46f)** (El Gran Senor (USA)) 9.6f **(76)**
Form - 0345
Record 2000 - 1st:0 2nd:0 3rd:1 Ran:4
Win Prizemoney £0 *Total Prizemoney* £863
2000 Turf 0-2: (7f, 8f) (g-f, frm) 2000 AW 0-2: (8f, 10f) (Equi 2)
Above-average colt. Turf high 72 (began Aug) - 3rd of 16 giving 5lb to Burning Sunset (5 Spt Lingfield 7f frm RF 4227). AW high 63 (began Spt) - 5th of 12 getting 11lb from Padhams Green (11 Oct Lingfield 8f Equi RF 4929). **R W Armstrong [0-4] Ahmed Al Shafar.*

SALEYMA RR 65f 5236[9]
2 b f Mtoto 11.5f **(71)** - Silk Braid (USA) (Danzig (USA)) 8.4f **(76)**
Form - 0
Record 2000 - 1st:0 2nd:0 3rd:0 Ran:1
2000 Turf 0-1: (7f) (g-s)
Currently average filly. **M A Jarvis [0-1] Sheikh Ahmed Al Maktoum.*

SALFORD FLYER BHB 79f **RR 79f** 896[7]
4 b g Pharly (FR) 11.5f **(64)** - Edge of Darkness **(52f)** (Vaigly Great) 7f **(58)**
Form - 27

Record 2000 - 1st:0 2nd:1 3rd:0 Ran:2
Pre2000 - 1st:3 2nd:3 3rd:1 Ran:17
Win Prizemoney £8,349 *Total Prizemoney* £17,144
Wins 1999 Jly Salisb (G-S) 14.1f 68 <
1999 Jun Yarmou (G-F) H 14.1f 65 68 <
1999 Jun Haydoc (G-S) C 11.9f 68 <
2000 Turf 0-2: (14f, 16f) (sft, gd)
Workmanlike, above-average gelding, effective 14 to 16f, best at 14f, acts on gd to frm, best on gd, excels at Yarmouth. Turf high 79 (1st run) - 2nd of 14 giving 11lb to Final Settlement (25 Mar Kempton 14f gd RF 0500). **D R C Elsworth [1-9] A J Thompson (from G Wragg [3-17] Oct 1999).*

SALIENT POINT (IRE) BHB 56f59a **RR 64f 59a** 5059[6]
3 gr f Sri Pekan (USA) - Tajarib (IRE) (Last Tycoon) 8.5f **(62)**
Form - 5704007P6
Record 2000 - 1st:0 2nd:0 3rd:0 Ran:9
Win Prizemoney £0 *Total Prizemoney* £212
2000 Turf 0-6: (7f 2, 8f, 10f 2, 14f) (sft, gd, g-f 4) 2000 AW 0-3: (8f, 10f, 13f) (Equi 2, Fibr)
Scopey, average filly, effective 8f, - acts on Fibr, likes left handed tracks, likes tight tracks. Turf high 67. AW high 65 (1st run) - 4th of 7 to Shady Point (9 Jun Southwell 8f Fibr RF 1856). Becoming disappointing. **S P C Woods [0-9] Leydens Farm Stud.*

SALIGO (IRE) BHB 63f **RR 62f** 1983[2]
5 b m Elbio 9f **(62)** - Doppio Filo (Vision (USA)) 9f **(64)**
Form - 0000342
Record 2000 - 1st:0 2nd:1 3rd:1 Ran:7
Pre2000 - 1st:3 2nd:4 3rd:2 Ran:26
Win Prizemoney £26,926 *Total Prizemoney* £37,034
Wins 1998 Oct York (GD) H 8.9f 76 79 <
1998 Jun Leices (GD) H 10f 73 77
1998 May Salisb (FRM) H 8f 67 73
2000 Turf 0-7: (7f, 8f 2, 9f 2, 10f 2) (sft, g-s, gd 2, g-f 2, frm)
Average filly, effective 8 to 10f, best at 8f, acted on gd to frm, best on gd, had worn blinkers, excelled at Salisbury. Turf high 62. (DEAD) **N Tinkler [0-8] Arthur Plant (from H Morrison [3-25] Oct 1999).*

SALIM BHB 78f **RR 86f** 4166[16]
3 b c Salse (USA) 10.9f **(71)** - Moviegoer (Pharly (FR)) 9.8f **(68)**
Form - 140430
Record 2000 - 1st:1 2nd:0 3rd:1 Ran:6
Pre2000 - 1st:0 2nd:0 3rd:0 Ran:1
Win Prizemoney £4,306 *Total Prizemoney* £6,186
Wins * 2000 May Thirsk (GD) 7f 86 <
2000 Turf 1-6: (6f, 7f 1-1, 8f, 9f 2, 10f) (gd 1-2, g-f 4)
Leggy, useful colt, effective 7 to 10f, acts on gd to g-f, has worn blinkers. Turf high 86 (1st run) - 1st of 11 giving 5lb to Thermal Spring (6 May Thirsk RF 1066). He made a winning reappearance in a Thirsk maiden, but has not progressed from that. **Sir Michael Stoute [1-7] Hamdan Al Maktoum.*

SALIX DANCER BHB 70f65a **RR 78f 65a** 5026[14]
3 b g Shareef Dancer (USA) 10.1f **(67)** - Willowbank (Gay Fandango (USA)) 8.5f **(59)**
Form - 3060
Record 2000 - 1st:0 2nd:0 3rd:1 Ran:4
Win Prizemoney £0 *Total Prizemoney* £696
2000 Turf 0-3: (8f 2, 10f) (g-s 2, gd) 2000 AW 0-1: (8f) (Fibr)
Leggy, above-average gelding. Turf high 78. **Pat Mitchell [0-4] The Hamilton Partnership.*

SALLY GARDENS BHB 52f48a **RR 47f 48a** 61[10]
3 b f Alzao (USA) 9.8f **(73)** - Polina **(62f)** (Polish Precedent (USA)) 10.2f **(60)**
Form - 070
Record 2000 - 1st:0 2nd:0 3rd:0 Ran:2
Pre2000 - 1st:1 2nd:0 3rd:0 Ran:7
Win Prizemoney £1,934 *Total Prizemoney* £1,934
Wins 1999 *Jly Wolver (STD) S 7f* 62 <
2000 AW 0-2: (6f, 8f) (Equi, Fibr)
Light-framed, moderate filly, effective 7f, - acts on Fibr, likes left handed tracks, likes tight tracks. AW high 27. Becoming disappointing. **T J Naughton [0-5] Ashley Carr Racing 3 (from M R Channon [1-4] Jly 1999).*

SALMON LADDER (USA) BHB 93f **RR 99f** 2114[16]
8 b h Bering 9.6f **(80)** - Ballerina Princess (USA) (Mr Prospector (USA)) 8.8f **(78)**
Form - 4740
Record 2000 - 1st:0 2nd:0 3rd:0 Ran:4
Pre2000 - 1st:10 2nd:7 3rd:4 Ran:37
Win Prizemoney £127,404 *Total Prizemoney* £192,124
Wins * 1999 Aug Cheste (G-S) LH 13.4f 96 101
* 1999 May Goodwo (GD) H 14f 92 96
* 1998 May Bath (GD) 10.2f 106
* 1998 May Hamilt (G-S) 9.2f 79+
* 1997 Aug Windso (G-F) 10f 106
* 1996 Oct Newbur (SFT) G3 12f 115 <
* 1996 Aug Goodwo (G-F) LH 12f 108 113
* 1996 Jun Ascot (G-F) H 10f 102 107
* 1996 Jun Hamilt (GD) 9.2f 88+
2000 Turf 0-4: (12f 3, 14f) (g-s, gd 3)
Very useful horse, effective 12 to 14f, acts on gd, has worn blinkers, likes left handed tracks. Turf high 99. Consistent. A grand campaigner, he enjoys front-running but is not the force of old. A free sweater, he has worn blinkers in the past. **P F I Cole [10-41] M Arbib.*

SALORY BHB 47f44a **RR 65f 44a** 4823[20]
4 b h Salse (USA) 10.9f **(71)** - Mory Kante (USA) (Icecapade (USA)) 11f **(62)**
Form - 030802000
Record 2000 - 1st:0 2nd:1 3rd:1 Ran:8
Pre2000 - 1st:0 2nd:0 3rd:0 Ran:6
Win Prizemoney £0 *Total Prizemoney* £1,233
2000 Turf 0-6: (7f, 8f 3, 10f 2) (g-f 3, frm 3) 2000 AW 0-2: (8f, 9f) (Equi, Fibr)
Workmanlike, average colt, effective 8f, acts on g-f, has worn blinkers, likes tight tracks. Turf high 65 - 2nd of 9 getting 5lb from Lake Sunbeam (26 Jly Sandown 8f g-f RF 3139). AW high 39. **Miss Jacqueline Doyle [0-12] Sanford Racing (from R T Phillips [0-2] Oct 1998).*

SALOUP **RR 58f** 4820[14]
2 b f Wolfhound (USA) 7.3f **(71)** - Sarcita (Primo Dominie) 6.2f **(80)**
Form - 0
Record 2000 - 1st:0 2nd:0 3rd:0 Ran:1
2000 Turf 0-1: (6f) (g-f)
Currently fair filly. **D R C Elsworth [0-1] Raymond Tooth.*

SALSA **RR 74f** 3839[3]
2 b c Salse (USA) 10.9f **(71)** - Lana Turrel (USA) (Trempolino (USA)) 12f **(71)**
Form - 53
Record 2000 - 1st:0 2nd:0 3rd:1 Ran:2
Win Prizemoney £0 *Total Prizemoney* £580
2000 Turf 0-2: (6f 2) (gd, g-f)
Currently above-average colt. Turf high 74 (began Jly) - 3rd of 15 giving 7lb to Zietunzeen (21 Aug Nottingham 6f g-f RF 3839). **W R Muir [0-2] Mrs J M Muir.*

SALSIFY BHB 24f **RR ?f** 3782[6]
4 b g Salse (USA) 10.9f **(71)** - Amaranthus (Shirley Heights) 10.3f **(74)**
Form - 6
Record 2000 - 1st:0 2nd:0 3rd:0 Ran:1
Pre2000 - 1st:0 2nd:0 3rd:0 Ran:2
2000 Turf 0-1: (14f) (frm)
Scopey, currently very poor gelding. **G A Ham [0-1] P A Dales (from R Charlton [0-2] Apr 1999).*

SALSKA BHB 44f45a **RR 54f 45a** 4630[7]
9 b m Salse (USA) 10.9f **(71)** - Anzeige (GER) (Soderini) 13.5f **(68)**
Form - 0054250667
Record 2000 - 1st:0 2nd:1 3rd:0 Ran:10
Pre2000 - 1st:8 2nd:7 3rd:3 Ran:58
Win Prizemoney £27,592 *Total Prizemoney* £42,928
Wins 1999 Jly Redcar (FRM) H 16f 67 64
1998 Jun Newcas (GD) H 16.1f 60 66 <
1998 Jun Nottin (GD) H 14.1f 60 66 <
1997 Jly Redcar (G-F) H 16f 58 61
1997 Jun Nottin (G-F) H 14.1f 56 61
1996 Jly Redcar (G-F) H 14.1f 46 57+

1996 Jly Warwic (G-F) H 14.9f 46 54+
2000 Turf 0-10: (16f 8, 17f 2) (g-s, gd 2, g-f, frm 6)
Fair mare, effective 16f, acts on gd to frm, best on frm, has worn blinkers, likes left handed tracks. Turf high 60. **P L Clinton [0-10] P L Clinton (from A Streeter [8-40] Oct 1999).*

SALTAIRE (IRE) RR 20f — 3151[9]

2 b f Idris (IRE) - Rahwah (Northern Baby (CAN)) 11.6f **(71)**
Form - 0
Record 2000 - 1st:0 2nd:0 3rd:0 Ran:1
2000 Turf 0-1: (5f) (g-f)
Currently little account filly. **Mrs P N Dutfield [0-1] Aidan Walsh.*

SALTRIO RR 76f — 5157[6]

2 b c Slip Anchor 12.7f **(75)** - Hills' Presidium (Presidium)
Form - 6
Record 2000 - 1st:0 2nd:0 3rd:0 Ran:1
2000 Turf 0-1: (8f) (sft)
Currently above-average colt.
**J H M Gosden [0-1] Dr Ornella Carlini Cozzi.*

SALTWOOD BHB 75f RR 79f — 4970[18]

2 b f Mujtahid (USA) 7.4f **(69)** - Actualite (Polish Precedent (USA)) 10.2f **(60)**
Form - 84100
Record 2000 - 1st:1 2nd:0 3rd:0 Ran:5
Win Prizemoney £4,426 *Total Prizemoney* £4,814
Wins * **2000** Spt Ayr (SFT) 7f 79 <
2000 Turf 1-5: (6f, 7f 1-3, 8f) (gd 1-2, g-f, frm 2)
Above-average filly. Turf high 79 (began Aug) - 1st of 9 getting 5lb from Irish Stream (14 Spt Ayr RF 4386). Got off the mark in an Ayr maiden on her third start when encountering soft ground for the first time. **B W Hills [1-5] Bodfari Stud Ltd.*

SALTY JACK (IRE) BHB 83f85a RR 87f 85a — 5240[18]

6 b h Salt Dome (USA) 6.5f **(59)** - Play The Queen (IRE) (King of Clubs) 7.1f **(57)**
Form - 10213000545130260
Record 2000 - 1st:2 2nd:2 3rd:2 Ran:16
Pre2000 - 1st:7 2nd:5 3rd:7 Ran:37
Win Prizemoney £47,807 *Total Prizemoney* £83,013
Wins * **2000** Jly Ascot (G-F) H 8f 79 84
* **2000** *Feb Lingfi (STD) H 8f 81 84*
* 1999 *Dec Lingfi (STD) H 7f 74 77*
* 1998 Oct Newmar (GD) H 7f 85 90 <
* 1998 Spt Doncas (GD) H 7f 81 84
* 1998 Jly Epsom (G-F) H 7f 75 78
* 1998 Apr Folkes (SFT) 6.9f 74
* 1997 *Dec Lingfi (STD) H 7f 65 69*
1996 Aug Salisb (GD) 6f 75
2000 Turf 1-12: (7f 3, 8f 1-8, 9f) (g-s 3, gd 6, g-f 1-2, frm) 2000 AW 1-4: (7f 3, 8f 1-1) (Equi 1-4)
Useful horse, effective 7 to 8f, best at 7f, acts on gd to frm - acts on Equi, likes left handed tracks, likes tight tracks, excels at Lingfield and does well at Ascot. Turf high 87 - also 1st of 15 giving 10lb to It's Magic (30 Jly Ascot RF 3229). AW high 84 - 1st of 7 giving 9lb to Ron's Pet (9 Feb Lingfield RF 0249). Suited by being held up in a fast-run race, those tactics were employed to perfection at Ascot in July.
**V Soane [8-47] Salts Of The Earth (from S Dow [1-6] Spt 1996).*

SALUEM BHB 80f RR 81f — 5091a[6]

3 b f Salse (USA) 10.9f **(71)** - Pat Or Else (Alzao (USA)) 7.1f **(68)**
Form - 32256
Record 2000 - 1st:0 2nd:2 3rd:1 Ran:5
Win Prizemoney £0 *Total Prizemoney* £3,810
2000 Turf 0-5: (10f, 12f 2, 14f, 15f) (sft, g-s, g-f 3)
Scopey, decent filly. Turf high 81 (1st run) - 3rd of 6 to Bella Lambada (16 Jun York 10f g-f RF 2037). Placed in maidens.
**R Guest [0-5].*

SALVA RR 56f — 4544[7]

4 b m Grand Lodge (USA) - Salvezza (IRE) **(83df)** (Superpower)
Form - 46007
Record 2000 - 1st:0 2nd:0 3rd:0 Ran:5
Pre2000 - 1st:0 2nd:0 3rd:1 Ran:2
Win Prizemoney £0 *Total Prizemoney* £720
2000 Turf 0-4: (8f 3, 10f) (sft, gd 2, frm) 2000 AW 0-1: (8f) (Fibr)
Unfurnished, fair filly, effective 8f, acts on gd, has worn blinkers, likes tight tracks. Turf high 56. **P J Makin [0-7] Mrs P J Makin.*

SALVAGE BHB 40f35a RR 47f 35a — 2672[5]

5 b g Kahyasi 12.9f **(74)** - Storm Weaver (USA) (Storm Bird (CAN)) 10.3f **(74)**
Form - 7378485
Record 2000 - 1st:0 2nd:0 3rd:1 Ran:7
Pre2000 - 1st:1 2nd:1 3rd:0 Ran:8
Win Prizemoney £2,967 *Total Prizemoney* £4,320
Wins * 1999 Oct Catter (SFT) H 15.8f 49 53 <
2000 Turf 0-6: (14f 3, 16f 2, 18f) (gd 3, frm 3) 2000 AW 0-1: (16f) (Fibr)
Moderate gelding, effective 14 to 16f, best at 16f, acts on gd to frm, best on gd, favours tight tracks. Turf high 47 - 4th of 6 giving 4lb to Noufari (13 Jun Redcar 16f frm RF 1914). Consistent.
**W W Haigh [2-19] Arnie Flower.*

SALVIANO RR 27f — 4828[21]

2 b g River Falls 8.2f **(56)** - Shiny Kay (Star Appeal) 9.6f **(65)**
Form - 00
Record 2000 - 1st:0 2nd:0 3rd:0 Ran:2
2000 Turf 0-2: (8f 2) (g-s, gd)
Currently little account gelding. Turf high 27 (began Aug).
**N Tinkler [0-2] Mrs Christine Cawley.*

SALVIATI (USA) BHB 87f RR 87f — 1690[13]

3 b c Lahib (USA) 8f **(69)** - Mother Courage (Busted) 10.2f **(61)**
Form - 20
Record 2000 - 1st:0 2nd:1 3rd:0 Ran:2
Pre2000 - 1st:1 2nd:0 3rd:1 Ran:2
Win Prizemoney £3,687 *Total Prizemoney* £6,601
Wins * 1999 Jly Folkes (G-F) 6f 73 <
2000 Turf 0-2: (6f 2) (g-f, frm)
Scopey, useful colt. Turf high 87 (1st run) - 2nd of 18 giving 8lb to Ravishing (20 May Newbury 6f g-f RF 1335). Showed plenty of promise on his debut at two before landing a Folkestone maiden, but was then off the track for ten months before being just caught in a competitive Newbury handicap in May.
**Mrs A J Perrett [1-4] Cyril Humphris.*

SALZGITTER BHB 67f RR 73f — 5220[3]

3 b f Salse (USA) 10.9f **(71)** - Anna of Brunswick **(71f)** (Rainbow Quest (USA)) 10.4f **(75)**
Form - 337603
Record 2000 - 1st:0 2nd:0 3rd:3 Ran:6
Pre2000 - 1st:0 2nd:0 3rd:0 Ran:1
Win Prizemoney £0 *Total Prizemoney* £1,447
2000 Turf 0-6: (7f, 10f 3, 12f 2) (sft, g-s, gd 2, frm 2)
Light-framed, above-average filly, effective 10f, acts on gd. Turf high 73 - 3rd of 13 to Revival (18 May Salisbury 10f gd RF 1267).
**H Candy [0-7] Major M G Wyatt.*

SAMADILLA (IRE) BHB 79f RR 82f — 4833[3]

2 b f Mujadil (USA) 7.7f **(70)** - Samnaun (USA) (Stop The Music (USA)) 9.2f **(71)**
Form - 1441043
Record 2000 - 1st:2 2nd:0 3rd:1 Ran:7
Win Prizemoney £7,137 *Total Prizemoney* £9,264
Wins * **2000** Aug Ripon (GD) H 6f 78 82 <
* **2000** Jly Pontef (GD) 5f 72+
2000 Turf 2-7: (5f 1-3, 6f 1-3, 7f) (sft, g-s, gd, frm 2-3, hrd)
Decent filly, effective 5 to 6f, acts on frm. Turf high 82 (began Jly) - 1st of 9 giving 4lb to Face D Facts (29 Aug Ripon RF 4062). **T D Easterby [2-7] W T Whittle.*

SAMARA MIDDLE EAST (FR) RR 86+f — 5308a[6]

2 b f Marju (IRE) 9.2f **(76)** - Modelliste (Machiavellian (USA))
Form - 616
Record 2000 - 1st:1 2nd:0 3rd:0 Ran:3
Win Prizemoney £3,542 *Total Prizemoney* £3,857
Wins * **2000** Oct Ayr (HVY) 8f 86+ <
2000 Turf 1-3: (7f, 8f 1-1, 10f) (hvy 1-2, gd)
Currently useful filly. Turf high 86 (began Spt) - 1st of 7 from Phoebe Robinson (10 Oct Ayr RF 4889).
**M R Channon [1-3].*

SAMARARDO BHB 55f54a **RR 57f 54a** 5161[4]
3 b g Son Pardo - Kinlet Vision (IRE) (Vision (USA)) 9f **(64)**
Form - 2035464214
Record 2000 - 1st:1 2nd:1 3rd:0 Ran:7
Pre2000 - 1st:1 2nd:1 3rd:1 Ran:10
Win Prizemoney £5,945 *Total Prizemoney* £8,024
Wins * **2000** Spt Goodwo (SFT) H 16f 49 52
* 1999 *Oct Wolver (STD) SH 8.5f 49 54* <
2000 Turf 1-7: (10f, 11f, 12f 2, 16f 1-3) (sft, g-s 1-1, g-f 2, frm 3)
Leggy, average gelding, effective 8f, - acts on Fibr, has worn blinkers, likes tight tracks. Turf high 57 (began Jly).
**N P Littmoden [2-17] Trojan Racing.*

SAMARA SONG BHB 53f45a **RR 57f 45a** 5116[3]
7 ch g Savahra Sound 7.8f **(55)** - Hosting (Thatching) 8f **(66)**
Form - 07526774O403
Record 2000 - 1st:0 2nd:1 3rd:1 Ran:12
Pre2000 - 1st:4 2nd:9 3rd:4 Ran:50
Win Prizemoney £25,838 *Total Prizemoney* £40,500
Wins * 1999 Jly York (G-F) H 7.9f 66 68 <
* 1999 May Salisb (G-F) H 7f 63 65
* 1998 Aug Sandow (GD) H 7.1f 59 63
* 1997 Spt Leices (G-F) H 7f 53 54
2000 Turf 0-11: (7f 4, 8f 6, 11f) (hvy, sft, gd, g-f 3, frm 4, hrd) 2000 AW 0-1: (8f) (Fibr)
Fair gelding, effective 7 to 8f, best at 7f, acts on gd to frm, has worn blinkers. Turf high 57. Best at seven furlongs, he is on a long losing run.
**Ian Williams [4-51] R J Turton (from W G M Turner [0-10] Oct 1996).*

SAMAWI (IRE) RR 70f 5100[8]
2 b c Pennekamp (USA) - Raaqiyya (USA) (Blushing Groom (FR)) 10.3f **(76)**
Form - 8
Record 2000 - 1st:0 2nd:0 3rd:0 Ran:1
2000 Turf 0-1: (7f) (gd)
Currently above-average colt.
**M P Tregoning [0-1] Hamdan Al Maktoum.*

SAMBAKONIG (GER) RR 106f 4944a[3]
7 h Turfkonig (GER) - 00
Form - 133
2000 Turf 1-3: (10f 1-2, 11f) (hvy, sft 1-1, g-s)
Pattern-class horse, effective 10 to 11f, best at 10f, acts on hvy to g-s, best on g-s. Turf high 106 (1st run) - 1st of 12 getting 5lb from Kalatos (9 Apr Gelsenkirchen-horst RF 0706a). Consistent.
**H Horwart in GER [1-15] A von Mulert.*

SAMEEAH (IRE) BHB 30f **RR 33f** 2391[7]
4 br m Perugino (USA) - Kayrava (Irish River (FR)) 8.6f **(78)**
Form - 67
Record 2000 - 1st:0 2nd:0 3rd:0 Ran:2
Pre2000 - 1st:0 2nd:0 3rd:0 Ran:1
2000 Turf 0-1: (6f) (g-f) 2000 AW 0-1: (9f) (Fibr)
Lengthy, currently very moderate filly.
**K Mahdi [0-3] Hamad Al-Mutawa.*

SAMIYAH (IRE) BHB 45f37a **RR 52f 37a** 417[13]
4 b m Anshan 8.2f **(63)** - Fujaiyrah (In Fijar (USA)) 7.5f **(70)**
Form - 0
Record 2000 - 1st:0 2nd:0 3rd:0 Ran:1
Pre2000 - 1st:0 2nd:0 3rd:0 Ran:6
Win Prizemoney £0 *Total Prizemoney* £219
2000 AW 0-1: (8f) (Fibr)
Leggy, fair filly.
**Mrs P Sly [0-3] Cameron Racing Partners (from Miss I Foustok [0-6] Aug 1999).*

SAMMAL (IRE) BHB 41f48a **RR 45f 48a** 4398[9]
4 b g Petardia 8.2f **(58)** - Prime Site (IRE) (Burslem) 8.8f **(53)**
Form - 005004620860
Record 2000 - 1st:0 2nd:1 3rd:0 Ran:12
Pre2000 - 1st:1 2nd:1 3rd:2 Ran:13
Win Prizemoney £3,195 *Total Prizemoney* £6,292
Wins * 1998 Apr Carlis (G-S) 5f 74 <
2000 Turf 0-10: (5f, 6f 9) (hvy, gd, g-f 3, frm 5) 2000 AW 0-2: (5f 2) (Fibr 2)
Leggy, moderate gelding, effective 5 to 6f, acts on g-f to hrd, has worn blinkers. Turf high 45. AW high 24.
**J A Glover [1-25] Mrs Andrea Mallinson.*

SAMMIE DUROSE (IRE) BHB 41f **RR 47f** 306[8]
3 b g Forest Wind (USA) - La Calera (Corvaro (USA)) 9f **(53)**
Form - 5208
Record 2000 - 1st:0 2nd:1 3rd:0 Ran:4
Pre2000 - 1st:0 2nd:0 3rd:0 Ran:3
Win Prizemoney £0 *Total Prizemoney* £430
2000 AW 0-4: (8f 2, 9f, 11f) (Fibr 4)
Moderate gelding, effective 9f, - acts on Fibr, has worn blinkers. AW high 42 - 2nd of 5 getting 1lb from Wilemmgeo (22 Jan Wolverhampton 9f Fibr RF 0143).
**R A Fahey [0-7] Mrs Elizabeth Pettinger.*

SAMMY'S SHUFFLE BHB 46f57a **RR 50f 57a** 4304[12]
5 b h Touch of Grey 8.1f **(47)** - Cabinet Shuffle (Thatching) 8f **(66)**
Form - 33251587153764O2232123580
Record 2000 - 1st:2 2nd:4 3rd:3 Ran:20
Pre2000 - 1st:4 2nd:3 3rd:3 Ran:30
Win Prizemoney £17,226 *Total Prizemoney* £27,228
Wins * **2000** Jly Epsom (GD) H 10.1f 41 44
* **2000** *Feb Lingfi (STD) H 10f 55 59* <
* 1999 *Dec Lingfi (STD) H 10f 55 57*
1998 *Dec Lingfi (STD) H 10f 37 47*
1998 Spt Bright (GD) H 10f 43 47
1998 Jly Bright (G-F) H 10f 30 35
2000 Turf 1-12: (8f 2, 9f, 10f 1-8, 12f) (gd 6, g-f 1-2, frm 4) 2000 AW 1-8: (10f 1-7, 12f) (Equi 1-8)
Fair colt, effective 8 to 10f, best at 10f, acts on gd - acts on Equi, mostly wears blinkers (effectively), likes left handed tracks, favours tight tracks, likes Lingfield. Turf high 50 - 2nd of 7 getting 26lb from Riberac (9 Aug Sandown 8f gd RF 3506). AW high 59 - 1st of 5 getting 9lb from Admirals Place (23 Feb Lingfield RF 0344). He runs regularly and wins in his turn on both Equitrack and turf. He is suited by a sharp left-handed track and scored in good style at Epsom in July. Best over ten furlongs.
**J R Poulton [3-30] Mrs G M Temmerman (from R M Flower [3-21] Feb 1999).*

SAMPOWER STAR BHB 116f82a **RR 119f 82a** 4608[1]
4 b h Cyrano de Bergerac 7.3f **(58)** - Green Supreme (Primo Dominie) 6.2f **(80)**
Form - 15221
Record 2000 - 1st:2 2nd:2 3rd:0 Ran:5
Pre2000 - 1st:5 2nd:3 3rd:2 Ran:22
Win Prizemoney £138,373 *Total Prizemoney* £227,837
Wins * **2000** Spt Ascot (SFT) G2 6f 109+
* **2000** May Longch (HVY) G3 5f 109
1999 May York (SFT) G3 6f 113+
1999 Apr Ascot (GD) L 6f 119+ <
1999 Apr Windso (G-F) 6f 90
1998 Jly Salisb (GD) 7f 82
1998 Jly Folkes (G-F) 6f 71+
2000 Turf 2-5: (5f 1-2, 6f 1-3) (g-s 1-3, gd 1-2)
Strong, high-class colt, effective 5 to 6f, best at 6f, acts on sft to frm, excels at Ascot and Haydock and Longchamp. Turf high 119 - 2nd of 13 giving 3lb to Pipalong (2 Spt Haydock 6f g-s RF 4157). He proved a shrewd purchase for the Goldophin team, winning two Group races including the Diadem Sakes. Effective on most types of ground but best over six furlongs on an easy surface, he will win a big sprint under suitable conditions this year.
**S bin Suroor [2-5] Godolphin (from R Hannon [3-13] Oct 1999).*

SAMSAAM (IRE) BHB 108f **RR 109f** 4985[7]
3 b c Sadler's Wells (USA) 11.3f **(87)** - Azyaa (Kris) 9.5f **(73)**
Form - 11132137
Record 2000 - 1st:4 2nd:1 3rd:2 Ran:8
Pre2000 - 1st:0 2nd:0 3rd:0 Ran:3
Win Prizemoney £32,357 *Total Prizemoney* £47,645
Wins * **2000** Jly Chanti (SFT) G3 15f 105+ <
* **2000** Jun Haydoc (G-S) H 14f 81 93
* **2000** May Doncas (G-S) H 14.6f 73 88++
* **2000** Apr Windso (HVY) H 11.6f 66 72
2000 Turf 4-8: (12f 1-1, 14f 1-2, 15f 2-3, 16f 2) (sft 1-1, g-s 2-2, gd 1-5)
Scopey, Pattern-class colt, effective 14 to 15f, best at 15f, acts on sft to gd, best on gd. Turf high 109 - 3rd of 5 giving 5lb to Alva

Glen (26 Aug Goodwood 14f gd RF 3983) - also 1st of 9 from Mister Kick (28 Jly Chantilly RF 3348a). He made a fine start to the season by completing a hat-trick and looking well suited by extended trips. Lost no caste in defeat at Ascot or Goodwood before landing a Chantilly Group Three in good style. Disappointing on his last two runs, he is suited by cut in the ground.
**J L Dunlop [4-11] Hamdan Al Maktoum.*

SAMUM (GER) RR 125+f
4846a[6]
3 ch c Monsun (GER) - Sacarina (GER) (Old Vic)
Form - 11116
2000 Turf 4-5: (9f 1-1, 10f 1-1, 12f 2-3) (hvy 2-2, sft 2-2, gd)
Top-class colt. Turf high 125 - 1st of 11 getting 7lb from Catella (3 Spt Baden-Baden RF 4289a) - also 1st of 20 from Subiaco (2 Jly Hamburg RF 2581a). Has claims to be the best middle-distance horse in Germany having won the German Derby and seen off a top-class field in a Group One at Baden-Baden in September. Ran with credit in the Arc and the Hong Kong Cup later in the year on ground rather faster than her prefers. Very much suited by soft going and the best of him may yet to be seen.
**A Schutz in GER [4-5].*

SAMWAR BHB 50f55a RR 49f 55a
5118[P]
8 b g Warning 8.1f **(77)** - Samaza (USA) (Arctic Tern (USA)) 8.9f **(69)**
Form - 811571406226063201225632635P

Record	**2000** -	1st:1	2nd:6	3rd:3	Ran:22
	Pre2000 -	1st:8	2nd:7	3rd:7	Ran:67

Win Prizemoney £38,736 — *Total Prizemoney* £63,232

Wins								
* **2000**	*May*	*Wolver*	*(STD)*	*S*	*5f*		*45*	
* 1999	*Dec*	*Southw*	*(SLW)*	*C*	*5f*		*75*	
* 1999	*Dec*	*Wolver*	*(STD)*	*H*	*5f*	*69*	*73*	
* 1999	*Nov*	*Southw*	*(STD)*	*C*	*5f*		*58*	
* 1999	*Aug*	*Wolver*	*(STD)*	*H*	*5f*	*62*	*68*	
* 1999	*Jly*	*Southw*	*(STD)*	*H*	*5f*	*59*	*61*	
* 1999	*Jun*	*Wolver*	*(STD)*	*S*	*5f*		*57+*	
1996	Aug	Ripon	(GD)	H	6f	78	89	<

2000 Turf 0-1: (6f) (g-f) 2000 AW 1-21: (5f 1-14, 6f 7) (Equi, Fibr 1-20)
Fair gelding, effective 5 to 6f, best at 5f, - acts on Fibr, often wears blinkers (extremely effectively). AW high 72 - 2nd of 11 giving 10lb to Eastern Trumpeter (10 Feb Wolverhampton 5f Fibr RF 0255). Consistent. **Mrs N Macauley [7-58] Andy Peake (from Miss Gay Kelleway [2-20] Jly 1998).*

SANAPTA RR 40f
5019[7]
2 b f Elmaamul (USA) 8.1f **(70)** - La Domaine (Dominion) 8.5f **(63)**
Form - 07

Record	**2000** -	1st:0	2nd:0	3rd:0	Ran:2

2000 Turf 0-1: (6f) (g-f) 2000 AW 0-1: (7f) (Fibr)
Currently moderate filly. **W R Muir [0-2] Larksborough Stud Ltd.*

SANDABAR BHB 51f RR 60f
4327[10]
7 b g Green Desert (USA) 7.8f **(78)** - Children's Corner (FR) (Top Ville) 11.7f **(68)**
Form - 0032156340

Record	**2000** -	1st:1	2nd:1	3rd:2	Ran:10
	Pre2000 -	1st:2	2nd:0	3rd:1	Ran:15

Win Prizemoney £13,702 — *Total Prizemoney* £18,984

Wins								
* **2000**	Jun	Mussel	(FRM)	H	16f	59	64	
* 1999	Jly	Ripon	(G-F)	H	10f	58	63	
1996	Apr	Folkes	(G-F)		6.9f		75	<

2000 Turf 1-10: (10f 2, 11f, 12f 4, 14f, 16f 1-2) (g-s, gd, g-f 2, frm 1-6)
Average gelding, effective 8 to 16f, acts on g-f to frm, best on frm, likes right handed tracks, favours tight tracks, excels at Musselburgh, does well at Redcar. Turf high 64 - 1st of 7 giving 32lb to Xellance (26 Jun Musselburgh RF 2272). **Mrs M Reveley [7-30] W Williams (from Sir Michael Stoute [1-6] Jun 1997).*

SANDAL RR 69f
2625[12]
2 b f Prince Sabo 6.6f **(64)** - Australia Fair (AUS) (Without Fear (FR)) 5.9f **(55)**
Form - 3450

Record	**2000** -	1st:0	2nd:0	3rd:1	Ran:4

Win Prizemoney £0 — *Total Prizemoney* £957
2000 Turf 0-4: (5f 2, 6f 2) (gd, frm 3)
Average filly, has worn blinkers. Turf high 69.
**R Hannon [0-4] The Queen.*

SANDBAGGEDAGAIN BHB 65f RR 68f
4535[7]
6 b g Prince Daniel (USA) 11.4f **(46)** - Paircullis (Tower Walk) 10f **(62)**
Form - 0552047

Record	**2000** -	1st:0	2nd:1	3rd:0	Ran:7
	Pre2000 -	1st:4	2nd:3	3rd:8	Ran:26

Win Prizemoney £26,393 — *Total Prizemoney* £42,571

Wins								
* 1998	Spt	Cheste	(GD)	H	15.9f	74	76	<
* 1998	Jly	Ascot	(G-F)	H	16.2f	64	68	
* 1998	Jly	Catter	(GD)	H	15.8f	62	63	
* 1997	Jun	York	(G-S)	H	11.9f		76+	

2000 Turf 0-7: (12f, 14f 3, 16f 3) (g-s 2, g-f 5)
Average gelding, effective 14f, acts on g-f, has worn blinkers, likes left handed tracks. Turf high 68. Consistent.
**M W Easterby [4-37] Mrs Christopher Hanbury.*

SAND BANKES BHB 72f RR 76?f
2887[5]
2 ch c Efisio 7.7f **(69)** - Isabella Sharp **(67f)** (Sharpo) 7.7f **(59)**
Form - 276121165

Record	**2000** -	1st:3	2nd:2	3rd:0	Ran:9

Win Prizemoney £6,748 — *Total Prizemoney* £7,928

Wins								
* **2000**	Jun	Mussel	(FRM)		7.1f		76?	<
* **2000**	Jun	Yarmou	(G-F)	S	7f		56	
* **2000**	May	Chepst	(HVY)	S	6.1f		56	

2000 Turf 3-7: (5f, 6f 1-2, 7f 2-4) (g-s 1-2, gd 2, g-f 1-1, frm 1-2) 2000 AW 0-2: (5f 2) (Fibr 2)
Above-average colt, effective 7f, acted on frm, often wore blinkers (extremely effectively). Turf high 76 - 1st of 5 giving 6lb to Mujalina (26 Jun Musselburgh RF 2270). AW high 56. (DEAD)
**W G M Turner [3-9] T Lightbowne.*

SAND HAWK BHB 54f65a RR 53f 65a
5185[2]
5 ch g Polar Falcon (USA) 9f **(74)** - Ghassanah (Pas de Seul) 9.1f **(67)**
Form - 122114235074176222

Record	**2000** -	1st:3	2nd:5	3rd:1	Ran:16
	Pre2000 -	1st:1	2nd:4	3rd:2	Ran:25

Win Prizemoney £13,268 — *Total Prizemoney* £25,052

Wins								
* **2000**	Aug	Catter	(G-S)	H	7f	41	44	
* **2000**	*Jan*	*Wolver*	*(STD)*	*H*	*7f*	*54*	*62*	<
* **2000**	*Jan*	*Southw*	*(STD)*	*H*	*7f*	*54*	*58*	
* 1999	*Dec*	*Wolver*	*(STD)*		*7f*		*59*	

2000 Turf 1-8: (6f, 7f 1-6, 8f) (hvy, g-s, gd, g-f 1-4, frm) 2000 AW 2-8: (6f 3, 7f 2-5) (Fibr 2-8)
Average gelding, effective 6 to 7f, best at 7f, - acts on Fibr, often wears blinkers (very effectively), prefers left handed tracks, prefers tight tracks, excels at Wolverhampton and Southwell. Turf high 53 (began Aug). AW high 70 - 2nd of 8 getting 2lb from Out of Sight (18 Feb Southwell 7f Fibr RF 0308) - also 1st of 12 getting 10lb from Ron's Pet (13 Jan Wolverhampton RF 0084). **D Shaw [4-41] J C Fretwell.*

SAN DIMAS (USA) BHB 51f RR 64f
1915[11]
3 gr g Distant View (USA) - Chrystophard (USA) (Lypheor) 12f **(71)**
Form - 07600

Record	**2000** -	1st:0	2nd:0	3rd:0	Ran:5
	Pre2000 -	1st:0	2nd:0	3rd:0	Ran:2

2000 Turf 0-5: (8f 2, 10f 3) (sft, gd, g-f, frm 2)
Scopey, average gelding, has worn blinkers. Turf high 64.
**Andrew Turnell [0-7] Dr John Hollowood.*

SANDLES BHB 68f RR 72f
5027[4]
2 b g Komaite (USA) 6.9f **(61)** - Miss Calculate (Mummy's Game) 8.2f **(60)**
Form - 15440754

Record	**2000** -	1st:1	2nd:0	3rd:0	Ran:8

Win Prizemoney £2,233 — *Total Prizemoney* £3,402

Wins								
* **2000**	*May*	*Wolver*	*(STD)*		*5f*		*65*	<

2000 Turf 0-7: (5f, 6f, 7f 3, 8f 2) (g-s 2, gd, g-f 2, frm 2) 2000 AW 1-1: (5f 1-1) (Fibr 1-1)
Above-average gelding, effective 5 to 8f, best at 7f, acts on g-s to frm - acts on Fibr. Turf high 72 (began Jly) - 4th of 12 getting 2lb from Port Moresby (17 Oct Yarmouth 8f g-s RF 5027). (1st run) - 1st of 12 from If By Chance (11 May Wolverhampton RF 1149). Consistent. **S C Williams [1-8] Chris Wright.*

SANDMASON BHB 105f RR 113?f
1278[2]
3 ch c Grand Lodge (USA) - Sandy Island (Mill Reef (USA)) 10.5f **(78)**
Form - 22

Record 2000 - 1st:0 2nd:2 3rd:0 Ran:2
Pre2000 - 1st:1 2nd:0 3rd:0 Ran:1
Win Prizemoney £3,615 *Total Prizemoney* £15,572
Wins * 1999 Spt Kempto (HVY) 8f 78+ <
2000 Turf 0-2: (10f 2) (gd, g-f)
Scopey, currently Group-class colt. Turf high 113 (1st run) - 2nd of 5 to Beat Hollow (5 May Newmarket 10f g-f RF 1046). He ran a couple of promising races in Listed company during the spring and looked like developing into a St Leger candidate. The fact that he was not seen after mid-May is a concern, but this likeable individual remains one to keep on the right side if all is well.
**H R A Cecil [1-3] Exors of the late Lord Howard de Walden.*

SANDMOOR CHAMBRAY BHB 68f RR 66df 1487[7]

0 ch g Most Welcome 8.6f **(66)** - Valadon (High Line) 10.3f **(70)**
Form - 07
Record 2000 - 1st:0 2nd:0 3rd:0 Ran:2
Pre2000 - 1st:8 2nd:12 3rd:8 Ran:65
Win Prizemoney £52,009 *Total Prizemoney* £95,333
Wins * 1999 Aug Pontef (GD) H 12f 72 73
* 1997 Spt Epsom (GD) H 10.1f 92 96+ <
* 1997 Aug Newcas (G-F) H 10.1f 80 85
* 1997 Jly Ripon (G-F) H 10f 77 81
* 1996 Jun York (GD) H 8.9f 73 77
2000 Turf 0-2: (12f 2) (gd, g-f)
Average gelding, effective 12f, acts on frm, has worn blinkers (very effectively), likes left handed tracks, likes tight tracks. Turf high 52. Becoming disappointing. **T D Easterby [5-46] Mrs Sue Tindall (from M H Easterby [3-21] Spt 1995).*

S AND O P RR 2672[7]

6 b g Arctic Lord 11.7f **(37)** - Beringa Bee (Sunley Builds)
Form - 7
Record 2000 - 1st:0 2nd:0 3rd:0 Ran:1
2000 Turf 0-1: (16f) (gd)
Formerly very poor gelding. **P D Evans [0-1] M A Lloyd.*

SANDORRA BHB 63f RR 63f 4965[25]

2 b f Emperor Jones (USA) - Oribi (Top Ville) 11.7f **(68)**
Form - 7640
Record 2000 - 1st:0 2nd:0 3rd:0 Ran:4
Win Prizemoney £0 *Total Prizemoney* £669
2000 Turf 0-4: (6f 2, 7f 2) (g-s, gd 2, g-f)
Average filly. Turf high 63 (began Jly). **M Brittain [0-4] Mel Brittain.*

SANDOWN CLANTINO BHB 24f RR 21f 5018[9]

3 b f Clantime 6.6f **(57)** - Tino Reppin (Neltino) 7.6f **(54)**
Form - 0800
Record 2000 - 1st:0 2nd:0 3rd:0 Ran:4
2000 Turf 0-3: (7f 2, 8f) (gd, frm 2) 2000 AW 0-1: (7f) (Fibr)
Scopey, little account filly. Turf high 21 (began Aug).
**J G Given [0-4] Sandown Park Stud.*

SAND PARTRIDGE (IRE) RR 100f 4521a[8]

3 b f Desert Style (IRE) - Pipe Opener (Prince Sabo) 7.2f **(62)**
Form - 727022108
2000 Turf 1-9: (7f 1-5, 8f 3, 10f) (sft, g-s 2, gd 1-4, g-f)
Very useful filly, effective 7 to 8f, best at 8f, acts on g-s to gd, best on gd, has worn blinkers, likes left handed tracks. Turf high 100 - 1st of 9 getting 5lb from Shoal Creek (17 Aug Tipperary RF 3875a).
**K Prendergast in IRE [2-17] Mrs Catherine McNulty.*

SAND PEBBLES (IRE) RR 3438[10]

3 b f Sadler's Wells (USA) 11.3f **(87)** - Clandestina (USA) (Secretariat (USA)) 9f **(79)**
Form - 0
Record 2000 - 1st:0 2nd:0 3rd:0 Ran:1
2000 Turf 0-1: (10f) (g-f)
Scopey, currently very poor filly. **J H M Gosden [0-1] R E Sangster.*

SANDPOINT BHB 36f RR 35f 3908[19]

4 b m Lugana Beach 7f **(63)** - Instinction (Never so Bold) 6.3f **(66)**
Form - 03000
Record 2000 - 1st:0 2nd:0 3rd:1 Ran:5
Pre2000 - 1st:0 2nd:0 3rd:0 Ran:6
Win Prizemoney £0 *Total Prizemoney* £330
2000 Turf 0-5: (5f 2, 6f 3) (gd, g-f, frm, hrd 2)
Neat, very moderate filly, effective 6f, acts on hrd, has worn blinkers. Turf high 35 - 3rd of 19 getting 8lb from Ones Enough (17 Jun Bath 6f hrd RF 2039). Inconsistent. **L G Cottrell [0-11] L G Cottrell.*

SANDROS BOY BHB 31f RR 55f 4455[6]

3 b g Alhijaz 7.7f **(57)** - Bearnaise (IRE) **(62f)** (Cyrano de Bergerac) 6f **(68)**
Form - 3206
Record 2000 - 1st:0 2nd:1 3rd:1 Ran:4
Win Prizemoney £0 *Total Prizemoney* £1,064
2000 Turf 0-4: (10f, 11f, 14f 2) (g-s, gd, g-f, frm)
Fair gelding. Turf high 55.
**M D Hammond [0-2] A Saccomando (from P D Evans [0-2] Jly 2000).*

SAN GLAMORE MELODY (FR) BHB 35f40a RR 42f 40a 347[3]

6 b g Sanglamore (USA) 12.9f **(67)** - Lyphantissima (FR) (Lightning (FR)) 7.9f **(74)**
Form - 033
Record 2000 - 1st:0 2nd:0 3rd:2 Ran:3
Pre2000 - 1st:0 2nd:4 3rd:3 Ran:21
Win Prizemoney £0 *Total Prizemoney* £5,961
2000 AW 0-3: (8f, 9f 2) (Fibr 3)
Moderate gelding, has worn blinkers. AW high 38.
**R Ingram [0-19] Alex Fraser (from J H M Gosden [0-5] Jly 1997).*

SANGRA (USA) BHB 55f RR 65f 5071[9]

3 b f El Gran Senor (USA) 8.9f **(85)** - Water Song (CAN) (Clever Trick (USA)) 6.6f **(77)**
Form - 425020
Record 2000 - 1st:0 2nd:2 3rd:0 Ran:6
Pre2000 - 1st:0 2nd:0 3rd:1 Ran:3
Win Prizemoney £0 *Total Prizemoney* £3,559
2000 Turf 0-6: (7f 3, 8f, 9f 2) (g-s, g-f, frm 4)
Scopey, average filly, effective 7f, acts on frm, has worn blinkers. Turf high 65. **N A Callaghan [0-9] M Tabor & Mrs John Magnier.*

SAN MICHEL (IRE) BHB 43f34a RR 47f 34a 3698[17]

8 b g Scenic 10.6f **(66)** - The Top Diesis (USA) (Diesis) 9.3f **(69)**
Form - 0637507543030
Record 2000 - 1st:0 2nd:0 3rd:2 Ran:8
Pre2000 - 1st:1 2nd:3 3rd:6 Ran:45
Win Prizemoney £3,082 *Total Prizemoney* £11,954
Wins 1996 Jly Leopar (GD) H 5f 66 58 <
2000 Turf 0-3: (6f 3) (gd, g-f 2) 2000 AW 0-5: (6f, 7f 3, 8f) (Fibr 5)
Moderate gelding, effective 6 to 7f, best at 6f, acts on hvy to g-f, mostly wears blinkers. Turf high 47 (1st run) - 3rd of 16 getting 6lb from Bowlers Boy (15 Jun Hamilton 6f g-f RF 1985). AW high 39. Inconsistent.
**J L Eyre [0-22] Whitestonecliffe Racing Partnership (from K O'Sullivan in IRE [1-27] Oct 1998).*

SANNAAN RR 57f 2644[8]

2 b c Robellino (USA) 9.5f **(68)** - Quest for the Best (Rainbow Quest (USA)) 10.4f **(75)**
Form - 8
Record 2000 - 1st:0 2nd:0 3rd:0 Ran:1
2000 Turf 0-1: (7f) (frm)
Currently fair colt. **M P Tregoning [0-1] Sheikh Ahmed Al Maktoum.*

SAN SALVADOR (USA) RR 101+f 1338[1]

3 b c Dayjur (USA) 6.8f **(79)** - Sheer Gold (USA) (Cutlass (USA)) 8.5f **(76)**
Form - 32111
Record 2000 - 1st:3 2nd:1 3rd:1 Ran:5
Win Prizemoney £44,044 *Total Prizemoney* £46,111
Wins * **2000** May Nottin (GD) 6.1f 89
* **2000** May Lingfi (G-S) H 6f 83 101+ <
* **2000** May Pontef (SFT) 6f 74+
2000 Turf 3-5: (5f, 6f 3-4) (g-s 1-1, gd 1-3, g-f 1-1)
Light-framed, very useful colt. Turf high 101 - 1st of 16 getting 15lb from Awake (13 May Lingfield RF 1194). He showed plenty of ability in maiden company before making the most of a straightforward task at Pontefract in May. Followed up with a hugely impressive victory in a Lingfield handicap, but did not impress when landing odds of 1/5 in a muddling event at Nottingham. Absent since, he still looks a high-class sprinter in the making.

**J Noseda [3-5] Lucayan Stud.*

SAN SEBASTIAN BHB 116f **RR 118f** 5212a[2]
6 ch g Niniski (USA) 13.2f **(67)** - Top of the League (High Top) 10.2f **(67)**
Form - 4643612
Record 2000 - 1st:1 2nd:1 3rd:1 Ran:7
Pre2000 - 1st:7 2nd:4 3rd:2 Ran:23
Win Prizemoney £116,204 *Total Prizemoney* £194,363
Wins * 2000 Oct Longch (GD) G1 20f 118 <
1999 Jun Ascot (G-F) 22.2f 98
1998 Jun Ascot (G-S) H 20f 84 91
1998 May Gowran (GD) H 14f 99
1997 Oct Cork (G-S) H 12f 72+
1997 Aug Wexfor (SFT) H 13f 72
1997 Jly Wexfor (FRM) H 13f 65
1997 Jun Sligo (FRM) H 11f 49
2000 Turf 1-7: (16f 4, 18f, 20f 1-2) (hvy, g-s 2, gd 1-2, g-f, frm)
High-class gelding, effective 16 to 20f, best at 16f, acts on hvy to g-f, best on gd, mostly wears blinkers (very effectively), prefers right handed tracks, excels at Longchamp, likes Ascot. Turf high 118 - 2nd of 11 to Amilynx (22 Oct Longchamp 16f hvy RF 5212a) - also 1st of 9 from Persian Punch (1 Oct Longchamp RF 4848a). Consistent. He cost his current connections 170,000gns at the end of 1999 and repaid a sizeable chunk of that outlay when winning the Group One Prix du Cadran in October. Probably best over distances in excess of two miles, he acts on any ground and is genuine despite the blinkers.
**J L Dunlop [1-7] Mrs Michael Wyatt (from M J Grassick in IRE [7-23] Oct 1999).*

SANS RIVALE BHB 28f47a **RR 12f 47a** 265[12]
5 ch m Elmaamul (USA) 8.1f **(70)** - Strawberry Song (Final Straw) 7.9f **(64)**
Form - 070
Record 2000 - 1st:0 2nd:0 3rd:0 Ran:3
Pre2000 - 1st:2 2nd:2 3rd:1 Ran:23
Win Prizemoney £4,818 *Total Prizemoney* £6,537
Wins 1998 Apr Catter (GD) 5f 60
1997 Aug Mussel (GD) S 5f 71 <
2000 AW 0-3: (6f 3) (Fibr 3)
Poor filly. AW high 7. Becoming disappointing.
**D W Chapman [0-7] David Mann (from J L Eyre [1-14] Apr 1999).*

SAN SURU (GER) RR 110f 706a[3]
6 b h Surumu (GER) - Sweet Virtue (USA) (Halo (USA)) 10.6f **(75)**
Form - 3
2000 Turf 0-1: (10f) (sft)
Group-class horse, has worn blinkers. (1st run) - 3rd of 12 giving 5lb to Sambakonig (9 Apr Gelsenkirchen-Horst 10f sft RF 0706a).
**C Von der Recke in GER [0-5] (from P Rau in GER [0-2] Jly 1997).*

SANTA ISOBEL RR 69f 5132[3]
2 ch f Nashwan (USA) 10.3f **(79)** - Atlantic Record (Slip Anchor) 9.8f **(73)**
Form - 33
Record 2000 - 1st:0 2nd:0 3rd:2 Ran:2
Win Prizemoney £0 *Total Prizemoney* £1,366
2000 Turf 0-2: (5f, 6f) (sft, frm)
Currently average filly. Turf high 69.
**I A Balding [0-2] Robert Hitchins.*

SANTA LUCIA BHB 41f36a **RR 60f 36a** 4213[13]
4 b m Namaqualand (USA) - Villasanta (Corvaro (USA)) 9f **(53)**
Form - 002601140
Record 2000 - 1st:2 2nd:1 3rd:0 Ran:8
Pre2000 - 1st:0 2nd:1 3rd:0 Ran:6
Win Prizemoney £4,952 *Total Prizemoney* £7,332
Wins * 2000 Jly Hamilt (G-F) C 11.1f 48
*** 2000** Jly Hamilt (G-F) C 11.1f 53 <
2000 Turf 2-8: (10f, 11f 2-2, 12f 3, 13f, 17f) (g-s, gd, g-f 2-4, frm 2)
Workmanlike, average filly, effective 11 to 12f, best at 11f, acts on g-f, prefers tight tracks. Turf high 60 - 2nd of 6 to Fee Mail (12 May Carlisle 12f g-f RF 1162) - also 1st of 5 giving 9lb to Rooftop Protest (4 Jly Hamilton RF 2493).
**M Dods [2-8] J A Wynn-Williams (from C W Thornton [0-6] Nov 1999).*

SANTANDRE BHB 46f65a **RR 48f 65a** 5122[14]
4 ch g Democratic (USA) - Smartie Lee (Dominion) 8.5f **(63)**
Form - 453076411507005063080
Record 2000 - 1st:2 2nd:0 3rd:1 Ran:18
Pre2000 - 1st:2 2nd:1 3rd:4 Ran:27
Win Prizemoney £20,004 *Total Prizemoney* £24,933
Wins * 2000 *Mar Southw (STD) H 7f 65 67*
*** 2000** *Mar Wolver (STD) 7f 68*
* 1999 *Spt Wolver (STD) H 6f 68 70*
* 1998 *Jly Thirsk (GD) H 5f 75+* <
2000 Turf 0-10: (6f, 7f 9) (g-s 2, gd, g-f 4, frm, hrd 2) 2000 AW 2-8: (6f 2, 7f 2-4, 8f, 9f) (Fibr 2-8)
Light-framed, average gelding, has broken blood-vessels, effective 6 to 8f, best at 7f, - acts on Fibr, prefers left handed tracks, likes tight tracks, excels at Wolverhampton. Turf high 48. AW high 68 - 1st of 8 getting 8lb from Rambo Waltzer (2 Mar Wolverhampton RF 0392) - also 1st of 15 getting 26lb from Blue Star (17 Mar Southwell RF 0460). Inconsistent. **R Hollinshead [4-45] Geoff Lloyd.*

SANTIBURI GIRL BHB 70f **RR 73f** 4616[6]
3 b f Casteddu 7.4f **(54)** - Lake Mistassiu (Tina's Pet) 6.8f **(59)**
Form - 06170237011248666
Record 2000 - 1st:3 2nd:2 3rd:1 Ran:17
Pre2000 - 1st:1 2nd:2 3rd:2 Ran:14
Win Prizemoney £18,878 *Total Prizemoney* £26,839
Wins * 2000 Aug Redcar (FRM) H 11f 66 71
*** 2000** Aug Newbur (G-F) H 10f 64 66
*** 2000** May Lingfi (G-S) 7f 73
* 1999 Jly Salisb (G-S) 7f 80 <
2000 Turf 3-17: (6f 4, 7f 1-4, 8f, 10f 1-4, 11f 1-1, 12f 2, 14f) (hvy, gd 1-4, g-f 1-2, frm 1-9, hrd)
Small, above-average filly, effective 7 to 14f, best at 7f, acts on gd to frm, likes left handed tracks, likes tight tracks. Turf high 73 - 1st of 9 getting 3lb from Distant Guest (20 May Lingfield RF 1326) - also 1st of 6 getting 18lb from Abuzaid (13 Aug Redcar RF 3616). Consistent. She found her form when stepped up in trip in August, winning over ten furlongs at Newbury and eleven furlongs at Redcar. Generally running well since despite rising in the weights. Suited by fast ground.
**J R Best [4-30] Alan Turner (from J J O'Neill [0-1] Mar 1999).*

SANTIBURI LAD (IRE) BHB 67f **RR 63+f** 5105[11]
3 b g Namaqualand (USA) - Suggia (Alzao (USA)) 7.1f **(68)**
Form - 1200
Record 2000 - 1st:1 2nd:1 3rd:0 Ran:4
Win Prizemoney £3,471 *Total Prizemoney* £4,191
Wins * 2000 Aug Ripon (G-F) 5f 63+ <
2000 Turf 1-4: (5f 1-1, 6f 2, 7f) (g-s 2, gd, g-f 1-1)
Lengthy, average gelding. Turf high 63 (1st run) (began Aug) - 1st of 10 giving 5lb to Amazed (19 Aug Ripon RF 3794).
**A Berry [1-4] E A Brook.*

SANTISIMA TRINIDAD (IRE) BHB 51f **RR 56f** 4382[11]
2 b f Definite Article - Brazilia **(63f 63a)** (Forzando) 7.6f **(59)**
Form - 050
Record 2000 - 1st:0 2nd:0 3rd:0 Ran:3
2000 Turf 0-3: (6f 2, 8f) (gd 3)
Currently fair filly. Turf high 55.
**T D Easterby [0-3] Chris & Antonia Deuters.*

SANTOLINA (USA) RR 99f 4644[7]
2 b f Boundary (USA) - Alamosa (Alydar (USA)) 9.1f **(76)**
Form - 12417
Record 2000 - 1st:2 2nd:1 3rd:0 Ran:5
Win Prizemoney £15,489 *Total Prizemoney* £22,564
Wins * 2000 Spt Kempto (GD) L 6f 99 <
*** 2000** Jun Leices (G-F) 6f 72++
2000 Turf 2-5: (6f 2-5) (gd, g-f 1-2, frm, hrd 1-1)
Very useful filly. Turf high 99 - 1st of 9 getting 5lb from Proceed With Care (3 Spt Kempton RF 4189). She looked unlucky in a Listed race on her second start and developed into a useful sprinting juvenile. Beaten but not discredited when tried in Group company, she may have to travel abroad in 2001.
**J H M Gosden [2-5] H Lascelles, Indian Creek & A Stroud.*

SAORSIE BHB 59f **RR 56f** 5218[3]
2 b g Emperor Jones (USA) - Exclusive Lottery (Presidium)

Form - 007813
Record 2000 - 1st:1 2nd:0 3rd:1 Ran:6
Win Prizemoney £3,031 *Total Prizemoney* £3,575
Wins * **2000** Oct Bright (SFT) H 7f 52 55 <
2000 Turf 1-6: (6f 3, 7f 1-1, 8f 2) (sft, g-s 1-1, g-f, frm 3)
Fair gelding, effective 7f, acts on g-s. Turf high 56 (began Aug) - also 1st of 17 getting 4lb from Jarv (19 Oct Brighton RF 5074).
**J C Fox [1-6] Lord Mutton Racing Partnership.*

SAPHIRE BHB 83f RR 89f 5127[16]

4 ch m College Chapel - Emerald Eagle (Sandy Creek) 8.9f **(59)**
Form - 05650248600
Record 2000 - 1st:0 2nd:1 3rd:0 Ran:11
Pre2000 - 1st:2 2nd:2 3rd:2 Ran:17
Win Prizemoney £8,667 *Total Prizemoney* £23,963
Wins * 1998 Jun York (G-S) 6f 70 <
* 1998 Jun Newcas (SFT) 5f 73 <
2000 Turf 0-11: (5f 10, 6f) (g-s 4, gd 4, g-f 3)
Scopey, useful filly, effective 5 to 6f, best at 5f, acts on gd. Turf high 89. Inconsistent. After a good juvenile season in which she ran well in Listed company, she has struggled at that level in the last couple of seasons, but is dropping down the handicap.
**C B B Booth [2-28] Mrs Marian Rogers.*

SAPPHIRE MILL RR 37f 2258[15]

3 gr f Petong 7.6f **(58)** - Amber Mill (Doulab (USA)) 9.8f **(65)**
Form - 60
Record 2000 - 1st:0 2nd:0 3rd:0 Ran:2
2000 Turf 0-2: (6f 2) (gd, frm)
Lengthy, currently very moderate filly. Turf high 37.
**M A Jarvis [0-2] T G & Mrs M E Holdcroft.*

SAPPHIRE SON (IRE) BHB 23f27a RR 33f 27a 693[14]

8 ch g Maelstrom Lake 8.8f **(53)** - Gluhwein (Ballymoss) 8.5f **(55)**
Form - 0
Record 2000 - 1st:0 2nd:0 3rd:0 Ran:1
Pre2000 - 1st:3 2nd:9 3rd:4 Ran:55
Win Prizemoney £8,604 *Total Prizemoney* £17,027
Wins 1997 Aug Lingfi (G-F) H 11.5f 46 48
2000 Turf 0-1: (12f) (gd)
Very moderate gelding, has worn blinkers. **J R Boot [0-1] D Cobb (from P Butler [0-1] Oct 1999).*

SARAFAN (USA) BHB 113f RR 116f 3985[6]

3 b c Lear Fan (USA) 10.4f **(80)** - Saraa Ree (USA) (Caro)
Form - 536
Record 2000 - 1st:0 2nd:0 3rd:1 Ran:3
Pre2000 - 1st:4 2nd:2 3rd:0 Ran:6
Win Prizemoney £26,237 *Total Prizemoney* £57,422
Wins * 1999 Spt Goodwo (G-F) L 8f 110+ <
* 1999 Jly Beverl (SFT) 7.5f 94
* 1999 Jun Pontef (GD) 6f 93+
* 1999 Jun Hamilt (G-S) 6f 77+
2000 Turf 0-3: (8f 2, 9f) (gd 3)
Well made, high-class colt, effective 7 to 8f, best at 8f, acts on gd to frm, best on g-f, likes tight tracks. Turf high 116 (1st run) - 5th of 11 to Giant's Causeway (20 Jun Ascot 8f gd RF 2111). Impressive when winning a Listed race on his final start in 1999, he attracted plenty of support before finishing fifth in the St James's Palace Stakes on his belated reappearance. Very disappointing in two subsequent outings, he may have a problem and is one to watch at present. **Sir Mark Prescott [4-9] Mrs Burnet Osborne House II.*

SARAH MADELINE RR 54?f 490[5]

3 b f Pelder (IRE) - Final Rush (Final Straw) 7.9f **(64)**
Form - 5
Record 2000 - 1st:0 2nd:0 3rd:0 Ran:1
2000 Turf 0-1: (7f) (gd)
Lengthy, currently fair filly. **T D Barron [0-1] R M West.*

SARA MOON CLASSIC (IRE) BHB 48f39a RR 44f 39a 20[8]

5 b g Fayruz 6.6f **(63)** - Irish Affaire (IRE) (Fairy King (USA)) 7.7f **(59)**
Form - 8
Record 2000 - 1st:0 2nd:0 3rd:0 Ran:1
Pre2000 - 1st:0 2nd:1 3rd:4 Ran:23
Win Prizemoney £0 *Total Prizemoney* £3,223
2000 AW 0-1: (9f) (Fibr)
Moderate gelding, often wears blinkers. Inconsistent.
**K McAuliffe [0-26] Aidan Ryan.*

SARATOV BHB 98f RR 92f 4818[9]

2 b c Rudimentary (USA) 8.2f **(66)** - Sarabah (IRE) (Ela-Mana-Mou) 10.1f **(70)**
Form - 31130
Record 2000 - 1st:2 2nd:0 3rd:2 Ran:5
Win Prizemoney £21,580 *Total Prizemoney* £25,710
Wins * **2000** Jly Ascot (G-F) 7f 92 <
* **2000** Jly York (GD) 7f 84
2000 Turf 2-5: (6f, 7f 2-3, 8f) (g-s, gd 1-2, g-f 1-2)
Useful colt. Turf high 92 (began Jly) - 1st of 12 giving 3lb to Swing Band (30 Jly Ascot RF 3226) - also 1st of 11 from Hurricane Floyd (14 Jly York RF 2825). A handsome individual, he had a couple of hard races in mid-summer and ran poorly on his final outing. Possibly unsuited by soft ground, he should stay a mile and make his mark in Listed company. **M Johnston [2-5] David Abell.*

SARENA PRIDE (IRE) BHB 68f68a RR 78f 68a 4224[14]

3 b f Persian Bold 10f **(69)** - Avidal Park (Horage) 10.3f **(61)**
Form - 7502438000
Record 2000 - 1st:0 2nd:1 3rd:1 Ran:10
Pre2000 - 1st:2 2nd:1 3rd:0 Ran:7
Win Prizemoney £6,714 *Total Prizemoney* £12,924
Wins * 1999 Aug Warwic (GD) H 6f 70 75
* 1999 Jun Windso (SFT) 6f 78+ <
2000 Turf 0-10. (6f 3, 7f 4, 8f 2, 9f) (g-s 2, gd, g-f 2, frm 5)
Leggy, above-average filly, effective 6 to 8f, best at 6f, acts on g-s to frm, best on g-s, likes left handed trackslikes right handed tracks, likes tight tracks, excels at Windsor, likes Kempton. Turf high 79 - 5th of 21 giving 3lb to Castle Sempill (10 Apr Windsor 6f frm RF 0655). Becoming disappointing.
**R J O'Sullivan [2-17] Sarena Mfg Ltd.*

SARENA SPECIAL BHB 69f60a RR 76f 60a 3259[12]

3 b c Lucky Guest - Lariston Gale (Pas de Seul) 9.1f **(67)**
Form - 2573040
Record 2000 - 1st:0 2nd:1 3rd:1 Ran:7
Pre2000 - 1st:0 2nd:2 3rd:0 Ran:5
Win Prizemoney £0 *Total Prizemoney* £5,084
2000 Turf 0-7: (6f, 7f 4, 8f 2) (sft, g-s, gd 2, g-f, frm 2)
Leggy, above-average colt, effective 6 to 7f, best at 7f, acts on sft to frm, has worn blinkers. Turf high 77 (1st run) - 2nd of 10 to Big Future (24 Apr Kempton 7f sft RF 0840).
**R J O'Sullivan [0-12] Sarena Mfg Ltd.*

SARMATIAN (USA) BHB 25f RR 24f 1685[12]

9 br g Northern Flagship (USA) 12.2f **(72)** - Tracy L (USA) (Bold Favorite (USA))
Form - 0000
Record 2000 - 1st:0 2nd:0 3rd:0 Ran:4
Pre2000 - 1st:3 2nd:5 3rd:4 Ran:34
Win Prizemoney £14,362 *Total Prizemoney* £26,973
Wins 1996 May Ayr (G-S) H 10f 69 77 <
2000 Turf 0-4: (8f 2, 9f, 11f) (gd, g-f 2, frm)
Little account gelding, has worn blinkers. Turf high 24. Becoming disappointing. **D A Nolan [0-4] F Jestin (from M D Hammond [7-35] Jly 1997).*

SARPEDON (IRE) BHB 26a RR 31f 545[7]

4 ch g Be My Chief (USA) 10.2f **(62)** - Sariza (Posse (USA)) 8.9f **(61)**
Form - 05085567
Record 2000 - 1st:0 2nd:0 3rd:0 Ran:8
Pre2000 - 1st:0 2nd:0 3rd:0 Ran:4
2000 Turf 0-1: (7f) (frm) 2000 AW 0-7: (6f, 7f, 8f 2, 12f 3) (Fibr 7)
Workmanlike, very moderate gelding, has worn blinkers. AW high 28.
**M C Chapman [0-14] R J Hayward (from L M Cumani [0-2] May 1999).*

SARSON BHB 67f RR 79f 5242[8]

4 b g Efisio 7.7f **(69)** - Sarcita (Primo Dominie) 6.2f **(80)**
Form - 800707468
Record 2000 - 1st:0 2nd:0 3rd:0 Ran:9
Pre2000 - 1st:1 2nd:4 3rd:0 Ran:11
Win Prizemoney £10,308 *Total Prizemoney* £29,823
Wins * 1998 Jly Sandow (G-S) L 5f 95 <

2000 Turf 0-9: (6f 4, 7f 5) (sft, g-s 4, g-f 3, frm)
Workmanlike, above-average gelding. Turf high 79. **R Hannon [1-20] Raymond Tooth.*

SARTEANO BHB 20f RR 4f — 295[5]

6 ch m Anshan 8.2f **(63)** - Daisy Girl (Main Reef) 9.6f **(57)**
Form - 6365
Record 2000 - 1st:0 2nd:0 3rd:1 Ran:4
Pre2000 - 1st:0 2nd:0 3rd:1 Ran:6
Win Prizemoney £0 *Total Prizemoney* £748
2000 AW 0-4: (8f, 9f, 12f, 16f) (Fibr 4)
Poor mare. AW high 18.
**D Shaw [0-5] S Taberner (from T W Donnelly [0-3] Jly 1998).*

SARTORIAL (IRE) BHB 98f80a RR 101f 80a — 4612[17]

4 b g Elbio 9f **(62)** - Madam Slaney (Prince Tenderfoot (USA)) 9f **(61)**
Form - 141870
Record 2000 - 1st:2 2nd:0 3rd:0 Ran:6
Pre2000 - 1st:0 2nd:2 3rd:1 Ran:4
Win Prizemoney £29,295 *Total Prizemoney* £32,886
Wins * 2000 May Newmar (GD) H 6f 95 101 <
*** 2000** Apr Haydoc (GD) 5f 91+
2000 Turf 2-6: (5f 1-4, 6f 1-2) (g-s 2, gd 2-3, g-f)
Very useful gelding, effective 5 to 6f, acts on gd, has worn blinkers. Turf high 101 - 1st of 29 giving 17lb to Cadeaux Cher (6 May Newmarket RF 1062). Still comparatively lightly raced, he bolted up in a Haydock maiden on his reappearance and may have found the ground too soft next time. Back to form when winning a valuable handicap at Newmarket, he was then off the track for three months. Effective over five furlongs, but probably better over six.
**P J Makin [2-10] Mrs Greta Sarfaty Marchant.*

SARUM BHB 20f25a RR 14f 25a — 368[9]

14 b g Tina's Pet 7.4f **(56)** - Contessa (HUN) (Peleid) 7.6f **(37)**
Form - 0
Record 2000 - 1st:0 2nd:0 3rd:0 Ran:1
Pre2000 - 1st:8 2nd:10 3rd:13 Ran:115
Win Prizemoney £19,785 *Total Prizemoney* £34,778
Wins 1996 *Mar Lingfi (STD) H 8f 50 49*
2000 AW 0-1: (7f) (Fibr)
Little account gelding, has worn blinkers. Inconsistent. Once a useful performer on sand at Lingfield, his best days are well and truly behind him.
**J E Long [0-37] Terry Waters (from C P Wildman [8-79] May 1996).*

SASEEDO (USA) BHB 28f31a RR 37?f 31a — 4585[15]

10 ch g Afleet (CAN) 6.2f **(83)** - Barbara's Moment (USA) (Super Moment (USA)) 6.2f **(92)**
Form - 008040886080
Record 2000 - 1st:0 2nd:0 3rd:0 Ran:10
Pre2000 - 1st:8 2nd:3 3rd:7 Ran:83
Win Prizemoney £60,859 *Total Prizemoney* £72,339
Wins * 1999 *Apr Lingfi (STD) S 10f 54*
1996 Jly Haydoc (GD) H 7.1f 86 90
1996 Jly Pontef (G-F) H 6f 86 90
1996 May Newmar (GD) H 7f 86 91 <
2000 Turf 0-3: (10f 3) (g-f 2, frm) 2000 AW 0-7: (8f, 10f 2, 12f 4) (Equi 6, Fibr)
Very moderate gelding, effective 8 to 10f, best at 10f, acts on frm - acts on Equi, has worn blinkers. Turf high 37. AW high 29.
**J J Bridger [1-31] J J Bridger (from K A Morgan [0-2] Feb 1999).*

SASH (IRE) BHB 47f52a RR 53f 52a — 5150[3]

3 b f Sabrehill (USA) 8.5f **(64)** - Lady Nash **(66f 50a)** (Nashwan (USA))
Form - 5750073
Record 2000 - 1st:0 2nd:0 3rd:1 Ran:7
Win Prizemoney £0 *Total Prizemoney* £420
2000 Turf 0-5: (7f, 8f 3, 9f) (gd 2, g-f, frm 2) 2000 AW 0-2: (8f, 10f) (Equi 2)
Scopey, fair filly, effective 9f, acts on frm. Turf high 53 (began Jly). AW high 49 (began Oct). **S Dow [0-7] Mrs Jean Coles.*

SASHA BHB 47f42a RR 47f 42a — 4748[10]

3 ch c Factual (USA) - Twice in Bundoran (IRE) **(47f 44a)** (Bold Arrangement)
Form - 40840
Record 2000 - 1st:0 2nd:0 3rd:0 Ran:5
Pre2000 - 1st:0 2nd:0 3rd:0 Ran:1
Win Prizemoney £0 *Total Prizemoney* £539
2000 Turf 0-5: (5f 5) (gd, g-f, frm 3)
Scopey, moderate colt, effective 5f, acts on g-f, has worn blinkers. Turf high 47 (began Jly) - 4th of 22 giving 11lb to Upper Chamber (2 Spt Thirsk 5f g-f RF 4174).
**J Balding [0-5] Ms Kim Jansen (from J L Eyre [0-1] Spt 1999).*

SASHA STAR (IRE) RR 35f — 2960[6]

2 b c Namaqualand (USA) - Trojan Relation (Trojan Fen) 8.1f **(62)**
Form - 86
Record 2000 - 1st:0 2nd:0 3rd:0 Ran:2
2000 Turf 0-2: (7f 2) (g-f 2)
Currently very moderate colt. Turf high 35 (began Jun).
**G Brown [0-2] T Curry.*

SASHAY RR 2f — 4629[13]

2 b f Bishop of Cashel - St James's Antigua (IRE) (Law Society (USA)) 9.9f **(70)**
Form - 0
Record 2000 - 1st:0 2nd:0 3rd:0 Ran:1
2000 Turf 0-1: (6f) (gd)
Currently very poor filly. **C G Cox [0-1] E J G Young.*

SATARRA BHB 72f75a RR 74f 75a — 4204[7]

3 ch c Lammtarra (USA) - Gemaasheh (Habitat) 9.4f **(70)**
Form - 247
Record 2000 - 1st:0 2nd:1 3rd:0 Ran:3
Win Prizemoney £0 *Total Prizemoney* £1,171
2000 Turf 0-2: (12f 2) (frm 2) 2000 AW 0-1: (10f) (Equi)
Scopey, currently above-average colt. Turf high 74 (began Jly). (1st run) - 2nd of 7 to Swinging Trio (27 Jun Lingfield 10f Equi RF 2301). **H R A Cecil [0-3] The Thoroughbred Corporation.*

SATEEN RR 60f — 954[5]

3 ch f Barathea (IRE) - Souk (IRE) (Ahonoora) 8.1f **(73)**
Form - 5
Record 2000 - 1st:0 2nd:0 3rd:0 Ran:1
2000 Turf 0-1: (8f) (sft)
Lengthy, currently average filly. **L M Cumani [0-1] Fittocks Stud.*

SATIRE BHB 40f35a RR 42f 35a — 5162[2]

3 br f Terimon 8.7f **(58)** - Salchow (Niniski (USA)) 10.6f **(65)**
Form - 50002
Record 2000 - 1st:0 2nd:1 3rd:0 Ran:5
Pre2000 - 1st:0 2nd:0 3rd:0 Ran:1
Win Prizemoney £0 *Total Prizemoney* £854
2000 Turf 0-3: (8f, 10f, 12f) (sft, gd, frm) 2000 AW 0-2: (8f, 14f) (Fibr 2)
Lengthy, moderate filly, effective 10f, acts on sft. Turf high 42 (began Jly) - 2nd of 14 getting 11lb from Lady Jones (24 Oct Nottingham 10f sft RF 5162). AW high 34.
**T J Etherington [0-6] R V Hughes and Partners.*

SATWA BOULEVARD BHB 34f26a RR 37f 26a — 4102[3]

5 ch m Sabrehill (USA) 8.5f **(64)** - Winnie Reckless (Local Suitor (USA)) 8.4f **(67)**
Form - 87000020073
Record 2000 - 1st:0 2nd:1 3rd:1 Ran:11
Pre2000 - 1st:0 2nd:1 3rd:1 Ran:8
Win Prizemoney £0 *Total Prizemoney* £2,366
2000 Turf 0-8: (6f, 7f, 8f 3, 10f, 12f 2) (gd, g-f, frm 5, hrd) 2000 AW 0-3: (8f 2, 10f) (Equi, Fibr 2)
Very moderate filly, effective 8f, acts on frm, likes left handed tracks, favours tight tracks. Turf high 37 - 2nd of 7 getting 28lb from Twenty First (19 Jun Brighton 8f frm RF 2089). AW high 41.
**P Mitchell [0-5] M Mason (from P Burgoyne [0-6] May 2000).*

SATYR RR 27f — 4807[15]

2 b c Pursuit of Love 9.5f **(69)** - Sardonic **(103df)** (Kris) 9.5f **(73)**
Form - 0
Record 2000 - 1st:0 2nd:0 3rd:0 Ran:1
2000 Turf 0-1: (7f) (g-s)
Currently little account colt.
**R Hannon [0-1] Exors of the late Lord Howard de Walden.*

SATZUMA (IRE) BHB 50f RR 58f — 4403[16]

3 ch g Lycius (USA) 8.8f **(71)** - Satz (USA) (The Minstrel (CAN)) 10f

(72)
Form - 0500
Record 2000 - 1st:0 2nd:0 3rd:0 Ran:4
Pre2000 - 1st:0 2nd:0 3rd:0 Ran:1
2000 Turf 0-4: (7f, 8f 3) (gd 3, g-f)
Fair gelding. Turf high 58. **C F Wall [0-5] Islanmore Stud.*

SAUCE TARTAR BHB 73f RR 74f 4334[3]
2 ch f Salse (USA) 10.9f **(71)** - Filly Mignonne (IRE) **(50f)** (Nashwan (USA))
Form - 61083
Record 2000 - 1st:1 2nd:0 3rd:1 Ran:5
Win Prizemoney £4,387 *Total Prizemoney* £5,086
Wins * 2000 Jly Folkes (GD-) 7f 70 <
2000 Turf 1-5: (6f, 7f 1-3, 8f) (g-s, gd, frm 1-3)
Above-average filly. Turf high 74 (began Jly) - 3rd of 15 giving 6lb to Dilly (12 Spt Yarmouth 7f frm RF 4334) - also 1st of 7 from Rambagh (31 Jly Folkestone RF 3244).
**N A Callaghan [1-5] Wafic Said.*

SAUDIA (USA) RR 78+f 1696[1]
2 b f Gone West (USA) 7.8f **(82)** - Bint Pasha (USA) (Affirmed (USA)) 9.3f **(79)**
Form - 1
Record 2000 - 1st:1 2nd:0 3rd:0 Ran:1
Win Prizemoney £3,640 *Total Prizemoney* £3,640
Wins * 2000 Jun Pontef (SFT) 6f 78+ <
2000 Turf 1-1: (6f 1-1) (gd 1-1)
Currently above-average filly. (1st run) - 1st of 5 from Forum Finale (4 Jun Pontefract RF 1696). She coped with the soft ground well when winning on her Pontefract debut and could be anything.
**P F I Cole [1-1] H R H Prince Fahd Salman.*

SAVANNAH QUEEN (USA) BHB 58f RR 59f 1915[13]
3 b br f Green Desert (USA) 7.8f **(78)** - Bay Queen **(75f)** (Damister (USA)) 9f **(73)**
Form - 58750
Record 2000 - 1st:0 2nd:0 3rd:0 Ran:5
2000 Turf 0-5: (6f 2, 7f, 8f, 10f) (g-s, gd 3, frm)
Light-framed, fair filly. Turf high 59 (1st run) - 5th of 14 to Cinnamon Court (30 Mar Leicester 7f gd RF 0567).
**M L W Bell [0-5] B J Warren.*

SAVANNA MISS BHB 34f RR 57df 5067[13]
2 b f Son Pardo - Havana Miss **(43f 34a)** (Cigar)
Form - 570600
Record 2000 - 1st:0 2nd:0 3rd:0 Ran:6
2000 Turf 0-6: (5f 5, 6f) (g-s 2, gd, g-f 2, frm)
Fair filly. Turf high 57. **B Palling [0-6] Mrs L Hedlund.*

SAVED BY THE BELLE RR 13f 4678[5]
3 b f Emarati (USA) 6.6f **(63)** - Belle Danseuse (Bellypha) 9.8f **(73)**
Form - 5
Record 2000 - 1st:0 2nd:0 3rd:0 Ran:1
2000 Turf 0-1: (8f) (g-s)
Workmanlike, currently poor filly. **L A Dace [0-1] L P Dace.*

SAVE THE PLANET BHB 47f RR 49f 3186[7]
3 b f Environment Friend 7.5f **(67)** - Geoffreys Bird (Master Willie) 7f **(70)**
Form - 00707
Record 2000 - 1st:0 2nd:0 3rd:0 Ran:5
2000 Turf 0-4: (7f, 8f, 11f 2) (g-s 2, gd 2) 2000 AW 0-1: (11f) (Fibr)
Lengthy, moderate filly, has worn blinkers. Turf high 49.
**J G Given [0-5] Mrs G A Jennings.*

SAVE THE POUND (USA) BHB 52f RR 52f 4428[6]
2 br c Northern Flagship (USA) 12.2f **(72)** - Key Bid (USA) (Key To The Mint (USA)) 9.4f **(75)**
Form - 5776
Record 2000 - 1st:0 2nd:0 3rd:0 Ran:4
2000 Turf 0-4: (7f 3, 8f) (gd 2, g-f, frm)
Fair colt. Turf high 52. **T D Easterby [0-4] C H Stevens.*

SAVING LIVES ATSEA (IRE) BHB 53f RR 51f 4001[7]
2 ch g Dolphin Street (FR) - Advantageous (Top Ville) 11.7f **(68)**
Form - 607
Record 2000 - 1st:0 2nd:0 3rd:0 Ran:3
Win Prizemoney £0 *Total Prizemoney* £189
2000 Turf 0-3: (5f, 6f 2) (g-f 3)
Currently fair gelding. Turf high 51.
**M H Tompkins [0-3] Yours For A Day Ltd.*

SAVOIRE VIVRE RR 116+f 3789[2]
3 b c Sadler's Wells (USA) 11.3f **(87)** - Oh So Sharp (Kris) 9.5f **(73)**
Form - 12
Record 2000 - 1st:1 2nd:1 3rd:0 Ran:2
Win Prizemoney £6,678 *Total Prizemoney* £20,478
Wins * 2000 Jly Ascot (G-F) 10f 95++ <
2000 Turf 1-2: (10f 1-1, 13f) (g-f 1-1, frm)
Well made, currently high-class colt. Turf high 116 (began Jly) - 2nd of 6 getting 11lb from Murghem (19 Aug Newbury 13f frm RF 3789). An imposing, blue-blooded colt, he won an Ascot maiden in July on his debut and ran a cracker behind Murghem in the Group 2 Geoffrey Freer Stakes the following month. Unable to run in the St Leger after suffering a late setback, he is clearly held in high regard and remains open to any amount of improvement. A tendency to pull hard aside, he is a first rate prospect.
**J H M Gosden [1-2] Sheikh Mohammed.*

SAVOIR FAIRE (IRE) BHB 27f RR 22f 3495[9]
4 b m College Chapel - Arctic Splendour (USA) (Arctic Tern (USA)) 8.9f **(69)**
Form - 0800
Record 2000 - 1st:0 2nd:0 3rd:0 Ran:4
Pre2000 - 1st:0 2nd:0 3rd:0 Ran:4
2000 Turf 0-4: (8f 3, 12f) (gd, g-f 2, frm)
Leggy, little account filly, has worn blinkers. Turf high 22.
**M A Buckley [0-8] Mrs D J Buckley.*

SAWBO LAD (IRE) BHB 68f63a RR 72f 63a 5010[4]
2 b c Namaqualand (USA) - Maafi Esm (Polish Precedent (USA)) 10.2f **(60)**
Form - 6000104
Record 2000 - 1st:1 2nd:0 3rd:0 Ran:7
Win Prizemoney £2,331 *Total Prizemoney* £2,331
Wins * 2000 Aug Folkes (G-F) S 7f 72 <
2000 Turf 1-6: (5f 2, 6f, 7f 1-2, 8f) (sft, gd 1-3, frm 2) 2000 AW 0-1: (7f) (Fibr)
Above-average colt, effective 7f, acts on gd. Turf high 72 - 1st of 14 from Kaluki (24 Aug Folkestone RF 3919).
**J Akehurst [1-3] Normandy Developments (London) (from R J O'Sullivan [0-4] Jun 2000).*

SAWLAJAN (USA) BHB 47f43a RR 37f 43a 1089[17]
9 ch g Woodman (USA) 9.7f **(77)** - Crafty Satin (USA) (Crimson Satan) 8f **(67)**
Form - 0
Record 2000 - 1st:0 2nd:0 3rd:0 Ran:1
Pre2000 - 1st:2 2nd:0 3rd:2 Ran:12
Win Prizemoney £10,237 *Total Prizemoney* £11,774
2000 Turf 0-1: (14f) (g-f)
Very moderate gelding. Becoming disappointing. **T R Watson [1-13] Miss S Hoare (from J L Dunlop [2-9] Spt 1994).*

SAWWAAH (IRE) BHB 90f RR 91f 5158[1]
3 b c Marju (IRE) 9.2f **(76)** - Just a Mirage (Green Desert (USA)) 8.6f **(78)**
Form - 61
Record 2000 - 1st:1 2nd:0 3rd:0 Ran:2
Pre2000 - 1st:0 2nd:1 3rd:1 Ran:2
Win Prizemoney £4,615 *Total Prizemoney* £6,688
Wins * 2000 Oct Nottin (SFT) 8.2f 67+ <
2000 Turf 1-2: (8f 1-2) (sft 1-1, frm)
Useful colt. Turf high 87. **E A L Dunlop [1-4] Hamdan Al Maktoum.*

SAYEDAH (IRE) BHB 100f RR 93f 4990[1]
2 b f Darshaan 11.9f **(81)** - Balaabel (USA) **(76f)** (Sadler's Wells (USA)) 10f **(76)**
Form - 221
Record 2000 - 1st:1 2nd:2 3rd:0 Ran:3
Win Prizemoney £29,000 *Total Prizemoney* £36,029
Wins * 2000 Oct Newmar (G-S) G2 7f 93 <
2000 Turf 1-3: (7f 1-3) (gd 1-2, frm)

Currently useful filly. Turf high 93 (began Aug) - 1st of 16 getting 3lb from Imagine (14 Oct Newmarket RF 4990). She made all to land the Rockfel Stakes on her third run. That event has become an informative guide to the 1000 Guineas, but she needs to show further improvement to figure in that Classic.

**M P Tregoning [1-3] Hamdan Al Maktoum.*

SCACHMATT BHB 82f **RR** 710a5

3 f

Form - 5

Record 2000 - 1st:0 2nd:0 3rd:0 Ran:1

2000 Turf 0-1: (8f) (hvy)

Currently very poor filly.

**L M Cumani [0-1].*

SCAFELL BHB 56f63a **RR 68f 63a** 5105[19]

3 b c Puissance 7.1f **(60)** - One Half Silver (CAN) (Plugged Nickle (USA)) 7.8f **(68)**

Form - 8205310800

Record	**2000** -	1st:1	2nd:1	3rd:1	Ran:10
	Pre2000 -	1st:0	2nd:2	3rd:2	Ran:8

Win Prizemoney £2,401 *Total Prizemoney* £7,060

Wins * **2000** Jun Hamilt (G-F) 5f 61 <

2000 Turf 1-9: (5f 1-4, 6f 2, 7f 3) (g-s, gd 3, g-f, frm 1-4) 2000 AW 0-1: (5f) (Equi)

Workmanlike, average colt, effective 5 to 6f, best at 5f, acts on g-f to frm, best on frm, has worn blinkers. Turf high 68. Inconsistent.

**C Smith [1-18] & Mrs T I Gourley.*

SCAPAVIA (FR) RR 48f 4821[14]

2 b f Alzao (USA) 9.8f **(73)** - Larrikin (USA) **(40f)** (Slew O' Gold (USA)) 8f **(75)**

Form - 00

Record 2000 - 1st:0 2nd:0 3rd:0 Ran:2

2000 Turf 0-2: (6f, 8f) (gd, g-f)

Currently moderate filly. Turf high 48 (began Spt).

**L M Cumani [0-2] Scuderia Rencati Srl.*

SCARLET LIVERY BHB 30f **RR 32f** 4650[13]

4 b m Saddlers' Hall (IRE) 10.5f **(65)** - Go For Red (IRE) (Thatching) 8f **(66)**

Form - 0000580

Record	**2000** -	1st:0	2nd:0	3rd:0	Ran:7
	Pre2000 -	1st:0	2nd:0	3rd:1	Ran:8

Win Prizemoney £0 *Total Prizemoney* £887

2000 Turf 0-6: (8f 3, 9f, 10f 2) (gd, g-f, frm 4) 2000 AW 0-1: (11f) (Fibr)

Very moderate filly, effective 7f, acts on frm, likes left handed tracks. Turf high 32.

**W H Tinning [0-7] W H Tinning (from C B B Booth [0-4] Oct 1999).*

SCARLETTA (USA) RR 88?f 1054[4]

3 b f Red Ransom (USA) 8.6f **(83)** - Snowtown (IRE) **(99f)** (Alzao (USA)) 7.1f **(68)**

Form - 4

Record	**2000** -	1st:0	2nd:0	3rd:0	Ran:1
	Pre2000 -	1st:0	2nd:2	3rd:0	Ran:2

Win Prizemoney £0 *Total Prizemoney* £2,358

2000 Turf 0-1: (11f) (gd)

Neat, currently useful filly.

**J H M Gosden [0-1] R E Sangster (from A G Foster [0-2] Oct 1999).*

SCARLETT RIBBON BHB 92f **RR 96+f** 4735[9]

3 b f Most Welcome 8.6f **(66)** - Scarlett Holly (Red Sunset) 8.2f **(63)**

Form - 8250

Record	**2000** -	1st:0	2nd:1	3rd:0	Ran:3
	Pre2000 -	1st:1	2nd:0	3rd:0	Ran:2

Win Prizemoney £3,160 *Total Prizemoney* £8,541

Wins * 1999 Nov Windso (G-S) 6f 96+ <

2000 Turf 0-3: (6f 2, 7f) (g-s, gd, g-f)

Unfurnished, very useful filly. Turf high 96 (1st run) - 2nd of 13 getting 12lb from Hot Tin Roof (13 May Lingfield 7f g-s RF 1192). Highly rated at two, she made an excellent start to her second season when chasing Hot Tin Roof home in a Listed event at Lingfield. A shade below that form in two sprint handicaps afterwards, she deserves another chance over seven furlongs.

**P J Makin [1-5] R Angelini-Hurll.*

SCARLET WOMAN RR 39f 1477[8]

3 b f Sri Pekan (USA) - Gara Yaka (IRE) **(66f)** (Soviet Star (USA))

Form - 08

Record 2000 - 1st:0 2nd:0 3rd:0 Ran:2

2000 Turf 0-1: (8f) (frm) 2000 AW 0-1: (11f) (Fibr)

Neat, currently very moderate filly.

**K R Burke [0-2] Mrs Elaine Burke.*

SCARPE ROSSE (IRE) RR 71f 4162[6]

2 b f Sadler's Wells (USA) 11.3f **(87)** - Red Comes Up (USA) (Blushing Groom (FR)) 10.3f **(76)**

Form - 56

Record 2000 - 1st:0 2nd:0 3rd:0 Ran:2

Win Prizemoney £0 *Total Prizemoney* £162

2000 Turf 0-2: (7f 2) (g-f 2)

Currently above-average filly. Turf high 71 (began Aug).

**J L Dunlop [0-2] Mrs Sonia Rogers.*

SCARROTTOO RR 47f 5224[7]

2 ch g Zilzal (USA) 8.5f **(79)** - Bold and Beautiful (Bold Lad (IRE)) 8.4f **(68)**

Form - 67

Record 2000 - 1st:0 2nd:0 3rd:0 Ran:2

Win Prizemoney £0 *Total Prizemoney* £195

2000 Turf 0-2: (7f, 8f) (gd 2)

Currently moderate gelding. Turf high 47 (began Oct).

**S C Williams [0-2] Michael Peacock.*

SCARTEEN FOX (IRE) BHB 109f **RR 110f** 2441[8]

3 ch c Foxhound (USA) - Best Swinger (IRE) (Ela-Mana-Mou) 10.1f **(70)**

Form - 40508

Record	**2000** -	1st:0	2nd:0	3rd:0	Ran:5
	Pre2000 -	1st:2	2nd:0	3rd:1	Ran:4

Win Prizemoney £25,451 *Total Prizemoney* £28,084

Wins	* 1999	Oct	Newmar (G-S)	L	7f	112	<
	* 1999	Spt	Newbur (G-S)		7f	96	

2000 Turf 0-5: (6f, 7f 2, 8f 2) (g-s, gd 3, frm)

Scopey, Group-class colt, effective 7f, acts on gd. Turf high 110. He has been disappointing since winning the Somerville Tattersalls Stakes in October 1999 and looks a horse without a trip. Sold for 160,000gns at Newmarket in October, he has moved to Peter Ho Leung and will be trained for the Hong Kong Derby.

**D R C Elsworth [2-9] McDowell Racing.*

SCARTEEN SISTER (IRE) RR 43f 3323[8]

2 ch f Eagle Eyed (USA) - Best Swinger (IRE) (Ela-Mana-Mou) 10.1f **(70)**

Form - 38

Record 2000 - 1st:0 2nd:0 3rd:1 Ran:2

Win Prizemoney £0 *Total Prizemoney* £554

2000 Turf 0-2: (6f, 7f) (g-f, frm)

Currently moderate filly. Turf high 43 (began Jly).

**D R C Elsworth [0-2] McDowell Racing.*

SCENE (IRE) BHB 78f75a **RR 82f 75a** 5240[6]

5 b m Scenic 10.6f **(66)** - Avebury Ring (Auction Ring (USA)) 8.6f **(65)**

Form - 01780700004136

Record	**2000** -	1st:2	2nd:0	3rd:1	Ran:14
	Pre2000 -	1st:6	2nd:2	3rd:6	Ran:38

Win Prizemoney £51,840 *Total Prizemoney* £67,120

Wins	* **2000**	Oct	Newmar (SFT)	H	8f	69	82 <
	2000	Apr	Leices (G-S)	H	8f	76	78+
	1999	Nov	Nottin (SFT)	H	10f	70	72
	1999	Jun	Epsom (G-S)	H	8.5f	74	81
	1999	Apr	Ascot (GD)	H	8f	70	75
	1998	Jly	Haydoc (G-F)	H	8.1f	72	77
	1998	Jun	Thirsk (SFT)	H	8f	68	76
	1997	Nov	Doncas (G-S)	H	7f	63	70

2000 Turf 2-14: (8f 2-9, 9f 2, 10f 3) (sft 3, g-s 3, gd 2-7, g-f)

Decent filly, effective 8 to 10f, best at 8f, acts on sft to frm, best on gd, has worn blinkers, excels at Ripon. Turf high 82 - 1st of 30 getting 4lb from Judicious (12 Oct Newmarket RF 4934) - also 1st of 6 getting 4lb from Nouf (6 Apr Leicester RF 0626).

**N P Littmoden [1-6] Paul Dixon (from J A Glover [6-34] Jun 2000).*

SCENIC LADY (IRE) BHB 26f **RR 22f** 4679[10]
4 b m Scenic 10.6f **(66)** - Tu Tu Maori (IRE) (Kings Lake (USA)) 10.8f **(67)**
Form - 002540
Record 2000 - 1st:0 2nd:1 3rd:0 Ran:6
Pre2000 - 1st:0 2nd:1 3rd:0 Ran:11
Win Prizemoney £0 *Total Prizemoney* £1,364
2000 Turf 0-5: (10f 2, 12f 3) (g-s, g-f 2, frm 2) 2000 AW 0-1: (12f) (Equi)
Neat, little account filly, has worn blinkers. Turf high 22. Inconsistent.
**L A Dace [0-15] Eddie Davess (from J J Sheehan [0-2] Spt 1998).*

SCENTED AIR RR 49f 5062[5]
3 b f Lion Cavern (USA) 7.5f **(74)** - Jungle Rose (Shirley Heights) 10.3f **(74)**
Form - 85
Record 2000 - 1st:0 2nd:0 3rd:0 Ran:2
2000 Turf 0-2: (8f, 10f) (sft, g-f)
Light-framed, currently moderate filly. Turf high 49 (began Spt).
**T R Watson [0-2] A F Heselton.*

SCHATZI BHB 47f50a **RR 58f 50a** 5191[4]
3 gr f Chilibang 7f **(55)** - Fluorescent Flo (Ballad Rock) 7.8f **(63)**
Form - 0200054
Record 2000 - 1st:0 2nd:1 3rd:0 Ran:7
Pre2000 - 1st:0 2nd:3 3rd:2 Ran:11
Win Prizemoney £0 *Total Prizemoney* £0,030
2000 Turf 0-7: (5f, 6f 4, 7f, 8f) (g-s 2, gd 2, g-f, frm, hrd)
Neat, fair filly, effective 5 to 6f, best at 6f, acts on gd to g-f, best on gd, has worn blinkers. Turf high 58 - 2nd of 18 getting 5lb from Cape Coast (2 May Nottingham 6f gd RF 0966). Inconsistent.
**D Moffatt [0-19] Mrs Jennie Moffatt.*

SCHEHERAZADE RR 57f 5098[19]
2 b f Sadler's Wells (USA) 11.3f **(87)** - Impatiente (USA) (Vaguely Noble) 10.1f **(72)**
Form - 0
Record 2000 - 1st:0 2nd:0 3rd:0 Ran:1
2000 Turf 0-1: (8f) (gd)
Currently fair filly.
**L M Cumani [0-1] Lindy Regis & Geoff Howard-Spink.*

SCHEMING BHB 71f **RR 79f** 5101[1]
3 br g Machiavellian (USA) 9.8f **(83)** - Alusha **(90+f)** (Soviet Star (USA))
Form - 16081
Record 2000 - 1st:2 2nd:0 3rd:0 Ran:5
Win Prizemoney £9,818 *Total Prizemoney* £9,818
Wins * **2000** Oct Doncas (GD) H 10.3f 65 69
* **2000** Aug Haydoc (GD) 11.9f 79 <
2000 Turf 2-5: (10f 1-2, 12f 1-2, 16f) (g-s 2, gd 2-3)
Strong, above-average gelding. Turf high 79 (1st run) (began Aug) - 1st of 9 from Shair (12 Aug Haydock RF 3586).
**W M Brisbourne [2-5] Christopher Chell.*

SCISSOR RIDGE BHB 42f52a **RR 54f 52a** 4924[8]
8 ch g Indian Ridge 7.6f **(74)** - Golden Scissors (Kalaglow) 9.8f **(67)**
Form - 1304324264023868505088
Record 2000 - 1st:0 2nd:3 3rd:2 Ran:18
Pre2000 - 1st:8 2nd:14 3rd:10 Ran:116
Win Prizemoney £25,519 *Total Prizemoney* £52,866

Wins								
	* 1999	*Nov*	*Lingfi*	*(STD)*	*H*	*7f*	*52*	*57*
	* 1998	Jly	Folkes	(GD)	H	6f	50	56
	* 1996	*Dec*	*Lingfi*	*(STD)*	*H*	*5f*	*60*	*65* <
	* 1996	*Nov*	*Lingfi*	*(STD)*	*H*	*6f*	*60*	*65* <
	* 1996	Spt	Goodwo	(G-F)	H	5f	58	60
	* 1996	Jun	Goodwo	(G-F)	H	6f	43	52

2000 Turf 0-10: (6f 2, 7f 6, 8f 2) (g-s, gd 4, g-f 2, frm 3) 2000 AW 0-8: (8f 7, 10f) (Equi 6, Fibr 2)
Fair gelding, effective 6 to 8f, acts on gd - acts on AW, best on Equi, has worn blinkers, likes left handed tracks, likes tight tracks, likes Lingfield. Turf high 54 - 3rd of 14 getting 10lb from Dolphinelle (31 May Newbury 7f gd RF 1588). AW high 61 - 2nd of 10 giving 9lb to Tufamore (27 Jan Wolverhampton 8f Fibr RF 0172). A fair handicapper at between seven furlongs and a mile on turf and Equitrack, but is on a very long losing run.
**J J Bridger [7-126] Donald Smith (from M R Channon [1-8] Aug 1994).*

SCONCED (USA) BHB 25f **RR 34f** 240[9]
5 ch g Affirmed (USA) 10.3f **(75)** - Quaff (USA) (Raise A Cup (USA)) 7.6f **(74)**
Form - 370
Record 2000 - 1st:0 2nd:0 3rd:0 Ran:2
Pre2000 - 1st:1 2nd:0 3rd:3 Ran:15
Win Prizemoney £3,468 *Total Prizemoney* £5,692
Wins 1998 Spt Hamilt (SFT) 9.2f 73 <
2000 AW 0-2: (15f, 16f) (Fibr 2)
Very moderate gelding, has worn blinkers. AW high 10.
**Martyn Wane [0-13] James S Kennerley and Miss Jenny Hall (from G Wragg [1-6] Oct 1998).*

SCORPION (USA) RR 5330a[9]
2 b f Seattle Slew (USA) 7.8f **(64)** - Petiteness (USA) (Chief's Crown (USA)) 9.0f **(72)**
Form - 0
2000 AW 0-1: (9f) (Dirt)
Currently useful.
**D W Lukas in USA [0-1] R Baker & D Cornstein & W Mack.*

SCOTISH LAW (IRE) BHB 73f **RR 75f** 4547[10]
2 ch g Case Law 6f **(64)** - Scotia Rose (Tap On Wood) 10.3f **(65)**
Form - 2100
Record 2000 - 1st:1 2nd:1 3rd:0 Ran:4
Win Prizemoney £3,542 *Total Prizemoney* £4,349
Wins * **2000** Aug Epsom (GD) 6f 71 <
2000 Turf 1-4: (6f 1-3, 8f) (g-s, g-f 1-2, frm)
Above-average gelding. Turf high 72 (1st run) (began Jly) - 2nd of 10 getting 2lb from Red Carpet (28 Jly Chepstow 6f frm RF 3169) - also 1st of 7 getting 3lb from Vislink (16 Aug Epsom RF 3690).
**P R Chamings [1-4] P R Chamings.*

SCOTLAND BAY BHB 37f37a **RR 39f 37a** 635[13]
5 b m Then Again 7.4f **(52)** - Down the Valley (Kampala) 8.4f **(56)**
Form - 0080
Record 2000 - 1st:0 2nd:0 3rd:0 Ran:2
Pre2000 - 1st:2 2nd:2 3rd:2 Ran:23
Win Prizemoney £4,260 *Total Prizemoney* £6,471
Wins 1998 Oct Folkes (G-S) S 7f 60 <
1998 Jan Lingfi (STD) H 7f 54 59
2000 Turf 0-1: (7f) (gd) 2000 AW 0-1: (9f) (Fibr)
Very moderate filly, has worn blinkers. **P Butler [0-14] Christopher Wilson (from R Hannon [2-12] Oct 1998).*

SCOTTISH MEMORIES (IRE) RR 104f 4528a[3]
4 ch g Houmayoun (FR) 7.1f **(79)** - Interj **00**
Form - 8363
2000 Turf 0-4: (8f 2, 9f, 10f) (sft, gd 2)
Very useful gelding, effective 8 to 10f, best at 9f, acts on g-f, prefers right handed tracks. Turf high 104 (began Aug) - 3rd of 13 giving 5lb to Shoal Creek (17 Spt Curragh 9f RF 4528a). He has an excellent record at The Curragh and made the frame in a Listed event there on his final start. Probably best around a mile and a quarter, he enjoys some give underfoot.
**J E Mulhern in IRE [2-9] Mrs Chryss O'Reilly (from F Ennis in IRE [0-4] May 1999).*

SCOTTISH SONG BHB 33f **RR 45df** 4445[13]
7 b g Niniski (USA) 13.2f **(67)** - Miss Saint-Cloud (Nonoalco (USA)) 8.5f **(66)**
Form - 0
Record 2000 - 1st:0 2nd:0 3rd:0 Ran:1
Pre2000 - 1st:2 2nd:0 3rd:0 Ran:7
Win Prizemoney £7,206 *Total Prizemoney* £7,206
Wins 1998 Jly Killar (GD) 14f 80+ <
1998 May Leopar (G-F) 16f 80
2000 Turf 0-1: (16f) (gd)
Moderate gelding. Inconsistent.
**Mrs M Reveley [0-1] J Walby (from T Stack in IRE [3-8] Jly 1999).*

SCOTTISH SPICE BHB 82f **RR 86f** 5159[3]
3 b f Selkirk (USA) 7.9f **(76)** - Dilwara (IRE) (Lashkari) 9.8f **(67)**
Form - 600530D203
Record 2000 - 1st:0 2nd:1 3rd:2 Ran:10
Pre2000 - 1st:2 2nd:0 3rd:0 Ran:4
Win Prizemoney £10,885 *Total Prizemoney* £19,633

Wins * 1999 Spt Newbur (G-F) H 7f 85 87 <
* 1999 Aug Folkes (G-S) 7f 83
2000 Turf 0-10: (8f 5, 9f 2, 10f 3) (sft, g-s 3, gd 2, g-f 2, frm 2)
Leggy, useful filly, effective 7 to 9f, best at 7f, acts on sft to frm, best on frm, likes tight tracks, likes Goodwood. Turf high 86 - 3rd of 17 giving 15lb to Greenaway Bay (24 Oct Nottingham 8f sft RF 5159). Consistent. **I A Balding [2-14] J C Smith.*

SCOTTY GUEST (IRE) BHB 76f **RR 60f** 1815[10]

3 b c Distinctly North (USA) 7.4f **(63)** - Tartan Lady (IRE) (Taufan (USA)) 7f **(57)**
Form - 00
Record 2000 - 1st:0 2nd:0 3rd:0 Ran:2
Pre2000 - 1st:1 2nd:0 3rd:0 Ran:2
Win Prizemoney £3,297 *Total Prizemoney* £3,297
Wins * 1999 Oct Yarmou (G-S) 8f 88+ <
2000 Turf 0-2: (8f, 10f) (gd, frm)
Leggy, average colt. Turf high 60. (DEAD)
**G G Margarson [1-4] John Guest.*

SCOTTY'S FUTURE (IRE) BHB 65f **RR 63f** 5318[9]

2 b c Namaqualand (USA) - Persian Empress (IRE) (Persian Bold) 9.3f **(66)**
Form - 080
Record 2000 - 1st:0 2nd:0 3rd:0 Ran:3
2000 Turf 0-3: (6f 3) (sft, g-s, gd)
Currently average colt. Turf high 63 (began Oct).
**A C Stewart [0-3] Collins, Saunders, Kinge & McGuinness.*

SCRAMBLE (USA) **RR 52f** 4964[3]

2 ch c Gulch (USA) 9.6f **(79)** - Syzygy (ARG) (Big Play (USA))
Form - 3
Record 2000 - 1st:0 2nd:0 3rd:1 Ran:1
Win Prizemoney £0 *Total Prizemoney* £1,435
2000 Turf 0-1: (7f) (gd)
Currently fair colt. **J H M Gosden [0-1] Stonerside Stables LLC.*

SCRATCH THE DOVE BHB 39f **RR 13f** 1054[6]

3 ch f Henbit (USA) 10.2f **(46)** - Coney Dove (Celtic Cone) 9.8f **(43)**
Form - 006
Record 2000 - 1st:0 2nd:0 3rd:0 Ran:3
2000 Turf 0-3: (7f, 8f, 11f) (hvy, gd 2)
Light-framed, currently poor filly. Turf high 13.
**C J Price [0-3] Cecil Price.*

SCREAMIN' GEORGINA BHB 65f **RR 66f** 4582[10]

2 b f Muhtarram (USA) - Carrie Kool **(61df)** (Prince Sabo) 7.2f **(62)**
Form - 7211050
Record 2000 - 1st:2 2nd:1 3rd:0 Ran:7
Win Prizemoney £4,102 *Total Prizemoney* £4,638
Wins * **2000** Jly Folkes (GD-) C 5f 65 <
* **2000** Jly Leices (G-F) S 5f 65 <
2000 Turf 2-7: (5f 2-7) (gd 2, g-f, frm 2-4)
Average filly, effective 5f, acts on frm. Turf high 66 - 5th of 9 getting 11lb from Nifty Alice (31 Aug Musselburgh 5f frm RF 4120) - also 1st of 6 getting 5lb from Justalord (31 Jly Folkestone RF 3243). **S C Williams [2-7] The Lager Khan.*

SCROOGE (IRE) BHB 43f47a **RR 42f 47a** 159[5]

4 b g Tirol 8.1f **(64)** - Gay Appeal (Star Appeal) 9.6f **(65)**
Form - 325
Record 2000 - 1st:0 2nd:1 3rd:1 Ran:3
Pre2000 - 1st:0 2nd:0 3rd:0 Ran:12
Win Prizemoney £0 *Total Prizemoney* £774
2000 AW 0-3: (7f 2, 8f) (Equi 2, Fibr)
Scopey, fair gelding, has worn blinkers. AW high 50.
**M H Tompkins [0-16] M P Bowring.*

SEA DANZIG BHB 40f60a **RR 51f 60a** 4810[8]

7 ch g Roi Danzig (USA) 10.5f **(62)** - Tosara (Main Reef) 9.6f **(57)**
Form - 57174221700004010500 78
Record 2000 - 1st:3 2nd:2 3rd:0 Ran:22
Pre2000 - 1st:8 2nd:9 3rd:8 Ran:80
Win Prizemoney £35,894 *Total Prizemoney* £55,521
Wins * **2000** Jly Salisb (FRM) H 14.1f 45 50
* **2000** *Mar Lingfi (STD)* *12f* *72*
* **2000** *Jan Lingfi (STD)* *10f* *67*
* 1999 Spt Epsom (GD) H 10.1f 55 59
* 1998 Jly Folkes (G-F) 9.7f 63
* 1998 Jun Goodwo (G-F) H 9f 52 61
* 1998 *Jan Lingfi (STD) H* *10f* *68 73* <
* 1998 *Jan Lingfi (STD) H* *10f* *68 73* <
* 1997 *Nov Lingfi (STD) H* *10f* *67 69*
* 1997 *Jan Lingfi (STD) H* *7f* *63 58*
* 1996 Oct Lingfi (GD) H 7f 62 66
2000 Turf 1-11: (10f 2, 12f 4, 14f 1-4, 17f) (sft, gd 2, g-f, frm 1-6, hrd)
2000 AW 2-11: (10f 1-5, 12f 1-5, 13f) (Equi 2-10, Fibr)
Above-average gelding, effective 10 to 12f, best at 10f, - acts on AW, best on Equi, has worn blinkers (very effectively), favours tight tracks, likes Lingfield. Turf high 51. AW high 72 - 1st of 4 giving 7lb to Pulau Pinang (29 Mar Lingfield RF 0551) - also 1st of 5 from Barbason (15 Jan Lingfield RF 0096). Effective on turf, but is probably better on Equitrack and scored twice on that surface last season. He is a bit of a character though, and needs to be left alone to do it his way.
**J J Bridger [11-91] P Cook (from P Howling [0-11] Jly 1996).*

SEA-DEER BHB 64f75a **RR 67f 75a** 3969[5]

11 ch g Hadeer 8.9f **(58)** - Hi-Tech Girl (Homeboy) 6.6f **(55)**
Form - 8006005
Record 2000 - 1st:0 2nd:0 3rd:0 Ran:7
Pre2000 - 1st:16 2nd:12 3rd:14 Ran:102
Win Prizemoney £62,775 *Total Prizemoney* £95,574
Wins 1999 Spt Yarmou (G-S) H 7f 66 76
1999 Spt Yarmou (G-F) S 7f 51
1998 Jly Newmar (G-F) H 6f 69 73
1997 Jun Yarmou (GD) 6f 87
1996 *Aug Wolver (STD) H* *6f* *74 77*
1996 Jly Newmar (GD) 5f 96 <
1996 Jun Yarmou (FRM) H 6f 73 71
1996 Jun Yarmou (FRM) H 6f 67 72
1996 May Catter (GD) C 5f 49
1996 May Newcas (GD) S 5f 60
2000 Turf 0-7: (6f 3, 7f 3, 8f) (g-f 3, frm 4)
Above-average gelding, effective 6 to 7f, acts on g-s to gd. Turf high 69. **J Pearce [0-5] M M Foulger (from C A Dwyer [8-62] Jun 2000).*

SEA DRIFT (FR) BHB 68f **RR 72f** 4729[7]

3 gr f Warning 8.1f **(77)** - Night At Sea (Night Shift (USA)) 7.2f **(69)**
Form - 5313027
Record 2000 - 1st:1 2nd:1 3rd:2 Ran:7
Pre2000 - 1st:0 2nd:0 3rd:0 Ran:1
Win Prizemoney £4,420 *Total Prizemoney* £6,412
Wins * **2000** Jly Newmar (G-F) 7f 72 <
2000 Turf 1-7: (7f 1-5, 8f 2) (gd 3, g-f 1-2, frm 2)
Unfurnished, above-average filly, effective 7f, acts on g-f. Turf high 72 - also 1st of 8 getting 5lb from Grampas (22 Jly Newmarket RF 3034). Gradually improved with each run and got off the mark in a Newmarket maiden in July, the form of which has worked out well. Fair effort under an inexperienced pilot in an amateur riders' event at Redcar next time. **L M Cumani [1-8] Lady Juliet Tadgell.*

SEA EMPEROR **RR 51f** 4277[4]

3 br g Emperor Jones (USA) - Blumarin (IRE) (Scenic)
Form - 03044304
Record 2000 - 1st:0 2nd:0 3rd:2 Ran:8
Pre2000 - 1st:0 2nd:0 3rd:0 Ran:3
Win Prizemoney £0 *Total Prizemoney* £1,130
2000 Turf 0-8: (7f 2, 8f 3, 9f, 10f, 11f) (hvy, gd, g-f 4, frm, hrd)
Light-framed, fair gelding, has worn blinkers. Turf high 51. Inconsistent. **Mrs G S Rees [0-11] Cross Farm Partnership.*

SEA GOD BHB 18f25a **RR 25a** 457[10]

9 ch g Rainbow Quest (USA) 11.2f **(81)** - Sea Pageant (Welsh Pageant) 10f **(65)**
Form - 0000
Record 2000 - 1st:0 2nd:0 3rd:0 Ran:3
Pre2000 - 1st:1 2nd:3 3rd:2 Ran:37
Win Prizemoney £3,077 *Total Prizemoney* £6,122
Wins * 1996 *Feb Southw (STD) H* *11f* *44 48* <
2000 AW 0-3: (8f, 11f, 16f) (Fibr 3)
Very poor gelding. AW high 5.
**M C Chapman [1-61] McCann Ltd (from B W Hills [0-3] May 1994).*

SEA HAZE BHB 56f **RR 69f** 4543[19]
3 ch g Emarati (USA) 6.6f **(63)** - Unveiled **(54f 48a)** (Sayf El Arab (USA)) 7.1f **(54)**
Form - 0288000
Record 2000 - 1st:0 2nd:1 3rd:0 Ran:7
Pre2000 - 1st:1 2nd:0 3rd:1 Ran:8
Win Prizemoney £2,808 *Total Prizemoney* £4,764
Wins 1999 Jun Bath (FRM) 5.7f 62 <
2000 Turf 0-7: (5f 3, 6f 4) (gd 2, g-f, frm 3, hrd)
Strong, average gelding, effective 5f, acts on gd, has worn blinkers. Turf high 69 - 2nd of 14 getting 5lb from Blue Holly (8 Jun Chepstow 5f gd RF 1799). Becoming disappointing.
**R J Baker [0-7] P Slade (from R J Hodges [1-8] Spt 1999).*

SEAHORSE BOY (IRE) BHB 40f **RR 52f** 4366[13]
3 b g Petardia 8.2f **(58)** - Million At Dawn (IRE) (Fayruz)
Form - 0074000000
Record 2000 - 1st:0 2nd:0 3rd:0 Ran:10
Win Prizemoney £0 *Total Prizemoney* £527
2000 Turf 0-10: (5f 4, 6f 3, 7f, 8f 2) (g-s, g-f 4, frm 3, hrd 2)
Lengthy, fair gelding, has worn blinkers. Turf high 52. Becoming disappointing. **J S Wainwright [0-10] Mrs D Drewery.*

SEA ISLE BHB 62f53a **RR 68f 53a** 4474[10]
4 ch m Selkirk (USA) 7.9f **(76)** - Miss Blitz (Formidable (USA)) 9.2f **(63)**
Form - 80
Record 2000 - 1st:0 2nd:0 3rd:0 Ran:2
Pre2000 - 1st:0 2nd:0 3rd:1 Ran:5
Win Prizemoney £0 *Total Prizemoney* £495
2000 AW 0-2: (8f 2) (Fibr 2)
Scopey, average filly, effective 7 to 8f, best at 7f, acts on g-f to frm, best on frm. AW high 39 (began Spt).
**I A Balding [0-7] George Strawbridge.*

SEALED BY FATE (IRE) BHB 42f48a **RR 51f 48a** 5122[20]
5 b g Mac's Imp (USA) 5.6f **(54)** - Fairy Don (Don) 7.7f **(64)**
Form - 57660445727070
Record 2000 - 1st:0 2nd:1 3rd:0 Ran:14
Pre2000 - 1st:1 2nd:5 3rd:5 Ran:39
Win Prizemoney £2,430 *Total Prizemoney* £9,274
Wins * 1999 Jun Carlis (GD) H 5f 58 61 <
2000 Turf 0-12: (5f 6, 6f 3, 7f 3) (g-s, gd 2, g-f 3, frm 5, hrd) 2000 AW 0-2: (6f 2) (Fibr 2)
Fair gelding, effective 5f, acts on g-f to frm, best on g-f, mostly wears blinkers, likes right handed tracks. Turf high 51. AW high 48. **J S Wainwright [1-53] Neil Harrison.*

SEA MARK BHB 84f **RR 83f** 4743[1]
4 br h Warning 8.1f **(77)** - Mettlesome (Lomond (USA)) 8.8f **(65)**
Form - 01
Record 2000 - 1st:1 2nd:0 3rd:0 Ran:2
Pre2000 - 1st:1 2nd:1 3rd:0 Ran:3
Win Prizemoney £10,020 *Total Prizemoney* £11,840
Wins *** 2000** Spt Newmar (GD) H 7f 80 83 <
* 1999 Oct Leices (G-S) 7f 67
2000 Turf 1-2: (7f 1-2) (gd, g-f 1-1)
Scopey, decent colt. Turf high 83 - 1st of 28 getting 1lb from Pays d'Amour (30 Spt Newmarket RF 4743). **B W Hills [2-5] K Abdulla.*

SEA MINSTREL BHB 30f **RR 16f** 1377[12]
4 b m Sea Raven (IRE) - Give Us a Treat (Cree Song)
Form - 0
Record 2000 - 1st:0 2nd:0 3rd:0 Ran:1
Pre2000 - 1st:0 2nd:0 3rd:1 Ran:14
Win Prizemoney £0 *Total Prizemoney* £756
2000 AW 0-1: (6f) (Fibr)
Scopey, poor filly. **M E Sowersby [0-18] M E Sowersby.*

SEAN'S HONOR (IRE) BHB 56f54a **RR 57f 54a** 4762[5]
2 b f Mukaddamah (USA) 7.6f **(74)** - Great Land (USA) (Friend's Choice (USA)) 8.6f **(57)**
Form - 54476255
Record 2000 - 1st:0 2nd:1 3rd:0 Ran:8
Win Prizemoney £0 *Total Prizemoney* £1,024
2000 Turf 0-7: (5f 7) (g-s, gd 2, g-f 3, frm) 2000 AW 0-1: (5f) (Fibr)
Fair filly, effective 5f, - acts on Fibr, has worn blinkers. Turf high 57. (1st run) - 5th of 12 getting 5lb from Acorn Catcher (30 Spt Wolverhampton 5f Fibr RF 4762). Consistent.
**C N Kellett [0-8] Sean Taylor.*

SEA RAY **RR 18f** 1011[8]
2 gr g Casteddu 7.4f **(54)** - Grey Twig (Godswalk (USA)) 7.3f **(58)**
Form - 08
Record 2000 - 1st:0 2nd:0 3rd:0 Ran:2
2000 Turf 0-2: (5f 2) (frm 2)
Currently poor gelding. Turf high 27. **J J Bridger [0-2] P Cook.*

SEARCH AND DESTROY (USA) BHB 58f **RR 57f** 5140[10]
2 b br c Sky Classic (CAN) 10f **(83)** - Hunt The Thimble (USA) (Turn and Count (USA)) 7.5f **(47)**
Form - 000
Record 2000 - 1st:0 2nd:0 3rd:0 Ran:3
2000 Turf 0-3: (6f 3) (g-s, gd 2)
Currently fair colt. Turf high 57 (began Spt).
**Sir Mark Prescott [0-3] McSwiney Osborne House.*

SEASAME PARK BHB 34f38a **RR 25f 38a** 1310[17]
3 b f Elmaamul (USA) 8.1f **(70)** - Holyrood Park (Sharrood (USA)) 10.5f **(72)**
Form - 703000
Record 2000 - 1st:0 2nd:0 3rd:1 Ran:5
Pre2000 - 1st:1 2nd:2 3rd:1 Ran:7
Win Prizemoney £1,871 *Total Prizemoney* £3,552
Wins * 1999 *Jun Wolvor (STD) S 7f 60* <
2000 Turf 0-2: (8f, 10f) (gd 2) 2000 AW 0-3: (8f, 9f 2) (Fibr 3)
Neat, very moderate filly, effective 7f, - acts on Fibr, has worn blinkers, likes left handed tracks, likes tight tracks. Turf high 18. AW high 31. **B Palling [1-12] The Saturday Seven.*

SEASONAL BHB 72f **RR 53f** 2640[7]
4 ch m Generous (IRE) 11.5f **(82)** - Ypha (USA) (Lyphard (USA)) 9.9f **(72)**
Form - 7
Record 2000 - 1st:0 2nd:0 3rd:0 Ran:1
2000 Turf 0-1: (12f) (frm)
Currently fair filly. **P R Webber [0-1] J Duggan & Mrs P Day.*

SEASONAL BLOSSOM (IRE) **RR 45f** 4552[10]
3 b f Fairy King (USA) 7.7f **(75)** - Temporary Lull (USA) (Super Concorde (USA)) 10.9f **(66)**
Form - 060
Record 2000 - 1st:0 2nd:0 3rd:0 Ran:3
2000 Turf 0-3: (6f, 7f, 10f) (g-s, gd 2)
Currently moderate filly. Turf high 45.
**B Smart [0-1] Adrienne and Michael Barnett (from D K Weld in IRE [0-2] Jly 2000).*

SEASON OF HOPE BHB 35f20a **RR 38f 20a** 219[9]
4 ch m Komaite (USA) 6.9f **(61)** - Honour and Glory (Hotfoot) 10.5f **(59)**
Form - 300
Record 2000 - 1st:0 2nd:0 3rd:1 Ran:3
Pre2000 - 1st:0 2nd:0 3rd:1 Ran:10
Win Prizemoney £0 *Total Prizemoney* £552
2000 AW 0-3: (11f 3) (Fibr 3)
Leggy, very moderate filly, effective 10f, acts on g-f, has worn blinkers, favours left handed tracks, favours tight tracks. AW high 32.
**D E Cantillon [0-12] Mrs Christine Willmott (from D J S Cosgrove [0-3] Jly 1998).*

SEASON'S GREETINGS (IRE) **RR 99f** 4563a[1]
2 b f Ezzoud (IRE) - Dream Season (USA) (Mr Prospector (USA)) 8.8f **(78)**
Form - 21
2000 Turf 1-2: (5f 1-1, 6f) (gd 1-2)
Currently very useful filly. Turf high 99 (began Aug) - 1st of 9 getting 3lb from Jack Spratt (15 Spt Chantilly RF 4563a). She showed plenty of speed to beat Jack Spratt in a Listed race at Chantilly in September. Bred to stay beyond the minimum trip, she should win a Group race this term.
**C Laffon-Parias in FR [1-2] Maktoum Al Maktoum.*

SEA SPOUSE BHB 29f40a **RR 27f 40a** 389[6]
9 ch g Jalmood (USA) 11.1f **(59)** - Bambolona (Bustino) 10.4f **(64)**

Form - 486
Record 2000 - 1st:0 2nd:0 3rd:0 Ran:3
Pre2000 - 1st:9 2nd:6 3rd:10 Ran:77
Win Prizemoney £23,378 *Total Prizemoney* £33,438
Wins * 1998 *Jun Lingfi (STD)* 8f 74 <
* 1998 *Jun Lingfi (STD)* 8f 63
* 1998 *Mar Southw (STD) H* 8f 58 61
* 1997 *Jan Southw (STD) H* 8f 61 66
* 1997 *Jan Southw (STD) H* 8f 61 66
* 1996 *Jun Southw (STD) H* 7f 57 64
* 1996 Mar Folkes (G-S) H 6.9f 41 45
* 1996 *Feb Southw (STD) H* 8f 48 59
2000 AW 0-3: (8f, 10f 2) (Equi 3)
Very moderate gelding, effective 10 to 11f, - acts on AW, favours left handed tracks, favours tight tracks. AW high 38. **M Blanshard [9-80] Seven Seas Racing.*

SEASQUILL (AUS) RR 93f 578a[14]

4 f
Form - 0
2000 Turf 0-1: (12f) (gd)
Currently useful. **G Rogerson in NZ [0-1].*

SEA SQUIRT (IRE) BHB 72f72a RR 76f 72a 4626[4]

3 b g Fourstars Allstar (USA) - Polynesian Goddess (IRE) (Salmon Leap (USA)) 11f **(61)**
Form - 22304162315204
Record 2000 - 1st:2 2nd:3 3rd:2 Ran:13
Pre2000 - 1st:0 2nd:2 3rd:0 Ran:3
Win Prizemoney £7,735 *Total Prizemoney* £15,436
Wins * **2000** Aug Newmar (G-F) C 8f 72
* **2000** Jun Carlis (FRM) 8f 74 <
2000 Turf 2-12: (8f 2-6, 9f, 10f, 11f, 12f 3) (sft, g-s 2, gd 2, g-f 2-5, frm 2) 2000 AW 0-1: (9f) (Fibr)
Lengthy, above-average gelding, effective 7 to 9f, best at 8f, acts on g-s to frm - acts on Fibr, likes right handed tracks. Turf high 78 - 2nd of 5 giving 5lb to Lady Helen (29 Jly Newcastle 9f g-f RF 3212) - also 1st of 4 getting 10lb from Supreme Salutation (18 Jun Carlisle RF 2070). (1st run) - 2nd of 7 to Royal Cavalier (25 Mar Wolverhampton 9f Fibr RF 0506). **M Johnston [2-16] M J Pilkington.*

SEA STAR RR 80+f 5186[3]

2 b c Distant Relative 7f **(69)** - Storm Card (Zalazl (USA))
Form - 3
Record 2000 - 1st:0 2nd:0 3rd:1 Ran:1
Win Prizemoney £0 *Total Prizemoney* £640
2000 Turf 0-1: (7f) (g-s)
Currently decent colt. (1st run) - 3rd of 16 to Halland (25 Oct Yarmouth 7f g-s RF 5186). **H R A Cecil [0-1] L Marinopoulos.*

SEA STORM (IRE) RR 28f 4169[13]

2 b g Dolphin Street (FR) - Prime Interest (IRE) (Kings Lake (USA)) 10.8f **(67)**
Form - 00
Record 2000 - 1st:0 2nd:0 3rd:0 Ran:2
2000 Turf 0-2: (5f, 7f) (gd 2)
Currently little account gelding. Turf high 50.
**R F Fisher [0-1] M W Chapman (from M Todhunter [0-1] Apr 2000).*

SEATTLE ART (USA) BHB 43f RR 59f 2329[5]

6 b g Seattle Slew (USA) 7.8f **(64)** - Artiste (Artaius (USA)) 9f **(69)**
Form - 605
Record 2000 - 1st:0 2nd:0 3rd:0 Ran:3
Pre2000 - 1st:0 2nd:2 3rd:1 Ran:7
Win Prizemoney £0 *Total Prizemoney* £2,785
2000 Turf 0-3: (13f, 16f, 17f) (frm 3)
Fair gelding. Turf high 43. Becoming disappointing. **P Monteith [1-16] I Bell (from H R A Cecil [0-5] Aug 1997).*

SEATTLE BAY (USA) RR 95f 1282a[2]

3 b f Opening Verse (USA) 11.8f **(70)** - Seattle Ways (FR) (Seattle Slew (USA)) 9.4f **(76)**
Form - 2
2000 Turf 0-1: (7f) (g-s)
Currently very useful filly. (1st run) - 2nd of 9 to Gold Round (12 May Saint-cloud 7f g-s RF 1282a).
**J E Pease in FR [0-2] G Strawbridge.*

SEATTLE PRINCE (USA) BHB 75f RR 79f 4970[14]

2 gr c Cozzene (USA) 10.1f **(87)** - Chicken Slew (USA) (Seattle Slew (USA)) 9.4f **(76)**
Form - 85360
Record 2000 - 1st:0 2nd:0 3rd:1 Ran:5
Win Prizemoney £0 *Total Prizemoney* £627
2000 Turf 0-5: (6f, 8f 2, 9f, 10f) (g-s, gd 2, g-f, frm)
Above-average colt. Turf high 79 (began Jly).
**R Hannon [0-5] Nicholas Hodges.*

SEA VIXEN RR 2026[1]

2 ch f Machiavellian (USA) 9.8f **(83)** - Hill Hopper (IRE) **(104f)** (Danehill (USA)) 10f **(72)**
Form - 1
Record 2000 - 1st:1 2nd:0 3rd:0 Ran:1
Win Prizemoney £2,785 *Total Prizemoney* £2,785
Wins * **2000** *Jun Southw (STD)* 6f 79 <
2000 AW 1-1: (6f 1-1) (Fibr 1-1)
Currently above-average filly. (1st run) - 1st of 9 from Jamila (16 Jun Southwell RF 2026). **Sir Mark Prescott [1-1] Cheveley Park Stud.*

SEA WAVE (IRE) BHB 112f RR 120f 2689[5]

5 b h Sadler's Wells (USA) 11.3f **(87)** - Three Tails (Blakeney) 10.5f **(64)**
Form - 3015
Record 2000 - 1st:1 2nd:0 3rd:0 Ran:3
Pre2000 - 1st:3 2nd:1 3rd:2 Ran:10
Win Prizemoney £80,242 *Total Prizemoney* £155,002
Wins * **2000** May Newbur (G-F) L 13.3f 111
* 1998 Aug York (G-F) G2 11.9f 119+ <
* 1998 Jun Leices (SFT) 11.8f 109+
* 1998 May Lingfi (GD) 10f 84
2000 Turf 1-3: (10f, 12f, 13f 1-1) (gd 2, g-f 1-1)
Very high-class colt, effective 12f, acts on g-f to frm, best on g-f. Turf high 111. He was limited to just three starts last season, finishing down the field in a valuable race in Singapore on his debut, but came back to winning form in a Newbury Listed event next time. Tied up quickly in the Princess Of Wales's Stakes and was not seen again.
**S bin Suroor [4-11] Godolphin (from S bin Suroor in UAE [0-2] Mar 2000).*

SEA YA MAITE BHB 32f62a RR 31f 62a 5006[13]

6 b g Komaite (USA) 6.9f **(61)** - Marina Plata (Julio Mariner) 7.2f **(57)**
Form - 180053156521650
Record 2000 - 1st:2 2nd:1 3rd:1 Ran:11
Pre2000 - 1st:4 2nd:3 3rd:6 Ran:43
Win Prizemoney £14,636 *Total Prizemoney* £21,725
Wins * **2000** *Feb Wolver (STD) H* 7f 60 66
* **2000** *Jan Southw (STD) H* 8f 52 58+
* 1999 *Nov Southw (STD) H* 7f 52 54
* 1998 *May Southw (STD) H* 8f 63 67 <
* 1997 *Oct Wolver (STD) H* 8.5f 58 65
* 1997 *Jly Southw (STD) H* 6f 52 56
2000 Turf 0-1: (8f) (frm) 2000 AW 2-10: (7f 1-3, 8f 1-6, 9f) (Fibr 2-10)
Average gelding, effective 7 to 8f, best at 7f, - acts on Fibr, has worn blinkers, likes left handed tracks, favours tight tracks. AW high 66 - 1st of 12 giving 4lb to Sacrementum (24 Feb Wolverhampton RF 0351) - also 1st of 12 giving 5lb to Godmersham Park (17 Jan Southwell RF 0106). **S R Bowring [6-54] S R Bowring.*

SEAZUN (IRE) BHB 107f RR 113f 4739[7]

3 b f Zieten (USA) - Sunset Cafe (IRE) (Red Sunset) 8.2f **(63)**
Form - 244847
Record 2000 - 1st:0 2nd:1 3rd:0 Ran:6
Pre2000 - 1st:2 2nd:1 3rd:0 Ran:4
Win Prizemoney £81,326 *Total Prizemoney* £115,670
Wins * 1999 Spt Newmar (G-S) G1 6f 107 <
* 1999 Apr Bright (GD) 5.3f 77+
2000 Turf 0-6: (7f, 8f 5) (g-s, gd 3, g-f, frm)
Scopey, Group-class filly, has broken blood-vessels, effective 6 to 8f, acts on g-s to g-f. Turf high 113. She won the Cheveley Park Stakes in 1999 and finished fourth in the English and Irish 1000 Guineas during May. Unable to improve on those performances later in the campaign, she is game but difficult to place.
**M R Channon [2-10] Katsumi Yoshida.*

SEBULBA (IRE) BHB 67f72a **RR 51f 72a** 5008[3]
2 b br g Dolphin Street (FR) - Twilight Calm (IRE) (Hatim (USA))
Form - 216053
Record 2000 - 1st:1 2nd:1 3rd:1 Ran:6
Win Prizemoney £2,254 *Total Prizemoney* £4,046
Wins * **2000** *Jly Southw (STD) 6f 69* <
2000 Turf 0-2: (7f, 8f) (gd, frm) 2000 AW 1-4: (6f 1-4) (Fibr 1-4)
Above-average gelding, effective 6f, - acts on Fibr. Turf high 51 (began Spt). AW high 69 - 1st of 12 giving 5lb to Spree Love (14 Jly Southwell RF 2817). **J G Given [1-6] A Clarke.*

SECOND AFFAIR (IRE) BHB 77f **RR 85f** 5058[2]
3 b f Pursuit of Love 9.5f **(69)** - Startino (Bustino) 10.4f **(64)**
Form - 32422
Record 2000 - 1st:0 2nd:3 3rd:1 Ran:5
Win Prizemoney £0 *Total Prizemoney* £1,660
2000 Turf 0-5: (8f, 10f 2, 12f 2) (sft, g-s, g-f 3)
Light-framed, useful filly. Turf high 85 - 2nd of 6 to Banco Suivi (5 Aug Doncaster 12f g-f RF 3387). **C F Wall [0-5] B McAllister.*

SECOND GENERATION (IRE) RR 45f 5242[16]
3 ch g Cadeaux Genereux 7.9f **(76)** - Title Roll (IRE) (Tate Gallery (USA)) 7.4f **(67)**
Form - 057000
Record 2000 - 1st:0 2nd:0 3rd:0 Ran:6
2000 Turf 0-6: (5f 3, 6f 2, 7f) (g-s, gd 2, g-f, frm 2)
Scopey, moderate gelding, has worn blinkers. Turf high 45 (began Jly). **D R C Elsworth [0-6] Graham Dalziel.*

SECOND PAIGE (IRE) BHB 74f67a **RR 74+f 67a** 5201[5]
3 b g Nicolotte - My First Paige (IRE) **(41f 48a)** (Runnett) 7f **(59)**
Form - 4722115
Record 2000 - 1st:2 2nd:2 3rd:0 Ran:7
Pre2000 - 1st:0 2nd:0 3rd:0 Ran:3
Win Prizemoney £6,827 *Total Prizemoney* £8,521
Wins * **2000** Jly Windso (GD) H 11.6f 69 74+ <
* **2000** Jun Windso (G-F) H 11.6f 62 71
2000 Turf 2-7: (8f, 10f 2, 12f 2-4) (gd 4, g-f 1-1, frm 1-2)
Workmanlike, above-average gelding, effective 12f, acts on g-f to frm, favours tight tracks. Turf high 74 - 1st of 10 giving 4lb to Skye Blue (17 Jly Windsor RF 2876) - also 1st of 10 getting 13lb from Fanfare (26 Jun Windsor RF 2286).
**N A Graham [2-10] Coronation Partnership.*

SECONDS AWAY BHB 20f22a **RR 35f 22a** 4184[6]
9 b g Hard Fought 8.9f **(51)** - Keep Mum (Mummy's Pet) 7.7f **(60)**
Form - 684243334333606
Record 2000 - 1st:0 2nd:1 3rd:6 Ran:15
Pre2000 - 1st:2 2nd:7 3rd:10 Ran:65
Win Prizemoney £4,964 *Total Prizemoney* £18,746
Wins * 1998 Jun Ayr (GD) SH 8f 31 36 <
* 1997 Jly Mussel (G-F) H 8f 30 35
2000 Turf 0-15: (8f, 9f 5, 11f 4, 12f, 14f 2, 16f 2) (g-s, g-f 7, frm 6, hrd)
Very moderate gelding, effective 8 to 11f, acts on g-f to frm, best on g-f, has worn blinkers, and does well at Ayr. Turf high 40. Consistent. Has a very poor wins to runs ratio.
**J S Goldie [2-86] J S Goldie (from A Harrison [0-9] Apr 1995).*

SECOND STRIKE RR 74f 4541[3]
2 b c Kris 10f **(75)** - Honeyspike (IRE) **(64f)** (Chief's Crown (USA)) 9.8f **(72)**
Form - 53
Record 2000 - 1st:0 2nd:0 3rd:1 Ran:2
Win Prizemoney £0 *Total Prizemoney* £1,182
2000 Turf 0-2: (6f, 7f) (gd, g-f)
Currently above-average colt. Turf high 74 (1st run) (began Spt) - 5th of 15 giving 11lb to Tickle (3 Spt York 6f g-f RF 4198).
**B Smart [0-2] The Family Partnership.*

SECOND VENTURE (IRE) RR 85?f 5102[4]
2 b c Petardia 8.2f **(58)** - Hilton Gateway (Hello Gorgeous (USA)) 9.7f **(63)**
Form - 732444
Record 2000 - 1st:0 2nd:1 3rd:1 Ran:6
Win Prizemoney £0 *Total Prizemoney* £4,102
2000 Turf 0-6: (5f, 6f 3, 7f 2) (sft, gd 4, frm)
Useful colt, effective 6f, acts on gd. Turf high 85 (began Jly) - 4th of 22 giving 5lb to Zietunzeen (20 Oct Doncaster 6f gd RF 5102).
**J R Weymes [0-6] C I North Racing Club.*

SECOND WIND BHB 82f **RR 86f** 3590[4]
5 ch g Kris 10f **(75)** - Rimosa's Pet (Petingo) 11f **(72)**
Form - 1500124054
Record 2000 - 1st:2 2nd:1 3rd:0 Ran:10
Pre2000 - 1st:3 2nd:1 3rd:1 Ran:23
Win Prizemoney £23,730 *Total Prizemoney* £34,734
Wins * **2000** Jun Newmar (G-F) H 7f 75 84 <
* **2000** Apr Leices (G-S) H 7f 70 79
* 1999 Jly Epsom (G-F) H 7f 61 70
1999 Jly Bright (FRM) C 7f 66
1997 Apr Newmar (G-F) 5f 79
2000 Turf 2-10: (6f, 7f 2-6, 8f 2, 10f) (sft, g-s, gd 1-4, g-f 2, frm 1-2)
Useful gelding, effective 7 to 10f, best at 7f, acts on sft to frm, does well at Newmarket. Turf high 85 - 4th of 19 getting 3lb from Tayseer (13 Jly Newmarket 7f gd RF 2774) - also 1st of 18 getting 19lb from Juno Marlowe (23 Jun Newmarket RF 2227). He is suited by a sharp downhill track. **C A Dwyer [3-18] John Purcell (from Miss Gay Kelleway [1-6] Jly 1999).*

SECRET AGENT BHB 98f **RR 103+f** 2606[15]
3 b c Machiavellian (USA) 9.8f **(83)** - Secret Obsession (USA) (Secretariat (USA)) 9f **(79)**
Form - 14230
Record 2000 - 1st:1 2nd:1 3rd:1 Ran:5
Pre2000 - 1st:1 2nd:1 3rd:0 Ran:2
Win Prizemoney £10,528 *Total Prizemoney* £23,675
Wins * **2000** Apr Windso (GD) 8.3f 95 <
* 1999 Spt Warwic (SFT) 7.7f 86+
2000 Turf 1-5: (8f 1-1, 9f, 10f 3) (g-s, gd 2, g-f, frm 1-1)
Light-framed, very useful colt, effective 8 to 10f, best at 10f, acts on g-s to frm. Turf high 103 - 3rd of 20 giving 15lb to Moon Solitaire (23 May Goodwood 9f g-s RF 1394) - also 1st of 7 getting 12lb from Welsh Wind (10 Apr Windsor RF 0654). He is consistent, and ran a cracker when third in a hot handicap at Goodwood. There should be more to come.
**Sir Michael Stoute [2-7] Sheikh Maktoum bin Mohammed Al Maktoum.*

SECRETARIO BHB 24f28a **RR 26f 28a** 4209[10]
3 b f Efisio 7.7f **(69)** - Lucidity **(59f 43a)** (Vision (USA)) 9f **(64)**
Form - 6600008050
Record 2000 - 1st:0 2nd:0 3rd:0 Ran:10
Pre2000 - 1st:0 2nd:0 3rd:0 Ran:2
2000 Turf 0-9: (7f, 8f 2, 9f 2, 10f 3, 16f) (g-s, gd 2, g-f 2, frm 4) 2000 AW 0-1: (8f) (Fibr)
Unfurnished, little account filly, has worn blinkers. Turf high 45.
**J Hetherton [0-7] C D Barber-Lomax (from C W Thornton [0-5] Jun 2000).*

SECRET CONQUEST BHB 57f **RR 64f** 4767[18]
3 b f Secret Appeal - Mohibbah (USA) (Conquistador Cielo (USA)) 8.8f **(69)**
Form - 006450000
Record 2000 - 1st:0 2nd:0 3rd:0 Ran:9
Pre2000 - 1st:3 2nd:2 3rd:1 Ran:10
Win Prizemoney £11,186 *Total Prizemoney* £14,651
Wins * 1999 Aug Catter (G-F) H 6f 72 79 <
* 1999 Jly Catter (GD) H 7f 69
* 1999 Jly Haydoc (G-S) S 6f 65
2000 Turf 0-9: (6f 3, 7f 5, 8f) (g-s, gd 2, g-f 3, frm 3)
Average filly, effective 6f, acts on frm, likes left handed tracks. Turf high 66. Becoming disappointing. **D W Barker [3-19] P Asquith.*

SECRET DESTINY (USA) BHB 90f **RR 92f** 4041[3]
3 b f Cozzene (USA) 10.1f **(87)** - Dramatrix (USA) (Forty Niner (USA))
Form - 51563
Record 2000 - 1st:1 2nd:0 3rd:1 Ran:5
Pre2000 - 1st:0 2nd:0 3rd:2 Ran:3
Win Prizemoney £3,835 *Total Prizemoney* £8,407
Wins * **2000** Jun Salisb (G-F) 8f 84 <
2000 Turf 1-5: (7f, 8f 1-1, 10f 3) (g-s, gd, frm 1-3)
Workmanlike, useful filly, effective 7 to 10f, best at 10f, acts on gd to frm, best on frm. Turf high 92 - also 1st of 12 from Seeking Success (18 Jun Salisbury RF 2083). Improving. Usually held-up, she won her maiden comfortably but struggled in Listed company.
**J H M Gosden [1-5] R E Sangster and B V Sangster (from A G Foster*

[0-2] Oct 1999).

SECRET DROP BHB 50f53a **RR 58df 53a** 5161[6]
4 b f Bustino 11f **(64)** - Safe House (Lyphard (USA)) 9.9f **(72)**
Form - 87P704336
Record 2000 - 1st:0 2nd:0 3rd:2 Ran:9
Pre2000 - 1st:0 2nd:0 3rd:1 Ran:5
Win Prizemoney £0 *Total Prizemoney* £1,482
2000 Turf 0-9: (12f 4, 14f, 16f 3, 18f) (sft, g-s, gd 4, g-f 2, frm)
Fair filly, effective 10f, acted on g-s, had worn blinkers, liked tight tracks. Turf high 58. (DEAD) **K McAuliffe [0-14] G E Amey.*

SECRETE CONTRACT RR 60f 4540[6]
2 b c Contract Law (USA) 8.9f **(54)** - Secret Account (Blakeney) 10.5f **(64)**
Form - 6
Record 2000 - 1st:0 2nd:0 3rd:0 Ran:1
2000 Turf 0-1: (8f) (gd)
Currently average colt.
**G L Moore [0-1] The Secrete Society Partnership.*

SECRET INDEX (IRE) BHB 92f **RR 92f** 5107[13]
2 b f Nicolotte - Deerussa (IRE) (Jareer (USA)) 5.9f **(75)**
Form - 115446800
Record 2000 - 1st:2 2nd:0 3rd:0 Ran:9
Win Prizemoney £9,022 *Total Prizemoney* £10,514
Wins * **2000** May Salisb (G-F) 5f 83+ <
* **2000** Apr Windso (HVY) 5f 76
2000 Turf 2-9: (5f 2-6, 6f 3) (g-s 1-1, gd 5, g-f 1-3)
Useful filly, effective 5f, acts on g-f. Turf high 92 - 4th of 10 giving 3lb to Strange Destiny (19 Aug Newbury 5f g-f RF 3788) - also 1st of 8 giving 3lb to Celtic Island (7 May Salisbury RF 1085). Probably unlucky not to make the frame in the Queen Mary at Royal Ascot, she lost her way in the second half of the season and will be difficult to place off her current mark.
**Mrs P N Dutfield [2-9] The Index Racing Partnership.*

SECRET PASSION BHB 57f **RR 60f** 4784[4]
2 gr f Petong 7.6f **(58)** - Jamarj (Tyrnavos) 10.1f **(55)**
Form - 664
Record 2000 - 1st:0 2nd:0 3rd:0 Ran:3
2000 Turf 0-2: (7f, 8f) (gd, g-f) 2000 AW 0-1: (8f) (Fibr)
Currently average filly. Turf high 60 (began Spt).
**K Mahdi [0-3] Miss Debbie Mountain.*

SECRET RENDEZVOUS (IRE) BHB 51f45a **RR 63f 45a** 1377[13]
3 br f Petong 7.6f **(58)** - Heaven-Liegh-Grey (Grey Desire) 8.7f **(50)**
Form - 000
Record 2000 - 1st:0 2nd:0 3rd:0 Ran:3
Pre2000 - 1st:0 2nd:0 3rd:0 Ran:4
2000 Turf 0-1: (6f) (g-s) 2000 AW 0-2: (6f 2) (Fibr 2)
Scopey, average filly. AW high 9.
**D Nicholls [0-3] Peter Dodd (from A T Murphy [0-4] Spt 1999).*

SECRET SENTIMENT RR 36f 5318[12]
2 b f Mark of Esteem (IRE) - Sahara Baladee (USA) (Shadeed (USA)) 8.2f **(70)**
Form - 0
Record 2000 - 1st:0 2nd:0 3rd:0 Ran:1
2000 Turf 0-1: (6f) (sft)
Currently very moderate filly.
**E A L Dunlop [0-1] Maktoum Al Maktoum.*

SECRET'S OUT BHB 72f **RR 71f** 2060[16]
4 b g Polish Precedent (USA) 9f **(73)** - Secret Obsession (USA) (Secretariat (USA)) 9f **(79)**
Form - 500
Record 2000 - 1st:0 2nd:0 3rd:0 Ran:3
Pre2000 - 1st:1 2nd:4 3rd:0 Ran:7
Win Prizemoney £3,831 *Total Prizemoney* £9,013
Wins 1999 Apr Windso (G-F) 10f 87 <
2000 Turf 0-3: (7f, 9f, 10f) (g-s, gd, g-f)
Scopey, above-average gelding, effective 10f, acts on frm, has worn blinkers. Turf high 71.
**J J Quinn [0-7] Brockhall Village Ltd (from Sir Michael Stoute [1-7] May 1999).*

SECRET SPRING (FR) BHB 75f85a **RR 82df 85a** 4484[13]
8 b g Dowsing (USA) 7f **(61)** - Nordica (Northfields (USA)) 9f **(72)**
Form - 172114775500
Record 2000 - 1st:0 2nd:0 3rd:0 Ran:7
Pre2000 - 1st:7 2nd:8 3rd:4 Ran:37
Win Prizemoney £28,292 *Total Prizemoney* £52,629
Wins * 1999 *Dec Lingfi (STD)* *8f* *76*
* 1999 *Dec Lingfi (STD) H* *8f 84 87* <
* 1999 *Nov Lingfi (STD) H* *8f 80 84*
1998 Jly Kempto (G-F) H 10f 82 87 <
1997 Oct Bright (G-F) 8f 81
1996 *Feb Lingfi (STD) H* *8f 82 83*
1996 *Feb Lingfi (STD)* *8f* *81*
2000 Turf 0-2: (8f, 10f) (g-s, g-f) 2000 AW 0-5: (7f 2, 8f, 10f 2) (Equi 5)
Useful gelding, effective 7 to 10f, acts on g-f to frm - acts on Equi, prefers left handed tracks, prefers tight tracks, excels at Lingfield. Turf high 62 (began Spt). AW high 87. Only bits and pieces of form on turf in recent seasons and has had rather more success on Equitrack. Suited by a mile, but stays further.
**Mrs L Richards [3-19] M K George (from P R Hedger [6-28] Oct 1998).*

SECRET STYLE BHB 73f **RR 74f** 5322[3]
5 b g Shirley Heights 12.1f **(76)** - Rosie Potts (Shareef Dancer (USA)) 9.9f **(73)**
Form - 3
Record 2000 - 1st:0 2nd:0 3rd:1 Ran:1
Pre2000 - 1st:2 2nd:0 3rd:0 Ran:9
Win Prizemoney £3,327 *Total Prizemoney* £5,779
Wins 1999 Jly Les La (G-F) H 15f 73 <
1999 Jun Nottin (GD) C 16f 70+
2000 Turf 0-1: (17f) (sft)
Above-average gelding, has broken blood-vessels, effective 15f, acts on g-f, has worn blinkers, prefers left handed tracks. Consistent. Won a Nottingham claimer in '99 before being sold to race in Jersey. Now with R. Hollinshead.
**R Hollinshead [0-4] Mrs B Ramsden (from Mrs A Malzard in JER [1-1] Jly 1999).*

SECURITY COUNCIL RR 62f 5310[5]
2 b c Polish Precedent (USA) 9f **(73)** - Set Fair (USA) **(89f)** (Alleged (USA)) 10f **(76)**
Form - 5
Record 2000 - 1st:0 2nd:0 3rd:0 Ran:1
2000 Turf 0-1: (7f) (g-s)
Currently average colt. **B W Hills [0-1] K Abdulla.*

SECURON DANCER BHB 59f **RR 62f** 5106[9]
2 b f Emperor Jones (USA) - Gena Ivor (USA) (Sir Ivor) 10.2f **(70)**
Form - 48600
Record 2000 - 1st:0 2nd:0 3rd:0 Ran:5
Win Prizemoney £0 *Total Prizemoney* £478
2000 Turf 0-5: (5f 2, 6f 2, 7f) (gd 2, g-f 2, frm)
Average filly. Turf high 62. **R Rowe [0-5] Mrs R A Proctor.*

SEDONA (IRE) BHB 54f50a **RR 56f 50a** 3430[R]
3 b g Namaqualand (USA) - Talahari (IRE) (Roi Danzig (USA))
Form - 5U30170RR
Record 2000 - 1st:1 2nd:0 3rd:1 Ran:9
Pre2000 - 1st:0 2nd:0 3rd:0 Ran:2
Win Prizemoney £1,976 *Total Prizemoney* £2,290
Wins * **2000** May Nottin (G-S) SH 8.2f 47 56 <
2000 Turf 1-6: (8f 1-2, 9f 2, 10f, 12f) (sft, gd 1-1, g-f, frm 3) 2000 AW 0-3: (6f, 7f, 8f) (Fibr 3)
Leggy, fair gelding, effective 8f, acts on gd, has worn blinkers, likes left handed tracks, likes tight tracks. Turf high 56 - 1st of 18 getting 5lb from Perfect Moment (19 May Nottingham RF 1310). AW high 46. Inconsistent.
**Andrew Turnell [1-11] Mrs Claire Hollowood.*

SEDUCTION RR 1611[7]
3 b f Pursuit of Love 9.5f **(69)** - Champagne 'n Roses (Chief Singer) 8.9f **(66)**
Form - 67
Record 2000 - 1st:0 2nd:0 3rd:0 Ran:2
2000 Turf 0-1: (16f) (g-f) 2000 AW 0-1: (12f) (Equi)
Workmanlike, currently poor filly. **C A Cyzer [0-2] R M Cyzer.*

SEDUCTIVE BHB 76f79a **RR 74f 79a** 4623[6]
2 b c Pursuit of Love 9.5f **(69)** - Full Orchestra (Shirley Heights) 10.3f **(74)**
Form - 823516
Record 2000 - 1st:1 2nd:1 3rd:1 Ran:6
Win Prizemoney £3,562 *Total Prizemoney* £5,385
Wins * 2000 *Spt Wolver (STD) 8.5f 77 <*
2000 Turf 0-5: (5f, 6f, 7f 2, 8f) (gd 3, frm 2) 2000 AW 1-1: (8f 1-1) (Fibr 1-1)
Above-average colt, effective 6 to 8f, acts on gd to frm - acts on Fibr. Turf high 74 (began Jly) - 3rd of 7 to Snowstorm (24 Jly Ayr 7f frm RF 3060). (1st run) - 1st of 10 from Carnival Lad (16 Spt Wolverhampton RF 4475).
**Sir Mark Prescott [1-6] Charles Walker & Jonathon Carroll.*

SEEK BHB 93f **RR 92f** 4611[11]
4 br c Rainbow Quest (USA) 11.2f **(81)** - Souk (IRE) (Ahonoora) 8.1f **(73)**
Form - 2510
Record 2000 - 1st:1 2nd:1 3rd:0 Ran:4
Pre2000 - 1st:1 2nd:1 3rd:0 Ran:2
Win Prizemoney £23,544 *Total Prizemoney* £27,584
Wins * 2000 Aug York (GD) H 11.9f 86 92 <
* 1999 Jly Pontef (G-S) 12f 75
2000 Turf 1-4: (10f, 12f 1-2, 14f) (g-s 2, gd 1-2)
Workmanlike, useful colt, effective 10 to 14f, acts on g-s to gd, best on gd. Turf high 92 - 1st of 18 giving 25lb to Morgans Orchard (22 Aug York RF 3854). He landed a punt at York's Ebor Meeting, but ran as if something was amiss on his next two starts. Sold for 50,000gns at Newmarket in October, he is now with Jim Old and could develop into a smart hurdler. **L M Cumani [2-6] Fittocks Stud.*

SEEKER BHB 73f **RR 69f** 4273[3]
3 ch f Rainbow Quest (USA) 11.2f **(81)** - Sarmatia (USA) (Danzig (USA)) 8.4f **(76)**
Form - 323
Record 2000 - 1st:0 2nd:1 3rd:2 Ran:3
Win Prizemoney £0 *Total Prizemoney* £2,668
2000 Turf 0-3: (11f, 12f 2) (gd, frm 2)
Workmanlike, currently average filly. Turf high 69 (began Jly).
**H R A Cecil [0-3] Exors of the late Lord Howard de Walden.*

SEEKING SANCTUARY BHB 43f38a **RR 42f 38a** 3565[5]
3 ch f Most Welcome 8.6f **(66)** - Tjakka (USA) (Little Missouri (USA))
Form - 7045
Record 2000 - 1st:0 2nd:0 3rd:0 Ran:4
Pre2000 - 1st:0 2nd:0 3rd:0 Ran:1
Win Prizemoney £0 *Total Prizemoney* £278
2000 Turf 0-4: (6f, 7f, 10f, 12f) (gd, g-f 2, hrd)
Scopey, moderate filly. Turf high 42.
**Dr J D Scargill [0-5] Mrs V Bayley.*

SEEKING SUCCESS (USA) BHB 79f **RR 82f** 4369[4]
3 b f Seeking the Gold (USA) 7.4f **(80)** - Testy Trestle (USA) (Private Account (USA)) 8.5f **(74)**
Form - 07226134
Record 2000 - 1st:1 2nd:2 3rd:1 Ran:8
Win Prizemoney £3,412 *Total Prizemoney* £8,372
Wins * 2000 Aug Pontef (G-F) 8f 75+ <
2000 Turf 1-8: (7f, 8f 1-7) (gd 3, g-f, frm 1-3, hrd)
Scopey, decent filly, effective 8f, acts on gd to frm, best on frm. Turf high 82 - 2nd of 12 to Secret Destiny (18 Jun Salisbury 8f frm RF 2083) - also 1st of 4 from Couture (9 Aug Pontefract RF 3500). After some promising efforts, she made all to win a Pontefract maiden in August, but has just looked held in handicap company since. **Sir Michael Stoute [1-8] R Barnett.*

SEEKING UTOPIA BHB 52f53a **RR 72f 53a** 5150[6]
3 b f Wolfhound (USA) 7.3f **(71)** - Sakura Queen (IRE) (Woodman (USA)) 9f **(74)**
Form - 5840P03306
Record 2000 - 1st:0 2nd:0 3rd:2 Ran:10
Pre2000 - 1st:1 2nd:3 3rd:1 Ran:7
Win Prizemoney £2,612 *Total Prizemoney* £8,704
Wins * 1999 Aug Mussel (G-S) 7.1f 73 <
2000 Turf 0-8: (8f, 9f, 10f 4, 12f 2) (gd, g-f, frm 5, hrd) 2000 AW 0-2: (8f, 10f) (Equi 2)
Workmanlike, above-average filly, effective 7 to 12f, best at 7f, acts on g-f to frm, best on frm. Turf high 75. AW high 43 (began Aug). Well held in 2000. **S P C Woods [1-17] Mrs J Roberts.*

SEEK THE LIGHT (USA) BHB 69f58a **RR 71f 58a** 4617[7]
3 b c Seeking the Gold (USA) 7.4f **(80)** - Jolypha (USA) (Lyphard (USA)) 9.9f **(72)**
Form - 647
Record 2000 - 1st:0 2nd:0 3rd:0 Ran:3
Win Prizemoney £0 *Total Prizemoney* £334
2000 Turf 0-3: (10f 2, 12f) (gd 2, g-f)
Scopey, currently above-average colt. Turf high 71.
**H R A Cecil [0-3] K Abdulla.*

SEE YOU LATER BHB 96f **RR 97f** 5324[6]
3 b f Emarati (USA) 6.6f **(63)** - Rivers Rhapsody (Dominion) 8.5f **(63)**
Form - 633001206
Record 2000 - 1st:1 2nd:1 3rd:2 Ran:9
Pre2000 - 1st:1 2nd:0 3rd:2 Ran:3
Win Prizemoney £12,168 *Total Prizemoney* £23,725
Wins * 2000 Aug Sandow (GD) H 5f 93 96 <
* 1999 Jun Sandow (GD) 5f 77+
2000 Turf 1-9: (5f 1-7, 6f 2) (sft, g-s 2, gd 1-3, g-f 2, frm)
Scopey, very useful filly, effective 5 to 6f, best at 5f, acts on g-s to frm. Turf high 97 - 2nd of 8 getting 6lb from Lord Kintyre (7 Spt Doncaster 5f frm RF 4278) - also 1st of 11 giving 5lb to Lago Di Varano (19 Aug Sandown RF 3805). She goes well at Sandown and gained a deserved win there in August. Second in a Listed race on her next start, she has plenty of early speed and probably handles any ground. **Major D N Chappell [2-12] Rex Mead.*

SEGAVIEW (IRE) BHB 58f **RR 60f** 4456[R]
4 b g Scenic 10.6f **(66)** - Little Sega (FR) (Bellypha) 9.8f **(73)**
Form - 4454R
Record 2000 - 1st:0 2nd:0 3rd:0 Ran:5
Pre2000 - 1st:1 2nd:1 3rd:0 Ran:11
Win Prizemoney £5,432 *Total Prizemoney* £8,272
Wins * 1999 Jun York (G-S) 11.9f 63 <
2000 Turf 0-5: (12f, 14f 2, 15f, 16f) (hvy, g-s, gd 2, g-f)
Leggy, average gelding, effective 12f, acts on g-s to gd. Turf high 60. **Mrs P Sly [1-16] Thorney Racing Club.*

SEL BHB 58f53a **RR 69f 53a** 6218[6]
2 b f Salse (USA) 10.9f **(71)** - Frog **(82f 74a)** (Akarad (FR)) 9f **(76)**
Form - 351251056
Record 2000 - 1st:2 2nd:1 3rd:1 Ran:9
Win Prizemoney £4,039 *Total Prizemoney* £4,938
Wins * 2000 Aug Bright (FRM) S 7f 69 <
2000 Jly Bright (G-S) S 7f 44
2000 Turf 2-9: (7f 2-7, 8f 2) (sft, g-s 2, gd 1-1, g-f 2, frm 1-3)
Average filly, effective 7f, acts on frm, mostly wears blinkers (extremely effectively), prefers tight tracks. Turf high 69 - 2nd of 7 giving 4lb to Violent (18 Jly Brighton 7f frm RF 2887) - also 1st of 5 giving 5lb to Golden Beach (30 Aug Brighton RF 4097).
**G L Moore [1-6] C F Sparrowhawk (from Sir Mark Prescott [1-3] Jly 2000).*

SELHURSTPARK FLYER (IRE) BHB 66f **RR 64f** 2549[6]
9 b g Northiam (USA) 6f **(69)** - Wisdom to Know (Bay Express) 7.1f **(60)**
Form - 006
Record 2000 - 1st:0 2nd:0 3rd:0 Ran:3
Pre2000 - 1st:10 2nd:5 3rd:6 Ran:61
Win Prizemoney £173,835 *Total Prizemoney* £203,805
Wins 1998 Jun Ascot (G-S) H 6f 92 105 <
1998 Jun Epsom (GD) H 6f 92 105 <
1997 Jun Ascot (G-S) H 6f 94 105 <
1996 Spt Epsom (G-F) 6f 94+
1996 Jun Epsom (GD) H 6f 79 86
1996 May Carlis (G-F) H 5.9f 70 75
2000 Turf 0-3: (6f 3) (sft, gd 2)
Average gelding, has worn blinkers. Turf high 64. He has been retired after a distinguished career. **A Berry [0-3] Chris & Antonia Deuters (from J Berry [10-61] Spt 1999).*

SELIANA BHB 77f **RR 81f** 4399[3]
4 b m Unfuwain (USA) 11.4f **(74)** - Anafi (Slip Anchor) 9.8f **(73)**
Form - 2347223

Record 2000 - 1st:0 2nd:3 3rd:2 Ran:7
Pre2000 - 1st:0 2nd:0 3rd:1 Ran:2
Win Prizemoney £0 *Total Prizemoney* £18,028
2000 Turf 0-7: (12f 2, 14f, 16f, 18f, 20f 2) (g-s 2, gd 4, g-f)
Lengthy, decent filly, effective 12 to 20f, best at 20f, acts on g-s to g-f, best on gd. Turf high 81 - 2nd of 8 giving 15lb to Laffah (2 Aug Goodwood 20f gd RF 3315). Still a maiden, she ran a cracker when runner-up in the competitive Ascot Stakes and clearly stays extra well. **G Wragg [0-9] L Marinopoulos.*

SELKING (IRE) BHB 103f95a **RR 105df 95a** 3578[8]
3 ch c Selkirk (USA) 7.9f **(76)** - Stay That Way (Be My Guest (USA)) 9.3f **(67)**
Form - 324728
Record 2000 - 1st:0 2nd:2 3rd:1 Ran:6
Pre2000 - 1st:1 2nd:1 3rd:2 Ran:7
Win Prizemoney £2,857 *Total Prizemoney* £20,517
Wins * 1999 Jun Carlis (G-F) 5f 78+ <
2000 Turf 0-6: (6f 2, 7f 4) (g-s, gd 4, g-f)
Scopey, Pattern-class colt, effective 7f, acts on gd. Turf high 105 - 2nd of 5 getting 7lb from Arctic Char (6 May Haydock 7f gd RF 1052). He ran some good races last season and is capable of winning a listed race at around seven furlongs.
**K R Burke [1-13] Nigel Shields.*

SELLINGER'S ROUND (IRE) BHB 34f **RR 61f** 5113[8]
4 ch g Lucky Guest - Cellophane (Coquelin (USA)) 8.4f **(58)**
Form - 003633808
Record 2000 - 1st:0 2nd:0 3rd:3 Ran:9
Pre2000 - 1st:0 2nd:0 3rd:0 Ran:3
Win Prizemoney £0 *Total Prizemoney* £1,085
2000 Turf 0-8: (7f 4, 8f 3, 9f) (g-s, gd, g-f 2, frm 3) 2000 AW 0-1: (8f) (Fibr)
Average gelding. Turf high 61.
**Mrs L C Jewell [0-2] I C Wallond (from Miss S Collins in IRE [0-10] Aug 2000).*

SELTITUDE (IRE) **RR 104f** 4845a[6]
4 b f Fairy King (USA) 7.7f **(75)** - Dunoof (Shirley Heights) 10.3f **(74)**
Form - 3306
2000 Turf 0-4: (5f 4) (gd 4)
Very useful filly, effective 5 to 6f, best at 5f, acts on sft to gd, best on gd. Turf high 104 (1st run) - 3rd of 11 giving 1lb to Sampower Star (14 May Longchamp 5f gd RF 1292a). A French-trained sprinter, she has shown some decent form in soft-ground Group events, but needs to be held up until the last possible moment.
**J E Hammond in FR [1-6] N P Bloodstock.*

SELTON HILL (IRE) BHB 63f **RR 66f** 850[2]
3 b g Bin Ajwaad (IRE) - Ivory Gull (USA) (Storm Bird (CAN)) 10.3f **(74)**
Form - 32
Record 2000 - 1st:0 2nd:1 3rd:1 Ran:2
Pre2000 - 1st:0 2nd:0 3rd:0 Ran:5
Win Prizemoney £0 *Total Prizemoney* £1,667
2000 Turf 0-2: (10f 2) (sft, gd)
Workmanlike, average gelding, effective 8 to 10f, best at 10f, acts on sft to g-f. Turf high 66 - 2nd of 13 giving 10lb to Ratified (24 Apr Nottingham 10f sft RF 0850). **N A Callaghan [0-7] Gallagher Equine Ltd.*

SELVORINE BHB 59f **RR 62f** 5069[11]
3 ch f Selkirk (USA) 7.9f **(76)** - Ivorine (USA) (Blushing Groom (FR)) 10.3f **(76)**
Form - 5060
Record 2000 - 1st:0 2nd:0 3rd:0 Ran:4
2000 Turf 0-4: (9f, 10f, 12f 2) (g-s 2, g-f, frm)
Workmanlike, average filly. Turf high 62 (began Aug).
**R Charlton [0-4] K Abdulla.*

SENATOR'S ALIBI **RR 34f** 5310[14]
2 b c Caerleon (USA) 10.9f **(79)** - Salul (Soviet Star (USA))
Form - 0
Record 2000 - 1st:0 2nd:0 3rd:0 Ran:1
2000 Turf 0-1: (7f) (g-s)
Currently average colt.
**Sir Mark Prescott [0-1] Barouche Stud Ltd.*

SENDAWAR (IRE) **RR 132f** 3735a[2]
4 b c Priolo (USA) 10.9f **(71)** - Sendana (FR) (Darshaan) 9.9f **(84)**
Form - 142
2000 Turf 1-3: (8f, 9f 1-1, 10f) (g-s 1-1, gd, g-f)
High-calibre colt, effective 8 to 9f, best at 8f, acts on g-s to g-f. Turf high 123 (1st run) - 1st of 5 from Indian Danehill (21 May Longchamp RF 1453a). A top-class French colt, he showed he had retained his ability with an easy victory over just short of ten furlongs in the Prix d'Ispahan, but an attempt to take on Dubai Millennium at Royal Ascot seemed to burst him, and he did not look quite the same horse when finishing second in the Jacques le Marois. He was retired to stud in France at 70,000 FF.
**A deRoyerDupre in FR [5-8] H H Aga Khan.*

Sendawar has since been retired to stud

SEND IT TO PENNY (IRE) BHB 54f53a **RR 54f 53a** 3312[13]
3 b f Marju (IRE) 9.2f **(76)** - Sparkish (IRE) (Persian Bold) 9.3f **(66)**
Form - 0020150010
Record 2000 - 1st:2 2nd:1 3rd:0 Ran:10
Pre2000 - 1st:0 2nd:0 3rd:0 Ran:4
Win Prizemoney £4,907 *Total Prizemoney* £5,559
Wins * **2000** Jly Thirsk (FRM) SH 8f 49 51
* **2000** *Jun Southw (STD) H 8f 44 53* <
2000 Turf 1-8: (7f 2, 8f 1-5, 10f) (sft, gd 2, g-f 4, hrd 1-1) 2000 AW 1-2: (7f, 8f 1-1) (Fibr 1-2)
Scopey, fair filly, effective 7 to 8f, best at 8f, acts on g-f to hrd - acts on Fibr, best on g-f, often wears blinkers (very effectively), prefers tight tracks. Turf high 54 - 2nd of 17 giving 2lb to Pix Me Up (31 May Ripon 8f g-f RF 1594) - also 1st of 16 from Granite City (28 Jly Thirsk RF 3193). AW high 53 (1st run) - 1st of 13 getting 1lb from Red Sonny (9 Jun Southwell RF 1857). Inconsistent.
**M W Easterby [2-14] Guy Reed.*

SEND ME AN ANGEL (IRE) BHB 67f **RR 70f** 4741[15]
3 ch f Lycius (USA) 8.8f **(71)** - Niamh Cinn Oir (IRE) (King of Clubs) 7.1f **(57)**
Form - 442263150
Record 2000 - 1st:1 2nd:2 3rd:1 Ran:9
Pre2000 - 1st:0 2nd:0 3rd:0 Ran:1
Win Prizemoney £3,542 *Total Prizemoney* £6,236
Wins * **2000** Aug Yarmou (G-F) H 14.1f 62 68 <
2000 Turf 1-9: (12f 3, 14f 1-4, 16f 2) (gd 1-3, g-f 3, frm 2, hrd)
Leggy, above-average filly, effective 14 to 16f, best at 14f, acts on gd to frm, prefers tight tracks. Turf high 70 - 5th of 13 getting 10lb from Hambleden (13 Spt Sandown 14f frm RF 4373) - also 1st of 11 getting 10lb from Elms Schoolgirl (27 Aug Yarmouth RF 4022). Won at Yarmouth, but held from a better mark.
**S P C Woods [1-10] Kaniz Bloodstock Investments Ltd.*

SENIOR MINISTER BHB 100f **RR 95f** 3916[2]
2 b c Lion Cavern (USA) 7.5f **(74)** - Crime Ofthecentury (Pharly (FR)) 9.8f **(68)**

Form - 212
Record 2000 - 1st:1 2nd:2 3rd:0 Ran:3
Win Prizemoney £3,750 *Total Prizemoney* £10,455
Wins * **2000** Aug Lingfi (G-F) 5f 87 <
2000 Turf 1-3: (5f 1-3) (frm 1-3)
Currently very useful colt. Turf high 95 (began Jly) - 2nd of 7 to Bouncing Bowdler (23 Aug York 5f frm RF 3916) - also 1st of 10 from Leozian (11 Aug Lingfield RF 3552). He improved with every start and lost nothing in defeat behind the subsequent Mill Reef Stakes winner, Bouncing Bowdler, at York in August. A scopey individual, he should improve during the close season and is a useful sprinter in the making. **J M P Eustace [1-3] R Carstairs.*

SENOR MIRO BHB 70f **RR 72f** 4443[9]

2 b c Be My Guest (USA) 10.2f **(66)** - Classic Moonlight (IRE) (Machiavellian (USA))
Form - 0540
Record 2000 - 1st:0 2nd:0 3rd:0 Ran:4
Win Prizemoney £0 *Total Prizemoney* £330
2000 Turf 0-4: (6f 3, 7f) (gd 3, g-f)
Above-average colt. Turf high 72 (began Jly).
**R F JohnsonHoughton [0-4] C W Sumner.*

SENSE OF FREEDOM (IRE) BHB 87f **RR 86+f** 4625[5]

3 ch f Grand Lodge (USA) - Greatest Pleasure (Be My Guest (USA)) 9.3f **(67)**
Form - 222315
Record 2000 - 1st:1 2nd:3 3rd:1 Ran:6
Win Prizemoney £6,922 *Total Prizemoney* £10,673
Wins * **2000** Aug Pontef (G-F) H 12f 80 86+ <
2000 Turf 1-6: (10f, 12f 1-4, 16f) (gd, g-f 2, frm 1-3)
Scopey, useful filly, effective 12f, acts on frm. Turf high 86 - 1st of 7 getting 10lb from Archie Babe (9 Aug Pontefract RF 3503).
**M Johnston [1-6] Salem Suhail.*

SENSIMELIA (IRE) BHB 60f **RR 65f** 3775[10]

2 b f Inzar (USA) - In the Papers (Aragon) 8.1f **(60)**
Form - 53650
Record 2000 - 1st:0 2nd:0 3rd:1 Ran:5
Win Prizemoney £0 *Total Prizemoney* £542
2000 Turf 0-5: (5f 4, 6f) (g-s, gd 2, frm 2)
Average filly. Turf high 65.
**Martyn Wane [0-5] Mrs David Hodgkinson.*

SEOMRA HOCHT (IRE) BHB 65f60a **RR 66?f 60a** 5058[6]

3 b g Standiford (USA) - Woodbury Princess (Never so Bold) 6.3f **(66)**
Form - 846
Record 2000 - 1st:0 2nd:0 3rd:0 Ran:3
Win Prizemoney £0 *Total Prizemoney* £236
2000 Turf 0-3: (9f, 10f, 12f) (sft, gd 2)
Lengthy, currently average gelding. Turf high 66 (began Spt).
**J G Given [0-3] Ray Monaghan.*

SEPTEMBER HARVEST (USA) BHB 33f31a **RR 31f 31a** 3715[7]

4 ch g Mujtahid (USA) 7.4f **(69)** - Shawgatny (USA) (Danzig Connection (USA)) 8f **(68)**
Form - 64400777
Record 2000 - 1st:0 2nd:0 3rd:0 Ran:8
Pre2000 - 1st:1 2nd:2 3rd:2 Ran:25
Win Prizemoney £3,730 *Total Prizemoney* £7,246
Wins * 1999 Aug Pontef (G-F) H 8f 54 56 <
2000 Turf 0-4: (8f, 10f 2, 11f) (g-s, g-f, frm 2) 2000 AW 0-4: (8f 2, 12f 2) (Fibr 4)
Workmanlike, very moderate gelding, effective 8f, acts on frm, has worn blinkers. Turf high 31. AW high 46.
**Mrs S Lamyman [1-22] P Lamyman (from B J Meehan [0-15] Jun 1999).*

SEQUOYAH (IRE) **RR 100+f** 4644[5]

2 b f Sadler's Wells (USA) 11.3f **(87)** - Brigid (USA)
Form - 31215
2000 Turf 2-5: (6f 2, 7f 2-3) (gd 1-3, g-f 1-2)
Very useful filly. Turf high 100 (began Jly) - 1st of 10 from Hotelgenie Dot Com (3 Spt Curragh RF 4252a). A high-class filly, she ran out a clear-cut winner of the Group One Moyglare Stud Stakes on her fourth start. The drop back to six in the Cheveley Park did not suit her, but she was beaten under two lengths into fifth. Looks a likely type for the Irish Guineas at this stage.
**A P O'Brien in IRE [2-5] Mrs John Magnier.*

SERAPHINA (IRE) BHB 96f **RR 96f** 4700[3]

3 ch f Pips Pride 6.7f **(70)** - Angelic Sounds (IRE) (The Noble Player (USA)) 6.5f **(67)**
Form - 762030083
Record 2000 - 1st:0 2nd:1 3rd:2 Ran:9
Pre2000 - 1st:1 2nd:1 3rd:1 Ran:8
Win Prizemoney £5,303 *Total Prizemoney* £39,457
Wins * 1999 Mar Doncas (GD) 5f 74 <
2000 Turf 0-9: (5f 5, 6f 3, 7f) (hvy, g-s 2, gd 3, g-f 3)
Strong, very useful filly, effective 5 to 6f, best at 5f, acts on g-s to g-f, best on gd, has worn blinkers. Turf high 96 - 2nd of 12 getting 9lb from Cassandra Go (2 May Bath 5f gd RF 0961). Inconsistent. Fourth in the Cheveley Park Stakes in 1999, she struggled last term but showed the ability is still there when finishing third in a Listed event at Newmarket on her final start. However, she remains difficult to place. **B A McMahon [1-17] Michael Stokes.*

SERENE VIEW (USA) **RR 101f** 5366a[2]

3 ch f Distant View (USA) - Navarene (USA) (Known Fact (USA)) 7.4f **(67)**
Form - 2
2000 Turf 0-1: (8f) (hvy)
Currently very useful filly. (1st run) - 2nd of 16 to Miss Riviera Golf (3 Nov Maisons-Laffitte 8f hvy RF 5366a). **in FR [0-1].*

SERENGETI BRIDE (USA) **RR 49f** 5186[7]

2 ch f Lion Cavern (USA) 7.5f **(74)** - Island Wedding (USA) (Blushing Groom (FR)) 10.3f **(76)**
Form - 7
Record 2000 - 1st:0 2nd:0 3rd:0 Ran:1
2000 Turf 0-1: (7f) (g-s)
Currently moderate filly. **E A L Dunlop [0-1] Maktoum Al Maktoum.*

SEREN HILL BHB 100f **RR 100f** 5323[3]

4 ch m Sabrehill (USA) 8.5f **(64)** - Seren Quest **(81f)** (Rainbow Quest (USA)) 10.4f **(75)**
Form - 7808280113
Record 2000 - 1st:2 2nd:1 3rd:1 Ran:9
Pre2000 - 1st:2 2nd:1 3rd:4 Ran:11
Win Prizemoney £27,420 *Total Prizemoney* £37,672
Wins * **2000** Oct Newmar (SFT) H 12f 80 90 <
* **2000** Oct York (SFT) 11.9f 88
* 1999 Spt Haydoc (SFT) H 14f 77 82+
* 1998 Nov Redcar (G-S) H 8f 69 76
2000 Turf 2-9: (12f 2-4, 13f, 14f 2, 16f 2) (sft 3, g-s 1-1, gd 1-4, g-f)
Unfurnished, very useful filly, effective 12f, acts on sft to gd, likes left handed tracks. Turf high 94 - 3rd of 20 giving 13lb to Batswing (4 Nov Doncaster 12f sft RF 5323) - also 1st of 20 getting 11lb from Flossy (12 Oct Newmarket RF 4936). A tough filly who stays well and loves soft ground, she landed handicaps at York and Newmarket before finishing third in the November Handicap.
**G A Butler [4-17] The Fairy Story Partnership (from J W Hills [0-3] Aug 1998).*

SEREN TEG BHB 43f54a **RR 44f 54a** 4180[7]

4 ch m Timeless Times (USA) 6.1f **(56)** - Hill of Fare (Brigadier Gerard) 9.3f **(58)**
Form - 14400064687
Record 2000 - 1st:1 2nd:0 3rd:0 Ran:11
Pre2000 - 1st:2 2nd:3 3rd:3 Ran:23
Win Prizemoney £5,986 *Total Prizemoney* £13,486
Wins * **2000** *Feb Lingfi (STD) C 5f 58*
1998 *Dec Lingfi (STD) C 6f 73* <
1998 *Nov Wolver (STD) 6f 69*
2000 Turf 0-7: (5f 2, 6f 5) (gd, g-f 2, frm 4) 2000 AW 1-4: (5f 1-2, 6f 2) (Equi 1-2, Fibr 2)
Workmanlike, average filly, effective 5 to 6f, best at 6f, acts on gd to frm - acts on Equi, has worn blinkers, likes tight tracks. Turf high 44. AW high 61. She is nothing special, but claiming races over sprint trips on sand are just about with in her reach.
**R M Flower [1-16] K & D Computers Ltd (from B Palling [2-18] Jly 1999).*

SERENUS (USA) BHB 73f **RR 74f** 831[5]
7 b g Sunshine Forever (USA) 13.2f **(76)** - Curl And Set (USA) (Nijinsky (CAN)) 10.3f **(77)**
Form - 5
Record 2000 - 1st:0 2nd:0 3rd:0 Ran:1
Pre2000 - 1st:1 2nd:1 3rd:2 Ran:6
Win Prizemoney £7,360 *Total Prizemoney* £10,748
Wins * 1999 May Kempto (G-F) H 12f 70 72 <
2000 Turf 0-1: (16f) (sft)
Above-average gelding. **N J Henderson [8-28] W V M W & Mrs E S Robins (from Lord Huntingdon [0-4] Spt 1996).*

SERGEANT IMP (IRE) BHB 37f39a **RR 31f 39a** 4221[7]
5 b g Mac's Imp (USA) 5.6f **(54)** - Genzyme Gene (Riboboy (USA)) 14f **(54)**
Form - 7335437
Record 2000 - 1st:0 2nd:0 3rd:3 Ran:6
Pre2000 - 1st:1 2nd:1 3rd:0 Ran:34
Win Prizemoney £2,550 *Total Prizemoney* £5,385
Wins * 1998 Apr Bright (GD) 6f 48 <
2000 AW 0-6: (8f, 10f 4, 12f) (Equi 6)
Moderate gelding, effective 7 to 10f, acts on g-f to frm - acts on Equi, has worn blinkers. AW high 40. **P Mitchell [1-40] W R Mann.*

SERGEANT SLIPPER BHB 48f67a **RR 46f 67a** 2655[12]
3 ch g Never so Bold 7.1f **(62)** - Pretty Scarce **(23a)** (Handsome Sailor)
Form - 81188170
Record 2000 - 1st:2 2nd:0 3rd:0 Ran:5
Pre2000 - 1st:2 2nd:1 3rd:0 Ran:12
Win Prizemoney £6,553 *Total Prizemoney* £7,065
Wins * **2000** *Apr Southw (STD) H 5f 60* 63 <
* 1999 *Dec Southw (SLW) S 5f* 62
* 1999 *Dec Wolver (STD) S 5f* 60
2000 Turf 0-3: (5f 3) (gd 2, g-f) 2000 AW 1-2: (5f 1-1, 6f) (Fibr 1-2)
Scopey, average gelding, effective 5f, - acts on Fibr, mostly wears blinkers (very effectively). Turf high 45. AW high 63 - 1st of 13 giving 2lb to Paddywack (11 Apr Southwell RF 0670).
**C Smith [3-17] C Smith.*

SERGEANT YORK BHB 73f **RR 85f** 4471[7]
4 b g Be My Chief (USA) 10.2f **(62)** - Metaphysique (FR) (Law Society (USA)) 9.9f **(70)**
Form - 05336045387
Record 2000 - 1st:0 2nd:0 3rd:3 Ran:11
Pre2000 - 1st:1 2nd:3 3rd:3 Ran:19
Win Prizemoney £3,436 *Total Prizemoney* £16,924
Wins * 1998 May Hamilt (SFT) 5f 69 <
2000 Turf 0-11: (7f, 8f 9, 9f) (g-s, gd 3, g-f 2, frm 5)
Workmanlike, useful gelding, effective 8 to 9f, acts on g-f to frm, has worn blinkers, likes right handed tracks. Turf high 87. Inconsistent. He is proving hard to win with and has faced some impossible tasks. **C Smith [1-30] A E Needham.*

SERGE LIFAR RR 84f 5099[3]
2 b c Shirley Heights 12.1f **(76)** - Ballet (Sharrood (USA)) 10.5f **(72)**
Form - 33
Record 2000 - 1st:0 2nd:0 3rd:2 Ran:2
Win Prizemoney £0 *Total Prizemoney* £1,097
2000 Turf 0-2: (7f, 8f) (g-s, gd)
Currently decent colt. Turf high 84 (began Spt).
**R Hannon [0-2] Lord Carnarvon.*

SERIAL (POL) RR 2092[12]
6 bl g Who Knows - Sajra (POL) (Miami Prince)
Form - 0
Record 2000 - 1st:0 2nd:0 3rd:0 Ran:1
2000 Turf 0-1: (7f) (frm)
Formerly very poor gelding. **Mrs D Thomson [0-4] Spit & Polish.*

SERINGA (GER) RR 103f 4414a[3]
3 b f Acatenango (GER) - Seldom (Wavering Monarch (USA)) 10.4f **(94)**
Form - 3
2000 Turf 0-1: (12f) (gd)
Currently very useful filly. (1st run) - 3rd of 8 to Moonlady (10 Spt Hanover 12f gd RF 4414a).
**P Rau in GER [0-1] Gestut Fahrhof Stiftung.*

SERPENT SYSTEMS BHB 27f **RR 16f** 5009[7]
3 b f Noble Patriarch 12.2f **(43)** - Takeall (Another Realm) 6.6f **(55)**
Form - 037
Record 2000 - 1st:0 2nd:0 3rd:1 Ran:3
Win Prizemoney £0 *Total Prizemoney* £319
2000 Turf 0-1: (7f) (g-f) 2000 AW 0-2: (6f, 7f) (Fibr 2)
Workmanlike, currently little account filly. AW high 26 (began Oct).
**D Shaw [0-3] M Wainman.*

SERRA NEGRA BHB 80f **RR 83f** 1534[2]
3 b f Kris 10f **(75)** - Congress (IRE) (Dancing Brave (USA)) 8.4f **(76)**
Form - 162
Record 2000 - 1st:1 2nd:1 3rd:0 Ran:3
Pre2000 - 1st:0 2nd:0 3rd:0 Ran:1
Win Prizemoney £2,913 *Total Prizemoney* £5,073
Wins * **2000** May Warwic (SFT) 7.7f 83 <
2000 Turf 1-3: (7f, 8f 1-2) (sft 1-1, g-s, gd)
Scopey, decent filly. Turf high 83 (1st run) - 1st of 10 getting 13lb from Spellbinder (1 May Warwick RF 0954). She won a soft-ground Warwick maiden in good style on her reappearance and was not disgraced in a competitive handicap on much faster ground at York. She still has improvement in her.
**W J Haggas [1-4] Cyril Humphris.*

SERVICEABLE BHB 73f **RR 74f** 5320[17]
2 ch f Pursuit of Love 9.5f **(69)** - Absaloute Service (Absalom) 7.2f **(58)**
Form - 31600
Record 2000 - 1st:1 2nd:0 3rd:1 Ran:5
Win Prizemoney £3,125 *Total Prizemoney* £3,797
Wins * **2000** Apr Warwic (HVY) 5f 74 <
2000 Turf 1-5: (5f 1-3, 6f, 7f) (hvy 1-1, sft, gd 2, g-f)
Above-average filly. Turf high 74 - 1st of 10 from Franica (12 Apr Warwick RF 0686). Put her experience to good use to win a heavy-ground Warwick maiden on her second start.
**J M P Eustace [1-5] Major M G Wyatt.*

SERVICE STAR (IRE) BHB 78f87a **RR 80f 87a** 463[9]
3 b br c Namaqualand (USA) - Shenley Lass (Prince Tenderfoot (USA)) 9f **(61)**
Form - 13210
Record 2000 - 1st:1 2nd:1 3rd:0 Ran:3
Pre2000 - 1st:1 2nd:2 3rd:1 Ran:8
Win Prizemoney £6,123 *Total Prizemoney* £12,420
Wins * **2000** *Mar Wolver (STD) H 9.4f 80* 85 <
* 1999 *Nov Southw (STD) 8f* 80
2000 AW 1-3: (9f 1-1, 10f 2) (Equi 2, Fibr 1-1)
Leggy, useful colt, effective 8 to 10f, acted on frm - acted on Equi to Fibr, best on Fibr, often wore blinkers (extremely effectively), preferred left handed tracks, liked tight tracks. AW high 85 - 1st of 7 giving 18lb to Church Farm Flyer (2 Mar Wolverhampton RF 0394). (DEAD) **M A Jarvis [2-11] N S Yong.*

SET THE FASHION (AUS) RR 106f 1157a[3]
4 br h Bellotto (USA)
Form - 3
2000 Turf 0-1: (10f) (gd)
Currently Pattern-class colt. (1st run) - 3rd of 14 to All The Way (7 May Kranji 10f gd RF 1157a). **in SIN [0-1].*

SEVEN BHB 50f60a **RR 51f 60a** 4275[5]
5 ch g Weldnaas (USA) 8.4f **(55)** - Polly's Teahouse (Shack (USA)) 5.8f **(53)**
Form - 2271547040835
Record 2000 - 1st:1 2nd:0 3rd:1 Ran:11
Pre2000 - 1st:1 2nd:5 3rd:1 Ran:19
Win Prizemoney £4,440 *Total Prizemoney* £8,085
Wins * **2000** *Jan Southw (STD) 6f* 60
1999 *Mar Southw (STD) C 7f* 71 <
2000 Turf 0-6: (6f 2, 7f 3, 8f) (gd 2, g-f 2, frm 2) 2000 AW 1-5: (6f 1-3, 7f 2) (Fibr 1-5)
Average gelding, effective 7f, - acts on Fibr, mostly wears blinkers, likes left handed tracks, likes tight tracks. Turf high 51. AW high 60.
**Miss S J Wilton [1-22] John Pointon and Sons (from B Smart [1-11] Mar 1999).*

SEVEN NO TRUMPS BHB 76f **RR 82f** 4384[15]
3 ch g Pips Pride 6.7f **(70)** - Classic Ring (IRE) (Auction Ring (USA)) 8.6f **(65)**
Form - 7708388000
Record 2000 - 1st:0 2nd:0 3rd:1 Ran:10
Pre2000 - 1st:2 2nd:3 3rd:1 Ran:10
Win Prizemoney £6,648 *Total Prizemoney* £17,386
Wins * 1999 May Newcas (G-F) 5f 78 <
* 1999 May Nottin (FRM) 6.1f 77
2000 Turf 0-10: (5f 3, 6f 6, 7f) (gd 5, g-f 3, frm 2)
Workmanlike, decent gelding, effective 6f, acts on g-s to gd, has worn blinkers. Turf high 97. Listed placed as a juvenile, he showed little last term despite plummeting in the ratings.
**B W Hills [?-20] Paul McNamara.*

SEVEN OF NINE (IRE) RR 52f 4472[4]
2 b br f Alzao (USA) 9.8f **(73)** - Sharakawa (IRE) (Darshaan) 9.9f **(84)**
Form - 4
Record 2000 - 1st:0 2nd:0 3rd:0 Ran:1
Win Prizemoney £0 *Total Prizemoney* £425
2000 Turf 0-1: (8f) (g-f)
Currently fair filly. **W R Muir [0-1] M J Caddy.*

SEVEN OF SPADES BHB 55f45a **RR 63f 45a** 5009[5]
3 h g Mistertopogigo (IRE) - Misty Arch (Starch Reduced) 11.5f **(52)**
Form - 0005
Record 2000 - 1st:0 2nd:0 3rd:0 Ran:4
Pre2000 - 1st:0 2nd:1 3rd:1 Ran:6
Win Prizemoney £0 *Total Prizemoney* £1,170
2000 Turf 0-3: (5f 3) (g-f 2, frm) 2000 AW 0-1: (6f) (Fibr)
Scopey, average gelding, effective 5f, acts on frm. Turf high 57.
**D Nicholls [0-1] B L Cassidy (from R A Fahey [0-9] Aug 2000).*

SEVEN O SEVEN BHB 50f30a **RR 8f 30a** 459[9]
7 b g Skyliner 6.8f **(51)** - Fille de Phaeton (Sun Prince) 12.4f **(52)**
Form - 670
Record 2000 - 1st:0 2nd:0 3rd:0 Ran:3
Pre2000 - 1st:0 2nd:0 3rd:1 Ran:6
Win Prizemoney £0 *Total Prizemoney* £1,196
2000 AW 0-3: (8f 2, 11f) (Fibr 3)
Little account gelding, effective 10f, - acts on Equi. AW high 21. Inconsistent. **P D Cundell [0-13] John Davies (Stonehill).*

SEVEN SING (USA) BHB 90f **RR 79f** 3788[10]
2 b f Machiavellian (USA) 9.8f **(83)** - Seven Springs (USA) (Irish River (FR)) 8.6f **(78)**
Form - 310
Record 2000 - 1st:1 2nd:0 3rd:1 Ran:3
Win Prizemoney £3,591 *Total Prizemoney* £4,481
Wins * **2000** Jly Thirsk (FRM) 6f 78 <
2000 Turf 1-3: (5f, 6f 1-2) (gd, g-f, hrd 1-1)
Currently above-average filly. Turf high 83 (began Jly) - also 1st of 5 from Forever Times (28 Jly Thirsk RF 3197). She showed ability on her Newmarket debut when third behind a very decent sort and got off the mark in a Thirsk maiden next time. Not particularly impressive there, but the ground was very fast.
**B W Hills [1-3] K Abdulla.*

SEVEN SPRINGS (IRE) BHB 38f **RR 33f** 4147[7]
4 b g Unblest - Zaydeen (Sassafras (FR)) 9.6f **(69)**
Form - 800062037000847
Record 2000 - 1st:0 2nd:1 3rd:1 Ran:13
Pre2000 - 1st:1 2nd:1 3rd:0 Ran:18
Win Prizemoney £1,882 *Total Prizemoney* £3,973
Wins * 1998 *Nov Wolver (STD) 6f 76* <
2000 Turf 0-8: (5f 3, 6f 3, 7f 2) (hvy, gd 2, g-f 3, frm 2) 2000 AW 0-5: (5f, 6f 2, 7f, 8f) (Fibr 5)
Workmanlike, very moderate gelding, has worn blinkers. Turf high 41. AW high 36. Inconsistent. **R Hollinshead [1-31] N Chapman.*

SEWARDS FOLLY BHB 35f **RR 33f** 2958[9]
4 b m Rudimentary (USA) 8.2f **(66)** - Anchorage (IRE) (Slip Anchor) 9.8f **(73)**
Form - 0080
Record 2000 - 1st:0 2nd:0 3rd:0 Ran:4
Pre2000 - 1st:0 2nd:0 3rd:0 Ran:7
Win Prizemoney £0 *Total Prizemoney* £258
2000 Turf 0-4: (10f 3, 12f) (g-s, gd, frm, hrd)
Light-framed, very moderate filly. Turf high 33. Becoming disappointing. **P Bowen [0-11] P Bowen (from J A R Toller [0-7] Aug 1999).*

SEYOOLL (IRE) RR 74f 4368[3]
2 b f Danehill (USA) 9.1f **(79)** - Andromaque (USA) **(106f)** (Woodman (USA)) 9f **(74)**
Form - 43
Record 2000 - 1st:0 2nd:0 3rd:1 Ran:2
Win Prizemoney £0 *Total Prizemoney* £919
2000 Turf 0-2: (8f 2) (frm 2)
Currently above-average filly. Turf high 72 (began Aug) - 3rd of 5 to Time Away (13 Spt Sandown 8f frm RF 4368).
**M R Channon [0-2] Sheikh Ahmed Al Maktoum.*

SHAANARA (IRE) BHB 79f **RR 71f** 5053[1]
2 b f Darshaan 11.9f **(81)** - Mochara (Last Fandango) 7.8f **(61)**
Form - 601
Record 2000 - 1st:1 2nd:0 3rd:0 Ran:3
Win Prizemoney £3,315 *Total Prizemoney* £3,315
Wins * **2000** Oct Newcas (HVY) 7f 71 <
2000 Turf 1-3: (7f 1-3) (sft 1-1, g-f 2)
Currently above-average filly. Turf high 71 (began Spt) - 1st of 14 from Follow A Dream (18 Oct Newcastle RF 5053).
**Andrew Turnell [1-3] Dr John Hollowood.*

SHAANDAR (IRE) RR 54f 5310[12]
2 br c Darshaan 11.9f **(81)** - Moon Parade (Welsh Pageant) 10f **(65)**
Form - 0
Record 2000 - 1st:0 2nd:0 3rd:0 Ran:1
2000 Turf 0-1: (7f) (g-s)
Currently fair colt. **J L Dunlop [0-1] G J Pinchen.*

SHAAN MADARY (FR) BHB 76f72a **RR 76f 72a** 3626[8]
3 b br f Darshaan 11.9f **(81)** - Madary (CAN) **(89f)** (Green Desert (USA)) 8.6f **(78)**
Form - 02148
Record 2000 - 1st:1 2nd:1 3rd:0 Ran:5
Pre2000 - 1st:0 2nd:0 3rd:0 Ran:1
Win Prizemoney £3,893 *Total Prizemoney* £5,343
Wins * **2000** Jly Thirsk (FRM) 7f 71 <
2000 Turf 1-5: (7f 1-1, 8f 3, 10f) (gd, g-f, frm 2, hrd 1-1)
Scopey, above-average filly, effective 7 to 8f, acts on frm to hrd. Turf high 76 - 4th of 7 getting 2lb from Adobe (5 Aug Thirsk 8f frm RF 3409) - also 1st of 6 getting 5lb from Honest Warning (28 Jly Thirsk RF 3194). Improving steadily, she landed a Thirsk maiden in July. **B W Hills [1-6] Hilal Salem.*

SHAANXI ROMANCE (IRE) BHB 48f51a **RR 53df 51a** 5159[15]
5 b g Darshaan 11.9f **(81)** - Easy Romance (USA) (Northern Jove (CAN)) 9.7f **(66)**
Form - 250055436611234060070
Record 2000 - 1st:2 2nd:2 3rd:2 Ran:21
Pre2000 - 1st:2 2nd:1 3rd:1 Ran:14
Win Prizemoney £13,793 *Total Prizemoney* £22,034
Wins * **2000** Aug Kempto (G-F) H 8f 43 46
* **2000** *Jly Southw (STD) H 8f 47 52*
1999 Aug Carlis (FRM) 6.9f 57
1998 *Mar Wolver (STD) 8.5f 67* <
2000 Turf 1-14: (7f 3, 8f 1-9, 12f 2) (sft, gd 2, g-f 1-5, frm 6) 2000 AW 1-7: (7f, 8f 1-5, 12f) (Fibr 1-7)
Fair gelding, effective 7 to 8f, best at 8f, acts on gd to frm - acts on Fibr, best on frm, often wears blinkers (effectively), likes left handed tracks, excels at Bath, does well at Southwell. Turf high 53 - 3rd of 8 getting 20lb from Minetta (8 Aug Bath 8f frm RF 3444). AW high 52 - 1st of 8 getting 8lb from Toyon (21 Jly Southwell RF 3017). Had shown signs of form in ordinary handicaps before hitting a rich vein in midsummer, winning on the Southwell Fibresand and at Kempton. Running well off higher marks since.
**M J Polglase [2-19] Mark Lewis (from I Semple [1-11] Apr 2000).*

SHAARD (IRE) BHB 100f **RR 99f** 5123[1]
2 b c Anabaa (USA) - Braari (USA) **(100f)** (Gulch (USA)) 8f **(81)**
Form - 1341
Record 2000 - 1st:2 2nd:0 3rd:1 Ran:4
Win Prizemoney £16,194 *Total Prizemoney* £23,064

Wins *** 2000** Oct Doncas (SFT) L 6f 99 <
*** 2000** Jly Bath (G-S) 5.7f 83+
2000 Turf 2-4: (6f 2-3, 7f) (g-s 1-1, gd 1-2, frm)
Very useful colt, always wears blinkers. Turf high 99 (began Jly) - 1st of 10 from Down To The Woods (21 Oct Doncaster RF 5123). He wore blinkers on his debut and certainly looked tricky on occasions. However, he did nothing wrong when short-heading Down To The Woods in a Listed race at Doncaster in October and deserves the benefit of doubt. Unlikely to stay beyond seven furlongs, he might struggle if tried in Group company.
**B W Hills [2-4] Hamdan Al Maktoum.*

SHABAASH (IRE) BHB 46f23a **RR 53f 23a** 421[12]

4 b h Mujadil (USA) 7.7f **(70)** - Folly Vision (IRE) (Vision (USA)) 9f **(64)**
Form - 530476700
Record **2000** - 1st:0 2nd:0 3rd:0 Ran:6
Pre2000 - 1st:2 2nd:1 3rd:4 Ran:28
Win Prizemoney £5,004 *Total Prizemoney* £8,154
Wins * 1999 *Feb Lingfi (STD) C 7f 59*
1998 Jly Folkes (G-F) H 5f 70 <
2000 AW 0-6: (9f, 10f, 11f, 12f 2, 13f) (Equi 3, Fibr 3)
Fair colt, effective 7f, - acts on Equi. AW high 27. **P Howling [1-25] S J Hammond (from G Lewis [1-9] Spt 1998).*

SHABLAM (USA) BHB 98f93a **RR 103f 93a** 4003[4]

3 b c Lear Fan (USA) 10.4f **(80)** - Awestamind (USA) (Flying Paster (USA))
Form - 54474
Record **2000** - 1st:0 2nd:0 3rd:0 Ran:5
Pre2000 - 1st:1 2nd:0 3rd:1 Ran:2
Win Prizemoney £5,691 *Total Prizemoney* £10,040
Wins * 1999 Spt Ayr (G-S) 7f 79 <
2000 Turf 0-5: (7f, 8f, 10f 2, 12f) (gd 4, g-f)
Well made, very useful colt, effective 7 to 10f, acts on gd to g-f, has worn blinkers. Turf high 103 - 4th of 8 to Merry Merlin (11 May Chester 10f g-f RF 1134). He has plenty of ability but has proved a little disappointing when the chips are down. Not an easy type to place. **Sir Michael Stoute [1-7] Saeed Suhail.*

SHADALHI RR 54f 2117[5]

2 ch f Alhijaz 7.7f **(57)** - Dangerous Shadow **(37f 47a)** (Absalom) 7.2f **(58)**
Form - 75
Record **2000** - 1st:0 2nd:0 3rd:0 Ran:2
2000 Turf 0-2: (5f, 6f) (frm, hrd)
Currently fair filly. Turf high 54 - 5th of 9 to Milltide (20 Jun Thirsk 6f frm RF 2117). **K A Ryan [0-2] The Shadowline Club Ltd.*

SHADED MEMOIR (USA) BHB 64f58a **RR 65f 58a** 5310[8]

2 ch f Woodman (USA) 9.7f **(77)** - Sam's Diary (USA) (Private Account (USA)) 8.5f **(74)**
Form - 678
Record **2000** - 1st:0 2nd:0 3rd:0 Ran:3
2000 Turf 0-3: (6f, 7f 2) (g-s 2, gd)
Currently average filly. Turf high 65 (began Aug).
**J H M Gosden [0-3] R E Sangster.*

SHADES OF LOVE BHB 43f60a **RR 35f 60a** 4922[13]

6 b h Pursuit of Love 9.5f **(69)** - Shadiliya (Red Alert) 7.6f **(66)**
Form - 0
Record **2000** - 1st:0 2nd:0 3rd:0 Ran:1
Pre2000 - 1st:3 2nd:2 3rd:2 Ran:25
Win Prizemoney £8,673 *Total Prizemoney* £11,555
Wins * 1999 *Jan Lingfi (STD) H 7f 70 71* <
* 1998 *Nov Lingfi (STD) H 7f 65 68*
* 1998 *Mar Southw (STD) H 7f 57 64*
2000 AW 0-1: (7f) (Equi)
Above-average horse, effective 7f, - acts on Equi, favours left handed tracks, favours tight tracks. Becoming disappointing.
**V Soane [3-26] The Pursuers.*

SHADIRWAN (IRE) BHB 35f **RR 8f** 2569[11]

9 b g Kahyasi 12.9f **(74)** - Shademah (Thatch (USA)) 9.8f **(62)**
Form - 0
Record **2000** - 1st:0 2nd:0 3rd:0 Ran:1
Pre2000 - 1st:2 2nd:3 3rd:0 Ran:28
Win Prizemoney £10,708 *Total Prizemoney* £20,134
Wins 1996 Mar Doncas (G-S) H 18f 70 83 <
2000 Turf 0-1: (18f) (g-f)
Very poor gelding, has broken blood-vessels, has worn blinkers. Becoming disappointing. **C L Popham [0-10] Mrs A E Baker (from Mrs A J Perrett [0-7] Spt 1998).*

SHADOWBLASTER (IRE) BHB 74f **RR 83f** 4769[4]

3 b c Wolfhound (USA) 7.3f **(71)** - Swame (USA) (Jade Hunter (USA))
Form - 52274
Record **2000** - 1st:0 2nd:2 3rd:0 Ran:5
Win Prizemoney £0 *Total Prizemoney* £2,706
2000 Turf 0-5: (7f, 8f 3, 10f) (g-s, gd, g-f 3)
Scopey, decent colt. Turf high 85 - 2nd of 8 to Dance West (19 Jly Yarmouth 7f g-f RF 2951).
**B Hanbury [0-5] Mrs Mette Campbell-Andenaes.*

SHADOW CASTER (USA) RR 5328a[13]

4 ch h Future Storm (USA) - Just Dance (USA) (Duck Dance (USA))
Form - 30
2000 AW 0-2: (6f 2) (Dirt 2)
Currently very useful colt. AW high 100.
**J P Terranova in USA [0-1] Gatsas Thoroughbred LLC (from C Assimakopoulos in USA [0-1] Jun 2000).*

SHADOWLESS BHB 100f **RR 88f** 4435[7]

2 b c Alzao (USA) 9.8f **(73)** - Warning Shadows (IRE) **(110f)** (Cadeaux Genereux)
Form - 47237
Record **2000** - 1st:0 2nd:1 3rd:1 Ran:5
Win Prizemoney £0 *Total Prizemoney* £10,130
2000 Turf 0-5: (6f 2, 7f, 8f 2) (gd 4, frm)
Useful colt. Turf high 88 - 3rd of 9 to Turnberry Isle (12 Aug Ascot 8f gd RF 3579). In the frame in decent company, he stays a mile and looks sure to find a race.
**C E Brittain [0-5] Sheikh Marwan Al Maktoum.*

SHADOW PRINCE BHB 80f **RR 84f** 4465[2]

3 ch g Machiavellian (USA) 9.8f **(83)** - Shadywood (Habitat) 9.4f **(70)**
Form - 57133752
Record **2000** - 1st:1 2nd:1 3rd:2 Ran:8
Pre2000 - 1st:0 2nd:0 3rd:0 Ran:1
Win Prizemoney £4,407 *Total Prizemoney* £12,857
Wins *** 2000** Jun Kempto (G-F) H 7f 72 76 <
2000 Turf 1-8: (7f 1-5, 8f 2, 9f) (sft, gd, g-f 4, frm 1-2)
Scopey, decent gelding, effective 7 to 8f, best at 7f, acts on g-f to frm, best on g-f, likes right handed tracks. Turf high 84 - 3rd of 12 getting 1lb from Rushmore (26 Jly Sandown 7f g-f RF 3141) - also 1st of 14 getting 12lb from Carlton (28 Jun Kempton RF 2345). Looked one to keep on the right side when scoring on his handicap debut at Kempton in June, and has continued to run well without always enjoying the breaks.
**R Charlton [1-9] Hippodrome Racing.*

SHADY DEAL BHB 41a **RR 49f** 4276[19]

4 b g No Big Deal - Taskalady (Touching Wood (USA)) 8.2f **(55)**
Form - 0747730002213480
Record **2000** - 1st:1 2nd:2 3rd:2 Ran:15
Pre2000 - 1st:0 2nd:2 3rd:1 Ran:18
Win Prizemoney £2,215 *Total Prizemoney* £7,458
Wins *** 2000** Jly Bath (G-S) H 5.1f 47 49 <
2000 Turf 1-9: (5f 1-7, 6f 2) (gd 1-2, g-f 3, frm 3, hrd) 2000 AW 0-6: (5f, 6f 3, 7f 2) (Equi 5, Fibr)
Neat, moderate gelding, effective 6 to 7f, acts on gd - acts on Equi. Turf high 49. AW high 42. Consistent.
**M D I Usher [1-33] G A Summers.*

SHADY POINT (IRE) BHB 75f **RR 81f** 4274[9]

3 b f Unfuwain (USA) 11.4f **(74)** - Warning Shadows (IRE) **(110f)** (Cadeaux Genereux)
Form - 7562176060
Record **2000** - 1st:1 2nd:1 3rd:0 Ran:10
Pre2000 - 1st:0 2nd:0 3rd:1 Ran:2
Win Prizemoney £2,756 *Total Prizemoney* £5,366
Wins *** 2000** *Jun Southw (STD) H 8f 67 68+* <
2000 Turf 0-9: (7f, 8f 5, 9f, 10f, 12f) (sft, gd 4, g-f 3, frm) 2000 AW 1-1: (8f 1-1) (Fibr 1-1)
Scopey, decent filly, often wears blinkers (very effectively). Turf

high 102. (1st run). Some fair efforts on turf, but her only victory so far came over a mile on Fibresand. She faced some impossible tasks during the summer, but was beaten under five lengths in a Newmarket Group Two.
**C E Brittain [1-12] Sheikh Marwan Al Maktoum.*

SHAFAQ (USA) BHB 72f **RR 77f** 3922[8]
3 b f Dayjur (USA) 6.8f **(79)** - Shemaq (USA) **(94f)** (Blushing John (USA))
Form - 06008
Record 2000 - 1st:0 2nd:0 3rd:0 Ran:5
Pre2000 - 1st:1 2nd:0 3rd:1 Ran:2
Win Prizemoney £3,850 *Total Prizemoney* £4,480
Wins * 1999 Jly Lingfi (G-F) 6f 76+ <
2000 Turf 0-5: (6f 2, 7f 2, 10f) (g-f 4, frm)
Scopey, above-average filly, effective 6 to 7f, acts on g-t to frm, has worn blinkers. Turf high 77 - 6th of 7 giving 5lb to Night Empress (4 Jly Yarmouth 7f g-f RF 2503). **R W Armstrong [1-7] Hamdan Al Maktoum.*

SHAFFISHAYES BHB 49f65a **RR 58f 65a** 4749[9]
8 ch g Clantime 6.6f **(57)** - Mischievous Miss (Niniski (USA)) 10.6f **(65)**
Form - 06546530670
Record 2000 - 1st:0 2nd:0 3rd:1 Ran:11
Pre2000 - 1st:7 2nd:8 3rd:7 Ran:45
Win Prizemoney £27,353 *Total Prizemoney* £43,557
Wins * 1999 Aug Ripon (GD) H 12.3f 62 67
* 1998 Spt Nottin (GD) 10f 73 <
* 1998 Apr Thirsk (G-S) 12f 73 <
* 1997 Jun Newmar (SFT) H 12f 68 70
* 1997 May Newcas (GD) H 12.4f 65 69
* 1996 Apr Pontef (G-F) 8f 66
2000 Turf 0-11: (10f 3, 11f 2, 12f 3, 14f 3) (sft, g-s 3, gd 3, g-f 3, frm)
Average gelding, effective 10 to 14f, acts on g-s to frm, best on g-f, likes left handed tracks, favours tight tracks, excels at Thirsk and Pontefract. Turf high 58. **Mrs M Reveley [7-56] P Davidson-Brown.*

SHAHED BHB 78f **RR 79f** 3052[3]
3 ch g Arazi (USA) 9.2f **(74)** - Nafhaat (USA) (Roberto (USA)) 10f **(76)**
Form - 63
Record 2000 - 1st:0 2nd:0 3rd:1 Ran:2
Pre2000 - 1st:0 2nd:0 3rd:1 Ran:3
Win Prizemoney £0 *Total Prizemoney* £1,817
2000 Turf 0-2: (7f, 8f) (sft, frm)
Strong, above-average gelding. Turf high 79.
**M P Tregoning [0-5] Hamdan Al Maktoum.*

SHAHIRAH (USA) BHB 86f **RR 81+f** 5128[8]
2 b f Diesis 9f **(80)** - Shemaq (USA) **(94f)** (Blushing John (USA))
Form - 108
Record 2000 - 1st:1 2nd:0 3rd:0 Ran:3
Win Prizemoney £4,368 *Total Prizemoney* £4,368
Wins * 2000 Aug Kempto (G-F) 7f 81+ <
2000 Turf 1-3: (7f 1-2, 8f) (sft, gd, frm 1-1)
Currently decent filly. Turf high 81 (1st run) (began Aug) - 1st of 9 from Bylaw (14 Aug Kempton RF 3621). Ready winner on her debut, she finished last in the Group One Fillies' Mile after being hampered. **M P Tregoning [1-3] Hamdan Al Maktoum.*

SHAIBANI BHB 84f **RR 86+f** 1484[4]
3 b c Muhtarram (USA) - Haboobti (Habitat) 9.4f **(70)**
Form - 4
Record 2000 - 1st:0 2nd:0 3rd:0 Ran:1
Pre2000 - 1st:1 2nd:0 3rd:0 Ran:1
Win Prizemoney £3,297 *Total Prizemoney* £4,129
Wins * 1999 Oct Yarmou (G-S) 7f 86+ <
2000 Turf 0-1: (10f) (gd)
Scopey, currently useful colt. **B W Hills [1-2] H R H Prince Fahd Salman & H Shaibani.*

SHAIR (USA) BHB 83f **RR 86f** 4552[1]
3 b br g Warning 8.1f **(77)** - Shaima (USA) (Shareef Dancer (USA)) 9.9f **(73)**
Form - 42221
Record 2000 - 1st:1 2nd:3 3rd:0 Ran:5
Win Prizemoney £4,416 *Total Prizemoney* £8,634
Wins * 2000 Spt Goodwo (SFT) 9.9f 80 <
2000 Turf 1-5: (10f 1-2, 12f 3) (g-s 1-1, gd 3, g-f)
Scopey, useful gelding. Turf high 86 (began Jly) - 2nd of 7 giving 5lb to Isadora (7 Spt Chepstow 12f gd RF 4273) - also 1st of 11 giving 5lb to Second Affair (21 Spt Goodwood RF 4552).
**J H M Gosden [1-5] Sheikh Mohammed.*

SHAKAKHAN BHB 80f **RR 62f** 4998[3]
2 ch f Night Shift (USA) 8.1f **(73)** - Sea Wedding **(61f)** (Groom Dancer (USA))
Form - 53
Record 2000 - 1st:0 2nd:0 3rd:1 Ran:2
Win Prizemoney £0 *Total Prizemoney* £260
2000 Turf 0-2: (6f 2) (g-s, gd)
Currently above-average filly. Turf high 62 (began Spt).
**B W Hills [0-2] Peter Law.*

SHAKESPEARE RR 105f 3645a[1]
3 b c Rainbow Quest (USA) 11.2f **(81)** - Silver Lane (USA) (Silver Hawk (USA)) 8.6f **(70)**
Form - 41831
2000 Turf 2-5: (9f 1-1, 10f 1-3, 12f) (sft, g-s 1-1, gd 1-2, g-f)
Pattern-class colt, effective 9f, acts on gd, has worn blinkers. Turf high 105 - also 1st of 6 giving 3lb to Islandagore (7 Aug Cork RF 3645a). Won a maiden on his only start at two, and finished last of four on his reappearance, reported to have finished distressed. Well beaten in the Irish Derby, he landed two minor races at Cork and remains and remains a promising colt.
**A P O'Brien in IRE [3-6] Mrs John Magnier.*

SHALARISE (IRE) BHB 47f60a **RR 45f 60a** 5188[11]
3 ch f Shalford (IRE) 7.8f **(63)** - Orthorising (Aragon) 8.1f **(60)**
Form - 00050200000
Record 2000 - 1st:0 2nd:1 3rd:0 Ran:11
Pre2000 - 1st:1 2nd:2 3rd:1 Ran:8
Win Prizemoney £3,403 *Total Prizemoney* £9,583
Wins * 1999 Aug Newcas (GD) 5f 70 <
2000 Turf 0-11: (5f 9, 6f 2) (gd 6, g-f 4, frm)
Strong, fair filly, effective 5f, acts on g-f to frm, best on frm, often wears blinkers. Turf high 58. Inconsistent. **Miss L A Perratt [1-19] Third Estate Racing Club.*

SHALBEEBLUE (IRE) BHB 56f58a **RR 62f 58a** 5016[2]
3 b g Shalford (IRE) 7.8f **(63)** - Alberjas (IRE) (Sure Blade (USA)) 11.3f **(67)**
Form - 350004742
Record 2000 - 1st:0 2nd:1 3rd:1 Ran:9
Win Prizemoney £0 *Total Prizemoney* £1,488
2000 Turf 0-8: (7f, 8f 2, 10f 4, 12f) (sft, g-s, gd, frm 4, hrd) 2000 AW 0-1: (9f) (Fibr)
Scopey, average gelding, effective 9 to 10f, acts on frm - acts on Fibr, has worn blinkers, prefers tight tracks. Turf high 64. (1st run) - 2nd of 11 getting 13lb from Faraway Look (17 Oct Wolverhampton 9f Fibr RF 5016). Inconsistent.
**B Ellison [0-3] Cotterill, Kimberley & Schofield (from J G Given [0-6] Spt 2000).*

SHALIMAR (IRE) BHB 88f **RR 88+f** 2690[8]
3 b f Indian Ridge 7.6f **(74)** - Athens Belle (IRE) (Groom Dancer (USA))
Form - 3118
Record 2000 - 1st:2 2nd:0 3rd:1 Ran:4
Pre2000 - 1st:0 2nd:1 3rd:0 Ran:2
Win Prizemoney £10,816 *Total Prizemoney* £12,405
Wins * 2000 Jly Newmar (G-F) H 8f 82 88+ <
*** 2000** Jun Salisb (G-F) 7f 63
2000 Turf 2-4: (7f 1-3, 8f 1-1) (gd 2, g-f 1-1, frm 1-1)
Scopey, useful filly, effective 7 to 8f, best at 7f, acts on gd to frm. Turf high 88 - 1st of 8 giving 1lb to Picture Puzzle (1 Jly Newmarket RF 2448). Showed ability before getting off the mark in a seven-furlong Salisbury maiden in June, but she resents being hit with the whip and requires some kidding.
**J H M Gosden [2-4] Lady Bamford (from A G Foster [0-1] Oct 1999).*

SHAMAH BHB 92f **RR 93++f** 1384[1]
3 ch f Unfuwain (USA) 11.4f **(74)** - Shurooq (USA) (Affirmed (USA)) 9.3f **(79)**
Form - 21
Record 2000 - 1st:1 2nd:1 3rd:0 Ran:2

Pre2000 - 1st:0 2nd:2 3rd:0 Ran:2
Win Prizemoney £4,277 *Total Prizemoney* £7,577
Wins *** 2000** May Windso (G-S) 8.3f 93++ <
2000 Turf 1-2: (8f 1-1, 10f) (g-f 1-1, frm)
Scopey, useful filly. Turf high 93 - 1st of 15 from Latour (22 May Windsor RF 1384). Second behind Petrushka as a juvenile, she was not seen out after making-all in a Windsor maiden during May. Highly rated, she stays a mile and a quarter and remains a useful prospect. **B W Hills [1-4] Hamdan Al Maktoum.*

SHAMAIEL (IRE) BHB 93f **RR 99f** 4963[11]
3 b f Lycius (USA) 8.8f **(71)** - Pearl Kite (USA) **(101df)** (Silver Hawk (USA)) 8.6f **(70)**
Form - 440430100
Record 2000 - 1st:1 2nd:0 3rd:1 Ran:9
Win Prizemoney £3,916 *Total Prizemoney* £11,235
Wins *** 2000** Spt Bath (GD) 11.7f 86+ <
2000 Turf 1-9: (10f 4, 12f 1-5) (gd 5, g-f, frm 1-3)
Workmanlike, very useful filly, effective 10 to 12f, acts on gd. Turf high 99 - 3rd of 5 getting 3lb from Sailing (12 Aug Ascot 12f gd RF 3580). She kept hot company for much of the season and made no mistake when winning a weak maiden at Bath in September. Outclassed in Listed and Group races thereafter, she will be difficult to place. **C E Brittain [1-9] Saeed Manana.*

SHAMAN BHB 63f67a **RR 68f 67a** 4676[7]
3 b g Fraam - Magic Maggie (Beveled (USA)) 9f **(59)**
Form - 041218132277
Record 2000 - 1st:2 2nd:3 3rd:1 Ran:9
Pre2000 - 1st:2 2nd:2 3rd:1 Ran:11
Win Prizemoney £8,689 *Total Prizemoney* £12,942
Wins *** 2000** Jun Bright (FRM) 10f 64
*** 2000** *Apr Lingfi (STD) S 10f 65+*
* 1999 *Dec Lingfi (STD) S 8f 60*
1999 Aug Folkes (G-S) S 7f 68 <
2000 Turf 1-6: (8f, 10f 1-3, 12f 2) (g-s, g-f, frm 1-3, hrd) 2000 AW 1-3: (10f 1-2, 12f) (Equi 1-3)
Workmanlike, average gelding, effective 6 to 10f, best at 6f, acts on g-s to frm - acts on Equi, likes left handed tracks, does well at Lingfield, likes Brighton. Turf high 66 - 2nd of 14 giving 23lb to Highcal (21 Aug Brighton 10f g-f RF 3837) - also 1st of 8 getting 7lb from Sharp Spice (19 Jun Brighton RF 2087). AW high 66 (1st run) - 2nd of 5 giving 11lb to Glenwhargen (8 Jan Lingfield 10f Equi RF 0047) - also 1st of 4 giving 5lb to Armenia (12 Apr Lingfield RF 0682). Consistent. **G L Moore [3-15] Mrs S M Redjep (from M R Channon [1-5] Aug 1999).*

SHAMEL BHB 70f65a **RR 74f 65a** 449[6]
4 b h Unfuwain (USA) 11.4f **(74)** - Narjis (USA) (Blushing Groom (FR)) 10.3f **(76)**
Form - 6
Record 2000 - 1st:0 2nd:0 3rd:0 Ran:1
Pre2000 - 1st:1 2nd:1 3rd:2 Ran:8
Win Prizemoney £3,054 *Total Prizemoney* £5,450
Wins 1999 Jun Yarmou (GD) H 14.1f 66 69+ <
2000 AW 0-1: (12f) (Fibr)
Scopey, above-average colt, effective 14f, acts on g-f. **D Shaw [0-2] J C Fretwell (from J L Dunlop [1-7] Jun 1999).*

SHAMOKIN BHB 24f37a **RR 16df 37a** 3495[14]
8 b g Green Desert (USA) 7.8f **(78)** - Shajan (Kris) 9.5f **(73)**
Form - 50
Record 2000 - 1st:0 2nd:0 3rd:0 Ran:2
Pre2000 - 1st:0 2nd:1 3rd:3 Ran:29
Win Prizemoney £0 *Total Prizemoney* £1,456
2000 Turf 0-1: (12f) (g-f) 2000 AW 0-1: (11f) (Fibr)
Little account gelding, effective 7 to 8f, - acts on Fibr, has worn blinkers, likes left handed tracks, likes tight tracks. **F Watson [0-31] F Watson.*

SHAMPOOED (IRE) BHB 49f **RR 47f** 972[2]
6 b m Law Society (USA) 11.6f **(71)** - White Caps (Shirley Heights) 10.3f **(74)**
Form - 32
Record 2000 - 1st:0 2nd:1 3rd:1 Ran:2
Pre2000 - 1st:2 2nd:1 3rd:1 Ran:13
Win Prizemoney £5,308 *Total Prizemoney* £8,049
Wins 1998 Jun Thurle (GD) 16f 72 <
1997 Jun Tralee (FRM) H 11f 60 63
2000 Turf 0-2: (14f, 15f) (hvy, gd)
Moderate mare, has worn blinkers. Turf high 45. Becoming disappointing.
**R Dickin [3-13] Warwick Members Racing Club (from J G Murphy in IRE [2-7] Jun 1998).*

SHAMROCK CITY (IRE) BHB 112f **RR 115f** 1882[1]
3 b c Rock City 8.8f **(62)** - Actualite (Polish Precedent (USA)) 10.2f **(60)**
Form - 6041
Record 2000 - 1st:1 2nd:0 3rd:0 Ran:4
Pre2000 - 1st:1 2nd:1 3rd:0 Ran:3
Win Prizemoney £20,588 *Total Prizemoney* £36,285
Wins *** 2000** Jun Newmar (G-F) L 10f 110+ <
* 1999 Spt Doncas (G-F) 8f 97+
2000 Turf 1-4: (8f 2, 10f 1-2) (gd 2, g-f, frm 1-1)
Scopey, high-class colt, effective 10f, acts on g-f to frm. Turf high 115 - 4th of 5 to Sakhee (17 May York 10f g-f RF 1263) - also 1st of 7 from Subtle Power (11 Jun Newmarket RF 1882). Nominated as a horse to follow by Kieren Fallon at the start of the campaign, he improved once stepped-up in trip, making-all over a mile and a quarter at Newmarket in June. Not seen out again, he has plenty of scope and could make a mark in Group races on the continent. Withdrawn on soft ground in the past, he has shown his best form on good to firm. **P Howling [2-7] Liam Sheridan.*

SHAMSAN (IRE) BHB 67a **RR 68f** 5016[4]
3 ch c Night Shift (USA) 8.1f **(73)** - Awayil (USA) **(78f)** (Woodman (USA)) 9f **(74)**
Form - 4103205223034
Record 2000 - 1st:1 2nd:3 3rd:3 Ran:12
Pre2000 - 1st:0 2nd:0 3rd:0 Ran:3
Win Prizemoney £4,056 *Total Prizemoney* £8,479
Wins *** 2000** *Jan Lingfi (STD) H 8f 63 68* <
2000 Turf 0-7: (8f 4, 10f, 11f 2) (hvy, g-s, g-f 3, frm, hrd) 2000 AW 1-5: (7f, 8f 1-1, 9f 2, 10f) (Equi 1-3, Fibr 2)
Neat, average colt, effective 8 to 11f, best at 8f, acts on g-s to frm - acts on AW, has worn blinkers, prefers tight tracks. Turf high 68 - 2nd of 14 giving 13lb to Rudetski (9 Aug Pontefract 8f frm RF 3505). AW high 68 (1st run) - 1st of 4 getting 5lb from Joely Green (5 Jan Lingfield RF 0027). Consistent. Looks rather better on sand than on turf and landed a four-runner handicap on the Lingfield Equitrack at the start of this year. A mile looks his optimum trip.
**M Johnston [1-13] A Al-Rostamani (from B Hanbury [0-2] Jly 1999).*

SHAM SHARIF BHB 55f50a **RR 65f 50a** 4785[9]
3 b f Be My Chief (USA) 10.2f **(62)** - Syrian Queen **(76f)** (Slip Anchor) 9.8f **(73)**
Form - 5185800
Record 2000 - 1st:1 2nd:0 3rd:0 Ran:7
Pre2000 - 1st:0 2nd:0 3rd:0 Ran:2
Win Prizemoney £2,800 *Total Prizemoney* £2,800
Wins *** 2000** Jun Ayr (G-F) 9.1f 65 <
2000 Turf 1-6: (9f 1-1, 10f 2, 11f, 12f 2) (sft, g-f, frm 1-4) 2000 AW 0-1: (9f) (Fibr)
Scopey, average filly, effective 9 to 12f, acts on frm, has worn blinkers, prefers tight tracks. Turf high 65 - 1st of 8 getting 3lb from Noble Splendour (1 Jun Ayr RF 1618). She got off the mark in a very modest Ayr maiden in June when racing on fast ground for the first time, but has been well held since.
**B W Hills [1-9] Wafic Said.*

SHAMWARI SONG BHB 47f42a **RR 50f 42a** 2571[8]
5 b g Sizzling Melody 6.3f **(49)** - Spark Out (Sparkler)
Form - 57002038740318
Record 2000 - 1st:1 2nd:1 3rd:2 Ran:13
Pre2000 - 1st:3 2nd:1 3rd:1 Ran:28
Win Prizemoney £10,862 *Total Prizemoney* £14,446
Wins *** 2000** Jun Carlis (G-F) H 6.9f 40 50
1998 May Newcas (G-F) H 8f 67 72 <
1998 May Beverl (G-F) C 7.5f 57
1997 Oct Newcas (G-F) 7f 63
2000 Turf 1-5: (7f 1-3, 8f 2) (gd, g-f 1-2, frm 2) 2000 AW 0-8: (7f 3, 8f 4, 10f) (Equi 5, Fibr 3)
Fair gelding, effective 7f, acts on g-f - acts on Equi, has worn blinkers, favours tight tracks. Turf high 50 - 1st of 15 getting 3lb from Dovebrace (29 Jun Carlisle RF 2366). AW high 42 - 3rd of 8 getting 5lb from Unchain My Heart (1 Mar Lingfield 7f Equi RF

0385).
K A Ryan [1-3] Gallagher Equine Ltd (from Mrs L C Jewell [0-19] May 2000).

SHANGHAI LADY RR ?f 4619[15]
4 b m Sabrehill (USA) 8.5f **(64)** - Session (Reform) 8.9f **(62)**
Form - 00
Record 2000 - 1st:0 2nd:0 3rd:0 Ran:2
Pre2000 - 1st:1 2nd:0 3rd:0 Ran:6
Win Prizemoney £3,382 *Total Prizemoney* £3,632
Wins 1999 Spt Bright (SFT) 8f 68+ <
2000 Turf 0-2: (7f, 9f) (gd 2)
Workmanlike, very poor filly, effective 8f, acts on g-s. (began Jly). Well beaten in nurseries in '99 after winning her maiden.
P W D'Arcy [0-2] Pacific Hawk (HK) Ltd (from J H M Gosden [1-6] Nov 1999).

SHANGHAI LIL BHB 28f40a **RR 20f 40a** 22[11]
8 b m Petong 7.6f **(58)** - Toccata (USA) (Mr Leader (USA)) 9.8f **(66)**
Form - 700
Record 2000 - 1st:0 2nd:0 3rd:0 Ran:1
Pre2000 - 1st:9 2nd:4 3rd:4 Ran:58
Win Prizemoney £22,918 *Total Prizemoney* £27,584
Wins 1999 *Oct Wolver (STD) H 12f 46 48*
1999 *Feb Lingfi (STD) H 10f 41 50*
1999 *Feb Lingfi (STD) H 12f 41 45*
1998 *Jun Wolver (STD) H 12f 44 46*
1998 *Mar Wolver (STD) C 12f 47*
1998 *Feb Lingfi (SLW) 10f 41*
1997 *Jan Lingfi (STD) H 8f 46 51* <
1996 *Dec Lingfi (STD) H 8f 40 45*
2000 AW 0-1: (12f) (Fibr)
Moderate mare, has broken blood-vessels, effective 10 to 13f, - acts on AW, best on Equi, has worn blinkers, favours left handed tracks. *P D Evans [0-3] J E Abbey (from M J Fetherston-Godley [9-56] Oct 1999).*

SHANNON DORE (IRE) BHB 74f **RR 78f** 4183[11]
3 b f Turtle Island (IRE) - Solas Abu (IRE) (Red Sunset) 8.2f **(63)**
Form - 4080
Record 2000 - 1st:0 2nd:0 3rd:0 Ran:4
Pre2000 - 1st:1 2nd:3 3rd:0 Ran:6
Win Prizemoney £3,947 *Total Prizemoney* £9,271
Wins * 1999 Spt Nottin (GD) 6.1f 78 <
2000 Turf 0-4: (5f, 6f 3) (g-s 2, g-f 2)
Scopey, above-average filly, effective 5 to 6f, best at 6f, acts on gd to frm. Turf high 78. Consistent. *B Hanbury [1-10] B Hanbury.*

SHANNON FLYER (USA) RR 24f 5140[15]
2 br c Irish River (FR) 9f **(77)** - Stormeor (CAN) (Lypheor) 12f **(71)**
Form - 0
Record 2000 - 1st:0 2nd:0 3rd:0 Ran:1
2000 Turf 0-1: (6f) (g-s)
Currently little account colt.
J W Hills [0-1] Freddy Bienstock and Martin Boase.

SHANNON'S DREAM BHB 32f **RR 37f** 5155[11]
4 b m Anshan 8.2f **(63)** - Jenny's Call (Petong) 6.6f **(58)**
Form - 000
Record 2000 - 1st:0 2nd:0 3rd:0 Ran:3
Pre2000 - 1st:0 2nd:0 3rd:0 Ran:2
2000 Turf 0-2: (10f 2) (frm 2) 2000 AW 0-1: (7f) (Equi)
Neat, very moderate filly. Turf high 37 (began Jly).
Mrs Barbara Waring [0-3] Mrs B Taylor (from G M McCourt [0-1] Oct 1998).

SHAPIRO RR 4366[18]
3 ch f Superlative 8.8f **(57)** - Lady Keyser (Le Johnstan) 7.4f **(55)**
Form - 0
Record 2000 - 1st:0 2nd:0 3rd:0 Ran:1
2000 Turf 0-1: (5f) (g-f)
Currently very poor filly. *N P Littmoden [0-1] Paul Sandy.*

SHAPOUR (IRE) BHB 78f **RR 80f** 3416[8]
3 b c Sadler's Wells (USA) 11.3f **(87)** - Sharamana (IRE) **(97+f)** (Darshaan) 9.9f **(84)**
Form - 048
Record 2000 - 1st:0 2nd:0 3rd:0 Ran:3
Pre2000 - 1st:0 2nd:1 3rd:0 Ran:2
Win Prizemoney £0 *Total Prizemoney* £1,749
2000 Turf 0-3: (10f, 12f 2) (gd, g-f, frm)
Well made, decent colt. Turf high 80 - 4th of 10 giving 7lb to Second Paige (17 Jly Windsor 12f frm RF 2876). (DEAD)
Sir Michael Stoute [0-5] H H Aga Khan.

SHARAF (IRE) BHB 47f44a **RR 52df 44a** 4766[6]
7 b g Sadler's Wells (USA) 11.3f **(87)** - Marie de Flandre (FR) (Crystal Palace (FR)) 12.5f **(76)**
Form - P423044726
Record 2000 - 1st:0 2nd:2 3rd:1 Ran:10
Pre2000 - 1st:2 2nd:6 3rd:4 Ran:37
Win Prizemoney £6,918 *Total Prizemoney* £19,963
Wins * 1998 Jly Bath (GD) H 17.2f 47 51
1996 Apr Folkes (G-F) 12f 80+ <
2000 Turf 0-8: (14f, 16f 4, 17f 2, 18f) (g-s 4, gd 3, g-f) 2000 AW 0-2: (16f 2) (Fibr 2)
Fair gelding, has broken blood-vessels, effective 15 to 18f, acts on g-s to g-f - acts on Fibr, best on g-s, has worn blinkers, likes left handed tracks, excels at Chepstow, likes Warwick. Turf high 52 - 4th of 12 giving 19lb to Xellance (6 Jly Chepstow 18f g-f RF 2569). AW high 47 - 4th of 16 giving 22lb to Aquavita (28 Jly Southwell 16f Fibr RF 3192). Stays well, but has a poor strike rate. Seems best on good or faster ground.
W R Muir [1-41] Mrs A E Chapman (from J L Dunlop [1-7] Jly 1996).

SHARAVAWN (IRE) BHB 32f **RR 18f** 1012[10]
3 b f College Chapel - My My Marie (Artaius (USA)) 9f **(69)**
Form - 080060
Record 2000 - 1st:0 2nd:0 3rd:0 Ran:2
Pre2000 - 1st:0 2nd:0 3rd:0 Ran:8
2000 Turf 0-2: (7f, 12f) (g-s, frm)
Unfurnished, little account filly, has worn blinkers. Turf high 18.
Miss A M Newton-Smith [0-2] Tallulah Racing (from N P Littmoden [0-8] Dec 1999).

SHARAZAN (IRE) BHB 52f42a **RR 59f 42a** 2242[12]
7 b g Akarad (FR) 9.7f **(73)** - Sharaniya (USA) (Alleged (USA)) 10f **(76)**
Form - 0300
Record 2000 - 1st:0 2nd:0 3rd:1 Ran:4
Pre2000 - 1st:2 2nd:3 3rd:1 Ran:16
Win Prizemoney £10,960 *Total Prizemoney* £17,164
Wins 1997 Jly Currag (GD) H 16f 94 109 <
1996 May Leopar (GD) 12f 70
2000 Turf 0-4: (16f 2, 18f, 20f) (g-s, gd 3)
Fair gelding, effective 18f, acts on gd, has worn blinkers, likes left handed tracks. Turf high 59 - 3rd of 14 getting 23lb from Eastwell Hall (8 Jun Chepstow 18f gd RF 1804). Inconsistent.
O O'Neill [3-24] Merry Fellows (from J Oxx in IRE [2-9] Aug 1997).

SHARED HARMONY (IRE) RR 60f 4300[10]
2 b c Common Grounds 8.1f **(66)** - Harmer (IRE) (Alzao (USA)) 7.1f **(68)**
Form - 60
Record 2000 - 1st:0 2nd:0 3rd:0 Ran:2
2000 Turf 0-2: (6f 2) (gd 2)
Currently average colt. Turf high 60 (began Aug).
P W Harris [0-2] The Charmers.

SHAREEF RR 95+f 1874[4]
3 b c Shareef Dancer (USA) 10.1f **(67)** - Bustling Nelly (Bustino) 10.4f **(64)**
Form - 1574
Record 2000 - 1st:1 2nd:0 3rd:0 Ran:4
Win Prizemoney £2,782 *Total Prizemoney* £3,848
Wins * 2000 *Feb Southw (STD) 12f 76+* <
2000 Turf 0-3: (6f, 12f 2) (g-s, gd, g-f) 2000 AW 1-1: (12f 1-1) (Fibr 1-1)
Workmanlike, very useful colt. Turf high 95. (1st run). He ran a remarkable race over six furlongs at Lingfield, but probably needs at least a mile and a quarter. Sold for 10,000gns at Newmarket in October, he will be difficult to place off his current mark.
P F I Cole [1-4] H R H Prince Fahd Salman.

SHAREEF KHAN (FR) BHB 65f **RR 71f** 4585[18]

3 b g Alzao (USA) 9.8f **(73)** - Sharenara (USA) (Vaguely Noble) 10.1f **(72)**
Form - 03360
Record 2000 - 1st:0 2nd:0 3rd:2 Ran:5
Pre2000 - 1st:0 2nd:0 3rd:0 Ran:1
Win Prizemoney £0 *Total Prizemoney* £1,034
2000 Turf 0-4: (10f 2, 12f 2) (g-f, frm 2, hrd) 2000 AW 0-1: (12f) (Equi)
Light-framed, above-average gelding, effective 10f, acts on frm, has worn blinkers. Turf high 71 - 3rd of 13 giving 5lb to Janet (19 Jun Windsor 10f frm RF 2108). **N A Graham [0-6] Fieldspring Racing.*

SHARMY (IRE) BHB 100f **RR 100f** 1537[5]

4 b h Caerleon (USA) 10.9f **(79)** - Petticoat Lane (Ela-Mana-Mou) 10.1f **(70)**
Form - 145
Record 2000 - 1st:1 2nd:0 3rd:0 Ran:3
Pre2000 - 1st:1 2nd:1 3rd:0 Ran:2
Win Prizemoney £11,062 *Total Prizemoney* £15,255
Wins * **2000** May Ascot (G-S) 8f 99 <
* 1999 Aug Sandow (G-S) 8.1f 82++
2000 Turf 1-3: (8f 1-2, 10f) (g-s 1-2, gd)
Scopey, very useful colt. Turf high 100 - 5th of 9 getting 8lb from Swallow Flight (29 May Sandown 8f g-s RF 1537) - also 1st of 7 from Cardiff Arms (3 May Ascot RF 1003). Lightly raced, he won well first time out at Ascot but was held in a couple of decent handicaps. Looks to require give in the ground and a truly-run mile. **Sir Michael Stoute [2-5] Saeed Suhail.*

SHAROURA BHB 66f **RR 75df** 5313[14]

4 ch m Inchinor 8.9f **(64)** - Kinkajoo (Precocious) 8.6f **(62)**
Form - 0082000300
Record 2000 - 1st:0 2nd:1 3rd:1 Ran:10
Pre2000 - 1st:2 2nd:1 3rd:0 Ran:11
Win Prizemoney £11,626 *Total Prizemoney* £15,175
Wins 1999 Spt Yarmou (G-F) H 5.2f 76 79
1999 Mar Doncas (G-S) 6f 83 <
2000 Turf 0-10: (5f 5, 6f 4, 7f) (sft, g-s 2, gd, g-f 3, frm 3)
Scopey, above-average filly, effective 5 to 6f, best at 5f, acts on gd to frm. Turf high 75 - 2nd of 7 giving 8lb to Poppy's Song (15 Jly Nottingham 5f frm RF 2842). **D Nicholls [0-10] Manor House Partnership (from K Mahdi [2-11] Oct 1999).*

SHARP ACT (USA) BHB 65f **RR 71f** 5106[10]

2 b br g Alydeed (CAN) 8f **(81)** - Cutty Cabin (CAN) (Vaguely Noble) 10.1f **(72)**
Form - 00550
Record 2000 - 1st:0 2nd:0 3rd:0 Ran:5
2000 Turf 0-5: (5f, 6f 3, 7f) (gd 2, g-f 2, frm)
Above-average gelding. Turf high 71.
**J W Hills [0-5] Wauchope,Sir Simon D Cottam.*

SHARP BELLINE (IRE) BHB 45f52a **RR 54f 52a** 5020[2]

3 b g Robellino (USA) 9.5f **(68)** - Moon Watch (Night Shift (USA)) 7.2f **(69)**
Form - 43404262
Record 2000 - 1st:0 2nd:2 3rd:1 Ran:8
Win Prizemoney £0 *Total Prizemoney* £2,717
2000 Turf 0-6: (8f, 10f 5) (g-s, g-f 3, frm 2) 2000 AW 0-2: (8f, 12f) (Fibr 2)
Scopey, average gelding, effective 10 to 12f, acts on g-f - acts on Fibr, has worn blinkers. Turf high 63. AW high 59 (began Spt) - 2nd of 12 getting 5lb from Mysterium (17 Oct Wolverhampton 12f Fibr RF 5020).
**J L Harris [0-6] Townville C C Racing Club (from M Johnston [0-2] Jly 2000).*

SHARP EDGE BOY BHB 46f37a **RR 48f 37a** 5122[21]

4 gr g Mystiko (USA) 7.7f **(59)** - Leap Castle (Never so Bold) 6.3f **(66)**
Form - 088770020070
Record 2000 - 1st:0 2nd:1 3rd:0 Ran:12
Pre2000 - 1st:2 2nd:1 3rd:3 Ran:22
Win Prizemoney £5,748 *Total Prizemoney* £9,233
Wins * 1999 Jun Haydoc (G-S) H 7.1f 62 66 <
* 1999 Mar Hamilt (HVY) H 6f 56 59
2000 Turf 0-10: (5f, 6f 6, 7f 3) (hvy, sft, g-s 2, gd 2, g-f, frm 3) 2000 AW 0-2: (6f 2) (Fibr 2)
Workmanlike, moderate gelding, effective 6 to 7f, best at 6f, acts on sft to frm, best on frm, has worn blinkers. Turf high 48. AW high 36. Becoming disappointing. **E J Alston [2-34] N Gilbert & A Shandley.*

SHARP GOSSIP (IRE) BHB 62f63a **RR 61+f 63a** 5185[1]

4 b g College Chapel - Idle Gossip (Runnett) 7f **(59)**
Form - 000072211
Record 2000 - 1st:2 2nd:2 3rd:0 Ran:9
Pre2000 - 1st:0 2nd:3 3rd:1 Ran:10
Win Prizemoney £9,604 *Total Prizemoney* £14,973
Wins * **2000** Oct Yarmou (SFT) H 7f 56 61
* **2000** *Oct Southw (STD) H 8f 56 62+* <
2000 Turf 1-8: (6f 4, 7f 1-1, 8f 3) (sft, g-s 1-2, g-f 2, frm 3) 2000 AW 1-1: (8f 1-1) (Fibr 1-1)
Average gelding, effective 6 to 8f, acts on hvy to frm - acts on Fibr, best on g-s, has worn blinkers, likes left handed tracks, likes Curragh. Turf high 61 - 1st of 17 giving 7lb to Sand Hawk (25 Oct Yarmouth RF 5185). (1st run) - 1st of 15 getting 4lb from Haunt The Zoo (16 Oct Southwell RF 5006).
**J A R Toller [2-9] Buckingham Thoroughbreds I (from D Gillespie in IRE [0-10] Oct 1999).*

SHARP HAT BHB 72f60a **RR 73f 60a** 5313[8]

6 ch g Shavian 7.7f **(67)** - Madam Trilby (Grundy) 10.3f **(65)**
Form - 1300342447205261163032303O8
Record 2000 - 1st:2 2nd:4 3rd:5 Ran:23
Pre2000 - 1st:4 2nd:3 3rd:3 Ran:40
Win Prizemoney £30,918 *Total Prizemoney* £62,875
Wins * **2000** Jly Ayr (G-F) H 5f 65 69
* **2000** Jly Newcas (G-F) H 5f 57 67
* 1999 *Nov Lingfi (STD) H 5f 57 58*
1997 May Newbur (SFT) H 6f 85 90 <
1996 Spt Doncas (G-F) H 6f 78 83
1996 Aug Warwic (GD) H 6f 70 67
2000 Turf 2-17: (5f 2-13, 6f 4) (g-s 3, gd 1-6, g-f 7, frm 1-1) 2000 AW 0-6: (6f 6) (Equi, Fibr 5)
Above-average gelding, effective 5 to 6f, best at 5f, acts on g-s to frm, has worn blinkers, excels at Haydock. Turf high 73 - 3rd of 17 giving 5lb to Polly Golightly (23 Spt Haydock 5f gd RF 4605) - also 1st of 9 getting 10lb from Xanadu (17 Jly Ayr RF 2873). AW high 60. Ended a long losing run on the Lingfield Equitrack at the end of '99 and continued to run well afterwards, if always finding one or two too good. Suddenly hit form in July with victories on fast ground over the minimum trip at Newcastle and Ayr.
**D W Chapman [3-27] Miss N F Thesiger (from T J Etherington [0-9] Oct 1999).*

SHARPINCH RR 57f 4725[6]

2 b c Beveled (USA) 6.9f **(64)** - Giant Nipper **(45f)** (Nashwan (USA))
Form - 6
Record 2000 - 1st:0 2nd:0 3rd:0 Ran:1
2000 Turf 0-1: (6f) (gd)
Currently fair colt. **P R Chamings [0-1] Mrs Ann Jenkins.*

SHARP LIFE (USA) BHB 75f **RR 77f** 2756[5]

3 b c Diesis 9f **(80)** - Liteup My Life (USA) (Green Dancer (USA)) 10.3f **(74)**
Form - 855
Record 2000 - 1st:0 2nd:0 3rd:0 Ran:3
2000 Turf 0-3: (6f, 8f, 10f) (gd, frm 2)
Scopey, currently above-average colt. Turf high 77.
**H R A Cecil [0-3] The Thoroughbred Corporation.*

SHARP MONKEY BHB 35f39a **RR 39a** 2923[9]

5 b g Man Among Men (IRE) 8f **(47)** - Sharp Thistle (Sharpo) 7.7f **(59)**
Form - 0
Record 2000 - 1st:0 2nd:0 3rd:0 Ran:1
Pre2000 - 1st:2 2nd:4 3rd:4 Ran:34
Win Prizemoney £4,171 *Total Prizemoney* £7,394
Wins 1998 *Feb Southw (STD) SH 8f 54 63* <
1998 *Jan Southw (STD) C 8f 63* <
2000 Turf 0-1: (12f) (frm)
Moderate gelding, effective 8f, - acts on Fibr, mostly wears blinkers. Inconsistent. **G M Moore [0-8] Anmaf Partnership (from Mrs N Macauley [2-34] Mar 1999).*

SHARP PEARL BHB 48f50a **RR 45f 50a** 5242[22]

7 ch g Sharpo 7.5f **(68)** - Silent Pearl (USA) (Silent Screen (USA)) 8.6f

(65)
Form - 0
Record 2000 - 1st:0 2nd:0 3rd:0 Ran:1
Pre2000 - 1st:3 2nd:3 3rd:4 Ran:40
Win Prizemoney £9,944 *Total Prizemoney* £17,691
Wins 1997 Aug Newmar (G-F) H 5f 77 79 <
1997 Apr Bright (FRM) H 5.3f 70 75
1996 Jun Bright (FRM) H 5.3f 70 75
2000 Turf 0-1: (7f) (g-s)
Fair gelding, often wears blinkers.
**S P C Woods [0-1] Dennis Yardy (from D J S Cosgrove [0-7] Apr 1999).*

SHARP PLAY BHB 100f **RR 103f** 4464^{6}

5 b g Robellino (USA) 9.5f **(68)** - Child's Play (USA) (Sharpen Up) 8.3f **(67)**
Form - 1042041006
Record 2000 - 1st:2 2nd:1 3rd:0 Ran:10
Pre2000 - 1st:4 2nd:1 3rd:1 Ran:10
Win Prizemoney £62,870 *Total Prizemoney* £85,092
Wins * **2000** Aug Goodwo (G-F) H 9.9f 96 101
* **2000** May Pontef (GD) C 8f 62++
* 1998 May Thirsk (G-F) 8f 109 <
* 1998 May Dielsd (G-S) 8f 85
* 1998 Apr Ripon (SFT) 9f 93
* 1997 Jly York (GD) 7f 80+
2000 Turf 2-10: (8f 1-3, 9f, 10f 1 6) (gd 6, g-f 2-4, frm)
Very useful gelding, effective 10f, acts on gd to g-f, best on g-f. Turf high 103 - 6th of 17 giving 18lb to Komistar (16 Spt Newbury 10f g-f RF 4464) - also 1st of 11 giving 7lb to Prairie Wolf (1 Aug Goodwood RF 3277). A useful handicapper, he finished fast to land a valuable handicap at Glorious Goodwood, although he was beaten there over a shorter trip two days later. Held off higher marks subsequently. **M Johnston [6-20] Mrs I Bird.*

SHARP REBUFF BHB 65f60a **RR 82df 60a** 4934^{30}

9 b h Reprimand 8.2f **(63)** - Kukri (Kris) 9.5f **(73)**
Form - 80
Record 2000 - 1st:0 2nd:0 3rd:0 Ran:2
Pre2000 - 1st:5 2nd:6 3rd:5 Ran:38
Win Prizemoney £21,511 *Total Prizemoney* £40,293
Wins 1998 Jun Sandow (G-S) H 7.1f 85 90 <
* 1997 Jun Warwic (GD) H 8f 79 83
* 1996 Jly Kempto (GD) H 8f 74 81
2000 Turf 0-2: (8f 2) (sft, gd)
Decent horse, effective 7 to 8f, acts on gd to g-f. Turf high 67. Becoming disappointing. **P J Makin [5-40] D M Ahier.*

SHARP RISK BHB 67f57a **RR 78f 57a** 2778^{5}

3 ch c Risk Me (FR) 8f **(53)** - Dara Dee (Dara Monarch) 8.8f **(59)**
Form - 530025
Record 2000 - 1st:0 2nd:1 3rd:1 Ran:6
Win Prizemoney £0 *Total Prizemoney* £1,048
2000 Turf 0-2: (8f, 10f) (gd, frm) 2000 AW 0-4: (8f 2, 9f, 11f) (Equi 2, Fibr 2)
Leggy, above-average colt. Turf high 78. AW high 53. **P Howling [0-6] R N Khan.*

SHARP SCOTCH BHB 50f65a **RR 53f 65a** 4745^{8}

7 b g Sharpo 7.5f **(68)** - Scotch Thistle (Sassafras (FR)) 9.6f **(69)**
Form - 8
Record 2000 - 1st:0 2nd:0 3rd:0 Ran:1
Pre2000 - 1st:6 2nd:1 3rd:4 Ran:27
Win Prizemoney £14,682 *Total Prizemoney* £16,515
Wins * 1999 *Mar Southw (STD) H 8f* 79 84 <
* 1999 *Feb Southw (STD) H 8f* 75 75
* 1999 *Jan Southw (STD) H 8f* 62 73
* 1999 *Jan Southw (STD) H 8f* 62 69
1998 *Nov Wolver (STD) H 9.4f* 57 59
1998 Jun Naas (SFT) H 8f 54 76
2000 Turf 0-1: (8f) (gd)
Fair gelding, effective 8f, - acts on Fibr, has worn blinkers, prefers left handed tracks, prefers tight tracks.
**D Carroll [4-15] J J Devaney (from D Carroll [1-3] Dec 1998).*

SHARP SECRET (IRE) BHB 72f **RR 75f** 4293^{10}

2 b f College Chapel - State Treasure (USA) (Secretariat (USA)) 9f **(79)**
Form - 5251220
Record 2000 - 1st:1 2nd:3 3rd:0 Ran:7
Win Prizemoney £3,575 *Total Prizemoney* £7,017
Wins * **2000** Aug Windso (GD) H 6f 62 75+ <
2000 Turf 1-6: (6f 1-5, 7f) (g-f 1-4, frm 2) 2000 AW 0-1: (5f) (Fibr)
Above-average filly, effective 6 to 7f, best at 6f, acts on g-f to frm, best on g-f. Turf high 75 (began Jly) - 1st of 10 getting 8lb from Quizzical Lady (14 Aug Windsor RF 3635). Won decisively on her nursery debut, but failed to handle the track when runner-up at Catterick four days later. **M Johnston [1-7] T T Bloodstocks.*

SHARP SHUFFLE (IRE) BHB 60f50a **RR 63f 50a** 4997^{10}

7 ch g Exactly Sharp (USA) 8.4f **(66)** - Style (Homing) 7.8f **(59)**
Form - 11027240023210 0
Record 2000 - 1st:1 2nd:4 3rd:1 Ran:12
Pre2000 - 1st:7 2nd:11 3rd:7 Ran:50
Win Prizemoney £25,705 *Total Prizemoney* £47,283
Wins * **2000** Aug Chepst (G-F) S 7.1f 56
* 1999 *Dec Wolver (STD) S 8.5f 47*
* 1999 *Nov Wolver (STD) S 7f 53*
1998 Aug Newmar (G-F) C 7f 71+
1998 Jly Newmar (G-F) S 8f 61
1997 Jun Goodwo (G-F) H 8f 75 78+ <
1997 Apr Bright (FRM) 8f 74
1996 Spt Kempto (GD) H 7f 68 74
2000 Turf 1-6: (6f, 7f 1-2, 8f 3) (hvy, g-f 3, frm 1-2) 2000 AW 0-6: (7f, 8f 5) (Fibr 6)
Average gelding, effective 7 to 8f, best at 7f, acts on g-f to frm - acts on Fibr, best on frm, does well at Wolverhampton. Turf high 63 - 2nd of 19 giving 2lb to My Emily (13 Jun Salisbury 7f g-f RF 1918) - also 1st of 12 from Zeppo (10 Aug Chepstow RF 3526). AW high 56 (1st run) - 2nd of 6 to Internal Affair (4 Jan Wolverhampton 8f Fibr RF 0017). Inconsistent. **Ian Williams [3-17] G A Gilbert (from Miss S J Wilton [0-3] Jan 2000).*

SHARP SMOKE BHB 21f **RR ?f** 2467^{14}

3 gr f Cigar 6.3f **(43)** - Abrasive (Absalom) 7.2f **(58)**
Form - 670
Record 2000 - 1st:0 2nd:0 3rd:0 Ran:3
Pre2000 - 1st:0 2nd:0 3rd:0 Ran:1
Win Prizemoney £0 *Total Prizemoney* £190
2000 Turf 0-2: (5f, 6f) (gd, frm) 2000 AW 0-1: (6f) (Fibr)
Leggy, very poor filly. **D W Barker [0-4] Mrs S J Barker.*

SHARP SPICE BHB 58f53a **RR 59f 53a** 5227^{3}

4 b m Lugana Beach 7f **(63)** - Ewar Empress (IRE) **(11f 35a)** (Persian Bold) 9.3f **(66)**
Form - 44452553031403
Record 2000 - 1st:1 2nd:1 3rd:3 Ran:14
Pre2000 - 1st:1 2nd:0 3rd:2 Ran:14
Win Prizemoney £8,724 *Total Prizemoney* £15,903
Wins * **2000** Spt Epsom (GD) H 12f 53 59 <
* 1999 Aug Goodwo (GD) H 9.9f 55 58
2000 Turf 1-13: (10f 9, 11f, 12f 1-3) (sft, g-s, gd 4, g-f 1-3, frm 3, hrd) 2000 AW 0-1: (12f) (Equi)
Light-framed, fair filly, effective 10 to 12f, acts on sft to hrd, has worn blinkers, likes left handed tracks, prefers tight tracks, excels at Haydock and Folkestone and Epsom. Turf high 59 - 1st of 22 getting 22lb from Batswing (6 Spt Epsom RF 4269). Pretty consistent in ordinary handicap company, often making the frame, but ended quite a long losing run when scoring at Epsom in September.
**D J Coakley [2-25] The Nags Head Racing Syndicate (from Lord Huntingdon [0-3] Nov 1998).*

SHARP STEEL BHB 45f54a **RR 26f 54a** 4763^{9}

5 ch g Beveled (USA) 6.9f **(64)** - Shift Over (USA) (Night Shift (USA)) 7.2f **(69)**
Form - 2562125320
Record 2000 - 1st:1 2nd:3 3rd:1 Ran:9
Pre2000 - 1st:1 2nd:2 3rd:1 Ran:12
Win Prizemoney £3,868 *Total Prizemoney* £7,601
Wins * **2000** *May Southw (STD) S 8f 60*
1998 *Mar Southw (STD) S 7f 61* <
2000 AW 1-9: (7f 4, 8f 1-3, 9f, 11f) (Fibr 1-9)
Average gelding, effective 7 to 8f, best at 8f, - acts on Fibr, has worn blinkers. AW high 60 - 1st of 16 from Canadian Approval (26 May Southwell RF 1480).

**Miss S J Wilton [1-15] John Pointon and Sons (from G L Moore [1-6] Mar 1998).*

SHARP STEPPER BHB 84f **RR 85f** 4936[13]
4 b m Selkirk (USA) 7.9f **(76)** - Awtaar (USA) **(35df)** (Lyphard (USA)) 9.9f **(72)**
Form - 1362140
Record 2000 - 1st:1 2nd:1 3rd:1 Ran:6
Pre2000 - 1st:1 2nd:1 3rd:2 Ran:8
Win Prizemoney £21,443 *Total Prizemoney* £28,063
Wins * **2000** Spt York (GD) H 13.9f 78 83 <
* 1999 *Nov Southw (STD) 12f* 66++
2000 Turf 1-6: (12f 3, 13f, 14f 1-1, 15f) (gd 2, g-f 1-3, frm)
Scopey, useful filly, effective 10 to 15f, best at 12f, acts on gd to frm, best on g-f. Turf high 85 - 4th of 18 getting 3lb from Flossy (26 Spt Newmarket 12f g-f RF 4647) - also 1st of 12 getting 12lb from Montalcino (3 Spt York RF 4197). A winner on Fibresand last year, he made a bleated return to action and eventually regained winning form over 14 furlongs at York in September. Likely to stay further, and appreciates a galloping track.
**J H M Gosden [2-14] Mrs Diane Snowden.*

SHARP VISION (IRE) RR 32f 5067[10]
2 b f Eagle Eyed (USA) - Day Dress (Ashmore (FR)) 8.5f **(65)**
Form - 80
Record 2000 - 1st:0 2nd:0 3rd:0 Ran:2
2000 Turf 0-2: (5f, 6f) (g-s, frm)
Currently very moderate filly. Turf high 32 (began Jly).
**J S Moore [0-2] Ernie Houghton.*

SHARVIE BHB 38f43a **RR 44f 43a** 3374[10]
3 b g Rock Hopper 10.6f **(54)** - Heresheis (Free State) 8.7f **(61)**
Form - 0060
Record 2000 - 1st:0 2nd:0 3rd:0 Ran:4
Pre2000 - 1st:0 2nd:0 3rd:0 Ran:1
2000 Turf 0-4: (10f, 14f, 16f 2) (gd, g-f 2, frm)
Workmanlike, moderate gelding. Turf high 44.
**J Pearce [0-5] Mrs Jennifer Marsh.*

SHARWAY LADY BHB 36f39a **RR 44f 39a** 323[6]
5 b m Shareef Dancer (USA) 10.1f **(67)** - Eladale (IRE) (Ela-Mana-Mou) 10.1f **(70)**
Form - 66
Record 2000 - 1st:0 2nd:0 3rd:0 Ran:2
Pre2000 - 1st:1 2nd:1 3rd:0 Ran:12
Win Prizemoney £1,738 *Total Prizemoney* £2,421
Wins 1998 *Jan Southw (STD) S 8f* 60 <
2000 AW 0-2: (9f, 12f) (Fibr 2)
Moderate filly, mostly wears blinkers. AW high 21. Becoming disappointing.
**S A Brookshaw [1-11] Sharway Contracts (from B A McMahon [1-12] Apr 1998).*

SHATHER (IRE) BHB 74f **RR 79f** 4753[10]
3 b br c Goofalik (USA) 15.4f **(66)** - Western Pride (GER) (Priamos (GER)) 11.1f **(61)**
Form - 03432250
Record 2000 - 1st:0 2nd:2 3rd:2 Ran:8
Win Prizemoney £0 *Total Prizemoney* £4,709
2000 Turf 0-7: (7f 5, 8f, 9f) (g-s, gd, g-f 2, frm 3) 2000 AW 0-1: (8f) (Fibr)
Workmanlike, above-average colt, effective 7f, acts on g-f to frm, best on frm. Turf high 81. **J W Hills [0-8] Ziad Galadari.*

SHATIN BEAUTY BHB 41f **RR 37f** 5188[9]
3 b f Mistertopogigo (IRE) - Starisk **(33f)** (Risk Me (FR)) 5.9f **(53)**
Form - 0000000
Record 2000 - 1st:0 2nd:0 3rd:0 Ran:7
Pre2000 - 1st:1 2nd:1 3rd:0 Ran:6
Win Prizemoney £2,737 *Total Prizemoney* £3,991
Wins * 1999 Jly Hamilt (FRM) 5f 69 <
2000 Turf 0-7: (5f 6, 6f) (sft, gd 3, g-f, frm 2)
Scopey, very moderate filly, effective 5f, acts on g-f to frm, best on frm. Turf high 39.
**Miss L A Perratt [1-13] Shatin Racing Group.*

SHATIN DOLLYBIRD (IRE) BHB 72f **RR 73f** 4697[13]
2 ch f Up and At 'em - Pumpona (USA) (Sharpen Up) 8.3f **(67)**
Form - 223318340
Record 2000 - 1st:1 2nd:2 3rd:3 Ran:9
Win Prizemoney £2,843 *Total Prizemoney* £6,397
Wins * **2000** Jly Hamilt (G-F) 5f 73 <
2000 Turf 1-9: (5f 1-8, 6f) (gd, g-f 1-5, frm 3)
Above-average filly, effective 5 to 6f, best at 5f, acts on gd to frm, best on frm, excels at Hamilton. Turf high 73 - 4th of 9 getting 6lb from Nifty Alice (31 Aug Musselburgh 5f frm RF 4120) - also 1st of 4 getting 3lb from Miss Verity (21 Jly Hamilton RF 2991).
**Miss L A Perratt [1-9] Shatin Racing Group.*

SHATIN LAW (IRE) RR 24f 1070[10]
2 b c Case Law 6f **(64)** - Janet Oliphant (Red Sunset) 8.2f **(63)**
Form - 0
Record 2000 - 1st:0 2nd:0 3rd:0 Ran:1
2000 Turf 0-1: (5f) (g-f)
Currently little account colt.
**Miss L A Perratt [0-1] Shatin Racing Group.*

SHATIN PLAYBOY (IRE) BHB 68f **RR 63f** 5296[7]
2 ch c Goldmark (USA) - Skinity (Rarity) 10.1f **(60)**
Form - 4472057
Record 2000 - 1st:0 2nd:1 3rd:0 Ran:7
Win Prizemoney £0 *Total Prizemoney* £1,723
2000 Turf 0-7: (5f, 6f 2, 7f 4) (hvy 2, g-s, gd 3, frm)
Average colt, effective 7f, acts on gd. Turf high 63 (began Jly).
**Miss L A Perratt [0-7] T P Finch.*

SHATIN VENTURE (IRE) BHB 87f **RR 97f** 4150[1]
3 b c Lake Coniston (IRE) - Justitia (Dunbeath (USA)) 7.8f **(70)**
Form - 3000501
Record 2000 - 1st:1 2nd:0 3rd:1 Ran:7
Pre2000 - 1st:1 2nd:1 3rd:0 Ran:4
Win Prizemoney £10,130 *Total Prizemoney* £16,373
Wins * **2000** Spt Haydoc (SFT) 6f 61+
* 1999 May Ayr (GD) 5f 91+ <
2000 Turf 1-7: (5f 2, 6f 1-2, 7f 3) (g-s 1-1, g-f 3, frm 3)
Well made, very useful colt, effective 5 to 7f, acts on gd to g-f. Turf high 97 (1st run) - 3rd of 17 giving 15lb to Rendition (16 May York 7f g-f RF 1217). An imposing individual, he seemed to appreciate soft ground when winning at Haydock in September. Worth another try over seven furlongs, he goes well fresh and is one to keep an eye on this spring. **Miss L A Perratt [2-11] Shatin Racing Group.*

SHATTERED SILENCE (USA) BHB 70f **RR 75f** 5058[4]
3 b f Cozzene (USA) 10.1f **(87)** - Sunday Bazaar (USA) (Nureyev (USA)) 8.7f **(78)**
Form - 733334
Record 2000 - 1st:0 2nd:0 3rd:4 Ran:6
Win Prizemoney £0 *Total Prizemoney* £2,806
2000 Turf 0-6: (8f, 10f 2, 11f, 12f 2) (sft, gd, g-f 2, frm 2)
Workmanlike, above-average filly, effective 10 to 12f, acts on g-f to frm, has worn blinkers. Turf high 75 - 3rd of 9 getting 5lb from Takwin (19 Jly Kempton 12f frm RF 2938). She has shown some ability, but looks short of toe and probably still needs more time.
**R Charlton [0-6] K Abdulla.*

SHATZ RR 2583a[2]
2 b c General Monash (USA) - Mandalika (USA) (Arctic Tern (USA)) 8.9f **(69)**
Form - 2
Record 2000 - 1st:0 2nd:1 3rd:0 Ran:1
Win Prizemoney £0 *Total Prizemoney* £2,863
2000 Turf 0-1: (6f) (g-f)
Currently unrated colt - 2nd of 5 to Royal Hawk (2 Jly San Siro 6f g-f RF 2583a). **L M Cumani [0-1].*

SHAW VENTURE BHB 38f54a **RR 53f 54a** 4877[14]
3 ch g Whittingham (IRE) - Al Shany (Burslem) 8.8f **(53)**
Form - 60675630
Record 2000 - 1st:0 2nd:0 3rd:1 Ran:8
Pre2000 - 1st:1 2nd:0 3rd:0 Ran:9
Win Prizemoney £2,827 *Total Prizemoney* £3,154
Wins * 1999 Jly Windso (G-F) 5f 73 <
2000 Turf 0-6: (7f, 8f 2, 10f 2, 12f) (g-s, g-f 2, frm 2, hrd) 2000 AW 0-2: (5f, 6f) (Fibr 2)

Scopey, fair gelding, effective 5f, acts on frm, has worn blinkers. Turf high 53. AW high 30. **B Palling [1-17] Mrs M M Palling.*

SHAYADI (IRE) RR 91f
4066a[1]

3 b c Kahyasi 12.9f **(74)** - Shayrdia **00**
Form - 2421
2000 Turf 1-4: (7f, 9f, 10f 1-2) (sft, gd, g-f, frm 1-1)
Useful colt. Turf high 91 - also 1st of 8 giving 5lb to Alexander Eliott (21 Aug Roscommon RF 4066a).
**J Oxx in IRE [1-4] H H Aga Khan.*

SHAYZAN (USA) BHB 48f50a RR 57df 50a
2012[12]

3 b c Shadeed (USA) 7.7f **(72)** - Espuela (USA) (Gone West (USA)) 6.5f **(75)**
Form - 46070

Record 2000 - 1st:0 2nd:0 3rd:0 Ran:3
Pre2000 - 1st:0 2nd:0 3rd:0 Ran:4
Win Prizemoney £0 *Total Prizemoney* £193
2000 Turf 0-2: (7f 2) (gd, g-f) 2000 AW 0-1: (7f) (Equi)
Workmanlike, fair colt. Turf high 32.
**W R Muir [0-7] Fayzad Thoroughbred Ltd.*

SHEARWATER BHB 65a RR
4653[1]

3 b f Shareef Dancer (USA) 10.1f **(67)** - Sea Ballad (USA) (Bering) 7.4f **(61)**
Form -
Record 2000 - 1st:1 2nd:0 3rd:0 Ran:0
Win Prizemoney £1,932 *Total Prizemoney* £1,932
Wins * 2000 *Spt Southw (STD) S* 7f 78+ <
2000 Turf 0-5: (g-s, frm 3, hrd) 2000 AW 1-1: (Fibr 1-1)
Above-average colt, - acts on Fibr. Turf high 63. (1st run) - 1st of 16 from Caliban (26 Spt Southwell RF 4653).
**B W Hills [1-6] R J Arculli.*

SHEBEG RR 38f
2940[10]

3 ch f Rudimentary (USA) 8.2f **(66)** - Oakbrook Tern (USA) (Arctic Tern (USA)) 8.9f **(69)**
Form - 0
Record 2000 - 1st:0 2nd:0 3rd:0 Ran:1
Pre2000 - 1st:0 2nd:0 3rd:0 Ran:1
2000 AW 0-1: (7f) (Equi)
Neat, currently very moderate filly. **Mrs L C Jewell [0-2] I C Wallond.*

SHEEP STEALER BHB 54f26a RR 48?f 26a
46[10]

12 gr g Absalom 7.1f **(56)** - Kilroe's Calin (Be Friendly) 9.3f **(53)**
Form - 0
Record 2000 - 1st:0 2nd:0 3rd:0 Ran:1
Pre2000 - 1st:0 2nd:0 3rd:0 Ran:9
2000 AW 0-1: (16f) (Equi)
Moderate gelding. Becoming disappointing.
**R E Peacock [1-27] R E Peacock.*

SHEER FACE BHB 60f52a RR 62f 52a
5072[5]

6 b g Midyan (USA) 9.9f **(64)** - Rock Face (Ballad Rock) 7.8f **(63)**
Form - 56548133501225
Record 2000 - 1st:2 2nd:2 3rd:2 Ran:14
Pre2000 - 1st:3 2nd:4 3rd:5 Ran:39
Win Prizemoney £19,270 *Total Prizemoney* £34,961
Wins * 2000 Aug Bright (GD) H 10f 53 59
* 2000 May Bright (FRM) C 10f 46
* 1998 Jun Goodwo (G-F) H 8f 69 74
* 1996 Spt Bath (G-F) H 8f 86 90 <
* 1996 Aug Bright (FRM) 7f 81+
2000 Turf 2-10: (8f, 10f 2-9) (g-s, gd 3, g-f 2-3, frm 3) 2000 AW 0-4: (8f 2, 9f, 11f) (Equi, Fibr 3)
Average gelding, effective 8f, acts on g-f to frm, best on frm, has worn blinkers, prefers left handed tracks, favours tight tracks, does well at Bath, excels at Brighton. Turf high 62. AW high 55.
**W R Muir [5-53] A J de V Patrick.*

SHEER FOCUS (IRE) BHB 64f64a RR 63f 64a
4653[1]

2 b c Eagle Eyed (USA) - Persian Danser (IRE) **(58f)** (Persian Bold) 9.3f **(66)**
Form - 057671
Record 2000 - 1st:1 2nd:0 3rd:0 Ran:6
Win Prizemoney £1,932 *Total Prizemoney* £1,932
Wins * 2000 *Spt Southw (STD) S* 7f 78+ <
2000 Turf 0-5: (6f 4, 7f) (g-s, frm 3, hrd) 2000 AW 1-1: (7f 1-1) (Fibr 1-1)
Above-average colt, effective 7f, - acts on Fibr. Turf high 63. (1st run) - 1st of 16 from Caliban (26 Spt Southwell RF 4653).
**B W Hills [1-6] R J Arculli.*

SHEER NATIVE BHB 60f69a RR 46f 69a
6[9]

4 b m In The Wings 11.2f **(77)** - Native Magic (Be My Native (USA)) 10.2f **(71)**
Form - 130
Record 2000 - 1st:0 2nd:0 3rd:0 Ran:1
Pre2000 - 1st:2 2nd:0 3rd:2 Ran:10
Win Prizemoney £4,686 *Total Prizemoney* £5,467
Wins 1999 *Nov Southw (STD) S* 8f 51+
1999 *Mar Lingfi (STD)* 10f 64++ <
2000 AW 0-1: (12f) (Equi)
Unfurnished, above-average filly, effective 10 to 12f, best at 10f, - acts on Equi, prefers tight tracks. Inconsistent.
**Miss Gay Kelleway [0-2] & Mrs Gary Pinchen (from B W Hills [2-9] Nov 1999).*

SHEERNESS ESSITY BHB 55f49a RR 63?f 49a
111[7]

3 b f Fraam - Reclusive (Sunley Builds)
Form - 887
Record 2000 - 1st:0 2nd:0 3rd:0 Ran:2
Pre2000 - 1st:1 2nd:1 3rd:0 Ran:7
Win Prizemoney £1,966 *Total Prizemoney* £2,926
Wins 1999 *Oct Wolver (STD) S* 8.5f 61 <
2000 AW 0-2: (8f 2) (Fibr 2)
Neat, average filly, effective 7 to 8f, best at 8f, acts on gd - acts on Fibr, has worn blinkers, favours left handed tracks, favours tight tracks. AW high 13. Becoming disappointing.
**M Dods [0-4] C A Lynch (from M R Channon [1-5] Oct 1999).*

SHEER PASSION BHB 72f RR 63f
4293[11]

2 b c Distant Relative 7f **(69)** - Yldizlar (Star Appeal) 9.6f **(65)**
Form - 800
Record 2000 - 1st:0 2nd:0 3rd:0 Ran:3
2000 Turf 0-3: (6f 3) (g-f 2, frm)
Currently average colt. Turf high 63 (began Aug).
**B W Hills [0-3] R J Arculli.*

SHEER SPIRIT (IRE) BHB 76f RR 86f
4485[9]

3 b f Caerleon (USA) 10.9f **(79)** - Sheer Audacity (Troy) 10.4f **(68)**
Form - 3140
Record 2000 - 1st:1 2nd:0 3rd:1 Ran:4
Win Prizemoney £4,186 *Total Prizemoney* £5,321
Wins * 2000 Jly Newmar (GD) 12f 81 <
2000 Turf 1-4: (8f, 12f 1-2, 14f) (g-s, g-f 1-1, frm 2)
Scopey, useful filly. Turf high 86 - also 1st of 5 getting 5lb from Shair (28 Jly Newmarket RF 3179). Won a twelve-furlong maiden on her second start. Like her half-brother Pelder, she could relish soft ground. **D R C Elsworth [1-4] Mrs Max Morris.*

SHEER TENBY (IRE) BHB 72f76a RR 72f 76a
1719[7]

3 b c Tenby 10.4f **(76)** - Take My Pledge (IRE) (Ahonoora) 8.1f **(73)**
Form - 40167
Record 2000 - 1st:1 2nd:0 3rd:0 Ran:5
Win Prizemoney £4,803 *Total Prizemoney* £5,379
Wins * 2000 *Feb Cagnes (STD)* 10f 68 <
2000 Turf 0-3: (10f 3) (g-s, gd 2) 2000 AW 1-2: (8f, 10f 1-1) (Fibr, Dirt 1-1)
Above-average colt. Turf high 72. AW high 68 - 1st of 12 from Field Master (23 Feb Cagnes-sur-mer RF 0397a). **R W Armstrong [1-5] R J Arculli.*

SHEER VIKING (IRE) BHB 93f RR 100f
5109[5]

4 b g Danehill (USA) 9.1f **(79)** - Schlefalora (Mas Media)
Form - 223200058475
Record 2000 - 1st:0 2nd:3 3rd:1 Ran:12
Pre2000 - 1st:2 2nd:2 3rd:1 Ran:14
Win Prizemoney £34,133 *Total Prizemoney* £75,398
Wins * 1998 Spt Doncas (GD) G2 5f 105 <
* 1998 May Newmar (G-S) 5f 90+
2000 Turf 0-12: (5f 8, 6f 4) (g-s 2, gd 6, g-f, frm 3)
Scopey, very useful gelding, effective 5 to 6f, best at 5f, acts on g-s to frm, has worn blinkers. Turf high 100 - 2nd of 19 giving 12lb to

Indian Spark (27 May Haydock 5f g-s RF 1489). Gelded over the winter, he put up some encouraging displays early on in the season but then seemed to lose his form. Much better efforts in the autumn, however. **B W Hills [2-26] R J Arculli.*

SHEPHERDS REST (IRE) BHB 37f42a RR 40f 42a 1204[10]

8 b g Accordion 11.3f **(75)** - Mandy's Last (Krayyan) 8.5f **(49)**
Form - 0
Record 2000 - 1st:0 2nd:0 3rd:0 Ran:1
Pre2000 - 1st:0 2nd:3 3rd:3 Ran:14
Win Prizemoney £0 *Total Prizemoney* £3,180
2000 AW 0-1: (14f) (Fibr)
Moderate gelding, effective 12 to 15f, acts on hvy to gd - acts on Fibr, has worn blinkers. Inconsistent. **S Mellor [6-56] The Odd Dozen.*

SHEPPARD'S WATCH BHB 103f RR 94f 3788[9]

2 b f Night Shift (USA) 8.1f **(73)** - Sheppard's Cross **(83f)** (Soviet Star (USA))
Form - 4110
Record 2000 - 1st:2 2nd:0 3rd:0 Ran:4
Win Prizemoney £10,731 *Total Prizemoney* £11,061
Wins * 2000 Aug Haydoc (GD) 6f 94 <
*** 2000** Aug Goodwo (G-F) 6f 82
2000 Turf 2-4: (5f 2, 6f 2-2) (gd 2-2, g-f 2)
Useful filly. Turf high 94 (began Jly) - 1st of 8 giving 3lb to Alinga (12 Aug Haydock RF 3582). She looked good when winning twice over six furlongs in August, but struggled when dropped back to the minimum trip. Likely to be happier over seven furlongs, she could yet make a mark in Group company.
**M P Tregoning [2-4] Major & Mrs R B Kennard and Partners.*

SHERATON HEIGHTS BHB 40f RR 43f 4877[10]

3 b f Deploy 11.4f **(67)** - Norbella (Nordico (USA)) 6.5f **(62)**
Form - 87700
Record 2000 - 1st:0 2nd:0 3rd:0 Ran:5
Pre2000 - 1st:0 2nd:0 3rd:0 Ran:3
2000 Turf 0-5: (7f, 8f, 10f 3) (g-s 2, g-f, frm 2)
Unfurnished, moderate filly. Turf high 43 (began Jly). Inconsistent.
**B R Millman [0-5] Philip Harvey (from K R Burke [0-3] Oct 1999).*

SHEREKIYA (IRE) RR 73f 4889[5]

2 b f Lycius (USA) 8.8f **(71)** - Sheriya (USA) (Green Dancer (USA)) 10.3f **(74)**
Form - 55
Record 2000 - 1st:0 2nd:0 3rd:0 Ran:2
2000 Turf 0-2: (7f, 8f) (hvy, g-s)
Currently above-average filly. Turf high 73 (began Spt).
**Sir Michael Stoute [0-2] H H Aga Khan.*

SHERGANZAR BHB 65f58a RR 73df 58a 62[13]

5 b g Shernazar 11.8f **(71)** - Victory Kingdom (CAN) (Viceregal (CAN)) 6.8f **(64)**
Form - 0
Record 2000 - 1st:0 2nd:0 3rd:0 Ran:1
Pre2000 - 1st:0 2nd:2 3rd:2 Ran:14
Win Prizemoney £0 *Total Prizemoney* £3,082
2000 AW 0-1: (12f) (Fibr)
Above-average gelding, has broken blood-vessels, has worn blinkers. Becoming disappointing.
**D J S ffrenchDavis [0-2] Ms C Taylor (from G L Moore [0-2] Spt 1999).*

SHERIFF BHB 55f65a RR 61+f 65a 5161[13]

9 b g Midyan (USA) 9.9f **(64)** - Daisy Warwick (USA) (Ribot) 15.4f **(65)**
Form - 02821034110
Record 2000 - 1st:3 2nd:2 3rd:1 Ran:11
Pre2000 - 1st:5 2nd:4 3rd:3 Ran:29
Win Prizemoney £24,207 *Total Prizemoney* £32,869
Wins * 2000 Oct Pontef (HVY) H 18f 51 61+
*** 2000** Spt Bath (SFT) H 17.2f 47 53
*** 2000** Jun Bath (G-F) H 17.2f 46 47
* 1998 *Feb Lingfi (SLW) H 16f 70 76* <
* 1998 *Feb Lingfi (SLW) H 16f 60 75+*
* 1998 *Jan Lingfi (STD) H 16f 53 59*
* 1996 *Feb Lingfi (STD) H 16f 52 56+*
2000 Turf 3-11: (14f, 15f, 16f 4, 17f 2-4, 18f 1-1) (sft, g-s 2-3, gd 2, g-f, frm, hrd 1-3)
Above-average gelding, effective 16f, - acts on Equi, has worn blinkers, prefers left handed tracks, favours tight tracks. Turf high 61. **J W Hills [14-62] The Sheriff Partnership.*

SHERIFF SONG BHB 55f RR 36f 5318[17]

2 br c Hernando (FR) - Zippy Zoe (Rousillon (USA)) 8.2f **(74)**
Form - 00
Record 2000 - 1st:0 2nd:0 3rd:0 Ran:2
2000 Turf 0-2: (5f, 6f) (sft, g-s)
Currently average colt. Turf high 36 (began Oct).
**M W Easterby [0-2] Yorkshire Racing Club III.*

SHERINGHAM (USA) BHB 75f RR 65f 5228[5]

3 b f Robin Des Pins (USA) 8f **(92)** - Kimberley (URU) (Paradise Bay) 6f **(75)**
Form - 15
Record 2000 - 1st:1 2nd:0 3rd:0 Ran:2
Win Prizemoney £1,701 *Total Prizemoney* £1,975
Wins * 2000 *Oct Southw (STD) 6f 75+* <
2000 Turf 0-1: (6f) (gd) 2000 AW 1-1: (6f 1-1) (Fibr 1-1)
Workmanlike, currently above-average filly. (1st run) - 1st of 9 getting 5lb from First Venture (16 Oct Southwell RF 5005).
**P J Makin [1-2] Mrs P J Makin.*

SHE ROCKS (IRE) BHB 93f RR 79f 2377[2]

2 b f Spectrum (IRE) - Liberty Song (IRE) (Last Tycoon) 8.5f **(62)**
Form - 142
Record 2000 - 1st:1 2nd:1 3rd:0 Ran:3
Win Prizemoney £2,968 *Total Prizemoney* £8,258
Wins * 2000 Jun Lingfi (G-S) 6f 72 <
2000 Turf 1-3: (6f 1-1, 7f 2) (gd, g-f 1-1, frm)
Currently above-average filly. Turf high 79 - 2nd of 3 to Celtic Island (29 Jun Salisbury 7f frm RF 2377) - also 1st of 10 getting 3lb from Quantum Lady (3 Jun Lingfield RF 1675).
**R Hannon [1-3] M Mulholland.*

SHERVANA BHB 37f RR 33f 2973[14]

4 b m Cigar 6.3f **(43)** - Marsdale (Royal Palace) 9f **(56)**
Form - 000
Record 2000 - 1st:0 2nd:0 3rd:0 Ran:3
2000 Turf 0-3: (10f 3) (frm 3)
Workmanlike, very moderate filly. Turf high 33.
**N A Smith [0-4] P E T Chandler.*

SHERZABAD (IRE) BHB 42f50a RR 54f 50a 5229[13]

3 b br g Doyoun 10.7f **(69)** - Sheriya (USA) (Green Dancer (USA)) 10.3f **(74)**
Form - 08000
Record 2000 - 1st:0 2nd:0 3rd:0 Ran:5
Pre2000 - 1st:0 2nd:0 3rd:0 Ran:2
2000 Turf 0-4: (8f, 10f 2, 12f) (g-s, gd, g-f 2) 2000 AW 0-1: (9f) (Fibr)
Workmanlike, fair gelding. Turf high 54 (began Aug).
**H J Collingridge [0-4] C V Lines (from Sir Michael Stoute [0-3] May 2000).*

SHE'S A DEVIL DUE (USA) RR 5326a[3]

2 b f Devil His Due (USA) - Fapulous Star (USA) (Fappiano (USA)) 8.7f **(77)**
Form - 3
2000 AW 0-1: (9f) (Dirt)
Currently very useful filly. (1st run) - 3rd of 12 to Caressing (4 Nov Churchill Downs 9f Dirt RF 5326a).
**K McPeek in USA [0-1] Brian Griggs & Mike Goetz.*

SHE'S GRAND RR 42f 2983[6]

2 b f Cyrano de Bergerac 7.3f **(58)** - Sunley Stars (Sallust) 8.4f **(63)**
Form - 6
Record 2000 - 1st:0 2nd:0 3rd:0 Ran:1
2000 Turf 0-1: (5f) (hrd)
Currently moderate filly. **T D Barron [0-1] J Falvey & G Williamson.*

SHE'S MAGIC BHB 42f36a RR 39f 36a 905[12]

3 b f Magic Ring (IRE) 6.5f **(64)** - Norfolk Serenade (Blakeney) 10.5f **(64)**
Form - 00
Record 2000 - 1st:0 2nd:0 3rd:0 Ran:2
Pre2000 - 1st:0 2nd:0 3rd:0 Ran:2

2000 Turf 0-1: (6f) (g-s) 2000 AW 0-1: (9f) (Fibr)
Neat, very moderate filly. **M Brittain [0-4] Northgate Magic.*

SHE'S SO LOVELY (ITY) RR 106f 3351a[8]

4 f
Form - 8
2000 Turf 0-1: (8f) (g-s)
Currently Pattern-class filly. **S Saggiamo in ITY [0-2].*

SHE WADI WADI RR 54f 5310[7]

2 b f Green Desert (USA) 7.8f **(78)** - Great Inquest **(79f)** (Shernazar) 10.2f **(73)**
Form - 07
Record 2000 - 1st:0 2nd:0 3rd:0 Ran:2
2000 Turf 0-2: (7f 2) (g-s, gd)
Currently fair filly. Turf high 54 (began Oct).
**A C Stewart [0-2] Lord Dalmeny.*

SHIBBOLETH (USA) BHB 114f RR 117f 2111[4]

3 b c Danzig (USA) 8.1f **(88)** - Razyana (USA) (His Majesty (USA)) 10.9f **(82)**
Form - 114
Record 2000 - 1st:2 2nd:0 3rd:0 Ran:3
Win Prizemoney £19,998 *Total Prizemoney* £33,498
Wins * 2000 Jun Newmar (G-F) L 7f 112 <
*** 2000** Apr Newmar (SFT) 7f 102++
2000 Turf 2-3: (7f 2-2, 8f) (gd 1 2, frm 1 1)
Scopey, currently high-class colt. Turf high 117 - 4th of 11 to Giant's Causeway (20 Jun Ascot 8f gd RF 2111) - also 1st of 9 from Observatory (3 Jun Newmarket RF 1689). A brother to Danehill, he was heavily touted during the spring and looked smart when winning a maiden and Listed event over seven furlongs at Newmarket on his first two starts. Moved up in trip and class for the St James's Palace Stakes, he had every chance at the furlong pole but weakened to finish fourth. Unraced thereafter, he should stay a mile this term and is an exciting prospect. Free of Group-race penalties, he will be a lively contender for Royal Ascot's Queen Anne Stakes. **H R A Cecil [2-3] K Abdulla.*

SHIBL RR 108f 2921a[1]

3 b c Arazi (USA) 9.2f **(74)** - Mahasin (USA) (Danzig (USA)) 8.4f **(76)**

Shibboleth won his first two starts

Form - 521211
2000 Turf 3-7: (8f 3-5, 9f, 10f) (sft, g-s 1-3, gd, g-f 2-2)
Pattern-class colt, effective 8f, acts on g-s to g-f. Turf high 108 - 1st of 6 from McDab (16 Jly Curragh RF 2921a) - also 1st of 10 giving 5lb to Margay (1 Jly Curragh RF 2525a). Improving. Progressed well last term, culminating in victory in a weakly-contested Group Three. **K Prendergast in IRE [3-8] Hamdan Al Maktoum.*

SHIBUNI'S FALCON RR 114f 5215a[4]

3 b c Polar Falcon (USA) 9f **(74)** - Shibuni (Damister (USA)) 9f **(73)**
Form - 11514
2000 Turf 2-4: (10f 2-2, 12f 2) (hvy 1-2, g-f 1-2)
Group-class colt, effective 12f, acts on hvy. Turf high 114 - 4th of 10 getting 6lb from Golden Snake (22 Oct San Siro 12f hvy RF 5215a). **M Guarnieri in ITY [3-6].*

SHII-TAKE'S GIRL BHB 73f RR 68f 5196[5]

2 ch f Deploy 11.4f **(67)** - Super Sally (Superlative) 7.2f **(56)**
Form - 385
Record 2000 - 1st:0 2nd:0 3rd:1 Ran:3
Win Prizemoney £0 *Total Prizemoney* £361
2000 Turf 0-3: (7f, 8f 2) (gd, g-f, frm)
Currently average filly. Turf high 68 (began Aug) - 5th of 16 to Jumaireyah (26 Oct Windsor 8f gd RF 5196).
**Mrs A J Perrett [0-3] Clive Batt & Mrs Elaine Batt.*

SHIMLA (IRE) BHB 55f53a RR 57f 53a 5004[2]

2 b f Rudimentary (USA) 8.2f **(66)** - Olivia Jane (IRE) (Ela-Mana-Mou) 10.1f **(70)**
Form - 80582
Record 2000 - 1st:0 2nd:1 3rd:0 Ran:5
Win Prizemoney £0 *Total Prizemoney* £984
2000 Turf 0-5: (6f, 7f 3, 8f) (g-s 2, g-f 2, frm)
Fair filly. Turf high 57 - 2nd of 20 to Leatherback (16 Oct Pontefract 8f g-s RF 5004). **R Hannon [0-5] Stonethorn Stud Farms Ltd.*

SHINBONE ALLEY BHB 72f66a RR 77f 66a 4150[12]

3 b c Lake Coniston (IRE) - Villota (Top Ville) 11.7f **(68)**
Form - 51700
Record 2000 - 1st:1 2nd:0 3rd:0 Ran:5
Pre2000 - 1st:0 2nd:2 3rd:0 Ran:5
Win Prizemoney £4,309 *Total Prizemoney* £6,359
Wins * 2000 Jun Doncas (G-F) 5f 77 <
2000 Turf 1-5: (5f 1-3, 6f 2) (g-s, g-f, frm 1-2, hrd)
Scopey, above-average colt, effective 5 to 6f, acts on gd to frm. Turf high 77. **A Berry [1-5] J Hanson (from J Berry [0-5] Aug 1999).*

SHINGHAAR (USA) BHB 63f RR 60?f 2108[5]

3 ch g Silver Hawk (USA) 11.2f **(85)** - Amal Hayati (USA) (Seattle Song (USA)) 9f **(77)**
Form - 005
Record 2000 - 1st:0 2nd:0 3rd:0 Ran:3
2000 Turf 0-3: (8f, 10f 2) (frm 3)
Currently average gelding. Turf high 60.
**P W D'Arcy [0-3] Abdulla Al Khalifa.*

SHINING OASIS (IRE) BHB 75f RR 75f 4040[2]

2 b f Mujtahid (USA) 7.4f **(69)** - Desert Maiden **(66f 70a)** (Green Desert (USA)) 8.6f **(78)**
Form - 43512
Record 2000 - 1st:1 2nd:1 3rd:1 Ran:5
Win Prizemoney £2,856 *Total Prizemoney* £5,870
Wins * 2000 Aug Folkes (G-F) H 7f 70 72 <
2000 Turf 1-5: (5f, 6f 2, 7f 1-2) (gd 1-2, frm 3)
Above-average filly. Turf high 75 - also 1st of 7 getting 2lb from El Maximo (18 Aug Folkestone RF 3751).
**P F I Cole [1-5] Elite Racing Club.*

SHINING STAR RR 61f 5141[5]

3 ch f Selkirk (USA) 7.9f **(76)** - Mystery Ship (Decoy Boy) 6.7f **(56)**
Form - 40504305
Record 2000 - 1st:0 2nd:0 3rd:1 Ran:8
Pre2000 - 1st:0 2nd:0 3rd:0 Ran:4
Win Prizemoney £0 *Total Prizemoney* £515
2000 Turf 0-8: (6f 5, 7f 3) (hvy, g-s, gd 4, g-f 2)
Scopey, average filly, effective 6f, acts on g-f. Turf high 61 - 3rd of 25 giving 9lb to Bound To Please (6 Oct Windsor 6f g-f RF 4825).
**J A Osborne [0-8] Andy Miller (from J Berry [0-4] Spt 1999).*

SHINNER BHB 65f64a RR 60f 64a 4555[9]

2 b f Charnwood Forest (IRE) - Trick (IRE) **(71f)** (Shirley Heights) 10.3f **(74)**
Form - 421400
Record 2000 - 1st:1 2nd:1 3rd:0 Ran:6
Win Prizemoney £3,737 *Total Prizemoney* £4,517
Wins * 2000 Jun Pontef (G-F) 6f 60 <
2000 Turf 1-4: (5f, 6f 1-1, 7f, 8f) (gd 2, g-f, frm 1-1) 2000 AW 0-2: (5f, 6f) (Fibr 2)
Average filly, effective 5 to 6f, acts on gd to frm. Turf high 60 - 1st of 16 getting 4lb from Meriden Mist (12 Jun Pontefract RF 1898). AW high 52.
**T D Easterby [1-6] Sandal Racing.*

SHIRAZI BHB 73f **RR 72f** 4203[9]
2 b c Mtoto 11.5f **(71)** - Al Shadeedah (USA) **(84f)** (Nureyev (USA)) 8.7f **(78)**
Form - 5630
Record 2000 - 1st:0 2nd:0 3rd:1 Ran:4
Win Prizemoney £0 *Total Prizemoney* £452
2000 Turf 0-4: (6f 2, 7f, 8f) (g-f, frm 3)
Above-average colt. Turf high 72 (began Jly) - 3rd of 9 giving 7lb to Ridgeway Dawn (17 Aug Salisbury 7f frm RF 3726).
**J W Hills [0-4] K Berry & D Kerr.*

SHIRLEY FONG (IRE) BHB 63f **RR 62f** 5121[10]
2 b f Bluebird (USA) 7.9f **(71)** - Decrescendo (IRE) (Polish Precedent (USA)) 10.2f **(60)**
Form - 7600
Record 2000 - 1st:0 2nd:0 3rd:0 Ran:4
2000 Turf 0-4: (5f, 6f, 7f 2) (g-s 2, g-f, frm)
Average filly. Turf high 62.
**C F Wall [0-2] Mrs Julie Mitchell (from J W Hills [0-2] Jun 2000).*

SHIRLEY NOT BHB 67f **RR 70f** 3688[18]
4 gr g Paris House 5.9f **(64)** - Hollia (Touch Boy) 5f **(66)**
Form - 03184755000
Record 2000 - 1st:1 2nd:0 3rd:1 Ran:11
Pre2000 - 1st:2 2nd:5 3rd:1 Ran:16
Win Prizemoney £10,226 *Total Prizemoney* £18,298

Wins								
* **2000**	May	Beverl	(G-F)	H	5f	65	65	
* 1998	Aug	Cheste	(G-S)	H	5.1f		73	<
1998	*Apr*	*Southw*	*(STD)*	*S*	*5f*		*51*	

2000 Turf 1-11: (5f 1-10, 6f) (sft 2, gd 2, g-f 3, frm 3, hrd 1-1)
Leggy, above-average gelding, effective 5f, acts on gd to hrd, best on g-f, has worn blinkers. Turf high 74 - 5th of 18 getting 17lb from Henry Hall (30 Jun Newcastle 5f g-f RF 2404) - also 1st of 20 giving 4lb to Bodfari Komaite (13 May Beverley RF 1187). Becoming disappointing. He took advantage of a good draw when getting up on the line to win at Beverley in May, but has not been able to cope with the resulting rise in the handicap since.
**S Gollings [2-24] Whinham-P Brown-J Stelling (from J Berry [1-3] May 1998).*

SHIRLEY OAKS (IRE) **RR 55f** 2811[5]
2 b f Sri Pekan (USA) - Duly Elected (Persian Bold) 9.3f **(66)**
Form - 05
Record 2000 - 1st:0 2nd:0 3rd:0 Ran:2
2000 Turf 0-2: (5f, 7f) (g-f 2)
Currently fair filly. Turf high 55.
**Miss Gay Kelleway [0-2] M Butler & R Paul.*

SHIVA (JPN) BHB 121f **RR 129f** 4989[9]
5 ch m Hector Protector (USA) 9f **(89)** - Lingerie (Shirley Heights) 10.3f **(74)**
Form - 71370
Record 2000 - 1st:1 2nd:0 3rd:1 Ran:5
Pre2000 - 1st:3 2nd:1 3rd:0 Ran:5
Win Prizemoney £109,680 *Total Prizemoney* £235,280

Wins							
* **2000**	May	Sandow	(HVY)	G3	10f	129	<
* 1999	May	Currag	(GD)	G1	10.5f	117	
* 1999	Apr	Newmar	(GD)	G3	8.5f	106	
* 1998	May	Kempto	(GD)		9f	89	

2000 Turf 1-5: (9f, 10f 1-3, 12f) (g-s 1-1, gd 3, frm)
Top-class mare, effective 10f, acts on g-s to frm. Turf high 129 - 1st of 8 giving 4lb to Border Arrow (30 May Sandown RF 1557). She had an in-and-out season, a brilliant winner of the Brigadier Gerard at Sandown but not getting the clearest of runs in the Eclipse, although it is unlikely that it cost her the race. She found the ground too fast and the trip too far in the King George, and was disappointing in the Dubai Champion Stakes, although she was struck into. It was reported after that race that she would be retired to stud. **H R A Cecil [4-10] Niarchos Family.*

SHOAL CREEK (IRE) **RR 117?f** 4528a[1]
3 b c Fairy King (USA) 7.7f **(75)** - Catalonia Express (USA) (Diesis) 9.3f **(69)**
Form - 5310241
2000 Turf 2-7: (7f, 8f 1-2, 9f 1-1, 10f 2, 12f) (sft 2, g-s 1-1, gd 3)
High-class colt, effective 9f, has worn blinkers. Turf high 117. Inconsistent. He acted as Giant's Causeway's pacemaker, but proved himself a smart performer when winning a Listed event at The Curragh in September. Aggressively ridden there, he will stay a mile and a quarter and is open to improvement.
**A P O'Brien in IRE [2-8] Michael Tabor.*

SHOESHINE BOY (IRE) BHB 99f **RR 91f** 3363[8]
2 b br g Prince Sabo 6.6f **(64)** - Susie Sunshine (IRE) (Waajib)
Form - 2111008
Record 2000 - 1st:3 2nd:1 3rd:0 Ran:7
Win Prizemoney £17,662 *Total Prizemoney* £19,414

Wins						
* **2000**	May	Ascot	(G-S)	5f	91	<
* **2000**	Apr	Newmar	(SFT)	5f	85	
* **2000**	Apr	Warwic	(SFT)	5f	76	

2000 Turf 3-7: (5f 3-7) (sft 1-1, gd 2-3, g-f, frm, hrd)
Useful gelding, effective 5f, acts on gd, has worn blinkers. Turf high 91 - 1st of 10 giving 4lb to Dominus (3 May Ascot RF 0998) - also 1st of 5 giving 7lb to Emms (20 Apr Newmarket RF 0807). The archetypal sharp two-year-old, he showed blinding speed to complete a hat-trick during the spring. Well beaten thereafter, he is unlikely to improve. **B J Meehan [3-7] Oneoneone Racing.*

SHOLTO **RR 48f** 2570[6]
2 b g Tragic Role (USA) 9.4f **(63)** - Rose Mill (Puissance)
Form - 006
Record 2000 - 1st:0 2nd:0 3rd:0 Ran:3
2000 Turf 0-3: (5f, 6f 2) (g-f, frm, hrd)
Currently moderate gelding, has worn blinkers. Turf high 48.
**B J Meehan [0-3] T Herbert-Jackson.*

SHONTAINE BHB 28f35a **RR 29f 35a** 4221[5]
7 b g Pharly (FR) 11.5f **(64)** - Hinari Televideo (Caerleon (USA)) 8.6f **(71)**
Form - 7516633300080045
Record 2000 - 1st:1 2nd:0 3rd:3 Ran:15
Pre2000 - 1st:11 2nd:9 3rd:12 Ran:95
Win Prizemoney £31,525 *Total Prizemoney* £45,822

Wins							
2000	*Jan*	*Southw*	*(STD)*	*H*	*8f*	*38*	*40*
1999	Jun	Ayr	(GD)	SH	8f	40	44
1998	*Feb*	*Southw*	*(STD)*	*H*	*8f*	*60*	*63*
1998	*Jan*	*Southw*	*(STD)*	*H*	*8f*	*51*	*56*
1997	Spt	Hamilt	(GD)	H	8.3f	55	59
1997	Aug	Thirsk	(G-F)	SH	8f	51	57
1997	May	Carlis	(FRM)	H	6.9f	50	56
1997	*Mar*	*Lingfi*	*(STD)*	*C*	*6f*		*52*
1996	*Nov*	*Southw*	*(STD)*	*H*	*7f*	*60*	*67*
1996	Jly	Catter	(GD)	SH	7f	60	64

2000 Turf 0-6: (7f, 8f 5) (g-s, gd 3, frm 2) 2000 AW 1-9: (8f 1-5, 9f 3, 10f) (Equi, Fibr 1-8)
Very moderate gelding, effective 7 to 9f, best at 8f, acts on gd to hrd - acts on Fibr, best on frm, has worn blinkers, excels at Ayr and does well at Musselburgh. Turf high 29. AW high 40 - 3rd of 10 getting 7lb from Mysterium (22 Jan Wolverhampton 9f Fibr RF 0144) - also 1st of 12 getting 19lb from Mutahadeth (10 Jan Southwell RF 0058).
**Mrs L Stubbs [0-8] D R Richards (from M Johnston [12-102] Feb 2000).*

SHOOFHA (IRE) BHB 57f52a **RR 72f 52a** 5070[10]
3 b f Bluebird (USA) 7.9f **(71)** - Courtesane (USA) (Majestic Light (USA)) 10.6f **(75)**
Form - 0
Record 2000 - 1st:0 2nd:0 3rd:0 Ran:1
Pre2000 - 1st:0 2nd:0 3rd:0 Ran:1
2000 Turf 0-1: (12f) (g-s)
Scopey, currently above-average filly.
**M P Tregoning [0-2] Sheikh Ahmed Al Maktoum.*

SHOOT AWAY **RR 3f** 5189[11]
2 b f Polar Falcon (USA) 9f **(74)** - Cut Clear (Kris) 9.5f **(73)**
Form - 0
Record 2000 - 1st:0 2nd:0 3rd:0 Ran:1
2000 Turf 0-1: (7f) (gd)
Currently moderate filly.
**R M H Cowell [0-1] Bottisham Heath Stud.*

SHORE VISION **RR 45f** 4726[9]
2 b c Efisio 7.7f **(69)** - South Shore (Caerleon (USA)) 8.6f **(71)**

Form - 0
Record 2000 - 1st:0 2nd:0 3rd:0 Ran:1
2000 Turf 0-1: (6f) (gd)
Currently moderate colt. **P W Harris [0-1] Beach Combers.*

SHOTACROSS THE BOW (IRE) BHB 63f63a **RR 68f 63a** 5072[18]

3 b c Warning 8.1f **(77)** - Nordica (Northfields (USA)) 9f **(72)**
Form - 0083230300
Record 2000 - 1st:0 2nd:1 3rd:3 Ran:10
Pre2000 - 1st:1 2nd:0 3rd:0 Ran:3
Win Prizemoney £3,468 *Total Prizemoney* £6,265
Wins * 1999 Spt Epsom (G-F) 6f 78 <
2000 Turf 0-8: (8f 2, 10f 4, 11f 2) (g-s 2, gd, g-f, frm 4) 2000 AW 0-2: (8f, 9f) (Equi, Fibr)
Leggy, average colt, effective 6f, acts on frm, likes left handed tracks, likes tight tracks. Turf high 68. AW high 67 (began Spt). Inconsistent. **B W Hills [1-13] C Wright & The Hon Mrs J M Corbett.*

SHOTLEY MARIE (IRE) BHB 22f **RR 10?f** 105[P]

5 b m Scenic 10.6f **(66)** - Hana Marie (Formidable (USA)) 9.2f **(63)**
Form - 5668P
Record 2000 - 1st:0 2nd:0 3rd:0 Ran:3
Pre2000 - 1st:0 2nd:0 3rd:0 Ran:15
2000 AW 0-3: (11f, 12f, 16f) (Fibr 3)
Poor filly, often wore blinkers. AW high 19. (DEAD)
**N Bycroft [0-19] J A Swinburne.*

SHOUF AL BADOU (USA) BHB 76f **RR 79f** 5014[1]

3 b c Sheikh Albadou 9.2f **(75)** - Millfit (USA) (Blushing Groom (FR)) 10.3f **(76)**
Form - 000650601
Record 2000 - 1st:1 2nd:0 3rd:0 Ran:9
Pre2000 - 1st:3 2nd:0 3rd:1 Ran:5
Win Prizemoney £14,120 *Total Prizemoney* £15,321
Wins * **2000** *Oct Wolver (STD) H 6f 69 77+*
* 1999 Nov Doncas (SFT) 8f 90+ <
* 1999 *Oct Wolver (STD) 6f 90*
* 1999 *Oct Wolver (STD) 6f 72+*
2000 Turf 0-7: (7f 5, 8f 2) (g-s 2, g-f 2, frm 3) 2000 AW 1-2: (6f 1-1, 9f) (Fibr 1-1, Dirt)
Scopey, very useful colt, effective 6 to 8f, acts on g-s - acts on Fibr, likes left handed tracks, prefers tight tracks. Turf high 81. AW high 98. He tumbled down the ratings before landing a gamble on the all-weather in October. Effective up to a mile, he was subsequently sold to David Nicholls for 37,000gns and should make a mark in decent handicaps this term. **B W Hills [4-14] Hilal Salem.*

SHOULDHAVEGONEHOME (IRE) BHB 47f47a **RR 45f 47a** 1840[R]

3 ch f Up and At 'em - Gentle Papoose (Commanche Run) 8.5f **(58)**
Form - 275756R
Record 2000 - 1st:0 2nd:0 3rd:0 Ran:5
Pre2000 - 1st:1 2nd:3 3rd:1 Ran:16
Win Prizemoney £2,766 *Total Prizemoney* £5,216
Wins 1999 Aug Mussel (G-F) S 5f 65 <
2000 Turf 0-1: (5f) (gd) 2000 AW 0-4: (6f 4) (Equi 2, Fibr 2)
Light-framed, moderate filly, effective 5f, acts on gd to g-f, best on g-f, has worn blinkers. AW high 45.
**J Balding [0-1] Men Behaving Badly (from P D Evans [1-20] Feb 2000).*

SHOWBOAT BHB 103f **RR 102df** 4597[23]

6 b h Warning 8.1f **(77)** - Boathouse (Habitat) 9.4f **(70)**
Form - 06303030430
Record 2000 - 1st:0 2nd:0 3rd:4 Ran:11
Pre2000 - 1st:5 2nd:2 3rd:4 Ran:26
Win Prizemoney £96,448 *Total Prizemoney* £157,398
Wins * 1999 Spt Newbur (G-F) 9f 102
* 1999 Jun Ascot (G-F) H 8f 92 108 <
* 1999 Apr Newmar (GD) H 7f 86 90
* 1997 Aug Salisb (G-F) 8f 93
* 1996 Oct Leices (G-F) 7f 93+
2000 Turf 0-10: (7f 5, 8f 4, 10f) (gd 5, g-f, frm 4) 2000 AW 0-1: (12f) (Dirt)
Group-class horse, effective 7 to 12f, acts on gd to frm - acts on Dirt, has worn blinkers, prefers left handed tracks, excels at Newmarket. Turf high 108 - 3rd of 9 to Arkadian Hero (1 Jly Newmarket 7f frm RF 2449). (1st run) - 6th of 11 to Rhythm Band (25 Mar Nad Al Sheba 12f Dirt RF 0579a). A runaway winner of the Royal Hunt Cup in 1999, he spent much of last season in Listed and Group company, acquitting himself with credit on several occasions. Best on fast ground, he will be difficult to place this term. **B W Hills [5-37] R D Hollingsworth.*

SHOWING BHB 40f55a **RR 60f 55a** 4471[14]

3 b c Owington - Sharanella (Shareef Dancer (USA)) 9.9f **(73)**
Form - 886000
Record 2000 - 1st:0 2nd:0 3rd:0 Ran:6
Pre2000 - 1st:0 2nd:0 3rd:0 Ran:2
2000 Turf 0-5: (7f 4, 8f) (gd, g-f 3, frm) 2000 AW 0-1: (6f) (Fibr)
Average colt. Turf high 60. Becoming disappointing.
**N A Graham [0-8] First Millennium Racing.*

SHOW ME THE MONEY (IRE) **RR 90f** 4521a[7]

4 b m Mujadil (USA) 7.7f **(70)** - Snappy Dresser (Nishapour (FR)) 9.1f **(61)**
Form - 770507
2000 Turf 0-6: (6f 2, 7f 4) (g-s 2, gd 2, g-f)
Useful filly, effective 6 to 7f, acts on sft to g-f. Turf high 91. Consistent. Successful in the Cornwallis Stakes back in 1998, she is on a long losing run and had a disappointing campaign.
**N Meade in IRE [5-19] L Queally.*

SHOW THE WAY **RR 48f** 5184[12]

2 ch c Hernando (FR) - Severine (USA) (Trempolino (USA)) 12f **(71)**
Form - 0
Record 2000 - 1st:0 2nd:0 3rd:0 Ran:1
2000 Turf 0-1: (8f) (g-s)
Currently moderate colt. **A P Jarvis [0-1] A P Jarvis.*

SHRIVAR (IRE) BHB 80f **RR 80f** 5323[11]

3 b g Sri Pekan (USA) - Kriva **(72df 61a)** (Reference Point) 6.8f **(70)**
Form - 0552464147421100
Record 2000 - 1st:3 2nd:2 3rd:0 Ran:16
Pre2000 - 1st:0 2nd:0 3rd:0 Ran:3
Win Prizemoney £14,737 *Total Prizemoney* £17,509
Wins * **2000** Spt Newmar (GD) H 10f 70 80 <
* **2000** Spt Pontef (G-S) 10f 80 <
* **2000** Jly Warwic (GD) H 10.5f 65 69
2000 Turf 3-16: (7f, 8f, 10f 2-5, 11f 1-3, 12f 4, 14f 2) (hvy, sft, g-s, gd 3-8, g-f 4, frm)
Scopey, decent gelding, effective 10f, acts on gd, has worn blinkers (extremely effectively), likes left handed tracks. Turf high 80 - 1st of 19 giving 3lb to Zagaleta (21 Spt Pontefract RF 4559) - also 1st of 22 getting 10lb from Barton Sands (29 Spt Newmarket RF 4734). He showed progressive form when tried in a visor in September, but was never going in testing ground when on to a hat-trick. Has a turn of foot. **M R Channon [3-19] P D Savill.*

SHUDDER BHB 60f **RR 60f** 3246[7]

5 b g Distant Relative 7f **(69)** - Oublier L'Ennui (FR) (Bellman (FR)) 8.4f **(77)**
Form - 43031637
Record 2000 - 1st:1 2nd:0 3rd:3 Ran:8
Pre2000 - 1st:2 2nd:1 3rd:2 Ran:12
Win Prizemoney £7,824 *Total Prizemoney* £31,641
Wins * **2000** Jun Folkes (FRM) C 6f 59
1999 Aug Haydoc (G-S) C 6f 80
1997 Aug Goodwo (G-F) 6f 85+ <
2000 Turf 1-8: (5f, 6f 1-3, 7f 4) (g-s, gd 2, g-f 1-3, frm 2)
Average gelding, effective 6f, acts on g-f, has worn blinkers (effectively). Turf high 64.
**R J Hodges [1-13] Footsteps Flyers (from W J Haggas [2-7] Aug 1999).*

SHUFFLE BHB 40f **RR 26f** 1477[5]

3 b c First Trump - Secret Dance (Sadler's Wells (USA)) 10f **(76)**
Form - 065
Record 2000 - 1st:0 2nd:0 3rd:0 Ran:3
2000 Turf 0-1: (10f) (g-s) 2000 AW 0-2: (8f, 11f) (Fibr 2)
Leggy, currently very moderate colt, often wears blinkers. AW high 36. **Mrs N Macauley [0-3] Mrs N Macauley.*

SHUSH BHB 88f **RR 87f** 5024[5]

2 b c Shambo - Abuzz (Absalom) 7.2f **(58)**
Form - 15601075
Record 2000 - 1st:2 2nd:0 3rd:0 Ran:8
Win Prizemoney £7,273 *Total Prizemoney* £7,910
Wins * **2000** Jly Leices (G-F) H 6f 87 <
* **2000** Apr Kempto (SFT) 5f 79
2000 Turf 2-8: (5f 1-3, 6f 1-3, 7f 2) (sft 1-1, g-s, gd 3, g-f, frm 1-2)
Useful colt, effective 5 to 6f, best at 5f, acts on sft to frm. Turf high 87 - 1st of 8 giving 17lb to Troubleshooter (20 Jly Leicester RF 2972) - also 1st of 9 from Princes Street (22 Apr Kempton RF 0827). Made a winning debut at Kempton and outclassed his opponents in a Leicester nursery. Held in decent company otherwise.
**C E Brittain [2-8] Mrs C E Brittain.*

SHUWAIB RR 108f
4842a[3]
3 b c Polish Precedent (USA) 9f **(73)** - Ajab Alzamaan (Rainbow Quest (USA)) 10.4f **(75)**
Form - 13143
Record 2000 - 1st:2 2nd:0 3rd:2 Ran:5
Win Prizemoney £17,349 *Total Prizemoney* £30,118
Wins * **2000** Aug Deauvi (G-F) L 15f 103 <
* **2000** Jun Goodwo (G-F) 12f 75+
2000 Turf 2-5: (12f 1-1, 14f, 15f 1-3) (hvy, sft, gd, g-f 2-2)
Scopey, Pattern-class colt. Turf high 108 - 3rd of 8 giving 4lb to Moonlady (1 Oct Dortmund 14f hvy RF 4842a) - also 1st of 4 from Bourgeois (16 Aug Deauville RF 3940a). He is a promising young stayer who appreciates easy ground.
**M R Channon [2-5] Darley Stud Management Inc.*

SHY PADDY (IRE) BHB 23f27a RR 32f 27a
1739[9]
8 b g Shy Groom (USA) 8.2f **(59)** - Griqualand (Connaught) 7.7f **(63)**
Form - 800
Record 2000 - 1st:0 2nd:0 3rd:0 Ran:3
Pre2000 - 1st:1 2nd:2 3rd:1 Ran:15
Win Prizemoney £2,658 *Total Prizemoney* £4,495
2000 Turf 0-1: (11f) (gd) 2000 AW 0-2: (12f, 16f) (Fibr 2)
Very moderate gelding, has worn blinkers. AW high 22.
**K O Cunningham-Brown [1-22] Danebury Racing Stables Ltd.*

SIAMO (GER) RR 92f
1285a[3]
3 gr c Java Gold (USA) 9.3f **(67)** - Suffinja (GER) (Windwurf (GER)) 12.7f **(72)**
Form - 33
2000 Turf 0-2: (8f, 9f) (hvy, gd)
Currently useful colt. Turf high 92 - 3rd of 11 to Pacino (14 May Cologne 8f gd RF 1285a).
**D Richardson in GER [0-2] Gestut Winterhauch.*

SIAMO DISPERATI BHB 69f59a RR 76?f 59a
5320[15]
2 ch c Aragon 7.7f **(58)** - Jambo **(64f)** (Rambo Dancer (CAN))
Form - 300260
Record 2000 - 1st:0 2nd:1 3rd:1 Ran:6
Win Prizemoney £0 *Total Prizemoney* £2,323
2000 Turf 0-6: (5f 3, 6f 2, 7f) (sft 2, gd 2, g-f, frm)
Above-average colt, effective 5f, acts on gd. Turf high 76.
**C B B Booth [0-6] Mrs Mary Burden.*

SIBELIUS RR 35f
944[14]
3 b c Suave Dancer (USA) 10.7f **(68)** - Photo Call (Chief Singer) 8.9f **(66)**
Form - 00
Record 2000 - 1st:0 2nd:0 3rd:0 Ran:2
2000 Turf 0-2: (8f, 12f) (g-s, gd)
Leggy, currently very moderate colt. Turf high 35.
**N P Littmoden [0-2] J R Good.*

SIBERTIGO BHB 36f RR 54f
4130[16]
4 b g Touch of Grey 8.1f **(47)** - Young Lady (Young Generation) 7.7f **(63)**
Form - 00700
Record 2000 - 1st:0 2nd:0 3rd:0 Ran:5
Pre2000 - 1st:0 2nd:0 3rd:0 Ran:2
2000 Turf 0-5: (7f, 8f 2, 10f, 12f) (gd, g-f 2, frm 2)
Workmanlike, fair gelding, has worn blinkers. Turf high 54.
**R M Flower [0-7] Richard Gurr.*

SIBLA BHB 84f RR 79f
4259[8]
2 b f Piccolo - Malibasta (Auction Ring (USA)) 8.6f **(65)**
Form - 5212518
Record 2000 - 1st:2 2nd:2 3rd:0 Ran:7
Win Prizemoney £5,701 *Total Prizemoney* £7,185
Wins * **2000** Aug Bath (FRM) 5.7f 79 <
* **2000** Jly Bath (FRM) 5.7f 75
2000 Turf 2-7: (6f 2-7) (gd, g-f 4, frm 1-1, hrd 1-1)
Above-average filly, effective 6f, acts on g-f to hrd. Turf high 79 - 2nd of 10 to Becky Simmons (15 Jly Salisbury 6f g-f RF 2845) - also 1st of 8 giving 3lb to Goldie (25 Aug Bath RF 3951). Will be suited by a step up to seven furlongs.
**Mrs P N Dutfield [2-7] D Bevan.*

SIEGE (IRE) BHB 107f RR 111f
3759[3]
4 br h Indian Ridge 7.6f **(74)** - Above Water (IRE) (Reference Point) 6.8f **(70)**
Form - 83
Record 2000 - 1st:0 2nd:0 3rd:1 Ran:2
Pre2000 - 1st:1 2nd:4 3rd:2 Ran:8
Win Prizemoney £3,712 *Total Prizemoney* £46,805
Wins 1999 May Kempto (G-F) 7f 89 <
2000 Turf 0-1: (7f) (g-f) 2000 AW 0-1: (8f) (Dirt)
Scopey, Group-class colt, effective 8 to 10f, acts on g-f. A very useful handicapper in '99, he was in good form in Dubai in the spring. Appeared just once in Britain, when a good third in the Hungerford Stakes at Newbury.
**S bin Suroor [0-1] Godolphin (from S bin Suroor in UAE [0-1] Mar 2000).*

SIEGFRIED BHB 50f RR 22f
2536[7]
4 ch g Magic Ring (IRE) 6.5f **(64)** - Spirit of The Wind (USA) (Little Current (USA)) 9.6f **(75)**
Form - 7
Record 2000 - 1st:0 2nd:0 3rd:0 Ran:1
Pre2000 - 1st:0 2nd:0 3rd:0 Ran:3
2000 Turf 0-1: (12f) (gd)
Leggy, little account gelding.
**G A Butler [0-1] H R H Princess Michael of Kent (from B W Hills [0-3] Jun 1999).*

SIENA STAR (IRE) BHB 77f RR 76+f
4623[4]
2 b g Brief Truce (USA) 9.1f **(73)** - Gooseberry Pie **(63f)** (Green Desert (USA)) 8.6f **(78)**
Form - 0044322174
Record 2000 - 1st:1 2nd:2 3rd:1 Ran:10
Win Prizemoney £6,240 *Total Prizemoney* £10,004
Wins * **2000** Aug Newmar (G-F) H 8f 73 76 <
2000 Turf 1-9: (5f 2, 7f 4, 8f 1-3) (gd 3, g-f 1-2, frm 4) 2000 AW 0-1: (6f) (Fibr)
Above-average gelding, effective 7 to 8f, best at 7f, acts on g-f to frm, best on frm. Turf high 76 - 2nd of 9 giving 4lb to Pasithea (17 Aug Beverley 7f frm RF 3719) - also 1st of 10 getting 12lb from Northfields Dancer (25 Aug Newmarket RF 3965).
**J L Eyre [1-10] Peel, Hopkinson, Binney.*

SIERRA STORM RR 37f
1317[6]
5 gr m Gods Solution - Iberian Start (King of Spain) 7.8f **(52)**
Form - 6
Record 2000 - 1st:0 2nd:0 3rd:0 Ran:1
2000 Turf 0-1: (8f) (gd)
Very moderate filly. **C Grant [0-6] J W Barker.*

SIFAT BHB 65f RR 66f
4446[13]
5 b m Marju (IRE) 9.2f **(76)** - Reine Maid (USA) (Mr Prospector (USA)) 8.8f **(78)**
Form - 511230
Record 2000 - 1st:2 2nd:1 3rd:1 Ran:6
Pre2000 - 1st:1 2nd:0 3rd:2 Ran:14
Win Prizemoney £8,075 *Total Prizemoney* £11,155
Wins * **2000** Jun Yarmou (GD) H 10.1f 54 65
* **2000** May Yarmou (GD) H 10.1f 54 58
1998 Oct Pontef (G-S) 8f 76 <
2000 Turf 2-6: (9f, 10f 2-4, 12f) (gd 1-3, g-f 1-1, frm 2)
Average filly, effective 9 to 10f, best at 10f, acts on g-s to hrd, best on gd, often wears blinkers (extremely effectively), prefers left handed tracks, prefers tight tracks, and excels at Yarmouth. Turf high 66 - 3rd of 13 giving 11lb to Paarl Rock (21 Aug Nottingham 10f gd RF 3843) - also 1st of 10 giving 5lb to Smarter Charter (7

Jun Yarmouth RF 1797). In fine form early in the summer, winning twice and arguably unlucky not to make it three.
**J R Jenkins [2-9] C N & Mrs J C Wright (from N A Graham [0-7] Oct 1999).*

SIGNATORY BHB 77f72a **RR 97f 72a** 4713a[7]

5 ch h King's Signet (USA) 7f **(51)** - Pearl Pet (Mummy's Pet) 7.7f **(60)**
Form - 27
2000 Turf 0-2: (8f 2) (sft, gd)
Very useful colt. Turf high 97 (1st run) (began Jly) - 2nd of 10 giving 9lb to Yorba Linda (23 Jly Dusseldorf 8f gd RF 3160a).
**U Suter in GER [1-4].*

SIGN OF HOPE BHB 94f **RR 109f** 5210a[1]

3 ch g Selkirk (USA) 7.9f **(76)** - Rainbow's End (My Swallow) 9.2f **(71)**
Form - 1121
2000 Turf 3-4: (8f 2-3, 9f 1-1) (gd, g-f 1-1, frm 2-2)
Scopey, Pattern-class gelding, effective 9f, acts on frm, has worn blinkers. Turf high 109 - 1st of 5 from David Copperfield (21 Oct Santa Anita RF 5210a). Touched off by El Gran Papa in Royal Ascotís Britannia Handicap, he was later transferred to Neil Drysdale in America and won the Grade 2 Oak Tree Derby at Santa Anita.
**N Drysdale in USA [1-1] Relatively Stable (from I A Balding [2-8] Jun 2000).*

SIGN OF NIKE **RR 103f** 5204a[1]

2 b c Mistertopogigo (IRE) - Infanta Maria (King of Spain) 7.8f **(52)**
Form - 311
2000 Turf 2-3: (6f 2-3) (hvy 1-1, g-s 1-1, gd)
Currently very useful colt. Turf high 103 (began Spt) - 1st of 7 getting 3lb from Distinctly Dancer (23 Spt San Siro RF 4715a) - also 1st of 5 giving 8lb to Nasmatt (18 Oct Deauville RF 5204a).
**D Richardson in GER [2-3] Stall Silvester.*

SIGN OF THE DRAGON BHB 42f **RR 47f** 4893[3]

3 b g Sri Pekan (USA) - Tartique Twist (USA) (Arctic Tern (USA)) 8.9f **(69)**
Form - 453
Record 2000 - 1st:0 2nd:0 3rd:1 Ran:3
Win Prizemoney £0 *Total Prizemoney* £912
2000 Turf 0-3: (7f, 8f, 10f) (hvy, g-s, frm)
Workmanlike, currently moderate gelding. Turf high 47.
**I Semple [0-3] Mrs E Chung.*

SIGN OF THE TIGER BHB 71f70a **RR 74f 70a** 3808[11]

3 b g Beveled (USA) 6.9f **(64)** - Me Spede (Valiyar) 8.5f **(73)**
Form - 31144231000
Record 2000 - 1st:3 2nd:1 3rd:1 Ran:10
Pre2000 - 1st:0 2nd:0 3rd:1 Ran:5
Win Prizemoney £9,984 *Total Prizemoney* £12,789

Wins								
*** 2000**	May	Newcas	(GD)	H	8f	68	72	
*** 2000**	*Feb*	*Wolver*	*(STD)*	*H*	*7f*	*57*	*76+*	<
*** 2000**	*Jan*	*Southw*	*(STD)*	*H*	*7f*	*57*	*64*	

2000 Turf 1-6: (7f, 8f 1-5) (gd 1-4, g-f, frm) 2000 AW 2-4: (7f 2-3, 9f) (Equi, Fibr 2-3)
Above-average gelding, effective 7 to 8f, best at 8f, acts on gd - acts on AW, likes left handed tracks, likes tight tracks. Turf high 74 - 3rd of 16 getting 5lb from Sovereign State (20 May Thirsk 8f gd RF 1350) - also 1st of 20 giving 11lb to Nowt Flash (25 May Newcastle RF 1441). AW high 76 - 1st of 7 giving 11lb to Lord Harley (3 Feb Wolverhampton RF 0213).
**P C Haslam [3-15] Mrs B M Hawkins.*

SIGNS AND WONDERS BHB 58f65a **RR 59f 65a** 551[3]

6 b m Danehill (USA) 9.1f **(79)** - Front Line Romance (Caerleon (USA)) 8.6f **(71)**
Form - 3
Record 2000 - 1st:0 2nd:0 3rd:1 Ran:1
Pre2000 - 1st:1 2nd:6 3rd:3 Ran:32
Win Prizemoney £3,460 *Total Prizemoney* £12,663

Wins								
* 1998	*Mar*	*Lingfi*	*(STD)*	*H*	*10f*	*62*	*66*	<

2000 AW 0-1: (12f) (Equi)
Average mare, effective 8 to 12f, best at 8f, acts on frm - acts on Equi. (1st run) - 3rd of 4 getting 5lb from Sea Danzig (29 Mar Lingfield 12f Equi RF 0551). Consistent.
**C A Cyzer [1-33] R M Cyzer.*

SIGN THE TRUCE (IRE) **RR 46f** 1472[6]

2 ch c Brief Truce (USA) 9.1f **(73)** - Sign of Peace (IRE) (Posen (USA))
Form - 76
Record 2000 - 1st:0 2nd:0 3rd:0 Ran:2
Win Prizemoney £0 *Total Prizemoney* £154
2000 Turf 0-2: (5f, 6f) (sft, g-f)
Moderate colt. Turf high 46. (DEAD) **T D Easterby [0-2] D F Sills.*

SIGY POINT BHB 25f **RR 13f** 4489[15]

3 b f King's Signet (USA) 7f **(51)** - Red Point **(5f)** (Reference Point) 6.8f **(70)**
Form - 000
Record 2000 - 1st:0 2nd:0 3rd:0 Ran:3
2000 Turf 0-3: (8f, 10f 2) (g-f 2, frm)
Lengthy, currently poor filly. Turf high 13 (began Jly).
**K Bishop [0-3] Mrs Maureen Emery.*

SIHAFI (USA) BHB 67f75a **RR 68f 75a** 4299[15]

7 ch g Elmaamul (USA) 8.1f **(70)** - Kit's Double (USA) (Spring Double) 6.8f **(76)**
Form - 043023618432458100
Record 2000 - 1st:2 2nd:2 3rd:3 Ran:18
Pre2000 - 1st:11 2nd:9 3rd:4 Ran:71
Win Prizemoney £46,934 *Total Prizemoney* £64,836

Wins								
*** 2000**	Aug	Mussel	(G-F)	H	5f	61	68	
*** 2000**	Jly	Lingfi	(G-F)	H	5f	56	57	
* 1998	*Oct*	*Wolver*	*(STD)*	*H*	*6f*	*75*	*77*	<
* 1998	Spt	Haydoc	(G-F)	H	5f	70	71	
* 1998	Jly	Sandow	(G-F)	H	5f	60	70+	
* 1998	Jly	Salisb	(GD)	H	5f	56	64	
* 1998	Jly	Lingfi	(G-F)	H	5f	46	53+	
* 1998	Jly	Folkes	(G-F)	H	5f	46	51+	
* 1998	Jly	Bath	(GD)	H	5.1f	46	61	
* 1998	Jun	Windso	(GD)	H	6f	41	54+	
* 1998	*Jan*	*Lingfi*	*(STD)*	*H*	*6f*	*61*	*64*	
1997	*Feb*	*Lingfi*	*(STD)*	*H*	*6f*	*56*	*57*	
1996	*Dec*	*Lingfi*	*(STD)*	*H*	*6f*	*50*	*51*	

2000 Turf 2-18: (5f 2-14, 6f 4) (g-s, gd 3, g-f 1-5, frm 1-8, hrd)
Decent gelding, has broken blood-vessels, effective 5f, acts on gd to frm, best on frm, has worn blinkers. Turf high 68 - 1st of 11 giving 5lb to Johayro (24 Aug Musselburgh RF 3931). He has had a brilliant 1998, and equalled the twentieth century record of nine handicap wins in a season when scoring on the Wolverhampton Fibresand in October. The fact that he has achieved this feat by winning races on turf, Equitrack and Fibresand pays testament to his versatility. After dropping in the handicap, he regained winning ways in the summer. **D Nicholls [11-65] John Gilbertson (from J M Carr [2-17] Aug 1997).*

SILCA BLANKA (IRE) BHB 91f82a **RR 97f 82a** 4817[3]

8 b h Law Society (USA) 11.6f **(71)** - Reality (Known Fact (USA)) 7.4f **(67)**
Form - 81110327603
Record 2000 - 1st:3 2nd:1 3rd:2 Ran:10
Pre2000 - 1st:6 2nd:6 3rd:2 Ran:51
Win Prizemoney £75,065 *Total Prizemoney* £112,925

Wins							
*** 2000**	Jun	Cheste	(G-S)	H	7f	84	93
*** 2000**	May	Cheste	(GD)	H	7.6f	81	85
*** 2000**	Apr	Bright	(G-S)	H	8f	75	79
* 1999	Jun	Epsom	(GD)	H	7f	84	87
* 1999	*Jan*	*Lingfi*	*(STD)*	*H*	*7f*	*82*	*83*
* 1998	Jly	Warwic	(G-F)		7f		86

2000 Turf 3-10: (6f, 7f 1-5, 8f 2-4) (g-s, gd 2-6, g-f 1-3)
Very useful horse, effective 7f, acts on g-s to g-f, prefers left handed tracks, likes tight tracks, does well at Chester. Turf high 97 - 2nd of 6 to Late Night Out (15 Jly Chester 7f g-f RF 2834) - also 1st of 10 giving 5lb to Nomore Mr Niceguy (7 Jun Chester RF 1782). He had a period at stud in 1997 and has already raced on the same card as his offspring. Still a useful handicapper around seven furlongs or a mile, he goes well on turning tracks and has an excellent record at Chester.
**A G Newcombe [6-41] Duckhaven Stud (from M R Channon [3-20] Aug 1996).*

SILCA FANTASY BHB 40f49a **RR 34f 49a** 2554[9]

3 b f Piccolo - Fantasy Racing (IRE) **(75f)** (Tirol)
Form - 444600

Record 2000 - 1st:0 2nd:0 3rd:0 Ran:6
Pre2000 - 1st:0 2nd:0 3rd:0 Ran:1
Win Prizemoney £0 *Total Prizemoney* £653
2000 Turf 0-2: (7f 2) (frm, hrd) 2000 AW 0-4: (7f 2, 8f 2) (Fibr 4)
Leggy, fair filly. Turf high 34. AW high 50.
**P Howling [0-6] Paul Howling Racing Syndicate 2 (from M R Channon [0-1] May 1999).*

SILCA LEGEND BHB 95f **RR 93f** 4747[17]

2 ch c Efisio 7.7f **(69)** - Silca-Cisa (Hallgate)
Form - 232422126170
Record 2000 - 1st:2 2nd:5 3rd:1 Ran:12
Win Prizemoney £9,546 *Total Prizemoney* £19,081
Wins * **2000** Aug Cheste (GD) 6.1f 93 <
* **2000** Jly Newcas (FRM) 6f 79
2000 Turf 2-12: (5f 6, 6f 2-6) (g-s 3, gd 1-5, g-f, frm 1-3)
Useful colt, effective 5 to 6f, acts on gd. Turf high 93 - 1st of 4 from River Raven (20 Aug Chester RF 3819). Consistent. He raced consistently through a busy season and was sold for 21,000gns at Newmarket in October. Unlikely to stay much beyond sprint distances, he will be difficult to place at home and may be better employed on the continent.
**M R Channon [2-12] Aldridge Racing Ltd.*

SILENT NIGHT BHB 63f **RR 64f** 3730[8]

3 gr f Night Shift (USA) 8.1f **(73)** - Catch The Sun (Kalaglow) 9.8f **(67)**
Form - 0508
Record 2000 - 1st:0 2nd:0 3rd:0 Ran:4
Pre2000 - 1st:1 2nd:0 3rd:0 Ran:3
Win Prizemoney £5,122 *Total Prizemoney* £5,342
Wins * 1999 Spt Kempto (G-F) 7f 80+ <
2000 Turf 0-4: (8f 2, 10f 2) (g-f 2, frm 2)
Scopey, average filly, effective 7f, acts on frm, has worn blinkers. Turf high 64. She made a winning debut at Kempton in September, but was all at sea on soft ground in two subsequent races.
**D R C Elsworth [1-7] C J Harper.*

SILENT SOUND (IRE) BHB 51f48a **RR 52f 48a** 4723[10]

4 b g Be My Guest (USA) 10.2f **(66)** - Whist Awhile (Caerleon (USA)) 8.6f **(71)**
Form - 048025340
Record 2000 - 1st:0 2nd:1 3rd:1 Ran:9
Pre2000 - 1st:1 2nd:2 3rd:1 Ran:16
Win Prizemoney £4,289 *Total Prizemoney* £7,852
Wins 1999 Aug Redcar (FRM) H 10f 51 53 <
2000 Turf 0-8: (9f, 10f 3, 11f, 12f 2, 14f) (gd 2, g-f 6) 2000 AW 0-1: (12f) (Equi)
Workmanlike, fair gelding, effective 10 to 14f, acts on g-s to frm, has worn blinkers (effectively), likes left handed tracks, excels at Yarmouth. Turf high 52 - 4th of 16 giving 6lb to Admirals Secret (31 May Yarmouth 11f g-f RF 1612). Consistent.
**Mrs A J Perrett [0-9] G Harwood (from P Calver [1-16] Oct 1999).*

SILENT VALLEY BHB 27a **RR 34f** 1720[8]

6 b m Forzando 7.2f **(63)** - Tremmin (Horage) 10.3f **(61)**
Form - 0878
Record 2000 - 1st:0 2nd:0 3rd:0 Ran:4
Pre2000 - 1st:1 2nd:2 3rd:3 Ran:27
Win Prizemoney £2,940 *Total Prizemoney* £5,431
Wins 1997 Jly Nottin (G-F) 10f 56 <
2000 Turf 0-3: (12f, 14f 2) (sft, gd 2) 2000 AW 0-1: (14f) (Fibr)
Moderate mare, often wears blinkers. Turf high 34.
**Mrs A M Naughton [0-5] Mrs S E Cooper (from Miss L C Siddall [3-26] Jly 1999).*

SILENT VOICE (IRE) **RR 75f** 4128[6]

3 ch c Unfuwain (USA) 11.4f **(74)** - Symeterie (USA) (Seattle Song (USA)) 9f **(77)**
Form - 176
Record 2000 - 1st:1 2nd:0 3rd:0 Ran:3
Win Prizemoney £4,880 *Total Prizemoney* £5,043
Wins * **2000** May San Si (GD) 12f 75 <
2000 Turf 1-3: (11f, 12f 1-1, 14f) (gd 1-1, frm 2)
Currently above-average colt. Turf high 75 (1st run) - 1st of 6 getting 4lb from Quim Di San Jore (27 May San Siro RF 1632a).
**J L Dunlop [1-3] Grundy Bloodstock Ltd.*

SILENT WARNING BHB 84f85a **RR 90+f 85a** 4987[13]

5 b g Ela-Mana-Mou 12.7f **(72)** - Buzzbomb (Bustino) 10.4f **(64)**
Form - 260
Record 2000 - 1st:0 2nd:1 3rd:0 Ran:3
Pre2000 - 1st:4 2nd:0 3rd:1 Ran:12
Win Prizemoney £15,402 *Total Prizemoney* £21,017
Wins * 1998 *Nov Southw (STD) H 14f 73 87+* <
* 1998 Nov Mussel (SFT) H 16f 73 79+
* 1998 Oct Leices (SFT) 11.8f 83
* 1998 *Oct Southw (STD) H 14f 69 75*
2000 Turf 0-3: (16f, 18f, 20f) (gd 2, g-f)
Useful gelding, effective 16f, acted on gd to g-f. Turf high 90 (1st run) (began Jly) - 2nd of 12 giving 7lb to Ski Run (28 Jly Ascot 16f g-f RF 3163). Beat all bar the impressive Ski Run on his belated return to action at Ascot but disappointed at Goodwood five days later. He was fatally injured on his hurdling debut. (DEAD).
**Sir Mark Prescott [4-15] Eclipse Thoroughbreds - Osborne House.*

SILK DAISY BHB 64f **RR 66f** 5242[17]

4 b m Barathea (IRE) - Scene Galante (FR) (Sicyos (USA))
Form - 4515150
Record 2000 - 1st:2 2nd:0 3rd:0 Ran:7
Pre2000 - 1st:0 2nd:1 3rd:3 Ran:6
Win Prizemoney £9,558 *Total Prizemoney* £12,845
Wins * **2000** Aug Nottin (G-F) H 8.2f 62 63 <
* **2000** Jun Goodwo (GD) H 7f 60 62
2000 Turf 2-7: (6f, 7f 1-2, 8f 1-4) (g-s 3, gd, g-f 2-2, frm)
Leggy, average filly, effective 7f, acts on g-f to frm. Turf high 63. Better over a mile than seven furlongs, she is suited by fast ground. **H Candy [2-13] Mrs C M Poland.*

SILKEN DALLIANCE BHB 78f72a **RR 82f 72a** 2462[11]

5 b m Rambo Dancer (CAN) 8.4f **(59)** - A Sharp (Sharpo) 7.7f **(59)**
Form - 870270
Record 2000 - 1st:0 2nd:1 3rd:0 Ran:6
Pre2000 - 1st:4 2nd:4 3rd:0 Ran:20
Win Prizemoney £72,437 *Total Prizemoney* £81,690
Wins 1998 Oct Newmar (GD) H 8f 79 83 <
1998 Spt Ascot (SFT) H 8f 74 76
1998 Spt Kempto (SFT) H 8f 67 74+
1998 Mar Southw (STD) 6f 56
2000 Turf 0-4: (8f 4) (g-s 2, g-f, frm) 2000 AW 0-2: (8f 2) (Fibr 2)
Decent filly, effective 8f, acts on g-s to frm, best on frm, has worn blinkers. Turf high 82 - 2nd of 11 getting 10lb from Silk St John (10 Jun Haydock 8f g-s RF 1878). AW high 43. Inconsistent.
**I A Balding [0-13] The C H F Partnership (from Lord Huntingdon [4-13] Nov 1998).*

SILKEN FOX (IRE) BHB 33f **RR 41f** 1908[14]

3 b g Foxhound (USA) - Crown Witness (Crowned Prince (USA)) 10.1f **(67)**
Form - 0070
Record 2000 - 1st:0 2nd:0 3rd:0 Ran:4
Pre2000 - 1st:0 2nd:0 3rd:0 Ran:3
2000 Turf 0-4: (7f 2, 10f, 12f) (g-s, gd 2, frm)
Scopey, moderate gelding, often wears blinkers. Turf high 24.
**J S Moore [0-7] Mrs Angela Speyer.*

SILKEN LADY **RR 23f** 5182[5]

4 br m Rock Hopper 10.6f **(54)** - Silk St James (Pas de Seul) 9.1f **(67)**
Form - 0003675855
Record 2000 - 1st:0 2nd:0 3rd:1 Ran:10
Pre2000 - 1st:0 2nd:0 3rd:0 Ran:3
Win Prizemoney £0 *Total Prizemoney* £386
2000 Turf 0-10: (8f 2, 10f 2, 11f 2, 12f 3, 14f) (sft, g-s 2, gd 2, g-f 2, frm 3)
Workmanlike, little account filly, effective 11f, acts on g-f, likes left handed tracks. Turf high 35 - 6th of 9 getting 32lb from Fahs (19 Jly Yarmouth 11f g-f RF 2952). **M J Ryan [0-13] Sez Les Partnership.*

SILKEN TOUCH **RR 53f** 1325[6]

2 b f Pivotal - Prima Silk **(62f 78a)** (Primo Dominie) 6.2f **(80)**
Form - 26
Record 2000 - 1st:0 2nd:1 3rd:0 Ran:2
Win Prizemoney £0 *Total Prizemoney* £812
2000 Turf 0-2: (5f, 6f) (sft, gd)
Currently fair filly. Turf high 53 (1st run) - 2nd of 5 getting 5lb from

Dayglow Dancer (24 Apr Nottingham 5f sft RF 0848).
**N A Callaghan [0-2] Norcroft Park Stud.*

SILKEN WHISPER (USA) BHB 88f **RR 87f** 4613[9]

3 b f Diesis 9f **(80)** - Yaguda (USA) (Green Dancer (USA)) 10.3f **(74)**
Form - 100
Record 2000 - 1st:1 2nd:0 3rd:0 Ran:3
Win Prizemoney £4,348 *Total Prizemoney* £4,348
Wins * **2000** Aug Sandow (GD) 10f 79+ <
2000 Turf 1-3: (10f 1-2, 12f) (g-s, gd 1-2)
Scopey, currently useful filly. Turf high 87 (began Aug) - also 1st of 5 getting 5lb from Azaan (9 Aug Sandown RF 3511).
**J H M Gosden [1-3] R E Sangster and B V Sangster.*

SILKEN WINGS (IRF) BHB 64f **RR 66f** 4728[11]

2 b f Brief Truce (USA) 9.1f **(73)** - Winged Victory (IRE) **(89f)** (Dancing Brave (USA)) 8.4f **(76)**
Form - 32200
Record 2000 - 1st:0 2nd:2 3rd:1 Ran:5
Win Prizemoney £0 *Total Prizemoney* £2,204
2000 Turf 0-5: (5f, 6f 2, 7f 2) (gd 2, g-f, frm, hrd)
Average filly. Turf high 66 (began Jly) - 2nd of 6 to Magical Flute (20 Jly Bath 6f hrd RF 2953).
**I A Balding [0-5] The C H F Partnership.*

SILK GLOVE (IRE) **RR 40f** 2223[7]

3 b c Hernando (FR) - Gwydion (USA) (Raise A Cup (USA)) 7.6f **(74)**
Form - 7
Record 2000 - 1st:0 2nd:0 3rd:0 Ran:1
2000 Turf 0-1: (9f) (g-f)
Leggy, currently moderate colt. **H R A Cecil [0-1] Niarchos Family.*

SILK LAW (IRE) BHB 82f **RR 78f** 4257[19]

2 ch f Barathea (IRE) - Jural **(95f)** (Kris) 9.5f **(73)**
Form - 11230
Record 2000 - 1st:2 2nd:1 3rd:1 Ran:5
Win Prizemoney £5,898 *Total Prizemoney* £10,228
Wins * **2000** Jun Warwic (G-F) 6.8f 76 <
* **2000** Jun Nottin (G-F) 6.1f 74
2000 Turf 2-5: (6f 1-2, 7f 1-3) (gd 2, g-f 2-3)
Above-average filly. Turf high 78 - 3rd of 12 getting 7lb from Saratov (30 Jly Ascot 7f g-f RF 3226) - also 1st of 7 giving 3lb to Jamila (28 Jun Warwick RF 2354). Was not suited by the drop back in trip when runner-up in an Ascot nursery, but ran well over seven next time. **A Berry [2-5] Kangaroo Courtiers.*

SILK ON SONG (USA) **RR** 5019[9]

2 b c Hazaam (USA) - Wazeerah (USA) (The Minstrel (CAN)) 10f **(72)**
Form - 0
Record 2000 - 1st:0 2nd:0 3rd:0 Ran:1
2000 AW 0-1: (7f) (Fibr)
Currently very poor colt. **B Smart [0-1] Paul Darling & Michael Broke.*

SILK SOUK **RR 9f** 2618[9]

2 ch f Dancing Spree (USA) 8f **(59)** - Silky Smooth (IRE) (Thatching) 8f **(66)**
Form - 00
Record 2000 - 1st:0 2nd:0 3rd:0 Ran:2
2000 Turf 0-2: (6f, 7f) (g-f, frm)
Currently very poor filly, often wears blinkers.
**R D Wylie [0-2] M R Johnson.*

SILK ST BRIDGET BHB 36f45a **RR 44f 45a** 5086[13]

3 b f Rock Hopper 10.6f **(54)** - Silk St James (Pas de Seul) 9.1f **(67)**
Form - 000088600
Record 2000 - 1st:0 2nd:0 3rd:0 Ran:9
Pre2000 - 1st:0 2nd:0 3rd:0 Ran:3
2000 Turf 0-9: (6f, 7f 4, 8f 4) (hvy, gd 2, g-f 2, frm 3, hrd)
Leggy, moderate filly, effective 8f, acts on g-f, has worn blinkers. Turf high 44 - 6th of 14 getting 26lb from Sadaka (19 Jly Yarmouth 8f g-f RF 2948).
**M J Ryan [0-12] The Bridget Partnership.*

SILK ST JOHN BHB 84f80a **RR 94df 80a** 5240[15]

6 b g Damister (USA) 9.1f **(66)** - Silk St James (Pas de Seul) 9.1f **(67)**
Form - 006513164080500
Record 2000 - 1st:2 2nd:0 3rd:1 Ran:15
Pre2000 - 1st:7 2nd:7 3rd:6 Ran:51
Win Prizemoney £51,880 *Total Prizemoney* £91,807
Wins * **2000** Jun Haydoc (G-S) H 8.1f 88 93
* **2000** May Haydoc (G-S) H 8.1f 85 88
* 1999 Jly Newbur (G-F) H 8f 92 93
* 1999 Apr Sandow (G-S) H 8.1f 92 95 <
* 1998 Aug Windso (G-F) H 8.3f 86 90
* 1998 Jly Newbur (GD) H 8f 82 87
* 1998 Jun Windso (GD) 8.3f 83
* 1998 May Chepst (G-F) 8.1f 83
* 1997 Aug Newmar (GD) H 8f 74 78
2000 Turf 2-15: (8f 2-15) (sft 2, g-s 2-6, gd 4, g-f 2, frm)
Useful gelding, effective 8 to 9f, best at 8f, acts on g-s to frm, best on g-s, likes right handed tracks, prefers tight tracks, excels at Haydock and Goodwood and Sandown. Turf high 94 - 4th of 18 getting 10lb from Caribbean Monarch (9 Jly Sandown 8f g-f RF 2658) - also 1st of 11 giving 10lb to Silken Dalliance (10 Jun Haydock RF 1878). A useful mile handicapper on his day, he won twice at Haydock during the summer. Effective on any ground, he has a useful turn-of-foot and is invariably held-up.
**M J Ryan [9-66] C R S Partners.*

SILK STOCKINGS (FR) BHB 48f **RR 71f** 4875[16]

3 b f Trempolino (USA) 11.9f **(77)** - Waaria (Shareef Dancer (USA)) 9.9f **(73)**
Form - 0307880P0
Record 2000 - 1st:0 2nd:0 3rd:1 Ran:9
Win Prizemoney £0 *Total Prizemoney* £1,155
2000 Turf 0-8: (7f, 8f 2, 10f 2, 11f, 12f, 16f) (g-s 3, gd, g-f 3, frm) 2000 AW 0-1: (16f) (Equi)
Above-average filly, effective 11f, acts on g-s. Turf high 71 - 3rd of 3 getting 14lb from First Fantasy (4 Jun Warwick 11f g-s RF 1705). Inconsistent. **C E Brittain [0-9] A J Richards.*

SILKY DAWN (IRE) **RR 88f** 4990[5]

2 b f Night Shift (USA) 8.1f **(73)** - Bluffing (IRE) (Darshaan) 9.9f **(84)**
Form - 35
Record 2000 - 1st:0 2nd:0 3rd:1 Ran:2
Win Prizemoney £0 *Total Prizemoney* £2,035
2000 Turf 0-2: (7f 2) (gd, g-f)
Currently useful filly. Turf high 88 (began Spt) - 5th of 16 to Sayedah (14 Oct Newmarket 7f gd RF 4990). Had a big home reputation prior to finishing third in a warm maiden on her debut. Fifth in a Group Three on her second run, she will come into her own over a mile. **H R A Cecil [0-2] Wafic Said.*

SILKY FINISH (USA) **RR** 3217[6]

3 ch f A P Indy (USA) - Hey Baba Lulu (USA) (Silent Screen (USA)) 8.6f **(65)**
Form - 6
Record 2000 - 1st:0 2nd:0 3rd:0 Ran:1
2000 Turf 0-1: (10f) (frm)
Light-framed, currently very poor filly. **B Hanbury [0-1] Abdullah Ali.*

SILLA (USA) BHB 95f **RR 94f** 5107[8]

2 br f Gone West (USA) 7.8f **(82)** - Silver Fling (USA) (The Minstrel (CAN)) 10f **(72)**
Form - 0311278
Record 2000 - 1st:2 2nd:1 3rd:1 Ran:7
Win Prizemoney £9,802 *Total Prizemoney* £14,047
Wins * **2000** Jly Kempto (G-F) H 5f 77+ <
* **2000** Jly Sandow (GD) 5f 75
2000 Turf 2-7: (5f 2-5, 6f 2) (gd 2, g-f 1-4, frm 1-1)
Useful filly, effective 5f, acts on g-f. Turf high 94 - 2nd of 10 to Strange Destiny (19 Aug Newbury 5f g-f RF 3788). Beautifully bred, she was unlucky in a Listed race at Newbury in August but ran a shade disappointingly on her last two starts. Open to improvement, her dam got better with age and she could develop into a Group-class sprinter. **I A Balding [2-7] George Strawbridge.*

SILLY GOOSE (IRE) **RR 70f** 4602[2]

2 b f Sadler's Wells (USA) 11.3f **(87)** - Ducking **(68f 60a)** (Reprimand)
Form - 62
Record 2000 - 1st:0 2nd:1 3rd:0 Ran:2
Win Prizemoney £0 *Total Prizemoney* £1,370
2000 Turf 0-2: (7f, 8f) (gd, g-f)
Currently above-average filly. Turf high 70 (began Aug) - 2nd of 8 to La Vita E Bella (23 Spt Haydock 8f gd RF 4602).

**J L Dunlop [0-2] Wafic Said.*

SILOGUE (IRE) RR 34f 3505[9]
3 b br g Distinctly North (USA) 7.4f **(63)** - African Bloom (African Sky) 7.7f **(50)**
Form - 7060
Record 2000 - 1st:0 2nd:0 3rd:0 Ran:4
2000 Turf 0-4: (6f 2, 8f 2) (frm 4)
Very moderate gelding. Turf high 34 (began Jly).
**O Brennan [0-4] O Brennan.*

SILVAANI (USA) RR 41f 5151[4]
2 gr c Dumaani (USA) - Ruby Silver (USA) (Silver Hawk (USA)) 8.6f **(70)**
Form - 4
Record 2000 - 1st:0 2nd:0 3rd:0 Ran:1
Win Prizemoney £0 *Total Prizemoney* £273
2000 Turf 0-1: (7f) (g-s)
Currently moderate colt.
**Miss Gay Kelleway [0-1] Lingfield Breakfast Club.*

SILVANO (GER) RR 115f 2384a[3]
4 b h Lomitas - Spirit of Eagals (Beau's Eagle (USA))
Form - 213
2000 Turf 1-3: (11f 1-2, 12f) (hvy, sft 1-1, gd)
High-class colt, effective 11 to 12f, best at 11f, acts on sft to gd, best on gd. Turf high 115 - 1st of 5 giving 4lb to Catella (4 Jun Baden-Baden RF 1824a). **A Wohler in GER [2-6].*

SILVER ARROW (USA) BHB 55f60a **RR 38f 60a** 4529a[30]
3 b br f Shadeed (USA) 7.7f **(72)** - Aneesati (Kris) 9.5f **(73)**
Form - 0400000
Record 2000 - 1st:0 2nd:0 3rd:0 Ran:7
Pre2000 - 1st:0 2nd:0 3rd:0 Ran:1
Win Prizemoney £0 *Total Prizemoney* £243
2000 Turf 0-6: (7f 4, 10f, 12f) (g-s, gd 3, g-f) 2000 AW 0-1: (7f) (Fibr)
Scopey, fair filly, has worn blinkers. Turf high 68. Becoming disappointing.
**F Flood in IRE [0-2] J L Doyle (from B W Hills [0-6] Jun 2000).*

SILVER AURIOLE BHB 27f **RR 38f** 2637[14]
3 gr f Absalom 7.1f **(56)** - Saltina (Bustino) 10.4f **(64)**
Form - 00700
Record 2000 - 1st:0 2nd:0 3rd:0 Ran:5
2000 Turf 0-5: (6f, 8f 3, 10f) (hvy, gd, frm 3)
Small, very moderate filly, has worn blinkers. Turf high 38.
**J R Arnold [0-5] Miss C M Green.*

SILVER BULLET RR 32f 2986[5]
4 gr g Grey Desire 9.3f **(49)** - Spanish Realm (King of Spain) 7.8f **(52)**
Form - 00705
Record 2000 - 1st:0 2nd:0 3rd:0 Ran:5
Pre2000 - 1st:0 2nd:0 3rd:0 Ran:3
2000 Turf 0-5: (7f 3, 8f, 10f) (g-s, gd 2, frm, hrd)
Leggy, very moderate gelding, often wears blinkers. Turf high 32. Inconsistent. **W W Haigh [0-8] Des Redhead.*

SILVER CHEVALIER (IRE) RR 49f 4969[25]
2 gr c Petong 7.6f **(58)** - Princess Eurolink (Be My Guest (USA)) 9.3f **(67)**
Form - 0
Record 2000 - 1st:0 2nd:0 3rd:0 Ran:1
2000 Turf 0-1: (8f) (gd)
Currently moderate colt. **C N Allen [0-1] Green Square Racing.*

SILVER CLOUD RR 35f 1904[18]
2 gr f Petong 7.6f **(58)** - Pepeke (Mummy's Pet) 7.7f **(60)**
Form - 000
Record 2000 - 1st:0 2nd:0 3rd:0 Ran:3
2000 Turf 0-3: (5f, 6f 2) (g-f 2, frm)
Currently very moderate filly, has worn blinkers. Turf high 35.
**W Jarvis [0-3] Yusuf Baig.*

SILVER COLOURS (USA) BHB 97f **RR 96+f** 769[12]
3 b br f Silver Hawk (USA) 11.2f **(85)** - Team Colors (USA) (Mr Prospector (USA)) 8.8f **(78)**
Form - 0
Record 2000 - 1st:0 2nd:0 3rd:0 Ran:1
Pre2000 - 1st:1 2nd:0 3rd:0 Ran:2
Win Prizemoney £10,841 *Total Prizemoney* £10,841
Wins * 1999 Oct Newmar (SFT) L 8f 96+ <
2000 Turf 0-1: (7f) (gd)
Scopey, currently very useful filly. Not knocked about on her Leicester two-year-old debut, she went on to land a Newmarket Listed race over a mile next time, winning with plenty in hand and handling the soft ground really well. Well beaten in the Nell Gwyn on her return. **L M Cumani [1-3] Christopher Wright.*

SILVER DAWN (IRE) BHB 40f **RR** 5005[7]
3 gr f Common Grounds 8.1f **(66)** - Nicea (IRE) (Dominion) 8.5f **(63)**
Form - 7
Record 2000 - 1st:0 2nd:0 3rd:0 Ran:1
2000 AW 0-1: (6f) (Fibr)
Scopey, currently very moderate filly.
**P W Harris [0-1] Mrs P W Harris.*

SILVER GREY LADY (IRE) RR 73f 5098[8]
2 gr f Saddlers' Hall (IRE) 10.5f **(65)** - Early Rising (USA) (Grey Dawn II) 11.1f **(72)**
Form - 38
Record 2000 - 1st:0 2nd:0 3rd:1 Ran:2
Win Prizemoney £0 *Total Prizemoney* £850
2000 Turf 0-2: (8f 2) (gd, g-f)
Currently above-average filly. Turf high 73 (began Spt).
**J L Dunlop [0-2] Mrs Philippa Cooper.*

SILVER GYRE (IRE) BHB 56f48a **RR 56f 48a** 346[6]
4 b m Silver Hawk (USA) 11.2f **(85)** - Kraemer (USA) (Lyphard (USA)) 9.9f **(72)**
Form - 66426
Record 2000 - 1st:0 2nd:1 3rd:0 Ran:4
Pre2000 - 1st:1 2nd:1 3rd:0 Ran:13
Win Prizemoney £2,775 *Total Prizemoney* £4,235
Wins * 1999 Jly Bath (G-F) H 17.2f 54 56 <
2000 AW 0-4: (12f, 16f 3) (Fibr 4)
Light-framed, fair filly, effective 12 to 17f, acts on sft to hrd, has worn blinkers, likes left handed tracks, favours tight tracks. AW high 47.
**D J Wintle [1-14] Mrs Joan Egan (from Mrs J R Ramsden [0-3] Oct 1998).*

SILVER INFERNO RR 45f 4055[7]
2 gr c Chocolat de Meguro (USA) - Miss Lakeland (Pongee)
Form - 07
Record 2000 - 1st:0 2nd:0 3rd:0 Ran:2
2000 Turf 0-2: (7f 2) (gd 2)
Currently moderate colt. Turf high 45.
**W de Best-Turner [0-2] W de Best-Turner.*

SILVER JORDEN BHB 100f **RR 94f** 4137a[4]
2 gr f Imp Society (USA) 7.1f **(63)** - Final Call (Town Crier) 10.2f **(55)**
Form - 11714
Record 2000 - 1st:3 2nd:0 3rd:0 Ran:5
Win Prizemoney £20,965 *Total Prizemoney* £23,270
Wins * **2000** Jly Sandow (G-F) L 7.1f 98 <
* **2000** Jun Yarmou (G-F) 6f 89+
* **2000** May Lingfi (HVY) 6f 67+
2000 Turf 3-5: (6f 2-3, 7f 1-2) (g-s 1-2, g-f 2-2, frm)
Useful filly. Turf high 98 - 1st of 12 from Hotelgenie Dot Com (27 Jly Sandown RF 3153) - also 1st of 7 giving 8lb to Sylvan Girl (15 Jun Yarmouth RF 1998). She was not particularly consistent, but is capable of useful form and connections will probably map out a continental plan of attack for her this year. Likely to stay a mile, she acts on any ground. **J L Dunlop [3-5].*

SILVER PRAIRIE (IRE) BHB 40f **RR 51f** 4813[12]
3 b f Common Grounds 8.1f **(66)** - Silver Slipper **(62f)** (Indian Ridge)
Form - 070
Record 2000 - 1st:0 2nd:0 3rd:0 Ran:3
2000 Turf 0-3: (7f, 8f 2) (sft, g-s, gd)
Light-framed, currently fair filly. Turf high 51 (began Spt).
**C R Egerton [0-3] Austin Allison.*

SILVER PRINCE BHB 25f **RR 17f** 190[7]

5 gr g Mystiko (USA) 7.7f **(59)** - Hawaiian Song (Henbit (USA)) 9f **(61)**
Form - 7
Record 2000 - 1st:0 2nd:0 3rd:0 Ran:1
Pre2000 - 1st:0 2nd:0 3rd:0 Ran:3
2000 AW 0-1: (7f) (Fibr)
Poor gelding. **D Nicholls [0-4] John Gilbertson.*

SILVER QUEEN BHB 53f **RR 62f** 4492[13]

3 ch f Arazi (USA) 9.2f **(74)** - Love of Silver (USA) (Arctic Tern (USA)) 8.9f **(69)**
Form - 088246080
Record 2000 - 1st:0 2nd:1 3rd:0 Ran:9
Pre2000 - 1st:0 2nd:0 3rd:0 Ran:5
Win Prizemoney £0 *Total Prizemoney* £1,495
2000 Turf 0-9: (8f 4, 10f 3, 12f 2) (gd, g-f 2, frm 5, hrd)
Light-framed, average filly, effective 8 to 10f, best at 10f, acts on gd to frm, has worn blinkers, prefers right handed tracks, likes tight tracks. Turf high 65 - 2nd of 13 getting 1lb from Common Consent (30 Jun Folkestone 10f g-f RF 2396). Becoming disappointing. Some ability in varied company so far, but has yet to win.
**C E Brittain [0-14] Ali Saeed.*

SILVER ROBIN (USA) BHB 95f **RR 98?f** 1314[2]

4 b br g Silver Hawk (USA) 11.2f **(85)** - Wedge Musical (What A Guest) 7f **(62)**
Form - 2
Record 2000 - 1st:0 2nd:1 3rd:0 Ran:1
Pre2000 - 1st:0 2nd:1 3rd:1 Ran:2
Win Prizemoney £0 *Total Prizemoney* £4,366
2000 Turf 0-1: (14f) (gd)
Scopey, currently very useful gelding. **N J Henderson [0-1] W V M W & Mrs E S Robins (from L M Cumani [0-2] Apr 1999).*

SILVER SECRET BHB 40f **RR 44f** 3589[5]

6 ro g Absalom 7.1f **(56)** - Secret Dance (Sadler's Wells (USA)) 10f **(76)**
Form - 0516868555
Record 2000 - 1st:1 2nd:0 3rd:0 Ran:10
Pre2000 - 1st:2 2nd:0 3rd:3 Ran:29
Win Prizemoney £8,117 *Total Prizemoney* £11,622
Wins * 2000 Jun Haydoc (G-S) H 10.5f 38 44
* 1999 Jly Newmar (G-F) H 8f 42 43
1997 Aug Folkes (G-F) 6f 60 <
2000 Turf 1-10: (8f 3, 10f 5, 11f 1-1, 12f) (g-s 1-1, gd, g-f 4, frm 4)
Moderate gelding, effective 8 to 11f, best at 8f, acts on g-s to frm, has worn blinkers, likes left handed tracks, excels at Haydock and Newmarket. Turf high 44 - 1st of 17 getting 11lb from Big Al (9 Jun Haydock RF 1848). Consistent. **S Gollings [2-29] Northern Bloodstock Racing (from M J Heaton-Ellis [1-11] Spt 1997).*

SILVER SKY BHB 33f33a **RR 26f 33a** 1703[19]

4 gr m Chilibang 7f **(55)** - Sizzling Sista (Sizzling Melody)
Form - 000000
Record 2000 - 1st:0 2nd:0 3rd:0 Ran:4
Pre2000 - 1st:0 2nd:0 3rd:0 Ran:5
2000 Turf 0-4: (6f 2, 7f, 11f) (g-s, g-f 2, frm)
Scopey, little account filly. Turf high 26. Inconsistent.
**M D I Usher [0-10] Bryan Fry.*

SILVER SOCKS BHB 39f **RR 43df** 3981[2]

3 gr g Petong 7.6f **(58)** - Tasmim (Be My Guest (USA)) 9.3f **(67)**
Form - 0062
Record 2000 - 1st:0 2nd:1 3rd:0 Ran:4
Pre2000 - 1st:0 2nd:0 3rd:0 Ran:4
Win Prizemoney £0 *Total Prizemoney* £639
2000 Turf 0-4: (6f 2, 10f 2) (g-f 2, frm 2)
Leggy, moderate gelding. Turf high 40. Inconsistent.
**M W Easterby [0-8] Miss V Foster.*

SILVER SPOON (IRE) BHB 42f **RR 39f** 1551[13]

3 b f College Chapel - Emmuska (USA) (Roberto (USA)) 10f **(76)**
Form - 8080
Record 2000 - 1st:0 2nd:0 3rd:0 Ran:4
2000 Turf 0-3: (8f, 10f, 14f) (sft, g-f, frm) 2000 AW 0-1: (8f) (Fibr)
Unfurnished, very moderate filly. Turf high 39.
**R Guest [0-4] The Escapologists.*

SILVER TONGUED BHB 26f **RR 30f** 4925[10]

4 b g Green Desert (USA) 7.8f **(70)** - Love of Silver (USA) (Arctic Tern (USA)) 8.9f **(69)**
Form - 70068400
Record 2000 - 1st:0 2nd:0 3rd:0 Ran:8
Pre2000 - 1st:0 2nd:0 3rd:0 Ran:5
Win Prizemoney £0 *Total Prizemoney* £318
2000 Turf 0-7: (6f 2, 7f 3, 8f, 10f) (g-s, gd, frm 4, hrd) 2000 AW 0-1: (7f) (Equi)
Lengthy, very moderate gelding. Turf high 30.
**J M Bradley [0-8] Mrs Kay Blandford (from C E Brittain [0-5] Spt 1999).*

SILVER TONIC **RR 51f** 2616[6]

4 gr h Petong 7.6f **(58)** - Princess Eurolink (Be My Guest (USA)) 9.3f **(67)**
Form - 76
Record 2000 - 1st:0 2nd:0 3rd:0 Ran:2
2000 Turf 0-2: (7f, 8f) (gd, g-f)
Scopey, currently fair colt. Turf high 51 (began Jun).
**K Mahdi [0-2] Miss Debbie Mountain.*

SILVERTOWN BHB 68f69a **RR 69f 69a** 4823[1]

5 b g Danehill (USA) 9.1f **(79)** - Docklands (USA) (Theatrical)
Form - 201100211
Record 2000 - 1st:4 2nd:1 3rd:0 Ran:7
Pre2000 - 1st:2 2nd:3 3rd:3 Ran:23
Win Prizemoney £21,736 *Total Prizemoney* £27,099
Wins * 2000 Oct Windso (G-S) H 10f 65 69 <
*** 2000** Spt Goodwo (GD) H 8f 58 64
*** 2000** *Mar Lingfi (STD) H 10f 55 68+*
*** 2000** *Feb Wolver (STD) H 9.4f 55 65+*
* 1999 Spt York (G-F) H 10.4f 51 53
* 1999 Aug Epsom (GD) H 10.1f 45 49
2000 Turf 2-5: (8f 1-2, 10f 1-2, 11f) (hvy, gd 1-2, g-f 1-1, frm) 2000 AW 2-2: (9f 1-1, 10f 1-1) (Equi 1-1, Fibr 1-1)
Average gelding, effective 8 to 10f, best at 10f, acts on gd to g-f - acts on AW. Turf high 69 - 1st of 21 giving 3lb to Thihn (6 Oct Windsor RF 4823) - also 1st of 21 getting 2lb from One Dinar (8 Spt Goodwood RF 4304). AW high 68 - 1st of 13 getting 3lb from Sea Danzig (1 Mar Lingfield RF 0387) - also 1st of 13 giving 9lb to Gablesea (22 Feb Wolverhampton RF 0338). Inconsistent. He has plenty of temperament and flashes his tail under pressure. He needs the kid-glove treatment and Jamie Spencer rode a peach of a race on him to win at Lingfield.
**B J Curley [6-25] Mrs B J Curley (from J H M Gosden [0-5] Jun 1998).*

SIMAND BHB 25f41a **RR 13f 41a** 3187[10]

8 b m Reprimand 8.2f **(63)** - Emmylou (Arctic Tern (USA)) 8.9f **(69)**
Form - 000
Record 2000 - 1st:0 2nd:0 3rd:0 Ran:3
Pre2000 - 1st:3 2nd:2 3rd:3 Ran:27
Win Prizemoney £8,430 *Total Prizemoney* £12,616
2000 Turf 0-2: (7f, 10f) (g-s, g-f) 2000 AW 0-1: (8f) (Fibr)
Poor mare, has worn blinkers. Turf high 13. Becoming disappointing.
**A Smith [0-3] Mrs S Setterington (from G M Moore [0-12] Aug 1996).*

SIMA'S GOLD (IRE) BHB 57f **RR 46f** 2484[1]

2 b f Goldmark (USA) - Mujadil Princess (IRE) (Mujadil (USA))
Form - 61
Record 2000 - 1st:1 2nd:0 3rd:0 Ran:2
Win Prizemoney £1,827 *Total Prizemoney* £1,827
Wins * 2000 *Jly Southw (STD) S 5f 61* <
2000 Turf 0-1: (5f) (g-f) 2000 AW 1-1: (5f 1-1) (Fibr 1-1)
Currently average filly. (1st run) - 1st of 8 getting 10lb from Some Dust (3 Jly Southwell RF 2484). **W R Muir [1-2] D J Kerwood.*

SIMBATU BHB 54f55a **RR 58f 55a** 4174[18]

3 b f Muhtarram (USA) - Kantado (Saulingo) 6.2f **(53)**
Form - 8650
Record 2000 - 1st:0 2nd:0 3rd:0 Ran:3
Pre2000 - 1st:0 2nd:0 3rd:1 Ran:4
Win Prizemoney £0 *Total Prizemoney* £414
2000 Turf 0-3: (5f 2, 6f) (g-f, frm 2)
Light-framed, fair filly, effective 5f, acts on g-f. Turf high 58 (began Jly). **Miss I Foustok [0-7] A Foustok.*

SIMLA BIBI **RR 68f** 4861[3]

2 ch f Indian Ridge 7.6f **(74)** - Scandalette (Niniski (USA)) 10.6f **(65)**
Form - 33
Record 2000 - 1st:0 2nd:0 3rd:2 Ran:2
Win Prizemoney £0 *Total Prizemoney* £1,624
2000 Turf 0-2: (8f 2) (sft, frm)
Currently average filly. Turf high 68 (began Spt) - 3rd of 7 getting 5lb from Tupgill Tango (7 Oct York 8f sft RF 4861).
**B J Meehan [0-2] Miss K Rausing.*

SIMPATICH (FR) BHB 86f RR 83f 4849a[1]

2 ch c First Trump - Arc Empress Jane (IRE) (Rainbow Quest (USA)) 10.4f **(75)**
Form - 436311
Record 2000 - 1st:2 2nd:0 3rd:2 Ran:6
Win Prizemoney £14,639 *Total Prizemoney* £16,210
Wins * **2000** Oct San Si (HVY) 7.5f 83 <
* **2000** Spt San Si (GD) 7.5f 78
2000 Turf 2-6: (6f, 7f 3, 8f 2-2) (hvy 1-1, gd 1-3, g-f 2)
Decent colt, effective 7 to 8f, best at 7f, acts on hvy to g-f. Turf high 83 (began Jly) - 1st of 4 giving 2lb to Betasito (1 Oct San Siro RF 4849a) - also 1st of 11 from King Of Lycius (16 Spt San Siro RF 4569a). **L M Cumani [2-6] Scuderia Rencati Srl.*

SIMPLE IDEALS (USA) BHB 45f RR 52f 4863[6]

6 bb g Woodman (USA) 9.7f **(77)** - Comfort and Style (Be My Guest (USA)) 9.3f **(67)**
Form - 0285565425246
Record 2000 - 1st:0 2nd:3 3rd:0 Ran:13
Pre2000 - 1st:3 2nd:2 3rd:7 Ran:36
Win Prizemoney £10,443 *Total Prizemoney* £24,074
Wins * 1999 Oct Redcar (GD) H 14.1f 43 46 <
* 1999 Aug Ayr (G-F) H 15f 33 41
* 1999 Aug Haydoc (G-S) H 11.9f 36 39
2000 Turf 0-13: (12f 5, 13f, 14f 5, 15f, 16f) (sft, g-s, gd 5, g-f, frm 4, hrd)
Fair gelding, effective 11 to 15f, best at 14f, acts on g-s to frm, best on gd, has worn blinkers, prefers left handed tracks, excels at Haydock and York and Doncaster, likes Redcar. Turf high 52 - 2nd of 11 getting 20lb from Capriolo (30 Aug York 12f gd RF 4104). Consistent. **Don Enrico Incisa [3-30] Don Enrico Incisa (from N Tinkler [0-11] May 1999).*

SIMPLICITY RR 95f 4796a[7]

3 b f Polish Precedent (USA) 9f **(73)** - Safita (Habitat) 9.4f **(70)**
Form - 1376877
2000 Turf 1-7: (8f, 10f, 12f 1-4, 14f) (g-s, gd 1-6)
Very useful filly, effective 12f, acts on g-s, has worn blinkers. Turf high 95 - 3rd of 9 getting 15lb from Katiykha (7 Jun Gowran Park 12f g-s RF 1934a). Listed placed on her second start, she lost her way in late summer and does not appear to have a trip.
**N Meade in IRE [1-7] Barouche Stud (Ireland) Ltd.*

SIMPLY BROKE RR 23f 2439[11]

2 br g Simply Great (FR) 11.9f **(61)** - Empty Purse (Pennine Walk) 8.5f **(61)**
Form - 00
Record 2000 - 1st:0 2nd:0 3rd:0 Ran:2
2000 Turf 0-2: (5f, 6f) (g-f, frm)
Currently little account gelding, has broken blood-vessels. Turf high 23.
**P C Haslam [0-2] Mrs J Trotter/Marquess Of Downshire.*

SIMPLY ERIC (IRE) BHB 63f RR 59f 4998[4]

2 b c Simply Great (FR) 11.9f **(61)** - Sanjana (GER) (Priamos (GER)) 11.1f **(61)**
Form - 244
Record 2000 - 1st:0 2nd:1 3rd:0 Ran:3
Win Prizemoney £0 *Total Prizemoney* £1,705
2000 Turf 0-3: (6f, 8f 2) (g-s, gd 2)
Currently fair colt. Turf high 59 (1st run) (began Aug) - 2nd of 8 to Smyslov (22 Aug Hamilton 8f gd RF 3845).
**J L Eyre [0-3] Pinnacle Great Partnership.*

SIMPLY NOBLE BHB 68f RR 77f 1592[8]

4 b h Noble Patriarch 12.2f **(43)** - Simply Candy (IRE) (Simply Great (FR)) 8.2f **(65)**
Form - 008
Record 2000 - 1st:0 2nd:0 3rd:0 Ran:3
Pre2000 - 1st:1 2nd:1 3rd:1 Ran:9
Win Prizemoney £2,738 *Total Prizemoney* £5,978
Wins * 1998 Spt Hamilt (SFT) 8.3f 81 <
2000 Turf 0-3: (10f 2, 13f) (g-s, gd, g-f)
Lengthy, above-average colt, effective 10 to 12f, acts on g-f to frm, prefers left handed tracks. Turf high 69.
**K McAuliffe [1-12] MCKPS Equine Ltd.*

SIMPLY REMY BHB 40f RR 30f 4727[14]

2 ch g Chaddleworth (IRE) - Exemplaire (FR) (Polish Precedent (USA)) 10.2f **(60)**
Form - 000
Record 2000 - 1st:0 2nd:0 3rd:0 Ran:3
2000 Turf 0-3: (6f 3) (gd, g-f, frm)
Currently very moderate gelding. Turf high 30.
**John Berry [0-3] Simply 2000.*

SIMPLY SENSATIONAL (IRE) BHB 67f RR 72f 5201[4]

3 ch c Cadeaux Genereux 7.9f **(76)** - Monaiya (Shareef Dancer (USA)) 9.9f **(73)**
Form - 4434
Record 2000 - 1st:0 2nd:0 3rd:1 Ran:4
Win Prizemoney £0 *Total Prizemoney* £1,480
2000 Turf 0-4: (8f 3, 12f) (g-s, gd 3)
Light-framed, above-average colt. Turf high 72 (began Aug).
**P F I Cole [0-4] M Arbib.*

SIMULCASTING (IRE) BHB 72f RR 75f 1524[4]

3 ch c College Chapel - Simply The Best (ITY) (Lidhame) 9.2f **(50)**
Form - 5034
Record 2000 - 1st:0 2nd:0 3rd:1 Ran:4
Win Prizemoney £0 *Total Prizemoney* £505
2000 Turf 0-4: (7f 2, 8f, 9f) (hvy, gd 2, g-f)
Above-average colt. Turf high 75 - 3rd of 17 to Autumn Rain (12 May Lingfield 7f gd RF 1172).
**L M Cumani [0-4] Allevamento Gialloblu.*

SINCERITY BHB 65f60a RR 81f 60a 5021[4]

3 b f Selkirk (USA) 7.9f **(76)** - Integrity (Reform) 8.9f **(62)**
Form - 72304
Record 2000 - 1st:0 2nd:1 3rd:1 Ran:5
Win Prizemoney £0 *Total Prizemoney* £1,758
2000 Turf 0-5: (7f 2, 8f 3) (g-s 2, gd 2, g-f)
Rangy, decent filly. Turf high 81 - 2nd of 13 getting 5lb from Mornings Minion (7 Jly Warwick 8f gd RF 2615).
**J R Fanshawe [0-5] Mrs Mary Watt.*

SING AND DANCE BHB 50f RR 52f 3927[5]

7 b m Rambo Dancer (CAN) 8.4f **(59)** - Musical Princess (Cavo Doro) 10.6f **(57)**
Form - 2553275
Record 2000 - 1st:0 2nd:2 3rd:1 Ran:7
Pre2000 - 1st:6 2nd:5 3rd:8 Ran:52
Win Prizemoney £20,571 *Total Prizemoney* £33,682
Wins 1999 Aug Hamilt (G-F) H 12.1f 50 52 <
1999 May Mussel (G-F) H 12f 48 52 <
1998 Oct Catter (G-S) H 12f 47 50
1998 Jly Newcas (GD) H 12.4f 44 46
1998 Jun Mussel (G-F) H 12f 39 42
1997 Aug Redcar (G-F) H 10f 38 44
2000 Turf 0-7: (12f 3, 13f 2, 14f 2) (gd, g-f, frm 5)
Fair mare, effective 11 to 14f, best at 12f, acts on gd to frm, best on frm, has worn blinkers, excels at Newcastle and likes Catterick and Hamilton. Turf high 52 - 2nd of 12 getting 15lb from Bhutan (8 Aug Catterick 14f frm RF 3450). Consistent.
**J R Weymes [0-7] Mrs N Napier (from E Weymes [6-52] Oct 1999).*

SING A SONG (IRE) RR 89f 4690[3]

2 b f Blues Traveller (IRE) - Raja Moulana (Raja Baba (USA)) 10f **(64)**
Form - 13
Record 2000 - 1st:1 2nd:0 3rd:1 Ran:2
Win Prizemoney £2,938 *Total Prizemoney* £4,123
Wins * **2000** Jly Windso (SFT) 5f 68+ <
2000 Turf 1-2: (5f 1-1, 6f) (gd 1-2)
Currently useful filly. Turf high 89 (began Jly) - 3rd of 6 getting 8lb from Inspector General (27 Spt Salisbury 6f gd RF 4690).
**R Hannon [1-2] Lady Davis.*

SING CHEONG (IRE) BHB 55f47a **RR 53f 47a** 1199[4]

4 b h Forest Wind (USA) - Lady Counsel (IRE) (Law Society (USA)) 9.9f **(70)**

Form - 243844

Record 2000 - 1st:0 2nd:0 3rd:0 Ran:3
Pre2000 - 1st:0 2nd:1 3rd:2 Ran:9

Win Prizemoney £0 *Total Prizemoney* £1,832

2000 Turf 0-1: (8f) (frm) 2000 AW 0-2: (7f, 8f) (Equi, Fibr)

Unfurnished, fair colt, effective 7f, acts on g-f, has worn blinkers. AW high 42. A very disappointing performer.

**G C H Chung [0-12] H C Chung.*

SING FOR ME (IRE) BHB 34f32a **RR 32f 32a** 2957[7]

5 b br m Songlines (FR) 5f **(68)** - Running For You (FR) (Pampabird) 7.5f **(73)**

Form - 0070884842450600657

Record 2000 - 1st:0 2nd:1 3rd:0 Ran:15
Pre2000 - 1st:1 2nd:1 3rd:3 Ran:51

Win Prizemoney £1,738 *Total Prizemoney* £3,665

Wins * 1998 *Feb Wolver (STD) S* *5f* *53* <

2000 Turf 0-3: (5f 3) (g-f, hrd 2) 2000 AW 0-12: (5f 5, 6f 5, 7f 2) (Fibr 12)

Very moderate filly, effective 5 to 6f, acts on gd - acts on Fibr, has worn blinkers. Turf high 27. AW high 38 - 2nd of 12 getting 16lb from Blushing Grenadier (28 Feb Southwell 6f Fibr RF 0372).

**R Hollinshead [1-66] Miss Sarah Hollinshead.*

SINGLE CURRENCY BHB 48f **RR 38f** 5079[6]

4 b h Barathea (IRE) - Kithanga (IRE) **(109f)** (Darshaan) 9.9f **(84)**

Form - 706

Record 2000 - 1st:0 2nd:0 3rd:0 Ran:3
Pre2000 - 1st:0 2nd:0 3rd:1 Ran:1

Win Prizemoney £0 *Total Prizemoney* £625

2000 Turf 0-3: (10f, 12f 2) (g-s, gd 2)

Well made, very moderate colt. Turf high 38.

**P Butler [0-1] Christopher Wilson (from P F I Cole [0-3] May 2000).*

SINGLE HONOUR BHB 100f **RR 90f** 4280[6]

2 b f Mark of Esteem (IRE) - Once Upon a Time (Teenoso (USA)) 9.9f **(72)**

Form - 5226

Record 2000 - 1st:0 2nd:2 3rd:0 Ran:4

Win Prizemoney £0 *Total Prizemoney* £2,257

2000 Turf 0-4: (6f, 7f, 8f 2) (gd, frm 3)

Useful filly. Turf high 90. Bred to improve (a half-sister to Arablan Story), she shaped with plenty of promise, finishing a creditable sixth in the Group 3 May Hill Stakes on her final start. Certain to win a maiden, she should stay a mile and a quarter.

**R Hannon [0-4] The Queen.*

SINGLE TRACK MIND BHB 79f **RR 62f** 5217[2]

2 b c Mind Games - Compact Disc (IRE) **(52f 55a)** (Royal Academy (USA))

Form - 052

Record 2000 - 1st:0 2nd:1 3rd:0 Ran:3

Win Prizemoney £0 *Total Prizemoney* £1,136

2000 Turf 0-3: (6f 3) (sft, gd, frm)

Currently decent colt. Turf high 62 (began Jly) - 2nd of 10 giving 5lb to Ecstatic (27 Oct Brighton 6f sft RF 5217).

**N Hamilton [0-3] John Hopkins (T/A So Racing).*

SINGSONG BHB 85f **RR 89f** 5127[6]

3 b g Paris House 5.9f **(64)** - Miss Whittingham (IRE) **(53f 55a)** (Fayruz)

Form - 437330006

Record 2000 - 1st:0 2nd:0 3rd:3 Ran:9
Pre2000 - 1st:2 2nd:1 3rd:1 Ran:8

Win Prizemoney £6,455 *Total Prizemoney* £16,147

Wins 1999 Jun Ripon (G-F) 5f 87 <
1999 Mar Doncas (G-S) 5f 80

2000 Turf 0-9: (5f 8, 6f) (g-s 2, gd 3, g-f 2, frm 2)

Neat, useful gelding, effective 5f, acts on g-s to frm, best on g-f, does well at Doncaster. Turf high 89 - 3rd of 14 giving 17lb to Xanadu (3 Jun Musselburgh 5f frm RF 1683). **A Berry [0-9] G L Tanner (from J Berry [2-8] Jly 1999).*

SINJAREE RR 69f 5075[5]

2 b c Mark of Esteem (IRE) - Forthwith **(94f)** (Midyan (USA)) 6f **(60)**

Form - 05

Record 2000 - 1st:0 2nd:0 3rd:0 Ran:2

2000 Turf 0-2: (7f, 8f) (g-s, frm)

Currently average colt. Turf high 69 (began Spt).

**E A L Dunlop [0-2] Mohammed Jaber.*

SINNDAR (IRE) RR 130+f 4846a[1]

3 b c Grand Lodge (USA) - Sinntara (IRE) (Lashkari) 9.8f **(67)**

Form - 211111

2000 Turf 5-6: (10f 1-2, 12f 4-4) (sft, gd 4-4, g-f 1-1)

High-calibre colt, effective 12f, acts on gd, does well at Curragh, likes Longchamp. Turf high 130 - 1st of 11 from Glyndebourne (2 Jly Curragh RF 2530a) - also 1st of 10 giving 3lb to Egyptband (1 Oct Longchamp RF 4846a). Inconsistent. Narrowly beaten by Grand Finale on his reappearance, there was plenty to like about his defeat of Bach in the Derrinstown Stud Derby Trial at Leopardstown next time and he relished the step up to a mile and a half when beating Sakhee in the Derby at Epsom. Followed up in emphatic style in the Irish version and was even more impressive when running away with the Prix Niel. He became the first horse ever to land the English, Irish Derby and Arc treble with an authoritative victory at Longchamp. Sadly, the Aga Khan continued his policy with his Derby winners by retiring him to stud after that race. Perhaps his achievements were slightly overshadowed in a year when there were colts such as Dubai Millennium, Montjeu, Giant's Causeway and Kalanisi in action, but nevertheless he had all the attributes of a Champion and fully deserved his place as top three-year-old in the International Classifications.

**J Oxx in IRE [7-8] Aga Khan.*

SINON (IRE) BHB 99f **RR 108f** 2853[7]

5 ch g Ela-Mana-Mou 12.7f **(72)** - Come In (Be My Guest (USA)) 9.3f **(67)**

Form - 1657

Sinndar, the first horse to win The English Derby, Irish Derby and Prix de l'Arc de Triomphe

Record 2000 - 1st:0 2nd:0 3rd:0 Ran:3
Pre2000 - 1st:3 2nd:0 3rd:0 Ran:7

Win Prizemoney £28,204 *Total Prizemoney* £34,099

Wins 1999 Nov Saint- (HVY) L 15.5f 108 <
* 1998 May York (GD) 13.9f 96
* 1997 Spt Redcar (FRM) 9f 85+

2000 Turf 0-3: (14f 3) (g-s, gd 2)

Pattern-class gelding. Turf high 103. Consistent. Lightly raced, he did not find his best in 2000.

**M Johnston [2-9] Ridings Racing (from M A Johnson [1-1] Nov 1999).*

SIONED LYN BHB 43f **RR 53f** 2050[12]
3 b br f Perpendicular - Lady Spider (Ring Bidder)
Form - 200300
Record 2000 - 1st:0 2nd:1 3rd:1 Ran:6
Win Prizemoney £0 *Total Prizemoney* £2,191
2000 Turf 0-6: (10f 4, 11f, 12f) (sft, g-s, gd 3, g-f)
Light-framed, fair filly, effective 11f, acts on sft. Turf high 70 (1st run) - 2nd of 8 to Bedara (3 Apr Warwick 11f sft RF 0594).
**D Burchell [0-6] Lyn Phillips.*

SIOUX CHEF BHB 67f **RR ?f** 5139[8]
3 b f Be My Chief (USA) 10.2f **(62)** - Sea Fret (Habat) 7.6f **(61)**
Form - 8
Record 2000 - 1st:0 2nd:0 3rd:0 Ran:1
Pre2000 - 1st:1 2nd:0 3rd:0 Ran:2
Win Prizemoney £3,571 *Total Prizemoney* £3,821
Wins 1999 Jly Bath (FRM) 5.7f 84 <
2000 Turf 0-1: (8f) (g-s)
Scopey, currently very poor filly.
**J A Osborne [0-1] Mountgrange Stud (from M R Channon [1-2] Jly 1999).*

SIPOWITZ BHB 38f35a **RR 27f 35a** 4477[11]
6 b g Warrshan (USA) 9.7f **(59)** - Springs Welcome (Blakeney) 10.5f **(64)**
Form - 58300
Record 2000 - 1st:0 2nd:0 3rd:1 Ran:5
Pre2000 - 1st:5 2nd:1 3rd:2 Ran:16
Win Prizemoney £14,226 *Total Prizemoney* £16,818
Wins * 1997 Oct Pontef (G-S) H 18f 56 64 <
* 1997 Oct Pontef (G-F) H 17.1f 53 57
* 1997 *Aug Lingfi (G-S) H 16f 46 50*
* 1997 Jly Lingfi (G-F) H 16f 44 52
* 1997 *Jun Wolver (STD) H 14.8f 44 41*
2000 Turf 0-1: (16f) (g-f) 2000 AW 0-4: (12f, 14f, 15f 2) (Fibr 4)
Moderate gelding. AW high 43. **C A Cyzer [5-21] R M Cyzer.*

SIPSI FAWR BHB 78f **RR 84f** 2448[7]
3 b f Selkirk (USA) 7.9f **(76)** - Sipsi Fach (Prince Sabo) 7.2f **(62)**
Form - 0137
Record 2000 - 1st:1 2nd:0 3rd:1 Ran:4
Win Prizemoney £3,835 *Total Prizemoney* £5,335
Wins * 2000 May Nottin (G-S) 8.2f 66 <
2000 Turf 1-4: (7f, 8f 1-2, 10f) (gd 1-2, g-f, frm)
Light-framed, decent filly. Turf high 84 - 3rd of 7 getting 18lb from Forbearing (16 Jun Goodwood 10f g-f RF 2016). A daughter of a useful racemare for the same stable, she was unraced at two but landed an ordinary Nottingham maiden on her second start in May. Probably put up a better performance when third in a Goodwood handicap next time. Ten furlongs looks her trip.
**M L W Bell [1-4] W H Joyce.*

SIPTITZ HEIGHTS (IRE) BHB 88f **RR 84f** 5128[6]
2 b f Zieten (USA) - The Multiyorker (IRE) **(68f)** (Digamist (USA))
Form - 50105756
Record 2000 - 1st:1 2nd:0 3rd:0 Ran:8
Win Prizemoney £6,119 *Total Prizemoney* £6,614
Wins * 2000 Jly Pontef (GD) 6f 77 <
2000 Turf 1-8: (5f 3, 6f 1-4, 7f) (sft, g-s, gd 5, frm 1-1)
Decent filly, effective 5 to 6f, acts on gd to frm. Turf high 84 - 5th of 12 getting 2lb from Vicious Dancer (14 Spt Ayr 5f gd RF 4383) - also 1st of 6 getting 11lb from Dayglow Dancer (3 Jly Pontefract RF 2475). She has ability, but could do with a drop in class.
**G C Bravery [1-7] The TT Partnership (from Trained [0-1] Oct 2000).*

SIR DESMOND RR 42f 4440[8]
2 gr c Petong 7.6f **(58)** - I'm Your Lady **(72f 66a)** (Risk Me (FR)) 5.9f **(53)**
Form - 88
Record 2000 - 1st:0 2nd:0 3rd:0 Ran:2
2000 Turf 0-2: (6f 2) (gd, g-f)
Currently moderate colt. Turf high 42 (began Aug).
**R Guest [0-2] The Quintessentials.*

SIR ECHO (FR) BHB 83f **RR 85f** 4647[12]
4 b g Saumarez 15.1f **(87)** - Echoes (FR) (Niniski (USA)) 10.6f **(65)**
Form - 0
Record 2000 - 1st:0 2nd:0 3rd:0 Ran:1
Pre2000 - 1st:1 2nd:1 3rd:0 Ran:8
Win Prizemoney £3,753 *Total Prizemoney* £5,925
Wins * 1999 Jun Newbur (GD) H 12f 78 85 <
2000 Turf 0-1: (12f) (g-f)
Workmanlike, useful gelding.
**H Candy [1-9] P A Deal & I M S Racing.*

SIR EDWARD BURROW (IRE) BHB 59f54a **RR 50f 54a** 5115[13]
2 b c Distinctly North (USA) 7.4f **(63)** - Alalja (IRE) (Entitled)
Form - 74080360
Record 2000 - 1st:0 2nd:0 3rd:1 Ran:8
Win Prizemoney £0 *Total Prizemoney* £800
2000 Turf 0-7: (5f, 6f, 7f 3, 8f, 10f) (g-s, gd, g-f 3, frm 2) 2000 AW 0-1: (8f) (Fibr)
Fair colt, effective 8f, acts on frm. Turf high 50. Inconsistent.
**R F Fisher [0-7] Mrs D Miller (from M Todhunter [0-1] May 2000).*

SIR EFFENDI (IRE) BHB 91f **RR 101f** 4303[7]
4 ch h Nashwan (USA) 10.3f **(79)** - Jeema (Thatch (USA)) 9.8f **(62)**
Form - 2717
Record 2000 - 1st:1 2nd:1 3rd:0 Ran:4
Pre2000 - 1st:1 2nd:1 3rd:0 Ran:3
Win Prizemoney £10,161 *Total Prizemoney* £15,502
Wins * 2000 Aug Chepst (G-F) 7.1f 101 <
* 1999 Jly Lingfi (G-F) 7.6f 88
2000 Turf 1-4: (7f 1-2, 9f, 10f) (gd, g-f 2, frm 1-1)
Very useful colt, effective 7 to 10f, acts on g-f to frm, best on frm. Turf high 101 (began Jly) - 1st of 6 giving 1lb to Welcome Friend (28 Aug Chepstow RF 4032). A big colt with plenty of scope, he did not make his reappearance until July, but ran a blinder to go down narrowly under a welter burden in a Newbury handicap. Disappointing next time, but made no mistake in a Chepstow conditions event in August. **M P Tregoning [2-7] Hamdan Al Maktoum.*

SIRENE BHB 45f53a **RR 47f 53a** 4655[15]
3 ch f Mystiko (USA) 7.7f **(59)** - Breakaway (Song) 7.2f **(61)**
Form - 10272080835770
Record 2000 - 1st:0 2nd:1 3rd:1 Ran:11
Pre2000 - 1st:1 2nd:1 3rd:0 Ran:6
Win Prizemoney £1,924 *Total Prizemoney* £3,598
Wins * 1999 *Nov Southw (STD) S 7f 57* <
2000 Turf 0-6: (6f 3, 7f 3) (g-f 2, frm 4) 2000 AW 0-5: (5f, 6f 4) (Fibr 5)
Strong, average filly, effective 6 to 7f, - acts on Fibr, often wears blinkers, likes left handed tracks, likes tight tracks. Turf high 47. AW high 67 - 2nd of 11 giving 7lb to Nowt Flash (10 Jan Southwell 6f Fibr RF 0061). **M J Polglase [1-17] Mark Bury.*

SIR FERBET (IRE) BHB 85f93a **RR 88f 93a** 5240[17]
3 b c Mujadil (USA) 7.7f **(70)** - Mirabiliary (USA) (Crow (FR)) 7.4f **(75)**
Form - 210710042500
Record 2000 - 1st:2 2nd:2 3rd:0 Ran:12
Pre2000 - 1st:0 2nd:0 3rd:1 Ran:2
Win Prizemoney £10,205 *Total Prizemoney* £14,254
Wins * 2000 Jun Newmar (G-F) H 8f 83 88 <
*** 2000** *Apr Wolver (STD) 8.5f 81++*
2000 Turf 1-10: (8f 1-10) (sft, g-s, gd 2, g-f 2, frm 1-3, hrd) 2000 AW 1-2: (8f 1-2) (Fibr 1-2)
Scopey, very useful colt, effective 6 to 8f, best at 8f, acts on g-f to hrd - acts on Fibr, best on frm, excels at Wolverhampton. Turf high 88 - 1st of 14 giving 1lb to Red Letter (11 Jun Newmarket RF 1881). AW high 86 (1st run) - 2nd of 5 to Petit Marquis (23 Mar Wolverhampton 8f Fibr RF 0481) - also 1st of 10 from Baileys Prize (15 Apr Wolverhampton RF 0742). An easy winner on the Wolverhampton Fibresand in April, he finally got his act together on turf in a Newmarket handicap in June. A mile and fast ground looks to suit him best.
**B W Hills [2-14] International Plywood Plc & R J C Upton.*

SIR FRANCIS (IRE) BHB 99f **RR 94+f** 5024[1]
2 b g Common Grounds 8.1f **(66)** - Red Note (Rusticaro (FR)) 8.2f **(65)**
Form - 521061321
Record 2000 - 1st:3 2nd:2 3rd:1 Ran:9
Win Prizemoney £12,422 *Total Prizemoney* £14,966
Wins * 2000 Oct Yarmou (SFT) 6f 94+ <

*** 2000** Aug Bright (G-F) H 6f 82 89
*** 2000** Apr Bright (G-S) 5.3f 76
2000 Turf 3-9: (5f 1-5, 6f 2-4) (sft, g-s 1-1, gd 1-3, g-f 1-2, frm, hrd)
Useful gelding, effective 6f, acts on g-s to g-f, has worn blinkers. Turf high 94 - 1st of 11 from Trillie (17 Oct Yarmouth RF 5024) - also 1st of 7 giving 6lb to Densim Blue (10 Aug Brighton RF 3518). He did not always look an easy ride, but stood up well to a busy campaign and seems to handle any ground. Best when ridden positively, he should stay seven furlongs
**J Noseda [3-9] L P Calvente.*

SIRINGAS (IRE) RR 94f 4236a[1]
2 b f Barathea (IRE) - In Unison (Bellypha) 9.8f **(73)**
Form - 1
2000 Turf 1-1: (8f 1-1) (gd 1-1)
Currently useful filly. (1st run) - 1st of 16 getting 5lb from Elbader (31 Aug Gowran Park RF 4236a). She ran away with a Gowran Park maiden in August (form worked out reasonably well) and looked a bright prospect. Not seen out again, she would be interesting in Listed company. **J S Bolger in IRE [1-1] Ms Charlotte Musgrave.*

SIRINNDI (IRE) BHB 50f RR 52f 4777[1]
6 b g Shahrastani (USA) 11.5f **(69)** - Sinntara (IRE) (Lashkari) 9.8f **(67)**
Form - 0500625681
Record 2000 - 1st:1 2nd:1 3rd:0 Ran:10
Pre2000 - 1st:2 2nd:1 3rd:2 Ran:9
Win Prizemoney £13,970 *Total Prizemoney* £18,318
Wins * 2000 Oct Catter (SFT) H 15.8f 46 51
1997 Aug Cork (GD) 12f 90 <
1997 Jly Currag (GD) 12f 85+
2000 Turf 1-9: (11f, 12f, 14f, 15f, 16f 1-5) (g-s 1-1, gd 4, g-f 2, frm 2)
2000 AW 0-1: (16f) (Fibr)
Fair gelding, effective 12 to 16f, best at 16f, acts on g-s to g-f. Turf high 52 - 2nd of 16 giving 8lb to Lost Spirit (24 Aug Folkestone 12f g-f RF 3923) - also 1st of 14 getting 9lb from Revenge (3 Oct Catterick RF 4777).
**B J Curley [1-10] P Byrne (from C Roche in IRE [0-5] Oct 1998).*

SIR JACK BHB 52f60a RR 50f 60a 2992[10]
4 b g Distant Relative 7f **(69)** - Frasquita (Song) 7.2f **(61)**
Form - 0082440630
Record 2000 - 1st:0 2nd:1 3rd:1 Ran:10
Pre2000 - 1st:1 2nd:1 3rd:0 Ran:6
Win Prizemoney £3,371 *Total Prizemoney* £5,770
Wins 1998 Spt Newcas (GD) 6f 75 <
2000 Turf 0-9: (5f, 6f 7, 7f) (g-s, gd 3, g-f, frm 4) 2000 AW 0-1: (7f) (Fibr)
Fair gelding, has worn blinkers. Turf high 52.
**D Nicholls [0-10] Lucayan Stud (from J Noseda [0-3] Jun 1999).*

SIR NICHOLAS BHB 111f RR 113f 3542a[7]
3 b c Cadeaux Genereux 7.9f **(76)** - Final Shot (Dalsaan) 9.8f **(64)**
Form - 12657
Record 2000 - 1st:1 2nd:1 3rd:0 Ran:5
Pre2000 - 1st:1 2nd:1 3rd:1 Ran:3
Win Prizemoney £10,073 *Total Prizemoney* £31,860
Wins * 2000 Apr Leices (G-S) 6f 106 <
* 1999 May Doncas (G-F) 6f 90+
2000 Turf 1-5: (5f, 6f 1-3, 7f) (gd 1-4, g-f)
Scopey, Group-class colt, effective 5 to 6f, best at 6f, acts on gd to frm, best on gd. Turf high 113 - 2nd of 8 to Mount Abu (3 May Ascot 6f gd RF 1002) - also 1st of 9 from Watching (6 Apr Leicester RF 0624). Consistent. He threatened to develop into a top sprinter during the spring, but was found wanting when tried in Group company. Genuine and consistent, he might need soft ground.
**J Noseda [2-8].*

SIR NINJA (IRE) BHB 98f RR 104f 4740[30]
3 b g Turtle Island (IRE) - The Poachers Lady (IRE) (Salmon Leap (USA)) 11f **(61)**
Form - 562600
Record 2000 - 1st:0 2nd:1 3rd:0 Ran:6
Pre2000 - 1st:2 2nd:3 3rd:0 Ran:9
Win Prizemoney £12,926 *Total Prizemoney* £24,936
Wins * 1999 Oct Ascot (G-S) 7f 104 <
* 1999 Aug Thirsk (SFT) 7f 87+
2000 Turf 0-6: (7f, 8f 2, 9f, 10f 2) (g-s 2, gd, g-f 3)
Scopey, very useful gelding, effective 7 to 8f, acts on g-s to gd, has worn blinkers. Turf high 104 - 2nd of 5 to Inglenook (27 May Kempton 8f g-s RF 1500). Inconsistent. Suited by soft ground, he chased home the useful Inglenook at Kempton in May but has run below that form since. **D J S ffrenchDavis [2-15] Hargood Ltd.*

SIROLO (ITY) RR 101f 1636a[6]
3 f
Form - 6
2000 Turf 0-1: (12f) (g-f)
Currently very useful. **F Camici in ITY [0-1].*

SIR SANDROVITCH (IRE) BHB 72f RR 72+f 2541[5]
4 b g Polish Patriot (USA) 7.8f **(70)** - Old Downie (Be My Guest (USA)) 9.3f **(67)**
Form - 7004185
Record 2000 - 1st:1 2nd:0 3rd:0 Ran:7
Pre2000 - 1st:1 2nd:1 3rd:0 Ran:10
Win Prizemoney £5,720 *Total Prizemoney* £7,852
Wins * 2000 Jun Ayr (G-F) H 5f 65 72+ <
* 1999 May Mussel (FRM) 5f 70
2000 Turf 1-7: (5f 1-7) (sft, gd 2, g-f 1-1, frm 2, hrd)
Workmanlike, above-average gelding, effective 5f, acts on g-f. Turf high 72 - 1st of 11 giving 21lb to Tick Tock (1 Jun Ayr RF 1615). Inconsistent. **R A Fahey [2-17] W G Moore & G Winton.*

SIR WALTER (IRE) BHB 30f30a RR 39f 30a 53[6]
7 b g The Bart (USA) - Glenbalda (Kambalda)
Form - 776
Record 2000 - 1st:0 2nd:0 3rd:0 Ran:1
Pre2000 - 1st:1 2nd:1 3rd:2 Ran:22
Win Prizemoney £2,750 *Total Prizemoney* £3,934
Wins 1998 Aug Tramor (G-F) H 9f 40 49 <
2000 AW 0-1: (9f) (Fibr)
Very moderate gelding, effective 8f, - acts on Fibr, has worn blinkers. Becoming disappointing.
**A T Murphy [0-23] A J Oliver (from Seamus Cotter in IRE [1-10] Aug 1998).*

SISAO (IRE) BHB 50f54a RR 53f 54a 758[14]
4 ch h College Chapel - Copt Hall Princess (Crowned Prince (USA)) 10.1f **(67)**
Form - 63218040
Record 2000 - 1st:1 2nd:0 3rd:0 Ran:5
Pre2000 - 1st:0 2nd:1 3rd:1 Ran:6
Win Prizemoney £2,847 *Total Prizemoney* £4,403
Wins * 2000 *Jan Wolver (STD) 6f 51 <*
2000 Turf 0-1: (6f) (g-s) 2000 AW 1-4: (6f 1-4) (Equi, Fibr 1-3)
Workmanlike, fair colt, effective 6f, - acts on AW, mostly wears blinkers (very effectively), likes left handed tracks, likes tight tracks. AW high 52 - also 1st of 11 giving 5lb to College Blue (6 Jan Wolverhampton RF 0034).
**Miss Gay Kelleway [1-11] K & W Racing Partnership.*

SISTER CELESTINE BHB 73f RR 74f 5103[6]
2 b f Bishop of Cashel - Pipistrelle (Shareef Dancer (USA)) 9.9f **(73)**
Form - 24146
Record 2000 - 1st:1 2nd:1 3rd:0 Ran:5
Win Prizemoney £3,051 *Total Prizemoney* £4,823
Wins * 2000 Spt Beverl (G-F) 7.5f 71 <
2000 Turf 1-5: (6f, 7f 1-2, 8f 2) (gd 3, g-f 1-1, frm)
Above-average filly. Turf high 74 (began Aug) - 4th of 21 getting 3lb from Regatta Point (13 Oct Newmarket 8f gd RF 4970) - also 1st of 10 getting 3lb from Marshal Bond (13 Spt Beverley RF 4362).
**W Jarvis [1-5] Sales Race 2000 Syndicate.*

SISTER KATE BHB 40f RR 40f 3250[14]
3 b f Barathea (IRE) - Norpella (Northfields (USA)) 9f **(72)**
Form - 7670
Record 2000 - 1st:0 2nd:0 3rd:0 Ran:4
Pre2000 - 1st:0 2nd:0 3rd:0 Ran:1
2000 Turf 0-4: (7f, 8f, 10f 2) (g-s, g-f, frm 2)
Scopey, moderate filly. Turf high 40. **N Tinkler [0-5] Mrs D Wright.*

SITARA BHB 66f RR 63f 5196[12]
2 ch f Salse (USA) 10.9f **(71)** - Souk (IRE) (Ahonoora) 8.1f **(73)**
Form - 880
Record 2000 - 1st:0 2nd:0 3rd:0 Ran:3

2000 Turf 0-3: (7f 2, 8f) (g-s, gd 2)
Currently average filly. Turf high 62 (began Spt).
**L M Cumani [0-3] Fittocks Stud.*

SITTING PRETTY BHB 22f RR 18f 4746[13]

4 b m Presidium 7.5f **(56)** - Malvern Madam (Reesh)
Form - P050000
Record 2000 - 1st:0 2nd:0 3rd:0 Ran:7
Pre2000 - 1st:0 2nd:0 3rd:0 Ran:3
2000 Turf 0-7: (7f, 8f 4, 10f, 12f) (gd 6, g-f)
Unfurnished, poor filly, has worn blinkers. Turf high 18.
**R Bastiman [0-7] Ten To Four (from D Nicholls [0-3] Jly 1999).*

SIX FOR LUCK BHB 24f RR 26f 2990[10]

8 b g Handsome Sailor 6.6f **(53)** - Fire Sprite (Mummy's Game) 8.2f **(60)**
Form - 00000
Record 2000 - 1st:0 2nd:0 3rd:0 Ran:5
Pre2000 - 1st:1 2nd:2 3rd:2 Ran:43
Win Prizemoney £2,348 *Total Prizemoney* £5,242
2000 Turf 0-5: (5f 2, 6f 3) (gd, g-f 2, frm 2)
Little account gelding, has worn blinkers. Turf high 26.
**D A Nolan [0-42] Mrs J McFadyen-Murray (from J Berry [1-6] Jun 1995).*

SIXTY SECONDS (IRE) BHB 97f RR 100+f 4733[12]

2 b c Definite Article - Damemill (IRE) (Danehill (USA)) 10f **(72)**
Form - 210
Record 2000 - 1st:1 2nd:1 3rd:0 Ran:3
Win Prizemoney £4,069 *Total Prizemoney* £5,653
Wins * 2000 Spt Leices (G-F) 7f 100+ <
2000 Turf 1-3: (7f 1-3) (gd, frm 1-2)
Currently very useful colt. Turf high 100 (began Jly) - 1st of 18 from Taabeer (5 Spt Leicester RF 4218). Runner-up to a decent sort on his Newmarket debut, he was impressive in a fair Leicester maiden next time. He finished distressed at Newmarket on his final run, but deserves a chance to make amends.
**J H M Gosden [1-3] The Smoking/Brady Partnership.*

SIZE DOESNT MATTER BHB 45f RR 41f 4114[11]

2 b g Greensmith - Singing Rock (IRE) **(63f)** (Ballad Rock) 7.8f **(63)**
Form - 0300
Record 2000 - 1st:0 2nd:0 3rd:1 Ran:4
Win Prizemoney £0 *Total Prizemoney* £492
2000 Turf 0-3: (5f, 6f, 7f) (sft, gd, frm) 2000 AW 0-1: (5f) (Equi)
Moderate gelding. Turf high 41. **J R Best [0-4] Mercato Ltd.*

SKELTON MONARCH (IRE) BHB 42f RR 41f 3533[13]

3 ch c Prince of Birds (USA) - Toda (Absalom) 7.2f **(58)**
Form - 663870330
Record 2000 - 1st:0 2nd:0 3rd:3 Ran:9
Pre2000 - 1st:0 2nd:0 3rd:0 Ran:5
Win Prizemoney £0 *Total Prizemoney* £1,049
2000 Turf 0-7: (7f, 8f 4, 10f 2) (g-s, gd 2, frm 4) 2000 AW 0-2: (7f, 9f) (Fibr 2)
Moderate colt, effective 7f, acts on frm, likes tight tracks. Turf high 41. AW high 46. **R Hollinshead [0-14] G Bailey.*

SKIBO (JPN) BHB 81f RR 81f 964[3]

3 b c Carnegie (IRE) - Dyna Avenue (JPN) (Northern Taste (CAN))
Form - 3
Record 2000 - 1st:0 2nd:0 3rd:1 Ran:1
Pre2000 - 1st:0 2nd:0 3rd:0 Ran:2
Win Prizemoney £0 *Total Prizemoney* £1,215
2000 Turf 0-1: (10f) (gd)
Strong, currently decent colt. (1st run) - 3rd of 15 to Fantasy Park (2 May Bath 10f gd RF 0964). In the frame in maidens, he will appreciate a mile and a half and should get off the mark before long. **M P Tregoning [0-3] Sheikh Mohammed.*

SKI FREE BHB 34f28a RR 10f 28a 5018[10]

3 b f Factual (USA) - Ski Blade **(16f)** (Niniski (USA)) 10.6f **(65)**
Form - 0568800
Record 2000 - 1st:0 2nd:0 3rd:0 Ran:5
Pre2000 - 1st:0 2nd:0 3rd:1 Ran:5
Win Prizemoney £0 *Total Prizemoney* £250
2000 Turf 0-2: (6f 2) (g-f 2) 2000 AW 0-3: (5f, 6f, 7f) (Equi, Fibr 2)
Neat, little account filly. Turf high 10 (began Jly).
**J L Harris [0-6] Mrs R Morley (from R Guest [0-4] Dec 1999).*

SKIMMER RR 5073[12]

2 b c Lake Coniston (IRE) - Mountain Bluebird (USA) (Clever Trick (USA)) 6.6f **(77)**
Form - 0
Record 2000 - 1st:0 2nd:0 3rd:0 Ran:1
2000 Turf 0-1: (7f) (g-s)
Currently very poor colt. **W R Muir [0-1] Chris van Hoorn.*

SKIMMING (USA) RR 211[4]

4 b h Nureyev (USA) 8.4f **(84)** - Skimble (USA) (Lyphard (USA)) 9.9f **(72)**
Form - 14
Record 2000 - 1st:1 2nd:0 3rd:0 Ran:2
Win Prizemoney £2,795 *Total Prizemoney* £3,302
Wins * 2000 *Jan Wolver (STD)* *8.5f* *70+* <
2000 AW 1-2: (8f 1-2) (Fibr 1-2)
Currently useful colt, has broken blood-vessels. AW high 91. He has ability but was not seen out after breaking a blood vessel at Wolverhampton in February. **B W Hills [1-2] K Abdulla.*

SKIMRA BHB 82f RR 85f 1821a[5]

3 b f Hernando (FR) - Skuld (Kris) 9.5f **(73)**
Form - 15
Record 2000 - 1st:1 2nd:0 3rd:0 Ran:2
Pre2000 - 1st:0 2nd:1 3rd:0 Ran:2
Win Prizemoney £2,758 *Total Prizemoney* £4,078
Wins * 2000 Apr Folkes (SFT) 12f 77 <
2000 Turf 1-2: (12f 1-2) (g-s 1-1, gd)
Lengthy, useful filly. Turf high 85 - 5th of 6 to Sadler's Flag (3 Jun Chantilly 12f gd RF 1821a) - also 1st of 7 from Busy Lizzie (18 Apr Folkestone RF 0764). **R Guest [1-4].*

SKIP (IRE) RR 102f 1819a[1]

6 b g Distinctly North (USA) 7.4f **(63)** - Etching (Auction Ring (USA)) 8.6f **(65)**
Form - 1
2000 Turf 1-1: (6f 1-1) (g-s 1-1)
Currently very useful gelding. (1st run) - 1st of 9 from Super Lover (2 Jun Baden-Baden RF 1819a). **U Suter in GER [1-1] L Plietzsch.*

SKIPPING RR 104f 3733a[2]

3 b c Rainbow Quest (USA) 11.2f **(81)** - Minskip (USA) (The Minstrel (CAN)) 10f **(72)**
Form - 2
2000 Turf 0-1: (10f) (gd)
Currently very useful colt. (1st run) - 2nd of 9 to Cheshire (12 Aug Deauville 10f gd RF 3733a). **in FR [0-1].*

SKI RUN RR 111+f 4613[10]

4 b m Petoski 10.4f **(56)** - Cut and Run **(54f)** (Slip Anchor) 9.8f **(73)**
Form - 01330
Record 2000 - 1st:1 2nd:0 3rd:2 Ran:5
Pre2000 - 1st:1 2nd:0 3rd:0 Ran:3
Win Prizemoney £16,265 *Total Prizemoney* £29,115
Wins * 2000 Jly Ascot (G-F) H 16.2f 75 84+ <
1999 Oct Bath (SFT) 11.7f 74
2000 Turf 1-5: (10f, 12f, 15f, 16f 1-2) (g-s, gd 2, g-f 1-2)
Scopey, Group-class filly, effective 15 to 16f, acts on gd. Turf high 111 - 3rd of 5 getting 8lb from Royal Rebel (22 Aug York 16f gd RF 3851). Inconsistent. Well treated when winning a handicap at Ascot in July, she looked unlucky when finishing third in the Lonsdale Stakes (saddle slipped) and Park Hill Stakes. Open to improvement, she stays well and will be interesting in races like the Sagaro Stakes this spring.
**G A Butler [1-5] T D Holland-Martin (from R F JohnsonHoughton [1-3] Oct 1999).*

SKITTLES (IRE) RR 51f 3091[P]

2 br f Topanoora 8.3f **(67)** - State (Dominion) 8.5f **(63)**
Form - 787P
Record 2000 - 1st:0 2nd:0 3rd:0 Ran:4
2000 Turf 0-4: (5f, 7f 3) (gd 2, frm 2)
Fair filly, has worn blinkers. Turf high 51.
**M H Tompkins [0-4] www raceworld co uk.*

SKI WELLS RR 48f 5309[12]

2 b c Sadler's Wells (USA) 11.3f **(87)** - Jet Ski Lady (USA) (Vaguely Noble) 10.1f **(72)**

Form - 00

Record 2000 - 1st:0 2nd:0 Ran:2

2000 Turf 0-2: (7f, 8f) (g-s, gd)

Currently moderate colt. Turf high 48 (began Spt).

**E A L Dunlop [0-2] Mohammed Ali.*

SKUKUSA RR 50f 2048[8]

2 b f Emarati (USA) 6.6f **(63)** - Glensara (Petoski) 5.7f **(62)**

Form - 8

Record 2000 - 1st:0 2nd:0 3rd:0 Ran:1

2000 Turf 0-1: (6f) (g-f)

Currently fair filly.

**R Guest [0-1] The Bricklayers Partnership.*

SKY CITY BHB 16f24a **RR 1f 24a** 3095[11]

4 b m Be My Chief (USA) 10.2f **(62)** - Pellinora (USA) (King Pellinore (USA)) 8.2f **(68)**

Form - 80075600080

Record 2000 - 1st:0 2nd:0 3rd:0 Ran:7

Pre2000 - 1st:0 2nd:1 3rd:0 Ran:10

Win Prizemoney £0 *Total Prizemoney* £1,140

2000 Turf 0-3: (8f, 12f, 14f) (frm 3) 2000 AW 0-4: (8f, 10f, 12f 2) (Equi 3, Fibr)

Leggy, little account filly, effective 10f, - acts on Equi, has worn blinkers. Turf high 1 (began Jly). AW high 28.

**P Howling [0-17] Manor Farm Packers Ltd.*

SKY DOME (IRE) BHB 68f **RR 75f** 4934[6]

7 ch g Bluebird (USA) 7.9f **(71)** - God Speed Her (Pas de Seul) 9.1f **(67)**

Form - 060230325456

Record 2000 - 1st:0 2nd:2 3rd:2 Ran:12

Pre2000 - 1st:5 2nd:3 3rd:1 Ran:34

Win Prizemoney £33,287 *Total Prizemoney* £48,073

Wins								
* 1999	May	Newmar	(GD)	H	8f	74	77	
* 1996	Aug	Goodwo	(GD)	H	8f	84	89	<
* 1996	Aug	Newmar	(GD)	H	8f	78	86	
* 1996	Apr	Newmar	(G-F)	H	7f	75	80	

2000 Turf 0-12: (7f, 8f 8, 9f 2, 10f) (gd 4, g-f 6, frm 2)

Above-average gelding, effective 7 to 9f, best at 8f, acts on g-s to frm, best on g-f, and excels at Kempton. Turf high 75 - 2nd of 18 getting 3lb from Muyassir (14 Jun Kempton 8f g-f RF 1963). Consistent. A tough and genuine performer at his best, he gained a well-deserved success at Newmarket in May '99 but has not won since. A couple of fair efforts so far this season however.

**M H Tompkins [5-47] www raceworld co uk.*

SKYE BLUE (IRE) BHB 56f **RR 70f** 4868[2]

3 b g Blues Traveller (IRE) - Hitopah (Bustino) 10.4f **(64)**

Form - 0530232056542

Record 2000 - 1st:0 2nd:3 3rd:2 Ran:12

Pre2000 - 1st:0 2nd:0 3rd:0 Ran:2

Win Prizemoney £0 *Total Prizemoney* £4,348

2000 Turf 0-12: (10f 4, 11f, 12f 5, 13f, 14f) (hvy, sft, g-s, gd 2, g-f 2, frm 5)

Unfurnished, above-average gelding, effective 10 to 14f, best at 12f, acts on sft to frm, prefers tight tracks. Turf high 70 - 3rd of 11 getting 10lb from Pompeii (1 May Warwick 12f sft RF 0956).

**M R Channon [0-14] W H Ponsonby.*

SKYERS A KITE BHB 65f34a **RR 60f 34a** 5085[7]

5 b m Deploy 11.4f **(67)** - Milady Jade (IRE) (Drumalis) 12f **(54)**

Form - 2065315215617

Record 2000 - 1st:3 2nd:2 3rd:1 Ran:13

Pre2000 - 1st:3 2nd:2 3rd:4 Ran:20

Win Prizemoney £21,385 *Total Prizemoney* £26,128

Wins								
* **2000**	Oct	York	(SFT)	C	10.4f		60	<
* **2000**	Aug	Hamilt	(SFT)	H	13f	43	51	
* **2000**	Jun	Beverl	(G-F)	C	12f		49	
* 1999	Spt	Beverl	(SFT)	H	9.9f	40	43	
* 1998	Oct	Catter	(gd,)	H	12f	42	45	
* 1998	Jly	Beverl	(GD)	SH	12f	40	45	

2000 Turf 3-13: (10f 1-2, 12f 1-8, 13f 1-1, 14f, 16f) (hvy, sft, g-s 1-2, gd 1-5, g-f 2, frm 1-2)

Average filly, effective 10 to 13f, acts on g-s to gd, likes right handed tracks. Turf high 60 - 1st of 20 getting 10lb from Prince Among Men (5 Oct York RF 4814) - also 1st of 9 getting 2lb from Papi Special (16 Aug Hamilton RF 3699).

**Ronald Thompson [6-39] G A W Racing Partnership.*

SKYERS FLYER (IRE) BHB 37f34a **RR 34f 34a** 5084[2]

6 b br m Magical Wonder (USA) 7.2f **(60)** - Siwana (IRE) (Dom Racine (FR)) 9.2f **(62)**

Form - 0000808672

Record 2000 - 1st:0 2nd:1 3rd:0 Ran:10

Pre2000 - 1st:5 2nd:6 3rd:8 Ran:52

Win Prizemoney £13,419 *Total Prizemoney* £25,375

Wins								
* 1999	Jly	Carlis	(GD)	H	5.9f	42	46	
* 1997	Aug	Newcas	(G-F)	S	6f		48	
* 1997	Apr	Nottin	(GD)	S	6.1f		68	
* 1996	Aug	Bright	(FRM)	H	5.3f	85	72	<
* 1996	May	Beverl	(G-F)	S	5f		47	

2000 Turf 0-8: (5f, 6f 3, 7f 2, 8f 2) (hvy, gd 2, g-f 2, frm 2, hrd) 2000 AW 0-2: (6f 2) (Fibr 2)

Very moderate mare, effective 5 to 6f, best at 6f, acts on g-f to frm, best on frm. Turf high 34. AW high 18. Consistent.

**Ronald Thompson [5-46] A Bell (from Martyn Wane [0-16] Oct 1998).*

SKY HOOK BHB 52f36a **RR 47f 36a** 4768[4]

3 ch g Superlative 8.8f **(57)** - Lady Eccentric (IRE) (Magical Wonder (USA))

Form - 5500884

Record 2000 - 1st:0 2nd:0 3rd:0 Ran:6

Pre2000 - 1st:0 2nd:0 3rd:1 Ran:7

Win Prizemoney £0 *Total Prizemoney* £487

2000 Turf 0-4: (6f, 8f 2, 10f) (g-s, g-f, frm 2) 2000 AW 0-2: (6f, 8f) (Fibr 2)

Leggy, moderate gelding, effective 6f, acts on gd, has worn blinkers. Turf high 47 (began Aug). AW high 38 (began Aug). Consistent.

**J A Osborne [0-6] Wilwyn Racing (WWW Wilwyn Com) (from N P Littmoden [0-7] Dec 1999).*

SKYLARK BHB 63f71a **RR 69f 71a** 3989[8]

3 ch f Polar Falcon (USA) 9f **(74)** - Boozy (Absalom) 7.2f **(58)**

Form - 74653008

Record 2000 - 1st:0 2nd:0 3rd:1 Ran:7

Pre2000 - 1st:0 2nd:1 3rd:2 Ran:6

Win Prizemoney £0 *Total Prizemoney* £3,226

2000 Turf 0-7: (5f 2, 6f 2, 7f 2, 8f) (g-s, gd, g-f 4, frm)

Scopey, average filly, effective 5 to 6f, best at 5f, acts on gd to frm, best on frm. Turf high 69.

**R Hannon [0-13] Heathavon Stables Ltd.*

SKY QUEST (IRE) RR 84f 3550[2]

2 b c Spectrum (IRE) - Rose Vibert (Caerleon (USA)) 8.6f **(71)**

Form - 2

Record 2000 - 1st:0 2nd:1 3rd:0 Ran:1

Win Prizemoney £0 *Total Prizemoney* £1,262

2000 Turf 0-1: (7f) (g-f)

Currently decent colt. (1st run) - 2nd of 8 to Zeloso (11 Aug Haydock 7f g-f RF 3550).

**P W Harris [0-1] Colourful Band.*

SLAM BID BHB 68a **RR 50df** 5071[13]

3 b g First Trump - Nadema (Artaius (USA)) 9f **(69)**

Form - 563800

Record 2000 - 1st:0 2nd:0 3rd:1 Ran:6

Pre2000 - 1st:0 2nd:0 3rd:0 Ran:2

Win Prizemoney £0 *Total Prizemoney* £356

2000 Turf 0-5: (7f 2, 8f 3) (g-s, gd, g-f 3) 2000 AW 0-1: (6f) (Fibr)

Unfurnished, fair gelding, has worn blinkers. Turf high 63 (began Jly). Becoming disappointing.

**M Wigham [0-1] Michael Wigham (from S Gollings [0-1] Spt 2000).*

SLANEYSIDE (IRE) BHB 50f45a **RR 68f 45a** 5294[13]

3 ch g Project Manager 7.2f **(47)** - Erneside (Lomond (USA)) 8.8f **(65)**

Form - 36781770680

Record 2000 - 1st:1 2nd:0 3rd:1 Ran:11

Pre2000 - 1st:0 2nd:0 3rd:1 Ran:6

Win Prizemoney £2,954 *Total Prizemoney* £3,584

Wins * **2000** Aug Mussel (G-F) 12f 68? <
2000 Turf 1-9: (10f 2, 11f, 12f 1-3, 13f, 14f, 15f) (hvy 2, sft, g-s 2, gd 3, frm 1-1) 2000 AW 0-2: (9f, 12f) (Fibr 2)
Average gelding, effective 9 to 14f, acts on hvy to frm, has worn blinkers, likes right handed tracks. Turf high 68 - 1st of 3 getting 8lb from Chaka Zulu (31 Aug Musselburgh RF 4118). AW high 52 .
**I Semple [1-8] Gordon McDowall (from J S Bolger in IRE [0-9] May 2000).*

SLAPY DAM BHB 30f30a **RR 24f 30a** 4306[16]
8 b g Deploy 11.4f - Key to the River(USA) (Irish River (FR)) 8.6f **(78)**
Form - 0000

Record	**2000 -**	1st:0	2nd:0	3rd:0	Ran:3
	Pre2000 -	1st:5	2nd:2	3rd:1	Ran:40

Win Prizemoney £16,406 *Total Prizemoney* £19,326

Wins	* 1999	Aug	Chepst	(G-S)	C	12.1f	56
	* 1999	Aug	Bright	(SFT)	C	11.9f	47

2000 Turf 0-2: (12f 2) (gd, g-f) 2000 AW 0-1: (11f) (Fibr)
Little account gelding, effective 12f, acts on gd to g-f, has worn blinkers, likes left handed tracks, favours tight tracks. Turf high 16. **D Burchell [2-7] Three Acres Racing (from J M Bradley [0-6] Nov 1999).*

SLASHER JACK (IRE) BHB 55f49a **RR 59?f 49a** 570[9]
9 b g Alzao (USA) 9.8f **(73)** - Sherkraine (Shergar) 10.4f **(66)**
Form - 0

Record	**2000 -**	1st:0	2nd:0	3rd:0	Ran:1
	Pre2000 -	1st:6	2nd:4	3rd:2	Ran:36

Win Prizemoney £24,031 *Total Prizemoney* £40,195

Wins	1998	Jly	Haydoc	(GD)	C	11.9f	59

2000 Turf 0-1: (16f) (gd)
Fair gelding, has worn blinkers.
**Mrs D Thomson [1-4] Discounted Cashflow (from K A Ryan [0-1] Apr 1999).*

SLEAVE SILK (IRE) BHB 39f52a **RR 39f 52a** 317[6]
5 b m Unfuwain (USA) 11.4f **(74)** - Shanira (Shirley Heights) 10.3f **(74)**
Form - 2816

Record	**2000 -**	1st:1	2nd:1	3rd:0	Ran:4
	Pre2000 -	1st:3	2nd:2	3rd:1	Ran:12

Win Prizemoney £10,103 *Total Prizemoney* £13,112

Wins	* **2000**	*Feb*	*Lingfi*	*(STD)*	*H*	*12f*	*49*	*50* <
	* 1999	*Mar*	*Lingfi*	*(STD)*	*H*	*16f*	*39*	*49*
	* 1999	*Feb*	*Lingfi*	*(STD)*	*H*	*16f*	*39*	*47*
	* 1999	*Jan*	*Lingfi*	*(STD)*	*H*	*12f*	*32*	*37*

2000 AW 1-4: (12f 1-3, 16f) (Equi 1-4)
Fair filly, effective 12 to 16f, best at 12f, - acts on Equi, favours tight tracks. AW high 50 - 1st of 5 getting 16lb from Mono Lady (16 Feb Lingfield RF 0294). She showed much-improved form when stepped up to middle distances on Equitrack, and has now proved that she gets two miles on that surface.
**W J Musson [4-16] Broughton Bloodstock.*

SLEW THE RED (USA) RR 111f 5094a[2]
3 bb c Red Ransom (USA) 8.6f **(83)** - Great Lady Slew (USA) (Seattle Slew (USA)) 9.4f **(76)**
Form - 2
2000 Turf 0-1: (12f) (sft)
Currently Group-class colt. (1st run) - 2nd of 5 to Crimson Quest (15 Oct Longchamp 12f sft RF 5094a). **A Fabre in FR [0-1].*

SLICKLY (FR) RR 121f 4989[8]
4 gr cLinamix (FR) 8.2f **(64)** - Slipstream Queen (USA) (Conquistador Cielo (USA)) 8.8f **(69)**
Form - 1718

Record	**2000 -**	1st:2	2nd:0	3rd:0	Ran:4
	Pre2000 -	1st:3	2nd:1	3rd:0	Ran:6

Win Prizemoney £247,497 *Total Prizemoney* £317,465

Wins	* **2000**	Spt	Longch	(GD)	G2	9.8f	121	<
	* **2000**	Jun	Longch	(GD)	G3	10f	116	
	1999	Jun	Longch	(GD)	G1	10f	121	<
	1999	Apr	Longch	(G-S)	G2	11f	104	
	1998	Spt	Chanti	(GD)	G3	8f	107	

2000 Turf 2-4: (10f 2-4) (g-s, gd 2-3)
Very high-class colt, effective 8 to 10f, best at 10f, acts on hvy to gd, best on gd, prefers right handed tracks. Turf high 121 - 1st of 4 from Albarahin (30 Spt Longchamp RF 4839a) - also 1st of 8 from Agol Lack (15 Jun Longchamp RF 2200a). Consistent. A Group 1 winner for Andre Fabre in 1999, he has been a decent recruit to the Godolphin team, landing La Coupe and Prix Dollar at Longchamp. Unhappy going left-handed in the Arlington Million, he enjoys forcing the pace and should do well again this term.
**S bin Suroor [2-4] Godolphin (from A Fabre in FR [3-6] Spt 1999).*

SLICK WILLIE (IRE) BHB 63f **RR 73df** 1900[9]
3 b g Up and At 'em - Perfectly Entitled (IRE) (Entitled)
Form - 0000

Record	**2000 -**	1st:0	2nd:0	3rd:0	Ran:4
	Pre2000 -	1st:1	2nd:3	3rd:4	Ran:15

Win Prizemoney £2,843 *Total Prizemoney* £9,021

Wins	* 1999	Jly	Beverl	(G-F)	5f	71	<

2000 Turf 0-4: (7f 2, 8f, 10f) (g-s, gd 2, frm)
Scopey, above-average gelding, effective 5 to 7f, best at 7f, acts on sft to frm, best on g-s, often wears blinkers (extremely effectively). Turf high 52. **T D Easterby [1-19] D H Brown.*

SLIEVE BLOOM (IRE) BHB 46f37a **RR 56df 37a** 5154[10]
3 b g Dancing Dissident (USA) 6.8f **(65)** - Full of Sparkle (IRE) (Persian Heights)
Form - 6050030

Record	**2000 -**	1st:0	2nd:0	3rd:1	Ran:7

Win Prizemoney £0 *Total Prizemoney* £332
2000 Turf 0-5: (6f, 7f 2, 8f, 11f) (g-s 2, gd 2, frm) 2000 AW 0-2: (8f, 12f) (Equi, Fibr)
Workmanlike, fair gelding. Turf high 58. AW high 24 (began Spt).
**T G Mills [0-7] Mrs Stephanie Merrydew.*

SLIP KILLICK BHB 53f **RR 63f** 2069[11]
3 b f Cosmonaut - Killick **(64f 55a)** (Slip Anchor) 9.8f **(73)**
Form - 60

Record	**2000 -**	1st:0	2nd:0	3rd:0	Ran:2
	Pre2000 -	1st:0	2nd:0	3rd:0	Ran:3

Win Prizemoney £0 *Total Prizemoney* £265
2000 Turf 0-2: (7f 2) (g-f 2)
Light-framed, average filly. Turf high 63.
**M Mullineaux [0-5] Esprit de Corps Racing.*

SLIPPERING RR 95f 4841a[3]
3 b f Shining Steel 7f **(46)** - Sectarine (FR) (Maelstrom Lake)
Form - 3
2000 Turf 0-1: (10f) (gd)
Currently very useful filly. (1st run) - 3rd of 12 to Tawasila (30 Spt Longchamp 10f gd RF 4841a). **in FR [0-1].*

SLIPPER ROSE BHB 45f49a **RR 34f 49a** 5295[6]
2 ch f Democratic (USA) - Brown Taw (Whistlefield) 5f **(55)**
Form - 430608780576

Record	**2000 -**	1st:0	2nd:0	3rd:1	Ran:12

Win Prizemoney £0 *Total Prizemoney* £722
2000 Turf 0-10: (5f 5, 6f 3, 7f, 8f) (g-s 2, gd 2, g-f, frm 4, hrd) 2000 AW 0-2: (6f, 8f) (Fibr 2)
Fair filly. Turf high 50. AW high 39 (began Oct).
**R Hollinshead [0-12] Mrs D A Hodson.*

SLIP STREAM (USA) BHB 113f **RR 116+f** 2789a[1]
4 ch h Irish River (FR) 9f **(77)** - Sous Entendu (USA) (Shadeed (USA)) 8.2f **(70)**
Form - 001

Record	**2000 -**	1st:1	2nd:0	3rd:0	Ran:3
	Pre2000 -	1st:2	2nd:1	3rd:1	Ran:6

Win Prizemoney £59,179 *Total Prizemoney* £90,202

Wins	* **2000**	Jly	Hoppeg	(GD)	G2	8f	116+	<
	* 1999	Jly	Goodwo	(FRM)	L	8f	116+	<
	1998	Oct	Leices	(SFT)		7f	88++	

2000 Turf 1-2: (8f 1-2) (gd 1-2) 2000 AW 0-1: (8f) (Dirt)
Scopey, high-class colt, effective 8 to 10f, best at 8f, acts on sft to g-f, best on gd, has worn blinkers. Turf high 116 - 1st of 5 from Up And Away (9 Jly Hoppegarten RF 2789a). He enjoys forcing the pace and was allowed to dictate when winning a Group Two at Hoppegarten in July. Best around a mile, he probably acts on any ground but may need to be campaigned on the continent to land another decent prize. **S bin Suroor [2-8] Godolphin*

SLIPSTREAM KING (FR) RR 112f 1290a[7]
3 gr c Linamix (FR) 8.2f **(64)** - Slipstream Queen (USA) (Conquistador

Cielo (USA)) 8.8f **(69)**
Form - 37
2000 Turf 0-2: (8f 2) (hvy, gd)
Currently Group-class colt. Turf high 112 (1st run) - 3rd of 8 to Berine's Son (23 Apr Longchamp 8f hvy RF 0890a).
**A Fabre in FR [0-2].*

SLOANE BHB 77f **RR 73f** 3960[1]

4 chhMachiavellian(USA)9.8f **(83)**-Gussy Marlowe(Final Straw)7.9f **(64)**
Form - 21

Record	**2000** -	1st:1	2nd:1	3rd:0	Ran:2
	Pre2000 -	1st:0	2nd:1	3rd:0	Ran:4

Win Prizemoney £3,662 *Total Prizemoney* £6,343
Wins * **2000** Aug Newcas (G-F) 7f 55 <
2000 Turf 1-2: (7f 1-1, 8f) (gd, hrd 1-1)
Scopey, above-average colt, effective 8f, acts on gd to frm. Turf high 73 (1st run) - 2nd of 15 giving 17lb to Auchonvillers (29 Mar Nottingham 8f gd RF 0557). A lightly-raced sort, he ran very well to finish runner-up at Nottingham on his reappearance and went one better on his next start at Newcastle five months later.
**M L W Bell [1-2] Mrs John Van Geest (from G Wragg [0-4] Oct 1999).*

SLUMBERING (IRE) BHB 73f69a **RR 74f 69a** 5242[14]

4 b g Thatching 7.8f **(69)** - Bedspread (USA) (Seattle Dancer (USA))
Form - 170000634885110

Record	**2000** -	1st:2	2nd:0	3rd:1	Ran:15
	Pre2000	1st:1	2nd:0	3rd:0	Ran:8

Win Prizemoney £17,710 *Total Prizemoney* £20,240

Wins	* **2000**	Oct	Nottin	(SFT)	H	6.1f	68	72	
	* **2000**	Spt	Sandow	(SFT)	H	7.1f	65	68	
	1998	Oct	York	(GD)		6f		84	<

2000 Turf 2-15: (6f 1-7, 7f 1-4, 8f 3, 10f) (sft 1-2, g-s 1-3, gd 5, frm 5)
Leggy, above-average gelding, effective 6 to 8f, acts on sft, has worn blinkers, likes right handed tracks, likes tight tracks. Turf high 80 (1st run) - 4th of 10 getting 3lb from Nimello (28 Apr Sandown 8f sft RF 0894) - also 1st of 14 giving 11lb to Amber Brown (18 Oct Nottingham RF 5061).
**B A Pearce [2-4] Mrs Christine Painting (from B J Meehan [1-19] Aug 2000).*

SMALL CHANGE (IRE) **RR 89+f** 4990[11]

2 b f Danzig (USA) 8.1f **(88)** - Blue Note (FR) (Habitat) 9.4f **(70)**
Form - 10
2000 Turf 1-2: (7f 1-2) (gd 1-2)
Scopey, currently useful filly. Turf high 89 (1st run) (began Spt) - 1st of 11 from Rockerlong (23 Spt Ascot RF 4599). Made a winning debut at Ascot, and is likely to winter in Dubai.
**D R Loder in FR [1-2] Godolphin C.*

SMALL FRY (IRE) **RR** 581[3]

2 b f Tagula (IRE) - Alaroos (IRE) (Persian Bold) 9.3f **(66)**
Form - 3

Record	**2000** -	1st:0	2nd:0	3rd:1	Ran:1

Win Prizemoney £0 *Total Prizemoney* £315
2000 AW 0-1: (5f) (Fibr)
Currently fair filly. **T D Easterby [0-1] The Four Ball Partnership.*

SMART DANCER (IRE) **RR 82f** 5103[10]

2 b c Spectrum (IRE) - Plessaya (USA) (Nureyev (USA)) 8.7f **(78)**
Form - 504410

Record	**2000** -	1st:1	2nd:0	3rd:0	Ran:6

Win Prizemoney £3,851 *Total Prizemoney* £4,331
Wins * **2000** Aug Thirsk (G-F) 7f 82 <
2000 Turf 1-6: (5f 2, 6f, 7f 1-2, 8f) (gd 3, g-f, frm 1-1, hrd)
Decent colt, effective 7f, acts on frm. Turf high 82 - 1st of 12 giving 6lb to Gone Too Far (25 Aug Thirsk RF 3973).
**T D Easterby [1-6] Bernard Hathaway.*

SMARTER CHARTER BHB 48f47a **RR 59f 47a** 5294[7]

7 br g Master Willie 9.2f **(67)** - Irene's Charter (Persian Bold) 9.3f **(66)**
Form - 1232232563774457

Record	**2000** -	1st:1	2nd:4	3rd:3	Ran:16
	Pre2000 -	1st:5	2nd:5	3rd:6	Ran:51

Win Prizemoney £20,511 *Total Prizemoney* £35,024

Wins	* **2000**	Apr	Pontef	(G-S)	H	10f	50	55	
	* 1999	Jun	Mussel	(GD)	H	9f	53	54	
	* 1998	Jly	Beverl	(G-F)	H	7.5f	60	65	
	* 1998	Jly	Kempto	(G-F)	H	8f	56	57	
	1996	Jly	Beverl	(G-F)	H	8.5f	70	75	<
	1996	May	Beverl	(G-F)	H	7.5f	58	61	

2000 Turf 1-16: (10f 1-11, 11f, 12f 4) (sft, g-s 1-4, gd 6, g-f 4, frm)
Fair gelding, effective 10 to 12f, best at 10f, acts on g-s to g-f, best on g-f, likes left handed tracks, favours tight tracks, excels at Yarmouth and Pontefract. Turf high 65 - 2nd of 9 giving 10lb to May King Mayhem (21 Jun Kempton 12f g-f RF 2160). Scored at Pontefract on his reappearance and has kept making the frame since, but has just been able to put his head in front where it matters. Best over ten furlongs though he does get further, he deserves another victory.
**Mrs L Stubbs [4-53] O J Williams (from Mrs J R Ramsden [2-14] Aug 1996).*

SMART PREDATOR BHB 86f **RR 87f** 4605[5]

4 gr g Polar Falcon (USA) 9f **(74)** - She's Smart (Absalom) 7.2f **(58)**
Form - 0030310520301325

Record	**2000** -	1st:2	2nd:2	3rd:4	Ran:16
	Pre2000 -	1st:1	2nd:3	3rd:0	Ran:10

Win Prizemoney £15,544 *Total Prizemoney* £36,871

Wins	* **2000**	Aug	Yarmou	(G-F)	H	5.2f	77	82	<
	* **2000**	May	Redcar	(G-S)		7f		74	
	* 1999	Spt	York	(G-F)		7.9f		81	

2000 Turf 2-16: (5f 1-4, 6f 6, 7f 1-6) (sft, gd 1-8, g-f 1-3, frm 4)
Workmanlike, useful gelding, effective 5 to 8f, best at 5f, acts on gd to frm, best on gd, excels at Yarmouth. Turf high 87 - 2nd of 18 giving 2lb to Dancing Mystery (12 Spt Yarmouth 5f frm RF 4332) - also 1st of 8 giving 1lb to Mizhar (27 Aug Yarmouth RF 4026).
**J J Quinn [3-26] B Shaw.*

SMART RIDGE BHB 98f **RR 101f** 4817[7]

3 ch c Indian Ridge 7.6f **(74)** - Guanhumara (Caerleon (USA)) 8.6f **(71)**
Form - 5720234057

Record	**2000** -	1st:0	2nd:2	3rd:1	Ran:10
	Pre2000 -	1st:3	2nd:1	3rd:0	Ran:10

Win Prizemoney £12,154 *Total Prizemoney* £33,950

Wins	1999	Aug	Bright	(G-F)	H	5.3f	84	86	<
	1999	Jly	Hamilt	(G-F)	H	6f		86	<
	1999	May	Bright	(FRM)		5.3f		79	

2000 Turf 0-10: (7f 6, 8f 4) (sft, g-s 3, gd 2, g-f 3, frm)
Unfurnished, very useful colt, effective 7 to 8f, best at 7f, acts on gd to frm, prefers tight tracks, excels at Brighton. Turf high 105 - 2nd of 16 giving 24lb to Rushmore (8 Jly Sandown 7f frm RF 2645). Inconsistent. He ran well in some warm races, but looked to be held by the handicapper.
**K R Burke [0-11] Achilles International (from M R Channon [3-9] Aug 1999).*

SMART SAVANNAH BHB 90f **RR 87f** 941[13]

4 b g Primo Dominie 7.2f **(67)** -High Savannah(Rousillon(USA))8.2f **(74)**
Form - 0

Record	**2000** -	1st:0	2nd:0	3rd:0	Ran:1
	Pre2000 -	1st:2	2nd:0	3rd:1	Ran:12

Win Prizemoney £11,023 *Total Prizemoney* £12,163

Wins	* 1999	Aug	Ascot	(SFT)	H	8f	93	99	<
	* 1998	Spt	Sandow	(GD)		7.1f		88+	

2000 Turf 0-1: (8f) (g-s)
Well made, useful gelding, effective 8 to 10f, best at 8f, acts on gd to frm, best on frm. Consistent. **R Charlton [2-13] George Ward.*

SMARTS MEGAN BHB 19f **RR 22f** 3996[9]

4 b mMarju(IRE)9.2f **(76)** -Taschkent(IRE)(Sure Blade (USA))11.3f **(67)**
Form - 00070

Record	**2000** -	1st:0	2nd:0	3rd:0	Ran:5
	Pre2000 -	1st:0	2nd:0	3rd:0	Ran:2

2000 Turf 0-4: (7f, 10f, 14f 2) (gd, g-f 2, frm) 2000 AW 0-1: (7f) (Fibr)
Workmanlike, little account filly, effective 14f, acts on frm. Turf high 22 - 7th of 15 getting 3lb from Italian Rose (29 Jly Nottingham 14f frm RF 3213).
**J G Given [0-2] & Mrs D J Smart (from Ian Williams [0-5] May 2000).*

SMART SPIRIT (IRE) BHB 42f **RR 47f** 650[9]

6 b m Persian Bold 10f **(69)** - Sharp Ego (USA) (Sharpen Up) 8.3f **(67)**
Form - 50

Record	**2000** -	1st:0	2nd:0	3rd:0	Ran:2
	Pre2000 -	1st:1	2nd:2	3rd:2	Ran:23

Win Prizemoney £2,868 *Total Prizemoney* £6,421
Wins * 1999 May Nottin (GD) H 10f 43 45+ <

2000 Turf 0-2: (10f, 12f) (g-s, g-f)
Moderate mare, effective 10f, acts on gd to g-f, best on g-f, prefers tight tracks. Turf high 35.
**Mrs M Reveley [5-34] Mrs Stephanie Smith.*

SMART SQUALL (USA) BHB 93f RR 87?f 880[11]
5 b h Summer Squall (USA) 7f **(80)** - Greek Wedding (USA) (Blushing Groom (FR)) 10.3f **(76)**
Form - 0
Record 2000 - 1st:0 2nd:0 3rd:0 Ran:1
Pre2000 - 1st:3 2nd:2 3rd:1 Ran:11
Win Prizemoney £26,668 *Total Prizemoney* £59,555
Wins 1997 Dec Toulou (HVY) L 8f 99 <
1997 Oct Ascot (HVY) H 7f 83 95+
1997 Spt Chepst (GD) 7.1f 81
2000 Turf 0-1: (10f) (sft)
Useful colt. **E Stanners [0-3] George Ward (from D J Coakley [0-1] Oct 1999).*

SMASHING TIME (USA) RR 68f 5136[8]
2 b f Smart Strike (CAN) - Broken Peace (USA) (Devil's Bag (USA)) 12.4f **(78)**
Form - 78
Record 2000 - 1st:0 2nd:0 3rd:0 Ran:2
2000 Turf 0-2: (7f, 8f) (g-s, g-f)
Currently average filly. Turf high 68 (began Spt).
**Mrs A J Perrett [0-2] Lady Harrison & Sir Eric Parker.*

SMILE ITS SHOWTIME BHB 46f RR 40f 1957[10]
3 b g Missed Flight - Treeline (High Top) 10.2f **(67)**
Form - 0880
Record 2000 - 1st:0 2nd:0 3rd:0 Ran:4
2000 Turf 0-3: (6f, 8f 2) (gd 2, frm) 2000 AW 0-1: (9f) (Fibr)
Workmanlike, moderate gelding. Turf high 40.
**R Guest [0-4] Miss Dawn Allen.*

SMIRFYS PARTY BHB 70f76a RR 70f 76a 5117[3]
2 ch c Clantime 6.6f **(57)** - Party Scenes (Most Welcome)
Form - 625533
Record 2000 - 1st:0 2nd:1 3rd:2 Ran:6
Win Prizemoney £0 *Total Prizemoney* £1,957
2000 Turf 0-4: (5f 3, 6f) (gd, g-f, frm, hrd) 2000 AW 0-2: (5f, 6f) (Fibr 2)
Above-average colt, effective 5 to 6f, acts on g-f - acts on Fibr. Turf high 70 - 2nd of 5 giving 5lb to Karitsa (15 Jly Chester 5f g-f RF 2832). AW high 78 (1st run) (began Spt) - 3rd of 13 giving 5lb to Ella's Pal (30 Spt Wolverhampton 6f Fibr RF 4760).
**B A McMahon [0-6] Mrs Dian Plant.*

SMIRK BHB 85f RR 90f 5132[2]
2 ch c Selkirk (USA) 7.9f **(76)** - Elfin Laughter **(72f)** (Alzao (USA)) 7.1f **(68)**
Form - 602
Record 2000 - 1st:0 2nd:1 3rd:0 Ran:3
Win Prizemoney £0 *Total Prizemoney* £1,570
2000 Turf 0-3: (6f 3) (sft, gd, frm)
Currently useful colt. Turf high 90 (began Spt) - 2nd of 19 to Prime Version (21 Oct Newbury 6f sft RF 5132).
**D R C Elsworth [0-3] M Tabor.*

SMITH AND WESTERN BHB 87f RR 90f 4690[4]
2 b c Factual (USA) - Temple Heights (Shirley Heights) 10.3f **(74)**
Form - 50123504
Record 2000 - 1st:1 2nd:1 3rd:1 Ran:8
Win Prizemoney £4,212 *Total Prizemoney* £8,863
Wins * 2000 Jly Epsom (G-S) 7f 80 <
2000 Turf 1-8: (5f, 6f 4, 7f 1-3) (gd 1-5, g-f, frm 2)
Useful colt, effective 6 to 7f, acts on gd. Turf high 90 - 4th of 6 getting 6lb from Inspector General (27 Spt Salisbury 6f gd RF 4690). Appreciated the step up to seven furlongs when getting off the mark in an Epsom maiden and has put in some fair efforts since.
**R Hannon [1-8] Paul Jubert.*

SMOKEY FROM CAPLAW BHB 43f RR 37f 5194[5]
6 b g Sizzling Melody 6.3f **(49)** - Mary From Dunlow (Nicholas Bill) 10.1f **(56)**
Form - 05
Record 2000 - 1st:0 2nd:0 3rd:0 Ran:2
Pre2000 - 1st:5 2nd:3 3rd:1 Ran:36
Win Prizemoney £16,780 *Total Prizemoney* £21,570
Wins 1998 Jly Carlis (G-F) H 6.9f 67 69
1997 Oct Redcar (G-F) H 7f 65 67
1997 May Thirsk (GD) H 6f 62 70 <
1997 May Newcas (GD) H 6f 62 64
1996 May Hamilt (G-F) C 6f 66
2000 Turf 0-2: (6f, 7f) (sft, gd)
Very moderate gelding, effective 8f, acts on g-f, has worn blinkers, likes tight tracks. Turf high 35 (began Oct).
**J S Goldie [0-2] Charles Johnston (from J J O'Neill [5-36] Jly 1999).*

SMOKIN BEAU BHB 80f75a RR 81f 75a 5199[10]
3 b g Cigar 6.3f **(43)** - Beau Dada (IRE) (Pine Circle (USA))
Form - 3153200280036110700
Record 2000 - 1st:2 2nd:2 3rd:2 Ran:16
Pre2000 - 1st:1 2nd:0 3rd:2 Ran:6
Win Prizemoney £18,688 *Total Prizemoney* £24,463
Wins * 2000 Aug Newbur (G-F) H 5.2f 79 81 <
*** 2000** Aug Goodwo (GD) H 5f 71 75
* 1999 *Nov Southw (STD) 5f 67+*
2000 Turf 2-13: (5f 2-8, 6f 5) (hvy, sft, g-s, gd 5, g-f 2-5) 2000 AW 0-3: (5f 2, 6f) (Fibr 3)
Decent gelding, effective 5 to 6f, best at 5f, acts on sft to g-f - acts on AW, best on g-f, has worn blinkers, excels at Southwell, does well at Wolverhampton. Turf high 81 - 1st of 6 getting 7lb from Brecongill Lad (19 Aug Newbury RF 3791) - also 1st of 17 getting 8lb from Travesty of Law (4 Aug Goodwood RF 3365). AW high 81 - 2nd of 5 giving 12lb to Kirsch (20 Jan Wolverhampton 5f Fibr RF 0122). Consistent. Best at five furlongs, he struck form in August with wins at Goodwood and Newbury. Fair efforts since.
**J Cullinan [3-22] Turf 2000 Ltd.*

SMOOTHIE (IRE) BHB 64f RR 64f 5004[10]
2 gr c Definite Article - Limpopo (Green Desert (USA)) 8.6f **(78)**
Form - 30540
Record 2000 - 1st:0 2nd:0 3rd:1 Ran:5
Win Prizemoney £0 *Total Prizemoney* £533
2000 Turf 0-5: (5f, 6f, 7f 2, 8f) (g-s, gd 2, g-f, frm)
Average colt. Turf high 64 (1st run) (began Aug) - 3rd of 5 to Lapwing (4 Aug Ayr 6f frm RF 3354). **P F I Cole [0-5] Ben Arbib.*

SMOOTH SAILING BHB 78f73a RR 84f 73a 4934[15]
5 gr g Beveled (USA) 6.9f **(64)** - Sea Farer Lake (Gairloch) 7f **(63)**
Form - 748051800
Record 2000 - 1st:1 2nd:0 3rd:0 Ran:9
Pre2000 - 1st:2 2nd:7 3rd:3 Ran:39
Win Prizemoney £12,361 *Total Prizemoney* £33,175
Wins * 2000 Aug Newmar (GD) H 8f 77 82 <
* 1998 Jun Leices (SFT) H 7f 78 80
* 1997 Apr Sandow (GD) 5f 78
2000 Turf 1-9: (7f, 8f 1-7, 9f) (sft, g-s, gd 4, g-f 1-1, frm 2)
Decent gelding, effective 7 to 8f, best at 8f, acts on gd to g-f, best on gd, has worn blinkers, likes left handed tracks, likes tight tracks. Turf high 84 - also 1st of 14 giving 4lb to Gwendoline (4 Aug Newmarket RF 3368). A clear-cut winner at Newmarket in August, he is suited by a truly-run race.
**K McAuliffe [4-50] A R Parrish.*

SMOOTH SAND (USA) BHB 75f RR 81f 4484[19]
3 b g Desert Secret (IRE) - Baby Smooth (USA) (Apalachee (USA)) 9.4f **(71)**
Form - 11360
Record 2000 - 1st:2 2nd:0 3rd:1 Ran:5
Pre2000 - 1st:0 2nd:0 3rd:0 Ran:3
Win Prizemoney £6,099 *Total Prizemoney* £7,477
Wins * 2000 Apr Bright (G-S) H 10f 70 79 <
*** 2000** Mar Mussel (GD) H 8f 67 71
2000 Turf 2-5: (8f 1-2, 10f 1-3) (g-s, gd 2-3, g-f)
Scopey, decent gelding, effective 6 to 10f, best at 10f, acts on gd. Turf high 81 - 3rd of 12 getting 4lb from Dancing Bay (3 May Pontefract 10f gd RF 1008) - also 1st of 20 giving 24lb to Ratified (13 Apr Brighton RF 0692). Inconsistent.
**M A Jarvis [2-8] Walter Grubmuller.*

SMUDGER SMITH BHB 50f RR 64f 3905[5]
3 ch g Deploy 11.4f **(67)** - Parfait Amour **(48f)** (Clantime)
Form - 834646255

Record 2000 - 1st:0 2nd:1 3rd:1 Ran:9
Pre2000 - 1st:0 2nd:1 3rd:1 Ran:5
Win Prizemoney £0 *Total Prizemoney* £2,773
2000 Turf 0-8: (10f, 12f 3, 14f, 15f, 16f, 17f) (gd, g-f 3, frm 4) 2000 AW 0-1: (12f) (Fibr)
Workmanlike, average gelding, effective 8 to 12f, acts on gd to g-f, has worn blinkers. Turf high 64 - 3rd of 15 giving 7lb to Penshiel (23 May Beverley 12f gd RF 1388). **B S Rothwell [0-14] S P Hudson.*

SMYSLOV BHB 80f **RR 80f** 4428^{4}

2 b c Rainbow Quest (USA) 11.2f **(81)** - Vlaanderen (IRE) **(54f)** (In The Wings)
Form - 84414
Record 2000 - 1st:1 2nd:0 3rd:0 Ran:5
Win Prizemoney £3,867 *Total Prizemoney* £5,137
Wins * 2000 Aug Hamilt (SFT) **8.3f** 82 <
2000 Turf 1-5: (7f 3, 8f 1-2) (gd 1-2, g-f 2, frm)
Decent colt. Turf high 80 (began Jly).
**J L Dunlop [1-5] Benny Andersson.*

SNAKE GODDESS **RR 33f** 5152^{10}

2 b f Primo Dominie 7.2f **(67)** - Shoshone **(46f 44a)** (Be My Chief (USA))
Form - 0
Record 2000 - 1st:0 2nd:0 3rd:0 Ran:1
2000 Turf 0-1: (7f) (g-s)
Currently very moderate filly.
**H Morrison [0-1] Angela McAlpine And Partners.*

SNAP CRACKER BHB 37f40a **RR 34f 40a** 3931^{11}

4 b m Inchinor 8.9f **(64)** - Valkyrie (Bold Lad (IRE)) 8.4f **(68)**
Form - 870020000000
Record 2000 - 1st:0 2nd:1 3rd:0 Ran:10
Pre2000 - 1st:3 2nd:1 3rd:2 Ran:24
Win Prizemoney £9,397 *Total Prizemoney* £14,713
Wins 1998 Jun Cheste (G-S) 5.1f 78 <
1998 Jun Leices (SFT) 5f 64+
1998 Apr Sandow (HVY) 5f 65
2000 Turf 0-6: (5f 3, 6f 3) (g-s, gd 3, g-f, frm) 2000 AW 0-4: (5f 3, 6f) (Fibr 4)
Scopey, very moderate filly, effective 6f, acts on gd. Turf high 34. AW high 38. Becoming disappointing. A winner of three of her first five starts at two, she has failed to score since. Acts on soft ground, but has disappointed recently, and a drop in class has not really seen much improvement.
**D W Chapman [0-12] David Chapman (from H S Howe [0-10] Nov 1999).*

SNATCH BHB 47f **RR 49f** 5150^{2}

3 b f Elmaamul (USA) 8.1f **(70)** - Tarkhana (IRE) (Dancing Brave (USA)) 8.4f **(76)**
Form - 640012
Record 2000 - 1st:1 2nd:1 3rd:0 Ran:6
Win Prizemoney £2,226 *Total Prizemoney* £3,066
Wins * 2000 Spt Yarmou (G-F) H 8f 40 49 <
2000 Turf 1-5: (8f 1-3, 10f 2) (g-f 1-2, frm 3) 2000 AW 0-1: (10f) (Equi)
Leggy, fair filly, effective 8 to 10f, acts on g-f - acts on Equi. Turf high 49 - 1st of 18 getting 19lb from Laraza (14 Spt Yarmouth RF 4402). (1st run) - 2nd of 13 getting 24lb from Fair Lady (23 Oct Lingfield 10f Equi RF 5150). **M L W Bell [1-6] Mrs G Rowland-Clark.*

SNETTERTON **RR 95f** $891a^{4}$

3 b c Machiavellian (USA) 9.8f **(83)** - Schezerade (USA) (Tom Rolfe) 9.4f **(75)**
Form - 4
2000 Turf 0-1: (11f) (hvy)
Currently very useful colt. **P Bary in FR [1-2].*

SNIZORT (USA) **RR 74f** 4969^{21}

2 b c Bahri (USA) - Ava Singstheblues (USA) (Dixieland Band (USA)) 7f **(74)**
Form - 40
Record 2000 - 1st:0 2nd:0 3rd:0 Ran:2
Win Prizemoney £0 *Total Prizemoney* £327
2000 Turf 0-2: (8f 2) (gd 2)
Currently above-average colt. Turf high 74 (began Spt).
**J D Bethell [0-2] M J Dawson.*

SNOW BUNTING **RR 79tf** 1332^{3}

2 ch c Polar Falcon (USA) 9f **(74)** - Marl **(81f)** (Lycius (USA))
Form - 3
Record 2000 - 1st:0 2nd:0 3rd:1 Ran:1
Win Prizemoney £0 *Total Prizemoney* £704
2000 Turf 0-1: (6f) (g-f)
Currently above-average colt. (1st run) - 3rd of 13 to Patsy's Double (20 May Newbury 6f g-f RF 1332).
**R Charlton [0-1] The Queen.*

SNOWEY MOUNTAIN BHB 81f **RR 76f** 4400^{1}

2 gr c Inchinor 8.9f **(64)** - Mrs Gray (Red Sunset) 8.2f **(63)**
Form - 6443631
Record 2000 - 1st:1 2nd:0 3rd:2 Ran:7
Win Prizemoney £3,029 *Total Prizemoney* £10,313
Wins * 2000 Spt Yarmou (G-F) H 8f 75 76 <
2000 Turf 1-7: (6f 4, 7f, 8f 1-2) (gd, g-f 1-3, frm 3)
Above-average colt, effective 6 to 8f, best at 6f, acts on g-f to frm, best on g-f. Turf high 76 - 1st of 10 giving 9lb to Dancing Venture (14 Spt Yarmouth RF 4400).
**N A Callaghan [1-7] Gallagher Equine Ltd.*

SNOW POLINA (USA) **RR 115f** $5329a^{4}$

5 ch m Trempolino (USA) 11.9f **(77)** - Snow House (IRE) (Vacarme (USA)) 8.5f **(68)**
Form - 14
2000 Turf 1-2: (10f 1-1, 11f) (g-s 1-1, frm)
High-class filly. Turf high 115 (began Aug) - 4th of 14 to Perfect Sting (4 Nov Churchill Downs 11f frm RF 5329a).
**W Mott in USA [1-2] G Tanaka (from J-C Rouget in FR [1-2] Nov 1998).*

SNOWSTORM BHB 98f **RR 93f** 5124^{10}

2 gr c Environment Friend 7.5f **(67)** - Choral Sundown (Night Shift (USA)) 7.2f **(69)**
Form - 261210
Record 2000 - 1st:2 2nd:2 3rd:0 Ran:6
Win Prizemoney £18,557 *Total Prizemoney* £20,532
Wins * 2000 Spt Doncas (G-F) H 8f 92 93 <
*** 2000** Jly Ayr (FRM) 7f 81
2000 Turf 2-6: (6f, 7f 1-2, 8f 1-3) (g-s, gd 2, g-f, frm 2-2)
Useful colt, effective 8f, acts on gd to frm. Turf high 93 - 1st of 15 giving 3lb to Northfields Dancer (7 Spt Doncaster RF 4283). Probably best on fast ground, he defied a big weight in a valuable nursery at Doncaster in September but was found out in the Racing Post Trophy. Likely to stay middle-distances, he could be a suitable type for the Italian Derby. **M L W Bell [2-6] Lord Blyth.*

SNUGFIT ROSIE (GER) BHB 55f **RR 64f** 5002^{2}

4 ch m Kris 10f **(75)** - Sorceress (FR) (Fabulous Dancer (USA)) 9.4f **(70)**
Form - 542
Record 2000 - 1st:0 2nd:1 3rd:0 Ran:3
Pre2000 - 1st:0 2nd:0 3rd:3 Ran:9
Win Prizemoney £0 *Total Prizemoney* £3,056
2000 Turf 0-3: (14f, 16f, 18f) (g-s 2, gd)
Scopey, average filly, effective 12 to 16f, acts on gd to frm. Turf high 60 (began Spt). Consistent.
**M W Easterby [4-8] A Greenwood (from M R Channon [0-9] Oct 1999).*

SOAKED BHB 61f63a **RR 58f 63a** 4098^{2}

7 b g Dowsing (USA) 7f **(61)** - Water Well (Sadler's Wells (USA)) 10f **(76)**
Form - 088078R21133402
Record 2000 - 1st:2 2nd:2 3rd:2 Ran:15
Pre2000 - 1st:10 2nd:4 3rd:4 Ran:55
Win Prizemoney £38,824 *Total Prizemoney* £48,711
Wins * 2000 Aug Bath (G-F) H 5.1f 50 60
*** 2000** Aug Windso (G-F) H 5f 50 55
* 1999 *Jan Lingfi (STD) H 5f 80 84* <
* 1998 *Nov Lingfi (STD) H 6f 70 82*
* 1998 *Nov Lingfi (STD) H 5f 70 75+*
* 1998 Spt Pontef (G-F) H 5f 56 63
* 1998 *Jun Southw (STD) H 5f 50 67*
* 1998 *Jun Southw (STD) H 5f 48 63+*
* 1998 Jun Hamilt (GD) H 6f 46 56

* 1998	May	Mussel	(G-S)	H	5f	46	57
* 1998	May	Mussel	(GD)	H	5f	35	44
* 1998	*Mar*	*Southw*	*(STD)*	*SH*	*6f*	*41*	*49*

2000 Turf 2-10: (5f 2-8, 6f 2) (gd, g-f 1-2, frm 1-5, hrd 2) 2000 AW 0-5: (5f 4, 6f) (Fibr 5)

Fair gelding, has broken blood-vessels, effective 5f, - acts on Equi, has worn blinkers (extremely effectively), likes left handed tracks. Turf high 60 (began Jly). AW high 58. Consistent. A real speedster from the stalls, he is effective on turf, Equitrack and Fibresand, and equalled the 20th century record of ten handicap wins in a season in '99. Very effective when gaining an uncontested early lead, though six furlongs looks to be right on the limit of his stamina.

**D W Chapman [12-65] David Chapman (from J R Fanshawe [0-5] Jly 1996).*

SOARING PHOENIX (USA) RR 14f 5151[11]

2 b. br c St Jovite (USA) 11.8f **(75)** - Pamzig (USA) (Danzig (USA)) 8.4f **(76)**

Form - 0

Record 2000 - 1st:0 2nd:0 3rd:0 Ran:1

2000 Turf 0-1: (7f) (g-s)

Currently poor colt. **B W Hills [0-1] Deln Ltd.*

SOBA JONES BHB 59f45a RR 59f 45a 4384[24]

3 b g Emperor Jones (USA) - Soba (Most Secret) 7.1f **(58)**

Form - 6602343153350

Record 2000 - 1st:1 2nd:1 3rd:4 Ran:13
Pre2000 - 1st:0 2nd:0 3rd:1 Ran:1

Win Prizemoney £3,328 *Total Prizemoney* £8,049

Wins * 2000 Jly Newcas (GD) 5f 56 <

2000 Turf 1-11: (5f 1-4, 6f 3, 7f 3, 8f) (gd, g-f 1-4, frm 6) 2000 AW 0-2: (5f, 6f) (Fibr 2)

Light-framed, fair gelding, effective 5 to 8f, best at 5f, acts on g-f to frm, best on frm, often wears blinkers (extremely effectively), excels at Thirsk and Carlisle. Turf high 59 - 3rd of 17 getting 5lb from Northern Svengali (25 Aug Thirsk 5f frm RF 3975) - also 1st of 4 from Kind Emperor (31 Jly Newcastle RF 3252). AW high 40. Consistent. **T D Easterby [1-14] Mrs M Hills.*

SOBER AS A JUDGE BHB 31f39a RR 39f 39a 5229[17]

3 b g Mon Tresor 7.9f **(60)** - Flicker Toa Flame (USA) (Empery (USA)) 11.2f **(69)**

Form - 0003008700

Record 2000 - 1st:0 2nd:0 3rd:1 Ran:10
Pre2000 - 1st:0 2nd:0 3rd:0 Ran:3

Win Prizemoney £0 *Total Prizemoney* £277

2000 Turf 0-9: (7f 2, 8f 5, 10f, 11f) (g-s, gd 2, g-f 2, frm 4) 2000 AW 0-1: (7f) (Fibr)

Leggy, moderate gelding, effective 7f, acts on frm. Turf high 47 - 3rd of 11 giving 5lb to Alabama Wurley (5 Jly Yarmouth 7f frm RF 2554). **J Pearce [0-7] M M Foulger (from C A Dwyer [0-6] Jun 2000).*

SOBER HILL BHB 44f RR 2419[4]

2 b g Komaite (USA) 6.9f **(61)** - Mamoda (Good Times (ITY)) 6.6f **(54)**

Form - 84

Record 2000 - 1st:0 2nd:0 3rd:0 Ran:2

2000 AW 0-2: (6f, 7f) (Fibr 2)

Currently very moderate gelding. AW high 33.

**D Shaw [0-2] M Wainman.*

SOBIESKI (IRE) RR 87f 4839a[4]

3 c

Form - 6134

2000 Turf 1-4: (10f 1-2, 11f, 12f) (hvy 1-2, gd 2)

Useful. Turf high 120 - 1st of 5 from Premier Pas (14 Jly Deauville RF 2979a). Winner of the Prix Eugene Adam, he appeared not to quite stay in the Prix Neil, and was dropped back in trip, but disappointed, in the Prix Dollar. **A Fabre in FR [1-4].*

SOBRIETY (IRE) RR 112f 3278[3]

3 b c Namaqualand (USA) - Scanno's Choice (IRE) (Pennine Walk) 8.5f **(61)**

Form - 106513

Record 2000 - 1st:2 2nd:0 3rd:1 Ran:6
Pre2000 - 1st:1 2nd:1 3rd:0 Ran:3

Win Prizemoney £97,580 *Total Prizemoney* £107,064

Wins	*** 2000**	Jly	York	(GD)	H	10.4f	100	110 <
	*** 2000**	May	Doncas	(G-S)		8f		98
	* 1999	Aug	Salisb	(SFT)		7f		84+

2000 Turf 2-6: (8f 1-4, 10f 1-1, 12f) (g-s, gd 2-3, g-f 2)

Scopey, Group-class colt, effective 10 to 12f, acts on gd to g-f. Turf high 112 - 3rd of 11 getting 3lb from Millenary (1 Aug Goodwood 12f g-f RF 3278) - also 1st of 22 giving 6lb to Man O'Mystery (15 Jly York RF 2854). An enthusiastic sort, he improved markedly once stepped-up in trip, winning the John Smith's Cup and finishing third in the Group 3 Gordon Stakes. Tough and genuine, he is reportedly continuing his career in America. **R F JohnsonHoughton [3-9] Anthony Pye-Jeary.*

SOCIAL CONTRACT BHB 82f RR 84f 4991[1]

3 b g Emarati (USA) 6.6f **(63)** - Just Buy Baileys **(63f)** (Formidable (USA)) 9.2f **(63)**

Form - 7713401

Record 2000 - 1st:2 2nd:0 3rd:1 Ran:7
Pre2000 - 1st:2 2nd:0 3rd:2 Ran:7

Win Prizemoney £15,956 *Total Prizemoney* £19,020

Wins	*** 2000**	Oct	Newmar	(G-S)	H	7f	78	84 <
	*** 2000**	Jun	Leices	(G-F)	H	7f	75	78
	1999	Aug	Lingfi	(GD)	H	7f	75	75
	1999	*Jly*	*Southw*	*(STD)*	*S*	*6f*		*80+*

2000 Turf 2-7: (6f, 7f 2-3, 8f 3) (g-s, gd 1-1, g-f 3, frm, hrd 1-1)

Decent gelding, effective 6 to 8f, acts on gd to hrd - acts on Fibr, has worn blinkers, excels at Newmarket. Turf high 84 - 1st of 29 getting 9lb from Lord Pacal (14 Oct Newmarket RF 4991) - also 1st of 18 giving 25lb to Chilworth (18 Jun Leicester RF 2072). Beat a big field with a bit to spare at Leicester in June.

**R Hannon [2-7] J G Lambton (from W J Haggas [1-3] Aug 1999).*

SOCIAL HARMONY (IRE) BHB 90f RR 110f 4521a[1]

6 b g Polish Precedent (USA) 9f **(73)** - Latest Chapter (IRE) (Ahonoora) 8.1f **(73)**

Form - 7204141

2000 Turf 2-7: (5f 2, 6f 1-3, 7f 1-1, 8f) (g-s, gd 3, g-f 1-2)

Group-class gelding, effective 5 to 7f, acts on g-f. Turf high 110 - 1st of 8 from Tarry Flynn (16 Spt Curragh RF 4521a) - also 1st of 7 getting 5lb from One Won One (19 Aug Fairyhouse RF 3883a). Best over six and seven furlongs nowadays, he gained a deserved big race win when landing the Group Three Boland Stakes at The Curragh in September. Effective when held-up or ridden positively, he is thoroughly genuine.

**D K Weld in IRE [8-22] S Creaven.*

SOCIALIST (USA) BHB 25f31a RR 13tf 31a 4649[4]

4 b g Hermitage (USA) 8.6f **(84)** - Social Missy (USA) (Raised Socially (USA))

Form - 630004

Record 2000 - 1st:0 2nd:0 3rd:1 Ran:6

Win Prizemoney £0 *Total Prizemoney* £318

2000 Turf 0-3: (12f 2, 14f) (gd 2, g-f) 2000 AW 0-3: (11f, 12f 2) (Fibr 3)

Very moderate gelding, effective 11f, - acts on Fibr, has worn blinkers. Turf high 13. AW high 33 - 4th of 16 getting 10lb from Be Warned (26 Spt Southwell 11f Fibr RF 4649).

**J A Osborne [0-6] The Woolfie and Tom Partnership.*

SOCIETY KING (IRE) BHB 46a RR 18f 5077[7]

5 b g Fairy King (USA) 7.7f **(75)** - Volga (USA) (Riverman (USA)) 9.1f **(76)**

Form - 07

Record 2000 - 1st:0 2nd:0 3rd:0 Ran:2
Pre2000 - 1st:0 2nd:0 3rd:1 Ran:9

Win Prizemoney £0 *Total Prizemoney* £450

2000 Turf 0-2: (8f, 10f) (g-s 2)

Poor gelding, has broken blood-vessels. Turf high 18 (began Oct).

**Mrs A E Johnson [0-2] Lifestyle Bloodstock (UK) Ltd (from J E Banks [0-9] Apr 1999).*

SOCIETY TIMES (USA) BHB 28f RR 30f 2420[7]

7 b g Imp Society (USA) 7.1f **(63)** - Mauna Loa (USA) (Hawaii) 9.4f **(66)**

Form - 507

Record 2000 - 1st:0 2nd:0 3rd:0 Ran:3
Pre2000 - 1st:0 2nd:0 3rd:0 Ran:3

2000 Turf 0-2: (8f, 11f) (frm 2) 2000 AW 0-1: (8f) (Fibr)

Very moderate gelding. Turf high 30.

**A Bailey [0-3] Sandybrow Stables Ltd (from D A Nolan [0-4] May*

1997).

SO DAINTY (IRE) BHB 43f57a **RR 21f 57a** 3910[17]
3 b br f Common Grounds 8.1f **(66)** - Naxos (USA) (Big Spruce (USA)) 11f **(71)**
Form - 000
Record 2000 - 1st:0 2nd:0 3rd:0 Ran:3
Pre2000 - 1st:0 2nd:0 3rd:1 Ran:5
Win Prizemoney £0 *Total Prizemoney* £281
2000 Turf 0-3: (8f 2, 9f) (g-f 2, frm)
Unfurnished, fair filly. Turf high 21 (began Jly). Becoming disappointing.
**Miss B Sanders [0-3] J M Quinn (from B W Hills [0-5] Oct 1999).*

SODFAHH RR 54f 3920[6]
2 ch f Lion Cavern (USA) 7.5f **(74)** - Balwa (USA) (Danzig (USA)) 8.4f **(76)**
Form - 6
Record 2000 - 1st:0 2nd:0 3rd:0 Ran:1
2000 Turf 0-1: (7f) (gd)
Currently fair filly. **M P Tregoning [0-1] Sheikh Ahmed Al Maktoum.*

SO DIVINE BHB 77f **RR 70f** 2931[5]
2 br f So Factual (USA) - Divina Mia **(65f)** (Dowsing (USA))
Form - 415
Record 2000 - 1st:1 2nd:0 3rd:0 Ran:3
Win Prizemoney £2,824 *Total Prizemoney* £0,050
Wins * 2000 Jly Ripon (G-S) 5f 70+ <
2000 Turf 1-3: (5f 1-3) (g-s 1-1, g-f, frm)
Currently above-average filly. Turf high 70 - 1st of 11 from New Wonder (10 Jly Ripon RF 2675).
**M Johnston [1-3] The 5th Middleham Partnership.*

SOFISIO BHB 60f68a **RR 63f 68a** 4925[2]
3 ch g Efisio 7.7f **(69)** - Legal Embrace (CAN) (Legal Bid (USA))
Form - 2144032450062
Record 2000 - 1st:0 2nd:2 3rd:1 Ran:9
Pre2000 - 1st:1 2nd:1 3rd:0 Ran:7
Win Prizemoney £2,127 *Total Prizemoney* £5,802
Wins * 1999 *Nov Lingfi (STD) 7f* 77 <
2000 Turf 0-6: (7f, 8f 4, 10f) (g-s, g-f 2, frm 3) 2000 AW 0-3. (7f 2, 8f) (Equi, Fibr 2)
Workmanlike, above-average gelding, effective 7 to 8f, - acts on Equi, has worn blinkers, likes left handed tracks, likes tight tracks. Turf high 64. AW high 70 (began Jun).
**W R Muir [1-16] North Farm Stud.*

SO FOXY BHB 44f **RR 39f** 4996[4]
2 b f So Factual (USA) - Miss Foxtrot (Bustino) 10.4f **(64)**
Form - 0074
Record 2000 - 1st:0 2nd:0 3rd:0 Ran:4
2000 Turf 0-2: (5f, 6f) (g-f, frm) 2000 AW 0-2: (7f, 8f) (Fibr 2)
Moderate filly. Turf high 39 (began Aug). AW high 45 (began Spt).
**J A Gilbert [0-4] Ms Tania Baybut.*

SOFT BREEZE RR 69+f 1221[3]
2 ch f Zafonic (USA) 9f **(83)** - Tropical **(103f)** (Green Desert (USA)) 8.6f **(78)**
Form - 3
Record 2000 - 1st:0 2nd:0 3rd:1 Ran:1
Win Prizemoney £0 *Total Prizemoney* £1,180
2000 Turf 0-1: (6f) (frm)
Currently average filly. (1st run) - 3rd of 8 to Barathiki (16 May York 6f frm RF 1221). **E A L Dunlop [0-1] Maktoum Al Maktoum.*

SOHAPARA RR 28[13]
5 ch m Arapahos (FR) - Mistress Boreen (Boreen (FR))
Form - 0
Record 2000 - 1st:0 2nd:0 3rd:0 Ran:1
2000 AW 0-1: (12f) (Equi)
Currently very poor filly. **L A Dace [0-2] Luke Dace.*

SOLAIA (USA) RR 107f 4963[10]
3 ch f Miswaki (USA) 8.1f **(81)** - Indian Fashion (USA) (General Holme (USA)) 5.7f **(63)**
Form - 4172440
Record 2000 - 1st:1 2nd:1 3rd:0 Ran:7
Pre2000 - 1st:1 2nd:0 3rd:0 Ran:4
Win Prizemoney £32,947 *Total Prizemoney* £48,148
Wins * 2000 May Cheste (GD) L 11.4f 99 <
* 1999 Jly Newmar (G-F) 7f 70+
2000 Turf 1-7: (8f, 10f, 11f 1-1, 12f 3, 15f) (sft, g-s, gd 4, g-f 1-1)
Well made, Pattern-class filly, effective 8 to 15f, acts on sft to g-f, best on gd. Turf high 107 - 2nd of 11 getting 13lb from Ela Athena (8 Jly Haydock 12f gd RF 2632) - also 1st of 5 from Inforapenny (10 May Chester RF 1130). Consistent. She appreciated the step up in trip when winning the Cheshire Oaks in May and has run pretty well in very decent company since. Twelve furlongs looks her best trip. **P F I Cole [2-11] Faisal Salman.*

SOLAR FLARE (IRE) RR 14f 4125[10]
2 b f Danehill (USA) 9.1f **(79)** - Cochineal (USA) (Vaguely Noble) 10.1f **(72)**
Form - 0
Record 2000 - 1st:0 2nd:0 3rd:0 Ran:1
2000 Turf 0-1: (7f) (frm)
Currently poor filly. **J H M Gosden [0-1] R E Sangster.*

SOLDIER ON (IRE) RR 84f 4742[6]
2 b g General Monash (USA) - Golden Form (Formidable (USA)) 9.2f **(63)**
Form - 7215571352216
Record 2000 - 1st:3 2nd:3 3rd:1 Ran:13
Win Prizemoney £18,505 *Total Prizemoney* £23,851
Wins * 2000 Spt Ayr (SFT) H 6f 84 84 <
*** 2000** Aug Goodwo (GD) H 5f 73 76
*** 2000** May Bright (FRM) 5.3f 73
2000 Turf 3-13: (5f 2-7, 6f 1-6) (gd 2-7, g-f 5, frm 1-1)
Decent gelding, effective 5 to 6f, best at 6f, acts on gd to g-f, best on gd, excels at Goodwood. Turf high 84 - 6th of 19 getting 5lb from Caustic Wit (30 Spt Newmarket 6f g-f RF 4742) - also 1st of 11 getting 4lb from Armagnac (15 Spt Ayr RF 4425). Improving.
**M R Channon [3-13] T S M Cunningham.*

SOLDIER POINT RR 72f 3502[2]
2 ch c Sabrehill (USA) 8.5f **(64)** - Reel Foyle (USA) (Irish River (FR)) 8.6f **(78)**
Form - 02
Record 2000 - 1st:0 2nd:1 3rd:0 Ran:2
Win Prizemoney £0 *Total Prizemoney* £1,100
2000 Turf 0-2: (6f 2) (frm 2)
Currently above-average colt. Turf high 72 - 2nd of 12 to Time To Remember (9 Aug Pontefract 6f frm RF 3502).
**P C Haslam [0-2] W J Gredley.*

SOLE SINGER (GER) BHB 53f **RR 49f** 131[5]
4 b g Slip Anchor 12.7f **(75)** - Singer on the Roof (Chief Singer) 8.9f **(66)**
Form - 325
Record 2000 - 1st:0 2nd:1 3rd:0 Ran:2
Pre2000 - 1st:0 2nd:1 3rd:2 Ran:8
Win Prizemoney £0 *Total Prizemoney* £2,239
2000 AW 0-2: (12f 2) (Fibr 2)
Scopey, fair gelding, has worn blinkers. AW high 53.
**D HaydnJones [0-5] Hugh O'Donnell (from I A Balding [0-5] Jun 1999).*

SOLITARY BHB 84f **RR 91f** 5111[5]
3 b c Sanglamore (USA) 12.9f **(67)** - Set Fair (USA) **(89f)** (Alleged (USA)) 10f **(76)**
Form - 22105
Record 2000 - 1st:1 2nd:2 3rd:0 Ran:5
Pre2000 - 1st:0 2nd:0 3rd:0 Ran:1
Win Prizemoney £4,173 *Total Prizemoney* £7,293
Wins * 2000 Aug Ripon (GD) 12.3f 80+ <
2000 Turf 1-5: (12f 1-4, 16f) (gd 3, g-f, frm 1-1)
Scopey, useful colt, effective 12 to 16f, acts on gd, often wears blinkers. Turf high 91 (1st run) - 2nd of 8 to Wellbeing (18 Apr Newmarket 12f gd RF 0767). He found life tough after winning a weak Ripon maiden, failing to stay two miles on his final start. Sold for 32,000gns at Newmarket in October, he will not be easy to place on the Flat. **B W Hills [1-6] K Abdulla.*

SOLLER BAY BHB 81f72a **RR 83+f 72a** 2649[9]
3 b g Contract Law (USA) 8.9f **(54)** - Bichette **(43f 47a)** (Lidhame) 9.2f

(50)
Form - 131010
Record 2000 - 1st:3 2nd:0 3rd:1 Ran:6
Pre2000 - 1st:0 2nd:1 3rd:0 Ran:1
Win Prizemoney £10,985 *Total Prizemoney* £12,670
Wins * 2000 Jun Ayr (GD) H 9.1f 76 83+ <
*** 2000** Apr Windso (HVY) H 8.3f 72 77
*** 2000** *Jan Wolver (STD) 9.4f 64*
2000 Turf 2-4: (8f 1-1, 9f 1-2, 10f) (g-s 1-2, g-f 1-1, frm) 2000 AW 1-2: (9f 1-1, 10f) (Equi, Fibr 1-1)
Scopey, decent gelding, effective 8 to 9f, acts on g-s to g-f, prefers tight tracks. Turf high 83 - 1st of 4 giving 11lb to Yenaled (24 Jun Ayr RF 2248) - also 1st of 15 giving 12lb to Pipssalio (17 Apr Windsor RF 0753). AW high 64 (1st run). Got off the mark in a maiden on the Wolverhampton Fibresand in January, and showed he could act on turf too when winning quite a competitive handicap on heavy ground at Windsor in April. Showed he retains his form when taking an easy race at Ayr in June.
**K R Burke [3-7] Mrs Melba Bryce.*

SOLLY'S PAL BHB 49f52a **RR 50f 52a** 4826[3]
5 gr g Petong 7.6f **(58)** - Petriece (Mummy's Pet) 7.7f **(60)**
Form - 0453103
Record 2000 - 1st:1 2nd:0 3rd:2 Ran:5
Pre2000 - 1st:0 2nd:0 3rd:0 Ran:5
Win Prizemoney £2,359 *Total Prizemoney* £2,898
Wins * 2000 *Jun Southw (STD) H 7f 45 48* <
2000 Turf 0-2: (6f, 7f) (g-f, frm) 2000 AW 1-3: (7f 1-3) (Equi, Fibr 1-2)
Fair gelding, effective 6 to 7f, acts on g-f - acts on Fibr, has worn blinkers. Turf high 42 (began Aug) - 3rd of 25 getting 11lb from Square Dancer (6 Oct Windsor 6f g-f RF 4826). AW high 48 - 1st of 16 getting 11lb from Sharp Steel (9 Jun Southwell RF 1854). He has a questionable attitude under pressure and should be treated with caution.
**P J Makin [1-8] Mrs Paul Levinson (from I A Balding [0-2] May 1998).*

SOLO BID **RR 59f** 3529[8]
3 ch f Rislan (USA) - Deauville Duchess (Ballad Rock) 7.8f **(63)**
Form - 48
Record 2000 - 1st:0 2nd:0 3rd:0 Ran:2
Win Prizemoney £0 *Total Prizemoney* £327
2000 Turf 0-2: (7f, 8f) (gd, frm)
Currently fair filly. Turf high 59 (began Jly).
**B R Millman [0-2] Rod Hamilton.*

SOLO DANCE BHB 42f **RR 52f** 4930[8]
2 b f Tragic Role (USA) 9.4f **(63)** - Dancing Heights (IRE) **(80f)** (High Estate)
Form - 448578
Record 2000 - 1st:0 2nd:0 3rd:0 Ran:6
Win Prizemoney £0 *Total Prizemoney* £502
2000 Turf 0-6: (7f 6) (gd, g-f 2, frm 3)
Fair filly, often wears blinkers. Turf high 52 (began Jly).
**T D Easterby [0-6] Exors of the late R Leah.*

SOLO FLIGHT BHB 80f **RR 87f** 5187[4]
3 gr g Mtoto 11.5f **(71)** - Silver Singer **(65f 55a)** (Pharly (FR)) 9.8f **(68)**
Form - 21004
Record 2000 - 1st:1 2nd:1 3rd:0 Ran:5
Pre2000 - 1st:0 2nd:0 3rd:0 Ran:2
Win Prizemoney £2,247 *Total Prizemoney* £3,998
Wins * 2000 May Bright (SFT) 10f 87 <
2000 Turf 1-5: (10f 1-4, 12f) (sft, gd 1-3, frm)
Leggy, useful gelding, effective 10f, acts on gd. Turf high 87 - 1st of 7 from El Zito (24 May Brighton RF 1423). Gradually improving, he got off the mark in a Brighton maiden in May.
**B W Hills [1-7] Lady Hardy.*

SOLOIST (IRE) BHB 35f **RR 53tf** 2882[9]
3 ch f Elmaamul (USA) 8.1f **(70)** - Alyara (USA) (Alydar (USA)) 9.1f **(76)**
Form - 70000
Record 2000 - 1st:0 2nd:0 3rd:0 Ran:5
Pre2000 - 1st:0 2nd:0 3rd:0 Ran:2
2000 Turf 0-5: (7f 2, 8f 2, 12f) (gd 2, g-f 1, frm 2)
Light-framed, fair filly. Turf high 53.
**J L Eyre [0-7] Mrs Angela Seed.*

SOLO PERFORMANCE (IRE) RR 76f 2460[1]
3 b f Sadler's Wells (USA) 11.3f **(87)** - Royal Heroine (Lypheor) 12f **(71)**
Form - 1
Record 2000 - 1st:1 2nd:0 3rd:0 Ran:1
Win Prizemoney £4,056 *Total Prizemoney* £4,056
Wins * 2000 Jly Goodwo (G-F) 12f 76 <
2000 Turf 1-1: (12f 1-1) (g-f 1-1)
Scopey, currently above-average filly. (1st run) - 1st of 6 from Bathwick Babe (2 Jly Goodwood RF 2460).
**J H M Gosden [1-1] R E Sangster.*

SOMALIA RR 4730[12]
3 b g Sanglamore (USA) 12.9f **(67)** - Nesaah (USA) (Topsider (USA)) 8.3f **(71)**
Form - 0
Record 2000 - 1st:0 2nd:0 3rd:0 Ran:1
2000 AW 0-1: (13f) (Equi)
Currently very poor gelding, always wears blinkers.
**B A Pearce [0-2] Mrs P Salter.*

SOME DUST BHB 60f **RR 69f** 2484[2]
2 ch c King's Signet (USA) 7f **(51)** - Some Dream (Vitiges (FR)) 8.2f **(59)**
Form - U8212
Record 2000 - 1st:1 2nd:2 3rd:0 Ran:5
Win Prizemoney £1,834 *Total Prizemoney* £2,883
Wins * 2000 Jun Yarmou (FRM) S 5.2f 69 <
2000 Turf 1-2: (5f 1-2) (gd, g-f 1-1) 2000 AW 0-3: (5f 3) (Equi, Fibr 2)
Average colt. Turf high 69 - 1st of 5 from Harry Junior (26 Jun Yarmouth RF 2290). AW high 69 - 2nd of 8 giving 10lb to Sima's Gold (3 Jly Southwell 5f Fibr RF 2484).
**W G M Turner [1-5] T O C S Ltd.*

SOME MIGHT SAY BHB 37f72a **RR 71?f 72a** 78[9]
5 b g Be My Chief (USA) 10.2f **(62)** - Willowbed (Wollow) 8.2f **(61)**
Form - 80
Record 2000 - 1st:0 2nd:0 3rd:0 Ran:1
Pre2000 - 1st:1 2nd:3 3rd:1 Ran:6
Win Prizemoney £3,355 *Total Prizemoney* £6,675
Wins 1998 *Mar Lingfi (SLW) 10f 76* <
2000 AW 0-1: (13f) (Equi)
Above-average gelding, has worn blinkers.
**N J Hawke [0-4] Trevor Heayns (from M Johnston [1-5] May 1998).*

SOMERS HEATH (IRE) BHB 61f **RR 75?f** 3719[6]
2 b f Definite Article - Glen Of Imaal (IRE) **(34f)** (Common Grounds)
Form - 701056
Record 2000 - 1st:1 2nd:0 3rd:0 Ran:6
Win Prizemoney £7,410 *Total Prizemoney* £7,410
Wins * 2000 Jun York (GD) S 6f 75 <
2000 Turf 1-6: (5f, 6f 1-3, 7f 2) (gd 2, g-f 1-2, frm 2)
Above-average filly, effective 6f, acts on g-f. Turf high 75 - 1st of 13 getting 5lb from Joint Instruction (16 Jun York RF 2033).
**T D Easterby [1-6] Mrs P E Needham.*

SOMESESSION BHB 69f59a **RR 64f 59a** 5317[17]
3 b c Prince Sabo 6.6f **(64)** - Session (Reform) 8.9f **(62)**
Form - 0717000
Record 2000 - 1st:1 2nd:0 3rd:0 Ran:7
Pre2000 - 1st:0 2nd:0 3rd:0 Ran:3
Win Prizemoney £6,900 *Total Prizemoney* £7,125
Wins 2000 Jly Currag (G-F) H 5f 53 <
2000 Turf 1-6: (5f 1-3, 6f 2, 7f) (sft, g-s, g-f 1-2, frm 2) 2000 AW 0-1: (6f) (Fibr)
Average colt, has worn blinkers (very effectively). Turf high 64.
**R A Fahey [0-2] R A Fahey (from Ms J Morgan in IRE [1-8] Aug 2000).*

SOMETHINGABOUTMARY (IRE) BHB 58f **RR 37f** 2294[3]
2 b f Fayruz 6.6f **(63)** - Cut it Fine (USA) (Big Spruce (USA)) 11f **(71)**
Form - 0703
Record 2000 - 1st:0 2nd:0 3rd:1 Ran:4
Win Prizemoney £0 *Total Prizemoney* £405
2000 Turf 0-4: (5f, 6f 2, 7f) (g-s, g-f, frm 2)
Very moderate filly. Turf high 37. **J S Wainwright [0-4] R Bond.*

SOME WILL BHB 60f **RR 51f** 3502[8]
2 b c Handsome Sailor 6.6f **(53)** - Bollin Sophie **(33f)** (Efisio)

Form - 048
Record 2000 - 1st:0 2nd:0 3rd:0 Ran:3
Win Prizemoney £0 *Total Prizemoney* £477
2000 Turf 0-3: (6f 2, 7f) (frm 3)
Currently fair colt. Turf high 51. **T D Easterby [0-3] Bill Toner.*

SONATINA RR 83+f 4397[1]

2 b f Distant Relative 7f **(69)** - Son Et Lumiere (Rainbow Quest (USA)) 10.4f **(75)**
Form - 11
Record 2000 - 1st:2 2nd:0 3rd:0 Ran:2
Win Prizemoney £8,212 *Total Prizemoney* £8,212
Wins * **2000** Spt Yarmou (G-F) 6f 83+ <
* **2000** Aug Folkes (G-F) 6f 81+
2000 Turf 2-2: (6f 2-2) (gd 1-1, g-f 1-1)
Currently decent filly. Turf high 83 (began Aug) - 1st of 7 getting 9lb from Greenwood (14 Spt Yarmouth RF 4397) - also 1st of 12 from Pleasure Dome (18 Aug Folkestone RF 3750). **J W Payne [2-2] Mrs R A C Vigors.*

SONBELLE BHB 46f62a RR 54f 62a 4491[19]

3 b f Son Pardo - Ty-With-Belle (Pamroy) 12.5f **(55)**
Form - 472000
Record 2000 - 1st:0 2nd:1 3rd:0 Ran:5
Pre2000 - 1st:1 2nd:0 3rd:0 Ran:6
Win Prizemoney £2,723 *Total Prizemoney* £3,451
Wins * 1999 Jun Bath (GD) 5.7f 72 <
2000 Turf 0-4: (6f 3, 7f) (gd, g-f, frm 2) 2000 AW 0-1: (8f) (Fibr)
Unfurnished, fair filly, effective 6f, acts on frm. Turf high 54. Becoming disappointing. **B Palling [1-11] Mrs M M Palling.*

SONDA (IRE) RR 98f 3351a[13]

3 ch f Dolphin Street (FR) - Isca **(73df)** (Caerleon (USA)) 8.6f **(71)**
Form - 70
2000 Turf 0-2: (8f 2) (sft, g-s)
Very useful filly. Turf high 98. **A Botti in ITY [2-5].*

SONG 'N DANCE BHB 54f52a RR 56f 52a 5067[7]

2 br f Dancing Spree (USA) 8f **(59)** - Don't Smile (Sizzling Melody)
Form - 856047
Record 2000 - 1st:0 2nd:0 3rd:0 Ran:6
2000 Turf 0-5: (5f 2, 6f 3) (g-s, gd, g-f 2, frm) 2000 AW 0-1: (5f) (Equi)
Average filly. Turf high 56 (began Jly).
**M D I Usher [0-6] The Magic And Dance Partnership.*

SONG OF SKYE BHB 66f73a RR 69f 73a 2757[6]

6 b m Warning 8.1f **(77)** - Song of Hope (Chief Singer) 8.9f **(66)**
Form - 22836007236
Record 2000 - 1st:0 2nd:1 3rd:2 Ran:9
Pre2000 - 1st:3 2nd:5 3rd:4 Ran:35
Win Prizemoney £16,951 *Total Prizemoney* £37,504
Wins * 1999 Jun Lingfi (G-F) H 7f 68 68
* 1999 May Sandow (GD) H 7.1f 65 66
* 1996 Jly Newbur (G-F) 5.2f 69 <
2000 Turf 0-6: (7f 4, 8f, 9f) (g-s, gd, g-f 2, frm 2) 2000 AW 0-3: (7f 2, 8f) (Equi 3)
Above-average mare, effective 6 to 8f, best at 7f, acts on g-f to frm - acts on AW, best on Equi, has worn blinkers, likes left handed tracks, and excels at Newbury and Lingfield. Turf high 69 - 3rd of 10 giving 18lb to Dovebrace (5 Jly Catterick 7f frm RF 2543). AW high 74 - 3rd of 11 giving 1lb to Foreign Editor (29 Jan Lingfield 7f Equi RF 0186). **T J Naughton [3-44] Exors of the late E J Fenaroli.*

SONGS OF PRAISE RR 53f 5065[11]

2 b g Sir Harry Lewis (USA) - Hymne D'Amour (USA) (Dixieland Band (USA)) 7f **(74)**
Form - 0
Record 2000 - 1st:0 2nd:0 3rd:0 Ran:1
2000 Turf 0-1: (8f) (g-s)
Currently fair gelding. **M P Tregoning [0-1] The Earl Cadogan.*

SONICOS BHB 25f RR 21f 2329[6]

4 ch g Cosmonaut - Bella Bambola (IRE) **(7f)** (Tate Gallery (USA)) 7.4f **(67)**
Form - 086
Record 2000 - 1st:0 2nd:0 3rd:0 Ran:3
Pre2000 - 1st:0 2nd:0 3rd:0 Ran:1
2000 Turf 0-1: (17f) (frm) 2000 AW 0-2: (12f, 15f) (Fibr 2)
Leggy, little account gelding. AW high 16. **J S Wainwright [0-4] S Pedersen.*

SONIQUE RR 5224[10]

2 b f Shaamit (IRE) - Dolly Bevan (Another Realm) 6.6f **(55)**
Form - 0
Record 2000 - 1st:0 2nd:0 3rd:0 Ran:1
2000 Turf 0-1: (8f) (gd)
Currently very poor filly. **I A Wood [0-1] John Purcell.*

SON OF A GUN BHB 83f RR 71f 3434[3]

6 b g Gunner B 11.2f **(45)** - Sola Mia (Tolomeo) 5.6f **(60)**
Form - 423
Record 2000 - 1st:0 2nd:1 3rd:1 Ran:3
Win Prizemoney £0 *Total Prizemoney* £2,083
2000 Turf 0-3: (10f, 14f 2) (g-s, gd, frm)
Above-average gelding. Turf high 71 - 2nd of 8 giving 19lb to Follow Lammtarra (9 Jun Haydock 14f g-s RF 1853). A bumper winner, he has been placed in maidens on the level and staying handicaps are where his future lies. **J Neville [1-9] Mrs P A Barratt.*

SON OF A PREACHER (IRE) RR 30f 1600[12]

2 ch c College Chapel - Kunuz (Ela-Mana-Mou) 10.1f **(70)**
Form - 000
Record 2000 - 1st:0 2nd:0 3rd:0 Ran:3
2000 Turf 0-3: (5f, 6f 2) (gd, g-f 2)
Currently very moderate colt. Turf high 30.
**D Shaw [0-3] J C Fretwell.*

SON OF SNURGE (FR) BHB 72f68a RR 77f 68a 3142[3]

4 b g Snurge - Swift Spring (FR) (Bluebird (USA)) 7.5f **(69)**
Form - 04043
Record 2000 - 1st:0 2nd:0 3rd:1 Ran:5
Pre2000 - 1st:2 2nd:3 3rd:1 Ran:14
Win Prizemoney £6,813 *Total Prizemoney* £14,889
Wins * 1999 Jly Sandow (G-F) H 14f 59 72 <
* 1999 Jly Bright (FRM) 11.9f 65
2000 Turf 0-5: (14f 3, 19f, 20f) (gd, g-f 4)
Strong, above-average gelding, effective 14 to 16f, acts on gd to frm, best on gd, has worn blinkers (extremely effectively), likes right handed tracks, excels at Sandown. Turf high 77 - 4th of 16 getting 3lb from Dominant Duchess (17 May York 14f g-f RF 1266). He had looked a disappointing sort until transformed by blinkers and the use of forcing tactics in the summer of 1999. He has not won so far this season, but has hinted at better to come. Stays well and is suited by fast ground. **P F I Cole [2-19] M Arbib.*

SONTIME BHB 47f53a RR 57df 53a 4826[16]

3 b f Son Pardo - Fact of Time (Known Fact (USA)) 7.4f **(67)**
Form - 08500
Record 2000 - 1st:0 2nd:0 3rd:0 Ran:5
Pre2000 - 1st:2 2nd:0 3rd:2 Ran:10
Win Prizemoney £4,178 *Total Prizemoney* £5,306
Wins * 1999 Jly Lingfi (G-F) C 6f 69
* 1999 Jun Lingfi (G-F) S 5f 78+ <
2000 Turf 0-4: (6f 3, 7f) (gd, g-f 2, frm) 2000 AW 0-1: (7f) (Equi)
Neat, fair filly, effective 5 to 6f, acts on frm. Turf high 57. Becoming disappointing. **B Palling [2-15] Mrs P K Chick.*

SOONA BHB 65f60a RR 80f 60a 3832[4]

2 ch f Royal Abjar (USA) - Presently **(45df)** (Cadeaux Genereux)
Form - 0555224
Record 2000 - 1st:0 2nd:2 3rd:0 Ran:7
Win Prizemoney £0 *Total Prizemoney* £1,729
2000 Turf 0-7: (5f 2, 6f, 7f 4) (g-s, gd, g-f 3, frm 2)
Decent filly, effective 7f, acts on g-f. Turf high 73 - 2nd of 10 getting 3lb from Carnot (9 Aug Brighton 7f g-f RF 3481).
**A P Jarvis [0-7] Christopher Shankland.*

SOOTY TIME BHB 58f60a RR 62f 60a 5067[3]

2 ch g Timeless Times (USA) 6.1f **(56)** - Gymcrak Gem (IRE) **(58f)** (Don't Forget Me) 8.3f **(74)**
Form - 6376623403
Record 2000 - 1st:0 2nd:1 3rd:3 Ran:10
Win Prizemoney £0 *Total Prizemoney* £1,448
2000 Turf 0-6: (5f 4, 6f 2) (g-s, g-f, frm 4) 2000 AW 0-4: (5f 4) (Equi 2,

Fibr 2)
Average gelding, effective 6f, acts on g-s. Turf high 62 (began Jly) - 3rd of 18 giving 5lb to Ivans Bride (19 Oct Bath 6f g-s RF 5067). AW high 40. Inconsistent. **J S Moore [0-10] A D Crook.*

SOPHALA BHB 65f RR 65f 5227[9]

3 b f Magical Wonder (USA) 7.2f **(60)** - Fujaiyrah (In Fijar (USA)) 7.5f **(70)**
Form - 3701340
Record 2000 - 1st:1 2nd:0 3rd:2 Ran:7
Pre2000 - 1st:0 2nd:0 3rd:0 Ran:1
Win Prizemoney £2,695 *Total Prizemoney* £4,104
Wins * 2000 Spt Bright (SFT) H 10f 60 65 <
2000 Turf 1-7: (8f, 10f 1-4, 12f 2) (g-s 1-3, gd 2, g-f 2)
Light-framed, average filly, effective 10f, acts on g-s. Turf high 65 (began Aug) - 1st of 20 giving 5lb to Twilight World (27 Spt Brighton RF 4677).
**C F Wall [1-7] T J Wells (from D Morris [0-1] Spt 1999).*

SOPHIELU RR 80+f 5319[4]

2 ch f Rudimentary (USA) 8.2f **(66)** - Aquaglow (Caerleon (USA)) 8.6f **(71)**
Form - 24
Record 2000 - 1st:0 2nd:1 3rd:0 Ran:2
Win Prizemoney £0 *Total Prizemoney* £944
2000 Turf 0-2: (5f, 6f) (sft, gd)
Currently decent filly. Turf high 80 (1st run) (began Oct) - 2nd of 12 to How Do I Know (24 Oct Redcar 5f gd RF 5163).
**M Johnston [0-2] Hertford Offset Ltd.*

SOPHOMORE BHB 51f51a RR 68f 51a 5166[5]

6 b g Sanglamore (USA) 12.9f **(67)** - Livry (USA) (Lyphard (USA)) 9.9f **(72)**
Form - 030601680020555
Record 2000 - 1st:1 2nd:1 3rd:1 Ran:15
Pre2000 - 1st:1 2nd:0 3rd:0 Ran:5
Win Prizemoney £6,325 *Total Prizemoney* £8,334
Wins * 2000 Jun Leices (G-S) C 8f 68
1996 Oct Doncas (GD) 7f 86 <
2000 Turf 1-11: (7f, 8f 1-7, 10f 3) (g-s, gd 1-2, g-f 2, frm 4, hrd 2) 2000 AW 0-4: (7f, 8f 2, 11f) (Fibr 4)
Average gelding, effective 8f, acts on gd. Turf high 68 - 1st of 12 giving 13lb to The Wild Widow (5 Jun Leicester RF 1715). AW high 67. He has had his problems, but managed to win a Leicester claimer in June when the ground was on the easy side. Modest form otherwise.
**J L Harris [1-17] J L Harris (from B W Hills [1-5] Oct 1997).*

SOPRAN GLAUMIX (ITY) RR 98+f 5214a[4]

2 gr c Linamix (FR) 8.2f **(64)** - Glauce (Superlative) 7.2f **(56)**
Form - 114
2000 Turf 2-3: (8f 2-3) (hvy 1-2, g-f 1-1)
Currently very useful colt. Turf high 98 (began Jly) - 1st of 6 giving 2lb to Lagudin (1 Oct San Siro RF 4850a) - also 1st of 6 from Barking Mad (6 Jly San Siro RF 2785a). He goes well under testing conditions and ran a fair race when fourth behind Count Dubois in the Group 1 Gran Criterium at San Siro in October. Possibly best around a mile, he should win Group races in Italy this year.
**B Grizzetti in ITY [2-3].*

SOPRANINO (USA) RR 92f 5355a[11]

3 ch f Theatrical 11.5f **(78)** - My Darling One (USA) (Exclusive Native (USA)) 9.1f **(81)**
Form - 03150
2000 Turf 1-5: (8f, 9f, 10f, 12f, 13f 1-1) (hvy, sft 2, gd, g-f 1-1)
Useful filly. Turf high 92 - 5th of 10 to Abikan (14 Oct Gowran Park 9f sft RF 5043a). **J Oxx in IRE [1-5] Sheikh Mohammed.*

SOPRAN MONTANELLI (IRE) RR 109f 5215a[6]

3 gr c Tenby 10.4f **(76)** - 00
Form - 8536
2000 Turf 0-4: (10f, 12f 2, 15f) (hvy, sft, g-f 2)
Pattern-class colt. Turf high 109. **L Camici in ITY [0-4].*

SOPRAN ZANCHI (IRE) RR 74+f 4577[4]

3 ch f College Chapel - Star Gazing (IRE) (Caerleon (USA)) 8.6f **(71)**
Form - 4
Record 2000 - 1st:0 2nd:0 3rd:0 Ran:1
Pre2000 - 1st:0 2nd:1 3rd:1 Ran:2
Win Prizemoney £0 *Total Prizemoney* £3,254
2000 Turf 0-1: (7f) (sft)
Currently above-average filly. **L M Cumani [0-3] Sant Uberto.*

SO PRECIOUS (IRE) RR 87f 5159[14]

3 b f Batshoof 9.5f **(66)** - Golden Form (Formidable (USA)) 9.2f **(63)**
Form - 470000
Record 2000 - 1st:0 2nd:0 3rd:0 Ran:6
Pre2000 - 1st:1 2nd:0 3rd:0 Ran:2
Win Prizemoney £3,078 *Total Prizemoney* £4,229
Wins * 1999 Spt Kempto (HVY) 7f 68 <
2000 Turf 0-6: (8f 3, 10f, 12f 2) (sft, g-s 3, gd, g-f)
Workmanlike, useful filly. Turf high 87. Winner of a heavy-ground maiden at Kempton at two, she finished well into fourth in a decent Listed event on her return, but was last in the Prix Saint-Alary and well beaten in the Oaks, looking as if she failed to stay.
**N P Littmoden [1-8] Joy and Valentine Feerick.*

SORAYAS QUEST (IRE) BHB 55f RR 60f 5053[9]

2 b f Royal Abjar (USA) - Trumped (IRE) **(61?f)** (Last Tycoon) 8.5f **(62)**
Form - 040
Record 2000 - 1st:0 2nd:0 3rd:0 Ran:3
Win Prizemoney £0 *Total Prizemoney* £225
2000 Turf 0-3: (6f, 7f 2) (sft, gd, g-f)
Currently average filly. Turf high 60 (began Aug).
**A B Mulholland [0-3] Ms C Pamphlett.*

SORBETT BHB 83f RR 88f 2852[21]

3 b c Dolphin Street (FR) - Midnight Imperial (Night Shift (USA)) 7.2f **(69)**
Form - 68400
Record 2000 - 1st:0 2nd:0 3rd:0 Ran:5
Pre2000 - 1st:1 2nd:0 3rd:0 Ran:1
Win Prizemoney £7,290 *Total Prizemoney* £7,961
Wins * 1999 Oct San Si (YLD) 7.5f
2000 Turf 0-5: (6f 2, 7f, 8f 2) (gd 4, frm)
Useful colt. Turf high 88. Won at San Siro on his only start as a juvenile, but has yet to cut much ice over here.
**L M Cumani [1-6] Scuderia Rencati Srl.*

SORRENTO KING BHB 43f RR 46f 4000[6]

3 ch g First Trump - Star Face (African Sky) 7.7f **(50)**
Form - 007236
Record 2000 - 1st:0 2nd:1 3rd:1 Ran:6
Pre2000 - 1st:0 2nd:0 3rd:0 Ran:6
Win Prizemoney £0 *Total Prizemoney* £1,724
2000 Turf 0-6: (10f 3, 12f 2, 14f) (gd 2, g-f 2, frm 2)
Neat, moderate gelding, often wears blinkers. Turf high 46.
**M W Easterby [0-12] B Padgett, K Bennett & A Davies.*

SO SOBER (IRE) BHB 79f RR 70f 5156[15]

2 b c Common Grounds 8.1f **(66)** - Femme Savante **(73f)** (Glenstal (USA)) 10.1f **(64)**
Form - 5427620
Record 2000 - 1st:0 2nd:2 3rd:0 Ran:7
Win Prizemoney £0 *Total Prizemoney* £2,372
2000 Turf 0-7: (5f 7) (g-s, gd 4, g-f, frm)
Above-average colt, effective 5f, acts on gd. Turf high 70 - 2nd of 15 to Leozian (29 Spt Lingfield 5f gd RF 4724).
**C F Wall [0-7] The Boardroom Syndicate.*

SOSSUS VLEI BHB 110f RR 111f 1557[3]

4 b h Inchinor 8.9f **(64)** - Sassalya (Sassafras (FR)) 9.6f **(69)**
Form - 513
Record 2000 - 1st:1 2nd:0 3rd:1 Ran:3
Pre2000 - 1st:2 2nd:2 3rd:0 Ran:7
Win Prizemoney £24,714 *Total Prizemoney* £40,181
Wins * 2000 May Cheste (GD) L 10.3f 110 <
* 1999 Spt Bath (SFT) 8f 103
* 1998 Aug Newmar (G-F) 7f 87
2000 Turf 1-3: (10f 1-3) (sft, g-s, g-f 1-1)
Workmanlike, Group-class colt, effective 8 to 10f, best at 10f, acts on hvy to g-f. Turf high 110 - 1st of 5 from Rain In Spain (11 May Chester RF 1136). A big attractive horse, he got up close home to

win a Listed event at Chester in May and ran creditably behind Shiva in a Group 3 at Sandown later that month. Missing for the rest of the campaign, he is at home on soft or heavy ground.
**G Wragg [3-10] A E Oppenheimer.*

SO TEMPTING RR 78f 5296[2]

2 b c So Factual (USA) - Persuasion **(49f 73a)** (Batshoof)
Form - 32
Record 2000 - 1st:0 2nd:1 3rd:1 Ran:2
Win Prizemoney £0 *Total Prizemoney* £1,121
2000 Turf 0-2: (6f, 7f) (sft, g-s)
Currently above-average colt. Turf high 78 (began Oct) - 2nd of 8 to Mayville Thunder (1 Nov Musselburgh 7f g-s RF 5296).
**J R Fanshawe [0-2] Countess of Lonsdale.*

SOTONIAN (HOL) BHB 54f56a RR 57f 50a 4027[12]

7 br g Statoblest 6.4f **(63)** - Visage (Vision (USA)) 9f **(64)**
Form - 05003766345365100
Record 2000 - 1st:1 2nd:0 3rd:3 Ran:17
Pre2000 - 1st:8 2nd:5 3rd:10 Ran:59
Win Prizemoney £26,326 *Total Prizemoney* £38,464

Wins							
* **2000**	*Aug Wolver*	*(STD)*	*H*	*5f*	*54*	*56*	
* 1999	May Catter	(G-F)	H	5f	60	65	<
* 1999	Apr Warwic	(GD)	H	5f	56	62	
* 1999	*Feb Lingfi*	*(STD)*	*H*	*5f*	*56*	*62*	
* 1999	*Feb Lingfi*	*(STD)*	*H*	*5f*	*56*	*58*	
* 1999	*Jan Wolver*	*(STD)*	*H*	*5f*	*50*	*52*	
* 1998	*Aug Wolver*	*(STD)*	*H*	*5f*	*36*	*46*	
* 1997	*Jan Wolver*	*(STD)*	*H*	*5f*	*30*	*44*	
* 1997	*Jan Wolver*	*(STD)*	*H*	*5f*	*30*	*44*	

2000 Turf 0-9: (5f 8, 6f) (gd 2, g-f 2, frm 4, hrd) 2000 AW 1-8: (5f 1-6, 6f 2) (Equi 2, Fibr 1-6)
Fair gelding, has broken blood-vessels, effective 5f, acts on g-s to frm - acts on AW, has worn blinkers, likes left handed tracks, and likes Lingfield. Turf high 57 - 3rd of 9 giving 15lb to Rude Awakening (19 Jly Catterick 5f frm RF 2924). AW high 62 - 5th of 11 getting 22lb from Dil (25 Jan Wolverhampton 5f Fibr RF 0155) - also 1st of 11 getting 3lb from Samwar (11 Aug Wolverhampton RF 3570). Consistent. A speedy sprinter on his day, he is effective on sand and on fast ground on turf.
**P S Felgate [9-73] Tim Dean (from Mrs L Stubbs [0-3] Jly 1996).*

SOUHAITE (FR) BHB 47f49a RR 45f 49a 5116[1]

4 b g Salse (USA) 10.9f **(71)** - Parannda (Bold Lad (IRE)) 8.4f **(68)**
Form - 1373701700101
Record 2000 - 1st:3 2nd:0 3rd:0 Ran:9
Pre2000 - 1st:1 2nd:0 3rd:2 Ran:7
Win Prizemoney £8,532 *Total Prizemoney* £9,038

Wins							
* **2000**	*Oct Wolver*	*(STD)*	*H*	*8.5f*	*42*	*50*	*<*
* **2000**	Spt Chepst	(G-S)	H	7.1f	41	45	
* **2000**	Jun Leices	(G-F)	H	8f	40	41	
* 1999	*Nov Southw*	*(STD)*	*H*	*12f*	*40*	*46*	

2000 Turf 2-6: (7f 1-3, 8f 1-3) (gd, g-f 1-2, frm, hrd 1-2) 2000 AW 1-3: (8f 1-2, 12f) (Fibr 1-3)
Scopey, fair gelding, effective 7 to 12f, acts on g-f to hrd - acts on Fibr. Turf high 45 - 1st of 19 getting 3lb from Sand Hawk (7 Spt Chepstow RF 4275) - also 1st of 17 getting 18lb from Derryquin (18 Jun Leicester RF 2073). AW high 50 - 1st of 12 getting 14lb from Bobbydazzle (20 Oct Wolverhampton RF 5116).
**W R Muir [4-16] J Bernstein.*

SOUND DOMINO (GER) RR 91f 4716a[3]

4 b g Dashing Blade 7.9f **(80)** - Swift Connection (USA) (Conquistador Cielo (USA)) 8.8f **(69)**
Form - 3
2000 Turf 0-1: (5f) (sft)
Currently useful gelding. (1st run) - 3rd of 7 getting 1lb from Trinidad (24 Spt Cologne 5f sft RF 4716a). **in GER [0-1].*

SOUND'S ACE BHB 40f37a RR 46f 37a 5118[6]

4 ch m Savahra Sound 7.8f **(55)** - Ace Girl (Stanford) 7.9f **(56)**
Form - 06037387076006
Record 2000 - 1st:0 2nd:0 3rd:2 Ran:14
Pre2000 - 1st:2 2nd:0 3rd:1 Ran:11
Win Prizemoney £6,583 *Total Prizemoney* £8,185

Wins							
* 1998	Oct Newmar	(G-S)	H	5f	64	67	<
* 1998	Aug Beverl	(G-F)	S	5f	64		

2000 Turf 0-13: (5f 11, 6f 2) (sft, gd 3, g-f 4, frm 4, hrd) 2000 AW 0-1: (6f) (Fibr)
Light-framed, moderate filly, often wears blinkers. Turf high 46.
**D Shaw [2-25] Paul Dixon.*

SOUNDS COOL BHB 32f22a RR 24f 22a 1019[12]

4 b g Savahra Sound 7.8f **(55)** - Lucky Candy (Lucky Wednesday) 8f **(50)**
Form - 00650400
Record 2000 - 1st:0 2nd:0 3rd:0 Ran:6
Pre2000 - 1st:0 2nd:1 3rd:2 Ran:17
Win Prizemoney £0 *Total Prizemoney* £1,124
2000 Turf 0-1: (7f) (gd) 2000 AW 0-5: (8f 2, 9f 2, 12f) (Fibr 5)
Leggy, little account gelding, effective 10f, acts on g-f, has worn blinkers. AW high 19.
**S R Bowring [0-24] Paul Dixon.*

SOUNDS CRAZY BHB 38f RR 43f 192[12]

3 b f Savahra Sound 7.8f **(55)** - Sugar Token (Record Token) 6.3f **(53)**
Form - 00200
Record 2000 - 1st:0 2nd:1 3rd:0 Ran:3
Pre2000 - 1st:0 2nd:0 3rd:0 Ran:8
Win Prizemoney £0 *Total Prizemoney* £622
2000 AW 0-3: (7f 2, 8f) (Fibr 3)
Unfurnished, moderate filly, often wears blinkers. AW high 38.
**S R Bowring [0-11] Paul Dixon.*

SOUNDS LUCKY BHB 45f53a RR 46f 53a 4180[10]

4 b g Savahra Sound 7.8f **(55)** - Sweet And Lucky (Lucky Wednesday) 8f **(50)**
Form - 604416050000
Record 2000 - 1st:1 2nd:0 3rd:0 Ran:12
Pre2000 - 1st:3 2nd:1 3rd:0 Ran:21
Win Prizemoney £9,801 *Total Prizemoney* £10,645

Wins							
* **2000**	*Feb Wolver*	*(STD)*	*H*	*5f*	*51*	*54*	
* 1999	May Lingfi	(G-F)	H	6f	58	62	<
* 1999	*Mar Wolver*	*(SLW)*	*H*	*6f*	*45*	*59*	
* 1999	*Mar Wolver*	*(STD)*	*SH*	*5f*	*45*	*59*	

2000 Turf 0-5: (5f 2, 6f 3) (gd, g-f, frm 2) 2000 AW 1-7: (5f 1-3, 6f 3, 7f) (Equi, Fibr 1-6)
Light-framed, fair gelding, effective 5 to 8f, best at 6f, acts on frm - acts on Fibr, has worn blinkers, likes left handed tracks, likes tight tracks. Turf high 46. AW high 54 - 1st of 8 getting 4lb from Off Hire (22 Feb Wolverhampton RF 0332).
**N P Littmoden [4-33] Paul Dixon.*

SOUNDS SOLO BHB 40f45a RR 45a 667[13]

4 b g Savahra Sound 7.8f **(55)** - Sola Mia (Tolomeo) 5.6f **(60)**
Form - 637600
Record 2000 - 1st:0 2nd:0 3rd:1 Ran:6
Pre2000 - 1st:1 2nd:1 3rd:0 Ran:4
Win Prizemoney £2,094 *Total Prizemoney* £3,020

Wins							
1998	*Oct Southw*	*(STD)*	*S*	*7f*		*56*	*<*

2000 Turf 0-1: (7f) (sft) 2000 AW 0-5: (6f, 7f 3, 8f) (Fibr 5)
Leggy, moderate gelding, always wears blinkers. AW high 48. Becoming disappointing.
**D Nicholls [0-6] Paul Dixon (from S R Bowring [1-4] Mar 1999).*

SOUNDS SPECIAL BHB 43f56a RR 54df 56a 3380[19]

3 b f Savahra Sound 7.8f **(55)** - Sola Mia (Tolomeo) 5.6f **(60)**
Form - 0000
Record 2000 - 1st:0 2nd:0 3rd:0 Ran:4
Pre2000 - 1st:0 2nd:0 3rd:0 Ran:2
2000 Turf 0-3: (6f 3) (gd, frm 2) 2000 AW 0-1: (8f) (Fibr)
Unfurnished, fair filly, has worn blinkers. Turf high 34.
**S R Bowring [0-6] Paul Dixon.*

SOUND THE TRUMPET (IRE) BHB 33f35a RR 37f 35a 2611[16]

8 b g Fayruz 6.6f **(63)** - Red Note (Rusticaro (FR)) 8.2f **(65)**
Form - 441387688006800
Record 2000 - 1st:0 2nd:0 3rd:0 Ran:10
Pre2000 - 1st:3 2nd:5 3rd:5 Ran:57
Win Prizemoney £8,242 *Total Prizemoney* £16,952

Wins						
* 1999	*Nov Lingfi*	*(STD)*	*H*	*8f*	*39*	*54*
* 1998	*Jan Lingfi*	*(STD)*	*H*	*5f*	*30*	*50*

2000 Turf 0-6: (6f 3, 7f 2, 8f) (gd 4, frm 2) 2000 AW 0-4: (7f, 8f 3) (Equi 2, Fibr 2)

Very moderate gelding, effective 8 to 10f, - acts on Equi, has worn blinkers, likes left handed tracks, likes tight tracks. Turf high 37. AW high 37. Becoming disappointing.

**R C Spicer [2-54] Mrs J A Nichols (from A Streeter [0-4] Oct 1995).*

SOUPERFICIAL BHB 40f40a **RR 47f 40a** 5083[16]

9 gr g Petong 7.6f **(58)** - Duck Soup (Decoy Boy) 6.7f **(56)**
Form - 0028646000

Record	**2000** -	1st:0	2nd:1	3rd:0	Ran:10
	Pre2000 -	1st:11	2nd:7	3rd:5	Ran:89

Win Prizemoney £32,372 *Total Prizemoney* £43,652

Wins	* 1999	Aug	Newcas	(GD)	H	6f	47	50
	* 1998	Jun	Hamilt	(SFT)	S	5f		56
	* 1998	Jun	Carlis	(G-S)	C	5.9f		56
	1997	Jly	Hamilt	(SFT)		6f		46
	1996	Spt	Leices	(FRM)	H	5f	50	52
	1996	Aug	Nottin	(G-F)	H	5.1f	46	47

2000 Turf 0-10: (5f, 6f 9) (hvy, sft, g-f 3, frm 3, hrd 2)
Moderate gelding, effective 5 to 6f, best at 6f, acts on sft to frm, best on g-f, often wears blinkers (effectively), excels at Hamilton, likes Newcastle. Turf high 47 - 4th of 13 to Naissant (14 Jly Hamilton 6f g-f RF 2805).

**Don Enrico Incisa [3-35] Mrs Christine Cawley (from N Tinkler [1-17] Oct 1997).*

SOUTHAMPTON BHB 23f32a **RR 32f 32a** 2627[12]

10 b g Ballacashtal (CAN) 7.9f **(51)** - Petingo Gold (Pitskelly) 8.5f **(53)**
Form - 0

Record	**2000** -	1st:0	2nd:0	3rd:0	Ran:1
	Pre2000 -	1st:0	2nd:0	3rd:1	Ran:14

Win Prizemoney £0 *Total Prizemoney* £562
2000 Turf 0-1: (18f) (frm)
Very moderate gelding, has worn blinkers.

**G B Balding [12-77] Highflyers.*

SOUTHERN DANCER **RR 75f** 5100[12]

2 b g Makbul - Bye-Bye (Superlative) 7.2f **(56)**
Form - 00

Record	**2000** -	1st:0	2nd:0	3rd:0	Ran:2

2000 Turf 0-2: (7f, 8f) (g-s, gd)
Currently above-average gelding. Turf high 75 (began Spt).

**R Hollinshead [0-2] R Hollinshead.*

SOUTHERN DOMINION BHB 51f57a **RR 52f 57a** 132[1]

8 ch g Dominion 8.9f **(65)** - Southern Sky (Comedy Star (USA)) 7.5f **(50)**
Form - 227431

Record	**2000** -	1st:1	2nd:0	3rd:1	Ran:2
	Pre2000 -	1st:7	2nd:13	3rd:9	Ran:100

Win Prizemoney £24,797 *Total Prizemoney* £41,782

Wins	*** 2000**	*Jan*	*Lingfi*	*(STD)*	*H*	*5f*	*56*	*60*	
	* 1998	Aug	Mussel	(GD)	H	5f	52	61	<
	* 1998	Jly	Mussel	(GD)	H	5f	48	51	
	* 1997	Nov	Doncas	(GD)	H	5f	51	56	
	* 1997	Oct	Ayr	(SFT)	H	5f	45	54	
	* 1997	May	Mussel	(G-F)	H	5f	40	40	

2000 AW 1-2: (5f 1-2) (Equi 1-1, Fibr)
Average gelding, effective 5 to 6f, best at 5f, acts on g-s to g-f - acts on AW, best on Fibr, often wears blinkers (effectively), prefers left handed tracks, prefers tight tracks. AW high 60 - 1st of 9 giving 6lb to Wishbone Alley (22 Jan Lingfield RF 0132). Inconsistent. Usually blazes from the stalls and it is just a question of whether he can hold on. Best suited by an easy five, he can act on sand as well.

**Miss J F Craze [6-60] Mrs Angela Wilson (from C N Allen [0-8] Oct 1996).*

SOUTH LANE BHB 45f **RR 46f** 1441[9]

3 br g Rock City 8.8f **(62)** - Steppey Lane (Tachypous) 8.6f **(55)**
Form - 50

Record	**2000** -	1st:0	2nd:0	3rd:0	Ran:2
	Pre2000 -	1st:0	2nd:0	3rd:0	Ran:2

2000 Turf 0-2: (7f, 8f) (gd 2)
Leggy, moderate gelding. Turf high 46.

**N Tinkler [0-2] R Midgley (from G P Kelly [0-2] Oct 1999).*

SOUTH SEA PEARL (USA) BHB 65f55a **RR 74f 55a** 5155[9]

3 b f Southern Halo (USA) - Naturalracer (USA) (Copelan (USA))
Form - 223600

Record	**2000** -	1st:0	2nd:2	3rd:1	Ran:6

Win Prizemoney £0 *Total Prizemoney* £3,000
2000 Turf 0-5: (10f 3, 12f 2) (gd, g-f, frm 3) 2000 AW 0-1: (7f) (Equi)
Rangy, above-average filly, effective 10 to 12f, acts on frm. Turf high 74 (began Aug) - 2nd of 4 to Clepsydra (17 Aug Epsom 12f frm RF 3724). **M Johnston [0-6] Ian Deane.*

SOVEREIGN ABBEY (IRE) BHB 60f54a **RR 72f 54a** 262[3]

4 b m Royal Academy (USA) 7.8f **(77)** - Elabella (Ela-Mana-Mou) 10.1f **(70)**
Form - 462143

Record	**2000** -	1st:1	2nd:1	3rd:1	Ran:4
	Pre2000 -	1st:0	2nd:0	3rd:2	Ran:6

Win Prizemoney £2,613 *Total Prizemoney* £4,942

Wins	*** 2000**	*Jan*	*Wolver*	*(STD)*	*9.4f*		*50*	<

2000 AW 1-4: (8f 2, 9f 1-1, 12f) (Fibr 1-4)
Leggy, above-average filly. AW high 59.

**Sir Mark Prescott [1-10] G S Shropshire.*

SOVEREIGNS COURT BHB 72f **RR 74f** 5134[12]

7 ch g Statoblest 6.4f **(63)** - Clare Celeste (Coquelin (USA)) 8.4f **(58)**
Form - 301620

Record	**2000** -	1st:1	2nd:1	3rd:1	Ran:6
	Pre2000 -	1st:3	2nd:2	3rd:2	Ran:22

Win Prizemoney £12,230 *Total Prizemoney* £17,861

Wins	*** 2000**	Jun	Bath	(G-S)	H	10.2f	67	70	
	* 1998	Jun	Newbur	(HVY)	H	10f	74	74	<
	* 1997	Nov	Nottin	(GD)	H	10f	65	73	
	* 1997	Oct	Nottin	(SFT)	H	8.2f	56	71	

2000 Turf 1-6: (9f, 10f 1-4, 12f) (sft 2, gd 1-3, g-f)
Above-average gelding, effective 10 to 12f, acts on gd, has worn blinkers. Turf high 74 - 2nd of 13 giving 9lb to Pheisty (20 Spt Goodwood 12f gd RF 4539) - also 1st of 18 giving 31lb to Vanborough Lad (2 Jun Bath RF 1643). Consistent. Missed the whole of last season, but regained winning form at Bath in June. Needs cut in the ground.

**L G Cottrell [4-21] E Gadsden (from Major D N Chappell [0-7] Oct 1996).*

SOVEREIGN STATE (IRE) BHB 70f **RR 80f** 4471[20]

3 b g Soviet Lad (USA) 9.4f **(63)** - Portree (Slip Anchor) 9.8f **(73)**
Form - 017546000

Record	**2000** -	1st:1	2nd:0	3rd:0	Ran:9
	Pre2000 -	1st:1	2nd:0	3rd:0	Ran:4

Win Prizemoney £8,657 *Total Prizemoney* £9,789

Wins	*** 2000**	May	Thirsk	(GD)	H	8f	73	80	<
	* 1999	Spt	Thirsk	(FRM)		8f		79	

2000 Turf 1-9: (6f, 7f, 8f 1-5, 9f, 10f) (g-s, gd 1-2, g-f 2, frm 4)
Decent gelding, effective 8f, acts on gd to hrd, best on gd, likes left handed tracks, likes tight tracks. Turf high 80 - 1st of 16 giving 16lb to Nowt Flash (20 May Thirsk RF 1350). Inconsistent.

**M A Jarvis [2-13] Mrs G R Smith.*

SOVIET FLASH (IRE) BHB 102f **RR 102f** 5225[6]

3 b c Warning 8.1f **(77)** - Mrs Moonlight (Ajdal (USA)) 9.2f **(89)**
Form - 246

Record	**2000** -	1st:0	2nd:1	3rd:0	Ran:3
	Pre2000 -	1st:1	2nd:0	3rd:0	Ran:2

Win Prizemoney £3,241 *Total Prizemoney* £7,362

Wins	* 1999	Aug	Leices	(G-F)	7f	83+	<

2000 Turf 0-3: (8f 2, 10f) (gd, g-f 2)
Lengthy, very useful colt. Turf high 102 (began Spt) - 4th of 12 getting 4lb from Hopeful Light (28 Spt Newmarket 8f g-f RF 4698). Missing for most of the season, he ran well in Listed company during the autumn. Probably best around a mile, he may be unsuited by soft ground. **E A L Dunlop [1-5] Khalifa Sultan.*

SO WILLING BHB 36f46a **RR 47f 46a** 1718[19]

4 gr g Keen 11.1f **(58)** - Sweet Whisper **(14f 46a)** (Petong) 6.6f **(58)**
Form - 07706030568000

Record	**2000** -	1st:0	2nd:0	3rd:1	Ran:11
	Pre2000 -	1st:1	2nd:2	3rd:1	Ran:19

Win Prizemoney £2,057 *Total Prizemoney* £4,632

Wins	* 1999	*Mar*	*Southw*	*(STD)*	*6f*	*62* <

2000 Turf 0-6: (6f, 7f 4, 8f) (gd 5, frm) 2000 AW 0-5: (6f 2, 7f 3) (Fibr 5)
Light-framed, moderate gelding, effective 6f, acts on sft - acts on

Fibr, has worn blinkers. Turf high 47. AW high 47. Becoming disappointing. *M Dods [1-30] Exors of the late A G Watson.*

SPACE QUEST RR 104f 4953a[1]
3 f Rainbow Quest (USA) 11.2f **(81)** - Apogee (Shirley Heights) 10.3f **(74)**
Form - 41
2000 Turf 1-2: (12f 1-1, 14f) (sft 1-1, g-s)
Currently very useful. Turf high 104 (1st run) (began Jly) - 4th of 8 to Interlude (30 Jly Deauville 14f g-s RF 3352a) - also 1st of 9 from Dream Quest (8 Oct Longchamp RF 4953a).
**A Fabre in FR [1-2] K Abdulla.*

SPACE RACE BHB 66f80a **RR 67f 80a** 404[5]
6 b g Rock Hopper 10.6f **(54)** - Melanoura (Imperial Fling (USA)) 7.1f **(58)**
Form - 20216225
Record 2000 - 1st:1 2nd:2 3rd:0 Ran:5
Pre2000 - 1st:2 2nd:6 3rd:0 Ran:21
Win Prizemoney £10,374 *Total Prizemoney* £19,929
Wins * **2000** *Jan Lingfi (STD) H 12f 76 78* <
* 1999 *Jan Lingfi (STD) H 12f 72 76*
* 1997 *May* Bath (GD) 8f 70
2000 AW 1-5: (12f 1-5) (Equi 1-5)
Above-average gelding, effective 10 to 12f, best at 12f, - acted on Equi, favoured left handed tracks, excelled at Lingfield. AW high 78 - 2nd of 8 giving 2lb to Ursa Major (23 Feb Lingfield 12f Equi RF 0341) - also 1st of 9 getting 5lb from Noukari (2 Jan Lingfield RF 0006). (DEAD) **C A Cyzer [3-26] R M Cyzer.*

SPA GULCH (USA) BHB 45f **RR 51f** 4727[15]
2 ch g Gulch (USA) 9.6f **(79)** - Carezza (USA) (Caro)
Form - 00
Record 2000 - 1st:0 2nd:0 3rd:0 Ran:2
2000 Turf 0-2: (6f, 7f) (gd, g-f)
Currently fair gelding. Turf high 51 (began Spt).
**I A Balding [0-2] George Strawbridge.*

SPAIN RR 66f 4271[12]
2 ch f Polar Falcon (USA) 9f **(74)** - Emaline (FR) (Empery (USA)) 11.2f **(69)**
Form - 50
Record 2000 - 1st:0 2nd:0 3rd:0 Ran:2
2000 Turf 0-2: (7f, 8f) (gd, g-f)
Currently average filly. Turf high 66 (1st run) (began Jun) - 5th of 6 to Rizerie (30 Jun Goodwood 7f gd RF 2400).
**P F I Cole [0-2] H R H Prince Fahd Salman.*

SPAIN (USA) RR 5325a[1]
3 f Thunder Gulch (USA) - Drina (USA) (Regal And Royal (USA))
Form - 11
2000 AW 2-2: (9f 2-2) (Dirt 2-2)
Currently high-class. AW high 117 (began Spt) - 1st of 9 from Surfside (4 Nov Churchill Downs RF 5325a).
**D W Lukas in USA [2-2] The Thoroughbred Corporation (from J L Bonde in USA [0-1] Nov 1999).*

SPA LANE BHB 29f40a **RR 44f 40a** 4648[7]
7 ch g Presidium 7.5f **(56)** - Sleekit (Blakeney) 10.5f **(64)**
Form - 5143325775887
Record 2000 - 1st:1 2nd:1 3rd:2 Ran:13
Pre2000 - 1st:5 2nd:9 3rd:3 Ran:50
Win Prizemoney £16,996 *Total Prizemoney* £31,931
Wins * **2000** May Beverl (G-F) H 16.2f 37 39
* 1999 May Pontef (G-F) H 12f 36 41
* 1999 *Jan Southw (STD) H 16f 34 38*
* 1998 May Beverl (GD) H 16.2f 35 40
1996 Aug Nottin (G-S) 14.1f 58 <
1996 Jun Nottin (G-F) 10f 54
2000 Turf 1-12: (12f 4, 14f, 16f 1-6, 17f) (sft, gd 2, g-f 3, frm 5, hrd 1-1)
2000 AW 0-1: (16f) (Fibr)
Moderate gelding, effective 12 to 17f, best at 16f, acts on gd to hrd - acts on Fibr, likes right handed tracks, and likes Pontefract. Turf high 44 - 3rd of 15 giving 2lb to Keep Ikis (31 May Ripon 16f g-f RF 1595) - also 1st of 19 getting 7lb from Kagoshima (13 May Beverley RF 1185).
**Mrs S Lamyman [4-43] Sotby Farming Company Ltd (from M P Bielby [0-11] Oct 1997).*

SPANISH SPUR BHB 81f **RR 81f** 5100[4]
2 b c Indian Ridge 7.6f **(74)** - Las Flores (IRE) **(96f)** (Sadler's Wells (USA)) 10f **(76)**
Form - 254
Record 2000 - 1st:0 2nd:1 3rd:0 Ran:3
Win Prizemoney £0 *Total Prizemoney* £1,584
2000 Turf 0-3: (7f, 8f 2) (gd 3)
Currently decent colt. Turf high 81 (began Spt).
**J H M Gosden [0-3] George Strawbridge.*

SPANISH STAR BHB 56f62a **RR 49f 62a** 4810[11]
3 b g Hernando (FR) - Desert Girl (Green Desert (USA)) 8.6f **(78)**
Form - 513686010
Record 2000 - 1st:2 2nd:0 3rd:1 Ran:9
Pre2000 - 1st:0 2nd:0 3rd:1 Ran:2
Win Prizemoney £4,612 *Total Prizemoney* £5,806
Wins 2000 *Spt Southw (STD) C 11f 66+* <
2000 *Feb Wolver (STD) 12f 66*
2000 Turf 0-4: (8f, 10f 2, 12f) (g-f 2, frm 2) 2000 AW 2-5: (10f, 11f 1-1, 12f 1-3) (Equi 2, Fibr 2-3)
Workmanlike, average gelding, effective 8 to 12f, acts on gd - acts on Fibr, prefers left handed tracks. Turf high 49. AW high 66 - 1st of 15 getting 7lb from Sharp Steel (26 Spt Southwell RF 4650) - also 1st of 8 from Le Cavalier (22 Feb Wolverhampton RF 0334).
**T D Barron [0-1] Nigel Shields (from W Jarvis [2-10] Spt 2000).*

SPANKER BHB 65f50a **RR 34f 50a** 28[/]
4 ch m Suave Dancer (USA) 10.7f **(68)** - Yawl **(93f)** (Rainbow Quest (USA)) 10.4f **(75)**
Form - 2307
Record 2000 - 1st:0 2nd:0 3rd:0 Ran:1
Pre2000 - 1st:0 2nd:1 3rd:2 Ran:8
Win Prizemoney £0 *Total Prizemoney* £2,175
2000 AW 0-1: (12f) (Equi)
Light-framed, fair filly, effective 12f, acts on frm, has worn blinkers, likes left handed tracks, likes tight tracks. Inconsistent.
**B W Hills [0-9] R D Hollingsworth.*

SPARKLING DOVE BHB 20f **RR** 685[14]
7 ch m Lighter 9.5f **(36)** - Nimble Dove (Starch Reduced) 11.5f **(52)**
Form - 8000
Record 2000 - 1st:0 2nd:0 3rd:0 Ran:4
2000 Turf 0-2: (7f, 15f) (hvy, gd) 2000 AW 0-2: (12f 2) (Fibr 2)
Formerly very poor mare, mostly wears blinkers.
**C J Price [1-14] Cecil J Price and P Crawford.*

SPARKLING ISLE BHB 48f **RR 42f** 4874[15]
3 ch f Inchinor 8.9f **(64)** - Brillante (FR) (Green Dancer (USA)) 10.3f **(74)**
Form - 000
Record 2000 - 1st:0 2nd:0 3rd:0 Ran:3
Pre2000 - 1st:0 2nd:0 3rd:0 Ran:4
Win Prizemoney £0 *Total Prizemoney* £468
2000 Turf 0-3: (8f 2, 10f) (g-s, gd, frm)
Unfurnished, moderate filly. Turf high 42 (began Aug).
**M Blanshard [0-7] The Cheapside Syndicate.*

SPARK OF LIFE RR 59f 4757[11]
3 b f Rainbows For Life (CAN) 9.3f **(64)** - Sparkly Girl (IRE) **(80f)** (Danehill (USA)) 10f **(72)**
Form - 03231130
Record 2000 - 1st:2 2nd:1 3rd:3 Ran:8
Pre2000 - 1st:0 2nd:0 3rd:0 Ran:3
Win Prizemoney £4,675 *Total Prizemoney* £7,178
Wins * **2000** Aug Kempto (G-F) H 9f 51 59 <
2000 Jly Bright (FRM) S 8f 47
2000 Turf 2-8: (7f, 8f 1-2, 9f 1-2, 10f 3) (g-s, g-f 2, frm 2-5)
Workmanlike, fair filly, effective 9f, acts on g-f to frm, mostly wears blinkers (extremely effectively), prefers tight tracks. Turf high 59 - 1st of 10 getting 8lb from Waverley Road (14 Aug Kempton RF 3619).
**T D McCarthy [1-3] A D Spence (from P R Chamings [1-8] Jly 2000).*

SPARKY BHB 56f **RR 59f** 2367[2]
6 b g Warrshan (USA) 9.7f **(59)** - Pebble Creek (IRE) (Reference Point)

6.8f **(70)**
Form - 2832
Record 2000 - 1st:0 2nd:2 3rd:1 Ran:4
Pre2000 - 1st:3 2nd:4 3rd:3 Ran:28
Win Prizemoney £7,966 *Total Prizemoney* £16,506
Wins * 1997 *Jun Southw (STD) H* 8f 57 60+
* 1996 Aug Beverl (FRM) H 7.5f 54 65 <
* 1996 Aug Bright (FRM) S 6f 65 <
2000 Turf 0-4: (8f, 9f 3) (g-f 3, frm)
Above-average gelding, mostly wears blinkers. Turf high 59.
**M W Easterby [5-45] Abbots Salford Carav Park.*

SPARTAN ROYALE BHB 67f **RR 68f** 527[4]
6 b g Shareef Dancer (USA) 10.1f **(67)** - Cormorant Creek (Gorytus (USA)) 7.8f **(60)**
Form - 4
Record 2000 - 1st:0 2nd:0 3rd:0 Ran:1
Pre2000 - 1st:1 2nd:6 3rd:2 Ran:20
Win Prizemoney £2,346 *Total Prizemoney* £12,512
Wins * 1998 Aug Carlis (G-S) H 17.2f 55 58 <
2000 Turf 0-1: (16f) (g-s)
Average gelding, effective 13 to 17f, best at 13f, acts on sft to gd. (1st run) - 4th of 15 giving 23lb to Swiftway (28 Mar Newcastle 16f g-s RF 0527).
**P Monteith [3-22] Allan Melville (from C E Brittain [0-5] Oct 1997).*

SPARTAN SAILOR RR 4532[12]
2 b g Handsome Sailor 6.6f **(53)** - Spartan Native (Native Bazaar) 6.9f **(62)**
Form - 0
Record 2000 - 1st:0 2nd:0 3rd:0 Ran:1
2000 Turf 0-1: (7f) (gd)
Currently very poor gelding.
**A Senior [0-1] G B Maher.*

SPEAKING OF TIME (USA) RR 5325a[8]
4 b m Gilded Time (USA) 7f **(76)** - Terrys Wild Again (USA) (Wild Again (USA))
Form - 8
2000 AW 0-1: (9f) (Dirt)
Currently very useful, always wears blinkers.
**B Abrams in USA [0-1] Nakkashian, Plan B Stable & Roberts.*

SPECIAL RR 56f 4821[10]
2 b f Polar Falcon (USA) 9f **(74)** - Shore Line (High Line) 10.3f **(70)**
Form - 0
Record 2000 - 1st:0 2nd:0 3rd:0 Ran:1
2000 Turf 0-1: (6f) (g-f).
Currently fair filly.
**Sir Michael Stoute [0-1] Cheveley Park Stud.*

SPECIAL DANCER RR 90f 1455a[17]
3 f
Form - 0
2000 Turf 0-1: (11f) (gd)
Currently useful filly. **A Tortorella in ITY [0-1].*

SPECIALIZE BHB 31f33a **RR 32?f 33a** 304[3]
8 b g Faustus (USA) 9.1f **(54)** - Scholastika (GER) (Alpenkonig (GER)) 10.8f **(76)**
Form - 03
Record 2000 - 1st:0 2nd:0 3rd:1 Ran:2
Pre2000 - 1st:0 2nd:1 3rd:1 Ran:13
Win Prizemoney £0 *Total Prizemoney* £1,264
2000 AW 0-2: (16f 2) (Fibr 2)
Very moderate gelding, has worn blinkers. AW high 35. Inconsistent. **K R Burke [7-43] P A Brazier.*

SPECIAL-K BHB 44f37a **RR 43f 37a** 2339[9]
8 br m Treasure Kay 6.5f **(53)** - Lissi Gori (FR) (Bolkonski) 7.6f **(64)**
Form - 20
Record 2000 - 1st:0 2nd:1 3rd:0 Ran:2
Pre2000 - 1st:7 2nd:4 3rd:7 Ran:58
Win Prizemoney £19,924 *Total Prizemoney* £29,225
Wins 1999 May Pontef (G-F) C 8f 42
1997 Jly Ripon (G-F) S 8f 50
1997 Jly Beverl (HVY) SH 7.5f 44 49

2000 Turf 0-2: (8f, 9f) (gd, g-f)
Moderate mare, effective 8 to 10f, best at 8f, acts on gd to frm, has worn blinkers, favours tight tracks, excels at Pontefract. Turf high 43 (1st run) - 2nd of 20 to Leonie Samual (3 May Pontefract 8f gd RF 1005).
**J R Weymes [0-2] G Falshaw (from E Weymes [7-48] Spt 1999).*

SPECIAL PROMISE (IRE) BHB 56f70a **RR 34f 70a** 5000[13]
3 ch g Anjiz (USA) 7f **(67)** - Woodenitbenice (USA) (Nasty And Bold (USA))
Form - 51111000
Record 2000 - 1st:4 2nd:0 3rd:0 Ran:7
Pre2000 - 1st:0 2nd:0 3rd:0 Ran:5
Win Prizemoney £11,726 *Total Prizemoney* £11,726
Wins *** 2000** *Feb Wolver (STD) H* 8.5f 67 79 <
*** 2000** *Feb Southw (STD) H* 8f 58 78+
*** 2000** *Jan Wolver (STD) H* 9.4f 58 62
*** 2000** *Jan Lingfi (STD) H* 10f 51 58
2000 Turf 0-2: (10f 2) (g-s, frm) 2000 AW 4-5: (8f 2-2, 9f 1-1, 10f 1-1, 12f) (Equi 1-1, Fibr 3-4)
Lengthy, above-average gelding, effective 8f, - acts on Fibr, prefers left handed tracks, prefers tight tracks. Turf high 35 (began Aug). AW high 79 - 1st of 9 giving 3lb to Noble Pasao (10 Feb Wolverhampton RF 0259) - also 1st of 5 giving 16lb to Niciara (4 Feb Southwell RF 0215). Becoming disappointing. He improved out of all recognition at the start of the year, reeling off a fine four-timer on sand. Ten furlongs looks to be his trip.
**P C Haslam [4-12] R Young.*

SPECIAL RING (USA) RR 105f 3347a[3]
3 b c Nureyev (USA) 8.4f **(84)** - Ring Beaune (USA) (Bering) 7.4f **(61)**
Form - 3
2000 Turf 0-1: (9f) (sft)
Currently Pattern-class colt. (1st run) - 3rd of 8 to Boutron (25 Jly Chantilly 9f sft RF 3347a).
**Mme C Head in FR [0-1] Wertheimer et Frere.*

SPECIFIC SORCEROR (IRE) BHB 92f **RR 88f** 4283[3]
2 ch c Definite Article - Mystic Dispute (IRE) (Magical Strike (USA))
Form - 5113
Record 2000 - 1st:2 2nd:0 3rd:1 Ran:4
Win Prizemoney £5,096 *Total Prizemoney* £7,406
Wins *** 2000** Aug Newcas (G-F) 8f 88 <
*** 2000** Jly Warwic (G-F) 7.1f 73
2000 Turf 2-4: (7f 1-2, 8f 1-2) (g-f 1-1, frm 2, hrd 1-1)
Useful colt. Turf high 88 (began Jly) - 3rd of 15 getting 4lb from Snowstorm (7 Spt Doncaster 8f frm RF 4283) - also 1st of 4 giving 9lb to Pathan (25 Aug Newcastle RF 3957).
**A P Jarvis [2-4] The Aston Partnership.*

SPECKLED GEM BHB 36f35a **RR 46f 35a** 115[4]
4 b m Precocious 7.2f **(54)** - My Diamond Ring (Sparkling Boy) 5f **(36)**
Form - 054
Record 2000 - 1st:0 2nd:0 3rd:0 Ran:2
Pre2000 - 1st:0 2nd:0 3rd:0 Ran:9
2000 AW 0-2: (6f 2) (Equi 2)
Leggy, moderate filly, has worn blinkers. AW high 33. Inconsistent.
**J R Best [0-3] Alan Turner (from R Rowe [0-2] Dec 1998).*

SPECTINA RR 8f 4873[11]
2 b f Spectrum (IRE) - Catina (Nureyev (USA)) 8.7f **(78)**
Form - 0
Record 2000 - 1st:0 2nd:0 3rd:0 Ran:1
2000 Turf 0-1: (7f) (g-s)
Currently very poor filly.
**J R Fanshawe [0-1] Chris Machin.*

SPECTRE BROWN RR 21f 4624[14]
10 b g Respect 5.7f **(44)** - My Goddess (Palm Track) 9.8f **(50)**
Form - 00
Record 2000 - 1st:0 2nd:0 3rd:0 Ran:2
2000 Turf 0-2: (11f, 12f) (gd, g-f)
Little account gelding. Turf high 21.
**D A Nolan [0-16] Mrs J McFadyen-Murray.*

SPECTROMETER BHB 75f **RR 81+f** 4306[12]

3 ch c Rainbow Quest (USA) 11.2f **(81)** - Selection Board (Welsh Pageant) 10f **(65)**
Form - 41120
Record 2000 - 1st:2 2nd:1 3rd:0 Ran:5
Pre2000 - 1st:0 2nd:0 3rd:0 Ran:3
Win Prizemoney £6,437 *Total Prizemoney* £7,816
Wins * **2000** Jly Hamilt (G-F) H 13f 65 76+
* **2000** Jly Bright (G-S) H 11.9f 65 80+ <
2000 Turf 2-5: (12f 1-3, 13f 1-1, 14f) (gd 1-2, g-f 1-2, frm)
Decent colt, effective 12 to 13f, best at 12f, acts on gd to frm, prefers tight tracks. Turf high 81 - 2nd of 2 giving 17lb to Rapid Deployment (7 Aug Carlisle 12f frm RF 3426) - also 1st of 9 giving 14lb to Baileys On Line (5 Jly Brighton RF 2536). Inconsistent. Improved once stepped up in trip and scored twice in July at Brighton and Hamilton. Unsuited by the muddling pace when beaten in a Carlisle match. **Sir Mark Prescott [2-8] Lord Derby.*

SPEEDFIT FREE (IRE) BHB 53f RR 50f 4168[11]

3 b g Night Shift (USA) 8.1f **(73)** - Dedicated Lady (IRE) (Pennine Walk) 8.5f **(61)**
Form - 00574413640
Record 2000 - 1st:1 2nd:0 3rd:1 Ran:11
Pre2000 - 1st:1 2nd:0 3rd:0 Ran:7
Win Prizemoney £6,284 *Total Prizemoney* £7,004
Wins * **2000** Jly Nottin (G-F) C 8.2f 48
1999 May Yarmou (FRM) 6f 75 <
2000 Turf 1-11: (5f, 6f, 7f 3, 8f 1-6) (gd, g-f 3, frm 1-7)
Fair gelding, effective 6f, acts on g-f, has worn blinkers. Turf high 61. Consistent. **M A Buckley [1-11] Mrs N W Buckley & G N Buckley (from G G Margarson [1-7] Spt 1999).*

SPEEDFIT TOO (IRE) BHB 105f RR 108f 3583[9]

5 b h Scenic 10.6f **(66)** - Safka (USA) (Irish River (FR)) 8.6f **(78)**
Form - 712370
Record 2000 - 1st:1 2nd:1 3rd:1 Ran:6
Pre2000 - 1st:3 2nd:1 3rd:2 Ran:13
Win Prizemoney £38,303 *Total Prizemoney* £65,651
Wins * **2000** Jun Salisb (G-F) H 8f 98 103 <
1998 May Kempto (G-F) L 8f 99+
1997 Aug Newmar (G-F) H 6f 97 97
1997 Aug Windso (GD) 6f 94
2000 Turf 1-6: (7f 2, 8f 1-3, 11f) (gd 3, g-f, frm 1-2)
Pattern-class colt, effective 8f, acts on gd to frm, has worn blinkers. Turf high 108 - 2nd of 18 giving 1lb to Caribbean Monarch (9 Jly Sandown 8f g-f RF 2658) - also 1st of 9 giving 27lb to Punishment (28 Jun Salisbury RF 2350). Consistent. A useful colt over here in '98, he was trained in Dubai the following season. Returned to join Clive Brittain at the start of last term, and ran a fine race when seventh in the Royal Hunt Cup, only collared inside the last, before winning at Salisbury. Good efforts in decent company since, but no show when stepped up to ten furlongs in a Haydock Group Three.
**C E Brittain [1-6] H E Sheikh Rashid Bin Mohammed (from G G Margarson [3-13] Aug 1998).*

SPEEDMASTER RR 99f 1454a[2]

14 b g Dunbeath (USA) 9.9f **(53)** - Hopeful Subject
Form - 2
2000 Turf 0-1: (10f) (sft)
Currently very useful gelding. (1st run) - 2nd of 8 to Samum (21 May Munich 10f sft RF 1454a).
**W Himmel in GER [0-1] Haras Chevotel.*

SPEED OF LIGHT (IRE) RR 52f 4964[4]

2 b c Spectrum (IRE) - Phylella (Persian Bold) 9.3f **(66)**
Form - 4
Record 2000 - 1st:0 2nd:0 3rd:0 Ran:1
Win Prizemoney £0 *Total Prizemoney* £652
2000 Turf 0-1: (7f) (gd)
Currently fair colt. **W R Muir [0-1] A J de V Patrick.*

SPEED ON BHB 73f RR 78f 5068[19]

7 b g Sharpo 7.5f **(68)** - Pretty Poppy (Song) 7.2f **(61)**
Form - 0630504600
Record 2000 - 1st:0 2nd:0 3rd:1 Ran:10
Pre2000 - 1st:4 2nd:2 3rd:3 Ran:29
Win Prizemoney £25,908 *Total Prizemoney* £34,383
Wins * 1999 Jun Chepst (G-F) H 5.1f 87 88
* 1999 Apr Newbur (G-F) H 5.2f 81 89
* 1998 Apr Bath (SFT) 5.1f 97 <
* 1996 May Beverl (G-F) 5f 83
2000 Turf 0-10: (5f 8, 6f 2) (g-s 2, gd 3, g-f 2, frm 3)
Above-average gelding, effective 5f, acts on g-f to frm, has worn blinkers. Turf high 78. Suited by the minimum trip, he has won on soft ground, but looks better on a fast surface. Dropping down the handicap, but apparently does not like big fields.
**H Candy [4-39] P A Deal.*

SPEED VENTURE BHB 64f61a RR 76f 61a 5069[4]

3 b g Owington - Jade Venture **(66f)** (Never so Bold) 6.3f **(66)**
Form - 422557404
Record 2000 - 1st:0 2nd:2 3rd:0 Ran:9
Win Prizemoney £0 *Total Prizemoney* £3,330
2000 Turf 0-8: (8f, 10f 4, 12f 3) (sft, g-s, gd 3, g-f 3) 2000 AW 0-1: (10f) (Equi)
Light-framed, above-average gelding, effective 10 to 12f, acts on gd to g-f. Turf high 76 - 2nd of 6 to Baldaquin (1 Jun Goodwood 10f gd RF 1626). **S P C Woods [0-9] Dr Frank Chao.*

SPEEDY GEE (IRE) BHB 95f RR 89f 4495[3]

2 b c Petardia 8.2f **(58)** - Champagne Girl (Robellino (USA)) 7.6f **(80)**
Form - 3617560463
Record 2000 - 1st:1 2nd:0 3rd:2 Ran:10
Win Prizemoney £3,412 *Total Prizemoney* £5,785
Wins * **2000** Jun Sandow (G-F) 5f 69 <
2000 Turf 1-10: (5f 1-7, 6f 3) (g-s, gd 2, g-f 4, frm 1-3)
Useful colt, effective 6f, acts on gd. Turf high 89.
**M R Channon [1-10] John Guest.*

SPEEDY JAMES (IRE) BHB 80f RR 51f 2209[29]

4 ch g Fayruz 6.6f **(63)** - Haraabah (USA) (Topsider (USA)) 8.3f **(71)**
Form - 6000
Record 2000 - 1st:0 2nd:0 3rd:0 Ran:4
Pre2000 - 1st:2 2nd:1 3rd:2 Ran:10
Win Prizemoney £8,156 *Total Prizemoney* £16,593
Wins 1998 Apr Newmar (SFT) 5f 98++ <
1998 Mar Newcas (G-S) 5f 84++
2000 Turf 0-4: (5f 2, 6f 2) (g-s, gd 2, g-f)
Fair gelding, has worn blinkers. Turf high 51.
**D Nicholls [0-5] Lucayan Stud (from J Berry [2-9] Aug 1999).*

SPELLBINDER (IRE) BHB 68f RR 78f 2448[8]

4 b m Magical Wonder (USA) 7.2f **(60)** - Shamanka (IRE) (Shernazar) 10.2f **(73)**
Form - 3228
Record 2000 - 1st:0 2nd:2 3rd:1 Ran:4
Pre2000 - 1st:0 2nd:0 3rd:0 Ran:1
Win Prizemoney £0 *Total Prizemoney* £2,180
2000 Turf 0-4: (7f, 8f 2, 10f) (sft, g-s, frm 2)
Workmanlike, above-average filly. Turf high 78 - 2nd of 10 giving 13lb to Serra Negra (1 May Warwick 8f sft RF 0954). She had yet to get off the mark, but has made the frame on a few occasions and looks the sort who will do better in time.
**G B Balding [0-5] Baldings (Training) Ltd.*

SPENCERS WOOD (IRE) BHB 107f RR 107f 4467[5]

3 b c Pips Pride 6.7f **(70)** - Ascoli (Skyliner) 7.3f **(53)**
Form - 14365
Record 2000 - 1st:1 2nd:0 3rd:1 Ran:5
Pre2000 - 1st:1 2nd:0 3rd:0 Ran:1
Win Prizemoney £13,673 *Total Prizemoney* £20,140
Wins * **2000** May Newmar (GD) 7f 101 <
* 1999 Oct Windso (G-S) 6f 79+
2000 Turf 1-5: (7f 1-1, 8f 2, 9f, 10f) (gd 2, g-f 2, frm 1-1)
Pattern-class colt, effective 7 to 10f, acts on gd to frm, best on gd. Turf high 107 - 5th of 6 giving 9lb to Compton Bolter (16 Spt Newbury 9f g-f RF 4467) - also 1st of 8 getting 4lb from Acrobatic (7 May Newmarket RF 1081). Placed in listed races after winning at Newmarket, he is likely to be suited by a strongly-run race.
**P J Makin [2-6] Four Seasons Racing Ltd.*

SPENDENT RR 109f 2205a[3]

4 ch h Generous (IRE) 11.5f **(82)** - Cattermole (USA) (Roberto (USA)) 10f **(76)**
Form - 33

2000 Turf 0-2: (12f 2) (sft, g-f)
Currently Pattern-class colt, often wears blinkers. Turf high 109.
**P Bary in FR [1-3] K Abdulla.*

SPETTRO (IRE) BHB 111f **RR 100f** 5214a[3]
2 b c Spectrum (IRE) - Overruled (IRE) **(80f)** (Last Tycoon) 8.5f **(62)**
Form - 51113
Record 2000 - 1st:3 2nd:0 3rd:1 Ran:5
Win Prizemoney £14,566 *Total Prizemoney* £33,223
Wins * **2000** Spt Haydoc (HVY) 8.1f 97 <
* **2000** Aug Nottin (GD) 8.2f 87
* **2000** Aug Catter (G-F) 7f 87+
2000 Turf 3-5: (5f, 7f 1-1, 8f 2-3) (hvy, sft 1-1, gd 1-2, frm 1-1)
Very useful colt. Turf high 100 - 3rd of 6 to Count Dubois (22 Oct San Siro 8f hvy RF 5214a) - also 1st of 4 giving 2lb to Lucayan Chief (2 Spt Haydock RF 4160). A thorough stayer, he made all to complete a hat-trick in late summer and battled back bravely when beaten three-parts of a length by Count Dubois in the Group 1 Gran Criterium at San Siro. Probably feeling those exertions when disappointing on his final start, he should win a middle-distance Group race on the continent. **P F I Cole [3-5] Luciano Gaucci.*

SPICE ISLAND BHB 62f **RR 73f** 5169[11]
2 b f Reprimand 8.2f **(63)** - Little Emmeline **(39df)** (Emarati (USA))
Form - 538710
Record 2000 - 1st:1 2nd:0 3rd:1 Ran:6
Win Prizemoney £3,263 *Total Prizemoney* £3,591
Wins * **2000** Oct Pontef (HVY) H 6f 53 73+ <
2000 Turf 1-6: (5f 2, 6f 1-4) (g-s 1-1, gd 2, g-f, frm 2)
Above-average filly, effective 6f, acts on g-s. Turf high 73 - 1st of 17 getting 20lb from Thomas Smythe (2 Oct Pontefract RF 4770).
**J A Glover [1-6] Mrs R Morley.*

SPIN A YARN **RR 80f** 3431[5]
3 b c Wolfhound (USA) 7.3f **(71)** - Green Flower (USA) (Fappiano (USA)) 8.7f **(77)**
Form - 805545
Record 2000 - 1st:0 2nd:0 3rd:0 Ran:6
Pre2000 - 1st:1 2nd:0 3rd:0 Ran:5
Win Prizemoney £6,190 *Total Prizemoney* £7,563
Wins * 1999 Aug Newbur (GD) H 7.3f 73 76 <
2000 Turf 0-6: (8f 5, 9f) (gd 3, frm 3)
Scopey, decent colt, effective 7 to 8f, best at 8f, acts on gd to frm, best on frm. Turf high 80 - 5th of 14 getting 1lb from Sir Ferbet (11 Jun Newmarket 8f frm RF 1881). Consistent.
**B W Hills [1-11] Maktoum Al Maktoum.*

SPINETAIL RUFOUS (IRE) BHB 48f58a **RR 30f 58a** 4762[4]
2 b c Prince of Birds (USA) - Miss Kinabalu **(34df)** (Shirley Heights) 10.3f **(74)**
Form - 0804
Record 2000 - 1st:0 2nd:0 3rd:0 Ran:4
2000 Turf 0-3: (5f, 6f 2) (gd, g-f, frm) 2000 AW 0-1: (5f) (Fibr)
Fair colt. Turf high 30 (began Aug). (1st run) - 4th of 12 to Acorn Catcher (30 Spt Wolverhampton 5f Fibr RF 4762).
**D W P Arbuthnot [0-4] Noel Cronin.*

SPINNER TOY BHB 28f **RR 12df** 2849[14]
5 ch g Seven Hearts - Priory Bay (Petong) 6.6f **(58)**
Form - 0
Record 2000 - 1st:0 2nd:0 3rd:0 Ran:1
Pre2000 - 1st:0 2nd:0 3rd:0 Ran:2
2000 Turf 0-1: (14f) (g-f)
Poor gelding. **J C Fox [0-3] Ground Force.*

SPINNING STAR BHB 65f68a **RR 63f 68a** 294[5]
4 ch m Arazi (USA) 9.2f **(74)** - Queen Midas (Glint of Gold) 9.3f **(66)**
Form - 15
Record 2000 - 1st:1 2nd:0 3rd:0 Ran:2
Pre2000 - 1st:0 2nd:0 3rd:1 Ran:5
Win Prizemoney £2,664 *Total Prizemoney* £3,280
Wins * **2000** *Jan Lingfi (STD) H 12f 61 63+* <
2000 AW 1-2: (12f 1-2) (Equi 1-2)
Average filly, effective 11 to 12f, best at 12f, acts on gd to frm - acts on Equi, prefers left handed tracks. AW high 63 (1st run) - 1st of 11 giving 32lb to Alberkinnie (22 Jan Lingfield RF 0138).
**C F Wall [1-7] S Fustok.*

SPINNING TOP **RR 101f** 2522a[7]
3 b f Alzao (USA) 9.8f **(73)** - Zenith (Shirley Heights) 10.3f **(74)**
Form - 127
Record 2000 - 1st:1 2nd:1 3rd:0 Ran:3
Win Prizemoney £3,087 *Total Prizemoney* £9,087
Wins * **2000** May Lingfi (G-S) 10f 90+ <
2000 Turf 1-3: (10f 1-3) (sft 1-1, g-s, gd)
Scopey, currently very useful filly. Turf high 101 - 2nd of 6 to Love Divine (24 May Goodwood 10f gd RF 1426). Unraced at two, she turned a Lingfield maiden into a procession on her debut but was held when raised in class. Should not be written off however, as she had valid excuses. **Sir Michael Stoute [1-3] The Queen.*

SPIRIT HOUSE (USA) **RR 71f** 3579[7]
2 b c Hansel (USA) 12.6f **(78)** - Ashwood Angel (USA) (Well Decorated (USA)) 7.6f **(64)**
Form - 27
Record 2000 - 1st:0 2nd:1 3rd:0 Ran:2
Win Prizemoney £0 *Total Prizemoney* £1,336
2000 Turf 0-2: (7f, 8f) (gd, g-f)
Currently above-average colt. Turf high 71 (began Jly). Ran green on his debut but showed promise for the future.
**M Johnston [0-2] David Abell.*

SPIRIT OF KHAMBANI (IRE) BHB 43f **RR 47df** 4694[13]
3 ch f Indian Ridge 7.6f **(74)** - Khambani (IRE) **(68f)** (Royal Academy (USA))
Form - 00842580240
Record 2000 - 1st:0 2nd:2 3rd:0 Ran:11
Pre2000 - 1st:0 2nd:0 3rd:1 Ran:2
Win Prizemoney £0 *Total Prizemoney* £1,804
2000 Turf 0-11: (6f, 7f, 8f 4, 9f, 10f, 11f 2, 12f) (gd 5, g-f 2, frm 4)
Lengthy, moderate filly, effective 8 to 12f, best at 8f, acts on gd to frm, best on frm, has worn blinkers, prefers right handed tracks, prefers tight tracks. Turf high 47 - 2nd of 13 giving 1lb to Wilemmgeo (18 Jly Beverley 8f frm RF 2886).
**M Johnston [0-13] M P Burke.*

SPIRIT OF LIGHT (IRE) BHB 60f55a **RR 73f 55a** 4676[10]
3 b g Unblest - Light Thatch (Thatch (USA)) 9.8f **(62)**
Form - 782300050
Record 2000 - 1st:0 2nd:1 3rd:1 Ran:9
Pre2000 - 1st:0 2nd:1 3rd:0 Ran:4
Win Prizemoney £0 *Total Prizemoney* £2,991
2000 Turf 0-9: (8f 6, 9f 2, 10f) (sft, g-s, gd 2, g-f 2, frm 3)
Scopey, above-average gelding, effective 8 to 9f, best at 8f, acts on sft to frm, prefers right handed tracks, likes tight tracks. Turf high 73 - 2nd of 8 getting 18lb from Common Place (22 Apr Kempton 9f sft RF 0833). Inconsistent.
**B R Johnson [0-1] Equality Racing (from M R Channon [0-12] Aug 2000).*

SPIRIT OF LOVE (USA) BHB 95f85a **RR 109f 85a** 4987[22]
5 ch g Trempolino (USA) 11.9f **(77)** - Dream Mary (USA) (Marfa (USA)) 14.9f **(73)**
Form - 1730324830
Record 2000 - 1st:0 2nd:1 3rd:3 Ran:9
Pre2000 - 1st:6 2nd:1 3rd:3 Ran:17
Win Prizemoney £112,025 *Total Prizemoney* £136,823
Wins * 1999 Nov Mulhei (HVY) L 18f 84+
* 1998 Oct Newmar (GD) H 18f 91 112+ <
* 1998 Spt Doncas (GD) H 14.6f 91 99
* 1998 Aug Ascot (G-F) H 16.2f 83 90
* 1998 May Doncas (G-F) H 14.6f 77 81
* 1998 *Jan Southw (STD) 11f 70*
2000 Turf 0-9: (14f, 16f 5, 18f 2, 22f) (sft, g-s, gd 4, g-f, frm 2)
Pattern-class gelding, effective 16f, acts on gd to g-f, best on gd, has worn blinkers. Turf high 110 - 4th of 5 getting 5lb from Royal Rebel (22 Aug York 16f gd RF 3851). A nine-length winner of the Cesarewitch in 1998 and successful in Listed company during 1999, he regressed last year. He will continue to be difficult to place unless the Handicapper relents.
**M Johnston [6-26] A W Robinson.*

SPIRIT OF PARK (IRE) BHB 60f **RR 61f** 4199[7]
3 b g Rashar (USA) - Rose Deer (Whistling Deer) 16.4f **(48)**

Form - 557
Record 2000 - 1st:0 2nd:0 3rd:0 Ran:3
2000 Turf 0-3: (10f 2, 12f) (gd, g-f, frm)
Workmanlike, average gelding. Turf high 61 (began Jly). Progressing nicely over hurdles, winner twice in Scotland in the autumn. **L Lungo [0-3] Mrs Ann Fortune.*

SPIRIT OF SONG (IRE) RR 70df 2515a[11]

2 b f Selkirk (USA) 7.9f **(76)** - Roxy Music (IRE) (Song) 7.2f **(61)**
Form - 440
Record 2000 - 1st:0 2nd:0 3rd:0 Ran:3
Win Prizemoney £0 *Total Prizemoney* £756
2000 Turf 0-3: (5f, 6f 2) (gd 3)
Currently above-average filly. Turf high 70. **M R Channon [0-3] Michael Hills.*

SPIRIT OF TENBY (IRE) BHB 63f64a RR 66f 64a 5069[16]

3 b g Tenby 10.4f **(76)** - Asturiana (Julio Mariner) 7.2f **(57)**
Form - 5603033047214500
Record 2000 - 1st:1 2nd:1 3rd:3 Ran:15
Pre2000 - 1st:0 2nd:0 3rd:1 Ran:6
Win Prizemoney £4,270 *Total Prizemoney* £7,952
Wins * **2000** Aug Epsom (G-F) H 12f 62 66 <
2000 Turf 1-15: (7f, 8f 5, 9f 2, 10f, 12f 1-6) (sft, g-s, gd 3, g-f 3, frm 1-6, hrd)
Workmanlike, average gelding, effective 7 to 12f, acts on frm. Turf high 67 - also 1st of 6 getting 10lb from After The Blue (17 Aug Epsom RF 3725). **S Dow [1-21] John Lever.*

SPIRIT OF TEXAS (IRE) BHB 60f57a RR 68f 57a 5160[1]

2 b g Namaqualand (USA) - Have A Flutter (Auction Ring (USA)) 8.6f **(65)**
Form - 808771
Record 2000 - 1st:1 2nd:0 3rd:0 Ran:6
Win Prizemoney £1,985 *Total Prizemoney* £1,985
Wins * **2000** Oct Nottin (SFT) S 8.2f 68 <
2000 Turf 1-6: (5f, 6f 2, 7f, 8f 1-2) (sft 1-1, g-s, gd, g-f, frm 2)
Average gelding, effective 8f, acts on sft, has worn blinkers. Turf high 68 - 1st of 15 from Tatty The Tank (24 Oct Nottingham RF 5160). **K McAuliffe [1-6] The Tri Nations Syndicate.*

SPLIT THE ACES (IRE) BHB 36f58a RR 56?f 58a 3445[7]

4 gr g Balla Cove - Hazy Lady (Habitat) 9.4f **(70)**
Form - 00550007
Record 2000 - 1st:0 2nd:0 3rd:0 Ran:8
Pre2000 - 1st:1 2nd:1 3rd:1 Ran:13
Win Prizemoney £2,332 *Total Prizemoney* £3,438
Wins * 1999 May Bath (GD) C 5.1f 61 <
2000 Turf 0-8: (5f 3, 6f 3, 7f 2) (gd 2, g-f, frm 3, hrd 2)
Neat, fair gelding, effective 5 to 6f, acts on gd, has worn blinkers. Turf high 56. Becoming disappointing. **R J Hodges [1-17] R J Hodges (from R Hannon [0-4] Dec 1998).*

SPONTANEITY (IRE) BHB 35f30a RR 34f 30a 3955[6]

4 ch m Shalford (IRE) 7.8f **(63)** - Mariyda (IRE) (Vayrann) 9.7f **(74)**
Form - 0625056
Record 2000 - 1st:0 2nd:1 3rd:0 Ran:7
Pre2000 - 1st:1 2nd:0 3rd:1 Ran:9
Win Prizemoney £3,805 *Total Prizemoney* £5,312
Wins * 1998 Aug Thirsk (G-F) 7f 78 <
2000 Turf 0-7: (10f 4, 12f 3) (gd, g-f 3, frm 2, hrd)
Scopey, fair filly, has worn blinkers. Turf high 36. **P D Evans [1-16] Colin Booth.*

SPORTING GESTURE BHB 68f RR 73f 4829[11]

3 ch g Safawan 6.6f **(60)** - Polly Packer (Reform) 8.9f **(62)**
Form - 000161070
Record 2000 - 1st:2 2nd:0 3rd:0 Ran:9
Pre2000 - 1st:1 2nd:0 3rd:0 Ran:7
Win Prizemoney £21,175 *Total Prizemoney* £21,175
Wins * **2000** Aug Cheste (GD) H 10.3f 70 73 <
* **2000** Jly York (GD) H 7.9f 65 69
* 1999 Spt Catter (G-F) H 7f 65 73+
2000 Turf 2-9: (7f, 8f 1-4, 10f 1-4) (sft, g-s, gd 1-3, g-f 1-3, hrd)
Leggy, above-average gelding, effective 7 to 10f, acts on gd to frm, prefers left handed tracks, likes tight tracks. Turf high 73 - 1st of 7 getting 9lb from Kaiapoi (18 Aug Chester RF 3745) - also 1st of 12 getting 7lb from Harmony Hall (14 Jly York RF 2821). Inconsistent. **M W Easterby [3-16] Steve Hull.*

SPORTING LAD (USA) BHB 103f RR 103df 1213[7]

4 b h Danzig (USA) 8.1f **(88)** - Lydara (USA) (Alydar (USA)) 9.1f **(76)**
Form - 7
Record 2000 - 1st:0 2nd:0 3rd:0 Ran:1
Pre2000 - 1st:2 2nd:2 3rd:0 Ran:11
Win Prizemoney £21,968 *Total Prizemoney* £30,120
Wins * 1999 May Cheste (G-F) H 7.6f 96 101 <
* 1998 Aug Cheste (GD) 7f 89
2000 Turf 0-1: (8f) (frm)
Scopey, very useful colt, effective 7 to 8f, acts on gd to g-f. **P F I Cole [2-12] M Arbib.*

SPORTING LADDER (USA) BHB 70f65a RR 79f 65a 4274[10]

3 b f Danzig (USA) 8.1f **(88)** - Lydara (USA) (Alydar (USA)) 9.1f **(76)**
Form - 4740
Record 2000 - 1st:0 2nd:0 3rd:0 Ran:4
Win Prizemoney £0 *Total Prizemoney* £268
2000 Turf 0-3: (8f, 9f, 10f) (g-s, gd, g-f) 2000 AW 0-1: (6f) (Fibr)
Lengthy, above-average filly. Turf high 79. **P F I Cole [0-4] M Arbib.*

SPORTS EXPRESS BHB 55f49a RR 51f 49a 3973[5]

2 ch f Then Again 7.4f **(52)** - Lady St Lawrence (USA) (Bering) 7.4f **(61)**
Form - 445
Record 2000 - 1st:0 2nd:0 3rd:0 Ran:3
2000 Turf 0-3: (6f, 7f 2) (frm 3)
Currently fair filly. Turf high 51 (began Jly). **W W Haigh [0-3] Tim Hawkins.*

SPORTY MO (IRE) BHB 71f79a RR 74f 79a 5139[5]

3 b g Namaqualand (USA) - Miss Fortunate (IRE) (Taufan (USA)) 7f **(57)**
Form - 45031131005
Record 2000 - 1st:3 2nd:0 3rd:2 Ran:11
Pre2000 - 1st:2 2nd:0 3rd:0 Ran:6
Win Prizemoney £10,798 *Total Prizemoney* £11,650
Wins * **2000** Apr Bright (G-S) 8f 74
* **2000** *Feb Lingfi (STD) C 8f 80+* <
* **2000** *Feb Lingfi (STD) C 10f 73*
* 1999 *Oct Southw (STD) S 7f 72*
* 1999 *May Southw (STD) S 6f 70+*
2000 Turf 1-5: (7f, 8f 1-4) (g-s, gd 1-2, g-f, frm) 2000 AW 2-6. (6f, 7f 2, 8f 1-2, 10f 1-1) (Equi 2-3, Fibr 3)
Tall, decent gelding, effective 6 to 10f, best at 8f, acts on gd - acts on AW, best on Equi, often wears blinkers, prefers left handed tracks, favours tight tracks. Turf high 74 - 1st of 10 giving 7lb to Inchinnan (13 Apr Brighton RF 0694). AW high 80 - 1st of 6 giving 17lb to Kigema (26 Feb Lingfield RF 0365) - also 1st of 6 giving 2lb to Finery (19 Feb Lingfield RF 0314). Becoming disappointing. **K R Burke [5-17] Maurice Charge.*

SPOSA (USA) BHB 41f55a RR 50f 55a 4603[9]

4 b m St Jovite (USA) 11.8f **(75)** - Barelyabride (USA) (Blushing Groom (FR)) 10.3f **(76)**
Form - 5382406375P811443770
Record 2000 - 1st:2 2nd:1 3rd:3 Ran:20
Pre2000 - 1st:1 2nd:0 3rd:1 Ran:2
Win Prizemoney £7,650 *Total Prizemoney* £11,258
Wins * **2000** Jly Leices (G-F) C 11.8f 45
* **2000** *Jly Southw (STD) S 12f 45++*
1999 Aug Tramor (G-F) 12f 58 <
2000 Turf 1-12: (12f 1-4, 13f, 14f 3, 15f, 16f, 18f, 20f) (sft, gd 5, g-f 2, frm 1-4) 2000 AW 1-8: (10f, 12f 1-3, 14f, 15f, 16f 2) (Equi, Fibr 1-7)
Average filly, effective 12 to 16f, acts on g-f - acts on Fibr. Turf high 50. AW high 68 - 2nd of 14 giving 11lb to Hetra Heights (6 Mar Southwell 16f Fibr RF 0415). **M J Polglase [2-20] The Lovatt Partnership (from M J Grassick in IRE [1-2] Aug 1999).*

SPOT BHB 62f56a RR 63f 56a 5155[10]

3 gr f Inchinor 8.9f **(64)** - Billie Grey **(61f 73a)** (Chilibang)
Form - 034770
Record 2000 - 1st:0 2nd:0 3rd:1 Ran:6
Win Prizemoney £0 *Total Prizemoney* £777
2000 Turf 0-3: (7f, 8f, 10f) (g-f, frm 2) 2000 AW 0-3: (6f, 7f, 8f) (Equi,

Fibr 2)
Workmanlike, average filly, effective 6f, - acts on Fibr. Turf high 63. AW high 61 (1st run) (began Jly) - 4th of 8 getting 5lb from Geronimo (13 Jly Wolverhampton 6f Fibr RF 2780).
**Andrew Reid [0-6] A S Reid.*

SPREE LOVE BHB 72f67a **RR 75f 67a** 5008[9]
2 b f Dancing Spree (USA) 8f **(59)** - Locorotondo (IRE) **(69f 63a)** (Broken Hearted)
Form - 2450
Record 2000 - 1st:0 2nd:1 3rd:0 Ran:4
Win Prizemoney £0 *Total Prizemoney* £1,484
2000 Turf 0-2: (7f 2) (gd, frm) 2000 AW 0-2: (6f 2) (Fibr 2)
Above-average filly. Turf high 75 (began Aug). AW high 59 (began Jly). **A G Newcombe [0-4] D Bass.*

SPREE VISION BHB 55f **RR 62?f** 5294[11]
4 b g Suave Dancer (USA) 10.7f **(68)** - Regent's Folly (IRE) (Touching Wood (USA)) 8.2f **(55)**
Form - 0074516500230
Record 2000 - 1st:1 2nd:1 3rd:1 Ran:13
Pre2000 - 1st:1 2nd:1 3rd:0 Ran:12
Win Prizemoney £8,164 *Total Prizemoney* £11,330
Wins * **2000** Jun Hamilt (GD) H 12.1f 49 55
1998 Oct Newcas (SFT) 8f 82 <
2000 Turf 1-13: (10f 3, 11f 2, 12f 1-3, 13f 4, 14f) (hvy, g-s 2, gd 5, g-f 2, frm 1-3)
Light-framed, average gelding, effective 10 to 12f, best at 12f, acts on g-f to frm, best on g-f, has worn blinkers, likes right handed tracks. Turf high 62. Inconsistent.
**P Monteith [1-16] I Bell (from S C Williams [1-12] Oct 1999).*

SPRING ANCHOR (FR) BHB 60f **RR 74?f** 395[6]
5 b g Slip Anchor 12.7f **(75)** - Swift Spring (FR) (Bluebird (USA)) 7.5f **(69)**
Form - 6
Record 2000 - 1st:0 2nd:0 3rd:0 Ran:1
Pre2000 - 1st:1 2nd:5 3rd:2 Ran:8
Win Prizemoney £2,490 *Total Prizemoney* £10,342
Wins 1998 Spt Lingfi (G-S) 11.5f 74 <
2000 AW 0-1: (12f) (Fibr)
Above-average gelding. (DEAD)
**P T Dalton [0-3] R A H Perkins (from P F I Cole [1-8] Spt 1998).*

SPRING BEACON BHB 25f25a **RR 12f 25a** 2480[7]
5 ch m Pharly (FR) 11.5f **(64)** - Vernair (USA) (Super Concorde (USA)) 10.9f **(66)**
Form - 67707
Record 2000 - 1st:0 2nd:0 3rd:0 Ran:5
Pre2000 - 1st:0 2nd:2 3rd:0 Ran:10
Win Prizemoney £0 *Total Prizemoney* £1,123
2000 AW 0-5: (7f 2, 8f 2, 11f) (Fibr 5)
Poor filly. AW high 15. **C N Allen [0-15] ShadowfaxRacing Com.*

SPRINGFIELDSUPREME RR 2954[15]
5 b g Jupiter Island 10.4f **(57)** - Altaghaderry Run (Deep Run) 18f **(46)**
Form - 0
Record 2000 - 1st:0 2nd:0 3rd:0 Ran:1
2000 Turf 0-1: (12f) (hrd)
Currently very poor gelding. **M Quinn [0-3] W Trezise.*

SPRING GIFT BHB 62f **RR 54f** 4326[10]
3 b f Slip Anchor 12.7f **(75)** - Belmez Melody **(68f)** (Belmez (USA))
Form - 6460
Record 2000 - 1st:0 2nd:0 3rd:0 Ran:4
Win Prizemoney £0 *Total Prizemoney* £300
2000 Turf 0-4: (8f 3, 10f) (g-f 3, frm)
Unfurnished, fair filly. Turf high 54 (began Jly).
**K Mahdi [0-4] Miss Debbie Mountain.*

SPRING PURSUIT BHB 59f **RR 88f** 5125[10]
4 b g Rudimentary (USA) 8.2f **(66)** - Pursuit of Truth (USA) (Irish River (FR)) 8.6f **(78)**
Form - 60213705000330
Record 2000 - 1st:1 2nd:1 3rd:3 Ran:14
Pre2000 - 1st:5 2nd:2 3rd:2 Ran:21
Win Prizemoney £40,939 *Total Prizemoney* £51,124
Wins * **2000** Apr Haydoc (HVY) H 11.9f 80 87 <
* 1999 Oct Lingfi (G-F) H 10f 67 75
* 1999 Oct Windso (G-S) H 10f 62 73+
* 1999 Oct York (SFT) H 8.9f 62 65
* 1999 Spt Bright (SFT) H 10f 56 59
1998 Jun Warwic (GD) 6f 85
2000 Turf 1-13: (8f, 10f 3, 12f 1-7, 14f 2) (hvy 1-1, sft 2, g-s 3, gd 2, g-f 2, frm 3) 2000 AW 0-1: (9f) (Fibr)
Neat, useful gelding, effective 10 to 12f, best at 12f, acts on hvy to gd, has worn blinkers, likes left handed tracks, prefers tight tracks. Turf high 88 - 3rd of 16 giving 28lb to Blue Style (1 May Kempton 12f g-s RF 0940) - also 1st of 15 getting 11lb from Lord Lamb (22 Apr Haydock RF 0825). He notched up a fine four-timer in soft ground in the autumn of '99, and bolted up over 12 furlongs in heavy ground at Haydock in April. Rose in the handicap subsequently and has somewhat lost his way.
**R J Price [5-28] E G Bevan (from R J Hodges [0-3] Jun 1999).*

SPRINGS NOBLEQUEST BHB 52f41a **RR 54f 41a** 471[6]
4 b m Noble Patriarch 12.2f **(43)** - Primum Tempus **(42df)** (Primo Dominie) 6.2f **(80)**
Form - 0666
Record 2000 - 1st:0 2nd:0 3rd:0 Ran:4
Pre2000 - 1st:1 2nd:1 3rd:3 Ran:16
Win Prizemoney £3,113 *Total Prizemoney* £5,551
Wins 1998 May Carlis (G-S) 5f 65 <
2000 AW 0-4: (6f 3, 7f) (Fibr 4)
Leggy, fair filly, effective 6 to 7f, best at 6f, acts on frm. AW high 38. **E J Alston [0-4] Springs Equestrian Ltd (from T D Easterby [1-16] Aug 1999).*

SPRING SYMPHONY (IRE) RR 66f 5098[15]
2 b f Darshaan 11.9f **(81)** - Well Head (IRE) (Sadler's Wells (USA)) 10f **(76)**
Form - 0
Record 2000 - 1st:0 2nd:0 3rd:0 Ran:1
2000 Turf 0-1: (8f) (gd)
Currently average filly. **Sir Michael Stoute [0-1] Lord Weinstock.*

SPRINGTIME LADY BHB 59f54a **RR 59f 54a** 3081[6]
4 ch m Desert Dirham (USA) - Affaire de Coeur (Imperial Fling (USA)) 7.1f **(58)**
Form - 5228223736
Record 2000 - 1st:0 2nd:2 3rd:2 Ran:6
Pre2000 - 1st:0 2nd:3 3rd:0 Ran:12
Win Prizemoney £0 *Total Prizemoney* £5,524
2000 Turf 0-3: (8f, 10f 2) (gd 2, frm) 2000 AW 0-3: (8f, 10f, 12f) (Equi 3)
Leggy, fair filly, effective 6 to 10f, best at 8f, acts on gd to g-f - acts on Equi, has worn blinkers. Turf high 59 (began Jly) - 3rd of 9 giving 1lb to Summer Song (13 Jly Folkestone 10f gd RF 2770). AW high 52. Consistent. **S Dow [0-18] Graham Brown.*

SPRINGWOOD JASMIN (IRE) BHB 48f **RR 40f** 4441[10]
2 b f Midhish - White Jasmin (Jalmood (USA)) 10.1f **(52)**
Form - 05670
Record 2000 - 1st:0 2nd:0 3rd:0 Ran:5
2000 Turf 0-5: (5f 2, 6f 2, 7f) (gd 3, g-f, frm)
Moderate filly. Turf high 40.
**D Carroll [0-5] The Springwood Syndicate.*

SPUNKIE BHB 85f **RR 87f** 5311[5]
7 ch g Jupiter Island 10.4f **(57)** - Super Sol (Rolfe (USA)) 12.1f **(65)**
Form - 5
Record 2000 - 1st:0 2nd:0 3rd:0 Ran:1
Pre2000 - 1st:3 2nd:1 3rd:1 Ran:11
Win Prizemoney £28,929 *Total Prizemoney* £45,600
Wins * 1999 Spt Newbur (G-S) H 16f 87 87+ <
* 1998 Spt Ascot (GD) H 16.2f 76 76
* 1998 Jly Salisb (GD) 14.1f 73
2000 Turf 0-1: (15f) (sft)
Useful gelding, effective 16f, acts on gd to g-f, best on gd.
**R F JohnsonHoughton [4-16] Jim Short.*

SPUR OF GOLD (IRE) BHB 45f **RR 42f** 5167[7]
2 b f Flying Spur (AUS) - Tony's Ridge (Indian Ridge)
Form - 667
Record 2000 - 1st:0 2nd:0 3rd:0 Ran:3

2000 Turf 0-3: (5f, 6f, 7f) (gd 2, g f)
Currently moderate filly. Turf high 42.
**J S Wainwright [0-3] Mrs Kay Harrison.*

SPY KNOLL BHB 72f RR 73f 1089[5]

6 b g Shirley Heights 12.1f **(76)** - Garden Pink (FR) (Bellypha) 9.8f **(73)**
Form - 5
Record 2000 - 1st:0 2nd:0 3rd:0 Ran:1
Pre2000 - 1st:1 2nd:2 3rd:3 Ran:13
Win Prizemoney £3,798 *Total Prizemoney* £10,535
Wins 1997 Spt Cheste (GD) 13.4f 83 <
2000 Turf 0-1: (14f) (g-f)
Above-average gelding, has worn blinkers.
**J R Poulton [0-1] M K George (from Mrs L Richards [0-5] Aug 1999).*

SPY MASTER BHB 81f RR 79f 5129[3]

2 b c Green Desert (USA) 7.8f **(78)** - Obsessive (USA) **(100f)** (Seeking the Gold (USA))
Form - 723413
Record 2000 - 1st:1 2nd:1 3rd:2 Ran:6
Win Prizemoney £3,068 *Total Prizemoney* £9,080
Wins * **2000** Spt Catter (SFT) 6f 77 <
2000 Turf 1-6: (6f 1-3, 7f 3) (sft, g-s 1-1, gd 2, g-f, frm)
Above-average colt, effective 6 to 7f, best at 7f, acts on g-s to frm, often wears blinkers. Turf high 79 (began Jly) - 4th of 10 giving 5lb to Lapwing (11 Spt Warwick 7f g-f RF 4325) - also 1st of 12 giving 5lb to Western Flame (16 Spt Catterick RF 4454). His win came in a very ordinary maiden on soft ground.
**Sir Michael Stoute [1-6] Cheveley Park Stud.*

SPYRO (IRE) RR 91f 1032a[6]

3 ch c Thatching 7.8f **(69)** - Nordic Success (IRE) (Nordico (USA)) 6.5f **(62)**
Form - 6
2000 Turf 0-1: (8f) (sft)
Currently useful colt.
**A Mataresi in ITY [0-2] (from M Quinlan [0-1] Jly 1999).*

SQUARE DANCER BHB 65a RR 59f 4992[3]

4 b g Then Again 7.4f **(52)** - Cubist (IRE) (Tate Gallery (USA)) 7.4f **(67)**
Form - 80005402605506013
Record 2000 - 1st:1 2nd:1 3rd:1 Ran:17
Pre2000 - 1st:2 2nd:3 3rd:1 Ran:18
Win Prizemoney £7,438 *Total Prizemoney* £14,244
Wins * **2000** Oct Windso (G-S) H 6f 59 58
* 1999 Aug Bright (SFT) 6f 70
* 1999 Jun Carlis (G-F) 5.9f 71 <
2000 Turf 1-16: (5f 4, 6f 1-8, 7f 3, 8f) (sft, gd, g-f 1-3, frm 9, hrd 2) 2000 AW 0-1: (6f) (Fibr)
Scopey, average gelding, effective 6f, acts on g-s to hrd - acts on Fibr, excels at Windsor. Turf high 59. (1st run) - 3rd of 13 giving 1lb to City Reach (14 Oct Wolverhampton 6f Fibr RF 4992).
**M Dods [3-30] A Mallen (from Mrs J R Ramsden [0-5] Oct 1998).*

SQUASQUAS (USA) RR 4851a[9]

3 f Hermitage (USA) 8.6f **(84)** - Seeking Glory (USA)
Form - 0
Record 2000 - 1st:0 2nd:0 3rd:0 Ran:1
2000 Turf 0-1: (9f) (hvy)
Currently very poor. **L M Cumani [0-1].*

SQUIRE CORRIE BHB 42f42a RR 29?f 42a 1044[P]

8 b g Distant Relative 7f **(69)** - Fast Car (FR) (Carwhite) 7.2f **(61)**
Form - 00P
Record 2000 - 1st:0 2nd:0 3rd:0 Ran:3
Pre2000 - 1st:11 2nd:10 3rd:12 Ran:103
Win Prizemoney £46,265 *Total Prizemoney* £71,199

Wins	* 1999	*Feb*	*Lingfi*	*(STD)*	*H*	*5f*	*55*	*56*
	* 1997	Jun	Ayr	(GD)	H	5f	71	82
	* 1997	Jun	York	(G-S)	H	5f	71	84 <
	* 1997	Jun	Hamilt	(GD)	H	5f	71	76
	* 1997	May	Thirsk	(GD)	H	5f	69	70
	* 1997	*Feb*	*Lingfi*	*(STD)*	*H*	*6f*	*68*	*69*
	* 1997	*Feb*	*Wolver*	*(STD)*	*H*	*5f*	*58*	*63*
	1996	Spt	Salisb	(FRM)	H	5f	57	63
	1996	Aug	Sandow	(GD)	H	5f	57	60
	1996	Jly	Sandow	(G-F)	H	5f	55	57

2000 Turf 0-1: (7f) (frm) 2000 AW 0-2: (5f, 6f) (Fibr 2)
Little account gelding, effective 5f, - acts on Equi, often wears blinkers, likes left handed tracks, likes tight tracks. Becoming disappointing. **D W Chapman [7-72] J M Chapman (from G Harwood [3-19] Oct 1996).*

SQUIRE TAT (IRE) RR 60f 2850[12]

2 b c Lake Coniston (IRE) - Classic Dilemma (Sandhurst Prince) 7.9f **(63)**
Form - 50
Record 2000 - 1st:0 2nd:0 3rd:0 Ran:2
2000 Turf 0-2: (6f 2) (gd, frm)
Currently average colt. Turf high 60 (began Jly).
**R A Fahey [0-2] J H Tattersall.*

SQUIRREL NUTKIN (IRE) BHB 83f RR 71f 823[4]

2 b br c Bluebird (USA) 7.9f **(71)** - Saltoki (Ballad Rock) 7.8f **(63)**
Form - 224
Record 2000 - 1st:0 2nd:2 3rd:0 Ran:3
Win Prizemoney £0 *Total Prizemoney* £2,235
2000 Turf 0-3: (5f 3) (hvy, gd 2)
Currently above-average colt. Turf high 71 - 2nd of 10 to Time N Time Again (8 Apr Hamilton 5f gd RF 0640).
**M L W Bell [0-3] Wilwyn Racing.*

STAFFORD KING (IRE) BHB 44f RR 48f 5162[9]

3 b c Nicolotte - Opening Day (Day Is Done) 6.3f **(67)**
Form - 7420076400
Record 2000 - 1st:0 2nd:1 3rd:0 Ran:10
Pre2000 - 1st:0 2nd:0 3rd:0 Ran:2
Win Prizemoney £0 *Total Prizemoney* £1,190
2000 Turf 0-10: (7f, 8f, 10f, 11f 2, 12f 5) (hvy, sft, g-s, gd 2, g-f 2, frm 3)
Moderate colt, effective 11f, acts on hvy, likes tight tracks. Turf high 57. Consistent. **J G M O'Shea [0-12] The Stafford Syndicate.*

STAFFORD PRINCE BHB 42f38a RR 52f 38a 2666[18]

3 br c Bin Ajwaad (IRE) - Petonellajill **(57f 50a)** (Petong) 6.6f **(58)**
Form - 800
Record 2000 - 1st:0 2nd:0 3rd:0 Ran:3
Pre2000 - 1st:0 2nd:0 3rd:0 Ran:5
2000 Turf 0-1: (12f) (gd) 2000 AW 0-2: (8f, 12f) (Fibr 2)
Unfurnished, fair colt, has worn blinkers. AW high 6.
**J G M O'Shea [0-8] The Stafford Syndicate.*

STAGE DIRECTION (USA) BHB 82f RR 84f 4262[5]

3 b c Theatrical 11.5f **(78)** - Carya (USA) (Northern Dancer) 9.6f **(80)**
Form - 44145
Record 2000 - 1st:1 2nd:0 3rd:0 Ran:5
Win Prizemoney £3,945 *Total Prizemoney* £5,191
Wins * **2000** Jly Haydoc (G-F) 10.5f 83 <
2000 Turf 1-5: (10f 4, 11f 1-1) (gd, g-f 2, frm 1-2)
Scopey, decent colt. Turf high 84 (1st run) - 4th of 20 to Subtle Power (20 May Newbury 10f g-f RF 1333) - also 1st of 9 getting 6lb from Helen's Day (16 Jly Haydock RF 2861). Won an ordinary maiden at Haydock on his third run and should make his mark in handicaps. Likely to stay twelve furlongs.
**J H M Gosden [1-5] K Abdulla.*

STAGE PASS BHB 85f RR 75f 1129[11]

7 ch h In The Wings 11.2f **(77)** - Sateen (FR) (Round Table) 9.5f **(81)**
Form - 0
Record 2000 - 1st:0 2nd:0 3rd:0 Ran:1
Pre2000 - 1st:0 2nd:1 3rd:1 Ran:2
Win Prizemoney £0 *Total Prizemoney* £20,685
2000 Turf 0-1: (19f) (g-f)
Above-average horse.
**G Barnett [1-4] J C Bradbury (from N Clement in FR [0-2] Jun 1996).*

STAGE PRESENCE (IRE) RR 70f 4599[8]

2 ch f Selkirk (USA) 7.9f **(76)** - Park Charger **(96f)** (Tirol)
Form - 08
Record 2000 - 1st:0 2nd:0 3rd:0 Ran:2
2000 Turf 0-2: (7f 2) (gd 2)
Currently above-average filly. Turf high 70 (began Spt).
**B W Hills [0-2] R E Sangster.*

STAGING POST (USA) RR 93f 5157[2]

2 b c Pleasant Colony (USA) 12.4f **(88)** - Interim **(103f)** (Sadler's Wells (USA)) 10f **(76)**
Form - 32
Record 2000 - 1st:0 2nd:1 3rd:1 Ran:2
Win Prizemoney £0 *Total Prizemoney* £2,014
2000 Turf 0-2: (7f, 8f) (sft, g-s)
Currently useful colt. Turf high 93 (began Aug) - 2nd of 17 to Random Quest (24 Oct Nottingham 8f sft RF 5157). A neat individual, he shaped encouragingly in two useful maidens and should have no difficulty winning a similar contest this year.
**H R A Cecil [0-2] K Abdulla.*

STAKIS CASINOS BOY (IRE) BHB 44f RR 5020[11]

6 ch g Magical Wonder (USA) 7.2f **(60)** - Hardiona (FR) (Hard To Beat) 10.1f **(67)**
Form - 0
Record 2000 - 1st:0 2nd:0 3rd:0 Ran:1
Pre2000 - 1st:1 2nd:1 3rd:0 Ran:9
Win Prizemoney £3,420 *Total Prizemoney* £4,771
Wins 1997 May Newcas (G-F) 10.1f 71 <
2000 AW 0-1: (12f) (Fibr)
Very poor gelding, has worn blinkers. Becoming disappointing.
**B Ellison [1-5] Ashley Carr Racing (from M Johnston [1-7] Oct 1997).*

STALLONE BHB 83f RR 81f 3431[3]

3 ch g Brief Truce (USA) 9.1f **(73)** - Bering Honneur (USA) (Bering) 7.4f **(61)**
Form - 4551113
Record 2000 - 1st:3 2nd:0 3rd:1 Ran:7
Win Prizemoney £13,338 *Total Prizemoney* £14,667
Wins * 2000 Jly Redcar (G-F) H 10f 79 81 <
*** 2000** Jly Newcas (G-F) H 8f 75 79
*** 2000** Jun Redcar (FRM) H 9f 70 74
2000 Turf 3-7: (7f 2, 8f 1-1, 9f 1-2, 10f 1-2) (g-s 2, gd 1-2, frm 2-3)
Scopey, decent gelding, effective 8 to 10f, acts on gd to frm, best on frm. Turf high 81 - 1st of 5 giving 13lb to Peteuresque (29 Jly Redcar RF 3222) - also 1st of 14 from Hadath (9 Jly Newcastle RF 2654). He has improved considerably since encountering fast ground and racing in handicap company, completing a hat-trick. Suited by at least a mile. **J Noseda [3-7] Lucayan Stud.*

STALWART MEMBER (USA) RR 5367a[1]

7 ch g Claramount (USA) - Ms Stalwart (USA) (Stalwart (USA)) 9.9f **(78)**
Form - 1
2000 AW 1-1: (7f 1-1) (Dirt 1-1)
Currently very useful gelding. (1st run) - 1st of 6 from Istintaj (4 Nov Aqueduct RF 5367a). **A Dutrow in USA [1-1] S Goldfarb.*

STAMFORD HILL BHB 17f RR 30?f 4815[14]

5 ch g Jendali (USA) - Laxay (Laxton)
Form - 0000560050000
Record 2000 - 1st:0 2nd:0 3rd:0 Ran:13
Win Prizemoney £0 *Total Prizemoney* £254
2000 Turf 0-13: (7f 2, 8f 3, 9f, 10f 2, 12f 4, 14f) (g-s 2, gd 6, g-f 2, frm 2, hrd)
Very moderate gelding. Turf high 30. Inconsistent.
**G P Kelly [0-13] A M McArdle.*

STAND ASIDE BHB 43f RR 49f 4546[4]

4 b g In The Wings 11.2f **(77)** - Honourable Sheba (USA) (Roberto (USA)) 10f **(76)**
Form - 5404
Record 2000 - 1st:0 2nd:0 3rd:0 Ran:4
Pre2000 - 1st:0 2nd:0 3rd:0 Ran:5
Win Prizemoney £0 *Total Prizemoney* £295
2000 Turf 0-4: (12f, 16f 3) (g-s, g-f 2, frm)
Tall, moderate gelding, has worn blinkers. Turf high 49 (began Aug). **Lady Herries [0-9] Chris Hardy.*

STAND BY BHB 56a RR 48f 5155[3]

3 b f Missed Flight - Ma Rivale (Last Tycoon) 8.5f **(62)**
Form - 5330013
Record 2000 - 1st:1 2nd:0 3rd:3 Ran:6
Pre2000 - 1st:0 2nd:0 3rd:0 Ran:3
Win Prizemoney £1,694 *Total Prizemoney* £2,779
Wins * 2000 *Oct Southw (STD) 6f 69+* <
2000 Turf 0-2: (7f, 8f) (gd, frm) 2000 AW 1-4: (6f 1-2, 7f 2) (Equi, Fibr 1-3)
Leggy, above-average filly, effective 6 to 7f, - acts on AW, prefers tight tracks. Turf high 19 (began Aug). AW high 69 - 1st of 9 getting 5lb from Carew Castle (16 Oct Southwell RF 5009). Inconsistent.
**B A Pearce [1-4] M O'Malley (from T D Easterby [0-5] Jan 2000).*

STANDIFORD GIRL (IRE) BHB 41f46a RR 36f 46a 4123[9]

3 b f Standiford (USA) - Pennine Girl (IRE) (Pennine Walk) 8.5f **(61)**
Form - 620073240
Record 2000 - 1st:0 2nd:2 3rd:1 Ran:9
Win Prizemoney £0 *Total Prizemoney* £1,336
2000 Turf 0-4: (8f 2, 10f 2) (g-s, gd, frm, hrd) 2000 AW 0-5: (8f 3, 9f 2) (Fibr 5)
Light-framed, fair filly, effective 8 to 9f, - acts on Fibr, likes left handed tracks. Turf high 36. AW high 50 - 2nd of 9 to Cyber Babe (4 May Wolverhampton 9f Fibr RF 1028).
**J G Given [0-9] Ray Monaghan.*

STANDS TO REASON RR 73f 5131[4]

2 gr g Hernando (FR) - Reason to Dance **(98df)** (Damister (USA)) 9f **(73)**
Form - 4
Record 2000 - 1st:0 2nd:0 3rd:0 Ran:1
Win Prizemoney £0 *Total Prizemoney* £392
2000 Turf 0-1: (6f) (sft)
Currently above-average gelding. **L G Cottrell [0-1] Mrs D Joly.*

ST ANTIM (IRE) BHB 78f RR 65f 4808[P]

2 b f Petardia 8.2f **(58)** - Efficient Funding (IRE) (Entitled)
Form - 15P
Record 2000 - 1st:1 2nd:0 3rd:0 Ran:3
Win Prizemoney £3,038 *Total Prizemoney* £3,306
Wins * 2000 Aug Haydoc (G-S) 6f 58 <
2000 Turf 1-3: (6f 1-2, 7f) (g-s, gd 1-2)
Currently average filly, has broken blood-vessels. Turf high 65 (began Aug) - also 1st of 18 getting 5lb from Track The Cat (10 Aug Haydock RF 3535). **J A Osborne [1-3] Mrs H J Clarke.*

STAPLOY RR 70+f 5312[3]

2 b f Deploy 11.4f **(67)** - Balliasta (USA) (Lyphard (USA)) 9.9f **(72)**
Form - 3
Record 2000 - 1st:0 2nd:0 3rd:1 Ran:1
Win Prizemoney £0 *Total Prizemoney* £615
2000 Turf 0-1: (8f) (g-s)
Currently above-average filly. **B W Hills [0-1] K Abdulla.*

STAR ATTRACTION RR 25f 3955[10]

3 b f Rambo Dancer (CAN) 8.4f **(59)** - Flying Fascination (Flying Tyke)
Form - 4850
Record 2000 - 1st:0 2nd:0 3rd:0 Ran:4
Win Prizemoney £0 *Total Prizemoney* £301
2000 Turf 0-4: (10f 3, 12f) (g-f 2, frm, hrd)
Scopey, little account filly. Turf high 25 (began Jly).
**M Quinn [0-4] Bright Sparks Racing.*

STARBECK (IRE) BHB 88f RR 80f 5123[9]

2 b f Spectrum (IRE) - Tide of Fortune (Soviet Star (USA))
Form - 410
Record 2000 - 1st:1 2nd:0 3rd:0 Ran:3
Win Prizemoney £6,581 *Total Prizemoney* £6,908
Wins * 2000 Oct York (SFT) 6f 80 <
2000 Turf 1-3: (6f 1-3) (g-s 1-2, frm)
Currently decent filly. Turf high 80 (began Aug) - 1st of 13 getting 5lb from Orientor (6 Oct York RF 4830). Handled the soft ground well when getting home by the minimum margin at York on her second start with the rest well beaten.
**J D Bethell [1-3] WWW Clarendon Racing Com.*

STARBOARD TACK (FR) BHB 45f47a RR 53f 47a 3732[16]

4 b m Saddlers' Hall (IRE) 10.5f **(65)** - North Wind (IRE) (Lomond (USA)) 8.8f **(65)**
Form - 0830R0
Record 2000 - 1st:0 2nd:0 3rd:1 Ran:6
Pre2000 - 1st:0 2nd:0 3rd:3 Ran:7
Win Prizemoney £0 *Total Prizemoney* £2,165

2000 Turf 0-4: (8f, 10f, 11f, 14f) (gd 2, frm 2) 2000 AW 0-2: (8f 2) (Fibr 2)
Well made, average filly, effective 8 to 12f, acts on g-f to hrd - acts on Fibr, prefers left handed tracks, favours tight tracks. Turf high 35. AW high 67 - 3rd of 7 giving 11lb to Shady Point (9 Jun Southwell 8f Fibr RF 1856). Becoming disappointing.
**R Brotherton [0-6] Roy Brotherton (from B W Hills [0-7] Spt 1999).*

STAR BRIEF BHB 55f RR 55f — 3919[10]
2 b c Cosmonaut - Valise **(32f)** (Salse (USA)) 7.5f **(66)**
Form - 040
Record 2000 - 1st:0 2nd:0 3rd:0 Ran:3
Win Prizemoney £0 *Total Prizemoney* £265
2000 Turf 0-3: (7f 3) (gd 2, frm)
Currently fair colt. Turf high 55 (began Jly).
**W J Musson [0-3] C D F Partnership.*

STAR CAST (IRE) RR 81f — 2601[3]
3 ch f In The Wings 11.2f **(77)** - Thank One's Stars (Alzao (USA)) 7.1f **(68)**
Form - 113
Record 2000 - 1st:2 2nd:0 3rd:1 Ran:3
Pre2000 - 1st:0 2nd:0 3rd:0 Ran:4
Win Prizemoney £12,350 *Total Prizemoney* £12,975
Wins * 2000 Jun Goodwo (GD) H 12f 68 75+ <
*** 2000** May Windso (G-S) H 11.6f 68 75
2000 Turf 2-3: (12f 2-3) (g-s, gd 1-1, g-f 1-1)
Neat, decent filly, effective 12f, acts on g-s to g-f. Turf high 81 - 3rd of 9 getting 5lb from Romantic Affair (7 Jly Salisbury 12f g-s RF 2601) - also 1st of 9 getting 7lb from Polar Red (1 Jun Goodwood RF 1623). Showed little at two, but really came into her own once being stepped up to middle distances last season, winning her first two starts in good style at Windsor and Goodwood. Looks progressive.
**Major D N Chappell [2-7] Mrs G C Maxwell.*

STARDARA (USA) RR 56f — 4472[5]
2 b f Theatrical 11.5f **(78)** - Lydara (USA) (Alydar (USA)) 9.1f **(76)**
Form - 65
Record 2000 - 1st:0 2nd:0 3rd:0 Ran:2
2000 Turf 0-2: (8f 2) (g-f, frm)
Currently fair filly. Turf high 56 (began Aug).
**P F I Cole [0-2] M Arbib.*

STARDREAMER (FR) BHB 48f RR 44f — 4014[2]
3 ch g Arazi (USA) 9.2f **(74)** - Hafwah (Gorytus (USA)) 7.8f **(60)**
Form - 062
Record 2000 - 1st:0 2nd:1 3rd:0 Ran:3
Win Prizemoney £0 *Total Prizemoney* £1,260
2000 Turf 0-3: (8f, 10f, 11f) (frm 3)
Lengthy, currently moderate gelding. Turf high 44 (began Jly) - 2nd of 10 to First Back (27 Aug Beverley 10f frm RF 4014).
**B Hanbury [0-3] Abdullah Ali.*

STAR DYNASTY (IRE) BHB 86f RR 88f — 1531[2]
3 b c Bering 9.6f **(80)** - Siwaayib (Green Desert (USA)) 8.6f **(78)**
Form - 322
Record 2000 - 1st:0 2nd:2 3rd:1 Ran:3
Pre2000 - 1st:0 2nd:0 3rd:0 Ran:1
Win Prizemoney £0 *Total Prizemoney* £6,434
2000 Turf 0-3: (8f, 10f 2) (gd 3)
Workmanlike, useful colt. Turf high 88 - 2nd of 8 to St Expedit (3 May Pontefract 10f gd RF 1007).
**E A L Dunlop [0-4] Maktoum Al Maktoum.*

STARFLEET RR 70f — 4737[7]
2 ch f Inchinor 8.9f **(64)** - Sunfleet (Red Sunset) 8.2f **(63)**
Form - 57
Record 2000 - 1st:0 2nd:0 3rd:0 Ran:2
2000 Turf 0-2: (6f 2) (g-f, frm)
Currently above-average filly. Turf high 70 (began Jly).
**P F I Cole [0-2] P F I Cole.*

STAR GLADE RR 41f — 5075[8]
2 b f Charnwood Forest (IRE) - Movieland (USA) (Nureyev (USA)) 8.7f **(78)**
Form - 08
Record 2000 - 1st:0 2nd:0 3rd:0 Ran:2
2000 Turf 0-2: (7f, 8f) (g-s, g-f)
Currently moderate filly. Turf high 41 (began Spt).
**G Brown [0-2] Mrs Carol Ann Brown.*

STARINE (FR) RR 106f — 1445a[2]
3 gr f Mendocino (USA) - Grisonnante (FR) (Kaldoun (FR)) 10.3f **(68)**
Form - 12
2000 Turf 0-1: (8f) (gd)
Currently Pattern-class filly. (1st run) - 2nd of 7 to England's Legend (17 May Saint-cloud 8f gd RF 1445a).
**Jean-Marc Capitte in FR [1-2].*

STARLIGHT BHB 63f RR 64f — 4729[13]
3 b f King's Signet (USA) 7f **(51)** - Petinata (Petong) 6.6f **(58)**
Form - 1015000
Record 2000 - 1st:2 2nd:0 3rd:0 Ran:7
Pre2000 - 1st:0 2nd:0 3rd:0 Ran:5
Win Prizemoney £4,450 *Total Prizemoney* £4,702
Wins * 2000 Jly Lingfi (GD) H 7f 62 68+
*** 2000** Apr Thirsk (G-S) 7f 74 <
2000 Turf 2-7: (7f 2-4, 8f 3) (gd 1-3, g-f 1-2, frm 2)
Unfurnished, average filly, effective 7f, acts on gd to g-f, best on gd. Turf high 74 (1st run) - 1st of 9 getting 17lb from Technician (15 Apr Thirsk RF 0737) - also 1st of 12 giving 19lb to Dancing Lily (12 Jly Lingfield RF 2743). Becoming disappointing. Won at Lingfield in July after a ten-week break.
**E A L Dunlop [2-11] Mrs Mollie Cooper Webster (from N A Graham [0-1] Jun 1999).*

STARLYTE GIRL (IRE) BHB 94f RR 92f — 3361[2]
3 b f Fairy King (USA) 7.7f **(75)** - Blushing Storm (USA) (Blushing Groom (FR)) 10.3f **(76)**
Form - 601212
Record 2000 - 1st:2 2nd:2 3rd:0 Ran:6
Pre2000 - 1st:1 2nd:1 3rd:1 Ran:4
Win Prizemoney £15,093 *Total Prizemoney* £31,155
Wins * 2000 Jly Windso (GD) H 8.3f 85 90 <
*** 2000** Jun Salisb (G-F) 9.9f 83+
* 1999 Aug Warwic (GD) 7.7f 78
2000 Turf 2-6: (8f 1-1, 9f, 10f 1-4) (g-s, gd, g-f 1-3, frm 1-1)
Leggy, useful filly, effective 8 to 10f, best at 10f, acts on g-f to frm, best on g-f, likes right handed tracks, prefers tight tracks. Turf high 92 - 2nd of 11 getting 11lb from Happy Diamond (4 Aug Goodwood 10f g-f RF 3361) - also 1st of 8 giving 11lb to Midnight Allure (17 Jly Windsor RF 2877). A tough front-runner, she stays a mile and a quarter and goes well on fast ground.
**R Hannon [3-10] Mohamed Suhail.*

STAR MANAGER (USA) BHB 34f54a RR 39f 54a — 4585[16]
10 b g Lyphard (USA) 10.6f **(75)** - Angel Clare (FR) (Mill Reef (USA)) 10.5f **(78)**
Form - 70
Record 2000 - 1st:0 2nd:0 3rd:0 Ran:2
Pre2000 - 1st:6 2nd:1 3rd:5 Ran:58
Win Prizemoney £44,761 *Total Prizemoney* £75,213
Wins 1998 Jun Epsom (GD) C 8.5f 71
1996 Apr Sandow (GD) H 8.1f 78 89 <
2000 Turf 0-1: (16f) (g-f) 2000 AW 0-1: (12f) (Equi)
Moderate gelding, has worn blinkers. **R C Spicer [0-30] John Purcell (from P F I Cole [6-51] Aug 1998).*

STAR OF AKKAR RR 116f — 3946a[2]
4 b m Distant Relative 7f **(69)** - Donna Star (Stately Don (USA))
Form - 2
2000 Turf 0-1: (10f) (g-f)
High-class filly, effective 9 to 11f, acts on g-s to gd, best on gd.
** J-C Rouget in FR [3-7].*

STAR OF WONDER RR 47f — 5196[10]
2 b f Celtic Swing - Meant to Be **(65f 70a)** (Morston (FR)) 9.4f **(55)**
Form - 00
Record 2000 - 1st:0 2nd:0 3rd:0 Ran:2
2000 Turf 0-2: (8f 2) (gd 2)
Currently moderate filly. Turf high 47 (began Spt).
**Lady Herries [0-2] Lady Mary Mumford.*

STAR PRINCESS RR 75f 4834[5]
3 b f Up and At 'em - Princess Sharpenup (Lochnager) 6f **(59)**
Form - 64224253305
Record 2000 - 1st:0 2nd:3 3rd:2 Ran:11
Pre2000 - 1st:0 2nd:1 3rd:1 Ran:4
Win Prizemoney £0 *Total Prizemoney* £8,933
2000 Turf 0-11: (5f 4, 6f 7) (sft, g-s 2, gd 3, g-f, frm 4)
Unfurnished, above-average filly, effective 5 to 6f, best at 6f, acts on hvy to frm, best on frm, has worn blinkers, excels at Yarmouth. Turf high 75 - 3rd of 18 getting 10lb from Dancing Mystery (12 Spt Yarmouth 5f frm RF 4332). Progressive form in maidens at two, but found the minimum too sharp on her comeback.
**K T Ivory [0-15] The Star Princess Partnership.*

STAR RAGE (IRE) BHB 82f85a **RR 85f 85a** 4317[7]
10 b g Horage 11.4f **(58)** - Star Bound (Crowned Prince (USA)) 10.1f **(67)**
Form - 60F22554217
Record 2000 - 1st:1 2nd:3 3rd:0 Ran:11
Pre2000 - 1st:19 2nd:15 3rd:10 Ran:81
Win Prizemoney £84,702 *Total Prizemoney* £119,729
Wins * 2000 Aug Thirsk (G-F) H 16f 79 78
* 1999 Spt Goodwo (G-F) H 16f 83 85 <
* 1999 Aug Beverl (GD) H 16.2f 79 80
* 1999 Jly Redcar (FRM) H 16f 75 77
* 1999 May Beverl (GD) H 16.2f 72 77
1999 *Feb Lingfi (STD) H 16f 80 83*
* 1998 *Apr Wolver (STD) H 14.8f 78 80*
* 1997 Aug Redcar (FRM) H 16f 75 77
2000 Turf 1-11: (14f, 15f, 16f 1-7, 18f, 19f) (gd 3, g-f 4, frm 1-4)
Useful gelding, effective 15 to 18f, best at 16f, acts on gd to frm - acts on Equi, best on g-f, likes right handed tracks, and excels at Thirsk and Beverley and Goodwood. Turf high 85 - 2nd of 5 giving 16lb to Renzo (19 May Thirsk 16f gd RF 1320) - also 1st of 4 giving 19lb to Embryonic (25 Aug Thirsk RF 3974). Consistent. Not getting any younger, but he retains ability. Suited by top of the ground and coming off a fast pace, he is a credit to connections.
**M Johnston [21-90] David Abell (from D R C Elsworth [1-7] Apr 1999).*

STARRY LADY (IRE) RR 86+f 5138[4]
2 b f Marju (IRE) 9.2f **(76)** - Caroline Lady (JPN) (Caro)
Form - 24
Record 2000 - 1st:0 2nd:1 3rd:0 Ran:2
Win Prizemoney £0 *Total Prizemoney* £1,216
2000 Turf 0-2: (7f, 8f) (g-s, gd)
Currently useful filly. Turf high 86 (began Spt).
**M R Channon [0-2] John Mckay.*

STARRY MARY BHB 61f56a **RR 66f 56a** 4615[3]
2 b f Deploy 11.4f **(67)** - Darling Splodge (Elegant Air) 13.2f **(61)**
Form - 84083
Record 2000 - 1st:0 2nd:0 3rd:1 Ran:5
Win Prizemoney £0 *Total Prizemoney* £252
2000 Turf 0-4: (6f 2, 7f, 8f) (gd 2, g-f 2) 2000 AW 0-1: (6f) (Fibr)
Average filly. Turf high 66 - 4th of 9 getting 4lb from Silk Law (17 Jun Nottingham 6f g-f RF 2048).
**E L James [0-5] The Westenholz Family.*

STAR SELECTION BHB 70f **RR 41f** 2061[16]
9 b g Rainbow Quest (USA) 11.2f **(81)** - Selection Board (Welsh Pageant) 10f **(65)**
Form - 0
Record 2000 - 1st:0 2nd:0 3rd:0 Ran:1
Pre2000 - 1st:1 2nd:4 3rd:1 Ran:16
Win Prizemoney £4,204 *Total Prizemoney* £17,704
2000 Turf 0-1: (12f) (g-f)
Moderate gelding. Inconsistent.
**J Mackie [6-39] R M Mitchell (from P F I Cole [1-8] Jun 1994).*

STAR TURN (IRE) BHB 62f58a **RR 71f 58a** 1306[8]
6 ch g Night Shift (USA) 8.1f **(73)** - Ringtail (Auction Ring (USA)) 8.6f **(65)**
Form - 18
Record 2000 - 1st:1 2nd:0 3rd:0 Ran:2
Pre2000 - 1st:2 2nd:3 3rd:2 Ran:23
Win Prizemoney £14,400 *Total Prizemoney* £18,424
Wins * 2000 May Newmar (GD) H 10f 57 71 <
* 1999 Aug Newmar (GD) H 10f 53 56
* 1999 *Jan Lingfi (STD) H 10f 48 55*
2000 Turf 1-2: (10f 1-2) (gd, g-f 1-1)
Above-average gelding, effective 10f, acts on g-f. Turf high 71 (1st run) - 1st of 18 getting 18lb from Pinchincha (5 May Newmarket RF 1045). Inconsistent. Came back from a seven-month break to win a lady amateur riders' race at Newmarket. Not particularly consistent.
**R M Flower [3-7] K & D Computers Ltd (from B J Llewellyn [0-3] Aug 1998).*

STATE APPROVAL BHB 26f38a **RR 37f 38a** 3192[8]
7 b g Pharly (FR) 11.5f **(64)** - Tabeeba (Diesis) 9.3f **(69)**
Form - 68007233685060308
Record 2000 - 1st:0 2nd:1 3rd:3 Ran:17
Pre2000 - 1st:12 2nd:9 3rd:3 Ran:51
Win Prizemoney £24,935 *Total Prizemoney* £35,083
Wins * 1999 *May Wolver (Std) C 9.4f 46*
1999 *Mar Southw (SLW) C 12f 68*
1998 *May Wolver (STD) S 12f 66+*
1998 *Apr Southw (STD) C 12f 64*
1998 *Apr Southw (STD) S 12f 66*
1998 *Mar Southw (STD) S 11f 55*
1998 *Jan Wolver (STD) S 12f 57+*
1998 *Jan Wolver (STD) S 12f 57+*
1997 *Jun Wolver (STD) H 12f 62 74* <
1997 *Mar Wolver (STD) H 12f 57 62*
1996 *Aug Wolver (STD) H 12f 56 68+*
1996 Aug Kempto (G-F) H 12f 58 61+
2000 Turf 0-1: (10f) (gd) 2000 AW 0-16: (8f, 9f, 11f 8, 12f 3, 16f 3) (Fibr 16)
Very moderate gelding, effective 9 to 12f, - acts on Fibr, favours left handed tracks. AW high 54. **D Shaw [1-25] K Nicholls (from Miss S J Wilton [6-11] Mar 1999).*

STATE OF CAUTION BHB 68f83a **RR 71f 83a** 1287a[2]
7 b g Reprimand 8.2f **(63)** - Hithermoor Lass (Red Alert) 7.6f **(66)**
Form - 2
2000 AW 0-1: (5f) (Dirt)
Very useful gelding, has broken blood-vessels, effective 5 to 6f, - acts on Dirt, mostly wears blinkers (effectively). (1st run) - 2nd of 10 to Rolo Tomasi (14 May Jagersro 5f Dirt RF 1287a). Inconsistent. Useful on the All-Weather, he is effective from five to seven furlongs and seems to have improved since being exported.
**C Bjorling in SWE [1-2] Aug 1999).*

STATE OPENING RR 5070[20]
3 ch f Absalom 7.1f **(56)** - Lightning Legend (Lord Gayle (USA)) 8.8f **(62)**
Form - 0
Record 2000 - 1st:0 2nd:0 3rd:0 Ran:1
2000 Turf 0-1: (12f) (g-s)
Scopey, currently very poor filly.
**Miss Z C Davison [0-1] Highly Charged Partnership.*

STATEROOM (USA) RR 55f 4607[7]
2 ch c Affirmed (USA) 10.3f **(75)** - Sleet (USA) (Summer Squall (USA))
Form - 7
Record 2000 - 1st:0 2nd:0 3rd:0 Ran:1
2000 Turf 0-1: (7f) (g-s)
Currently fair colt. **J A R Toller [0-1] Lady Sophia Topley.*

STATE SHINTO (USA) RR 119f 3736a[9]
4 br h Pleasant Colony (USA) 12.4f **(88)** - Sha Tha (USA) (Mr Prospector (USA)) 8.8f **(78)**
Form - 830
Record 2000 - 1st:0 2nd:0 3rd:1 Ran:3
Pre2000 - 1st:3 2nd:3 3rd:0 Ran:6
Win Prizemoney £70,115 *Total Prizemoney* £127,557
Wins 1999 Oct Longch (HVY) G2 9.8f 119 <
1999 Spt Longch (SFT) G3 10f 115
1998 Nov Saint- (HVY) L 8f 95+
2000 Turf 0-3: (10f, 12f 2) (sft, gd 2)
High-class colt, effective 10f, acts on hvy to gd, has worn blinkers. Turf high 116 - 3rd of 8 to Greek Dance (30 Jly Munich 10f sft RF 3353a). A dual Group winner when trained by Andre Fabre in 1999, he was lightly raced for Saeed bin Suroor last year, running his best race when short-headed by Greek Dance in a Group One at

Munich. He seems not to stay a mile and a half and needs soft or heavy ground. **S bin Suroor [0-3] (from A Fabre in FR [3-6] Oct 1999).*

STATE WIND (IRE) BHB 30f35a **RR 38f 35a** 1203[25]

4 ch g Forest Wind (USA) - Kowalski (IRE) (Cyrano de Bergerac) 6f **(68)**
Form - 0605800
Record 2000 - 1st:0 2nd:0 3rd:0 Ran:7
Pre2000 - 1st:0 2nd:2 3rd:2 Ran:15
Win Prizemoney £0 *Total Prizemoney* £2,103
2000 Turf 0-4: (6f, 7f, 8f, 9f) (g-s, g-f, frm 2) 2000 AW 0-3: (7f, 8f 2) (Fibr 3)
Leggy, very moderate gelding, effective 7f, - acts on Fibr, often wears blinkers (effectively), likes left handed tracks, likes tight tracks. Turf high 38. AW high 33. Inconsistent.
**D Shaw [0-7] The Denton Partnership (from N P Littmoden [0-15] Aug 1999).*

STATOSILVER RR 37f 5052[13]

2 b c Puissance 7.1f **(60)** - Silver Blessings (Statoblest)
Form - 50
Record 2000 - 1st:0 2nd:0 3rd:0 Ran:2
2000 Turf 0-2: (5f, 6f) (sft, gd)
Currently very moderate colt. Turf high 37 (began Oct).
**Mrs A Duffield [0-2] T Shaw & S Smith.*

STATOYORK BHB 62f46a **RR 64f 46a** 5003[16]

7 b g Statoblest 6.4f **(63)** - Ultimate Dream (Kafu) 6f **(47)**
Form - 0050700721415000
Record 2000 - 1st:2 2nd:1 3rd:0 Ran:16
Pre2000 - 1st:5 2nd:5 3rd:6 Ran:63
Win Prizemoney £34,320 *Total Prizemoney* £45,427

Wins								
* 2000	Spt	Haydoc	(HVY)	H	5f	59	64	
* 2000	Aug	Carlis	(GD)	H	5f	52	58	
* 1999	Jun	Ripon	(G-F)	H	5f	65	69+	<
* 1999	May	Ripon	(G-S)	H	5f	60	61	
* 1999	May	Carlis	(FRM)		5f		59	
* 1998	Aug	Pontef	(G-F)	H	5f	52	57	
1996	Jun	Ayr	(G-F)		7f		48+	

2000 Turf 2-16: (5f 2-14, 6f 2) (g-s 1-2, gd 4, g-f 5, frm 1-5)
Average gelding, has broken blood-vessels, effective 5 to 6f, best at 5f, acts on g-s to frm, best on g-f, has worn blinkers, excels at Carlisle and Ripon. Turf high 64 - 1st of 16 getting 11lb from Sharp Hat (2 Spt Haydock RF 4161). **D Shaw [6-65] M Torley (from B W Hills [1-14] Jly 1997).*

STATUE GALLERY (IRE) BHB 79f **RR 75f** 4673[6]

2 ch c Cadeaux Genereux 7.9f **(76)** - Kinlochewe **(99f)** (Old Vic)
Form - 5216
Record 2000 - 1st:1 2nd:1 3rd:0 Ran:4
Win Prizemoney £3,432 *Total Prizemoney* £4,497
Wins * **2000** Aug Bright (FRM) 6f 74 <
2000 Turf 1-4: (6f 1-4) (g-s, g-f, frm 1-2)
Above-average colt. Turf high 74 (began Aug) - 1st of 6 from Kaluki (30 Aug Brighton RF 4096). Not impressive when landing the odds at Brighton. **J A R Toller [1-4] Duke of Devonshire.*

STAY BEHIND RR 82+f 4191[3]

2 ch f Elmaamul (USA) 8.1f **(70)** - I Will Lead (USA) (Seattle Slew (USA)) 9.4f **(76)**
Form - 3
Record 2000 - 1st:0 2nd:0 3rd:1 Ran:1
Win Prizemoney £0 *Total Prizemoney* £669
2000 Turf 0-1: (8f) (g-f)
Currently decent filly. (1st run) - 3rd of 15 getting 5lb from Hill Country (3 Spt Kempton 8f g-f RF 4191).
**Mrs A J Perrett [0-1] K Abdulla.*

STAYIN ALIVE (USA) BHB 83f **RR 67f** 804[16]

3 b br c Sword Dance 9.4f **(67)** - Marilyn's Mystique (USA) (Dearest Doctor (USA))
Form - 1880
Record 2000 - 1st:0 2nd:0 3rd:0 Ran:3
Pre2000 - 1st:1 2nd:0 3rd:0 Ran:3
Win Prizemoney £3,468 *Total Prizemoney* £4,099
Wins * 1999 *Dec Lingfi (STD)* *7f* *95+* <
2000 Turf 0-1: (6f) (gd) 2000 AW 0-2: (8f, 10f) (Equi, Dirt)

Workmanlike, very useful colt, effective 7f, - acts on Equi. AW high 78. **G A Butler [1-4] Gary Seidler (from A G Foster [0-1] Oct 1999).*

STEALTHY TIMES BHB 55f80a **RR 65f 80a** 5105[12]

3 ch f Timeless Times (USA) 6.1f **(56)** - Stealthy (Kind of Hush) 10.1f **(62)**
Form - 00005540070
Record 2000 - 1st:0 2nd:0 3rd:0 Ran:11
Pre2000 - 1st:1 2nd:0 3rd:0 Ran:1
Win Prizemoney £3,202 *Total Prizemoney* £3,514
Wins * 1999 Jly Nottin (GD) 6.1f 86+ <
2000 Turf 0-10: (6f 2, 7f 5, 8f 3) (g-s, gd 4, g-f 4, frm) 2000 AW 0-1: (6f) (Fibr)
Neat, average filly, effective 6f, acts on g-f. Turf high 77. Becoming disappointing. **J G Given [1-12] John Wills.*

STEAMROLLER STANLY BHB 42f52a **RR 52df 52a** 3575[8]

7 b g Shirley Heights 12.1f **(76)** - Miss Demure (Shy Groom (USA)) 10f **(66)**
Form - 43335246807412208
Record 2000 - 1st:1 2nd:3 3rd:1 Ran:14
Pre2000 - 1st:8 2nd:2 3rd:11 Ran:39
Win Prizemoney £34,037 *Total Prizemoney* £50,626

Wins								
* **2000**	*Jun*	*Southw*	*(STD)*	*C*	*14f*		*50+*	
1999	*Jun*	*Southw*	*(STD)*	*C*	*16f*		*84*	
1999	*Apr*	*Wolver*	*(STD)*	*H*	*14.8f*	*90*	*85*	
1999	*Feb*	*Lingfi*	*(SLW)*		*10f*		*93*	<
1998	*Feb*	*Lingfi*	*(SLW)*		*10f*		*91*	
1997	*Feb*	*Lingfi*	*(STD)*		*10f*		*90*	
1997	*Jan*	*Lingfi*	*(STD)*	*H*	*12f*	*80*	*90*	
1996	*Nov*	*Lingfi*	*(STD)*		*12f*		*84*	
1996	Jun	Newbur	(G-F)	H	13.3f	65	69	

2000 Turf 0-1: (11f) (g-s) 2000 AW 1-13: (12f 3, 13f, 14f 1-2, 15f, 16f 6) (Equi 2, Fibr 1-11)
Fair gelding, effective 12 to 16f, - acts on Fibr, has worn blinkers, favours left handed tracks, favours tight tracks. AW high 67. Formerly smart on the Flat and especially on Equitrack, he can still win staying events on sand when able to dominate, but he has also been beaten at very short prices and may not be completely trustworthy these days.
**D W Chapman [1-11] David Chapman (from K R Burke [2-19] Jan 2000).*

STEEL BAND BHB 91f **RR 87f** 4488[2]

2 b c Kris 10f **(75)** - Quaver (USA) (The Minstrel (CAN)) 10f **(72)**
Form - 312
Record 2000 - 1st:1 2nd:1 3rd:1 Ran:3
Win Prizemoney £3,493 *Total Prizemoney* £5,426
Wins * **2000** Aug Chepst (G-F) 8.1f 87 <
2000 Turf 1-3: (7f 2, 8f 1-1) (g-f, frm 1-2)
Currently useful colt. Turf high 87 (began Aug) - 2nd of 5 to Cafeteria Bay (18 Spt Leicester 7f g-f RF 4488) - also 1st of 9 from Kings of Europe (28 Aug Chepstow RF 4030).
**H Candy [1-3] Girsonfield Ltd.*

STEEL TRADER RR 40?f 1727[5]

3 b c Bin Ajwaad (IRE) - Miss Gorgeous (IRE) (Damister (USA)) 9f **(73)**
Form - 5
Record 2000 - 1st:0 2nd:0 3rd:0 Ran:1
2000 Turf 0-1: (8f) (gd)
Leggy, currently moderate colt. **M Brittain [0-1] Mel Brittain.*

STEINITZ RR 79+f 3397[7]

2 ch c Nashwan (USA) 10.3f **(79)** - Circe's Isle (Be My Guest (USA)) 9.3f **(67)**
Form - 27
Record 2000 - 1st:0 2nd:1 3rd:0 Ran:2
Win Prizemoney £0 *Total Prizemoney* £2,240
2000 Turf 0-2: (7f 2) (g-f, frm)
Currently above-average colt. Turf high 79 (1st run) (began Jly) - 2nd of 12 to No Excuse Needed (8 Jly Sandown 7f frm RF 2644).
**J L Dunlop [0-2] Benny Andersson.*

STEPASTRAY BHB 51f **RR 54f** 4199[9]

3 gr g Alhijaz 7.7f **(57)** - Wandering Stranger (Petong) 6.6f **(58)**
Form - 08363380

Record 2000 - 1st:0 2nd:0 3rd:3 Ran:8
Pre2000 - 1st:0 2nd:0 3rd:0 Ran:3
Win Prizemoney £0 *Total Prizemoney* £1,889
2000 Turf 0-8: (9f, 10f 4, 11f 3) (g-f 3, frm 4, hrd)
Leggy, fair gelding, effective 9 to 11f, acts on g-f to hrd, prefers left handed tracks, prefers tight tracks. Turf high 54 - 3rd of 6 getting 3lb from Winged Angel (23 Jly Redcar 11f g-f RF 3056). Consistent.
**R E Barr [0-8] D Thomson (from P G Murphy [0-3] Aug 1999).*

STEP ON DEGAS BHB 49f51a **RR 47f 51a** 4147[15]

7 b m Superpower 6.6f **(58)** - Vivid Impression (Cure The Blues (USA)) 9.5f **(63)**
Form - 080
Record 2000 - 1st:0 2nd:0 3rd:0 Ran:3
Pre2000 - 1st:4 2nd:9 3rd:5 Ran:52
Win Prizemoney £9,998 *Total Prizemoney* £21,008
Wins * 1998 May Bright (FRM) H 6f 54 58
1997 Aug Bright (G-F) 7f 54
1997 *Jan Lingfi (STD) H 7f 63 63*
1996 Jun Warwic (FRM) H 5f 63 64 <
2000 Turf 0-3: (7f, 8f, 11f) (sft, g-f 2)
Fair mare, effective 6 to 8f, best at 7f, acts on gd to frm - acts on Fibr, best on g-f, has worn blinkers, excels at Epsom. Turf high 47. Inconsistent. On a lengthy losing run since scoring at Brighton in May '98.
**Mrs A L M King [1-29] Mrs Pennie Muir (from M J Fetherston-Godley [3-22] Nov 1997).*

STEPPIN OUT BHB 65f60a **RR 66f 60a** 4384[27]

3 ch f First Trump - Mo Stopher **(31f)** (Sharpo) 7.7f **(59)**
Form - 170
Record 2000 - 1st:1 2nd:0 3rd:0 Ran:3
Win Prizemoney £3,575 *Total Prizemoney* £3,575
Wins * 2000 Jly Salisb (G-S) 6f 66 <
2000 Turf 1-3: (5f, 6f 1-1, 7f) (gd 1-2, g-f)
Workmanlike, currently average filly. Turf high 66 (1st run) (began Jly) - 1st of 8 from Ulysses Daughter (7 Jly Salisbury RF 2603).
**W Jarvis [1-3] Canisbay Bloodstock Ltd.*

STERLING GUARANTEE (USA) **RR 78+f** 4646[4]

2 b c Silver Hawk (USA) 11.2f **(85)** - Sterling Pound (USA) (Seeking the Gold (USA))
Form - 4
Record 2000 - 1st:0 2nd:0 3rd:0 Ran:1
Win Prizemoney £0 *Total Prizemoney* £439
2000 Turf 0-1: (8f) (g-f)
Currently above-average colt. **J H M Gosden [0-1] Cliveden Stud.*

STERLING HIGH (IRE) BHB 32f43a **RR 34f 43a** 5085[6]

5 b g Mujadil (USA) 7.7f **(70)** - Verusa (IRE) (Petorius) 7.3f **(61)**
Form - 7403548000076
Record 2000 - 1st:0 2nd:0 3rd:1 Ran:13
Pre2000 - 1st:3 2nd:0 3rd:2 Ran:26
Win Prizemoney £7,650 *Total Prizemoney* £8,824
Wins 1999 Spt Tramor (G-S) H 9f 47 51
1999 Spt Dundal (FRM) H 9f 41 47
1998 Aug Roscom (G-S) H 7f 53 71 <
2000 Turf 0-6: (7f, 8f, 10f 3, 11f) (hvy 2, sft, gd 2, frm) 2000 AW 0-7: (8f 4, 9f 3) (Fibr 7)
Moderate gelding, effective 8 to 9f, best at 9f, acts on g-s to frm - acts on Fibr, has worn blinkers. Turf high 34. AW high 51 - 3rd of 14 giving 12lb to Nice Balance (28 Jan Southwell 8f Fibr RF 0181). Inconsistent.
**D Carroll [0-13] Shamrock Society (from M Halford in IRE [3-26] Oct 1999).*

STEVAL BHB 57f45a **RR 57f 45a** 5171a[11]

3 ch f Efisio 7.7f **(69)** - Vannozza (Kris) 9.5f **(73)**
Form - 4013010
Record 2000 - 1st:2 2nd:0 3rd:1 Ran:7
Pre2000 - 1st:0 2nd:0 3rd:0 Ran:3
Win Prizemoney £6,870 *Total Prizemoney* £7,571
Wins * 2000 Spt Down R (GD) H 5f 57 <
2000 Jun Catter (SFT) 6f 39
2000 Turf 2-5: (5f 1-2, 6f 1-1, 8f 2) (hvy, sft, g-s 1-1, gd 1-1, g-f) 2000 AW 0-2: (5f 2) (Equi, Fibr)
Leggy, fair filly, effective 5f, acts on gd. Turf high 57 - 1st of 12 giving 9lb to Maghas (30 Spt Down Royal RF 4801a). AW high 30.
**Patrick Flynn in IRE [1-4] Mrs Geraldine Reilly-Maloney (from R Guest [1-6] Jun 2000).*

ST EXPEDIT BHB 108f **RR 109df** 3583[6]

3 b c Sadler's Wells (USA) 11.3f **(87)** - Miss Rinjani **(88f)** (Shirley Heights) 10.3f **(74)**
Form - 27127386
Record 2000 - 1st:1 2nd:2 3rd:1 Ran:8
Pre2000 - 1st:0 2nd:0 3rd:1 Ran:1
Win Prizemoney £7,085 *Total Prizemoney* £18,710
Wins * 2000 May Pontef (SFT) 10f 89 <
2000 Turf 1-8: (10f 1-4, 11f, 12f 3) (g-s, gd 1-6, g-f)
Scopey, Pattern-class colt, effective 10 to 12f, acts on g-s to gd, prefers tight tracks. Turf high 109. Inclined to pull in his early starts, he just went down to Roscius after a protracted struggle in the Predominate Stakes at Goodwood and did as well as could be expected when seventh in the Derby. May have found the ground too fast when third of five in a Haydock Listed event and down the field at Goodwood. **G Wragg [1-9] J L C Pearce.*

ST FLORENT (USA) BHB 63f **RR 69f** 4203[7]

2 b f Thunder Gulch (USA) - Honfleur (IRE) **(97f)** (Sadler's Wells (USA)) 10f **(76)**
Form - 28007
Record 2000 - 1st:0 2nd:1 3rd:0 Ran:5
Win Prizemoney £0 *Total Prizemoney* £1,100
2000 Turf 0-5: (7f 3, 8f 2) (g-f 3, frm 2)
Average filly, has worn blinkers. Turf high 69 (began Jly).
**J H M Gosden [0-5] R E Sangster.*

ST GEORGE'S BOY BHB 34f **RR 36f** 3095[8]

3 b g Inchinor 8.9f **(64)** - Deanta in Eirinn (Red Sunset) 8.2f **(63)**
Form - 06002458
Record 2000 - 1st:0 2nd:1 3rd:0 Ran:7
Pre2000 - 1st:0 2nd:0 3rd:0 Ran:3
Win Prizemoney £0 *Total Prizemoney* £675
2000 Turf 0-4: (8f, 11f, 14f, 16f) (gd, frm 3) 2000 AW 0-3: (8f, 9f, 12f) (Equi, Fibr 2)
Very moderate gelding, effective 11f, acts on frm, has worn blinkers, likes left handed tracks, likes tight tracks. Turf high 36 - 2nd of 12 getting 25lb from Penshiel (14 Jun Lingfield 11f frm RF 1967). AW high 24.
**H Morrison [0-4] John Goddard (from J Wharton [0-6] Mar 2000).*

ST HELENSFIELD BHB 87f80a **RR 92f 80a** 3761[2]

5 ch g Kris 10f **(75)** - On Credit (FR) (No Pass No Sale) 11.9f **(85)**
Form - 03032201182
Record 2000 - 1st:2 2nd:3 3rd:2 Ran:11
Pre2000 - 1st:2 2nd:1 3rd:2 Ran:12
Win Prizemoney £18,403 *Total Prizemoney* £33,485
Wins * 2000 Jly Newcas (FRM) H 14.4f 85 92 <
*** 2000** Jly Ripon (G-F) H 12.3f 81 85
* 1999 Jly Newcas (FRM) H 10.1f 85 86
* 1997 Spt Bath (G-F) 10.2f 86+
2000 Turf 2-10: (10f 4, 12f 1-3, 13f, 14f 1-2) (gd 3, g-f 2-5, frm, hrd)
2000 AW 0-1: (12f) (Equi)
Useful gelding, effective 9 to 14f, acts on gd to hrd, best on g-f, has worn blinkers, excels at Newcastle. Turf high 92 - 1st of 2 giving 21lb to Maraha (29 Jly Newcastle RF 3208) - also 1st of 5 giving 9lb to Original Spin (22 Jly Ripon RF 3038). Consistent. He improved for front-running tactics in the second half of the season. Suited by fast ground, he probably stays a mile and three-quarters and is game.
**M Johnston [4-23] Paul Dean.*

STICIBOOTS BHB 52f52a **RR 52a** 1179[14]

3 b g Batshoof 9.5f **(66)** - Satiric (IRE) (Doyoun) 9f **(69)**
Form - 5570
Record 2000 - 1st:0 2nd:0 3rd:0 Ran:4
2000 Turf 0-1: (14f) (g-f) 2000 AW 0-3: (8f, 12f 2) (Fibr 3)
Fair gelding, has broken blood-vessels. AW high 53.
**N P Littmoden [0-4] Wetherby Racing Bureau 43.*

STICKS **RR 55f** 1910[P]

2 ch f Aragon 7.7f **(58)** - Petiller (Monsanto (FR)) 6.5f **(59)**
Form - 3P
Record 2000 - 1st:0 2nd:0 3rd:1 Ran:2

Win Prizemoney £0 *Total Prizemoney* £390
2000 Turf 0-2: (6f, 7f) (gd, frm)
Fair filly. Turf high 55 (1st run) - 3rd of 13 getting 5lb from Time Maite (25 May Newcastle 6f gd RF 1440). (DEAD)
**C B B Booth [0-2] C B B Booth.*

STICKS AND STONES (IRE) BHB 30f **RR 34f** 3520[9]

8 b g Waajib 8.9f **(67)** - Maiacourt (Malacate (USA)) 8.8f **(63)**
Form - 720040
Record 2000 - 1st:0 2nd:1 3rd:0 Ran:6
Pre2000 - 1st:1 2nd:0 3rd:0 Ran:8
Win Prizemoney £3,739 *Total Prizemoney* £5,537
2000 Turf 0-4: (10f, 12f 2, 14f) (gd, g-f, frm 2) 2000 AW 0-2: (8f, 12f) (Fibr 2)
Very moderate gelding, has worn blinkers. Turf high 34. AW high 34. Inconsistent.
**J A Gilbert [0-6] Terry Connors (from Mrs J Cecil [1-8] Jun 1996).*

STILL IN LOVE BHB 70f **RR 73df** 2258[3]

3 b f Emarati (USA) 6.6f **(63)** - In Love Again (IRE) **(67f)** (Prince Rupert (FR))
Form - 253
Record 2000 - 1st:0 2nd:1 3rd:1 Ran:3
Pre2000 - 1st:0 2nd:0 3rd:1 Ran:1
Win Prizemoney £0 *Total Prizemoney* £1,715
2000 Turf 0 3: (6f, 7f 2) (gd, g-f, frm)
Workmanlike, above-average filly. Turf high 73 (1st run) - 2nd of 6 getting 5lb from Noblenor (4 May Redcar 7f gd RF 1022).
**H R A Cecil [0-4] W H Ponsonby.*

STILL WATERS BHB 51a **RR 49?f** 2819[3]

5 b g Rainbow Quest (USA) 11.2f **(81)** - Krill (Kris) 9.5f **(73)**
Form - 70600313
Record 2000 - 1st:1 2nd:0 3rd:2 Ran:7
Pre2000 - 1st:1 2nd:1 3rd:0 Ran:9
Win Prizemoney £3,926 *Total Prizemoney* £5,585
Wins * **2000** *Jun Southw (STD) H* 7f 45 49
1999 *Jan Southw (STD) H* 8f 62 68 <
2000 Turf 0-1: (7f) (hrd) 2000 AW 1-6: (7f 1-3, 8f 3) (Fibr 1-6)
Fair gelding, effective 8f, - acts on Fibr, likes left handed tracks. AW high 49. Inconsistent.
**I A Wood [1-10] Neardown Stables (from K Bell [1-4] Apr 1999).*

STILMEMAITE BHB 52f **RR 64f** 2033[4]

2 b f Komaite (USA) 6.9f **(61)** - Stilvella (Camden Town) 9.3f **(53)**
Form - 35774
Record 2000 - 1st:0 2nd:0 3rd:1 Ran:5
Win Prizemoney £0 *Total Prizemoney* £1,193
2000 Turf 0-5: (5f 3, 6f 2) (sft, g-s, gd, g-f 2)
Average filly. Turf high 64. **N Bycroft [0-5] J A Swinburne.*

STINGER (JPN) **RR 113f** 1286a[1]

4 m
Form - 01
2000 Turf 1-1: (7f 1-1) (frm 1-1)
Currently Group-class. (1st run) - 1st of 18 getting 9lb from Black Hawk (14 May Fuchu RF 1286a). **K Fujisawa in JPN [1-2] T Yoshida.*

STITCH IN TIME BHB 47f60a **RR 46f 60a** 5020[3]

4 ch g Inchinor 8.9f **(64)** - Late Matinee (Red Sunset) 8.2f **(63)**
Form - 22338205433323
Record 2000 - 1st:0 2nd:4 3rd:6 Ran:14
Pre2000 - 1st:0 2nd:0 3rd:0 Ran:7
Win Prizemoney £0 *Total Prizemoney* £4,792
2000 Turf 0-11: (7f 2, 8f 3, 9f, 10f 4, 12f) (g-s 2, gd 3, g-f 3, frm 3) 2000 AW 0-3: (8f 2, 12f) (Fibr 3)
Leggy, average gelding, effective 7 to 10f, best at 8f, acts on g-s to g-f - acts on Fibr, has worn blinkers, prefers left handed tracks, prefers tight tracks, does well at Brighton. Turf high 47 - 2nd of 18 giving 1lb to Danzas (13 Apr Brighton 7f gd RF 0696). AW high 49 (began Jly) - 3rd of 13 giving 1lb to Robbies Dream (19 Aug Wolverhampton 8f Fibr RF 3812).
**G C Bravery [0-21] H P Carrington.*

ST IVES BHB 34f42a **RR 40f 42a** 5005[9]

3 b c Puissance 7.1f **(60)** - Clan Scotia **(46f)** (Clantime)
Form - 06004080
Record 2000 - 1st:0 2nd:0 3rd:0 Ran:8
Pre2000 - 1st:0 2nd:0 3rd:0 Ran:3
2000 Turf 0-6: (6f 2, 7f, 8f 3) (g-s, g-f 3, frm 2) 2000 AW 0-2: (6f 2) (Equi, Fibr)
Light-framed, moderate colt, has worn blinkers. Turf high 40. AW high 31. **V Soane [0-11] Mrs M Watts And Miss R Hatley.*

ST LAWRENCE (CAN) BHB 34f51a **RR 37f 51a** 3430[10]

6 gr g With Approval (CAN) 8.7f **(80)** - Mingan Isle (USA) (Lord Avie (USA)) 5.3f **(61)**
Form - 672312213370240
Record 2000 - 1st:2 2nd:4 3rd:3 Ran:13
Pre2000 - 1st:0 2nd:4 3rd:2 Ran:24
Win Prizemoney £3,475 *Total Prizemoney* £12,022
Wins * **2000** *Feb Southw (STD) H* 16f 42 56 <
2000 *Jan Southw (STD) H* 12f 41 46
2000 Turf 0-2: (12f, 16f) (gd, frm) 2000 AW 2-11: (11f, 12f 1-2, 14f 2, 16f 1-6) (Equi, Fibr 2-10)
Fair gelding, effective 10 to 16f, acts on g-f - acts on Fibr, has worn blinkers, likes left handed tracks, favours tight tracks. Turf high 37. AW high 56 - 2nd of 12 getting 17lb from French Spice (10 Feb Wolverhampton 12f Fibr RF 0253) - also 1st of 9 getting 10lb from Fearsome Factor (18 Feb Southwell RF 0311). He is an effective stayer in modest company on Fibresand these days.
**B S Rothwell [1-13] Northern Cladding Ltd (from N Tinkler [1-12] Jan 2000).*

ST MATTHEW (USA) **RR 45f** 5110[8]

2 b c Lear Fan (USA) 10.4f **(80)** - Social Crown (USA) (Chief's Crown (USA)) 9.8f **(72)**
Form - 8
Record 2000 - 1st:0 2nd:0 3rd:0 Ran:1
2000 Turf 0-1: (8f) (gd)
Currently moderate colt. **J W Hills [0-1] George Tong.*

ST NICHOLAS BHB 50f **RR 57f** 5102[14]

2 b g Komaite (USA) 6.9f **(61)** - Nikoola Eve (Roscoe Blake) 11f **(66)**
Form - 70050
Record 2000 - 1st:0 2nd:0 3rd:0 Ran:5
2000 Turf 0-4: (6f 2, 7f, 8f) (g-s, gd 3) 2000 AW 0 1: (7f) (Fibr)
Fair gelding. Turf high 57 (began Jly). **D Shaw [0-5] D C G Cooper.*

STOCK PROOF **RR 61f** 4702[12]

2 b c Green Desert (USA) 7.8f **(78)** - Kissing Gate (USA) **(47f 59a)** (Easy Goer (USA))
Form - 0
Record 2000 - 1st:0 2nd:0 3rd:0 Ran:1
2000 Turf 0-1: (7f) (g-f)
Currently average colt. **Sir Michael Stoute [0-1] The Queen.*

STOLEN MUSIC (IRE) BHB 35f **RR 39f** 2251[8]

7 b m Taufan (USA) 8.3f **(65)** - Causa Sua (Try My Best (USA)) 7.6f **(67)**
Form - 7328
Record 2000 - 1st:0 2nd:1 3rd:1 Ran:4
Pre2000 - 1st:5 2nd:1 3rd:3 Ran:44
Win Prizemoney £15,216 *Total Prizemoney* £19,051
Wins * 1999 Aug Catter (FRM) H 13.8f 43 47 <
* 1999 Jun Redcar (FRM) H 14.1f 32 35
* 1998 Oct Redcar (HVY) H 14.1f 33 36
* 1998 Spt Beverl (G-F) H 9.9f 29 33
* 1998 Aug Beverl (G-F) H 9.9f 25 30
2000 Turf 0-4: (14f 3, 16f) (gd, frm 3)
Very moderate mare, effective 14 to 16f, best at 14f, acts on gd to frm, has worn blinkers, favours left handed tracks, favours tight tracks. Turf high 39 - 3rd of 6 getting 9lb from Night City (9 Jun Catterick 14f gd RF 1837). Inconsistent.
**R E Barr [5-46] P Cartmell (from Major D N Chappell [0-3] Spt 1996).*

STOLI (IRE) **RR 74f** 4466[6]

2 ch c Spectrum (IRE) - Crystal City (Kris) 9.5f **(73)**
Form - 86
Record 2000 - 1st:0 2nd:0 3rd:0 Ran:2
2000 Turf 0-2: (7f 2) (sft, g-f)
Currently above-average colt. Turf high 74 (began Spt).
**P J Makin [0-2] Brian Brackpool.*

STONE COLD BHB 48f **RR 55df** 4749[12]
3 ch g Inchinor 8.9f **(64)** - Vaula (Henbit (USA)) 9f **(61)**
Form - 0
Record 2000 - 1st:0 2nd:0 3rd:0 Ran:1
Pre2000 - 1st:0 2nd:0 3rd:0 Ran:3
2000 Turf 0-1: (10f) (gd)
Light-framed, fair gelding.
**T D Easterby [0-4] Six Diamonds Partnership.*

STONEY GARNETT BHB 63f60a **RR 69f 60a** 4809[14]
3 b f Emarati (USA) 6.6f **(63)** - Etourdie (USA) (Arctic Tern (USA)) 8.9f **(69)**
Form - 12600
Record 2000 - 1st:1 2nd:1 3rd:0 Ran:5
Pre2000 - 1st:0 2nd:1 3rd:3 Ran:8
Win Prizemoney £2,731 *Total Prizemoney* £5,486
Wins * **2000** May Bright (SFT) H 5.3f 65 69 <
2000 Turf 1-5: (5f 1-2, 6f 3) (g-s, gd 1-2, frm 2)
Scopey, average filly, effective 5 to 6f, best at 6f, acts on gd to frm, best on frm, has worn blinkers. Turf high 69 (1st run) - 1st of 6 giving 10lb to Tick Tock (26 May Brighton RF 1462). Inconsistent.
**M S Saunders [1-13] David Chown.*

STOP BY (IRE) **RR 108f** 4416a[4]
5 gr h
Form - 44
2000 Turf 0-2: (12f 2) (gd 2)
Currently Pattern-class, has worn blinkers. Turf high 108 (began Jly). He had the distinction of acting as Montjeu's pacemaker.
**J E Hammond in FR [0-3].*

STOPPES BROW BHB 70f80a **RR 74f 80a** 4824[7]
8 b g Primo Dominie 7.2f **(67)** - So Bold (Never so Bold) 6.3f **(66)**
Form - 400652563447
Record 2000 - 1st:0 2nd:1 3rd:1 Ran:12
Pre2000 - 1st:12 2nd:12 3rd:10 Ran:80
Win Prizemoney £48,100 *Total Prizemoney* £78,490
Wins * 1999 Aug Epsom (GD) H 8.5f 77 80
* 1999 Jun Kempto (GD) H 8f 69 71
* *1999 Apr Lingfi (STD) H 7f 65 75*
* *1999 Apr Lingfi (STD) H 8f 65 74*
* 1998 May Goodwo (G-F) H 8f 67 72
* 1996 May Newbur (SFT) H 6f 70 71
2000 Turf 0-11: (8f 5, 9f 5, 10f) (sft, g-s 2, gd 4, g-f 4) 2000 AW 0-1: (9f) (Fibr)
Above-average gelding, effective 7 to 9f, best at 9f, acts on g-s to frm - acts on AW, best on g-f, mostly wears blinkers (effectively), favours tight tracks, and likes Lingfield. Turf high 75 - 5th of 11 giving 19lb to Adobe (23 Jun Goodwood 8f g-f RF 2220). (1st run) - 4th of 7 to Pantar (11 Mar Wolverhampton 9f Fibr RF 0434). He ran some fine races last season, but was unable to force his head in front. **G L Moore [12-92] Bryan Pennick.*

STOP THE TRAFFIC (IRE) BHB 39f41a **RR 61f 41a** 5018[2]
3 b f College Chapel - Miss Bagatelle (Mummy's Pet) 7.7f **(60)**
Form - 4252285580805567882
Record 2000 - 1st:0 2nd:4 3rd:0 Ran:19
Pre2000 - 1st:0 2nd:0 3rd:2 Ran:4
Win Prizemoney £0 *Total Prizemoney* £5,533
2000 Turf 0-8: (6f 3, 7f 3, 8f 2) (g-s, gd 2, g-f 2, frm 3) 2000 AW 0-11: (5f, 6f 6, 7f 4) (Equi 2, Fibr 9)
Unfurnished, average filly, effective 6 to 7f, best at 6f, acts on g-s - acts on Fibr, has worn blinkers, likes left handed tracks, prefers tight tracks. Turf high 61 (1st run) - 5th of 15 giving 11lb to Printsmith (4 Jun Warwick 7f g-s RF 1706). AW high 68 - 2nd of 12 getting 11lb from Dancing Empress (4 May Wolverhampton 6f Fibr RF 1025). **C N Allen [0-23] Kentavr (UK) Ltd.*

STOPWATCH (IRE) BHB 38f70a **RR 41f 70a** 317[7]
5 b g Lead on Time (USA) 7.5f **(69)** - Rose Bonbon (FR) (High Top) 10.2f **(67)**
Form - 7
Record 2000 - 1st:0 2nd:0 3rd:0 Ran:1
Pre2000 - 1st:1 2nd:1 3rd:1 Ran:14
Win Prizemoney £3,767 *Total Prizemoney* £5,791
Wins 1998 Apr Cork (G-S) 8f 90 <
2000 AW 0-1: (16f) (Equi)
Moderate gelding, has worn blinkers. Becoming disappointing.
**Mrs L C Jewell [1-12] The Stopwatch Partnership (from T Stack in IRE [1-10] Spt 1998).*

STORM CRY (USA) BHB 58f56a **RR 31f 56a** 4275[19]
5 b g Hermitage (USA) 8.6f **(84)** - Doonesbury Lady (USA) (Doonesbury (USA)) 7.7f **(99)**
Form - 00000
Record 2000 - 1st:0 2nd:0 3rd:0 Ran:5
Pre2000 - 1st:2 2nd:1 3rd:1 Ran:17
Win Prizemoney £6,011 *Total Prizemoney* £8,849
Wins * 1999 Spt Lingfi (HVY) H 7f 63 65 <
1998 May Bath (FRM) 8f 64+
2000 Turf 0-3: (7f 3) (gd, g-f, frm) 2000 AW 0-2: (7f, 8f) (Fibr 2)
Moderate gelding, effective 8f, acts on g-s, has worn blinkers. Turf high 31. AW high 41. Inconsistent.
**M S Saunders [1-16] Brian McFadzean (from Major D N Chappell [1-6] Jly 1998).*

STORMDANCER (IRE) BHB 58f **RR 56f** 956[9]
3 ch c Bluebird (USA) 7.9f **(71)** - Unspoiled (Tina's Pet) 6.8f **(59)**
Form - 0
Record 2000 - 1st:0 2nd:0 3rd:0 Ran:1
Pre2000 - 1st:0 2nd:0 3rd:0 Ran:3
2000 Turf 0-1: (12f) (sft)
Strong, fair colt. **R Hannon [0-4] J A Forsyth.*

STORM DREAM (IRE) **RR 109f** 1584a[3]
3 b f Catrail (USA) - Mamara Reef **(57df)** (Salse (USA)) 7.5f **(66)**
Form - 23
2000 Turf 0-2: (8f 2) (g-s, g-f)
Pattern-class filly. Turf high 109 - 3rd of 13 to Crimplene (28 May Curragh 8f g-s RF 1584a). Still a maiden, but ran a blinder when beaten a short head by Preseli in the Leopardstown 1000 Guineas Trial before finishing third in the Irish Guineas.
**K Prendergast in IRE [0-4] Mrs Isobel Foley.*

STORM FROM HEAVEN (IRE) BHB 52a **RR 52a** 4993[8]
2 b br g Mujadil (USA) 7.7f **(70)** - Lady of Man (So Blessed) 8.7f **(67)**
Form - 48
Record 2000 - 1st:0 2nd:0 3rd:0 Ran:2
2000 AW 0-2: (6f 2) (Fibr 2)
Currently fair gelding. AW high 53 (began Oct).
**P C Haslam [0-2] P C Haslam.*

STORM HILL (IRE) BHB 73f **RR 74f** 1964[U]
4 b h Caerleon (USA) 10.9f **(79)** - Jackie Berry (Connaught) 7.7f **(63)**
Form - 082U
Record 2000 - 1st:0 2nd:1 3rd:0 Ran:4
Pre2000 - 1st:0 2nd:0 3rd:1 Ran:4
Win Prizemoney £0 *Total Prizemoney* £2,080
2000 Turf 0-4: (10f, 12f 3) (gd 2, g-f 2)
Light-framed, above-average colt, effective 10 to 12f, acts on gd to g-f. Turf high 74 - 8th of 15 giving 3lb to Wait For The Will (18 May Salisbury 12f gd RF 1274).
**J H M Gosden [0-4] R E Sangster & A K Collins (from A G Foster [0-1] Oct 1999).*

STORMING FOLEY BHB 61f **RR 63f** 1600[8]
2 ch c Makbul - Cute Dancer (Remainder Man) 11.2f **(45)**
Form - 4258
Record 2000 - 1st:0 2nd:1 3rd:0 Ran:4
Win Prizemoney £0 *Total Prizemoney* £913
2000 Turf 0-4: (5f 3, 6f) (gd 2, g-f, frm)
Average colt. Turf high 63.
**W G M Turner [0-4] Foley Steelstock.*

STORMING HOME BHB 100f **RR 98f** 4733[9]
2 b c Machiavellian (USA) 9.8f **(83)** - Try To Catch Me (USA) (Shareef Dancer (USA)) 9.9f **(73)**
Form - 0120
Record 2000 - 1st:1 2nd:1 3rd:0 Ran:4
Win Prizemoney £4,251 *Total Prizemoney* £11,151
Wins * **2000** Aug Newmar (GD) 7f 91 <
2000 Turf 1-4: (7f 1-4) (gd, g-f 1-2, frm)
Very useful colt. Turf high 98 (began Jly) - 2nd of 7 to King's Ironbridge (19 Aug Sandown 7f g-f RF 3802) - also 1st of 10 from

Canada (4 Aug Newmarket RF 3371). He looked a shade unlucky when second behind Kingís Ironbridge in the Group 3 Solario Stakes, but did nothing for the form when unplaced at Newmarket in September. He will probably struggle in Group company this year. **B W Hills [1-4] Maktoum Al Maktoum.*

STORM KING (IRE) BHB 60f RR 63f 2858[5]

2 b c Mukaddamah (USA) 7.6f **(74)** - Busker (Bustino) 10.4f **(64)**
Form - 805
Record 2000 - 1st:0 2nd:0 3rd:0 Ran:3
2000 Turf 0-3: (6f 3) (gd, frm 2)
Currently average colt. Turf high 63. **A Berry [0-3] Andy Miller.*

STORMLESS BHB 40f RR 41f 5277[7]

9 b g Silly Prices 6.8f **(51)** - Phyl's Pet (Aberdeen) 9.4f **(55)**
Form - 7

Record	**2000** -	1st:0	2nd:0	3rd:0	Ran:1
	Pre2000 -	1st:4	2nd:4	3rd:3	Ran:31

Win Prizemoney £14,585 *Total Prizemoney* £20,598

Wins								
1998	May	Hamilt	(SFT)	H	8.3f	58	69	<
1997	May	Hamilt	(SFT)	H	8.3f	53	59	
1996	Aug	Ayr	(G-F)	H	10f	48	54	
1996	Jun	Ayr	(G-F)	H	10f	43	47	

2000 Turf 0-1: (16f) (g-s)
Moderate gelding, had broken blood-vessels. Consistent. (DEAD)
**J S Haldane [0-12] D St Clair (from J S Goldie [1-10] May 1998).*

STORM PRINCE (IRE) BHB 56f65a RR 40f 65a 4364[13]

3 ch g Prince of Birds (USA) - Petersford Girl (IRE) **(70f)** (Taufan (USA)) 7f **(57)**
Form - 680000

Record	**2000** -	1st:0	2nd:0	3rd:0	Ran:6
	Pre2000 -	1st:1	2nd:1	3rd:0	Ran:6

Win Prizemoney £2,220 *Total Prizemoney* £3,285
Wins 1999 Spt Leices (FRM) SH 8f 63 73 <
2000 Turf 0-4: (8f 2, 10f, 12f) (gd 2, g-f 2) 2000 AW 0-2: (8f, 9f) (Fibr 2)
Workmanlike, above-average gelding, effective 8f, acts on frm, has worn blinkers. Turf high 40. AW high 57. Becoming disappointing.
**J L Spearing [0-7] D J Oseman (from S C Williams [1-5] Spt 1999).*

STORMSWELL BHB 48f RR 51f 5195[7]

3 ch f Persian Bold 10f **(69)** - Stormswept (USA) (Storm Bird (CAN)) 10.3f **(74)**
Form - 003153048487

Record	**2000** -	1st:1	2nd:0	3rd:2	Ran:12
	Pre2000 -	1st:0	2nd:0	3rd:0	Ran:4

Win Prizemoney £3,835 *Total Prizemoney* £4,658
Wins 2000 Jun Hamilt (GD) H 8.3f 49 51 <
2000 Turf 1-12: (7f 3, 8f 1-5, 9f 2, 10f, 11f) (sft 2, g-s 2, gd 2, g-f 2, frm 1-4)
Fair filly. Turf high 52.
**J Hetherton [0-3] Exors of the late M J Paver (from R A Fahey [1-13] Aug 2000).*

STORMVILLE (IRE) BHB 60f RR 61f 4498[9]

3 b g Catrail (USA) - Haut Volee (Top Ville) 11.7f **(68)**
Form - 6408260

Record	**2000** -	1st:0	2nd:1	3rd:0	Ran:7
	Pre2000 -	1st:0	2nd:0	3rd:1	Ran:4

Win Prizemoney £0 *Total Prizemoney* £5,709
2000 Turf 0-7: (7f 2, 8f 2, 9f 2, 10f) (g-s, gd 3, frm 3)
Scopey, average gelding, effective 6 to 7f, acts on gd. Turf high 63. Inconsistent.
**M Brittain [0-11] Northgate Gold.*

STORM WIZARD (IRE) BHB 65f RR 77f 5201[6]

3 b g Catrail (USA) - Society Ball (Law Society (USA)) 9.9f **(70)**
Form - 34220066

Record	**2000** -	1st:0	2nd:2	3rd:1	Ran:8
	Pre2000 -	1st:0	2nd:0	3rd:0	Ran:1

Win Prizemoney £0 *Total Prizemoney* £3,872
2000 Turf 0-8: (9f, 10f 4, 11f, 12f 2) (sft 2, g-s 4, gd, g-f)
Scopey, above-average gelding, effective 10f, acts on g-s, likes tight tracks. Turf high 77 - 2nd of 9 giving 4lb to Fanfare (30 May Sandown 10f g-s RF 1555). Becoming disappointing. A fair maiden, he has looked rather one-paced.
**M R Channon [0-9] BEL Leisure Ltd.*

STORMY CREST (IRE) RR 32f 5296[8]

2 b c Catrail (USA) - Broken Wave (Bustino) 10.4f **(64)**
Form - 88
Record 2000 - 1st:0 2nd:0 3rd:0 Ran:2
2000 Turf 0-2: (5f, 7f) (g-s, gd)
Currently very moderate colt. Turf high 32 (began Oct).
**John Berry [0-2] J McCarthy.*

STORMY RAINBOW BHB 67f65a RR 65f 65a 4929[8]

3 b c Red Rainbow - Stormy Heights **(9f 44a)** (Golden Heights)
Form - 2258

Record	**2000** -	1st:0	2nd:2	3rd:0	Ran:4
	Pre2000 -	1st:0	2nd:0	3rd:0	Ran:1

Win Prizemoney £0 *Total Prizemoney* £1,510
2000 Turf 0-1: (7f) (g-s) 2000 AW 0-3: (8f 3) (Equi 2, Fibr)
Workmanlike, average colt. (1st run) - 5th of 16 giving 1lb to Slumbering (30 Spt Sandown 7f g-s RF 4753). AW high 69 (1st run) - 2nd of 6 to Bonaguil (26 Feb Lingfield 8f Equi RF 0361).
**V Soane [0-4] Michael Hancock (from R Simpson [0-1] Jun 1999).*

STORMY SKYE (IRE) BHB 72f RR 81df 4987[12]

4 b g Bluebird (USA) 7.9f **(71)** - Canna (Caerleon (USA)) 8.6f **(71)**
Form - 32460

Record	**2000** -	1st:0	2nd:1	3rd:1	Ran:5
	Pre2000 -	1st:0	2nd:1	3rd:1	Ran:7

Win Prizemoney £0 *Total Prizemoney* £5,776
2000 Turf 0-4: (12f, 14f, 18f 2) (gd 4) 2000 AW 0-1: (13f) (Equi)
Scopey, decent gelding, effective 18f, acts on gd, has worn blinkers. Turf high 81 - 2nd of 14 getting 4lb from Eastwell Hall (8 Jun Chepstow 18f gd RF 1804). Still a maiden on the level, he ran well when tackling a marathon trip at Chepstow in June. Goes well with some cut in the ground.
**G L Moore [1-11] Mrs Higson, Agnew, Pollock (from A J McNae [0-7] May 1999).*

STORMY VOYAGE RR 47f 2810[7]

2 b c Storm Bird (CAN) 8.5f **(82)** - Vivid Imagination (USA) (Raise A Man (USA)) 7.8f **(78)**
Form - 47
Record 2000 - 1st:0 2nd:0 3rd:0 Ran:2
Win Prizemoney £0 *Total Prizemoney* £275
2000 Turf 0-2: (6f 2) (g-f, frm)
Currently moderate colt. Turf high 56.
**E A L Dunlop [0-2] Abdullah Ali.*

STORNOWAY RR 50f 5060[2]

2 b f Catrail (USA) - Heavenly Waters (Celestial Storm (USA))
Form - 2
Record 2000 - 1st:0 2nd:1 3rd:0 Ran:1
Win Prizemoney £0 *Total Prizemoney* £822
2000 Turf 0-1: (6f) (sft)
Currently fair filly. **G C Bravery [0-1] The Iona Stud.*

STORYTELLER (IRE) BHB 79f RR 84f 2820[5]

6 b g Thatching 7.8f **(69)** - Please Believe Me (Try My Best (USA)) 7.6f **(67)**
Form - 0704305

Record	**2000** -	1st:0	2nd:0	3rd:1	Ran:7
	Pre2000 -	1st:8	2nd:7	3rd:1	Ran:34

Win Prizemoney £34,129 *Total Prizemoney* £52,988

Wins									
*	1999	Jun	Salisb	(Gd)	H	5f	80	83	
*	1999	May	Doncas	(G-F)		6f		79	
*	1998	Jly	Pontef	(G-F)	H	5f	77	84	<
*	1998	Jly	Beverl	(GD)	H	5f	65	76	
*	1998	Jly	Haydoc	(GD)	H	5f	65	67	
*	1998	Jun	Ayr	(GD)	H	5f	58	62	
*	1998	Jun	Carlis	(G-S)	H	5f	58	61	
	1997	Jly	Doncas	(GD)	H	5f	50	54	

2000 Turf 0-7: (5f 5, 6f 2) (gd 5, g-f 2)
Decent gelding, effective 5 to 6f, best at 5f, acts on g-f to frm, best on g-f, mostly wears blinkers (effectively). Turf high 83 - 3rd of 22 getting 7lb from Henry Hall (16 Jun York 5f g-f RF 2032).
**M Dods [7-30] Mrs Karen Pratt (from Mrs J R Ramsden [1-10] Oct 1997).*

ST PACOKISE (IRE) BHB 45f RR 40f 5086[7]

3 b f Brief Truce (USA) 9.1f **(73)** - Classic Opera (Lomond (USA)) 8.8f **(65)**
Form - 0757
Record 2000 - 1st:0 2nd:0 3rd:0 Ran:4
Pre2000 - 1st:0 2nd:0 3rd:0 Ran:3
2000 Turf 0-4: (7f 3, 9f) (hvy, frm 3)
Scopey, moderate filly. Turf high 40 (began Jly).
**A B Mulholland [0-7] Silent Running Syndicate.*

STRACHIN BHB 70f **RR 93?f** 1523[9]

6 b g Salse (USA) 10.9f **(71)** - Collage (Ela-Mana-Mou) 10.1f **(70)**
Form - 0
Record 2000 - 1st:0 2nd:0 3rd:0 Ran:1
Pre2000 - 1st:1 2nd:2 3rd:1 Ran:5
Win Prizemoney £3,566 *Total Prizemoney* £11,820
Wins 1998 Apr Carlis (G-S) 8f 80 <
2000 Turf 0-1: (8f) (gd)
Useful gelding. **K C Bailey [0-6] The Sporting Has Beens (from L M Cumani [1-5] Oct 1998).*

STRAHAN (IRE) BHB 98f **RR 105f** 4732[2]

3 b c Catrail (USA) - Soreze (IRE) **(92?f)** (Gallic League)
Form - 12230402
Record 2000 - 1st:1 2nd:3 3rd:1 Ran:8
Pre2000 - 1st:1 2nd:1 3rd:1 Ran:3
Win Prizemoney £14,298 *Total Prizemoney* £44,334
Wins * **2000** Apr Newmar (SFT) H 6f 87 93 <
* 1999 Oct York (G-S) 6f 82
2000 Turf 1-8: (6f 1-2, 7f 6) (gd 1-7, g-f)
Scopey, Pattern-class colt, effective 6 to 7f, best at 7f, acts on gd, and likes Goodwood. Turf high 105 - 2nd of 17 giving 14lb to Capricho (29 Spt Newmarket 7f gd RF 4732). Consistent. A winner at Newmarket on his reappearance, he was not beaten far in some competitive handicaps later, but might be in the handicapper's grip now. **J H M Gosden [2-11] Sheikh Mohammed.*

STRAND OF GOLD BHB 56f52a **RR 70f 52a** 5122[3]

3 b g Lugana Beach 7f **(63)** - Miss Display (Touch Paper) 6.8f **(57)**
Form - 558507783
Record 2000 - 1st:0 2nd:0 3rd:1 Ran:9
Pre2000 - 1st:0 2nd:1 3rd:0 Ran:4
Win Prizemoney £0 *Total Prizemoney* £1,727
2000 Turf 0-9: (6f 2, 7f 7) (g-s 2, gd 4, g-f 2, frm)
Workmanlike, above-average gelding, effective 5 to 7f, acts on g-s to gd, has worn blinkers. Turf high 70 - 5th of 8 to Last Symphony (27 May Haydock 7f g-s RF 1493). **R Hannon [0-13] R Hannon.*

STRANGE DESTINY BHB 99f **RR 95f** 3788[1]

2 b f Mujadil (USA) 7.7f **(70)** - Blue Birds Fly (Rainbow Quest (USA)) 10.4f **(75)**
Form - 31461
Record 2000 - 1st:2 2nd:0 3rd:1 Ran:5
Win Prizemoney £15,067 *Total Prizemoney* £19,912
Wins * **2000** Aug Newbur (G-F) L 5.2f 95 <
* **2000** Jun Warwic (G-S) 5f 75
2000 Turf 2-5: (5f 2-4, 6f) (g-s 1-1, gd 2, g-f 1-1, frm)
Very useful filly. Turf high 95 - 1st of 10 from Silla (19 Aug Newbury RF 3788). She lacks scope but, like her half-brother For Old Times Sake, was a useful juvenile. Successful in a Listed race at Newbury in August. She was then sold to America.
**A Berry [2-5] Team Valor.*

STRASBOURG (USA) BHB 75f **RR 77f** 5101[18]

3 ch c Dehere (USA) - Pixie Erin (Golden Fleece (USA)) 7.9f **(74)**
Form - 0022008060
Record 2000 - 1st:0 2nd:2 3rd:0 Ran:10
Pre2000 - 1st:1 2nd:1 3rd:0 Ran:3
Win Prizemoney £3,192 *Total Prizemoney* £9,841
Wins 1999 Spt Chepst (GD) 7.1f 82+ <
2000 Turf 0-10: (7f 2, 8f 7, 10f) (g-s 2, gd 2, g-f 3, frm 3)
Scopey, above-average colt, effective 7 to 8f, best at 8f, acts on gd to frm, best on frm. Turf high 96 - 2nd of 11 giving 15lb to Falconidae (1 Jly Bath 8f frm RF 2424). Inconsistent. He proved very disappointing in the second half of the season and is one to watch at present.
**N Tinkler [0-6] James Marshall & Mrs Susan Marshall (from J H M Gosden [0-4] Jly 2000).*

STRATEGIC CHOICE (USA) BHB 94f **RR 92f** 2823[7]

9 b h Alleged (USA) 11.8f **(81)** - Danlu (USA) (Danzig (USA)) 8.4f **(76)**
Form - 07
Record 2000 - 1st:0 2nd:0 3rd:0 Ran:2
Pre2000 - 1st:6 2nd:5 3rd:5 Ran:32
Win Prizemoney £338,403 *Total Prizemoney* £828,912
Wins * 1997 Spt Velief (FRM) 12f 113+
* 1996 Aug Deauvi (GD) G2 12.5f 118
* 1996 Jun San Si (GD) G1 12f 116
2000 Turf 0-2: (12f 2) (gd 2)
Useful horse, has worn blinkers. Turf high 92 (began Jly). Consistent. High-class in his prime (won the Group 1 Gran Premio de Milano in 1996), he has reached the veteran stage and is a bit player in decent handicaps. **P F I Cole [6-34] M Arbib.*

STRATEGIC DANCER (USA) BHB 61f **RR 66f** 1541[9]

3 b c Gulch (USA) 9.6f **(79)** - Danlu (USA) (Danzig (USA)) 8.4f **(76)**
Form - 6000
Record 2000 - 1st:0 2nd:0 3rd:0 Ran:4
2000 Turf 0-4: (8f, 10f 2, 12f) (g-s, gd 2, frm)
Rangy, average colt. Turf high 66. **P F I Cole [0-4] M Arbib.*

STRATH FILLAN BHB 54f **RR 63f** 4400[5]

2 b f Dolphin Street (FR) - Adarama (IRE) (Persian Bold) 9.3f **(66)**
Form - 0005
Record 2000 - 1st:0 2nd:0 3rd:0 Ran:4
2000 Turf 0-4: (6f, 7f 2, 8f) (gd, g-f, frm 2)
Average filly. Turf high 63. **W J Musson [0-4] Mrs P A Linton.*

STRAT'S QUEST BHB 43f30a **RR 49f 30a** 1803[18]

6 b m Nicholas (USA) 6.1f **(63)** - Eagle's Quest (Legal Eagle) 7.3f **(54)**
Form - 56580180580570
Record 2000 - 1st:1 2nd:0 3rd:0 Ran:13
Pre2000 - 1st:3 2nd:2 3rd:1 Ran:39
Win Prizemoney £11,098 *Total Prizemoney* £14,435
Wins * **2000** Apr Warwic (SFT) C 6.8f 49
* 1999 *Mar Southw (STD) SH 6f 41 48*
* 1997 May Windso (SFT) H 6f 64 58
* 1996 Oct Chepst (SFT) H 6.1f 64 64 <
2000 Turf 1-9: (5f 2, 6f 3, 7f 1-4) (hvy, sft 1-1, g-s 2, gd 4, g-f) 2000 AW 0-4: (6f, 7f 2, 8f) (Fibr 4)
Moderate mare, effective 6 to 7f, best at 7f, acts on sft to g-s - acts on Fibr, has worn blinkers (effectively), prefers left handed tracks, prefers tight tracks. Turf high 49 - 1st of 13 getting 19lb from Agent Mulder (3 Apr Warwick RF 0596). AW high 31.
**D W P Arbuthnot [4-52] Jack Blumenow.*

STRATTON (IRE) BHB 58f54a **RR 66df 54a** 5064[11]

3 b g Fairy King (USA) 7.7f **(75)** - Golden Bloom (Main Reef) 9.6f **(57)**
Form - 4030
Record 2000 - 1st:0 2nd:0 3rd:1 Ran:4
Pre2000 - 1st:0 2nd:0 3rd:0 Ran:1
Win Prizemoney £0 *Total Prizemoney* £701
2000 Turf 0-4: (6f 2, 8f 2) (sft, g-s, gd, frm)
Workmanlike, average gelding. Turf high 66.
**C F Wall [0-5] Peter Willmott.*

STRAVSEA BHB 36f51a **RR 33f 51a** 2194[14]

5 b m Handsome Sailor 6.6f **(53)** - La Stravaganza (Slip Anchor) 9.8f **(73)**
Form - 7103511635742700
Record 2000 - 1st:2 2nd:1 3rd:2 Ran:14
Pre2000 - 1st:2 2nd:8 3rd:4 Ran:33
Win Prizemoney £9,836 *Total Prizemoney* £18,158
Wins * **2000** *Jan Southw (STD) H 8f 48 60* <
* **2000** *Jan Southw (STD) H 8f 48 53*
* 1999 *Dec Southw (STD) H 8f 43 46*
* 1999 *Jly Southw (STD) H 8f 45 49*
2000 AW 2-14: (7f, 8f 2-11, 11f 2) (Fibr 2-14)
Fair filly, effective 8f, - acts on Fibr, favours left handed tracks, favours tight tracks. AW high 60 - 1st of 7 getting 14lb from My Tess (31 Jan Southwell RF 0193) - also 1st of 11 getting 8lb from Bobbydazzle (24 Jan Southwell RF 0145).
**R Hollinshead [4-25] E Bennion (from B P J Baugh [0-22] Mar 1999).*

STRAWBERRY DAWN **RR 56f** 4096[5]

2 gr f Fayruz 6.6f **(63)** - Alasib **(86f)** (Siberian Express (USA)) 8.8f **(65)**

Form - 45
Record 2000 - 1st:0 2nd:0 3rd:0 Ran:2
Win Prizemoney £0 *Total Prizemoney* £280
2000 Turf 0-2: (5f, 6f) (frm 2)
Currently fair filly. Turf high 56 (began Aug).
**N Hamilton [0-2] John Hopkins (T/A So Racing).*

STRAWMAN BHB 60f **RR 66f** 5058[9]
3 b g Ela-Mana-Mou 12.7f **(72)** - Oatfield (Great Nephew) 9.9f **(64)**
Form - 70650
Record 2000 - 1st:0 2nd:0 3rd:0 Ran:5
2000 Turf 0-5: (8f, 10f, 11f 2, 12f) (sft 2, g-s, gd, frm)
Lengthy, average gelding. Turf high 66.
**B W Hills [0-5] Mrs E Roberts.*

STREAK OF DAWN BHB 24f **RR 29f** 4228[7]
3 b f Old Vic 12.8f **(72)** - Nafla (FR) (Arctic Tern (USA)) 8.9f **(69)**
Form - 8000057
Record 2000 - 1st:0 2nd:0 3rd:0 Ran:7
Pre2000 - 1st:0 2nd:0 3rd:0 Ran:2
2000 Turf 0-6: (6f, 10f, 12f 2, 16f 2) (gd, g-f 3, frm 2) 2000 AW 0-1: (12f) (Equi)
Leggy, little account filly. Turf high 29.
**John Berry [0-7] J B J Richards (from K A Ryan [0-2] Jly 1999).*

STRECCIA BHB 38f **RR 55f** 4583[11]
3 b f Old Vic 12.8f **(72)** - Hills' Presidium (Presidium)
Form - 6480
Record 2000 - 1st:0 2nd:0 3rd:0 Ran:4
Win Prizemoney £0 *Total Prizemoney* £287
2000 Turf 0-2: (10f, 12f) (gd, g-f) 2000 AW 0-2: (9f, 16f) (Equi, Fibr)
Unfurnished, fair filly. Turf high 55. (began Jly).
**M Blanshard [0-4] Dr Ornella Carlini Cozzi.*

STREET CRY (IRE) RR 5330a[3]
2 br f Machiavellian (USA) 9.8f **(83)** - Helen Street (Troy) 10.4f **(68)**
Form - 3
2000 AW 0-1: (9f) (Dirt)
Currently very useful. (1st run) - 3rd of 14 to Macho Uno (4 Nov Churchill Downs 9f Dirt RF 5330a).
**E G Harty in USA [0-1] Godolphin Racing Inc.*

STREET LIFE (IRE) BHB 68f **RR 66f** 5310[4]
2 ch g Dolphin Street (FR) - Wolf Cleugh (IRE) **(58f)** (Last Tycoon) 8.5f **(62)**
Form - 004
Record 2000 - 1st:0 2nd:0 3rd:0 Ran:3
Win Prizemoney £0 *Total Prizemoney* £256
2000 Turf 0-3: (6f 2, 7f) (g-s, gd 2)
Currently average gelding. Turf high 66 (began Oct).
**W J Musson [0-3] Howard Spooner & Partners (I).*

STREET WALKER (IRE) BHB 39f **RR 43f** 3743[8]
4 b m Dolphin Street (FR) - Foolish Dame (USA) (Foolish Pleasure (USA)) 8.9f **(72)**
Form - 400648
Record 2000 - 1st:0 2nd:0 3rd:0 Ran:6
Pre2000 - 1st:0 2nd:2 3rd:1 Ran:9
Win Prizemoney £0 *Total Prizemoney* £2,481
2000 Turf 0-6: (12f 2, 13f, 14f 2, 16f) (sft, g-f, frm 4)
Neat, moderate filly, effective 8 to 10f, acts on gd to g-f, has worn blinkers, likes left handed tracks, likes tight tracks. Turf high 49.
**S Mellor [0-11] P E Logan Ltd (from C F Wall [0-9] Spt 1999).*

STREGONE (IRE) BHB 100f **RR 87f** 4259[7]
2 b g Namaqualand (USA) - Sabonis (USA) (The Minstrel (CAN)) 10f **(72)**
Form - 16522842767
Record 2000 - 1st:1 2nd:3 3rd:0 Ran:11
Win Prizemoney £2,717 *Total Prizemoney* £21,888
Wins * **2000** Mar Windso (G-F) 5f 74 <
2000 Turf 1-11: (5f 1-4, 6f 6, 7f) (sft, g-s, gd 5, g-f 1-3, hrd)
Useful gelding, effective 6f, acts on gd to hrd, has worn blinkers. Turf high 87. Consistent. Won on his debut, but has been a stranger to the winner's enclosure since. However, he has run with credit in some good races and deserves to score again.
**B J Meehan [1-11] A Rovai.*

STRENSALL BHB 30f **RR 23f** 4746[15]
3 b g Beveled (USA) 6.9f **(64)** - Payvashooz (Ballacashtal (CAN)) 5.3f **(50)**
Form - 0
Record 2000 - 1st:0 2nd:0 3rd:0 Ran:1
Pre2000 - 1st:0 2nd:0 3rd:0 Ran:2
2000 Turf 0-1: (7f) (gd)
Scopey, currently little account gelding.
**R E Barr [0-1] R E Barr (from M Brittain [0-2] Jun 1999).*

STRETFORD LASS (USA) BHB 66a **RR 66a** 367[3]
3 b f Woodman (USA) 9.7f **(77)** - Ladanum (USA) (Green Dancer (USA)) 10.3f **(74)**
Form - 313
Record 2000 - 1st:1 2nd:0 3rd:2 Ran:3
Win Prizemoney £2,743 *Total Prizemoney* £3,541
Wins * **2000** *Feb Lingfi (STD) 8f 61* <
2000 AW 1-3: (8f 1-2, 10f) (Equi 1-2, Fibr)
Light-framed, currently average filly. AW high 64 (1st run) - 3rd of 10 getting 20lb from Crimson Glory (27 Jan Wolverhampton 8f Fibr RF 0170) - also 1st of 10 from Maid To Love (19 Feb Lingfield RF 0313). **J Noseda [1-3] John Sikura.*

STRETTON (IRE) BHB 70f65a **RR 82f 65a** 4193[10]
2 br c Doyoun 10.7f **(69)** - Awayil (USA) **(78f)** (Woodman (USA)) 9f **(74)**
Form - 03200
Record 2000 - 1st:0 2nd:1 3rd:1 Ran:5
Win Prizemoney £0 *Total Prizemoney* £1,328
2000 Turf 0-5: (6f 4, 7f) (gd, g-f 2, frm 2)
Decent colt. Turf high 73. **J D Bethell [0-5] M J Dawson.*

STRICTLY PLEASURE BHB 52f **RR 49f** 4816[7]
2 b g Reprimand 8.2f **(63)** - Curlew Calling (IRE) (Pennine Walk) 8.5f **(61)**
Form - 607
Record 2000 - 1st:0 2nd:0 3rd:0 Ran:3
2000 Turf 0-3: (6f 2, 7f) (g-s, g-f, frm)
Currently moderate gelding. Turf high 48.
**M Brittain [0-3] Phil Hankins & Brian Gaynor.*

STRICTLY SPEAKING (IRE) BHB 60f65a **RR 62+f 65a** 4621[3]
3 b c Sri Pekan (USA) - Gaijin (Caerleon (USA)) 8.6f **(71)**
Form - 0668123
Record 2000 - 1st:1 2nd:1 3rd:1 Ran:7
Pre2000 - 1st:0 2nd:0 3rd:1 Ran:4
Win Prizemoney £1,809 *Total Prizemoney* £3,857
Wins * **2000** *Aug Wolver (STD) H 12f 54 66* <
2000 Turf 0-6: (8f 2, 11f 2, 12f 2) (hvy, g-s, gd 3, frm) 2000 AW 1-1: (12f 1-1) (Fibr 1-1)
Scopey, average colt, effective 8 to 12f, acts on g-s to gd - acts on Fibr, has worn blinkers, likes left handed tracks, favours tight tracks. Turf high 62 - 2nd of 18 giving 1lb to Kid'z'play (14 Spt Ayr 11f gd RF 4387). (1st run) - 1st of 11 giving 18lb to Topaz (19 Aug Wolverhampton RF 3807). **P F I Cole [1-11] P F I Cole Ltd.*

STRIDHANA BHB 52f **RR 50f** 3568[9]
4 ch m Indian Ridge 7.6f **(74)** - French Gift **(92f)** (Cadeaux Genereux)
Form - 00400
Record 2000 - 1st:0 2nd:0 3rd:0 Ran:5
Pre2000 - 1st:1 2nd:0 3rd:1 Ran:7
Win Prizemoney £4,592 *Total Prizemoney* £5,393
Wins * 1999 Aug Lingfi (G-F) 6f 72 <
2000 Turf 0-5: (6f 4, 7f) (gd, g-f 2, frm 2)
Unfurnished, fair filly, effective 6f, acts on g-f to frm, has worn blinkers. Turf high 50. **D R C Elsworth [1-12] Raymond Tooth.*

STRIDING KING BHB 40f60a **RR 42df 60a** 2392[F]
5 ch g King's Signet (USA) 7f **(51)** - Stride Home (Absalom) 7.2f **(58)**
Form - 00F
Record 2000 - 1st:0 2nd:0 3rd:0 Ran:3
Pre2000 - 1st:0 2nd:2 3rd:3 Ran:12
Win Prizemoney £0 *Total Prizemoney* £3,162
2000 Turf 0-3: (6f 2, 7f) (g-f 3)
Fair gelding, had worn blinkers. Turf high 19. (DEAD)
**M Madgwick [0-3] Peter Taplin (from M R Channon [0-12] Jly 1999).*

STROMNESS (USA) **RR 101f** 3940a[3]
3 f Trempolino (USA) 11.9f **(77)** - Caithness (USA) (Roberto (USA)) 10f **(76)**
Form - 3
2000 Turf 0-1: (15f) (g-f)
Currently very useful. (1st run) - 3rd of 4 to Shuwaib (16 Aug Deauville 15f g-f RF 3940a). Now hurdling with Alan King. *in FR [0-1].*

STROMSHOLM (IRE) BHB 66f65a **RR 71+f 65a** 3609[9]
4 ch g Indian Ridge 7.6f **(74)** - Upward Trend (Salmon Leap (USA)) 11f **(61)**
Form - 486324230
Record 2000 - 1st:0 2nd:2 3rd:2 Ran:9
Pre2000 - 1st:0 2nd:1 3rd:0 Ran:2
Win Prizemoney £0 *Total Prizemoney* £6,075
2000 Turf 0-8: (7f, 8f, 9f, 10f 5) (sft, gd 2, g-f 2, frm 2, hrd) 2000 AW 0-1: (6f) (Fibr)
Lengthy, above-average gelding, effective 8 to 10f, best at 10f, acts on g-f to hrd, best on g-f, prefers tight tracks. Turf high 71 - 2nd of 15 giving 8lb to Octane (9 Jly Sandown 10f g-f RF 2657).
J R Fanshawe [0-11] Paul & Jenny Green.

STRONG PRESENCE BHB 84f **RR 85+f** 4050[1]
3 b c Anshan 8.2f **(63)** - Lazybird Blue (IRE) (Bluebird (USA)) 7.5f **(69)**
Form - 121
Record 2000 - 1st:2 2nd:1 3rd:0 Ran:3
Pre2000 - 1st:0 2nd:0 3rd:0 Ran:1
Win Prizemoney £11,154 *Total Prizemoney* £12,332
Wins * 2000 Aug Ripon (GD) H 8f 80 85+ <
*** 2000** Jly Newmar (G-F) 6f 74
2000 Turf 2-3: (6f 1-2, 8f 1-1) (gd 1-1, frm 1-2)
Useful colt. Turf high 85 (began Jly) - 1st of 12 getting 6lb from Indian Plume (28 Aug Ripon RF 4050). Landed a four-runner Newmarket maiden over six furlongs on his seasonal debut and had no trouble with the step up to a mile when winning a decent handicap at Ripon in August with a great deal in hand. Still looks to be improving. **T P Tate [2-4] T P Tate.*

STRUDEL FITZ (ARG) **RR** 580a[11]
5 ch h Fitzcarraldo (USA) - Miss Con Strued (USA) (Forli (ARG)) 9.6f **(67)**
Form - 530
2000 AW 0-3: (10f 2, 17f) (Dirt 3)
Currently very useful colt. AW high 97. **J Veitch in SAR [0-3].*

STRUMPET BHB 71f **RR 76f** 5218[8]
2 bl f Tragic Role (USA) 9.4f **(63)** - Fee (Mandamus) 12.6f **(56)**
Form - 271638868
Record 2000 - 1st:1 2nd:1 3rd:1 Ran:9
Win Prizemoney £3,354 *Total Prizemoney* £7,279
Wins * 2000 Jun Salisb (G-F) 5f 72 <
2000 Turf 1-9: (5f 1-2, 6f 4, 7f 2, 8f) (sft, gd 4, g-f 3, frm 1-1)
Above-average filly, effective 5f, acts on gd to frm. Turf high 76 - also 1st of 11 from Lady Eberspacher (28 Jun Salisbury RF 2348). Ran well on her debut and won a Salisbury maiden on her third start. Fair form in nurseries since and may worth a try over seven.
**R F JohnsonHoughton [1-9] Lady Rothschild.*

STUNNING (USA) **RR 97f** 5365a[2]
2 b f Nureyev (USA) 8.4f **(84)** - Gorgeous (USA) (Slew O' Gold (USA)) 8f **(75)**
Form - 32
2000 Turf 0-2: (7f 2) (hvy, g-s)
Currently very useful filly. Turf high 97 (began Oct) - 2nd of 5 getting 3lb from Amiwain (3 Nov Maisons-laffitte 7f hvy RF 5365a).
**Mme C Head in FR [0-2] R N Clay.*

STUTTER **RR 81f** 4935[5]
2 ch c Polish Precedent (USA) 9f **(73)** - Bright Spells (Salse (USA)) 7.5f **(66)**
Form - 55
Record 2000 - 1st:0 2nd:0 3rd:0 Ran:2
2000 Turf 0-2: (6f 2) (gd 2)
Currently decent colt. Turf high 81 (began Jly).
**W J Haggas [0-2] B Haggas & Wentworth Racing (PTY) Ltd.*

STYLE DANCER (IRE) BHB 73f61a **RR 74f 61a** 4609[13]
6 b g Dancing Dissident (USA) 6.8f **(65)** - Showing Style (Pas de Seul) 9.1f **(67)**
Form - 033754847117731020
Record 2000 - 1st:3 2nd:1 3rd:1 Ran:14
Pre2000 - 1st:3 2nd:3 3rd:10 Ran:54
Win Prizemoney £37,337 *Total Prizemoney* £58,733
Wins * 2000 Spt York (GD) H 7f 69 72
*** 2000** Jly Beverl (GD) H 8.5f 60 66
*** 2000** Jly Doncas (GD) H 8f 60 64
* 1999 Jly Haydoc (G-S) H 7.1f 60 61
* 1998 Jly York (FRM) H 7f 70 73 <
* 1996 Oct Redcar (G-F) H 6f 70 72
2000 Turf 3-14: (7f 1-2, 8f 2-12) (sft, g-s, gd 3, g-f 2-5, frm 1-3, hrd)
Above-average gelding, effective 7 to 8f, best at 8f, acts on gd to frm, best on g-f, often wears blinkers (effectively). Turf high 74 - 2nd of 11 getting 1lb from Great News (16 Spt Ayr 8f gd RF 4452) - also 1st of 24 giving 6lb to Cusin (3 Spt York RF 4195). He looks very much a summer horse, ending a long losing run at Doncaster in July and followed up with a game victory at Beverley. Scored again in a big field at York in September. Best when coming late off a strong pace. **R M Whitaker [6-68] Mrs C A Hodgetts.*

STYLISH FELLA (USA) BHB 49f **RR 49f** 4215[6]
2 b c Irish River (FR) 9f **(77)** - Dariela (USA) (Manila (USA)) 9.3f **(71)**
Form - 0066
Record 2000 - 1st:0 2nd:0 3rd:0 Ran:4
2000 Turf 0-4: (6f 2, 7f, 8f) (gd 2, frm 2)
Moderate colt. Turf high 49 (began Jly). **P F I Cole [0-4] M Arbib.*

STYLISH WAYS (IRE) BHB 66f62a **RR 66f 62a** 4195[23]
8 b g Thatching 7.8f **(69)** - Style Of Life (USA) (The Minstrel (CAN)) 10f **(72)**
Form - 06253000
Record 2000 - 1st:0 2nd:1 3rd:1 Ran:8
Pre2000 - 1st:4 2nd:4 3rd:8 Ran:49
Win Prizemoney £20,706 *Total Prizemoney* £47,789
Wins * 1998 Oct Haydoc (SFT) H 6f 71 76
* 1998 Aug Newmar (G-F) H 6f 67 69
2000 Turf 0-8: (6f 6, 7f 2) (gd 2, g-f 3, frm 3)
Average gelding, effective 6f, acts on g-f. Turf high 66. Becoming disappointing.
**J Pearce [2-41] Ian Hall (from Miss S E Hall [0-8] Nov 1996).*

SUANCES **RR 119+f** 1826a[1]
3 ch c Most Welcome 8.6f **(66)** - Prayer Wheel (High Line) 10.3f **(70)**
Form - 11
2000 Turf 2-2: (9f 2-2) (g-s 1-1, gd 1-1)
Currently high-class colt. Turf high 119 - 1st of 7 from Bach (4 Jun Chantilly RF 1826a). An imposing individual, he created a tremendous impression when winning the Group 1 Prix Jean Prat by six lengths at Chantilly in June. Bought by American owners before that success, he is open to further improvement and could develop into a cracking four-year-old.
**M Delcher-Sanchez in SPA [2-2] J Cohen.*

SUAVE FRANKIE BHB 38f35a **RR 53df 35a** 1701[10]
4 ch g Suave Dancer (USA) 10.7f **(68)** - Francia **(58f)** (Legend of France (USA)) 9.5f **(61)**
Form - 0
Record 2000 - 1st:0 2nd:0 3rd:0 Ran:1
Pre2000 - 1st:0 2nd:2 3rd:0 Ran:9
Win Prizemoney £0 *Total Prizemoney* £1,724
2000 Turf 0-1: (10f) (gd)
Unfurnished, fair gelding, effective 16f, acts on frm, has worn blinkers. Becoming disappointing.
**A Smith [0-1] Rufus 2 Partnership (from S C Williams [0-9] Oct 1999).*

SUAVE NATIVE (USA) **RR 98+f** 5140[1]
2 ch c Shuailaan (USA) - Courtly Courier (USA) (Raise A Native) 11.2f **(69)**
Form - 1
Record 2000 - 1st:1 2nd:0 3rd:0 Ran:1
Win Prizemoney £4,225 *Total Prizemoney* £4,225
Wins * 2000 Oct Yarmou (HVY) 6f 98+ <
2000 Turf 1-1: (6f 1-1) (g-s 1-1)

Currently very useful colt. (1st run) - 1st of 15 giving 5lb to Matron (22 Oct Yarmouth RF 5140). **A C Stewart [1-1] Roy Clemons.*

SUAVE PERFORMER BHB 48f49a RR 54f 49a 2769[5]

3 b g Suave Dancer (USA) 10.7f **(68)** - Francia **(58f)** (Legend of France (USA)) 9.5f **(61)**
Form - 74542445
Record 2000 - 1st:0 2nd:1 3rd:0 Ran:8
Win Prizemoney £0 *Total Prizemoney* £1,971
2000 Turf 0-5: (9f, 10f, 12f 3) (gd 4, frm) 2000 AW 0-3: (5f, 6f, 7f) (Fibr 3)
Small, fair gelding, effective 10 to 12f, best at 12f, acts on gd, favours tight tracks. Turf high 54. AW high 45. Consistent.
**S C Williams [0-8] D A Shekells.*

SUAVE SHOT RR 1090[18]

3 br f Suave Dancer (USA) 10.7f **(68)** - Optaria (Song) 7.2f **(61)**
Form - 0
Record 2000 - 1st:0 2nd:0 3rd:0 Ran:1
2000 Turf 0-1: (6f) (g-f)
Light-framed, currently very poor filly. **I A Balding [0-1] J C Smith.*

SUBADAR MAJOR BHB 27f30a RR 30a 3015[6]

3 b g Komaite (USA) 6.9f **(61)** - Rather Gorgeous (Billion (USA)) 12f **(43)**
Form - 0076
Record 2000 - 1st:0 2nd:0 3rd:0 Ran:0
Pre2000 - 1st:0 2nd:0 3rd:0 Ran:1
2000 AW 0-3: (7f, 8f, 12f) (Fibr 3)
Little account gelding. AW high 22.
**Mrs G S Rees [0-4] Major Peter Bailey.*

SUBIACO (GER) RR 113f 4717a[8]

3 b c Monsun (GER) - So Sedulous (USA) **(96f)** (The Minstrel (CAN)) 10f **(72)**
Form - 12338
2000 Turf 1-5: (11f 1-2, 12f 3) (sft 3, gd 1-2)
Group-class colt. Turf high 113 - 3rd of 9 getting 9lb from Catella (13 Aug Gelsenkirchen-horst 12f gd RF 3736a). He was overshadowed by his stablemate Samum, but is a smart colt in his own right. Likely to stay beyond middle-distances, he should win a Group race in Germany this term. **A Schutz in GER [1-5].*

SUBSTANTIVE (USA) RR 25f 2061[8]

3 ch f Distant View (USA) - Substance (USA) (Diesis) 9.3f **(69)**
Form - 8
Record 2000 - 1st:0 2nd:0 3rd:0 Ran:1
2000 Turf 0-1: (7f) (g-f)
Light-framed, currently little account filly.
**H R A Cecil [0-1] K Abdulla.*

SUBTLE INFLUENCE (IRE) BHB 70f RR 75f 4892[2]

6 b g Sadler's Wells (USA) 11.3f **(87)** - Campestral (USA) (Alleged (USA)) 10f **(76)**
Form - 82
Record 2000 - 1st:0 2nd:1 3rd:0 Ran:2
Pre2000 - 1st:0 2nd:0 3rd:1 Ran:7
Win Prizemoney £0 *Total Prizemoney* £6,583
2000 Turf 0-2: (13f, 17f) (hvy, gd)
Above-average gelding, has worn blinkers. Turf high 75 (began Spt). Inconsistent. Good run at Ayr in October on his second run back after a long absence. **J S Goldie [0-2] Martin Delaney (from N A Callaghan [0-7] Jly 1998).*

SUBTLE POWER (IRE) BHB 111f RR 118f 5331a[10]

3 b c Sadler's Wells (USA) 11.3f **(87)** - Mosaique Bleue (Shirley Heights) 10.3f **(74)**
Form - 12150
2000 Turf 2-5: (10f 1-2, 12f 1-3) (gd 1-2, g-f 1-1, frm 2)
Scopey, high-class colt. Turf high 118 - also 1st of 7 from Zafonium (23 Jun Ascot RF 2206). He was given a shrewd ride when winning a weak renewal of Royal Ascot's Group 2 King Edward VII Stakes, and showed little in the Great Voltgeur at York in August. Transferred to Bill Mott in America thereafter, he made no show in the Breeders' Cup Turf.
**W Mott in USA [0-1] The Thoroughbred Corporation (from H R A Cecil [2-4] Aug 2000).*

SUCCESSFUL APPEAL (USA) RR 5328a[7]

4 m Valid Appeal (USA) - Successful Dancer (USA) (Fortunate Dancer (USA))
Form - 7
2000 AW 0-1: (6f) (Dirt)
Currently Group-class.
**J Kimmel in USA [0-2] Starview Stable & Walmac International.*

SUCH BOLDNESS BHB 46f58a RR 47f 58a 3557[3]

6 b g Persian Bold 10f **(69)** - Bone China (IRE) (Sadler's Wells (USA)) 10f **(76)**
Form - 00883
Record 2000 - 1st:0 2nd:0 3rd:1 Ran:5
Pre2000 - 1st:2 2nd:4 3rd:6 Ran:21
Win Prizemoney £4,260 *Total Prizemoney* £10,616
Wins * 1999 *Jan Lingfi (STD) 12f 66+* <
* 1999 *Jan Southw (STD) H 12f 58 61*
2000 Turf 0-4: (9f, 10f 2, 11f) (gd 2, frm 2) 2000 AW 0-1: (10f) (Equi)
Average gelding, effective 12 to 13f, best at 12f, - acts on AW, best on Equi, likes left handed tracks, favours tight tracks. Turf high 47 (began Jly). Inconsistent.
**Miss Gay Kelleway [2-23] Mrs M E O'Shea (from R Akehurst [0-3] Jly 1997).*

SUCH FLAIR (USA) BHB 73f72a RR 71f 72a 5220[1]

3 b f Kingmambo (USA) 10.9f **(85)** - Lady Fairfax **(93df)** (Sharrood (USA)) 10.5f **(77)**
Form - 30411
Record 2000 - 1st:2 2nd:0 3rd:1 Ran:5
Pre2000 - 1st:0 2nd:0 3rd:0 Ran:1
Win Prizemoney £6,838 *Total Prizemoney* £7,428
Wins * **2000** Oct Bright (SFT) H 10f 66 71 <
* **2000** Oct Pontef (HVY) H 10f 66 70
2000 Turf 2-4: (8f 2, 10f 2-2) (sft 1-2, g-s 1-1, g-f) 2000 AW 0-1: (8f) (Fibr)
Leggy, above-average filly, effective 8 to 10f, best at 10f, acts on sft to g-s - acts on Fibr. Turf high 71 - 1st of 4 getting 3lb from Guarded Secret (27 Oct Brighton RF 5220) - also 1st of 18 giving 2lb to Rutland Chantry (16 Oct Pontefract RF 5000). (1st run) - 4th of 13 giving 6lb to Bahrain (16 Spt Wolverhampton 8f Fibr RF 4474). **J Noseda [2-6] Sanford Robertson.*

SUCHITA (IRE) RR 95f 1455a[15]

3 f
Form - 00
2000 Turf 0-2: (8f, 11f) (sft, gd)
Currently very useful filly, often wears blinkers. Turf high 95.
**L Bietolini in ITY [0-2].*

SUDDEN FLIGHT (IRE) BHB 85f RR 87f 4385[6]

3 b c In The Wings 11.2f **(77)** - Ma Petite Cherie (USA) (Caro)
Form - 137252126
Record 2000 - 1st:2 2nd:3 3rd:1 Ran:9
Pre2000 - 1st:1 2nd:0 3rd:1 Ran:6
Win Prizemoney £10,912 *Total Prizemoney* £21,167
Wins * **2000** Aug Haydoc (GD) H 14f 78 84 <
* **2000** Apr Thirsk (G-S) 12f 78
* 1999 Spt Yarmou (SFT) H 8f 62 67
2000 Turf 2-9: (12f 1-5, 14f 1-3, 15f) (sft, g-s, gd 2-6, g-f)
Workmanlike, useful colt, effective 12 to 14f, best at 14f, acts on sft to gd, best on gd, likes left handed tracks, prefers tight tracks, excels at Haydock. Turf high 87 - 2nd of 14 getting 7lb from Majestic Bay (2 Spt Haydock 14f sft RF 4156) - also 1st of 12 getting 13lb from Seren Hill (12 Aug Haydock RF 3585). He has not always looked the easiest of rides, but he showed the right attitude to win at Haydock in August.
**E A L Dunlop [3-15] Maktoum Al Maktoum.*

SUDDEN SPIN BHB 21f26a RR 31f 26a 1040[5]

10 b g Doulab (USA) 7.4f **(61)** - Lightning Legacy (USA) (Super Concorde (USA)) 10.9f **(66)**
Form - 05865
Record 2000 - 1st:0 2nd:0 3rd:0 Ran:3
Pre2000 - 1st:6 2nd:1 3rd:6 Ran:45
Win Prizemoney £18,061 *Total Prizemoney* £22,143
Wins 1997 *Jan Southw (STD) H 16f 61 67* <
1996 Apr Beverl (G-F) H 16.2f 42 50

2000 Turf 0-1: (16f) (frm) 2000 AW 0-2: (16f 2) (Fibr 2)
Very moderate gelding, has worn blinkers. AW high 15. Won a moderate event at Southwell in January, but he was well beaten on two subsequent All-Weather starts and on turf.
**J L Eyre [0-7] Billy Parker (from J Norton [2-20] Mar 1998).*

SUDEST (IRE) BHB 60f80a **RR 59f 80a** 2621[3]

6 b g Taufan (USA) 8.3f **(65)** - Frill (Henbit (USA)) 9f **(61)**
Form - 003
Record 2000 - 1st:0 2nd:0 3rd:1 Ran:2
Pre2000 - 1st:6 2nd:4 3rd:1 Ran:29
Win Prizemoney £17,843 *Total Prizemoney* £24,244
Wins 1999 *Jan Wolver (STD) H 16.2f 75 80*
1999 *Jan Wolver (STD) H 14.8f 64 81* <
1999 *Jan Wolver (STD) H 16.2f 64 72*
1997 Jun Bath (G-F) 11.7f 73
1997 May Bath (G-F) H 17.2f 64 69
1997 May Warwic (FRM) H 12.5f 59 64
2000 Turf 0-2: (14f, 16f) (gd, g-f)
Very useful gelding, effective 16f, - acts on Fibr, has worn blinkers, prefers left handed tracks, favours tight tracks. Turf high 59. Becoming disappointing.
**J L Harris [1-6] Dr C W Ashpole (from I A Balding [7-31] Aug 1999).*

SUDRA BHB 78f **RR 73f** 4005[9]

3 b g Indian Ridge 7.6f **(74)** - Bunting **(90f)** (Shaadi (USA))
Form - 0800
Record 2000 - 1st:0 2nd:0 3rd:0 Ran:4
Pre2000 - 1st:1 2nd:0 3rd:1 Ran:3
Win Prizemoney £4,391 *Total Prizemoney* £5,013
Wins * 1999 Aug Thirsk (G-F) 6f 94+ <
2000 Turf 0-4: (6f 2, 8f 2) (g-s, gd 2, g-f)
Scopey, above-average gelding, effective 6f, acts on hrd. Turf high 73. **E A L Dunlop [1-7] Mohammed Al Nabouda.*

SUE ME (IRE) BHB 58f42a **RR 57f 42a** 4384[6]

8 b or br g Contract Law (USA) 8.9f **(54)** - Pink Fondant (Northfields (USA)) 9f **(72)**
Form - 0607176
Record 2000 - 1st:1 2nd:0 3rd:0 Ran:5
Pre2000 - 1st:8 2nd:6 3rd:8 Ran:75
Win Prizemoney £31,619 *Total Prizemoney* £43,086
Wins * **2000** May Mussel (FRM) S 5f 57
* 1999 Spt Ayr (G-S) H 5f 57 59
* 1999 *Jan Southw (STD) C 6f 67*
* 1998 *Spt Southw (STD) H 6f 56 58*
* 1998 Jly Doncas (G-F) H 5f 62 68
* 1998 Apr Pontef (G-S) H 5f 59 62
* 1998 *Feb Southw (STD) H 6f 43 49*
* 1998 *Jan Southw (STD) H 6f 44 45*
2000 Turf 1-4: (5f 1-3, 6f) (gd, frm 1-3) 2000 AW 0-1: (6f) (Fibr)
Fair gelding, effective 5 to 6f, best at 6f, acts on g-s to frm - acts on Fibr, has worn blinkers. Turf high 57. Inconsistent. He ended a very long losing run when winning a six-furlong handicap on the Southwell Fibresand in January, and followed up in a better race over the same course and distance the following month. He unfortunately finished lame next time, but has bounced back to take two apprentice events on turf, and obviously goes well for an inexperienced rider.
**D Nicholls [8-50] T G Meynell (from W R Muir [1-30] Jan 1997).*

SUEZ TORNADO (IRE) BHB 54f50a **RR 49f 50a** 2160[8]

7 ch g Mujtahid (USA) 7.4f **(69)** - So Stylish (Great Nephew) 9.9f **(64)**
Form - 88
Record 2000 - 1st:0 2nd:0 3rd:0 Ran:2
Pre2000 - 1st:4 2nd:2 3rd:6 Ran:57
Win Prizemoney £14,155 *Total Prizemoney* £24,131
Wins 1999 Spt Newmar (G-S) C 12f 55
1999 Jly Ayr (GD) H 9.1f 47 50
1997 Jun Newmar (G-S) H 8f 61 63
1996 Jly Killar (GD) 8.5f 68 <
2000 Turf 0-2: (10f, 12f) (g-f, frm)
Average gelding, effective 9 to 12f, best at 10f, acts on gd to frm, best on frm, has worn blinkers (extremely effectively), prefers right handed tracks. Turf high 48. **P Bowen [0-5] & Mrs Don Last & & Mrs Bill Yates (from E J Alston [3-50] Oct 1999).*

SUGAR CUBE TREAT BHB 45f **RR 53f** 4894[15]

4 b m Lugana Beach 7f **(63)** - Fair Eleanor (Saritamer (USA)) 9.5f **(63)**
Form - 070350000
Record 2000 - 1st:0 2nd:0 3rd:1 Ran:9
Pre2000 - 1st:1 2nd:0 3rd:3 Ran:17
Win Prizemoney £3,369 *Total Prizemoney* £6,000
Wins * 1999 Oct Ayr (SFT) H 6f 50 55 <
2000 Turf 0-9: (5f 3, 6f 5, 7f) (sft, g-s, gd 2, frm 5)
Light-framed, fair filly, effective 5 to 6f, best at 6f, acts on sft to g-f. Turf high 53 - 3rd of 6 getting 20lb from Lago Di Varano (8 Jun Haydock 5f gd RF 1809). **M Mullineaux [1-26] Abbey Racing.*

SUGARFOOT BHB 114f **RR 118f** 5369a[6]

6 ch h Thatching 7.8f **(69)** - Norpella (Northfields (USA)) 9f **(72)**
Form - 1551005336
Record 2000 - 1st:2 2nd:0 3rd:2 Ran:10
Pre2000 - 1st:7 2nd:5 3rd:3 Ran:25
Win Prizemoney £176,483 *Total Prizemoney* £249,039
Wins * **2000** Jly Ascot (GD) L 8f 114
* **2000** Apr Doncas (G-S) G3 7f 116
* 1999 Spt Doncas (G-F) G3 8f 117 <
* 1999 Aug York (GD) H 7.9f 105 116
* 1999 May York (SFT) LH 7.9f 104 106
* 1998 Oct York (GD) H 7.9f 99 104
* 1998 Aug York (FRM) H 7.9f 92 97
* 1998 Jly Ascot (G-F) H 8f 87 92
* 1996 Jly Ayr (G-F) 6f 82+
2000 Turf 2-10: (7f 1-3, 8f 1-7) (hvy, sft 2, gd 2-5, g-f 2)
High-class horse, effective 7 to 8f, best at 8f, acts on hvy to g-f, best on g-f, excels at Doncaster and York, does well at Longchamp. Turf high 118 - 5th of 7 to Aljabr (20 May Newbury 8f g-f RF 1331) - also 1st of 5 from Tumbleweed Ridge (29 Apr Doncaster RF 0907). Consistent. This grand campaigner retains all his ability and landed another Listed and Group 3 last year. Effective over seven furlongs or a mile, he handles any ground and can go well when fresh. **N Tinkler [9-35].*

SUGAR ROLO BHB 43f48a **RR 55f 48a** 5237[4]

2 b f Bin Ajwaad (IRE) - Spriolo **(12f)** (Priolo (USA))
Form - 6540304
Record 2000 - 1st:0 2nd:0 3rd:1 Ran:7
Win Prizemoney £0 *Total Prizemoney* £551
2000 Turf 0-6: (7f 4, 8f 2) (g-s, gd 2, frm 3) 2000 AW 0-1: (7f) (Fibr)
Fair filly. Turf high 55 (began Jly). **D Morris [0-7] W J Palmer.*

SUGGEST BHB 28f **RR 30f** 4766[7]

5 b g Midyan (USA) 9.9f **(64)** - Awham (USA) (Lear Fan (USA)) 8.5f **(73)**
Form - 7
Record 2000 - 1st:0 2nd:0 3rd:0 Ran:1
Pre2000 - 1st:2 2nd:1 3rd:2 Ran:28
Win Prizemoney £6,630 *Total Prizemoney* £9,138
Wins * 1997 Aug Newmar (G-F) S 7f 70 <
* 1997 Aug Thirsk (GD) C 7f 70 <
2000 Turf 0-1: (17f) (g-s)
Very moderate gelding, has worn blinkers.
**W Storey [7-41] Mrs M Tindale (from M Meade [0-1] Jly 1997).*

SUHAIL (IRE) BHB 37f43a **RR 36f 43a** 4812[18]

4 b g Wolfhound (USA) 7.3f **(71)** - Sharayif (IRE) (Green Desert (USA)) 8.6f **(78)**
Form - 0
Record 2000 - 1st:0 2nd:0 3rd:0 Ran:1
Pre2000 - 1st:0 2nd:1 3rd:0 Ran:7
Win Prizemoney £0 *Total Prizemoney* £806
2000 Turf 0-1: (8f) (g-s)
Scopey, fair gelding, effective 8f, - acts on Fibr. Becoming disappointing.
**Jane Southcombe [0-1] Mrs G M S Slater (from P L Gilligan [0-5] Jun 1999).*

SULTAN GAMAL RR 823[1]

2 b c Mind Games - Jobiska (Dunbeath (USA)) 7.8f **(70)**
Form - 1
Record 2000 - 1st:1 2nd:0 3rd:0 Ran:1
Win Prizemoney £2,975 *Total Prizemoney* £2,975
Wins * **2000** Apr Haydoc (HVY) 5f 74 <
2000 Turf 1-1: (5f 1-1) (hvy 1-1)
Currently very poor colt. (1st run) - 1st of 13 giving 5lb to Franica

(22 Apr Haydock RF 0823). **B A McMahon [1-1] G S D Imports Ltd.*

SULU (IRE) BHB 62f **RR 70f** 5055[19]
4 b g Elbio 9f **(62)** - Foxy Fairy (IRE) (Fairy King (USA)) 7.7f **(59)**
Form - 07010000
Record 2000 - 1st:1 2nd:0 3rd:0 Ran:8
Pre2000 - 1st:0 2nd:1 3rd:3 Ran:7
Win Prizemoney £4,862 *Total Prizemoney* £7,488
Wins * 2000 May Thirsk (GD) H 5f 63 70 <
2000 Turf 1-8: (5f 1-4, 6f 3, 7f) (hvy, sft 2, gd 1-5)
Unfurnished, above-average gelding, effective 5 to 7f, acts on gd to frm, best on frm. Turf high 70 - 1st of 24 getting 11lb from Blessingindisguise (6 May Thirsk RF 1069). Becoming disappointing. He made the frame several times early in his career, but did not get off the mark until causing a bit of a surprise in a handicap at Thirsk in May.
**M W Easterby [1-9] Bodfari Stud & Winton Bloodstock (from I A Balding [0-7] Spt 1999).*

SUMITAS (GER) RR 120f 4956a[2]
4 br h Lomitas - Subia (GER) (Konigsstuhl (GER)) 11.2f **(76)**
Form - 62252
2000 Turf 0-5: (8f, 10f 4) (sft 2, gd 3)
Very high-class colt, effective 8 to 12f, acts on sft to gd, best on sft, likes right handed tracks, does well at Cologne. Turf high 120. Consistent. German trained, he took the German 2000 Guineas in 1999 and, following a defeat at Cologne, has raced exclusively in Group One company, both home and abroad since then, often running well but failing to win in that grade.
**P Schiergen in GER [3-13] Baron G Von Ullmann.*

SUMITRA BHB 37f **RR 37f** 3245[7]
4 b m Tragic Role (USA) 9.4f **(63)** - Nipotina (Simply Great (FR)) 8.2f **(65)**
Form - 057
Record 2000 - 1st:0 2nd:0 3rd:0 Ran:3
Pre2000 - 1st:0 2nd:1 3rd:1 Ran:5
Win Prizemoney £0 *Total Prizemoney* £1,096
2000 Turf 0-3: (11f, 12f, 15f) (gd, frm, hrd)
Leggy, very moderate filly, effective 11 to 16f, acts on g-s to gd. Turf high 37 (began Jly). Becoming disappointing.
**Major D N Chappell [0-8] C V Cruden.*

SUMMER BOUNTY BHB 60f49a **RR 64?f 49a** 1139[12]
4 b g Lugana Beach 7f **(63)** - Tender Moment (IRE) (Caerleon (USA)) 8.6f **(71)**
Form - 06072000
Record 2000 - 1st:0 2nd:1 3rd:0 Ran:8
Pre2000 - 1st:1 2nd:1 3rd:2 Ran:10
Win Prizemoney £3,021 *Total Prizemoney* £8,077
Wins 1999 *Feb Lingfi (STD) 10f 71+* <
2000 Turf 0-2: (10f, 12f) (gd, g-f) 2000 AW 0-6: (9f 4, 12f, 13f) (Equi, Fibr 5)
Well made, average gelding, effective 10f, acts on gd - acts on Equi, has worn blinkers, favours tight tracks. Turf high 41. AW high 54. Inconsistent. **F Jordan [0-11] Mrs S J Le Gros (from B W Hills [1-10] Aug 1999).*

SUMMER CHERRY (USA) BHB 53f48a **RR 60f 48a** 5229[24]
3 b g Summer Squall (USA) 7f **(80)** - Cherryrob (USA) (Roberto (USA)) 10f **(76)**
Form - 4463680
Record 2000 - 1st:0 2nd:0 3rd:1 Ran:7
Pre2000 - 1st:0 2nd:0 3rd:0 Ran:2
Win Prizemoney £0 *Total Prizemoney* £798
2000 Turf 0-7: (7f, 8f 2, 9f, 10f 2, 12f) (g-s, gd 2, g-f 3, frm)
Well made, average gelding, effective 7 to 10f, acts on g-s to frm. Turf high 60 (1st run) - 4th of 10 giving 14lb to Presto (31 May Newbury 10f g-s RF 1591). Consistent.
**J R Poulton [0-1] Miss M S Walker (from D J Murphy [0-3] Spt 2000).*

SUMMER DREAMS (IRE) RR 72f 5070[5]
3 b f Sadler's Wells (USA) 11.3f **(87)** - Marie de Beaujeu (FR) (Kenmare (FR)) 6.5f **(72)**
Form - 235
Record 2000 - 1st:0 2nd:1 3rd:1 Ran:3
Win Prizemoney £0 *Total Prizemoney* £1,960
2000 Turf 0-3: (10f 2, 12f) (g-s, gd, frm)
Scopey, currently above-average filly. Turf high 80 (1st run) (began Aug) - 2nd of 6 to Gweneira (18 Aug Sandown 10f frm RF 3770). **Major D N Chappell [0-3] Mrs B Woodford.*

SUMMERHILL PARKES RR 62+f 3197[3]
2 b f Zafonic (USA) 9f **(83)** - Summerhill Spruce (Windjammer (USA)) 7f **(59)**
Form - 3
Record 2000 - 1st:0 2nd:0 3rd:1 Ran:1
Win Prizemoney £0 *Total Prizemoney* £552
2000 Turf 0-1: (6f) (hrd)
Currently average filly. **A Berry [0-1] Joseph Heler.*

SUMMER JAZZ RR 54f 5246[2]
3 b f Alhijaz 7.7f **(57)** - Salvezza (IRE) **(83df)** (Superpower)
Form - 52
Record 2000 - 1st:0 2nd:1 3rd:0 Ran:2
Win Prizemoney £0 *Total Prizemoney* £892
2000 Turf 0-1: (8f) (g-s) 2000 AW 0-1: (8f) (Fibr)
Workmanlike, currently fair filly. (1st run) - 2nd of 12 to Ipanema Beach (28 Oct Wolverhampton 8f Fibr RF 5246).
**P J Makin [0-2] Mrs P J Makin.*

SUMMER KEY (IRE) BHB 43f **RR 40f** 5152[14]
2 b f Doyoun 10.7f **(69)** - Summer Silence (USA) (Stop The Music (USA)) 9.2f **(71)**
Form - 000
Record 2000 - 1st:0 2nd:0 3rd:0 Ran:3
2000 Turf 0-3: (6f, 7f 2) (g-s, g-f 2)
Currently moderate filly. Turf high 40 (began Spt).
**R Guest [0-3] Mrs Jane Poulter.*

SUMMER SHADES BHB 68f **RR 65f** 3785[4]
2 b f Green Desert (USA) 7.8f **(78)** - Sally Slade **(79?f 75a)** (Dowsing (USA))
Form - 364
Record 2000 - 1st:0 2nd:0 3rd:1 Ran:3
Win Prizemoney £0 *Total Prizemoney* £894
2000 Turf 0-3: (5f, 6f 2) (frm 3)
Currently average filly. Turf high 65 (began Jly).
**C A Cyzer [0-3] Mrs E A Cyzer.*

SUMMER SOLSTICE (IRE) RR 106f 4417a[7]
3 f
Form - 7
2000 Turf 0-1: (12f) (gd)
Currently Pattern-class filly. **J E Pease in FR [0-1].*

SUMMER SONG BHB 90f **RR 91+f** 4931[9]
3 b f Green Desert (USA) 7.8f **(78)** - High Standard **(73f)** (Kris) 9.5f **(73)**
Form - 453111311170
Record 2000 - 1st:6 2nd:0 3rd:2 Ran:12
Pre2000 - 1st:1 2nd:0 3rd:0 Ran:1
Win Prizemoney £28,605 *Total Prizemoney* £32,229
Wins * 2000 Spt Thirsk (GD) H 12f 86 91+ <
*** 2000** Aug Beverl (G-F) H 9.9f 82 87+
*** 2000** Aug Ripon (G-F) H 10f 76 81
*** 2000** Jly Redcar (G-F) 9f 73
*** 2000** Jly Folkes (GD) H 9.7f 70 74+
*** 2000** Jun Windso (G-F) H 10f 68 75
* 1999 Oct Newmar (GD) 7f 66+
2000 Turf 6-12: (7f, 8f 2, 9f 1-1, 10f 4-6, 12f 1-2) (sft, g-s 2, gd 2-3, g-f 2-4, frm 2-2)
Scopey, useful filly, effective 10 to 12f, best at 10f, acts on gd to frm, best on frm, prefers tight tracks. Turf high 91 - 1st of 8 giving 12lb to Warning Reef (2 Spt Thirsk RF 4171) - also 1st of 9 giving 7lb to Bollin Roberta (27 Aug Beverley RF 4013). A hold-up handicapper, she enjoyed a wonderful season, being well placed to win six times. Effective up to a mile and a half, she was still improving physically at the end of the campaign and is worth a try in Listed company. **E A L Dunlop [7-13] Maktoum Al Maktoum.*

SUMMER SYMPHONY (IRE) BHB 100f **RR 96f** 4595[2]
2 gr f Caerleon (USA) 10.9f **(79)** - Summer Sonnet (Baillamont (USA)) 7f **(78)**
Form - 122

Record 2000 - 1st:1 2nd:2 3rd:0 Ran:3
Win Prizemoney £5,164 *Total Prizemoney* £58,364
Wins * 2000 Jly Newmar (GD) 7f 87+ <
2000 Turf 1-3: (7f 1-2, 8f) (gd, g-f 1-2)
Currently very useful filly. Turf high 96 (began Jly) - 2nd of 9 to Crystal Music (23 Spt Ascot 8f gd RF 4595) - also 1st of 11 from Flight of Fancy (30 Jly Newmarket RF 3231). She probably hit the front too soon when second in a Group 3 at Goodwood in August, and did not enjoy a clear run behind Crystal Music in Ascot's Group One Fillies' Mile the following month. Likely to stay beyond a mile, she has a sharp turn-of-foot and is capable of making the frame in the 1000 Guineas. **L M Cumani [1-3] Gerald Leigh.*

SUMMER VIEW (USA) BHB 110f **RR 115f** 4967^{2}

3 ch c Distant View (USA) - Miss Summer (Luthier) 9.8f **(71)**
Form - 1132
Record 2000 - 1st:2 2nd:1 3rd:1 Ran:4
Win Prizemoney £11,335 *Total Prizemoney* £18,363
Wins * 2000 Aug Salisb (G-F) 8f 99+ <
*** 2000** Jly Kempto (G-F) 8f 87++
2000 Turf 2-4: (8f 2-3, 9f) (gd, g-f, frm 2-2)
Well made, high-class colt. Turf high 115 (began Jly) - 2nd of 11 getting 8lb from Albarahin (13 Oct Newmarket 9f gd RF 4967). Unraced at two, he won a Kempton maiden and a Salisbury classified race in his first two starts, but was just unable to cope with stronger opposition in a Doncaster conditions event. Produced an improved performance when faced with easy ground for the first time at Newmarket, and should be able to win in Pattern company. **R Charlton [2-4] K Abdulla.*

SUMMONER BHB 112f **RR 115+f** 3393^{2}

3 b c Inchinor 8.9f **(64)** - Sumoto (Mtoto)
Form - 10412
Record 2000 - 1st:2 2nd:1 3rd:0 Ran:5
Pre2000 - 1st:1 2nd:0 3rd:0 Ran:2
Win Prizemoney £17,476 *Total Prizemoney* £24,411
Wins * 2000 Jly Doncas (G-F) 8f 115 <
*** 2000** Mar Doncas () 8f 106
* 1999 Nov Doncas (SFT) 8f 82+
2000 Turf 2-5: (8f 2-5) (gd 1-3, g-f, frm 1-1)
Scopey, high-class colt, effective 8f, acts on gd to frm. Turf high 115 - 1st of 5 giving 1lb to Pythios (19 Jly Doncaster RF 2932) - also 1st of 9 getting 2lb from Zyz (25 Mar Doncaster RF 0496). A good-looking individual, he suffered an interrupted preparation before finishing ninth in the 2000 Guineas. Back to his best when giving older horses weight and a beating at Doncaster in July, he probably hit the front too soon when caught by Adilabad in a Listed heat at Goodwood the following month. Still lightly raced, he is open to improvement and can win a Group race around a mile this term. **R Charlton [3-7] Michael Pescod.*

SUMTHINELSE BHB 72f **RR 78f** 5014^{12}

3 ch g Magic Ring (IRE) 6.5f **(64)** - Minne Love (Homeric) 9.8f **(67)**
Form - 54021460300
Record 2000 - 1st:1 2nd:1 3rd:1 Ran:11
Pre2000 - 1st:0 2nd:0 3rd:2 Ran:5
Win Prizemoney £4,101 *Total Prizemoney* £8,717
Wins * 2000 Jun Cheste (G-F) H 7f 73 75 <
2000 Turf 1-9: (6f 5, 7f 1-4) (g-s, gd 3, g-f 2, frm 1-3) 2000 AW 0-2: (6f, 7f) (Fibr 2)
Small, above-average gelding, effective 5 to 7f, acts on g-f to frm - acts on Fibr, best on frm, has worn blinkers, prefers left handed tracks, prefers tight tracks. Turf high 79 - also 1st of 11 from Royal Cavalier (28 Jun Chester RF 2335). AW high 74 (1st run) (began Spt) - 3rd of 10 getting 6lb from Hand Chime (2 Spt Wolverhampton 7f Fibr RF 4177). **N P Littmoden [1-16] Hanibel Racing Partnership.*

SUN BIRD (IRE) **RR 60f** 5004^{5}

2 ch c Prince of Birds (USA) - Summer Fashion (Moorestyle) 6.9f **(64)**
Form - 505875
Record 2000 - 1st:0 2nd:0 3rd:0 Ran:6
2000 Turf 0-5: (6f 3, 8f, 10f) (g-s 2, g-f 2, frm) 2000 AW 0-1: (5f) (Fibr)
Average colt, effective 8f, acts on g-s, has worn blinkers. Turf high 60 (began Jly) - 5th of 20 giving 7lb to Leatherback (16 Oct Pontefract 8f g-s RF 5004). **Sir Mark Prescott [0-6] Sturt Osborne House IV.*

SUN CHARM (USA) BHB 97f **RR 99f** 2647^{8}

3 b br c Gone West (USA) 7.8f **(82)** - Argon Laser (Kris) 9.5f **(73)**
Form - 38
Record 2000 - 1st:0 2nd:0 3rd:1 Ran:2
Pre2000 - 1st:1 2nd:0 3rd:0 Ran:2
Win Prizemoney £5,547 *Total Prizemoney* £7,837
Wins 1999 Oct Leices (GD) 7f 86+ <
2000 Turf 0-2: (8f, 10f) (g-s, frm)
Workmanlike, very useful colt, has worn blinkers. Turf high 99. He acted as a pacemaker in the Eclipse, but has basically been disappointing since leaving Sir Michael Stoute. **S bin Suroor [0-2] Godolphin (from Sir Michael Stoute [1-2] Oct 1999).*

SUNDAY RAIN (USA) BHB 67f **RR 70f** 1179^{5}

3 b g Summer Squall (USA) 7f **(80)** - Oxava (FR) (Antheus (USA))
Form - 42245
Record 2000 - 1st:0 2nd:2 3rd:0 Ran:5
Pre2000 - 1st:0 2nd:0 3rd:0 Ran:5
Win Prizemoney £0 *Total Prizemoney* £3,137
2000 Turf 0-5: (10f, 12f 2, 14f, 15f) (gd 2, g-f, frm 2)
Scopey, above-average gelding, effective 8 to 12f, acts on g-s to frm, best on g-s, has worn blinkers, prefers left handed tracks, likes tight tracks. Turf high 75 - 2nd of 10 giving 3lb to Merryvale Man (29 Mar Catterick 12f frm RF 0549). Consistent. **P F I Cole [0-10] H R H Prince Fahd Salman.*

SUNDERLAND (GER) **RR 106f** $4954a^{3}$

3 b c Emarati (USA) 6.6f **(63)** - See Me Well (GER) (Common Grounds)
Form - 133
2000 Turf 1-3: (6f, 7f 1-2) (sft, gd 1-2)
Currently Pattern-class colt. Turf high 106 (began Jly) - 3rd of 7 getting 3lb from Tertullian (8 Oct Munich 7f sft RF 4954a) - also 1st of 8 from Arc Royal (22 Jly Hoppegarten RF 3158a). **A Wohler in GER [1-3] Stall Schwindelfrei.*

SUNDOWN **RR 79f** 4820^{3}

2 b f Polish Precedent (USA) 9f **(73)** - Ruby Setting (Gorytus (USA)) 7.8f **(60)**
Form - 03
Record 2000 - 1st:0 2nd:0 3rd:1 Ran:2
Win Prizemoney £0 *Total Prizemoney* £449
2000 Turf 0-2: (6f, 7f) (g-f 2)
Currently above-average filly. Turf high 79 (began Aug). **M P Tregoning [0-2] R J McCreery.*

SUNGIO BHB 70f **RR 72f** 5298^{2}

2 b c Halling (USA) - Time Or Never (FR) (Dowsing (USA))
Form - 6062
Record 2000 - 1st:0 2nd:1 3rd:0 Ran:4
Win Prizemoney £0 *Total Prizemoney* £1,085
2000 Turf 0-4: (7f, 8f 3) (g-s 3, gd)
Above-average colt. Turf high 72 (began Spt). **L M Cumani [0-4] Scuderia Rencati Srl.*

SUNLEY SCENT BHB 65f **RR 62f** 5131^{8}

2 ch f Wolfhound (USA) 7.3f **(71)** - Brown Velvet (Mansingh (USA)) 7.4f **(55)**
Form - 88
Record 2000 - 1st:0 2nd:0 3rd:0 Ran:2
2000 Turf 0-2: (6f 2) (sft, g-f)
Currently average filly. Turf high 62 (began Oct). **M R Channon [0-2] John Sunley.*

SUNLEY SENSE BHB 77f **RR 86f** 5003^{5}

4 b g Komaite (USA) 6.9f **(61)** - Brown Velvet (Mansingh (USA)) 7.4f **(55)**
Form - 08220020066465
Record 2000 - 1st:0 2nd:3 3rd:0 Ran:14
Pre2000 - 1st:2 2nd:4 3rd:1 Ran:16
Win Prizemoney £8,758 *Total Prizemoney* £33,922
Wins * 1998 Spt Newbur (GD) H 5.2f 76 91 <
* 1998 Spt Sandow (G-S) H 5f 76 80
2000 Turf 0-14: (5f 12, 6f 2) (g-s 2, gd 7, g-f 3, frm 2)
Scopey, useful gelding, effective 5f, acts on gd to frm, has worn blinkers. Turf high 86 - 2nd of 12 getting 5lb from Damalis (11 May Chester 5f g-f RF 1133). Some decent performances to make the frame in decent sprint handicaps last season, but is not particularly consistent. Shows plenty of dash.

**M R Channon [2-30] John Sunley.*

SUNLEY'S PICC BHB 50f53a **RR 52f 53a** 3898[12]
3 b f Piccolo - Pharsical **(73f)** (Pharly (FR)) 9.8f **(68)**
Form - 067580
Record 2000 - 1st:0 2nd:0 3rd:0 Ran:6
Pre2000 - 1st:0 2nd:0 3rd:0 Ran:1
2000 Turf 0-5: (6f 2, 7f 2, 8f) (gd 2, g-f, frm, hrd) 2000 AW 0-1: (6f) (Fibr)
Neat, fair filly. Turf high 52.
**C Weedon [0-3] Mrs J M Jeyes (from M R Channon [0-4] Apr 2000).*

SUNNY GLENN BHB 79f **RR 72f** 4726[1]
2 ch c Rock Hopper 10.6f **(54)** - La Ballerine (Lafontaine (USA)) 8.7f **(49)**
Form - 051
Record 2000 - 1st:1 2nd:0 3rd:0 Ran:3
Win Prizemoney £3,461 *Total Prizemoney* £3,700
Wins * **2000** Spt Lingfi (SFT) 6f 72 <
2000 Turf 1-3: (6f 1-1, 7f, 8f) (sft, g-s, gd 1-1)
Currently above-average colt. Turf high 72 (began Spt) - 1st of 15 from Breaking News (29 Spt Lingfield RF 4726).
**N P Littmoden [1-3] Mrs H F Mahr.*

SUNNY STROKA BHB 30f **RR 16f** 5067[16]
2 b f Whittingham (IRE) - Luckley Brake (Quiet Fling (USA)) 11.8f **(36)**
Form - 000
Record 2000 - 1st:0 2nd:0 3rd:0 Ran:3
2000 Turf 0-3: (5f, 6f 2) (g-s, gd, frm)
Currently poor filly. Turf high 16 (began Aug).
**J C Tuck [0-3] B Higham.*

SUNRIDGE ROSE BHB 48f **RR 46f** 4993[10]
2 b f Piccolo - Floral Spark **(61f 72a)** (Forzando) 7.6f **(59)**
Form - 360
Record 2000 - 1st:0 2nd:0 3rd:1 Ran:3
Win Prizemoney £0 *Total Prizemoney* £420
2000 Turf 0-1: (5f) (g-f) 2000 AW 0-2: (5f, 6f) (Fibr 2)
Currently moderate filly. AW high 47 (began Spt).
**P C Haslam [0-3] R Young.*

SUNRISE (IRE) BHB 52f45a **RR 60f 45a** 744[9]
3 b br f Sri Pekan (USA) - Grade A Star (IRE) (Alzao (USA)) 7.1f **(68)**
Form - 000
Record 2000 - 1st:0 2nd:0 3rd:0 Ran:3
Pre2000 - 1st:0 2nd:0 3rd:1 Ran:3
Win Prizemoney £0 *Total Prizemoney* £507
2000 Turf 0-2: (7f 2) (gd 2) 2000 AW 0-1: (9f) (Fibr)
Unfurnished, average filly. Turf high 42. **W R Muir [0-6] D G Clarke.*

SUNRISE GIRL BHB 35f35a **RR 35a** 2355[20]
3 ch f King's Signet (USA) 7f **(51)** - Dawn Ditty (Song) 7.2f **(61)**
Form - 06000
Record 2000 - 1st:0 2nd:0 3rd:0 Ran:5
2000 Turf 0-3: (5f 2, 6f) (gd 2, g-f) 2000 AW 0-2: (5f 2) (Fibr 2)
Scopey, poor filly. AW high 11.
**A G Hobbs [0-5] Unity Farm Holiday Centre Ltd.*

SUNSET GLOW RR 76f 2170[3]
3 gr c Rainbow Quest (USA) 11.2f **(81)** - Oscura (USA) (Caro)
Form - 3
Record 2000 - 1st:0 2nd:0 3rd:1 Ran:1
Pre2000 - 1st:0 2nd:0 3rd:0 Ran:1
Win Prizemoney £0 *Total Prizemoney* £956
2000 Turf 0-1: (12f) (g-f)
Tall, currently above-average colt. **B W Hills [0-2] K Abdulla.*

SUNSET HARBOUR (IRE) BHB 41f44a **RR 47f 44a** 5112[24]
7 br m Prince Sabo 6.6f **(64)** - City Link Pet (Tina's Pet) 6.8f **(59)**
Form - 2416360568600080
Record 2000 - 1st:1 2nd:1 3rd:1 Ran:16
Pre2000 - 1st:5 2nd:5 3rd:9 Ran:58
Win Prizemoney £17,049 *Total Prizemoney* £27,896
Wins * **2000** Jun Bright (FRM) H 5.3f 42 47
1998 Aug Catter (GD) H 5f 47 50 <
1998 May Newcas (G-F) H 5f 42 44
1998 *Apr Wolver (STD) H 5f 37 40*
1997 Jun Beverl (G-S) H 5f 40 41
1996 Jly Redcar (FRM) SH 5f 44 45
2000 Turf 1-16: (5f 1-14, 6f 2) (gd 4, g-f 5, frm 1-7)
Moderate mare, effective 5f, acts on g-f to frm - acts on Equi, has worn blinkers, prefers left handed tracks, likes tight tracks. Turf high 47 - 1st of 9 getting 22lb from Knockemback Nellie (15 Jun Brighton RF 1976). Inconsistent. **J M Bradley [1-16] Mrs Kay Blandford (from S E Kettlewell [5-40] Aug 1999).*

SUNSET LADY (IRE) BHB 47f60a **RR 51f 60a** 1471[9]
4 b br m Red Sunset 9f **(57)** - Lady of Man (So Blessed) 8.7f **(67)**
Form - 0030
Record 2000 - 1st:0 2nd:0 3rd:1 Ran:4
Pre2000 - 1st:3 2nd:2 3rd:1 Ran:16
Win Prizemoney £9,690 *Total Prizemoney* £13,261
Wins 1998 Oct Ayr (SFT) H 8f 65 74 <
1998 Spt Pontef (G-F) H 8f 61 66
1998 Jun Thirsk (GD) S 6f 66
2000 Turf 0-4: (8f, 10f 2, 12f) (gd 2, g-f 2)
Unfurnished, fair filly, effective 8f, acts on gd, likes left handed tracks. Turf high 51. Inconsistent.
**J S Wainwright [0-4] Ms Julie French (from P C Haslam [3-17] Aug 1999).*

SUNSET SHORE RR 3220[P]
2 b f Hernando (FR) - Shimmering Sea (Slip Anchor) 9.8f **(73)**
Form - P
Record 2000 - 1st:0 2nd:0 3rd:0 Ran:1
2000 Turf 0-1: (6f) (frm)
Pulled up on debut. (DEAD) **Sir Mark Prescott [0-1] Miss K Rausing.*

SUNSETTER (USA) RR 88f 4644[9]
2 ch f Diesis 9f **(80)** - Hushi (USA) (Riverman (USA)) 9.1f **(76)**
Form - 0
Record 2000 - 1st:0 2nd:0 3rd:0 Ran:1
2000 Turf 0-1: (6f) (g-f)
Currently useful filly. **G A Butler [0-1] Des Swan.*

SUNSHINE N'SHOWERS RR 69f 3582[5]
2 b f Spectrum (IRE) - Mainly Dry (The Brianstan) 5.9f **(55)**
Form - 35
Record 2000 - 1st:0 2nd:0 3rd:1 Ran:2
Win Prizemoney £0 *Total Prizemoney* £557
2000 Turf 0-2: (6f 2) (gd, frm)
Currently average filly. Turf high 69 (began Jly).
**A Berry [0-2] Mrs David Brown.*

SUN SILK (USA) BHB 67f **RR 68f** 4730[5]
3 b f Gone West (USA) 7.8f **(82)** - Silk Slippers (USA) (Nureyev (USA)) 8.7f **(78)**
Form - 8575
Record 2000 - 1st:0 2nd:0 3rd:0 Ran:4
2000 Turf 0-3: (7f, 8f, 10f) (g-s, frm 2) 2000 AW 0-1: (13f) (Equi)
Scopey, average filly. Turf high 68.
**J H M Gosden [0-4] R E Sangster.*

SUNSTONE RR 63f 5098[17]
2 b f Caerleon (USA) 10.9f **(79)** - Chita Rivera **(44f 37a)** (Chief Singer) 8.9f **(66)**
Form - 0
Record 2000 - 1st:0 2nd:0 3rd:0 Ran:1
2000 Turf 0-1: (8f) (gd)
Currently average filly. **M R Channon [0-1] Mrs M J Vincent.*

SUPERBIT BHB 55f52a **RR 56f 52a** 4558[10]
8 b g Superpower 6.6f **(58)** - On A Bit (Mummy's Pet) 7.7f **(60)**
Form - 06180
Record 2000 - 1st:1 2nd:0 3rd:0 Ran:5
Pre2000 - 1st:6 2nd:4 3rd:13 Ran:73
Win Prizemoney £17,750 *Total Prizemoney* £27,846
Wins * **2000** Jly Nottin (G-F) S 6.1f 48
* 1999 Oct Nottin (SFT) 6.1f 56
* 1998 Aug Ripon (GD) SH 5f 50 54
* 1997 Jun Nottin (SFT) H 6.1f 60 64 <
* 1996 Oct Nottin (GD) 5.1f 60
* 1996 Spt Haydoc (GD) SH 6f 49 53
2000 Turf 1-4: (5f 2, 6f 1-2) (gd 3, frm 1-1) 2000 AW 0-1: (6f) (Fibr)

Fair gelding, effective 6f, acts on gd to frm, has worn blinkers. Turf high 56 - also 1st of 20 from Sealed By Fate (15 Jly Nottingham RF 2838). **B A McMahon [7-74] Neville Smith (from J G FitzGerald [0-4] Spt 1994).*

SUPERCHIEF BHB 49f71a **RR 39f 71a** 5155[5]

5 b g Precocious 7.2f **(54)** - Rome Express (Siberian Express (USA)) 8.8f **(65)**

Form - 030344211150088235

Record 2000 - 1st:3 2nd:2 3rd:1 Ran:13
Pre2000 - 1st:0 2nd:0 3rd:2 Ran:16

Win Prizemoney £5,989 *Total Prizemoney* £8,533

Wins * **2000** *Feb Lingfi (STD) H 8f* 51 58 <
* **2000** *Feb Lingfi (STD) H 7f* 44 48
* **2000** *Feb Lingfi (STD) H 7f* 39 53

2000 Turf 0-2: (6f, 8f) (frm 2) 2000 AW 3-11: (7f 2-5, 8f 1-6) (Equi 3-11)

Average gelding, effective 7 to 10f, best at 7f, - acts on Equi, has worn blinkers, prefers left handed tracks, prefers tight tracks, excels at Lingfield. Turf high 39 (began Jly). AW high 58 - 1st of 9 getting 6lb from Border Glen (26 Feb Lingfield RF 0366) - also 1st of 12 getting 5lb from Beguile (2 Feb Lingfield RF 0202). Inconsistent. Has a good record at around a mile on Equitrack but did not stay further. **Miss B Sanders [3-22] Copy Xpress Ltd (from J E Banks [0-7] Spt 1998).*

SUPER DOMINION BHB 53f58a **RR 41f 58a** 5005[5]

3 ch c Superpower 6.6f **(58)** - Smartie Lee (Dominion) 8.5f **(63)**

Form - 4336005

Record 2000 - 1st:0 2nd:0 3rd:2 Ran:7

Win Prizemoney £0 *Total Prizemoney* £1,581

2000 Turf 0-6: (7f 5, 12f) (g-s, gd, g-f, frm 2, hrd) 2000 AW 0-1: (6f) (Fibr)

Fair colt. Turf high 43. **R Hollinshead [0-7] Mrs Norman Hill.*

SUPERFRILLS BHB 39f34a **RR 40f 34a** 5083[2]

7 b m Superpower 6.6f **(58)** - Pod's Daughter (IRE) (Tender King) 6.8f **(54)**

Form - 02087400502

Record 2000 - 1st:0 2nd:2 3rd:0 Ran:11
Pre2000 - 1st:3 2nd:4 3rd:4 Ran:48

Win Prizemoney £7,899 *Total Prizemoney* £15,354

Wins * 1998 Oct Newcas (SFT) H 5f 45 47 <
* 1998 Aug Hamilt (SFT) H 5f 39 47 <
* 1998 Jun Hamilt (G-S) H 5f 33 40

2000 Turf 0-5: (5f 3, 6f 2) (hvy, gd 3, hrd) 2000 AW 0-6: (5f, 6f 5) (Fibr 6)

Moderate mare, effective 5 to 6f, acts on hvy to g-f. Turf high 40 - 2nd of 19 getting 22lb from Bowlers Boy (19 Oct Newcastle 6f hvy RF 5083). AW high 37. **Miss L C Siddall [3-59] Podso Racing.*

SUPER GOLDLUCK (IRE) **RR 107f** 1157a[2]

4 b h Fairy King (USA) 7.7f **(75)** - Perfect Welcome (Taufan (USA)) 7f **(57)**

Form - 2

2000 Turf 0-1: (10f) (gd)

Currently Pattern-class colt. (1st run) - 2nd of 14 to All The Way (7 May Kranji 10f gd RF 1157a). **in SIN [0-1].*

SUPERIOR PREMIUM BHB 120f **RR 119f** 2181[1]

6 br h Forzando 7.2f **(63)** - Devils Dirge (Song) 7.2f **(61)**

Form - 800161

Record 2000 - 1st:2 2nd:0 3rd:0 Ran:6
Pre2000 - 1st:9 2nd:5 3rd:2 Ran:36

Win Prizemoney £213,744 *Total Prizemoney* £250,387

Wins * **2000** Jun Ascot (G-F) G2 6f 119 <
* **2000** May Goodwo (G-S) 6f 111
* 1999 Oct Newbur (G-S) H 6f 109 110
* 1999 Oct Ascot (G-S) H 5f 104 108
* 1999 Jun Taby (FRM) L 9.8f 102
* 1998 Aug Goodwo (GD) H 6f 99 105
* 1998 Jly Haydoc (GD) 6f 95
* 1998 Jun Cheste (G-S) H 6.1f 94 98
* 1997 Mar Haydoc (SFT) L 5f 100
* 1996 Oct Haydoc (SFT) 5f 90
* 1996 Apr Nottin (G-S) 5.1f 79

2000 Turf 2-6: (5f 3, 6f 2-3) (g-s 1-3, gd 1-3)

High-class horse, effective 6f, acts on g-s to g-f, has worn blinkers, excels at Ascot. Turf high 119 - 1st of 16 from Sampower Star (22 Jun Ascot RF 2181) - also 1st of 6 getting 4lb from Tomba (23 May Goodwood RF 1395). Inconsistent. He has an excellent record at Ascot and put up a career best performance when springing a 20-1 shock in the Cork And Orrery Stakes at the Royal Meeting. Effective over five (on a stiff track) and six furlongs, he probably acts on any ground, is usually held up and has a sharp turn-of-foot. **R A Fahey [11-42] J C Parsons.*

SUPER KIM BHB 43f **RR 33f** 2451[6]

3 b f Superpower 6.6f **(58)** - Kimble Blue (Blue Refrain)

Form - 006

Record 2000 - 1st:0 2nd:0 3rd:0 Ran:3
Pre2000 - 1st:0 2nd:0 3rd:0 Ran:3

2000 Turf 0-3: (8f, 10f 2) (g-s, g-f, frm)

Neat, very moderate filly. Turf high 33.
**P L Gilligan [0-6] The Angel Partnership.*

SUPERLAO (BEL) BHB 33f29a **RR 27f 29a** 248[8]

8 b m Bacalao (USA) 5f **(27)** - Princess of Import (Import) 6.6f **(68)**

Form - 6758

Record 2000 - 1st:0 2nd:0 3rd:0 Ran:3
Pre2000 - 1st:1 2nd:1 3rd:8 Ran:65

Win Prizemoney £3,096 *Total Prizemoney* £7,752

Wins * 1997 Jun Lingfi (SFT) H 5f 38 41 <

2000 AW 0-3: (6f 3) (Equi 3)

Little account mare, has worn blinkers. AW high 23. **J J Bridger [1-62] J J Bridger (from Andre Hermans in BEL [0-6] Jan 1996).*

SUPER LOVER (GER) **RR 101f** 1819a[2]

4 m

Form - 32

2000 Turf 0-2: (6f 2) (g-s, gd)

Very useful. Turf high 101 - 2nd of 9 to Skip (2 Jun Baden-Baden 6f g-s RF 1819a).
**W Baltromei in GER [0-2] Euro-American Bet Ve Gmbh (from H Hiller in GER [0-2] Spt 1999).*

SUPER MONARCH BHB 49f56a **RR 47f 56a** 4275[11]

6 ch g Cadeaux Genereux 7.9f **(76)** - Miss Fancy That (USA) (The Minstrel (CAN)) 10f **(72)**

Form - 004707020

Record 2000 - 1st:0 2nd:1 3rd:0 Ran:9
Pre2000 - 1st:2 2nd:4 3rd:1 Ran:35

Win Prizemoney £11,117 *Total Prizemoney* £22,105

Wins 1998 Oct Newmar (GD) H 8f 68 78 <
1998 Feb Lingfi (SLW) 7f 56

2000 Turf 0-7: (7f 2, 8f 4, 9f) (g-s, gd, g-f 3, frm 2) 2000 AW 0-2: (7f, 8f) (Equi 2)

Fair gelding, effective 7 to 8f, best at 8f, acts on g-f to frm - acts on Equi, has worn blinkers. Turf high 54. AW high 57. **L A Dace [0-9] Auld Firm Partnership (from K R Burke [1-20] Oct 1999).*

SUPERSONIC BHB 58f57a **RR 62f 57a** 5072[17]

4 b m Shirley Heights 12.1f **(76)** - Bright Landing (Sun Prince) 12.4f **(52)**

Form - 4604030380

Record 2000 - 1st:0 2nd:0 3rd:2 Ran:10
Pre2000 - 1st:0 2nd:3 3rd:1 Ran:9

Win Prizemoney £0 *Total Prizemoney* £4,811

2000 Turf 0-7: (10f 7) (g-s, gd 2, g-f 2, frm 2) 2000 AW 0-3: (10f, 12f 2) (Equi 2, Fibr)

Scopey, average filly, effective 8 to 11f, best at 10f, acts on gd to frm, best on frm, prefers tight tracks, excels at Windsor and Bath. Turf high 66 - 4th of 9 to The Green Grey (24 Jly Windsor 10f frm RF 3081). AW high 60. Inconsistent. **R F JohnsonHoughton [0-19] J W Rowles.*

SUPERSTAR LEO (IRE) BHB 120f **RR 115f** 4845a[2]

2 b f College Chapel - Council Rock (General Assembly (USA)) 10f **(68)**

Form - 21111212

Record 2000 - 1st:5 2nd:3 3rd:0 Ran:8

Win Prizemoney £138,515 *Total Prizemoney* £192,713

Wins * **2000** Spt Doncas (G-F) G2 5f 105 <
* **2000** Jly Newbur (G-F) 5.2f 105 <
* **2000** Jun Ascot (G-F) G3 5f 89
* **2000** Jun Catter (G-S) 5f 85+

* 2000	Jun	Catter	(GD)	5f	59++

2000 Turf 5-8: (5f 5-7, 6f) (gd 2-4, g-f, frm 2-2, hrd 1-1)
High-class filly, effective 5f, acts on gd to hrd, excels at Catterick. Turf high 115 - 2nd of 11 getting 21lb from Namid (1 Oct Longchamp 5f gd RF 4845a). Originally part-owned by Lester Piggott, she stamped herself a very useful juvenile with decisive wins in both the Norfolk Stakes and Weatherbys Super Sprint. Ran creditably when stepped up to six furlongs in the Heinz 57 Phoenix Stakes, if well beaten by Minardi, and ended the season with an excellent effort against the older sprinters in the Prix de l'Abbaye. She might find things harder at three.
**W J Haggas [5-8] Lael Stable.*

SUPER STORY BHB 27f RR 2f 5200[11]
3 b f Superlative 8.6f **(57)** - Princess Story (Prince de Galles)
Form - 00

Record	**2000 -**	1st:0	2nd:0	3rd:0	Ran:2
	Pre2000 -	1st:0	2nd:0	3rd:0	Ran:1

2000 Turf 0-2: (10f 2) (g-s, gd)
Scopey, currently very poor filly. Turf high 2 (began Spt).
**M Madgwick [0-3] W V Roker.*

SUPER TASSA (IRE) RR 105f 5215a[8]
4 ch m Lahib (USA) 8f **(69)** - Center Moriches (IRE) (Magical Wonder (USA))
Form - 1388
2000 Turf 1-4: (11f 1-1, 12f 2, 13f) (hvy, gd 1-2, g-f)

Superstar Leo was the top rated juvenile filly in Europe

Pattern-class filly. Turf high 105 (1st run) - 1st of 5 from War Game (17 May Saint-cloud RF 1446a).
**V Valiani in ITY [1-5] (from V Renzetti in ITY [0-1] Spt 2000).*

SUPER VALUE RR 57f 4222[8]
2 ch f Polar Falcon (USA) 9f **(74)** - Superstore (USA) (Blushing Groom (FR)) 10.3f **(76)**
Form - 08

Record	**2000 -**	1st:0	2nd:0	3rd:0	Ran:2

2000 Turf 0-2: (7f 2) (g-f, frm)
Currently fair filly. Turf high 57 (began Aug).
**Mrs A J Perrett [0-2] K Abdulla.*

SUPLIZI (IRE) BHB 37f RR 67f 5161[10]
9 b h Alzao (USA) 9.8f **(73)** - Sphinx (GER) (Alpenkonig (GER)) 10.8f **(76)**
Form - 4000606800

Record	**2000 -**	1st:0	2nd:0	3rd:0	Ran:10
	Pre2000 -	1st:3	2nd:4	3rd:2	Ran:18

Win Prizemoney £28,324 *Total Prizemoney* £53,022

Wins	1996	Apr	Ripon	(GD)		12.3f		100

2000 Turf 0-10: (9f, 10f, 11f, 12f 5, 16f 2) (sft, gd, g-f 4, frm 4)
Average horse, effective 12f, acts on gd, has worn blinkers, likes left handed tracks, likes tight tracks. Turf high 67 (1st run) - 4th of 9 to Rapier (8 Jun Haydock 12f gd RF 1805).
**P Bowen [0-16] T G Price (from B J Llewellyn [0-3] May 1998).*

SUPPLY AND DEMAND BHB 103f94a RR 103f 94a 1860[1]
6 b g Belmez (USA) 11.4f **(65)** - Sipsi Fach (Prince Sabo) 7.2f **(62)**
Form - 7221

Record	**2000 -**	1st:1	2nd:2	3rd:0	Ran:4
	Pre2000 -	1st:3	2nd:5	3rd:2	Ran:28

Win Prizemoney £74,455 *Total Prizemoney* £111,136

Wins	*** 2000**	Jun	Epsom	(GD)	H	10.1f	90	103	<
	1998	Jly	Goodwo	(GD)	H	9.9f	94	99	
	1997	May	Lingfi	(SFT)	H	9f	90	93	
	1997	Apr	Epsom	(GD)		8.5f		75	

2000 Turf 1-4: (10f 1-4) (sft, g-s, gd 1-2)
Very useful gelding, effective 10f, acts on g-s to gd, has worn blinkers (effectively). Turf high 103 - 1st of 14 giving 12lb to Gentleman Venture (10 Jun Epsom RF 1860). Runner-up in a couple of decent handicaps in May, he bolted up at Epsom on Derby day but did not reappear. He is very able when conditions are right.
**J H M Gosden [1-4] Action Bloodstock (from G L Moore [5-32] Aug 1999).*

SUPREME ANGEL BHB 63f63a RR 67f 63a 5199[7]
5 b m Beveled (USA) 6.9f **(64)** - Blue Angel (Lord Gayle (USA)) 8.8f **(62)**
Form - 3174013500707

Record	**2000 -**	1st:2	2nd:0	3rd:2	Ran:13
	Pre2000 -	1st:3	2nd:2	3rd:1	Ran:22

Win Prizemoney £24,076 *Total Prizemoney* £28,018

Wins	**2000**	May	Lingfi	(G-S)	H	5f	59	62	
	*** 2000**	*Mar*	*Southw*	*(STD)*	*H*	*5f*	*59*	*61*	
	* 1998	May	Kempto	(GD)	H	6f	82	84	<
	* 1997	Oct	Haydoc	(HVY)	H	5f	75	81	
	* 1997	Apr	Newbur	(G-F)		5.2f		69	

2000 Turf 1-10: (5f 1-6, 6f 4) (g-s, gd 1-5, g-f 3, frm) 2000 AW 1-3: (5f 1-3) (Fibr 1-3)
Average filly, effective 5f, acts on gd - acts on Fibr, has worn blinkers. Turf high 67 - 3rd of 10 giving 4lb to Eastern Trumpeter (20 May Lingfield 5f gd RF 1327) - also 1st of 15 getting 5lb from Polly Golightly (12 May Lingfield RF 1173). AW high 61 - 1st of 12 giving 2lb to Jack To A King (14 Mar Southwell RF 0444). Consistent. She took advantage of a favourable mark to win at Lingfield in May.
**M P Muggeridge [5-35] Least Moved Partners.*

SUPREMELY DEVIOUS BHB 56f46a RR 62f 46a 107[3]
3 ch f Wolfhound (USA) 7.3f **(71)** - Clearly Devious **(74f)** (Machiavellian (USA))
Form - 62633

Record	**2000 -**	1st:0	2nd:0	3rd:2	Ran:2
	Pre2000 -	1st:0	2nd:2	3rd:0	Ran:10

Win Prizemoney £0 *Total Prizemoney* £2,334
2000 AW 0-2: (7f 2) (Equi, Fibr)
Neat, average filly, effective 6f, acts on frm, often wears blinkers. AW high 46. **R M H Cowell [0-12] Bottisham Heath Stud.*

SUPREME SALUTATION BHB 75f RR 79f 4743[7]
4 ch g Most Welcome 8.6f **(66)** - Cardinal Press **(88df)** (Sharrood (USA)) 10.5f **(72)**
Form - 60627673553427

Record	**2000 -**	1st:0	2nd:2	3rd:2	Ran:14
	Pre2000 -	1st:2	2nd:3	3rd:1	Ran:10

Win Prizemoney £8,665 *Total Prizemoney* £20,785

Wins	* 1999	Aug	Thirsk	(SFT)	H	8f	72	79	<
	* 1999	Jly	Catter	(GD)	H	7f	62	72	

2000 Turf 0-14: (7f 10, 8f 4) (sft, g-s 2, gd 3, g-f 3, frm 5)
Workmanlike, above-average gelding, effective 7 to 8f, best at 7f, acts on gd to frm, best on gd, excels at Ayr and Newmarket, does well at Thirsk. Turf high 79 - 2nd of 16 giving 5lb to Great News (15 Spt Ayr 7f gd RF 4430). Consistent. He has his own ideas and is hard to win with, but has been running well in the autumn.
**T D Barron [2-24] J Baggott.*

SUPREME SILENCE (IRE) BHB 51f55a RR 53f 55a 4923[1]
3 b c Bluebird (USA) 7.9f **(71)** - Why so Silent (Mill Reef (USA)) 10.5f **(78)**
Form - 0070701

Record	**2000 -**	1st:1	2nd:0	3rd:0	Ran:7

Win Prizemoney £2,320 *Total Prizemoney* £2,320

Wins	*** 2000**	*Oct*	*Lingfi*	*(STD)*	*H*	*16f*	*47*	*56*	<

2000 Turf 0-6: (8f 2, 10f 2, 12f, 16f) (gd, g-f 3, frm 2) 2000 AW 1-1: (16f 1-1) (Equi 1-1)
Strong, fair colt, effective 12 to 16f, acts on g-f - acts on Equi, prefers tight tracks. Turf high 54. (1st run) - 1st of 14 getting 18lb from Destination (11 Oct Lingfield RF 4923).
**P W Harris [1-7] Mrs P W Harris.*

SUPREME TRAVEL BHB 48f **RR 47f** 4614[9]

2 b c Piccolo - Salinas (Bay Express) 7.1f **(60)**
Form - 000
Record 2000 - 1st:0 2nd:0 3rd:0 Ran:3
2000 Turf 0-3: (5f, 7f, 8f) (gd 2, g-f)
Currently moderate colt. Turf high 47. Has shown little so far.
**J Pearce [0-3] Bridge Veasey Whatley Partnership.*

SURE DANCER (USA) BHB 100f **RR 103f** 4309[9]

5 b h Affirmed (USA) 10.3f **(75)** - Danlu (USA) (Danzig (USA)) 8.4f **(76)**
Form - 620
Record 2000 - 1st:0 2nd:1 3rd:0 Ran:3
Pre2000 - 1st:2 2nd:0 3rd:0 Ran:3
Win Prizemoney £10,329 *Total Prizemoney* £12,738
Wins * 1999 Jly Doncas (G-F) 8f 112 <
* 1999 Apr Leices (GD) 10f 84+
2000 Turf 0-3: (8f 2, 9f) (gd 2, frm)
Very useful colt, effective 8f, acts on gd to frm, has worn blinkers. Turf high 103 (1st run) (began Jly) - 6th of 9 getting 5lb from Sugarfoot (15 Jly Ascot 8f gd RF 2827). Well beaten in an Ascot Listed event on his belated return to action, he was beaten pointless by Albarahin in a Sandown conditions event next time. Making his handicap debut and sporting first-time blinkers, he was well down the field at Doncaster in September.
**P F I Cole [2-6] M Arbib.*

SURE FUTURE BHB 40f **RR 45f** 4269[8]

4 b g Kylian (USA) 8.1f **(66)** - Lady Ever-so-Sure (Malicious) 8.7f **(50)**
Form - 07558
Record 2000 - 1st:0 2nd:0 3rd:0 Ran:5
Pre2000 - 1st:0 2nd:1 3rd:0 Ran:7
Win Prizemoney £0 *Total Prizemoney* £916
2000 Turf 0-5: (10f, 11f, 12f 2, 16f) (gd, g-f 3, frm)
Leggy, moderate gelding, often wears blinkers. Turf high 45.
**J R Best [0-7] James Hill (from A C Stewart [0-7] Spt 1999).*

SURE QUEST BHB 61f58a **RR 63f 58a** 4994[3]

5 b m Sure Blade (USA) 10.6f **(66)** - Eagle's Quest (Legal Eagle) 7.3f **(54)**
Form - 234111223423
Record 2000 - 1st:3 2nd:4 3rd:3 Ran:12
Pre2000 - 1st:1 2nd:0 3rd:2 Ran:13
Win Prizemoney £15,654 *Total Prizemoney* £25,192
Wins * 2000 May Bath (G-S) H 11.7f 52 59
*** 2000** Apr Windso (GD) H 11.6f 49 50
*** 2000** *Mar Wolver (STD) S 12f 46+*
* 1998 Aug Folkes (G-F) H 9.7f 57 61 <
2000 Turf 2-6: (10f, 12f 2-5) (g-s, gd 1-1, g-f, frm 1-3) 2000 AW 1-6: (9f 2, 11f, 12f 1-3) (Fibr 1-6)
Average filly, effective 8 to 12f, best at 12f, acts on gd to frm - acts on Fibr, best on frm, has worn blinkers, excels at Bath and likes Windsor. Turf high 63 - 3rd of 8 giving 17lb to Dizzy Tilly (3 Jly Windsor 12f frm RF 2489) - also 1st of 11 getting 16lb from Pulau Pinang (2 May Bath RF 0962). AW high 61 - 3rd of 12 giving 17lb to Town Gossip (14 Oct Wolverhampton 12f Fibr RF 4994). Consistent. She has not looked back since winning a seller on the Wolverhampton Fibresand in March, going on to complete a hat-trick with further wins in much better company on turf at Windsor and Bath. **D W P Arbuthnot [4-25] Miss P E Decker.*

SURE TO DREAM (IRE) BHB 38f45a **RR 37f 45a** 267[P]

7 b m Common Grounds 8.1f **(66)** - Hard to Stop (Hard Fought) 8.8f **(62)**
Form - 804P
Record 2000 - 1st:0 2nd:0 3rd:0 Ran:2
Pre2000 - 1st:3 2nd:2 3rd:2 Ran:22
Win Prizemoney £7,269 *Total Prizemoney* £9,607
Wins * 1999 *May Southw (STD) H 7f 52 55* <
* 1998 *May Southw (STD) H 6f 49 54*
* 1997 *Nov Lingfi (STD) 6f 41*
2000 AW 0-2: (7f, 8f) (Equi, Fibr)
Very moderate mare, effective 6 to 7f, - acted on Equi to Fibr, had worn blinkers, favoured left handed tracks, favoured tight tracks. AW high 34. Inconsistent. (DEAD)
**R T Phillips [3-24] Dozen Dreamers Partnership.*

SURFSIDE (USA) RR 5325a[2]

3 f Seattle Slew (USA) 7.8f **(64)** - Flanders (USA) **(108f)** (Seeking the Gold (USA))
Form - 2
2000 AW 0-1: (9f) (Dirt)
Currently Group-class, often wears blinkers. (1st run) - 2nd of 9 to Spain (4 Nov Churchill Downs 9f Dirt RF 5325a).
**D W Lukas in USA [0-2] Overbrook Farm.*

SURPRISED BHB 78f **RR 80f** 4449[4]

5 b g Superpower 6.6f **(58)** - Indigo (Primo Dominie) 6.2f **(80)**
Form - 001544134
Record 2000 - 1st:2 2nd:0 3rd:1 Ran:9
Pre2000 - 1st:1 2nd:4 3rd:1 Ran:15
Win Prizemoney £29,717 *Total Prizemoney* £39,168
Wins * 2000 Aug Goodwo (GD) H 6f 70 75 <
*** 2000** Jun Hamilt (GD) 6f 68
* 1999 Jun Pontef (GD) H 6f 64 66
2000 Turf 2-9: (5f 3, 6f 2-6) (gd 1-4, g-f 2, frm 1-3)
Decent gelding, effective 6f, acts on gd to frm, best on gd, has worn blinkers (extremely effectively), excels at Goodwood. Turf high 80 - 4th of 29 giving 3lb to Lady Boxer (16 Spt Ayr 6f gd RF 4449) - also 1st of 21 getting 16lb from Marsad (26 Aug Goodwood RF 3984). Worth watching out for when the money is down.
**R A Fahey [3-17] D R Brotherton (from Mrs J R Ramsden [0-7] Jly 1998).*

SURPRISE ENCOUNTER BHB 86f **RR 86f** 4115[1]

4 ch g Cadeaux Genereux 7.9f **(76)** - Scandalette (Niniski (USA)) 10.6f **(65)**
Form - 005421
Record 2000 - 1st:1 2nd:1 3rd:0 Ran:6
Pre2000 - 1st:1 2nd:0 3rd:0 Ran:5
Win Prizemoney £7,271 *Total Prizemoney* £9,116
Wins * 2000 Aug Lingfi (G-F) H 7f 79 86 <
* 1999 Apr Kempto (G-F) 7f 81
2000 Turf 1-6: (7f 1-4, 8f 2) (sft, gd, g-f, frm 1-3)
Workmanlike, useful gelding, effective 7f, acts on gd to frm. Turf high 86 - 1st of 10 getting 5lb from Volontiers (31 Aug Lingfield RF 4115). Landed a Kempton maiden in April of last year before running with some credit in a couple of decent handicaps, but was off for almost a year before finishing down the field at Kempton on his return. Gradually found his form, and got off the mark for the season at Lingfield in August, breaking the track record in the process. **E A L Dunlop [2-11] Ahmed Ali.*

SURVEYOR BHB 65f **RR 67f** 5141[8]

5 ch g Lycius (USA) 8.8f **(71)** - Atacama (Green Desert (USA)) 8.6f **(78)**
Form - 00878
Record 2000 - 1st:0 2nd:0 3rd:0 Ran:5
Pre2000 - 1st:2 2nd:1 3rd:1 Ran:11
Win Prizemoney £7,211 *Total Prizemoney* £11,848
Wins 1997 Spt Kempto (GD) H 6f 90 93 <
1997 Aug Lingfi (G-F) 6f 83+
2000 Turf 0-5: (6f 3, 7f 2) (g-s, gd, frm 3)
Average gelding. Turf high 67. Consistent. He has never quite lived up to expectations and seems to have lost his form completely.
**C N Allen [0-5] NewmarketConnections com (from J L Dunlop [2-11] Spt 1999).*

SUSAN'S DOWRY BHB 39f **RR 40f** 5054[3]

4 b m Efisio 7.7f **(69)** - Adjusting (IRE) (Busted) 10.2f **(61)**
Form - 000403
Record 2000 - 1st:0 2nd:0 3rd:1 Ran:6
Pre2000 - 1st:1 2nd:0 3rd:0 Ran:6
Win Prizemoney £3,615 *Total Prizemoney* £4,249
Wins 1998 Jun Pontef (SFT) 6f 76+ <
2000 Turf 0-6: (8f 2, 10f 2, 11f, 12f) (sft, g-s, gd 3, frm)
Scopey, moderate filly. Turf high 40 (began Jly). Inconsistent.
**Andrew Turnell [0-7] Mrs Claire Hollowood (from T D Easterby [1-5] Jly 1998).*

SUSAN'S PRIDE (IRE) BHB 73f **RR 79f** 4433[13]

4 b g Pips Pride 6.7f **(70)** - Piney Pass (Persian Bold) 9.3f **(66)**

Form - 4107303475450

Record					
	2000 -	1st:1	2nd:0	3rd:2	Ran:13
	Pre2000 -	1st:3	2nd:1	3rd:1	Ran:14

Win Prizemoney £13,975 *Total Prizemoney* £22,059

Wins								
* **2000**	Mar	Catter	(GD)	H	7f	75	82	<
* 1999	Oct	Bright	(G-S)	C	7f		68	
* 1999	Oct	Doncas	(SFT)	C	7f		77	
* 1999	May	Nottin	(GD)		6.1f		75	

2000 Turf 1-13: (6f, 7f 1-12) (sft 2, gd 3, g-f 3, frm 1-5)

Workmanlike, above-average gelding, effective 7f, acts on sft to frm, has worn blinkers, likes left handed tracks, likes tight tracks. Turf high 82 - 1st of 16 giving 14lb to Foreign Editor (29 Mar Catterick RF 0547). Inconsistent. **B J Meehan [4-27] Mrs Susan Roy.*

SUSIE'S FLYER (IRE) BHB 75f **RR 58f** 2265[6]

3 br f Frimaire - Wisdom to Know (Bay Express) 7.1f **(60)**

Form - 5006

Record					
	2000 -	1st:0	2nd:0	3rd:0	Ran:4
	Pre2000 -	1st:2	2nd:1	3rd:0	Ran:5

Win Prizemoney £10,040 *Total Prizemoney* £11,070

Wins								
1999	Spt	Newbur	(G-F)	H	5.2f	77	90+	<
1999	Aug	Lingfi	(GD)		5f		72	

2000 Turf 0-4: (5f 2, 6f 2) (hvy, gd, g-f, frm)

Light-framed, fair filly, effective 5f, acts on frm. Turf high 58. Consistent. Made all to win at Lingfield on her third start at two, despite hanging badly left in the closing stages, and followed up in a Newbury nursery. Well held in heavy ground since.

**A Berry [0-4] Mrs U O'Reilly (from J Berry [2-5] Spt 1999).*

SUSIE THE FLOOSIE (IRE) BHB 43f38a **RR 52f 38a** 5247[8]

2 b f General Monash (USA) - Cala-Holme (IRE) **(24f)** (Fools Holme (USA))

Form - 07808

Record					
	2000 -	1st:0	2nd:0	3rd:0	Ran:5

2000 Turf 0-3: (6f, 7f, 8f) (gd 2, g-f) 2000 AW 0-2: (8f 2) (Fibr 2)

Fair filly. Turf high 52 (began Jly). AW high 25 (began Oct).

**B Smart [0-5] Coriolan Partnership.*

SUSSEX LAD BHB 74f68a **RR 79f 68a** 5317[12]

3 b g Prince Sabo 6.6f **(64)** - Pea Green (Try My Best (USA)) 7.6f **(67)**

Form - 740646160

Record					
	2000 -	1st:1	2nd:0	3rd:0	Ran:9
	Pre2000 -	1st:0	2nd:0	3rd:0	Ran:2

Win Prizemoney £2,782 *Total Prizemoney* £3,029

Wins								
* **2000**	Aug	Salisb	(G-F)	H	6f	72	77	<

2000 Turf 1-9: (5f 3, 6f 1-5, 7f) (sft, gd 2, g-f 4, frm 1-2)

Workmanlike, above-average gelding, effective 5 to 6f, best at 6f, acts on gd to frm. Turf high 79 - also 1st of 11 getting 4lb from Referendum (17 Aug Salisbury RF 3727). Consistent. He was running fairly well prior to winning an apprentice handicap at Salisbury in August. **R Hannon [1-11] Peter Crane.*

SUSY WELLS (IRE) BHB 30f **RR 30f** 3069[11]

5 b m Masad (IRE) - My Best Susy (IRE) (Try My Best (USA)) 7.6f **(67)**

Form - 005500

Record					
	2000 -	1st:0	2nd:0	3rd:0	Ran:6
	Pre2000 -	1st:0	2nd:1	3rd:1	Ran:16

Win Prizemoney £0 *Total Prizemoney* £1,215

2000 Turf 0-6: (6f 2, 7f 2, 8f, 14f) (gd 3, g-f 2, frm)

Very moderate filly, has worn blinkers. Turf high 30. Is very disappointing and her form promises little. **J Parkes [0-22] C W Moore.*

SUTTON COMMON (IRE) BHB 70f68a **RR 86f 68a** 4177[9]

3 b g Common Grounds 8.1f **(66)** - Fadaki Hawaki (USA) (Vice Regent (CAN)) 8.7f **(74)**

Form - 2021000

Record					
	2000 -	1st:1	2nd:2	3rd:0	Ran:7
	Pre2000 -	1st:0	2nd:0	3rd:0	Ran:2

Win Prizemoney £3,477 *Total Prizemoney* £6,110

Wins								
* **2000**	Jun	Beverl	(G-S)		7.5f		86	<

2000 Turf 1-6: (6f, 7f 1-4, 8f) (g-s, gd 1-2, g-f, frm 2) 2000 AW 0-1: (7f) (Fibr)

Workmanlike, useful gelding, effective 7f, acts on gd to frm, best on gd. Turf high 86 - 1st of 4 from Golden Chance (7 Jun Beverley RF 1779). Becoming disappointing.

**K A Ryan [1-9] The North Broomhill Racing Syndicate.*

SWAGGER BHB 63a **RR 66+f** 1301[1]

4 ch g Generous (IRE) 11.5f **(82)** - Widows Walk (Habitat) 9.4f **(70)**

Form - 11141

Record					
	2000 -	1st:4	2nd:0	3rd:0	Ran:5
	Pre2000 -	1st:1	2nd:0	3rd:1	Ran:9

Win Prizemoney £11,283 *Total Prizemoney* £11,619

Wins								
* **2000**	May	Hamilt	(G-F)	H	13f	58	66	<
2000	*Jan*	*Southw*	*(STD)*	*H*	*12f*	*52*	*65*	
2000	*Jan*	*Southw*	*(STD)*	*H*	*12f*	*42*	*53+*	
2000	*Jan*	*Southw*	*(STD)*	*H*	*11f*	*42*	*47*	
1999	*Spt*	*Southw*	*(STD)*	*H*	*14f*	*39*	*41*	

2000 Turf 1-1: (13f 1-1) (g-f 1-1) 2000 AW 3-4: (11f 1-1, 12f 2-2, 16f) (Fibr 3-4)

Strong, average gelding, effective 12 to 16f, acted on g-f - acted on Fibr, liked left handed tracks, favoured tight tracks, excelled at Southwell. (1st run) - 1st of 9 giving 23lb to Happy Days (19 May Hamilton RF 1301). AW high 65 - 1st of 11 giving 30lb to Wellcome Inn (28 Jan Southwell RF 0176). (DEAD)

**A Dickman [1-1] Mike Smallman (from Sir Mark Prescott [4-13] Feb 2000).*

SWALDO BHB 44f59a **RR 56df 59a** 3632[8]

3 ch g Muhtarram (USA) - Ethel Knight (Thatch (USA)) 9.8f **(62)**

Form - 7888

Record					
	2000 -	1st:0	2nd:0	3rd:0	Ran:4
	Pre2000 -	1st:0	2nd:1	3rd:1	Ran:4

Win Prizemoney £0 *Total Prizemoney* £906

2000 Turf 0-3: (8f, 9f, 12f) (g-f, frm 2) 2000 AW 0-1: (8f) (Fibr)

Leggy, fair gelding, effective 8f, acts on gd, has worn blinkers, prefers tight tracks. Turf high 32 (began Jly).

**M P Muggeridge [0-2] London Bridge II (from N E Berry [0-2] Jly 2000).*

SWALLOW FLIGHT (IRE) BHB 120f **RR 123f** 4698[5]

4 b h Bluebird (USA) 7.9f **(71)** - Mirage (Red Sunset) 8.2f **(63)**

Form - 21131345

Record					
	2000 -	1st:3	2nd:1	3rd:2	Ran:8
	Pre2000 -	1st:2	2nd:4	3rd:4	Ran:14

Win Prizemoney £85,558 *Total Prizemoney* £156,872

Wins								
* **2000**	Jly	Goodwo	(G-F)	L	8f		123+	<
* **2000**	May	Sandow	(HVY)	H	8.1f	108	111	
* **2000**	May	Windso	(G-F)	L	8.3f		96	
* 1999	Spt	Doncas	(G-F)		8f		101+	
* 1999	May	York	(G-S)	H	7f	94	96	

2000 Turf 3-8: (7f, 8f 3-7) (g-s 1-1, gd, g-f 1-3, frm 1-3)

Scopey, very high-class colt, effective 8f, acts on gd to frm, likes left handed trackslikes right handed tracks, likes tight tracks, excels at Doncaster. Turf high 123 - 1st of 2 giving 3lb to Duck Row (2 Jly Goodwood RF 2465). Probably best over a mile, he acts on any ground and won a listed event at Windsor in good style in May. Followed up in a hot handicap at Sandown before running a blinder when third in a Group Two at Royal Ascot. Regained winning ways in a two-horse race at Goodwood. Continued to perform well in Pattern company later in the season, and looks capable of scoring at Group Three level next term. **G Wragg [5-22] Mollers Racing.*

SWALLOW JAZ BHB 47f **RR 60?f** 3331[19]

3 b g Alhijaz 7.7f **(57)** - Marguerite Bay (IRE) **(84f)** (Darshaan) 9.9f **(84)**

Form - 0

Record					
	2000 -	1st:0	2nd:0	3rd:0	Ran:1
	Pre2000 -	1st:0	2nd:0	3rd:0	Ran:4

2000 Turf 0-1: (8f) (g-f)

Light-framed, average gelding.

**P S Felgate [0-1] Foreneish Racing (from T J Etherington [0-4] Spt 1999).*

SWALLOW MAGIC (IRE) RR 5156[16]

2 b c Magic Ring (IRE) 6.5f **(64)** - Scylla **(36f 33a)** (Rock City)

Form - 0

Record					
	2000 -	1st:0	2nd:0	3rd:0	Ran:1

2000 Turf 0-1: (5f) (g-s)

Currently very poor colt. **P S Felgate [0-1] Foreneish Racing.*

SWAMPY (IRE) BHB 60f32a **RR 66f 32a** 235[11]

4 b g Second Set (IRE) 9.2f **(67)** - Mystery Lady (USA) (Vaguely Noble) 10.1f **(72)**
Form - 7540
Record 2000 - 1st:0 2nd:0 3rd:0 Ran:3
Pre2000 - 1st:0 2nd:3 3rd:1 Ran:15
Win Prizemoney £0 *Total Prizemoney* £2,884
2000 AW 0-3: (7f, 8f 2) (Fibr 3)
Average gelding, effective 8 to 10f, acts on hvy to gd, best on gd. AW high 36.
**R F Marvin [0-2] Wetherby Racing Bureau 41 (from J Wharton [0-2] Jan 2000).*

SWANDALE FLYER BHB 24f22a **RR 28f 22a** 4119[7]
8 ch g Weldnaas (USA) 8.4f **(55)** - Misfire (Gunner B) 11.2f **(58)**
Form - 0057217
Record 2000 - 1st:1 2nd:1 3rd:0 Ran:7
Pre2000 - 1st:0 2nd:1 3rd:1 Ran:33
Win Prizemoney £2,247 *Total Prizemoney* £4,516
Wins * **2000** Aug Carlis (GD) H 17.2f 15 28 <
2000 Turf 1-7: (12f 2, 13f, 14f, 16f 2, 17f 1-1) (g-f, frm 1-5, hrd)
Very moderate gelding, has broken blood-vessels, effective 17f, acts on frm, likes right handed tracks. Turf high 28 - 1st of 10 getting 29lb from Jordan's Ridge (23 Aug Carlisle RF 3905).
**N Bycroft [2-56] Barrie Abbott.*

SWAN HUNTER BHB 50f50a **RR 45f 50a** 163[7]
7 b h Sharrood (USA) 11.1f **(67)** - Cache (Bustino) 10.4f **(64)**
Form - 2527
Record 2000 - 1st:0 2nd:1 3rd:0 Ran:2
Pre2000 - 1st:6 2nd:6 3rd:0 Ran:31
Win Prizemoney £15,926 *Total Prizemoney* £28,832
Wins * 1998 *Jan Wolver (STD) H 12f 77 84* <
* 1997 *Dec Wolver (STD) H 12f 68 74+*
* 1997 *Nov Wolver (STD) H 14.8f 62 67*
* 1997 Oct Catter (SFT) C 12f 57+
* 1997 Oct Leices (G-S) C 11.8f 62
* 1996 Apr Mussel (GD) 11.1f 63
2000 AW 0-2: (15f, 16f) (Equi, Fibr)
Moderate horse, effective 12f, - acts on Equi, has worn blinkers, favours left handed tracks. AW high 48.
**D J S Cosgrove [6-33] Derrick Yarwood.*

SWAN KNIGHT (USA) BHB 95f84a **RR 95f 84a** 5240[25]
4 b br h Sadler's Wells (USA) 11.3f **(87)** - Shannkara (IRE) (Akarad (FR)) 9f **(76)**
Form - 26018030
Record 2000 - 1st:1 2nd:1 3rd:1 Ran:8
Pre2000 - 1st:1 2nd:0 3rd:0 Ran:2
Win Prizemoney £10,669 *Total Prizemoney* £16,291
Wins 2000 Spt Bath (SFT) 8f 82+ <
1999 Apr Newmar (GD) 8f 77t
2000 Turf 1-8: (7f 2, 8f 1-4, 9f, 10f) (hvy, sft, g-s 1-3, gd, g-f 2)
Scopey, very useful colt, effective 8 to 9f, acts on sft to gd. Turf high 95 (began Jly) - 3rd of 11 giving 2lb to Cornelius (21 Oct Newbury 9f sft RF 5133). Inconsistent. Best on soft ground, he is capable but inconsistent. Still unproven over a mile and a quarter, he is probably best left alone.
**M Quinn [0-1] & Mrs Gary Pinchen (from J L Dunlop [1-7] Oct 2000).*

SWAN LAKE (FR) BHB 36a **RR 44f** 4584[9]
4 b m Lyphard (USA) 10.6f **(75)** - Dame Au Faucon (USA) (Silver Hawk (USA)) 8.6f **(70)**
Form - 00
Record 2000 - 1st:0 2nd:0 3rd:0 Ran:1
Pre2000 - 1st:0 2nd:0 3rd:0 Ran:10
2000 AW 0-1: (10f) (Equi)
Moderate filly. Inconsistent. Looks more of a goose on what she has shown so far. **K O Cunningham-Brown [0-11] A J Richards.*

SWAN PRINCE BHB 30f **RR 12f** 2565[15]
3 b g King's Signet (USA) 7f **(51)** - Princess Tallulah **(15f 30a)** (Chief Singer) 8.9f **(66)**
Form - 0
Record 2000 - 1st:0 2nd:0 3rd:0 Ran:1
Pre2000 - 1st:0 2nd:0 3rd:0 Ran:6
2000 Turf 0-1: (8f) (g-f)
Light-framed, poor gelding. **W G M Turner [0-7] Vale Racing.*

SWANTON ABBOT (IRE) BHB 70f **RR 67f** 4283[15]
2 b c Charnwood Forest (IRE) - Shaping Up (USA) (Storm Bird (CAN)) 10.3f **(74)**
Form - 8050
Record 2000 - 1st:0 2nd:0 3rd:0 Ran:4
2000 Turf 0-4: (5f, 6f, 8f 2) (gd, frm 3)
Average colt. Turf high 70 (began Aug).
**M H Tompkins [0-4] J H Ellis.*

SWEET ANGELINE BHB 68f **RR 67f** 5072[19]
3 b f Deploy 11.4f **(67)** - Fiveofive (IRE) (Fairy King (USA)) 7.7f **(59)**
Form - 075431230
Record 2000 - 1st:1 2nd:1 3rd:2 Ran:9
Pre2000 - 1st:0 2nd:0 3rd:1 Ran:7
Win Prizemoney £3,373 *Total Prizemoney* £7,507
Wins * **2000** Aug Thirsk (GD) H 12f 60 64 <
2000 Turf 1-9: (8f, 10f 4, 11f 2, 12f 1-2) (g-s, gd 2, g-f 4, frm 1-2)
Scopey, average filly, effective 8 to 12f, acts on g-f to frm, best on frm, likes tight tracks. Turf high 67 - 3rd of 12 getting 5lb from Double Blade (26 Aug Redcar 11f g-f RF 3999).
**G G Margarson [1-7] Mrs T A Foreman (from A T Murphy [0-9] May 2000).*

SWEET AS A NUT (IRE) BHB 50f65a **RR 47f 65a** 2893[8]
4 ch m Pips Pride 6.7f **(70)** - My First Paige (IRE) **(41f 48a)** (Runnett) 7f **(59)**
Form - 0008
Record 2000 - 1st:0 2nd:0 3rd:0 Ran:4
Pre2000 - 1st:3 2nd:3 3rd:1 Ran:21
Win Prizemoney £8,213 *Total Prizemoney* £11,538
Wins 1998 Jly Doncas (FRM) H 5f 83 <
1998 Jun Hamilt (SFT) C 5f 75
1998 Jun Beverl (GD) C 5f 58
2000 Turf 0-2: (6f, 7f) (gd, frm) 2000 AW 0-2: (6f 2) (Fibr 2)
Leggy, moderate filly, effective 6f, acts on g-s, likes left handed tracks, likes tight tracks. Turf high 41 (began Jly). Inconsistent.
**G L Moore [0-2] Wessex House Racing (from D Carroll [0-2] Feb 2000).*

SWEET CICELY (IRE) BHB 60f **RR 67f** 3707[8]
3 b f Darshaan 11.9f **(81)** - Glendora (Glenstal (USA)) 10.1f **(64)**
Form - 3588
Record 2000 - 1st:0 2nd:0 3rd:1 Ran:4
Pre2000 - 1st:0 2nd:0 3rd:0 Ran:2
Win Prizemoney £0 *Total Prizemoney* £475
2000 Turf 0-4: (10f 3, 12f) (sft, g-f 2, frm)
Workmanlike, average filly, effective 10f, acts on g-f. Turf high 67 - 5th of 14 getting 11lb from Lidakiya (8 Jun Newbury 10f g-f RF 1814). **D R C Elsworth [0-6] Colin Brown Racing.*

SWEET ENVIRONMENT RR 2276[10]
3 gr f Environment Friend 7.5f **(67)** - Sweets (IRE) (Persian Heights)
Form - 0
Record 2000 - 1st:0 2nd:0 3rd:0 Ran:1
2000 Turf 0-1: (8f) (g-f)
Light-framed, currently very poor filly.
**Mrs M Bridgwater [0-1] R W Neale.*

SWEET HAVEN BHB 40f41a **RR 49f 41a** 4874[7]
3 b f Lugana Beach 7f **(63)** - Sweet Enough (Caerleon (USA)) 8.6f **(71)**
Form - 08002807
Record 2000 - 1st:0 2nd:1 3rd:0 Ran:8
Pre2000 - 1st:1 2nd:0 3rd:0 Ran:7
Win Prizemoney £2,372 *Total Prizemoney* £3,092
Wins 1999 Apr Beverl (G-F) 5f 72 <
2000 Turf 0-7: (7f, 8f 6) (g-s 2, gd, g-f 3, frm) 2000 AW 0-1: (7f) (Fibr)
Light-framed, moderate filly, effective 5 to 6f, acts on g-f to frm, has worn blinkers. Turf high 49.
**C G Cox [0-12] P G Horrocks (from M J Heaton-Ellis [1-3] May 1999).*

SWEET MAGIC BHB 39f46a **RR 55f 46a** 3742[8]
9 ch g Sweet Monday 8.3f **(43)** - Charm Bird (Daring March) 7.1f **(61)**
Form - 606400404147777008
Record 2000 - 1st:1 2nd:0 3rd:0 Ran:17
Pre2000 - 1st:5 2nd:6 3rd:3 Ran:46
Win Prizemoney £21,119 *Total Prizemoney* £36,302
Wins * **2000** *May Wolver (STD) S 5f 47*

* 1999 Jun Catter (G-F) H 5f 57 59
* 1999 *Apr Wolver (STD) S 5f 64*
1997 Aug Sandow (G-S) H 5f 59 63
2000 Turf 0-8: (5f 8) (sft, gd 2, g-f 2, frm 3) 2000 AW 1-9: (5f 1-9) (Equi, Fibr 1-8)
Fair gelding, effective 5f, acts on gd to frm - acts on Fibr, has worn blinkers. Turf high 56. AW high 48. He has been a good sprint handicapper in the past, but has not had a great deal of success in recent seasons.
**L R Lloyd-James [3-32] Miss Kate Waddington (from P Howling [1-20] Jun 1998).*

SWEET PATOOPIE BHB 44f54a **RR 46f 54a** 5063[14]
6 b m Indian Ridge 7.6f **(74)** - Patriotic (Hotfoot) 10.5f **(59)**
Form - 00
Record 2000 - 1st:0 2nd:0 3rd:0 Ran:1
Pre2000 - 1st:1 2nd:3 3rd:2 Ran:14
Win Prizemoney £2,733 *Total Prizemoney* £6,175
Wins 1999 *May Lingfi (STD) H 12f 59 68* <
2000 Turf 0-1: (10f) (sft)
Fair mare, effective 12f, - acts on AW, has worn blinkers. Becoming disappointing. Able in modest handicap company on turf, but her best form in the last couple of seasons has been on sand.
**Mrs P Ford [0-10] Advantage Chemicals Holdings Ltd (from B Hanbury [1-11] Jun 1000).*

SWEET PROSPECT BHB 89f **RR 84f** 4738[5]
2 b f Shareef Dancer (USA) 10.1f **(67)** - Vayavaig (Damister (USA)) 9f **(73)**
Form - 01455
Record 2000 - 1st:1 2nd:0 3rd:0 Ran:5
Win Prizemoney £3,591 *Total Prizemoney* £12,204
Wins * 2000 Jly Kempto (G-F) 6f 72 <
2000 Turf 1-5: (6f 1-4, 7f) (gd 2, g-f, frm 1-2)
Decent filly. Turf high 84. Held in better company since her Kempton win. **C F Wall [1-5] The Silver and Blue Horse Racing Club.*

SWEET REWARD BHB 68f **RR 74f** 4484[1]
5 ch g Beveled (USA) 6.9f **(64)** - Sweet Revival (Claude Monet (USA))
Form - 44735331
Record 2000 - 1st:1 2nd:0 3rd:3 Ran:8
Pre2000 - 1st:1 2nd:2 3rd:6 Ran:19
Win Prizemoney £8,228 *Total Prizemoney* £20,724
Wins * 2000 Spt Kempto (SFT) H 8f 64 71
* 1997 Jun Leices (GD) 6f 72 <
2000 Turf 1-8: (8f 1-1, 10f 6, 12f) (g-s 1-1, gd, g-f 5, frm)
Above-average gelding, effective 8 to 10f, best at 10f, acts on hvy to frm, likes right handed tracks, does well at Sandown. Turf high 74 - also 1st of 19 getting 2lb from Pagan King (18 Spt Kempton RF 4484). Consistent. His win at Kempton was his first since his two-year-old days.
**J G Smyth-Osbourne [2-28] Mrs Andria Dorler & Partners.*

SWEET SORROW (IRE) BHB 102f **RR 104df** 1262[6]
5 b m Lahib (USA) 8f **(69)** - So Long Boys (FR) (Beldale Flutter (USA)) 9.7f **(71)**
Form - 26
Record 2000 - 1st:0 2nd:1 3rd:0 Ran:2
Pre2000 - 1st:2 2nd:1 3rd:6 Ran:15
Win Prizemoney £7,448 *Total Prizemoney* £26,533
Wins * 1999 Jun Goodwo (G-F) 12f 81 <
* 1999 May Ayr (GD) 10f 78
2000 Turf 0-2: (10f 2) (sft, g-f)
Very useful filly, effective 10 to 12f, best at 12f, acts on sft to gd, best on sft. Turf high 104 (1st run) - 2nd of 8 getting 5lb from Right Wing (24 Apr Kempton 10f sft RF 0836). Consistent. Ran well in a listed race on her reappearance but was well held next time and that was it for the season. **C F Wall [2-17] Mrs Yoshiko Allan.*

SWEET TEDDY BHB 45f65a **RR 45f 65a** 4168[10]
3 b f Namaqualand (USA) - Nashville Blues (IRE) **(74f)** (Try My Best (USA)) 7.6f **(67)**
Form - 0000
Record 2000 - 1st:0 2nd:0 3rd:0 Ran:4
Pre2000 - 1st:0 2nd:0 3rd:0 Ran:3
Win Prizemoney £0 *Total Prizemoney* £428
2000 Turf 0-3: (8f 3) (gd, g-f, frm) 2000 AW 0-1: (8f) (Fibr)
Scopey, moderate filly, effective 6f, acts on g-f. Turf high 46.
**J W Hills [0-7] Freddy Bienstock.*

SWEET VELETA BHB 44f44a **RR 44a** 4996[8]
2 b f Cosmonaut - Redgrave Design (Nebbiolo) 8.1f **(75)**
Form - 34408
Record 2000 - 1st:0 2nd:0 3rd:1 Ran:5
Win Prizemoney £0 *Total Prizemoney* £262
2000 AW 0-5: (6f 2, 7f 2, 8f) (Fibr 5)
Moderate filly. AW high 43. **R M Whitaker [0-5] Christopher Cooke.*

SWEMBY BHB 40f **RR 47f** 4204[11]
3 ch f Mizoram (USA) - Equilibrium **(52f 43a)** (Statoblest)
Form - 770
Record 2000 - 1st:0 2nd:0 3rd:0 Ran:3
2000 Turf 0-3: (10f, 11f, 12f) (gd 2, frm)
Leggy, currently moderate filly. Turf high 47.
**W R Muir [0-3] North Farm Stud.*

SWIFT BHB 51f59a **RR 61f 59a** 4863[12]
6 ch g Sharpo 7.5f **(68)** - Three Terns (USA) (Arctic Tern (USA)) 8.9f **(69)**
Form - 007600
Record 2000 - 1st:0 2nd:0 3rd:0 Ran:5
Pre2000 - 1st:9 2nd:7 3rd:6 Ran:72
Win Prizemoney £34,992 *Total Prizemoney* £49,971
Wins * 1999 May York (SFT) H 13.9f 66 68
* 1999 Apr Warwic (GD) H 10.8f 57 76
* 1999 Mar Nottin (G-S) H 10f 57 67
* 1999 *Mar Southw (STD) H 12f 68 77* <
* 1999 *Mar Southw (STD) H 12f 65 65*
* 1997 Jun Redcar (GD) H 7f 62 66
* 1997 May Ripon (G-F) H 6f 57 63
* 1997 *Mar Wolver (STD) 8.5f 61*
* 1996 Oct Catter (GD) 5f 61
2000 Turf 0-2: (10f, 14f) (sft, gd) 2000 AW 0-3: (11f, 12f 2) (Fibr 3)
Average gelding, effective 10 to 14f, acts on sft to gd - acts on Fibr, favours left handed tracks. Turf high 5 (began Spt). AW high 61. Inconsistent. **M J Polglase [10-80] Gen Sir Geoffrey Howlett.*

SWIFT DISPERSAL BHB 81f **RR 84f** 1427[3]
3 gr f Shareef Dancer (USA) 10.1f **(67)** - Minsden's Image (Dancers Image (USA)) 9.3f **(71)**
Form - 001023
Record 2000 - 1st:1 2nd:1 3rd:1 Ran:6
Win Prizemoney £3,542 *Total Prizemoney* £9,986
Wins * 2000 Apr Pontef (G-S) 6f 71 <
2000 Turf 1-4: (6f 1-1, 7f 2, 9f) (g-s 1-2, gd, g-f) 2000 AW 0-2: (6f, 7f) (Fibr 2)
Workmanlike, decent filly, effective 7f, acts on gd to g-f. Turf high 84 - 3rd of 18 getting 7lb from Camberley (24 May Goodwood 7f gd RF 1427). AW high 23. Unraced as a juvenile, he started with two unpromising efforts on Fibresand early in the year. He was transformed on his turf debut however, running on resolutely to cause a 50/1 shock in a Pontefract maiden. **S C Williams [1-6] Mrs Marion Southcott.*

SWIFT MAIDEN BHB 50f **RR** 66[8]
7 gr m Sharrood (USA) 11.1f **(67)** - Gunner Girl (Gunner B) 11.2f **(58)**
Form - 8
Record 2000 - 1st:0 2nd:0 3rd:0 Ran:1
Pre2000 - 1st:1 2nd:0 3rd:2 Ran:10
Win Prizemoney £3,168 *Total Prizemoney* £4,189
Wins * 1996 May Newbur (SFT) C 10f 73+ <
2000 AW 0-1: (9f) (Fibr)
Very moderate mare. Inconsistent. **J Neville [1-10] F J Ayres (from Mrs L A Murphy [0-5] Nov 1995).*

SWIFTMAR **RR 61f** 5196[6]
2 b f Marju (IRE) 9.2f **(76)** - Swift Spring (FR) (Bluebird (USA)) 7.5f **(69)**
Form - 36
Record 2000 - 1st:0 2nd:0 3rd:1 Ran:2
Win Prizemoney £0 *Total Prizemoney* £545
2000 Turf 0-2: (8f 2) (hvy, gd)
Currently average filly. Turf high 61 (began Oct).
**P F I Cole [0-2] M Arbib.*

SWIFTUR BHB 38f **RR 36f** 2426[4]
3 b f Snurge - Swift Spring (FR) (Bluebird (USA)) 7.5f **(69)**
Form - 8004
Record 2000 - 1st:0 2nd:0 3rd:0 Ran:4
Pre2000 - 1st:0 2nd:0 3rd:0 Ran:1
2000 Turf 0-3: (7f, 8f, 10f) (g-s, frm 2) 2000 AW 0-1: (8f) (Fibr)
Unfurnished, very moderate filly, has worn blinkers. Turf high 36 - 4th of 16 getting 1lb from Chaka Zulu (1 Jly Bath 10f frm RF 2426).
**P F I Cole [0-5] Ben Arbib.*

SWIFTWAY BHB 45f **RR 47f** 4431[11]
6 ch g Anshan 8.2f **(63)** - Solemn Occasion (USA) (Secreto (USA)) 8.7f **(72)**
Form - 150
Record 2000 - 1st:1 2nd:0 3rd:0 Ran:3
Pre2000 - 1st:1 2nd:1 3rd:4 Ran:20
Win Prizemoney £5,889 *Total Prizemoney* £9,495
Wins * 2000 Mar Newcas (G-S) H 16.1f 44 47
* 1998 Jly Beverl (G-F) H 16.2f 44 49 <
2000 Turf 1-3: (16f 1-2, 17f) (g-s 1-1, gd, g-f)
Moderate gelding. Turf high 47 (1st run) - 1st of 15 getting 16lb from Cinder Hills (28 Mar Newcastle RF 0527).
**K W Hogg [5-29] Anthony White.*

SWING ALONG BHB 59f57a **RR 59f 57a** 1986[9]
5 ch m Alhijaz 7.7f **(57)** - So it Goes (Free State) 8.7f **(61)**
Form - 16241005333480200
Record 2000 - 1st:1 2nd:2 3rd:3 Ran:15
Pre2000 - 1st:1 2nd:2 3rd:3 Ran:14
Win Prizemoney £3,900 *Total Prizemoney* £11,089
Wins * 2000 *Jan Wolver (STD) H 9.4f 65 65 <*
1999 Nov Wolver (STD) H 7f 59 65 <
2000 Turf 0-4: (8f 2, 10f 2) (hvy, g-s, g-f, frm) 2000 AW 1-11: (7f, 8f 4, 9f 1-2, 11f 3, 12f) (Equi, Fibr 1-10)
Fair filly, effective 7 to 11f, acts on hvy to g-f - acts on Fibr, excels at Leicester and likes Southwell. Turf high 59 - 2nd of 16 giving 15lb to Hoh Gem (27 May Warwick 8f hvy RF 1509). AW high 65 - 1st of 13 giving 32lb to Ei Ei (27 Jan Wolverhampton RF 0165). She fluffed several chances before winning a modest handicap on the Wolverhampton Fibresand in November and added an equally moderate amateur riders' event at the same track in January.
**R Guest [1-16] A B Coogan (from C F Wall [1-13] Nov 1999).*

SWING BAND BHB 95f **RR 88f** 4752[5]
2 b c Celtic Swing - Inchkeith **(79f 69a)** (Reference Point) 6.8f **(70)**
Form - 1245
Record 2000 - 1st:1 2nd:1 3rd:0 Ran:4
Win Prizemoney £5,356 *Total Prizemoney* £11,039
Wins * 2000 Jly Newbur (G-F) 7f 88 <
2000 Turf 1-4: (7f 1-3, 8f) (g-s, g-f 1-2, frm)
Useful colt. Turf high 88 (1st run) (began Jly) - 1st of 17 from Northfields Dancer (16 Jly Newbury RF 2866).
**G B Balding [1-4] The Swingers.*

SWING BAR BHB 33f **RR 37f** 4694[4]
7 b m Sadeem (USA) - Murex (Royalty) 11.4f **(49)**
Form - 0077784
Record 2000 - 1st:0 2nd:0 3rd:0 Ran:7
Pre2000 - 1st:1 2nd:1 3rd:0 Ran:8
Win Prizemoney £2,210 *Total Prizemoney* £3,300
Wins * 1999 Aug Beverl (GD) H 9.9f 48 51 <
2000 Turf 0-7: (8f, 10f 6) (g-s, gd 2, g-f, frm, hrd 2)
Very moderate mare, effective 10f, acts on frm, favours tight tracks. Turf high 37. **J M Bradley [2-21] Miss S Howell.*

SWING CITY (IRE) BHB 46f **RR 48f** 5022[10]
3 ch f Indian Ridge 7.6f **(74)** - Menominee (Soviet Star (USA))
Form - 0030000
Record 2000 - 1st:0 2nd:0 3rd:1 Ran:7
Pre2000 - 1st:0 2nd:0 3rd:0 Ran:3
Win Prizemoney £0 *Total Prizemoney* £905
2000 Turf 0-7: (5f 2, 6f 3, 7f 2) (g-s 2, gd 2, frm 3)
Workmanlike, moderate filly. Turf high 48. Becoming disappointing. **J G Given [0-2] Mrs J Holder (from R Guest [0-8] Jun 2000).*

SWINGING THE BLUES (IRE) BHB 52f45a **RR 56f 45a** 5316[3]
6 b g Bluebird (USA) 7.9f **(71)** - Winsong Melody (Music Maestro) 7.7f **(66)**
Form - 00180073
Record 2000 - 1st:1 2nd:0 3rd:1 Ran:8
Pre2000 - 1st:3 2nd:3 3rd:3 Ran:26
Win Prizemoney £12,394 *Total Prizemoney* £18,532
Wins * 2000 Jun Yarmou (FRM) H 10.1f 54 56
* 1999 Oct Redcar (GD) H 9f 52 54
* 1998 Oct Redcar (g-s) H 9f 62 66 <
1998 Jly Nottin (G-F) H 8.2f 53 56
2000 Turf 1-7: (8f 2, 9f, 10f 1-2, 11f, 12f) (g-s, g-f 1-2, frm 4) 2000 AW 0-1: (12f) (Fibr)
Fair gelding, effective 8 to 10f, acts on gd to frm, has worn blinkers (effectively), prefers left handed tracks, prefers tight tracks. Turf high 56 - 1st of 10 getting 13lb from Rogue Spirit (26 Jun Yarmouth RF 2293). Won on fast ground at Yarmouth in June but is not altogether consistent.
**C A Dwyer [3-23] S B Components (International) Ltd (from J W Hills [1-6] Spt 1998).*

SWINGING TRIO (USA) BHB 62a **RR 55f** 2491[10]
3 b c Woodman (USA) 9.7f **(77)** - Las Meninas (IRE) **(110f)** (Glenstal (USA)) 10.1f **(64)**
Form - 00410
Record 2000 - 1st:1 2nd:0 3rd:0 Ran:5
Pre2000 - 1st:0 2nd:0 3rd:0 Ran:1
Win Prizemoney £2,782 *Total Prizemoney* £2,782
Wins * 2000 *Jun Lingfi (STD) 10f 83 <*
2000 Turf 0-3: (8f, 10f 2) (gd, frm 2) 2000 AW 1-2: (9f, 10f 1-1) (Equi 1-1, Fibr)
Workmanlike, decent colt, effective 10f, - acts on Equi. Turf high 55. AW high 83 - 1st of 7 from Satarra (27 Jun Lingfield RF 2301).
**T G Mills [1-6] T G Mills.*

SWING JOB BHB 43f35a **RR 46f 35a** 3836[3]
4 b m Ezzoud (IRE) - Leave Her Be (USA) (Known Fact (USA)) 7.4f **(67)**
Form - 03
Record 2000 - 1st:0 2nd:0 3rd:1 Ran:2
Pre2000 - 1st:0 2nd:0 3rd:0 Ran:9
Win Prizemoney £0 *Total Prizemoney* £590
2000 Turf 0-2: (7f 2) (g-f, frm)
Unfurnished, moderate filly, has worn blinkers. Turf high 46 (began Aug). Inconsistent.
**P S McEntee [0-2] Shipman Racing (from T G Mills [0-9] Aug 1999).*

SWINO BHB 41f52a **RR 56f 52a** 4277[16]
6 b g Forzando 7.2f **(63)** - St Helena (Monsanto (FR)) 6.5f **(59)**
Form - 4082468044607808270800
Record 2000 - 1st:0 2nd:1 3rd:0 Ran:18
Pre2000 - 1st:4 2nd:11 3rd:4 Ran:67
Win Prizemoney £26,276 *Total Prizemoney* £45,679
Wins * 1998 May Haydoc (GD) H 6f 80 84
* 1998 Apr Thirsk (G-S) H 5f 72 84
* 1997 Oct Redcar (G-F) 5f 66
* 1996 Aug Carlis (FRM) 5f 85 <
2000 Turf 0-16: (5f 3, 6f 10, 7f 2, 8f) (hvy 2, g-f 3, frm 11) 2000 AW 0-2: (6f, 7f) (Fibr 2)
Fair gelding, effective 6f, acts on gd, often wears blinkers. Turf high 56. AW high 42. Is on a massive losing run dating back to May 1998, and recent form offers little hope that it will end.
**P D Evans [4-85] Swinnerton Transport Ltd.*

SWISS ALPS (IRE) BHB 40f30a **RR 58f 30a** 5016[9]
3 b g Common Grounds 8.1f **(66)** - Lady of Zurich (IRE) (Danehill (USA)) 10f **(72)**
Form - 00000
Record 2000 - 1st:0 2nd:0 3rd:0 Ran:5
Pre2000 - 1st:0 2nd:0 3rd:0 Ran:1
2000 Turf 0-3: (8f 3) (gd 2, frm) 2000 AW 0-2: (6f, 9f) (Fibr 2)
Neat, fair gelding, often wears blinkers. Turf high 58. AW high 24.
**R W Armstrong [0-6] Mrs Johnny Mckeever.*

SWOOSH BHB 40f51a **RR 51a** 1791[8]
5 gr g Absalom 7.1f **(56)** - Valldemosa (Music Boy) 6.8f **(57)**
Form - 08
Record 2000 - 1st:0 2nd:0 3rd:0 Ran:2
Pre2000 - 1st:1 2nd:1 3rd:1 Ran:19
Win Prizemoney £2,250 *Total Prizemoney* £3,719

Wins 1998 Jun Nottin (GD) SH 8.2f 54 56 <
2000 Turf 0-2: (7f, 10f) (sft, frm)
Very poor gelding, has worn blinkers.
**C Parker [0-4] and Mrs M C MacKenzie (from J A Glover [1-14] Oct 1998).*

SWORD LOCAL (GER) RR 112f 4842a[7]

3 ch c Local Suitor (USA) 9.7f **(58)** - Sappho (GER) (Windwurf (GER)) 12.7f **(72)**
Form - 157
2000 Turf 1-3: (11f 1-1, 12f, 14f) (hvy, sft 1-2)
Currently Group-class colt. Turf high 112 (1st run) (began Aug) - 1st of 5 from Indian Ruby (27 Aug Baden-Baden RF 4136a).
**M Hofer in GER [1-3].*

S W THREE RR 80f 3567[2]

2 b f Slip Anchor 12.7f **(75)** - Anna Karietta (Precocious) 8.6f **(62)**
Form - 2
Record 2000 - 1st:0 2nd:1 3rd:0 Ran:1
Win Prizemoney £0 *Total Prizemoney* £1,174
2000 Turf 0-1: (7f) (g-f)
Currently decent filly. **M P Tregoning [0-1] The Earl Cadogan.*

SWYNFORD DREAM BHB 51f51a RR 59f 51a 4266[10]

7 b g Statoblest 6.4f **(63)** - Qualitair Dream (Dreams to Reality (USA)) 6.4f **(73)**
Form - 852042670050
Record 2000 - 1st:0 2nd:2 3rd:0 Ran:11
Pre2000 - 1st:6 2nd:6 3rd:2 Ran:59
Win Prizemoney £26,186 *Total Prizemoney* £41,785
Wins 1999 Apr Mussel (GD) H 5f 57 60
* 1998 Jly Catter (GD) H 5f 55 57
1996 Oct Newmar (G-F) H 5f 79 82
2000 Turf 0-11: (5f 11) (gd 2, g-f 2, frm 6, hrd)
Fair gelding, effective 5f, acts on gd to frm, best on gd, has worn blinkers. Turf high 59 - 2nd of 16 giving 11lb to Cool Prospect (5 May Musselburgh 5f frm RF 1038).
**J Hetherton [1-34] Qualitair Holdings Ltd (from T J Etherington [1-10] Jly 1999).*

SWYNFORD ELEGANCE BHB 43f RR 48f 5229[12]

3 ch f Charmer 9f **(59)** - Qualitairess (Kampala) 8.4f **(56)**
Form - 588270002400
Record 2000 - 1st:0 2nd:2 3rd:0 Ran:10
Pre2000 - 1st:0 2nd:0 3rd:0 Ran:5
Win Prizemoney £0 *Total Prizemoney* £2,156
2000 Turf 0-10: (6f, 7f 2, 8f 7) (sft, g-s, gd 2, g-f 3, frm 3)
Leggy, moderate filly, effective 7 to 8f, acts on gd to g-f. Turf high 48 - 2nd of 16 getting 21lb from Anthemion (8 Jun Haydock 7f gd RF 1810). Inconsistent. **J Hetherton [0-15] Qualitair Holdings Ltd.*

SWYNFORD PLEASURE BHB 47f36a RR 51f 36a 5192[4]

4 b m Reprimand 8.2f **(63)** - Pleasuring (Good Times (ITY)) 6.6f **(54)**
Form - 844713253343003044
Record 2000 - 1st:1 2nd:1 3rd:5 Ran:17
Pre2000 - 1st:0 2nd:3 3rd:1 Ran:15
Win Prizemoney £3,542 *Total Prizemoney* £13,117
Wins * 2000 Jun Hamilt (GD) H 9.2f 39 38 <
2000 Turf 1-17: (7f 2, 8f 7, 9f 1-7, 10f) (gd 2, g-f 4, frm 1-11)
Scopey, fair filly, effective 7 to 9f, acts on g-f to frm, best on frm, has worn blinkers, prefers right handed tracks, prefers tight tracks, excels at Hamilton. Turf high 51. Consistent.
**J Hetherton [1-26] Qualitair Holdings Ltd (from T J Etherington [0-6] Jly 1999).*

SWYNFORD WELCOME BHB 42f40a RR 46df 40a 5086[10]

4 b m Most Welcome 8.6f **(66)** - Qualitair Dream (Dreams to Reality (USA)) 6.4f **(73)**
Form - 000000000108000
Record 2000 - 1st:1 2nd:0 3rd:0 Ran:11
Pre2000 - 1st:2 2nd:2 3rd:1 Ran:20
Win Prizemoney £9,183 *Total Prizemoney* £13,707
Wins * 2000 Jly Haydoc (G-F) H 7.1f 43 46
1999 Oct Bright (G-S) H 6f 44 51
* 1998 Jly Redcar (G-F) 6f 76 <
2000 Turf 1-11: (5f 2, 6f 2, 7f 1-3, 8f 4) (hvy, g-s, gd 2, g-f 4, frm 1-3)
Scopey, moderate filly, effective 6 to 7f, acts on gd to frm, has worn blinkers, likes left handed tracks, likes tight tracks. Turf high 46 - 1st of 16 getting 11lb from Pengamon (6 Jly Haydock RF 2571). Becoming disappointing.
**J Hetherton [2-19] Qualitair Holdings Ltd (from J Pearce [1-7] Dec 1999).*

SYCAMORE LODGE (IRE) BHB 43f45a RR 45f 45a 3449[9]

9 ch g Thatching 7.8f **(69)** - Bell Tower (Lyphard's Wish (FR)) 9f **(74)**
Form - 08034068300
Record 2000 - 1st:0 2nd:0 3rd:2 Ran:11
Pre2000 - 1st:4 2nd:8 3rd:6 Ran:47
Win Prizemoney £9,896 *Total Prizemoney* £22,420
Wins * 1999 Jly Catter (GD) H 7f 59 66
* 1999 Jly Catter (FRM) S 6f 57
* 1999 May Catter (G-F) C 6f 54
1996 Jun Doncas (G-F) H 6f 67 67 <
2000 Turf 0-11: (6f 5, 7f 6) (g-s 2, gd, g-f, frm 5, hrd 2)
Moderate gelding, effective 6 to 7f, best at 7f, acts on g-f to frm, best on frm, has worn blinkers, prefers left handed tracks, prefers tight tracks. Turf high 45. Consistent.
**D Nicholls [3-33] The David Nicholls Racing Club (from M A Peill [0-7] Nov 1997).*

SYLVA LEGEND (USA) BHB 63f56a RR 72f 56a 3834[10]

4 b g Lear Fan (USA) 10.4f **(80)** - Likeashot (CAN) (Gun Shot) 12f **(74)**
Form - 56733000
Record 2000 - 1st:0 2nd:0 3rd:2 Ran:8
Pre2000 - 1st:0 2nd:1 3rd:3 Ran:12
Win Prizemoney £0 *Total Prizemoney* £9,258
2000 Turf 0-5: (7f, 8f 2, 10f 2) (gd, g-f 3, frm) 2000 AW 0-3: (8f, 10f, 11f) (Equi 2, Fibr)
Scopey, above-average gelding, effective 8 to 9f, acts on gd to frm, has worn blinkers. Turf high 72. AW high 57.
**C E Brittain [0-20] Eddy Grimstead Honda.*

SYLVAN GIRL (IRE) BHB 65a RR 68f 5019[2]

2 ch f Case Law 6f **(64)** - Nordic Living (IRE) (Nordico (USA)) 6.5f **(62)**
Form - 3253840052
Record 2000 - 1st:0 2nd:2 3rd:2 Ran:10
Win Prizemoney £0 *Total Prizemoney* £6,772
2000 Turf 0-8: (6f 6, 7f 2) (gd 2, g f 3, frm 3) 2000 AW 0-2: (6f, 7f) (Equi, Fibr)
Above-average filly, effective 6 to 7f, best at 6f, acts on gd to frm - acts on Fibr. Turf high 68. AW high 69 (began Oct) - 2nd of 9 giving 6lb to Monte Mayor Golf (17 Oct Wolverhampton 7f Fibr RF 5019). **C N Allen [0-10] ShadowfaxRacing Com.*

SYLVA PARADISE (IRE) BHB 72f RR 71f 4098[7]

7 b g Dancing Dissident (USA) 6.8f **(65)** - Brentsville (USA) (Arctic Tern (USA)) 8.9f **(69)**
Form - 845030107
Record 2000 - 1st:1 2nd:0 3rd:1 Ran:9
Pre2000 - 1st:2 2nd:5 3rd:8 Ran:48
Win Prizemoney £17,369 *Total Prizemoney* £60,076
Wins * 2000 Aug Bright (FRM) H 5.3f 68 71
* 1996 Jly Yarmou (FRM) H 6f 84 93 <
2000 Turf 1-9: (5f 1-5, 6f 3, 7f) (gd 3, g-f 1-3, frm 3)
Above-average gelding, effective 5 to 6f, best at 6f, acts on gd to frm, best on g-f, often wears blinkers (extremely effectively), excels at Goodwood. Turf high 71.
**C E Brittain [3-57] Eddy Grimstead Honda.*

SYLVA STORM (USA) RR 72f 3048[4]

2 ch c Miswaki (USA) 8.1f **(81)** - Sudden Storm Bird (USA) (Storm Bird (CAN)) 10.3f **(74)**
Form - 4
Record 2000 - 1st:0 2nd:0 3rd:0 Ran:1
Win Prizemoney £0 *Total Prizemoney* £348
2000 Turf 0-1: (7f) (frm)
Currently above-average colt.
**C E Brittain [0-1] Peter Head Racing Ltd.*

SYRAH BHB 25f27a RR 41?f 27a 3448[2]

4 b m Minshaanshu Amad (USA) 11.3f **(53)** - La Domaine (Dominion) 8.5f **(63)**
Form - 6802
Record 2000 - 1st:0 2nd:1 3rd:0 Ran:4

Pre2000 - 1st:0 2nd:0 3rd:0 Ran:7
Win Prizemoney £0 *Total Prizemoney* £516
2000 Turf 0-3: (12f 2, 16f) (g-f, frm 2) 2000 AW 0-1: (11f) (Fibr)
Moderate filly. Turf high 41. Inconsistent.
**W R Muir [0-4] Larksborough Stud Ltd (from R T Phillips [0-1] Nov 1999).*

SYRINGA RR 76f 5156[6]
2 b f Lure (USA) - Tass (Soviet Star (USA))
Form - 66
Record 2000 - 1st:0 2nd:0 3rd:0 Ran:2
2000 Turf 0-2: (5f, 6f) (g-s, g-f)
Currently above-average filly. Turf high 76 (began Oct).
**B J Meehan [0-2] Fieldspring Racing.*

TAABEER BHB 92f **RR 97f** 4218[2]
2 b c Caerleon (USA) 10.9f **(79)** - Himmah (USA) (Habitat) 9.4f **(70)**
Form - 722
Record 2000 - 1st:0 2nd:2 3rd:0 Ran:3
Win Prizemoney £0 *Total Prizemoney* £2,503
2000 Turf 0-3: (7f 2, 8f) (g-f 2, frm)
Currently very useful colt. Turf high 97 (began Jly) - 2nd of 18 to Sixty Seconds (5 Spt Leicester 7f frm RF 4218). A scopey individual, he ran well in two hot maidens and should not be troubled to win a similar contest this spring. Likely to stay beyond a mile, he tries hard and could develop into a useful handicapper.
**E A L Dunlop [0-3] Hamdan Al Maktoum.*

TABBETINNA BLUE BHB 34f34a **RR 41f 34a** 4398[11]
3 b f Interrex (CAN) 7.7f **(51)** - True Is Blue (Gabitat) 5f **(44)**
Form - 702060
Record 2000 - 1st:0 2nd:1 3rd:0 Ran:6
Pre2000 - 1st:0 2nd:0 3rd:0 Ran:1
Win Prizemoney £0 *Total Prizemoney* £550
2000 Turf 0-3: (6f 2, 7f) (gd 2, g-f) 2000 AW 0-3: (6f 2, 8f) (Equi, Fibr 2)
Light-framed, moderate filly, effective 7f, acts on gd. Turf high 41 (1st run) - 2nd of 13 getting 23lb from Northern Times (7 Apr Lingfield 7f gd RF 0638). AW high 23.
**J W Payne [0-7] Vetsango Partnership.*

TABHEEJ (IRE) BHB 94f **RR 97f** 4735[5]
3 ch f Mujtahid (USA) 7.4f **(69)** - Abhaaj (Kris) 9.5f **(73)**
Form - 60065
Record 2000 - 1st:0 2nd:0 3rd:0 Ran:5
Pre2000 - 1st:2 2nd:0 3rd:2 Ran:4
Win Prizemoney £11,191 *Total Prizemoney* £21,987
Wins * 1999 Spt Doncas (G-F) 6f 90 <
* 1999 May Haydoc (GD) 5f 71+
2000 Turf 0-5: (5f, 6f 4) (gd 3, g-f, hrd)
Lengthy, very useful filly, effective 6 to 7f, acts on gd to frm. Turf high 97. Consistent. Just short of Group class in 1999, she failed to progress last year.
**B W Hills [2-9] Hamdan Al Maktoum.*

TABORITE (USA) BHB 17f **RR 8f** 304[9]
6 gr g Gulch (USA) 9.6f **(79)** - Ziska (USA) (Danzig (USA)) 8.4f **(76)**
Form - 80
Record 2000 - 1st:0 2nd:0 3rd:0 Ran:2
Pre2000 - 1st:0 2nd:0 3rd:0 Ran:4
2000 AW 0-2: (12f, 16f) (Fibr 2)
Very poor gelding.
**A G Newcombe [0-2] Wetherby Racing Bureau 32 (from G Woodward [0-1] Oct 1998).*

TACHOMETER (IRE) RR 59f 3438[4]
6 b m Jurado (USA) - Tacheo (Tachypous) 8.6f **(55)**
Form - 484
Record 2000 - 1st:0 2nd:0 3rd:0 Ran:3
Win Prizemoney £0 *Total Prizemoney* £630
2000 Turf 0-3: (8f, 10f 2) (gd, g-f 2)
Fair mare. Turf high 59 (began Jly).
**H S Howe [0-16] Richard Garrard.*

TACTFUL REMARK (USA) BHB 83f **RR 101f** 4968[20]
4 ch h Lord At War (ARG) 6.6f **(67)** - Right Word (USA) (Verbatim (USA)) 8.5f **(64)**
Form - 05403000
Record 2000 - 1st:0 2nd:0 3rd:1 Ran:8
Pre2000 - 1st:2 2nd:0 3rd:2 Ran:9
Win Prizemoney £10,731 *Total Prizemoney* £16,362
Wins 1999 Jly Newbur (G-F) H 9f 82 90+ <
1999 Apr Kempto (GD) H 9f 77 80+
2000 Turf 0-8: (8f 4, 9f, 10f 3) (sft, g-s, gd 4, g-f, frm)
Scopey, very useful colt, effective 9 to 10f, acts on gd to frm, prefers left handed tracks. Turf high 101 - 5th of 8 giving 5lb to Amalia (18 May York 10f gd RF 1280). A front-runner, he appeared to be in the handicappe's grip in 2000.
**J A Osborne [0-8] Dr D B A & Mrs Heather Silk (from J H M Gosden [2-9] Spt 1999).*

TADEO BHB 75f **RR 77df** 4691[9]
7 ch g Primo Dominie 7.2f **(67)** - Royal Passion (Ahonoora) 8.1f **(73)**
Form - 03800350
Record 2000 - 1st:0 2nd:0 3rd:2 Ran:8
Pre2000 - 1st:9 2nd:7 3rd:6 Ran:58
Win Prizemoney £81,222 *Total Prizemoney* £116,062
Wins * 1998 Aug Fairyh (G-F) L 6f 102
* 1998 May Haydoc (G-S) H 5f 97 105 <
* 1997 Spt Nottin (GD) 5.1f 95
* 1997 Aug Ripon (G-F) H 6f 95 101
* 1997 Jly Newmar (GD) H 5f 92 93
* 1996 Oct Ascot (GD) H 5f 91 95
* 1996 Oct Haydoc (SFT) 5f 93
2000 Turf 0-8: (5f 5, 6f 3) (gd 4, g-f 3, frm)
Above-average gelding, effective 5f, acts on frm. Turf high 91 (began Jun). Becoming disappointing. A Listed winner in his prime, he was beaten in claimers last year. Sold to Milton Bradley for just 6,000gns at Newmarket in October, he is well treated if the change of scenery sparks a revival.
**M Johnston [8-53] J R Good (from B J Meehan [0-6] Jly 1999).*

TADREEJ (IRE) BHB 65f **RR 57f** 1390[16]
3 b g Fairy King (USA) 7.7f **(75)** - Rose Bonbon (FR) (High Top) 10.2f **(67)**
Form - 700
Record 2000 - 1st:0 2nd:0 3rd:0 Ran:3
Pre2000 - 1st:0 2nd:1 3rd:1 Ran:3
Win Prizemoney £0 *Total Prizemoney* £1,699
2000 Turf 0-3: (8f, 10f, 12f) (sft, g-s, gd)
Neat, average gelding. Turf high 57.
**M R Channon [0-6] Sheikh Ahmed Al Maktoum.*

TAFFETA (IRE) RR 66f 3836[1]
3 ch f Barathea (IRE) - Almela (IRE) (Akarad (FR)) 9f **(76)**
Form - 576401
Record 2000 - 1st:1 2nd:0 3rd:0 Ran:6
Win Prizemoney £3,835 *Total Prizemoney* £4,152
Wins * **2000** Aug Bright (FRM) 7f 55+ <
2000 Turf 1-6: (7f 1-6) (gd, g-f 1-3, frm 2)
Workmanlike, average filly, effective 7f, acts on frm. Turf high 66.
**J L Dunlop [1-6] Capt J Macdonald-Buchanan.*

TAFFRAIL BHB 49f **RR 51f** 5100[13]
2 b g Slip Anchor 12.7f **(75)** - Tizona (Pharly (FR)) 9.8f **(68)**
Form - 00
Record 2000 - 1st:0 2nd:0 3rd:0 Ran:2
2000 Turf 0-2: (7f 2) (g-s, gd)
Currently fair gelding. Turf high 51 (began Oct).
**J L Dunlop [0-2] Sir David Sieff.*

TAFFS WELL BHB 60f **RR 75f** 5165[15]

7 b g Dowsing (USA) 7f **(61)** - Zahiah (So Blessed) 8.7f **(67)**

Form - 474260000070

Record 2000 - 1st:0 2nd:1 3rd:0 Ran:12
Pre2000 - 1st:4 2nd:5 3rd:2 Ran:35

Win Prizemoney £27,782 *Total Prizemoney* £41,153

Wins * 1999 Jun Newcas (GD) H 8f 77 78+ <
* 1999 May Haydoc (GD) H 8.1f 69 76+
* 1999 May Cheste (G-F) H 7.6f 57 69
* 1999 Apr Mussel (G-F) H 7.1f 57 63

2000 Turf 0-12: (7f 2, 8f 10) (sft, g-s 2, gd 3, g-f 5, frm)

Above-average gelding, effective 7 to 8f, best at 8f, acts on g-s to frm, best on gd, likes left handed tracks, prefers tight tracks, excels at Haydock and Chester. Turf high 75 - 4th of 17 getting 8lb from Silca Blanka (11 May Chester 8f g-f RF 1138). Scored four times early on last season and, though running well on several occasions since, has been unable to force his head in front where it matters. Suited by a mile and needs to be produced late.

**B Ellison [4-28] The Breach Partnership (from Mrs J R Ramsden [0-13] Oct 1998).*

TAGANO SILENCE (JPN) RR 575a[6]

7 m

Form - 6

2000 AW 0-1: (8f) (Dirt)

Currently very useful. (1st run) - 6th of 13 to Conflict (25 Mar Nad Al Sheba 8f Dirt RF 0575a). **T Hashimoto in JPN [0-1].*

TAIKI BRIDLE (JPN) RR 113f 1286a[3]

5 b h Thrill Snow (USA) - Submission (IRE) (Darshaan) 9.9f **(84)**

Form - 3

2000 Turf 0-1: (7f) (frm)

Currently Group-class colt. (1st run) - 3rd of 18 giving 5lb to Stinger (14 May Fuchu 7f frm RF 1286a). **in JPN [0-1].*

TAJAR (USA) BHB 36f40a **RR 39f 40a** 5154[5]

8 b g Slew O' Gold (USA) 10.2f **(73)** - Mashaarif (USA) (Mr Prospector (USA)) 8.8f **(78)**

Form - 680831738025

Record 2000 - 1st:1 2nd:1 3rd:2 Ran:12
Pre2000 - 1st:4 2nd:3 3rd:7 Ran:44

Win Prizemoney £13,869 *Total Prizemoney* £22,066

Wins * 2000 Jun Ripon (G-F) H 12.3f 34 36
* 1999 May Windso (G-F) H 11.6f 48 50
* 1998 Aug Warwic (G-F) 10.8f 52 <
* 1998 Jly Pontef (G-F) H 10f 40 45
* 1997 Jly Chepst (G-F) H 12.1f 30 35

2000 Turf 1-10: (10f 3, 11f 2, 12f 1-5) (hvy, g-s, g-f 3, frm 1-5) 2000 AW 0-2: (12f 2) (Equi 2)

Moderate gelding, effective 10 to 12f, best at 10f, acts on g-s to frm - acts on Equi, best on frm, has worn blinkers, excels at Nottingham. Turf high 39. AW high 48 (1st run) (began Spt) - 2nd of 16 to Chalcedony (29 Spt Lingfield 12f Equi RF 4723). Wins in his turn but has not always looked keen.

**T Keddy [5-46] The Veg Chef Partnership (from M Dods [0-5] Apr 1997).*

TAJOUN (FR) RR 117f 5212a[3]

6 b g General Holme (USA) 5.7f **(58)** - Taeesha (Mill Reef (USA)) 10.5f **(78)**

Form - 363

2000 Turf 0-3: (16f 2, 20f) (hvy, g-s, gd)

High-class gelding, effective 16 to 20f, best at 16f, acts on hvy to gd, best on gd, favours Longchamp. Turf high 117 (began Spt) - 3rd of 11 to Amilynx (22 Oct Longchamp 16f hvy RF 5212a). Consistent. He is a hard ride and looked unenthusiastic when finishing third in the Group 1 Prix Royal-Oak. Dropped in class when winning a Listed event at Saint-Cloud in November, he goes well on heavy ground but is not one to trust.

**A deRoyerDupre in FR [5-14] H H Aga Khan.*

TAKALI (IRE) RR 113f 3891a[1]

3 ch c Kris 10f **(75)** - Takarouna (USA) (Green Dancer (USA)) 10.3f **(74)**

Form - 2144511

2000 Turf 3-7: (10f 2-5, 12f 1-2) (sft, g-s 1-3, gd 1-2, g-f 1-1)

Strong, Group-class colt, effective 10f, acts on g-s to g-f, prefers right handed tracks. Turf high 113 - also 1st of 5 giving 3lb to Molomo (20 Aug Curragh RF 3891a). He helped make the pace for Sinndar in the Irish Derby, but proved himself a smart performer when going on to win the Group Three Meld Stakes and Group Two Royal Whip. Likely to improve when moved back up to a mile and a half (he could stay further), he is an interesting prospect.

**J Oxx in IRE [3-7] H H Aga Khan.*

TAKAMAKA BAY (IRE) BHB 80f **RR 81f** 4893[1]

3 ch c Unfuwain (USA) 11.4f **(74)** - Stay Sharpe (USA) (Sharpen Up) 8.3f **(67)**

Form - 221

Record 2000 - 1st:1 2nd:2 3rd:0 Ran:3

Win Prizemoney £3,997 *Total Prizemoney* £6,467

Wins * 2000 Oct Ayr (HVY) 10f 65+ <

2000 Turf 1-3: (9f, 10f 1-2) (hvy 1-1, g-f, frm)

Workmanlike, currently decent colt. Turf high 81 - 2nd of 7 to Aranyi (11 Jun Ripon 9f g-f RF 1891).

**M Johnston [1-3] The Chaps Partnership.*

TAKARIAN (IRE) RR 116+f 579a[8]

5 b h Doyoun 10.7f **(69)** - Takarouna (USA) (Green Dancer (USA)) 10.3f **(74)**

Form - 8

2000 AW 0-1: (12f) (Dirt)

High-class colt.

**C B Greely in USA [0-1] (from J Oxx in IRE [2-7] Jly 1998).*

TAKAROA BHB 84f **RR 91f** 5121[13]

2 b c Tagula (IRE) - Mountain Harvest (FR) (Shirley Heights) 10.3f **(74)**

Form - 3310150

Record 2000 - 1st:2 2nd:0 3rd:2 Ran:7

Win Prizemoney £7,975 *Total Prizemoney* £10,412

Wins * 2000 Spt Salisb (SFT) 7f 91 <
* 2000 Aug Thirsk (G-F) 6f 91 <

2000 Turf 2-7: (6f 1-2, 7f 1-5) (g-s 2, gd 1-3, g-f, frm 1-1)

Useful colt, effective 6 to 7f, acts on gd to frm. Turf high 91 (began Jly) - 1st of 12 from Proletariat (25 Aug Thirsk RF 3970) - also 1st of 3 giving 5lb to Barathiki (27 Spt Salisbury RF 4693). He lost his form on his last two starts, but had looked quite useful over six and seven furlongs earlier in the campaign. Open to some improvement physically, he should pick up a handicap this year.

**I A Balding [2-7] Robert Hitchins.*

TAKE ACTION (IRE) BHB 32f38a **RR 35f 38a** 2046[10]

3 b g Shalford (IRE) 7.8f **(63)** - Action Belle (Auction Ring (USA)) 8.6f **(65)**

Form - 58000

Record 2000 - 1st:0 2nd:0 3rd:0 Ran:5
Pre2000 - 1st:0 2nd:0 3rd:0 Ran:5

2000 Turf 0-2: (10f, 14f) (g-s, g-f) 2000 AW 0-3: (8f, 9f, 12f) (Fibr 3)

Workmanlike, very moderate gelding, has worn blinkers. Turf high 31. AW high 58. Becoming disappointing. **F Jordan [0-10] D Pugh.*

TAKE ANOTHER BOW (USA) RR 84f 4300[4]

2 ch c Theatrical 11.5f **(78)** - Shy Princess (USA) (Irish River (FR)) 8.6f **(78)**

Form - 34

Record 2000 - 1st:0 2nd:0 3rd:1 Ran:2

Win Prizemoney £0 *Total Prizemoney* £1,063

2000 Turf 0-2: (6f, 7f) (gd, g-f)

Currently decent colt. Turf high 84 (began Aug).

**J H M Gosden [0-2] Mrs Diane Snowden.*

TAKE A TURN BHB 46f54a **RR 47f 54a** 2013[7]

5 br g Forzando 7.2f **(63)** - Honeychurch (USA) (Bering) 7.4f **(61)**

Form - 67

Record 2000 - 1st:0 2nd:0 3rd:0 Ran:2
Pre2000 - 1st:2 2nd:3 3rd:3 Ran:29

Win Prizemoney £8,732 *Total Prizemoney* £13,804

Wins 1998 Jly Salisb (G-F) H 8f 69 75
1997 Aug Cheste (SFT) H 7f 77 79 <

2000 Turf 0-2: (10f 2) (g-s, g-f)

Above-average gelding, often wears blinkers. Turf high 37.

**M J Wilkinson [0-2] The Dann, Gomersall & Pullan Partnership (from Miss Gay Kelleway [3-19] Aug 1999).*

TAKE FLITE BHB 71f **RR 79f** 5139[7]

3 b g Cadeaux Genereux 7.9f **(76)** - Green Seed (IRE) **(78f)** (Lead on Time (USA)) 8f **(65)**

Form - 28031607

Record					
2000 -	1st:1	2nd:1	3rd:1	Ran:8
Pre2000 -	1st:0	2nd:0	3rd:2	Ran:5

Win Prizemoney £2,769 *Total Prizemoney* £6,556

Wins						
* **2000**	Jly	Folkes	(GD)	7f	78	<

2000 Turf 1-8: (6f, 7f 1-5, 8f 2) (g-s 2, gd 1-3, g-f, frm 2)

Scopey, above-average gelding, effective 6 to 7f, best at 7f, acts on gd to frm, best on g-f. Turf high 79 (1st run) - 2nd of 15 to Peaceful Promise (1 May Doncaster 7f g-f RF 0936) - also 1st of 9 giving 5lb to Harmonic (13 Jly Folkestone RF 2766). Made the frame in varied company before landing a Folkestone maiden in July, but looked a hard ride there and is hardly progressive.

**W R Muir [1-13] The Wheet Partnership.*

TAKE MANHATTAN (IRE) BHB 69f65a **RR 73+f 65a** 5139[6]

3 b br g Hamas (IRE) 8f **(72)** - Arab Scimetar (IRE) (Sure Blade (USA)) 11.3f **(67)**

Form - 70661108001664826

Record				
2000 -	1st:3	2nd:1	3rd:0	Ran:17
Pre2000 -	1st:0	2nd:0	3rd:0	Ran:1

Win Prizemoney £10,299 *Total Prizemoney* £11,680

Wins								
* **2000**	Jly	Bright	(FRM)	H	8f	65	68	
* **2000**	May	Carlis	(FRM)	H	8f	56	73+	<
* **2000**	May	Nottin	(G-S)	H	8.2f	57	68	

2000 Turf 3-16: (6f, 7f, 8f 3-13, 9f) (hvy, sft, g-s 2, gd 1-4, g-f 1-7, frm 1-1) 2000 AW 0-1: (6f) (Fibr)

Scopey, above-average gelding, effective 8f, acts on gd to frm, best on g-f, likes left handed trackslikes right handed tracks, likes tight tracks. Turf high 73 - 1st of 18 getting 6lb from Sign of The Tiger (12 May Carlisle RF 1164) - also 1st of 7 getting 15lb from Aranyi (25 Jly Brighton RF 3087). Inconsistent.

**M R Channon [3-18] M G St Quinton.*

TAKE NOTICE BHB 23f36a **RR 8f 36a** 2804[6]

7 b g Warning 8.1f **(77)** - Metair (Laser Light) 9f **(68)**

Form - 066

Record				
2000 -	1st:0	2nd:0	3rd:0	Ran:3
Pre2000 -	1st:0	2nd:0	3rd:2	Ran:26

Win Prizemoney £0 *Total Prizemoney* £1,237

2000 Turf 0-3: (5f, 6f, 8f) (g-f 2, frm)

Very poor gelding, has worn blinkers. Turf high 8. Has done little over hurdles, having been pulled up more often than not. Equally ordinary on the flat, there is little for punters to get enthuiastic about.

**Martyn Wane [0-24] J P Slattery (from R M McKellar [0-7] May 1997).*

TAKER CHANCE BHB 28f35a **RR 35f 35a** 5054[9]

4 b g Puissance 7.1f **(60)** - Flower Princess (Slip Anchor) 9.8f **(73)**

Form - 0088776862000700

Record				
2000 -	1st:0	2nd:1	3rd:0	Ran:16
Pre2000 -	1st:1	2nd:0	3rd:1	Ran:13

Win Prizemoney £2,416 *Total Prizemoney* £4,028

Wins							
* 1999	Aug	Beverl	(GD)	C	7.5f	50	<

2000 Turf 0-14: (6f, 7f 5, 8f 5, 9f, 10f 2) (sft, g-s 2, gd 3, g-f 2, frm 5, hrd) 2000 AW 0-2: (7f, 9f) (Fibr 2)

Light-framed, very moderate gelding, effective 7f, acts on frm, has worn blinkers, likes right handed tracks. Turf high 40.

**J Hetherton [1-30] Eureka Racing (from W J Haggas [0-4] Oct 1998).*

TAKESMYBREATHAWAY (USA) **RR 57f** 3756[7]

2 ch f Gone West (USA) 7.8f **(82)** - Oscillate (USA) (Seattle Slew (USA)) 9.4f **(76)**

Form - 67

Record				
2000 -	1st:0	2nd:0	3rd:0	Ran:2

2000 Turf 0-2: (6f 2) (g-f, frm)

Currently fair filly. Turf high 57 (began Jun).

**J L Dunlop [0-2] Neil Jones.*

TAKE TO TASK (USA) BHB 93f **RR 95f** 5100[2]

2 b br c Conquistador Cielo (USA) 9.8f **(67)** - Tash (USA) (Never Bend) 13.1f **(70)**

Form - 222

Record				
2000 -	1st:0	2nd:3	3rd:0	Ran:3

Win Prizemoney £0 *Total Prizemoney* £3,778

2000 Turf 0-3: (7f 3) (gd 2, g-f)

Currently very useful colt. Turf high 95 - 2nd of 21 to Aldebaran (20 Oct Doncaster 7f gd RF 5100).

**M Johnston [0-3] F Gillespie.*

TAKHLID (USA) BHB 55f67a **RR 58f 67a** 2420[3]

9 b h Nureyev (USA) 8.4f **(84)** - Savonnerie (USA) (Irish River (FR)) 8.6f **(78)**

Form - 2311647225366501331З

Record				
2000 -	1st:2	2nd:2	3rd:4	Ran:15
Pre2000 -	1st:18	2nd:5	3rd:10	Ran:77

Win Prizemoney £56,165 *Total Prizemoney* £72,149

Wins								
* **2000**	*Jun*	*Lingfi*	*(STD)*	*C*	*7f*		*54*	
* **2000**	*May*	*Wolver*	*(STD)*	*C*	*6f*		*66*	
* 1999	*Dec*	*Wolver*	*(STD)*	*C*	*7f*		*75+*	
* 1999	*Dec*	*Wolver*	*(STD)*	*C*	*6f*		*86*	<
* 1999	*Oct*	*Wolver*	*(STD)*	*C*	*7f*		*68+*	
* 1999	*Jly*	*Wolver*	*(STD)*	*C*	*8.5f*		*72+*	
* 1999	*Jly*	*Southw*	*(STD)*	*C*	*7f*		*80+*	
* 1999	*Jun*	*Wolver*	*(STA)*	*C*	*7f*		*80*	
* 1999	*May*	*Southw*	*(STD)*	*C*	*7f*		*82*	
* 1999	*Apr*	*Wolver*	*(STD)*	*C*	*6f*		*76+*	
* 1999	*Feb*	*Lingfi*	*(STD)*	*H*	*8f*	*70*	*79*	
* 1999	*Jan*	*Lingfi*	*(STD)*		*7f*		*71*	
* 1999	*Jan*	*Southw*	*(STD)*	*H*	*8f*	*63*	*70*	
* 1998	Jun	Hamilt	(SFT)	H	8.3f	61	72+	
* 1998	Jun	Thirsk	(GD)	H	8f	57	62	
* 1997	*Spt*	*Wolver*	*(STD)*	*H*	*6f*	*68*	*73*	
* 1997	*Apr*	*Southw*	*(STD)*	*H*	*8f*	*63*	*69*	
* 1997	*Mar*	*Wolver*	*(STD)*	*H*	*6f*	*61*	*59*	

2000 Turf 0-3: (7f, 8f 2) (sft, g-s, gd) 2000 AW 2-12: (6f 1-5, 7f 1-4, 8f 3) (Equi 1-1, Fibr 1-11)

Average horse, effective 6 to 8f, - acts on AW, best on Fibr, favours left handed tracks, prefers tight tracks, excels at Lingfield and does well at Wolverhampton. Turf high 59. AW high 66. Prolific winner on sand, he appears to have gone off the boil this year. Effective from six furlongs to a mile, but is probably best over seven.

**D W Chapman [18-85] S B Clark (from H ThomsonJones [2-7] Spt 1995).*

TAKING (FR) BHB 53f **RR 39f** 2695[8]

4 gr g Take Risks (FR) - Sonning (FR) (Moulin)

Form - 08

Record				
2000 -	1st:0	2nd:0	3rd:0	Ran:2

2000 Turf 0-2: (10f 2) (frm, hrd)

Very moderate gelding. Turf high 39. **C N Kellett [0-6] Sean Taylor.*

TAKRIR (IRE) **RR 84+f** 1307[1]

3 b c Bahri (USA) - Ice House (Northfields (USA)) 9f **(72)**

Form - 1

Record				
2000 -	1st:1	2nd:0	3rd:0	Ran:1

Win Prizemoney £4,043 *Total Prizemoney* £4,043

Wins						
* **2000**	May	Newbur	(G-F)	8f	84	<

2000 Turf 1-1: (8f 1-1) (gd 1-1)

Workmanlike, currently decent colt. (1st run) - 1st of 15 from Grey Eminence (19 May Newbury RF 1307).

**J L Dunlop [1-1] Hamdan Al Maktoum.*

TAKWIN (IRE) BHB 97f **RR 97f** 4647[7]

3 b c Alzao (USA) 9.8f **(73)** - Gale Warning (IRE) (Last Tycoon) 8.5f **(62)**

Form - 032211017

Record				
2000 -	1st:3	2nd:2	3rd:1	Ran:9

Win Prizemoney £26,835 *Total Prizemoney* £30,673

Wins								
* **2000**	Spt	Doncas	(G-F)	H	12f	92	97	<
* **2000**	Jly	Sandow	(G-F)	H	14f	82	95	
* **2000**	Jly	Kempto	(G-F)		12f		87+	

2000 Turf 3-9: (10f 2, 12f 2-4, 14f 1-3) (gd 3, g-f 1-3, frm 2-3)

Scopey, very useful colt, effective 12 to 14f, best at 12f, acts on g-f to frm, best on frm. Turf high 97 - 1st of 15 getting 16lb from Mowelga (9 Spt Doncaster RF 4308) - also 1st of 5 giving 15lb to Typhoon Tilly (27 Jly Sandown RF 3154). A powerful front-runner, he developed into a smart middle-distance hadicapper. Open to improvement over long distances, he was sold for 220,000gns at Newmarket in October and will continue his career in Saudi Arabia.

**B Hanbury [3-9] Hamdan Al Maktoum.*

Takwin (right) has been sold to race in Saudi Arabia

TALAASH (IRE) BHB 106f **RR 107+f** 4840a[0]
3 b c Darshaan 11.9f **(81)** - Royal Ballet (IRE) (Sadler's Wells (USA)) 10f **(76)**
Form - 136106
Record 2000 - 1st:2 2nd:0 3rd:1 Ran:6
Win Prizemoney £16,622 *Total Prizemoney* £18,442
Wins * **2000** Aug Claire (GD) L 12f 107+ <
* **2000** Jun Goodwo (GD) 12f 91
2000 Turf 2-6: (10f, 12f 2-3, 15f 2) (gd 2-3, g-f 2, frm)
Scopey, Pattern-class colt, effective 10 to 12f, acts on gd to g-f. Turf high 107 - also 1st of 6 getting 4lb from Crimson Quest (26 Aug Clairefontaine RF 4134a). Unraced at two, he was an easy winner over 12 furlongs at Goodwood on his debut, but may not have been suited by the step down to ten furlongs at Doncaster next time. Not disgraced in the Gordon Stakes, just what he achieved in winning a Listed race at Clairefontaine is anyone's guess. He was found wanting in the St Leger. **M R Channon [2-6].*

TALAQI RR 73f 909[6]
3 b f Nashwan (USA) 10.3f **(79)** - Na-Ayim (IRE) (Shirley Heights) 10.3f **(74)**
Form - 6
Record 2000 - 1st:0 2nd:0 3rd:0 Ran:1
2000 Turf 0-1: (10f) (gd)
Scopey, currently above-average filly.
**E A L Dunlop [0-1] Hamdan Al Maktoum.*

TALARIA (IRE) BHB 62f60a **RR 67f 60a** 5155[8]
4 ch m Petardia 8.2f **(58)** - Million At Dawn (IRE) (Fayruz)
Form - 601004056118
Record 2000 - 1st:3 2nd:0 3rd:0 Ran:12
Pre2000 - 1st:1 2nd:0 3rd:0 Ran:9
Win Prizemoney £11,425 *Total Prizemoney* £12,682
Wins 2000 *Oct Lingfi (STD) C* 7f *43+*
2000 Spt Leices (G-S) C 6f 56+
2000 May Nottin (G-S) H 6.1f 62 67
1999 Jly Newmar (G-F) 6f 80 <
2000 Turf 2-10: (6f 2-9, 8f) (sft, gd 1-4, g-f 1-3, frm, hrd) 2000 AW 1-2: (7f 1-2) (Equi 1-2)
Scopey, average filly, effective 6f, acts on frm, has worn blinkers. Turf high 67. AW high 49 (began Oct).
**M Quinn [0-1] R M Ellis (from J Pearce [1-1] Oct 2000).*

TALAT BHB 49f **RR 43f** 3920[9]
2 b f Missed Flight - Tawnais (Artaius (USA)) 9f **(69)**
Form - 060
Record 2000 - 1st:0 2nd:0 3rd:0 Ran:3
2000 Turf 0-3: (6f, 7f 2) (gd, g-f, frm)
Currently moderate filly. Turf high 43 (began Jly).
**M J Ryan [0-3] Mrs G Singh.*

TALBIYA (IRE) RR 27f 810[9]
3 ch f Mujtahid (USA) 7.4f **(69)** - Talwara (USA) (Diesis) 9.3f **(69)**
Form - 0
Record 2000 - 1st:0 2nd:0 3rd:0 Ran:1
2000 Turf 0-1: (7f) (sft)
Scopey, currently little account filly.
**Sir Michael Stoute [0-1] H H Aga Khan.*

TALBOT AVENUE BHB 73f **RR 68f** 4932[18]
2 b c Puissance 7.1f **(60)** - Dancing Daughter (Dance In Time (CAN)) 8.9f **(59)**
Form - 4430
Record 2000 - 1st:0 2nd:0 3rd:1 Ran:4
Win Prizemoney £0 *Total Prizemoney* £1,117
2000 Turf 0-4: (5f, 6f 3) (gd, g-f, frm 2)
Average colt. Turf high 68 - 3rd of 9 to Whale Beach (26 Aug Windsor 6f g-f RF 4001).
**R F JohnsonHoughton [0-4] Mrs C S Wilson.*

TALECA SON (IRE) BHB 30f20a **RR 28f 20a** 2818[5]
5 b g Conquering Hero (USA) 10.6f **(50)** - Lady Taleca (IRE) (Exhibitioner) 8.7f **(61)**
Form - 8434225400065475
Record 2000 - 1st:0 2nd:2 3rd:0 Ran:12
Pre2000 - 1st:0 2nd:2 3rd:4 Ran:44
Win Prizemoney £0 *Total Prizemoney* £4,059
2000 Turf 0-3: (10f 2, 12f) (sft, g-f, frm) 2000 AW 0-9: (8f, 9f, 11f 3, 12f 4) (Fibr 9)
Very moderate gelding, effective 7 to 12f, best at 11f, acts on sft to gd - acts on Fibr, has worn blinkers. Turf high 28. AW high 42 (1st run) - 2nd of 14 giving 3lb to Mice Ideas (3 Jan Southwell 11f Fibr RF 0009). Inconsistent.
**D Carroll [0-16] The Green Army (from P Matthews in IRE [0-45] Oct 1999).*

TALENTS LITTLE GEM BHB 42f40a **RR 50f 40a** 3331[7]
3 b f Democratic (USA) - Le Saule D'Or (Sonnen Gold) 6.6f **(47)**
Form - 00458507
Record 2000 - 1st:0 2nd:0 3rd:0 Ran:6
Pre2000 - 1st:0 2nd:0 3rd:1 Ran:6
Win Prizemoney £0 *Total Prizemoney* £537
2000 Turf 0-6: (7f, 8f 5) (gd, g-f 4, frm)
Workmanlike, fair filly. Turf high 50.
**A W Carroll [0-6] Talent Entertainment (from V Soane [0-5] Dec 1999).*

TALENT STAR BHB 50f **RR 50?f** 4206[8]
3 b g Mizoram (USA) - Bells of Longwick **(51f 50a)** (Myjinski (USA)) 9.5f **(54)**
Form - 0468
Record 2000 - 1st:0 2nd:0 3rd:0 Ran:4

Win Prizemoney £0 *Total Prizemoney* £330
2000 Turf 0-4: (6f, 7f, 8f, 10f) (g-f, frm 3)
Workmanlike, fair gelding. Turf high 50.
**A W Carroll [0-4] Talent Entertainment.*

TALES OF BOUNTY (IRE) BHB 54f **RR 59f** 1592[12]
5 b g Ela-Mana-Mou 12.7f **(72)** - Tales of Wisdom (Rousillon (USA)) 8.2f **(74)**
Form - 80

Record	**2000 -**	1st:0	2nd:0	3rd:0	Ran:2
	Pre2000 -	1st:0	2nd:0	3rd:2	Ran:11

Win Prizemoney £0 *Total Prizemoney* £1,262
2000 Turf 0-2: (13f, 14f) (g-s, g-f)
Fair gelding. Turf high 59. Consistent.
**D R C Elsworth [1-21] Mrs Michael Meredith.*

TALIB (USA) BHB 14f43a **RR 33tf 43a** 345[6]
6 b g Silver Hawk (USA) 11.2f **(85)** - Dance For Lucy (USA) (Dance Bid (USA)) 11.6f **(71)**
Form - 0486

Record	**2000 -**	1st:0	2nd:0	3rd:0	Ran:3
	Pre2000 -	1st:1	2nd:1	3rd:0	Ran:22

Win Prizemoney £2,388 *Total Prizemoney* £3,959
Wins 1998 Jun Windso (GD) C 11.6f 58 <
2000 AW 0-3: (16f 3) (Fibr 3)
Very moderate gelding. AW high 20.
**P W Hiatt [0-20] P W Hiatt (from P Mitchell [0-6] Apr 1999).*

TALIBAN (IRE) BHB 50f **RR 41f** 1317[10]
4 b h Bigstone (IRE) - Aunt Hester (IRE) (Caerleon (USA)) 8.6f **(71)**
Form - 600
Record 2000 - 1st:0 2nd:0 3rd:0 Ran:3
2000 Turf 0-3: (7f, 8f 2) (g-s, gd 2)
Currently moderate colt. Turf high 41.
**G Wragg [0-3] Mollers Racing.*

TALISKER BAY BHB 70f **RR 77f** 5163[6]
2 b c Clantime 6.6f **(57)** - Fabulous Rina (FR) (Fabulous Dancer (USA)) 9.4f **(70)**
Form - 75536
Record 2000 - 1st:0 2nd:0 3rd:1 Ran:5
Win Prizemoney £0 *Total Prizemoney* £806
2000 Turf 0-5: (5f 5) (gd 2, frm 3)
Above-average colt. Turf high 77 (began Jly).
**C Smith [0-5] Mrs N Stewart.*

TALK TO MOJO **RR 72f** 2868[1]
3 ch c Deploy 11.4f **(67)** - Balnaha (Lomond (USA)) 8.8f **(65)**
Form - 1
Record 2000 - 1st:1 2nd:0 3rd:0 Ran:1
Win Prizemoney £4,134 *Total Prizemoney* £4,134
Wins * 2000 Jly Newbur (G-F) 12f 72 <
2000 Turf 1-1: (12f 1-1) (g-f 1-1)
Scopey, currently above-average colt. (1st run) - 1st of 8 from Tufty Hopper (16 Jly Newbury RF 2868). Made a winning debut at Newbury in the colours of Liverpool star Michael Owen.
**J H M Gosden [1-1] Owen Promotions Ltd.*

TALLULAH BELLE BHB 67f81a **RR 68f 81a** 403[7]
7 b m Crowning Honors (CAN) 9.9f **(36)** - Fine a Leau (USA) (Youth (USA)) 9.8f **(64)**
Form - 361500427

Record	**2000 -**	1st:0	2nd:1	3rd:0	Ran:4
	Pre2000 -	1st:12	2nd:10	3rd:13	Ran:81

Win Prizemoney £42,785 *Total Prizemoney* £74,836

Wins								
* 1999	*Nov*	*Wolver*	*(STD)*	*H*	*9.4f*	*83*	*84*	
* 1999	*Jun*	*Wolver*	*(STA)*	*H*	*9.4f*	*80*	*86*	<
* 1999	May	Hamilt	(SFT)	H	9.2f	68	70	
* 1999	*Apr*	*Lingfi*	*(STD)*		*12f*		*79*	
* 1998	Aug	Yarmou	(FRM)		10.1f		68	
* 1998	Jly	Goodwo	(G-S)	H	9f	61	65	
* 1998	*May*	*Lingfi*	*(STD)*	*H*	*10f*	*69*	*71*	
* 1997	Oct	Redcar	(G-F)		10f		68	
* 1997	Spt	Kempto	(G-F)	H	11.1f	56	65	
* 1997	Apr	Beverl	(G-F)	H	9.9f	57	56	
* 1997	*Feb*	*Lingfi*	*(STD)*	*H*	*10f*	*57*	*66*	
* 1997	*Jan*	*Wolver*	*(STD)*		*9.4f*		*56*	

2000 AW 0-4: (8f, 10f 3) (Equi 3, Fibr)
Decent mare, effective 9 to 12f, best at 9f, - acts on AW, best on Fibr, has worn blinkers, likes left handed tracks, favours tight tracks, does well at Lingfield, likes Wolverhampton. AW high 80 - 2nd of 8 getting 7lb from Zanay (26 Feb Lingfield 10f Equi RF 0363). She is just below the very best on artificial surfaces.
**N P Littmoden [12-88] Trojan Racing.*

TALLYWHACKER BHB 39f **RR 28f** 2[6]
3 b f Bon Secret (IRE) - Nomadic Rose (Nomination) 7f **(60)**
Form - 06

Record	**2000 -**	1st:0	2nd:0	3rd:0	Ran:1
	Pre2000 -	1st:0	2nd:0	3rd:0	Ran:2

2000 AW 0-1: (8f) (Equi)
Currently little account filly. **T J Naughton [0-3] T J Naughton.*

TAL-Y-LLYN (IRE) BHB 30f38a **RR 32f 38a** 1512[8]
6 ch g Common Grounds 8.1f **(66)** - Welsh Fantasy (Welsh Pageant) 10f **(65)**
Form - 8

Record	**2000 -**	1st:0	2nd:0	3rd:0	Ran:1
	Pre2000 -	1st:1	2nd:1	3rd:0	Ran:18

Win Prizemoney £3,533 *Total Prizemoney* £4,840
Wins 1997 May Newbur (SFT) 7.3f 79 <
2000 Turf 0-1: (11f) (hvy)
Very moderate gelding, has worn blinkers.
**N E Berry [0-9] The Purple People Racing Partnership (from B W Hills [1-10] Oct 1997).*

TAMASHAN BHB 40f **RR 43f** 788[15]
4 b g Puissance 7.1f **(60)** - Wild Truffes (IRE) **(28df)** (Danehill (USA)) 10f **(72)**
Form - 80

Record	**2000 -**	1st:0	2nd:0	3rd:0	Ran:2
	Pre2000 -	1st:0	2nd:0	3rd:0	Ran:4

2000 Turf 0-2: (7f, 8f) (g-s, gd)
Light-framed, moderate gelding. Turf high 37.
**G C H Chung [0-6] H C Chung.*

TAMBOURINAIRE (IRE) BHB 83f **RR 77f** 503[1]
3 gr g Kendor (FR) 12.2f **(66)** - Rotina (FR) (Crystal Glitters (USA)) 11.3f **(79)**
Form - 1

Record	**2000 -**	1st:1	2nd:0	3rd:0	Ran:1
	Pre2000 -	1st:0	2nd:0	3rd:2	Ran:3

Win Prizemoney £4,251 *Total Prizemoney* £5,486
Wins * 2000 Mar Kempto (GD) 6f 77 <
2000 Turf 1-1: (6f 1-1) (gd 1-1)
Scopey, above-average gelding. (1st run) - 1st of 12 from Port St Charles (25 Mar Kempton RF 0503). (DEAD)
**B J Meehan [1-4] Abbott Racing Ltd.*

TAMBURLAINE (IRE) BHB 100f **RR 101f** 5124[2]
2 b c Royal Academy (USA) 7.8f **(77)** - Well Bought (IRE) (Auction Ring (USA)) 8.6f **(65)**
Form - 2212
Record 2000 - 1st:1 2nd:3 3rd:0 Ran:4
Win Prizemoney £5,707 *Total Prizemoney* £51,697
Wins * 2000 Spt Newmar (G-S) 8f 95+ <
2000 Turf 1-4: (7f, 8f 1-3) (g-s, g-f 1-2, frm)
Very useful colt. Turf high 101 (began Aug) - 2nd of 10 to Dilshaan (21 Oct Doncaster 8f g-s RF 5124) - also 1st of 15 from Painted Room (26 Spt Newmarket RF 4646). Beaten a neck by Nayef at Newbury in September, he powered clear in a Newmarket maiden and was only caught close home by Dilshaan in the Group 1 Racing Post Trophy. Held in high regard by Richard Hannon, he has a high cruising speed and should give a good account of himself in the 2000 Guineas. However he fares there, this likeable individual will surely win a Group race in 2001.
**R Hannon [1-4] Jeffen Racing.*

TAMIAMI TRAIL (IRE) BHB 82f **RR 81f** 4631[2]
2 ch c Indian Ridge 7.6f **(74)** - Eurobird (Ela-Mana-Mou) 10.1f **(70)**
Form - 0052
Record 2000 - 1st:0 2nd:1 3rd:0 Ran:4
Win Prizemoney £0 *Total Prizemoney* £1,051
2000 Turf 0-4: (6f, 7f, 8f, 10f) (g-s, g-f 2, frm)

Decent colt. Turf high 81 - 2nd of 9 to Capal Garmon (25 Spt Bath 10f g-s RF 4631). **B J Meehan [0-4] Mrs Susan Roy.*

TAMILIA (IRE) BHB 54f49a **RR 57f 49a** 5115[9]
2 b f Ridgewood Ben - Nellie's Away (IRE) (Magical Strike (USA))
Form - 00040
Record 2000 - 1st:0 2nd:0 3rd:0 Ran:5
2000 Turf 0-4: (6f 3, 7f) (g-s, g-f 3) 2000 AW 0-1: (8f) (Fibr)
Fair filly. Turf high 57 (began Aug).
**D W P Arbuthnot [0-5] The Tamilia Partnership.*

TAMING (IRE) BHB 77f **RR 80f** 4987[16]
4 ch g Lycius (USA) 8.8f **(71)** - Black Fighter (USA) (Secretariat (USA)) 9f **(70)**
Form - 0440
Record 2000 - 1st:0 2nd:0 3rd:0 Ran:4
Pre2000 - 1st:1 2nd:0 3rd:1 Ran:3
Win Prizemoney £3,712 *Total Prizemoney* £5,376
Wins 1999 Jly Kempto (G-F) 12f 77+ <
2000 Turf 0-3: (12f, 16f, 18f) (gd 2, frm) 2000 AW 0-1: (12f) (Equi)
Scopey, decent gelding. Turf high 80 - 4th of 9 getting 11lb from Bangalore (15 Spt Newbury 16f frm RF 4438). Lightly raced, he won his only start of '99 before showing ability for a drifferent yard over hurdles. Has changed stables again, finishing fourth in a couple of handicaps.
**I A Balding [0-3] Oakview Racing (from D G Bridgwater [0-3] Mar 2000).*

TAMMAM (IRE) BHB 75f72a **RR 86f 72a** 4740[26]
4 b g Priolo (USA) 10.9f **(71)** - Bristle (Thatch (USA)) 9.8f **(62)**
Form - 07853446680
Record 2000 - 1st:0 2nd:0 3rd:1 Ran:11
Pre2000 - 1st:1 2nd:1 3rd:4 Ran:8
Win Prizemoney £8,367 *Total Prizemoney* £14,278
Wins 1999 May Cheste (G-F) 10.3f 88 <
2000 Turf 0-11: (7f, 8f 7, 9f 2, 10f) (g-s 2, gd 5, g-f 3, frm)
Scopey, useful gelding, effective 8 to 10f, best at 10f, acts on g-s to g-f, has worn blinkers, prefers tight tracks. Turf high 86. He ran some fair races last term but is proving hard to win with.
**Mrs L Stubbs [0-11] Maurice Parker (from B Hanbury [1-4] Aug 1999).*

TAMORA (FR) RR 100f 4851a[1]
3 b f Linamix (FR) 8.2f **(64)** - Tyramisou (FR) (Fabulous Dancer (USA)) 9.4f **(70)**
Form - 1
2000 Turf 1-1: (9f 1-1) (hvy 1-1)
Currently very useful filly. (1st run) - 1st of 9 giving 6lb to Masaniella (1 Oct San Siro RF 4851a).
**B Grizzetti in ITY [1-1] Scuderia Belforte.*

TAM O'SHANTER BHB 40f42a **RR 58f 42a** 57[6]
6 gr g Persian Bold 10f **(69)** - No More Rosies (Warpath) 12.3f **(52)**
Form - 6
Record 2000 - 1st:0 2nd:0 3rd:0 Ran:1
Pre2000 - 1st:0 2nd:1 3rd:0 Ran:6
Win Prizemoney £0 *Total Prizemoney* £748
2000 AW 0-1: (16f) (Fibr)
Fair gelding.
**J G M O'Shea [1-9] Foley Steelstock (from C W Thornton [0-6] Dec 1997).*

TANCRED ARMS BHB 46f42a **RR 48f 42a** 5083[4]
4 b m Clantime 6.6f **(57)** - Mischievous Miss (Niniski (USA)) 10.6f **(65)**
Form - 0223000302037044
Record 2000 - 1st:0 2nd:3 3rd:3 Ran:16
Pre2000 - 1st:1 2nd:4 3rd:1 Ran:26
Win Prizemoney £3,629 *Total Prizemoney* £11,205
Wins * 1999 Jly Catter (GD) H 6f 57 68 <
2000 Turf 0-15: (6f 11, 7f 4) (hvy, g-s 3, gd 2, g-f 2, frm 4, hrd 3) 2000 AW 0-1: (6f) (Fibr)
Leggy, moderate filly, effective 6f, acts on g-f, has worn blinkers, likes left handed tracks. Turf high 53.
**D W Barker [1-42] Miss A Clift.*

TANCRED TIMES BHB 55f45a **RR 55f 45a** 5188[5]
5 ch m Clantime 6.6f **(57)** - Mischievous Miss (Niniski (USA)) 10.6f **(65)**
Form - 2678357532411552676205
Record 2000 - 1st:2 2nd:3 3rd:2 Ran:20
Pre2000 - 1st:3 2nd:4 3rd:4 Ran:41
Win Prizemoney £18,391 *Total Prizemoney* £27,245
Wins * **2000** Jly Hamilt (G-F) H 5f 46 50
* **2000** Jun Hamilt (G-F) C 5f 46
* 1998 Aug Carlis (G-S) H 5.9f 56 62
* 1997 Jly Catter (G-F) H 7f 68 <
* 1997 Jun Thirsk (GD) S 6f 64
2000 Turf 2-16: (5f 2-11, 6f 5) (sft, gd 3, g-f 1-6, frm 1-6) 2000 AW 0-4: (6f 4) (Fibr 4)
Fair filly, effective 5 to 6f, best at 5f, acts on gd to frm, best on g-f, has worn blinkers, excels at Hamilton. Turf high 55 - 2nd of 24 getting 14lb from Chorus (6 Oct Windsor 5f g-f RF 4827) - also 1st of 8 getting 26lb from Riberac (4 Jly Hamilton RF 2495). AW high 45.
**D W Barker [5-52] D W Barker (from J Cullinan [0-9] Jun 1999).*

TANCRED WALK RR 49f 4200[13]
2 b f Clantime 6.6f **(57)** - Mischievous Miss (Niniski (USA)) 10.6f **(65)**
Form - 760
Record 2000 - 1st:0 2nd:0 3rd:0 Ran:3
2000 Turf 0-3: (5f, 6f 2) (g-f, frm 2)
Currently moderate filly. Turf high 49 (began Jly).
**D W Barker [0-3] Red Card Racing Partnership.*

TANGERINE BHB 42f **RR 46f** 3686[5]
3 ch f Primo Dominie 7.2f **(67)** - Sweet Jaffa (Never so Bold) 6.3f **(66)**
Form - 0000705
Record 2000 - 1st:0 2nd:0 3rd:0 Ran:7
Pre2000 - 1st:1 2nd:0 3rd:0 Ran:4
Win Prizemoney £3,777 *Total Prizemoney* £3,777
Wins 1999 Spt Bath (G-S) 5.7f 73? <
2000 Turf 0-7: (5f 2, 6f 2, 7f, 8f, 10f) (g-s, gd, g-f 2, frm 3)
Lengthy, moderate filly, effective 6f, acts on gd, has worn blinkers. Turf high 46. Inconsistent.
**M W Easterby [0-7] Winton Bloodstock & Guy Reed (from B W Hills [1-4] Oct 1999).*

TANGERINE FLYER BHB 42f49a **RR 29f 49a** 1366[12]
5 ch g Presidium 7.5f **(56)** - Factuelle (Known Fact (USA)) 7.4f **(67)**
Form - 0600
Record 2000 - 1st:0 2nd:0 3rd:0 Ran:4
Pre2000 - 1st:3 2nd:2 3rd:2 Ran:18
Win Prizemoney £8,451 *Total Prizemoney* £11,071
Wins 1998 *Jan Lingfi (STD) C 5f 80+* <
1998 *Jan Lingfi (STD) H 5f 73 80+* <
1997 *Dec Lingfi (STD) 5f 72*
2000 Turf 0-2: (5f, 7f) (frm 2) 2000 AW 0-2: (5f, 6f) (Fibr 2)
Very moderate gelding. Turf high 29. AW high 30.
**P D Evans [0-10] Mike Nolan (from J Berry [3-12] May 1998).*

TANGO TWO THOUSAND (IRE) BHB 84f **RR 82f** 3319[5]
3 b br f Sri Pekan (USA) - Run Bonnie (Runnett) 7f **(59)**
Form - 5215
Record 2000 - 1st:1 2nd:1 3rd:0 Ran:4
Win Prizemoney £4,257 *Total Prizemoney* £5,559
Wins * **2000** Jly Windso (SFT) 8.3f 74 <
2000 Turf 1-4: (8f 1-2, 9f 2) (gd 1-3, g-f)
Decent filly. Turf high 82 - also 1st of 14 from Berzoud (10 Jly Windsor RF 2684).
**J H M Gosden [1-4] Mrs C A Waters And Ms Rachel D S Hood.*

TANTALUS BHB 94f **RR 104f** 4741[6]
3 ch c Unfuwain (USA) 11.4f **(74)** - Water Quest (IRE) (Rainbow Quest (USA)) 10.4f **(75)**
Form - 1340636
Record 2000 - 1st:1 2nd:0 3rd:2 Ran:7
Pre2000 - 1st:0 2nd:1 3rd:0 Ran:1
Win Prizemoney £4,075 *Total Prizemoney* £16,440
Wins * **2000** Mar Doncas (GD) 10.3f 91 <
2000 Turf 1-7: (10f 1-3, 12f 2, 14f, 15f) (g-s, gd 1-2, g-f 3, frm)
Scopey, very useful colt, effective 12f, acts on g-f to frm. Turf high 104 - 3rd of 8 to Millenary (9 May Chester 12f g-f RF 1111). Put up a workmanlike performance to win a Doncaster maiden on his reappearance and was not beaten far when third in the Chester Vase next time. Disappointing in decent company since but ran quite well at Doncaster in September. He is now hurdling with Oliver Sherwood. **B W Hills [1-8] K Abdulla.*

TANTISPER BHB 21f **RR 37f** 438[8]
4 ch g Anshan 8.2f **(63)** - Fine Asset (Hot Spark) 7.6f **(62)**
Form - 568
Record 2000 - 1st:0 2nd:0 3rd:0 Ran:2
Pre2000 - 1st:0 2nd:0 3rd:0 Ran:4
2000 AW 0-2: (12f, 14f) (Fibr 2)
Scopey, very moderate gelding, has worn blinkers. AW high 11.
**Mrs A Duffield [0-6] Brooke Rankin.*

TANZILLA BHB 92f **RR 97f** 4963[15]
3 b f Warning 8.1f **(77)** - Tanz (IRE) (Sadler's Wells (USA)) 10f **(76)**
Form - 1230000
Record 2000 - 1st:1 2nd:1 3rd:1 Ran:7
Win Prizemoney £5,330 *Total Prizemoney* £14,330
Wins * 2000 Apr Newbur (SFT) 7f 94 <
2000 Turf 1-7: (7f 1-1, 8f 2, 11f 3, 12f) (sft, g-s 1-1, gd 4, g-f)
Scopey, very useful filly, effective 7 to 11f, best at 11f, acts on sft to g-f. Turf high 101 - 2nd of 7 to Lady Upstage (22 Apr Kempton 8f sft RF 0829) - also 1st of 14 from Velvet Lady (14 Apr Newbury RF 0715). She made a winning debut in a field of unraced fillies at Newbury before making the frame in a couple of Listed races, but has looked out of her depth since.
**C E Brittain [1-7] Abdullah Saeed Bul Hab.*

TAP BHB 69f78a **RR 69f 78a** 5316[13]
3 b c Emarati (USA) 6.6f **(63)** - Pubby (Doctor Wall)
Form - 1605670
Record 2000 - 1st:1 2nd:0 3rd:0 Ran:7
Pre2000 - 1st:0 2nd:1 3rd:0 Ran:1
Win Prizemoney £2,646 *Total Prizemoney* £3,746
Wins 2000 Apr Folkes (SFT) 7f 91 <
2000 Turf 1-6: (7f 1-3, 8f 2, 10f) (g-s 1-3, gd 2, frm) 2000 AW 0-1: (7f) (Fibr)
Neat, above-average colt, effective 7f, acts on g-s. Turf high 91 (1st run) - 1st of 13 from Al-King Slayer (18 Apr Folkestone RF 0761). He went backwards after sprinting clear to win a weak Folkestone maiden. Happy on easy ground, he is well treated and worth keeping an eye on this spring.
**Mrs A J Perrett [0-1] G Harwood (from J A R Toller [1-7] Oct 2000).*

TAPAGE (IRE) BHB 65f63a **RR 70f 63a** 4924[1]
4 b g Great Commotion (USA) 9.2f **(80)** - Irena (Bold Lad (IRE)) 8.4f **(68)**
Form - 301111621571
Record 2000 - 1st:6 2nd:1 3rd:0 Ran:10
Pre2000 - 1st:1 2nd:3 3rd:1 Ran:14
Win Prizemoney £21,897 *Total Prizemoney* £26,423
Wins * 2000 *Oct Lingfi (STD) H 8f 59 64*
*** 2000** Aug Windso (GD) H 8.3f 60 65
*** 2000** Jly Bright (FRM) H 8f 55 63
*** 2000** *Jun Lingfi (STD) H 8f 48 51*
*** 2000** May Bath (G-F) H 8f 51 53
*** 2000** *May Lingfi (STD) H 8f 46 47*
1998 *Nov Lingfi (STD) 7f 77* <
2000 Turf 3-6: (8f 3-5, 9f) (gd, g-f 1-1, frm 2-4) 2000 AW 3-4: (8f 3-4) (Equi 3-3, Fibr)
Above-average gelding, effective 8f, acts on g-f to frm - acts on Equi, best on frm, has worn blinkers, favours tight tracks, and does well at Lingfield. Turf high 66 - 2nd of 8 getting 8lb from Minetta (8 Aug Bath 8f frm RF 3444) - also 1st of 15 getting 10lb from Legal Set (14 Aug Windsor RF 3636). AW high 64 - 1st of 12 getting 10lb from Hail The Chief (11 Oct Lingfield RF 4924). He has been with a few trainers in his time and started off his career in Ireland. He has been in fine form since joining Andrew Reid during the summer, winning five times including three on Equitrack. Another successful story for his in-form yard.
**Andrew Reid [6-16] A S Reid (from W R Muir [0-6] Aug 1999).*

TAPATCH (IRE) BHB 40f55a **RR 55a** 2693[17]
12 b g Thatching 7.8f **(69)** - Knees Up (USA) (Dancing Champ (USA)) 8.8f **(80)**
Form - 0
Record 2000 - 1st:0 2nd:0 3rd:0 Ran:1
Pre2000 - 1st:2 2nd:3 3rd:5 Ran:27
Win Prizemoney £5,330 *Total Prizemoney* £13,708
Wins * 1998 Jun Pontef (GD) H 10f 45 49 <
2000 Turf 0-1: (10f) (frm)
Very poor gelding, has worn blinkers.
**M W Easterby [5-36] Miss V Foster (from J S Wainwright [0-1] Feb 1995).*

TAPAUA (IRE) BHB 46f42a **RR 47f 42a** 35[6]
4 b g Common Grounds 8.1f **(66)** - Tap The Line (Tap On Wood) 10.3f **(65)**
Form - 776
Record 2000 - 1st:0 2nd:0 3rd:0 Ran:2
Pre2000 - 1st:0 2nd:1 3rd:1 Ran:12
Win Prizemoney £0 *Total Prizemoney* £1,041
2000 AW 0-2: (7f 2) (Fibr 2)
Light-framed, moderate gelding, effective 6 to 7f, acts on g-f to frm, has worn blinkers. AW high 38. **M Dods [0-14] A G Watson.*

TARABAYA (IRE) BHB 86f **RR 89f** 4027[5]
3 b f Warning 8.1f **(77)** - Tarakana (USA) (Shahrastani (USA)) 8.8f **(72)**
Form - 6135
Record 2000 - 1st:1 2nd:0 3rd:1 Ran:4
Win Prizemoney £4,231 *Total Prizemoney* £5,813
Wins * 2000 Jun Kempto (G-F) 9f 78+ <
2000 Turf 1-4: (8f, 9f 1-1, 10f 2) (gd 2, g-f 1-2)
Unfurnished, useful filly. Turf high 89 - 5th of 6 getting 3lb from Welsh Main (27 Aug Yarmouth 10f gd RF 4027). Unraced at two, she won an ordinary Kempton maiden on her second run.
**Sir Michael Stoute [1-4] H H Aga Khan.*

TARABELA (FR) RR 100f 4953a[3]
3 ch f Johann Quatz (FR) - Muirfield (FR) (Crystal Glitters (USA)) 11.3f **(79)**
Form - 3
2000 Turf 0-1: (12f) (sft)
Currently very useful filly. (1st run) - 3rd of 9 to Space Quest (8 Oct Longchamp 12f sft RF 4953a). **in FR [0-1].*

TARA GOLD (IRE) BHB 82f **RR 76f** 4643[13]
2 b f Royal Academy (USA) 7.8f **(77)** - Soha (USA) (Dancing Brave (USA)) 8.4f **(76)**
Form - 4340
Record 2000 - 1st:0 2nd:0 3rd:1 Ran:4
Win Prizemoney £0 *Total Prizemoney* £1,409
2000 Turf 0-4: (6f, 7f 3) (gd, g-f 2, frm)
Above-average filly. Turf high 76 (began Aug).
**R Hannon [0-4] Tom Gaffney.*

TARA HALL BHB 51f **RR 55f** 4868[1]
3 b f Saddlers' Hall (IRE) 10.5f **(65)** - Katie Scarlett (Lochnager) 6f **(59)**
Form - 751
Record 2000 - 1st:1 2nd:0 3rd:0 Ran:3
Pre2000 - 1st:0 2nd:0 3rd:0 Ran:6
Win Prizemoney £2,769 *Total Prizemoney* £2,769
Wins * 2000 Oct Ayr (HVY) C 10.9f 45+ <
2000 Turf 1-3: (11f 1-1, 12f, 15f) (hvy 1-1, gd, frm)
Unfurnished, fair filly, has worn blinkers, likes left handed tracks, likes tight tracks. Turf high 45. Inconsistent.
**W M Brisbourne [1-3] John Pugh (from N P Littmoden [0-6] Oct 1999).*

TARAS EMPEROR (IRE) BHB 100f **RR 97f** 5107[9]
2 b g Common Grounds 8.1f **(66)** - Strike It Rich (FR) (Rheingold) 10.4f **(62)**
Form - 414105800
Record 2000 - 1st:2 2nd:0 3rd:0 Ran:9
Win Prizemoney £15,333 *Total Prizemoney* £16,380
Wins * 2000 May Sandow (HVY) L 5f 97 <
*** 2000** Apr Newcas (SFT) 5f 78
2000 Turf 2-9: (5f 2-7, 6f 2) (sft 1-1, g-s 1-1, gd 4, g-f, frm 2)
Very useful gelding, effective 5f, acts on g-s. Turf high 97 - 1st of 6 from Stregone (30 May Sandown RF 1556). He was in good form on soft ground during the spring, winning the Listed National Stakes at Sandown. Disappointing thereafter, he could bounce back under testing conditions. **J J Quinn [2-9] Tara Leisure.*

TARA'S GIRL (IRE) RR 92f 4161[10]
3 b f Fayruz 6.6f **(63)** - Florissa (FR) (Persepolis (FR)) 6.4f **(67)**
Form - 3500000000
Record 2000 - 1st:0 2nd:0 3rd:1 Ran:10
Pre2000 - 1st:2 2nd:2 3rd:0 Ran:9
Win Prizemoney £11,128 *Total Prizemoney* £21,926

Wins * 1999 Jun Beverl (GD) 5f 91 <
* 1999 Apr Beverl (G-F) 5f 71
2000 Turf 0-10: (5f 6, 6f 4) (hvy, g-s 2, gd 3, g-f 2, frm 2)
Unfurnished, useful filly, effective 5f, acts on gd. Turf high 92. Becoming disappointing. Fourth in the Queen Mary Stakes in 1999, she failed to train on and became very disappointing.
**J J Quinn [2-19] Tara Leisure.*

TARAS TIPPLE (IRE) RR 35f 5163[7]

2 b g College Chapel - Lady Portobello (Porto Bello) 8.9f **(43)**
Form - 07
Record 2000 - 1st:0 2nd:0 3rd:0 Ran:2
2000 Turf 0-2: (5f, 7f) (gd 2)
Very moderate gelding. Turf high 35 (began Spt). (DEAD)
**J J Quinn [0-2] Tara Leisure.*

TARAWAN BHB 70f76a RR 77f 76a 4036[7]

4 ch g Nashwan (USA) 10.3f **(79)** - Soluce (Junius (USA)) 7.7f **(65)**
Form - 00005007
Record 2000 - 1st:0 2nd:0 3rd:0 Ran:8
Pre2000 - 1st:2 2nd:7 3rd:1 Ran:16
Win Prizemoney £15,061 *Total Prizemoney* £28,651
Wins * 1999 Oct Sandow (SFT) H 8.1f 85 90 <
* 1999 Aug Newcas (GD) 8f 81
2000 Turf 0-7: (8f 2, 9f, 10f 3, 12f) (sft, gd 4, g-f 2) 2000 AW 0-1: (8f) (Fibr)
Scopey, above-average gelding, effective 8 to 10f, best at 8f, acts on g-s to frm, best on frm, often wears blinkers, excels at Sandown and Newbury. Turf high 77. Becoming disappointing.
**I A Balding [2-25] Robert Hitchins.*

TARBOUSH BHB 90f RR 87f 2058[1]

3 b c Polish Precedent (USA) 9f **(73)** - Barboukh (Night Shift (USA)) 7.2f **(69)**
Form - 031
Record 2000 - 1st:1 2nd:0 3rd:1 Ran:3
Win Prizemoney £4,270 *Total Prizemoney* £4,910
Wins * **2000** Jun Sandow (G-F) 10f 78 <
2000 Turf 1-3: (10f 1-3) (gd, g-f 1-1, frm)
Currently useful colt. Turf high 87 - 3rd of 19 to Rasm (3 Jun Newmarket 10f frm RF 1693) - also 1st of 6 from Kaliypour (17 Jun Sandown RF 2058). **H R A Cecil [1-3] Wafic Said.*

TARCOOLA BHB 51f RR 53f 4021[16]

3 ch c Pursuit of Love 9.5f **(69)** - Miswaki Belle (USA) **(64+f)** (Miswaki (USA)) 9f **(81)**
Form - 0F000
Record 2000 - 1st:0 2nd:0 3rd:0 Ran:5
Pre2000 - 1st:0 2nd:0 3rd:0 Ran:2
Win Prizemoney £0 *Total Prizemoney* £325
2000 Turf 0-5: (7f, 8f 3, 10f) (gd, g-f 2, frm 2)
Scopey, fair colt. Turf high 53.
**V Soane [0-7] Michael Abdallah and Steve Herbert.*

TAR FIH (USA) BHB 77f RR 75f 4322[4]

2 b f Gone West (USA) 7.8f **(82)** - Najiya **(95f)** (Nashwan (USA))
Form - 434
Record 2000 - 1st:0 2nd:0 3rd:1 Ran:3
Win Prizemoney £0 *Total Prizemoney* £1,188
2000 Turf 0-3: (5f, 6f, 7f) (g-f 2, frm)
Currently above-average filly. Turf high 75 (began Jly) - 4th of 17 to Lilium (11 Spt Warwick 7f g-f RF 4322).
**J L Dunlop [0-3] Hamdan Al Maktoum.*

TARFSHI BHB 94f RR 85f 4752[1]

2 b f Mtoto 11.5f **(71)** - Pass the Peace (Alzao (USA)) 7.1f **(68)**
Form - 131
Record 2000 - 1st:2 2nd:0 3rd:1 Ran:3
Win Prizemoney £10,121 *Total Prizemoney* £11,314
Wins * **2000** Spt Sandow (SFT) 8.1f 85 <
* **2000** Aug Doncas (G-F) 7f 84+
2000 Turf 2-3: (7f 1-2, 8f 1-1) (g-s 1-1, g-f, frm 1-1)
Currently useful filly. Turf high 85 (began Aug) - 1st of 8 getting 5lb from Worthily (30 Spt Sandown RF 4752) - also 1st of 13 getting 5lb from Alnahaam (5 Aug Doncaster RF 3386).
**M A Jarvis [2-3] Sheikh Ahmed Al Maktoum.*

TARRADALE BHB 41f37a RR 43f 37a 5166[10]

6 br g Interrex (CAN) 7.7f **(51)** - Encore L'Amour (USA) (Monteverdi) 6.5f **(61)**
Form - 0000
Record 2000 - 1st:0 2nd:0 3rd:0 Ran:4
Pre2000 - 1st:1 2nd:5 3rd:4 Ran:34
Win Prizemoney £2,983 *Total Prizemoney* £9,316
Wins * 1998 Jun Hamilt (G-S) H 8.3f 32 35 <
2000 Turf 0-4: (8f 3, 10f) (gd 3, frm)
Moderate gelding, effective 8 to 9f, best at 8f, acts on hvy to hrd, best on gd, likes left handed tracks. Turf high 33. Inconsistent.
**C B B Booth [1-40] J A Porteous.*

TARRANAKI KNIGHT (IRE) BHB 43f RR 43f 4323[15]

2 b c Brief Truce (USA) 9.1f **(73)** - Yo (IRE) **(38tf)** (Glow (USA)) 6.7f **(71)**
Form - 000
Record 2000 - 1st:0 2nd:0 3rd:0 Ran:3
2000 Turf 0-3: (6f 2, 7f) (gd, g-f 2)
Currently moderate colt. Turf high 43 (began Aug).
**T J Naughton [0-3] J L Knight Roadworks Ltd.*

TARRIFA (IRE) BHB 39f RR 41f 5062[8]

3 ch f Mujtahid (USA) 7.4f **(69)** - Gibraltar Heights (High Top) 10.2f **(67)**
Form - 08
Record 2000 - 1st:0 2nd:0 3rd:0 Ran:2
Pre2000 - 1st:0 2nd:0 3rd:0 Ran:1
2000 Turf 0-2: (10f 2) (sft, g-f)
Workmanlike, currently moderate filly. Turf high 13.
**J G Smyth-Osbourne [0-3] J H Henderson.*

TARRY FLYNN (IRE) RR 109f 5286a[11]

6 br g Kenmare (FR) 9.6f **(76)** - Danzig Lass (USA) 00
Form - 524600240
2000 Turf 0-9: (7f 3, 8f 4, 9f, 10f) (hvy, sft 3, g-s 2, gd 2)
Pattern-class gelding, effective 7 to 8f, best at 7f, acts on g-f, best on gd, often wears blinkers, and excels at Leopardstown. Turf high 109 - 2nd of 8 to Social Harmony (16 Spt Curragh 7f RF 4521a). Inconsistent. One of Ireland's best handicappers, this tough performer failed by just three parts of a length to beat Giant's Causeway at the Curragh in April.
**D K Weld in IRE [6-24] Mrs C L Weld.*

TARSHEEH (USA) RR 59f 955[7]

3 b br f Mr Prospector (USA) 8.6f **(88)** - Oumaldaaya (USA) (Nureyev (USA)) 8.7f **(78)**
Form - 87
Record 2000 - 1st:0 2nd:0 3rd:0 Ran:2
2000 Turf 0-2: (7f, 8f) (sft, gd)
Workmanlike, currently fair filly. Turf high 59.
**J L Dunlop [0-2] Hamdan Al Maktoum.*

TARSKI BHB 40f RR 48f 4928[13]

6 ch g Polish Precedent (USA) 9f **(73)** - Illusory (Kings Lake (USA)) 10.8f **(67)**
Form - 70335460
Record 2000 - 1st:0 2nd:0 3rd:2 Ran:8
Pre2000 - 1st:2 2nd:3 3rd:1 Ran:21
Win Prizemoney £11,981 *Total Prizemoney* £19,561
Wins * 1999 Jun Goodwo (G-F) H 9.9f 51 54
1996 Jly Sandow (G-F) 7.1f 92+ <
2000 Turf 0-7: (8f, 9f 2, 10f 3, 12f) (gd 3, g-f 2, frm, hrd) 2000 AW 0-1: (12f) (Equi)
Moderate gelding, effective 9 to 10f, best at 10f, acts on gd to hrd, has worn blinkers, favours tight tracks. Turf high 48 - 5th of 9 getting 18lb from The Green Grey (24 Jly Windsor 10f frm RF 3081). Consistent.
**L G Cottrell [1-25] E Gadsden (from H R A Cecil [1-4] Spt 1997).*

TARTAN ISLAND (IRE) BHB 43f RR 51f 3429[18]

3 b g Turtle Island (IRE) - Welsh Harp (Mtoto)
Form - 0025470
Record 2000 - 1st:0 2nd:1 3rd:0 Ran:7
Pre2000 - 1st:0 2nd:0 3rd:0 Ran:3
Win Prizemoney £0 *Total Prizemoney* £1,049
2000 Turf 0-7: (5f 4, 6f 3) (g-f 3, frm 4)
Fair gelding, effective 5f, acts on frm, often wears blinkers (very

effectively). Turf high 52 - 2nd of 6 giving 5lb to Paradise Yangshuo (26 Jun Musselburgh 5f frm RF 2273). Inconsistent.

**I Semple [0-10] Mrs E Chung.*

TARWILA (IRE) RR 97f $5355a^{3}$

3 ch f In The Wings 11.2f **(77)** - Tarwiya (IRE) (Dominion) 8.5f **(63)**

Form - 301152713

2000 Turf 3-9: (9f 1-1, 10f 3, 11f 1-1, 12f 1-4) (hvy, g-s 1-1, gd 1-4, g-f 1-3)

Very useful filly, effective 10 to 12f, acts on hvy to gd, likes right handed tracks. Turf high 97 - 3rd of 12 getting 10lb from Jammaal (30 Oct Leopardstown 10f hvy RF 5355a) - also 1st of 15 getting 7lb from Golden Fact (22 Oct Naas RF 5180a).

**J Oxx in IRE [3-11] H H Aga Khan.*

TARXIEN BHB 81f RR 83f 500^{8}

6 b g Kendor (FR) 12.2f **(66)** - Tanz (IRE) (Sadler's Wells (USA)) 10f **(76)**

Form - 8

Record 2000 - 1st:0 2nd:0 3rd:0 Ran:1
Pre2000 - 1st:5 2nd:3 3rd:3 Ran:24

Win Prizemoney £17,547 *Total Prizemoney* £25,802

Wins 1998 Jun Goodwo (G-F) H 14f 85 88 <
1998 May Newbur (GD) H 13.3f 73 86
1998 May Haydoc (G-S) H 14f 73 77+
1997 Spt Pontef (G-S) 12f 68
1997 Aug Haydoc (G-F) H 11.9f 62 68

2000 Turf 0-1: (14f) (gd)

Decent gelding.

**Mrs Merrita Jones [0-7] F J Sainsbury (from K R Burke [5-22] Oct 1998).*

TASSO DANCER BHB 39f RR 37f 3213^{9}

4 gr m Dilum (USA) 7.1f **(56)** - Dancing Diana (Raga Navarro (ITY)) 8f **(64)**

Form - P7050

Record 2000 - 1st:0 2nd:0 3rd:0 Ran:5
Pre2000 - 1st:0 2nd:0 3rd:0 Ran:1

2000 Turf 0-5: (8f 2, 10f 2, 14f) (g-s, g-f, frm 2, hrd)

Scopey, very moderate filly. Turf high 37.

**Ian Williams [0-5] Mrs J Tredwell (from B J Meehan [0-1] Oct 1998).*

TATANTE (IRE) RR 72f 4821^{3}

2 gr f Highest Honor (FR) 10.9f **(72)** - Tamnia **(100f)** (Green Desert (USA)) 8.6f **(78)**

Form - 03

Record 2000 - 1st:0 2nd:0 3rd:1 Ran:2

Win Prizemoney £0 *Total Prizemoney* £447

2000 Turf 0-2: (5f, 6f) (gd, g-f)

Currently above-average filly. Turf high 72 (began Spt) - 3rd of 19 to Princess Chloe (6 Oct Windsor 6f g-f RF 4821).

**Sir Mark Prescott [0-2] S Frisby.*

TATE VENTURE BHB 60f RR 61f 5125^{16}

3 b g Deploy 11.4f **(67)** - Tasseled (USA) (Tate Gallery (USA)) 7.4f **(67)**

Form - 831080

Record 2000 - 1st:1 2nd:0 3rd:1 Ran:6

Win Prizemoney £2,219 *Total Prizemoney* £2,541

Wins * 2000 *May Southw (STD) 8f 65* <

2000 Turf 0-3: (8f, 10f, 12f) (g-s, gd, frm) 2000 AW 1-3: (7f, 8f 1-1, 12f) (Equi, Fibr 1-2)

Unfurnished, average gelding, effective 8f, - acts on Fibr. Turf high 61. AW high 65 - 1st of 10 giving 5lb to Most Stylish (8 May Southwell RF 1093). He has shown ability on Fibresand and got off the mark with a narrow victory at Southwell in May.

**S P C Woods [1-6] Dr Frank Chao.*

TATTENHAM STAR BHB 68f64a RR 71f 64a 1326^{3}

3 b c Mistertopogigo (IRE) - Candane **(77f)** (Danehill (USA)) 10f **(72)**

Form - 357363

Record 2000 - 1st:0 2nd:0 3rd:2 Ran:3
Pre2000 - 1st:0 2nd:0 3rd:1 Ran:7

Win Prizemoney £0 *Total Prizemoney* £1,109

2000 Turf 0-3: (6f 2, 7f) (gd 2, g-f)

Workmanlike, above-average colt, effective 7f, acts on gd. Turf high 71. Consistent.

**M J Haynes [0-10] David Butler.*

TATTOO BHB 20a RR 20a 62^{11}

5 b m Casteddu 7.4f **(54)** - Ebony Park (Local Suitor (USA)) 8.4f **(67)**

Form - 080

Record 2000 - 1st:0 2nd:0 3rd:0 Ran:2
Pre2000 - 1st:0 2nd:0 3rd:0 Ran:1

2000 AW 0-2: (12f 2) (Equi, Fibr)

Currently very poor filly.

**K Mahdi [0-3] Hamad Al-Mutawa.*

TATTY THE TANK BHB 57f47a RR 66f 47a 5160^{2}

2 b c Tragic Role (USA) 9.4f **(63)** - Springfield Girl (Royal Vulcan)

Form - 82

Record 2000 - 1st:0 2nd:1 3rd:0 Ran:2

Win Prizemoney £0 *Total Prizemoney* £567

2000 Turf 0-1: (8f) (sft) 2000 AW 0-1: (7f) (Fibr)

Currently average colt. (1st run) - 2nd of 15 to Spirit of Texas (24 Oct Nottingham 8f sft RF 5160).

**M C Pipe [0-2] Sandicroft Stud Syndicate.*

TAUFAN BOY BHB 55f65a RR 52f 65a 500^{6}

7 b g Taufan (USA) 8.3f **(65)** - Lydia Maria (Dancing Brave (USA)) 8.4f **(76)**

Form - 6

Record 2000 - 1st:0 2nd:0 3rd:0 Ran:1
Pre2000 - 1st:2 2nd:3 3rd:5 Ran:32

Win Prizemoney £7,123 *Total Prizemoney* £17,481

Wins * 1998 May Haydoc (G-S) H 14f 58 63

2000 Turf 0-1: (14f) (gd)

Above-average gelding, effective 14f, acts on g-s, has worn blinkers.

**G B Balding [4-30] Supreme Team (from P W Harris [1-22] Oct 1997).*

TAUFAN'S MELODY BHB 102f RR 104f 4731^{7}

9 b g Taufan (USA) 8.3f **(65)** - Glorious Fate (Northfields (USA)) 9f **(72)**

Form - 072357

Record 2000 - 1st:0 2nd:1 3rd:1 Ran:6
Pre2000 - 1st:10 2nd:12 3rd:2 Ran:34

Win Prizemoney £474,231 *Total Prizemoney* £606,086

Wins * 1998 Oct Caulfi (GD) G1 12f 114 <
* 1998 Spt Baden- (GD) L 16f 103
* 1997 Nov Lyon P (HVY) L 12f 111
* 1997 Nov Doncas (SFT) L 12f 114 <
* 1997 May Lingfi (G-F) 11.5f 103+
* 1996 Jun Lingfi (G-F) 11.5f 110

2000 Turf 0-6: (12f 3, 13f 2, 14f) (hvy, g-s, gd 3, g-f)

Very useful gelding, has worn blinkers. Turf high 104. Unraced in '99 after his Australian exploits the previous autumn, he failed to show his best in three runs in the spring. Much better run on his return at Chester in August, but well held on two subsequent starts.

**Lady Herries [10-40] All At Sea.*

TAVERNER SOCIETY (IRE) BHB 60f RR 61f 1735^{4}

5 b g Imp Society (USA) 7.1f **(63)** - Straw Boater (Thatch (USA)) 9.8f **(62)**

Form - 044

Record 2000 - 1st:0 2nd:0 3rd:0 Ran:3
Pre2000 - 1st:1 2nd:2 3rd:2 Ran:16

Win Prizemoney £3,387 *Total Prizemoney* £11,401

Wins 1997 Spt Kempto (G-F) 8f 81 <

2000 Turf 0-2: (8f, 10f) (g-s, gd) 2000 AW 0-1: (7f) (Equi)

Average gelding, has worn blinkers. Turf high 56.

**M S Saunders [0-7] M S Saunders (from R W Armstrong [1-12] Oct 1998).*

TAWASILA (IRE) RR 95f $4841a^{1}$

3 b f Turtle Island (IRE) - Tazmeen (Darshaan) 9.9f **(84)**

Form - 1

2000 Turf 1-1: (10f 1-1) (gd 1-1)

Currently very useful filly. (1st run) - 1st of 12 getting 4lb from Ghyraan (30 Spt Longchamp RF 4841a).

**A deRoyerDupre in FR [1-1] H H Aga Khan.*

TAWN AGAIN BHB 45f RR 44f 3040^{2}

4 b g Then Again 7.4f **(52)** - Tawny (Grey Ghost) 9.9f **(60)**

Form - 000022

Record 2000 - 1st:0 2nd:2 3rd:0 Ran:6

Pre2000 - 1st:0 2nd:0 3rd:0 Ran:1
Win Prizemoney £0 *Total Prizemoney* £2,172
2000 Turf 0-6: (5f 2, 6f 4) (gd, g-f, frm 4)
Leggy, fair gelding, effective 5 to 6f, acts on g-f to frm. Turf high 44 - 2nd of 19 getting 17lb from Fly More (22 Jly Ripon 6f g-f RF 3040).
**T D Barron [0-7] B Elsworth.*

TAW PARK BHB 64f **RR 52f** 3529[6]
6 b g Inca Chief (USA) 5.6f **(45)** - Parklands Belle (Stanford) 7.9f **(56)**
Form - 566
Record 2000 - 1st:0 2nd:0 3rd:0 Ran:3
2000 Turf 0-3: (7f, 10f, 11f) (g-f, frm 2)
Currently fair gelding. Turf high 52 (began Jly).
**R J Baker [0-3] Miss Linda Bacon.*

TAXI-FOR-ROBBO (IRE) BHB 47f **RR 40df** 5158[8]
3 b f Shalford (IRE) 7.8f **(63)** - Miromaid (Simply Great (FR)) 8.2f **(65)**
Form - 8
Record 2000 - 1st:0 2nd:0 3rd:0 Ran:1
Pre2000 - 1st:0 2nd:0 3rd:1 Ran:4
Win Prizemoney £0 *Total Prizemoney* £270
2000 Turf 0-1: (8f) (sft)
Neat, moderate filly.
**I A Wood [0-1] The First Thursday Club (from J L Eyre [0-4] Oct 1999).*

TAXMERE BHB 30f **RR 24f** 3528[13]
3 ch f Lake Coniston (IRE) - Maculatus (USA) (Sharpen Up) 8.9f **(67)**
Form - 0000
Record 2000 - 1st:0 2nd:0 3rd:0 Ran:4
Pre2000 - 1st:0 2nd:0 3rd:0 Ran:2
2000 Turf 0-4: (7f, 8f, 12f 2) (hvy, gd 2, frm)
Light-framed, little account filly. Turf high 24.
**A T Murphy [0-6] Exmoor Racing Partnership.*

TAYAR RR 430[9]
4 gr h Mystiko (USA) 7.7f **(59)** - Tahnee (Cadeaux Genereux)
Form - 0
Record 2000 - 1st:0 2nd:0 3rd:0 Ran:1
2000 AW 0-1: (8f) (Fibr)
Currently very poor colt.
**H Akbary [0-1] & Mrs Kantis.*

TAYEED (USA) RR 4680[6]
3 b c Dixieland Band (USA) 10.1f **(80)** - Alsharta (USA) (Mr Prospector (USA)) 8.8f **(78)**
Form - 6
Record 2000 - 1st:0 2nd:0 3rd:0 Ran:1
2000 Turf 0-1: (8f) (hvy)
Scopey, currently very poor colt.
**R W Armstrong [0-1] Hamdan Al Maktoum.*

TAYIF BHB 86f **RR 77f** 2949[10]
4 gr h Taufan (USA) 8.3f **(65)** - Rich Lass (Broxted) 6.7f **(65)**
Form - 00000
Record 2000 - 1st:0 2nd:0 3rd:0 Ran:5
Pre2000 - 1st:3 2nd:1 3rd:1 Ran:7
Win Prizemoney £16,421 *Total Prizemoney* £18,289

Wins									
	* 1999	Aug	Newcas	(GD)	H	7f	90	94+	<
	* 1999	Jly	Sandow	(G-F)	H	7.1f	86	89+	
	* 1999	Apr	Nottin	(G-S)	H	5.1f		92+	

2000 Turf 0-5: (7f 5) (gd 3, g-f, frm)
Workmanlike, above-average colt, effective 5 to 7f, best at 7f, acts on sft to frm. Turf high 77. Consistent.
**J W Payne [3-12] G Jabre.*

TAYOVULLIN (IRE) BHB 46f47a **RR 45f 47a** 2432[10]
6 ch m Shalford (IRE) 7.8f **(63)** - Fifth Quarter (Cure The Blues (USA)) 9.5f **(63)**
Form - 0800652250
Record 2000 - 1st:0 2nd:2 3rd:0 Ran:9
Pre2000 - 1st:3 2nd:5 3rd:3 Ran:33
Win Prizemoney £8,289 *Total Prizemoney* £15,571

Wins									
	1999	*May*	*Wolver*	*(Std)*	*H*	*7f*	*51*	*54*	
	1998	Jun	Newmar	(GD)	H	7f	44	48	
	1997	*Apr*	*Southw*	*(STD)*	*H*	*7f*	*56*	*63*	<

2000 Turf 0-7: (6f, 7f 4, 8f 2) (gd 2, frm 5) 2000 AW 0-2: (6f, 8f) (Fibr 2)
Moderate mare, effective 7f, - acts on Fibr, has worn blinkers, likes left handed tracks, likes tight tracks. Turf high 45. AW high 21.
**K A Ryan [0-10] The Gloria Darley Racing Partnership (from H Morrison [3-31] Aug 1999).*

TAYSEER (USA) BHB 113f93a **RR 108f 93a** 4608[2]
6 ch g Sheikh Albadou 9.2f **(75)** - Millfit (USA) (Blushing Groom (FR)) 10.3f **(76)**
Form - 005303131772
Record 2000 - 1st:2 2nd:1 3rd:3 Ran:12
Pre2000 - 1st:6 2nd:2 3rd:1 Ran:23
Win Prizemoney £152,751 *Total Prizemoney* £205,242

Wins									
	*** 2000**	Aug	Goodwo	(GD)	H	6f	86	102	<
	*** 2000**	Jly	Newmar	(G-S)	H	7f	86	93	
	* 1999	Oct	Newmar	(SFT)	H	8f	80	90+	
	* 1999	Spt	Ayr	(G-S)	H	8f	72	87	
	1999	Spt	Bright	(G-F)	C	8f		60	
	1998	*Nov*	*Southw*	*(STD)*	*C*	*6f*		*70*	
	1997	May	York	(GD)	H	7f	89	95	
	1996	Nov	Redcar	(G-F)		7f		95	

2000 Turf 2-12: (6f 1-5, 7f 1-4, 8f 2, 9f) (g-s 3, gd 1-6, g-f 1-2, frm)
Pattern-class gelding, effective 6f, acts on g-s to g-f. Turf high 108 - 2nd of 11 to Sampower Star (24 Spt Ascot 6f g-s RF 4608) - also 1st of 30 giving 9lb to Bon Ami (5 Aug Goodwood RF 3395). Gradually recaptured his form before landing the Bunbury Cup in good style. Slightly unlucky in Ascot's Tote International Handicap, he came with a tremendous late spurt to land the Stewards' Cup. Handicaps are out now, but he finished second in the Group Two Diadem Stakes on his final start.
**D Nicholls [4-14] Sammy Doo Racing (from W R Muir [2-14] Spt 1999).*

Stewards' Cup winner Tayseer

TEA FOR TEXAS BHB 45f48a **RR 55f 48a** 5064[12]
3 ch f Weldnaas (USA) 8.4f **(55)** - Polly's Teahouse (Shack (USA)) 5.8f **(53)**

Form - 4352716800430
Record 2000 - 1st:1 2nd:1 3rd:2 Ran:12
Pre2000 - 1st:0 2nd:0 3rd:0 Ran:1
Win Prizemoney £2,284 *Total Prizemoney* £3,579
Wins 2000 May Bright (FRM) C 7f 55 <
2000 Turf 1-8: (6f 2, 7f 1-4, 8f 2) (sft, gd, g-f 4, frm 1-1, hrd) 2000 AW 0-4: (5f, 6f, 7f 2) (Equi 3, Fibr)
Neat, fair filly, effective 6 to 7f, acts on frm - acts on Equi, likes left handed tracks, likes tight tracks. Turf high 55 (1st run) - 1st of 11 getting 9lb from Welcome Shade (9 May Brighton RF 1107). AW high 48 - 2nd of 8 getting 5lb from Itsgottabdun (16 Feb Lingfield 6f Equi RF 0293).
**P L Clinton [0-1] The Buckers (from J Akehurst [0-6] Spt 2000).*

TEAM OF THREE BHB 20f **RR 25f** 106[11]
4 b g Jumbo Hirt (USA) 15.8f **(44)** - Dominance (Dominion) 8.5f **(63)**
Form - 00
Record 2000 - 1st:0 2nd:0 3rd:0 Ran:2
Pre2000 - 1st:0 2nd:0 3rd:0 Ran:3
2000 AW 0-2: (8f, 15f) (Fibr 2)
Light-framed, little account gelding. **D Shaw [0-5] J Roundtree.*

TE ANAU BHB 32f44a **RR 16f 44a** 5025[14]
3 b f Reprimand 8.2f **(63)** - Neenah (Bold Lad (IRE)) 8.4f **(68)**
Form - 70070
Record 2000 - 1st:0 2nd:0 3rd:0 Ran:5
Pre2000 - 1st:0 2nd:0 3rd:1 Ran:4
Win Prizemoney £0 *Total Prizemoney* £263
2000 Turf 0-2: (10f, 11f) (g-s 2) 2000 AW 0-3: (6f, 8f, 12f) (Equi, Fibr 2)
Light-framed, very moderate filly, effective 7f, - acts on Fibr, likes left handed tracks, likes tight tracks. Turf high 16. AW high 32. Becoming disappointing.
**W J Musson [0-5] W J Musson (from B J McMath [0-4] Aug 1999).*

TEAPOT ROW (IRE) BHB 100f **RR 106df** 4462[6]
5 b h Generous (IRE) 11.5f **(82)** - Secrage (USA) (Secreto (USA)) 8.7f **(72)**
Form - 5036
Record 2000 - 1st:0 2nd:0 3rd:1 Ran:4
Pre2000 - 1st:4 2nd:4 3rd:0 Ran:14
Win Prizemoney £91,757 *Total Prizemoney* £116,240

Wins	* 1999	Jly	Newbur	(G-F)		7.3f		105+	
	* 1997	Spt	Ascot	(G-F)	G2	8f		107	<
	* 1997	Spt	Doncas	(G-F)		7f		102	
	* 1997	Aug	Newmar	(GD)		6f		93+	

2000 Turf 0-4: (6f 3, 7f) (gd 3, g-f)
Pattern-class colt, effective 6 to 8f, best at 8f, acts on gd to frm, best on gd. Turf high 101. Consistent. Not a bad effort to finish fifth in the Abernant on his return considering the six-furlong trip would have been on the short side, and two further runs at that trip have suggested that he really needs further. Ran a lacklustre race over seven on his final start, however.
**J A R Toller [4-18] Duke of Devonshire.*

TECHNICIAN (IRE) BHB 62f62a **RR 68f 62a** 5248[5]
5 ch g Archway (IRE) 8.5f **(60)** - How It Works (Commanche Run) 8.5f **(58)**
Form - 0052001232220005
Record 2000 - 1st:1 2nd:5 3rd:1 Ran:16
Pre2000 - 1st:0 2nd:10 3rd:8 Ran:40
Win Prizemoney £4,030 *Total Prizemoney* £24,083
Wins * 2000 Jun Carlis (FRM) H 5.9f 49 53 <
2000 Turf 1-13: (6f 1-9, 7f 4) (sft, g-s, gd 3, g-f 1-4, frm 4) 2000 AW 0-3: (6f, 7f 2) (Fibr 3)
Average gelding, effective 6 to 7f, best at 7f, acts on gd to frm, mostly wears blinkers (effectively). Turf high 75 - 2nd of 9 giving 17lb to Starlight (15 Apr Thirsk 7f gd RF 0737). AW high 44. Becoming disappointing. A fair handicapper who runs at distances ranging from six furlongs to a mile, and finally got off the mark over six at Carlisle. Has run well since despite climbing the handicap. Seems to handle most ground and, is suited by a turning track.
**E J Alston [1-48] All Saints Racing (from M A Jarvis [0-8] Feb 1998).*

TEDBURROW BHB 113f **RR 113f** 4608[4]
8 b g Dowsing (USA) 7f **(61)** - Gwiffina (Welsh Saint) 7.6f **(64)**
Form - 0070813724
Record 2000 - 1st:1 2nd:1 3rd:1 Ran:9
Pre2000 - 1st:17 2nd:4 3rd:3 Ran:56
Win Prizemoney £224,399 *Total Prizemoney* £276,895

Wins	* 2000	Jly	Newcas	(FRM)	L	6f		113	<
	* 1999	Spt	Leopar	(SFT)	G3	5f		113+	
	* 1999	Jly	Cheste	(G-F)	L	6.1f		98	
	* 1999	Jly	Cheste	(G-F)	L	5.1f		105	
	* 1999	Mar	Doncas	(G-S)	L	6f		113	<
	* 1998	Spt	Leopar	(SFT)	G3	5f		110+	
	* 1998	Jly	Cheste	(G-F)	L	5.1f		110	
	* 1998	Apr	Newmar	(G-S)	L	6f		110	
	* 1997	Spt	Ascot	(G-F)	H	5f	105	108	
	* 1997	Jly	Cheste	(G-F)		5.1f		100	
	* 1997	Jun	York	(G-S)	H	6f	95	98	
	* 1997	May	Haydoc	(G-S)	H	5f	88	94	
	1996	Jly	Newmar	(G-F)	H	5f	88	91	

2000 Turf 1-9: (5f 3, 6f 1-6) (g-s, gd 5, g-f 2, frm 1-1)
Group-class gelding, effective 5 to 6f, best at 6f, acts on g-s to frm, best on gd, excels at Leopardstown, likes Chester. Turf high 113 - 1st of 11 giving 4lb to Cretan Gift (1 Jly Newcastle RF 2441). He took longer than usual to find his form, but won a Listed race in July before being touched off in close finishes to the Group 3 Flying Five at Leopardstown and Group 2 Diadem Stakes at Ascot. Effective at five or six furlongs, he can sweat up but is tremendously game. Usually ridden with restraint, he has an excellent record at Chester.
**E J Alston [12-37] Philip Davies (from Mrs A M Naughton [5-25] Oct 1996).*

Tedburrow dug deep at Newcastle

TE-DEUM (IRE) BHB 55f **RR 62f** 5161[9]
3 ch c Ridgewood Ben - Tabessa (USA) (Shahrastani (USA)) 8.8f **(72)**
Form - 05010
Record 2000 - 1st:1 2nd:0 3rd:0 Ran:5
Pre2000 - 1st:0 2nd:0 3rd:1 Ran:3
Win Prizemoney £3,107 *Total Prizemoney* £3,573
Wins * 2000 Spt Salisb (SFT) H 14.1f 55 58 <
2000 Turf 1-5: (8f, 12f 2, 14f 1-1, 16f) (sft, g-s, gd 1-2, frm)
Scopey, average colt. Turf high 62.
**J C Fox [1-8] Lord Mutton Racing Partnership.*

TEDSTALE (USA) BHB 78f **RR 78f** 4970[17]
2 ch c Irish River (FR) 9f **(77)** - Carefree Kate (USA) (Lyphard (USA)) 9.9f **(72)**
Form - 744350
Record 2000 - 1st:0 2nd:0 3rd:1 Ran:6
Win Prizemoney £0 *Total Prizemoney* £1,427
2000 Turf 0-6: (7f 4, 8f 2) (g-s 2, gd, g-f 3)
Above-average colt, effective 7 to 8f, acts on g-f. Turf high 84 (began Aug). **L M Cumani [0-6] M J Dawson.*

TEE CEE BHB 71f **RR 69f** 4277[1]
3 b f Lion Cavern (USA) 7.5f **(74)** - Hawayah (IRE) **(33f)** (Shareef Dancer (USA)) 9.9f **(73)**
Form - 533431
Record 2000 - 1st:1 2nd:0 3rd:3 Ran:6

Win Prizemoney £2,240 *Total Prizemoney* £4,209
Wins * **2000** Spt Chepst (G-S) H 7.1f 65 69 <
2000 Turf 1-6: (6f, 7f 1-3, 8f 2) (gd 2, g-f 1-3, frm)
Light-framed, average filly, effective 7f, acts on g-f to frm. Turf high 69 - 1st of 18 giving 14lb to Davis Rock (7 Spt Chepstow RF 4277). **R Guest [1-6] Matthews Breeding and Racing.*

TEEHEE (IRE) BHB 83f **RR 80f** 5167[3]
2 b c Anita's Prince 6f **(62)** - Regal Charmer (Royal And Regal (USA)) 9.5f **(60)**
Form - 5533
Record 2000 - 1st:0 2nd:0 3rd:2 Ran:4
Win Prizemoney £0 *Total Prizemoney* £1,186
2000 Turf 0-4: (7f 3, 8f) (gd, g-f 2, frm)
Decent colt. Turf high 80 (began Aug) - 3rd of 7 to Lanesborough (24 Oct Redcar 7f gd RF 5167). **B Palling [0-4] Celtic Racing.*

TEEJAY'N'AITCH (IRE) BHB 20f **RR 29f** 1076[8]
8 b g Maelstrom Lake 8.8f **(53)** - Middle Verde (USA) (Sham (USA)) 9.5f **(68)**
Form - 8
Record 2000 - 1st:0 2nd:0 3rd:0 Ran:1
Pre2000 - 1st:0 2nd:1 3rd:4 Ran:30
Win Prizemoney £0 *Total Prizemoney* £3,484
2000 Turf 0-1: (9f) (g-f)
Little account gelding, has worn blinkers.
**J S Goldie [6-80] Mrs Alice Goldie (from R Ingram [0-3] Jly 1994)*

TEENAWON (IRE) BHB 53f **RR 54f** 3919[13]
2 ch f Polar Falcon (USA) 9f **(74)** - Oasis (Valiyar) 8.5f **(73)**
Form - 320
Record 2000 - 1st:0 2nd:1 3rd:1 Ran:3
Win Prizemoney £0 *Total Prizemoney* £808
2000 Turf 0-3: (6f 2, 7f) (gd 2, frm)
Currently fair filly. Turf high 54 (began Jly) - 2nd of 8 to Delta Song (11 Aug Lingfield 6f frm RF 3553).
**K R Burke [0-3] Haydn Kelly.*

TEEPLOY GIRL BHB 22f32a **RR 32a** 322[11]
5 b m Deploy 11.1f **(67)** - Intoxication (Great Nephew) 9.9f **(64)**
Form - 60
Record 2000 - 1st:0 2nd:0 3rd:0 Ran:2
Pre2000 - 1st:0 2nd:0 3rd:1 Ran:6
Win Prizemoney £0 *Total Prizemoney* £273
2000 AW 0-2: (9f, 12f) (Fibr 2)
Very poor filly, has worn blinkers.
**D Burchell [0-3] D N Carey (from J P Smith [0-1] Oct 1999).*

TEFI BHB 62f **RR 69f** 4998[6]
2 ch g Efisio 7.7f **(69)** - Masuri Kabisa (USA) **(46f)** (Ascot Knight (CAN))
Form - 5322306
Record 2000 - 1st:0 2nd:2 3rd:2 Ran:7
Win Prizemoney £0 *Total Prizemoney* £2,761
2000 Turf 0-7: (5f, 6f 4, 7f 2) (g-s, gd, g-f 3, frm 2)
Average gelding, effective 6 to 7f, acts on g-f to frm. Turf high 66 - 2nd of 8 to Galaxy Returns (2 Aug Carlisle 6f g-f RF 3309).
**T D Easterby [0-7] T E F Freight (Scarborough) Ltd.*

TEGGIANO (IRE) BHB 110f **RR 109f** 2918a[10]
3 b f Mujtahid (USA) 7.4f **(69)** - Tegwen (USA) **(81df)** (Nijinsky (CAN)) 10.3f **(77)**
Form - 20
Record 2000 - 1st:0 2nd:1 3rd:0 Ran:2
Pre2000 - 1st:3 2nd:0 3rd:0 Ran:4
Win Prizemoney £140,520 *Total Prizemoney* £171,927
Wins 1999 Spt Ascot (HVY) G1 8f 101+
1999 Spt Doncas (G-F) G3 8f 108+ <
1999 Aug Newbur (GD) 6f 87+
2000 Turf 0-2: (12f 2) (g-f 2)
Workmanlike, Pattern-class filly, effective 8 to 12f, best at 8f, acts on sft to g-f, best on g-f. Turf high 109 (1st run) - 2nd of 9 to Miletrian (22 Jun Ascot 12f g-f RF 2178). A leading two-year-old in '99, she joined Godolphin over the winter and finished a staying-on second to Bintalreef in one of their public trials. She was declared for the Oaks, but was a late absentee due to a minor injury and then a temperature. Made an encouraging comeback in the Ribblesdale, but failed to build on that in the Irish Oaks.
**S bin Suroor [0-2] Godolphin (from C F Brittain [3-4] Spt 1999).*

TELECASTER (IRE) BHB 58f74a **RR 35+f 74a** 5014[8]
4 ch g Indian Ridge 7.6f **(74)** - Monashee (USA) (Sovereign Dancer (USA)) 11.2f **(68)**
Form - 311211528
Record 2000 - 1st:4 2nd:2 3rd:1 Ran:9
Pre2000 - 1st:0 2nd:0 3rd:0 Ran:3
Win Prizemoney £13,856 *Total Prizemoney* £16,371
Wins * **2000** *Mar Wolver (STD) H* 6f 59 70 <
* **2000** *Feb Southw (STD) H* 6f 59 62
* **2000** *Jan Southw (STD) H* 6f 46 58
* **2000** *Jan Wolver (STD) H* 6f 40 48+
2000 AW 4-9: (5f, 6f 4-7, 7f) (Fibr 4-9)
Lengthy, above-average gelding, effective 5 to 6f, best at 6f, - acts on Fibr, often wears blinkers (very effectively), prefers left handed tracks, favours tight tracks. AW high 72 - 2nd of 8 giving 6lb to Eastern Trumpeter (16 Mar Wolverhampton 5f Fibr RF 0448) - also 1st of 11 getting 2lb from Days of Grace (2 Mar Wolverhampton RF 0391). He improved beyond all recognition last year, winning four times on Fibresand and taking a hike up the handicap as a result. Suited by six furlongs, he also has a commendable attitude in a battle. **C R Egerton [4-12] Casting Partners B.*

TELLION BHB 46f59a **RR 30f 59a** 355[7]
6 b g Mystiko (USA) 7.7f **(59)** - Salchow (Niniski (USA)) 10.6f **(65)**
Form - 37
Record 2000 - 1st:0 2nd:0 3rd:1 Ran:2
Pre2000 - 1st:0 2nd:0 3rd:2 Ran:13
Win Prizemoney £0 *Total Prizemoney* £1,820
2000 AW 0-2: (8f, 12f) (Fibr 2)
Moderate gelding, has worn blinkers. AW high 47. Inconsistent.
**J R Jenkins [1-18] Mrs Wendy Jenkins (from Major W R Hern [0-7] Oct 1997).*

TEMERAIRE (USA) BHB 76f83a **RR 82df 83a** 5141[12]
5 b g Dayjur (USA) 6.8f **(79)** - Key Dancer (USA) (Nijinsky (CAN)) 10.3f **(77)**
Form - 51702004237000
Record 2000 - 1st:0 2nd:2 3rd:1 Ran:11
Pre2000 - 1st:4 2nd:3 3rd:0 Ran:23
Win Prizemoney £22,206 *Total Prizemoney* £35,405
Wins * 1999 *Nov Lingfi (STD)* 7f 87
* 1999 Spt Newbur (G-F) H 7.3f 78 85
1998 Jly Lingfi (G-F) 7.6f 93 <
1998 Jun Windso (G-F) 8.3f 84+
2000 Turf 0-11: (6f, 7f 8, 8f 2) (g-s, gd 5, g-f 4, frm)
Useful gelding, effective 7f, acts on gd to frm - acts on Equi, has worn blinkers, prefers right handed tracks, likes tight tracks. Turf high 82. Becoming disappointing. He is kept busy and wins from time to time, but has a moderate strike rate.
**D J S Cosgrove [2-19] Global Racing Club (from R Ingram [0-11] Jly 1999).*

TEMESIDE TINA BHB 43f34a **RR 38f 34a** 26[4]
4 ch m Tina's Pet 7.4f **(56)** - Expletive (Shiny Tenth) 9.2f **(56)**
Form - 064
Record 2000 - 1st:0 2nd:0 3rd:0 Ran:1
Pre2000 - 1st:0 2nd:0 3rd:0 Ran:6
Win Prizemoney £0 *Total Prizemoney* £189
2000 AW 0-1: (8f) (Equi)
Unfurnished, very moderate filly. **P D Evans [0-7] H M Thursfield.*

TEMPER TANTRUM BHB 70a **RR 70a** 5019[8]
2 b g Pursuit of Love 9.5f **(69)** - Queenbird **(63f 52a)** (Warning)
Form - 8
Record 2000 - 1st:0 2nd:0 3rd:0 Ran:1
2000 AW 0-1: (7f) (Fibr)
Currently average gelding. **Andrew Reid [0-1] A S Reid.*

TEMPEST BHB 116f **RR 112f** 4988[3]
2 b c Zafonic (USA) 9f **(83)** - Pidona (Baillamont (USA)) 7f **(78)**
Form - 41263
Record 2000 - 1st:1 2nd:1 3rd:1 Ran:5
Win Prizemoney £4,446 *Total Prizemoney* £31,108
Wins * **2000** Aug Newbur (G-F) 7f 83+ <
2000 Turf 1-5: (7f 1-5) (gd 3, g-f 1-2)

Group-class colt. Turf high 112 (began Aug) - 3rd of 10 to Tobougg (14 Oct Newmarket 7f gd RF 4988). The subject of glowing reports after an easy win at Newbury in August, he looked overrated until finishing third in the Dewhurst Stakes on his final start. Waiting tactics may have been responsible for that improvement and, provided he continues to relax through the early stages of a race, there is a major prize to be won with this colt.
**Sir Michael Stoute [1-5] Cheveley Park Stud.*

TEMPLES TIME (IRE) BHB 72f **RR 72f** 5218[5]
2 b f Distinctly North (USA) 7.4f **(63)** - Midnight Patrol (Ashmore (FR)) 8.5f **(65)**
Form - 436105
Record 2000 - 1st:1 2nd:0 3rd:1 Ran:6
Win Prizemoney £1,767 *Total Prizemoney* £2,793
Wins * 2000 Spt Bright (G-S) 8f 70 <
2000 Turf 1-6: (5f, 6f, 7f, 8f 1-3) (sft, gd 1-4, frm)
Above-average filly, effective 7 to 8f, acts on gd to frm. Turf high 72 - also 1st of 10 getting 2lb from Midnight Creek (24 Spt Brighton RF 4614). **R Hannon [1-6] J B Kavanagh.*

TEMPLE WAY BHB 93f **RR 93f** 4295[5]
4 b g Shirley Heights 12.1f **(76)** - Abbey Strand (USA) (Shadeed (USA)) 8.2f **(70)**
Form - 0222105
Record 2000 - 1st:1 2nd:3 3rd:0 Ran:7
Pre2000 - 1st:1 2nd:1 3rd:1 Ran:9
Win Prizemoney £36,298 *Total Prizemoney* £72,644
Wins * 2000 Aug Goodwo (G-F) H 14f 88 93 <
* 1999 Jly Chepst (G-F) H 16.2f 69 75
2000 Turf 1-7: (12f, 14f 1-3, 15f, 16f 2) (gd 2, g-f 1-3, frm 2)
Workmanlike, useful gelding, effective 14 to 16f, acts on gd to frm, best on g-f, often wears blinkers (effectively), prefers left handed tracks. Turf high 93 - 5th of 13 giving 7lb to Romantic Affair (8 Spt Doncaster 15f g-f RF 4295) - also 1st of 17 giving 11lb to Jardines Lookout (1 Aug Goodwood RF 3275). Improving. Much improved last year, he launched his challenge a stride too late in the Northumberland Plate, but gained compensation when running away with a valuable handicap at Goodwood in August. Worth another try over two miles, he enjoys fast ground and is genuine.
**R Charlton [2-16] The Queen.*

TEMPRAMENTAL (IRE) BHB 46f36a **RR 54f 36a** 3191[8]
4 ch m Midhish - Musical Horn (Music Boy) 6.8f **(57)**
Form - 75537225333141578
Record 2000 - 1st:2 2nd:2 3rd:3 Ran:12
Pre2000 - 1st:1 2nd:0 3rd:3 Ran:24
Win Prizemoney £10,267 *Total Prizemoney* £14,258
Wins * 2000 Jun Redcar (G-F) H 8f 51 53
*** 2000** May Pontef (GD) H 10f 45 52
1998 Aug Chepst (G-F) H 5.1f 54 60 <
2000 Turf 2-8: (8f 1-4, 10f 1-4) (g-s, gd, g-f 1-2, frm 1-4) 2000 AW 0-4: (8f 2, 12f 2) (Fibr 4)
Strong, fair filly, effective 8 to 10f, best at 10f, acts on g-s to frm - acts on AW, best on g-f, has worn blinkers. Turf high 54 - 4th of 15 getting 2lb from Sifat (31 May Yarmouth 10f g-f RF 1613) - also 1st of 19 giving 8lb to Tayovullin (13 Jun Redcar RF 1912). AW high 43. Consistent.
**S R Bowring [2-12] Roland Wheatley (from D HaydnJones [1-24] Dec 1999).*

TEMPTING FATE (IRE) BHB 100f **RR 91f** 4990[4]
2 b f Persian Bold 10f **(69)** - West of Eden (Crofter (USA)) 8.4f **(56)**
Form - 2114
Record 2000 - 1st:2 2nd:1 3rd:0 Ran:4
Win Prizemoney £14,354 *Total Prizemoney* £19,024
Wins * 2000 Aug Salisb (G-F) 6f 89 <
*** 2000** Aug Newbur (G-F) 6f 81+
2000 Turf 2-4: (6f 2-3, 7f) (gd 2, frm 2-2)
Useful filly. Turf high 90 (began Aug) - 4th of 16 to Sayedah (14 Oct Newmarket 7f gd RF 4990) - also 1st of 5 from Innit (31 Aug Salisbury RF 4126). Successful twice on fast ground last season, she may have mistimed her run and not got home in the Rockfel on her last run. She is usually held up and possesses a nice turn of foot, so can be given another chance.
**J W Hills [2-4] Michael Kerr-Dineen & Partners.*

TENACIOUS MELODY BHB 43f **RR 39f** 2108[9]
4 b g Tina's Pet 7.4f **(56)** - High Run (HOL) (Runnymede) 9.3f **(50)**
Form - 000
Record 2000 - 1st:0 2nd:0 3rd:0 Ran:3
Pre2000 - 1st:0 2nd:0 3rd:1 Ran:1
Win Prizemoney £0 *Total Prizemoney* £4,126
2000 Turf 0-3: (8f, 10f 2) (gd 2, frm)
Very moderate gelding. Turf high 39.
**M P Muggeridge [0-3] L & Mrs A Chamberlain (from A Tortorella in ITY [0-1] Oct 1998).*

TENBY HEIGHTS (IRE) BHB 20f **RR 4f** 4328[16]
4 b g Tenby 10.4f **(76)** - Alpine Spring (Head for Heights) 9.6f **(55)**
Form - 700
Record 2000 - 1st:0 2nd:0 3rd:0 Ran:3
Pre2000 - 1st:0 2nd:0 3rd:0 Ran:10
Win Prizemoney £0 *Total Prizemoney* £483
2000 Turf 0-3: (12f 2, 16f) (gd, g-f, hrd)
Scopey, very poor gelding. Turf high 4 (began Aug).
**H S Howe [0-4] The Trojan Partnership (from R Hollinshead [0-10] Jun 1999).*

TENDERFOOT **RR 26f** 5075[6]
2 b f Be My Chief (USA) 10.2f **(62)** - Kelimutu (Top Ville) 11.7f **(68)**
Form - 6
Record 2000 - 1st:0 2nd:0 3rd:0 Ran:1
2000 Turf 0-1: (8f) (g-s)
Currently moderate filly. **J Pearce [0-1] Jim Furlong.*

TENDER TRAP (IRE) **RR 82f** 5157[5]
2 b c Sadler's Wells (USA) 11.3f **(87)** - Shamiyda (USA) (Sir Ivor) 10.2f **(70)**
Form - 5
Record 2000 - 1st:0 2nd:0 3rd:0 Ran:1
2000 Turf 0-1: (8f) (sft)
Currently decent colt. **T G Mills [0-1] T G Mills.*

TENERIFE FLYER BHB 55f **RR 55f** 5004[16]
2 ch f Rock City 8.8f **(62)** - Nobleata **(8f)** (Dunbeath (USA)) 7.8f **(70)**
Form - 60467440
Record 2000 - 1st:0 2nd:0 3rd:0 Ran:8
Win Prizemoney £0 *Total Prizemoney* £236
2000 Turf 0-7: (5f, 7f 2, 8f 4) (g-s 3, gd 2, g-f, frm) 2000 AW 0-1: (5f) (Fibr)
Fair filly, effective 8f, acts on gd. Turf high 55 - 4th of 13 getting 7lb from Cynara (21 Spt Pontefract 8f gd RF 4555).
**J Norton [0-8] D J Jarvis.*

TENNESSEE WALTZ BHB 54f **RR 51f** 5236[16]
2 b f Caerleon (USA) 10.9f **(79)** - Military Tune (IRE) (Nashwan (USA))
Form - 000
Record 2000 - 1st:0 2nd:0 3rd:0 Ran:3
2000 Turf 0-3: (7f 2, 8f) (g-s, gd, frm)
Currently fair filly. Turf high 51 (began Spt).
**E A L Dunlop [0-3] Geoff Howard-Spink & Lindy Regis.*

TEN PAST SIX BHB 20f37a **RR 27f 37a** 3699[9]
8 ch g Kris 10f **(75)** - Tashinsky (USA) (Nijinsky (CAN)) 10.3f **(77)**
Form - 0567080
Record 2000 - 1st:0 2nd:0 3rd:0 Ran:7
Pre2000 - 1st:5 2nd:7 3rd:0 Ran:35
Win Prizemoney £13,139 *Total Prizemoney* £24,983
Wins * 1998 Aug Carlis (G-S) C 12f 57
* 1998 Jun Hamilt (G-S) C 11.1f 56
* 1998 *May Southw (STD) C 11f 64*
* 1997 Apr Ripon (GD) S 10f 59
2000 Turf 0-4: (11f, 12f, 13f 2) (gd, g-f 2, frm) 2000 AW 0-3: (11f 2, 12f) (Fibr 3)
Little account gelding, effective 12f, acts on g-f, has worn blinkers (effectively). Turf high 27. AW high 26.
**Martyn Wane [4-49] James S Kennerley and Miss Jenny Hall (from B W Hills [1-6] Spt 1995).*

TENSILE (IRE) BHB 85f **RR 90f** 4987[9]
5 b g Tenby 10.4f **(76)** - Bonnie Isle (Pitcairn) 9.5f **(60)**
Form - 68743350
Record 2000 - 1st:0 2nd:0 3rd:2 Ran:8
Pre2000 - 1st:1 2nd:3 3rd:1 Ran:16

Win Prizemoney £3,938 *Total Prizemoney* £17,547
Wins 1998 Apr Beverl (SFT) H 9.9f 77 87 <
2000 Turf 0-8: (14f, 15f, 16f 2, 18f, 19f 2, 22f) (g-s, gd 3, g-f 3, frm)
Useful gelding, effective 14 to 22f, acts on g-s to frm, best on g-f, has worn blinkers, excels at Ascot and Chester. Turf high 90 - 3rd of 5 giving 17lb to Fait Le Jojo (25 Aug Newmarket 15f g-f RF 3967). Consistent. He has a poor strike rate for one of his ability and looks a better horse over hurdles nowadays.
**M C Pipe [0-4] D Charlesworth (from J R Fanshawe [1-10] Jly 2000).*

TEODORA (IRE) BHB 77f **RR 86f** 4743[17]
3 b f Fairy King (USA) 7.7f **(75)** - Pinta (IRE) (Ahonoora) 8.1f **(73)**
Form - 50762700700
Record 2000 - 1st:0 2nd:1 3rd:0 Ran:11
Pre2000 - 1st:1 2nd:0 3rd:1 Ran:4
Win Prizemoney £3,668 *Total Prizemoney* £40,773
Wins * 1999 Jly Windso (G-F) 6f 79t <
2000 Turf 0-11: (6f, 7f 8, 8f 2) (sft, g-s, gd 4, g-f 3, frm 2)
Workmanlike, useful filly, effective 7f, acts on gd to g-f. Turf high 89 - 2nd of 8 getting 3lb from Out of Reach (11 Jly Newmarket 7f gd RF 2690). **S Dow [1-15] G Steinberg.*

TEOFILIO (IRE) BHB 66f68a **RR 67f 68a** 5245[2]
6 ch h Night Shift (USA) 8.1f **(73)** - Rivoltade (USA) (Sir Ivor) 10.2f **(70)**
Form - 16070023004540222
Record 2000 - 1st:1 2nd:4 3rd:1 Ran:17
Pre2000 - 1st:4 2nd:5 3rd:2 Ran:25
Win Prizemoney £29,002 *Total Prizemoney* £48,047
Wins * **2000** *Feb Lingfi (STD)* H *8f* 62 67+
* 1999 Jun Newmar (G-F) H 7f 64 72
* 1999 Jun Sandow (GD) H 7.1f 64 75 <
* 1999 *Feb Lingfi (STD)* *8f* *59*
1997 Apr Beverl (G-F) 8.5f 74
2000 Turf 0-11: (7f 9, 8f 2) (gd 2, g-f 4, frm 5) 2000 AW 1-6: (6f, 7f, 8f 1-4) (Equi 1-2, Fibr 4)
Average horse, effective 7f, acts on gd to frm, often wears blinkers (very effectively), and excels at Newmarket. Turf high 72 - 2nd of 14 getting 3lb from Yeast (8 Jly Leicester 7f frm RF 2639). AW high 68. Best when able to be covered up and produced late, he is suited by seven furlongs on turf, but gets a mile on Equitrack and scored back under those conditions at the start of last year.
**A J McNae [4-36] L R Gotch (from D R Loder [1-6] Jun 1997).*

TE QUIERO RR 66f 4807[8]
2 gr c Bering 9.6f **(80)** - Ma Lumiere (FR) (Niniski (USA)) 10.6f **(65)**
Form - 8
Record 2000 - 1st:0 2nd:0 3rd:0 Ran:1
2000 Turf 0-1: (7f) (g-s)
Currently average colt. **Miss Gay Kelleway [0-1] A P Griffin.*

TEREED ELHAWA BHB 83f **RR 75f** 5024[4]
2 b f Cadeaux Genereux 7.9f **(76)** - Dimakya (USA) **(83df)** (Dayjur (USA))
Form - 63144
Record 2000 - 1st:1 2nd:0 3rd:1 Ran:5
Win Prizemoney £4,368 *Total Prizemoney* £6,253
Wins * **2000** Jly Nottin (G-F) 6.1f 65+ <
2000 Turf 1-5: (6f 1-5) (g-s, gd, g-f 2, frm 1-1)
Above-average filly. Turf high 75. **E A L Dunlop [1-5] Khalifa Sultan.*

TERIMON'S DREAM RR 50f 4486[11]
3 gr g Terimon 8.7f **(58)** - I Have A Dream (SWE) (Mango Express)
Form - 0
Record 2000 - 1st:0 2nd:0 3rd:0 Ran:1
2000 Turf 0-1: (12f) (g-s)
Scopey, currently fair gelding. **A W Carroll [0-1] John McKenna.*

TERM OF ENDEARMENT BHB 45f **RR 45f** 4874[17]
3 b f First Trump - Twilight Secret (Vaigly Great) 7f **(58)**
Form - 005605208213000
Record 2000 - 1st:1 2nd:2 3rd:1 Ran:15
Pre2000 - 1st:1 2nd:0 3rd:0 Ran:10
Win Prizemoney £5,202 *Total Prizemoney* £8,232
Wins 2000 Aug Leices (G-F) S 7f 45
1999 Jun Bath (GD) 5.1f 74 <
2000 Turf 1-13: (6f 3, 7f 1-5, 8f 5) (hvy, g-s, gd 2, g-f, frm 1-6, hrd 2)
2000 AW 0-2: (7f, 10f) (Equi, Fibr)
Moderate filly, effective 5 to 6f, acts on g-f to frm. Turf high 45. AW high 47.
**L R James [0-1] Miss Kate Waddington (from J Pearce [1-19] Spt 2000).*

TERRA NOVA BHB 63f60a **RR 67df 60a** 4652[9]
3 ch f Polar Falcon (USA) 9f **(74)** - Tarsa (Ballad Rock) 7.8f **(63)**
Form - 3030
Record 2000 - 1st:0 2nd:0 3rd:2 Ran:4
Pre2000 - 1st:0 2nd:2 3rd:0 Ran:6
Win Prizemoney £0 *Total Prizemoney* £4,899
2000 Turf 0-3: (6f 2, 7f) (g-s, g-f 2) 2000 AW 0-1: (7f) (Fibr)
Scopey, average filly, effective 7f, acts on frm. Turf high 65. Becoming disappointing. **R W Armstrong [0-10] P J Vela.*

TERRAZZO (USA) BHB 56f54a **RR 58df 54a** 2367[7]
5 b g Nureyev (USA) 8.4f **(84)** - Diese (USA) (Diesis) 9.3f **(69)**
Form - 7
Record 2000 - 1st:0 2nd:0 3rd:0 Ran:1
Pre2000 - 1st:1 2nd:1 3rd:1 Ran:6
Win Prizemoney £2,598 *Total Prizemoney* £4,040
Wins * 1999 May Mussel (FRM) H 9f 56 58 <
2000 Turf 0-1: (8f) (g-f)
Fair gelding, effective 9 to 12f, acts on g-f to frm - acts on Fibr.
**J G FitzGerald [1-9] & Mrs Raymond Anderson Green.*

TERRE A TERRE (ITY) RR 104f 5366a[3]
3 b f Kaldounevees (FR) - Toujours Juste (ITY) (Always Fair (USA))
Form - 13
2000 Turf 1-2: (8f 1-2) (hvy, gd 1-1)
Currently very useful filly. Turf high 104 (began Spt) - 3rd of 16 giving 5lb to Miss Riviera Golf (3 Nov Maisons-laffitte 8f hvy RF 5366a) - also 1st of 10 getting 4lb from Peony (27 Spt Saint-cloud RF 4836a). **E Libaud in FR [1-2] Spt 2000).*

TERRESTRIAL (USA) RR 86+f 4969[1]
2 ch c Theatrical 11.5f **(78)** - Stellaria (USA) (Roberto (USA)) 10f **(76)**
Form - 1
Record 2000 - 1st:1 2nd:0 3rd:0 Ran:1
Win Prizemoney £7,800 *Total Prizemoney* £7,800
Wins * **2000** Oct Newmar (SFT) 8f 86+ <
2000 Turf 1-1: (8f 1-1) (gd 1-1)
Currently useful colt. (1st run) - 1st of 29 from Painted Room (13 Oct Newmarket RF 4969). **J H M Gosden [1-1] K Abdulla.*

TERRE VIERGE (FR) RR 91f 5205a[1]
3 b f Common Grounds 8.1f **(66)** - Divine Madness (FR) (Carwhite) 7.2f **(61)**
Form - 1
2000 Turf 1-1: (9f 1-1) (hvy 1-1)
Currently useful filly. (1st run) - 1st of 11 from Muschana (19 Oct Longchamp RF 5205a). **E Lellouche in FR [1-1] Ecurie Ferdane.*

TERROIR (IRE) RR 104f 1820a[4]
5 b h Fairy King (USA) 7.7f **(75)** - Terracotta Hut (Habitat) 9.4f **(70)**
Form - 34
2000 Turf 0-2: (5f, 6f) (hvy, gd)
Currently very useful colt, often wears blinkers. Turf high 104 - 4th of 5 to Nuclear Debate (3 Jun Chantilly 5f gd RF 1820a).
**Mlle I Turc in FR [0-3] .*

TERTULLIAN (USA) RR 115f 4954a[1]
5 ch h Miswaki (USA) 8.1f **(81)** - Turbaine (USA) (Trempolino (USA)) 12f **(71)**
Form - 33351
2000 Turf 1-5: (6f 2, 7f 1-3) (sft 1-2, g-s, gd 2)
High-class colt, effective 6 to 7f, best at 7f, acts on sft to gd, excels at Hoppegarten and Munich. Turf high 110 - 1st of 7 giving 5lb to Gaelic Storm (8 Oct Munich RF 4954a). Consistent.
**P Schiergen in GER [4-12] Gestut Schlenderhan.*

TEST THE WATER (IRE) BHB 50f44a **RR 42f 44a** 2261[7]
6 ch h Maelstrom Lake 8.8f **(53)** - Baliana (CAN) (Riverman (USA)) 9.1f **(76)**
Form - 0807
Record 2000 - 1st:0 2nd:0 3rd:0 Ran:4
Pre2000 - 1st:2 2nd:5 3rd:3 Ran:28

Win Prizemoney £11,620 *Total Prizemoney* £19,966
Wins 1998 Jly Sandow (G-F) C 8.1f 74
1996 Oct Ascot (GD) H 7f 85 90 <
2000 Turf 0-2: (9f, 11f) (gd 2) 2000 AW 0-2: (8f, 10f) (Equi 2)
Moderate horse, effective 8f, acts on frm, has worn blinkers. Turf high 42. AW high 35. Consistent. Has plenty of ability, but is by no means consistent. His best form is on fast ground.
**T J Arnold [0-4] Steppey Lane Bloodstock (from R Hannon [2-28] Jly 1999).*

TEXALINA (FR) RR 103f 2005a[10]
3 b f
Form - 120
2000 Turf 0-2: (8f, 11f) (hvy, gd)
Very useful filly. Turf high 103. **J deRoualle in FR [2-4].*

TEXANNIE BHB 52f RR 4470[7]
3 b f Inchinor 8.9f **(64)** - Texanne (BEL) **(45f)** (Efisio)
Form - 07
Record 2000 - 1st:0 2nd:0 3rd:0 Ran:2
2000 Turf 0-2: (8f, 10f) (g-f 2)
Currently very poor filly. (began Spt).
**S C Williams [0-2] Stuart Williams.*

TEYAAR BHB 74f76a RR 78df 76a 3856[18]
4 b g Polar Falcon (USA) 9f **(74)** - Music in My Life (IRE) (Law Society (USA)) 9.9f **(70)**
Form - 517112522200
Record 2000 - 1st:3 2nd:4 3rd:0 Ran:12
Pre2000 - 1st:0 2nd:1 3rd:1 Ran:6
Win Prizemoney £8,381 *Total Prizemoney* £16,521
Wins * 2000 *Apr Wolver (STD) H 6f 67 71* <
*** 2000** *Mar Southw (STD) 6f 65*
*** 2000** *Feb Southw (STD) 6f 65*
2000 Turf 0-5: (5f, 6f 4) (sft, gd 2, g-f 2) 2000 AW 3-7: (5f, 6f 3-5, 7f) (Fibr 3-7)
Workmanlike, above-average gelding, effective 5 to 6f, best at 6f, acts on gd to g-f - acts on Fibr, has worn blinkers, prefers left handed tracks, prefers tight tracks, excels at Southwell and Wolverhampton. Turf high 78 - 2nd of 20 getting 7lb from Manorbier (20 May Thirsk 6f gd RF 1346). AW high 75 - 2nd of 13 giving 2lb to Cartmel Park (21 Jun Wolverhampton 5f Fibr RF 2175). Showed some ability on turf, but did very well last year for his new trainer, winning three times over six furlongs on Fibresand. He ran well on turf last season without managing to force his head in front. Suited by forcing the pace.
**D Shaw [3-13] Justin Aaron (from J L Dunlop [0-5] Jun 1999).*

T G'S GIRL BHB 45f RR 32f 4767[17]
3 gr f Selkirk (USA) 7.9f **(76)** - River's Rising (FR) (Mendez (FR))
Form - 060
Record 2000 - 1st:0 2nd:0 3rd:0 Ran:3
Pre2000 - 1st:0 2nd:0 3rd:0 Ran:3
Win Prizemoney £0 *Total Prizemoney* £282
2000 Turf 0-3: (5f, 7f, 8f) (g-s 2, g-f)
Leggy, very moderate filly. Turf high 32.
**D Nicholls [0-2] Mrs Caroline Parker (from R Hannon [0-4] Jun 2000).*

THAILAND RR 43f 2540[9]
2 ch f Lycius (USA) 8.8f **(71)** - Tigwa **(66f)** (Cadeaux Genereux)
Form - 000
Record 2000 - 1st:0 2nd:0 3rd:0 Ran:3
2000 Turf 0-3: (5f, 6f, 7f) (frm 3)
Currently moderate filly. Turf high 43. **B W Hills [0-3] W J Gredley.*

THAMAN (IRE) BHB 75f RR 71f 2228[1]
3 b c Sri Pekan (USA) - Shaping Up (USA) (Storm Bird (CAN)) 10.3f **(74)**
Form - 01
Record 2000 - 1st:1 2nd:0 3rd:0 Ran:2
Win Prizemoney £3,776 *Total Prizemoney* £3,776
Wins * 2000 Jun Newmar (G-F) C 8f 71 <
2000 Turf 1-2: (7f, 8f 1-1) (gd, frm 1-1)
Neat, currently above-average colt. Turf high 71 - 1st of 18 giving 21lb to Spark of Life (23 Jun Newmarket RF 2228).
**B Hanbury [1-2] B Hanbury.*

THAMES DANCER (USA) BHB 79f68a RR 82f 68a 2153[4]
4 ch h Green Dancer (USA) 11.9f **(77)** - Hata (FR) (Kaldoun (FR)) 10.3f **(68)**
Form - 74134
Record 2000 - 1st:1 2nd:0 3rd:1 Ran:5
Pre2000 - 1st:0 2nd:1 3rd:1 Ran:6
Win Prizemoney £3,094 *Total Prizemoney* £8,095
Wins * 2000 May Lingfi (G-S) H 16f 69 73 <
2000 Turf 1-4: (12f, 14f, 16f 1-1, 20f) (g-s 2, gd 1-2) 2000 AW 0-1: (14f) (Fibr)
Workmanlike, decent colt, effective 14 to 20f, acts on g-s to gd, best on gd. Turf high 82 - 4th of 24 getting 5lb from Barba Papa (21 Jun Ascot 20f gd RF 2153) - also 1st of 20 giving 25lb to Sharaf (20 May Lingfield RF 1323). He was a long-standing maiden before winning a handicap over two miles at Lingfield in May.
**K McAuliffe [1-11] Mrs Mary O'Connor.*

THANKS MAX (IRE) BHB 75f70a RR 71f 70a 4869[10]
2 b g Goldmark (USA) - Almost A Lady (IRE) (Entitled)
Form - 0510
Record 2000 - 1st:1 2nd:0 3rd:0 Ran:4
Win Prizemoney £3,094 *Total Prizemoney* £3,094
Wins * 2000 Spt Hamilt (SFT) 5f 71 <
2000 Turf 1-4: (5f 1-1, 6f, 7f, 8f) (sft, g-s 1-1, frm 2)
Above-average gelding. Turf high 71 (began Aug) - 1st of 6 getting 4lb from Fantasy Believer (3 Spt Hamilton RF 4181).
**Miss L A Perratt [1-4] T P Finch.*

THARI (USA) BHB 102f RR 101+f 5323[14]
3 b br c Silver Hawk (USA) 11.2f **(85)** - Magic Slipper (Habitat) 9.4f **(70)**
Form - 76310
Record 2000 - 1st:1 2nd:0 3rd:1 Ran:5
Pre2000 - 1st:1 2nd:1 3rd:1 Ran:4
Win Prizemoney £17,222 *Total Prizemoney* £23,389
Wins * 2000 Spt Newmar (GD) H 14f 95 101+ <
1999 Spt Chepst (GD) 7.1f 79+
2000 Turf 1-5: (10f 2, 12f, 13f, 14f 1-1) (sft, g-f 1-4)
Workmanlike, very useful colt, effective 7 to 14f, acts on sft to g-f, best on g-f, has worn blinkers. Turf high 101 - 1st of 17 giving 25lb to Lord Alaska (30 Spt Newmarket RF 4741). A strong colt, he bounced back well from a mid-season lay-off and developed into a smart handicapper. Worth a try over two miles, he is open to some improvement but may not be at his best on heavy ground.
**B Hanbury [1-5] Hamdan Al Maktoum (from P T Walwyn [1-4] Oct 1999).*

THATCHAM (IRE) BHB 59f48a RR 61f 48a 5122[18]
4 ch g Thatching 7.8f **(69)** - Calaloo Sioux (USA) (Our Native (USA)) 11.2f **(63)**
Form - 3200412340
Record 2000 - 1st:1 2nd:2 3rd:2 Ran:10
Pre2000 - 1st:0 2nd:0 3rd:0 Ran:6
Win Prizemoney £2,938 *Total Prizemoney* £6,405
Wins * 2000 Jun Yarmou (G-F) H 6f 46 56 <
2000 Turf 1-6: (6f 1-3, 7f 2, 10f) (g-s, gd 2, g-f 1-2, frm) 2000 AW 0-4: (6f, 8f 2, 10f) (Equi 2, Fibr 2)
Workmanlike, average gelding, effective 6f, acts on g-f to frm, best on g-f, has worn blinkers (extremely effectively). Turf high 61 - 3rd of 10 giving 10lb to Muja's Magic (5 Jly Yarmouth 6f frm RF 2556) - also 1st of 14 getting 8lb from Be My Wish (15 Jun Yarmouth RF 1997). AW high 50. **R W Armstrong [1-16] Mrs John Davall.*

THATCHED (IRE) BHB 44f RR 50df 4626[10]
10 b g Thatching 7.8f **(69)** - Shadia (USA) (Naskra (USA)) 8.8f **(69)**
Form - 506756302400
Record 2000 - 1st:0 2nd:1 3rd:1 Ran:12
Pre2000 - 1st:10 2nd:7 3rd:11 Ran:96
Win Prizemoney £35,452 *Total Prizemoney* £54,290
Wins * 1998 May Redcar (G-F) H 9f 41 44
* 1997 Apr Carlis (GD) H 8f 51 56
* 1996 Oct Redcar (G-F) H 8f 48 52
* 1996 Spt Beverl (G-F) H 8.5f 47 43
* 1996 Jly Beverl (G-F) H 7.5f 43 46
2000 Turf 0-12: (7f 4, 8f 3, 9f 5) (gd, g-f 3, frm 7, hrd)
Fair gelding, effective 8 to 9f, best at 8f, acts on g-f to hrd, has worn blinkers. Turf high 52.
**R E Barr [10-105] R E Barr (from C F Wall [0-9] Spt 1993).*

THATCHED COTTAGE RR 60f 4201[6]

2 b f Thatching 7.8f **(69)** - Attaproffitt (Batshoof)
Form - 6
Record 2000 - 1st:0 2nd:0 3rd:0 Ran:1
2000 Turf 0-1: (5f) (frm)
Currently average filly. **B Palling [0-1] Merthyr Motor Auctions.*

THATCHING LAD RR 13[15]
7 gr g Belfort (FR) 6.7f **(53)** - Sing Out Loud (Thatching) 8f **(66)**
Form - 80
Record 2000 - 1st:0 2nd:0 3rd:0 Ran:1
Pre2000 - 1st:0 2nd:0 3rd:0 Ran:1
2000 AW 0-1: (8f) (Fibr)
Poor gelding. **D Eddy [0-6] Equiname Ltd.*

THATCHMASTER (IRE) BHB 60f **RR 65df** 4544[9]
9 b g Thatching 7.8f **(69)** - Key Maneuver (USA) (Key To Content (USA)) 8f **(54)**
Form - 00270
Record 2000 - 1st:0 2nd:1 3rd:0 Ran:5
Pre2000 - 1st:6 2nd:4 3rd:4 Ran:42
Win Prizemoney £22,733 *Total Prizemoney* £31,025

Wins								
* 1999	Aug	Goodwo	(GD)	H	9f	63	65	
* 1998	Jly	Windso	(G-F)	H	11.6f	63	67	<
* 1998	Jun	Windso	(GD)	H	11.6f	60	62	
* 1997	Aug	Goodwo	(G-F)	CH	10f	59	67	<
* 1996	Aug	Goodwo	(G-F)	CH	10f	52	58	
* 1996	Jly	Sandow	(G-F)	SH	8.1f	46	51	

2000 Turf 0-5: (8f, 9f 2, 10f, 12f) (gd 4, frm)
Average gelding, effective 9 to 12f, best at 12f, acts on gd to frm, best on gd, has worn blinkers. Turf high 59 (began Aug).
**C A Horgan [6-47] Mrs B Sumner.*

THAT MAN AGAIN BHB 64f72a **RR 73f 72a** 4372[1]
8 ch g Prince Sabo 6.6f **(64)** - Milne's Way (The Noble Player (USA)) 6.5f **(67)**
Form - 00001084380531
Record 2000 - 1st:2 2nd:0 3rd:2 Ran:14
Pre2000 - 1st:9 2nd:5 3rd:6 Ran:68
Win Prizemoney £58,389 *Total Prizemoney* £78,430

Wins							
* **2000**	Spt	Sandow	(G-F)	C	5f		57
* **2000**	Jun	Salisb	(G-F)	H	5f	66	73
* 1999	Jly	Newmar	(GD)	H	5f	68	79
* 1999	Jly	Sandow	(GD)	H	5f	68	69
* 1998	Aug	Lingfi	(G-F)	C	5f		65
* 1998	Jun	Folkes	(G-F)	H	5f	71	77?

2000 Turf 2-14: (5f 2-14) (g-s, gd 4, g-f 5, frm 2-4)
Above-average gelding, effective 5f, acts on frm, often wears blinkers. Turf high 73 - 1st of 11 getting 5lb from Mungo Park (18 Jun Salisbury RF 2081). He landed a gamble at Salisbury in June when he finally had his favoured fast ground. At his best when able to dominate.
**S C Williams [6-51] J T Duffy & R E Duffy (from G Lewis [5-31] Spt 1996).*

THATS ALL FOLKS BHB 73f **RR 62f** 275[5]
3 b c Alhijaz 7.7f **(57)** - So it Goes (Free State) 8.7f **(61)**
Form - 33125
Record 2000 - 1st:1 2nd:1 3rd:0 Ran:3
Pre2000 - 1st:0 2nd:0 3rd:2 Ran:4
Win Prizemoney £2,470 *Total Prizemoney* £5,915
Wins * **2000** *Jan Lingfi (STD) 8f 76* <
2000 AW 1-3: (8f 1-1, 10f 2) (Equi 1-3)
Above-average colt, effective 8 to 10f, - acts on Equi, prefers left handed tracks. AW high 76 - 2nd of 5 giving 2lb to Kathakali (29 Jan Lingfield 10f Equi RF 0183) - also 1st of 10 giving 5lb to Royal Ivy (5 Jan Lingfield RF 0025). **P J Makin [1-7] Arron Banks.*

THATS ALL JAZZ BHB 50f **RR 51f** 4198[8]
2 b f Prince Sabo 6.6f **(64)** - Gate of Heaven **(15f 23a)** (Starry Night (USA))
Form - 00608
Record 2000 - 1st:0 2nd:0 3rd:0 Ran:5
2000 Turf 0-5: (5f 2, 6f 3) (sft, g-f 2, frm 2)
Fair filly, has worn blinkers. Turf high 51.
**C A Dwyer [0-2] John Purcell (from T T Clement [0-3] Aug 2000).*

THAT'S JAZZ BHB 72f **RR 76f** 3402[10]
2 b f Cool Jazz - Miss Mercy (IRE) **(65f 54a)** (Law Society (USA)) 9.9f **(70)**
Form - 8220
Record 2000 - 1st:0 2nd:2 3rd:0 Ran:4
Win Prizemoney £0 *Total Prizemoney* £3,050
2000 Turf 0-4: (5f, 6f 2, 7f) (gd, g-f 2, frm)
Above-average filly. Turf high 76 - 2nd of 13 getting 6lb from Brilliantrio (29 Jly Newcastle 7f g-f RF 3209).
**M L W Bell [0-4] Billy Maguire.*

THATS LIFE BHB 59f64a **RR 51f 64a** 199[9]
5 b g Mukaddamah (USA) 7.6f **(74)** - Run Faster (IRE) (Commanche Run) 8.5f **(58)**
Form - 30
Record 2000 - 1st:0 2nd:0 3rd:0 Ran:1
Pre2000 - 1st:3 2nd:0 3rd:3 Ran:17
Win Prizemoney £6,941 *Total Prizemoney* £8,085

Wins							
1999	*Jly*	*Lingfi*	*(STD)*	*C*	*5f*	*71*	
1999	*Feb*	*Lingfi*	*(STD)*	*S*	*6f*	*71+*	
1998	Jly	Folkes	(G-F)		6f	74	<

2000 AW 0-1: (6f) (Fibr)
Above-average gelding, effective 5 to 6f, best at 6f, - acts on AW, best on Equi, prefers left handed tracks, prefers tight tracks. He is suited by both fast ground on turf and by Equitrack.
**R Bastiman [0-4] Peter Beaton-Brown (from T G Mills [3-14] Jly 1999).*

THATS LOGIC (IRE) RR 92f 5286a[15]
6 b g Cyrano de Bergerac 7.3f **(58)** - Allberry (Alzao (USA)) 7.1f **(68)**
Form - 4104400
2000 Turf 1-6: (8f 1-5, 9f) (hvy, sft 1-2, g-s, gd 2)
Useful gelding, effective 7 to 8f, best at 8f, acts on sft to gd, has worn blinkers. Turf high 92 - also 1st of 26 giving 10lb to Zelden (26 Mar Curragh RF 0540a). Inconsistent. He won the Irish Lincoln at The Curragh in March and promptly took a hike in the ratings. Suited by easy ground, he will find life hard until the handicapper relents. **D Hassett in IRE [6-36] D M Murphy.*

THE ANGEL GABRIEL BHB 36f **RR** 1684[8]
5 ch h My Generation 6.5f **(68)** - Minsk **(30df)** (Kabour)
Form - 08
Record 2000 - 1st:0 2nd:0 3rd:0 Ran:2
Pre2000 - 1st:0 2nd:0 3rd:0 Ran:4
2000 Turf 0-2: (5f, 6f) (g-f, frm)
Very poor colt. **D A Nolan [0-6] Mrs J McFadyen-Murray.*

THEATRE KING RR 106f 2000a[3]
6 b g Old Vic 12.8f **(72)** - Draft Board (Rainbow Quest (USA)) 10.4f **(75)**
Form - 23
2000 Turf 0-1: (15f) (sft)
Pattern-class gelding. (1st run) - 3rd of 5 getting 6lb from Three Cheers (9 Jun Maisons-Laffitte 15f sft RF 2000a).
**Mme M Bollack-Badel in FR [0-4].*

THEATRE LADY (IRE) RR 64f 5053[3]
2 b f King's Theatre (IRE) - Littlepace (Indian King (USA)) 7.4f **(64)**
Form - 43
Record 2000 - 1st:0 2nd:0 3rd:1 Ran:2
Win Prizemoney £0 *Total Prizemoney* £782
2000 Turf 0-2: (7f, 8f) (hvy, sft)
Currently average filly. Turf high 64 (began Oct) - 3rd of 14 to Shaanara (18 Oct Newcastle 7f sft RF 5053).
**M Johnston [0-2] John Keaney.*

THEATRELAND (USA) BHB 71f **RR 72f** 1719[6]
3 b g Dynaformer (USA) 12f **(82)** - Mime (Cure The Blues (USA)) 9.5f **(63)**
Form - 06
Record 2000 - 1st:0 2nd:0 3rd:0 Ran:2
Pre2000 - 1st:0 2nd:0 3rd:0 Ran:3
2000 Turf 0-2: (10f 2) (gd, g-f)
Scopey, above-average gelding, has worn blinkers. Turf high 72.
**Sir Michael Stoute [0-5] Highclere Thoroughbred Racing Ltd.*

THEATRE SCRIPT (USA) RR 85+f 4261[1]
2 ch c Theatrical 11.5f **(78)** - Gossiping (USA) (Chati (USA))
Form - 1
Record 2000 - 1st:1 2nd:0 3rd:0 Ran:1

Win Prizemoney £4,251 *Total Prizemoney* £4,251
Wins * **2000** Spt Doncas (GD) 8f 85+ <
2000 Turf 1-1: (8f 1-1) (gd 1-1)
Currently useful colt. (1st run) - 1st of 10 from Persian Pride (6 Spt Doncaster RF 4261). Made a winning debut at Doncaster despite running as green as grass. There looks to be plenty of improvement to come. **J H M Gosden [1-1] R E Sangster & A K Collins.*

THEATRO DANIELLI (IRE) RR 58f 594[8]
3 b f Bluebird (USA) 7.9f **(71)** - Harry's Irish Rose (USA) (Sir Harry Lewis (USA))
Form - 8
Record **2000** - 1st:0 2nd:0 3rd:0 Ran:1
Pre2000 - 1st:0 2nd:0 3rd:0 Ran:1
2000 Turf 0-1: (11f) (sft)
Currently fair filly.
**R A Fahey [0-1] Cathal Ryan (from K Prendergast in IRE [0-1] Spt 1999).*

THEBAN (IRE) BHB 63f63a RR 65f 63a 3189[4]
2 b g Inzar (USA) - Phoenix Forli (USA) (Forli (ARG)) 9.6f **(67)**
Form - 5434
Record **2000** - 1st:0 2nd:0 3rd:1 Ran:4
Win Prizemoney £0 *Total Prizemoney* £678
2000 Turf 0-3: (5f, 7f 2) (gd, g-f, frm) 2000 AW 0-1: (6f) (Fibr)
Average gelding. Turf high 65. **D Nicholls [0-4] Neil Smith.*

THE BARGATE FOX BHB 47f54a RR 51f 54a 4479[12]
4 b g Magic Ring (IRE) 6.5f **(64)** - Hithermoor Lass (Red Alert) 7.6f **(66)**
Form - 17413403007300
Record **2000** - 1st:0 2nd:0 3rd:3 Ran:10
Pre2000 - 1st:2 2nd:0 3rd:0 Ran:8
Win Prizemoney £3,921 *Total Prizemoney* £5,218
Wins * 1999 *Dec Wolver (STD) H 8.5f 50 54* <
* 1999 *Nov Wolver (STD) H 9.4f 47 50*
2000 Turf 0-4: (8f, 10f 2, 12f) (gd, g-f, frm 2) 2000 AW 0-6: (8f, 9f 3, 12f 2) (Fibr 6)
Strong, fair gelding, effective 8 to 12f, - acts on Fibr, favours left handed tracks, favours tight tracks. Turf high 51. AW high 56 (1st run) - 3rd of 11 giving 24lb to Manful (4 Jan Wolverhampton 12f Fibr RF 0021).
**D J G MurraySmith [2-18] The Joiners Arms Racing Club Quarndon.*

THE BARNSLEY BELLE (IRE) BHB 39f50a RR 31f 50a 3187[1]
7 b m Distinctly North (USA) 7.4f **(63)** - La Tanque (USA) (Last Raise (USA)) 7f **(51)**
Form - 4571
Record **2000** - 1st:1 2nd:0 3rd:0 Ran:4
Pre2000 - 1st:3 2nd:5 3rd:4 Ran:49
Win Prizemoney £9,404 *Total Prizemoney* £15,206
Wins * **2000** *Jly Southw (STD) C 8f 45*
1999 *Feb Southw (STD) H 8f 36 39*
1997 *Apr Southw (STD) 7f 63* <
1996 *Nov Southw (STD) H 7f 47 49*
2000 AW 1-4: (7f, 8f 1-3) (Fibr 1-4)
Moderate mare, effective 8f, - acts on Fibr, favours left handed tracks. AW high 45 - 1st of 11 giving 10lb to Standiford Girl (28 Jly Southwell RF 3187). She seems to be more effective on Fibresand than on turf, but her strike-rate is fairly moderate.
**J Balding [1-2] K Meynell (from G Woodward [1-13] Jan 2000).*

THE BARNSLEY CHOP RR 39f 3739[10]
2 b g Ezzoud (IRE) - Ariadne (GER) (Kings Lake (USA)) 10.8f **(67)**
Form - 00
Record **2000** - 1st:0 2nd:0 3rd:0 Ran:2
2000 Turf 0-2: (7f 2) (gd, g-f)
Currently very moderate gelding. Turf high 39 (began Aug).
**N Tinkler [0-2] Bezwell Fixings Ltd.*

THE BIZZ RR 1105[18]
7 b m Devon Missile - Kingmon's Girl (Saucy Kit) 6f **(43)**
Form - 0
Record **2000** - 1st:0 2nd:0 3rd:0 Ran:1
Pre2000 - 1st:0 2nd:0 3rd:0 Ran:1
2000 Turf 0-1: (10f) (frm)
Formerly very poor mare. **B A Pearce [0-2] J F Panvert.*

THE BLUE BRAZIL (IRE) BHB 20f RR 1908[13]
4 b g Thatching 7.8f **(69)** - Approche (FR) (Sharpman) 11.3f **(66)**
Form - 000
Record **2000** - 1st:0 2nd:0 3rd:0 Ran:2
Pre2000 - 1st:0 2nd:0 3rd:1 Ran:8
Win Prizemoney £0 *Total Prizemoney* £553
2000 Turf 0-2: (11f, 12f) (g-f, frm)
Lengthy, very poor gelding, has worn blinkers.
**R Curtis [0-2] Kate Curtis & David Auer (from Denys Smith [0-9] Dec 1999).*

THE BLUES ACADEMY (IRE) BHB 60f RR 64f 1595[12]
5 b g Royal Academy (USA) 7.8f **(77)** - She's the Tops (Shernazar) 10.2f **(73)**
Form - 0
Record **2000** - 1st:0 2nd:0 3rd:0 Ran:1
Pre2000 - 1st:1 2nd:2 3rd:2 Ran:18
Win Prizemoney £3,533 *Total Prizemoney* £8,728
Wins * 1998 Jly Bath (GD) H 17.2f 67 71 <
2000 Turf 0-1: (16f) (g-f)
Average gelding, effective 16f, acts on frm to hrd, has worn blinkers, prefers tight tracks.
**M A Buckley [1-18] C C Buckley (from M Johnston [0-3] Oct 1997).*

THE BOXER (IRE) BHB 40f RR 41f 2268[9]
4 b m Brief Truce (USA) 9.1f **(73)** - Bean Siamsa (Solinus) 9f **(71)**
Form - 0
Record **2000** - 1st:0 2nd:0 3rd:0 Ran:1
Pre2000 - 1st:1 2nd:0 3rd:1 Ran:14
Win Prizemoney £4,468 *Total Prizemoney* £4,836
Wins 1999 Jly Galway (G-F) H 8.5f 45 49 <
2000 Turf 0-1: (8f) (frm)
Moderate filly, effective 8f, acts on sft to g-f, often wears blinkers (very effectively), prefers right handed tracks.
**K A Morgan [0-2] John Sheridan (from E Lynam in IRE [1-11] Oct 1999).*

THE BOY KING (IRE) BHB 36f RR 63f 4648[14]
8 ch g Roi Danzig (USA) 10.5f **(62)** - Susie Spangles (USA) (Solford (USA)) 13f **(71)**
Form - 0
Record **2000** - 1st:0 2nd:0 3rd:0 Ran:1
Pre2000 - 1st:1 2nd:0 3rd:0 Ran:6
Win Prizemoney £4,140 *Total Prizemoney* £4,140
Wins 1999 Spt Tramor (G-S) H 14f 36 41 <
2000 AW 0-1: (16f) (Fibr)
Average gelding, has worn blinkers.
**P R Chamings [0-4] R V Shaw (from R V Shaw in IRE [2-21] Oct 1999).*

THE BROKER (IRE) RR 48f 4271[13]
2 b c Rainbows For Life (CAN) 9.3f **(64)** - Roberts Pride (Roberto (USA)) 10f **(76)**
Form - 0
Record **2000** - 1st:0 2nd:0 3rd:0 Ran:1
2000 Turf 0-1: (8f) (g-f)
Currently moderate colt. **M Blanshard [0-1] Mrs C J Ward.*

THE BUTTERWICK KID BHB 66f70a RR 74df 70a 4863[8]
7 ch g Interrex (CAN) 7.7f **(51)** - Ville Air (Town Crier) 10.2f **(55)**
Form - 8468
Record **2000** - 1st:0 2nd:0 3rd:0 Ran:4
Pre2000 - 1st:8 2nd:4 3rd:5 Ran:33
Win Prizemoney £32,746 *Total Prizemoney* £43,063
Wins * 1999 Mar Hamilt (HVY) H 11.1f 70 72 <
* 1998 May Redcar (G-F) H 14.1f 62 66+
* 1998 *Jan Southw (STD) H 11f 59 60*
* 1997 May Mussel (G-S) H 12f 54 57+
* 1997 May Cheste (HVY) H 12.3f 52 59
* 1997 Apr Nottin (G-F) H 14.1f 45 49
* 1996 Spt Hamilt (GD) H 12.1f 44 45
2000 Turf 0-4: (12f 2, 14f, 16f) (sft, g-s, gd, g-f)
Above-average gelding, effective 11 to 13f, acts on hvy, has worn blinkers, prefers tight tracks. Turf high 72 (began Aug).
**R A Fahey [10-48] Robert Chambers & Mrs M W Kenyon.*

THE BYSTANDER (IRE) BHB 82f RR 84f 5102[2]

2 b f Bin Ajwaad (IRE) - Dilwara (IRE) (Lashkari) 9.8f **(67)**
Form - 712
Record 2000 - 1st:1 2nd:1 3rd:0 Ran:3
Win Prizemoney £7,400 *Total Prizemoney* £14,964
Wins * **2000** Oct York (SFT) 7.9f 76 <
2000 Turf 1-3: (6f, 8f 1-2) (g-s 1-2, gd)
Currently decent filly. Turf high 84 (began Spt) - 2nd of 22 to Zietunzeen (20 Oct Doncaster 6f gd RF 5102) - also 1st of 22 getting 5lb from Lord Protector (6 Oct York RF 4828).
**N P Littmoden [1-3] Mrs D E Sharp.*

THE CASTIGATOR BHB 28f **RR 28f** 5311[9]

3 b g Reprimand 8.2f **(63)** - Summer Eve (Hotfoot) 10.5f **(59)**
Form - 60000000050780
Record 2000 - 1st:0 2nd:0 3rd:0 Ran:14
Pre2000 - 1st:0 2nd:0 3rd:0 Ran:3
Win Prizemoney £0 *Total Prizemoney* £444
2000 Turf 0-14: (6f 2, 7f 3, 8f 4, 9f, 10f, 12f 2, 15f) (hvy, sft 2, g-s 3, gd 3, g-f, frm 4)
Little account gelding. Turf high 28.
**R Bastiman [0-14] Peter Julian (from J J O'Neill [0-3] Aug 1999).*

THE CHOCOLATIER (IRE) BHB 66f **RR 68f** 4737[8]

2 b f Inzar (USA) - Clover Honey (King of Clubs) 7.1f **(57)**
Form - 658
Record 2000 - 1st:0 2nd:0 3rd:0 Ran:3
2000 Turf 0-3: (6f 2, 7f) (gd, g-f 2)
Currently average filly. Turf high 68.
**P L Gilligan [0-3] Treasure Seekers 2000.*

THE COTTONWOOL KID BHB 26f34a **RR 34a** 311[3]

8 b g Blakeney 11.9f **(53)** - Relatively Smart (Great Nephew) 9.9f **(64)**
Form - 13
Record 2000 - 1st:1 2nd:0 3rd:1 Ran:2
Pre2000 - 1st:0 2nd:0 3rd:2 Ran:19
Win Prizemoney £1,527 *Total Prizemoney* £2,429
Wins * **2000** *Feb Wolver (STD) SH 16.2f 15 31* <
2000 AW 1-2: (16f 1-2) (Fibr 1-2)
Very moderate gelding, effective 16f, - acts on Fibr, has worn blinkers (effectively), likes left handed tracks. AW high 31 (1st run) - 1st of 10 getting 6lb from Bobona (10 Feb Wolverhampton RF 0256).
**Mrs Merrita Jones [1-2] Mrs S E Cooper (from Mrs A M Naughton [0-9] Aug 1999).*

THE DARK LADY BHB 50f **RR 38f** 1511[7]

2 b f Definite Article - Nuthatch (IRE) **(31f 30a)** (Thatching) 8f **(66)**
Form - 07
Record 2000 - 1st:0 2nd:0 3rd:0 Ran:2
2000 Turf 0-2: (5f 2) (hvy, gd)
Currently very moderate filly. Turf high 38.
**M D I Usher [0-2] P Sweeting.*

THE DIDDLER BHB 36a **RR 30f** 3191[11]

3 b g Presidium 7.5f **(56)** - Sakosan (Absalom) 7.2f **(58)**
Form - 707000
Record 2000 - 1st:0 2nd:0 3rd:0 Ran:6
2000 Turf 0-3: (7f 2, 8f) (gd, frm, hrd) 2000 AW 0-3: (5f, 8f 2) (Fibr 3)
Light-framed, very moderate gelding. Turf high 30.
**M J Polglase [0-6] Mrs Victor Pulleyn.*

THE DOCTOR (IRE) BHB 54f **RR 59f** 5151[16]

2 b c Dr Devious (IRE) 9.9f **(74)** - Night Spell (IRE) **(74f)** (Fairy King (USA)) 7.7f **(59)**
Form - 070
Record 2000 - 1st:0 2nd:0 3rd:0 Ran:3
2000 Turf 0-3: (7f 2, 10f) (g-s 2, g-f)
Currently fair colt. Turf high 59 (began Spt).
**P F I Cole [0-3] Alessandro Gaucci.*

THE DOWNTOWN FOX BHB 66f81a **RR 64f 81a** 4866[14]

5 br g Primo Dominie 7.2f **(67)** - Sara Sprint (Formidable (USA)) 9.2f **(63)**
Form - 100867002040
Record 2000 - 1st:1 2nd:1 3rd:0 Ran:12
Pre2000 - 1st:2 2nd:2 3rd:2 Ran:24
Win Prizemoney £23,376 *Total Prizemoney* £29,893
Wins * **2000** *Jan Wolver (STD) H 6f 76 85*
* 1999 Oct York (SFT) 6f 74
* 1998 Apr Leices (SFT) H 7f 82 88 <
2000 Turf 0-8: (5f, 6f, 7f 4, 8f 2) (sft 2, g-s, gd, g-f 2, frm 2) 2000 AW 1-4: (6f 1-4) (Fibr 1-4)
Above-average gelding, effective 6f, - acts on Fibr, often wears blinkers. Turf high 64. AW high 85 (1st run) - 1st of 12 getting 3lb from Cherish Me (13 Jan Wolverhampton RF 0081). Not particularly consistent, and although bolting up on the Wolverhampton Fibresand at the start of last year, the moderate performances far outweigh the good ones. **B A McMahon [3-36] Mrs J McMahon.*

THE EXHIBITION FOX BHB 67f **RR 77f** 4578[9]

4 b g Be My Chief (USA) 10.2f **(62)** - Swift Return (Double Form) 7.3f **(58)**
Form 03000000
Record 2000 - 1st:0 2nd:0 3rd:1 Ran:8
Pre2000 - 1st:1 2nd:1 3rd:0 Ran:7
Win Prizemoney £7,002 *Total Prizemoney* £9,771
Wins * 1999 Jun York (G-S) 7.9f 86 <
2000 Turf 0-8: (7f 4, 8f 3, 10f) (sft, g-s, gd 3, g-f 2, frm)
Scopey, above-average gelding, effective 8 to 10f, best at 8f, acts on g-s to gd, best on gd, likes tight tracks. Turf high 77 - 3rd of 11 getting 12lb from Silk St John (10 Jun Haydock 8f g-s RF 1878).
**B A McMahon [1-15] J D Graham.*

THE FAIRY FLAG (IRE) BHB 56f **RR 50f** 4993[6]

2 ch f Inchinor 8.9f **(64)** - Good Reference (IRE) (Reference Point) 6.8f **(70)**
Form - 856
Record 2000 - 1st:0 2nd:0 3rd:0 Ran:3
2000 Turf 0-2: (7f, 8f) (gd, frm) 2000 AW 0-1: (6f) (Fibr)
Currently fair filly. Turf high 50 (began Spt).
**R M Beckett [0-3] Eric Perry.*

THE FANCY MAN (IRE) BHB 62f **RR 64f** 5004[12]

2 ch g Definite Article - Fanciful (IRE) **(32f)** (Mujtahid (USA))
Form - 4060100
Record 2000 - 1st:1 2nd:0 3rd:0 Ran:7
Win Prizemoney £2,492 *Total Prizemoney* £2,835
Wins * **2000** Spt Beverl (G-F) SH 7.5f 57 64 <
2000 Turf 1-7: (5f, 6f 2, 7f 1-2, 8f, 10f) (g-s 2, g-f 1-3, frm 2)
Average gelding, effective 7f, acts on g-f, often wears blinkers. Turf high 64 - 1st of 16 giving 1lb to Petit Tor (13 Spt Beverley RF 4360). **N Tinkler [1-7] P D Savill.*

THE FINAL WORD BHB 39f46a **RR 23f 46a** 1183[15]

3 ch f Cosmonaut - Jolizal (Good Times (ITY)) 6.6f **(54)**
Form - 578070
Record 2000 - 1st:0 2nd:0 3rd:0 Ran:6
Pre2000 - 1st:0 2nd:0 3rd:0 Ran:1
2000 Turf 0-3: (8f, 10f, 12f) (sft, gd, hrd) 2000 AW 0-3: (9f 2, 12f) (Fibr 3)
Small, very moderate filly. Turf high 23. AW high 37.
**R Hollinshead [0-7] P J Corns.*

THE FLYER (IRE) BHB 58f **RR 67f** 4327[20]

3 b g Blues Traveller (IRE) - National Ballet (Shareef Dancer (USA)) 9.9f **(73)**
Form - 602080
Record 2000 - 1st:0 2nd:1 3rd:0 Ran:6
Pre2000 - 1st:0 2nd:0 3rd:0 Ran:1
Win Prizemoney £0 *Total Prizemoney* £705
2000 Turf 0-5: (8f 2, 11f 2, 12f) (sft, gd 2, g-f, hrd) 2000 AW 0-1: (12f) (Fibr)
Light-framed, average gelding, effective 8f, acts on gd, has worn blinkers. Turf high 67 - 2nd of 14 giving 11lb to Ronni Pancake (30 May Leicester 8f gd RF 1542).
**Miss S J Wilton [0-3] John Pointon and Sons (from P F I Cole [0-4] May 2000).*

THE FOSSICK (IRE) BHB 23f29a **RR 1f 29a** 2674[16]

4 ch g Forest Wind (USA) - Rose of Summer (IRE) (Taufan (USA)) 7f **(57)**
Form - 6000
Record 2000 - 1st:0 2nd:0 3rd:0 Ran:4
Pre2000 - 1st:0 2nd:0 3rd:0 Ran:1

2000 Turf 0-2: (8f, 10f) (g-s, frm) 2000 AW 0-2: (12f 2) (Fibr 2)
Angular, poor gelding. Turf high 1. AW high 10.
**B D Leavy [0-2] H M de B Lipscomb (from M A Peill [0-3] Mar 2000).*

THE FROG QUEEN BHB 48f60a **RR 58f 60a** 4489[2]

3 b f Bin Ajwaad (IRE) - The Frog Lady (IRE) **(50f 41a)** (Al Hareb (USA))
Form - 04037532

Record		1st	2nd	3rd	Ran
2000 -		1st:0	2nd:1	3rd:2	Ran:8
Pre2000 -		1st:1	2nd:0	3rd:2	Ran:5

Win Prizemoney £2,102 *Total Prizemoney* £4,307
Wins * 1999 *Spt Southw (STD) S 7f 66* <
2000 Turf 0-8: (10f 4, 12f 4) (g-s, gd, g-f, frm 4, hrd)
Scopey, average filly, effective 6 to 7f, best at 6f, acts on g-f to frm - acts on Fibr. Turf high 58.
**D W P Arbuthnot [1-13] Mrs Sheila Crown.*

THE FUGATIVE BHB 82f56a **RR 94f 56a** 3164[16]

7 b m Nicholas (USA) 6.1f **(63)** - Miss Runaway (Runnett) 7f **(59)**
Form - 88456340

Record	1st	2nd	3rd	Ran
2000 -	1st:0	2nd:0	3rd:1	Ran:7
Pre2000 -	1st:8	2nd:5	3rd:3	Ran:45

Win Prizemoney £29,855 *Total Prizemoney* £50,086

Wins	Year	Month	Course	Going	Type	Dist			
	* 1999	Jun	Epsom	(GD)	H	6f	82	83	<
	* 1999	Apr	Epsom	(SFT)	H	6f	72	81	
	* 1998	Jun	Epsom	(GD)	H	6f	70	72	
	* 1998	May	Lingfi	(GD)	H	6f	65	68	
	* 1998	Apr	Folkes	(SFT)		5f		73	
	* 1997	Jly	Folkes	(GD)	H	5f	61	66	
	* 1997	Jun	Folkes	(SFT)	H	5f	50	60	
	* 1997	Jun	Epsom	(G-S)	H	6f	50	56	

2000 Turf 0-6: (6f 5, 7f) (sft, g-s, gd 2, g-f, frm) 2000 AW 0-1: (6f) (Fibr)
Useful mare, effective 6 to 7f, acts on sft to g-s, likes left handed tracks, likes tight tracks. Turf high 94 - 5th of 13 to Hot Tin Roof (13 May Lingfield 7f g-s RF 1192). Something of an Epsom specialist, she was not at her best last year. Effective from five to seven furlongs, she has slipped to a decent mark and is one to look out for at Epsom's Spring Meeting. **P Mitchell [8-52] J A Redmond.*

THE GAMBOLLER (USA) BHB 39f **RR 38f** 2559[6]

5 b g Irish Tower (USA) 7.3f **(69)** - Lady Limbo (USA) (Dance Spell (USA)) 9.6f **(75)**
Form - 06

Record	1st	2nd	3rd	Ran
2000 -	1st:0	2nd:0	3rd:0	Ran:2
Pre2000 -	1st:1	2nd:1	3rd:0	Ran:10

Win Prizemoney £2,427 *Total Prizemoney* £3,306
Wins 1998 Jly Leices (GD) 10f 69 <
2000 Turf 0-2: (16f, 18f) (g-f, frm)
Very moderate gelding, has worn blinkers. Turf high 38.
**M E Sowersby [3-18] The Wolds Partnership (from Mrs A J Perrett [1-8] Oct 1998).*

THE GAY FOX BHB 72f **RR 71f** 5061[6]

6 b gr g Never so Bold 7.1f **(62)** - School Concert (Music Boy) 6.8f **(57)**
Form - 53724100466

Record	1st	2nd	3rd	Ran
2000 -	1st:1	2nd:1	3rd:1	Ran:11
Pre2000 -	1st:4	2nd:4	3rd:4	Ran:53

Win Prizemoney £32,346 *Total Prizemoney* £57,835

Wins	Year	Month	Course	Going	Type	Dist			
	*** 2000**	Jly	York	(GD)	H	6f	71	72	
	* 1998	Apr	Sandow	(HVY)	H	5f	87	90	<
	* 1997	Jly	Cheste	(G-F)	H	5.1f	81	83	
	* 1997	Jun	Newmar	(SFT)	H	5f	74	76	
	* 1997	May	Warwic	(FRM)	H	7f	73	70	

2000 Turf 1-11: (5f 4, 6f 1-6, 8f) (sft, g-s, gd 1-5, g-f 2, frm 2)
Above-average gelding, effective 5 to 6f, best at 5f, acts on gd to frm, best on frm. Turf high 72 - 1st of 23 giving 12lb to Peppiatt (15 Jly York RF 2855). Consistent. He is quite a useful sprint handicapper on his day, and his best performances in recent seasons have been when there has been plenty of cut in the ground.
**B A McMahon [5-64] Mrs J McMahon.*

THE GENERALS LADY (IRE) **RR 40f** 3272[14]

2 gr f General Monash (USA) - Brooks Masquerade **(27df 24a)** (Absalom) 7.2f **(58)**
Form - 00
Record 2000 - 1st:0 2nd:0 3rd:0 Ran:2
2000 Turf 0-2: (5f 2) (gd, hrd)
Currently moderate filly. Turf high 40 (began Jly).

**B S Rothwell [0-2] Mrs D E Sharp.*

THE GIRLS' FILLY BHB 46f57a **RR 51f 57a** 3089[10]

3 b f Emperor Jones (USA) - Sioux City (Simply Great (FR)) 8.2f **(65)**
Form - 23007260

Record	1st	2nd	3rd	Ran
2000 -	1st:0	2nd:2	3rd:1	Ran:8
Pre2000 -	1st:0	2nd:0	3rd:1	Ran:4

Win Prizemoney £0 *Total Prizemoney* £3,012
2000 Turf 0-3: (8f, 10f 2) (gd, frm 2) 2000 AW 0-5: (7f, 8f, 10f, 12f 2) (Equi 5)
Scopey, fair filly, effective 7 to 12f, - acts on Equi, likes left handed tracks, likes tight tracks. Turf high 45. AW high 53 - 2nd of 10 getting 13lb from Able Native (27 Jun Lingfield 12f Equi RF 2305).
**Miss B Sanders [0-8] T J Blake (from J H M Gosden [0-4] Spt 1999).*

THE GLEN **RR 72f** 4969[9]

2 gr c Mtoto 11.5f **(71)** - Silver Singer **(65f 55a)** (Pharly (FR)) 9.8f **(68)**
Form - 0
Record 2000 - 1st:0 2nd:0 3rd:0 Ran:1
2000 Turf 0-1: (8f) (gd)
Currently above-average colt.
**B W Hills [0-1] John Grant.*

THE GREEN GREY BHB 80f90a **RR 74f 90a** 4810[1]

6 gr g Environment Friend 7.5f **(67)** - Pea Green (Try My Best (USA)) 7.6f **(67)**
Form - 00610715254311

Record	1st	2nd	3rd	Ran
2000 -	1st:4	2nd:1	3rd:1	Ran:14
Pre2000 -	1st:6	2nd:4	3rd:1	Ran:27

Win Prizemoney £38,548 *Total Prizemoney* £45,407

Wins	Year	Month	Course	Going	Type	Dist			
	*** 2000**	*Oct*	*Lingfi*	*(STD)*	*H*	*12f*	*71*	*79+*	<
	*** 2000**	*Spt*	*Lingfi*	*(STD)*		*12f*		*68*	
	*** 2000**	Jly	Windso	(G-F)	H	10f	66	70+	
	*** 2000**	Jun	Windso	(G-F)	H	10f	60	68+	
	1998	*Nov*	*Lingfi*	*(STD)*	*H*	*8f*	*52*	*60*	
	1998	Spt	Kempto	(GD)	H	8f	67	70	
	1998	Spt	Bright	(FRM)	C	8f		68	
	1998	Aug	Bath	(FRM)	S	8f		61	
	1998	Aug	Yarmou	(G-F)	SH	8f	43	49	
	1997	Spt	Bath	(G-F)	H	8f	42	51	

2000 Turf 2-12: (8f 2, 9f 2, 10f 2-5, 12f 2, 14f) (gd 3, g-f 5, frm 2-4) 2000 AW 2-2: (12f 2-2) (Equi 2-2)
Useful gelding, effective 10 to 14f, acts on g-f to frm - acts on Equi, has worn blinkers, likes tight tracks, and does well at Windsor. Turf high 74 - 2nd of 11 getting 11lb from Mynah (13 Aug Ascot 10f g-f RF 3602) - also 1st of 9 from No Mercy (24 Jly Windsor RF 3081). AW high 79 (began Spt) - 1st of 13 giving 14lb to Noble Calling (4 Oct Lingfield RF 4810). He is an effective sort on fast ground and scored twice over ten furlongs at Windsor last summer. Showed some very decent form on the Lingfield Equitrack in the autumn.
**L MontagueHall [4-16] J Daniels (from Derrick Morris [2-6] Jan 1999).*

THE GROOVER BHB 40f **RR 39f** 1512[10]

4 ch g Beveled (USA) 6.9f **(64)** - Taffidale (Welsh Pageant) 10f **(65)**
Form - 0

Record	1st	2nd	3rd	Ran
2000 -	1st:0	2nd:0	3rd:0	Ran:1
Pre2000 -	1st:0	2nd:0	3rd:0	Ran:2

2000 Turf 0-1: (11f) (hvy)
Leggy, currently very moderate gelding.
**G M McCourt [0-3] J F Watson.*

THE IMPOSTER (IRE) BHB 39f58a **RR 43f 58a** 3132[9]

5 ch g Imp Society (USA) 7.1f **(63)** - Phoenix Dancer (IRE) (Gorytus (USA)) 7.8f **(60)**
Form - 180875070

Record	1st	2nd	3rd	Ran
2000 -	1st:1	2nd:0	3rd:0	Ran:9
Pre2000 -	1st:1	2nd:2	3rd:2	Ran:15

Win Prizemoney £4,234 *Total Prizemoney* £6,008
Wins *** 2000** *Mar Wolver (STD) 8.5f 63* <
1999 *May Wolver (STD) S 8.5f 56*
2000 Turf 0-5: (7f, 8f, 10f, 11f 2) (hvy, gd, g-f, frm 2) 2000 AW 1-4: (8f 1-4) (Fibr 1-4)
Moderate gelding, effective 8f, - acts on Fibr, has worn blinkers. Turf high 43. AW high 63 (1st run) - 1st of 10 getting 2lb from Be Warned (23 Mar Wolverhampton RF 0480). Inconsistent. Acts on Fibresand, with the extended mile at Wolverhampton looking his optimum conditions.

**Miss S J Wilton [1-11] John Pointon and Sons (from D J G MurraySmith [1-13] May 1999).*

THE JAM SAHEB BHB 40f **RR 43f** 5229[18]
3 b c Petong 7.6f **(58)** - Reem El Fala (FR) (Fabulous Dancer (USA)) 9.4f **(70)**
Form - 6000
Record 2000 - 1st:0 2nd:0 3rd:0 Ran:4
Pre2000 - 1st:0 2nd:0 3rd:0 Ran:2
2000 Turf 0-4: (6f, 7f, 8f 2) (g-s, gd 2, frm)
Workmanlike, moderate colt. Turf high 37.
**J R Poulton [0-4] Michael WingfieldDigby (from Lady Herries [0-2] Oct 1999).*

THE JUDGE RR 50f 4159[10]
2 b c Polish Precedent (USA) 9f **(73)** - Just Speculation (IRE) (Ahonoora) 8.1f **(73)**
Form - 0
Record 2000 - 1st:0 2nd:0 3rd:0 Ran:1
2000 Turf 0-1: (7f) (sft)
Currently fair colt. **P F I Cole [0-1] The Hon Mrs J M Corbett.*

THE LAD BHB 24f36a **RR 23f 36a** 3168[6]
11 b g Bold Owl 9.7f **(47)** - Solbella (Starch Reduced) 11.5f **(52)**
Form - 06
Record 2000 - 1st:0 2nd:0 3rd:0 Ran:2
Pre2000 - 1st:3 2nd:0 3rd:0 Ran:11
Win Prizemoney £8,147 *Total Prizemoney* £8,358
Wins 1996 Jly Chepst (G-F) H 12.1f 44 52 <
1996 Apr Folkes (FRM) H 15.4f 36 48
1996 Feb Lingfi (STD) H 16f 27 32
2000 Turf 0-2: (12f, 16f) (g-f, frm)
Little account gelding. Turf high 23 (began Jly).
**J M Bradley [0-2] Treberth Partnership (from Mrs L Stubbs [0-2] Jun 1998).*

THE LAMBTON WORM BHB 30f28a **RR 34f 28a** 442[5]
6 b g Superpower 6.6f **(58)** - Springwell (Miami Springs) 9.9f **(59)**
Form - 465
Record 2000 - 1st:0 2nd:0 3rd:0 Ran:3
Pre2000 - 1st:1 2nd:3 3rd:1 Ran:29
Win Prizemoney £3,493 *Total Prizemoney* £8,761
Wins 1996 Jly Ayr (GD) 6f 77 <
2000 AW 0-3: (11f 2, 12f) (Fibr 3)
Very moderate gelding, effective 11f, - acts on Fibr, has worn blinkers, likes tight tracks. AW high 32 (1st run) - 4th of 13 getting 24lb from Western Command (21 Feb Southwell 11f Fibr RF 0329). Consistent.
**N Bycroft [0-17] G J Allison (from Denys Smith [1-23] Jly 1998).*

THE LAST RAMBO BHB 42f34a **RR 41f 34a** 2621[13]
3 b g Rambo Dancer (CAN) 8.4f **(59)** - Under the Wing (Aragon) 8.1f **(60)**
Form - 7800
Record 2000 - 1st:0 2nd:0 3rd:0 Ran:4
Pre2000 - 1st:0 2nd:0 3rd:0 Ran:1
2000 Turf 0-3: (7f, 10f, 16f) (gd 2, g-f) 2000 AW 0-1: (9f) (Fibr)
Scopey, moderate gelding. Turf high 41. **J L Eyre [0-5] J Bladen.*

THE LONELY WIGEON BHB 33f38a **RR 34f 38a** 5162[7]
3 b g Rudimentary (USA) 8.2f **(66)** - Lonely Shore (Blakeney) 10.5f **(64)**
Form - 050657
Record 2000 - 1st:0 2nd:0 3rd:0 Ran:6
2000 Turf 0-4: (8f 2, 9f, 10f) (sft, g-s, gd, frm) 2000 AW 0-2: (7f, 8f) (Fibr 2)
Strong, very moderate gelding. Turf high 34. AW high 38.
**R M H Cowell [0-6] The Wild Fowlers.*

THE LOOSE SCREW (IRE) BHB 59f **RR 47f** 4781[7]
2 b g Bigstone (IRE) - Princess of Dance (IRE) (Dancing Dissident (USA))
Form - 6707
Record 2000 - 1st:0 2nd:0 3rd:0 Ran:4
2000 Turf 0-3: (5f, 6f, 7f) (sft, g-s, frm) 2000 AW 0-1: (5f) (Fibr)
Moderate gelding. Turf high 47. **J L Eyre [0-4] Sykes Distribution Ltd.*

THE MARSHALL BHB 53f **RR 60f** 5008[13]
2 ch c Clantime 6.6f **(57)** - Shaft of Sunlight (Sparkler)
Form - 7000
Record 2000 - 1st:0 2nd:0 3rd:0 Ran:4
2000 Turf 0-3: (5f 3) (gd 2, frm) 2000 AW 0-1: (6f) (Fibr)
Average colt, has worn blinkers. Turf high 60.
**J W Hills [0-4] Jampot Partners, T Morning & T Milson.*

THE MERRY WIDOW (IRE) BHB 46f44a **RR 49f 44a** 4783[9]
2 ch f Brief Truce (USA) 9.1f **(73)** - Classic Opera (Lomond (USA)) 8.8f **(65)**
Form - 08880
Record 2000 - 1st:0 2nd:0 3rd:0 Ran:5
2000 Turf 0-3: (6f, 7f 2) (g-f, frm 2) 2000 AW 0-2: (7f, 8f) (Fibr 2)
Moderate filly. Turf high 48 (began Jly). AW high 39 (began Spt).
**B S Rothwell [0-5] Mrs Liz Hunt.*

THE NAMES BOND BHB 67f **RR 75f** 4460[9]
2 b g Tragic Role (USA) 9.4f **(63)** - Artistic Licence (High Top) 10.2f **(67)**
Form - 3140008
Record 2000 - 1st:1 2nd:0 3rd:1 Ran:7
Win Prizemoney £3,737 *Total Prizemoney* £4,940
Wins * **2000** May Carlis (FRM) 5f 75 <
2000 Turf 1-7: (5f 1-3, 6f, 7f 2, 8f) (g-s 2, gd 3, frm 1-2)
Above-average gelding, effective 5f, acts on frm. Turf high 75 - also 1st of 15 from Joint Instruction (12 May Carlisle RF 1161).
**Andrew Turnell [1-7] Mrs Claire Hollowood.*

THE NOBLEMAN (USA) BHB 25f26a **RR 35f 26a** 1199[28]
4 b g Quiet American (USA) 7.9f **(60)** - Furajet (USA) (The Minstrel (CAN)) 10f **(72)**
Form - 85330
Record 2000 - 1st:0 2nd:0 3rd:2 Ran:5
Pre2000 - 1st:0 2nd:0 3rd:0 Ran:1
Win Prizemoney £0 *Total Prizemoney* £536
2000 Turf 0-1: (8f) (frm) 2000 AW 0-4: (8f, 11f, 12f 2) (Fibr 4)
Very moderate gelding. AW high 31.
**T J Etherington [0-6] Mrs J E Todd (from Sir Michael Stoute [0-1] Oct 1998).*

THE OLD SOLDIER BHB 56f **RR 53f** 4998[8]
2 b c Magic Ring (IRE) 6.5f **(64)** - Grecian Belle (Ilium)
Form - 708
Record 2000 - 1st:0 2nd:0 3rd:0 Ran:3
2000 Turf 0-3: (6f, 8f 2) (g-s, gd, g-f)
Currently fair colt. Turf high 53 (began Aug).
**E J O'Neill [0-3] A D Simmons.*

THE O'MALLEY RR 514[7]
3 b f Risk Me (FR) 8f **(53)** - Farrh Nouriya (IRE) (Lomond (USA)) 8.8f **(65)**
Form - 7
Record 2000 - 1st:0 2nd:0 3rd:0 Ran:1
2000 AW 0-1: (7f) (Fibr)
Leggy, currently very poor filly. **R Ford [0-1] Mrs N O'Malley.*

THEORETICALLY (USA) RR 109f 4140a[2]
3 b f Theatrical 11.5f **(78)** - Aspern (FR) (Riverman (USA)) 9.1f **(76)**
Form - 36842
2000 Turf 0-5: (8f 2, 9f 2, 12f) (g-s, gd, g-f 2, frm)
Pattern-class filly, effective 8 to 9f, best at 9f, acts on gd to frm. Turf high 109 - 2nd of 9 to No Matter What (27 Aug Del Mar 9f frm RF 4140a). Winner of a Curragh Group Three as a juvenile, she finished third in the Leopardstown 1000 Guineas Trial on her return and did not run at all badly in the Irish Guineas. Found wanting in the Irish Oaks, she ended her season by finishing second in a Grade One at Del Mar. **D K Weld in IRE [2-8].*

THEO'S LAD (IRE) BHB 53f **RR 48f** 4768[16]
3 b g Shareef Dancer (USA) 10.1f **(67)** - Inshirah (USA) (Caro)
Form - 571730
Record 2000 - 1st:1 2nd:0 3rd:1 Ran:6
Pre2000 - 1st:1 2nd:0 3rd:0 Ran:5
Win Prizemoney £5,207 *Total Prizemoney* £5,683
Wins * **2000** Jly Hamilt (G-F) S 6f 46
1999 May Catter (FRM) S 6f 52+ <
2000 Turf 1-6: (5f, 6f 1-2, 7f 3) (g-s, g-f 1-1, frm 4)

Moderate gelding, effective 6 to 7f, best at 6f, acts on g-f to frm, best on frm, has worn blinkers, likes tight tracks. Turf high 48 - 3rd of 11 getting 11lb from Mytton's Again (24 Aug Musselburgh 7f frm RF 3930).
**R Allan [1-6] London Gold (Fanway Ltd) (from R Guest [1-5] Spt 1999).*

THE PRIEST RR 6f 4774^{8}
3 b g College Chapel - Pharazini **(69f)** (Pharly (FR)) 9.8f **(68)**
Form - 8
Record 2000 - 1st:0 2nd:0 3rd:0 Ran:1
2000 Turf 0-1: (6f) (g-s)
Currently very poor gelding. **J A Osborne [0-1] C R Buttery.*

THE PRINCE BHB 88f93a **RR 89f 93a** 2151^{12}
6 b g Machiavellian (USA) 9.8f **(83)** - Mohican Girl (Dancing Brave (USA)) 8.4f **(76)**
Form - 18560
Record 2000 - 1st:1 2nd:0 3rd:0 Ran:5
Pre2000 - 1st:3 2nd:3 3rd:2 Ran:18
Win Prizemoney £50,440 *Total Prizemoney* £62,856
Wins * 2000 *Mar Wolver (STD) H 8.5f 90 94 <*
1999 Spt Hamilt (G-F) H 8.3f 85 90+
1999 May Lingfi (G-F) 7.6f 92
1997 May Newmar (G-F) 8f 82
2000 Turf 0-4: (7f, 8f 3) (g-s, gd 2, g-f) 2000 AW 1-1: (8f 1-1) (Fibr 1-1)
Useful gelding, effective 8f, acts on g-s to frm - acts on Fibr, prefers tight tracks, excels at Windsor and York. Turf high 89 - 6th of 9 getting 17lb from Swallow Flight (29 May Sandown 8f g-s RF 1537). (1st run) - 1st of 13 getting 3lb from River Times (11 Mar Wolverhampton RF 0435). Best when ridden patiently, he is a smart mile handicapper on the Flat and has already shown a decent level of form over hurdles. Possibly unsuited by heavy ground, he seems genuine nowadays.
**Ian Williams [1-5] Patrick Kelly (from R M H Cowell [2-12] Oct 1999).*

THE PROOF BHB 43f **RR 43f** 4486^{13}
3 b g Rudimentary (USA) 8.2f **(66)** - Indubitable (Sharpo) 7.7f **(59)**
Form - 00
Record 2000 - 1st:0 2nd:0 3rd:0 Ran:2
Pre2000 - 1st:0 2nd:0 3rd:0 Ran:3
2000 Turf 0-2: (10f, 12f) (g-s, gd)
Leggy, moderate gelding. Turf high 43 (began Aug).
**G B Balding [0-5] Miss B Swire.*

THE PROSECUTOR BHB 64f71a **RR 65f 71a** 4551^{7}
3 b c Contract Law (USA) 8.9f **(54)** - Elsocko (Swing Easy (USA)) 6.5f **(55)**
Form - 16150014487
Record 2000 - 1st:2 2nd:0 3rd:0 Ran:10
Pre2000 - 1st:1 2nd:2 3rd:1 Ran:7
Win Prizemoney £11,564 *Total Prizemoney* £13,390
Wins * 2000 May Haydoc (SFT) H 6f 62 65
*** 2000** *Mar Southw (STD) H 6f 73 82 <*
* 1999 *Nov Wolver (STD) 6f 70*
2000 Turf 1-7: (6f 1-2, 7f 5) (sft, g-s, gd 1-3, g-f, frm) 2000 AW 1-3: (6f 1-1, 7f, 8f) (Fibr 1-3)
Scopey, decent colt, effective 6f, - acts on Fibr. Turf high 65. AW high 82 - 1st of 7 giving 3lb to Oscar Pepper (17 Mar Southwell RF 0462). **B A McMahon [3-17] Whiston Management Ltd.*

THE PUZZLER (IRE) BHB 77f **RR 80f** 1893^{11}
9 b or br g Sharpo 7.5f **(68)** - Enigma (Ahonoora) 8.1f **(73)**
Form - 3000
Record 2000 - 1st:0 2nd:0 3rd:1 Ran:4
Pre2000 - 1st:4 2nd:2 3rd:4 Ran:38
Win Prizemoney £32,896 *Total Prizemoney* £44,508
Wins * 1999 Apr Sandow (G-S) H 5f 77 90
* 1997 Oct Newmar (G-S) H 5f 98 99
* 1996 Oct Newbur (SFT) H 6f 100 106 <
2000 Turf 0-4: (5f 2, 6f 2) (g-s 2, gd 2)
Decent gelding, effective 5f, acts on g-s, has worn blinkers. Turf high 80. A one-time useful sprinter, he is not easy to train and usually wears bandages.
**B W Hills [3-35] Lady Richard Wellesley (from M Kauntze in IRE [0-3] Jun 1995).*

THE REPUBLICAN BHB 25f **RR 28f** 3035^{10}
3 b g Democratic (USA) - Loving You (Thatch (USA)) 9.8f **(62)**
Form - 00000
Record 2000 - 1st:0 2nd:0 3rd:0 Ran:5
Pre2000 - 1st:0 2nd:0 3rd:0 Ran:2
2000 Turf 0-5: (6f, 8f 2, 9f, 10f) (gd, g-f 3, hrd)
Unfurnished, little account gelding, has worn blinkers. Turf high 28. **W Storey [0-7] Gremlin Racing.*

THERESA GREEN (IRE) BHB 67f **RR 70f** 4257^{10}
2 b f Charnwood Forest (IRE) - In Your Dreams (IRE) **(48f)** (Suave Dancer (USA))
Form - 7038140
Record 2000 - 1st:1 2nd:0 3rd:1 Ran:7
Win Prizemoney £4,231 *Total Prizemoney* £4,967
Wins * 2000 Aug Kempto (G-F) H 6f 64 70 <
2000 Turf 1-7: (5f 2, 6f 1-3, 7f 2) (g-s, gd 4, g-f, frm 1-1)
Above-average filly, effective 5 to 6f, acts on gd to frm. Turf high 70 - 4th of 10 getting 6lb from Blakeshall Boy (9 Aug Sandown 5f gd RF 3507) - also 1st of 9 getting 15lb from Imperial Measure (2 Aug Kempton RF 3324). **Mrs P N Dutfield [1-7] M Bevan.*

THERE'S TWO (IRE) BHB 89f **RR 84f** 4690^{5}
2 b f Ashkalani (IRE) - Sudden Interest (FR) (Highest Honor (FR))
Form - 3105
Record 2000 - 1st:1 2nd:0 3rd:1 Ran:4
Win Prizemoney £4,192 *Total Prizemoney* £5,247
Wins * 2000 Aug Goodwo (GD) 6f 70 <
2000 Turf 1-4: (6f 1-3, 8f) (gd, g-f 1-1, frm 2)
Decent filly. Turf high 84 (began Aug).
**M R Channon [1-4] Timberhill Racing Partnership.*

THERE WITH ME (USA) RR 65f 5191^{3}
3 b f Distant View (USA) - Breeze Lass (USA) (It's Freezing (USA)) 10f **(83)**
Form - 33
Record 2000 - 1st:0 2nd:0 3rd:2 Ran:2
Win Prizemoney £0 *Total Prizemoney* £906
2000 Turf 0-2: (7f, 8f) (g-s, gd)
Light-framed, currently average filly. Turf high 65 (began Oct).
**J H M Gosden [0-2] Bernard Gover Bloodstock Trading Ltd.*

THERMAL SPRING BHB 76f **RR 79f** 2567^{9}
3 ch f Zafonic (USA) 9f **(83)** - Seven Springs (USA) (Irish River (FR)) 8.6f **(78)**
Form - 240
Record 2000 - 1st:0 2nd:1 3rd:0 Ran:3
Pre2000 - 1st:0 2nd:0 3rd:0 Ran:1
Win Prizemoney £0 *Total Prizemoney* £1,860
2000 Turf 0-3: (7f, 8f, 10f) (gd 2, g-f)
Neat, above-average filly. Turf high 79 (1st run) - 2nd of 11 getting 5lb from Salim (6 May Thirsk 7f gd RF 1066). Ordinary form in maidens. **H R A Cecil [0-4] K Abdulla.*

THE ROBSTER (USA) BHB 57f **RR 64f** 2090^{5}
3 ch c Woodman (USA) 9.7f **(77)** - Country Cruise (USA) (Riverman (USA)) 9.1f **(76)**
Form - 02005
Record 2000 - 1st:0 2nd:1 3rd:0 Ran:5
Pre2000 - 1st:0 2nd:0 3rd:0 Ran:2
Win Prizemoney £0 *Total Prizemoney* £1,175
2000 Turf 0-5: (7f 3, 8f 2) (gd, g-f 2, frm 2)
Leggy, average colt, effective 7f, acts on g-f, has worn blinkers. Turf high 64 - 2nd of 9 to Mister Clinton (17 May Brighton 7f g-f RF 1257).
**B J Meehan [0-7] R L Harding.*

THE RORT (USA) RR 93f $4343a^{3}$
3 b c Diesis 9f **(80)** - Free Thinker (USA) (Shadeed (USA)) 8.2f **(70)**
Form - 314353
2000 Turf 1-6: (7f, 8f 1-3, 9f, 10f) (g-s 1-3, gd 2, g-f)
Useful colt, effective 8f, acts on gd. Turf high 93 - 3rd of 4 to Worldly Treasure (6 Aug Galway 8f gd RF 3480a). Probably best around a mile on easy ground, he did well for an inexperienced horse last season and is open to improvement.
**M J Grassick in IRE [1-6] Mrs Michael Watt.*

THE ROXBURGH (USA) RR 74f 1090^{4}

3 b br c Known Fact (USA) 8.3f **(72)** - Musical Precedent (USA) (Seattle Song (USA)) 9f **(77)**
Form - 4
Record 2000 - 1st:0 2nd:0 3rd:0 Ran:1
Win Prizemoney £0 *Total Prizemoney* £248
2000 Turf 0-1: (6f) (g-f)
Currently above-average colt. **J A R Toller [0-1] Duke of Devonshire.*

THESAURUS (USA) RR 91f 578a[13]
6 m
Form - 0
2000 Turf 0-1: (12f) (gd)
Currently useful. **C Dickey in USA [0-1].*

THE SCAFFOLDER BHB 70f70a RR 57f 70a 5156[5]
2 b g Tachyon Park - Fallal (IRE) **(49f 34a)** (Fayruz)
Form - 65
Record 2000 - 1st:0 2nd:0 3rd:0 Ran:2
2000 Turf 0-2: (5f 2) (g-s, gd)
Currently above-average gelding. Turf high 57 (began Oct).
**D Carroll [0-2] J J Devaney.*

THE SHADOW BHB 66a RR 42f 5012[12]
4 br g Polar Falcon (USA) 9f **(74)** - Shadiliya (Red Alert) 7.6f **(66)**
Form - 80578330
Record 2000 - 1st:0 2nd:0 3rd:2 Ran:8
Pre2000 - 1st:1 2nd:0 3rd:1 Ran:7
Win Prizemoney £2,944 *Total Prizemoney* £4,222
Wins * 1999 *Jly Wolver (STD) H 9.4f 63 65* <
2000 Turf 0-6: (8f, 10f 3, 12f 2) (gd 3, g-f, frm 2) 2000 AW 0-2: (12f, 14f) (Fibr 2)
Scopey, average gelding, effective 9 to 12f, - acts on Fibr, has worn blinkers, prefers left handed tracks, favours tight tracks. Turf high 42. AW high 67 (1st run) (began Oct) - 3rd of 11 giving 11lb to Failed To Hit (3 Oct Wolverhampton 12f Fibr RF 4779).
**D W P Arbuthnot [1-15] Mrs B J Lee.*

THE SHEIKH (IRE) BHB 51f RR 31f 2952[9]
3 b g Sri Pekan (USA) - Arabian Dream (IRE) (Royal Academy (USA))
Form - 250
Record 2000 - 1st:0 2nd:1 3rd:0 Ran:3
Pre2000 - 1st:0 2nd:0 3rd:0 Ran:3
Win Prizemoney £0 *Total Prizemoney* £675
2000 Turf 0-1: (11f) (g-f) 2000 AW 0-2: (8f 2) (Fibr 2)
Leggy, fair gelding, effective 8f, - acts on Fibr. AW high 59 (1st run) - 2nd of 14 giving 4lb to Just The Job Too (21 Feb Southwell 8f Fibr RF 0324). **M L W Bell [0-6] The Fitzrovians.*

THE STAGER (IRE) BHB 49f73a RR 41f 73a 3017[7]
8 b g Danehill (USA) 9.1f **(79)** - Wedgewood Blue (USA) (Sir Ivor) 10.2f **(70)**
Form - 0211451007
Record 2000 - 1st:3 2nd:0 3rd:0 Ran:8
Pre2000 - 1st:4 2nd:3 3rd:1 Ran:33
Win Prizemoney £22,262 *Total Prizemoney* £27,005
Wins * 2000 *Mar Southw (STD) H 8f 70 74*
* 2000 *Jan Southw (STD) H 8f 58 74+*
* 2000 *Jan Southw (STD) H 8f 58 59*
* 1999 *Apr Southw (STD) H 8f 54 56*
* 1998 *Nov Southw (STD) H 8f 49 53*
* 1996 May Newmar (GD) 7f 75 <
2000 AW 3-8: (8f 3-7, 10f) (Equi, Fibr 3-7)
Above-average gelding, effective 8f, - acts on Fibr, has worn blinkers, favours left handed tracks. AW high 74 - 1st of 10 getting 4lb from One Dinar (14 Mar Southwell RF 0439) - also 1st of 12 giving 24lb to Preposition (17 Jan Southwell RF 0101).
**J R Jenkins [7-46] J B Wilcox.*

THE TATLING (IRE) BHB 104f RR 104f 2110[13]
3 b c Perugino (USA) - Aunty Eileen (Ahonoora) 8.1f **(73)**
Form - 0380
Record 2000 - 1st:0 2nd:0 3rd:1 Ran:4
Pre2000 - 1st:2 2nd:3 3rd:1 Ran:9
Win Prizemoney £6,306 *Total Prizemoney* £48,576
Wins * 1999 Aug Bright (SFT) 5.3f 95+ <
* 1999 Jly Yarmou (G-F) 5.2f 87
2000 Turf 0-4: (5f 3, 6f) (g-s, gd 3)
Very useful colt, effective 5 to 6f, best at 6f, acts on g-s to gd, best on gd. Turf high 104 - 3rd of 9 to Jarn (19 May Newbury 6f gd RF 1302). Lightly raced at three, he struggled to make an impact against some top sprinters.
**M L W Bell [2-13] Messrs McGee.*

THE THIRD CURATE (IRE) BHB 47f45a RR 47f 45a 5185[13]
5 b g Fairy King (USA) 7.7f **(75)** - Lassalia (Sallust) 8.4f **(63)**
Form - 08071100
Record 2000 - 1st:2 2nd:0 3rd:0 Ran:6
Pre2000 - 1st:1 2nd:0 3rd:0 Ran:13
Win Prizemoney £9,220 *Total Prizemoney* £9,408
Wins * **2000** Jly Bright (FRM) H 7f 45 47
* **2000** *Jly Southw (STD) H 8f 39 46*
1999 Jun Currag (GD) H 7f 70 63 <
2000 Turf 1-4: (7f 1-2, 8f, 10f) (g-s 2, frm 1-1, hrd) 2000 AW 1-2: (6f, 8f 1-1) (Fibr 1-2)
Moderate gelding, effective 7f, acts on g-f, has worn blinkers (extremely effectively), likes left handed tracks, likes tight tracks. Turf high 47. AW high 46. Winner of a seven-furlong event at the Curragh for Dermot Weld, he is now with Barney Curley and was well beaten on his early English starts, but landed a gamble on the Southwell Fibresand in July.
**B J Curley [2-14] P Byrne (from D K Weld in IRE [1-5] Jun 1999).*

THE TRADER (IRE) BHB 104f RR 98f 5107[11]
2 ch c Selkirk (USA) 7.9f **(76)** - Snowing **(87f)** (Tate Gallery (USA)) 7.4f **(67)**
Form - 332211340
Record 2000 - 1st:2 2nd:2 3rd:3 Ran:9
Win Prizemoney £6,682 *Total Prizemoney* £13,460
Wins * **2000** Aug Folkes (G-F) 5f 76 <
* **2000** Aug Nottin (G-F) 5.1f 73
2000 Turf 2-9: (5f 2-7, 6f 2) (sft, gd 1-3, g-f 1-1, frm 4)
Very useful colt, effective 5f, acts on frm. Turf high 98 - 3rd of 9 giving 4lb to Reel Buddy (29 Aug Ripon 5f frm RF 4064). A poor mover, he handles all types of ground and improved with almost every start last year. However, handicaps are a thing of the past off his current mark and he may be difficult to place.
**M Blanshard [2-9] Mrs C J Ward.*

THE TUBE (IRE) RR 5015[9]
2 b f Royal Abjar (USA) - Grandeur And Grace (USA) **(67f)** (Septieme Ciel (USA))
Form - 0
Record 2000 - 1st:0 2nd:0 3rd:0 Ran:1
2000 AW 0-1: (6f) (Fibr)
Currently poor filly.
**Andrew Reid [0-1] A S Reid.*

THE WALL BHB 33f RR 52f 5237[13]
2 b f Mistertopogigo (IRE) - Lady Pennington (Blue Cashmere) 6.4f **(54)**
Form - 858008000
Record 2000 - 1st:0 2nd:0 3rd:0 Ran:9
2000 Turf 0-7: (5f 3, 6f, 7f 2, 8f) (g-s, gd 3, g-f 2, frm) 2000 AW 0-2: (5f 2) (Equi, Fibr)
Fair filly. Turf high 52. AW high 33.
**J A Gilbert [0-9] The Black & White Partnership.*

THE WALRUS (IRE) BHB 49f38a RR 58df 38a 2481[2]
3 b g Sri Pekan (USA) - Cathy Garcia (IRE) (Be My Guest (USA)) 9.3f **(67)**
Form - 03307552
Record 2000 - 1st:0 2nd:1 3rd:2 Ran:8
Win Prizemoney £0 *Total Prizemoney* £1,237
2000 Turf 0-5: (10f 2, 11f 2, 12f) (gd 2, frm 3) 2000 AW 0-3: (9f 2, 11f) (Fibr 3)
Light-framed, fair gelding, effective 10f, acts on gd. Turf high 58 (1st run) - 3rd of 13 to French Master (31 Mar Southwell 10f gd RF 0586). AW high 32. **N P Littmoden [0-8] Wilwyn Racing.*

THEWAYSHEWALKS BHB 20f RR 3080[18]
3 b f Mizoram (USA) - My Diamond Ring (Sparkling Boy) 5f **(36)**
Form - 7000
Record 2000 - 1st:0 2nd:0 3rd:0 Ran:4
2000 Turf 0-2: (8f, 12f) (gd, frm) 2000 AW 0-2: (8f, 11f) (Fibr 2)

Lengthy, formerly very poor filly. (began Jly).
**K Bell [0-4] S J Edwards.*

THEWHIRLINGDERVISH (IRE) BHB 66f **RR 69f** 4428[10]
2 ch c Definite Article - Nomadic Dancer (IRE) **(17f 36a)** (Nabeel Dancer (USA))
Form - 003200
Record 2000 - 1st:0 2nd:1 3rd:1 Ran:6
Win Prizemoney £0 *Total Prizemoney* £2,220
2000 Turf 0-6: (6f 2, 7f 2, 8f 2) (g-s, gd 2, frm 3)
Average colt, effective 7f, acts on frm. Turf high 69 - 2nd of 6 getting 1lb from Dominaite (29 Jly Redcar 7f frm RF 3221).
**T D Easterby [0-6] Major I C Straker.*

THE WHISTLING TEAL BHB 77f85a **RR 83f 85a** 4740[33]
4 b h Rudimentary (USA) 8.2f **(66)** - Lonely Shore (Blakeney) 10.5f **(64)**
Form - 703700
Record 2000 - 1st:0 2nd:0 3rd:1 Ran:6
Pre2000 - 1st:2 2nd:3 3rd:2 Ran:12
Win Prizemoney £9,439 *Total Prizemoney* £24,331
Wins * 1999 *Aug Wolver (STD) H* *8.5f 80 89* <
* 1999 Apr Windso (G-F) H 8.3f 74 76
2000 Turf 0-5: (8f 4, 9f) (sft, g-s, gd, g-f 2) 2000 AW 0-1: (8f) (Fibr)
Workmanlike, useful colt, effective 8 to 10f, best at 8f, acts on sft to gd - acts on Fibr, prefers left handed tracks, prefers tight tracks, excels at Wolverhampton. Turf high 83 - 3rd of 19 giving 6lb to Yarob (11 Apr Pontefract 8f g-s RF 0662). Able on both turf and sand, he was running well in the spring but was well held in July on his return from a break.
**J G Smyth-Osbourne [2-18] Mrs F A Veasey.*

THE WIFE BHB 79f **RR 82f** 2821[5]
3 b f Efisio 7.7f **(69)** - Great Steps **(70f)** (Vaigly Great) 7f **(58)**
Form - 00355
Record 2000 - 1st:0 2nd:0 3rd:1 Ran:5
Pre2000 - 1st:2 2nd:2 3rd:1 Ran:8
Win Prizemoney £11,350 *Total Prizemoney* £16,652
Wins * 1999 Spt York (G-F) H 7.9f 80 89 <
* 1999 Jun Beverl (G-F) 7.5f 75
2000 Turf 0-5: (8f 3, 9f, 10f) (gd 2, g-f 2, frm)
Leggy, decent filly, effective 8 to 10f, acts on g-f to frm, best on frm, likes left handed tracks. Turf high 82 - 5th of 6 getting 4lb from Gralmano (24 Jun Redcar 10f frm RF 2252). She ran her best race of last season under her ideal conditions to finish third in a very competitive handicap at York in June.
**T D Easterby [2-13] Jonathan Gill.*

THE WILD WIDOW BHB 77f75a **RR 87?f 75a** 4306[5]
6 gr m Saddlers' Hall (IRE) 10.5f **(65)** - No Cards (No Mercy) 8f **(61)**
Form - 70222111185
Record 2000 - 1st:4 2nd:3 3rd:0 Ran:10
Pre2000 - 1st:2 2nd:4 3rd:3 Ran:25
Win Prizemoney £19,407 *Total Prizemoney* £26,695
Wins * **2000** Jly Chepst (G-F) H 10.2f 68 87+ <
* **2000** Jun Kempto (G-F) H 9f 50 65+
* **2000** Jun Leices (G-F) H 8f 50 70
* **2000** Jun Newbur (G-F) H 10f 50 70?
1999 Aug Warwic (GD) S 10.5f 54
1999 *Feb Wolver (STD) S 9.4f 50*
2000 Turf 4-8: (8f 1-2, 9f 1-2, 10f 2-2, 11f, 12f) (hvy, gd 2, g-f 2-3, frm 1-1, hrd 1-1) 2000 AW 0-2: (8f, 9f) (Fibr 2)
Useful mare, effective 10f, acts on frm, often wears blinkers (very effectively). Turf high 87 - 1st of 5 giving 19lb to Parisian Lady (8 Jly Chepstow RF 2630). AW high 42.
**M C Pipe [4-7] Mrs Pam Pengelly & Mrs Helen Stoneman (from Miss S J Wilton [1-17] May 2000).*

THE WOODSTOCK LADY BHB 81f **RR 91f** 5104[13]
3 ch f Barathea (IRE) - Howlin' (USA) (Alleged (USA)) 10f **(76)**
Form - 0724800
Record 2000 - 1st:0 2nd:1 3rd:0 Ran:7
Pre2000 - 1st:1 2nd:0 3rd:0 Ran:1
Win Prizemoney £3,752 *Total Prizemoney* £7,776
Wins * 1999 Oct Leices (G-S) 7f 79+ <
2000 Turf 0-7: (8f, 10f, 12f 2, 14f, 15f, 16f) (g-s 2, gd 3, g-f 2)
Leggy, useful filly, effective 12 to 16f, acts on g-s to gd. Turf high 91 - 2nd of 8 getting 9lb from Riddlesdown (10 Jun Haydock 12f g-s RF 1874). Consistent. Highly tried in the spring, she only ran to form once last season and is basically disappointing.
**B W Hills [1-8] Gareth Thomas.*

THIEVES WELCOME BHB 50f40a **RR 60f 40a** 5166[17]
3 b f Most Welcome 8.6f **(66)** - Miss Tealeaf (USA) (Lear Fan (USA)) 8.5f **(73)**
Form - 0700
Record 2000 - 1st:0 2nd:0 3rd:0 Ran:4
Pre2000 - 1st:0 2nd:0 3rd:1 Ran:2
Win Prizemoney £0 *Total Prizemoney* £337
2000 Turf 0-3: (8f 3) (gd 3) 2000 AW 0-1: (12f) (Fibr)
Scopey, average filly. Turf high 52.
**J R Weymes [0-4] John Weymes Racing (from E Weymes [0-2] Aug 1999).*

THIHN (IRE) BHB 65f **RR 66f** 5299[2]
5 ch g Machiavellian (USA) 9.8f **(83)** - Hasana (USA) (Private Account (USA)) 8.5f **(74)**
Form - 28368023122852
Record 2000 - 1st:1 2nd:5 3rd:2 Ran:14
Pre2000 - 1st:0 2nd:2 3rd:1 Ran:8
Win Prizemoney £3,594 *Total Prizemoney* £11,503
Wins * **2000** Spt Beverl (G-F) H 8.5f 53 62+ <
2000 Turf 1-14: (7f, 8f 1-7, 9f, 10f 4, 11f) (sft, g-s 3, gd 3, g-f 1-3, frm 3, hrd)
Average gelding, effective 7 to 10f, best at 8f, acts on g-s to g-f, best on g-f, prefers right handed tracks, likes tight tracks. Turf high 66 - 2nd of 21 getting 3lb from Silvertown (6 Oct Windsor 10f g-f RF 4823) - also 1st of 15 getting 3lb from Route Sixty Six (13 Spt Beverley RF 4361). Consistent. Despite several placings, it took him a long time to get off the mark but he managed to do so in a handicap at Beverley in September.
**J L Spearing [1-10] Messrs P Cowan, S Daniels & B Beale (from N E Berry [0-12] Jly 2000).*

THIRTY SIX CEE BHB 41f41a **RR 49f 41a** 4054[12]
3 b f Rudimentary (USA) 8.2f **(66)** - Dear Person (Rainbow Quest (USA)) 10.4f **(75)**
Form - 80505000
Record 2000 - 1st:0 2nd:0 3rd:0 Ran:7
Pre2000 - 1st:0 2nd:0 3rd:0 Ran:7
Win Prizemoney £0 *Total Prizemoney* £246
2000 Turf 0-5: (6f, 10f 3, 11f) (gd 3, frm 2) 2000 AW 0-2: (8f, 9f) (Fibr 2)
Leggy, fair filly, effective 5f, acts on gd. Turf high 49. AW high 36.
**A W Carroll [0-14] Triumph International Ltd.*

THOMAS HENRY (IRE) BHB 44f35a **RR 47f 35a** 5154[14]
4 br g Petardia 8.2f **(58)** - Hitopah (Bustino) 10.4f **(64)**
Form - 1600668550035836463510
Record 2000 - 1st:1 2nd:0 3rd:3 Ran:20
Pre2000 - 1st:2 2nd:0 3rd:1 Ran:15
Win Prizemoney £7,117 *Total Prizemoney* £9,250
Wins * **2000** Oct Yarmou (SFT) SH 11.5f 39 47
* 1999 *Nov Lingfi (STD) S 10f 58*
* 1999 *Jan Lingfi (STD) 7f 59* <
2000 Turf 1-11: (8f 3, 10f 6, 11f 1-1, 12f) (hvy, g-s 1-2, gd 4, g-f, frm 3)
2000 AW 0-9: (8f 2, 10f 4, 12f 3) (Equi 8, Fibr)
Light-framed, moderate gelding, effective 7 to 8f, acts on frm - acts on Equi, has worn blinkers, likes tight tracks. Turf high 59. AW high 40. **J S Moore [3-35] J S Moore.*

THOMAS SMYTHE (IRE) BHB 75f73a **RR 80f 73a** 5115[2]
2 ch c College Chapel - Red Barons Lady (IRE) (Electric) 10.1f **(61)**
Form - 7226322
Record 2000 - 1st:0 2nd:4 3rd:1 Ran:7
Win Prizemoney £0 *Total Prizemoney* £4,079
2000 Turf 0-5: (5f, 6f 4) (sft, g-s 2, gd, frm) 2000 AW 0-2: (6f, 8f) (Fibr 2)
Decent colt, effective 8f, - acts on Fibr, likes left handed tracks, likes tight tracks. Turf high 80. AW high 72 (began Jly) - 2nd of 13 giving 7lb to Forum Finale (20 Oct Wolverhampton 8f Fibr RF 5115). **N P Littmoden [0-7] Richard Green (Fine Paintings).*

THORNCLIFF FOX (IRE) BHB 58f **RR 62f** 4366[12]
3 ch g Foxhound (USA) - Godly Light (FR) (Vayrann) 9.7f **(74)**
Form - 0483603300
Record 2000 - 1st:0 2nd:0 3rd:3 Ran:10

Pre2000 - 1st:0 2nd:0 3rd:2 Ran:4
Win Prizemoney £0 *Total Prizemoney* £2,267
2000 Turf 0-10: (5f 7, 6f, 7f 2) (sft, gd, g-f 4, frm 3, hrd)
Average gelding, effective 5 to 6f, acts on gd, mostly wears blinkers (effectively). Turf high 62 - 4th of 12 getting 4lb from Morgan Le Fay (19 May Thirsk 6f gd RF 1319).
**J A Glover [0-14] P and S Partnership.*

THORNTOUN DANCER BHB 62f RR 68f 5004[3]
2 b f Unfuwain (USA) 11.4f **(74)** - Westry (Gone West (USA)) 6.5f **(75)**
Form - 70563823
Record 2000 - 1st:0 2nd:1 3rd:2 Ran:8
Win Prizemoney £0 *Total Prizemoney* £2,217
2000 Turf 0-8: (5f 2, 6f, 7f, 8f 4) (hvy, g-s, gd 3, frm 3)
Average filly, effective 8f, acts on hvy to g-s. Turf high 63 - 3rd of 20 giving 7lb to Leatherback (16 Oct Pontefract 8f g-s RF 5004).
**J S Goldie [0-8] W M Johnstone.*

THORNTOUN DIVA BHB 64f RR 64f 5081[11]
2 ch f Wolfhound (USA) 7.3f **(71)** - Al Guswa (Shernazar) 10.2f **(73)**
Form - 3020860
Record 2000 - 1st:0 2nd:1 3rd:1 Ran:7
Win Prizemoney £0 *Total Prizemoney* £1,574
2000 Turf 0-7: (5f 4, 6f 3) (hvy, sft 2, gd 3, g-f)
Average filly, effective 5f, acts on sft, has worn blinkers. Turf high 68 - 2nd of 10 getting 5lb from Taras Emperor (24 Apr Newcastle 5f sft RF 0841).
**J S Goldie [0-7] W M Johnstone.*

THORNTOUN GOLD (IRE) BHB 41f RR 46f 4426[9]
4 ch m Lycius (USA) 8.8f **(71)** - Gold Braisim (IRE) (Jareer (USA)) 5.9f **(75)**
Form - 4010023552000
Record 2000 - 1st:1 2nd:2 3rd:1 Ran:13
Pre2000 - 1st:1 2nd:1 3rd:1 Ran:18
Win Prizemoney £7,358 *Total Prizemoney* £11,542
Wins * **2000** Jun Pontef (G-F) H 8f 44 46 <
* 1999 Jly Thirsk (FRM) SH 8f 39 44
2000 Turf 1-13: (8f 1-5, 9f 4, 10f, 11f 3) (gd, g-f 4, frm 1-7, hrd)
Strong, moderate filly, effective 7 to 11f, acts on gd to hrd, best on frm, has worn blinkers, prefers left handed tracks, favours tight tracks, excels at Thirsk, does well at Ayr, likes Pontefract. Turf high 46 - 1st of 10 giving 3lb to Swynford Pleasure (25 Jun Pontefract RF 2268).
**J S Goldie [2-28] Tough Construction Ltd (from M Johnston [0-3] Jly 1998).*

THORNTOUN HOUSE (IRE) BHB 25f30a RR 6f 30a 5082[6]
7 b g Durgam (USA) 12.3f **(53)** - Commanche Song (Commanche Run) 8.5f **(58)**
Form - 6
Record 2000 - 1st:0 2nd:0 3rd:0 Ran:1
Pre2000 - 1st:0 2nd:0 3rd:0 Ran:5
2000 Turf 0-1: (16f) (hvy)
Very poor gelding, has worn blinkers.
**J S Goldie [6-36] W M Johnstone.*

THREAT BHB 71f RR 70f 5068[3]
4 br g Zafonic (USA) 9f **(83)** - Prophecy (IRE) **(99f)** (Warning)
Form - 000006070513573
Record 2000 - 1st:1 2nd:0 3rd:2 Ran:15
Pre2000 - 1st:1 2nd:1 3rd:1 Ran:6
Win Prizemoney £10,772 *Total Prizemoney* £17,700
Wins * **2000** Spt Doncas (G-F) H 5f 64 70
1998 Jly Goodwo (G-S) 6f 97+ <
2000 Turf 1-15: (5f 1-9, 6f 2, 7f 4) (g-s 4, gd 6, g-f 1-3, frm 2)
Workmanlike, above-average gelding, effective 6f, acts on g-f to frm. Turf high 85. Consistent. Dropped dramatically in the handicap and eventually returned to winning form at Doncaster in September. Not altogether consistent.
**S C Williams [1-15] Pertemps Flexipeople Owners Syndicate (from J H M Gosden [1-6] Jly 1999).*

THREE ANGELS (IRE) RR 69f 3969[15]
5 b g Houmayoun (FR) 7.1f **(79)** - Mullaghroe (Tarboosh (USA)) 10f **(55)**
Form - 25080
Record 2000 - 1st:0 2nd:1 3rd:0 Ran:5
Pre2000 - 1st:2 2nd:6 3rd:5 Ran:27
Win Prizemoney £5,648 *Total Prizemoney* £18,365
Wins * 1998 Jun Haydoc (GD) H 7.1f 61 75 <
* 1998 May Folkes (G-F) 7f 70
2000 Turf 0-5: (6f, 7f 4) (gd, g-f, frm 3)
Average gelding, effective 7 to 8f, best at 7f, acts on g-f to frm, best on frm, has worn blinkers, prefers tight tracks, excels at Musselburgh. Turf high 69 (1st run) - 2nd of 14 giving 18lb to Erupt (22 May Musselburgh 7f frm RF 1367).
**M H Tompkins [2-32] M Sakal and Mrs B Cross.*

THREE CHEERS (IRE) RR 114f 4848a[8]
6 b br g Slip Anchor 12.7f **(75)** - Three Tails (Blakeney) 10.5f **(64)**
Form - 127358
Record 2000 - 1st:1 2nd:1 3rd:1 Ran:6
Pre2000 - 1st:3 2nd:3 3rd:2 Ran:16
Win Prizemoney £52,267 *Total Prizemoney* £125,551
Wins * **2000** Jun Maison (SFT) L 15f 114 <
* 1997 Oct Longch (GD) G3 15f 110
* 1997 Jly Newmar (G-F) L 14.8f 97
* 1997 May Newmar (G-F) 14f 78
2000 Turf 1-6: (15f 1-2, 16f, 18f, 20f, 22f) (sft 1-1, g-s, gd 3, frm)
Group-class gelding, effective 15 to 20f, best at 20f, acts on sft to frm, mostly wears blinkers (extremely effectively). Turf high 114 - 8th of 9 to San Sebastian (1 Oct Longchamp 20f gd RF 4848a) - also 1st of 5 giving 6lb to Mr Academy (9 Jun Maisons-laffitte RF 2000a). Consistent. He has a stack of ability, but keeps most of it to himself and was gaining his first win for almost three years when landing a Listed race at Maisons-Laffitte In June. Not disgraced in Group company thereafter, he stays extreme distances but is best left alone for betting purposes.
**J H M Gosden [4-22].*

THREE CHERRIES BHB 27f RR 39?f 5164[7]
4 ch m Formidable (USA) 7.8f **(60)** - Mistral's Dancer (Shareef Dancer (USA)) 9.9f **(73)**
Form - 40800084564507
Record 2000 - 1st:0 2nd:0 3rd:0 Ran:14
Pre2000 - 1st:0 2nd:0 3rd:0 Ran:4
Win Prizemoney £0 *Total Prizemoney* £416
2000 Turf 0-14: (7f, 8f 4, 9f 3, 10f, 11f 2, 12f 3) (gd 2, g-f 5, frm 6, hrd)
Workmanlike, very moderate filly. Turf high 39.
**R E Barr [0-14] P Cartmell (from R Hannon [0-4] Spt 1999).*

THREEFORTYCASH (IRE) BHB 30f48a RR 42f 48a 3714[7]
3 b g Balla Cove - Tigeen (Habitat) 9.4f **(70)**
Form - 4500607057
Record 2000 - 1st:0 2nd:0 3rd:0 Ran:10
Pre2000 - 1st:0 2nd:0 3rd:0 Ran:2
2000 Turf 0-8: (7f 2, 8f 3, 10f, 12f, 16f) (sft, g-f, frm 4, hrd 2) 2000 AW 0-2: (7f, 8f) (Fibr 2)
Scopey, moderate gelding. Turf high 42. AW high 40.
**Andrew Turnell [0-12] Mrs Claire Hollowood.*

THREE GREEN LEAVES (IRE) BHB 85f RR 91f 4308[15]
4 ch m Environment Friend 7.5f **(67)** - Kick the Habit (Habitat) 9.4f **(70)**
Form - 08810366200
Record 2000 - 1st:1 2nd:1 3rd:1 Ran:11
Pre2000 - 1st:5 2nd:1 3rd:2 Ran:13
Win Prizemoney £47,253 *Total Prizemoney* £55,080
Wins * **2000** Jun Newmar (G-F) 12f 89 <
* 1998 Oct Pontef (SFT) L 8f 84
* 1998 Oct Cork (G-S) 7f 84+
* 1998 Spt Newcas (GD) 8f 84+
* 1998 Jly Beverl (G-F) 7.5f 77
* 1998 Jun Beverl (GD) 7.5f 77
2000 Turf 1-11: (10f, 12f 1-7, 13f, 14f 2) (hvy, gd 3, g-f 3, frm 1-3, hrd)
Scopey, useful filly, effective 12 to 14f, best at 12f, acts on gd to hrd, best on g-f, does well at York. Turf high 91 - 8th of 17 giving 19lb to Inch Perfect (16 May York 12f g-f RF 1216) - also 1st of 7 getting 3lb from Westender (3 Jun Newmarket RF 1691). She has suffered her share of problems, but bounced back well last year, landing a decent conditions event at Newmarket. Yet to win a handicap, she struggles to stay a mile and three-quarters.
**M Johnston [6-24] R N Pennell.*

THREE LEADERS (IRE) BHB 40f40a RR 41f 40a 2967[5]
4 ch g Up and At 'em - Wolviston (Wolverlife) 9.3f **(54)**

Form - 06000480405

Record **2000 -** 1st:0 2nd:0 3rd:0 Ran:11
Pre2000 - 1st:1 2nd:1 3rd:1 Ran:15

Win Prizemoney £2,189 *Total Prizemoney* £3,730

Wins 1999 Jun Beverl (G-F) H 5f 55 56 <

2000 Turf 0-9: (5f, 6f 2, 7f, 8f, 9f 2, 10f 2) (gd, g-f 5, frm 3) 2000 AW 0-2: (7f, 8f) (Fibr 2)

Scopey, moderate gelding, effective 5 to 6f, acts on g-f, has worn blinkers. Turf high 41. AW high 13.

**E J Alston [0-11] RJH Ltd & Heath Private & Commercial (from D Nicholls [1-15] Oct 1999).*

THREE LIONS BHB 80f RR 79+f 5201[1]

3 ch g Jupiter Island 10.4f **(57)** - Super Sol (Rolfe (USA)) 12.1f **(65)**

Form - 0164101

Record 2000 - 1st:3 2nd:0 3rd:0 Ran:7
Pre2000 - 1st:0 2nd:0 3rd:0 Ran:3

Win Prizemoney £11,245 *Total Prizemoney* £11,938

Wins * **2000** Oct Windso (HVY) H 11.6f 72 79+ <
* **2000** Spt Kempto (GD) H 14.4f 67 75
* **2000** Jly Beverl (G-F) 9.9f 68

2000 Turf 3-7: (10f 1-3, 12f 1-1, 14f 1-3) (gd 1-2, g-f 2-3, frm 2)

Above-average gelding, effective 12 to 14f, acts on gd to g-f, prefers tight tracks. Turf high 79 (began Jly) - 1st of 7 giving 1lb to Dickie Deadeye (26 Oct Windsor RF 5201) - also 1st of 12 giving 13lb to Able Seaman (3 Spt Kempton RF 4192). Consistent. Stays well and still looks to be improving.

**R F JohnsonHoughton [3-10] Jim Short.*

THREE OWLS (IRE) BHB 76f RR 78+f 5078[5]

3 b f Warning 8.1f **(77)** - Three Terns (USA) (Arctic Tern (USA)) 8.9f **(69)**

Form - 315

Record 2000 - 1st:1 2nd:0 3rd:1 Ran:3

Win Prizemoney £3,282 *Total Prizemoney* £3,932

Wins * **2000** Spt Bright (SFT) 8f 78+ <

2000 Turf 1-3: (7f, 8f 1-2) (hvy 1-1, g-s, gd)

Currently above-average filly. Turf high 78 (began Aug) - 1st of 8 from Ardanza (27 Spt Brighton RF 4680).

**L M Cumani [1-3] Mrs A Rothschild.*

THREE POINTS BHB 113f RR 115f 4139a[1]

3 b c Bering 9.6f **(80)** - Trazl (IRE) **(86f)** (Zalazl (USA))

Form - 3244121

Record 2000 - 1st:2 2nd:2 3rd:1 Ran:7
Pre2000 - 1st:2 2nd:0 3rd:1 Ran:3

Win Prizemoney £38,370 *Total Prizemoney* £71,257

Wins * **2000** Aug Deauvi (G-S) G3 6f 115 <
* **2000** Jly Newbur (G-F) 7f 114+
* 1999 Aug Nottin (G-F) 8.2f 95+
* 1999 Aug Kempto (G-F) 7f 79

2000 Turf 2-7: (6f 1-1, 7f 1-3, 9f 2, 10f) (g-s 1-1, gd 3, g-f 2, frm 1-1)

Scopey, high-class colt, effective 6 to 7f, best at 7f, acts on g-s to frm. Turf high 115 - 1st of 10 from Danger Over (27 Aug Deauville RF 4139a) - also 1st of 10 getting 3lb from Glad Master (21 Jly Newbury RF 2997). Consistent. He pulled far too hard over nine and ten furlongs at the start of the campaign and clearly appreciated being ridden aggressively over shorter trips. Sharp enough to make-all in the Group Three six furlong Prix de Meautry at Deauville in August, he could improve again this year.

**J L Dunlop [4-10] Hesmonds Stud.*

THREE WHITE SOX BHB 66f RR 66f 3492[1]

3 ch f Most Welcome 8.6f **(66)** - Empty Purse (Pennine Walk) 8.5f **(61)**

Form - 832551

Record 2000 - 1st:1 2nd:1 3rd:1 Ran:6
Pre2000 - 1st:0 2nd:0 3rd:0 Ran:1

Win Prizemoney £2,938 *Total Prizemoney* £4,981

Wins * **2000** Aug Leices (G-F) 11.8f 66 <

2000 Turf 1-6: (10f 2, 11f, 12f 1-2, 14f) (gd 2, g-f, frm 1-3)

Lengthy, average filly, effective 11 to 12f, best at 12f, acts on frm, prefers tight tracks. Turf high 66 - 1st of 9 getting 3lb from Malarkey (9 Aug Leicester RF 3492). Had been improving with her racing before winning a classified event at Leicester. The third won his next two races, so the form looks reasonable.

**P W Harris [1-7] Les McLaughlin.*

THREEZEDZZ BHB 92f RR 91f 4742[2]

2 ch c Emarati (USA) 6.6f **(63)** - Exotic Forest **(68df)** (Dominion) 8.5f **(63)**

Form - 1263402

Record 2000 - 1st:1 2nd:2 3rd:1 Ran:7

Win Prizemoney £2,926 *Total Prizemoney* £18,883

Wins * **2000** Apr Windso (GD) 5f 75 <

2000 Turf 1-7: (5f 1-4, 6f 3) (gd 2, g-f 2, frm 1-2, hrd)

Useful colt, effective 6f, acts on g-f. Turf high 91 - 2nd of 19 getting 2lb from Caustic Wit (30 Spt Newmarket 6f g-f RF 4742). A late foal, he did well last year, running a cracking race behind Caustic Wit in a valuable nursery on his final start. Likely to be difficult to place off his current mark, he has yet to race on ground softer than good.

**J G Portman [1-7] Steve Evans.*

THROUGH THE RYE BHB 89f RR 87f 1807[7]

4 ch h Sabrehill (USA) 8.5f **(64)** - Baharlilys (Green Dancer (USA)) 10.3f **(74)**

Form - 7

Record 2000 - 1st:0 2nd:0 3rd:0 Ran:1
Pre2000 - 1st:1 2nd:0 3rd:1 Ran:8

Win Prizemoney £5,277 *Total Prizemoney* £9,611

Wins 1999 Jun Newcas (G-F) 8f 69+ <

2000 Turf 0-1: (11f) (gd)

Scopey, useful colt.

**M C Pipe [2-5] W J Gredley (from B W Hills [1-8] Oct 1999).*

THROWER BHB 47f53a RR 50f 53a 4535[3]

9 b g Thowra (FR) 11.2f **(47)** - Atlantic Line (Capricorn Line) 14.6f **(62)**

Form - 145803

Record 2000 - 1st:1 2nd:0 3rd:1 Ran:6
Pre2000 - 1st:2 2nd:2 3rd:1 Ran:16

Win Prizemoney £8,007 *Total Prizemoney* £12,064

Wins 2000 *Feb Southw (STD) H 16f 50 55* <
1999 Apr Nottin (SFT) H 10f 45 50
1999 Apr Leices (G-S) H 11.8f 26 46

2000 Turf 0-3: (10f, 11f, 16f) (g-s, gd, frm) 2000 AW 1-3: (12f, 16f 1-2) (Fibr 1-3)

Fair gelding, effective 10 to 16f, best at 16f, acts on g-s to gd - acts on Fibr, favours tight tracks. Turf high 49. AW high 55 (1st run) - 1st of 11 giving 8lb to St Lawrence (7 Feb Southwell RF 0234).

**P D Evans [0-5] C M & S J Owen (from S A Brookshaw [7-12] Mar 2000).*

THUNDERED (USA) RR 43f 4482[10]

2 gr c Thunder Gulch (USA) - Lady Lianga (USA) (Secretariat (USA)) 9f **(79)**

Form - 70

Record 2000 - 1st:0 2nd:0 3rd:0 Ran:2

2000 Turf 0-2: (7f, 8f) (g-s, frm)

Currently moderate colt. Turf high 43 (began Aug).

**E J O'Neill [0-2] J D Martin.*

THUNDERING PAPOOSE BHB 28f RR 25f 3843[11]

5 b m Be My Chief (USA) 10.2f **(62)** - Thunder Bug (USA) (Secreto (USA)) 8.7f **(72)**

Form - 0

Record 2000 - 1st:0 2nd:0 3rd:0 Ran:1
Pre2000 - 1st:0 2nd:0 3rd:0 Ran:5

2000 Turf 0-1: (10f) (gd)

Little account filly.

**J R Jenkins [0-1] C N & Mrs J C Wright (from N A Graham [0-2] Jun 1998).*

THUNDERING SURF BHB 82f RR 84f 5187[2]

3 b c Lugana Beach 7f **(63)** - Thunder Bug (USA) (Secreto (USA)) 8.7f **(72)**

Form - 78135432

Record 2000 - 1st:1 2nd:1 3rd:2 Ran:8
Pre2000 - 1st:0 2nd:0 3rd:0 Ran:1

Win Prizemoney £7,507 *Total Prizemoney* £12,775

Wins * **2000** Jly Sandow (GD) H 10f 75 81 <

2000 Turf 1-8: (8f, 10f 1-7) (sft, g-s, gd 2, g-f 2, frm 1-2)

Scopey, decent colt, effective 10f, acts on sft to frm. Turf high 84 - 2nd of 8 giving 1lb to Generous Diana (25 Oct Yarmouth 10f sft RF 5187) - also 1st of 14 giving 5lb to Rich Vein (8 Jly Sandown RF 2649). Consistent. Scored at Sandown in July on his debut in handicap company but paid for it in the weights.

**J R Jenkins [1-8] C N & Mrs J C Wright (from N A Graham [0-1] Oct*

1999).

THUNDERMILL (USA) BHB 76f73a **RR 86f 73a** 4547[8]
2 ch c Thunder Gulch (USA) - Specifically (USA) (Sky Classic (CAN))
Form - 5368
Record 2000 - 1st:0 2nd:0 3rd:1 Ran:4
Win Prizemoney £0 *Total Prizemoney* £697
2000 Turf 0-4: (7f 2, 8f 2) (g-s, gd 2, frm)
Useful colt. Turf high 72 (began Jly).
**T G Mills [0-4] Resplendent Racing Ltd.*

THUNDER SKY BHB 74f **RR 76f** 4375[7]
4 b h Zafonic (USA) 9f **(83)** - Overcast (IRE) (Caerleon (USA)) 8.6f **(71)**
Form - 04510857
Record 2000 - 1st:1 2nd:0 3rd:0 Ran:8
Pre2000 - 1st:0 2nd:0 3rd:0 Ran:4
Win Prizemoney £2,996 *Total Prizemoney* £7,756
Wins * 2000 Jun Folkes (FRM) 7f 75 <
2000 Turf 1-7: (7f 1-3, 8f 3, 10f) (gd 2, g-f 1-3, frm 2) 2000 AW 0-1: (8f) (Dirt)
Well made, above-average colt, often wears blinkers (very effectively). Turf high 76. Consistent. The drop back to seven and application of a visor did the trick at Folkestone in June, but that has been by far his best effort to date. Suited by fast ground.
**C E Brittain [1-12] Ali Saeed.*

THWAAB BHB 56f53a **RR 55f 53a** 3616[7]
8 b g Dominion 8.9f **(65)** - Velvet Habit (Habitat) 9.4f **(70)**
Form - 061117
Record 2000 - 1st:3 2nd:0 3rd:0 Ran:6
Pre2000 - 1st:4 2nd:5 3rd:5 Ran:50
Win Prizemoney £24,684 *Total Prizemoney* £37,848
Wins * 2000 Aug Redcar (FRM) H 8f 54 55
*** 2000** Jly Redcar (G-F) H 8f 41 52
*** 2000** Jly Carlis (FM) H 6.9f 41 49
* 1998 Jly Doncas (FRM) H 7f 56 58
* 1996 Aug Redcar (G-F) H 6f 59 61 <
* 1996 Jly Ayr (G-F) H 6f 52 56
* 1996 Jun Ayr (G-F) H 6f 45 50
2000 Turf 3-6: (6f, 7f 1-3, 8f 2-2) (g-f 1-2, frm 2, hrd 2-2)
Fair gelding, effective 7 to 8f, best at 8f, acts on g-f to hrd, best on hrd, often wears blinkers (effectively). Turf high 55 - 1st of 6 getting 20lb from Pentagon Lad (12 Aug Redcar RF 3597) - also 1st of 29 giving 1lb to Saifan (23 Jly Redcar RF 3054).
**F Watson [7-56] F Watson.*

TIBBIE **RR 60f** 5065[5]
2 b f Slip Anchor 12.7f **(75)** - Circe (Main Reef) 9.6f **(57)**
Form - 05
Record 2000 - 1st:0 2nd:0 3rd:0 Ran:2
2000 Turf 0-2: (6f, 8f) (g-s, g-f)
Currently average filly. Turf high 60 (began Spt).
**R M Beckett [0-2] A D G Oldrey.*

TICCATOO (IRE) BHB 56f60a **RR 62f 60a** 5060[10]
2 br f Dolphin Street (FR) - Accountancy Jewel (IRE) **(63a)** (Pennine Walk) 8.5f **(61)**
Form - 100827040
Record 2000 - 1st:1 2nd:1 3rd:0 Ran:9
Win Prizemoney £2,299 *Total Prizemoney* £3,461
Wins * 2000 *Apr Southw (STD) 5f 63 <*
2000 Turf 0-7: (5f 4, 6f 3) (sft, gd, g-f 4, frm) 2000 AW 1-2: (5f 1-2) (Fibr 1-2)
Average filly, effective 5f, acts on frm - acts on Fibr. Turf high 56. AW high 63 (1st run) - 1st of 11 getting 2lb from Beverley Macca (11 Apr Southwell RF 0665). **R Hollinshead [1-9] John Marriott.*

TICKER **RR 62f** 1637[6]
2 b c Timeless Times (USA) 6.1f **(56)** - Lady Day (FR) (Lightning (FR)) 7.9f **(74)**
Form - 36
Record 2000 - 1st:0 2nd:0 3rd:1 Ran:2
Win Prizemoney £0 *Total Prizemoney* £402
2000 Turf 0-2: (5f, 6f) (g-f, frm)
Currently average colt. Turf high 62.
**Denys Smith [0-2] Duke of Sutherland.*

TICKLE BHB 80f **RR 80f** 4808[1]
2 b f Primo Dominie 7.2f **(67)** - Funny Choice (IRE) **(55f)** (Commanche Run) 8.5f **(58)**
Form - 02211
Record 2000 - 1st:2 2nd:2 3rd:0 Ran:5
Win Prizemoney £9,249 *Total Prizemoney* £11,698
Wins * 2000 Oct Lingfi (SFT) H 6f 73 80 <
*** 2000** Spt York (GD) 6f 72
2000 Turf 2-5: (5f, 6f 2-4) (g-s 1-1, g-f 1-4)
Decent filly. Turf high 80 (began Jly) - 1st of 19 giving 5lb to Captain Gibson (4 Oct Lingfield RF 4808) - also 1st of 15 getting 5lb from Halcyon Magic (3 Spt York RF 4198).
**P J Makin [2-5] Mrs Derek Strauss.*

TICKLISH BHB 69a **RR 61f** 877[7]
4 b m Cadeaux Genereux 7.9f **(76)** - Exit Laughing (Shaab)
Form - 37
Record 2000 - 1st:0 2nd:0 3rd:1 Ran:2
Pre2000 - 1st:3 2nd:1 3rd:3 Ran:16
Win Prizemoney £11,080 *Total Prizemoney* £14,038
Wins * 1999 Aug Warwic (GD) H 6.8f 67 68
* 1998 Spt Bright (GD) H 6f 66 69 <
* 1998 Spt Ripon (HVY) H 6f 61 67
2000 Turf 0-2: (6f, 7f) (sft, gd)
Average filly, effective 7f, acts on gd. Turf high 61. Consistent.
**W J Haggas [3-18] Michael Brower.*

TICK TOCK **RR 57f** 5112[8]
3 ch f Timeless Times (USA) 6.1f **(56)** - Aquiletta **(26f 42a)** (Bairn (USA)) 7.7f **(59)**
Form - 7722000408638
Record 2000 - 1st:0 2nd:2 3rd:1 Ran:13
Pre2000 - 1st:0 2nd:1 3rd:0 Ran:5
Win Prizemoney £0 *Total Prizemoney* £3,003
2000 Turf 0-13: (5f 12, 6f) (sft, gd 5, g-f 5, frm 2)
Neat, fair filly, effective 5f, acts on gd to frm, has worn blinkers. Turf high 57 - 2nd of 6 getting 10lb from Stoney Garnett (26 May Brighton 5f gd RF 1462). **M Mullineaux [0-18] Frank Chadwick.*

TIC TAC MAC BHB 28f **RR 10f** 1970[11]
3 b c Mac's Fighter - Tickle Me Too (Tickled Pink) 6.5f **(59)**
Form - 000
Record 2000 - 1st:0 2nd:0 3rd:0 Ran:1
Pre2000 - 1st:0 2nd:0 3rd:0 Ran:5
2000 Turf 0-1: (11f) (frm)
Workmanlike, poor colt. **L A Dace [0-6] Miss Nicola Pfann.*

TIERRA DEL FUEGO BHB 18f **RR 14f** 440[7]
6 b m Chilibang 7f **(55)** - Dolly Bevan (Another Realm) 6.6f **(55)**
Form - 07
Record 2000 - 1st:0 2nd:0 3rd:0 Ran:2
Pre2000 - 1st:0 2nd:0 3rd:0 Ran:9
2000 AW 0-2: (8f, 11f) (Fibr 2)
Poor mare, effective 8f, - acts on Fibr, has worn blinkers, likes left handed tracks, likes tight tracks. AW high 4.
**H J Collingridge [0-11] The Headquarters Partnership V.*

TIGER GRASS (IRE) BHB 52f **RR 58df** 2357[6]
4 gr g Ezzoud (IRE) - Rustic Lawn (Rusticaro (FR)) 8.2f **(65)**
Form - 06
Record 2000 - 1st:0 2nd:0 3rd:0 Ran:2
Pre2000 - 1st:0 2nd:2 3rd:0 Ran:11
Win Prizemoney £0 *Total Prizemoney* £2,726
2000 Turf 0-2: (10f, 12f) (gd, g-f)
Light-framed, fair gelding, has worn blinkers. Turf high 41.
**W R Muir [1-16] M J Caddy.*

TIGER GROOM **RR 93f** 2203a[1]
8 Arazi (USA) 9.2f **(74)** - Rifada (Ela-Mana-Mou) 10.1f **(70)**
Form - 51
2000 Turf 1-2: (11f, 12f 1-1) (hvy, gd 1-1)
Currently useful. Turf high 93 - 1st of 9 from Allen Park (18 Jun Frauenfeld RF 2203a). **R Collet in FR [1-2] R Collet.*

TIGER IMP (IRE) BHB 66f **RR 70df** 4276[11]
4 b g Imp Society (USA) 7.1f **(63)** - Mrs Merry Man (Bellypha) 9.8f **(73)**
Form - 06010

Record 2000 - 1st:1 2nd:0 3rd:0 Ran:5
Pre2000 - 1st:0 2nd:2 3rd:1 Ran:3
Win Prizemoney £2,772 *Total Prizemoney* £5,770
Wins * 2000 Aug Folkes (G-F) 5f 61 <
2000 Turf 1-5: (5f 1-5) (gd 1-2, g-f 3)
Scopey, above-average gelding, effective 6 to 7f, best at 7f, acts on g-f to frm, best on g-f. Turf high 61.
**I A Balding [1-8] Mrs Angela Brodie.*

TIGER PRINCESS RR 39[14]

3 b f Bin Ajwaad (IRE) - Penny Dip **(86f)** (Cadeaux Genereux)
Form - 0
Record 2000 - 1st:0 2nd:0 3rd:0 Ran:1
2000 AW 0-1: (7f) (Fibr)
Neat, currently very poor filly. **M A Jarvis [0-1] N S Yong.*

TIGER ROYAL (IRE) RR 105f 5285a[2]

4 gr g Royal Academy (USA) 7.8f **(77)** - Lady Redford (Bold Lad (IRE)) 8.4f **(68)**
Form - 26644332132
2000 Turf 1-11: (5f 1-7, 6f 4) (hvy, sft 1-2, g-s, gd 4, g-f, frm)
Pattern-class gelding, effective 5 to 6f, best at 6f, acts on hvy to g-s, mostly wears blinkers (very effectively). Turf high 102 - 2nd of 10 getting 10lb from Gaelic Storm (28 Oct Leopardstown 6f hvy RF 5285a) - also 1st of 13 giving 6lb to Eveam (30 Spt Curragh RF 4795a). He raced with tremendous consistency through a hectic campaign. Probably best on easy ground, he struggles to stay beyond six furlongs. **D K Weld in IRE [2-18] Peter Jones.*

TIGER TALK BHB 37f RR 48f 3979[8]

4 ch g Sabrehill (USA) 8.5f **(64)** - Tebre (USA) (Sir Ivor) 10.2f **(70)**
Form - 0000058
Record 2000 - 1st:0 2nd:0 3rd:0 Ran:7
Pre2000 - 1st:2 2nd:2 3rd:0 Ran:11
Win Prizemoney £11,334 *Total Prizemoney* £13,048
Wins 1999 Apr Sandow (SFT) H 8.1f 84 89 <
1999 Mar Folkes (SFT) 7f 89 <
2000 Turf 0-7: (7f, 8f, 10f, 11f 2, 12f 2) (g-s, gd 3, g-f, frm 2)
Scopey, moderate gelding, effective 7 to 8f, acts on sft to g-s, has worn blinkers. Turf high 48.
**M E Sowersby [0-2] Racing Ladies (from N P Littmoden [0-7] Jly 2000).*

TIGHTROPE BHB 52f65a RR 50f 65a 744[13]

5 b g Alzao (USA) 9.8f **(73)** - Circus Act (Shirley Heights) 10.3f **(74)**
Form - 282463801000
Record 2000 - 1st:1 2nd:0 3rd:1 Ran:8
Pre2000 - 1st:2 2nd:4 3rd:0 Ran:17
Win Prizemoney £14,503 *Total Prizemoney* £20,041
Wins * 2000 *Mar Lingfi (STD) H 10f 62 69*
1999 Spt Yarmou (G-S) S 10.1f 51+
1997 Oct Leices (G-F) H 8f 70 79+ <
2000 Turf 0-2: (9f, 10f) (g-s, gd) 2000 AW 1-6: (9f 4, 10f 1-2) (Equi 1-2, Fibr 4)
Average gelding, effective 9 to 10f, best at 9f, - acts on AW, best on Fibr, has worn blinkers, prefers left handed tracks, favours tight tracks, excels at Lingfield, likes Wolverhampton. Turf high 9. AW high 69 - 1st of 13 getting 14lb from Anemos (4 Mar Lingfield RF 0403). Becoming disappointing. Won a seller for Sir Mark Prescott on turf last year and is now with Nick Littmoden. Rather inconsistent on sand, he showed what he could do when in the mood by bolting up in a competitive handicap on the Lingfield Equitrack in March. He suffers with a fibrillating heart and cannot be relied upon to reproduce his best.
**N P Littmoden [1-12] Wilwyn Racing (from Sir Mark Prescott [2-13] Oct 1999).*

TIGONTIME RR 4458[8]

3 b f Tigani - Molly Brazen (Risk Me (FR)) 5.9f **(53)**
Form - 08
Record 2000 - 1st:0 2nd:0 3rd:0 Ran:2
2000 Turf 0-2: (7f, 10f) (g-s, frm)
Rangy, currently very poor filly. (began Aug).
**N Wilson [0-2] Geoff Pickering.*

TIGRE BHB 81f RR 83f 3616[3]

3 b c Mujtahid (USA) 7.4f **(69)** - Vice Vixen (CAN) (Vice Regent (CAN)) 8.7f **(74)**
Form - 408213
Record 2000 - 1st:1 2nd:1 3rd:1 Ran:6
Pre2000 - 1st:0 2nd:4 3rd:0 Ran:5
Win Prizemoney £3,575 *Total Prizemoney* £12,058
Wins * 2000 Jly Ripon (G-F) 10f 81 <
2000 Turf 1-6: (7f, 9f, 10f 1-3, 11f) (g-s 2, gd, frm 1-3)
Scopey, decent colt, effective 7 to 11f, best at 10f, acts on gd to frm, best on frm, prefers left handed tracks, likes tight tracks, excels at Ayr. Turf high 83 - 2nd of 5 giving 5lb to Delamere (17 Jly Ayr 10f frm RF 2874) - also 1st of 12 from Scachmatt (30 Jly Ripon RF 3241). **B W Hills [1-11] Guy Reed & J Hanson.*

TIHEROS GLENN BHB 40f RR 51?f 750[15]

4 ch g Toxotis - Warthill Girl (Anfield) 8.5f **(59)**
Form - 0
Record 2000 - 1st:0 2nd:0 3rd:0 Ran:1
Pre2000 - 1st:0 2nd:0 3rd:0 Ran:4
Win Prizemoney £0 *Total Prizemoney* £344
2000 Turf 0-1: (8f) (sft)
Workmanlike, fair gelding.
**Miss J F Craze [0-1] Mrs H F Mahr (from D McCain [0-4] Nov 1998).*

TIJIYR (IRE) RR 114f 3734a[2]

4 gr h Primo Dominie 7.2f **(67)** - Tijara (IRE) (Darshaan) 9.9f **(84)**
Form - 22
2000 Turf 0-2: (10f 2) (sft, gd)
Group-class colt. Turf high 114 (began Jly) - 2nd of 8 to Agol Lack (12 Aug Deauville 10f gd RF 3734a). He has speed and stamina in his pedigree, but shapes like a stayer and is worth a try over a mile and a half. **A deRoyerDupre in FR [0-4] H H Aga Khan.*

TIKRAM BHB 87f RR 88f 5058[1]

3 ch c Lycius (USA) 8.8f **(71)** - Black Fighter (USA) (Secretariat (USA)) 9f **(79)**
Form - 731
Record 2000 - 1st:1 2nd:0 3rd:1 Ran:3
Win Prizemoney £3,445 *Total Prizemoney* £4,124
Wins * 2000 Oct Nottin (SFT) 10f 88 <
2000 Turf 1-3: (10f 1-3) (sft 1-1, g-s, frm)
Scopey, currently useful colt. Turf high 88 - 1st of 9 giving 5lb to Second Affair (18 Oct Nottingham RF 5058).
**H R A Cecil [1-3] Buckram Oak Holdings.*

TILER (IRE) BHB 77f80a RR 75f 80a 2092[P]

8 br g Ballad Rock 7.2f **(63)** - Fair Siobahn (Petingo) 11f **(72)**
Form - P
Record 2000 - 1st:0 2nd:0 3rd:0 Ran:1
Pre2000 - 1st:7 2nd:10 3rd:9 Ran:76
Win Prizemoney £44,551 *Total Prizemoney* £82,372
Wins * 1999 Apr Newcas (GD) H 7f 76 83
* 1998 Aug Cheste (G-S) H 7.6f 73 74
* 1997 Jly Ayr (G-F) H 6f 74 75
* 1996 Jly Thirsk (FRM) H 6f 78 83
2000 Turf 0-1: (7f) (frm)
Above-average gelding, had worn blinkers. (DEAD)
**M Johnston [7-77] Mrs C Robinson.*

TILIA RR 32f 2539[11]

4 b m Primo Dominie 7.2f **(67)** - Bermuda Lily (Dunbeath (USA)) 7.8f **(70)**
Form - 00
Record 2000 - 1st:0 2nd:0 3rd:0 Ran:2
Pre2000 - 1st:0 2nd:0 3rd:0 Ran:11
2000 Turf 0-2: (5f, 6f) (gd, frm)
Scopey, very moderate filly, effective 6f, acts on gd, has worn blinkers (very effectively). Turf high 32. Consistent.
**R Hannon [0-13] Mrs W H GibsonFleming.*

TILLERMAN BHB 111f RR 114+f 3759[6]

4 b h In The Wings 11.2f **(77)** - Autumn Tint (USA) (Roberto (USA)) 10f **(76)**
Form - 35016
Record 2000 - 1st:1 2nd:0 3rd:1 Ran:5
Pre2000 - 1st:2 2nd:0 3rd:0 Ran:2
Win Prizemoney £96,525 *Total Prizemoney* £100,891
Wins * 2000 Jly Ascot (G-F) H 7f 103 114 <
* 1999 Oct Newmar (G-S) 8f 99

* 1999	Aug Lingfi	(G-F)	9f	84+

2000 Turf 1-5: (7f 1-3, 8f 2) (g-s, gd 1-3, g-f)

Scopey, Group-class colt, effective 7 to 8f, acts on gd. Turf high 114 - 1st of 24 giving 14lb to El Gran Papa (29 Jly Ascot RF 3202). He was heavily backed before the Royal Hunt Cup, but may not have stayed that stiff mile and finished fifth. Impressive when dropped back to seven furlongs for the valuable Tote International Handicap at Ascot in July, he is lightly raced and should make the transition to Group company this year.

**Mrs A J Perrett [3-7] K Abdulla.*

TIMAHS BHB 108f **RR 108f** 4131a[8]

Tillerman, impressive at Ascot

4 b h Mtoto 11.5f **(71)** - Shomoose (Habitat) 9.4f **(70)**

Form - 18

Record	**2000** -	1st:1	2nd:0	3rd:0	Ran:2
	Pre2000 -	1st:2	2nd:1	3rd:1	Ran:6

Win Prizemoney £182,050 — *Total Prizemoney* £197,384

Wins					
2000	Mar Kranji	(GD)	10f	105	
* 1999	Spt Doncas	(G-F)	10.3f	108	<
1998	Spt Newmar	(GD)	8f	93+	

2000 Turf 1-2: (10f 1-2) (gd 1-2)

Strong, Pattern-class colt, effective 10 to 12f, best at 10f, acts on gd to g-f, best on g-f. Turf high 105 (1st run) - 1st of 14 from Graf Philipp (5 Mar Kranji RF 0428a).

**S bin Suroor [1-5] (from S bin Suroor in UAE [1-1] Mar 2000).*

TIMBOROA **RR 117f** 3735a[5]

4 b h Salse (USA) 10.9f **(71)** - Kisumu (FR) (Damister (USA)) 9f **(73)**

Form - 15

2000 Turf 1-2: (8f, 10f 1-1) (gd 1-1, g-f)

High-class colt. Turf high 117 (1st run) - 1st of 9 from Crisos II Monaco (14 May Capannelle RF 1284a).

**A deRoyerDupre in FR [0-1] (from R Brogi in ITY [1-4] May 2000).*

TIME AND AGAIN BHB 27a **RR 18f** 4123[13]

4 ch m Timeless Times (USA) 6.1f **(56)** - Busted Love (Busted) 10.2f **(61)**

Form - 080

Record	**2000** -	1st:0	2nd:0	3rd:0	Ran:2
	Pre2000 -	1st:0	2nd:0	3rd:1	Ran:11

Win Prizemoney £0 — *Total Prizemoney* £461

2000 Turf 0-1: (8f) (frm) 2000 AW 0-1: (7f) (Fibr)

Workmanlike, poor filly. Becoming disappointing.

**D W Chapman [0-3] A Rhodes (from Mrs G S Rees [0-10] Oct 1999).*

TIME AWAY (IRE) **RR 80f** 4368[1]

2 b f Darshaan 11.9f **(81)** - Not Before Time (IRE) (Polish Precedent (USA)) 10.2f **(60)**

Form - 21

Record	**2000** -	1st:1	2nd:1	3rd:0	Ran:2

Win Prizemoney £4,231 — *Total Prizemoney* £5,731

Wins					
* **2000**	Spt Sandow	(G-F)	8.1f	78+	<

2000 Turf 1-2: (7f, 8f 1-1) (g-f, frm 1-1)

Currently decent filly. Turf high 80 (1st run) (began Aug) - 2nd of 12 to Karasta (25 Aug Newmarket 7f g-f RF 3963) - also 1st of 5 from Gay Heroine (13 Spt Sandown RF 4368). Found Karasta too good on her debut but made no mistake in a small field at Sandown. Could well make up into an Oaks filly.

**J L Dunlop [1-2] R Barnett.*

TIME BOMB BHB 47f **RR 58f** 5198[2]

3 b f Great Commotion (USA) 9.2f **(80)** - Play For Time (Comedy Star (USA)) 7.5f **(50)**

Form - 4006000002

Record	**2000** -	1st:0	2nd:1	3rd:0	Ran:10
	Pre2000 -	1st:0	2nd:0	3rd:0	Ran:1

Win Prizemoney £0 — *Total Prizemoney* £1,218

2000 Turf 0-10: (5f, 6f 4, 7f 3, 8f 2) (hvy, g-s, gd, g-f 5, frm 2)

Lengthy, fair filly. Turf high 58. **B R Millman [0-11] Wild Beef Racing.*

TIME CAN TELL BHB 42f50a **RR 38f 50a** 3192[10]

6 ch g Sylvan Express 9.6f **(45)** - Stellaris (Star Appeal) 9.6f **(65)**

Form - 450551342030

Record	**2000** -	1st:1	2nd:1	3rd:2	Ran:9
	Pre2000 -	1st:3	2nd:7	3rd:7	Ran:49

Win Prizemoney £9,535 — *Total Prizemoney* £21,610

Wins							
* **2000**	*Mar Southw*	*(STD)*	*H*	*16f*	*40*	*40*	
* 1999	*Apr Wolver*	*(STD)*	*H*	*16.2f*	*55*	*63*	
1998	*Jan Lingfi*	*(STD)*	*C*	*13f*		*69*	<
1996	Oct Nottin	(GD)	S	8.2f		62	

2000 Turf 0-1: (12f) (frm) 2000 AW 1-8: (14f, 16f 1-7) (Fibr 1-8)

Fair gelding, effective 13 to 16f, best at 16f, - acts on AW, best on Fibr, has worn blinkers, favours left handed tracks, favours tight tracks. AW high 51. Consistent.

**A G Juckes [2-23] A C W Price (from R T Juckes [0-8] Jun 1998).*

TIME FOR MUSIC (IRE) BHB 62f57a **RR 69f 57a** 4484[16]

3 b g Mukaddamah (USA) 7.6f **(74)** - Shrewd Girl (USA) (Sagace (FR)) 8f **(124)**

Form - 0000

Record	**2000** -	1st:0	2nd:0	3rd:0	Ran:4
	Pre2000 -	1st:1	2nd:2	3rd:0	Ran:5

Win Prizemoney £2,988 — *Total Prizemoney* £4,805

Wins						
* 1999	Aug Nottin	(G-F)	H	6.1f	77	80 <

2000 Turf 0-4: (5f, 6f, 8f 2) (g-s, g-f, frm 2)

Workmanlike, average gelding, effective 6 to 7f, acts on frm. Turf high 69 (began Aug). Consistent.

**T G Mills [1-9] Shipman Racing Ltd.*

TIME FOR THE CLAN BHB 35f **RR 39f** 5228[9]

3 ch g Clantime 6.6f **(57)** - Fyas (Sayf El Arab (USA)) 7.1f **(54)**

Form - 000006050008080

Record	**2000** -	1st:0	2nd:0	3rd:0	Ran:16
	Pre2000 -	1st:0	2nd:0	3rd:0	Ran:7

2000 Turf 0-16: (5f 4, 6f 3, 7f 2, 8f 4, 9f, 10f 2) (hvy, sft, g-s, gd 4, g-f 5, frm 2, hrd 2)

Leggy, very moderate gelding, effective 6f, acts on g-f, has worn blinkers. Turf high 39.

**R Bastiman [0-16] Mrs C B Bastiman (from J J O'Neill [0-7] Aug 1999).*

TIME IS MONEY (IRE) BHB 36f32a **RR 38df 32a** 3224[22]

8 br g Sizzling Melody 6.3f **(49)** - Tiempo (King of Spain) 7.8f **(52)**

Form - 000

Record	**2000** -	1st:0	2nd:0	3rd:0	Ran:3
	Pre2000 -	1st:0	2nd:1	3rd:2	Ran:18

Win Prizemoney £0 — *Total Prizemoney* £1,577

2000 Turf 0-2: (5f, 7f) (g-f, frm) 2000 AW 0-1: (7f) (Fibr)

Very moderate gelding, effective 7f, acts on frm, has worn blinkers. Turf high 5. Becoming disappointing.

**M H Tompkins [0-21] Camden Town Typesetters.*

TIMELESS CHICK BHB 52f38a **RR 51f 38a** 3898[10]

3 ch f Timeless Times (USA) 6.1f **(56)** - Be My Bird **(55f 42a)** (Be My Chief (USA))

Form - 0043751060

Record	**2000** -	1st:1	2nd:0	3rd:1	Ran:10

Pre2000 - 1st:0 2nd:0 3rd:0 Ran:5
Win Prizemoney £2,144 *Total Prizemoney* £2,427
Wins 2000 Jly Warwic (GD) SH 7.7f 47 51 <
2000 Turf 1-8: (7f, 8f 1-6, 10f) (gd 1-4, g-f, frm 2, hrd) 2000 AW 0-2: (8f, 9f) (Fibr 2)
Leggy, fair filly, effective 8f, acts on gd to g-f, often wears blinkers (very effectively), likes left handed tracks, likes tight tracks. Turf high 51 - also 1st of 19 getting 2lb from Red Cafe (7 Jly Warwick RF 2611). AW high 36.
**B A McMahon [0-3] G S D Imports Ltd (from Andrew Reid [1-12] Jly 2000).*

TIMELESS FARRIER BHB 65f69a RR 61f 69a 5013[4]
2 b g Timeless Times (USA) 6.1f **(56)** - Willrack Farrier **(60f 50a)** (Lugana Beach)
Form - 66774
Record 2000 - 1st:0 2nd:0 3rd:0 Ran:5
2000 Turf 0-4: (5f 4) (g-f 2, frm 2) 2000 AW 0-1: (6f) (Fibr)
Above-average gelding. Turf high 61. (1st run) - 4th of 9 to Moyne Pleasure (17 Oct Wolverhampton 6f Fibr RF 5013).
**B Smart [0-5] Willrackers.*

TIMELESS QUEST BHB 40f53a RR 38f 53a 1548[14]
3 ch f Timeless Times (USA) 6.1f **(56)** - Animate (IRE) (Tate Gallery (USA)) 7.4f **(67)**
Form - 000
Record 2000 - 1st:0 2nd:0 3rd:0 Ran:3
Pre2000 - 1st:0 2nd:1 3rd:0 Ran:5
Win Prizemoney £0 *Total Prizemoney* £590
2000 Turf 0-2: (6f, 8f) (gd, g-f) 2000 AW 0-1: (7f) (Fibr)
Workmanlike, average filly, effective 7f, - acts on Fibr, has worn blinkers, likes tight tracks. Turf high 27. Becoming disappointing.
**T J Etherington [0-8] G J Harris.*

TIME LOSS BHB 40f RR 48f 3696[11]
5 ch g Kenmare (FR) 9.6f **(76)** - Not Before Time (IRE) (Polish Precedent (USA)) 10.2f **(60)**
Form - 0540000
Record 2000 - 1st:0 2nd:0 3rd:0 Ran:7
Pre2000 - 1st:1 2nd:1 3rd:0 Ran:9
Win Prizemoney £3,566 *Total Prizemoney* £4,346
Wins 1998 Jun Chepst (G-S) 10.2f 82 <
2000 Turf 0-7: (9f, 10f 3, 11f, 12f, 14f) (g-s, gd 3, g-f, frm 2)
Moderate gelding, effective 11f, acts on g-f, has worn blinkers, favours tight tracks. Turf high 48. Becoming disappointing.
**J L Eyre [0-7] Black Combe Racing (from Mrs A Duffield [0-4] Spt 1999).*

TIME MAITE BHB 75f RR 78f 5081[1]
2 b g Komaite (USA) 6.9f **(61)** - Martini Time (Ardoon) 7.3f **(53)**
Form - 4313531301
Record 2000 - 1st:3 2nd:0 3rd:4 Ran:10
Win Prizemoney £9,508 *Total Prizemoney* £12,079
Wins * 2000 Oct Newcas (HVY) H 5f 68 78 <
*** 2000** Aug Haydoc (G-S) H 5f 63 68
*** 2000** May Newcas (GD) C 6f 63
2000 Turf 3-9: (5f 2-6, 6f 1-3) (hvy 1-1, g-s 2, gd 2-5, g-f) 2000 AW 0-1: (5f) (Fibr)
Above-average gelding, effective 5f, acts on hvy to gd. Turf high 78 - 1st of 16 giving 13lb to Patrician Fox (19 Oct Newcastle RF 5081). **M W Easterby [3-10] Tom Beston & Bernard Bargh.*

TIME MARCHES ON RR 5163[12]
2 b g Timeless Times (USA) 6.1f **(56)** - Tees Gazette Girl (Kalaglow) 9.8f **(67)**
Form - 0
Record 2000 - 1st:0 2nd:0 3rd:0 Ran:1
2000 Turf 0-1: (5f) (gd)
Currently very poor gelding. **Mrs M Reveley [0-1] Mrs M B Thwaites.*

TIME N TIME AGAIN BHB 85f RR 76f 4383[10]
2 b g Timeless Times (USA) 6.1f **(56)** - Primum Tempus **(42df)** (Primo Dominie) 6.2f **(80)**
Form - 10870
Record 2000 - 1st:1 2nd:0 3rd:0 Ran:5
Win Prizemoney £3,558 *Total Prizemoney* £3,558
Wins * 2000 Apr Hamilt (GD) 5f 71 <
2000 Turf 1-5: (5f 1-5) (gd 1-4, frm)
Above-average gelding. Turf high 76 - also 1st of 10 from Squirrel Nutkin (8 Apr Hamilton RF 0640).
**E J Alston [1-5] Springs Equestrian Ltd.*

TIME ON MY HANDS BHB 57a RR 28f 57a 1019[16]
4 b g Most Welcome 8.6f **(66)** - Zareeta (Free State) 8.7f **(61)**
Form - 8P02000060
Record 2000 - 1st:0 2nd:1 3rd:0 Ran:7
Pre2000 - 1st:1 2nd:0 3rd:1 Ran:15
Win Prizemoney £2,024 *Total Prizemoney* £2,893
Wins 1999 *May Southw (STD) C 8f 59* <
2000 Turf 0-3: (7f, 8f, 12f) (g-s, gd 2) 2000 AW 0-4: (8f, 12f 3) (Fibr 4)
Scopey, moderate gelding, effective 8f, - acts on Fibr, has worn blinkers. Turf high 28. AW high 44.
**S R Bowring [0-14] J Doxey (from C W Thornton [1-8] May 1999).*

TIME PROOF BHB 53f RR 53f 4553[12]
2 b g Clantime 6.6f **(57)** - Off Camera (Efisio)
Form - 700
Record 2000 - 1st:0 2nd:0 3rd:0 Ran:3
2000 Turf 0-3: (6f, 7f 2) (gd, frm 2)
Currently fair gelding. Turf high 53 (began Aug).
**R A Fahey [0-3] Mrs J Hazell.*

TIMES SQUARE BHB 84f RR 87f 4325[8]
2 b c Timeless Times (USA) 6.1f **(56)** - Alaskan Princess (IRE) **(49f)** (Prince Rupert (FR))
Form - 4317188
Record 2000 - 1st:2 2nd:0 3rd:1 Ran:7
Win Prizemoney £9,831 *Total Prizemoney* £10,621
Wins * 2000 Aug Newbur (G-F) H 7.3f 78 87 <
*** 2000** Jly Catter (G-F) 6f 73
2000 Turf 2-7: (5f 2, 6f 1-2, 7f 1-3) (g-s, g-f 4, frm 2-2)
Useful colt, effective 7f, acts on g-f to frm, has worn blinkers. Turf high 87 - 1st of 9 giving 12lb to Analyze (19 Aug Newbury RF 3792). Returned from a three-month break to scrape home at Catterick and added a Newbury nursery.
**G C H Chung [2-7] Ian Pattle.*

TIME TEMPTRESS BHB 48f50a RR 55f 50a 2923[2]
4 b m Timeless Times (USA) 6.1f **(56)** - Tangalooma (Hotfoot) 10.5f **(59)**
Form - 07822
Record 2000 - 1st:0 2nd:2 3rd:0 Ran:5
Pre2000 - 1st:1 2nd:1 3rd:2 Ran:17
Win Prizemoney £3,956 *Total Prizemoney* £7,892
Wins * 1999 May Newcas (G-F) H 8f 60 64 <
2000 Turf 0-3: (8f, 10f, 12f) (g-s, frm 2) 2000 AW 0-2: (8f 2) (Fibr 2)
Leggy, fair filly, effective 8 to 9f, best at 8f, acts on frm. Turf high 53. AW high 19. Inconsistent.
**G M Moore [1-22] Middleham Racing Bureau/G Heap.*

TIME TO FLY BHB 40f62a RR 42f 62a 5126[8]
7 b g Timeless Times (USA) 6.1f **(56)** - Dauntless Flight (Golden Mallard) 5.7f **(38)**
Form - 005040060008
Record 2000 - 1st:0 2nd:0 3rd:0 Ran:12
Pre2000 - 1st:6 2nd:6 3rd:4 Ran:47
Win Prizemoney £14,752 *Total Prizemoney* £23,600
Wins * 1999 *Apr Lingfi (STD) H 6f 65 66*
* 1998 *Jan Lingfi (STD) H 6f 68 72* <
* 1998 *Jan Wolver (STD) H 5f 52 70*
* 1998 *Jan Wolver (STD) H 6f 52 61*
* 1997 *Jun Southw (STD) H 6f 42 46*
* 1997 *Apr Wolver (STD) H 5f 32 43*
2000 Turf 0-12: (5f 8, 6f 3, 7f) (g-s 3, gd 3, g-f, frm 4, hrd)
Average gelding, effective 6f, - acts on Equi, often wears blinkers, likes left handed tracks, likes tight tracks. Turf high 42.
**B W Murray [6-59] B Murray.*

TIME TO REMEMBER (IRE) RR 74f 4193[6]
2 b c Pennekamp (USA) - Bequeath (USA) (Lyphard (USA)) 9.9f **(72)**
Form - 3146
Record 2000 - 1st:1 2nd:0 3rd:1 Ran:4
Win Prizemoney £3,575 *Total Prizemoney* £5,628
Wins * 2000 Aug Pontef (G-F) 6f 74+ <

2000 Turf 1-4: (6f 1-3, 7f) (gd, g-f, frm 1-2)
Above-average colt. Turf high 74 (began Jly) - 4th of 13 getting 17lb from Imperial Dancer (22 Aug York 7f gd RF 3855) - also 1st of 12 from Soldier Point (9 Aug Pontefract RF 3502).
**T D Easterby [1-4] Reg Griffin and Jim McGrath.*

TIME TO SKIP BHB 32f **RR 41f** 4054[16]
3 b f Timeless Times (USA) 6.1f **(56)** - North Pine (Import) 6.6f **(68)**
Form - 00
Record 2000 - 1st:0 2nd:0 3rd:0 Ran:2
Pre2000 - 1st:0 2nd:0 3rd:0 Ran:5
2000 Turf 0-2: (8f, 11f) (gd, g-f)
Unfurnished, moderate filly. (began Aug).
**A W Carroll [0-2] Miss D L Martin (from R Hannon [0-5] Spt 1999).*

TIME TO WYN BHB 40f41a **RR 42f 41a** 5195[4]
4 b g Timeless Times (USA) 6.1f **(56)** - Wyn-Bank (Green God) 9.6f **(68)**
Form - 00562
Record 2000 - 1st:0 2nd:1 3rd:0 Ran:5
Pre2000 - 1st:2 2nd:1 3rd:2 Ran:17
Win Prizemoney £5,030 *Total Prizemoney* £7,352
Wins * 1999 Jun Carlis (G-F) 8f 63 <
* 1998 Spt Beverl (G-F) SH 7.5f 52 57
2000 Turf 0-4: (8f 2, 9f, 11f) (sft, gd 2, g-f) 2000 AW 0-1: (8f) (Fibr)
Neat, moderate gelding, effective 8f, acts on frm to hrd, likes right handed tracks, likes tight tracks. Turf high 40 (began Aug). Inconsistent. **J G FitzGerald [2-22] Mike Browne.*

TIME VALLY BHB 67f **RR 73f** 5064[14]
3 ch f Timeless Times (USA) 6.1f **(56)** - Fort Vally **(47f)** (Belfort (FR)) 6.8f **(63)**
Form - 71055400
Record 2000 - 1st:1 2nd:0 3rd:0 Ran:8
Pre2000 - 1st:0 2nd:0 3rd:0 Ran:3
Win Prizemoney £7,182 *Total Prizemoney* £7,554
Wins * **2000** Jun Newmar (G-F) H 7f 64 73 <
2000 Turf 1-8: (7f 1-4, 8f 3, 9f) (sft, g-f 4, frm 1-3)
Workmanlike, above-average filly, effective 7 to 8f, acts on frm. Turf high 73 - 1st of 8 getting 1lb from Sangra (11 Jun Newmarket RF 1883). She scored at Newmarket in June and has continued to run with credit. She stays a mile. **S Dow [1-11] Mrs M Lingwood.*

TIMI RR 107f 4847a[12]
3 f b Alzao (USA) 9.8f **(73)** - Timiram (IRE) (Runnett) 7f **(59)**
Form - 210
2000 Turf 1-3: (8f, 10f, 11f 1-1) (sft, gd 1-2)
Pattern-class. Turf high 107 (1st run) - 2nd of 18 to Xua (30 Apr Capannelle 8f sft RF 1031a) - also 1st of 18 from Polar Charge (21 May San Siro RF 1455a). **L Brogi in ITY [2-4].*

TIMIDJAR (IRE) BHB 50f **RR 72f** 21[10]
7 b g Doyoun 10.7f **(69)** - Timissara (USA) (Shahrastani (USA)) 8.8f **(72)**
Form - 0
Record 2000 - 1st:0 2nd:0 3rd:0 Ran:1
Pre2000 - 1st:2 2nd:0 3rd:0 Ran:5
Win Prizemoney £6,378 *Total Prizemoney* £6,378
Wins 1996 Jly Killar (GD) H 11f 77 72+ <
1996 Jly Roscom (G-F) H 12f 72 68
2000 AW 0-1: (12f) (Fibr)
Above-average gelding, has worn blinkers.
**D Burchell [0-3] Three Acres Racing (from J Oxx in IRE [2-5] Jly 1996).*

TIMOTE (IRE) RR 106f 1926a[7]
4 ch m Indian Ridge 7.6f **(74)** - Across the Ice (USA) (General Holme (USA)) 5.7f **(63)**
Form - 557
2000 Turf 0-3: (5f, 6f 2) (g-s 2, gd)
Pattern-class filly, effective 5 to 6f, best at 5f, acts on g-s to frm, has worn blinkers, excels at Curragh. Turf high 100 - 5th of 9 getting 3lb from Namid (27 May Curragh 6f g-s RF 1575a). Developed into a high-class sprinter in '99, but did not fire in a limited campaign last year. **D K Weld in IRE [3-14] Michael Smurfit.*

TINA'S ROYALE BHB 25f **RR 31f** 4398[16]
4 b m Prince Sabo 6.6f **(64)** - Aventina (Averof) 8.2f **(62)**

Form - 500000060
Record 2000 - 1st:0 2nd:0 3rd:0 Ran:9
Pre2000 - 1st:0 2nd:1 3rd:2 Ran:12
Win Prizemoney £0 *Total Prizemoney* £2,687
2000 Turf 0-8: (5f 3, 6f 5) (gd, g-f 3, frm 3, hrd) 2000 AW 0-1: (6f) (Fibr)
Neat, very moderate filly, effective 5f, acts on g-f. Turf high 35.
**J Pearce [0-9] Jeff Pearce (from H Candy [0-12] Oct 1999).*

TING (IRE) BHB 57f50a **RR 51f 50a** 4474[5]
3 b g Magical Wonder (USA) 7.2f **(60)** - Rozmiyn (Caerleon (USA)) 8.6f **(71)**
Form - 54605
Record 2000 - 1st:0 2nd:0 3rd:0 Ran:4
Pre2000 - 1st:0 2nd:0 3rd:0 Ran:4
Win Prizemoney £0 *Total Prizemoney* £250
2000 AW 0 4: (7f, 8f 3) (Equi, Fibr 3)
Leggy, fair gelding. AW high 50. **P C Haslam [0-8] Mrs S V Milner.*

TINKERS CLOUGH (IRE) BHB 25f **RR** 2778[9]
3 b g Never so Bold 7.1f **(62)** - Swivel **(72f)** (Salse (USA)) 7.5f **(66)**
Form - 800
Record 2000 - 1st:0 2nd:0 3rd:0 Ran:3
2000 Turf 0-1: (10f) (gd) 2000 AW 0-2: (6f, 9f) (Fibr 2)
Currently very poor gelding. **A Senior [0-3] A Senior.*

TINKER'S SURPRISE (IRE) BHB 40f39a **RR 42f 39a** 410[4]
6 b g Cyrano de Bergerac 7.3f **(58)** - Lils Fairy (Fairy King (USA)) 7.7f **(59)**
Form - 06536564
Record 2000 - 1st:0 2nd:0 3rd:1 Ran:6
Pre2000 - 1st:2 2nd:7 3rd:4 Ran:51
Win Prizemoney £6,235 *Total Prizemoney* £14,192
Wins * 1999 *Jan Wolver (STD) H 5f 46 51*
1996 Jun Goodwo (G-F) S 5f 69 <
2000 AW 0-6: (5f 5, 6f) (Fibr 6)
Moderate gelding, effective 5f, - acts on Fibr, often wears blinkers (effectively), likes left handed tracks, likes tight tracks. AW high 43.
**J Balding [1-46] Classic Racing (from B J Meehan [1-11] Spt 1996).*

TINSEL MOON (IRE) RR 93f 4528a[5]
3 b f River Falls 8.2f **(56)** - Fordes Cross (Ya Zaman (USA))
Form - 642225
2000 Turf 0-6: (9f 2, 10f 3, 12f) (g-s 2, gd 2, frm)
Useful filly. Turf high 93. **C Collins in IRE [0-6] Mrs Riddell Martin.*

TINSEL WHISTLE BHB 65f **RR 66f** 2934[7]
3 b c Piccolo - Pewter Lass **(24f)** (Dowsing (USA))
Form - 0667
Record 2000 - 1st:0 2nd:0 3rd:0 Ran:4
Pre2000 - 1st:2 2nd:1 3rd:1 Ran:10
Win Prizemoney £3,940 *Total Prizemoney* £5,472
Wins * 1999 Jly Yarmou (FRM) S 6f 74 <
* 1999 Jun Yarmou (G-F) S 5.2f 72
2000 Turf 0-4: (6f 4) (g-f, frm 3)
Neat, average colt, effective 5 to 6f, best at 6f, acts on g-f to frm, best on g-f, has worn blinkers. Turf high 66. Inconsistent.
**M A Jarvis [2-14] Yusof Sepiuddin.*

TINY MIND BHB 19f **RR** 4044[11]
2 b g Factual (USA) - Lady Louise (IRE) (Lord Americo)
Form - 07080
Record 2000 - 1st:0 2nd:0 3rd:0 Ran:5
2000 Turf 0-3: (6f 2, 8f) (g-s 2, hrd) 2000 AW 0-2: (5f, 6f) (Fibr 2)
Formerly very poor gelding, has worn blinkers.
**Miss A Stokell [0-5] A Saccomando.*

TINY TIM (IRE) BHB 60f **RR 62f** 4728[17]
2 b g Brief Truce (USA) 9.1f **(73)** - Nonnita (Welsh Saint) 7.6f **(64)**
Form - 6480
Record 2000 - 1st:0 2nd:0 3rd:0 Ran:4
2000 Turf 0-4: (6f, 7f 3) (gd, g-f, frm, hrd)
Average gelding. Turf high 62 (began Jly).
**I A Balding [0-4] D H Caslon.*

TIPPERARY SUNSET (IRE) BHB 62f57a **RR 63f 57a** 5165[16]
6 gr g Red Sunset 9f **(57)** - Chapter And Verse (Dancers Image (USA))

9.3f **(71)**
Form - 072366541400
Record 2000 - 1st:1 2nd:1 3rd:1 Ran:12
Pre2000 - 1st:6 2nd:4 3rd:7 Ran:40
Win Prizemoney £26,119 *Total Prizemoney* £40,057
Wins * **2000** Aug Beverl (FRM) H 7.5f 59 62
1999 Jun Beverl (GD) H 7.5f 61 64 <
1998 Aug Hamilt (SFT) H 8.3f 54 55
1997 Nov Doncas (G-S) H 8f 56 64 <
1997 Oct Newmar (G-F) H 9f 54 58
1997 Aug Ripon (G-F) H 10f 41 48
1997 Aug Pontef (G-F) H 8f 35 44
2000 Turf 1-12: (7f 1-5, 8f 7) (sft, gd 6, frm 1-3, hrd 2)
Average gelding, effective 7 to 8f, best at 8f, acts on gd to frm, best on gd, has worn blinkers (effectively), excels at Leicester, likes Beverley. Turf high 63 - 4th of 20 giving 6lb to Unchain My Heart (5 Spt Leicester 7f frm RF 4217) - also 1st of 14 getting 2lb from Calcavella (26 Aug Beverley RF 3977). Consistent. He is hard to win with.
**D Shaw [1-12] Harold Bray (from J J Quinn [6-41] Nov 1999).*

TIP THE SCALES BHB 62f **RR 61f** 3559[2]
2 b g Dancing Spree (USA) 8f **(59)** - Keen Melody (USA) (Sharpen Up) 8.3f **(67)**
Form - 0572
Record 2000 - 1st:0 2nd:1 3rd:0 Ran:4
Win Prizemoney £0 *Total Prizemoney* £1,060
2000 Turf 0-4: (6f, 7f 3) (gd, g-f, frm 2)
Average gelding, often wears blinkers. Turf high 61 - 2nd of 7 to Chauntry Gold (11 Aug Newmarket 7f frm RF 3559).
**R M Whitaker [0-4] G F Pemberton.*

TIRANA (IRE) BHB 49a **RR 34f** 5115[4]
2 b c Brief Truce (USA) 9.1f **(73)** - Cloche du Roi (FR) (Fairy King (USA)) 7.7f **(59)**
Form - 0074
Record 2000 - 1st:0 2nd:0 3rd:0 Ran:4
2000 Turf 0-3: (5f, 6f 2) (gd, g-f 2) 2000 AW 0-1: (8f) (Fibr)
Fair colt. Turf high 34. (1st run) - 4th of 13 getting 14lb from Forum Finale (20 Oct Wolverhampton 8f Fibr RF 5115).
**D Shaw [0-4] J C Fretwell.*

TISSALY BHB 82f **RR 79f** 4377[6]
2 b f Pennekamp (USA) - Island Ruler (Ile de Bourbon (USA)) 10.1f **(67)**
Form - 236
Record 2000 - 1st:0 2nd:1 3rd:1 Ran:3
Win Prizemoney £0 *Total Prizemoney* £2,726
2000 Turf 0-3: (5f, 6f, 7f) (gd, g-f, frm)
Currently above-average filly. Turf high 79 (1st run) (began Jly) - 2nd of 6 getting 6lb from Dance On (31 Jly Yarmouth 5f gd RF 3262). **C E Brittain [0-3] Saeed Manana.*

TISSIFER BHB 94f **RR 105f** 4647[9]
4 b g Polish Precedent (USA) 9f **(73)** - Ingozi **(74f)** (Warning)
Form - 220040330
Record 2000 - 1st:0 2nd:2 3rd:2 Ran:9
Pre2000 - 1st:3 2nd:2 3rd:0 Ran:8
Win Prizemoney £17,960 *Total Prizemoney* £35,737
Wins * 1999 Apr Thirsk (GD) 8f 112+ <
* 1998 Spt Kempto (SFT) 7f 82
* 1998 Aug Epsom (G-F) 6f 81+
2000 Turf 0-9: (7f, 8f 3, 10f 4, 12f) (g-s, gd 5, g-f 3)
Unfurnished, Pattern-class gelding, effective 8 to 10f, best at 10f, acts on gd to frm, best on gd, has worn blinkers, likes left handed tracks. Turf high 105 - 2nd of 6 getting 7lb from King Adam (10 Jun Doncaster 10f gd RF 1870). He ran pretty well in a couple of conditions events early on in the season, but basically falls between handicap and Pattern company and is proving difficult to place.
**M Johnston [3-17] M P Burke.*

TITAN BHB 38f34a **RR 38f 34a** 3526[5]
5 b g Lion Cavern (USA) 7.5f **(74)** - Sutosky (Great Nephew) 9.9f **(64)**
Form - 607005005
Record 2000 - 1st:0 2nd:0 3rd:0 Ran:7
Pre2000 - 1st:1 2nd:3 3rd:1 Ran:25
Win Prizemoney £4,110 *Total Prizemoney* £8,603
Wins 1997 Spt Goodwo (GD) H 7f 74 76 <
2000 Turf 0-4: (7f 2, 8f 2) (sft, gd 2, frm) 2000 AW 0-3: (7f, 8f 2) (Equi 3)
Very moderate gelding, effective 8f, acts on gd, likes left handed tracks, likes tight tracks. Turf high 38. AW high 30. Inconsistent.
**M P Muggeridge [0-1] The Titanic Partnership (from N E Berry [0-8] Jly 2000).*

TITAN LAD BHB 20f **RR 27f** 3955[12]
3 b g Puissance 7.1f **(60)** - Sister Sal (Bairn (USA)) 7.7f **(59)**
Form - 0070
Record 2000 - 1st:0 2nd:0 3rd:0 Ran:4
Pre2000 - 1st:0 2nd:0 3rd:0 Ran:6
2000 Turf 0-4: (7f, 10f, 12f 2) (gd, g-f, frm, hrd)
Workmanlike, very moderate gelding. Turf high 27.
**G A Ham [0-10] The Smudge Racing Partnership.*

TITIAN ANGEL (IRE) BHB 72f **RR 86?f** 1468[4]
3 ch f Brief Truce (USA) 9.1f **(73)** - Kuwah (IRE) (Be My Guest (USA)) 9.3f **(67)**
Form - 674
Record 2000 - 1st:0 2nd:0 3rd:0 Ran:3
Pre2000 - 1st:0 2nd:1 3rd:0 Ran:1
Win Prizemoney £0 *Total Prizemoney* £1,358
2000 Turf 0-3: (10f 2, 12f) (sft, g-s, frm)
Scopey, useful filly. Turf high 86. **C N Allen [0-4] Conrad's Angels.*

TITUS BRAMBLE BHB 45f **RR 43f** 3955[5]
3 b g Puissance 7.1f **(60)** - Norska (Northfields (USA)) 9f **(72)**
Form - 000681415
Record 2000 - 1st:2 2nd:0 3rd:0 Ran:9
Pre2000 - 1st:0 2nd:0 3rd:0 Ran:5
Win Prizemoney £3,773 *Total Prizemoney* £3,988
Wins * **2000** Aug Windso (GD) S 11.6f 43 <
* **2000** Jly Yarmou (GD) S 10.1f 42
2000 Turf 2-8: (8f, 10f 1-3, 12f 1-4) (g-s, gd, g-f 2-2, frm 3, hrd) 2000 AW 0-1: (12f) (Equi)
Leggy, moderate gelding, has worn blinkers, likes tight tracks. Turf high 51. **B R Millman [2-14] Henry Rix.*

TIYE BHB 35f **RR 27f** 3807[8]
5 b m Salse (USA) 10.9f **(71)** - Kiya (USA) (Dominion) 8.5f **(63)**
Form - 08
Record 2000 - 1st:0 2nd:0 3rd:0 Ran:2
Pre2000 - 1st:0 2nd:1 3rd:1 Ran:8
Win Prizemoney £0 *Total Prizemoney* £1,491
2000 Turf 0-1: (10f) (g-f) 2000 AW 0-1: (12f) (Fibr)
Little account filly, has worn blinkers. Becoming disappointing.
**D L Williams [0-11] P F Moore (from R Hannon [0-5] May 1998).*

TIYOUN (IRE) BHB 83f **RR 84f** 4818[4]
2 b g Kahyasi 12.9f **(74)** - Taysala (IRE) (Akarad (FR)) 9f **(76)**
Form - 3214
Record 2000 - 1st:1 2nd:1 3rd:1 Ran:4
Win Prizemoney £3,965 *Total Prizemoney* £6,021
Wins * **2000** Spt Pontef (G-S) 8f 84 <
2000 Turf 1-4: (8f 1-4) (g-s, gd 1-2, hrd)
Decent gelding. Turf high 84 (began Aug) - 1st of 12 from Mr Combustible (21 Spt Pontefract RF 4557).
**D W Barker [1-4] Miss Sharon Long.*

TIZNOW (USA) **RR 129a** 5332a[1]
3 b c Cee's Tizzy (USA) - Cee's Song (USA) (Seattle Slew (USA)) 9.4f **(76)**
Form - 1
2000 AW 1-1: (10f 1-1) (Dirt 1-1)
Currently top-class colt. (1st run) - 1st of 13 from Giant's Causeway (4 Nov Churchill Downs RF 5332a). Came out best after a titanic struggle with Giant's Causeway in the Breeders Cup Classic at Churchill Downs.
**J M Robbins in USA [1-1] Michael Cooper & Cecilia Straub Rubens.*

TOBARANAMA (IRE) **RR 95f** 5043a[4]
3 b f Sadler's Wells (USA) 11.3f **(87)** - Ridge The Times (USA) (Riva Ridge (USA)) 8.2f **(68)**
Form - 145034
2000 Turf 1-6: (9f 1-2, 10f, 12f 2, 14f) (sft 1-2, g-s, gd 3)
Very useful filly, effective 9 to 12f, acts on sft to gd, has worn

blinkers. Turf high 95 - 3rd of 9 getting 10lb from Dolydille (30 Spt Curragh 10f gd RF 4796a). Just below Listed class, she stays a mile and a half but is difficult to place.
**D K Weld in IRE [1-7] Ballylinch Stud.*

TOBLERSONG BHB 40f56a **RR 39f 56a** 4378[14]
5 b g Tirol 8.1f **(64)** - Winsong Melody (Music Maestro) 7.7f **(66)**
Form - 4006442040300
Record 2000 - 1st:0 2nd:1 3rd:1 Ran:13
Pre2000 - 1st:2 2nd:4 3rd:1 Ran:29
Win Prizemoney £7,805 *Total Prizemoney* £16,789
Wins 1997 Oct Yarmou (GD) 6f 93 <
1997 Jly Epsom (SFT) 6f 77+
2000 Turf 0-13: (6f 3, 7f 5, 8f 5) (sft, g-s, gd 2, g-f 2, frm 6, hrd)
Moderate gelding, effective 6 to 8f, best at 7f, acts on gd to hrd, best on g-f, has worn blinkers, likes left handed tracks, likes tight tracks. Turf high 49.
**Mrs L Stubbs [0-13] Mrs Mary Wooltorton (from C A Dwyer [0-20] Oct 1999).*

TOBOUGG (IRE) **RR 115+f** 4988[1]
2 b c Barathea (IRE) - Lacovia (USA) (Majestic Light (USA)) 10.6f **(75)**
Form - 111
Record 2000 - 1st:3 2nd:0 3rd:0 Ran:3
Win Prizemoney £169,618 *Total Prizemoney* £169,618
Wins * 2000 Oct Newmar (G-S) G1 7f 115+ <
* 2000 Spt Longch (G-S) G1 7f 115+ <
* 2000 Aug York (GD) 7f 92+
2000 Turf 3-3: (7f 3-3) (gd 3-3)
Currently high-class colt. Turf high 115 (began Aug) - 1st of 10 from Noverre (14 Oct Newmarket RF 4988) - also 1st of 4 from Honours List (16 Spt Longchamp RF 4566a). A handsome individual, he recovered well from a sluggish start to make a successful debut and went on to record a Group 1 double in the Prix de la Salamandre and Dewhurst Stakes. A fine mover, he was awarded third spot among European juveniles on the International Classifications and is currently quoted second favourite behind Nayef for the 2000 Guineas. Out of the 1986 French Oaks winner Lacovia, he should stay 10 furlongs but is not short of pace and seems certain to give a good account of himself in the first colts' Classic.
**M R Channon [3-3] Sheikh Ahmod Al Maktoum.*

TOBY GRIMES (IRE) BHB 35f **RR 44f** 4584[10]
3 ch g Forest Wind (USA) - Emma Grimes (IRE) **(39f)** (Nordico (USA))

Tobougg, prominent in the 2000 Guineas betting

6.5f **(62)**
Form - 00
Record 2000 - 1st:0 2nd:0 3rd:0 Ran:2
Pre2000 - 1st:0 2nd:0 3rd:0 Ran:3
2000 Turf 0-1: (11f) (gd) 2000 AW 0-1: (10f) (Equi)
Leggy, moderate gelding. **J S Moore [0-5] J K Grimes.*

TOBYTOO BHB 32f **RR 28f** 5228[11]
2 b c Perpendicular - Mostimus (Doulab (USA)) 9.8f **(65)**
Form - 00000000
Record 2000 - 1st:0 2nd:0 3rd:0 Ran:8
2000 Turf 0-7: (6f 3, 7f 3, 8f) (gd 2, g-f 2, frm 3) 2000 AW 0-1: (5f) (Fibr)
Little account colt, has worn blinkers. Turf high 28.
**C Smith [0-8] A E Moss.*

TODAYS MAN **RR** 3130[5]
3 b g Bigstone (IRE) - Snowgirl (IRE) (Mazaad) 7.1f **(45)**
Form - 5
Record 2000 - 1st:0 2nd:0 3rd:0 Ran:1
2000 Turf 0-1: (14f) (frm)
Workmanlike, currently very poor gelding.
**Mrs Dianne Sayer [0-1] A Slack.*

TOEJAM BHB 38f **RR 36f** 3683[9]
7 ch g Move Off - Cheeky Pigeon (Brave Invader (USA))
Form - 70150460
Record 2000 - 1st:1 2nd:0 3rd:0 Ran:8
Pre2000 - 1st:0 2nd:0 3rd:0 Ran:6
Win Prizemoney £1,848 *Total Prizemoney* £2,489
Wins * 2000 Jun Redcar (FRM) H 8f 30 42 <
2000 Turf 1-8: (7f 2, 8f 1-3, 10f 3) (gd, g-f 4, frm 1-3)
Very moderate gelding, has worn blinkers. Turf high 42. Consistent. **R E Barr [1-15] Mrs R E Barr.*

TOFFEE NOSED **RR 79f** 5236[2]
2 ch f Selkirk (USA) 7.9f **(76)** - Ever Welcome (Be My Guest (USA)) 9.3f **(67)**
Form - 42
Record 2000 - 1st:0 2nd:1 3rd:0 Ran:2
Win Prizemoney £0 *Total Prizemoney* £1,807
2000 Turf 0-2: (7f 2) (g-s, g-f)
Currently above-average filly. Turf high 79 (began Spt) - 2nd of 22 to Good Standing (28 Oct Newmarket 7f g-s RF 5236).
**B W Hills [0-2] W J Gredley.*

TOKEN BHB 77f **RR 80f** 5218[10]
2 b c Mark of Esteem (IRE) - Kindergarten (Trempolino (USA)) 12f **(71)**
Form - 8430
Record 2000 - 1st:0 2nd:0 3rd:1 Ran:4
Win Prizemoney £0 *Total Prizemoney* £826
2000 Turf 0-4: (7f 2, 8f 2) (sft, g-s 2, frm)
Decent colt. Turf high 80 (began Aug).
**M P Tregoning [0-4] Sheikh Mohammed.*

TOLDYA BHB 68f65a **RR 68f 65a** 5313[6]
3 b f Beveled (USA) 6.9f **(64)** - Run Amber Run (Run The Gantlet (USA)) 12.1f **(59)**
Form - 22432132416
Record 2000 - 1st:2 2nd:3 3rd:2 Ran:10
Pre2000 - 1st:0 2nd:1 3rd:0 Ran:4
Win Prizemoney £6,107 *Total Prizemoney* £10,519
Wins * 2000 Oct Lingfi (SFT) H 6f 62 68 <
2000 *Feb Lingfi (STD) H 5f 55 60*
2000 Turf 1-4: (5f 2, 6f 1-2) (g-s 1-2, gd, frm) 2000 AW 1-6: (5f 1-3, 6f 2, 7f) (Equi 1-5, Fibr)
Neat, average filly, effective 5 to 6f, best at 6f, acts on g-s to frm - acts on Equi, has worn blinkers. Turf high 68 (began Aug) - 1st of 19 giving 1lb to Cryfield (4 Oct Lingfield RF 4809). AW high 60 - 1st of 8 getting 7lb from Pips Star (16 Feb Lingfield RF 0292).
**M Kettle [1-4] G Montgomery (from E A Wheeler [1-10] Feb 2000).*

TOLERATION BHB 76f **RR 81f** 3446[12]
3 b f Petong 7.6f **(58)** - Dancing Chimes (London Bells (CAN)) 5.8f **(53)**
Form - 000
Record 2000 - 1st:0 2nd:0 3rd:0 Ran:3
Pre2000 - 1st:1 2nd:0 3rd:0 Ran:2
Win Prizemoney £3,403 *Total Prizemoney* £3,753
Wins * 1999 Oct Windso (G-S) 6f 81 <
2000 Turf 0-3: (5f, 6f 2) (gd, g-f, frm)
Leggy, decent filly. Turf high 81.
**D R C Elsworth [1-5] Miss Juliet Reed.*

TOLSTOY BHB 79f **RR 89df** 4624[2]
3 b c Nashwan (USA) 10.3f **(79)** - Millazure (USA) **(62f)** (Dayjur (USA))
Form - 522222
Record 2000 - 1st:0 2nd:5 3rd:0 Ran:6
Pre2000 - 1st:0 2nd:2 3rd:0 Ran:2
Win Prizemoney £0 *Total Prizemoney* £9,856
2000 Turf 0-6: (8f, 10f 4, 12f) (gd, g-f, frm 4)
Well made, useful colt, effective 8 to 10f, best at 8f, acts on gd to

frm, best on frm, likes tight tracks. Turf high 89 - 2nd of 17 giving 5lb to Jalisco (5 Spt Leicester 10f frm RF 4216). A professional bridesmaid and is not one to trust.
**Sir Michael Stoute [0-8] Mrs John Magnier & M Tabor.*

TOMAMIE BHB 39f **RR 38f** 3628[9]
2 b f Tina's Pet 7.4f **(56)** - Springhead **(56df)** (Komaite (USA))
Form - 870000
Record 2000 - 1st:0 2nd:0 3rd:0 Ran:6
2000 Turf 0-5: (5f 3, 7f 2) (hvy, g-s, gd, frm 2) 2000 AW 0-1: (5f) (Fibr)
Very moderate filly. Turf high 38.
**J Norton [0-6] G A Hancock & A Parsonage.*

TOMASINO BHB 81f **RR 82f** 5080[1]
2 br c Celtic Swing - Bustinetta (Bustino) 10.4f **(64)**
Form - 461
Record 2000 - 1st:1 2nd:0 3rd:0 Ran:3
Win Prizemoney £3,435 *Total Prizemoney* £3,757
Wins * 2000 Oct Newcas (HVY) 8f 72 <
2000 Turf 1-3: (8f 1-3) (hvy 1-1, g-s, gd)
Currently decent colt. Turf high 82 (1st run) (began Spt) - 4th of 6 getting 12lb from Harrier (16 Spt Ayr 8f gd RF 4447).
**M Johnston [1-3] P D Savill.*

TOMASZEWSKI (FR) BHB 50f **RR 55f** 4205[15]
5 b g Polish Precedent (USA) 9f **(73)** - Circus Plume (High Top) 10.2f **(67)**
Form - 7650
Record 2000 - 1st:0 2nd:0 3rd:0 Ran:4
Pre2000 - 1st:0 2nd:0 3rd:0 Ran:3
2000 Turf 0-4: (10f, 11f, 13f, 14f) (gd 2, frm 2)
Fair gelding. Turf high 55. **P W Harris [0-7] Mrs P W Harris.*

TOMBA BHB 114f **RR 116f** 5095a[7]
6 ch h Efisio 7.7f **(69)** - Indian Love Song (Be My Guest (USA)) 9.3f **(67)**
Form - 27350387
Record 2000 - 1st:0 2nd:1 3rd:2 Ran:8
Pre2000 - 1st:13 2nd:4 3rd:5 Ran:37
Win Prizemoney £242,208 *Total Prizemoney* £357,260

Wins								
	1999	Oct Munich	(SFT)	G3	6.5f		107	
	1999	Jly Haydoc	(G-S)		6f		113	
	1998	Oct Longch	(HVY)	G1	7f		118	<
	1998	Oct Munich	(SFT)	G3	6.5f		115	
	1998	Jun Ascot	(SFT)	G2	6f		117	
	1997	Aug Hoppeg	(GD)	G3	6.5f		111	
	1997	Jun Newcas	(HVY)	L	6f		115	
	1997	May Haydoc	(G-S)	LH	6f	109	109	
	1997	May Newbur	(G-S)		6f		107	
	1997	May Haydoc	(SFT)		6f		98	
	1996	Nov Evry	(HLD)	L	6f		104	
	1996	Oct Salisb	(G-S)		6f		106	
	1996	Aug Epsom	(GD)		6f		80	

2000 Turf 0-8: (6f 6, 7f 2) (hvy, sft, g-s 4, g-f 2)
High-class horse, effective 6 to 7f, best at 6f, acts on sft to frm, has worn blinkers, excels at Haydock. Turf high 116 - 3rd of 13 giving 3lb to Pipalong (2 Spt Haydock 6f g-s RF 4157). He revels in the mud and had ideal conditions when finishing third in the Group One Stanley Leisure Sprint Cup at Haydock in September. Mainly disappointing apart from that effort, he is usually outpaced and needs strong driving.
**M A Jarvis [0-8] (from B J Meehan [13-37] Oct 1999).*

TOM DOUGAL BHB 65f **RR 70f** 4626[7]
5 b h Ron's Victory (USA) 9.2f **(52)** - Fabulous Rina (FR) (Fabulous Dancer (USA)) 9.4f **(70)**
Form - 085007
Record 2000 - 1st:0 2nd:0 3rd:0 Ran:6
Pre2000 - 1st:3 2nd:2 3rd:2 Ran:26
Win Prizemoney £31,638 *Total Prizemoney* £43,458

Wins								
	* 1999	May Ayr	(GD)		8f		86	
	* 1998	May York	(GD)	H	7.9f	83	90+	<
	* 1998	May Newmar	(GD)	H	8f	75	86	

2000 Turf 0-6: (8f 6) (g-s, gd 2, g-f 2, frm)
Above-average colt, effective 8 to 9f, best at 8f, acts on gd to frm, best on gd, prefers left handed tracks. Turf high 70. He is able but has a moderate strike rate. **C Smith [3-32] Mrs N Stewart.*

TOMENOSO RR 60f 3809[10]
2 b c Teenoso (USA) 10.5f **(62)** - Guarded Expression **(45f)** (Siberian Express (USA)) 8.8f **(65)**
Form - 70
Record 2000 - 1st:0 2nd:0 3rd:0 Ran:2
2000 Turf 0-1: (7f) (g-f) 2000 AW 0-1: (6f) (Fibr)
Currently average colt. **W G M Turner [0-2] D & J Racing.*

TOMMY CARSON BHB 40f **RR 52f** 4306[14]
5 b g Last Tycoon 9.4f **(73)** - Ivory Palm (USA) (Sir Ivor) 10.2f **(70)**
Form - 625040680
Record 2000 - 1st:0 2nd:1 3rd:0 Ran:9
Pre2000 - 1st:0 2nd:2 3rd:3 Ran:8
Win Prizemoney £0 *Total Prizemoney* £3,901
2000 Turf 0-9: (11f, 12f 6, 13f, 14f) (gd 2, g-f 4, frm 3)
Fair gelding, often wears blinkers. Turf high 52.
**J R Poulton [0-19] J Logan (from D R C Elsworth [0-11] Aug 1999).*

TOMMY LORNE BHB 73f **RR 76f** 5312[7]
2 b c Inchinor 8.9f **(64)** - Actress (Known Fact (USA)) 7.4f **(67)**
Form - 637
Record 2000 - 1st:0 2nd:0 3rd:1 Ran:3
Win Prizemoney £0 *Total Prizemoney* £600
2000 Turf 0-3: (7f, 8f 2) (g-s, gd, g-f)
Currently above-average colt. Turf high 76 (began Aug).
**J L Dunlop [0-3] J L Dunlop.*

TOMMY SMITH BHB 56f **RR 60f** 4182[11]
2 ch g Timeless Times (USA) 6.1f **(56)** - Superstream (Superpower)
Form - 784116500
Record 2000 - 1st:2 2nd:0 3rd:0 Ran:9
Win Prizemoney £4,767 *Total Prizemoney* £4,767

Wins							
	* 2000	Jly Hamilt	(G-F)	S	6f	60	<
	* 2000	Jun Mussel	(FRM)	S	5f	60	<

2000 Turf 2-9: (5f 1-7, 6f 1-2) (g-s, gd 2, g-f 1-1, frm 1-4, hrd)
Average gelding, effective 5 to 6f, acts on g-f to frm, has worn blinkers. Turf high 60 - 1st of 6 giving 5lb to Italian Affair (26 Jun Musselburgh RF 2269) - also 1st of 4 giving 11lb to Miss Equinox (4 Jly Hamilton RF 2494). **J S Wainwright [2-9] T W Heseltine.*

TOM'S DEAL RR 4111[4]
6 ch m Broadsword (USA) - Darrington Deal (Rymer)
Form - 4
Record 2000 - 1st:0 2nd:0 3rd:0 Ran:1
Win Prizemoney £0 *Total Prizemoney* £222
2000 Turf 0-1: (11f) (frm)
Formerly very poor mare. **G Prodromou [0-4] K J Walls.*

TOM TAILOR (GER) RR 54f 4692[10]
6 b g Beldale Flutter (USA) 10.2f **(62)** - Thoughtful (Northfields (USA)) 9f **(72)**
Form - 0
Record 2000 - 1st:0 2nd:0 3rd:0 Ran:1
Pre2000 - 1st:2 2nd:2 3rd:1 Ran:20
Win Prizemoney £10,260 *Total Prizemoney* £14,038

Wins								
	* 1999	Jly Sandow	(G-F)	H	16.4f	55	58	
	* 1997	May Windso	(SFT)		10f		74	<

2000 Turf 0-1: (14f) (gd)
Fair gelding, effective 12 to 16f, best at 16f, acts on gd to frm, best on g-f, favours tight tracks. Consistent.
**D R C Elsworth [4-31] The A A Partnership.*

TOMTHEVIC BHB 81f **RR 80f** 3995[1]
2 ch g Emarati (USA) 6.6f **(63)** - Madame Bovary (Ile de Bourbon (USA)) 10.1f **(67)**
Form - 4732101
Record 2000 - 1st:2 2nd:1 3rd:1 Ran:7
Win Prizemoney £7,007 *Total Prizemoney* £8,932

Wins						
	* 2000	Aug Redcar	(FRM)	5f	80	<
	* 2000	Aug Thirsk	(G-F)	5f	80	<

2000 Turf 2-7: (5f 2-4, 6f 3) (gd, g-f 1-1, frm 4, hrd 1-1)
Decent gelding, effective 5 to 6f, best at 5f, acts on g-f to hrd. Turf high 80 - 1st of 10 getting 2lb from Only One Legend (26 Aug Redcar RF 3995) - also 1st of 10 giving 5lb to Forever Times (5 Aug Thirsk RF 3405). **J J Quinn [2-7] Derrick Bloy.*

TOM TUN BHB 73f72a **RR 74f 72a** 4449[11]

5 b g Bold Arrangement 8.7f **(57)** - B Grade (Lucky Wednesday) 8f **(50)**
Form - 26523005001100
Record 2000 - 1st:2 2nd:1 3rd:1 Ran:12
Pre2000 - 1st:8 2nd:3 3rd:3 Ran:30
Win Prizemoney £41,786 *Total Prizemoney* £55,499
Wins * **2000** Aug Hamilt (SFT) H 6f 70 74
* **2000** Aug Leices (G-F) 6f 65
* 1999 Jly Doncas (G-F) 6f 77 <
* 1999 May Doncas (G-F) H 6f 68 73
* 1999 Mar Newcas (G-S) H 5f 57 61
* 1999 *Feb Southw (STD) H 6f 68 74*
* 1999 *Jan Southw (STD) H 6f 62 65*
* 1998 *Nov Lingfi (STD) H 5f 53 58*
* 1998 Spt Newcas (GD) H 6f 49 50
* 1998 *Jly Southw (STD) H 6f 42 44*
2000 Turf 2-10: (5f 3, 6f 2-6, 7f) (sft, gd 1-3, g-f 1-2, frm 4) 2000 AW 0-2: (5f, 6f) (Fibr 2)
Above-average gelding, effective 5 to 6f, best at 6f, acts on gd to hrd - acts on Fibr, does well at Ayr and likes Southwell. Turf high 75 - also 1st of 18 from Treasure Touch (16 Aug Hamilton RF 3698). AW high 71. A pretty decent sprinter on turf and sand, he was high in the handicap at the start of the season, but returned to form with victories at Leicester and Hamilton in August. Seems equally suited by either five or six furlongs and is a notably tough performer. **Miss J F Craze [10-42] Mrs O Tunstall.*

TONDYNE BHB 55f RR 54f 1661[6]
3 b g Owington - Anodyne (Dominion) 8.5f **(63)**
Form - 716
Record 2000 - 1st:1 2nd:0 3rd:0 Ran:3
Pre2000 - 1st:0 2nd:0 3rd:0 Ran:2
Win Prizemoney £3,062 *Total Prizemoney* £3,062
Wins * **2000** Mar Nottin (GD) H 6.1f 44 54 <
2000 Turf 1-2: (6f 1-2) (g-f 1-1, frm) 2000 AW 0-1: (8f) (Fibr)
Workmanlike, fair gelding. Turf high 54 (1st run) - 1st of 16 getting 10lb from Paddywack (29 Mar Nottingham RF 0558).
**T D Easterby [1-5] Dr M Gelfand.*

TONG ROAD BHB 37f30a RR 35f 30a 4894[14]
4 gr g Petong 7.6f **(58)** - Wayzgoose (USA) (Diesis) 9.3f **(69)**
Form - 8000020
Record 2000 - 1st:0 2nd:1 3rd:0 Ran:6
Pre2000 - 1st:0 2nd:0 3rd:0 Ran:10
Win Prizemoney £0 *Total Prizemoney* £985
2000 Turf 0-4: (5f 2, 6f 2) (sft, gd, g-f, hrd) 2000 AW 0-2: (5f, 7f) (Fibr 2)
Scopey, very moderate gelding, effective 5f, acts on g-f, has worn blinkers. Turf high 35 (began Aug) - 2nd of 22 getting 1lb from Upper Chamber (2 Spt Thirsk 5f g-f RF 4174).
**D W Chapman [0-6] J B Wilcox (from B R Cambidge [0-10] Nov 1999).*

TONIC BHB 75f RR 78f 3454a[20]
4 b g Robellino (USA) 9.5f **(68)** - Alyara (USA) (Alydar (USA)) 9.1f **(76)**
Form - 0743160
Record 2000 - 1st:1 2nd:0 3rd:1 Ran:7
Pre2000 - 1st:1 2nd:1 3rd:1 Ran:5
Win Prizemoney £6,107 *Total Prizemoney* £8,067
Wins 2000 Jun Windso (G-F) C 11.6f 74
1999 Apr Ripon (G-S) 8f 81 <
2000 Turf 1-7: (7f, 10f, 12f 1-3, 16f, 20f) (sft, gd 4, g-f, frm 1-1)
Leggy, above-average gelding, effective 8 to 12f, best at 12f, acts on gd to frm, best on gd. Turf high 78 - also 1st of 14 giving 10lb to Mutadarra (12 Jun Windsor RF 1908).
**Edward Hales in IRE [0-1] L Queally (from J A Osborne [0-1] Jun 2000).*

TONIGHT'S PRIZE (IRE) BHB 73f RR 79f 4167[16]
6 b g Night Shift (USA) 8.1f **(73)** - Bestow (Shirley Heights) 10.3f **(74)**
Form - 14670
Record 2000 - 1st:1 2nd:0 3rd:0 Ran:5
Pre2000 - 1st:2 2nd:5 3rd:3 Ran:25
Win Prizemoney £15,128 *Total Prizemoney* £26,302
Wins * **2000** May Windso (G-F) 10f 79
* 1998 Aug Pontef (G-F) H 8f 82 87 <
* 1997 Oct Pontef (G-F) 8f 72
2000 Turf 1-5: (10f 1-5) (gd, g-f 3, frm 1-1)
Above-average gelding, effective 8 to 10f, best at 10f, acts on gd to frm, best on g-f, prefers left handed tracks. Turf high 79 (1st run) - 1st of 12 from Prince Slayer (15 May Windsor RF 1210). He put up a fine performance to win at Windsor on his reappearance and met trouble in running at Nottingham next time. Ran at excellent race at long odds in the John Smith's Cup at York.
**C F Wall [3-30] Hintlesham Thoroughbreds.*

TONKOV (ITY) RR 98f 1283a[2]
3 b c
Form - 32
2000 Turf 0-1: (6f) (gd)
Currently very useful colt. (1st run) - 2nd of 9 getting 10lb from Barrow Creek (14 May Capannelle 6f gd RF 1283a).
**R Brogi in ITY [0-2] Scuderia Itaca.*

TONTO O'REILLY BHB 62f57a RR 59f 57a 5318[11]
2 gr c Mind Games - Most Uppitty **(47f 49a)** (Absalom) 7.2f **(58)**
Form - 700
Record 2000 - 1st:0 2nd:0 3rd:0 Ran:3
2000 Turf 0-3: (6f 3) (sft, g-s 2)
Currently fair colt. Turf high 59 (began Oct).
**B Smart [0-3] Mrs Julie Martin and David R Martin.*

TONY BHB 48f RR 52f 5004[20]
2 b c Marju (IRE) 9.2f **(76)** - Present Imperfect **(55f)** (Cadeaux Genereux)
Form - 0000
Record 2000 - 1st:0 2nd:0 3rd:0 Ran:4
2000 Turf 0-4: (5f, 6f 2, 8f) (g-s, gd, g-f 2)
Fair colt. Turf high 52 (began Jly).
**M W Easterby [0-4] Guy Reed.*

TONY DANCER BHB 36f30a RR 42f 30a 5160[4]
2 ch g Forzando 7.2f **(63)** - Capricious Lady (IRE) (Capricorn Line) 14.6f **(62)**
Form - 004
Record 2000 - 1st:0 2nd:0 3rd:0 Ran:3
2000 Turf 0-2: (6f, 8f) (sft, frm) 2000 AW 0-1: (6f) (Fibr)
Currently moderate gelding. Turf high 42 (began Jly).
**K Bell [0-3] Mines A Double Club.*

TONY TIE BHB 86f80a RR 92f 80a 5317[14]
4 b g Ardkinglass 5f **(64)** - Queen of the Quorn **(51df 45a)** (Governor General)
Form - 06223182021222800300
Record 2000 - 1st:2 2nd:7 3rd:2 Ran:19
Pre2000 - 1st:3 2nd:1 3rd:1 Ran:15
Win Prizemoney £31,627 *Total Prizemoney* £61,271
Wins * **2000** Jly Newcas (G-F) H 7f 85 87
* **2000** Jun Ayr (G-F) H 10f 81 85
* 1999 Nov Doncas (SFT) H 8f 69 81
1998 Aug Cheste (G-S) H 7f 87 89 <
1998 May Salisb (G-S) 5f 79
2000 Turf 2-19: (6f, 7f 1-5, 8f 9, 9f 2, 10f 1-2) (sft 2, g-s 3, gd 7, g-f 1-4, frm 1-3)
Unfurnished, useful gelding, effective 7 to 10f, best at 8f, acts on g-s to frm, has worn blinkers, likes left handed tracks, excels at Newcastle and Haydock, does well at Ayr. Turf high 92 - 2nd of 11 giving 10lb to Adobe (12 Aug Haydock 8f gd RF 3587) - also 1st of 11 giving 1lb to Karameg (29 Jly Newcastle RF 3210). A tough handicapper, he stays a mile and a quarter and probably acts on any turf going.
**J S Goldie [3-27] Frank Brady (from W G M Turner [2-7] Nov 1998).*

TOORAK (USA) BHB 70f RR 78f 2601[8]
3 b c Irish River (FR) 9f **(77)** - Just Juliet (USA) (What A Pleasure (USA)) 8.4f **(61)**
Form - 788
Record 2000 - 1st:0 2nd:0 3rd:0 Ran:3
Pre2000 - 1st:0 2nd:0 3rd:0 Ran:1
2000 Turf 0-3: (8f, 10f, 12f) (g-s, gd, g-f)
Scopey, above-average colt. Turf high 70. **J W Hills [0-4] D J Deer.*

TOOTORIAL (IRE) RR 5009[4]
3 b c College Chapel - Touche-A-Tout (IRE) (Royal Academy (USA))
Form - 4
Record 2000 - 1st:0 2nd:0 3rd:0 Ran:1
2000 AW 0-1: (6f) (Fibr)
Workmanlike, currently very moderate colt.

**A C Stewart [0-1] Racing For Gold.*

TOPAZ BHB 25f26a **RR 37f 26a** 4723[7]
5 b g Alhijaz 7.7f **(57)** - Daisy Topper (Top Ville) 11.7f **(68)**
Form - 0408267
Record 2000 - 1st:0 2nd:1 3rd:0 Ran:7
Pre2000 - 1st:0 2nd:0 3rd:0 Ran:13
Win Prizemoney £0 *Total Prizemoney* £517
2000 Turf 0-2: (10f, 14f) (gd 2) 2000 AW 0-5: (12f 3, 15f, 16f) (Equi, Fibr 4)
Very moderate gelding. Turf high 37. AW high 34.
**H J Collingridge [0-16] The Topaz Partnership (from J W Hills [0-4] Jun 1998).*

TOP BANANA BHB 55f54a **RR 58f 54a** 4277[10]
9 ch g Pharly (FR) 11.5f **(64)** - Oxslip (Owen Dudley) 8.3f **(61)**
Form - 080
Record 2000 - 1st:0 2nd:0 3rd:0 Ran:3
Pre2000 - 1st:4 2nd:6 3rd:5 Ran:45
Win Prizemoney £19,435 *Total Prizemoney* £54,893
Wins * 1996 Jun Newmar (G-F) H 5f 91 95 <
2000 Turf 0-2: (7f 2) (gd, g-f) 2000 AW 0-1: (7f) (Fibr)
Fair gelding, effective 6f, acts on g-s to gd, has worn blinkers. Turf high 45. **H Candy [4-48] Henry Candy.*

TOP CEES BHB 99f **RR 98f** 1129[P]
10 b g Shirley Heights 12.1f **(76)** - Sing Softly (Luthier) 9.8f **(71)**
Form - P
Record 2000 - 1st:0 2nd:0 3rd:0 Ran:1
Pre2000 - 1st:9 2nd:7 3rd:2 Ran:38
Win Prizemoney £179,142 *Total Prizemoney* £231,568
Wins * 1999 Oct Newmar (GD) H 17.3f 95 98 <
* 1999 Spt Ayr (G-S) H 13.1f 95 98 <
1998 Aug Pontef (G-F) H 12f 96 98 <
1998 Jun Ayr (G-F) H 15f 93 96+
1997 Spt Ayr (GD) H 13.1f 90 97
1997 May Cheste (SFT) H 18.7f 87 98 <
1996 Jly Newmar (G-F) H 14.8f 82 88+
2000 Turf 0-1: (19f) (g-f)
Very useful gelding. Consistent. Retired after getting injured in the Chester Cup. Retired after getting injured in the Chester Cup.
**I A Balding [2-4] Charlton Bloodstock Ltd (from Mrs J R Ramsden [9-39] Aug 1998).*

TOP HAND BHB 50f **RR 61f** 4364[8]
3 ch f First Trump - Gold Luck (USA) (Slew O' Gold (USA)) 8f **(75)**
Form - 400888
Record 2000 - 1st:0 2nd:0 3rd:0 Ran:6
Pre2000 - 1st:1 2nd:0 3rd:0 Ran:2
Win Prizemoney £2,489 *Total Prizemoney* £2,844
Wins 1999 Oct Bath (SFT) 8f 71 <
2000 Turf 0-6: (9f, 10f 3, 12f 2) (sft, gd, g-f 2, frm 2)
Light-framed, average filly, effective 8f, acts on gd. Turf high 68. Becoming disappointing.
**E W Tuer [0-2] E Tuer (from B W Hills [1-6] Jly 2000).*

TOPLESS IN TUSCANY BHB 35f60a **RR 39f 60a** 4925[7]
3 b f Lugana Beach 7f **(63)** - Little Scarlett **(23f 44a)** (Mazilier (USA))
Form - 036004007
Record 2000 - 1st:0 2nd:0 3rd:1 Ran:9
Win Prizemoney £0 *Total Prizemoney* £845
2000 Turf 0-7: (5f, 6f 2, 7f 3, 8f) (gd 3, g-f 4) 2000 AW 0-2: (6f, 7f) (Equi, Fibr)
Lengthy, very moderate filly, effective 6f, acts on gd. Turf high 59 - 3rd of 8 to Steppin Out (7 Jly Salisbury 6f gd RF 2603). AW high 24 (began Jly). **P W Hiatt [0-10] Jeremy Arnold.*

TOPMAN BHB 21f **RR** 5070[16]
3 ch c Komaite (USA) 6.9f **(61)** - Top Yard (Teekay)
Form - 0500
Record 2000 - 1st:0 2nd:0 3rd:0 Ran:4
Pre2000 - 1st:0 2nd:0 3rd:0 Ran:1
2000 Turf 0-3: (11f, 12f 2) (g-s, g-f, frm) 2000 AW 0-1: (16f) (Equi)
Small, formerly very poor colt. (began Aug) - 16th of 20 to Maniatis (19 Oct Bath 12f g-s RF 5070).
**M P Muggeridge [0-4] George Smith (from G F H Charles-Jones [0-1] Apr 1999).*

TOP NOLANS (IRE) BHB 69f **RR 72f** 4040[9]
2 ch c Topanoora 8.3f **(67)** - Lauretta Blue (IRE) (Bluebird (USA)) 7.5f **(69)**
Form - 7333840
Record 2000 - 1st:0 2nd:0 3rd:3 Ran:7
Win Prizemoney £0 *Total Prizemoney* £1,722
2000 Turf 0-7: (5f, 6f 5, 7f) (gd 2, g-f 2, frm 3)
Above-average colt, effective 5 to 6f, best at 6f, acts on gd to frm, best on g-f, has worn blinkers. Turf high 68 - 4th of 7 giving 3lb to Scotish Law (16 Aug Epsom 6f g-f RF 3690).
**M H Tompkins [0-7] Flint Fairyhouse Partnership.*

TOP OF THE CHARTS BHB 33f **RR 38f** 5082[9]
4 b g Salse (USA) 10.9f **(71)** - Celebrity (Troy) 10.4f **(68)**
Form - 581740
Record 2000 - 1st:1 2nd:0 3rd:0 Ran:6
Pre2000 - 1st:0 2nd:0 3rd:0 Ran:7
Win Prizemoney £3,103 *Total Prizemoney* £3,302
Wins * **2000** Aug Mussel (GD) SH 16f 32 37 <
2000 Turf 1-6: (14f, 16f 1-4, 17f) (hvy, g-s, g-f, frm 1-3)
Scopey, very moderate gelding, effective 14 to 16f, best at 16f, acts on g-s to frm, best on frm, often wears blinkers (very effectively), likes left handed tracks, prefers tight tracks. Turf high 38 - 4th of 14 getting 8lb from Sirinndi (3 Oct Catterick 16f g-s RF 4777) - also 1st of 7 giving 1lb to Victor Laszlo (2 Aug Musselburgh RF 3335).
**Mrs M Reveley [1-8] P D Savill (from J Noseda [0-7] Jly 1999).*

TOP OF THE CLASS (IRE) BHB 52f **RR 60f** 5192[8]
3 b f Rudimentary (USA) 8.2f **(66)** - School Mum **(6f)** (Reprimand)
Form - 00030008
Record 2000 - 1st:0 2nd:0 3rd:1 Ran:8
Pre2000 - 1st:1 2nd:0 3rd:3 Ran:11
Win Prizemoney £7,766 *Total Prizemoney* £10,012
Wins * 1999 Spt Ayr (G-S) H 6f 64 67 <
2000 Turf 0-8: (6f 2, 7f 2, 8f 3, 9f) (hvy, g-s, gd 2, g-f, frm 3)
Leggy, average filly, effective 5 to 7f, best at 6f, acts on g-s to frm, best on gd, has worn blinkers, excels at Ayr. Turf high 60 - 3rd of 15 giving 9lb to Printsmith (4 Jun Warwick 7f g-s RF 1706).
**Martyn Wane [1-21] B & J Racing & Breeding Syndicate II.*

TOP OF THE PARKES BHB 57f49a **RR 62f 49a** 4992[10]
3 b f Mistertopogigo (IRE) - Bella Parkes **(53f 80a)** (Tina's Pet) 6.8f **(59)**
Form - 372830
Record 2000 - 1st:0 2nd:1 3rd:2 Ran:6
Pre2000 - 1st:0 2nd:0 3rd:1 Ran:3
Win Prizemoney £0 *Total Prizemoney* £2,389
2000 Turf 0-3: (5f 2, 6f) (gd, g-f 2) 2000 AW 0-3: (6f 3) (Fibr 3)
Workmanlike, average filly, effective 6f, acts on frm. Turf high 52 (began Aug). AW high 62 (began Jly).
**N P Littmoden [0-9] Tim Godkin.*

TOP OF THE POPS (IRE) BHB 59f56a **RR 61f 56a** 903[2]
4 b g Ballad Rock 7.2f **(63)** - Summerhill (Habitat) 9.4f **(70)**
Form - 2
Record 2000 - 1st:0 2nd:1 3rd:0 Ran:1
Pre2000 - 1st:0 2nd:0 3rd:0 Ran:6
Win Prizemoney £0 *Total Prizemoney* £640
2000 AW 0-1: (7f) (Fibr)
Rangy, average gelding, effective 6f, acts on gd to g-f.
**C W Thornton [0-7] Guy Reed.*

TOPO'S GUEST BHB 60f **RR 60f** 5102[11]
2 b f Mistertopogigo (IRE) - Arctic Guest (IRE) **(62f 56a)** (Arctic Tern (USA)) 8.9f **(69)**
Form - 540
Record 2000 - 1st:0 2nd:0 3rd:0 Ran:3
Win Prizemoney £0 *Total Prizemoney* £403
2000 Turf 0-3: (6f 3) (gd, g-f 2)
Currently average filly. Turf high 60 (began Aug).
**J G Given [0-3] John Starbuck and Swallow Homes.*

TOPOSHEES RR 45f 2741[6]
3 b c Mistertopogigo (IRE) - Golden Crown (Main Reef) 9.6f **(57)**
Form - 6

Record 2000 - 1st:0 2nd:0 3rd:0 Ran:1
2000 Turf 0-1: (5f) (g-f)
Workmanlike, moderate colt. (DEAD)
**B Smart [0-1] Mrs Sheila Nelson.*

TOP QUALITY BHB 49f **RR 52f** 5053[10]

2 br f Simply Great (FR) 11.9f **(61)** - Qurrat Al Ain (Wolver Hollow) 8f **(56)**
Form - 500
Record 2000 - 1st:0 2nd:0 3rd:0 Ran:3
2000 Turf 0-3: (7f 2, 8f) (sft, g-s, hrd)
Currently fair filly. Turf high 52 (began Aug).
**T D Easterby [0-3] T H Bennett.*

TOPSY MORNING (IRE) **RR 95f** 4795a[10]

3 b f Lahib (USA) 8f **(69)** - Grand Morning 00
Form - 8360200
2000 Turf 0-7: (5f, 7f, 8f 4, 9f) (sft 2, g-s, gd 2, g-f)
Very useful filly, effective 7 to 8f, acts on g-s to gd. Turf high 95 - 3rd of 10 to Kermiyana (8 Jly Leopardstown 8f gd RF 2722a). She proved disappointing after a mid-summer break and does not seem to have a trip.
**Patrick Prendergast in IRE [1-9] Mrs Susan Whitehead.*

TOPTON (IRE) BHB 75f92a **RR 76f 92a** 5317[2]

6 b g Royal Academy (USA) 7.8f **(77)** - Circo (High Top) 10.2f **(67)**
Form - 0232420107020050823518600102
Record 2000 - 1st:2 2nd:4 3rd:2 Ran:24
Pre2000 - 1st:8 2nd:9 3rd:8 Ran:58
Win Prizemoney £35,187 *Total Prizemoney* £70,857

Wins	* **2000**	Jly	Yarmou	(G-F)	H	7f	72	74	
	* **2000**	*Feb*	*Lingfi*	*(STD)*	*H*	*8f*	*85*	*94*	<
	* 1999	Aug	Yarmou	(FRM)	H	7f	74	78	
	* 1999	Jly	Doncas	(G-F)	H	7f	67	70+	
	* 1999	Jun	Doncas	(GD)	H	7f	65	67	
	* 1999	*Jan*	*Lingfi*	*(STD)*	*H*	*7f*	*80*	*83*	
	* 1998	*Nov*	*Lingfi*	*(STD)*	*H*	*7f*	*69*	*73*	
	* 1998	*Nov*	*Southw*	*(STD)*	*H*	*7f*	*61*	*69*	
	* 1998	Jun	Doncas	(GD)	H	7f	69	74	
	1997	Oct	Folkes	(GD)		6f		74	

2000 Turf 1-17: (7f 1-8, 8f 9) (sft, g-s 2, gd 3, g-f 5, frm 1-6) 2000 AW 1-7: (7f 3, 8f 1-3, 10f) (Equi 1-5, Fibr 2)
Useful gelding, effective 8f, - acts on Equi, mostly wears blinkers, likes Doncaster and Yarmouth and Lingfield. Turf high 77. AW high 94 - 1st of 9 giving 15lb to Crimson Glory (5 Feb Lingfield RF 0227). Vigorously campaigned, he is very tough but difficult to win with. Best over seven furlongs or a mile, he wears blinkers and must be held-up.
**P Howling [9-74] Liam Sheridan (from I A Balding [1-8] Oct 1997).*

TORGAU (IRE) BHB 111f **RR 108f** 1080[7]

3 b f Zieten (USA) - Snoozy Time (Cavo Doro) 10.6f **(57)**
Form - 7
Record 2000 - 1st:0 2nd:0 3rd:0 Ran:1
Pre2000 - 1st:2 2nd:2 3rd:0 Ran:5
Win Prizemoney £26,430 *Total Prizemoney* £89,070

Wins	* 1999	Jly	Newmar	(GD)	G2	6f		97	<
	* 1999	Jun	Catter	(GD)		5f		79+	

2000 Turf 0-1: (8f) (frm)
Pattern-class filly, effective 6 to 7f, acts on g-f. She did her small yard proud, landing the Cherry Hinton Stakes at two, but was exported to America after finishing seventh in the 1000 Guineas. Disappointed on her debut for Jenine Sahadi at Hollywood Park.
**G C Bravery [2-6] Team Valor & Heiligbrodt Racing Stable.*

TORMENTOSO BHB 47f47a **RR 53f 47a** 4634[8]

3 b g Catrail (USA) - Chita Rivera **(44f 37a)** (Chief Singer) 8.9f **(66)**
Form - 4605058
Record 2000 - 1st:0 2nd:0 3rd:0 Ran:7
Pre2000 - 1st:0 2nd:0 3rd:0 Ran:3
Win Prizemoney £0 *Total Prizemoney* £475
2000 Turf 0-5: (7f, 8f, 12f, 13f, 16f) (g-s, g-f 2, frm 2) 2000 AW 0-2: (9f 2) (Fibr 2)
Workmanlike, fair gelding. Turf high 53. AW high 47. Becoming disappointing.
**D Burchell [0-3] D N Carey (from M R Channon [0-7] May 2000).*

TORNADO PRINCE (IRE) BHB 83f63a **RR 91+f 63a** 5240[14]

5 ch g Caerleon (USA) 10.9f **(79)** - Welsh Flame (Welsh Pageant) 10f **(65)**
Form - 014427100
Record 2000 - 1st:2 2nd:1 3rd:0 Ran:9
Pre2000 - 1st:4 2nd:1 3rd:2 Ran:30
Win Prizemoney £44,774 *Total Prizemoney* £50,894

Wins	* **2000**	Spt	Ascot	(SFT)	H	8f	70	91+	<
	* **2000**	Jun	Thirsk	(FRM)	H	7f	60	67	
	* 1999	Spt	Pontef	(G-F)	SH	8f	56	63+	
	* 1999	Spt	Thirsk	(FRM)	S	8f		56	
	* 1999	Jly	Ripon	(G-F)	S	8f		56	
	1998	Jly	Folkes	(G-F)	H	9.7f	62	69+	

2000 Turf 2-9: (7f 1-2, 8f 1-7) (g-s 1-2, gd 3, g-f, frm 1-3)
Useful gelding, effective 8f, acts on g-s, likes tight tracks. Turf high 91 - 1st of 24 getting 14lb from Salty Jack (24 Spt Ascot RF 4609). Scored at Thirsk in June and was only just beaten in the ladies' race at Ascot on Diamond day, but bolted up in the Mail On Sunday Series Final at the same track. Suited by coming from off a strong pace.
**E J Alston [5-31] Mrs J R Ramsden (from N A Callaghan [1-8] Aug 1998).*

TOROCA (USA) **RR 97f** 4644[2]

2 ch f Nureyev (USA) 8.4f **(84)** - Grand Falls (USA) (Ogygian (USA))
Form - 362
2000 Turf 0-3: (6f 2, 7f) (gd, g-f)
Currently very useful filly. Turf high 97 (began Spt) - 2nd of 13 to Regal Rose (26 Spt Newmarket 6f g-f RF 4644). Having run only a fair sixth to stable companion Black Minnaloushe in a listed race in Ireland, she was a 50/1 outsider when second in the Cheveley Park. Front-running tactics seemed to suit her on that occasion, but it is difficult to assess whether she can repeat that level of form next season.
**A P O'Brien in IRE [0-3] Mrs E M Stockwell.*

TORRENT BHB 68f70a **RR 73f 70a** 5313[9]

5 ch g Prince Sabo 6.6f **(64)** - Maiden Pool (Sharpen Up) 8.3f **(67)**
Form - 321133655304444463331335183000
Record 2000 - 1st:2 2nd:0 3rd:8 Ran:25
Pre2000 - 1st:5 2nd:4 3rd:5 Ran:34
Win Prizemoney £23,935 *Total Prizemoney* £30,917

Wins	* **2000**	Spt	Pontef	(G-S)	H	5f	67	73	
	* **2000**	Aug	Bright	(FRM)		5.3f		60	
	* 1999	*Dec*	*Lingfi*	*(STD)*	*H*	*5f*	*67*	*69*	
	* 1999	*Dec*	*Lingfi*	*(STD)*	*H*	*6f*	*60*	*64*	
	* 1999	Jly	Beverl	(G-F)		5f		68	
	1998	May	Thirsk	(G-F)	H	5f	78	83	<
	1998	Apr	Catter	(GD)		6f		79	

2000 Turf 2-21: (5f 2-20, 6f) (g-s 3, gd 1-8, g-f 2, frm 7, hrd 1-1) 2000 AW 0-4: (5f 4) (Equi 3, Fibr)
Above-average gelding, has broken blood-vessels, effective 5 to 6f, best at 5f, acts on gd to frm - acts on Equi, often wears blinkers, likes left handed tracks, likes tight tracks, likes Lingfield. Turf high 73 - 1st of 17 giving 8lb to Maromito (21 Spt Pontefract RF 4558). AW high 67. Kept very busy, he is an effective sprinter at a modest level.
**D W Chapman [5-41] Mrs J Hazell (from T D Barron [2-14] Jun 1999).*

TORRID KENTAVR (USA) BHB 80f83a **RR 87f 83a** 4761[1]

3 b c Trempolino (USA) 11.9f **(77)** - Torrid Tango (USA) (Green Dancer (USA)) 10.3f **(74)**
Form - 3318051
Record 2000 - 1st:2 2nd:0 3rd:2 Ran:7
Win Prizemoney £7,910 *Total Prizemoney* £9,452

Wins	* **2000**	*Spt*	*Wolver*	*(STD)*	*H*	*12f*	*83*	*88*	<
	* **2000**	Jly	Bath	(FRM)		11.7f		73+	

2000 Turf 1-6: (10f 3, 12f 1-3) (gd 2, frm 1-4) 2000 AW 1-1: (12f 1-1) (Fibr 1-1)
Scopey, useful colt, effective 10 to 12f, best at 12f, acts on gd to frm - acts on Fibr. Turf high 87 - 8th of 14 getting 2lb from Hannibal Lad (15 Jly Ascot 12f gd RF 2826). (1st run) - 1st of 12 giving 17lb to Sure Quest (30 Spt Wolverhampton RF 4761). Had one run in Italy at two, and was placed twice at ten furlongs this term before a step-up in trip did the trick at Bath. Added a victory on the Wolverhampton Fibresand.
**T G Mills [2-7] Kentavr (UK) Ltd.*

TORROS STRAITS (USA) RR 74df 567^{11}
3 b f Boundary (USA) - Preparation (USA) (Easy Goer (USA))
Form - 0
Record 2000 - 1st:0 2nd:0 3rd:0 Ran:1
Pre2000 - 1st:0 2nd:0 3rd:0 Ran:1
Win Prizemoney £0 *Total Prizemoney* £332
2000 Turf 0-1: (7f) (gd)
Currently above-average filly. Pulled too hard, spoiling her chances, when fourth in what should be a decent maiden over six furlongs at Newmarket's July meeting.
**N A Callaghan [0-2] M Tabor & Mrs John Magnier.*

TORTUGUERO (IRE) BHB 104f **RR 94f** 4643^{4}
2 b gr c Highest Honor (FR) 10.9f **(72)** - Rahaam (USA) (Secreto (USA)) 8.7f **(72)**
Form - 061124474
Record 2000 - 1st:2 2nd:1 3rd:0 Ran:9
Win Prizemoney £6,435 *Total Prizemoney* £40,655
Wins * **2000** Jly Salisb (G-S) H 7f 86 <
* **2000** Jun Ayr (GD) 7f 77
2000 Turf 2-9: (6f 2, 7f 2-6, 8f) (gd 1-2, g-f 1-5, frm 2)
Useful colt, effective 7 to 8f, best at 7f, acts on gd to frm. Turf high 94 - also 1st of 9 getting 3lb from Zeloso (7 Jly Salisbury RF 2599). Improving. Tough if a shade one-paced, he ran a series of solid races and could improve over a mile next term. That said, he is not Group class and could be difficult to place.
**B W Hills [2-9] Trevor Stewart.*

TORY BOY BHB 58f44a **RR 64f 44a** 311^{4}
5 b g Deploy 11.4f **(67)** - Mukhayyalah (Dancing Brave (USA)) 8.4f **(76)**
Form - 434
Record 2000 - 1st:0 2nd:0 3rd:0 Ran:1
Pre2000 - 1st:1 2nd:2 3rd:2 Ran:13
Win Prizemoney £3,235 *Total Prizemoney* £5,819
Wins * 1998 Jun Warwic (SFT) 10.8f 76 <
2000 AW 0-1: (16f) (Fibr)
Average gelding, has broken blood-vessels, effective 16f, acts on g-f, has worn blinkers (very effectively), favours left handed tracks, favours tight tracks.
**Ian Williams [4-21] Mary Ann Properties Ltd.*

TOSHIBA TIMES BHB 28f **RR 30df** 1957^{15}
4 b g Persian Bold 10f **(69)** - Kirkby Belle (Bay Express) 7.1f **(60)**
Form - 000
Record 2000 - 1st:0 2nd:0 3rd:0 Ran:3
Pre2000 - 1st:0 2nd:0 3rd:0 Ran:6
2000 Turf 0-3: (8f 3) (g-f, frm 2)
Leggy, very moderate gelding, has worn blinkers. Becoming disappointing. **B Ellison [0-9] Toshiba (UK) Ltd.*

TOTAL CARE BHB 75f70a **RR 83f 70a** 2633^{14}
3 br c Caerleon (USA) 10.9f **(79)** - Totality **(103f)** (Dancing Brave (USA)) 8.4f **(76)**
Form - 22210
Record 2000 - 1st:1 2nd:3 3rd:0 Ran:5
Win Prizemoney £4,192 *Total Prizemoney* £8,410
Wins * **2000** Jun Kempto (G-F) 12f 83 <
2000 Turf 1-5: (10f, 11f, 12f 1-3) (g-s 2, gd, g-f 1-2)
Scopey, decent colt. Turf high 83 - 2nd of 22 giving 5lb to Bezzaaf (8 May Windsor 10f g-f RF 1101) - also 1st of 7 from Armen (14 Jun Kempton RF 1966). Unraced at two, he found one too good in each of his first three starts before finally getting off the mark in a Kempton maiden. Looks a stayer. **H R A Cecil [1-5] K Abdulla.*

TOTAL DELIGHT BHB 72f77a **RR 81f 77a** 4306^{11}
4 b g Mtoto 11.5f **(71)** - Shesadelight (Shirley Heights) 10.3f **(74)**
Form - 10041208040
Record 2000 - 1st:2 2nd:1 3rd:0 Ran:11
Pre2000 - 1st:0 2nd:1 3rd:1 Ran:4
Win Prizemoney £8,274 *Total Prizemoney* £12,664
Wins * **2000** Jun Sandow (G-F) H 14f 80 81 <
* **2000** Mar Leices (GD) H 10f 74 79
2000 Turf 2-10: (10f 1-2, 12f 4, 14f 1-3, 16f) (sft, gd 3, g-f 2-4, frm 2)
2000 AW 0-1: (12f) (Equi)
Scopey, decent gelding, effective 10 to 14f, best at 14f, acts on gd to g-f, best on g-f, has worn blinkers, prefers right handed tracks, likes tight tracks. Turf high 86 - 2nd of 4 giving 19lb to Fait Le Jojo (30 Jun Goodwood 14f gd RF 2399) - also 1st of 6 giving 21lb to Cheek To Cheek (17 Jun Sandown RF 2057). Inconsistent. A winner over ten furlongs on his Leicester reappearance, he was stepping up to 14 furlongs when winning at Sandown in June, but ran some very poor races as well last term and does not look particularly consistent. **Lady Herries [2-15] D Heath.*

TOTAL LOVE BHB 91f **RR 97df** 4732^{16}
3 ch f Cadeaux Genereux 7.9f **(76)** - Favorable Exchange (USA) (Exceller (USA)) 12.5f **(74)**
Form - 8253400
Record 2000 - 1st:0 2nd:1 3rd:1 Ran:7
Pre2000 - 1st:1 2nd:2 3rd:3 Ran:9
Win Prizemoney £3,457 *Total Prizemoney* £31,628
Wins * 1999 May Leices (GD) 6f 80 <
2000 Turf 0-7: (7f 3, 8f 3, 10f) (g-s 2, gd 3, g-f, frm)
Neat, very useful filly, effective 7 to 8f, best at 7f, acts on gd. Turf high 104. She is a useful performer but is a 'twilight' filly for whom winning opportunities are hard to find.
**E A L Dunlop [1-16] John Brown & Megan Dennis.*

TOTALLY COMMITTED (IRE) BHB 76f **RR 81f** 4283^{4}
2 b c Turtle Island (IRE) - Persian Light (IRE) (Persian Heights)
Form - 0323684
Record 2000 - 1st:0 2nd:1 3rd:2 Ran:7
Win Prizemoney £0 *Total Prizemoney* £3,262
2000 Turf 0-7: (5f, 6f 2, 7f 2, 8f 2) (g-s, gd, g-f 4, frm)
Decent colt, effective 6 to 8f, best at 6f, acts on g-f to frm, best on g-f. Turf high 81 - 3rd of 21 getting 3lb from Man of Distinction (14 Jun Kempton 6f g-f RF 1961).
**R Hannon [0-7] The Schedule Partnership.*

TOTALLY SCOTTISH BHB 34f **RR 42f** 4445^{10}
4 b g Mtoto 11.5f **(71)** - Glenfinlass (Lomond (USA)) 8.8f **(65)**
Form - 856570
Record 2000 - 1st:0 2nd:0 3rd:0 Ran:6
Pre2000 - 1st:0 2nd:0 3rd:0 Ran:3
Win Prizemoney £0 *Total Prizemoney* £196
2000 Turf 0-6: (10f, 13f, 15f, 16f 2, 17f) (gd 2, frm 4)
Small, moderate gelding, effective 13 to 16f, acts on frm, favours tight tracks. Turf high 45 - 5th of 6 getting 3lb from Love Bitten (23 Jun Ayr 13f frm RF 2217). **Mrs M Reveley [0-9] P D Savill.*

TOTAL MAGIC RR 53f 959^{8}
2 ch c Pivotal - Inherent Magic (IRE) **(92f 84a)** (Magical Wonder (USA))
Form - 8
Record 2000 - 1st:0 2nd:0 3rd:0 Ran:1
2000 Turf 0-1: (5f) (gd)
Currently fair colt. **I A Balding [0-1] Harris Allport Tuckerman.*

TOTAL TROPIX BHB 25f **RR 44?f** 1040^{7}
5 b m Saddlers' Hall (IRE) 10.5f **(65)** - Ivana (IRE) (Taufan (USA)) 7f **(57)**
Form - 07
Record 2000 - 1st:0 2nd:0 3rd:0 Ran:2
Pre2000 - 1st:0 2nd:0 3rd:0 Ran:6
2000 Turf 0-1: (16f) (frm) 2000 AW 0-1: (8f) (Fibr)
Moderate filly, has worn blinkers.
**Mrs S C Bradburne [0-22] J G Bradburne (from B J Meehan [0-1] May 1998).*

TOTEM DANCER BHB 48f38a **RR 62f 38a** 5193^{3}
7 b m Mtoto 11.5f **(71)** - Ballad Opera (Sadler's Wells (USA)) 10f **(76)**
Form - 000010242863003
Record 2000 - 1st:1 2nd:2 3rd:2 Ran:15
Pre2000 - 1st:3 2nd:8 3rd:5 Ran:36
Win Prizemoney £14,606 *Total Prizemoney* £39,672
Wins * **2000** May Nottin (G-S) H 14.1f 51 54
* 1998 Aug Cheste (GD) H 12.3f 75 79 <
* 1997 Spt Hamilt (GD) H 12.1f 69 76
* 1996 Oct Nottin (GD) 14.1f 76
2000 Turf 1-13: (12f, 13f 2, 14f 1-6, 15f, 16f 3) (sft 2, g-s 2, gd 1-4, g-f 2, frm 3) 2000 AW 0-2: (12f 2) (Equi, Fibr)
Average mare, effective 10 to 12f, acts on gd to frm, has worn blinkers. Turf high 62. AW high 27. Inconsistent. She ended a long losing run when winning over 14 furlongs at Nottingham in May. A

couple of fair efforts on fast ground since, but is better suited by some cut in the ground. **J L Eyre [4-52] G Lloyd.*

TO THE LAST MAN BHB 40f **RR 48f** 5056[8]

4 b g Warrshan (USA) 9.7f **(59)** - Shirley's Touch (Touching Wood (USA)) 8.2f **(55)**
Form - 7008
Record 2000 - 1st:0 2nd:0 3rd:0 Ran:4
Pre2000 - 1st:2 2nd:2 3rd:1 Ran:23
Win Prizemoney £5,704 *Total Prizemoney* £8,801
Wins 1999 Aug Bright (G-S) 8f 60+
1999 Jun Salisb (GD) H 8f 57 62+ <
2000 Turf 0-4: (8f 2, 10f 2) (sft, g-s, g-f, frm)
Light-framed, moderate gelding, effective 8 to 11f, best at 8f, acts on gd to g-f, best on gd, has worn blinkers, likes tight tracks. Turf high 35 (began Aug). Becoming disappointing.
**G M Moore [0-9] N B Atkinson (from M D I Usher [2-23] Oct 1999).*

TO THE ROOF (IRE) BHB 104f **RR 103f** 2833[8]

8 b g Thatching 7.8f **(69)** - Christine Daae (Sadler's Wells (USA)) 10f **(76)**
Form - 8
Record 2000 - 1st:0 2nd:0 3rd:0 Ran:1
Pre2000 - 1st:7 2nd:10 3rd:5 Ran:47
Win Prizemoney £99,277 *Total Prizemoney* £137,424
Wins * 1999 Jun Epsom (CD,) LH 5f 108 109 <
* 1999 May Beverl (GD) 5f 108
* 1998 Spt Ascot (SFT) H 5f 102 106
* 1996 Jun Epsom (G-F) LH 5f 90 92
* 1996 May Thirsk (G-F) H 6f 84 90
* 1996 May Bath (G-F) H 5.1f 79 87
* 1996 Apr Mussel (GD) H 5f 67 69
2000 Turf 0-1: (5f) (g-f)
Very useful gelding, effective 5f, acted on gd to frm, best on gd. (DEAD) **P W Harris [7-48] Mrs P W Harris.*

TO THE STARS (IRE) BHB 30f **RR 6f** 2083[10]

3 b f Zieten (USA) - Rocket Alert (Red Alert) 7.6f **(66)**
Form - 000
Record 2000 - 1st:0 2nd:0 3rd:0 Ran:3
2000 Turf 0-3: (6f, 8f, 10f) (gd, g-f, frm)
Light-framed, currently very poor filly. Turf high 6.
**B R Millman [0-3] Mrs Maureen Shenkin.*

TOTOM BHB 65f74a **RR 73f 74a** 4616[9]

5 b m Mtoto 11.5f **(71)** - A Lyph (USA) (Lypheor) 12f **(71)**
Form - 43445470
Record 2000 - 1st:0 2nd:0 3rd:1 Ran:8
Pre2000 - 1st:5 2nd:2 3rd:1 Ran:18
Win Prizemoney £17,143 *Total Prizemoney* £27,256
Wins * 1999 Aug Lingfi (G-F) H 11.5f 69 72
* 1999 Jly Windso (G-F) H 10f 63 67
* 1999 Jun Windso (G-F) 10f 61
* 1999 *Feb Lingfi (STD) H 10f 68 75+* <
1998 *Nov Lingfi (STD) 10f 65*
2000 Turf 0-7: (10f 3, 12f, 13f, 14f 2) (gd, g-f 4, frm 2) 2000 AW 0-1: (12f) (Equi)
Above-average filly, effective 10 to 14f, best at 10f, acts on g-f to frm - acts on Equi, has worn blinkers, and excels at Windsor and Newbury. Turf high 73 (1st run) - 4th of 12 getting 3lb from Tonight's Prize (15 May Windsor 10f frm RF 1210). (1st run) - 3rd of 10 giving 3lb to Pluralist (3 Jun Lingfield 12f Equi RF 1679). Consistent.
**J R Fanshawe [4-18] Chris van Hoorn (from Lord Huntingdon [1-8] Dec 1998).*

TOUCH FOR GOLD (USA) BHB 67f **RR 64+f** 4013[9]

3 br f Mr Prospector (USA) 8.6f **(88)** - Daijin (USA) (Deputy Minister (CAN)) 7.4f **(80)**
Form - 710
Record 2000 - 1st:1 2nd:0 3rd:0 Ran:3
Win Prizemoney £3,770 *Total Prizemoney* £3,770
Wins * **2000** Aug Newcas (GD) 9f 64+ <
2000 Turf 1-3: (8f, 9f 1-1, 10f) (g-s, g-f 1-1, frm)
Scopey, currently average filly. Turf high 64 - 1st of 5 getting 5lb from Tough Times (9 Aug Newcastle RF 3496).
**Sir Michael Stoute [1-3] Teruya Yoshida.*

TOUCH OF FAIRY (IRE) BHB 84f **RR 72f** 4743[27]

4 b h Fairy King (USA) 7.7f **(75)** - Decadence (Vaigly Great) 7f **(58)**
Form - 0400
Record 2000 - 1st:0 2nd:0 3rd:0 Ran:4
Pre2000 - 1st:0 2nd:1 3rd:0 Ran:1
Win Prizemoney £0 *Total Prizemoney* £1,137
2000 Turf 0-4: (5f, 6f 2, 7f) (g-s, gd 2, g-f)
Scopey, above-average colt. Turf high 91.
**K Mahdi [0-5] Hamad Al-Mutawa.*

TOUCH OF THE BLUES (FR) RR 112f 5095a[5]

3 b c Cadeaux Genereux 7.9f **(76)** - Silabteni (USA) (Nureyev (USA)) 8.7f **(78)**
Form - 415
2000 Turf 1-3: (7f 1-2, 8f) (sft, gd 1-2)
Group-class colt. Turf high 112. **C Laffon-Parias in FR [2-5].*

TOUCH THE SKY RR 1084[P]

3 b f Terimon 8.7f **(58)** - Topcliffe (Top Ville) 11.7f **(68)**
Form - P
Record 2000 - 1st:0 2nd:0 3rd:0 Ran:1
2000 Turf 0-1: (6f) (g-f)
Leggy, very poor filly. (DEAD) **B R Millman [0-1] Mrs V A Tory.*

TOUCHY FEELINGS (IRE) RR 67f 3567[8]

2 b f Ashkalani (IRE) - Adjalisa (IRE) (Darshaan) 9.9f **(84)**
Form - 38
Record 2000 - 1st:0 2nd:0 3rd:1 Ran:2
Win Prizemoney £0 *Total Prizemoney* £657
2000 Turf 0-2: (7f 2) (g-f, frm)
Currently average filly. Turf high 67. **R Hannon [0-2] Teviot Stud.*

TOUGH GUY (IRE) RR 92f 3539a[2]

4 b h Namaqualand (USA) - Supreme Crown (USA) (Chief's Crown (USA)) 9.8f **(72)**
Form - 32
2000 Turf 0-1: (7f) (sft) 2000 AW 0-1: (9f) (Dirt)
Scopey, useful colt, effective 7 to 9f, best at 7f, acts on sft to gd - acts on Dirt. (1st run) - 2nd of 14 getting 2lb from Rolo Tomasi (3 Aug Ovrevoll 7f sft RF 3539a). (1st run) - 3rd of 11 to Stato One (14 May Jagersro 9f Dirt RF 1280a). **M Kahn in SWE [0-2].*

TOUGH MEN (USA) BHB 93f **RR 92+f** 2429[1]

3 b c Woodman (USA) 9.7f **(77)** - Rhumba Rage (USA) (Nureyev (USA)) 8.7f **(78)**
Form - 521
Record 2000 - 1st:1 2nd:1 3rd:0 Ran:3
Win Prizemoney £4,387 *Total Prizemoney* £5,549
Wins * **2000** Jly Doncas (G-F) 10.3f 92+ <
2000 Turf 1-3: (8f, 9f, 10f 1-1) (g-s, frm 1-2)
Scopey, currently useful colt. Turf high 92 - 1st of 7 giving 5lb to Banco Suivi (1 Jly Doncaster RF 2429). He cost 350,000gns as a yearling but did not look to be enjoying himself when scrambling home in a Doncaster maiden in July. Probably open to improvement, he was not seen out in the second half of the season and may have a problem.
**H R A Cecil [1-3] The Thoroughbred Corporation.*

TOUGH SPEED (USA) BHB 106f **RR 103f** 1689[5]

3 b c Miswaki (USA) 8.1f **(81)** - Nature's Magic (USA) (Nijinsky (CAN)) 10.3f **(77)**
Form - 5
Record 2000 - 1st:0 2nd:0 3rd:0 Ran:1
Pre2000 - 1st:1 2nd:1 3rd:0 Ran:3
Win Prizemoney £6,035 *Total Prizemoney* £12,265
Wins * 1999 Spt Doncas (G-F) 7f 95+ <
2000 Turf 0-1: (7f) (frm)
Tall, very useful colt. Fifth in a listed race on his reappearance, having given trouble at the start, he did not reappear.
**Sir Michael Stoute [1-4] Saeed Suhail.*

TOUGH TIMES (IRE) BHB 58f **RR 68f** 4426[10]

3 b g Ezzoud (IRE) - Shahaamh (IRE) (Reference Point) 6.8f **(70)**
Form - 5602500
Record 2000 - 1st:0 2nd:1 3rd:0 Ran:7
Win Prizemoney £0 *Total Prizemoney* £1,160
2000 Turf 0-7: (7f 2, 8f, 9f 2, 10f 2) (gd 3, g-f 3, frm)

Rangy, average gelding, effective 9f, acts on g-f, has worn blinkers. Turf high 68 - 2nd of 5 giving 5lb to Touch For Gold (9 Aug Newcastle 9f g-f RF 3496). **T D Easterby [0-7] C H Stevens.*

TOUJOURS RIVIERA BHB 56f58a **RR 56f 58a** 5244[2]
10 ch g Rainbow Quest (USA) 11.2f **(81)** - Miss Beaulieu (Northfields (USA)) 9f **(72)**
Form - 00151262
Record 2000 - 1st:2 2nd:2 3rd:0 Ran:8
Pre2000 - 1st:8 2nd:7 3rd:8 Ran:66
Win Prizemoney £54,670 *Total Prizemoney* £76,719
Wins * 2000 Spt Thirsk (GD) S 8f 56
*** 2000** Aug Newmar (GD) S 8f 37
* 1998 *Jan Lingfi (STD) H 12f 73 77*
* 1997 Spt Bright (FRM) H 8f 74 81
* 1997 Aug Hamilt (G-F) H 8.3f 71 74
2000 Turf 2-6: (7f, 8f 2-5) (gd 1-3, g-f 1-2, frm) 2000 AW 0-2: (12f 2) (Fibr 2)
Average gelding. Turf high 56 (began Jly). AW high 60 (began Spt).
**J Pearce [10-71] The Fantasy Fellowship (from G Wragg [0-4] Oct 1993).*

TOUS LES JOURS (USA) BHB 61f **RR 64f** 1912[13]
4 b m Dayjur (USA) 6.8f **(79)** - Humility (USA) (Cox's Ridge (USA)) 8f **(68)**
Form - 280
Record 2000 - 1st:0 2nd:1 3rd:0 Ran:3
Pre2000 - 1st:2 2nd:1 3rd:4 Ran:24
Win Prizemoney £6,355 *Total Prizemoney* £13,711
Wins 1999 Jly Catter (GD) 7f 57
1998 Aug Beverl (G-F) H 7.5f 67 74 <
2000 Turf 0-3: (7f 2, 8f) (frm 3)
Scopey, average filly, effective 6 to 8f, best at 7f, acts on g-f to frm, best on frm, has worn blinkers. Turf high 64 (1st run) - 2nd of 21 giving 6lb to Mother Corrigan (15 May Redcar 7f frm RF 1200).
**J S Goldie [0-3] J S Morrison (from M Johnston [2-24] Oct 1999).*

TOUT CHARMANT (USA) RR 118f 5329a[2]
4 b m Slewvescent (USA) - Charm A Gendarme (USA) (Batonnier (USA))
Form - 2
2000 Turf 0-1: (11f) (frm)
Currently high-class filly. (1st run) - 2nd of 14 to Perfect Sting (4 Nov Churchill Downs 11f frm RF 5329a).
**R McAnally in USA [0-2] Stonerside Stable.*

TOWER OF SONG (IRE) BHB 38f40a **RR 60f 40a** 1599[7]
3 ch g Perugino (USA) - New Rochelle (IRE) (Lafontaine (USA)) 8.7f **(49)**
Form - 14205423504007
Record 2000 - 1st:0 2nd:1 3rd:1 Ran:11
Pre2000 - 1st:1 2nd:2 3rd:1 Ran:10
Win Prizemoney £2,029 *Total Prizemoney* £5,574
Wins 1999 *Nov Southw (STD) S 8f 68 <*
2000 Turf 0-3: (7f 2, 10f) (g-s, gd 2) 2000 AW 0-8: (7f, 8f 3, 9f, 11f 2, 12f) (Fibr 8)
Scopey, average gelding, effective 7 to 8f, best at 8f, acts on g-f - acts on Fibr, has worn blinkers, likes left handed tracks, likes tight tracks. Turf high 38. AW high 62. Becoming disappointing.
**D W Chapman [0-14] K Nicholls (from M R Channon [1-7] Nov 1999).*

TOWN GIRL (IRE) RR 71f 1885[7]
3 ch f Lammtarra (USA) - Greektown (Ela-Mana-Mou) 10.1f **(70)**
Form - 7
Record 2000 - 1st:0 2nd:0 3rd:0 Ran:1
Pre2000 - 1st:0 2nd:0 3rd:0 Ran:1
2000 Turf 0-1: (10f) (frm)
Leggy, currently above-average filly.
**Sir Michael Stoute [0-2] Lord Weinstock.*

TOWN GOSSIP (IRE) BHB 51f56a **RR 62f 56a** 4994[1]
3 ch f Indian Ridge 7.6f **(74)** - Only Gossip (USA) (Trempolino (USA)) 12f **(71)**
Form - 750731
Record 2000 - 1st:1 2nd:0 3rd:1 Ran:6
Pre2000 - 1st:0 2nd:0 3rd:0 Ran:1
Win Prizemoney £2,723 *Total Prizemoney* £3,055
Wins * 2000 *Oct Wolver (STD) H 12f 43 59 <*
2000 Turf 0-4: (8f 2, 11f, 12f) (gd 2, frm 2) 2000 AW 1-2: (12f 1-1, 15f) (Fibr 1-2)
Average filly, effective 12f, - acts on Fibr. Turf high 62. AW high 59 (began Spt) - 1st of 12 getting 1lb from Maiden Aunt (14 Oct Wolverhampton RF 4994).
**P J Makin [1-7] Admin of the late C Stelling.*

TOYON (IRE) BHB 65f62a **RR 74f 62a** 4824[8]
3 b g Catrail (USA) - Princess Toy (Prince Tenderfoot (USA)) 9f **(61)**
Form - 606522340758
Record 2000 - 1st:0 2nd:2 3rd:1 Ran:12
Win Prizemoney £0 *Total Prizemoney* £2,302
2000 Turf 0-7: (5f, 6f 2, 7f 3, 8f) (gd 4, g-f 2, hrd) 2000 AW 0-5: (6f, 7f, 8f 3) (Fibr 5)
Rangy, above-average gelding, effective 7f, acts on g-f. Turf high 74 - 2nd of 14 giving 3lb to Anyhow (12 Jly Lingfield 7f g-f RF 2742). AW high 64 (began Jun). Steadily improving and should be able to find a race. **Sir Mark Prescott [0-12] Roger Ferris.*

TOY STORY (FR) BHB 45f36a **RR 57f 36a** 534[8]
4 b g Fijar Tango (FR) - Grundygold (FR) (Grundy) 10.3f **(65)**
Form - 263308
Record 2000 - 1st:0 2nd:0 3rd:2 Ran:5
Pre2000 - 1st:0 2nd:1 3rd:0 Ran:4
Win Prizemoney £0 *Total Prizemoney* £1,282
2000 AW 0-5: (12f 2, 13f, 14f, 16f) (Equi, Fibr 4)
Workmanlike, fair gelding, has worn blinkers. AW high 43.
**Miss Gay Kelleway [0-11] M Butler & R Paul.*

TRACK THE CAT RR 63f 3535[2]
2 b c Catrail (USA) - Snowtop (Thatching) 8f **(66)**
Form - 2
Record 2000 - 1st:0 2nd:1 3rd:0 Ran:1
Win Prizemoney £0 *Total Prizemoney* £868
2000 Turf 0-1: (6f) (gd)
Currently average colt. (1st run) - 2nd of 18 giving 5lb to St Antim (10 Aug Haydock 6f gd RF 3535). **B A McMahon [0-1] J C Fretwell.*

TRAGIC LADY BHB 34f **RR 30f** 2212[11]
4 b m Tragic Role (USA) 9.4f **(63)** - Rainbow Lady (Jaazeiro (USA)) 9.2f **(54)**
Form - 0
Record 2000 - 1st:0 2nd:0 3rd:0 Ran:1
Pre2000 - 1st:0 2nd:0 3rd:0 Ran:3
2000 Turf 0-1: (8f) (frm)
Light-framed, very moderate filly.
**W McKeown [0-1] I Fox (from M G Meagher [0-3] Jly 1999).*

TRAGIC LOVER RR 91f 4794a[1]
4 b g Tragic Role (USA) 9.4f **(63)** - Wild Lover (USA) (Lyphard (USA)) 9.9f **(72)**
Form - 2611
2000 Turf 2-3: (10f, 12f 1-1, 16f 1-1) (gd 2-2)
Useful gelding, effective 12 to 16f, acts on gd, has worn blinkers. Turf high 91 - 1st of 24 giving 18lb to Hill Port (30 Spt Curragh RF 4794a) - also 1st of 15 getting 12lb from Bamford Castle (2 Jly Curragh RF 2533a).
**D Kinsella in IRE [2-3] D Kinsella (from D Hanley in IRE [1-4] Nov 1999).*

TRAHERN BHB 98f **RR 105df** 4464[16]
3 b c Cadeaux Genereux 7.9f **(76)** - Tansy **(71df)** (Shareef Dancer (USA)) 9.9f **(73)**
Form - 4214000
Record 2000 - 1st:1 2nd:1 3rd:0 Ran:7
Win Prizemoney £2,964 *Total Prizemoney* £12,078
Wins * 2000 May Redcar (G-S) 10f 77+ <
2000 Turf 1-7: (8f, 10f 1-5, 12f) (gd 4, g-f 1-2, frm)
Neat, Pattern-class colt, effective 12f, acts on gd, has worn blinkers. Turf high 105 - 4th of 7 to Subtle Power (23 Jun Ascot 12f gd RF 2206). Unraced at two, he easily won a Redcar maiden before finishing fourth in a substandard Group Two at Ascot. Reported lame after finishing down the field in a hot Sandown handicap and did not figure on his last two runs.
**J H M Gosden [1-7] Sheikh Mohammed.*

TRAIKEY (IRE) BHB 34f **RR 46f** 4497[9]
8 b g Scenic 10.6f **(66)** - Swordlestown Miss (USA) (Apalachee (USA)) 9.4f **(71)**
Form - 80
Record 2000 - 1st:0 2nd:0 3rd:0 Ran:2
Pre2000 - 1st:1 2nd:0 3rd:1 Ran:8
Win Prizemoney £5,250 *Total Prizemoney* £6,761
2000 Turf 0-2: (7f, 8f) (g-s, frm)
Moderate gelding. Turf high 31 (began Aug). Inconsistent.
**Mrs S Lamyman [0-12] P Lamyman (from J E Banks [1-2] May 1995).*

TRAJAN (IRE) BHB 65f60a **RR 76f 60a** 5009[6]
3 b g Dolphin Street (FR) - Lavezzola (IRE) (Salmon Leap (USA)) 11f **(61)**
Form - 4767244006
Record 2000 - 1st:0 2nd:1 3rd:0 Ran:10
Pre2000 - 1st:0 2nd:2 3rd:0 Ran:8
Win Prizemoney £0 *Total Prizemoney* £6,457
2000 Turf 0-8: (6f 2, 7f 4, 8f 2) (gd, g-f 4, frm 3) 2000 AW 0-2: (6f, 7f) (Equi, Fibr)
Light-framed, above-average gelding, effective 6 to 7f, best at 6f, acts on gd to frm, has worn blinkers. Turf high 76 (1st run) - 7th of 16 giving 8lb to Persian Fayre (1 Jun Ayr 7f frm RF 1617). AW high 45. **A P Jarvis [0-18] Mrs D B Brazier.*

TRAMLINE BHB 60f54a **RR 64df 54a** 685[9]
7 b h Shirley Heights 12.1f **(76)** - Tramphip (High Line) 10.3f **(70)**
Form - 0
Record 2000 - 1st:0 2nd:0 3rd:0 Ran:1
Pre2000 - 1st:4 2nd:3 3rd:1 Ran:24
Win Prizemoney £15,673 *Total Prizemoney* £22,831

Wins								
* 1999	Aug	Sandow	(GD)	H	16.4f	65	66	
* 1999	Jun	Doncas	(G-F)	H	14.6f	57	58	
* 1999	Jun	Sandow	(GD)	H	14f	51	54	
* 1997	Jun	Newmar	(G-S)		14.8f		82	<

2000 Turf 0-1: (15f) (hvy)
Average horse, effective 15 to 16f, best at 16f, acts on gd to frm, likes right handed tracks. Becoming disappointing.
**M Blanshard [4-25] H C Promotions Ltd.*

TRAMWAY RR 83+f 5099[2]
2 ch c Lycius (USA) 8.8f **(71)** - Black Fighter (USA) (Secretariat (USA)) 9f **(79)**
Form - 2
Record 2000 - 1st:0 2nd:1 3rd:0 Ran:1
Win Prizemoney £0 *Total Prizemoney* £1,070
2000 Turf 0-1: (7f) (gd)
Currently decent colt. (1st run) - 2nd of 22 to Harmony Row (20 Oct Doncaster 7f gd RF 5099). **H R A Cecil [0-1] Buckram Oak Holdings.*

TRANQUILITY LAKE (USA) RR 110f 5329a[8]
5 b m Rahy (USA) 9.1f **(80)** - Winters' Love (USA) (Danzig (USA)) 8.4f **(76)**
Form - 8
2000 Turf 0-1: (11f) (frm)
Currently Group-class. **J Canani in USA [0-1] & Mrs M Wygod.*

TRANS ISLAND BHB 115f **RR 121f** 5095a[11]
5 b h Selkirk (USA) 7.9f **(76)** - Khubza (Green Desert (USA)) 8.6f **(78)**
Form - 22140
Record 2000 - 1st:1 2nd:2 3rd:0 Ran:5
Pre2000 - 1st:6 2nd:5 3rd:1 Ran:14
Win Prizemoney £180,475 *Total Prizemoney* £276,517

Wins							
* 2000	Jun	Epsom	(GD)	G3	8.5f	119+	<
* 1999	Oct	Longch	(HVY)	G2	8f	117	
* 1999	Spt	Newbur	(G-S)	L	7.3f	104	
* 1999	Spt	Leopar	(SFT)	H	7f	107+	
* 1997	Aug	Deauvi	(SFT)	L	7f	91+	
* 1997	Jly	Newbur	(G-F)		7f	93	
* 1997	Jun	Newbur	(G-F)		6f	86	

2000 Turf 1-5: (7f, 8f 3, 9f 1-1) (hvy, sft 2, gd 1-1, g-f)
Very high-class colt, effective 7 to 9f, best at 8f, acts on g-f, and excels at Newbury. Turf high 121 - 2nd of 7 to Aljabr (20 May Newbury 8f g-f RF 1331) - also 1st of 5 giving 5lb to Duck Row (10 Jun Epsom RF 1862). He improved towards the end of 1999, putting up a game effort when beating Sugarfoot by a neck in the Prix du Rond-Point at Longchamp in October. A good second to Indian Lodge on his reappearance, he reversed the form with that horse when finishing runner-up to Aljabr in the Lockinge. Made all to win the Diomed at Epsom, showing fine battling qualities. He has a grand attitude, but appeared to struggle twice on heavy ground in France later in the season. He has been retired to stud in Ireland, and his breeding suggests there could be some fast sorts among his progeny. **I A Balding [7-19].*

TRAPPER (TUR) RR 99f 4412a[3]
6 ch h Knight Line Dancer - Elemis (USA) (Sir Ivor) 10.2f **(70)**
Form - 3
2000 Turf 0-1: (12f) (gd)
Currently very useful horse. **H Sav in TUR [0-1].*

TRAPPER NORMAN BHB 35f30a **RR 34f 30a** 4333[14]
8 b g Mazilier (USA) 8.5f **(56)** - Free Skip (Free State) 8.7f **(61)**
Form - 000
Record 2000 - 1st:0 2nd:0 3rd:0 Ran:3
Pre2000 - 1st:0 2nd:1 3rd:3 Ran:16
Win Prizemoney £0 *Total Prizemoney* £1,866
2000 Turf 0-3: (6f, 7f, 8f) (g-f 2, frm)
Very moderate gelding, effective 6 to 7f, best at 6f, acts on frm. Turf high 34. Consistent.
**C Smith [0-12] Brian Culley (from R Ingram [0-10] Jan 1997).*

TRAVELLERS DREAM (IRE) BHB 60f **RR 64f** 4822[16]
2 b g Blues Traveller (IRE) - Helen's Dream (Troy) 10.4f **(68)**
Form - 03000
Record 2000 - 1st:0 2nd:0 3rd:1 Ran:5
Win Prizemoney £0 *Total Prizemoney* £624
2000 Turf 0-5: (6f, 7f 2, 8f, 10f) (gd, g-f 3, frm)
Average gelding. Turf high 64.
**B R Millman [0-5] Mrs G Austen-Smith.*

TRAVELLERS REST BHB 60f **RR 68f** 4692[18]
3 b g Nomadic Way (USA) - Rest (Dance In Time (CAN)) 8.9f **(59)**
Form - 0500
Record 2000 - 1st:0 2nd:0 3rd:0 Ran:4
2000 Turf 0-4: (10f 2, 11f, 14f) (gd 2, g-f, frm)
Workmanlike, average gelding. Turf high 68 (began Jly).
**J G Smyth-Osbourne [0-4] R N Richmond-Watson.*

TRAVELLING BAND (IRE) RR 66+f 931[5]
2 b c Blues Traveller (IRE) - Kind of Cute (Prince Sabo) 7.2f **(62)**
Form - 5
Record 2000 - 1st:0 2nd:0 3rd:0 Ran:1
2000 Turf 0-1: (5f) (g-f)
Currently average colt. **I A Balding [0-1] Park House Partnership.*

TRAVELLING LITE (IRE) BHB 76f **RR 83f** 4755[11]
3 b c Blues Traveller (IRE) - Lute and Lyre (IRE) (The Noble Player (USA)) 6.5f **(67)**
Form - 34203400
Record 2000 - 1st:0 2nd:1 3rd:2 Ran:8
Pre2000 - 1st:1 2nd:1 3rd:0 Ran:7
Win Prizemoney £3,240 *Total Prizemoney* £9,486

Wins								
* 1999	Spt	Lingfi	(G-F)	H	7f	72	75	<

2000 Turf 0-8: (8f 6, 9f, 10f) (g-s, gd 2, g-f 3, frm 2)
Workmanlike, decent colt, effective 7 to 10f, best at 8f, acted on gd to frm, had worn blinkers, excelled at Newbury. Turf high 83 (1st run) - 3rd of 7 to Common Place (25 Mar Kempton 9f gd RF 0501). (DEAD) **B R Millman [1-15] The Three Bears Racing II.*

TRAVELMATE BHB 109f **RR 110f** 1000[7]
6 b g Persian Bold 10f **(69)** - Ustka (Lomond (USA)) 8.8f **(65)**
Form - 7
Record 2000 - 1st:0 2nd:0 3rd:0 Ran:1
Pre2000 - 1st:5 2nd:4 3rd:0 Ran:16
Win Prizemoney £29,543 *Total Prizemoney* £121,935

Wins								
* 1998	Spt	Newmar	(GD)	H	12f	91	93	<
* 1998	Aug	Newmar	(G-F)	H	14.8f	81	84+	
* 1998	Jun	Newmar	(GD)	H	12f	76	79	
* 1997	Jun	Newmar	(G-S)	H	12f	73	74	
* 1997	May	Nottin	(GD)	H	10f	66	74+	

2000 Turf 0-1: (16f) (g-s)
Group-class gelding. Made his reappearance in the transferred Sagaro Stakes at Newmarket, but ran poorly and that was the last

seen of him. **J R Fanshawe [5-17] Barford Bloodstock II.*

TRAVEL TARDIA (IRE) BHB 83f83a **RR 78f 83a** 5243[1]

2 br c Petardia 8.2f **(58)** - Annie's Travels (IRE) (Mac's Imp (USA))
Form - 021
Record 2000 - 1st:1 2nd:1 3rd:0 Ran:3
Win Prizemoney £2,261 *Total Prizemoney* £2,781
Wins * 2000 *Oct Wolver (STD) 6f 86+* <
2000 Turf 0-2: (6f, 7f) (g-s 2) 2000 AW 1-1: (6f 1-1) (Fibr 1-1)
Currently useful colt. Turf high 78 (began Oct) - 2nd of 10 giving 6lb to Captain Gibson (16 Oct Pontefract 6f g-s RF 4998). (1st run) - 1st of 12 from In Spirit (28 Oct Wolverhampton RF 5243).
**I A Wood [1-3] Neardown Stables.*

TRAVESTY OF LAW (IRE) BHB 80f **RR 84f** 5199[13]

3 ch g Case Law 6f **(64)** - Bold As Love (Lomond (USA)) 8.8f **(65)**
Form - 000003255470
Record 2000 - 1st:0 2nd:1 3rd:1 Ran:12
Pre2000 - 1st:2 2nd:1 3rd:0 Ran:12
Win Prizemoney £6,515 *Total Prizemoney* £13,529
Wins * 1999 Jun Windso (G-F) 5f 93+ <
* 1999 May Salisb (G-F) 5f 86+
2000 Turf 0-12: (5f 11, 6f) (gd 6, g-f 3, frm 3)
Neat, decent gelding, effective 5f, acts on g-f to frm, best on frm, has worn blinkers. Turf high 97. He has tremendous early pace, but seems happier under waiting tactics nowadays. Best around five furlongs, he is well treated on the pick of his form but may have to drop into claiming company for a confidence boosting win. **B J Meehan [2-24] Stephen Molloy.*

TRAWLING BHB 48f **RR 60f** 97[10]

4 b m Mtoto 11.5f **(71)** - Ghost Tree (IRE) (Caerleon (USA)) 8.6f **(71)**
Form - 880
Record 2000 - 1st:0 2nd:0 3rd:0 Ran:2
Pre2000 - 1st:1 2nd:2 3rd:1 Ran:7
Win Prizemoney £3,161 *Total Prizemoney* £4,961
Wins 1999 *Feb Lingfi (STD) 8f 75+* <
2000 AW 0-2: (7f, 8f) (Equi 2)
Unfurnished, average filly, effective 8f, - acts on Equi. AW high 38. Becoming disappointing.
**C A Dwyer [0-3] A Joannou (from B W Hills [1-6] Jly 1999).*

TREASURE CHEST (IRE) BHB 48a **RR 67f** 4923[P]

5 b g Last Tycoon 9.4f **(73)** - Sought Out (IRE) (Rainbow Quest (USA)) 10.4f **(75)**
Form - 088405860P
Record 2000 - 1st:0 2nd:0 3rd:0 Ran:10
Pre2000 - 1st:0 2nd:3 3rd:3 Ran:15
Win Prizemoney £0 *Total Prizemoney* £8,157
2000 Turf 0-9: (15f, 16f 5, 18f 2, 20f) (hvy, g-s, gd 4, g-f 2, frm) 2000 AW 0-1: (16f) (Equi)
Average gelding, effective 16 to 18f, best at 16f, acts on gd to frm, best on frm, often wears blinkers. Turf high 67 - 4th of 14 getting 14lb from Eastwell Hall (8 Jun Chepstow 18f gd RF 1804).
**M C Pipe [0-31] S A Helaissi (from M P Tregoning [0-6] Oct 1998).*

TREASURE TOUCH (IRE) BHB 71f55a **RR 71f 55a** 5317[3]

6 b g Treasure Kay 6.5f **(53)** - Bally Pourri (IRE) (Law Society (USA)) 9.9f **(70)**
Form - 780113013137124040513
Record 2000 - 1st:6 2nd:1 3rd:4 Ran:22
Pre2000 - 1st:5 2nd:2 3rd:3 Ran:30
Win Prizemoney £40,968 *Total Prizemoney* £48,932

Wins								
* **2000**	Oct	Redcar	(SFT)	H	7f	68	71	
* **2000**	Aug	Carlis	(FRM)	C	5.9f		68	
* **2000**	Jly	Leices	(G-F)	H	6f	64	69	
2000	Jun	Carlis	(G-F)	S	5.9f		50+	
2000	Jun	Catter	(G-S)	H	6f	54	59	
2000	Jun	Catter	(GD)	C	6f		51	
1997	May	Thirsk	(GD)	H	5f	85	85+	
1997	Apr	Newmar	(G-F)	H	6f	72	86	<
1997	Apr	Nottin	(G-F)	H	6.1f	63	78+	
1997	Mar	Nottin	(G-F)	H	6.1f	63	71+	
1997	*Feb*	*Southw*	*(STD)*		*6f*		*69+*	

2000 Turf 6-19: (5f 4, 6f 5-10, 7f 1-4, 8f) (sft, g-s, gd 2-6, g-f 1-6, frm 3-5) 2000 AW 0-3: (5f 2, 6f) (Fibr 3)
Above-average gelding, effective 6 to 7f, best at 6f, acts on gd to frm, best on gd, has worn blinkers, likes left handed tracks, likes tight tracks, excels at Catterick and Carlisle. Turf high 74 - 2nd of 18 to Tom Tun (16 Aug Hamilton 6f gd RF 3698) - also 1st of 17 giving 3lb to Rex Is Okay (24 Oct Redcar RF 5165). AW high 38.
**P D Evans [3-14] David Oxley & James Mitchell (from D Nicholls [7-31] Jun 2000).*

TREBLE RED BHB 40f **RR 43f** 5237[16]

2 b f Shareef Dancer (USA) 10.1f **(67)** - Bilad (USA) (Riverman (USA)) 9.1f **(76)**
Form - 600
Record 2000 - 1st:0 2nd:0 3rd:0 Ran:3
2000 Turf 0-3: (7f, 8f 2) (g-s, gd 2)
Currently moderate filly. Turf high 43 (began Spt).
**M R Channon [0-3] A Merza.*

TREMEZZO RR 58f 4628[11]

2 b c Mind Games - Rosa Van Fleet (Sallust) 8.4f **(63)**
Form - 30
Record 2000 - 1st:0 2nd:0 3rd:1 Ran:2
Win Prizemoney £0 *Total Prizemoney* £644
2000 Turf 0-2: (6f 2) (g-s, gd)
Currently fair colt. Turf high 58 (began Spt).
**B J Meehan [0-2] G Battocchi.*

TREMOR RR 10f 5237[12]

2 ch c Zilzal (USA) 8.5f **(79)** - Happydrome (Ahonoora) 8.1f **(73)**
Form - 0
Record 2000 - 1st:0 2nd:0 3rd:0 Ran:1
2000 Turf 0-1: (8f) (g-s)
Currently moderate colt. **W R Muir [0-1] Mrs J M Muir.*

TRES RAVI (GER) RR 109f 4847a[11]

3 br f Monsun (GER) - Tres Magnifique
Form - 220
2000 Turf 0-3: (10f 2, 11f) (sft, gd, g-f)
Currently Pattern-class filly. Turf high 109 - 2nd of 6 to Di Moi Oui (19 Aug Deauville 10f g-f RF 3945a). **A Wohler in GER [0-3].*

TRESS BHB 75f63a **RR 79f 63a** 4820[4]

2 ch f Wolfhound (USA) 7.3f **(71)** - Splice **(101f)** (Sharpo) 7.7f **(59)**
Form - 74
Record 2000 - 1st:0 2nd:0 3rd:0 Ran:2
Win Prizemoney £0 *Total Prizemoney* £224
2000 Turf 0-2: (6f 2) (g-f, frm)
Currently above-average filly. Turf high 79 (began Spt).
**J R Fanshawe [0-2] Cheveley Park Stud.*

TREVERRICK BHB 46f **RR 37f** 5164[12]

5 b g Formidable (USA) 7.8f **(60)** - Jenny Mere (Brigadier Gerard) 9.3f **(58)**
Form - 50
Record 2000 - 1st:0 2nd:0 3rd:0 Ran:2
Pre2000 - 1st:1 2nd:0 3rd:2 Ran:9
Win Prizemoney £4,795 *Total Prizemoney* £5,587
Wins 1997 Oct Cork (SFT) 9f 79 <
2000 Turf 0-2: (10f, 11f) (g-s, gd)
Very moderate gelding. Turf high 37 (began Oct). Consistent.
**R M H Cowell [0-2] & Mrs D A Gamble (from W P Mullins in IRE [1-9] Jly 1998).*

TREWORNAN BHB 70f **RR 82f** 1895[10]

3 b f Midyan (USA) 9.9f **(64)** - Miss Silca Key (Welsh Saint) 7.6f **(64)**
Form - 00
Record 2000 - 1st:0 2nd:0 3rd:0 Ran:2
Pre2000 - 1st:1 2nd:0 3rd:0 Ran:3
Win Prizemoney £3,631 *Total Prizemoney* £3,962
Wins 1999 Oct Bright (G-S) 6f 82 <
2000 Turf 0-2: (7f, 8f) (gd, g-f)
Leggy, decent filly. Turf high 34.
**J L Dunlop [0-2] Mrs M E Slade (from D R C Elsworth [1-3] Oct 1999).*

TRIBAL PEACE (IRE) BHB 36f35a **RR 36df 35a** 2300[11]

8 ch g Red Sunset 9f **(57)** - Mirabiliary (USA) (Crow (FR)) 7.4f **(75)**
Form - 0000
Record 2000 - 1st:0 2nd:0 3rd:0 Ran:2
Pre2000 - 1st:5 2nd:5 3rd:5 Ran:54
Win Prizemoney £21,403 *Total Prizemoney* £31,738

Wins 1997 Jly Goodwo (G-F) H 9f 60 64
1997 *Jan Lingfi (STD) H* 10f *65 70*
1996 *Jan Lingfi (STD) C* 10f *67*
2000 AW 0-2: (10f 2) (Equi 2)
Very moderate gelding, has worn blinkers. AW high 16.
**B A Pearce [0-6] Richard Gray (from B Gubby [5-52] Dec 1999).*

TRIBAL PRINCE BHB 76f RR 78f 4934[8]

3 b g Prince Sabo 6.6f **(64)** - Tshusick **(77f)** (Dancing Brave (USA)) 8.4f **(76)**
Form - 08134208
Record 2000 - 1st:1 2nd:1 3rd:1 Ran:8
Pre2000 - 1st:0 2nd:2 3rd:0 Ran:5
Win Prizemoney £3,024 *Total Prizemoney* £8,489
Wins * **2000** Aug Folkes (G-F) H 7f 70 75 <
2000 Turf 1-8: (7f 1-5, 8f 3) (sft, g-s, gd 1-2, g-f 2, frm, hrd)
Tall, above-average gelding, effective 5 to 8f, best at 7f, acts on gd to frm, best on g-f, has worn blinkers. Turf high 78 - 4th of 24 giving 4lb to Style Dancer (3 Spt York 7f g-f RF 4195) - also 1st of 14 from Rule of Thumb (18 Aug Folkestone RF 3752).
**P W Harris [1-13] The Tribe.*

TRICCOLO BHB 81f RR 84+f 4734[6]

3 b c Piccolo - Tribal Lady (Absalom) 7.2f **(58)**
Form - 81513156
Record 2000 - 1st:3 2nd:0 3rd:1 Ran:8
Pre2000 - 1st:0 2nd:0 3rd:0 Ran:2
Win Prizemoney £18,024 *Total Prizemoney* £18,819
Wins * **2000** Jly Nottin (G-F) H 8.2f 77 84 <
* **2000** Jun Sandow (G-F) H 8.1f 74 78
* **2000** May Salisb (GD) H 8f 66 71++
2000 Turf 3-8: (6f, 8f 3-6, 10f) (g-s, gd 1-2, g-f, frm 2-4)
Scopey, decent colt, effective 8 to 10f, best at 8f, acts on gd to frm, best on frm. Turf high 84 - 1st of 8 getting 5lb from Hadath (29 Jly Nottingham RF 3216) - also 1st of 6 giving 6lb to Kirovski (16 Jun Sandown RF 2022). Three times a winner over a mile last term, he likes fast ground but shot up the handicap.
**A C Stewart [3-10] Bruce Corman.*

TRICKS (IRE) BHB 53f60a RR 54f 60a 1102[5]

4 b m First Trump - Party Line **(57f 60a)** (Never so Bold) 6.3f **(66)**
Form - 5
Record 2000 - 1st:0 2nd:0 3rd:0 Ran:1
Pre2000 - 1st:1 2nd:1 3rd:1 Ran:9
Win Prizemoney £2,814 *Total Prizemoney* £3,930
Wins 1998 *Dec Lingfi (STD)* 7f *73* <
2000 Turf 0-1: (8f) (g-f)
Neat, above-average filly, has worn blinkers.
**D J Coakley [0-1] Chris van Hoorn (from I A Balding [0-5] Aug 1999).*

TRICKSY (IRE) RR 29f 3135[9]

2 b f Dr Devious (IRE) 9.9f **(74)** - Shoof Althahab (Sadler's Wells (USA)) 10f **(76)**
Form - 0
Record 2000 - 1st:0 2nd:0 3rd:0 Ran:1
2000 Turf 0-1: (7f) (frm)
Currently little account filly. **M A Jarvis [0-1] J Shack.*

TRILLIE BHB 88f RR 83f 5228[7]

2 b f Never so Bold 7.1f **(62)** - Trull **(100f)** (Lomond)
Form - 116027
Record 2000 - 1st:2 2nd:1 3rd:0 Ran:6
Win Prizemoney £7,656 *Total Prizemoney* £9,848
Wins * **2000** Aug Salisb (GD) 7f 89 <
* **2000** Jly Salisb (FRM) 6f 61t
2000 Turf 2-6: (6f 1-3, 7f 1-3) (g-s, gd, g-f 2, frm 2-2)
Decent filly, effective 7f, acts on frm. Turf high 89 (began Jly) - 1st of 7 giving 2lb to Repulse Bay (16 Aug Salisbury RF 3706). Won both of her first two races at Salisbury, but found the step up to Group Three company too much for her at Goodwood.
**D R C Elsworth [2-6] Sir Stanley and Lady Grinstead.*

TRILLIONAIRE RR 72f 5106[11]

2 ch g Dilum (USA) 7.1f **(56)** - Madam Trilby (Grundy) 10.3f **(65)**
Form - 0640
Record 2000 - 1st:0 2nd:0 3rd:0 Ran:4
Win Prizemoney £0 *Total Prizemoney* £330
2000 Turf 0-4: (7f 3, 8f) (gd, g-f 2, frm)
Above-average gelding. Turf high 72 (began Jly).
**R Hannon [0-4] J C Smith.*

TRINCULO (IRE) BHB 113f RR 109f 4608[3]

3 b c Anita's Prince 6f **(62)** - Fandangerina (USA) (Grey Dawn II) 11.1f **(72)**
Form - 0734048073
Record 2000 - 1st:0 2nd:0 3rd:2 Ran:10
Pre2000 - 1st:1 2nd:0 3rd:2 Ran:5
Win Prizemoney £2,931 *Total Prizemoney* £41,669
Wins * 1999 Aug Leices (G-F) 6f 79 <
2000 Turf 0-9: (5f, 6f 7, 7f) (g-s, gd 5, g-f 2, frm) 2000 AW 0-1: (9f) (Dirt)
Rangy, Pattern-class colt, effective 6f, acts on g-s to frm, has worn blinkers. Turf high 109 - 3rd of 8 to Mount Abu (3 May Ascot 6f gd RF 1002). He ran with credit in Listed and Group events last season. Just seems unable to get home over six when the ground is soft but ran a cracker in those conditions at Ascot on his final start. **N P Littmoden [1-15] Joy and Valentine Feerick.*

TRINIDAD (GER) RR 97+f 4716a[1]

3 ch f Big Shuffle (USA) - Tirajana (GER) (Riboprince (USA))
Form - 1
2000 Turf 1-1: (5f 1-1) (sft 1-1)
Currently very useful filly. (1st run) - 1st of 7 giving 4lb to Rozel (24 Spt Cologne RF 4716a).
**U Ostmann in GER [1-1] H Schroer-Dreesmann.*

TRINITY (IRE) RR 64f 4449[25]

4 b h College Chapel - Kaskazi (Dancing Brave (USA)) 8.4f **(76)**
Form - 0064000
Record 2000 - 1st:0 2nd:0 3rd:0 Ran:7
Pre2000 - 1st:1 2nd:3 3rd:1 Ran:18
Win Prizemoney £2,853 *Total Prizemoney* £14,159
Wins * 1999 May Doncas (G-F) 5f 84 <
2000 Turf 0-7: (5f 3, 6f 4) (gd 2, g-f 4, frm)
Light-framed, average colt, effective 5f, acts on frm. Turf high 64.
**M Brittain [1-25] Miss Debi Woods.*

TRINITY BAY RR 3794[10]

3 b f Governor General 6.8f **(45)** - Eucharis (Tickled Pink) 6.5f **(59)**
Form - 0
Record 2000 - 1st:0 2nd:0 3rd:0 Ran:1
2000 Turf 0-1: (5f) (g-f)
Leggy, currently very poor filly. **J Balding [0-1] John Balding.*

TRIPLE BLUE (IRE) BHB 104f RR 97f 5108[6]

2 ch c Bluebird (USA) 7.9f **(71)** - Persian Tapestry (Tap On Wood) 10.3f **(65)**
Form - 11352453406
Record 2000 - 1st:2 2nd:1 3rd:2 Ran:11
Win Prizemoney £9,624 *Total Prizemoney* £25,779
Wins * **2000** May Kempto (SFT) 6f 90+ <
* **2000** May Lingfi (G-S) 5f 78+
2000 Turf 2-11: (5f 1-2, 6f 1-7, 7f 2) (g-s 1-1, gd 1-6, g-f 3, hrd)
Very useful colt, effective 5 to 6f, best at 6f, acts on g-s to g-f, best on g-f, excels at Kempton. Turf high 97 - 3rd of 9 giving 5lb to Santolina (3 Spt Kempton 6f g-f RF 4189) - also 1st of 3 giving 4lb to Barakana (27 May Kempton RF 1496). Consistent. He ran creditably in Listed and Group company after winning twice in the spring, but falls short at that level. Still unproven beyond six furlongs, he looks too high in the handicap and may have to be campaigned on the continent. **R Hannon [2-11] J C Smith.*

TRIPLE DASH BHB 88f RR 91f 4740[5]

4 ch g Nashwan (USA) 10.3f **(79)** - Triple Joy **(104f 98a)** (Most Welcome)
Form - 570007405
Record 2000 - 1st:0 2nd:0 3rd:0 Ran:9
Pre2000 - 1st:2 2nd:1 3rd:2 Ran:7
Win Prizemoney £9,934 *Total Prizemoney* £26,535
Wins * 1999 Jly Sandow (GD) 8.1f 110 <
* 1998 Oct Newcas (SFT) 6f 74+
2000 Turf 0-9: (7f 2, 8f 4, 9f, 10f 2) (sft, g-s 3, gd 3, g-f 2)
Strong, useful gelding, effective 8f, acts on hvy to g-f, has worn blinkers, likes right handed tracks. Turf high 91. Rated a Classic contender in his youth, he is a frustrating individual. Often the

subject of inspired but unsuccessful gambles, he was sold for 72,000gns at Newmarket in October and ran a poor race for Venetia Williams on his hurdling debut three months later.
**Sir Mark Prescott [2-16] Neil Greig Osborne House II.*

TRIPLE SHARP BHB 77f **RR 79f** 5101[6]
3 ch f Selkirk (USA) 7.9f **(76)** - Drei (USA) **(74f)** (Lyphard (USA)) 9.9f **(72)**
Form - 4106
Record 2000 - 1st:1 2nd:0 3rd:0 Ran:4
Win Prizemoney £3,965 *Total Prizemoney* £4,294
Wins * 2000 Jun Chepst (GD) 10.2f 79 <
2000 Turf 1-4: (8f 2, 10f 1-2) (g-s, gd 1-2, g-f)
Well made, above-average filly. Turf high 79 - 1st of 14 from Twin Logic (8 Jun Chepstow RF 1800). Improved from her debut to land a ten-furlong Chepstow maiden in June and looked as though she would be suited by further. **L M Cumani [1-4] Robert Smith.*

TRIPLE WOOD (USA) BHB 66f **RR 65f** 3977[10]
3 b br f Woodman (USA) 9.7f **(77)** - Triple Kiss (Shareef Dancer (USA)) 9.9f **(73)**
Form - 5431080
Record 2000 - 1st:1 2nd:0 3rd:1 Ran:7
Pre2000 - 1st:0 2nd:1 3rd:0 Ran:2
Win Prizemoney £4,075 *Total Prizemoney* £6,180
Wins * 2000 Jly Carlis (FM) 6.9f 59++ <
2000 Turf 1-7: (7f 1-3, 8f 3, 10f) (gd, g-f 2, frm 3, hrd 1-1)
Scopey, average filly. Turf high 80. Consistent. Showed ability in maiden company before making the most of a straightforward task on fast ground at Carlisle in July, but was well beaten in a decent event at Glorious Goodwood. **B Hanbury [1-9] Hilal Salem.*

TRIPPI (USA) RR 5328a[9]
3 b c End Sweep (USA) - Jealous Appeal (USA) (Valid Appeal (USA)) 8.9f **(78)**
Form - 0
2000 AW 0-1: (6f) (Dirt)
Currently very useful colt. **T Pletcher in USA [0-1] Dogwood Stable.*

TRIPPITAKA BHB 53f **RR 38f** 4573[3]
3 b f Ezzoud (IRE) - Bluish (USA) (Alleged (USA)) 10f **(76)**
Form - 783
Record 2000 - 1st:0 2nd:0 3rd:1 Ran:3
Win Prizemoney £0 *Total Prizemoney* £673
2000 Turf 0-3: (10f 2, 11f) (sft, g-f, frm)
Lengthy, currently very moderate filly. Turf high 38.
**N A Graham [0-3] W J de Ruiter.*

TRISTACENTURY (NZ) BHB 60f **RR 72f** 4625[9]
7 b g Stylish Century (AUS) - Taj Mistress (NZ) (Sir Tristram) 10.7f **(76)**
Form - 4450
Record 2000 - 1st:0 2nd:0 3rd:0 Ran:4
Win Prizemoney £0 *Total Prizemoney* £1,362
2000 Turf 0-4: (9f, 12f, 14f, 16f) (gd 3, frm)
Above-average gelding. Turf high 72 (began Aug).
**M A Buckley [0-4] Eddis,J Kottler,B Sc Sweeting.*

TROILUS (USA) RR 80f 5104[10]
3 ch c Bien Bien (USA) - Nakterjal (Vitiges (FR)) 8.2f **(59)**
Form - 832210
Record 2000 - 1st:1 2nd:2 3rd:1 Ran:6
Pre2000 - 1st:0 2nd:0 3rd:0 Ran:2
Win Prizemoney £4,706 *Total Prizemoney* £7,655
Wins * 2000 Aug Newmar (G-F) 12f 80 <
2000 Turf 1-6: (10f, 11f, 12f 1-3, 15f) (gd 2, g-f, frm 1-3)
Decent colt, effective 11 to 12f, best at 12f, acts on g-f to frm, best on frm, has worn blinkers. Turf high 80 - also 1st of 4 giving 5lb to Seeker (12 Aug Newmarket RF 3588). Consistent. He was beginning to look expensive to follow, but had little trouble landing a four-runner Newmarket maiden in August.
**J H M Gosden [1-6] J Toffan & T McCaffery (from A G Foster [0-1] Oct 1999).*

TROIS BHB 55f75a **RR 61f 75a** 4493[7]
4 b g Efisio 7.7f **(69)** - Drei (USA) **(74f)** (Lyphard (USA)) 9.9f **(72)**
Form - 110300504521007
Record 2000 - 1st:2 2nd:1 3rd:1 Ran:14
Pre2000 - 1st:1 2nd:0 3rd:0 Ran:5
Win Prizemoney £9,934 *Total Prizemoney* £12,424
Wins * 2000 *Aug Wolver (STD) H* *9.4f* *70* *75* <
2000 *Jan Wolver (STD) H* *9.4f* *67* *69*
1999 *Dec Wolver (STD)* *9.4f* *66*
2000 Turf 0-10: (8f 2, 9f, 10f 6, 12f) (sft, g-s, gd 3, g-f, frm 3, hrd) 2000 AW 2-4: (9f 2-4) (Fibr 2-4)
Above-average gelding, effective 9f, - acts on Fibr, prefers left handed tracks, prefers tight tracks. Turf high 61. AW high 75 - 1st of 13 getting 3lb from Joondey (19 Aug Wolverhampton RF 3808) - also 1st of 9 giving 19lb to Western Rainbow (6 Jan Wolverhampton RF 0032).
**J G Given [1-12] Mrs Jo Hardy (from G Woodward [2-3] Jan 2000).*

TROIS ELLES BHB 39f35a **RR 47f 35a** 1606[5]
4 b g Elmaamul (USA) 8.1f **(70)** - Ca Ira (IRE) **(24f)** (Dancing Dissident (USA))
Form - 03605
Record 2000 - 1st:0 2nd:0 3rd:1 Ran:5
Pre2000 - 1st:1 2nd:4 3rd:2 Ran:19
Win Prizemoney £2,018 *Total Prizemoney* £7,881
Wins * 1999 *Jan Lingfi (STD) H* *7f* *29* *34* <
2000 Turf 0-3: (8f, 10f 2) (g-s, gd, frm) 2000 AW 0-2: (8f 2) (Equi, Fibr)
Moderate gelding, effective 8 to 10f, best at 8f, acts on gd to hrd, likes tight tracks. Turf high 26. AW high 29.
**R C Spicer [1-24] Mrs A Grayson.*

TROJAN HERO (SAF) BHB 44a **RR 20f** 2880[13]
9 ch g Raise A Man (USA) 7.3f **(63)** - Helleness (SAF) (Northfields (USA)) 9f **(72)**
Form - 6218045370686000
Record 2000 - 1st:0 2nd:0 3rd:1 Ran:11
Pre2000 - 1st:4 2nd:10 3rd:5 Ran:47
Win Prizemoney £9,033 *Total Prizemoney* £19,771
Wins * 1999 *Dec Southw (STD) S* *6f* *46*
1998 *Jun Warwic (GD)* *7f* *64*
1997 *Nov Wolver (STD) H* *7f* *54* *59+*
1997 *Jun Leices (G-F) C* *8f* *70+* <
2000 Turf 0-3: (5f, 6f 2) (gd, frm 2) 2000 AW 0-8: (6f 8) (Equi, Fibr 7)
Very moderate gelding, effective 6 to 7f, best at 7f, - acts on Fibr, has worn blinkers, likes left handed tracks, likes tight tracks. Turf high 12. AW high 52. Becoming disappointing.
**K C Comerford [1-14] G J Sargent (from M A Buckley [0-10] Nov 1999).*

TROJAN PRINCE (USA) RR 81df 4305[4]
2 b br g Known Fact (USA) 8.3f **(72)** - Helen V (USA) (Slewacide (USA))
Form - 0725604
Record 2000 - 1st:0 2nd:1 3rd:0 Ran:7
Win Prizemoney £0 *Total Prizemoney* £1,437
2000 Turf 0-7: (5f 2, 6f 4, 7f) (gd 5, g-f, frm)
Decent gelding, effective 6f, acts on gd. Turf high 81 - 2nd of 12 to Blueberry Forest (27 May Doncaster 6f gd RF 1482).
**B W Hills [0-7] Stephen Crown.*

TROJAN WOLF BHB 52f69a **RR 32f 69a** 3517[12]
5 ch g Wolfhound (USA) 7.3f **(71)** - Trojan Lady (USA) (Irish River (FR)) 8.6f **(78)**
Form - 111453000800615O
Record 2000 - 1st:2 2nd:0 3rd:1 Ran:14
Pre2000 - 1st:2 2nd:2 3rd:0 Ran:19
Win Prizemoney £7,680 *Total Prizemoney* £12,026
Wins * 2000 *Jly Southw (STD) C* *8f* *64*
*** 2000** *Jan Wolver (STD) H* *8.5f* *70* *72* <
* 1999 *Nov Southw (STD) H* *11f* *57* *72* <
* 1999 *Nov Southw (STD) H* *8f* *57* *67*
2000 Turf 0-4: (7f 2, 9f, 10f) (gd, g-f 2, frm) 2000 AW 2-10: (7f, 8f 2-8, 12f) (Equi, Fibr 2-9)
Average gelding, effective 8 to 11f, best at 8f, - acts on Fibr, has worn blinkers, likes left handed tracks, likes tight tracks. Turf high 32. AW high 72 (1st run) - 1st of 12 giving 25lb to Lilanita (4 Jan Wolverhampton RF 0016) - also 1st of 12 giving 3lb to Pippas Pride (21 Jly Southwell RF 3016). Inconsistent. He has taken extremely well to racing on Fibresand, competing a hat-trick at the turn of the year. Effective from a mile to 11 furlongs, he is suited by forcing tactics and goes well for an inexperienced rider.

**P Howling [4-16] Max Pocock (from D Sasse [0-9] Oct 1999).*

TROOPER BHB 65a **RR 35f** 3738[9]
6 b g Rock Hopper 10.6f **(54)** - Silica (USA) (Mr Prospector (USA)) 8.8f **(78)**
Form - 0
Record 2000 - 1st:0 2nd:0 3rd:0 Ran:1
Pre2000 - 1st:0 2nd:3 3rd:0 Ran:10
Win Prizemoney £0 *Total Prizemoney* £2,799
2000 Turf 0-1: (12f) (g-f)
Very moderate gelding, has worn blinkers. Inconsistent. He has finished runner-up in some moderate handicaps on turf and sand.
**M D Hammond [2-10] S T Brankin (from R Akehurst [0-7] Oct 1997).*

TROPICAL BEACH BHB 39f67a **RR 39f 67a** 2893[14]
7 b g Lugana Beach 7f **(63)** - Hitravelscene (Mansingh (USA)) 7.1f **(66)**
Form - 066080
Record 2000 - 1st:0 2nd:0 3rd:0 Ran:6
Pre2000 - 1st:10 2nd:4 3rd:6 Ran:68
Win Prizemoney £29,277 *Total Prizemoney* £36,601

Wins									
*	1999	Jly	Lingfi	(G-F)	H	7.6f	51	53	
*	1999	Jun	Newmar	(G-F)	H	8f	48	51	
*	*1998*	*Dec*	*Wolver*	*(SLW)*	*H*	*9.4f*	*65*	*68*	<
*	*1998*	*Nov*	*Wolver*	*(STD)*	*H*	*8.5f*	*60*	*64*	
*	*1998*	*Oct*	*Wolver*	*(STD)*	*H*	*8.5f*	*55*	*58*	
	1997	Jly	Carlis	(GD)	H	5f	55	61	
	1996	Aug	Hamilt	(G-F)	H	5f	57	62	
	1996	Aug	Thirsk	(G-F)	SH	6f	57	61	
	1996	Jun	Hamilt	(GD)	H	5f	53	56	

2000 Turf 0-6: (7f 2, 8f 3, 11f) (g-s, gd 2, g-f, frm 2)
Fair gelding, effective 8f, acts on frm, often wears blinkers. Turf high 39. **J Pearce [5-35] A J Thompson (from J Berry [5-39] Spt 1997).*

TROPICAL KING (IRE) BHB 60a **RR 57f** 5171a[21]
3 b g Up and At 'em - Princess Gay (IRE) **(9f)** (Fairy King (USA)) 7.7f **(59)**
Form - 42521167060
Record 2000 - 1st:2 2nd:2 3rd:0 Ran:11
Pre2000 - 1st:0 2nd:0 3rd:0 Ran:4
Win Prizemoney £3,659 *Total Prizemoney* £5,825

Wins								
	2000	*Mar*	*Southw*	*(STD)*	*S*	*5f*	*59*	
	2000	*Mar*	*Wolver*	*(STD)*	*S*	*5f*	*65*	<

2000 Turf 0-4: (5f 3, 7f) (hvy, sft, g-s) 2000 AW 2-7: (5f 2-3, 6f 4) (Fibr 2-7)
Average gelding, effective 5f, - acts on Fibr. Turf high 57 (began Aug). AW high 65. Inconsistent.
**Emmanuel Hughes in IRE [0-4] Mrs A Hughes (from D Carroll [2-7] Mar 2000).*

TROPICAL RIVER (IRE) BHB 49f44a **RR 55f 44a** 5132[18]
2 b c Lahib (USA) 8f **(69)** - Tropical Dance (USA) **(88f)** (Thorn Dance (USA))
Form - 600
Record 2000 - 1st:0 2nd:0 3rd:0 Ran:3
2000 Turf 0-3: (5f, 6f 2) (sft, g-s, frm)
Currently fair colt. Turf high 55. **E Stanners [0-3] George Ward.*

TROTTER'S FUTURE **RR 49f** 5312[20]
2 b c Emperor Jones (USA) - Miss Up N Go (Gorytus (USA)) 7.8f **(60)**
Form - 00
Record 2000 - 1st:0 2nd:0 3rd:0 Ran:2
2000 Turf 0-2: (7f, 8f) (g-s 2)
Currently moderate colt. Turf high 49 (began Oct).
**A C Stewart [0-2] McGuinness, Saunders Collins.*

TROUBADOUR GIRL BHB 60f53a **RR 74?f 53a** 5117[6]
2 b f Clantime 6.6f **(57)** - Nilu (IRE) (Ballad Rock) 7.8f **(63)**
Form - 087386
Record 2000 - 1st:0 2nd:0 3rd:1 Ran:6
Win Prizemoney £0 *Total Prizemoney* £280
2000 Turf 0-4: (6f 4) (gd, g-f, frm 2) 2000 AW 0-2: (5f 2) (Fibr 2)
Above-average filly. Turf high 74. AW high 37 (began Jly).
**M A Jarvis [0-6] The Merchants.*

TROUBLE BHB 37f **RR 55df** 4649[13]
4 b g Kris 10f **(75)** - Ringlet (USA) **(53f 54a)** (Secreto (USA)) 8.7f **(72)**
Form - 00
Record 2000 - 1st:0 2nd:0 3rd:0 Ran:2
Pre2000 - 1st:0 2nd:0 3rd:0 Ran:4
2000 Turf 0-1: (11f) (g-f) 2000 AW 0-1: (11f) (Fibr)
Scopey, fair gelding.
**P W Hiatt [0-2] Red Lion (Chipping Norton) Partnership (from B W Hills [0-4] Spt 1999).*

TROUBLE MOUNTAIN (USA) BHB 91f **RR 93f** 5133[6]
3 br c Mt Livermore (USA) 7.7f **(90)** - Trouble Free (USA) (Nodouble (USA)) 8.8f **(68)**
Form - 650086
Record 2000 - 1st:0 2nd:0 3rd:0 Ran:6
Pre2000 - 1st:2 2nd:1 3rd:1 Ran:4
Win Prizemoney £10,024 *Total Prizemoney* £24,133

Wins							
*	1999	Jly	Doncas	(G-F)	7f	95	<
*	1999	Jly	Haydoc	(FRM)	6f	92+	

2000 Turf 0-6: (7f 4, 8f, 9f) (sft, gd, g-f 2, frm 2)
Light-framed, useful colt, effective 6f, acts on frm. Turf high 101. Consistent. He did well as a juvenile, but cut little ice in handicap company last term. **B W Hills [2-10] Maktoum Al Maktoum.*

TROUBLE NEXT DOOR (IRE) **RR 13f** 5224[9]
2 b c Persian Bold 10f **(69)** - Adjacent (IRE) (Doulab (USA)) 9.8f **(65)**
Form - 0
Record 2000 - 1st:0 2nd:0 3rd:0 Ran:1
2000 Turf 0-1: (8f) (gd)
Currently fair colt. **N P Littmoden [0-1] Mrs Linda Francis.*

TROUBLESHOOTER BHB 69f **RR 71tf** 4808[13]
2 b c Ezzoud (IRE) - Oublier L'Ennui (FR) (Bellman (FR)) 8.4f **(77)**
Form - 60282762630
Record 2000 - 1st:0 2nd:3 3rd:1 Ran:11
Win Prizemoney £0 *Total Prizemoney* £3,743
2000 Turf 0-11: (5f 4, 6f 6, 7f) (g-s, gd 2, g-f 5, frm 3)
Above-average colt, effective 6f, acts on frm, often wears blinkers. Turf high 71. **W R Muir [0-11] Trouble Free Partnership.*

TROYS GUEST (IRE) BHB 68f **RR 66f** 4574[8]
2 gr f Be My Guest (USA) 10.2f **(66)** - Troja (Troy) 10.4f **(68)**
Form - 53368
Record 2000 - 1st:0 2nd:0 3rd:2 Ran:5
Win Prizemoney £0 *Total Prizemoney* £1,089
2000 Turf 0-5: (6f 4, 7f) (sft, gd 3, frm)
Average filly. Turf high 66 (began Jly) - 3rd of 12 getting 5lb from Time To Remember (9 Aug Pontefract 6f frm RF 3502).
**E J Alston [0-5] Trevor Hemmings.*

TRUDIE BHB 56f **RR 59f** 5081[14]
2 b f Komaite (USA) 6.9f **(61)** - Irish Limerick (Try My Best (USA)) 7.6f **(67)**
Form - 6030
Record 2000 - 1st:0 2nd:0 3rd:1 Ran:4
Win Prizemoney £0 *Total Prizemoney* £420
2000 Turf 0-3: (5f 3) (hvy, gd, g-f) 2000 AW 0-1: (5f) (Fibr)
Fair filly. Turf high 59 (began Spt).
**Miss J F Craze [0-4] Mrs S E Cooper.*

TRUE CRYSTAL (IRE) BHB 86f **RR 89f** 4260[11]
3 b f Sadler's Wells (USA) 11.3f **(87)** - State Crystal (IRE) **(107f)** (High Estate)
Form - 1040
Record 2000 - 1st:1 2nd:0 3rd:0 Ran:4
Win Prizemoney £4,329 *Total Prizemoney* £4,865

Wins							
*	**2000**	Jun	Kempto	(G-F)	10f	84	<

2000 Turf 1-4: (10f 1-1, 12f 2, 15f) (gd, g-f, frm 1-2)
Scopey, useful filly. Turf high 89 - 4th of 5 getting 9lb from Fair Warning (19 Aug Newbury 12f frm RF 3793) - also 1st of 8 from Amneris (28 Jun Kempton RF 2342). Unraced at two, she ran green when winning a Newcastle maiden on her debut. Found wanting since, but is obviously held in some regard.
**H R A Cecil [1-4] Michael Poland.*

TRUE NIGHT BHB 80f **RR 73f** 3909[1]
3 b c Night Shift (USA) 8.1f **(73)** - Dead Certain (Absalom) 7.2f **(58)**
Form - 41
Record 2000 - 1st:1 2nd:0 3rd:0 Ran:2
Win Prizemoney £3,016 *Total Prizemoney* £3,303

Wins *** 2000** Aug Lingfi (G-F) 6f 73+ **<**
2000 Turf 1-2: (6f 1-2) (frm 1-2)
Scopey, currently above-average colt. Turf high 73 (began Jly) - 1st of 14 from Amjad (23 Aug Lingfield RF 3909).
**H Candy [1-2] The Hon Mrs M A Marten.*

TRUE NOTE RR 39f
5132[16]
2 b g So Factual (USA) - Singer on the Roof (Chief Singer) 8.9f **(66)**
Form - 0
Record 2000 - 1st:0 2nd:0 3rd:0 Ran:1
2000 Turf 0-1: (6f) (sft)
Currently very moderate gelding. **D R C Elsworth [0-1] J C Smith.*

TRUE OBSESSION (USA) BHB 65f RR 62f
2196[8]
3 br c Lear Fan (USA) 10.4f **(80)** - Valid Fixation (USA) (Valid Appeal (USA)) 8.9f **(78)**
Form - 058
Record 2000 - 1st:0 2nd:0 3rd:0 Ran:3
Pre2000 - 1st:1 2nd:2 3rd:2 Ran:8
Win Prizemoney £2,853 *Total Prizemoney* £7,483
Wins *** 1999** *Jun Southw (STD) 7f 84* **<**
2000 Turf 0-2: (8f, 10f) (gd 2) 2000 AW 0-1: (12f) (Fibr)
Workmanlike, decent colt, effective 7f, acts on g-f to frm - acts on Fibr, best on g-f. Turf high 62. Becoming disappointing.
**P F I Cole [1-11] Tony Feng.*

TRUE ROMANCE BHB 20f22a RR 39f 22a
2288[5]
4 b g Rainbow Quest (USA) 11.2f **(81)** - First Kiss (Kris) 9.5f **(73)**
Form - 07005
Record 2000 - 1st:0 2nd:0 3rd:0 Ran:5
Pre2000 - 1st:0 2nd:0 3rd:0 Ran:1
2000 Turf 0-2: (14f 2) (gd, g-f) 2000 AW 0-3: (7f, 12f 2) (Equi, Fibr 2)
Very moderate gelding, has worn blinkers. Turf high 39. AW high 17.
**Miss D A McHale [0-2] Yusuf Baig (from C A Dwyer [0-3] Feb 2000).*

TRUE THUNDER RR 88f
2443[1]
3 b c Bigstone (IRE) - Puget Dancer (USA) (Seattle Dancer (USA))
Form - 1
Record 2000 - 1st:1 2nd:0 3rd:0 Ran:1
Win Prizemoney £6,743 *Total Prizemoney* £6,743
Wins *** 2000** Jly Newcas (FRM) 8f 88 **<**
2000 Turf 1-1: (8f 1-1) (frm 1-1)
Scopey, currently useful colt. (1st run) - 1st of 8 from Tolstoy (1 Jly Newcastle RF 2443). **H R A Cecil [1-1] Buckram Oak Holdings.*

TRUMPET BLUES (USA) BHB 40f48a RR 23f 48a
4173[12]
4 br g Dayjur (USA) 6.8f **(79)** - Iosifa (Top Ville) 11.7f **(68)**
Form - 030000
Record 2000 - 1st:0 2nd:0 3rd:1 Ran:6
Pre2000 - 1st:0 2nd:1 3rd:0 Ran:3
Win Prizemoney £0 *Total Prizemoney* £1,856
2000 Turf 0-4: (6f 4) (g-f 3, frm) 2000 AW 0-2: (6f, 7f) (Fibr 2)
Neat, moderate gelding. Turf high 23. AW high 40. Becoming disappointing.
**D Nicholls [0-6] Roddy Owen (from J L Dunlop [0-3] Apr 1999).*

TRUMPET SOUND (IRE) BHB 104f RR 109f
4967[10]
3 b c Theatrical 11.5f **(78)** - Free At Last (Shirley Heights) 10.3f **(74)**
Form - 174260
Record 2000 - 1st:1 2nd:1 3rd:0 Ran:6
Pre2000 - 1st:0 2nd:0 3rd:0 Ran:1
Win Prizemoney £4,972 *Total Prizemoney* £11,558
Wins *** 2000** May Bright (G-F) 10f 85 **<**
2000 Turf 1-6: (8f, 9f, 10f 1-3, 11f) (g-s, gd, g-f 2, frm 1-2)
Scopey, Pattern-class colt, effective 10f, acts on g-f to frm. Turf high 109 - 2nd of 6 getting 5lb from Claxon (22 Jly Newbury 10f g-f RF 3025). Winner of a Brighton maiden on his return, he has since reached the frame in pattern company and there should be a listed race for him, probably over ten furlongs.
**L M Cumani [1-7] Gerald Leigh.*

TRUMPINGTON BHB 73f RR 76f
4822[1]
2 ch f First Trump - Brockton Flame **(65f)** (Emarati (USA))
Form - 8310471
Record 2000 - 1st:2 2nd:0 3rd:1 Ran:7
Win Prizemoney £7,232 *Total Prizemoney* £8,005
Wins *** 2000** Oct Windso (G-S) H 10f 69 76 **<**
*** 2000** Jly Newbur (G-F) 7f 75
2000 Turf 2-7: (6f, 7f 1-4, 8f, 10f 1-1) (gd, g-f 1-3, frm 1-3)
Above-average filly, effective 7 to 10f, acts on g-f to frm. Turf high 76 - 1st of 21 giving 3lb to Homelife (6 Oct Windsor RF 4822) - also 1st of 11 from Trustthunder (21 Jly Newbury RF 2998).
**I A Balding [2-7] Park House Partnership.*

TRUMP STREET BHB 42f40a RR 55f 40a
4826[22]
4 b m First Trump - Pepeke (Mummy's Pet) 7.7f **(60)**
Form - 7025010007000
Record 2000 - 1st:1 2nd:1 3rd:0 Ran:13
Pre2000 - 1st:0 2nd:1 3rd:1 Ran:7
Win Prizemoney £3,883 *Total Prizemoney* £7,005
Wins *** 2000** May Chepst (HVY) H 6.1f 48 55 **<**
2000 Turf 1-11: (5f 2, 6f 1-5, 7f 2, 8f 2) (sft, g-s 1-3, gd 2, g-f 3, frm 2)
2000 AW 0-2: (5f, 7f) (Fibr 2)
Scopey, fair filly, effective 6 to 8f, acts on sft to g-s, has worn blinkers. Turf high 55 - 1st of 8 getting 17lb from Dancing Empress (29 May Chepstow RF 1520). AW high 10. Becoming disappointing.
**S G Knight [1-13] Richard Withers (from N A Graham [0-7] Spt 1999).*

TRUSTED MOLE (IRE) BHB 65f61a RR 67f 61a
4203[12]
2 b c Eagle Eyed (USA) - Orient Air **(37f 45a)** (Prince Sabo) 7.2f **(62)**
Form - 66374480
Record 2000 - 1st:0 2nd:0 3rd:1 Ran:8
Win Prizemoney £0 *Total Prizemoney* £1,001
2000 Turf 0-6: (5f, 6f 2, 7f 2, 8f) (gd, g-f 3, frm 2) 2000 AW 0-2: (6f, 7f) (Fibr 2)
Average colt, effective 7f, acts on gd, has worn blinkers. Turf high 67 - 4th of 9 getting 14lb from Tortuguero (7 Jly Salisbury 7f gd RF 2599). AW high 33. **J A Osborne [0-8] Desmond de Silva.*

TRUST IN PAULA (USA) BHB 66f RR 70f
4820[8]
2 b f Arazi (USA) 9.2f **(74)** - Trust In Dixie (USA) (Dixieland Band (USA)) 7f **(74)**
Form - 708
Record 2000 - 1st:0 2nd:0 3rd:0 Ran:3
2000 Turf 0-3: (6f, 7f 2) (g-f 2, frm)
Currently above-average filly. Turf high 70 (began Aug).
**D HaydnJones [0-3] S Hunter.*

TRUSTTHUNDER BHB 87f RR 79f
4965[7]
2 ch f Selkirk (USA) 7.9f **(76)** - Royal Cat (Royal Academy (USA))
Form - 722017
Record 2000 - 1st:1 2nd:2 3rd:0 Ran:6
Win Prizemoney £3,484 *Total Prizemoney* £5,817
Wins *** 2000** Spt Lingfi (SFT) 6f 77+ **<**
2000 Turf 1-6: (6f 1-3, 7f 3) (gd 1-2, g-f, frm 3)
Above-average filly, effective 6 to 7f, best at 6f, acts on gd to frm, best on gd. Turf high 79 - 7th of 30 getting 3lb from Goodie Twosues (13 Oct Newmarket 6f gd RF 4965) - also 1st of 15 getting 5lb from Mysteri Dancer (29 Spt Lingfield RF 4725). Showed ability in her early starts, but was impressive the first time she encountered soft ground when easily winning a Lingfield maiden.
**N P Littmoden [1-6] Tallulah Racing.*

TRUTH BE KNOWN RR 5f
4002[11]
2 gr g Bin Ajwaad (IRE) - Fair Minded (Shareef Dancer (USA)) 9.9f **(73)**
Form - 00
Record 2000 - 1st:0 2nd:0 3rd:0 Ran:2
2000 Turf 0-2: (5f, 6f) (gd, g-f)
Currently very poor gelding, often wears blinkers. Turf high 5 (began Jly). **E L James [0-2] Miss Lawson Johnston.*

TRY PARIS (IRE) BHB 34f38a RR 36f 38a
2358[8]
4 b g Paris House 5.9f **(64)** - Try My Rosie (Try My Best (USA)) 7.6f **(67)**
Form - 000448
Record 2000 - 1st:0 2nd:0 3rd:0 Ran:6
Pre2000 - 1st:0 2nd:0 3rd:0 Ran:10
2000 Turf 0-5: (8f, 10f 2, 12f 2) (gd 2, g-f 2, frm) 2000 AW 0-1: (9f) (Fibr)
Very moderate gelding, effective 10f, acts on gd to g-f, often wears blinkers (very effectively), likes left handed tracks, prefers tight tracks. Turf high 36 - 4th of 19 getting 6lb from Sheer Face (17 May

Brighton 10f g-f RF 1255).
**H J Collingridge [0-6] The Headquarters Partnership II (from Mrs L C Jewell [0-6] Oct 1999).*

TRYSOR BHB 53f **RR 53f** 3847[1]
4 b h Then Again 7.4f **(52)** - Zahiah (So Blessed) 8.7f **(67)**
Form - 0770021
Record 2000 - 1st:1 2nd:1 3rd:0 Ran:7
Win Prizemoney £2,618 *Total Prizemoney* £3,483
Wins * **2000** Aug Hamilt (SFT) SH 8.3f 47 53 <
2000 Turf 1-7: (5f, 7f 2, 8f 1-4) (hvy, g-s, gd 1-2, g-f, frm 2)
Scopey, fair colt, effective 8f, acts on gd to frm, has worn blinkers. Turf high 53 - 1st of 16 giving 9lb to Claim Gebal Claim (22 Aug Hamilton RF 3847). **S C Williams [1-7] Tyrnest Ltd.*

TSUNAMI BHB 70f **RR 55f** 1375[3]
4 b m Beveled (USA) 6.9f **(64)** - Alvecote Lady (Touching Wood (USA)) 8.2f **(55)**
Form - 06683
Record 2000 - 1st:0 2nd:0 3rd:1 Ran:5
Pre2000 - 1st:0 2nd:0 3rd:1 Ran:13
Win Prizemoney £0 *Total Prizemoney* £2,263
2000 Turf 0-1: (7f) (frm) 2000 AW 0-4: (8f 2, 9f, 10f) (Equi, Fibr 3)
Fair filly, effective 7 to 8f, acts on gd to g-f. AW high 34. Becoming disappointing.
**P D Evans [0-5] M W Lawrence (from D R C Elsworth [0-12] Oct 1999).*

TSWALU BHB 51f **RR 57f** 4387[18]
3 b f Cosmonaut - Madam Taylor (Free State) 8.7f **(61)**
Form - 0
Record 2000 - 1st:0 2nd:0 3rd:0 Ran:1
Pre2000 - 1st:0 2nd:0 3rd:1 Ran:3
Win Prizemoney £0 *Total Prizemoney* £517
2000 Turf 0-1: (11f) (gd)
Workmanlike, fair filly. **M Mullineaux [0-4] Michael Mullineaux.*

TUCSON (IRE) BHB 32f **RR** 2738[14]
3 ch g Gabitat 8.5f **(44)** - Gabibti (IRE) (Dara Monarch) 8.8f **(59)**
Form - 00
Record 2000 - 1st:0 2nd:0 3rd:0 Ran:2
Pre2000 - 1st:0 2nd:0 3rd:0 Ran:1
2000 AW 0-2: (7f, 10f) (Equi 2)
Workmanlike, currently poor gelding. AW high 15.
**B Gubby [0-3] Brian Gubby Ltd.*

TUDOR REEF (IRE) BHB 102f **RR 89f** 5315[1]
2 b c Mujadil (USA) 7.7f **(70)** - Exciting (Mill Reef (USA)) 10.5f **(78)**
Form - 046411
Record 2000 - 1st:2 2nd:0 3rd:0 Ran:6
Win Prizemoney £8,970 *Total Prizemoney* £9,538
Wins * **2000** Nov Doncas (HVY) 8f 89 <
* **2000** Oct Bright (SFT) 8f 80
2000 Turf 2-6: (6f, 7f 3, 8f 2-2) (g-s 2-2, g-f 2, frm 2)
Useful colt, effective 7 to 8f, best at 8f, acts on g-s to frm, best on g-s. Turf high 89 - 1st of 6 from Dayglow Dancer (3 Nov Doncaster RF 5315) - also 1st of 9 giving 5lb to English Harbour (19 Oct Brighton RF 5075). Ended the season by winning a Brighton maiden and a Doncaster conditions event.
**J Noseda [2-3] B E Nielsen (from M R Channon [0-3] Aug 2000).*

TUDOR ROMANCE BHB 18f **RR** 4723[14]
15 b g Aragon 7.7f **(58)** - Dovey (Welsh Pageant) 10f **(65)**
Form - 00
Record 2000 - 1st:0 2nd:0 3rd:0 Ran:2
Pre2000 - 1st:1 2nd:0 3rd:0 Ran:4
Win Prizemoney £2,616 *Total Prizemoney* £2,616
2000 Turf 0-1: (10f) (g-f) 2000 AW 0-1: (12f) (Equi)
Very poor gelding.
**T J Arnold [0-2] T J Arnold (from L A Dace [0-2] Jun 1998).*

TUFAMORE (USA) BHB 38f51a **RR 38f 51a** 2674[8]
4 ch g Mt Livermore (USA) 7.7f **(90)** - Tufa (Warning)
Form - 421053358
Record 2000 - 1st:1 2nd:1 3rd:2 Ran:9
Pre2000 - 1st:0 2nd:0 3rd:1 Ran:8
Win Prizemoney £2,802 *Total Prizemoney* £5,021
Wins * **2000** *Jan Wolver (STD) H 8.5f 46 54* <
2000 Turf 0-2: (10f 2) (g-s, frm) 2000 AW 1-7: (8f 1-4, 9f 2, 12f) (Equi, Fibr 1-6)
Fair gelding, effective 8 to 9f, - acts on Fibr, often wears blinkers (effectively), likes left handed tracks. Turf high 38. AW high 63 - 2nd of 11 giving 1lb to Bachelors Pad (20 Jan Wolverhampton 9f Fibr RF 0121) - also 1st of 10 getting 9lb from Scissor Ridge (27 Jan Wolverhampton RF 0172).
**K R Burke [1-18] D G & D J Robinson.*

TUFTY HOPPER BHB 65f56a **RR 67f 56a** 5119[2]
3 b g Rock Hopper 10.6f **(54)** - Melancolia (Legend of France (USA)) 9.5f **(61)**
Form - 64422433222745332662
Record 2000 - 1st:0 2nd:7 3rd:4 Ran:20
Pre2000 - 1st:0 2nd:0 3rd:0 Ran:1
Win Prizemoney £0 *Total Prizemoney* £9,505
2000 Turf 0-14: (11f 4, 12f 4, 13f, 14f 4, 15f) (g-s, gd 2, g-f 7, frm 4)
2000 AW 0-6: (9f, 12f 4, 16f) (Equi, Fibr 5)
Workmanlike, average gelding, effective 11 to 14f, best at 14f, acts on gd to frm, best on g-f, has worn blinkers, excels at Yarmouth. Turf high 71 - 2nd of 4 to Zafonic's Song (4 Jly Yarmouth 11f g-f RF 2498). AW high 59. Consistent.
**P Howling [0-20] Exors of the late G H Tufts (from J Pearce [0-1] Oct 1999).*

TUI BHB 35f28a **RR 39f 28a** 2101[3]
5 b m Tina's Pet 7.4f **(56)** - Curious Feeling (Nishapour (FR)) 9.1f **(61)**
Form - 515403
Record 2000 - 1st:1 2nd:0 3rd:1 Ran:6
Pre2000 - 1st:2 2nd:2 3rd:1 Ran:27
Win Prizemoney £10,521 *Total Prizemoney* £13,079
Wins * **2000** May Bright (FRM) H 11.9f 30 34
* 1998 Aug Newmar (G-F) H 12f 51 56 <
* 1998 Jly Beverl (GD) H 9.9f 42 47
2000 Turf 1-6: (11f, 12f 1-3, 15f, 16f) (hvy, g-s, gd, g-f 1-2, frm)
Very moderate filly, effective 12 to 16f, acts on hvy to g-f, best on g-f, prefers left handed tracks, likes tight tracks. Turf high 39 - 3rd of 13 getting 4lb from Renaissance Lady (19 Jun Warwick 16f g-f RF 2101) - also 1st of 11 getting 32lb from Elms Schoolgirl (17 May Brighton RF 1256). A winner twice in 1998 on varying ground, she has not shown much until winning at Brighton in May. Apparently needs time between her races.
**P Bowen [6-45] Dragon Racing (from K McAuliffe [0-4] Aug 1997).*

TUIGAMALA BHB 25f31a **RR 31a** 4585[14]
9 b g Welsh Captain 7.2f **(54)** - Nelliellamay (Super Splash (USA)) 7.3f **(54)**
Form - 0
Record 2000 - 1st:0 2nd:0 3rd:0 Ran:1
Pre2000 - 1st:3 2nd:1 3rd:1 Ran:34
Win Prizemoney £8,145 *Total Prizemoney* £10,258
Wins * 1996 *Feb Lingfi (STD) H 8f 55 58* <
2000 AW 0-1: (12f) (Equi)
Very moderate gelding. **R Ingram [3-35] Adrian O'Halloran.*

TULSA (IRE) BHB 33f39a **RR 38f 39a** 5154[13]
6 b g Priolo (USA) 10.9f **(71)** - Lagrion (USA) (Diesis) 9.3f **(69)**
Form - 552700
Record 2000 - 1st:0 2nd:1 3rd:0 Ran:6
Pre2000 - 1st:1 2nd:1 3rd:3 Ran:27
Win Prizemoney £2,053 *Total Prizemoney* £5,386
Wins * 1999 *Jly Lingfi (STD) H 10f 35 39* <
2000 Turf 0-5: (12f 4, 16f) (g-f 3, frm 2) 2000 AW 0-1: (12f) (Equi)
Very moderate gelding, effective 10 to 16f, best at 12f, acts on g-f to frm - acts on Equi, best on frm, has worn blinkers, likes Windsor. Turf high 38 (began Jly) - 5th of 19 getting 8lb from Mysterium (31 Jly Windsor 12f frm RF 3260).
**L MontagueHall [1-16] Miss J D Anstee & Partners 2 (from B Gubby [0-22] Oct 1998).*

TUMBLEWEED GLEN (IRE) BHB 62f **RR 63df** 4546[13]
4 ch g Mukaddamah (USA) 7.6f **(74)** - Mistic Glen (IRE) (Mister Majestic)
Form - 0
Record 2000 - 1st:0 2nd:0 3rd:0 Ran:1
Pre2000 - 1st:2 2nd:0 3rd:2 Ran:15
Win Prizemoney £9,715 *Total Prizemoney* £13,350

Wins 1999 Spt Leices (GD) S 10f 61
1998 Spt Warwic (G-F) H 8f 75 75 <
2000 Turf 0-1: (16f) (g-s)
Well made, average gelding, effective 9 to 10f, best at 10f, acts on gd to frm, best on gd, has worn blinkers.
**N A Twiston-Davies [0-8] Peter Kelsall (from B J Meehan [2-17] Spt 1999).*

TUMBLEWEED QUARTET (USA) BHB 73f RR 71f 1306[11]

4 b g Manila (USA) 10f **(81)** - Peggy's String (USA) (Highland Park (USA))
Form - 5600
Record 2000 - 1st:0 2nd:0 3rd:0 Ran:4
Pre2000 - 1st:1 2nd:0 3rd:2 Ran:11
Win Prizemoney £6,257 *Total Prizemoney* £17,824
Wins * 1998 Jun Newbur (SFT) 6f 71+ <
2000 Turf 0-4: (8f 3, 10f) (gd 4)
Scopey, above-average gelding, has worn blinkers. Turf high 78.
**B J Meehan [1-15] The Tumbleweed Partnership.*

TUMBLEWEED RIDGE BHB 113f91a RR 115f 91a 3759[P]

7 ch h Indian Ridge 7.6f **(74)** - Billie Blue (Ballad Rock) 7.8f **(63)**
Form - 231374P
Record 2000 - 1st:1 2nd:1 3rd:2 Ran:7
Pre2000 - 1st:8 2nd:7 3rd:4 Ran:40
Win Prizemoney £160,743 *Total Prizemoney* £240,905
Wins * 2000 Jun Leopar (G-F) G3 7f 113+
* 1999 Spt Epsom (GD) L 7f 118 <
* 1999 Jun Longch (GD) G3 7f 113
* 1999 Jun Leopar (GD) G3 7f 111
* 1998 Jun Leopar (SFT) G3 7f 109
* 1998 Apr Newmar (SFT) H 7f 101 106
* 1997 Jly Newmar (G-F) H 7f 94 101
2000 Turf 1-7: (7f 1-7) (gd 3, g-f 1-3, frm)
High-class horse, effective 7f, acts on gd to g-f, best on gd, has worn blinkers, likes left handed tracks, excels at Leopardstown, does well at Longchamp. Turf high 115 - 3rd of 9 giving 3lb to Josr Algarhoud (25 Jun Longchamp 7f gd RF 2388a) - also 1st of 7 giving 16lb to Bashkir (14 Jun Leopardstown RF 2131a). A seven furlong specialist, he made all when winning Leopardstown's Group Three Ballycorus Stakes for the third year in succession. Pulled-up and dismounted at Newbury in August, he may have a problem.
**B J Meehan [9-47] The Tumbleweed Partnership.*

TUMBLEWEED RIVER (IRE) BHB 75f RR 76f 5122[7]

4 ch g Thatching 7.8f **(69)** - Daphne Indica (IRE) (Ballad Rock) 7.8f **(63)**
Form - 000207
Record 2000 - 1st:0 2nd:1 3rd:0 Ran:6
Pre2000 - 1st:1 2nd:1 3rd:0 Ran:5
Win Prizemoney £4,188 *Total Prizemoney* £8,874
Wins * 1999 Spt Haydoc (SFT) 7.1f 77+ <
2000 Turf 0-6: (7f 5, 8f) (sft, g-s 3, gd, frm)
Scopey, above-average gelding, effective 6 to 7f, best at 7f, acts on g-s to gd, best on gd, has worn blinkers. Turf high 76 - 2nd of 16 giving 9lb to Slumbering (30 Spt Sandown 7f g-s RF 4753).
**B J Meehan [1-11] The Fourth Tumbleweed Partnership.*

TUMBLEWEED TENOR (IRE) BHB 74f78a RR 71f 78a 5015[1]

2 b g Mujadil (USA) 7.7f **(70)** - Princess Carmen (IRE) (Arokar (FR))
Form - 52831
Record 2000 - 1st:1 2nd:1 3rd:1 Ran:5
Win Prizemoney £1,750 *Total Prizemoney* £3,194
Wins * 2000 *Oct Wolver (STD)* 6f 80 <
2000 Turf 0-4: (5f 3, 7f) (gd, frm 3) 2000 AW 1-1: (6f 1-1) (Fibr 1-1)
Decent gelding. Turf high 71 - 3rd of 16 giving 8lb to Chaweng Beach (5 Spt Lingfield 7f frm RF 4223). (1st run) - 1st of 9 from A C Azure (17 Oct Wolverhampton RF 5015).
**B J Meehan [1-5] The Seventh Tumbleweed Partnership.*

TUMBLEWEED TOR BHB 89f RR 92f 4465[10]

3 b g Rudimentary (USA) 8.2f **(66)** - Hilly (Town Crier) 10.2f **(55)**
Form - 7310636330
Record 2000 - 1st:1 2nd:0 3rd:4 Ran:10
Pre2000 - 1st:0 2nd:0 3rd:1 Ran:3
Win Prizemoney £6,730 *Total Prizemoney* £15,135
Wins * 2000 May Nottin (G-S) 8.2f 91 <
2000 Turf 1-10: (8f 1-8, 9f, 10f) (sft 2, gd 1-3, g-f 3, frm 2)
Workmanlike, useful gelding, effective 8f, acts on gd to frm, best on gd. Turf high 95 - 3rd of 13 giving 13lb to Chapel Royale (13 Jly Newmarket 8f gd RF 2772) - also 1st of 8 from Dare Hunter (19 May Nottingham RF 1311). Consistent. He is in the Handicapper's grip, but tries hard and was consistent last year. Worth another try beyond a mile, he lacks finishing speed and is probably best under aggressive tactics.
**B J Meehan [1-13] The Sixth Tumbleweed Partnership.*

TUMBLEWEED WIZARD BHB 56f RR 58f 2666[15]

3 ch g Magic Ring (IRE) 6.5f **(64)** - Chiquitita (Reliance II) 9.9f **(58)**
Form - 760
Record 2000 - 1st:0 2nd:0 3rd:0 Ran:3
Pre2000 - 1st:0 2nd:0 3rd:0 Ran:3
2000 Turf 0-3: (12f 2, 14f) (gd 2, frm)
Workmanlike, fair gelding, has worn blinkers. Turf high 58.
**B J Meehan [0-6] The Second Tumbleweed Partnership.*

TUNEFUL MELODY BHB 40f RR 5117[8]

2 b f Merdon Melody 6.8f **(56)** - Royal Scots Greys (Blazing Saddles (AUS)) 6.7f **(46)**
Form - 8
Record 2000 - 1st:0 2nd:0 3rd:0 Ran:1
2000 AW 0-1: (5f) (Fibr)
Currently moderate filly.
**R A Fahey [0-1] Derrick Bloy.*

TUPGILL CENTURION BHB 54f49a RR 47f 49a 4651[8]

2 b g Emperor Jones (USA) - Elisa War (Warning)
Form - 458
Record 2000 - 1st:0 2nd:0 3rd:0 Ran:3
Win Prizemoney £0 *Total Prizemoney* £263
2000 Turf 0-2: (7f, 8f) (g-f, frm) 2000 AW 0-1: (8f) (Fibr)
Currently moderate gelding. Turf high 47 (began Aug).
**S E Kettlewell [0-3] The Tupgill Partnership.*

TUPGILL FLIGHT (IRE) BHB 42f RR 38f 4651[5]

2 b f Be My Chief (USA) 10.2f **(62)** - Wing Partner (IRE) **(64f)** (In The Wings)
Form - 80005
Record 2000 - 1st:0 2nd:0 3rd:0 Ran:5
2000 Turf 0-4: (5f, 6f, 7f 2) (sft, gd, g-f 2) 2000 AW 0-1: (8f) (Fibr)
Very moderate filly. Turf high 38.
**S E Kettlewell [0-5] The Tupgill Partnership.*

TUPGILL TANGO BHB 80f RR 75f 5001[6]

2 ch g Presidium 7.5f **(56)** - Tangalooma (Hotfoot) 10.5f **(59)**
Form - 016
Record 2000 - 1st:1 2nd:0 3rd:0 Ran:3
Win Prizemoney £6,669 *Total Prizemoney* £6,993
Wins * 2000 Oct York (HVY) 7.9f 75 <
2000 Turf 1-3: (7f, 8f 1-2) (sft 1-1, g-s, g-f)
Currently above-average gelding. Turf high 75 (began Spt) - 1st of 7 from Art Expert (7 Oct York RF 4861).
**S E Kettlewell [1-3] The Tupgill Partnership.*

TUPGILL TIPPLE BHB 42f52a RR 49f 52a 5295[9]

2 b f Emperor Jones (USA) - Highest Baby (FR) (Highest Honor (FR))
Form - 2340050
Record 2000 - 1st:0 2nd:1 3rd:1 Ran:7
Win Prizemoney £0 *Total Prizemoney* £998
2000 Turf 0-4: (5f 3, 6f) (g-s, gd, g-f, frm) 2000 AW 0-3: (5f 2, 6f) (Fibr 3)
Average filly, has worn blinkers. Turf high 49 (began Jly). AW high 63.
**S E Kettlewell [0-7] The Tupgill Partnership.*

TUPGILL TURBO RR 56f 3249[5]

2 ch g Rudimentary (USA) 8.2f **(66)** - Persian Alexandra (Persian Bold) 9.3f **(66)**
Form - 35
Record 2000 - 1st:0 2nd:0 3rd:1 Ran:2
Win Prizemoney £0 *Total Prizemoney* £1,740
2000 Turf 0-2: (6f, 7f) (gd, g-f)
Currently fair gelding. Turf high 56 (began Jly).
**S E Kettlewell [0-2] The Tupgill Partnership.*

TURAATH (IRE) BHB 85f **RR 88f** 5134^{14}
4 b g Sadler's Wells (USA) 11.3f **(87)** - Diamond Field (USA) (Mr Prospector (USA)) 8.8f **(78)**
Form - 7720
Record 2000 - 1st:0 2nd:1 3rd:0 Ran:4
Pre2000 - 1st:1 2nd:0 3rd:1 Ran:3
Win Prizemoney £4,201 *Total Prizemoney* £8,834
Wins 1999 Mar Doncas (G-S) 10.3f 84+ <
2000 Turf 0-4: (10f 3, 12f) (sft 2, g-s, gd)
Scopey, useful gelding. Turf high 88 - 2nd of 4 giving 1lb to Forbearing (7 Jly Salisbury 10f g-s RF 2602).
**G M McCourt [0-1] Mrs Kathy Stuart (from B W Hills [1-6] Jly 2000).*

TURBO BLUE (IRE) BHB 46f **RR 59f** 5160^{11}
2 ch f Dolphin Street (FR) - Ferrovia (Never so Bold) 6.3f **(66)**
Form - 88000
Record 2000 - 1st:0 2nd:0 3rd:0 Ran:5
2000 Turf 0-5: (5f, 6f 3, 8f) (sft, g-s, gd, frm 2)
Fair filly. Turf high 59.
**G G Margarson [0-5] G G Margarson.*

TURBOTIERE (FR) RR 108f $4837a^{7}$
5 br m Turgeon (USA) - Victoria Dee (FR) (Rex Magna (FR))
Form - 3337
2000 Turf 0-4: (11f, 12f, 13f 2) (hvy, gd 3)
Pattern-class filly, effective 11 to 15f, best at 15f, acts on sft to gd, best on gd. Turf high 108 - 7th of 11 giving 10lb to Mouramara (30 Spt Longchamp 13f gd RF 4837a).
**E Libaud in FR [0-6] .*

TURGENEV (IRE) BHB 32f27a **RR 41f 27a** 5182^{2}
11 b g Sadler's Wells (USA) 11.3f **(87)** - Tilia (ITY) (Dschingis Khan) 11.3f **(75)**
Form - 000050664002
Record 2000 - 1st:0 2nd:1 3rd:0 Ran:11
Pre2000 - 1st:8 2nd:7 3rd:2 Ran:55
Win Prizemoney £54,459 *Total Prizemoney* £74,311
Wins * 1998 Jun Sandow (SFT) H 14f 60 68
* 1997 Aug Sandow (GD) H 14f 64 70
* 1997 Jly Haydoc (GD) H 14f 60 65
* 1997 May Haydoc (SFT) H 14f 63 69
* 1996 Jun Haydoc (G-S) H 14f 58 66
2000 Turf 0-9: (12f, 13f, 14f 3, 16f 4) (sft, g-s, gd 3, g-f, frm 2, hrd) 2000 AW 0-2: (14f, 16f) (Fibr 2)
Moderate gelding, effective 14f, acts on sft to frm, has worn blinkers, likes left handed tracks, likes tight tracks. Turf high 41.
**R Bastiman [5-50] Mrs P Bastiman (from J H M Gosden [3-16] Aug 1993).*

TURKU BHB 88f **RR 92f** 5224^{2}
2 b c Polar Falcon (USA) 9f **(74)** - Princess Zepoli (Persepolis (FR)) 6.4f **(67)**
Form - 132
Record 2000 - 1st:1 2nd:1 3rd:1 Ran:3
Win Prizemoney £4,013 *Total Prizemoney* £7,651
Wins * 2000 Spt Haydoc (HVY) 7.1f 80+ <
2000 Turf 1-3: (7f 1-2, 8f) (g-s, gd 1-2)
Currently useful colt. Turf high 92 (began Spt) - 2nd of 10 to Welsh Border (27 Oct Newmarket 8f gd RF 5224).
**M Johnston [1-3] J R Good.*

TURNBERRY ISLE (IRE) RR 101f $5330a^{6}$
2 ch c Deputy Minister (CAN) 9.2f **(71)** - Blush with Pride (USA) (Blushing Groom (FR)) 10.3f **(76)**
Form - 11216
2000 Turf 3-4: (7f 1-1, 8f 2-3) (g-s 1-2, gd 2-2) 2000 AW 0-1: (9f) (Dirt)
Very useful colt. Turf high 101 - 2nd of 8 to Atlantis Prince (24 Spt Ascot 8f g-s RF 4610) - also 1st of 6 from Sligo Bay (15 Oct Curragh RF 5046a). (1st run) - 6th of 14 to Macho Uno (4 Nov Churchill Downs 9f Dirt RF 5330a). Described as a 'tough but lazy' individual by his trainer, he went close in the Royal Lodge Stakes and gained compensation in the Group 3 Beresford Stakes at The Curragh in October. A staying on sixth in the Breeders Cup Juvenile the following month, he is a smart middle-distance colt in the making but probably lacks the speed required to win a Classic.
**A P O'Brien in IRE [3-5] Mrs John Magnier.*

TURNED OUT WELL BHB 43f39a **RR 49f 39a** 3776^{4}
3 b g Robellino (USA) 9.5f **(68)** - In the Shade (Bustino) 10.4f **(64)**
Form - 55134
Record 2000 - 1st:1 2nd:0 3rd:1 Ran:5
Pre2000 - 1st:0 2nd:0 3rd:0 Ran:3
Win Prizemoney £3,107 *Total Prizemoney* £3,509
Wins * **2000** Jly Beverl (G-F) H 16.2f 40 44 <
2000 Turf 1-3: (16f 1-3) (gd, g-f 1-2) 2000 AW 0-2: (7f, 11f) (Fibr 2)
Workmanlike, moderate gelding, effective 16f, acts on g-f, favours tight tracks. Turf high 49 (began Jly) - also 1st of 17 getting 6lb from Niciara (24 Jly Beverley RF 3066). AW high 34.
**P C Haslam [1-8] Middleham Park Racing XVIII.*

TURNING LEAF (IRE) RR 100f $2579a^{2}$
3 b f Last Tycoon 9.4f **(73)**
Form - 32
2000 Turf 0-2: (8f 2) (hvy, gd)
Strong, currently very useful filly. Turf high 100 - 2nd of 16 giving 1lb to Kirona (30 Jun Hamburg 8f hvy RF 2579a).
**A Wohler in GER [0-2].*

TURNPOLE (IRE) BHB 75f **RR 78f** 5322^{10}
9 br g Satco (FR) 14.2f **(57)** - Mountain Chase (Mount Hagen (FR)) 8.4f **(70)**
Form - 8641400
Record 2000 - 1st:1 2nd:0 3rd:0 Ran:7
Pre2000 - 1st:6 2nd:6 3rd:0 Ran:19
Win Prizemoney £101,833 *Total Prizemoney* £123,232
Wins * **2000** Jly Newmar (GD) H 16.1f 74 78
* 1998 Mar Doncas (GD) H 18f 82 87 <
* 1997 Oct Newmar (GD) H 18f 74 82
* 1997 May York (GD) H 13.9f 70 78
* 1997 Apr Hamilt (G-S) 12.1f 69
2000 Turf 1-7: (15f, 16f 1-3, 17f 2, 18f) (sft, gd 1-5, g-f)
Above-average gelding. Turf high 78. The 1997 Cesarewitch winner, he has been lightly raced on the Flat in the last couple of seasons and scored at the Newmarket July meeting.
**Mrs M Reveley [11-40] & Mrs W J Williams.*

TURN TO STONE (IRE) BHB 30f **RR 32f** 455^{5}
6 b g West China - Marronzina (IRE) (Burslem) 8.8f **(53)**
Form - 05
Record 2000 - 1st:0 2nd:0 3rd:0 Ran:2
Pre2000 - 1st:0 2nd:0 3rd:0 Ran:9
2000 AW 0-2: (9f, 12f) (Fibr 2)
Very moderate gelding, has broken blood-vessels, has worn blinkers. AW high 14.
**N P Littmoden [0-2] George Moore (from P A Fahy in IRE [0-4] Mar 1999).*

TURQUOISE GEM (IRE) BHB 54f **RR 60f** 2353^{7}
3 b f Fayruz 6.6f **(63)** - Pepilin (Coquelin (USA)) 8.4f **(58)**
Form - 7
Record 2000 - 1st:0 2nd:0 3rd:0 Ran:1
Pre2000 - 1st:0 2nd:0 3rd:0 Ran:4
2000 Turf 0-1: (7f) (frm)
Scopey, average filly. **V Soane [0-5] M Nelmes-Crocker.*

TURTLE BHB 37f59a **RR 31f 59a** 5054^{10}
4 b g Turtle Island (IRE) - Kate Marie (USA) (Bering) 7.4f **(61)**
Form - 00
Record 2000 - 1st:0 2nd:0 3rd:0 Ran:2
Pre2000 - 1st:1 2nd:0 3rd:3 Ran:15
Win Prizemoney £2,490 *Total Prizemoney* £4,243
Wins 1999 Jun Pontef (G-S) S 10f 55 <
2000 Turf 0-2: (9f, 10f) (sft, frm)
Strong, fair gelding, effective 10f, acts on gd, likes left handed tracks, likes tight tracks. Turf high 30 (began Aug). Becoming disappointing.
**W Storey [0-9] Mrs Jean Jarvis (from M Johnston [1-11] Jun 1999).*

TURTLE SOUP (IRE) BHB 76f **RR 78f** 2017^{5}
4 b g Turtle Island (IRE) - Lisa's Favourite (Gorytus (USA)) 7.8f **(60)**
Form - 15
Record 2000 - 1st:1 2nd:0 3rd:0 Ran:2
Pre2000 - 1st:1 2nd:1 3rd:0 Ran:7
Win Prizemoney £6,020 *Total Prizemoney* £7,621

Wins * 2000 May Newbur (SFT) H 13.3f 74 77 <
1999 Jly Ayr (SFT) H 10.9f 67 69
2000 Turf 1-2: (13f 1-1, 14f) (g-s 1-1, g-f)
Workmanlike, above-average gelding, effective 10 to 14f, best at 12f, acts on g-s to frm, excels at Newmarket. Turf high 77 (1st run) - 1st of 13 giving 5lb to Achilles Wings (31 May Newbury RF 1592). Consistent.
**Mrs L Richards [1-2] M K George (from L M Cumani [1-7] Oct 1999).*

TURTLE'S RISING (IRE) BHB 63f RR 62f 2639[10]
4 b m Turtle Island (IRE) - Zabeta (Diesis) 9.3f **(69)**
Form - 0300
Record 2000 - 1st:0 2nd:0 3rd:1 Ran:4
Pre2000 - 1st:2 2nd:1 3rd:2 Ran:17
Win Prizemoney £7,007 *Total Prizemoney* £10,337
Wins 1999 Aug Lingfi (GD) H 7f 65 69
1998 Jly Sandow (G-F) 5f 78 <
2000 Turf 0-4: (6f, 7f 2, 8f) (frm 4)
Workmanlike, average filly, effective 7 to 8f, best at 7f, acts on gd to frm, best on gd, has worn blinkers. Turf high 62 - 3rd of 10 giving 20lb to Thorntoun Gold (25 Jun Pontefract 8f frm RF 2268). Inconsistent.
**M Mullineaux [0-4] Total (Bloodstock) Ltd (from B J Meehan [2-17] Oct 1999).*

TURTLE VALLEY (IRE) BHB 93f90a RR 94f 90a 1808[3]
4 b g Turtle Island (IRE) - Primrose Valley (Mill Reef (USA)) 10.5f **(78)**
Form - 77023
Record 2000 - 1st:0 2nd:1 3rd:1 Ran:5
Pre2000 - 1st:3 2nd:3 3rd:0 Ran:19
Win Prizemoney £25,147 *Total Prizemoney* £33,423
Wins * 1999 Jun Salisb (GD) H 14.1f 90 92 <
* 1999 May Newbur (SFT) H 12f 74 91
* 1999 May York (G-S) 13.9f 87
2000 Turf 0-4: (14f, 16f 3) (sft, g-s 2, gd) 2000 AW 0-1: (12f) (Fibr)
Useful gelding, effective 12 to 16f, best at 16f, acts on g-s to g-f, best on gd, has worn blinkers, likes left handed tracks, excels at Newbury. Turf high 94 - 2nd of 10 giving 9lb to Wave of Optimism (27 May Kempton 16f g-s RF 1497). Notably tough, he relishes the mud and must always be considered under those conditions. Already a dual winner over hurdles, he stays well and is probably best when ridden close to the pace.
**S Dow [3-19] Cazanove Clear Height Racing (from J L Dunlop [0-6] Spt 1998).*

TUSCAN (IRE) BHB 60f62a RR 56f 62a 4780[11]
2 b f Charnwood Forest (IRE) - Madam Loving (Vaigly Great) 7f **(58)**
Form - 460240
Record 2000 - 1st:0 2nd:1 3rd:0 Ran:6
Win Prizemoney £0 *Total Prizemoney* £981
2000 Turf 0-5: (5f, 6f 3, 7f) (g-f 3, frm 2) 2000 AW 0-1: (6f) (Fibr)
Average filly, effective 5f, acts on frm. Turf high 56 (began Jly).
**B G Powell [0-2] Mrs John Weld (from M R Channon [0-4] Aug 2000).*

TUSCAN DREAM BHB 77f70a RR 78f 70a 4266[3]
5 b g Clantime 6.6f **(57)** - Excavator Lady (Most Secret) 7.1f **(58)**
Form - 0051240353
Record 2000 - 1st:1 2nd:1 3rd:2 Ran:10
Pre2000 - 1st:4 2nd:4 3rd:3 Ran:20
Win Prizemoney £22,347 *Total Prizemoney* £30,511
Wins * 2000 Jun Ripon (G-F) H 5f 70 71 <
1999 Spt Epsom (G-F) H 5f 67 71 <
1999 Jun Lingfi (G-F) H 5f 59 63
1999 May Wolver (STD) C 5f 61
1999 May Mussel (G-F) S 5f 43
2000 Turf 1-9: (5f 1-9) (gd 3, g-f 2, frm 1-4) 2000 AW 0-1: (5f) (Fibr)
Above-average gelding, effective 5f, acts on gd to frm, best on g-f, has worn blinkers, and excels at Epsom. Turf high 78 - 3rd of 13 giving 4lb to Forgotten Times (6 Spt Epsom 5f g-f RF 4266) - also 1st of 11 giving 6lb to Bollin Ann (22 Jun Ripon RF 2186). Consistent.
**A Berry [1-10] Chris & Antonia Deuters (from J Berry [4-20] Spt 1999).*

TUSCAN FLYER BHB 60f RR 63f 5163[9]
2 b g Clantime 6.6f **(57)** - Excavator Lady (Most Secret) 7.1f **(58)**
Form - 8580
Record 2000 - 1st:0 2nd:0 3rd:0 Ran:4
2000 Turf 0-4: (5f 4) (gd 3, g-f)
Average gelding. Turf high 63.
**A Berry [0-4] Chris & Antonia Deuters.*

TUSHNA (IRE) RR 100f 4805a[8]
3 b c Erins Isle 8.3f **(76)** - Smaointeach 00
Form - 10152861225208
2000 Turf 2-13: (6f 2, 7f 4, 8f 2-4, 9f 3) (sft 3, g-s 1-2, gd 1-6, g-f)
Very useful colt, effective 7 to 8f, best at 8f, acts on sft to gd, prefers right handed tracks, and excels at Galway. Turf high 100 - 2nd of 16 giving 14lb to Tarakan (9 Spt Leopardstown 7f gd RF 4353a) - also 1st of 17 from Bibi Karam (1 Aug Galway RF 3458a). Consistent. **J S Bolger in IRE [4-19] D H W Dobson.*

TUSSLE BHB 94f RR 97f 3202[21]
5 b g Salse (USA) 10.9f **(71)** - Crime Ofthecentury (Pharly (FR)) 9.8f **(68)**
Form - 020
Record 2000 - 1st:0 2nd:1 3rd:0 Ran:3
Pre2000 - 1st:1 2nd:1 3rd:0 Ran:12
Win Prizemoney £4,077 *Total Prizemoney* £31,907
Wins * 1997 Oct Newmar (G-F) 6f 95+ <
2000 Turf 0-3: (5f, 6f, 7f) (g-s, gd 2)
Very useful gelding, effective 6f, acts on gd to frm. Turf high 97 - 2nd of 29 getting 13lb from Harmonic Way (23 Jun Ascot 6f gd RF 2209). **M L W Bell [1-15] Lordship Stud.*

TWEED BHB 57a RR 57f 5294[2]
3 ch g Barathea (IRE) - In Perpetuity (Great Nephew) 9.9f **(64)**
Form - 0742
Record 2000 - 1st:0 2nd:1 3rd:0 Ran:4
Pre2000 - 1st:0 2nd:0 3rd:0 Ran:3
Win Prizemoney £0 *Total Prizemoney* £978
2000 Turf 0-3: (8f, 11f, 12f) (hvy, g-s, frm) 2000 AW 0-1: (12f) (Fibr)
Workmanlike, fair gelding, has worn blinkers. Turf high 55.
**Jedd O'Keeffe [0-1] Richard Johnson (from R Charlton [0-6] May 2000).*

TWEED MILL BHB 76f RR 86df 4604[11]
3 b f Selkirk (USA) 7.9f **(76)** - Island Mill (Mill Reef (USA)) 10.5f **(78)**
Form - 210080
Record 2000 - 1st:1 2nd:1 3rd:0 Ran:6
Pre2000 - 1st:0 2nd:0 3rd:1 Ran:1
Win Prizemoney £4,270 *Total Prizemoney* £5,665
Wins * 2000 Apr Epsom (HVY) 8.5f 89 <
2000 Turf 1-6: (7f, 8f 4, 9f 1-1) (sft 1-1, g-s, gd 2, frm 2)
Scopey, useful filly, effective 8 to 9f, acts on sft to frm. Turf high 89 - 1st of 10 getting 5lb from Glory Quest (26 Apr Epsom RF 0881). Gradually improving, she got off the mark when bolting up in a maiden at Epsom in April. That win was in heavy ground, but she has shown ability on a much faster surface.
**I A Balding [1-7] D H Back.*

TWENTY FIRST BHB 61f RR 67f 2089[1]
4 ch m Inchinor 8.9f **(64)** - Picnicing (Good Times (ITY)) 6.6f **(54)**
Form - 8601
Record 2000 - 1st:1 2nd:0 3rd:0 Ran:4
Pre2000 - 1st:0 2nd:1 3rd:1 Ran:6
Win Prizemoney £2,982 *Total Prizemoney* £4,287
Wins * 2000 Jun Bright (FRM) H 8f 60 63 <
2000 Turf 1-4: (8f 1-1, 10f 3) (gd, g-f, frm 1-2)
Scopey, average filly, effective 8 to 10f, acts on gd to frm, prefers left handed tracks, favours tight tracks. Turf high 67 - also 1st of 7 giving 28lb to Satwa Boulevard (19 Jun Brighton RF 2089).
**G Wragg [1-10] Bloomsbury Stud.*

TWICE BHB 65f69a RR 60df 69a 5154[3]
4 b g Rainbow Quest (USA) 11.2f **(81)** - Bolas **(110f)** (Unfuwain (USA))
Form - 8053
Record 2000 - 1st:0 2nd:0 3rd:1 Ran:4
Pre2000 - 1st:0 2nd:0 3rd:0 Ran:3
Win Prizemoney £0 *Total Prizemoney* £1,060
2000 Turf 0-3: (10f 2, 12f) (sft, gd, frm) 2000 AW 0-1: (12f) (Equi)
Scopey, above-average gelding, effective 10f, acts on gd, likes tight tracks. Turf high 35.
**G L Moore [0-9] Trotters Independent Racing (from B W Hills [0-3] Spt*

1999).

TWICE AS SHARP BHB 86f82a **RR 86f 82a** 502[14]
8 ch h Sharpo 7.5f **(68)** - Shadiliya (Red Alert) 7.6f **(66)**
Form - 0
Record 2000 - 1st:0 2nd:0 3rd:0 Ran:1
Pre2000 - 1st:4 2nd:6 3rd:6 Ran:47
Win Prizemoney £37,275 *Total Prizemoney* £60,010
Wins * 1997 May York (GD) H 5f 83 86
* 1996 Jun Newcas (FRM) H 5f 84 88 <
2000 Turf 0-1: (6f) (gd)
Useful horse, effective 6f, acts on g-s to frm, best on frm. Consistent. **P W Harris [4-48] Formula Twelve.*

TWICE BLESSED (IRE) BHB 67f72a **RR 58f 72a** 927[11]
3 ch c Thatching 7.8f **(69)** - Fairy Blesse (IRE) (Fairy King (USA)) 7.7f **(59)**
Form - 210
Record 2000 - 1st:0 2nd:0 3rd:0 Ran:1
Pre2000 - 1st:1 2nd:1 3rd:0 Ran:4
Win Prizemoney £2,703 *Total Prizemoney* £3,571
Wins * 1999 *Dec Lingfi (STD) 7f* 72 <
2000 Turf 0-1: (8f) (sft)
Scopey, above-average colt. Beat the useful Buggy Ride in an Equitrack maiden at the end of 1999. **R Hannon [1-5] J C Smith.*

TWICKERS BHB 46f57a **RR 57f 57a** 2814[9]
4 b m Primo Dominie 7.2f **(67)** - Songstead (Song) 7.2f **(61)**
Form - 0600000680
Record 2000 - 1st:0 2nd:0 3rd:0 Ran:10
Pre2000 - 1st:0 2nd:2 3rd:1 Ran:8
Win Prizemoney £0 *Total Prizemoney* £2,957
2000 Turf 0-8: (5f 8) (gd 2, g-f, frm 3, hrd 2) 2000 AW 0-2: (5f 2) (Fibr 2)
Scopey, fair filly, effective 5f, acts on gd to g-f, has worn blinkers. Turf high 57. AW high 32.
**D W Chapman [0-10] J Bayram (from R Guest [0-8] Spt 1999).*

TWILIGHT DANCER (IRE) BHB 58f **RR 58f** 5157[10]
2 b f Sri Pekan (USA) - Manhattan Sunset (USA) **(62f)** (El Gran Senor (USA)) 9.6f **(76)**
Form - 650
Record 2000 - 1st:0 2nd:0 3rd:0 Ran:3
2000 Turf 0-2: (8f 2) (sft, g-f) 2000 AW 0-1: (8f) (Fibr)
Currently fair filly. Turf high 58 (began Spt).
**P W Harris [0-3] The Manhattan Club.*

TWILIGHT HAZE **RR 37f** 4969[29]
2 b c Darshaan 11.9f **(81)** - Hiwaayati (Shadeed (USA)) 8.2f **(70)**
Form - 0
Record 2000 - 1st:0 2nd:0 3rd:0 Ran:1
2000 Turf 0-1: (8f) (gd)
Currently above-average colt. **E A L Dunlop [0-1] Maktoum Al Maktoum.*

TWILIGHT MISTRESS BHB 70f **RR 76f** 5156[10]
2 b f Bin Ajwaad (IRE) - By Candlelight (IRE) **(80f)** (Roi Danzig (USA))
Form - 08430
Record 2000 - 1st:0 2nd:0 3rd:1 Ran:5
Win Prizemoney £0 *Total Prizemoney* £631
2000 Turf 0-5: (5f 3, 6f 2) (g-s, g-f, frm 3)
Above-average filly. Turf high 76 (began Jly).
**D W P Arbuthnot [0-5] The Twilight Team.*

TWILIGHT WORLD BHB 59f53a **RR 58f 53a** 4785[7]
3 b g Night Shift (USA) 8.1f **(73)** - Masskana (IRE) (Darshaan) 9.9f **(84)**
Form - 1327
Record 2000 - 1st:1 2nd:1 3rd:1 Ran:4
Pre2000 - 1st:0 2nd:0 3rd:0 Ran:3
Win Prizemoney £4,270 *Total Prizemoney* £5,498
Wins * **2000** Jly Mussel (G-S) H 9f 47 52 <
2000 Turf 1-3: (9f 1-2, 10f) (g-s, gd 1-1, hrd) 2000 AW 0-1: (9f) (Fibr)
Strong, fair gelding, effective 9 to 10f, acts on g-s to gd. Turf high 58 (began Jly) - 2nd of 20 getting 5lb from Sophala (27 Spt Brighton 10f g-s RF 4677) - also 1st of 6 getting 19lb from Bold State (10 Jly Musselburgh RF 2670).
**Sir Mark Prescott [1-7] Fishpool Osborne House.*

TWIN LOGIC (USA) BHB 88f **RR 90f** 3704[7]
3 ch f Diesis 9f **(80)** - Indigenous (USA) **(55+f)** (Lyphard (USA)) 9.9f **(72)**
Form - 543217
Record 2000 - 1st:1 2nd:1 3rd:1 Ran:6
Win Prizemoney £4,114 *Total Prizemoney* £6,175
Wins * **2000** Jly Epsom (G-S) 10.1f 80+ <
2000 Turf 1-6: (7f, 8f, 10f 1-4) (sft, g-s, gd 1-3, frm)
Unfurnished, useful filly, effective 10f, acts on gd to frm. Turf high 90 - 7th of 10 getting 8lb from First Fantasy (16 Aug Salisbury 10f frm RF 3704). She lacks scope, but is genuine and seemed to improve with racing. Probably best around a mile and a quarter, she will find life tough in handicaps.
**J H M Gosden [1-6] K Abdulla.*

TWIN SET (GER) **RR 99f** 5202a[1]
3 b f Second Set (IRE) 9.2f **(67)** - Tosca Rhea (GER) (Song) 7.2f **(61)**
Form - 1
2000 Turf 1-1: (7f 1-1) (hvy 1-1)
Currently very useful filly. (1st run) - 1st of 14 from Castiya (16 Oct Deauville RF 5202a).
**P Lautner in GER [1-1] Mme E Hilger.*

TWIN TIME BHB 65a **RR 67f** 3444[4]
6 b m Syrtos 8.1f **(57)** - Carramba (CZE) (Tumble Wind (USA)) 7.5f **(57)**
Form - 4231434
Record 2000 - 1st:1 2nd:1 3rd:2 Ran:7
Pre2000 - 1st:3 2nd:3 3rd:4 Ran:23
Win Prizemoney £12,348 *Total Prizemoney* £21,779
Wins * **2000** Jun Goodwo (G-F) H 7f 64 64
* 1999 Jly Bath (FRM) H 10.2f 62 65 <
* 1999 May Bath (GD) H 8f 61 64
* 1998 Aug Bath (GD) H 10.2f 63 60
2000 Turf 1-7: (7f 1-2, 8f 5) (sft, gd 1-2, g-f, frm 3)
Average mare, effective 7 to 10f, best at 8f, acts on gd to frm, best on frm, likes left handed tracks, favours tight tracks, excels at Kempton, does well at Bath. Turf high 67 - 3rd of 10 getting 4lb from Eastern Spice (27 Jly Bath 8f frm RF 3148) - also 1st of 10 giving 1lb to Just Nick (30 Jun Goodwood RF 2397).
**J S King [4-27] Dajam Ltd (from M J Heaton-Ellis [0-6] Aug 1997).*

TWIST **RR 65f** 3557[8]
3 b c Suave Dancer (USA) 10.7f **(68)** - Reason to Dance **(98df)** (Damister (USA)) 9f **(73)**
Form - 85858258
Record 2000 - 1st:0 2nd:1 3rd:0 Ran:8
Pre2000 - 1st:0 2nd:0 3rd:0 Ran:3
Win Prizemoney £0 *Total Prizemoney* £1,371
2000 Turf 0-8: (7f, 8f 3, 9f, 11f, 12f 2) (g-f, frm 6, hrd)
Workmanlike, average colt, effective 8 to 12f, best at 8f, acts on gd to hrd, has worn blinkers. Turf high 65. Consistent.
**W R Muir [0-11] John O'Mulloy.*

TWOFORTEN BHB 31f28a **RR 42f 28a** 4679[5]
5 b g Robellino (USA) 9.5f **(68)** - Grown At Rowan (Gabitat) 5f **(44)**
Form - 75766700365007603005
Record 2000 - 1st:0 2nd:0 3rd:2 Ran:18
Pre2000 - 1st:0 2nd:1 3rd:4 Ran:20
Win Prizemoney £0 *Total Prizemoney* £3,484
2000 Turf 0-16: (7f, 8f, 9f 2, 10f 6, 12f 6) (g-s, gd 6, g-f 4, frm 5) 2000 AW 0-2: (10f, 13f) (Equi 2)
Moderate gelding, effective 8 to 12f, acts on gd to frm, often wears blinkers, likes right handed tracks. Turf high 42. AW high 25.
**P Butler [0-11] P Butler (from M Madgwick [0-28] Jun 2000).*

TWO JACKS (IRE) BHB 42f **RR 47f** 4174[14]
3 b g Fayruz 6.6f **(63)** - Kaya (GER) (Young Generation) 7.7f **(63)**
Form - 0080
Record 2000 - 1st:0 2nd:0 3rd:0 Ran:4
Pre2000 - 1st:0 2nd:0 3rd:0 Ran:2
2000 Turf 0-4: (5f 2, 6f 2) (g-s, gd, g-f, frm)
Moderate gelding. Turf high 47.
**W S Cunningham [0-6] Mrs Ann Bell.*

TWO'S BETTER BHB 50f **RR 64f** 2433[7]
3 br g Rock City 8.8f **(62)** - Miss Pin Up **(63f 50a)** (Kalaglow) 9.8f **(67)**
Form - 03607
Record 2000 - 1st:0 2nd:0 3rd:1 Ran:5

Pre2000 - 1st:0 2nd:0 3rd:0 Ran:3
Win Prizemoney £0 *Total Prizemoney* £336
2000 Turf 0-5: (10f, 11f, 12f 3) (gd 2, g-f, frm 2)
Light-framed, average gelding, effective 12f, acted on gd, favoured tight tracks. Turf high 64 - 3rd of 11 giving 3lb to Cross Dall (2 May Windsor 12f gd RF 0974). (DEAD)
**G L Moore [0-8] Heart Of The South Racing (4).*

TWO SOCKS BHB 62f57a **RR 66f 57a** 5069[14]
7 ch g Phountzi (USA) 9.6f **(60)** - Mrs Feathers (Pyjama Hunt) 11.1f **(38)**
Form - 61410200
Record 2000 - 1st:2 2nd:1 3rd:0 Ran:8
Pre2000 - 1st:3 2nd:7 3rd:3 Ran:38
Win Prizemoney £17,941 *Total Prizemoney* £27,510
Wins * **2000** Jun Kempto (G-F) H 12f 60 65
* **2000** May Bright (FRM) H 11.9f 57 60
* 1999 Jun Kempto (G-F) H 12f 70 67 <
* 1998 Jun Warwic (GD) H 10.8f 66 67 <
1996 Jly Lingfi (FRM) H 11.5f 57 59
2000 Turf 2-8: (10f, 12f 2-7) (g-s 2, gd 2, g-f 1-2, frm 1-2)
Average gelding, effective 10 to 12f, best at 12f, acts on gd to frm, has worn blinkers, likes right handed tracks, likes tight tracks, excels at Salisbury and Kempton. Turf high 66 - 2nd of 18 giving 12lb to Coughlan's Gift (27 Spt Salisbury 10f gd RF 4695) - also 1st of 10 giving 5lb to My Pledge (14 Jun Kempton RF 1964).
**J S King [4-27] Mrs Satu Marks (from P Burgoyne [0-2] Oct 1996).*

TWO STEP BHB 43f43a **RR 41f 43a** 5118[5]
4 b m Mujtahid (USA) 7.4f **(69)** - Polka Dancer **(95f)** (Dancing Brave (USA)) 8.4f **(76)**
Form - 760001057325
Record 2000 - 1st:1 2nd:1 3rd:1 Ran:9
Pre2000 - 1st:0 2nd:0 3rd:0 Ran:3
Win Prizemoney £2,261 *Total Prizemoney* £3,431
Wins * **2000** *Jly Southw (STD) H 5f 28 35* <
2000 Turf 0-6: (5f, 6f 4, 7f) (gd, g-f 3, frm 2) 2000 AW 1-3: (5f 1-1, 6f 2) (Fibr 1-3)
Lengthy, moderate filly, effective 5 to 6f, best at 6f, acts on g-f - acts on Fibr. Turf high 41 - 2nd of 17 getting 15lb from American Cousin (14 Spt Yarmouth 6f g-f RF 4398). AW high 42 (began Jly) - 5th of 12 getting 8lb from Puppet Play (20 Oct Wolverhampton 6f Fibr RF 5118) - also 1st of 15 getting 16lb from Mujagem (14 Jly Southwell RF 2814). Inconsistent.
**R M H Cowell [1-12] Bottisham Heath Stud.*

TYCANDO BHB 68f68a **RR 79?f 68a** 2940[6]
3 ch g Forzando 7.2f **(63)** - Running Tycoon (IRE) **(42f)** (Last Tycoon) 8.5f **(62)**
Form - 2205806
Record 2000 - 1st:0 2nd:0 3rd:0 Ran:5
Pre2000 - 1st:1 2nd:3 3rd:2 Ran:10
Win Prizemoney £2,339 *Total Prizemoney* £5,904
Wins 1999 *Oct Wolver (STD) C 6f 74+* <
2000 Turf 0-1: (7f) (frm) 2000 AW 0-4: (6f 2, 7f 2) (Equi 2, Fibr 2)
Workmanlike, above-average gelding, effective 6 to 7f, best at 6f, acts on g-f - acts on AW, has worn blinkers, likes tight tracks. AW high 57. Inconsistent.
**K R Burke [0-7] Nigel Shields (from R Hannon [1-8] Oct 1999).*

TYCOON'S LAST BHB 58f56a **RR 64f 56a** 5162[6]
3 b f Nalchik (USA) 12.6f **(44)** - Royal Tycoon (Tycoon II) 8.7f **(47)**
Form - 3577435304106
Record 2000 - 1st:1 2nd:0 3rd:3 Ran:13
Pre2000 - 1st:0 2nd:0 3rd:0 Ran:7
Win Prizemoney £11,017 *Total Prizemoney* £13,161
Wins * **2000** Spt Haydoc (HVY) H 10.5f 36 56 <
2000 Turf 1-12: (10f 3, 11f 1-1, 12f 5, 13f, 14f, 16f) (sft, g-s, gd 1-4, g-f 2, frm 4) 2000 AW 0-1: (12f) (Fibr)
Leggy, average filly, effective 11f, acts on gd. Turf high 64 - also 1st of 6 getting 18lb from Queen's Pageant (23 Spt Haydock RF 4606). **W M Brisbourne [1-20] L R Owen.*

TYCOON TINA BHB 27f28a **RR 22f 28a** 330[6]
6 b m Tina's Pet 7.4f **(56)** - Royal Tycoon (Tycoon II) 8.7f **(47)**
Form - 36
Record 2000 - 1st:0 2nd:0 3rd:1 Ran:2
Pre2000 - 1st:3 2nd:6 3rd:1 Ran:39
Win Prizemoney £8,232 *Total Prizemoney* £14,568
Wins * 1998 Apr Beverl (SFT) H 9.9f 53 58 <
* 1998 Mar Hamilt (HVY) H 12.1f 49 52
* 1997 May Mussel (G-S) H 8f 46 51
2000 AW 0-2: (9f, 11f) (Fibr 2)
Little account mare, has worn blinkers. AW high 21.
**W M Brisbourne [3-48] Mrs Mary Brisbourne.*

TYLERS GREEN RR 92f 1634a[7]
4 f
Form - 7
2000 Turf 0-1: (12f) (g-f)
Currently useful. **A Peraino in ITY [0-1].*

TYLER'S TOAST BHB 62f70a **RR 74df 70a** 1906[10]
4 ch g Grand Lodge (USA) - Catawba (Mill Reef (USA)) 10.5f **(78)**
Form - 2111050
Record 2000 - 1st:3 2nd:1 3rd:0 Ran:7
Pre2000 - 1st:0 2nd:0 3rd:1 Ran:5
Win Prizemoney £8,266 *Total Prizemoney* £9,630
Wins * **2000** *Mar Wolver (STD) H 9.4f 67 72* <
* **2000** *Feb Wolver (STD) H 9.4f 56 66*
* **2000** *Feb Wolver (STD) 9.4f 66*
2000 Turf 0-3: (9f, 10f 2) (g-s, gd, frm) 2000 AW 3-4: (9f 3-4) (Fibr 3-4)
Lengthy, above-average gelding, effective 9f, - acts on Fibr, prefers left handed tracks, prefers tight tracks. Turf high 60. AW high 72 - 1st of 11 giving 11lb to Bread Winner (4 Mar Wolverhampton RF 0408) - also 1st of 7 giving 5lb to Ahouod (10 Feb Wolverhampton RF 0254). Inconsistent. Showed a little bit of ability on turf, but was in sparkling form on Fibresand at the start of the year, winning three times over the extended nine furlongs at Wolverhampton. He did not transfer the improvement on to turf.
**S Dow [3-7] S Dow (from W Jarvis [0-5] Spt 1999).*

TYPE ONE (IRE) BHB 74f **RR 72f** 3424[4]
2 b c Bigstone (IRE) - Isca **(73df)** (Caerleon (USA)) 8.6f **(71)**
Form - 034
Record 2000 - 1st:0 2nd:0 3rd:1 Ran:3
Win Prizemoney £0 *Total Prizemoney* £547
2000 Turf 0-3: (5f 2, 6f) (g-f 2, frm)
Currently above-average colt. Turf high 72 (began Jly).
**T G Mills [0-3] Mrs A K Petersen.*

TYPHOON GINGER (IRE) BHB 62f57a **RR 59f 57a** 5314[3]
5 ch m Archway (IRE) 8.5f **(60)** - Pallas Viking (Viking (USA)) 6.7f **(65)**
Form - 66205363
Record 2000 - 1st:0 2nd:1 3rd:2 Ran:8
Pre2000 - 1st:0 2nd:2 3rd:3 Ran:13
Win Prizemoney £0 *Total Prizemoney* £7,374
2000 Turf 0-8: (7f, 8f 2, 10f 4, 12f) (sft 2, gd 3, g-f, frm 2)
Fair filly, effective 7 to 10f, best at 10f, acts on sft to frm, best on sft, likes left handed tracks, and does well at York. Turf high 59 - 3rd of 15 to Coughlan's Gift (18 Oct Nottingham 10f sft RF 5063). She has shown ability in varied company, but always seems to find one or two to beat her. **G Woodward [0-21] Andrew Lloyd.*

TYPHOON TILLY BHB 71f **RR 76f** 3585[6]
3 b g Hernando (FR) - Meavy **(77f)** (Kalaglow) 9.8f **(67)**
Form - 311126
Record 2000 - 1st:3 2nd:1 3rd:1 Ran:6
Pre2000 - 1st:0 2nd:0 3rd:0 Ran:3
Win Prizemoney £9,367 *Total Prizemoney* £11,504
Wins * **2000** Jly Nottin (G-F) H 14.1f 63 71 <
* **2000** Jly Yarmou (G-F) H 14.1f 51 68+
* **2000** Jun Yarmou (FRM) H 14.1f 51 65
2000 Turf 3-6: (12f, 14f 3-5) (gd 2, g-f 1-2, frm 2-2)
Scopey, above-average gelding, effective 14f, acts on g-f to frm, best on frm, prefers tight tracks. Turf high 76 - 2nd of 5 getting 15lb from Takwin (27 Jly Sandown 14f g-f RF 3154) - also 1st of 9 getting 11lb from Hambleden (15 Jly Nottingham RF 2839).
**C F Wall [3-9] M Tilbrook.*

TYRA BHB 42f **RR 32f** 1509[16]
4 b m Lion Cavern (USA) 7.5f **(74)** - Lara (USA) (Lyphard (USA)) 9.9f **(72)**
Form - 8700
Record 2000 - 1st:0 2nd:0 3rd:0 Ran:4

Pre2000 - 1st:0 2nd:1 3rd:0 Ran:1
Win Prizemoney £0 *Total Prizemoney* £1,214
2000 Turf 0-4: (8f 2, 10f, 12f) (hvy, gd 2, g-f)
Scopey, very moderate filly, has worn blinkers. Turf high 32.
**D Burchell [0-5] Riverside Racing Partnership (from H R A Cecil [0-1] Aug 1999).*

TYROLEAN LOVE (IRE) BHB 33f **RR 34f** 1720[12]
4 b m Tirol 8.1f **(64)** - Paradise Forum (Prince Sabo) 7.2f **(62)**
Form - 760
Record 2000 - 1st:0 2nd:0 3rd:0 Ran:3
Pre2000 - 1st:0 2nd:0 3rd:0 Ran:5
Win Prizemoney £0 *Total Prizemoney* £193
2000 Turf 0-3: (12f 2, 13f) (gd, frm 2)
Scopey, very moderate filly. Turf high 34.
**C A Horgan [0-8] Mrs B Sumner.*

UBITOO BHB 32f34a **RR 26f 34a** 4374[11]
3 b g Puissance 7.1f **(60)** - Cassiar (Connaught) 7.7f **(63)**
Form - 0700053070800
Record 2000 - 1st:0 2nd:0 3rd:1 Ran:10
Pre2000 - 1st:0 2nd:0 3rd:0 Ran:4
Win Prizemoney £0 *Total Prizemoney* £269
2000 Turf 0-10: (6f 2, 7f 4, 8f 2, 10f, 11f) (gd, g-f 4, frm 5)
Unfurnished, very moderate gelding, often wears blinkers. Turf high 34. **R M Flower [0-14] T J Lowe & P Wager.*

UHOOMAGOO BHB 79f **RR 79f** 4313[5]
2 b c Namaqualand (USA) - Point of Law (Law Society (USA)) 9.9f **(70)**
Form - 21131345
Record 2000 - 1st:3 2nd:1 3rd:2 Ran:8
Win Prizemoney £9,708 *Total Prizemoney* £12,376
Wins * **2000** Aug Catter (G-S) H 6f 74 77 <
* **2000** *May Southw (STD) C 5f 64*
* **2000** Apr Thirsk (G-S) C 5f 64
2000 Turf 2-7: (5f 1-2, 6f 1-3, 7f 2) (gd 1-2, g-f 1-3, frm 2) 2000 AW 1-1: (5f 1-1) (Fibr 1-1)
Above-average colt, effective 6f, acts on g-f. Turf high 79 - 4th of 11 giving 17lb to My American Beauty (3 Spt York 6f g-f RF 4193) - also 1st of 6 giving 6lb to Sharp Secret (18 Aug Catterick RF 3740). (1st run). Only plating class, but has won a couple of small events on turf and Fibresand.
**D Nicholls [3-7] The David Nicholls Racing Club (from R A Fahey [0-1] Mar 2000).*

ULSHAW BHB 31f **RR 39f** 3905[4]
3 ch g Salse (USA) 10.9f **(71)** - Kintail (Kris) 9.5f **(73)**
Form - 0370744
Record 2000 - 1st:0 2nd:0 3rd:1 Ran:7
Pre2000 - 1st:0 2nd:0 3rd:0 Ran:2
Win Prizemoney £0 *Total Prizemoney* £633
2000 Turf 0-7: (12f, 14f 4, 16f, 17f) (gd, g-f 2, frm 3, hrd)
Strong, very moderate gelding, has worn blinkers. Turf high 46. Consistent. **J D Bethell [0-9] WWW Clarendon Racing Co UK.*

ULTIMAJUR (USA) BHB 58f **RR** 806[10]
2 br c Dayjur (USA) 6.8f **(79)** - Crystal Lady (CAN) (Stop The Music (USA)) 9.2f **(71)**
Form - 0
Record 2000 - 1st:0 2nd:0 3rd:0 Ran:1
2000 Turf 0-1: (5f) (gd)
Currently fair colt. **Miss Gay Kelleway [0-1] Roger Paul.*

ULTIMATE CHOICE BHB 55a **RR 61f 55a** 5243[5]
2 b c Petong 7.6f **(58)** - Jay Gee Ell (Vaigly Great) 7f **(58)**
Form - 75
Record 2000 - 1st:0 2nd:0 3rd:0 Ran:2
2000 Turf 0-1: (7f) (g-s) 2000 AW 0-1: (6f) (Fibr)
Currently average colt.
**W J Haggas [0-2] A A Goodman.*

ULTRA CALM (IRE) BHB 42f47a **RR 29f 47a** 2680[9]
4 ch g Doubletour (USA) 12f **(46)** - Shyonn (IRE) (Shy Groom (USA)) 10f **(66)**
Form - 0380600220
Record 2000 - 1st:0 2nd:2 3rd:1 Ran:9
Pre2000 - 1st:3 2nd:2 3rd:0 Ran:15
Win Prizemoney £7,195 *Total Prizemoney* £10,738
Wins 1999 Apr Ripon (G-F) H 10f 54 61+
1999 *Mar Wolver (SLW) 8.5f 63* <
1999 *Jan Wolver (STD) C 9.4f 54*
2000 Turf 0-3: (8f, 9f, 10f) (gd 3) 2000 AW 0-6: (8f, 9f 3, 11f 2) (Fibr 6)
Leggy, moderate gelding, effective 8 to 10f, best at 8f, acts on g-s to g-f - acts on Fibr, has worn blinkers, does well at Wolverhampton. Turf high 29. AW high 62 (1st run) - 3rd of 9 giving 10lb to Areish (18 Jan Wolverhampton 9f Fibr RF 0110).
**Miss K M George [0-1] Exterior Profiles Ltd (from P C Haslam [3-23] Jun 2000).*

ULUNDI BHB 98f **RR 100+f** 4611[10]
5 b g Rainbow Quest (USA) 11.2f **(81)** - Flit (USA) (Lyphard (USA)) 9.9f **(72)**
Form - 1130825210
Record 2000 - 1st:3 2nd:2 3rd:2 Ran:11
Win Prizemoney £16,961 *Total Prizemoney* £24,990
Wins * **2000** Spt Kempto (GD) H 12f 92 100 <
* **2000** Mar Windso (G-F) 10f 87
* **2000** *Mar Wolver (STD) 8.5f 77*
2000 Turf 2-10: (10f 1-7, 12f 1-3) (g-s 2, gd 3, g-f 1-4, frm 1-1) 2000 AW 1-1: (8f 1-1) (Fibr 1-1)
Very useful gelding, effective 10 to 12f, best at 10f, acts on g-f, prefers tight tracks. Turf high 100 - 1st of 7 giving 11lb to Riyafa (3 Spt Kempton RF 4190). (1st run). A decent hurdler, he has run some good races in decent company since returning to the level and was successful on Fibresand and turf at the start of the season. Bounced back to form when winning quite a valuable handicap at Kempton in September. Suited by 12 furlongs.
**Lady Herries [7-18] D Heath.*

ULYSSES DAUGHTER (IRE) BHB 76f **RR 76f** 5313[18]
3 ch f College Chapel - Trysinger (IRE) (Try My Best (USA)) 7.6f **(67)**
Form - 4215420
Record 2000 - 1st:1 2nd:2 3rd:0 Ran:7
Win Prizemoney £3,799 *Total Prizemoney* £6,766
Wins * **2000** Spt Bath (GD) 5.7f 71+ <
2000 Turf 1-7: (5f 3, 6f 1-4) (g-s 3, gd, g-f, frm 1-2)
Scopey, above-average filly, effective 5 to 6f, best at 5f, acts on g-s to frm. Turf high 76 - 2nd of 20 giving 2lb to Mr Stylish (10 Oct Bath 5f g-s RF 5068) - also 1st of 10 from Our First Lady (4 Spt Bath RF 4206). **G A Butler [1-7] The Travellers.*

UMBOPA (USA) RR 38f 4765[9]
2 b c Gilded Time (USA) 7f **(76)** - How Fortunate (USA) (What Luck (USA)) 8.1f **(79)**
Form - 00
Record 2000 - 1st:0 2nd:0 3rd:0 Ran:2
2000 Turf 0-2: (8f, 10f) (g-s, gd)
Currently very moderate colt. Turf high 38 (began Spt).
**M L W Bell [0-2] Thurloe Thoroughbreds V.*

UMBRIAN GOLD (IRE) BHB 73f **RR 80f** 2732[11]
4 b m Perugino (USA) - Golden Sunlight (Ile de Bourbon (USA)) 10.1f **(67)**
Form - 2080
Record 2000 - 1st:0 2nd:1 3rd:0 Ran:4
Pre2000 - 1st:1 2nd:4 3rd:0 Ran:7
Win Prizemoney £5,498 *Total Prizemoney* £11,481
Wins * 1999 Aug Ascot (SFT) 7f 75 <
2000 Turf 0-4: (8f 2, 9f, 10f) (gd 3, g-f)
Workmanlike, decent filly, effective 7 to 8f, best at 7f, acts on gd to frm, best on gd. Turf high 80 (1st run) - 2nd of 7 giving 20lb to Den's-Joy (2 May Windsor 8f gd RF 0975).
**J A R Toller [1-11] Mrs R W Gore-Andrews.*

UMISTIM BHB 115f **RR 118f** 5126[1]
3 ch c Inchinor 8.9f **(64)** - Simply Sooty (Absalom) 7.2f **(58)**
Form - 16527271
Record 2000 - 1st:2 2nd:2 3rd:0 Ran:8
Pre2000 - 1st:3 2nd:0 3rd:1 Ran:5
Win Prizemoney £63,535 *Total Prizemoney* £93,666
Wins * **2000** Oct Doncas (SFT) 7f 95+
* **2000** Apr Newmar (SFT) G3 8f 118 <
* 1999 Oct Newbur (G-S) G3 7.3f 104
* 1999 Aug Windso (HVY) 6f 94+

* 1999 Jly Newbur (G-F) 7.3f 85
2000 Turf 2-8: (7f 1-4, 8f 1-3, 9f) (g-s 1-2, gd 1-4, g-f 2)
Workmanlike, high-class colt, effective 7 to 8f, best at 7f, acts on gd to g-f, best on gd, excels at Newbury. Turf high 118 (1st run) - 1st of 6 from King's Best (20 Apr Newmarket RF 0803). He kicked his three-year-old campaign off in style, beating King's Best in the Group Three Craven Stakes. Flattered by that result (the runner-up hit the front too soon and hung), he ran unaccountably badly at Kempton in May and is not particularly consistent. Smart at his best, he goes well on a straight track and probably handles any ground. **R Hannon [5-13] Mrs S Joint.*

UNAWARE BHB 86f **RR 94f** 4469[4]

3 b c Unfuwain (USA) 11.4f **(74)** - Rainbow Lake (Rainbow Quest (USA)) 10.4f **(75)**
Form - 534834
Record 2000 - 1st:0 2nd:0 3rd:2 Ran:6

Umistim started and ended the season in the winner's enclosure

Pre2000 - 1st:1 2nd:0 3rd:0 Ran:4
Win Prizemoney £3,582 *Total Prizemoney* £8,764
Wins * 1999 Aug Chepst (G-S) 8.1f 91+ <
2000 Turf 0-6: (11f, 12f 4, 14f) (hvy, gd, g-f 2, frm 2)
Well made, useful colt, effective 8 to 12f, best at 12f, acts on gd to frm. Turf high 94 - 3rd of 10 giving 17lb to Kaiapoi (10 May Chester 12f g-f RF 1132). He looked unlucky on a couple of occasions during the spring and was the subject of an inspired gamble at Goodwood in August. Disappointing there, he does not seem to finish his races and could have a problem.
**R Charlton [1-10] K Abdulla.*

UNCHAIN MY HEART BHB 61f57a **RR 59f 57a** 4929[10]

4 b m Pursuit of Love 9.5f **(69)** - Addicted to Love **(66f)** (Touching Wood (USA)) 8.2f **(55)**
Form - 1301630814110
Record 2000 - 1st:4 2nd:0 3rd:1 Ran:10
Pre2000 - 1st:1 2nd:3 3rd:6 Ran:18
Win Prizemoney £13,655 *Total Prizemoney* £19,116
Wins * **2000** Spt Leices (G-F) H 7f 57 59 <
* **2000** Aug Kempto (G-F) H 7f 53 57
* **2000** Jly Doncas (G-F) H 7f 50 52
* ***2000*** *Mar Lingfi (STD) C 7f 49*
* *1999 Nov Lingfi (STD) 8f 57*
2000 Turf 3-6: (7f 3-6) (frm 3-6) 2000 AW 1-4: (7f 1-2, 8f 2) (Equi 1-4)
Scopey, fair filly, effective 7 to 8f, best at 8f, acts on g-f to frm - acts on Equi, best on frm, often wears blinkers (extremely effectively). Turf high 59 - 1st of 20 getting 10lb from Adelphi Boy (5 Spt Leicester RF 4217). AW high 49 (1st run).
**B J Meehan [5-28] Mascalls Stud.*

UNCLE DOUG BHB 40f45a **RR 25f 45a** 4459[13]

9 b g Common Grounds 8.1f **(66)** - Taqa (Blakeney) 10.5f **(64)**
Form - 0
Record 2000 - 1st:0 2nd:0 3rd:0 Ran:1
Pre2000 - 1st:3 2nd:5 3rd:2 Ran:34
Win Prizemoney £11,120 *Total Prizemoney* £19,416
Wins 1996 Aug Ripon (HVY) H 16f 55 60 <
1996 May Thirsk (G-F) H 16f 49 56
2000 Turf 0-1: (16f) (g-s)
Little account gelding. Becoming disappointing.
**J L Eyre [0-8] D D Saul (from Mrs M Reveley [6-39] Oct 1997).*

UNCLE EXACT BHB 65f70a **RR 62f 70a** 2364[9]

3 b g Distant Relative 7f **(69)** - True Precision **(61f 59a)** (Presidium)
Form - 000050
Record 2000 - 1st:0 2nd:0 3rd:0 Ran:6
Pre2000 - 1st:1 2nd:1 3rd:1 Ran:10
Win Prizemoney £3,436 *Total Prizemoney* £5,637
Wins 1999 May Hamilt (G-F) 5f 79+ <
2000 Turf 0-5: (5f 3, 6f 2) (gd, g-f 3, frm) 2000 AW 0-1: (5f) (Fibr)
Neat, average gelding, effective 5f, acts on gd to g-f. Turf high 62.
**K A Ryan [0-13] Uncle Jacks Pub (from J Berry [1-3] May 1999).*

UNCLE FOLDING (IRE) BHB 47f **RR 41f** 4400[8]

2 b c Danehill (USA) 9.1f **(79)** - Bubbling Danseuse (USA) (Arctic Tern (USA)) 8.9f **(69)**
Form - 6008
Record 2000 - 1st:0 2nd:0 3rd:0 Ran:4
2000 Turf 0-4: (6f, 7f 2, 8f) (gd, g-f 2, frm)
Moderate colt. Turf high 41. **J A Osborne [0-4] J D Martin.*

UNCLE OBERON BHB 41f **RR 40f** 1182[13]

4 b g Distant Relative 7f **(69)** - Fairy Story (IRE) **(75f 64a)** (Persian Bold) 9.3f **(66)**
Form - 67400
Record 2000 - 1st:0 2nd:0 3rd:0 Ran:5
Pre2000 - 1st:0 2nd:0 3rd:0 Ran:4
2000 Turf 0-3: (6f, 7f 2) (gd, frm 2) 2000 AW 0-2: (7f, 9f) (Fibr 2)
Workmanlike, moderate gelding, has worn blinkers. Turf high 40. AW high 21. Inconsistent.
**C A Dwyer [0-5] Mrs Shelley Dwyer (from G A Butler [0-4] Jun 1999).*

UNDENIABLE BHB 64f **RR 71f** 5309[9]

2 b g Unfuwain (USA) 11.4f **(74)** - Shefoog **(89f)** (Kefaah (USA))
Form - 70
Record 2000 - 1st:0 2nd:0 3rd:0 Ran:2
2000 Turf 0-2: (7f, 8f) (sft, g-s)
Currently above-average gelding. Turf high 71 (began Oct).
**J L Dunlop [0-2] J L Dunlop.*

UNDERCOVER GIRL (IRE) BHB 54f **RR 55f** 5074[7]

2 b f Barathea (IRE) - Les Trois Lamas (IRE) (Machiavellian (USA))
Form - 5087
Record 2000 - 1st:0 2nd:0 3rd:0 Ran:4
2000 Turf 0-4: (7f 4) (g-s 2, g-f 2)
Fair filly. Turf high 55. **W R Muir [0-4] M J Caddy.*

UNDERMINE (USA) RR 4571a[3]

4 br m Miner's Mark (USA) - Sweet Willa (USA) (Assert) 10.6f **(85)**
Form - 3
2000 AW 0-1: (9f) (Dirt)
Currently useful filly. (1st run) - 3rd of 9 to Spain (16 Spt Turfway Park 9f Dirt RF 4571a).
**in USA [0-1].*

UNDER THE SAND (IRE) BHB 75f **RR 80+f** 4749[10]

3 b g Turtle Island (IRE) - Occupation (Homing) 7.8f **(59)**
Form - 077420160
Record 2000 - 1st:1 2nd:1 3rd:0 Ran:9
Win Prizemoney £3,248 *Total Prizemoney* £5,072
Wins * **2000** Aug Haydoc (G-S) H 10.5f 68 80 <
2000 Turf 1-9: (7f 2, 10f 3, 11f 1-1, 12f 3) (g-s 2, gd 1-5, g-f 2)
Workmanlike, decent gelding, effective 11f, acts on gd, likes tight tracks. Turf high 80 - 1st of 14 giving 24lb to Katie Komaite (19

Aug Haydock RF 3780). Got off the mark with a fine victory against older horses under top weight in a Haydock handicap in August.
**M A Jarvis [1-9] David Barker.*

UNDERWOOD FERN (FR) RR 38f 5318[14]

2 b c Charnwood Forest (IRE) - Dame Solitaire (CAN) (Halo (USA)) 10.6f **(75)**
Form - 0
Record 2000 - 1st:0 2nd:0 3rd:0 Ran:1
2000 Turf 0-1: (6f) (sft)
Currently very moderate colt. **H R A Cecil [0-1] Niarchos Family.*

UNDETERRED BHB 87f RR 92f 4164[21]

4 ch h Zafonic (USA) 9f **(83)** - Mint Crisp (IRE) (Green Desert (USA)) 8.6f **(78)**
Form - 0364100
Record 2000 - 1st:1 2nd:0 3rd:1 Ran:7
Pre2000 - 1st:2 2nd:0 3rd:1 Ran:9
Win Prizemoney £21,128 *Total Prizemoney* £28,229
Wins * 2000 Jly Chepst (G-F) 6.1f 88
* 1998 Oct York (GD) L 6f 99 <
* 1998 Aug Yarmou (FRM) 6f 69
2000 Turf 1-7: (6f 1-4, 7f 3) (sft, gd 2, g-f 3, frm 1-1)
Useful colt, effective 7f, acts on g-f. Turf high 92. Successful in Listed company as a juvenile in 1998, he is just a useful handicapper nowadays. Probably best over six furlongs, he is best on a fast surface **C F Wall [3-16] S Fustok.*

UNFORTUNATE BHB 52f47a RR 52f 47a 2642[12]

3 ch f Komaite (USA) 6.9f **(61)** - Honour and Glory (Hotfoot) 10.5f **(59)**
Form - 721465376001440
Record 2000 - 1st:1 2nd:0 3rd:1 Ran:11
Pre2000 - 1st:1 2nd:1 3rd:0 Ran:8
Win Prizemoney £4,010 *Total Prizemoney* £5,278
Wins * 2000 Jun Leices (G-S) SH 6f 46 45+ <
* 1999 *Dec Southw (STD) S 6f 45*
2000 Turf 1-6: (6f 1-5, 7f) (gd 1-3, frm 3) 2000 AW 0-5: (5f, 6f 2, 7f 2) (Fibr 5)
Workmanlike, fair filly, effective 5 to 6f, best at 6f, acts on gd to frm - acts on Fibr, has worn blinkers (very effectively). Turf high 52 - 4th of 13 getting 16lb from Lord Omni (20 Jun Thirsk 6f frm RF 2118) - also 1st of 22 getting 13lb from Bayonet (5 Jun Leicester RF 1718). AW high 47. **Miss J F Craze [2-19] P T Walton.*

UNICORN STAR (IRE) BHB 44f47a RR 48f 47a 3905[8]

3 b g Persian Bold 10f **(69)** - Highland Warning **(36f 44a)** (Warning)
Form - 843625238
Record 2000 - 1st:0 2nd:2 3rd:2 Ran:8
Pre2000 - 1st:0 2nd:0 3rd:0 Ran:3
Win Prizemoney £0 *Total Prizemoney* £2,217
2000 Turf 0-8: (10f, 12f 5, 16f, 17f) (gd 3, frm 4, hrd)
Leggy, moderate gelding, has worn blinkers. Turf high 48. Consistent.
**J S Wainwright [0-11] P Wong & T Leung.*

UNIMPEACHABLE (IRE) BHB 46f RR 60f 3575[12]

3 b f Namaqualand (USA) - Bourbon Topsy (Ile de Bourbon (USA)) 10.1f **(67)**
Form - 008526442250
Record 2000 - 1st:0 2nd:3 3rd:0 Ran:12
Pre2000 - 1st:1 2nd:0 3rd:1 Ran:5
Win Prizemoney £2,092 *Total Prizemoney* £4,754
Wins 1999 Oct Nottin (GD) S 8.2f 65 <
2000 Turf 0-11: (8f, 10f 3, 11f 3, 12f 3, 16f) (hvy, g-s 2, gd 2, g-f 2, frm 4) 2000 AW 0-1: (15f) (Fibr)
Light-framed, average filly, effective 7 to 11f, acts on g-s to g-f, best on g-s, likes left handed tracks, favours tight tracks. Turf high 60 - 2nd of 16 getting 2lb from Perfect Moment (2 Jun Nottingham 10f g-s RF 1665).
**G M McCourt [0-2] Stephen Hillen (from J M Bradley [0-10] Jly 2000).*

UNITED FRONT BHB 28f RR 45f 1707[14]

8 br g Be My Chief (USA) 10.2f **(62)** - Julia Flyte (Drone) 10.3f **(74)**
Form - 000
Record 2000 - 1st:0 2nd:0 3rd:0 Ran:3
Pre2000 - 1st:1 2nd:1 3rd:0 Ran:5
Win Prizemoney £4,204 *Total Prizemoney* £5,429
2000 Turf 0-3: (14f, 16f 2) (g-s, gd, g-f)
Moderate gelding, has worn blinkers. Turf high 45. Inconsistent.
**J Neville [0-10] T Beresford (from R J O'Sullivan [0-2] Oct 1995).*

UNITED PASSION BHB 51f62a RR 26f 62a 2814[6]

3 b f Emarati (USA) 6.6f **(63)** - Miriam **(48df 50a)** (Forzando) 7.6f **(59)**
Form - 27736
Record 2000 - 1st:0 2nd:1 3rd:1 Ran:5
Win Prizemoney £0 *Total Prizemoney* £1,235
2000 Turf 0-1: (5f) (sft) 2000 AW 0-4: (5f 4) (Fibr 4)
Average filly. AW high 50. **D Shaw [0-5] J C Fretwell.*

UNLIKELY BHB 60f RR 74f 4751[9]

2 ch c Aragon 7.7f **(58)** - Homebeforemidnight (Fools Holme (USA))
Form - 3070
Record 2000 - 1st:0 2nd:0 3rd:1 Ran:4
Win Prizemoney £0 *Total Prizemoney* £1,140
2000 Turf 0-4: (5f 2, 6f 2) (g-s, gd, g-f 2)
Above-average colt. Turf high 74 (1st run) - 3rd of 13 giving 5lb to Somers Heath (16 Jun York 6f g-f RF 2033).
**J A Osborne [0-4] The Woolfie and Tom Partnership.*

UNMASKED BHB 24f RR 28f 3355[12]

4 ch m Safawan 6.6f **(60)** - Unveiled **(54f 48a)** (Sayf El Arab (USA)) 7.1f **(54)**
Form - 780080333070
Record 2000 - 1st:0 2nd:0 3rd:3 Ran:12
Pre2000 - 1st:0 2nd:0 3rd:0 Ran:3
Win Prizemoney £0 *Total Prizemoney* £1,343
2000 Turf 0-12: (5f 4, 7f 4, 8f, 9f 3) (gd 5, g-f 4, frm 3)
Neat, little account filly, effective 8f, acts on gd, has worn blinkers, likes right handed tracks, likes tight tracks. Turf high 28.
**J S Goldie [0-13] William Burns (from J Berry [0-2] Jly 1998).*

UNPARALLELED BHB 67f57a RR 69f 57a 4773[12]

2 b f Primo Dominie 7.2f **(67)** - Sharp Chief (Chief Singer) 8.9f **(66)**
Form - 2270
Record 2000 - 1st:0 2nd:2 3rd:0 Ran:4
Win Prizemoney £0 *Total Prizemoney* £2,366
2000 Turf 0-4: (5f, 6f 2, 7f) (g-s, gd, frm)
Average filly, has worn blinkers. Turf high 69 (1st run) (began Jly) - 2nd of 18 getting 5lb from Greenwood (31 Jly Windsor 6f frm RF 3258). **I A Balding [0-4] J C Smith.*

UNSEEDED BHB 89f RR 98f 4936[20]

3 ch f Unfuwain (USA) 11.4f **(74)** - Sesame (Derrylin) 8.8f **(54)**
Form - 10600
Record 2000 - 1st:1 2nd:0 3rd:0 Ran:5
Pre2000 - 1st:0 2nd:0 3rd:0 Ran:2
Win Prizemoney £3,874 *Total Prizemoney* £4,147
Wins * 2000 Apr Doncas (G-S) 10.3f 88++ <
2000 Turf 1-5: (10f 1-2, 12f 3) (gd 1-3, g-f 2)
Scopey, very useful filly, effective 10f, acts on gd. Turf high 98. Out of that grand mare Sesame, she proved bitterly disappointing after strolling home in a Doncaster maiden in April. She is one to avoid until showing a revival. **J L Dunlop [1-7] Christopher Spence.*

UNSHADED (USA) RR 4135a[1]

3 b c Unbridled (USA) - Shade The Flame (USA) (Caucasus (USA)) 8.2f **(74)**
Form - 31
2000 AW 1-2: (10f 1-1, 12f) (Dirt 1-2)
Currently high-class colt. AW high 117 - 1st of 9 from Albert The Great (26 Aug Saratoga RF 4135a). Normally ridden patiently, he reversed Belmont Stakes form with Commendable at Saratoga in August and may be best around a mile and a quarter.
**C Nafzger in USA [1-2] J Tafel.*

UNSHAKEN BHB 63f60a RR 69f 60a 5055[20]

6 b h Environment Friend 7.5f **(67)** - Reel Foyle (USA) (Irish River (FR)) 8.6f **(78)**
Form - 024070070010500
Record 2000 - 1st:1 2nd:1 3rd:0 Ran:15
Pre2000 - 1st:6 2nd:4 3rd:7 Ran:44
Win Prizemoney £43,475 *Total Prizemoney* £62,573
Wins * 2000 Aug Carlis (GD) 6.9f 66
* 1999 Jun Newcas (G-F) H 6f 75 81

* 1999 May Hamilt (GD) H 6f 73 80
* 1999 Apr Hamilt (HVY) H 6f 68 73
* 1998 Jun Hamilt (G-S) 6f 67
* 1998 May Carlis (G-S) H 5.9f 46 56
1996 Oct Folkes (G-S) 5f 86 <

2000 Turf 1-15: (5f 5, 6f 6, 7f 1-4) (sft 3, g-s, gd 4, g-f 2, frm 1-5)

Average horse, effective 5 to 6f, best at 6f, acts on hvy to frm, has worn blinkers, excels at Hamilton. Turf high 75. Inconsistent.

**E J Alston [6-52] G G Sanderson & M Twentyman & A J Picton (from J R Fanshawe [1-7] Jly 1997).*

UNSIGNED (USA) BHB 83f RR 78f 5151[3]

2 b br c Cozzene (USA) 10.1f **(87)** - Striata (USA) (Gone West (USA)) 6.5f **(75)**

Form - 743

Record 2000 - 1st:0 2nd:0 3rd:1 Ran:3

Win Prizemoney £0 *Total Prizemoney* £1,083

2000 Turf 0-3: (7f 2, 8f) (g-s, gd, g-f)

Currently above-average colt. Turf high 78 (began Spt).

**J R Fanshawe [0-3] Great Cumberland Pals.*

UNTOLD STORY (USA) BHB 27f23a RR 24f 23a 4054[18]

5 b g Theatrical 11.5f **(78)** - Committed Miss (USA) (Key To Content (USA)) 8f **(54)**

Form - 0664600

Record 2000 - 1st:0 2nd:0 3rd:0 Ran:7
Pre2000 - 1st:0 2nd:0 3rd:1 Ran:13

Win Prizemoney £0 *Total Prizemoney* £446

2000 Turf 0-1: (11f) (gd) 2000 AW 0-6: (6f, 9f 3, 12f 2) (Equi, Fibr 5)

Little account gelding, has worn blinkers. AW high 28. He has shown precious little so far.

**G A Ham [0-1] Colin Taylor (from T Keddy [0-10] Feb 2000).*

UNVEIL BHB 48f50a RR 51f 50a 4727[4]

2 b f Rudimentary (USA) 8.2f **(66)** - Magical Veil (Majestic Light (USA)) 10.6f **(75)**

Form - 4466503404

Record 2000 - 1st:0 2nd:0 3rd:1 Ran:10

Win Prizemoney £0 *Total Prizemoney* £340

2000 Turf 0-7: (5f 3, 6f 3, 8f) (gd 3, g-f, frm 3) 2000 AW 0-3: (5f 2, 7f) (Fibr 3)

Fair filly, effective 6f, acts on gd. Turf high 51 - 4th of 18 getting 25lb from Clanbroad (29 Spt Lingfield 6f gd RF 4727). AW high 48.

**G M McCourt [0-10] The Antwick Partnership.*

UP AND AWAY (GER) RR 112f 4713a[3]

6 b g Le Glorieux - Ultima Ratio (GER) (Vice Regal (NZ))

Form - 23

2000 Turf 0-2: (8f 2) (sft, gd)

Group-class gelding. Turf high 112 (began Jly) - 3rd of 10 getting 2lb from Bernardon (23 Spt Cologne 8f sft RF 4713a).

**Frau E Mader in GER [0-4] Stall Arc.*

UP IN FLAMES (IRE) BHB 32f17a RR 51f 17a 5056[3]

9 br g Nashamaa 8.1f **(58)** - Bella Lucia (Camden Town) 9.3f **(53)**

Form - 8070203563

Record 2000 - 1st:0 2nd:1 3rd:2 Ran:10
Pre2000 - 1st:5 2nd:5 3rd:4 Ran:56

Win Prizemoney £25,525 *Total Prizemoney* £34,541

Wins 1998 *Jan Southw (STD) H 8f 47 55*
1997 *Dec Wolver (STD) H 9.4f 41 46*
1997 Nov Nottin (GD) H 8.2f 43 46

2000 Turf 0-6: (7f, 8f 3, 10f 2) (sft, gd 2, frm 3) 2000 AW 0-4: (9f 3, 12f) (Fibr 4)

Fair gelding, effective 7f, acts on gd, has worn blinkers. Turf high 51 (1st run) - 2nd of 23 to Mybotye (4 May Redcar 7f gd RF 1019). AW high 32. Inconsistent.

**Mrs G S Rees [0-7] WWW Mark-Kilner-Raci (17) (from R Simpson [0-3] Jan 2000).*

UPLIFTING BHB 57f RR 51f 4618[15]

5 b m Magic Ring (IRE) 6.5f **(64)** - Strapless (Bustino) 10.4f **(64)**

Form - 8000

Record 2000 - 1st:0 2nd:0 3rd:0 Ran:4
Pre2000 - 1st:2 2nd:4 3rd:2 Ran:19

Win Prizemoney £9,604 *Total Prizemoney* £17,909

Wins * 1999 May Goodwo (GD) H 6f 66 68
* 1998 Jly Leices (GD) 5f 74+ <

2000 Turf 0-4: (6f 3, 7f) (gd 2, g-f, frm)

Fair filly, effective 6f, acts on gd to frm, best on gd, has worn blinkers. Turf high 51. Consistent. **L G Cottrell [2-23] H C Seymour.*

UP ON POINTS RR 85f 4129[1]

2 ch f Royal Academy (USA) 7.8f **(77)** - Champagne 'n Roses (Chief Singer) 8.9f **(66)**

Form - 21

Record 2000 - 1st:1 2nd:1 3rd:0 Ran:2

Win Prizemoney £5,024 *Total Prizemoney* £5,924

Wins * **2000** Aug Salisb (G-F) 7f 85 <

2000 Turf 1-2: (7f 1-2) (frm 1-2)

Currently useful filly. Turf high 85 (began Aug) - 1st of 11 from Nafisah (31 Aug Salisbury RF 4129).

**R Hannon [1-2] Vernon Carl Matalon.*

UPPER BULLENS BHB 60f55a RR 59df 55a 4387[17]

3 ch g Rock City 8.8f **(62)** - Monstrosa (Monsanto (FR)) 6.5f **(59)**

Form - 700

Record 2000 - 1st:0 2nd:0 3rd:0 Ran:3
Pre2000 - 1st:0 2nd:0 3rd:0 Ran:3

Win Prizemoney £0 *Total Prizemoney* £522

2000 Turf 0-2: (10f, 11f) (gd, frm) 2000 AW 0-1: (9f) (Fibr)

Workmanlike, fair gelding. (began Spt). **A Bailey [0-6] R Farrington.*

UPPER CHAMBER BHB 38f39a RR 37?f 39a 5188[7]

4 b g Presidium 7.5f **(56)** - Vanishing Trick (Silly Season) 9.7f **(56)**

Form - 0078517

Record 2000 - 1st:1 2nd:0 3rd:0 Ran:7
Pre2000 - 1st:0 2nd:2 3rd:1 Ran:15

Win Prizemoney £3,201 *Total Prizemoney* £5,603

Wins * **2000** Spt Thirsk (GD) H 5f 35 36 <

2000 Turf 1-7: (5f 1-5, 6f 2) (gd, g-f 1-2, frm 3, hrd)

Unfurnished, very moderate gelding, effective 5f, acts on g-f, has worn blinkers. Turf high 37. **J G FitzGerald [1-22] J G FitzGerald.*

UPSTREAM BHB 72f RR 67f 4747[23]

2 b f Prince Sabo 6.6f **(64)** - Rivers Rhapsody (Dominion) 8.5f **(63)**

Form - 4430

Record 2000 - 1st:0 2nd:0 3rd:1 Ran:4

Win Prizemoney £0 *Total Prizemoney* £1,048

2000 Turf 0-4: (5f 2, 6f 2) (gd, g-f 2, frm)

Average filly. Turf high 67. The form of her debut fourth now reads really well, but she has not really progressed from that.

**Major D N Chappell [0-4] Major P G Pusinelli.*

UP TEMPO (IRE) BHB 93f RR 94f 3433[2]

2 b c Flying Spur (AUS) - Musical Essence (Song) 7.2f **(61)**

Form - 2132232

Record 2000 - 1st:1 2nd:4 3rd:2 Ran:7

Win Prizemoney £2,814 *Total Prizemoney* £19,360

Wins * **2000** May Mussel (FRM) 5f 65 <

2000 Turf 1-7: (5f 1-6, 6f) (g-s, gd, frm 1-4, hrd)

Useful colt. Turf high 94. A tough customer, he ran a cracking race when third behind Superstar Leo in the Weatherbys Super Sprint at Newbury in July. Likely to be difficult to place this term, he may prove best around six furlongs. **T D Easterby [1-7] T H Bennett.*

UP THE KYBER BHB 72f RR 74f 1816[8]

3 b c Missed Flight - Najariya (Northfields (USA)) 9f **(72)**

Form - 388

Record 2000 - 1st:0 2nd:0 3rd:1 Ran:3
Pre2000 - 1st:0 2nd:0 3rd:0 Ran:2

Win Prizemoney £0 *Total Prizemoney* £607

2000 Turf 0-3: (7f 2, 8f) (hvy, sft, frm)

Lengthy, above-average colt. Turf high 74 (1st run) - 3rd of 19 to My Retreat (12 Apr Warwick 8f hvy RF 0684).

**R F JohnsonHoughton [0-5] Lady Lloyd Webber.*

URBAN MYTH RR 69f 5066[11]

2 b c Shaamit (IRE) - Nashville Blues (IRE) **(74f)** (Try My Best (USA)) 7.6f **(67)**

Form - 0

Record 2000 - 1st:0 2nd:0 3rd:0 Ran:1

2000 Turf 0-1: (8f) (g-s)

Currently average colt.
**J W Hills [0-1] Freddy Bienstock and Martin Boase.*

URBAN OCEAN (FR) RR 115+f 3306a[6]
4 ch h Bering 9.6f **(80)** - Urban Sea (USA) **(119f)** (Miswaki (USA)) 9f **(81)**
Form - 15076
2000 Turf 1-5: (10f 1-2, 11f, 12f, 14f) (sft 1-1, g-s, gd 2, g-f)
Strong, high-class colt, effective 10f, acts on sft to g-s, prefers right handed tracks. Turf high 115 (1st run) - 1st of 6 giving 8lb to Quws (1 May Curragh RF 1118a). Becoming disappointing. He has been used as a pacemaker in the past and seems to lose interest once headed nowadays. **A P O'Brien in IRE [4-12] David Tsui.*

URGENT REPLY (USA) BHB 22f **RR 26f** 3245[8]
7 b g Green Dancer (USA) 11.9f **(77)** - Bowl of Honey (USA) (Lyphard (USA)) 9.9f **(72)**
Form - 08066268

Record	**2000 -**	1st:0	2nd:1	3rd:0	Ran:8
	Pre2000 -	1st:6	2nd:2	3rd:0	Ran:35

Win Prizemoney £16,163 *Total Prizemoney* £19,071

Wins								
	* 1999	Jun	Warwic	(HVY)	H	16.1f	38	42
	* 1998	Jly	Chepst	(GD)	H	12.1f	44	51
	* 1998	Jun	Mussel	(SFT)	H	16f	44	49
	* 1998	Jun	Hamilt	(SFT)	H	13f	40	44
	* 1997	Aug	Catter	(G-F)	C	12f		51
	* 1997	Jly	Hamilt	(G-F)	C	12.1f		52

2000 Turf 0-8: (11f, 14f, 15f, 16f 5) (g-s, gd 2, g-f 2, frm 3)
Little account gelding, effective 16f, acts on g-s to g-f, has worn blinkers. Turf high 26. **C A Dwyer [6-49] Mrs Christine Rawson.*

URGENT SWIFT BHB 60f65a **RR 66f 65a** 4022[10]
7 ch g Beveled (USA) 6.9f **(64)** - Good Natured (Troy) 10.4f **(68)**
Form - 351440171247580

Record	**2000 -**	1st:3	2nd:1	3rd:0	Ran:14
	Pre2000 -	1st:3	2nd:6	3rd:8	Ran:42

Win Prizemoney £21,180 *Total Prizemoney* £38,565

Wins									
	*** 2000**	Jun	Goodwo	(G-F)	H	14f	65	66	
	*** 2000**	*May*	*Southw*	*(STD)*	*H*	*14f*	*63*	*68*	
	*** 2000**	*Feb*	*Southw*	*(STD)*	*H*	*12f*	*60*	*65*	
	* 1999	Jly	Haydoc	(G-S)	H	14f	70	76+	<
	* 1999	May	Salisb	(G-F)	H	12f	63	66	
	* 1996	Spt	Redcar	(FRM)	H	10f	67	71	

2000 Turf 1-10: (12f, 13f, 14f 1-6, 15f, 16f) (gd 2, g-f 1-5, frm 3) 2000 AW 2-4: (12f 1-2, 14f 1-1, 16f) (Fibr 2-4)
Average gelding, has broken blood-vessels, effective 12 to 16f, best at 16f, acts on gd to frm - acts on Fibr, best on frm, has worn blinkers, likes tight tracks, and excels at Goodwood. Turf high 67 - 2nd of 5 getting 9lb from Fiori (24 Jun Ayr 15f g-f RF 2246). AW high 68 - 1st of 15 giving 32lb to Manful (15 May Southwell RF 1204). Consistent. He scored his first two victories of last term on the Southwell Fibresand. Returned to winning form on turf with a battling victory at Goodwood in June. Stays 14 furlongs, but is not altogether consistent.
**A P Jarvis [6-52] A P Jarvis (from M Pitman [0-8] Jun 1998).*

URSA MAJOR BHB 73f81a **RR 59f 81a** 463[12]
6 b g Warning 8.1f **(77)** - Double Entendre (Dominion) 8.5f **(63)**
Form - 0482121160

Record	**2000 -**	1st:3	2nd:2	3rd:0	Ran:7
	Pre2000 -	1st:6	2nd:2	3rd:3	Ran:41

Win Prizemoney £45,374 *Total Prizemoney* £53,900

Wins									
	*** 2000**	*Feb*	*Lingfi*	*(STD)*	*H*	*12f*	*78*	*81*	
	*** 2000**	*Feb*	*Lingfi*	*(STD)*	*H*	*12f*	*67*	*80+*	
	*** 2000**	*Jan*	*Lingfi*	*(STD)*	*H*	*10f*	*62*	*67*	
	* 1999	Spt	York	(G-F)	H	7f	57	59	
	* 1998	*Feb*	*Lingfi*	*(SLW)*	*H*	*8f*	*82*	*87+*	<
	* 1998	*Jan*	*Lingfi*	*(STD)*	*H*	*8f*	*70*	*87+*	<
	1998	*Jan*	*Southw*	*(STD)*	*C*	*8f*		*82+*	
	1998	*Jan*	*Southw*	*(STD)*	*C*	*8f*		*69*	
	1996	*Dec*	*Lingfi*	*(STD)*		*6f*		*70+*	

2000 AW 3-7: (8f, 10f 1-3, 12f 2-3) (Equi 3-7)
Decent gelding, effective 12f, - acts on Equi, has worn blinkers, likes left handed tracks. AW high 81 - 1st of 8 getting 2lb from Space Race (23 Feb Lingfield RF 0341) - also 1st of 9 getting 1lb from Chalcedony (12 Feb Lingfield RF 0274). He is a winner on turf, but is a much better performer on Equitrack. Suited by forcing tactics, he has shown that he gets twelve furlongs really well and a very effective front runner.
**C N Allen [6-33] Newmarket Connections Ltd (from A Kelleway [2-5] Jan 1998).*

US AND THEM (IRE) RR 29f 1178[12]
3 ch f Pips Pride 6.7f **(70)** - Tasskeen (FR) (Lyphard (USA)) 9.9f **(72)**
Form - 0

Record	**2000 -**	1st:0	2nd:0	3rd:0	Ran:1
	Pre2000 -	1st:0	2nd:0	3rd:0	Ran:1

2000 Turf 0-1: (8f) (g-f)
Scopey, currently little account filly, often wears blinkers.
**Mrs N Macauley [0-2] T J Bird.*

USTIMONA (GER) RR 103f 5090a[2]
3 b f Mondrian (GER) - Well Known (GER) (Konigsstuhl (GER)) 11.2f **(76)**
Form - 32
2000 Turf 0-2: (10f, 11f) (hvy, gd)
Currently very useful filly. Turf high 106 - 2nd of 13 getting 4lb from Claxon (15 Oct Capannelle 10f hvy RF 5090a).
**H Blume in GER [0-2] Gestut Rottgen.*

UTAH (IRE) BHB 36f36a **RR 28f 36a** 534[7]
6 b g High Estate 10.5f **(66)** - Easy Romance (USA) (Northern Jove (CAN)) 9.7f **(66)**
Form - 07432807

Record	**2000 -**	1st:0	2nd:1	3rd:1	Ran:7
	Pre2000 -	1st:0	2nd:1	3rd:0	Ran:10

Win Prizemoney £0 *Total Prizemoney* £1,656
2000 AW 0-7: (7f 3, 8f 2, 9f, 12f) (Equi 2, Fibr 5)
Little account gelding, effective 7 to 8f, best at 7f, - acts on AW, best on Fibr, has worn blinkers (effectively). AW high 43 - 2nd of 11 getting 3lb from Itch (7 Feb Southwell 7f Fibr RF 0235).
**A G Juckes [0-2] A C W Price (from G L Moore [0-6] Feb 2000).*

UTMOST (IRE) BHB 35f **RR 27f** 3739[12]
2 ch f Most Welcome 8.6f **(66)** - Bint Alhabib **(30f)** (Nashwan (USA))
Form - 000

Record	**2000 -**	1st:0	2nd:0	3rd:0	Ran:3

2000 Turf 0-3: (5f, 6f, 7f) (g-f 2, frm)
Currently little account filly. Turf high 27.
**P D Evans [0-3] Mrs H Raw.*

UZY BHB 26f **RR 15f** 4374[12]
4 ch g Common Grounds 8.1f **(66)** - Loch Clair (IRE) (Lomond (USA)) 8.8f **(65)**
Form - 0000

Record	**2000 -**	1st:0	2nd:0	3rd:0	Ran:4
	Pre2000 -	1st:0	2nd:2	3rd:1	Ran:12

Win Prizemoney £0 *Total Prizemoney* £2,576
2000 Turf 0-4: (5f, 7f, 8f, 10f) (gd, frm 3)
Workmanlike, poor gelding, effective 6f, acts on frm, has worn blinkers (effectively). Turf high 15. Inconsistent.
**M J Ryan [0-7] Peter Scott & Mike Bromley (from I A Balding [0-9] Aug 1999).*

VACAMONTE BHB 112f **RR 107f** 4988[6]
2 ch c Caerleon (USA) 10.9f **(79)** - Bahamian (Mill Reef (USA)) 10.5f **(78)**
Form - 156

Record	**2000 -**	1st:1	2nd:0	3rd:0	Ran:3

Win Prizemoney £12,818 *Total Prizemoney* £16,043

Wins	*** 2000**	Jly	Newmar	(G-S)	L	7f	96++	<

2000 Turf 1-3: (7f 1-3) (gd 1-2, g-f)
Currently Pattern-class colt. Turf high 107 (began Jly) - 6th of 10 to Tobougg (14 Oct Newmarket 7f gd RF 4988). Withdrawn after refusing to enter the stalls on his intended debut, he looked a star when quickening clear in a Listed contest at Newmarket's July Meeting. Bitterly disappointing in the Solario Stakes on his next start, he redeemed himself to some extent when finishing a close sixth in the Dewhurst Stakes. Warm and unimpressive to look at there, he is open to plenty of improvement over middle-distances and must not be written off yet. **H R A Cecil [1-3] K Abdulla.*

VAHORIMIX (FR) RR 93f 4712a[2]
2 gr c Linamix (FR) 8.2f **(64)** - Vadsa Honor (FR) **(99f)** (Highest Honor (FR))

Form - 2
2000 Turf 0-1: (8f) (sft)
Currently useful colt. (1st run) - 2nd of 6 to Okawango (20 Spt Chantilly 8f sft RF 4712a). **A Fabre in FR [0-1] J-L Lagardere.*

VAIL PEAK (USA) BHB 62f **RR 65f** 4441[5]
2 b c Peaks and Valleys (USA) - Search Committee (USA) (Roberto (USA)) 10f **(76)**
Form - 505
Record 2000 - 1st:0 2nd:0 3rd:0 Ran:3
2000 Turf 0-3: (5f, 6f, 7f) (g-s 2, gd)
Currently average colt. Turf high 65.
**J Noseda [0-3] Sanford Robertson.*

VALDERO BHB 60f **RR 44tf** 4364[11]
3 ch g Arazi (USA) 9.2f **(74)** - Vale of Truth (USA) (Lyphard's Wish (FR)) 9f **(74)**
Form - 04000
Record 2000 - 1st:0 2nd:0 3rd:0 Ran:5
Win Prizemoney £0 *Total Prizemoney* £348
2000 Turf 0-5: (8f 3, 10f, 12f) (g-s, gd 2, g-f 2)
Scopey, moderate gelding. Turf high 75. **W R Muir [0-5] J Haim.*

VALDESCO (IRE) BHB 75f **RR 73f** 3838[4]
2 ch c Bluebird (USA) 7.9f **(71)** - Allegheny River (USA) (Lear Fan (USA)) 8.5f **(73)**
Form - 34104
Record 2000 - 1st:1 2nd:0 3rd:1 Ran:5
Win Prizemoney £3,380 *Total Prizemoney* £4,355
Wins * **2000** Jly Bright (G-F) 6f 67 <
2000 Turf 1-5: (5f 2, 6f 1-2, 7f) (gd, g-f 2, frm 1-2)
Above-average colt. Turf high 73 - also 1st of 4 from Moonlight Dancer (18 Jly Brighton RF 2888). Got off the mark in a four-runner Brighton maiden on his third start, though the form may not add up to much. **M A Jarvis [1-5] D Fisher.*

VALENTINE BAND (USA) RR 97+f 2477[1]
3 b f Dixieland Band (USA) 10.1f **(80)** - Shirley Valentine (Shirley Heights) 10.3f **(74)**
Form - 1
Record 2000 - 1st:1 2nd:0 3rd:0 Ran:1
Pre2000 - 1st:0 2nd:0 3rd:0 Ran:1
Win Prizemoney £3,542 *Total Prizemoney* £3,676
Wins * **2000** Jly Pontef (GD) 10f 97+ <
2000 Turf 1-1: (10f 1-1) (frm 1-1)
Scopey, currently very useful filly. (1st run) - 1st of 4 from Drama Class (3 Jly Pontefract RF 2477). Sixth in a Listed race on her only start in 1999, she ran out the easy winner of a Pontefract maiden in July but was not seen out again. Highly regarded, she will stay a mile and a half and remains an interesting prospect.
**R Charlton [1-2] K Abdulla.*

VALENTINES VISION BHB 44f50a **RR 44f 50a** 5018[1]
3 b g Distinctly North (USA) 7.4f **(63)** - Sharp Anne (Belfort (FR)) 6.8f **(63)**
Form - 0341
Record 2000 - 1st:1 2nd:0 3rd:1 Ran:4
Pre2000 - 1st:0 2nd:0 3rd:0 Ran:3
Win Prizemoney £1,939 *Total Prizemoney* £2,252
Wins * **2000** *Oct Wolver (STD) S 7f 54* <
2000 Turf 0-1: (7f) (frm) 2000 AW 1-3: (7f 1-1, 8f, 9f) (Equi, Fibr 1-2)
Leggy, fair gelding, effective 7f, - acts on Fibr. AW high 54 (began Aug) - 1st of 12 giving 5lb to Stop The Traffic (17 Oct Wolverhampton RF 5018).
**N P Littmoden [1-7] Alan Miller & Mrs Maggie McClean.*

VALENTINO BHB 116f **RR 120f** 4596[10]
3 ch c Nureyev (USA) 8.4f **(84)** - Divine Danse (FR) (Kris) 9.5f **(73)**
Form - 32720
Record 2000 - 1st:0 2nd:2 3rd:1 Ran:5
Pre2000 - 1st:1 2nd:0 3rd:0 Ran:2
Win Prizemoney £7,002 *Total Prizemoney* £97,970
Wins 1999 Jly Ascot (G-F) 6f 80+ <
2000 Turf 0-5: (8f 5) (gd 4, frm)
Scopey, very high-class colt, effective 8f, acts on gd to frm, best on gd. Turf high 120 - 2nd of 11 to Giant's Causeway (20 Jun Ascot 8f gd RF 2111). Lightly raced, he was a good third to Bachir in the French Guineas on his reappearance. Seemed set to land the St James's Palace Stakes next time, but was caught close home by Giant's Causeway. He was a little disappointing in subsequent efforts, and seemd to be outbattled when beaten by Distant Music at Doncaster. May well improve for another winter, and the ability is certainly there.
**J H M Gosden [0-5] A E Oppenheimer (from P W Chapple-Hyam [1-2] Spt 1999).*

VALEUREUX RR 34f 5131[15]
2 ch c Cadeaux Genereux 7.9f **(76)** - La Strada (Niniski (USA)) 10.6f **(65)**
Form - 0
Record 2000 - 1st:0 2nd:0 3rd:0 Ran:1
2000 Turf 0-1: (6f) (sft)
Currently very moderate colt. **D R C Elsworth [0-1] Miss K Rausing.*

VALHALLA GOLD RR 9f 1473[12]
6 ch g Golden Lahab (USA) 14.4f **(32)** - Key Harvest (Deep Diver) 6.6f **(62)**
Form - 0
Record 2000 - 1st:0 2nd:0 3rd:0 Ran:1
2000 Turf 0-1: (8f) (g-f)
Currently very poor gelding.
**B Ellison [0-1] Ms Glynis Purcell-Brydon.*

VALIANT HALORY (USA) RR 5328a[12]
3 b c Valiant Nature (USA) - Private Reply (USA) (Private Terms (USA))
Form - 0
2000 AW 0-1: (6f) (Dirt)
Currently very useful colt. **N Zito in USA [0-1] Celtic Pride Stable.*

VALLEY CHAPEL (IRE) RR 107f 4422a[1]
4 ch h Selkirk (USA) 7.9f **(76)**
Form - 311
2000 Turf 2-3: (9f 1-1, 12f 1-2) (sft 1-1, gd 1-2)
Pattern-class colt. Turf high 107 (began Aug) - 1st of 10 giving 9lb to Barrier Reef (10 Spt Taby RF 4422a) - also 1st of 14 from Martellian (27 Aug Ovrevoll RF 4141a).
**W Neuroth in NOR [2-5] Stall Perlen.*

VALLEY OF DREAMS (IRE) RR 59f 4466[12]
2 b f Fairy King (USA) 7.7f **(75)** - Capegulch (USA) (Gulch (USA)) 8f **(81)**
Form - 0
Record 2000 - 1st:0 2nd:0 3rd:0 Ran:1
2000 Turf 0-1: (7f) (g-f)
Currently fair filly. **P Howling [0-1] Liam Sheridan.*

VALS RING RR 4926[12]
2 ch c King's Signet (USA) 7f **(51)** - Factuelle (Known Fact (USA)) 7.4f **(67)**
Form - 0
Record 2000 - 1st:0 2nd:0 3rd:0 Ran:1
2000 AW 0-1: (6f) (Equi)
Currently little account colt.
**J Gallagher [0-1] Horses Away Racing Club.*

VANADIUM ORE BHB 38f **RR 41f** 3253[6]
7 b g Precious Metal 9.3f **(42)** - Rockefillee (Tycoon II) 8.7f **(47)**
Form - 6
Record 2000 - 1st:0 2nd:0 3rd:0 Ran:1
Pre2000 - 1st:4 2nd:3 3rd:1 Ran:29
Win Prizemoney £12,155 *Total Prizemoney* £15,896
Wins 1998 Jun Newcas (GD) H 10.1f 52 60 <
1998 Jun Ayr (G-F) H 10.9f 52 56
1998 Jun Cheste (GD) H 10.3f 50 53
1997 Oct Newcas (G-F) H 10.1f 48 52
2000 Turf 0-1: (12f) (g-f)
Moderate gelding, effective 12f, acts on frm, has worn blinkers, likes tight tracks.
**D Eddy [0-1] Garth Ormond (from W McKeown [4-30] Oct 1999).*

VANBOROUGH LAD BHB 34f41a **RR 39f 41a** 3696[P]
11 b g Precocious 7.2f **(54)** - Lustrous (Golden Act (USA)) 8.8f **(67)**
Form - 50021708P

Record 2000 - 1st:1 2nd:1 3rd:0 Ran:9
Pre2000 - 1st:8 2nd:10 3rd:8 Ran:90
Win Prizemoney £24,673 *Total Prizemoney* £42,433
Wins * 2000 Jun Warwic (G-S) SH 10.5f 31 36
1999 Jun Haydoc (SFT) H 10.5f 47 52
1999 May Bath (GD) H 10.2f 44 45
1998 Jly Windso (G-F) H 10f 42 44
1997 May Bath (GD) H 8f 37 39
2000 Turf 1-9: (9f, 10f 3, 11f 1-3, 12f 2) (hvy, g-s 1-2, gd 4, g-f, frm)
Very moderate gelding, effective 10 to 12f, acted on gd to frm, had worn blinkers. Turf high 39. (DEAD)
**Dr J R J Naylor [1-13] Mrs S P Elphick (from M J Bolton [6-58] Aug 1999).*

VANISHING DANCER (SWI) BHB 68f70a **RR 71f 70a** 5207[8]

3 ch g Llandaff (USA) - Vanishing Prairie (USA) (Alysheba (USA)) 9f **(84)**
Form - 30331288
Record 2000 - 1st:1 2nd:1 3rd:3 Ran:8
Pre2000 - 1st:0 2nd:0 3rd:0 Ran:2
Win Prizemoney £2,990 *Total Prizemoney* £5,276
Wins 2000 *Jly Lingfi (STD) H 12f 59 64* <
2000 Turf 0-5: (10f, 12f, 14f, 15f, 16f) (g-s 3, gd, g-f) 2000 AW 1-3: (10f, 12f 1-2) (Equi 1-2, Fibr)
Well made, above-average gelding, effective 12 to 14f, acts on g-f - acts on Equi, has worn blinkers, likes left handed tracks, favours tight tracks. Turf high 71 - 2nd of 10 giving 2lb to Jack Dawson (26 Aug Redcar 14f g-f RF 4000). AW high 64 - 1st of 8 getting 3lb from Dont Worry Bout Me (14 Jly Lingfield RF 2809).
**A Dickman [0-3] Mike Smallman (from K R Burke [1-7] Jly 2000).*

VANITY (IRE) RR 15f 5198[6]

3 b f Thatching 7.8f **(69)** - Penny Fan **(34f)** (Nomination) 7f **(60)**
Form - 6
Record 2000 - 1st:0 2nd:0 3rd:0 Ran:1
2000 Turf 0-1: (6f) (gd)
Scopey, currently poor filly. **G B Balding [0-1] Theo Waddington.*

VANNUCCI (IRE) RR 34tf 977[9]

3 b g Perugino (USA) - Confirmed Friend (Wolverlife) 9.3f **(54)**
Form - 0
Record 2000 - 1st:0 2nd:0 3rd:0 Ran:1
2000 Turf 0-1: (8f) (gd)
Workmanlike, very moderate gelding. (DEAD)
**J C Fox [0-1] Lord Mutton Racing Partnership.*

VANTAGE POINT BHB 42f **RR 50f** 5161[17]

4 b h Casteddu 7.4f **(54)** - Rosie Dickins (Blue Cashmere) 6.4f **(54)**
Form - 33220
Record 2000 - 1st:0 2nd:0 3rd:0 Ran:1
Pre2000 - 1st:1 2nd:4 3rd:4 Ran:18
Win Prizemoney £4,659 *Total Prizemoney* £10,076
Wins * 1999 Aug Folkes (G-S) H 12f 45 49 <
2000 Turf 0-1: (16f) (sft)
Scopey, fair colt, effective 11 to 16f, best at 12f, acts on gd to frm - acts on AW, favours tight tracks, excels at Lingfield. Consistent.
**K McAuliffe [1-19] The Hare and Hounds Partnership.*

VARIEGATION BHB 68f **RR 32f** 5310[15]

2 ch g Spectrum (IRE) - Ninotchka (USA) **(102f)** (Nijinsky (CAN)) 10.3f **(77)**
Form - 00
Record 2000 - 1st:0 2nd:0 3rd:0 Ran:2
2000 Turf 0-2: (7f 2) (g-s 2)
Currently fair gelding. Turf high 32 (began Oct).
**J L Dunlop [0-2] J L Dunlop.*

VARIETY (USA) BHB 63f **RR 71f** 5069[15]

3 ch f Theatrical 11.5f **(78)** - Kamsi (USA) (Afleet (CAN))
Form - 03630
Record 2000 - 1st:0 2nd:0 3rd:2 Ran:5
Win Prizemoney £0 *Total Prizemoney* £2,339
2000 Turf 0-5: (10f 2, 11f, 12f 2) (g-s, gd, g-f 3)
Leggy, above-average filly. Turf high 71.
**J R Fanshawe [0-5] Philip Newton.*

VARIETY SHOP (USA) BHB 90f **RR 90+f** 4303[4]

4 b m Mr Prospector (USA) 8.6f **(88)** - Nimble Feet (USA) (Danzig (USA)) 8.4f **(76)**
Form - 14
Record 2000 - 1st:1 2nd:0 3rd:0 Ran:2
Pre2000 - 1st:0 2nd:1 3rd:0 Ran:1
Win Prizemoney £3,367 *Total Prizemoney* £5,152
Wins * 2000 Jly Ripon (G-S) 8f 85 <
2000 Turf 1-2: (7f, 8f 1-1) (g-s 1-1, gd)
Scopey, currently useful filly. Turf high 90 (began Jly) - 4th of 8 giving 2lb to Blue Mountain (8 Spt Goodwood 7f gd RF 4303) - also 1st of 5 giving 9lb to Latour (10 Jly Ripon RF 2679). Very lightly raced, she broke her duck at Ripon in July but was outpaced when stepped-up a grade on her only subsequent start. She may be happier back over a mile, but will not be easy to place.
**H R A Cecil [1-3] K Abdulla.*

VASARI (IRE) BHB 55f56a **RR 51f 56a** 5165[6]

6 ch g Imperial Frontier (USA) 7f **(65)** - Why Not Glow (IRE) (Glow (USA)) 6.7f **(71)**
Form - 06
Record 2000 - 1st:0 2nd:0 3rd:0 Ran:1
Pre2000 - 1st:1 2nd:1 3rd:4 Ran:27
Win Prizemoney £7,112 *Total Prizemoney* £14,356
Wins 1996 May Cheste (GD) 5.1f 83+ <
2000 AW 0-1: (7f) (Equi)
Average gelding, effective 6f, acts on g-f, has worn blinkers.
**J R Poulton [0-1] J R Poulton (from John Harris [0-2] Nov 1999).*

VEGAS BHB 30f35a **RR 35a** 1104[16]

4 ch m Then Again 7.4f **(52)** - Cazanove's Pet **(45f 52a)** (Tina's Pet) 6.8f **(59)**
Form - 880
Record 2000 - 1st:0 2nd:0 3rd:0 Ran:3
Pre2000 - 1st:0 2nd:0 3rd:0 Ran:4
2000 Turf 0-2: (12f 2) (gd, frm) 2000 AW 0-1: (8f) (Equi)
Workmanlike, fair filly. **J S Moore [0-7] Western Solvents Ltd.*

VEIL OF AVALON (USA) BHB 100f **RR 101f** 4282[2]

3 b f Thunder Gulch (USA) - Wind in Her Hair (IRE) **(109f)** (Alzao (USA)) 7.1f **(68)**
Form - 621622
Record 2000 - 1st:1 2nd:3 3rd:0 Ran:6
Pre2000 - 1st:2 2nd:0 3rd:1 Ran:4
Win Prizemoney £21,553 *Total Prizemoney* £35,455
Wins * 2000 Aug Goodwo (GD) 7f 98 <
* 1999 Spt Newbur (G-F) 7f 88
* 1999 Aug Lingfi (GD) 6f 76+
2000 Turf 1-6: (7f 1-4, 8f 2) (g-s, gd, g-f 1-3, frm)
Scopey, very useful filly, effective 7f, acts on g-f to frm, best on g-f. Turf high 101 - 2nd of 9 getting 8lb from Nicobar (1 Spt Epsom 7f g-f RF 4145) - also 1st of 9 from Kashra (5 Aug Goodwood RF 3398). Consistent. Gradually found her form last season, landing a classified event at Glorious Goodwood. Runner-up in two listed races in September, she is a seven-furlong filly.
**R Charlton [3-10] Jeffen Racing.*

VELMEZ BHB 54f68a **RR 48f 68a** 2264[11]

7 ch g Belmez (USA) 11.4f **(65)** - Current Raiser (Filiberto (USA)) 9.5f **(66)**
Form - 0
Record 2000 - 1st:0 2nd:0 3rd:0 Ran:1
Pre2000 - 1st:0 2nd:0 3rd:0 Ran:4
Win Prizemoney £0 *Total Prizemoney* £478
2000 Turf 0-1: (18f) (frm)
Moderate gelding, has worn blinkers.
**B J Llewellyn [1-2] Thomas Leonard (from R Guest [0-4] Jly 1996).*

VELVET GLADE (USA) BHB 95f **RR 83f** 4595[6]

2 b f Kris S (USA) 9.3f **(76)** - Vailmont (USA) (Diesis) 9.3f **(69)**
Form - 316
Record 2000 - 1st:1 2nd:0 3rd:1 Ran:3
Win Prizemoney £3,038 *Total Prizemoney* £7,286
Wins * 2000 Spt Lingfi (G-F) 7f 83 <
2000 Turf 1-3: (6f, 7f 1-1, 8f) (gd, g-f, frm 1-1)
Currently decent filly. Turf high 83 (began Jly) - 1st of 11 from Fille de Bucheron (5 Spt Lingfield RF 4226). Third behind Regal Rose in a useful race on her debut and won readily at Lingfield second time up. **I A Balding [1-3] George Strawbridge.*

VELVET JONES BHB 30f34a **RR 30f 34a** 2792[12]
7 b gr g Sharrood (USA) 11.1f **(67)** - Cradle of Love (USA) (Roberto (USA)) 10f **(76)**
Form - 0
Record 2000 - 1st:0 2nd:0 3rd:0 Ran:1
Pre2000 - 1st:0 2nd:4 3rd:4 Ran:42
Win Prizemoney £0 *Total Prizemoney* £5,105
2000 Turf 0-1: (8f) (frm)
Very moderate gelding, has worn blinkers. Consistent.
**G F H Charles-Jones [0-42] Mrs Jessica Charles-Jones (from P F I Cole [0-6] Spt 1995).*

VELVET LADY BHB 104f95a **RR 111df 95a** 5366a[8]
3 b f Nashwan (USA) 10.3f **(79)** - Velvet Moon (IRE) **(102f)** (Shaadi (USA))
Form - 26518
Record 2000 - 1st:1 2nd:1 3rd:0 Ran:5
Win Prizemoney £6,711 *Total Prizemoney* £12,101
Wins * 2000 Jly Ascot (G-F) 8f 100+ <
2000 Turf 1-5: (7f, 8f 1-3, 10f) (hvy, g-s, gd, g-f 1-1, frm)
Scopey, Group-class filly. Turf high 111. An eye-catching sixth in the 1000 Guineas, she proved disappointing and does not seem to be finishing her races. **P F I Cole [1-5].*

VENDOME (IRE) BHB 83f **RR 83f** 5129[16]
2 b c General Monash (USA) - Kealbra Lady **(16f)** (Petong) 6.6f **(58)**
Form - 0003312230
Record 2000 - 1st:1 2nd:2 3rd:3 Ran:10
Win Prizemoney £7,289 *Total Prizemoney* £12,948
Wins * 2000 Aug Beverl (G-F) H 5f 74 77 <
2000 Turf 1-10: (5f 1-8, 6f 2) (sft, gd 2, g-f 3, frm 1-3, hrd)
Decent colt, effective 5f, acts on gd to hrd. Turf high 83 - 2nd of 9 giving 1lb to Nifty Alice (31 Aug Musselburgh 5f frm RF 4120) - also 1st of 12 from Rough Shoot (27 Aug Beverley RF 4010). Took time finding his form and eventually got off the mark at Beverley in August, though he only just held on. Decent efforts in nurseries since. Best when allowed to bowl along in front.
**J A Osborne [1-10] John Livock.*

VENIKA VITESSE BHB 54f63a **RR 66f 63a** 3600[5]
4 b g Puissance 7.1f **(60)** - Vilanika (FR) (Top Ville) 11.7f **(68)**
Form - 08000005
Record 2000 - 1st:0 2nd:0 3rd:0 Ran:8
Pre2000 - 1st:3 2nd:0 3rd:2 Ran:10
Win Prizemoney £9,605 *Total Prizemoney* £10,548
Wins * 1999 Aug Nottin (G-F) H 6.1f 68 69
* 1999 Jun Carlis (G-F) H 5.9f 64 66
* 1999 *Jan Lingfi (STD) 5f* 73 <
2000 Turf 0-8: (5f 2, 6f 6) (gd 2, g-f 2, frm 2, hrd 2)
Workmanlike, above-average gelding, effective 5 to 6f, best at 6f, acts on gd to frm - acts on Equi. Turf high 66.
**T D Barron [3-18] Kevin Shaw.*

VENTO DEL ORENO (FR) RR 67f 5299[7]
3 ch f Lando (GER) - Very Sweet (Bellypha) 9.8f **(73)**
Form - 56004257
Record 2000 - 1st:0 2nd:1 3rd:0 Ran:8
Win Prizemoney £0 *Total Prizemoney* £819
2000 Turf 0-8: (8f 5, 10f 3) (g-s 3, gd 2, g-f 2, frm)
Average filly, effective 8f, acts on g-s to g-f, prefers tight tracks. Turf high 67. Inconsistent. **L M Cumani [0-8] Mrs Luca Cumani.*

VENTO DEL ORENO (ITY) RR 818a[6]
3 f
Form - 6
Record 2000 - 1st:0 2nd:0 3rd:0 Ran:1
2000 Turf 0-1: (8f) (hvy)
Currently very poor filly. **L M Cumani [0-1].*

VENTURE CAPITALIST BHB 66f **RR 58f** 1167[14]
11 ch g Never so Bold 7.1f **(62)** - Brave Advance (USA) (Bold Laddie (USA)) 5.6f **(69)**
Form - 00
Record 2000 - 1st:0 2nd:0 3rd:0 Ran:2
Pre2000 - 1st:9 2nd:13 3rd:11 Ran:88
Win Prizemoney £114,322 *Total Prizemoney* £178,951
Wins * 1999 Jly Catter (GD) C 5f 52
* 1998 Jly Doncas (G-F) 6f 92
* 1996 May York (G-F) G3 6f 106 <
2000 Turf 0-2: (6f 2) (g-s, frm)
Fair gelding, effective 5 to 6f, acted on gd to hrd, had worn blinkers (very effectively). Turf high 26. (DEAD)
**D Nicholls [5-57] P S Platt (from R Hannon [4-33] Oct 1994).*

VERBOSE (USA) BHB 95f **RR 95f** 4282[10]
3 b f Storm Bird (CAN) 8.5f **(82)** - Alvernia (USA) (Alydar (USA)) 9.1f **(76)**
Form - 12500
Record 2000 - 1st:1 2nd:1 3rd:0 Ran:5
Pre2000 - 1st:0 2nd:0 3rd:0 Ran:1
Win Prizemoney £2,782 *Total Prizemoney* £7,386
Wins * 2000 Mar Windso (G-F) 8.3f 90+ <
2000 Turf 1-5: (7f 2, 8f 1-2, 9f) (g-s 2, gd, frm 1-2)
Scopey, very useful filly, effective 8f, acts on g-s to frm. Turf high 95 - 2nd of 12 to Embraced (3 May Ascot 8f g-s RF 0999) - also 1st of 8 from Tweed Mill (27 Mar Windsor RF 0518). She capitalised on a fitness advantage when finishing second in a Listed race at Ascot during April. Disappointing thereafter, she is unlikely to improve. **J H M Gosden [1-6] K Abdulla.*

VERDURA BHB 62f60a **RR 63?f 60a** 4785[12]
3 b f Green Desert (USA) 7.8f **(78)** - Spirit of The Wind (USA) (Little Current (USA)) 9.6f **(75)**
Form - 647020
Record 2000 - 1st:0 2nd:1 3rd:0 Ran:6
Pre2000 - 1st:0 2nd:0 3rd:0 Ran:1
Win Prizemoney £0 *Total Prizemoney* £1,094
2000 Turf 0-4: (7f, 8f, 9f, 10f) (gd 2, g-f, frm) 2000 AW 0-2: (8f, 9f) (Equi, Fibr)
Scopey, average filly, has worn blinkers. Turf high 63. AW high 45 (began Aug).
**G A Butler [0-6] H R H Princess Michael of Kent (from B W Hills [0-1] Spt 1999).*

VERIDIAN RR 88f 4015[2]
7 b g Green Desert (USA) 7.8f **(78)** - Alik (FR) (Targowice (USA)) 11.4f **(70)**
Form - 1342
Record 2000 - 1st:1 2nd:1 3rd:1 Ran:4
Pre2000 - 1st:3 2nd:3 3rd:0 Ran:16
Win Prizemoney £22,274 *Total Prizemoney* £40,936
Wins * 2000 May Cheste (GD) H 12.3f 76 78
1997 Jly Cheste (G-F) H 12.3f 73 80 <
1997 May Doncas (GD) H 12f 68 78
1996 Aug Lingfi (G-S) H 11.5f 70 75
2000 Turf 1-4: (12f 1-4) (gd 2, g-f 1-2)
Useful gelding. Turf high 88 - 3rd of 20 getting 19lb from Katiykha (20 Jun Ascot 12f gd RF 2114). Consistent. Lightly raced in the Flat, he was successful at Chester on his reappearance.
**N J Henderson [3-16] Thurloe Thoroughbreds III (from P W Harris [3-16] Oct 1997).*

VERSATILITY BHB 46f53a **RR 47f 53a** 2569[9]
7 b m Teenoso (USA) 10.5f **(62)** - Gay Criselle (Decoy Boy) 6.7f **(56)**
Form - 53105630
Record 2000 - 1st:1 2nd:0 3rd:2 Ran:8
Pre2000 - 1st:1 2nd:0 3rd:1 Ran:10
Win Prizemoney £6,216 *Total Prizemoney* £7,805
Wins * 2000 Apr Folkes (SFT) H 15.4f 47 62 <
1999 May Warwic (SFT) H 14.6f 45 55
2000 Turf 1-8: (14f 2, 15f 1-1, 16f 3, 17f, 18f) (g-s 1-3, gd 2, g-f 2, hrd)
Moderate mare, effective 15f, acts on sft to g-s, likes tight tracks. Turf high 62 - 1st of 16 getting 3lb from Sheriff (18 Apr Folkestone RF 0763). Consistent.
**Dr J R J Naylor [1-8] Magno-Pulse Ltd (from G M McCourt [2-7] Oct 1999).*

VETORITY BHB 53f **RR 71f** 5070[11]
3 b f Vettori (IRE) - Celerite (USA) (Riverman (USA)) 9.1f **(76)**
Form - 353040
Record 2000 - 1st:0 2nd:0 3rd:2 Ran:6
Win Prizemoney £0 *Total Prizemoney* £1,321
2000 Turf 0-6: (10f 4, 12f 2) (g-s 2, g-f 3, frm)
Scopey, above-average filly, effective 10f, acts on g-f to frm. Turf

high 71 - 3rd of 15 to Eurolink Artemis (20 Jly Leicester 10f frm RF 2973). *B Smart [0-6] Alvarez Cervera.

VIA CAMP BHB 83f **RR 87f** 4262[9]
3 b f Kris 10f **(75)** - Honeyspike (IRE) **(64f)** (Chief's Crown (USA)) 9.8f **(72)**
Form - 4620
Record 2000 - 1st:0 2nd:1 3rd:0 Ran:4
Pre2000 - 1st:1 2nd:0 3rd:1 Ran:3
Win Prizemoney £3,647 *Total Prizemoney* £8,867
Wins * 1999 Aug Beverl (GD) 7.5f 87 <
2000 Turf 0-4: (7f, 8f, 10f 2) (gd 4)
Unfurnished, useful filly, effective 7 to 10f, best at 7f, acts on gd to frm, best on frm. Turf high 87 - 2nd of 6 getting 7lb from Welsh Main (27 Aug Yarmouth 10f gd RF 4027).
*E A L Dunlop [1-7] Coutinho Nogueira.

VIA RODEO (IRE) RR 86f 5355a[9]
3 ch c Erins Isle 8.3f **(76)** - Closette (FR) (Fabulous Dancer (USA)) 9.4f **(70)**
Form - 041320300740
2000 Turf 1-12: (8f 2, 10f 1-2, 12f 8) (hvy, sft, g-s 3, gd 4, g-f 1-2, frm)
Useful colt, effective 10 to 12f, best at 12f, acts on g-s to frm, has worn blinkers, likes right handed tracks. Turf high 92 - 3rd of 13 getting 8lb from Media Puzzle (13 Jly Down Royal 12f frm RF 2905a) - also 1st of 8 from Worldly Treasure (9 May Navan RF 1229a). Tried over a variety of trips, he has yet to prove he stays beyond a mile and a half. *J S Bolger in IRE [1-16] D H W Dobson.

VICE PRESIDENTIAL BHB 37f43a **RR 37f 43a** 5083[8]
5 ch g Presidium 7.5f **(56)** - Steelock (Lochnager) 6f **(59)**
Form - 102508458408
Record 2000 - 1st:0 2nd:1 3rd:0 Ran:10
Pre2000 - 1st:4 2nd:0 3rd:2 Ran:28
Win Prizemoney £9,734 *Total Prizemoney* £11,395
Wins * 1999 *Nov Southw (STD) C 6f 55*
1998 Jun Mussel (SFT) C 7.1f 62+
1998 Jun Warwic (SFT) C 7f 77
1997 May Hamilt (SFT) 5f 93+ <
2000 Turf 0-3: (6f 2, 7f) (hvy, gd 2) 2000 AW 0-7: (6f 6, 7f) (Fibr 7)
Fair gelding, effective 6 to 7f, best at 6f, - acts on Fibr, likes left handed tracks, prefers tight tracks. Turf high 28. AW high 55.
*J G Given [1-18] A Clarke (from M P Bielby [0-7] Oct 1998).

VICIOUS CIRCLE BHB 109f **RR 108+f** 4985[4]
6 b g Lahib (USA) 8f **(69)** - Tight Spin (High Top) 10.2f **(67)**
Form - 44
Record 2000 - 1st:0 2nd:0 3rd:0 Ran:2
Pre2000 - 1st:4 2nd:2 3rd:1 Ran:9
Win Prizemoney £166,923 *Total Prizemoney* £178,294
Wins * 1999 Spt Ascot (HVY) H 12f 101 106+ <
* 1999 Aug York (GD) H 13.9f 90 97
* 1999 Jun Newcas (GD) 10.1f 87
* 1998 Oct Ayr (HVY) 10f 97+
2000 Turf 0-2: (12f, 16f) (gd, g-f)
Pattern-class gelding, effective 12f, acts on sft to g-f. Turf high 108 (1st run) (began Aug) - 4th of 7 getting 1lb from Murghem (4 Aug Goodwood 12f g-f RF 3364). Lightly raced, he ran well in a Listed handicap at Goodwood on his belated return but was well held in the Jockey Club Cup. *L M Cumani [4-11] D Metcalf And J Samuel.

VICIOUS DANCER BHB 100f **RR 94f** 5107[15]
2 b g Timeless Times (USA) 6.1f **(56)** - Yankeedoodledancer (Mashhor Dancer (USA)) 10f **(65)**
Form - 76110
Record 2000 - 1st:2 2nd:0 3rd:0 Ran:5
Win Prizemoney £16,723 *Total Prizemoney* £16,723
Wins * **2000** Spt Ayr (SFT) L 5f 94 <
* **2000** Spt York (GD) 6f 83+
2000 Turf 2-5: (5f 1-2, 6f 1-3) (gd 1-2, g-f 1-1, frm 2)
Useful gelding. Turf high 94 (began Jly) - 1st of 12 from Red Millennium (14 Spt Ayr RF 4383). A progressive individual, he had a tough race to win the listed Harry Rosebery Stakes at Ayr in September. Probably feeling the effects of that when unplaced in the Group 3 Cornwallis Stakes on his only subsequent start, he should stay seven furlongs but does not look Group class at present. *R M Whitaker [2-5] Mrs C Samuel.

VICIOUS KNIGHT BHB 100f **RR 93f** 4001[6]
2 b c Night Shift (USA) 8.1f **(73)** - Myth (Troy) 10.4f **(68)**
Form - 6126
Record 2000 - 1st:1 2nd:1 3rd:0 Ran:4
Win Prizemoney £4,134 *Total Prizemoney* £13,134
Wins * 2000 Jly Beverl (G-F) 7.5f 93+ <
2000 Turf 1-4: (7f 1-2, 8f 2) (gd 2, g-f 1-1, frm)
Useful colt. Turf high 93 (began Jly) - 1st of 4 from Sabana (24 Jly Beverley RF 3068). He looked progressive when winning a four-runner novice event at Beverley on his second start and was unlucky not to win the Shergar Cup Juvenile next time. He disappointed on rain-softened ground at Goodwood.
*L M Cumani [1-4] D Metcalf And J Samuel.

VICKY SCARLETT RR 10f 4008[11]
3 gr f Missed Flight - Just Greenwich **(43f)** (Chilibang)
Form - 00
Record 2000 - 1st:0 2nd:0 3rd:0 Ran:2
2000 Turf 0-2: (7f, 8f) (gd, frm)
Strong, currently poor filly. Turf high 10 (began Aug).
*W M Brisbourne [0-2] Mrs E A Dawson.

VICKY VETTORI BHB 23f **RR** 596[13]
3 b f Vettori (IRE) - Key West (FR) (Highest Honor (FR))
Form - 0500
Record 2000 - 1st:0 2nd:0 3rd:0 Ran:3
Pre2000 - 1st:0 2nd:0 3rd:0 Ran:5
2000 Turf 0-1: (7f) (sft) 2000 AW 0-2: (7f, 8f) (Equl, Fibr)
Unfurnished, little account filly. AW high 24.
*A G Newcombe [0-8] P A Bedford.

VICTEDDU RR 50f 2048[7]
2 b f Casteddu 7.4f **(54)** - Glint of Victory (Glint of Gold) 9.3f **(66)**
Form - 67
Record 2000 - 1st:0 2nd:0 3rd:0 Ran:2
2000 Turf 0-2: (5f, 6f) (gd, g-f)
Currently fair filly. Turf high 50. *M G Quinlan [0-2] Roy Matthews.

VICTOIRE BHB 58a **RR 38f** 2948[13]
4 b m Makbul - Boxit (General Ironside)
Form - 80000
Record 2000 - 1st:0 2nd:0 3rd:0 Ran:5
Pre2000 - 1st:0 2nd:0 3rd:0 Ran:4
Win Prizemoney £0 *Total Prizemoney* £197
2000 Turf 0-3: (8f 3) (gd, g-f 2) 2000 AW 0-2: (7f, 8f) (Fibr 2)
Light-framed, very moderate filly, effective 8f, acts on frm, has worn blinkers. Turf high 38. AW high 19.
*H Akbary [0-9] Michael Whatley.

VICTORIA CROSS (IRE) RR 73f 4935[8]
2 b f Mark of Esteem (IRE) - Glowing With Pride (Ile de Bourbon (USA)) 10.1f **(67)**
Form - 8
Record 2000 - 1st:0 2nd:0 3rd:0 Ran:1
2000 Turf 0-1: (6f) (gd)
Currently above-average filly. *G Wragg [0-1] A E Oppenheimer.

VICTORIAN LADY BHB 35f **RR 44f** 3374[16]
3 b f Old Vic 12.8f **(72)** - Semperflorens (Don) 7.7f **(64)**
Form - 7740
Record 2000 - 1st:0 2nd:0 3rd:0 Ran:4
Win Prizemoney £0 *Total Prizemoney* £296
2000 Turf 0-4: (10f 2, 11f, 16f) (gd, g-f 2, frm)
Scopey, moderate filly. Turf high 44.
*R M H Cowell [0-4] C S Tateson.

VICTORIET BHB 47f45a **RR 56?f 45a** 5116[4]
3 ch f Hamas (IRE) 8f **(72)** - Wedgewood (USA) (Woodman (USA)) 9f **(74)**
Form - 557444474
Record 2000 - 1st:0 2nd:0 3rd:0 Ran:9
Pre2000 - 1st:0 2nd:0 3rd:0 Ran:7
Win Prizemoney £0 *Total Prizemoney* £1,503
2000 Turf 0-8: (7f, 8f 5, 9f 2) (g-f 4, frm 4) 2000 AW 0-1: (8f) (Fibr)
Scopey, fair filly, has worn blinkers. Turf high 63. Consistent.
*A T Murphy [0-16] & Mrs Peter Foden.

VICTORIOUS BHB 63a **RR 62f** 5245[3]
4 ch g Formidable (USA) 7.8f **(60)** - Careful Dancer (Gorytus (USA)) 7.8f **(60)**
Form - 11005003
Record 2000 - 1st:2 2nd:0 3rd:1 Ran:8
Pre2000 - 1st:1 2nd:0 3rd:0 Ran:11
Win Prizemoney £9,806 *Total Prizemoney* £10,440
Wins * **2000** Apr Thirsk (SFT) H 7f 58 59
2000 *Mar Wolver (STD) H 7f 58 68* <
1999 Aug Haydoc (G-S) H 7.1f 63 66
2000 Turf 1-6: (7f 1-6) (hvy, sft, g-s 1-1, gd 2, frm) 2000 AW 1-2: (7f 1-2) (Fibr 1-2)
Lengthy, average gelding, effective 7f, acts on g-s to frm - acts on Fibr, prefers left handed tracks, prefers tight tracks. Turf high 62 - 5th of 16 giving 3lb to Persian Fayre (1 Jun Ayr 7f frm RF 1617) - also 1st of 15 getting 9lb from Kass Alhawa (14 Apr Thirsk RF 0722). AW high 68 (1st run) - 1st of 12 getting 10lb from Royal Artist (23 Mar Wolverhampton RF 0484). Inconsistent.
**R A Fahey [1-7] Tommy Staunton (from B A McMahon [2-12] Mar 2000).*

VICTOR LASZLO BHB 32f37a **RR 30f 37a** 3335[2]
8 b g Ilium 11.7f **(46)** - Report 'em (USA) (Staff Writer (USA)) 10f **(54)**
Form - 2
Record 2000 - 1st:0 2nd:1 3rd:0 Ran:1
Pre2000 - 1st:1 2nd:0 3rd:1 Ran:12
Win Prizemoney £3,252 *Total Prizemoney* £4,727
Wins * 1996 May Hamilt (G-F) H 13f 36 41 <
2000 Turf 0-1: (16f) (frm)
Very moderate gelding, has worn blinkers.
**R Allan [2-25] Mrs L A Ogilvie (from J D Bethell [0-4] Nov 1995).*

VICTOR POWER BHB 28f **RR 23f** 4272[15]
5 ro g Superpower 6.6f **(58)** - Vico Equense (Absalom) 7.2f **(58)**
Form - 000
Record 2000 - 1st:0 2nd:0 3rd:0 Ran:3
2000 Turf 0-3: (8f 2, 12f) (g-f, frm, hrd)
Little account gelding. Turf high 23 (began Jly).
**P Bowen [0-6] T M Morris.*

VICTOR'S CROWN (IRE) BHB 53f **RR 61f** 4402[9]
3 b c Desert Style (IRE) - Royal Wolff (Prince Tenderfoot (USA)) 9f **(61)**
Form - 06000
Record 2000 - 1st:0 2nd:0 3rd:0 Ran:5
Pre2000 - 1st:0 2nd:1 3rd:0 Ran:4
Win Prizemoney £0 *Total Prizemoney* £584
2000 Turf 0-5: (6f 3, 7f, 8f) (g-f 3, frm 2)
Workmanlike, average colt, effective 6f, acts on frm. Turf high 61 (began Aug). Becoming disappointing.
**M H Tompkins [0-9] Mrs Brian Grice.*

VICTORY DAY (IRE) BHB 105f **RR 100df** 1061[21]
3 b c Fairy King (USA) 7.7f **(75)** - Inanna (Persian Bold) 9.3f **(66)**
Form - 0
Record 2000 - 1st:0 2nd:0 3rd:0 Ran:1
Pre2000 - 1st:2 2nd:2 3rd:0 Ran:6
Win Prizemoney £16,090 *Total Prizemoney* £30,045
Wins 1999 Jly Cheste (G-F) 5.1f 100+ <
1999 May Windso (GD) 5f 89+
2000 Turf 0-1: (5f) (gd)
Well made, very useful colt, effective 5f, acts on g-f. A decent juvenile, he changed stables before last season, but showed nothing in his only start.
**D Nicholls [0-1] Mrs Monica Caine (from J Noseda [2-6] Oct 1999).*

VICTORY ROLL BHB 55f **RR 69f** 5063[6]
4 b h In The Wings 11.2f **(77)** - Persian Victory (IRE) (Persian Bold) 9.3f **(66)**
Form - 02606
Record 2000 - 1st:0 2nd:1 3rd:0 Ran:5
Win Prizemoney £0 *Total Prizemoney* £1,344
2000 Turf 0-5: (10f 4, 12f) (sft, g-s, gd 2, frm)
Tall, average colt. Turf high 69.
**Miss E C Lavelle [0-5] Sir Gordon Brunton.*

VICTORY STAR BHB 42f **RR 42f** 171[5]
5 ch g Soviet Star (USA) 8.6f **(74)** - Victoriana (USA) (Storm Bird (CAN)) 10.3f **(74)**
Form - 5
Record 2000 - 1st:0 2nd:0 3rd:0 Ran:1
Pre2000 - 1st:0 2nd:0 3rd:0 Ran:5
2000 AW 0-1: (12f) (Fibr)
Moderate gelding, has worn blinkers.
**M C Pipe [1-11] E Reitel (from Lady Herries [0-5] Jly 1999).*

VIEWFORTH BHB 70f **RR 81f** 4869[11]
2 b c Emarati (USA) 6.6f **(63)** - Miriam **(48df 50a)** (Forzando) 7.6f **(59)**
Form - 4300
Record 2000 - 1st:0 2nd:0 3rd:1 Ran:4
Win Prizemoney £0 *Total Prizemoney* £713
2000 Turf 0-4: (5f 2, 6f 2) (sft, gd 2, frm)
Decent colt. Turf high 81 (began Aug).
**Miss L A Perratt [0-4] Alex Penman Builders Ltd.*

VIKING PRINCE BHB 50f42a **RR 62f 42a** 2086[11]
3 b g Chilibang 7f **(55)** - Fire Sprite (Mummy's Game) 8.2f **(60)**
Form - 88000
Record 2000 - 1st:0 2nd:0 3rd:0 Ran:5
Pre2000 - 1st:0 2nd:0 3rd:0 Ran:5
2000 Turf 0-4: (6f 2, 7f, 8f) (gd, g-f 2, frm) 2000 AW 0-1: (6f) (Equi)
Neat, average gelding. Turf high 62. Inconsistent.
**J R Poulton [0-5] Glendale Partnership Ltd (from M Quinn [0-5] Oct 1999).*

VILLA CARLOTTA BHB 80f **RR 77+f** 5236[3]
2 ch f Rainbow Quest (USA) 11.2f **(81)** - Subya **(99f)** (Night Shift (USA)) 7.2f **(69)**
Form - 303
Record 2000 - 1st:0 2nd:0 3rd:2 Ran:3
Win Prizemoney £0 *Total Prizemoney* £1,608
2000 Turf 0-3: (7f 3) (g-s 2, g-f)
Currently above-average filly. Turf high 77 (began Spt) - 3rd of 22 to Good Standing (28 Oct Newmarket 7f g-s RF 5236).
**J L Dunlop [0-3] Prince A A Faisal.*

VILLAGE NATIVE (FR) BHB 46f46a **RR 51f 46a** 4946a[0]
7 ch g Village Star (FR) 5.7f **(61)** - Zedative (FR) (Zeddaan) 9f **(76)**
Form - 87000707620000
Record 2000 - 1st:0 2nd:1 3rd:0 Ran:14
Pre2000 - 1st:7 2nd:5 3rd:3 Ran:56
Win Prizemoney £18,523 *Total Prizemoney* £24,923
Wins * 1999 Jun Salisb (G-F) C 8f 66
* 1998 *Spt Wolver (STD) H 6f 56 59*
* 1998 Jly Bath (GD) C 5.1f 61
* 1998 May Sandow (G-S) C 8.1f 52
* 1997 *Nov Wolver (STD) H 5f 54 57*
* 1997 *Aug Wolver (STD) H 5f 52 59*
2000 Turf 0-7: (6f 3, 7f, 8f 2, 9f) (sft, g-f, frm 4, hrd) 2000 AW 0-7: (6f 2, 7f 2, 8f, 9f, 12f) (Equi 3, Fibr 4)
Fair gelding, effective 7 to 8f, best at 7f, acts on g-f - acts on AW, often wears blinkers. Turf high 51. AW high 39. Inconsistent.
**K O Cunningham-Brown [7-70].*

VILLA ROMANA BHB 55f45a **RR 67f 45a** 5018[3]
3 b f Komaite (USA) 6.9f **(61)** - Keep Quiet **(30a)** (Reprimand)
Form - 076583
Record 2000 - 1st:0 2nd:0 3rd:1 Ran:5
Pre2000 - 1st:1 2nd:1 3rd:2 Ran:12
Win Prizemoney £3,165 *Total Prizemoney* £5,987
Wins 1999 Oct Bright (G-F) H 7f 69 73 <
2000 Turf 0-2: (7f, 8f) (g-f, frm) 2000 AW 0-3: (6f 2, 7f) (Fibr 3)
Light-framed, average filly, effective 5 to 7f, acts on gd to frm, best on gd. Turf high 25 (began Aug). AW high 55 (began Spt). Inconsistent. **W M Brisbourne [0-5] Great Taste Foods Ltd (from A Bailey [1-12] Nov 1999).*

VILLA VIA (IRE) BHB 65f **RR 74f** 4703[12]
3 b f Night Shift (USA) 8.1f **(73)** - Joma Kaanem (Double Form) 7.3f **(58)**
Form - 53221000
Record 2000 - 1st:1 2nd:2 3rd:1 Ran:8
Win Prizemoney £3,893 *Total Prizemoney* £6,563
Wins * **2000** Aug Beverl (FRM) 5f 54 <
2000 Turf 1-8: (5f 1-4, 6f 4) (gd 3, g-f 4, frm 1-1)

Above-average filly, effective 5 to 6f, acts on gd. Turf high 74.
**J A R Toller [1-8] Harry McCalmont.*

VILLEGGIATURA BHB 46f **RR 20f** 3147[11]

7 b g Machiavellian (USA) 9.8f **(83)** - Hug Me (Shareef Dancer (USA)) 9.9f **(73)**
Form - 80
Record 2000 - 1st:0 2nd:0 3rd:0 Ran:2
Pre2000 - 1st:1 2nd:4 3rd:1 Ran:15
Win Prizemoney £3,808 *Total Prizemoney* £9,680
2000 Turf 0-2: (12f, 17f) (frm, hrd)
Little account gelding, has worn blinkers. Turf high 20 (began Jly). Becoming disappointing.
**W G M Turner [0-5] P A N Bailey (from C McCready in JER [0-1] Jly 1998).*

VILLIAN BHB 60f **RR 69f** 4204[6]

5 b m Kylian (USA) 8.1f **(66)** - Shotsville (Random Shot) 11.4f **(52)**
Form - 346
Record 2000 - 1st:0 2nd:0 3rd:1 Ran:3
Win Prizemoney £0 *Total Prizemoney* £964
2000 Turf 0-3: (12f 3) (g-f, frm 2)
Average filly. Turf high 69 (began Aug).
**J G Smyth-Osbourne [0-3] Mrs Helen Mobley.*

VINCENT BHB 40f65a **RR 41f 65a** 5011[2]

5 b g Anshan 8.2f **(63)** - Top-Anna (IRE) **(52f)** (Ela-Mana-Mou) 10.1f **(70)**
Form - 1013441152
Record 2000 - 1st:4 2nd:1 3rd:1 Ran:10
Pre2000 - 1st:2 2nd:1 3rd:2 Ran:24
Win Prizemoney £12,351 *Total Prizemoney* £15,868
Wins * **2000** *Spt Southw (STD) H 16f 55 61* <
* **2000** *Spt Wolver (STD) 14.8f 56*
* **2000** *Jly Wolver (STD) H 16.2f 51 52*
* **2000** *May Southw (STD) H 16f 46 51*
* 1999 *Jly Wolver (STD) H 16.2f 45 50*
* 1999 *Jan Southw (STD) H 12f 47 55*
2000 Turf 0-4: (16f 2, 17f 2) (g-s 2, frm, hrd) 2000 AW 4-6: (14f, 15f 1-1, 16f 3-4) (Fibr 4-6)
Average gelding, effective 12 to 16f, - acts on Fibr, has worn blinkers, prefers left handed tracks, favours tight tracks, excels at Wolverhampton, does well at Southwell. Turf high 41. AW high 62 - 2nd of 16 giving 14lb to Furness (16 Oct Southwell 14f Fibr RF 5011) - also 1st of 16 giving 16lb to Monacle (26 Spt Southwell RF 4648). He is extremely inconsistent, but can win modest events on Fibresand when he wants to. **J L Harris [6-34] P Caplan.*

VINCENTIA BHB 73f **RR 72f** 5293[3]

2 ch f Komaite (USA) 6.9f **(61)** - Vatersay (USA) (Far North (CAN)) 9.7f **(75)**
Form - 0443
Record 2000 - 1st:0 2nd:0 3rd:1 Ran:4
Win Prizemoney £0 *Total Prizemoney* £933
2000 Turf 0-4: (6f, 7f 3) (g-s 2, gd, frm)
Above-average filly. Turf high 72. **C Smith [0-4] The Brave Few.*

VINCENZO DANTE **RR 92f** 1635a[3]

5 b h Sharpo 7.5f **(68)** - Maiden Eileen (Stradavinsky) 12.5f **(64)**
Form - 3
2000 Turf 0-1: (7f) (g-f)
Currently useful colt. (1st run) - 3rd of 11 to Fay Breeze (28 May Capannelle 7f g-f RF 1635a). **in ITY [0-1].*

VINE COURT (IRE) BHB 49f44a **RR 49f 44a** 5074[17]

2 b f Turtle Island (IRE) - Foxrock (Ribero) 9.3f **(56)**
Form - 76750
Record 2000 - 1st:0 2nd:0 3rd:0 Ran:5
2000 Turf 0-5: (5f 3, 6f, 7f) (g-s 3, gd 2)
Moderate filly. Turf high 49. **T G Mills [0-5] Albert Soden Ltd.*

VINTAGE PREMIUM BHB 101f **RR 105f** 4740[27]

3 b c Forzando 7.2f **(63)** - Julia Domna **(18f 34a)** (Dominion) 8.5f **(63)**
Form - 214022160230
Record 2000 - 1st:2 2nd:4 3rd:1 Ran:12
Pre2000 - 1st:1 2nd:2 3rd:0 Ran:4
Win Prizemoney £20,240 *Total Prizemoney* £49,886
Wins * **2000** Jly Doncas (GD) 10.3f 101 <
* **2000** Apr Newbur (SFT) H 8f 86 89
* 1999 Spt Beverl (GD) 7.5f 84
2000 Turf 2-12: (8f 1-4, 9f, 10f 1-5, 11f 2) (sft 2, g-s 1-2, gd 3, g-f 1-4, frm)
Scopey, Pattern-class colt, effective 8 to 11f, best at 10f, acts on sft to g-f, likes left handed tracks, likes tight tracks, does well at Haydock. Turf high 105 - 2nd of 9 to Polar Red (2 Spt Haydock 11f sft RF 4155) - also 1st of 6 getting 3lb from Blue Gold (2 Jly Doncaster RF 2457). Consistent. He had fitness on his side when running away with a competitive handicap on soft ground at Newbury in April and has continued to run well since, including a fine victory at Doncaster in July. Appreciates a soft surface.
**R A Fahey [3-16] J C Parsons.*

VIOLENT BHB 60f59a **RR 68f 59a** 4334[12]

2 b f Deploy 11.4f **(67)** - Gentle Irony **(61f 46a)** (Mazilier (USA))
Form - 070212040
Record 2000 - 1st:1 2nd:2 3rd:0 Ran:9
Win Prizemoney £2,236 *Total Prizemoney* £4,888
Wins * **2000** Jly Bright (G-F) C 7f 68 <
2000 Turf 1-8: (5f 2, 6f, 7f 1-5) (gd, g-f 3, frm 1-4) 2000 AW 0-1: (8f) (Fibr)
Average filly, effective 7f, acts on frm, often wears blinkers (extremely effectively). Turf high 68 - 1st of 7 getting 4lb from Sel (18 Jly Brighton RF 2887). Won a Brighton claimer in July and is basically modest. **Andrew Reid [1-9] A S Reid.*

VIOLET (IRE) BHB 41f49a **RR 45f 49a** 4826[10]

4 b m Mukaddamah (USA) 7.6f **(74)** - Scanno's Choice (IRE) (Pennine Walk) 8.5f **(61)**
Form - 080076017506000
Record 2000 - 1st:1 2nd:0 3rd:0 Ran:12
Pre2000 - 1st:1 2nd:1 3rd:1 Ran:13
Win Prizemoney £7,279 *Total Prizemoney* £8,651
Wins * **2000** Jly Epsom (G-S) H 6f 44 46
1999 *Jan Wolver (STD) 8.5f 65* <
2000 Turf 1-12: (5f 3, 6f 1-3, 7f 3, 8f 3) (g-s, gd 1-3, g-f 5, frm 2, hrd)
Unfurnished, moderate filly, effective 8f, - acts on Fibr, has worn blinkers, likes left handed tracks, likes tight tracks. Turf high 46. Becoming disappointing. Formerly trained by Lord Huntingdon, she turned a Wolverhampton Fibresand maiden into a procession at the start of last year, but has done little since apart from a shock victory at Epsom in July. Suited by easy ground.
**R C Spicer [1-14] John Purcell (from Miss Gay Kelleway [0-5] Nov 1999).*

VIRGIN SOLDIER (IRE) BHB 65a **RR 96f** 4295[10]

4 ch g Waajib 8.9f **(67)** - Never Been Chaste (Posse (USA)) 8.9f **(61)**
Form - 11112182421330
Record 2000 - 1st:2 2nd:2 3rd:2 Ran:9
Pre2000 - 1st:6 2nd:2 3rd:2 Ran:17
Win Prizemoney £30,768 *Total Prizemoney* £64,758
Wins * **2000** Aug Newmar (G-F) H 16.1f 85 90 <
* **2000** May Newcas (GD) H 16.1f 78 83
* 1999 *Nov Southw (STD) H 14f 65 89++*
* 1999 *Nov Wolver (STD) H 16.2f 60 76++*
* 1999 *Nov Southw (STD) H 14f 49 68+*
* 1999 *Nov Lingfi (STD) H 16f 49 63*
* 1999 Nov Mussel (GD) H 16f 46 58+
* 1999 *Oct Lingfi (STD) H 12f 45 55*
2000 Turf 2-9: (14f 2, 15f, 16f 2-4, 19f, 20f) (gd 1-2, g-f 3, frm 1-4)
Unfurnished, very useful gelding, effective 14 to 20f, best at 14f, acts on gd to frm - acts on Fibr, best on frm, has worn blinkers, likes left handed tracks, excels at York and Southwell, likes Lingfield. Turf high 96 - 3rd of 22 to Give The Slip (23 Aug York 14f frm RF 3914) - also 1st of 9 giving 29lb to Generous Ways (11 Aug Newmarket RF 3558). Consistent. He improved out of all recognition towards the end of 1999, winning six on the bounce during October and November, of which five were on sand. He came back to win in good style at Newcastle in May, despite having taken a big hike in the weights. He was well fancied for the Northumberland Plate, but was swallowed up after being kicked into a clear lead. However, he made amends by winning at Newmarket the following month and finished a creditable third in the Ebor.
**M Johnston [8-17] David Abell (from T J Etherington [0-9] Jly 1999).*

VIRTUAL REALITY BHB 75f70a **RR 74f 70a** 4102[1]
9 b g Diamond Shoal 9.8f **(79)** - Warning Bell (Bustino) 10.4f **(64)**
Form - 0551
Record 2000 - 1st:1 2nd:0 3rd:0 Ran:4
Pre2000 - 1st:5 2nd:8 3rd:4 Ran:39
Win Prizemoney £29,553 *Total Prizemoney* £56,875
Wins * **2000** Aug Bright (FRM) C 8f 74
* 1999 Jly Warwic (G-F) 7.7f 85 <
* 1998 Aug Salisb (G-F) H 8f 78 84
* 1998 May Bath (GD) H 8f 75 78
2000 Turf 1-4: (8f 1-3, 9f) (gd, g-f, frm 1-2)
Above-average gelding, effective 8f, acts on g-f to hrd, has worn blinkers, prefers left handed tracks, prefers tight tracks. Turf high 74. A mile on fast ground are his ideal conditions so everything was just right for him when he bolted up in a Brighton claimer in August. He struggles in handicap company though.
**J A R Toller [4-24] G B Partnership (from A Hide [2-19] Oct 1995).*

VISCARIA (IRE) RR 90f 1578a[3]
3 b f Barathea (IRE) - Zivania (IRE) (Shernazar) 10.2f **(73)**
Form - 123
2000 Turf 1-3: (10f 1-3) (sft 1-1, g-s 2)
Useful filly. Turf high 90 - 2nd of 14 getting 3lb from Just Wondering (19 May Cork 10f g-s RF 1410a) - also 1st of 15 giving 8lb to Sammagefromtenesse (1 May Curragh RF 1117a). She won a ten furlong handicap at The Curragh on her reappearance and was also placed in a couple of similar races later in the month.
**J S Bolger in IRE [2-5] Mrs A G Kavanagh.*

VISCOUNT BANKES BHB 60f **RR 40f** 2811[13]
2 ch c Clantime 6.6f **(57)** - Bee Dee Dancer (Ballacashtal (CAN)) 5.3f **(50)**
Form - 400
Record 2000 - 1st:0 2nd:0 3rd:0 Ran:3
Win Prizemoney £0 *Total Prizemoney* £438
2000 Turf 0-3: (5f 2, 7f) (gd, g-f, frm)
Currently moderate colt. Turf high 70.
**W G M Turner [0-3] T Lightbowne.*

VISHNU (GER) RR 102f 4289a[11]
5 b h Shareef Dancer (USA) 10.1f **(67)** - Vinca (GER) (King Of Macedon) 8.1f **(59)**
Form - 370
2000 Turf 0-3: (12f 2, 16f) (hvy, gd 2)
Very useful colt, effective 16f, acts on gd, often wears blinkers (very effectively). Turf high 102. **C Von der Recke in GER [0-6].*

VISION AND VERSE (USA) RR 5332a[8]
4 b h Storm Cat (USA) 7f **(86)** - Bunting (Private Account (USA)) 8.5f **(74)**
Form - 8
2000 AW 0-1: (10f) (Dirt)
Currently very high-class colt, often wears blinkers. He ran really well when touched off in the Belmont Stakes in 1999, but was never in the hunt in the Breeders' Cup Classic.
**W Mott in USA [0-3] B Lunsford & Y Ito.*

VISION OF NIGHT BHB 111f **RR 114f** 4157[10]
4 b h Night Shift (USA) 8.1f **(73)** - Dreamawhile (Known Fact (USA)) 7.4f **(67)**
Form - 110
Record 2000 - 1st:2 2nd:0 3rd:0 Ran:3
Pre2000 - 1st:4 2nd:1 3rd:2 Ran:11
Win Prizemoney £61,232 *Total Prizemoney* £95,199
Wins * **2000** Aug Newmar (G-F) L 6f 112 <
* **2000** Aug Yarmou (GD) 6f 101+
* 1999 Aug Deauvi (GD) G3 6f 109
* 1999 May Newbur (GD) 6f 111
* 1998 Spt Doncas (GD) 6f 93+
* 1998 Aug Ripon (G-F) 6f 89+
2000 Turf 2-3: (6f 2-3) (g-s, g-f 2-2)
Light-framed, Group-class colt, effective 6 to 7f, best at 6f, acts on hvy to g-f, best on g-f, excels at Ascot and Deauville. Turf high 112 (began Aug) - 1st of 8 giving 8lb to Littlefeather (25 Aug Newmarket RF 3966). Consistent. He proved disappointing in America and rejoined his former trainer, John Dunlop, in the summer. Successful in a Yarmouth conditions race and Listed contest at Newmarket, he probably found the ground too heavy when unplaced in Haydock's Stanley Leisure Sprint Cup. Best around six furlongs, he falls shy of the top class but can win another Group race on the continent. **J L Dunlop [6-14] Hesmonds Stud.*

VISITATION RR 71f 4283[13]
2 b f Bishop of Cashel - Golden Envoy (USA) **(72f)** (Dayjur (USA))
Form - 01270
Record 2000 - 1st:1 2nd:1 3rd:0 Ran:5
Win Prizemoney £1,862 *Total Prizemoney* £2,597
Wins 2000 *Jly Southw (STD) S 7f 51+ <*
2000 Turf 0-4: (6f, 7f 2, 8f) (gd, frm 3) 2000 AW 1-1: (7f 1-1) (Fibr 1-1)
Above-average filly. Turf high 71 (began Jly) - 2nd of 12 getting 5lb from Harrier (4 Aug Thirsk 7f frm RF 3383). (1st run).
**K A Ryan [0-3] Tony Fawcett (from M L W Bell [1-2] Jly 2000).*

VISLINK (IRE) BHB 70f65a **RR 74f 65a** 5008[15]
2 br c Shalford (IRE) 7.8f **(63)** - Wide Outside (IRE) **(18f 28a)** (Don't Forget Me) 8.3f **(74)**
Form - 070020
Record 2000 - 1st:0 2nd:1 3rd:0 Ran:6
Win Prizemoney £0 *Total Prizemoney* £1,090
2000 Turf 0-5: (6f 3, 7f 2) (gd 2, g-f 3) 2000 AW 0-1: (6f) (Fibr)
Above-average colt, effective 6f, acts on g-f. Turf high 70 - 2nd of 7 giving 3lb to Scottish Law (16 Aug Epsom 6f g-f RF 3690).
**A P Jarvis [0-6] A L R Morton.*

VITA SPERICOLATA (IRE) BHB 103f **RR 101f** 4966[8]
3 b f Prince Sabo 6.6f **(64)** - Ahonita (Ahonoora) 8.1f **(73)**
Form - 2483384258
Record 2000 - 1st:0 2nd:2 3rd:2 Ran:10
Pre2000 - 1st:2 2nd:1 3rd:1 Ran:9
Win Prizemoney £14,055 *Total Prizemoney* £42,720
Wins * 1999 Jly Sandow (GD) L 5f 88 <
* 1999 May Mussel (FRM) S 5f 60+
2000 Turf 0-10: (5f 7, 6f 2, 7f) (g-s 2, gd 3, g-f 3, frm 2)
Scopey, very useful filly, effective 5 to 6f, best at 5f, acts on g-s to g-f, has worn blinkers, likes Newmarket. Turf high 101 (1st run) - 2nd of 8 getting 9lb from Monkston Point (27 May Kempton 5f g-s RF 1499). Consistent. She won a Musselburgh seller on her juvenile debut, but has proved herself much better than a plater. She did not win at three, but ran some good races in listed company.
**J S Wainwright [2-19] The Blue Check Partnership.*

VITESSE (IRE) RR 62f 5223[7]
2 b f Royal Academy (USA) 7.8f **(77)** - Brentsville (USA) (Arctic Tern (USA)) 8.9f **(69)**
Form - 07
Record 2000 - 1st:0 2nd:0 3rd:0 Ran:2
2000 Turf 0-2: (6f 2) (gd, g-f)
Currently average filly. Turf high 62 (began Aug).
**J Pearce [0-2] Paul Sandy.*

VITUS BERING (USA) RR 3831[8]
3 b g Bering 9.6f **(80)** - Most Precious (USA) (Nureyev (USA)) 8.7f **(78)**
Form - 8
Record 2000 - 1st:0 2nd:0 3rd:0 Ran:1
2000 Turf 0-1: (8f) (hrd)
Lengthy, currently very poor gelding.
**D J Murphy [0-1] Colin Booth.*

VODKA (IRE) BHB 55f **RR 42f** 3535[10]
2 b g Inzar (USA) - Clear Glade (Vitiges (FR)) 8.2f **(59)**
Form - 560
Record 2000 - 1st:0 2nd:0 3rd:0 Ran:3
2000 Turf 0-3: (5f, 6f 2) (gd 2, hrd)
Currently moderate gelding. Turf high 42.
**P C Haslam [0-3] Mrs B M Hawkins.*

VOLATA (IRE) RR 94+f 4988[9]
2 b c Flying Spur (AUS) - Musianica (Music Boy) 6.8f **(57)**
Form - 10
Record 2000 - 1st:1 2nd:0 3rd:0 Ran:2
Win Prizemoney £5,252 *Total Prizemoney* £5,252
Wins * **2000** Jun Newmar (G-F) 6f 94+ <
2000 Turf 1-2: (6f 1-1, 7f) (gd, frm 1-1)
Currently useful colt. Turf high 94 (1st run) - 1st of 17 giving 5lb to

Arhaaff (3 Jun Newmarket RF 1687). He was a surprise winner of a fair Newmarket maiden, despite missing the break, on his debut, but was up against it when finishing down the field on his next start in the Dewhurst. **M H Tompkins [1-2] J Ellis.*

VOLONTIERS (FR) BHB 87f82a RR 89f 82a 4732[4]

5 b g Common Grounds 8.1f **(66)** - Senlis (USA) (Sensitive Prince (USA)) 9.1f **(60)**

Form - 250416822702734

Record 2000 - 1st:1 2nd:3 3rd:1 Ran:13
Pre2000 - 1st:2 2nd:3 3rd:2 Ran:17

Win Prizemoney £36,613 *Total Prizemoney* £52,719

Wins * 2000 May Thirsk (GD) H 8f 76 81
* 1999 Jun Epsom (GD) L 7f 101 <
* 1998 May Haydoc (G-S) 7.1f 95

2000 Turf 1-13: (7f 6, 8f 1-7) (g-s, gd 1-5, g-f 3, frm 4)

Useful gelding, effective 7 to 8f, best at 7f, acts on gd to frm - acts on Equi, best on gd, likes left handed tracks, excels at Doncaster, does well at Lingfield. Turf high 89 - 3rd of 16 giving 9lb to Floating Charge (15 Spt Newbury 7f frm RF 4433) - also 1st of 18 getting 1lb from Tony Tie (6 May Thirsk RF 1067). Consistent. An able handicapper, he scored at Thirsk in May and can pick up another race at around a mile. **P W Harris [3-30] The Commoners.*

VOLTE FACE RR 59f 4935[21]

2 ch f Polar Falcon (USA) 9f **(74)** - Kramenia (Kris) 9.5f **(73)**

Form - 0

Record 2000 - 1st:0 2nd:0 3rd:0 Ran:1

2000 Turf 0-1: (6f) (gd)

Currently fair filly. **R Hannon [0-1] Lord Roborough.*

VOLVORETA RR 122f 4846a[3]

3 ch f Suave Dancer (USA) 10.7f **(68)** - Robertiya (FR) (Don Roberto (USA))

Form - 1213

2000 Turf 2-4: (11f 1-2, 12f 1-2) (sft 1-1, gd 1-3)

Very high-class filly. Turf high 122 - 1st of 11 from Reve D'Oscar (10 Spt Longchamp RF 4417a) - also 1st of 6 from Reve D'Oscar (12 Apr Saint-cloud RF 0814a). She enjoyed a tremendous season, figuring behind only Egyptband and Petrushka among three-year-old fillies on the International Classifications. A brave third in the Arc, she is ultra consistent and should win a major prize if kept in training as a four-year-old. **C Lerner in FR [3-5].*

VOSBURGH BHB 49f45a RR 48f 45a 10[P]

4 br g Petong 7.6f **(58)** - Pour Moi (Bay Express) 7.1f **(60)**

Form - 0P

Record 2000 - 1st:0 2nd:0 3rd:0 Ran:1
Pre2000 - 1st:0 2nd:2 3rd:2 Ran:13

Win Prizemoney £0 *Total Prizemoney* £2,533

2000 AW 0-1: (7f) (Fibr)

Scopey, moderate gelding, effective 6 to 7f, acts on g-f to frm, has worn blinkers. Inconsistent.

**D Carroll [0-2] Miss Diane Allman (from P Calver [0-12] Spt 1999).*

VRIN (IRE) BHB 75f RR 74f 4047[4]

5 b g Mukaddamah (USA) 7.6f **(74)** - Traumerei (GER) (Surumu (GER)) 10f **(83)**

Form - 04

Record 2000 - 1st:0 2nd:0 3rd:0 Ran:2
Pre2000 - 1st:1 2nd:0 3rd:0 Ran:2

Win Prizemoney £4,425 *Total Prizemoney* £4,706

Wins * 1998 Jun York (G-S) 11.9f 83 <

2000 Turf 0-2: (12f, 14f) (g-s, gd)

Above-average gelding. Turf high 74 (began Jly).

**L M Cumani [1-4] T Cooper, P Kent & R Stevenson.*

WADENHOE (IRE) BHB 43f RR 56f 5229[23]

3 b f Persian Bold 10f **(69)** - Frill (Henbit (USA)) 9f **(61)**

Form - 678800

Record 2000 - 1st:0 2nd:0 3rd:0 Ran:6
Pre2000 - 1st:1 2nd:1 3rd:0 Ran:7

Win Prizemoney £3,522 *Total Prizemoney* £4,824

Wins 1999 Jun Ayr (G-S) 7f 81 <

2000 Turf 0-6: (8f 2, 10f, 12f 2, 16f) (sft, g-s, gd 3, frm)

Unfurnished, fair filly, effective 7f, acts on gd to frm, likes tight tracks. Turf high 56. Becoming disappointing.

**M S Saunders [0-2] Mrs Margaret Hall (from M R Channon [1-11] Aug 2000).*

WADI BHB 65f58a RR 67f 58a 3700[3]

5 b g Green Desert (USA) 7.8f **(78)** - Eternal (Kris) 9.5f **(73)**

Form - 067417143

Record 2000 - 1st:2 2nd:0 3rd:1 Ran:9
Pre2000 - 1st:3 2nd:2 3rd:3 Ran:16

Win Prizemoney £14,169 *Total Prizemoney* £17,823

Wins * 2000 Jly Hamilt (G-F) H 11.1f 58 65
* 2000 Jun Folkes (FRM) H 12f 52 59
1999 Jly Salisb (FRM) C 9.9f 68
1999 Jly Warwic (G-F) SH 12.3f 54 59+
1998 Jly Pontef (G-F) 10f 79 <

2000 Turf 2-9: (10f 2, 11f 1-3, 12f 1-4) (gd 2, g-f 2-5, frm 2)

Average gelding, has broken blood-vessels, effective 10 to 12f, acts on gd to frm, best on frm, has worn blinkers, likes right handed tracks, favours tight tracks, excels at Hamilton. Turf high 67 - 4th of 19 giving 20lb to Mysterium (31 Jly Windsor 12f frm RF 3260) - also 1st of 7 giving 16lb to Ocean Drive (20 Jly Hamilton RF 2969). Consistent.

**Dr J R J Naylor [2-11] Mrs S P Elphick (from G M McCourt [2-9] Jly 1999).*

WAFFIGG (IRE) BHB 87f RR 85f 3136[5]

3 b c Rainbow Quest (USA) 11.2f **(81)** - Celtic Ring (Welsh Pageant) 10f **(65)**

Form - 51035

Record 2000 - 1st:1 2nd:0 3rd:1 Ran:5

Win Prizemoney £3,818 *Total Prizemoney* £4,873

Wins * 2000 May Chepst (HVY) 12.1f 84 <

2000 Turf 1-5: (11f, 12f 1-3, 16f) (sft, g-s 1-1, gd 2, frm)

Workmanlike, useful colt. Turf high 85 - also 1st of 6 from Kadoun (29 May Chepstow RF 1517). Unraced at two, he got off the mark in heavy ground at Chepstow on his second start, but did not seem to get home when stepped up to two miles in the Queen's Vase.

**M A Jarvis [1-5] Sheikh Ahmed Al Maktoum.*

WAFFLES OF AMIN BHB 66f75a RR 73f 75a 4217[17]

3 b c Owington - Alzianah **(102f)** (Alzao (USA)) 7.1f **(68)**

Form - 167848750

Record 2000 - 1st:0 2nd:0 3rd:0 Ran:7
Pre2000 - 1st:1 2nd:2 3rd:1 Ran:7

Win Prizemoney £2,788 *Total Prizemoney* £5,673

Wins * 1999 *Nov Wolver (STD) 5f* 78 <

2000 Turf 0-7: (6f 4, 7f 2, 8f) (g-s, g-f 3, frm 3)

Workmanlike, above-average colt, effective 5 to 7f, acts on gd to frm - acts on Fibr, prefers left handed tracks, prefers tight tracks. Turf high 73 - 4th of 7 getting 9lb from Elmhurst Boy (2 Jun Brighton 7f frm RF 1654).

**R Hannon [1-13] Sheikh Amin Dahlawi (from J D Bethell [0-1] Jun 1999).*

WAFF'S FOLLY BHB 54f51a RR 58f 51a 5112[4]

5 b m Handsome Sailor 6.6f **(53)** - Shirl (Shirley Heights) 10.3f **(74)**

Form - 70353244

Record 2000 - 1st:0 2nd:1 3rd:2 Ran:8
Pre2000 - 1st:1 2nd:0 3rd:4 Ran:16

Win Prizemoney £2,070 *Total Prizemoney* £5,693

Wins 1998 Apr Folkes (GD) 6f 65 <

2000 Turf 0-8: (5f 4, 6f 4) (gd 3, g-f 2, frm 3)

Fair filly, effective 5 to 6f, best at 6f, acts on gd to frm, excels at Windsor, does well at Nottingham, likes Salisbury. Turf high 58 - 2nd of 17 giving 4lb to American Cousin (31 Aug Salisbury 5f frm RF 4124).

**D J S ffrenchDavis [0-8] P H Wafford (from G F H Charles-Jones [1-16] Nov 1999).*

WAFIR (IRE) BHB 47f50a RR 56f 50a 3738[5]

8 b g Scenic 10.6f **(66)** - Taniokey (Grundy) 10.3f **(65)**

Form - 432642135

Record 2000 - 1st:1 2nd:2 3rd:2 Ran:9
Pre2000 - 1st:4 2nd:3 3rd:4 Ran:37

Win Prizemoney £20,341 *Total Prizemoney* £39,514

Wins * 2000 Jly Hamilt (G-F) H 11.1f 43 56
1999 Jun Redcar (FRM) C 10f 60
1998 Aug Newcas (GD) 12.4f 79
1997 May Ayr (G-F) H 10f 80 83+ <

1996 Aug Ripon (HVY) H 10f 80 83
2000 Turf 1-7: (11f 1-1, 12f 3, 14f 2, 16f) (gd, g-f 1-3, frm 2, hrd) 2000 AW 0-2: (12f, 14f) (Fibr 2)
Fair gelding, effective 10 to 12f, best at 12f, acts on gd to frm - acts on Fibr, best on frm, has worn blinkers, likes right handed tracks, favours tight tracks, excels at Ripon. Turf high 59 (1st run) - 4th of 18 giving 9lb to Haya Ya Kefaah (5 Apr Ripon 12f gd RF 0617) - also 1st of 10 giving 1lb to Ocean Drive (14 Jly Hamilton RF 2802). AW high 56 (1st run) - 2nd of 14 giving 2lb to Wilton (8 May Southwell 12f Fibr RF 1092).
**T A K Cuthbert [1-3] T A K Cuthbert (from D Nicholls [1-15] Jun 2000).*

WAHJ (IRE) BHB 98f **RR 101f** 4376[7]
5 ch g Indian Ridge 7.6f **(74)** - Sabaah (USA) (Nureyev (USA)) 8.7f **(78)**
Form - 0112017
Record 2000 - 1st:3 2nd:1 3rd:0 Ran:7
Pre2000 - 1st:2 2nd:0 3rd:1 Ran:7
Win Prizemoney £29,646 *Total Prizemoney* £34,238
Wins * **2000** Aug Newbur (G-F) H 7f 95 100
* **2000** Jly Haydoc (G-F) H 7.1f 88 93
* **2000** Jun Haydoc (G-S) 7.1f 89
1998 Aug Chepst (G-F) 7.1f 103 <
1998 Aug Windso (G-F) 8.3f 82++
2000 Turf 3-7: (6f, 7f 3-5, 8f) (g-s 1-1, gd 2, g-f 2-3, frm)
Very useful gelding, effective 7f, acts on g-f. Turf high 101 - 2nd of 13 giving 21lb to Willoughby's Boy (19 Jly Yarmouth 7f g-f RF 2949) - also 1st of 9 giving 9lb to Aljawf (19 Aug Newbury RF 3787). His drop in the handicap helped him recapture his best form, and he made all over seven furlongs on three occasions.
**C A Dwyer [3-7] S B Components (International) Ltd (from Sir Michael Stoute [2-7] Oct 1999).*

WAIKIKI BEACH (USA) BHB 42f38a **RR 36f 38a** 5077[3]
9 ch g Fighting Fit (USA) 7.9f **(70)** - Running Melody (Rheingold) 10.4f **(62)**
Form - 401088470620603
Record 2000 - 1st:0 2nd:1 3rd:1 Ran:12
Pre2000 - 1st:9 2nd:7 3rd:8 Ran:64
Win Prizemoney £33,626 *Total Prizemoney* £45,106
Wins * *1999 Dec Wolver (STD) S 8.5f 56*
* *1999 Mar Lingfi (STD) H 8f 54 65*
* *1998 Nov Lingfi (STD) S 10f 60+*
* *1998 Apr Southw (STD) H 8f 56 61*
* *1996 Dec Lingfi (STD) C 10f 69*
* *1996 Jun Lingfi (STD) 8f 80+*
* *1996 Apr Wolver (STD) 8.5f 65*
2000 Turf 0-5: (8f, 9f, 10f 3) (g-s, gd 2, frm 2) 2000 AW 0-7: (7f, 8f 4, 10f, 12f) (Equi 3, Fibr 4)
Moderate gelding, effective 8f, - acts on AW, best on Equi, has worn blinkers, favours left handed tracks, favours tight tracks. Turf high 36. AW high 42. Inconsistent. He has won on Fibresand, but looks better on Equitrack. Good ride for an amateur.
**G L Moore [9-76] Mrs J Moore.*

WAIKIKI DANCER (IRE) BHB 53f **RR 49f** 5013[6]
2 br f General Monash (USA) - Waikiki (GER) (Zampano (GER))
Form - 0006
Record 2000 - 1st:0 2nd:0 3rd:0 Ran:4
2000 Turf 0-3: (6f, 7f, 8f) (g-s, frm 2) 2000 AW 0-1: (6f) (Fibr)
Moderate filly. Turf high 52 (began Aug). **B Palling [0-4] B Reynolds.*

WAINAK (USA) BHB 82f **RR 78f** 4172[2]
2 b c Silver Hawk (USA) 11.2f **(85)** - Cask **(103f)** (Be My Chief (USA))
Form - 02232
Record 2000 - 1st:0 2nd:3 3rd:1 Ran:5
Win Prizemoney £0 *Total Prizemoney* £4,075
2000 Turf 0-5: (7f 4, 8f) (gd 2, g-f, frm 2)
Above-average colt. Turf high 78 - 2nd of 7 giving 5lb to Min Mirri (2 Spt Thirsk 8f gd RF 4172). **J L Dunlop [0-5] Hamdan Al Maktoum.*

WAIT FOR THE WILL (USA) BHB 85f **RR 87f** 3854[14]
4 ch g Seeking the Gold (USA) 7.4f **(80)** - You'd Be Surprised (USA) (Blushing Groom (FR)) 10.3f **(76)**
Form - 001223130
Record 2000 - 1st:2 2nd:2 3rd:2 Ran:9
Pre2000 - 1st:1 2nd:0 3rd:1 Ran:8
Win Prizemoney £15,644 *Total Prizemoney* £26,145
Wins * **2000** Jly Ascot (G-F) H 12f 80 87 <
* **2000** May Salisb (GD) H 12f 73 76
* 1999 Jly Salisb (G-F) H 12f 75 78
2000 Turf 2-9: (12f 2-6, 13f, 14f 2) (g-s, gd 2-4, g-f 4)
Scopey, useful gelding, effective 12 to 14f, best at 12f, acts on gd to frm, best on g-f, has worn blinkers (effectively), excels at Salisbury and Goodwood and Newbury, likes Ascot. Turf high 87 - 1st of 8 getting 11lb from Gallery God (29 Jly Ascot RF 3206). Got off the mark in an amateur riders' event at Salisbury over 12 furlongs in 1999 and he scored over the same course and distance in May. Consistent efforts since, including a victory in a decent Ascot handicap in July.
**G L Moore [3-16] Richard Green (Fine Paintings) (from I A Balding [0-2] Spt 1998).*

WAITING KNIGHT (USA) BHB 56f43a **RR 66f 43a** 1480[4]
5 b br h St Jovite (USA) 11.8f **(75)** - Phydilla (FR) (Lyphard (USA)) 9.9f **(72)**
Form - 0040022234
Record 2000 - 1st:0 2nd:3 3rd:1 Ran:8
Pre2000 - 1st:1 2nd:6 3rd:2 Ran:24
Win Prizemoney £3,572 *Total Prizemoney* £12,746
Wins * *1999 Feb Lingfi (STD) 8f 68* <
2000 AW 0-8: (7f 2, 8f 6) (Fibr 8)
Average colt, effective 6 to 8f, - acts on AW, often wears blinkers. AW high 42.
**Mrs N Macauley [1-22] Mrs N Macauley (from B Hanbury [0-10] Spt 1998).*

WAJINA (FR) **RR 106f** 4407a[2]
4 b m Rainbow Quest (USA) 11.2f **(81)** - Wajd (USA) (Northern Dancer) 9.6f **(80)**
Form - 22
2000 Turf 0-2: (15f, 16f) (g-s 2)
Pattern-class filly, has worn blinkers. Turf high 106 (1st run) (began Aug) - 2nd of 7 getting 3lb from Persian Punch (20 Aug Deauville 15f g-s RF 3949a). **A Fabre in FR [1-4] Sheikh Mohammed.*

WAKI MUSIC (USA) BHB 100f **RR 93f** 4280[5]
2 b f Miswaki (USA) 8.1f **(81)** - Light Music (USA) (Nijinsky (CAN)) 10.3f **(77)**
Form - 135
Record 2000 - 1st:1 2nd:0 3rd:1 Ran:3
Win Prizemoney £4,524 *Total Prizemoney* £9,124
Wins * **2000** Aug Kempto (G-F) 7f 85+ <
2000 Turf 1-3: (7f 1-2, 8f) (g-f 1-2, frm)
Currently useful filly. Turf high 93 (began Aug) - 5th of 12 to Karasta (7 Spt Doncaster 8f frm RF 4280) - also 1st of 9 from Johnson's Point (2 Aug Kempton RF 3323). She looked a filly with a future when scoring on her debut at Kempton and went on to finish third in the Prestige Stakes, before finishing a fair fifth in the May Hill on her final start. **R Charlton [1-3] K Abdulla.*

WALDOR **RR 62f** 2452[9]
2 b c Exit To Nowhere (USA) 8.7f **(77)** - Seek the Pearl **(90df)** (Rainbow Quest (USA)) 10.4f **(75)**
Form - 80
Record 2000 - 1st:0 2nd:0 3rd:0 Ran:2
2000 Turf 0-2: (5f, 7f) (gd, frm)
Currently average colt. Turf high 62. **C A Dwyer [0-2] Mrs J Parvizi.*

WALKSLIKEADUCK (USA) **RR 114f** 5327a[12]
3 br c Blushing John (USA) 8.9f **(75)** - Nabla (USA) (Theatrical)
Form - 0
2000 Turf 0-1: (8f) (frm)
Currently Group-class colt.
**P Gallagher in USA [0-1] D Bienstock, M Parks, C Winner et al.*

WALLY MCARTHUR BHB 84f **RR 83f** 4932[11]
2 b c Puissance 7.1f **(60)** - Giddy **(49f 41a)** (Polar Falcon (USA))
Form - 8321184230
Record 2000 - 1st:2 2nd:2 3rd:2 Ran:10
Win Prizemoney £10,065 *Total Prizemoney* £32,397
Wins * **2000** Jly Doncas (G-F) 6f 74 <
* **2000** Jly Beverl (GD) 5f 74 <
2000 Turf 2-10: (5f 1-3, 6f 1-7) (gd 3, g-f 4, frm 2-3)
Decent colt, effective 5 to 6f, best at 6f, acts on gd to frm. Turf high 83 - 11th of 22 giving 2lb to Idle Power (12 Oct Newmarket 6f gd RF

4932) - also 1st of 14 giving 5lb to Extra Guest (7 Jly Beverley RF 2587). Inconsistent. Ran a couple of fine races in September, staying on well into third in the Redcar Two-Year-Old Trophy.
**A Berry [2-10] T Herbert-Jackson.*

WALNUT WONDER RR 13f — 634[18]

3 b f Pyramus (USA) - Super Style (Artaius (USA)) 9f **(69)**
Form - 0
Record 2000 - 1st:0 2nd:0 3rd:0 Ran:1
Pre2000 - 1st:0 2nd:0 3rd:0 Ran:1
2000 Turf 0-1: (6f) (gd)
Leggy, currently poor filly.
**W G M Turner [0-2] Walnut Revellers Racing Club.*

WALTER THE WHISTLE BHB 38f RR 44f — 2565[11]

3 b c Pips Pride 6.7f **(70)** - Fleur de Lyphard (USA) (Lyphard (USA)) 9.9f **(72)**
Form - 54000
Record 2000 - 1st:0 2nd:0 3rd:0 Ran:5
Pre2000 - 1st:0 2nd:0 3rd:0 Ran:1
2000 Turf 0-5: (7f, 8f 3, 11f) (gd 2, g-f 2, frm)
Scopey, moderate colt, has worn blinkers. Turf high 44.
**J A Osborne [0-5] Mrs Julie Mitchell (from A P Jarvis [0-1] Aug 1999).*

WA-NAAM RR 43f — 5223[15]

2 ch c Cadeaux Genereux 7.9f **(76)** - Na-Ayim (IRE) (Shirley Heights) 10.3f **(74)**
Form - 0
Record 2000 - 1st:0 2nd:0 3rd:0 Ran:1
2000 Turf 0-1: (6f) (gd)
Currently moderate colt. **E A L Dunlop [0-1] Hamdan Al Maktoum.*

WANNABE AROUND BHB 84f RR 82f — 5309[4]

2 b c Primo Dominie 7.2f **(67)** - Noble Peregrine (Lomond (USA)) 8.8f **(65)**
Form - 6324
Record 2000 - 1st:0 2nd:1 3rd:1 Ran:4
Win Prizemoney £0 *Total Prizemoney* £1,925
2000 Turf 0-4: (7f 4) (g-s 2, g-f, frm)
Decent colt. Turf high 82 (began Jly) - 2nd of 18 to Asian Heights (23 Oct Lingfield 7f g-s RF 5151). **T G Mills [0-4] T G Mills.*

WANNABE BOLD (IRE) RR 37f — 3190[10]

2 b f Persian Bold 10f **(69)** - Chiltern Show **(18f 39a)** (Rambo Dancer (CAN))
Form - 000
Record 2000 - 1st:0 2nd:0 3rd:0 Ran:3
2000 Turf 0-2: (5f, 6f) (sft, g-f) 2000 AW 0-1: (7f) (Fibr)
Currently very moderate filly. Turf high 37.
**P C Haslam [0-3] Mrs B M Hawkins.*

WANNA SHOUT BHB 70f70a RR 57f 70a — 1655[2]

2 b f Missed Flight - Lulu **(33f)** (Polar Falcon (USA))
Form - 552
Record 2000 - 1st:0 2nd:1 3rd:0 Ran:3
Win Prizemoney £0 *Total Prizemoney* £660
2000 Turf 0-3: (5f 3) (hvy, sft, frm)
Currently above-average filly. Turf high 57 - 2nd of 13 to Superstar Leo (2 Jun Catterick 5f frm RF 1655). **R Dickin [0-3] Alscot Racing.*

WAQUAAS RR 98f — 4421a[1]

4 br g Green Desert (USA) 7.8f **(78)** - Hamaya (USA) (Mr Prospector (USA)) 8.8f **(78)**
Form - 31
2000 Turf 1-2: (6f 1-2) (gd 1-1)
Currently very useful gelding. Turf high 98 (began Jly) - 1st of 10 from El Gran Lode (10 Spt Taby RF 4421a). One of Scandinavia's best sprinters. **E Nordling in SWE [1-2] G Hesse.*

WAR BABY BHB 28f25a RR 46df 25a — 2395[9]

4 b m Warrshan (USA) 9.7f **(59)** - Dutch Czarina (Prince Sabo) 7.2f **(62)**
Form - 7000
Record 2000 - 1st:0 2nd:0 3rd:0 Ran:4
Pre2000 - 1st:0 2nd:0 3rd:0 Ran:6
2000 Turf 0-2: (12f 2) (g-f, frm) 2000 AW 0-2: (10f, 13f) (Equi 2)
Leggy, moderate filly, has worn blinkers. Turf high 10. AW high 28. Becoming disappointing. **Miss B Sanders [0-10] Mrs J M Laycock.*

WAR CHANT (USA) RR — 5327a[1]

3 br c Danzig (USA) 8.1f **(88)** - Hollywood Wildcat (USA) **(122df)** (Kris S (USA)) 7.9f **(71)**
Form - 1
2000 Turf 1-1: (8f 1-1) (frm 1-1)
Strong, currently very poor colt. (1st run) - 1st of 14 getting 3lb from North East Bound (4 Nov Churchill Downs RF 5327a). Swooped late to win the Breeders' Cup Mile.
**N Drysdale in USA [1-1] Marjorie Cowan & Irving Cowan.*

WARDAT ALLAYL (IRE) BHB 89f RR 86f — 1989[7]

3 b f Mtoto 11.5f **(71)** - Society Lady (USA) (Mr Prospector (USA)) 8.8f **(78)**
Form - 7
Record 2000 - 1st:0 2nd:0 3rd:0 Ran:1
Pre2000 - 1st:1 2nd:0 3rd:1 Ran:4
Win Prizemoney £10,514 *Total Prizemoney* £12,163
Wins * 1999 Jly Newbur (G-F) 7f 86 <
2000 Turf 0-1: (10f) (g-f)
Leggy, useful filly. **M R Channon [1-5] Sheikh Ahmed Al Maktoum.*

WARDEN WARREN BHB 88f RR 88f — 4742[5]

2 b c Petong 7.6f **(58)** - Silver Spell **(56f)** (Aragon) 8.1f **(60)**
Form - 01265
Record 2000 - 1st:1 2nd:1 3rd:0 Ran:5
Win Prizemoney £4,891 *Total Prizemoney* £6,904
Wins *** 2000** Jun Newmar (G-F) 6f 75 <
2000 Turf 1-5: (6f 1-5) (g-f 3, frm 1-2)
Useful colt. Turf high 88. Showed the benefit of his debut when taking a Newmarket maiden next time. Ran well to be second in a decent conditions race but seemed to hang fire in a nursery.
**M A Jarvis [1-5] John Sims.*

WAR GAME (FR) RR 105f — 2982a[1]

4 b m Caerleon (USA) 10.9f **(79)** - Walensee (Troy) 10.4f **(68)**
Form - 21
2000 Turf 1-2: (11f, 13f 1-1) (sft 1-1, gd)
Currently Pattern-class filly. Turf high 105 - 1st of 5 giving 10lb to Herculano (16 Jly Maisons-laffitte RF 2982a).
**A Fabro in FR [1-2] D Wildenstein.*

WARJAN (FR) RR 92f — 707a[6]

3 b c Beaudelaire (USA) - Twilight Mood (USA) (Devil's Bag (USA)) 12.4f **(78)**
Form - 6
2000 Turf 0-1: (11f) (hvy)
Currently useful colt. **P Bary in FR [0-2].*

WARLINGHAM (IRE) BHB 76f76a RR 77f 76a — 4305[12]

2 b c Catrail (USA) - Tadjnama (USA) (Exceller (USA)) 12.5f **(74)**
Form - 463621430
Record 2000 - 1st:1 2nd:1 3rd:2 Ran:9
Win Prizemoney £3,428 *Total Prizemoney* £7,464
Wins *** 2000** Jly Yarmou (GD) 5.2f 77 <
2000 Turf 1-8: (5f 1-7, 6f) (gd 4, g-f 1-1, frm 3) 2000 AW 0-1: (6f) (Fibr)
Above-average colt, effective 5f, acts on g-f to frm. Turf high 77 - 1st of 8 giving 5lb to Racina (19 Jly Yarmouth RF 2947). Consistent. **Miss Gay Kelleway [1-9] Martin Butler.*

WARNINGFORD BHB 112f RR 113f — 5239[3]

6 b h Warning 8.1f **(77)** - Barford Lady (Stanford) 7.9f **(56)**
Form - 242631583
Record 2000 - 1st:1 2nd:2 3rd:2 Ran:9
Pre2000 - 1st:6 2nd:5 3rd:1 Ran:26
Win Prizemoney £81,085 *Total Prizemoney* £141,145

Wins								
*** 2000**	Spt	Newbur	(G-F)	L	7.3f		113	<
* 1999	Jun	Haydoc	(GD-)	L	7.1f		104	
* 1999	Apr	Leices	(HVY)	G3	7f		110	
* 1999	Apr	Warwic	(GD)		7f		104	
* 1998	Spt	Goodwo	(SFT)	H	7f	99	104	
* 1998	Jly	Yarmou	(G-F)	H	7f	97	99	
* 1997	Jun	Sandow	(G-F)		7.1f		90	

2000 Turf 1-9: (6f 2, 7f 1-5, 8f 2) (sft, g-s 3, gd 3, g-f 1-2)
Group-class horse, effective 6 to 7f, best at 6f, acts on sft to g-f, best on gd, has worn blinkers, likes left handed tracks, excels at Newbury and Longchamp. Turf high 113 - 1st of 9 from Umistim

(16 Spt Newbury RF 4462). Consistent. Best over six and seven furlongs, he stood up well to another hectic campaign, winning a Listed heat at Newbury in September. Usually held-up, he goes well on easy ground and is genuine.

**J R Fanshawe [7-35] Barford Bloodstock.*

WARNING REEF BHB 66f65a **RR 69f 65a** 5323[16]

7 b g Warning 8.1f **(77)** - Horseshoe Reef (Mill Reef (USA)) 10.5f **(78)**

Form - 456533312142400

Record 2000 - 1st:2 2nd:2 3rd:3 Ran:15
Pre2000 - 1st:3 2nd:9 3rd:9 Ran:49

Win Prizemoney £39,762 *Total Prizemoney* £80,094

Wins * **2000** Aug Newmar (G-F) H 12f 59 66+ <
* **2000** Jly Kempto (G-F) H 12f 55 57
* 1998 Aug Ascot (G-F) H 12f 57 60
* 1998 Jly Sandow (GD) H 11.4f 53 54
* 1998 Jun Carlis (G-S) H 12f 49 51

2000 Turf 2-15: (10f 4, 12f 2-11) (sft 2, g-s, gd 4, g-f 1-6, frm 1-2)

Average gelding, effective 10 to 12f, best at 12f, acts on gd to frm, best on g-f, has worn blinkers, excels at Thirsk and York, likes Chester. Turf high 69 - 2nd of 8 getting 12lb from Summer Song (2 Spt Thirsk 12f gd RF 4171) - also 1st of 7 getting 28lb from Mardani (18 Aug Newmarket RF 3768). A winner twice in the summer, he is best on fast ground and disappointed twice in testing conditions in the autumn.

**E J Alston [5-44] Valley Paddocks Racing Ltd (from P Eccles [0-7] Aug 1997).*

WARRING BHB 43f39a **RR 45f 39a** 4544[17]

6 b g Warrshan (USA) 9.7f **(59)** - Emerald Ring (Auction Ring (USA)) 8.6f **(65)**

Form - 50300341380

Record 2000 - 1st:1 2nd:0 3rd:3 Ran:11
Pre2000 - 1st:2 2nd:5 3rd:0 Ran:33

Win Prizemoney £14,647 *Total Prizemoney* £24,829

Wins * **2000** Aug Bath (GD) H 8f 38 45
* 1998 Aug Windso (G-F) H 8.3f 54 60 <
* 1998 Jly Windso (G-F) H 8.3f 46 54

2000 Turf 1-11: (7f, 8f 1-10) (sft, gd 2, g-f 1-4, frm 2, hrd 2)

Moderate gelding, effective 8f, acts on gd to g-f, best on gd, likes left handed tracks, likes tight tracks. Turf high 45 - 1st of 9 getting 32lb from Barabaschi (20 Aug Bath RF 3814). Inconsistent.

**M S Saunders [3-41] Chris Scott (from M R Channon [0-4] Oct 1996).*

WARRIOR KING (IRE) BHB 23f30a **RR 13f 30a** 277[6]

6 b g Fairy King (USA) 7.7f **(75)** - It's All Academic (IRE) (Mazaad) 7.1f **(45)**

Form - 80750086

Record 2000 - 1st:0 2nd:0 3rd:0 Ran:6
Pre2000 - 1st:1 2nd:3 3rd:1 Ran:33

Win Prizemoney £3,241 *Total Prizemoney* £5,740

Wins 1997 Aug Mussel (GD) H 7.1f 47 53 <

2000 AW 0-6: (7f, 8f, 9f, 11f 2, 12f) (Fibr 6)

Poor gelding, had worn blinkers. AW high 30. (DEAD)

**Mrs S Lamyman [0-13] P Lamyman (from K Mahdi [0-2] Nov 1998).*

WARRIOR QUEEN (USA) RR 104f 3276[13]

3 b f Quiet American (USA) 7.9f **(60)** - Call Me Fleet (USA) (Afleet (CAN))

Form - 7720

2000 Turf 0-4: (5f 3, 6f) (gd 3, g-f)

Very useful filly, effective 5 to 6f, acts on gd to g-f, has worn blinkers. Turf high 104. An edgy sort, she takes a strong hold and has given trouble at the start. She did not perform at all badly when dropped to five in the King's Stand on her return but failed to build on that. **A P O'Brien in IRE [2-9] Mrs Hyde,Mrs Paul Shanah Murphy.*

WASEEM BHB 77f70a **RR 78f 70a** 4063[10]

3 ch c Polar Falcon (USA) 9f **(74)** - Astolat (Rusticaro (FR)) 8.2f **(65)**

Form - 188210310

Record 2000 - 1st:3 2nd:1 3rd:1 Ran:9

Win Prizemoney £14,520 *Total Prizemoney* £16,805

Wins * **2000** Aug Thirsk (G-F) H 12f 75 78 <
* **2000** Jun Pontef (G-F) H 10f 70 75
* **2000** *Feb Wolver (STD) 7f 62+*

2000 Turf 2-8: (8f 2, 10f 1-3, 11f, 12f 1-2) (gd 2, g-f 2, frm 2-4) 2000 AW 1-1: (7f 1-1) (Fibr 1-1)

Scopey, above-average colt, effective 10 to 12f, best at 10f, acts on gd to frm, best on frm, prefers left handed tracks. Turf high 78 - 1st of 3 giving 4lb to Desert Fighter (5 Aug Thirsk RF 3410) - also 1st of 10 getting 3lb from Rum Punch (12 Jun Pontefract RF 1900). (1st run). Has steadily got it together on turf, winning a couple of handicaps in determined fashion under a positive ride.

**M Johnston [3-9] A Al-Rostamani.*

WASEYLA (IRE) BHB 65f52a **RR 73f 52a** 5142[13]

3 b f Sri Pekan (USA) - Lady Windley (Baillamont (USA)) 7f **(78)**

Form - 70

Record 2000 - 1st:0 2nd:0 3rd:0 Ran:2
Pre2000 - 1st:0 2nd:0 3rd:0 Ran:3

Win Prizemoney £0 *Total Prizemoney* £255

2000 Turf 0-2: (11f, 12f) (g-s, g-f)

Workmanlike, above-average filly, has worn blinkers. Turf high 67.

**A C Stewart [0-2] Sheikh Ahmed Al Maktoum (from J H M Gosden [0-3] Nov 1999).*

WASP RANGER (USA) BHB 78f75a **RR 79f 75a** 4308[9]

6 b g Red Ransom (USA) 8.6f **(83)** - Lady Climber (USA) (Mount Hagen (FR)) 8.4f **(70)**

Form - 722316220

Record 2000 - 1st:1 2nd:4 3rd:1 Ran:9
Pre2000 - 1st:2 2nd:3 3rd:1 Ran:21

Win Prizemoney £19,302 *Total Prizemoney* £43,790

Wins * **2000** Jly Sandow (GD) H 11.4f 75 77
* 1999 Jly Kempto (G-F) H 10f 69 72
1997 May Goodwo (GD) 8f 78 <

2000 Turf 1-9: (10f 2, 11f 1-2, 12f 5) (g-s, gd 2, g-f 1-3, frm 3)

Above-average gelding, effective 10 to 12f, best at 12f, acts on gd to frm, best on frm, has worn blinkers (very effectively), excels at Newmarket, likes Kempton. Turf high 79 - 2nd of 9 giving 17lb to Rare Talent (28 Aug Epsom 12f gd RF 4036) - also 1st of 11 giving 9lb to Just Gifted (9 Jly Sandown RF 2660). Returned to winning form at Sandown in July, but his win record is very poor despite some other fair efforts this season. Best when held up for a late run.

**G L Moore [2-19] Rodger Sargent (from P F I Cole [1-11] Spt 1997).*

WASSL STREET (IRE) BHB 45f **RR 61f** 763[5]

8 b g Dancing Brave (USA) 10.4f **(78)** - One Way Street (Habitat) 9.4f **(70)**

Form - 5

Record 2000 - 1st:0 2nd:0 3rd:0 Ran:1
Pre2000 - 1st:0 2nd:0 3rd:0 Ran:3

2000 Turf 0-1: (15f) (g-s)

Average gelding, often wears blinkers.

**K A Morgan [3-13] Rex Norton (from J H M Gosden [0-3] Spt 1995).*

WATCHING BHB 116f **RR 114f** 4845a[10]

3 ch c Indian Ridge 7.6f **(74)** - Sweeping (Indian King (USA)) 7.4f **(64)**

Form - 2122014450

Record 2000 - 1st:2 2nd:3 3rd:0 Ran:10
Pre2000 - 1st:1 2nd:3 3rd:3 Ran:9

Win Prizemoney £39,360 *Total Prizemoney* £92,581

Wins * **2000** Jly Sandow (GD) L 5f 110 <
* **2000** Apr Haydoc (HVY) L 5f 108
* 1999 Jun Cheste (SFT) 5.1f 83+

2000 Turf 2-10: (5f 2-9, 6f) (hvy 1-1, gd 7, g-f, frm 1-1)

Workmanlike, Group-class colt, effective 5 to 6f, best at 5f, acts on hvy to frm. Turf high 114 - also 1st of 10 getting 1lb from Lord Kintyre (8 Jly Sandown RF 2646). A pacey individual, he was always prominent when winning Listed heats at Haydock and Sandown. Suited by soft ground, he is best over five furlongs and can win a Group race granted favourable conditions.

**R Hannon [3-19] Mrs Dare Wigan.*

WATCHKEEPER (IRE) RR 66+f 4226[4]

2 b f Rudimentary (USA) 8.2f **(66)** - Third Watch (Slip Anchor) 9.8f **(73)**

Form - 4

Record 2000 - 1st:0 2nd:0 3rd:0 Ran:1

Win Prizemoney £0 *Total Prizemoney* £233

2000 Turf 0-1: (7f) (frm)

Currently average filly. **J L Dunlop [0-1] Hesmonds Stud.*

WATER BABE BHB 67f **RR 66f** 3924[11]

3 b f Lake Coniston (IRE) - Isabella Sharp **(67f)** (Sharpo) 7.7f **(59)**

Form - 41710
Record 2000 - 1st:2 2nd:0 3rd:0 Ran:5
Pre2000 - 1st:0 2nd:0 3rd:0 Ran:3
Win Prizemoney £7,605 *Total Prizemoney* £7,605
Wins * 2000 Aug Yarmou (G-F) H 6f 64 66 <
*** 2000** Jly Leices (G-F) H 6f 59 63
2000 Turf 2-5: (6f 2-5) (gd, g-f 1-1, frm 1-3)
Neat, average filly, effective 6f, acts on g-f to frm, best on frm. Turf high 66 - 1st of 8 getting 2lb from First Draw (16 Aug Yarmouth RF 3713) - also 1st of 14 getting 1lb from Muffled (8 Jly Leicester RF 2642). **J W Payne [2-8] Raymond Tooth.*

WATER FLOWER BHB 57f **RR 71f** 4987[31]
0 b m Environment Friend 7.5f **(67)** - Flower Girl (Pharly (FR)) 9.8f **(68)**
Form - 71800080
Record 2000 - 1st:1 2nd:0 3rd:0 Ran:8
Pre2000 - 1st:4 2nd:1 3rd:1 Ran:13
Win Prizemoney £16,297 *Total Prizemoney* £17,574
Wins * 2000 Jun Salisb (G-F) H 12f 68 71 <
* 1999 Aug Chepst (G-F) H 12.1f 68 71 <
* 1999 Jly Chepst (G-F) H 12.1f 65 67
* 1999 Jun Salisb (GD) H 12f 62 65
1997 Oct Newmar (G-F) C 12f 58
2000 Turf 1-8: (12f 1-6, 14f, 18f) (gd 2, g-f 2, frm 1-4)
Above-average mare, effective 12f, acts on g-f to frm, best on frm, has worn blinkers, likes left handed tracks, prefers tight tracks. Turf high 71 - 1st of 7 giving 4lb to Happy Go Lucky (18 Jun Salisbury RF 2082). Twelve furlongs and fast ground seem her ideal conditions.
**B R Millman [4-15] Avalon Surfacing Ltd (from J R Fanshawe [1-6] Oct 1997).*

WATERFORD SPIRIT (IRE) BHB 50f **RR 60f** 5003[9]
4 ch g Shalford (IRE) 7.8f **(63)** - Rebecca's Girl (IRE) (Nashamaa) 7.1f **(66)**
Form - 0000000700
Record 2000 - 1st:0 2nd:0 3rd:0 Ran:10
Pre2000 - 1st:1 2nd:2 3rd:0 Ran:12
Win Prizemoney £7,064 *Total Prizemoney* £10,063
Wins 1999 May Thirsk (G-S) H 5f 73 74 <
2000 Turf 0-10: (5f 10) (g-s, gd 4, g-f 3, frm 2)
Scopey, average gelding, effective 5f, acts on gd, has worn blinkers. Turf high 60.
**D Nicholls [0-2] W G Swiers (from T D Barron [1-20] Jun 2000).*

WATERFRONT (IRE) BHB 42f32a **RR 47f 32a** 442[9]
4 b g Turtle Island (IRE) - Rising Tide (Red Alert) 7.6f **(66)**
Form - 00
Record 2000 - 1st:0 2nd:0 3rd:0 Ran:2
Pre2000 - 1st:0 2nd:1 3rd:0 Ran:11
Win Prizemoney £0 *Total Prizemoney* £1,048
2000 AW 0-2: (8f, 11f) (Fibr 2)

Watching's rivals never got a look-in at Sandown

Workmanlike, moderate gelding, effective 7f, acts on g-f, has worn blinkers, likes left handed tracks, likes tight tracks. AW high 5. Becoming disappointing.
**R Bastiman [0-8] J R Swift (from P W Chapple-Hyam [0-5] Jun 1999).*

WATERGOLD (IRE) BHB 38f **RR 57f** 4995[8]
3 ch g Shalford (IRE) 7.8f **(63)** - Trust Sally (Sallust) 8.4f **(63)**
Form - 50000608
Record 2000 - 1st:0 2nd:0 3rd:0 Ran:8
Pre2000 - 1st:0 2nd:0 3rd:0 Ran:3
2000 Turf 0-7: (6f 2, 7f 2, 8f 3) (gd 2, g-f, frm 4) 2000 AW 0-1: (7f) (Fibr)
Workmanlike, fair gelding, often wears blinkers. Turf high 57.
**I Semple [0-11] Patersons of Greenoakhill.*

WATERGRASSHILL BHB 53f56a **RR 64f 56a** 1211[5]
3 b f Terimon 8.7f **(58)** - Party Game (Red Alert) 7.6f **(66)**
Form - 2545285
Record 2000 - 1st:0 2nd:1 3rd:0 Ran:4
Pre2000 - 1st:0 2nd:1 3rd:0 Ran:6
Win Prizemoney £0 *Total Prizemoney* £3,039
2000 Turf 0-4: (6f 4) (sft, g-f, frm 2)
Scopey, average filly, effective 6f, acts on frm. Turf high 64 - 2nd of 21 getting 18lb from Castle Sempill (10 Apr Windsor 6f frm RF 0655). **N A Callaghan [0-10] A R G Else, M P Jones & N A Callaghan.*

WATER JUMP (IRE) BHB 95f **RR 103f** 3361[3]
3 b c Suave Dancer (USA) 10.7f **(68)** Jolies Faux (Shirley Heights) 10.3f **(74)**
Form - 123
Record 2000 - 1st:1 2nd:1 3rd:1 Ran:3
Pre2000 - 1st:1 2nd:2 3rd:0 Ran:3
Win Prizemoney £10,212 *Total Prizemoney* £27,599
Wins * 2000 May Salisb (G-F) H 9.9f 85 93 <
* 1999 Spt Hamilt (SFT) 8.3f 74
2000 Turf 1-3: (10f 1-2, 12f) (g-f 1-3)
Scopey, very useful colt, effective 10 to 12f, acts on g-f. Turf high 103 - 2nd of 16 getting 5lb from Give The Slip (22 Jun Ascot 12f g-f RF 2182). He made a winning reappearance in a decent Salisbury handicap and only found one too good in the King George V Handicap at Royal Ascot. The drop back to ten furlongs found him out at Goodwood. Lightly raced, he still has room for improvement. **J L Dunlop [2-6] The Earl Cadogan.*

WATER LOUP BHB 32f39a **RR 32f 39a** 3996[3]
4 b m Wolfhound (USA) 7.3f **(71)** - Heavenly Waters (Celestial Storm (USA))
Form - 67807622263
Record 2000 - 1st:0 2nd:3 3rd:1 Ran:11
Pre2000 - 1st:0 2nd:0 3rd:1 Ran:9
Win Prizemoney £0 *Total Prizemoney* £3,028
2000 Turf 0-9: (8f 3, 9f, 10f, 12f, 13f, 14f 2) (g-s, gd 3, g-f 3, frm, hrd)
2000 AW 0-2: (8f, 12f) (Fibr 2)
Scopey, very moderate filly, effective 8f, acts on frm, has worn blinkers. Turf high 32. AW high 27. **W R Muir [0-20] J Haim.*

WATERPARK BHB 76f **RR 77f** 2694[10]
2 b f Namaqualand (USA) - Willisa **(66f)** (Polar Falcon (USA))
Form - 632110
Record 2000 - 1st:2 2nd:1 3rd:1 Ran:6
Win Prizemoney £5,826 *Total Prizemoney* £7,253
Wins * 2000 Jun Ayr (G-F) 6f 77 <
*** 2000** May Haydoc (G-S) C 5f 60+
2000 Turf 2-5: (5f 1-3, 6f 1-2) (gd 1-3, g-f 1-1, frm) 2000 AW 0-1: (5f) (Fibr)
Above-average filly, effective 6f, acts on g-f. Turf high 77 - 1st of 11 getting 2lb from Distinctly Chic (1 Jun Ayr RF 1614).
**M Dods [2-6] Russ Mould.*

WATHBAT MUJTAHID BHB 80f **RR 81f** 1519[6]
3 ch c Mujtahid (USA) 7.4f **(69)** - Wathbat Mtoto **(88f)** (Mtoto)
Form - 56
Record 2000 - 1st:0 2nd:0 3rd:0 Ran:2
Pre2000 - 1st:0 2nd:1 3rd:1 Ran:3
Win Prizemoney £0 *Total Prizemoney* £1,527
2000 Turf 0-2: (7f, 8f) (g-s, gd)
Scopey, decent colt. Turf high 81 (1st run) - 5th of 11 to Salim (6 May Thirsk 7f gd RF 1066).

**A C Stewart [0-5] Sheikh Ahmed Al Maktoum.*

WATTNO ELJOHN (IRE) BHB 65f65a **RR 70f 65a** 5320[4]
2 b c Namaqualand (USA) - Caroline Connors (Fairy King (USA)) 7.7f **(59)**
Form - 000163534
Record 2000 - 1st:1 2nd:0 3rd:2 Ran:9
Win Prizemoney £2,163 *Total Prizemoney* £4,001
Wins * 2000 Jly Bath (G-S) S 5.1f 69 <
2000 Turf 1-9: (5f 1-3, 6f 3, 7f 3) (sft, g-s, gd 1-4, g-f 2, frm)
Above-average colt, effective 5 to 7f, acts on sft to g-f. Turf high 70 - also 1st of 6 giving 5lb to One Beloved (10 Jly Bath RF 2663).
**D W P Arbuthnot [1-9] Essandess Partners.*

WATTREY RR 53f 4602[4]
2 b f Royal Academy (USA) 7.8f **(77)** - Raneen Alwatar (Sadler's Wells (USA)) 10f **(76)**
Form - 4
Record 2000 - 1st:0 2nd:0 3rd:0 Ran:1
Win Prizemoney £0 *Total Prizemoney* £342
2000 Turf 0-1: (8f) (gd)
Currently fair filly. **M A Jarvis [0-1] Sheikh Ahmed Al Maktoum.*

WAVE OF OPTIMISM BHB 90f **RR 88f** 5297[6]
5 ch g Elmaamul (USA) 8.1f **(70)** - Ballerina Bay **(68f 63a)** (Myjinski (USA)) 9.5f **(54)**
Form - 01100026
Record 2000 - 1st:2 2nd:1 3rd:0 Ran:8
Pre2000 - 1st:2 2nd:2 3rd:2 Ran:8
Win Prizemoney £23,674 *Total Prizemoney* £50,815
Wins * 2000 May Kempto (SFT) H 16f 79 83 <
*** 2000** Apr Doncas (G-S) H 16.5f 74 77
* 1999 Apr Sandow (G-S) H 16.4f 72 75
* 1998 Oct Nottin (SFT) 14.1f 80
2000 Turf 2-8: (12f, 14f, 16f 1-4, 17f 1-1, 18f) (g-s 1-2, gd 1-5, g-f)
Useful gelding, effective 16 to 18f, acts on g-s to gd, likes right handed tracks. Turf high 88 - 2nd of 33 getting 1lb from Heros Fatal (14 Oct Newmarket 18f gd RF 4987) - also 1st of 10 getting 9lb from Turtle Valley (27 May Kempton RF 1497). A winner twice in the spring, he was very slowly away next time. No show in a couple of starts after returning from a summer break. He stays well. **J Pearce [4-16] Wave of Optimism Partnership.*

WAVERLEY ROAD BHB 60f62a **RR 61f 62a** 4493[2]
3 ch g Pelder (IRE) - Lillicara (FR) (Caracolero (USA)) 8.2f **(57)**
Form - 50658262
Record 2000 - 1st:0 2nd:2 3rd:0 Ran:8
Pre2000 - 1st:0 2nd:0 3rd:0 Ran:1
Win Prizemoney £0 *Total Prizemoney* £1,812
2000 Turf 0-8: (8f 2, 9f, 10f 5) (gd 2, g-f, frm 4, hrd)
Leggy, average gelding. Turf high 66. Consistent.
**A P Jarvis [0-9] All Four Corners.*

WAX LYRICAL BHB 65f **RR 66f** 3333[7]
4 b m Safawan 6.6f **(60)** - Hannah's Music (Music Boy) 6.8f **(57)**
Form - 70077
Record 2000 - 1st:0 2nd:0 3rd:0 Ran:5
Pre2000 - 1st:1 2nd:0 3rd:0 Ran:2
Win Prizemoney £3,208 *Total Prizemoney* £3,208
Wins 1999 May Salisb (G-F) 6f 84+ <
2000 Turf 0-5: (6f 4, 7f) (g-s, gd 2, g-f 2)
Lengthy, average filly, effective 6f, acts on frm, has worn blinkers. Turf high 66.
**M A Jarvis [0-5] Magno-Pulse Ltd (from J A R Toller [1-2] Spt 1999).*

WAY OUT WEST BHB 30f **RR 49f** 2474[11]
3 b f Distant Relative 7f **(69)** - Mohican (Great Nephew) 9.9f **(64)**
Form - 08000
Record 2000 - 1st:0 2nd:0 3rd:0 Ran:5
2000 Turf 0-4: (7f 2, 8f, 12f) (gd, frm 3) 2000 AW 0-1: (8f) (Fibr)
Rangy, moderate filly. Turf high 39.
**C W Thornton [0-5] Guy Reed.*

WAZARO (IRE) RR 100f 2789a[4]
3 f
Form - 4
2000 Turf 0-1: (8f) (gd)
Currently very useful, always wears blinkers.
**H Blume in GER [0-1].*

WEALTHY STAR (IRE) BHB 85f **RR 90f** 941[12]
5 b h Soviet Star (USA) 8.6f **(74)** - Catalonda (African Sky) 7.7f **(50)**
Form - 0550
Record 2000 - 1st:0 2nd:0 3rd:0 Ran:4
Pre2000 - 1st:1 2nd:0 3rd:0 Ran:6
Win Prizemoney £4,467 *Total Prizemoney* £5,388
Wins * 1998 Jun Nottin (GD) 8.2f 92 <
2000 Turf 0-4: (7f 2, 8f 2) (g-s, gd 3)
Useful colt, effective 7f, acts on gd. Turf high 90 - 5th of 21 giving 3lb to Present Laughter (19 Apr Newmarket 7f gd RF 0794).
**B Hanbury [1-10] Ahmed Ali.*

WEE BARNEY BHB 30f **RR 25f** 3339[11]
3 b g Balnibarbi - Never so True **(37f 37a)** (Never so Bold) 6.3f **(66)**
Form - 00000
Record 2000 - 1st:0 2nd:0 3rd:0 Ran:5
Pre2000 - 1st:0 2nd:1 3rd:0 Ran:6
Win Prizemoney £0 *Total Prizemoney* £536
2000 Turf 0-5: (7f, 8f 4) (gd, frm 3, hrd)
Leggy, little account gelding, effective 7f, acts on frm, has worn blinkers, likes left handed tracks, likes tight tracks. Turf high 25.
**Martyn Wane [0-5] James Kennerley (from B Ellison [0-6] Nov 1999).*

WEE JIMMY BHB 27f **RR 20df** 3213[15]
4 b g Lugana Beach 7f **(63)** - Cutlass Princess (USA) (Cutlass (USA)) 8.5f **(76)**
Form - 70
Record 2000 - 1st:0 2nd:0 3rd:0 Ran:2
Pre2000 - 1st:0 2nd:0 3rd:0 Ran:5
Win Prizemoney £0 *Total Prizemoney* £589
2000 Turf 0-1: (14f) (frm) 2000 AW 0-1: (9f) (Fibr)
Light-framed, little account gelding, has worn blinkers.
**B A McMahon [0-13] Michael Sturgess.*

WEET-A-MINUTE (IRE) BHB 75f94a **RR 90f 94a** 5125[17]
7 ro h Nabeel Dancer (USA) 6.1f **(65)** - Ludovica (Bustino) 10.4f **(64)**
Form - 8122225600543800
Record 2000 - 1st:0 2nd:4 3rd:1 Ran:14
Pre2000 - 1st:6 2nd:11 3rd:9 Ran:59
Win Prizemoney £41,967 *Total Prizemoney* £108,534
Wins 1999 *Dec Wolver (STD) H 9.4f 96 97*
1999 *Mar Wolver (STD) H 9.4f 95 96*
1998 *Dec Wolver (STD) H 9.4f 88 93*
2000 Turf 0-10: (8f 2, 9f 3, 10f 4, 12f) (g-s, gd 3, g-f 5, frm) 2000 AW 0-4: (8f 2, 9f 2) (Fibr 4)
Very useful horse, effective 8 to 10f, best at 8f, acts on gd to frm - acts on Fibr, has worn blinkers, favours left handed tracks, likes tight tracks, and excels at Wolverhampton. Turf high 95 (1st run) - 5th of 8 giving 5lb to Hasty Words (23 Mar Doncaster 8f frm RF 0476). AW high 97 (1st run) - 2nd of 5 to Welville (13 Jan Wolverhampton 8f Fibr RF 0082). Becoming disappointing. He is effective between a mile and ten furlongs on both turf and Fibresand and is very hardy. He is capable of handling any ground but lacks a telling turn-of-foot and usually has to settle for minor honours.
**N P Littmoden [0-8] Ed Weetman (Haulage & Storage) Ltd (from R Hollinshead [6-65] May 2000).*

WEET AND SEE BHB 55f45a **RR 47?f 45a** 337[13]
6 b g Lochnager 6.9f **(50)** - Simply Style (Bairn (USA)) 7.7f **(59)**
Form - 0
Record 2000 - 1st:0 2nd:0 3rd:0 Ran:1
Pre2000 - 1st:1 2nd:1 3rd:1 Ran:13
Win Prizemoney £2,277 *Total Prizemoney* £3,878
Wins 1997 *Mar Wolver (STD) H 8.5f 63 64* <
2000 AW 0-1: (9f) (Fibr)
Moderate gelding.
**T Wall [3-26] Ed Weetman (Haulage & Storage) Ltd (from R Hollinshead [1-11] Oct 1997).*

WEET A WHILE (IRE) BHB 58f52a **RR 69f 52a** 5310[10]
2 b c Lahib (USA) 8f **(69)** - Takeshi (IRE) **(62f 51a)** (Cadeaux Genereux)
Form - 075770

Record 2000 - 1st:0 2nd:0 3rd:0 Ran:6
2000 Turf 0-6: (6f 5, 7f) (g-s 2, gd, g-f 2, frm)
Average colt. Turf high 66 (began Jly).
**R Hollinshead [0-6] Ed Weetman (Haulage & Storage) Ltd.*

WEET FOR ME BHB 80f88a RR 80f 88a 5322[7]

4 b h Warning 8.1f **(77)** - Naswara (USA) (Al Nasr (FR)) 9.3f **(68)**
Form - 703816307
Record 2000 - 1st:1 2nd:0 3rd:2 Ran:9
Pre2000 - 1st:1 2nd:3 3rd:0 Ran:12
Win Prizemoney £8,205 *Total Prizemoney* £16,294
Wins * 2000 Jly Doncas (G-F) H 14.6f 75 77
* 1999 Jly Haydoc (FRM) 10.5f 81 <
2000 Turf 1-9: (14f 3, 15f 1-2, 16f, 17f, 18f 2) (hvy, sft, g-s, gd 4, g-f, frm 1-1)
Leggy, useful colt, effective 11 to 16f, acts on g-s to frm, prefers left handed tracks. Turf high 80 - 3rd of 12 giving 12lb to Sudden Flight (12 Aug Haydock 14f gd RF 3585) - also 1st of 8 getting 3lb from Sharp Stepper (1 Jly Doncaster RF 2431). An able stayer, he enjoyed his favoured fast ground when winning over 14 furlongs at Doncaster in July.
**R Hollinshead [2-21] Ed Weetman (Haulage & Storage) Ltd.*

WEETMAN'S WEIGH (IRE) BHB 66f85a RR 69f 85a 5242[1]

7 b h Archway (IRE) 8.5f **(60)** - Indian Sand (Indian King (USA)) 7.4f **(64)**
Form - 2464808056486581
Record 2000 - 1st:1 2nd:0 3rd:0 Ran:15
Pre2000 - 1st:12 2nd:15 3rd:7 Ran:66
Win Prizemoney £60,116 *Total Prizemoney* £93,765

Wins								
* 2000	Oct	Newmar	(SFT)	H	7f	62	68	
* 1999	*Feb*	*Wolver*	*(STD)*	*H*	*8.5f*	*90*	*94*	<
* 1999	*Jan*	*Southw*	*(STD)*	*H*	*7f*	*85*	*91*	
* 1998	Oct	Newmar	(SFT)	H	7f	72	77	
* 1998	Aug	Newcas	(GD)	H	7f	67	72	
* 1998	*Feb*	*Wolver*	*(STD)*	*H*	*7f*	*79*	*84*	
* 1997	Jun	Thirsk	(FRM)		7f		81	
* 1997	May	Redcar	(G-F)		7f		81	
* 1997	May	Thirsk	(G-F)	H	7f	73	76	
* 1996	Mar	Leices	(SFT)	H	6f	68	75	
* 1996	*Jan*	*Wolver*	*(STD)*	*H*	*6f*	*74*	*74*	
* 1996	*Jan*	*Southw*	*(STD)*	*H*	*6f*	*64*	*65*	

2000 Turf 1-11: (7f 1-4, 8f 7) (g-s 1-2, gd 3, g-f 4, frm 2) 2000 AW 0-4: (7f, 8f 3) (Fibr 4)
Useful horse, effective 7 to 8f, best at 8f, - acts on Fibr. Turf high 69. AW high 87. A fairly useful handicapper on turf and sand, he broke a long losing run when coming good at Newmarket in October. **R Hollinshead [13-81] Ed Weetman (Haulage & Storage) Ltd.*

WEETRAIN (IRE) BHB 51f35a RR 30f 35a 393[8]

4 b m Fayruz 6.6f **(63)** - Mantlepiece (IRE) (Common Grounds)
Form - 0608
Record 2000 - 1st:0 2nd:0 3rd:0 Ran:3
Pre2000 - 1st:0 2nd:0 3rd:2 Ran:11
Win Prizemoney £0 *Total Prizemoney* £548
2000 AW 0-3: (5f 2, 6f) (Fibr 3)
Very moderate filly, effective 5f, acts on g-s. AW high 28.
**J G Given [0-10] Maltby Sporting Club (from M Cunningham in IRE [0-4] Oct 1998).*

WELCH'S DREAM (IRE) BHB 55f63a RR 64f 63a 3827[13]

3 b f Brief Truce (USA) 9.1f **(73)** - Swift Chorus (Music Boy) 6.8f **(57)**
Form - 4245607600
Record 2000 - 1st:0 2nd:0 3rd:0 Ran:7
Pre2000 - 1st:1 2nd:2 3rd:1 Ran:10
Win Prizemoney £3,126 *Total Prizemoney* £6,452
Wins 1999 May Ripon (G-F) 5f 66 <
2000 Turf 0-6: (5f 4, 6f 2) (g-f 4, frm, hrd) 2000 AW 0-1: (5f) (Fibr)
Leggy, above-average filly, effective 5 to 6f, best at 5f, acts on g-f to frm - acts on Fibr, best on frm, has worn blinkers. Turf high 64.
**E J Alston [0-6] David Hall (from A Berry [0-1] Jan 2000).*

WELCOME ABOARD BHB 70f RR 65f 1900[7]

3 ch f Be My Guest (USA) 10.2f **(66)** - Loreef (Main Reef) 9.6f **(57)**
Form - 3017
Record 2000 - 1st:1 2nd:0 3rd:1 Ran:4
Win Prizemoney £2,541 *Total Prizemoney* £3,163
Wins * 2000 May Leices (SFT) 8f 65 <
2000 Turf 1-4: (7f, 8f 1-2, 10f) (hvy, gd 1-1, g-f, frm)
Workmanlike, average filly. Turf high 65 - 1st of 10 from Prinisha (29 May Leicester RF 1524). **J G Given [1-4] J W Rowles.*

WELCOME BACK BHB 35a RR 38f 4179[10]

3 ch g Most Welcome 8.6f **(66)** - Villavina **(49f)** (Top Ville) 11.7f **(68)**
Form - 70553630
Record 2000 - 1st:0 2nd:0 3rd:2 Ran:8
Pre2000 - 1st:0 2nd:0 3rd:0 Ran:4
Win Prizemoney £0 *Total Prizemoney* £928
2000 Turf 0-7: (8f 3, 11f, 12f, 14f 2) (gd 2, g-f 3, frm, hrd) 2000 AW 0-1: (12f) (Fibr)
Unfurnished, very moderate gelding. Turf high 41.
**K A Ryan [0-12] J J Stephenson.*

WELCOME FRIEND (USA) BHB 100f RR 101f 4303[2]

3 b c Kingmambo (USA) 10.9f **(85)** - Kingscote (Kings Lake (USA)) 10.8f **(67)**
Form - 122
Record 2000 - 1st:1 2nd:2 3rd:0 Ran:3
Win Prizemoney £3,233 *Total Prizemoney* £7,919
Wins * 2000 May Salisb (G-F) 6f 83 <
2000 Turf 1-3: (6f 1-1, 7f 2) (gd, g-f 1-1, frm)
Well made, currently very useful colt. Turf high 101 - 2nd of 8 giving 3lb to Blue Mountain (8 Spt Goodwood 7f gd RF 4303). From a useful family, he did not race at two and beat a big field of maidens on his Salisbury debut in May, but was off the track for three months before finishing runner-up in a Chepstow conditions event. Another good effort on his final run.
**R Charlton [1-3] K Abdulla.*

WELCOME GIFT BHB 69a RR 61f 69a 1589[9]

4 b g Prince Sabo 6.6f **(64)** - Ausonia (Beldale Flutter (USA)) 9.7f **(71)**
Form - 222160
Record 2000 - 1st:1 2nd:2 3rd:0 Ran:5
Pre2000 - 1st:0 2nd:1 3rd:0 Ran:1
Win Prizemoney £2,730 *Total Prizemoney* £4,857
Wins * 2000 *Feb Wolver (STD) 6f 66* <
2000 Turf 0-2: (6f, 7f) (g-s, gd) 2000 AW 1-3: (6f 1-1, 7f 2) (Fibr 1-3)
Scopey, average gelding, effective 6 to 7f, best at 7f, - acts on Fibr. Turf high 61. AW high 66 - 1st of 6 giving 15lb to Tropical King (1 Feb Wolverhampton RF 0197). **W J Haggas [1-6] M H Wilson.*

WELCOME HEIGHTS BHB 42f45a RR 41f 45a 4559[16]

6 b g Most Welcome 8.6f **(66)** - Mount Ida (USA) (Conquistador Cielo (USA)) 8.8f **(69)**
Form - 00
Record 2000 - 1st:0 2nd:0 3rd:0 Ran:1
Pre2000 - 1st:4 2nd:4 3rd:4 Ran:36
Win Prizemoney £14,155 *Total Prizemoney* £19,376

Wins							
1998	May	Leices	(GD)	H	8f	55	64 <
1997	*Dec*	*Lingfi*	*(STD)*	*H*	*10f*	*57*	*60*
1997	Jly	Doncas	(GD)	H	7f	48	55
1997	Jly	Chepst	(G-S)	H	6.1f	38	44

2000 Turf 0-1: (10f) (gd)
Moderate gelding, effective 8 to 11f, best at 8f, acts on sft to frm, prefers left handed tracks. Becoming disappointing.
**R C Spicer [0-6] Robert McNamara (from M J Fetherston-Godley [4-34] Oct 1999).*

WELCOME SHADE BHB 47f53a RR 61f 53a 2778[7]

3 gr g Green Desert (USA) 7.8f **(78)** - Grey Angel (Kenmare (FR)) 6.5f **(72)**
Form - 14207877
Record 2000 - 1st:0 2nd:1 3rd:0 Ran:6
Pre2000 - 1st:1 2nd:0 3rd:0 Ran:5
Win Prizemoney £2,290 *Total Prizemoney* £2,943
Wins 1999 *Nov Lingfi (STD) H 6f 63 62* <
2000 Turf 0-4: (7f, 8f, 11f, 12f) (g-f 2, frm, hrd) 2000 AW 0-2: (7f, 9f) (Fibr 2)
Scopey, average gelding, effective 6 to 7f, best at 6f, acts on frm - acts on Equi, has worn blinkers, prefers left handed tracks, prefers tight tracks. Turf high 61 (1st run) - 2nd of 11 giving 9lb to Tea For Texas (9 May Brighton 7f frm RF 1107). AW high 38. Becoming disappointing.
**L A Dace [0-5] M C S D Racing Ltd (from R Hannon [1-6] May 2000).*

WELCOME TO UNOS BHB 60f58a RR 63f 58a 4498[5]

3 ch g Exit To Nowhere (USA) 8.7f **(77)** - Royal Loft (Homing) 7.8f **(59)**
Form - 863027655
Record 2000 - 1st:0 2nd:1 3rd:1 Ran:9
Pre2000 - 1st:0 2nd:1 3rd:0 Ran:3
Win Prizemoney £0 *Total Prizemoney* £2,615
2000 Turf 0-8: (6f 3, 7f 4, 8f) (sft, g-s, g-f 3, frm 3) 2000 AW 0-1: (8f) (Fibr)
Leggy, average gelding, effective 6f, acts on g-f to frm, prefers left handed tracks, likes tight tracks. Turf high 63 - 3rd of 8 giving 10lb to Maron (6 Jly Catterick 6f g-f RF 2563). Consistent.
**M Dods [0-12] J & M Leisure / Unos Restaurant.*

WELDUNFRANK BHB 49f RR 57f 2802[8]

7 b g Weld - Damsong (Petong) 6.6f **(58)**
Form - 085608
Record 2000 - 1st:0 2nd:0 3rd:0 Ran:6
2000 Turf 0-6: (10f, 11f 2, 12f 2, 14f) (gd 2, g-f 3, frm)
Fair gelding. Turf high 57.
**W M Brisbourne [0-12] Mrs J P McCormack.*

WELLBEING BHB 115f RR 118f 5130[1]

3 b c Sadler's Wells (USA) 11.3f **(87)** - Charming Life (NZ) (Sir Tristram) 10.7f **(76)**
Form - 11511
Record 2000 - 1st:4 2nd:0 3rd:0 Ran:5
Pre2000 - 1st:0 2nd:0 3rd:1 Ran:1
Win Prizemoney £48,061 *Total Prizemoney* £75,275
Wins * 2000 Oct Newbur (HVY) G3 12f 118+ <
*** 2000** Spt Newmar (GD) L 12f 116+
*** 2000** May Newmar (GD) 12f 100
*** 2000** Apr Newmar (G-S) 12f 92+
2000 Turf 4-5: (12f 4-5) (sft 1-1, gd 3-4)
Well made, high-class colt, effective 12f, acts on sft to gd. Turf high 118 - 1st of 7 from Marienbard (21 Oct Newbury RF 5130) - also 1st of 7 getting 4lb from Pawn Broker (29 Spt Newmarket RF 4731). He appreciated the step up in trip when winning over 12 furlongs at Newmarket on his return. Followed up over course and distance before finishing fifth, beaten a fair way, in the Derby. Off for more than three months afterwards, before landing a Newmarket listed race and the St Simon Stakes at Newbury (run in 2000 as the Perpetual Stakes), he is a useful four-year-old prospect. **H R A Cecil [4-6] Exors of the late Lord Howard de Walden.*

WELLCOME INN BHB 34f39a RR 28f 39a 3016[10]

6 ch g Most Welcome 8.6f **(66)** - Mimining (Tower Walk) 10f **(62)**
Form - 7022334140
Record 2000 - 1st:1 2nd:2 3rd:2 Ran:9
Pre2000 - 1st:1 2nd:2 3rd:1 Ran:19
Win Prizemoney £4,826 *Total Prizemoney* £8,402
Wins * 2000 *Mar Wolver (STD) H 9.4f 35 38*
1997 Aug Beverl (G-S) 12f 64 <
2000 Turf 0-1: (8f) (g-f) 2000 AW 1-8: (8f, 9f 1-2, 11f, 12f 3, 16f) (Fibr 1-8)
Very moderate gelding, effective 9 to 12f, best at 9f, acts on frm - acts on Fibr. AW high 38 - 1st of 11 getting 7lb from Midnight Watch (28 Mar Wolverhampton RF 0531).
**G Woodward [1-18] Burntwood Sports Ltd (from J O'Reilly [1-8] Nov 1997).*

WELL MADE (GER) RR 110f 5215a[5]

3 br c Mondrian (GER) - Well Known (GER) (Konigsstuhl (GER)) 11.2f **(76)**
Form - 355
2000 Turf 0-3: (10f, 11f, 12f) (hvy, sft, gd)
Strong, currently Group-class colt. Turf high 110.
**H Blume in GER [0-3].*

WE'LL MAKE IT (IRE) BHB 70f RR 71f 4547[12]

2 b c Spectrum (IRE) - Walliser (Niniski (USA)) 10.6f **(65)**
Form - 6000
Record 2000 - 1st:0 2nd:0 3rd:0 Ran:4
2000 Turf 0-4: (6f, 7f, 8f 2) (g-s, g-f 2, frm)
Above-average colt. Turf high 71 (began Jly).
**G L Moore [0-4] C F Sparrowhawk.*

WELL MINDED (GER) RR 105f 4414a[2]

3 br f Monsun (GER) - Well Proved (GER) (Prince Ippi (GER)) 10.4f **(68)**
Form - 352
2000 Turf 0-3: (11f 2, 12f) (gd 3)
Pattern-class filly. Turf high 105 - 2nd of 8 to Moonlady (10 Spt Hanover 12f gd RF 4414a). **H Blume in GER [0-4] Gestut Rottgen.*

WELODY BHB 49f58a RR 54f 58a 4782[3]

4 ch g Weldnaas (USA) 8.4f **(55)** - The Boozy News (USA) (L'Emigrant (USA)) 10.5f **(62)**
Form - 421004008880003
Record 2000 - 1st:1 2nd:1 3rd:1 Ran:15
Pre2000 - 1st:0 2nd:0 3rd:0 Ran:4
Win Prizemoney £2,418 *Total Prizemoney* £4,192
Wins * 2000 *Mar Wolver (STD) 8.5f 69* <
2000 Turf 0-9: (7f, 8f 5, 10f 2, 12f) (g-s, gd, g-f 4, frm 3) 2000 AW 1-6: (7f, 8f 1-4, 9f) (Fibr 1-6)
Rangy, average gelding, effective 8f, - acts on Fibr, often wears blinkers (effectively). Turf high 54. AW high 69 - 1st of 9 giving 23lb to Marju Guest (11 Mar Wolverhampton RF 0430).
**K Mahdi [1-19] Prospect Estates Ltd.*

WELSH BORDER RR 92f 5224[1]

2 ch c Zafonic (USA) 9f **(83)** - Welsh Daylight (Welsh Pageant) 10f **(65)**
Form - 11
Record 2000 - 1st:2 2nd:0 3rd:0 Ran:2
Win Prizemoney £9,607 *Total Prizemoney* £9,607
Wins * 2000 Oct Newmar (SFT) 8f 92 <
*** 2000** Spt Nottin (G-S) 8.2f 70+
2000 Turf 2-2: (8f 2-2) (gd 2-2)
Currently useful colt. Turf high 92 (began Spt) - 1st of 10 from Turku (27 Oct Newmarket RF 5224). **H R A Cecil [2-2] K Abdulla.*

WELSH DREAM BHB 70f RR 71+f 4621[2]

3 b c Mtoto 11.5f **(71)** - Morgannwg (IRE) (Simply Great (FR)) 8.2f **(65)**
Form - 112
Record 2000 - 1st:2 2nd:1 3rd:0 Ran:3
Pre2000 - 1st:0 2nd:0 3rd:0 Ran:3
Win Prizemoney £8,148 *Total Prizemoney* £9,074
Wins * 2000 Aug Bright (FRM) H 11.9f 61 71 <
*** 2000** Aug Newmar (GD) H 12f 53 63
2000 Turf 2-3: (12f 2-3) (gd, frm 1-1, hrd 1-1)
Scopey, above-average colt, effective 12f, acts on gd to hrd. Turf high 71 (began Aug) - 2nd of 8 giving 1lb to Perfect Moment (24 Spt Brighton 12f gd RF 4621) - also 1st of 8 getting 4lb from Alpha Rose (23 Aug Brighton RF 3897).
**A C Stewart [2-6] K J Mercer & Mrs S Mercer.*

WELSH MAIN RR 98+f 4027[1]

3 br c Zafonic (USA) 9f **(83)** - Welsh Daylight (Welsh Pageant) 10f **(65)**
Form - 11
Record 2000 - 1st:2 2nd:0 3rd:0 Ran:2
Win Prizemoney £11,006 *Total Prizemoney* £11,006
Wins * 2000 Aug Yarmou (G-F) 10.1f 98 <
*** 2000** Jly Windso (G-F) 10f 82
2000 Turf 2-2: (10f 2-2) (gd 1-1, frm 1-1)
Scopey, currently very useful colt. Turf high 98 (began Jly) - 1st of 6 giving 7lb to Via Camp (27 Aug Yarmouth RF 4027). He won his maiden at Windsor on his debut despite showing signs of greenness and followed up from more experienced sorts at Yarmouth.
**H R A Cecil [2-2] K Abdulla.*

WELSH PLOY BHB 62f65a RR 50f 65a 5229[20]

3 b f Deploy 11.4f **(67)** - Safe House (Lyphard (USA)) 9.9f **(72)**
Form - 12000
Record 2000 - 1st:0 2nd:0 3rd:0 Ran:3
Pre2000 - 1st:1 2nd:2 3rd:1 Ran:8
Win Prizemoney £2,640 *Total Prizemoney* £4,978
Wins * 1999 *Dec Lingfi (STD) H 8f 73 81* <
2000 Turf 0-3: (8f, 9f, 10f) (sft, gd 2)
Scopey, above-average filly, effective 7 to 8f, best at 7f, acts on g-s to gd - acts on AW, prefers tight tracks. Turf high 35 (began Spt). Becoming disappointing. **K McAuliffe [1-11] G E Amey.*

WELSH VALLEY (USA) BHB 68a RR 64f 1706[8]

3 b f Irish River (FR) 9f **(77)** - Sweet Snow (USA) (Lyphard (USA)) 9.9f **(72)**
Form - 2748

Record 2000 - 1st:0 2nd:1 3rd:0 Ran:4
Pre2000 - 1st:0 2nd:1 3rd:0 Ran:2
Win Prizemoney £0 *Total Prizemoney* £2,056
2000 Turf 0-2: (7f 2) (g-s, gd) 2000 AW 0-2: (5f, 6f) (Fibr 2)
Average filly, effective 6f, - acts on Fibr. Turf high 64. AW high 65 (1st run) - 2nd of 14 getting 5lb from Lord Yasmin (17 Mar Southwell 6f Fibr RF 0458). **M L W Bell [0-6] Usk Valley Stud.*

WELSH WIND (IRE) BHB 92f **RR 92f** 4556[8]

4 b g Tenby 10.4f **(76)** - Bavaria (Top Ville) 11.7f **(68)**
Form - 22042238
Record 2000 - 1st:0 2nd:4 3rd:1 Ran:8
Pre2000 - 1st:1 2nd:0 3rd:2 Ran:8
Win Prizemoney £3,781 *Total Prizemoney* £17,253
Wins 1999 Jly Leopar (G-F) 10f 87+ <
2000 Turf 0-8: (8f 5, 9f, 10f 2) (gd 6, g-f, frm)
Useful gelding, effective 8 to 12f, acts on g-s to frm, likes right handed tracks, excels at Windsor. Turf high 92 - 2nd of 15 getting 3lb from Pantar (8 Spt Goodwood 9f gd RF 4302). Formerly trained in Ireland, he changed stables again during the summer and put up some good performances in decent handicaps without being able to get his head in front.
**D J Murphy [0-5] The Barracuda Boys (from R Ingram [0-3] Jun 2000).*

WELVILLE BHB 78f101a **RR 74f 101a** 82[1]

7 b g Most Welcome 8.6f **(66)** - Miss Top Ville (FR) (Top Ville) 11.7f **(68)**
Form - 1
Record 2000 - 1st:1 2nd:0 3rd:0 Ran:1
Pre2000 - 1st:4 2nd:3 3rd:0 Ran:14
Win Prizemoney £27,684 *Total Prizemoney* £41,248
Wins * **2000** *Jan Wolver (STD)* *8.5f* *98* <
* 1999 *Apr Wolver (STD) H* *8.5f* *93 96*
* 1999 *Feb Lingfi (STD) H* *8f* *87 90*
* 1999 *Feb Lingfi (STD) H* *8f* *75 88*
2000 AW 1-1: (8f 1-1) (Fibr 1-1)
Very useful gelding, effective 8f, - acts on AW, best on Fibr. (1st run) - 1st of 5 from Weet-A-Minute (13 Jan Wolverhampton RF 0082). Improving. He has a fine record on sand and his win at Wolverhampton in January was an especially fine effort after an eight-month break. Best suited by a mile, he is at his best when able to dominate. **P J Makin [5-15] T G Warner.*

WEND'S DAY (IRE) BHB 65f **RR 66f** 1592[4]

5 br g Brief Truce (USA) 9.1f **(73)** - Iswara (USA) (Alleged (USA)) 10f **(76)**
Form - 4
Record 2000 - 1st:0 2nd:0 3rd:0 Ran:1
Pre2000 - 1st:0 2nd:0 3rd:1 Ran:4
Win Prizemoney £0 *Total Prizemoney* £895
2000 Turf 0-1: (13f) (g-s)
Average gelding. (1st run) - 4th of 13 getting 9lb from Turtle Soup (31 May Newbury 13f g-s RF 1592).
**S E H Sherwood [1-6] Andrew Cohen (from S E Sherwood [0-2] Jun 1998).*

WENSUM DANCER BHB 40f **RR 49f** 4868[5]

3 b f Shareef Dancer (USA) 10.1f **(67)** - Burning Ambition (Troy) 10.4f **(68)**
Form - 040647425
Record 2000 - 1st:0 2nd:1 3rd:0 Ran:9
Win Prizemoney £0 *Total Prizemoney* £1,545
2000 Turf 0-9: (8f 2, 10f 4, 11f, 12f 2) (hvy, gd 2, g-f 2, frm 4)
Scopey, moderate filly, effective 8 to 12f, acts on g-f to frm. Turf high 49 - 2nd of 16 getting 11lb from Final Lap (28 Spt Newmarket 12f g-f RF 4696). **R Guest [0-9] Mrs B P Cannell.*

WE'RE NOT JOKEN BHB 45f **RR 43f** 3425[14]

3 b f Foxhound (USA) - We're Joken **(51f 43a)** (Statoblest)
Form - 8080
Record 2000 - 1st:0 2nd:0 3rd:0 Ran:4
Pre2000 - 1st:0 2nd:0 3rd:0 Ran:5
2000 Turf 0-4: (5f 2, 6f, 7f) (g-f 2, frm 2)
Moderate filly, has worn blinkers. Turf high 43 (began Jly).
**Mrs N Macauley [0-9] T J Bird.*

WERE NOT STOPPIN BHB 57f47a **RR 60f 47a** 4864[12]

5 b g Mystiko (USA) 7.7f **(59)** - Power Take Off (Aragon) 8.1f **(60)**
Form - 0057511141360
Record 2000 - 1st:4 2nd:0 3rd:1 Ran:13
Pre2000 - 1st:0 2nd:0 3rd:0 Ran:4
Win Prizemoney £11,713 *Total Prizemoney* £13,066
Wins * **2000** Jly Pontef (GD) H 10f 53 58 <
* **2000** May Redcar (G-S) H 9f 47 52
* **2000** May Redcar (G-F) H 8f 40 45
* **2000** Apr Beverl (HVY) S 8.5f 34
2000 Turf 4-8: (8f 2-2, 9f 1-3, 10f 1-3) (sft, g-s 1-1, gd 2, g-f 1-1, frm 2-3) 2000 AW 0-5: (8f 3, 11f 2) (Fibr 5)
Average gelding, effective 9 to 10f, best at 10f, acts on gd to frm, best on frm, excels at Beverley and Redcar. Turf high 60 - 3rd of 7 getting 14lb from Kind Regards (17 Aug Beverley 10f frm RF 3718) - also 1st of 18 giving 6lb to Annadawi (11 Jly Pontefract RF 2693). AW high 29. Showed big improvement to land a hat-trick in the spring at Beverley and Redcar (twice). He was set a bit too much to do when going for a four-timer, but returned to winning form in a Pontefract amateur riders' event. Suited by trips from a mile to ten furlongs, but has given trouble at the stalls.
**R Bastiman [4-18] I B Barker.*

WESLEY'S LAD (IRE) BHB 44f49a **RR 54f 49a** 253[5]

6 b br g Classic Secret (USA) 8.8f **(56)** -Galouga (FR)(Lou Piguet (FR))
Form - 5
Record 2000 - 1st:0 2nd:0 3rd:0 Ran:1
Pre2000 - 1st:0 2nd:0 3rd:2 Ran:10
Win Prizemoney £0 *Total Prizemoney* £799
2000 AW 0-1: (12f) (Fibr)
Fair gelding.
**D Burchell [3-20] Brian Williams (from J Neville [0-8] Jly 1997).*

WESTBROOK (IRE) BHB 50f **RR 58f** 400[8]

4 b g Fairy King (USA) 7.7f **(75)** - Abury (IRE) (Law Society (USA)) 9.9f **(70)**
Form - 8
Record 2000 - 1st:0 2nd:0 3rd:0 Ran:1
Pre2000 - 1st:0 2nd:0 3rd:0 Ran:5
2000 AW 0-1: (10f) (Equi)
Fair gelding, has worn blinkers.
**C N Kellett [0-7] Sean Taylor (from P W Chapple-Hyam [0-1] Aug 1999).*

WESTCOURT MAGIC BHB 59f **RR 71f** 4537[6]

7 b g Emarati (USA) 6.6f **(63)** -Magic Milly (Simply Great (FR)) 8.2f **(65)**
Form - 000006
Record 2000 - 1st:0 2nd:0 3rd:0 Ran:6
Pre2000 - 1st:11 2nd:5 3rd:1 Ran:60
Win Prizemoney £71,037 *Total Prizemoney* £95,585
Wins * 1999 Spt Cheste (HVY) H 5.1f 74 75
* 1998 Aug Cheste (G-S) H 5.1f 83 87
* 1998 May Cheste (G-F) H 5.1f 87 89
* 1998 Mar Newcas (G-S) H 5f 80 85
* 1997 Aug Cheste (SFT) H 5.1f 80 88
* 1996 Apr Haydoc (GD) L 5f 103
2000 Turf 0-6: (5f 6) (g-s, gd 2, g-f, frm 2)
Above-average gelding, effective 5f, acts on g-s to g-f, likes left handed tracks, likes tight tracks. Turf high 71.
**M W Easterby [11-66] K Hodgson & Mrs J Hodgson.*

WEST END DANCER (USA) BHB 28f40a **RR 41f 40a** 5227[10]

3 b f West by West (USA) - Chateau Dancer (USA) (Giacometti) 11.2f **(56)**
Form - 500057338040
Record 2000 - 1st:0 2nd:0 3rd:2 Ran:10
Pre2000 - 1st:0 2nd:0 3rd:0 Ran:2
Win Prizemoney £0 *Total Prizemoney* £544
2000 Turf 0-8: (10f, 11f 2, 12f 3, 14f 2) (sft, g-s, gd 2, g-f, frm 2, hrd)
2000 AW 0-2: (10f, 12f) (Equi 2)
Leggy, moderate filly, effective 12f, acts on frm, has worn blinkers, likes tight tracks. Turf high 41. AW high 4.
**P S McEntee [0-7] Miss Rosalynd Sweeney (from G C H Chung [0-9] Aug 2000).*

WESTENDER (FR) BHB 96f **RR 99f** 3912[16]

4 b g In The Wings 11.2f **(77)** - Trude (GER) (Windwurf (GER)) 12.7f **(72)**
Form - 2257210

Record 2000 - 1st:1 2nd:3 3rd:0 Ran:7
Pre2000 - 1st:2 2nd:2 3rd:1 Ran:6
Win Prizemoney £20,588 *Total Prizemoney* £38,402
Wins * 2000 Aug Newbur (G-F) H 11f 93 99 <
* 1999 Aug Ripon (GD) H 10f 80 87
* 1999 Jly Yarmou (G-F) 7f 75
2000 Turf 1-7: (10f 4, 11f 1-1, 12f 2) (gd 4, g-f 1-1, frm 2)
Workmanlike, very useful gelding, effective 10 to 12f, acts on gd to frm, best on gd, likes Ascot. Turf high 99 - 1st of 6 giving 16lb to Cracow (18 Aug Newbury RF 3758). Consistent. Genuine and consistent, he deserved his victory at Newbury in August following a string of good efforts in high-class handicaps. He is suited by ten furlongs and a sound surface. **W J Haggas [3-13] Khalifa Dasmal.*

WESTERN APPEAL (USA) RR 96f
5202a[3]
3 br f Gone West (USA) 7.8f **(82)** - Zaizafon (USA)(The Minstrel (CAN)) 10f **(72)**
Form - 3
2000 Turf 0-1: (7f) (hvy)
Currently very useful filly. (1st run) - 3rd of 14 to Twin Set (16 Oct Deauville 7f hvy RF 5202a). **in FR [0-1].*

WESTERN BAY (IRE) BHB 54a RR 55f
4779[11]
4 b g Midhish - Redington Belle (Ahonoora) 8.1f **(73)**
Form - 68700
Record 2000 - 1st:0 2nd:0 3rd:0 Ran:5
2000 Turf 0-4: (8f, 10f 2, 14f) (gd, frm 3) 2000 AW 0-1: (12f) (Fibr)
Fair gelding. Turf high 55.
**D W P Arbuthnot [0-5] Eastwind Racing Ltd.*

WESTERN COMMAND (GER) BHB 43f58a RR 46f 58a
5007[3]
4 b g Saddlers' Hall (IRE) 10.5f **(65)** - Western Friend (USA) (Gone West (USA)) 6.5f **(75)**
Form - 62214573362168346451862868353
Record 2000 - 1st:2 2nd:2 3rd:5 Ran:25
Pre2000 - 1st:3 2nd:5 3rd:3 Ran:22
Win Prizemoney £10,486 *Total Prizemoney* £20,713
Wins * 2000 *May Southw (STD) H 14f 59 64*
*** 2000** *Feb Southw (STD) H 11f 62 66*
***** 1999 *Dec Wolver (STD) H 12f 63 66*
1999 *Mar Southw (STD) H 12f 63 73* <
1999 *Mar Southw (SLW) H 11f 63 70*
2000 Turf 0-4: (12f 2, 14f, 16f) (gd, g-f, frm 2) 2000 AW 2-21: (11f 1-5, 12f 12, 14f 1-2, 15f, 16f) (Equi, Fibr 2-20)
Workmanlike, average gelding, effective 11 to 14f, best at 11f, - acts on Fibr, has worn blinkers, favours left handed tracks, favours tight tracks. Turf high 46. AW high 66 - 1st of 13 giving 31lb to Irsal (21 Feb Southwell RF 0329) - also 1st of 13 giving 12lb to Time Can Tell (26 May Southwell RF 1476).
**Mrs N Macauley [3-40] Andy Peake (from Sir Mark Prescott [2-7] Mar 1999).*

WESTERN EDGE (USA) BHB 71f RR 87f
5320[22]
2 b f Woodman (USA) 9.7f **(77)** - Star Pastures (Northfields (USA)) 9f **(72)**
Form - 5630
Record 2000 - 1st:0 2nd:0 3rd:1 Ran:4
Win Prizemoney £0 *Total Prizemoney* £497
2000 Turf 0-4: (7f 2, 8f 2) (sft, g-s 2, frm)
Useful filly. Turf high 87 (began Spt).
**J H M Gosden [0-4] R E Sangster.*

WESTERN FLAME (USA) BHB 68f RR 70f
4932[22]
2 b f Zafonic (USA) 9f **(83)** - Samya's Flame (Artaius (USA)) 9f **(69)**
Form - 5200
Record 2000 - 1st:0 2nd:1 3rd:0 Ran:4
Win Prizemoney £0 *Total Prizemoney* £944
2000 Turf 0-4: (6f 3, 7f) (g-s 2, gd, g-f)
Above-average filly. Turf high 70 (began Jly) - 2nd of 12 getting 5lb from Spy Master (16 Spt Catterick 6f g-s RF 4454).
**R Guest [0-4] Matthews Breeding and Racing.*

WESTERN GENERAL BHB 34f RR 37f
2493[5]
9 ch g Cadeaux Genereux 7.9f **(76)** - Patsy Western (Precocious) 8.6f **(62)**
Form - 055
Record 2000 - 1st:0 2nd:0 3rd:0 Ran:3
Pre2000 - 1st:3 2nd:6 3rd:2 Ran:26
Win Prizemoney £14,997 *Total Prizemoney* £25,725
Wins * 1996 Jun Hamilt (GD) H 8.3f 71 71
2000 Turf 0-3: (9f 2, 11f) (gd, g-f 2)
Very moderate gelding, has worn blinkers. Turf high 37. Becoming disappointing.
**Miss Kate Milligan [2-29] J D Gordon (from Miss S E Hall [1-7] Oct 1995).*

WESTERN HERO (IRE) BHB 78f RR 76f
4751[7]
2 ch c Lake Coniston (IRE) - Miss Pickpocket (IRE) **(68f 46a)** (Petorius) 7.3f **(61)**
Form - 332157
Record 2000 - 1st:1 2nd:1 3rd:2 Ran:6
Win Prizemoney £2,951 *Total Prizemoney* £5,068
Wins * 2000 Jly Windso (GD) 5f 71 <
2000 Turf 1-6: (5f 1-4, 6f 2) (g-s, gd 2, frm 1-3)
Above-average colt, effective 5f, acts on frm. Turf high 76 - also 1st of 13 from Avery Ring (17 Jly Windsor RF 2875). His Windsor win was not coming out of turn. Fast ground may not be ideal for him. **R Hannon [1-6] Michael Pescod.*

WESTERNMOST BHB 53f RR 41f
3845[6]
2 b g Most Welcome 8.6f **(66)** -Dakota Girl **(48f)** (Northern State (USA))
Form - 006
Record 2000 - 1st:0 2nd:0 3rd:0 Ran:3
2000 Turf 0-3: (5f, 6f, 8f) (gd, frm 2)
Currently moderate gelding. Turf high 41 (began Jly).
**T D Barron [0-3] Mrs J Hazell.*

WESTERN RAINBOW (IRE) BHB 48f59a RR 35f 59a
3468a[18]
4 b g Rainbows For Life (CAN) 9.3f **(64)** - Miss Galwegian (Sandford Lad) 7.8f **(54)**
Form - 222241260
Record 2000 - 1st:1 2nd:3 3rd:0 Ran:7
Pre2000 - 1st:0 2nd:2 3rd:0 Ran:9
Win Prizemoney £2,205 *Total Prizemoney* £5,626
Wins 2000 *Feb Lingfi (STD) 13f 45+* <
2000 Turf 0-1: (12f) (gd) 2000 AW 1-6: (9f, 12f 3, 13f 1-1, 16f) (Equi 1-1, Fibr 5)
Fair gelding, effective 12f, - acts on Fibr, has worn blinkers, prefers left handed tracks, prefers tight tracks. AW high 59 - 2nd of 8 giving 10lb to Ichi Beau (19 Feb Wolverhampton 12f Fibr RF 0323).
**R O'Leary in IRE [0-1] Mrs R O'Leary (from P D Evans [1-9] Mar 2000).*

WESTERN RIDGE (FR) BHB 85f RR 90df
5142[12]
3 b c Darshaan 11.9f **(81)** -Helvellyn (USA)(Gone West (USA)) 6.5f **(75)**
Form - 0
Record 2000 - 1st:0 2nd:0 3rd:0 Ran:1
Pre2000 - 1st:0 2nd:0 3rd:0 Ran:2
Win Prizemoney £0 *Total Prizemoney* £815
2000 Turf 0-1: (11f) (g-s)
Scopey, currently useful colt. **L M Cumani [0-3] Robert Smith.*

WESTERN SUMMER (USA) BHB 104f RR 102f
1060[13]
3 ch c Summer Squall (USA) 7f **(80)** - Mrs West (USA) (Gone West (USA)) 6.5f **(75)**
Form - 40
Record 2000 - 1st:0 2nd:0 3rd:0 Ran:2
Pre2000 - 1st:1 2nd:0 3rd:0 Ran:1
Win Prizemoney £3,720 *Total Prizemoney* £4,908
Wins * 1999 Oct Nottin (GD) 8.2f 89+ <
2000 Turf 0-2: (8f, 9f) (gd 2)
Workmanlike, currently very useful colt. Turf high 102.
**H R A Cecil [1-3] S Khaled.*

WESTERN VENTURE (IRE) BHB 26f27a RR 34f 27a
1076[6]
7 ch g Two Timing (USA) 7.1f **(58)** - Star Gazing (IRE) (Caerleon (USA)) 8.6f **(71)**
Form - 6
Record 2000 - 1st:0 2nd:0 3rd:0 Ran:1
Pre2000 - 1st:2 2nd:2 3rd:3 Ran:31
Win Prizemoney £6,599 *Total Prizemoney* £9,488

Wins 1997 Aug Hamilt (G-F) SH 9.2f 27 31
2000 Turf 0-1: (9f) (g-f)
Moderate gelding, has worn blinkers.
**I Semple [0-1] P Macrae (from Martyn Wane [1-13] Spt 1999).*

WESTGATE RUN BHB 70f RR 72f 4311[13]

3 b f Emperor Jones (USA) - Glowing Reference (Reference Point) 6.8f **(70)**
Form - 71133112100
Record 2000 - 1st:5 2nd:1 3rd:2 Ran:11
Pre2000 - 1st:0 2nd:1 3rd:1 Ran:10
Win Prizemoney £15,281 *Total Prizemoney* £19,514
Wins * 2000 Aug Ayr (G-F) H 10.9f 61 71 <
*** 2000** Jly Nottin (G-F) H 10f 61 71 <
*** 2000** Jly Bright (FRM) 11.9f 63
*** 2000** Jun Hamilt (G-F) H 9.2f 54 60+
*** 2000** Jun Warwic (G-F) H 10.5f 54 62
2000 Turf 5-11: (6f, 9f 1-1, 10f 1-3, 11f 2-2, 12f 1-4)(gd, g-f 1-2, frm 4-8)
Scopey, above-average filly, effective 7 to 12f, acts on gd to frm, best on frm, prefers left handed tracks, prefers tight tracks. Turf high 72 - 2nd of 9 getting 6lb from Najjm (30 Jly Ripon 12f frm RF 3242) - also 1st of 12 giving 4lb to Sacrementum (29 Jly Nottingham RF 3218). Improved dramatically when stepped up to middle distances and was in irresistible form last year, winning five times and maintaining her form well despite rising in the weights. Suited by fast ground. **R A Fahey [5-21] Mark Leatham.*

WESTLIFE (IRE) BHB 41f RR 30f 2193[6]

2 b f Mind Games - Enchantica **(62f 56a)** (Timeless Times (USA))
Form - 76
Record 2000 - 1st:0 2nd:0 3rd:0 Ran:2
2000 Turf 0-1: (5f) (g-s) 2000 AW 0-1: (5f) (Fibr)
Currently very moderate filly. **H J Collingridge [0-2] D Burke.*

WESTMINSTER CITY (USA) BHB 46f64a RR 52f 64a 2792[5]

4 b g Alleged (USA) 11.8f **(81)** - Promanade Fan (USA) (Timeless Moment (USA)) 6f **(72)**
Form - 5803212U0440405
Record 2000 - 1st:1 2nd:2 3rd:1 Ran:12
Pre2000 - 1st:1 2nd:0 3rd:1 Ran:14
Win Prizemoney £5,168 *Total Prizemoney* £8,472
Wins 2000 *Jan Wolver (STD) S 8.5f 55*
1998 May Lingfi (GD) 5f 76 <
2000 Turf 0-9: (8f 2, 9f, 10f 2, 12f 4) (sft, g-s 2, gd, g-f, frm 4) 2000 AW 1-3: (8f 1-1, 9f 2) (Fibr 1-3)
Light-framed, fair gelding, effective 8 to 12f, acts on frm - acts on Fibr, often wears blinkers, likes tight tracks. Turf high 56 (1st run) - 2nd of 20 getting 1lb from Zorro (27 Mar Windsor 12f frm RF 0521). AW high 55 - 1st of 12 getting 5lb from Billichang (13 Jan Wolverhampton RF 0083).
**D R C Elsworth [0-9] K Costello (from K O Cunningham-Brown [1-8] Jan 2000).*

WESTON HILLS (IRE) BHB 65f RR 73f 4321[10]

2 b c Robellino (USA) 9.5f **(68)** - Magic Milly (Simply Great (FR)) 8.2f **(65)**
Form - 780
Record 2000 - 1st:0 2nd:0 3rd:0 Ran:3
2000 Turf 0-3: (5f, 7f, 8f) (gd 2, g-f)
Currently above-average colt. Turf high 73.
**K R Burke [0-3] Mrs M Dower.*

WEST ORDER (USA) RR 85+f 4964[1]

2 ch c Gone West (USA) 7.8f **(82)** - Irish Order (USA) (Irish River (FR)) 8.6f **(78)**
Form - 11
Record 2000 - 1st:2 2nd:0 3rd:0 Ran:2
Win Prizemoney £12,983 *Total Prizemoney* £12,983
Wins * 2000 Oct Newmar (SFT) 7f 85+ <
*** 2000** Spt Newbur (G-F) 7f 85+ <
2000 Turf 2-2: (7f 2-2) (gd 1-1, g-f 1-1)
Currently useful colt. Turf high 85 (began Spt) - 1st of 6 giving 3lb to Cafe Grande (13 Oct Newmarket RF 4964) - also 1st of 22 from Halawan (16 Spt Newbury RF 4466). Showed battling qualities when making a winning debut at Newbury, but had nothing to beat when following up in the Houghton.
**R Hannon [2-2] Monsun Investments Ltd.*

WESTSIDE FLYER BHB 40f35a RR 5f 35a 41[8]

4 ch m Risk Me (FR) 8f **(53)** - Celtic River (IRE) (Caerleon (USA)) 8.6f **(71)**
Form - 8
Record 2000 - 1st:0 2nd:0 3rd:0 Ran:1
Pre2000 - 1st:1 2nd:1 3rd:1 Ran:20
Win Prizemoney £2,097 *Total Prizemoney* £3,459
Wins 1999 *Jan Southw (STD) C 6f 51* <
2000 AW 0-1: (6f) (Fibr)
Neat, fair filly, effective 6f, - acts on AW, has worn blinkers, likes left handed tracks, likes tight tracks.
**J C McConnochie [0-3] Miss B J Herring (from A Kelleway [1-18] Jly 1999).*

WESTWOOD VIEW BHB 35f23a RR 32f 23a 62[7]

4 b m Puissance 7.1f **(80)** - Long View (Persian Bold) 9.3f **(66)**
Form - 0457
Record 2000 - 1st:0 2nd:0 3rd:0 Ran:2
Pre2000 - 1st:0 2nd:0 3rd:3 Ran:19
Win Prizemoney £0 *Total Prizemoney* £1,391
2000 AW 0-2: (11f, 12f) (Fibr 2)
Scopey, very moderate filly, effective 6f, acts on g-f to frm, has worn blinkers. AW high 27. Inconsistent.
**Ronald Thompson [0-6] I Fox (from J J Quinn [0-15] Spt 1999).*

WETHAAB (USA) BHB 52f RR 55f 4000[7]

3 b c Pleasant Colony (USA) 12.4f **(88)** - Binntastic (USA) (Lyphard's Wish (FR)) 9f **(74)**
Form - 8471607
Record 2000 - 1st:1 2nd:0 3rd:0 Ran:7
Pre2000 - 1st:0 2nd:0 3rd:0 Ran:1
Win Prizemoney £2,415 *Total Prizemoney* £2,960
Wins 2000 Jun Warwic (G-F) H 12.3f 50 55 <
2000 Turf 1-7: (7f, 10f, 12f 1-4, 14f) (gd 3, g-f 1-2, frm 2)
Neat, fair colt, effective 12f, acts on g-f, often wears blinkers (very effectively), favours tight tracks. Turf high 55 - 1st of 11 getting 1lb from Lunar Lord (28 Jun Warwick RF 2357).
**G M Moore [0-2] A J Racehorses (from B W Hills [1-6] Jly 2000).*

WHALAH (USA) RR 58f 3963[10]

2 ch f Dixieland Band (USA) 10.1f **(80)** - Firm Stance (USA) (Affirmed (USA)) 9.3f **(79)**
Form - 0
Record 2000 - 1st:0 2nd:0 3rd:0 Ran:1
2000 Turf 0-1: (7f) (g-f)
Currently fair filly.
**C E Brittain [0-1] Prince Abdul Aziz Bin Saud.*

WHALE BEACH (USA) BHB 88f RR 89f 4970[3]

2 b c Known Fact (USA) 8.3f **(72)** - Zulu Dance (USA) (Danzatore (CAN)) 8.5f **(86)**
Form - 7123
Record 2000 - 1st:1 2nd:1 3rd:1 Ran:4
Win Prizemoney £3,705 *Total Prizemoney* £6,973
Wins * 2000 Aug Windso (G-F) 6f 72 <
2000 Turf 1-4: (6f 1-2, 7f, 8f) (gd, g-f 1-1, frm 2)
Useful colt. Turf high 89 (began Aug) - 3rd of 21 giving 11lb to Regatta Point (13 Oct Newmarket 8f gd RF 4970).
**B W Hills [1-4] C Wright & The Hon Mrs J M Corbett.*

WHARFEDALE CYGNET BHB 48f RR 36f 3334[7]

2 b f King's Signet (USA) 7f **(51)** - Your Care (FR) **(37f)** (Caerwent)
Form - 647
Record 2000 - 1st:0 2nd:0 3rd:0 Ran:3
Win Prizemoney £0 *Total Prizemoney* £215
2000 Turf 0-3: (5f 3) (g-f, frm 2)
Currently very moderate filly. Turf high 36.
**W T Kemp [0-3] Drakemyre Racing.*

WHARFEDALE GHOST RR 19f 2270[5]

2 gr c King Among Kings 7.4f **(49)** - Heavenly Pet (Petong) 6.6f **(58)**
Form - 005
Record 2000 - 1st:0 2nd:0 3rd:0 Ran:3
2000 Turf 0-2: (5f, 7f) (frm 2) 2000 AW 0-1: (5f) (Fibr)
Currently poor colt. Turf high 19.
**W T Kemp [0-3] Drakemyre Racing.*

WHARFEDALE LADY BHB 48f **RR 55f** 4381[13]
2 b f Charmer 9f **(59)** - Ladysave (Stanford) 7.9f **(56)**
Form - 770860
Record 2000 - 1st:0 2nd:0 3rd:0 Ran:6
2000 Turf 0-6: (5f 2, 6f 2, 7f, 8f) (gd 2, g-f, frm 3)
Fair filly. Turf high 55. **W T Kemp [0-6] Drakemyre Racing.*

WHATA BRAINSTORM (USA) RR 109f 4835a[2]
3 br c Honor Grades (USA) - What A Future (USA) (Roberto (USA)) 10f **(76)**
Form - 2
2000 Turf 0-1: (12f) (frm)
Currently Pattern-class colt. (1st run) - 2nd of 10 getting 8lb from Ciro (24 Spt Belmont Park 12f frm RF 4835a). **in USA [0-1].*

WHAT A CRACKER BHB 30f **RR 38f** 4228[9]
3 b f Bustino 11f **(64)** - Moon Spin (Night Shift (USA)) 7.2f **(69)**
Form - 6000
Record 2000 - 1st:0 2nd:0 3rd:0 Ran:4
Pre2000 - 1st:0 2nd:0 3rd:0 Ran:3
2000 Turf 0-3: (12f, 14f, 16f) (g-f 2, frm) 2000 AW 0-1: (12f) (Equi)
Scopey, very moderate filly. Turf high 37 (began Aug).
**M P Tregoning [0-7] Mrs Hugh Dalgety.*

WHAT-A-DANCER (IRE) BHB 54f **RR 51f** 3960[6]
3 b g Dancing Dissident (USA) 6.8f **(65)** - Cool Gales (Lord Gayle (USA)) 8.8f **(62)**
Form - 726
Record 2000 - 1st:0 2nd:1 3rd:0 Ran:3
Win Prizemoney £0 *Total Prizemoney* £912
2000 Turf 0-3: (7f, 9f, 10f) (frm 2, hrd)
Unfurnished, currently fair gelding. Turf high 51 (began Jly) - 2nd of 10 giving 5lb to Berzoud (13 Aug Redcar 9f frm RF 3613).
**W W Haigh [0-3] Alan Swinbank.*

WHAT A FUSS BHB 41f51a **RR 42f 51a** 658[16]
7 b g Great Commotion (USA) 9.2f **(80)** - Hafwah (Gorytus (USA)) 7.8f **(60)**
Form - 0
Record 2000 - 1st:0 2nd:0 3rd:0 Ran:1
Pre2000 - 1st:2 2nd:3 3rd:1 Ran:15
Win Prizemoney £6,305 *Total Prizemoney* £9,210
Wins 1997 Jly Yarmou (GD) H 11.5f 58 61
1997 Jan Wolver (STD) H 7f 64 67 <
2000 Turf 0-1: (10f) (g-s)
Average gelding. Becoming disappointing.
**M W Easterby [2-10] Mrs Denise Shefras (from B Hanbury [2-13] Jly 1997).*

WHATSITSNAME BHB 28f28a **RR 28a** 387[13]
4 br g Tragic Role (USA) 9.4f **(63)** - Princess Yasmin (USA) (Le Fabuleux) 11.4f **(76)**
Form - 85000
Record 2000 - 1st:0 2nd:0 3rd:0 Ran:2
Pre2000 - 1st:0 2nd:0 3rd:0 Ran:4
2000 AW 0-2: (9f, 10f) (Equi, Fibr)
Leggy, poor gelding. AW high 19. **J L Eyre [0-6] T S Ely.*

WHATTA MADAM BHB 51f43a **RR 48f 43a** 1458[7]
4 gr m Whittingham (IRE) - Sylvan Song (Song) 7.2f **(61)**
Form - 644057
Record 2000 - 1st:0 2nd:0 3rd:0 Ran:4
Pre2000 - 1st:0 2nd:3 3rd:3 Ran:18
Win Prizemoney £0 *Total Prizemoney* £2,809
2000 Turf 0-2: (6f 2) (gd, frm) 2000 AW 0-2: (6f 2) (Equi, Fibr)
Light-framed, moderate filly, effective 6f, acts on g-s to hrd, has worn blinkers. Turf high 48. AW high 31.
**G L Moore [0-22] Mark Barrett.*

WHEN IN ROME RR 93f 4610[6]
2 b c Saddlers' Hall (IRE) 10.5f **(65)** - Seasonal Splendour (IRE) **(80f)** (Prince Rupert (FR))
Form - 636
Record 2000 - 1st:0 2nd:0 3rd:1 Ran:3
Win Prizemoney £0 *Total Prizemoney* £427
2000 Turf 0-3: (8f 3) (g-s, g-f 2)
Currently useful colt. Turf high 93 (began Aug).
**C A Cyzer [0-3] Mrs E A Cyzer.*

WHENWILLIEMETHARRY BHB 60f46a **RR 69f 46a** 1254[13]
3 b f Sabrehill (USA) 8.5f **(64)** - William's Bird (USA) (Master Willie) 7f **(70)**
Form - 60
Record 2000 - 1st:0 2nd:0 3rd:0 Ran:2
Pre2000 - 1st:0 2nd:0 3rd:0 Ran:6
Win Prizemoney £0 *Total Prizemoney* £260
2000 Turf 0-2: (8f, 10f) (gd, g-f)
Unfurnished, average filly, effective 7 to 10f, acts on gd to g-f. Turf high 69 (1st run) - 6th of 15 getting 4lb from Bless The Bride (2 May Bath 10f gd RF 0965). **D R C Elsworth [0-8] Harry Redknapp.*

WHERE'S CHARLOTTE BHB 47f43a **RR 70f 43a** 3[6]
3 b f Sure Blade (USA) 10.6f **(66)** - One Degree (Crooner) 9.9f **(49)**
Form - 3006
Record 2000 - 1st:0 2nd:0 3rd:0 Ran:1
Pre2000 - 1st:0 2nd:1 3rd:1 Ran:10
Win Prizemoney £0 *Total Prizemoney* £1,142
2000 AW 0-1: (6f) (Equi)
Scopey, above-average filly. Inconsistent.
**R Hannon [0-11] Peter Crane.*

WHERE'S JASPER (IRE) BHB 92f **RR 89f** 4747[5]
2 ch g Common Grounds 8.1f **(66)** - Stifen (Burslem) 8.8f **(53)**
Form - 2120105
Record 2000 - 1st:2 2nd:2 3rd:0 Ran:7
Win Prizemoney £10,534 *Total Prizemoney* £17,534
Wins * 2000 Aug Haydoc (GD) 6f 89 <
*** 2000** Jun Haydoc (G-S) 6f 76
2000 Turf 2-7: (5f 2, 6f 2-5) (g-s 1-1, gd 4, g-f 1-1, hrd)
Useful gelding, effective 6f, acts on gd to g-f. Turf high 89 - also 1st of 5 giving 5lb to Galapagos Girl (11 Aug Haydock RF 3549). Won well on his second start before a useful effort at Goodwood. Finished in midfield in a warm race at Newbury before winning at Haydock. Well beaten in a Doncaster sales race.
**K A Ryan [2-7] Jimm Racing.*

WHERE THE HEART IS BHB 76f **RR 84f** 4970[19]
2 ch c Efisio 7.7f **(69)** - Luminary (Kalaglow) 9.8f **(67)**
Form - 3540
Record 2000 - 1st:0 2nd:0 3rd:1 Ran:4
Win Prizemoney £0 *Total Prizemoney* £880
2000 Turf 0-4: (6f, 7f 2, 8f) (gd 3, frm)
Decent colt. Turf high 84 (began Jly).
**M H Tompkins [0-4] www raceworld co uk.*

WHISKY NINE RR 41f 4725[7]
2 b c Makbul - Indivisible (Remainder Man) 11.2f **(45)**
Form - 7
Record 2000 - 1st:0 2nd:0 3rd:0 Ran:1
2000 Turf 0-1: (6f) (gd)
Currently moderate colt. **M A Jarvis [0-1] Miss V C Arnold.*

WHISTLER RR 92+f 5127[3]
3 ch g Selkirk (USA) 7.9f **(76)** - French Gift **(92f)** (Cadeaux Genereux)
Form - 2412153
Record 2000 - 1st:2 2nd:2 3rd:1 Ran:7
Pre2000 - 1st:0 2nd:1 3rd:1 Ran:4
Win Prizemoney £8,986 *Total Prizemoney* £16,649
Wins * 2000 Spt Newmar (GD) H 5f 79 82 <
*** 2000** Jly Salisb (FRM) 6f 76
2000 Turf 2-7: (5f 1-4, 6f 1-3) (g-s, gd 2, g-f 1-2, frm 1-1, hrd)
Leggy, useful gelding, effective 5f, acts on g-s to g-f. Turf high 92 (began Jly) - 3rd of 18 getting 11lb from Dancing Mystery (21 Oct Doncaster 5f g-s RF 5127). Improving. Progressing well, he beat a big field in a Newmarket handicap in September.
**R Hannon [2-11] Raymond Tooth.*

WHISTLING DIXIE (IRE) BHB 46f39a **RR 49f 39a** 4764[6]
4 ch g Forest Wind (USA) - Camden's Gift (Camden Town) 9.3f **(53)**
Form - 2601415306
Record 2000 - 1st:2 2nd:1 3rd:1 Ran:10
Pre2000 - 1st:0 2nd:2 3rd:1 Ran:19
Win Prizemoney £5,201 *Total Prizemoney* £9,774
Wins * 2000 Jly Lingfi (GD) H 10f 40 47 <
*** 2000** Jly Pontef (GD) H 10f 40 44

2000 Turf 2-8: (10f 2-6, 12f 2) (g-s, gd, g-f 1-3, frm 1-3) 2000 AW 0-2: (11f, 14f) (Fibr 2)
Leggy, moderate gelding, has worn blinkers, likes left handed tracks, likes tight tracks. Turf high 49. AW high 36.
**D Nicholls [2-10] Mrs P D Savill (from T J Etherington [0-14] Oct 1999).*

WHISTLING JACK (IRE) BHB 50f RR 617[18]

4 b g Roi Danzig (USA) 10.5f **(62)** - Candy's Sister (Great Nephew) 9.9f **(64)**
Form - 0
Record 2000 - 1st:0 2nd:0 3rd:0 Ran:1
Pre2000 - 1st:1 2nd:0 3rd:1 Ran:6
Win Prizemoney £2,532 *Total Prizemoney* £2,918
Wins * 1998 Oct Nottin (SFT) 10f 68 <
2000 Turf 0-1: (12f) (gd)
Scopey, average gelding. **D J Moohan [1-9] R J Meehan.*

WHITE AMIT RR 39f 4475[10]

2 b f Shaamit (IRE) - White African (Carwhite) 7.2f **(61)**
Form - 80
Record 2000 - 1st:0 2nd:0 3rd:0 Ran:2
2000 Turf 0-1: (7f) (g-f) 2000 AW 0-1: (8f) (Fibr)
Currently very moderate filly. **J A Gilbert [0-2] James Gilbert.*

WHITE EMIR BHB 66f RR 66f 4619[1]

7 b g Emarati (USA) 6.6f **(63)** - White African (Carwhite) 7.2f **(61)**
Form - 8321401
Record 2000 - 1st:2 2nd:1 3rd:1 Ran:6
Pre2000 - 1st:4 2nd:9 3rd:8 Ran:59
Win Prizemoney £23,388 *Total Prizemoney* £61,116
Wins * **2000** Spt Bright (SFT) H 7f 61 66
* **2000** Jly Kempto (G-F) H 7f 59 64
1997 Jun Salisb (G-S) H 5f 80 80 <
1997 Jun Sandow (G-F) C 5f 80 <
2000 Turf 2-6: (7f 2-5, 8f) (gd 1-2, g-f 2, frm 1-2)
Average gelding, effective 6 to 8f, best at 7f, acts on gd to frm, best on frm, has worn blinkers (extremely effectively), likes left handed tracks. Turf high 66 - 1st of 16 getting 8lb from Padhams Green (24 Spt Brighton RF 4619) - also 1st of 16 getting 3lb from Pengamon (19 Jly Kempton RF 2936). Consistent.
**L G Cottrell [2-6] Miss D M Stafford (from B R Millman [0-23] Dec 1999).*

WHITEFOOT RR 106f 2178[5]

3 b f Be My Chief (USA) 10.2f **(62)** - Kelimutu (Top Ville) 11.7f **(68)**
Form - 4105
Record 2000 - 1st:1 2nd:0 3rd:0 Ran:4
Pre2000 - 1st:1 2nd:0 3rd:1 Ran:3
Win Prizemoney £18,743 *Total Prizemoney* £24,044
Wins * **2000** May Newbur (G-F) L 10f 106 <
1999 Spt Sandow (G-F) 8.1f 90
2000 Turf 1-4: (10f 1-2, 12f 2) (sft, g-s, gd 1-1, g-f)
Unfurnished, Pattern-class filly, effective 10f, acts on gd. Turf high 106 - 1st of 14 from Circle of Light (19 May Newbury RF 1305). She stayed on dourly from behind a strong pace when winning a Listed heat at Newbury in May, but looked slow in the Oaks and Ribblesdale Stakes. She may be open to improvement over two miles. **G A Butler [1-4] Gary Tanaka (from J Pearce [1-3] Oct 1999).*

WHITEGATE WAY BHB 45f RR 64f 4202[11]

3 b f Greensmith - Lady Longmead (Crimson Beau) 9.8f **(52)**
Form - 804700
Record 2000 - 1st:0 2nd:0 3rd:0 Ran:6
Win Prizemoney £0 *Total Prizemoney* £315
2000 Turf 0-6: (7f 3, 8f 3) (gd 2, frm 3, hrd)
Unfurnished, average filly. Turf high 64. **A Bailey [0-6] J E Bownes.*

WHITE HOUSE BHB 77f RR 82f 5323[20]

3 b f Pursuit of Love 9.5f **(69)** - Much Too Risky (Bustino) 10.4f **(64)**
Form - 443100
Record 2000 - 1st:1 2nd:0 3rd:1 Ran:6
Pre2000 - 1st:0 2nd:0 3rd:0 Ran:1
Win Prizemoney £4,060 *Total Prizemoney* £5,494
Wins * **2000** Aug Ayr (G-F) 10f 82 <
2000 Turf 1-6: (9f, 10f 1-3, 12f, 14f) (sft 2, gd, g-f, frm 1-2)
Workmanlike, decent filly, effective 10f, acts on gd to frm. Turf high 82 - 1st of 3 getting 6lb from Golden Chance (4 Aug Ayr RF 3359). Winner of a three-runner Ayr maiden, she should stay a mile and a half. **W Jarvis [1-7] J M Greetham.*

WHITE MAGIC (IRE) RR 28f 3632[9]

3 b f Rainbows For Life (CAN) 9.3f **(64)** - Shamanka (IRE) (Shernazar) 10.2f **(73)**
Form - 00
Record 2000 - 1st:0 2nd:0 3rd:0 Ran:2
Pre2000 - 1st:0 2nd:0 3rd:0 Ran:1
2000 Turf 0-2: (8f, 12f) (g-f, frm)
Neat, currently little account filly. Turf high 10 (began Jly).
**G B Balding [0-3] Baldings (Training) Ltd.*

WHITE MARVEL BHB 67f RR 77f 3079[7]

2 b f Polar Falcon (USA) 9f **(74)** - Million Heiress (Auction Ring (USA)) 8.6f **(65)**
Form - 637
Record 2000 - 1st:0 2nd:0 3rd:1 Ran:3
Win Prizemoney £0 *Total Prizemoney* £318
2000 Turf 0-3: (5f, 6f 2) (g-f 2, frm)
Currently above-average filly. Turf high 77 - 3rd of 6 to Young Alex (6 Jly Chepstow 6f g-f RF 2564).
**N P Littmoden [0-1] Richard Green (Fine Paintings) (from W J Haggas [0-2] Jly 2000).*

WHITE PLAINS (IRE) BHB 58f70a RR 45f 70a 4761[11]

7 b g Nordico (USA) 8.2f **(59)** - Flying Diva (Chief Singer) 8.9f **(66)**
Form - 433114833350O
Record 2000 - 1st:1 2nd:0 3rd:3 Ran:9
Pre2000 - 1st:12 2nd:6 3rd:9 Ran:61
Win Prizemoney £55,670 *Total Prizemoney* £77,554
Wins 2000 *Jan Lingfi (STD)* H *10f 79 90* <
1999 *Dec Lingfi (STD)* H *12f 79 85*
1999 *Feb Lingfi (STD)* *10f 89*
1998 *Feb Southw (STD)* *12f 84*
1997 *Dec Lingfi (STD)* H *10f 72 90+*
1997 *Dec Lingfi (STD)* H *10f 69 75+*
1997 Jly Hamilt (G-S) C 9.2f 81
1997 Apr Nottin (G-F) H 10f 75 80
1996 Spt Lingfi (FRM) H 10f 70 74
1996 Spt Leices (FRM) H 10f 71 75+
1996 Aug Newcas (G-F) 9f 72
1996 Jun Lingfi (FRM) H 10f 68 74
2000 AW 1-9: (9f, 10f 1-4, 12f 4) (Equi 1-7, Fibr 2)
Decent gelding, effective 10 to 12f, best at 10f, - acts on AW, best on Equi, favours left handed tracks, favours tight tracks, excels at Lingfield. AW high 90 (1st run) - 1st of 13 giving 10lb to Anemos (2 Jan Lingfield RF 0005). Inconsistent. A smart performer on sand on his day, especially Equitrack, his performances lacked consistency last year and he tended to struggle against the better sand performers.
**T D Barron [0-1] Nigel Shields (from K R Burke [7-49] Mar 2000).*

WHITE SANDS BHB 35f38a RR 31f 38a 4221[8]

3 b f Green Desert (USA) 7.8f **(78)** - Carte Blanche **(47f 57a)** (Cadeaux Genereux)
Form - 0006008
Record 2000 - 1st:0 2nd:0 3rd:0 Ran:7
Pre2000 - 1st:0 2nd:0 3rd:0 Ran:1
2000 Turf 0-3: (7f, 8f 2) (gd, g-f, frm) 2000 AW 0-4: (6f, 8f, 10f, 12f) (Equi 3, Fibr)
Scopey, very moderate filly. Turf high 31. AW high 31.
**C A Cyzer [0-8] R M Cyzer.*

WHITE SETTLER BHB 52f49a RR 50f 49a 4875[10]

7 b g Polish Patriot (USA) 7.8f **(70)** - Oasis (Valiyar) 8.5f **(73)**
Form - 3100
Record 2000 - 1st:1 2nd:0 3rd:1 Ran:4
Pre2000 - 1st:3 2nd:3 3rd:5 Ran:29
Win Prizemoney £10,839 *Total Prizemoney* £16,223
Wins * **2000** Spt Yarmou (G-F) S 7f 49
* 1998 Spt Chepst (G-S) S 8.1f 56+
1998 Apr Leices (SFT) S 7f 63
1996 Jly Chepst (G-F) H 7.1f 64 67 <
2000 Turf 1-4: (7f 1-2, 8f 2) (g-s, g-f, frm 1-2)
Fair gelding, has worn blinkers. Turf high 50 (began Aug). Ran his best race of '97 so far when third at Salisbury in July.
**Miss S J Wilton [2-13] John Pointon and Sons (from R J Hodges [2-17]*

Apr 1998).

WHITE STAR LADY BHB 59f RR 62f 5102[16]

2 ch f So Factual (USA) - Cottonwood (Teenoso (USA)) 9.9f **(72)**
Form - 5850130
Record 2000 - 1st:1 2nd:0 3rd:1 Ran:7
Win Prizemoney £2,716 *Total Prizemoney* £3,176
Wins * **2000** Aug Mussel (G-F) S 5f 62 <
2000 Turf 1-6: (5f 1-4, 6f 2) (g-s, gd, g-f 1-2, frm, hrd) 2000 AW 0-1: (5f) (Fibr)
Average filly, effective 5 to 6f, acts on g-f. Turf high 62 (began Jly) - 3rd of 19 getting 10lb from Lady Kinvarrah (18 Spt Leicester 6f g-f RF 4490) - also 1st of 10 getting 5lb from Amamackemmush (24 Aug Musselburgh RF 3926). **J R Weymes [1-7] White Star Racing.*

WHITE SUMMIT BHB 39f RR 46f 5112[20]

3 b g Mistertopogigo (IRE) - White Heat **(41f 46a)** (Last Tycoon) 8.5f **(62)**
Form - 0006700
Record 2000 - 1st:0 2nd:0 3rd:0 Ran:7
Pre2000 - 1st:0 2nd:0 3rd:0 Ran:4
2000 Turf 0-7: (5f 5, 6f 2) (gd 2, g-f, frm 4)
Scopey, moderate gelding, has worn blinkers. Turf high 46 (began Jly). Inconsistent. **B Palling [0-11] Whitehall Barn Racing Partnership.*

WHITE WATERS (IRE) BHB 48f RR 51f 689[17]

4 b g Great Commotion (USA) 9.2f **(80)** - Water Spirit (USA) (Riverman (USA)) 9.1f **(76)**
Form - 60
Record 2000 - 1st:0 2nd:0 3rd:0 Ran:2
Pre2000 - 1st:0 2nd:0 3rd:0 Ran:3
2000 Turf 0-1: (11f) (hvy) 2000 AW 0-1: (7f) (Equi)
Leggy, fair gelding.
**Mrs P Townsley [0-4] The Village Idiot Partnership (from C A Dwyer [0-3] May 1999).*

WHITE WILLOW BHB 35f58a RR 1f 58a 2839[9]

11 br g Touching Wood (USA) - Dimant Blanche (USA) (Gummo (USA))
Form - 40
Record 2000 - 1st:0 2nd:0 3rd:0 Ran:2
Pre2000 - 1st:4 2nd:6 3rd:6 Ran:36
Win Prizemoney £13,040 *Total Prizemoney* £26,756
2000 Turf 0-1: (14f) (frm) 2000 AW 0-1: (16f) (Fibr)
Very poor gelding, has worn blinkers. Becoming disappointing.
**R Brotherton [0-2] Paul Stringer (from T Wall [0-2] Jan 1997).*

WHITGIFT ROSE BHB 77f RR 76f 3052[2]

3 b br f Polar Falcon (USA) 9f **(74)** - Celtic Wing (Midyan (USA)) 6f **(60)**
Form - 842
Record 2000 - 1st:0 2nd:1 3rd:0 Ran:3
Win Prizemoney £0 *Total Prizemoney* £1,658
2000 Turf 0-3: (8f 2, 10f) (gd, frm 2)
Unfurnished, currently above-average filly. Turf high 74 - 2nd of 9 getting 5lb from Summer View (23 Jly Kempton 8f frm RF 3052).
**Lady Herries [0-3] Whitgift Racing Ltd.*

WHITLEYGRANGE GIRL BHB 35f30a RR 19f 30a 4774[6]

3 b f Rudimentary (USA) 8.2f **(66)** - Choir's Image **(10f)** (Lochnager) 6f **(59)**
Form - 67576
Record 2000 - 1st:0 2nd:0 3rd:0 Ran:5
2000 Turf 0-2: (6f, 7f) (g-s 2) 2000 AW 0-3: (7f 2, 8f) (Equi, Fibr 2)
Leggy, poor filly. Turf high 19 (began Spt). AW high 10.
**J L Eyre [0-5] Mrs Carole Sykes.*

WHIZZ RR 5314[6]

3 b f Salse (USA) 10.9f **(71)** - Cut Ahead (Kalaglow) 9.8f **(67)**
Form - 6
Record 2000 - 1st:0 2nd:0 3rd:0 Ran:1
2000 Turf 0-1: (10f) (sft)
Currently very poor filly. **R Charlton [0-1] Lady Rothschild.*

WHIZZ KID BHB 64f49a RR 67f 49a 5068[17]

6 b m Puissance 7.1f **(60)** -Panienka (POL)(Dom Racine (FR)) 9.2f **(62)**
Form - 70512312601008000057260
Record 2000 - 1st:3 2nd:3 3rd:1 Ran:22
Pre2000 - 1st:6 2nd:1 3rd:4 Ran:52
Win Prizemoney £36,715 *Total Prizemoney* £44,254

Wins								
* **2000**	Jly	Chepst	(G-F)	H	5.1f	67	69	<
* **2000**	*May*	*Wolver*	*(STD)*	*H*	*6f*	*37*	*43*	
* **2000**	Apr	Warwic	(HVY)	H	5f	56	61	
* 1999	Oct	Newcas	(G-S)	H	5f	57	58	
* 1999	Jly	Ayr	(GD)	H	5f	57	59	
* 1999	May	Chepst	(G-S)	H	5.1f	53	59	
* 1999	Apr	Redcar	(G-S)	H	5f	46	47	
* 1999	Apr	Ripon	(G-S)	H	5f	34	43	
1996	Jun	Windso	(G-F)	S	5f		67	

2000 Turf 2-19: (5f 2-17, 6f 2) (hvy 1-1, g-s 4, gd 4, g-f 1-6, frm 3, hrd)
2000 AW 1-3: (5f 2, 6f 1-1) (Fibr 1-3)
Average mare, effective 5f, acts on hvy to g-f, has worn blinkers, does well at Chepstow and Redcar. Turf high 69 - 1st of 10 getting 6lb from Eastern Trumpeter (6 Jly Chepstow RF 2568) - also 1st of 20 giving 13lb to Seven Springs (24 Apr Warwick RF 0858). AW high 43. She missed the whole of 1998, but won five times last season and regained winning ways last year at Warwick in April and has won twice since, one of which was on Fibresand. She can handle fast ground, but ideally needs some cut, the minimum trip, and a strongly-run race.
**J M Bradley [8-43] B Paling (from J J Bridger [1-31] Dec 1997).*

WHO CARES WINS BHB 73f RR 75f 2826[14]

4 ch h Kris 10f **(75)** - Anne Bonny (Ajdal (USA)) 9.2f **(89)**
Form - 000340
Record 2000 - 1st:0 2nd:0 3rd:1 Ran:6
Pre2000 - 1st:1 2nd:1 3rd:2 Ran:6
Win Prizemoney £3,616 *Total Prizemoney* £13,434
Wins * 1999 Jun Cheste (G-F) 13.4f 69 <
2000 Turf 0-6: (11f, 12f 2, 13f, 14f 2) (gd 2, g-f 4)
Scopey, above-average colt, effective 11 to 14f, best at 14f, acts on gd to g-f, best on g-f, has worn blinkers. Turf high 75 - 3rd of 6 getting 5lb from Total Delight (17 Jun Sandown 14f g-f RF 2057).
**C E Brittain [1-12] Khalifa Dasmal.*

WHO DA LEADER (IRE) BHB 43f RR 58f 3484[15]

3 b g Brief Truce (USA) 9.1f **(73)** - Lingdale Lass (Petong) 6.6f **(58)**
Form - 0506800
Record 2000 - 1st:0 2nd:0 3rd:0 Ran:7
Pre2000 - 1st:0 2nd:1 3rd:0 Ran:6
Win Prizemoney £0 *Total Prizemoney* £1,395
2000 Turf 0-7: (7f, 8f 5, 10f) (gd, g-f 3, frm 3)
Neat, fair gelding, effective 5f, acts on frm, has worn blinkers. Turf high 58. **R Hannon [0-13] Buddy Hackett.*

WHO GOES THERE BHB 33a RR 56f 4188[16]

4 ch m Wolfhound (USA) 7.3f **(71)** - Challanging (Mill Reef (USA)) 10.5f **(78)**
Form - 50002003816170
Record 2000 - 1st:2 2nd:1 3rd:1 Ran:14
Pre2000 - 1st:0 2nd:3 3rd:1 Ran:16
Win Prizemoney £5,715 *Total Prizemoney* £9,823
Wins * **2000** Aug Lingfi (G-F) H 7f 52 56 <
* **2000** Jly Chepst (FRM) H 7.1f 46 50
2000 Turf 2-12: (6f, 7f 2-8, 8f 2, 10f) (gd 5, g-f 2, frm 2-4, hrd) 2000 AW 0-2: (8f, 10f) (Equi 2)
Neat, fair filly, effective 7 to 9f, best at 7f, acts on g-s to frm, best on frm. Turf high 56 - 1st of 18 giving 5lb to Cappellina (11 Aug Lingfield RF 3554) - also 1st of 18 giving 10lb to Mujkari (28 Jly Chepstow RF 3171). AW high 27.
**T M Jones [2-30] The Rest Hill Partnership.*

WHYOME (IRE) BHB 105f RR 105f 733[3]

3 b c Owington - Al Corniche (IRE) **(45f 37a)** (Bluebird (USA)) 7.5f **(69)**
Form - 3
Record 2000 - 1st:0 2nd:0 3rd:1 Ran:1
Pre2000 - 1st:2 2nd:3 3rd:1 Ran:8
Win Prizemoney £11,682 *Total Prizemoney* £48,039
Wins * 1999 Aug Pontef (GD) 8f 88+
* 1999 Jun Nottin (GD) 6.1f 93+ <
2000 Turf 0-1: (8f) (gd)
Workmanlike, Pattern-class colt, effective 8f, acts on g-f.
**M L W Bell [2-9] Thurloe Thoroughbreds IV.*

WICKHAM BHB 38f RR 16tf 3191[10]

4 b m Thowra (FR) 11.2f **(47)** - Lizzy Cantle (Homing) 7.8f **(59)**

Form - 00000
Record 2000 - 1st:0 2nd:0 3rd:0 Ran:5
Pre2000 - 1st:0 2nd:0 3rd:0 Ran:1
2000 Turf 0-4: (7f, 8f 2, 12f) (gd, g-f 3) 2000 AW 0-1: (8f) (Fibr)
Strong, poor filly, has worn blinkers. Turf high 16.
**G G Margarson [0-5] Brian Cantle (from R Simpson [0-1] Oct 1998).*

WIDAR RR 100f 463[3]
6 b h Soviet Star (USA) 8.6f **(74)** - Waseela (IRE) (Ahonoora) 8.1f **(73)**
Form - 3
2000 AW 0-1: (10f) (Equi)
Very useful horse. (1st run) - 3rd of 14 to Zanay (18 Mar Lingfield 10f Equi RF 0463). This German raider was a fine third in the Winter Derby at Lingfield.
**A Lowe in GER [1-4] Niklas Kaloudis Reih Ubber.*

WIGMAN LADY (IRE) BHB 57f **RR 73df** 1389[8]
3 b f Tenby 10.4f **(76)** - Height of Elegance (Shirley Heights) 10.3f **(74)**
Form - 58
Record 2000 - 1st:0 2nd:0 3rd:0 Ran:2
Pre2000 - 1st:0 2nd:0 3rd:1 Ran:1
Win Prizemoney £0 *Total Prizemoney* £247
2000 Turf 0-2: (7f, 10f) (gd 2)
Leggy, currently above-average filly. Turf high 44.
**M Brittain [0-3] & Mrs J M Swinglehurst & Partners.*

WILBY WILLIE RR 37f 2973[15]
4 bl g Bob's Return (IRE) - Kev's Lass (IRE) (Kemal (FR))
Form - 0
Record 2000 - 1st:0 2nd:0 3rd:0 Ran:1
Pre2000 - 1st:0 2nd:0 3rd:0 Ran:1
2000 Turf 0-1: (10f) (frm)
Light-framed, currently very moderate gelding.
**C M Kinane [0-1] Exors of the late G A Hubbard (from G A Hubbard [0-1] Jly 1999).*

WILCOY WARRIER RR 742[P]
4 ch g Desert Dirham (USA) - Noirianna (Morston (FR)) 9.4f **(55)**
Form - 0P
Record 2000 - 1st:0 2nd:0 3rd:0 Ran:2
Pre2000 - 1st:0 2nd:0 3rd:0 Ran:1
2000 AW 0-2: (8f, 9f) (Fibr 2)
Light-framed, very poor gelding. (DEAD)
**P Eccles [0-3] Wilson & Coyle.*

WILCUMA BHB 77f **RR 84f** 5125[8]
9 b g Most Welcome 8.6f **(66)** -Miss Top Ville (FR) (Top Ville) 11.7f **(68)**
Form - 01553838
Record 2000 - 1st:1 2nd:0 3rd:2 Ran:8
Pre2000 - 1st:7 2nd:2 3rd:5 Ran:38
Win Prizemoney £105,733 *Total Prizemoney* £125,108
Wins * 2000 *Jan Wolver (STD) H 16.2f 80 84*
* 1996 Dec Evry (HLD) L 10f 109 <
* 1996 Oct Newbur (SFT) H 9f 100 107
* 1996 Jly York (GD) H 10.4f 89 97
2000 Turf 0-5: (12f 2, 13f 2, 14f) (hvy, g-s, gd 2, g-f) 2000 AW 1-3: (11f, 16f 1-2) (Fibr 1-3)
Decent gelding, effective 13 to 16f, acts on gd to g-f - acts on Fibr, best on gd, has worn blinkers, likes tight tracks. Turf high 84 - 3rd of 14 giving 23lb to Exalted (8 Apr Hamilton 13f gd RF 0642). AW high 84 - 1st of 6 giving 9lb to Fiori (22 Jan Wolverhampton RF 0141). Inconsistent. The 1996 Magnet Cup winner, he had been in the doldrums for a while, but was dramatically stepped up in trip for his sand debut at Wolverhampton in January and it did the trick. Has been running over shorter trips on Turf, but there is probably another little staying handicap in him.
**P J Makin [8-46] T G Warner.*

WILD COLONIAL BOY (IRE) BHB 27f **RR 28f** 4112[15]
5 b g Warning 8.1f **(77)** - Loch Clair (IRE) (Lomond (USA)) 8.8f **(65)**
Form - 4470060
Record 2000 - 1st:0 2nd:0 3rd:0 Ran:7
Pre2000 - 1st:0 2nd:2 3rd:3 Ran:18
Win Prizemoney £0 *Total Prizemoney* £4,007
2000 Turf 0-5: (14f, 16f 2, 18f, 20f) (gd 3, g-f, frm) 2000 AW 0-2: (16f 2) (Equi 2)
Moderate gelding, effective 16f, - acts on Equi, has worn blinkers, likes left handed tracks, likes tight tracks. Turf high 34. AW high 40 (1st run) - 4th of 7 getting 32lb from Harik (19 Feb Lingfield 16f Equi RF 0317). He has a long name but appears not to be long on talent.
**G P Enright [0-10] The Jack Duggan Trio (from R Hannon [0-15] Oct 1998).*

WILDERNESS (USA) RR 46f 4128[7]
3 b f Gilded Time (USA) 7f **(76)** - Dark of The Moon (Dancing Brave (USA)) 8.4f **(76)**
Form - 07
Record 2000 - 1st:0 2nd:0 3rd:0 Ran:2
Pre2000 - 1st:0 2nd:0 3rd:0 Ran:1
2000 Turf 0-2: (14f 2) (g-f, frm)
Leggy, moderate filly. Turf high 46 (began Jly).
**A J McNae [0-2] J Willoughby (from I A Balding [0-1] Aug 1999).*

WILD FLIGHT BHB 40f **RR 37f** 1552[9]
3 b g Alflora (IRE) - Absolutely Nuts (Absalom) 7.2f **(58)**
Form - 00
Record 2000 - 1st:0 2nd:0 3rd:0 Ran:1
Pre2000 - 1st:0 2nd:0 3rd:0 Ran:2
2000 Turf 0-1: (10f) (g-f)
Light-framed, very moderate gelding. (DEAD)
**T P Tate [0-3] T P Tate.*

WILDFLOWER BHB 78f **RR 79f** 4753[3]
3 b f Namaqualand (USA) - Fajjoura (IRE) **(88f)** (Fairy King (USA)) 7.7f **(59)**
Form - 1700413
Record 2000 - 1st:2 2nd:0 3rd:1 Ran:7
Win Prizemoney £8,622 *Total Prizemoney* £9,968
Wins * 2000 Spt Goodwo (SFT) H 7f 68 75 <
*** 2000** Apr Kempto (SFT) 7f 68
2000 Turf 2-7: (5f, 6f, 7f 2-5) (sft 1-1, g-s 1-2, g-f 2, frm 2)
Scopey, above-average filly, effective 7f, acts on g-s. Turf high 79 - 3rd of 16 giving 9lb to Slumbering (30 Spt Sandown 7f g-s RF 4753) - also 1st of 12 getting 2lb from Cape Coast (21 Spt Goodwood RF 4551).
**R Charlton [2-7] Anglia Bloodstock Syndicate 1998.*

WILD IMAGINATION (USA) RR 1628a[3]
6 b g Wild Again (USA) 10.7f **(69)** - La Fantastique (USA) (Le Fabuleux) 11.4f **(76)**
Form - 3
2000 AW 0-1: (9f) (Dirt)
Currently very useful gelding. **in USA [0-1].*

WILD MAGIC RR 27f 1647[14]
3 ch f Magic Ring (IRE) 6.5f **(64)** - Wild Humour (IRE) **(47f)** (Fayruz)
Form - 0
Record 2000 - 1st:0 2nd:0 3rd:0 Ran:1
Pre2000 - 1st:0 2nd:0 3rd:0 Ran:1
2000 Turf 0-1: (5f) (gd)
Workmanlike, currently little account filly.
**W R Muir [0-2] Mrs J A Hubbard.*

WILD NETTLE BHB 34f23a **RR 42f 23a** 2078[12]
6 ch m Beveled (USA) 6.9f **(64)** - Pink Pumpkin (Tickled Pink) 6.5f **(59)**
Form - 00087420
Record 2000 - 1st:0 2nd:1 3rd:0 Ran:7
Pre2000 - 1st:0 2nd:4 3rd:3 Ran:36
Win Prizemoney £0 *Total Prizemoney* £5,602
2000 Turf 0-4: (8f 3, 10f) (g-s, gd 2, hrd) 2000 AW 0-3: (8f, 9f, 10f) (Equi 2, Fibr)
Moderate mare, effective 8 to 10f, acts on gd - acts on Equi, has worn blinkers. Turf high 42. AW high 20. Inconsistent.
**J C Fox [0-43] Mrs J A Cleary.*

WILD RICE BHB 78f34a **RR 39f 34a** 417[12]
8 b g Green Desert (USA) 7.8f **(78)** -On Show (Welsh Pageant) 10f **(65)**
Form - 486080
Record 2000 - 1st:0 2nd:0 3rd:0 Ran:4
Pre2000 - 1st:4 2nd:0 3rd:2 Ran:17
Win Prizemoney £21,000 *Total Prizemoney* £23,370
2000 AW 0-4: (8f 2, 10f, 12f) (Equi, Fibr 3)
Moderate gelding, has worn blinkers. AW high 43. Inconsistent.

**L A Dace [0-5] Trojan Racing (from P Winkworth [0-2] Nov 1999).*

WILD RIVER (IRE) BHB 50f **RR 46f** 3496[5]
3 b g Sadler's Wells (USA) 11.3f **(87)** - Mystical River (USA) (Riverman (USA)) 9.1f **(76)**
Form - 845
Record 2000 - 1st:0 2nd:0 3rd:0 Ran:3
Win Prizemoney £0 *Total Prizemoney* £259
2000 Turf 0-3: (9f, 12f 2) (gd, g-f 2)
Currently moderate gelding. Turf high 40.
**M Johnston [0-3] Andy Peake & David Jackson.*

WILD SIDE (GER) RR 108f 4717a[9]
3 b f Sternkonig (IRE) - Wild Romance (GER) **(100f)** (Alkalde (GER))
Form - 310
2000 Turf 1-3: (11f, 12f 1-2) (sft 2, gd 1-1)
Currently Pattern-class filly. Turf high 108 - 1st of 4 getting 4lb from Indian Ruby (13 Aug Hoppegarten RF 3737a).
**P Rau in GER [1-3].*

WILD SKY (IRE) BHB 70f **RR 70f** 2865[5]
6 br g Warning 8.1f **(77)** - Erwinna (USA) (Lyphard (USA)) 9.9f **(72)**
Form - 0005
Record 2000 - 1st:0 2nd:0 3rd:0 Ran:4
Pre2000 - 1st:2 2nd:5 3rd:3 Ran:27
Win Prizemoney £10,738 *Total Prizemoney* £31,472
Wins 1999 May Leices (GD) H 8f 80 83 <
1997 Nov Newmar (G-F) H 7f 72 76
2000 Turf 0-4: (7f, 8f 2, 10f) (gd, g-f 2, frm)
Above-average gelding, effective 8f, acts on gd to g-f, has worn blinkers. Turf high 70.
**C G Cox [0-6] The Gold Partnership (from M J Heaton-Ellis [2-25] Jly 1999).*

WILD SPIRIT BHB 48f **RR 51f** 4440[9]
2 b g Salse (USA) 10.9f **(71)** - Signs **(94f)** (Risk Me (FR)) 5.9f **(53)**
Form - 560
Record 2000 - 1st:0 2nd:0 3rd:0 Ran:3
2000 Turf 0-3: (6f 3) (gd, frm 2)
Currently fair gelding. Turf high 51 (began Aug).
**D W P Arbuthnot [0-3] Derrick Broomfield.*

WILD THING BHB 55f59a **RR 52f 59a** 49[F]
4 b h Never so Bold 7.1f **(62)** - Tame Duchess (Saritamer (USA)) 9.5f **(63)**
Form - 2003F
Record 2000 - 1st:0 2nd:0 3rd:0 Ran:1
Pre2000 - 1st:1 2nd:4 3rd:2 Ran:12
Win Prizemoney £2,253 *Total Prizemoney* £6,384
Wins 1999 *Oct Southw (STD)* 6f *59* <
2000 AW 0-1: (6f) (Equi)
Workmanlike, fair colt, effective 5 to 8f, - acted on Equi to Fibr, best on Equi, had worn blinkers, preferred left handed tracks, preferred tight tracks. Inconsistent. (DEAD)
**J J Bridger [0-4] K J Walls (from R Hannon [1-9] Nov 1999).*

WILEMMGEO BHB 62f54a **RR 66f 54a** 5072[2]
3 b f Emarati (USA) 6.6f **(63)** - Floral Spark **(61f 72a)** (Forzando) 7.6f **(59)**
Form - 818212185050801141102
Record 2000 - 1st:6 2nd:3 3rd:0 Ran:18
Pre2000 - 1st:1 2nd:1 3rd:1 Ran:7
Win Prizemoney £22,998 *Total Prizemoney* £26,101
Wins * 2000 Oct Pontef (HVY) H 8f 51 63 <
*** 2000** Spt Sandow (SFT) H 10f 51 56
2000 Jly Beverl (G-F) H 7.5f 45 50
2000 Jly Beverl (G-F) H 8.5f 45 47
2000 *Feb Southw (STD) S 8f 53*
2000 *Jan Wolver (STD) S 9.4f 48+*
1999 *Nov Wolver (STD) S 8.5f 55*
2000 Turf 4-13: (6f, 7f 1-2, 8f 2-4, 10f 1-6) (g-s 2-4, gd 2, g-f 1-3, frm 1-4) 2000 AW 2-5: (8f 1-3, 9f 1-2) (Fibr 2-5)
Scopey, average filly, effective 7 to 10f, acts on g-s to hrd - acts on Fibr, best on g-s, has worn blinkers, prefers tight tracks, excels at Beverley and likes Wolverhampton. Turf high 66 - 2nd of 20 getting 11lb from Greyfield (19 Oct Bath 10f g-s RF 5072) - also 1st of 18 getting 25lb from Judicious (2 Oct Pontefract RF 4767). AW high 57 - 2nd of 6 getting 5lb from Castlebridge (8 Feb Wolverhampton 9f Fibr RF 0245). She is no world-beater, but managed to win six times on Sand and Turf last year.
**P D Evans [2-5] R J Hayward (from M C Chapman [2-9] Jly 2000).*

WILFRAM BHB 63f **RR 63f** 4493[1]
3 b g Fraam - Ming Blue (Primo Dominie) 6.2f **(80)**
Form - 08031632451
Record 2000 - 1st:2 2nd:1 3rd:2 Ran:11
Pre2000 - 1st:0 2nd:0 3rd:0 Ran:3
Win Prizemoney £5,326 *Total Prizemoney* £8,984
Wins * 2000 Spt Leices (G-S) 8f 63 <
*** 2000** Jly Chepst (G-F) H 6.1f 53 54
2000 Turf 2-11: (6f 1-2, 7f 4, 8f 1-2, 9f, 10f 2) (sft, gd 2, g-f 1-2, frm 1-6)
Average gelding, effective 8f, acts on g-f. Turf high 63. Consistent.
**J M Bradley [2-14] R D Willis.*

WILLIAMSHAKESPEARE (IRE) BHB 72f65a **RR 74f 65a** 5026[15]
4 b h Slip Anchor 12.7f **(75)** - Rostova (Blakeney) 10.5f **(64)**
Form - 00
Record 2000 - 1st:0 2nd:0 3rd:0 Ran:2
Pre2000 - 1st:0 2nd:4 3rd:2 Ran:8
Win Prizemoney £0 *Total Prizemoney* £6,610
2000 Turf 0-2: (10f, 12f) (g-s, gd)
Neat, above-average colt, effective 10 to 12f, best at 12f, acts on g-f to frm, best on frm. Turf high 74.
**D Morris [0-1] W J Gredley (from B W Hills [0-9] Apr 2000).*

WILLIAMS NEWS (USA) RR 125f 5331a[13]
5 b g Alleged (USA) 11.8f **(81)** - Wooden Crown (USA) (His Majesty (USA)) 10.9f **(82)**
Form - 20
2000 Turf 0-2: (12f 2) (frm 2)
Currently top-class gelding. Turf high 125 (1st run) (began Oct) - 2nd of 12 to Mutafaweq (15 Oct Woodbine 12f frm RF 5097a).
**T Amoss in USA [0-2] On Target Racing Stables.*

WILLIAM'S WELL BHB 78f60a **RR 79f 60a** 4832[13]
6 ch g Superpower 6.6f **(58)** - Catherines Well (Junius (USA)) 7.7f **(65)**
Form - 760143655222116000
Record 2000 - 1st:3 2nd:3 3rd:1 Ran:18
Pre2000 - 1st:4 2nd:7 3rd:7 Ran:49
Win Prizemoney £43,414 *Total Prizemoney* £59,518
Wins * 2000 Aug Ripon (G-F) H 6f 75 79 <
*** 2000** Aug Pontef (G-F) H 5f 70 77
*** 2000** May Nottin (GD) H 5.1f 60 63
* 1999 Jly Catter (FRM) H 5f 57 60
* 1999 Jly Carlis (GD) H 5f 53 54
* 1997 Jun Mussel (GD) H 5f 51 53
* 1997 Jun Catter (GD) H 5f 43 44
2000 Turf 3-18: (5f 2-12, 6f 1-6) (sft, g-s, gd 5, g-f 2-3, frm 1-7, hrd)
Above-average gelding, effective 5 to 6f, best at 6f, acts on g-f to frm, best on frm, mostly wears blinkers (effectively). Turf high 79 - 1st of 22 getting 14lb from Blue Mountain (19 Aug Ripon RF 3796) - also 1st of 17 giving 15lb to Quite Happy (9 Aug Pontefract RF 3501). Ran well last term prior to his cosy win at Pontefract in August, and followed up in the Great St Wilfrid at Ripon, a race his dam had won. **M W Easterby [7-67] K Hodgson & Mrs J Hodgson.*

WILLIAM THE LION BHB 45f **RR 51tf** 3714[10]
3 b g Puissance 7.1f **(60)** - Last Note (Welsh Pageant) 10f **(65)**
Form - 05527400
Record 2000 - 1st:0 2nd:1 3rd:0 Ran:8
Pre2000 - 1st:0 2nd:0 3rd:0 Ran:3
Win Prizemoney £0 *Total Prizemoney* £1,078
2000 Turf 0-8: (7f, 8f, 9f, 10f, 12f, 13f, 14f, 16f) (gd 2, g-f, frm 5)
Strong, fair gelding, effective 9 to 13f, acts on g-f to frm, best on frm, prefers tight tracks. Turf high 53 - 2nd of 6 getting 15lb from Love Bitten (23 Jun Ayr 13f frm RF 2217).
**A Berry [0-8] Chris & Antonia Deuters (from J Berry [0-3] Aug 1999).*

WILLIE CONQUER BHB 70f71a **RR 75f 71a** 4810[4]
8 ch g Master Willie 9.2f **(67)** - Maryland Cookie (USA) (Bold Hour) 10f **(81)**
Form - 10017111234
Record 2000 - 1st:5 2nd:1 3rd:1 Ran:11

Pre2000 - 1st:4 2nd:2 3rd:3 Ran:29
Win Prizemoney £34,085 *Total Prizemoney* £51,346

Wins	* **2000**	Aug	Bright	(FRM)	C	10f		55+
	* **2000**	Aug	Yarmou	(GD)	C	10.1f		55+
	* **2000**	Jly	Salisb	(FRM)	C	9.9f		71
	* **2000**	Jly	Bright	(G-S)	C	10f		61+
	2000	May	Bright	(FRM)	S	10f		54+
	1999	Jun	Bright	(GD)	H	11.9f	80	85+
	1996	Oct	Newmar	(G-F)	H	12f	84	92 <
	1996	Spt	Goodwo	(G-F)		12f		82
	1996	Aug	Newbur	(GD)		12f		80

2000 Turf 5-10: (9f, 10f 5-8, 12f) (gd 1-3, g-f 2-3, frm 2-4) 2000 AW 0-1: (12f) (Equi)
Above-average gelding, effective 12 to 15f, best at 12f, acts on gd to frm, best on gd, prefers tight tracks, excels at Brighton. Turf high 75. Enjoyed a fine season in selling and claiming company.
**Andrew Reid [1-10] A S Reid (from D R C Elsworth [2-9] May 2000).*

WILL IVESON (IRE) BHB 59f62a RR 63f 62a 1147^{4}

3 b g Mukaddamah (USA) 7.6f **(74)** - Cherlinoa (FR) (Crystal Palace (FR)) 12.5f **(76)**
Form - 655121014
Record 2000 - 1st:3 2nd:1 3rd:0 Ran:6
Pre2000 - 1st:0 2nd:0 3rd:0 Ran:8
Win Prizemoney £6,910 *Total Prizemoney* £8,296

Wins	* **2000**	May	Hamilt	(G-F)	C	9.2f		59
	* **2000**	*Jan*	*Lingfi*	*(STD)*	*H*	*8f*	*58*	*63* <
	* **2000**	*Jan*	*Wolver*	*(STD)*	*H*	*8.5f*	*53*	*57*

2000 Turf 1-2: (9f 1-1, 10f) (gd, g-f 1-1) 2000 AW 2-4: (8f 2-4) (Equi 1-2, Fibr 1-2)
Workmanlike, average gelding, effective 5 to 9f, acts on gd to frm - acts on AW, has worn blinkers. Turf high 59 - 1st of 10 getting 3lb from Merly Notty (7 May Hamilton RF 1072). AW high 63 - 1st of 9 giving 6lb to Lord Harley (29 Jan Lingfield RF 0182) - also 1st of 7 getting 2lb from Colombe d'Or (11 Jan Wolverhampton RF 0072).
**P C Haslam [3-14] Lord Bolton.*

WILLOUGHBY'S BOY (IRE) BHB 87f RR 90f 4736^{10}

3 b c Night Shift (USA) 8.1f **(73)** - Andbell (Trojan Fen) 8.1f **(62)**
Form - 0316162010
Record 2000 - 1st:3 2nd:1 3rd:1 Ran:10
Win Prizemoney £17,572 *Total Prizemoney* £20,375

Wins	* **2000**	Spt	Sandow	(G-F)		8.1f		87+
	* **2000**	Jly	Yarmou	(GD)	H	7f	78	90+ <
	* **2000**	May	Beverl	(GD)		7.5f		89

2000 Turf 3-10: (7f 2-7, 8f 1-3) (gd 1-4, g-f 1-4, frm 1-2)
Workmanlike, useful colt, effective 7 to 8f, best at 7f, acts on gd to frm, prefers tight tracks. Turf high 90 - 1st of 13 getting 21lb from Wahj (19 Jly Yarmouth RF 2949) - also 1st of 14 from Sutton Common (23 May Beverley RF 1386). Unraced at two, he hit the target three times last season, showing he gets the mile with a win at Sandown in September. **B Hanbury [3-10] Mrs G E M Brown.*

WILLOW MAGIC BHB 50f45a RR 63f 45a 4618^{10}

3 b f Petong 7.6f **(58)** - Love Street (Mummy's Pet) 7.7f **(60)**
Form - 25843834344500
Record 2000 - 1st:0 2nd:0 3rd:3 Ran:13
Pre2000 - 1st:0 2nd:1 3rd:0 Ran:4
Win Prizemoney £0 *Total Prizemoney* £2,290
2000 Turf 0-11: (5f 5, 6f 4, 7f 2) (gd 4, g-f 3, frm 4) 2000 AW 0-2: (5f, 6f) (Equi 2)
Workmanlike, average filly, effective 5 to 6f, best at 5f, acts on gd to frm - acts on Equi, prefers left handed tracks, prefers tight tracks. Turf high 63 - 3rd of 6 getting 2lb from Kinsman (19 Jun Brighton 6f frm RF 2088). AW high 46. Becoming disappointing.
**S Dow [0-14] Mrs Anne Malby (from A J McNae [0-3] Oct 1999).*

WILLRACK TIMES BHB 39f47a RR 39f 47a 4366^{15}

3 b f Timeless Times (USA) 6.1f **(56)** - Willrack Farrier **(60f 50a)** (Lugana Beach)
Form - 500000450
Record 2000 - 1st:0 2nd:0 3rd:0 Ran:9
Pre2000 - 1st:0 2nd:0 3rd:1 Ran:5
Win Prizemoney £0 *Total Prizemoney* £832
2000 Turf 0-7: (5f 5, 6f 2) (gd, g-f 2, frm, hrd 3) 2000 AW 0-2: (5f, 6f) (Fibr 2)
Moderate filly, effective 5f, acts on g-f. Turf high 39. AW high 49. Inconsistent. **B A McMahon [0-14] Willrackers.*

WILLY BANG BANG BHB 42f RR 21f 1597^{7}

3 b g Contract Law (USA) 8.9f **(54)** - Megan's Move (Move Off) 15f **(41)**
Form - 807
Record 2000 - 1st:0 2nd:0 3rd:0 Ran:3
2000 Turf 0-3: (8f, 10f, 11f) (gd, g-f 2)
Rangy, currently little account gelding. Turf high 21.
**W Storey [0-3] H S Hutchinson.*

WILOMENO BHB 20f RR 219^{13}

4 b m Efisio 7.7f **(69)** - Tzarina (USA) (Gallant Romeo (USA)) 8.4f **(64)**
Form - 70
Record 2000 - 1st:0 2nd:0 3rd:0 Ran:1
Pre2000 - 1st:0 2nd:0 3rd:0 Ran:2
2000 AW 0-1: (11f) (Fibr)
Workmanlike, formerly very poor filly. **Mrs L C Jewell [0-6] K Hay.*

WILSON BLYTH BHB 77f RR 77f 4833^{6}

2 b c Puissance 7.1f **(60)** - Pearls (Mon Tresor)
Form - 22143426
Record 2000 - 1st:1 2nd:3 3rd:1 Ran:8
Win Prizemoney £2,769 *Total Prizemoney* £7,880

Wins	* **2000**	Jun	Hamilt	(G-F)		6f		77 <

2000 Turf 1-8: (5f 4, 6f 1-4) (g-s, gd, g-f 1-4, frm, hrd)
Above-average colt, effective 5 to 6f, best at 5f, acts on g-f to hrd, best on g-f. Turf high 77 - 1st of 4 getting 1lb from Last Impression (28 Jun Hamilton RF 2340). Consistent.
**A Berry [1-8] Dennis Blyth & Owen Wilson.*

WILTON BHB 61f57a RR 59f 57a 5168^{4}

5 ch g Sharpo 7.5f **(68)** - Poyle Amber (Sharrood (USA)) 10.5f **(72)**
Form - 3011817054
Record 2000 - 1st:3 2nd:0 3rd:1 Ran:10
Pre2000 - 1st:4 2nd:3 3rd:1 Ran:19
Win Prizemoney £26,751 *Total Prizemoney* £30,979

Wins	**2000**	*May*	*Southw*	*(STD)*	*C*	*12f*		*58*
	2000	Apr	Pontef	(HVY)	H	10f	67	70
	2000	Apr	Hamilt	(GD)		8.3f		71
	1998	*Nov*	*Lingfi*	*(STD)*	*H*	*8f*	*74*	*75* <
	1998	Oct	Redcar	(HVY)	H	8f	62	70
	1998	Oct	Pontef	(G-S)	H	8f	52	60
	1997	*Nov*	*Southw*	*(STD)*		*6f*		*68*

2000 Turf 2-7: (8f 1-2, 10f 1-4, 12f) (sft 1-1, g-s 3, gd 1-3) 2000 AW 1-3: (8f 2, 12f 1-1) (Fibr 1-3)
Fair gelding, effective 8 to 10f, acts on sft to gd, favours tight tracks. Turf high 71 (1st run) - 1st of 11 from Bold Amusement (8 Apr Hamilton RF 0644) - also 1st of 18 giving 25lb to Noirie (17 Apr Pontefract RF 0751). AW high 59. Consistent. He was in fine form last spring, winning over a mile at Hamilton and following up in heavy ground over an extra two furlongs at Pontefract before winning at Southwell the following month. Like his sire he goes particularly well in testing conditions.
**Miss S J Wilton [0-4] John Pointon and Sons (from J Hetherton [7-25] May 2000).*

WINDCHILL BHB 59f RR 64f 3614^{4}

2 ch f Handsome Sailor 6.6f **(53)** - Baroness Gymcrak (Pharly (FR)) 9.8f **(68)**
Form - 07221134
Record 2000 - 1st:2 2nd:2 3rd:1 Ran:8
Win Prizemoney £9,135 *Total Prizemoney* £11,806

Wins	* **2000**	Jun	Newcas	(FRM)	S	6f		64+ <
	* **2000**	Jun	Redcar	(G-F)	S	7f		57

2000 Turf 2-8: (5f 3, 6f 1-3, 7f 1-2) (gd 4, g-f 1-1, frm 1-3)
Average filly, effective 6 to 7f, best at 7f, acts on g-f to frm, best on frm. Turf high 64 - 1st of 12 getting 5lb from Orchard Raider (30 Jun Newcastle RF 2406) - also 1st of 10 from Bula Rose (13 Jun Redcar RF 1910).
**T D Easterby [2-8] Mrs Bridget Tranmer.*

WIND CHIME (IRE) BHB 70f60a RR 73f 60a 4484^{10}

3 ch c Arazi (USA) 9.2f **(74)** - Shamisen (Diesis) 9.3f **(69)**
Form - 200220
Record 2000 - 1st:0 2nd:3 3rd:0 Ran:6
Pre2000 - 1st:0 2nd:1 3rd:0 Ran:2
Win Prizemoney £0 *Total Prizemoney* £4,859
2000 Turf 0-6: (6f, 7f 4, 8f) (g-s, gd, g-f 2, frm 2)

Leggy, above-average colt, effective 6 to 7f, best at 7f, acts on gd to frm. Turf high 73 (1st run) - 2nd of 16 to Diamond Look (7 Apr Lingfield 7f gd RF 0636). Consistent.
**C E Brittain [0-8] Saeed Manana.*

WINDFALL BHB 58f **RR 60tf** 3922[6]
3 b g Polish Precedent (USA) 9f **(73)** - Captive Heart (Conquistador Cielo (USA)) 8.8f **(69)**
Form - 8380806
Record 2000 - 1st:0 2nd:0 3rd:1 Ran:7
Pre2000 - 1st:0 2nd:0 3rd:0 Ran:1
Win Prizemoney £0 *Total Prizemoney* £581
2000 Turf 0-7: (7f, 8f, 9f 2, 10f, 11f, 12f) (gd, g-f 4, frm 2)
Unfurnished, average gelding, has worn blinkers. Turf high 60.
**C A Cyzer [0-8] R M Cyzer.*

WINDMILL BHB 59f **RR 78f** 4364[12]
3 b f Ezzoud (IRE) - Bempton (Blakeney) 10.5f **(64)**
Form - 414470
Record 2000 - 1st:1 2nd:0 3rd:0 Ran:6
Win Prizemoney £2,205 *Total Prizemoney* £3,294
Wins * **2000** Jly Catter (G-F) 13.8f 47+ <
2000 Turf 1-6: (10f, 12f 3, 14f 1-1, 16f) (gd, g-f 1-4, frm)
Unfurnished, above-average filly, effective 10f, acts on gd, has worn blinkers. Turf high 78 (1st run) - 4th of 10 to Abscond (23 May Beverley 10f gd RF 1389).
**T D Easterby [1-6] Lord Halifax.*

WINDMILL LANE BHB 50f54a **RR 66df 54a** 4459[11]
3 b f Saddlers' Hall (IRE) 10.5f **(65)** - Alpi Dora (Valiyar) 8.5f **(73)**
Form - 263721735050
Record 2000 - 1st:1 2nd:2 3rd:2 Ran:12
Pre2000 - 1st:0 2nd:0 3rd:0 Ran:5
Win Prizemoney £2,320 *Total Prizemoney* £6,282
Wins * **2000** Jun Carlis (G-F) H 17.2f 53 58 <
2000 Turf 1-9: (12f 4, 16f 4, 17f 1-1) (g-s 2, gd 2, g-f 3, frm 1-2) 2000 AW 0-3: (11f, 12f 2) (Fibr 3)
Scopey, average filly, effective 16f, acts on g-f, has worn blinkers. Turf high 69 - 3rd of 7 getting 9lb from High Topper (15 Jly Chester 16f g-f RF 2836). AW high 52.
**B S Rothwell [1-12] B Valentine (from A P Jarvis [0-5] Oct 1999).*

WINDRUSH BOY BHB 36f39a **RR 36f 39a** 4276[14]
10 br g Dowsing (USA) 7f **(61)** - Bridge Street Lady (Decoy Boy) 6.7f **(56)**
Form - 087444670
Record 2000 - 1st:0 2nd:0 3rd:0 Ran:9
Pre2000 - 1st:5 2nd:6 3rd:3 Ran:68
Win Prizemoney £15,132 *Total Prizemoney* £21,529
Wins * 1999 Jly Bath (FRM) C 5.1f 51
* 1998 Jun Lingfi (GD) H 5f 38 41
1996 Aug Warwic (GD) C 5f 57 <
2000 Turf 0-9: (5f 9) (gd 3, g-f, frm 3, hrd 2)
Very moderate gelding, effective 5f, acts on g-f, likes left handed tracks. Turf high 36.
**M R Bosley [2-37] Girls On Top Racing 2000 (from J R Bosley [3-33] Jan 1997).*

WINDSHIFT (IRE) BHB 50f64a **RR 26f 64a** 4745[23]
4 b g Forest Wind (USA) - Beautyofthepeace (IRE) (Exactly Sharp (USA))
Form - 0531600000
Record 2000 - 1st:1 2nd:0 3rd:1 Ran:9
Pre2000 - 1st:4 2nd:1 3rd:2 Ran:17
Win Prizemoney £19,823 *Total Prizemoney* £24,409
Wins * **2000** *Jan Wolver (STD) H 8.5f 74 76*
* 1999 Mar Warwic (G-S) H 8f 70 74
* 1999 *Mar Southw (STD) H 8f 70 78* <
* 1999 *Feb Southw (STD) H 8f 63 69*
* 1998 *Dec Southw (STD) H 8f 51 57*
2000 Turf 0-5: (8f 3, 9f, 10f) (sft 2, gd 2, g-f) 2000 AW 1-4: (8f 1-3, 9f) (Fibr 1-4)
Leggy, above-average gelding, effective 8 to 9f, best at 8f, acts on g-s - acts on Fibr, mostly wears blinkers (extremely effectively), prefers left handed tracks, prefers tight tracks, and excels at Southwell. Turf high 26. AW high 76 - 1st of 10 giving 7lb to Hannibal Lad (22 Jan Wolverhampton RF 0142). Becoming disappointing.

**D Shaw [5-26] G E Griffiths.*

WINDSOR BOY (IRE) BHB 106f **RR 105f** 1636a[2]
3 b c Mtoto 11.5f **(71)** - Fragrant Belle (USA) **(87f)** (Al Nasr (FR)) 9.3f **(68)**
Form - 22
Record 2000 - 1st:0 2nd:2 3rd:0 Ran:2
Pre2000 - 1st:1 2nd:0 3rd:0 Ran:3
Win Prizemoney £3,582 *Total Prizemoney* £135,290
Wins * 1999 Aug Beverl (GD) 8.5f 84+ <
2000 Turf 0-2: (12f 2) (g-f 2)
Workmanlike, Pattern-class colt. Turf high 105 - 2nd of 20 to Kallisto (28 May Capannelle 12f g-f RF 1636a). Just caught by Millenary in the Chester Vase, he finished runner-up in the German Derby next time but that was it for the season. He looks a useful stayer in the making. **P F I Cole [1-5] H R H Prince Fahd Salman.*

WINFIELD (IRE) BHB 64f **RR 69f** 4747[22]
2 ch c Catrail (USA) - Burishki (Chilibang)
Form - 04000
Record 2000 - 1st:0 2nd:0 3rd:0 Ran:5
2000 Turf 0-5: (6f 5) (sft, gd 3, frm)
Average colt, has worn blinkers. Turf high 69 (began Jly).
**C G Cox [0-5] S P Lansdown Racing.*

WINGED ANGEL BHB 53f57a **RR 58f 57a** 4499[13]
3 ch g Prince Sabo 6.6f **(64)** - Silky Heights (IRE) **(59f 61a)** (Head for Heights) 9.6f **(55)**
Form - 408001500
Record 2000 - 1st:1 2nd:0 3rd:0 Ran:9
Win Prizemoney £7,215 *Total Prizemoney* £7,438
Wins * **2000** Jly Redcar (G-F) H 11f 55 58 <
2000 Turf 1-8: (6f, 7f, 8f 2, 10f, 11f 1-3) (g-s 2, gd 2, g-f 1-2, frm 2) 2000 AW 0-1: (7f) (Fibr)
Rangy, fair gelding, effective 11f, acts on g-f, has worn blinkers, likes left handed tracks, likes tight tracks. Turf high 64 - also 1st of 6 getting 20lb from Fantastic Fantasy (23 Jly Redcar RF 3056). Showed little in his early starts, but seemed to appreciate the step up in trip when winning a modest 11-furlong Redcar handicap by the minimum margin in July.
**Miss J A Camacho [1-9] Bernard Bloom.*

WINGED GREYBIRD BHB 35f **RR 34f** 4923[13]
6 gr m Batshoof 9.5f **(66)** - To Oneiro (Absalom) 7.2f **(58)**
Form - 0
Record 2000 - 1st:0 2nd:0 3rd:0 Ran:1
Pre2000 - 1st:0 2nd:0 3rd:1 Ran:4
Win Prizemoney £0 *Total Prizemoney* £350
2000 AW 0-1: (16f) (Equi)
Moderate mare. **Miss A M Newton-Smith [0-7] Ian Moody.*

WINGED HUSSAR RR 97f 4092a[7]
7 b g In The Wings 11.2f **(77)** - Akila 00
Form - 315847
2000 Turf 1-6: (12f 1-3, 14f 2, 22f) (g-s 1-2, gd 4)
Very useful gelding, effective 12 to 22f, best at 12f, acts on g-s to gd, best on gd, has worn blinkers. Turf high 97 - 4th of 12 giving 6lb to Grand Finale (13 Aug Leopardstown 12f gd RF 3673a) - also 1st of 13 giving 1lb to Catch The Dragon (28 May Curragh RF 1586a). A smart handicapper, he won a handicap over a mile and a half at The Curragh in May and then raced unsuccessfully in Listed company during the summer.
**J Oxx in IRE [4-19] Dundalk Racing Club.*

WINGS AS EAGLES RR 21tf 2868[7]
3 gr c Bedford (USA) - Biddesden Merelina (My Swanee) 7.6f **(52)**
Form - 77
Record 2000 - 1st:0 2nd:0 3rd:0 Ran:2
2000 Turf 0-2: (9f, 12f) (g-f 2)
Leggy, currently little account colt. Turf high 21.
**R M Beckett [0-2] Mrs E M Hudson.*

WINGS OF SOUL (USA) RR 80+f 5110[3]
2 b c Thunder Gulch (USA) - Party Cited (USA)(Alleged (USA)) 10f **(76)**
Form - 3
Record 2000 - 1st:0 2nd:0 3rd:1 Ran:1
Win Prizemoney £0 *Total Prizemoney* £1,254

2000 Turf 0-1: (8f) (gd)
Currently decent colt. (1st run) - 3rd of 11 getting 3lb from Aldwych (20 Oct Newbury 8f gd RF 5110).
**P F I Cole [0-1] Andy Smith.*

WINLEAH BHB 20f **RR 24f** 85[13]
4 gr h Petong 7.6f **(58)** - Tower Glades (Tower Walk) 10f **(62)**
Form - 00
Record 2000 - 1st:0 2nd:0 3rd:0 Ran:1
Pre2000 - 1st:0 2nd:0 3rd:0 Ran:7
2000 AW 0-1: (11f) (Fibr)
Leggy, little account colt. Becoming disappointing.
**A G Newcombe [0-8] Advanced Marketing Services Ltd.*

WINNING PLEASURE (IRE) BHB 75f **RR 67f** 5309[7]
2 b c Ashkalani (IRE) - Karamana (Habitat) 9.4f **(70)**
Form - 007
Record 2000 - 1st:0 2nd:0 3rd:0 Ran:3
2000 Turf 0-3: (7f 3) (g-s 2, g-f)
Currently average colt. Turf high 67 (began Spt).
**A P Jarvis [0-3] Mrs B A Headon.*

WINNING VENTURE RR 110f 4549[5]
3 b c Owington - Push a Button (Bold Lad (IRE)) 8.4f **(68)**
Form - 302307005
Record 2000 - 1st:0 2nd:1 3rd:2 Ran:9
Pre2000 - 1st:1 2nd:2 3rd:3 Ran:6
Win Prizemoney £5,284 *Total Prizemoney* £47,375
Wins * 1999 Aug Kempto (SFT) 7f 79 <
2000 Turf 0-9: (6f 5, 7f 3, 8f) (g-s 2, gd 5, g-f, frm)
Well made, Group-class colt, effective 6 to 8f, best at 7f, acts on gd to g-f, best on gd, has worn blinkers. Turf high 111 (1st run) - 3rd of 7 to Barathea Guest (18 Apr Newmarket 7f gd RF 0766).
**S P C Woods [1-15] Seiichi Wada.*

WINNIPEG (IRE) BHB 25f **RR** 4680[8]
4 ch m Mac's Imp (USA) 5.6f **(54)** - Cadasi (Persian Bold) 9.3f **(66)**
Form - 808
Record 2000 - 1st:0 2nd:0 3rd:0 Ran:1
Pre2000 - 1st:0 2nd:0 3rd:0 Ran:2
2000 Turf 0-1: (8f) (hvy)
Workmanlike, currently poor filly.
**Mrs N Smith [0-1] Mrs N Smith (from B Gubby [0-2] Dec 1999).*

WINS FICTION (GER) RR 119f 5212a[10]
5 b g Platini (GER) - Win Hands Down (Ela-Mana-Mou) 10.1f **(70)**
Form - 180
2000 Turf 1-3: (12f, 16f 1-2) (hvy, gd 1-2)
High-class gelding. Turf high 106. **P Remmert in GER [1-5].*

WINSOME GEORGE BHB 28f23a **RR 37f 23a** 5012[13]
5 b g Marju (IRE) 9.2f **(76)** - June Moon (IRE) (Sadler's Wells (USA)) 10f **(76)**
Form - 2330747506864100
Record 2000 - 1st:1 2nd:1 3rd:2 Ran:17
Pre2000 - 1st:3 2nd:3 3rd:4 Ran:35
Win Prizemoney £14,039 *Total Prizemoney* £22,965
Wins * 2000 Spt Hamilt (SFT) H 12.1f 21 27
1998 May Redcar (G-F) H 11f 70 82 <
1998 May Beverl (GD) H 12f 70 76
1997 Jun Ayr (GD) 7f 77
2000 Turf 1-13: (11f, 12f 1-8, 13f, 14f 2, 17f) (g-s 2, gd 1-1, g-f 3, frm 6, hrd) 2000 AW 0-4: (12f, 14f 3) (Fibr 4)
Very moderate gelding, often wears blinkers. Turf high 48. AW high 46.
**M Quinn [1-9] M B Clemence (from C W Fairhurst [3-43] Jly 2000).*

WINSTON BHB 33f28a **RR 32f 28a** 2382a[1]
7 b g Safawan 6.6f **(60)** - Lady Leman (Pitskelly) 8.5f **(53)**
Form - 8801
Record 2000 - 1st:1 2nd:0 3rd:0 Ran:4
Pre2000 - 1st:2 2nd:2 3rd:5 Ran:37
Win Prizemoney £8,007 *Total Prizemoney* £14,225
Wins * 2000 Jun Les La (G-F) H 9f 32
* 1996 May Newcas (GD) H 8f 60 62 <
* 1996 Apr Nottin (G-F) H 8.2f 56 52
2000 Turf 1-2: (8f, 9f 1-1) (g-f 1-1, frm) 2000 AW 0-2: (8f, 12f) (Fibr 2)
Very moderate gelding, has worn blinkers (extremely effectively). Turf high 32. Inconsistent. **J D Bethell [3-41] Mrs James Bethell.*

WINTER DOLPHIN (IRE) BHB 58f **RR 65f** 5117[4]
2 b f Dolphin Street (FR) - Winter Tern (USA) (Arctic Tern (USA)) 8.9f **(69)**
Form - 06604
Record 2000 - 1st:0 2nd:0 3rd:0 Ran:5
2000 Turf 0-4: (5f 3, 6f) (g-s, gd, g-f, frm) 2000 AW 0-1: (5f) (Fibr)
Average filly. Turf high 65 (began Aug).
**I A Wood [0-5] David Hammond.*

WINTER JASMINE BHB 73f **RR 69f** 1961[7]
2 b f Robellino (USA) 9.5f **(68)** - Wild Truffes (IRE) **(28df)** (Danehill (USA)) 10f **(72)**
Form - 047
Record 2000 - 1st:0 2nd:0 3rd:0 Ran:3
Win Prizemoney £0 *Total Prizemoney* £385
2000 Turf 0-3: (5f 2, 6f) (g-f 3)
Currently average filly. Turf high 69.
**B J Meehan [0-3] Mrs Susan Roy.*

WINTER SOLSTICE RR 96f 5308a[7]
2 b f Unfuwain (USA) 11.4f **(74)** - Hunt The Sun (Rainbow Quest (USA)) 10.4f **(75)**
Form - 277
2000 Turf 0-3: (8f 2, 10f) (hvy, gd 2)
Currently very useful filly. Turf high 96 (began Spt).
**Mme C Head in FR [0-3].*

WINTZIG BHB 53f58a **RR 70f 58a** 4492[4]
3 b f Piccolo - Wrangbrook (Shirley Heights) 10.3f **(74)**
Form - 0525033044
Record 2000 - 1st:0 2nd:1 3rd:2 Ran:10
Pre2000 - 1st:1 2nd:0 3rd:0 Ran:4
Win Prizemoney £3,262 *Total Prizemoney* £6,062
Wins * 1999 Spt Pontef (GD) H 8f 65 65 <
2000 Turf 0-9: (8f 6, 10f 2, 12f) (gd 2, g-f 3, frm 4) 2000 AW 0-1: (9f) (Fibr)
Scopey, above-average filly, effective 8f, acts on g-f, likes left handed tracks, likes tight tracks. Turf high 70 - 2nd of 11 getting 12lb from Sign of Hope (26 May Pontefract 8f g-f RF 1470).
**M L W Bell [1-14] Baron F C Oppenheim.*

WISHBONE ALLEY (IRE) BHB 44f43a **RR 46f 43a** 3961[8]
5 b g Common Grounds 8.1f **(66)** - Dul Dul (USA) (Shadeed (USA)) 8.2f **(70)**
Form - 7222132042030800730508
Record 2000 - 1st:1 2nd:3 3rd:3 Ran:19
Pre2000 - 1st:2 2nd:8 3rd:5 Ran:40
Win Prizemoney £13,729 *Total Prizemoney* £25,943
Wins * 2000 *Jan Lingfi (STD) H 5f 45 47*
* 1999 Jun Newcas (GD) H 6f 51 53
* 1998 Aug Thirsk (G-F) H 5f 59 63 <
2000 Turf 0-11: (5f, 6f 8, 7f, 8f) (gd, g-f 3, frm 5, hrd 2) 2000 AW 1-8: (5f 1-5, 6f 3) (Equi 1-6, Fibr 2)
Fair gelding, effective 5 to 6f, best at 6f, acts on g-s to frm - acts on AW, best on frm, often wears blinkers, and excels at Newcastle. Turf high 46. AW high 52 - 2nd of 8 giving 14lb to Arab Gold (4 Mar Lingfield 6f Equi RF 0405) - also 1st of 8 getting 8lb from Palacegate Jack (12 Jan Lingfield RF 0073).
**M Dods [3-59] Doug Graham.*

WISHEDHADGONEHOME (IRE) BHB 31f44a **RR 33f 44a** 4007[9]
3 b f Archway (IRE) 8.5f **(60)** - Yavarro (Raga Navarro (ITY)) 8f **(64)**
Form - 8026305600440
Record 2000 - 1st:0 2nd:0 3rd:1 Ran:9
Pre2000 - 1st:0 2nd:1 3rd:0 Ran:11
Win Prizemoney £0 *Total Prizemoney* £1,443
2000 Turf 0-5: (6f, 7f 2, 8f 2) (frm 4, hrd) 2000 AW 0-4: (7f, 8f 3) (Equi, Fibr 3)
Light-framed, moderate filly, effective 5f, acts on g-f, often wears blinkers. Turf high 33 (began Jly). AW high 47.
**J Balding [0-5] Men Behaving Badly (from P D Evans [0-15] Feb 2000).*

WISHFUL THINKER BHB 49f **RR 55f** 5200[4]
3 b g Prince Sabo 6.6f **(64)** - Estonia (Kings Lake (USA)) 10.8f **(67)**
Form - 800381204
Record 2000 - 1st:1 2nd:1 3rd:1 Ran:9
Pre2000 - 1st:0 2nd:1 3rd:1 Ran:6
Win Prizemoney £1,904 *Total Prizemoney* £4,972
Wins * **2000** Jly Redcar (G-F) S 11f 40+ <
2000 Turf 1-9: (8f 4, 9f, 10f 2, 11f 1-2) (gd 4, g-f, frm 1-4)
Scopey, fair gelding, effective 6f, acts on frm. Turf high 57.
**N Tinkler [1-6] Mrs Marie Tinkler (from J W Hills [0-5] Jun 2000).*

WITCH'S BREW BHB 55f **RR 50f** 1010[7]
3 b f Simply Great (FR) 11.9f **(61)** - New Broom (IRE) **(49f)** (Brush Aside (USA))
Form - 7
Record 2000 - 1st:0 2nd:0 3rd:0 Ran:1
Pre2000 - 1st:0 2nd:0 3rd:0 Ran:3
2000 Turf 0-1: (12f) (gd)
Leggy, fair filly. **T D Easterby [0-4] Mrs Bridget Tranmer.*

WITH A WILL BHB 70f **RR 68f** 4934[12]
6 b g Rambo Dancer (CAN) 8.4f **(59)** - Henceforth (Full of Hope) 8.5f **(64)**
Form - 3314110
Record 2000 - 1st:3 2nd:0 3rd:2 Ran:7
Pre2000 - 1st:3 2nd:0 3rd:2 Ran:23
Win Prizemoney £19,166 *Total Prizemoney* £21,739

Wins								
* **2000**	Aug	Salisb	(G-F)	H	8f	66	68	<
* **2000**	Aug	Windso	(G-F)	H	8.3f	61	62	
* **2000**	Jly	Windso	(Gd)		10f		61	
* 1998	Jun	Lingfi	(GD)	H	9f	58	62	
* 1998	May	Kempto	(GD)	H	9f	56	59	
* 1997	Jly	Chepst	(G-F)	H	8.1f	61	66	

2000 Turf 3-7: (8f 2-4, 9f, 10f 1-2) (g-s, gd 3, g-f 1-1, frm 2-2)
Average gelding, effective 8 to 10f, best at 8f, acts on g-f to frm, best on frm, likes tight tracks. Turf high 68 - 1st of 18 giving 16lb to Thihn (31 Aug Salisbury RF 4130) - also 1st of 18 giving 7lb to Caution (7 Aug Windsor RF 3437). **H Candy [6-30] Henry Candy.*

WITHIN THE LAW **RR 16f** 4867[4]
2 b f Contract Law (USA) 8.9f **(54)** - Fyas (Sayf El Arab (USA)) 7.1f **(54)**
Form - 04
Record 2000 - 1st:0 2nd:0 3rd:0 Ran:2
Win Prizemoney £0 *Total Prizemoney* £290
2000 Turf 0-2: (5f, 7f) (hvy, gd)
Currently poor filly. Turf high 16 (began Oct).
**W Storey [0-2] S Hogg.*

WITHOUT FRIENDS (IRE) BHB 29f30a **RR 31f 30a** 389[11]
6 b g Thatching 7.8f **(69)** - Soha (USA) (Dancing Brave (USA)) 8.4f **(76)**
Form - 768440
Record 2000 - 1st:0 2nd:0 3rd:0 Ran:4
Pre2000 - 1st:8 2nd:3 3rd:7 Ran:52
Win Prizemoney £18,290 *Total Prizemoney* £22,157

Wins								
* 1999	*Mar*	*Southw*	*(STD)*	H	*8f*	*51*	*54*	
1998	*Mar*	*Lingfi*	*(SLW)*		*8f*		*66*	
1998	*Feb*	*Lingfi*	*(SLW)*	SH	*8f*	*50*	*64*	
1998	*Feb*	*Lingfi*	*(SLW)*	S	*8f*		*61*	
1997	Mar	Newcas	(GD)	S	6f		56	
1996	Jly	Chepst	(G-F)	C	6.1f		71	<
1996	May	Goodwo	(GD)	C	6f		63	
1996	Apr	Folkes	(FRM)	S	5f		63	

2000 AW 0-4: (8f, 10f 2, 12f) (Equi 2, Fibr 2)
Very moderate gelding, effective 8f, - acts on Fibr, has worn blinkers. AW high 34. He is fairly useful, if exposed, in sellers and claimers, but had a very productive time over a mile on the Lingfield Equitrack earlier in the year, winning three modest events.
**Mrs N Macauley [1-22] Joe Macari (from Miss Gay Kelleway [0-2] Feb 1999).*

WITH RESPECT (USA) BHB 46a **RR 40f** 4402[16]
3 b f Rakeen (USA) - Low Approach (Artaius (USA)) 9f **(69)**
Form - 005400
Record 2000 - 1st:0 2nd:0 3rd:0 Ran:6
Pre2000 - 1st:0 2nd:0 3rd:0 Ran:2
Win Prizemoney £0 *Total Prizemoney* £322
2000 Turf 0-4: (8f 2, 9f, 10f) (g-f 2, frm 2) 2000 AW 0-2: (12f 2) (Fibr 2)
Leggy, moderate filly. Turf high 40. AW high 30 (began Jly).
**J G Given [0-8] K H Benson.*

WITNEY ROYALE (IRE) BHB 77f **RR 72f** 4313[20]
2 ch g Royal Abjar (USA) - Collected (IRE) (Taufan (USA)) 7f **(57)**
Form - 1400
Record 2000 - 1st:1 2nd:0 3rd:0 Ran:4
Win Prizemoney £3,136 *Total Prizemoney* £3,470
Wins * **2000** Jun Doncas (G-F) 6f 68 <
2000 Turf 1-4: (6f 1-2, 7f 2) (g-s, g-f, frm 1-2)
Above-average gelding. Turf high 72 - also 1st of 12 from El Maximo (10 Jun Doncaster RF 1867).
**J S Moore [1-4] Ernie Houghton.*

WITTON WOOD (IRE) BHB 45f **RR 45f** 111[6]
3 b g Bluebird (USA) 7.9f **(71)** -Leyete Gulf (IRE) (Slip Anchor) 9.8f **(73)**
Form - 36
Record 2000 - 1st:0 2nd:0 3rd:1 Ran:2
Pre2000 - 1st:0 2nd:0 3rd:0 Ran:3
Win Prizemoney £0 *Total Prizemoney* £313
2000 AW 0-2: (8f, 10f) (Equi, Fibr)
Workmanlike, moderate gelding, has worn blinkers. AW high 48.
**M H Tompkins [0-5] www raceworld co uk.*

WODHILL FOLLY **RR 56f** 5142[9]
3 ch f Faustus (USA) 9.1f **(54)** - Muarij (Star Appeal) 9.6f **(65)**
Form - 60
Record 2000 - 1st:0 2nd:0 3rd:0 Ran:2
2000 Turf 0-2: (8f, 11f) (g-s, g-f)
Currently fair filly. Turf high 56 (began Aug).
**N A Callaghan [0-2] Miss S Graham.*

WOLF VENTURE BHB 74f **RR 84f** 4932[15]
2 ch c Wolfhound (USA) 7.3f **(71)** - Relatively Sharp (Sharpen Up) 8.3f **(67)**
Form - 43580
Record 2000 - 1st:0 2nd:0 3rd:1 Ran:5
Win Prizemoney £0 *Total Prizemoney* £874
2000 Turf 0-4: (6f 2, 7f 2) (g-s, gd, g-f 2) 2000 AW 0-1: (6f) (Fibr)
Decent colt. Turf high 84 (began Spt).
**S P C Woods [0-5] Dr Frank Chao.*

WONDERFUL MAN BHB 45f **RR 50f** 3977[14]
4 ch g Magical Wonder (USA) 7.2f **(60)** - Gleeful (Sayf El Arab (USA)) 7.1f **(54)**
Form - 600
Record 2000 - 1st:0 2nd:0 3rd:0 Ran:3
Pre2000 - 1st:0 2nd:0 3rd:0 Ran:6
Win Prizemoney £0 *Total Prizemoney* £205
2000 Turf 0-3: (7f, 8f, 11f) (gd, frm 2)
Leggy, fair gelding, effective 8f, acts on g-f to frm. Turf high 50 (1st run) - 6th of 28 giving 1lb to Derryquin (15 May Redcar 8f frm RF 1199).
**R D E Woodhouse [0-3] M K Oldham (from M J Heaton-Ellis [0-6] May 1999).*

WONDERGREEN BHB 73f **RR 63f** 4818[7]
2 ch c Wolfhound (USA) 7.3f **(71)** - Tenderetta (Tender King) 6.8f **(54)**
Form - 600317
Record 2000 - 1st:1 2nd:0 3rd:1 Ran:6
Win Prizemoney £3,051 *Total Prizemoney* £4,082
Wins * **2000** Spt Beverl (G-F) 7.5f 63 <
2000 Turf 1-6: (5f 2, 6f, 7f 1-1, 8f 2) (g-s, gd, g-f 1-2, frm, hrd)
Average colt, effective 7 to 8f, acts on gd to g-f. Turf high 63 (began Jly) - 1st of 9 getting 9lb from Heathyards Guest (13 Spt Beverley RF 4359). **T D Easterby [1-6] Health Mail Ltd.*

WONDERLAND (IRE) BHB 40f **RR 46f** 2215[12]
3 b f Dolphin Street (FR) - Smart Pet **(68f)** (Petong) 6.6f **(58)**
Form - 07500
Record 2000 - 1st:0 2nd:0 3rd:0 Ran:5
Pre2000 - 1st:0 2nd:0 3rd:0 Ran:3
2000 Turf 0-5: (7f, 8f, 9f, 10f, 11f) (hvy, g-s, gd, g-f, frm)
Scopey, moderate filly, has worn blinkers. Turf high 46. Inconsistent. **J J O'Neill [0-8] Carlton Appointments (Aberdeen) Ltd.*

WONTCOSTALOTBUT BHB 55f45a **RR 52f 45a** 1804[11]

6 b m Nicholas Bill 9.8f **(56)** - Brave Maiden (Three Legs) 11.1f **(54)**
Form - 200
Record 2000 - 1st:0 2nd:1 3rd:0 Ran:3
Pre2000 - 1st:1 2nd:0 3rd:1 Ran:9
Win Prizemoney £3,150 *Total Prizemoney* £6,228
Wins * 1999 Apr Folkes (HVY) H 15.4f 47 57 <
2000 Turf 0-3: (16f 2, 18f) (sft, gd 2)
Fair mare, effective 15 to 16f, best at 15f, acts on hvy to sft, best on hvy. Turf high 52 (1st run) - 2nd of 9 getting 9lb from Renzo (28 Apr Sandown 16f sft RF 0896). A useful hurdler, she also managed a runaway victory in a Folkestone stayers' event last spring.
**M J Wilkinson [5-42] Wontcostalot Partnership.*

WOODBASTWICK CHARM BHB 37f **RR 39f** 3981[6]

8 b g Charmer 9f **(59)** - Miss Mint (Music Maestro) 7.7f **(66)**
Form - 0007056
Record 2000 - 1st:0 2nd:0 3rd:0 Ran:7
Pre2000 - 1st:0 2nd:0 3rd:0 Ran:1
2000 Turf 0-7: (7f, 8f, 10f 4, 12f) (gd, g-f, frm 5)
Leggy, very moderate gelding. Turf high 44.
**N P Littmoden [0-4] The Wayfarers (from J Pearce [0-4] May 2000).*

WOODCUT (IRE) BHB 25a **RR 30f** 374[9]

4 ch g Woods of Windsor (USA) - Lady of State (IRE) (Petong) 6.6f **(58)**
Form - 700
Record 2000 - 1st:0 2nd:0 3rd:0 Ran:3
Pre2000 - 1st:0 2nd:0 3rd:0 Ran:8
2000 AW 0-3: (6f 2, 7f) (Fibr 3)
Scopey, very moderate gelding. AW high 35.
**P S Felgate [0-11] Yorkshire Racing Club Owners Group 1990.*

WOODEN DOLL (USA) **RR 98f** 4566a[3]

2 ch f Woodman (USA) 9.7f **(77)** - Kingscote (Kings Lake (USA)) 10.8f **(67)**
Form - 23
2000 Turf 0-2: (7f 2) (g-s, gd)
Currently very useful filly. Turf high 98 (began Aug). A Group-class filly, she struggled to go the early pace but finished to good effect when third behind Tobougg in the Prix de la Salamandre, and will get further as a three-year-old.
**Mme C Head in FR [0-2] K Abdulla.*

WOODFIELD BHB 79f **RR 78f** 4643[19]

2 b c Zafonic (USA) 9f **(83)** - Top Society (High Top) 10.2f **(67)**
Form - 8370
Record 2000 - 1st:0 2nd:0 3rd:1 Ran:4
Win Prizemoney £0 *Total Prizemoney* £1,050
2000 Turf 0-4: (7f 4) (gd, g-f 3)
Above-average colt. Turf high 78 (began Jly).
**C E Brittain [0-4] Wyck Hall Stud.*

WOODLAND RIVER (USA) BHB 83f **RR 78f** 3233[10]

3 ch c Irish River (FR) 9f **(77)** - Wiener Wald (USA) (Woodman (USA)) 9f **(74)**
Form - 00210
Record 2000 - 1st:1 2nd:1 3rd:0 Ran:5
Win Prizemoney £2,990 *Total Prizemoney* £4,054
Wins * **2000** Jly Warwic (GD) 7.7f 78 <
2000 Turf 1-5: (7f 2, 8f 1-3) (gd 1-3, g-f 2)
Scopey, above-average colt. Turf high 78 - 1st of 12 giving 5lb to Shaan Madary (7 Jly Warwick RF 2616). Gradually improving, he won a Warwick maiden in good style in July and can go on to better things. **J R Fanshawe [1-5] Car Colston Hall Stud.*

WOODLANDS BHB 60f **RR 38f** 4378[15]

3 b g Common Grounds 8.1f **(66)** - Forest of Arden (Tap On Wood) 10.3f **(65)**
Form - 3080
Record 2000 - 1st:0 2nd:0 3rd:1 Ran:4
Pre2000 - 1st:0 2nd:0 3rd:1 Ran:3
Win Prizemoney £0 *Total Prizemoney* £893
2000 Turf 0-4: (6f 2, 7f 2) (g-s, frm 3)
Workmanlike, very moderate gelding. Turf high 38.
**N A Graham [0-4] The 1 2 3 Partnership (from R McGhin [0-3] Oct 1999).*

WOODLANDS LAD TOO BHB 20f28a **RR 11f 28a** 3080[16]

8 b g Risk Me (FR) 8f **(53)** - Hallowed (Wolver Hollow) 8f **(56)**
Form - 000
Record 2000 - 1st:0 2nd:0 3rd:0 Ran:3
Pre2000 - 1st:0 2nd:0 3rd:1 Ran:5
Win Prizemoney £0 *Total Prizemoney* £600
2000 Turf 0-3: (8f, 12f 2) (gd, frm 2)
Poor gelding. Turf high 11 (began Jly).
**P A Pritchard [0-27] Woodlands (Worcestershire) Ltd.*

WOOD POUND (USA) BHB 83f87a **RR 80f 87a** 185[5]

4 b h Woodman (USA) 9.7f **(77)** - Poundzig (USA) (Danzig (USA)) 8.4f **(76)**
Form - 125
Record 2000 - 1st:1 2nd:1 3rd:0 Ran:3
Pre2000 - 1st:0 2nd:1 3rd:0 Ran:3
Win Prizemoney £2,831 *Total Prizemoney* £5,456
Wins * **2000** *Jan Southw (STD)* *12f* *79* <
2000 AW 1-3: (11f, 12f 1-2) (Equi, Fibr 1-2)
Workmanlike, useful colt. AW high 87 - 2nd of 9 giving 19lb to Chalcedony (17 Jan Southwell 11f Fibr RF 0104) - also 1st of 15 from Oro Street (10 Jan Southwell RF 0062).
**R Hollinshead [1-3] Peter Wetzel (from Sir Michael Stoute [0-3] Oct 1999).*

WOODWIND DOWN BHB 47f54a **RR 50f 54a** 3312[5]

3 b f Piccolo - Bint El Oumara (Al Nasr (FR)) 9.3f **(68)**
Form - 20707325
Record 2000 - 1st:0 2nd:2 3rd:1 Ran:8
Pre2000 - 1st:0 2nd:0 3rd:0 Ran:2
Win Prizemoney £0 *Total Prizemoney* £2,079
2000 Turf 0-7: (7f 2, 8f 4, 9f) (sft, gd, g-f 3, frm, hrd) 2000 AW 0-1: (7f) (Equi)
Scopey, fair filly, effective 7 to 8f, acts on g-f - acts on Equi, prefers tight tracks. Turf high 53. (1st run) - 2nd of 7 getting 5lb from Air Mail (8 Mar Lingfield 7f Equi RF 0422).
**M Todhunter [0-2] Domino Racing (from M R Channon [0-8] Jun 2000).*

WOODYATES BHB 50f **RR 52f** 5200[1]

3 b f Naheez (USA) - Night Mission (IRE) (Night Shift (USA)) 7.2f **(69)**
Form - 0685801
Record 2000 - 1st:1 2nd:0 3rd:0 Ran:7
Win Prizemoney £1,907 *Total Prizemoney* £1,907
Wins * **2000** Oct Windso (HVY) S 10f 46 <
2000 Turf 1-7: (7f 2, 9f, 10f 1-3, 12f) (g-s, gd 1-2, g-f 3, frm)
Scopey, fair filly, effective 10f, acts on gd to g-f. Turf high 52 - 5th of 19 giving 1lb to Night Diamond (27 Aug Goodwood 10f g-f RF 4021) - also 1st of 11 from Ariala (26 Oct Windsor RF 5200).
**D R C Elsworth [1-7] D R C Elsworth.*

WOODY'S BOY (IRE) BHB 60f **RR 63f** 3558[P]

6 gr g Roi Danzig (USA) 10.5f **(62)** - Smashing Gale (Lord Gayle (USA)) 8.8f **(62)**
Form - 56P
Record 2000 - 1st:0 2nd:0 3rd:0 Ran:3
Pre2000 - 1st:2 2nd:2 3rd:2 Ran:13
Win Prizemoney £10,338 *Total Prizemoney* £13,441
Wins 1998 Aug Newmar (FRM) H 16.1f 60 65 <
1998 May Newmar (G-F) H 14f 58 61
2000 Turf 0-3: (12f, 16f 2) (frm 3)
Average gelding. Turf high 63 - 6th of 8 getting 12lb from Bid Me Welcome (21 Jly Newbury 16f frm RF 3000). Consistent. (DEAD)
**C G Cox [0-3] Vic Woodason (from M J Heaton-Ellis [2-16] Aug 1998).*

WOOLFE BHB 68f **RR 75f** 5158[4]

3 ch f Wolfhound (USA) 7.3f **(71)** - Brosna (USA) (Irish River (FR)) 8.6f **(78)**
Form - 33204
Record 2000 - 1st:0 2nd:1 3rd:2 Ran:5
Win Prizemoney £0 *Total Prizemoney* £2,831
2000 Turf 0-5: (8f 4, 10f) (sft, gd, g-f 3)
Scopey, above-average filly, has worn blinkers. Turf high 75 (began Jly) - 3rd of 7 getting 5lb from Polar Challenge (7 Aug Windsor 8f g-f RF 3439). **J H M Gosden [0-5] K Abdulla.*

WOOLLY WINSOME BHB 35f35a **RR 38f 35a** 4925[5]

4 br g Lugana Beach 7f **(63)** - Gay Ming (Gay Meadow)

Form - 065380067505
Record 2000 - 1st:0 2nd:0 3rd:1 Ran:9
Pre2000 - 1st:0 2nd:2 3rd:2 Ran:13
Win Prizemoney £0 *Total Prizemoney* £3,288
2000 Turf 0-5: (6f 2, 8f, 10f, 11f) (hvy, g-s, gd, g-f 2) 2000 AW 0-4: (7f 2, 8f 2) (Equi, Fibr 3)
Very moderate gelding, effective 8f, - acts on Equi, has worn blinkers (effectively), likes left handed tracks, favours tight tracks. Turf high 38. AW high 39.
**Dr J R J Naylor [0-5] W Clifford (from B Smart [0-17] Apr 2000).*

WOORE LASS (IRE) BHB 43f33a **RR 46f 33a** 5056[14]
4 ch m Persian Bold 10f **(69)** - Miss Ballylea (Junius (USA)) 7.7f **(65)**
Form - 00024500
Record 2000 - 1st:0 2nd:1 3rd:0 Ran:8
Pre2000 - 1st:2 2nd:2 3rd:0 Ran:22
Win Prizemoney £5,473 *Total Prizemoney* £9,893
Wins 1999 May Bright (FRM) H 8f 64 73 <
1998 Jun Salisb (G-S) 6f 64
2000 Turf 0-8: (7f, 8f 5, 9f 2) (sft, frm 7)
Workmanlike, moderate filly, effective 8 to 10f, acts on gd to g-f, likes left handed tracks, likes tight tracks. Turf high 55. Inconsistent.
**Don Enrico Incisa [0-7] Don Enrico Incisa (from N Tinkler [0-1] May 2000).*

WORK OF FICTION (USA) BHB 58f **RR 64f** 2936[10]
3 b c Known Fact (USA) 8.3f **(72)** - Sahara Forest (Green Desert (USA)) 8.6f **(78)**
Form - 04440
Record 2000 - 1st:0 2nd:0 3rd:0 Ran:5
Win Prizemoney £0 *Total Prizemoney* £321
2000 Turf 0-5: (7f 3, 8f 2) (gd 2, frm 3)
Workmanlike, average colt. Turf high 66.
**R Hannon [0-5] Cliveden Stud.*

WORLD CLEEK (JPN) RR 580a[6]
5 gr h Magic Mirror - Keishu Herb (JPN) (Mississipian (USA))
Form - 166
2000 AW 0-2: (10f, 11f) (Dirt 2)
Currently Group-class colt. AW high 111. **A Hitoshi in JPN [1-3].*

WORLDLY MANNER (USA) RR 93f 1894[3]
4 b h Riverman (USA) 9.7f **(78)** - Lady Pastor (USA) (Flying Paster (USA))
Form - 2073
Record 2000 - 1st:0 2nd:1 3rd:1 Ran:4
Pre2000 - 1st:0 2nd:0 3rd:0 Ran:1
Win Prizemoney £0 *Total Prizemoney* £1,158
2000 Turf 0-2: (8f 2) (gd, g-f) 2000 AW 0-2: (9f, 10f) (Dirt 2)
Useful colt, has worn blinkers. Turf high 93. AW high 87. Godolphin's representative in the 1999 Kentucky Derby, he was in action in Dubai in the spring and finished down the field in the World Cup. He finished last in the Lockinge, was subsequently beaten in a conditions race at Doncaster, and has clearly failed to reach the heights once expected of him.
**S bin Suroor [0-2] Godolphin (from S bin Suroor in UAE [0-2] Mar 2000).*

WORLDLY TREASURE (USA) RR 95f 3480a[1]
3 bb c Ghazi (USA) - Kitten's First (USA) 00
Form - 2211
2000 Turf 2-4: (8f 1-1, 10f 1-3) (g-s, gd 2-2, g-f)
Very useful colt. Turf high 95 - 1st of 4 giving 5lb to Sand Partridge (6 Aug Galway RF 3480a). He broke his duck at Roscommon over ten furlongs and followed up at Galway where he made all the running.
**D K Weld in IRE [2-4] Kenneth Ramsey.*

WORSTED BHB 63f **RR 62f** 3774[2]
3 ch f Whittingham (IRE) - Calamanco **(65f 66a)** (Clantime)
Form - 352
Record 2000 - 1st:0 2nd:1 3rd:1 Ran:3
Pre2000 - 1st:0 2nd:0 3rd:0 Ran:2
Win Prizemoney £0 *Total Prizemoney* £1,647
2000 Turf 0-3: (5f 3) (g-f 3)
Strong, average filly. Turf high 61 (began Jly) - 2nd of 10 giving 2lb to Premium Princess (18 Aug Sandown 5f g-f RF 3774).

**Major D N Chappell [0-5] Mrs D Ellis.*

WORTH A GAMBLE BHB 50f **RR 47f** 5132[12]
2 ch c So Factual (USA) - The Strid (IRE) (Persian Bold) 9.3f **(66)**
Form - 000
Record 2000 - 1st:0 2nd:0 3rd:0 Ran:3
2000 Turf 0-3: (6f 3) (sft, gd, frm)
Currently moderate colt. Turf high 47 (began Spt).
**H E Haynes [0-3] F J Sainsbury.*

WORTH A RING BHB 36f39a **RR 27f 39a** 4930[20]
2 b f Chaddleworth (IRE) - Ring of Pearl (Auction Ring (USA)) 8.6f **(65)**
Form - 0580
Record 2000 - 1st:0 2nd:0 3rd:0 Ran:4
2000 Turf 0-1: (7f) (gd) 2000 AW 0-3: (5f, 6f, 7f) (Fibr 3)
Moderate filly. AW high 48. **J Cullinan [0-4] Turf 2000 Ltd.*

WORTHILY (USA) BHB 100f **RR 101f** 5238[1]
2 b br c Northern Spur (IRE) - Worth's Girl (USA) (Devil's Bag (USA)) 12.4f **(78)**
Form - 051211
Record 2000 - 1st:3 2nd:1 3rd:0 Ran:6
Win Prizemoney £28,712 *Total Prizemoney* £31,121
Wins * 2000 Oct Newmar (SFT) L 10f 101 <
* 2000 Oct Pontef (HVY) L 8f 95
* 2000 Spt Kempto (SFT) 8f 99
2000 Turf 3-6: (7f 2, 8f 2-3, 10f 1-1) (sft, g-s 3-4, gd)
Very useful colt, effective 8 to 10f, best at 8f, acts on g-s. Turf high 101 (began Jly) - 1st of 9 giving 5lb to Capal Garmon (28 Oct Newmarket RF 5238) - also 1st of 10 from King's Secret (18 Spt Kempton RF 4482). Clearly suited by soft ground, he improved steadily last autumn, taking a Listed event in brave fashion at Pontefract and following up in the Zetland Stakes in similarly testing conditions. **M R Channon [3-6] Salem Suhail.*

WORTH THE RISK BHB 27f40a **RR 35f 40a** 4868[8]
3 b f Chaddleworth (IRE) - Bay Risk **(37f)** (Risk Me (FR)) 5.9f **(53)**
Form - 357828
Record 2000 - 1st:0 2nd:1 3rd:1 Ran:6
Pre2000 - 1st:0 2nd:0 3rd:0 Ran:8
Win Prizemoney £0 *Total Prizemoney* £1,076
2000 Turf 0-6: (8f, 9f, 10f, 11f, 14f 2) (hvy, g-s, g-f, frm 2, hrd)
Light-framed, very moderate filly. Turf high 43.
**Don Enrico Incisa [0-7] Don Enrico Incisa (from B J Meehan [0-7] Oct 1999).*

WRANGEL (FR) BHB 44f **RR 47f** 4648[6]
6 ch g Tropular - Swedish Princess (Manado) 9.6f **(63)**
Form - 7016
Record 2000 - 1st:1 2nd:0 3rd:0 Ran:4
Win Prizemoney £2,383 *Total Prizemoney* £2,383
Wins 2000 Aug Catter (G-F) C 12f 47 <
2000 Turf 1-3: (10f, 12f 1-2) (g-s, gd, frm 1-1) 2000 AW 0-1: (16f) (Fibr)
Moderate gelding. Turf high 47 - 1st of 11 from Field of Vision (8 Aug Catterick RF 3451).
**B J Llewellyn [0-3] Mrs Jayne Lewis (from J G FitzGerald [2-18] Aug 2000).*

WRAY (IRE) RR 92f 4528a[11]
8 ch g Sharp Victor (USA) 10f **(56)** - Faye (Monsanto (FR)) 6.5f **(59)**
Form - 243680000
2000 Turf 0-8: (7f, 8f 3, 9f 3, 10f) (sft, g-s 2, gd 3, g-f)
Useful gelding, effective 6 to 9f, best at 7f, acts on sft to g-f, best on g-s, and likes Curragh. Turf high 101 (1st run) - 4th of 11 giving 7lb to Giant's Causeway (9 Apr Curragh 7f g-s RF 0674a). Consistent. **L Browne in IRE [6-37] B Cunningham.*

WROTHAM ARMS (IRE) BHB 30f **RR 26f** 2409[8]
3 b f Second Set (IRE) 9.2f **(67)** - Usance (GER) (Kronenkranich (GER)) 6f **(97)**
Form - 088
Record 2000 - 1st:0 2nd:0 3rd:0 Ran:3
Pre2000 - 1st:0 2nd:0 3rd:0 Ran:1
2000 Turf 0-2: (7f, 10f) (gd, g-f) 2000 AW 0-1: (9f) (Fibr)
Leggy, little account filly, has worn blinkers. Turf high 26.
**Dr J D Scargill [0-4] A C Edwards.*

WRY ARDOUR BHB 38f26a **RR 32f 26a** 262[11]
4 b g Pursuit of Love 9.5f **(69)** - Wryneck (Niniski (USA)) 10.6f **(65)**
Form - 000
Record 2000 - 1st:0 2nd:0 3rd:0 Ran:1
Pre2000 - 1st:0 2nd:0 3rd:0 Ran:10
2000 AW 0-1: (8f) (Fibr)
Workmanlike, very moderate gelding. Becoming disappointing.
**A G Newcombe [0-11] Advanced Marketing Services Ltd.*

WURFSPIEL (GER) RR 91f 5208a[2]
3 b f Lomitas - Wurfbahn (GER) (Frontal) 6.4f **(64)**
Form - 2
2000 Turf 0-1: (10f) (sft)
Currently useful filly. (1st run) - 2nd of 11 giving 4lb to Nicara (21 Oct Gelsenkirchen-horst 10f sft RF 5208a).
**H Remmert in GER [0-1].*

WURZEL BHB 84f **RR 81f** 712[8]
3 ch c Weldnaas (USA) 8.4f **(55)** - Down the Valley (Kampala) 8.4f **(56)**
Form - 8
Record 2000 - 1st:0 2nd:0 3rd:0 Ran:1
Pre2000 - 1st:1 2nd:0 3rd:1 Ran:3
Win Prizemoney £2,983 *Total Prizemoney* £3,483
Wins *1999 Oct Bright (G-F) 7f 81 <
2000 Turf 0-1: (8f) (g-s)
Scopey, decent colt. (DEAD) **R Hannon [1-4] J R Shannon.*

WUXI VENTURE BHB 66f60a **RR 61f 60a** 1188[11]
5 b g Wolfhound (USA) 7.3f **(71)** - Push a Button (Bold Lad (IRE)) 8.4f **(68)**
Form - 78808800
Record 2000 - 1st:0 2nd:0 3rd:0 Ran:8
Pre2000 - 1st:3 2nd:5 3rd:4 Ran:28
Win Prizemoney £15,900 *Total Prizemoney* £34,977
Wins 1998 Spt Hamilt (SFT) H 8.3f 88 91 <
1998 Aug Haydoc (GD) H 8.1f 85 88
1998 Apr Ripon (SFT) 8f 86
2000 Turf 0-5: (8f 3, 10f 2) (g-s 2, gd 2, hrd) 2000 AW 0-3: (7f, 8f 2) (Fibr 3)
Average gelding, effective 8f, acts on gd, has worn blinkers, likes left handed tracks. Turf high 61. AW high 55.
**D Nicholls [0-8] R G Leatham (from S P C Woods [3-28] Oct 1999).*

WYN BHB 42f47a **RR 66f 47a** 1520[6]
5 b m Gildoran 11.6f **(58)** - Its A Romp (Hotfoot) 10.5f **(59)**
Form - 6
Record 2000 - 1st:0 2nd:0 3rd:0 Ran:1
Pre2000 - 1st:0 2nd:1 3rd:0 Ran:7
Win Prizemoney £0 *Total Prizemoney* £852
2000 Turf 0-1: (6f) (g-s)
Average filly.
**M D I Usher [0-3] A J Owen (from C A Dwyer [0-7] Spt 1998).*

XALOC BAY (IRE) BHB 72f **RR 76f** 5183[7]
2 br c Charnwood Forest (IRE) - Royal Jade **(63f)** (Last Tycoon) 8.5f **(62)**
Form - 22007
Record 2000 - 1st:0 2nd:2 3rd:0 Ran:5
Win Prizemoney £0 *Total Prizemoney* £2,081
2000 Turf 0-5: (5f 2, 6f 3) (g-s, gd, g-f, frm 2)
Above-average colt. Turf high 76 - 2nd of 9 to Xipe Totec (16 Jly Haydock 6f frm RF 2858). Runner-up on his first two starts, but outpaced in a listed race. **K R Burke [0-5] Mrs Melba Bryce.*

XANADU BHB 79f **RR 78f** 4449[29]
4 ch g Casteddu 7.4f **(54)** - Bellatrix (Persian Bold) 9.3f **(66)**
Form - 0011201012436020
Record 2000 - 1st:4 2nd:3 3rd:1 Ran:16
Pre2000 - 1st:2 2nd:0 3rd:1 Ran:10
Win Prizemoney £36,298 *Total Prizemoney* £42,356
Wins *** 2000** Jly Haydoc (G-F) H 5f 68 75 <
*** 2000** Jun Mussel (FRM) H 5f 64 68
*** 2000** May Hamilt (FRM) 6f 65
*** 2000** May Hamilt (G-F) H 6f 53 64
* 1999 Aug Carlis (FRM) H 5.9f 44 54
* 1999 Jly Hamilt (FRM) S 6f 43
2000 Turf 4-16: (5f 2-9, 6f 2-7) (gd 1-6, g-f 1-4, frm 2-6)
Strong, above-average gelding, effective 5f, acts on gd to frm, likes Hamilton. Turf high 78 - 2nd of 9 giving 10lb to Sharp Hat (17 Jly Ayr 5f frm RF 2873) - also 1st of 16 giving 9lb to Bollin Rita (8 Jly Haydock RF 2636). A winner four times last season, he is very much suited by very fast ground, conditions under which he won twice at Hamilton in May and broke a very old course record when winning over the minimum trip at Musselburgh in June.
**Miss L A Perratt [6-26] Mrs Meta Sutherland.*

XANIA BHB 51f45a **RR 42f 45a** 4907a[6]
3 b f Mujtahid (USA) 7.4f **(69)** - Polish Honour (USA) (Danzig Connection (USA)) 8f **(68)**
Form - 800806
Record 2000 - 1st:0 2nd:0 3rd:0 Ran:5
Pre2000 - 1st:0 2nd:0 3rd:0 Ran:3
2000 Turf 0-4: (7f, 8f, 9f, 13f) (g-s, gd, g-f) 2000 AW 0-1: (7f) (Fibr)
Neat, moderate filly, has worn blinkers. Turf high 42 (began Jly).
**P F McEnery in IRE [0-4] Mrs A M Burns (from M Johnston [0-4] Jan 2000).*

XATIVA (IRE) BHB 50f45a **RR 63f 45a** 687[17]
3 b f Thatching 7.8f **(69)** - Abergwrle (Absalom) 7.2f **(58)**
Form - 0840
Record 2000 - 1st:0 2nd:0 3rd:0 Ran:4
Pre2000 - 1st:0 2nd:0 3rd:0 Ran:3
2000 Turf 0-1: (7f) (hvy) 2000 AW 0-3: (6f, 7f, 8f) (Equi, Fibr 2)
Scopey, average filly. AW high 40.
**J A Osborne [0-2] A Edward (from M R Channon [0-5] Jan 2000).*

XELLANCE (IRE) BHB 73f51a **RR 75f 51a** 4399[4]
3 b g Be My Guest (USA) 10.2f **(66)** - Excellent Alibi (USA) (Exceller (USA)) 12.5f **(74)**
Form - 151U7111221412314
Record 2000 - 1st:8 2nd:3 3rd:1 Ran:17
Pre2000 - 1st:0 2nd:0 3rd:0 Ran:3
Win Prizemoney £23,157 *Total Prizemoney* £28,010
Wins *** 2000** Aug Warwic (GD) H 16.2f 70 74 <
*** 2000** Jly Redcar (G-F) H 16f 62 67
*** 2000** Jly Chepst (G-F) H 18f 52 65
*** 2000** Jun Redcar (FRM) H 14.1f 40 50
*** 2000** *Jun Southw (STD) H 12f 48 48*
*** 2000** Jun Mussel (FRM) H 14f 45 48
*** 2000** *May Wolver (STD) H 12f 42 46*
*** 2000** *Feb Southw (STD) H 11f 35 37*
2000 Turf 5-13: (12f 2, 14f 2-3, 16f 2-6, 18f 1-2) (gd 1-3, g-f 2-6, frm 2-4) 2000 AW 3-4: (10f, 11f 1-1, 12f 2-2) (Equi, Fibr 3-3)
Workmanlike, above-average gelding, effective 16 to 18f, best at 16f, acts on gd to frm, prefers left handed tracks, excels at Southwell and Redcar, likes Yarmouth. Turf high 75 - 4th of 4 getting 9lb from King Flyer (14 Spt Yarmouth 18f g-f RF 4399) - also 1st of 6 getting 6lb from Palua (28 Aug Warwick RF 4058). AW high 48. Improving. He proved most progressive in staying events last term, winning eight times in all.
**M Johnston [8-20] T T Bloodstocks.*

XENOS BHB 51f44a **RR 62f 44a** 365[4]
3 b g Owington - Little Change (Grundy) 10.3f **(65)**
Form - 8756304
Record 2000 - 1st:0 2nd:0 3rd:1 Ran:6
Pre2000 - 1st:0 2nd:0 3rd:0 Ran:4
Win Prizemoney £0 *Total Prizemoney* £260
2000 AW 0-6: (6f, 7f, 8f 2, 9f, 11f) (Equi 2, Fibr 4)
Scopey, average gelding, has worn blinkers. AW high 47.
**P Howling [0-7] Mrs P Reditt (from M R Channon [0-3] Jun 1999).*

XIBALBA BHB 68f **RR 71f** 3619[U]
3 b c Zafonic (USA) 9f **(83)** - Satanic Dance (FR) (Shareef Dancer (USA)) 9.9f **(73)**
Form - 1400U
Record 2000 - 1st:1 2nd:0 3rd:0 Ran:5
Pre2000 - 1st:0 2nd:0 3rd:0 Ran:3
Win Prizemoney £2,177 *Total Prizemoney* £2,533
Wins *** 2000** May Nottin (GD) H 8.2f 67 70 <
2000 Turf 1-5: (8f 1-1, 9f, 10f 2, 12f) (gd 1-2, g-f, frm 2)
Workmanlike, above-average colt, effective 8 to 10f, acts on gd, has worn blinkers. Turf high 71 - 4th of 10 getting 7lb from Original Spin (5 Jun Leicester 10f gd RF 1719) - also 1st of 16 getting 9lb from Compatriot (20 May Nottingham RF 1343). Won a moderate

maiden handicap on his seasonal return, but did not do too badly when stepped up in class next time. **C E Brittain [1-8] R Meredith.*

XIPE TOTEC BHB 80f **RR 77f** 3614[6]
2 ch c Pivotal - Northern Bird **(60+f)** (Interrex (CAN))
Form - 0136
Record 2000 - 1st:1 2nd:0 3rd:1 Ran:4
Win Prizemoney £3,753 *Total Prizemoney* £4,289
Wins * **2000** Jly Haydoc (G-F) 6f 77 <
2000 Turf 1-4: (6f 1-4) (frm 1-3, hrd)
Above-average colt. Turf high 77 - also 1st of 9 from Xaloc Bay (16 Jly Haydock RF 2858). **R A Fahey [1-4] Mrs Brigitte Pollard.*

XSYNNA BHB 49f53a **RR 48f 53a** 4476[10]
4 b g Cyrano de Bergerac 7.3f **(58)** - Rose Ciel (IRE) (Red Sunset) 8.2f **(63)**
Form - 54267000
Record 2000 - 1st:0 2nd:1 3rd:0 Ran:7
Pre2000 - 1st:1 2nd:1 3rd:3 Ran:16
Win Prizemoney £2,872 *Total Prizemoney* £6,072
Wins 1998 *Dec Lingfi (STD) H* 6f 62 64 <
2000 Turf 0-2: (6f, 8f) (gd, frm) 2000 AW 0-5: (6f 4, 7f) (Equi, Fibr 4)
Workmanlike, fair gelding, effective 6f, - acts on Fibr, has worn blinkers, likes left handed tracks, likes tight tracks. Turf high 13. AW high 58 - 2nd of 12 giving 9lb to Press Ahead (18 Jan Wolverhampton 6f Fibr RF 0112). Becoming disappointing.
**J A Gilbert [0-1] Ms Tania Baybut (from T T Clement [0-7] Jun 2000).*

XTRA RR 87f 5224[3]
2 b c Sadler's Wells (USA) 11.3f **(87)** - Oriental Mystique (Kris) 9.5f **(73)**
Form - 03
Record 2000 - 1st:0 2nd:0 3rd:1 Ran:2
Win Prizemoney £0 *Total Prizemoney* £1,082
2000 Turf 0-2: (8f 2) (gd 2)
Currently useful colt. Turf high 87 (began Oct) - 3rd of 10 getting 2lb from Welsh Border (27 Oct Newmarket 8f gd RF 5224).
**L M Cumani [0-2] M J Dawson.*

XUA (IRE) RR 108f 5364a[2]
3 b f Fairy King (USA) 7.7f **(75)** - Bold Starlet (Precocious) 8.6f **(62)**
Form - 10802
2000 Turf 1-5: (7f, 8f 1-3, 11f) (hvy, sft 1-1, g-s, gd 2)
Pattern-class filly, effective 7 to 8f, best at 8f, acts on hvy to gd. Turf high 108 (1st run) - 1st of 18 from Timi (30 Apr Capannelle RF 1031a). **B Grizzetti in ITY [1-8] Jly 2000).*

XYLEM (USA) BHB 20f34a **RR 40f 34a** 3080[14]
9 ch g Woodman (USA) 9.7f **(77)** - Careful (USA) (Tampa Trouble (USA)) 8f **(87)**
Form - 32372305400
Record 2000 - 1st:0 2nd:2 3rd:3 Ran:11
Pre2000 - 1st:2 2nd:1 3rd:4 Ran:37
Win Prizemoney £6,554 *Total Prizemoney* £13,205
Wins 1997 Oct Newcas (G-F) H 8f 69 70
2000 Turf 0-4: (12f 2, 14f, 16f) (gd, g-f, frm 2) 2000 AW 0-7: (12f 3, 13f, 14f, 16f 2) (Equi, Fibr 6)
Moderate gelding, effective 10 to 16f, acts on g-s to g-f - acts on AW, best on Fibr, has worn blinkers, likes left handed tracks, favours tight tracks, excels at Lingfield and Wolverhampton. Turf high 40. AW high 43 - 3rd of 14 giving 7lb to Irish Cream (14 Mar Southwell 14f Fibr RF 0438). Inconsistent.
**J Pearce [0-25] Mrs Anne Holman-Chappell (from J H M Gosden [1-17] Spt 1998).*

YABINT EL SHAM BHB 47f48a **RR 43f 48a** 4997[5]
4 b m Sizzling Melody 6.3f **(49)** - Dalby Dancer (Bustiki) 8.7f **(78)**
Form - 0152307000877075
Record 2000 - 1st:0 2nd:1 3rd:1 Ran:14
Pre2000 - 1st:2 2nd:0 3rd:0 Ran:12
Win Prizemoney £7,541 *Total Prizemoney* £10,119
Wins * 1999 *Dec Wolver (STD) H* 5f 60 63
* 1998 Aug Leices (GD) 5f 85 <
2000 Turf 0-4: (5f 2, 6f 2) (g-f 2, frm 2) 2000 AW 0-10: (5f 6, 6f 3, 8f) (Fibr 10)
Neat, moderate filly, effective 5 to 6f, best at 5f, - acts on Fibr, likes left handed tracks, likes tight tracks. Turf high 43. AW high 68 - 2nd of 11 getting 25lb from Dil (25 Jan Wolverhampton 5f Fibr RF 0155).
**B A McMahon [2-26] G S D Imports Ltd.*

YAFA BHB 35f **RR 31f** 2195[8]
4 ch g Elmaamul (USA) 8.1f **(70)** - Mousaiha (USA) (Shadeed (USA)) 8.2f **(70)**
Form - 0008
Record 2000 - 1st:0 2nd:0 3rd:0 Ran:4
2000 Turf 0-3: (8f, 9f, 10f) (sft 2, gd) 2000 AW 0-1: (7f) (Fibr)
Scopey, very moderate gelding, has worn blinkers. Turf high 31.
**N A Graham [0-4] Paul Jacobs.*

YAGLI (USA) RR 123f 1153a[3]
7 ch h Jade Hunter (USA) 10.4f **(72)**
Form - 3
2000 Turf 0-1: (9f)
Currently very high-class horse. (1st run) - 3rd of 8 giving 6lb to Manndar (6 May Churchill Downs 9f RF 1153a).
**W Mott in USA [0-3] Nov 1999).*

YAHESKA (IRE) BHB 32f **RR 42f** 2815[11]
3 b f Prince of Birds (USA) - How Ya Been (IRE) (Last Tycoon) 8.5f **(62)**
Form - 5880
Record 2000 - 1st:0 2nd:0 3rd:0 Ran:4
Pre2000 - 1st:0 2nd:0 3rd:0 Ran:3
2000 Turf 0-2: (10f, 12f) (g-f, frm) 2000 AW 0-2: (7f, 10f) (Equi, Fibr)
Leggy, moderate filly, has worn blinkers. Turf high 42. AW high 14.
**E J O'Neill [0-7] Mrs Patrick O'Neill.*

YAKAREEM (IRE) BHB 92f93a **RR 98f 93a** 4105[9]
4 b h Rainbows For Life (CAN) 9.3f **(64)** - Brandywell (Skyliner) 7.3f **(53)**
Form - 045880
Record 2000 - 1st:0 2nd:0 3rd:0 Ran:5
Pre2000 - 1st:1 2nd:2 3rd:1 Ran:13
Win Prizemoney £3,596 *Total Prizemoney* £22,008
Wins * 1999 *Mar Wolver (STD) 9.4f 94 <*
2000 Turf 0-5: (7f, 9f 2, 10f 2) (gd 3, g-f 2)
Strong, very useful colt, effective 9f, acts on gd, likes left handed tracks, likes tight tracks. Turf high 98. Inconsistent.
**K Mahdi [1-18] Hamad Al-Mutawa.*

YALAIL (IRE) BHB 33f30a **RR 46f 30a** 4228[10]
4 b h Perugino (USA) - Cristalga (High Top) 10.2f **(67)**
Form - 070840
Record 2000 - 1st:0 2nd:0 3rd:0 Ran:3
Pre2000 - 1st:0 2nd:0 3rd:0 Ran:7
2000 Turf 0-1: (7f) (frm) 2000 AW 0-2: (12f 2) (Equi, Fibr)
Light-framed, moderate colt. AW high 30 (began Aug).
**K Mahdi [0-10] Hamad Al-Mutawa.*

YANKEE DANCER BHB 26f **RR 31f** 5011[14]
5 b m Groom Dancer (USA) 9.5f **(75)** - Yakin (USA) (Nureyev (USA)) 8.7f **(78)**
Form - 00000870
Record 2000 - 1st:0 2nd:0 3rd:0 Ran:8
Pre2000 - 1st:0 2nd:1 3rd:1 Ran:3
Win Prizemoney £0 *Total Prizemoney* £877
2000 Turf 0-5: (10f, 12f 3, 14f) (g-s, gd, g-f, frm 2) 2000 AW 0-3: (8f, 14f, 15f) (Fibr 3)
Very moderate filly. Turf high 31. AW high 24 (began Jly). Inconsistent.
**R Hollinshead [0-8] Leslie Laverty (from C Roche in IRE [0-3] Nov 1998).*

YANUS BHB 50f **RR 53f** 4726[13]
2 b c Inchinor 8.9f **(64)** - Birsay (Bustino) 10.4f **(64)**
Form - 000
Record 2000 - 1st:0 2nd:0 3rd:0 Ran:3
2000 Turf 0-3: (6f 2, 7f) (gd, g-f, frm)
Currently fair colt. Turf high 53 (began Aug).
**M L W Bell [0-3] Kenneth MacPherson.*

YAQOOTAH (USA) RR 72f 4377[7]
2 ch f Gone West (USA) 7.8f **(82)** - Sweet Roberta (USA) (Roberto (USA)) 10f **(76)**
Form - 7

Record 2000 - 1st:0 2nd:0 3rd:0 Ran:1
2000 Turf 0-1: (6f) (frm)
Currently above-average filly.
**E A L Dunlop [0-1] Hamdan Al Maktoum.*

YARA (IRE) RR 105f 3306a[2]
3 b f Sri Pekan (USA) - Your Village (IRE) (Be My Guest (USA)) 9.3f **(67)**
Form - 2271632
2000 Turf 1-7: (7f, 8f 2, 9f 1-1, 10f 3) (sft 2, g-s 1-3, g-f 2)
Pattern-class filly, effective 9 to 10f, acts on g-s to g-f. Turf high 105 - 2nd of 9 getting 3lb from Takali (29 Jly Curragh 10f g-f RF 3306a) - also 1st of 8 getting 5lb from Raypour (10 Jun Curragh RF 1940a). An amazing filly who has finished runner-up on no fewer than ten occasions and, when she actually 'won' a race (a Curragh maiden), had the misfortune to be disqualified subsequently. She seems genuine enough, but just lacks a turn of foot when it matters, and must have walked under several ladders in her short life.
**K Prendergast in IRE [1-15] Mrs Chryss O'Reilly.*

YAROB (IRE) BHB 82f90a **RR 92f 90a** 4814[8]
7 ch g Unfuwain (USA) 11.4f **(74)** - Azyaa (Kris) 9.5f **(73)**
Form - 710102606068
Record 2000 - 1st:2 2nd:1 3rd:0 Ran:12
Pre2000 - 1st:2 2nd:3 3rd:0 Ran:24
Win Prizemoney £26,310 *Total Prizemoney* £44,739
Wins * 2000 May Doncas (G-S) H 10.3f 82 91 <
*** 2000** Apr Pontef (G-S) H 8f 77 82
* 1999 May Doncas (G-F) H 10.3f 77 81
2000 Turf 2-12: (7f, 8f 1-5, 10f 1-5, 12f) (sft, g-s 1-2, gd 1-5, g-f 3, frm)
Useful gelding, effective 8 to 10f, best at 10f, acts on g-s to g-f, likes left handed tracks. Turf high 92 - 2nd of 13 giving 14lb to Noukari (9 May Chester 10f g-f RF 1112) - also 1st of 15 from Mindanao (1 May Doncaster RF 0934). Gelded during the winter, he was hampered on his Catterick reappearance but made no mistake when winning in good style at Pontefract next time. He added another victory at Doncaster in May and was just touched off at Chester later the same month. Best suited by ten furlongs these days, he ideally likes a bit of cut in the ground.
**D Nicholls [3-22] Lucayan Stud (from D R Loder [0-3] Mar 1998).*

YA TARRA RR 76f 5314[2]
3 ch f Unbridled (USA) - Snow Bride (USA) (Blushing Groom (FR)) 10.3f **(76)**
Form - 32
Record 2000 - 1st:0 2nd:1 3rd:1 Ran:2
Win Prizemoney £0 *Total Prizemoney* £2,690
2000 Turf 0-2: (10f 2) (sft 2)
Leggy, currently above-average filly. Turf high 76 (1st run) (began Oct) - 3rd of 9 getting 5lb from Tikram (18 Oct Nottingham 10f sft RF 5058). **S bin Suroor [0-2] Godolphin.*

YATTARNA (IRE) BHB 52f **RR 53f** 2359[4]
4 b g Be My Guest (USA) 10.2f **(66)** - Kindpiano (USA) (Fappiano (USA)) 8.7f **(77)**
Form - 544
Record 2000 - 1st:0 2nd:0 3rd:0 Ran:3
Pre2000 - 1st:1 2nd:0 3rd:0 Ran:6
Win Prizemoney £3,093 *Total Prizemoney* £3,392
Wins 1999 Jly Wexfor (G-F) H 13f 60 46 <
2000 Turf 0-2: (14f, 16f) (gd, g-f) 2000 AW 0-1: (12f) (Fibr)
Fair gelding, effective 13 to 16f, acts on gd to g-f, best on g-f, has worn blinkers. Turf high 53 (1st run) - 4th of 15 getting 2lb from Zincalo (12 Jun Nottingham 14f gd RF 1896).
**Ian Williams [1-5] P B R Abrasives (W'ton) Ltd (from K Prendergast in IRE [1-8] Spt 1999).*

YAVANA'S PACE (IRE) BHB 114f **RR 120f** 4717a[2]
8 ch g Accordion 11.3f **(75)** - Lady in Pace (Burslem) 8.8f **(53)**
Form - 601843226522
Record 2000 - 1st:1 2nd:4 3rd:1 Ran:11
Pre2000 - 1st:8 2nd:8 3rd:4 Ran:35
Win Prizemoney £172,622 *Total Prizemoney* £418,339
Wins * 2000 Apr Haydoc (HVY) G3 11.9f 115 <
* 1999 Spt Epsom (GD) G3 12f 114
* 1999 Aug Goodwo (GD) L 14f 115 <
* 1999 Jun Leices (G-S) L 11.8f 115 <
* 1998 Nov Doncas (SFT) H 12f 105 114
* 1998 Spt Galway (HVY) L 12f 90
* 1998 Jly Sandow (GD) H 10f 88 92
* 1998 May Ayr (GD) H 10f 83 87
1996 Jun Leopar (GD) H 7f 90 75
2000 Turf 1-11: (12f 1-8, 13f, 14f, 16f) (hvy 1-1, sft, g-s 2, gd 5, g-f 2)
Very high-class gelding, effective 12 to 14f, best at 12f, acts on hvy to frm, likes right handed tracks, does well at Newmarket. Turf high 120 - 2nd of 11 to Golden Snake (24 Spt Cologne 12f sft RF 4717a) - also 1st of 11 getting 2lb from Capri (22 Apr Haydock RF 0821). This remarkably tough gelding won the Group Three John Porter Stakes at Haydock in April and was still in top form when touched off in a Group One at Cologne six months later. Effective up to a mile and three-quarters, he acts on anything from good-firm to heavy ground and seems to run well when getting stirred-up in the preliminaries.
**M Johnston [8-31] Mrs Joan Keaney (from M A Johnson [0-1] Spt 1999).*

YAZAIN (IRE) BHB 65f **RR 68f** 4618[16]
4 b h Pips Pride 6.7f **(70)** - Trust Sally (Sallust) 8.4f **(63)**
Form - 3000
Record 2000 - 1st:0 2nd:0 3rd:1 Ran:4
Win Prizemoney £0 *Total Prizemoney* £428
2000 Turf 0-4: (6f, 7f 2, 8f) (gd 2, g-f, frm)
Scopey, average colt. Turf high 68 (1st run) (began Jun) - 3rd of 8 to Thunder Sky (30 Jun Folkestone 7f g-f RF 2393).
**K Mahdi [0-4] Hamad Al-Mutawa.*

Globetrotting Yavana's Pace

YAZMIN (IRE) BHB 95f **RR 88f** 1192[10]
3 b f Green Desert (USA) 7.8f **(78)** - All My Heart (USA) (Sharpen Up) 8.3f **(67)**
Form - 60
Record 2000 - 1st:0 2nd:0 3rd:0 Ran:2
Pre2000 - 1st:1 2nd:1 3rd:1 Ran:4
Win Prizemoney £3,824 *Total Prizemoney* £5,702
Wins * 1999 Aug Windso (G-F) 6f 72 <
2000 Turf 0-2: (7f 2) (g-s 2)
Light-framed, useful filly, effective 6f, acts on g-f. Turf high 82.
**J L Dunlop [1-6] & Mrs Gary Pinchen.*

YEAST BHB 75f **RR 77f** 3003[2]
8 b g Salse (USA) 10.9f **(71)** - Orient (Bay Express) 7.1f **(60)**
Form - 020112
Record 2000 - 1st:2 2nd:2 3rd:0 Ran:6
Pre2000 - 1st:8 2nd:4 3rd:2 Ran:33
Win Prizemoney £126,867 *Total Prizemoney* £138,987
Wins * 2000 Jly Leices (G-F) 7f 77
*** 2000** Jun Lingfi (G-F) 7.6f 74
* 1999 Aug Ripon (GD) C 8f 77+

* 1999	Jun	Salisb	(G-F)	H	8f	80	84	
* 1999	May	Chepst	(GD)		8.1f		80	
* 1996	Oct	Newmar	(G-F)	L	8f		108	<
* 1996	Jly	Ascot	(G-F)	H	8f	97	107	
* 1996	Jun	Ascot	(G-F)	H	8f	87	102	
* 1996	May	Ascot	(G-F)	H	7f	80	87	
* 1996	Mar	Newcas	(G-S)		8f		83	

2000 Turf 2-6: (7f 1-2, 8f 1-4) (sft, gd, g-f 1-3, frm 1-1)
Above-average gelding, effective 7 to 8f, best at 8f, acts on gd to frm. Turf high 77 - 1st of 14 giving 3lb to Teofilio (8 Jly Leicester RF 2639). A one-time very useful handicapper, winner of the 1996 Hunt Cup and a winner in Listed company, he was disappointing for a couple of seasons, but rediscovered the winning thread in 1999, and added to that last term with victories over seven furlongs. He remains well handicapped on his best form and is suited by forcing tactics.
**W J Haggas [10-39] The Not Over Big Partnership.*

YELLOW TRUMPET RR 70f
3901[1]
2 b f Petong 7.6f **(58)** - Daffodil Fields (Try My Best (USA)) 7.6f **(67)**
Form - 1
Record 2000 - 1st:1 2nd:0 3rd:0 Ran:1
Win Prizemoney £2,879 *Total Prizemoney* £2,879
Wins * 2000 Aug Carlis (GD) 5f 70 <
2000 Turf 1-1: (5f 1-1) (frm 1-1)
Currently above-average filly. (1st run) - 1st of 12 from Silken Wings (23 Aug Carlisle RF 3901).
**M L W Bell [1-1] Cheveley Park Stud.*

YENALED BHB 64f RR 63f
5299[3]
3 gr g Rambo Dancer (CAN) 8.4f **(59)** - Fancy Flight (FR) (Arctic Tern (USA)) 8.9f **(69)**
Form - 316246225103
Record 2000 - 1st:2 2nd:3 3rd:2 Ran:12
Pre2000 - 1st:0 2nd:1 3rd:3 Ran:10
Win Prizemoney £7,221 *Total Prizemoney* £14,120
Wins * 2000 Spt Mussel (G-S) H 7.1f 59 63 <
* 2000 May Mussel (FRM) H 8f 59 62
2000 Turf 2-12: (7f 1-2, 8f 1-6, 9f, 10f, 11f 2) (g-s, gd 1-3, g-f 4, frm 1-4)
Small, average gelding, effective 7 to 10f, acts on gd to frm, best on g-f, likes left handed trackslikes right handed tracks, prefers tight tracks. Turf high 66 - 2nd of 4 getting 11lb from Soller Bay (24 Jun Ayr 9f g-f RF 2248) - also 1st of 14 giving 1lb to Bodfari Anna (24 Spt Musselburgh RF 4627). Consistent. He took his time in getting off the mark, but managed to do so in a modest fast-ground Musselburgh handicap in May and scored at the same track in September. Suited by coming late off a strong pace.
**J S Goldie [2-22] Martin Delaney.*

YERTLE (IRE) BHB 56f RR 65f
4823[9]
3 b c Turtle Island (IRE) - Minatina (IRE) **(71?f)** (Ela-Mana-Mou) 10.1f **(70)**
Form - 883600
Record 2000 - 1st:0 2nd:0 3rd:1 Ran:6
Win Prizemoney £0 *Total Prizemoney* £268
2000 Turf 0-6: (7f, 8f 4, 10f) (g-s, gd 2, g-f, frm 2)
Average colt. Turf high 83.
**J A R Toller [0-6] Gerald Cooper.*

YES KEEMO SABEE BHB 47f37a RR 56f 37a
4456[2]
5 b g Arazi (USA) 9.2f **(74)** - Nazeera (FR) (Lashkari) 9.8f **(67)**
Form - 6000878253302082
Record 2000 - 1st:0 2nd:3 3rd:2 Ran:16
Pre2000 - 1st:1 2nd:5 3rd:0 Ran:14
Win Prizemoney £7,337 *Total Prizemoney* £17,288
Wins * 1999 May Thirsk (G-S) H 16f 65 68 <
2000 Turf 0-14: (12f 3, 14f 2, 15f, 16f 6, 17f 2) (sft, g-s, gd 7, g-f, frm 3, hrd) 2000 AW 0-2: (12f, 16f) (Fibr 2)
Fair gelding, effective 11 to 18f, best at 16f, acts on g-s to g-f - acts on Fibr, best on gd, has worn blinkers, likes right handed tracks. Turf high 56. Consistent.
**D Shaw [1-25] M Torley (from B A McMahon [0-5] Dec 1998).*

YETTI BHB 67f RR 73f
4808[5]
2 ch f Aragon 7.7f **(58)** - Willyet (Nicholas Bill) 10.1f **(56)**
Form - 225365
Record 2000 - 1st:0 2nd:2 3rd:1 Ran:6
Win Prizemoney £0 *Total Prizemoney* £2,109
2000 Turf 0-6: (5f 2, 6f 4) (g-s, g-f 2, frm 2, hrd)
Above-average filly, effective 5 to 6f, best at 6f, acts on g-f to frm, best on frm. Turf high 73 - 2nd of 11 getting 2lb from Sibla (1 Jly Bath 6f frm RF 2422).
**H Candy [0-6] Henry Candy.*

YNYSMON BHB 75f RR 83f
5129[11]
2 b c Mind Games - Florentynna Bay (Aragon) 8.1f **(60)**
Form - 574010
Record 2000 - 1st:1 2nd:0 3rd:0 Ran:6
Win Prizemoney £3,672 *Total Prizemoney* £4,136
Wins * 2000 Spt Mussel (G-S) 5f 83 <
2000 Turf 1-6: (5f 1-3, 6f 3) (sft, gd 1-1, g-f, frm, hrd 2)
Decent colt, effective 5f, acts on gd. Turf high 83 (began Jly) - 1st of 14 giving 5lb to Micklow Magic (24 Spt Musselburgh RF 4622). A winner at Musselburgh on his fifth start, he probably has ideas of his own. **A Berry [1-6] The Boursot Judges.*

YORBA LINDA (IRE) BHB 91f RR 89f
3160a[1]
5 ch m Night Shift (USA) 8.1f **(73)** - Allepolina (USA) (Trempolino (USA)) 12f **(71)**
Form - 475871
Record 2000 - 1st:1 2nd:0 3rd:0 Ran:6
Pre2000 - 1st:2 2nd:3 3rd:2 Ran:16
Win Prizemoney £18,722 *Total Prizemoney* £23,190
Wins * 2000 Jly Dussel (GD) L 7.5f 89 <
1999 Jly Currag (G-F) H 5f 81 81+
1997 Spt Currag (SFT) 5f 71
2000 Turf 1-6: (5f 4, 8f 1-1, 10f) (g-s, gd 1-1, g-f, frm 2, hrd)
Useful filly, effective 6 to 8f, acts on gd, has worn blinkers. Turf high 89 - also 1st of 10 getting 9lb from Signatory (23 Jly Dusseldorf RF 3160a).
**E J O'Neill [1-6] T F Brennan (from P Martin in IRE [1-7] Oct 1999).*

YORK CLIFF RR 84f
5184[3]
2 b c Marju (IRE) 9.2f **(76)** - Azm **(61f)** (Unfuwain (USA))
Form - 3
Record 2000 - 1st:0 2nd:0 3rd:1 Ran:1
Win Prizemoney £0 *Total Prizemoney* £605
2000 Turf 0-1: (8f) (g-s)
Currently decent colt. (1st run) - 3rd of 17 to Caughnawaga (25 Oct Yarmouth 8f g-s RF 5184). **J H M Gosden [0-1] R Van Gelder.*

YORKER (USA) BHB 68f RR 54f
5156[8]
2 b c Boundary (USA) - Shallows (USA) (Cox's Ridge (USA)) 8f **(68)**
Form - 008
Record 2000 - 1st:0 2nd:0 3rd:0 Ran:3
2000 Turf 0-3: (5f 3) (g-s, g-f, hrd)
Currently fair colt. Turf high 54 (began Aug).
**J M P Eustace [0-3] Michael Scott.*

YORKIES BOY BHB 100f RR 99f
5324[10]
5 ro h Clantime 6.6f **(57)** - Slipperose (Persepolis (FR)) 6.4f **(67)**
Form - 0522041671040760
Record 2000 - 1st:2 2nd:2 3rd:0 Ran:16
Pre2000 - 1st:3 2nd:4 3rd:1 Ran:28
Win Prizemoney £54,400 *Total Prizemoney* £87,609
Wins * 2000 Aug Cheste (GD) L 6.1f 96
* 2000 Jly Haydoc (G-F) 6f 99
1998 May Newmar (G-S) G3 5f 113 <
1998 Apr Newmar (SFT) L 5f 109
1997 Jun Cheste (G-F) 5.1f 76+
2000 Turf 2-16: (5f 6, 6f 2-8, 7f 2) (sft, g-s 3, gd 3, g-f 2-8, hrd)
Very useful colt, effective 5 to 7f, best at 6f, acts on gd to frm, best on gd, has worn blinkers. Turf high 104 - 4th of 9 giving 4lb to Nicobar (1 Spt Epsom 7f g-f RF 4145). A tough sprinter, he ran creditably in a couple of conditions events earlier this season and returned to winning form in such an event at Haydock in July, his first win over six furlongs. Has added another win over that trip at Chester.
**A Berry [2-16] Mrs M Beddis (from B A McMahon [3-28] Nov 1999).*

YORKIE TOO BHB 40f39a RR 36f 39a
5037a[9]
4 b g Prince Sabo 6.6f **(64)** - Petonica (IRE) (Petoski) 5.7f **(62)**
Form - 085000
Record 2000 - 1st:0 2nd:0 3rd:0 Ran:6
Pre2000 - 1st:0 2nd:0 3rd:0 Ran:7

Win Prizemoney £0 *Total Prizemoney* £492
2000 Turf 0-4: (6f 2, 7f, 9f) (sft, gd, g-f, frm) 2000 AW 0-2: (6f, 7f) (Fibr 2)
Scopey, very moderate gelding, often wears blinkers. Turf high 36. AW high 28.
**J G Cromwell in IRE [0-1] M & G K Syndicate (from H J Collingridge [0-12] Jun 2000).*

YORKSHIRE (IRE) BHB 105f **RR 112f** 5311[4]

6 ch g Generous (IRE) 11.5f **(82)** - Ausherra (USA) (Diesis) 9.3f **(69)**
Form - 5304
Record 2000 - 1st:0 2nd:0 3rd:1 Ran:4
Pre2000 - 1st:2 2nd:3 3rd:1 Ran:13
Win Prizemoney £15,512 *Total Prizemoney* £66,087
Wins * 1998 May Newbur (G-F) L 13.3f 107 <
* 1996 Oct Salisb (G-S) 8f 97+
2000 Turf 0-4: (13f, 14f, 15f, 19f) (sft, g-f, frm 2)
Group-class gelding. Turf high 112 (began Aug) - 3rd of 6 to Murghem (19 Aug Newbury 13f frm RF 3789). He went missing for 21 months after finishing a close fifth in the 1998 Melbourne Cup, but showed he retains his ability when running third in the Group Three Geoffrey Freer Stakes. Worth another try over two miles, he has a poor strike rate and does not find much off the bridle.
**P F I Cole [2-17] H R H Prince Fahd Salman.*

YORKSHIRE ROSE (IRE) RR 76+f 4807[2]

2 b f Sadler's Wells (USA) 11.3f **(87)** - Bush Rose (Rainbow Quest (USA)) 10.4f **(75)**
Form - 2
Record 2000 - 1st:0 2nd:1 3rd:0 Ran:1
Win Prizemoney £0 *Total Prizemoney* £1,090
2000 Turf 0-1: (7f) (g-s)
Currently above-average filly. (1st run) - 2nd of 18 to Paiyda (4 Oct Lingfield 7f g-s RF 4807). Likely to appreciate middle distances as a three-year-old, and should have little difficulty winning a maiden before possibly going on to better things.
**H R A Cecil [0-1] M P Burke.*

YORK WHINE (IRE) BHB 59f **RR 33f** 5223[17]

2 ch f Tagula (IRE) - Cwm Deri (IRE) (Alzao (USA)) 7.1f **(68)**
Form - 0
Record 2000 - 1st:0 2nd:0 3rd:0 Ran:1
2000 Turf 0-1: (6f) (gd)
Currently average filly.
**W Jarvis [0-1] Bernard Gover Bloodstock Trading Ltd.*

YOU ARE THE ONE BHB 90f **RR 88f** 4931[8]

3 b f Unfuwain (USA) 11.4f **(74)** - Someone Special (Habitat) 9.4f **(70)**
Form - 108
Record 2000 - 1st:1 2nd:0 3rd:0 Ran:3
Win Prizemoney £4,992 *Total Prizemoney* £4,992
Wins * 2000 Aug Newmar (G-F) 8f 75+ <
2000 Turf 1-3: (8f 1-1, 10f 2) (gd 2, g-f 1-1)
Workmanlike, currently useful filly. Turf high 88 (began Aug). Unraced at two, she just got up to make a winning debut in a Newmarket maiden in August, but was well beaten in a Yarmouth Listed event. **L M Cumani [1-3] Helena Springfield Ltd.*

YOU DA MAN (IRE) BHB 76f75a **RR 78f 75a** 3693[3]

3 b c Alzao (USA) 9.8f **(73)** - Fabled Lifestyle (Kings Lake (USA)) 10.8f **(67)**
Form - 42241251763
Record 2000 - 1st:2 2nd:3 3rd:1 Ran:11
Pre2000 - 1st:0 2nd:0 3rd:0 Ran:4
Win Prizemoney £8,333 *Total Prizemoney* £11,855
Wins * 2000 Jun Newmar (G-F) H 12f 73 76 <
*** 2000** *Mar Lingfi (STD) 10f 73*
2000 Turf 1-6: (8f, 9f, 10f 2, 12f 1-2) (sft, g-s, g-f 2, frm 1-2) 2000 AW 1-5: (7f, 9f, 10f 1-2, 12f) (Equi 1-3, Fibr 2)
Scopey, above-average colt, effective 8 to 12f, acts on g-f to frm - acts on AW, has worn blinkers, likes left handed tracks, likes tight tracks, excels at Windsor. Turf high 78 - 3rd of 9 getting 3lb from Flight Sequence (16 Aug Epsom 10f g-f RF 3693) - also 1st of 6 getting 6lb from Just Gifted (23 Jun Newmarket RF 2225). AW high 75 - 2nd of 5 giving 5lb to Fair Lady (5 Feb Wolverhampton 9f Fibr RF 0231) - also 1st of 10 getting 21lb from Donatus (4 Mar Lingfield RF 0400).
**R Hannon [2-15] Buddy Hackett.*

YOUHADYOURWARNING (USA) BHB 73f65a **RR 81f 65a** 5142[2]

3 f Warning 8.1f **(77)** - Youm Jadeed (IRE) **(104f)** (Sadler's Wells (USA)) 10f **(76)**
Form - 32
Record 2000 - 1st:0 2nd:1 3rd:1 Ran:2
Pre2000 - 1st:0 2nd:0 3rd:1 Ran:1
Win Prizemoney £0 *Total Prizemoney* £1,610
2000 Turf 0-2: (8f, 11f) (g-s, g-f)
Currently decent filly. Turf high 81.
**E A L Dunlop [0-1] Maktoum Al Maktoum (from S bin Suroor [0-1] May 2000).*

YOUNG ALEX (IRE) BHB 69f69a **RR 79f 69a** 5008[5]

2 ch g Midhish - Snipe Hunt (IRE) (Stalker)
Form - 01145
Record 2000 - 1st:2 2nd:0 3rd:0 Ran:5
Win Prizemoney £4,473 *Total Prizemoney* £4,743
Wins * 2000 Jly Chepst (G-F) C 6.1f 79 <
*** 2000** Jun Bright (FRM) C 6f 54+
2000 Turf 2-4: (5f, 6f 2-2, 7f) (gd, g-f 1-1, frm 1-2) 2000 AW 0-1: (6f) (Fibr)
Above-average gelding. Turf high 79 - 1st of 6 giving 3lb to Joint Instruction (6 Jly Chepstow RF 2564).
**K R Burke [2-5] D G & D J Robinson.*

YOUNG BEN (IRE) BHB 32f32a **RR 25f 32a** 2984[0]

8 ch g Fayruz 6.6f **(63)** - Jive (Ahonoora) 8.1f **(73)**
Form - 0500
Record 2000 - 1st:0 2nd:0 3rd:0 Ran:4
Pre2000 - 1st:1 2nd:3 3rd:7 Ran:47
Win Prizemoney £3,731 *Total Prizemoney* £9,461
Wins * 1997 Jly Beverl (G-F) H 5f 36 43 <
2000 Turf 0-3: (5f, 6f, 7f) (frm 2, hrd) 2000 AW 0-1: (6f) (Fibr)
Very moderate gelding, mostly wears blinkers. Turf high 25. Consistent.
**J S Wainwright [1-51] J S Wainwright.*

YOUNG BIGWIG (IRE) BHB 47f44a **RR 56f 44a** 5248[6]

6 b g Anita's Prince 6f **(62)** - Humble Mission (Shack (USA)) 5.8f **(53)**
Form - 000060345334030046
Record 2000 - 1st:0 2nd:0 3rd:4 Ran:15
Pre2000 - 1st:7 2nd:7 3rd:6 Ran:66
Win Prizemoney £31,654 *Total Prizemoney* £70,588
Wins * 1999 *Oct Wolver (STD) H 6f 64 67*
* 1999 *Oct Wolver (STD) H 6f 57 62+*
* 1999 Jun Redcar (FRM) H 6f 62 64
* 1998 Jun Hamilt (SFT) H 5f 73 76
* 1998 May Thirsk (GD) H 5f 70 75
1996 Jly Goodwo (G-F) H 6f 96 <
1996 *May Wolver (STD) 5f 65*
2000 Turf 0-7: (6f 7) (sft, g-f, frm 4, hrd) 2000 AW 0-8: (6f 7, 7f) (Equi, Fibr 7)
Fair gelding, effective 5 to 7f, acts on g-s to frm - acts on Fibr, has worn blinkers, does well at Wolverhampton. Turf high 57. AW high 53.
**D W Chapman [5-65] David Chapman (from J Berry [2-16] Oct 1997).*

YOUNG BUTT BHB 24f50a **RR 24?f 50a** 693[13]

7 ch g Bold Owl 9.7f **(47)** - Cymbal (Ribero) 9.3f **(56)**
Form - P0
Record 2000 - 1st:0 2nd:0 3rd:0 Ran:2
Pre2000 - 1st:2 2nd:1 3rd:2 Ran:21
Win Prizemoney £10,310 *Total Prizemoney* £12,240
Wins 1996 May Goodwo (G-S) H 8f 58 69 <
2000 Turf 0-1: (12f) (gd) 2000 AW 0-1: (12f) (Fibr)
Little account gelding. Becoming disappointing. He seemed to appreciate the yielding ground when scoring at Goodwood.
**L A Dace [0-3] D Newman (from B A Pearce [0-7] Jun 1999).*

YOUNG IBNR (IRE) BHB 52f44a **RR 51f 44a** 5118[11]

5 b g Imperial Frontier (USA) 7f **(65)** - Zalatia (Music Boy) 6.8f **(57)**
Form - 5337568144380 1500
Record 2000 - 1st:2 2nd:0 3rd:1 Ran:14
Pre2000 - 1st:1 2nd:3 3rd:4 Ran:30
Win Prizemoney £7,094 *Total Prizemoney* £11,473

Wins * **2000** Aug Ripon (GD) SH 5f 47 51
* **2000** *Mar Wolver (STD) S 5f 50*
1997 Apr Pontef (G-F) 5f 82 <

2000 Turf 1-2: (5f 1-2) (gd, frm 1-1) 2000 AW 1-12: (5f 1-10, 6f 2) (Fibr 1-12)

Fair gelding, effective 5f, acts on frm - acts on Fibr, has worn blinkers. Turf high 51 (1st run) (began Aug) - 1st of 19 getting 3lb from Pisces Lad (7 Aug Ripon RF 3429). AW high 50 - 1st of 9 from Legal Venture (4 Mar Wolverhampton RF 0410).

**B A McMahon [2-17] Roy Penton (from P D Evans [1-27] Dec 1998).*

YOUNG JACK BHB 66f61a **RR 63f 61a** 5197[6]

2 b g Reprimand 8.2f **(63)** - Chadenshe (Taufan (USA)) 7f **(57)**

Form - 52356

Record 2000 - 1st:0 2nd:1 3rd:1 Ran:5

Win Prizemoney £0 *Total Prizemoney* £1,546

2000 Turf 0-5: (6f 3, 7f 2) (gd 3, g-f, frm)

Average gelding. Turf high 63 - 2nd of 12 to Co Dot Uk (31 May Southwell 6f gd RF 1600). **W Jarvis [0-5] D G Wright.*

YOUNG MONASH (IRE) RR 1095[4]

2 b g General Monash (USA) - Sound Pet (Runnett) 7f **(59)**

Form - 4

Record 2000 - 1st:0 2nd:0 3rd:0 Ran:1

2000 AW 0-1: (5f) (Fibr)

Currently moderate gelding. **B S Rothwell [0-1] John Price.*

YOUNG PRECEDENT BHB 75f **RR 80f** 1963[17]

6 b g Polish Precedent (USA) 9f **(73)** - Guyum (Rousillon (USA)) 8.2f **(74)**

Form - 00

Record 2000 - 1st:0 2nd:0 3rd:0 Ran:2
Pre2000 - 1st:5 2nd:1 3rd:2 Ran:24

Win Prizemoney £43,971 *Total Prizemoney* £51,733

Wins * 1998 Oct Leices (SFT) H 7f 86 92 <
* 1998 Jly York (G-F) H 7.9f 85 88
* 1998 May Haydoc (GD) H 8.1f 83 85
* 1997 Aug Newbur (G-F) H 7.3f 81 82
* 1997 May Thirsk (G-F) 7f 71

2000 Turf 0-2: (8f 2) (g-s, g-f)

Decent gelding, effective 8f, acts on frm. Turf high 26. Becoming disappointing. **P W Harris [5-26] Pendley Knights.*

YOUNG ROOSTER BHB 40f **RR 37f** 2572[6]

3 b g Timeless Times (USA) 6.1f **(56)** - Jussoli (Don) 7.7f **(64)**

Form - 6

Record 2000 - 1st:0 2nd:0 3rd:0 Ran:1
Pre2000 - 1st:0 2nd:0 3rd:0 Ran:2

2000 Turf 0-1: (7f) (frm)

Currently very moderate gelding. **Miss S E Hall [0-3] C Platts.*

YOUNG ROSEIN BHB 57f **RR 58f** 5299[10]

4 b m Distant Relative 7f **(69)** - Red Rosein (Red Sunset) 8.2f **(63)**

Form - 003806113030

Record 2000 - 1st:2 2nd:0 3rd:3 Ran:12
Pre2000 - 1st:1 2nd:1 3rd:0 Ran:12

Win Prizemoney £9,072 *Total Prizemoney* £11,363

Wins * **2000** Aug Carlis (GD) H 8f 57 58 <
* **2000** Aug Haydoc (GD) H 8.1f 51 54
* 1999 Aug Mussel (G-F) H 7.1f 52 55

2000 Turf 2-12: (7f, 8f 2-10, 9f) (g-s 3, gd, g-f 1-2, frm 1-6)

Scopey, fair filly, effective 6 to 8f, best at 8f, acts on g-s to frm, best on g-f, likes tight tracks. Turf high 58 - 1st of 12 giving 18lb to Mai Tai (23 Aug Carlisle RF 3904) - also 1st of 18 giving 4lb to Yenaled (11 Aug Haydock RF 3551). A genuine filly, she completed a double in August, both wins coming over a mile on good ground. **Mrs G S Rees [3-24] J W Gittins.*

YOUNG TERN BHB 62f **RR 73?f** 5320[16]

2 b c Young Ern - Turnaway (Runnett) 7f **(59)**

Form - 00880

Record 2000 - 1st:0 2nd:0 3rd:0 Ran:5

2000 Turf 0-5: (6f 4, 7f) (sft, gd 3, g-f)

Above-average colt. Turf high 73 (began Jly). **C G Cox [0-5] P G Horrocks.*

YOUNG-UN BHB 62f73a **RR 63f 73a** 4823[10]

5 b h Efisio 7.7f **(69)** - Stardyn (Star Appeal) 9.6f **(65)**

Form - 760D272557073000

Record 2000 - 1st:0 2nd:2 3rd:1 Ran:16
Pre2000 - 1st:3 2nd:1 3rd:2 Ran:24

Win Prizemoney £10,078 *Total Prizemoney* £18,054

Wins * 1999 Nov Redcar (G-S) H 10f 59 62 <
* 1999 Aug Nottin (G-F) H 10f 43 53
* 1999 Aug Newcas (GD) H 9f 46 48

2000 Turf 0-16: (8f, 9f 2, 10f 13) (g-s 2, gd 4, g-f 8, frm, hrd)

Decent colt, effective 9 to 10f, best at 10f, acts on g-s to frm, best on g-f, has worn blinkers, prefers left handed tracks, and excels at Redcar and Yarmouth. Turf high 66.

**M J Ryan [3-33] M F Kentish (from S Dow [0-7] Oct 1998).*

YOU'RE SPECIAL (USA) BHB 79f70a **RR 78+f 70a** 5297[1]

3 b g Northern Flagship (USA) 12.2f **(72)** - Pillow Mint (USA) (Stage Door Johnny) 10.3f **(84)**

Form - 2100768111

Record 2000 - 1st:4 2nd:0 3rd:0 Ran:9
Pre2000 - 1st:0 2nd:2 3rd:0 Ran:5

Win Prizemoney £21,816 *Total Prizemoney* £23,403

Wins * **2000** Nov Mussel (G-S) H 16f 62 78+ <
* **2000** Oct Nottin (SFT) H 16f 58 73+
* **2000** Oct Newcas (HVY) H 16.1f 58 64
* **2000** *Jan Wolver (STD) 9.4f 70*

2000 Turf 3-7: (8f, 10f 2, 12f, 16f 3-3) (hvy 1-1, sft 1-1, g-s 1-1, gd, g-f, frm 2) 2000 AW 1-2: (9f 1-1, 12f) (Fibr 1-2)

Scopey, decent gelding, effective 6 to 16f, acts on sft to gd - acts on Fibr, has worn blinkers, likes left handed tracks, likes tight tracks, excels at Wolverhampton. Turf high 78 - 1st of 10 getting 11lb from Mane Frame (1 Nov Musselburgh RF 5297) - also 1st of 17 giving 4lb to Alcayde (24 Oct Nottingham RF 5161). AW high 70 (1st run) - 1st of 9 from Atalya (13 Jan Wolverhampton RF 0080). Got off the mark in a modest maiden on the Wolverhampton Fibresand at the start of the year. Looked a stayer on that occasion and ended the season in fine form over staying trips.

**P C Haslam [4-14] Les Buckley.*

YOUR THE LADY (IRE) BHB 74f **RR 77f** 3922[2]

3 b f Indian Ridge 7.6f **(74)** - Edwina (IRE) **(55f)** (Caerleon (USA)) 8.6f **(71)**

Form - 0851172

Record 2000 - 1st:2 2nd:1 3rd:0 Ran:7
Pre2000 - 1st:0 2nd:0 3rd:0 Ran:1

Win Prizemoney £6,538 *Total Prizemoney* £7,778

Wins * **2000** Jly Bright (FRM) 8f 64
* **2000** Jly Chepst (G-F) H 8.1f 70 73 <

2000 Turf 2-7: (8f 2-5, 10f 2) (sft, g-f 3, frm 2-2)

Above-average filly, effective 8 to 10f, best at 8f, acts on g-f to frm, best on g-f. Turf high 77 - 2nd of 9 getting 1lb from Keltic Bard (24 Aug Folkestone 10f g-f RF 3922) - also 1st of 8 giving 7lb to Sofisio (14 Jly Chepstow RF 2795).

**M R Channon [2-5] John Mckay (from P Hughes in IRE [0-2] Apr 2000).*

Y TO KMAN (IRE) BHB 93f **RR 97f** 5183[1]

2 b c Mujadil (USA) 7.7f **(70)** - Hazar (IRE) (Thatching) 8f **(66)**

Form - 124061

Record 2000 - 1st:2 2nd:1 3rd:0 Ran:6

Win Prizemoney £7,683 *Total Prizemoney* £9,965

Wins * **2000** Oct Yarmou (SFT) H 5.2f 85 97 <
* **2000** Mar Kempto (GD) 5f 78

2000 Turf 2-6: (5f 2-4, 6f 2) (g-s 1-2, gd 1-2, g-f 2)

Very useful colt, effective 5f, acts on g-s. Turf high 97 - 1st of 7 giving 3lb to Princess of Garda (25 Oct Yarmouth RF 5183). Made a winning debut in a Kempton maiden in March, though the form is difficult to evaluate. Off for a long time between his third and fourth starts. **R Hannon [2-6] The Cayman 'A' Team.*

YUKA SAN (IRE) BHB 54f51a **RR 57f 51a** 4324[5]

2 ch f General Monash (USA) - Smilin N Wishin (USA) **(80f 75a)** (Lyphard's Wish (FR)) 9f **(74)**

Form - 60475

Record 2000 - 1st:0 2nd:0 3rd:0 Ran:5

Win Prizemoney £0 *Total Prizemoney* £267

2000 Turf 0-5: (5f 3, 6f 2) (g-s, g-f, frm 2, hrd)

Fair filly. Turf high 57.

**C G Cox [0-5] P G Lowe.*

YURA MADAM BHB 25f **RR 15f** 4930[29]
2 b f Cosmonaut - Joyful Escapade (Precocious) 8.6f **(62)**
Form - 050
Record 2000 - 1st:0 2nd:0 3rd:0 Ran:3
2000 Turf 0-3: (7f 3) (gd 2, frm)
Currently poor filly. Turf high 15 (began Aug).
**P S McEntee [0-3] Ms Clare Sharp.*

ZAAJER (USA) RR 112f 4450[5]
4 ch h Silver Hawk (USA) 11.2f **(85)** - Crown Quest (USA) (Chief's Crown (USA)) 9.8f **(72)**
Form - 3315
Record 2000 - 1st:1 2nd:0 3rd:2 Ran:4
Pre2000 - 1st:2 2nd:1 3rd:0 Ran:7
Win Prizemoney £39,811 *Total Prizemoney* £50,951
Wins * **2000** Aug Cheste (GD) LH 13.4f 109 112 <
* 1999 May York (SFT) L 10.4f 106+
* 1998 Oct Ascot (SFT) 7f 97
2000 Turf 1-4: (10f, 11f, 13f 1-2) (sft, gd 1-2, g-f)
Scopey, Group-class colt, effective 10 to 13f, best at 13f, acts on sft to g-f, best on gd. Turf high 112 - 1st of 4 giving 1lb to Lightning Arrow (20 Aug Chester RF 3821). A heavy-topped individual, he needs soft ground and was given a good ride when winning a Listed handicap at Chester in August. Disappointing over a mile and a quarter (needs further) at Ayr the following month, he will be difficult to place.
**E A L Dunlop [3-11] Hamdan Al Maktoum.*

ZABIONIC (IRE) BHB 50f54a **RR 61f 54a** 3269[7]
3 ch g Zafonic (USA) 9f **(83)** - Scene Galante (FR) (Sicyos (USA))
Form - 4707067
Record 2000 - 1st:0 2nd:0 3rd:0 Ran:7
Pre2000 - 1st:0 2nd:0 3rd:0 Ran:3
Win Prizemoney £0 *Total Prizemoney* £325
2000 Turf 0-6: (7f, 8f 2, 10f 2, 11f) (hvy, gd 2, g-f 3) 2000 AW 0-1: (8f) (Fibr)
Strong, average gelding, has worn blinkers. Turf high 63.
**M E Sowersby [0-1] The Southwold Set (from B A McMahon [0-9] Jun 2000).*

ZAFARELLI BHB 42f **RR 37df** 763[9]
6 gr g Nishapour (FR) 11.1f **(58)** - Voltigeuse (USA) (Filiberto (USA)) 9.5f **(66)**
Form - 0
Record 2000 - 1st:0 2nd:0 3rd:0 Ran:1
Pre2000 - 1st:1 2nd:1 3rd:0 Ran:6
Win Prizemoney £3,122 *Total Prizemoney* £3,802
Wins * 1997 Jly Folkes (SFT) H 15.4f 54 57 <
2000 Turf 0-1: (15f) (g-s)
Very moderate gelding, has worn blinkers.
**J R Jenkins [3-28] R M Ellis (from S C Williams [0-2] May 1997).*

ZAFFIA BHB 72f **RR 76f** 1816[10]
3 b f Zilzal (USA) 8.5f **(79)** - Zeffirella (Known Fact (USA)) 7.4f **(67)**
Form - 80
Record 2000 - 1st:0 2nd:0 3rd:0 Ran:2
Pre2000 - 1st:0 2nd:1 3rd:0 Ran:2
Win Prizemoney £0 *Total Prizemoney* £785
2000 Turf 0-2: (7f, 8f) (gd, frm)
Leggy, above-average filly. Turf high 76 (1st run) - 8th of 14 getting 5lb from Foreign Secretary (19 May Newbury 8f gd RF 1308).
**P R Chamings [0-4] Twenty Twenty Research.*

ZAFILLY BHB 55f **RR 57f** 4930[13]
2 ch f Zafonic (USA) 9f **(83)** - Rifada (Ela-Mana-Mou) 10.1f **(70)**
Form - 070
Record 2000 - 1st:0 2nd:0 3rd:0 Ran:3
2000 Turf 0-3: (7f 3) (gd 2, g-f)
Currently fair filly. Turf high 57 (began Spt).
**G L Moore [0-3] J B R Leisure Ltd.*

ZAFONIC'S SONG (FR) BHB 101f **RR 107f** 4436[7]
3 br c Zafonic (USA) 9f **(83)** - Savoureuse Lady (Caerleon (USA)) 8.6f **(71)**
Form - 35127
Record 2000 - 1st:1 2nd:1 3rd:1 Ran:5
Pre2000 - 1st:0 2nd:0 3rd:0 Ran:1
Win Prizemoney £3,848 *Total Prizemoney* £18,889
Wins * **2000** Jly Yarmou (FRM) 11.5f 73++ <
2000 Turf 1-5: (10f 2, 11f 1-2, 12f) (sft, gd 2, g-f 1-1, frm)
Pattern-class colt, effective 11 to 12f, acts on gd to frm. Turf high 107. By no means disgraced behind Sakhee in the Sandown Classic Trial, he won a maiden at 1/6 next time before going down fighting in a warm handicap at Goodwood. Well beaten in a listed race on his last run. **Sir Michael Stoute [1-6] Satish Sanan.*

ZAFONIUM (USA) BHB 104f **RR 107f** 4731[6]
3 ch c Zafonic (USA) 9f **(83)** - Bint Pasha (USA) (Affirmed (USA)) 9.3f **(79)**
Form - 24766
Record 2000 - 1st:0 2nd:1 3rd:0 Ran:5
Pre2000 - 1st:1 2nd:0 3rd:1 Ran:2
Win Prizemoney £7,018 *Total Prizemoney* £41,568
Wins * 1999 Oct York (SFT) 7.9f 86 <
2000 Turf 0-5: (11f, 12f 4) (gd 3, g-f, frm)
Scopey, Pattern-class colt, effective 11 to 12f, acts on gd to frm, has worn blinkers. Turf high 109 - 6th of 7 to Pawn Broker (15 Spt Newbury 11f frm RF 4436). He looked tremendously well when finishing second in the King Edward VII Stakes on his belated reappearance, but failed to progress and became disappointing.
**P F I Cole [1-7] H R H Prince Fahd Salman.*

ZAGALETA BHB 69f **RR 71f** 4559[2]
3 b f Sri Pekan (USA) - Persian Song (Persian Bold) 9.0f **(00)**
Form - 00021232
Record 2000 - 1st:1 2nd:3 3rd:1 Ran:8
Pre2000 - 1st:0 2nd:2 3rd:1 Ran:3
Win Prizemoney £3,984 *Total Prizemoney* £10,039
Wins * **2000** Aug Ayr (GD) H 10f 63 65 <
2000 Turf 1-8: (6f, 8f 2, 10f 1-5) (gd 4, g-f, frm 1-3)
Workmanlike, above-average filly, effective 6 to 10f, best at 10f, acts on gd to frm, best on gd, likes left handed tracks, likes tight tracks. Turf high 71 - 3rd of 14 giving 14lb to Middlethorpe (7 Spt Chepstow 10f gd RF 4274). Improving.
**Andrew Turnell [1-11] Dr John Hollowood.*

ZAHA (IRE) BHB 54f56a **RR 61f 56a** 5007[8]
5 b h Lahib (USA) 8f **(69)** - Mayaasa (USA) (Lyphard (USA)) 9.9f **(72)**
Form - 600140078
Record 2000 - 1st:1 2nd:0 3rd:0 Ran:9
Pre2000 1st:2 2nd:2 3rd:3 Ran:18
Win Prizemoney £8,285 *Total Prizemoney* £12,670
Wins * **2000** May Nottin (G-S) H 10f 52 60
* 1999 Aug Yarmou (GD) 10.1f 57
* 1999 *Feb Southw (STD) 11f 64* <
2000 Turf 1-7: (10f 1-5, 11f, 12f) (hvy, gd 1-2, g-f 2, frm, hrd) 2000 AW 0-2: (12f 2) (Fibr 2)
Average colt, effective 10 to 11f, best at 10f, acts on hvy to hrd - acts on AW, has worn blinkers, prefers right handed tracks, prefers tight tracks, excels at Leicester and likes Beverley. Turf high 61 - 4th of 18 giving 18lb to Mice Ideas (14 Jun Beverley 10f hrd RF 1952) - also 1st of 17 giving 8lb to Annadawi (19 May Nottingham RF 1315). AW high 48.
**J Pearce [3-23] Exclusive Three Partnership (from R W Armstrong [0-4] Jly 1998).*

ZAHEEMAH (USA) BHB 100f **RR 91f** 3771[2]
2 b f El Prado (IRE) 8f **(74)** - Port of Silver (USA) (Silver Hawk (USA)) 8.6f **(70)**
Form - 6452
Record 2000 - 1st:0 2nd:1 3rd:0 Ran:4
Win Prizemoney £0 *Total Prizemoney* £4,588
2000 Turf 0-4: (6f 3, 8f) (gd 3, frm)
Useful filly. Turf high 91 - 2nd of 4 getting 3lb from Crystal Music (18 Aug Sandown 8f frm RF 3771). Last of six in a decent race on her debut, she then ran a cracker to finish fourth to Dora Carrington at Newmarket and was subsequently sent to Ascot and Sandown to race against some smart fillies. She deserves to be given a chance in a maiden on turf.
**C E Brittain [0-4] Saeed Manana.*

ZALAL (IRE) BHB 97f **RR 91f** 4794a[3]
5 b h Darshaan 11.9f **(81)** - Zallaka (IRE) (Shardari) 11f **(46)**
Form - 0050000003

2000 Turf 0-10: (8f, 9f 2, 12f 6, 16f) (hvy, g-s 2, gd 5, g-f, frm)
Useful colt, effective 12f, acts on gd, has worn blinkers, likes right handed tracks. Turf high 91. Inconsistent.
**L Comer in IRE [0-10] L Comer (from L M Cumani [3-8] Jun 1999).*

ZAMAT BHB 44f **RR 37?f** 5054[7]
4 b g Slip Anchor 12.7f **(75)** - Khandjar (Kris) 9.5f **(73)**
Form - 0487
Record 2000 - 1st:0 2nd:0 3rd:0 Ran:4
Pre2000 - 1st:0 2nd:0 3rd:0 Ran:1
Win Prizemoney £0 *Total Prizemoney* £547
2000 Turf 0-4: (6f, 7f, 10f 2) (hvy, sft, gd, g-f)
Scopey, very moderate gelding. Turf high 37 (began Spt).
**P Monteith [0-4] I Bell (from W Jarvis [0-1] Spt 1999).*

ZANAY BHB 88f108a **RR 85f 108a** 2151[9]
4 b h Forzando 7.2f **(63)** - Nineteenth of May (Homing) 7.8f **(59)**
Form - 41111040
Record 2000 - 1st:3 2nd:0 3rd:0 Ran:6
Pre2000 - 1st:2 2nd:2 3rd:1 Ran:8
Win Prizemoney £56,939 *Total Prizemoney* £60,765
Wins * **2000** *Mar Lingfi (STD) L 10f 106*
* **2000** *Feb Lingfi (STD) 10f 96+*
* **2000** *Feb Lingfi (STD) H 10f 95 119* <
* 1999 *Dec Lingfi (STD) 10f 97*
* 1999 Oct Nottin (GD) 8.2f 81
2000 Turf 0-3: (8f 2, 10f) (gd 3) 2000 AW 3-3: (10f 3-3) (Equi 3-3)
Scopey, high-class colt, effective 10f, - acts on Equi, has worn blinkers, prefers left handed tracks, prefers tight tracks. Turf high 85. AW high 119 (1st run) - 1st of 6 giving 27lb to Ursa Major (2 Feb Lingfield RF 0205). An All-Weather specialist, he made hard work of winning the Listed Winter Derby at Lingfield in March. A fair eighth in the Royal Hunt Cup, he probably prefers give underfoot when racing on the Turf.
**Miss Jacqueline Doyle [5-10] Sanford Racing (from K Bell [0-1] Aug 1999).*

ZANDEED (IRE) RR 65f 2075[9]
2 b c Inchinor 8.9f **(64)** - Persian Song (Persian Bold) 9.3f **(66)**
Form - 50
Record 2000 - 1st:0 2nd:0 3rd:0 Ran:2
2000 Turf 0-2: (6f 2) (frm, hrd)
Currently average colt. Turf high 65. **E A L Dunlop [0-2] Ahmed Ali.*

ZANDO'S CHARM BHB 60f **RR 66f** 4930[28]
2 b f Forzando 7.2f **(63)** - Silver Charm (Dashing Blade)
Form - 501300
Record 2000 - 1st:1 2nd:0 3rd:1 Ran:6
Win Prizemoney £2,247 *Total Prizemoney* £3,337
Wins 2000 Aug Salisb (GD) C 7f 66 <
2000 Turf 1-6: (6f 2, 7f 1-4) (gd 2, g-f, frm 1-3)
Average filly, effective 7f, acts on frm. Turf high 66 (began Jly) - 1st of 12 getting 3lb from Fazzani (16 Aug Salisbury RF 3703).
**J Akehurst [0-3] The Plan Flow Leasing Partnership (from R Hannon [1-3] Aug 2000).*

ZANGOOEY BHB 30f **RR 9f** 5315[6]
2 ch g Polar Falcon (USA) 9f **(74)** - Villota (Top Ville) 11.7f **(68)**
Form - 806
Record 2000 - 1st:0 2nd:0 3rd:0 Ran:3
2000 Turf 0-3: (6f, 7f, 8f) (g-s 3)
Currently very poor gelding. Turf high 9 (began Oct).
**J S Wainwright [0-3] Barry Ross.*

ZANZIBAR (IRE) BHB 79f **RR 77f** 5098[3]
2 b f In The Wings 11.2f **(77)** - Isle of Spice (USA) **(73f)** (Diesis) 9.3f **(69)**
Form - 523
Record 2000 - 1st:0 2nd:1 3rd:1 Ran:3
Win Prizemoney £0 *Total Prizemoney* £1,926
2000 Turf 0-3: (7f, 8f, 9f) (gd 2, g-f)
Currently above-average filly. Turf high 77 (began Aug). Has shown enough in maiden events to suggest that she can find a race. **M L W Bell [0-3] Mrs G Rowland Clark & Usk Valley Stud.*

ZARAGOSSA BHB 55f48a **RR 61f 48a** 5120[10]
4 gr m Paris House 5.9f **(64)** - Antonia's Folly **(53f 53a)** (Music Boy) 6.8f **(57)**
Form - 507507600
Record 2000 - 1st:0 2nd:0 3rd:0 Ran:9
Pre2000 - 1st:1 2nd:0 3rd:1 Ran:12
Win Prizemoney £3,821 *Total Prizemoney* £5,913
Wins 1998 Aug Thirsk (GD) 5f 73+ <
2000 Turf 0-7: (5f 7) (gd, g-f 3, frm 3) 2000 AW 0-2: (6f 2) (Fibr 2)
Unfurnished, average filly, effective 5f, acts on g-f. Turf high 61. AW high 33 (began Spt). Inconsistent.
**A Berry [0-9] Slatch Farm Stud (from J Berry [1-12] Spt 1999).*

ZARKIYA (IRE) RR 117+f 5095a[6]
3 b f Catrail (USA) - Zarkana (IRE) (Doyoun) 9f **(69)**
Form - 4146
2000 Turf 1-4: (7f, 8f 1-3) (sft, gd 1-3)
High-class filly. Turf high 117 (1st run) - 4th of 11 to Bluemamba (14 May Longchamp 8f gd RF 1291a) - also 1st of 13 from Penny's Gold (4 Jun Chantilly RF 1827a). She was unlucky when a fast-finishing fourth in the French 1000 Guineas and gained some compensation in the Group Three Prix de Sandringham. Put in her place in the Coronation Stakes and Prix de la Foret, she lacks scope and is unlikely to improve. **A deRoyerDupre in FR [1-4].*

ZATOPEK BHB 25f38a **RR 25f 38a** 1352[5]
8 b or br g Reprimand 8.2f **(63)** - Executive Lady (Night Shift (USA)) 7.2f **(69)**
Form - 5
Record 2000 - 1st:0 2nd:0 3rd:0 Ran:1
Pre2000 - 1st:0 2nd:4 3rd:2 Ran:27
Win Prizemoney £0 *Total Prizemoney* £4,267
2000 AW 0-1: (12f) (Fibr)
Little account gelding, has worn blinkers. Becoming disappointing. **R Lee [0-6] Richard Lee (from J Cullinan [0-22] Aug 1997).*

ZAZA TOP (GER) RR 96f 4955a[2]
2 ch f Lomitas - Zorina **(25f)** (Shirley Heights) 10.3f **(74)**
Form - 2
2000 Turf 0-1: (8f) (sft)
Currently very useful filly. (1st run) - 2nd of 12 to Innit (8 Oct San Siro 8f sft RF 4955a). **A Wohler in GER [0-1] Stall Steigenberger.*

ZECHARIAH BHB 35f30a **RR 41df 30a** 5056[4]
4 b g Kasakov - Runfawit Pet (Welsh Saint) 7.6f **(64)**
Form - 46564004
Record 2000 - 1st:0 2nd:0 3rd:0 Ran:8
Pre2000 - 1st:1 2nd:2 3rd:2 Ran:17
Win Prizemoney £1,479 *Total Prizemoney* £4,267
Wins * 1998 *Nov Wolver (STD) S 8.5f 65* <
2000 Turf 0-8: (7f 4, 8f 4) (sft, g-s, gd 4, frm, hrd)
Unfurnished, moderate gelding, effective 7f, acts on frm, likes tight tracks. Turf high 49. Consistent. **J L Eyre [1-25] John Ashcroft.*

ZEITING (IRE) RR 111f 1291a[6]
3 b f
Form - 16
2000 Turf 0-1: (8f) (gd)
Currently Group-class filly. (1st run) - 6th of 11 to Bluemamba (14 May Longchamp 8f gd RF 1291a). **R Collet in FR [1-2].*

ZELBECK BHB 34f30a **RR 45?f 30a** 201[12]
4 b m Komaite (USA) 6.9f **(61)** - Kakisa (Forlorn River) 7.3f **(54)**
Form - 800
Record 2000 - 1st:0 2nd:0 3rd:0 Ran:3
Pre2000 - 1st:0 2nd:0 3rd:0 Ran:3
2000 AW 0-3: (6f 2, 7f) (Equi 2, Fibr)
Small, moderate filly, has worn blinkers. AW high 19.
**P D Evans [0-6] Treble Chance Partnership.*

ZELOSO BHB 88f **RR 88f** 5001[7]
2 b c Alzao (USA) 9.8f **(73)** - Silk Petal (Petorius) 7.3f **(61)**
Form - 03021437
Record 2000 - 1st:1 2nd:1 3rd:2 Ran:8
Win Prizemoney £4,101 *Total Prizemoney* £7,499
Wins * **2000** Aug Haydoc (GD) 7.1f 88 <
2000 Turf 1-8: (6f 2, 7f 1-3, 8f 3) (sft, g-s 2, gd 2, g-f 1-2, frm)
Useful colt, effective 6 to 8f, best at 7f, acts on g-s to frm, has worn blinkers. Turf high 88 - 1st of 8 from Sky Quest (11 Aug

Haydock RF 3550). Inconsistent. He got off the mark in a Haydock maiden in August after a couple of decent efforts earlier on, but was well beaten in heavy ground next time. Fair effort at Chester.
**J L Dunlop [1-8] Tom Wilson.*

ZENDIUM (IRE) RR 63f 2850[9]

2 b g Earl of Barking (IRE) - Speedy Action (Horage) 10.3f **(61)**
Form - 0
Record 2000 - 1st:0 2nd:0 3rd:0 Ran:1
2000 Turf 0-1: (6f) (gd)
Currently average gelding. **T D Easterby [0-1] Mrs Jennifer Pallister.*

ZEPPO (IRE) BHB 61f56a RR 60f 56a 4207[9]

5 ch g Fayruz 6.6f **(63)** - Chase Paperchase (Malinowski (USA)) 10f **(56)**
Form - 84064452130
Record 2000 - 1st:1 2nd:1 3rd:1 Ran:11
Pre2000 - 1st:2 2nd:2 3rd:1 Ran:25
Win Prizemoney £13,233 *Total Prizemoney* £17,814
Wins * **2000** Aug Lingfi (G-F) SH 6f 56 58
* 1999 Aug Chepst (G-F) H 6.1f 56 56
* 1998 Jun Lingfi (G-F) H 6f 60 62 <
2000 Turf 1-11: (5f, 6f 1-7, 7f 3) (gd 2, g-f 3, frm 1-6)
Average gelding, effective 5 to 7f, best at 6f, acts on g-f to frm, best on frm, has worn blinkers, and does well at Lingfield. Turf high 60 - 3rd of 16 to Contrary Mary (1 Spt Epsom 7f g-f RF 4147) - also 1st of 20 giving 16lb to Miss Money Spider (23 Aug Lingfield RF 3908). Consistent. He is a fair sprint handicapper, but has a moderate wins to runs ratio.
**B R Millman [3-33] The Plyform Syndicate (from M J Heaton-Ellis [0-3] Spt 1997).*

ZERO GRAVITY BHB 68f RR 76?f 2868[6]

3 b g Cosmonaut - Comfort (Chief Singer) 8.9f **(66)**
Form - 636
Record 2000 - 1st:0 2nd:0 3rd:1 Ran:3
Win Prizemoney £0 *Total Prizemoney* £636
2000 Turf 0-3: (10f, 12f 2) (gd, g-f, frm)
Scopey, currently above-average gelding. Turf high 76.
**D J S ffrenchDavis [0-3] Mrs Jenny Phillips.*

ZESTRIL BHB 61f RR 70f 3630[5]

3 ch f Zilzal (USA) 8.5f **(79)** - Rynavey **(60a)** (Rousillon (USA)) 8.2f **(74)**
Form - 0066085
Record 2000 - 1st:0 2nd:0 3rd:0 Ran:7
Pre2000 - 1st:1 2nd:0 3rd:0 Ran:3
Win Prizemoney £3,566 *Total Prizemoney* £3,795
Wins * 1999 Jun Carlis (G-F) 5.9f 76+ <
2000 Turf 0-7: (5f, 6f 4, 7f, 8f) (g-f 6, frm)
Tall, above-average filly, effective 6f, acts on frm, has worn blinkers. Turf high 70. **Denys Smith [1-10] Duke of Sutherland.*

ZETAGALOPON RR 37f 4581[13]

2 b f Petong 7.6f **(58)** - Azola (IRE) (Alzao (USA)) 7.1f **(68)**
Form - 0
Record 2000 - 1st:0 2nd:0 3rd:0 Ran:1
2000 Turf 0-1: (6f) (gd)
Currently very moderate filly.
**J A Osborne [0-1] Miss Deborah Bullion.*

ZEYAARAH (USA) BHB 80f RR 83f 4373[12]

3 ch f Rahy (USA) 9.1f **(80)** - Princess Haifa (USA) (Mr Prospector (USA)) 8.8f **(78)**
Form - 310
Record 2000 - 1st:1 2nd:0 3rd:1 Ran:3
Pre2000 - 1st:0 2nd:0 3rd:1 Ran:2
Win Prizemoney £2,892 *Total Prizemoney* £4,176
Wins * **2000** Aug Lingfi (G-F) 11.5f 73+ <
2000 Turf 1-3: (11f 1-1, 12f, 14f) (gd, frm 1-2)
Decent filly. Turf high 73 (began Aug).
**M P Tregoning [1-5] Sheikh Ahmed Al Maktoum.*

ZHITOMIR BHB 85f RR 85f 5129[13]

2 ch c Lion Cavern (USA) 7.5f **(74)** - Treasure Trove (USA) (The Minstrel (CAN)) 10f **(72)**
Form - 64861230
Record 2000 - 1st:1 2nd:1 3rd:1 Ran:8
Win Prizemoney £4,290 *Total Prizemoney* £7,273
Wins * **2000** Spt Epsom (GD) 6f 81 <
2000 Turf 1-8: (5f, 6f 1-6, 7f) (sft 2, g-s, g-f 1-4, frm)
Useful colt, effective 6f, acts on g-s to g-f, best on g-f. Turf high 85 - 3rd of 19 getting 7lb from Caustic Wit (30 Spt Newmarket 6f g-f RF 4742) - also 1st of 6 giving 5lb to Bouchra (6 Spt Epsom RF 4263). Inconsistent. Running well in the autumn, he seemed not to stay when tried at seven furlongs. **S Dow [1-8] G Steinberg.*

ZIBAK (USA) BHB 29f RR 33f 3429[11]

6 b br g Capote (USA) 9.1f **(84)** - Minifah (USA) (Nureyev (USA)) 8.7f **(78)**
Form - 06547680
Record 2000 - 1st:0 2nd:0 3rd:0 Ran:8
Pre2000 - 1st:2 2nd:1 3rd:3 Ran:24
Win Prizemoney £6,327 *Total Prizemoney* £8,800
Wins * 1999 Jly Thirsk (FRM) SH 6f 36 39 <
* 1999 Jly Ayr (GD) SH 7f 33 36
2000 Turf 0-8: (5f 2, 6f 3, 7f 3) (gd, g-f 3, frm 4)
Very moderate gelding, effective 6 to 7f, best at 6f, acts on gd to frm. Turf high 33 - 5th of 16 getting 16lb from Bowlers Boy (15 Jun Hamilton 6f g-f RF 1985).
**J S Goldie [2-29] Mrs Lisa Olley (from B J McMath [0-3] Apr 1998).*

ZIBELINE (IRE) BHB 83f RR 86f 4734[20]

3 b c Cadeaux Genereux 7.9f **(76)** - Zia (USA) (Shareef Dancer (USA)) 9.9f **(73)**
Form - 724415230
Record 2000 - 1st:1 2nd:2 3rd:1 Ran:9
Pre2000 - 1st:0 2nd:0 3rd:0 Ran:4
Win Prizemoney £3,900 *Total Prizemoney* £12,792
Wins * **2000** Jly Chepst (G-F) H 10.2f 78 80 <
2000 Turf 1-9: (7f, 8f, 10f 1-4, 11f, 12f 2) (g-s, gd 4, g-f 1-4)
Scopey, useful colt, effective 8 to 12f, best at 10f, acts on gd to g-f, best on g-f. Turf high 86 - 5th of 13 getting 7lb from Moon Solitaire (12 Jly Newmarket 10f gd RF 2747) - also 1st of 10 giving 3lb to Astronaut (6 Jly Chepstow RF 2567). Consistent. A consistent performer, he gained reward for some fair events when coming out best in a bunch finish at Chepstow in July.
**C E Brittain [1-13] Sheikh Marwan Al Maktoum.*

ZIBET RR 77f 5223[3]

2 b f Kris 10f **(75)** - Zonda (Fabulous Dancer (USA)) 9.4f **(70)**
Form - 3
Record 2000 - 1st:0 2nd:0 3rd:1 Ran:1
Win Prizemoney £0 *Total Prizemoney* £706
2000 Turf 0-1: (6f) (gd)
Currently above-average filly. (1st run) - 3rd of 21 getting 5lb from Heretic (27 Oct Newmarket 6f gd RF 5223).
**E A L Dunlop [0-1] Mohammed Al Nabouda.*

ZIBILENE BHB 98f RR 100f 5366a[12]

3 b f Rainbow Quest (USA) 11.2f **(81)** - Brocade (Habitat) 9.4f **(70)**
Form - 21530
Record 2000 - 1st:1 2nd:1 3rd:1 Ran:5
Win Prizemoney £3,493 *Total Prizemoney* £8,325
Wins * **2000** Jly Pontef (GD) 12f 68+ <
2000 Turf 1-5: (8f, 10f 2, 12f 1-2) (hvy, gd, g-f, frm 1-2)
Scopey, very useful filly. Turf high 100 - 3rd of 12 getting 5lb from Katy Nowaitee (12 Oct Newmarket 10f gd RF 4931). She was not disgraced in a Listed race after winning an ordinary maiden at Pontefract and appeared to need ten furlongs plus.
**L M Cumani [1-5].*

ZIDAC BHB 62f55a RR 62f 55a 5077[2]

8 b or br g Statoblest 6.4f **(63)** - Sule Skerry (Scottish Rifle) 10f **(55)**
Form - 002622
Record 2000 - 1st:0 2nd:3 3rd:0 Ran:6
Pre2000 - 1st:6 2nd:3 3rd:3 Ran:37
Win Prizemoney £16,455 *Total Prizemoney* £23,505
Wins * 1999 Oct Bright (GD) SH 10f 58 68+
* 1999 Jun Bath (GD) C 10.2f 63
* 1999 *Feb Lingfi (STD) 10f 62*
* 1998 Spt Warwic (G-F) CH 10.8f 59 63
* 1996 May Lingfi (G-F) H 10f 70 74 <
* 1996 Apr Leices (GD) H 10f 64 72
2000 Turf 0-5: (10f 4, 11f) (g-s 2, gd 2, frm) 2000 AW 0-1: (10f) (Equi)
Average gelding, effective 10f, acts on g-s to g-f - acts on Equi,

favours tight tracks. Turf high 62 - 2nd of 20 giving 14lb to Wilemmgeo (30 Spt Sandown 10f g-s RF 4757).
**P J Makin [6-46] Brian Brackpool.*

ZIETING (IRE) BHB 56f **RR 60f** 4495[4]
2 b c Zieten (USA) - Ball Cat (FR) (Cricket Ball (USA))
Form - 054
Record 2000 - 1st:0 2nd:0 3rd:0 Ran:3
Win Prizemoney £0 *Total Prizemoney* £283
2000 Turf 0-3: (5f 2, 6f) (g-s, frm 2)
Currently average colt. Turf high 60 (began Jly).
**K R Burke [0-3] Nigel Shields.*

ZIETUNZEEN (IRE) BHB 95f **RR 93f** 5102[1]
2 b f Zieten (USA) - Hawksbill Special (IRE) (Taufan (USA)) 7f **(57)**
Form - 233551521
Record 2000 - 1st:2 2nd:2 3rd:2 Ran:9
Win Prizemoney £22,680 *Total Prizemoney* £67,396
Wins * 2000 Oct Doncas (GD) 6f 84 <
*** 2000** Aug Nottin (GD) 6.1f 75
2000 Turf 2-9: (5f 4, 6f 2-5) (g-s, gd 1-6, g-f 1-1, hrd)
Useful filly, effective 6f, acts on gd. Turf high 93 - 2nd of 23 giving 3lb to Dim Sums (30 Spt Redcar 6f gd RF 4747) - also 1st of 22 from The Bystander (20 Oct Doncaster RF 5102). She ran well in some decent events early on, including in the Windsor Castle and Weatherbys Super Sprint, but did not get off the mark until landing a Nottingham maiden auction event in August. Slowly away in a listed race next time. **A Berry [2-9] Chris & Antonia Deuters.*

ZIETZIG (IRE) BHB 77f72a **RR 79f 72a** 4866[11]
3 b c Zieten (USA) - Missing You (Ahonoora) 8.1f **(73)**
Form - 7557064810700
Record 2000 - 1st:1 2nd:0 3rd:0 Ran:13
Pre2000 - 1st:1 2nd:1 3rd:0 Ran:7
Win Prizemoney £40,533 *Total Prizemoney* £50,653
Wins * 2000 Aug Goodwo (GD) H 7f 75 82 <
*** 1999** Aug York (GD) S 6f 74
2000 Turf 1-12: (6f 5, 7f 1-5, 8f 2) (sft, g-s 2, gd 4, g-f 1-4, frm) 2000 AW 0-1: (6f) (Fibr)
Unfurnished, above-average colt, effective 6 to 7f, best at 7f, acts on gd to frm, best on g-f, excels at Newmarket. Turf high 82 - 1st of 18 getting 9lb from Capricho (4 Aug Goodwood RF 3360). Landed a valuable handicap at Glorious Goodwood, but has looked a character at times. **K R Burke [2-20] Nigel Shields.*

ZIGGY'S DANCER (USA) BHB 65f65a **RR 74f 65a** 4832[11]
9 b h Ziggy's Boy (USA) 6.1f **(61)** - My Shy Dancer (USA) (Northjet) 10.3f **(74)**
Form - 7843340400800600
Record 2000 - 1st:0 2nd:0 3rd:2 Ran:15
Pre2000 - 1st:8 2nd:18 3rd:13 Ran:112
Win Prizemoney £39,366 *Total Prizemoney* £112,801
Wins * 1998 *Feb Southw (STD) C 6f 76+*
* 1997 Jun Cheste (G-F) H 5.1f 81 82
2000 Turf 0-11: (5f 9, 6f 2) (g-s, gd 4, g-f 4, frm 2) 2000 AW 0-4: (5f 3, 6f) (Fibr 4)
Above-average horse, effective 5f, acts on frm. Turf high 74. AW high 66. Probably best over five and six furlongs nowadays, he is tough and genuine but difficult to win with.
**E J Alston [8-116] J Connor (from R W Armstrong [0-11] Oct 1994).*

ZIGGY STARDUST (IRE) BHB 33f28a **RR 38f 28a** 3147[4]
5 b g Roi Danzig (USA) 10.5f **(62)** - Si Princess (Coquelin (USA)) 8.4f **(58)**
Form - 34324
Record 2000 - 1st:0 2nd:1 3rd:2 Ran:5
Pre2000 - 1st:0 2nd:3 3rd:2 Ran:19
Win Prizemoney £0 *Total Prizemoney* £5,221
2000 Turf 0-5: (12f 2, 16f, 17f, 18f) (gd, g-f, frm 3)
Very moderate gelding, effective 10 to 12f, best at 10f, acts on g-f to frm, best on frm. Turf high 38 - 4th of 34 getting 5lb from May King Mayhem (11 Jun Newmarket 12f frm RF 1880). Consistent.
**Mrs A J Bowlby [0-24] Joe Cool Partnership.*

ZIG ZIG (IRE) BHB 68f72a **RR 73f 72a** 3615[13]
3 b g Perugino (USA) - Queen of Erin (IRE) (King of Clubs) 7.1f **(57)**
Form - 310
Record 2000 - 1st:1 2nd:0 3rd:1 Ran:3
Pre2000 - 1st:0 2nd:0 3rd:0 Ran:1
Win Prizemoney £2,821 *Total Prizemoney* £3,420
Wins * **2000** *Jun Southw (STD) 6f 70 <*
2000 Turf 0-2: (7f 2) (frm, hrd) 2000 AW 1-1: (6f 1-1) (Fibr 1-1)
Leggy, above-average gelding. Turf high 73 (1st run) - 3rd of 7 to Adawar (14 Jun Beverley 7f hrd RF 1953). (1st run) - 1st of 10 from Geronimo (30 Jun Southwell RF 2417). Got off the mark in a maiden on the Southwell Fibresand in June, but it was a very poor race.
**Mrs A Duffield [1-4] Miss Betty Duxbury.*

ZILARATOR (USA) BHB 97f **RR 95f** 5321[2]
4 b g Zilzal (USA) 8.5f **(79)** - Allegedly (USA) (Sir Ivor) 10.2f **(70)**
Form - 616152
Record 2000 - 1st:2 2nd:1 3rd:0 Ran:6
Pre2000 - 1st:1 2nd:1 3rd:1 Ran:8
Win Prizemoney £21,373 *Total Prizemoney* £31,397
Wins * 2000 Spt Kempto (SFT) 12f 95 <
*** 2000** Apr Epsom (HVY) H 12f 85 91
* 1999 Apr Leices (HVY) 10f 72+
2000 Turf 2-6: (10f, 12f 2-4, 14f) (sft 1-2, g-s 1-3, g-f)
Leggy, very useful gelding, effective 12 to 15f, best at 12f, acts on sft to g-f, likes right handed tracks, likes tight tracks, likes Newmarket. Turf high 95 - also 1st of 9 giving 9lb to Purple Heather (18 Spt Kempton RF 4485). Consistent. Twice a winner last season, he won the Great Metropolitan at Epsom and a handicap at Kempton in September. He signed off by chasing home Boreas in a Listed event at Doncaster, and soft ground is clearly a must with this horse. **W J Haggas [3-14] Wentworth Racing (Pty) Ltd.*

ZILCH BHB 100f **RR 98f** 5318[1]
2 ch c Zilzal (USA) 8.5f **(79)** - Bunty Boo **(84f)** (Noalto) 5.7f **(49)**
Form - 242341
Record 2000 - 1st:1 2nd:2 3rd:1 Ran:6
Win Prizemoney £3,363 *Total Prizemoney* £38,730
Wins * 2000 Nov Doncas (HVY) 6f 86 <
2000 Turf 1-6: (5f 2, 6f 1-4) (sft 1-1, g-s, g-f, frm 3)
Very useful colt, effective 5 to 6f, acts on frm. Turf high 98 - 3rd of 11 to Superstar Leo (9 Spt Doncaster 5f frm RF 4312). Out of a useful sprinter, he made the frame in the Gimcrack and the Flying Childers and finally got off the mark in a maiden on the last day of the turf season at Doncaster.
**R Hannon [1-6] Mary Mayall, Linda C Martin.*

ZILINA (IRE) **RR 97f** 5285a[5]
5 b m Pips Pride 6.7f **(70)** - Tatra (Niniski (USA)) 10.6f **(65)**
Form - 17438035
2000 Turf 1-8: (5f 1-5, 6f 3) (hvy, sft 1-2, g-s 2, gd 2, frm)
Very useful filly, effective 5f, acts on sft to gd, best on sft. Turf high 97 - also 1st of 12 getting 4lb from Tiger Royal (26 Mar Curragh RF 0541a). She won a five furlong handicap at The Curragh under a big weight on her reappearance, but found life tougher in Pattern-class races later in the season.
**C Collins in IRE [5-33] G O'Kane.*

ZILKHA BHB 50f **RR 48f** 4821[16]
2 gr f Petong 7.6f **(58)** - Peperonata (IRE) **(71df)** (Cyrano de Bergerac) 6f **(68)**
Form - 000
Record 2000 - 1st:0 2nd:0 3rd:0 Ran:3
2000 Turf 0-3: (5f 2, 6f) (gd, g-f, frm)
Currently moderate filly. Turf high 48 (began Spt).
**I A Balding [0-3] Anthony & Valerie Hogarth.*

ZILUTTE (IRE) BHB 57f **RR 48f** 4173[6]
3 b g Zieten (USA) - Jungle Book (IRE) (Ballad Rock) 7.8f **(63)**
Form - 456
Record 2000 - 1st:0 2nd:0 3rd:0 Ran:3
Win Prizemoney £0 *Total Prizemoney* £256
2000 Turf 0-3: (5f 2, 6f) (g-f 3)
Rangy, currently moderate gelding. Turf high 48 (began Jly).
**John Berry [0-3] Twinacre Nurseries Ltd.*

ZINCALO (USA) BHB 46f **RR 57f** 5137[11]
4 gr g Zilzal (USA) 8.5f **(79)** -Silver Glitz (USA)(Grey Dawn II) 11.1f **(72)**
Form - 0481336000
Record 2000 - 1st:1 2nd:0 3rd:2 Ran:10

Pre2000 - 1st:0 2nd:2 3rd:0 Ran:7
Win Prizemoney £2,930 *Total Prizemoney* £6,424
Wins * **2000** Jun Nottin (G-F) H 14.1f 56 57 <
2000 Turf 1-9: (14f 1-6, 15f, 16f 2) (sft, g-s, gd 1-2, g-f, frm 4) 2000 AW 0-1: (13f) (Equi)
Scopey, fair gelding, effective 14f, acts on gd to g-f, has worn blinkers, likes left handed tracks, likes tight tracks. Turf high 60. He was second past the post at Nottingham in May, and was very fortunate to get the race in the Stewards' Room. Looks very slow and needs a severe test of stamina. **C E Brittain [1-17] C E Brittain.*

ZINDABAD (FR) BHB 113f RR 116f 2344[3]

4 b c Shirley Heights 12.1f **(76)** - Miznah (IRE) (Sadler's Wells (USA)) 10f **(76)**
Form - 33
Record 2000 - 1st:0 2nd:0 3rd:2 Ran:2
Pre2000 - 1st:4 2nd:2 3rd:0 Ran:9
Win Prizemoney £56,190 *Total Prizemoney* £89,710
Wins * 1999 Aug Windso (GD) G3 10f 112 <
* 1999 Jly Ascot (G-F) H 10f 104 112 <
* 1999 Jly Newmar (GD) H 10f 100 102
* 1998 Spt Pontef (G-F) 8f 97+
2000 Turf 0-2. (10f, 12f) (frm, hrd)
Scopey, high-class colt, effective 10 to 12f, best at 10f, acts on gd to hrd, best on frm, likes right handed tracks. Turf high 116 - 3rd of 4 giving 3lb to Island House (28 Jun Kempton 10f frm RF 2344). Most progressive in 1999 (he completed a hat-trick when winning the Group Three Winter Hill Stakes), he ran a couple of promising races during June but was not seen out again. Best when forcing the issue on fast ground, he should stay a mile and a half.
**B Hanbury [4-11] Abdullah Ali.*

ZIRCONI (FR) BHB 68f RR 77df 5122[9]

4 b g Zieten (USA) - Muirfield (FR) (Crystal Glitters (USA)) 11.3f **(79)**
Form - 4033800
Record 2000 - 1st:0 2nd:0 3rd:2 Ran:7
Pre2000 - 1st:0 2nd:2 3rd:4 Ran:10
Win Prizemoney £0 *Total Prizemoney* £37,625
2000 Turf 0-7: (6f 3, 7f 4) (g-s, gd 2, g-f, frm 3)
Above-average gelding, effective 6f, acts on gd to frm, has worn blinkers. Turf high 77 - 3rd of 14 to Pips Magic (12 Jly Doncaster 6f frm RF 2731).
**D Nicholls [0-9] P D Savill (from Mme C Head in FR [0-8] Oct 1999).*

ZOENA BHB 60f62a RR 47f 62a 4372[11]

3 ch f Emarati (USA) 6.6f **(63)** - Exotic Forest **(68df)** (Dominion) 8.5f **(63)**
Form - 7045637530
Record 2000 - 1st:0 2nd:0 3rd:2 Ran:9
Pre2000 - 1st:0 2nd:0 3rd:1 Ran:6
Win Prizemoney £0 *Total Prizemoney* £1,669
2000 Turf 0-9: (5f 6, 6f 3) (gd, g-f 3, frm 4, hrd)
Workmanlike, average filly, effective 6f, acts on frm. Turf high 54.
**J G Portman [0-15] Mrs R Pease.*

ZOE'S NEWSBOX BHB 26a RR 26a 133[7]

6 b m Inca Chief (USA) 5.6f **(45)** - Let's Go Lochy (Lochnager) 6f **(59)**
Form - 0007
Record 2000 - 1st:0 2nd:0 3rd:0 Ran:2
Pre2000 - 1st:0 2nd:0 3rd:0 Ran:2
2000 AW 0-2: (5f, 6f) (Equi, Fibr)
Little account mare. AW high 11. **A G Newcombe [0-4] A J Harley.*

ZOLA (IRE) BHB 20f30a RR 20f 30a 5011[15]

4 ch g Indian Ridge 7.6f **(74)** - Fluella (Welsh Pageant) 10f **(65)**
Form - 05000000
Record 2000 - 1st:0 2nd:0 3rd:0 Ran:8
Pre2000 - 1st:2 2nd:2 3rd:1 Ran:20
Win Prizemoney £4,541 *Total Prizemoney* £6,912
Wins * 1999 *Aug Lingfi (STD) H 16f 40 41*
* 1999 May Yarmou (FRM) C 16f 52 <
2000 Turf 0-4: (14f, 17f 2, 18f) (g-f, frm 2, hrd) 2000 AW 0-4: (12f, 14f, 16f 2) (Equi 2, Fibr 2)
Scopey, very moderate gelding, effective 10 to 16f, acts on frm - acts on AW, has worn blinkers, favours left handed tracks, favours tight tracks. Turf high 20. AW high 31. Does not have the ability or speed of his illustrious namesake.
**M Quinn [2-30] M Quinn (from M R Channon [0-2] Spt 1998).*

ZOMARADAH BHB 117f RR 118f 4542[4]

5 b m Deploy 11.4f **(67)** - Jawaher (IRE) (Dancing Brave (USA)) 8.4f **(76)**
Form - 4
Record 2000 - 1st:0 2nd:0 3rd:0 Ran:1
Pre2000 - 1st:6 2nd:1 3rd:1 Ran:12
Win Prizemoney £289,913 *Total Prizemoney* £379,677
Wins * 1999 Spt Capann (GD) G2 10f 113
* 1999 Aug Currag (GD) G2 10f 118 <
* 1999 Jun Doncas (G-S) 10.3f 114
* 1998 Oct Woodbi (FRM) 10f 113
* 1998 May San Si (HVY) G1 11f 103+
* 1998 Apr Bright (GD) 10f 66+
2000 Turf 0-1: (10f) (gd)
High-class filly, effective 10 to 11f, best at 10f, acts on gd to frm, best on frm. Consistent. Returned from the paddocks to finish fourth in a Goodwood listed event in September.
**L M Cumani [6-13] Sheikh Mohammed Obaid Al Maktoum.*

ZONING BHB 110f RR 113f 1060[4]

3 b c Warning 8.1f **(77)** - Zonda (Fabulous Dancer (USA)) 9.4f **(70)**
Form - 34
Record 2000 - 1st:0 2nd:0 3rd:1 Ran:2
Pre2000 - 1st:2 2nd:0 3rd:0 Ran:4
Win Prizemoney £12,079 *Total Prizemoney* £44,070
Wins 1999 Oct York (G-S) 7f 91 <
1999 Aug Yarmou (GD) 6f 87+
2000 Turf 0-1: (8f) (gd) 2000 AW 0-1: (8f) (Dirt)
Workmanlike, Group-class colt. An honest individual, he ran a sound race when fourth in the 2000 Guineas but was not seen out again. Unlikely to stay beyond a mile, he is capable of winning a Group race on the continent.
**S bin Suroor [0-1] Godolphin (from S bin Suroor in UAE [0-1] Feb 2000).*

ZORBA BHB 53f39a RR 61df 39a 856[6]

6 b g Shareef Dancer (USA) 10.1f **(67)** - Zabelina (USA) (Diesis) 9.3f **(69)**
Form - 6
Record 2000 - 1st:0 2nd:0 3rd:0 Ran:1
Pre2000 - 1st:5 2nd:6 3rd:9 Ran:40
Win Prizemoney £13,428 *Total Prizemoney* £22,889
Wins 1998 *May Southw (STD) C 11f 54*
1998 Mar Hamilt (HVY) C 9.2f 47
1997 Oct Ayr (SFT) H 9f 60 64
1997 Jun Redcar (GD) C 10f 69 <
1997 Jun Hamilt (GD) S 9.2f 64
2000 Turf 0-1: (11f) (hvy)
Average gelding, has worn blinkers. Becoming disappointing.
**J G M O'Shea [0-23] The Cross Racing Club (from J Hetherton [3-21] May 1998).*

ZORRO BHB 55f56a RR 56f 56a 521[1]

6 gr g Touch of Grey 8.1f **(47)** - Snow Huntress (Shirley Heights) 10.3f **(74)**
Form - 11
Record 2000 - 1st:1 2nd:0 3rd:0 Ran:1
Pre2000 - 1st:2 2nd:3 3rd:2 Ran:18
Win Prizemoney £7,532 *Total Prizemoney* £10,756
Wins * **2000** Mar Windso (G-F) H 11.6f 52 56
* 1999 *Dec Lingfi (STD) H 13f 50 53*
1997 Jun Yarmou (FRM) H 10.1f 51 57 <
2000 Turf 1-1: (12f 1-1) (frm 1-1)
Fair gelding. (1st run) - 1st of 20 giving 1lb to Westminster City (27 Mar Windsor RF 0521). Consistent.
**J R Poulton [2-3] Mrs G M Temmerman (from R M Flower [1-16] May 1998).*

ZOUDIE RR 72f 5236[5]

2 b f Ezzoud (IRE) - Patsy Western (Precocious) 8.6f **(62)**
Form - 5
Record 2000 - 1st:0 2nd:0 3rd:0 Ran:1
2000 Turf 0-1: (7f) (g-s)
Currently above-average filly. (1st run) - 5th of 22 to Good Standing (28 Oct Newmarket 7f g-s RF 5236).
**J Noseda [0-1] B McAllister.*

ZOZARHARRY (IRE) BHB 77f **RR 74f** 5140^{5}
2 b c Nicolotte - Miss Butterfield (Cure The Blues (USA)) 9.5f **(63)**
Form - 005
Record 2000 - 1st:0 2nd:0 3rd:0 Ran:3
2000 Turf 0-3: (6f 2, 7f) (g-s, frm 2)
Currently above-average colt. Turf high 74 (began Aug).
**D J S Cosgrove [0-3] Colin Davey.*

ZSARABAK BHB 46f **RR 49f** 4764^{11}
3 br g Soviet Lad (USA) 9.4f **(63)** - Moorefield Girl (IRE) (Gorytus (USA)) 7.8f **(60)**
Form - 00
Record 2000 - 1st:0 2nd:0 3rd:0 Ran:2
Pre2000 - 1st:0 2nd:0 3rd:0 Ran:4
2000 Turf 0-2: (12f 2) (g-s, g-f)
Leggy, moderate gelding. Turf high 18 (began Aug).
**J J O'Neill [1-5] C D Carr (from B S Rothwell [0-4] Spt 1999).*

ZUCCHERO RR 85f 4732^{6}
4 br g Dilum (USA) 7.1f **(56)** - Legal Sound (Legal Eagle) 7.3f **(54)**
Form - 61655436
Record 2000 - 1st:1 2nd:0 3rd:1 Ran:8
Pre2000 - 1st:3 2nd:1 3rd:0 Ran:9
Win Prizemoney £14,713 *Total Prizemoney* £26,389
Wins * **2000** Jly Newbur (G-F) H 7.3f 76 80+ <
* 1999 Jly Newmar (G-F) H 7f 65 73+
* 1999 Jly Lingfi (G-F) H 7f 53 66
* 1999 Jly Chepst (G-F) H 6.1f 53 68
2000 Turf 1-8: (6f, 7f 1-6, 8f) (gd 2, g-f 2, frm 1-4)
Leggy, useful gelding, effective 7f, acts on gd to frm, best on frm, often wears blinkers, likes Ascot and Newbury. Turf high 85 (began Jly) - 3rd of 26 getting 12lb from Duke of Modena (23 Spt Ascot 7f gd RF 4597) - also 1st of 8 getting 2lb from Surprise Encounter (21 Jly Newbury RF 3002). Consistent. He was in fair form last term, winning at Newbury in July. Likes to bowl along in front. **D W P Arbuthnot [4-17] Philip Banfield.*

ZUHAIR BHB 84f80a **RR 84f 80a** 4865^{11}
7 ch g Mujtahid (USA) 7.4f **(69)** - Ghzaalh (USA) (Northern Dancer) 9.6f **(80)**
Form - 70000003315057180
Record 2000 - 1st:2 2nd:0 3rd:2 Ran:17
Pre2000 - 1st:6 2nd:5 3rd:3 Ran:47
Win Prizemoney £76,844 *Total Prizemoney* £94,071
Wins * **2000** Spt Goodwo (GD) H 6f 79 84
* **2000** Aug Goodwo (G-F) H 5f 72 82
* 1999 Aug York (GD) H 6f 83 88 <
* 1999 Jly Goodwo (G-F) H 6f 72 83
* 1999 Jly Goodwo (G-F) H 5f 72 74
* 1999 Jun Lingfi (G-F) H 5f 66 71
1997 *May Wolver (STD) C 6f 66*
2000 Turf 2-17: (5f 1-7, 6f 1-10) (sft, gd 2-9, g-f 5, frm 2)
Decent gelding, effective 5 to 6f, best at 6f, acts on gd to g-f, best on g-f, has worn blinkers, excels at Goodwood. Turf high 84 - 1st of 16 getting 7lb from Molly Brown (9 Spt Goodwood RF 4316) - also 1st of 19 giving 13lb to Sihafi (2 Aug Goodwood RF 3321). Consistent. He came back to the boil last year when landing a Goodwood handicap in August with something to spare and scored again there in September. Suited by coming from behind off a strong pace and obviously likes the Sussex track.
**D Nicholls [6-34] The Gardening Partnership (from D McCain [1-27] Oct 1998).*

ZULFAA (USA) BHB 88f **RR 87f** 4447^{2}
2 b f Bahri (USA) - Haniya (IRE) **(86f)** (Caerleon (USA)) 8.6f **(71)**
Form - 412
Record 2000 - 1st:1 2nd:1 3rd:0 Ran:3
Win Prizemoney £2,530 *Total Prizemoney* £4,217
Wins * **2000** Aug Lingfi (G-F) 7.6f 82+ <
2000 Turf 1-3: (7f, 8f 1-2) (gd, g-f, frm 1-1)
Currently useful filly. Turf high 87 (began Jly) - 2nd of 6 getting 11lb from Harrier (16 Spt Ayr 8f gd RF 4447) - also 1st of 17 from Dubai Seven Stars (23 Aug Lingfield RF 3907).
**J L Dunlop [1-3] Hamdan Al Maktoum.*

ZULU DAWN (USA) RR 79f 5069^{13}
4 b g El Gran Senor (USA) 8.9f **(85)** - Celtic Loot (USA) (Irish River (FR)) 8.6f **(78)**
Form - 33085700
Record 2000 - 1st:0 2nd:0 3rd:2 Ran:8
Pre2000 - 1st:1 2nd:1 3rd:1 Ran:8
Win Prizemoney £5,572 *Total Prizemoney* £10,419
Wins * 1999 Spt Newbur (G-F) 8f 80 <
2000 Turf 0-8: (8f 7, 12f) (g-s 2, g-f 3, frm 3)
Scopey, above-average gelding, effective 7 to 8f, best at 8f, acts on gd to frm, best on frm, has worn blinkers. Turf high 79 (1st run) - 3rd of 6 giving 3lb to Madam Alison (12 Jun Windsor 8f frm RF 1907). **J W Hills [1-16] The Jampot Partnership.*

ZURS (IRE) BHB 54f75a **RR 67df 75a** 5079^{9}
7 b g Tirol 8.1f **(64)** - Needy (High Top) 10.2f **(67)**
Form - 00
Record 2000 - 1st:0 2nd:0 3rd:0 Ran:2
Pre2000 - 1st:6 2nd:4 3rd:9 Ran:50
Win Prizemoney £18,354 *Total Prizemoney* £34,880
Wins * 1999 May Sandow (GD) H 10f 68 72 <
* 1998 Spt Salisb (HVY) H 9.9f 67 67
* 1998 Aug Sandow (G-F) H 8.1f 64 66
* 1997 Spt Folkes (FRM) H 6.9f 52 65
* 1997 Spt Leices (G-F) 8f 58
1997 *Feb Lingfi (STD) 8f 56+*
2000 Turf 0-2: (10f, 12f) (g-s 2)
Above-average gelding, effective 8 to 10f, best at 10f, acts on g-s to frm, has worn blinkers. Turf high 21 (began Spt).
**J R Poulton [6-41] Mrs M Liston (from Miss Gay Kelleway [1-16] Aug 1997).*

ZYDECO (IRE) BHB 83f **RR 84f** 5134^{4}
5 b g Darshaan 11.9f **(81)** - Cajun Melody (Cajun) 5.2f **(54)**
Form - 4
Record 2000 - 1st:0 2nd:0 3rd:0 Ran:1
Pre2000 - 1st:0 2nd:3 3rd:0 Ran:5
Win Prizemoney £0 *Total Prizemoney* £3,833
2000 Turf 0-1: (10f) (sft)
Decent gelding.
**Mrs A J Perrett [0-1] James Hartnett (from M C Pipe [0-3] Jun 1998).*

ZYZ BHB 103f **RR 104f** 4740^{9}
3 b c Unfuwain (USA) 11.4f **(74)** - Girette (USA) (General Assembly (USA)) 10f **(68)**
Form - 233050
Record 2000 - 1st:0 2nd:1 3rd:2 Ran:6
Pre2000 - 1st:1 2nd:1 3rd:1 Ran:3
Win Prizemoney £4,272 *Total Prizemoney* £18,947
Wins * 1999 Spt Leices (FRM) 7f 88 <
2000 Turf 0-6: (8f 2, 9f, 10f 2, 12f) (sft, gd 3, g-f 2)
Scopey, very useful colt, effective 7 to 10f, best at 8f, acts on sft to g-f. Turf high 104. Improving. He finished third in the Easter Stakes at Kempton, where he got himself into a real state, and in the Dee Stakes at Chester, where he appreciated the step up in trip. Out of his depth in the Derby, he was not disgraced in the Cambridgeshire on his final run. **B W Hills [1-9] W J Gredley.*

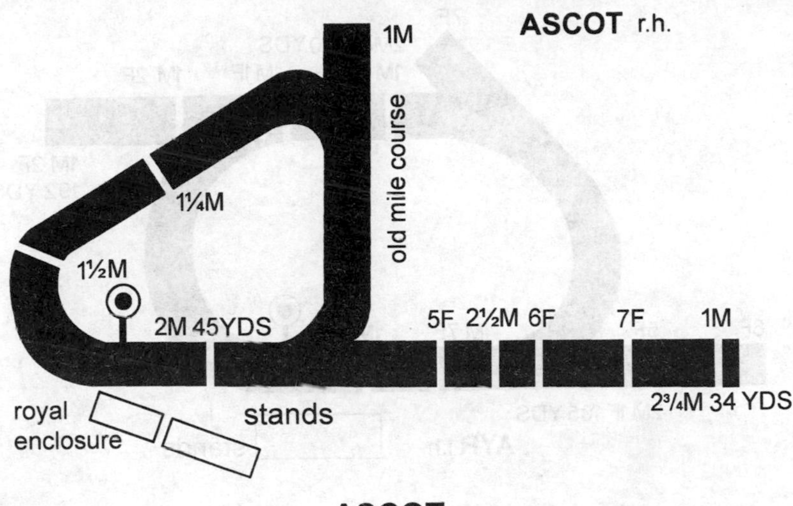

ASCOT

Address: Ascot Racecourse, Ascot, Berkshire SL5 7JN Tel: (01344) 622211 **Fax:** (01344) 624978
E-mail: AscotatITL.Net **Internet:** http://www.sportinglife.co.uk/ascot/
A triangular course of 1m 6f 34y. The course goes downhill from the mile and a half start for three furlongs into Swinley Bottom (the lowest part of the track): it soon joins the Old Mile (which starts on a chute) and is then uphill with a straight run-in of two and a half furlongs, the last 100y being level. The straight mile (Royal Hunt Cup Course) is downhill from the start, rises to the five furlong gate and then falls slightly to the junction of the courses. The whole course is of a galloping nature with easy turns but is nevertheless a testing one, especially on soft going.
Clerk of the Course: Mr N. Cheyne, Ascot Racecourse, Ascot, Berkshire SL5 7JN. Tel: (01344) 874567.
Chief Executive: Mr D. Erskine-Crum
Going Reports: Day (01344) 874567/ Eve (07885) 505407 (Mobile)
Free stabling: shavings, straw or paper Tel: 01344 25630/Fax: 01344 873751
By Car: West of the town on the A329. Easy access from the M3 (Junc 3) and the M4 (Junc 6). Car parking adjoining the course and Ascot Heath. Contact the Secretary, Ascot Authority. Tel: (01344) 876456.
By Rail: Regular service from Waterloo to Ascot (500y from the racecourse).
By Air: Helicopter landing facility at the course. London (Heathrow) Airport 15 miles, White Waltam Airfield 12 miles.

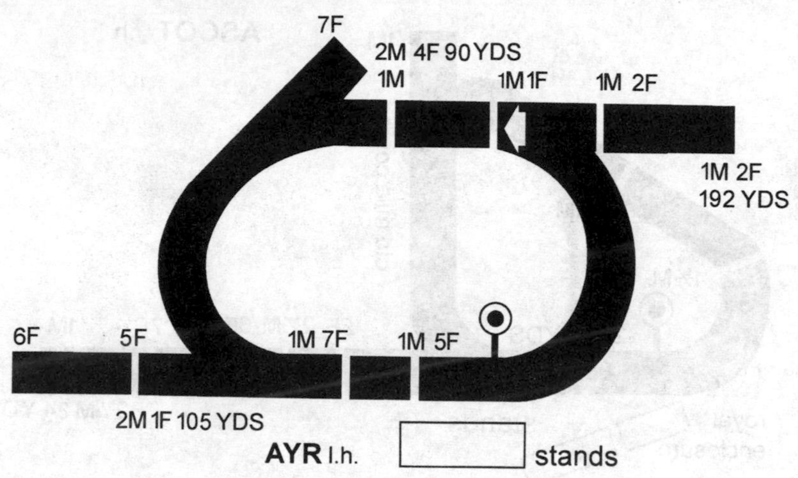

AYR

Address: Ayr Racecourse, Whitletts Road, Ayr KA8 0JE Tel: (01292) 264179 **Fax:** (01292) 610140
Internet: www.ayr-racecourse.com
A wide, relatively flat oval track of just over 1m 4f. An extension to the back straight provides a 1m 3f course with a sweeping turn at the top of the track tojoin the straight course four furlongs from the winning post. The straight six furlongs falls slightly for some three and a half furlongs and then rises slightly. In general, this is a very fair galloping course.
Clerk of the Course and Manager: Mr Richard Pridham, Racecourse Office, 2 Whitletts Road, Ayr. Tel: (01292) 264179. Mobile: (0468) 651261 or (07771) 522800.
Free stabling and accommodation for lads and lasses. Tel: (01292) 264179.
By Car: East of the town on the A758. Free parking for buses and cars.
By Rail: Ayr Station (trains on the half hour from Glasgow Central). Journey time 55 minutes. Buses and taxis also to the course.
By Air: Prestwick International Airport (10 minutes by car). Glasgow Airport (1hour).

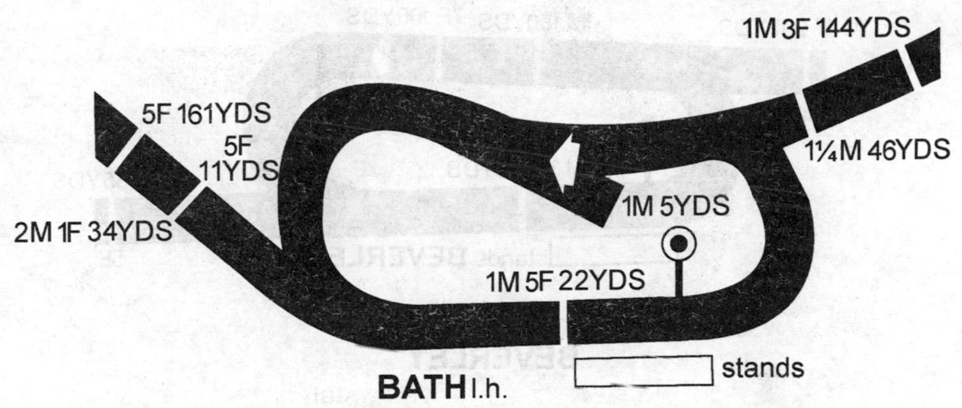

BATH

Address: The Racecourse, Lansdown, Bath Tel: Office (01291) 622260 Racedays (01225) 424609

An oval track of 1m 4f 25y with 1m 3f 144y, 1m 2f 46y and 1m 5y starts set on chutes from the back straight and an uphill run-in of four furlongs, which bends to the left. There is no straight course but an extension provides for races of five furlongs and of 5f 167y, which run generally uphill and left-handed to a distinct left-handed curve about a furlong from the winning post.

Clerk of the Course: Mr R. D. Farrant, Tylers Farm, Gravel Hill Road, Yate, Bristol BS37 7BN. Tel: (01398) 332410 Mobile (07788) 101250 Fax: 01398 332411.

Secretary: Miss S.J. Wilcox, Hopkins Farm, Lower Tysoe, Warwick, CV35 0BN Tel: (01295) 688030/Fax: (01295) 688211.

Free stabling and accommodation for lads and lasses. Tel: (01225) 444274

By Car: 2 miles North-West of the City (M4 Junc 18) at Lansdown. Unlimited free car and coach parking space immediately behind the stands. Special bus services operate from Bath to the racecourse.

By Rail: Bath Station (from Paddington), regular bus service from Bath to the course (3 miles).

By Air: Bristol or Colerne Airports. (no landing facilities at the course).

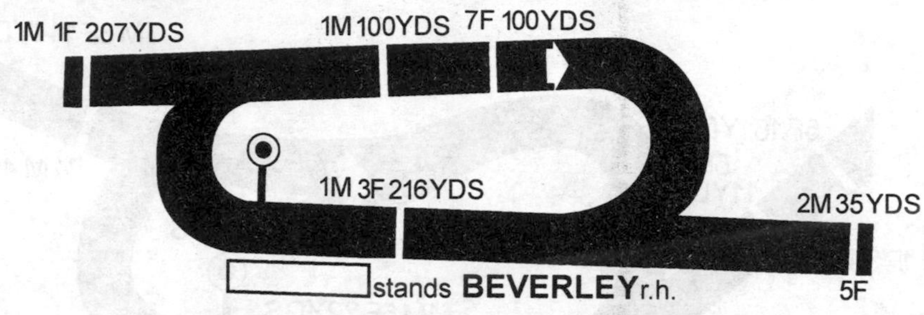

BEVERLEY

Address: Beverley Race Co. Ltd, York Road, Beverley, E.Yorkshire HU17 8QZ

Tel: (01482) 867488/882645 **Fax:** (01482) 863892

An oval course of 1m 3f set on two levels. A chute to the back straight provides a mile and a quarter course, which has a straight run of some five furlongs to a steep downhill bend into the home turn and an uphill run-in of two and a half furlongs. The five furlong course, which rises throughout with a distinct jink after a furlong and a slight bend to the right at halfway, provides a severe test for juveniles at the start of the season. The downhill turn into the straight and the short run-in prevent this from being an entirely galloping track.

Racecourse Manager: Sally Iggulden, The Racecourse, York Road, Beverley, E.Yorkshire. Tel: (01482) 867488/882645 (Course Office) Mobile:(07850) 458605.

Clerk of the Course: Mr J.M.Hutchinson. (01765) 602156, Mobile (0860) 679904).

Free stabling. Tel: (01482) 867488 or 882645

By Car: 7 miles from the M62 (Junc 38) off the A1035. Free car parking opposite the course. Owners and Trainers use a separate enclosure.

By Rail: Beverley Station (Hull-Scarborough line). Occasional bus service to the course (1 mile).

By Air: Helicopter landings by prior arrangement. Light aircraft landing facilities at Linley Hill, Leven airport.

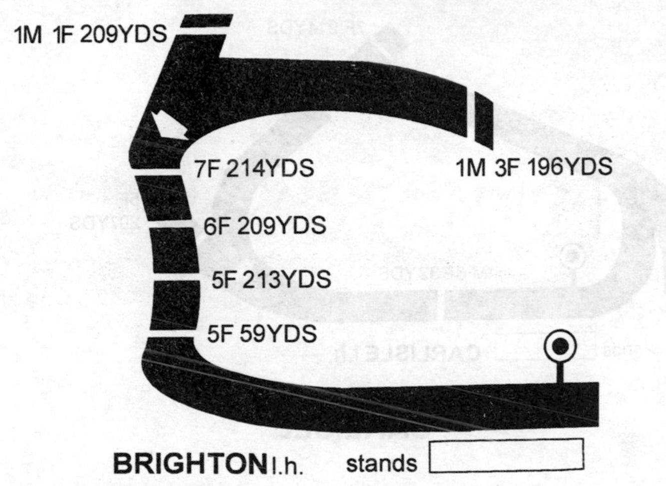

BRIGHTON

Address: Brighton Racecourse, Freshfield Road, Brighton, Sussex BN2 2XZ
Tel: (01273) 603580 **Fax:** (01273) 673267 **E-mail:** 1016111.141@compuserve.com
The course forms a horseshoe of 1m 4f round with easy turns and a run-in of three and a half furlongs. The first three furlongs are slightly uphill. Then there is a gentle descent and rise to about four furlongs from home. From there the ground falls steeply until about two furlongs out; then a sharp rise with the last 100y level. This sharp track, reminiscent of Epsom with its pronounced gradients, is unsuitable for big, long-striding animals, but it suits sharp sorts and is something of a specialists' course.
Clerk of the Course: Mr Jeremy Martin Tel. (0411) 739103 (mobile)
Stabling and accommodation available on request. Tel: (01273) 603580
By Car: East of the city on the A27 (Lewes Road). There is a car park adjoining the course.
By Rail: Brighton Station (from Victoria on the hour, London Bridge or Portsmouth). Special bus service to the course from the station (approx 2 miles) and to the sea front.
By Air: No racecourse facilities.

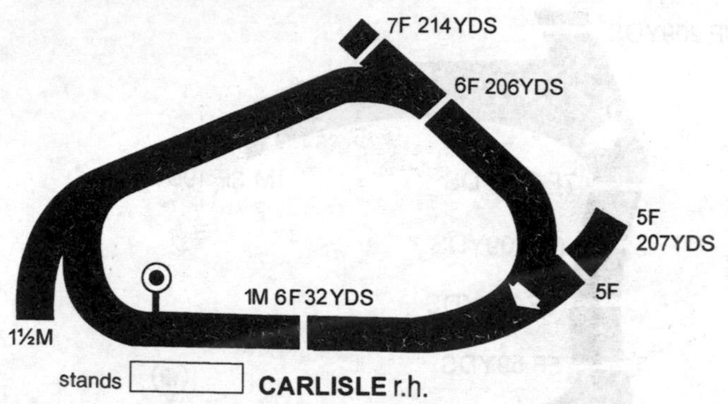

CARLISLE

Address: Carlisle Racecourse, Durdar Road, Carlisle CA2 4TS
Tel: (01228) 522973 **Fax:** Office (01228) 591827 Weighing room (01228) 523751

A pear-shaped, undulating course of 1m 5f with an extension for a mile and a half start and a straight uphill run-in of three and a half furlongs. The six furlong course (which includes the five furlong) starts on a chute, bears right for the first furlong and a half and again at the turn into the straight. The rise to the winning post, although it begins to level out from `the distance', makes it a stiff test of stamina.

Clerk of the Course: Mr J. E. Fenwicke-Clennell Tel: (01694) 26589 (home) Mobile: (0860) 737729.

General Manager: I. R. Duff Esq, Grandstand Office, Carlisle Racecourse, Durdar Road, Carlisle, Cumbria CA2 4TS. Tel: (01228) 522973 Fax: (01228) 591827.

Club Secretary: Mrs S. L. Mortensen. Tel: (01228) 591827.

Stabling and accommodation available on request. Please Please phone Head Groundsman on (01228) 546188, or Stable Office on (01228) 549489 by 5pm day before racing.

By Car: 2 miles south of the town (Durdar Road). Easy access from the M6 (Junc 42). The car park is free (adjacent to the course). Trackside car parking £3 (except Saturdays & Bank Holidays £5).

By Rail: Carlisle Station (2 miles from the course).

By Air: Helicopter landing facility by prior arrangement.

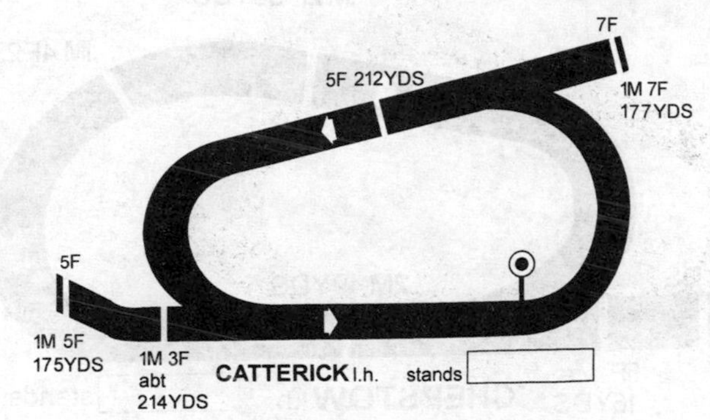

CATTERICK

Address: The Racecourse, Catterick Bridge, Richmond, North Yorkshire DL10 7PE Tel: (01748) 811478 **Fax:** (01748) 811082

An oval, undulating course of 1m 180y with two chutes, one for seven furlong and another for five furlong starts, and a straight run-in of three furlongs. The five furlong course is downhill throughout, sharply at first, and jinks left-handed at the junction of the courses. The seven furlong track joins the round course at the six furlong gate and is slightly downhill to the home turn. This sharp track is entirely unsuitable for long-striding gallopers and is often a specialists' track for both horse and jockey.

Clerk of the Course: (Flat) Mr J. Gundill, c/o The Racecourse, Catterick Bridge, Richmond, North Yorkshire DL10 7PE Tel: Mobile (07770) 613049.

Secretary: International Racecourse Management Ltd., c/o The Racecourse, Catterick Bridge, Richmond, North Yorkshire DL10 7PE. Tel: (01748) 811478. Fax: (01748) 811082.

Boxes are allotted on arrival. Contact Mr Adrian Swingler, Racecourse Lodge, Catterick. Tel: (01748) 811478.

By Car: The course is adjacent to the A1, 1 mile North-West of the town on the A6136. There is a free car park.

By Rail: Darlington Station (special buses to course - 14 mile journey).

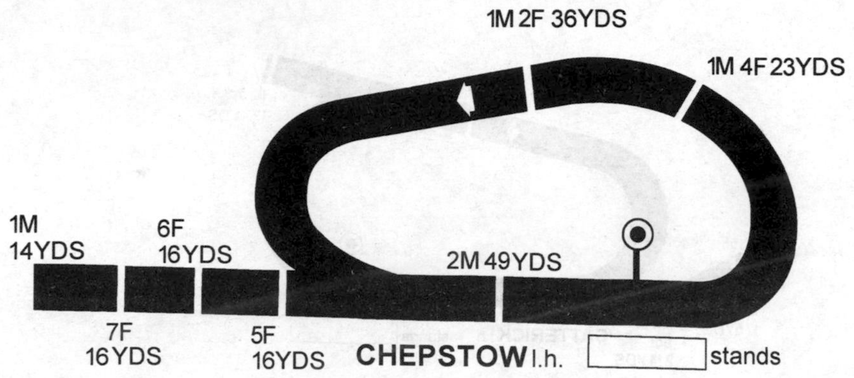

CHEPSTOW

Address: Chepstow Racecourse, Chepstow, Gwent NP6 5YH Tel: (01291) 622260 **Fax:** (01291) 625550

An oval, undulating course, about 2m in circumference with a straight run-in of five furlongs, which extends to make a straight mile. All races of up to a mile are run on the latter, which is downhill to the five furlong start and then rises sharply for two and a half furlongs before levelling out to the winning post. The changing gradients prevent this from being a really galloping track.

Clerk of the Course and Manager: Major D. McAllister BS37 7BN. Tel: Office (01283) 711233 Home (01889) 562221 Mobile (0860) 286003.

Managing Director: Mr G. C. Francis, 17 Welsh Street, Chepstow, Gwent NP6 5YH.

Stabling: 109 boxes, allotted on arrival. Limited accommodation for lads and lasses. Apply: (01291) 623414.

By Car: 1 mile North-West of the town on the A466. (1 mile from Junc 22 of the M4 (Severn Bridge)). There is a Free public car park opposite the Stands entrance.

By Rail: Chepstow Station (from Paddington, change at Gloucester or Newport). The course is 1 mile from station.

By Air: Helicopter landing facility in the centre of the course.

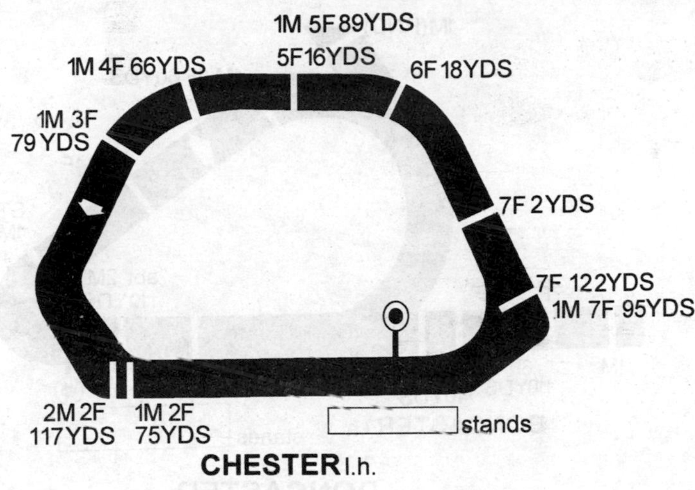

CHESTER

Address: The Racecourse, Chester CH1 2LY Tel: (01244) 323170
Fax: (01244) 344971

A perfectly flat, circular course, 1m 73y in circumference, with a sharp bend to a straight run-in of 230y. Long distance events are an extreme test of stamina, but for middle-distance races and sprints, the course greatly favours a sharp-actioned horse. Horses with previous winning form on this track are worthy of note.

Clerk of the Course: Mr R. Thomas. Tel: (01244) 323170 (racedays).
Racecourse Manager: Mr R. Walls Tel. (01244) 327171
Secretaries: Messrs Kidsons Impey, Steam Mill, Chester. CH3 5AN Tel: (01244) 327171.

Free stabling (175 boxes) and accommodation. Apply: (01244) 324880 (racedays) or (01244) 323170.

By Car: The course is near the centre of the city on the A548 (Queensferry Road). The Owners and Trainers car park is adjacent to the County Stand. There is a public car park in the centre of the course.

By Rail: Chester Station (3/4 mile from the course). Services from Euston, Paddington and Northgate.

By Air: Hawarden Airport (2 miles).

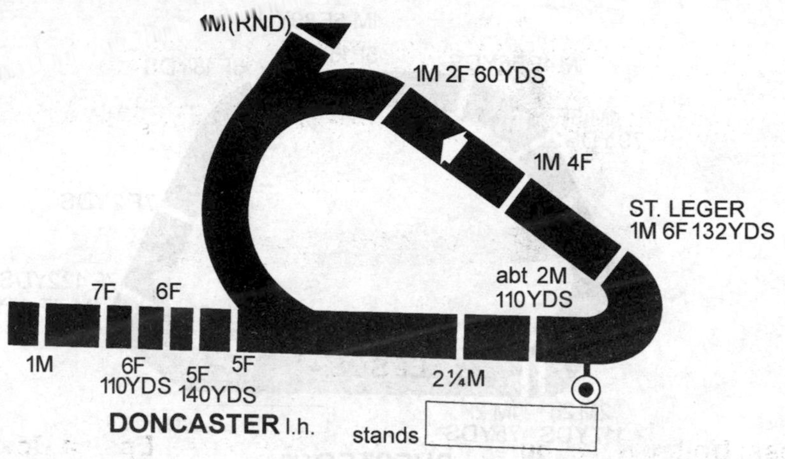

DONCASTER

Address: Doncaster Racecourse, Grand Stand, Leger Way, Doncaster DN2 6BB
Tel: (01302) 320066 **Fax:** (01302) 323271 **E-mail:** info@britishracing.com
Internet: www.britishracing.com
A pear-shaped track, about 1m 7f 110y in circumference with a distinct rise and fall to the mile marker. There is a level run-in of four and a half furlongs, extending to a straight mile, which tapers from a width of 88ft at the five-furlong pole to 60ft at the winning post. A round mile joins the straight course at a tangent. This good galloping track is suitable for strongly-built stayers and calls for stamina and courage.
Chief Executive & Clerk of Course (Flat): Mr J. Sanderson, International Racecourse Management Ltd., Grandstand, Leger Way, Doncaster DN2 6BB. Tel: (01302) 320066. Fax: Office (01673) 843434
Free stabling and accommodation Tel: (01302) 349337
By Car: East of the town, off the A638 (M18 Junc 3 & 4). Club members car park reserved. Large public car park free and adjacent to the course. **By Rail:** Doncaster Central Station (from King's Cross). Special bus service from the station (1 mile).
By Air: Helicopter landing facility by prior arrangement only.

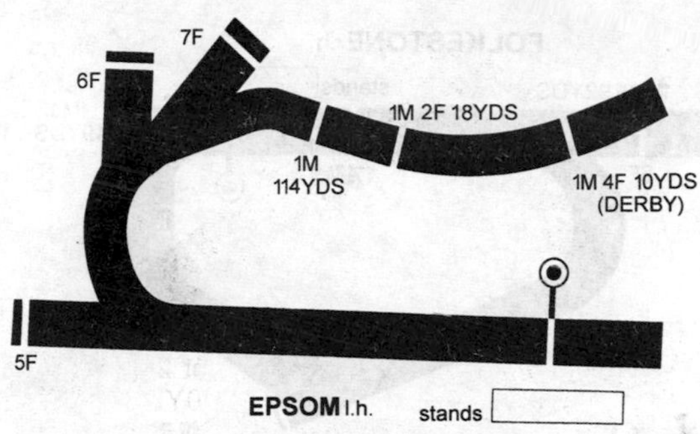

EPSOM

Address: United Racecourses Ltd., The Racecourse, Epsom Downs, Surrey KT18 5LQ Tel: (01372) 726311 **Fax:** (01372) 748253

From the Derby start at the top of the Downs, the course climbs steadily for the first gently-bending four furlongs, then levels out for nearly two furlongs before falling sharply round the bend to Tattenham Corner and into the straight. This is of less than four furlongs and ends with a fairish rise of just over a furlong to the winning post. The City and Suburban course and the Epsom Mile are, respectively, the last 1m 2f 15y and the last 1m 110y of the Derby course. The five furlong course (Egmont Course) is perfectly straight and, running sharply downhill to the junction with the round course, is the fastest in the world. The Derby course is a unique test for the thoroughbred, the frequently fast early pace demanding stamina, and the bends and gradients calling for a faultless action. Well-balanced, medium-sized, handy sorts seem to do best over five furlongs.

Clerk of the Course: Mr A. J. Cooper, The Grandstand, Epsom Downs, Surrey KT18 5LQ. Tel: (01372) 726311, Mobile (0374) 230850

Free stabling and accommodation Tel: (01372) 725794

By Car: 2 miles South of the town on the B290 (M25 Junc 8 & 9). For full car park particulars apply to: The Club Secretary, The Racecourse, Epsom Downs, Surrey KT18 5LQ. Tel: (01372) 726311.

By Rail: Epsom, Epsom Downs or Tattenham Corner Stations (trains from London Bridge, Waterloo, Victoria). Regular bus services run to the course from Epsom and Morden Underground Station.

By Air: London (Heathrow) and London (Gatwick) are both within 20 miles of the course. Heliport (Derby Meeting only) apply to Hascombe Aviation Tel: (01279) 680291.

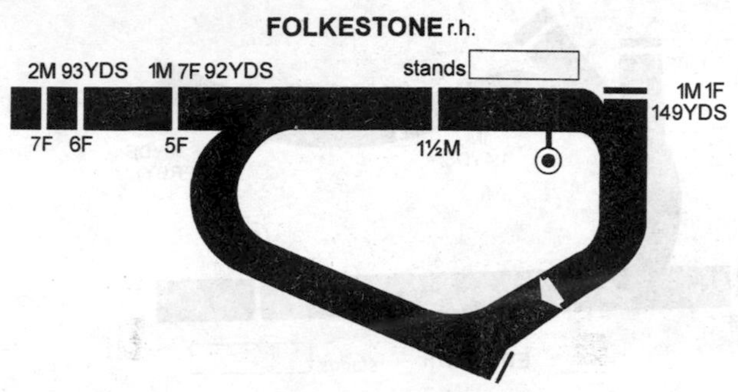

FOLKESTONE

Address: Folkestone Racecourse, Westenhanger, Hythe, Kent CT21 4HX

Tel: (01303) 266407 **Fax:** (01303) 260185 **E-mail:** 1016111.141@compuserve.com

A circuit of 1m 3f, somewhat undulating, with a straight run-in of two and a half furlongs. Five and six furlong races start on an extension which joins the round course about three furlongs from the line and has a slight rise over the final furlong. Despite its gentle turns and its width, Folkestone can not be described as a galloping track.

Director of Racing: Mr C. G. Stickels, Lingfield Park (1991) Ltd., Lingfield, Surrey RH7 6PQ. Tel: (01342) 834800 or (01303) 266407 (racedays) Mobile: (07970) 621440.

Clerk of the Course: Mr F. I. W. Cameron, Lingfield Park 1991 Ltd., Lingfield, Surrey.

Stabling: 90 boxes allotted in rotation. Advance notice required for overnight accommodation, before 12 noon on the day prior to racing Tel: 01303 268449 (racedays).

By Car: 6 miles West of town at Westenhanger. Easy access from Junc 11 of the M20. Car park adjoins stands. (Free, except course enclosure £4).

By Rail: Westenhanger Station adjoins course. Trains from Charing Cross.

By Air: Helicopter landing facility by prior arrangement.

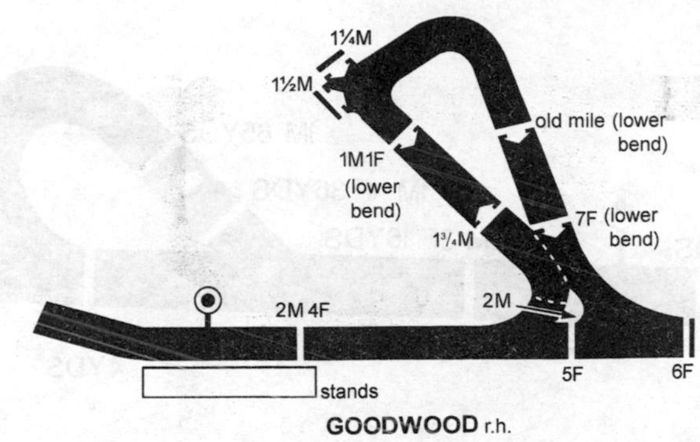

GOODWOOD

Address: Goodwood Racecourse Ltd., Goodwood, Chichester, West Sussex PO18 0PX Tel: (01243) 755022 **Fax:** (01243) 755025
Internet: http://www.demon.co.uk/racenews/goodwood
Set on the edge of the Downs, a straight six furlongs with a triangular loop on one side provides a variety of courses with the possibility of re-entering just above or below the five furlong gate. The Cup Course of about two and a half miles starts on a chute adjacent to the five furlong track and, running the reverse way of the course, turns left after about four furlongs and returns to the straight five furlong run-in by the top bend. The Stakes Course is the last 2m 3f, the Bentinck Course the last 1m 6f and the Gratwicke Course the last 1m 4f of the Cup Course. The Craven Course is 1m 2f, starting in almost the same spot as the Gratwicke Course but running in the reverse direction and returning to the five furlong run-in by the top bend. The Old Mile and seven furlong courses start on the Cup Course and join the five furlong course on the lower bend. The five and six furlong (Stewards' Cup) courses are perfectly straight, the first furlong of the latter being uphill and then slightly undulating to the finish. The sharp bends and downhill gradients suit the handy, well-balanced, neat-actioned sort over middle-distances and are against the big, long-striding horse.
Clerk of the Course and General Manager: Mr R. N. Fabricius, Goodwood Racecourse Limited, Chichester, Sussex. Tel: (01243) 755022 or (0374) 100223
Free stabling and accommodation for runners (110 well equipped boxes at Goodwood House). Subsidised canteen and recreational facilities.Tel: (01243) 755022/Mobile (0860) 951375.
By Car: 6 miles North of Chichester between the A286 & A285. There is a car park adjacent to the course. Ample free car and coach parking.
By Rail: Chichester Station (from Victoria or London Bridge). Regular bus service to the course (6 miles).
By Air: Helicopter landing facility by prior arrangement with Stephenson Aviation. Tel: (01243) 779222. Goodwood Airport 2 miles (taxi to the course).

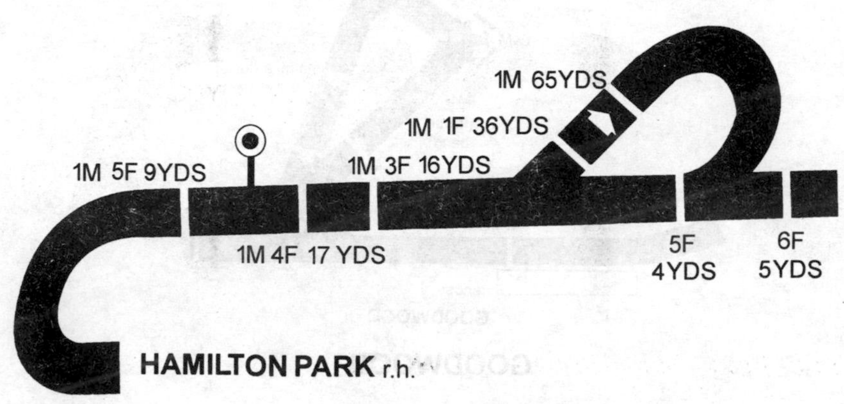

HAMILTON

Address: Hamilton Park Racecourse, Bothwell Road, Hamilton, Lanarkshire ML3 0DW Tel: (01698) 283806 **Fax:** (01698) 286621

A straight six furlongs with a pear-shaped loop course of 1m 5f from a start in front of the stands and a run-in of five and a half furlongs. The turns are easy on the loop. The track is undulating with a dip (which can be very testing in wet weather) about three furlongs out and then rises to level out for the last 150y. A course where judgement and experience can make a considerable difference. Races are usually run at a true gallop here and form can be relied upon.

Clerk of the Course: Hazel Peplinski, The Racecourse, Bothwell Road, Hamilton ML3 0DW Tel: (0131) 333 4891 Mobile (0374) 116733.

Chief Executive: Morag Gray, The Racecourse, Bothwell Road, Hamilton ML3 0DW. Tel: (01698) 283806. Fax: (01698) 286621. Mobile: (0777) 613 6677

Going details Tel: (0850) 609037 (mobile) Head Groundsman.

Free stabling (120 boxes) and accommodation on request. Tel: (01698) 284892.

By Car: Off the A74 on the B7071 (Hamilton-Bothwell road). (M74 Junc). Free parking for cars and buses.

y Rail: Hamilton West Station (1 mile).

Air: Glasgow Airport (20 miles).

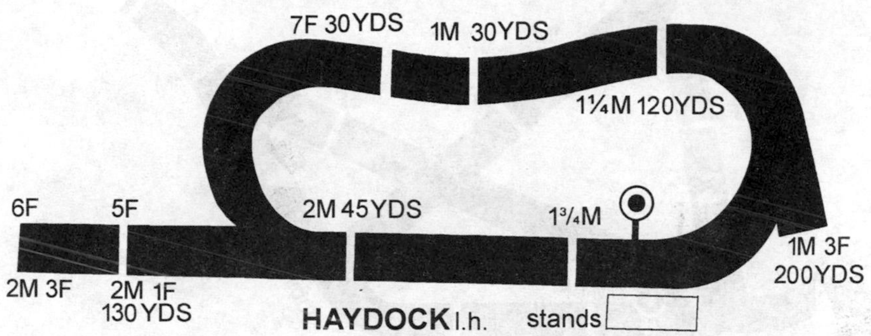

HAYDOCK

Address: Haydock Park Racecourse, Newton-le-Willows, Merseyside WA12 0HQ
Tel: (01942) 725963 **Fax:** (01942) 270879
An almost flat, oval track, 1m 5f round, with a run-in of four and a half furlongs and a straight six furlong course. The 1m 4f gate is set on a short chute. This course, which is of a galloping nature, suits the long-striding horse. On rain-affected turf, the going down the stands' rail in the straight is often faster and horses have often won races by being brought over to that side.
Clerk of the Course: Mr W. K. Tellwright. Tel: (01942) 725963.
General Manager: Mr A. J. P Waterworth, Haydock Park Racecourse, Newton-le-Willows, Merseyside WA12 0HQ. Tel: (01942) 725963 or (01942) 402615 (racedays).
Applications to be made to the Racecourse for stabling (140 boxes) and accommodation for lads/girls.
By Car: The course is on the A49 near Junc 23 of the M6.
By Rail: Newton-le-Willows Station (Manchester-Liverpool line) is 21/2 miles from the course. Earlstown 3 miles from the course. Warrington Bank Quay and Wigan are on the London to Carlisle/ Glasgow line.
By Air: Landing facilities in the centre of the course for helicopters and planes not exceeding 10,000lbs laden weight. Apply to the Sales Office

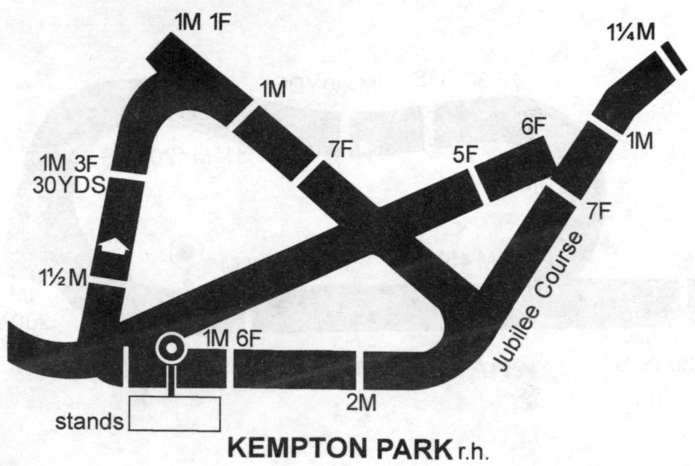

KEMPTON

Address: Kempton Park Racecourse, Sunbury-on-Thames, Middlesex TW16 5AQ Tel: (01932) 782292 **Fax:** (01932) 782044
Raceday Fax: (01932) 779525
Internet: http://www.demon.co.uk/.racenews/rht
A 1m 5f triangular course with a three and a half furlong straight run-in. The 1m 2f Jubilee Course starts on an extension to the round course and sprint races are run over a separate diagonal course. Kempton is a perfectly flat track which can not be described as either sharp or galloping.
Clerk of the Course: Mr A. J. Cooper, Kempton Park, Sunbury-on-Thames. Tel: (01932) 782292.
General Manager: Mr J. M. Thick, Kempton Park, Sunbury-on-Thames. Tel: (01932) 782292.
Stabling allocated on arrival (99 boxes). Prior booking required for overnight stay
Tel: (01932) 783334
By Car: On the A308 near Junc 1 of the M3. Main car park £2, Silver Ring and centre car park free.
By Rail: Kempton Park Station (from Waterloo).
By Air: London (Heathrow) Airport 6 miles.

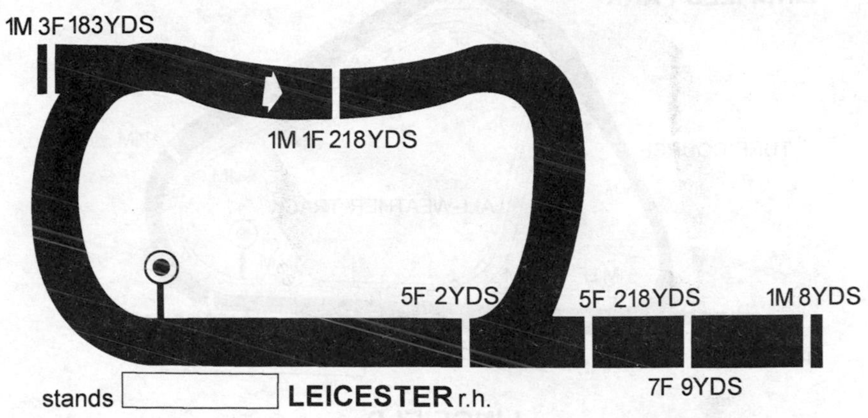

LEICESTER

Address: Leicester Racecourse, Oadby, Leicester LE2 3QH Tel: (01162) 2716515

An oval track of approximately 1m 5f with a straight run-in of five furlongs. Races of a mile and less are run on a dead straight course which joins the round course five furlongs from the finish, the first half being downhill, followed by an ascent gradually levelling off to the winning post. The bends into the straight and after the winning post have been cambered to make a more galloping track.

Clerk of the Course: Captain N. E. S. Lees, Westfield House, The Links, Newmarket, Suffolk CB8 0TG. Tel: (0116) 2716515 Newmarket (01638) 662933 or Home (01284) 386651.

Manager: Mr Russell Parrott, Leicester Racecourse Co. Ltd., The Racecourse, Leicester. Tel: (0116) 2716515.

Going details Tel: Head Groundsman (0116) 271 2115 or (07774) 497281 (mobile)

109 boxes allocated on arrival. Accommodation for one attendant per horse only Tel: (01162) 712115 Canteen opens at 7.30a.m.

By Car: The course is 21/2 miles South-East of the City on the A6 (M1, Junc 21). The car park is free.

By Rail: Leicester Station (from St Pancras) is 21/2 miles.

By Air: Helicopter landing facility in the centre of the course.

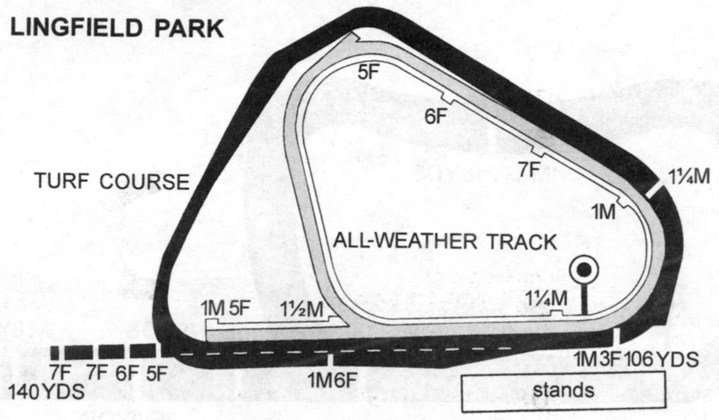

LINGFIELD

Address: Lingfield Park Racecourse, Lingfield, Surrey RH7 6PQ
Tel: (01342) 831720 **Fax:** (01342) 832833 **E-mail:** 1016111.141@compuserve.com

A 7f 140y straight course with a downhill gradient for about five furlongs, a slight rise and then a gradual fall to the winning post. The round turf course joins the straight at the four furlong post and then follows round the outside of the All-Weather tracks to the summit of a slight hill before turning downhill into the straight. The Derby Trial Course (1m 3f 106y) is very similar to the Epsom Derby Course and provides a good test for the Classic. The re-alignment of the turf course to accomodate the All-Weather tracks has made the turn out of the back straight much less pronounced. However, most of the characteristics remain. The Equitrack course favours the keen, free-running, sharp-actioned horse, particularly so in sprints, which are run on the turn.

Clerks of the Course: Mr F. I. W. Cameron (address as above),
180 boxes available. For details of accommodation apply to the Manager, Mr W. Sutton (01342) 831720. Advance notice for overnight accommodation required before 12 noon on the day before racing.

By Car: South-East of the town off the A22 (M25 Junc 6). Ample free parking. Reserved car park £3.

By Rail: Lingfield Station (regular services from London Bridge and Victoria). 1/2m walk to the course.

By Air: London (Gatwick) Airport 10 miles. Helicopter landing facility south of wind-sock.

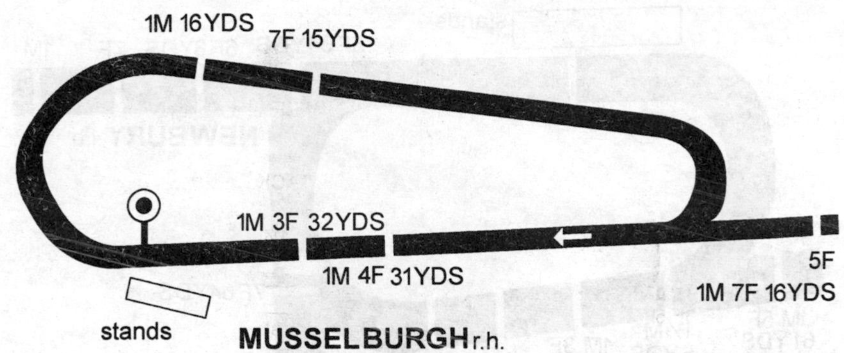

MUSSELBURGH

Address: Musselburgh Racecourse, Linkfield Road, Musselburgh, East Lothian Tel: (0131) 665 2859 Racecourse (01292) 264179 **Fax:** (0131) 653 2083

An oval of 1m 2f, with sharp bends and a straight, slightly undulating run-in of four furlongs. An extension provides a five furlong course, which bears slightly left and makes a distinct right-hand inclination after a furlong. Musselburgh is virtually flat but, with the turns being very sharp, handiness and manoeuvrability are at a premium.

Clerk of the Course & Manager: Mr M. Kershaw, Racecourse Office, 2 Whitletts Road, Ayr. Tel: Office (01292) 264179 Racedays (0131) 6652859 Mobile (0850) 464258 Fax: (01292) 610140. Free stabling Tel: (0131) 665 4955. Racedays (0131) 665 2796.

By Car: Musselburgh, 5 miles East of Edinburgh on the A1. Car park adjoining course, free for buses and cars.

By Rail: Waverley Station (Edinburgh). Local Rail service to Musselburgh.

By Air: Edinburgh (Turnhouse) Airport 30 minutes by car.

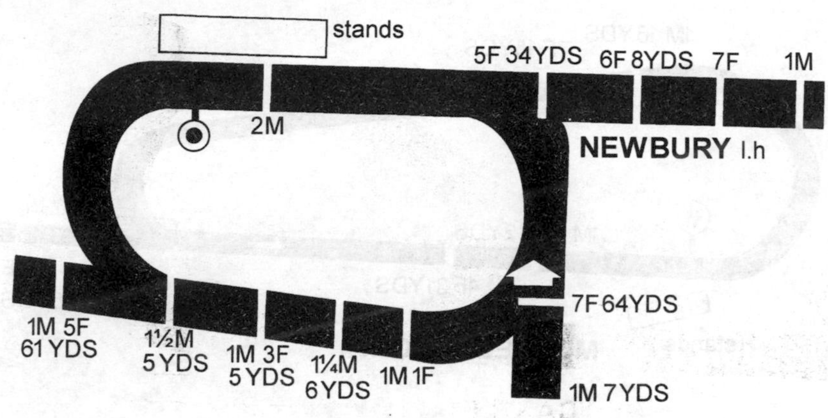

NEWBURY

Address: The Racecourse, Newbury, Berkshire RG14 7NZ
Tel: (01635) 40015 or 550354 **Fax:** (01635) 528354
Internet: http://www.raceweb.com/newbury **E-mail:** newbury@raceweb.com

An oval track of about 1m 7f, 80 feet wide with a slightly undulating straight mile. The round mile and 7f 60y starts are set on a chute from the round course and both join the straight about five furlongs from the finish. Newbury is a good, galloping track, which is efficiently watered during dry periods.

Clerk of the Course: Mr M. Kershaw, Racecourse Office (01635) 40015 or 550354.

Chief Executive, Secretary and Club Secretary: Major General J. D. G. Pank, C.B. Tel: (01635) 40015.

Free stabling (127 boxes) and accommodation for lads and lasses.

By Car: East of the town off the A34 (M4, Junc 12 or 13). Car park, adjoining enclosures, free, except Southmead £2

By Rail: Newbury Racecourse Station, adjoins course.

By Air: Light Aircraft landing strip East/West. 830 metres by 30 metres wide. Helicopter landing facilities.

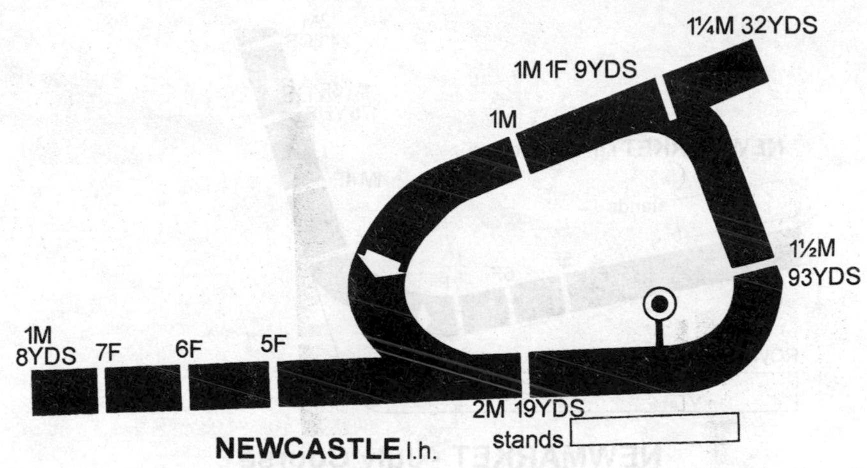

NEWCASTLE

Address: High Gosforth Park, Newcastle-Upon-Tyne NE3 5HP Tel: (0191) 236 2020 **Fax:** (0191) 236 7761

An oval course of 1m 6f with a chute to provide a 1m 2f start and a straight run-in of four furlongs, gradually rising until levelling off in the final 100y. The run-in extends to allow a straight mile, which is against the collar all the way. Newcastle is a galloping track with the final climb making it a test of stamina and is not one for short runners.

Clerk of the Course: Major David McAllister c/o High Gosforth Park Ltd, High Gosforth Park, Newcastle-upon-Tyne. NE3 5HP. Tel: (0191) 236 2020 Mobile (0860) 286003.

Head Groundsman: (0860) 274289.

Chairman: Mr S. W. Clarke C.B.E. Tel. (0191) 2362020

Free stabling (120 boxes). It is essential to book accommodation in advance. Apply to the Manager. Tel: (0191) 217 0060 the day before racing, or the Racecourse Office otherwise.

By Car: 4 miles North of the city on the A6125 (near the A1). Car and coach park free.

By Rail: Newcastle Central Station (from King's Cross), a free bus service operates from South Gosforth and Regent Centre Metro Station.

By Air: Helicopter landing facility by prior arrangement. The Airport is 4 miles from the course.

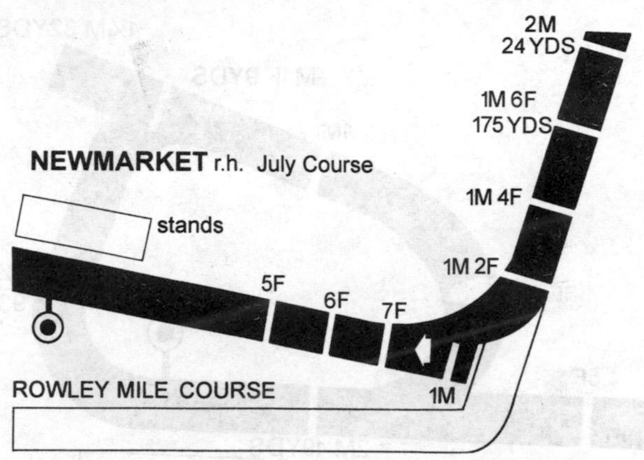

NEWMARKET - July Course

Address: Newmarket Racecourse, Newmarket, Suffolk CB8 0TG
Tel: Main Office (01638) 662933 July (01638) 662752
Fax: (01638) 663044
(July Course) - All races up to a mile inclusive are run on the straight Bunbury Mile, which has a steadily increasing downhill gradient after two furlongs, the final furlong being uphill. Races further than a mile start on the Cesarewitch course and turn right into the straight mile. Like the Rowley Mile course, this is a wide, galloping track.
Clerk of the Course: Mr M. Prosser. Tel: (01638) 662933.
Manager: Mrs Lisa Hancock Tel: (01638) 663482
100 boxes and free accommodation available at the Links Stables Tel: (01638) 662200
By Car: South-West of the town on the A1304 London Road (M11 Junc 9). Free car parking at the rear of the enclosure. Members car park £1 all days; Free courtesy bus service from Newmarket Station, Bus Station and High Street, commencing 90 minutes prior to the first race, and return trips up to 60 minutes after the last race.
By Rail: Infrequent rail service to Newmarket Station from Cambridge (Liverpool Street) or direct bus service from Cambridge (13 mile journey).
By Air: Landing facilities for light aircraft and helicopters on racedays at both racecourses. See Flight Guide. Cambridge Airport 11 miles.

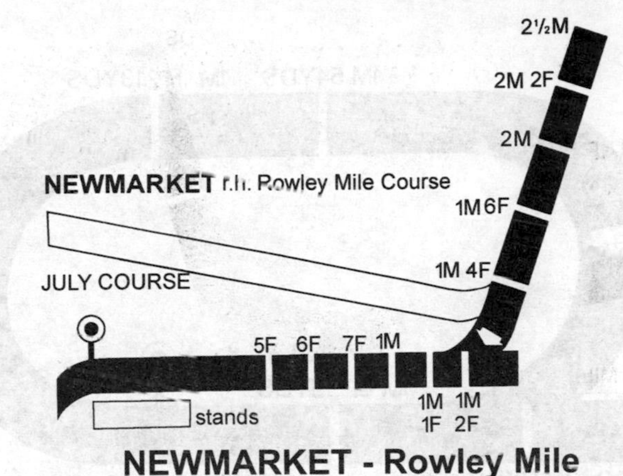

NEWMARKET - Rowley Mile

Address: Newmarket Racecourse, Newmarket, Suffolk CB8 0TG
Tel: Main Office (01638) 662933 Rowley (01638) 662524
Fax: (01638) 663044
(Rowley Mile Course) - There is a straight course of ten furlongs with slight undulations as far as 'The Bushes', about two furlongs from the finish. From that point it is downhill for a furlong to 'The Dip', the final furlong being uphill. The Cesarewitch course starts on the Beacon Course, which turns right into the straight. The ten furlong straight is a wide, galloping track ideal for long-striding horses.
Clerk of the Course: Mr M. Prosser. Tel: (01638) 662933
Manager: Mrs Lisa Hancock Tel: (01638) 662933.
100 boxes and free accommodation available at the Links Stables Tel: (01638) 662200
By Car: South-West of the town on the A1304 London Road (M11 Junc 9). Free car parking at the rear of the enclosure. Members car park £1 all days; Free courtesy bus service from Newmarket Station, Bus Station and High Street, commencing 90 minutes prior to the first race, and return trips up to 60 minutes after the last race.
By Rail: Infrequent rail service to Newmarket Station from Cambridge (Liverpool Street) or direct bus service from Cambridge (13 mile journey).
By Air: Landing facilities for light aircraft and helicopters on racedays at both racecourses. See Flight Guide. Cambridge Airport 11 miles.

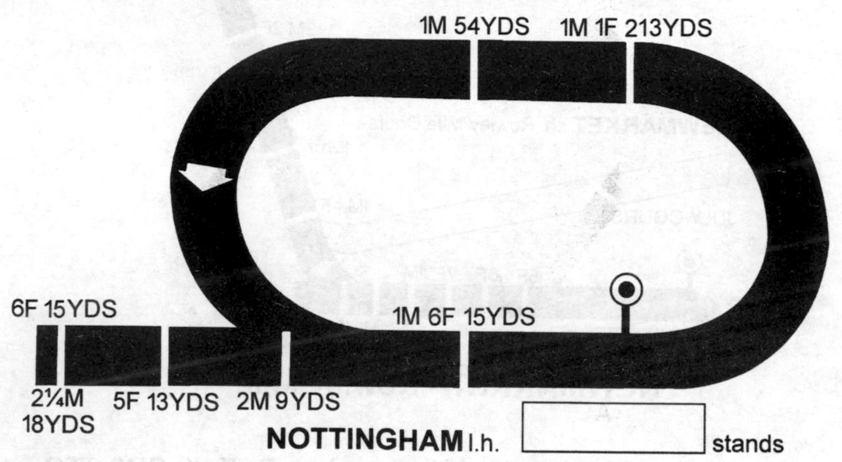

NOTTINGHAM

Address: Nottingham Racecourse, Colwick Park, Nottingham NG2 4BE

Tel: (0115) 958 0620 **Fax:** (0115) 958 4515

A galloping oval track with a straight run-in of about five furlongs, from which a chute provides a straight six furlongs. The turns on this flat course are easy.

Clerk of the Course: Major C. Moore, Hamilton House, Toft-next-Newton, Market Rasen, Lincolnshire LN8 3NE. Tel: (01673) 843434 (office) (01673) 878575 (home).

Manager: Miss Sally Westcott, The Racecourse Office, Colwick Park, Nottingham NG2 4BE Tel: (0115) 958 0620

Free stabling. 120 boxes allotted on arrival. New hostel for lads and lasses Tel: (0115) 950 1198

By Car: 2 miles East of the City on the B686. The car park is free. Silver Ring Picnic Car Park £12 (admits car and four occupants).

By Rail: Nottingham (Midland) Station. Regular bus service to course (2 miles).

By Air: Helicopter landing facility in the centre of the course.

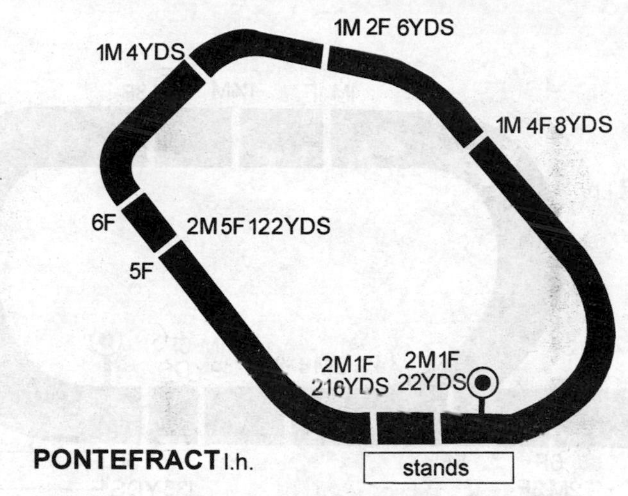

PONTEFRACT

Address: Pontefract Park Race Co. Ltd., The Park, Pontefract, West Yorkshire
Tel: Admin Office (01977) 703224 Racedays (01977) 702210
Fax: Admin Office (01977) 600577 Racedays (01977) 702210
An oval, undulating course of 2m 133y with two sharp bends and a straight run-in of only two furlongs. There is a steep ascent over the last three furlongs. The undulations make it unsuitable for a long-striding horse, although a degree of stamina is called for. There have been a number of course specialists at Pontefract.
Clerk of the Course and Secretary: Mr J. N. Gundill, 33 Ropergate, Pontefract, West Yorkshire. WF8 1LE Tel: Office (01977) 703224 Home (01977) 620649 Racedays (01977) 702210.
116 boxes available. Stabling and accommodation must be reserved. They will be allocated on a first come-first served basis. Tel: (01977 702323)
By Car: 1 mile North of the town on the A639. Junc 32 of M62. Free car park adjacent to the course.
By Rail: Pontefract Station (Baghill), 11/2 miles from the course. Regular bus service from Leeds.
By Air: Helicopters by arrangement only. (Nearest airfield: Doncaster, Sherburn-in-Elmet, Yeadon (Leeds/Bradford).

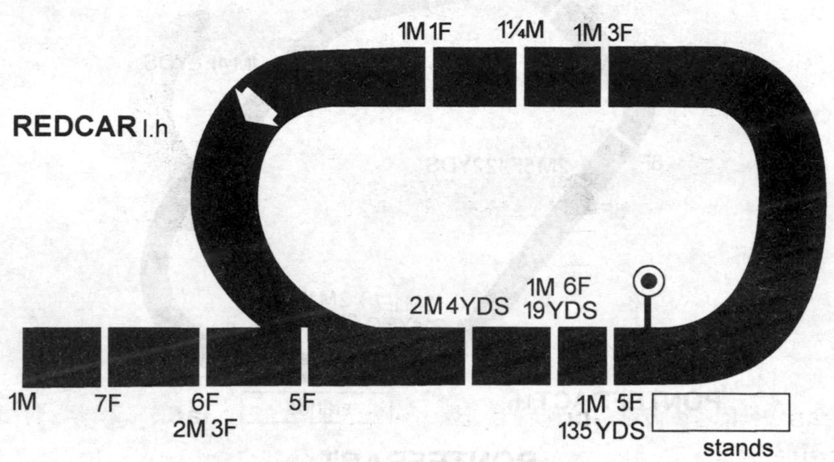

REDCAR

Address: Redcar Racecourse, Redcar, Cleveland TS10 2BY Tel: (01642) 484068 **Fax:** (01642) 488272

A perfectly flat, narrow, oval course of two miles with a straight run-in of five furlongs, which extends backwards to make a straight mile.

Despite two very tight bends into and out of the back straight, Redcar is an excellent galloping course.

Clerk of the Course & General Manager: Mr J. Gundill, Racecourse Office, The Racecourse, Redcar, Cleveland TS10 2BY. Tel: (01642) 484068 or (01482) 867488 Mobile (0370) 613049.

Groundsman: Mr J. Berry, The Racecourse, Redcar, Cleveland. Tel: (01642) 489861 Stables Tel: (on racedays only) (01642) 484254 OR (01642) 484068.

By Car: In town off the A1085. Free parking adjoining the course for buses and cars.

By Rail: Redcar Station (1/4 mile from the course).

By Air: Landing facilities at Turners Arms Farm (600y runway) Yearby, Cleveland. 2 miles South of the racecourse - transport available. Teeside airport (18 miles west of Redcar).

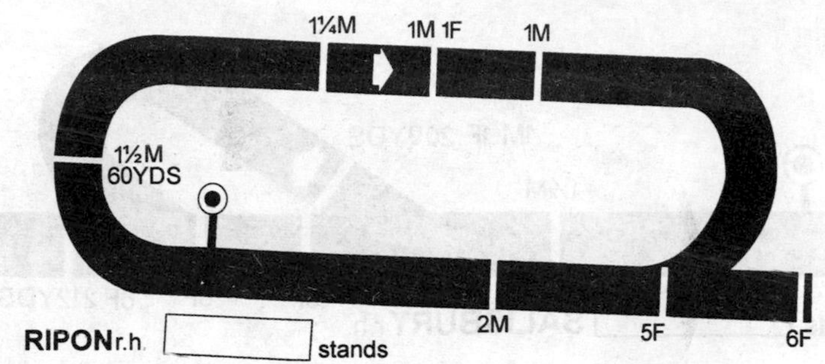

RIPON

Address: Ripon Racecourse, Boroughbridge Road, Ripon, North Yorkshire
HG4 3UG Tel: (01765) 602156 **Fax:** (01765) 690018
E-mail: mail@hutchbuch.demon.co.uk

An oval course of 1m 5f, joined to a straight six furlongs by a tightish bend at the five furlong point. The straight course is slightly on the ascent except for a shallow dip at the 'distance' and, in general, this is a rather sharp track, a course where experience can be decisive.

Clerk of the Course: Mr J. M. Hutchinson, 77 North Street, Ripon HG4 1DS. Tel: (01765) 602156 Evenings (01845) 567378 Mobile (0860) 679904.

Non-racedays: Admin Office, 77, North Street, Ripon HG4 1DS. Tel: (01765) 602156. Fax (01765) 690018. Racedays: The Racecourse, Boroughbridge Road, Ripon HG4 3UG. Tel: (01765) 603696.

Trainers requiring stabling (104 boxes available) are requested to contact Mr P. Bateson, The Racecourse, Ripon prior to 11a.m. the day before racing. Tel: (01765) 603696.

By Car: The course is situated 2 miles South-East of the city, on the B6265. There is ample free parking for cars and coaches. For reservations apply to the Secretary.

By Rail: Harrogate Station (11 miles), or Thirsk (15 miles). Bus services to Ripon.

By Air: Helicopters only on the course. Otherwise Leeds/Bradford airport.

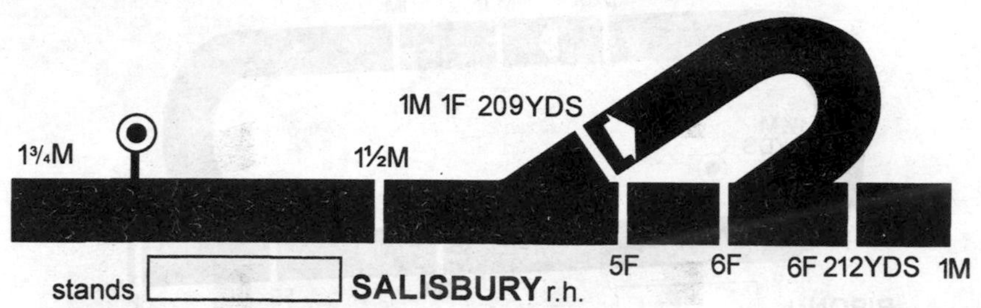

SALISBURY

Address: Salisbury Racecourse, Netherhampton, Salisbury, Wiltshire SP2 8PN

Tel: (01722) 326461 **Fax:** (01722) 412710

The course consists of a loop with an arm of about four furlongs for the finish of all races. Contests of up to a mile are almost straight except for a slight right-hand bend at halfway. On the 1m 6f course, horses start opposite the stands, turn to the left around the loop and re-enter the straight at the seven furlong starting gate. The last half-mile is uphill, providing a stiff test of stamina.

Clerk of the Course: Mr R. I. Renton, Salisbury Racecourse, Netherhampton, Salisbury, Wiltshire SP2 8PN. Tel: (01722) 326461 Mobile (07836) 784543.

Secretary: The Bibury Club, Salisbury Racecourse, Netherhampton, Salisbury, Wiltshire. Tel: (01722) 326461.

Free stabling (112 boxes) and accommodation for lads and lasses, apply to the Stabling Manager Tel: (01722) 327327.

By Car: 3 miles South-West of the city on the A3094 at Netherhampton. Free car park adjoins the course.

By Rail: Salisbury Station is 31/2 miles (from Waterloo). Bus service to the course.

By Air: Helicopter landing facility near the ten furlong start.

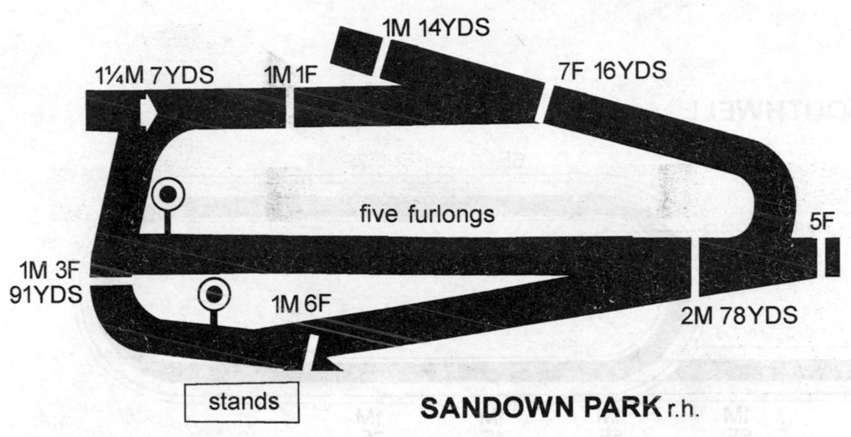

SANDOWN

Address: Sandown Park Racecourse, Esher, Surrey KT10 9AJ
Tel: (01372) 463072 **Fax:** (01372) 470427
An oval course of 1m 5f with a straight run-in of four furlongs. The ground is almost level until entering the straight, where it rises to the winning post. Five furlong contests are run on a separate straight course which cuts diagonally across the inside of the main circuit and is uphill all the way. The track suits long-striding horses and is a real test of stamina.
Clerk of the Course: Mr A. J. Cooper, Sandown Park, Esher, Surrey. Tel: (01372) 463072 Mobile (0374) 230850.
Managing Director: Mrs S. C. Ellen (address & tel as above).
Going Line Tel: (01372) 461212
108 boxes available. Free stabling and accommodation for lads and lasses Tel: (01372) 463511.
By Car: 4 miles South-West of Kingston-on-Thames, on the A307 (M25 Junc 10). The members' car park in More Lane £2. All other car parking is free.
By Rail: Esher Station (from Waterloo) adjoins the course.
By Air: London (Heathrow) Airport 12 miles.

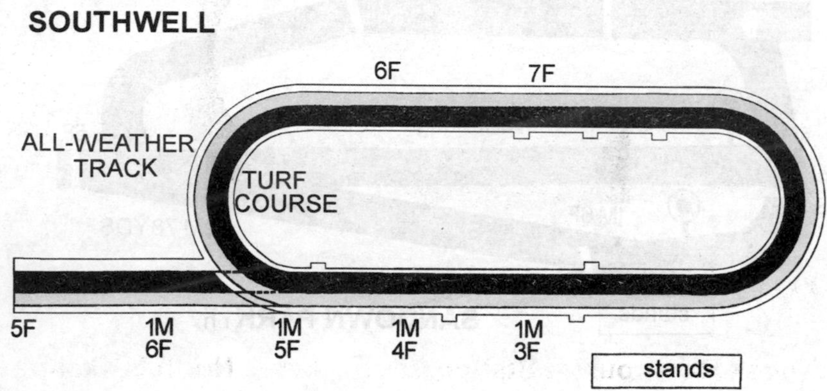

SOUTHWELL

Address: Southwell Racecourse, Rolleston, Newark, Nottinghamshire NG25 0TS
Tel: (01636) 814481 **Fax:** (01636) 812271
The All-Weather Fibresand track consists of an oval circuit, 1m 2f in circumference, with a three furlong straight and a spur to provide a five furlong straight All-Weather track. The turf tracks are on the inside of the All-Weather track. A sharp, flat circuit, Southwell suits the keen, front-running sort.
Clerk of the Course: Mr M. Prosser, Wolverhampton Racecourse Tel. (01902) 421421, Mobile (07971) 531162, Fax (01902) 421621
Going details Tel: (07968) 306378 Head Groundsman
110 boxes at the course. Applications for staff and horse accommodation to be booked by noon the day before racing on (01636) 814481
By Car: The course is situated at Rolleston, 3 miles South of Southwell, 5 miles from Newark.
By Rail: Rolleston Station (Nottingham-Newark line) adjoins the course.

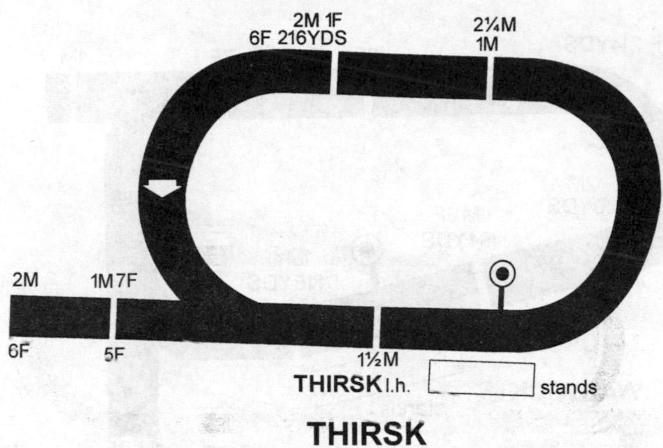

THIRSK

Address: Thirsk Racecourse, Station Road, Thirsk, North Yorkshire YO7 1QL

Tel: (01845) 522276 **Fax:** (01845) 525353

An oval track of 1m 2f, with fairly tight turns and an undulating run-in of four furlongs. Races of five and six furlongs start on a straight, more undulating two furlong extension of the run-in. Though the turns on the round course are comparatively easy, the track is somewhat sharp. The going seldom rides heavy.

Managing Director & Clerk of the Course: Mr Christopher Tetley, The Racecourse, Station Road, Thirsk, North Yorkshire YO7 1QL. Tel: (01845) 522276.

Club Secretary: Mr D. Whitehead, Thirsk Racecourse Limited, The Racecourse, Station Road, Thirsk, North Yorkshire YO7 1QL. Tel: (01845) 522276 Fax: (01845) 525353.

112 boxes available. For stabling and accommodation apply to, The Racecourse, Station Road, Thirsk, North Yorkshire. Tel: (01845) 522276 Racedays (01845) 522096.

By Car: West of the town on the A61. Free car park adjacent to the course for buses and cars.

By Rail: Thirsk Station (from King's Cross). 1/2 mile from the course.

By Air: Helicopters only, landing on the hockey pitch. Prior arrangement required.Tel: Racecourse (01845) 522276. Fixed wing aircraft can land at RAF Leeming. Tel: (01677) 423041. Light aircraft at Bagby. Tel: (01845) 597385 or (01845) 537555.

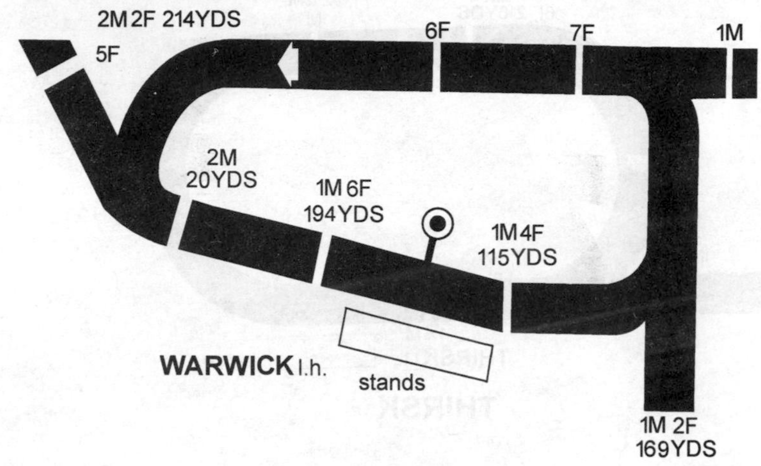

WARWICK

Address: Warwick Racecourse, Hampton Street, Warwick CV34 6HN

Tel: (01926) 491553 **Fax:** (01926) 403223

A nearly circular track, 1m 6f 32y in circumference, with a distinct rise and fall levelling off a mile from home, and a run-in of about two and a half furlongs. The five furlong course has a left-hand elbow at the junction with the round course. The mile course, straight for the first five furlongs, then turns into the home straight. This sharp track favours handiness and speed rather than staying power.

Racecourse Manager: Mr C. R. Leech, Warwick Racecourse, Hampton Street, Warwick CV34 6HN. Tel: (01926) 491553. Fax (01926) 403223.

Clerk of the Course: Mr H. Bevan, Warwick Racecourse, Hampton Street, Warwick CV34 6HN. Tel: Racedays (01926) 491553.

112 boxes allocated on arrival or by reservation Tel: (01526) 493803.

By Car: West of the town on the B4095 adjacent to Junc 15 of the M40. Free parking (except the Members' Car Park, £5 to Daily Club Members).

By Rail: Warwick or Leamington Spa Station.

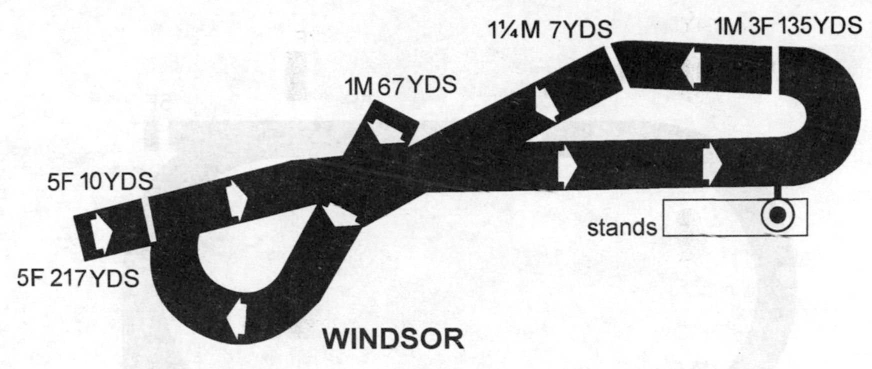

WINDSOR

Address: Royal Windsor Racecourse, Maidenhead Road, Windsor, Berkshire SL4 5JJ Tel: (01753) 498400 **Fax:** (01753) 830156

In the form of a figure eight, Windsor has a circuit of 1m 4f 110y. Although both left and right-hand turns are met in races of a mile and a half, only right-hand turns occur in races up to 1m 70y. The five furlong course bends slightly to the right approaching halfway but is otherwise straight. The track is perfectly flat and its sharpness is largely offset by the long run-in.

Clerk of the Course: Mr C. G. Stickels. Tel: (01753) 498400. Mobile: (07970) 621440.

Racecourse Manager: Mrs S. Dingle, The Racecourse, Windsor, Berkshire. Tel: (01753) 498400 or (01753) 498404 (going reports).

Stabling: reservation required for overnight stay and accommodation only. Tel: (01753) 498400 or (01753) 498405 (racedays only).

By Car: North of the town on the A308 (M4 Junc 6). Car parks adjoin the course (£1, £1.50, £2).

By Rail: Windsor Central Station (from Paddington) or Windsor & Eton Riverside Station (from Waterloo).

By Air: London (Heathrow) Airport 15 minutes by car via the M4. Also White Waltham Airport (West London Aero Club) 15 minutes.

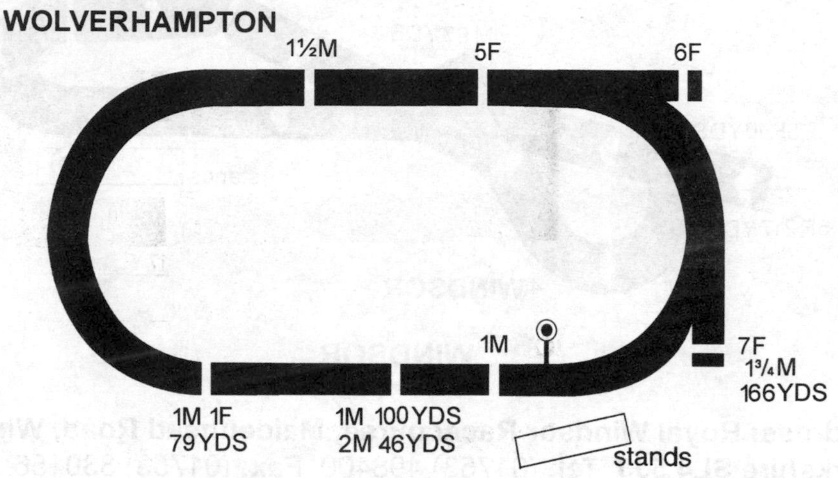

WOLVERHAMPTON

Address: Wolverhampton Racecourse, Dunstall Park, Gorsebrook Road, Wolverhampton WV6 0PE Tel: (01902) 421421 **Fax:** (01902) 716626

An oval circuit, a mile in circumference with a run-in of 380y. The Fibresand surface consists of a blended mixture of silica sand and synthetic fibres set in a re-enforced sub-base.A turf track for hurdles and chases is situated on the outside of the All-Weather track.

Clerk of the Course: Mr M. Prosser, Wolverhampton Racecourse Tel. (01902) 421421, Mobile (07971) 531162, Fax (01902) 421621

74 boxes allotted on arrival. Applications for lads and lasses, and overnight stables must be made to Racecourse by noon on the day before racing. Tel: (01902) 421421. Fax: (01902) 421621.

By Car: 1 mile North of city on the A449 (M54 Junc 2 or M6 Junc 12). Car parking free of charge.

By Rail: Wolverhampton Station (from Euston) 1 mile.

By Air: Halfpenny Green Airport 8 miles.

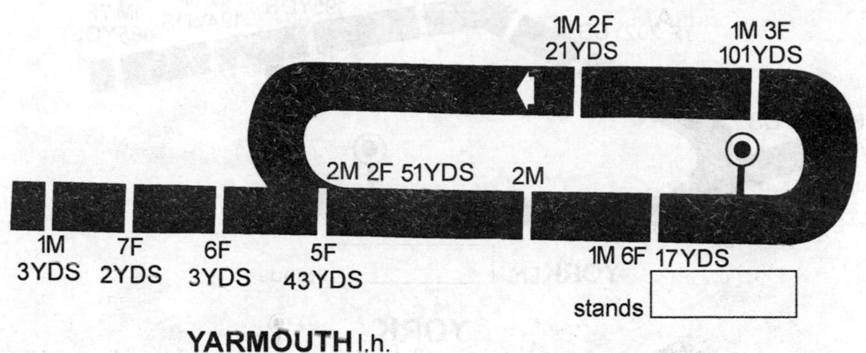

YARMOUTH

Address: The Racecourse, Jellicoe Road, Great Yarmouth, Norfolk NR30 4AU
Tel: (01493) 842527 **Fax:** (01493) 843254
An oblong course of about 1m 4f with a slight fall to a run-in of five furlongs. The straight mile joins the round course at the run-in and is perfectly level. The five, six and seven furlong courses form part of the straight mile.
Clerk of the Course: Mr D. C. Henson, F.R.I.C.S., 2 Lower Mounts, Northampton NN1 3DE. Tel: (01327) 861061. Fax: (01327) 861062.
Manager: Mr David Thompson, The Racecourse, Jellicoe Road, Great Yarmouth, Norfolk NR30 4AU. Tel: (01493) 842527 Fax: (01493) 843254.
Stabling allocated on arrival. Tel: (01493) 855651.
By Car: 1 mile East of town centre (well sign-posted from A47 & A12). Large car park adjoining course £1.
By Rail: Great Yarmouth Station (1 mile). Bus service to the course.
By Air: Helicopter landing facilities available 300y from the course at North Denes Airfield. Tel: (01493) 851500. Fixed wing aircraft landing facilities are available at a private airfield in Ludham. Prior permission is required through Mr R. Collins. Tel: (01493) 843211. Fax: (01493) 859555.

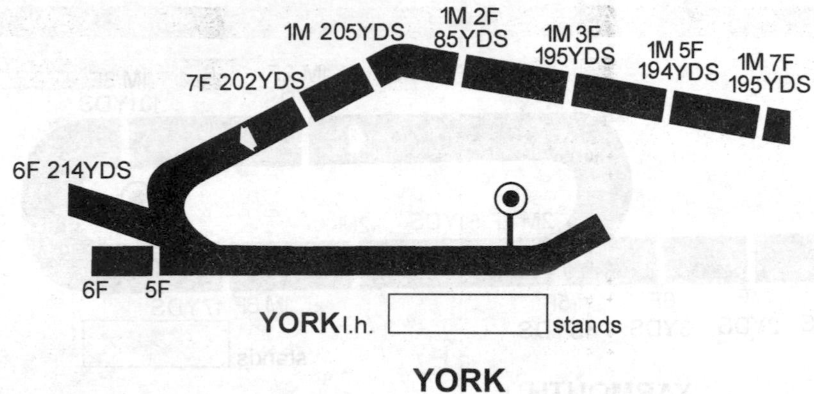

YORK

Address: The Racecourse, York YO23 1EX Tel: (01904) 620911 **Fax:** (01904) 611071

From the two mile start at the bottom of the Knavesmire, this wide, U-shaped course runs parallel with the Tadcaster Road for five furlongs before bending left to pass under Knavesmire Wood and join the straight six furlongs round a sweeping turn in front of the five furlong gate. A new two furlong extension, set at a tangent, also joins the round course here and caters for seven furlong events. A fair, galloping course which calls for stamina and courage, especially in the wet weather when the going can be very testing. Because of the watering system, when the going is soft, much better ground can be found by racing wide in the back straight.

Manager, Clerk of the Course and Secretary: Mr J. L. Smith F.C.A., The Racecourse, York YO2 1EX. Tel: (01904) 620911 Home (01759) 368455. Fax: (01904) 611071.

Free stabling (200 boxes) Tel: Racedays (01904) 706317.

By Car: 1 mile South-East of the city on the A1036. Car parking bookings can be made prior to race meetings (except August) for reserved car park (£2 (inc. VAT) per day). All other parking is free.

By Rail: 1 1/2 miles York Station (from King's Cross). Special bus service from station to the course.

By Air: Light aircraft and helicopter landing facilities available at Rufforth aerodrome (5,000ft tarmac runway). £20 landing fee-transport arranged to course. Leeds/Bradford airport (25 miles).

LEADING JOCKEYS AT ASCOT (SINCE 1995)

	Total W-R	Per cent	£1 Level stake
L. Dettori	62-269	23.0	**+ 103.62**
M. J. Kinane	35-226	15.0	**+ 1.48**
Pat Eddery	33-307	10.0	- 96.33
T. Quinn	32-260	12.0	- 37.62
K. Fallon	30-209	14.0	- 46.78
J. Reid	27-271	9.0	- 3.67
R. Hills	27-211	12.0	- 69.76
K. Darley	14-140	10.0	**+ 2.13**
O. Peslier	13-111	11.0	**+ 59.83**
R. Hughes	12-181	6.0	- 42.00
Dane O'Neill	10-111	9.0	**+ 37.50**
J. Murtagh	10-52	19.0	**+ 47.41**
M. Hills	10-183	5.0	- 72.67
D. Holland	10-111	9.0	**+ 2.75**
M. Roberts	9-140	6.0	- 22.75
J. Fortune	8-89	8.0	- 13.36
S. Sanders	7-92	7.0	**+ 4.50**
Gary Stevens	5-38	13.0	- 2.50
J. Weaver	5-93	5.0	- 67.88
W. Supple	3-32	9.0	- 6.67
N. Pollard	3-41	7.0	- 10.50
P. Robinson	3-61	4.0	- 49.67
Martin Dwyer	3-66	4.0	- 28.00
W. Ryan	3-71	4.0	- 58.25
G. Duffield	3-44	6.0	- 25.88

LEADING JOCKEYS AT AYR (SINCE 1995)

	Total W-R	Per cent	£1 Level stake
K. Darley	30-216	13.0	- 30.48
D. Holland	22-144	15.0	- 42.87
K. Fallon	22-124	17.0	- 7.03
J. Fortune	21-153	13.0	- 5.35
J. Weaver	21-139	15.0	- 45.18
A. Culhane	19-153	12.0	**+ 35.28**
J. Carroll	18-243	7.0	- 117.01
L. Charnock	12-114	10.0	**+ 22.00**
N. Kennedy	12-125	9.0	**+ 15.83**
R. Hughes	10-27	37.0	**+ 35.85**
J. F. Egan	10-76	13.0	**+ 41.25**
Dean McKeown	10-114	8.0	- 35.46
J. Fanning	10-90	11.0	- 2.65
G. Duffield	9-111	8.0	- 70.04
F. Lynch	8-54	14.0	- 1.17
S. Sanders	7-38	18.0	- 6.84
J. Bramhill	7-67	10.0	**+ 0.50**
M. Fenton	7-57	12.0	**+ 9.03**
M. Hills	7-34	20.0	- 2.26
Darren Moffatt	7-57	12.0	- 14.50
W. Supple	6-76	7.0	- 1.00
M. Roberts	6-23	26.0	**+ 22.50**
G. Carter	6-53	11.0	- 19.35
F. Norton	5-43	11.0	**+ 17.50**
T. Williams	5-95	5.0	- 63.25

LEADING JOCKEYS AT BATH (SINCE 1995)

	Total W-R	Per cent	£1 Level stake
R. Hughes	29-165	17.0	**+ 14.97**
T. Quinn	28-189	14.0	- 48.98
Pat Eddery	23-119	19.0	- 28.47
J. Reid	19-142	13.0	- 24.05
T. Sprake	18-169	10.0	**+ 1.00**
M. Hills	18-87	20.0	**+ 39.49**
Martin Dwyer	18-121	14.0	**+ 30.00**
K. Fallon	16-67	23.0	**+ 5.23**
L. Dettori	13-56	23.0	**+ 13.29**
S. Whitworth	13-134	9.0	- 54.06
S. Sanders	13-153	8.0	**+ 31.83**
M. Henry	12-72	16.0	**+ 8.83**
A. Clark	12-112	10.0	- 32.92
M. Roberts	11-61	18.0	**+ 30.00**
R. Ffrench	9-74	12.0	**+ 12.63**
P. P. Murphy	9-76	11.0	**+ 6.95**
Paul Eddery	9-79	11.0	- 49.89
J. Quinn	8-83	9.0	**+ 7.15**
S. Drowne	8-187	4.0	- 90.13
C. Rutter	7-93	7.0	- 38.26
B. Thomson	7-20	35.0	**+ 30.50**
Dane O'Neill	7-118	5.0	- 61.75
J. F. Egan	6-56	10.0	- 2.75
D. Sweeney	6-64	9.0	- 20.40
B. Doyle	6-43	13.0	**+ 29.00**

LEADING JOCKEYS AT BEVERLEY (SINCE 1995)

	Total W-R	Per cent	£1 Level stake
K. Darley	56-307	18.0	- 53.85
K. Fallon	30-174	17.0	- 50.99
A. Culhane	26-241	10.0	- 50.46
J. Carroll	25-195	12.0	- 71.43
J. Fortune	19-138	13.0	- 40.31
L. Charnock	18-231	7.0	- 98.48
J. Weaver	16-162	9.0	- 58.88
D. Holland	14-99	14.0	- 16.32
R. Winston	13-169	7.0	- 66.92
Dean McKeown	13-181	7.0	- 69.00
G. Duffield	12-135	8.0	- 89.34
J. Fanning	12-108	11.0	- 25.65
G. Carter	12-89	13.0	- 23.05
M. Fenton	11-92	11.0	- 10.50
F. Lynch	11-136	8.0	- 44.92
T. Williams	11-143	7.0	- 48.38
W. Ryan	11-51	21.0	- 18.42
D. Mernagh	10-119	8.0	- 45.83
Pat Eddery	10-38	26.0	**+ 7.34**
C. Lowther	9-72	12.0	- 9.50
J. Quinn	8-102	7.0	- 19.75
R. Lappin	7-91	7.0	- 26.50
M. Hills	7-28	25.0	- 3.21
L. Dettori	7-31	22.0	- 13.66
P. Fessey	6-91	6.0	- 35.50

LEADING JOCKEYS AT BRIGHTON

(SINCE 1995)

	Total W-R	Per cent	£1 Level stake
T. Quinn	62-238	26.0	+ **32.72**
Dane O'Neill	35-239	14.0	- 19.84
S. Sanders	31-217	14.0	- 18.34
Martin Dwyer	19-129	14.0	- 8.60
S. Whitworth	19-172	11.0	- 27.25
R. Hughes	19-154	12.0	- 19.55
J. Reid	18-108	16.0	- 3.22
R. Ffrench	17-114	14.0	- 1.14
D. Sweeney	16-120	13.0	+ **17.71**
T. Sprake	15-117	12.0	- 3.42
M. Roberts	13-80	16.0	+ **11.45**
D. Harrison	13-90	14.0	- 13.50
M. Fenton	13-73	17.0	+ **6.50**
N. Pollard	12-81	14.0	+ **16.25**
G. Duffield	11-97	11.0	- 28.68
A. Daly	11-137	8.0	+ **8.75**
D. Holland	10-58	17.0	- 12.75
J. F. Egan	10-116	8.0	- 38.92
A. Clark	10-163	6.0	- 62.21
J. Quinn	10-139	7.0	- 26.47
P. Doe	9-131	6.0	- 47.44
M. Henry	9-81	11.0	- 24.00
G. Bardwell	9-129	6.0	- 0.50
F. Norton	9-69	13.0	+ **11.16**
A. Nicholls	8-69	11.0	- 12.84

LEADING JOCKEYS AT CARLISLE

(SINCE 1995)

	Total W-R	Per cent	£1 Level stake
K. Darley	31-139	22.0	- 7.13
J. Carroll	19-181	10.0	- 66.41
J. Fortune	16-109	14.0	- 28.24
A. Culhane	15-130	11.0	- 42.25
R. Winston	12-102	11.0	+ **0.25**
J. Weaver	12-69	17.0	+ **4.94**
K. Fallon	12-64	18.0	+ **5.08**
W. Supple	10-69	14.0	+ **21.50**
J. Fanning	10-100	10.0	- 40.75
C. Lowther	9-50	18.0	+ **5.10**
T. Williams	7-85	8.0	- 15.81
G. Duffield	7-90	7.0	- 62.01
Dean McKeown	6-101	5.0	- 16.50
J. F. Egan	5-64	7.0	- 29.00
P. Fessey	5-76	6.0	- 41.75
F. Norton	4-19	21.0	+ **2.00**
M. Fenton	4-28	14.0	- 10.33
L. Charnock	4-97	4.0	- 65.90
N. Callan	3-11	27.0	- 0.90
A. Nicholls	3-17	17.0	+ **16.00**
P. Goode	3-17	17.0	+ **10.00**
J. McAuley	3-43	6.0	- 9.00
P. Robinson	3-21	14.0	- 8.92
R. Lappin	3-52	5.0	- 21.25
N. Kennedy	3-44	6.0	- 11.00

LEADING JOCKEYS AT CATTERICK

(SINCE 1995)

	Total W-R	Per cent	£1 Level stake
K. Darley	35-205	17.0	- 47.42
J. Fortune	21-119	17.0	- 5.73
J. Carroll	20-177	11.0	- 43.64
A. Culhane	20-193	10.0	- 21.67
F. Lynch	16-84	19.0	+ **9.09**
D. Holland	14-55	25.0	- 5.95
L. Charnock	13-194	6.0	- 49.45
J. Weaver	13-75	17.0	- 17.24
T. Williams	12-169	7.0	- 72.25
G. Duffield	11-106	10.0	- 32.69
J. F. Egan	10-60	16.0	+ **2.75**
K. Fallon	10-38	26.0	+ **7.63**
Alex Greaves	10-64	15.0	- 12.94
P. Fessey	9-124	7.0	- 49.13
R. Winston	8-83	9.0	- 44.35
O. Pears	7-99	7.0	- 10.00
G. Carter	7-36	19.0	+ **0.85**
C. Lowther	7-68	10.0	+ **28.75**
A. Nicholls	6-36	16.0	+ **22.00**
R. Mullen	6-26	23.0	+ **11.86**
R. Lappin	6-70	8.0	- 12.75
J. Lowe	6-56	10.0	- 13.09
G. Parkin	6-94	6.0	- 51.75
Dale Gibson	6-120	5.0	- 82.38
D. Mernagh	5-49	10.0	- 16.50

LEADING JOCKEYS AT CHEPSTOW

(SINCE 1995)

	Total W-R	Per cent	£1 Level stake
S. Drowne	13-121	10.0	- 41.50
S. Sanders	12-97	12.0	- 31.04
J. Reid	11-78	14.0	- 36.48
R. Havlin	9-68	13.0	+ **20.38**
S. Whitworth	9-82	10.0	- 29.50
Dane O'Neill	9-85	10.0	- 21.45
L. Dettori	8-22	36.0	+ **1.54**
T. Quinn	8-77	10.0	- 50.84
Pat Eddery	8-43	18.0	- 17.01
R. Hughes	8-57	14.0	- 24.28
L. Newman	7-28	25.0	+ **4.00**
K. Fallon	7-26	26.0	+ **7.10**
C. Rutter	7-81	8.0	- 39.92
G. Carter	6-42	14.0	- 8.03
R. Ffrench	6-32	18.0	+ **2.08**
R. Hills	6-31	19.0	+ **1.35**
R. Price	6-41	14.0	+ **7.50**
G. Duffield	5-30	16.0	- 11.12
J. P. Spencer	4-11	36.0	+ **3.64**
P. Fitzsimons	4-33	12.0	- 7.00
J. Weaver	4-18	22.0	- 2.50
A. Clark	4-59	6.0	- 28.75
J. D. Smith	4-22	18.0	- 3.25
G. Hind	4-45	8.0	- 23.50
D. Harrison	4-40	10.0	+ **8.00**

LEADING JOCKEYS AT CHESTER
(SINCE 1995)

	Total W-R	Per cent	£1 Level stake
K. Fallon	21-123	17.0	- 28.91
J. F. Egan	20-145	13.0	+ **6.75**
K. Darley	16-123	13.0	- 22.39
D. Holland	16-85	18.0	- 5.88
M. Hills	15-99	15.0	- 7.98
J. Fortune	14-109	12.0	- 34.40
J. Reid	14-77	18.0	- 6.70
Pat Eddery	12-71	16.0	- 10.63
R. Hughes	12-58	20.0	- 2.75
J. Carroll	11-110	10.0	- 53.00
M. Roberts	9-47	19.0	- 8.23
L. Dettori	9-56	16.0	- 11.88
W. Supple	8-85	9.0	- 21.67
S. Sanders	8-34	23.0	+ **5.25**
R. Hills	8-41	19.0	- 13.46
D. Wright	7-48	14.0	- 5.67
T. Quinn	7-77	9.0	- 24.29
W. Ryan	6-37	16.0	- 7.40
F. Norton	6-66	9.0	- 32.83
Paul Eddery	5-33	15.0	- 17.20
A. Culhane	5-37	13.0	- 9.00
A. Mackay	5-39	12.0	+ **48.13**
M. Fenton	5-23	21.0	+ **16.00**
J. Quinn	5-50	10.0	- 11.00
J. Weaver	4-37	10.0	- 15.75

LEADING JOCKEYS AT DONCASTER
(SINCE 1995)

	Total W-R	Per cent	£1 Level stake
M. Hills	45-231	19.0	+ **3.95**
K. Fallon	41-247	16.0	- 48.08
K. Darley	38-349	10.0	- 51.68
L. Dettori	38-212	17.0	- 22.18
Pat Eddery	29-240	12.0	- 64.22
J. Fortune	28-252	11.0	- 70.76
T. Quinn	26-182	14.0	- 25.52
D. Holland	21-130	16.0	- 6.51
R. Hills	21-122	17.0	- 33.64
J. Carroll	19-205	9.0	- 84.72
J. Reid	19-220	8.0	- 92.33
W. Ryan	19-145	13.0	- 49.75
R. Hughes	15-116	12.0	- 4.00
M. Roberts	14-109	12.0	- 6.93
G. Carter	14-144	9.0	- 45.60
S. Sanders	13-119	10.0	- 15.54
J. Weaver	12-166	7.0	- 54.80
A. Culhane	12-202	5.0	- 41.93
J. Quinn	12-142	8.0	- 64.79
G. Hind	10-73	13.0	- 7.25
R. Winston	9-83	10.0	+ **9.00**
G. Duffield	9-191	4.0	- 92.80
D. Harrison	8-74	10.0	- 27.00
C. Lowther	7-103	6.0	- 39.90
F. Lynch	7-90	7.0	- 4.25

LEADING JOCKEYS AT EPSOM
(SINCE 1995)

	Total W-R	Per cent	£1 Level stake
K. Fallon	20-88	22.0	+ **4.37**
Pat Eddery	18-109	16.0	- 30.02
T. Quinn	16-155	10.0	- 77.74
S. Sanders	13-107	12.0	- 36.21
L. Dettori	13-77	16.0	- 25.51
M. Roberts	11-75	14.0	+ **2.08**
Dane O'Neill	9-96	9.0	- 60.67
J. Fortune	8-38	21.0	+ **8.83**
R. Hughes	8-76	10.0	- 13.10
M. Hills	8-60	13.0	- 13.34
R. Hills	7-47	14.0	+ **18.00**
W. Ryan	7-58	12.0	- 9.38
J. Weaver	6-35	17.0	- 5.75
A. Daly	6-46	13.0	+ **3.91**
G. Carter	6-33	18.0	+ **33.13**
P. Doe	5-71	7.0	- 40.29
M. Tebbutt	5-24	20.0	+ **13.00**
Martin Dwyer	5-61	8.0	- 30.17
M. Henry	5-42	11.0	+ **8.50**
S. Whitworth	5-47	10.0	- 25.92
J. Quinn	5-58	8.0	- 20.00
D. Holland	5-66	7.0	- 42.13
J. Reid	5-87	5.0	- 58.03
M. J. Kinane	5-39	12.0	+ **3.00**
A. Beech	4-11	36.0	+ **13.00**

LEADING JOCKEYS AT FOLKESTONE
(SINCE 1995)

	Total W-R	Per cent	£1 Level stake
S. Sanders	22-160	13.0	- 8.43
T. Quinn	21-137	15.0	- 19.23
Dane O'Neill	18-128	14.0	+ **37.10**
Paul Eddery	14-96	14.0	- 16.00
G. Duffield	14-82	17.0	- 20.29
Martin Dwyer	13-89	14.0	+ **41.75**
J. Quinn	12-134	8.0	- 13.01
S. Drowne	12-92	13.0	- 6.63
A. Whelan	10-59	16.0	- 0.84
A. Clark	9-128	7.0	- 79.38
R. Ffrench	8-61	13.0	- 19.02
C. Rutter	8-72	11.0	+ **9.96**
M. Hills	7-18	38.0	+ **19.04**
K. Fallon	7-34	20.0	+ **0.85**
S. Whitworth	7-69	10.0	- 25.75
R. Hughes	7-54	12.0	- 24.83
M. Fenton	7-64	10.0	+ **12.75**
Pat Eddery	7-38	18.0	+ **3.12**
F. Norton	7-45	15.0	+ **53.00**
N. Callan	6-27	22.0	+ **1.22**
J. F. Egan	6-68	8.0	- 20.76
D. Harrison	6-50	12.0	+ **14.73**
G. Carter	6-55	10.0	- 15.68
P. Robinson	6-66	9.0	- 33.50
N. Pollard	5-46	10.0	+ **23.50**

LEADING JOCKEYS AT GOODWOOD

(SINCE 1995)

	Total W-R	Per cent	£1 Level stake
L. Dettori	53-222	23.0	- 1.84
T. Quinn	50-371	13.0	- 81.98
Pat Eddery	38-249	15.0	- 72.86
K. Fallon	37-186	19.0	**+ 18.47**
J. Reid	37-304	12.0	- 112.04
R. Hills	35-205	17.0	- 1.02
R. Hughes	26-243	10.0	- 3.39
K. Darley	23-171	13.0	**+ 3.03**
Dane O'Neill	21-223	9.0	- 17.63
J. Fortune	19-113	16.0	**+ 3.73**
M. Roberts	16-151	10.0	- 49.54
M. Hills	16-159	10.0	- 15.22
D. Holland	15-106	14.0	**+ 17.25**
J. Quinn	14-140	10.0	- 38.45
S. Sanders	14-208	6.0	- 109.25
O. Peslier	11-41	26.0	**+ 54.75**
W. Ryan	11-99	11.0	- 46.52
J. Weaver	11-96	11.0	- 0.31
G. Carter	10-108	9.0	- 30.17
S. Drowne	9-94	9.0	- 11.50
M. J. Kinane	9-47	19.0	**+ 6.35**
R. Ffrench	8-61	13.0	- 8.38
G. Duffield	8-79	10.0	- 31.59
Paul Eddery	8-139	5.0	- 94.75
Gary Stevens	7-27	25.0	**+ 11.50**

LEADING JOCKEYS AT HAMILTON

(SINCE 1995)

	Total W-R	Per cent	£1 Level stake
J. Weaver	30-128	23.0	**+ 12.52**
K. Darley	30-179	16.0	- 29.24
J. Carroll	26-246	10.0	- 108.67
A. Mackay	24-136	17.0	- 29.75
J. Fortune	23-129	17.0	- 19.47
T. Williams	18-158	11.0	- 48.38
G. Duffield	18-113	15.0	- 24.75
A. Culhane	17-160	10.0	- 65.08
K. Fallon	17-91	18.0	- 8.04
J. Fanning	16-151	10.0	**+ 16.96**
N. Kennedy	15-143	10.0	**+ 2.75**
L. Charnock	14-130	10.0	- 32.00
Dean McKeown	13-184	7.0	- 34.75
C. Lowther	12-98	12.0	**+ 58.17**
D. Holland	12-56	21.0	- 10.06
R. Winston	10-113	8.0	- 57.93
O. Pears	9-111	8.0	- 60.90
A. Beech	8-28	28.0	**+ 15.58**
J. McAuley	8-125	6.0	- 55.00
Dale Gibson	8-107	7.0	**+ 2.00**
P. Fessey	8-146	5.0	- 95.42
F. Lynch	7-50	14.0	- 23.02
T. Quinn	7-14	50.0	- 0.67
R. Lappin	7-78	8.0	- 28.25
D. Mernagh	6-47	12.0	**+ 19.38**

LEADING JOCKEYS AT HAYDOCK

(SINCE 1995)

	Total W-R	Per cent	£1 Level stake
K. Darley	35-269	13.0	- 90.54
Pat Eddery	34-153	22.0	- 5.22
J. Carroll	28-303	9.0	- 135.48
K. Fallon	25-143	17.0	- 14.66
L. Dettori	24-110	21.0	- 10.83
J. Weaver	21-159	13.0	- 12.12
J. Reid	20-122	16.0	- 21.90
T. Quinn	19-75	25.0	**+ 36.67**
W. Ryan	19-89	21.0	**+ 8.70**
R. Hills	18-114	15.0	- 38.34
A. Culhane	15-167	8.0	- 42.50
P. Robinson	15-86	17.0	**+ 8.83**
J. F. Egan	14-150	9.0	- 0.63
J. Fortune	12-163	7.0	- 95.67
G. Carter	12-106	11.0	- 5.38
M. Hills	11-66	16.0	**+ 35.75**
S. Sanders	10-84	11.0	- 6.88
D. Holland	10-90	11.0	- 28.10
D. Harrison	10-60	16.0	**+ 11.46**
M. Roberts	10-78	12.0	- 21.03
Dean McKeown	9-131	6.0	- 21.50
G. Hind	9-89	10.0	- 37.88
Paul Eddery	9-65	13.0	- 14.34
G. Duffield	7-105	6.0	- 34.60
W. Supple	6-89	6.0	- 61.40

LEADING JOCKEYS AT KEMPTON

(SINCE 1995)

	Total W-R	Per cent	£1 Level stake
Pat Eddery	47-228	20.0	**+ 13.89**
T. Quinn	34-228	14.0	- 1.92
J. Reid	31-181	17.0	**+ 1.58**
R. Hughes	23-181	12.0	**+ 21.53**
L. Dettori	23-102	22.0	- 7.94
R. Hills	17-123	13.0	- 6.31
K. Fallon	16-105	15.0	- 25.54
M. Hills	16-129	12.0	- 36.05
S. Sanders	14-178	7.0	- 77.17
J. Fortune	11-67	16.0	- 9.34
N. Pollard	11-83	13.0	**+ 7.00**
Dane O'Neill	11-156	7.0	- 90.50
M. Roberts	9-82	10.0	- 31.13
R. Mullen	7-42	16.0	**+ 16.83**
W. Ryan	7-104	6.0	- 74.25
G. Hind	6-81	7.0	- 23.75
P. Robinson	6-68	8.0	- 12.00
A. Clark	6-140	4.0	- 37.00
L. Newman	5-40	12.0	- 7.25
S. Whitworth	5-98	5.0	- 26.25
D. Harrison	5-90	5.0	- 43.25
O. Peslier	4-21	19.0	**+ 14.41**
R. Ffrench	4-53	7.0	**+ 1.00**
D. Holland	4-32	12.0	- 15.67
O. Urbina	4-30	13.0	**+ 2.50**

LEADING JOCKEYS AT LEICESTER (SINCE 1995)

	Total W R	Per cent		£1 Level stake
L. Dettori	35-131	26.0	-	1.61
Pat Eddery	34-175	19.0	-	36.01
K. Fallon	26-153	16.0	-	3.96
T. Quinn	22-167	13.0	-	56.87
W. Ryan	21-130	16.0	-	17.40
G. Carter	18-170	10.0	-	38.88
Dane O'Neill	17-160	10.0	-	34.50
J. Reid	17-149	11.0	-	47.90
M. Roberts	15-99	15.0	+	**15.68**
R. Hills	15-110	13.0	-	5.91
J. Fortune	15-98	15.0	-	15.74
D. Holland	15-103	14.0	+	**57.96**
G. Duffield	14-121	11.0	-	38.25
M. Hills	13-136	9.0	-	55.50
C. Rutter	10-138	7.0	-	32.00
S. Sanders	9-95	9.0	-	21.38
K. Darley	9-88	10.0	-	46.36
M. Fenton	9-141	6.0	-	70.63
F. Lynch	8-83	9.0	-	20.00
S. Drowne	8-143	5.0	-	73.50
J. Weaver	8-92	8.0	-	24.00
J. Quinn	8-143	5.0	-	65.77
M. Tebbutt	7-80	8.0	-	36.75
A. Mackay	7-80	8.0	-	24.00
Martin Dwyer	7-83	8.0	+	**9.62**

LEADING JOCKEYS AT LINGFIELD- All Weather (SINCE 1995)

	Total W-R	Per cent		£1 Level stake
A. Clark	87-628	13.0	-	30.89
J. Weaver	68-321	21.0	-	16.74
S. Sanders	59-482	12.0	-	78.24
S. Whitworth	54-387	13.0	-	117.78
J. Quinn	53-659	8.0	-	292.24
D. Holland	43-191	22.0	+	**25.46**
W. Ryan	41-211	19.0	+	**9.13**
Dean McKeown	33-207	15.0	+	**13.23**
L. Dettori	33-148	22.0	-	21.24
F. Norton	32-314	10.0	+	**18.13**
P. Doe	29-318	9.0	-	108.45
Dane O'Neill	29-300	9.0	-	140.36
Martin Dwyer	27-290	9.0	-	127.01
D. Harrison	27-202	13.0	-	46.35
A. Culhane	26-172	15.0	+	**13.76**
G. Carter	26-215	12.0	-	74.53
D. Sweeney	25-174	14.0	-	9.77
N. Callan	22-138	15.0	-	24.73
A. Daly	20-208	9.0	+	**11.50**
M. Hills	19-79	24.0	-	2.08
D. Biggs	19-213	8.0	-	71.47
K. Fallon	18-79	22.0	-	16.78
G. Duffield	18-156	11.0	-	79.76
C. Rutter	18-217	8.0	-	36.67
R. Ffrench	16-92	17.0	-	12.43

LEADING JOCKEYS AT LINGFIELD- Turf (SINCE 1995)

	Total W-R	Per cent		£1 Level stake
K. Fallon	34-95	35.0	+	**36.05**
Pat Eddery	29-125	23.0	-	10.01
S. Sanders	27-221	12.0	-	48.21
J. Reid	22-136	16.0	-	7.16
R. Hills	22-96	22.0	-	0.51
Dane O'Neill	20-198	10.0	-	69.88
T. Quinn	20-174	11.0	-	94.42
R. Hughes	15-132	11.0	-	40.05
G. Carter	13-102	12.0	-	21.54
Martin Dwyer	12-136	8.0	-	22.25
C. Rutter	12-130	9.0	-	6.93
J. Weaver	12-90	13.0	+	**19.83**
W. Ryan	11-111	9.0	-	27.72
R. Mullen	11-67	16.0	+	**2.30**
R. Perham	10-105	9.0	+	**38.88**
A. McGlone	10-86	11.0	-	44.71
N. Pollard	9-82	10.0	-	17.17
D. Holland	9-71	12.0	-	22.71
F. Norton	9-85	10.0	+	**17.75**
A. Daly	9-107	8.0	-	43.06
G. Hind	9-87	10.0	-	28.20
P. Robinson	8-64	12.0	-	22.67
M. Tebbutt	8-72	11.0	-	9.00
M. Henry	8-66	12.0	+	**10.00**
L. Dettori	8-49	16.0	-	28.22

LEADING JOCKEYS AT MUSSELBURGH (SINCE 1995)

	Total W-R	Per cent		£1 Level stake
K. Darley	33-203	16.0	-	38.15
A. Culhane	29-225	12.0	-	55.00
J. Carroll	27-220	12.0	+	**9.45**
R. Winston	24-149	16.0	+	**77.50**
K. Fallon	19-90	21.0	-	9.43
J. Fortune	17-157	10.0	-	78.58
F. Lynch	15-73	20.0	+	**26.25**
L. Charnock	15-131	11.0	-	28.34
J. F. Egan	14-105	13.0	-	48.43
D. Holland	14-50	28.0	+	**21.48**
M. Fenton	12-63	19.0	+	**67.08**
P. Fessey	12-152	7.0	-	48.26
G. Duffield	12-107	11.0	-	20.24
C. Lowther	11-90	12.0	-	6.50
T. Williams	11-157	7.0	-	27.88
J. Fanning	10-128	7.0	-	25.75
G. Carter	9-37	24.0	+	**1.23**
R. Lappin	9-91	9.0	+	**29.50**
J. Weaver	9-82	10.0	-	61.80
W. Supple	8-71	11.0	+	**44.88**
T. E. Durcan	7-24	29.0	+	**15.25**
F. Norton	7-38	18.0	-	2.77
Dean McKeown	6-131	4.0	-	104.38
J. Bramhill	5-57	8.0	-	23.75
O. Pears	5-95	5.0	-	59.00

LEADING JOCKEYS AT NEWBURY (SINCE 1995)

	Total W-R	Per cent	£1 Level stake
T. Quinn	46-327	14.0	+ **23.40**
Pat Eddery	43-347	12.0	- 106.71
J. Reid	42-313	13.0	- 14.75
L. Dettori	41-212	19.0	+ **8.05**
K. Fallon	35-199	17.0	- 34.74
R. Hills	31-199	15.0	- 1.06
M. Hills	24-239	10.0	- 31.28
R. Hughes	19-245	7.0	- 88.69
J. Fortune	14-97	14.0	- 19.46
Dane O'Neill	13-233	5.0	- 80.58
W. Ryan	13-103	12.0	- 3.13
S. Sanders	12-170	7.0	- 80.00
D. Harrison	11-111	9.0	+ **22.50**
M. Roberts	10-116	8.0	- 33.80
P. Robinson	9-73	12.0	+ **70.63**
K. Darley	8-93	8.0	- 54.02
D. Holland	7-76	9.0	- 11.25
S. Whitworth	7-89	7.0	- 25.50
O. Peslier	6-34	17.0	+ **11.25**
P. Doe	6-53	11.0	- 14.75
J. Quinn	6-89	6.0	- 41.00
G. Hind	6-51	11.0	+ **6.25**
A. Clark	6-77	7.0	+ **15.00**
M. J. Kinane	6-45	13.0	- 22.24
C. Rutter	6-99	6.0	- 57.13

LEADING JOCKEYS AT NEWCASTLE (SINCE 1995)

	Total W-R	Per cent	£1 Level stake
K. Darley	49-295	16.0	- 59.04
K. Fallon	28-152	18.0	- 14.87
J. Weaver	26-151	17.0	- 4.83
D. Holland	22-121	18.0	- 25.08
G. Duffield	21-168	12.0	- 19.25
J. Carroll	21-246	8.0	- 106.73
J. Fortune	21-173	12.0	- 46.88
A. Culhane	21-227	9.0	- 33.88
L. Charnock	15-175	8.0	- 2.00
M. Hills	11-36	30.0	+ **2.51**
T. Williams	11-158	6.0	- 53.50
J. Fanning	10-134	7.0	- 55.37
R. Winston	9-119	7.0	- 34.75
G. Carter	9-70	12.0	- 10.88
L. Dettori	9-40	22.0	- 15.54
R. Hills	9-35	25.0	+ **19.63**
M. Fenton	9-55	16.0	+ **3.71**
W. Supple	8-91	8.0	- 32.88
Dean McKeown	8-146	5.0	- 75.25
J. Reid	7-53	13.0	- 19.38
G. Hind	7-33	21.0	+ **28.00**
F. Lynch	6-119	5.0	- 93.69
W. Ryan	6-27	22.0	- 6.18
T. Quinn	6-37	16.0	- 10.73
J. Quinn	6-74	8.0	- 11.17

LEADING JOCKEYS AT NEWMARKET- Rowley (SINCE 1995)

	Total W-R	Per cent	£1 Level stake
L. Dettori	59-348	16.0	- 101.59
K. Fallon	44-249	17.0	- 10.63
Pat Eddery	41-313	13.0	- 103.27
R. Hills	40-274	14.0	+ **29.08**
M. Hills	29-304	9.0	- 27.21
T. Quinn	26-303	8.0	- 143.35
J. Reid	25-331	7.0	- 140.19
M. J. Kinane	21-129	16.0	+ **14.08**
R. Hughes	14-161	8.0	- 65.78
J. Fortune	11-144	7.0	- 51.24
S. Sanders	11-132	8.0	- 5.00
W. Ryan	10-119	8.0	- 42.92
K. Darley	9-168	5.0	- 85.00
G. Carter	9-140	6.0	- 25.25
Dane O'Neill	8-129	6.0	- 31.00
P. Robinson	8-106	7.0	+ **12.83**
M. Roberts	8-130	6.0	- 39.50
D. Holland	8-106	7.0	- 48.88
D. Harrison	7-106	6.0	- 14.25
M. Fenton	7-90	7.0	- 40.02
R. Ffrench	6-91	6.0	- 28.00
O. Peslier	6-58	10.0	- 25.56
G. Duffield	6-77	7.0	- 42.75
J. Weaver	5-125	4.0	- 92.67
W. Supple	4-46	8.0	+ **33.00**
A. Clark	4-84	4.0	+ **10.57**

LEADING JOCKEYS AT NEWMARKET- July (SINCE 1995)

	Total W-R	Per cent	£1 Level stake
L. Dettori	55-255	21.0	+ **3.43**
Pat Eddery	52-326	15.0	- 110.39
K. Fallon	47-203	23.0	+ **31.13**
R. Hills	38-244	15.0	- 57.65
M. Hills	34-268	12.0	+ **16.91**
T. Quinn	33-258	12.0	- 36.97
J. Reid	21-159	13.0	+ **51.67**
J. Fortune	17-159	10.0	- 43.58
W. Ryan	17-195	8.0	- 83.01
M. Roberts	16-143	11.0	- 23.00
J. Quinn	14-117	11.0	- 24.21
Dane O'Neill	14-170	8.0	- 35.38
S. Sanders	12-98	12.0	+ **35.88**
R. Hughes	12-160	7.0	- 46.13
J. Weaver	12-122	9.0	- 31.72
G. Carter	12-119	10.0	- 18.43
D. Harrison	11-85	12.0	- 22.13
M. J. Kinane	11-89	12.0	- 34.45
D. Holland	11-126	8.0	- 52.62
P. Robinson	10-170	5.0	- 82.75
M. Fenton	9-145	6.0	- 62.50
P. Doe	8-61	13.0	+ **27.75**
D. R. McCabe	8-42	19.0	+ **54.33**
R. Ffrench	7-87	8.0	1.78
T. Sprake	7-65	10.0	- 9.17

LEADING JOCKEYS AT NOTTINGHAM
(SINCE 1995)

	Total W-R	Per cent	£1 Level stake
K. Fallon	45-221	20.0	- 27.24
Pat Eddery	25-118	21.0	- 19.02
T. Quinn	25-158	15.0	+ **2.90**
T. Sprake	25-207	12.0	+ **35.60**
G. Duffield	23-168	13.0	- 27.68
W. Ryan	21-139	15.0	- 40.59
L. Dettori	20-93	21.0	- 2.79
R. Hills	18-100	18.0	- 17.58
G. Carter	17-228	7.0	- 116.08
J. Quinn	15-206	7.0	- 24.83
D. Holland	15-101	14.0	+ **46.63**
P. Robinson	14-108	12.0	+ **66.58**
J. Weaver	14-143	9.0	- 38.37
J. Fortune	13-121	10.0	- 34.67
M. Fenton	13-136	9.0	- 40.48
K. Darley	12-129	9.0	- 75.66
S. Sanders	12-145	8.0	- 41.88
Dean McKeown	12-146	8.0	- 70.75
D. Harrison	12-104	11.0	- 3.68
J. Reid	12-118	10.0	- 38.50
S. Drowne	11-171	6.0	- 55.00
A. Culhane	11-144	7.0	- 79.97
A. Clark	11-120	9.0	- 43.92
G. Hind	10-118	8.0	- 46.55
R. Mullen	10-90	11.0	- 19.13
J. Carroll	8-94	8.0	- 9.46

LEADING JOCKEYS AT REDCAR
(SINCE 1995)

	Total W-R	Per cent	£1 Level stake
K. Darley	60-321	18.0	- 49.62
J. Weaver	26-122	21.0	- 7.37
A. Culhane	23-268	8.0	- 93.27
J. Carroll	22-192	11.0	+ **5.50**
G. Duffield	21-179	11.0	- 66.76
G. Carter	21-101	20.0	- 6.64
K. Fallon	20-99	20.0	- 16.48
J. Fortune	19-182	10.0	- 66.73
L. Charnock	16-224	7.0	+ **9.50**
Dean McKeown	13-177	7.0	- 73.75
W. Ryan	11-65	16.0	- 10.08
G. Hind	10-39	25.0	+ **21.00**
D. Holland	9-49	18.0	+ **3.63**
G. Parkin	9-108	8.0	+ **9.25**
J. Fanning	9-155	5.0	- 85.01
M. Fenton	9-98	9.0	- 12.25
F. Norton	8-59	13.0	- 1.75
F. Lynch	8-116	6.0	- 62.00
P. Fessey	8-126	6.0	- 52.25
L. Dettori	8-36	22.0	- 10.09
W. Supple	7-86	8.0	- 24.10
Kim Tinkler	7-198	3.0	- 80.00
R. Winston	6-118	5.0	- 64.50
O. Pears	6-94	6.0	- 69.80
S. Sanders	6-42	14.0	- 20.58

LEADING JOCKEYS AT PONTEFRACT
(SINCE 1995)

	Total W-R	Per cent	£1 Level stake
K. Darley	49-325	15.0	- 23.04
K. Fallon	44-213	20.0	+ **41.45**
Pat Eddery	26-83	31.0	+ **29.86**
J. Fortune	22-192	11.0	- 39.68
A. Culhane	18-200	9.0	- 11.42
L. Dettori	13-69	18.0	- 5.07
J. Carroll	12-198	6.0	- 82.75
J. Weaver	11-130	8.0	- 59.54
L. Charnock	11-145	7.0	- 30.00
F. Lynch	10-113	8.0	- 36.33
M. Hills	10-47	21.0	- 8.45
W. Ryan	10-74	13.0	- 39.48
G. Duffield	10-125	8.0	- 39.27
M. Roberts	9-54	16.0	+ **22.42**
D. Holland	9-105	8.0	- 43.75
W. Supple	8-107	7.0	- 46.50
R. Winston	8-92	8.0	- 20.75
D. Mernagh	8-80	10.0	+ **11.88**
T. Quinn	8-36	22.0	+ **17.44**
J. F. Egan	7-86	8.0	- 15.75
A. Clark	7-42	16.0	+ **35.00**
J. Quinn	7-80	8.0	- 22.00
S. Sanders	7-72	9.0	- 17.58
T. Williams	7-131	5.0	- 79.00
R. Hills	7-60	11.0	- 44.06

LEADING JOCKEYS AT RIPON
(SINCE 1995)

	Total W-R	Per cent	£1 Level stake
K. Darley	42-216	19.0	+ **17.25**
J. Weaver	25-137	18.0	+ **48.10**
K. Fallon	25-111	22.0	+ **22.82**
J. Carroll	15-171	8.0	- 79.15
D. Holland	14-77	18.0	+ **17.72**
L. Charnock	14-154	9.0	- 57.53
J. Fanning	14-147	9.0	- 39.87
A. Culhane	13-185	7.0	- 73.17
G. Carter	12-74	16.0	+ **3.60**
G. Hind	12-54	22.0	- 7.73
J. Fortune	12-141	8.0	- 74.13
R. Ffrench	10-47	21.0	+ **17.45**
W. Ryan	10-48	20.0	- 11.77
Dean McKeown	9-156	5.0	- 72.38
T. Williams	8-135	5.0	- 64.50
T. Quinn	6-20	30.0	+ **16.17**
S. Sanders	6-43	13.0	- 22.79
L. Dettori	6-11	54.0	+ **11.25**
F. Lynch	6-71	8.0	- 29.80
G. Duffield	6-64	9.0	- 20.91
R. Hills	5-22	22.0	- 1.22
D. Mernagh	4-59	6.0	- 1.00
Iona Wands	4-25	16.0	- 1.84
R. Havlin	4-21	19.0	- 12.27
P. Fessey	4-78	5.0	- 32.00

LEADING JOCKEYS AT SALISBURY

(SINCE 1995)

	Total W-R	Per cent	£1 Level stake
R. Hughes	36-176	20.0	- 2.56
T. Quinn	32-160	20.0	- 26.00
Dane O'Neill	22-205	10.0	- 69.92
L. Dettori	21-79	26.0	+ **2.47**
J. Reid	19-174	10.0	- 78.92
T. Sprake	19-208	9.0	- 69.26
Pat Eddery	19-112	16.0	- 32.51
G. Duffield	14-65	21.0	+ **23.50**
K. Fallon	13-49	26.0	+ **40.70**
R. Hills	13-69	18.0	+ **4.43**
W. Ryan	13-69	18.0	- 16.20
S. Drowne	12-179	6.0	- 62.75
C. Rutter	11-148	7.0	- 50.68
B. Doyle	10-44	22.0	+ **71.11**
S. Sanders	10-150	6.0	- 105.58
L. Newman	8-67	11.0	+ **12.73**
M. Hills	8-76	10.0	- 9.33
M. Roberts	8-64	12.0	+ **32.08**
D. Harrison	8-100	8.0	- 42.90
N. Pollard	7-114	6.0	- 65.15
D. Sweeney	7-51	13.0	+ **92.00**
M. Henry	7-68	10.0	- 3.56
D. Holland	7-31	22.0	+ **15.50**
A. Clark	6-137	4.0	- 81.00
I. Mongan	5-22	22.0	+ **10.25**

LEADING JOCKEYS AT SANDOWN

(SINCE 1995)

	Total W-R	Per cent	£1 Level stake
Pat Eddery	60-303	19.0	- 35.14
L. Dettori	51-255	20.0	- 62.16
T. Quinn	33-255	12.0	- 62.23
K. Fallon	28-176	15.0	- 20.79
J. Reid	25-210	11.0	- 77.46
Dane O'Neill	24-219	10.0	- 62.13
R. Hills	21-139	15.0	- 19.12
M. Roberts	20-152	13.0	- 28.34
M. Hills	17-151	11.0	- 42.60
S. Sanders	16-194	8.0	- 71.00
G. Carter	12-72	16.0	+ **32.96**
J. Fortune	11-64	17.0	+ **21.10**
J. Weaver	11-66	16.0	+ **15.83**
Gary Stevens	10-38	26.0	+ **8.03**
T. Sprake	10-105	9.0	+ **23.30**
R. Hughes	10-137	7.0	- 57.27
P. Robinson	10-80	12.0	+ **22.50**
K. Darley	9-73	12.0	- 18.67
C. Rutter	9-79	11.0	+ **50.00**
D. Holland	8-63	12.0	+ **15.83**
D. Harrison	8-76	10.0	- 6.30
M. J. Kinane	8-55	14.0	+ **1.13**
G. Duffield	7-54	12.0	- 8.92
W. Ryan	7-115	6.0	- 81.93
B. Doyle	7-122	5.0	- 52.50

LEADING JOCKEYS AT SOUTHWELL

(SINCE 1995)

	Total W-R	Per cent	£1 Level stake
J. Weaver	50-299	16.0	- 11.65
G. Duffield	48-319	15.0	- 115.10
J. Quinn	48-556	8.0	- 250.67
A. Culhane	38-444	8.0	- 174.51
F. Norton	34-340	10.0	- 44.15
Dean McKeown	34-513	6.0	- 289.92
L. Charnock	34-416	8.0	- 166.32
C. Lowther	29-207	14.0	+ **2.53**
D. Holland	29-143	20.0	+ **39.08**
F. Lynch	28-226	12.0	- 14.67
C. Teague	27-306	8.0	- 100.67
R. Fitzpatrick	26-202	12.0	+ **22.38**
D. Sweeney	26-201	12.0	- 29.67
K. Fallon	24-109	22.0	+ **39.40**
P. McCabe	24-204	11.0	+ **29.55**
Martin Dwyer	23-164	14.0	+ **27.25**
J. Fanning	23-276	8.0	- 33.99
M. Tebbutt	22-168	13.0	- 15.94
S. Sanders	22-193	11.0	- 45.67
G. Carter	22-263	8.0	- 109.60
T. G. McLaughlin	22-258	8.0	- 75.88
P. M. Quinn	21-178	11.0	+ **21.98**
S. Whitworth	21-228	9.0	- 64.88
A. Clark	20-245	8.0	- 92.53
T. Sprake	19-179	10.0	- 36.81

LEADING JOCKEYS AT THIRSK

(SINCE 1995)

	Total W-R	Per cent	£1 Level stake
K. Darley	37-166	22.0	- 20.59
A. Culhane	23-207	11.0	- 39.02
J. Carroll	22-206	10.0	- 96.34
J. Weaver	21-104	20.0	- 2.73
G. Duffield	20-118	16.0	+ **19.46**
J. Fortune	18-116	15.0	- 16.55
G. Carter	16-114	14.0	- 22.96
F. Lynch	12-91	13.0	- 12.25
K. Fallon	12-45	26.0	+ **8.90**
W. Ryan	11-42	26.0	+ **13.50**
L. Charnock	11-182	6.0	- 97.52
Dean McKeown	11-119	9.0	- 27.42
S. Sanders	10-40	25.0	+ **31.03**
D. Holland	10-53	18.0	- 11.43
J. F. Egan	9-67	13.0	+ **15.00**
C. Lowther	8-75	10.0	+ **16.00**
D. Mernagh	7-66	10.0	+ **19.88**
Alex Greaves	6-80	7.0	- 24.88
D. Harrison	6-33	18.0	+ **1.66**
P. Fessey	6-84	7.0	- 34.25
Dale Gibson	6-110	5.0	- 56.75
J. Stack	6-62	9.0	- 37.88
Paul Eddery	6-28	21.0	- 7.80
T. Williams	6-131	4.0	- 69.00
D. Sweeney	5-37	13.0	+ **14.18**

LEADING JOCKEYS AT WARWICK (SINCE 1995)

	Total W-R	Per cent	£1 Level stake
M. Hills	20-66	30.0	+ **29.62**
T. Quinn	19-83	22.0	+ **4.75**
G. Carter	16-100	16.0	- 26.59
Pat Eddery	14-46	30.0	+ **7.01**
R. Hughes	13-60	21.0	+ **13.17**
T. Sprake	13-108	12.0	- 28.81
J. Reid	13-79	16.0	- 13.16
D. Harrison	9-51	17.0	+ **8.67**
F. Norton	9-83	10.0	- 20.90
M. Fenton	9-120	7.0	- 23.50
G. Bardwell	9-71	12.0	+ **32.75**
S. Drowne	9-130	6.0	- 74.13
G. Duffield	8-58	14.0	+ **2.50**
S. Whitworth	8-70	11.0	+ **33.75**
C. Rutter	8-101	7.0	- 47.88
J. Fortune	7-23	30.0	+ **24.50**
K. Fallon	7-36	19.0	- 11.47
Martin Dwyer	7-75	9.0	- 42.38
Paul Eddery	7-57	12.0	- 21.08
A. Clark	7-81	8.0	- 21.25
J. Tate	6-50	12.0	+ **10.25**
J. Carroll	6-50	12.0	- 18.88
S. Sanders	6-72	8.0	+ **2.16**
N. Adams	6-64	9.0	- 2.30
J. F. Egan	5-82	6.0	- 49.88

LEADING JOCKEYS AT WINDSOR (SINCE 1995)

	Total W-R	Per cent	£1 Level stake
Pat Eddery	50-282	17.0	- 84.20
L. Dettori	38-172	22.0	- 31.49
J. Reid	30-191	15.0	- 40.10
T. Quinn	26-215	12.0	- 23.38
R. Hughes	23-181	12.0	- 37.34
Dane O'Neill	21-219	9.0	- 48.51
K. Fallon	17-116	14.0	- 32.40
S. Sanders	16-203	7.0	- 49.25
Martin Dwyer	15-164	9.0	+ **2.21**
M. Roberts	13-104	12.0	- 15.91
T. Sprake	11-149	7.0	- 51.42
W. Ryan	11-84	13.0	- 24.26
M. Hills	10-128	7.0	- 63.42
R. Hills	9-74	12.0	+ **5.22**
P. Doe	9-117	7.0	- 45.88
J. Fortune	9-102	8.0	- 30.75
S. Drowne	9-175	5.0	- 95.00
M. Fenton	9-91	9.0	- 4.50
C. Rutter	9-157	5.0	- 83.13
D. Holland	9-74	12.0	- 7.13
B. Doyle	8-68	11.0	+ **14.00**
J. Quinn	7-145	4.0	- 70.50
P. Robinson	7-100	7.0	- 40.18
L. Newman	6-56	10.0	+ **16.80**
P. Fitzsimons	6-31	19.0	+ **34.00**

LEADING JOCKEYS AT WOLVERHAMPTON (SINCE 1995)

	Total W-R	Per cent	£1 Level stake
S. Sanders	57-375	15.0	- 10.62
T. G. McLaughlin	50-384	13.0	+ **8.07**
J. Weaver	48-272	17.0	+ **30.25**
Dean McKeown	44-463	9.0	- 197.81
G. Duffield	44-280	15.0	- 50.02
J. Quinn	38-489	7.0	- 103.84
F. Lynch	35-355	9.0	- 142.42
D. Holland	33-165	20.0	- 6.69
J. F. Egan	32-212	15.0	+ **50.57**
S. Whitworth	32-302	10.0	- 135.48
N. Callan	31-202	15.0	- 4.98
G. Carter	30-249	12.0	- 70.73
A. Culhane	29-386	7.0	- 138.86
T. Sprake	28-245	11.0	- 57.86
M. Tebbutt	28-216	12.0	+ **7.23**
D. Sweeney	27-226	11.0	- 94.60
J. Tate	27-181	14.0	+ **9.86**
F. Norton	25-249	10.0	- 22.00
A. Clark	25-241	10.0	- 35.85
S. Drowne	24-339	7.0	- 80.13
C. Lowther	23-181	12.0	- 69.51
T. Williams	23-250	9.0	- 116.39
A. McCarthy	21-179	11.0	- 11.00
K. Fallon	20-128	15.0	- 40.12
K. Darley	20-88	22.0	+ **25.50**

LEADING JOCKEYS AT YARMOUTH (SINCE 1995)

	Total W-R	Per cent	£1 Level stake
L. Dettori	38-116	32.0	- 3.89
R. Hills	36-167	21.0	+ **6.71**
W. Ryan	27-183	14.0	- 43.49
M. Hills	27-195	13.0	- 10.01
Pat Eddery	23-102	22.0	- 20.26
K. Fallon	19-116	16.0	- 39.74
T. Quinn	19-80	23.0	+ **5.91**
S. Sanders	18-105	17.0	+ **84.49**
M. Roberts	17-103	16.0	+ **4.18**
J. Reid	13-99	13.0	- 41.75
P. Robinson	13-122	10.0	+ **28.75**
R. Hughes	11-63	17.0	+ **0.94**
G. Carter	11-108	10.0	- 56.38
D. Holland	11-69	15.0	- 1.04
M. Fenton	11-104	10.0	- 33.42
G. Duffield	10-98	10.0	- 54.09
B. Doyle	10-66	15.0	- 3.00
D. Harrison	10-77	12.0	- 6.50
R. Mullen	9-99	9.0	- 18.47
K. Darley	9-53	16.0	- 12.45
J. Quinn	9-142	6.0	- 81.38
A. Clark	8-51	15.0	+ **39.25**
G. Bardwell	8-127	6.0	- 39.00
J. F. Egan	7-65	10.0	- 14.50
J. Stack	7-51	13.0	- 6.75

LEADING JOCKEYS AT YORK

(SINCE 1995)

	Total W-R	Per cent		£1 Level stake
L. Dettori	43-218	19.0	-	19.64
Pat Eddery	37-250	14.0	-	27.90
K. Fallon	36-278	12.0	-	77.54
K. Darley	30-302	9.0	-	49.84
M. J. Kinane	29-144	20.0	+	**1.07**
T. Quinn	26-228	11.0	-	82.04
R. Hills	19-150	12.0	+	**3.13**
J. Fortune	19-167	11.0	-	24.62
M. Hills	19-209	9.0	-	34.87
J. Reid	17-187	9.0	-	78.77
D. Holland	16-114	14.0	+	**32.25**
R. Hughes	10-90	11.0	+	**32.50**
W. Ryan	10-81	12.0	-	28.86
M. Roberts	9-102	8.0	-	48.42
J. Weaver	8-175	4.0	-	56.00
L. Charnock	7-112	6.0	-	62.13
D. Mernagh	6-55	10.0	+	**23.00**
R. Winston	6-69	8.0	+	**16.00**
A. Culhane	6-113	5.0	-	73.25
G. Duffield	6-92	6.0	-	49.33
Gary Stevens	5-22	22.0	+	**4.90**
J. Murtagh	5-18	27.0	+	**8.00**
Dean McKeown	5-78	6.0	-	28.00
J. F. Egan	5-89	5.0	-	28.50
M. Fenton	5-68	7.0	-	45.25

LEADING FLAT TRAINERS AT ASCOT (SINCE 1995)

	Total W-R	2yo Stks	3yo Stks	Other Stks	2yo H'caps	3yo H'caps	Other H'caps	App'ce	Amateurs	Per cent	£1 Level stake
S bin Suroor	30-130	5-13	3-36	21-72	0-0	0-3	1-6	0-0	0-0	23.1	**+ 39.55**
J. H. M. Gosden	29-173	5-25	9-45	4-33	0-0	5-22	6-48	0-0	0-0	16.8	**+ 21.23**
J. L. Dunlop	28-194	5-31	2-23	12-55	1-4	2-19	6-61	0-1	0-0	14.4	**+ 21.46**
R. Hannon	24-246	8-91	4-72	3-29	6-14	1-31	2-58	0-1	0-0	9.8	**+ 1.08**
Sir Michael Stoute	23-195	3-32	5-36	8-63	0-1	2-25	5-37	0-0	0-1	11.8	- 60.97
M. Johnston	22-158	5-24	1-7	5-38	0-3	5-19	6-67	0-0	0-0	13.9	**+ 69.75**
H. R. A. Cecil	20-131	4-18	8-36	5-48	0-0	2-15	1-14	0-0	0-0	15.3	- 42.58
P. F. I. Cole	18-141	9-44	2-13	3-22	0-3	0-16	4-42	0-1	0-0	12.8	- 20.10
L. M. Cumani	12-84	4-13	1-15	2-22	0-2	1-8	4-23	0-1	0-0	14.3	- 11.29
D. R. Loder	11-71	7-21	3-11	1-16	0-0	0-10	0-13	0-0	0-0	15.5	**+ 14.48**
B. W. Hills	11-166	6-46	1-25	2-35	0-7	1-17	1-36	0-0	0-0	6.6	- 82.43
A. P. O'Brien,Ireland	9-59	6-27	2-14	1-16	0-0	0-1	0-1	0-0	0-0	15.3	- 1.97
M. R. Channon	8-127	3-53	1-12	1-11	0-8	1-14	2-29	0-0	0-0	6.3	- 45.25
R. Charlton	8-69	0-9	1-10	3-16	0-0	1-9	2-24	0-0	1-1	11.6	- 13.75
A. C. Stewart	7-36	0-0	2-6	2-8	0-0	1-3	2-19	0-0	0-0	19.4	**+ 12.50**
E. A. L. Dunlop	7-74	4-16	0-9	0-11	0-1	0-10	3-27	0-0	0-0	9.5	- 29.64

LEADING FLAT TRAINERS AT AYR (SINCE 1995)

	Total W-R	2yo Stks	3yo Stks	Other Stks	2yo H'caps	3yo H'caps	Other H'caps	App'ce	Amateurs	Per cent	£1 Level stake
B. W. Hills	30-108	13-32	3-8	7-23	4-10	1-10	2-22	0-0	0-3	27.8	**+ 12.31**
M. Johnston	29-222	10-71	1-3	4-15	2-22	2-15	9-92	1-3	0-1	13.1	- 100.41
Miss L. A. Perratt	21-347	4-70	0-8	0-31	1-17	1-32	14-173	0-6	1-10	6.1	- 18.00
J. S. Goldie	18-258	2-23	0-2	0-22	2-20	1-22	11-150	1-4	1-15	7.0	- 97.05
J. L. Dunlop	15-55	6-15	1-2	4-9	1-7	1-2	2-19	0-0	0-1	27.3	- 1.24
A. Bailey	14-129	2-13	2-5	0-14	0-12	2-9	8-68	0-3	0-5	10.9	- 43.59
M. R. Channon	11-76	5-27	1-4	0-2	3-7	0-11	2-23	0-2	0-0	14.5	- 11.88
D. Nicholls	10-127	0-2	0-1	1-12	0-1	0-5	9-101	0-1	0-4	7.9	**+ 24.00**
Mrs M. Reveley	9-88	0-6	0-0	4-21	0-0	0-3	4-49	0-1	1-8	10.2	- 37.61
P. Calver	9-37	0-2	0-0	0-1	0-3	2-4	7-26	0-0	0-1	24.3	**+ 38.25**
Sir Mark Prescott	9-41	4-11	1-7	1-4	3-10	0-4	0-5	0-0	0-0	22.0	- 18.33
W. J. Haggas	8-20	0-4	1-1	1-3	0-2	1-2	4-7	1-1	0-0	40.0	**+ 7.33**
M. Dods	8-72	1-8	0-3	0-3	0-2	0-9	7-46	0-1	0-0	11.1	- 7.00
S. E. Kettlewell	8-52	0-3	1-2	0-7	0-0	1-5	6-29	0-1	0-5	15.4	**+ 21.75**
T. D. Easterby	7-73	3-14	0-0	0-3	2-19	2-6	0-29	0-1	0-1	9.6	- 2.50
Sir Michael Stoute	7-27	1-7	1-1	4-12	1-1	0-0	0-6	0-0	0-0	25.9	- 4.09

LEADING FLAT TRAINERS AT BATH (SINCE 1995)

	Total W-R	2yo Stks	3yo Stks	Other Stks	2yo H'caps	3yo H'caps	Other H'caps	App'ce	Amateurs	Per cent	£1 Level stake
M. R. Channon	23-184	9-64	4-22	6-24	0-7	2-17	2-50	0-0	0-0	12.5	- 44.68
I. A. Balding	22-131	4-25	1-15	4-19	1-2	4-11	8-53	0-6	0-0	16.8	- 0.27
R. Hannon	19-169	9-67	3-23	4-22	2-10	0-14	1-31	0-2	0-0	11.2	- 60.78
B. W. Hills	17-106	7-34	5-22	2-22	0-1	0-6	3-20	0-1	0-0	16.0	**+ 7.92**
P. F. I. Cole	16-77	2-14	4-12	3-8	2-7	0-11	5-22	0-3	0-0	20.8	- 10.82
R. Charlton	15-72	3-19	3-13	8-21	0-4	0-3	1-9	0-3	0-0	20.8	- 8.09
J. W. Hills	15-88	1-15	4-17	2-11	1-2	1-9	6-34	0-0	0-0	17.1	**+ 18.58**
W. R. Muir	14-124	0-27	1-16	3-10	1-3	0-8	7-53	2-7	0-0	11.3	- 10.00
R. J. Hodges	11-171	1-21	1-10	4-42	0-1	1-8	4-82	0-7	0-0	6.4	- 87.05
J. S. King	9-55	0-0	0-6	0-3	0-0	0-1	8-43	1-2	0-0	16.4	**+ 11.50**
J. A. R. Toller	9-61	2-11	1-10	1-9	0-0	1-3	4-26	0-2	0-0	14.8	**+ 7.60**
L. M. Cumani	8-22	0-1	3-10	5-9	0-0	0-1	0-1	0-0	0-0	36.4	**+ 9.49**
J. L. Dunlop	8-49	0-7	2-12	1-4	0-4	2-8	3-14	0-0	0-0	16.3	- 20.37
D. R. C. Elsworth	8-82	3-17	1-10	4-20	0-2	0-5	0-28	0-0	0-0	9.8	- 7.25
P. J. Makin	8-43	2-10	0-7	2-5	0-0	1-5	3-14	0-2	0-0	18.6	**+ 29.25**
B. J. Meehan	8-94	4-46	0-10	1-3	1-7	0-12	2-15	0-1	0-0	8.5	- 19.51

LEADING FLAT TRAINERS AT BEVERLEY (SINCE 1995)

	Total W-R	2yo Stks	3yo Stks	Other Stks	2yo H'caps	3yo H'caps	Other H'caps	App'ce	Amateurs	Per cent	£1 Level stake
M. Johnston	37-191	13-52	2-13	2-13	4-6	3-33	13-71	0-3	0-0	19.4	**+ 5.40**
T. D. Easterby	35-298	12-84	0-7	4-21	3-18	5-47	9-110	2-9	0-2	11.7	- 65.34
M. W. Easterby	20-305	6-118	0-4	1-13	2-14	6-37	5-101	0-17	0-1	6.6	- 165.17
Mrs M. Reveley	17-106	0-3	0-2	5-16	0-1	0-8	12-74	0-2	0-0	16.0	- 17.55
J. L. Dunlop	16-63	1-20	3-6	0-3	0-1	5-17	7-16	0-0	0-0	25.4	- 6.93
J. L. Eyre	15-183	1-22	0-7	1-11	0-5	2-25	10-100	0-8	1-5	8.2	- 85.63
D. R. Loder	13-28	7-13	2-3	3-4	0-0	1-4	0-4	0-0	0-0	46.4	- 2.73
H. R. A. Cecil	12-25	5-9	1-3	5-9	0-0	0-2	1-2	0-0	0-0	48.0	**+ 0.78**
L. M. Cumani	11-25	2-5	2-4	5-9	0-0	1-3	1-4	0-0	0-0	44.0	**+ 10.93**
E. A. L. Dunlop	11-45	5-15	0-5	2-10	0-0	2-5	1-9	1-1	0-0	24.4	**+ 7.39**
N. Tinkler	10-134	2-42	0-14	3-18	1-4	1-11	3-40	0-3	0-2	7.5	- 60.25
D. Nicholls	10-140	0-6	0-4	1-25	0-2	0-9	7-86	2-7	0-1	7.1	- 64.96
Sir Mark Prescott	9-38	7-24	0-3	0-3	0-1	2-4	0-3	0-0	0-0	23.7	- 7.68
Sir Michael Stoute	9-36	2-10	2-3	3-10	0-0	2-8	0-5	0-0	0-0	25.0	- 7.06
D. W. Chapman	8-73	0-1	0-1	2-4	0-1	0-4	5-56	1-5	0-1	11.0	- 6.13
B. W. Hills	8-66	3-17	0-6	2-13	0-1	2-18	1-9	0-0	0-2	12.1	- 39.72

LEADING FLAT TRAINERS AT BRIGHTON (SINCE 1995)

	Total W-R	2yo Stks	3yo Stks	Other Stks	2yo H'caps	3yo H'caps	Other H'caps	App'ce	Amateurs	Per cent	£1 Level stake
R. Hannon	48-305	20-77	9-41	4-48	3-28	3-33	8-76	1-2	0-0	15.7	- 40.00
G. L. Moore	41-357	2-28	1-14	13-87	2-10	2-31	18-163	2-15	1-9	11.5	- 103.44
M. R. Channon	26-173	10-54	3-16	3-21	1-14	4-16	4-49	1-3	0-0	15.0	- 23.78
S. Dow	25-201	4-17	3-16	3-30	0-7	4-25	10-102	1-3	0-1	12.4	- 35.52
Miss Gay Kelleway	20-126	2-10	1-10	6-33	0-5	0-8	10-53	1-7	0-0	15.9	**+ 10.84**
B. J. Meehan	20-160	13-60	1-17	2-15	1-16	3-20	0-30	0-0	0-2	12.5	- 61.78
W. R. Muir	17-84	2-16	1-9	8-19	0-3	1-7	4-29	1-1	0-0	20.2	**+ 41.55**
K. T. Ivory	16-91	4-16	0-2	2-9	0-3	2-13	8-48	0-0	0-0	17.6	**+ 42.75**
Sir Mark Prescott	14-56	2-18	2-4	3-10	2-7	2-8	3-9	0-0	0-0	25.0	**+ 0.45**
J. Pearce	13-117	2-9	0-4	4-26	0-6	0-5	7-57	0-4	0-6	11.1	**+ 43.75**
J. L. Dunlop	13-55	5-14	2-7	2-8	2-5	1-8	1-12	0-0	0-1	23.6	- 3.91
M. L. W. Bell	12-61	4-22	1-3	3-8	0-4	2-10	2-13	0-1	0-0	19.7	**+ 6.12**
K. R. Burke	11-74	1-8	1-2	3-17	0-3	0-5	6-34	0-2	0-3	14.9	**+ 1.48**
J. M. Bradley	11-170	0-1	0-1	1-36	0-0	1-5	8-109	1-18	0-0	6.5	- 78.75
P. F. I. Cole	11-81	3-17	0-7	4-17	0-7	1-13	3-19	0-1	0-0	13.6	- 36.46
S. P. C. Woods	11-63	0-4	3-11	3-20	0-3	0-3	4-17	1-4	0-1	17.5	- 22.30

LEADING FLAT TRAINERS AT CARLISLE (SINCE 1995)

	Total W-R	2yo Stks	3yo Stks	Other Stks	2yo H'caps	3yo H'caps	Other H'caps	App'ce	Amateurs	Per cent	£1 Level stake
M. Johnston	17-93	2-22	1-6	3-12	0-0	4-21	7-30	0-2	0-0	18.3	**+ 16.25**
M. R. Channon	15-39	6-11	0-2	7-12	0-0	2-10	0-4	0-0	0-0	38.5	**+ 13.77**
J. L. Eyre	15-95	1-9	1-3	0-17	0-0	3-14	8-45	2-6	0-1	15.8	**+ 41.75**
Mrs M. Reveley	12-67	1-3	1-1	4-18	0-0	1-8	5-33	0-2	0-2	17.9	- 3.00
E. J. Alston	11-84	0-5	0-1	3-18	0-0	1-9	7-48	0-3	0-0	13.1	**+ 19.00**
M. Dods	9-89	0-9	0-3	3-26	0-0	0-7	5-38	1-6	0-0	10.1	- 14.50
T. D. Easterby	8-109	3-27	2-6	1-11	0-0	0-26	1-36	1-3	0-0	7.3	- 70.98
D. Nicholls	8-89	0-4	0-3	2-26	0-0	0-13	5-37	1-5	0-1	9.0	- 34.75
Miss L. A. Perratt	7-77	1-10	0-4	2-12	0-0	2-9	1-33	1-7	0-2	9.1	**+ 10.38**
Sir Mark Prescott	7-32	3-9	0-1	3-11	0-0	0-8	1-3	0-0	0-0	21.9	- 12.29
P. D. Evans	7-69	4-22	0-2	3-16	0-0	0-8	0-18	0-3	0-0	10.1	- 45.53
R. A. Fahey	6-56	0-8	0-3	4-13	0-0	1-11	1-21	0-0	0-0	10.7	- 14.50
M. H. Tompkins	6-41	2-8	0-2	1-13	0-0	2-7	0-10	0-0	1-1	14.6	- 2.00
M. W. Easterby	6-68	2-17	0-1	1-3	0-0	0-21	3-22	0-4	0-0	8.8	- 32.13
K. R. Burke	5-16	2-2	0-0	0-2	0-0	0-1	3-11	0-0	0-0	31.3	**+ 6.60**
E. Weymes	5-38	1-8	2-3	0-11	0-0	0-3	2-10	0-3	0-0	13.2	- 5.50

LEADING FLAT TRAINERS AT CATTERICK (SINCE 1995)

	Total W-R	2yo Stks	3yo Stks	Other Stks	2yo H'caps	3yo H'caps	Other H'caps	App'ce	Amateurs	Per cent	£1 Level stake
D. Nicholls	25-170	0-4	0-2	11-56	1-2	1-9	10-87	2-10	0-0	14.7	- 14.09
Mrs M. Reveley	21-126	0-4	3-7	10-32	0-1	0-12	7-64	1-4	0-2	16.7	- 42.17
B. W. Hills	20-68	5-14	7-14	5-11	0-4	1-7	2-15	0-2	0-1	29.4	**+ 10.25**
M. Johnston	20-124	5-36	3-9	4-14	1-15	3-17	2-28	2-5	0-0	16.1	- 31.19
M. W. Easterby	20-201	2-34	0-4	0-6	3-29	3-36	12-89	0-2	0-1	10.0	- 47.38
T. D. Easterby	17-140	3-34	2-9	2-17	1-18	7-24	0-30	2-7	0-1	12.1	**+ 17.03**
T. D. Barron	17-88	5-12	0-3	6-18	1-8	1-9	3-35	1-3	0-0	10.3	**+ 93.73**
J. L. Eyre	15-170	1-19	2-10	0-32	0-10	1-16	10-71	1-11	0-1	8.8	- 16.00
P. D. Evans	14-118	4-28	0-3	2-23	2-11	2-13	3-30	0-7	1-3	11.9	- 29.75
D. W. Barker	11-77	1-8	0-5	1-16	4-10	2-5	2-31	0-1	1-1	14.3	- 10.13
J. Pearce	10-37	0-1	1-3	0-6	1-3	0-1	5-16	1-3	2-4	27.0	**+ 46.82**
M. R. Channon	10-64	5-18	3-7	0-4	0-13	0-4	2-15	0-3	0-0	15.6	- 24.66
Sir Michael Stoute	8-18	3-6	4-6	1-3	0-0	0-2	0-1	0-0	0-0	44.4	**+ 1.60**
Sir Mark Prescott	7-48	4-23	0-2	0-5	2-8	0-4	1-5	0-1	0-0	14.6	- 17.93
P. F. I. Cole	7-16	4-6	0-3	2-3	0-0	0-4	0-0	1-1	0-0	43.8	- 1.22
R. Hollinshead	7-77	1-9	2-9	0-17	0-0	0-11	4-28	0-3	0-0	9.1	- 19.50

LEADING FLAT TRAINERS AT CHEPSTOW (SINCE 1995)

	Total W-R	2yo Stks	3yo Stks	Other Stks	2yo H'caps	3yo H'caps	Other H'caps	App'ce	Amateurs	Per cent	£1 Level stake
R. Hannon	18-149	4-48	2-10	5-18	2-9	2-14	2-48	1-2	0-0	12.1	- 42.13
J. M. Bradley	15-185	0-7	0-9	0-16	0-1	1-7	13-133	0-0	1-12	8.1	- 83.50
Sir Michael Stoute	14-38	5-10	6-10	2-13	0-0	0-3	1-2	0-0	0-0	36.8	- 2.91
L. M. Cumani	11-28	2-4	3-9	4-8	0-0	2-6	0-1	0-0	0-0	39.3	**+ 7.24**
J. L. Dunlop	11-65	5-28	2-7	1-6	0-2	3-12	0-9	0-0	0-1	16.9	- 24.03
D. W. P. Arbuthnot	10-58	2-12	0-0	0-5	1-3	1-4	4-30	0-0	2-4	17.2	**+ 77.50**
B. R. Millman	9-63	2-11	0-4	0-8	0-2	0-7	6-28	0-1	1-2	14.3	**+ 6.73**
M. C. Pipe	9-58	0-5	1-7	4-8	0-0	1-4	3-28	0-1	0-5	15.5	- 21.75
P. F. I. Cole	8-65	1-24	1-9	3-11	0-0	2-12	1-9	0-0	0-0	12.3	- 30.46
H. Candy	8-52	2-5	1-9	2-9	0-0	1-6	2-22	0-0	0-1	15.4	**+ 8.08**
L. MontagueHall	7-11	0-0	0-0	0-0	0-0	0-0	4-8	3-3	0-0	63.6	**+ 28.75**
J. H. M. Gosden	7-40	2-10	1-9	1-10	0-0	0-2	3-9	0-0	0-0	17.5	- 16.92
Sir Mark Prescott	7-28	3-14	0-0	1-3	1-1	1-6	1-4	0-0	0-0	25.0	- 12.74
W. R. Muir	7-79	1-7	0-6	0-13	0-3	0-5	6-40	0-2	0-3	8.9	- 24.75
M. R. Channon	7-106	3-41	1-9	0-4	0-2	1-11	2-36	0-2	0-1	6.6	- 63.50
B. W. Hills	6-43	2-11	2-7	1-6	0-1	0-10	1-7	0-0	0-1	14.0	- 15.88

LEADING FLAT TRAINERS AT CHESTER (SINCE 1995)

	Total W-R	2yo Stks	3yo Stks	Other Stks	2yo H'caps	3yo H'caps	Other H'caps	App'ce	Amateurs	Per cent	£1 Level stake
B. W. Hills	22-121	4-18	7-37	4-22	0-5	2-16	5-23	0-0	0-0	18.2	**+ 9.96**
P. D. Evans	21-224	0-42	0-8	3-16	5-23	4-25	8-99	1-11	0-0	9.4	- 23.50
Sir Michael Stoute	18-78	4-12	4-22	4-16	0-1	3-14	3-13	0-0	0-0	23.1	- 3.59
E. J. Alston	17-170	3-28	0-1	5-22	0-5	0-12	9-97	0-5	0-0	10.0	- 49.13
J. L. Dunlop	14-44	3-9	1-10	3-5	0-0	0-2	7-18	0-0	0-0	31.8	**+ 5.25**
R. Hannon	12-83	8-27	0-5	1-10	1-12	1-17	1-12	0-0	0-0	14.5	- 20.38
M. R. Channon	11-74	3-20	1-4	0-3	2-10	2-9	3-26	0-2	0-0	14.9	- 2.67
B. A. McMahon	11-86	4-20	1-6	3-7	0-2	2-13	1-36	0-2	0-0	12.8	- 7.29
M. W. Easterby	10-45	0-0	0-1	0-0	1-7	1-3	7-33	1-1	0-0	22.2	**+ 9.75**
M. Johnston	10-74	2-11	1-5	0-5	0-4	2-13	5-36	0-0	0-0	13.5	- 23.56
H. R. A. Cecil	9-37	2-3	3-10	4-15	0-0	0-2	0-7	0-0	0-0	24.3	- 15.65
B. Hanbury	8-45	1-3	1-11	2-4	0-0	1-9	3-18	0-0	0-0	17.8	**+ 18.88**
P. F. I. Cole	8-50	1-8	2-12	0-4	0-4	1-8	4-14	0-0	0-0	16.0	- 0.34
M. C. Pipe	7-33	0-0	0-0	4-8	1-1	0-2	2-21	0-1	0-0	21.2	- 10.37
G. Wragg	7-32	1-1	3-12	2-4	0-0	1-4	0-11	0-0	0-0	21.9	- 12.86
J. H. M. Gosden	7-39	1-3	1-13	2-10	0-1	3-9	0-3	0-0	0-0	18.0	- 7.43

LEADING FLAT TRAINERS AT DONCASTER (SINCE 1995)

	Total W-R	2yo Stks	3yo Stks	Other Stks	2yo H'caps	3yo H'caps	Other H'caps	App'ce	Amateurs	Per cent	£1 Level stake
B. W. Hills	59-321	21-105	8-52	19-63	5-30	1-12	5-56	0-2	0-1	18.4	+ **22.12**
J. L. Dunlop	41-208	16-82	4-17	8-39	3-14	3-17	6-38	1-1	0-0	19.7	- 5.27
J. H. M. Gosden	36-195	11-66	5-17	12-57	1-8	3-7	4-38	0-2	0-0	18.5	+ **5.57**
H. R. A. Cecil	30-138	10-33	4-24	14-64	0-0	0-4	2-13	0-0	0-0	21.7	- 12.73
M. Johnston	23-235	6-54	3-18	5-37	1-25	4-21	4-78	0-2	0-0	9.8	- 122.20
Sir Michael Stoute	21-111	8-43	1-13	8-37	0-2	1-2	2-13	1-1	0-0	18.9	+ **18.20**
S bin Suroor	20-55	6-13	9-15	5-22	0-2	0-1	0-2	0-0	0-0	36.4	+ **23.68**
D. Nicholls	18-203	0-8	0-3	1-20	0-4	0-9	12-140	5-19	0-0	8.9	- 75.50
R. Hannon	18-250	6-63	1-18	5-45	1-47	1-19	4-48	0-10	0-0	7.2	- 65.13
P. F. I. Cole	14-93	2-22	2-14	3-21	0-4	2-9	5-23	0-0	0-0	15.1	+ **0.64**
M. R. Channon	14-143	6-53	0-18	4-9	1-10	0-14	3-36	0-3	0-0	9.8	- 22.00
T. D. Easterby	12-166	0-38	0-3	5-10	4-28	1-19	2-65	0-3	0-0	7.2	- 78.18
R. Charlton	12-65	3-25	5-10	2-15	0-0	1-5	1-9	0-1	0-0	18.5	+ **1.50**
J. L. Eyre	11-203	0-15	0-2	0-10	1-5	3-20	7-124	0-23	0-4	5.4	- 103.25
I. A. Balding	11-108	2-25	1-5	1-14	1-11	0-4	6-45	0-4	0-0	10.2	- 36.92
Miss Gay Kelleway	11-73	0-9	1-4	2-10	0-0	0-4	6-36	2-10	0-0	15.1	+ **23.00**

LEADING FLAT TRAINERS AT EPSOM (SINCE 1995)

	Total W-R	2yo Stks	3yo Stks	Other Stks	2yo H'caps	3yo H'caps	Other H'caps	App'ce	Amateurs	Per cent	£1 Level stake
R. Hannon	21-173	11-48	4-17	3-25	3-10	0-27	0-43	0-3	0-0	12.1	- 54.16
M. Johnston	17-74	7-22	0-3	3-7	1-2	0-7	6-33	0-0	0-0	23.0	+ **12.67**
P. F. I. Cole	13-75	4-13	3-17	2-10	0-2	1-5	2-26	1-2	0-0	17.3	- 12.72
J. L. Dunlop	12-52	2-9	1-11	5-11	0-2	2-7	2-12	0-0	0-0	23.1	- 8.62
I. A. Balding	11-94	1-8	3-12	4-16	0-2	1-10	2-45	0-1	0-0	11.7	- 44.97
H. R. A. Cecil	10-39	0-0	7-17	3-13	0-0	0-2	0-7	0-0	0-0	25.6	- 2.21
S. Dow	10-134	1-19	0-8	1-13	0-4	2-12	3-71	3-7	0-0	7.5	- 45.31
D. R. C. Elsworth	9-42	1-6	0-3	5-8	0-1	1-4	2-19	0-1	0-0	21.4	+ **21.88**
P. W. Harris	8-58	0-2	3-6	0-7	0-1	0-6	5-36	0-0	0-0	13.8	- 2.38
G. L. Moore	8-89	0-6	0-1	1-12	1-2	0-10	6-53	0-5	0-0	9.0	- 19.50
B. J. Meehan	7-68	2-20	2-8	1-7	0-4	0-5	2-24	0-0	0-0	10.3	- 21.17
J. W. Hills	7-44	1-5	0-4	2-7	1-2	0-4	3-21	0-1	0-0	15.9	+ **4.75**
Sir Michael Stoute	7-60	0-2	2-15	4-22	0-2	0-11	1-8	0-0	0-0	11.7	- 39.79
W. R. Muir	6-37	0-3	0-0	2-12	0-2	0-0	4-20	0-0	0-0	16.2	- 0.33
N. A. Callaghan	6-29	2-8	0-2	0-3	0-3	0-2	4-10	0-1	0-0	20.7	+ **3.25**
P. Mitchell	6-43	0-4	0-2	0-3	0-0	0-2	5-29	1-3	0-0	14.0	- 9.30

LEADING FLAT TRAINERS AT FOLKESTONE (SINCE 1995)

	Total W-R	2yo Stks	3yo Stks	Other Stks	2yo H'caps	3yo H'caps	Other H'caps	App'ce	Amateurs	Per cent	£1 Level stake
R. Hannon	16-146	7-57	4-18	1-20	1-8	0-10	3-28	0-5	0-0	11.0	- 30.21
S. C. Williams	13-59	3-12	1-7	3-7	0-2	2-11	4-16	0-4	0-0	22.0	+ **29.03**
J. L. Dunlop	12-60	4-20	1-7	4-14	0-2	1-11	2-5	0-1	0-0	20.0	- 15.13
J. Pearce	11-77	0-7	0-0	4-16	0-0	1-3	3-44	1-4	2-3	14.3	+ **8.00**
G. L. Moore	11-112	2-18	1-4	0-18	0-3	1-7	5-51	2-5	0-6	9.8	- 55.07
Miss Gay Kelleway	10-66	2-8	0-2	6-18	0-2	0-4	1-28	0-3	1-1	15.2	- 9.50
N. A. Callaghan	10-42	3-13	0-1	1-5	1-5	2-12	2-5	1-1	0-0	23.8	+ **27.54**
W. R. Muir	10-62	3-17	2-8	4-15	0-3	0-3	1-15	0-1	0-0	16.1	- 2.54
M. R. Channon	10-99	4-35	4-15	1-12	0-4	0-11	1-15	0-7	0-0	10.1	- 55.13
Sir Mark Prescott	9-41	4-22	0-0	3-7	0-3	1-4	0-4	0-0	1-1	22.0	- 6.85
P. F. I. Cole	9-64	2-22	1-5	0-9	1-3	2-12	2-9	1-3	0-1	14.1	- 3.25
J. M. Bradley	9-65	0-2	1-2	4-21	0-0	0-0	2-29	1-7	1-4	13.9	- 14.13
C. A. Horgan	8-39	0-3	0-3	1-6	0-0	0-2	7-23	0-1	0-1	20.5	+ **6.25**
P. W. Harris	7-46	2-10	1-2	1-4	0-3	0-4	3-22	0-1	0-0	15.2	+ **11.50**
D. R. C. Elsworth	7-40	1-8	0-4	2-11	0-0	0-2	4-12	0-2	0-1	17.5	+ **35.83**
M. L. W. Bell	7-54	3-16	1-8	2-8	0-2	1-8	0-7	0-5	0-0	13.0	- 19.75

LEADING FLAT TRAINERS AT GOODWOOD (SINCE 1995)

	Total W-R	2yo Stks	3yo Stks	Other Stks	2yo H'caps	3yo H'caps	Other H'caps	App'ce	Amateurs	Per cent	£1 Level stake
R. Hannon	42-435	17-127	6-42	5-50	3-37	4-60	7-115	0-2	0-2	9.7	- 170.51
J. H. M. Gosden	41-189	9-37	14-48	8-39	0-0	1-21	9-42	0-1	0-1	21.7	+ 19.49
P. F. I. Cole	36-167	13-51	5-24	5-19	2-9	5-30	6-34	0-0	0-0	21.6	+ 23.18
Sir Michael Stoute	30-130	4-15	6-31	8-31	0-1	7-26	5-26	0-0	0-0	23.1	+ 3.11
H. R. A. Cecil	29-122	10-24	6-27	7-10	0-0	3-11	3-20	0-0	0-0	23.8	- 6.74
S bin Suroor	27-74	2-7	15-20	9-39	0-0	0-2	1-6	0-0	0-0	36.5	+ 23.06
J. L. Dunlop	26-276	7-82	7-38	3-48	0-12	1-43	8-53	0-0	0-0	9.4	- 134.63
M. R. Channon	21-198	8-62	5-13	2-13	1-19	1-27	3-57	0-6	1-1	10.6	- 3.75
M. Johnston	20-137	0-15	0-5	7-27	4-9	3-25	6-54	0-2	0-0	14.6	+ 24.00
G. L. Moore	19-182	1-15	1-6	0-10	1-6	1-13	14-116	0-6	1-10	10.4	+ 8.00
I. A. Balding	19-183	0-28	1-14	4-17	3-8	1-24	10-89	0-3	0-0	10.4	- 39.88
E. A. L. Dunlop	17-94	3-16	4-21	3-15	1-2	2-14	3-25	1-1	0-0	18.1	+ 9.76
D. R. C. Elsworth	16-124	1-19	3-20	4-20	0-2	1-8	5-50	2-5	0-0	12.9	- 16.15
D. Nicholls	15-83	0-0	0-0	1-4	0-0	1-4	12-69	1-6	0-0	18.1	+ 39.42
L. M. Cumani	13-111	5-18	3-26	1-15	0-3	2-23	2-26	0-0	0-0	11.7	- 44.31
R. Charlton	13-83	4-13	4-25	2-10	0-4	1-10	2-21	0-0	0-0	15.7	+ 2.84

LEADING FLAT TRAINERS AT HAMILTON (SINCE 1995)

	Total W-R	2yo Stks	3yo Stks	Other Stks	2yo H'caps	3yo H'caps	Other H'caps	App'ce	Amateurs	Per cent	£1 Level stake
Miss L. A. Perratt	49-512	8-53	0-11	8-66	2-9	3-19	18-267	5-52	5-35	9.6	+ 27.67
M. Johnston	42-221	10-72	1-8	7-18	4-11	2-11	17-94	1-7	0-0	19.0	- 43.09
J. S. Goldie	20-263	0-20	0-2	1-39	0-6	0-7	14-149	5-23	0-17	7.6	- 94.25
P. C. Haslam	20-114	4-15	3-7	3-8	0-3	1-8	9-61	0-9	0-3	17.5	+ 75.68
D. W. Chapman	19-117	0-1	0-0	1-7	0-2	0-1	10-76	3-14	5-16	16.2	+ 156.25
M. R. Channon	18-77	9-25	1-13	2-9	1-1	1-6	3-20	1-3	0-0	23.4	+ 18.00
Mrs M. Reveley	17-117	1-5	2-5	6-24	0-0	0-2	7-76	1-4	0-1	14.5	- 44.02
D. HaydnJones	15-83	1-9	0-0	2-5	0-3	3-6	9-51	0-6	0-3	18.1	- 16.75
Sir Mark Prescott	12-41	6-17	0-1	2-6	0-1	2-6	1-9	1-1	0-1	29.3	3.33
J. Hetherton	12-74	0-5	1-4	4-17	0-0	0-1	6-43	1-3	0-1	16.2	+ 13.50
R. A. Fahey	11-63	1-10	0-2	3-4	1-2	1-5	4-34	0-4	1-2	17.5	+ 6.75
J. Pearce	11-52	1-2	0-0	1-9	0-0	0-0	6-30	0-1	3-10	21.2	+ 5.88
D. A. Nolan	11-299	0-4	0-2	1-56	0-0	0-1	8-178	1-29	1-29	3.7	- 209.75
S. C. Williams	11-27	2-3	3-7	2-2	0-4	0-3	4-7	0-1	0-0	40.7	+ 32.25
J. L. Eyre	11-134	0-8	0-1	3-26	0-1	1-4	7-82	0-4	0-8	8.2	- 67.34
R. M. McKellar	11-160	0-5	1-3	0-17	0-2	0-4	7-94	2-21	1-14	6.9	- 34.50

LEADING FLAT TRAINERS AT HAYDOCK (SINCE 1995)

	Total W-R	2yo Stks	3yo Stks	Other Stks	2yo H'caps	3yo H'caps	Other H'caps	App'ce	Amateurs	Per cent	£1 Level stake
J. L. Dunlop	39-149	14-41	3-12	5-28	0-0	9-32	8-36	0-0	0-0	26.2	+ 22.02
B. W. Hills	29-144	10-36	7-20	6-31	0-3	2-29	4-25	0-0	0-0	20.1	+ 10.14
J. H. M. Gosden	26-132	4-21	6-32	7-32	0-0	4-20	5-25	0-0	0-2	19.7	6.41
H. R. A. Cecil	21-59	6-8	3-13	8-23	0-0	2-7	2-8	0-0	0-0	35.6	+ 11.21
T. D. Easterby	18-166	4-57	1-9	5-16	0-7	2-25	6-48	0-4	0-0	10.8	- 87.18
B. J. Meehan	15-74	6-25	2-8	3-11	1-5	2-8	1-15	0-0	0-2	20.3	- 4.55
Mrs M. Reveley	14-109	0-8	0-4	4-15	0-1	0-6	10-72	0-2	0-1	12.8	- 34.64
M. A. Jarvis	14-62	3-19	2-14	4-11	0-0	3-7	2-11	0-0	0-0	22.6	+ 22.70
R. Hannon	14-165	7-50	2-19	1-31	0-7	2-32	2-25	0-1	0-0	8.5	- 96.13
M. Johnston	14-163	6-40	0-11	3-23	0-3	3-33	2-49	0-4	0-0	8.6	- 65.07
E. A. L. Dunlop	13-76	2-17	3-14	4-14	1-1	2-15	1-15	0-0	0-0	17.1	- 11.88
R. A. Fahey	13-68	2-15	1-3	2-9	0-4	4-17	3-15	1-5	0-0	19.1	+ 48.25
L. M. Cumani	12-63	1-3	4-15	2-19	0-0	1-14	3-11	1-1	0-0	19.1	- 12.08
P. F. I. Cole	12-93	5-19	0-10	2-14	0-0	3-24	2-26	0-0	0-0	12.9	- 28.75
B. A. McMahon	12-163	1-28	2-13	0-20	0-7	3-22	5-68	1-4	0-1	7.4	- 54.38
Sir Michael Stoute	11-73	4-18	4-23	3-15	0-0	0-10	0-7	0-0	0-0	15.1	- 33.27
P. W. Harris	10-65	2-14	1-4	2-8	0-0	0-16	5-23	0-0	0-0	15.4	+ 15.75

LEADING FLAT TRAINERS AT KEMPTON (SINCE 1995)

	Total W-R	2yo Stks	3yo Stks	Other Stks	2yo H'caps	3yo H'caps	Other H'caps	App'ce	Amateurs	Per cent	£1 Level stake
R. Hannon	38-334	16-103	8-50	3-33	0-10	3-41	6-86	2-11	0-0	11.4	- 66.94
J. L. Dunlop	21-144	5-49	8-39	5-13	1-1	0-15	2-27	0-0	0-0	14.6	- 48.70
Sir Michael Stoute	20-119	4-37	10-41	4-22	0-0	0-4	2-15	0-0	0-0	16.8	- 28.09
H. R. A. Cecil	19-78	2-8	14-44	1-16	0-0	0-1	2-9	0-0	0-0	24.4	**+ 3.83**
B. J. Meehan	16-142	4-48	3-17	2-11	2-7	1-18	4-41	0-0	0-0	11.3	- 14.02
D. R. C. Elsworth	15-121	3-31	1-24	2-12	2-4	1-4	6-42	0-4	0-0	12.4	**+ 1.50**
P. F. I. Cole	15-100	6-30	2-25	2-14	0-0	0-6	5-24	0-1	0-0	15.0	**+ 16.08**
J. R. Fanshawe	13-81	2-12	5-27	2-9	0-1	0-5	4-27	0-0	0-0	16.1	**+ 23.74**
R. Charlton	12-76	3-15	2-27	1-10	0-0	1-7	5-17	0-0	0-0	15.8	**+ 11.94**
J. H. M. Gosden	12-85	5-21	3-33	2-14	0-0	2-9	0-6	0-2	0-0	14.1	35.78
I. A. Balding	11-117	3-26	4-23	0-10	1-3	0-11	2-37	1-7	0-0	9.4	- 69.25
C. F. Wall	9-50	1-7	1-9	2-5	0-1	2-7	3-20	0-1	0-0	18.0	**+ 15.83**
B. Hanbury	9-60	1-7	5-20	1-7	0-1	0-7	2-18	0-0	0-0	15.0	- 17.22
P. W. Harris	9-117	3-28	2-26	1-12	0-0	1-5	1-45	1-1	0-0	7.7	- 51.54
M. R. Channon	9-121	4-40	2-21	1-8	0-3	2-19	0-27	0-3	0-0	7.4	- 0.79
Mrs A. J. Perrett	8-33	0-4	2-6	2-4	0-0	1-1	3-18	0-0	0-0	24.2	**+ 59.83**

LEADING FLAT TRAINERS AT LEICESTER (SINCE 1995)

	Total W-R	2yo Stks	3yo Stks	Other Stks	2yo H'caps	3yo H'caps	Other H'caps	App'ce	Amateurs	Per cent	£1 Level stake
J. L. Dunlop	33-189	13-87	4-24	5-29	0-6	8-27	3-16	0-0	0-0	17.5	**+ 6.14**
R. Hannon	32-227	9-63	9-43	2-32	3-23	4-21	5-40	0-5	0-0	14.1	**+ 39.64**
Sir Michael Stoute	23-89	11-48	5-12	6-20	0-0	1-4	0-4	0-1	0-0	25.8	**+ 1.00**
P. F. I. Cole	19-137	5-46	2-29	5-23	1-8	4-17	2-12	0-2	0-0	13.9	- 45.48
H. R. A. Cecil	18-71	11-31	3-14	4-18	0-0	0-2	0-6	0-0	0-0	25.4	- 8.65
B. W. Hills	18-100	9-47	2-10	5-12	1-5	0-13	0-10	1-3	0-0	18.0	- 20.20
J. H. M. Gosden	18-85	4-32	5-14	8-20	0-2	0-4	1-8	0-5	0-0	21.2	**+ 2.28**
B. J. Meehan	13-104	4-33	4-20	2-13	1-13	1-13	1-12	0-0	0-0	12.5	**+ 9.90**
B. Hanbury	12-46	2-7	2-12	4-11	1-2	2-3	0-9	1-2	0-0	26.1	**+ 7.65**
L. M. Cumani	12-59	2-18	4-16	1-8	0-0	0-5	4-9	1-3	0-0	20.3	- 19.19
J. L. Harris	12-73	0-4	1-7	4-20	1-2	0-1	4-33	2-6	0-0	16.4	**+ 65.00**
M. R. Channon	11-93	2-25	4-15	1-8	0-10	2-11	2-23	0-1	0-0	11.8	8.00
D. R. Loder	10-29	7-19	3-6	0-3	0-0	0-1	0-0	0-0	0-0	34.5	**+ 0.32**
R. Hollinshead	10-162	4-32	0-25	1-31	0-11	1-14	4-45	0-4	0-0	6.2	- 39.50
M. L. W. Bell	10-98	4-36	0-14	1-7	1-8	1-16	2-15	1-2	0-0	10.2	- 31.13
Sir Mark Prescott	9-54	1-25	1-5	2-9	2-3	1-4	2-6	0-1	0-1	16.7	- 7.38

LEADING FLAT TRAINERS AT LINGFIELD- Turf (SINCE 1995)

	Total W-R	2yo Stks	3yo Stks	Other Stks	2yo H'caps	3yo H'caps	Other H'caps	App'ce	Amateurs	Per cent	£1 Level stake
R. Hannon	35-288	22-119	2-19	3-45	4-20	3-43	1-41	0-1	0-0	12.2	- 109.55
J. L. Dunlop	28-148	13-76	5-14	4-20	0-8	4-17	2-12	0-0	0-1	18.9	- 65.88
H. R. A. Cecil	20-57	5-14	4-11	11-29	0-0	0-3	0-0	0-0	0-0	35.1	- 10.37
Sir Michael Stoute	18-79	7-33	3-12	7-24	0-0	1-3	0-7	0-0	0-0	22.8	**+ 19.71**
B. J. Meehan	15-107	10-47	1-5	0-5	1-5	3-22	0-21	0-0	0-2	14.0	- 28.38
C. F. Wall	13-58	2-9	1-6	0-8	0-4	3-10	4-15	2-5	1-1	22.4	**+ 10.83**
M. L. W. Bell	12-82	4-33	0-2	1-9	0-10	4-14	2-9	1-5	0-0	14.6	- 30.49
C. E. Brittain	12-104	2-18	0-14	2-23	0-3	3-16	3-27	2-3	0-0	11.5	**+ 2.30**
K. T. Ivory	12-106	2-28	0-2	0-7	0-5	1-17	8-42	1-4	0-1	11.3	**+ 32.25**
B. W. Hills	11-57	3-17	2-10	4-14	0-3	1-7	1-6	0-0	0-0	19.3	- 0.16
S. Dow	11-171	0-45	2-17	2-21	0-5	0-19	5-56	2-4	0-4	6.4	- 23.50
D. R. C. Elsworth	10-69	2-21	1-8	2-12	0-0	1-6	3-19	0-1	1-2	14.5	- 17.00
Sir Mark Prescott	10-74	2-35	2-5	1-5	1-4	1-11	3-13	0-1	0-0	13.5	- 44.20
G. L. Moore	10-170	4-35	1-9	0-28	0-2	2-18	2-64	1-11	0-3	5.9	- 91.18
M. R. Channon	10-117	3-47	1-4	2-12	1-12	1-21	2-19	0-2	0-0	8.6	- 31.50
B. Hanbury	9-46	1-9	2-5	1-13	0-1	1-6	4-12	0-0	0-0	19.6	**+ 4.08**

LEADING FLAT TRAINERS AT LINGFIELD- All Weather (SINCE 1995)

	Total W-R	2yo Stks	3yo Stks	Other Stks	2yo H'caps	3yo H'caps	Other H'caps	App'ce	Amateurs	Per cent	£1 Level stake
G. L. Moore	123-840	7-27	8-50	30-212	2-18	10-55	52-391	4-42	10-45	14.6	- 144.14
Miss Gay Kelleway	54-380	1-10	5-23	17-111	0-9	4-18	22-182	4-21	1-6	14.2	- 133.19
M. Johnston	54-312	3-20	12-35	12-52	6-17	10-67	10-112	1-9	0-0	17.3	- 50.91
R. Hannon	45-264	11-39	5-33	6-46	5-27	8-35	6-72	3-8	1-4	17.1	- 50.98
K. R. Burke	41-296	2-3	3-12	13-87	0-8	2-14	17-148	3-19	1-5	13.9	- 48.85
S. Dow	40-450	0-11	4-30	6-77	0-10	7-42	20-230	0-23	3-21	8.9	- 152.00
C. A. Cyzer	37-255	0-4	1-13	14-76	0-2	3-15	17-131	2-8	0-6	14.6	- 21.21
R. Ingram	34-267	0-10	2-14	14-68	0-4	0-12	16-140	1-12	1-7	12.7	- 4.97
D. W. Chapman	32-167	0-0	0-0	3-16	0-1	1-7	25-131	0-2	3-10	19.2	**+ 40.51**
T. G. Mills	32-150	1-10	3-9	12-37	0-7	2-17	10-60	3-8	1-2	21.3	**+ 5.46**
R. J. O'Sullivan	32-258	0-2	0-4	12-57	0-3	0-5	18-165	0-8	2-14	12.4	- 53.36
T. J. Naughton	30-245	1-16	6-38	10-56	1-8	6-27	5-86	0-8	1-6	12.2	- 88.03
P. C. Haslam	30-152	1-2	10-22	1-16	0-1	10-49	7-52	1-9	0-1	19.7	- 6.01
P. D. Evans	25-239	0-13	0-19	6-37	1-10	1-24	10-109	4-13	3-14	10.5	- 66.00
Miss B. Sanders	25-180	0-4	0-3	3-29	0-1	0-5	17-112	2-8	3-18	13.9	- 48.65
J. J. Bridger	25-506	1-19	0-33	8-157	1-8	0-11	13-234	1-19	1-25	4.9	- 194.25

LEADING FLAT TRAINERS AT MUSSELBURGH (SINCE 1995)

	Total W-R	2yo Stks	3yo Stks	Other Stks	2yo H'caps	3yo H'caps	Other H'caps	App'ce	Amateurs	Per cent	£1 Level stake
M. Johnston	25-151	8-33	2-3	2-12	1-7	2-15	9-78	1-3	0-0	16.6	- 40.74
J. S. Goldie	22-227	1-14	0-2	2-10	1-11	2-9	14-161	2-15	0-5	9.7	- 16.00
Mrs M. Reveley	22-135	0-7	2-6	7-24	0-2	0-1	11-89	2-6	0-0	16.3	- 37.48
M. L. W. Bell	13-31	1-4	2-3	2-4	0-1	1-4	6-13	1-2	0-0	41.9	**+ 42.95**
M. W. Easterby	12-60	3-13	0-0	0-3	0-7	2-6	7-28	0-3	0-0	20.0	**+ 27.25**
Sir Mark Prescott	12-37	2-11	1-1	1-5	1-5	4-7	3-7	0-1	0-0	32.4	- 1.34
E. J. Alston	11-87	1-9	1-1	3-11	0-3	0-8	5-53	1-2	0-0	12.6	- 16.63
M. R. Channon	11-48	3-15	0-1	1-10	3-5	0-3	4-14	0-0	0-0	22.9	**+ 6.79**
A. Berry	10-55	4-13	0-0	3-7	1-8	0-2	2-23	0-1	0-1	18.2	**+ 0.88**
P. D. Evans	10-97	6-31	0-0	0-8	1-10	0-9	2-36	1-2	0-1	10.3	- 63.45
J. L. Eyre	10-155	0-14	0-4	2-12	0-5	0-10	8-101	0-6	0-3	6.5	- 54.00
D. Nicholls	10-88	0-8	0-1	3-14	0-3	2-9	3-47	2-4	0-2	11.4	- 30.50
T. D. Easterby	9-43	1-8	1-1	1-5	0-4	1-7	4-17	1-1	0-0	20.9	**+ 19.83**
S. C. Williams	9-48	0-4	1-6	1-5	1-6	1-9	5-17	0-1	0-0	18.8	- 5.13
N. Tinkler	9-56	3-15	0-3	3-5	0-1	0-8	3-23	0-0	0-1	16.1	- 20.12
T. J. Etherington	8-45	1-7	1-1	1-2	0-2	0-6	5-26	0-0	0-1	17.8	**+ 12.49**

LEADING FLAT TRAINERS AT NEWBURY (SINCE 1995)

	Total W-R	2yo Stks	3yo Stks	Other Stks	2yo H'caps	3yo H'caps	Other H'caps	App'ce	Amateurs	Per cent	£1 Level stake
J. H. M. Gosden	38-180	13-44	10-59	11-35	0-2	2-12	2-28	0-0	0-0	21.1	**+ 64.92**
J. L. Dunlop	32-238	2-87	10-41	9-32	0-13	5-24	6-41	0-0	0-0	13.5	- 58.33
P. F. I. Cole	28-200	9-56	5-31	6-37	2-8	3-27	3-40	0-1	0-0	14.0	**+ 51.35**
R. Hannon	26-532	11-198	6-82	1-47	2-35	1-44	5-113	0-13	0-0	4.9	- 342.86
H. R. A. Cecil	24-124	4-14	10-55	6-33	0-0	1-5	3-17	0-0	0-0	19.4	**+ 4.48**
I. A. Balding	22-237	10-73	2-36	4-25	1-4	1-25	4-72	0-2	0-0	9.3	- 102.86
B. W. Hills	22-296	13-133	1-50	3-33	1-8	0-17	4-54	0-1	0-0	7.4	- 150.63
R. Charlton	16-134	4-31	6-45	2-16	0-2	1-11	3-26	0-3	0-0	11.9	- 52.01
B. J. Meehan	14-258	5-105	3-37	1-17	1-28	2-18	2-50	0-3	0-0	5.4	- 100.00
D. R. C. Elsworth	14-169	3-44	2-26	2-16	1-6	1-7	4-62	1-8	0-0	8.3	- 73.55
Sir Michael Stoute	14-113	2-23	3-30	7-37	0-3	1-7	1-13	0-0	0-0	12.4	- 21.75
M. R. Channon	14-238	7-90	1-34	0-7	2-28	1-17	3-56	0-6	0-0	5.9	- 126.90
L. M. Cumani	13-62	2-8	5-22	3-15	1-1	0-5	2-11	0-0	0-0	21.0	- 7.31
G. B. Balding	10-78	1-16	1-6	0-2	0-4	0-5	6-38	2-7	0-0	12.8	**+ 38.83**
M. Johnston	10-66	2-12	1-2	1-10	1-5	0-6	5-30	0-1	0-0	15.2	**+ 1.75**
E. A. L. Dunlop	9-67	3-17	1-12	0-9	1-1	1-7	3-20	0-1	0-0	13.4	- 13.88

LEADING FLAT TRAINERS AT NEWCASTLE (SINCE 1995)

	Total W-R	2yo Stks	3yo Stks	Other Stks	2yo H'caps	3yo H'caps	Other H'caps	App'ce	Amateurs	Per cent	£1 Level stake
M. Johnston	44-246	14-76	1-9	8-38	1-9	2-27	18-85	0-2	0-0	17.9	- 24.96
J. L. Dunlop	22-76	8-16	2-8	4-15	0-3	3-11	5-23	0-0	0-0	29.0	- 1.41
T. D. Easterby	18-189	6-57	0-4	2-12	1-16	3-34	6-65	0-0	0-1	9.5	- 71.22
M. L. W. Bell	16-61	2-13	3-6	3-10	2-5	3-9	2-17	1-1	0-0	26.2	**+ 35.60**
Mrs M. Reveley	16-156	0-14	0-6	2-27	0-0	2-13	11-88	1-8	0-0	10.3	- 47.75
Sir Michael Stoute	14-65	6-18	2-7	4-14	0-0	1-9	1-17	0-0	0-0	21.5	- 22.04
H. R. A. Cecil	13-32	1-5	2-5	8-14	0-0	0-0	2-8	0-0	0-0	40.6	**+ 15.95**
R. A. Fahey	12-80	4-21	0-1	1-3	0-0	3-11	4-44	0-0	0-0	15.0	**+ 18.50**
M. W. Easterby	12-180	4-45	0-1	0-5	1-14	2-27	5-87	0-1	0-0	6.7	- 89.07
Sir Mark Prescott	10-46	4-20	0-1	3-10	1-4	2-5	0-5	0-1	0-0	21.7	**+ 5.00**
J. L. Eyre	10-115	1-22	0-3	3-10	0-3	1-12	5-61	0-3	0-1	8.7	**+ 14.00**
M. R. Channon	8-52	6-20	1-3	1-5	0-5	0-6	0-13	0-0	0-0	15.4	- 24.43
B. W. Hills	8-57	5-13	0-5	1-12	1-6	1-6	0-14	0-1	0-0	14.0	- 30.03
P. W. Harris	7-24	0-2	0-1	3-5	1-2	1-2	2-12	0-0	0-0	29.2	**+ 26.25**
M. Brittain	7-100	3-23	0-1	0-8	0-3	1-13	3-51	0-1	0-0	7.0	- 4.50
D. R. Loder	7-22	4-10	1-2	1-5	0-0	0-0	1-5	0-0	0-0	31.8	- 2.88

LEADING FLAT TRAINERS AT NEWMARKET- Rowley (SINCE 1995)

	Total W-R	2yo Stks	3yo Stks	Other Stks	2yo H'caps	3yo H'caps	Other H'caps	App'ce	Amateurs	Per cent	£1 Level stake
H. R. A. Cecil	49-206	9-36	30-100	8-45	0-0	0-6	2-19	0-0	0-0	23.8	**+ 9.24**
B. W. Hills	30-325	10-87	3-75	5-44	2-15	3-34	7-70	0-0	0-0	9.2	- 69.50
R. Hannon	24-336	9-88	3-42	3-48	1-35	4-48	4-71	0-4	0-0	7.1	- 107.26
J. H. M. Gosden	23-199	8-62	8-61	4-30	0-3	1-13	2-28	0-2	0-0	11.6	- 46.10
S bin Suroor	22-91	8-22	10-35	4-30	0-1	0-0	0-3	0-0	0-0	24.2	**+ 22.15**
Sir Michael Stoute	22-227	4-54	9-83	6-48	0-3	1-15	2-24	0-0	0-0	9.7	- 118.41
J. L. Dunlop	21-245	7-62	3-44	5-47	0-8	0-27	6-57	0-0	0-0	8.6	- 80.13
D. R. Loder	20-86	13-39	3-14	2-18	1-4	1-3	0-8	0-0	0-0	23.3	**+ 10.65**
L. M. Cumani	18-152	3-36	3-47	7-27	0-3	3-17	2-21	0-1	0-0	11.8	- 68.57
P. F. I. Cole	13-129	8-40	0-20	3-17	1-8	0-18	1-26	0-0	0-0	10.1	- 57.54
M. L. W. Bell	12-133	3-37	1-19	1-11	1-13	3-25	2-23	1-5	0-0	9.0	- 46.02
E. A. L. Dunlop	11-123	3-42	2-23	2-16	4-9	0-9	0-21	0-3	0-0	8.9	- 74.30
J. R. Fanshawe	11-114	1-14	0-17	3-23	3-6	0-8	4-44	0-2	0-0	9.7	- 38.88
C. E. Brittain	11-176	1-37	6-45	3-29	0-6	0-17	1-41	0-1	0-0	6.3	- 53.79
M. R. Channon	10-110	6-36	0-11	0-9	0-12	3-17	0-21	1-4	0-0	9.1	**+ 15.23**
G. Wragg	9-104	0-31	2-34	3-17	0-0	2-6	1-15	1-1	0-0	8.7	- 59.51

LEADING FLAT TRAINERS AT NEWMARKET- July (SINCE 1995)

	Total W-R	2yo Stks	3yo Stks	Other Stks	2yo H'caps	3yo H'caps	Other H'caps	App'ce	Amateurs	Per cent	£1 Level stake
J. H. M. Gosden	39-208	9-71	14-51	10-40	0-1	3-24	3-20	0-1	0-0	18.8	- 10.97
J. L. Dunlop	36-239	13-101	4-20	10-44	2-11	2-24	5-39	0-0	0-0	15.1	- 32.32
H. R. A. Cecil	35-155	11-29	12-51	7-47	0-0	2-11	3-17	0-0	0-0	22.6	- 25.98
R. Hannon	31-328	5-87	3-37	9-51	4-39	4-61	5-49	1-4	0-0	9.5	- 108.63
L. M. Cumani	28-171	8-55	8-43	5-28	0-1	2-13	5-30	0-1	0-0	16.4	- 20.65
B. W. Hills	21-232	7-83	2-35	2-32	1-10	4-32	4-39	1-1	0-0	9.1	- 68.96
B. Hanbury	20-126	6-32	2-16	5-20	0-1	3-14	4-41	0-0	0-2	15.9	**+ 59.41**
Sir Michael Stoute	19-155	7-65	2-25	6-34	0-0	1-14	3-17	0-0	0-0	12.3	- 70.09
E. A. L. Dunlop	18-142	7-43	4-18	2-17	0-7	1-17	4-39	0-1	0-0	12.7	- 13.31
P. F. I. Cole	16-124	10-38	1-18	2-18	1-11	1-21	1-17	0-1	0-0	12.9	- 28.47
J. R. Fanshawe	14-116	1-15	3-11	0-21	1-3	0-21	9-45	0-0	0-0	12.1	- 34.71
M. Johnston	13-110	1-13	1-8	3-16	1-10	1-19	6-42	0-2	0-0	11.8	- 7.53
M. L. W. Bell	13-181	5-53	2-16	1-12	2-16	2-29	1-50	0-5	0-0	7.2	- 64.50
B. J. Meehan	13-144	3-39	3-18	0-12	0-13	2-30	5-31	0-0	0-1	9.0	- 48.74
W. J. Musson	12-123	0-7	0-12	0-6	0-0	1-4	9-80	2-13	0-1	9.8	- 14.50
D. R. C. Elsworth	11-66	5-15	3-8	0-13	0-1	1-10	2-19	0-0	0-0	16.7	**+ 4.46**

LEADING FLAT TRAINERS AT NOTTINGHAM (SINCE 1995)

	Total W-R	2yo Stks	3yo Stks	Other Stks	2yo H'caps	3yo H'caps	Other H'caps	App'ce	Amateurs	Per cent	£1 Level stake
J. L. Dunlop	30-176	10-63	2-22	6-22	0-5	8-36	4-28	0-0	0-0	17.1	- 39.17
H. R. A. Cecil	22-75	10-31	7-21	5-19	0-0	0-3	0-1	0-0	0-0	29.3	- 18.91
M. L. W. Bell	17-115	7-37	1-14	3-15	0-4	4-20	1-21	1-4	0-0	14.8	- 12.37
B. J. Meehan	16-98	6-35	5-18	2-8	1-7	2-18	0-11	0-1	0-0	16.3	**+ 25.57**
J. R. Fanshawe	16-80	2-15	3-19	4-15	1-1	2-8	4-22	0-0	0-0	20.0	**+ 43.03**
E. A. L. Dunlop	15-71	7-31	2-14	4-9	0-1	1-7	1-8	0-1	0-0	21.1	- 1.21
R. Hollinshead	15-184	2-34	0-23	1-26	0-5	4-43	7-46	1-7	0-0	8.2	- 63.75
B. A. McMahon	14-197	1-36	2-22	7-38	0-5	0-18	4-73	0-5	0-0	7.1	- 49.00
M. R. Channon	14-110	6-34	4-13	1-13	0-8	3-24	0-16	0-2	0-0	12.7	- 16.87
Sir Mark Prescott	12-59	3-22	3-12	2-5	1-2	2-5	1-11	0-2	0-0	20.3	**+ 33.03**
J. H. M. Gosden	11-67	4-25	4-15	0-11	0-0	2-7	1-9	0-0	0-0	16.4	- 4.43
B. Palling	11-132	4-30	1-11	1-16	0-11	1-12	3-48	1-4	0-0	8.3	**+ 29.00**
Mrs M. Reveley	11-103	0-1	0-2	3-18	0-0	1-11	7-65	0-6	0-0	10.7	- 48.34
P. W. Harris	11-98	3-24	0-8	2-10	1-2	1-12	4-40	0-2	0-0	11.2	- 30.88
C. E. Brittain	10-70	4-22	1-5	0-10	0-1	1-12	3-17	1-3	0-0	14.3	**+ 21.25**
B. R. Millman	10-43	4-12	1-3	1-3	2-2	0-10	2-12	0-1	0-0	23.3	**+ 66.50**

LEADING FLAT TRAINERS AT PONTEFRACT (SINCE 1995)

	Total W-R	2yo Stks	3yo Stks	Other Stks	2yo H'caps	3yo H'caps	Other H'caps	App'ce	Amateurs	Per cent	£1 Level stake
Mrs M. Reveley	17-140	0-5	0-8	5-32	0-4	1-3	10-82	0-5	1-1	12.1	- 38.73
J. L. Eyre	17-231	2-28	1-8	1-18	0-13	1-24	11-121	1-18	0-1	7.4	- 80.50
M. Johnston	17-150	5-41	1-8	3-18	4-16	2-20	2-44	0-3	0-0	11.3	- 41.65
D. Nicholls	16-153	0-6	0-5	2-16	0-3	0-4	12-108	2-11	0-0	10.5	- 8.25
J. L. Dunlop	15-65	2-11	1-6	6-20	0-7	2-11	4-8	0-2	0-0	23.1	- 1.71
I. A. Balding	13-69	3-11	3-14	0-5	1-6	3-7	3-23	0-2	0-1	18.8	**+ 17.83**
T. D. Easterby	12-147	8-44	1-11	0-9	0-17	0-19	3-47	0-0	0-0	8.2	- 56.63
B. W. Hills	12-68	4-15	2-11	2-11	0-8	1-9	3-14	0-0	0-0	17.7	**+ 23.29**
J. J. Quinn	12-85	1-16	0-1	3-9	0-6	2-5	6-45	0-3	0-0	14.1	- 1.67
M. W. Easterby	12-142	1-28	0-1	0-6	0-29	0-5	8-59	3-14	0-0	8.5	- 50.00
R. A. Fahey	11-74	4-17	3-7	0-8	2-7	0-5	2-28	0-2	0-0	14.9	**+ 22.00**
L. M. Cumani	10-45	1-4	1-11	7-22	0-0	0-1	1-6	0-1	0-0	22.2	- 11.14
H. R. A. Cecil	10-34	0-1	1-8	9-19	0-0	0-2	0-4	0-0	0-0	29.4	**+ 14.52**
N. Tinkler	9-82	1-21	0-8	3-6	2-10	0-2	3-33	0-2	0-0	11.0	- 0.50
M. Dods	9-124	1-4	0-6	1-22	0-7	1-2	6-78	0-5	0-0	7.3	- 15.15
Sir Michael Stoute	9-42	2-7	3-13	2-12	0-0	0-6	2-4	0-0	0-0	21.4	- 15.84

LEADING FLAT TRAINERS AT REDCAR (SINCE 1995)

	Total W-R	2yo Stks	3yo Stks	Other Stks	2yo H'caps	3yo H'caps	Other H'caps	App'ce	Amateurs	Per cent	£1 Level stake
Mrs M. Reveley	31-336	0-25	1-15	14-60	0-14	2-21	13-183	1-9	0-9	9.2	- 162.96
M. Johnston	28-174	10-65	1-2	5-17	0-7	4-22	8-58	0-2	0-1	16.1	- 3.50
J. H. M. Gosden	24-69	6-20	2-8	8-18	0-0	5-10	3-12	0-1	0-0	34.8	**+ 28.68**
J. L. Dunlop	20-80	8-24	0-1	3-9	2-5	1-14	6-27	0-0	0-0	25.0	- 2.13
J. L. Eyre	20-196	3-31	0-6	1-22	1-11	1-18	12-92	0-9	2-7	10.2	- 37.56
M. W. Easterby	19-204	3-54	0-0	0-8	4-34	3-29	8-65	1-6	0-8	9.3	- 31.50
T. D. Easterby	13-198	7-66	0-9	0-5	1-13	2-32	3-61	0-3	0-9	6.6	- 82.00
T. D. Barron	13-107	6-27	0-2	0-3	0-9	3-11	3-47	1-4	0-4	12.2	- 17.13
E. A. L. Dunlop	12-46	3-13	0-1	5-11	0-2	4-6	0-13	0-0	0-0	26.1	- 11.36
Sir Mark Prescott	12-57	4-26	2-4	1-3	0-3	3-9	2-11	0-0	0-1	21.1	- 17.88
E. J. Alston	10-91	0-5	0-3	1-13	0-3	2-11	6-49	1-4	0-3	11.0	**+ 22.50**
J. J. Quinn	9-59	2-13	0-3	2-5	0-2	2-4	2-25	1-4	0-3	15.3	**+ 15.13**
D. W. Chapman	9-99	0-0	0-0	2-13	1-5	1-12	3-53	0-5	2-11	9.1	- 10.50
M. L. W. Bell	9-64	4-18	0-2	2-9	0-3	3-17	0-13	0-1	0-1	14.1	- 14.69
D. Nicholls	9-123	0-7	0-4	3-24	0-3	0-8	5-66	1-6	0-5	7.3	- 75.00
C. A. Dwyer	8-37	0-6	0-1	1-3	0-2	2-8	4-14	1-1	0-2	21.6	**+ 9.25**

LEADING FLAT TRAINERS AT RIPON (SINCE 1995)

	Total W-R	2yo Stks	3yo Stks	Other Stks	2yo H'caps	3yo H'caps	Other H'caps	App'ce	Amateurs	Per cent	£1 Level stake
M. Johnston	30-163	8-39	3-14	5-17	0-1	3-32	10-57	1-3	0-0	18.4	+ **14.19**
T. D. Easterby	24-225	8-62	0-10	2-20	1-4	4-51	8-72	1-6	0-0	10.7	- 107.24
J. L. Dunlop	18-69	7-7	2-12	1-3	0-1	4-25	4-21	0-0	0-0	26.1	+ **3.27**
H. R. A. Cecil	16-37	0-0	4-8	10-20	0-0	0-3	2-6	0-0	0-0	43.2	+ **2.72**
B. W. Hills	15-74	2-9	5-14	7-20	0-1	0-15	1-15	0-0	0-0	20.3	- 16.76
M. W. Easterby	13-194	2-49	0-7	0-6	1-6	5-41	5-73	0-12	0-0	6.7	- 106.75
L. M. Cumani	12-58	3-6	3-15	3-18	0-0	0-9	3-10	0-0	0-0	20.7	- 22.15
M. R. Channon	10-55	1-19	2-3	0-0	0-2	4-16	3-13	0-2	0-0	18.2	+ **19.38**
J. M. Bradley	9-71	0-1	0-0	1-11	0-0	1-4	5-43	2-12	0-0	12.7	+ **43.00**
S. P. C. Woods	9-35	0-1	1-4	4-10	0-0	2-6	2-13	0-1	0-0	25.7	- 0.97
Mrs M. Reveley	9-92	0-4	0-4	1-13	0-0	1-8	7-60	0-3	0-0	9.8	- 16.42
J. L. Eyre	9-137	0-18	0-5	0-16	0-1	2-22	5-62	2-13	0-0	6.6	- 48.00
W. J. Haggas	8-33	1-4	1-2	1-4	1-1	0-6	4-15	0-1	0-0	24.2	- 0.88
Sir Michael Stoute	8-45	0-2	5-16	2-16	0-0	0-5	1-6	0-0	0-0	17.8	- 21.16
J. H. M. Gosden	8-57	0-3	2-15	6-29	0-0	0-7	0-3	0-0	0-0	14.0	- 38.79
J. S. Goldie	7-40	1-4	0-0	0-1	0-1	1-7	3-23	2-4	0-0	17.5	+ **42.50**

LEADING FLAT TRAINERS AT SALISBURY (SINCE 1995)

	Total W-R	2yo Stks	3yo Stks	Other Stks	2yo H'caps	3yo H'caps	Other H'caps	App'ce	Amateurs	Per cent	£1 Level stake
R. Hannon	53-452	23-174	11-45	7-49	0-0	6-54	5-110	1-17	0-3	11.7	- 133.16
J. L. Dunlop	33-162	12-75	3-17	5-26	0-1	7-23	6-20	0-0	0-0	20.4	- 32.50
M. R. Channon	19-215	7-78	1-22	0-13	0-0	2-23	7-66	2-12	0-1	8.8	- 83.43
R. Charlton	18-87	6-34	4-14	3-16	0-0	4-10	1-13	0-0	0-0	20.7	- 17.75
I. A. Balding	16-165	5-46	4-28	3-21	0-1	1-22	3-37	0-7	0-3	9.7	- 82.06
P. F. I. Cole	16-110	8-39	4-20	2-19	0-0	0-14	2-13	0-5	0-0	14.6	- 53.78
J. H. M. Gosden	14-78	3-24	5-20	4-17	0-0	0-4	2-11	0-2	0-0	18.0	- 29.71
D. R. C. Elsworth	13-186	8-40	1-35	0-29	0-0	0-18	4-55	0-6	0-3	7.0	- 115.98
G. L. Moore	13-69	0-6	0-3	1-5	0-0	2-7	6-32	2-11	2-5	18.8	+ **52.25**
Sir Michael Stoute	12-52	2-14	2-11	7-17	0-0	1-9	0-1	0-0	0-0	23.1	- 5.07
Miss Gay Kelleway	11-101	2-14	0-14	3-13	0-0	1-6	4-48	1-6	0-0	10.9	+ **31.63**
B. J. Meehan	10-117	5-53	0-7	1-6	0-0	1-15	3-28	0-1	0-7	8.6	- 44.17
R. F. JohnsonHoughton	10-37	3-11	0-1	1-4	0-0	1-4	4-15	0-0	1-2	27.0	+ **84.00**
S. Dow	10-109	2-18	0-10	1-7	0-0	3-15	1-46	1-7	2-6	9.2	- 19.42
A. P. Jarvis	9-48	4-17	0-6	1-1	0-0	1-5	2-13	1-5	0-1	18.8	+ **28.60**
H. R. A. Cecil	9-35	1-2	4-16	4-13	0-0	0-2	0-2	0-0	0-0	25.7	- 15.76

LEADING FLAT TRAINERS AT SANDOWN (SINCE 1995)

	Total W-R	2yo Stks	3yo Stks	Other Stks	2yo H'caps	3yo H'caps	Other H'caps	App'ce	Amateurs	Per cent	£1 Level stake
Sir Michael Stoute	39-171	10-27	8-31	12-56	0-1	2-22	7-33	0-0	0-1	22.8	+ **3.19**
R. Hannon	34-360	17-110	2-25	5-47	2-14	3-76	5-78	0-9	0-1	9.4	- 106.73
J. L. Dunlop	24-148	10-41	4-11	1-29	0-1	5-32	4-33	0-0	0-1	16.2	- 29.40
H. R. A. Cecil	21-104	5-17	5-28	7-43	0-0	3-9	1-7	0-0	0-0	20.2	- 22.53
J. H. M. Gosden	21-128	4-22	6-34	8-46	0-1	1-15	2-10	0-0	0-0	16.4	- 40.85
P. F. I. Cole	20-102	6-33	4-14	1-15	0-1	5-21	4-18	0-0	0-0	19.6	+ **34.24**
I. A. Balding	20-130	5-34	0-10	6-26	0-1	5-21	4-38	0-0	0-0	15.4	- 20.83
D. R. C. Elsworth	19-129	4-23	3-25	5-36	0-1	2-8	5-36	0-0	0-0	14.7	+ **8.13**
B. J. Meehan	17-173	8-60	1-12	3-18	1-13	1-34	3-35	0-0	0-1	9.8	- 17.24
M. Johnston	14-70	2-11	0-0	3-20	0-3	4-10	4-25	1-1	0-0	20.0	+ **55.58**
J. R. Fanshawe	13-75	1-4	5-14	5-19	0-0	0-11	2-27	0-0	0-0	17.3	+ **46.45**
S bin Suroor	11-30	4-6	1-2	5-21	0-0	1-1	0-0	0-0	0-0	36.7	+ **6.48**
M. R. Channon	11-142	5-49	0-9	1-11	3-12	2-30	0-29	0-2	0-0	7.8	- 74.13
B. W. Hills	10-109	4-39	1-9	1-16	0-2	3-23	1-18	0-2	0-0	9.2	- 50.00
J. R. Poulton	8-31	0-0	0-0	0-6	0-0	1-3	6-17	1-5	0-0	25.8	+ **66.00**
S. C. Williams	8-28	0-2	1-2	2-3	0-0	0-5	5-15	0-1	0-0	28.6	+ **24.13**

LEADING FLAT TRAINERS AT SOUTHWELL (SINCE 1995)

	Total W-R	2yo Stks	3yo Stks	Other Stks	2yo H'caps	3yo H'caps	Other H'caps	App'ce	Amateurs	Per cent	£1 Level stake
S. R. Bowring	65-537	1-20	0-32	10-82	2-6	8-42	35-304	7-39	2-12	12.1	- 64.45
R. Hollinshead	57-554	4-38	5-63	23-153	1-12	4-43	17-205	3-37	0-3	10.3	- 158.58
J. L. Eyre	56-442	0-15	0-21	12-57	0-5	2-15	32-253	4-25	6-51	12.7	- 124.81
M. Johnston	55-279	3-38	9-30	6-31	2-17	12-57	18-90	4-10	1-6	19.7	**+ 73.00**
D. Nicholls	55-389	2-9	1-22	23-107	0-5	0-29	22-185	4-23	3-9	14.1	- 89.79
Sir Mark Prescott	53-136	5-30	1-5	7-14	4-12	9-23	10-00	1-2	10-11	39.0	**+ 22.03**
Mrs N. Macauley	50-517	0-29	8-44	19-144	0-2	3-27	20-251	0-14	0-6	9.7	- 79.18
D. W. Chapman	43-647	0-6	0-10	10-109	1-12	1-22	26-400	0-38	5-50	6.7	- 345.69
T. D. Barron	38-208	4-22	7-21	4-33	1-8	8-33	13-84	1-5	0-2	18.3	**+ 19.49**
P. C. Haslam	33-202	2-23	4-21	2-14	0-15	14-51	11-61	0-10	0-7	16.3	- 53.25
M. J. Ryan	31-198	0-7	0-0	6-39	0-1	0-10	23-119	0-4	2-18	15.7	- 7.03
K. R. Burke	25-174	2-10	0-9	8-39	0-5	0-7	12-83	3-13	0-8	14.4	- 19.88
W. R. Muir	23-158	1-16	1-13	13-45	1-7	1-14	6-54	0-6	0-3	14.6	- 5.41
Miss S. J. Wilton	22-114	0-0	0-1	16-69	0-0	0-0	3-32	3-10	0-2	19.3	**+ 46.33**
P. D. Evans	22-215	4-37	3-11	3-30	2-7	1-18	6-90	1-10	2-12	10.2	- 94.94
N. P. Littmoden	22-343	3-31	2-27	2-68	0-11	3-18	8-131	4-33	0-24	6.4	- 108.18

LEADING FLAT TRAINERS AT THIRSK (SINCE 1995)

	Total W-R	2yo Stks	3yo Stks	Other Stks	2yo H'caps	3yo H'caps	Other H'caps	App'ce	Amateurs	Per cent	£1 Level stake
D. Nicholls	25-244	1-16	0-7	6-36	0-2	2-16	13-156	3-11	0-0	10.3	- 76.40
J. L. Eyre	21-210	2-29	0-8	3-38	1-3	1-18	12-104	2-10	0-0	10.0	**+ 3.75**
M. Johnston	20-108	4-24	3-14	0-15	0-1	2-10	11-43	0-1	0-0	18.5	- 23.69
T. D. Easterby	17-216	6-67	0-13	2-27	1-6	2-23	5-75	1-5	0-0	7.9	- 129.92
T. D. Barron	16-157	1-23	0-6	0-10	2-6	6-15	6-91	1-6	0-0	10.2	- 47.00
Sir Michael Stoute	14-40	0-3	8-15	4-15	0-0	0-1	2-6	0-0	0-0	35.0	**+ 18.49**
M. W. Easterby	14-241	2-101	0-2	0-8	1-6	2-17	9-101	0-6	0-0	5.8	- 112.52
J. L. Dunlop	12-38	0-10	6-11	2-4	0-0	2-7	2-6	0-0	0-0	31.6	- 0.67
B. W. Hills	12-31	3-5	5-13	2-7	0-0	0-2	2-4	0-0	0-0	38.7	**+ 3.44**
H. R. A. Cecil	10-27	0-0	4-14	6-11	0-0	0-0	0-2	0-0	0-0	37.0	- 2.87
M. R. Channon	10-46	10-24	0-0	0-6	0-1	0-4	0-11	0-0	0-0	21.7	**+ 2.32**
J. R. Fanshawe	9-32	2-6	1-3	2-7	0-0	1-3	3-13	0-0	0-0	28.1	**+ 23.78**
P. D. Evans	9-87	4-22	0-0	0-5	2-6	0-9	3-38	0-7	0-0	10.3	- 34.63
J. M. Bradley	8-97	0-1	0-1	0-5	0-0	1-7	7-66	0-17	0-0	8.3	- 34.00
Mrs M. Reveley	8-63	0-3	0-3	5-19	0-0	0-0	3-38	0-0	0-0	12.7	- 22.59
J. H. M. Gosden	7-24	0-2	5-9	2-10	0-0	0-0	0-3	0-0	0-0	29.2	- 2.79

LEADING FLAT TRAINERS AT WARWICK (SINCE 1995)

	Total W-R	2yo Stks	3yo Stks	Other Stks	2yo H'caps	3yo H'caps	Other H'caps	App'ce	Amateurs	Per cent	£1 Level stake
B. W. Hills	17-66	2-14	4-6	4-16	1-5	2-9	3-14	1-1	0-1	25.8	**+ 32.50**
P. F. I. Cole	14-75	4-20	2-9	3-11	2-5	2-12	1-15	0-3	0-0	18.7	- 3.24
M. C. Pipe	12-45	1-6	0-1	0-2	0-1	1-5	9-28	1-2	0-0	26.7	**+ 7.79**
B. J. Meehan	12-91	5-34	3-9	0-12	1-5	1-18	2-11	0-0	0-2	13.2	- 16.97
J. R. Fanshawe	12-50	4-14	0-4	5-22	0-1	1-3	2-6	0-0	0-0	24.0	**+ 2.08**
R. Hannon	11-115	9-44	1-8	0-19	1-8	0-15	0-18	0-3	0-0	9.6	- 67.86
B. A. McMahon	11-69	0-9	0-3	0-19	0-1	2-6	7-28	2-2	0-1	15.9	**+ 33.75**
J. M. Bradley	10-162	0-3	1-2	1-25	0-0	0-7	6-94	1-24	1-7	6.2	- 67.75
M. R. Channon	10-80	4-26	0-6	2-13	1-2	1-17	2-13	0-3	0-0	12.5	- 19.13
J. Pearce	9-61	0-4	0-2	3-9	0-2	0-3	5-35	0-3	1-3	14.8	**+ 20.63**
J. L. Dunlop	9-50	1-13	1-1	1-7	0-2	1-13	5-13	0-1	0-0	18.0	**+ 4.72**
R. Charlton	7-21	1-4	1-2	3-6	0-0	1-4	1-4	0-1	0-0	33.3	**+ 6.40**
B. Smart	7-37	3-13	0-3	0-2	0-2	0-1	2-12	1-2	1-2	18.9	**+ 63.68**
P. J. Makin	7-46	0-9	1-4	1-16	0-0	0-3	5-13	0-1	0-0	15.2	- 4.50
J. W. Hills	7-40	3-12	1-4	3-10	0-0	0-6	0-7	0-1	0-0	17.5	- 11.55
A. Berry	6-20	2-7	1-2	1-4	0-1	0-1	1-4	1-1	0-0	30.0	**+ 8.71**
W. J. Haggas	6-26	1-9	1-1	3-5	0-0	1-2	0-5	0-4	0-0	23.1	- 7.38
M. Johnston	6-40	1-6	1-4	1-6	0-3	0-6	3-14	0-0	0-1	15.0	- 6.00

LEADING FLAT TRAINERS AT WINDSOR (SINCE 1995)

	Total W-R	2yo Stks	3yo Stks	Other Stks	2yo H'caps	3yo H'caps	Other H'caps	App'ce	Amateurs	Per cent	£1 Level stake
R. Hannon	53-384	26-156	1-15	7-52	4-15	7-67	8-75	0-4	0-0	13.8	- 89.68
Sir Michael Stoute	21-75	0-11	9-26	10-27	0-0	1-6	1-5	0-0	0-0	28.0	**+ 12.42**
B. J. Meehan	21-202	11-88	1-11	6-14	0-13	2-44	1-30	0-2	0-0	10.4	- 112.04
I. A. Balding	18-122	1-28	1-19	4-17	1-1	5-24	6-30	0-3	0-0	14.8	- 17.15
J. H. M. Gosden	17-88	1-7	9-33	5-27	0-0	1-13	1-8	0-0	0-0	19.3	- 35.05
P. F. I. Cole	17-128	5-33	0-22	5-22	1-4	5-25	1-22	0-0	0-0	13.3	- 8.06
D. R. C. Elsworth	13-102	1-24	4-8	2-23	0-2	0-7	6-37	0-1	0-0	12.8	**+ 2.63**
C. F. Wall	12-99	1-15	0-11	1-9	0-1	6-30	4-33	0-0	0-0	12.1	- 20.25
H. R. A. Cecil	11-49	0-2	6-19	5-24	0-0	0-1	0-3	0-0	0-0	22.5	**+ 2.22**
K. T. Ivory	10-113	2-30	0-1	1-8	0-3	3-23	3-46	1-2	0-0	8.9	- 31.50
B. R. Millman	10-72	3-14	0-6	2-5	0-6	1-15	4-23	0-3	0-0	13.9	**+ 5.50**
W. R. Muir	10-128	1-28	0-16	5-19	0-1	1-25	3-38	0-1	0-0	7.8	- 50.86
M. L. W. Bell	10-94	5-41	0-3	0-8	0-4	0-17	4-17	1-4	0-0	10.6	- 31.75
B. W. Hills	9-84	6-33	0-11	2-18	0-2	1-9	0-11	0-0	0-0	10.7	- 43.63
W. J. Musson	9-98	0-15	0-5	0-13	0-1	0-6	8-56	1-2	0-0	9.2	- 39.75
J. R. Fanshawe	8-73	0-9	1-17	3-21	0-1	1-7	3-17	0-1	0-0	11.0	- 16.50

LEADING FLAT TRAINERS AT WOLVERHAMPTON (SINCE 1995)

	Total W-R	2yo Stks	3yo Stks	Other Stks	2yo H'caps	3yo H'caps	Other H'caps	App'ce	Amateurs	Per cent	£1 Level stake
N. P. Littmoden	85-614	18-112	4-57	17-127	1-8	10-49	32-237	3-13	0-11	13.8	- 46.56
R. Hollinshead	81-770	6-77	9-80	20-203	1-10	8-66	37-309	0-17	0-8	10.5	- 260.26
M. Johnston	52-309	13-48	7-22	7-41	2-13	7-57	16-120	0-5	0-3	16.8	- 53.77
Sir Mark Prescott	51-177	16-53	3-17	9-26	1-8	5-22	15-48	1-2	1-1	28.8	- 20.60
P. D. Evans	45-571	9-85	1-29	13-137	0-11	1-43	18-225	1-10	2-31	7.9	- 190.48
P. C. Haslam	44-264	5-51	13-28	4-25	1-14	12-54	6-79	2-9	1-4	16.7	- 19.28
B. A. McMahon	42-334	6-40	7-21	8-84	0-3	2-23	19-159	0-3	0-1	12.6	**+ 89.87**
D. W. Chapman	35-336	0-6	0-5	12-58	0-2	1-17	18-212	0-6	4-30	10.4	- 96.22
Mrs N. Macauley	30-320	1-15	2-16	7-85	0-2	1-23	19-175	0-3	0-1	9.4	- 87.65
J. L. Eyre	29-243	1-16	3-11	3-40	2-3	3-17	15-131	0-4	2-21	11.9	- 79.35
J. Pearce	28-171	0-5	0-1	9-44	0-1	0-6	15-97	0-2	4-15	16.4	**+ 40.12**
D. Nicholls	23-157	0-3	2-7	11-56	0-0	0-6	10-79	0-3	0-3	14.7	- 35.38
M. L. W. Bell	23-101	3-14	2-13	8-19	0-2	7-24	3-26	0-3	0-0	22.8	**+ 8.19**
D. HaydnJones	20-224	1-10	0-10	2-35	0-0	1-6	15-159	1-4	0-0	8.9	- 39.00
T. D. Barron	17-85	2-8	1-8	6-20	0-0	0-12	8-36	0-1	0-0	20.0	**+ 11.75**
W. R. Muir	17-163	0-21	1-13	9-43	0-4	3-12	3-65	1-4	0-1	10.4	- 74.77

LEADING FLAT TRAINERS AT YARMOUTH (SINCE 1995)

	Total W-R	2yo Stks	3yo Stks	Other Stks	2yo H'caps	3yo H'caps	Other H'caps	App'ce	Amateurs	Per cent	£1 Level stake
H. R. A. Cecil	33-108	13-35	6-22	11-42	0-0	1-3	2-6	0-0	0-0	30.6	- 25.49
M. L. W. Bell	23-135	8-33	1-7	3-10	1-7	3-19	4-48	3-11	0-0	17.0	**+ 8.28**
C. E. Brittain	20-213	2-38	4-25	5-40	0-9	4-21	5-72	0-7	0-1	9.4	- 55.17
J. H. M. Gosden	20-125	8-34	4-31	3-31	1-5	2-7	2-16	0-1	0-0	16.0	- 37.74
C. A. Dwyer	19-167	5-47	0-7	2-15	3-9	0-13	8-72	1-3	0-1	11.4	- 63.33
E. A. L. Dunlop	17-98	5-44	0-11	5-18	3-5	1-5	3-14	0-1	0-0	17.4	**+ 1.03**
Sir Michael Stoute	16-104	5-49	3-13	5-20	1-3	0-5	2-14	0-0	0-0	15.4	- 46.87
L. M. Cumani	15-71	3-19	4-16	5-16	2-4	0-0	1-16	0-0	0-0	21.1	- 6.45
J. L. Dunlop	14-52	4-7	1-6	3-10	1-7	4-13	1-9	0-0	0-0	26.9	- 6.60
N. A. Callaghan	14-74	2-16	0-6	1-7	2-9	2-4	7-30	0-2	0-0	18.9	**+ 15.80**
D. R. Loder	14-49	10-27	2-7	1-7	0-2	0-3	1-3	0-0	0-0	28.6	- 12.64
J. R. Fanshawe	14-104	2-23	4-17	2-21	0-1	1-8	5-34	0-0	0-0	13.5	- 37.38
J. Pearce	14-138	0-5	1-9	2-23	1-6	0-5	10-81	0-8	0-1	10.1	- 8.75
B. Hanbury	13-83	3-14	2-13	3-20	0-2	0-6	5-28	0-0	0-0	15.7	- 3.20
M. R. Channon	12-80	5-20	0-5	0-4	0-9	2-12	5-27	0-3	0-0	15.0	- 9.72
W. J. Haggas	11-82	2-27	2-11	1-7	0-4	3-5	3-26	0-1	0-1	13.4	**+ 15.07**

LEADING FLAT TRAINERS AT YORK (SINCE 1995)

	Total W-R	2yo Stks	3yo Stks	Other Stks	2yo H'caps	3yo H'caps	Other H'caps	App'ce	Amateurs	Per cent	£1 Level stake
Sir Michael Stoute	31-166	4-21	13-31	6-40	1-4	4-23	3-47	0-0	0-0	18.7	- 36.58
H. R. A. Cecil	26-111	5-14	7-26	8-36	0-0	0-5	5-30	0-0	0-0	22.5	- 12.62
M. Johnston	25-217	6-44	1-6	4-26	4-15	2-22	7-99	1-5	0-0	11.5	- 10.51
P. F. I. Cole	21-154	15-50	2-15	2-14	0-6	1-20	1-40	0-3	0-0	13.6	- 72.45
J. L. Dunlop	19-122	10-26	1-11	3-24	0-3	1-12	4-46	0-0	0-0	15.6	- 00.06
B. W. Hills	18-202	9-53	0-23	3-29	1-12	2-32	3-53	0-0	0-0	8.9	- 87.73
T. D. Easterby	17-197	6-51	0-4	2-16	3-26	1-22	5-77	0-1	0-0	8.6	- 73.13
L. M. Cumani	17-93	4-13	1-11	8-25	0-2	0-13	4-28	0-1	0-0	18.3	- 14.50
R. Hannon	16-138	6-45	1-3	4-22	1-12	0-22	4-34	0-0	0-0	11.6	**+ 9.75**
S bin Suroor	14-54	0-6	5-15	9-30	0-0	0-0	0-3	0-0	0-0	25.9	- 3.56
I. A. Balding	14-116	4-17	0-5	2-15	2-4	2-22	4-53	0-0	0-0	12.1	- 28.05
M. W. Easterby	13-181	0-25	0-0	1-3	1-26	0-6	10-110	1-11	0-0	7.2	- 37.67
D. R. Loder	12-44	5-13	0-7	2-8	1-2	2-2	2-12	0-0	0-0	27.3	**+ 9.23**
J. H. M. Gosden	12-92	4-21	6-24	0-12	0-2	0-7	2-26	0-0	0-0	13.0	- 53.30
D. Nicholls	11-174	0-4	0-0	2-19	0-2	1-7	8-136	0-6	0-0	6.3	- 62.00
M. R. Channon	10-86	6-32	0-3	0-5	1-7	1-13	2-26	0-0	0-0	11.6	**+ 26.75**

Five-Season Draw Analysis For British Flat Tracks

The following table shows the record of draw position categories over each distance on each track over the past five seasons. Distances which have not had a sufficient number of races run over them to produce a meaningful statistic are not shown.

ASCOT

Distance : *Flat 5f*

Draw Category	Winners	% Winners/Races
Low	17	30
Middle	17	30
High	23	40

Distance : *Flat 6f*

Draw Category	Winners	% Winners/Races
Low	23	39
Middle	18	31
High	18	31

Distance : *Flat 7f*

Draw Category	Winners	% Winners/Races
Low	21	34
Middle	22	36
High	18	30

Distance : *Str 1m*

Draw Category	Winners	% Winners/Races
Low	18	34
Middle	19	36
High	16	30

Distance : *Rnd 1m*

Draw Category	Winners	% Winners/Races
Low	15	25
Middle	24	41
High	20	34

Distance : *Flat 1m 2f*

Draw Category	Winners	% Winners/Races
Low	10	26
Middle	15	39
High	13	34

Distance : *Flat 1m 4f*

Draw Category	Winners	% Winners/Races
Low	20	24
Middle	35	43
High	27	33

Distance : *Flat 2m 45y*

Draw Category	Winners	% Winners/Races
Low	11	35
Middle	9	29
High	11	35

AYR

Distance : *Flat 5f*

Draw Category	Winners	% Winners/Races
Low	12	24
Middle	29	58
High	9	18

Distance : *Flat 6f*

Draw Category	Winners	% Winners/Races
Low	18	24
Middle	36	47
High	22	29

Distance : *Flat 7f*

Draw Category	Winners	% Winners/Races
Low	15	20
Middle	42	55
High	19	25

Distance : *Flat 1m*

Draw Category	Winners	% Winners/Races
Low	24	41
Middle	25	42
High	10	17

Distance : *Flat 1m 2f*

Draw Category	Winners	% Winners/Races
Low	7	14
Middle	23	47
High	19	39

Distance : *Flat 1m 2f 192y*

Draw Category	Winners	% Winners/Races
Low	6	20
Middle	14	47
High	10	33

Distance : *Flat 1m 5f 13y*

Draw Category	Winners	% Winners/Races
Low	7	26
Middle	11	41
High	9	33

BATH

Distance : *Flat 5f 11y*

Draw Category	Winners	% Winners/Races
Low	28	28
Middle	41	41
High	32	32

Distance : *Flat 5f 161y*

Draw Category	Winners	% Winners/Races
Low	25	32
Middle	25	32
High	27	35

Distance : *Flat 1m 5y*

Draw Category	Winners	% Winners/Races
Low	35	35
Middle	38	38
High	26	26

Distance : *Flat 1m 2f 46y*

Draw Category	Winners	% Winners/Races
Low	18	26
Middle	30	43
High	22	31

Distance : *Flat 1m 3f 144y*

Draw Category	Winners	% Winners/Races
Low	13	28
Middle	19	41
High	14	30

Distance : *Flat 2m 1f 34y*

Draw Category	Winners	% Winners/Races
Low	12	31
Middle	16	41
High	11	28

BEVERLEY

Distance : *Flat 5f*

Draw Category	Winners	% Winners/Races
Low	25	16
Middle	43	28
High	84	55

Distance : *Flat 7f 100y*

Draw Category	Winners	% Winners/Races
Low	33	23
Middle	61	42
High	52	36

Distance : *Flat 1m 100y*

Draw Category	Winners	% Winners/Races
Low	9	12
Middle	34	47
High	30	41

Distance : *Flat 1m 1f 207y*

Draw Category	Winners	% Winners/Races
Low	24	24
Middle	33	33
High	43	43

Distance : *Flat 1m 3f 216y*

Draw Category	Winners	% Winners/Races
Low	23	32
Middle	30	42
High	18	25

Distance : *Flat 2m 35y*

Draw Category	Winners	% Winners/Races
Low	8	22
Middle	14	39
High	14	39

BRIGHTON

Distance : *Flat 5f 59y*

Draw Category	Winners	% Winners/Races
Low	27	34
Middle	27	34
High	26	33

Distance : *Flat 5f 213y*

Draw Category	Winners	% Winners/Races
Low	34	32
Middle	48	45
High	24	23

Distance : *Flat 6f 209y*

Draw Category	Winners	% Winners/Races
Low	48	35
Middle	47	34
High	43	31

Distance : *Flat 7f 214y*

Draw Category	Winners	% Winners/Races
Low	24	19
Middle	50	39
High	53	42

Distance : *Flat 1m 1f 209y*

Draw Category	Winners	% Winners/Races
Low	29	33
Middle	34	39
High	25	28

Distance : *Flat 1m 3f 196y*

Draw Category	Winners	% Winners/Races
Low	32	31
Middle	41	40
High	29	28

CARLISLE

Distance : *Flat 5f*

Draw Category	Winners	% Winners/Races
Low	13	21
Middle	27	44
High	22	35

Distance : *Flat 5f 207y*

Draw Category	Winners	% Winners/Races
Low	13	22
Middle	29	50
High	16	28

Distance : *Flat 6f 206y*

Draw Category	Winners	% Winners/Races
Low	16	33
Middle	19	39
High	14	29

Distance : *Flat 7f 214y*

Draw Category	Winners	% Winners/Races
Low	11	21
Middle	24	46
High	17	33

Distance : *Flat 1m 4f*

Draw Category	Winners	% Winners/Races
Low	9	28
Middle	12	38
High	11	34

CATTERICK

Distance : *Flat 5f*

Draw Category	Winners	% Winners/Races
Low	23	26
Middle	34	38
High	33	37

Distance : *Flat 5f 212y*

Draw Category	Winners	% Winners/Races
Low	26	33
Middle	22	28
High	31	39

Distance : *Flat 7f*

Draw Category	Winners	% Winners/Races
Low	38	27
Middle	58	42
High	43	31

Distance : *Flat 1m 3f 214y*

Draw Category	Winners	% Winners/Races
Low	26	37
Middle	24	34
High	20	29

Distance : *Flat 1m 5f 175y*

Draw Category	Winners	% Winners/Races
Low	8	18
Middle	22	49
High	15	33

Distance : *Flat 1m 7f 177y*

Draw Category	Winners	% Winners/Races
Low	10	33
Middle	12	40
High	8	27

CHEPSTOW

Distance : *Flat 5f 16y*

Draw Category	Winners	% Winners/Races
Low	8	25
Middle	18	56
High	6	19

Distance : *Flat 6f 16y*

Draw Category	Winners	% Winners/Races
Low	19	35
Middle	23	43
High	12	22

Distance : *Flat 7f 16y*

Draw Category	Winners	% Winners/Races
Low	16	28
Middle	19	33
High	22	39

Distance : *Flat 1m 14y*

Draw Category	Winners	% Winners/Races
Low	18	31
Middle	19	32
High	22	37

Distance : *Flat 1m 2f 36y*

Draw Category	Winners	% Winners/Races
Low	13	27
Middle	19	40
High	16	33

Distance : *Flat 1m 4f 23y*

Draw Category	Winners	% Winners/Races
Low	13	33
Middle	18	45
High	9	23

CHESTER

Distance : *Flat 5f 16y*

Draw Category	Winners	% Winners/Races
Low	29	41
Middle	33	46
High	9	13

Distance : *Flat 6f 18y*

Draw Category	Winners	% Winners/Races
Low	15	42
Middle	16	44
High	5	14

Distance : *Flat 7f 2y*

Draw Category	Winners	% Winners/Races
Low	27	51
Middle	16	30
High	10	19

Distance : *Flat 7f 122y*

Draw Category	Winners	% Winners/Races
Low	12	34
Middle	19	54
High	4	11

Distance : *Flat 1m 2f 75y*

Draw Category	Winners	% Winners/Races
Low	18	38
Middle	17	36
High	12	26

Distance : *Flat 1m 4f 66y*

Draw Category	Winners	% Winners/Races
Low	15	34
Middle	21	48
High	8	18

DONCASTER

Distance : *Flat 5f*

Draw Category	Winners	% Winners/Races
Low	36	37
Middle	34	35
High	27	28

Distance : *Flat 6f*

Draw Category	Winners	% Winners/Races
Low	26	24
Middle	47	44
High	35	32

Distance : *Flat 7f*

Draw Category	Winners	% Winners/Races
Low	37	31
Middle	45	37
High	39	32

Distance : *Str 1m*

Draw Category	Winners	% Winners/Races
Low	27	40
Middle	21	31
High	19	28

Distance : *Rnd 1m*

Draw Category	Winners	% Winners/Races
Low	18	28
Middle	24	38
High	22	34

Distance : *Flat 1m 2f 60y*

Draw Category	Winners	% Winners/Races
Low	29	33
Middle	43	48
High	17	19

Distance : *Flat 1m 4f*

Draw Category	Winners	% Winners/Races
Low	22	35
Middle	22	35
High	19	30

Distance : *Flat 1m 6f 132y*

Draw Category	Winners	% Winners/Races
Low	14	39
Middle	11	31
High	11	31

EPSOM

Distance : *Flat 5f*

Draw Category	Winners	% Winners/Races
Low	3	20
Middle	6	40
High	6	40

Distance : *Flat 6f*

Draw Category	Winners	% Winners/Races
Low	11	20
Middle	28	51
High	16	29

Distance : *Flat 7f*

Draw Category	Winners	% Winners/Races
Low	21	33
Middle	28	44
High	14	22

Distance : *Flat 1m 114y*

Draw Category	Winners	% Winners/Races
Low	31	48
Middle	17	26
High	17	26

Distance : *Flat 1m 2f 18y*

Draw Category	Winners	% Winners/Races
Low	14	26
Middle	22	41
High	18	33

Distance : *Flat 1m 4f 10y*

Draw Category	Winners	% Winners/Races
Low	19	31
Middle	31	51
High	11	18

FOLKESTONE

Distance : *Flat 5f*

Draw Category	Winners	% Winners/Races
Low	20	31
Middle	25	39
High	19	30

Distance : *Flat 6f*

Draw Category	Winners	% Winners/Races
Low	25	34
Middle	22	30
High	27	36

Distance : *Rnd 6f 189y*

Draw Category	Winners	% Winners/Races
Low	15	28
Middle	17	32
High	21	40

Distance : *Str 7f*

Draw Category	Winners	% Winners/Races
Low	16	31
Middle	18	35
High	17	33

Distance : *Flat 1m 1f 149y*

Draw Category	Winners	% Winners/Races
Low	14	27
Middle	17	33
High	20	39

Distance : *Flat 1m 4f*

Draw Category	Winners	% Winners/Races
Low	12	22
Middle	26	47
High	17	31

GOODWOOD

Distance : *Flat 5f*

Draw Category	Winners	% Winners/Races
Low	19	37
Middle	16	31
High	17	33

Distance : *Flat 6f*

Draw Category	Winners	% Winners/Races
Low	39	31
Middle	44	35
High	41	33

Distance : *Flat 7f*

Draw Category	Winners	% Winners/Races
Low	31	25
Middle	43	35
High	50	40

Distance : *Flat 1m*

Draw Category	Winners	% Winners/Races
Low	16	15
Middle	45	42
High	46	43

Distance : *Flat 1m 1f*

Draw Category	Winners	% Winners/Races
Low	13	25
Middle	24	46
High	15	29

Distance : *Flat 1m 1f 192y*

Draw Category	Winners	% Winners/Races
Low	10	18
Middle	23	42
High	22	40

Distance : *Flat 1m 2f*

Draw Category	Winners	% Winners/Races
Low	10	28
Middle	13	36
High	13	36

Distance : *Flat 1m 4f*

Draw Category	Winners	% Winners/Races
Low	17	27
Middle	21	34
High	24	39

Distance : *Flat 1m 6f*

Draw Category	Winners	% Winners/Races
Low	7	26
Middle	9	33
High	11	41

Distance : *Flat 2m*

Draw Category	Winners	% Winners/Races
Low	8	40
Middle	10	50
High	2	10

HAMILTON

Distance : *Flat 5f 4y*

Draw Category	Winners	% Winners/Races
Low	21	20
Middle	41	40
High	41	40

Distance : *Flat 6f 5y*

Draw Category	Winners	% Winners/Races
Low	22	20
Middle	31	28
High	57	52

Distance : *Flat 1m 65y*

Draw Category	Winners	% Winners/Races
Low	16	18
Middle	40	44
High	34	38

Distance : *Flat 1m 1f 36y*

Draw Category	Winners	% Winners/Races
Low	15	21
Middle	34	47
High	23	32

Distance : *Flat 1m 3f 16y*

Draw Category	Winners	% Winners/Races
Low	14	27
Middle	15	29
High	22	43

Distance : *Flat 1m 4f 17y*

Draw Category	Winners	% Winners/Races
Low	11	24
Middle	19	41
High	16	35

Distance : *Flat 1m 5f 9y*

Draw Category	Winners	% Winners/Races
Low	14	29
Middle	22	46
High	12	25

HAYDOCK

Distance : *Flat 5f*

Draw Category	Winners	% Winners/Races
Low	21	23
Middle	25	28
High	44	49

Distance : *Flat 6f*

Draw Category	Winners	% Winners/Races
Low	27	24
Middle	46	41
High	39	35

Distance : *Flat 7f 30y*

Draw Category	Winners	% Winners/Races
Low	37	39
Middle	30	32
High	28	29

Distance : *Flat 1m 30y*

Draw Category	Winners	% Winners/Races
Low	22	27
Middle	30	36
High	31	37

Distance : *Flat 1m 2f 120y*

Draw Category	Winners	% Winners/Races
Low	24	28
Middle	28	33
High	34	40

Distance : *Flat 1m 3f 200y*

Draw Category	Winners	% Winners/Races
Low	24	27
Middle	33	38
High	31	35

Distance : *Flat 1m 6f*

Draw Category	Winners	% Winners/Races
Low	11	21
Middle	23	44
High	18	35

KEMPTON

Distance : *Flat 5f*

Draw Category	Winners	% Winners/Races
Low	8	35
Middle	11	48
High	4	17

Distance : *Flat 6f*

Draw Category	Winners	% Winners/Races
Low	25	30
Middle	22	27
High	35	43

Distance : *Jub 7f*

Draw Category	Winners	% Winners/Races
Low	23	30
Middle	26	34
High	27	36

Distance : *Jub 1m*

Draw Category	Winners	% Winners/Races
Low	19	33
Middle	22	39
High	16	28

Distance : *Rnd 1m 1f*

Draw Category	Winners	% Winners/Races
Low	10	32
Middle	11	35
High	10	32

Distance : *Jub 1m 2f*

Draw Category	Winners	% Winners/Races
Low	15	38
Middle	13	33
High	11	28

Distance : *Flat 1m 4f*

Draw Category	Winners	% Winners/Races
Low	14	27
Middle	27	53
High	10	20

LEICESTER

Distance : *Flat 5f 2y*

Draw Category	Winners	% Winners/Races
Low	17	28
Middle	24	40
High	19	32

Distance : *Flat 5f 218y*

Draw Category	Winners	% Winners/Races
Low	26	26
Middle	41	41
High	33	33

Distance : *Flat 7f 9y*

Draw Category	Winners	% Winners/Races
Low	38	27
Middle	58	41
High	46	32

Distance : *Flat 1m 8y*

Draw Category	Winners	% Winners/Races
Low	32	27
Middle	44	37
High	43	36

Distance : *Flat 1m 1f 218y*

Draw Category	Winners	% Winners/Races
Low	27	28
Middle	31	33
High	37	39

Distance : *Flat 1m 3f 183y*

Draw Category	Winners	% Winners/Races
Low	16	19
Middle	45	54
High	23	27

LINGFIELD AW

Distance : *Equi 5f*

Draw Category	Winners	% Winners/Races
Low	49	34
Middle	60	41
High	36	25

Distance : *Equi 6f*

Draw Category	Winners	% Winners/Races
Low	64	32
Middle	74	37
High	61	31

Distance : *Equi 6f*

Draw Category	Winners	% Winners/Races
Low	64	32
Middle	74	37
High	61	31

Distance : *Equi 7f*

Draw Category	Winners	% Winners/Races
Low	61	23
Middle	109	41
High	99	37

Distance : *Equi 1m*

Draw Category	Winners	% Winners/Races
Low	84	28
Middle	120	41
High	91	31

Distance : *Equi 1m 2f*

Draw Category	Winners	% Winners/Races
Low	102	31
Middle	140	43
High	82	25

Distance : *Equi 1m 4f*

Draw Category	Winners	% Winners/Races
Low	41	27
Middle	59	38
High	54	35

Distance : *Equi 1m 5f*

Draw Category	Winners	% Winners/Races
Low	16	25
Middle	26	41
High	22	34

Distance : *Equi 2m*

Draw Category	Winners	% Winners/Races
Low	16	20
Middle	39	48
High	26	32

LINGFIELD TURF

Distance : *Flat 5f*

Draw Category	Winners	% Winners/Races
Low	29	31
Middle	37	40
High	27	29

Distance : *Flat 6f*

Draw Category	Winners	% Winners/Races
Low	25	19
Middle	47	36
High	59	45

Distance : *Flat 7f*

Draw Category	Winners	% Winners/Races
Low	29	22
Middle	54	42
High	46	36

Distance : *Flat 7f 140y*

Draw Category	Winners	% Winners/Races
Low	7	13
Middle	31	57
High	16	30

Distance : *Flat 1m 1f*

Draw Category	Winners	% Winners/Races
Low	6	20
Middle	12	40
High	12	40

Distance : *Flat 1m 2f*

Draw Category	Winners	% Winners/Races
Low	20	33
Middle	25	42
High	15	25

Distance : *Flat 1m 3f 106y*

Draw Category	Winners	% Winners/Races
Low	23	37
Middle	23	37
High	16	26

MUSSELBURGH

Distance : *Flat 5f*

Draw Category	Winners	% Winners/Races
Low	38	29
Middle	55	42
High	37	28

Distance : *Flat 7f 30y*

Draw Category	Winners	% Winners/Races
Low	16	20
Middle	36	45
High	28	35

Distance : *Flat 1m*

Draw Category	Winners	% Winners/Races
Low	26	34
Middle	34	44
High	17	22

Distance : *Flat 1m 4f 31y*

Draw Category	Winners	% Winners/Races
Low	13	25
Middle	26	51
High	12	24

Distance : *Flat 2m*

Draw Category	Winners	% Winners/Races
Low	9	23
Middle	20	50
High	11	28

NEWBURY

Distance : *Flat 5f 34y*

Draw Category	Winners	% Winners/Races
Low	12	20
Middle	26	44
High	21	36

Distance : *Flat 6f 8y*

Draw Category	Winners	% Winners/Races
Low	27	28
Middle	31	32
High	38	40

Distance : *Str 7f*

Draw Category	Winners	% Winners/Races
Low	15	21
Middle	29	41
High	26	37

Distance : *Rnd 7f 64y*

Draw Category	Winners	% Winners/Races
Low	18	32
Middle	18	32
High	21	37

Distance : *Str 1m*

Draw Category	Winners	% Winners/Races
Low	8	18
Middle	19	43
High	17	39

Distance : *Flat 1m 2f 6y*

Draw Category	Winners	% Winners/Races
Low	24	29
Middle	30	36
High	30	36

Distance : *Flat 1m 4f 5y*

Draw Category	Winners	% Winners/Races
Low	10	23
Middle	18	41
High	16	36

Distance : *Flat 1m 5f 61y*

Draw Category	Winners	% Winners/Races
Low	9	30
Middle	11	37
High	10	33

Distance : *Flat 2m*

Draw Category	Winners	% Winners/Races
Low	6	23
Middle	12	46
High	8	31

NEWCASTLE

Distance : *Flat 5f*

Draw Category	Winners	% Winners/Races
Low	29	36
Middle	25	31
High	27	33

Distance : *Flat 6f*

Draw Category	Winners	% Winners/Races
Low	27	31
Middle	29	34
High	30	35

Distance : *Flat 7f*

Draw Category	Winners	% Winners/Races
Low	26	29
Middle	35	38
High	30	33

Distance : *Str 1m 3y*

Draw Category	Winners	% Winners/Races
Low	6	17
Middle	12	33
High	18	50

Distance : *Rnd 1m*

Draw Category	Winners	% Winners/Races
Low	11	21
Middle	27	52
High	14	27

Distance : *Flat 1m 2f 32y*

Draw Category	Winners	% Winners/Races
Low	18	31
Middle	25	42
High	16	27

Distance : *Flat 1m 4f 93y*

Draw Category	Winners	% Winners/Races
Low	10	24
Middle	20	49
High	11	27

Distance : *Flat 2m 19y*

Draw Category	Winners	% Winners/Races
Low	10	32
Middle	9	29
High	12	39

NEWMARKET JULY

Distance : *Jly 5f*

Draw Category	Winners	% Winners/Races
Low	11	31
Middle	12	34
High	12	34

Distance : *Jly 6f*

Draw Category	Winners	% Winners/Races
Low	44	29
Middle	66	43
High	43	28

Distance : *Jly 7f*

Draw Category	Winners	% Winners/Races
Low	45	27
Middle	65	40
High	54	33

Distance : *Jly 1m*

Draw Category	Winners	% Winners/Races
Low	31	28
Middle	44	40
High	36	32

Distance : *Jly 1m 2f*

Draw Category	Winners	% Winners/Races
Low	19	23
Middle	34	41
High	30	36

Distance : *Jly 1m 4f*

Draw Category	Winners	% Winners/Races
Low	18	26
Middle	35	51
High	16	23

Distance : *Jly 1m 6f 175y*

Draw Category	Winners	% Winners/Races
Low	7	33
Middle	7	33
High	7	33

NEWMARKET ROWLEY

Distance : *Rwly 5f*

Draw Category	Winners	% Winners/Races
Low	14	31
Middle	18	40
High	13	29

Distance : *Rwly 6f*

Draw Category	Winners	% Winners/Races
Low	27	35
Middle	30	39
High	20	26

Distance : *Rwly 7f*

Draw Category	Winners	% Winners/Races
Low	28	24
Middle	53	45
High	38	32

Distance : *Rwly 1m*

Draw Category	Winners	% Winners/Races
Low	26	30
Middle	28	32
High	33	38

Distance : *Rwly 1m 1f*

Draw Category	Winners	% Winners/Races
Low	6	27
Middle	10	45
High	6	27

Distance : *Rwly 1m 2f*

Draw Category	Winners	% Winners/Races
Low	16	27
Middle	25	42
High	18	31

Distance : *Rwly 1m 4f*

Draw Category	Winners	% Winners/Races
Low	13	27
Middle	14	29
High	21	44

NOTTINGHAM

Distance : *Flat 5f 13y*

Draw Category	Winners	% Winners/Races
Low	32	36
Middle	29	32
High	29	32

Distance : *Flat 1m 54y*

Draw Category	Winners	% Winners/Races
Low	65	31
Middle	75	36
High	68	33

Distance : *Flat 1m 1f 213y*

Draw Category	Winners	% Winners/Races
Low	50	33
Middle	55	37
High	45	30

Distance : *Flat 1m 6f 15y*

Draw Category	Winners	% Winners/Races
Low	25	30
Middle	30	36
High	28	34

Distance : *Flat 2m 9y*

Draw Category	Winners	% Winners/Races
Low	13	36
Middle	18	50
High	5	14

PONTEFRACT

Distance : *Flat 5f*

Draw Category	Winners	% Winners/Races
Low	12	18
Middle	21	31
High	34	51

Distance : *Flat 6f*

Draw Category	Winners	% Winners/Races
Low	37	27
Middle	55	40
High	47	34

Distance : *Flat 1m 4y*

Draw Category	Winners	% Winners/Races
Low	35	33
Middle	41	38
High	31	29

Distance : *Flat 1m 2f 6y*

Draw Category	Winners	% Winners/Races
Low	40	33
Middle	35	29
High	47	39

Distance : *Flat 1m 4f 8y*

Draw Category	Winners	% Winners/Races
Low	19	38
Middle	20	40
High	11	22

Distance : *Flat 2m 1f 22y*

Draw Category	Winners	% Winners/Races
Low	4	20
Middle	10	50
High	6	30

REDCAR

Distance : *Flat 5f*

Draw Category	Winners	% Winners/Races
Low	16	24
Middle	28	41
High	24	35

Distance : *Flat 6f*

Draw Category	Winners	% Winners/Races
Low	28	26
Middle	37	34
High	43	40

Distance : *Flat 7f*

Draw Category	Winners	% Winners/Races
Low	40	34
Middle	45	38
High	34	29

Distance : *Flat 1m*

Draw Category	Winners	% Winners/Races
Low	15	24
Middle	22	35
High	26	41

Distance : *Flat 1m 1f*

Draw Category	Winners	% Winners/Races
Low	7	22
Middle	10	31
High	15	47

Distance : *Flat 1m 2f*

Draw Category	Winners	% Winners/Races
Low	22	31
Middle	21	30
High	28	39

Distance : *Flat 1m 3f*

Draw Category	Winners	% Winners/Races
Low	9	18
Middle	19	39
High	21	43

Distance : *Flat 1m 6f 19y*

Draw Category	Winners	% Winners/Races
Low	13	25
Middle	24	46
High	15	29

RIPON

Distance : *Flat 5f*

Draw Category	Winners	% Winners/Races
Low	21	27
Middle	25	32
High	31	40

Distance : *Flat 6f*

Draw Category	Winners	% Winners/Races
Low	28	30
Middle	34	37
High	31	33

Distance : *Flat 1m*

Draw Category	Winners	% Winners/Races
Low	16	21
Middle	26	33
High	36	46

Distance : *Flat 1m 1f*

Draw Category	Winners	% Winners/Races
Low	9	36
Middle	9	36
High	7	28

Distance : *Flat 1m 2f*

Draw Category	Winners	% Winners/Races
Low	20	25
Middle	26	33
High	34	43

Distance : *Flat 1m 4f 60y*

Draw Category	Winners	% Winners/Races
Low	20	29
Middle	32	46
High	18	26

SALISBURY

Distance : *Flat 5f*

Draw Category	Winners	% Winners/Races
Low	9	23
Middle	14	36
High	16	41

Distance : *Flat 6f*

Draw Category	Winners	% Winners/Races
Low	31	32
Middle	33	34
High	34	35

Distance : *Flat 6f 212y*

Draw Category	Winners	% Winners/Races
Low	27	24
Middle	50	45
High	34	31

Distance : *Flat 1m*

Draw Category	Winners	% Winners/Races
Low	21	26
Middle	36	45
High	23	29

Distance : *Flat 1m 1f 209y*

Draw Category	Winners	% Winners/Races
Low	14	29
Middle	21	44
High	13	27

Distance : *Flat 1m 4f*

Draw Category	Winners	% Winners/Races
Low	14	29
Middle	22	45
High	13	27

Distance : *Flat 1m 6f 15y*

Draw Category	Winners	% Winners/Races
Low	11	25
Middle	18	41
High	15	34

SANDOWN

Distance : *Flat 5f 6y*

Draw Category	Winners	% Winners/Races
Low	31	22
Middle	49	34
High	64	44

Distance : *Flat 7f 16y*

Draw Category	Winners	% Winners/Races
Low	24	26
Middle	36	39
High	32	35

Distance : *Flat 1m 14y*

Draw Category	Winners	% Winners/Races
Low	34	31
Middle	47	42
High	30	27

Distance : *Flat 1m 2f 7y*

Draw Category	Winners	% Winners/Races
Low	27	27
Middle	37	37
High	37	37

Distance : *Flat 1m 6f*

Draw Category	Winners	% Winners/Races
Low	12	27
Middle	21	47
High	12	27

Distance : *Flat 2m 78y*

Draw Category	Winners	% Winners/Races
Low	4	19
Middle	11	52
High	6	29

SOUTHWELL AW

Distance : *Fibr 5f*

Draw Category	Winners	% Winners/Races
Low	33	25
Middle	61	46
High	40	30

Distance : *Fibr 6f*

Draw Category	Winners	% Winners/Races
Low	86	29
Middle	124	42
High	88	30

Distance : *Fibr 7f*

Draw Category	Winners	% Winners/Races
Low	87	30
Middle	115	39
High	93	32

Distance : *Fibr 1m*

Draw Category	Winners	% Winners/Races
Low	79	22
Middle	155	43
High	129	36

Distance : *Fibr 1m 3f*

Draw Category	Winners	% Winners/Races
Low	51	31
Middle	64	38
High	54	32

Distance : *Fibr 1m 4f*

Draw Category	Winners	% Winners/Races
Low	38	21
Middle	72	41
High	67	38

Distance : *Fibr 1m 6f*

Draw Category	Winners	% Winners/Races
Low	16	25
Middle	27	42
High	21	33

Distance : *Fibr 2m*

Draw Category	Winners	% Winners/Races
Low	19	30
Middle	28	44
High	20	32

THIRSK

Distance : *Flat 5f*

Draw Category	Winners	% Winners/Races
Low	15	18
Middle	37	44
High	33	39

Distance : *Flat 6f*

Draw Category	Winners	% Winners/Races
Low	16	20
Middle	26	32
High	39	48

Distance : *Flat 7f*

Draw Category	Winners	% Winners/Races
Low	31	32
Middle	36	38
High	29	30

Distance : *Flat 1m*

Draw Category	Winners	% Winners/Races
Low	30	29
Middle	44	43
High	28	27

Distance : *Flat 1m 4f*

Draw Category	Winners	% Winners/Races
Low	9	16
Middle	29	53
High	17	31

WARWICK

Distance : *Flat 5f*

Draw Category	Winners	% Winners/Races
Low	22	37
Middle	17	28
High	21	35

Distance : *Flat 6f*

Draw Category	Winners	% Winners/Races
Low	9	30
Middle	15	50
High	6	20

Distance : *Flat 7f*

Draw Category	Winners	% Winners/Races
Low	29	34
Middle	36	42
High	20	24

Distance : *Flat 1m*

Draw Category	Winners	% Winners/Races
Low	26	37
Middle	22	31
High	23	32

Distance : *Flat 1m 2f*

Draw Category	Winners	% Winners/Races
Low	23	30
Middle	28	36
High	26	34

Distance : *Flat 1m 4f*

Draw Category	Winners	% Winners/Races
Low	15	41
Middle	14	38
High	8	22

WINDSOR

Distance : *Flat 5f 10y*

Draw Category	Winners	% Winners/Races
Low	19	21
Middle	32	35
High	41	45

Distance : *Flat 6f*

Draw Category	Winners	% Winners/Races
Low	40	30
Middle	39	30
High	53	40

Distance : *Flat 1m 67y*

Draw Category	Winners	% Winners/Races
Low	28	22
Middle	51	40
High	48	38

Distance : *Flat 1m 2f 7y*

Draw Category	Winners	% Winners/Races
Low	19	17
Middle	52	46
High	43	38

Distance : *Flat 1m 3f 135y*

Draw Category	Winners	% Winners/Races
Low	29	32
Middle	34	38
High	27	30

WOLVERHAMPTON AW

Distance : *Fibr 5f*

Draw Category	Winners	% Winners/Races
Low	51	26
Middle	66	34
High	80	41

Distance : *Fibr 6f*

Draw Category	Winners	% Winners/Races
Low	77	27
Middle	109	39
High	96	34

Distance : *Fibr 6f*

Draw Category	Winners	% Winners/Races
Low	77	27
Middle	109	39
High	96	34

Distance : *Fibr 7f*

Draw Category	Winners	% Winners/Races
Low	83	33
Middle	92	37
High	76	30

Distance : *Fibr 1m 100y*

Draw Category	Winners	% Winners/Races
Low	75	29
Middle	91	36
High	90	35

Distance : *Fibr 1m 1f 79y*

Draw Category	Winners	% Winners/Races
Low	65	28
Middle	81	35
High	85	37

Distance : *Fibr 1m 4f*

Draw Category	Winners	% Winners/Races
Low	45	23
Middle	78	40
High	70	36

Distance : *Fibr 1m 6f 166y*

Draw Category	Winners	% Winners/Races
Low	18	27
Middle	25	37
High	24	36

Distance : *Fibr 2m 46y*

Draw Category	Winners	% Winners/Races
Low	10	19
Middle	20	37
High	24	44

YARMOUTH

Distance : *Flat 5f 43y*

Draw Category	Winners	% Winners/Races
Low	9	24
Middle	15	41
High	13	35

Distance : *Flat 6f 3y*

Draw Category	Winners	% Winners/Races
Low	22	19
Middle	55	47
High	39	34

Distance : *Flat 7f 3y*

Draw Category	Winners	% Winners/Races
Low	37	28
Middle	46	34
High	51	38

Distance : *Flat 1m 3y*

Draw Category	Winners	% Winners/Races
Low	27	32
Middle	31	37
High	26	31

Distance : *Flat 1m 2f 21y*

Draw Category	Winners	% Winners/Races
Low	28	33
Middle	42	50
High	14	17

Distance : *Flat 1m 3f 101y*

Draw Category	Winners	% Winners/Races
Low	18	49
Middle	8	22
High	11	30

Distance : *Flat 1m 6f 17y*

Draw Category	Winners	% Winners/Races
Low	12	28
Middle	22	51
High	9	21

YORK

Distance : *Flat 5f*

Draw Category	Winners	% Winners/Races
Low	12	27
Middle	24	53
High	9	20

Distance : *Flat 6f*

Draw Category	Winners	% Winners/Races
Low	33	28
Middle	45	38
High	42	35

Distance : *Flat 6f 214y*

Draw Category	Winners	% Winners/Races
Low	14	23
Middle	20	33
High	26	43

Distance : *Flat 7f 202y*

Draw Category	Winners	% Winners/Races
Low	29	43
Middle	23	34
High	16	24

Distance : *Flat 1m 2f 85y*

Draw Category	Winners	% Winners/Races
Low	25	33
Middle	32	43
High	18	24

Distance : *Flat 1m 3f 195y*

Draw Category	Winners	% Winners/Races
Low	23	38
Middle	27	45
High	10	17

Distance : *Flat 1m 5f 194y*

Draw Category	Winners	% Winners/Races
Low	17	38
Middle	14	31
High	14	31

Five-Season Front Runners Analysis For British Flat Tracks

The following table shows the record of front runners over each distance on each track over the last five seasons. Horses are included in the winners column if they have made all or most of the running. The Impact Value or 'IV' is the strike rate of front runners as against random chance. i.e. an IV of 1.0 would mean that front runners have won as often as they are entitled, 2.0 means they have won twice as often (a bias towards front runners) and 0.5 means they have won half as often (a bias against front runners). Distances which have not had a sufficient number of races run over them to produce a meaningful statistic are not shown.

ASCOT

Distance	Winners	Races	% Winners	IV
5f	6	57	11	1.85
6f	9	59	15	2.30
7f	9	61	15	2.24
1m Str	7	53	13	2.82
1m Rnd	7	59	12	1.07
1m 2f	3	38	8	0.78
1m 4f	7	82	9	1.01
2m 45y	1	31	3	0.44

AYR

Distance	Winners	Races	% Winners	IV
5f	9	50	18	3.71
6f	13	76	17	3.62
7f	13	76	17	2.84
1m	14	59	24	4.19
1m 2f	7	49	14	1.62
1m 2f 192y	0	30	0	0.00
1m 5f 13y	5	27	19	2.28

BATH

Distance	Winners	Races	% Winners	IV
5f 11y	15	101	15	2.16
5f 161y	7	77	9	1.51
1m 5y	13	99	13	2.01
1m 2f 46y	14	70	20	2.52
1m 3f 144y	6	46	13	1.61
2m 1f 34y	2	39	5	0.51

BEVERLEY

Distance	Winners	Races	% Winners	IV
5f	33	152	22	3.79
7f 100y	34	146	23	3.97
1m 100y	17	73	23	4.09
1m 1f 207y	12	100	12	2.11
1m 3f 216y	9	71	13	2.04
2m 35y	2	36	6	0.88

BRIGHTON

Distance	Winners	Races	% Winners	IV
5f 59y	18	80	23	2.02
5f 213y	22	106	21	2.18
6f 209y	20	138	14	1.69
7f 214y	23	127	18	1.93
1m 1f 209y	14	88	16	1.99
1m 3f 196y	18	102	18	1.73

CARLISLE

Distance	Winners	Races	% Winners	IV
5f	13	62	21	3.13
5f 207y	7	58	12	2.46
6f 206y	5	49	10	1.85
7f 214y	5	52	10	1.91
1m 4f	5	32	16	1.96

CATTERICK

Distance	Winners	Races	% Winners	IV
5f	14	90	16	2.67
5f 212y	12	79	15	2.23
7f	14	139	10	2.04
1m 3f 214y	11	70	16	2.18
1m 5f 175y	6	45	13	1.54
1m 7f 177y	3	30	10	1.53

CHEPSTOW

Distance	Winners	Races	% Winners	IV
5f 16y	9	32	28	3.24
6f 16y	10	54	19	2.26
7f 16y	6	57	11	1.88
1m 14y	17	59	29	4.30
1m 2f 36y	5	48	10	1.12
1m 4f 23y	5	40	13	1.31

CHESTER

Distance	Winners	Races	% Winners	IV
5f 16y	21	71	30	4.27
6f 18y	11	36	31	3.56
7f 2y	12	53	23	3.38
7f 122y	7	35	20	4.07
1m 2f 75y	4	47	9	1.23
1m 4f 66y	10	44	23	2.24

DONCASTER

Distance	Winners	Races	% Winners	IV
5f	20	97	21	4.26
6f	22	108	20	3.86
7f	16	121	13	3.11
1m Str	5	67	7	1.64
1m Rnd	5	64	8	1.70
1m 2f 60y	10	89	11	2.03
1m 4f	8	63	13	2.25
1m 6f 132y	4	36	11	1.36

EPSOM

Distance	Winners	Races	% Winners	IV
5f	3	15	20	3.22
6f	9	55	16	1.75
7f	10	63	16	1.73
1m 114y	7	65	11	1.14
1m 2f 18y	12	54	22	2.09
1m 4f 10y	4	61	7	0.71

FOLKESTONE

Distance	Winners	Races	% Winners	IV
5f	17	64	27	2.39
6f	13	74	18	1.97
6f 189y	8	53	15	1.67
7f	14	51	27	3.38
1m 1f 149y	8	51	16	1.87
1m 4f	9	55	16	1.80

GOODWOOD

Distance	Winners	Races	% Winners	IV
5f	6	52	12	1.39
6f	18	124	15	1.98
7f	19	124	15	1.81
1m	18	107	17	2.17
1m 1f	6	52	12	1.60
1m 1f 192y	11	55	20	2.02
1m 2f	9	36	25	2.73
1m 4f	6	62	10	0.83
1m 6f	6	27	22	2.31
2m	5	20	25	2.50

HAMILTON

Distance	Winners	Races	% Winners	IV
5f 4y	23	103	22	2.90
6f 5y	14	110	13	1.70
1m 65y	10	90	11	1.75
1m 1f 36y	16	72	22	3.20
1m 3f 16y	12	51	24	3.27
1m 4f 17y	7	46	15	2.26
1m 5f 9y	3	48	6	0.99

HAYDOCK

Distance	Winners	Races	% Winners	IV
5f	19	90	21	3.60
6f	22	112	20	3.52
7f 30y	25	95	26	4.16
1m 30y	8	83	10	1.71
1m 2f 120y	14	86	16	1.92
1m 3f 200y	8	88	9	1.14
1m 6f	7	52	13	2.02

KEMPTON

Distance	Winners	Races	% Winners	IV
5f	2	23	9	0.78
6f	14	82	17	2.36
7f Jub	15	76	20	2.71
1m Jub	6	57	11	1.29
1m 1f	0	31	0	0.00
1m 2f Jub	4	39	10	1.34
1m 4f	5	51	10	1.20

LEICESTER

Distance	Winners	Races	% Winners	IV
5f 2y	7	60	12	1.77
5f 218y	9	100	9	1.69
7f 9y	27	142	19	3.21
1m 8y	8	119	7	1.41
1m 1f 218y	7	95	7	1.60
1m 3f 183y	12	84	14	1.87

LINGFIELD AW

Distance	Winners	Races	% Winners	IV
5f	33	145	23	1.95
6f	41	199	21	2.08
7f	36	269	13	1.42
1m	32	295	11	1.05
1m 2f	39	324	12	1.20
1m 4f	10	154	6	0.65
1m 5f	3	64	5	0.50
2m	5	81	6	0.61

LINGFIELD TURF

Distance	Winners	Races	% Winners	IV
5f	31	93	33	3.78
6f	18	131	14	1.80
7f	21	129	16	2.30
7f 140y	8	54	15	1.67
1m 1f	8	30	27	2.70
1m 2f	9	60	15	1.57
1m 3f 106y	12	62	19	1.86

MUSSELBURGH

Distance	Winners	Races	% Winners	IV
5f	34	130	26	3.45
7f 30y	15	80	19	2.52
1m	12	77	16	2.06
1m 4f 31y	6	51	12	1.72
2m	1	40	3	0.30

NEWBURY

Distance	Winners	Races	% Winners	IV
5f 34y	8	59	14	1.76
6f 8y	8	96	8	1.16
7f Str	4	70	6	0.78
7f 64y Rnd	8	57	14	1.74
1m Str	4	44	9	1.18
1m 2f 6y	9	84	11	1.40
1m 3f 5y	2	13	15	1.26
1m 4f 5y	5	44	11	1.29
1m 5f 61y	4	30	13	1.33
2m	3	26	12	1.21

NEWCASTLE

Distance	Winners	Races	% Winners	IV
5f	20	81	25	4.21
6f	15	86	17	3.32
7f	13	91	14	2.75
1m 3y Str	9	36	25	4.03
1m Rnd	4	52	8	1.37
1m 2f 32y	11	59	19	2.93
1m 4f 93y	2	41	5	0.41
2m 19y	2	31	6	1.32

NEWMARKET JULY

Distance	Winners	Races	% Winners	IV
5f	3	35	9	1.63
6f	26	153	17	2.51
7f	20	164	12	2.07
1m	9	111	8	1.64
1m 2f	7	83	8	1.53
1m 4f	9	69	13	1.58
1m 6f 175y	3	21	14	1.45

NEWMARKET ROWLEY

Distance	Winners	Races	% Winners	IV
5f	10	45	22	4.09
6f	11	77	14	2.88
7f	12	119	10	2.41
1m	9	87	10	2.51
1m 1f	2	22	9	1.76
1m 2f	5	59	8	1.56
1m 4f	4	48	8	1.46

NOTTINGHAM

Distance	Winners	Races	% Winners	IV
5f 13y	18	90	20	3.22
6f 15y	29	171	17	3.51
1m 54y	26	208	13	2.04
1m 1f 213y	8	150	5	0.93
1m 6f 15y	2	83	2	0.46
2m 9y	3	36	8	1.21

PONTEFRACT

Distance	Winners	Races	% Winners	IV
5f	13	67	19	4.26
6f	29	139	21	4.07
1m 4y	13	107	12	2.94
1m 2f 6y	16	122	13	2.36
1m 4f 8y	5	50	10	1.34
2m 1f 22y	3	20	15	2.70

REDCAR

Distance	Winners	Races	% Winners	IV
5f	15	68	22	3.81
6f	12	108	11	2.05
7f	12	119	10	1.69
1m	6	63	10	2.48
1m 1f	2	32	6	0.98
1m 2f	5	71	7	1.07
1m 3f	2	49	4	0.63
1m 6f 19y	3	52	6	0.86

RIPON

Distance	Winners	Races	% Winners	IV
5f	29	77	38	5.81
6f	21	93	23	4.92
1m	13	78	17	3.17
1m 1f	8	25	32	3.75
1m 2f	13	80	16	2.35
1m 4f 60y	10	70	14	2.05

SALISBURY

Distance	Winners	Races	% Winners	IV
5f	11	39	28	3.39
6f	13	98	13	1.87
6f 212y	10	111	9	1.34
1m	11	80	14	1.87
1m 1f 209y	8	48	17	2.00
1m 4f	10	49	20	2.70
1m 6f 15y	7	44	16	2.94

SANDOWN

Distance	Winners	Races	% Winners	IV
5f 6y	30	144	21	2.21
7f 16y	15	92	16	1.72
1m 14y	12	111	11	1.15
1m 2f 7y	14	101	14	1.53
1m 6f	6	45	13	1.25
2m 78y	1	21	5	0.52

SOUTHWELL AW

Distance	Winners	Races	% Winners	IV
5f	27	134	20	3.46
6f	46	296	16	2.43
7f	43	293	15	2.32
1m	37	357	10	1.69
1m 3f	15	167	9	1.40
1m 4f	26	177	15	1.88
1m 6f	5	64	8	1.24
2m	5	63	8	1.05

THIRSK

Distance	Winners	Races	% Winners	IV
5f	20	85	24	4.41
6f	20	81	25	4.98
7f	18	96	19	3.20
1m	12	102	12	1.94
1m 4f	7	55	13	1.41

WARWICK

Distance	Winners	Races	% Winners	IV
5f	10	60	17	2.35
6f	7	30	23	3.00
7f	20	85	24	3.19
1m	5	71	7	1.24
1m 2f	8	77	10	2.02
1m 4f	6	35	17	1.45

WINDSOR

Distance	Winners	Races	% Winners	IV
5f 10y	16	92	17	2.29
6f	17	132	13	2.17
1m 67y	22	127	17	2.75
1m 2f 7y	15	114	13	1.84
1m 3f 135y	11	90	12	1.63

WOLVERHAMPTON

Distance	Winners	Races	% Winners	IV
5f	32	197	16	2.32
6f	47	282	17	2.32
7f	42	251	17	2.14
1m 100y	30	256	12	1.59
1m 1f 79y	28	231	12	1.55
1m 4f	21	193	11	1.28
1m 6f 166y	4	67	6	0.68
2m 46y	9	54	17	1.70

YARMOUTH

Distance	Winners	Races	% Winners	IV
5f 43y	11	37	30	2.96
6f 3y	28	116	24	2.84
7f 3y	35	134	26	3.40
1m 3y	14	84	17	2.97
1m 2f 21y	6	84	7	1.00
1m 3f 101y	4	37	11	1.11
1m 6f 17y	3	43	7	0.75

YORK

Distance	Winners	Races	% Winners	IV
5f	6	45	13	2.55
6f	12	120	10	2.22
6f 214y	8	60	13	2.80
7f 202y	9	68	13	2.87
1m 205y	3	20	15	4.55
1m 2f 85y	11	75	15	2.81
1m 3f 195y	6	60	10	1.53
1m 5f 194y	2	45	4	0.85

RACEFORM MEDIAN TIMES FLAT 2001

ASCOT

5f	1m2
6f	1m16.2
7f	1m29.9
1m Round	1m43.2
1m Straight	1m41.9
1m2f	2m8.9
1m4f	2m34.1
2m45yds	3m34.8
2m4f	4m23.9
2m6f34yds	4m57.7

AYR

5f	1m0.6
6f	1m13.7
7f	1m29.4
1m	1m43
1m1f	1m56.4
1m2f	2m12.2
1m2f192yds	2m23.6
1m5f13yds	2m55.9
1m7f	3m23.7
2m1f105yds	3m59.4

BATH

5f11yds	1m2.5
5f161yds	1m11.4
1m5yds	1m41.2
1m2f46yds	2m11
1m3f144yds	2m30.4
1m5f22yds	2m51.3
2m1f34yds	3m49.6

BEVERLEY

5f	1m4.2
7f100yds	1m34.4
1m100yds	1m47.4
1m1f207yds	2m7
1m3f216yds	2m38.1
2m35yds	3m39.4

BRIGHTON

5f59yds	1m2.3
5f213yds	1m10
6f209yds	1m22.7
7f214yds	1m34.9
1m1f209yds	2m2.5
1m3f196yds	2m31.9

CARLISLE

5f	1m1.6
5f207yds	1m14.6
6f206yds	1m27.6
7f214yds	1m40.7
1m1f61yds	1m58.1
1m4f	2m34.8
1m6f32yds	3m7.3
2m1f52yds	3m49.7

CATTERICK

5f	1m0.8
5f212yds	1m14.4
7f	1m27.7
1m3f214yds	2m40.2
1m5f175yds	3m4.9
1m7f177yds	3m32.2

CHEPSTOW

5f16yds	59.5
6f16yds	1m12.2
7f16yds	1m23.3
1m14yds	1m35.9
1m2f36yds	2m9.2
1m4f23yds	2m38.3
2m49yds	3m38.3
2m2f	4m

CHESTER

5f16yds	1m2.3
6f18yds	1m15.9
7f2yds	1m28.7
7m122yds	1m35.6
1m2f75yds	2m13.8
1m3f79yds	2m26.4

1m4f66yds	2m41
1m5f89yds	2m56.2
1m7f195yds	3m33.9
2m2f147yds	4m6.5

DONCASTER

5f	1m1.3
5f140yds	1m7.9
6f	1m14.3
6f110yds	1m20.7
7f	1m27.7
1m Round	1m40.4
1m Straight	1m41.3
1m2f60yds	2m11.8
1m4f	2m35.3
1m6f132yds	3m9.7
2m110yds	3m41.8
2m2f	3m57.7

EPSOM

5f	55.9
6f	1m10.6
7f	1m23.7
1m114yds	1m45.5
1m2f18yds	2m8.7
1m4f10yds	2m38.5

FOLKESTONE

5f	1m0.8
6f	1m13.7
7f	1m28.1
1m1f149yds	2m4.8
1m4f	2m39.8
1m7f92yds	3m27.2
2m93yds	3m40.3

GOODWOOD

5f	59.1
6f	1m13
7f	1m28.2
1m	1m40.5
1m1f	1m57.1
1m1f192yds	2m8.4
1m4f	2m39.1
1m6f	3m4.2
2m	3m30.8
2m4f	4m20.9

HAMILTON

5f4yds	1m1.3
6f5yds	1m13
1m65yds	1m49.3
1m1f36yds	1m59
1m3f16yds	2m25.9
1m4f17yds	2m39.5
1m5f9yds	2m52.6

HAYDOCK

5f	1m2.1
6f	1m14.7
7f30yds	1m32.2
1m30yds	1m45.6
1m2f120yds	2m17.8
1m3f200yds	2m35.6
1m6f	3m6.6
2m45yds	3m38.7

KEMPTON

5f	1m1.6
6f	1m13.3
7f Jubilee	1m27.1
7f	1m26.6
1m Jubilee	1m40.5
1m	1m39.8
1m1f	1m54.8
1m2f Jubilee	2m6.1
1m3f30yds	2m22.4
1m4f	2m35
1m6f92yds	3m10.7
2m	3m30.4

LEICESTER

5f2yds	1m1.1
5f218yds	1m13.5
7f9yds	1m26
1m8yds	1m39.2
1m1f218yds	2m8.8
1m3f183yds	2m35.3

LINGFIELD (Turf)

5f	59.1
6f	1m11.6
7f	1m24.3
7f140yds	1m31.4

1m1f	1m55.6
1m2f	2m9.4
1m3f106yds	2m29.2
1m6f	3m6.9
2m	3m33.1

LINGFIELD (AW)

5f	59.9
6f	1m13.3
7f	1m26.3
1m	1m39.8
1m2f	2m7.6
1m4f	2m34.2
1m5f	2m48.5
2m	3m34.8

MUSSELBURGH

5f	1m0.6
7f15yds	1m30.3
1m	1m43.1
1m200yds	1m54.2
1m4f31yds	2m39.6
1m6f	3m6.1
2m	3m34.7

NEWBURY

5f34yds	1m2.9
6f8yds	1m14.5
7f	1m27.9
7f64yds Round	1m31.3
1m	1m41.3
1m7yds Round	1m38.7
1m1f	1m54.6
1m2f6yds	2m8.7
1m3f5yds	2m23.8
1m4f5yds	2m36.7
1m5f61yds	2m51.8
2m	3m36.3

NEWCASTLE

5f	1m1.6
6f	1m15.2
7f	1m28
1m Round	1m43.9
1m3yds	1m41
1m1f9yds	1m57.8
1m2f32yds	2m12
1m4f93yds	2m43.1
2m19yds	3m35.2

NEWMARKET (Rowley)

5f	1m0.5
6f	1m13.1
7f	1m26.4
1m	1m39.4
1f	1m51.9
1m2t	2m5.6
1m4f	2m23.7
1m6f	3m1.1
2m	3m26.2
2m2f	3m52.6

NEWMARKET (July)

5f	59.8
6f	1m13.2
7f	1m26.7
1m1f	1m51.9
1m2f	2m5.6
1m4f	2m23.7
1m6f	3m1.1
2m	3m26.2
2m2f	3m52.6

NOTTINGHAM

5f13yds	1m1.8
6f15yds	1m14.8
1m54yds	1m46.3
1m1f213yds	2m9.5
1m6f15yds	3m7.1
2m9yds	3m33.4

PONTEFRACT

5f	1m3.8
6f	1m17.4
1m4yds	1m45.8
1m2f6yds	2m14.1
1m4f8yds	2m40.4
2m1f22y	3m52
2m1f216y	4m3
2m5f122y	5m0.8

SALISBURY

5f	1m1.6

6f	1m15.2
6f212yds	1m29.2
1m	1m43.2
1m1f198yds	2m8.5
1m4f	2m36.2
1m6f15yds	3m6.2

SANDOWN

5f6yds	1m2.2
7f16yds	1m31.1
1m14yds	1m43.9
1m1f	1m56.5
1m2f7yds	2m10.2
1m3f91yds	2m28.2
1m6f	3m4.3
2m78yds	3m38.3

SOUTHWELL (AW)

5f	1m0.4
6f	1m16.9
7f	1m30.9
1m	1m44.7
1m3f	2m29
1m4f	2m42
1m6f	3m10.1
2m	3m53.3

THIRSK

5f	1m0.1
6f	1m12.6
7f	1m27.3
1m	1m39.7
1m4f	2m35.2
2m	3m30.9

WARWICK

New distances introduced in 1999/2000.
No medians available.

WINDSOR

5f10yds	1m1.2
6f	1m12.9
1m67yds	1m45.4
1m2f7yds	2m7.7
1m3f135yds	2m29.8

WOLVERHAMPTON (AW)

5f	1m2.9
6f	1m15.8
7f	1m30.3
1m100yds	1m51
1m1f79yds	2m2.9
1m4f	2m41.9
1m6f166yds	3m20.7
2m46yds	3m42.3

YARMOUTH

5f43yds	1m2.7
6f3yds	1m13.6
7f3yds	1m26.6
1m3yds	1m39.7
1m2f21yds	2m7.9
1m3f101yds	2m27.5
1m6f17yds	3m5.4
2m	3m31.8
2m2f51yds	4m6.9

YORK

5f	59.3
6f	1m12.7
6f214yds	1m25.5
7f202yds	1m39.6
1m205yds	1m52.5
1m2f85yds	2m12.1
1m3f195yds	2m31.7
1m5f194yds	2m58.9
1m7f195yds	3m24.6

Winners of Principal Races

Group One Races

2000 GUINEAS

2000 King's Best
1999 Island Sands
1998 King of Kings
1997 Entrepreneur
1996 Mark of Esteem
1995 Pennekamp
1994 Mister Baileys
1993 Zafonic
1992 Rodrigo de Triano
1991 Mystiko

CORONATION CUP

2000 Daliapour
1000 Daylami
1998 Silver Patriarch
1997 Singspiel
1996 Swain
1995 Sunshack
1994 Apple Tree
1993 Opera House
1992 Saddlers' Hall
1991 In the Groove

1000 GUINEAS

2000 Lahan
1999 Wince
1998 Cape Verdi
1997 Sleepytime
1996 Bosra Sham
1995 Harayir
1994 Las Meninas
1993 Sayyedati
1992 Hatoof
1991 Shadayid

LOCKINGE STKS

2000 Aljabr
1999 Fly To the Stars
1998 Cape Cross
1997 First Island
1996 Soviet Line
1995 Soviet Line
1994 Emperor Jones
1993 Swing Low
1992 Selkirk
1991 Polar Falcon

ST JAMES'S PALACE STKS

2000 Giant's Causeway
1999 Sendawar
1998 Dr Fong
1997 Starborough
1996 Bijou d'Inde
1995 Bahri
1994 Grand Lodge
1993 Kingmambo
1992 Brief Truce
1991Marju

PRINCE OF WALES'S STKS

2000 Dubai Millennium
1999 Lear Spear
1998 Faithful Son
1997 Bosra Sham
1996 First Island
1995 Muhtarram
1994 Muhtarram
1993 Placerville
1992 Perpendicular
1991 Stagecraft

DERBY

2000 Sinndar
1999 Oath
1998 High-Rise
1997 Benny The Dip
1996 Shaamit
1995 Lammtarra
1994 Erhaab
1993 Commander in Chief
1992 Dr Devious
1991 Generous

CORONATION STKS

2000 Crimplene
1999 Balisada
1998 Exclusive
1997 Rebecca Sharp
1996 Shake the Yoke
1995 Ridgewood Pearl
1994 Kissing Cousin
1993 Gold Splash
1992 Marling
1991 Kooyonga

OAKS

2000 Love Divine
1999 Ramruma
1998 Shahtoush
1997 Reams of Verse
1996 Lady Carla
1995 Moonshell
1994 Balanchine
1993 Intrepidity
1992 User Friendly
1991 Jet Ski Lady

GOLD CUP

2000 Kayf Tara
1999 Enzeli
1998 Kayf Tara
1997 Celeric
1996 Classic Cliche
1995 Double Trigger
1994 Arcadian Heights
1993 Drum Taps
1992 Drum Taps
1001 Indian Queen

CORAL-ECLIPSE STKS

2000 Giant's Causeway
1999 Compton Admiral
1998 Daylami
1997 Pilsudski
1996 Halling
1995 Halling
1994 Ezzoud
1993 Opera House
1992 Kooyonga
1991 Environment Friend

JUDDMONTE INTERNATIONAL

2000 Giant's Causeway
1999 Royal Anthem
1998 One So Wonderful
1997 Singspiel
1996 Halling
1995 Halling
1994 Ezzoud
1993 Ezzoud
1992 Rodrigo de Triano
1991 Terimon

JULY CUP

2000 Agnes World
1999 Stravinsky
1998 Elnadim
1997 Compton Place
1996 Anabaa
1995 Lake Coniston
1994 Owington
1993 Hamas
1992 Mr Brooks
1991 Polish Patriot

YORKSHIRE OAKS

2000 Petrushka
1999 Ramruma
1998 Catchascatchcan
1997 My Emma
1996 Key Change
1995 Pure Grain
1994 Only Royale
1993 Only Royale
1992 User Friendly
1991 Magnificent Star

KING GEORGE VI & QUEEN ELIZABETH DIAMOND STKS

2000 Montjeu
1999 Daylami
1998 Swain
1997 Swain
1996 Pentire
1995 Lammtarra
1994 King's Theatre
1993 Opera House
1992 St Jovite
1991 Generous

NUNTHORPE STKS

2000 Nuclear Debate
1999 Stravinsky
1998 Lochangel
1997 Coastal Bluff & Ya Malak (d/heat)
1996 Pivotal
1995 So Factual
1994 Piccolo (Blue Siren disq.)
1993 Lochsong
1992 Lyric Fantasy
1991 Sheikh Albadou

SUSSEX STKS

2000 Giant's Causeway
1999 Aljabr
1998 Among Men
1997 Ali-Royal

NASSAU STKS

2000 Crimplene
1999 Zahrat Dubai
1998 Alborada
1997 Ryafan

1996 First Island
1995 Sayyedati
1994 Distant View
1993 Bigstone
1992 Marling
1991 Second Set

1996 Last Second
1995 Caramba
1994 Hawajiss
1993 Lyphard's Delta
1992 Ruby Tiger
1991 Ruby Tiger

STANLEY LEISURE SPRINT CUP

2000 Pipalong
1999 Diktat
1998 Tamarisk
1997 Royal Applause
1996 Iktamal
1995 Cherokee Rose
1994 Lavinia Fontana
1993 Wolfhound
1992 Sheikh Albadou
1991 Polar Falcon

QUEEN ELIZABETH II STKS

2000 Observatory
1999 Dubai Millennium
1998 Desert Prince
1997 Air Express
1996 Mark of Esteem
1995 Bahri
1994 Maroof
1993 Bigstone
1992 Lahib
1991 Selkirk

DUBAI CHAMPION STKS

2000 Kalanisi
1999 Alborada
1998 Alborada
1997 Pilsudski
1996 Bosra Sham
1995 Spectrum
1994 Dernier Empereur
1993 Hatoof
1992 Rodrigo de Triano
1991 Tel Quel

ST LEGER

2000 Millenary
1999 Mutafaweq
1998 Nedawi
1997 Silver Patriarch
1996 Shantou
1995 Classic Cliche
1994 Moonax
1993 Bob's Return
1992 User Friendly
1991 Toulon

Group Two Races

TEMPLE STKS

2000 Perryston View
1999 Tipsy Creek
1998 Bolshoi
1997 Croft Pool
1996 Mind Games
1995 Mind Games
1994 Lochsong
1993 Paris House
1992 Snaadee
1991 Elbio

DANTE STKS

2000 Sakhee
1999 Salford Express
1998 Saratoga Springs
1997 Benny The Dip
1996 Glory of Dancer
1995 Classic Cliche
1994 Erhaab
1993 Tenby
1992 Alnasr Alwasheek
1991 Environment Friend

YORKSHIRE CUP

2000 Kayf Tara
1999 Churlish Charm
1998 Busy Flight
1997 Celeric
1996 Classic Cliche
1995 Moonax
1994 Key To My Heart
1993 Assessor
1992 Rock Hopper
1991 Arzanni

QUEEN ANNE STKS

2000 Kalanisi
1999 Cape Cross
1998 Intikhab
1997 Allied Forces
1996 Charnwood Forest
1995 Nicolotte
1994 Barathea
1993 Alflora
1992 Lahib
1991 Sikeston

SANDOWN MILE

2000 Indian Lodge
1999 Handsome Ridge
1998 Almushtarak
1997 Wixim
1996 Gabr
1995 Missed Flight
1994 Penny Drops
1993 Alhijaz
1992 Rudimentary
1991 In the Groove

JOCKEY CLUB STKS

2000 Blueprint
1999 Silver Patriarch
1998 Romanov
1997 Time Allowed
1996 Riyadian
1995 Only Royale
1994 Silver Wisp
1993 Zinaad
1992 Sapience
1991 Rock Hopper

RIBBLESDALE STKS

2000 Miletrian
1999 Fairy Queen
1998 Bahr
1997 Yashmak
1996 Tulipa
1995 Phantom Gold
1994 Bolas
1993 Thawakib
1992 Armarama
1991 Third Watch

HARDWICKE STKS

2000 Fruits of Love
1999 Fruits of Love
1998 Posidonas
1997 Predappio
1996 Oscar Schindler
1995 Beauchamp Hero
1994 Bobzao
1993 Jeune
1992 Rock Hopper
1991 Rock Hopper (Topanoora disq.)

KING'S STAND STKS

2000 Nuclear Debate
1999 Mitcham
1998 Bolshoi
1997 Don't Worry Me
1996 Pivotal
1995 Piccolo
1994 Lochsong
1993 Elbio
1992 Sheikh Albadou
1991 Elbio

KING EDWARD VII STKS

2000 Subtle Power
1999 Mutafaweq
1998 Royal Anthem
1997 Kingfisher Mill
1996 Amfortas
1995 Pentire
1994 Foyer
1993 Beneficial
1992 Beyton
1991 Saddlers' Hall

CORK & ORRERY STKS

2000 Superior Premium
1999 Bold Edge
1998 Tomba
1997 Royal Applause
1996 Atraf
1995 So Factual
1994 Owington
1993 College Chapel
1992 Shalfordl
1991 Polish Patriot

PRINCESS OF WALES'S STKS

2000 Little Rock
1999 Craigsteel
1998 Fruits of Love
1997 Shantou
1996 Posidonas
1995 Beauchamp Hero
1994 Wagon Master
1993 Desert Team
1992 Saddlers' Hall
1991 Rock Hopper

GOODWOOD CUP

2000 Royal Rebel
1999 Kayf Tara
1998 Double Trigger
1997 Double Trigger
1996 Gey Shot
1995 Double Trigger
1994 Tioman Island
1993 Sonus
1992 Further Flight
1991 Further Flight

GREAT VOLTIGEUR STKS

2000 Air Marshall
1999 Fantastic Light
1998 Sea Wave
1997 Stowaway
1996 Dushyantor
1995 Pentire
1994 Sacrament
1993 Bob's Return
1992 Bonny Scot
1991 Corrupt

CHALLENGE STKS
2000 Last Resort
1999 Susu
1998 Decorated Hero
1997 Kahal
1996 Charnwood Forest
1995 Harayir
1994 Zieten
1993 Catrail
1992 Selkirk
1991 Mystiko

FALMOUTH STKS
2000 Alshakr
1999 Ronda
1998 Lovers Knot
1997 Ryafan
1996 Sensation
1995 Caramba
1994 Lemon Souffle
1993 Niche
1992 Gussy Marlowe
1991 Only Yours

CELEBRATION MILE
2000 Medicean
1999 Cape Cross
1998 Muhtathir
1997 Among Men
1996 Mark of Esteem
1995 Harayir
1994 Mehthaaf
1993 Swing Low
1992 Selkirk
1991 Bold Russian

DIADEM STKS
2000 Sampower Star
1999 Bold Edge
1998 Bianconi
1997 Elnadim
1996 Diffident
1995 Cool Jazz
1994 Lake Coniston
1993 Catrail
1992 Wolfhound
1991 Shalford

SUN CHARIOT STKS
2000 Danceabout
1999 Lady In Waiting
1998 Kissogram
1997 One So Wonderful
1996 Last Second
1995 Warning Shadows
1994 La Confederation
1993 Talented
1992 Red Slippers
1991 Ristna

GEOFFREY FREER STKS
2000 Murghem
1999 Silver Patriarch
1998 Multicoloured
1997 Dushyantor
1996 Phantom Gold
1995 Presenting
1994 Red Route
1993 Azzilfi
1992 Shambo
1991 Drum Taps

Top Two-Year-Old Races

MIDDLE PARK STKS
2000 Minardi
1999 Primo Valentino
1998 Lujain
1997 Hayil
1996 Bahamian Bounty
1995 Royal Applause
1994 Fard
1993 First Trump
1992 Zieten
1991 Rodrigo de Triano

DEWHURST STKS
2000 Tobougg
1999 Distant Music
1998 Mujahid
1997 Xaar
1996 In Command
1995 Alhaarth
1994 Pennekamp
1993 Grand Lodge
1992 Zafonic
1991 Dr Devious

FILLIES' MILE
2000 Crystal Music
1999 Teggiano
1998 Sunspangled
1997 Glorosia
1996 Reams of Verse
1995 Bosra Sham
1994 Aqaarid
1993 Fairy Heights
1992 Ivanka
1991 Culture Vulture

RACING POST TROPHY
2000 Dilshaan
1999 Aristotle
1998 Commander Collins
1997 Saratoga Springs
1996 Medaaly
1995 Beauchamp King
1994 Celtic Swing
1993 King's Theatre
1992 Armiger
1991 Seattle Rhyme

CHEVELEY PARK STKS
2000 Regal Rose
1999 Seazun
1998 Wannabe Grand
1997 Embassy
1996 Pas De Reponse
1995 Blue Duster
1994 Gay Gallanta
1993 Prophecy
1992 Sayyedati
1991 Marling

COVENTRY STKS
2000 Cd Europe
1999 Fasliyev
1998 Red Sea
1997 Harbour Master
1996 Verglas
1995 Royal Applause
1994 Sri Pekan
1993 Stonehatch
1992 Petardia
1991 Dilum

GIMCRACK STKS
2000 Bannister
1999 Mull Of Kintyre
1998 Josr Algarhoud
1997 Carrowkeel
1996 Abou Zouz
1995 Royal Applause
1994 Chilly Billy
1993 Turtle Island
1992 Splendent
1991 River Falls

SOLARIO STKS
2000 King's Ironbridge
1999 Best of The Bests
1998 Raise A Grand
1997 Little Indian
1996 Brave Act
1995 Alhaarth
1994 Lovely Millie
1993 Island Magic
1992 White Crown
1991 Chicmond

QUEEN MARY STKS
2000 Romantic Myth
1999 Shining Hour
1998 Bint Allayl
1997 Nadwah
1996 Dance Parade
1995 Blue Duster
1994 Gay Gallanta
1993 Risky
1992 Lyric Fantasy
1991 Marling

NORFOLK STKS
2000 Superstar Leo
1999 Warm Heart
1998 Rosselli
1997 Tippitt Boy
1996 Tipsy Creek
1995 Lucky Lionel
1994 Mind Games
1993 Turtle Island
1992 Niche
1991 Magic Ring

CHERRY HINTON STKS
2000 Dora Carrington
1999 Torgau
1998 Wannabe Grand
1997 Asfurah
1996 Dazzle
1995 Applaud
1994 Red Carnival
1993 Lemon Souffle
1992 Sayyedati
1991 Musicale

CHAMPAGNE VINTAGE STKS
2000 No Excuse Needed
1999 Ekraar
1998 Aljabr
1997 Central Park
1996 Putra
1995 Alhaarth
1994 Eltish
1993 Mister Baileys
1992 Maroof
1991 Dr Devious

ROYAL LODGE STKS
2000 Atlantis Prince
1999 Royal Kingdom
1998 Mutaahab
1997 Teapot Row
1996 Benny The Dip
1995 Mons
1994 Eltish
1993 Mister Baileys
1992 Desert Secret
1991 Made of Gold

LOWTHER STKS
2000 Enthused
1999 Jemima
1998 Bint Allayl
1997 Cape Verdi
1996 Bianca Nera
1995 Dance Sequence
1994 Harayir
1993 Velvet Moon
1992 Niche
1991 Culture Vulture

RICHMOND STKS

2000 Endless Summer
1999 Bachir
1998 Muqtarib
1997 Daggers Drawn
1996 Easycall
1995 Polaris Flight
1994 Sri Pekan
1993 First Trump
1992 Son Pardo
1991 Dilum

FLYING CHILDERS STKS

2000 Superstar Leo
1999 Mrs P
1998 Sheer Viking
1997 Land of Dreams
1996 Easycall
1995 Cayman Kai
1994 Raah Algharb
1993 Imperial Bailiwick
1992 Poker Chip
1991 Paris House

MILL REEF STKS

2000 Bouncing Bowdler
1999 Primo Valentino
1998 Golden Silca
1997 Arkadian Hero
1996 Indian Rocket
1995 Kahir Almaydan
1994 Princely Hush
1993 Polish Laughter
1992 Forest Wind
1991 Showbrook

CHAMPAGNE STKS

2000 Noverre
1999 Distant Music
1998 Auction House
1997 Daggers Drawn
1996 Bahhare
1995 Alhaarth
1994 Sri Pekan
1993 Unblest
1992 Petardia
1991 Rodrigo de Triano

Major Handicaps

LINCOLN H'CAP

2000 John Ferneley
1999 Right Wing
1998 Hunters of Brora
1997 Kuala Lipis
1996 Stone Ridge
1995 Roving Minstrel
1994 Our Rita
1993 High Premium
1992 High Low
1991 Amenable

EBOR H'CAP

2000 Give The Slip
1999 Vicious Circle
1998 Tuning
1997 Far Ahead
1996 Clerkenwell
1995 Sanmartino
1994 Hasten to Add
1993 Sarawat
1992 Quick Ransom
1991 Deposki

AYR GOLD CUP

2000 Bahamian Pirate
1999 Grangeville
1998 Always Alight
1997 Wildwood Flower
1996 Coastal Bluff
1995 Royale Figurine
1994 Daring Destiny
1993 Hard to Figure
1992 Lochsong
1991 Sarcita

CAMBRIDGESHIRE H'CAP

2000 Katy Nowaitee
1999 She's Our Mare
1998 Lear Spear
1997 Pasternak
1996 Clifton Fox
1995 Cap Juluca
1994 Halling
1993 Penny Drops
1992 Rambo's Hall
1991 Mellottie

CESAREWITCH H'CAP

2000 Heros Fatal
1999 Top Cees
1998 Spirit of Love
1997 Turnpole
1996 Inchcailloch
1995 Old Red
1994 Captain's Guest
1993 Aahsaylad
1992 Vintage Crop
1991 Go South

ROYAL HUNT CUP

2000 Caribbean Monarch
1999 Showboat
1998 Refuse To Lose
1997 Red Robbo
1996 Yeast
1995 Realities
1994 Face North
1993 Imperial Ballet
1992 Colour Sergeant
1991 Eurolink the Lad

WOKINGHAM H'CAP

2000 Harmonic Way
1999 Deep Space
1998 Selhurstpark Flyer
1997 Selhurstpark Flyer
1996 Emerging Market
1995 Astrac
1994 Venture Capitalist
1993 Nagida
1992 Red Rosein
1991 Amigo Menor

NORTHUMBERLAND PLATE

2000 Bay Of Islands
1999 Far Cry
1998 Cyrian
1997 Windsor Castle
1996 Celeric
1995 Bold Gait
1994 Quick Ransom
1993 Highflying
1992 Witness Box
1991 Tamarpour

TOTE EXACTA H'CAP
(formerly Hong Kong Trophy)

2000 Lady Angharad
1999 Moutahddee
1998 Yavana's Pace
1997 Hawksley Hill
1996 Sheer Danzig
1995 Yoush
1994 Knowth
1993 Smarginato
1992 Fire Top
1991 You Know the Rules

WILLIAM HILL MILE

2000 Persiano
1999 Lonesome Dude
1998 For Your Eyes Only
1997 Fly To The Stars
1996 Moscow Mist
1995 Khayrapour
1994 Fraam
1993 Philidor
1992 Little Bean
1991 Sky Cloud

STEWARDS' CUP

2000 Tayseer
1999 Harmonic Way
1998 Superior Premium
1997 Danetime
1996 Coastal Bluff
1995 Shikari's Son
1994 For the Present
1993 King's Signet
1992 Lochsong
1991 Notley

JOHN SMITH'S CUP

2000 Sobriety
1999 Achilles
1998 Porto Foricos
1997 Pasternak
1996 Wilcuma
1995 Naked Welcome
1994 Cezanne
1993 Baron Ferdinand
1992 Mr Confusion
1991 Halkopous

STAMINA OF SIRES' PROGENY

The following table gives the average distance in furlongs of races won at three-year-old and upwards by the progeny of the stallions named for the period 1990-1999. The mean average distance is the figure shown immediately after the stallion's name. The following two figures are the shortest and longest distances at which a sire's progeny were successful during the period 7/11/99 - 4/11/2000.

A

Absalom	7.1f	5.1	12.0
Acatenango (GER)		8.0	12.0
Accordion	11.3f	10.0	11.9
Affirmed (USA)	10.3f	11.7	11.7
Ajraas (USA)	7f	8.5	8.5
Al Nasr (FR)	9.9f	21.6	21.6
Alhijaz	7.7f	5.0	9.4
Alleged (USA)	11.8f	8.5	16.2
Alnasr Alwasheek	9.4f	9.9	10.0
Always Fair (USA)	14f	8.0	8.0
Alzao (USA)	9.8f	8.0	16.4
Anita's Prince	6f	5.0	8.0
Anjiz (USA)	7f	8.0	10.0
Anshan	8.2f	5.0	17.1
Approach The Bench (GB)		7.0	7.0
Aragon	7.7f	5.0	14.1
Arapahos (FR)		11.9	11.9
Arazi (USA)	9.2f	7.0	14.0
Archway (IRE)	8.5f	5.0	12.0
Ardkinglass	5f	5.0	14.0
Astronef (GB)	7.9f	5.0	5.0

B

Bahri (USA)		6.0	10.4
Bairn (USA)	9.4f	16.4	16.4
Balla Cove (GB)		8.0	13.0
Ballacashtal (CAN)	7.9f	8.0	8.0
Ballad Rock	7.2f	8.0	9.4
Bandmaster (USA)		5.0	5.1
Barathea (IRE)		7.0	14.4
Barrys Gamble	7f	6.0	6.0
Batshoof	9.5f	6.0	16.0
Be My Chief (USA)	10.2f	6.0	16.2
Be My Guest (USA)	10.2f	8.0	18.0
Belmez (USA)	11.4f	10.1	10.1
Bering (GB)	9.6f	5.0	10.5
Beveled (USA)	6.9f	5.0	14.0
Bien Bien (USA)		10.0	12.0
Big Shuffle (USA)		5.0	8.5
Bigstone (IRE)		6.0	8.5
Bin Ajwaad (IRE)		7.0	16.5
Binary Star (USA)		11.5	11.5
Blakeney	11.9f	11.9	16.2
Bluebird (USA)	7.9f	8.0	16.0
Blues Traveller (IRE)		5.1	11.7
Blush Rambler (USA)		11.0	11.0
Bob Back (USA)	11.5f	9.0	9.0
Bob's Return (IRE)		8.5	8.5
Bold Arrangement	8.7f	5.0	7.0
Brief Truce (USA)	9.1f	7.1	16.2
Broad Brush (USA)		12.0	12.0
Brocco (USA)		10.0	10.0
Broken Hearted	10.1f	6.0	8.1
Brunswick (USA)		6.0	6.0

C

Cadeaux Genereux	7.9f	5.0	12.0
Caerleon (USA)	10.9f	5.0	16.1
Cahill Road (USA)	8.5f	7.0	7.0
Capote (USA)	9.1f	8.5	8.5
Case Law	6f	7.0	16.0
Casteddu	7.4f	5.0	16.0
Catrail (USA)		6.0	9.9
Cee's Tizzy		10.0	10.0
Chaddleworth (IRE)		10.5	10.5
Charmer	9f	6.0	11.0
Chief Singer	8.6f	10.0	10.0
Chief's Crown (USA)	10.2f	6.0	8.0
Chilibang	7f	5.0	10.0
Cigar	6.3f	5.0	5.2
Clantime	6.6f	5.0	8.0
Claramount		7.0	7.0
Classic Music (USA)	7.2f	5.0	7.0
Clever Trick (USA)	7.6f	8.1	8.1
College Chapel		5.0	8.0
Colonel Collins (USA)		5.0	5.0
Common Grounds	8.1f	5.0	16.0
Conquering Hero (USA)	10.6f	12.3	12.3
Contract Law (USA)	8.9f	5.0	11.0
Convinced		12.0	12.0
Cosmonaut		7.0	11.9
Cox's Ridge (USA)	9.4f	15.4	16.2
Cozzene (USA)	10.1f	8.0	13.9
Crowning Honors (CAN)	9.9f	9.4	9.4
Cryptoclearance (USA)		10.0	12.0
Cyrano de Bergerac	7.3f	5.0	14.1

D

Damister (USA)	9.1f	8.1	8.1
Dancing Dissident (USA)	6.8f	5.0	10.0
Danehill (USA)	9.1f	5.0	18.7
Danzig (USA)	8.1f	5.0	12.0
Darshaan	11.9f	7.0	16.2
Dashing Blade (GB)	7.9f	8.0	8.0
Dayjur (USA)	6.8f	5.0	7.0
Dehere (USA)		6.0	6.0
Democratic (USA)		7.0	7.0
Deploy	11.4f	7.0	17.2
Desert Secret (IRE)		8.0	10.0
Desert Style (IRE)		6.0	8.0
Desse Zenny (USA)	12f	15.8	15.8
Devil's Bag (USA)	9.3f	7.6	7.6
Diamond Shoal	9.8f	8.0	8.0
Diesis (GB)	9f	7.1	14.0
Dilum (USA)	7.1f	5.0	10.0
Distant Relative	7f	5.0	13.0
Distant View (USA)		5.0	9.4
Distinctly North (USA)	7.4f	5.0	12.0
Dixieland Band (USA)	10.1f	7.0	10.5
Dolphin Street (FR)		6.0	13.1
Dominion	8.9f	5.0	16.0
Domynsky	7.8f	6.0	6.0
Don't Forget Me	9.5f	5.0	12.1
Double Bed (FR)	13.9f	8.0	10.0
Doulab (USA)	7.4f	8.2	14.1
Dowsing (USA)	7f	5.0	8.0
Doyoun	10.7f	7.0	16.0
Dunbeath (USA)	9.9f	13.0	13.0
Dynaformer (USA)	12f	7.0	12.3

E

Eagle Eyed (USA)		6.0	8.0
Efisio	7.7f	5.0	15.0
El Gran Senor (USA)	8.9f	7.6	9.0
El Prado (IRE)	8f	6.0	6.0
Ela-Mana-Mou (GB)	12.7f	5.7	15.5
Elbio	9f	5.0	8.0
Elmaamul (USA)	8.1f	5.0	16.5
Emarati (USA)	6.6f	5.0	14.0
Emperor Jones (USA)		5.0	12.0
Environment Friend	7.5f	6.9	12.0
Erins Isle (GB)	8.3f	8.5	10.0
Exactly Sharp (USA)	8.4f	7.0	10.1
Exbourne (USA)		8.0	8.0
Exit To Nowhere (USA)	8.7f	7.0	12.0
Explosive Red (CAN)		5.0	5.0
Ezzoud (IRE)		6.0	18.2

F

Factual (USA)		5.0	6.0
Fairy King (USA)	7.7f	6.0	10.4
Farma Way (USA)	12f	12.0	12.0
Faustus (USA)	9.1f	10.1	12.0
Fayruz	6.6f	5.0	11.0
Fighting Fit (USA)	7.9f	8.5	8.5
First Trump (GB)		5.0	16.2
Fools Holme (USA)	10.3f	12.4	14.1
Forest Wind (USA)		8.5	12.0
Formidable (USA)	7.8f	5.0	12.0
Forzando	7.2f	5.0	10.3
Fourstars Allstar (USA)		8.0	14.6
Foxhound (USA)		6.0	10.0
Fraam		5.0	14.0

G

Geiger Counter (USA)	7.8f	5.0	6.1
General Meeting (GB)		9.0	10.0
Generous (IRE)	11.5f	8.0	16.2
Ghazi		8.0	10.0
Goldeneyev (USA)		5.5	5.5
Gone West (USA)	7.8f	7.0	14.4
Grand Lodge (USA)		6.0	13.1
Great Commotion (USA)	9.2f	6.0	12.0
Green Dancer (USA)	11.9f	8.0	16.0
Green Desert (USA)	7.8f	5.0	16.0
Green Tune (USA)		11.9	12.0
Greinton	15.8f	11.0	11.0
Grey Dawn II	6.8f	6.0	7.0
Grey Desire	9.3f	7.0	7.5
Groom Dancer (USA)	9.5f	8.0	10.0
Gulch (USA)	9.6f	8.0	14.0
Gunner B	11.2f	12.0	12.1

H

Hadeer	8.9f	12.0	12.0
Hamas (IRE)	8f	7.0	10.5
Handsome Sailor	6.6f	8.0	8.0
Hansel (USA)	12.6f	8.0	12.0
Hector Protector (USA)	9f	10.0	10.0
Hermitage (USA)	8.6f	7.7	8.0
Hernando (FR)		8.0	15.8
Hero's Honor (USA)	9.2f	10.0	18.0
High Estate (GB)	10.5f	5.0	13.0
Hi[illegible]est Honor (FR)	10.9f	7.0	12.0
[illegible]me de Loi (IRE)		10.0	12.0
Horage	11.4f	16.0	16.0
Housebuster (USA)	7f	5.0	12.0
Hubbly Bubbly (USA)	9.5f	11.9	12.3

I

Imp Society (USA)	7.1f	5.0	15.8
Imperial Falcon (CAN)	9.2f	12.0	12.0
Imperial Frontier (USA)	7f	5.0	9.3
In The Wings	11.2f	7.0	14.0
Inca Chief (USA)	5.6f	5.0	5.0
Inchinor	8.9f	5.0	17.5
Indian Ore (USA)		12.0	12.0
Indian Ridge	7.6f	5.0	12.0
Interrex (CAN)	7.7f	10.0	11.0
Irish River (FR)	9f	7.0	12.0

J

Jareer (USA)	10.2f	12.0	12.0
Java Gold (USA)	9.3f	6.0	12.0
Jester	8.5f	7.1	8.0
Joli Wasfi (USA)	11.7f	11.8	11.8
Jung (GB)		10.0	10.0
Jupiter Island	10.4f	9.9	16.1

K

Kabour	6.1f	5.0	14.6
Kahyasi	12.9f	9.0	18.0
Kalaglow	11.2f	8.0	16.0
Kaldoun	9.9f	8.0	8.0
Kaldounevees		8.0	8.0
Kasakov		6.0	6.0
Keen	11.1f	6.0	9.4
Kefaah (USA)	11.2f	10.0	12.4
Kendor (FR)	12.2f	6.0	6.0
Kenmare (FR)	9.6f	12.3	16.4
King's Signet (USA)	7f	6.0	10.0
Kingmambo (USA)	10.9f	6.0	10.4
Kleven (USA)		6.0	6.0
Known Fact (USA)	8.3f	8.5	12.0
Komaite (USA)	6.9f	5.0	12.0
Kris	10f	7.0	16.0
Kris S	9.3f	12.0	12.0
Kylian (USA)	8.1f	11.6	16.0

L

Lahib (USA)	8f	5.0	14.1
Lake Coniston (IRE)		5.0	8.1
Lammtarra (USA)		8.0	14.0
Last Tycoon	9.4f	6.0	14.0
Law Society (USA)	11.6f	7.0	14.1
Layal (GB)		14.0	14.0
Lear Fan (USA)	10.4f	5.1	12.0
Lesotho (USA)	6f	10.0	10.0
Linamix	8.2f	8.5	15.5
Lion Cavern (USA)	7.5f	6.0	9.9
Lively One (USA)		10.0	10.0
Llandaff (USA)		12.0	12.0
Loach		7.0	7.0
Local Suitor (USA)	9.7f	8.0	11.0
Lode		6.0	12.0
Lomitas (GB)		11.0	11.0
Lomond (USA)	9.9f	11.0	11.0
Lord At War (ARG)	6.6f	12.0	12.0
Lord Avie (USA)		10.0	10.0
Lost World (IRE)		8.5	8.5
Lucky Guest		6.0	8.0
Lugana Beach	7f	5.0	12.0
Lure (USA)		7.0	8.0
Lycius (USA)	8.8f	6.0	14.1

M

Mac's Imp (USA)	5.6f	5.0	8.0
Machiavellian (USA)	9.8f	7.0	16.0
Magic Mirror (GB)		10.0	10.0
Magic Ring (IRE)	6.5f	5.0	9.4
Magical Wonder (USA)	7.2f	8.0	12.1
Major Jacko		11.1	11.9
Makbul		5.0	5.1
Marju (IRE)	9.2f	8.0	16.2
Master Willie	9.2f	9.9	10.1
Mazaad	8.5f	8.0	8.0
Mazilier (USA)	8.5f	5.0	7.0
Mendocino (USA)		10.0	10.0
Merdon Melody	6.8f	5.0	10.0
Midhish		5.0	10.0
Midyan (USA)	9.9f	5.0	18.0
Mille Balles (FR)		9.0	9.0
Minshaanshu Amad (USA)	11.3f	7.0	12.0
Missed Flight		6.0	8.5
Mister Baileys		8.0	10.0
Miswaki (USA)	8.1f	6.5	12.0
Mizaaya		6.0	6.0
Mizoram (USA)		8.0	8.1
Moment of Hope (USA)	6.9f	7.0	7.0
Mon Tresor	7.9f	5.0	6.0
Mondrian (GER)		12.0	12.0
Monsun		8.5	12.0
Most Welcome	8.6f	5.0	16.2
Mountain Cat (USA)		16.0	16.0
Move Off		8.0	8.0
Mr Prospector	8.6f	8.0	10.0
Mt Livermore (USA)	7.7f	6.0	10.0
Mtoto (GB)	11.5f	8.0	17.1
Muhtarram (USA)		10.0	12.4
Mujadil (USA)	7.7f	5.0	20.0
Mujtahid (USA)	7.4f	5.0	16.0
Mukaddamah (USA)	7.6f	5.0	12.0
Music Boy	6.5f	6.0	6.0
Mystiko (USA)	7.7f	5.0	12.0

N

Nabeel Dancer (USA)	6.1f	5.0	9.4
Naevus (USA)	7.2f	7.0	7.1
Naheez (USA)		10.0	10.0
Nalchik (USA)	12.6f	10.5	10.5
Namaqualand (USA)		5.0	16.0
Nashwan (USA)	10.3f	7.1	14.0
Nawwar		5.0	5.0
Nebos		10.0	10.0
Never so Bold	7.1f	5.0	13.0
Nicholas (USA)	6.1f	5.0	8.5
Nicolotte		5.0	11.6
Night Shift (USA)	8.1f	5.0	12.1
Niniski (USA)	13.2f	12.0	20.0
Nishapour (FR)	11.1f	12.0	12.0
No Big Deal		5.1	5.1
Noble Patriarch	12.2f	10.2	12.0
Nomination	7.3f	8.0	10.5
Nordico (USA)	8.2f	6.0	12.0
Northern Flagship (USA)	12.2f	9.4	16.1
Northern Park (USA)	10f	11.9	16.2
Northern Score (USA)		8.0	8.0
Not in Doubt (USA)		10.0	16.0
Nureyev (USA)	8.4f	6.0	9.9

O

Old Vic (GB)	12.8f	12.5	22.2
Opening Verse (USA)	11.8f	10.0	10.0
Owington		5.1	9.9

P

Panoramic (GB)		8.0	8.0
Paris House	5.9f	5.0	8.0
Pelder (IRE)		8.2	12.0
Persian Bold	10f	8.0	16.2
Persian Heights	10.5f	7.0	16.4
Perugino (USA)		5.3	10.0
Petardia	8.2f	6.0	11.5
Peteski (CAN)		10.0	10.0
Petit Loup (USA)		10.5	14.6
Petong	7.6f	5.0	14.0
Petorius	8f	6.0	13.0
Petoski	10.4f	6.0	16.2
Pharly (FR)	11.5f	8.0	10.0
Phountzi (USA)	9.6f	11.5	12.0
Piccolo		5.0	9.9
Pine Bluff (USA)		9.0	13.3
Pips Pride	6.7f	5.0	10.0
Pistolet Bleu (IRE)		14.0	14.8
Platini (GER)		10.5	16.0
Pleasant Colony	12.4f	8.0	12.3
Polar Falcon (USA)	9f	5.0	16.0
Polish Patriot (USA)	7.8f	5.0	13.8
Polish Precedent (USA)	9f	6.0	15.0
Precocious	7.2f	6.0	10.5
Presidium	7.5f	5.0	16.2
Primo Dominie	7.2f	5.0	12.0
Prince Sabo	6.6f	5.0	12.0
Prince of Birds (USA)		7.0	15.0
Priolo (USA)	10.9f	8.0	12.3
Private Account	10.1f	10.0	10.0
Project Manager	7.2f	12.0	12.0
Puissance	7.1f	5.0	11.6
Pursuit of Love	9.5f	6.0	12.3
Pyramus (USA)		13.8	13.8

Q

Quest for Fame	12.8f	7.6	12.0

R

Rahy (USA)	9.1f	10.0	12.0
Rainbow Quest (USA)	11.2f	6.9	14.6
Rainbows For Life (CAN)	9.3f	8.0	17.1
Raise A Man (USA)	7.3f	6.0	6.0
Rambo Dancer (CAN)	8.4f	5.9	11.0
Red Ransom (USA)	8.6f	8.0	11.4
Red Sunset	9f	7.5	9.0
Reprimand	8.2f	5.0	12.0
Rich Charlie	5.9f	6.0	6.0
Richard of York (GB)		12.0	12.0
Ridgewood Ben		13.0	14.1
Risk Me (FR)	8f	5.0	12.1
River Falls	8.2f	6.0	6.0
River God (USA)	6f	9.4	10.0
River Special (USA)		8.0	8.0
Riverman (USA)	9.7f	7.9	13.0
Robellino (USA)	9.5f	7.0	16.2
Robin Des Pins (USA)	8f	6.0	6.0
Rock City	8.8f	5.0	12.0
Rock Hopper	10.6f	8.0	12.5
Roi Danzig (USA)	10.5f	9.0	16.0
Rolfe (USA)	11.2f	12.0	12.0
Ron's Victory (USA)	9.2f	10.0	10.0
Rousillon (USA)	10.4f	9.9	9.9
Royal Academy (USA)	7.8f	5.0	13.0
Rudimentary (USA)	8.2f	5.0	12.0
Runnett	6.7f	11.7	11.7
Rymer		8.0	8.0

S

Sabrehill (USA)	8.5f	10.0	12.0
Saddlers' Hall (IRE)	10.5f	6.1	18.0
Sadler's Wells (USA)	11.3f	7.0	20.0
Safawan	6.6f	7.9	10.3
Salse (USA)	10.9f	6.0	16.0
Salt Dome (USA)	6.5f	6.0	8.0
Sanglamore (USA)	12.9f	8.0	18.7
Satco (FR)	14.2f	16.1	16.1
Savahra Sound	7.8f	5.0	5.0
Sayf El Arab (USA)	8.2f	5.0	12.0
Scenic	10.6f	7.0	14.0
Sea Raven (IRE)		5.0	5.0
Seattle Dancer (USA)	10.1f	13.3	14.1
Second Set (IRE)	9.2f	7.0	7.0
Secret Appeal		8.3	9.2
Secreto (USA)	9.9f	11.5	11.5
Seeking the Gold (USA)	7.4f	8.0	12.0
Selkirk (USA)	7.9f	5.0	13.9
Septieme Ciel (USA)		8.0	10.0
Shaadi (USA)	8.1f	6.0	6.0
Shadeed (USA)	7.7f	8.0	8.0
Shahrastani (USA)	11.5f	15.8	15.8
Shalford (IRE)	7.8f	5.0	7.0
Shareef Dancer (USA)	10.1f	6.0	17.1
Sharpo	7.5f	6.0	12.0
Shavian	7.7f	5.0	7.0
Sheikh Albadou	9.2f	5.1	12.0
Shernazar (GB)	11.8f	10.0	16.2
Shining Steel (GB)	7f	7.5	7.5
Shirley Heights	12.1f	8.0	17.1
Shuailaan (USA)		10.0	10.0
Siberian Express (USA)	9f	7.0	12.0
Sicyos (USA)	7f	9.0	9.0
Silent King		6.0	6.0
Sillery (USA)		10.0	10.0
Silver Hawk (USA)	11.2f	8.0	20.0
Silver Kite (USA)	10.2f	6.0	6.0
Simply Great (FR)	11.9f	7.0	7.0
Simply Majestic (USA)	7.8f	7.9	8.0
Sir Harry Lewis (USA)		16.0	16.4
Sizzling Melody	6.3f	5.0	12.1
Skyliner	6.8f	5.0	5.0
Slew O' Gold (USA)	10.2f	12.3	12.3
Slip Anchor	12.7f	10.0	15.0
Son Pardo		16.0	16.0
Son of Silver		16.0	16.0
Southern Halo (USA)		8.0	8.0
Soviet Lad (USA)	9.4f	6.0	16.0
Soviet Star (USA)	8.6f	8.0	8.0
Sri Pekan (USA)		5.0	12.0
St Jovite (USA)	11.8f	11.8	12.0
Standaan (FR)	5.4f	5.1	5.1
Star de Naskra (USA)	8.8f	9.3	9.3
Statoblest	6.4f	5.0	10.2
Sternkonig (IRE)		10.0	12.0
Storm Bird (CAN)	8.5f	8.2	8.3
Storm Cat (USA)	7f	6.0	10.4
Strolling Along (USA)		12.0	12.6
Suave Dancer (USA)	10.7f	7.0	14.1
Summer Squall (USA)	7f	10.3	10.3
Sunday Silence (USA)		10.0	12.0
Superlative	8.8f	5.0	14.0
Superpower	6.6f	5.0	8.0
Supreme Leader	10.9f	10.0	16.0
Sure Blade (USA)	10.6f	6.0	12.0
[illegible]umu (GER)		11.6	11.6
[illegible]onday	8.3f	5.0	5.0
[illegible]s	9.6f	16.0	18.0
[illegible]	8.1f	7.0	8.0

T

Tate Gallery (USA)	8.2f	7.0	7.0
Taufan (USA)	8.3f	5.0	14.8
Teenoso (USA)	10.5f	15.4	15.4
Tel Quel		10.0	10.0
Tenby	10.4f	6.0	12.0
Thatching	7.8f	5.0	12.0
Theatrical (GB)	11.5f	7.0	12.3
Then Again	7.4f	6.0	11.0
Thowra (FR)	11.2f	6.0	16.0
Thunder Gulch (USA)		7.0	9.0
Timeless Times (USA)	6.1f	5.0	8.0
Tina's Pet	7.4f	5.0	11.9
Tirol	8.1f	6.0	6.0
Totem (USA)	5f	5.0	6.1
Touch of Grey	8.1f	10.0	13.0
Tragic Role (USA)	9.4f	5.7	16.0
Treasure Kay	6.5f	5.9	10.0
Trempolino (USA)	11.9f	7.0	18.0
Tropular (GB)		9.0	12.0
Turfkonig		10.0	10.0
Turtle Island (IRE)		6.0	16.2
Two Punch		6.0	6.0

U

Unblest		5.0	10.0
Unbridled (USA)		9.5	10.0
Uncle Pokey	10f	13.8	14.1
Unfuwain (USA)	11.4f	6.0	16.0
Up and At 'em		5.0	18.0

V

Vacarme (USA)		16.0	16.0
Vettori (IRE)		10.0	14.0
Vision (USA)	10.4f	12.0	12.0

W

Waajib	8.9f	7.0	16.2
Warning	8.1f	5.0	14.6
Warrshan (USA)	9.7f	6.0	14.0
Weldnaas (USA)	8.4f	5.0	17.2
Whittingham (IRE)		5.0	6.0
Winged Love (IRE)		12.0	12.0
With Approval (CAN)	8.7f	8.0	16.0
Wolfhound (USA)	7.3f	5.0	16.2
Woodman (USA)	9.7f	6.9	16.2
Woods of Windsor (USA)		7.1	8.0

Y

Yachtie (AUS)		9.0	9.0

Z

Zafonic (USA)	9f	5.0	11.5
Zieten (USA)		7.0	10.9
Zilzal (USA)	8.5f	6.0	14.1